The Penguin

English Student's Dictionary

Edited by L A Hill

PENGUIN ENGLISH

PENGUIN BOOKS

Published by the Penguin Group
Penguin Books, 27 Wrights Lane, London W8 5TZ, England
Viking Penguin, a division of Penguin Books USA Inc.
375 Hudson Street, New York, New York 10014, USA
Penguin Books Australia Ltd, Ringwood, Victoria, Australia
Penguin Books Canada Ltd, 2801 John Street, Markham, Ontario, Canada L3R 1B4
Penguin Books (NZ) Ltd, 182–190 Wairau Road, Auckland 10, New Zealand

Penguin Books Ltd, Registered Offices: Harmondsworth, Middlesex, England

First published 1991
1 3 5 7 9 10 8 6 4 2

Assistant editors
Robert Cameron
Elana Katz
Charlotte Martin
James Phillips

Assistants
Katharine Mendelsohn
Rosemary Sansome
Anne Vinden

Secretarial assistance from
Doreen Clarkson
Julia Donahue
Mollie Phipps

Filmset in
Scantext 7/7.5 pt Times
by Joshua Associates Ltd, Oxford

Made and printed in Great Britain by
Clays Ltd, St Ives plc

Contents

Introduction

The *Penguin English Student's Dictionary* has been carefully prepared for people studying and using English as a foreign or second language. It is based on many years of experience of teaching English, training teachers of English and writing textbooks for students and teachers.

This dictionary pays as much attention to English phrases and expressions as to the meanings of individual words. It helps the student to understand the meaning *and* usage of a word or expression when he/she is listening or reading or writing. If the student hears or reads '*Helen is on business in our town. She is in business in London.*' and wants to know the difference between '*in* business' and '*on* business', he/she should look up **business** in the dictionary and then find *in business* and *on business*.

The main word (called a 'headword') is given in **bold** letters and words with the same spelling but different meanings are numbered ¹,² etc. Changes in the part of speech of a word (e.g adjective, noun, and verb) are listed in alphabetical order and marked ▷.

Pronunciation for each word is given in phonetic symbols (e.g **seat** /si:t/). For the meaning of these symbols and practice in using them, ⇨ page viii.

After the pronunciation, the part of speech is given (e.g *adj*, *adv*, *c.n*, *u.n*, *tr.v*, *intr.v* etc). For explanations of these abbreviations and the part of speech, ⇨ page x.

If the headword is a noun that does not form its plural by adding -*s* or -*es*, the plural form is given (e.g **body** (*pl* -*ies*) means that the plural of 'body' is 'bodies'; **child** (*pl children*) means that the plural of 'child' is 'children').

If the comparative or superlative of an adjective or adverb is not formed with -*er*, -*est* or -*r*, -*st*, the forms are given (e.g **tiny** (-*ier*, -*iest*) means that the forms are 'tinier' and 'tiniest'; **big** (-*ger*, -*gest*) means that the forms are 'bigger', 'biggest').

Any unusual verb forms are also given (e.g **swim** (-*mm*-, *p.t swam*, *p.p swum*) means that we write 'swimming' in the present tense, 'swam' in the past tense and 'swum' as the past participle; **cancel** (-*ll*-, US -*l*-) means that in British English we write 'cancelling', 'cancelled' etc and in American English we write 'canceling', 'canceled' etc).

There is information if a word is used only in certain situations (e.g *formal*, *informal*, *slang* or *med*, *law*, *tech*). For an explanation of these abbreviations, ⇨ page xii.

The meaning of the word is then given, often with one or more examples. Different meanings of the same word are numbered **1, 2** etc. Detailed help is given with usage. For example, a word may be used in a particular phrase or group of words (e.g **abstain** is often used in '*abstain from* (*doing*) *s.t*').

At the end and after all the meanings have been given, there is a list of idioms in which the word is used (e.g at the end of **come** we find *come across s.o/s.t*, *come into money* etc).

A word that comes from the same root as another but has a suffix added to it is grouped under the headword (e.g the adjective '**bearable**' comes from the verb '**bear**' with the suffix '**-able**'; ⇨ Appendix 2 for details). If the word comes in a different alphabetical order when grouped in this way, it also appears in its correct alphabetical position with an arrow, ⇨ meaning 'look up . . .', to show where to find it (e.g 'showy' is explained under **show**, and between **shower** and **shrank** we find **showy** ⇨ show). If the pronunciation does not present any difficulties, these words do not have a full phonetic transcription but stress-markers only (e.g **'yellowness**). If there is a major change in pronunciation, the full phonetic transcription is given (e.g **ratification** /ˌrætɪfɪˈkeɪʃən/ from **ratify** /ˈrætɪˌfaɪ/; **pleasure** /ˈpleʒə/ from **please** /pliːz/). For explanations of stress-markers, ⇨ page ix.

After the main dictionary, there are very useful appendices on irregular verbs, common affixes and roots, punctuation, the family, geographical names, numbers, times and dates, money, weights and measures, mathematical signs and symbols and ranks in the armed forces.

Phonetic symbols

Vowels

iː	keep	ɔː	all	əʊ	bone	aɪə	fire
ɪ	lip	ʊ	full	aʊ	how	ɔɪə	lawyer
e	end	uː	food	ɔɪ	toy	aʊə	tower
æ	sat	ɔ	away	ɪə	clear	əʊə	lower
ʌ	up	ɜː	nerve	eə	pair		
ɑː	star	eɪ	make	ʊə	sure		
ɒ	pot	aɪ	side	eɪə	player		

For more practice, ⇨ the end of this section.

Consonants

b	bed	k	came	v	van	tʃ	chip
d	do	l	lost	w	went	ʃ	sheep
f	fish	m	man	s	sat	θ	think
g	great	n	now	z	zoo	ð	there
h	hit	p	pill	ŋ	sing	dʒ	gentle
j	you	r	run	t	time	ʒ	pleasure

For more practice, ⇨ the end of this section.

Note: Linking r. When the letter r appears between vowel sounds, it is pronounced /r/; we do not point this out each time in this dictionary. Compare, for example, gather /ˈgaeðə/ and gathering /ˈgaeðərɪŋ/; come here /ˌkam ˈhɪə/ and here it is /ˌhɪər it ˈɪz/.

Stress-markers

ˈ (showing main or primary stress), e.g ˈ**perfect** (*adj*), perˈ**fect** (*verb*).

ˌ (showing secondary (less important) stress), e.g ˌunimˈ**portant**, ˈ**recogˌnize**, ˌ**reconˌciliˈation**, ˌ**interˈnationaˌlize**.

Note: Rhythm is very important in spoken English and in this dictionary there is maximum help by a liberal use of secondary stress-marks.

Sound examples to use for practice

iː	these, tea, keen, receive, people, key, machine, field, quay, phoenix.	eɪ	lake, aid, date, break, eight, they, gaol, gauge, fête, ballet, fiancée.
ɪ	village, captain, Friday, married, exact, coffee, foreign, abbey, mirror, carriage, women, minute, build, city.	əʊ	sew, home, road, toe, blow, owe, brooch, soul, chauffeur, beau.
		aɪ	either, eye, bite, die, guide, buy, type, goodbye, my, light, aisle, ay, aye, geyser.
e	bed, any, said, says, very, head, leisure, leopard, friend, bury, guess, hæmorrhage.	aʊ	house, out, cow.
		ɔɪ	oil, foil, boy, buoy.
æ	map, apple, valley, plait, guarantee.	ɪə	here, dear, beer, area, happier, museum, theory, courteous, pier, companion, curious, souvenir, medium, diarrhoea.
ʌ	study, above, doesn't, blood, courage.		
ɑː	car, bazaar, aunt, clerk, heart, guard.	eə	care, air, prayer, mayor, there, bear, their, aeroplane.
ɒ	lot, forest, quarrel, sausage, rendezvous, knowledge, cough.	ʊə	tour, sure, February, influence.
		eɪə	player, playable, abeyance, greyer.
ɔː	more, door, four, warm, tall, August, extraordinary, law, awe, bought.	aɪə	hire, dial, quiet, lion, tyre, flyer.
		ɔɪə	lawyer, employer, joyous.
ʊ	put, woman, wolf, book, could.	aʊə	flower, our, coward.
uː	June, blue, fruit, chew, move, shoe, too, soup, manoeuvre, rheumatism.	əʊə	mower, sower, coalesce.
		b	bad, dabble.
ə	arrange, basement, action, original, cupboard, sergeant, bigger, honour, figure, surgeon, courageous, chauffeur, gracious, tortoise.	d	day, middle.
		f	fat, suffer, enough, photograph.
		g	get, gone, gear, beggar, ghost.
		h	hat, who.
ɜː	bird, serve, word, burn, early, connoisseur, colonel, journey, myrtle.	j	yet, hallelujah.

k	cat, acclaim, character, back, racket, saccharin, kill, cheque, khaki.
l	self, fall.
m	man, hammer, hymn.
n	nail, penny.
p	pen, shepherd, happy, hiccough.
r	red, marry, diarrhoea.
v	very, voice, of.
w	way, what.
s	city, gas, dress, scene, muscle, schism, waltz.
z	zoom, dogs, his, dissolve, xylophone.
ŋ	bang, anchor.
t	ten, Thomas, butter, baked.
tʃ	chap, question, nature, catch, cello.
ʃ	ship, mission, action, social, machine, conscious, schedule, chalet, fuchsia.
dʒ	edge, judge, gem, gaol, suggest, adjust, soldier, jam, sandwich.
ʒ	garage, measure, vision, azure.
θ	thick, thin, thistle, cloth, north, worth.
ð	bathe, the, than, these, clothe, clothes, worthy.

Abbreviations

abbr abbreviation, e.g **CID** *abbr* Criminal Investigation Department.

adj adjective, e.g *This is a big place. This place is big.*

adv adverb, e.g *He walks quickly. This place is very big. This hat is big enough for me. Come home soon. She is not in today.*

attrib attributive (of an adj), i.e that comes before a noun or pron and not after a verb, e.g *a big tree.*

aux.v auxiliary verb, i.e one used to form a tense of a verb, e.g *He was reading a book. I have finished. It may rain soon.*

chem.symb chemical symbol, e.g **ammonia** (*chem.symb* NH₃).

c.n countable noun, i.e one that can be used after 'a(n)' and that has a plural, e.g *horse; woman; answer.*

comp comparative (of adjs and advs), e.g *bigger; better; more beautiful.*

conj conjunction, e.g *You and I. Come in or shut the door.*

def.n definite noun, i.e one that is used with 'the' before it, e.g *north; seaside.*

def.pl.n definite plural noun, i.e one that is used with 'the' before it and that takes a plural verb; e.g *tropics; Philippines.*

derog derogatory, e.g *It is derog to say that an adult is 'childish'.*

det determiner, i.e a word that qualifies a noun or pronoun and comes before any adjs that also qualify it, e.g *this small girl; every day.*

e.g for example.

esp especially.

etc et cetera.

fig figurative, i.e not used in its literal sense, e.g *What an animal that man is!*

i.e that is; in other words.

interj interjection, e.g *Hi! Sh! What!*

intr.v verb that does not take a direct object, e.g *go; live; garden.*

n noun; e.g *policeman; physics; women.*

neg negative.

pers person, e.g *3rd pers sing pres.t* =
third person singular present tense.

pl plural.

pl.n plural noun, e.g *deer*; *cacti*; *cattle*.
The government have decided to
change the law.

poss possessive, e.g *Jack's*; *monkeys'*;
women's.

poss.adj possessive adjective, e.g *my*;
your.

poss.pron possessive pronoun, e.g
mine; *yours*; *someone's*.

p.p past participle, e.g *finished*; *grown*;
swum.

pred predicative (of an adj.), i.e one
that follows a verb, e.g *He is ill*.

prep preposition, e.g *She is not at*
home. What are you looking at?

pres.t present tense, e.g *I live here. I am*
listening to some music.

pron pronoun, e.g *I*; *you*; *everyone*.
Some like it, some don't.

p.t past tense, e.g *lived*; *was*; *swam*.

refl.v reflexive verb, i.e one that takes a
pronoun in *-self/-selves* as its object;
e.g *enjoy oneself*.

Scot Scots English.

sing singular.

sing.n noun that can be used after 'a(n)'
but cannot be used in the plural, e.g
an abundance of birds. She is a match
for any of us.

s.o someone.

s.t something.

superl superlative (of adjs and advs),
e.g *biggest*; *best*; *most beautiful*.

s.w somewhere.

symb symbol; e.g **H** *symb* Hydrogen.

t.n trade name, e.g *hoover*.

tr.v transitive verb; i.e one that takes a
direct object, e.g *get*; *outdo*.

UK British English.

u.n uncountable noun, i.e one that is
not used after 'a(n)' nor in the plural,
but which can be used after 'some'
/səm/ or 'any', e.g *water*; *modesty*.

unique n singular noun that is neither a
c.n ($\Rightarrow$ above) nor a *def.n* ($\Rightarrow$ above),
nor a *u.n* ($\Rightarrow$ above), e.g *England*;
mathematics. School begins at
9 o'clock.

US American English.

usu usually.

v verb, e.g *receive*; *ought*.

written abbr written abbreviation, e.g
Ave *written abbr* Avenue.

$\triangleright$ change of part of speech in an entry.

$\Rightarrow$ see, e.g **advocate** ... $\Rightarrow$ attorney.

/ or, e.g *each/every* means *each or*
every.

= is the same as, e.g *anyone* = *anybody*.

To save space, changes that occur in
words when they are put in the
plural, in the past tense etc are not
always shown in full. The following
'abbreviations' are used:

doubling e.g **rob** (*-bb-*) means that
when a suffix other than *-s* is added to
'rob', the *b* is doubled, producing
'robbing' and 'robbed'.

plurals **tomato** (*pl -es*) means that the
plural of tomato is tomatoes; **motto** (*pl*
-s) means that the plural of motto is
mottos.

Grammatical markers used in full

collective noun/name noun or name that is singular in form but takes a plural verb, e.g *The crowd are drinking and singing.*

command = imperative.

direct object person, animal or thing that the action of a verb is directed to, e.g *I saw him.*

imperative form of a verb that gives an order, e.g *Stop!*

indirect object person, animal or thing that is the beneficiary or sufferer of an action that consists of verb + direct object, e.g *I gave him a book.*

object direct object of a verb, or person, animal or thing governed by a preposition, e.g *There's nothing in it.*

objective case form of a pronoun that is used when it is the object, e.g *me*, *him*, *us*, *them*.

prefix part of a word that comes at the beginning of it, has an individual meaning, but cannot be used as a word by itself, e.g '*un*easy'; '*pre*historic'. ⇨ Appendix 2.

suffix part of a word that comes at the end of it and cannot be used as a word by itself. Many suffixes change one part of speech into another, '*good*ness'; '*easi*ly'; '*green*ish'. ⇨ Appendix 2.

Style markers used in full

showing style, areas of use or origin

commerce	*literary*
formal	*mathematics*
French	*French in origin.*	*medicine*
German	*German in origin.*	*military*
Greek	*Greek in origin.*	*old use*
informal	*proverb*
joking	*religion*
Latin	*Latin in origin.*	*slang*
law	*technical*

Aa

A, a /eɪ/ c/unique n **1** 1st letter of the English alphabet.

▷ det (strong form /eɪ/, weak form /ə/) **2** (used before a word that begins with a consonant sound): a cat; a horse; a useful book; a one-eyed man. Compare an. **3** one example of, when one is not contrasting (⇒ contrast(4)) this with two, three etc: 'Have you got a match?' 'Yes, I've got one match but I need it myself.' **4** any, every, example of: A cat is an animal. **5** a certain, usu one that one does not know: There is a Mr Grant to see you. **6** a kind of: This is a bread I like very much. **7** one cup etc of: I had a coffee at 10 o'clock. **8** each; every: They say that an apple a day keeps the doctor away. **9** a person/animal/thing like: The cat was a lion when it defended its young. **10** a painting etc by: There is a Rubens in our museum. **a brother** etc **of mine, yours, Mary's** etc = one of my etc brothers etc.

▷ symb **11 (A)** (used with a number) major road: the A40 to Oxford. ⇒ M(14).

A1 /ˌeɪ 'wʌn/ adj **1** of the best kind. **2** in the best condition.

AA /ˌeɪ 'eɪ/ def.n abbr Automobile Association.

AAA /ˌeɪ eɪ 'eɪ/ def.n abbr Amateur Athletic(1) Association.

aback /ə'bæk/ adv **take s.o, be taken, aback** surprise s.o, be surprised, greatly.

abandon /ə'bændən/ tr.v **1** leave (s.o/s.t) without intending to return: The car was found abandoned in a field. **2** give (s.t) up; stop trying to do (s.t): They abandoned the attempt.

a'bandonment u.n.

abashed /ə'bæʃt/ adj feeling shy or ashamed. Compare unabashed.

abate /ə'beɪt/ intr.v (formal) become less (strong): We waited till the storm abated before starting.

a'batement u.n.

abattoir /'æbə,twɑː/ c.n official place where animals, e.g cows, are killed; slaughterhouse.

abbess /'æbɪs/ c.n woman who is the head of a convent.

abbey /'æbɪ/ n **1** c/unique n name by which some big churches are known: Westminster Abbey. **2** c.n (old use) monastery or convent. **3** c.n building that used to be an abbey(2).

abbot /'æbət/ c.n man who is the head of a monastery.

abbreviate /ə'briːvɪ,eɪt/ tr.v make (a word etc) short(er).

abbreviation /ə,briːvɪ'eɪʃən/ c.n short form, usu of words: 'Mon' is an abbreviation of 'Monday'.

ABC /ˌeɪ biː 'siː/ def.n **1** alphabet, usu when being learnt by small children. **2** children's book with pictures illustrating(1) the ABC(1). **as easy as ABC** very easy.

abdicate /'æbdɪ,keɪt/ v **1** intr.v give up being king, queen etc. **2** tr.v give up (a claim, responsibility etc).

abdication /ˌæbdɪ'keɪʃən/ c/u.n.

abdomen /'æbdəmən/ c.n **1** part of one's body that is between the chest and the top of one's legs. **2** (in insects) last section(1) of the body.

abdominal /əb'dɒmɪnl/ adj of or referring to the abdomen: abdominal pains.

abduct /əb'dʌkt/ tr.v take (s.o) away unlawfully.

abduction /əb'dʌkʃən/ u.n.

aberrant /æ'berənt/ adj not right or normal: aberrant behaviour.

aberration /ˌæbə'reɪʃən/ c/u.n (example of the) act of not doing what is right or normal, usu without thinking. **in (a moment of) aberration** as a result of (a short) aberration: She drank his coffee in a moment of aberration.

abet /ə'bet/ tr.v (-tt-) (usu **aid and — s.o** (in doing, to do, s.t)) help and/or encourage (s.o) to do s.t wrong.

abeyance /ə'beɪəns/ u.n (often **fall into, be in, —**) (formal) (of a law, rule etc) state of temporarily not being in use/operation.

abhor /əb'hɔː/ tr.v (-rr-) (formal) hate (s.t); be disgusted by (s.t): We all abhor cruelty to animals.

abhorrence /əb'hɒrəns/ u.n.

abhorrent /əb'hɒrənt/ adj that causes hatred or disgust.

abide /ə'baɪd/ v (p.t,p.p abode /ə'bəʊd/, abided) **1** intr.v (usu — in s.w) (old use; literary) live (in a place). **2** tr.v (formal) be able to suffer (s.o/s.t) patiently; tolerate (s.o/s.t): I can't abide the way that man boasts. **abide by s.t** be faithful to s.t; not change s.t: I abide by what I have already promised.

a'biding attrib. adj: an abiding love.

ability ⇒ able.

abject /'æbdʒekt/ adj (of conditions of living etc) extremely poor and miserable: abject poverty.

abjure /əb'dʒʊə/ tr.v (formal) promise to give (s.t) up, stop doing (s.t): Those men have abjured all violence.

ablaze /ə'bleɪz/ pred.adj **1** on fire; burning. **2** (fig) (sometimes — with s.t) shining brightly (because of s.t): The castle was ablaze with lights. **3** (fig) (often — with s.t) very excited (because of anger etc).

able /'eɪbl/ adj **1** (pred) (often — to do s.t) having the skill, strength etc needed (to do s.t): I wasn't able to lift the box. Opposite unable. **2** clever; skilful: an able lawyer.

ability /ə'bɪlɪtɪ/ c/u.n (pl -ies) **1** (often the — to do s.t) skill, strength etc needed (to do s.t). **2** u.n (often a person etc of —) (a person etc who has) cleverness, skill. Opposite inability.

able-'bodied adj fit and strong in one's body.

able-,bodied 'seaman c.n (also **able 'seaman**) fully trained sailor who is not an officer of any kind.

'ably adv.

abnormal /æb'nɔːml/ adj not normal.

abnormality /ˌæbnɔː'mælɪtɪ/ n (pl -ies) **1** u.n fact or quality of being abnormal. **2** c.n thing that is abnormal.

ab'normally adv.

aboard /ə'bɔːd/ adv/prep on or in (a boat, aeroplane etc): The ship left port as soon as all the passengers were aboard.

abode¹ /ə'bəʊd/ c.n (formal or old use) place where one lives. **of no fixed abode** not living at any permanent address. **take up one's abode** begin to live in a place.

abode² /ə'bəʊd/ *p.t,p.p* of abide.
abolish /ə'bɒlɪʃ/ *tr.v* stop (s.t) permanently: *Most of us would like to see taxes abolished.*
abolition /,æbə'lɪʃən/ *u.n.*
A-bomb /'eɪ ,bɒm/ *c.n* (*informal*) atomic bomb.
abominate /ə'bɒmɪ,neɪt/ *tr.v* (*formal*) hate (s.o/s.t); feel disgust for (s.o/s.t): *I abominate rudeness.*
abominable /ə'bɒmɪnəbl/ *adj* **1** disgusting. **2** (*informal*) very unpleasant: *We had abominable weather during our holidays.*
a,bominable 'snowman *c/def.n* (*also* **yeti**) (*informal*) big creature supposed to live in high mountains in central Asia and look like a person with long hair on its body.
a'bominably *adv.*
abomination /ə,bɒmɪ'neɪʃən/ *n* **1** *u.n* disgust. **2** *c.n* disgusting thing: *Cruelty to animals is an abomination.* **hold s.o/s.t in abomination** feel disgust for s.o/s.t.
aboriginal /,æbə'rɪdʒɪnl/ *adj* **1** (*technical*) having existed in that place from the earliest known times.
Aborigine /,æbə'rɪdʒɪ,ni:/ *unique n* (also *attrib*) original inhabitant of Australia: *the Aborigine culture.*
abort /ə'bɔ:t/ *tr/intr.v* **1** (cause (a baby or young animal) to) be born too soon so that it dies. **2** (cause (a plan, a space flight etc) to) come to an end before the planned time.
abortion /ə'bɔ:ʃən/ *c/u.n* **1** (example of the) removal or loss of a baby before it is born, usu before the end of the 28th week of pregnancy(2), so that the baby dies: *Vanessa had to have an abortion because the foetus was not normal.* ⇨ miscarriage(1), premature(1). **2** (*fig; informal*) event, thing, that is completely unsuccessful: *That dinner party was a total abortion.*
a'bortive *adj* (*formal*) unsuccessful: *He made several abortive attempts to start the engine.*
abound /ə'baʊnd/ *intr.v* (*formal*) exist in great numbers or quantities. **abound in/with s.t** have great numbers or quantities of s.t: *This lake abounds in fish.*
abundance /ə'bʌndəns/ *n* **1** *u.n* plenty; more than enough. **2** *sing.n* (often *an — of* s.t) number or quantity (of s.t) that is more than enough.
a'bundant *adj* existing in numbers or quantities that are more than enough.
a'bundantly *adv.*
about /ə'baʊt/ *adv* **1** here and there; to one side and another or the other; on any side: *The children were running about. The ship was rolling about in the rough sea.* **2** here and there (sometimes suggesting that one is idle): *Don't stand about; come and help!* **3** present; in this/ that place: *Is there anyone about?* **4** present or in your office at 8 a.m? **about turn** (order given to soldiers etc to turn and face in the opposite direction).
▷ *prep* **4** here and there in, on, (s.t): *Stop running about the room!* **5** here and there but suggesting that one is idle: *There were men standing about the place waiting.* **6** present; in this/that place: *Mr Jones is somewhere about the office.* **7** (often *just — s.t*) more or less (s.t); not exactly, but close to (s.t): *It's just about 3 o'clock.* **8** with regard to; on the subject of: *What do you know about this letter?* **9** (becoming *old use*) (a)round: *She was*

wearing pearls about her neck. **10** (while) doing: *Wash these dishes up, and be quick about it! I'm baking a cake and while I'm about it I'll bake some biscuits.* **about to do s.t** going to do s.t very soon: *I can't see Mr Smith just now; I'm about to leave for London.* **have s.t about one** be carrying s.t, usu in a pocket. For verb, noun etc + 'about', e.g *beat about the bush, be on about s.t, know one's way about* (s.t), ⇨ the verb/noun.
above /ə'bʌv/ *adv* Opposite below. **1** (also *up —*) vertically up from s.o/s.t; upstairs; directly over: *I sat above and threw the apples down to him. We looked at the stars above.* Opposite beneath(1). **2** higher than its line or upper surface: *Half the rock was under the water and half above.* **3** (also *up —*) higher without being directly over: *When we looked up at the mountain we could see the top high above.* **4** higher in rank etc: *The invitations are for captains and above.* **5** higher up a river: *We sailed up the Thames to Windsor and places above.* **6** higher on a page; earlier in a book, magazine etc: *See page 4, above.* **7** more in number, age etc: *children of 11 and above.* **8** from below up onto the deck, to a higher place, of a ship: *The captain has gone above to check the sails.* **from above** from a higher position: *Something fell on me from above.* **Heavens above!** ⇨ heaven.
▷ *prep* Opposite **9–14** below. **9** (also *up —*) vertically up from; directly over: *Sue lives in the flat above John.* **10** higher than the line or upper surface of; at a level higher than: *The plane flew above the clouds. The water came above my knees.* **11** higher than without being directly over: *A few trees were growing above the valley.* **12** higher than in rank, social position etc: *A general is above a colonel.* **13** further up a river than: *Windsor is above London.* **14** more in number, age etc than: *To get in, you must be above 16 years of age.* **15** louder than: *One can hear the water running past above the sound of voices.* **16** (often *— s.o's head*) too difficult for (s.o to understand): *This book is above me.* **17** too good, high, important etc to be affected by (s.t): *be above criticism/suspicion* (i.e so good that no one could criticize or suspect one/it). **above all** ⇨ all(*pron*). **above board** ⇨ board¹. **above one's station** ⇨ station. **be above doing s.t** be too good to do s.t bad. **from above s.o/s.t** from over, higher up, than s.o/s.t: *From above the clouds the sky is deep blue.* **over and above s.t** ⇨ over(*prep*).
a,bove-'mentioned *adj* mentioned above(6).
abrasive /ə'breɪsɪv/ *adj* **1** rough and able to scratch things or wear them away: *Don't clean the bath with anything abrasive.* **2** (*fig; derog*) (of a person, a way of talking etc) rude; unpleasant: *What an abrasive man Mr Jones is!*
▷ *c.n* **3** abrasive(1) thing, material.
a'brasively *adv.* **a'brasiveness** *u.n.*
abreast /ə'brest/ *adv* side by side: *Our soldiers marched three abreast.* **be/keep abreast of s.t** (continue) to know all the latest information about s.t.
abridge /ə'brɪdʒ/ *tr.v* make (s.t written) shorter.
a'bridgment *c/u.n* (also **a'bridgement**).
abroad /ə'brɔ:d/ *adv* **1** in, to, one or more foreign countries: *When are you going abroad?* **2** widely; to many or all places: *The good news was spread*

abroad. **from abroad** from one or more foreign countries.

abrogate /'æbrəgeɪt/ *tr.v* (*formal*) make (s.t) stop being the law, rule etc: *We can't just abrogate our treaties with other countries!*

abrogation /ˌæbrə'geɪʃən/ *c/u.n.*

abrupt /ə'brʌpt/ *adj* 1 (very) sudden: *Our pleasant days at school came to an abrupt end with the arrival of the new head teacher.* 2 impolitely quick, without trying to be pleasant: *an abrupt manner of speaking.*

a'bruptly *adv.* **a'bruptness** *u.n.*

abscess /'æbses/ *c.n* part of the body that has been attacked by bacteria so that there is pus under the skin.

abscond /əb'skɒnd/ *intr.v* (often — *from s.w*) (*with s.t*) (*formal*) go away secretly and unlawfully (from a place) (taking s.t with one).

absent /'æbsənt/ *adj* 1 (often — *from s.t*) not present (at s.t, usu s.t one ought to be present at); not in this/that place: *He's been absent from work all week.* 2 (showing that one is) not paying attention or listening: *an absent look in someone's eyes.* 3 lacking: *The male bird has red on its head but in the female this is absent.*

▷ *tr.v* /əb'sent/ 4 **absent oneself (from s.t)** (*formal*) not go to s.t that one ought, was expected, to go to.

absence /'æbsəns/ *c/u.n* (often — *from s.t*) fact or state of being absent(1) (from s.t): *Your absence was noted.* **absence of mind** (*formal*) lack of attention; forgetfulness.

absentee /ˌæbsən'tiː/ *c.n* person who is absent(1).

'absently *adv* in an absent(2) way.

ˌabsent-'minded *adj* not paying attention or listening: *The absent-minded professor came to college without his socks on.*

ˌabsent-'mindedly *adv.* **ˌabsent-'mindedness** *u.n.*

absolute /'æbsəluːt/ *adj* 1 complete; perfect: *We have absolute confidence in the pilot of the plane.* 2 allowing no doubt: *You must have absolute proof before you make an accusation.* 3 (of a ruler, her/his power etc) not limited in any way: *Modern kings and queens are no longer absolute rulers.* **absolute gem** ⇒ gem. **decree absolute** ⇒ decree.

'abso,lutely *adv.*

ˌabso'lute ma,jority *c.n* (*pl -ies*) a majority of more than 50 per cent (⇒ per).

ˌabsolute 'zero *unique n* the lowest temperature so far known to be possible; −273.13° Centigrade.

absolve /əb'zɒlv/ *tr.v* (*formal*) 1 (often — *s.o/ s.t from s.t*) declare (s.o/s.t) to be free (from s.t): *After asking many questions, the police absolved Judy of all blame for the accident.* 2 (of a priest) give (s.o) absolution(1).

absolution /ˌæbsə'luːʃən/ *n* 1 *u.n* (often *give s.o, receive*(6), — (*for s.t*)) forgiveness by a priest (for the bad things he/she has done). 2 *c.n* statement by a priest in a church giving the congregation absolution(1).

absorb /əb'zɔːb/ *tr.v* 1 take (a liquid etc) in: *Blotting paper absorbs ink.* 2 (*fig*) understand (an idea etc): *Did you absorb everything the teacher said?* 3 make (s.t) part of oneself/

itself: *Big companies absorb smaller ones to stop competition.* 4 make (shock, force etc) less.

ab'sorbed *adj* (often — *in s.t*) so busy (doing s.t) that one thinks of nothing else.

ab'sorbent *adj* that absorbs(1) ink, water etc.

ab'sorbing *adj* so interesting that one cannot think about anything else.

absorption /əb'zɔːpʃən/ *u.n.*

abstain /əb'steɪn/ *intr.v* (often — *from* (*doing*) *s.t*) not do (s.t): *500 members voted for Mrs Jones, 452 for Miss Robinson and 12 abstained (from voting).*

ab'stainer *c.n* person who abstains from doing s.t, often from drinking alcoholic(1) drinks.

abstention /əb'stenʃən/, **abstinence** /'æbstɪnəns/ *u.n.*

abstemious /əb'stiːmɪəs/ *adj* (*formal*) moderate, esp in eating and drinking.

ab'stemiously *adv.* **ab'stemiousness** *u.n.*

abstention, abstinence ⇒ abstain.

abstract¹ /'æbstrækt/ *adj* 1 (of or referring to s.t) that cannot be seen, touched etc; not made of matter: *abstract thought*. Opposite concrete(3). 2 that concerns abstract art.

▷ *c.n* 3 example of abstract art. **in the abstract** in general; without looking at particular cases: *It is no use agreeing to a holiday in the abstract; it depends on where you are willing to go.*

ˌabstract 'art *u.n* form of art that does not try to represent things as they really look.

abstraction¹ /əb'strækʃən/ *c.n* thing that is abstract¹(1).

ˌabstract 'noun *c.n* noun that is the name of a quality or state, not the name of s.t one can touch, see etc: *'Size' and 'wickedness' are abstract nouns.* Compare concrete noun.

abstract² /əb'strækt/ *tr.v* (*technical*; *formal*) (often — *s.t from s.t*) remove (s.t) (from s.t), usu by a special process(1).

ab'straction² *u.n* fact or act of abstracting² (s.t).

abstraction³ /əb'strækʃən/ *u.n* (*formal*) absentmindedness.

abstruse /əb'struːs/ *adj* (*formal*) difficult to understand: *an abstruse argument.*

ab'strusely *adv.* **ab'struseness** *u.n.*

absurd /əb'sɜːd/ *adj* foolish; not reasonable.

ab'surdity *c/u.n* (*pl -ies*). **ab'surdly** *adv.*

abundance, abundant(ly) ⇒ abound.

abuse¹ /ə'bjuːs/ *u.n* 1 rude, unkind or cruel etc things said or written. **a stream of abuse** a lot of abuse¹(1).

▷ *tr.v* /ə'bjuːz/ 2 say or write rude, unkind or cruel things to/about (s.o/s.t).

abusive /ə'bjuːsɪv/ *adj* (of a person, what he/ she says or writes etc) full of abuse¹(1): *an abusive letter.*

a'busively *adv.* **a'busiveness** *u.n.*

abuse² /ə'bjuːs/ *c/u.n* 1 (often *an — of s.t*) cruel or dishonest use (of s.t): *an abuse of one's power.*

▷ *tr.v* /ə'bjuːz/ 2 use (one's position, power etc) wrongly, often dishonestly.

abut /ə'bʌt/ *intr.v* (*-tt-*) **abut (up)on s.t** (*formal*) be next to, or touching, s.t: *Mrs Smith's land abuts on ours.*

abysmal /ə'bɪzməl/ *adj* (*informal*) very bad: *abysmal weather*; *an abysmal lack of knowledge.*

a'bysmally adv.

abyss /ə'bɪs/ c.n very deep hole in the ground. (in) **an abyss of s.t** (fig) (in) a state of feeling s.t unpleasant (e.g despair) very strongly.

AC /,eɪ 'siː/ u.n abbr alternating current.

a/c written abbr account(1).

acacia /ə'keɪʃə/ c.n kind of tree from which one gets a kind of gum¹(1) for sticking things.

academy /ə'kædəmɪ/ c/unique n (pl -ies) (often with capital A; an/the — of s.t) **1** college for teaching a particular thing: the Royal Academy of Music. **2** group of professional people connected with a particular subject: the Royal Academy of Arts. ⇨ military academy.

academic /,ækə'demɪk/ adj **1** of or referring to a university, college etc, the things studied there etc: an academic life. **2** of or referring to subjects that provide information and training for the mind rather than for the hands or for practical purposes: academic studies. Compare technical(1). **3** (derog) not practical; not useful in real life: Those objections are purely academic. ▷ c.n **4** person who teaches and studies at a university or college.

,aca'demically adv.

accede /ək'siːd/ intr.v (often — to s.t) (formal) **1** agree (to s.t); accept (s.t): We have acceded to the government's call for help. **2** become a member of s.t: Spain and Portugal have acceded to the EEC. **3** become king, chairperson etc of s.t after the one before has died, retired etc: accede to the throne.

accession /ək'seʃən/ u.n fact or act of acceding.

accelerate /ək'selə,reɪt/ v **1** tr/intr.v (cause (s.t) to) move faster: John was late so he accelerated and drove the rest of the way at 100 kilometres an hour. **2** tr.v (formal) cause (s.t) to happen sooner: We are accelerating the building of the new houses.

acceleration /ək,selə'reɪʃən/ u.n **1** act or fact of accelerating (s.t). **2** ability to accelerate(1); rate at which s.t accelerates(1).

ac'cele,rator n **1** c.n device in a car etc that one presses etc to make it go faster. **2** u.n (technical) substance that makes a chemical change happen faster. **3** c.n (technical) machine for greatly increasing the speed of particles(1) to produce power.

accent /'æksənt/ n **1** c/u.n way of speaking a language by people from a particular part of a country, a particular social class etc: Ian has a very strong Scots accent. **2** c.n emphasis(2) on a (part of a) word: The main accent on 'accentuation' is on the fourth syllable. **3** c.n mark put above some letters in some languages: In the French phrase(1) 'très gêné', all the e's have accents. ▷ tr.v /ək'sent/ **4** pronounce (s.t) with emphasis(2): We accent the first syllable of 'agriculture'.

accentuate /ək'sentju,eɪt/ tr.v make (s.t) seem more important by giving emphasis(1) to it: Her sunburnt skin accentuates the fairness of her hair.

accentuation /ək,sentju'eɪʃən/ c/u.n.

accept /ək'sept/ v **1** tr/intr.v agree to take (s.o/s.t who/that is offered); receive (s.t) and agree to do what is asked: I accept your invitation with great pleasure. He was soon accepted into the family.

2 tr.v (often — that . . .) agree to (s.t, or that . . .): I accept that I made a mistake. **3** tr.v take responsibility for (s.t): I accept the blame for the accident.

acceptability /ək,septə'bɪlɪtɪ/ u.n (often the — of s.t (as s.t)) fact of (s.t) being acceptable (as s.t).

ac'ceptable adj that can be accepted(1). Opposite unacceptable.

ac'ceptance n **1** c/u.n (often the — of s.t) fact of accepting (⇨ accept(v)) (s.t): the acceptance of his offer. **2** c/u.n approval. **3** c.n (commerce) agreement to pay (a bill etc).

access /'ækses/ u.n (often — to s.o/s.t) **1** way of getting into a place, reaching s.o/s.t. **2** opportunity to get, use etc, s.t: Students need to have access to a good library. ▷ tr.v **3** (in computers) get access(1) to (stored information in printed form or on a screen).

accessibility /ək,sesɪ'bɪlɪtɪ/ u.n.

accessible /ək'sesɪbl/ adj able to be reached, got, used etc. Opposite inaccessible.

'access ,road c.n road that gives access(1) to a motorway, a group of houses etc.

accessary ⇨ accessory(2).

accession ⇨ accede.

accessory /ək'sesərɪ/ c.n (pl -ies) **1** (often pl) thing that is not absolutely necessary but that helps to make other things more beautiful, comfortable etc: This white dress would look particularly fine with blue accessories like gloves, belt and shoes. Compare extra(4). **2** (also **ac'cessary**) (law) person who was not present at the time of a crime but helped the criminal(s) before and/or after it. **accessory after/before the fact** person who hides facts about a crime or helps to plan a crime but is not there while the crime is being committed.

accident /'æksɪdənt/ c.n (usu unfortunate) thing that happens for no clear reason, e.g a crash between two cars. **by accident** as a result of an accident; not intentionally: We didn't come together – it was quite by accident that we arrived together.

accidental /,æksɪ'dentl/ adj happening by chance, not intentionally: an accidental meeting.

,acci'dentally adv.

acclaim /ə'kleɪm/ u.n (formal) **1** applause and/ or praise: a film greeted with acclaim. ▷ tr.v **2** greet (s.o/s.t) with acclaim(1). **3** (often — s.o/s.t as s.o/s.t) declare publicly that (s.o/s.t) is particularly good: Shakespeare is acclaimed as England's best dramatist.

acclamation /,æklə'meɪʃən/ u.n (formal) **1** shouts of approval; applause. **2** public declaration by shouting: Nicola was elected president of our club by acclamation.

acclimatize, -ise /ə'klaɪmə,taɪz/ tr/intr.v (cause (s.o/s.t) to) become used to a new climate.

acclimatization, -isation /ə,klaɪmətaɪ'zeɪʃən/ u.n.

accolade /'ækə,leɪd/ c.n great praise; public approval: The film won the accolade of the newspapers.

accommodate /ə'komə,deɪt/ tr.v **1** provide lodging for (s.o). **2** allow enough space for (s.o/ s.t): This seat accommodates three people comfortably. **accommodate to s.t** (formal) change in such a way as to fit s.t: *Young people accommodate easily to new conditions.*

ac'commodating *adj* willing to fit in with others.

accommodation /ə,kɒmə'deɪʃən/ *u.n* house, room(s) etc in which to live; lodging(s). *accommodation to s.t* (*formal*) changing in such a way as to fit in with s.t.

accompany /ə'kʌmpənɪ/ *tr.v* (*-ies, -ied*) **1** go s.w with (s.o/s.t): *I shall accompany you as far as the station.* **2** happen, exist, at the same time as (s.t): *Lack of wind is often accompanied by fog here.* **3** play music to support (one or more singers, a soloist etc): *Maureen accompanied the singer on the piano.*

ac'companiment *c/u.n* thing that accompanies (1–3) s.o/s.t. *to the accompaniment of s.t* (*formal*) accompanied (2,3) by s.t: *Joe won the race to the accompaniment of cheers from his friends.*

ac'companist *c.n* person who accompanies (3) s.o.

accomplice /ə'kʌmplɪs/ *c.n* partner in doing s.t bad.

accomplish /ə'kʌmplɪʃ/ *tr.v* complete (s.t), do (s.t), successfully: *accomplish a difficult job.*

ac'complished *adj* very skilful: *an accomplished tennis player.*

ac'complishment *n* **1** *u.n* fact or act of accomplishing (s.t). **2** *c.n* thing accomplished (⇒ accomplish). **3** *c.n* thing that one is accomplished at; skill: *One of Mary's accomplishments is playing the violin.*

accord /ə'kɔːd/ *c/u.n* (*formal*) agreement: *The two countries have reached (an) accord on trade. of one's own accord* without being forced or told to by anyone else; freely. *with one accord* all together.

ac'cordance *u.n in accordance with s.t* (*formal*) in agreement with s.t; following what is said or ordered in s.t: *in accordance with the rules.*

ac'cording *adv* **1** *according to s.o/s.t* (a) as stated, shown, by s.o/s.t: *According to Diana, it snowed here last week.* (b) in a way that depends on s.o/s.t: *We dress according to the weather.* **2** *according as . . .* (*formal*) in so far as . . .; to the extent that . . .; depending on the extent to which . . .: *According as something becomes more transparent it becomes less easy to see.*

ac'cordingly *adv* **1** therefore; so: *I was told to hurry; accordingly, I came by train.* **2** in the way that has been said, indicated etc: *I thought it was going to snow so I dressed accordingly.*

accordion /ə'kɔːdɪən/ *c.n* kind of musical instrument that is carried and played by pressing from the sides to push air in and out.

accost /ə'kɒst/ *tr.v* (*formal*) **1** go up to (s.o, usu a stranger) and speak to (her/him) first. **2** go up to (s.o) and ask for s.t, usu money.

account /ə'kaʊnt/ *c.n* **1** (*written abbr* a/c) statement of money owed and paid or paid in and out. **2** (often (*give*) *an — of s.t*), report, story, (about s.t) in speech or writing. *current/deposit/joint/ savings account* ⇒ current etc. *bring/call s.o to account (for s.t)* (a) make s.o explain s.t, usu s.t bad he/she has done. (b) punish s.o (for s.t). *by/ from all accounts* according to what everyone says. *have an account with s.o* keep money with a bank etc. *leave s.o/s.t out of account*

not include s.o/s.t in one's calculations. *not on any account; on no account* not for any reason. *of some, no* etc *account* having some, no etc importance. *on account of s.o/ s.t* because of s.o/s.t. *open/close an account* start/end an account(1) at a bank etc. *put s.t down to one's/s.o's account* buy s.t without paying for it at once, so that the account(1) is sent in later. *put/turn s.t to (good) account* use s.t to one's advantage. *render an account (to s.o)* prepare and send an account(1) (to s.o). *settle an account, accounts, (with s.o)* (a) pay what is owing (to s.o). (b) get revenge or satisfaction (from s.o) for s.t bad he or she has done. *take (no) account of s.o/s.t* pay (no) attention to s.o/s.t. *take s.o/s.t into account* include s.o/s.t in one's calculations.
▷ *intr.v* (usu *— (to s.o) for s.t*) **3** give an explanation (to s.o) (of s.t one has done etc). **4** be responsible (to s.o) (for s.t).

ac'countable *adj* **1** (often *— (to s.o) for s.t*) responsible (to s.o) (for s.t): *I hold you accountable for what happened.* **2** having to give an explanation. Compare account(3).

ac'countancy *u.n* job of an accountant.

ac'countant *c.n* person whose job is to keep and/or examine accounts(1). *chartered accountant* ⇒ charter.

accredited /ə'kredɪtɪd/ *adj* (*formal*) having an official right and duty to represent s.o, a company, a government etc.

accretion /ə'kriːʃən/ *n* (*formal*) **1** *u.n* growing by having additions made. **2** *c.n* thing that is added in this way.

accrue /ə'kruː/ *intr.v* (often *— to s.t*) (*formal*) increase by being added (to s.t). *accrue to s.o* come to s.o as a result of accruing.

accumulate /ə'kjuː,mjuːleɪt/ *tr/intr.v* (cause (s.t) to) become greater in number or quantity: *Rubbish accumulates quickly if you don't clear it regularly.*

accumulation /ə,kjuː,mjuː'leɪʃən/ *n* **1** *u.n* fact or act of accumulating (s.t). **2** *c.n* thing accumulated: *an accumulation of jobs to do.*

ac'cumu,lator *c.n* (*technical*) cell in which electricity is stored.

accurate /'ækjʊrət/ *adj* exact; correct. Opposite inaccurate.

'accuracy *u.n.* **'accurately** *adv.*

accursed /ə'kɜːst/ *adj* (*formal*) **1** hated. **2** suffering under a curse.

accusative /ə'kjuːzətɪv/ *adj/c.n* (*grammar*) (of the) form of a word when it is the direct object of a sentence: *The accusative form of the pronoun 'he' is 'him' as in 'I love him'.* ⇒ nominative.

accuse /ə'kjuːz/ *tr.v* (often *— s.o/s.t of (doing) s.t*) say that (s.o/s.t) has done, is doing, s.t wrong, wicked etc.

accusation /,ækjʊ'zeɪʃən/ *n* **1** *u.n* act or fact of accusing (s.o/s.t of (doing) s.t). **2** *c.n* thing of which one accuses s.o/s.t: *an accusation of dishonesty.*

ac'cused *def.n* (*law*) person in a court of law who is accused of a crime.

ac'cuser *c.n* person who accuses s.o/s.t.

ac'cusing *adj* in a way that accuses s.o/s.t: *an accusing look.*

ac'cusingly *adv.*

accustom /ə'kʌstəm/ *tr.v accustom oneself/*

s.o/s.t to s.t cause oneself, another person, an animal, to become used(2) to s.t.

ac'customed *adj* usual: *Pauline went to her accustomed restaurant for lunch.* **accustomed to (doing) s.t** used(2) to (doing) s.t: *The children are quite accustomed to travelling by bus now.*

ace /eɪs/ *c.n* 1 (usu *the — of hearts, spades* etc) playing card with the highest value or with the value of one. 2 person who is very good at s.t, usu a sport: *a cycling ace.*

acetone /'æsɪˌtəʊn/ *u.n* kind of liquid used as a solvent², e.g to remove nail-polish, *chem.form* CH₃COCH₃.

acetylene /ə'setɪˌliːn/ *u.n* (also *attrib*) kind of gas that burns very brightly and is used for melting and cutting metal, *chem.form* C₂H₂: *an acetylene torch.*

ache /eɪk/ *c.n* 1 (used in combinations; often *have an — (in s.t)*) dull continuous pain (in one of one's ears etc): *have a headache; have (a) toothache; have an ache in your heel.*
▷ *intr.v* 2 (of a person, a (part of the) body) have an ache(1): *I'm aching all over. My head aches.*

achieve /ə'tʃiːv/ *tr.v* 1 complete (s.t) successfully: *Helen has achieved her ambition to become a doctor.* 2 get, reach, (s.t, usu s.t difficult): *Einstein achieved great fame as a scientist.*
a'chievable *adj* that can be achieved.
a'chievement *n* 1 *u.n* (often *the — of s.t*) act or fact of achieving (s.t). 2 *c.n* thing achieved.

acid /'æsɪd/ *adj* 1 sour to the taste: *Lemon juice is acid.* 2 of or referring to acid(4), an acid(5). 3 (*fig*) (of a person, her/his way of speaking etc) unpleasant; sour(1): *an acid remark.*
▷ *n* 4 *c/u.n* (*technical*) substance that gives off hydrogen when it is put with water. 5 *c.n* substance, usu a liquid, that has an acid(1) taste. 6 *u.n* (*slang*) LSD(1).
acidity /ə'sɪdɪtɪ/ *u.n* 1 fact or quality of being acid(1). 2 unpleasant feeling in one's stomach caused by acid(5).
'acidly *adv* in an acid(3) way.

acknowledge /ək'nɒlɪdʒ/ *tr.v* 1 (often *— that, what, how* etc . . .) admit that (s.t) is true: *He acknowledged that he was wrong.* 2 (also *— receipt of (s.t)*) say that (s.t) has been received: *She acknowledged (receipt of) the letter from the company.* 3 show one's appreciation(1) of support, praise etc from people.
ack'nowledgement *c/u.n* (also **ack'nowledgment**) (example of the) fact or act of acknowledging (s.t). **in acknowledgement (of s.t) (a)** as a means of acknowledging (s.t): *I sent John a telegram in acknowledgement of his parcel.* **(b)** as a reward for s.t: *Sue has been made a CBE in acknowledgement of her services.*

acme /'ækmɪ/ *c/def.n* (often *the — of s.t*) highest point (of development etc).

acne /'æknɪ/ *u.n* disease, usu of young people, marked by unpleasant spots on the face, back etc.

acorn /'eɪkɔːn/ *c.n* fruit of the oak(1).

acoustic /ə'kuːstɪk/ *adj* of or referring to sound or hearing.
a'coustically *adv.*
a'coustics *n* 1 *u.n* science of sound. 2 *pl.n* qualities of a building etc that affect how well sounds can be heard in it.

acquaint /ə'kweɪnt/ *tr.v* **acquaint oneself/s.o with s.t** make oneself/s.o familiar with s.t; give oneself/s.o information about s.t.

ac'quaintance *n* 1 *u.n* (often (*have*) *some* etc *— with s.t*) knowledge that one has gained (about s.t). 2 *c.n* person one has met but is not (yet) a friend. **a passing acquaintance** person one has met but only for a short time. **make s.o's acquaintance; make the acquaintance of s.o** meet s.o (and get to know her/him).
ac'quainted *adj* (often *— with s.o*) in a state of knowing each other (or s.o).

acquiesce /ˌækwɪ'es/ *intr.v* (*formal*) agree; give in: *He acquiesced and said he would come.*
ˌacqui'escent *adj.*

acquire /ə'kwaɪə/ *tr.v* gain, get, obtain(1), (s.t): *acquire a good knowledge of French.*
ac'quired *adj* gained through one's own efforts: *an acquired taste.*
Acquired Immune Deficiency Syndrome /əˌkwaɪəd ɪ'mjuːn dɪˌfɪʃənsɪ ˌsɪndrəʊm/ *u.n* (*abbr* AIDS) disease passed from person to person through the blood or sexual intercourse and causing the body to stop being able to resist diseases.
ac'quirement *n* (also **acquisition** /ˌækwɪ'zɪʃən/) 1 *u.n.* fact or act of acquiring (s.t). 2 *c.n* thing acquired (⇒ acquire).
acquisitive /ə'kwɪzɪtɪv/ *adj* (often *derog*) who likes to acquire a lot of things.
ac'quisitively *adv.* **ac'quisitiveness** *u.n.*

acquit /ə'kwɪt/ *tr.v* (*-tt-*) (often *— s.o of s.t*) (usu in a court of law) declare that (s.o) is not guilty (of s.t).
ac'quittal *c/u.n.*

acre /'eɪkə/ *c.n* unit of measure of area equalling 4840 square yards²(1) or about 4000 square metres. ⇒ hectare.
acreage /'eɪkrɪdʒ/ *u.n* area of land measured in acres.

acrid /'ækrɪd/ *adj* 1 having a sharp bitter smell or taste. 2 (*derog*) (of a person, her/his way of speaking etc) sharp and unpleasant.

acrimony /'ækrɪmənɪ/ *u.n* (of an argument, a way of speaking etc) bitterness; annoyance.
acrimonious /ˌækrɪ'məʊnɪəs/ *adj* full of acrimony.
ˌacri'moniously *adv.*

acrobat /'ækrəˌbæt/ *c.n* person who performs difficult gymnastic(1) acts, e.g in a circus.
ˌacro'batic *adj* of or like an acrobat.
ˌacro'batically *adv.*
ˌacro'batics *n* 1 *u.n* skill of an acrobat. 2 *pl.n* acts performed by an acrobat.

across /ə'krɒs/ *adv* 1 from one side to the other; from one corner to the opposite one; in a direction forming a cross: *This river is deep; how do we get across?* 2 (often *— from s.t*) on the other side: *My house isn't on this side of the road; it is across from here.* **get/put s.t across (to s.o)** ⇒ get, put. **five metres** etc **across** five metres etc measured from one side to the other.
▷ *prep* 3 from one side of (s.t) to the other; from one corner of (s.t) to the opposite one; in a direction forming a cross with (s.t): *How do we get across this road safely?* ⇒ across(1). 4 (often *— s.t from s.t*) on the other side of (s.t): *My house is across the road from the post office.* ⇒ across(2). **across country** ⇒ country. **come/run across s.o/s.t** ⇒ come, run. **cut across s.t** ⇒ cut. **from across s.t**

from the other side of s.t: *That cat is from across the river.*

a,cross-the-'board *attrib.adj* so as to affect everybody/everything: *an across-the-board increase in taxes.*

acrylic /ə'krɪlɪk/ *adj* made by man from *acrylic acid* (a kind of liquid that is used to make synthetic cloth, plastics(3) or resins(2)).

act /ækt/ *c.n* **1** thing that one does; action; deed: *It would be a kind act to let that sick pupil go home.* **2** (often with capital **A**) one of the main parts into which a play is divided: *Act 1 of Shakespeare's 'Hamlet'.* ⇨ scene(1). **3** one of the parts of a show, e.g in a circus. **4** (often with capital **A**) law passed by parliament etc. **5** (*derog; informal*) pretence: *That little boy hasn't really got a headache; it's just an act to get out of work.* (**catch s.o**) **in the act** (**of doing s.t**) (catch s.o) while he/she is actually doing s.t, usu s.t bad. **get in on the/s.o's act** (*informal*) manage to share s.t that s.o else is doing, usu in such a way that one gains from this. **put on an act** pretend. Compare act(5,9).

▷ *v* **6** *intr.v* do s.t; perform an action: *Unless we act quickly it will be too late.* **7** *intr.v* be an actor/ actress in a play. **8** *tr.v* act(7) as (s.o) in a play: *Carol is acting Juliet in our school play.* **9** *tr/ intr.v* (*derog*) behave as if one were acting(7,8) (a part) in a play: *Don't pay any attention to John's complaints; he's just acting (the hurt husband).* ⇨ overact. **act as s.o/s.t** do the job, duties, of s.o/s.t. **act for s.o** represent s.o, e.g in a law case. **act s.t out** express s.t, e.g what one is feeling, in actions not words. **act up** (*informal*) behave badly. **act** (**up**)**on s.o/s.t** (e.g of a medicine) have an effect(1) on s.o/s.t. **act** (**up**)**on s.t** do what is suggested by s.o./s.t.

'acting *attrib.adj* doing the duties of the person whose name follows: *the acting manager.*

action /'ækʃən/ *n* **1** *c.n* thing done; deed; act(1). ⇨ inaction. **2** *def.n* (often *the — of s.t*) way s.t, e.g the brakes of a car, act(6); way of doing s.t. **3** *c.n* (often *the — of s.t*) parts of a clock etc that move. **4** *c.n* (often *the — of s.t*) effect, workings, (of s.t): *Chlorophyll is produced in plants by the action of light.* **5** *c.n* (often *an — for s.t*) (*law*) case[1](6). **6** *c/u.n* fight(ing) in a war etc: *killed in action.* **7** *c.n* events in a film, book etc. **8** *def.n* (*informal*) excitement; interest: *Don't stay here; come out into the streets where the action is!* **bring s.t into action** start using s.t. **go into action** start fighting, working. **in action** (**a**) busy doing s.t. (**b**) taking part in a battle. **out of action** no longer working, often because of damage. **put s.o/s.t out of action** stop s.o/s.t working: *An electric fault put our computer out of action.* **set s.t in action** start s.t working: *You set the machine in action by pressing this button.* **swing into action** begin doing s.t quickly and efficiently. **take action** begin to act(6). **take action against s.o/s.t** start to do s.t against s.o/s.t. **take evasive action** ⇨ evasive.

'actionable *adj* (*law*) that gives a good case for starting an action(5): *an actionable statement.*

activate /'æktɪ,veɪt/ *tr.v* make (s.t) active; put (s.t) into operation: *activate a machine.*

activation /,æktɪ'veɪʃən/ *u.n.*

active /'æktɪv/ *adj* **1** who/that is working, able and/or very willing to work: *Peter is a very active*

member of our club. Opposite inactive(1,2). **2** that is (still) able to produce certain results: *an active volcano* (i.e one that can still erupt(1)). Opposite inactive(3); extinct(2). **3** (*grammar*) (of a verb) the subject[1](4) of which does the action: *In 'I saw him', the verb is active; in 'I was seen by him' it is passive*(3). **under active consideration** ⇨ consideration.

▷ *def.n* **4** (*grammar*) (verb in the) active voice.

,active 'service *u.n* (often *on —*) taking part in fighting as a member of the armed services.

,active 'voice *def.n.* (*grammar*) form of a verb in a sentence used when the subject[1](4) does the action, e.g 'My brother *took* the photograph', 'Who *broke* the window?' ⇨ passive voice.

'actively *adv.*

'activist *c.n* person who takes an active(1) part in s.t, often politics.

ac'tivity *n* (*pl -ies*) **1** *u.n.* fact of being active(1). **2** *c.n* thing in which one is active(1). **3** *c.n* (often *pl*) (often *the — of s.o*) action; deed.

,act of 'God *c.n* natural happening such as a storm or earthquake that cannot be prevented.

actor /'æktə/ *c.n* man or boy who acts(7) in a play.

actress /'æktrɪs/ *c.n* woman or girl who acts(7) in a play.

actual /'æktʃʊəl/ *adj* real; really existing: *the actual cost.* **in** (**actual**) **fact** ⇨ fact.

'actually *adv* **1** really; truly: *I don't believe anything actually happened.* **2** although it may seem strange: *I actually saw a small boy with white hair yesterday!*

actuary /'æktʃʊərɪ/ *c.n* (*pl -ies*) person whose job is to work out risks using statistics(1) and then advise insurance companies how much to charge for them.

actuate /'æktʃʊ,eɪt/ *tr.v* cause (s.t) to start working: *Pressing this button actuates the bell.*

acumen /'ækju:mən/ *u.n* (*formal*) ability to understand things quickly and well.

acupuncture /'ækjʊ,pʌŋktʃə/ *u.n* act, process, system, of putting fine needles into the skin to cure diseases.

acute /ə'kju:t/ *adj* **1** (of pain etc) very strong or severe. **2** dangerously great: *an acute lack of engineers.* **3** (of the brain, hearing etc) very sharp and efficient: *Many animals have an acute sense of smell.* **4** (of an illness) quickly reaching a severe state. ⇨ chronic. **5** (of a sound) unpleasantly high in pitch[1](4). **6** (of an angle in geometry) less than 90°. Compare obtuse(3).

a'cute ,accent *c.n* kind of accent that is on the e's in French 'été'. ⇨ circumflex, grave[3].

a'cutely *adv.* **a'cuteness** *u.n.*

ad /æd/ *c.n* (*informal*) advertisement(2).

AD /,eɪ 'di:/ *abbr* Anno Domini: *1066 AD.* Compare BC.

adamant /'ædəmənt/ *adj* absolutely determined; not willing to change at all.

'adamantly *adv.*

Adam's apple /'ædəmz ,æpl/ *c.n* part of the front of a man's throat that sticks out in a lump and moves up and down when one swallows or speaks.

adapt /ə'dæpt/ *v* **1** *tr/intr.v* (*— (oneself/s.o/s.t) to s.t*) (cause (oneself/s.o/s.t) to) fit, become more suited to, new conditions: *The young adapt to change easily.* **2** *tr.v* (usu *— s.t (from s.t) for/to s.t*) take (a play etc) (from another country, language etc) and fit it to other needs: *His book has now been adapted for television.*

a,dapta'bility *u.n* (often *the — of s.o/s.t to s.t*) fact or quality of (s.o/s.t) being adaptable (to s.t).

a'daptable *adj* who/that can adapt(1) s.t or be adapted (easily).

adaptation /ˌædəp'teɪʃən/ *n* **1** *u.n* (often *— (of s.t) to s.t*) act or fact of (s.t) adapting or being adapted (to s.t, e.g a new climate). **2** *c.n* thing that has (been) adapted.

a'dapter /ə'dæptə/ *c.n* (also **a'daptor**) person or thing who/that adapts (s.t): *an adapter that allows one to use an English plug(3) in an American socket.*

ADC /ˌeɪ di: 'si:/ *c.n abbr* aide-de-camp .

add /æd/ *tr.v* (often *— s.t to s.t*) put (s.t) with s.t else to produce a larger number or amount of it. **add s.t and s.t together** put two or more things together. **add up** (**a**) increase in quantity, value etc: *If you save regularly every month it soon adds up.* (**b**) (*informal*) make sense: *She was once happy and now suddenly she's very sad — it just doesn't add up.* **add s.t up** find the total of s.t: *If you add 5, 7 and 8 up, you get 20.*

addition /ə'dɪʃən/ *n* **1** *u.n* act or fact of adding (s.t). **2** *c.n* thing that is added or joined to s.t. **in addition** (**to s.o/s.t**) including; as well (as s.o/s.t).

ad'ditional *adj* extra; that has been added to s.t: *additional information.*

ad'ditionally *adv.*

additive /'ædɪtɪv/ *c.n* substance that one adds in small amounts to s.t else to improve its taste, colour etc: *food/petrol additives.*

adder /'ædə/ *c.n* kind of small poisonous snake found in Europe etc; viper(1).

addict /'ædɪkt/ *c.n* person who has an addiction to s.t, esp a drug(2).

addicted /ə'dɪktɪd/ *adj* (often *— to s.t*) having an addiction to s.t.

addiction /ə'dɪkʃən/ *c/u.n* (often *— to s.t*) fact of not being able to free oneself from a harmful habit: drug(2) *addiction*; *addiction to smoking.*

ad'dictive *adj* (of a drug(1,2) etc) that it is easy to become addicted to.

addition(al(ly), additive ⇒ add.

addled /'ædld/ *adj* **1** (of an egg) that has gone bad. **2** (of a person's brain) that has become confused, usu through thinking for too long.

address /ə'dres/ *c.n* **1** details of where one lives, e.g the name of the street and town and the number of the house. **2** formal speech to an audience. **3** code(4) etc that finds particular information on a computer.

▷ *tr.v* **4** (often *— s.t to s.o/s.t*) write the name and address(1) (of s.o/s.t) on (an envelope etc). **5** give an address(2) to (an audience etc). **6** (*formal*) speak to (s.o).

addressee /ˌædre'si:/ *c.n* person to whom a letter etc is addressed(4).

adenoids /'ædəˌnɔɪdz/ *pl.n* soft masses that grow at the back of one's nose and throat and can make it difficult to breathe and hear if they become too big.

adept /'ædept/ *adj* **1** (often *— at (doing) s.t*) very skilful (at (doing) s.t).

▷ *c.n* **2** (often *— at (doing) s.t*) person adept(1) (at (doing) s.t).

adequate /'ædɪkwɪt/ *adj* (often *— for s.o/s.t*) **1** enough (for s.o/s.t) (but no more). **2** good enough (for s.t). Opposite inadequate.

'adequacy *u.n.* **'adequately** *adv.*

adhere /əd'hɪə/ *intr.v* (often *— to s.t*) (*formal*) stick (to s.t) with glue etc. **adhere to s.t** (*fig*; *formal*) join a political party etc and support it firmly; hold an opinion etc firmly.

ad'herence *u.n.*

ad'herent *c.n* (*formal*) person who adheres to a political party etc.

adhesion /əd'hi:ʒən/ *n* **1** *u.n* (*formal*) fact of adhering (to s.t). **2** *c/u.n* (*medical*) joining together of parts inside one's body that should not join together, often after an operation(1).

adhesive /əd'hi:sɪv/ *adj* **1** that can adhere easily.

▷ *c/u.n* **2** adhesive(1) substance, e.g glue.

adieu /ə'dju:/ *interj/c.n* (*French*) goodbye.

adj *written abbr* adjective.

adjacent /ə'dʒeɪsnt/ *adj* (often *— to s.o/s.t*) who/that is very near (s.o/s.t): *When the fire began, all adjacent buildings were evacuated.*

adjective /'ædʒəktɪv/ *c.n* (*written abbr* adj) (*grammar*) word that describes s.o/s.t represented by a noun or pronoun: *In 'This is a small house', 'This house is small' and 'It is cold today', 'small' and 'cold' are adjectives.*

adjectival /ˌædʒək'taɪvl/ *adj* (*grammar*) of or referring to an adjective.

adjourn /ə'dʒɜ:n/ *tr/intr.v* (often *— (s.t) for s.t, till/until s.t*) stop (s.t) with the intention of starting it again at a later time (in order to do s.t else): *Shall we adjourn for lunch now?*

a'djournment *c/u.n.*

adjudge /ə'dʒʌdʒ/ *tr.v* (*law or formal*) (often *— that . . .; — s.o/s.t (to be) s.t*) decide or state officially or by law (that . . . etc): *George was adjudged to be responsible for the accident.*

adjudicate /ə'dʒu:dɪˌkeɪt/ *tr/intr.v* (*law or formal*) (often *— (up)on s.t*) act as a judge (in (s.t)); give an official decision or judgement (about (s.t)).

adjudication /əˌdʒu:dɪ'keɪʃən/ *u.n.*

a'djudi,cator *c.n* person who adjudicates (s.t).

adjunct /'ædʒʌŋkt/ *c.n* **1** thing that is added to s.t without this being necessary. **2** (*grammar*) adverb or adverbial phrase.

adjust /ə'dʒʌst/ *v* **1** *tr/intr.v* (often *— (s.t) to s.t*) change (s.t), usu a little, in order to fit in with s.t else: *You can adjust the temperature in your room to your taste.* **2** *tr.v* arrange (s.t, e.g one's tie) in the proper way.

a'djustable *adj* that can be adjusted(1): *adjustable seats in a car.*

a,djustable 'spanner *c.n* spanner with a screw that can be turned to make the opening wider or narrower to fit nuts(2) and bolts²(2) of different sizes.

a'djustment *n* **1** *u.n* act or fact of adjusting (s.t). **2** *c.n* thing done to adjust (s.t): *The mirror needs an adjustment.*

adjutant /'ædʒətənt/ *c.n* officer in a regiment(1) etc who looks after the office work.

Adm *written abbr* Admiral.

administer /əd'mɪnɪstə/ *tr.v* **1** control, manage, (the affairs of a company etc). **2** (often *— s.t to* s.o) give (a medicine etc) (to s.o). **administer an oath (to s.o)** ⇒ oath(1).

administration /ədˌmɪnɪˈstreɪʃən/ n **1** u.n (often the — of s.t) control or management (of a company etc). **2** u.n (often the — of s.t) fact or act of administering (s.t). **3** c/def.n (often with capital **A**) government.

administrative /ədˈmɪnɪstrətɪv/ adj of or referring to (the) administration.

adˈministratively adv.

administrator /ədˈmɪnɪˌstreɪtə/ c.n **1** person who administers (s.t). **2** person who has been officially given the job of administering(1) s.o else's affairs, usu because he/she is too old, ill etc to do it herself/himself.

admirable ⇒ admire.

admiral /ˈædmɪrəl/ c.n (written abbr **Adm**) (in the British navy) officer of the second highest rank. **red admiral** ⇒ red.

ˌadmiral of the ˈfleet c.n (in the British navy) officer of the highest rank.

ˈAdmiralty def.n (also attrib) branch of the civil service that is in charge of the Royal Navy.

admire /ədˈmaɪə/ tr.v (often — s.o/s.t for s.t) look at or treat (s.o/s.t) with pleasure and respect (because of s.t): admire the view; admire a person for her/his honesty.

admirable /ˈædmɪrəbl/ adj who/that deserves to be admired.

ˈadmirably adv.

admiration /ˌædmɪˈreɪʃən/ u.n (often — for s.o/s.t) feeling of pleasure and respect (for s.o/s.t). **the admiration of s.o** the person/thing admired by s.o: Her beauty and charm make her the admiration of all who see her.

adˈmirer c.n (often — of s.o/s.t) person who admires s.o/s.t.

adˈmiring adj (usu attrib) feeling or showing admiration: admiring looks.

admit /ədˈmɪt/ tr.v (-tt-) **1** (often — s.o/s.t in(to s.t); — s.o to s.t) allow (s.o/s.t) to enter or come in(to s.t): Children are only admitted if accompanied(1) by an adult. **2** (often — that . . . ; — s.t to be true etc) confess or agree (that s.t bad is true): The man finally admitted that he had not stopped after hitting someone with his car. **3** (usu — of s.t) (formal) allow (s.t); leave the possibility of (s.t): The facts you have just told us admit of other explanations than the one you have given. **admit to (doing) s.t** admit(2) (that one has done) s.t.

adˌmissiˈbility u.n fact of being admissible.

adˈmissible adj that can be accepted (for discussion), esp in a court of law: Hearsay evidence(2) is not admissible. Opposite inadmissible.

admission /ədˈmɪʃən/ n **1** c/u.n act or fact of admitting(1) (s.o/s.t): an admission to a meeting. **2** u.n price for being admitted(1), e.g to a cinema or museum. **3** c/u.n act or fact of admitting(2) s.t: an admission of guilt.

adˈmittance u.n (often — to s.t) = admission(1). **gain admittance** manage to enter.

adˈmittedly adv one has to admit that . . . : I like Caroline; admittedly, she can be very rude but she has never been that to me.

ado /əˈduː/ u.n **1 without further/more/much ado** without delaying, worrying etc any/much more. **2 much ado about nothing** a lot of

fuss(1) about s.t that is really not at all important.

adolescent /ˌædəˈlesnt/ adj **1** of or referring to an adolescent(3). **2** (derog) = childish.

▷ c.n **3** person who is no longer a child but is not yet an adult. **4** (derog) adult who behaves like a child.

ˌadoˈlescence u.n time between childhood and becoming an adult.

adopt /əˈdɒpt/ tr.v **1** make (s.o, usu a child) legally a member of one's family: If you can't have any children yourselves, why don't you adopt one? Compare foster(1). **2** take (s.o else's idea, way of dressing etc) and use or follow it oneself: Before you adopt these new methods make sure they suit you. **3** accept (a suggestion, a plan, a candidate(1) for an election etc).

adoption /əˈdɒpʃən/ u.n.

aˈdoptive attrib.adj (formal) who has adopted(1) s.o: Jane is William's adoptive mother.

adore /əˈdɔː/ tr.v **1** worship (s.o, e.g God); love (s.o) strongly and respectfully. **2** (informal) like (s.o/s.t) very much: I adore grapes!

aˈdorable adj **1** who/that deserves to be adored(1). **2** (informal) attractive; very pleasing: What an adorable little house!

aˈdorably adv.

adoration /ˌædəˈreɪʃən/ u.n (often — of s.o). **aˈdorer** c.n person who adores s.o/s.t.

aˈdoring adj (usu attrib) feeling or showing adoration: an adoring look.

adorn /əˈdɔːn/ tr.v (often — s.o/s.t with s.t) (formal) put s.t on (s.o/s.t), add s.t to (s.t), to make her/him/it more beautiful, interesting etc.

aˈdornment n **1** u.n act or fact of adorning s.o/s.t. **2** c.n thing that adorns (s.o/s.t).

adrenalin /əˈdrenəlɪn/ u.n **1** substance produced by one's body when one is angry, afraid etc; it makes one's heart beat faster and allows one to act more quickly and violently than usual. **2** (medical) substance of this kind produced from animals.

adrift /əˈdrɪft/ pred.adj/adv **1** (of a boat etc) not tied up, usu when it should be, and therefore drifting⁴. **2** (fig) not properly controlled, helped etc.

adroit /əˈdrɔɪt/ adj (often — at/in s.t) (formal) quick and skilful or clever (at/in s.t).

aˈdroitly adv. **aˈdroitness** u.n.

adulation /ˌædjʊˈleɪʃən/ u.n great, often too much, praise.

adult /ˈædʌlt/ adj **1** of a person or animal who/ that is fully grown: She's not adult enough to understand.

▷ c.n **2** person who is treated as a mature person, esp by the law, because he/she has reached a certain age. ⇒ adolescent(3). **3** animal that has reached a certain age.

ˈadulthood u.n state of being an adult.

adulterate /əˈdʌltəˌreɪt/ tr.v (often — s.t with s.t) spoil (s.t) by adding s.t less good, pure etc to it: They have adulterated the good soil with a poor variety.

adultery /əˈdʌltərɪ/ u.n act of having sex with a person who is not one's own husband/wife. **commit adultery** have sex in this way.

aˈdulterer c.n man who commits adultery.

aˈdulteress c.n woman who commits adultery.

aˈdulterous adj of or referring to adultery.

adulthood ⇨ adult.

adv *written abbr* adverb.

advance /ədˈvɑːns/ *attrib.adj* **1** that comes, goes, before s.o/s.t: *advance warning of a meeting*; *an advance party in the army*.

▷ *c.n* **2** (often — *of s.t*) movement forward; progress: *an advance of 10 metres*; *the advance of the expedition*(2). **3** (often — *in s.t*) improvement (in a field of study, investigation etc): *advances in education*. **4** (often *an* — *of* £20 etc (*on one's wages* etc)) money given to s.o before he/she is due to receive it. **an advance on s.t** an improvement compared with s.t: *The motor vehicle was a great advance on the horse and carriage*. **in advance** (**of s.o/s.t**) before (s.o/s.t) in time or place: *We had some meetings of our committee in advance of the conference*.

▷ *v* **5** *tr/intr.v* (often — *against/* (*up*) *on s.o/s.t*) (cause (s.o/s.t, e.g an army) to) move forward (against s.o/s.t, e.g an enemy). **6** *tr/intr.v* (often — (*s.o/s.t*) *to s.t*) move (s.o/s.t) to a better, higher, more important etc, position; (cause (s.o/s.t) to) make progress: *Philip has been advanced to captain*. Compare promote(1). **7** *tr.v* (often — *s.t to s.t*) change the time of (s.t) to a later time: *Clocks must be advanced one hour at midnight*. Compare back(11), forward(9). **8** *tr.v* (often — *s.o/s.t*) give s.o (s.t, usu money) as an advance(4).

adˈvanced *adj* **1** very modern. **2** (of education etc) at a high level: *advanced studies*. Opposite elementary(1).

adˈvancement *u.n* act or fact of advancing(5,6).

advantage /ədˈvɑːntɪdʒ/ *c.n* (often — (*over s.o/ s.t*); *have the* — *of s.t*) thing that helps one, could help one, to be successful in s.t (as against s.o/s.t else). **Advantage Graf** etc (in tennis) Miss Graf etc has won a point after deuceˈ(1). **be to s.o's advantage** be s.t that helps s.o to get what he/ she needs or wants. **take advantage of s.o** cheat s.o, usu by using her/his kindness unfairly. **take (full) advantage of s.t** use s.t in a way that gives one an (excellent) advantage.

advantageous /ˌædvənˈteɪdʒəs/ *adj* useful; helpful; that gives one an advantage.

ˌadvanˈtageously *adv*.

adventure /ədˈventʃə/ *n* **1** *c.n* happening, activity etc that is unusual, exciting and sometimes dangerous: *For the children, their first trip to a big city was quite an adventure*. **2** *u.n* excitement, often with some danger as well: *live a life of adventure*.

adˈventurer *c.n* **1** person who enjoys adventure(s). **2** person who tries to become rich, important etc, either by taking risks or (*derog*) by bad means, e.g by trying to win the love of a rich woman whom he does not love.

adˈventuresome *adj* bold; feeling or showing a love of adventure(2).

adˈventuress *c.n* (*derog*) female adventurer(2).

adˈventurous *adj* bold; adventuresome.

adˈventurously *adv*.

adverb /ˈædvɜːb/ *c.n* (*written abbr* adv) (*grammar*) word that adds s.t to the meaning of a verb, adjective, other adverb, phrase(1) or sentence: *In 'see well', 'well trained', 'well inside (the town)', 'well' is an adverb; and in 'Unfortunately, I can't come', 'unfortunately' is an adverb too*.

adverbial /ædˈvɜːbɪəl/ *adj* (*grammar*) of or referring to an adverb.

adˈverbial ˌparticle *c.n* (*grammar*) particle(2) that is an adverb used as part of a phrasal verb.

adˈverbial ˌphrase *c.n* (*grammar*) phrase(1) that contains an adverb.

adverse /ˈædvɜːs/ *adj* (*formal*) that is against one; unfavourable: *adverse winds*; *adverse publicity*(2).

adversary /ˈædvəsərɪ/ *c.n* (*pl* -ies) enemy; person against whom one is playing a match etc.

adˈversity *c/u.n* (*pl* -ies) (piece of) bad luck, trouble or misfortune.

advert /ˈædvɜːt/ *c.n* (*informal*) advertisement(2).

advertise /ˈædvətaɪz/ *tr/intr.v* (often — *for s.o/ s.t*; — *that . . .*) state publicly, often in newspapers, on television etc that one wants to sell, buy etc (s.t): *We are advertising for more staff. You can advertise that you've got something for sale in our shop window*.

advertisement /ədˈvɜːtɪsmənt/ *n* (*informal* ad(vert)) **1** *u.n* fact or act of advertising (⇨ advertise). **2** *c.n* notice stating what one is advertising (⇨ advertise).

ˈadverˌtiser *c.n* person or business who/that advertises.

ˈadverˌtising *u.n* business of preparing and producing advertisements.

advice /ədˈvaɪs/ *n* **1** *u.n* thing said or written to suggest what s.o else should do: *My advice (to you) is not to buy that house because it is too expensive*. **2** *c.n* (usu *pl*) (*commerce*) written statement warning a company etc that s.t has been sent to them and giving details. **follow/take s.o's advice** do what s.o advises(1). **ignore s.o's advice** not do what s.o advises(1).

adˌvisaˈbility *u.n* (often *the* — *of* (*doing*) *s.t*) fact of being advisable.

advisable /ədˈvaɪzəbl/ *adj* that is a wise thing to do: *It is advisable to listen when people who know more than you do are talking*. Opposite inadvisable.

advise /ədˈvaɪz/ *tr.v* **1** (often — *s.o about/on s.t, to do s.t, what/where* etc *to do s.t*) give (s.o) advice(1) (about s.t, what to do etc). **2** (often — *s.o of s.t, that/where* etc . . .) (*formal*) inform (s.o) (about s.t, that etc . . .): *Are you going to advise Mrs Jones of your expected time of arrival?* ⇨ ill-advised, well-advised.

adˈviser *c.n* person who gives advice.

adˈvisory *adj* (usu *attrib*) **1** who/that gives advice as (part of) her/his/its job. **2** that contains advice, not orders; recommended.

advocate /ˈædvəkət/ *c.n* **1** lawyer whose job is to represent people in a court of law. ⇨ attorney, barrister, solicitor. **2** (often *an* — *of s.t*) person who advocates(3) s.t.

▷ *tr.v*/ˈædvəˌkeɪt/ **3** (often — *doing s.t*) (*formal*) support, speak/write in support of, (an argument, idea etc): *Do you advocate accepting the offer?*

advocacy /ˈædvəkəsɪ/ *u.n*.

aegis /ˈiːdʒɪs/ *def.n* **under the aegis of s.o/s.t** that has the support of s.o, a government, the church etc.

aerial /ˈeərɪəl/ *attrib.adj* **1** that is in, comes from, the air: *aerial pollution*.

▷ *c.n* **2** device to receive radio or television signals.

aerobatics /ˌeərəˈbætɪks/ *u.n* trick flying, usu

by planes as a performance for the public or as
a means of escaping an enemy plane.

aerodrome /ˈeərəˌdrəʊm/ c.n kind of small
airport, usu for the airforce or private planes.
⇒ airfield.

aerodynamics /ˌeərədaɪˈnæmɪks/ u.n (technical) study of the forces that affect, are caused by,
gases, esp air and esp with reference to planes.

aeronautics /ˌeərəˈnɔːtɪks/ u.n (technical) science of flight, mostly of planes.

aeroplane /ˈeərəˌpleɪn/ c.n (US **ˈairˌplane**) =
plane¹(2).

aerosol /ˈeərəˌsɒl/ c.n kind of can in which a
liquid is under great pressure, so that when it
comes out it does so in a fine mist(1); this liquid
itself.

aesthetic /iːsˈθetɪk/ adj (US **esˈthetic**) of,
referring to, having, the appreciation(1) of beautiful things.
aesˈthetically adv (US **esˈthetically**).
aesˈthetics u.n (US **esˈthetics**) study of
beauty.

afar /əˈfɑː/ adv (often from —) (literary) a long
distance away: People come from afar to see our
beautiful village.

affable /ˈæfəbl/ adj (formal) (showing that one
is) ready and willing to be polite and pleasant:
an affable manner.
affability /ˌæfəˈbɪlɪtɪ/ u.n. **ˈaffably** adv.

affair /əˈfeə/ c.n 1 (often pl) thing that s.o has
done, is doing, is going to do etc, ought to do etc;
business; matter(3): Stop interfering in my affairs!
This is my affair; it doesn't concern you at all.
John's business affairs are in a very confused state.
2 thing that happens; event: The wedding was a
very enjoyable affair for all. 3 (often have an —
(with s.o)) sexual intercourse (with s.o, with each
other) when not married to each other. **current
affairs** ⇒ current. **settle one's affairs** pay your
rent, debts, bills etc and put things in order. **state
of affairs** ⇒ state(n).
afˌfairs of ˈstate pl.n government business.

affect¹ /əˈfekt/ tr.v 1 cause some result in (s.o/
s.t); have an effect(1) on (s.o/s.t): Very hot weather
affects some people badly. 2 make (s.o) feel an
emotion(1), e.g of love or pity: The death of Joe's
grandfather affected him deeply.
afˈfection u.n love that is not very strong but is
good and kind. **have an affection for s.o/s.t** like
s.o/s.t.
affectionate /əˈfekʃənɪt/ adj feeling or showing
affection.
afˈfectionately adv.

affect² /əˈfekt/ tr.v (formal) (often — to do s.t)
pretend to have, feel etc (s.t): When I told George
about my sister, he affected disinterest(2) but I
knew he was really deeply interested.
affectation /ˌæfekˈteɪʃən/ c/u.n (example of)
affected behaviour etc.
afˈfected adj (derog) behaving, talking etc in
an unpleasantly artificial way, usu to try to make
people think one is more important etc than one
really is.

affidavit /ˌæfɪˈdeɪvɪt/ c.n (law) written statement that one has officially sworn to be true.

affiliate /əˈfɪlɪˌeɪt/ tr/intr.v (often — to/with s.t)
(cause (s.o/s.t, e.g a club) to) join (s.t, e.g another
club).
affiliation /əˌfɪlɪˈeɪʃən/ c/u.n.

affinity /əˈfɪnɪtɪ/ n (pl -ies) 1 c/u.n (often —
between s.o/s.t and s.o/s.t; — with s.o/s.t) relationship, similarity(1) or connection (between s.o/
s.t and s.o/s.t etc), sometimes by marriage: The
affinities between the British and the Irish are
great. 2 c.n (often — for/to s.o, between s.o and
s.o) attraction (for s.o/s.t etc); strong feeling of
liking and understanding (for s.o/s.t etc): Joan
has an affinity for clever men.

affirm /əˈfɜːm/ v 1 tr.v (often — that . . .) say
(s.t) firmly; declare(3) (s.t): Can you really and
honestly affirm that you were not there at the
time? 2 intr.v (law) promise to tell the truth
but without taking an oath because one believes
that it is wicked.
affirmation /ˌæfəˈmeɪʃən/ c/u.n.
affirmative /əˈfɜːmətɪv/ adj 1 that means 'Yes':
an affirmative answer. Opposite negative(1).
▷ def.n 2 meaning 'Yes'. **answer in the affirmative**
answer in a way that means 'Yes'. Opposite
negative(6).
afˈfirmatively adv.

affix /əˈfɪks/ tr.v (often — s.t to s.t) (formal) stick,
fix etc (a stamp etc) on(to a letter etc).

afflict /əˈflɪkt/ tr.v (often — s.o with s.t) trouble
(s.o) (with s.t); make (s.o) feel pain, sadness
etc (because of s.t): afflicted with rheumatism/
remorse.
afˈfliction n 1 u.n state of being afflicted. 2 c.n
thing that afflicts s.o.

affluent /ˈæfluənt/ adj rich; wealthy: the affluent
society.
ˈaffluence u.n.

afford /əˈfɔːd/ tr.v (often — to do s.t) have enough
money or time (to buy, get, do etc (s.t)): Can you
afford a new car? I'm sorry, but I can't come to the
cinema with you because I can't afford the time.
ill afford (to do) s.t ⇒ ill(adv).

affray /əˈfreɪ/ c.n (law; formal) public fight that
causes a disturbance and trouble.

affront /əˈfrʌnt/ c.n 1 (often an — to s.o/s.t)
insult.
▷ tr.v 2 insult (s.o/s.t).

afield /əˈfiːld/ adv **far afield** far away, usu from
home.

afloat /əˈfləʊt/ pred.adj 1 floating on water, air
etc: The little boat is still afloat. 2 at sea; as a
sailor etc: Ted's life afloat lasted 30 years. 3 (often
— with s.t) flooded (with s.t): After the heavy rain
our garden was afloat with muddy water. **keep
(oneself/s.o) afloat** (fig) keep (oneself/s.o) out
of debt: I need a loan to keep me afloat until the
end of the month.

aforementioned /əˈfɔːˌmenʃənd/ adj (also
aforesaid /əˈfɔːˌsed/) 1 (formal) who/that
has been mentioned before.
▷ def.n 2 person, animal or thing who/that has been
mentioned before.

aforethought /əˈfɔːˌθɔːt/ ⇒ malice.

afraid /əˈfreɪd/ pred.adj 1 (often — of s.o/s.t)
frightened, feeling fear, (because of s.o/s.t).
2 (often — of doing s.t) worried, anxious,
(about doing s.t) in case one does wrong, makes
a mistake etc: afraid of saying the wrong thing.
3 (often — (that) . . .; — so/not) sorry but . . .:
I'm afraid I'm going to be late. 'Are you having
any snow this year?' 'I'm afraid so/not.' **be afraid
to do s.t** not want to do s.t because of fear.

afresh /əˈfreʃ/ adv (formal) (starting) again:

If you've made a mistake you must start afresh.

aft /ɑ:ft/ *adj/adv* at, in, towards, the back part, esp of a boat. Opposite fore(1,2). **fore and aft** ⇒ fore(*adv*).

after /'ɑ:ftə/ *adv* 1 (often *an hour* etc —; *soon* —) later in time, sometimes immediately following, sometimes not: *I got there at 10 and Harry arrived soon after.* 2 behind: *A bus passed with several cars following after.*

▷ *prep* 3 later in time than, sometimes immediately following, sometimes not: *The day after tomorrow is Saturday.* Compare after(1), before(2). 4 behind: *They followed each other down the stairs one after the other.* Compare after(2), before(5). 5 chasing; trying to get/catch (s.o/ s.t): *I've got a job but I'm after a better one.* 6 when one has passed, completed: *After a few kilometres the road crosses a river.* 7 later than the beginning of: *after dark.* 8 next in order of importance to: *After water, sleep is our most important need.* 9 following and as a result of: *After the way the boy behaved I was not surprised his mother was angry with him.* 10 following and in spite of: *It is surprising that she still talks to him after the way he behaved last week.* 11 (of a work of art etc) in the manner of: *This painting is after Rembrandt.* **after a fashion/manner** not well but well enough to be recognized for what it is supposed to be. **after all** ⇒ all(*pron*). **after tax** ⇒ tax(1). **day after day**, **time after time**, **mistake after mistake** etc one day etc after another, often with the suggestion of it being tiring or boring. For verb + 'after', e.g *ask after s.o/s.t*, *hunger after s.t*, *look after s.o/s.t*, *name s.o/s.t after s.o/s.t*, ⇒ the verb.

'**after,birth** *def.n* placenta and membranes that come out of a woman's vagina after childbirth.

'**after-ef,fect** *c.n* (often *pl*) (usu unpleasant) thing that is the result of s.t but does not happen immediately after it: *John is suffering from the after-effects of his big meal last night.*

'**afters** *pl.n* (*informal*) course that comes after the main one of a meal; it is usu sweet.

'**after-,sale** *attrib.adj* happening after a sale(1): *after-sale service.*

'**after,thought** *c.n* thing one thinks of, adds, later.

'**afterwards** /'ɑ:ftəwədz/ *adv* later.

afternoon /ˌɑ:ftə'nu:n/ *c/unique n* (also *attrib*) time between midday and evening: *It will be afternoon soon and then we can rest. I like an afternoon rest.*

again /ə'geɪn, ə'gen/ *adv* 1 once more; another time: *Goodbye, come again soon.* 2 in the place, state etc in which he/she/it was before: *If you take something you should put it back again when you finish with it.* 3 (usu *and* (then) —) also: *You can't go swimming today because it's too cold; and then again you have work to do.* **again and again** repeatedly. **as many/much again** the same number/amount as before: *She sold all her fruit in ten minutes and could have sold five times as much again if she had had it.* (**every**) **now and again** ⇒ now. **once/yet again** ⇒ once, yet. (**the**) **same again** ⇒ same(*pron*). **time and** (**time**) **again** ⇒ time(*n*).

against /ə'geɪnst, ə'genst/ *adv* 1 not in favour; opposed: *When we had a vote, there were 120 for*

and only 23 against. 2 (of chances or likelihood) that s.t will not happen etc: *The chances of an accident are a million to one against.*

▷ *prep* 3 not in favour of; opposed to: *I'm against your buying a car.* ⇒ against(1). 4 in the opposite direction to: *swim against the current.* Opposite with(11). 5 towards; so as to touch or be stopped by: *I hit my head against a wall.* 6 (of chances etc) that (s.t) will not happen etc: *The* odds(3) *are ten to one against your horse.* ⇒ against(2). 7 in front of and often contrasted(5) with (a background etc): *The island stood out clearly against the white clouds behind it.* 8 opposite: *That mark against your name means that you have passed your examination.* 9 in comparison with: *The discomfort of the* operation(1) *is nothing against the relief you will feel afterwards.* **have** (**got**) **something**, **nothing**, **not anything**, **against s.o/s.t** feel, not feel, dislike, hatred, etc for s.o/s.t: *What have you got against him? He's very pleasant. I haven't got anything against you personally.* For verb, adverb or noun + 'against', e.g *borrow* (*money* etc) *against s.t*, *hope against hope* (*that . . .*), *race against time*, ⇒ the verb, adverb or noun.

age /eɪdʒ/ *n* 1 *c/u.n* number of years, months etc during which a person or animal has been alive, or during which s.t has existed: *What was your age last birthday?* 2 *u.n* (fact of having reached a) late part of one's life or of the life of s.t: *You can see plenty of signs of age in this building.* 3 *c.n* (also *attrib*) (often with capital **A**) (people of a) time in history lasting a (large) number of years: *the Stone Age*; *the age of the Roman emperors*; *ages to come.* 4 *c.n* (often *pl*) (*informal*) (thing that seems a) very long time: *It's an age* (or *It's ages*) *since I had a real holiday.* **be of age** be old enough for s.t, e.g to vote etc. **come of age** reach this age. **in this day and age** ⇒ day. **for ages** (**and ages**) for a long time: *I've been waiting for ages.* **middle/old age** the middle/late years of one's life. **over/under age** too old/young for s.t.

▷ *tr/intr.v* 5 (cause (s.o/s.t) to) become old; show signs of age(2): *Poor Fred is ageing fast.* 6 (cause (wine etc) to) become better by keeping or treating it.

aged /eɪdʒd/ *adj* 1 having (been) aged (⇒ age(6)). **aged 45** etc having the age(1) of 45 etc.

▷ *attrib.adj/def.pl.n* /'eɪdʒəd/ 2 very old: *an aged woman*; *the sick and the aged.*

'**age-,group** *c.n* group of people of (almost) the same age: *People of my age-group are mostly retired.*

'**ageless** *adj* 1 who/that never becomes, never seems to become, old(er). 2 that never stops being true, the same etc: *the ageless needs of human beings.*

'**age-,long** *adj* lasting for a very long time.

,**age of con'sent** *def.n* age at which a person is allowed by law to marry or to have sex with another person.

'**age-,old** *adj* that has existed for a very long time.

agency ⇒ agent.

agenda /ə'dʒendə/ *c.n* (*pl* -s) list of things to be dealt with at a meeting etc.

agent /'eɪdʒənt/ *c.n* 1 person who acts for, represents, s.o else, a company etc. 2 person whose job is to bring buyers and sellers together for business. **3** = secret agent. **4** (often — *of s.t*) thing that causes a change in s.t: *a chemical agent.*

'agency *n* (*pl -ies*) **1** *c.n* job, business or office of an agent(1,2): *An employment agency finds work for people and workers for employers.* **2** *u.n* (often *through the — of s.t*) action of an agent(4).

age-old ⇨ age.

aggravate /'ægrəˌveɪt/ *tr.v* **1** make (s.t, e.g an illness) worse. **2** (*informal*) make (s.o) angry; annoy (s.o).

aggravation /ˌægrə'veɪʃən/ *u.n.*

aggression /ə'greʃən/ *n* **1** *c/u.n* (usu unjust) attack(s). **2** *u.n* wish to attack. ⇨ non-aggression.

ag'gressive /ə'gresɪv/ *adj* **1** (always) wanting, ready, to attack: *It is good to be a little aggressive in business but people who are aggressive in social life are not popular.* **2** (of a weapon etc) intended for use in attack. Opposite defensive(1).

ag'gressor *c.n* person, country etc who/that makes the first (usu unjust) attack.

aggro /'ægrəʊ/ *u.n* (*slang*) aggressive(1) behaviour.

aggrieved /ə'griːvd/ *adj* (often — *at/over s.t*) feeling that one is being, has been, treated unjustly (in s.t): *Sarah is rightly aggrieved at her dismissal.*

aghast /ə'gɑːst/ *adj* (often — *at s.t*) shocked (at s.t); suddenly feeling afraid or surprised in a very unpleasant way (by s.t).

agile /'ædʒaɪl/ *adj* active; able to move very quickly and easily.

'agilely *adv.*

agility /ə'dʒɪlɪti/ *u.n.*

agitate /'ædʒɪˌteɪt/ *v* **1** *tr.v* shake (s.t, often a container of liquid). **2** *tr.v* make (s.o) feel worried or anxious. **3** *intr.v* (often — *against/for s.t*) argue strongly and publicly (against/for s.t).

'agi,tated *adj* worried or anxious.

agitation /ˌædʒɪ'teɪʃən/ *u.n.*

'agi,tator *c.n* person who agitates(3): *political agitators.*

AGM /ˌeɪ dʒiː 'em/ *c.n abbr* Annual General Meeting.

agnostic /æg'nɒstɪk/ *c.n* (also *attrib*) person who believes that one cannot prove that God exists or does not exist. Compare atheist.

agnosticism /æg'nɒstɪˌsɪzəm/ *u.n.*

ago /ə'gəʊ/ *adv* in the past (from now): *I started this work a year ago.* Compare before(2). **long ago** = long(*adv*).

agony /'ægəni/ *c/u.n* (*pl -ies*) (often *in —*) great pain of body or mind. **pile/put/turn on the agony** (*fig*; *informal*) describe s.t in a way that makes it seem much worse than it really is.

agonize, -ise /'ægəˌnaɪz/ *intr.v* (often — *about/over s.t*) be very worried or concerned (about s.t): *Stop agonizing over something you can do nothing about.*

'ago,nized, -ised *adj* that shows that s.o is in agony.

'ago,nizing, -ising *adj* causing agony.

'agony ,column *c.n* (*joking*) part of a newspaper, magazine etc where people write personal letters that are answered by a journalist.

agoraphobia /ˌægərə'fəʊbɪə/ *u.n* (*medical*) fear of being in a big open space. Compare claustrophobia.

agree /ə'griː/ *v* **1** *intr.v* (often — *to s.t*; — *to do*

s.t) accept (s.t); say that one will do (s.t): *She agreed to pay for the repairs.* **2** *intr.v* (often — (*with s.o*) *about/(up)on s.t, that . . .*) say that one is of the same opinion (as s.o) (about s.t, that . . .): *I agree with you that it is warm enough to swim today.* **3** *intr.v* be able to live, work etc together in harmony(2). **4** *tr.v* (*informal*) accept (s.t), usu after arguments or discussions: *We have agreed new wages with the employers at last.* **agree to differ** stop trying to make each other change her/his mind and remain friends in spite of having different ideas.

a'greeable *adj* **1** pleasant. **2** (usu *pred*; often — *to* (*doing*) *s.t*) willing (to accept, do etc s.t).

a'greeably *adv* pleasantly: *I was agreeably surprised by her offer to help.*

a'greed-up,on *attrib.adj* (also **a'greed**) that has been accepted: *We shall meet at the agreed (-upon) place at 6 this evening.* ⇨ agree(2).

a'greement *n* **1** *u.n* fact or state of agreeing. **2** *c.n* (often *arrive at, come to, make, an — with s.o* (*for s.t, to do s.t*)) thing agreed with each other by people. **3** *u.n* (*grammar*) fact of a noun etc having a form that fits with that of a verb etc: *If the subject is 'I' you must have 'am' after it, not 'are' or 'is', so as to have agreement.* **break an agreement** not do what one has agreed to do. **in agreement (a)** (often — *with s.o/s.t*) in such a way that one agrees(2,3) (with s.o/s.t). **(b)** showing agreement(1): *When I said it was time to go the children nodded in agreement.*

agriculture /'ægrɪˌkʌltʃə/ *u.n* cultivation of the soil and sometimes also other farming work.

,agri'cultural *adj* of or referring to agriculture.

aground /ə'graʊnd/ *pred.adj* (often *run —*) (of a ship etc) onto the bottom, rocks etc in the sea etc.

ah /ɑː/ *interj* (sound showing (pleased) surprise, sadness, pain etc): *Ah, here's our dinner at last!*

aha /ɑː'hɑː/ *interj* (sound showing (pleased) surprise, satisfaction etc): *Aha, I've found it.*

ahead /ə'hed/ *adv* **1** (often — *of s.o/s.t*) further towards the front, further forward, (than s.o/s.t), e.g in a race: *Our horse was several metres ahead of the next one. The road ahead is quite dark. There is a river ahead of us.* Opposite behind(1). **2** in, towards, the future: *look ahead.* **ahead of s.o/s.t (a)** ⇨ ahead(1). **(b)** better than s.o/s.t because of having made more progress. **get/go ahead** ⇨ get, go.

ahem /ə'hem/ *interj* (sound like a small cough showing that one wants s.o to listen to what one is going to say, or showing some doubt etc).

AI /ˌeɪ 'aɪ/ *abbr* Artificial Insemination.

aid /eɪd/ *c/u.n* **1** help; thing that helps. ⇨ hearing aid, audiovisual aid. **come/go to s.o's aid** come/go to help s.o.

▷ *tr.v* **2** help (s.o/s.t).

aide-de-camp /ˌeɪd də 'kɒŋ/ *c.n* (*pl aides-de-camp* /ˌeɪd də 'kɒŋ/) (*French*) officer in the armed forces whose job is to help a senior(1) officer.

AIDS /eɪdz/ *u.n abbr* Acquired Immune Deficiency Syndrome (⇨ acquire).

ailment /'eɪlmənt/ *c.n* (*formal*) illness.

aim /eɪm/ *n* **1** *u.n* pointing of a weapon at s.o/s.t, usu with the intention of trying to shoot, hit etc her/him/it: *Luckily the man's aim was not good and his shot missed.* **2** *u.n* directing of words

at s.o/s.t, sometimes with the purpose of being critical or rude: *Lynne's aim was good and the man was soon ashamed of himself.* **3** *c.n* (often *s.o's* — *in* (*doing*) *s.t*) purpose (in (doing) s.t): *John's main aim in life is to make money.* **take aim (at s.o/s.t)** aim(4,5) a gun etc (at s.o/s.t).
▷ *tr/intr.v* **4** (often — (*s.t*) *at* s.o/s.t; — *for* s.o/s.t) point (a weapon) at s.o/s.t, usu with the purpose of trying to shoot etc her/him/it. ⇒ aim(1). **5** (often — (*s.t*) *at* s.o) direct (words) at s.o/s.t: *Was that remark aimed at me?* ⇒ aim(2). **aim to do s.t** have s.t as one's purpose/goal.
'aimless *adj* (*derog*) not having any aim(3).
'aimlessly *adv.* **'aimlessness** *u.n.*
ain't /eɪnt/ *aux.v* (do not use!) am/are/is not; have/has not.
air /eə/ *n* **1** *u.n* substance that we breathe and that surrounds the earth; it is a mixture of gases. **2** *def.n* space above the ground: *I jumped high into the air.* **3** *u.n* (also *attrib*) plane: *go on holiday by air*; *air travel.* **4** *c.n* (often — *of* s.t) appearance (of s.t); manner; feeling caused: *That man has an air of importance.* **5** *c.n* (*music*) tune. **clear the air** (a) make the air fresh by opening a window etc. (b) (*fig*) stop people feeling suspicious, doubtful etc by explaining things. **in the air** (a) above the ground. (b) (*fig*) not certain; not yet agreed: *Our plans are still in the air.* (c) (*fig*) being talked about: *There are interesting new ideas in the air.* **disappear into thin air** (*fig*) disappear completely and mysteriously. **on/off the air** broadcasting, not broadcasting, on radio/television. **take the air** (*formal*) go for a walk, drive etc to get fresh air. **tread on air** ⇒ tread(v).
▷ *tr.v* **6** let air(1) get (in) to (a bed, a room etc) to make it dry or fresh. **7** talk about, give, (an opinion etc): *Anyone can air their views at our meetings.*
'air,bed *c.n* rubber bed filled with air(1).
'air,borne *adj* carried by air(1,3): *an airborne disease*; *airborne army units.*
,Air ,Chief/Vice 'Marshal *c.n* (also **,Air 'Marshal**) officer of high rank in the Royal Air Force.
,Air 'Commo,dore *c.n* officer of high rank in the Royal Air Force above a Group Captain but below an Air Vice Marshal.
,air-con'ditioned *adj* supplied with air that is kept at the temperature one wants.
,air-con'ditioning *u.n* (system for) keeping a room etc air-conditioned.
'air ,cover *u.n* planes used to protect troops on the ground.
'air,craft *c.n* (*pl aircraft*) planc.
'air,craft ,carrier *c.n* (also **'carrier**) naval ship carrying planes that can take off and land on it.
'air,craftsman *c.n* (*pl -men*) lowest rank for men in the Royal Air Force.
'aircrafts,woman *c.n* (*pl -,women*) lowest rank for women in the Royal Air Force.
'air-,crew *c.n* people who fly a plane, e.g the pilot, navigator, engineer.
'air ,cushion *c.n* rubber cushion filled with air(1).
'air,field *c.n* flat area of land, smaller and less important than an airport, where planes take off and land. ⇒ aerodrome.
'air,force *c.n* branch of the armed forces that uses aircraft to fight. Compare army(1); navy(1).
'airfreight *u.n* **1** carriage of goods by air.

▷ *tr.v* **2** send (goods) by air. ⇒ freight.
'air,gun *c.n* gun that fires shots by air pressure.
'air ,hostess *c.n* woman who looks after the passengers in a plane.
airing /'eərɪŋ/ *c.n* (often *get*, *give s.t*, *an —*) **1** drying of clothes etc by dry air, heat etc. **2** (*fig*) (of opinions etc) chance to be heard by other people.
'airing-,cupboard *c.n* warm cupboard for drying clothes etc.
'airless *adj* **1** without fresh air. **2** (of weather) without any wind.
'air ,letter *c.n* letter made of thin paper to be folded and sent by air; it is already stamped.
'air,line *c.n* company that operates passenger planes.
'air,liner *c.n* big plane for passengers.
'air,mail *u.n* letters etc carried by planes.
'airman *c.n* (*pl -men*) **1** man who flies planes. **2** man in the airforce who is not an officer.
'air,plane *c.n* (US) plane.
'air,port *c.n* place where passengers get into and off planes, and where big planes take off and land. ⇒ aerodrome, airfield.
'air ,raid *c.n* attack by planes with bombs.
'air ,rifle *c.n* = airgun.
,air-,sea 'rescue *c/u.n* (example of) work of saving people from the sea using boats, helicopters etc.
'air,ship *c.n* large long balloon filled with gas, used to carry passengers and cargo.
'air ,space *u.n* air above a country that is controlled by it.
'air ,terminal *c.n* place in a city, airport etc from/to which passengers are taken to/from planes.
'air,tight *adj* that does not allow air through: *an airtight joint.*
,air-to-'air *adj* (of a missile(1)) fired by one plane to try to hit another in the air.
,air-to-'ground *adj* (of a missile(1)) fired by a plane to try to hit s.t on the ground.
'air,way *c.n* wide stretch of the sky along which planes fly.
'air,woman *c.n* (*pl -,women*) **1** woman who flies a plane. **2** woman in the airforce who is not an officer.
'air,worthiness *u.n* state or fact of being airworthy.
'air,worthy *adj* (*-ier, -iest*) (of a plane) in a fit and safe state for flying.
'airy *adj* (*-ier, -iest*) **1** of, like or in the air(1,2). **2** having plenty of fresh air.
aisle /aɪl/ *c.n* passage between rows of seats in a church, theatre, plane etc.
aitch /eɪtʃ/ *c.n* letter H, h. **drop one's aitches** not pronounce the h's at the beginnings of words, e.g say ' 'ouse' instead of 'house'.
ajar /ə'dʒɑ:/ *pred.adj* slightly open.
à la carte /,ɑ: lɑ: 'kɑ:t/ *adj* **1** (*French*) that one chooses from a list in a restaurant etc and pays for according to what one has: *an à la carte meal.* Opposite table d'hôte.
▷ *adv* **2** (*French*) choosing à la carte(1).
alacrity /ə'lækrɪtɪ/ *u.n* (often *do s.t with —*) cheerful willingness.
alarm /ə'lɑ:m/ *n* **1** *u.n* (often — *at* s.t) state of sudden fear (because of s.t). **2** *c.n* sound, sign, e.g a flashing red light, that warns of danger. **3** *c.n*

= alarm clock or the device on it that causes it to ring. **burglar alarm** ⇨ burglar. **false alarm** ⇨ false. **give/raise/sound the alarm** ring a bell etc as a warning of danger. **in alarm** because one is suddenly frightened: *jump up in alarm*. **set an alarm** arrange the alarm(3) on a clock to ring at a certain time.
▷ *tr.v* 4 make (s.o, an animal) feel sudden fear.
a**'larm ,clock** *c.n* clock that can ring at any time one wants it to wake one up etc.
a**'larming** *adj* that frightens one.
a**'larmingly** *adv*.
a**'larmist** *c.n* (*derog*) person who causes unnecessary alarm(1).
alas /ə'læs/ *interj* (expressing sadness or pity) unfortunately.
album /'ælbəm/ *c.n* empty book into which one can put photographs, stamps etc: *a photograph/ stamp album*.
alcohol /'ælkə,hɒl/ *u.n* kind of chemical compound(1) of carbon(1) and hydrogen that makes wine, beer, whisky(1) etc able to make a person drunk.
,**alco'holic** *adj* 1 containing alcohol: *alcoholic drinks*. 2 of or referring to, caused by, alcohol: *alcoholic depression*(1). ⇨ non-alcoholic.
▷ *c.n* 3 person who drinks too much alcohol and cannot stop doing so.
alcove /'ælkəʊv/ *c.n* small area in a room etc that is set back in a wall and in which one can put a bed, a small table, some shelves etc.
alderman /'ɔːldəmən/ *c.n* (*pl -men /-mən/*) one of the chief elected members of a city etc council; councillor.
ale /eɪl/ *u.n* kind of beer.
alert /ə'lɜːt/ *adj* 1 fully awake and watchful. 2 having/showing a quick mind.
▷ *c.n* 3 warning of danger, e.g of an air raid. Compare all clear(2). 4 time during which people are on the alert. **on the alert** = alert(1).
▷ *tr.v* 5 (often — *s.o to s.t*) warn (s.o of s.t, e.g danger): *The barking of the dog alerted them to their danger*.
a**'lertly** *adv*. a**'lertness** *u.n*.
algae /'ældʒiː/ *pl.n* very simple plants that grow in or near water.
algebra /'ældʒɪbrə/ *u.n* kind of mathematics that uses letters and numbers, e.g 2x + 3y = 12.
,**alge'braic** /,ældʒɪ'breɪk/ *adj* (also ,**alge'braical**).
alias /'eɪlɪəs/ *adv* 1 also called; also calling herself/himself, often for a criminal purpose: *Henry Jones, alias Henry James, alias the Red*.
▷ *c.n* 2 false name; name that is not one's real one.
alibi /'ælɪ,baɪ/ *c.n* 1 statement that a person accused of a crime etc was at a different place when it happened so that he/she cannot be guilty. 2 (*informal*) excuse.
alien /'eɪlɪən/ *adj* 1 belonging to another country; foreign. 2 (often — *to s.t*) (very) different in nature or character (from s.t): *I don't believe Jack did it; violence is alien to his nature*.
▷ *c.n* 3 person from another country; person living in a country that is not her/his own; foreigner.
alienate /'eɪlɪə,neɪt/ *tr.v* cause (s.o/s.t) to stop being friendly: *alienate s.o's affections* (i.e make s.o stop loving one).
alienation /,eɪlɪə'neɪʃən/ *u.n*.

alight[1] /ə'laɪt/ *pred.adj* burning; on fire: *It was difficult to get the damp wood alight*.
alight[2] /ə'laɪt/ *intr.v* (*formal*) (often — *from s.t*) get down (from a train, bus etc).
align /ə'laɪn/ *tr.v* (often — *s.o/s.t with s.o/s.t*) 1 place (s.o/s.t) in line (with s.o/s.t): *Please align the words on this page with each other*. 2 join (a country, political opinion etc) to form a group. Compare non-aligned.
a**'lignment** *u.n*. Compare non-alignment.
alike /ə'laɪk/ *pred.adj* like each other: *The two sisters are very alike*.
alimentary canal /,ælɪ,mentərɪ kə'næl/ *c.n* tube or passage in the body that carries food to be digested(3).
alimony /'ælɪmənɪ/ *u.n* money a husband has to pay his divorced/separated wife.
alive /ə'laɪv/ *pred.adj* 1 (still) living: *Is your grandmother alive?* Opposite dead. 2 lively; active: *Graham still looks very alive at 80*. 3 still being practised, talked about etc: *The old customs are still alive in our village*. **alive and kicking** (*informal*) in good health and with lots of energy(1). **alive to s.t** knowing s.t (well): *I am well alive to the dangers of this line of action*. **alive with s.t** having many insects etc in or on one/it: *The poor child's hair was alive with* lice (⇨ louse(1)). **keep s.t alive** prevent s.t, e.g an old custom, from dying.
alkali /'ælkə,laɪ/ *c/u.n* kind of chemical substance, e.g bicarbonate of soda, that neutralizes acids.
'**alka,line** *adj* of, referring to, consisting of, alkali.
all /ɔːl/ *adj* 1 (often — *the*, *my*, *this* etc money etc ; — *the*, *my*, *these* etc books etc ; *it*, *they* etc —) the full number or quantity of: *All foreign money must be changed into pounds. All books must be handed in to the library. 'Is all this bread for us?' 'Have you got all your children at home?' 'Yes, they're all here.'* 2 the greatest possible: *with all haste/speed*. 3 any possibility of: *beyond all doubt*. 4 nothing except: *Patricia is all heart* (i.e she has very strong kind feelings). **all the family** etc (**that**) . . . the only family etc (that) . . .: *For many children in Hong Kong, a small boat is all the home they have ever known*. **at all events** ⇨ event. **of all people** surprisingly, among all the possible people: *Why did you choose Andy to help you of all people when you know he's the most useless person in the college?* **on all fours** ⇨ four.
▷ *adv* 5 completely; quite(1): *all alone*. **all along** (*informal*) during the whole of the time: *I knew all along that we would be late*. **all but** nearly: *The boy all but fell into the river*. **all for (doing) s.t** (*informal*) completely in favour of (doing) s.t. **all in** (*informal*) (**a**) very tired. (**b**) (of the cost of s.t) including everything: *Our holiday cost £120 all in*. **all out** (*informal*) using all one's possible strength etc: *We must go all out till we succeed*. **all over** completely finished. **all over s.o** (*fig*) very, sometimes too, friendly, polite, to s.o: *The children are all over me when they want something*. **all over (s.t)** so as to cover, visit, the whole of s.t: *The table was wet all over. Have you been all over the house?* **all right** (also **alright** (*informal*)) (**a**) well; in a satisfactory state. (**b**) (in answer to a question) I agree; yes: *'Will you help?' 'All right.'* **all that/those** the whole number, amount,

all the better, less, more, more beautiful etc (**for s.t**) (that) much better, more etc (because of s.t): *Have a rest; you'll feel all the readier for a busy evening then.* **all the same** in spite of that/anything/everything else: *I've got a headache but I'm going to the party all the same.* **all the same to/with s.o** not causing any annoyance, trouble etc to s.o: *If it's all the same with you, I'd like to stay at home this evening.* **all there** (*informal*) quick, sensible or alert(2) in one's mind: *Mary's over 100 but she's still very much all there.* **all told** in total: *There were 25 of us at the party all told.* **all up** (**with s.o/s.t**) (*informal*) finished; over, sometimes with the result being defeat, death etc: *When the soldiers saw that it was all up with them they dropped their guns and ran.* **three** etc **all** both teams etc having scored three etc goals, points etc so that the result is a draw(2).

▷ *pron* **6** (often — *of it/us* etc; — *I know* etc) everybody, everything (of it etc); the total number/amount (of it etc): *You can have all of this food; eat all you can.* **above all** more than anything else: *You must be careful and above all avoid catching cold.* **after all** in spite of everything: *Charles said he was busy but he's coming to see us after all.* **all in all** after considering everything: *All in all, I think we should stay where we are.* **all the best** ⇒ best(*pron*). **at all** (in negative sentences or questions) in any way: *Is Vanessa at all likely to be here? John isn't at all pleased with his job. 'Do you mind if I come in?' 'No, not at all.'* **in all** as the total: *We have 20 workers in all.* **last of all** ⇒ last(*adv*). **once and for all** ⇒ once. **all together** all the people, things etc as a group taken together: *Come on, let's sing it again and this time all together.* Compare altogether.

‚**all 'clear** *adj* **1** without any danger (any more).
▷ *def.n* **2** signal, e.g a siren(1), that there is no longer any danger.

'**all-con,suming** *adj* taking up all of one's desire, feelings etc: *an all-consuming passion.*

‚**all-'female** *adj* for, used by etc women only: *an all-female prison.*

‚**all-in'clusive** *adj* including all the costs, fees etc: *an all-inclusive price.*

‚**all-'male** *adj* for, used by etc men only: *an all-male choir.*

‚**all-'round** *attrib.adj* good at many skills, often in different sports: *an all-round athlete.*

‚**all-'rounder** *c.n* person who is good at many skills, often in different sports.

‚**all-'star** *attrib.adj* including famous film-stars etc.

Allah /'ælə/ *unique n* Muslim name for God.

allay /ə'leɪ/ *tr.v* (*formal*) calm (s.t); make (s.t) less (strong): *allay his fears.*

allege /ə'ledʒ/ *tr.v* (often — *that* . . .) (*formal*) say (s.t, that . . .) as a reason or excuse; claim(5) (s.t): *Peter alleges that you broke his bicycle.*

allegation /‚ælə'geɪʃən/ *c.n*.

al'leged *adj* stated but not yet proved: *the alleged murderer.*

allegedly /ə'ledʒɪdlɪ/ *adv*.

allegiance /ə'liːdʒəns/ *u.n* (often — *to s.o/s.t*) loyalty (to s.o): *Soldiers owe allegiance to their country.*

allegory /'ælɪgərɪ/ *c/u.n* (*pl -ies*) (kind of) story, picture etc in which abstract[1](1) ideas such as

patience and truth are represented as people, animals etc.

allegorical /‚ælɪ'gɒrɪkl/ *adj* (also ‚**alle'goric**) of or referring to allegory.

alleluia /‚ælɪ'luːjə/ *interj* (also ‚**halle'lujah**) (usu in religious songs) praise God.

allergy /'ælədʒɪ/ *c.n* (*pl -ies*) state in which a person is sensitive to certain substances that make her/him ill or irritate(2) her/his skin etc.

allergic /ə'lɜːdʒɪk/ *adj* (often — *to s.t*) **1** having an allergy (caused by a particular substance). **2** (*informal*) disliking (s.t) very much.

alleviate /ə'liːvɪ‚eɪt/ *tr.v* relieve (s.t, often pain or suffering); make (s.t) less strong or painful: *This medicine will alleviate your sore throat.*

alleviation /ə‚liːvɪ'eɪʃən/ *u.n*.

alley /'ælɪ/ *c.n* (also '**alley‚way**) narrow passage between buildings. **blind alley** ⇒ blind[1].

alliance ⇒ ally.

alligator /'ælɪ‚geɪtə/ *c.n* kind of animal like a crocodile(1) but with a shorter rounder nose, found in warm lakes and rivers in America.

alliterate /ə'lɪtə‚reɪt/ *intr.v* (of two or more syllables near each other in a sentence) have the same sound at the beginning of both/all; e.g *Around the rugged rocks the ragged rascal ran.*

alliteration /ə‚lɪtə'reɪʃən/ *u.n*.

alliterative /ə'lɪtərətɪv/ *adj*.

allocate /'ælə‚keɪt/ *tr.v* (often — *s.t to s.o/s.t*; — *s.o/s.t s.t*) give (s.t) to s.o/s.t as her/his/its share, for a purpose: *The teacher allocated each pupil a seat in the theatre.*

allocation /‚ælə'keɪʃən/ *n* **1** *u.n* act or fact of allocating (s.t). **2** *c.n* share allocated.

allot /ə'lɒt/ *tr.v* (*-tt-*) (often — *s.t to s.o/s.t*; — *s.o/s.t s.t*) = allocate.

al'lotment *n* **1** *u.n* act or fact of allotting s.t. **2** *c.n* share allotted. **3** *c.n* small area of land allotted to s.o for growing her/his vegetables etc on.

allow /ə'laʊ/ *tr.v* (often —*s.o/s.t to do s.t*) **1** let (s.o/s.t) (do s.t, go in(to) s.t) etc); permit (s.o/s.t) (to do s.t): *I was allowed to go to the meeting. Do they allow children in? My parents won't allow me out late at night.* **2** make it possible for (s.o) (to do s.t): *This window allows one to watch the boats on the sea.* **allow for s.t** take s.t into consideration: *To allow for the possibility of fog we'd better get to London the day before our flight.* **allow s.o s.t** give s.o s.t as an allowance(1).

al'lowable *adj* that can be allowed(1).

al'lowance *c.n* **1** amount of money etc given to s.o, usu regularly, sometimes for a particular purpose: *That student gets an allowance of £20 a week. Our company gives us a travel allowance for getting to and from work.* **2** (often an — *for s.t*) money taken off what one has to pay for s.t (because of s.t): *get an allowance for s.t.* Compare discount(1). **make allowances**, (**an**) **allowance**, **for s.o/s.t** take s.t into consideration, usu because it makes one think less unpleasantly of s.o/s.t: *We must make allowances for the fact that John lives a long way from school.*

alloy /'ælɔɪ/ *c/u.n* mixture or combination of two or more different metals.

all-round(er) ⇒ all.

allude /ə'luːd/ *intr.v* **allude to s.o/s.t** (*formal*) refer to s.o/s.t; mean s.o/s.t in what one says: *When Dorothy said she liked her neighbours she was alluding particularly to the Smiths.*

allusion /ə'lu:ʒən/ c.n (often *an — to s.o/s.t*) indirect(3) reference (to s.o/s.t).

allure /ə'luə/ u.n (often *— of s.o/s.t*) attraction; charm. ⇨ lure.

al'luring adj very attractive or tempting.

al'luringly adv.

ally c.n /'ælaɪ/ (pl *-ies*) **1** person, country etc who/that helps or supports another. Opposite enemy.

▷ tr/intr.v /ə'laɪ/ (*-ies, -ied*) **2** (often *— (oneself) with s.o/s.t*) join (s.o/s.t) as an ally: *In the election, the* Liberals(5) *allied themselves with the* Social Democrats.

alliance /ə'laɪəns/ n **1** u.n act or fact of allying(2) oneself with s.o/s.t. **2** c.n example of this. **3** c.n group of people, countries etc that are allied(2).

almighty /ɔːl'maɪtɪ/ adj **1** (often with capital **A**) having complete power over everybody and everything: *Almighty God*; *God Almighty*. **2** (*attrib*) (*informal*) very big, loud etc: *an almighty crash*.

▷ def.n **3** (with capital **A**) God.

almond /'ɑːmənd/ c.n (also *attrib*) **1** kind of nut that one eats: *almond* icing(1). **2** (also **'almond ,tree**) tree on which almonds(1) grow.

almost /'ɔːlməʊst/ adv (very) nearly; very close to; not quite; a very small distance, amount etc from: *It is almost time for lunch. The flowers on this tree are almost open. Almost all our friends were there.* **almost no one, none, nothing, never** etc hardly any (people etc), anything, ever: *Almost nobody came*.

alms /ɑːmz/ pl.n (*old use*) money etc given to beggars or other poor people.

alone /ə'ləʊn/ pred.adj/adv **1** without anyone or anything else; without help: *Don't leave me alone. Please come to the meeting alone. I can't do this alone.* **2** only: *Rita alone knows where the letter is. Time alone can cure such sorrows.* **leave/let s.o/s.t alone (a)** ⇨ alone(1). **(b)** allow s.o/s.t to stay as he/she/it is without interference(1).

along /ə'lɒŋ/ adv **1** on in the direction in which he/she/it is moving: *Come along, we haven't much time!* **2** moving in one's company: *Can David come along to the cinema with us?* **all along** ⇨ all(adv). **along with s.o/s.t** together with s.o/s.t: *Emma went to church along with the other children.* For verb + 'along', e.g bring s.o/ s.t along, come along, go along with s.o/s.t, invite s.o along, run along, ⇨ the verb. **s.o will be along** (*informal*) s.o will arrive: *John will be along in a few minutes.*

▷ prep **3** following the line of; through the whole length of; parallel(1) to (the length of): *The road runs along the river here.* **along the usual lines** in the usual way: *Please prepare a report of the meeting along the usual lines.*

a,long'side adv/prep beside; close to, in line with, the side of: *The ship came alongside (the harbour wall).*

aloof /ə'luːf/ adj/adv (often *— from s.o/s.t*) staying at a distance (from s.o/s.t); not joining in (with s.o/s.t): *Bill keeps aloof from the other boys in his class.*

a'loofly adv. **a'loofness** u.n.

aloud /ə'laʊd/ adv **1** so that one can hear it: *Don't just read the letter to yourself; read it aloud.* Opposite silently. Compare loudly. **2** loudly: *Surprise made him cry aloud.*

alpha /'ælfə/ c.n **1** first letter (**A, α**) of the Greek alphabet. **2** (often *get, give s.o, an —*) good marks in an examination. **alpha plus** very good marks.

alphabet /'ælfə,bet/ c.n set of letters of a language arranged in order (in English A, B, C etc to X, Y, Z).

,alpha'betical adj (also **,alpha'betic**) of, in the order of, the alphabet (**in**) **alphabetical order** according to the order of letters in the alphabet. Compare numerical.

alpine /'ælpaɪn/ adj **1** of, referring to, found in, high mountains, e.g the Alps in Switzerland, France and Italy: *alpine flowers.*

▷ c.n **2** alpine(1) plant.

already /ɔːl'redɪ/ adv by/before now or another particular time: *It is only February but there are already flowers in the garden. It was only 5 a.m but the children were already awake.* Opposite not yet (⇨ yet(1)).

alright = all right (⇨ all(adv)).

Alsatian /æl'seɪʃən/ c.n kind of big dog that looks like a wolf(1) and is used by the police etc.

also /'ɔːlsəʊ/ adv in addition; besides; too(1): *Mary is kind and also clever* (or *and clever also*). **not only . . . but also . . .** ⇨ not.

'also-,ran c.n (*derog; informal*) **1** horse etc that did not come first, second, third (or fourth) in a race. **2** person who is not successful.

altar /'ɔːltə/ c.n **1** (thing like a) table in a holy place on which things are offered to a god(dess). **2** table in a church on which the bread and wine are blessed in the Communion(3) service.

alter /'ɔːltə/ tr/intr.v (cause (s.o/s.t) to) change or become different: *Someone has altered the date on this letter.*

alteration /ˌɔːltə'reɪʃən/ c/u.n.

alternate /ɔːl'tɜːnɪt/ adj **1** by turns; first one, then the other etc: *Yesterday we had alternate sunshine and rain.* **2** leaving out one in between each time: *He works on alternate weekends* (i.e one weekend he works, the next he does not etc).

▷ tr/intr.v /'ɔːltə,neɪt/ **3** (often *— (s.t) with s.t*) (cause (s.t) to) happen by turns, first one and then the other: *Betty alternates hard work with complete rest.* **4** (often *— between s.t and s.t*) (cause (s.t) to) change from one state to another and then back again etc: *Joe's mood*[1](1) *alternates between hope and despair.*

alternately /ɔːl'tɜːnɪtlɪ/ adv.

alter,nating 'current u.n (*abbr AC*) flow of electricity which changes direction regularly and very fast. Opposite direct current.

alternation /ˌɔːltə'neɪʃən/ c/u.n.

alternative /ɔːl'tɜːnətɪv/ adj **1** that is, gives, a choice out of two things: *What is the alternative treatment for this illness? There is an alternative way of getting to London from here.*

▷ c.n **2** thing that one can choose out of two or more possibilities: *As John would not accept the salary I could offer, I had no alternative but to give the job to someone else.* **have the alternative of (doing) s.t or (doing) s.t** have a choice between (doing) s.t and (doing) s.t.

al'ternatively adv.

although /ɔːl'ðəʊ/ conj (also **though**) in spite of the fact that: *Although I worked hard, I (still) failed my examination* (= I worked hard but I (still) failed my examination).

altimeter /'æltɪˌmiːtə/ c.n (technical) instrument that shows one's height above sea-level or above any other level that one sets it for.

altitude /'æltɪˌtjuːd/ c.n height above sea-level or any other level, e.g that of the ground, that one has chosen.

alto /'æltəʊ/ c.n (pl -s) (also attrib) **1** woman's singing voice lower than a soprano(1). **2** woman with such a singing voice. **3** man's or boy's singing voice higher than a tenor¹(1). **4** man or boy with such a singing voice. ⇨ treble²(2). Compare contralto.

▷ adj/adv **5** having the musical range of an alto(1): an alto saxophone. She sings alto.

altogether /ˌɔːltə'geðə/ adv **1** completely; quite(1): Our holiday was altogether successful. She was not altogether sorry. **2** taking everything into consideration: We had sun, good food and good company; altogether, a very happy holiday. Compare all together (⇨ all(pron)).

altruism /'æltruːˌɪzəm/ u.n concern for the good of others before one's own; being unselfish.
'altruist c.n unselfish person.
ˌaltru'istic adj showing altruism.
ˌaltru'istically adv.

aluminium /ˌæljʊ'mɪnɪəm/ u.n (US **a'luminum** /ə'luːmɪnəm/) kind of white metal that is light in weight, chem.symb Al.

always /'ɔːlweɪz, 'ɔːlwɪz/ adv **1** at all times; without exception: Henry is always late. **2** for ever; without end in time: He said he would remember that moment always.

am (strong form /æm/, weak form /əm/) 1st pers sing pres.t of 'be': I'm here!' 'So am I!'

am /eɪ 'em/ adv abbr (also ˌa.'m.) (Latin) ante meridiem (before noon; in the morning): It's now 10.30 am. ⇨ pm.

amalgamate /ə'mælgəˌmeɪt/ tr/intr.v (cause (s.o/s.t) to) form into a complete whole, unite into one: The different sports groups amalgamated into one main club.
amalgamation /əˌmælgə'meɪʃən/ c/u.n.

amass /ə'mæs/ tr.v collect (s.t) together; produce (s.t) by collecting together the parts of which it is composed: Elizabeth amassed her fortune in a very short time.

amateur /'æmətə, ˌæmət'ɜː/ adj **1** (attrib) taking part in a sport etc for pleasure, not for money: an amateur tennis player. Opposite professional(1). **2** having limited knowledge and/or skill in s.t: I don't know much about stamps; I'm a very amateur collector. His whole approach is very amateur.

▷ c.n **3** amateur(1) person.
'amateurish adj not having, showing, much knowledge and/or skill.
'amateuˌrism u.n fact or state of being amateur(1,2).

amaze /ə'meɪz/ tr.v surprise (s.o) very much; astonish (s.o): It amazes me to see how well small children swim now.
a'mazed adj (often — at s.t; — to do s.t) feeling amazement (because of s.t or when one does s.t): He was amazed at his own stupidity (or to remember how stupid he had been).
a'mazement u.n great surprise; astonishment. **in amazement** feeling amazed: I looked at her in amazement when she told me she was 60.
a'mazing adj causing amazement.

a'mazingly adv **1** in an amazing way. **2** and this was amazing: Amazingly, no one was hurt in the crash.

ambassador /əm'bæsədə/ c.n highest rank of a person who is sent to a foreign country to represent her/his own country there. ⇨ embassy, High Commissioner.

ambassadress /əm'bæsədrɪs/ c.n female ambassador.

amber /'æmbə/ u.n (also attrib) **1** kind of clear yellow-brown substance, used to make jewellery etc: an amber necklace. **2** yellow-brown colour. **3** yellow traffic light.

ambidextrous /ˌæmbi'dekstrəs/ adj (also ˌambi'dexterous) able to use either hand equally well. Compare left/right-handed.

ambience /'æmbɪəns/ c.n (formal) feeling one gets from the surroundings of s.o/s.t: The church had a peaceful ambience.

ambiguous /æm'bɪgjʊəs/ adj that could mean two or more different things; not clear in meaning.
ambiguity /ˌæmbɪ'gjuːɪtɪ/ n (pl -ies) **1** u.n fact of being ambiguous. **2** c.n thing that is ambiguous.
am'biguously adv.

ambition /æm'bɪʃən/ n **1** c/u.n strong desire to be successful. **2** c.n object or goal of this desire.
ambitious /æm'bɪʃəs/ adj (often — to do s.t) having/showing ambition(1) (that consists of trying to do s.t). **2** showing, needing, a great amount of hard work, skill etc, perhaps more than one really has: Isn't it ambitious of such a small boy to try to swim that river?
am'bitiously adv. **am'bitiousness** u.n.

amble /'æmbl/ intr.v walk at a comfortably slow speed.

ambulance /'æmbjʊləns/ c.n vehicle for taking sick or wounded people to hospital.

ambush /'æmbʊʃ/ c.n **1** act of waiting secretly to attack an enemy when he/she comes past. **lie in ambush (for s.o/s.t)** wait (for s.o/s.t) in this way.

▷ tr.v **2** wait for (s.o/s.t) secretly (and then attack her/him/it).

ameliorate /ə'miːlɪəˌreɪt/ tr/intr.v (formal) (cause (s.t) to) become better.
amelioration /əˌmiːlɪə'reɪʃən/ c/u.n.

amen /eɪ'men, ɑː'men/ interj (word used at the end of a prayer) let it be truly so.

amenable /ə'miːnəbl/ adj (often — to s.t) (formal) **1** willing to do what one is asked to do: The children are quite amenable to gentle persuasion. **2** able to be tested (by s.t): I don't believe anything unless it is amenable to scientific testing.

amend /ə'mend/ tr.v make (s.t) better or bring (it) up to date by making changes in it, removing mistakes etc: The government have decided to amend the laws on street trading.
a'mendment n **1** u.n act or fact of amending s.t. **2** c.n change made while amending s.t: an amendment to a law.

amends /ə'mendz/ pl.n (usu make – (to s.o) (for s.t)) thing done in order to compensate(2) (s.o) (for s.t bad one has done): Fred made amends to Anne for his rudeness by bringing her some flowers.

amenity /ə'miːnɪtɪ/ c.n (pl -ies) **1** (often pl) thing that one can enjoy and that makes one's life more pleasant: One of the amenities tourists enjoy in *our town is a free bus service from the hotels to the beaches.* **2** (often *the — of s.t*) (*formal*) fact or state of being pleasant.

amethyst /ˈæmɪθɪst/ *n* **1** *c.n* (also *attrib*) kind of purple precious stone used in jewellery. **2** *c.n* jewel made from such a stone. **3** *u.n* (also *attrib*) purple colour of this stone.

amiable /ˈeɪmɪəbl/ *adj* friendly; pleasant: *an amiable person/manner.*
amiability /ˌeɪmɪəˈbɪlɪtɪ/ *u.n.* ˈ**amiably** *adv.*

amicable /ˈæmɪkəbl/ *adj* (*formal*) peaceful; friendly; without any unpleasant arguments etc: *an amicable solution to a* conflict(1).
amicability /ˌæmɪkəˈbɪlɪtɪ/ *u.n.* ˈ**amicably** *adv.*

amid /əˈmɪd/ *prep* (also **aˈmidst**) (*literary; formal*) **1** in, near, to, the middle of; among: *There were a few flowers amid the corn.* **2** (fig) in; surrounded by: *Amidst the* stillness *of the night, we could hear an occasional distant train.*

amiss /əˈmɪs/ *pred.adj/adv* (*formal*) **1** wrong: *What's that shouting? I hope nothing's amiss.* **2** (in negative sentences and questions) bad; unsuitable: *A bit of advice to the newly married pair would not be amiss.* **take s.t amiss** feel angry or hurt by s.t s.o has said, done etc, usu because one has misunderstood it.

amity /ˈæmɪtɪ/ *u.n* (*formal*) friendship; friendly relations.

ammonia /əˈməʊnɪə/ *u.n* kind of gas that has no colour and a very strong smell; it is used in refrigerators and was once sometimes used to make people who had fainted conscious again, *chem.form* NH₃.

ammonium /əˈməʊnɪəm/ *adj* of, containing, ammonia.

ammunition /ˌæmjuˈnɪʃən/ *u.n* **1** things shot out of guns, dropped from planes etc to kill people or animals, to damage things etc: *Our ammunition consists of shells, bullets, bombs and explosives.* **2** (fig) facts, ideas etc used for attacking s.o/s.t: *I need some ammunition about price rises for my speech next week.*

amnesia /æmˈniːzɪə/ *u.n* loss of memory: *Peter is suffering from amnesia.*

amnesty /ˈæmnɪstɪ/ *c.n* (*pl -ies*) general pardon given to political prisoners, criminals etc.

amoeba /əˈmiːbə/ *c.n* (*pl -s*, or, less usu, *-ae* /əˈmiːbiː/*) (US **aˈmeba**) very small creature consisting of only one cell(4); it lives in water.

amok /əˈmɒk/ *adv* **run amok** run about wildly and violently out of control.

among /əˈmʌŋ/ *prep* (also **aˈmongst**) **1** (so as to be) surrounded by (people, animals, things): *walk among the trees.* **2** (fig) in association with, in connection with, (people or animals): *She has worked for many years as a nurse among the poor.* **3** so as to give shares to three or more people etc: *Divide this food fairly among you.* ⇒ between(8). **4** (referring to action towards each other by members of a group): *They decided among themselves where they should go first.* ⇒ between(11). **5** in the group of: *I saw several of my friends, among them Joan and Bob.* **6** by the combined action of: *None of them could move the table alone but they managed it among them.* ⇒ between(12). **among(st) others (a)** among(st) their number: *You can get plenty of fruit here — apples, grapes and bananas amongst others.* **(b)** among other, different ones: *My favourite*

sports are football and tennis; amongst others, I prefer swimming to riding. **from among(st) s.o/ s.t** out of the number of certain people/animals/things.

amoral /eɪˈmɒrəl/ *adj* neither moral nor immoral; lacking moral sense or knowledge.

amorous /ˈæmərəs/ *adj* (*formal*) (easily) feeling or showing love, usu sexual love.
ˈ**amorously** *adv.* ˈ**amorousness** *u.n.*

amorphous /əˈmɔːfəs/ *adj* (*formal*) shapeless; having no proper shape.

amount /əˈmaʊnt/ *c.n* **1** (often *a large* etc — *of s.t*) quantity (of s.t). **2** total quantity: *The bicycle cost £120 and Sam could not afford to pay that amount.*
▷ *intr.v* **3 amount to s.t** reach the amount(2) of s.t; add up to s.t: *What he finally owed the bank amounted to more than £500.*

amp /æmp/ *c.n abbr* ampere.

ampere /ˈæmpeə/ *c.n* (*abbr* **amp**) (*technical*) unit for measuring the rate at which electricity passes through a particular place.

amphetamine /æmˈfetəˌmiːn/ *u.n* kind of medicine that causes a feeling of excitement and pleasure, and that gives one quick energy(1) of mind.

amphibian /æmˈfɪbɪən/ *c.n* (also *attrib*) animal that can live both on land and in water.
amˈphibious *adj* able to live both on land and in water.
amˌphibious ˈvehicle *c.n* vehicle that can go across both land and water.

amphitheatre /ˈæmfɪˌθɪətə/ *c.n* (US **amphiˌtheater**) large building without a roof that has a round empty space in the middle and seats that rise above and behind each other round it.

ample /ˈæmpl/ *adj* quite (large etc) enough: *There was ample room in the bus for more passengers. Mary has ample money for her needs.*
amplification /ˌæmplɪfɪˈkeɪʃən/ *n* **1** *u.n* act or fact of amplifying s.t. **2** *c.n* (*formal*) thing that is the result of amplifying s.t: *Could I have some amplifications of your reasons for suggesting this?*
amplifier /ˈæmplɪˌfaɪə/ *c.n* machine etc for amplifying sound.
amplify /ˈæmplɪˌfaɪ/ *v* (*-ies, -ied*) **1** *tr.v* make (s.t) larger, stronger etc: *This device amplifies sound.* **2** *tr/intr.v* (often *— (up)on s.t*) (*formal*) give more details of (s.t): *The speaker then amplified upon what he had started by saying . . .*
ˈ**amply** *adv* in a generous way: *He was amply rewarded for his efforts.*

ampoule /ˈæmpuːl/ *c.n* small glass container for medicine, esp for injections.

amputate /ˈæmpjuˌteɪt/ *tr.v* (usu by a doctor) cut off (an arm, leg, hand etc).
amputation /ˌæmpjuˈteɪʃən/ *c/u.n.*

amulet /ˈæmjulɪt/ *c.n* thing some people wear to protect themselves from bad luck, illness etc.

amuse /əˈmjuːz/ *tr.v* **1** make (oneself/s.o) laugh, feel happy etc (by doing s.t): *What the woman said amused us a lot.* **2** keep (oneself/s.o) busy in a pleasant, happy way: *I told the children to go and amuse themselves while I cooked the meal.*
aˈmusement *n* **1** *u.n.* state or feeling of being amused(1). **2** *c.n* thing that amuses s.o. **for amusement** in order to amuse oneself.

a'musement ,park *c.n* place in which people can find different things (e.g swings, roundabouts(3), games etc) to amuse them.

a'musing *adj* who/that amuses s.o.

a'musingly *adv*.

an (strong form /æn/, weak form /ən/) *det* form of a(2–10) used before words that begin with a vowel sound: *an apple*; *an hour*; *an SOS*.

anachronism /əˈnækrəˌnɪzəm/ *c.n* **1** mistake consisting of putting s.t into a story etc about a certain time in history at which it did not exist: *To talk of Shakespeare using his typewriter would be an anachronism.* **2** thing that is thought to be out of date (⇒ date¹) or too old-fashioned: *Some people think that it is an anachronism to still have titles like 'lord' in the 20th century.*

a,nachro'nistic *adj* that is or contains an anachronism.

anaemia /əˈniːmɪə/ *u.n* (US **a'nemia**) lack or poor quality of the red blood cells.

a'naemic *adj* (US also **a'nemic**) **1** having anaemia. **2** lacking interest or excitement.

anaesthesia /ˌænəsˈθiːzɪə/ *u.n* (US **,anes-'thesia**) stopping, lessening, of pain or feeling, usu as a result of having an anaesthetic; loss of consciousness.

anaesthetic /ˌænəsˈθetɪk/ *c/u.n* (also *attrib*) (US **,anes'thetic**) substance, usu a liquid or a gas, used to make a person unconscious (*a general anaesthetic*) or to prevent her/him feeling anything in part of her/his body (*a local anaesthetic*), usu before an operation.

anaesthetist /əˈniːsθətɪst/ *c.n* (US **a'nesthetist**) person who gives an anaesthetic, usu before an operation.

anaesthetize, -ise /əˈniːsθəˌtaɪz/ *tr.v* (US **a'nesthe,tize**) (give s.o, an animal) an anaesthetic.

anagram /ˈænəˌgræm/ *c.n* word(s) made by changing the order of the letters in another word or other words without adding any or taking any away: *'Ache' is an anagram of 'each'.*

anal(ly) ⇒ anus.

analgesic /ˌænəlˈdʒiːzɪk/ *u.n* (also *attrib*) medicine that stops one feeling pain or that makes one feel less pain, e.g aspirin.

analogy /əˈnælədʒɪ/ *n* (*pl -ies*) **1** *c.n* (often *an — between s.t and s.t*; *an — to/with s.t*) amount of being like s.t; amount of likeness/similarity(1) (to s.t etc): *There is an analogy between the nostrils in our nose and the* gills¹ *of fish.* **2** *u.n* comparison with s.t analogous. **on the analogy of s.t** using s.t as an analogy(1) or comparison.

analogous /əˈnæləgəs/ *adj* (*formal*) (often — *to/with s.t*) nearly the same (as s.t) in certain ways.

analyse /ˈænəˌlaɪz/ *tr.v* (US also **'ana,lyze**) **1** (*science*; *grammar*) (often — *s.t into s.t*) divide (a substance, a sentence etc) (into separate parts). **2** examine (s.t) very carefully: *If we analyse what the minister said, we find there is nothing really new in it.* **3** = psychoanalyse.

analysis /əˈnælɪsɪs/ *n* (*pl analyses* /əˈnælɪˌsiːz/) **1** *u.n* act or fact of analysing s.t. **2** *c.n* example of this. **3** *c/u.n* result of analysing s.t. **4** *c.n* analysing(2) (s.t) and giving one's opinions etc about it. **5** *u.n* = psychoanalysis.

analyst /ˈænəlɪst/ *c.n* **1** person who analyses things, usu as a job. **2** = psychoanalyst.

analytical /ˌænəˈlɪtɪkl/ *adj* (also **,ana'lytic**) of, referring to, using, analysis(1,4). ⇒ psychoanalytical.

,ana'lytically *adv*.

anarchy /ˈænəkɪ/ *u.n* state of being without government, order or discipline; state of not being under the control of law.

anarchic /əˈnɑːkɪk/ *adj* (also **a'narchical**) that is in, or causes, a state of anarchy.

a'narchically *adv*.

anarchism /ˈænəˌkɪzəm/ *u.n* belief that society should not have any form of government.

'anarchist *c.n* person who believes in anarchism.

anathema /əˈnæθəmə/ *u.n* (often — *to s.o*) (*formal*) thing that is hated (by s.o): *Cruelty to animals is anathema to me.*

anatomy /əˈnætəmɪ/ *n* (*pl -ies*) **1** *u.n* act of cutting up of dead bodies in order to study their various parts. **2** *u.n* science of the study of the different parts of the body. **3** *c.n* body of a person or animal or its parts. **4** *u.n* (often *the — of s.t*) (*fig*) way in which s.t, e.g human society, is built up.

anatomical /ˌænəˈtomɪkl/ *adj* of or referring to anatomy(1–3).

a'natomist *c.n* person who studies, is skilled in, anatomy(1,2).

ancestor /ˈænsestə/ *c.n* person from whom one is directly descended.

ancestral /ænˈsestrəl/ *adj* of or referring to one or more ancestors: *my ancestral home.*

ancestress /ˈænsestrɪs/ *c.n* woman ancestor.

'ancestry *c/u.n* (*pl -ies*) line of ancestors.

anchor /ˈæŋkə/ *c.n* **1** heavy piece of iron, usu with two curved arms, which is tied to a rope or chain and dropped to the bottom of the sea etc to keep a ship in one place. **be/lie/ride at anchor** be anchored(2). **cast/drop anchor**; **lower, let go, the anchor** put one's anchor(1) down so as to keep the ship etc in one place. **come to anchor** stop and let down one's anchor(1). **weigh anchor** pull up one's anchor(1) from the bottom of the sea etc (and start to move).

▷ *tr/intr.v* **2** put down the anchor(1) (of a ship etc). **3** (*fig*) (cause (s.t) to) become firmly fixed: *The wind was so strong that we had to anchor the garden furniture to the ground.*

anchorage /ˈæŋkərɪdʒ/ *n* **1** *c.n* place where ships can anchor(2). **2** *c/u.n* (*fig*) thing to which s.t is anchored(3).

'anchorman *c.n* (*pl -men*) person who keeps the work of a group of people together, e.g on television or the radio.

anchovy /ˈæntʃəvɪ/ *c/u.n* (*pl -ies*) (also *attrib*) small fish with a strong taste, often used in sauces or pastes.

ancient /ˈeɪnʃənt/ *adj* **1** that existed a long time ago; that has existed from early times: *ancient Greece*; *our ancient rights.* **2** (*fig*) (very) old: *I can see an ancient man sitting in the sun.*

,ancient 'history *u.n* history(1) of ancient(1) times.

ancillary /ænˈsɪlərɪ/ *adj* who/that helps to support other (more important) people/things: *ancillary workers in a hospital*; *ancillary services.*

and (strong form /ænd/, weak form /ənd/) *conj* (used for joining words, parts of sentences or whole sentences) together with; as well as: *There* *were three horses and two cows, and they all lived in the same farm.*

anecdote /ˈænəkˌdəʊt/ *c.n* short story with an important or amusing point.

anemone /əˈnemənɪ/ *c.n* kind of small flower with dull purple, pink or blue flowers. **sea anemone** ⇒ sea.

anesthesia, anesthetic, anesthetist, anesthetize ⇒ anaesthesia.

anew /əˈnjuː/ *adv* (*literary*) again and/or in a different way: *The old man forgot what he was trying to say and had to start anew.*

angel /ˈeɪndʒəl/ *c.n* messenger from God, usu shown as a person with big wings. **2** (*fig*) very kind and/or beautiful person: *Sheila has been an angel to us.*

angelic /ænˈdʒelɪk/ *adj* **1** of or referring to an angel(1) or angels. **2** like an angel(2): *What an angelic baby!*

an'gelically *adv*.

anger /ˈæŋgə/ *u.n* **1** very strong (and violent) feeling of bad temper or annoyance against s.o/ s.t which sometimes makes one want to hurt her/ him/it: *John was filled with anger when he saw what had been done to his bicycle.*

▷ *tr.v* **2** cause (s.o, an animal) to feel anger(1): *Don't anger that goat or it will butt³(2) you.*

'angrily *adv* in an angry way.

'angry *adj* (-*ier*, -*iest*) (often — (*with s.o*) *about s.t*) feeling, showing, anger(1) (against s.o) (about s.t).

angle¹ /ˈæŋgl/ *c.n* **1** space between two lines or surfaces that meet or cross: *an angle of 35°; a right angle.* **2** corner: *a sharp angle in the road.* **3** point of view: *I can't see it from your angle I am afraid.* **at an angle** not vertical or horizontal but sloping.

▷ *tr.v* **4** (often — *s.t at/towards s.o/s.t*) put (a radio or television programme etc) in a way that will interest or attract (s.o, s.o's attention): *His speech was angled towards the older people in the audience.*

'angular /ˈæŋgjʊlə/ *adj* having sharp corners; pointed, not curved.

angularity /ˌæŋgjʊˈlærɪtɪ/ *u.n*.

angle² /ˈæŋgl/ *intr.v* fish with a hook and line.

'angler *c.n* person who angles².

Anglo- /ˈæŋgləʊ/ *c.n* form of English/British used as the first part of other words: *an Anglo-American committee* (i.e a committee composed of English/British and American people).

anglophile /ˈæŋgləʊˌfaɪl/ *c.n* (also *attrib*) person who likes England, the English/British.

anglophobe /ˈæŋgləʊˌfəʊb/ *c.n* (also *attrib*) person who does not like England, the English/British.

Anglo-Saxon /ˌæŋgləʊ ˈsæksn/ *c.n* (also *attrib*) **1** person, language, of England before 1066 AD. **2** person of English descent.

angrily, angry ⇒ anger.

anguish /ˈæŋgwɪʃ/ *u.n* great pain or anxiety.

'anguished *adj* feeling/showing anguish: *an anguished look on s.o's face.*

angular(ity) ⇒ angle¹.

animal /ˈænɪməl/ *c.n* (also *attrib*) **1** living creature that is not a plant, that has feeling and that can move when and where it wants: *Man is one of the animals.* **2** animal(1) that is not a person, e.g a cat, chicken, ant. **3** mammal. **4** (*fig; informal*)

very badly behaved person: *What an animal that man is!*

'animal ˌkingdom *def.n* all the animals in the world. ⇒ mineral kingdom, plant kingdom.

animate /ˈænɪmɪt/ *adj* living; alive.

animated /ˈænɪˌmeɪtɪd/ *adj* very full of life; lively; excited: *an animated child/conversation.*

ˌaniˌmated car'toon *c.n* = cartoon(2).

animation /ˌænɪˈmeɪʃən/ *u.n* **1** state or fact of being animated. **2** way of producing films by photographing drawings. Compare cartoon(2).

animosity /ˌænɪˈmɒsɪtɪ/ *c/u.n* (*pl* -*ies*) (often — *against/towards s.o/s.t*; — *between s.o/s.t and s.o/ s.t*) hatred (towards etc s.o/s.t); strong dislike: *I can't understand Ted's animosity towards his boss.*

aniseed /ˈænɪˌsiːd/ *u.n* kind of strong-flavoured seed used for flavouring food and drinks.

ankle /ˈæŋkl/ *c.n* joint connecting the foot to the rest of the leg.

'anklet /ˈæŋklɪt/ *c.n*. thing worn round the ankle, usu as an ornament.

annals /ˈænlz/ *pl.n* record of events written year by year.

annex /əˈneks/ *tr.v* take possession of (s.t, usu another country); take (s.t) over against its owner's, people's, will. **annex s.t to s.t** add s.t smaller to s.t bigger so that it becomes part of it.

annexation /ˌænekˈseɪʃən/ *u.n*.

'annexe /ˈæneks/ *c.n* (also **'annex**) smaller building added or connected to a larger one: *This hotel has an annexe for extra guests in the summer.*

annihilate /əˈnaɪəˌleɪt/ *tr.v* destroy (s.o/s.t) completely.

annihilation /əˌnaɪəˈleɪʃən/ *u.n*.

anniversary /ˌænɪˈvɜːsərɪ/ *c.n* (*pl* -*ies*) (also *attrib*) yearly return of a certain date or the celebration of s.t that happened on that date: *Our wedding anniversary is January 12th.*

Anno Domini /ˌænəʊ ˈdɒmɪˌnaɪ/ *adv* (*abbr* AD) year since the birth of Christ: *1988 AD is the one thousand nine hundred and eighty-eighth year after the birth of Christ.* ⇒ BC.

annotate /ˈænəˌteɪt/ *tr.v* add notes to (s.t) to explain it.

annotation /ˌænəˈteɪʃən/ *c/u.n*.

announce /əˈnaʊns/ *tr.v* make (s.t) known; declare (the presence, arrival, of s.o/s.t): *Train arrivals are announced over the* loudspeaker *at the station.*

an'nouncement *n* **1** *u.n* act or fact of announcing s.t. **2** *c.n* thing that is announced.

an'nouncer *c.n* person who announces things, esp on television or the radio.

annoy /əˈnɔɪ/ *tr.v* make (s.o, an animal) angry; cause trouble to (s.o, an animal).

annoyance /əˈnɔɪəns/ *n* **1** *u.n* fact or state of being annoyed. **2** *c.n* thing that annoys one.

an'noying *adj* causing annoyance(1).

annual /ˈænjʊəl/ *adj* **1** happening once a year; lasting one year and repeated every year; of one year: *one's annual salary.*

▷ *c.n* **2** book that is produced every year. **3** plant that comes up in one year only.

ˌAnnual ˌGeneral 'Meeting *c.n* (*abbr* AGM) official meeting held once a year by a company, club etc.

annuity /əˈnjuːɪtɪ/ *c.n* (*pl* -*ies*) fixed sum of

money paid to s.o every year: *Bob receives an annuity of £3000 from his insurance company.*

annul /ə'nʌl/ *tr.v* (*-ll-*) declare (s.t) to be no longer in existence or valid(1); put an end to (s.t); cancel (s.t): *The judge annulled the marriage.*

an'nulment *c/u.n.*

anode /'ænəʊd/ *c.n* (*technical*) point from which electric current enters an electrical system, e.g a battery. Compare cathode(1), electrode.

anoint /ə'nɔɪnt/ *tr.v* put oil on (s.o/s.t), esp in a religious ceremony.

a'nointment *u.n.*

anomalous /ə'nɒmələs/ *adj* that is an exception to a rule; not normal or regular: *an anomalous verb such as 'have'.*

a'nomalously *adv.*

a'nomaly *c.n* (*pl -ies*) person or thing who/that is anomalous: *Is it an anomaly that police officers are paid more than nurses?*

anonymous /ə'nɒnɪməs/ *adj* **1** (of a writer) not admitting to having written s.t: *the anonymous* author(1) *of a poem.* **2** (of a piece of writing) not having the writer's name on it: *an anonymous letter.*

anonymity /ˌænə'nɪmɪtɪ/ *u.n.*

anopheles /ə'nɒfɪˌliːz/ *c.n* (also **a,nophe,les mos'quito**) kind of mosquito that can carry malaria.

anorak /'ænəˌræk/ *c.n* short coat that keeps out wind and rain and has a hood(1) joined to it.

another /ə'nʌðə/ *adj/pron* **1** one more; one in addition: *Can I have another (piece of cake, please)?* **2** a different (one): *Can I have another (pen), please? This one's broken.* **one another** ⇨ one.

ans *written abbr* answer.

answer /'ɑːnsə/ *c.n* (often *— to s.o/s.t*) **1** word(s) one gives when one has been asked a question or in reply to an argument, an accusation etc: *Have you had an answer to your letter yet?* **2** action done in return for another or for s.t said: *Peter's only answer to Henry's kick was an angry look.* **3** solution to a problem: *12 × 12 answer: 144.* **4** (usu *pl*) written work done by students in an examination. **in answer (to s.t)** as an answer(1,2) (to s.t).

▷ *tr/intr.v* **5** (often *— (s.o) (s.t) with s.t*) give an answer(1,2) or answers (to (s.o/s.t) (by doing s.t)): *I'd like you to answer me a few questions, please. Julia answered with a smile.* **6** (often *— the bell, door, telephone* etc) do what is necessary (about s.t): *I rang the bell but no one answered. There's someone at the door; will you please answer it, Dick?* (i.e will you go and see what the person who has knocked etc wants?). *The telephone's ringing; is no one going to answer it?* **7** (often *— for s.t*) be suitable (for (s.t)); do what is needed, wanted, fit (s.t); fulfil (s.t): *This flat rock will answer (our needs) for a table while we have lunch in the forest.* **8** (often *— to s.t*) fit (s.t); be the same as (s.t): *The police questioned everyone who answered (to) the description of the wanted man.* **answer back** give a rude, usu cheeky, answer. **answer (to s.o) for s.t** (a) be, make oneself, responsible (to s.o) for s.t. (b) be, run the risk of being, punished (by s.o) for s.t: *You'll answer for any mistakes, I warn you!*

answerable /'ɑːnsərəbl/ *adj* **1** that can be answered. Opposite unanswerable. **2** (often

— (to s.o) for s.t) responsible (to s.o) (for s.t).

ant /ænt/ *c.n* kind of small insect that lives in large groups, either under the ground or in an ant hill; it is well known as a very good worker.

'ant ,hill *c.n* place built by ants above the ground to live in.

antagonism /æn'tægəˌnɪzəm/ *c/u.n* (often *— towards s.o/s.t*; *— between s.o/s.t and s.o/s.t*) (example of) active opposition (to s.o/s.t etc).

an'tagonist *c.n* **1** person who fights, argues etc against s.o/s.t; opponent(3). **2** character in a play, story etc who opposes the main character. ⇨ protagonist(1).

an,tago'nistic *adj* (often *— to(wards) s.o/s.t*) against (s.o/s.t); opposed (to s.o/s.t).

an,tago'nistically *adv.*

antagonize, -ise /æn'tægəˌnaɪz/ *tr.v* make an enemy of (s.o/s.t); make (s.o/s.t) angry, annoyed.

Antarctic /æn'tɑːktɪk/ *def.n* (also *attrib*) very cold most southern area of the world. Compare Arctic(1,3).

antecedent /ˌæntɪ'siːdənt/ *adj* **1** (*formal*) that happens or happened before (s.t else).

▷ *c.n* **2** (*formal*) person or thing who/that comes or came before (s.o/s.t else): *To find out why Joe behaves like this one needs to look at his antecedents.*

,ante'cedence *u.n.*

,ante'cedents *pl.n* (*formal*) (often *the — of s.o/ s.t*) **1** ancestors. **2** past history.

antedate /ˌæntɪ'deɪt/ *tr.v* **1** write a date that is earlier than the true one on (s.t): *Why have you antedated this cheque?* Opposite postdate(1). **2** happen, exist, earlier than (s.t): *The arrival of man in Britain antedated the Ice Age.* Opposite postdate(2).

antelope /'æntɪˌləʊp/ *c.n* kind of animal that is like a deer.

ante meridiem /ˌæntɪ mə'rɪdɪəm/ *adv* (*Latin*) (*abbr* am, a.m.) (*formal*) before noon: *9 am.* Compare post meridiem.

antenatal /ˌæntɪ'neɪtl/ *attrib.adj* existing, happening, before birth: *an antenatal examination of the mother by a doctor.*

antenna¹ /æn'tenə/ *c.n* (*pl -e* /æn'teniː/) feeler(1) on the head of an insect or a shellfish.

antenna² /æn'tenə/ *c.n* (*pl -s*) aerial(2) for a radio or television.

anterior /æn'tɪərɪə/ *adj* (*formal*) (often *— to s.o/ s.t*) **1** further forward (than s.o/s.t): *We found the animal in the anterior part of the cave.* **2** earlier in time (than s.o/s.t): *during the anterior part of the last century.* **3** of or near the head (of an insect etc): *the anterior wings.*

anteroom /'æntɪˌrʊm/ *c.n* small room that acts as an entrance to a bigger one; waiting-room.

anthem /'ænθəm/ *c.n* **1** song for singing in a church. **2** song of praise or gladness. **national anthem** ⇨ national(1).

anthology /æn'θɒlədʒɪ/ *c.n* (*pl -ies*) collection of the writings, often the poems, of one writer or of several.

anthracite /'ænθrəˌsaɪt/ *u.n* kind of coal that is very hard, burns slowly and does not produce smoke.

anthropology /ˌænθrə'pɒlədʒɪ/ *u.n* scientific

study of human beings, their society, religion, race, development etc.

anthropological /ˌænθrəpəˈlɒdʒɪkl/ *adj* of or referring to anthropology.

anthropologist /ˌænθrəˈpɒlədʒɪst/ *c.n* person who studies, is skilled in, anthropology.

anti /ˈæntɪ/ *adv/prep* (often as the first part of a word) not in favour of: *anti-war. Are you pro*[1] *the idea or anti?* ⇒ pro[1].

anti-aircraft /ˌæntɪ ˈeəkrɑːft/ *adj* used against enemy aircraft: *anti-aircraft guns.*

antibiotic /ˌæntɪbaɪˈɒtɪk/ *c/u.n* (also *attrib*) chemical substance, e.g penicillin, produced by bacteria etc that can kill or keep back other dangerous ones.

antibody /ˈæntɪˌbɒdɪ/ *c.n* (*pl* -ies) substance produced by the blood that destroys dangerous bacteria or prevents them causing disease.

antic /ˈæntɪk/ *c.n* (usu *pl*) amusing strange action.

anticipate /ænˈtɪsɪˌpeɪt/ *v* 1 *tr.v* look forward to (s.t) with pleasure, fear etc; expect (s.t, that . . .): *I anticipate a lot of snow this winter.* 2 *tr.v* see the need for (s.t) in advance (and then do what is necessary): *The nurse anticipated what the doctor wanted and passed her the notes.* 3 *tr.v* (often — *doing s.t*) expect (to do s.t): *We anticipated having more customers than this.* 4 *tr.v* do s.t before (s.o else): *I hoped to buy the house yesterday but someone else anticipated me and it was already sold when I arrived.* 5 *tr/intr.v* say (s.t) before the right time for it: *The story has a sad ending but I won't anticipate; I'll tell it to you from the beginning.*

anticipation /ænˌtɪsɪˈpeɪʃən/ *u.n* act or fact of anticipating(1–3,5) s.t. **in anticipation** (**of s.t**) expecting, waiting for, s.t: *I bought a bicycle in anticipation of high petrol prices.*

anticipatory /ænˈtɪsɪˌpeɪtərɪ/ *adj* that anticipates(1,3) s.t.

anticlimax /ˌæntɪˈklaɪmæks/ *c.n* thing that disappoints one after one has had high hopes of success, amusement etc.

anti-clockwise /ˌæntɪˈklɒkˌwaɪz/ *adj/adv* (US **ˌcounter-ˈclockˌwise**) going in the opposite direction to the hands of a clock. Opposite clockwise.

anticyclone /ˌæntɪˈsaɪkləʊn/ *c.n* area where air pressure is high, producing quiet, settled and usu fine weather conditions. Opposite cyclone(2).

antidote /ˈæntɪˌdəʊt/ *c.n* (often *an* — *to s.t*) 1 kind of medicine to stop (poison in the body) from working. 2 (*fig*) thing that acts against (s.t else) to stop it: *Television is many people's main antidote to boredom.*

antifreeze /ˈæntɪˌfriːz/ *u.n* kind of chemical substance put in the water system of a car etc to stop the water freezing.

antimony /ˈæntɪmənɪ/ *u.n* kind of white silvery metal used in some alloys, *chem.symb* Sb.

antipathy /ænˈtɪpəθɪ/ *c/u.n* (*pl* -ies) (often — *to/towards s.o/s.t*; — *between s.o/s.t and s.o/s.t*) strong feeling of dislike (for s.o/s.t etc): *Many small boys have a strong antipathy to soap and water.*

antipathetic /ˌæntɪpəˈθetɪk/ *adj* (often — *to/towards s.o/s.t*) 1 feeling/causing antipathy (against s.o/s.t). 2 opposed (to s.t).

antipersonnel /ˌæntɪˌpɜːsəˈnel/ *adj* (of bombs

etc) made to be used against people, not planes, ships, buildings etc.

Antipodes /ænˈtɪpəˌdiːz/ *def.pl.n* Australia and New Zealand.

antiquarian, antiquary ⇒ antique.

antiquated /ˈæntɪˌkweɪtɪd/ *adj* very old-fashioned; out-of-date (⇒date[1]).

antique /ænˈtiːk/ *adj* 1 ancient; belonging to, from, the past and therefore probably valuable: *antique furniture.*
▷ *c.n* 2 piece of antique(1) furniture etc, usu more than 100 years old.

antiquarian /ˌæntɪˈkweərɪən/ *adj* 1 of or referring to the study, collection and/or sale of antiquities(3).
▷ *c.n* 2 (also **antiquary** /ænˈtɪkwərɪ/) person who studies, collects and/or sells antiquities(3).

antiquity /ænˈtɪkwɪtɪ/ *n* (*pl* -ies) 1 *u.n* fact of being very ancient or very old; great age. 2 *u.n* ancient times, usu before the 12th century AD. 3 *c.n* statue, building etc remaining from ancient times.

antirrhinum /ˌæntɪˈraɪnəm/ *c.n* (also **ˈsnap-ˌdragon**) kind of plant grown in gardens for its pretty flowers.

anti-Semitic /ˌæntɪ səˈmɪtɪk/ *adj* feeling, showing, hatred of the Jews.

anti-Semitism /ˌæntɪ ˈsemɪˌtɪzəm/ *u.n.*

antiseptic /ˌæntɪˈseptɪk/ *c/u.n* (also *attrib*) substance used to clean wounds.

antisocial /ˌæntɪˈsəʊʃəl/ *adj* 1 against the rules and accepted behaviour of society: *antisocial behaviour.* 2 harmful to the interests of others; selfish: *Smoking in a small restaurant is antisocial.* 3 liking to be alone than be with others.
ˌantiˈsocially *adv.*

antitank /ˌæntɪˈtæŋk/ *adj* used against tanks(2): *an antitank gun.*

antithesis /ænˈtɪθəsɪs/ *c.n* (*pl* antitheses /ænˈtɪθəˌsiːz/) (often *an* — *to s.t*; *an* — *between s.t and s.t*) fact of being a/the direct opposite (of s.t): *Death is the antithesis of life.*

antithetical /ˌæntɪˈθetɪkl/ *adj* (also **antiˈthet-ic**).
ˌantiˈthetically *adv.*

antitoxin /ˈæntɪˌtɒksɪn/ *c.n* substance, esp in the blood, that prevents or cures a disease.

antler /ˈæntlə/ *c.n* branched horn on the head of some kinds of male deer.

antonym /ˈæntəˌnɪm/ *c.n* word that is exactly opposite in meaning to another: *'Good' is the antonym of 'bad'.* Opposite synonym.

anus /ˈeɪnəs/ *c.n* (*medical*) lower opening of the alimentary canal through which we defecate.
ˈanal *adj* of, referring to, in, the anus.
ˈanally *adv.*

anvil /ˈænvɪl/ *c.n* block of iron on which one hammers hot metal to shape it into horseshoes, tools, etc.

anxious /ˈæŋkʃəs/ *adj* 1 (often — *about/for s.o/ s.t*) feeling worried or uncomfortable in one's mind (about s.o/s.t): *I'm anxious about the examinations next week.* 2 causing worry or anxiety(2): *an anxious wait for news.* 3 (*informal*) (often — *for s.t*; — *that* . . .; — (*for s.o/s.t*) *to do s.t*) eager (for s.t etc); wanting (s.t) very much: *I'm anxious for everybody to have finished by 9 o'clock. We were anxious that the train should arrive on time.*

anxiety /æŋ'zaɪətɪ/ n (pl -ies) **1** u.n (often — about/for s.o/s.t) state of being anxious(1) (about s.o/s.t): *anxiety about/for the future.* **2** c.n feeling of being anxious(1). **3** c.n thing that makes one anxious(1): *Jim's illness is just another anxiety for his poor mother.* **4** u.n (usu — to do s.t) strong desire or wish (to do s.t): *Anne's anxiety to help.*
'anxiously adv.

any /'enɪ/ adv **1** to any degree or extent; at all: *If it gets any colder I shall have to get myself a warmer coat. Is this old hat any good to you?*
▷ det **2** (in negative sentences and questions) a number/amount of (s.t) (at all): *Are there any chairs there? There isn't any water left.* Compare some(2). **3** it does not matter which; any example of; every individual of: *You can borrow any book in this room. Any student in this school can answer that question.* **4** (informal) a/an/one: *There isn't any refrigerator to put our food in!* **any amount/number/quantity (of s.t)** a large amount etc (of s.t): *We won't go hungry because there's any amount of food in the house.* **any . . . else** ⇨ else. **any . . . (that) . . .** as much . . . as . . .; whatever . . .: *I shall be grateful for any advice (that) you can give me.* **in any case; at any rate** whatever may happen: *I'll come by bus or train or something; in any case, I won't be late.*
▷ pron (often — of it, them, us etc) **5** (in negative sentences and questions) any(2) persons/animals/thing(s): *'Are the teachers here yet?' 'No, I haven't seen any.' Have you still got any of that bread you bought yesterday?* Compare some(7). **6** it does not matter which; any quantity, number, individual(s), example(s): *You can take any of these books. I need milk, so please bring me any you can find.* **if any** and perhaps no/none: *We have few if any problems with our car.*

anybody /'enɪbɒdɪ/ pron (also **'any,one**) **1** (in negative sentences and questions) any(2) person: *Does anybody know the way to the station? I haven't seen anybody here.* Compare somebody(2), nobody(2). **2** any(3) person at all: *You can ask anybody and you'll get the same answer.* **anybody else** ⇨ else. **anybody's guess** (informal) thing that is not at all certain: *'When is Dorothy going to arrive?' 'That's anybody's guess.'* **if anybody** and perhaps nobody at all: *Linda will know the answer to that question if anybody. If anybody, it was Nick that broke that lamp.*

anyhow /'enɪhaʊ/ adv **1** in any way: *The car stopped and I couldn't start it anyhow.* **2** carelessly: *He put the things in the bag anyhow and some got broken.* **3** (also **'any,way**) in any case; in spite of that: *I don't think it will work but I'll try anyhow.* **4** (used when speaking to show that one is changing the subject): *Well, anyhow, it was nice talking to you but I've got to go now.*
anymore /,enɪ'mɔː/ adv (also **any more**) (not) ever again. ⇨ any more (⇨ more(pron)).
anyone /'enɪwʌn/ pron = anybody.
anything /'enɪθɪŋ/ pron **1** (in negative sentences and questions) any(2) thing: *Have you anything I could use to clean the floor?* **2** any(3) thing at all: *You can take anything you like from the food table.* **3** (in negative sentences and questions) important/serious thing: *'What's that in the middle of the road?' 'Don't be afraid; it isn't anything; just a paper bag.'* **anything but (. . .)** not

at all (. . .): *Jane is anything but stupid. 'Is Fred ill?' 'Anything but!'* **anything else** ⇨ else. **as easy** etc **as anything** very easy etc. **if anything** if there is in fact any such thing: *John's eyes aren't brown; if anything, they're green.* **like anything** (informal) very much, hard etc: *It's raining like anything.* **not make anything of s.o/s.t** not understand s.o/s.t at all. **not think anything of s.o/s.t** have a very low opinion of s.o/s.t. **or anything** or any other thing, action etc that may be wanted etc: *If you want a drink or anything the kitchen is through there.*
anyway /'enɪweɪ/ adv (informal) = anyhow(3,4).
anywhere /'enɪweə/ adv **1** (in negative sentences and questions) in, to, any(2) place: *Have you seen my bag anywhere?* **2** in, to, any(3) place: *You can go anywhere you want with this special ticket.* Compare somewhere, nowhere. **anywhere between s.t and s.t; anywhere from s.t to s.t** at any point in the number that starts with s.t and ends with s.t: *I'd say she's anywhere between 35 and 45 years old.* **anywhere else** ⇨ else. **anywhere near as . . . as . . .** at all as . . . as . . .: *Peter isn't anywhere near as old as you think he is.* **anywhere near (doing) s.t** at all close to (doing) s.t): *I'm not anywhere near finishing yet.* **if anywhere** more probably than in any other place, although perhaps nowhere at all: *You'll find Don in the garden, if anywhere.* **or anywhere** or in, to, some other place: *If you want to go to the theatre or anywhere, let me know.*
a.o.b. /,eɪ əʊ 'biː/ abbr (also **,AO'B**) any other business (as used on an agenda).
aorta /eɪ'ɔːtə/ c.n biggest blood vessel in one's body which carries blood away from one's heart.
apart /ə'pɑːt/ pred.adj or adj following the n/ pron **1** (often — from s.o/s.t) separate (from s.o/s.t); not like s.o/s.t; divided; separated: *The books are apart from the rest of the collection. These rooms in the hotel are a place apart — only for the very rich who want the greatest comfort. John and I are very far apart in our needs.* **worlds apart** ⇨ world.
▷ adv **2** (often — from s.o/s.t) (distant) from each other: *The bus stops are about a kilometre apart (or apart from each other).* **3** in such a way as to be separated: *Mary pulled the fighting dogs apart.* **4** into pieces: *tear it apart.* **5** separated from each other: *Rachel and her husband now live apart.* **6** to one side: *I'll take Bill apart and warn him to be careful.* **7** except for; not included or considered: *A few little things apart, the evening was a great success.* **apart from s.o/s.t** except s.o/s.t. **joking apart** ⇨ joke(4). **know/tell s.o/s.t apart** know which of s.o/s.t is which: *I just can't tell those twins apart.* **put/set s.t apart** put s.t on one side; reserve s.t. **take s.o apart** attack s.o with blows or criticism. ⇨ apart(6). **take s.t apart** separate s.t into its parts.
apartheid /ə'pɑːthaɪt, ə'pɑːtheɪt/ u.n (government policy(1) for the) separation of racial(1) groups in South Africa.
apartment /ə'pɑːtmənt/ c.n **1** room in a house. **2** (esp US) flat(13).
apathy /'æpəθɪ/ u.n state of not having strong feelings, sympathy, interest etc: *The apathy of most people here about politics is the result of*

*thinking there is nothing much they can do about
things.*

apathetic /ˌæpəˈθetɪk/ *adj* feeling/showing
apathy.

ˌapaˈthetically *adv.*

ape /eɪp/ *c.n* 1 kind of large monkey with no tail
or a very short one.

▷ *tr.v* 2 imitate, copy, (s.o/s.t), often as a joke.

ˈapish *adj* 1 of, like, an ape(1). 2 who/that imitates (s.o/s.t).

aperient /əˈpɪərɪənt/ *c.n* (*formal*) laxative(2).

aperitif /əˌperəˈtiːf/ *c.n* (*French*) alcoholic(1)
drink taken before a meal.

aperture /ˈæpətʃə/ *c.n* hole, gap or small opening, sometimes one that lets the light into a
camera for taking photographs.

apex /ˈeɪpeks/ *c.n* (*pl* **-es** or, less usu, *apices*
/ˈeɪpɪˌsiːz/) (often *the* — *of s.t*) 1 (*geometry*) top,
highest, point: *the apex of a triangle.* Opposite
base²(2). 2 (*fig*) highest point reached in s.t, e.g
one's career(1).

Apex /ˈeɪpeks/ *abbr* (also **ˈAPEX**) Advance Purchase Excursion(1) (a cheap ticket for a journey
by air).

aphid /ˈeɪfɪd/ *c.n* (also *aphis* /ˈeɪfɪs/, *pl aphides*
/ˈeɪfɪˌdiːz/) kind of small insect that feeds on the
juice of plants.

aphorism /ˈæfəˌrɪzəm/ *c.n* maxim.

aphrodisiac /ˌæfrəˈdɪzɪæk/ *c/u.n* (also *attrib*)
kind of medicine or substance that excites or is
supposed to excite one sexually.

apiary /ˈeɪpɪərɪ/ *c.n* (*pl* **-ies**) place where bees
are kept, usu in several hives(1).

ˈapiarist *c.n* person who keeps bees.

apiece /əˈpiːs/ *adv* each: *We were given £2
apiece.*

apish ⇒ ape.

aplomb /əˈplɒm/ *u.n* calm confidence, usu in
difficult situations.

apology /əˈpɒlədʒɪ/ *c.n* (*pl* **-ies**) (often — (*to
s.o*) *for s.t*) statement (to s.o) that one is sorry
(for a mistake, being rude etc). *an apology for
s.t* (a) ⇒ apology. (b) (*informal*) a very poor and
not really acceptable example of s.t: *The girl was
wearing an apology for a bathing dress.*

apologetic /əˌpɒləˈdʒetɪk/ *adj* saying/showing
that one is sorry for a mistake etc.

aˌpoloˈgetically *adv.*

aˈpologist *c.n* (*formal*) person who defends an
opinion by argument.

apologize, -ise /əˈpɒləˌdʒaɪz/ *intr.v* (often —
(*to s.o*) *for s.t*) say (to s.o) that one is sorry (for a
mistake etc): *I won't help her until she apologizes
for her rudeness.*

apostle /əˈpɒsl/ *c.n* 1 (often with capital **A**) one
of the 12 men sent out into the world by Christ to
preach Christianity. 2 (often *the* — *of s.t*) leader
(of a new (religious) movement).

apostrophe /əˈpɒstrəfɪ/ *c.n* (sign ' showing)
1 that a letter/number or letters/numbers has/
have been left out, e.g *it's = it is*; *'03 = 1903, 1803*
etc. 2 possession, e.g *the boy's/boys' brother.* 3 the
plural of letters and numbers, e.g *There are four
s's in possessive and two 5's in 554.* 4 length of
time in dates, e.g *the 1900's, the 1960's.*

apothecary /əˈpɒθəkərɪ/ *c.n* (*pl* **-ies**) (*old use*)
person who prepares and sells medicines.

appal /əˈpɔːl/ *tr.v* (**-ll-**) (US also **apˈpall**) cause
(s.o) great fear, unhappiness or shock.

apˈpalling *adj* frightening and horrible.

apˈpallingly *adv.*

apparatus /ˌæpəˈreɪtəs/ *c.n* instrument(s),
machine(s), used for some particular purpose:
*The scientist used a complicated apparatus for
her experiments.*

apparel /əˈpærəl/ *u.n* (*old use*; *literary*) clothing;
dress(4).

apparent(ly), apparition ⇒ appear.

appeal /əˈpiːl/ *n* 1 *c.n* (often — *to s.o* (*for, to do,
s.t*)) strong/serious request (to s.o) (for, to do,
s.t): *The chairman made an appeal to the audience
for quiet* (or *to be quiet*). *They organized an
appeal for money to help the homeless.* 2 *c/
u.n* (*law*) request to a higher court for the
decision of a lower one to be changed: *the
right of appeal.* 3 *c.n* (in games and sports)
request for an umpire(1), a judge etc to make
a certain decision. 4 *c/u.n* (often *the* — *of s.o/
s.t*) attraction, charm, (of s.o/s.t): *the appeal of
the sea on a hot day.*

▷ *intr.v* 5 (often — (*to s.o*) *for s.t*; — *to s.o to do s.t*)
make an appeal(1) (to s.o) (for s.t, to do s.t).
6 (often — *against s.t*) ask for a decision to be
changed, taken. ⇒ appeal(2,3). 7 (often — *to s.o*)
be attractive (to s.o): *Such films appeal mostly to
children.*

apˈpealing *adj* attractive; causing feelings of
sympathy. Opposite unappealing.

apˈpealingly *adv.*

appear /əˈpɪə/ *intr.v* 1 come into view; begin to
be seen: *As the fog cleared, big cliffs appeared
ahead.* 2 seem (that…); look, sound etc as if: *John
appears (to be) tired this morning. It appears that
he did not get to bed until 3 am.* 3 exist; be found;
(of a book, an actor etc) be published(1), be
shown, show oneself, to people, sometimes for
the first time: *Anne's poems appeared in the first
time in a magazine. Tom is appearing in a new
play next week. This word appears for the first
time in 14th century books.* 4 (of a person in a
law court) be present officially: *appear before a
judge; appear for a person* (*as her/his lawyer*).

apparent /əˈpærənt/ *adj* 1 that can be clearly
seen or understood: *When he explained, the
answer was quite apparent.* 2 not necessarily real:
*The fact that she was ill explained her apparent
unwillingness to speak to us.*

apˈparently *adv* (so) it seems or appears(2):
Apparently, he left before we got there.

apparition /ˌæpəˈrɪʃən/ *c.n* 1 sudden and unexpected appearance(1) of s.o/s.t, esp a dead
person. 2 person or thing who/that appears in
this way; ghost(1).

apˈpearance *n* 1 *c.n* act or fact of appear-
ing(1,3,4). 2 *c/u.n* what s.o/s.t looks like: *The
place had an appearance of calm but this was
only appearance; underneath there was a terrible
struggle for existence.* **by/from/to all appearances** judging only from what one can see, know
etc. **keep up appearances** hide s.t bad, poor
etc behind an appearance(2) of being as good,
successful etc as before. **make an appearance**
appear.

appease /əˈpiːz/ *tr.v* (*formal*) 1 make (s.t) less
painful, uncomfortable etc: *appease one's hunger
by having a piece of bread and cheese.* 2 make
(s.o) calm, quiet or less angry: *appease a crying
baby with milk.*

ap'peasement *u.n*.

append /ə'pend/ *tr.v* (often — *s.t to s.t*) (*formal*) add (s.t) (to s.t); put (one's signature etc) at the end/bottom of a letter etc.

ap'pendage *c.n* thing added on (to s.t): *You could call a monkey's tail an appendage.*

appendix /ə'pendɪks/ *c.n* (*pl -es, appendices* /ə'pendɪˌsiːz/) **1** thing added, esp at the end of a book to give more information. **2** very small organ on the alimentary canal that is often removed when one has appendicitis.

appendicitis /əˌpendɪ'saɪtɪs/ *u.n* painful illness often making it necessary to have an operation to remove one's appendix(2).

appertain /ˌæpə'teɪn/ *intr.v* (often — *to s.o/ s.t*) (*formal*) rightfully belong (to s.o/s.t): *There are several rights and duties appertaining to this position.*

appurtenance /ə'pɜːtɪnəns/ *c.n* (often — *of s.o/ s.t*) (*formal*) thing that appertains (to s.o/s.t).

appetite /'æpəˌtaɪt/ *c.n* (often (*have, give s.o*) *an — for s.t*) desire for or fact of wanting (food etc). **lose one's appetite** (*for s.t*) stop wanting s.t, esp food (of a certain kind). **whet s.o's appetite** (*for s.t*) make s.o want (more of) s.t. **work up an appetite** make one want to eat: *go for a long walk to work up an appetite before lunch*.

'appe,tizer, -iser *c.n* small thing eaten at the beginning of a meal to increase one's appetite.

'appe,tizing, -ising *adj* causing one to have an appetite; tasty. Opposite unappetizing.

'appe,tizingly, -isingly *adv*.

applaud /ə'plɔːd/ *tr/intr.v* show approval (of (s.o/s.t)) by clapping(3) or by words of praise.

applause /ə'plɔːz/ *u.n*. (often *a round of* —) clapping by all those present to show approval of s.o/s.t.

apple /'æpl/ *c/u.n* (also *attrib*) kind of hard round fruit that is white inside and usu red, yellow or green outside: *an apple tree*. **Adam's apple** ⇒ Adam's apple. **the apple of s.o's eye** the person/animal/thing s.o loves more than anything else.

'apple ,cart *c.n* **upset s.o's/the apple cart** (*fig; informal*) do s.t that spoils s.o's plans.

apply /ə'plaɪ/ *v* (*-ies, -ied*) **1** *intr.v* (often — (*to s.o*) *for s.t*) ask (s.o) (for s.t), often in writing: *I have applied to the theatre for tickets for the play.* **2** *tr.v* (often — *s.t to s.t*) put (s.t) on (s.t): *Apply the paint to the metal surface with this brush.* **3** *intr.v* (often — *to s.o/s.t*) concern s.o/ s.t; have to do with s.o/s.t; be relevant to s.o/s.t: *This rule applies only to people under 18 years old.* **4** *tr.v* (often — *s.t to s.t*) make use of s.t (in s.t): *Vera applied her knowledge of chemistry to the problem.* **5** *tr.v* bring (s.t) into operation; make (s.t) start to work: *Apply the brakes and the car will stop.* **apply oneself** (**to s.t**) work hard (at s.t).

appliance /ə'plaɪəns/ *c.n* machine, instrument etc used for doing s.t: *fire appliance* (i.e one used for fighting fires); *household appliance* (machine etc used in one's house, e.g a washing machine).

applicable /ə'plɪkəbl/ *adj* (often — *to s.o/s.t*) that can be applied(3) (to s.o/s.t); that is suitable (for s.o/s.t): *That rule is not applicable to people over 18*. Opposite inapplicable.

applicant /'æplɪkənt/ *c.n* person who applies(1) for s.t, esp a job.

application /ˌæplɪ'keɪʃən/ *n* **1** *c.n* (often *an* — (*to s.o*) *for s.t*) request (to s.o) (for s.t), usu in writing. **2** *u.n* (often — *for s.t*) requesting of s.t. **3** *c/u.n* (often — (*of s.t*) *to s.t*) putting (of polish etc) (on metal etc). **4** *u.n* thing that one puts on in an application(3). **5** *u.n* (often — *to s.t*) attention, effort, (put into doing s.t): *George lacks application* (*to his studies*). **6** *c.n* (often *an — (of s.t) to s.t*) making practical use (of s.t) (for a situation etc): *We must find an application of this new discovery in our work.*

appli'cation ,form *c.n* piece of paper on which one writes one's application(1) for s.t, esp a job.

ap'plied *adj* (of science) practical; used for practical purposes. Compare pure(6).

appoint /ə'pɔɪnt/ *tr.v* **1** (often — *s.o* (*as*) *s.t, to do s.t*) give (s.o) a job or position (as s.t etc): *The head has appointed Mary* (*as*) *captain of the team*. **2** set up (a committee etc); create(1) (s.t). **3** (*formal*) fix, choose or set (s.t): *Will you please appoint a day for our next meeting.*

ap'pointed *adj* **1** that has been agreed or fixed: *the appointed day*. **2** who has been chosen.

appointee /ˌæpɔɪn'tiː/ *c.n* (*formal*) person who is appointed(1) to a job or position.

ap'pointment 1 *c.n* (often — *to do s.t*) agreed fixing of a time and place for a meeting etc (to do s.t): *I made an appointment to see him tomorrow*. **2** *c.n* meeting at a time and place agreed before: *Don't be late for our appointment.* **3** *c/u.n* (often — (*of s.o*) *as/to s.t*) choosing (of s.o) (for a job or position): *We are very pleased about Ruth's appointment to the chair of English.* **4** *c.n* job: *Lynne got a local government appointment after leaving university*. **by appointment** as a result of making an appointment(1): *Our doctor only sees patients by appointment.* **by appointment to the Queen** etc (sign on a shop etc showing that the Queen etc buys things from there).

apportion /ə'pɔːʃən/ *tr.v* (often — *s.t among/ between s.o*) (*formal*) divide (s.t) into shares (among/between s.o): *The inquiry apportioned the blame equally between the two departments.*

ap'portionment *u.n*.

apposition /ˌæpə'zɪʃn/ *u.n* (often *in* — (*to s.t*)) (*grammar*) use of a word or phrase(1), esp a noun (phrase(1)), to give a fuller explanation of another: *In 'Dr Smith, our new doctor, comes from Scotland', 'our new doctor' is in apposition to 'Dr Smith'.*

appraise /ə'preɪz/ *tr.v* decide what (s.t) is worth. **appraise s.t at s.t** decide that s.t is worth s.t.

ap'praisal *c/u.n* (often — *of s.o/s.t*) **1** act or fact of appraising (s.t). **2** analysis(1,2) or judgment (of s.o/s.t): *The teacher's appraisal of her new class was quite favourable.*

appreciate /ə'priːʃɪˌeɪt/ *v* **1** *tr.v* realize the quality, value etc of (s.o/s.t) (and enjoy or feel grateful for it): *I appreciate good music.* **2** *tr.v* realize or understand (s.t): *I quite appreciate your worries about the future.* **3** *intr.v* increase in value: *The value of my house has appreciated by £5000 in one year.* Opposite depreciate.

appreciable /ə'priːʃəbl/ *adj* large enough to be noticed, seen, measured etc: *an appreciable increase in value.*

appreciation /əˌpriːʃɪ'eɪʃən/ *n* **1** *u.n* act or fact of appreciating(1,2) s.o/s.t: *They showed their appreciation for her bravery by collecting £500* *for her.* **2** *c.n* written or sometimes spoken account of the good and sometimes also the bad points of s.t: *The manager wrote an appreciation of Rosa's work for her.* **3** *c.n* increase in value. ⇒ appreciate(3). Opposite depreciation. **in appreciation of s.t** as a sign of one's gratitude for s.t: *Peter received a gold watch in appreciation of his services to the company.*

appreciative /ə'pri:ʃɪətɪv/ *adj* (often — *of* s.o/ s.t) feeling or showing that one appreciates(1) s.o/ s.t; grateful.

apprehend[1] /ˌæprɪ'hend/ *tr.v* (becoming *old use*) understand (s.t).

apprehension[1] /ˌæprɪ'henʃən/ *n* **1** *u.n* (often *pl* with *sing* meaning) fear about the future; anxiety: *I have so many apprehensions about his future.* **2** *c/u.n* (*formal*) fact of apprehending[1] (s.t); understanding (of s.t).

apprehensive /ˌæprɪ'hensɪv/ *adj* feeling apprehension[1](1) (about s.t).

apprehend[2] /ˌæprɪ'hend/ *tr.v* (*formal*) arrest (s.o).

apprehension[2] /ˌæprɪ'henʃən/ *u.n.*

apprentice /ə'prentɪs/ *c.n* person, usu a young one, who is learning a trade, e.g building, and has agreed to work for the person teaching her/him for some years in return for being taught.

ap'prentice,ship *u.n* time or state of being an apprentice.

appro /'æprəʊ/ *u.n* **on appro** (*informal*) on approval (⇒ approve).

approach /ə'prəʊtʃ/ *n* (often — *to* s.o/s.t) **1** *u.n* act of coming near(er) (to s.o/s.t): *The cat's approach to the birds was slow and silent.* **2** *c.n* way that leads to s.t: *The approach to the farm was always very muddy in winter.* **3** *c.n* act of speaking (to s.o) for the first time, usu to try to get to know her/him: *We made several approaches to her but she always ignored us.* **4** *c.n* way of doing or starting s.t: *We need a new approach to our problems of cost.*
▷ *v* **5** *tr.v* move towards (s.o/s.t); come or go near(er) (s.o/s.t): *The police warned the public not to approach the man if they saw him.* **6** *intr.v* come near(er) in time: *As summer approaches, the days become longer.* **7** *tr.v* become close(r) to (s.t) in quality etc: *The fruit is approaching* ripeness *at last.* **8** *tr.v* (often — s.o *about* s.t) go to (s.o) with a request, suggestion etc (about s.t): *Shall I approach the manager about a holiday?* **9** *tr.v* (begin) to deal with (s.t): *We have to approach the question of our costs in a new way.*

ap'proachable *adj* friendly; easy to approach(8).

approbation /ˌæprə'beɪʃən/ *u.n* (*formal*) (praise showing) official approval.

appropriate[1] /ə'prəʊprɪət/ *adj* (often — *for* s.o/ s.t) suitable (to a particular person, situation etc): *an appropriate dress for this weather; an appropriate answer to such a request.* Opposite inappropriate.

ap'propriately *adv.* **ap'propriateness** *u.n.*

appropriate[2] /ə'prəʊprɪ,eɪt/ *tr.v* (*formal*) **1** take (s.t) for oneself; steal (s.t). **2** (often — s.t *for* s.t) set (s.t) aside (for a particular purpose): *A sum of £50 000 was appropriated for the new* swimming pool.

appropriation /ə,prəʊprɪ'eɪʃən/ **1** *u.n* act or

fact of appropriating[2](1,2) s.t. **2** *c.n* thing appropriated[2](1,2): *We are hoping for an appropriation of £10 000 for new furniture.*

approve /ə'pru:v/ *tr/intr.v* agree (to (s.t), usu formally): *The government have approved our plans.* **approve of s.o/s.t** think that s.o/s.t is good, right etc: *Do you approve of free music lessons for children?*

ap'proval *u.n* act or fact of approving (of s.o/s.t); feeling or showing that one is satisfied or pleased (with s.o/s.t). **on approval** (*informal on appro*) (when one buys s.t in a shop) with the agreement that one can take it back and have one's money returned if one does not like it, it is not suitable etc.

ap,proved 'school *c/unique n* special kind of boarding school (⇒ board[2]) to which young people who have been found guilty of crimes are sent by a judge etc.

ap'provingly *adv* in a way that shows approval.

approx /ə'prɒks/ *adv* approximate(ly).

approximate *adj* /ə'prɒksɪmɪt/ **1** close to being the correct or accurate one: *The approximate time of the accident was 10.30 am.*
▷ *tr/intr.v* /ə'prɒksɪ,meɪt/ **2** (often — *to* s.t) (cause (s.t) to) come very near: *What Peter said approximated to the truth.*

ap'proximately *adv.*

approximation /ə,prɒksɪ'meɪʃən/ *c/u.n.*

appurtenance ⇒ appertain.

Apr *written abbr* April.

apricot /'eɪprɪ,kɒt/ *n* **1** *c/u.n* (also *attrib*) kind of soft orange or yellow fruit with a stone inside; it is smaller than a peach(1): *an apricot tree.* **2** *u.n* (also *attrib*) light orange-yellow colour.

April /'eɪprəl/ *c/unique n* (*written abbr* Apr) 4th month of the year: *There are thirty days in April. I was born on 6 April* (say 'the sixth of April' or 'April the sixth'). *It was a wet April afternoon.*

,April 'fool *c.n* **1** person who has a trick played on her/him on 1 April (*April Fools' Day*).
▷ *interj* **2** (words said to a person who has just been tricked on this day).

apron /'eɪprən/ *c.n* piece of cloth worn in front of one's body while cooking etc to keep one's clothes clean.

apse /æps/ *c.n* end part of a church, usu in the shape of half a circle, behind the altar(2).

apt /æpt/ *adj* **1** fit; suitable: *Ben would be an apt subject for this test because he is clever.* **2** (often — *at* s.t) clever or skilful (in s.t). **apt to do s.t** likely to do s.t; having a tendency to do s.t: *When one is tired one is apt to make mistakes.*

aptitude /'æptɪ,tjuːd/ *c/u.n* (also *attrib*) (often — *for* s.t) natural ability (for s.t): *an aptitude for learning languages.*

'aptitude ,test *c.n* test to find out whether one has an aptitude for s.t.

'aptly *adv.* **'aptness** *u.n.*

aqualung /'ækwə,lʌŋ/ *c.n* device for supplying air to s.o swimming under water without air pipes to the surface.

aquamarine /ˌækwəmə'riːn/ *n* **1** *c.n* (also *attrib*) precious stone, blue-green in colour, used for making jewellery. **2** *c.n* jewel made from such a stone. **3** *u.n* (also *attrib*) blue-green colour.

aquarium /ə'kweərɪəm/ *c.n* (*pl* -s or, less usu, aquaria /ə'kweərɪə/) **1** tank with glass sides in which fish and other water creatures are kept. **2** building containing a collection of such tanks.

Aquarius /ə'kweərɪəs/ *n* **1** *unique n* one of the 12 signs of the zodiac. **2** *c.n* person born under this sign.

aquatic /ə'kwætɪk/ *adj* **1** (of creatures) living in the water. **2** (of sports) happening in or on water, e.g swimming and rowing.

aqueduct /'ækwɪˌdʌkt/ *c.n* thing made for water to run along from one place to another, often like a bridge, e.g across a valley.

aqueous /'ækwɪəs/ *adj* (*technical*) of, referring to, like, in or containing water: *an aqueous solution*(1).

Arabic numeral /'ærəbɪk ˌnjuːmərəl/ *c.n* one of the numbers 1, 2, 3, 4, 5, 6, 7, 8, 9, 0. Compare Roman numeral.

arable /'ærəbl/ *adj* (of land) suitable for ploughing and the growing of crops.

arbiter /'ɑːbɪtə/ *c.n* **1** person who arbitrates. **2** (usu *an — of s.t*) person who has absolute control or great influence (over s.t): *Irene is the arbiter of fashion in our group.*

arbitration /ˌɑːbɪ'treɪʃən/ *u.n* (also (*formal*) **arbitrament** /ɑː'bɪtrəmənt/) deciding of an argument between two groups by a person chosen by both groups to act as judge.

arbitrate /'ɑːbɪˌtreɪt/ *tr/intr.v* (often — *between s.o and s.o*) decide (an argument) (between groups who have opposite views).

'arbiˌtrator *c.n* = arbiter(1).

arbour /'ɑːbə/ *c.n* (US **'arbor**) shelter in a garden, usu made by making plants or trees grow over a frame.

arc /ɑːk/ *c.n* **1** part of a circle: *A rainbow forms an arc in the sky.* **2** strong electric current flowing across the space between two electrodes.

'arc-ˌlamp/-ˌlight *c.n* kind of very bright light using an arc(2).

arcade /ɑː'keɪd/ *c.n* path with an arched ceiling over it and often with shops etc on both sides: *an amusement arcade; a shopping arcade.*

arch¹ /ɑːtʃ/ *c.n* **1** curved part of a building, often over a door or window, which supports the weight above it. **2** curved part that supports (part of) a bridge. **3** arched part under the centre of the foot.

▷ *tr/intr.v* **4** (cause (s.t) to) become shaped like an arch¹(1): *arch one's back.*

arched *adj* having the shape of an arch¹(1).

'archˌway *c.n* **1** passage with an arched roof. **2** entrance arch¹(1) often built as an ornament.

arch² /ɑːtʃ/ *adj* **1** = coy. **2** = supercilious.

'archly *adv.* **'archness** *u.n.*

archaeology /ˌɑːkɪ'ɒlədʒɪ/ *u.n* scientific study of the remains of ancient buildings etc.

archaeological /ˌɑːkɪə'lɒdʒɪkl/ *adj* of or referring to archaeology.

archaeologist /ˌɑːkɪ'ɒlədʒɪst/ *c.n* person who studies, is skilled in, archaeology.

archaic /ɑː'keɪɪk/ *adj* belonging to an ancient or much earlier age; no longer in common use: *an archaic word.*

archangel /'ɑːkˌeɪndʒəl/ *c.n* angel(1) of high rank.

archbishop /ˌɑːtʃ'bɪʃəp/ *c.n* high rank of Christian(1) priest above a bishop(1).

ˌarch'bishopric *c.n* **1** rank of an archbishop.

2 (also **archdiocese** /ˌɑːtʃ'daɪəsɪs/) area controlled by an archbishop.

archdeacon /ˌɑːtʃ'diːkən/ *c.n* Christian(1) priest lower in rank than a bishop(1) but higher than a vicar.

archer /'ɑːtʃə/ *c.n* person who shoots arrows from a bow.

'archery *u.n* sport in which one shoots arrows at a target(1).

archetype /'ɑːkɪˌtaɪp/ *c.n* (often — *of s.t*) **1** original model from which other things are made: *This was the archetype on which all later models were based.* **2** perfect example (of s.t): *This is an archetype of* Impressionist *painting.*

archipelago /ˌɑːkɪ'pelɪɡəʊ/ *c.n* (*pl* -(e)s) **1** large group of islands. **2** sea containing an archipelago(1).

architect /'ɑːkɪˌtekt/ *c.n* **1** person who makes the plans for buildings and checks the work as it is going on. **2** (*fig*) person who makes the plans (of s.t else, e.g a government policy(1)).

architectural /ˌɑːkɪ'tektʃərəl/ *adj* of or referring to architecture.

ˌarchi'tecturally *adv.*

architecture /'ɑːkɪˌtektʃə/ *u.n* **1** art and science of building. **2** way and/or style(2) of building (of a particular building, a city, an age etc): Roman(1) *architecture; the architecture of the* Pyramids(2).

archives /'ɑːkaɪvz/ *pl.n* **1** place where historical records are kept. **2** historical records kept in archives(1).

archivist /'ɑːkɪvɪst/ *c.n* keeper of archives(2).

archway ⇒ arch¹.

Arctic /'ɑːktɪk/ *adj* **1** of or referring to the very cold most northern area of the world: *arctic exploration.* **2** extremely cold: *an Arctic wind.*

▷ *def.n* **3** very cold most northern area of the world. Compare Antarctic.

ardour /'ɑːdə/ *u.n* (US **'ardor**) (often — *for s.o/ s.t*) very strong feeling, usu of love, admiration etc (for s.o/s.t).

ardent /'ɑːdnt/ *adj* full of ardour: *an ardent admirer of a film-star.*

'ardently *adv.*

arduous /'ɑːdjʊəs/ *adj* (*formal*) needing a lot of effort: *an arduous climb.*

'arduously *adv.* **'arduousness** *u.n.*

are (strong form /ɑː/, weak form /ə/) *2nd pers sing*, and *1st, 2nd* and *3rd pers pl pres. t* of 'be': *Are you/we/they ready?*

aren't /ɑːnt/ = are not.

area /'eərɪə/ *n* **1** *c/u.n* size of a surface which one finds by multiplying the length by the width. **2** *c.n* amount of space within certain limits: *There isn't much working area in this small office.* **3** *c.n* part of the earth's surface: *The area of sea between France and England is called the English Channel.* **4** *c.n* field of activity, study etc: *Her main work lies in the area of youth care.*

arena /ə'riːnə/ *c.n* **1** central area on which games are played etc and which is surrounded by rows of seats rising above and behind each other. **2** (*fig*) place where a competition, struggle etc takes place: *an arena of war.*

aren't = are not.

argue /'ɑːgjuː/ *v* **1** *intr.v* (often — (*with s.o*) *about/ over s.t*; — *against/for s.t*) give (strong) reasons to support one's own ideas (about s.t etc) and oppose(2) s.o else's; quarrel. **2** *tr.v* (often — *that*

. . .) support (s.t) by arguing(1)(that . . .): *Hilda is arguing that we should stay at home this evening.*
argue s.o into, **out of**, **(doing) s.t** use arguments to persuade s.o to do, not to do, s.t: *Peter wanted to hit the man but Alexander argued him out of it.*

arguable /ˈɑːgjuəbl/ *adj* **1** that can be supported by (reasonable) arguments: *It is arguable that this cold winter will have helped the garden by killing harmful insects.* **2** that can be argued against; doubtful: *Ted thinks we don't need help but I think that is arguable.*

'arguably *adv* it is possible to argue that . . .: *Arguably, the best thing to do is to sell the shop.*

'argument *n* **1** *u.n* act or fact of arguing(1). **2** *c.n* (often — against/for (doing) s.t) reason put forward to attack/support an idea. **3** *c.n* (often have an — (with s.o) about/over s.o/s.t) angry discussion (with s.o) (about s.t).

argumentative /ˌɑːgjuˈmentətɪv/ *adj* liking to argue(1).

aria /ˈɑːrɪə/ *c.n* song for singing by one person, esp in an opera(1).

arid /ˈærɪd/ *adj* **1** (of a place, climate etc) very dry; not having enough rain: *an arid part of Africa.* **2** (of an idea etc) boring; not useful: *an arid discussion.*

aridity /əˈrɪdɪtɪ/ *u.n.*

'aridly *adv* in an arid(2) way.

Arles /ˈɑːriːz/ *unique n* **1** one of the 12 signs of the zodiac. **2** *c.n* person born under this sign.

arise /əˈraɪz/ *intr.v* (*p.t* arose /əˈrəʊz/, *p.p* arisen /əˈrɪzən/) **1** appear; begin (to be noticed or to exist): *A problem arose when the car wouldn't start.* **2** (*formal*) = rise(9). **arise from**, **out of**, **s.t** be a result of s.t: *The whole trouble arose from a misunderstanding.*

aristocrat /əˈrɪstəˌkræt/ *c.n* member of the highest, the most powerful, class in society, usu a social class consisting of lords, ladies etc.

aristocracy /ˌærɪˈstɒkrəsɪ/ *n* (*pl* -ies) **1** *c/ def.pl.n* group of aristocrats in a country; upper class(2): *The French and Russian aristocracies were destroyed by* revolutions' (⇒ revolt (*v*)). **2** *u.n* government by an aristocracy(1). **3** *c.n* country ruled by an aristocracy(1).

aristocratic /ˌærɪstəˈkrætɪk/ *adj* **1** of or referring to aristocracy or aristocrats. **2** distinguished in manner, behaviour etc.

ˌaristoˈcratically *adv.*

arithmetic /əˈrɪθmətɪk/ *u.n* **1** science of numbers. **2** using numbers for counting etc.

ark /ɑːk/ *def.n* (also **ˌNoah's 'ark** *unique n*) (in the Bible(1)) big wooden ship in which Noah, his family and two of every kind of animal escaped the Flood(2).

arm¹ /ɑːm/ *c.n* **1** one of the two parts of one's upper body which stretch from the shoulders(1) to (the ends of) the hands. **2** thing that looks or is used like an arm¹(1): *an arm of the sea*; *the arm of a* crane²(1). **3** part of a piece of clothing that covers one's arm¹(1). **4** part of a chair etc on which one can rest one's arm¹(1). **at arm's length** (**a**) as far away as the length of one's arm¹(1). (**b**) at a safe distance away. **keep s.o at arm's length** (*fig*) avoid getting unpleasantly close to or familiar with s.o. **the (long) arm of the law** the power of the law, often as represented by the police. **twist s.o's arm** (try to) make s.o do s.t, agree

etc: *I don't really want to go but you can twist my arm.* **under one's arm** held in one's armpit. **with open arms** eagerly; willingly: *He welcomed me with open arms.*

'arm,band *c.n* (also **'armlet**) band of cloth etc worn round the arm as a sign of s.t, e.g a black band after s.o has died.

'arm,chair *c.n* chair that has arms'(4).

'arm,hole *c.n* opening in a shirt etc through which one puts one's arm'(1) when dressing.

'armlet *c.n* = armband.

ˌarm-in-'arm *adv* (often *walk* —) (of two or more people) beside each other, each with an arm round the arm of another.

'arm,pit *c.n* hollow part under one's shoulder where one's arm'(1) joins the rest of one's body.

arm² /ɑːm/ *c.n* **1** weapon for fighting or hunting with. ⇒ arms²(1).
▷ *v* **2** *tr.v* (often — s.o with s.t) supply (s.o/s.t) with arms²(1). **3** *intr.v* prepare for war etc by collecting supplies of arms²(1). **4** *tr.v* (often — s.o with s.t) supply (s.o) with s.t he/she needs for s.t: *William went into the meeting armed with plans for the future.*

armament /ˈɑːməmənt/ *n* **1** *u.n* act or fact of arming²(2,3) a country etc. **2** *c.n* (often *pl*) arms²(1) with which (parts of) the armed forces are supplied.

armed *adj* having a weapon or weapons: *an armed robber.*

ˌarmed 'forces/'services *def.pl.n* soldiers, sailors and airmen of a country; army, navy and airforce; people whose job is to defend a country against its enemies with weapons.

arms *pl.n* **1** weapons of war or sport. ⇒ firearm. **2** = coat of arms. **lay down one's arms** completely stop fighting; surrender(2). **small arms** guns that can be carried in one's hands. **take up arms** (**against s.o**) start to fight (s.o). **under arms** supplied with weapons and ready to fight: *The whole country is under arms and ready to fight for its freedom.* **up in arms** (*fig*) angry (and ready to fight in order to protect s.t): *The whole village was up in arms over the proposal for a new road through it.*

'arms ,race *c/def.n* competition between countries to produce or get more weapons than each other so as to be stronger in case of war.

arm³ /ɑːm/ *c.n* branch of the armed forces etc: *the air arm.*

armada /ɑːˈmɑːdə/ *c.n* big group of ships, usu warships; fleet²(1).

armament ⇒ arm².

armature /ˈɑːmətʃə/ *c.n* (*technical*) moving part of a dynamo which makes the electricity in it.

armband, **armchair** ⇒ arm¹.

armed ⇒ arm².

armhole, **arm-in-arm** ⇒ arm¹.

armistice /ˈɑːmɪstɪs/ *c.n* agreement between enemies during a war to stop fighting for a time.

armlet ⇒ arm¹.

armour /ˈɑːmə/ *u.n* **1** metal covering of warships, tanks etc to protect them from enemy shells. **2** (in history) metal covering to protect the body during fighting: *a suit of armour.*

'armoured *adj* **1** covered or protected with armour(1,2): *an armoured vehicle.* **2** consisting of armoured(1) vehicles: *an armoured* division(4).

,armoured 'car *c.n* army vehicle that is protected with armour(1) and runs on wheels not tracks.

'armour ,plate *u.n* metal plates out of which armour(1) for ships, tanks etc is made.

'armour-,plated *adj* protected with armour plate.

'armoury *c.n* (*pl -ies*) (US **'armory**) place where arms²(1) are kept.

armpit ⇒ arm¹.

arms ⇒ arm².

army /'ɑːmɪ/ *c.n* (*pl -ies*) **1** branch of the armed forces that fights on the land. Compare airforce, navy(1). **2** large group of men and women who form an organized part of the army(1) of a country. **3** (often — *of s.t*) large organized group (of people or animals): *We had an army of willing helpers to pull our boats ashore.*

'army ,corps *c.n* one of the main parts into which an army(1) is divided.

aroma /ə'rəʊmə/ *c.n* (often — *of s.t*) pleasant smell (of s.t).

aromatic /,ærə'mætɪk/ *adj* having a strong pleasant smell.

arose /ə'rəʊz/ *p.t* of arise.

around /ə'raʊnd/ = round(*adv*/*prep*)(4–14).

arouse /ə'raʊz/ *tr.v* **1** awaken (s.o, an animal) from sleep. **2** stir (s.t) up; cause (a feeling etc) to begin: *His interest in farming was aroused by a visit to the country when he was a child.* **3** cause sexual excitement in (s.o).

arr *written abbr* arrival; arrive(s).

arraign /ə'reɪn/ *tr.v* (often — *s.o for s.t*) (*law*; *formal*) accuse (s.o) (of s.t); bring (s.o) before a court of law for trial (for s.t).

ar'raignment *u.n.*

arrange /ə'reɪndʒ/ *v* **1** *tr.v* put (s.t) into some kind of order: *Helen arranged the plants in her garden in neat rows.* **2** *tr*/*intr.v* prepare (s.t); make plans (with s.o) (for etc s.t); come to an agreement: *We arranged with our friends to visit them on Sunday. We arranged to be there* (or *that we'd be there*) *at six o'clock.* **3** *tr.v* (often — *s.t for the piano* etc) change (a piece of music) (to make it suitable for the piano etc).

ar'rangement *n* **1** *c*/*u.n* act or fact of arranging(1) (s.t). **2** *c.n* (usu *pl*) (often *the —s for s.t*) plan. **3** *c.n* agreement: *My arrangement with the company was that they should pay me in advance.* **4** *c*/*u.n* changing of a piece of music to make it suitable for an instrument, instruments, voice or voices. **5** *c.n* piece of music after it has been arranged(3). **make an arrangement**; **make arrangements** arrange(2) a meeting, time etc.

array /ə'reɪ/ *c*/*u.n* (usu *sing*) (*formal*) **1** (often *an — of s.t*) collection (of s.t): *There was a distinguished array of people in the audience.* **2** clothes; dress: *Mandy was in her holiday array.* **3** order, esp for battle: *The army was drawn up in battle array.*

arrears /ə'rɪəz/ *pl.n* **1** money owed and not yet paid: *arrears of salary.* **2** work that should already have been done but has not. **fall into arrears (with s.t)** start to be in arrears (with s.t). **in arrears (with s.t)** (a) owing money (on s.t). (b) late (with s.t).

arrest /ə'rest/ *c*/*u.n* **1** act of stopping s.o/s.t. **2** act of stopping and holding s.o for a crime etc he/ she is thought to have committed: *Have the police*

made an arrest in connection with the robbery yet? **under arrest** made a prisoner, usu of the police: *'Where's Fred?' 'At the police station; he's under arrest.'* **place**/**put s.o under arrest** (usu of the police) arrest(3) s.o.

▷ *tr.v* **3** (usu of the police) stop and hold (s.o who is suspected of doing s.t wrong): *He was arrested on suspicion of murder.* **4** (*formal*) stop (s.t); prevent (s.t) continuing: *The doctor managed to arrest the bleeding.* **arrest s.o's attention** ⇒ attention.

ar'resting *adj* that attracts attention: *an arresting dress*/*sight.*

arrive /ə'raɪv/ *intr.v* (*written abbr* arr) **1** (often — *at s.w*) come (to a place); reach a place, esp after a journey or after some time: *Our guests arrived late. We arrived at the hotel at last after midnight. The day of our examination arrived all too soon.* **2** (of a baby) be born. **3** (*informal*) be successful: *At last he has arrived as an actor.* **arrive at s.t** (a) ⇒ arrive(1). (b) reach (a decision etc).

ar'rival *n* **1** *u.n* (*written abbr* arr) (often — *at s.t*/*s.w*) act or fact of arriving(1,2) (at s.t/s.w). **2** *c.n* person or thing who/that arrives: *a late arrival.* **on arrival** when one arrives: *He was so tired that he went straight to bed on arrival.*

arrogant /'ærəgənt/ *adj* in a rudely proud way.

'arrogance *u.n.* **'arrogantly** *adv.*

arrow /'ærəʊ/ *c.n* **1** sign ⇒ used to show a position or direction: *If you follow the arrows, you'll find our office.* **2** thin piece of wood or sometimes metal, sharp at one end and with feathers at the other, for shooting from a bow.

arse /ɑːs/ *c.n* (*slang*; do not use!) buttocks.

arsenal /'ɑːsənl/ *c.n* **1** building in which weapons, bullets etc are made and/or stored. **2** (often — *of s.t*) collection (of weapons): *The police found a whole arsenal of guns in the house.*

arsenic /'ɑːsnɪk/ *u.n* kind of poisonous chemical substance used in making medicines and glass, killing rats etc, *chem.symb* As.

arson /'ɑːsn/ *u.n* act or fact of criminally setting fire to s.t.

'arsonist *c.n* person who is guilty of arson.

art¹ /ɑːt/ *n* **1** *u.n* making or producing s.t, e.g a painting, that is beautiful or that arouses feelings of pleasure, satisfaction etc: *Jane is studying art at her college.* **2** *c.n* (often *the — of s.t*) skill (of s.t) that is the result of study and practice: *He became very good at the art of public speaking.* **3** *u.n* way of making s.t, esp s.t beautiful or difficult that can be seen, e.g a work of art. **4** (usu *pl*) subject of study which is not an exact science, e.g literature, languages and history. **Bachelor**/**Master of Arts** ⇒ bachelor, master. **the fine arts** ⇒ fine¹. **work of art** ⇒ work.

'artful *adj* (*derog*) clever, usu in a bad way; deceitful.

'artfully *adv.* **'artfulness** *u.n.*

'art ,gallery *c.n* building where works of art are on show.

'artiness *u.n* (usu *derog*) fact or quality of being arty.

artisan /,ɑːtɪ'zæn/ *c.n* skilled worker or mechanic.

artist *c.n* person who practises any form of art¹(1), esp painting or drawing.

artiste /,ɑː'tiːst/ *c.n* professional performer on radio or television, in the theatre etc.

artistic /,ɑː'tɪstɪk/ *adj* **1** (of s.t in the fine arts (⇒

fine¹)) done with skill: *an artistic flower arrangement*. **2** (of a person) who has skill in, a good understanding of, the fine arts: *Elizabeth is very artistic*.

ar'tistically *adv*.

'artistry *u.n* artistic(1) skill.

'artless *adj* sincere; not trying to deceive; without being artificial(3): *the artless charm of a child*.

'artlessly *adv*. **'artlessness** *u.n*.

'art ˌschool *c.n* college where the fine arts are taught.

'arty *adj* (**-ier, -iest**) (usu *derog*) pretending to be artistic; exaggeratedly artistic.

ˌarty-'crafty *adj* (*informal*; usu *derog*) of, using, making, handmade articles, esp when they seem silly.

art² /ɑːt/ (*old use*) *2nd pers sing pres.t* of 'be', usu found with 'thou': *Art thou ready?*

artery /'ɑːtərɪ/ *c.n* (*pl* **-ies**) **1** one of the pipes that carry blood to various parts of the body from the heart. Compare vein(1). **2** (*fig*) main road, shipping route(1) etc.

arterial /ɑː'tɪərɪəl/ *adj* of or referring to an artery(1) or arteries.

arˌterial 'road *c.n* important main road.

arteriosclerosis /ɑː'tɪərɪəʊsklə,rəʊsɪs/ *u.n* kind of disease in the walls of the arteries(1) which causes them to become hard, so that they prevent a good blood flow.

artesian well /ɑː'tiːzɪən ˌwel/ *c.n* kind of well sunk to below the level that the supply of water comes from, so that the water rises to the surface without pumping.

artful(ly/ness) ⇒ art¹.

arthritis /ɑː'θraɪtɪs/ *u.n* kind of disease of the joints of the body causing swelling, pain and difficulty in moving.

arthritic /ɑː'θrɪtɪk/ *adj* referring to, or suffering from, arthritis: *an arthritic shoulder*.

artichoke /'ɑːtɪ,tʃəʊk/ *c.n* **1** (also **'globe ˌartichoke**) plant with a thick leafy flower that is cooked and eaten as a vegetable. **2** (also **Je'rusalem ˌartichoke**) plant whose thick roots look like potatoes and are cooked and eaten as a vegetable.

article /'ɑːtɪkl/ *c.n* **1** particular thing or object: *an article of clothing* (e.g a hat or coat). **2** complete piece of writing in a newspaper, magazine etc. **definite/indefinite article** ⇒ definite, indefinite. **leading article** ⇒ leading.

articulate /ɑː'tɪkjʊlɪt/ *adj* **1** (of speech) in which the different sounds and words are divided clearly. **2** (of a person) able to express oneself easily, clearly and exactly. Opposite inarticulate.

▷ *tr/intr.v* /ɑː'tɪkjʊ,leɪt/ **3** pronounce (words) clearly; express (things) clearly in words.

articulation¹ /ɑː,tɪkjʊ'leɪʃən/ *u.n* manner of speaking, pronouncing, sounds and words.

articulated /ɑː'tɪkjʊ,leɪtɪd/ *adj* connected by joints: *an articulated lorry*.

arˌticu'lation² *c.n* (*formal*) joint; connection by means of a joint or joints, esp in one's body.

artifice /'ɑːtɪfɪs/ *c/u.n* (*formal*) **1** way of doing s.t skilfully: *The hall was furnished with great artifice*. **2** clever, esp deceitful, ways: *the artifices of a cunning(1) child*.

artificer /ɑː'tɪfɪsə/ *c.n* **1** (*formal*) skilled worker; artisan. **2** rank of skilled engineer officer in the Royal Navy.

artificial /ˌɑːtɪ'fɪʃəl/ *adj* **1** made by human skill; not natural: *artificial silk*. **2** done in a way that is not the natural one: *artificial* insemination/respiration. **3** (*derog*) (of a person, her/his behaviour) not sincere.

artificiality /ˌɑːtɪ,fɪʃɪ'ælɪtɪ/ *u.n*. **ˌarti'ficially** *adv*.

artillery /ɑː'tɪlərɪ/ *u.n* **1** large guns on wheels or in tracked vehicles. **2** branch of the army trained to use these.

artiness, artisan, artist, artiste, artistic-(ally), artistry, artless(ly/ness), arty-(crafty) ⇒ art¹.

arum /'eɪrəm/ *c.n* (also **'arum ˌlily**) kind of tall white lily.

as (strong form /æz/, weak form /əz/) *adv* **1** equally; no less: *You think I've got a lot of books but you've really got just as many.* ⇒ as . . . as . . . **2** looked at in the way (of being): *Norway, as described in this advertisement, seems to be a wonderful place for a holiday.* **3** (*formal*) for example; such as; like(2): *There are still several kingdoms in Europe, as Britain, Belgium and Spain.* **as . . . as . . .** (in which the second 'as' is a *conj*) equally . . . with . . .; no less . . . than . . .; with the same degree of . . . that . . . does, has etc: *Paul's house is as big as ours. John can run as quickly as Peter.* **as far as . . .** ⇒ far(*adv*). **as is/are** etc . . . and so is/are: *Elaine is old, as is her husband.* **as/so far as s.o/s.t is concerned** ⇒ far(*adv*). **as/so long as . . .** ⇒ long(*adv*). **as much** that; so: *'George didn't go to the meeting.' 'I expected as much.'* **as soon as . . .** ⇒ soon. **as s.t go(es), is/are** etc compared with the way s.t is/ are etc now: *This rent is cheap as rents go today.* **as well as . . .** ⇒ well.

▷ *conj* **4** at the time that: *I met him as he was leaving his house.* **5** because: *Charles couldn't come as he had another appointment.* **6** in the way that: *You must do (it) as your teacher tells you.* **7** although: *Old as I am, I can still walk fast.* **8** however much: *Try as I can, I can't open this door.* **s.t is to s.t as s.t is to s.t; as s.t is to s.t, (so) s.t is to s.t** the proportion(2) of s.t to s.t is the same as that of s.t to s.t: *4 is to 16 as 2 is to 8.* **as against s.o/s.t** compared with s.o/s.t. **as for/to s.o/s.t** with reference to, regard to, s.o/s.t; about s.o/ s.t. **as from/of s.t** starting/counting from s.t: *As from January 1st, all salaries go up by 6%.* ⇒ as of now. **as good as gold/new** ⇒ gold, new(*adj*). **as if/though . . .** (a) as he/she/it would be, do etc if . . .: *Neil behaves as if he owned the place! It looks as if it's going to rain.* (b) (used in an exclamation(2) to mean the opposite of what is said): *As if I mind what silly people say about me!* (I don't mind at all . . .). **as it is; as things are** under the present conditions: *I would have liked to have finished by March, but as it is, that is impossible.* **as it were** in a manner of speaking; as one way of saying it: *Greece is, as it were, my dream country.* **as of now** ⇒ now. **as of right** by right; according to law. **as much** ⇒ much(*pron*). **as opposed to s.o/s.t** ⇒ oppose. **as . . . as . . .** ⇒ as(*adv*). **as well** ⇒ well¹(*adv*). **as yet** ⇒ yet. **the same (. . .) as . . .** ⇒ same. **so/such (. . .) as . . .** ⇒ so¹(*adv*), such.

▷ *prep* **9** in the capacity, job, condition etc of: *Use* *this slice of bread as a plate. Lisa is looking for a job as a teacher.* **10** like; as if he/she/it was: *He was treated as a thief.* **11** with the purpose of its being: *What shall I send him as a reply to his message?* **12** when he/she/it is, was etc: *I used to eat a lot as a child but as an adult I eat little.* **as a consequence/result of s.t; as a (general) rule; as a matter of fact** ⇨ consequence, rule(*n*), fact.

▷ *pron* **13** which is s.t: *As you have heard, Helen has passed her examination.* **14** whatever or which fits in: *'Can I spend the night here?' 'Just as you wish.'.*

asbestos /æs'bestɒs/ *u.n* (also *attrib*) kind of mineral substance used in making materials that resist fire and heat: *asbestos gloves.*

ascend /ə'send/ *tr/intr.v* (*formal*) go/climb up (s.t); rise; go upwards: *I ascended the steps one by one.* Opposite descend.

ascension /ə'senʃən/ *u.n.*
A'scension *unique n* (also **A'scension ,Day**) Thursday 40 days after Easter when Christ ascended to Heaven.

a'scent *c.n* **1** (often *the — of s.t*) act or fact of ascending (s.t): *the first ascent of Everest.* **2** way up to s.t: *a difficult ascent to the top.* Opposite descent.

ascertain /ˌæsə'teɪn/ *tr.v* (often — *that, where* etc ...) (*formal*) find (s.t) out; get to know (s.t): *Have you ascertained what they want us to do here?*
ˌascer'tainable *adj* that can be ascertained.

ascetic /ə'setɪk/ *adj* **1** in favour of leading a simple strict life without any of the normal pleasures.
▷ *c.n* **2** person who leads an ascetic(1) life.
a'scetically *adv.* **asceticism** /ə'setɪˌsɪzəm/ *u.n.*

ascribe /ə'skraɪb/ *tr.v* (usu — *s.t to s.t*) (*formal*) consider s.t to be the cause of, or the reason for, s.t: *I ascribe Tom's silence to shyness.*

aseptic /æ'septɪk/ *adj* (*medical*) free from bacteria; completely clean.

ash¹ /æʃ/ *u.n* grey powder that remains after s.t has burnt: *cigarette ash.*
'ash-,bin/-,can *c.n* container for ash¹ and other waste materials from a house.
ashes /'æʃəz/ *pl.n* = ash¹.
'ash,tray *c.n* glass, metal etc dish or bowl for putting cigarette ash¹/stubs(1) etc in.
'ashy *adj* (-*ier*, -*iest*) made of, looking like, ash(es)¹.

ash² /æʃ/ *n* (also *attrib*) **1** *c.n* kind of tree that has a silvery grey trunk and hard wood. **2** *u.n* wood of this tree.

ashamed /ə'ʃeɪmd/ *adj* (often — *of s.o/s.t; — that...*) having feelings of shame or guilt (caused by s.o/s.t): *The mother was ashamed of her children's behaviour.* **ashamed to do s.t** not willing to do s.t because it would make one feel ashamed: *I am ashamed to say that I have never been to Scotland.*

ashore /ə'ʃɔː/ *adv* on, to, the shore. **be driven ashore** be forced onto the shore: *The ship was driven ashore by the storm.* **run (s.t) ashore** (cause (a ship etc) to) go onto the shore.

ashy ⇨ ash¹.

aside /ə'saɪd/ *adv* **1** on, to, one side; apart: *Put your books aside for a few minutes and have a rest.* **aside from s.o/s.t** apart from s.o/s.t:

Aside from our son there are no children here.
▷ *c.n* **2** remark spoken in such a way that only one person, or a few people, can hear it while others cannot. **3** remark spoken by an actor/actress to the audience and not to the other actors/actresses.

asinine /'æsɪˌnaɪn/ *adj* (*derog*) silly; stupid.

ask /ɑːsk/ *v* **1** *tr.v* try to get an answer to (a question) (from s.o): *Ask Elizabeth if she is ready. I'll ask him when he can come.* **2** *tr/intr.v* (often — (s.o) *about s.o/s.t*) try to get an answer to a question (about s.o/s.t) (from s.o): *I'm going to ask Jim about his school.* **3** *tr/intr.v* (often — (s.o) *for s.o/s.t, to do s.t*) try to get s.t (from s.o) by speaking or writing to her/him: *Could you please ask Mary to close the door.* **4** *tr.v* (often — *s.t from/of s.o; — that...*) try to get/require(2) (s.t) from s.o: *Could I ask a favour of you? I only ask that you should be quiet while I am working.* **5** *tr.v* invite (s.o) (to s.t etc): *Shall we ask Mrs Jones to tea today? Do ask your mother up to the office. I'll ask her for dinner.* **ask after s.o/s.t** try to find out about s.o/s.t by asking (s.o else): *I saw John last night and he was asking after you.* **ask for it/trouble** (*fig*) do s.t that is likely to cause trouble: *It's asking for trouble to go out in that old boat on such a rough sea.*
'asking ,price *c/def.n* price that s.o asks when selling s.t; bargaining price.

askew /ə'skjuː/ *adv* not straight; not at the normal angle: *Your tie is askew.*

aslant /ə'slɑːnt/ *adv* sloping: *Keith likes wearing his hat aslant.*

asleep /ə'sliːp/ *pred.adj* sleeping; not awake: *She's asleep in bed.* **fall asleep** start to sleep. **be/fall fast asleep** be in, fall into, a deep sleep: *Don't disturb him, he's fast asleep.* **sound asleep** completely asleep.

asparagus /ə'spærəgəs/ *c/u.n* (*pl* asparagus) kind of plant whose stems are cooked and eaten as a vegetable when they are young.

aspect /'æspekt/ *c.n* **1** direction in which a house etc faces: *Our house has a southerly aspect.* **2** (*literary*) appearance; look: *Geraldine had a sickly*(3) *aspect that day.* **3** particular part or side of s.t: *We must consider all aspects of the plan before deciding.*

aspen /'æspən/ *c.n* kind of tree whose leaves seem to be moving all the time unless there is absolutely no wind at all.

asperity /æ'sperɪtɪ/ *u.n* (*formal*) **1** roughness of surface, weather etc; severity(2). **2** roughness of manner; severity(1): *Maud spoke to the children with some asperity.*

aspersion /ə'spɜːʃən/ *c.n* **cast aspersions** ((**up**)**on s.o/s.t**) (*formal*) make unkind and/or damaging criticisms (of s.o/s.t): *I don't like people casting aspersions on my cooking.*

asphalt /'æsfælt/ *u.n* (also *attrib*) kind of black sticky substance mixed with sand etc and allowed to get hard when making road surfaces etc.

asphyxiate /ə'sfɪksɪˌeɪt/ *tr/intr.v* (cause (s.o, an animal) to) die or come near death because air does not reach her/his/its lungs: *The people who died in the fire were all asphyxiated by smoke.*
asphyxiation /əˌsfɪksɪ'eɪʃən/ *u.n.*

aspic /'æspɪk/ *u.n* clear brown jelly(3) made from meat bones.

aspirate /ˈæspɪrɪt/ c.n 1 (technical) sound produced just by breathing, e.g /h/.
▷ tr.v /ˈæspɪˌreɪt/ 2 (technical) say (s.t) with an /h/ sound: In English the 'h' in 'hour' is not aspirated.
aspiration[1] /ˌæspɪˈreɪʃən/ u.n.
aspire /əˈspaɪə/ intr.v (formal) 1 **aspire to** (**be/do**) **s.t** have hopes, plans, ambitions etc to be, do get etc s.t: Zoe aspires to be an actress. 2 **aspire after s.t** have aspirations[2] to be/do s.t: Peter aspires after a job in a bank.
aspirant /ˈæspɪrənt/ c.n (often — to s.t) person aspiring to s.t.
aspiration[2] /ˌæspɪˈreɪʃən/ c.n (often pl, have —s to become s.t) hopes, ambition, (to become s.t).
aspirin /ˈæsprɪn/ c/u.n (tablet of a) kind of white chemical substance that reduces pain or fever. ⇨ analgesic.
ass /æs/ c.n 1 kind of animal like a horse but with taller ears and usu smaller. ⇨ donkey(1). 2 (derog) foolish person: Don't be an ass. 3 (US slang; do not use!) buttocks.
assail /əˈseɪl/ tr.v (often — s.o/s.t with s.t) (formal) attack (s.o/s.t) violently (with blows, words etc).
as'sailant c.n person who assails s.o/s.t.
assassin /əˈsæsɪn/ c.n murderer, esp for political reasons.
assassinate /əˈsæsɪˌneɪt/ tr.v kill (s.o, esp an important politician or ruler).
assassination /əˌsæsɪˈneɪʃən/ u.n.
assault /əˈsɔːlt/ n (often — on s.o/s.t) 1 c.n sudden violent attack (on s.o/s.t). 2 c/u.n (law) (often charge s.o with —) unlawful hitting of, threatening to hit, s.o.
▷ tr.v 3 make an assault on (s.o/s.t).
as,sault and 'battery u.n (law) actual attack with blows, not just a threat of this.
assemble /əˈsembl/ v 1 tr/intr.v collect (s.o/s.t) together; come, meet, together: We assembled at the station before catching the train. 2 tr.v put the parts of (s.t) together: This is where the parts of the cars are assembled into the finished vehicles.
assemblage /əˈsemblɪdʒ/ c.n (formal) collection of people or things: an assemblage of old carriages(1).
as'sembly n (pl -ies) 1 c/u.n meeting together of people for a particular purpose: There is a school assembly at the beginning of each day. 2 u.n act or fact of assembling s.t. 3 c/def.n (often with capital A) group of people elected or appointed to make laws; (lower house of a) parliament.
as'sembly ,hall c.n large room where the students and teachers of a school assemble(1) for prayers etc.
as'sembly ,line c.n place in a factory where machines, cars etc are assembled(2) on a moving belt.
as'sembly ,room c.n public hall where meetings, dances etc are held.
assent /əˈsent/ u.n 1 (often give one's — to s.t) (formal) (esp by a ruler or government) agreement (to s.t). **with one assent** without anyone disagreeing.
▷ intr.v 2 (often — to s.t) (formal) agree (to a proposal etc).
assert /əˈsɜːt/ tr.v (often — that . . .) declare (s.t) to be true; claim (s.t): James asserted that

he had never intended to visit us. **assert oneself** show one's power and confidence: Don't let your friends have their own way; assert yourself!
assertion /əˈsɜːʃən/ c/u.n.
assertive /əˈsɜːtɪv/ adj making strong statements or claims; wanting to have one's own way.
as'sertively adv. **as'sertiveness** u.n.
assess /əˈses/ tr.v determine the value of (s.o/s.t) or the amount, quality etc of (s.t): The farmers are assessing the damage to their crops after the storm. **assess s.t at s.t** determine the value of s.t to be s.t: They assessed the damage at £200. **assess s.o/s.t for tax** etc; **assess the tax** etc on **s.t** determine what the tax etc to be paid by s.o on s.t should be.
as'sessment c/u.n.
as'sessor c.n person who assesses s.t.
asset /ˈæset/ c.n 1 (often pl) valuable possession: Fred has enough assets to cover anything he owes. 2 thing that adds to the value of (s.t): A good appearance is an asset in many jobs. 3 (usu pl) (commerce) all the things a company owns, including property, money etc: The company's assets did not cover its liabilities(2).
assiduous /əˈsɪdjʊəs/ adj (formal) paying careful attention to what one is doing: Dominic is an assiduous student.
assiduity /ˌæsɪˈdjuːɪtɪ/ u.n. **as'siduously** adv.
assign /əˈsaɪn/ tr.v 1 (often — s.o/s.t (to) s.o/s.t) give (s.o/s.t) as her/his/its share or part of s.t: The company has assigned me ten new shares (or assigned ten new shares to me). 2 (often — s.t (to) s.o) appoint (s.t) (for s.o); give s.o (s.t) as her/his job: Your manager will assign you your work for today. 3 appoint, fix, decide on, (s.t): I am going to assign a date in November for our next meeting. **assign s.o to s.t** give s.o s.t as her/his job.
as'signment n 1 u.n act of assigning(1,2) s.o to s.t or s.t to s.o. 2 c.n job, work etc assigned(2) to s.o.
assignation /ˌæsɪɡˈneɪʃən/ c.n arrangement to meet, often in secret. Compare rendezvous(1,2).
assimilate /əˈsɪmɪˌleɪt/ v 1 tr.v digest(3) (s.t). 2 tr.v take in (s.o/s.t from a different social etc group) and make (her/him) part of oneself: The UK has assimilated many foreigners. 3 intr.v (often — (in) to s.t) become part of s.t. 4 tr.v (fig) understand (s.t), usu by a gradual process(2): Henry finds it difficult to assimilate what he reads.
assimilation /əˌsɪmɪˈleɪʃən/ u.n.
assist /əˈsɪst/ tr/intr.v (formal) help (s.o/s.t).
as'sistance u.n help. **be of assistance** (**to s.o**); **give assistance to s.o** help (s.o). **come to s.o's assistance** come to help s.o.
as'sistant adj (written abbr asst) 1 who assists s.o/s.t; not having the full rank of: a shop assistant; an assistant teacher.
▷ c.n 2 person who helps s.o who is higher in rank.
assoc written abbr 1 associated (⇨ associate(4)). 2 (also **assn**) association(2).
associate /əˈsəʊʃɪət/ attrib.adj 1 lower in rank; having fewer rights or powers; not full: an associate professor/judge; an associate member of a club.
▷ c.n /əˈsəʊʃɪət/ 2 person with whom one works. 3 person who has an associate(1) position.

▷ *tr/intr.v* /əˈsəʊʃɪˌeɪt/ **4** (often — (s.o) with s.o) (cause (s.o) to) join or work together (with s.o) as friends or in the same business: *Do you associate much with the other parents at your child's school?* **associate oneself with s.o/s.t** support s.o/s.t: *I associate myself fully with what the last speaker said.* **associate s.o/s.t with s.o/ s.t** think of s.o/s.t as being connected with s.o/ s.t: *I don't associate teaching with a lazy life!*

association /ə,səʊsɪˈeɪʃən/ *n* **1** *u.n* (often — with s.o/s.t) act or fact of joining, being joined, (to s.o/s.t) for a purpose. **2** *c.n* (often — of s.t) group (of people etc) who have joined together for a particular purpose: *an association of building companies.* **3** *u.n* act or fact of associating s.o/ s.t with s.o/s.t. **in association (with s.o/s.t)** together (with s.o/s.t): *We are doing this work in association with two other companies.*
As,soci,ation ˈfoot,ball *u.n* (*formal*) = football.

assorted /əˈsɔːtɪd/ *adj* of different sorts, all together: *a bag of assorted sweets.*

asˈsortment *c.n* (often — of s.t) collection of different sorts (of s.t) all together.

asst *written abbr* assistant.

assuage /əˈsweɪdʒ/ *tr.v* (*formal*) make (s.t, usu pain or suffering) less.

assume /əˈsjuːm/ *tr.v* (often — that . . .) **1** treat (s.t) as true but without proof: *I assume that you agree with what Mike has just said.* **2** take (s.t) on; start being responsible for (s.t): *Jane assumed control of the business when her mother died.*

assumption /əˈsʌmpʃən/ *c/u.n* (example of the) fact or state of assuming s.t: *What you say is just an assumption based on little proof. Her assumption of control of the business began when her mother died.* **on the assumption that . . .** if one assumes(1) that . . . : *I am buying four tickets on the assumption that we are all going.*

assure /əˈʃʊə/ *tr.v* **1** (often — s.o of s.t; — s.o that . . .) try to make (s.o) feel sure, certain or confident (about s.t, that . . .): *I assure you that I will not say a word about this to anyone.* **2** insure (s.o/s.t), esp against death. **assure oneself of s.t, that . . .** make sure (of s.t, that . . .): *Before letting the children use the machine, I assured myself of its safety* (or *that it was safe*).

asˈsurance *n* **1** *c.n* (often *pl* with *sing* meaning) (often — of s.t) promise (about s.t); statement intended to make s.o confident (of s.t): *I give you my assurance that I shall not be late.* **2** *u.n* = self-assurance. **3** *u.n* (*commerce*) = insurance: *life assurance.*

asˈsured *adj* **1** certain; sure; promised. **2** = self-assured. **rest assured that . . .** feel/be confident that . . . : *Rest assured that I shall be there to help.*

asˈsuredly /əˈʃʊərɪdlɪ/ *adv.*

aster /ˈæstə/ *c.n* kind of plant that has pink, white or purple flowers with yellow centres.

asterisk /ˈæstərɪsk/ *c.n* sign with the shape of a star * used (**a**) to refer to a note at the bottom of the page; (**b**) to show that letters are missing in a word, e.g 'd*** it' for 'damn(3) it'; (**c**) to show that the word or phrase(1) that follows is wrong, e.g We say 'gave', not *gived.

astern /əˈstɜːn/ *adv* at, towards, the back of a ship etc. **go astern** (of a ship etc) go backwards.

lie astern (of a ship etc) be in a position behind (a ship etc).

asteroid /ˈæstəˌrɔɪd/ *c.n* one of the many small planets between Mars(1) and Jupiter(1).

asthma /ˈæsmə/ *u.n* disease that causes difficulty in breathing from time to time.

asthmatic /æsˈmætɪk/ *adj* **1** (sounding as if one is) suffering from asthma.
▷ *c.n* **2** person who suffers from asthma.

astigmatism /əˈstɪgməˌtɪzəm/ *u.n* fault in the shape of an eye that makes it difficult to see normally.

astir /əˈstɜː/ *adv* **1** up (out of bed) and moving about: *The children were already astir when I woke up.* **2** (often — at/with s.t) in a state of movement and/or excitement (caused by s.t): *The village was astir at the news of the Queen's visit.*

astonish /əˈstɒnɪʃ/ *tr.v* fill (s.o) with surprise or wonder.

aˈstonished *adj* (often — at s.t; — to hear etc s.t) feeling very surprised (because of s.t): *I was astonished at the news.*

aˈstonishing *adj* very surprising; remarkable.

aˈstonishingly *adv.* **aˈstonishment** *u.n.*

astound /əˈstaʊnd/ *tr.v* make (s.o) feel very astonished, extremely surprised; shock (s.o).

aˈstounding *adj* that astounds (s.o).

aˈstoundingly *adv.*

astral /ˈæstrəl/ *adj* of, referring to, from, the stars.

astray /əˈstreɪ/ *adj/adv* off, out of, the right way or course. **go astray** (**a**) lose one's way; go in the wrong direction. (**b**) start to behave badly. **lead s.o astray** cause s.o to start behaving badly.

astride /əˈstraɪd/ *prep/adv* (often *sitting* — *a horse* etc) with one leg on each side (of an animal, a wall etc).

astringent /əˈstrɪndʒənt/ *adj* **1** that causes the skin to tighten. **2** that stops bleeding. **3** (of s.t said, written etc) nasty; bitter; severe: *astringent criticisms.*
▷ *c/u.n* **4** (*medical*) astringent(1,2) substance.

astrology /əˈstrɒlədʒɪ/ *u.n* art of telling the future by studying the stars etc.

aˈstrologer *c.n* person who studies and uses astrology.

astrological /ˌæstrəˈlɒdʒɪkl/ *adj* of or referring to astrology.

astronaut /ˈæstrəˌnɔːt/ *c.n* person who travels beyond the air around the earth in a space vehicle. ⇒ cosmonaut.

astronomy /əˈstrɒnəmɪ/ *u.n* scientific study of the stars, the sun etc.

aˈstronomer *c.n* person who studies, is skilled in, astronomy.

astronomical /ˌæstrəˈnɒmɪkl/ *adj* **1** of, referring to, astronomy. **2** (*fig*) extremely large: *the astronomical costs of modern weapons.*

ˌastroˈnomically *adv.*

astute /əˈstjuːt/ *adj* very clever; quick at understanding things and making good use of them.

aˈstutely *adv.* **aˈstuteness** *u.n.*

asunder /əˈsʌndə/ *adv* (*literary*) into two or more pieces; apart(3): *The giant(2) split the tree asunder with one blow of his axe.*

asylum /əˈsaɪləm/ *n* **1** *c.n* (*old use*) mental hospital. **2** *c.n* safe place. **3** *u.n* (usu *political* —) safety provided by an asylum(2): *The* *man has asked for political asylum in the US.*

asymmetrical /ˌeɪsɪ'metrɪkl/ *adj* (also ˌasym'metric) not having **symmetry**. Opposite **symmetrical**.

at (strong form /æt/, weak form /ət/) *prep* **1** (when the exact position is not important) near; in; on; under etc: *Let's meet at the bridge. Mary's at her aunt's just now* (i.e at her aunt's house). *I live at No. 5, Green Street.* **2** (with the names of places thought of as spots on the map rather than as places with a big area): *Does this plane stop at London?* **3** sitting behind (a table etc) in the position one is in when using it for s.t: *The pupils were already at their desks when the teacher came in.* **4** near (a door etc) for the purpose of using it for its normal purpose: *There's someone at the window; what does he want?* **5** in, on etc (s.t) for a purpose connected with it: *Susan is at the cinema just now* (i.e she is seeing a film or working there). (Compare *Susan is in the cinema just now; she is hiding from her friends there.*) **6** (introducing the object to/against which action is aimed): *Look at your dirty hands! Stop throwing stones at that car! Our first attempts at a solution were unsuccessful.* **7** (introducing the way by which one comes in, goes out etc): *I went in at the front door and came out at the back.* **8** in the field of; on the subject of; as regards: *Jane is very good at languages. Peter is an* expert(2) *at tennis. We beat the Town School at football last year. John is a kind man at heart although he can seem rude.* **9** (introducing a time): *Come at 6 pm. At no time have I said such a thing.* **10** busy doing; engaged in: *at work/play/breakfast/war.* **11** during the course of: *We met at the match last week.* **12** present at: *Jack isn't here; he's at a meeting.* **13** engaged in the activity that concerns: *We left London in Alex's car but with Dorothy at the wheel* (i.e driving the car). **14** (introducing a speed or rate): *We were travelling at 100 kilometres an hour. We pay rent at a rate of £2500 a year.* **15** (introducing a distance, a height etc): *We dived down and found the wreck at a depth of 40 metres.* **16** (introducing a price or value): *They are selling potatoes at 20p a kilo here.* **17** (introducing an age): *Polly could already read at five years of age.* **18** (introducing a particular point in a* series(1)): *Water boils at 100° Centigrade.* **19** (introducing the cause of a feeling): *angry at s.t; pleasure at s.t; wonder at s.t.* **20** (introducing the state or condition in which s.t is): *You are at liberty to go now.* **21** at the time of; on the occasion of, sometimes with a suggestion that it is also the cause: *At his death, my uncle was a general. At these words, the children all began to laugh.* **22** subject to; under the control of: *I am at your service, madam. The prisoners were at the king's mercy.* **23** (showing relative(1) position): *The walls are at right angles to each other.* **at it** (*informal*) busy; working; fighting: *She's been hard at it all day, writing letters to all her friends.* **at one** (**with s.o/s.t**) (**about s.t**) ⇒ one. **at that** ⇒ that. For expressions introduced by 'at', e.g *at first, at a glance, at all events* or verb + 'at', e.g *play at s.t, get at s.o,* ⇒ the noun, pronoun or verb.

ate /et/ *p.t* of eat.

atheism /'eɪθɪˌɪzəm/ *u.n* not believing that God exists. Compare agnosticism.

'atheist *c.n* person who does not believe that God exists. Compare agnostic.

ˌathe'istic *adj* of, referring to, supporting, atheism.

ˌathe'istically *adv.*

athlete /'æθliːt/ *c.n* person skilled in taking part in sports and games.

ˌathlete's 'foot *u.n* kind of disease causing painful breaking of the skin between the toes.

athletic /æθ'letɪk/ *adj* **1** of, referring to, athletes and/or athletics: *an athletic meeting.* **2** (of a person, her/his body etc) strong; having skill in sports: *He's very athletic for his age.*

ath'letically *adv.*

ath'letics *u.n* (also *attrib*) practice of sports such as running, jumping and throwing things in competition with other people.

atishoo /ə'tɪʃuː/ *interj* (word used to represent the sound of a sneeze).

atlas /'ætləs/ *c.n* book of maps.

atmosphere /'ætməsˌfɪə/ *n* **1** c/def.n gases that surround the earth, a planet etc. **2** c/u.n (often *an — of s.t*) feeling (of s.t) one gets from a place, a group of people etc: *There was a very peaceful atmosphere* (or *an atmosphere of peace*) *in the church.*

atmospheric /ˌætməs'ferɪk/ *adj* of, referring to, the atmosphere(1).

ˌatmos'pherics *pl.n* unpleasant noises on radios which are caused by electricity in the atmosphere(1).

atoll /'ætɒl/ *c.n* island made of coral(1) which has the shape of a ring and (nearly) encloses a lagoon.

atom /'ætəm/ *c.n* **1** smallest part of an element(1) that still has the chemical character of the element. **2** (*fig*) (often *an — of s.t*) smallest amount (of s.t): *There isn't an atom of truth in what he says.*

atomic /ə'tɒmɪk/ *adj* of, referring to, an atom(1), atomic bombs or atomic energy.

atomic bomb *c.n* ((*informal*) **'A-ˌbomb**) extremely powerful bomb that is made to explode by splitting an atom(1).

aˌtomic 'energy/'power *u.n* = nuclear energy/power.

aˌtomic 'weight *u.n* (*technical*) weight of an atom(1) of s.t compared with the weight of an atom(1) of oxygen, which is given the atomic weight of 16.

atomize, -ise /'ætəˌmaɪz/ *tr.v* change (a liquid) into a spray(1) by forcing it through a very small hole.

'atoˌmizer, -iser *c.n* device for atomizing (s.t).

atone /ə'təun/ *intr.v* (usu *— for s.t*) (*formal*) make up for s.t bad one has done, a mistake etc by doing s.t good; make amends (for s.t).

a'tonement *u.n. in atonement for s.t* as a means of atoning for s.t.

atrocious /ə'trəuʃəs/ *adj* **1** (*derog*) very wicked or cruel. **2** (*informal*) very bad: *atrocious weather.*

a'trociously *adv.*

atrocity /ə'trɒsɪtɪ/ *n* (*pl -ies*) **1** *u.n* (often *the — of s.t*) fact or quality of being atrocious(1). **2** *c.n* atrocious(1) act: commit *atrocities against the* civil(2) *population.*

atrophy /'ætrəfɪ/ *u.n* (often *the — of s.t*) **1** wasting away (of part of the body). **2** (*fig; formal*) weakening (of one's will to succeed etc), sometimes until it disappears completely.

▷ *tr/intr.v* (*-ies, -ied*) **3** (*formal*) (cause (a muscle(1) etc or one's determination etc) to) waste away.

attach /ə'tætʃ/ *tr.v* **1** (often — *s.o/s.t to s.o/ s.t*) fasten or join (s.o/s.t) (to s.o/s.t): *Attach a photograph to your application form.* **2** (often — *s.o to s.o/s.t*) give (s.o) a job (working with s.o/s.t), usu for a short time: *Helen is attached to the accounts department for a month.* **attach oneself to s.o/s.t** join s.o/s.t, usu for a short time: *The lost boys attached themselves to our group till we got back to town.*

attaché /ə'tæʃeɪ/ *c.n* person who is one of the staff of an ambassador etc in a foreign country: *a naval attaché.*

at'taché ₁case *c.n* small flat case for holding papers etc.

at'tached *adj* **1** fixed to this letter: *Please see the attached list of members.* Compare enclosed. **2** (usu *become* — *to s.o/s.t*) having an attachment(3) for s.o/s.t.

at'tachment *n* **1** *u.n* (often — *to s.o/s.t*) act or fact of attaching (s.o/s.t); state of being attached (to s.o/s.t). **2** *c.n* thing that attaches(1) (s.t) or is attached(1) (to s.t). **3** *c.n* (often *have an* — (*to s.o/ s.t*)) liking (for s.o/s.t); friendship.

attack /ə'tæk/ *n* **1** *c.n* (often *make an* — *on s.o./ s.t*) violent act done to hurt and/or defeat s.o/s.t: *The soldiers made a strong attack on the enemy.* **2** *c.n* (often *make an* — *on s.o/s.t*) words said/ written against s.o/s.t: *an attack on the government.* **3** *c.n* (often *have an* — *of s.t*) (usu of an illness) case of (a disease etc), usu one that starts suddenly: *a bad attack of flu; a heart attack.* **4** *c/ u.n* (strong) way of beginning or dealing with s.t: *When playing this piece of music you need plenty of attack!*

▷ *v* **5** *tr/intr.v* make an attack(1,2) (on/against s.o /s.t); begin a fight (against s.o/s.t). **6** *tr.v* (of a disease etc) begin to affect (s.o/s.t); do damage to (s.t): *Our roses are being attacked by some kind of disease.* **7** *tr.v* start (s.t) eagerly and/or strongly: *When Mollie is given a new job, she attacks it with great energy(1).*

at'tacker *c.n* person who attacks(1,2) s.o/s.t.

attain /ə'teɪn/ *tr.v* reach (s.t); manage to arrive at (s.t): *attain one's ambition to become a doctor.* **attain to s.t** (*formal*) = attain s.t.

at'tainable *adj* that can be attained. Opposite unattainable.

at'tainment *n* **1** *u.n* (often *the* — *of s.t*) act or fact of attaining (s.t). **2** *c.n* thing attained; skill.

attempt /ə'tempt/ *c.n* **1** act of trying to do s.t. **make an attempt at s.t** try to do s.t. **make an attempt on s.o's life** try to kill s.o.

▷ *tr.v* **2** (often — *to do s.t*; — *doing s.t*) try (to do s.t, doing s.t).

attend /ə'tend/ *v* **1** *intr.v* (often — *to s.t, what . . .*) pay attention (to s.t); listen carefully (to s.t); direct one's mind (to s.t): *Please attend to what I am now going to tell you.* **2** *tr.v* look after (s.o); wait on (s.o): *I've been attended by this doctor for many years.* **3** *tr.v* be present at (s.t): *The football match was well attended* (i.e a lot of people attended it). **attend to s.o** help s.o; serve s.o: *In the shop, the assistant(1) said, 'Are you being attended to, sir?'*

at'tendance *n* **1** *u.n* (often — *at s.t*) act or fact

of attending(3) (s.t): *attendance at a meeting.* **2** *c.n* (often — *at s.t*) number of people attending(3) (s.t): *The attendance at the match was good.* **3** *u.n* (often — (*up*)*on s.o*) act or fact of attending(2) (s.o): *attendance upon a king.* **in attendance** present (at a meeting etc).

at'tendant *c.n* person who accompanies and/or helps or looks after s.o/s.t: *a lavatory attendant.*

attention /ə'tenʃən/ *u.n* act of careful thinking about s.t: *This matter needs urgent attention.* **Attention!** order to soldiers etc to stand straight and still with their heels together. **attract (s.o's) attention** make s.o/people interested: *This new play is attracting a lot of attention.* **bring s.t to s.o's attention** cause s.o to notice s.t. **come to s.o's attention** begin to be noticed by s.o. **pay attention (to s.o/s.t, what . . .)** listen carefully (to s.o/s.t, what . . .). **stand at attention** (of soldiers etc) stand straight and still with heels together.

at'tentive *adj* (often — *to s.o/s.t*) giving careful attention (to s.o/s.t). Opposite inattentive.

attic /'ætɪk/ *c.n* (also *attrib*) space or room below the sloping roof of a building: *an attic bedroom.*

attire /ə'taɪə/ *u.n* (*formal*) **1** clothes; dress(4).

▷ *tr.v* **2** (usu — *s.o in s.t*) dress (s.o) (in certain clothes).

attitude /'ætɪ₁tjuːd/ *c.n* **1** position or way of holding one's body: *David was sitting in an awkward attitude.* **2** (often — *to/towards s.o/s.t*) way of thinking, feeling etc (about s.o/s.t): *What is your attitude towards Sunday trading?*

attorney /ə'tɜːnɪ/ *c.n* (US) lawyer. **power of attorney** official power(3) given to s.o to act lawfully for s.o else who is away, ill etc.

At₁torney-'General *c/def.n* (pl *Attorneys-General*) chief law officer of a country who represents it in law cases. ⇨ Lord Chancellor.

attract /ə'trækt/ *tr.v* **1** make (s.o, an animal) like one or want to come near: *These flowers attract a lot of butterflies.* **2** pull (s.t) towards one: *A magnet(1) attracts metal.* **attract (s.o's) attention** ⇨ attention.

attraction /ə'trækʃən/ *n* **1** *u.n* act or fact of attracting s.o/s.t. **2** *c.n* thing that attracts(1) s.o/ s.t: *There are many attractions in a big city.*

attractive /ə'træktɪv/ *adj* **1** who/that attracts(1) s.o. **2** pleasant to look at; pretty; handsome: *Betty is a very attractive girl.*

at'tractively *adv.* **at'tractiveness** *u.n.*

attrib *written abbr* attributive.

attribute /'ætrɪ₁bjuːt/ *c.n* **1** quality, either good or bad, that is part of the nature of s.o/s.t: *Michael's best attribute is his kindness.*

▷ *tr.v* /ə'trɪbjuːt/ **2** (usu — *s.t to s.o/s.t*) believe, say etc that s.o/s.t is caused by (s.t): *I attribute the poor harvest this year to all the rain we have had.* **3** **attribute s.t to s.o** believe, say etc that s.o is the person who said, wrote etc s.t.

at'tributable /ə'trɪbjuːtəbl/ *adj* (usu — *to s.o/s.t*) that can be attributed (to s.o/s.t).

attribution /₁ætrɪ'bjuːʃən/ *u.n* act or fact of attributing s.t to s.o/s.t.

attributive /ə'trɪbjutɪv/ *adj* (*written abbr* attrib) (*grammar*) (of an adjective) placed before the noun or pronoun it describes, e.g 'small' in 'a small boy'. Compare predicative.

attrition /ə'trɪʃən/ *u.n* (*formal*) **1** wearing away by rubbing: *The attrition of tyres when one drives over rocky desert is terrible.* **2** (*fig*) weakening and tiring: *a war of attrition* (i.e in which each side waits for the other to wear itself out).

attune /ə'tjuːn/ *tr.v* (often — *s.o/s.t to s.t*) make (s.o/s.t) used to s.t and therefore able to understand and deal with it: *My ears gradually became attuned to the strange music. You must become attuned to life in a big city.*

aubergine /'əʊbəʒiːn/ *c/u.n* = eggplant.

auburn /'ɔːbən/ *adj* (of a person's hair) redbrown in colour.

auction /'ɔːkʃən/ *c/u.n* **1** public sale of things in which the person who offers the biggest amount of money for s.t gets it. **put s.t up for auction** ; **sell s.t by auction** (offer to) sell s.t in an auction (1).
▷ *tr.v* **2** (often — *s.t off*) sell (s.t) by auction (1).

auctioneer /ˌɔːkʃə'nɪə/ *c.n* **1** person who sells things for people at an auction (1). **2** (also ˌauctio'neer's) shop, company etc of an auctioneer (1).

audacious /ɔː'deɪʃəs/ *adj* (*formal*) **1** very, sometimes foolishly, bold: *an audacious attack on a bank.* **2** boldly rude: *an audacious remark.*
au'daciously *adv.* **audacity** /ɔː'dæsɪtɪ/ *u.n.*

audible /'ɔːdɪbl/ *adj* able to be heard; loud enough to be heard. Opposite inaudible.
audibility /ˌɔːdɪ'bɪlɪtɪ/ *u.n.* **'audibly** *adv.*

audience /'ɔːdɪəns/ *n* **1** *c/def.pl.n* group of people listening to (and watching) a lecture, play etc. **2** *c.n* formal meeting with a ruler etc: *The Queen gave the prime minister an audience.*

audiovisual aid /ˌɔːdɪəʊˌvɪʒʊəl 'eɪd/ *c.n* (*abbr* AV aid) thing that one can see and hear, e.g a film, which is used as a help in teaching.

audit /'ɔːdɪt/ *c.n* **1** official examination of the accounts of a company etc to make sure they are correct.
▷ *tr.v* **2** examine (the accounts of a company etc) officially; carry out an audit (1) (of s.t).
auditor /'ɔːdɪtə/ *c.n* person who audits (2) accounts.

audition /ɔː'dɪʃən/ *c.n* **1** trial given to an actress/ actor etc before choosing her/him for a part in a play etc.
▷ *tr/intr.v* **2** (often — *for s.t*) (cause (an actor/actress etc) to) show what he/she can do in an audition (1) (to try to get a certain part in a play etc).

auditorium /ˌɔːdɪ'tɔːrɪəm/ *c.n* part of a public hall, theatre etc in which the audience (1) sits.

Aug *written abbr* August.

auger /'ɔːgə/ *c.n* kind of tool for making large holes in wood, the ground etc.

augment /ɔːg'ment/ *tr/intr.v* (*formal*) (cause (s.t) to) increase in size, amount etc: *Jim augments his wages by delivering newspapers.*
augmentation /ˌɔːgmen'teɪʃən/ *n* **1** *u.n* act or fact of augmenting s.t. **2** *c.n* thing added in order to augment s.t.

augur /'ɔːgə/ *intr.v* (often — *s.t for s.o/s.t*) (*formal*) be a sign (of s.t) (for s.o/s.t's future). **augur ill/well for s.o/s.t** be a bad/good sign for the future of s.o/s.t.

August /'ɔːgəst/ *c/unique n* (also *attrib*) (*written abbr* Aug) 8th month of the year: *There are thirty-one days in August. He came on 10 August* (say 'August the tenth' or 'the tenth of August'). *It was a windy August evening.*

august² /ɔː'gʌst/ *adj* (*formal*) noble; causing feelings of respect: *an august appearance.*

aunt /ɑːnt/ *c.n* ((*informal* **'auntie, 'aunty**

(*pl-ies*)) **1** sister of one's mother or father or wife of one's uncle: *my aunt Sarah.* **2** woman whose brother/sister has a son/ daughter: *Mary has just become an aunt.* **3** woman friend etc who is old enough to be a young child's aunt (1). ⇒ maiden aunt.

au pair /ˌəʊ 'peə/ *c.n* (also *attrib*) (*French*) person, esp a foreign girl, who helps with the housework in return for free lodging in the house, free time for studying and usu a small wage.

aura /'ɔːrə/ *c.n* atmosphere (2) round a person/ thing which seems to come from her/him/it: *There was an aura of holiness about her.*

aural /'ɔːrəl/ *adj* of, referring to, coming to one by, hearing.
'aurally *adv.*

auspices /'ɔːspɪsɪz/ *pl.n* (usu *under the* — *of s.o/ s.t*) help and support: *Professor Smith is here under the auspices of the Ministry of Education.*

auspicious /ɔː'spɪʃəs/ *adj* giving favourable signs for future success: *auspicious signs.* Opposite inauspicious.
au'spiciously *adv.* **au'spiciousness** *u.n.*

austere /ɔː'stɪə/ *adj* **1** (of a person) very serious; severe; strict; self-disciplined. **2** (of a place, way of living etc) very simple and without comforts. ⇒ ascetic (1).
au'sterely *adv.* **austerity** /ɔː'sterɪtɪ/ *u.n.*

authentic /ɔː'θentɪk/ *adj* that has been proved to be the real or genuine (1) thing: *an authentic 16th-century glass.*
au'thentically *adv.*

authenticate /ɔː'θentɪˌkeɪt/ *tr.v* prove, declare, (s.t) to be true or genuine (1).
authentication /ɔːˌθentɪ'keɪʃən/ *u.n.*
authenticity /ˌɔːθen'tɪsɪtɪ/ *u.n* quality or fact of being authentic.

author /'ɔːθə/ *c.n* (often *the* — *of s.t*) **1** writer (of a book, an article in a newspaper etc). **2** person who starts or invents s.t: *Jane was the original author of the plan.*
'authoress *c.n* woman author (1).
'author,ship *u.n* **1** profession of being an author (1). **2** (often *the* — *of s.t*) fact of being, identity (1) of, the author (of s.t): *The authorship of this article is still in doubt.*

authority /ɔː'θɒrɪtɪ/ *n* (*pl -ies*) **1** *u.n* power to force obedience and give orders: *The teacher has the authority to punish naughty pupils.* **2** *c.n* (often *pl*) person or group of people who has/ have authority (1): *sports authorities. The local authority have changed the day on which rents are due.* **3** *u.n* (often *have* (*the*) — *to do s.t*) official right (to do s.t): *The police have* (*the*) *authority to stop and search people.* **4** *u.n* proof that one has authority (3): *Where is your authority to search my house?* **5** *u.n* (often *have* — *with s.o*) influence (with s.o): *Although Sally is only a clerk, she has a lot of authority with the manager because she is so clever.* **6** *c.n* (often *an* — *on s.o/s.t*) person who has a reputation for knowing a lot (about s.o/s.t): *The professor was an authority on Greek art.*

authoritarian /ɔːˌθɒrɪ'teərɪən/ *adj* **1** (often *derog*) of, referring to, supporting, authority (1), sometimes too strongly.
▷ *c.n* **2** (often *derog*) authoritarian (1) person.

authoritative /ɔː'θɒrɪtətɪv/ *adj* **1** having, showing that one has, authority (1): *He spoke in an* *authoritative manner*. **2** that can be trusted to be correct: *an authoritative* edition(1) *of Shakespeare's plays*.

authorization, -isation /ˌɔːθəraɪˈzeɪʃən/ *u.n* formal or official permission: *You need special authorization to enter this building*.

authorize, -ise /ˈɔːθəˌraɪz/ *tr.v* **1** give authority(3) for (s.t): *Who authorized this payment?* **authorize s.o to do s.t** give s.o authority(3) to do s.t.

authorship ⇨ author.

autistic /ɔːˈtɪstɪk/ *adj* (usu of a child) having an illness of the mind that prevents one taking part in or associating with the real world.

autobiography /ˌɔːtəbaɪˈɒɡrəfɪ/ *n* (*pl -ies*) **1** *c.n* book written by a person about (things in) her/his own life. **2** *u.n* books or writings of this kind.

ˌautobiˈographer *c.n* person who writes an autobiography(1).

autobiographical /ˌɔːtəˌbaɪəˈɡræfɪkl/ *adj* (also **ˌautobioˈgraphic**) **1** of, referring to, autobiography(2). **2** based on events in one's own life.

autocrat /ˈɔːtəˌkræt/ *c.n* **1** absolute ruler. **2** (*derog*) person who gives orders without consideration for other people.

autocracy /ɔːˈtɒkrəsɪ/ *n* (*pl -ies*) **1** *u.n* absolute power in government. **2** *c.n* government ruled by an autocrat(1).

autocratic /ˌɔːtəˈkrætɪk/ *adj* of, referring to, like, an autocrat or (an) autocracy.

ˌautoˈcratically *adv*.

autograph /ˈɔːtəˌɡrɑːf/ *c.n* **1** person's own handwriting, esp when he/she signs his/her own name.

▷ *tr.v* **2** sign (s.t); write one's own name on (s.t): *The writer will autograph copies for anyone who buys his book in our bookshop*.

automatic /ˌɔːtəˈmætɪk/ *adj* **1** that works, happens by itself, without needing to be controlled or arranged by a person: *an automatic gear-change on a car; an automatic increase in pay every year*. **2** done without thinking, usu because it has become a habit: *Babies have to learn to balance when they start walking but this soon becomes automatic*.

▷ *c.n* **3** kind of gun held in the hand which can fire several shots one after the other without having to load again. **4** car with automatic(1) gears: *Some people who drive a lot in town prefer automatics*.

automated /ˈɔːtəˌmeɪtɪd/ *adj* (of a factory, a way of making s.t etc) worked by automatic(1) means.

ˌautoˈmatically *adv*.

automation /ˌɔːtəˈmeɪʃən/ *u.n* automatic(1) control of making things with machines, in which one does not need workers to operate them.

automaton /ɔːˈtɒmətən/ *c.n* **1** robot(1). **2** person who appears to act without thinking.

automobile /ˈɔːtəməˌbiːl/ *c.n* (US) motor car. **ˈAutomoˌbile Asˌsociˈation** *def.n* (*abbr* AA) British club for car owners which helps them if they break down, provides them with maps, services etc.

autonomous /ɔːˈtɒnəməs/ *adj* that governs itself; free; independent: *The Channel Islands are an autonomous part of the British Isles*.

auˈtonomously *adv*. **auˈtonomy** *u.n*.

autopsy /ˈɔːtɒpsɪ/ *c.n* (*pl -ies*) examination of a dead body by cutting it up.

autumn /ˈɔːtəm/ *c/u.n* (also *attrib*) **1** (often with capital **A**) season of the year, between summer and winter: *autumn leaves. It gets colder in (the) autumn*.

▷ *intr.v* **2** (usu — (*in*) *s.w*) spend the autumn (s.w): *We autumned in Greece*.

autumnal /ɔːˈtʌmnəl/ *adj* of, like, autumn: *autumnal weather*. ⇨ equinox.

auxiliary /ɔːɡˈzɪlɪərɪ, ɔːɡˈzɪlɪərɪ/ *adj* **1** who/that helps and supports (others): *auxiliary workers*. Compare ancillary.

▷ *c.n* **2** auxiliary(1) person or thing: *a nursing auxiliary* (i.e one who helps nurses in a hospital). **3** (*grammar*) = auxiliary verb.

auˌxiliary ˈverb *c.n* (*written abbr* aux.v) (*grammar*) verb such as 'can', 'will' or a form of 'be' or 'have' that is used with a main verb to show tense², mode(4) etc: *In 'It might have been seen', 'might', 'have' and 'been' are auxiliary verbs*.

aux.v *written abbr* auxiliary verb.

av /ˌeɪ ˈviː/ *abbr* **1** audiovisual (aid). ▷ *written abbr* **2** average. **3** avoirdupois.

avail /əˈveɪl/ *u.n* **1 to little/no avail** (*literary*) with little/no good result: *Peter's attempts to start his car were of no avail and he had to go by bus*.

▷ *reflex.v* **2 avail oneself of s.t** (*formal*) use s.t for one's advantage: *You should avail yourself of every chance to practise your French while you are in France*.

aˌvailaˈbility *u.n* (often *the* — *of s.o/s.t*) fact or state of (s.o/s.t) being available.

aˈvailable *adj* able to be found; ready to be used, spoken to etc: *Materials for cleaning your room are available downstairs. The professor is available for* consultation *from 9 to 12 every morning*. Opposite unavailable.

avalanche /ˈævəˌlɑːntʃ/ *c.n* **1** heavy fall or slide of snow (and ice) down a mountain side. **2** (*fig*) (usu *an* — *of s.t*) large amount or number (of s.t) all coming at the same time: *We had an avalanche of letters after our visit to America*.

avarice /ˈævərɪs/ *u.n* (*formal*) greed, usu for getting or keeping money.

avaricious /ˌævəˈrɪʃəs/ *adj* (*formal*) having or showing avarice.

ˌavaˈriciously *adv*.

Ave *written abbr* Avenue(1).

avenge /əˈvendʒ/ *tr.v* **1** (often — *s.t* (*up*)*on s.o/s.t*) get/take revenge for (s.t) (by doing s.t against s.o/s.t): *Harry avenged the insult by refusing to give money to the* scheme(1). **2** get, take, revenge for s.t that has been done to (s.o): *The boy avenged his father by killing the man who had murdered him*. **avenge oneself** ((*up*)*on s.o/s.t*) get, take, revenge for s.t that has been done to one (by doing s.t to/against s.o/s.t).

aˈvenger *c.n* person who avenges s.o/s.t.

avenue /ˈævɪˌnjuː/ *c.n* **1** (with capital **A**) (*written abbr* Ave) (name for a) wide street in a town: *Kensington Avenue*. **2** road in the country with trees on both sides and often leading to a big house. **3** (*fig*) (often — *to s.t*) way of reaching (success etc).

average /ˈævərɪdʒ/ *adj* (*written abbr* av) **1** usual; ordinary; neither specially good etc nor specially bad etc: *an average student*. **2** found by working out the average(3): *The average age of our students is 20.6 years.*

▷ *c.n* **3** result of adding a group of quantities or numbers together and dividing by the total number of items(1): *The average of 3, 4 and 8 is 5.* **above/below average** better/higher etc or worse/lower etc than the average(3). **on (an/the) average** generally; usually; in the average(1,2) case: *Each of our horses runs in twenty races a year on average.*

▷ *tr.v* **4** be, come to, (a certain number or amount) on average: *Rainfall here averages 119 millimetres in October.* **5** do (s.t) on average: *Our car averages 550 kilometres a week.*

averse /ə'vɜːs/ *adj* (*usu* — *to* (*doing*) *s.t*) (*formal*) against (doing) s.t; not liking (to do) s.t: *I am averse to long lectures.*

aversion /ə'vɜːʃən/ *c/u.n* (*formal*) (often — *to s.o/s.t*) strong feeling of dislike (for s.o/s.t). **s.o's pet aversion** the thing s.o dislikes particularly.

avert /ə'vɜːt/ *tr.v* **1** prevent (s.t) from happening: *Bill managed to avert an accident by putting the brakes on hard.* **2** (*formal*) (often — *s.t from s.t*) turn (one's eyes, one's mind etc) away (from s.t) so as not to see, think about etc, it.

aviary /'eɪvɪərɪ/ *c.n* (*pl* -*ies*) large cage for keeping birds, in which they are able to fly about.

aviation /ˌeɪvɪ'eɪʃən/ *u.n* art or science of flying planes.

avid /'ævɪd/ *adj* (often — *for s.t*) (*formal*) eager (to have/get s.t): *avid readers of adventure stories. The parents were avid for news of their missing children.*

avidity /ə'vɪdɪtɪ/ *u.n.* **'avidly** *adv.*

AVM *written abbr* Air Vice Marshal.

avocado /ˌævə'kɑːdəʊ/ *n* (*pl* -*s*) (also *attrib*) (also ˌavo,cado 'pear) **1** *c/u.n* fruit that looks like a pear and grows on a tree in hot countries; it has a big stone inside and oily green flesh that is soft and smooth but not sweet. **2** *c.n* tree on which such fruit grows: *an avocado tree.*

avocation /ˌævə'keɪʃən/ *c.n* (*formal*) hobby.

avoid /ə'vɔɪd/ *tr.v* (often — *doing s.t*) get, keep, away from (s.o/s.t, doing s.t); have nothing to do with (s.o/s.t, doing s.t): *I have tried to avoid Colin since our fight.*

a'voidable *adj* that can be avoided. Opposite unavoidable.

a'voidance *u.n.*

avoirdupois /ˌævədə'pɔɪz/ *u.n* (*written abbr* av) standard system of weights used, or that used to be used, in Britain and some other countries where English is spoken; it uses pounds[1](2), ounces(1) etc instead of kilograms etc.

avowal /ə'vaʊəl/ *c.n* (*usu an* — *of s.t*) (*formal*) public declaration, admission(3), (of s.t): *an avowal of responsibility.*

avowed /ə'vaʊd/ *adj* (*formal*) publicly declared, admitted(2): *their avowed intention to stop him.*

avowedly /ə'vaʊɪdlɪ/ *adv.*

await /ə'weɪt/ *tr.v* **1** wait for (s.o/s.t). **2** be waiting, ready for, (s.o/s.t): *A surprise awaited us on our arrival at the castle.*

awake /ə'weɪk/ *pred.adj* **1** not asleep; having woken up: *Are the children awake yet?* **awake to s.t** (*fig*; *formal*) conscious of s.t; knowing about s.t: *I am fully awake to the dangers you mention.* **wide awake** ⇨ wide(*adv*).

▷ *tr/intr.v* (*formal*) **2** (*p.t* awoke /ə'wəʊk/, awaked, *p.p* awoken /ə'wəʊkən/, awaked) (often — (s.o, an animal) *from s.t*) (cause (s.o, an animal) to) stop sleeping (after s.t); wake[1](2) (s.o, an animal): *She was awoken by the loud crash.* **3** (cause (s.t) to) begin (to operate etc): *The film about Greece awoke pleasant memories of holidays in the sun.* **awake to s.t** begin to realize s.t.

a'waken *tr/intr.v* **awaken (s.o) to s.t** (cause(s.o) to) realize s.t.

award /ə'wɔːd/ *c.n* **1** (often *make an* — *for s.t*; *the* — *of s.t* (*to s.o*)) thing, often a prize, given to s.o (for s.t he/she has done particularly well). **2** (often — *of s.t*) amount (of money etc) given to s.o by a court of law, or the decision to do this: *win an award of £10 000 damages against s.o.* **3** amount of money given to s.o to enable her/him to study. ⇨ bursary(2), exhibition(3), scholarship(2).

▷ *tr.v* **4** (often — *s.o s.t*; — *s.t to s.o*) give (s.o) (s.t) as an award.

aware /ə'weə/ *adj* **1** (usu *pred*) (often — *of s.t*; — *that/how* . . .) knowing, conscious of, (s.t): *Are you aware how late it is?* **2** (following an adv) having knowledge, understanding or consciousness about s.t (that is shown by the adv): *a sexually aware child.*

a'wareness *u.n* (often — *of s.t*; — *that* . . .).

awash /ə'wɒʃ/ *pred.adj* **1** (often — *with s.t*) having water etc level with, flowing over, its surface: *After the accident, the street was awash with petrol.* **2** floating about free on the sea etc and pushed by the waves.

away /ə'weɪ/ *adv* **1** (often — *from s.o/s.t*) from a place, to a distance, (from s.o/s.t): *Come away from that fire!* **2** (often (*far*) — *from s.o/s.t*) distant (from s.o/s.t): *Keep away from that fire!* **3** (also *adj*) (often — *from s.t*) absent; not here/there: *'Is Elizabeth at home?' 'No, she's away (from home) for a week.' The team is playing away this week. It is an away game* (played at another ground). ⇨ home(3). **4** so as to remove s.t from being part of or from touching s.t: *We cut away half the hill to build the road. Please sweep away that dirt.* **5** (often — *from s.o/s.t*) out of one's/s.o's own possession: *Paul has given a lot of his money away to the poor. Take that needle away from the baby!* **6** aside; so as to store it: *She put her winter clothes away.* **7** from one direction to another: *When I looked at her she turned away and began to sew a button onto her coat.* **8** from the state or condition in which one/it was into nothing or to an end, usu gradually: *The tyres wore away until they burst. The sound of music died away as we drove on.* **9** forwards in time; continuously: *We still work away in our garden every weekend.* **10** (*fig*) out of one's everyday life: *The beautiful music carried us away into a happier land of dreams.* **away with s.o/s.t!** may s.o/s.t go away, or be removed!: *Away with the government! Away with all worries, let us enjoy ourselves!* For verb, noun or adverb + 'away', e.g **do away with s.o**, **get away** (*from s.o/s.t*), **get away with murder**, **right/straight away**, ⇨ the verb, noun or adverb.

awe /ɔː/ *u.n* **1** respectful fear. **stand in awe** (**of s.o/s.t**) feel great respect for (s.o/s.t).

▷ *tr.v* **2** (usu — *s.o into s.t*) fill (s.o) with awe(1) (so that he/she does s.t, e.g stops talking): *The* *children were awed into silence by the beauty of the place.*

'awe-in,spiring *adj* (also **'awesome**) that fills one with awe(1).

'awesomely *adv.* **'awesomeness** *u.n.*

'awe-,stricken, 'awe-,struck *adj* (suddenly) filled with awe(1).

awful /'ɔːfəl/ *adj* 1 terrible; shocking: *awful behaviour.* 2 (*informal*) very bad: *awful weather.* 3 (*informal*) very great: *I've got an awful lot of work to do.*

'awfully *adv* (*informal*) very: *That's awfully kind of you.*

'awfulness *u.n* fact or state of being awful(1,2).

awhile /ə'waɪl/ *adv* (*literary*; *formal*) for a short time: *Stay awhile and we'll have some tea.*

awkward /'ɔːkwəd/ *adj* 1 causing difficulty in use: *This door handle is in an awkward position.* 2 having little skill: *The young child was still awkward on its feet.* 3 causing discomfort of mind or embarrassment(1): *There was an awkward silence before he answered the question.* 4 (of a person) troublesome; difficult.

,awkward 'customer *c.n* awkward(4) person.

'awkwardly *adv.* **'awkwardness** *u.n.*

awl /ɔːl/ *c.n* kind of small tool with a sharp point for making holes in leather etc.

awning /'ɔːnɪŋ/ *c.n* covering made from strong material to give shelter from sun, rain etc, e.g over a door, a shop window or the deck of a ship.

awoke /ə'wəʊk/ *p.t* of awake (*v*).

awoken /ə'wəʊkən/ *p.p* of awake (*v*).

AWOL /'eɪwɒl or ,eɪ ,dʌbljuː ,əʊ 'el/ *abbr* (*military*) absent without leave: *go AWOL*.

awry /ə'raɪ/ *pred.adj/adv* not straight; not arranged as it should be; askew. **go awry** (*fig*) go wrong: *All our plans have gone awry.*

axe /æks/ *c.n* (US **ax**) (*pl axes* /'æksəz/) 1 kind of tool on a handle with an iron head that is sharp at one end, used for cutting down trees, cutting up wood etc. **get, give s.o, the axe** (*fig*; *informal*) be dismissed, dismiss s.o, from a job. **have an axe to grind** (*fig*; *informal*) have reasons for doing s.t which are one's own and often selfish: *Don't listen to Maurice's advice; you can't trust it because he has an axe to grind.*

▷ *tr.v* 2 remove, dismiss, get rid of, (s.o/s.t), often suddenly: *The company is losing money so a quarter of our staff has to be axed.*

axes *pl.n* 1 /'æksəz/ *pl* of axe. 2 /'æksiːz/ *pl* of axis.

axiom /'æksɪəm/ *c.n* statement that does not need proof or argument because it is generally accepted: *It is an axiom of our family that if anything goes wrong it must be my fault.*

axiomatic /,æksɪə'mætɪk/ *adj* of, referring to, containing, an axiom.

,axio'matically *adv.*

axis /'æksɪs/ *c.n* (*pl axes* /'æksiːz/) 1 imaginary line about which an object turns or spins: *the earth's axis.* 2 (*geometry*) line dividing a regular figure into two equal parts with the same shape as each other. 3 group, alliance(3), of countries that work together, esp in foreign affairs, war etc.

axle /'æksəl/ *c.n* rod on which a wheel or two wheels turn(s).

aye /aɪ/ *interj* 1 yes: *Aye, aye, captain!*

▷ *c.n* 2 vote in favour (of s.t). Opposite nay.

azalea /ə'zeɪlɪə/ *c.n* 1 kind of bush grown in gardens for its shiny leaves, which are green all year and for its flowers in spring. 2 red or pink flower of this bush.

azure /'æʒə/ *u.n* (also *attrib*) bright blue colour, esp of the sky.

Bb

B, b /biː/ *c/unique n* 1 2nd letter of the English alphabet.

▷ *written abbr* 2 born. 3 breadth. 4 (**B**) Bay². 5 (**B**) 6 British.

▷ *symb* 7 (**B**) softness of lead(3): *a 2B pencil.* ⇒ H, HB.

BA /,biː 'eɪ/ *abbr* 1 Bachelor of Arts. 2 British Airways.

baa /bɑː/ *c.n.*1 cry of a sheep.

▷ *intr.v* (*p.t,p.p baaed*) 2 make this sound.

babble /'bæbl/ *c/u.n* 1 talk that is foolish or does not have any meaning: *the babble of babies before they learn to speak properly.* 2 pleasant sound of water running, usu in a small stream.

▷ *v* 3 *intr.v* (often — *away/on*) talk in a babble(1) (for a long time). 4 *tr.v* (often – *s.t out*) say (s.t) while babbling(3). 5 *intr.v* (often — *along/away/on*) (of a stream of water) make a babble(2).

'babbler *c.n* person who babbles(3).

babe /beɪb/ *c.n.* 1 (*literary*) baby. 2 (*slang*; esp US) girl.

baboon /bə'buːn/ *c.n* kind of big monkey with a face like a dog.

baby /'beɪbɪ/ *n* (*pl -ies*) 1 *c.n* (also *attrib*) very young person or animal: *a baby girl/elephant.* 2 *def.n* (often *the — of s.t*) youngest person or animal (in a group): *Although Helen is 11, she is still treated as the baby of the family.* 3 (*derog*) person who is not a baby(1) but behaves like one, e.g by crying a lot. 4 (*slang*; usu US) person, usu female.

'baby ,carriage *c.n* (esp US) = pram.

'baby,hood *u.n* state or time of being a baby(1).

'babyish *adj* (*derog*) behaving like a baby(3).

'baby-,minder *c.n* person who looks after s.o's baby(1), usu for money while the parents are busy.

'baby-,sit *intr.v* (*-tt-*, *p.t,p.p -sat*/ *-,sæt*/) stay in a house, usu in the evening when the parents are out, to look after a child.

'baby-,sitter *c.n* person who baby-sits.

'baby-,talk *u.n* 1 = babble(1). 2 way of talking, sometimes used by adults when they are talking to children.

bachelor /'bætʃələ/ *c.n* 1 man who has never been married. Compare spinster(1). 2 = Bachelor of Arts/Science.

,Bachelor of 'Arts *c.n* (*abbr BA*) person who

has passed a first degree in an arts(4) subject. Compare Master of Arts.

,Bachelor of 'Science *c.n* (*abbr* BSc) person who has passed a first degree in a science subject. Compare Master of Science.

bacillus /bəˈsɪləs/ *c.n* (*pl bacilli* /bəˈsɪlaɪ/) small bacterium with the shape of a rod.

back /bæk/ *attrib.adj* **1** that is behind s.t: *the back door of the house.* Opposite front(1). **2** (of money) still owed from before: *The workers were given two months back pay yesterday.* **3** (of a magazine etc) earlier than the last one produced: *You won't find the report of your talk in today's newspaper; it will be in a back number.* **take a back seat** (*fig*) take an unimportant role as a member of a group (having had a more active role).

▷ *adv* **4** in the opposite direction, so as to return to the place where one started (without stopping on the way): *Joe went to the shops this morning and came back at 11. I ran back to get my coat.* **5** (showing the result of a return to a former position/condition): *Mary is back in London again. John was better last week but now he is back where he was a month ago with his illness.* **6** away from the front, or the forward position; towards/in a position that is to the rear'(2): *Keep back! After advancing for several kilometres, the climbers had to go back half a kilometre to find shelter. You'll find your name three pages back in the hotel book.* Compare ahead(1), forward(6). **7** in a state of being prevented from moving forward (easily): *The police kept the crowds back while the firemen were busy.* **8** away from the present or closed position: *Pull back the curtains and give us some light.* **9** in return for s.t received: *Have you paid back the money you borrowed?* **10** so as to return to a former condition: *John has gone back to his old habits now that his wife is not here.* **11** (of clocks, watches) so as to show an earlier time: *put a watch back an hour.* Compare advance(7). **12** in(to) time past: *This custom goes back to the 16th century. Back in the 17th century there were no trains or buses.* **13** to a later time: *Our holidays have been put back a week.* Opposite forward(8). **back and forth** ⇒ forth(1). Compare backwards and forwards. For verb/noun + 'back', e.g *come back, fall back, fall back on s.o/s.t, go back on s.t, take s.t back*, ⇒ the verb/noun.

▷ *n* **14** *c.n* back(1) part of the human body that is between the neck and the legs: *lie on one's back in the sun.* **15** *c.n* top part of an animal's body, from the neck to the beginning of the tail (or where the tail would be if the animal had one). **16** *c/def.n* part of a chair etc against which one can lean one's back(14). **17** *c/def.n* side of s.t, e.g a cheque or a knife, that one does not usu use. **18** *c/def.n* part of s.t that is furthest from the front(1,2): *Our bedroom was at the back of the hotel.* **19** *c.n* (in football etc) player whose position is nearest the goal, but who is not the goalkeeper. ⇒ half-back. **at s.o's back** (*fig*) supporting s.o; behind(11) s.o. **the back of beyond** (*informal*) a place that is very far away (from civilization). **back to back** with the backs to each other: *standing back to back.* ⇒ facing(2). **break the back of s.t** (*fig*) get most of s.t finished: *Well, we've broken the back of this work so we can have a rest.* **get/put s.o's back up** (*fig*; *informal*) annoy, antagonize,

s.o. **glad , pleased** etc **to see the back of s.o** (*fig*; *informal*) glad etc when s.o goes away. (**go** etc) **behind s.o's back** (*fig*; *informal*) (do s.t, e.g talk to s.o in a higher position) secretly and without telling s.o what one is doing. **have one's back to the wall** (*fig*; *informal*) be in a very difficult or dangerous position. **know a place like the back of one's hand** (*informal*) know a place very well. **on one's back** (*fig*; *informal*) ill in bed. **pat on the back (for (doing) s.t)** ⇒ pat(*n*). **pat s.o on the back** ⇒ pat(*v*). **put one's back into s.t** (*fig*; *informal*) work really hard at s.t. **turn one's back on s.o/s.t** (**a**) turn away from s.o/s.t rudely. (**b**) (*fig*) refuse to have anything (more) to do with s.o/ s.t.

▷ *v* **20** *tr/intr.v* (cause (s.t, e.g a car) to) go backwards. **21** *tr.v* (often — *s.o up* (*in s.t*)) support (s.o/s.t) (in s.t, e.g what he/she demands). **22** *tr.v* bet(3) on (s.o/s.t, e.g a horse in a race). **23** *tr.v* (often — *s.t with s.t*) put s.t on the back of (s.t), e.g to strengthen it; line (s.t, e.g a skirt) (with s.t, e.g silk). **24** *intr.v* (of wind etc) slowly change the direction from which it is coming, moving in an anti-clockwise direction. **back away (from s.o/s.t)** move backwards away from s.o/s.t, sometimes because one is afraid. **back down** (*fig*) admit that one was wrong, or stop arguing, (even though one knows one was right). **back onto s.t** have s.t close to it at the back: *Our house backs onto a farm.* **back out (from /of s.t)** (*fig*) do not do what one had promised etc to do (about s.t). **back s.o/s.t up** support s.o/s.t. ⇒ backup.

'back,ache *c/u.n* pain in one's back(14).

,back 'bench *def.n* (usu *pl*) ('back-, ,bench when *attrib*) less important members of parliament who sit in the back(6) seats: *She's a back-bench MP.* Compare frontbench.

,back'bencher *c.n* back-bench member of parliament. Compare frontbencher.

'back,bone *c.n* **1** *c/def.n* (*informal*) = spine(1). **2** *def.n* (often *the* — *of s.t*) people or thing who/that provide(s) the main support for, and strength of, s.t. **3** *u.n* strength of character: *Steve has no backbone and never tries hard.* **to the backbone** completely.

,back'date *tr.v* make (s.t) start on an earlier date: *In March we received an increase in pay backdated to January.* Compare postdate.

,back 'door *c.n* **1** door at the back of a house. ⇒ front door. **2** way of getting a job etc by using unfair means.

'backer *c.n* person who backs(21) s.o/s.t.

backfire /ˈbækˌfaɪə/ *c.n* **1** explosion in a cylinder(2) of a car engine before the piston has reached the top so that it does not help to turn the wheels.

▷ *intr.v*/ˌbækˈfaɪə/ **2** explode because of a backfire(1). **3** (*fig*) (of a plan etc) have a bad result that is the opposite of the one that was hoped for.

'back,ground *n* **1** *c.n* what can be seen behind s.t, sometimes in a picture. Opposite foreground. **2** *c.n* conditions under which s.t happens or exists. **3** *u.n* information about the background(2) of s.t. **4** *c.n* family from which s.o comes, way in which he/she has been educated, conditions in which he/she lives etc: *Mary comes from a* socially privileged *background*. **against a background of s.t** in conditions of s.t: *I had to speak against a background of noise.* Compare background(2). **in the background** in a position where one is not noticed: *The real power in this company lies with Mr Robinson but he always stays in the background.*

,background ,infor'mation *u.n* = background(3).

'back,hand *c.n* (also *attrib*) tennis, squash[2] etc stroke made with the front of the hand facing backward. Opposite forehand.

,back'hander *c.n* **1** indirect(3) attack, criticism etc. **2** bribe(1).

'backing *n* **1** *u.n* support. Compare back(21). **2** *c.n* thing that is put behind s.t, e.g to strengthen it, or that is used as the back of s.t. Compare back(23). **3** *c.n* music to support the main singer(s) or player(s), esp in popular music.

'back,lash *c.n* **1** sudden violent movement backwards following one forwards, e.g when a car stops suddenly. **2** (*fig*) (usu delayed but) strong reaction(1) to s.t, e.g a belief or way of doing things.

'back,log *c.n* work that should have been done before but has not, so that it still has to be done.

'back,most *adj* farthest back.

,back 'number *c.n* **1** issue(2) of a magazine etc from an earlier date. **2** (*fig*) old-fashioned person.

'back,pack *c.n* = haversack.

,back,room 'boy *c.n* (*informal*) person who does important work but who is not seen by the public.

,back,seat 'driver *c.n* (*derog*) passenger in a car, whether sitting in a front or a back seat, who is always telling the driver what to do.

'back,side *c.n* (*informal*) buttocks.

,back'stage *attrib.adj* **1** secret; in the background: *backstage help from a friend.*
▷ *adv* **2** behind the stage of a theatre etc: *go backstage.* **3** secretly.

'back ,street *c.n* unimportant street in a town etc that is away from the big important ones.

'back,up *u.n* support. ⇨ back s.o/s.t up.

backward /'bækwəd/ *adj* (US **'backwards**) **1** towards the back; towards what is behind one; towards the place one has just come from. **2** towards the past. Opposite forward(2). **3** not getting on as quickly or as fast as the average: *a backward learner/nation.* ⇨ forward(3); developing world; retarded(2).

'backward-,looking *adj* often thinking of the past. Opposite forward-looking.

'backwardness *u.n.*

backwards /'bækwədz/ *adv* **1** towards the back; towards what is behind one; towards the place one has just come from. **2** towards the past. **3** the wrong way round: *The man put his leather coat on backwards to protect himself from the rain on his* motorbike. **backwards and forwards** in one direction and then in the opposite one (again and again); back and forth ⇨ back(*adv*). **bend/ lean over backwards (to do s.t)** (*fig*; *informal*) try extremely, even too, hard (to do s.t). **know s.t backwards** (*fig*; *informal*) know s.t perfectly.

'back,water *c.n* **1** part of a river etc where the water is (almost) not moving. **2** (*fig*) place that is very quiet and untouched by civilization, progress etc.

bacon /'beɪkən/ *u.n* salted or smoked meat of a pig. **bring home the bacon** (*fig*; *informal*) be successful in getting s.t, esp earning a living. **save one's/s.o's bacon** (*fig*; *informal*) manage to save oneself/s.o from danger etc.

bacterium /bæk'tɪərɪəm/ *c.n* (*pl* **bacteria** /bæk'tɪərɪə/) kind of simple plant that is so small that it cannot be seen except with a microscope; some kinds are useful, others cause disease etc.

bac'terial *adj* of, referring to, bacteria.

bacteriologist /bæk,tɪərɪ'ɒlədʒɪst/ *c.n* person who studies, or is skilled in, bacteriology.

bacteriology /bæk,tɪərɪ'ɒlədʒɪ/ *u.n* scientific study of bacteria.

bad /bæd/ *adj* (*comp* **worse** /wɜːs/, *superl* **worst** /wɜːst/) **1** morally wrong; wicked; evil: *It is bad to tell lies.* **2** not doing what one is told: *a bad boy.* **3** not suitable for the situation in which it is used: *bad language* (using swearwords). **4** nasty; unpleasant: *a bad smell.* **5** serious in its results; severe: *a bad attack of flu.* **6** poor; rotten; not right; not of the quality needed or wanted: *This egg is bad. The light is too bad for taking photographs.* **7** (often — *for s.o/s.t*) not having a good result, or the result wanted, on s.o/s.t: *Smoking is bad for you* (or *your health*). *This soap has had a bad* effect(1) *on my skin.* **8** not in good health; sick: *John's off work with a bad back.* **9** unfortunate; not lucky: *It's bad that you can't come to my party.* **10** sad; unhappy; ashamed: *Don't feel bad about what happened; it wasn't your fault.* **11** not correct: *bad grammar.* **12** false; that has no value because it is not what it is supposed to be: *a bad £5 note*; *a bad cheque.* **call s.o bad names**; **give s.o a bad name** ⇨ name (*n*). **give s.o/s.t up as a bad job** ⇨ job. **go bad** become rotten. **go from bad to worse** ⇨ go from (⇨ go(*v*)). **in a bad way** ⇨ way. **make the best of a bad job** ⇨ job. **not bad** (*informal*) quite good: *Her new car is not bad!* **not half bad** (*informal*) very good: *This food's not half bad!* **not half bad (at s.t)** (*informal*) very good at (doing) s.t: *She's not half bad at tennis.* **too bad** (very) unfortunate. Compare bad(9). **with (a) bad grace** ⇨ grace(*n*).

,bad 'blood/'feeling ⇨ feeling(*n*).

,bad 'debt *c.n* money that is owed but not likely to be paid.

'baddy *c.n* (*pl* **-ies**) (often *pl*) (*informal*) bad(1) person, esp in a play, film etc: *Why is it that the baddies always get killed in old films?* Opposite goody(2).

,bad 'egg/'hat/'lot/'penny/'type *c.n* (*old use*; *slang*) bad(1) person.

,bad 'faith *u.n* dishonesty. **in bad faith** dishonestly.

,bad 'form *u.n* (*formal*) behaviour that is not suitable in good society.

'badly *adv.* **'badness** *u.n.*

'bad 'temper *c/u.n* ⇨ temper(*n*).

,bad-'tempered *adj* having, in, a bad temper.

bade /bæd, beɪd/ *p.t* of bid(*v*).

badge /bædʒ/ *c.n* thing worn on one's clothes, put on one's car etc, to show what one is or belongs to.

badger[1] /'bædʒə/ *c.n* kind of black and white

animal that lives in holes in the ground and comes out at night.

badger² /'bædʒə/ *tr.v* trouble (s.o) by asking too many questions.

badminton /'bædmɪntən/ *u.n* game like tennis but played with a shuttlecock and a high net.

baffle /'bæfl/ *tr.v* puzzle (s.o) completely so that one cannot find an answer.

bag /bæg/ *c.n* **1** container made of paper, cloth, leather, plastic etc that is open at the top and in which one puts things: *a paper/plastic bag.* ⇨ handbag. **2** (also **'bagful**) amount a bag(1) can hold. **3** number of birds etc caught or shot. *a bag of bones* (*fig*; *informal*) a very thin person or animal. *have bags under one's eyes* look tired. *in the bag* (*slang*) successfully done or arranged. *pack one's bags* ⇨ pack(*v*). *the whole bag of tricks* (*slang*) all of it/them.
▷ *tr.v* (*-gg-*) **4** put (s.t) in a bag(1) or bags. **5** (in hunting or shooting) catch or shoot (s.t). Compare bag(3). **6** (*slang*) steal (s.t): *I bagged her pen and ran.* **7** (*slang*) reserve (a seat in a cinema etc) informally: *Could you get there early and bag a place for us?*

,bag and 'baggage *adv* taking everything one possesses with one.

'bagful *c.n* = bag(2).

'baggage *u.n* = luggage.

'baggy *adj* (*-ier, -iest*) (of clothes) hanging loosely on one's body.

'bag,pipes *pl/def.pl.n* kind of musical instrument with a bag and pipes on it, esp used in Scotland.

bags *pl.n* bags of s.t (*informal*) lots of s.t.

bah /bɑː/ *interj* (sound showing that one does not like or believe s.t).

bail¹ /beɪl/ *u.n* **1** (*law*) money paid to a court of law to allow an accused person to stay out of prison until her/his trial. *go/stand bail for s.o* pay this money for s.o to be allowed to stay out of prison until trial. (*out*) *on bail* (of an accused person) free after bail¹(1) has been paid until one's trial. *forfeit one's bail* lose one's bail¹(1) because the person does not come to her/his trial. *surrender to one's bail* come for trial after having been (out) on bail.
▷ *tr.v* **2** (usu — *s.o out*) pay the bail¹(1) for s.o.

bail² /beɪl/ *c.n* one of two small pieces of wood put across the top of the stumps(4) in the game of cricket¹.

bail³ /beɪl/ *tr/intr.v* (also **bale**) **1** (often — *a boat etc out*) empty water out of (an open boat), using a bucket etc. **2** (often — *water etc out* (of s.t)) empty (water etc) out (of s.t, e.g a boat), using a bucket etc.

bailiff /'beɪlɪf/ *c.n* **1** officer of the law, esp one who seizes property etc on the orders of a judge etc. **2** person who works for the owner of land as her/his manager, collecting rents etc.

bait¹ /beɪt/ *n* **1** *sing/u.n* food, or thing that is made to look like it, used to catch fish, animals etc. **2** *c/u.n* (*fig*) thing that is used to attract s.o, e.g to persuade people to come into a shop. *rise to the bait*; *take the bait* accept the bait¹(1,2) without realizing that it is dangerous and so put oneself in danger.
▷ *tr.v* **3** put bait¹(1) on/in (s.t, e.g a hook or trap).

bait² /beɪt/ *tr.v* (try to) make (s.o, an animal) angry; tease(2) (s.o, an animal).

bake /beɪk/ *v* **1** *tr/intr.v* (cause (s.t) to) cook in an oven. **2** *tr/intr.v* (cause (s.t, e.g clay) to) become hard in the sun or other heat. **3** *intr.v* (*informal*) be very hot: *It's a baking day today; let's go for a swim.* ⇨ half-baked.

'baker *c.n* **1** person who bakes(1) bread etc as a job; person who has a bakery. **2** (also **'baker's**) shop where bread etc is sold.

,baker's 'dozen *c.n* thirteen.

'bakery *c.n* (*pl -ies*) place that bakes and/or sells bread and other baked(1) food as a business.

'baking ,powder *u.n* kind of powder used while making cake etc so that it rises(13).

balance /'bæləns/ *n* **1** *u.n* state of being able to remain in one position without falling to any side; equilibrium(1): *To cross the river on this rope needs very good balance.* **2** *u.n* (*fig*) state of being able to remain in a mental state without being influenced to change it by anything: *balance of mind.* **3** *u.n* state in which both sides of s.t are equal because they weigh etc the same: *We must try to keep the balance between successful teaching and happy students.* **4** *c.n* machine or device used for weighing things, esp when one wants very exact weights as in science. ⇨ scales (⇨ scale¹). **5** *c.n* part of a watch, clock etc that one can change to make it go faster or slower. **6** *c.n* (in accounts) difference between the totals of money that comes in and that goes out: *After paying for the carpets, I have a balance of £135.93 in my account.* **7** *c.n* (often *the* — of s.t) amount (of s.t) that still remains: *I can take 10 days off a month and I've had five already, so I have a balance of another five to come.* (*hang*) *in the balance* (be) in an uncertain state with the possibility that it will come to an end: *His life is hanging in the balance after an accident.* *hold the balance* (*between s.o/s.t and s.o/s.t*) be the person or thing who/that can make s.t swing to one side or the other. *keep/lose one's balance* manage/fail to remain in a state of balance(1,2). *off balance* in danger of falling because one has not got one's proper balance(1). *on balance* when one compares or considers everything: *On balance, I think Jill's plan is a good one.* *regain one's balance/footing* get one's balance(1)/footing again after nearly falling over. *strike a balance* (*between s.o/s.t and s.o/s.t*) reach a state which is fair both to s.o/s.t and to s.o/s.t.
▷ *v* **8** *tr/intr.v* (cause (s.o/s.t) to) be or remain in a position where one/it does not fall down on either side: *That man can balance a ball on one finger. Mary balanced on one hand at the edge of the pool and then dived in.* ⇨ overbalance. **9** *tr.v* compare (two or more things) with each other to try to make them equal: *We must balance the needs of the farmers and the city people in this country.* **10** *tr/intr.v* (cause (s.t) to) be of the same weight etc (as s.t, or as each other). **11** *tr/intr.v* (cause (an account etc) to) be equal on both sides (the credit(2) and the debit(1)): *balance one's books/budget(2).* **12** *tr.v* go through (an account) to see what the balance(6) is.

'balanced *adj* (of a person, her/his mind etc) sensible. Opposite unbalanced.

,balanced 'diet *c.n* diet(1) that contains the right kinds and amounts of different foods to keep one healthy.

,balance of 'payments/'trade *def.n* comparison between money coming into a country and money going out.

,balance of 'power *def.n* **1** relative(1) power of two or more countries etc. **2** situation in which different countries, political parties etc are equally strong.

'balance ,sheet *c.n* account showing credits(2), debits(1) and the balance(6).

balcony /'bælkənɪ/ *c.n* (*pl -ies*) **1** flat place, usu without a roof, that sticks out from a building and usu has a railing or low wall round the front and sides. **2** (in a theatre etc) higher level of seats, above the stalls (⇨ stall¹).

bald /bɔːld/ *adj* **1** not having hair where one expects it to grow: *a person's bald head*; *the bald necks of some birds.* **2** without decoration: *a bald pattern of red lines.* **3** plain; frank¹: *a bald statement of the truth.*

'baldly *adv* in a bald(3) way: *He stated baldly that he did not agree.*

'baldness *u.n.*

bale¹ /beɪl/ *c.n* **1** (often — *of s.t*) bundle (of hay, cloth etc), usu tied with strong string.
▷ *tr.v* **2** tie (s.t) in bales(1).

bale² /beɪl/ *tr/intr.v* = bail³.

bale³ /beɪl/ *intr.v* **bale out** jump out of a plane to save one's life.

balk /bɔːk/ *v* (also **baulk**) **1** *tr.v* prevent s.o doing (s.t) he/she wants to do; stop (s.t, e.g a plan). **2** *intr.v* (usu — *at s.t*) refuse to do s.t unpleasant.

ball¹ /bɔːl/ *c.n* **1** round thing, either hollow or filled with s.t, used for throwing, hitting or kicking in some games. **2** (often — *of s.t*) mass (of material, e.g wool or cotton), in the shape of a ball(1). **3** round piece of metal to be fired from a gun. ⇨ cannonball. **4** round part of s.t, esp of a person's body: *the ball of one's foot.* ⇨ eyeball. **5** throw of a ball(1): *a fast ball from the* bowler (⇨ bowl²). **the ball is in s.o's court** (*fig*) it is s.o's turn to deal with s.t. **keep the ball rolling** (*fig*) not allow s.t to stop. **on the ball** (*fig; informal*) efficient; quick in understanding or noticing things. **play ball** (**with s.o**) **(a)** (usu of children) use a ball to play games. **(b)** (*fig; informal*) (be willing to) work with s.o helpfully. **get/set/start the ball rolling** (*fig*) begin s.t, e.g a discussion.

,ball 'bearing *c.n* **1** ring of small metal balls round an axle to help it to turn more easily. **2** one of these balls.

'ball,cock *c.n* device, a round object on a rod, that controls the water running into a tank etc.

'ball,point *c.n* (also **,ball,point 'pen**) kind of pen that has a small ball instead of a nib.

balls *interj/u.n* **1** (*slang*; do not use!) nonsense.
▷ *pl.n* **2** (*slang*; do not use!) testicles.

'balls-,up *c.n* (*slang*; do not use!) failure, usu caused by inefficiency.

ball² /bɔːl/ *c.n* formal party at which there is dancing. **have a ball** (*fig; slang*) have a very enjoyable time.

'ball,room *c.n* room where balls² and other big parties are held.

'ball,room ,dancing *u.n* formal kind of dancing popular at balls².

ballad /'bæləd/ *c.n* **1** simple popular song, usu about love. **2** short story in verse.

ballast /'bæləst/ *u.n* **1** heavy material, e.g stones and/or sand, put in a ship to help keep it steady in rough seas. **2** material, usu stones and broken rock, used as a base for roads or railways.
▷ *tr.v* **3** load (s.t) with ballast(1).

ballet /'bæleɪ/ *n* **1** *c.n* dance given on a stage etc with music but not words, although the movements of the dancers tell a story. **2** *c.n* music for such a dance. **3** *u/def.n* (also *attrib*) this kind of dancing as an art form. **4** *c.n* group of dancers who work together in ballet(3).

ballerina /,bælə'riːnə/ *c.n* female ballet(3) dancer.

ballocks ⇨ bollocks(2).

balloon /bə'luːn/ *c.n* **1** bag made of a very light material, sometimes rubber, and filled with air or a gas lighter than air, either as a child's toy, or to carry passengers in a basket underneath, or to find out what the weather is. **2** thing that has the shape of a balloon(1), e.g one that is drawn as coming out of a person's mouth in a cartoon(1), with the words the person is supposed to be saying inside it. **when the balloon goes up** (*fig; informal*) when s.t, usu bad, that one is expecting starts to happen.
▷ *intr.v* **3** (often — *out/up*) become bigger and bigger, or rounder and rounder in shape.

ballot /'bælət/ *n* **1** *c.n* piece of paper used in secret voting. **2** *c.n* (often — *on s.t*) secret vote (to decide s.t). **3** *def.n* arrangement to elect s.o or choose s.t by a secret vote. **4** *def.n* right to have a secret vote.
▷ *v* **5** *intr.v* (often — *for s.o/s.t*) choose s.o/s.t by a secret vote. **6** *tr.v* (often — *s.o about/on s.t*) ask (a group of people, members etc) to decide or vote (about s.t) using a ballot(2): *Members of the union were balloted on whether to strike.*

ballpoint ⇨ ball¹.

ballroom ⇨ ball².

balls(-up) ⇨ ball¹.

ballyhoo /,bælɪ'huː/ *u.n* noisy unpleasant ways of advertising or of attracting attention.

balm /bɑːm/ *u.n* **1** kind of oily substance with a pleasant smell, used for lessening pain etc. **2** words etc that heal hurt feelings.

'balmy *adj* (*-ier, -iest*) **1** having a pleasant scent; healing. **2** (of wind or air) soft and warm; mild.

balsam /'bɔːlsəm/ *u.n* kind of balm(1).

balustrade /'bælə,streɪd/ *c.n* line of wooden, stone etc posts joined together on top by a rail etc, used round the edge of a staircase or balcony. Compare banister.

bamboo /bæm'buː/ *n* **1** *c/u.n* (also *attrib*) kind of tall plant with thick hard hollow stems that grows mostly in hot countries: *bamboo chairs*. **2** *c.n* stem of this plant. Compare cane(1).

ban /bæn/ *c.n* **1** (often — *on s.t*) order forbidding s.t.
▷ *tr.v* (*-nn-*) **2** order that (s.t) must not be done; forbid (s.t).

banana /bə'nɑːnə/ *c/u.n* (also *attrib*) kind of long fruit which has a thick skin, is yellow when ripe and grows in hot countries: *a banana tree.*

band¹ /bænd/ *c.n* **1** long narrow strip of material, e.g one to fasten one's hair or to hold things together. ⇨ armband, rubber band. **2** strip of a different material or colour running through, or at the edge of, s.t: *My cup was white, with a gold band round the top.* **3** one of a number of things that run parallel(3) with each other, e.g a range(7) of radio frequencies(2): *You will find the radio station you are looking for in the 31 metre band.* Compare wave band.

▷ *tr.v* **4** put a band(1,2) in or on (s.t): *a green skirt banded with yellow.*

'band ,aid *c.n(t.n)* plaster(3).

band² /bænd/ *c.n* **1** (often — of s.t) group (of people) who have joined together to do s.t: *a band of robbers.* **2** group of musicians who play together: *a* jazz(1) *band*; *a* brass(4) *band.* Compare orchestra.

▷ *intr.v* (usu — *together*; — *into* s.t) join (together) (to form a group).

'band ,master *c.n* conductor(2) of a band(2) playing military music or of a brass(4) band.

'bandsman *c.n* (*pl* -men) person who plays in a band(2).

'band ,stand *c.n* raised place, usu with a roof, on which a band(2) plays out-of-doors.

'band ,wagon *def.n* **jump on the bandwagon** (*fig*) join the side, party etc that is the most popular, or the most likely to be successful; do what everyone else is doing.

bandage /'bændɪdʒ/ *c/u.n* **1** long strip of cloth for covering a wound etc. Compare blindfold.

▷ *tr.v* **2** (often — *s.t. up*) cover (a wounded limb etc) with a bandage(1). **3** (often — *s.o up*) put a bandage(1) on the wounds of (s.o).

band aid ⇨ band¹.

bandit /'bændɪt/ *c.n* thief or robber, esp one who wanders about in the country or robs banks etc.

'banditry *u.n* activities of bandits.

bandmaster, bandsman, bandstand, bandwagon ⇨ band².

bandy¹ /'bændɪ/ *adj* (-ier, -iest) **1** (esp of legs) bent/curved outwards. **2** (also **bandy-legged** /'bændɪ ,legd/) having bandy(1) legs. Compare knock-kneed.

bandy² /'bændɪ/ *intr.v* (-ies, -ied) (often — *s.t. about*) say (s.t), talk about (s.t), in a careless or dishonest way. **2** *tr.v* exchange (words, insults, blows etc). **bandy words** (**with s.o**) argue unpleasantly (with s.o).

bane /beɪn/ *def.n* **the bane of s.o's life** *etc* the thing that keeps on causing s.o the most trouble.

bang /bæŋ/ *adv* **1** (*informal*) right; exactly: *Martin phoned bang in the middle of our dinner.* **bang on** (*informal*) exactly right, esp in one's guess, calculations.

▷ *c.n* **2** sudden loud noise, e.g of a gun firing. **3** sharp blow. Compare bump(1). **with a bang** (*fig*; *informal*) energetically: *The party started off with a bang.*

▷ *v* **4** *tr/intr.v* (often — *into* s.o/s.t) hit (s.o/s.t) sharply. Compare bump(7). **5** *tr/intr.v* (cause (s.t) to) hit s.t, often with a bang(3): *Joe banged his head against the wall as he leant forward.* **bang shut** close with a bang(2).

'banger *c.n* (*informal*) **1** = sausage(1). **2** kind of noisy firework. **3** old car that no longer goes well.

bangle /'bæŋgl/ *c.n* kind of metal etc ornament worn round one's wrist, or sometimes ankle.

banish /'bænɪʃ/ *tr.v* **1** send (s.o) away from her/his own country as a punishment. **2** (usu — *s.t from one's mind*) stop thinking of (s.t).

'banishment *u.n.*

banister /'bænɪstə/ *c.n* **1** vertical pole made of wood or metal that is part of some banisters. **2** = banisters.

'banisters *pl.n* row of banisters(1) joined at the top, used round the edge of a staircase etc. Compare balustrade.

banjo /'bændʒəʊ/ *c.n* (*pl* -(e)s) musical instrument with a round body and strings that are played with one's fingers, not a bow.

bank¹ /bæŋk/ *c.n* **1** land along each side of a river, canal etc. **2** sloping pile of earth, sand etc, sometimes forming an edge to s.t. **3** part of the bed of the sea etc which is higher than the rest. ⇨ sandbank. **4** (usu — *of* s.t) mass (of cloud, snow etc).

▷ *v* **5** *intr.v* (of a plane, car etc) go along with one side higher than the other in order to make a turn safely. **6** *tr.v* (usu — *s.t up*) pile, heap, s.t up in or on (s.t): *If you bank up the fire before you go to bed, it will burn slowly till the morning.*

bank² /bæŋk/ *n* **1** *c.n* (also *attrib*) business that receives and looks after customers' money, gives them cheque books so that they can draw their money out, lends money etc; building in which such work is done: *a bank manager.* **2** *c.n* store for keeping supplies of s.t for when they are needed: *a blood bank* (in which blood is kept ready for transfusions). **3** *c/def.n* (in games of chance) supply of money etc for paying people who win. **a run on a/the bank** ⇨ run(*n*). **break the bank** cause a bank²(1,3) to close by taking out, or winning, all the money in it.

▷ *v* **4** *tr.v* put (money) in a bank²(1). **5** *intr.v* (usu — *with* s.o/s.t) keep one's money in a particular bank²(1)). **bank (up)on s.o (to do s.t)** trust s.o (to do s.t); depend on s.o (to do s.t). **bank (up)on s.t** depend on s.t happening etc: *I was banking on his support.*

'bank ,bill/ ,**draft** *c.n* (also **'banker's ,draft**) piece of paper from one bank²(1) telling another (often in another country) to pay some money.

'bank ,card *c.n* (also **'cheque ,card**) plastic card showing that s.o is a customer of a bank²(1) and can draw money from any of its branches.

'banker *n* **1** *c.n* person who owns or controls (part of) a bank²(1). **2** *def.n* person holding the bank²(3) in a game.

,bank 'holiday *c.n* official public holiday that is not a Saturday or Sunday when banks²(1) and most other companies are closed.

'banking *u.n* business done by banks²(1).

'bank ,note *c.n* piece of paper money issued(4) by the main bank²(1) of a country and used by the public for buying things.

'bank ,rate *c/def.n* official rate at which interest is paid to people who lend money.

'bank ,robber *c.n* person who steals money from a bank²(1).

bankrupt /'bæŋkrʌpt/ *adj* **1** unable to pay one's debts; broke(1); insolvent. **2** (usu — *of* s.t) (*derog*) (of a person's mind etc) without useful ideas, plans etc.

▷ *c.n* **3** person who is bankrupt(1).

▷ *tr.v* **4** make (s.o/s.t) bankrupt(1).

'bankruptcy *c/u.n.*

banner /'bænə/ *c.n* (long) piece of cloth with words and/or pictures on it, esp one carried in a procession on one pole or between two poles.

under the banner of s.t (*fig*) for the cause of s.t, e.g a political idea.
,**banner 'head,line** *c.n* (in a newspaper) very big headline that spreads over several columns.

banns /bænz/ *pl.n* public announcement(2) by a priest in a church that two people are going to marry each other soon. *publish the banns* make such an announcement.

banquet /'bæŋkwɪt/ *c.n* 1 large formal meal. 2 rich meal; feast.
'**banqueting ,hall** *c.n* big room in which banquets(1) are held.

bantam /'bæntəm/ *c.n* kind of small chicken.
'**bantam,weight** *c.n* (also *attrib*) boxer weighing between 112 and 118 pounds¹(2).

banter /'bæntə/ *u.n* 1 joking talk.
▷ *intr.v* 2 use banter(1) when speaking.

baptism /'bæp,tɪzəm/ *c/u.n* religious ceremony in which water is put on s.o, or in which he/she is put in water, to make him/her pure and to admit him/her as a member of the Christian(1) Church etc. *a baptism of fire* (a) the first time a person, e.g a soldier, is fired at by an enemy. (b) the first time s.o has s.t unpleasant done to her/him.
baptize, -ise /bæp'taɪz/ *tr.v* carry out the ceremony of baptism on (s.o). *baptize s.o s.t* give s.o the name of s.t when baptizing her/him: *I baptize you Helen.*

bar /bɑː/ *n* 1 *c.n* long solid piece of metal etc, often one used for fastening or closing s.t. 2 *c.n* (often *a — to s.o/s.t*) thing that stops s.o/s.t moving forward, or makes it difficult to do so: *a bar to progress.* ⇨ barrier(2). 3 *c.n* (often — *of s.t*) shaped piece (of soap, chocolate etc) the length of which is usu greater than its width. 4 *c.n* (often — *of s.t*) strip (of s.t, e.g colour or cloud). 5 *c.n* bank¹(3), often across the mouth of a river etc. 6 *c.n* place, either a room or a long thing like a table in it, where drinks, and sometimes also kinds of food, are sold: *a coffee/wine bar*; *the public/saloon bar* (i.e in a pub). ⇨ snack bar. 7 *c.n* place with a long counter² where one can get shoes mended quickly, keys made etc: *a shoe bar.* 8 *c.n* (in written or printed music) group of notes divided from other such groups by vertical lines; one of these vertical lines. 9 *c.n* (in a court of law) line separating the judge, lawyers and other officials from the prisoner and the public. 10 *def.n* (with capital **B**) (a) the profession of barrister. (b) the people who belong to this profession. *be called to the Bar* become a barrister. *behind bars* in prison. *the prisoner at the bar* the person being tried in a court of law.
▷ *tr.v* (*-rr-*) 11 (often — *s.t off*) close (s.t) (off) with one or more bars(1). 12 (often — *s.o from* (*doing*) *s.t*) prevent (s.o) from (doing) s.t. 13 mark (s.t) with a bar(4): *a blue flag barred with red.* 14 not allow (s.t). *bar s.o/s.t in/out* keep s.o/s.t in/out with bars(1), a barrier(1) etc. *no holds barred* ⇨ hold(*n*).
▷ *prep* 15 (also '**barring**) except (for): *Alison is my best friend bar none. We shall be home at 7, barring accidents.*
'**bar,maid** *c.n* woman who works in a bar(6) of a pub.
'**barman** *c.n* (*pl -men*) man who works in a bar(6) of a pub.

barrister /'bærɪstə/ *c.n* lawyer who is allowed to do her/his job in the higher courts in the UK. Compare solicitor.
'**bar,tender** *c.n* = barman.

barb /bɑːb/ *c.n* sharp point of a fish hook, arrow etc which has a shape that is curved in such a way that it is difficult to pull the hook etc out.
,**barbed 'wire** *u.n* wire with short sharp points on it.

barbarian /bɑː'beərɪən/ *c.n* person who is not civilized, or who behaves as if he/she were not.
barbaric /bɑː'bærɪk/ *adj* 1 of, referring to, like, barbarians. 2 very cruel.
barbarism /'bɑːbə,rɪzəm/ *u.n.*
barbarity /bɑː'bærɪtɪ/ *c/u.n* (*pl -ies*) terrible (act of) cruelty.
barbarous /'bɑːbərəs/ *adj* 1 not civilized. 2 very cruel.

barbecue /'bɑːbɪ,kjuː/ *c.n* 1 iron framework for cooking things on a grill over wood, charcoal(1) etc, usu out-of-doors. 2 meal at which food is cooked on a barbecue(1) and usu eaten out-of-doors.
▷ *tr.v* 3 cook (s.t) on a barbecue(1).

barber /'bɑːbə/ *c.n* 1 person who cuts men's hair (and shaves them); men's hairdresser. 2 (also '**barber's**) place where a barber(1) works.

bard /bɑːd/ *c.n* (*literary*) poet.

bare /beə/ *adj* 1 not having any clothes, leaves, ornaments etc on; not covered: *walk in one's bare feet; go out in the rain with one's head bare.* 2 (often — *of s.t*) empty (and therefore not having s.t in, on, s.t): *The cupboard was bare of all food.* 3 (*attrib*) not more than; mere: *We have only the bare essentials for our journey. Joe earns a bare living* (i.e only just enough to live on). *There is a bare possibility that it will rain this evening* (i.e it is just possible, but not likely). *lay s.t bare* (a) take the covering off s.t. (b) (*fig*) make s.t known after it has been a secret.
▷ *tr.v* 4 take the covering off (s.t): *bare one's head.* 5 (*fig*) (often — *s.t to s.o*) let (s.t) be known (to s.o) after it has been a secret: *bare one's heart/soul to s.o. bare one's teeth* ⇨ tooth.
'**bare,back** *attrib.adj/adv* (in riding) without a saddle.
'**bare-,faced** *attrib.adj* without shame; cheeky: *a bare-faced lie.*
'**bare,foot** *adj/adv* without shoes or socks.
,**bare-'headed** *adj/adv* without anything on one's head.
,**bare-'legged** *adj/adv* without any clothing on one's legs.
'**barely** *adv* 1 in a bare(3) way: *We have barely enough to live on.* 2 only just: *We could barely see the distant ship. Barely had I sat down when the telephone rang.* Compare hardly(1), scarcely.
'**bareness** *u.n.*

bargain /'bɑːgɪn/ *c.n* 1 (often *make a — (to do s.t)*) agreement (to buy, sell, exchange etc), usu made after some discussion. 2 thing offered for sale, or bought, cheaply: *This coat was a real bargain; I got it for only £20! a bargain's a bargain* when one has agreed to s.t, one should not break one's promise. *a bad/good bargain* a bargain(1) that is in the other person's, one's own, favour. *drive a hard bargain* (try to) get a bargain(1) that is very much in one's own favour. *into the bargain* as well; in addition:

John's clever, and he's good at sports into the bargain. **strike a bargain** make a bargain(1).

▷ *intr.v* **3** (often — *with s.o* (*about/for s.t*)) talk (with s.o) to try to make a bargain(1) (for, to get, s.t). **get more than one bargained for** get more of s.t unpleasant than one had expected.

'**bargain** ,**price** *c.n* price that is a bargain(2).

'**bargain** ,**hunter** *c.n* person who tries to get the best bargains(2), usu by going from shop to shop.

barge¹ /bɑːdʒ/ *c.n* kind of long low vessel used to move heavy goods on a canal, the sea etc.

bargee /bɑːˈdʒiː/ *c.n* person who owns, or is in charge of, a barge¹.

'**barge** ,**pole** *c.n* long pole for pushing against the bottom of a canal etc to make a barge¹ move. *I wouldn't touch it/s.t with a barge pole* (*fig*; *informal*) I don't want to have anything to do with it/s.t, usu because it is bad, dangerous etc.

barge² /bɑːdʒ/ *intr.v* **1** (often — *into s.o/s.t*) move about without being careful (and hit s.o/s.t as a result). **2** (often — *in(to s.t*)) interrupt (a conversation etc), esp with some rudeness: *He just barged in when I was talking to her.*

baritone /ˈbærɪˌtəʊn/ *c.n* (also *attrib*) **1** man's singing voice lower than a tenor. **2** man with such a voice. Compare alto(3), bass¹.

▷ *adj/adv* **3** having the musical range of a baritone(1): *He sings baritone.*

bark¹ /bɑːk/ *c/u.n* hard outer layer of the trunks and branches of trees.

bark² /bɑːk/ *c.n* **1** sharp cry made by a dog etc as a warning etc. **2** sound like a bark²(1) made by a gun, or when s.o coughs etc. **3** person's voice that sounds like a bark²(1), or words spoken with such a voice. *s.o's bark is worse than her/his bite* (*informal*) s.o is not so fierce as she/he sounds, looks etc.

▷ *v* **4** *intr.v* (often — *at s.o/s.t*) make the sound of a bark²(1) (to warn s.o/s.t). **5** *intr.v* make the sound of a bark²(2,3). **6** *tr.v* (often — *s.t out*) say (s.t) in a barking²(5) voice. *bark up the wrong tree* (*fig*; *informal*) get a mistaken idea in one's mind.

barley /ˈbɑːlɪ/ *u.n* (also *attrib*) kind of grain used for feeding animals, in soups, making beer etc.

'**barley-**,**sugar** *u.n* kind of hard orange-coloured sweet made from boiled sugar.

barmaid, barman ⇒ bar.

barmy /ˈbɑːmɪ/ *adj* (-*ier*, -*iest*) (*slang*) mad.

barn /bɑːn/ *c.n* building used to store hay, corn, tools, farm vehicles etc.

'**barn**,**yard** *c.n* space in front of a barn, farm etc.

barometer /bəˈrɒmɪtə/ *c.n* **1** instrument used for measuring air pressure to help in finding out what the weather is going to be like. **2** (*fig*) (often — *of s.t*) thing that shows the state (of s.t, e.g public opinion) (and gives some idea of what it is going to be like in the future): *Their anger is a barometer of public opinion on this issue.*

baron /ˈbærən/ *c.n* **1** (*written abbr Bn*) lowest rank of lord. **2** (*fig*) person with great power because of wealth, position etc: *a newspaper baron* (person who has great power because he owns a newspaper or newspapers).

'**baroness** *c.n* **1** wife of a baron(1). **2** woman with the same rank as a baron(1).

baronial /bəˈrəʊnɪəl/ *adj* **1** of, referring to,

like, a baron(1). **2** large and grand: *They live in a baronial hall.*

'**barony** *c.n* (*pl* -*ies*) title or rank of a baron(1).

baronet /ˈbærənɪt/ *c.n* (*abbr Bart*, after the person's name) person who has the title 'Sir' before his name, and whose eldest son inherits(1) it: *Sir William James, Bart.* Compare knight(3).

'**baronetcy** *c.n* (*pl* -*ies*) title or rank of a baronet.

barrack /ˈbærək/ *tr/intr.v* interrupt (s.o, a speech etc) by calling out noisily.

barracks /ˈbærəks/ *c.n* (*pl* barracks) **1** block of buildings where soldiers etc live (and train). **2** (*derog*) big plain ugly block of buildings. **confined to barracks** (of a soldier etc) not allowed to go out of the barracks(1) as a punishment.

barrage /ˈbærɑːʒ/ *c.n* **1** bank etc built across a river etc for storing water. ⇒ dam(1). **2** heavy fire from guns. **3** (often *a* — *of s.t*) (*fig*) large number of questions, statements etc all coming at the same time, or very quickly one after the other.

'**barrage bal**,**loon** *c.n* big long balloon hanging in the air to make it difficult for enemy aircraft to fly low and attack s.t.

barrel /ˈbærəl/ *c.n* **1** round container made of wood etc for holding wine, beer, oil, some kinds of food etc. **2** (also '**barrelful**) amount that a barrel(1) holds. **3** part of a gun etc that is in the form of a tube, and through which the bullets etc go. **4** container that is shaped like a tube. (*have s.o*) *over a barrel* (*fig*; *informal*) (have s.o) in a position where they cannot resist.

'**barrelful** *c.n* = barrel(2).

'**barrel** ,**organ** *c.n* mechanical musical instrument from which music comes when one turns a handle.

barren /ˈbærən/ *adj* Opposite fertile. **1** (of land) not able to produce crops. **2** (of a plant) that does not produce fruit, seeds etc. **3** (of a woman or female animal) unable to have babies or young. **4** (*fig*) (of ideas etc) without value, use or interest: *a barren discussion.*

'**barrenness** *u.n.*

barricade /ˌbærɪˈkeɪd/ *c.n* **1** barrier(1) put up, e.g across a road, to try to stop people, vehicles etc.

▷ *tr.v* **2** put up a barricade(1) to block (s.t, e.g a street). *barricade oneself in(to s.t*) put up barricades(1) to try to prevent people reaching one (inside a place, building etc).

barrier /ˈbærɪə/ *c.n* **1** thing put up or built to prevent people coming in or going out (freely): *After you get out of the train you have to show your ticket at the barrier.* Compare barricade(1). **2** (often — *to s.t*) thing that makes s.t difficult: *Lack of education is a barrier to progress.* Compare bar(2), obstacle. *sound barrier* ⇒ sound².

barring, barrister ⇒ bar.

barrow /ˈbærəʊ/ *c.n.* **1** kind of small cart that is pulled or pushed by hand. **2** = wheelbarrow.

'**barrow** ,**boy**/,**man** *c.n* man who sells things in the street from a barrow(1).

Bart /bɑːt/ *abbr* baronet.

bartender ⇒ bar.

barter /ˈbɑːtə/ *u.n* **1** trading without the use of money; exchange of goods.

▷ *tr/intr.v* **2** (often — (*s.t*) (*with s.o*) *for s.t*) exchange (goods) (with s.o) without using money (receiving s.t in return).

basalt /ˈbæsɔːlt/ *u.n* kind of rock that originally came up from under the earth in a melted state.

base¹ /beɪs/ *adj* dishonourable.

,**base 'metal** *c/u.n* metal that is not one of the precious ones such as gold.

'**basely** *adv.* '**baseness** *u.n.*

base² /beɪs/ *c.n* **1** bottom of s.t, esp the part it sits/rests on: *the base of a marble column.* **2** (*geometry*) line at the bottom of a figure: *the base of a triangle.* Opposite apex(1). **3** (also *attrib*) place that is used as the home of s.t, or the point from which it starts out and to which it returns: *an army base; the base camp from which people climb a mountain.* **4** main substance of s.t to which other things can be added: *All these soups have the same potato base.* **5** (*chemistry*) substance that, with an acid, forms a salt and water. **at base** = basically.

▷ *tr.v* **6 base s.t (up)on s.t** give information etc to support an argument, opinion etc: *What do you base your accusations on?*

'**base,ball** *u.n* game between two teams in which a player can score points by hitting a ball and running around a diamond-shaped field with four base(3) points.

'**baseless** *adj* that has no basis(1).

'**base,line** *c.n* **1** (in tennis etc) back line at each end of the court. **2** line from which one starts s.t.

'**basement** *c.n* room(s) below ground level in a house. ⇒ cellar(1).

basic /ˈbeɪsɪk/ *adj* **1** that forms a basis(1); necessary for s.t; essential: *basic rules; basic ingredients for a cake.* Compare fundamental.

▷ *unique n* (also '**BASIC**) **2** simple language used in computers (it stands for 'Beginner's All-purpose Symbolic Instruction Code').

'**basically** *adv* really; when one looks at it thoroughly and gets right to the bottom of it; fundamentally: *Basically Tom's a kind person but he often gets angry.*

'**basics** *pl.n* (often *the — of s.t*) simplest but most important parts (of an activity etc).

basis /ˈbeɪsɪs/ *c.n* (*pl bases* /ˈbeɪsiːz/) **1** (often *a — for s.t; the — of s.t*) thing on which s.t is based²(6): *What is the basis for your accusations?* **2** (often *the — of s.t*) = base²(4): *the basis of a good soup.* **on the basis of s.t** using s.t as one's basis(1): *On the basis of this information, I agree with Harry.*

bash /bæʃ/ (*informal*) *c.n* **1** (often *give s.o/s.t a* —) hard hit/blow. **have a bash (at (doing) s.t)** (*slang*) try to do s.t.

▷ *tr.v* **2** hit (s.o/s.t) hard.

bashful /ˈbæʃful/ *adj* shy.

'**bashfully** *adv.* '**bashfulness** *u.n.*

basic(ally) ⇒ base².

basin /ˈbeɪsn/ *c.n* **1** bowl for washing (things) in, mixing and/or keeping food in etc. ⇒ washbasin. **2** hollow part of s.t where there is (sometimes) water: *the basin of a fountain*(1). **3** deep part of a harbour, where big ships can go. **4** (almost) circular valley. **5** area of country from which the water runs down into one river. ⇒ river basin.

basis ⇒ base².

bask /bɑːsk/ *intr.v* (usu *— in s.t*) **1** sit or lie (in the warmth (of the sun)). **2** (*fig*) enjoy (s.o's

approval, the glory of s.t etc): *The famous football player basked in his popularity.*

basket /ˈbɑːskɪt/ *c.n* **1** container, usu woven out of sticks, for carrying things in. **2** (also '**basketful**) amount that a basket(1) holds. **3** net with a hole in the bottom into which one tries to throw the ball in the game of basketball. **put all one's eggs in one basket** ⇒ egg.

'**basket,ball** *u.n* game between two teams in which one scores points by throwing the ball into a basket(3) on a tall pole.

'**basketful** *c.n* = basket(2).

bass¹ /beɪs/ *c.n* (also *attrib*) **1** man's lowest singing voice. **2** man with such a singing voice. Compare baritone, contralto. **double bass** ⇒ double.

▷ *adj/adv* **3** having the musical range of a bass(1): *He sings bass.*

,**bass 'clef** *c.n* (*music*) sign𝄢: showing that the notes that follow are below middle C. Compare treble clef.

bass² /bæs/ *c.n* (*pl -(es)*) *c.n* kind of fish found in the sea, a river etc used as food.

bassoon /bəˈsuːn/ *c.n* kind of big wooden musical instrument that makes deep sounds when one blows it.

bastard /ˈbɑːstəd/ *c.n* (also *attrib*) **1** child born of parents who are not married. Compare illegitimate(1). **2** (*slang*; do not use!) very unpleasant person. **3** (*slang*) (showing liking) person; fellow.

baste¹ /beɪst/ *tr.v* (in cooking) pour melted fat over (meat etc) while it is cooking.

baste² /beɪst/ *tr.v* (in dressmaking) join (pieces of cloth) together with long stitches(2) before sewing them properly, after which the stitches(2) are taken out.

bastion /ˈbæstɪən/ *c.n* **1** part of the wall of a fort that sticks out further than the rest of it. **2** (*fig*) (usu *— of s.t*) (a) place where s.t is defended strongly; stronghold(2): *That country is a bastion of hope in a dangerous world.* (b) person who defends a principle strongly.

bat¹ /bæt/ *c.n* creature like a mouse with wings that lives in dark places during the day, and flies at night. **as blind as a bat** (*informal*) not able to see well, or bad at noticing things. **have bats in the belfry** (*fig*; *informal*) be mad. **vampire bat** *c.n* ⇒ vampire(3).

bat² /bæt/ *c.n* **1** solid wooden instrument used for hitting the ball in some games, e.g cricket¹. Compare racket¹. (**do s.t**) **off one's own bat** (*fig*; *informal*) (do s.t) without any suggestion or help from anyone else.

▷ *intr.v* (*-tt-*) **2** be the batsman.

'**batsman** *c.n* (*pl -men*) person whose turn it is to hit the ball in a game of cricket¹.

bat³ /bæt/ *tr.v* (*-tt-*) **not bat an eyelid** not show shock or surprise at all: *When Joan asked to borrow Susan's new car, Susan never batted an eyelid.*

batch /bætʃ/ *c.n* (often *— of s.t*) set or collection (of people or things) that is of the same kind, or that is made, comes, at the same time.

bath /bɑːθ/ *c.n* (*pl -s* /bɑːθs, bɑːðz/) **1** big container for washing oneself or s.o, e.g a baby, in. **2** water in a bath(1): *Your bath's ready!* **3** (often *have/take a* —; *give s.o a* —) (carry out etc an) act of putting oneself or s.o else in water to wash all over. **4** container for a liquid in which s.t is put to clean it etc. **5** liquid in a bath(4). **6** (usu *pl*) = swimming bath. **run (oneself/s.o) a bath** put water in a bath(1) (so that one can wash oneself/s.o).

▷ *v* **7** *intr.v* have a bath(3). **8** *tr.v* give (s.o, e.g a baby) a bath(3).

bathe /beɪð/ *c.n* **1** (often *go for a —; have a —*) act of going into the sea, a bathing pool etc for pleasure.

▷ *v* **2** *intr.v* have a bathe(1). **3** *tr.v* wash (s.t, e.g one's eyes) gently with a liquid, e.g water. **be bathed in/with s.t** be wet all over with s.t, e.g sweat, or be covered all over with s.t, e.g warm sun.

'bathing, costume/,suit *c.n* clothing worn by women or girls for having a bathe(1).

'bathing ,pool *c.n* swimming pool, esp one in the open air, or a place in a river etc where it is deep enough to have a bathe(1).

'bath,mat *c.n* mat put at the side of a bath(1) to step on when one gets out of it.

'bath,robe *c.n* loose soft thing like a coat, often made of the same cloth as a towel, worn before and after bathing.

'bath,room *c.n* **1** room in which one can wash, have a bath(3), and sometimes also go to the lavatory. **2** (US) lavatory.

baths /bɑːθs, bɑːðz/ *c.n* (*pl baths*) (often *pl* with *sing* meaning) = swimming bath.

'bath ,salts *pl.n* kind of salts with perfume used in bath water.

'bath,tub *c.n* (also **tub**) (esp US) = bath(1).

'bath,water *u.n* water in a bath(1).

batman /'bætmən/ *c.n* (*pl -men*) personal servant of an army officer.

baton /'bætn/ *c.n* **1** short thick stick carried by a police officer as a weapon. **2** thin stick used by the conductor(2) of an orchestra etc. **3** short thick stick used as a sign of rank or authority. **4** hollow tube used in a relay race for passing on from one runner to the next.

batsman ⇒ bat².

battalion /bə'tælɪən/ *c.n* army unit of usu between 500 and 1000 soldiers forming part of a regiment(2) or brigade(1).

batten /'bætn/ *c.n* **1** strip of wood used to hold s.t in position.

▷ *tr.v* **2 batten s.t down** fasten s.t with battens(1).

batter¹ /'bætə/ *u.n* mixture of milk, eggs, flour etc used for cooking pancakes etc.

batter² /'bætə/ *tr/intr.v* (often *— (away) at/on s.o/s.t; — s.t to pieces*) hit (s.o/s.t) hard and again and again, sometimes causing damage or breakage(s).

'battered *adj* showing a lot of signs of wear and damage; knocked out of shape: *a battered old hat.*

,battered 'baby/'wife *c.n* baby/wife who has been hit, treated very badly, by a parent/husband (or another adult).

'battery¹ u.n assault and battery ⇒ assault.

battery² /'bætərɪ/ *c.n* (*pl -ies*) thing for producing electricity, consisting of a number of cells(6) joined together.

battery³ /'bætərɪ/ *c.n* (*pl -ies*) **1** (*military*) group of big guns, sometimes with the people who look after and fire them. **2** group or set (of tools, cameras, questions etc): *When the film-star came out, she faced a battery of cameras.* **3** (also *attrib*) set of boxes in which chickens etc live: *battery hens.* Compare freerange.

battiness ⇒ batty.

battle /'bætl/ *n* **1** *c.n* fight, esp between groups of people, or against s.t, e.g strong winds. **2** *u.n* fighting. **be half the battle** be half of the problem or difficulty dealt with successfully: *Recognizing that there is a problem is half the battle.* **do battle with s.o/s.t; give battle to s.o/s.t** fight s.o/s.t.

▷ *intr.v* **3** (often *— (away/on) against/with s.o/s.t*): *Though the situation looked hopeless they battled on against the enemy.* **battle for s.t** fight to get or keep s.t, e.g life.

'battle,dress *u.n* normal clothes worn by a soldier or officer.

'battle,field *c.n* (also **'battle,ground**) **1** place where a battle is, or has been, fought. **2** (*fig*) place where strong arguments take place.

'battlements *pl. n* wall built round the roof of a castle etc, with spaces through which one can shoot at an enemy.

'battle,ship *c.n* kind of large warship.

batty /'bætɪ/ *adj* (*-ier, -iest*) (*slang*) mad.

'battiness *u.n.*

bauble /'bɔːbl/ *c.n* ornament, decoration etc that looks pretty but is worth little.

baulk /bɔːk/ = balk(1,2).

bauxite /'bɔːksaɪt/ *u.n* kind of ore from which aluminium is made.

bawl /bɔːl/ *v* **1** *intr.v* (*informal*) cry loudly: *The baby's bawling again.* **2** *tr/intr.v* (often *— (s.t) out; — at s.o*) shout (s.t) loudly and unpleasantly.

bay¹ /beɪ/ *n* **1** *u.n* (also *attrib*) (usu of horses) colour between red and yellow. **2** *c.n* horse of this colour.

bay² /beɪ/ *c.n* (with capital **B** in names) (name for an) area of sea, lake etc which has land round a lot of it: *the Bay of Biscay; Colwyn Bay.*

bay³ /beɪ/ *c.n* (also *attrib*) **1** part of a room that sticks out further than the rest: *a bay window.* **2** part of a room etc that is divided off from the rest by s.t: *In a public library the books are on shelves in bays.*

bay⁴ /beɪ/ *c.n* (also **'bay ,tree**) kind of tree whose leaves are used in cooking.

'bay ,leaf *c.n* leaf of a bay⁴ (used in cooking).

bay⁵ /beɪ/ *c.n* **1** deep bark of some kinds of hound(1). **at bay** facing the person or animal who/that is attacking one and ready to resist. **hold/keep s.o/s.t at bay** (a) prevent s.o/s.t from coming forward to attack one. (b) not allow s.t, e.g an illness, to attack one.

▷ *intr.v* **2** (often *— at s.o/s.t*) (of a hound(1)) bark (at s.o/s.t) with a voice that is a bay⁵(1). **3** (of people, usu in a crowd) make a noise like that of baying⁵(2), esp when chasing or attacking s.o/s.t.

bayonet /'beɪənɪt/ *c.n* **1** sharp instrument like a long knife that a soldier puts at the end of his rifle for fighting.

▷ *tr.v* **2** stick a bayonet(1) into (s.o/s.t).

bazaar /bə'zɑː/ *c.n* **1** market in Asia/Africa. **2** sale of things, often for charity(2), not profit.

B & B /,biː ən 'biː/ *abbr* bed and breakfast(⇒ bed).

BBC /,biː biː 'siː/ *def.n abbr* British Broadcasting Corporation.

BC /ˌbiː ˈsiː/ abbr Before Christ (used in dates): *1500 BC* (i.e 1500 years before Christ was born). Compare AD.

be aux.v (restrong form /biː/, weak form /bɪ/) (*1st pers sing pres.t* am (strong form /æm/, weak form /əm/), *2nd pers sing pres.t* are (strong form /ɑː/, weak form /ə/), *3rd pers sing pres.t is* /ɪz/; *pres.t pl* (all persons) are; *pres.p* being /ˈbiːɪŋ/; *1st and 3rd pers sing p.t* was (strong form /wɒz/, weak form /wəz/), *2nd pers sing p.t* and *p.t pl* (all persons) were (strong form /wɜː/, weak form /wə/); negative forms am not, are not or aren't /ɑːnt/, is not or isn't /ɪznt/, was not or wasn't /wɒznt/, were not or weren't /wɜːnt/; 'I am' can be *I'm* /aɪm/, 'you are' can be *you're* /juə/, 'he/she is' can be *he's/she's* /hiːz, ʃiːz/, 'it is' can be *it's* /ɪts/, 'we are' can be *we're* /wɪə/, 'they are' can be *they're* /ðeə/) **1** (used with other verbs to form tenses²) **(a)** (continuous tenses): *I am, was, will be, reading.* **(b)** (passives): *Mary is/was being helped.* **(c)** (future tense): *Helen is to have her baby next month.* **(d)** (future tense in the past): *We thought all was going well but we were soon to find out that we were wrong.* **(e)** (future tense in the past when s.t expected did not happen): *I was to have been home by now, but the train arrived very late.* **2** ('be' is followed by the infinitive of a verb with *to*, showing **(a)** obligation(1)): *Your mother says that you are to stop that noise at once!* **(b)** (advisability): *Where are we to go now?* **(c)** (purpose): *This money is to help you get a job.* **is/was not/nowhere to be found, seen** etc cannot, could not, be found, seen etc (anywhere). **if s.o/s.t was/were to do s.t**; **were s.o/s.t to do s.t** (in clauses of imaginary condition): *If I were to tell you all I know* (or *Were I to tell you all I know*), *you would not believe it.*

▷ v (verb forms and pronunciations are the same as aux.v) **3** (joining the subject¹(4) of a clause(1) and s.t that gives more information about it) **(a)** a noun (phrase(1)): *This is John. He is my brother.* **(b)** a pron: *That coat is his. 'Who is that?' 'It's me'* (formal 'It is I'). **(c)** an adj (phrase(1)): *Our teacher is nice. She is kind to her pupils.* **(d)** an adv: *She is here.* **(e)** a prep phrase(1): *Our manager is in her room.* **(f)** an -ing form (phrase(1)): *Her work is looking after the school.* **(g)** an infinitive (phrase(1)) with 'to': *My work is to help her.* **(h)** a noun clause(1): *The difficulty is that I haven't had much experience.* **4** (after 'there') ⇒ there³(1). **5** (literary) exist: *To be or not to be, that is the question.* **let s.o/s.t be** not trouble or disturb s.o/s.t: *Sam is sleeping; let him be.*

being /ˈbiːɪŋ/ adj **1 for the time being** for now but not for long after this: *I am still living with my parents for the time being until my new house is ready.*

▷ n **2** u.n life; existence. **3** c.n living creature: *a human being.* **in being** that exists. **bring/call s.t into being** cause s.t to begin to exist. **come into being** begin to exist.

beach /biːtʃ/ c/u.n **1** land beside the sea, a lake etc with sand, stones etc on it, sometimes where people go to bathe etc.

▷ tr.v **2** cause (a boat etc) to go (partly) out of the water onto the shore.

beacon /ˈbiːkən/ c.n light or fire used as a signal, often to warn of danger.

bead /biːd/ c.n **1** small ball made of wood, glass etc with a hole in the middle through which one puts string etc to join it with other beads; it is used mostly as an ornament but sometimes for counting prayers. **2** drop, e.g of sweat.

'beady adj (-ier, -iest) (usu of eyes) small round and bright like beads.

beagle /ˈbiːgl/ c.n small hound(1) used in packs for hunting hares(1) etc.

beak /biːk/ c.n hard mouth of a bird.

beaker /ˈbiːkə/ c.n container made of glass, plastic etc, usu with no handle, used in scientific experiments, for drinking out of etc.

beam /biːm/ c.n **1** horizontal piece of wood or metal supporting a floor or ceiling. **2** greatest width of a ship. **3** ray of light: *a sun beam.* **4** radio signal used to guide aircraft. **on/off the beam** (fig) following, not following, the correct course (of action etc).

▷ v **5** intr.v give out bright light. **6** intr.v smile happily: *beam with happiness.* **7** tr.v (often — s.t to s.o/s.t) direct (a beam(4), a broadcast) (to s.o/s.t).

bean /biːn/ c.n (also attrib) **1** kind of plant producing seeds in pods(1). ⇒ broad bean, haricot bean, soya bean. Compare pea. **2** seed of a bean(1) plant. **3** pod of a bean(1) plant with the seeds in it. **full of beans** (fig; informal) lively and energetic. **not have a bean** (fig; informal) have no money at all; be very poor. **spill the beans** (fig; informal) tell s.t that was a secret.

'bean,feast c.n (also **beano** /ˈbiːnəʊ/) (UK informal) very good meal; feast(1).

bear¹ /beə/ c.n **1** kind of big wild animal with thick rough fur. ⇒ grizzly (bear), polar bear. **2** (commerce) (on a Stock Exchange) person who sells shares(3) in the hope of lowering the price so that he/she can buy again cheaply. Opposite bull¹(4). **like a bear with a sore head** having, in, a bad temper.

bear² /beə/ tr.v (p.t bore /bɔː/, p.p borne /bɔːn/) **1** (be able to) support (s.t), hold (s.t) up: *What weight will this beam bear?* **2** (formal) (often — s.o/s.t away/off to s.o/s.t)) carry (s.o/s.t) from one place to another: *We were borne off to the party in our host's car.* **3** produce (s.t, e.g fruit). **4** (p.p born in passive) give birth to (a baby). ⇒ born(2). **5** put up with (s.o/s.t, e.g pain); be able to tolerate (s.o/s.t): *I can't bear Alex; he's so rude!* **6** have or show (s.t): *Mary still bears the marks of her fall from her bicycle.* **7** (often — s.o/s.t) have (s.t) in mind; feel (s.t) (towards s.o): *I bear Peter no ill feeling for what he has done to us.* **8** be able to have s.t done to it: *Elizabeth's ideas may sound reasonable but they won't bear examination.*

bear down (up)on s.o/s.t (a) come towards s.o/ s.t in a dangerous way. **(b)** be a heavy burden(2) on s.o/s.t. **(c)** punish s.o severely.

bear fruit ⇒ fruit(n).

bear a grudge ⇒ grudge.

bear s.t in mind ⇒ mind¹.

bear oneself well etc **(a)** hold one's body upright etc. **(b)** behave well etc.

bear s.t out be evidence(1) that supports s.t.

bear up stop being sad; cheer up. **bear s.o up** support, help, s.o in difficulties. **bear up under s.t (a)** support s.t, e.g a weight, without breaking. **(b)** remain strong, cheerful etc in spite of s.t, e.g s.o's death.

bear (up)on s.t have a connection with s.t; be relevant to s.t.

bear with s.o/s.t treat s.o/s.t patiently.

'bearable *adj* that can be borne(⇒ bear²(5)). Opposite unbearable.

'bearer *n* **1** *def.n* (usu *the — of s.t*) person who carries (s.t, e.g news). **2** *c.n* one of the people carrying a dead body at a funeral. **3** *c.n* (*commerce*) person who holds a cheque etc and can therefore get the money for it.

'bearing *n* **1** *sing/u.n* way of holding oneself. Compare bear oneself well etc(a). **2** *c.n* (usu *have a — (up)on s.t*) connection; relevance. Compare bear (up)on s.t. **3** *c.n* direction as shown by a compass(1) etc. **4** *c.n* part of a machine in which a rod is held as it turns or which turns on a fixed rod. ⇒ ball bearing (⇒ ball¹). **beyond/past bearing** too much to be able to bear²(5). **lose one's bearings** no longer know one's direction or position. **take bearings** use a compass(1) and/or landmarks(1) to find one's direction.

beard /bɪəd/ *c.n* **1** hair that grows on a man's chin (and cheeks). Compare moustache. **2** hair like a beard(1) on an animal, e.g a goat. **3** long hairs on a plant, e.g barley.

'bearded *adj* having a beard(1,2).

'beardless *adj* not having a beard(1,2).

beast /biːst/ *c.n* **1** (*literary*) animal, esp one with four legs. **2** (*derog*) unpleasant or cruel person; brute(2). **a beast of a man, job** etc a beastly man, job etc. ⇒ bestial.

,beast of 'burden *c.n* animal, e.g a horse, used for carrying things,

'beastliness *u.n* fact or state of being beastly.

'beastly *adj* (*-ier, -iest*) (*derog*) unpleasant; nasty.

beat /biːt/ *pred.adj* **1** (often *dead —*) (*slang*) very tired: *We were dead beat after the walk.* ⇒ dead(9).

▷ *n* **2** *c.n* (sound of a) hit on a drum, pulsation of a person's heart etc; movement made as a signal, e.g by a conductor(2) to a band. ⇒ drum beat, heart beat. **3** *c.n* (often *the — of s.t*) (sound of the) regularly repeated hitting (of s.t, e.g a drum or s.o's heart). **4** *c/def.n* regular timing or rhythm(1) in music or verse: *Some people find it difficult to follow the beat when they are playing music.* **5** *c.n* regular course followed by s.o, e.g a police officer. **off, out of, s.o's beat** (*informal*) not what s.o is used to (doing). Compare off-beat.

▷ *v* (*p.t beat, p.p beaten* /'biːtn/) **7** *tr.v* hit (s.o/s.t) many times as a punishment, to produce a sound etc: *beat a naughty boy*; *beat a drum.* **8** *tr.v* shape (s.t, e.g gold) by beating(7) it. **9** *tr/intr.v* (cause (s.t) to) move up and down, in and out etc regularly; pulsate; vibrate: *A bird beats its wings. His heart is still beating.* **10** *tr.v* (often *— s.t up*) mix s.t, e.g a raw egg, by beating(7) it with an instrument such as a fork. **11** *tr.v* defeat (s.o/s.t); win in a fight etc against (s.o/s.t).

beat about for s.t search eagerly for s.t. **beat about the bush** ⇒ bush.

beat against s.o/s.t (e.g of rain) keep on hitting s.o/s.t.

beat down (on s.o/s.t) (usu of rain or the heat of the sun) fall hard (on s.o/s.t). **beat s.o down** persuade s.o to bring the price for s.t down. **beat s.t down** (a) hit s.t so that it falls flat. (b) bring the price of s.t down by bargaining.

beat s.t out cause a fire, flames etc to stop burning by beating it/them with s.t. **beat it** (*slang*) go

away quickly: *The police officers told the boys to beat it.*

beat s.o/s.t off stop s.o who is attacking one, an attack etc: *After heavy fighting we managed to beat off the enemy* (or *the enemy's attack*).

beat out a tune etc play a tune etc in a rhythmical way on drums etc.

beat time ⇒ time(*n*).

beat s.o up (*slang*) hurt s.o badly by hitting her/him. **beat s.t up** ⇒ beat(10).

'beaten *adj* **1** (of metal) shaped by beating(8) it. **2** defeated. **off the beaten track** ⇒ track(*n*).

'beater *c.n* **1** instrument used for beating(8,10): *an egg beater.* **2** person who drives wild birds or animals towards people who are waiting to shoot them.

'beating *c.n* (often *get a —*; *give s.o a —*) **1** act of hitting s.o, usu as a punishment. Compare beat(7). **2** defeat(*n*).

beau /bəʊ/ *c.n* (*pl -s, beaux* /bəʊz/) (*old use*) boyfriend.

beauty /'bjuːtɪ/ *n* (*pl -ies*) **1** *u.n* (also *attrib*) combination of qualities that pleases one's eyes, ears, mind etc: *the beauty of a child's face*; *the beauty of a small lake surrounded by trees.* **2** *c.n* person (usu female) or thing that has beauty(1): *Marilyn is our village's great beauty. I showed the visitors the beauties of this part of the country.* **3** *c.n* (*informal*) very good example of s.t, whether of s.t good or s.t bad etc: *The blow Eric gave Sam in the fight was a real beauty!* **the beauty of s.t** (*informal*) the good thing about s.t: *The beauty of Sarah's plan was that we could carry it all out without anyone else knowing.*

beauteous /'bjuːtɪəs/ *adj* (*literary*) beautiful.

'beauteously *adv.*

beautician /bjuːˈtɪʃən/ *c.n* person whose job is to make people beautiful by doing things to their skin, hair etc.

'beautiful *adj* **1** having beauty(1): *a beautiful woman/smile.* Compare handsome, pretty. **2** (*informal*) very good: *beautiful weather*; *a beautiful piece of cheese.*

'beautifully *adv.*

beautify /'bjuːtɪˌfaɪ/ *tr.v* (*-ies, -ied*) make (s.o/s.t) beautiful.

'beauty ,parlour/,salon *c.n* (US **'beauty ,parlor**) place that gives beauty treatments to women.

'beauty ,queen *c.n* woman or girl who wins a competition for the most beautiful contestant.

'beauty ,sleep *u.n* (usu *joking*) sleep before midnight, which is supposed to be better for one's health and beauty than sleep later in the night.

'beauty ,spot *c.n* **1** dark spot on a woman's face that some people consider beautiful. **2** place that has particularly beautiful scenery.

beaver /'biːvə/ *n* **1** *c.n* kind of animal of the rat family that has a wide flat tail and spends a lot of time in water. **2** *u.n* (also *attrib*) fur of this animal. **eager beaver** ⇒ eager.

▷ *intr.v* **3** **beaver away (at s.t)** (*informal*) work very hard and/or for a long time (at some job, activity etc): *They beavered away at clearing the garden but it took a whole week.*

becalmed /bɪˈkɑːmd/ *adj* (of a sailing ship) unable to move because there is no wind.

became /bɪˈkeɪm/ *p.t* of become.

because /bɪ'kɒz/ *conj* for the reason that; on account of the fact that; as(5); since(5): *I don't want it because it's too big. Because you are sorry I'll forgive you.* **because of s.t** as a result of s.t: *We went home because of the rain.*

beckon /'bekən/ *tr/intr.v* (often — (to) *s.o to do s.t*) give (s.o) a sign (to do s.t), usu with one's hand or finger: *Mary went forward quietly, beckoning (to) the children to follow her.*

become /bɪ'kʌm/ *v* (*p.t* became /bɪ'keɪm/, *p.p* become) **1** change to being; stop being and start being: *Children become men and women surprisingly quickly. The weather is becoming warmer.* **2** *tr.v* (*literary*) be suitable or right for: *Such behaviour does not become a person in your position.* **What**(ever) **became**, **will become**, **of s.o/s.t?** What happened, will happen, to s.o/s.t? What was, will be, the fate of s.o/s.t?

be'coming *adj* suiting s.o well; going well with s.o's clothes etc; right: *a becoming smile.* ⇒ become(2). Opposite unbecoming.
be'comingly *adv.*

bed /bed/ *n* **1** *c.n* piece of furniture made for sleeping on. **2** *c.n* part of a garden in which flowers, vegetables etc are grown. ⇒ flowerbed. **3** *c.n* bottom of the sea, a river etc: *a dry river bed in the summer.* **4** *c.n* base on which a road etc is built. **5** *c.n* rock stratum(1). *a bed of roses* ⇒ rose¹. *get out of bed on the wrong side* (*fig*; *informal*) be in a bad temper. *go to bed* get into one's bed, usu to sleep, or sometimes because one is ill. *go to bed with s.o* (*informal*) have sexual intercourse with s.o. *make a/one's/ the bed* arrange the sheets, blankets etc tidily on a bed. *You have made your bed and you must lie on it* (*saying*) It is your own fault that s.t unfortunate is happening to you so you have to accept it, put up with it. *wet one's/the bed* urinate in one's bed (while one is asleep).
▷ *tr.v* (*-dd-*) **6** (often — *s.t in s.t*) build or fix (s.t) on a bed(4) of s.t. **7** (usu — *s.t out*) put (young plants) in a bed(2), usu after they have been in pots. *bed* (*s.o*, *an animal*) *down* (cause (s.o, an animal) to) find a place where one/s.o/it can sleep, but not on a bed.

,bed and 'board *u.n* lodging and food; board and lodging (⇒ board²).

,bed and 'breakfast *u.n* (*abbr* B & B) place to sleep for one night and breakfast the next morning.

'bed,bug *c.n* kind of flat insect that sucks people's blood, esp at night.

'bed,clothes *pl.n* sheets, blankets etc put on beds.

'bedding *u.n* **1** bedclothes. **2** things on which a person or an animal can sleep, e.g straw.

'bed ,linen *u.n* sheets and pillowcases but not blankets etc. Compare bedclothes.

'bed,pan *c.n* container into which one urinates or defecates without getting out of bed, usu when one is in hospital.

'bed,ridden *adj* too ill, old etc to be able to get out of bed.

'bed,rock *u.n* **1** solid rock under loose rocks, earth etc. **2** (*fig*) basis on which one's ideas etc are built.

'bed,room *attrib.adj* **1** (of scenes in a film etc) showing or dealing with sex in a bedroom(2).
▷ *c.n* **2** room in which one sleeps.

,bed'settee *c.n* sofa bed.

'bed,side *c.n* (also *attrib*) (often *at s.o's* —) side of (s.o's) bed: *a bedside table.*

,bedside 'manner *c.n* way in which a doctor behaves and talks when visiting a patient.

,bed-'sitting ,room *c.n* (also ,bed-'sitter, ,bed-'sit (*informal*)) room in s.o's house in which one lives and sleeps and for which one usu pays rent.

'bed,sore *c.n* sore caused by having to remain lying for a long time.

'bed,spread *c.n* cloth put over a bed after it has been made (to make it look pretty).

bedstead /'bed,sted/ *c.n* framework of a bed, without the mattress etc.

'bed,time *c/unique n* usual or suitable time for going to sleep.

'bed,time ,story *c.n* (*pl -ies*) story read to small children before they go to bed.

bee /biː/ *c.n* kind of insect that has four wings and can sting people, esp the kind that makes honey. ⇒ bumblebee, wasp. *as busy as a bee* ⇒ busy. *have a bee in one's bonnet* (*about s.t*) (*fig*; *informal*) have a fixed idea (about s.t) which other people find strange or silly.

'bee,hive *c.n* = hive(1).

'bee,line *c.n* *make a beeline for s.o/s.t* (*informal*) go straight towards s.o/s.t quickly.

'bees,wax *u.n* wax made by bees that is used for making candles, polish for wood etc.

beech /biːtʃ/ *n* **1** *c.n* (also 'beech ,tree) kind of tree with a smooth bark and shiny leaves. **2** *u.n* (also *attrib*) wood from this tree: *beech chairs.*

beef¹ /biːf/ *u.n* **1** meat from a cow, bull¹(1) or ox. Compare veal. **2** strength of muscle(1).

'beef,burger *c.n* = hamburger.

'Beef,eater *c.n* warder of the Tower of London.

'beef,steak *c/u.n* steak(1,2) from the meat of a cow etc.

'beefy *adj* (*-ier*, *-iest*) (*informal*) big strong (and fat).

beef² /biːf/ *c.n* **1** (*derog*; *slang*) (annoying) complaint.
▷ *intr.v* **2** (often — *about s.o/s.t*) (*derog*; *slang*) complain (about s.o/s.t) in an annoying way.

beehive, beeline ⇒ bee.

been (strong form /biːn/, weak form /bɪn/) *p.p* of be. *been and (gone and) done s.t* (*informal*) done s.t surprising or dangerous: *Betty's been and married a film-star! Now you've been and gone and done it!*

beer /bɪə/ *n* (also *attrib*) **1** *u.n* kind of brown alcoholic(1) drink made from malt etc that is usu bitter. **2** *c.n* glass etc of beer(1). **3** *u.n* kind of brown drink that is not beer(1) and is usu not alcoholic(1): ginger beer. *small beer* ⇒ small.

'beery *adj* (*-ier*, *-iest*) (*derog*) caused by beer(1): *a person with beery breath.*

beeswax ⇒ bee.

beet /biːt/ *u.n* = sugar beet.

beetle /'biːtl/ *c.n* kind of insect that has hard wing cases.

beetroot /'biːt,ruːt/ *c/u.n* (also *attrib*) plant that has a big round dark red root, used as food: *beetroot soup. as red as a beetroot* (*informal*) very red, usu because one is blushing(2).

befall /bɪ'fɔːl/ *tr/intr.v* (*p.t* befell /bɪ'fel/, *p.p* befallen /bɪ'fɔːlən/) (*formal*) happen to (s.o/ s.t), usu in a bad way as a result of bad luck:

The ship is very late; let us hope nothing terrible has befallen (it).

befit /bɪˈfɪt/ *tr.v* (-tt-) *(formal)* be suitable or right for (s.o/s.t): *It does not befit you to be rude about someone who has helped you so often.*

beˈfitting *adj*. **beˈfittingly** *adv*.

before /bɪˈfɔː/ *adv* **1** earlier in time; previously: *Had you ever seen snow before?*

▷ *conj* **2** before(4) the time when: *I got home before Alex did.* **3** rather than; in preference to: *Charlotte said she would go out and work as a waitress before she would stay another moment in her parents' house.*

▷ *prep* **4** earlier in time (than): *We shall be home before evening.* Compare after(3). **5** when one has not yet reached: *As you go up the hill you will see a big white house; the small grey one before it is mine.* Compare after(6). **6** in front of: *The accident happened before my own eyes! The waiter set the food before them and then left.* **7** in front of s.o/s.t who/that is more important or powerful than one is oneself: *Peter was brought before a judge and accused of stealing a car.* **8** *(fig)* facing: *The problem before us is what to do about the furniture.* **9** in front of, in time: *We have all this week before us to enjoy ourselves.* **10** in preference to; rather than: *Death before surrender*(1)! **before long** ⇒ long¹(*n*).

beˈforeˌhand *adv* before(1); in advance: *You can have friends to visit you whenever you like but tell me beforehand.*

befriend /bɪˈfrend/ *tr.v* treat (s.o who is poorer, weaker etc than one is oneself) kindly and help her/him.

beg /beg/ *v* (-gg-) **1** *tr/intr.v* (often — (s.o) for s.t; — s.o to do s.t) ask (s.o) for s.t, to do s.t, often in a humble or earnest way: *'What does that man do?' 'He begs (for money/food).'* *Dorothy begged Norah to help her.* **2** *tr.v* (often — s.t from/ of s.o) ask (s.o) for (s.t) in a humble or earnest way: *She begged milk from her neighbour for her children. I beg of you to think carefully before putting money in that business. May I beg a favour of you?* **3** *intr.v* (of a dog) sit on its bottom with its front legs near its chest (as if begging(1)). **4** *tr.v* avoid dealing with (s.t, usu a difficulty): *Henry's idea seems a good one but it begs the question of how to get the money to put it into practice.* **beg for s.t** ⇒ beg(1). **go begging** not be accepted, bought etc by anybody: *Lots of jobs in this town go begging because people think themselves too good for them.* **I beg your pardon** (**a**) = pardon(*n*). (**b**) I am sorry but I did not understand, hear you etc.

beggar /ˈbegə/ *c.n* **1** person who begs(1). **2** *(informal)* person: *You silly beggar!* **Beggars can't be choosers** *(saying)* If you haven't enough money, power etc to choose what to do etc, you must accept whatever you can get.

▷ *tr.v* **3** make (s.o) very poor.

ˈbeggarliness *u.n* fact of being beggarly.

ˈbeggarly *adj* **1** of or referring to a beggar(1). **2** much too little: *a beggarly wage.*

begin /bɪˈgɪn/ *tr/intr.v* (*p.t* began /bɪˈgæn/, *p.p* begun /bɪˈgʌn/ (often — to do s.t; — (by) doing s.t) start ((doing or to do) s.t); take the first step (of (s.t)): *She began to cry. He began by thanking me for the invitation. We began singing as the lights went on.* **to begin with** (**a**) at first: *To begin*

with Peter didn't like school but now he enjoys it. (**b**) as the first reason (for s.t): *Julian isn't a good driver; to begin with, he's impatient, and also he can't see very well.*

beˈginner *c.n* person who is just beginning s.t for the first time.

beˈginning *c.n* point where s.t begins. **at/ in the beginning** when s.t first began. **from beginning to end** during the whole of s.t.

begonia /bɪˈgəʊnɪə/ *c.n* kind of plant grown in gardens for its beautiful leaves and waxy(1) flowers.

begrudge /bɪˈgrʌdʒ/ *tr.v* = grudge(2).

beguile /bɪˈgaɪl/ *tr.v* *(formal)* **1** charm (s.o). **2** (often — s.o into, out of, (doing) s.t) cheat (s.o) (so that he/she does (not) do s.t).

beˈguiling *adj* *(formal)* who/that is very pleasant or charming: *He has a beguiling manner.*

beˈguilingly *adj*. **beˈguilement** *u.n*.

begun /bɪˈgʌn/ *p.p* of begin.

behalf /bɪˈhɑːf/ *unique n* **on behalf of s.o**; **on s.o's behalf** in the interests, or as a representative, of s.o.

behave /bɪˈheɪv/ *intr.v* **1** (of a person, or sometimes an animal) act; do things: *Christine always behaves very politely when she is at school.* **2** (of a person, or sometimes an animal) behave(1) in a way that is suitable to the society in which one is: *Dick, you're not behaving! Sit down and be quiet!* **3** (of things) work; act: *Our new water pump is behaving well.* ⇒ misbehave . **behave oneself** = behave(2).

-behaved *adj* (of a person) behaving(1) in the way described by the first part of the word: *badly-behaved; well-behaved.*

behaviour /bɪˈheɪvjə/ *u.n* (US **beˈhavior**) way in which s.o/s.t behaves(1,3). **be on one's best behaviour** try to behave(2) as well as one can.

beˈhavioural *adj* of or referring to behaviour.

behead /bɪˈhed/ *tr.v* cut the head off (a person, an animal, a statue, a flower etc).

beheld /bɪˈheld/ *p.t,p.p* of behold.

behest /bɪˈhest/ *c.n* **at s.o's behest** *(formal)* at the command or strong request of s.o.

behind /bɪˈhaɪnd/ *adv* **1** not so far forward; in the rear¹(2) of s.t moving or standing still: *The big boys walked in front and the small ones came behind.* Opposite ahead(1). **2** in a place that has been left by the others: *Joan left her umbrella behind at the restaurant.* **3** backwards; towards the rear(2): *Look behind; there's a car following us.* **4** less advanced: *At half time our team was one goal behind.* Opposite ahead(1). ⇒ in front (of s.o/s.t) (⇒ front(*n*)). **5** (often — with s.t) late (with a payment): *Mr Smith is behind with his rent this week.*

▷ *prep* **6** not so far forward as; in the rear¹(2) of: *A man stood behind each visitor, holding an umbrella.* Opposite in front of (⇒ front(*n*)). **7** in a place that has been left by: *I stayed behind the others to wait for Steven.* **8** beyond or at the back of so as to be hidden, protected: *Hide behind that wall!* **9** backwards from; towards the rear of: *Look behind you; there's someone watching us.* Opposite in front of (⇒ front(*n*)). **10** less advanced than: *Peter is behind Mary in geography.* Opposite ahead of. **11** supporting or helping: *We are all behind Fred in his attempt to improve the food here.* **12** *(fig)* hidden at the back of: *I don't like Jim's latest suggestion; I think there's something else behind it.* **behind s.o's back** ⇨ back(*n*). **behind the scenes** ⇨ scene. **behind time** ⇨ time(*n*). **behind the times** ⇨ times(*pl.n*).

▷ *c.n* **13** (*informal*) buttocks.

be'hind,hand *adv* (often — *with s.t*) **1** late (esp with the payment of s.t): *Graham was behindhand with his rent last month.* **2** (often — *in doing s.t*) slow or reluctant (to do s.t): *Sheila is never behindhand in telling other people what to do but she never seems to do anything herself.*

behold /bɪˈhəʊld/ *tr/intr.v* (*p.t,p.p* **beheld** /bɪˈheld/) (*literary; old use*) look (at (s.o/s.t)); see (s.o/s.t).

be'holden *pred.adj* **beholden to s.o** (*formal*) having a debt or an obligation(1) to s.o: *I do not like being beholden to anybody for anything.*

be'holder *c.n* (*formal*) person who looks at s.o/s.t: *Beauty is in the eye of the beholder* (i.e whether s.o thinks s.t beautiful depends on the person looking at it, not on the thing itself).

beige /beɪʒ/ *u.n* (also *attrib*) pale yellow-brown colour.

being ⇨ be.

belated /bɪˈleɪtɪd/ *adj* (*formal*) coming very/too late: *a belated apology.*

be'latedly *adv*.

belch /beltʃ/ *c.n* **1** act or sound of bringing wind up from one's stomach and letting it come up into one's mouth. **2** (often — *of s.t*) thick cloud etc (of s.t, e.g smoke) coming out of s.t strongly.

▷ *v* **3** *intr.v* give a belch(1). **4** *tr/intr.v* (often — (*s.t*) *forth/out*) (cause (s.t, e.g smoke) to) come out in a belch(2): *factory chimneys belching smoke.*

belfry /ˈbelfrɪ/ *c.n* (*pl -ies*) (part of a) tower in which there is a bell. **have bats in the belfry** ⇨ bat¹.

believe /bɪˈliːv/ *v* **1** *tr.v* (often — *that* . . .) think that (s.t) is true or that (s.o) is telling the truth: *Ted seems to believe everyone, and everything they tell him. I believe that Helen will pass her examination.* **2** *intr.v* be a believer. **believe in s.o/s.t** (a) have faith in s.o/s.t; trust s.o/s.t. (b) believe(1) that s.o/s.t exists: *A lot of children believe in* Father Christmas. (c) think that s.t is a good thing: *I believe in taking plenty of exercise to remain in good health.* **believe so/not** believe(1) that it is true, not true: *'Is Frances coming this evening?' 'I believe so/not.'*

belief /bɪˈliːf/ *n* **1** *sing/u.n* (often — *in s.o/s.t*) fact of believing ((in) s.o/s.t). **2** *c.n* thing, idea, that one believes(1). **beyond belief** impossible to believe(1) because it is so strange.

be'lievable *adj* that can be believed(1). Opposite unbelievable.

be'liever *c.n* (often — *in s.o/s.t*) person who believes ((in) s.o/s.t).

Belisha beacon /bəˌliːʃə ˈbiːkən/ *c.n* (UK) round orange lamp on top of a post in the street that flashes to warn vehicles of a zebra crossing for pedestrians(3).

bell /bel/ *c.n* **1** hollow metal shape that makes a musical sound when one hits it: *a bicycle bell.* **2** thing shaped like a bell: *a diving bell for going down into deep water in.* **3** (often *pl*) sound made on a bell on a ship every half hour to give the time; the counting starts at midnight and then again after every four hours: *Four bells has just*

struck (i.e it is 2, 6 or 10 o'clock). **as sound as a bell** (*informal*) in perfect health or condition.

'bell,boy *c.n* boy or man in a hotel etc who carries people's luggage, gives them messages etc.

'bell-,push *c.n* button that rings an electric bell when one pushes it.

bellicose /ˈbelɪkəʊs/ *adj* (*formal*) having/ showing a liking for fighting or quarrelling.

bellicosity /ˌbelɪˈkɒsɪtɪ/ *u.n*.

belligerent /bəˈlɪdʒərənt/ *adj* **1** wanting a fight or quarrel; showing that s.o wants a fight or quarrel. **2** engaged in fighting a war.

▷ *c.n* **3** country that is fighting a war.

bel'ligerence, bel'ligerency *u.n*.

bellow /ˈbeləʊ/ *c.n* **1** loud deep angry cry (like that) of a bull¹(1).

▷ *v* **2** *intr.v* (often — *with s.t*) give a bellow(1), (because of s.t, e.g pain or anger). **3** *tr.v* (often — *s.t out*) shout (s.t) in a bellow(1).

bellows /ˈbeləʊz/ *c.n* (*pl* bellows) (often *a pair of* —) device for blowing air strongly, e.g to make a fire burn brightly or to produce the musical notes on an organ.

bell-push ⇨ bell.

belly /ˈbelɪ/ *c.n* (*pl -ies*) **1** (*informal*) stomach. **2** abdomen(1). **3** under part of an animal. **4** thing that has the round shape of a person's stomach, e.g part of some musical instruments that have strings.

belong /bɪˈlɒŋ/ *intr.v* **belong to s.o** be the property of s.o; be owned by s.o. **belong to s.t** (a) be a native of a place; come from a place. (b) be a member of s.t, e.g a secret society. (c) form part of, be connected with, s.t: *This screw belongs to that clock.* **belong in, on** etc **s.t** have its right place s.w: *This table belongs in the kitchen.*

be'longings *pl.n* property; things that belong to s.o.

beloved /bɪˈlʌvd/ *adj* **1** (usu — *by s.o*, or (*formal*) — *of s.o*) much loved.

▷ *c/pl.n* /bɪˈlʌvɪd/ **2** much loved person/people.

below /bɪˈləʊ/ *adv* Opposite above. **1** (often *down* —) directly down from s.o/s.t; downstairs; directly under: *You climb up the tree and I'll stand below and catch the apples as you drop them.* **2** lower than its line or upper surface: *Some of the wood was above the surface of the water and the rest was below.* **3** (often *down* —) lower without being directly under: *From the top of the mountain you can see all the villages below.* **4** lower in rank etc: *The meeting is for captains and below.* **5** lower down a river: *We sailed down to Henley and a few places below.* **6** lower on a page; later in a book, magazine etc: *Continued on page 42, below.* **7** less in amount, age etc: *children of 16 and below.* Compare over(8), under(2). **8** in, from the deck down into, the inside of a ship: *The captain has gone below.* **from below** upwards; from lower down: *The trees look very tall from below.*

▷ *prep* Opposite above. **9** (often *down* — *s.t*) directly down from: *John lives in the flat below Sue.* **10** lower than the line or upper surface of; at a level lower than: *Most of the wood is below the surface of the water. We stood in water below our knees.* **11** lower than without being directly under: *The clouds are below the mountain tops.* **12** lower than in rank etc: *A captain is below a* major. **13** further down a river than: *The harbour is below the second bridge.* **14** less in amount, age etc than: *Persons below the age of 18 are not allowed in here.* **from below s.t** from under, lower down than, s.t; upwards from s.t: *The noise came from below the stairs.*

belt /belt/ *c.n* **1** flat strip of leather etc worn round one's waist to keep trousers up etc. **2** flat strip of leather etc that goes round wheels continuously to drive a machine. **3** wide strip of land. *below the belt* (*fig; informal*) (of a remark that makes) unfair use of information to hurt, criticize s.o: *It was a bit below the belt to blame her son's failure on her.* **hit (s.o) below the belt** (*fig; informal*) treat s.o unfairly. **conveyor belt** ⇒ conveyor. **green belt** ⇒ green. **safety/seat belt** ⇒ safe. **tighten one's belt** (*fig*) spend less money; be more careful about spending money.
▷ *tr.v* **4** (often — *s.t up*) use a belt(1) to fasten (one's trousers etc): *He belted his trousers up after putting on his shirt.* **5** (*slang*) hit (s.o) with a belt(1) or with one's hand(s): *If you don't keep quiet I'll belt you!* **belt up** (often as an order) (*slang*) (demand that s.o should) stop talking: *Belt up! I'm trying to listen to the news.* **belt (oneself) up** use a safety belt in a car, plane etc.

bench /bentʃ/ *n* **1** *c.n* long flat seat made of wood, stone etc; it is often found in parks. **2** *c.n* strong table for working at, e.g when making things out of wood. **3** *def.n* (with capital **B**) judges and magistrates: *The man appeared before the Bench, accused of murder.* **back/front bench** ⇒ back, front.

bend /bend/ *c.n* **1** curve; shape that is not straight, but turns: *Nicholas drove round a bend in the road too fast and turned his car over.* **2** action of getting into, making s.o/s.t get into, a bend(1). **round the bend** (*informal*) mad.
▷ *v* (*p.t,p.p* **bent** /bent/) **3** *tr/intr.v* (cause (s.o/s.t) to) get into, or out of, the shape of a bend(1): *You can bend this wire easily into a circle and then bend it straight again.* **bend over backwards (to do s.t)** ⇒ backwards.

bends *def.pl.n* (*informal*) painful sickness that a diver suffers from when he/she comes to the surface too quickly.

bent *adj* **1** (*slang*) dishonest: *a bent police officer.* Compare straight(4). **be bent on s.t** be determined to do s.t: *She's bent on becoming an actress.*
▷ *c.n* **2** (often *have a — for s.t*) skill; natural ability. **follow one's bent** do what one is interested in and good at.

beneath /bɪˈniːθ/ *adv* **1** down from, in a lower position than, s.o/s.t, sometimes directly below, sometimes not, sometimes touching, sometimes not: *We looked down from the plane/mountain at the plains beneath.* Opposite above(1). **from beneath** from a lower position: *If you look up from beneath, it looks like an umbrella.*
▷ *prep* **2** down from, in a lower position than, sometimes directly below, sometimes not, sometimes touching, sometimes not: *We sat beneath the tree/wall having our lunch.* **3** covered, hidden, by: *He always wears a* vest *beneath his shirt.* Opposite over(14). **4** lower than the surface of: *These animals live beneath the ground.* Compare above(10), under. **5** (*fig*) under and controlled

by: *Beneath the teacher's guiding hand the children made great progress.* **6** lower in, into a lower, rank etc than: *Dorothy's parents think she has married beneath her.* Compare above(12). **7** not good, important, worthy(1) etc enough for: *Such details are beneath the manager's notice; they should be dealt with by the clerks.* Compare above(17). **beneath (one's) contempt** ⇒ contempt. **from beneath s.t** from a lower position than s.t: *Two children crawled out from beneath the table.*

benediction /ˌbenɪˈdɪkʃən/ *c/def.n* blessing given by a priest at the end of a church service.

benefaction /ˌbenɪˈfækʃən/ *c/u.n* (*formal*) (act of giving) money etc for charity(2).

benefactor /ˈbenɪˌfæktə/ *c.n* person who helps others, e.g by giving a benefaction.

benefactress /ˈbenɪˌfæktrɪs/ *c.n* female benefactor.

beneficent /bɪˈnefɪsnt/ *adj* (*formal*) generous; doing good; kind.
beˈneficence *u.n.* **beˈneficently** *adv.*

benefit /ˈbenɪfɪt/ *n* **1** *c.n* advantage; help; thing that produces good results: *A good education is an enormous benefit.* **2** *c/u.n* money received from the government or an insurance company when one is out of work etc: *unemployment benefit.* **3** *c.n* (also *attrib*) performance in a theatre, football match etc in which the money taken goes to charity(2) or to a particular player etc: *a benefit match.* **give s.o the benefit of the doubt** decide in s.o's favour if there is any doubt about her/his guilt.
▷ *v* **4** *tr.v* give benefit(1) to (s.o/s.t); do good to (s.o/ s.t): *Warm dry weather benefits people with weak chests.* **5** *intr.v* (often — *from s.t*) get benefit(1) (from s.t): *You'd benefit from a long holiday.*

beneficial /ˌbenɪˈfɪʃəl/ *adj* (often — *to s.o/ s.t*) helpful, useful, (to s.o/s.t); producing good results (for s.o/s.t).
ˌbeneˈficially *adv.*
ˌbeneˈficiary *c.n* (*pl* -ies) (often — *of s.t*) person who receives benefit(1) (from s.t, esp from the will of s.o who has died).

benevolent /bɪˈnevələnt/ *adj* (*formal*) kind; helpful; doing good to others.
beˈnevolence *u.n.* **beˈnevolently** *adv.*

bent /bent/ **1** *p.t,p.p* of bend(*v*). **2** *adj/c.n* ⇒ bend(*n*).

benzene /ˈbenziːn/ *u.n.* kind of liquid that has no colour, is made from coal and is used in making certain chemicals, *chem.form* C_6H_6.

benzine /ˈbenziːn/ *u.n.* kind of liquid made from petroleum and used for some engines, dry-cleaning clothes etc.

bequeath /bɪˈkwiːθ/ *tr.v* leave (money, property etc) to s.o after one's death.

bequest /bɪˈkwest/ *c.n* thing that is bequeathed to s.o.

bereaved /bɪˈriːvd/ *adj* **1** having just lost s.o, esp a close relative who has died.
▷ *def.pl.n* **2** bereaved(1) people.
beˈreavement *c/u.n.*

bereft /bɪˈreft/ *adj* (usu *pred*, — *of s.o/s.t*) (*formal*) without (s.o/s.t): *I was bereft of all hope.*

beret /ˈbereɪ/ *c.n* (*French*) kind of flat, usu round, soft cap without a peak(5).

berry /ˈberɪ/ *c.n* (*pl* -ies) one of many kinds of

small juicy fruit that has seeds in it but no stone.
⇒ blackberry, elderberry, raspberry, strawberry.

berserk /bə'sɜːk/ *pred.adj* (usu *go* —) violently angry (and without control).

berth /bɜːθ/ *c.n* **1** place where a ship lies in a harbour etc. **2** sleeping place in a ship, train etc. **give s.o/s.t a wide berth** (*fig*; *informal*) keep well away from s.o/s.t.

▷ *tr/intr.v* **3** (cause (a ship) to) come into port to be tied up.

beseech /bɪ'siːtʃ/ *tr.v* (*p.t,p.p besought* /bɪ'sɔːt/, *beseeched*) (*formal*) (*often — s.o to do s.t*) ask (s.o) very strongly (to do s.t etc); beg (s.t)(from s.o).

beset /bɪ'set/ *tr.v* (-tt-, *p.t,p.p beset*) (*often — s.o/ s.t with s.t*) (*formal*) surround (s.o/s.t); close (s.o/ s.t) in from all round, sometimes in preparation for attacking.

beside /bɪ'saɪd/ *prep* **1** at the side of; close to; near; by: *We live beside the river.* **2** compared with: *Beside other girls in the class, Chris is a good tennis player.* **be beside the point** ⇒ point(*n*). **beside oneself** (*fig*) extremely worried.

besides /bɪ'saɪdz/ *adv* **1** in addition; as well: *I paid the taxi driver and gave him a pound besides for his help.* **2** (introducing some more facts, information etc) also; further: *I didn't eat anything because I didn't like the food, and besides, I wasn't at all hungry.*

▷ *prep* **3** in addition to; as well as: *Besides us, there were twelve people at the party.* **4** (used in negative sentences and questions) except: *There was nothing in the refrigerator besides milk.*

besiege /bɪ'siːdʒ/ *tr.v* **1** surround (a town, building etc) with soldiers etc to prevent those inside from escaping. **2** (*fig*) crowd round (s.o/s.t) with requests etc.
be'sieger *c.n* person who besieges(1) (s.t).

besought /bɪ'sɔːt/ *p.t,p.p* of beseech.

best /best/ *adj* (*superl* of good) **1** of the most excellent quality; having the greatest skill, success, moral qualities etc; that cannot be beaten: *Mary is the best student in our class.* **may the best man win** ⇒ man(*n*). **the best part of s.t** ⇒ part(*n*). **make the best use of s.t.** ⇒ use(*n*).

▷ *adv* (*superl* of well) **2** in the most excellent way: *Helen works best under pressure.* **3** (often used in combinations) most: *Raymond is the best-liked student in our school. What fruit do you like best?* **as best one can** in the best way one is able: *The house was very dirty but we cleaned it as best we could.* **at best** if conditions are as favourable as possible: *You can earn £100 a week here at best.* **had best do s.t** ought to do s.t; should do s.t: *You had best tell your mother that you'll be late.*

▷ *pron* **4** person/animal/thing of the highest quality: *This is the best I can do.* **5** (often *the — of s.t*) most excellent part (of s.t): *The best of the summer is over now.* **all the best** (said to s.o when leaving) I wish you every happiness, success etc. **at one's/ its best** in one's/its best state: *Our part of the country is at its best in May.* **at the best of times** ⇒ times. **do one's (level) best** try as hard as one can. **get/have the best of s.o** defeat s.o. **get/have the best of s.t** win s.t: *The politician got the best of the argument.* **(have) the best of both worlds** ⇒ world. **hope for the best** ⇒ hope(*v*). **make the best of a bad job** ⇒ job. **make the best of s.t** put up with s.t although it is not perfect. **one's**

(**Sunday**) **best** one's best clothes. **the best of friends** as friendly as possible: *Diana and I have been the best of friends for years.* **to the best of s.o's belief/knowledge** as far as s.o believes/ knows: *To the best of my knowledge, the train leaves at about 11.30.* **with the best** as well as any other does: *The old man was still able to keep up with the best when out walking.*

,best 'man *c/def.n* male friend of a man who is about to get married; the best man helps him at the wedding ceremony.

,best 'seller *c.n* book that is sold in very large numbers.

,best-'selling *attrib.adj.*

bestial /'bestɪəl/ *adj* of or referring to a beast(1,2): *bestial behaviour/cruelty.*
bestiality /,bestɪ'ælɪtɪ/ *u.n.* **'bestially** *adv.*

bestow /bɪ'stəʊ/ *tr.v* (usu — *s.t* (*up*)*on s.o*) (*formal*) give (s.t) (to s.o).

best seller, best-selling ⇒ best.

bet /bet/ *c.n* (often — *on s.t*), **1** agreement with s.o that one will give her/him s.t, usu a certain amount of money, and that then, if a certain thing happens, she/he will give one back more than one gave her/him; but if it does not happen, she/ he will keep it: *I have a bet of £5 on that horse at 10 to 1* (i.e if the horse wins I shall get my £5 back and also another £50, but if it loses I shall lose my £5). *I lost/won my bet.* **2** agreement etc with s.o that whoever loses an argument will pay the winner: *I have a bet of £5 with Joe that I will pass my examinations.*

▷ *v* (-tt-, *p.t,p.p bet* (ted)) **3** *intr.v* (often — *on s.t*) make a bet (about s.t): *Do you ever bet on horses?* **4** *tr.v* (often — *s.t on s.t*) offer, pay, (a certain amount of money etc) as a bet (on s.t): *How much did you bet on that horse?* **bet s.o** (*any money*) **that . . .** (a) make a bet that . . . (b) (*informal*) feel sure that . . .: *I bet it'll rain this afternoon.* **I bet!** (*informal*) I don't think so: '*John will be here on time today.' 'I bet!'*

'better[1] *c.n* person who bets(3).

betray /bɪ'treɪ/ *tr.v* **1** be unfaithful to (s.o/s.t) who trusts one. **2** (often — *s.t to s.o*) (*formal*) tell (s.t secret) (to s.o): *The man betrayed our plans to the enemy.* **3** show (s.t that one wants to hide): *The look on her face betrayed her real feelings.* **betray s.o to s.o** tell s.o where he/she can find s.o, usu so as to arrest, kill etc her/him.
be'trayal *u.n* act of betraying s.o/s.t.
be'trayer *c.n* person who betrays s.o/s.t.

betroth /bɪ'trəʊð/ *tr.v* **betroth oneself to s.o** (*formal*) promise to marry s.o.
be'trothal *c/u.n* (*formal*) engagement(2).
be'trothed *n* (*formal*) **1** *c.n* person to whom one is betrothed. **2** *def.pl.n* two people who are betrothed to each other.

better[1] ⇒ bet.

better[2] /'betə/ *adj* (*comp* of good) **1** of higher quality, degree etc; greater in skill, success, moral quality etc; more suitable: *This is a better job than being a teacher.* **2** improved in health, esp after an illness. **for better or for worse** whether one has good fortune or bad fortune, e.g good health or bad health. **one's/s.o's better half** ⇒ half(*n*). **the better part of s.t** ⇒ part(*n*).

▷ *adv* (*comp* of well) **3** more successfully, skilfully etc; in a better[2](1) way: *Peter's younger sister can read better than he can.* **better off** (a) having more money. **(b)** being in a better(1) condition or situation: *You'll be much better off if you stop smoking.* **had better do s.t** ought to do s.t; should do s.t: *You'd better apologize.* **know better** not accept s.t because one knows it is not true: *Harry says he will be there but I know better.* **know better than to do s.t** be sensible enough not to do s.t: *Surely you know better than to throw stones at passing cars!* **think better of (doing) s.t** decide not to do s.t after all.

▷ *def.n* **4 get the better of s.o/s.t** defeat s.o/s.t.

▷ *tr.v* **5** make (s.t) better(1); improve (s.t): *A new battery will better the car's performance.* **6** do better than (s.t): *Dorothy bettered the record by 2.54 seconds.* **better oneself** improve one's position by getting a higher salary, a better education etc.

'betters *pl.n* **one's elders and betters** ⇒ elders (⇒ elder¹).

between /bɪ'twiːn/ *adv* (often *in* —) **1** (referring to position or motion, and introducing two or more points, lines or areas that are on opposite or surrounding sides): *In this picture Joe is on the left, Lisa is on the right, and their baby is* (in) *between.* **2** (*fig*) s.w on the line joining two limits: *It isn't rain and it isn't snow; it's something* (in) *between.* **3** at some, during the whole, time during the period(1) after one point in time and before another: *'Does the lesson start at 10 or 11?' 'Neither; it usually starts at some time* (in) *between.'*

▷ *prep* **4** (often *in* —) (referring to position or motion and two or more points etc that are) (in) between(1): *There is a field between our house and our neighbour's.* **5** (*fig*) s.w on a scale joining two or more points: *Peter must be between 70 and 80 years old. Good teachers are neither too strict nor too weak; they are somewhere between these two.* **6** at some, during the whole, time: *You will always find me here between 2 and 5.30 in the afternoon.* Compare between(3). **7** (introducing people/ animals/things that one can choose from): *You have a choice between this horse and that one for your ride.* **8** (showing division and/or sharing in which two or more people, groups etc take part): *The children divided the sweets equally between them.* ⇒ among(st)(3). **9** (referring to relations of comparison, difference etc): *There was little difference in height between the various children.* **10** (referring to action or relation of two or more people etc to each other): *There was a fight between the cats for the food.* **11** (introducing two or more people to whom s.t is limited, usu because it is a secret): *Between ourselves, I don't like our new manager at all.* ⇒ among(st)(4). **12** by the combined action of: *Between them the children soon finished the job.* ⇒ among(st)(6). **read between the lines** ⇒ line(n).

bevel /'bevl/ *c.n* **1** surface of glass etc which meets another surface at an angle and so does not form a sharp edge, e.g at the side of a mirror.

▷ *tr.v* **2** make a bevel(1) on (s.t, e.g a sheet of glass).

beverage /'bevərɪdʒ/ *c.n* (*formal*) drink, esp tea or coffee, but not water: *hot beverages*.

bevy /'bevɪ/ *c.n* (*pl -ies*) (often — *of* s.t) group, e.g of girls.

bewail /bɪ'weɪl/ *tr.v* (*formal*) show sorrow about (s.t); cry loudly over (s.t).

beware /bɪ'weə/ *tr/intr.v* (often — *of* s.o/s.t) be

careful (of s.o/s.t dangerous); take care (because of s.o/s.t): *Beware of the dog!*

bewilder /bɪ'wɪldə/ *tr.v* confuse, puzzle, (s.o, an animal).

be'wildering *adj.* **be'wilderingly** *adv.*
be'wilderment *u.n.*

bewitch /bɪ'wɪtʃ/ *tr.v* **1** affect (s.o/s.t) by magic(3) or witchcraft. **2** charm (s.o); delight (s.o).

beyond /bɪ'jɒnd/ *adv* **1** to, towards, on, the farther side; farther away; past so as to leave s.o/s.t behind: *This train stops at Rome and all stations beyond.*

▷ *prep* **2** to, towards, on the farther side of; farther away than; past so as to leave behind: *Our school is beyond that wood.* **3** outside the limit(s) of; out of the reach of: *That piece of work is beyond* (*the ability of*) *our students at present.* Opposite within(4). (*live*) **beyond one's means** ⇒ means.

▷ *def.n* **4** (also with capital **B**; often *the great* —) life after one has died. **the back of beyond** ⇒ back(*n*).

bias /'baɪəs/ *c/u.n* **1** (often — *against/towards* s.o/ s.t) (usu unfair) feeling (against, in favour of, s.o/ s.t).

▷ *tr.v* (*-s-* or *-ss-*) **2** (often — s.o *against, towards, in favour of,* s.o/s.t) give a bias(1) to (s.o) (against etc s.o/s.t).

bib /bɪb/ *c.n* cloth worn by a child under its chin to protect its clothes from spilt food, drink etc.

bible /'baɪbl/ *n* **1** *c/def.n* (usu with capital **B**) (copy of the) book of the sacred or holy writings of the Christians(3) or Jews. **2** *c.n* (*informal*) book, guide, person etc that/who s.o follows or admires very closely: *He treats the grammar book as his bible.*

biblical /'bɪblɪkl/ *adj* of, referring to, from, the Bible(1).

bibliography /ˌbɪblɪ'ɒgrəfɪ/ *n* (*pl -ies*) **1** *c.n* list of books concerned with one particular subject, writer etc. **2** *u.n* study of the history of books and other writings.

ˌbibli'ographer *c.n* person concerned with bibliography(2) or who prepares a bibliography(1).

bicarbonate /baɪ'kɑːbənɪt/ *u.n* (also **bi,carbonate of 'soda**) salt used in cooking and as a medicine to help relieve an acid stomach, *chem.form* HCO₃.

bicentenary /ˌbaɪsen'tiːnərɪ/ *c.n* (*pl -ies*) 200th year after an event in the past.

bicentennial /ˌbaɪsen'tenɪəl/ *adj* **1** happening every 200 years. **2** lasting 200 years. **3** of or referring to a bicentenary.

▷ *c.n* **4** = bicentenary.

biceps /'baɪseps/ *c.n* (*pl biceps*) muscle(1) on the front of the upper arm.

bicker /'bɪkə/ *intr.v* (often — *with* s.o) about/over s.o/s.t) (*derog*) quarrel, argue, (with s.o) about s.t unimportant.

'bickering *u.n.*

bicycle /'baɪsɪkl/ *c.n* (also *attrib*) (*informal* **bike** /baɪk/) **1** machine with two wheels which is used for riding on and is moved by pedalling(2) with one's feet. ⇒ cycle(4). Compare motorbike.

by bicycle on a bicycle: *go/travel by bicycle*.

▷ *intr.v* **2** go, travel, on a bicycle(1); cycle(5).

'bicy,clist *c.n* person who rides a bicycle; cyclist.

bid /bɪd/ *c.n* **1** (often — *for* s.t) price offered (for s.t), esp at an auction(1), or for doing a certain piece of work. **2** (in some card games, e.g bridge²) statement of the number of tricks one intends to win in a game. **3** (often — *to do s.t*) (*informal*) attempt (to do s.t). **make a bid for s.t (a)** ⇒ bid(1). **(b)** try to get s.t: *The general made a bid for political power.*

▷ *tr/intr.v* (-dd-, *p.t* **bade** /bæd, beɪd/, **bid**; *p.p* **bidden** /ˈbɪdn/, **bid**) **4** (often — *(s.t) for s.t*) make a bid(1) (of s.t, usu money) to try to get s.t, usu at an auction(1), or when trying to get a certain piece of work to do. ⇒ underbid. **5** (in some card games, e.g bridge²) make a bid(2): *I bid four diamonds.* **bid s.o do s.t** (*old use*) tell s.o to do s.t. **bid s.o goodbye** *etc* (becoming *old use*) say goodbye etc to s.o.
'**bidder** *c.n* person who bids(4,5) for s.t.
'**bidding** *u.n* bids(1) at an auction(1), or for doing a certain job etc. **do s.o's bidding** (becoming *old use*) do what s.o tells one to do.

bide /baɪd/ *tr.v* **bide one's time** wait for a suitable chance (to do s.t).

bidet /ˈbiːdeɪ/ *c.n* (*French*) low basin with hot and cold water on which one sits to wash one's buttocks, genitals etc.

biennial /baɪˈenɪəl/ *adj* **1** happening every two years. **2** lasting two years.
▷ *c.n* **3** plant that lives for two years and produces seeds in the second year.

bier /bɪə/ *c.n* kind of table on which a dead body or a coffin is put before burial.

bifocal /baɪˈfəʊkl/ *adj* (of glasses) having two areas of glass, one for looking at things that are far away and the other for looking at things that are near.
bi'focals *pl.n* bifocal glasses.

big /bɪg/ *adj* (-gg-) **1** large or great in size, mass, importance etc: *a big dog/salary/occasion.* **a big eater, spender** *etc* a person who eats, spends etc a lot. **be big of s.o (to do s.t)** (*informal*) be generous of s.o (to do s.t). **be/get/grow too big for one's boots** ⇒ boots. **have big ideas** ⇒ idea.
▷ *adv* **2 talk big** boast. **3 think big** have ambitious plans.
,**big 'game** *u.n* large wild animals, e.g lions, tigers, elephants, that are hunted as game(7).
,**big-'headed** *adj* (*derog*) too pleased with oneself; too proud.
'**bigness** *u.n.*
,**big 'noise/'shot** *c.n* (*informal*) important or powerful person, esp one who is conceited.

bigamy /ˈbɪgəmɪ/ *u.n* (in countries where one is only allowed to have one husband/wife at a time) crime of marrying s.o when one is already lawfully married.
'**biga,mist** *c.n* person who does this.
'**bigamous** *adj* of, referring to, committing, bigamy.

bigot /ˈbɪgət/ *c.n* (*derog*) person who believes in s.t, esp political, racial or religious, very strongly and refuses to listen to good arguments about it.
'**bigoted** *adj* (*derog*) who is, shows that one is, a bigot.
'**bigotry** *u.n.*

bike /baɪk/ *c.n* (*informal*) bicycle.

bikini /bɪˈkiːnɪ/ *c.n* (*pl* -s) bathing suit for women, consisting of two small pieces.

bilateral /baɪˈlætərəl/ *adj* of, on, belonging to,

two sides; referring to relations between two countries: *a bilateral agreement.*

bile /baɪl/ *u.n* kind of brown-yellow liquid that is made in the liver(1) to help it in breaking down food; it tastes very bitter.

bilious /ˈbɪlɪəs/ *adj* **1** caused by too much bile: *a bilious attack.* **2** suffering from bilious attacks. **3** (*fig*) having, in, a bad temper.
'**biliousness** *u.n.*

bilge /bɪldʒ/ *n* **1** *c.n* bottom of a ship. **2** *u.n* (also '**bilge ,water**) dirty water that collects in a ship's bilge(1). **3** *u.n* (*slang*) nonsense: *Stop talking bilge!*

bilingual /baɪˈlɪŋgwəl/ *adj* **1** (often — *in s.t* and *s.t*) using two languages (which are s.t and s.t) like a native: *I'm bilingual in Japanese and Spanish.* **2** written in two languages: *a bilingual dictionary.*

bilious(ness) ⇒ bile.

bill¹ /bɪl/ *c.n* **1** written statement of the cost of goods or services, e.g in a shop or restaurant. **2** written or printed advertisement for the theatre etc. **3** (often with capital **B**) proposed law presented by a government for discussion in parliament. **4** (US) bank note. **fill/fit the bill (for s.t)** (*informal*) be suitable. **foot the bill** ⇒ foot(*v*).
▷ *tr.v* **5** (often — *s.o for s.t*) give, send, (s.o) a bill¹(1) (for s.t).
,**bill of ex'change** *c.n* order to a bank to pay a certain amount of money to s.o on a certain date.
,**bill of 'lading** *c.n* ⇒ lading.

bill² /bɪl/ *c.n* beak of a bird.

billet /ˈbɪlɪt/ *c.n* **1** private house etc in which soldiers are put to live, usu for a short time.
▷ *tr.v* **2** (often — *s.o on s.o*) place (soldiers etc) in a billet(1) (that is s.o's home).

billiards /ˈbɪlɪədz/ *u.n* game played on a table covered with green cloth and having six pockets; one tries to hit balls with the tip of a long stick (cue(3)) so that they go into a pocket. Compare snooker(1), pool³.
'**billiard-,player** *c.n* person who plays billiards.
'**billiard-,table** *c.n* table on which one plays billiards.

billion /ˈbɪlɪən/ *det/pron* (*cardinal number*) (used with 'a' (*a billion*) unless there is another det, e.g *one billion, his billion*; *pl* **billion** after another number, e.g *two billion*, otherwise *billions*, e.g *billions of flies*) **1** thousand million. **2** (*old use*) million million. **3** great number: *billions of ants.*

billow /ˈbɪləʊ/ *c.n* **1** (large) wave on the sea. **2** mass (of smoke) etc that moves like a billow(1).
▷ *intr.v* **3** rise and move like a large wave.

billy goat /ˈbɪlɪ ,gəʊt/ *c.n* male goat. ⇒ nanny goat.

bimonthly /baɪˈmʌnθlɪ/ *adj/adv* **1** happening twice a month. **2** happening once in every two months.

bin /bɪn/ *c.n* **1** container with a lid for keeping corn, coal, bread etc. ⇒ dustbin. **2** wooden frame for storing bottles of wine in.

binary /ˈbaɪnərɪ/ *adj* of, referring to, a pair of s.t.
'**binary no,tation/,system** *u.n* system of numbers using 2 as a base and only the numbers 0 and 1; it is used in computers.

bind /baɪnd/ c.n **1** (often a bit of a —) (informal) something that causes a problem or difficulty: It was (a bit of) a bind having to stay in all day for the electrician to come.
▷ tr.v (p.t,p.p bound /baʊnd/) **2** (often — s.t to s.t, together (with s.t)) tie or fasten s.t (to s.t, together) (with s.t). **bind a book**, **magazine** etc fasten the leaves of a book etc together at one edge in a cover. **bind oneself to do s.t** (formal) promise to do s.t.
'binder c.n **1** person who binds s.t, esp books. **2** machine that binds s.t.
'binding adj **1** (usu pred) (of an agreement etc) that one has promised not to break.
▷ n **2** u.n act of binding s.t. **3** c.n cover holding the leaves of a book etc together. **4** u.n material used to bind a book etc.
bingo /'bɪŋgəʊ/ u.n game of chance played by covering numbers on a card when they are called out in an order that results from chance.
binnacle /'bɪnəkl/ c.n box containing a ship's compass(1).
binoculars /bɪ'nɒkjʊləz/ pl.n (often a pair of —) glasses that, when looked through, make things seem nearer.
biochemistry /ˌbaɪəʊ'kemɪstrɪ/ u.n study of the chemistry of living things.
ˌbio'chemist c.n person who studies, is skilled in, biochemistry.
biodegradable /ˌbaɪəʊdɪ'greɪdəbl/ adj (of a substance, e.g plastic) that can rot or break down naturally or biologically.
biography /baɪ'ɒgrəfɪ/ n (pl -ies) **1** c.n story of a person's life. **2** u.n branch of literature that concerns biographies(1).
bi'ographer c.n person who writes one or more biographies.
biographical /ˌbaɪə'græfɪkl/ adj (also **bio-'graphic**) of, referring to, (a) biography.
biology /baɪ'ɒlədʒɪ/ u.n science of living things.
biological /ˌbaɪə'lɒdʒɪkl/ adj of, referring to, biology.
ˌbio'logically adv.
ˌbio,logical 'war,fare u.n spreading of dangerous diseases as a way of fighting a war.
bi'ologist c.n person who studies, is skilled in, biology.
biped /'baɪped/ c.n (technical) animal with two legs, e.g a bird or a human being.
birch /bɜːtʃ/ c.n **1** (also **'birch ,tree**) kind of tree that grows mostly in northern countries and has smooth bark and thin branches. **2** (old use) bunch of these branches tied together and used for beating people as a punishment.
▷ tr.v **3** (old use) beat (s.o) with a birch(2).
bird /bɜːd/ c.n **1** any kind of creature with feathers, wings and two legs; most kinds are able to fly. **2** (slang; do not use!) woman or girl. **A bird in the hand is worth two in the bush** (proverb) Something small or not very wonderful that one has now is better than something bigger or more wonderful that one may perhaps never get. **Birds of a feather (flock together)** (proverb) People of the same kind (keep together). **an early bird** (fig; informal) a person who gets up, arrives s.w, early (and therefore gets an advantage). **The early bird catches/gets the worm** (proverb) A person who gets up, or arrives s.w, early has an advantage. **get, give**

s.o, the bird (slang) be shouted, whistled etc at, shout etc at s.o, with disapproval. **kill two birds with one stone** (manage to) do two things at the same time.
'birdie c.n **1** (informal) child's word for a bird. **2** (in golf) score for a hole that is one less than a good player is expected to get. Compare bogey(2), eagle(2), par(2).
'bird,life u.n conditions, types etc of the lives of birds.
ˌbird of 'prey c.n bird that kills and eats small animals, fish etc.
ˌbird's-,eye 'view c.n (often — of s.t) wide view (of s.t) seen from above.
'bird,watcher c.n person who observes(1) birds.
'bird,watching u.n.
biro /'baɪərəʊ/ c.n (pl -s) (t.n) = ballpoint (pen) (⇒ ball¹). **in biro** written with a ballpoint pen.
birth /bɜːθ/ c/u.n act of being born, coming into the world. **by birth** in origin; as a result of where one was born or who one's parents were: I'm French by birth. **give birth (to s.o/s.t)** produce s.o/s.t, e.g a baby or an idea. **virgin birth** ⇒ virgin.
'birth con,trol u.n way of preventing the conception(3) of babies that are not wanted.
'birth,day c.n (anniversary of the) day of one's birth.
'birth,mark c.n mark on a person's body that he/she was born with.
'birth,place c.n (often the — of s.o/s.t) place where (s.o/s.t, e.g a famous person or an idea) was born.
'birth,rate c.n number of births in a year etc compared to the total population: A birthrate of 10 in 1000.
'birth,right c.n thing that is one's right because of where one was born or who one's parents are.
biscuit /'bɪskɪt/ c.n flat firm dry kind of cake; some are sweet, others not. **take the biscuit** (slang) be very astonishing; be the most astonishing.
bisect /baɪ'sekt/ tr.v cut, divide, (s.t) into two, usu equal, parts.
bisexual /baɪ'seksjʊəl/ adj **1** having both male and female sex organs. **2** (of a person) attracted to people of both sexes. Compare heterosexual(2), homosexual(2).
▷ c.n **3** person who is bisexual(2).
bishop /'bɪʃəp/ c.n **1** Christian(1) priest of high rank who is responsible for the work of his Church in a city or large area. ⇒ archbishop. **2** one of the pieces in the game of chess.
'bishopric c.n office or rank of a bishop(1), or the area he is responsible for. Compare diocese.
bismuth /'bɪzməθ/ u.n chemical used in alloys and medicine; chem.symb Bi.
bison /'baɪsn/ c.n kind of wild animal like a large bull¹(1) that used to be very common in Europe and North America but is now very rare.
bistro /'biːstrəʊ/ c.n (pl -s) small bar or restaurant.
bit¹ /bɪt/ c.n **1** (often — of s.t) small piece (of s.t): a bit of dirt. **2** part of a tool that cuts when it is turned. **3** metal bar, sometimes jointed in

the middle, that is put across inside a horse's mouth and used to help control it when one is riding. **4** unit of information in a computer shown as a choice between two possibilities. **a bit** (*informal*) a short time: *If you wait a bit, I'll come with you.* **a bit much/steep/stiff/strong/thick**, ⇨ much(*pron*), steep, stiff(6), strong, thick. **a bit small**, **late** etc (*informal*) rather small etc. **a bit of a fool**, **idiot** etc (*informal*) rather a fool etc. **bit by bit**; **a bit at a time** (*informal*) by degrees; not all at once. **bits and pieces (of s.t)** (*informal*) small things of various kinds: *If you'll wait a moment I'll collect my bits and pieces up and join you.* **champ at the bit** ⇨ champ¹. **do one's bit** (*informal*) do one's share of a job etc. **every bit as good** etc **as . . .** (*informal*) just as good etc as...: *Ronald is every bit as excited about the news as you are.* **in bits** in (small) pieces: *The engine of the car lay in bits all over the garage floor.* **not a bit (of it)** not at all. **to bits** into pieces: *It was blown to bits by a bomb.*
'bitty *adj* (-ier, -iest) (*informal*) with too many small bits (of information etc) that are not very well connected: *I found his talk rather bitty.*
bit² /bɪt/ *p.t* of bite.
bitch /bɪtʃ/ *c.n* **1** female dog. **2** (*derog*; *informal*; do not use!) nasty unkind woman.
'bitchily *adv* in a bitchy way.
'bitchiness *u.n* quality or fact of being bitchy.
'bitchy *adj* (-ier, -iest) (*derog*) nasty; unkind; full of spite(1): *a bitchy remark.*
bite /baɪt/ *n* **1** *c.n* act or fact of biting(8) (s.o/s.t). **2** *c.n* (often — of *s.t*) piece bitten off (s.t). **3** *c.n* wound, mark etc caused by being bitten(8,9). **4** *c.n* (of a fish) act of biting (⇨ bite(10)). **5** *c.n* (have a — of *s.t*) small quantity (of s.t); mouthful (of s.t). **6** *u.n* hold; grip(1): *This screw has plenty of bite.* ⇨ bite(11). **7** *c.n* sting; sharpness; painful effect(1): *In winter there is often a bite in the air.*
▷ *v* (*p.t* bit /bɪt/, *p.p* bitten /bɪtn/) **8** *tr/intr.v* (often — into *s.t*) cut into (s.o/s.t) with one's teeth: *I bit into an apple.* **9** *tr/intr.v* (of an insect, e.g a mosquito) sting (s.o, an animal). **10** *intr.v* (of a fish) bite(1) the food etc on a hook. **11** *intr.v* (often — into *s.t*) get a firm hold (on s.t): *His boots bit into the rock as he climbed.* **12** *intr.v* have a strong effect: *As the new rules began to bite, the town became a safer place at night.* **13** *intr.v* (*fig*; *informal*) show interest (in s.t): *I tried to get the bank manager interested in putting money into my company but he wouldn't bite.*
be bitten with s.t (*informal*) be very interested in s.t; want to do s.t very much.
bite at s.o/s.t try to bite(1) s.o/s.t.
bite s.t away = bite s.t off (s.t).
bite s.t back; **bite one's lip** ⇨ lip.
bite s.o's head off ⇨ head(*n*).
bite off more than one can chew take on more than one has time, energy(1) for. **bite s.t off (s.t)** remove s.t (from s.t) by biting (⇨ bite(1)).
bite the dust ⇨ dust(*n*).
bite the hand that feeds one ⇨ hand(*n*).
have s.t to bite on have s.t real to do.
'biting *adj* having a bite(7); sharp; stinging: *a biting wind*; *a biting attack on the government.*
bitter /'bɪtə/ *adj* **1** tasting like strong black coffee with no sugar. Compare sour(1), sweet(1). **2** (*fig*) unpleasant; painful; causing sorrow: *Nigel has bitter memories of his childhood.* **3** showing,

caused by, hate, envy, disappointment etc: *a bitter argument.* **4** very cold: *a bitter wind.* **a bitter pill to swallow** ⇨ pill. **to/until the bitter end** ⇨ end(*n*).
▷ *u.n* **5** bitter(1) beer: *A pint of bitter, please.*
'bitterly *adv.* **'bitterness** *u.n.*
'bitter-,sweet *adj* **1** both bitter(1) and sweet(1) in taste. **2** (*fig*) pleasant as well as unpleasant: *bitter-sweet memories.*
bitty ⇨ bit¹.
bitumen /'bɪtjʊmɪn/ *u.n* kind of sticky black substance often used in making road surfaces.
biweekly /baɪ'wiːklɪ/ *adj/adv* **1** happening twice a week. **2** happening once in every two weeks.
blab /blæb/ *v* (-bb-) **1** *intr.v* talk foolishly. **2** *tr/intr.v* tell (s.t secret).
black /blæk/ *adj* **1** having the colour of the inside of a completely dark room. **2** (of coffee) without milk or cream in it. **3** (of a person) of a race that has a black skin. Compare white(4). **4** very dirty: *Your hands are black.* **5** (of news, feelings etc) very bad: *black despair.* **go black** (of s.t one is looking at) disappear, either because the light has gone out or because one loses consciousness. **not as black as s.o/s.t is painted** not as bad as people say he/she/it is.
▷ *n* **6** *c/u.n* black(1) colour. **7** *c.n* (often with capital **B**) black(3) person. **in the black** having money, usu in one's bank account. Opposite in the red (⇨ red(*n*)). **in black** wearing black clothes: *dressed in black.* **in black and white** (stated clearly) in writing or printing: *If you don't put it down in black and white no one will ever believe your story.*
▷ *tr.v* **8** make (s.t, e.g one's face) black(1). **9** (usu of a trade union) advise or tell people not to trade with, or work for, (a company etc) because of a disagreement, to try to force it to change its policy etc: *The workers blacked any company that continued to supply their employer during their dispute(1).* **black out** lose one's memory or consciousness for a short time: *The pilot blacked out as the plane dived steeply.* ⇨ blackout(2).
,black and 'blue *adj* covered with bruises.
blackberry /'blækbərɪ/ *c.n* (*pl* -ies) (also *attrib*) kind of black berry that usu grows wild on very thorny bushes: *blackberry jam.*
'black,bird *c.n* kind of bird found in Europe and America; the male is (almost) black.
'black,board *c.n* board on which a teacher writes and/or draws with chalk.
,black'currant *c.n* (also *attrib*) kind of small black berry that grows in groups on a bush: *blackcurrant ice-cream.*
'blacken /'blækən/ *v* **1** *tr/intr.v* (cause (s.t) to) become black(1). **2** *tr.v* (*fig*) give (s.o/s.t) a bad reputation.
,black 'eye *c.n* bruise round a person's eye caused by a blow.
blackguard /'blægɑːd/ *c.n* (*derog*) bad dishonourable man.
'black,head *c.n* spot on one's skin which has a black centre; it is a blocked pore¹.
,black 'ice *u.n* ice on roads that one cannot see easily so that it is dangerous.
'blacking *u.n* **1** kind of liquid or paste used for making things, e.g shoes, black(1). **2** (often the — of *s.t*) ⇨ black(9): *the blacking of a factory.*

'**black,leg** c.n person who works when the other workers are officially on strike; scab(2).

'**black,list** c.n 1 list of names of people, companies etc considered bad or dangerous.

▷ tr.v 2 put the name of (s.o/s.t) on a blacklist(1).

,**black 'magic** u.n = witchcraft.

'**black,mail** u.n 1 act of demanding money from s.o for keeping secret s.t that could be damaging if it was made known. 2 money paid for this purpose.

▷ tr.v 3 (try to) make (s.o) pay blackmail(2).

'**black,mailer** c.n (derog) person who blackmails(3) (s.o).

,**black 'market** c/u.def.n unlawful trading in goods, money etc. ⇨ under-the-counter.

black marketeer /ˌblæk ˌmɑːkɪ'tɪə/ c.n person who trades on the black market.

'**blackness** u.n fact or state of being black(1,5).

'**black,out** c.n 1 (in war) keeping of buildings etc dark at night with curtains etc so that they cannot be seen from the air. 2 loss of memory or consciousness for a short time. 3 failure of the electricity supply of a town etc, esp at night.

,**black 'sheep** c.n (pl black sheep) (usu the — of the family) person who does not behave well like the rest of her/his family or group; bad person in a group.

'**black,smith** c.n 1 person who makes things out of iron by heating and hammering it. 2 (also '**black,smith's**) place where a blacksmith(1) works.

'**black,thorn** c.n (also attrib) kind of tree with black branches, white flowers and small fruits like a plum. ⇨ sloe.

bladder /'blædə/ c.n 1 kind of bag in one's body that holds urine. 2 rubber bag inside a football which is filled with air.

blade /bleɪd/ c.n 1 flat part of a knife, which is the part that cuts. 2 flat part of anything else, e.g an oar or a propeller. 3 flat narrow leaf: a blade of grass.

blame /bleɪm/ u.n 1 (often bear/take the — for s.t; lay/put the — (for s.t) on s.o/s.t) responsibility (for a mistake, crime etc). 2 criticism; finding fault.

▷ tr.v 3 (often — s.o/s.t for s.t) put the blame(1) (for s.t) on (s.o/s.t). 4 (often — s.t on s.o/s.t) put the blame(1) for (s.t) on s.o/s.t.

'**blameless** adj free from blame(1); guiltless.

'**blamelessly** adv. '**blamelessness** u.n.

'**blame,worthiness** u.n fact or state of being blameworthy.

'**blame,worthy** adj deserving blame(1).

blanch /blɑːntʃ/ v 1 tr/intr.v (cause (s.t) to) become white, e.g by removal from light. 2 tr.v (in cooking) put (s.t) in boiling water or fat for a short time. 3 intr.v (of a person) become pale, usu through fear.

blancmange /blə'mɒnʒ/ c/u.n (French) kind of sweet that is like a jelly(1) but has milk in it.

bland /blænd/ adj 1 gentle in manner, not showing strong feelings, esp for the purpose of making oneself liked. 2 (of food, drink etc) not having a strong taste.

'**blandly** adv in a bland(1) way.

'**blandness** u.n.

blandishment /'blændɪʃmənt/ c.n (often pl) (formal) attempt to get s.o to agree to s.t by being pleasant to her/him.

blank /blæŋk/ adj 1 not having any writing or marks on it. 2 (usu go —) (of one's memory, mind) empty: I knew the man's name but the moment I met him my mind went blank and I had to ask him what it was. 3 (of a person's face etc) not showing any feeling or interest. **come up against a blank wall** ⇨ wall(n).

▷ c.n 4 empty place on a page etc, sometimes left to be filled in later. 5 ticket in a draw which does not win a prize. 6 piece of metal, wood etc which has been cut to size, shape etc before being treated further. 7 = blank cartridge. **become a blank** = go blank(2). **draw a blank** get nothing; get no information. **s.o's mind went blank** ⇨ mind¹.

,**blank 'cartridge** c.n cartridge(1) that has no bullet in it.

,**blank 'cheque** c.n signed cheque on which the amount of money has to be filled in by the person who cashes(3) it. **give s.o a blank cheque** (fig) allow s.o to do whatever he/she wants.

,**blank 'verse** u.n kind of poetry with long lines that do not rhyme(4): Shakespeare used blank verse in many scenes of his plays.

blanket /'blæŋkɪt/ attrib.adj 1 that covers all kinds and groups: a blanket insurance.

▷ c.n 2 (thick) woollen covering put on a bed to keep one warm. 3 (often — of s.t) (fig) thick mass (of cloud, fog etc). **wet blanket** ⇨ wet.

▷ tr.v 4 cover (s.t) completely (as if) with a blanket(2): Snow blanketed the hills. The town was blanketed with advertisements for the show.

blare /bleə/ sing.n 1 (often the — of s.t) loud unpleasant sound (of s.t, e.g a trumpet, a car horn).

▷ v 2 intr.v (often — out) make the sound of a blare(1). 3 tr.v (often — s.t out) produce (music, words etc) in a blaring(2) way.

blasé /'blɑːzeɪ/ adj (often — about s.t) (French) so bored by pleasure and/or success that one no longer enjoys it/them.

blaspheme /blæs'fiːm/ intr.v say bad things about God or other sacred persons or things; use bad language about s.o/s.t.

blas'phemer c.n person who blasphemes.

blasphemy /'blæsfəmɪ/ c/u.n.

blast /blɑːst/ c.n 1 (often — of s.t) strong rush (of wind etc). 2 strong rush of air, gas etc caused by an explosion: a bomb blast. 3 loud sound made by a wind instrument, e.g a trumpet, or by a horn.

▷ interj (also '**blast ,it**) 4 (expression showing anger): Blast (it)! I've forgotten my keys.

▷ tr.v 5 blow (s.t) up with explosives: The rocks were blasted out of the side of the mountain. 6 destroy (s.t): He failed the examination and blasted his hopes of becoming a doctor. 7 (slang) scold (s.o): The teacher blasted the students for their careless work. 8 curse (s.o/s.t): Blast this razor! It's cut me again! ⇨ blast(4). **blast off** (of a spacecraft) begin to go up into the air. ⇨ blast-off.

'**blasted** adj (used as a mild curse): This delay is a blasted nuisance. ⇨ blast(4,8).

'**blast ,furnace** c.n big oven in a factory in which metal is made by melting substances in great heat with a current of air.

'**blast-,off** c/unique n act of a spacecraft beginning to go up into the air.

blatant /'bleɪtnt/ adj unpleasantly, and often also intentionally, noticeable; without shame: blatant interference in her personal affairs.

'blatancy *u.n.* **'blatantly** *adv.*

blaze /bleɪz/ *c.n* **1** bright fire or flame. **2** area of light or bright colour: *The roses make a blaze of colour in the garden.* **3** (usu *in a — of s.t*) sudden burst (of strong feeling, e.g anger). **4** white mark on a horse's face. **go to blazes** (*slang*) = go to hell (⇒ **hell**). **work** *etc* **like blazes** (*slang*) work *etc* very hard.

▷ *intr.v* **5** burn with a strong flame. **6** burn or shine brightly: *The sun blazed down on the beach.* **7** (*fig*) show strong feeling: *His eyes blazed at me angrily.* **blaze a/the trail** (**for s.o/s.t**) ⇒ trail(*n*). **blaze away** fire a gun quickly and usu wildly. **blaze up** burst into flame.

'blazer *c.n* kind of informal jacket(1), esp one made in the colours of a club, college *etc* and with a badge on the top left-hand pocket.

Bldg(s) *written abbr* (usu in a name) building(s): *London Bldgs, 5 Green Street.*

bleach /bliːtʃ/ *u.n* **1** kind of chemical substance that removes the colour from materials.

▷ *tr/intr.v* **2** (cause (s.t) to) become white/paler through sun or chemical action.

bleak /bliːk/ *adj* **1** (of weather) cold and unpleasant. **2** (of a place) bare of shelter (and therefore cold and windy). **3** (*fig*) not at all encouraging: *His chances of getting another job were now bleak.*

'bleakly *adv.* **'bleakness** *u.n.*

bleary /'blɪərɪ/ *adj* (-ier, -iest) (of one's sight) not clear: *My eyes were so bleary just after I got up that I couldn't find the door.*

'blearily *adv.* **'bleariness** *u.n.*

,bleary-'eyed *adj* not able to see clearly.

bleat /bliːt/ *c.n* **1** cry of a sheep, goat *etc.*

▷ *v* **2** *intr.v* give a bleat(1). **3** *tr/intr.v* speak (s.t) in a voice that sounds like bleating(2). **4** *intr.v* (usu *— (on) about s.o/s.t*) (*informal*) complain (a lot about s.o/s.t).

bleed /bliːd/ *v* (*p.t,p.p* bled /bled/) **1** *intr.v* lose blood: *I bled a lot when I cut my arm.* **2** *tr.v* draw blood out of (s.o/s.t). **3** *tr.v* take air, water *etc* out of (s.t, e.g a hot water system). **4** *tr.v* (often *— s.o for/of s.t*) (*fig*) make (s.o) give one money for no just reason. **bleed for s.o/s.t** (*fig*) feel very sorry for s.o/s.t: *Our hearts bled for the poor child.* **bleed s.o white** (*informal*) bleed(4) s.o of all her/his money.

'bleeding *attrib.adj* (*slang*; do not use!) = bloody(3,4).

bleep /bliːp/ *c.n* **1** short high sound given out by a radio *etc* as a warning, to call a doctor *etc.*

▷ *v* **2** *intr.v* give a bleep(1). **3** *tr.v* call (s.o, often a doctor or nurse) by bleeping(2).

'bleeper *c.n* device that bleeps(2).

blemish /'blemɪʃ/ *c.n* **1** mark that lessens the perfection of s.t. **2** (*fig*) thing that makes a person's character less good: *Julia left the court room without a blemish on her reputation.*

▷ *tr.v* **3** put a blemish(1,2) on (s.t).

blend /blend/ *c.n* **1** mixture of two or more different substances/things to form a complete whole: *a new blend of coffee.*

▷ *v* **2** *tr/intr.v* (often *— s.t and s.t together; — s.t with s.t*) (cause (s.t) to) mix (with s.t *etc*). **3** *intr.v* (often *— (well etc) with s.t*) (esp of colours) go well *etc* together.

'blender *c.n* kitchen appliance used for blending(2) foods, liquids *etc.*

bless /bles/ *tr.v* **1** ask God's favour for (s.o/ s.t): *The priest blesses the people at the end of the service. Bless you, you have been very kind to me.* **2** call (s.t) holy: *Let us bless the name of the Lord.* **3** make (s.t) holy: *During the service the priest blesses the bread and wine.* **be blessed with s.t** be fortunate enough to have s.t: *Linda is blessed with brains.* **Bless me!** (exclamation showing surprise).

blessed /'blesɪd/ *adj* **1** holy; sacred. **2** (usu /blesd/) happy; fortunate. **3** (*attrib*) (*slang*) (mild swear word): *I've missed the blessed train again!*

'blessedness *u.n.*

'blessing *c.n* **1** prayer for God's favour: *The priest gives the blessing at the end of the service.* **2** advantage; thing one should be grateful for: *What a blessing I've got my umbrella now that it's started to rain!* **3** (usu *give s.t one's —*) (*informal*) approval. **a blessing in disguise** a thing or state that seemed bad at first but proves to be really good.

blew /bluː/ *p.t* of blow²(*v*).

blight /blaɪt/ *n* **1** *u.n* kind of disease in plants that causes them to grow poorly: *potato blight.* **2** *c.n* (usu *— on s.t*) bad influence (that affects s.o's character, reputation *etc*).

▷ *tr.v* **3** affect (s.t) with blight(1). **4** damage, spoil, (s.t); reduce s.o's chances of (s.t, e.g success).

blighter /'blaɪtə/ *c.n* (*slang*; becoming *old use*) **1** (*derog*) annoying person. **2** person: *You lucky blighter!*

blimey /'blaɪmɪ/ *interj* (*slang*; becoming *old use*) (expression showing surprise).

blind¹ /blaɪnd/ *adj* **1** who/that cannot see; without sight. **2** (*pred*) (often *— to s.t*) (*fig*) unable to understand or judge (s.t) clearly: *How blind I've been all these years not to see that he is a cheat! Peter is blind to his children's faults.* **3** (*attrib*) (*informal*) without thinking or being careful: *Joe was in such a blind hurry that he left his books behind.* **4** (usu in flying a plane) not being able to see outside: *a blind landing in fog using instruments only.* **5** (*attrib*) not guided by reason: *the blind forces of nature.* **6** (usu *attrib*) in which one cannot see far: *Go slowly round this blind corner because you can't see cars coming the other way.* **as blind as a bat** ⇒ bat¹. **turn a blind eye** (**to s.t**) ⇒ eye(*n*).

▷ *adv* **7** (usu in flying a plane) without being able to see outside: *We are flying blind now.* ⇒ blind¹(4).

▷ *tr.v* **8** make (s.o, an animal) blind¹(1,2).

,blind 'alley *c.n* **1** road that is closed at one end. **2** (*fig*) job *etc* that offers no chance of progress.

,blind 'date *c.n* arrangement to meet s.o socially whom one has not met before.

,blind 'drunk *adj* (*slang*) extremely drunk(1).

'blind,fold *c.n* cloth *etc* that covers one's eyes so that one cannot see anything.

▷ *tr.v* **2** put a blindfold(1) on (s.o).

'blindly *adv* in a blind(3) way: *He followed the instructions blindly.*

,blind ,man's 'buff *u.n* game in which one person is blindfolded(2) and has to catch one of the other players and say who he/she is.

'blindness *u.n.*

'blind ,spot *c.n* **1** spot in one's eye which does

not sense light. **2** area behind a vehicle which the driver cannot see in her/his mirror. **3** (*fig*) lack of ability to understand one particular thing properly: *Jim is a good student but he has a blind spot for mathematics.*

blind² /blaɪnd/ *c.n* cloth etc used to cover a window, usu to keep out the sun; it usu rolls up when not needed. ⇒ venetian blind.

blink /blɪŋk/ *c.n* **1** act of blinking(2,3). **on the blink** (*informal*) (of a machine etc) not working properly.
▷ *v* **2** *tr/intr.v* open and shut (one's eyes) quickly: *When I first went out into the bright sun I blinked* (*my eyes*). **3** *intr.v* (seem to) go on and off: *The ships' lights were blinking in the harbour.*
'**blinkers** *pl.n* things put at the sides of a horse's eyes so that it can only see in front of it.
'**blinking** *attrib.adj* (*informal*) (mild swear word): *What a blinking shame that Dorothy can't come!*

blip /blɪp/ *c.n* spot of light on a radar screen that shows that s.t, e.g a ship, is there.

bliss /blɪs/ *u.n* absolute happiness.
'**blissful** *adj* causing or feeling bliss.
'**blissfully** *adv*. '**blissfulness** *u.n*.

blister /'blɪstə/ *c.n* **1** small swelling under one's skin which is filled with liquid. **2** swelling on metal, a painted surface etc.
▷ *tr/intr.v* **3** (cause (s.t) to) come out in one or more blisters(1,2).

blithe /blaɪð/ *adj* (usu *literary*) happy; joyful.
'**blithely** *adv* without (really) caring: *He blithely ignored my advice.*

blithering /'blɪðərɪŋ/ *attrib.adj* (*slang*) (mild swear word): *You blithering fool!*

blitz /blɪts/ *c.n* **1** sudden violent attack, esp from the air. **have a blitz on s.t** (*informal*) work very hard at s.t, esp cleaning a place or clearing up an untidy place.
▷ *tr.v* **2** attack (s.t) suddenly, esp from the air.

blizzard /'blɪzəd/ *c.n* storm in which snow is driven along by a strong wind.

bloated /'bləʊtɪd/ *adj* (often — *with* s.t) swollen (with s.t), usu through eating too much. **bloated with pride** (*fig*) too proud.

blob /blɒb/ *c.n* (often — *of* s.t) small drop (of liquid, paint etc).

bloc /blɒk/ *c.n* combination of countries, parties, groups etc in order to work together: *the Eastern bloc countries* (USSR, Poland, Hungary etc).

block /blɒk/ *c.n* **1** solid piece of wood, stone etc, sometimes shaped for a particular purpose, e.g for shaping hats on. **2** piece of metal or wood with letters, patterns etc cut into it which is used for printing. **3** frame for holding pulleys. ⇒ block and tackle. **4** group of buildings joined together; one big building divided into parts: *an office block*; *a block of flats.* **5** (esp US) area of buildings separated from others by streets on all sides. **6** groups of seats in a theatre etc. **7** (usu *pl*) cube(2) of wood etc used as a child's toy for building. **8** thing that stops movement: *a road block put up by the police to check cars.* **knock s.o's block off** (*fig*; *slang*) hit s.o hard. **traffic block** ⇒ traffic.
▷ *tr.v* **9** make movement difficult or impossible in (s.t, e.g a pipe). **10** stop, interfere with, (s.t, e.g the flow of water in a stream). **11** prevent (s.t, e.g a plan) being carried out (successfully). **block**

s.t in/out make a rough drawing of s.t, e.g the plan of a house. **block s.t off/up** block(9,10) s.t completely. **block s.t out** stop s.t being seen.

blockade /blɒ'keɪd/ *c.n* **1** (almost) complete shutting off of a harbour, country etc to prevent it from having contacts with the rest of the world. **raise a blockade** end a blockade(1). **run a blockade** get through a blockade(1).
▷ *tr.v* **2** make a blockade(1) around (s.t).

blockage /'blɒkɪdʒ/ *c.n* **1** state of being blocked(9,10). **2** thing that blocks(9,10) (s.t).

,**block and 'tackle** *sing/u.n* device consisting of blocks(3) and ropes, used for lifting heavy things.

'**block,buster** *c.n* (*informal*) film, play, book etc that is heavily advertised and (so likely to be) successful.

,**block 'capitals**/'**letters** *pl.n* (often *in* —) capital letters, each of which is clear and separate like this: BLOCK LETTERS.

'**block,head** *c.n* (*informal*) stupid person.

bloke /bləʊk/ *c.n* (*informal*) man.

blond /blɒnd/ *adj* **1** fair in colour. **2** (of a male) having fair hair.
▷ *c.n* **3** male person who has fair hair.

blonde *adj* **1** fair in colour. **2** (of a female) having fair hair.
▷ *c.n* **3** female person who has fair hair.

blood /blʌd/ *u.n* **1** red liquid that goes through the blood vessels of one's body. **2** family relationship: *It is better if people of the same blood do not marry each other.* **be/run in s.o's/the blood** be s.t inherited(2). **Blood is thicker than water** (*saying*) Family relationships are closer than ones outside a family. **s.o's blood is up** s.o has become angry. **(do s.t) in cold blood** (do s.t) coldly and without feeling. **flesh and blood** ⇒ flesh(*n*). **fresh/new blood** (*fig*) new person(s) coming into s.t, e.g a family or a company. **make s.o's blood boil**; **one's blood boils** (*fig*) make s.o very angry; one is/becomes very angry. **make s.o's blood run cold** make s.o feel very afraid or disgusted. **(related) by blood** (related) by being descended from the same ancestors. Compare by marriage.

'**blood ,bank** *c.n* place where blood(1) is stored for use in operations etc.

'**blood ,count** *c.n* number of red and white corpuscles in a certain amount of blood(1).

'**blood-,curdling** *adj* that makes one very frightened.

'**blood ,donor** *c.n* person who gives blood(1) so that it can be used for patients in hospital etc.

'**blood ,group** *c.n* (also '**blood ,type**) one of several kinds of different blood(1) found in persons or animals.

'**blood-,heat** *u.n* usual temperature of the blood(1) of a living person or animal.

'**blood,hound** *c.n* big kind of hound(1) used for tracking people etc because of its strong sense of smell.

'**bloodiness** *u.n* state or fact of being bloody(1).

'**bloodless** *adj* **1** having no blood(1) in it. **2** pale. **3** without bloodshed: *a bloodless coup.*

'**blood-,poisoning** *u.n* dangerous condition caused by poison entering the blood.

'**blood ,pressure** *c/u.n* force with which the blood(1) travels through one's body.

,**blood 'red** *adj* having the colour of blood(1).

'blood re,lation *c.n* person related by blood(2).

'blood,shed *u.n* killing or wounding of people.

'blood-,shot *adj* (of the white part of an eye) red, usu after crying, or because of dust etc.

'blood,stained *adj* stained with blood(1).

'blood,thirstily *adv* in a bloodthirsty way.

'blood,thirstiness *u.n* state or fact of being bloodthirsty.

'blood,thirsty *adj* eager to kill or to see killing; getting pleasure from cruelty.

'blood trans,fusion *c.n* passing of blood(1) from one person to another.

'blood ,vessel *c.n* vein(1) or artery(1) through which blood(1) flows.

'bloody *adj* (-ier, -iest) **1** covered with blood(1). **2** producing bloodshed: *a bloody fight.* **3** (*slang*; do not use!): *You're a bloody fool!*

▷ *adv* **4** (*slang*; do not use!) very: *We bloody nearly turned over as we went round the corner too fast.* **not bloody likely!** (*slang*; do not use!) (as an angry answer to a request etc) certainly not!

,bloody-'minded *adj* (*derog*) not willing (usu without a good reason) to do what one is asked or expected to do; obstinate(1).

,bloody-'mindedly *adv.* **,bloody-'mindedness** *u.n.*

bloom /blu:m/ *n* **1** *c.n* flower, esp one used for decoration. **2** *u.n* (often *in the — of s.t*) time of greatest beauty, perfection etc: *in the bloom of youth.* **in bloom** blooming ⇨ bloom(3). **in full bloom** at one's/its best.

▷ *intr.v* **3** produce or have flowers. **4** (*fig*) be in one's best condition: *Jane was blooming with health after her holiday.*

'blooming *attrib.adj/adv* (*informal*) (mild swear word): *Don't be so blooming silly! It's blooming cold today.*

blossom /'blɒsəm/ *c.n* **1** flower, esp of a tree that produces fruit. **2** mass of flowers on such a tree. **in blossom** (a) blossoming(3). (b) that is blossoming(4).

▷ *intr.v* **3** produce flowers; bloom(3). **4** (often — (out) into s.t) develop (into s.t); make progress (resulting in s.t): *Their friendship blossomed into love and finally marriage.*

blot /blɒt/ *c.n* **1** spot or stain: *blots of ink.* **2** (often — on s.t) fault; thing that spoils s.t (esp one's character or reputation) that is otherwise good. **a blot on the landscape** an ugly thing (e.g a factory) that spoils the beauty of a scene.

▷ *tr.v* (-tt-) **3** make a blot(1,2) or blots on (s.t). **4** dry (ink) with blotting paper. **blot one's copybook** (*fig*; *informal*) do s.t that is a blot(2) on one's reputation. **blot s.t out** hide s.t from view.

'blotter *c.n* device with sheets of blotting paper in it, used for blotting(4) ink.

'blotting ,paper *u.n* kind of thick soft absorbent paper used to dry wet ink quickly.

blotch /blɒtʃ/ *c.n* **1** ugly spot or mark on one's skin; dirty spot of ink, colour etc on paper etc.

▷ *tr.v* **2** make one or more blotches(1) on (s.t).

blouse /blauz/ *c.n* light piece of clothing from the neck to the waist that has sleeves and is worn mostly by women and girls.

blow¹ /bləʊ/ *c.n* **1** hard hit or stroke. **2** (often a — to s.o) shock (to s.o); unfortunate happening (for s.o/s.t). **come to blows** start to fight each other. **cushion the blow** ⇨ cushion(*v*). **exchange blows** fight each other. **strike a blow**

against/for s.o/s.t do s.t important in opposition to, in support of, s.o/s.t. **without (striking) a blow** without having to fight at all.

,blow-by-'blow *attrib.adj* **a blow-by-blow account (of s.t)** a detailed description (of events) giving them in the order in which they happened and leaving none out.

blow² /bləʊ/ *c.n* **1** forcing of air through one's nose or mouth: *Give your nose a blow; it's running.* **2** (*informal*) strong wind.

▷ *v* (*p.t blew* /blu:/, *p.p blown*) **3** *intr.v* (of wind, air etc) move along; flow: *The wind was blowing down the valley.* **4** *tr.v* (often — s.t about, around, off etc (s.o/s.t)) (cause (s.t) to) move by blowing²(1) (it) (about etc): *The force of the explosion blew my hat off.* **5** *intr.v* (often — on s.t) send a (strong) current of air out (onto s.t). **6** produce, give a shape to, (s.t) by blowing(5): *This man blows glass; he has just blown me a beautiful vase.* **7** *tr/intr.v* (cause (s.t, e.g a trumpet or a car horn) to) make a noise by means of air. **8** *intr.v* (often *puff and* —) breathe with short breaths, usu because one is out of breath. **9** *tr/intr.v* (cause (a fuse¹(1)) to) stop working because of too great loading of the electrical circuit(4). **10** *tr.v* (*slang*) (often — s.t on s.t) spend (money etc) wastefully (on s.t). **11** *tr.v* lose (one's chance to do s.t etc) by behaving foolishly. **12** *intr.v* (*slang*) go away from somewhere suddenly and quickly; escape: *Let's blow!*

blow (s.t) down (cause (s.t) to) fall down by blowing(5) on it. **Blow me down!** (*informal*) (expression of surprise).

blow the gaff ⇨ gaff.

blow hot and cold (about s.t) (*fig*; *informal*) keep changing one's mind (about s.t).

blow in (*slang*) arrive when one is not expected.

Blow it! (*informal*) (expression of anger or annoyance).

blow (s.o) a kiss ⇨ kiss(*n*).

blow the lid off s.t ⇨ lid.

blow one's nose ⇨ nose(*n*).

blow off (*slang*) fart(3). **blow off steam** ⇨ steam.

blow on s.t ⇨ blow²(5). **blow s.t on s.t** ⇨ blow²(10). **blow the whistle on s.o/s.t** ⇨ whistle.

blow out (of a tyre etc) burst. **blow (s.t) out** (cause s.t, e.g a candle, to) stop burning by blowing it.

blow (s.t) to (cause (s.t) to) shut by wind blowing on it: *The wind blew the open door to.*

blow one's top ⇨ top¹.

blow up be destroyed by an explosion. **blow s.o up** (*informal*) scold s.o. **blow s.o/s.t up** destroy s.o/s.t by an explosion. **blow s.t up** make a photograph etc bigger; enlarge s.t. **blow (up) a gale/storm** (*informal*) (of a gale/storm) (begin to) blow²(3) violently.

'blow-,dry *tr.v* (-ies, -ied) dry (s.t, usu hair) by passing warm air over it. ⇨ hair-drier.

'blower *c.n* **1** machine for forcing air into or through s.t. **2** (often in combinations) person who makes s.t by blowing: *a glass-blower.* **3** (*informal*; becoming *old use*) telephone: *Please get Smith on the blower.*

'blow,lamp *c.n* (also **'blow,torch**) machine with a strong flame, used to remove paint from surfaces by melting it.

blubber¹ /ˈblʌbə/ *u.n* fat from whales and other large sea creatures.

blubber² /ˈblʌbə/ *v* (*derog*) **1** *intr.v* cry noisily. **2** *tr.v* (often — *s.t out*) say (s.t) while blubbering²(1).

blue /bluː/ *adj* **1** having the colour of the sky on a clear day when the sun is shining. **2** (*informal*) sad; unhappy. **3** very rude in an immoral way; obscene: *a blue joke*.

▷ *n* **4** *c/u.n* blue(1) colour. **5** *c.n* right to wear special clothes to show that one has represented either Oxford or Cambridge University in a match between the two. **6** *c.n* person who has a blue(5). **a bolt from the blue** ⇨ bolt²(*n*). **in blue** having blue clothes on: *She's (dressed) in blue*. **out of the blue** when one/it is not expected. **till/until s.o is blue in the face** (saying s.t etc) again and again, without success.

ˈblue ˌbell *c.n* kind of plant with small blue flowers shaped like bells.

ˌblue ˈblood *u.n* fact or quality of being of a noble family.

ˌblue-ˈblooded *adj* being of a noble family.

ˈblue ˌbottle *c.n* kind of large fly.

ˌblue-ˈcollar *adj* (usu *attrib*) **1** working with her/his hands rather than her/his brain: *Tom is a blue-collar worker in our factory*. **2** done by people who work with their hands rather than their brains: *He has a blue-collar job in the factory*. Compare white-collar.

ˈblueness *u.n.*

ˈblue ˌprint *c.n* **1** plan, esp for a building, machine etc which has white lines on blue paper. **2** (*fig*) plan.

ˈbluish *adj* rather blue.

bluff¹ /blʌf/ *adj* (of a person, her/his behaviour etc) rough, simple and cheerful, sometimes in a way that hurts people's feelings.

bluff² /blʌf/ *c.n* high steep slope.

bluff³ /blʌf/ *u.n* **1** pretence; way of trying to make s.o believe s.t that is not true. **call s.o's bluff** show that s.o is bluffing(2) by telling her/him to do what she/he was threatening to do.

▷ *intr.v* **2** pretend; hide the truth: *He said he had a gun but I knew he was only bluffing*. **bluff s.o into doing s.t** get s.o to do s.t by using bluff(1). **bluff it out** succeed in avoiding s.t unpleasant by using bluff(1). **bluff one's way out of, through**, **s.t** manage to get out of, through, s.t by bluff(1).

bluish ⇨ blue.

blunder /ˈblʌndə/ *c.n* **1** silly or careless mistake.

▷ *intr.v* **2** make a silly or careless mistake. **3** (often — *into s.t*) move about without any clear sense of direction (hitting against s.t). **blunder into s.t (a)** ⇨ blunder(3). **(b)** get into a difficult situation as a result of a blunder(1).

ˈblunderer *c.n* (*derog*) person who blunders(2,3).

blunt /blʌnt/ *adj* **1** not having a sharp point or edge. **2** (of a person, her/his way of speaking etc) frank(1) and not taking care to be polite or gentle.

▷ *tr.v* **3** make (s.t) blunt(1). **4** make (feelings etc) less sensitive.

ˈbluntly *adv* in a blunt(2) way: *He told her bluntly that he didn't believe her*.

ˈbluntness *u.n.*

blur /blɜː/ *c.n* **1** thing that one cannot see the outlines of clearly: *In the fog, the house was a blur*.

▷ *v* (*-rr-*) **2** *tr.v* make it difficult to see the outlines of (s.o/s.t) clearly: *Rain on the window blurred the view outside*. **3** *intr.v* become a blur(1).

blurt /blɜːt/ *tr.v* (often — *s.t out*) say (s.t) suddenly and without thinking first; give away (s.t that was a secret).

blush /blʌʃ/ *c.n* **1** red colour in the face caused by shame etc.

▷ *intr.v* **2** become red in the face through shame etc: *She blushed as she accepted her prize*.

bluster /ˈblʌstə/ *u.n* **1** noise of strong wind and/ or waves. **2** (*fig*) noisy empty boasts or threats.

▷ *intr.v* **3** blow or storm violently. **4** (*fig*) act or speak in a boastful and/or threatening way. **bluster one's way through s.t** get through s.t by using bluster(2).

ˈblustery *adj* (of weather) very windy; stormy.

BMA /ˌbiː em ˈeɪ/ *def.n abbr* British Medical Association.

Bn *written abbr* Baron(1).

BO /ˌbiː ˈəʊ/ *abbr* **1** body odour. **2** (*written abbr*) Box Office (⇨ box¹(*n*)).

boa /ˈbəʊə/ *c.n* (also **boa constrictor** /ˈbəʊə kənˌstrɪktə/) kind of very big snake found in South America which is not poisonous but kills creatures by winding itself round them and crushing them.

boar /bɔː/ *c.n* male pig, either wild or on a farm. Compare hog(1), sow¹, wild boar.

board¹ /bɔːd/ *c.n* **1** long thin flat piece of wood used for making floors, ships' decks etc. **2** flat piece of wood etc for putting notices on. ⇨ notice board. **3** (usu *the* —) = blackboard. **4** flat surface with patterns etc on it on which games, e.g chess, are played. **5** thick stiff paper often used to make hard covers for books. **above board** open(ly); without trying to cheat. **across the board** (**across-the-board** when *attrib*) including everybody: *an across-the-board increase in salaries and wages*. **go by the board** fail; be abandoned(2). **sweep the board** (*fig*) win everything; be completely successful.

▷ *tr.v* **6** provide, cover, (s.t, e.g a floor) with boards¹(1). **board s.t up** close s.t with boards¹(1).

ˈboard ˌgame *c.n* game, e.g chess, draughts, that uses a board¹(4).

ˈboarding *u.n* boards¹(1) laid together closely to form a flat surface, e.g a floor.

board² /bɔːd/ *u.n* **1** food provided for s.o, esp by the week, month etc: *Michelle gets free board in her job at this hotel*.

▷ *v* **2** *intr.v* receive one's meals with lodging: *John boards with his uncle during term time*. **3** *tr.v* provide (s.o) with meals as well as lodging.

ˌboard and ˈlodging *u.n* food and lodging, e.g in a boarding-house.

ˈboarder *c.n* **1** person who boards²(2). **2** student who lives and eats at school during term time.

ˈboarding-ˌhouse *c.n* house like a small hotel that provides board and lodging.

ˈboarding ˌschool *c.n* school, usu a private one, for students who board²(2). Compare day school.

board³ /bɔːd/ *c.n* (often — *of directors*) group (of persons who control a company).

ˈboard ˌroom *c.n* room in which a board³ meets.

board⁴ /bɔːd/ *unique n* **1 on board** (*a ship/ plane*) on or in a ship/plane. **2 go on board** (*a ship/plane*) get into or on a ship/plane. ⇨ inboard, outboard.

▷ *tr/intr.v* **3** get into or on (a ship/plane).
'boarding-,card/-,pass *c.n* card etc needed in order to board⁴(3) a plane/ship.

boast /bəʊst/ *c.n* **1** proud words about oneself, one's family etc. **2** reason for being satisfied; thing that one is proud of: *It was Peter's boast that he had never been caught cheating at cards.*

▷ *v* **3** *intr.v* praise oneself or s.o/s.t that one supports. **4** *tr.v* be fortunate enough to have (s.t): *Kathy's house boasts an indoor swimming pool.*
'boaster *c.n* (usu *derog*) person who boasts(3).
'boastful *adj* full of boasts(1).
'boastfully *adv.* **'boastfulness** *u.n.*

boat /bəʊt/ *c.n* **1** small vessel, usu one that does not have a deck and which one rows or sails. ⇨ motorboat. Compare ship(1). **2** dish shaped like a boat(1) and used for holding sauce etc: *a gravy boat.* **be** (*all*) **in the same boat** (*fig*) share the same difficulties. **burn one's boats** ⇨ burn (*v*). **miss the boat** ⇨ miss². **rock the boat** cause difficulties, quarrels etc in a situation. **take to the boats** go into the lifeboats, usu to escape from a sinking ship.
'boat,house *c.n* building near the water in which one or more boats are kept.
boatswain /'bəʊsn/ *c.n* (also **'bosun**) (rank of a) chief seaman on a ship.
'boat ,train *c.n* train that takes passengers to and from a passenger ship.

bob¹ /bɒb/ *c.n* **1** quick down and up movement.

▷ *intr.v* (**-bb-**) **2** move down and up in one or more short quick movements. **bob up** (*fig*; *informal*) appear suddenly and when one/it is not expected.

bob² /bɒb/ *c.n* (*old use*) shilling(1).

bob³ /bɒb/ *c.n* **1** (*old use*) way of cutting a woman's hair which leaves it loose and (rather) short.

▷ *tr.v* (**-bb-**) **2** (*old use*) cut (hair) in this way.

bobby /'bɒbɪ/ *c.n* (*pl* **-ies**) (*informal*; becoming *old use*) British policeman.

bobsled /'bɒb,sled/ *c.n* (also **bobsleigh** /'bɒb,sleɪ/) kind of sled for three or four people that can be steered and is used in racing.

bode /bəʊd/ *intr.v* **bode ill/well** (**for s.o/s.t**) be a bad/good sign for the future (of s.o/s.t): *Wendy's good results in her test bode well for her examinations next month.*

bodice /'bɒdɪs/ *c.n* upper part of a woman's dress or underclothing that fits tightly.

bodily ⇨ body.

bodkin /'bɒdkɪn/ *c.n* big blunt needle with a big eye, used for threading ribbon etc.

body /'bɒdɪ/ *c.n* (*pl* **-ies**) **1** whole of the parts of a person or animal that one can see, feel etc. Compare mind¹, soul(1). **2** dead body(1); corpse: *The bodies of the soldiers were buried where they fell.* **3** main part of a body(1) without the head, arms and legs. **4** main part of s.t, e.g a building. **5** group of people with the same interests, purpose etc: *the student body of a university.* **6** (often — *of s.t*) collection, quantity etc (of s.t, e.g information about s.t). **body and soul** completely. **heavenly body** ⇨ heavenly. **in a body** all together. **keep**

body and soul together get enough food etc to stay alive.
'bodily *adj* **1** of or referring to the body(1).

▷ *adv* **2** as a whole; completely; all together: *Jim was able to lift all the bags bodily onto the truck.*
'body,guard *c/pl.n* person(s) who protect(s) s.o, esp an important person, from danger, attack etc.
'body ,odour *u.n* (*abbr BO*) natural smell of one's body (unpleasant if one does not wash oneself regularly).
'body,work *u.n* main part, esp of a vehicle, i.e without the wheels, engine etc.

bog /bɒg/ *c.n* **1** area of soft very wet ground. **2** (*slang*; do not use!) lavatory.

▷ *tr/intr.v* (**-gg-**) **3 bog** (**s.o/s.t**) **down** (**in s.t**); **get bogged down** (**in s.t**) (**a**) (cause (s.o/s.t) to) get stuck in a bog(1) so that he/she/it cannot move. (**b**) (*fig*) (cause s.o/s.t to) be unable to make progress because of difficulties.
'boggy *adj* (**-ier, -iest**) (of land) soft and very wet.

bogey /'bəʊgɪ/ *c.n* (also **'bogie, 'bogy**) (*pl* **-eys, -ies**) **1** person or thing who/that frightens people. **2** (in golf) score for a hole that is one more than a good player is expected to get. Compare birdie(2), eagle(2), par(2).
'bogey,man *c.n* (*pl* **-men**) bogey(1) in human form.

boggle /'bɒgl/ *intr.v* **the mind boggles**; **mind-boggling** ⇨ mind¹.

boggy ⇨ bog.

boil¹ /bɔɪl/ *c.n* hard poisoned swelling just below one's skin which is often red and painful.

boil² /bɔɪl/ *v* **1** *tr/intr.v* (often — *s.t up*) (cause (a liquid) to) reach the temperature at which it produces bubbles(2) because the liquid is turning into steam or gas: *At sea level water boils at 100°* Centigrade. **2** *tr.v* cook (s.t) by boiling²(1) (it). **3** *intr.v* (*fig*) be/become very excited and/or angry. **boil away** (**a**) continue to boil²(1). (**b**) boil²(1) until there is no liquid left. **boil down to s.t** (**a**) be reduced to s.t. (**b**) (*fig*; *informal*) really mean s.t when one leaves out the unimportant or misleading parts. **boil s.t down** (**to s.t**) (**a**) make s.t less by boiling²(1) it (until it becomes s.t). (**b**) (*fig*) reduce s.t (until it becomes s.t). **boil over** boil²(1) and flow over the side of a pan etc. **one's blood boils** ⇨ blood.

▷ *def.n* **4** (often **bring s.t to the —; come to the —**) ((cause (s.t) to) reach the) temperature at which s.t boils²(1). **on the boil** (**a**) boiling²(1). (**b**) (*fig*) happening.
'boiler *c.n* **1** metal container in which liquid is boiled²(1), esp for making steam in an engine. **2** hot water tank for supplying a house etc.
,boiling 'hot *adj* (**'boiling-,hot** when *attrib*) (*informal*) very hot: *On boiling-hot days we stay indoors until evening.*
'boiling-,point *n* **1** *c.n* temperature at which a liquid boils²(1). **2** *unique n* (often **reach —**) point at which people get so angry etc that they become violent.

boisterous /'bɔɪstrəs/ *adj* rough; violent; noisily and happily excited: *boisterous children.*
'boisterously *adv.* **boisterousness** *u.n.*

bold /bəʊld/ *adj* **1** brave; not having any fear; daring. **2** shameless; forward(4). **3** very clear; that can be seen easily. **4** (in printing) using boldface.

as bold as brass rude(ly); shameless(ly). **be/make bold to do s.t**; **make so bold as to do s.t** dare to do s.t. **make bold with s.t** use s.t that belongs to s.o else without asking permission.

'**bold,face** u.n thick dark letters like this: **BOLDFACE**.

'**boldly** adv. '**boldness** u.n.

bollard /'bɒləd/ c.n **1** short metal post beside a harbour etc or on the deck of a ship, to which ropes etc can be tied. **2** short metal post on a traffic island, to stop cars going into a street etc.

bollocks /'bɒləks/ interj/u.n **1** (slang; do not use!) nonsense; balls(1).
▷ pl.n **2** (also '**ballocks**) (slang; do not use!) testicles; balls(2).

bolster[1] /'bəʊlstə/ c.n long round pillow that is put under other pillows on a bed.

bolster[2] /'bəʊlstə/ tr.v (often — s.o/s.t up) support (s.o/s.t).

bolt[1] /bəʊlt/ adv **bolt upright** (often sit —) absolutely vertical, erect(1).

bolt[2] /bəʊlt/ c.n **1** sliding metal rod that fits into a hole, used for fastening doors, windows etc. **2** metal rod with a head at one end and a thread like a screw at the other that is screwed into a nut(2) to fasten things together. **3** flash of lightning(2) followed by thunder. **4** roll of cloth. **a bolt from the blue** (fig; informal) a thing that happens suddenly as a complete surprise.
▷ tr.v **5** close (s.t, e.g a door) with a bolt[2](1). **6** (often — s.t to s.t; — s.t together) fasten (s.t) with a bolt[2](2) or bolts.

bolt[3] /bəʊlt/ c.n **1** (often do a —) (informal) act of running away. **make a bolt for it** run away to try to escape.
▷ v **2** intr.v (often of a frightened horse) run away (out of control). **3** tr.v (often — s.t down) eat, swallow, (s.t) too quickly.

bomb /bɒm/ c.n **1** container filled with explosive material or gas that explodes on hitting the ground or is set off by a time device. ⇨ nuclear bomb. **go like a bomb** (informal) be very successful; work very well. **cost/make a bomb** (informal) cost/make a lot of money.
▷ tr/intr.v **2** attack (s.o/s.t) with a bomb(1) or bombs, esp from the air.

'**bomb di,sposal** u.n (also attrib) dealing with bombs(1) that have not exploded.

'**bomber** c.n **1** kind of plane built for bombing(2). **2** person who places or throws bombs(1).

'**bomb-,proof** adj giving protection from exploding bombs(1).

'**bomb,shell** c.n **1** explosive shell(4) or bomb(1). **2** (fig) sudden unexpected and usu unpleasant news or event; unpleasant surprise.

bombard /bɒm'bɑːd/ tr.v **1** attack (s.o/s.t) continuously with shells from big guns. **2** (fig) (often — s.o with s.t) throw questions, complaints etc at (s.o).

bom'bardment c/u.n.

bombardier /,bɒmbə'dɪə/ c.n army rank equivalent(1) in the artillery(2) of the rank of corporal(2).

bombast /'bɒmbæst/ u.n (formal) talk, speech, that sounds important but is not sincere and does not mean much.

bom'bastic adj using, containing, bombast.
bom'bastically adv.

bomber, bomb-proof, bombshell ⇨ bomb.

bond /bɒnd/ c.n **1** thing that binds or joins things together. **2** (fig) (often — between s.o and s.o) friendship (between s.o and s.o); close relationship, e.g between a parent and a child. **3** state of being joined: Make sure the glue has set so that it makes a strong bond between the pieces of wood. **4** agreement that s.o must obey, esp in law: sign a bond. **5** printed paper given out by a government etc which says that it has been lent money and that it promises to pay it back with interest. ⇨ stock(10). **in bond** held officially by customs(2) until duties are paid or it is exported(3) again.
▷ tr.v **6** (often — s.t to s.t; — s.t together) join (s.t) (to s.t etc) with a bond(3).

bondage /'bɒndɪdʒ/ u.n state of having to work for s.o without being paid; slavery(1). **in bondage** in the state of being, or as if being, a slave.

bone /bəʊn/ n **1** c.n one of the hard parts of the body of a person or animal; one part of the skeleton(2): Henry broke a bone in his arm when he fell on the ice. **2** u.n (also attrib) material of which a bone(1) is made: a bone comb. **a bone of contention** ⇨ contention. **cut s.t to the bone** (fig) cut s.t (e.g costs) down to the lowest point possible. **as dry as a bone** extremely dry. **feel (s.t) in one's bones** (fig) feel sure about s.t without having any proof. **frozen to the bone** extremely cold. **funny bone** ⇨ funny. **have a bone to pick with s.o** (fig; informal) have s.t to argue, complain, about with s.o. **make no bones about (doing) s.t** have no hesitation or doubts about doing s.t. **skin and bone(s)** ⇨ skin(n).
▷ tr.v **3** remove the bones from (s.t, e.g a fish). **bone up on s.t** (informal) study s.t very hard, usu before an examination or test.

,**bone-'dry** adj extremely dry.
,**bone-'idle/'lazy** adj very lazy.

'**bony** adj (-ier, -iest) **1** full of small bones: bony fish. **2** having big bones that can be clearly seen under the skin: bony hands.

bonfire /'bɒn,faɪə/ c.n large fire in the open air on which garden rubbish is burnt or which is used to celebrate s.t.

bonnet /'bɒnɪt/ c.n **1** woman's or young child's round hat that is often tied under the chin. **2** cover over a car engine. ⇨ hood(3). **have a bee in one's bonnet (about s.t)** ⇨ bee.

bonny /'bɒnɪ/ adj (-ier, -iest) pretty; looking healthy: a bonny baby.

bonus /'bəʊnəs/ c.n **1** payment in addition to a wage or salary: This company always pays its workers a holiday bonus. **2** advantage that was not expected: Edward's arrival at the party was a bonus because we were one man short. **no claim(s) bonus** reduction in payment for the insurance of a car if no claims for payment have been made during the past year(s).

bony ⇨ bone.

boo /buː/ interj/c.n **1** sound made to show disapproval. ⇨ goose(n).
▷ tr/intr.v **2** show disapproval of (s.o/s.t) by boos(1).

boob /buːb/ c.n **1** (usu make a —) (informal) silly unnecessary mistake. **2** (slang; do not use!) woman's breast.
▷ intr.v **3** (informal) make a boob(1).

booby /'buːbɪ/ c.n (pl -ies) (informal; becoming old use) silly stupid person.

'**booby ,prize** c.n small prize of little value given to the person who is last in a race etc.

'booby ,trap c.n 1 thing that seems to be harmless but explodes when it is touched. 2 thing that is placed s.w to surprise s.o, e.g a book balanced on top of a door which falls on s.o's head when he/she comes in.

book /buk/ c.n 1 number of sheets of paper, usu with writing on them, which are bound together along one edge. ⇒ hardback, paperback. 2 work of literature etc: *I enjoy reading travel books.* 3 one of the main parts of a big book(1,2): *The Book of Genesis begins the* Bible(1). 4 packet of the same things fastened together: *a book of matches/ stamps.* 5 list of bets(1). *be a closed book (to s.o)* (*fig*) be a subject about which s.o knows (almost) nothing. *bring s.o to book* make s.o explain her/his actions. *go by the book/rules* follow the rules exactly, even when they are not relevant. *suit s.o's book* suit s.o. *take a leaf out of s.o's book* ⇒ leaf(*n*).
▷ *v* 6 *tr/intr.v* reserve (seats, tickets etc) on a train, in a theatre etc. 7 *tr.v* enter (s.t, the name of (s.o)) in a book: *The man was taken to the police station and booked for hitting a police officer.* 8 *tr.v* get the services of (s.o, e.g a speaker for a meeting). *book (s.o)* reserve a place (for oneself/s.o) in a hotel etc; sign one's/s.o's name at a hotel so that one/he/she can stay there. *book (s.o) out* sign etc that one/s.o is leaving a hotel. (*fully*) *booked*; *booked up* (of a restaurant, plane etc) having no more seats free.

'book,case c.n piece of furniture with shelves for books.

'book ,club c.n organization that sells books to its members at a reduced price in return for a promise to buy not less than a certain number of books every year etc.

'book ,end c.n (usu *pl*; often *a pair(1) of — s*) heavy ornament supporting one end of a row of books.

'bookie c.n (*informal*) bookmaker.

'booking c.n (often *make a —*) booking (⇒ book(6)) of a seat etc.

'booking ,clerk c.n person who sells tickets and/or reserves seats for people, esp at a railway station.

'booking ,office c.n (*abbr BO*) place where one buys tickets for travel, the theatre etc.

'bookish adj (often *derog*) more interested in books and reading than in practical things.

'bookishness u.n.

'book-,keeper c.n person who keeps the accounts(1) of a company.

'book-,keeping u.n (skill in, system of) keeping accounts(1).

booklet /'buklit/ c.n small book, usu with paper covers.

'book,maker c.n (*informal* 'bookie) person whose job is taking bets(1) at horse races etc.

'book,mark c.n (also 'book,marker) thing placed between the pages of a book to mark a certain place, usu one that a reader has reached.

books pl.n (often *keep the —*) accounts etc, usu of a company. *be in s.o's bad/good books* be disapproved/approved of by s.o. *cook the books* (*commerce*; *informal*) make false statements in the accounts(1) in order to deceive people, hide the bad state of affairs, steal money etc.

'book,seller c.n person whose trade is selling books.

'book,shelf c.n. shelf for books.

'book,stall c.n kind of small shop, often in a railway station etc, where books, newspapers etc are sold.

'book ,token c.n gift voucher allowing s.o to buy books to the value shown on it.

'book,worm c.n (*fig*) person who is very fond of reading.

boom[1] /bu:m/ c.n 1 barrier(1) of logs, chains etc across a river or harbour entrance to stop ships etc getting in or out. 2 long pole at the bottom of a sail. 3 pole used for lifting things on a ship. 4 long arm to which a microphone is fixed.

boom[2] /bu:m/ c.n 1 deep hollow sound, e.g of big guns. *sonic boom* ⇒ sonic.
▷ *intr.v* 2 (often *— out*) make the sound of a boom[2](1).

boom[3] /bu:m/ c.n 1 (often *— in s.t*) rapid increase (in s.t, e.g business).
▷ *intr.v* 2 (often of business) increase rapidly: *Sales are booming.*

boomerang /'bu:mə,ræŋ/ c.n 1 curved weapon made of hard wood which can be thrown in such a way that it comes back to the place where it started.
▷ *intr.v* 2 (often *— on s.o*) (*fig*) (of s.t s.o does) not work in the expected way but come back and affect s.o badly: *His lies about them boomeranged (on him) and he was shown to be untruthful.*

boon /bu:n/ c.n (*formal*) advantage; thing that one should be thankful for.

,boon com'panion c.n favourite companion, esp when one is having fun together.

boor /buə/ c.n (*derog*) rude person who has bad manners.

'boorish adj (*derog*) rude; having bad manners.

'boorishly adv. 'boorishness u.n.

boost /bu:st/ c.n 1 (often *— from s.o/s.t*; *give s.o/ s.t a —*) encouragement (from s.o/s.t); help to increase, improve etc.
▷ *tr.v* 2 give (s.o/s.t) a boost(1). 3 increase the value, popularity etc of (s.o/s.t).

'booster c.n (also *attrib*) 1 thing that gives extra power or efficiency, e.g in a rocket(3) or an electrical system. 2 injection given to prevent an earlier one losing its power.

boot /bu:t/ c.n 1 thing made of leather, rubber etc that is worn on one's foot and goes up higher than one's ankle. Compare shoe(1), wellington. 2 (in a car, usu at the back) place where luggage is put. ⇒ trunk(4). (*as*) *tough as old boots* ⇒ tough. *be/ get/grow too big for one's boots* (*fig*; *informal*) be/become too proud; (begin to) think that one is more important than one really is. *get, give s.o, the boot* (*slang*) be dismissed, dismiss s.o, usu from one's job. *put the boot in* (*slang*) (a) kick s.o in a fight, esp when he/she is lying on the ground. (b) (*fig*) make a bad situation even worse for s.o.
▷ *tr.v* 3 kick (s.o/s.t). *boot s.o out* (*slang*) dismiss s.o, usu from her/his job.

bootee /bu:'ti:/ c.n 1 knitted woollen boot for a baby. 2 short boot worn by a woman, often warmly lined.

'boot,lace c.n string or strip of leather used for fastening a boot by putting it through holes.

booth /buː:ð/ *c.n* **1** shelter made of light material that keeps out water, esp one where goods are sold in a market etc. **2** = telephone booth. **listening booth** ⇒ listening. **polling booth** ⇒ polling.

booty /'buː:tɪ/ *u.n* things taken by thieves or from an enemy in war.

booze /buːz/ *u.n* **1** (*slang*) alcoholic(1) drink. **be/go on the booze** be/start drinking heavily.

▷ *intr.v* **2** (*slang*) drink booze(1), esp too much of it.

'boozer *c.n* (*slang*) **1** person who boozes(2). **2** pub.

'boozy *adj* (*-ier, -iest*) (*slang*) drunk(en): *a boozy weekend.*

boracic acid /bəˌræsɪk 'æsɪd/ (also **,boric 'acid** /ˌbɒrɪk/) *u.n* kind of white powder used as a very weak antiseptic, *chem.form* H₃BO₃.

border /'bɔː:də/ *c.n* **1** (often *the — of s.t*) edge/ side (of s.t). **2** land, line, between two countries, states etc. **3** strip of ground forming the edge of a garden. **4** edge to a piece of cloth.

▷ *tr.v* **5** form a border to (s.t). **border (up)on s.t** (**a**) be next to s.t. (**b**) (*fig*) be/seem nearly the same as s.t: *His remarks bordered on rudeness.*

'border,land *c.n* **1** area of land near, on either side of, a border(2). **2** (*fig*) condition that is between two conditions: *the borderland between sleep and waking.*

'border,line *c.n* **1** line that marks a border(2). **2** (also *attrib*) area that is in a borderland(2): *John is a borderline case; his examination results were poor but so near a pass that he has been allowed to continue his studies.*

bore¹ /bɔː:/ *c.n* **1** (*derog*) person or thing who/ that is not at all interesting: *Charles is a bore; he is always talking about how important his job is. We have to stay at home and work instead of going to the cinema; what a bore!*

▷ *tr.v* **2** make (s.o) feel tired in mind and not at all interested: *The whole subject bores me.* **bore s.o stiff, to death/tears** (*fig*) bore¹(2) s.o very much.

'boredom *u.n* state or fact of being bored¹(2).

'boring *adj* who/that bores¹(2) s.o: *a boring person/talk.*

bore² /bɔː:/ *c.n* **1** hole made by drilling into the ground, e.g to try to find water. **2** distance across the inside of a gun barrel, etc.

▷ *tr/intr.v* **3** make a hole in, through, (s.t) with a tool or tools.

'bore-,hole *c.n* hole drilled into the ground to try to find oil etc.

'borer *c.n* insect/tool/person that/who drills holes.

bore³ /bɔː:/ *c.n* high tidal wave that is found in some rivers: *the Severn bore.*

bore⁴ /bɔː:/ *p.t* of bear².

boric acid ⇒ boracic acid.

born /bɔː:n/ *attrib.adj* **1** natural; perfect: *a born swimmer.*

▷ *v* **2 be born** (*p.p* in the passive of bear²(4)): *I was born in 1972. Sophie was born German but became British by marriage.* **be born of s.o** (*formal*) have s.o as one's parent(s) or ancestors. **be born of s.t** (*formal*) be the result of s.t: *John's criminal activities were born of poverty and hunger.* **be born to do s.t** be destined(3) to do s.t; having as one's fate to do s.t.

borne /bɔː:n/ *p.p* of bear².

borough /'bʌrə/ *c.n* (part of) town that has its own mayor, council and officials.

borrow /'bɒrəʊ/ *tr/intr.v* (often *— (s.t) from s.o/s.t*) **1** receive (s.t) (from s.o/s.t) on loan for some time with the duty of returning it again after that; get/use (s.t) for a short time with the owner's permission. **2** take and use (s.t, e.g s.o's ideas, a word from another language). **borrow (money etc) against s.t** borrow(1) (money) using s.t as security(3) if one fails to repay the loan.

'borrower *c.n* person who borrows (s.t).

'borrowing *c.n* (often *— from s.o/s.t*) thing borrowed(2) (from s.o/s.t).

borstal /'bɔː:stəl/ *c/u.n* (also with capital **B**) kind of prison to which young people who are guilty of crimes are sent by a judge.

bosh /bɒʃ/ *u.n* (*slang*; becoming *old use*) nonsense: *Don't talk bosh!*

bosom /'bʊzəm/ *c.n* **1** human chest, esp of a woman. **2** one of a woman's breasts(1). **3** centre, inner part, in which one feels sadness, happiness etc. **in the bosom of one's family** in the close friendship of one's family.

boss¹ /bɒs/ *c.n* **1** (*informal*) employer; manager; leader.

▷ *tr.v* **2** (often *— s.o about/around*) give (s.o) orders, usu in an unpleasant way.

'bossy *adj* (*-ier, -iest*) fond of giving orders, usu in an unpleasant way.

boss² /bɒs/ *c.n* round piece of decoration, usu made of metal, esp in the centre of a shield.

bosun /'bəʊsn/ *c.n* boatswain.

botany /'bɒtənɪ/ *u.n* scientific study of plants.

botanical /bə'tænɪkl/ *adj* of or referring to botany.

bo,tanical 'gardens *pl.n* place where plants are grown for scientific study and for people to come and look at them.

'botanist *c.n* person who studies, is skilled in, botany.

botch /bɒtʃ/ *tr.v* spoil (s.t) by doing it carelessly or without skill, often in an attempt to repair it.

both /bəʊθ/ *adj* **1** (of two persons/animals/ things) the two; the one and the other: *She was unable to get both (the) cars into the garage.*

▷ *conj* **2 both . . . and . . .** not only . . . but also . . .: *Both Mary and Fred are here. I both saw and heard them.*

▷ *pron* **3** (often *— of them, us, the girls* etc) the two (of them etc); the one and also the other (of them etc): *'I want those two books.' 'You can have one but not both (of them).'* **we, you, those men** etc **both** the two of us, you etc: *The twins both want to come to the cinema this evening.*

bother /'bɒðə/ *n* **1** *u.n* worry; trouble; nuisance: *Did you have much bother finding the theatre?* **2** *c.n* person or thing who/that causes bother(1): *My bad tooth is a bother to me.*

▷ *v* **3** *tr.v* annoy (s.o); cause trouble to (s.o). **4** *intr.v* (often *— to do s.t*) worry oneself; take trouble (to do s.t): *Don't bother to shut the door; I'm going out in a few moments.* **5** (expression showing annoyance): *Bother this weather! Bother (it)!* **bother one's head about s.t** be worried about s.t. **hot and bothered** ⇒ hot(*adj*). **I'm sorry to bother you, but . . .** (said when one wants s.t from s.o) I'm sorry to disturb or inconvenience(2) you, but . . .

'bothersome *adj* annoying; troublesome.

bottle /'bɒtl/ c.n **1** container, usu made of glass, that has a narrow neck and is for holding liquids: *a milk bottle*; *a wine bottle*. **2** (also **'bottleful**) as much as a bottle(1) holds: *I drank a bottle of milk*. **be fond of the bottle** (*informal*) like alcoholic(1) drinks very much. **hit the bottle** begin drinking alcohol.
▷ *tr.v* **3** put (s.t) in a bottle(1), sometimes for storing: *bottle fruit*. **bottle s.t up** (*fig*) keep control of s.t; prevent s.t, e.g anger, showing itself.
'bottle-,feed *tr/intr.v* (*p.t,p.p* bottle-fed/-fed/) feed (a baby) with milk from a special bottle. Compare breast-feed.
'bottleful c.n = bottle(2).
,bottle 'green *adj/u.n* dark green.
'bottle,neck c.n (*fig*) **1** narrow part of a road or a place in a road where it is being repaired that slows traffic down. **2** part of a production system etc where there are problems that cause delays.

bottom /'bɒtəm/ *attrib.adj* **1** lowest: *Please put that book on the bottom shelf.*
▷ *c.n* **2** (often *the — of s.t*) lowest or deepest part (of s.t). **3** (*informal*) part of one's body which one sits on; buttocks. **3** seat (of a chair etc). **4** bed (of the sea, a river etc). **5** underpart of a ship. **6** lowest place or position, e.g in a class. **at bottom** (*fig*) really; underneath all the appearances: *At bottom he's a kind man.* **at the bottom of s.t** the cause, basis, of s.t; responsible for s.t: *Who is at the bottom of all this trouble?* **from the bottom of s.o's heart** (*fig*) truly; sincerely. **from top to bottom** ⇒ top¹(n). **get to the bottom of s.t** (*informal*) find out the real cause of, reason for, s.t. **knock the bottom out of s.t** (*fig*) prove that s.t is not true or valuable. **rock-bottom** ⇒ rock¹. **touch bottom** (a) (of a ship etc) run aground. (b) (*fig*) reach a point where things cannot get worse.
'bottomless *adj* very deep; so deep that one cannot reach the bottom. **2** (*fig*) that never finishes or runs out: *Chris seems to have a bottomless supply of energy*(1).

bough /baʊ/ c.n big branch of a tree.
bought /bɔ:t/ *p.t,p.p* of buy.
boulder /'bəʊldə/ c.n large stone or piece of rock, often one that has been shaped by water or the weather.

bounce /baʊns/ *n* **1** c/u.n act or fact of bouncing(3,6). **2** u.n ability to bounce(3): *There is still plenty of bounce in this old ball.*
▷ *v* **3** *tr/intr.v* (cause (s.o/s.t) to) spring back after hitting s.t: *Dorothy is good at bouncing a ball off a wall and catching it*. **4** *tr/intr.v* (cause (s.o/s.t) to) move up and down quickly and violently: *Children love bouncing on their beds.* **5** *intr.v* get up quickly: *The students bounced out of their chairs when the headteacher came in.* **6** *intr.v* move about, along, quickly and noisily: *Peter bounced angrily from one office to another looking for the manager.* **7** (*informal*) (of a cheque) be returned by a bank because there is not enough money in the account to pay it. **bounce back** (*fig*) return cheerfully after a piece of bad luck.
bound¹ /baʊnd/ *adj* (of a book) having its leaves fixed together at one side inside covers. Opposite unbound. **bound for s.w** going s.w; in the direction of s.t. **bound to do s.t** (a) certain to do s.t: *Doris is bound to pass by here on her way*

to work. (b) forced, obliged(1), to do s.t by law, custom etc. **bound up in/with s.t** busy with s.t. **bound up with s.o/s.t** closely connected with s.o/s.t. **homeward bound** going home.
bound² /baʊnd/ c.n **1** sudden upward and/or forward movement; jump: *With one bound the cat was on the wall.*
▷ *intr.v* **2** jump upward and/or forward. **by leaps and bounds** ⇒ leap(n).
bound³ /baʊnd/ *tr.v* limit (s.t); be the boundary of (s.t): *Britain is bounded by sea on all sides.*
bounds *pl.n* limits; boundaries; ends: *There are no bounds to the things Alexander will do to succeed.* **in bounds** (**to s.o**) within the limits of the place where s.o is allowed. **out of bounds** (**to s.o**) outside the limits allowed. Compare unbounded.
'boundless *adj* not having any limits; infinite(1).
bound⁴ /baʊnd/ *p.t,p.p* of bind(2).
boundary /'baʊndərɪ/ c.n (*pl -ies*) **1** thing that marks the limit of s.t; dividing line. **2** (in cricket¹) (a) line round the total area in which the game is played. (b) hit over the boundary(2a), which scores four or six runs(8).
bounty /'baʊntɪ/ (*pl. -ies*) (*formal*) **1** u.n freedom in giving; generosity. **2** c.n gift. **3** c.n payment offered to encourage s.o to do s.t: *We received a generous bounty for capturing the escaped prisoner.*
bounteous /'baʊntɪəs/ *adj* (also **'bountiful**) (*literary* or *formal*) **1** generous; giving a lot. **2** plentiful.
'bounteously *adv* (also **'bountifully**).
'bounteousness *u.n* (also **'bountifulness**).
bouquet /bʊ'keɪ/ *c.n* **1** c.n bunch of flowers, usu for carrying by hand. **2** c/u.n smell of wine etc.
bourgeois /'bʊəʒwɑ:/ c.n (also *attrib*) (*French*) **1** (often *derog*) member of the middle class, esp s.o working in trade. **2** (*derog*) capitalist(2). **3** (*derog*) lacking good breeding(2) or culture(2).
bourgeoisie /,bʊəʒwɑ:'zi:/ *def/def.pl.n* (used with sing or pl v) bourgeois(1,2) people.
bout /baʊt/ c.n **1** limited time of doing s.t or of s.t happening: *a bout of flu.* **2** (esp in boxing) fight.
boutique /bu:'ti:k/ c.n (*French*) small shop, part of a big shop, in which fashionable clothes etc are sold.
bovine /'bəʊvaɪn/ *adj* **1** of or referring to cattle. **2** (*fig*) dull; stupid.
bow¹ /baʊ/ c.n **1** (often in *pl*) front/forward part of a boat, ship or plane. **2** person who rows nearest the bow¹(1) of a rowing boat.
bow² /baʊ/ c.n **1** act of bending the head and/ or body to show respect and/or to greet s.o formally.
▷ *v* **2** *intr.v* bend one's head and/or body in a bow²(1): *He bowed politely.* **3** *tr.v* bend (one's head) downwards in a bow²(1): *He bowed his head in shame.* **4** *intr.v* (usu passive) bend down: *The branches were bowed with the weight of fruit on them.* **bow and scrape** (**to s.o**) (*derog*; *fig*) be too obedient (to s.o). **bow s.o in/out** bow as s.o comes in, goes out. **bow to s.o's opinion, knowledge** etc (*fig*) accept s.o's opinion etc because one thinks her/him wiser etc than oneself.
bow³ /bəʊ/ c.n **1** weapon used for shooting arrows; it is usu made of a piece of wood that is bent into a curve and kept in that position by a tightly stretched string. **2** long thin piece of

wood with horsehair stretched from end to end of it, used for playing a violin etc. **3** kind of big knot tied in a ribbon, string etc as a decoration: *The little girl had a pretty white bow in her hair.* **4** curve. ⇨ rainbow. **have more than one string to one's bow**; **have a second string to one's bow** ⇨ string.

bowlegged /ˌbəʊˈlegɪd/ *adj* having legs that curve outwards above the knees and then back inwards below them. ⇨ bandy-legged (⇨ bandy¹). Compare knock-kneed.

ˌbow ˈlegs *pl.n* legs that curve outwards and then inwards: *We bought a chair with bow legs.* Compare bow-legged.

ˈbowˌtie *c.n* tie(1) knotted round the neck with a bow(3) in the front.

ˌbow ˈwindow *c.n* curved window that sticks out from the wall of a building. Compare bay³(1).

bowel /ˈbaʊəl/ *c.n* (usu *pl*) part of the alimentary canal that joins the stomach to the anus. ⇨ intestine.

ˈbowels *pl.n* **1** ⇨ bowel. **2** (*fig*) (often *the — of s.t*) inner part (of s.t, e.g a mountain). **keep one's bowels open** defecate regularly.

bower /ˈbaʊə/ *c.n* (*literary*) shady place in a garden, formed by trees, climbing plants etc.

bowl¹ /bəʊl/ *c.n* **1** round deep hollow dish used for holding or mixing liquids, food etc. **2** (also ˈbowlful) amount a bowl¹(1) holds. **3** basin, e.g for washing in. **4** thing shaped like a bowl¹(1): *Joe put some tobacco in the bowl of his pipe.*
ˈbowlful *c.n* = bowl¹(2).

bowl² /bəʊl/ *c.n* **1** hard wooden ball that has a weight on one side so that it will run in a curve on the ground in the game of bowls.
▷ *v* **2** *intr.v* play bowls. **3** *tr/intr.v* (in cricket¹) send (a ball) to the batsman by moving one's arm over the shoulder. **bowl along** move smoothly and usu quickly. **bowl s.o (out)** (in cricket¹) hit a wicket(1) so that he/she is out(19). **bowl s.o/s.t over (a)** knock s.o/s.t over. **(b)** (*fig*) surprise or shock s.o very much.

ˈbowler *c.n* **1** (in cricket¹) person who bowls²(3). **2** (also ˌbowler ˈhat) kind of formal, usu black, hard hat.

bowls *u.n* game played, usu on grass, by two people or teams who try to roll bowls (⇨ bowl²(1)) as near a small white ball as possible.

bowwow /ˈbaʊˌwaʊ/ *c.n* **1** (small child's word for) dog.
▷ *interj* /ˌbaʊˈwaʊ/ **2** (small child's imitation of a) dog's bark.

box¹ /bɒks/ **1** container, usu made of wood or cardboard and usu with a lid, used for holding solid objects. ⇨ matchbox, toolbox. **2** (also ˈboxful) as much as a box¹(1) contains. **3** (a container with) a wide hole for posting letters etc. ⇨ letterbox, postbox. **4** separate little space in a theatre etc which has several chairs in it. **5** part of a law court which is used for a particular purpose: *the* jury(1) *box*; *the* witness(2) *box*. **6** separate part in a stable²(1) or railway truck for a horse. ⇨ horsebox. **7** small hut or shelter for a guard: *a* sentry box. **8** (*slang*) coffin. **a (post office) box (number)** (*abbr PO Box*) (the number of) a box in a post office to which letters can be sent, to be collected from there.
▷ *tr.v* **9** (often *— s.t up*) put (s.t) in a box¹(1). **box s.o/s.t in/up** (*fig*) enclose s.o/s.t in a small space.

ˌbox ˈcamera *c.n* kind of camera that is shaped like a box¹(1).

ˈboxful *c.n* = box¹(2).

ˈbox-ˌkite *c.n* kite that is made in the shape of two boxes¹(1) joined together with rods.

ˈbox ˌoffice *c.n* (*written abbr BO*) place in a theatre etc where tickets are sold.

box² /bɒks/ *tr/intr.v* fight (s.o) wearing gloves over one's hands as a kind of sport. **box s.o's ears** hit s.o on the ears with one's open hands.

ˈboxer *c.n* **1** person who boxes². **2** kind of dog that has smooth brown hair and a flat face.

ˈboxing *u.n* (also *attrib*) sport in which people box²: *boxing gloves.*

box³ /bɒks/ *c.n* (also ˈbox ˌtree) kind of small evergreen(1) tree.

Boxing Day /ˈbɒksɪŋ ˌdeɪ/ *unique n* day after Christmas.

boy /bɔɪ/ *c.n* **1** baby or child of the male sex. **2** young man: *She is shy with boys.* **3** (*informal*) son of any age: *There were three boys and two girls in the family.* **man and boy** ⇨ man(n). **one of the boys** (*informal*) member of a group of young men who do things together: *John can't be one of the boys yet because he hasn't got a motorbike.*

ˈboyˌfriend *c.n* boy or man with whom a girl or woman is friendly, with whom she goes out etc. Compare girlfriend(1).

ˈboyˌhood *u.n* length of time when one is a boy.

ˈboyish /ˈbɔɪɪʃ/ *adj* of/like a boy; acting/looking like a boy, esp when one is an older man or when one is a girl or woman: *Helen has a boyish look.*
ˈboyishly *adv.* ˈboyishness *u.n.*

ˌBoy ˈScout *c.n* (*old use*) = Scout(1).

boycott /ˈbɔɪkɒt/ *c.n* **1** joining with others in refusing to deal, trade, or have anything to do, with another person, company, country etc.
▷ *tr.v* **2** join together to treat (s.o, a company etc) in this way.

bra /brɑː/ *c.n* (*formal* = brassiere) piece of underclothing, for supporting a woman's breasts(1).

brace¹ /breɪs/ *c.n* **1** thing that supports or strengthens (s.t), that makes it firm or solid. **2** (often *pl*) metal wire etc fastened around teeth to make them grow straight. **3** sign { or } used in writing and printing to enclose words, numbers etc. ⇨ bracket(2).
▷ *tr.v* **4** support or strengthen (s.t); make (s.t) firm, solid. **brace oneself (a)** place one's feet firmly and prepare to resist s.t. **(b)** (*fig*) get ready for s.t difficult or unpleasant. **brace (s.o) up** (cause (s.o) to) stop being lazy or careless.

ˈbracing *adj* that causes one to become more energetic: *a cold bracing climate.*

brace² /breɪs/ *c.n* tool that holds and turns a bit¹(2) for drilling holes.

ˌbrace and ˈbit *c.n* tool consisting of a brace² and a bit¹(2).

brace³ /breɪs/ *c.n* (often *a — of s.t*) two (dogs, wild birds such as partridge that are hunted and shot, or shotguns).

bracelet /ˈbreɪslɪt/ *c.n* band or chain worn round one's wrist or arm as an ornament.

braces /ˈbreɪsɪz/ *pl.n* (US susˈpenders) two strips of material, leather etc that go over one's shoulders to keep one's trousers up; they are fastened to the front and back of the trousers, usu with buttons or clips(1).

bracken /'brækən/ *u.n* (mass of a) kind of large fern that grows in forests, on rough land etc.

bracket /'brækɪt/ *c.n* **1** support, usu made of metal or wood, for a shelf on a wall. **2** sign (or), [or], used in writing or printing to enclose words, numbers etc: *round brackets* (i.e ( )); *square brackets* (i.e [ ]). ⇒ braces¹(3), parenthesis(1). **3** groups of people who are classified together: *an age bracket* (i.e all the people who are between certain ages); *an income bracket* (i.e all the people whose incomes are between certain amounts). *in brackets* having a bracket(2) before and another one after it.

▷ *tr.v* **4** enclose (s.t) in brackets(2). **5** join (s.o/s.t) by brackets(2). *bracket s.t off (from s.t)* separate s.t (from s.t) by brackets(2). *bracket s.o/s.t together; brackets.o/s.t with s.o/s.t (informal)* put s.o/s.t together to show a connection or equality: *Emily and Mary are bracketed together at the top of our class.*

brackish /'brækɪʃ/ *adj* (of water) tasting slightly salty.

bradawl /'bræd,ɔːl/ *c.n* kind of tool for making holes in wood etc, usu for nails or screws to be put in to start them.

brag /bræg/ *intr.v* (-gg-) (often — *about/of* s.t) boast.

braid /breɪd/ *n* **1** *c.n* number of separate pieces of hair which are woven together: *The little girl usually wore her hair in a braid.* **2** *u.n* band of woven threads, esp of gold or silver, used to edge cloth or for decoration: *The officer had gold braid on his shoulders and his cap.*

▷ *tr.v* **3** put (hair) into one or more braids(1). **4** make (s.t) into braid(2). **5** edge (s.t) with braid(2).

braille /breɪl/ *u.n* system of printing that uses raised dots so that blind people can read it by touch.

brain /breɪn/ *n* **1** *c/u.n* soft grey substance in the head of persons and animals which controls the nervous system. **2** *c/u.n* brain(1) used as food: *sheep's brains.* **3** *c/u.n* mind; intelligence: *Use your brain!* **4** *c.n* (*informal*) intelligent person. *have s.t on one's/the brain* think about s.t (almost) all the time. *tax s.o's brain* have, give s.o, s.t to do that needs a lot of hard thought.

▷ *tr.v* **5** (*informal*) hit (s.o) on the head: *I'll brain you if you do that again!*

'**brain ,drain** *c/def.n* movement of scientists and other clever people to another country for better pay, opportunities etc.

'**brainless** *adj* (*derog*) very stupid.

brains *pl.n* = brain(2–4). *beat/rack one's brains (about s.t)* think very hard (about s.t). *blow one's brains out* kill oneself by shooting oneself in the head. *the brains of the family* etc (*informal*) the cleverest person in the family etc. *pick s.o's brains* get information from s.o else instead of studying or learning it oneself.

'**brain,wash** *tr.v* make (s.o) forget what he/she knew before and believe new things by using clever psychological(2) pressure.

'**brain,wave** *c.n* (*informal*) sudden clever idea.

'**brainy** *adj* (-ier, -iest) (*informal*) intelligent.

braise /breɪz/ *tr.v* cook (meat etc) slowly in a covered pan.

brake /breɪk/ *c.n* **1** device that reduces the speed or movement of a vehicle or machine. *apply the brake; put the brake on* make the brake start to operate. *release the brake* take the pressure off the brake so that it allows the vehicle etc to move normally again. *jam/slam on the brake(s)* (*informal*) use the brakes hard and suddenly.

▷ *tr/intr.v* **2** (cause (a vehicle etc) to) stop by putting the brake(s) on: *The car/driver in front of me braked suddenly.*

'**brake-,light** *c.n* one of a pair of red lights at the back of a vehicle that lights up when one uses the brakes(1).

'**brake ,shoe** *c.n* = shoe(3).

bramble /'bræmbl/ *c.n* kind of wild plant, esp the wild blackberry, which has a lot of sharp thorns on its long shoots.

bran /bræn/ *u.n* (also *attrib*) outer covering of grain which is taken off before flour is made, used as a coarse food: *bran* flakes.

branch /brɑːntʃ/ *c.n* **1** long part that grows out of the trunk of a tree. **2** long part that is joined to the main part of a railway, river etc. **3** part of s.t, e.g a family, a language or a subject such as history, that can be considered separately from the rest. **4** local part of a company etc that is separate from the main/central part: *Our bank has branches all over the country.*

▷ *intr.v* **5** put out branches(1). **6** (often — *out*) separate, divide, into branches(1,2,4). *branch off (from s.t)* leave s.t, e.g a main road, and go off s.w else, e.g along a side road; take a new direction. *branch out (into s.t)* (of a person, company etc) start doing one or more new or different things.

brand /brænd/ *c.n* **1** particular make of s.t: *I like this brand of coffee.* **2** trademark printed on s.t. **3** particular kind of s.t: *I don't like David's brand of joke because it is cruel.* **4** mark made on an animal by pressing a red-hot iron on its skin to show who owns it.

▷ *tr.v* **5** mark (s.t) with a brand(2,4). *brand s.o/s.t (as) s.t* (*fig*) call s.o/s.t s.t as a criticism: *He was branded (as) a liar. brand s.t on s.o's memory* (*fig*) make a deep impression on s.o so that it cannot be forgotten.

'**brand ,name** *c.n* name for a brand(1,2) of s.t, esp one given or owned by a company.

,**brand-'new** *adj* absolutely new; never having been used.

brandish /'brændɪʃ/ *tr.v* wave (s.t, e.g a sword) about in order to show it or as a threat.

brandy /'brændɪ/ *n* (*pl* -ies) (also *attrib*) **1** *c/ u.n* (type of) strong alcoholic(1) drink: *cherry(1) brandy; brandy glasses.* **2** *c.n* portion of brandy(1): *Two brandies, please.*

brash /bræʃ/ *adj* (*derog*) **1** foolishly bold and hasty. **2** rudely proud without good reason.

'**brashly** *adv.* '**brashness** *u.n.*

brass /brɑːs/ *u.n* (also *attrib*) **1** *u.n* kind of bright yellow metal made by mixing copper(1) and zinc. **2** *def/u.n* (*fig*) cheek(2); nerve(3): *Joe had the brass to ask his new girlfriend to lend him £10.* **3** *u.n* (*slang*) money. **4** *def.n* the musical instruments that are made of brass, e.g trumpets. *as bold as brass* ⇒ bold.

,**brass 'band** *c.n* band of musicians who play brass instruments.

,**brass 'plate** *c.n* piece of metal etc fixed on a door or gate with the name and profession of s.o, e.g a doctor or lawyer.

brassiere, brassière /ˈbræsɪə/ *c.n* (*formal*) ⇒ bra.

brat /bræt/ *c.n* (*derog*) unpleasant spoilt child.

bravado /brəˈvɑːdəʊ/ *u.n* show of boldness whose purpose is to win admiration or to pretend that one is not afraid: *an act of bravado.*

brave /breɪv/ *adj* without fear; courageous; bold.
'**bravely** *adv*. **bravery** /ˈbreɪvəri/ *u.n*.

bravo /brɑːˈvəʊ/ *interj* well done; very good; excellent.

brawl /brɔːl/ *c.n* 1 noisy quarrel, argument or fight.
▷ *intr.v* 2 quarrel, argue or fight noisily.

brawn /brɔːn/ *u.n* 1 strength; power of one's muscles(1). 2 cooked pork pressed in a pot with jelly(3).
'**brawny** *adj* (-*ier*, -*iest*) strong in body; having strong muscles(1).

bray /breɪ/ *c.n* 1 cry of a donkey. 2 sound like a bray(1), e.g made by trumpets.
▷ *intr.v* 3 make a sound of, like, a bray(1).

brazen /ˈbreɪzn/ *adj* 1 made of, like, brass(1). 2 (*fig*; *derog*) not having any shame; shameless.
'**brazenly** *adv* in a brazen(2) way. '**brazenness** *u.n*.

brazier /ˈbreɪzɪə/ *c.n* open iron framework like a basket on legs, used for burning coal in for keeping warm and/or cooking outdoors.

Brazil /brəˈzɪl/ *c.n* (also **Bra'zil ,nut**) kind of very hard dark-brown nut.

breach /briːtʃ/ *c.n* 1 (often *a — of s.t*) breaking (of a rule, agreement, promise etc). 2 opening, gap, made in a wall etc, esp by enemy guns. *a breach of the peace* (*law*) unlawful fighting in a public place. *breach of contract* failure to carry out (some part of) a contract(1) (and so running the risk of legal action). *breach of promise* (*law*) refusal to marry after having agreed to do so. *fill the breach*; *step into the breach* (*fig*) come forward to help when s.o who should be doing the job fails to do so.
▷ *tr.v* 3 make a breach(1,2) in (s.t); break (through) (s.t).

bread /bred/ *u.n* 1 kind of food made by mixing flour, water and usu yeast and then baking the mixture in an oven: *a loaf of brown bread.* 2 (*informal*) food of any kind. 3 (*slang*) money. *one's daily bread* (*fig*) one's regular earnings for making a living. *earn one's bread* earn money to live on. *know which side one's bread is buttered on* know what is to one's advantage or in one's interests. *take the bread out of s.o's mouth* take away s.o's way of earning a living.
,**bread and 'butter** *u.n* 1 slice(s) of bread spread with butter. 2 (*fig*; *informal*) way of earning a living.
'**bread,board** *c.n* board, usu made of wood, on which one cuts or slices bread.
'**bread,crumb** *c.n* small bit of bread, used in cooking, e.g to cover fish before frying it.
'**bread,line** *def.n* **on the breadline** very poor; with only just enough money to live.
'**bread,winner** *c.n* person who supports a family by her/his earnings.

breadth /bredθ/ *u.n* 1 distance from one side or edge of s.t to the other; width. Compare length(1). 2 (of a person's mind) wide range(7): *Her breadth of understanding of world problems*

was extraordinary. Compare broad(4). *the length and breadth of s.t* ⇒ length.

break /breɪk/ *n* 1 *c.n* (often — *in s.t*) place where (s.t) is divided or separated into two parts, usu as a result of force: *Harry had two breaks in the bones of his left arm after the accident.* 2 *c/u.n* (often — *in s.t*) interruption (of s.t): *There was one break in our discussions of ten minutes while our manager was on the telephone.* 3 *c/u.n* time for resting; short holiday: *We only have half an hour for our lunch break. The travel company is offering cheap winter breaks.* 4 *c.n* (often *a — in s.t*) change (in s.t): *There was a break in the fine weather yesterday and we had rain.* 5 *c.n* (in cricket') change of direction of the ball after it hits the ground after having been bowled²(3). 6 *c.n* (in billiards or snooker(1)) continuous score of one player: *a break of 90.* 7 *c.n* (*informal*) piece of luck: *a bad break* (i.e a piece of bad luck). (*at*) *break of day* (at) daybreak. ⇒ break(15). *get, give s.o, a break* (*informal*) get, give s.o, a chance to improve things. *without a break* continuously: *We worked ten hours without a break*
▷ *v* (*p.t* broke /brəʊk/, *p.p* broken /ˈbrəʊkən/) 8 *tr/ intr.v* (cause (s.t) to) divide or separate into parts by force: *The ball hit the window and broke it. The jar fell on the floor and broke.* 9 *tr.v* have an accident in which one breaks(8) (s.t): *Simon has broken one of his legs.* 10 *tr.v* cause (s.t) to stop working by damaging a part of it: *Mary broke her watch by winding it too much.* 11 *tr.v* force (s.o) to do, say etc s.t he/she had refused to do, etc: *After several hours the police broke the man and he confessed.* 12 *tr.v* (often — *s.t in*) train (an animal, esp a horse) that has never been trained before, to allow itself to be ridden, driven etc. 13 *tr.v* interrupt (s.t); stop (s.t) for a short time: *break one's journey in Bombay.* 14 *tr.v* do s.t that is against (a law, a rule etc). 15 *intr.v* (of the day) begin: *Day breaks at 5 now* (i.e dawn(1) is at 5). ⇒ daybreak. 16 *intr.v* (of a boy's voice) change in quality on reaching puberty: *John's voice broke when he was 14.* 17 *intr.v* (of a voice) not be able to be controlled because of deep feelings: *The man's voice broke as he tried to tell us the terrible news.* 18 *intr.v* (of a storm) begin. 19 *intr.v* (of a wave) change into foam(1) on top. ⇒ breaker(2). 20 *intr.v* (of weather) (start to) change.
break away (**from s.o/s.t**) (**a**) go away, escape, (from s.o/s.t) suddenly. (**b**) form a separate (smaller) group after belonging to a large one: *The miners who worked have broken away from those who supported the strike.* ⇒ breakaway.
break away (**from s.t**) break(1) and fall (from s.t): *A branch broke away in the storm.*
break the back of s.t ⇒ back(*n*).
break the bank ⇒ bank²(*n*).
break camp ⇒ camp¹(*n*).
break cover ⇒ cover(*n*).
break down (**a**) become useless; stop working: *My car's broken down.* ⇒ breakdown(1). (**b**) fail; stop: *Talks between the two governments have broken down.* ⇒ breakdown(2). (**c**)become weak in body or mind: *He was breaking down under the pressure.* ⇒ breakdown(3). **break down** (**in(to**) **s.t**) become affected by deep feelings, usu so that one begins to cry. **break s.o down** = break(11).
break s.t down (**a**) make s.t, e.g a door, fall down by hitting it. (**b**) force s.t, e.g opposition(1), to yield:

We must first break down the enemy's resistance.
(c) divide s.t, e.g accounts, into parts; classify s.t
⇨ breakdown(4). (d) (*chemistry*) change s.t, e.g
the food one eats, into simpler substances.
break even ⇨ even(*adj*).
break faith with s.o ⇨ faith.
break s.o's fall ⇨ fall(1).
break the force of s.t ⇨ force(*n*).
break fresh/new ground ⇨ ground¹(*n*).
break a/the habit (of doing s.t) ⇨ habit.
break s.o's heart ⇨ heart(*n*).
break the ice ⇨ ice(*n*).
break in(to s.t) (a) enter (s.t) by breaking s.t,
e.g a door. ⇨ break-in. (b) interrupt (s.t, e.g
a conversation). **break s.o/s.t in** train s.o, an
animal, to do s.t new. **break (s.t) in two** ⇨ two.
break into a gallop, **run** etc ⇨ gallop(*n*), run(*n*).
break into laughter ⇨ laughter.
break loose ⇨ loose(1).
break the news to s.o ⇨ news.
break off stop talking: *He was telling them something but he broke off when he saw me.* **break (s.t)
off** (a) (cause s.t to) come off by breaking (it): *He
broke the handle off the cup. The handle broke
off.* (b) stop (s.t) suddenly and usu for a short
time only: *Let's break off for lunch. The talks have
been broken off.*
break (s.t) open ⇨ open(*adj*).
break out (of a fire, war etc) start suddenly. ⇨
outbreak. **break out (from/of s.t)** escape (from
a prison, from an enemy surrounding(2) one etc).
⇨ break-out. **break out in s.t** suddenly become
covered with s.t, e.g spots caused by an illness.
break out on s.t (of spots etc caused by illness)
suddenly appear on one's skin etc.
break over s.o/s.t (of the sea, a wave etc) cover
s.o/s.t as it breaks(19).
break a record ⇨ record³.
break step ⇨ step(*n*).
break a strike ⇨ strike(1).
break through (s.t) (a) force one's way through
(s.t, e.g an enemy position); make a way, hole,
through (s.t). ⇨ breakthrough(1). (b) suddenly
appear (from behind s.t): *The sun broke through
the clouds.* (c) overcome (s.t, e.g a person's
shyness): *He's so quiet that it's difficult to break
through (his reserve).*
break up (a) (of school) end a term and begin
holidays. (b) (of weather) end, to be followed by
s.t different. **break (s.o) up** (cause s.o to) become
weak, esp mentally: *The pressure is breaking him
up.* **break s.o/s.t up** force a group of people
etc to scatter: *The police moved in to break the
crowd up.* **break (s.t) up** (a) (cause s.t to) come to
pieces: *The ship broke up on the rocks.* (b) (cause
s.t, e.g a meeting, to) come to an end: *The meeting
broke up without any agreement.* (c) (cause s.t,
e.g an agreement, a marriage, to) end: *He was the
man who broke up their marriage.* ⇨ break-up.
break wind ⇨ wind¹.
break with s.o finish, end, one's friendship with
s.o. **break with s.t** stop following s.t, e.g tradi-
tion(1); give s.t up.
ˈbreakable *adj* easily broken (⇨ break(8)).
Opposite unbreakable.
ˈbreakables *pl.n* things that are breakable.
breakage /ˈbreɪkɪdʒ/ *n* 1 *u.n* act of break-
ing(8) (s.t). 2 *c.n* (often — *in s.t*) place
(in s.t) where s.t has broken (⇨ break(8)).

3 *c.n* (usu *pl*) an object that gets broken (⇨
break(8)).
ˈbreakˌaway *attrib.adj* that has broken away (⇨
break away(b)): *a breakaway group/union.*
ˈbreakˌdown *c.n* 1 mechanical failure, e.g of
a car. 2 failure; stoppage: *a breakdown in the
talks.* 3 weakening of the body or mind: *a nervous
breakdown.* 4 (often — *of s.t*) analysis(2) (of s.t);
classification (of s.t) into its parts.
ˈbreaker *c.n* 1 person or thing who/that
breaks(8) s.t. 2 large wave that breaks(19) into
foam(1). ⇨ ice-breaker(1).
ˈbreak-ˌin *c.n* entry into a building by force.
ˈbreak-ˌout *c.n* escape from a prison, from
enemy forces surrounding(2) one etc.
ˈbreakˌthrough *c.n* 1 forcing of one's way
through an enemy's forces. 2 important advance
or discovery, esp in science.
ˈbreak-ˌup *c.n* end; destruction: *the break-up of
a marriage.*
ˈbreakˌwater *c.n* stone wall etc that is built out
to sea etc to break the force of waves.
ˈbroken *attrib. adj* 1 ⇨ broke.
▷ *v* 2 *p.p* of break.
breakfast /ˈbrekfəst/ *c/u.n* 1 first meal of the
day.
▷ *intr.v* 2 have breakfast(1).
breast /brest/ *c.n* 1 one of the two organs of a
woman's body that produce milk. 2 upper part
of the front of a human or animal body; chest(1).
3 (*fig*) part of one's body where one's feelings
of love etc are supposed to be; heart(2). 4 =
chimney-breast. **make a clean breast of s.t** (*fig*)
make a full confession of s.t.
ˈbreast-ˌfeed *tr/intr.v* feed (a baby) from the
breast(1). Compare bottle-feed.
ˌbreast-ˈhigh *adj* (of water etc) coming up as
high as one's chest.
ˈbreastˌstroke *u.n* kind of way of swimming in
which one lies on one's chest and one's arms
move forward together and are then swung to
the sides of one's body at the same time.
breath /breθ/ *n* 1 *u.n* air taken into and sent
out of one's lungs. 2 *c.n* one act of doing this.
3 *c.n* movement of air: *There wasn't a breath
of air that day.* 4 *u.n* (*fig*; *literary*) life: *When
we found him the breath had already gone out
of him.* 5 *c.n* (often *a — of s.t*) (*fig*) slightest
suggestion, idea, sign, (of s.t): *You mustn't let
anyone hear a breath of our plans.* **bad breath**
breath with an unpleasant smell. **catch one's
breath** stop breathing suddenly for a short
time, e.g because of surprise. **get one's breath
(again/back)** return to normal breathing after
having been out of breath. **hold one's breath**
stop breathing for a time. **in the same breath**
(*fig*) at the same time. **lose one's breath** have
difficulty in breathing easily, e.g because one
is hurrying. **out of breath** not being able to
breathe easily, usu because one has been running
etc. **under one's breath** in a whisper. **take a
(deep) breath** breathe in (deeply). **take s.o's
breath away** surprise s.o. **waste (one's) breath
(doing s.t, on s.o/s.t)** talk to s.o who does not
understand or does not take any notice.
breathalyser /ˈbreθəˌlaɪzə/ *c.n* instrument
used to test s.o's breath to find out how
much alcohol he/she has drunk, esp in cases
of suspected drunken driving. ⇨ breath test.

breathe /bri:ð/ v 1 intr.v take air into one's lungs and send it out again. 2 intr.v (literary) be alive. 3 tr.v say (s.t) very quietly or in a whisper. 4 tr.v tell (s.t that is a secret): You mustn't breathe a word of our plans to a soul. 5 intr.v rest: You have to let your horse breathe from time to time. 6 intr.v (of wind) blow gently. 7 intr.v (of wine) get air into it. **breathe again** feel/show relief after danger etc. **breathe down s.o's neck** ⇒ neck(n). **breathe freely (again)** recover(1) from fear etc. **breathe in/out** take air into, push air out of, one's lungs. **breathe s.t into s.o** (fig) inspire(1) s.o with s.t, give s.o courage.

breathing /'bri:ðɪŋ/ u.n acts of taking air into the lungs and sending it out again.

'**breathing ,space** c.n (usu sing) (fig) short time during which one can rest.

'**breathless** adj 1 not able to breathe(1) easily because of having run fast or because of fright etc. 2 with no movement of the wind: a breathless quiet in a forest.

'**breath ,test** c.n test of the amount of alcohol(1) there is in a person's breath. ⇒ breathalyser.

bred /bred/ p.t,p.p of breed.

breech /bri:tʃ/ c.n back part of a gun into which one puts the bullets/shells.

breeches /'brɪtʃɪz/ pl.n (often a pair of —) clothes that cover the lower part of the body and the legs to just below the knees. ⇒ riding breeches.

breed /bri:d/ c.n 1 (often — of s.t) kind, sort, variety, (of animal etc): This breed of sheep has very good wool.

▷ v (p.t,p.p bred /bred/) 2 tr.v keep (animals, plants etc) in order to produce young, seeds etc, esp when one chooses the parents carefully: Anne has bred cats for years and has won many prizes. 3 intr.v give birth to young: Wild rabbits breed very quickly. 4 tr.v educate, train, (s.o); bring (s.o) up: This school breeds successful students. ⇒ ill-bred, well-bred. Compare inbred(1). 5 be the cause of (s.t); give rise to (s.t): A very hot climate can breed laziness.

'**breeder** c.n 1 person who breeds(2) animals. 2 (also ,**fast 'breeder (re,actor)**) machine, nuclear reactor, that produces more radioactive material than is put into it.

'**breeding** u.n 1 act of breeding (⇒ breed(2)) s.t. 2 knowing how to behave properly as a result of how one has been bred(4). **a person of good breeding** a person who knows how to behave well because of good breeding(2).

breeze /bri:z/ c/u.n light gentle wind.

'**breeze,block** c.n building block that is light in weight and is made from concrete(4) and cinders.

'**breezily** adv in a breezy(2) way.

'**breeziness** u.n fact or state of being breezy.

'**breezy** adj (-ier, -iest) 1 having a pleasantly strong breeze: a breezy day. 2 (fig) cheerful and lively.

Bren /bren/ c.n (also '**Bren ,gun**) kind of light machine-gun.

brethren /'breðrən/ pl.n (old use) brothers.

breve /bri:v/ c.n (music) note in music that is equal to two semibreves.

brevity /'brevɪtɪ/ u.n (of time, the way of saying s.t etc) shortness; quality of saying etc things in a short way. ⇒ brief¹.

brew /bru:/ c.n 1 drink, liquid, made by brewing (2,3).

▷ v 2 tr/intr.v (often — (s.t) up) make (tea etc) by putting boiling water on tea leaves etc. 3 tr.v make (beer) by mixing grain with water etc and fermenting(2) it. 4 intr.v (fig) (of s.t bad) be getting ready to start: Trouble is brewing in our office. 5 tr.v (often — s.t up) prepare (s.t bad): The children are brewing something up for tonight, I feel sure.

'**brewer** c.n person who brews(2) beer.

'**brewery** c.n (pl -ies) place where beer is brewed(3).

bribe /braɪb/ c.n 1 (often give/offer (s.o) a —) money etc given/offered to s.o to do s.t that he/she knows is not right or lawful.

▷ tr.v 2 (often — s.o to do s.t) give/offer (s.o) a bribe(1) (to do s.t).

'**bribery** u.n.

brick /brɪk/ n 1 c/u.n (block of) earth or clay that has been baked in an oven or in the sun so that it can be used in building. 2 c.n wooden or plastic block used by children as a toy. 3 c.n thing shaped like a brick(1): an ice-cream brick. 4 c.n (slang) kind helpful person. **come down (on s.o) like a ton of bricks** ⇒ ton. **drop a brick** (slang) do/say s.t stupid that then makes one feel ashamed.

▷ tr.v 5 (usu — s.t in/up) close, block, (s.t) with bricks(1).

'**brick,layer** c.n person who builds and repairs brickwork.

'**brick,laying** u.n job or skill of a bricklayer.

'**brick,work** c.n piece of building work in which bricks(1) are used.

'**brick,works** c.n (pl brickworks) place where bricks(1) are made.

bride /braɪd/ c.n woman who is just going to be, or has just been, married.

'**bridal** adj of or referring to a bride or a wedding.

'**bride,groom** c.n (also **groom**) man who is just going to be, or has just been, married.

'**brides,maid** c.n girl or young unmarried woman who attends a bride at her wedding.

bridge¹ /brɪdʒ/ c.n 1 structure(2) built of stone, iron, wood etc that carries a road, railway etc over a river, another road etc. 2 raised deck across a ship, usu near the front but sometimes at the back (e.g in oil tankers), from which the captain etc controls the ship. 3 upper bony(2) part of one's nose: Peter always has his glasses balanced on the bridge of his nose. 4 system for keeping false teeth from coming out by fastening them to natural teeth. 5 piece of wood etc over which the strings of a violin etc are stretched. **burn one's bridges** ⇒ burn(v).

▷ tr.v 6 join the sides of (s.t) with a bridge¹(1); build a bridge¹(1) over (s.t). 7 (fig) get over (difficulties etc): We have to find a way to bridge the gap between what we earn and what we spend.

bridge² /brɪdʒ/ u.n kind of card game played by four players in which one player attempts to get the number of tricks(7) he/she bids(5).

bridle /'braɪdl/ c.n 1 thing made of strips of leather that a horse wears on its head and that the rider uses to control it.

▷ v 2 tr.v put a bridle(1) on (a horse). 3 intr.v (often — at s.t) show one's annoyance (at s.t s.o has said or done): *He bridled at her suggestion that he needed to dress more neatly.* ⇨ unbridled.

brief[1] /briːf/ *adj* lasting for a short time only. *in brief* in a few words
'**briefly** *adv.* '**briefness** *u.n.* ⇨ brevity.
briefs *pl.n* very short underpants or panties.

brief[2] /briːf/ *c.n* **1** (*law*) short account of the facts of a case for use by a barrister. **2** advice, information, orders, given to s.o in advance: *My brief is to find out as much as I can about the other side's plans without giving away any of ours.*
▷ *tr.v* **3** employ (a barrister). **4** give (s.o) a brief(2). Compare debrief.
'**brief,case** *c.n* flat leather case used for carrying papers in.
'**briefing** *c.n* advice etc given in a brief[2](2). Compare debriefing.

Brig *written abbr* brigadier.

brigade /brɪˈgeɪd/ *c.n* **1** army unit consisting of about 5000 soldiers. **2** group of people who form an organization for a particular purpose: *the fire brigade.*
brigadier /ˌbrɪɡəˈdɪə/ *c.n* (*written abbr* Brig) army officer of high rank, above a colonel but below a major-general.

brigand /ˈbrɪɡənd/ *c.n* (*literary*; *formal*) armed robber, usu a member of a band of robbers who attack people travelling in mountains etc.

bright /braɪt/ *adj* **1** shining; giving out, reflecting, a lot of light. **2** (of a colour) strong and clear: *bright blue.* **3** happy; cheerful; lively(1): *a bright smile.* **4** clever; intelligent: *bright students.* *look on the bright side (of s.t)* ⇨ side(*n*).
'**brighten** *tr/intr.v* (cause (s.t) to) become bright(er)(1). **brighten (s.o/s.t) up** (cause (s.o/s.t) to) become bright(er)(1,3).
'**brightly** *adv.* '**brightness** *u.n.*

brilliant /ˈbrɪlɪənt/ *adj* **1** very bright(1–4).
▷ *c.n* **2** diamond of the best quality and cut.
'**brilliancy** *u.n.* '**brilliantly** *adv.*

brim /brɪm/ *c.n* **1** edge of a cup, glass etc. **2** part that sticks out round the lower part of a hat and gives shade. *full to the brim* completely full.
▷ *intr.v* (*-mm-*) **3** *brim over (with s.t)* (a) be so full (of s.t) that some spills over the top. (b) (*fig*) be very happy and lively (because of s.t).
'**brimful** *pred.adj* (usu — *of/with s.t*) (a) full (of s.t) up to the brim(1). (b) (*fig*) very full (of s.t, e.g new ideas).

brine /braɪn/ *u.n* salty water.

bring /brɪŋ/ *tr.v* (*p.t,p.p* brought /brɔːt/) **1** (often — s.o/s.t in(to s.t), out (of s.t) etc) carry (s.t) when one comes (in etc); come (in etc) with (s.o/s.t). **2** cause (s.o/s.t) to come: *Heavy rain often brings floods. The baby's cries brought its parents running.* **3** get (a certain amount of money) as its price when sold: *Our old furniture brought several hundred pounds in the sale.* Compare fetch(2). **4** (often — *a charge, complaint*, (*against* s.o)) make (a charge etc) (against s.o) in a court of law.
bring s.o. s.t earn s.t for s.o: *Renting out these flats brings me over £1000 a month.*
bring s.t about cause s.t to happen.
bring s.o/s.t back return with s.o/s.t. **bring s.t back** introduce s.t again: *Many people want the death* penalty(1) *brought back.* **bring s.t back (to s.o)** cause s.o to remember s.t. **bring s.o back to health** ⇨ health.

bring s.o/s.t down cause s.o/s.t to fall; shoot s.o/s.t down out of the sky. **bring s.t down** reduce s.t, e.g the price of s.t. **bring the house down** ⇨ house.
bring s.o/s.t forth (*old use*) produce s.o/s.t, e.g a baby. **bring s.t forth** (*formal*) bring s.t with it: *I wonder what the next few weeks will bring forth.*
bring s.t forward (a) cause s.t to be seen, talked about etc. (b) cause s.t to happen earlier.
bring s.o in (of police) arrest s.o and take her/him to the police station. **bring s.o/s.t in** go in with s.o/s.t. **bring s.t in** (a) introduce s.t, e.g a new law. (b) produce s.t as a profit, income. **bring in a verdict of (not) guilty** ⇨ verdict.
bring s.o/s.t into line ⇨ line(*n*).
bring s.o/s.t off manage to save, rescue, s.o/s.t, e.g from a sinking ship. **bring s.t off** succeed in doing s.t difficult.
bring s.t on (a) cause, produce, s.t: *The child's stomach pains were brought on by eating too many green apples.* (b) cause s.t to advance or make progress.
bring s.o out (a) cause s.o to become less shy. (b) cause workers to strike. **bring s.t out** (a) make s.t appear: *The sun and rain have brought out the flowers.* (b) make s.t clear or easy to understand: *The notes brought out the deeper meaning of the painting.* (c) produce a book, magazine etc.
bring s.o over (to s.t) persuade s.o to think differently (about s.t).
bring s.o round make s.o conscious again. **bring s.o round (to s.t)** persuade s.o to think the same as one does oneself.
bring s.o through prevent s.o from dying; save s.o.
bring s.o to make s.o conscious again. **bring oneself/s.o to do s.t** persuade oneself/s.o to do s.t, usu with difficulty: *I can't bring myself to stop the children because they are enjoying themselves so much.* **bring s.o to book** ⇨ book(*n*). **bring s.t to an end** ⇨ end(*n*). **bring s.t home to s.o** ⇨ home(*adv*). **bring s.t to a head** ⇨ head(*n*). **bring s.t to light** ⇨ light[1](*n*). **bring s.o/s.t to mind** ⇨ mind[1](*n*). **bring s.t to pass** (*formal*) cause s.t to happen. **bring s.o to her/his senses** ⇨ senses.
bring s.o/s.t under manage to control s.o/s.t.
bring s.o up educate, raise, s.o. **bring (s.t) up** be sick; vomit(3) (s.t). **bring s.t up** raise s.t for consideration. **bring up the rear (of s.t)** ⇨ rear[1](*n*).
bring s.o/s.t with one be accompanied by s.o/s.t that one brings(1,2).

brink /brɪŋk/ *c.n* **1** (often *on the* — (*of s.t*)) extreme edge (of s.t). **2** (*fig*) position very close to s.t, often s.t dangerous. *on the brink of (doing)* **s.t** very close to (doing) s.t.

briquette /brɪˈket/ *c.n* (also **bri'quet**) block of tightly packed coal dust shaped like a brick etc and used for burning in fires.

brisk /brɪsk/ *adj* active; lively(2); moving quickly; vigorous.
'**briskly** *adv.* '**briskness** *u.n.*

bristle /ˈbrɪsl/ *c/u.n* **1** short stiff hair.
▷ *intr.v* **2** (of an animal) raise its bristles(1) in anger or fear. **3** (*fig*) (of a person) feel/show anger or annoyance. **bristle with s.t** (*fig*) (a) feel/show anger or annoyance as a result of s.t: *Vivian bristles with anger when she sees cruelty to animals.* (b) be full of s.t, esp problems or difficulties.

'bristly adj (-ier, -iest) like, full of, bristles(1).

British /'brɪtɪʃ/ adj **1** of, referring to, belonging to, Great Britain: the British people. I'm British. **2** of, referring to, belonging to, the ancient Britons.

▷ def.pl.n **3** British(1) people: The British always talk about the weather.

,British 'Broadcasting ,Corpor,ation def.n (abbr BBC) UK public radio and television service paid for by licences(1). Compare ITV.

Briton /'brɪtn/ c.n **1** native of Britain. **2** native of ancient Britain.

brittle /'brɪtl/ adj hard and easily broken: Egg shells are very brittle.

'brittleness u.n.

broach /brəʊtʃ/ tr.v introduce (a subject) for discussion.

broad /brɔːd/ adj **1** wide; large from one side to the other: a broad street. Opposite narrow(1). **2** measured from one side to the other: This river is over 100 metres broad here. **3** general; having wide application; not limited: the broad lines of a plan, the details of which will be filled in later. **4** (of a person's mind) willing to listen to and/or accept very different ideas; tolerant. **5** (of speech) showing clearly that one comes from a certain part of the country; showing strong signs of dialect. It is as broad as it's long (fig) It does not matter which you choose because both are the same in their effects. ⇒ breadth.

,broad 'bean c.n kind of large flat bean that is eaten as a vegetable.

,broad 'day,light u.n **in broad daylight** during the day (when it is fully light).

'broaden tr/intr.v (cause (s.t) to) become broad(er)(1,3,4).

,broad 'hint c.n (often give s.o a —) very clear suggestion, without actually saying the thing directly.

'broadly adv.

,broad'minded adj prepared to listen to other points of view; tolerant. Opposite small-minded.

,broad'mindedness u.n.

'broadness u.n.

,broad 'out,line c.n (often in —) general account, without any details. Compare broad(3).

broadcast /'brɔːd,kɑːst/ c.n **1** speech, music, pictures etc sent out on radio or television.

▷ v (p.t,p.p broadcast, broadcasted) **2** tr/intr.v send (one or more programmes) out on radio or television. **3** tr.v make (s.t) known very clearly, esp by one's words or actions: He broadcast his intention to hit me by raising his hand.

'broad,caster c.n person who controls or appears in a radio or television broadcast(1).

'broad,casting u.n.

broadside /'brɔːd,saɪd/ adv **1** broadside on(to s.t) with a side facing s.t, or going first: The car hit the wall broadside on.

▷ c.n **2** firing of all the guns on one side of a ship at the same time. **3** (fig) strong attack in speech or writing.

brocade /brə'keɪd/ u.n kind of heavy silk material with raised patterns, esp ones made of gold or silver thread.

broccoli /'brɒkəlɪ/ c/u.n plant like a cauliflower(1) with small white or purple flowers, eaten as a vegetable.

brochure /'brəʊʃə/ c.n small book with paper covers, esp one used for advertising: a holiday/travel brochure.

broke /brəʊk/ pred.adj **1** (slang) not having any money. **flat/stony broke** having no money at all; penniless.

▷ v **2** p.t of break.

broken /'brəʊkən/ p.p of break(v).

,broken 'English etc u.n English etc spoken with a lot of mistakes, often by foreigners.

,broken-'hearted attrib.adj ⇒ heartbroken.

,broken 'home c.n home where the parents are separated or divorced.

,broken 'marriage c.n marriage that has failed.

broker /'brəʊkə/ c.n **1** person who buys and sells things, esp stocks(10) and shares(3), for other people. **2** official who sells the property of other people to get money to pay off their debts.

brolly /'brɒlɪ/ c.n (pl -ies) umbrella(1).

bromide /'brəʊmaɪd/ u.n **1** chemical used in photography; chem.symb AgBr. **2** (medical) chemical used to calm people; chem.symb HBr.

bronchial /'brɒŋkɪəl/ adj of, referring to, affecting, the bronchi.

bronchitis /brɒŋ'kaɪtɪs/ u.n inflammation of the bronchi.

bronchus /'brɒŋkəs/ c.n (pl bronchi /'brɒŋkaɪ/) one of two main branches of the windpipe leading to the lungs.

bronze /brɒnz/ n **1** u.n kind of yellow-orange metal made by mixing copper(1) and tin. **2** u.n (also attrib) yellow-orange colour of bronze(1). **3** c.n work of art etc made of bronze(1). **4** c.n = bronze medal.

'Bronze ,Age def.n period in the past between the Stone Age and Iron Age when weapons and tools were made of bronze(1).

'bronze ,medal c.n medal given for coming third in a race or contest.

brooch /brəʊtʃ/ c.n ornament made of metal, jewels etc which has a pin on it so that it can be fastened to a dress etc.

brood /bruːd/ c.n **1** family of young birds that came out of the eggs in a nest at the same time. **2** (fig) family of children.

▷ intr.v **3** (of a bird) sit on eggs to keep them warm until the young birds come out of them. **4** (fig) (often — on/over s.t) think deeply and often unhappily (about s.t).

'broodily adv in a broody(2,3) way.

'broodiness u.n state or fact of being broody.

'broody adj (-ier, -iest) **1** (of a bird) wanting to sit on eggs. **2** (informal) (of a woman) wanting to have babies. **3** (fig) (of a person) unhappy.

brook¹ /brʊk/ c.n small stream.

brook² /brʊk/ tr.v (usu with negatives) (formal) put up with (s.t); bear (s.t): Martin can't brook any opposition.

broom /bruːm, brʊm/ n **1** c.n kind of brush with a long handle, used for sweeping floors etc. **2** u.n kind of big plant like a bush which has yellow flowers and usu grows in sandy places. **a new broom** (fig) a person who has just got a job and who wants to change things.

Bros written abbr Brothers, usu in the name of a shop, office etc: Levin Bros.

broth /brɒθ/ u.n thin soup made by boiling meat, vegetables etc.

brothel /'brɒθl/ c.n place where prostitutes are hired for sexual intercourse.

brother /'brʌðə/ attrib.adj **1** belonging to the same group, association etc: our brother officers.
▷ n **2** c.n male child of the same parents (as oneself): Joan has two brothers and one sister. ⇒ half-brother, stepbrother. **3** c/unique n (with capital **B** in names) man who belongs to a religious order; monk: Brother Jonathan. ⇒ sister(4). **4** c.n man who is in the same group, e.g a trade union or political movement: We must join together in the fight for our rights, brothers! ⇒ sister(5).

'**brother,hood** n **1** u.n feeling that a brother(2–4) has, or should have, towards another: the brotherhood of man. **2** c.n group of people who are brothers(4).

'**brother-in-,law** c.n (pl brothers-in-law) brother of one's husband, wife; husband of one's sister or sister-in-law. ⇒ sister-in-law.

'**brotherliness** u.n feeling of being brotherly.

'**brotherly** adj of, like, a brother; like what a loving brother would be/do.

brought /brɔːt/ p.t,p.p of bring.

brow /braʊ/ c.n **1** (usu pl) = eyebrow. **2** = forehead. **3** edge of a steep cliff, hill etc. **4** top of a rise in a road etc after which it goes down again on the other side. **knit one's brows** frown(2), usu to show that one is thinking hard, or that one is worried or not pleased.

brown /braʊn/ adj **1** having the colour of earth or of strong tea: a brown coat; brown paint. **2** (of a person's skin) having become suntanned: She was very brown after her holiday in Greece.
▷ n **3** c/u.n brown(1) colour. **in brown** having brown clothes on: dressed in brown.
▷ tr/intr.v **4** (cause (s.o/s.t) to) become brown, e.g by cooking, being in the sun: First, brown the meat under the grill(2). She browns very easily.

,**brown 'bread** u.n kind of bread made from flour that has not been (completely) refined(1).

,**browned 'off** adj (usu pred) (fig; informal) **1** very bored: He had nothing to do and felt very browned off. **2** (usu — with s.o/s.t) very annoyed (with s.o/s.t): I get really browned off with all your complaints.

'**brownish** adj rather brown.

'**brownness** u.n.

,**brown 'paper** u.n kind of thick paper that is brown in colour and is used for wrapping things in etc.

,**brown 'sugar** u.n sugar that has not been (completely) refined(1).

browse /braʊz/ intr.v **1** (of an animal) feed on grass, leaves etc. **2** (of a person) read parts of one or more books without any particular purpose except enjoyment: I often browse in a bookshop during my lunch hour.

bruise /bruːz/ c.n **1** change in the colour of the skin of a person or a fruit etc, caused by a knock or blow, but without any breaking of the skin.
▷ v **2** tr.v make a bruise(1) on (s.o/s.t). **3** intr.v show the results of being bruised(2): Peter doesn't play rough games because he bruises very easily.

brunch /brʌntʃ/ c/u.n (informal) meal eaten in the middle of the morning in place of both breakfast and lunch.

brunette /bruː'net/ adj **1** (of a girl or woman) having dark red-brown hair.
▷ c.n **2** girl or woman who has dark red-brown hair.

brunt /brʌnt/ def.n **bear the brunt (of s.t)** suffer the main part (of s.t bad, e.g an attack or bad weather).

brush /brʌʃ/ n **1** c.n instrument made of bristles(1), hair etc fixed into a handle and used for sweeping, brushing(4) hair, painting etc. ⇒ hairbrush, nailbrush, paintbrush, toothbrush. **2** c.n quick slight touch while passing. ⇒ brush(5). **3** u.n (also '**brush,wood**) (area of land on which there are) rough bushes and small trees; pieces of such bushes and trees. **give s.t a brush** brush(4) s.t. (**have**) **a brush with s.o** (have) a short argument or fight, unfriendly meeting (with s.o). **tarred with the same brush** ⇒ tar(v).
▷ v **4** tr.v use a brush(1) to tidy (one's hair) or to clean, polish etc (s.o/s.t). **5** tr/intr.v (often (s.t) — against s.o/s.t) touch (s.o/s.t) lightly in passing. **brush s.o/s.t aside/away/off** (fig; informal) dismiss s.o/s.t quickly and rudely. ⇒ brush-off. **brush s.t away/off** remove s.t by brushing(4) it or by rubbing it with one's hand. **brush s.o/s.t down** clean s.o/s.t with a brush(1) or one's hand(s). **brush s.t up** (**a**) clean s.t away with a brush(1) or one's hand(s). (**b**) (fig) get back one's former skill in s.t: I must brush up my Italian before I go to Italy this summer.

'**brush-,off** def.n (slang) (usu get, give s.o, the —) rude refusal to talk/listen to s.o.

'**brush,wood** u.n = brush(3).

brusque /bruːsk/ adj rough and short in one's way of speaking or behaving.

'**brusquely** adv. '**brusqueness** u.n.

Brussels sprout /,brʌslz 'spraʊt/ c.n (usu pl) vegetable shaped like a very small cabbage that grows in groups on a stalk and is eaten as a vegetable.

brute /bruːt/ c.n **1** (often derog) animal, esp a large unpleasant one. **2** (derog) person who has a bad temper, is cruel, selfish etc.

'**brutal** adj (derog) cruel; rough.

brutality /bruː'tælɪtɪ/ u.n. '**brutally** adv.

,**brute 'force/'strength** u.n (usu by/with —) (using) great strength and nothing much else.

'**brutish** adj (derog) like a brute(1,2).

'**brutishly** adv. '**brutishness** u.n.

BSc /,biː es 'siː/ abbr Bachelor of Science.

Bt written abbr baronet.

bubble /'bʌbl/ c.n **1** round film of liquid filled with air or gas that can float in the air: soap bubbles. **2** ball of gas or air that rises to the surface of a liquid, e.g when it boils. **3** small ball of gas or air in s.t solid that was liquid before: glass with bubbles in it. **4** round shape like a bubble(1,2) on a painted surface etc. **5** (often the — of s.t) sound or appearance (of s.t that is bubbling(6)).
▷ intr.v **6** form, rise in, bubbles(2). **7** make the sound of, give the appearance of, bubbles(5). **bubble over** make bubbles(1,2) flow out over the top of s.t, e.g when a liquid boils. **bubble over (with s.t)** (fig) show happiness, excitement etc. **bubble up** rise to the surface in bubbles(2).

'**bubble ,bath** n **1** c.n bath whose water has a mass of small bubbles on the surface which are made by adding liquid soap etc. **2** u.n liquid soap used to make a bubble bath(1).

'**bubble,gum** u.n soft kind of chewing gum

that can be chewed and then blown into bubbles.

'bubbly adj (-ier, -iest) **1** full of bubbles(1,2). **2** (fig) very lively(1) and cheerful.

▷ u.n **3** (informal) champagne.

buccaneer /ˌbʌkəˈnɪə/ c.n (literary) **1** pirate(1). **2** adventurer(1).

buck¹ /bʌk/ c.n **1** male of certain animals, e.g rabbits, deer. Compare doe. **2** (US) (slang) dollar. **pass the buck** (slang) put responsibility for s.t onto s.o else. **The buck stops here** (slang) This is the place where final responsibility is taken.

,buck 'teeth pl.n upper teeth that stick out in front like a rabbit's.

buck² /bʌk/ intr.v (usu of a horse) jump suddenly off the four feet, usu to try to throw a rider off. **buck s.o off** (usu of a horse) throw a rider off by bucking. **buck (s.o) up** (informal) **(a)** (cause s.o to) become more cheerful, confident etc. **(b)** (cause s.o to) go faster or to speed up.

bucket /'bʌkɪt/ c.n **1** kind of container made of metal, plastic, wood etc that is open on top and usu has a curved handle; it is used for holding and carrying water, sand etc. **2** (also **'bucketful**) as much as a bucket(1) holds. **kick the bucket** (slang) die. **rain buckets** (fig) rain hard.

'bucketful c.n = bucket(2).

'bucket ,seat c.n seat with a round back, made for one person, and usu in a car or plane.

buckle /'bʌkl/ c.n **1** kind of fastener made of metal, plastic etc which has one or more sharp points that go through one or more holes in a leather belt etc to hold it tight.

▷ v **2** tr.v fasten (s.t) with a buckle(1). Opposite unbuckle. **3** intr.v be fastened with a buckle(1): This belt buckles across one's chest. **4** tr/intr.v (cause (s.t) to) bend out of shape under pressure, through heat etc: Railway lines sometimes buckle in very hot weather. **buckle down (to s.t)** (fig) begin to do (s.t) hard or seriously: Now that the holidays are over we must buckle down to some work. **buckle s.t on (to s.o/s.t)** fasten s.t (to s.o/ s.t) with a buckle(1).

bud /bʌd/ c.n **1** new flower, leaf or stem before it opens out or starts to grow properly. **in bud** that has buds(1) on it. **nip s.t in the bud** ⇒ nip(v).

▷ intr.v (-dd-) **2** produce buds(1).

'budding attrib.adj just beginning to develop (into s.t): Mary is a budding engineer.

Buddhism /'bʊdɪzəm/ u.n religion started by Buddha in North India in the 5th century BC. **'Buddhist** c.n (also attrib) person who follows Buddhism.

buddy /'bʌdɪ/ c.n (pl -ies) (slang) friend.

budge /bʌdʒ/ tr/intr.v (often — (s.o/s.t) from s.t) **1** (cause (s.o/s.t) to) move a little (away from s.t). **2** (fig) (cause (s.o) to) change her/his ideas etc a little. **not budge/give an inch** ⇒ inch(n).

budgerigar /'bʌdʒərɪˌgɑː/ c.n (informal budgie) kind of small brightly coloured bird from Australia which looks like a small parrot(1).

budget /'bʌdʒɪt/ attrib.adj **1** (informal) (usu in advertisements) sold, offered etc as a bargain(2): budget prices.

▷ c.n **2** calculation of how much money a person, company, government etc is going to receive and how much he/she/it is going to spend, usu in a year, week etc. **3** money in a budget(2): We have a budget of £30 a week for food.

▷ intr.v **4** prepare a budget(2). **budget for s.t** allow for s.t; take s.t into consideration when preparing a budget(2).

'budget ac,count c.n account with a bank to which money is transferred from another account when necessary to pay one's electricity bills etc.

budgetary /'bʌdʒɪtərɪ/ adj of or referring to a budget(2) or budgets(2).

budgie /'bʌdʒɪ/ c.n (informal) budgerigar.

buff¹ /bʌf/ u.n (also attrib) dull yellow-brown colour.

buff² /bʌf/ u.n thick soft yellow leather made from the skin of a cow etc. **in the buff** (informal) wearing no clothes; naked(1). **strip to the buff** (informal) take all one's clothes off.

buff³ /bʌf/ c.n (informal) person who is very interested in, knows a lot about, s.t; enthusiast: a railway buff.

buff⁴ /bʌf/ tr.v **buff s.t up** polish (s.t, usu metal) with s.t soft.

buffalo /'bʌfəˌləʊ/ (pl -(es)) c.n **1** kind of large black, often wild, animal like a cow/bull¹(1) found mostly in Asia and Africa. **2** = bison.

buffer /'bʌfə/ c.n metal pad with a spring inside it which is fitted to the front and back of a railway engine or carriage in pairs, and used to make the shock less strong when carriages etc hit each other.

buffet¹ /'bʊfeɪ/ c.n (French) **1** place, e.g at a railway station, where one can buy light refreshments. **2** table in a restaurant etc where refreshments, often cold ones, are served to guests.

'buffet-,car c.n carriage in a train in which one can have light refreshments.

buffet² /'bʌfɪt/ tr.v **1** hit (s.o/s.t) once or more than once: The corn was buffeted by wind and rain. **2** (fig) (of fate, misfortunes etc) attack (s.o).

buffoon /bə'fuːn/ c.n person who says and does silly things, usu to amuse others.

buf'foonery u.n things done or said by buffoons.

bug /bʌg/ c.n **1** small insect. **2** (informal) germ(1) that causes disease. **3** (informal) fault in a machine or computer that stops it working (properly). **4** (slang) small hidden microphone used to listen to people secretly.

▷ tr.v (-gg-) (slang) **5** put a bug(4) into (a room etc). **6** listen to what (s.o) is saying, using a bug(4). **7** annoy (s.o).

'bug,bear c.n thing that worries or frightens (s.o).

bugger /'bʌgə/ c.n (do not use!) **1** man who has sex with another person through the anus; sodomite. **2** (slang) person or animal: Look what you've done, you silly bugger! Those birds have nothing to eat, poor buggers. **3** (slang) thing or action that causes trouble or difficulty: Getting this screw out is a real bugger.

▷ tr.v **4** have sex with (s.o) through the anus. **5** (slang) (often — s.t up) ruin (s.t). **6** (slang) (expression showing anger etc): Oh, bugger (it), I've dropped my money in the river! **bugger about/around** (slang) behave foolishly. **bugger s.o about** (slang) cause s.o trouble. **bugger off** (slang) go away.

,bugger-'all *unique n* (*slang*; do not use!) nothing at all: '*What have you had to eat today?*' '*Bugger-all.*'

'buggery *u.n* (do not use!) act of buggering(4) (s.o). *like buggery* (*slang*) very much: *My tooth's hurting like buggery.*

bugle /'bjuːgl/ *c.n* kind of metal wind instrument like a trumpet but smaller and usu without keys; it is often used by the armed forces.

'bugler *c.n* person, often a soldier, who blows a bugle.

build /bɪld/ *u.n* 1 shape; structure(1): *a person of powerful build* (i.e who has a powerful body).

▷ *v* (*p.t,p.p* built/bɪlt/) 2 *tr/intr.v* (often — *s.t from*, (*out*) *of*, *s.t*) make (s.t) by putting things together. **build s.t in(to s.t)** make s.t a part of s.t larger: *We are having some cupboards built into our bedroom.* ⇨ built-in(1). **build s.t into s.t** fit parts together to make s.t: *The child built his bricks into a castle.* **build s.t on(to s.t)** add s.t to s.t by building (⇨ build(2)). **build up** collect together to form a mass: *Traffic always builds up here when people start to go home in the evening.* **build s.o/s.t up** (*fig*) make a person, an event etc seem more important: *Joan's reputation as a singer was built up by favourable reports in the newspapers.* **build s.t up** (**a**) make s.t get bigger, better etc gradually: *This doctor has built up a good reputation over the years.* (**b**) collect s.t together, sometimes as a store: *The farmers built up their supplies of winter food for their animals.* (**c**) cover s.t with buildings(2). ⇨ built-up area. **build** (*up*)**on s.t** (*fig*) base one's hopes etc on s.t.

'builder *c.n* person who builds and repairs buildings(2) etc.

'building *n* 1 *u.n* (also *attrib*) work of building (⇨ build(2)) things: *building land/site* (i.e land etc for building on); *building materials.* 2 *c.n* thing that is built, e.g a house.

'building e,state *c.n* area of land on which a lot of houses are built.

'building so,ciety *c.n* company that lends money to help people build or buy their houses, using money that the company borrows from other people.

,built-'in *adj* (usu *attrib*) 1 that has been built as a fixed part of s.t: *built-in cupboards.* ⇨ build s.t in(to s.t). 2 (*fig*) natural: *a built-in sense of what is right and wrong.*

,built-,up 'area *c.n* area that has many buildings on it: *You must not drive faster than 50 kilometres an hour through a built-up area.*

bulb /bʌlb/ *c.n* 1 round part at the bottom of the stem of certain plants, e.g onions. 2 = light bulb. 3 thing that has the shape of a bulb(1), e.g the round part at the bottom of some thermometers.

'bulbous *adj* shaped like a bulb(1).

bulge /bʌldʒ/ *c.n* 1 part of s.t that sticks out further than the rest; swelling: *There was a bulge on the bed where the cat had got under the blanket.* 2 temporary(1) increase in size or numbers: *There was a bulge in the population here in the 1950s.*

▷ *intr.v* 3 swell out, grow, to more than the usual size.

bulk /bʌlk/ *n* 1 *u.n* great size, mass or quantity. 2 *c.n* large fat, often badly shaped, body: *The man was so fat that he had trouble getting his bulk into a seat on a plane.* 3 *u.n* rough food needed to keep one's bowels(1) working

properly; roughage. 4 *def.n* (often *the — of s.t*) the greater part (of s.t): *The bulk* (*of our food*) *comes from abroad.* **in bulk** (**a**) in large quantities or numbers at a time: *It is cheaper to buy in bulk.* (**b**) loose, not packed in separate containers.

'bulkiness *u.n* fact or state of being bulky.

'bulky *adj* (*-ier, -iest*) taking up a lot of space; large and awkward to move or carry.

bulkhead /'bʌlkhed/ *c.n* watertight dividing wall in a ship.

bull¹ /bʊl/ *c.n* 1 male of the cattle family. ⇨ bullock, cow¹(1), ox. 2 male of some other kinds of animals, e.g elephants. 3 man who is like a bull¹(1) because he is big, strong and often with a thick neck. 4 (*commerce*) (on a Stock Exchange(1)) person who buys stocks(10) and/ or shares(3) hoping that they will go up in value so that he/she can sell them at a profit. Opposite bear¹(2). (*like*) *a red rag to a bull* ⇨ rag¹. *take the bull by the horns* (*fig*; *informal*) meet a difficult or dangerous situation bravely, without trying to avoid it.

'bull,fight *c.n* fight between a bull(1) and men for public entertainment, esp in Spain and Mexico.

'bull,fighter *c.n* person who fights bulls(1).

'bull,fighting *u.n*.

'bull,finch *c.n* kind of small bird with a thick neck, the male of which has a red throat, found in Europe. ⇨ finch.

'bull,frog *c.n*. kind of large frog which croaks(2) loudly.

bullock /'bʊlək/ *c.n* young castrated bull.

'bull,ring *c.n* place where bullfights take place.

bull² /bʊl/ *u.n* (*slang*) 1 (in the armed forces) too much cleaning, polishing, unnecessary discipline. 2 (also 'bull,shit; do not use!) nonsense: *Don't give me that bull!*

bulldog /'bʊl,dɒg/ *c.n* kind of strong dog with a short thick neck and a flat face which is known for its courage.

bulldozer /'bʊl,dəʊzə/ *c.n* powerful machine that is used to level ground or remove things that are in the way.

bullet /'bʊlɪt/ *c.n* shaped piece of metal, usu made of lead, which is fired from a gun.

'bullet-,proof *adj* able to stop bullets going through.

bulletin /'bʊlɪtɪn/ *c.n* short public or official statement, e.g about the health of an important person: *a news bulletin.*

bullfight(er) ⇨ bull¹.

bullion /'bʊlɪən/ *u.n* gold or silver in the form of bars.

bullock, bullring ⇨ bull¹.

bull's-eye /'bʊlz ,aɪ/ *c.n* 1 centre area of a target(1). 2 shot that hits the bull's-eye(1).

bullshit ⇨ bull²(2).

bully /'bʊlɪ/ *c.n* (*pl -ies*) 1 person who frightens or hurts s.o who is weaker than he/she is.

▷ *tr.v* (*-ies, -ied*) 2 frighten or hurt (s.o) by using one's greater strength, size etc. *bully s.o into doing s.t* force s.o to do s.t by bullying(2) her/ him.

bulrush /'bʊl,rʌʃ/ *c.n* kind of tall plant of the reed(1) family, usu found in or near water and having a long soft brown head.

bulwark /'bʊlwək/ *c.n* 1 wall of earth etc, esp one built for protection against attack. 2 (*fig*) (often *— against s.o/s.t*) strong defence or protection (against s.o/s.t). **3** side or wall of a ship above deck level.

bum¹ /bʌm/ *attrib.adj* (*slang*) **1** bad; useless; that does not work properly: *This is a bum radio.*

▷ *c.n* (*slang*) **2** lazy person. **3** person who has no job or home.

bum² /bʌm/ *c.n* (*slang*) buttocks; bottom(3).

bumblebee /'bʌmblˌbiː/ *c.n* kind of big wild bee that makes a loud buzz(1).

bump /bʌmp/ *c.n* **1** blow, knock or shock. **2** sound of such a blow etc. **3** place on a road etc where the surface is raised: *Our teeth shook as the car went over the bumps.* **4** swelling caused by a bump(1): *Susan had a nasty bump on her knee after her fall.* **5** natural raised place on a person's head. **6** downward or upward movement of a plane caused by changes in air pressure.

▷ *v* **7** *tr/intr.v* (often — (*s.t*) *against/on s.o/s.t, into s.o/s.t, together*) hit (s.t) (against etc s.o/s.t). **8** *intr.v* (often — *along* (*s.t*)) go along (s.t) with irregular up and down movements: *We bumped along the rough road for hours.* **bump into s.o** **(a)** ⇨ bump(7). **(b)** (*fig; informal*) meet s.o by chance. **bump s.o off** (*fig; slang*) kill s.o. **bump s.t up** increase s.t, e.g a price, sharply.

'bumper *attrib.adj* **1** very good: *a bumper crop/harvest.*

▷ *c.n* **2** (US **'fender**) bar along the front and back of a vehicle to protect it when it hits s.t.

'bumpiness *u.n* fact or state of being bumpy.

'bumpy *adj* (-*ier*, -*iest*) full of bumps(3,5,6).

bumptious /'bʌmpʃəs/ *adj* (*derog*) rude and thinking one is much more important than one is.

'bumptiously *adv.* **'bumptiousness** *u.n.*

bun /bʌn/ *c.n* **1** kind of small round soft, often sweet, cake. **2** knot of hair at the back of s.o's, usu a woman's, neck: *Betty wears her hair in a bun.*

bunch /bʌntʃ/ *c.n* (often — *of s.t*) **1** group (of things of the same kind) which grow or are fastened/held together: *a bunch of grapes/flowers/keys.* **2** group (of people, esp bad ones). **the pick of the bunch** ⇨ pick¹(1).

▷ *tr/intr.v* **3** (often — (*s.o/s.t*) *together*) (cause (s.o/s.t) to) form a bunch(1,2).

bundle /'bʌndl/ *c.n* **1** (often — *of s.t*) collection (of things, e.g clothes) that have been gathered together. **a bundle of nerves** ⇨ nerves.

▷ *tr.v* **2 bundle s.t together/up** gather s.t together to form a bundle(1). **3 bundle s.o/s.t away, out, into s.t** get/put s.o/s.t away etc in a hurry.

bung /bʌŋ/ *c.n* **1** piece of wood, cork etc put in the hole in a barrel to stop the liquid coming out.

▷ *tr.v* **2** put a bung(1) in (s.t). **3** (*informal*) throw (s.t). **bung s.t up (with s.t)** (*informal*) fill s.t (with s.t).

bungalow /'bʌŋgələʊ/ *c.n* house with only one floor that is at ground level.

bungle /'bʌŋgl/ *c.n* **1** poor piece of work; mistake.

▷ *tr/intr.v* **2** do (s.t) badly; make one or more mistakes (in (s.t)).

'bungler *c.n* (*derog*) person who bungles(2).

bunion /'bʌnɪən/ *c.n* painful swelling, usu on the big joint of one's big toe.

bunk¹ /bʌŋk/ *c.n* (also ˌbunk 'bed) narrow bed, often on a ship or train, sometimes in a group of two or three above each other.

bunk² /bʌŋk/ *u.n* (also **bunkum** /'bʌŋkəm/) (*slang*) nonsense.

bunk³ /bʌŋk/ *c.n* **1 do a bunk** (*slang*) escape; run away.

▷ *tr/intr.v* **2** (often — *off s.t*) stay away (from s.w) without permission or a good reason: *Let's bunk (off) school today! John's bunking.*

bunker /'bʌŋkə/ *c.n* **1** large container for coal, oil etc, esp on a ship. **2** sandy hollow on a golf course which can cause difficulties for a player if her/his ball gets into it. **3** underground shelter against bombs, shells(4) etc in war.

bunkum ⇨ bunk².

bunny /'bʌnɪ/ *c.n* (*pl* -*ies*) (child's name for a) rabbit.

Bunsen burner /ˌbʌnsn 'bɜːnə/ *c.n* device used in chemical experiments which burns a mixture of air and gas to produce a flame.

bunting /'bʌntɪŋ/ *u.n* **1** kind of light cloth used mostly for making flags and street decorations. **2** flags and decorations made of bunting(1).

buoy /bɔɪ/ *c.n* **1** object that floats in the water and is anchored to the sea, river etc bed; it is used for tying boats or ships to, or to mark dangers. ⇨ lifebuoy.

▷ *tr.v* **2** mark the position of (s.t) with one or more buoys(1). **buoy s.o/s.t up (a)** keep s.o/s.t floating. **(b)** (*fig*) keep/make s.o cheerful.

'buoyancy *u.n* fact or state of being buoyant(1,2).

'buoyant *adj* **1** able to float. **2** (*fig*) cheerful; lighthearted.

'buoyantly *adv.*

burble /'bɜːbl/ *c.n* **1** gentle bubbling(7) sound, e.g made by a happy baby or by a small stream running over rocks.

▷ *intr.v* **2** make the sound of burbles(1).

burden /'bɜːdn/ *c.n* **1** heavy load that s.o/s.t has to carry. **2** (*fig*) thing that is unpleasant or difficult to bear: *Dorothy was tired of the burden of looking after so many children.* **be a burden to s.o/s.t** cause s.o/s.t trouble, expense etc. **beast of burden** ⇨ beast. **the burden of proof** the responsibility for proving s.t.

▷ *tr.v* **3** (often — *s.o/s.t with s.o/s.t*) put a burden(1,2) (consisting of s.o/s.t) on (s.o/s.t). Compare unburden.

'burdensome *adj* that is a burden(1,2).

bureau /'bjʊərəʊ/ *c.n* (*pl* -**s**, **bureaux** /'bjʊərəʊz/) (*French*) **1** writing desk with drawers and a top that folds down so that one can write on it. **2** (often with capital **B**) office or department for a particular purpose: *an Information/Tourist Bureau.*

bureaucrat /'bjʊərəˌkræt/ *c.n* (often *derog*) official who works in a government office, esp one who follows the rules closely without considering whether they are suitable to a particular case.

bureaucracy /bjʊə'rɒkrəsɪ/ *u.n* (often *derog*) (government of a country, city etc by) officials who are appointed, not elected, and who often use a system that is slow, complicated and inefficient.

bureaucratic /ˌbjʊərə'krætɪk/ *adj* of, referring to, like, bureaucrats or bureaucracy.

ˌbureau'cratically *adv.*

burgle /'bɜːgl/ *tr.v* **1** enter (a building), esp at

night, by force to steal from it. **2** (try to) steal from (s.o) by burgling(1): *We were burgled twice last year.*

burglar /ˈbɜːglə/ *c.n* person who enters a house, esp at night, by breaking a window etc in order to steal.

'burglar-a,larm *c.n* device that gives a warning when s.o enters a building when he/she is not supposed to.

'burglary *n* (*pl -ies*) **1** *u.n* fact of burgling. **2** *c.n* example of burgling.

burial (ground) ⇒ bury.

burlesque /bɜːˈlesk/ *c/u.n* amusing imitation of a person's way of talking, behaving etc, or of events in a book, play etc, in a (distorted(2)) way.

burly /ˈbɜːlɪ/ *adj* (*-ier, -iest*) (of a person) strong and heavily built: *a burly football player; a burly policeman.*

'burliness *u.n.*

burn /bɜːn/ *c.n* **1** mark or hurt on the body caused by fire, heat or acid: *The pilot received terrible burns on his face when his plane crashed.*

▷ *v* (*p.t,p.p* burned, burnt /bɜːnt/) **2** *tr.v* damage, destroy, (s.o/s.t) by fire, heat or acid. **3** *tr.v* use (s.t, e.g coal, gas) as fuel(1): *This stove burns wood.* **4** *intr.v* be on fire; be alight'/shining: *Fires were burning on all the hills. The street lights burn all night.* **5** *intr.v* be able to burn: *This wood is dry so it burns easily.* **6** *intr.v* be burnt(2): *I have lost my books; they all burnt in the fire last week.* **7** *intr.v* feel very hot: *My cheeks are burning after that walk in the cold wind.*

be burning to do s.t (*fig*) want to do s.t very much; be very eager to do s.t.

burn away (a) continue burning: *The fire was burning away cheerfully in the fireplace.* (b) become less/smaller, be destroyed, by burning: *We'll need some more candles; the others have nearly burnt away.* **burn s.t away** destroy s.t by burning it.

burn one's boats/bridges (*fig; informal*) do s.t that one cannot change again so that one is forced to continue in the same way.

burn the candle at both ends ⇒ candle.

burn (s.t) down (cause (s.t, e.g a building) to) burn until it is all gone.

burn one's fingers; **get one's fingers burnt** ⇒ finger(*n*).

burn a hole in one's pocket ⇒ hole.

burn low (of a lamp etc) burn less brightly, e.g because the oil is nearly finished.

burn the midnight oil ⇒ oil(*n*).

burn out (a) stop burning because of lack of fuel(1). (b) (of an electric motor etc) stop working because of damage from too strong an electric current. **burn oneself out** damage one's health, make oneself very tired etc by working too much etc. **burn s.t out** reduce s.t to a shell(2) by burning it: *Only the walls of the house were left standing after it had been burnt out.*

burnt to a frazzle ⇒ frazzle.

burn up flame up. **burn s.t up** get rid of s.t by burning it.

burn with s.t have very strong feelings, e.g of anger or eagerness, caused by s.t: *The children are burning with curiosity to see whether our new neighbours have children too.*

'burner *c.n* part of a lamp, stove etc from which flames come.

'burning *adj* **1** on fire. **2** (*attrib*) (*fig*) very strong: *Mary has always had a burning desire to succeed.* **3** (*attrib*) (*fig*) much talked about: *The burning question this week is who is going to win the match on Saturday.* **4** (*attrib*) (*fig*) (of thirst) great.

burnish /ˈbɜːnɪʃ/ *tr.v* polish (s.t, esp a metal) to make it shine.

burp /bɜːp/ *c.n* **1** (*informal*) = belch(1).

▷ *v* **2** *intr.v* (*informal*) belch(3). **3** *tr.v* make (a baby) burp(2) by tapping its back.

burr /bɜː/ *c.n* **1** case in which the seeds of some plants grow and which sticks to clothes, the hair of animals etc. **2** rough edge left on metal after it has been cut. **3** humming (⇒ hum) sound, e.g made by a machine as it spins.

burrow /ˈbʌrəʊ/ *c.n* **1** hole in the ground, esp one made by rabbits to live in.

▷ *intr.v* **2** dig. **burrow into s.t** (a) make a hole in s.t. (b) (*fig*) examine s.t deeply.

bursar /ˈbɜːsə/ *c.n* **1** school or college treasurer. **2** student who has a bursary(2).

'bursary *c.n* (*pl -ies*) **1** bursar's(1) office. **2** money given to a student to (help) support her/him during her/his studies, usu because she/he is a particularly good student. ⇒ award(3), exhibition(3), scholarship(2).

burst /bɜːst/ *c.n* **1** explosion. **2** split or hole caused by pressure of water, ice etc: *There was a burst in one of our pipes as a result of last week's frost*(1). **3** (usu a — *of s.t*) sudden beginning (of s.t, e.g laughter or applause). **4** short violent effort: *When Tom is preparing for an examination he works in short bursts of a few hours at a time.* **5** number of shots fired quickly out of a gun.

▷ *v* (*p.t,p.p* burst) **6** *tr/intr.v* (cause (s.t) to) explode or to split apart (violently): *The bomb burst when it hit the ground. John has burst a blood vessel.* **7** *tr/intr.v* break outwards (through s.t): *After the heavy rain the river banks have burst* (or *the river has burst its banks*). **8** *intr.v* (of a balloon, bubble(1) etc) break.

burst forth (**into song** etc) suddenly begin (to do s.t, e.g to sing).

burst in (**(up)on s.o/s.t**) arrive suddenly (while s.o is doing s.t); interrupt (s.o/s.t).

burst into s.t (a) enter s.t suddenly. (b) begin to do s.t: *burst into flower.* ⇒ burst forth (into s.t).

burst into flame(s) ⇒ flame(*n*).

burst open open suddenly.

burst out crying, laughing etc suddenly begin to cry etc. **burst out** (**of s.t**) escape (from s.t) suddenly.

burst through (**s.t**) get through (s.t) suddenly.

burst with s.t (usu with an '*-ing*' form) be very full of s.t: *Mollie's basket was bursting with good things to eat. The children are bursting with excitement about the holidays.*

bury /ˈberɪ/ *tr.v* (*-ies, -ied*) **1** put (s.o/s.t) under the earth; cover (s.o/s.t) with earth etc, often to hide her/him/it: *Dogs bury bones.* **2** put (a dead person) in a grave, or into the sea when at sea. **bury oneself in the country** go into the country in order to have peace and quiet. **bury oneself in one's books, studies** etc spend a lot of time reading, studying etc. **bury one's hands in one's pockets** (*fig*) put one's hands deep into one's

pockets. **bury one's face/head in one's hands**
(*fig*) put one's face/head between one's hands.
bury one's head in the sand ⇒ head(*n*). **bury
the hatchet** ⇒ hatchet.
'**burial** *c/u.n* act of burying(1,2) (s.o/s.t).
'**burial** ,**ground** *c.n* place where people are
buried(2); cemetery.

bus /bʌs/ *c.n* (*pl* buses) **1** vehicle that travels
along the same roads on each trip and that picks
passengers up and puts them down at particular
stops. **by bus** in a bus: *We go/travel to work by
bus.* **catch a/the bus** (**to s.w**) (manage to) get on
a bus and go (to s.w). **miss a/the bus** arrive after
a/the bus has already left. **miss the bus** (*fig*) ⇒
miss(*v*).
▷ *v* **2** *intr.v* (usu — *into town* etc) travel by bus. **3** *tr.v*
send (s.o) by bus, e.g to school.
'**bus con**,**ductor** *c.n* ⇒ conductor(3).
'**bus con**,**ductress** *c.n* ⇒ conductress.

bush /buʃ/ *n* **1** plant that is like a small
tree. **2** *u/def.n* wild country, esp in Africa and
Australia. **beat about the bush** (*fig*; *informal*)
avoid saying s.t directly.
'**bushy** *adj* (-*ier*, -*iest*) **1** covered with bushes(1).
2 growing with thick rough hairs: *bushy eyebrows.*

busier, busiest, busily ⇒ busy.

business /'bɪznɪs/ *n* (also *attrib*) **1** *c/u.n* job;
work; way of earning money: *What sort of business do you do?* **2** *u.n* trade; buying and selling:
*We do business with a lot of countries. How's busi-
ness these days?* **3** *c.n* commercial firm, company,
shop etc: *John owns his own business.* **4** *sing.n*
duty; responsibility: *My business is making sure
everyone works properly.* **5** *u.n* right: *You have
no business to be here at this hour instead of at
school.* **6** *sing.n* matter; subject: *What's all this
business of a visit to France next week?* **7** *sing.n*
(*informal*) difficulty: *Changing a tyre is a terrible
business!* **funny business** ⇒ funny. **get down to
business** start doing s.t seriously: *Well, we've
had our tea so let's get down to business again.* **go
into business** (**as s.t**) start a business(3) (doing
a certain job). **go out of business** stop having a
business(3), usu because one, the company etc
is not successful. **in business** having a busi-
ness(2) job. **like nobody's business** ⇒ nobody.
mean business be serious and determined. **mind
one's own business** (*informal*) not interfere
in other people's private business(6): '*What are
you doing?*' '*Mind your own business!*' *I was just
minding my own business when this man started
shouting at me.* **monkey business** ⇒ monkey. **on
business** in order to do business(2): *Eric is here
on business, not for pleasure.*
'**business** ,**hours** *pl.n* times during which
business(2) is done, e.g 9 a.m to 5.30
p.m.
'**business**,**like** *adj* showing, using, a careful
system; efficient.
'**business**,**man** *c.n* (*pl* -**men**) man who works
in business(2).
'**business**,**woman** *c.n* (*pl* -,**women**) woman
who works in business(2).

busker /'bʌskə/ *c.n* musician or actor who performs in the street for money, often to people in
a queue.

bust[1] /bʌst/ *c.n* **1** statue of the human head
and shoulders made out of stone, metal etc.

2 woman's chest(1). **3** measurement around a
woman's chest and back.

bust[2] /bʌst/ *v* (*p.t,p.p* bust) (*slang*) **1** *tr/intr.v*
(cause (s.t) to) break, burst: *I dropped my clock
and bust it.* **2** *tr.v* (*informal*) (of police) catch
and arrest (s.o): *The man was busted for theft.* **go
bust** (*slang*) be ruined; run out of money.

bustle /'bʌsl/ *c/u.n* **1** (often *in a* —) (state of)
busy excited activity.
▷ *intr.v* **2** (often — *about/around*) move about
quickly in a busy excited way. **bustle with activity**,
life etc be full of busy activity etc.

busy /'bɪzɪ/ *adj* (-*ier*, -*iest*) **1** (often — *doing s.t*)
actively engaged (in doing s.t): *Don't go in there:
they're busy discussing things.* **2** full of activity: *We
had a busy day's work yesterday.* **3** (of a telephone
line etc) in use; engaged: *I tried ringing Fred but
his line was busy.* **4** (*derog*) (of a picture etc) too
full of small details that are not interesting. **as
busy as a bee** very busy. **get busy** start doing
s.t.
▷ *reflex.v* **2** (-*ies*, -*ied*) **5** (often — *oneself doing/with
s.t*) keep (oneself) busy(1) (doing/with s.t): *Paula
busies herself with her garden at weekends.*
'**busily** *adv.*
'**busy**,**body** *c.n* (*pl* -*ies*) (*derog*) person who
interferes in other people's business(6).
'**busyness** *u.n.*

but (strong form /bʌt/, weak form /bət/) *adv*
1 (*literary*) only; just: *Christina was but a baby
when her mother died.* **all but** ⇒ all.
▷ *conj* **2** and in spite of that/this; however; yet(4);
only(8): *We tried to arrive on time but were
unable to.* **3** except for the fact that; if it had
not been for the fact that: *We wanted to go out
but it rained.* **4** (in negative sentences) (*literary*)
without it happening that: *I can never go to
London but I remember my happy youth there.*
5 (in negative sentences) (*literary*) that: *There's
no doubt/question but it was Edward that broke
the window.* **6** instead; rather: *The boy ate not
one plate of the food but three!* **7** and in spite of
that; yet also: *John is rich but unhappy.* **8** (used in
exclamations to show disagreement, protest(1) or
surprise): *'It's time to go to bed, children.' 'But we
don't want to!' 'Lisa's coming home tomorrow!'
'But that's wonderful news!'* **9** (showing that one
is changing the subject): *But now we'd better get
down to business.* **but then** (**again**) on the other
hand; in another way: *The sea is usually warm
here in summer, but then currents sometimes
bring cold water in.* **not only . . . but** (**also**) . . .
⇒ not.
▷ *prep* **10** except: *All but one of the guests have
arrived. Who but a fool would say such a thing!*
but for s.o/s.t if s.o/s.t had not done s.t: *But
for the help of another boy, George might have
drowned.* **who/what . . . but . . .** surprisingly, . . .:
*We were invited to meet a new arrival in the town
and who did it prove to be but our very old friend
Andrew from Australia!*
buts *pl.n.* **ifs and buts** ⇒ if(5).

butane /'bjuːteɪn/ *u.n* (also '**butane** ,**gas**) kind
of gas often used to fill cigarette lighters or for
cooking or lighting, *chem.form* C_4H_{10}.

butch /butʃ/ *adj* (*slang*) **1** (of a woman) who
behaves, looks, dresses etc like a man. **2** (of a
man) who behaves etc in an excessively male
way.

butcher /'bʊtʃə/ *c.n* **1** person whose business is killing, cutting up, animals and selling the meat as food. **2** (also **'butcher's**) shop where meat is prepared and sold. **3** (*derog*) person who kills cruelly and/or unnecessarily.

▷ *tr.v* **4** kill (an animal) for food. **5** kill (s.o) cruelly and/or unnecessarily: *The soldiers butchered all the people in the village.*

'butchery *u.n* **1** trade of a butcher(1). **2** cruel and/or unnecessary killing.

butler /'bʌtlə/ *c.n* chief male staff member in a household who is in charge of the wine etc.

butt¹ /bʌt/ *c.n* **1** large barrel for wine, beer etc. **2** = water butt.

butt² /bʌt/ *c.n* **1** thick end (of a weapon or tool): *The soldier rested the butt of his rifle on the ground.* **2** end of a smoked cigarette or used candle which remains after the rest has been burnt. **3** (*fig*) (often *the — of s.t*) person who is the victim(1) of criticism, a joke etc.

butt³ /bʌt/ *c.n* **1** violent push or blow with one's head: *The goat gave the cat a butt when it came too close to its young.*

▷ *tr/intr.v* **2** give (s.o/s.t) a butt(1). **butt in** (**on s.t**) (*informal*) interrupt (a conversation etc).

butter /'bʌtə/ *u.n* **1** kind of fatty yellow food product made from cream and used for spreading on bread, in cooking etc. **Butter wouldn't melt in s.o's mouth** (*informal*) S.o pretends that he/she would never do anything wrong.

▷ *tr.v* **2** cover (s.t) with butter(1); spread butter(1) on (s.t, usu a slice of bread). **butter s.o up** (*informal*) praise s.o to try to get s.t one wants from her/him; flatter(1) s.o.

'butter,fingers *c.n* (*pl* **butterfingers**) (*informal*) person who cannot hold things without dropping them, esp when trying to catch them.

'butter,milk *u.n* liquid left after butter has been made from milk.

'butter,scotch *u.n* kind of sweet made by boiling butter and sugar together.

buttercup /'bʌtə,kʌp/ *c.n* kind of small wild plant with bright yellow flowers; it is often found in grassy fields.

butterfly /'bʌtə,flaɪ/ *c.n* (*pl* **-ies**) kind of insect that flies during the day and has four wings that are often brightly coloured. Compare moth. **have butterflies in one's stomach** (*fig*; *informal*) feel very nervous about s.t one is going to do.

buttermilk, butterscotch ⇨ butter.

buttocks /'bʌtəks/ *pl.n* the part of one's body which one sits on; bottom(3); one of the two parts is a buttock.

button /'bʌtn/ *c.n* **1** small round piece of bone, metal etc which is sewn onto clothing and used to fasten one part to another by passing it through a buttonhole(1). **2** small round object shaped like a button: *a button one pushes to ring an electric bell.* ⇨ pushbutton.

▷ *v* **3** *tr.v* (often *— s.t up*) fasten (s.t) with one or more buttons(1). Opposite unbutton. **4** *intr.v* be able to be buttoned(3): *This coat buttons right up to the chin.* **button s.t up** (a) ⇨ button(3). (b) (*fig*; *informal*) finish s.t completely and successfully.

'button,hole *c.n* **1** hole made in a piece of clothing for passing a button through to fasten s.t up. **2** flower worn in the top buttonhole(1) of a coat etc.

▷ *tr.v* **3** approach (s.o) in order to talk to her/him: *I was buttonholed by a stranger who wanted to tell me his life story.*

buttress /'bʌtrɪs/ *c.n* **1** piece built, usu of stone or bricks, to support a wall. **2** (*fig*) support: *Our political party is a buttress against violent change.*

▷ *tr.v* **3** support (s.t, usu a wall) (as if) with a buttress(1). **4** (*fig*; *formal*) support (s.o/s.t): *Their help and advice buttressed her during that difficult time.*

buxom /'bʌksəm/ *adj* (of a woman) attractively fat.

buy /baɪ/ *c.n* **1** bargain(2): *That shirt was a good/ real buy; I only paid £2 for it!*

▷ *tr.v* **3** (*p.t,p.p* bought /bɔːt/) **2** (often *— s.t for £5 etc, with s.t*) get (s.t) by paying (s.t, usu money) or giving s.t, e.g help, for it: *I bought this coat for £25 ten years ago. Our soldiers bought our freedom with their lives.* **3** be able to buy or get: *A pound now buys half what it did only a few years ago.* **buy s.t back** buy s.t again after having sold it. **buy s.t in** (a) buy a supply of s.t: *The baker always buys in large amounts of flour at the beginning of each week.* (b) (of a seller at an auction(1)) prevent anyone else buying s.t by buying it oneself because the offers are too low. **buy s.o off/over** bribe s.o. **buy s.o out** buy s.o's whole business, interest in s.t etc. **buy s.t up** buy all of a supply, business etc.

'buyer *c.n* **1** person who buys s.t. **2** person whose job is to buy goods to be sold in a shop.

'buyers' ,market *c.n* time when more people are trying to sell things than to buy them so that prices are low. Compare sellers' market.

buzz /bʌz/ *c.n* **1** sound (like that) of bees; sound of many people talking so that one cannot hear clearly what any of them are saying; sound of machines that are spinning round: *a buzz of conversation.* **give s.o a buzz** (*informal*) phone s.o.

▷ *v* **2** *intr.v* (often *— with s.t*) make the sound of a buzz(1) (because of s.t, often excitement). **3** *tr.v* (*informal*) call (s.o) by using a buzzer or phone. **4** *tr.v* (of a plane or its pilot) fly dangerously close to (s.o/s.t). **buzz off** (*slang*) go away.

'buzzer *c.n* electrical device used to make a buzz(1), esp to call s.o, get her/his attention etc.

buzzard /'bʌzəd/ *c.n* kind of large bird of prey(1) of the hawk¹(1) family.

by /baɪ/ *adv* **1** (also *close —*) near in position: *Several people were standing by, watching the men work.* **2** so as to pass in place or time: *Several people walked by. After an hour had gone by, they returned.* **3** aside; out of the way; out of use for the present: *We are setting some money by for our holidays next summer.* **by and by** eventually; at last: *By and by we arrived at a large building on a corner.* **by and large** on the whole; considering all the facts: *I enjoy this work by and large.*

▷ *prep* **4** (also *close —*) near in position; next to: *I sat by the fire reading. There was a child by her side.* **5** (introducing a means) using the method(1) of; by means of: *You can get there by sea or by air. You can see by looking at it that the child is happy.* **6** (introducing the difference resulting from comparing things): *We won the match by seven points.* **7** before the end of (a time): *You must be here by five p.m (at the latest).*

8 passing; so as to pass: *Several people walked by the sick man without stopping.* **9** joining the length, breadth etc of s.t: *Our garden is 20 metres by 16.* **10** (introducing the part of s.t to which one does s.t): *Jenny took the child by the hand and led him across the road. Always hold it by the handle.* **11** (introducing the person/animal/thing who/that does, makes etc s.t): *This play is by Shakespeare. This bird was killed by our cat. Our house was damaged by fire.* **12** (also — *way of s.t*) through; via(1): *The children came in by the back door.* **13** because of; through: *by mistake; by order of the judge.* **14** in a way that is counted in units of: *They sell potatoes here by the kilogram.* **15** (introducing s.t that serves as a sign or means of recognition): *You will recognize Peter by his red hair.* **16** according to: *It is 11.23 by my watch.* **17** (introducing the conditions in which s.t happens): *Reading by bad light is not good for one's eyes.* **begin**, **finish** etc **by doing s.t** do s.t as one's beginning, finish etc. **by car**, **bus** etc ⇒ car(1), bus etc. **by far** ⇒ far(*adv*). **by all means**; **by no/not any/means** ⇒ means. **by the by/way** (used when changing the subject of conversation) incidentally(2): *Well, that finishes our work. By the by, are you free for lunch?* For noun + 'by', e.g *by birth, by heart, by day/night, by far, little by little, side by side*, or verb + 'by', e.g *call by, get by, live by, swear by s.t,* ⇒ the noun or verb.

'by-e,lection *c.n* election caused by the death, resignation etc of a member of parliament and not held as part of a general election.

'by,gone *adj* of or referring to a time or times now past: *Old people often remember bygone days with pleasure.*

'by,gones *pl.n* **let bygones be bygones** (*informal*) forget about unpleasant times in the past so that one forgives people for anything bad they have done.

'by-,law *c.n* (also **'bye-,law**) local law made by a town council etc.

'by,pass *c.n* **1** wide road built round a town etc so that traffic does not have to pass through it. **2** small pipe allowing gas, oil etc through when the main pipe is closed.
▷ *tr.v* **3** avoid (s.t), e.g by using a bypass(1,2): *Let's bypass that problem and come back to it later.*

'by,path *c.n* less important or direct path than the main one(s).

'by-,product *c.n* thing produced at the same time as s.t more important: *One of the by-products one gets during the production of gas from coal is tar(1).*

'by,road *c.n* small less important road.

'by,stander *c.n* person standing near, but not taking part in, an activity: *There were several bystanders at the scene of the accident.*

,by,way *c.n* = bypath/byroad.

'by,ways *pl.n* (often *the* — *of s.t*) less important or less well known parts (of s.t, e.g history).

'by,word *c.n* (often — *for s.t*) example (of s.t) that is so typical of it that one immediately thinks of that thing when the name is mentioned: *Ancient Rome became a byword for glory and power.*

bye¹ /baɪ/ *c.n* **1** situation in which one does not have to play against another person/team in that particular round of a competition, so that one goes straight into the next round.

2 (in cricket¹) run(8) scored when the ball passes the batsman without her/him hitting it.

bye² /baɪ/ *interj* (also **bye-bye** /,baɪ 'baɪ/) (*informal*) goodbye.

bye-byes /'baɪ ,baɪz/ *pl.n* **go to bye-byes** (expression used by, or when speaking to, a small child) go to bed.

bye-law ⇒ by-law.

Cc

C, c /siː/ *c/unique n* **1** 3rd letter of the English alphabet.
▷ *written abbr* **2** cent(s). **3** (**c**) centimetre(s). **4** (**C**) century; centuries: *the 19th C.* **5** (**c**) circa. ⇒ ca. **6** (**C**) Conservative(3).
▷ *symbol* **7** Roman numeral for 100. **8** (**C**) Celsius. **9** (**C**) Centigrade. **10** (**C**) (*music*) note in a musical scale: middle C.

CA *written abbr* chartered accountant.

ca *written abbr* circa ⇒ C, c(5).

cab /kæb/ *c.n* **1** car for hire; taxi. **2** separate place where the driver of a railway engine or a lorry sits.

'cab ,driver *c.n* (*informal* **'cabbie**, **'cabby**) person who drives a cab(1).

'cab ,rank/,stand *c.n* = taxi rank.

cabaret /'kæbə,reɪ/ *c/u.n* (example of the) performance of music, singing, dancing etc which one watches while having a meal or drinks in a restaurant, nightclub etc.

cabbage /'kæbɪdʒ/ *n* (also *attrib*) **1** *c.n* kind of vegetable with green or red leaves which grow in the shape of a ball. **2** *u.n* this vegetable prepared and cooked for eating.

cabbie, cabby /'kæbɪ/ *c.n* (*pl* -ies) (*informal*) cab driver.

caber /'keɪbə/ *c.n* long piece of a trunk of a tree which athletes in Scotland throw as far as they can in a competition. **toss the caber** throw a caber in this competition.

cabin /'kæbɪn/ *c.n* **1** small house or hut, usu made of logs. **2** room in a ship for passengers or members of the crew to sleep in. **3** part of an aircraft where the crew or the passengers sit.

'cabin ,cruiser *c.n* motorboat used for pleasure which has one or more cabins(2) in it.

cabinet /'kæbɪnɪt/ *n* **1** *c.n* kind of cupboard with drawers and shelves, used for storing or showing things. **2** *c/def.n* (often with capital **C**) group of ministers, esp in the UK, who run the government. **filing cabinet** ⇒ file³.

'cabinet ,minister *c.n* member of a/the cabinet(2).

cable /'keɪbl/ *c.n* **1** thick strong rope made of steel, nylon etc, used for tying ships to the side of docks, to pull or hold very heavy things etc. **2** group of metal wires that carry electricity from place to place, either above the ground on poles (pylons) or underground. **3** group of metal wires that carry telephone or other messages from place to place: *a new telephone cable across the Atlantic.* **4** (also **'cable₁gram**) message sent by means of a cable(3): *I got a cable telling me my mother was ill.*

▷ *v* **5** *intr.v* send a cable(4): *A letter won't get there in time so we'd better cable.* **6** *tr.v* send a cable(4) to (s.o): *He cabled his office with the news.*

'cable-₁car *c.n* kind of carriage for passengers that hangs from a cable(1) and that goes up and down a steep hill or mountain.

'cable₁gram *c.n* ⇨ cable(4).

'cable-₁railway *c.n* railway that uses cables(1) to go up and down a steep hill or mountain.

₁cable₁tele'vision *u.n* (also **₁cable₁T'V**) television broadcasts that are sent to the home by a cable(3) instead of radio waves.

cacao /kə'kɑːəʊ/ *n* (*pl* -s) **1** *c/u.n* seed from which chocolate is made. **2** *c.n* (also **ca'cao ₁tree**) tree on which these seeds grow.

cachet /'kæʃeɪ/ *n* **1** *c.n* special mark on s.t to show that it is of good quality or value: *Each bottle of scent had a cachet on it showing that it had come from a famous manufacturer.* **2** *u.n* good position in society: *There is a great deal of cachet to be gained by being made a lord.*

cackle /'kækl/ *n* **1** *u.n* noise made by a hen, usu after it has laid an egg. **2** *c.n* loud silly, foolish talk. **cut the cackle** (*slang*) stop wasting time and start doing s.t (useful).

▷ *intr.v* **3** (of hens) make the sound of a cackle(1). **4** (often — *with laughter*) laugh or talk loudly.

cacophony /kə'kɒfənɪ/ *c/u.n* (*pl* -*ies*) (example of the) mixture of sounds that do not go together or are out of tune: *the cacophony of road drills, cars* hooting(5) *and people shouting.*

cacophonous /kə'kɒfənəs/ *adj.*

cactus /'kæktəs/ *c.n* (*pl* -es, cacti /'kæktaɪ/) plant with thick stems and often prickles on it, that grows in a desert.

cad /kæd/ *c.n* (*old use*; *joking*) person, usu a man, who behaves in a dishonourable way: *He's a bit of a cad and I wouldn't trust him with my money.*

'caddish *adj* behaving like a cad.

caddy¹ /'kædɪ/ *c.n* (*pl* -*ies*) (also **'caddie**) **1** person who carries the golf clubs for a player.

▷ *intr.v* (-*ies*, -*ied*) (also **'caddie**) **2** (often — *for s.o*) be a caddie(1) for s.o; do a job (for a player).

caddy² /'kædɪ/ *c.n* (*pl* -*ies*) tea caddy.

cadence /'keɪdəns/ *n* (*formal*) **1** *u.n* regular beat in sound. **2** *c.n* rise and fall of a voice, e.g in speaking a sentence. **3** *c.n* (*music*) group of sounds at the end of a piece of music.

cadenza /kə'denzə/ *c.n* (*music*) piece of music played by one musician among a group, usu towards the end of a longer piece of music.

cadet /kə'det/ *c.n* young person who is being trained for the armed forces, the police etc: *an army cadet; a police cadet.*

ca'det ₁corps /kɔː/ *c.n* (*pl* cadet corps /kɔː/z/) group in some UK schools which receives training for the armed forces.

cadge /kædʒ/ *def.n* **1** **be on the cadge** be engaged in cadging(2): *He's always on the cadge but don't ever give him anything.*

▷ *intr/tr.v* (*informal*) **2** (usu — (*s.t*) *from/off s.o*) get

(s.t, esp money) or borrow (from s.o) in a begging way: *I tried to cadge a lift off them but they were going in a different direction.*

cadre /'kɑːdə/ *c.n* **1** (*military*) small group of people in the armed forces who have had special training in s.t. **2** small, usu political, group of people who have special powers and responsibilities inside a larger group: *The government set up cadres of local officials to run the state farms.*

Caesarean /sɪ'zeərɪən/ *c.n* (also **Cae'sarian**; **Cæ'sarian ₁birth**; US **Ce'sarean**, **Ce'sarian**) (*medical*) operation in which a mother's body is cut open (*Caesarean section*) and a baby taken out of the womb rather than having it delivered in the normal way, usu because it would be difficult or dangerous.

café, cafe /'kæfeɪ/ *c.n* (*pl* -s) small inexpensive restaurant: *a motorway café.*

cafeteria /₁kæfɪ'tɪərɪə/ *c.n* (*pl* -s) restaurant (esp in a shop, office or factory) where people serve themselves, using trays which they then take to a table.

caffeine /'kæfiːn/ *u.n* substance found in coffee and tea which makes people active (and sometimes unable to sleep).

caftan /'kæftæn/ *c.n* (also **'kaftan**) kind of long loose dress worn by people in the Middle East and also by some people in western countries.

cage /keɪdʒ/ *c.n* **1** box with bars or wires on the sides (and top and bottom) in which animals and birds are kept: *a lion's cage; a bird cage.* **2** lift which has bars at the side and is used in a mine¹(1).

▷ *tr.v* **3** put (animals or birds) in a cage(1). **be/feel caged in** (of a person) be/feel that one cannot escape from a place or situation: *I was beginning to feel caged in in my job as there were no signs that I would be promoted.*

cagey /'keɪdʒɪ/ *adj* (-ier, -iest) (*informal*) not wanting to talk about s.t which one is doing etc; secretive: *He's very cagey about his plans because he's afraid someone will steal his ideas.*

'cagily *adv.* **'caginess** *u.n.*

cahoots /kə'huːts/ *pl.n* **be in cahoots with s.o** (*informal*) do or plan s.t (usu s.t wrong) in secret with s.o: *He's in cahoots with the local police force which is as corrupt as he is.*

Cain /keɪn/ *unique n* **raise Cain** ⇨ raise(*v*).

cairn /keən/ *c.n* pile of stones, usu placed on a hill or mountain, to show direction, remind people of a famous event etc.

cajole /kə'dʒəʊl/ *tr.v* (usu — *s.o into*, *out of*, (*doing*) *s.t*) make s.o do s.t (not do s.t) by continuous persuasion, esp when he/she is unwilling at the beginning: *Oliver cajoled Tracy into joining the tennis club.*

ca'jolery *u.n.*

cake /keɪk/ *n* **1** *u.n* kind of sweet food made by cooking flour, eggs, milk, sugar and other things together: *chocolate cake; a piece/slice of cake.* **2** *c.n* piece of this food in a particular shape or size: *a birthday cake.* **3** *c.n* piece of other kinds of food shaped like a cake(2): *fish cakes; potato cakes.* **4** *c.n* hard piece of s.t shaped like a cake(2): *a cake of soap.* **be a piece of cake** ⇨ piece(*n*). (*go/sell*) **like hot cakes** (*informal*) be sold very easily and quickly: *The new personal computer is selling like hot cakes.* **have one's cake and eat it** (*fig*; *informal*) get or have s.t, e.g an advantage, without any disadvantages. (**have/get**) **a slice of the cake** (*fig*; *informal*) (have/get) a share in s.t that brings a profit or is to one's advantage.

▷ *v* **5** *tr.v* (often — *s.t with s.t*) cover the surface of (s.t) (with s.t that then may dry on it): *The villagers caked the walls of their houses with mud.* **6** *intr.v* become hard; become covered with s.t: *As he walked across the field, mud caked on his trousers.*

calamine /'kæləˌmaɪn/ *u.n* (also **'calaˌmine ˌlotion**) pink liquid put on one's skin when it has become red and sore from sunburn etc.

calamity /kə'læmɪtɪ/ *c.n* (*pl* **-ies**) **1** bad thing that happens to s.o and esp the feeling of misery and loss that this brings: *It was a great calamity for Wendy to lose her husband in a road accident.* **2** great, often natural, event that brings misfortune etc: *The people suffered a* series(1) *of calamities, first an earthquake, then floods and finally disease.*

ca'lamitous *adj* of or referring to misery, misfortune etc.

calcium /'kælsɪəm/ *u.n* (*chemistry*) white metal that is an element(1) found in various substances such as chalk, bones and teeth, *chem.symb* Ca.

calculate /'kælkjʊˌleɪt/ *tr.v* **1** work out (a sum), find (a result) by using numbers: *He calculated the total cost at £2000.* **2** guess or estimate(2) (s.t) on the basis of the facts or numbers that one has: *I calculated that it would take us three years to pay back the loan.* **calculate on s.t** hope in advance for s.t to happen; base one's decisions on s.t: *We hadn't calculated on a railway strike and so we missed our flight.*

calculable /'kælkjʊləbl/ *adj* (*formal*) that can be measured, valued. Opposite incalculable.

'calcuˌlated *adj* (usu *attrib*) (of an action etc) thought out in advance; planned and intended, esp to hurt s.o: *It was a calculated insult that Ann was not prepared for.* **calculated risk** ⇒ risk.

'calcuˌlating *adj* (*derog*) (of a person) thinking in a clear but cold way how to do s.t, get a result etc: *She's an unpleasant and calculating woman who always wants her own way.*

'calcuˌlating maˌchine *c.n* machine that does sums mechanically or electronically.

calculation /ˌkælkjʊ'leɪʃən/ *c/u.n* **1** (example of the amount or sum found by the) act of calculating (⇒ calculate(1)) s.t. **2** opinion after serious thought: *Their calculation was that he would not oppose them.*

'calcuˌlator *c.n* **1** (also **'pocket ˌcalcuˌlator**) machine that does calculations(1). **2** person who does calculations.

calculus /'kælkjʊləs/ *u.n* (*mathematics*) system of mathematics that deals with quantities that can change (i.e which vary).

caldron ⇒ cauldron.

calendar /'kælɪndə/ *c.n* **1** system of days, months and dates arranged in a particular way: *the* Christian/Jewish/Muslim *calendars.* **2** list of such dates, usu with one month printed on each sheet. **3** list of future events that refer to a particular subject: *the sporting calendar.*

ˌcalendar 'month *c.n* whole month from the first to the last day as arranged in a calendar(2). Compare lunar month.

calf /kɑːf/ *n* (*pl* calves /kɑːvz/) **1** *c.n* young cow or bull. **2** *c.n* young animal of certain other kinds:

an elephant calf; a seal[1] *calf.* **3** *u.n* (also **'calf,-skin**) kind of soft leather made from the skin of a calf(1). **4** *c.n* rounded flesh at the back of the leg between the knee and the ankle. **be in/with calf** (of a cow and other animals) be pregnant. **kill the fatted calf** ⇒ fatted.

'calf ˌlove *u.n* love that a young, usu inexperienced, person has.

'calf,skin *u.n* ⇒ calf(3).

calve /kɑːv/ *intr.v* give birth to a baby cow or other animal.

calibrate /'kælɪˌbreɪt/ *tr.v* (*technical*) **1** measure the inside width of (a tube or gun). **2** mark or check (a series of measurements) on a scale or measuring instrument.

calibration /ˌkælɪ'breɪʃən/ *n* **1** *c.n* act of calibrating s.t. **2** *c.n* mark on a scale or measuring instrument.

calibre /'kælɪbə/ *n* (US **'caliber**) **1** *c.n* (*technical*) inside width (of a tube or gun). **2** *c.n* (*technical*) size of a bullet or shell, usu measured in millimetres. **3** *c/u.n* special quality, value or importance of s.o or s.t: *People in government should be of high moral calibre.*

calico /'kælɪˌkəʊ/ *u.n* kind of heavy cotton cloth.

calipers ⇒ callipers.

calk /kɔːk/ ⇒ caulk.

call /kɔːl/ *n* **1** *c.n* thing said in a loud voice, usu to attract attention: *We heard many calls for help from people trapped in the building.* **2** *c.n* sound made by an animal or a bird, or an imitation of this: *I could hear the call of a wild dog in the distance. He could imitate the calls of many birds.* **3** *c.n* visit, esp one for an official or business reason: *The doctor had several calls to make to patients' homes.* **4** *c.n* use of the telephone to talk to s.o: *There's a call for you from New York. I'd like a call at 7 o'clock* (i.e to be woken up then). **5** *c.n* (*commerce*) official request for money that has been promised but not paid to a company as part of its capital. **6** *c.n* (in card games) what a player says he/she is going to do; bid(2): *It's your call, partner.* **7** *def.n* (usu *the — of the s.t*) thing that attracts s.o, esp in nature: *Alex felt the call of the sea.* **a call on s.t** (*formal*) a claim that needs to be met; s.t that needs one's time, attention etc: *Having just got married and having bought a new house, they had many calls on their limited* resources(1). **at/on call** available to do s.t when asked, if necessary etc: *Firemen have to be on call 24 hours of the day.* **be no call for s.o to do s.t** be no need or reason for s.o to do s.t, esp s.t that may annoy others: *There's no call for you to get angry about what Jack said.* **be no call for s.t** be no need or demand for s.t: *There's no call for these old-fashioned tools nowadays.* **be/stay within call** remain close enough to hear a call(1) from s.o. **pay a call (on s.o)** visit s.o.

▷ *v* **8** *tr/intr.v* speak in a loud voice; shout (s.t): *Did you hear someone calling (me)? 'Be careful!' he called.* ⇒ call (s.t) out. **9** *tr.v* send (s.o) a message to come and do s.t: *I'm not feeling very well so could you call a doctor?* **10** *tr/intr.v* use a telephone to speak to (s.o): *I called (you) earlier this morning but you were in a meeting.* ⇒ call (s.o) back, call s.o up. **11** *intr.v* make a visit: *I'm sorry that I was out when you called.* ⇒ call about s.t, call (in) at s.w, call by ((at) s.w), call for s.o/s.t, call on s.o, call round (at s.w). **12** *tr.v* make a statement, usu an official one, that (s.t) is going to happen: *The government decided to call an election. The union called a strike.* **13** *intr.v* (in card games) make a call(6): *It's your turn to call, partner.* **14** *tr.v* (usu — s.o/s.t) give (s.o) a name: *They decided to call the baby James. My daughter's name is Philippa but everybody calls her Phil.* Compare call s.o names (⇒ name(*n*)). **15** *tr.v* (usu — s.o/s.t s.t) consider (s.o/s.t) to be s.o/s.t; describe (s.o/ s.t) as being s.o/s.t: *You may call his* methods *businesslike but I call them dishonest.*

call about s.t visit s.o's house in order to talk about s.t or to do s.t etc: *There's a man at the door who says he's calling about the leak in the roof.*

call s.o to account ⇒ account(*n*).

call at s.w ⇒ call (in) (at s.w).

call s.o away ask s.o, esp a doctor, to go s.w urgently (as a result of which he/she is not available for other things): *I'm afraid you won't be able to see Dr Green now as she's been called away on an urgent case.*

call back make another visit at a later time: *As they were not at home he put a note through the letterbox saying he would call back later.* **call (s.o) back** make a telephone call (to s.o) in answer to one which he/she has already made: *I'm sorry, I'm busy now. Do you mind if I call (you) back in half an hour?* **call s.o back** ask s.o to return just as he/she is leaving a place.

call the banns ⇒ banns.

call s.o's bluff ⇒ bluff³(*n*).

call by ((at) s.w) visit s.w on the way to s.w else: *Mr and Mrs Mason called by (our house) on their way to church.*

call it a day ⇒ day.

call for s.o/s.t (a) go s.w in order to collect s.o/ s.t: *He said he would call for me at 7 o'clock tonight.* (b) ask s.o for s.o/s.t (to do s.t): *He called for the bill (or for the waiter to give him the bill).* (c) need/demand some special kind of person or action: *The present situation calls for a leader of the strongest kind.* ⇒ uncalled-for. **call for s.o/s.t (to do s.t).**

call s.o forward ask s.o to come nearer the speaker, esp from a group of people: *I was called forward to be presented to the mayor.*

call (in) (at s.w) (a) visit s.w, esp s.o's house. (b) (of a ship etc) stop for a short time at a port.

call s.o in (a) ask s.o to come into a room: *Call the next patient in, please.* (b) ask s.o, esp s.o with professional experience, to come and do s.t: *The government is calling in* economic(1) experts(2) *to help with its problems.* **call s.t in** ask for s.t to be returned because it can no longer be used or does not work properly etc: *The manufacturers are calling in the new model because a serious fault has been discovered.*

call s.o/s.t to mind ⇒ mind¹(*n*).

call s.o names ⇒ name(*n*).

call s.o off order s.o to stop doing s.t or to keep away from s.o/s.t: *He asked the police to call off the bodyguards as he objected to them following him everywhere.* **call s.t off** order that s.t should be stopped: *The search for the missing aeroplane was called off.*

call on s.o visit s.o, usu for official or business reasons. **call on s.t** use s.t, esp one's own strength

or brain, in a time of need: *He called on his last remaining strength to try to gain the lead in the race.* ⇒ call (up)on s.o (for, to do, s.t).

call s.o/s.t to order ⇒ order(*n*).

call s.o out (a) order s.o, esp an official organization, to do s.t, usu in a time of trouble: *The government called out the police to stop the violence spreading.* (b) (of a trade union etc) order a group of people to stop work or to go on strike: *The employers refused to increase pay so the union called its members out.* **call (s.t) out** speak, say s.t, in a loud voice; shout: *'Don't touch the paint as it's wet', he called out. He called out the names of the people who had won prizes.*

call it quits ⇒ quits.

call round (at s.w) make a visit (to s.o's house, office etc): *I'll call round (at your house) and collect the tools.*

call a spade a spade ⇒ spade¹.

call s.o up (a) telephone s.o: *Why don't you call him up on the telephone and invite him to dinner?* (b) order s.o to become a member of the armed forces or to become a member again after an absence. ⇒ call-up. **call s.t up** remember s.t, bring s.t back to the memory: *After all these years, it is difficult to call up scenes of my childhood.*

call (up)on s.o (for, to do, s.t) (a) ask s.o for an answer, to make a speech etc: *The chairperson called on the secretary to read the letter.* (b) urge s.o to do s.t, make a special effort etc: *The government called on the people for patience (or to be patient).*

'call-,box *c.n* small cubicle in a street or public place where one can make a telephone call.

'caller *c.n* person who makes a call(3,4).

'call-,girl *c.n* prostitute who uses the telephone to arrange to meet men.

'calling *c.n* (*formal*) job; profession.

'call-,up *c.n* act of ordering people to join the armed forces. ⇒ call s.o up(b).

calligraphy /kə'lɪgrəfɪ/ *u.n* art and practice of writing beautifully.

cal'ligrapher *c.n* (also **cal'ligraphist**) person who writes beautifully (as a special skill).

calling ⇒ call.

callipers /'kælɪpəz/ *pl.n* (also **calipers**) **1** (often *a pair of* —) (*technical*) instrument for measuring the inside or outside diameter of a round object or tube. **2** kind of metal support for the legs of people who have suffered an accident or who have a disease.

callous /'kæləs/ *adj* (often — *to/towards s.o*) (*derog*) showing no pity (for the suffering of others); showing unkindness or cruel feeling (to s.o): *His callous behaviour to his children was heavily criticized.*

'callously *adv*. **'callousness** *u.n*.

call-up ⇒ call.

callus /'kæləs/ *c.n* (*pl -es*) hard piece of skin, esp on the hands, through work.

calm /kɑːm/ *adj* **1** (of weather, the sea) still; not violent: *The weather is expected to be calm after yesterday's storm. The sea was calm for our crossing.* **2** (of a person, the mind) free from anxiety, not disturbed: *Paul remained totally calm during the storm.*

▷ *n* **3** *c.n* (of weather, the sea) (time of) stillness, lack of violence: *There was a calm before the storm.*

4 *u.n* peace; quietness; freedom from anxiety: *There was a moment of calm before everybody started shouting at once.*

▷ *tr/intr.v* **5** (often — (s.o) *down*) (cause (s.o) to) become calm(2): *When she became angry, he tried to calm her down. Now, calm down and tell me what happened.*

'calmly *adv* in a calm(2) way (and sometimes causing surprise to other people): *While we stood there he quite calmly walked off with our bags.*

'calmness *u.n.*

Calor gas /ˈkælə ˌgæs/ *unique n (t.n)* kind of gas, usu sold in metal containers for use in houses, caravans(1) etc, or for travelling and camping where there is no regular supply.

calorie /ˈkælərɪ/ *c.n* **1** unit for the measurement of heat: *A calorie is the quantity of heat which is needed to raise the temperature of 1 gram of water by 1 degree at 15 degrees* Centigrade. ⇨ joule. **2** unit of energy(2) which is provided by food: *Young children between the ages of two and five require about 2000 calories a day.*

calorific /ˌkæləˈrɪfɪk/ *adj* that provides heat or energy(2).

ˌcaloˈrific ˌvalue *c.n* amount of ability to provide heat or energy(2).

calumny /ˈkæləmnɪ/ *c/u.n (pl -ies) (formal)* (example of the) act of saying s.t bad or slanderous about s.o/s.t: *His speech was full of calumnies about his* opponent(3).

calve ⇨ calf.

calypso /kəˈlɪpsəʊ/ *c.n (pl -es)* kind of song sung esp in the Caribbean, often based on recent pieces of news.

cam /kæm/ *c.n (technical)* piece of metal on a wheel or rod which, when the wheel/rod turns, changes a circular movement into a vertical or horizontal one.

'camˌshaft *c.n* long rod, e.g in a car engine, that has a cam on it.

camber /ˈkæmbə/ *c.n (technical)* curve in the surface of a road which allows water to run away to the side.

came /keɪm/ *p.t* of come.

camel /ˈkæml/ *c.n* kind of large animal with either one hump(1) (a dromedary) or two humps on the top of its back, used mostly in deserts for riding or for carrying things.

'camelˌhair *u.n (also attrib)* **1** smooth yellow-brown cloth: *a camelhair coat.* **2** very fine hair used for artists' paintbrushes.

camellia /kəˈmiːlɪə/ *c.n* (kind of plant with) big, usu red, white or pink flowers.

cameo /ˈkæmɪəʊ/ *c.n (pl -s)* **1** (also *attrib*) piece of jewellery which has a design or figure on it. **2** *(formal)* short piece of writing; short play.

camera /ˈkæmrə/ *c.n* mechanical or electronic instrument for taking pictures on photographic film or for sending by radio waves: *a 35mm camera; a television camera; a video camera.* **in camera** *(Latin)* in secret, not in public, esp in court cases: *The court met in camera.* **on camera** (of a person) in front of a television camera and so being seen in a broadcast.

'cameraˌman *c.n (pl -ˌmen)* person who operates a camera, esp one for a film or for television.

camouflage /ˈkæməˌflɑːʒ/ *n* **1** *c/u.n* natural way in which the colouring of animals etc

prevents them being seen easily: *The leopard's spots are a natural camouflage for it when it is hunting other animals among the trees.* **2** *u.n (military)* use of paint, nets, branches, leaves etc to prevent soldiers, guns, tanks etc being seen by an enemy.

▷ *tr.v* **3** *(military)* try to hide (one's soldiers, guns etc) by using camouflage(2). **4** *(fig)* try to hide (what one feels, intends to do etc): *David camouflaged his real intentions with talk about how we must work for the good of the company.*

camp¹ /kæmp/ *c.n* **1** place where tents are put up and where people stay for a short time in them (e.g for a holiday or special purpose): *an army camp.* **2** place with huts or other buildings where people can go and stay for a short time: *a holiday camp.* **3** group of people who hold the same political, religious etc views, esp against other groups: *Though they were in the same political party, they were in opposite camps on capital punishment.* **(be) in camp** (be) living in tents. **break/strike camp** take down and pack tents in order to go s.w else. **concentration camp** ⇨ concentrate. **make/pitch camp** put up tents in order to live in them.

▷ *intr.v* **4** go and live in tents for a short time, e.g as a holiday: *They camped in a field for the night.* **camp out** use tents for sleeping in etc: *We camped out for two nights as the hotels were full.* ⇨ go camping(⇨ camping).

ˌcamp-'bed/-'chair/-'stool *c.n* folding bed/chair/stool used in a camp(1).

'camper *c.n* **1** person who camps(4). **2** kind of van with a small kitchen, beds etc in it for use when going camping.

'campˌfire *c.n* large fire in a campsite to cook food or keep warm when camping (⇨ camp(4)).

'campˌground *c.n (also* **'campˌsite***)* place where one can put up tents.

'camping *u.n* act of living or having a holiday in tents: *I don't like camping because it's too uncomfortable.* **go camping** use tents for living, sleeping in, esp for a holiday: *We went camping in France last year.*

camp² /kæmp/ *adj (derog; informal)* **1** (of a man) acting, speaking like a woman, esp in a very exaggerated way: *I find his behaviour a bit camp.* **2** old-fashioned: *a camp design for such a modern room.*

▷ *tr.v* **3 camp it/s.t up** (a) act, say s.t, in a very exaggerated way, esp when performing a play, being in front of an audience etc: *He camped his lines up and spoiled the play for the rest of the actors.* (b) behave in a camp²(1) way.

campaign /kæmˈpeɪn/ *c.n* **1** *(military)* one or more actions, usu in one place, by the armed forces in a war, the purpose of which is to get a result, gain ground etc: *The campaign to cross the river was successful in the end.* **2** (often — *against/for s.t*) one or more plans or organized events that are intended to get a certain result: *a campaign against/for a new road; an election campaign* (i.e by a political party in order to get elected); *an advertising campaign.*

▷ *intr.v* **3** take part in a campaign. **campaign against/for s.o/s.t** have, take part in, a campaign(2) against/for s.o/s.t: *He's been campaigning against* nuclear(2) *weapons for years.*

cam'paigner *c.n* person who takes part in a campaign(2).

camper, campfire, campground, camping, campsite ⇨ camp¹.

campus /'kæmpəs/ *c.n* (*pl -es*) place where there are the buildings and grounds of a university or college, usu separate from a town: *The new university campus is two miles from the town.* **on campus** in such a place, esp to live and study: *Sheila lives in a flat on campus during the term.*

camshaft ⇨ cam.

can¹ *aux. v* (strong form /kæn/, weak form /kən/) (*pres.t* all persons) can; no *pres.p*; *p.t* **could** (strong form /kud/, weak form /kəd/); no *p.p*; negative forms cannot /'kænɒt/ or can't /kɑːnt/, could not or couldn't /kudnt/; 'could have' can be could've /'kudəv/; 'can' is followed by the infinitive of a verb without *to*) **1** am/are/is able to (do s.t) sometimes as a result of knowing how to do it: *I can speak six languages. She can swim but Simon can't. He could run 100 metres in 11 seconds when he was only fifteen.* **2** (with verbs of seeing, hearing, smelling, tasting etc) am/are/is able to (see, hear etc): *I can hear somebody shouting. Can you see the sea?* **3** have/ has permission, am/are/is allowed, to (do s.t): *You can go now. Can we go to the cinema, mum?* Compare may(3). **4** am/are/is allowed to (do s.t) according to certain rules: *You can't smoke in this cinema.* **5** (in polite requests) please; will (you do s.t): *Can you (or Could you) help me with this suitcase as it's rather heavy?* **6** (in emphatic(2) questions, showing surprise, anger etc): *What can he be up to? Where can she be?* **7** (often can/could be s.t) am/are/is/was/ were sometimes in the state that is described, mentioned: *The North Sea can get very rough. Mike could be very annoying sometimes.* **could do s.t** am/are/is able to do s.t (but do/does/did not do it): *You could at least help us.* **could have done s.t** was/were able to do s.t (but did not do it): *Why couldn't you have helped us?* For 'can' as a main verb, ⇨ can²(4, 5).

can² /kæn/ *c.n* **1** metal or plastic container, often with a lid, for holding things, esp liquids: *a watering can* (for the garden); *an oil-can.* **2** small round closed container for certain liquids or foods: *a can of beer; a can of soup.* ⇨ tin(2). **3** (*informal*) round metal or plastic box in which (cinema) film is stored. **carry the can** (**for s.o/s.t**) (*informal*) be blamed for s.t that one has (not) done (instead of s.o else who is not blamed): *Why should I carry the can for all the mistakes that you made?* **in the can** (of cinema or video film) already shot and ready for showing.

▷ *tr.v* (**-nn-**) **4** put (food or liquids) in a can²(2): *This factory cans fish.* **5** (*informal*) criticize (s.t) very severely: *The new play was canned by the newspapers the next morning.*

canned *adj* **1** (usu *attrib*) (of food etc) put in cans²(2): *canned beer/soup.* **2** (*pred*) (*informal*) very drunk: *I got/was canned last night.*

,canned 'music *u.n* music that has been recorded and is played over loudspeakers, esp in a public place.

'cannery *c.n* (*pl -ies*) factory where food is put into cans²(2).

'can-,opener ⇨ tin-opener.

canal /kə'næl/ *c.n* **1** (with capital **C** in names) kind of river that has been specially made or dug to carry ships and boats: *the Panama/Suez Canal. We went for a holiday on the canals of France.* **2** specially dug ditch or channel(1) for carrying water from place to place, esp for growing crops: *an irrigation canal.* **3** tube in the body that carries food. ⇨ alimentary canal.

ca'nal ,boat *c.n* (also **ca'nal ,barge**) long narrow barge¹/boat that can go on canals(1).

canalize, -ise /'kænəlaɪz/ *tr.v* (*formal*) **1** make (s.t, e.g a river) into a canal(1). **2** (*fig*) direct (one's attention, efforts etc) towards s.t; channel(9) (s.t): *It is up to us to canalize their energies(1) in the right direction.*

ca'nal ,lock *c.n* lock¹(2) in a canal.

canary /kə'neərɪ/ *n* (*pl -ies*) **1** *c.n* kind of small yellow bird that sings, and is often kept as a pet in a cage. **2** *u.n* (also *attrib*) yellow colour.

cancel /'kænsl/ *v* (**-ll-**, US **-l-**) **1** *tr.v* decide not to do (s.t which has been arranged earlier): *At the last minute he cancelled the meeting. I cancelled my order for the computer as the manufacturers couldn't give me a delivery date.* **2** *intr.v* say that one will not do s.t, or not continue with s.t, after having promised: *He said he would be at the meeting but he cancelled at the last minute.* **3** *tr.v* make a mark on (a postage stamp on a letter) to prevent it being used again. **cancel** (**s.t**) **out** (**a**) (*mathematics*, of two sets of figures) be equal (to each other), balance (each other): *The two sides of the equation*(1) *cancel out.* (**b**) (*fig*) (of opposing forces, arguments, thoughts etc) be or become equal (to each other) so that there is no advantage: *The other team had bigger players but we had faster players and it was felt that the two things cancelled each other out.*

cancellation /,kænsə'leɪʃən/ *c/u.n* (example of the) act of cancelling(1) s.t: *The theatre received many cancellations after the bad reviews of the play.*

cancer /'kænsə/ *n* **1** *u.n* disease in the body that grows by destroying cells(4) and that can cause death: *breast cancer; cancer of the throat.* **2** *c.n* example of this: *a cancer found near the eye.* **3** *c.n* (*fig*) bad thing that attacks society from within: *Crimes of violence are a growing cancer in our modern civilization.*

'cancerous *adj* having, like, cancer: *a cancerous growth.*

Cancer /'kænsə/ *n* **1** *unique n* ⇨ Tropic of Cancer. **2** *unique n* one of the 12 signs of the zodiac. **3** *c.n* person born under the sign of Cancer(2).

candid /'kændɪd/ *adj* (of a person, s.t said) who/ that is honest and does not try to hide anything: *He gave me his candid opinion of what was wrong with me. Lynne was very candid in her views.*

'candidly *adv.* **'candidness** *u.n.*

candour /'kændə/ *u.n* (US **'candor**) fact or state of being candid: *Politicians are not known for their candour.*

candidate /'kændɪdeɪt/ *c.n* **1** person who proposes herself/himself, or who is proposed by others, for an official position (in an election etc): *The Party expects to have nearly 500 candidates in the next election.* **2** person who is examined in an examination: *Candidates are requested to hand in their examination papers as soon as they have finished.*

candidacy /ˈkændɪdəsɪ/, **candidature** /ˈkændɪdətʃə/ u.n fact or act of being a candidate(1).

candied ⇨ candy.

candle /ˈkændl/ c.n long round piece of wax with a length of string (wick) through the middle that is lit to give a steady light. **burn the candle at both ends** (fig) work too hard, esp by continually starting early in the morning and finishing late at night.

ˈ**candle,light** u.n light given by candles.

ˈ**candle,lit** adj. with a light from a candle/candles.

ˈ**candle,stick** c.n holder for a candle.

candour ⇨ candid.

candy /ˈkændɪ/ n (pl -ies) **1** u.n sugar that is boiled and mixed with other ingredients(1) to make a sweet: I like sugar candy. **2** c.n (US) sweet(1).

▷ tr.v (-ies, -ied) **3** cover (fruit) with candy(1) and so preserve it: candy ginger(1).

ˈ**candied** adj (of fruit) preserved with candy(1): candied orange.

ˈ**candy ,floss** u.n sugar that is beaten until it is like threads that are then wrapped round a stick and eaten, esp at fairs²(2).

cane /keɪn/ n **1** u.n type of long hollow stem of some tall grasses or reeds(1): bamboo(1) cane; sugar cane. **2** c.n piece of cane(1), esp one cut and used as a support: He used a cane because his left leg was injured(1). **3** c.n piece of cane(1) or stick that is used to hit s.o as a punishment. **get, give s.o, the cane** be punished, punish s.o, with a cane(3): He got the cane for disobeying a teacher.

▷ tr.v **4** use a cane(3) on (s.o): Teachers are not allowed to cane children in Britain.

ˈ**cane ,sugar** u.n sugar made from the substance inside a sugar cane(1).

ˈ**caning** u.n act of punishing s.o with a cane(3): Caning is now banned in schools in Britain.

canine /ˈkeɪnaɪn/ adj of or referring to a dog or dogs: canine behaviour.

,**canine 'tooth** c.n one of four pointed teeth found at the sides of the front of the mouth.

canister /ˈkænɪstə/ c.n **1** small metal box with a lid, used for holding food such as tea. **2** (round) hollow metal object with gas etc in it that can be thrown or fired from a gun so that it bursts and spreads its contents: teargas canisters.

cannabis /ˈkænəbɪs/ u.n drug(2) made from Indian hemp(1), used e.g in cigarettes; hashish; marijuana.

canned, cannery ⇨ can².

cannibal /ˈkænɪbl/ c.n **1** person who eats the flesh of human beings. **2** animal or fish that eats others of its own kind.

ˈ**canniba,lism** u.n act, practice, of a cannibal.

,**canniba'listic** adj of, like, a cannibal.

cannibalize, -ise /ˈkænɪbə,laɪz/ tr.v take pieces (from one or more machines, engines etc which then will not work) and use them in another machine, engine etc to make it work: He reconstructed(1) the engine using parts which had been cannibalized from two other engines.

cannon /ˈkænən/ c.n (pl cannon(s)) (military) **1** (old use) kind of large gun with a long metal tube that fires a round metal or stone ball (⇨ cannonball). **2** modern automatic(1) gun that fires shells, esp from an aircraft: The new fighter was fitted with 30mm cannons.

▷ intr.v **3** cannon into/off s.o/s.t meet or hit s.o/s.t violently and without expecting it: Someone cannoned into him as he came out of the cinema.

ˈ**cannon,ball** c.n round metal or stone ball fired from a cannon(1).

ˈ**cannon ,fodder** /,fɒdə/ u.n soldiers etc who are used in battles regardless of the number who are killed.

cannot ⇨ can¹.

canny /ˈkænɪ/ adj (-ier, -iest) clever, cautious or careful, esp about money: Chris has a reputation for being canny with money.

ˈ**cannily** adv. ˈ**canniness** u.n.

canoe /kəˈnuː/ c.n **1** kind of long narrow boat for one or more people, made of wood, canvas or plastic, and moved by a paddle or paddles.

▷ intr.v **2** use a canoe(1): John canoed down the river.

ca'**noeing** u.n art of using a canoe(1).

ca'**noeist** c.n person who uses a canoe(1).

canon /ˈkænən/ c.n **1** law of the Christian(1) Church. **2** (with capital C in names) (title of a) Christian(1) priest who works in a cathedral. **3** group of books, esp the Bible(1), that is approved or known to be written by one person: the Shakespearean canon. **4** (formal) generally approved standard (of behaviour etc): He offends against every canon of good taste.

canonical /kəˈnɒnɪkl/ adj of or referring to a canon(1,2).

canonization, -isation /,kænənaɪˈzeɪʃən/ c/ u.n (example of) canonizing s.o.

ˈ**cano,nize, -ise** tr.v (in the Christian(1), esp the Roman Catholic, Church) declare officially (s.o who is dead) to be a saint(1).

canopy /ˈkænəpɪ/ c.n (pl -ies) **1** kind of covering of cloth or other substance which is held above s.o or above s.t else (e.g a bed, throne(1) etc) as a protection. **2** (technical) kind of usu transparent cover over the cockpit(1) of some aircraft. **3** (fig) any kind of covering: a canopy of branches.

cant¹ /kænt/ c.n **1** (formal) slope: a steep cant in the road.

▷ tr/intr.v **2** (often — over) (formal) (cause (s.t) to) move from a vertical position to one at an angle: The ship canted (over) as the wave hit it.

cant² /kænt/ u.n (formal) **1** special kind of language used by a group of people to prevent others outside the group from understanding them: thieves' cant. **2** talk that is not honest or genuine(2).

can't /kɑːnt/ = cannot. ⇨ can¹.

cantankerous /kænˈtæŋkərəs/ adj (derog; formal) having a bad temper; easily able to get annoyed: He's a cantankerous old man.

can'**tankerously** adv. can'**tankerousness** u.n.

cantata /kænˈtɑːtə/ c.n (music) music sung by soloists and a choir(1) which usu tells a story.

canteen /kænˈtiːn/ c.n **1** restaurant in a factory or large office. **2** set of several knives, forks and spoons, usu in a box: a canteen of cutlery. **3** (military) set of plate, knives, forks and spoons for one soldier. **4** set of pots, usu made of metal, used by campers(1) etc.

canter /ˈkæntə/ c.n **1** speed at which a horse moves that is faster than a trot(1) but slower than a gallop(1). **at a canter** moving at this speed. **break into a canter** begin to move at this speed.

▷ *tr/intr.v* **2** (cause (a horse) to) move at this speed: *The riders cantered (their horses) down the road.*

cantilever /ˈkæntɪˌliːvə/ *c.n* (*technical*) kind of support that sticks out from a wall or other vertical surface and holds up s.t above it (e.g a balcony).

ˌcantiˈlever ˈbridge *c.n* bridge that has one or more vertical columns that support the horizontal beams.

canvas /ˈkænvəs/ *n* **1** *u.n* kind of strong rough cloth used for sails, tents, bags etc and for painting pictures on: *a sack made of canvas. When using oils, I usually paint on canvas.* **2** *c.n* example of a painting on this cloth: *The artist had several canvases in his exhibition.* **under canvas** (**a**) (staying, living) in tents. (**b**) (of a sailing ship, boat) with the sail(s) open and being blown by the wind.

canvass /ˈkænvəs/ *c.n* **1** visit to s.o in order to get support for s.o/s.t: *a canvass for the local candidate(1) in an election.*

▷ *v* **2** *tr.v* visit (people) in order to get them to vote in a certain way in an election. **3** *intr.v* act in this way in support of a candidate(1) or a political party: *I spent the last election canvassing for the Labour Party.* **4** *tr/intr.v* try to get (support, an order etc) for s.t by visiting people: *They canvassed support for the new road. The sales representative was canvassing (for) orders.*

ˈ**canvasser** *c.n* person who canvasses.

canyon /ˈkænjən/ *c.n* valley with high, steep cliffs on either side and through which a river usu runs.

cap /kæp/ *c.n* **1** kind of soft hat with no brim(2) but with a peak(5), usu worn by boys and men: *a school cap; a cloth cap.* **2** special kind of cap(1) given to a member of a sports team to show he/she plays for it: *Emma has had three caps for playing hockey for England.* **3** covering for the head that is worn as a protection: *a sailor's cap.* **4** covering put on the top of a container to prevent liquid getting out: *Can you get the cap off this bottle?* (**come/go) cap/hat in hand (to s.o)** (*fig; informal*) visit s.o in a humble way (in order to obtain s.t): *The workers went cap in hand to the management over improvements in working conditions.* **dutch cap** ⇨ dutch. **if the cap fits (wear it)** (*fig; informal*) if s.o thinks that what s.o else has said (usu a criticism) applies to her/him, then she/he should accept it. **put one's thinking cap on** (*fig; informal*) stop and think hard and seriously (about s.t). **set one's cap at s.o** be determined to win s.o's love.

▷ *tr.v* (-pp-) **5** put a cap(4) on (a container): *The milk bottles were capped with silver* foil. **6** *tr.v* give a cap(2) to (s.o): *He has been capped six times for Scotland* (i.e has played in the Scottish team six times). **7** *tr.v* provide a natural covering to (s.t which is high): *Snow capped the mountains.* ⇨ snow-capped. **cap s.o's story, joke** etc do or say s.t better than s.o else has done: *Jerry always feels he has to cap my stories with what he thinks are better ones.* **to cap it all** as the final thing, usu the last and most annoying thing of a number of wrong things that have been done or said: *To cap it all, after having burnt the dinner and dropped six plates, Boris knocked the table over.*

cap(s) /kæp(s)/ *abbr* capital(s)(6).

capable /ˈkeɪpəbl/ *adj* (*formal*) Opposite incapable. **1** clever, able to do s.t, e.g a job, well: *She's a very capable teacher.* **2** (often — of (doing) s.t) having or showing an ability to do s.t, esp if necessary: *He's quite capable of getting a first-class degree.* **3** (often — of (doing) s.t) (*formal*) easily able to do s.t, to happen: *The situation is capable of change* (or *of changing*) *at any moment.*

ˌcapaˈbility */c/u.n* (*pl* -ies) (*formal*) **1** (example of the) quality of one's mind or body that makes one able to do s.t: *Sarah has the capability to become a leading politician. Francis has shown great capabilities in his job.* **2** (possession of the) means to do or use s.t, esp in connection with war: *Several countries now have* (*a*) nuclear(3) *capability* (i.e have nuclear(2) weapons).

ˈ**capably** *adv* in a capable(1) way.

capacious /kəˈpeɪʃəs/ *adj* (*formal*) **1** very large; with plenty of space inside: *a capacious room.* **2** having a lot of s.t, esp an ability: *a capacious mind/memory.*

caˈpaciously *adv.* caˈpaciousness *u.n.*

capacity /kəˈpæsɪti/ *n* (*pl* -ies) **1** *u.n* ability to take a number of people or things who/that will fill all the available space, seats etc: *The football ground has the capacity to hold 100 000 people. The jug has a capacity of 2 litres.* **2** *u.n* ability to produce a number of things: *The new factory has the capacity to make 5000 television sets a month.* **3** */c/u.n* (usu — for (doing), to do, s.t) (*formal*) (example of the) ability or power (in s.t, to do s.t): *She has a great capacity for getting things wrong. He has shown very little capacity to handle this kind of work.* (**do s.t**) **in one's capacity as s.o/s.t** (act) according to one's position or title: *In my capacity as mayor, I declare this meeting open.* **filled to capacity** so full of people that there is no more room. **seating capacity (of 500** etc) (of a building, hall, sports ground etc) the total number of seats that people can occupy: *The seating capacity in the new hall is 500.*

cape /keɪp/ *c.n* **1** (with capital **C** in names) land on the coast that sticks out and has the sea on two sides: *the Cape of Good Hope* (in South Africa). **2** kind of loose cloak(1) that hangs down from the shoulders.

caper¹ /ˈkeɪpə/ *c.n* **1** (*formal*) act of jumping or dancing about in a playful or silly way: *We watched the capers of the clowns(1) with amusement.* **2** mischievous behaviour: *I'd like to know what caper he is up to now.*

▷ *intr.v* **3** (often — about/around) (*formal*) jump, dance, (about) in a playful or silly way: *He capered about in front of us trying to make us laugh.*

caper² /ˈkeɪpə/ *c.n* (kind of plant with a) sour flower that is dried and used in cooking.

capital /ˈkæpɪtl/ *attrib.adj* **1** of, referring to, death or execution(1) according to the law: *a capital crime/offence.* ⇨ capital punishment. **2** chief (city of a country): *The capital city of Australia is Canberra.* ⇨ capital(5). **3** of the shape of written or printed letters like THIS or THIS: *Write the title in capital letters.* ⇨ capital(6). **4** (often as an *interj*) (*old use*) good; excellent: *What a capital idea!*

▷ *n* **5** */c/def.n* capital(2) city: *Canberra is the capital of Australia.* **6** *c.n* (*abbr* cap) capital(3) letter, as used in writing the beginning of a name, sentence etc: *Start every sentence with a capital.* **7** *u.n* (*commerce*) wealth in the form of buildings, machines etc that is used to make more wealth. **8** *u.n* (*commerce*) wealth etc used to start a business: *He had very little capital when he started.* **9** *c.n* top part of a column(1): *The column had a decorated capital in the Greek* style(2). **make capital** (**out**) **of s.t** (*fig*) gain some advantage from s.t: *He made capital out of the fact that I had not been to any of the recent meetings.*

,**capital** '**assets** *pl.n* buildings, machines etc that have a value in money (for a business).

,**capital** '**gain** *c.n* (usu *pl*) profit made from the sale of buildings and investments(2).

,**capital** '**gains** ,**tax** *c.n* tax paid to the government on sales of buildings and investments(2).

'**capita,lism** *u.n* (belief in the) system of trade run by private owners of capital(7) with little or no control, ownership or interference by a government.

'**capita,list** *adj* **1** (sometimes *derog*) of, referring to, in favour of, capitalism: *capitalist countries/ economies.*
▷ *c.n* **2** (sometimes *derog*) person who believes in capitalism.

,**capita'listic** *adj* = capitalist(1).

capitalization, -isation /,kæpɪtəlaɪˈzeɪʃən/ *u.n* **1** use of capitals(6) in writing or printing. **2** (*commerce*) amount of money available in a business as a result of capitalizing; act of changing goods etc into capital(7): *The capitalization of the company amounted to £250 000.*

'**capita,lize, -ise** *tr/intr.v* (*commerce*) change (goods, money etc) into capital(7); provide money for this purpose: *The company capitalized part of its profits. The bank agreed to capitalize the new company.* **capitalize on s.t** (*fig*) gain from, take advantage of, s.t: *Fred was able to capitalize on the mistakes made by others.*

'**capital** ,**punishment** *u.n* execution(1) of s.o for a serious crime according to the law.

capitulate /kəˈpɪtjuˌleɪt/ *intr.v* stop fighting or quarrelling and surrender(2), usu after agreeing to certain conditions: *The strikers(1) capitulated and were allowed to leave the factory.*

capitulation /kəˌpɪtjuˈleɪʃən/ *u.n.*

capon /ˈkeɪpɒn/ *c.n* male chicken that has had its sexual organs removed allowing it to become fat and good for eating.

caprice /kəˈpriːs/ *c/u.n* (*formal*) (example of) behaviour that changes suddenly and without much reason: *It is difficult to follow his reasoning as most of his decisions appear to be based on caprice.*

capricious /kəˈprɪʃəs/ *adj* (*formal*) **1** (of a person, behaviour) often changing without a reason. **2** often changing in a sudden way: *In the autumn the weather can be very capricious.*

ca'priciously *adv.* **ca'priciousness** *u.n.*

Capricorn /ˈkæprɪˌkɔːn/ *n* **1** *unique n* zodiac sign. **2** *c.n* person born under the sign of Capricorn(1). **3** Tropic of Capricorn ⇒ tropic.

caps *abbr* capitals(6).

capsicum /ˈkæpsɪkəm/ *c.n* = pepper(3).

capsize /kæpˈsaɪz/ *tr/intr.v* (cause (a ship, boat) to) turn completely over in the water so that the bottom is at the top.

capstan /ˈkæpstən/ *c.n* (*technical*) upright device shaped like a drum that is turned by hand or by power and that winds a rope around

it in order to pull or lift s.t, e.g an anchor on a ship.

capsule /ˈkæpsjuːl/ *c.n* **1** small container for medicine that can be swallowed. **2** part of a spacecraft that can be separated from the main part and that contains instruments, people etc. **3** (*technical*) container (for seeds) on a plant.

capt *written abbr* captain(1-3).

captain /ˈkæptɪn/ *c/unique n* (with capital **C** in names) **1** chief person or leader of a group, esp a sports team: *Tom is* (*the*) *captain of the local football team.* **2** person in charge of a ship, aircraft etc. **3** (*military*) (title of an) officer in the armed forces (in the army between a lieutenant(1) and a major(2); in the navy between a commander(1) and a commodore; in the (British) airforce a group captain is between a wing commander and an air commodore).
▷ *tr.v* **4** be, act as, the captain(1,2) of (a team, ship etc): *He captained the local football team. He captained the ship while the captain was ill.*

caption /ˈkæpʃən/ *c.n* group of words printed near a picture, photograph etc in a newspaper, book etc describing the picture etc.

captivate /ˈkæptɪˌveɪt/ *tr.v* (of a person, place etc) attract or interest (s.o) because of one's/its charm, beauty etc.

captivation /,kæptɪˈveɪʃən/ *u.n.*

captive /ˈkæptɪv/ *attrib.adj* **1** (of a person, animal) having been made a prisoner or having been caught. **hold/take s.o captive** keep/make s.o a prisoner.
▷ *c.n* **2** person who has become a prisoner, esp in a war.

,**captive** '**audience** *c.n* group of people willing to listen to or watch s.o/s.t, or not able to avoid doing so, (e.g at home watching television or at the cinema watching a film) and therefore open to persuasion (from advertising etc).

captivity /kæpˈtɪvɪtɪ/ *u.n* (of a person, animal) state of being a prisoner or of having been caught. (**be**) **in captivity** (be) in this state for some time.

capture /ˈkæptʃə/ *n* **1** *u.n* act or state of being made a prisoner or of being caught. **2** *c.n* person or animal caught.
▷ *tr.v* **3** make (s.o) a prisoner; catch (a wild animal etc) and put (it) in a cage etc. **4** (in war) take possession of (a town, place etc) from an enemy. **5** interest or attract (s.o, her/his imagination etc). **6** describe or make a record of (s.t) in words, pictures etc so that its essence is shown: *Her latest book has captured the charm of London.*

car /kɑː/ *c.n* **1** vehicle with an engine and wheels which carries a driver and passengers and is used for private or business travel. **2** (mainly US) railway carriage. **3** vehicle shaped like a box, used by passengers or goods and which is part of a travel system such as a lift, cable railway etc. **dining car** ⇒ dine. **sleeping-car** ⇒ sleep.

'**car-,ferry** *c.n* (*pl* -**ies**) ship which carries cars and people across a river, the sea etc.

'**car,park** *c.n* private or public land or building where cars can remain for a time, usu on payment of a sum of money.

'**car,port** *c.n* kind of garage for a car with a roof but usu no sides, built near or at the side of a house.

'car,sick *adj* feeling ill in a car because of the movement.
'car,sickness *u.n.*

carafe /kə'ræf/ *c.n* **1** glass bottle used for serving wine or water at table. **2** quantity of wine or water in such a bottle.

caramel /'kærəməl/ *n* **1** *u.n* (also *attrib*) boiled or burnt sugar used to flavour food or in a pudding(1): *caramel custard.* **2** *c.n* kind of yellow-brown sweet made from burnt sugar.

carat /'kærət/ *c.n* (US also **'karat**) **1** unit of measurement for the purity of gold (24 carats is pure gold): *Bob bought Julia a watch with an 18 carat gold case.* **2** unit of weight (200 milligrams) for jewels: *a diamond weighing 10 carats.*

caravan /'kærə,væn/ *c.n* **1** vehicle with beds, tables, seats, places for cooking and washing etc which is pulled by a car, used esp for touring holidays. **2** vehicle or cart with similar contents but usu pulled by a horse and used by people such as gypsies for living in. **3** (in the Middle East and Asia) people, vehicles and animals travelling together in a group (usu with goods for trade) in order to protect themselves.
'cara,vanning *u.n* (often *go* —) act of having a holiday in a caravan(1).

carbohydrate /,kɑː'bəʊ'haɪdreɪt/ *c/u.n* **1** one of a group of compounds(1) made up of carbon(1), hydrogen and oxygen which is present in sugar, starch(1), cellulose(1) etc and provides living things with energy(1). **2** (usu *pl*) food such as bread, potatoes etc that contain these substances: *Eating too many carbohydrates will make me fat.*

carbolic /kɑː'bɒlɪk/ *adj* made from carbon(1) present in coal: *carbolic soap.*

carbon /'kɑːbən/ *n* **1** *u.n* (*chemistry*) simple substance or element(1) found in pure form in diamonds, graphite etc which in organic compounds forms the basis of all living matter, *chem.symb* C. **2** *c.n* (also **'carbon ,paper**) sheet of thin paper with a special coloured (usu black) coating on it that is put between two sheets of typing or writing paper to make a copy on the second sheet. **3** *c.n* (also **'carbon ,copy**) **(a)** copy (of s.t) typed or written using a carbon(2). **(b)** (*fig*) exact copy (of s.o or s.t): *The crime was a carbon copy of one that happened two years ago.*
'carbon ,copy ⇒ carbon(3).
'carbon ,dating *u.n* (*technical*) process(1) for discovering the age of very old objects by the amount of carbon(1) in them.
,carbon di'oxide *u.n* (*chemistry*) gas without colour that is produced when carbon(1) burns and/or when animals and humans breathe out, *chem.form* CO_2.
,carbon mon'oxide *u.n* (*chemistry*) poisonous gas produced when petrol etc burns, e.g in a car engine, *chem.form* CO.
'carbon ,paper ⇒ carbon(2).

carbonated /'kɑːbə,neɪtɪd/ *adj* containing a lot of carbon dioxide, esp in order to make a drink full of gas: *carbonated drinks.*

carbuncle /'kɑː,bʌŋkl/ *c.n* painful red swelling on the skin.

carburettor /,kɑːbjʊ'retə/ *c.n* (also **,carbu-'retter**, US **,carbu'retor**) (*technical*) part of an engine, esp in a car, that mixes petrol and air and makes them ready for burning.

carcass /'kɑːkəs/ *c.n* (also **'carcase**) **1** body of a dead animal, esp one to be used as meat. **2** (*informal*; *joking*) body of a person, esp if it is big, in the way etc: *If you move your carcass, I'll be able to see better.* **3** remains (of s.t): *The carcass of an old ship was lying in the mud.*

card /kɑːd/ *n* **1** *u.n* kind of thick stiff paper, used esp for drawing or painting: *He drew the picture on a card so it wouldn't be damaged easily.* **2** *c.n* small, usu oblong, piece of stiff paper with information about s.o/s.t on it: *a membership card*; *a business card* (i.e one that has one's name, position, business address etc on it). **3** *c.n* piece of stiff paper, usu folded in two, often with a picture on the front and space for a message inside, sent to s.o on certain special occasions: *a birthday card*; *a Christmas card*; *a get-well card.* **4** *c.n* = postcard. **5** *c.n* (also **'playing ,card**) one of a set of fifty-two pieces of stiff paper or plastic with special pictures, shapes, numbers etc on them, used to play many kinds of games. **6** *c.n* small, usu oblong, piece of plastic with s.o's name and a number on it, provided by a bank or shop or business. ⇒ bank card, cash card, cheque card, credit card. **7** *c.n* printed list of special, usu sporting events: *a sports card*; *a racing card* (i.e one that lists a number of horse races). **8** *c.n* kind of instrument, shaped like a comb, used for preparing and straightening wool, cotton etc before it is spun. **9** *c.n* (*informal*) amusing person who behaves in strange ways: *Ben's a bit of a card and is always playing practical jokes on people.* **have a card up one's sleeve** (*fig*) keep s.t, e.g information, secret so that one can use it later to one's advantage. **play one's best/strongest card** (*fig*) say or do s.t that one has been saving or keeping secret in order to gain an advantage.
▷ *tr.v* **10** prepare and straighten (wool, cotton etc) using a card(8). **11** list or arrange (information, facts etc) on a card(7).

'card,board *u.n* (also *attrib*) kind of stiff thick material made from paper, used for making boxes for protecting things or as wrapping paper etc: *a cardboard box.*

'card ,index *c.n* pieces of card(1) arranged in alphabetical order, usu in a box, with information (words, names, addresses etc) on them.

'card ,player *c.n* person who plays(1) cards.

cards *pl.n* set of cards(5). **(be) on the cards** (*fig*) (be) likely to happen. **lay/put one's cards on the table** (*fig*) openly show what one knows, intends to do etc. **play cards** play games using cards(5). **play one's cards right/well** (*fig*) act in a way that gains an advantage.

'card ,sharp *c.n* (also **'card ,sharper**) (*derog*) person who cheats when he/she plays cards(5) in order to win money.

'card-,table *c.n* special table, often with a green cloth on it, used for playing cards on.

'card ,vote *c/u.n* vote taken at a meeting by people who represent others e.g in a trade union, and who have cards(2) on which is written how many people they represent: *The proposal was defeated by a card vote.*

cardamom /'kɑːdəməm/ *c/u.n* (also *attrib*) (plant grown in Asia with a) seed which is used for flavouring food and as a medicine.

cardiac /'kɑːdɪˌæk/ *adj* (*usu attrib*) (*medical*) of or referring to the heart in one's body: *cardiac muscles*(1); *cardiac arrest/failure* (= the stopping of one's heart because of disease etc).

cardigan /'kɑːdɪgən/ *c.n* article of knitted clothing with sleeves(1) and usu no collar, open in the front and with either buttons or a zip-fastener, worn over a shirt, dress etc.

cardinal /'kɑːdɪnl/ *adj* (*usu attrib*) 1 (*formal*) first in importance; main (thing): *the four cardinal virtues* (i.e prudence, justice(1), temperance, fortitude).
▷ *c.n* 2 (with capital **C** in names) priest in the Roman Catholic(1) Church with the highest rank below the Pope. 3 = cardinal number.
,**cardinal 'number** *c.n* any of the ordinary numbers one, two, three etc, esp as compared with ordinal numbers (first, second, third etc).
,**cardinal 'point** *c.n* one of the four points (north, south, east, west) on a compass(1).

cards, cardsharp(er) ⇨ card.

care /keə/ *n* 1 *u.n* proper and full attention or effort: *You must do your homework with more care next time.* 2 *u.n* watchfulness and attention so that there is no harm or damage: *You must use care when handling these dangerous chemicals.* 3 *c/u.n* (example of) worry or anxiety: *His face was full of care. He goes around as though all the cares of the world rest on his shoulders.* **care of s.o** (usu written c/o) (in an address on an envelope etc) sent to one person named at her/his address who will give it to the person for whom it is intended: *Mr J Smith, c/o Mr and Mrs Green, 5 Oxford St, Bath.* **in care** (of a child) having been taken into care. **in the care of s.o** be the responsibility of s.o: *While they were away, they left their house in the care of their neighbours.* **take care** show proper care(2) to avoid danger etc: *You must take care when crossing the road.* **take (good etc) care of s.o/s.t** be responsible for s.o/s.t: *I'll take care of the children while you're in hospital.* **take s.o into care** (of an official) remove s.o, esp a child, from her/his family because she/he is not being looked after properly or she/he has problems, and put her/him in a special home.
▷ *v* 4 *tr/intr.v* (often — *about s.o/s.t*) be interested, concerned or worried (about (s.o/s.t etc)): *James doesn't care (about) what happens to him. 'You won't have the money if you don't work.' 'I don't care!'* 5 *intr.v* (often — *for s.t; — to do s.t*) (*formal*) (usu negative or in questions) like (s.t), be willing (to do s.t etc): *Would you care for a drink* (or *care to come and have a drink*)? **care for s.o** look after s.o, esp by providing her/him with food, money, a house etc: *The government has a responsibility to care for the poorer members of society.* **care for s.o/s.t** (a) ⇨ care(5). (b) like or feel an interest in s.o/s.t: *She showed she really cared for him. I don't care for popular music.* **not care a damn**; **not care less (about s.o/s.t)** (*informal*) have or show complete lack of interest (in s.o/s.t): *I don't care a damn what you do. He couldn't care less about the future.* ⇨ hoot(*n*).
carefree /'keəˌfriː/ *adj* having/showing no worry or anxiety.
'**careful** *adj* 1 doing s.t with care(1) or attention: *He should be more careful in his work.* 2 (of s.t) done with care(1): *It was a very careful piece of*

work. 3 showing or exercising great care(2) so as not to harm or damage s.t: *Careful! That vase is very delicate.*
'**carefully** *adv.* '**carefulness** *u.n.*
'**careless** *adj* (*derog*) 1 not doing s.t with care(1) or attention: *She's very careless in her work.* 2 (of s.t) done without much care(1): *It was a very careless piece of work.* 3 (often — *about/of* s.t) (*formal*) not worried or concerned; free from care(3): *He's careless about his reputation.*
'**carelessly** *adv.* '**carelessness** *u.n.*
'**care,taker** *c.n* 1 person who looks after a building, esp a school, office, block of flats etc. 2 person who looks after s.o's house while the owner is away.
,**caretaker 'government** *c.n* government that runs a country for a short time before a new government is appointed.
careworn /'keəˌwɔːn/ *adj* (*formal*) showing signs of worry or anxiety: *There were careworn lines on his face from his struggle to bring up a large family on a very low income.*
career /kə'rɪə/ *n* 1 *c.n* job or profession one chooses or does for the whole or part of one's working life: *He chose a career in medicine.* 2 *c.n* one's whole working life, esp from the point of view of its successes and failures: *He had a very successful career.*
▷ *intr.v* 3 (usu — *about/around* etc) move quickly or suddenly: *The car careered off the road and ended up in a ditch.*
ca'reerist *c.n* (*derog*) person who puts all her/his attention and energy into developing a career(1).
carefree, careful(ly/ness), careless(ly/ness) ⇨ care.
caress /kə'res/ *c.n* 1 gentle touching or stroking of s.o whom one loves.
▷ *tr.v* 2 touch (s.o) gently to show love.
caretaker, careworn ⇨ care.
car-ferry ⇨ car.
cargo /'kɑːgəʊ/ *c/u.n* (*pl* -es) (example of a) load of goods carried by a ship or plane: *The ship carried cargoes of steel across the Atlantic.*
caricature /'kærɪkəˌtjʊə/ *n* 1 *c.n* written or spoken description or picture (of s.o) showing her/him in an unfavourable, but often amusing, way. 2 *u.n* art of doing this.
▷ *tr.v* 3 describe (s.o) in a caricature(1).
'**carica,turist** *c.n* person who does caricatures(1) as a profession.
caries /'keəriːz/ *u.n* (*technical*) decay or rotting in bones, esp teeth: *dental caries.*
carnage /'kɑːnɪdʒ/ *u.n* (*formal*) killing of many people, esp in a battle.
carnal /'kɑːnl/ *adj* (*formal*) of or referring to the body, esp in terms of sexual activity or desires: *carnal sins.*
,**carnal 'knowledge** *u.n* experience of having sex with s.o, esp for the first time.
carnation /kɑː'neɪʃən/ *n* 1 *c.n* kind of plant with small white, pink or red flowers. 2 *c.n* flower of this plant. 3 *u.n* (also *attrib*) bright pink colour: *walls painted in carnation.*
carnival /'kɑːnɪvl/ *n* 1 *c.n* public event in which there are processions, dancing, music, feasting, drinking etc. 2 *u.n* time when this event takes place.

carnivorous /kɑːˈnɪvərəs/ *adj* (*technical*) eating the flesh of animals as food.

carnivore /ˈkɑːnɪˌvɔː/ *c.n* animal, person that eats the flesh of other animals as food. ⇨ herbivore, omnivore.

carol /ˈkærəl/ *c.n* 1 Christian(1) song of joy sung at Christmas time.

▷ *tr/intr.v* (*-ll-*, US *-l-*) 2 sing carols(1); sing (s.t) joyfully. **go carolling** go from house to house at Christmas time and sing carols outside, usu in order to collect money for charity(2).

carousel /ˌkærəˈsel/ *c.n* 1 (US) roundabout(3). 2 circular moving belt on which luggage is placed in an airport after it comes off a plane so that passengers can collect their own.

carp[1] /kɑːp/ *n* (*pl* —(s)) 1 *c.n* kind of large fish that lives in rivers, lakes or ponds. 2 *u.n* this fish as food.

carp[2] /kɑːp/ *intr.v* (usu — (on) at s.o/about s.t) complain (about s.o/s.t) in a continuous way, esp over small and not important things: *He was always carping at her about not keeping the room tidy.*

carpenter /ˈkɑːpɪntə/ *c.n* 1 person who makes things with wood, e.g cupboards, doors, in a house or building. Compare woodcarver. 2 (also **'carpenter's**) shop, place of work, of a carpenter(1).

carpentry /ˈkɑːpɪntrɪ/ *u.n* art or work of a carpenter(1).

carpet /ˈkɑːpɪt/ *n* 1 *u.n* covering for a floor, stairs etc made of wool or other similar material. 2 *c.n* piece of carpet(1). 3 *c.n* (usu — of s.t) things (usu plants) that cover the ground like a carpet(2): *a carpet of flowers.* (**be**) **on the carpet** (*fig; informal*) (be) criticized or blamed for s.t one has done wrong. **sweep s.t under the carpet** (*informal*) hide s.t that has been done so that no one can be blamed or criticized.

▷ *tr.v* 4 cover (a floor, stairs etc) with carpet(1). 5 (*fig; informal*) bring (s.o) in front of one and criticize or blame (her/him) for bad work etc: *His boss carpeted him for his mistakes.*

'carpet ,slipper *c.n* (*old use*) = slipper.

'carpet ,sweeper *c.n* machine pushed by hand which cleans carpets(2).

'carpet ,tile *c.n* square piece of carpet(1) that can be put on a floor with other similar pieces to make a carpet(2) and that can be replaced when worn out.

carport ⇨ car.

carriage /ˈkærɪdʒ/ *n* 1 *c.n* (*old use*) vehicle with usu four wheels which is pulled by one or more horses: *a carriage and pair* (i.e with two horses). 2 *c.n* part of a railway train with compartments(1) and seats for passengers. 3 *u.n* act of carrying goods (and usu the cost of doing so) from one place to another. 4 *c.n* part of a vehicle with wheels that carries s.t: *a gun carriage.* ⇨ undercarriage. 5 *c.n* part of a machine that moves: *a typewriter carriage.* 6 *sing/u.n* way one holds or moves one's body or parts of it: *Francis has a rather awkward carriage.*

'carriage,way *c.n* part of a road on which vehicles drive. **dual carriageway** ⇨ dual.

carrier /ˈkærɪə/ *c.n* 1 person or company carrying people or goods from one place to another for money. 2 metal frame on a vehicle (e.g a bicycle, car etc) for carrying

bags etc on. 3 person/animal with a disease who/that can give it to another person/animal without suffering it herself/himself/itself. **aircraft carrier** ⇨ aircraft. **troop carrier** ⇨ troop(*n*).

,carrier 'bag *c.n* large paper or plastic bag used for shopping. Compare shopping bag.

'carrier ,pigeon *c.n* pigeon(1) that carries messages usu in a cylinder(3) fixed to one of its legs.

carrion /ˈkærɪən/ *u.n* dead and rotting flesh of animals.

carrot /ˈkærət/ *n* (also *attrib*) 1 *c.n* kind of plant that has an orange root. 2 *c.n* root of this plant as food: *Would you buy some carrots when you go shopping?* 3 *u.n* this root when prepared for eating: *carrot soup.* **hold out a carrot to s.o** (*fig*) offer s.o an advantage in order to get her/him to do s.t (esp by suggesting that the offer may be taken away if she/he does not act quickly).

'carroty *adj* (*old use*) (esp of s.o's hair on the head) having a red colour.

carry /ˈkærɪ/ *v* (*-ies*, *-ied*) 1 *tr.v* hold (s.o/s.t) in one's hands or arms or on one's back and take (her/him/it) s.w: *He carried her across the stream.* 2 *tr.v* have (s.t) on one's person: *Some police in Britain are starting to carry guns.* 3 *tr.v* (of things, vehicles etc) hold and take (s.o/s.t) from one place to another: *The ship carries both cargo and passengers. Water is carried across the desert in pipes.* 4 *tr.v* (of people, animals etc) have (a disease) in one's body and take (it) s.w: *Some pets carry diseases which affect children.* 5 *tr.v* support the weight of (s.t): *These walls carry the main weight of the floor above.* 6 *tr.v* have and sell (goods etc): *The local shop carries only a small stock of food.* 7 *tr.v* (of newspapers, broadcasts etc) contain, mention, (s.t): *The newspaper carried a report on the murder.* 8 *tr.v* have, lead to, (a certain result): *His position carries heavy responsibilities.* 9 *tr.v* capture (a place) by force: *The soldiers carried the position in their first attack.* 10 *tr.v* win or gain (s.t), persuade (s.o): *They carried the motion by a show of hands. He carried his audience with him.* 11 *tr.v* (*mathematics*) take (one number) from one column and add (it) to the next on the left: *26 + 9 is: 6 (from 26) + 9 = 15, so 5 carry 1; 1 + 2 (from 26) = 3; 3 and 5 are written 35.* 12 *intr.v* (of bullets, shells etc) go, travel, (a certain distance): *The guns couldn't carry as far as the enemy positions.* 13 *intr.v* (of voices, sounds) be heard (at a certain distance): *His powerful voice carried to every corner of the hall.*

be/get carried away (**by s.t**) be/become excited, lose control, (because of s.t): *Norman got carried away by the music.*

carry s.t about (**with one**) have s.t on one's person as a usual thing: *He always carries an umbrella about with him whatever the weather.*

carry s.o along (**with one**) persuade s.o to agree with one's own views, actions etc.

carry s.o back (**to s.t/s.w**) remind s.o (of s.t/s.w), come to the memory of s.o: *The sight of his face carried me back to my childhood.*

carry all/everything before one win a victory; succeed completely: *In the election she carried all before her.*

carry the can (**for s.o/s.t**) ⇨ can[2].

carry the day ⇨ day.

carry s.t forward/over (*commerce*) (*written abbr c.f*) take a total (a number or amount) from the bottom of one page to the top of the next.

carry s.o off (of illness, disease) cause s.o to die. **carry s.o off** (**to s.w**) seize s.o and take her/him (to a place): *The soldiers carried off all the children.* **carry s.t off** (**a**) do s.t successfully (sometimes after first making a mistake or having difficulties): *She tried to pretend she was old enough but couldn't quite carry it off.* (**b**) win or gain s.t and take it away with one: *She carried off most of the prizes in the competition.*

carry on (**about s.o/s.t**) (*informal*) talk in a complaining way, behave in a very excited way, (about s.o/s.t): *He was always carrying on about his wife's cooking.* ⇨ carryings-on, carry-on. **carry on** (**doing s.t/with s.t**) continue (doing s.t) that one has already started: *Carry on with your work.* **carry on** (**with s.o**) (*informal*) have a love affair (with s.o): *Bill was carrying on with his best friend's wife.*

carry s.t out do or complete s.t, esp s.t one has decided earlier: *He carried out his threat to tell her parents.*

carry s.t over ⇨ carry s.t forward/over.

carry s.o through (**s.t**) help s.o to overcome, get through, (difficulties, an illness etc).

carry s.t/things too far do or say s.t/things to excess, to the point of annoying other people: *He loves playing practical jokes but sometimes he carries things too far.*

carry weight (**with s.o**) ⇨ weight.

carry s.o with one persuade s.o, get s.o, to agree with what one is doing: *He carried the people with him by the force of his arguments.*

'carry,cot *c.n* kind of small bed with sides and handles in which a baby can be put and carried from place to place.

,carryings-'on *pl.n* (*informal*) noisy excited behaviour that disturbs other people: *We were kept awake all night by the carryings-on in the house next door.*

,carry-'on *c.n* (*informal*) act of loud crying or complaining that continues for some time: *What a carry-on; you would have thought he had broken his leg when it was only a little bruise!*

carsick(ness) ⇨ car.

cart /kɑːt/ *c.n* **1** vehicle with two or four wheels that is pulled by a horse and carries goods. **2** small vehicle with wheels that has an engine and can be driven or that is pulled by hand: *a golf cart.* **put the cart before the horse** (*fig*) deal, concern oneself, with the effect of s.t and not with its cause: *Dennis argued that spending more money on defence was putting the cart before the horse and that we needed to* disarm(2) *to preserve peace.*

▷ *tr.v* **3** carry (goods etc) in a cart(1). **4** (often — *s.t around* (*with one*)) (*informal*) hold, carry, (s.o/s.t) by hand as a usual thing: *She carts the baby around with her wherever she goes.* **cart s.o/s.t away/off** (**to s.w**) take s.o/s.t from one place (to another) in a cart(1) or any other kind of vehicle: *The men carted the rubbish away. He was carted off to prison.*

'cart,horse *c.n* kind of big strong horse, used for pulling a cart(1) etc.

'cart,load *c.n* all that can be carried in a cart(1).

'cart-,track *c.n* rough road made by the wheels of a cart(1).

'cart,wheel *c.n* **1** circular and sideways movement of the body in which the hands touch the ground while the body goes up in the air and over until the feet meet the ground again; somersault. **turn cartwheels** do this action.

▷ *intr. v* **2** do a cartwheel(1)

carte blanche /ˌkɑːt ˈblɑːnʃ/ *u.n* (*French*) complete freedom to do what one wants, esp in matters of money, politics etc and as a result of s.o else's permission: *I was given/got carte blanche to spend the money on what I wanted to.*

cartel /kɑːˈtel/ *c.n* (*commerce*) group of organizations, companies etc acting together to control prices, stop competition and make profit.

carthorse ⇨ cart.

cartilage /ˈkɑːtɪlɪdʒ/ *n* (*technical*) **1** *u.n* strong, white substance that acts like bones in the bodies of young people and animals and that is also found in older people and animals. **2** *c.n* piece of this substance.

cartload ⇨ cart.

cartography /kɑːˈtɒɡrəfɪ/ *u.n* art or practice of making maps.

cartographer /kɑːˈtɒɡrəfə/ *c.n* person who is skilled in making maps.

cartographical /ˌkɑːtəˈɡræfɪkl/ *adj.*

carton /ˈkɑːtn/ *c.n* (often — *of s.t*) box made of cardboard or material like it, used for packing and holding goods: *a carton of cigarettes.*

cartoon /kɑːˈtuːn/ *c.n* **1** funny drawing of a person, event etc, usu one that is in the news. **2** (also **'ani,mated car,toon**) cinema film made up from a number of drawings or paintings of people and/or things each in different positions that are photographed one after another so that when the film is played the people/things appear to move. **strip cartoon** ⇨ strip.

car'toonist *c.n* person who draws cartoons.

cart-track ⇨ cart.

cartridge /ˈkɑːtrɪdʒ/ *c.n* **1** metal or paper tube containing explosive material and a bullet or shot for use in a gun or rifle. **2** small case with a needle fixed so that it fits onto the end of a pick-up arm in a record player. **3** case containing an audio or video tape(2) for playing in a machine.

'cartridge ,paper *u.n* kind of strong thick paper used for writing, drawing etc.

cartwheel ⇨ cart.

carve /kɑːv/ *v* **1** *tr.v* (often — *s.t from, out of, s.t*) make (a shape, figure etc) by cutting (wood, stone etc): *He carved a horse in wood. He carved the wood into the shape of a horse.* **2** *intr.v* carve(1) as a profession: *He carves for a living.* **3** *tr.v* make (letters, a design(2) etc) on a surface with a knife etc: *He carved his name on the tree.* **4** *tr.v* slice (cooked meat) with a knife: *He carved the chicken.* **5** *intr.v* slice meat: *Will you carve or shall I?* **carve s.t out for oneself** (*fig*) get a certain job by hard work: *Sue carved out a very responsible position for herself in the company.* **carve s.o up** (*fig; informal*) cut and hurt s.o badly with a knife. **carve s.t up** (**a**) = carve(4). (**b**) divide s.t (esp goods, parts of a country etc) among a group of people: *After the death of the owner, his sons carved up the business among themselves.*

'carver *c.n* **1** person who carves(4). **2** = wood-carver. **3** = carving-knife.

'carving *n* **1** *u.n* art or practice of making shapes, statues etc by carving (carve(1)) them. **2** *c.n* shape etc that has been carved(1).

'carving-,knife *c.n* (*pl knives*) kind of long knife used to carve(4) meat etc.

cascade /kæs'keɪd/ *c.n* **1** small waterfall or part of one. **2** thing that falls or appears to fall like water: *They were greeted with a cascade of flowers as they came into the town.*
▷ *intr.v* **3** fall like water.

case¹ /keɪs/ *c.n* (often — of *s.t* except 6,7) **1** single example of s.t, esp an event: *It was a case of love at first sight.* **2** appearance of a disease: *There were many cases of influenza.* **3** person suffering from illness or disease: *The doctor had many cases to see.* **4** event that needs action (by the police or other officials): *The police are looking into several cases of robbery in the area.* **5** matter to be decided in a court of law: *The judge will be hearing my case tomorrow.* **6** facts or arguments to be used in a court of law: *The police had a strong case against the accused.* **7** (*grammar*) form of a noun, pronoun or adjective or any change in it, showing its connection with other words in a sentence: *'Him' is the objective case of 'he'.* **a case in point** an example that is typical or relevant. **be the case** be true; be the real facts: *If that is the case, I can understand why you don't like him.* **have a case (for s.t)** have good strong arguments, reasons etc in one's favour: *I have to admit he has a very strong case for not liking her.* **in any case** whatever happens or has happened: *Don't get angry — in any case, there's nothing you can do now.* **in case of s.t** if s.t should happen: *In case of fire, break the glass and press the button.* **in the first etc case** referring to the first etc of two or more persons or events mentioned earlier: *In the first case he was lying and in the second case he deceived his wife.* **in that/this case** if that/this is true; if that/this happens: *'He may attack you.' 'In that case I would call the police.'* **in which case** if that happens. **(just) in case (. . .)** as a precaution (if s.t should happen): *If I were you, I would take a raincoat just in case (it rains).* **make (out) a case against/for s.o/s.t** succeed in producing good reasons, arguments etc against, in support of, s.o/s.t. **put the case against/for s.o/s.t** produce reasons, arguments etc in support of, against, s.o/s.t.

'case,book *c.n* collection of notes on a person made by a doctor, the police etc.

,case 'history *c.n* (*pl -ies*) record of past events relating to a person made by a doctor, the police etc.

'case ,law *u.n* law based on past decisions of cases'(5) made by judges. Compare statute law.

'case ,study *c.n* (*pl. -ies*) examination of groups of people, the way they live etc in order to find out facts about them.

'case,work *u.n* work concerning a person, family etc in relation to their social problems.

case² /keɪs/ *c.n* **1** box made of wood, cardboard etc for holding things: *a case of wine.* **2** = suitcase. **3** container of any kind used for holding things: *a jewel case; a packing case; a pillowcase.*
▷ *tr.v* **4** make, put, a case²(1) around (s.t). **5** ⇨ lower case, upper case.

'casement /'keɪsmənt/ *c.n* (also **'casement ,window**) type of window that opens sideways (and not up or down). Compare sash window.

cash /kæʃ/ *u.n* **1** money in the form of coins and paper notes: *I've very little cash on me so will you accept a cheque?* **2** money in any form, esp as showing one's wealth or lack of it: *Tony's loaded with cash but refuses to spend anything on his family.* **cash down** immediate payment in cash(1) for goods. **petty cash** ⇨ petty.
▷ *tr.v* **3** change (a cheque etc) into coins and/or paper notes: *I'll have to stop at the bank and cash a cheque.* **cash in (on s.t)** make a profit (on s.t), usu when things are to one's own advantage: *Shops are cashing in on the demand for the new fashions.*

,cash and 'carry *c.n* (*pl -ies*) (also *attrib*) (large shop where) goods (are) bought for cash(1) and taken away by the buyer, usu at a lower price than at other kinds of shops.

'cash ,card *c.n* special plastic card(6) used to get money out of, put money into, a cash dispenser.

'cash ,crop *c.n* food grown by farmers for sale and not for their own use. Compare subsistence crop.

'cash ,desk *c.n* place in a shop etc where people pay for goods.

,cash 'discount *c.n* amount by which the price of goods is reduced in return for payment in cash(1) instead of by cheque or credit(1).

'cash ,dispenser *c.n* machine inside or outside a bank that provides cash(1) in the form of paper notes when a cash card is put in it.

'cash ,flow *sing/u.n* (*commerce*) movement of money into, or out of, a business in payment of goods and services.

,cash on de'livery *u.n* (*abbr* COD) payment (to be made) for goods when they arrive.

'cash ,register *c.n* machine in a shop etc that records sales and has drawers for money and cheques.

cashier /kæ'ʃɪə/ *c.n* person who deals with money in a bank, shop etc.

cashew /'kæʃuː/ *c.n* (also *attrib*) **1** kind of American tree with small curved nuts. **2** (also **'cashew ,nut**) nut from this tree as food.

cashier ⇨ cash.

cashmere /'kæʃmɪə/ *u.n* (also *attrib*) kind of soft wool made from the hair of goats, used in clothing: *a cashmere coat.*

casing /'keɪsɪŋ/ *c.n* protective rigid(1) cover for s.t.

casino /kə'siːnəʊ/ *c.n* (*pl -s*) place or building where card and other games are played for money (gambling).

cask /kɑːsk/ *c.n* **1** container shaped like a barrel, used for holding liquids such as beer, wine etc. **2** (also **'caskful**) amount of liquid held by a cask(1).

casket /'kɑːskɪt/ *c.n* small box used for holding precious things such as jewellery.

cassava /kə'sɑːvə/ *n* (also *attrib*) **1** *c.n* kind of plant with thick, fleshy roots that is grown in hot climates. **2** *u.n* root of this plant made into a kind of flour.

casserole /'kæsə,rəʊl/ *c.n* (also *attrib*) **1** kind of dish or bowl, usu with a lid, used in cooking: *a casserole dish.* **2** food (meat, vegetables etc) cooked in this dish: *a vegetable casserole.*

cassette /kə'set/ *c.n* **1** plastic container holding an audio or video tape(2) that is played in a tape recorder, video or computer. **2** plastic or metal container holding a roll of film in a camera.
cas'sette ,deck *c.n* part of a high-fidelity system containing the cassette player.
cas'sette ,player/re,corder *c.n* machine that plays audio cassettes(1) and records sounds (voices, music etc). ⇨ video cassette.
cassock /'kæsək/ *c.n* kind of long loose article of clothing worn by priests of the Christian(1) Church and by people who help at their religious services.
cast /kɑːst/ *c.n* **1** group of actors who perform in a play, film etc. **2** act of throwing (a fishing-line or fishing-net): *They made several casts before they caught any fish.* **3** act of throwing (dice(1)) in a game: *He lost all his money on a single cast of the dice.* **4** special shape or mould¹(1) into which hot metal is poured. **5** casing put round a broken bone while it heals. **6** (*formal*) particular shape or quality (in one's body, mind etc): *I am not sure that I like his cast of mind.* **7** kind of squint(1) in one's eye.
▷ *v* (*p.t,p.p* cast) **8** *tr/intr.v* choose (actors) who are going to perform in (a play, film etc): *The producer is already casting (parts) for the new film. The producer is casting (the new play).* **9** *tr.v* throw (a fishing-line or fishing-net): *He cast his line at the deepest part of the pool.* **10** *tr.v* (*formal*) throw (s.t): *She cast the letter into the fire.* **11** *tr.v* make (a shape or object) by pouring hot metal into a mould(1): *The statue was cast in a mixture of copper and tin.* **12** *tr.v* (also — *s.t* off) lose, get rid of, (a skin etc): *Some snakes cast (off) their skins once a year.*
be cast away be left at a place, esp a lonely island, as a result of a shipwreck. ⇨ castaway.
cast s.o as s.o give s.o the part of s.o in a play, film etc. ⇨ cast(8).
cast about/around for s.t look, search, for s.t in many places.
cast anchor ⇨ anchor(2).
cast s.o/s.t aside get rid of s.o/s.t.
cast doubts on s.t ⇨ doubt(*n*).
be cast down be unhappy/upset.
cast an/one's eye over s.t ⇨ eye(*n*).
cast a glance/look at s.o look towards s.o quickly or suddenly.
cast lots ⇨ lot¹(3).
cast s.o off (*formal*) get rid of s.o; abandon s.o.
cast (s.t) off (**a**) untie the rope(s) holding a boat to the land. (**b**) get rid of s.t. ⇨ cast-off, cast-offs. (**c**) (in knitting) finish making s.t in wool by taking the last row of stitches(3) off the needle.
cast (s.t) on (in knitting) start making s.t in wool by putting the first row of stitches on the needle.
cast s.o out (*formal*) make s.o leave a house, a place etc because he/she is not wanted any longer.
cast a/one's vote (**against/for s.o/s.t**) (decide to) vote (against/for s.o/s.t). ⇨ casting vote.
'casta,way *c.n* person whose ship has been wrecked or who is forced to leave it and who comes to land, esp a lonely island.
'casting *n* **1** *c.n* piece of metal etc made in a shape from a mould(1). ⇨ cast(4,11). **2** *u.n* act of choosing actors for a play, film etc. ⇨ cast(1,8).

'casting ,vote *c.n* final vote to decide s.t, usu made by a chairperson at a meeting when the other votes for and against s.t are equal.
,cast 'iron *u.n* special hard kind of iron made in a mould(1).
,cast-'iron² *attrib.adj* **1** made of cast iron. **2** (of a person, mind etc) very hard and tough: *Alan must have a cast-iron stomach considering the amount he eats and drinks.* **3** (of a statement, fact etc) very strong and unlikely to be changed: *The police have a cast-iron case against him.*
'cast-,off *attrib.adj* (usu of clothes) no longer wanted or used (and sometimes then used by other people).
'cast-,offs *pl.n* cast-off clothes: *Sally was wearing her sister's cast-offs.*
castanets /,kæstə'nets/ *pl.n* (often *a pair of* —) musical instruments made from two wooden, plastic etc shells joined by a string which are hit together to make a sound.
castaway ⇨ cast.
caste /kɑːst/ *c.n* one of the groups of society into which people are divided according to Hindu religion in India and other places.
caster /'kɑːstə/ *c.n* (also **'castor**) **1** small wheel fixed to the bottom or leg of a piece of furniture so that it can be moved easily. **2** small container made of metal, plastic etc with holes at the top so that sugar, salt etc can be poured from it.
'caster ,sugar *u.n* very fine white sugar.
castigate /'kæstɪ,geɪt/ *tr.v* (*formal*) criticize (s.o) very strongly; punish (s.o).
castigation /,kæstɪ'geɪʃən/ *u.n*.
casting, cast-iron, cast iron ⇨ cast.
castle /'kɑːsl/ *c.n* **1** large strong building or group of buildings with thick walls, built in former times to protect people from attack by enemies. **2** (in chess) one of the two pieces usu shaped like a tower; rook².
▷ *intr.v* **3** (in chess) move the king from its normal position two squares to the right or left and move the castle(2) on that side to the square on the other side of the king.
cast-off(s) ⇨ cast.
castor /'kɑːstə/ *c.n* = caster.
,castor 'oil *u.n* kind of thick yellow oil made from the beans of a plant, used as a medicine to get rid of stomach upsets.
castrate /kæ'streɪt/ *tr.v* remove part or the whole of the sexual organs of (a male animal, person), esp in order to stop it/him from producing sperm(2).
castration /kæ'streɪʃən/ *u.n*.
casual /'kæʒjuəl/ *adj* **1** not careful; not with great attention: *She gave me a casual look but didn't recognize me.* **2** by chance; without being intended: *a casual remark; a casual meeting.* **3** (of clothes etc) informal (e.g when one is not working): *Liz was dressed in casual clothes.* **4** not caring; without showing much interest: *His behaviour was very casual — he didn't pay us the slightest attention.* **5** (of work, people who work) not working all the time but only now and then: *As she has children to look after, she can only take on casual work. He's a casual labourer.*
'casually *adv*. **'casualness** *u.n*.
casualty /'kæʒjuəltɪ/ *n* (*pl* -ies) **1** *c.n* person who is hurt or killed in an accident: *There were hundreds of casualties in the train crash.* **2** *c.n*

person who is wounded or killed in fighting: *The enemy suffered heavy casualties but* civilian *casualties were slight.* **3** *c.n* person or thing affected or stopped or removed by the action of others: *He and his department were the first casualties in the government's cuts.* **4** *unique n* (also **'casualty de,partment/,ward**) part of a hospital where people injured in accidents are treated: *Ambulances rushed the* injured(3) *to casualty.*

cat¹ /kæt/ *c.n* **1** kind of small animal with short or long fur and sharp claws(1), often kept as a pet: *Cats catch mice and birds.* **2** wild animal with claws like a cat(1), such as a lion, tiger etc. **3** (*derog*) unpleasant, nasty woman. ⇨ catty. (**lead**) **a cat and dog life** (esp of a husband and wife) (have) a life full of quarrels and fights. **let the cat out of the bag** (*fig*) say, perhaps by mistake, s.t that should have been kept secret. **like a cat on hot bricks, on a hot tin roof** in a way that is excited or nervous. (**not have enough**) **room to swing a cat** (be in a) place, e.g a room, which is very small or crowded. **play cat and mouse** (**with s.o**) watch for the time to attack or escape (from s.o). **put the cat among the pigeons** (*fig*) do or say s.t that causes people to become annoyed, upset etc. **rain cats and dogs** (*fig*) rain very heavily.

'cat ,burglar *c.n* thief who climbs up walls etc in order to get into a building.

,cat-o-'nine ,tails *c.n* whip with nine ropes with knots in them which was once used for punishing people, esp sailors.

'cat's ,cradle *u.n* children's game using a piece of string held by the fingers of each hand to make different patterns.

'cat's-,eye *c.n* one of a number of small objects placed in the middle or at the side of a road, which reflect the lights of a car and so help to guide the car in the dark.

'cattery *c.n* (*pl -ies*) place where cats'(1) may be left while the owners are on holiday. ⇨ kennels.

'cattily *adv* in a catty way.

'catti,ness *u.n* (*derog*) (esp of a woman) behaviour which is full of spite or complaints against other people.

'catty *adj* (*-ier, -iest*) (*derog*) behaving in a spiteful way, esp with complaints that hurt s.o.

cat² /kæt/ *c.n* (*informal*) caterpillar tractor.

cataclysm /'kætə,klɪzəm/ *c.n* sudden and extraordinary event or change, such as an earthquake, political or social upset etc.

cataclysmic /,kætə'klɪzmɪk/ *adj.*

catacombs /'kætə,ku:mz/ *pl.n* underground place or rooms where people are buried.

catalogue /'kætə,lɒg/ (US **'cata,log**) *c.n* **1** (often — *of s.t*) (printed) list of things (names, objects, places etc) arranged in a certain way so that they can be looked up easily: *a catalogue of paintings.*
▷ *tr.v* **2** make such a list of (things).

catalyst /'kætə,lɪst/ *c.n* **1** (*chemistry*) substance that makes another substance change in a chemical way without changing itself. **2** (*fig*) person or thing who/that brings about a change: *He acted as the catalyst in the change in public opinion.*

catalytic /,kætə'lɪtɪk/ *adj.*

catamaran /,kætəmə'ræn/ *c.n* kind of sailing boat with two separate hulls joined by a deck. ⇨ trimaran.

catapult /'kætə,pʌlt/ *c.n* **1** small stick shaped like a Y with a rubber band between the two ends that children use to shoot stones etc with. **2** machine used in former times in war to shoot large stones etc at walls in order to break them down. **3** machine on a ship used to help planes take off.
▷ *v* **4** *tr.v* shoot (a stone) from a catapult(1). **5** *tr/intr.v* (cause (s.o/s.t) to) move suddenly through the air: *The car stopped suddenly and I was almost catapulted through the window.* **6** *tr.v* cause (s.o) to become famous, successful etc very quickly: *The television programme catapulted her to stardom.*

cataract /'kætə,rækt/ *c.n* **1** large kind of waterfall. **2** substance growing on the surface of an eye that stops light entering and can lead to blindness.

catarrh /kə'tɑ:/ *u.n* **1** kind of illness in the nose and throat that produces a flow of thick liquid as in a cold. **2** liquid that is produced in this way.

catarrhal /kə'tɑ:rəl/ *adj.*

catastrophe /kə'tæstrəfɪ/ *c.n* **1** sudden event such as an earthquake, flood, explosion etc that causes great destruction, loss of life etc. **2** sudden harmful event of any kind: *It was a catastrophe for his family when Brian lost his job.*

catastrophic /,kætə'strɒfɪk/ *adj.*

,cata'strophically *adv.*

catcall /'kæt,kɔ:l/ *c.n* **1** loud sound of disapproval (e.g a whistle or shout), esp made by s.o at a meeting etc.
▷ *intr.v* **2** make a catcall(1).

catch /kætʃ/ *c.n* **1** act of getting hold of s.t (esp a ball in a game) when it is moving in the air: *He made a fine catch.* **2** thing or things that s.o gets hold of or traps: *The boats brought back a good catch of fish.* **3** person whom it would be good to marry (because he/she is rich etc): *Vicky'll make a good catch for some lucky man.* **4** hook or part of a lock which holds a door, box etc closed: *The catch on his* suitcase *broke and all his clothes fell out.* **5** hidden difficulty, sometimes one that is there on purpose: *His offer seems too good and there must be a catch in it.*
▷ *v* (*p.t,p.p* **caught** /kɔ:t/) **6** *tr.v* get hold of (s.o/ s.t), esp when he/she/it is moving through the air: *He caught the ball. The dog caught the stick in its mouth. She caught my arm to stop me stepping in front of a bus.* **7** *tr.v* (in cricket') put (a player) out by getting hold of a ball he/ she has hit before it reaches the ground. **8** *tr.v* trap, seize, (s.o, an animal etc) before he/she/it can escape: *The police caught the thief. Cats are good at catching mice.* **9** *tr.v* (get to s.w in time in order to) get onto (a train, plane etc before it leaves): *I was just in time to catch the last plane to London.* **10** *tr/intr.v* (cause (s.t) to) become hooked on, trapped in, s.t: *I caught my trousers on the wire* (or *My trousers caught on the wire*) *as I was getting over the fence.* **11** *tr.v* hit (s.o) either by intention or by accident: *His blow caught me on the side of the head.* **12** *tr.v* get (an illness): *It's easy to catch a cold in this weather.* **13** *intr.v* (of a fire, an engine etc) begin to do s.t (e.g burn, work): *The engine caught on the third try.* **14** *tr.v* hear or understand (what s.o has said etc): *I'm sorry, I didn't catch your last remark, could you repeat it?*

catch s.o in the act ⇨ act(*n*).

catch at s.t try to get hold of s.t or to do s.t in order to save oneself: *He was catching at any opportunity to get himself out of his difficulties.*

catch s.o at/doing s.t find s.o doing s.t, esp s.t he/she should not be doing: *If I catch you at the biscuits* (or *eating the biscuits*) *again, I'll punish you.*

catch s.o's attention/eye etc be noticed, seen etc by s.o because of s.t one does, s.t that happens etc: *Valerie was so beautiful she caught everybody's attention. A small picture in the corner of the room caught my eye.*

catch one's breath ⇨ breath.

catch fire ⇨ fire(*n*). ⇨ catch(13).

catch hold of s.o/s.t ⇨ hold(*n*).

catch it (*informal*) be punished, hit, criticized etc: *If you do that again, you'll catch it from your father.*

catch on understand s.t, usu suddenly: *I had to repeat the joke before he finally caught on.* **catch on** (**with s.o**) become fashionable (with s.o, a group of people etc): *The new dance quickly caught on.*

catch s.o out show that s.o has made a mistake, done s.t wrong, esp when he/she has tried to hide it.

catch sight of s.o/s.t ⇨ sight(*n*).

catch (**s.o**) **up** (**a**) walk, run etc fast until one reaches s.o. (**b**) work hard until one has reached the same position as s.o else. **catch up** (**on s.t**) do, complete, (work etc) that has not been done: *As Teddy was ill last term, he has a lot of catching up to do if he hopes to pass the examinations.* **catch up** (**with s.o/s.t**) (**a**) = catch (s.o) up. (**b**) in competition, trade, standards etc) become equal (to s.o/s.t): *Our nation must catch up with its competitors in international trade.*

'**catcher** *c.n* person, esp in a game, who catches s.t, e.g a ball.

'**catching** *adj* (*informal*) (of a disease) easily moving from one person to another; infectious(1).

'**catchment** ,**area** *c.n* **1** place from which a river, lake etc gets its water. **2** place that has public services such as a school/hospital to which people in that place go.

'**catch,phrase/,word** *c.n* saying/word that becomes popular and is used by a lot of people.

'**catchy** /'kætʃɪ/ *adj* (-*ier*, -*iest*) (*informal*) (esp of a musical tune) easy to remember; likely to attract attention.

catechism /'kætɪ,kɪzəm/ *u.n* information about the beliefs of esp the Christian(1) religion arranged in the form of questions and answers.

categorical /,kætɪ'gɒrɪkl/ *adj* (esp of s.t one says, states etc) very firm and not to be changed: *The government made a categorical statement that it would not accept the proposals.*

category /'kætɪgərɪ/ *c.n* (*pl* -*ies*) class or group of people/things in a whole system of classification: *They divided the population into several categories.*

categorize, -ise /'kætɪgə,raɪz/ *tr.v* put, place, (s.o/s.t) in a category or categories.

cater /'keɪtə/ *intr.v* provide food and drink for payment, usu by taking them to a place (e.g a house, public building etc): *We will need to get*

a firm to cater at the wedding. **cater for s.o/s.t** (**a**) = cater. (**b**) consider and provide what one thinks people need: *Television tries to cater for all possible tastes.* **cater to s.o/s.t** provide what is needed or wanted by s.o/s.t, esp in order to attract as many people as possible: *The new book caters to the worst kind of person and the worst kind of humour.*

'**caterer** *c.n* **1** person who caters. **2** (also '**caterer's**) business of a caterer(1); place where a caterer(1) works.

caterpillar /'kætə,pɪlə/ *c.n* **1** kind of small long creature like a worm with many legs; it eats leaves and changes into a butterfly or moth. **2** = caterpillar tractor.

'**caterpillar** ,**tractor** *c.n* (*informal cat*) vehicle with a belt of steel plates moving over groups of wheels so that it can work on rough ground, e.g in farming, road building etc.

catfish /'kæt,fɪʃ/ *c.n* (*pl catfish*) kind of fish with long growths around the mouth.

catgut /'kæt,gʌt/ *u.n* kind of strong string made from parts of the stomach of animals and used in musical instruments, tennis rackets[1] etc.

cathedral /kə'θiːdrəl/ *c.n* large Christian(1) Church building which has a bishop who is in charge of the area around it (the diocese).

catherine wheel /'kæθrɪn ,wiːl/ *c.n* kind of firework with a round shape that spins round and round when lit.

cathode /'kæθəud/ *c.n* (*technical*) **1** part of an instrument (the negative terminal, usu marked '−') from which electrons come when an electric current goes through it, as in a battery[2] or cell(6). Compare anode. **2** part of an electron gun from which the electrons come in a cathode ray tube.

'**cathode** ,**rays** *pl.n* group of electrons that move at high speed when made hot in a vacuum(1).

,**cathode** '**ray** ,**tube** *c.n* glass tube without any air in it in which cathode rays act to form a picture on a screen, e.g in a television set.

catholic /'kæθlɪk/ *adj* **1** having or showing interest in many things: *He was a man of catholic tastes.*

▷ *c.n* (also *attrib*) **2** (with capital **C**; also ,**Roman** '**Catholic**) person who believes in, belongs to, the Roman Catholic Church.

,**Catholic** '**Church** *def.n* = Roman Catholic Church.

Catholicism /kə'θɒlɪ,sɪzəm/ *u.n* (also ,**Roman** **Ca'thol,icism**) religion and beliefs of Catholics.

catkin /'kætkɪn/ *c.n* kind of long hairy flower which hangs down from some trees such as a birch(1) or willow(1).

catnap /'kæt,næp/ *c.n* **1** short, light sleep.

▷ *intr.v* **2** sleep in this way.

cat-o'-nine-tails, cattery, cattily, catti-ness ⇨ cat.

cattle /'kætl/ *pl.n* **1** cows, bulls[1](1), oxen etc, esp when on a farm: *He has over 1000 head of cattle on his farm.* **2** (*derog*) people considered or treated as inferior(1): *He thinks his workers are cattle and is always rude to them.*

'**cattle** ,**grid** *c.n* group of bars placed over a hole in the ground in a road, at an entrance etc to stop cattle from crossing.

catty ⇨ cat.

Caucasian /kɔː'keɪzɪən/ *adj* **1** (*technical*) of, referring to, Caucasians(2).

▷ *c.n* **2** (*technical*) person of a race that has a light skin colour.

caucus /ˈkɔːkəs/ *c.n* (*pl* -es) **1** meeting in which members of a political party decide who to elect, what things to do etc. **2** small group of people in a political party, organization etc who (try to) control it.

caught /kɔːt/ *p.t,p.p* of catch.

cauldron /ˈkɔːldrən/ *c.n* (also **ˈcaldron**) kind of large pot used for boiling or cooking things over a fire.

cauliflower /ˈkɒlɪˌflaʊə/ *n* (also *attrib*) **1** *c.n* kind of vegetable with green leaves round a large central part with white hard heads. **2** *u.n* this vegetable cooked as food.

caulk /kɔːk/ *tr.v* (also **calk**) put a waterproof substance such as tar(1) or fibre(3) between (the wooden planks(1) of a boat or ship) to stop water coming in.

cause /kɔːz/ *n* **1** *c.n* event, act, person that/who makes s.t else happen or leads to a certain result: *The cause of the fire was a burning cigarette.* **2** *u.n* reason (why s.t happens or might happen): *You have very little cause for complaint as it's your own fault.* **3** *c.n* thing, e.g a purpose, social movement, political belief, that one supports: *She spends her life working for good causes.* **lost cause** s.t that has no possibility of success.

▷ *tr.v* **4** (often — s.o/s.t to do s.t) make (s.t) happen; be the reason why (s.t happens): *She caused a great deal of trouble to everybody. The lack of rain caused my plants to die.*

causeway /ˈkɔːzˌweɪ/ *c.n* road or path that is higher than the land or water around it, esp to avoid being flooded.

caustic /ˈkɔːstɪk/ *adj* **1** (*chemistry*) (of a chemical substance) able to burn or eat away (another substance). **2** (*derog*; *fig*) (of a person, what he/she says etc) unpleasant, unfriendly: *Sam can be very caustic when he wants to so it's not surprising that he has few friends.*

ˌcaustic ˈsoda *c.n* chemical substance used in soap, *chem.form* NaOH.

ˈcaustically *adv* in a caustic(2) manner.

cauterize, -ise /ˈkɔːtəˌraɪz/ *tr.v* burn (a wound etc) using a very hot piece of iron or a caustic(1) substance in order to stop infection.

cauterization, -isation /ˌkɔːtəraɪˈzeɪʃən/ *u.n.*

caution /ˈkɔːʃən/ *n* **1** *u.n* (state of) taking care; (act of) paying careful attention: *He showed great caution in his dealings with the enemy.* **2** *c.n* word(s) of warning (not to do s.t again), esp from a judge, a police officer etc (to s.o who may have done s.t wrong): *The police let him go after giving him a caution.* **fling/throw caution to the wind(s)** stop being careful and start behaving or talking in ways that might be dangerous or unwise.

▷ *tr.v* **3** (of a judge) warn (s.o who has done s.t wrong) not to do s.t wrong again: *She cautioned the man and let him go.* **caution s.o against (doing) s.t, against s.o** warn or advise s.o not to do s.t, not to listen to s.o.

cautionary /ˈkɔːʃənrɪ/ *adj* (usu *attrib*) having or showing a warning: *It was a cautionary story about how a man ended up in prison.*

cautious /ˈkɔːʃəs/ *adj* (of a person) showing or using great care. Opposite incautious.

ˈcautiously *adv.* **ˈcautiousness** *u.n.*

cavalcade /ˌkævlˌkeɪd/ *c.n* procession of people riding on horses, in cars etc (through the streets of a town etc).

cavalier /ˌkævəˈlɪə/ *adj* **1** (*derog*; *formal*) (acting) without thought or care; (treating s.o) in a careless way: *Steve got very cavalier treatment from the officials when he complained.*

▷ *c.n* **2** (*old use*) gentleman or knight(1) trained to fight on horseback.

cavalry /ˈkævlrɪ/ *u/def.n* (also *attrib*) (*military*; *old use*) soldiers who fought on horseback.

cave /keɪv/ *c.n* **1** large hollow space in the side of a hill or mountain or under the ground, usu big enough for people to stand up in.

▷ *intr.v* **cave in 2** (of the roof, sides of a building etc) fall down. **3** (*informal*) (of a person) give up, accept defeat, (under pressure from s.o).

ˈcaveˌman *c.n* (*pl* -ˌmen) person who lived in caves in prehistoric times.

cavern /ˈkævən/ *c.n* very large cave.

ˈcavernous *adj* (*formal*) **1** (of a place) having many caverns; shaped like a cavern. **2** (of a sound, a space etc) deep and hollow.

caviar /ˈkævɪɑː/ *u.n* (also **ˈcaviare**) salted black or grey eggs (roe) of certain kinds of fish, esp the sturgeon(1), eaten as food.

cavil /ˈkævɪl/ *intr.v* (-ll-, US -l-) (usu — at s.t) (*formal*) complain (about s.t), usu in an unnecessary way.

cavity /ˈkævɪtɪ/ *c.n* (*pl* -ies) small hole or space inside s.t solid: *He had several cavities in his teeth which needed to be filled by the dentist.*

ˈcavity ˌwall *c.n* wall of a building consisting of two separate walls with a small hollow space in between to help keep out the cold, noise etc.

cavort /kəˈvɔːt/ *intr.v* (often — about/around) jump about, behave, in a noisy way.

caw /kɔː/ *c.n* **1** sound made by some birds, such as a crow(1) or a rook[1].

▷ *intr.v* **2** (of a crow(1), rook[1] etc) make the sound of a caw(1).

cayenne /keɪˈen/ *u.n* (also **cayˈenne ˌpepper**) ⇒ pepper(2).

CB /ˌsiː ˈbiː/ *c.n/abbr* **1** Companion of the Order of the Bath (a British honorary(2) award). **2** Citizens' Band (radio); radio wavelength used by people (esp when driving lorries or cars) to talk to each other over short distances.

CBE /ˌsiː biː ˈiː/ *abbr* Commander of the British Empire (a British honorary(2) award).

CC, cc /ˌsiː ˈsiː(z)/ *abbr* **1** cubic centimetre(s). **2** cubic capacity.

CD /ˌsiː ˈdiː/ *abbr* **1** Corps Diplomatique. **2** compact disc.

Cdr *written abbr* Commander.

CE *written abbr* **1** Church of England. **2** civil engineer.

c/f *written abbr* (*commerce*) carried forward. ⇒ carry.

cease /siːs/ *u.n* **1** **without cease** (*formal*) without ever stopping; without coming to an end.

▷ *v* (*formal*) **2** *tr.v* stop (s.t): *Cease this noise immediately!* **3** *intr.v* (often — (from) doing, to do, s.t) stop; come to an end: *The noise finally ceased. In the end he ceased to complain about his problems.* **cease fire** ⇒ fire(*n*).

ˌcease-ˈfire *c.n* (*military*) agreement between two armies etc to stop shooting or fighting (for a certain amount of time).

'ceaseless *adj* (*formal*) without stopping; continuing all the time. ⇨ incessant.
'ceaselessly *adv.* **'ceaselessness** *u.n.*
cessation /se'seɪʃən/ *u.n* (*formal*) act of stopping (s.t) for either a short time or completely: *After the cessation of* hostilities, *a peace agreement was signed.*
cedar /'siːdə/ *n* (also *attrib*) **1** *c.n* kind of large evergreen tree with hard red wood. **2** *u.n* (also **'cedar,wood**) wood from this tree, esp used in making furniture etc.
cede /siːd/ *tr.v* (often — *s.t to s.o*) (*formal*) give up (s.t, esp land or rights in s.t) (to s.o else, esp another country): *After the war, the government was forced to cede a large part of the country to the enemy.* ⇨ concede, concession.
ceiling /'siːlɪŋ/ *c.n* **1** top part of a room above one's head. **2** greatest height to which an aircraft can go: *The new fighter can reach its ceiling in under ten minutes.* **3** the height above the ground of the bottom of a cloud or group of clouds. **4** (also *attrib*) limit, esp one fixed by a government, above which prices, wages etc should not go: *The new government has fixed a ceiling on spending by its departments.* ⇨ Compare floor(5). **hit the ceiling** (*fig.*) rise very high: *House prices have hit the ceiling.*
celebrate /'selɪˌbreɪt/ *v* **1** *tr.v* mark (a special day, occasion) by doing s.t enjoyable: *He celebrated his birthday by giving a large party.* **2** *intr.v* enjoy oneself, have a good time, (because of s.t one has done etc): *Jenny decided to celebrate when she got the job.* **3** *tr.v* (*formal*) praise (s.o, s.o's actions) in words or writing: *His book celebrates the deeds of famous women.* **celebrate Mass** (in the Roman Catholic Church, of a priest) perform the ceremony of the Mass[2](1).
'cele,brated *adj* famous: *a celebrated scientist.*
celebration /ˌselɪ'breɪʃən/ *c.n* (example of the) act of celebrating s.t.
celebrity /sɪ'lebrɪtɪ/ *n* (*pl -ies*) **1** *u.n* fame, honour. **2** *c.n* famous person, esp one who performs in public: *a television celebrity.*
celery /'selərɪ/ *n* (also *attrib*) **1** *c.n* kind of plant with white or pale green stems and leaves on the top. **2** this plant as food: *a stick of celery*; *celery soup.*
celestial /sɪ'lestɪəl/ *adj* (*formal*) **1** of or referring to the sky; of things seen from Earth: *a celestial body* (e.g the Sun, Moon, a star). **2** (in religion) of or referring to Heaven where God is said to live: *the celestial* angels(1).
celibate /'selɪbət/ *adj* **1** not married, usu as a definite or conscious decision, e.g for religious reasons.
▷ *c.n* **2** celibate(1) person.
'celibacy *u.n.*
cell /sel/ *c.n* **1** small room, usu for one person to live and sleep in, in a religious building such as a monastery or convent. **2** small room in which one or more prisoners are kept: *a prison cell*; *the police cells.* **3** small group of people who act together, usu in secret, within a larger political organization, esp a socialist or communist one. **4** (*science*) very small unit of matter that forms the basis of all living things: *a plant cell*; *the red and white blood cells in the human body.* **5** very small, usu hollow, part of a larger substance: *The honeycomb(1)*

built by bees *is made up of thousands of cells.* **6** (*technical*) battery or part of it that produces electric current through chemical action: *a* fuel(1) *cell.*
cellular /'seljʊlə/ *adj* **1** of or referring to a cell(4). **2** (esp of woven material such as cotton or wool) made with many holes or spaces: *a cellular blanket.*
cellar /'selə/ *c.n* **1** space or room below the ground floor of a house or building, usu where things such as coal, wine etc are stored. **2** (*formal*) (amount or quality of) wine stored by s.o for drinking later: *He keeps a very good cellar.*
cello /'tʃeləʊ/ *c.n* (*pl -s*) (*formal* violoncello) kind of very large musical instrument with four strings that is held between the knees and played with a bow; it produces deep sounds.
cellist /'tʃelɪst/ *c.n* (*formal* violoncellist) person who plays the cello.
cellophane /'seləˌfeɪn/ *u.n* (*t.n*) very thin plastic transparent material used esp for wrapping things.
cellular ⇨ cell.
cellulose /'seljʊˌləʊs/ *u.n* **1** (*science*) natural substance found in the cell(4) walls of plants, used esp in the making of cotton, paper etc. **2** (also **,cellulose 'ace,tate**) kind of plastic substance used in industry for making photographic film, explosives etc.
Celsius /'selsɪəs/ *unique n* (*science*) symb C. = Centigrade. ⇨ Fahrenheit.
cement /sɪ'ment/ *u.n* **1** grey powdery substance (clay and lime[1](1)) that becomes hard when mixed with water and usu sand, used in building and to make concrete(4). **2** (kind of) liquid substance which becomes hard and is used to fill holes (e.g in teeth) or to stick things together.
▷ *tr.v* **3** use cement(1) to build or cover (s.t): *cement bricks together. He cemented the garden path to stop weeds growing.* **4** *tr.v* (*fig*) make (s.t) stronger or closer: *The friendship between the two countries was cemented by the signing of the agreement.*
ce'ment ,mixer *c.n* kind of machine with a hollow drum that turns round and round and mixes cement(1), sand, water and stones in order to make concrete(4).
cemetery /'semɪtrɪ/ *c.n* (*pl -ies*) (usu public) area or place where people are buried.
cenotaph /'senəˌtɑːf/ *c.n* memorial built to honour those who died in a war and are buried in other places.
censor /'sensə/ *c.n* **1** official who examines films, books etc and decides if they are suitable for the public or if certain parts need to be removed (e.g because they are obscene, too violent, critical of the government etc). **2** (in time of war) official who examines letters, articles or newspapers etc and removes parts or stops them altogether so that the enemy or the public does not learn anything it should not know.
▷ *tr.v* **3** act as a censor (of s.t).
censorious /sen'sɔːrɪəs/ *adj* (*derog*; *formal*) (too fond of) finding fault with s.o/s.t; too critical.
cen'soriously *adv.* **cen'soriousness** *u.n.*
'censor,ship *u.n.* act, office, duties, of a censor.
censure /'senʃə/ *u.n* (*formal*) **1** act of blaming or criticizing s.o.

▷ *tr.v* **2** (usu — *s.o* for *s.t*) (*formal*) blame or criticize (s.o) (for s.t he/she has done or not done).

census /ˈsensəs/ *c.n* official counting of the number of people (and sometimes the collection of other information about them) in a country.

cent /sent/ *c.n* coin that is one of the hundred equal parts of a decimal system, e.g in the US, with the bigger unit usu called a dollar. *per cent* ⇒ per.

centenary /senˈtiːnərɪ/ *c.n* (*pl -ies*) (also *attrib*) day or year one hundred years after an event, esp one to be celebrated.

centenarian /ˌsentəˈneərɪən/ *c.n* person who is one hundred or more years old.

centennial /senˈtenɪəl/ *c.n* (also *attrib*) (esp US) = centenary. ⇒ bicentennial.

center ⇒ centre.

Centigrade /ˈsentɪˌɡreɪd/ *unique n* (also *attrib*) scale of temperature in which the freezing-point of water is taken as 0° (degrees) and its boiling point as 100° (degrees), *symb* C. ⇒ Celsius, Fahrenheit.

centigram /ˈsentɪˌɡræm/ *c.n* (also **centi-gramme**) (*written abbr cg*) one hundredth part of a gram.

centilitre /ˈsentɪˌliːtə/ *c.n* (US **centi-liter**) (*written abbr cl*) one hundredth part of a litre.

centimetre /ˈsentɪˌmiːtə/ *c.n* (US **centi-meter**) (*written abbr cm*) one hundredth part of a metre.

centipede /ˈsentɪˌpiːd/ *c.n* kind of small long creature with many joints each of which has a pair of legs. Compare millipede.

central /ˈsentrəl/ *adj* **1** in, at or near the centre (of a place): *the central shopping area.* **2** (of ideas, acts etc) most important; main: *His central purpose was to get into politics.*

central government *c/u.n* government of the whole country. ⇒ local government.

central heating *u.n* (*written abbr c.h.*) system of warming a building from one boiler with hot air or water in pipes going from it to each room.

Central Intelligence Agency *def/unique n* (*abbr CIA*) the US federal government department responsible for spying and intelligence(2).

centralization, -isation /ˌsentrəlaɪˈzeɪʃən/ *u.n* act of centralizing s.t, or state of being central-ized.

centralize, -ise *tr.v* bring (s.o/s.t) under one central control: *The government has centralized responsibility for food in one department.*

centrally *adv.*

central nervous system *c/def.n* main con-trolling part of the group of nerves(1) in the body, consisting of the brain and the spinal cord.

central processing unit *c.n* (*abbr CPU*) main part of a computer system that processes(3) information.

centre /ˈsentə/ *c.n* (US **center**) **1** (often *the — of s.t*) exact middle or middle point (of s.t): *the centre of a circle.* **2** main or most important place where s.t happens: *the town centre.* **3** (group of) buildings where a certain activity takes place: *an arts centre.* **4** (usu *the — of s.t*) person or thing who/that attracts the main interest: *He was the centre of attention wherever he went.* **5** *c/ def.n* (also *attrib*) (also with capital **C**) middle political party, group within a political party,

which is not extreme (i.e not to the left or the right): *The centre party gained a large number of seats in the election.* **6** (football etc) player who plays in or near the middle of the playing field. ⇒ centre forward. *at/in the centre of s.t* (**a**) in the middle of s.t that is happening around one: *His boat was in the centre of the storm.* (**b**) (taking part) in the main matter of interest, concern etc: *Christine was at the centre of the political row.*

▷ *tr.v* **7** put or place (s.t) at or near the centre(1) of s.t: *He centred the picture between two lights.* **8** (in football etc) kick or pass (the ball) to the middle of the playing field, esp in front of the goal. *centre (up)on s.o/s.t* (of s.o's thoughts, attention etc) become interested in, fixed on, s.o/ s.t: *His whole interest centred on how he could attract her notice.*

centre forward *c.n* (in football etc) player who plays in or near the middle of the playing field and whose main job is to try to score goals; striker(2).

centre of gravity *c.n* (*technical*) point in an object at which it will balance and not move down on the right or the left.

centrifugal /senˈtrɪfjʊɡl/ *adj* (*technical*) (of a force, motion) moving away from a central point. Opposite centripetal.

centrifugal force *c/u.n* (*technical*) force that makes an object move away from a central point (esp when it is spun around).

centurion /senˈtjʊərɪən/ *c.n* (*military*) officer in the ancient Roman army who commanded one hundred soldiers.

century /ˈsentʃərɪ/ *c.n* (*pl -ies*) (*written abbr C*) **1** one hundred years. **2** (often with capital **C**) (one of the group of) one hundred years counting backwards or forwards from the year when Christ was supposed to be born: *the 5th century* BC (i.e 500 – 401 years before Christ was born); *the 19th century* (= 1800 – 1899 AD). **3** (in cricket[1]) score of one hundred runs by a person batting: *He hit a century in 65 minutes.* (*at*) *the turn of the century* ⇒ turn(*n*).

ceramic /sɪˈræmɪk/ *adj* of, referring to, the art of making and decorating objects in clay.

ceramics *n* **1** *u.n* ceramic art. **2** *n pl* objects (*e.g pots, plates etc*) made and decorated in clay.

cereal /ˈsɪərɪəl/ *n* (also *attrib*) **1** *u.n* kind of plant that produces grain. **2** *c.n* (one of a number of plants such as) wheat, barley, rye(1), rice etc grown as food: *Farmers are growing more cereals.* **3** *c/u.n* (one of a number of foods from) grain specially prepared for eating at breakfast time: *Come on, eat your cereal.*

cerebral /ˈserɪbrəl/ *adj* **1** (*medical*) of or refer-ring to the brain, esp in connection with illness: *cerebral damage.* **2** (*formal*) thinking clearly (and not allowing one's emotions to control one): *He's too cerebral.*

ceremony /ˈserɪmənɪ/ *n* (*pl -ies*) **1** *u.n* formal or special rule(s) or behaviour for a public or private event: *The service was conducted with proper ceremony.* **2** *c.n* (religious or official) act or event performed according to certain rules: *The owner was present at the ceremony to open the new factory.* ⇒ Master of Ceremonies. (*not*) *stand (up)on ceremony* (*formal*) (not) do s.t in a formal way or according to fixed social rules: *There is no need for you to stand on ceremony with us — consider yourself as part of the family.*

ceremonial /ˌserɪˈməʊnɪəl/ *adj* (usu *attrib*) **1** of or referring to a formal event or ceremony(2): *a ceremonial occasion.*

▷ *n* **2** *u.n* formal or special rules; ceremony(1): *Ceremonial demanded that everyone knelt before the king.* **3** *c.n* = ceremony(2): *There was a special ceremonial to mark the end of the war.*

ˌcereˈmonially *adv.*

ceremonious /ˌserɪˈməʊnɪəs/ *adj* acting in a ceremonial(1) way. ⇨ unceremonious.

ˌcereˈmoniously *adv.* **ˌcereˈmoniousness** *u.n.*

cerise /səˈriːs/ *adj* **1** of, referring to, a light red colour.

▷ *u.n* **2** light red colour.

cert /sɜːt/ *c.n* (*informal*) **1** (often *a dead —*) certainty(2), esp in the opinion of the speaker and usu about s.t that will happen, succeed etc: *He claimed that his horse was a dead cert* (an absolute certainty(2)) *to win the race.* **2** certificate(1).

certain /ˈsɜːtn/ *adj* **1** (*attrib*) sure; known and proved: *The new medicine is claimed to be an almost certain remedy for this disease.* **2** that cannot be avoided: *She went into the final tennis match facing certain defeat.* **3** (*attrib*) fixed or settled (amount etc): *The new proposal provided him with a certain share of the profits.* **4** (*pred*) very sure; definite, free from doubt: *Are you certain about his ability to handle the job? I'm not certain what he meant. I'm no longer certain of the future. It is almost certain (that) there will be higher taxes next year.* Opposite uncertain. **for certain** without any doubt: *I can't say for certain what will happen.* **make certain (of s.t/(that) . . .)** (**a**) find out in advance and make sure (about s.t, that s.t will happen etc): *You'd better make certain that she'll be there.* (**b**) do s.t early enough (so that one gets s.t etc): *Have you made certain of your tickets as there's always a rush at the last minute?* **certain to do s.t** having no possibility of not doing s.t: *He is certain to fail his examinations.*

▷ *det* **5** having some amount or degree (of s.t) but only to a limited extent: *She has a certain charm once you get to know her.* **6** not named but possibly known to the speaker or known to exist: *Certain members of the government are not happy with the present situation.* **7** (of a person) known by name only: *A certain Mr Green phoned while you were out.*

▷ *pron* **8** (usu *— of us, his friends, our books* etc) (of a group of people, things etc) some but not all (of us etc): *They all complained but certain of them did so more loudly than others.*

ˈcertainly *adv* **1** without any doubt: *I'll certainly do it as soon as I can.* **2** (in answer to a question) yes; of course; I agree: *'Can I borrow your spade?' 'Certainly.'* **certainly not** (a strong way of saying 'no'): *'Can I have some more sweets?' 'Certainly not!'*

ˈcertainty *n* (*pl -ies*) Opposite uncertainty. **1** *u.n* state of being very sure and free from doubt: *There's no certainty that Nigel will succeed.* **2** *c.n* thing that is sure to happen: *There are very few certainties in this life.* ⇨ cert(1).

certifiable ⇨ certify.

certificate /səˈtɪfɪkɪt/ *c.n* **1** written or printed statement about certain facts that are declared to be true by an official writing or signing it: *a birth/death/marriage certificate. She had certificates to show the courses she had attended.*

▷ *tr.v* /səˈtɪfɪˌkeɪt/ **2** make, draw up, a certificate(1) about (s.t).

certification /ˌsɜːtɪfɪˈkeɪʃən/ *u.n* act of providing a certificate(1) (about s.t).

certify /ˈsɜːtɪfaɪ/ *tr.v* (*-ies, -ied*) **1** (often *— s.t to be s.t; — that . . .*) declare formally in speech or writing (s.t to be true etc): *I certify that this statement is correct.* **2** (*medical*) declare officially (s.o to be mad or insane(1)): *The doctors certified Mark ((as) mad) and he was sent to a special hospital.*

certifiable /ˈsɜːtɪˌfaɪəbl/ *adj* **1** that can be proved or shown to be true. **2** (of a person) (considered to be) mad and ready to be certified(2): *He's almost certifiable with his terrible temper.* Opposite uncertifiable.

certitude /ˈsɜːtɪˌtjuːd/ *u.n* (*formal*) state of being sure or certain (esp in one's own opinion).

cervix /ˈsɜːvɪks/ *c.n* (*pl -es, cervices* /sɜːˈvɪˌsiːz/) (*medical*) narrow opening to the womb.

cervical /ˈsɜːvɪkl/ *adj* of, referring to, the cervix.

ˌcervical ˈcancer *c.n* cancer(1) in the cervix.

ˌcervical ˈsmear ˌtest *c.n* test that takes a substance as a smear(2) from the cervix in order to check for cancer(1).

Cesarean, Cesarian ⇨ Caesarean.

cessation ⇨ cease.

cesspit /ˈsesˌpɪt/ *c.n* (also **cesspool** /ˈsesˌpuːl/) **1** place or hole, usu underground, where waste from a house, and esp waste from the body, is put. **2** (*derog*) dirty place: *This room is a cesspit!*

cf /ˌsiː ˈef/ *abbr* compare (s.t with s.t else) (from the Latin 'confer').

CFE /ˌsiː ˌef ˈiː/ *abbr* College of Further Education.

CH /ˌsiː ˈeɪtʃ/ *written abbr* Companion of Honour.

c.h. *written abbr* central heating.

ch *written abbr* chapter(s).

chafe /tʃeɪf/ *c.n* **1** sore on the body made by chafing(3).

▷ *v* (*formal*) **2** *tr.v* rub (a part of the body) in order to make it warm: *He chafed her frozen hands to get back the circulation(1).* **3** *tr/intr.v* (of clothes etc) (cause (a part of the body, one's skin) to) become sore by rubbing: *The wet raincoat chafed his neck. Her fair skin chafes badly in cold weather.* **chafe at/under s.t** (*fig; formal*) be, become, annoyed about s.t, esp because it prevents one doing s.t, causes a delay etc: *He chafed at the delay at the airport.*

chaff /tʃɑːf/ *u.n* **1** outer covering of seeds of grain that is removed when the grain is threshed. **2** worthless thing or object. **3** (*formal*) joking talk (among a group of people or aimed at one person). **4** very thin pieces of metal fired from a plane, ship etc to stop it being seen by radar or being hit by missiles(1). **separate the wheat from the chaff** ⇨ wheat.

▷ *tr.v* **5** talk in a joking way to (s.o); make fun of (s.o): *Mandy chaffed her brother about his new girlfriend.*

chaffinch /ˈtʃæfɪntʃ/ *c.n* kind of small bird with black and white wings, found in Europe.

chagrin /'ʃægrɪn/ *u.n* (*formal*) sense of disappointment or annoyance, e.g because s.t has gone wrong, one has failed to do s.t: *To his great chagrin, he failed his driving test.*

chain /tʃeɪn/ *c.n* **1** (number of) (usu metal) rings joined together to make a length for holding or pulling or lifting s.t, or as a decoration: *The anchor chain broke. Doris was wearing a gold chain around her neck.* **2** (number of) things that are connected to each other: *a mountain chain* (i.e a long line of mountains); *a chain of events* (i.e things that happen one after the other). **3** (*old use*) measure of length, esp of land, equal to 66 feet (about 20 metres).
▷ *tr.v* **4** (often — *s.o/s.t to s.o/s.t*; — *s.o/s.t up*) tie (s.o/s.t) with a chain so that he/she/it cannot escape or it cannot be taken away: *She chained the dog up* (or *chained it to the railings*) *before she went into the shop.*
'chain ,gang *c.n* number of prisoners joined together with chains(1) so that they cannot escape when working outside a prison.
'chain ,mail *u.n* (*old use*) armour for the body made of a large number of small metal rings.
,chain re'action *c.n* **1** (*chemistry*) number of chemical changes in substances or atoms that happen one after another, each one causing the next one to happen, esp as happens in a nuclear(2) explosion. **2** number of things that happen one after another, each causing the next one to happen.
'chain ,saw *c.n* kind of saw with a motor that drives an endless belt of teeth that can cut through wood very quickly.
'chain-,smoke *tr/intr.v* smoke (cigarettes) one after the other with only short breaks.
'chain-,smoker *c.n* person who chain-smokes.
'chain ,store *c.n* one of a number of large shops owned by one person or company.

chair /tʃeə/ *n* **1** *c.n* piece of furniture with a seat, a back and four legs on which one can sit. ⇨ armchair. **2** *c/def.n* (often with capital **C**) (seat for a person who holds an) office or most important position, esp at a meeting: *Who will be in the chair for tonight's meeting?* **3** = chairperson. **4** *c.n* (usu *the* — *of s.t*) position of a professor (of a subject) in a university: *He holds the chair of physics.* **5** *def.n* = electric chair. **take the chair** (start to) act as the person who runs a meeting.
▷ *tr.v* **6** put (s.o) in a chair or hold (s.o) as though in a chair and carry (her/him) high in the air, esp as a celebration: *He was chaired by the crowd when his horse came in first.* **7** (be the person chosen to) organize and run (an official meeting).
'chair ,lift *c.n* moving metal ropes with seats hanging down from them which carry people up and down mountains.
'chairman *c.n* (*pl -men*) **1** person who controls a meeting. **2** person who holds the most important position in a company, a committee etc: *the chairman of the* board³.
'chairperson *c.n* = chairman(1) or chairwoman.
'chair,woman *c.n* (*pl -,women*) woman who controls a meeting.

chalet /'ʃæleɪ/ *c.n* **1** kind of wooden house or hut with a steep roof. **2** small house usu of one floor only; small hut, esp one found at the seaside, in a holiday camp etc.

chalice /'tʃælɪs/ *c.n* special cup, usu made of gold or silver, with a stem, that is used esp in Christian(1) religious services.

chalk /tʃɔːk/ *n* **1** *u.n* soft white natural substance found in the ground as a rock, used as lime¹(1) and for writing or drawing. **2** *u/c.n* (piece of) this substance, usu made into white or coloured sticks, used for writing or drawing.
▷ *tr.v* **3** write or draw with chalk(2); make (s.t) white with chalk(2). **chalk s.t out** draw s.t, esp the outer lines of s.t, on the ground: *He chalked out the playing area.* **chalk s.t up** (*informal*) (a) gain a victory, an advantage; score points in a game etc: *The team chalked up yet another victory.* (b) (in a shop etc) charge or add an amount to what s.o owes when he/she buys s.t by writing it down against her/his name: *Could you chalk it up as I haven't got any money with me?*
'chalkiness *u.n* state of being chalky.
'chalky *adj* (-ier, -iest) **1** made of, containing, chalk: *chalky soil.* **2** (esp of one's skin, face) white and pale, e.g because of illness, shock etc.

challenge /'tʃælɪndʒ/ *n* **1** *c.n* formal demand or request to s.o to take part in s.t, e.g a race or fight, to see who is better or stronger, to see if he/she can succeed in doing s.t etc: *He offered a challenge to anybody to come and try to beat him at chess.* **2** *c.n* spoken demand by a soldier to s.o who is coming near to stop and say who he/she is: *As he got closer to the enemy camp, he was met by a challenge.* **3** *c/u.n* (example of the) quality of having or needing more demanding work or mental(1) power: *The new job was a real challenge.*
▷ *tr.v* **4** (usu — *s.o to s.t*) formally ask (s.o) to do s.t to show who is better, stronger etc: *He challenged him to a fight.* **5** (of a soldier) ask (s.o) to stop and say who he/she is. **6** (of work, a job etc) demand special or more effort from (s.o) or (her/his) mind: *The new position challenged his mind.* **7** ask (s.o) to prove s.t; say that (s.t) is not true: *The lawyer challenged his statement.*
'challenger *c.n* person who challenges(4) s.o.
'challenging *adj* **1** (of work, a job etc) demanding special or more effort. **2** (of a statement, argument etc) needing serious thought or attention.

chamber /'tʃeɪmbə/ *c.n* **1** (*old use*) room in a house, esp a bedroom. **2** (also with capital **C**) hall where members of parliament sit and pass laws: *The chamber was full for the Minister's speech.* **3** hollow space in a part of the body: *the chambers of the heart.* **4** hollow space in a machine. **5** hollow space in a gun into which a bullet goes. **Lower Chamber** ⇨ lower. **Upper Chamber** ⇨ upper.
chamberlain /'tʃeɪmbəlɪn/ *c.n* official who looks after the running of a royal household.
'chamber,maid *c.n* woman whose job is to clean bedrooms, esp in a hotel.
'chamber ,music *u.n* music for a small group of musicians and instruments, usu played in a small room or small hall.
,chamber of 'commerce *c.n* organization of a group of business people in a country or town who work together to improve trade.
'chamber ,orchestra *c.n* group of musicians who play chamber music.
'chamber,pot *c.n* round vessel for waste from the body which is kept in a bedroom.
'chambers *pl.n* (*law*) **1** room where a judge

decides about matters of law in private. **2** rooms
or office(s) where people, esp barristers, work. *in*
chambers in a judge's or barrister's room: *Let's*
discuss it in chambers.

chameleon /kə'mi:lɪən/ *c.n* **1** kind of lizard
which changes the colour of its skin according
to the surroundings it is in. **2** (*fig*; usu *derog*)
person who changes what he/she says, does etc
as he/she wishes or according to the situation
he/she is in.

chamois /'ʃæmwɑː/ *c.n* (*pl chamois*) kind of
small goat that lives in mountains in Europe
and southwest Asia.

chamois leather /'ʃæmɪ ˌleðə/ *n* **1** *u.n* soft
leather made from the skin of a chamois. **2** *c.n*
(also **shammy** (**leather**)) piece of this leather,
esp as used for cleaning glass etc.

champ¹ /tʃæmp/ *v* **1** *tr.v* (of a horse) bite (food,
hay etc) with its teeth. **2** *intr.v* (often *be* —*ing to*
do s.t) be eager (to do s.t): *They were champing*
to get going. **champ at/on s.t** (**a**) = champ¹(1).
(**b**) be impatient about s.t: *They were champing*
at the delay. **champ at the bit** (*fig*) be impatient,
esp because one cannot start doing s.t one wants
to do.

champ² /tʃæmp/ *c.n* (*informal*) champion(3).

champagne /ʃæm'peɪn/ *u.n* kind of expensive
(usu white) wine with bubbles(2) in it, from the
Champagne area of France.

champion /'tʃæmpɪən/ *adj* **1** (*informal*) very
good: *She's a champion gardener.*
▷ *c.n* **2** (usu — *of s.o/s.t*) person who supports or
defends s.o, an ideal, belief etc: *Martin was a*
champion of liberty. **3** (also *attrib*) person or
animal who/that wins a competition, race etc:
His team became the football champions.
▷ *tr.v* **4** support or defend (s.o, an ideal, belief etc):
She championed their right to vote.
champion,ship *n* **1** *u.n* (often *the* — *of s.t*)
act or fact of supporting or defending s.t etc:
the championship of civil rights. **2** *c.n* (often *pl*)
competition, race etc held to find a winner(1):
They took part in the European championships.
3 *c.n* position of being the winners(1) of such a
competition: *Liverpool won the football champi-*
onship for the third time.

chance /tʃɑːns/ *attrib.adj* **1** happening by luck
or accident: *It was a chance meeting.*
▷ *n* **2** *u.n* thing that appears to happen without a
known cause or reason: *It was pure chance that I*
met him. **3** *c.n* favourable situation; opportunity:
It was his one big chance to succeed. **4** *c.n* (often
— *of s.t*) thing that might happen; possibility:
There's a chance of meeting him if you hurry.
5 *c.n* thing that is doubtful; risk: *He took many*
chances in his attempt to win the race. **by chance**
happening by luck or accident. (**have/with an**
eye to) **the main chance** ⇨ main chance. **not**
have/stand the ghost of a chance (**of doing s.t**)
⇨ ghost. **on the off chance** (**of s.t**) in the hope,
however small, (of s.t succeeding, happening etc):
I went to the station on the off chance of meeting
him. **stand a** (**good** etc) **chance** (**of** (doing) **s.t**)
be in a position where one is (very etc) likely (to
do s.t, to succeed etc): *He stands very little chance*
of being elected. **take one's chance(s)** accept
and make use of whatever opportunities one gets.
the chance of a lifetime a good opportunity that
will probably not come again. **wait one's chance**

(**to do s.t**) wait until one has an opportunity (to
do s.t).
▷ *v* **6** *tr.v* use (s.t) in a way that is not certain to produce the result one wants; risk (s.t): *He chanced*
his money on a horse that came in last. **7** *intr.v*
(usu — *to do s.t*) (*formal*) happen by luck (to
do s.t, be s.w etc): *They chanced to meet on the*
steps of the hotel. **chance it**; **chance one's arm**
(*informal*) take a risk that s.t will happen to one's
advantage. **chance** (**up**)**on s.o/s.t** (*formal*) meet
s.o, find s.t, by accident or luck.
chancy *adj* (*-ier*, *-iest*) (*informal*) uncertain; full
of risk: *a chancy business opportunity.*

chancel /'tʃɑːnsl/ *c.n* eastern part of a Chris-
tian(1) church building where the altar(2) is and
where the priest sits or stands.

chancellor /'tʃɑːnsələ/ *c.n* (often with capital
C) **1** chief minister of a government in some
countries. **2** (UK) official head of some universities. **Lord Chancellor** ⇨ lord. **Vice-Chancellor**
⇨ vice³.
,Chancellor of the Ex'chequer *c/def.n* (UK)
official in charge of the Exchequer.

chancery /'tʃɑːnsərɪ/ *n* (*pl -ies*) **1** *u.n* (UK)
special division of the High Court of Justice
controlled by the office of the Lord Chancellor
that deals with cases that may need changes
in the law. **2** *c.n* office where official records
are kept. *in chancery* (referring to cases of
law) being dealt with by the office of the Lord
Chancellor.

chancy ⇨ chance.

chandelier /ˌʃændə'lɪə/ *c.n* ornamental frame
made of metal, glass etc with a number of
branches that usu hangs from the ceiling of a
room, used for holding lights or candles.

chandler /'tʃɑːndlə/ *c.n* (*old use*) person who
makes or sells candles, soap, oil etc. ⇨ ship's
chandler.

change /tʃeɪndʒ/ *n* **1** *c/u.n* (example of the) act
of becoming different or making s.t different: *He*
lived through a time of great social change. She has
seen many changes during her life. **2** *c.n* (often —
of s.t) replacing of s.t old or dirty with s.t new or
clean: *a change of clothes*; *a change of oil* (i.e in
an engine). **3** *c.n* different thing one does, e.g
in order to get a rest or more variety in one's
life: *You need a change; why not take a short*
holiday? **4** *u.n* (often *small* —) coins or notes
of small value when compared with larger ones:
Have you got any change because I need to make
a phone call? **5** *u.n* amount, usu in small coins
or notes, given back to a buyer when he/she
offers coins or notes greater than the price of
the thing(s) he/she is buying: *This is the wrong*
change! I gave you a £10 note, not a £5 one. ⇨
short-change. *a change of air/climate* a move
from one place to another, esp because it is
healthier, one needs a rest etc. *a change for*
the better/worse a change(1) to s.t better/worse
than what existed before, e.g in one's health, the
weather: *The doctors said that during the night*
her condition has shown a change for the worse.
have a change of heart decide not to do s.t
or to do s.t else, usu because it is better etc: *The*
government had a change of heart and gave the
nurses an extra pay rise. (**just**) *for a change* in
order to do s.t different; to do s.t that is different
from the usual thing: *Let's walk instead of getting*

the bus for a change. *For a change Roy didn't say exactly what he thought.* **get no** etc **change out of s.o** (*informal*) be unable to persuade s.o, to make her/him agree with one etc: *You'll get very little change out of him because he's the owner's son.* **loose change** money as coins and not notes. **make a change** be a different method, place, activity etc from the usual one. **ring the changes (on s.t)** change(6) the way one does something that is usual or regular in one's life, e.g wear different shoes instead of the usual ones. **small change** ⇨ small.

▷ *v* **6** *tr.v* make (s.t) different: *He changed the time of the meeting.* **7** *tr.v* replace (s.t one has got or uses) with s.t else, often of the same kind: *She changed her bank* (i.e moved her bank account from one bank to another). *He's changed his job.* **8** *tr/intr.v* take off (clothes, sheets on a bed etc) and put on different or fresh ones: *I must change (my shirt) before we go out.* **9** *tr.v* leave (one place where one lives) to go and live in another: *I've changed my address since I last saw you.* **10** *tr.v* give or receive (smaller coins or notes, or ones of a different country) for a note or notes, or a coin or coins, one has got: *Can you change this £20 note for me?* ⇨ change s.t for s.t. **11** *intr.v* (of a person, idea etc) become different in some way: *Have you noticed how Eric has changed since he became so rich?* ⇨ unchanged. **12** *tr/intr.v* (often — (trains etc) at s.w) get off (one train etc, usu at a station or stop) and get into (another): *You have to change at the next station if you want to go to London.*
All change! (request by an official that) everybody should get out of a train or bus, e.g because it is going no further.
change course ⇨ course(1).
change down/up move the gear(1) of a car or truck into a lower/higher position (and so go slower/faster).
change for the better/worse get better/worse, esp in health, the weather etc. **change s.t for s.t** give s.t and receive s.t else instead: *Can you change these pounds for dollars?* ⇨ change(10).
change (from s.t) (in)to s.t (a) take off (clothes etc) and put on different or fresh ones: *As it was cold she changed into warmer clothes.* ⇨ change(8). (b) become different (from what s.t was before): *The traffic lights changed from yellow to red.*
change gear(s) ⇨ gear(1).
change hands ⇨ hand(n).
change (s.t) into s.t (a) (cause s.t to) move from one state to another state: *Scientists can now change many substances into different ones.* Caterpillars(1) *change into butterflies.* (b) give one kind of money and receive a different kind: *Can you change these pounds into dollars?* ⇨ change(10), change s.t for s.t.
change one's mind (about s.o/s.t) ⇨ mind(n).
change over (from s.t) (to s.t) move (from doing one thing) to doing s.t different, esp an activity, a system etc: *Britain changed over to decimal currency in 1971.* ⇨ changeover.
change places (with s.o) ⇨ place(n).
change sides ⇨ side(n).
change the subject ⇨ subject¹.
change trains ⇨ change(12).
change one's tune ⇨ tune(n).

change up ⇨ change down/up.
chop and change ⇨ chop(v).
changeability /ˌtʃeɪndʒəˈbɪlɪtɪ/ *u.n* fact or state of being changeable.
'changeable *adj* **1** (of weather) not settled; likely to change. **2** (of a person, an idea etc) often changing.
'changeableness *u.n* = changeability.
'changeless *adj* not changing at all or ever.
,change of 'life *def.n* (*informal*) menopause.
'change,over *c.n* (often the — of s.t) move from one activity, system etc to another: *The changeover of power was handled smoothly.* ⇨ change over (from s.t) (to s.t).

channel /'tʃænl/ *c.n* **1** U-shaped passage for a stream of water or other kinds of liquid. **2** deeper part of a river, harbour etc, sometimes dug out specially to let ships in. **3** (with capital **C** in names) narrow area of sea with land on both sides and joining two other seas: *the English Channel* (i.e between England and France). **4** U-shaped cut in wood, metal etc into which s.t fits: *Cut a channel in the upright and fit the shelf into it.* **5** one of a number of television stations broadcasting on certain radio waves: *Britain has four main television channels.* **6** (often *pl*) manner or way in which information moves from one place or person to another: *Richard has his own channels of information.* **through/ via the official, usual** etc **channels** following, the official etc ways of getting information, arranging meetings with officials etc: *I'm afraid there will be some delay as your letter has to go through the official channels.*
▷ *tr.v* (-ll-, US -l-) **7** make (water or liquid) flow in a channel(1). **8** (of water or liquid) find (a way) to get s.w: *The river channelled a way under the ground.* **9** make (one's or s.o's ideas, activities etc) go in a certain direction: *To take her mind off her problems, he tried to channel her* energies(1) *into doing something useful.*

chant /tʃɑːnt/ *c.n* **1** kind of religious song in which words or syllables are sung mostly on one note. **2** word(s) which is/are repeated over and over again as though in a song, esp by a group of people: *The chant of the football crowd could be heard a mile away.*
▷ *tr/intr.v* **3** sing (a chant(1)): *The priests chanted on their way to the church.* **4** (of a group of people) shout out (words) over and over again: *The crowd was chanting 'We want jobs'.*

chaos /'keɪɒs/ *u.n* (often in —) condition or state of complete confusion: *The country was in a state of chaos* (or *There was chaos*) *after the war.*
chaotic /keɪˈɒtɪk/ *adj* being in this state: *Traffic conditions were chaotic as a result of the accident.*
cha'otically *adv.*

chap¹ /tʃæp/ *c.n* (*informal; old use*) man or boy: *Come on, chaps, let's get going.*
chap² /tʃæp/ *c.n* **1** small sore or crack on the skin, esp the face, lips or hands, because of cold or wet weather.
▷ *tr/intr.v* (-pp-) **2** (cause (one's skin) to) become rough or sore: *Her hands had become chapped through washing.*
chap³ *written abbr* chapter(s).
chapel /'tʃæpl/ *n* **1** *c.n* small church or room in a building, e.g a house, school, prison etc that

is used for Christian(1) religious services. **2** *c.n* separate place in a Christian(1) church with its own altar(2). **3** *c.n* church, esp in England and Wales, which does not belong to the Church of England or the Roman Catholic Church. **4** *u.n* (form of) religious service held in chapels(1–3): *They go to chapel every Sunday.* **5** *c.n* branch of a trade union: *He joined the local chapel when he started work.*

chaperon /ˈʃæpəˌrəʊn/ *c.n* (also **ˈchaperone**) **1** older person, who looks after a younger person or group of young people when they go out, e.g to a dance.
▷ *tr.v* **2** act as a chaperon(1) to (s.o).

chaplain /ˈtʃæplɪn/ *c.n* Christian(1) priest or minister, esp one who works in the armed forces or for a person or group of people.
ˈchaplaincy *n* (*pl* -ies) **1** *u.n* position of a chaplain. **2** *c.n* place where a chaplain lives or works.

chapter /ˈtʃæptə/ *c.n* **1** (*written abbr* ch, chap) one of the large sections into which a story or book is divided, usu numbered and often given a title. **2** period of history, esp one when s.t special happened in a country: *The war was one of the worst chapters in our history.* **3** (meeting of) canons(2) of a cathedral or monastery. **a chapter of accidents** a number of bad or unfortunate things which happen one after the other. (**give**, **quote** etc) **chapter and verse** (**for s.t**) (say, write) the exact place where information can be found, usu in a book etc, esp in order to support or defend one's argument.
ˈchapter ˌhouse *c.n* building where a chapter(3) meets.

char¹ /tʃɑː/ *c.n* **1** (*informal*) charwoman.
▷ *intr.v* (-rr-) **2** (often — for s.o) do the job of a charwoman (for s.o).
ˈchar ˌwoman *c.n* (*pl* -ˌwomen) (also **ˈchar ˌlady** (*pl* -ies)) (*informal* char) woman whose job is to clean offices, houses etc.

char² /tʃɑː/ *u.n* (*slang*) tea: *I'd like a cup of char.*

char³ /tʃɑː/ *tr/intr.v* (-rr-) (cause (s.t. made of wood) to) become black by burning: *The wood charred under the fierce heat.*

character /ˈkærɪktə/ *attrib.adj* **1** of or showing the special qualities needed to act the part of s.o in a play: *a character actor.*
▷ *n* **2** *u.n* mental(1) or moral quality or nature of a person: *He showed his true character when faced with defeat.* **3** *u.n* good moral quality or strength of a person: *Linda showed real character in her handling of the difficult situation.* **4** *u.n* (good or bad) quality or essence of s.t, esp of a place, building etc: *The town has a lot of character.* **5** *u.n* (good) reputation: *The newspapers tried to destroy his character.* **6** *c.n* person in a play, book, film etc: *All the characters in his latest book just don't seem real.* **7** *c.n* (*informal*) person who is strange, different etc in some way: *Phil's a bit of a character, especially in the way he dresses.* **8** *c.n* (*informal*) person whom one does not know or name: *There was this character who won £500 000 and spent it in one year.* **9** *c.n* letter or sign used in writing, typing or printing: *Special characters are used to show pronunciation in this dictionary.* (**act/be**) **in**, **out of**, **character** (of a person) (do things/behave) in a way which

other people expect, do not expect. **defamation of character** ⇒ defame.

characteristic /ˌkærɪktəˈrɪstɪk/ *adj* **1** of, showing, one's usual nature, behaviour etc: *It was characteristic of him to refuse the honour.*
▷ *c.n* **2** special quality (of s.o/s.t): *One of the characteristics of the new metal is that it is twice as strong as steel.*
ˌcharacteˈristically *adv.*

characterization, -isation /ˌkærɪktəraɪˈzeɪʃən/ *c/u.n* (act of) characterizing(1) s.o/s.t.
ˈcharacteˌrize, -ise *tr.v* **1** describe or show (the nature of s.o/s.t): *He characterized her performance as dull and not interesting.* **2** show or be an example of (the real or normal nature of s.t): *The woods and low hills characterize the area.*
ˈcharacterless *adj* (*derog*) (of a person, thing, place etc) showing no character(2–4); without interest.

charade /ʃəˈrɑːd/ *c.n* pretence of doing s.t; doing s.t that is known or seen by oneself or others to be false: *He went through the whole charade of saying that he really loved her.*
chaˈrades *pl.n* (usu *play* —) game in which each syllable of a word and then the whole word is made the basis of a number of acts of a play so that the audience have to guess the word.

charcoal /ˈtʃɑːˌkəʊl/ *u.n* (also *attrib*) **1** (pieces of a) black substance made by burning wood slowly in an enclosed space, used in fires, for drawing pictures etc. **2** drawing or picture made with this substance: *a drawing in charcoal*; *a charcoal drawing.*
ˈcharcoal ˌburner *c.n* **1** person who makes charcoal(1). **2** oven or stove which uses charcoal(1).

charge /tʃɑːdʒ/ *n* **1** *c.n* (often *a* — (*of £10* etc) *for* s.t) amount of money demanded for s.t, e.g goods, services etc: *There is a charge of £5 for delivery outside London.* **2** *c.n* sudden violent attack, e.g by soldiers, animals: *He led the charge on horseback.* **3** *c.n* (often — *of doing* s.t) official statement or accusation that s.o has done s.t wrong, broken the law etc: *He faced two charges of stealing.* ⇒ bring a charge (of s.t) against s.o. **4** *c.n* (*technical*) amount of electricity in a substance or device: *The battery contains* negative(4) *and* positive(11) *charges.* **5** *c.n* (*technical*) (amount of) explosive material used to make an explosion, e.g in a gun: *He placed the charge on the bottom of the ship to blow it up.* **6** *u.n* (usu — *of* s.t) care or responsibility (for s.o/s.t): *He had charge of the whole area.* ⇒ in charge of s.o/ s.t. **7** *c.n* (*formal*) person or thing whom/that one is responsible for: *The children became his charge when their parents died.* **in charge of s.o/ s.t** responsible for s.o/s.t: *He was* (*put*) *in charge of the whole department.* **bring a charge** (**of s.t**) **against s.o** make an official accusation against s.o (that he/she has done s.t wrong): *The police brought a charge of murder against her.* **free of charge** ⇒ free(*adv*). **reverse the charges** ask for the cost of a telephone call to be charged(8) to the person one is telephoning. **take charge (of s.o/s.t)** become responsible (for s.o/s.t): *When he took charge (of the team), there were only five good players.*
▷ *v* **8** *tr.v* (usu — (s.o) s.t for s.t) ask (an amount of money) (from s.o) (for goods, services etc): *They*

charged (*us*) *£10 for admission.* ⇒ overcharge, undercharge. **9** *tr/intr.v* (often — *at s.o/s.t*) make a charge(2) towards (s.o/s.t): *At the last moment the elephant charged* (*at*) *us.* **10** *tr.v* (often -- *s.o with s.t*) make an official charge(3) against (s.o) (of having done s.t wrong etc): *He was brought to the police station and charged* (*with causing a disturbance*). **11** *tr.v* put a charge(4) into (a battery etc): *The car battery had run down so he had to charge it.* ⇒ recharge. **12** *tr.v* (often — *s.o with s.t*) (*formal*) complain about (s.o); say that (s.o) has done s.t wrong: *He charged me with neglecting his interests.* **charge s.o with s.t** (**a**) ⇒ charge(10,12). (**b**) (*formal*) give s.o the responsibility for s.t: *He was charged with the duty of carrying out their decision.* **charge s.t** (**up**) **to s.o/s.t** put the price, cost of s.t as a debt in s.o's special record or account: *'Shall I charge the bill to your account?' 'Yes, charge it up to me.'*
'chargeable *adj* **1** that can be charged(10); open to an official accusation: *The police warned him that it was a chargeable offence.* **2** (often — *to s.o/s.t*) (of an amount of money) that can be charged(8), put to s.o's debt or to an account: *My expenses are chargeable to the company.*
'charge ˌsheet *c.n* written record of charges(3) kept at a police station.
chargé d'affaires /ˌʃɑːʒeɪ dæˈfeə/ *c.n* (*pl* **chargés d'affaires** /dæfeəz/) (*French*) official who acts in the place of an ambassador when he/she is absent or when none has been appointed.
chariot /ˈtʃærɪət/ *c.n* (also *attrib*) carriage, usu with two wheels and no seats, pulled by a horse or horses in ancient times during battles, races etc: *chariot races.*
charioteer /ˌtʃærɪəˈtɪə/ *c.n* chariot driver.
charisma /kəˈrɪzmə/ *u.n* ability of a person to be loved and admired by other people because of her/his special qualities, leadership etc.
charismatic /ˌkærɪzˈmætɪk/ *adj* having or showing charisma.
ˌcharisˈmatically *adv.*
charity /ˈtʃærɪtɪ/ *n* (*pl* *-ies*) **1** *u.n* kindness towards other people: *He was full of charity towards his neighbours.* **2** *u.n* (also *attrib*) help, esp money, food, clothes etc, given to the poor or those in need: *In her will she left all her money to charity.* **3** *c.n* group or organization that helps the poor etc: *The local charities organized food and shelter for those whose houses had been destroyed.* **4** *u.n* (in Christian(1) belief) love for all people. *Charity begins at home* (*saying*) One must first look after one's own family (or one's own country) before looking after others.
'charitable *adj* **1** having or showing charity(1,2) to others. Opposite uncharitable. **2** (of an organization, a cause etc) helping the poor etc: *He belongs to several charitable committees.* **3** able or worthy to be considered a charity(3): *Should private schools be allowed charitable status(1)?*
'charitably *adv.*
charlady ⇒ char¹.
charlatan /ˈʃɑːlətn/ *c.n* (*derog*) person who pretends to have special skills, knowledge etc, esp in medical matters, that he/she does not have: *He's a charlatan — he collects a lot of money by claiming he has a cure for the common cold.*
charm /tʃɑːm/ *n* **1** *u.n* quality of a person, thing

or place that pleases or attracts s.o: *Susan has a great deal of charm and is always popular at parties.* **2** *c.n* example of charm(1): *She used all her charms to try to attract him.* **3** *c.n* act or speech that works as if by magic(3): *In some stories the princess is sent to sleep by a charm.* **4** *c.n* small object, often worn on the body, that is thought to protect one from evil etc, bring good luck etc. **work like a charm** (of a plan, an action etc) be completely successful.
▷ *tr.v* **5** please or attract (s.o): *She charmed him with her conversation.* **6** affect (s.o/s.t) (as if) by using a charm(3). **have/lead a charmed life** escape from dangerous situations as if protected by magic(3).
'charmer *c.n* (*informal*) person who pleases or attracts s.o: *Helen's a real charmer.* ⇒ snake charmer.
'charming *adj* having or showing charm(1).
'charmingly *adv.*
chart /tʃɑːt/ *c.n* **1** map of the sea showing depths, coasts, rocks etc. **2** sheet of paper with information on it in a visual or graphic(1) form: *a weather chart; a sales chart.*
▷ *tr.v* **3** make a map of (the sea). **4** make a record of (s.t) as it happens: *The doctor charted the progress of his illness.*
charter /ˈtʃɑːtə/ *c.n* **1** formal written statement made by a ruler, government etc that gives s.o, an organization, a city etc certain rights or the freedom to do certain things: *The town's charter dates from the time of King Henry VIII.* **2** (also *attrib*) special hiring of a ship, plane etc for a certain time, to go s.w, carry certain things, people etc: *The company arranges ship charters. We flew to Spain on a charter flight.* ⇒ scheduled flight.
▷ *tr.v* **3** hire (a ship, plane etc).
ˌchartered acˈcountant *c.n* (*written abbr* CA) accountant who has passed the examinations (of the Institute(1) of Accountants) in Great Britain and has become a member.
charwoman ⇒ char¹.
chary /ˈtʃeərɪ/ *adj* (*-ier, -iest*) (usu — *about/of* (*doing*) *s.t*) wanting to avoid ((doing) s.t), not willing to risk ((doing) s.t): *He was chary about agreeing to the proposal.*
'charily *adv.*
chase /tʃeɪs/ *n* **1** *c.n* act of running after, following after, s.o/s.t in order to catch her/him/it: *He caught the dog after a long chase.* **2** *def.n* sport of hunting animals, e.g foxes(1), esp on horseback. **give chase** (*formal*) start to run after s.o/s.t: *The police gave chase but the thief got away.* **wild-goose chase** ⇒ wild-goose.
▷ *tr.v* **3** run after, follow after, (s.o/s.t) to try to catch her/him/it: *They chased the thief down the road.* **chase after s.o/s.t** (**a**) run towards s.o/s.t who/that is running away in order to catch her/him/it. (**b**) use all one's efforts in order to get s.o/s.t: *The company is chasing after a large order for its new machines.*
chasm /ˈkæzəm/ *c.n* (*formal*) **1** very deep opening or split in the ground. **2** (*fig*) very wide division (of opinions, beliefs etc) between people, nations etc: *A chasm developed between the two political parties.*
chassis /ˈʃæsɪ/ *c.n* (*pl* **chassis** /ˈʃæsɪz/) main framework (of a car, radio, television etc)

onto which are put other parts, e.g the motor.

chaste /tʃeɪst/ *adj* (of a person) pure and full of virtue; celibate(1).
'**chastely** *adv.*
chastity /'tʃæstɪtɪ/ *u.n* (also '**chasteness**) state of being chaste.

chasten /'tʃeɪsn/ *tr.v* (*formal*) make (s.o) better or less likely to do wrong because of s.t bad that it caused her/him: *The whole experience had chastened Chris and he promised never to do it again.*

chastise /tʃæs'taɪz/ *tr.v* (*formal*) punish or criticize (s.o) severely: *He was a hard father and often chastised his children.*
chas'tisement *c/u.n.*

chat /tʃæt/ *n* (*informal*) **1** *c.n* (often have a — (with s.o)) friendly talk (with s.o): *We'll have a longer chat the next time we meet.* **2** *u.n* act of doing this: *There's far too much chat going on in this office; we need to work, not talk.*
▷ *intr.v* (-tt-) **3** (often — (away) with s.o) talk in a friendly way (with s.o): *He introduced them to each other and they were soon chatting happily away.* **chat s.o up** (*informal*) talk to (s.o) in order to persuade her/him to become one's girlfriend or boyfriend.
'**chatty** *adj* (-ier, -iest) (fond of) talking in a friendly way, talking a lot: *You're very chatty today.*

chateau, château /'ʃætəʊ/ *c.n* (*pl* -s, chateaux, châteaux /'ʃætəʊz/) (*French*) castle or large country house in France.

chattel /'tʃætl/ *c.n* (often *pl*) (*law*) thing that one owns and which can be moved. **goods and chattels** ⇒ goods.

chatter /'tʃætə/ *u.n* (often the — of s.o/s.t) **1** idle, foolish or unimportant talk: *I can't stand the chatter of these stupid people.* **2** continuous sound of teeth knocking together, esp from the cold or fear: *The chatter of her teeth made him realize how cold she was.* **3** continuous noise made by animals, machines etc: *The chatter of the typewriters drove him mad.*
▷ *intr.v* **4** (often — away/on (about s.t)) talk in an idle or foolish way for a long time etc: *She chattered on about her children.* **5** (of the teeth) knock together, esp from the cold or fear: *Her teeth were chattering from the shock.* **6** (of animals, machines etc) make a continuous noise: *The birds were chattering in the forest.*
'**chatter,box** *c.n* (*derog*) person, usu a child, who is always talking, esp about things that are not important.

chatty ⇒ chat.

chauffeur /'ʃəʊfə/ *c.n* person whose job is to drive s.o's car.

chauvinism /'ʃəʊvɪ,nɪzəm/ *u.n* (usu *derog*) strong and unreasoning(1) belief that one's country is better than others.
'**chauvin,ist** *c.n* person with such a belief. **male chauvinism; male chauvinist (pig)** ⇒ male.
,**chauvi'nistic** *adv.* ,**chauvi'nistically** *adv.*

cheap /tʃiːp/ *adj* **1** not costing very much; low in price, esp when compared to other times, other things etc: *Fruit is very cheap in the summer.* Opposite dear(1), expensive. **2** of not very good quality: *Lisa was wearing a cheap dress.* **3** (of a person, action)

unpleasant: *I thought his behaviour towards her was very cheap.* **4** without value; not sincere: *She didn't like his type of cheap conversation.*
▷ *adv* **5** cheaply; for a low price: *They're selling tomatoes cheap in the market today.* **dirt cheap** ⇒ dirt. **feel cheap** (*informal*) feel ashamed.
▷ *def.n* **6** **on the cheap** at a low price: *He got his furniture on the cheap.*
'**cheapen** *tr.v* make (oneself, s.t, s.o) appear less good, of lower quality, value etc: *She cheapened herself with her attempts to attract him.*
'**cheaply** *adv.* '**cheapness** *u.n.*

cheat /tʃiːt/ *n* **1** (*derog*) person who does s.t dishonest, esp in a competition, a game etc: *Larry's a cheat and I wouldn't play cards with him.* **2** dishonest trick: *It was a cheat; I didn't get what I paid for.*
▷ *v* **3** *tr.v* (often — s.o out of s.t) act in a dishonest way towards (s.o) (by taking s.t, e.g money, from her/him): *He cheated Margaret out of all her savings.* **4** *intr.v* (esp — at s.t) act in a dishonest way (in a competition, game etc): *He cheats at cards.*

check /tʃek/ *n* **1** *c.n* act of examining s.t to see if it is correct, in working order etc: *The manufacturer is carrying out checks on all the new cars.* **2** *c.n* act of stopping or controlling s.t: *The bank of earth acted as a check against floods.* **3** *c.n* (esp US) ticket given in exchange for s.t: *a cloakroom*(1) *check* (i.e when one leaves one's coat in a cloakroom). **4** *c.n* (often *pl*) pattern of coloured squares on materials, clothes etc. **5** *c/u.n* (usu be in —) (chess) position when the king is attacked by another piece or pieces. ⇒ checkmate(1). **6** *c.n* (US) = cheque. **hold/keep s.o/s.t in check** stop or control s.t, esp so that he/she/it does no further harm: *The doctors were trying to keep the disease in check.* **keep a check on s.o/s.t** watch s.o, a situation etc, for some time.
▷ *tr.v* **7** examine (s.t) to see if s.t is wrong, if it is correct etc: *Have you checked the windows* (i.e to see if they are locked etc)? **8** stop or control (s.t): *They checked the enemy's advance.* ⇒ unchecked(2). **9** (chess) directly attack the king by moving one's own piece or pieces into a position where the king has to move. ⇒ checkmate(2). **check in (at s.w)** report (to an airline desk, a hotel desk etc) that one has arrived. ⇒ check-in. **check s.o/s.t off** make a note or mark against s.o's name, an item etc in a list to show that he/she/it is present, that s.t is correct etc. **check out (of s.w)** pay one's bill and leave (a hotel). ⇒ check-out(2). **check (up) on s.o/s.t** inquire about s.o/s.t, esp to find out if he/she is honest, not doing s.t wrong, if the facts are true etc. Compare check-up.
'**checked** *adj* (of material) having checks(4) printed on it: *a checked cloth.*
'**checker** *c.n* person who checks(7) goods to see if they are correct, in working order etc.
'**checkers** /'tʃekəz/ *u.n.* (US) draughts.
'**check-,in** *c.n* (also '**check-,in ,desk**) place, desk etc at an airport, hotel etc where one reports one's arrival for a flight, room etc.
'**check ,list** *c.n* list of names, things, instructions etc used to make sure that everybody or everything is present, that everything has been done correctly, is in the correct order etc.

'check,mate n 1 u.n (informal **mate**) (chess) position when the king is attacked by another piece or pieces and is unable to escape (and so the game ends).
▷ tr.v 2 put (a king) in checkmate(1) (and so end the game).

'check-,out c.n (also **'check-,out ,desk**) 1 counter² in a self-service shop or supermarket where goods are paid for. 2 place or desk in a hotel where one checks out.

'check,point c.n place, esp on a road, where people, goods etc are stopped and examined, e.g at a frontier(1).

'check-,up c.n (informal) examination by a doctor to see if one is healthy.

cheek /tʃiːk/ n 1 c.n one of the two fleshy parts of the face on either side of the nose. 2 u.n rude behaviour, showing of disrespect: He showed a lot of cheek towards her. **have the cheek/nerve to do s.t** do s.t in a bold or shameless way: He had the cheek to tell me I was wrong! **tongue in cheek; with one's tongue in one's cheek** ⇨ tongue.

'cheek,bone c.n one of the two bones below the eyes.

'cheekily adv acting in a cheeky way.

'cheekiness u.n fact of being cheeky.

'cheeky adj (-ier, -iest) (derog) showing disrespect (usu because of what one says): a cheeky little boy. It was very cheeky of Gregory to talk to his mother like that.

cheep /tʃiːp/ c.n 1 small sound like a squeak(1) made by young birds. **not (have/hear) a cheep (from, out of, s.o)** (informal) not (hear) a sound or word (coming from s.o); not (receive) any information (from s.o) for some time: There hasn't been a cheep from the children since they went to bed.
▷ intr.v 2 make the sound of a cheep(1).

cheer /tʃɪə/ c.n 1 shout(s) of encouragement, praise, approval etc: the cheers of the crowd.
▷ tr.v 2 encourage, praise, approve of, (s.o) by shouting: The crowd cheered the winner. **cheer up** (usu interj) (try to) become happier: Cheer up! The worst is over. **cheer s.o up** make s.o happier by encouragement: The good news cheered him up.

'cheerful adj feeling happy; without any cares.

'cheerfully adv. **cheerfulness** u.n.

'cheerily adv in a cheery way.

'cheeriness u.n fact of being cheery.

'cheering adj 1 bringing happiness or encouragement: cheering news.
▷ u.n 2 (many) cheers(1).

Cheerio /,tʃɪərɪ'əʊ/ interj (informal) Goodbye.

Cheers! interj (informal) (esp when starting to drink beer, wine etc with s.o) I wish you good health.

'cheery adj (-ier, -iest) (informal) showing happiness and encouragement: a cheery greeting.

cheese /tʃiːz/ n (also attrib) 1 u.n kind of solid or soft food made from the curds in the milk of cows (or goats, sheep): cheese pie. 2 c.n piece or kind of cheese(1): cheeses from many countries.

'cheese,cake c/u.n (piece of) sweet food made with pastry outside and containing cheese, eggs and sometimes fruit or other things.

,cheesed 'off pred.adj (slang) annoyed, bored

or angry: He's cheesed off with all these complaints.

'cheese,cloth u.n (also attrib) 1 kind of very fine thin cloth for covering cheeses. 2 kind of fine thin cloth used for shirts etc.

cheetah /'tʃiːtə/ c.n kind of very fast animal with dark spots, of the cat¹ family, found in Africa.

chef /ʃef/ c.n (pl -s) skilled (usu chief) cook, esp in hotels and restaurants.

chef-d'oeuvre /ʃe 'dɜːvrə/ c.n (pl chefs-d'oeuvre) (French; formal) a person's most important work, showing her/his best skills: The last book he wrote was his chef-d'oeuvre.

chemistry /'kemɪstrɪ/ u.n (also attrib) science dealing with the study of how substances are made, how they act together or separately, how they can be mixed etc: a chemistry teacher.

chemical /'kemɪkl/ adj 1 of or referring to chemistry: They made a number of chemical tests.
▷ c.n 2 substance produced by chemistry.

'chemically adv.

,chemical 'warfare u.n fighting an enemy by using poison gases, harmful chemicals(2) etc.

'chemist n (also attrib) 1 c.n scientist experienced in chemistry. 2 c.n person running a shop selling medicines and other goods such as soap, cosmetics(3), special food etc. ⇨ pharmacist. 3 c.n (also **'chemist's**) shop of a chemist(2). ⇨ pharmacy(1).

cheque /tʃek/ c.n (US **check**) special printed form provided by a bank and used to pay money from a person's bank account: He gave her a cheque for £50. **blank cheque** ⇨ blank. **cash a cheque** get money (from a bank) by using a cheque giving money to oneself. **pay (for s.t) by cheque** write a cheque (in order to buy s.t) instead of using cash.

'cheque,book c.n number of unused¹ cheques fastened together inside a cover.

'cheque ,card c.n special plastic card provided by a bank to prove who the owner of a cheque-book is and stating that cheques up to a certain amount will be paid.

cherish /'tʃerɪʃ/ tr.v (formal) 1 protect and care for (s.o/s.t) in a loving way: She cherished her children. 2 keep alive (a hope, memory etc): She cherished the memory of her dead husband.

cherry /'tʃerɪ/ n (pl -ies) (also attrib) 1 c.n kind of small round red, yellow or black fruit with a hard seed (stone) in the centre that grows in bunches (on a cherry tree). 2 u.n wood from this tree. 3 u.n bright red colour: cherry lips.

,cherry-'red adj/u.n deep red colour: The fire was cherry-red.

cherub /'tʃerəb/ c.n 1 (pl cherubim /'tʃerə,bɪm/) one of the groups of angels(1) in the Christian(1) Church (often shown in paintings or statues as a small beautiful child with wings). 2 (pl cherubs) (old use) (in the opinion of the speaker) small beautiful child: Isn't he a little cherub!

cherubic /tʃe'ruːbɪk/ adj (formal) showing or having the beauty of a child: a cherubic face.

chess /tʃes/ u.n (also attrib) game for two players played on a board, each player having 16 pieces which move on the squares in order to trap the other's 'king': a chess piece; a chess player. ⇨ checkmate. **play chess** (know how to) play this game: Do you play chess?

'chess,board *c.n* board on which this game is played.

'chess,man *c.n* (*pl* -,*men*) one of the pieces used in this game.

chest /tʃest/ *c.n* **1** upper part of the front of the body below the neck that holds the heart and the lungs. **2** large strong box, usu made of wood or metal and with a lid, that is used to store things, put goods into etc: *a chest for storing clothes*; *a tea chest.* **get s.t off one's chest** (*fig*; *informal*) speak about s.t which one was being secret about, which one was worrying about etc.

,chest of 'drawers *c.n* piece of furniture which has several drawers in it.

chestnut /'tʃesnʌt/ *n* (also *attrib*) **1** *c.n* hard red-brown nut with an outside green covering which has a number of prickles(1) on it; one kind (*sweet chestnut*) can be eaten and the other kind (*horse chestnut*) cannot be eaten. **2** *u.n* wood from the chestnut(1) tree. **3** *c.n* horse with a red-brown colour. **4** *u.n* red-brown colour: *chestnut hair.*

chevron /'ʃevrən/ *c.n* (*military*) V-shaped line on the sleeve of a soldier's uniform to show rank.

chew /tʃuː/ *c.n* **1** act of chewing(2) s.t.
▷ *tr/intr.v* **2** break (food) in one's mouth using the teeth before swallowing it: *She chewed* (*her food*) *slowly.* **bite off more than one can chew** ⇒ bite off (⇒ bite(*v*)). **chew the cud** ⇒ cud. **chew s.t over** (*informal*) think, usu for some time, about (a problem, a course of action etc) before deciding what to do.

'chewiness *u.n* fact of being chewy.

'chewing-,gum *c/u.n* kind of sweet sticky substance like rubber that is chewed for enjoyment but not swallowed.

'chewy *adj* (-ier, -iest) **1** (*derog*) that is difficult to chew(2): *chewy meat.* **2** pleasant to chew(2) for flavour: *chewy sweets.*

chic /ʃiːk/ *adj* **1** (of a person, esp a woman, clothes etc) showing good taste, fashionable: *a chic dress.*
▷ *u.n* **2** good taste in clothes, the way one carries oneself etc: *She has a lot of chic.*

chicanery /ʃɪ'keɪnərɪ/ *u.n* (*formal*) dishonest or deceitful behaviour or actions: *Robert was accused of chicanery when he got the job.*

chick /tʃɪk/ *c.n* young bird, esp a young chicken.

chicken /'tʃɪkɪn/ *pred.adj* **1** (also **,chicken-'hearted**) (*derog*; *slang*) cowardly; not ready to accept responsibility for doing s.t.
▷ *n* (also *attrib*) **2** *c.n* young hen (or cock): *a chicken farm.* **3** *u.n* meat of a chicken(2) as food: *We're having roast chicken for lunch.*
▷ *intr.v* **4** **chicken out** (**of doing s.t**) (*slang*) decide not to (do s.t) because one is afraid, cowardly etc.

'chicken,feed *u.n* (*fig*; *informal*) very small amount of money, esp in comparison with larger amounts: *His earnings were chickenfeed when compared with hers.*

,chicken-'hearted *adj* ⇒ chicken(1).

'chicken ,pox *u.n* kind of disease, esp among young children, that produces red spots on the skin and a fever.

chickpea /'tʃɪkpiː/ *c.n* (also *attrib*) (kind of bush producing a) large yellow seed like a pea and used in cooking: *chickpea soup.*

chicory /'tʃɪkərɪ/ *u.n* (also *attrib*) **1** plant with green leaves that are used in salads(1). **2** root of this plant roasted and added to coffee or used to replace it.

chide /tʃaɪd/ *tr/intr.v* (*p.t,p.p* chided, chid /tʃɪd/) (*formal*) scold or gently criticize (s.o, esp a child): *Tessa chided her son for his bad behaviour.*

chief /tʃiːf/ *attrib.adj* **1** most important: *The chief thing you've got to think about is getting a job.* **2** (of a person) highest in order of rank (esp in an office): *the chief officer of police.*
▷ *c.n* **3** (often the — of s.t) leader or ruler of a group: *the chief of the tribe.*

'chiefly *adv* most importantly; mainly: *I'm angry chiefly because you lied to me.*

chieftain /'tʃiːftən/ *c.n* chief(3), esp of a tribe or clan(1).

chiffon /'ʃɪfɒn/ *u.n* (also *attrib*) kind of fine soft cloth used for scarves, dresses etc.

chilblain /'tʃɪl,bleɪn/ *c.n* painful, usu red, swelling on the toes or fingers that happens in cold weather.

child /tʃaɪld/ *c.n* (*pl* children /'tʃɪldrən/) **1** young person of either sex: *There were thirty children in the class.* **2** son or daughter of any age in a family: *I have only one child.* **3** (*derog*) person without experience; person who behaves as though he/she is still a child(1): *He's a child when it comes to dealing with women.* **be child's play** (be) something that is very easy to do: *Flying a plane isn't child's play, you know.* **be an only child** have no brothers or sisters.

'child,birth *u.n* act of giving birth to a child.

'child,hood *u.n* length of time, state, when one is a child: *He couldn't remember his childhood.*

'childish *adj* **1** of or like a child: *He had a childish voice.* **2** (*derog*) behaving like a child (when one should be more adult): *Stop that childish behaviour!*

'childless *adj* not having a child or children.

'child,like *adj* having or showing the best qualities of a child, e.g simplicity, innocence(2).

'child,minder *c.n* person who looks after a child or children when the parents are not at home.

chile, chill ⇒ chile, chilli.

chill /tʃɪl/ *attrib.adj* **1** cold: *a chill wind.* **2** (*fig*) not friendly: *a chill reply.*
▷ *n* **3** *sing.n* certain amount or feeling of coldness (in the weather or the air): *During the night the temperature dropped and there was a chill in the air when he woke up.* **4** *c.n* illness caused by cold or wet weather and shown by shaking of the body: *I caught a chill from going out without my coat on.* **5** *sing.n* (*fig*) (show of an) unpleasant cold feeling (in the mind): *He noticed a chill in the audience when he started talking.* **cast a chill over s.t** (*fig*) cause a chill(5) to be felt during or about s.t: *The bad news cast a chill over the meeting.*
▷ *tr/intr.v* **6** (cause (s.o/s.t) to) become cold: *The wine needs to be chilled before being served.*

'chilliness *u.n* fact of being chilly.

'chilling *adj* (usu *attrib*) frightening: *a chilling story.*

'chilly *adj* (-ier, -iest) **1** (of weather etc) cold. **2** (of a person, behaviour etc) not friendly: *He got a chilly welcome when he arrived after midnight.*

chilli /'tʃɪlɪ/ *n* (*pl* -(e)s) (also *attrib*) (also **chile**, **'chili**) **1** *c.n* dried seed case of the red pepper(2) plant, used as a food and to give a hot flavour. **2** *u.n* chillis(1) made into a powder: *chilli powder.*

chime /tʃaɪm/ *c.n* **1** group of bells (esp in a church): *a bell chime.* **2** sound of a bell or bells: *the chime of the church bells.* **3** sound like a bell made by a clock, usu marking the hours, quarters of an hour etc.
▷ *v* **4** *tr.v* (esp of a clock) mark (the hour, quarter of an hour etc) by making a sound like a bell: *The clock chimed six o'clock.* **5** *intr.v* make this sound: *The church bells chimed.* **chime in** (**on s.t**) (**with s.t**) (*informal*) interrupt, break into, (the conversation of others) (with a remark of one's own): *'I disagree', he chimed in.*

chimney /'tʃɪmnɪ/ *c.n* (*pl* **-s**) **1** hollow passage up through the wall and roof of a house (and usu standing beyond the roof) through which smoke from a fire goes. **2** tall column carrying smoke, gases etc from a factory, power station etc: *factory chimneys pouring smoke into the air.*
'**chimney-,breast** *c.n* wall or walls that are round a fireplace in a room.
'**chimney,pot** *c.n* hollow round pipe on the roof at the top of a chimney(1).
'**chimney,stack** *c.n* group of chimneypots on the roof of a building.
'**chimney,sweep** *c.n* (also '**chimney-,sweeper**) person whose job is to clean chimneys(1) by pushing brushes up them and removing the soot(1).

chimp /tʃɪmp/ *c.n* (*informal*) chimpanzee.

chimpanzee /,tʃɪmpæn'ziː/ *c.n* (*informal* chimp) large animal of the ape(1) family, found in Africa.

chin /tʃɪn/ *c.n* front part of the face below the mouth: *She hit him on the chin.*

china /'tʃaɪnə/ *u.n* (also *attrib*) **1** kind of very fine white clay baked to a high temperature, glazed(1) and often decorated, used to make plates, cups, vases etc: *a vase made of china; a china cup.* **2** plates, cups etc made from china(1) or from substances like it: *Amy only used her best china when she had visitors.*

chink /tʃɪŋk/ *c.n* **1** small narrow opening or crack: *He could just see them through a chink in the curtains.* **2** small noise of things made of metal, glass etc hitting one another; clink(1): *From the next room came the chink of glasses.*
▷ *tr/intr.v* **3** (cause (s.t) to) make a chink(2) or chinks(2); clink(2): *He chinked the coins in his pocket. The coins chinked together as he ran.*

chip /tʃɪp/ *c.n* **1** small piece (of s.t, esp wood, brick, stone etc) that has come away or broken off from a larger piece: *When he had finished cutting up the wood there were chips everywhere.* **2** (damaged) place from which a chip(1) has broken off, esp on a glass, cup, plate etc: *Don't buy that plate; it's got a chip in it.* **3** (often *pl*) long thin piece cut from a potato and then fried in fat: *fish and chips.* **4** = microchip. **5** round or square flat plastic object used in some games and also to take the place of money. **a chip off the old block** (*old use*; *joking*) a person who is thought to be like one of her/his parents in her/his character. **have a chip on one's shoulder** (*fig*; *informal*) be discontented, feel bitter, because of other people's better advantages, because of some wrong which one thinks one has suffered

etc: *Andy's got a chip on his shoulder because he didn't get the job.*
▷ *v* (**-pp-**) **6** *tr.v* break a small piece off (s.t, e.g wood, brick, stone): *She chipped the cup when she dropped it.* **7** *intr.v* (of s.t) have a piece broken off: *This vase may chip if you don't hold it carefully.* **chip s.t away** gradually remove or destroy s.t by breaking it into bits: *He chipped the old plaster away.* **chip away at s.t** try to remove or destroy s.t by hitting it again and again: *He chipped away at the old plaster.* **chip in** (**with s.t**) (*informal*) (**a**) interrupt a conversation (with a remark of one's own): *He tried to chip in with his own views but no one listened to him.* (**b**) add (one's own money) to a collection: *When she fell ill and there was a collection in the office, he chipped in with £5.*

'**chip,board** *u.n* kind of board made from chips(1) of wood glued together, used for shelves, furniture etc.

chipmunk /'tʃɪp,mʌŋk/ *c.n* kind of small animal like a squirrel with a long bushy tail and black and grey-white bands on its back, found in North America.

chiropodist /kɪ'rɒpə,dɪst/ *c.n* **1** person who looks after and treats people's feet and toes. **2** (also **chi'ropodist's**) place where a chiropodist treats people.

chiropody /kɪ'rɒpədɪ/ *u.n* treatment by, work of, a chiropodist.

chirp /tʃɜːp/ *c.n* (also **chirrup** /'tʃɪrəp/) **1** short sharp sound made by some birds and insects.
▷ *intr.v* (also '**chirrup**) **2** make the sound of a chirp(1).
'**chirpily** *adv* in a chirpy way.
'**chirpiness** *u.n* fact of being chirpy.
'**chirpy** *adj* (**-ier, -iest**) (*informal*) cheerful: *Paula's very chirpy as she had some good news.*

chisel /'tʃɪzl/ *c.n* **1** kind of steel tool with a handle and a blade which has a sharp end, used to cut into or shape wood, stone etc.
▷ *tr.v* (**-ll-**, US **-l-**) **2** use this tool to cut (s.t), make (a shape) etc: *He chiselled a hole in the wood.* **chisel s.o** (**out of s.t**) (*informal*) cheat, trick, s.o (and get money etc from her/him).

chit /tʃɪt/ *c.n* (often — *for s.t*) short written and signed note, esp one showing that one owes money (for s.t, e.g food, drinks).

chitchat /'tʃɪt,tʃæt/ *u.n* (*informal*) idle conversation: *Stop that chitchat and get on with your work.*

chivalry /'ʃɪvlrɪ/ *u.n* (*formal*) **1** (of a man) showing of special kindness, good manners etc to women. **2** beliefs, practices and social behaviour of knights(1) in the Middle Ages.
chivalrous /'ʃɪvlrəs/ *adj* (of a man) showing chivalry(1). Opposite unchivalrous.
'**chivalrously** *adv.* '**chivalrousness** *u.n.*

chive /tʃaɪv/ *c.n* kind of plant with thin green leaves, used to give a flavour of onions to food.

chlorine /'klɔːriːn/ *u.n* green-yellow strong-smelling gas that is an element(1) and is used to get rid of germs(1), *chem.symb* Cl: *Public swimming pools often have so much chlorine in them that it makes one's eyes sting.*
chlorinate /'klɔːrɪ,neɪt/ *tr.v* put chlorine into (s.t, esp water).
chlorination /,klɔːrɪ'neɪʃən/ *u.n.*

chloroform /'klɒrə,fɔːm/ *u.n* colourless

strong-smelling liquid that can be changed into a gas; when it is breathed in it makes a person unconscious, *chem.form* CHC₃.

chlorophyll /'klɒrə,fɪl/ *u.n* substance in plants that gives them their green colour and which helps them to get energy(2) from sunlight.

choc /tʃɒk/ *c.n* (*informal*) chocolate(2).

'choc-,ice *c.n* ice-cream with chocolate on it.

chock /tʃɒk/ *c.n* piece of wood placed in front of or behind a wheel of a vehicle or an aircraft to stop it from moving.

chock-a-block /,tʃɒk ə 'blɒk/ *adj/adv* (also **chock-full** /,tʃɒk 'fʊl/) (often — with *s.o/s.t*) (*informal*) very crowded (with people, things) so that one cannot move: *The airport was chock-a-block with passengers waiting for their flights.*

chocolate /'tʃɒklɪt, 'tʃɒkəlɪt/ *n* (also *attrib*) **1** *u.n* sweet, usu dark brown, substance (made from the seeds of the cacao tree and) eaten as a sweet, often in the form of a bar: *Have some chocolate. Have a piece of chocolate. I like chocolate cakes.* ⇒ milk chocolate, plain chocolate. **2** *c.n* (*informal* **choc**) one of a number of sweets or nuts of different kinds with a covering of chocolate(1) on them: *a box of chocolates.* **3** *u.n* (hot) drink made from chocolate(1). **4** *u.n* dark brown colour: *The walls were painted in chocolate (or in a chocolate colour).*

choice /tʃɔɪs/ *adj* **1** (usu *attrib*) of the best quality, having been chosen from others: *choice bananas.*
▷ *n* **2** *u.n* power or ability to choose s.t: *You have some/little/no choice in the matter.* **3** *c.n* act or result of choosing s.t: *He was the people's choice.* **4** *c.n* one of a number of people or things one can choose: *There were several choices of jobs open to her.* ⇒ choose.

choir /kwaɪə/ *n* **1** *c.n* group of people who sing together, esp in a church or in front of the public. **2** *c.n* part of a church where the choir(1) sings. ⇒ chorus(1), choral.

choke /tʃəʊk/ *c.n* **1** act of choking(3). **2** mechanism in an engine, e.g of a car, that controls the flow of air, esp when starting it: *Many cars now have automatic(1) chokes.*
▷ *v* **3** *tr/reflex.v* stop the breathing of (s.o/oneself) either by stopping air getting into the nose, mouth and lungs or by some substance or object getting in the way: *He put his hands round her neck and nearly choked her to death. I choked myself by swallowing a bone.* **4** *intr.v* (often — on *s.t*) choke(3) oneself (when eating s.t): *I choked on a bone in my throat.* **5** *tr.v* fill (a space, an area etc) so that it is blocked, nothing can move etc: *Cars choked the road. Leaves had choked the pipes.* **choke s.t back/down** stop s.t that one is starting to do from happening: *She choked back her tears.* **choke to death (on s.t)** die because of choking(4) (when eating s.t). **(be) choked with s.t (a)** (of a space, an area etc) be full of s.t and so become blocked: *The roads were choked with cars.* **(b)** be full of a feeling, anger, love, and so be overcome: *Carol was choked with anger at Jason's rudeness.*

cholera /'kɒlərə/ *u.n* kind of disease found mostly in hot countries that attacks the stomach and bowels(1) of people and often causes death.

cholesterol /kə'lestə,rɒl/ *u.n* substance present in the cells(4) of the body and thought to cause medical problems such as heart disease if there is too much of it present.

choose /tʃuːz/ *v* (*p.t* chose /tʃəʊz/, *p.p* chosen /tʃəʊzn/) **1** *tr.v* take (s.o/s.t), decide to have (s.o/ s.t), from a number of people or things: *Have you chosen a new car yet? He was chosen to play for England.* **2** *intr.v* make a choice; decide on s.o/ s.t: *I can't decide which to have so you choose.* ⇒ choice(4). **choose between s.o/s.t and s.o/s.t** decide which of two people or things to take or have: *There's little or nothing to choose between the two of them so I don't mind which you have.* **choose to do s.t** decide, be determined, to do s.t: *He chose not to act on the information.* **pick and choose** ⇒ pick¹.

'choosy *adj* (*-ier, -iest*) (*informal*) careful about who/what one chooses and therefore difficult to please: *She's very choosy about the people she invites to dinner.*

chop /tʃɒp/ *c.n* **1** short sharp blow or hit, esp with an axe or a hand: *It took several chops to cut off the branch of the tree. He knocked him down with one chop of his hand.* **2** thick slice of meat, usu with a bone in it: lamb(2)/pork *chops.* **get the chop** (*fig*; *informal*) **(a)** lose one's job. **(b)** (of a plan, work etc) be suddenly stopped: *Building of the new aircraft is getting the chop as it is too expensive.*
▷ *tr.v* (*-pp-*) **3** (often — *s.o/s.t up*) cut (s.o/s.t) again and again into small pieces with an axe, a knife etc: *She chopped (up) the onions.* **chop and change** (*fig*; *informal*) be always changing one's mind, what one wants to do etc. **chop s.t down** cut s.t with an axe so that it falls to the ground: *He chopped down the old apple tree.* **chop s.t off (from s.t)** cut s.t with an axe etc and so remove it from the main part of s.t: *He chopped a branch off the tree.*

'chopper *c.n* **1** kind of small axe used for cutting up wood. **2** (*informal*) = helicopter.

'choppiness *u.n* fact or state of being choppy.

'choppy *adj* (*-ier, -iest*) (of the sea) rough, with many short waves going in different directions.

'chop,stick *c.n* (often *a pair of —s*) one of two long narrow sticks held in the hand and used in some countries to pick up food in order to eat it.

choral ⇒ chorus.

chord /kɔːd/ *c.n* **1** (*geometry*) straight line joining two points on a circle or curve. **2** two or more musical notes sounded or played together. **3** = cord(3).

chore /tʃɔː/ *c.n* small, dull piece of work, esp one which one would like to avoid: *the household chores* (i.e cleaning, dusting etc).

choreography /,kɒrɪ'ɒgrəfɪ/ *u.n* art of arranging patterns of dancing, esp for a ballet(1) or a musical(4).

,chore'ographer *c.n* person who does choreography.

chortle /'tʃɔːtl/ *intr.v* laugh in a way that shows personal pleasure (about one's success etc).

chorus /'kɔːrəs/ *c.n* (*pl* -es) **1** group of people who sing together either on their own or as a background to other singers. **2** part of a song following after the main part (sung by one or more special singers) that can be sung by others and can be repeated: *They all joined in the chorus.*

3 thing that is said, shouted, written etc by many people at the same time: *a chorus of praise.*

▷ *tr/intr.v* **4** (of many people) speak, shout etc (s.t) at the same time: *They choursed their agreement to the proposals.*

choral /ˈkɔːrl/ *adj* of or referring to a chorus(1) or choir(1): *choral music; a choral society.*

chose, chosen ⇒ choose.

Christ /kraɪst/ *unique n* ⇒ Jesus.

Christian /ˈkrɪstjən/ *adj* (usu *attrib*) **1** of, referring to, belonging to, the religion established by Christ and his followers: *the Christian Church.* **2** of or referring to the beliefs, practices etc of the Christian(1) religion: *Christian virtues.*

▷ *c.n* **3** person who believes in, or is a member of, the Christian(1) religion.

Christianity /ˌkrɪstɪˈænɪtɪ/ *u.n* belief in, practice of, the Christian(1) religion.

ˈChristian ˌname *c.n* first name given to a person at, or soon after, birth; forename.

christen /ˈkrɪsn/ *tr.v* **1** make (s.o, esp a baby) a member of the Christian(1) Church by the ceremony of baptism and usu give (the baby) a name or names at the same time: *The priest christened her Philippa Alice Mary.* **2** give a name to (a new ship): *The ship was christened Mary Rose.*

ˈchristening *c.n* (also *attrib*) ceremony of baptism and naming a baby.

Christmas /ˈkrɪsməs/ *c/unique n* (*pl* **-es**) (also *attrib*) time every year (the days around 25 December) when the birth of Christ is remembered and celebrated: *the Christmas holidays; Christmas presents.*

ˈChristmas ˌbox *c.n* present given to s.o at Christmas.

ˈChristmas cake *c/u.n* special kind of cake using lots of raisins etc, cooked and eaten at Christmas.

ˈChristmas ˌcard *c.n* special (folded) card with a picture and a message in it that is sent at Christmas.

ˌChristmas ˈcracker ⇒ cracker (⇒ crack).

ˌChristmas ˈDay *unique n* 25th December.

ˌChristmas ˈEve *unique n* day and evening before Christmas Day (i.e 24th December).

ˈChristmas ˌtree *c.n* fir tree (or an imitation) decorated with lights and other decorations which is usu set up in a house at Christmas.

chrome /krəʊm/ *u.n* (also *attrib*) **1** kind of hard shiny metal alloy made with chromium and steel, used to cover and protect objects. **2** (often — *yellow*) yellow colouring substance used in paints etc: *a chrome painting.*

chromium /ˈkrəʊmɪəm/ *u.n* (also *attrib*) hard metal that is an element(1), used to cover and protect other metals, esp on cars, bathroom fittings etc, *chem.symb* Cr.

chromosome /ˈkrəʊməˌsəʊm/ *c.n* very small part of a cell(4) of a living thing; it is shaped like a thread that carries genes that give living things their shape and character.

chronic /ˈkrɒnɪk/ *adj* **1** (of a disease, illness) going on for a long time: *She suffers from a chronic illness.* **2** (*derog; informal*) very bad: *That joke you told was pretty chronic!*

chronicle /ˈkrɒnɪkl/ *c.n* **1** (*formal*) list or description of usu historical events arranged in the order in which they take place.

▷ *tr.v* **2** write, make, an organized list or description: *He chronicled the main points of the discussions.*

chronology /krəˈnɒlədʒɪ/ *n* (*pl* **-ies**) (*formal*) **1** *u.n* science and study of the times and dates when things happened. **2** *c.n* list of times and dates in chronological order.

chronological /ˌkrɒnəˈlɒdʒɪkl/ *adj* (arranged) according to the date and time when things happen: *We need to put things in chronological order before we can decide exactly when he died.*

ˌchronoˈlogically *adv.*

chronometer /krəˈnɒmɪtə/ *c.n* kind of special watch or clock that keeps time very accurately (and is used esp on ships).

chrysalis /ˈkrɪsəˌlɪs/ *c.n* (*pl* **-es**) (*science*) state or form of a certain kind of insect (such as a butterfly) when it wraps itself in a case of threads (after being a larva and before becoming a butterfly etc).

chrysanthemum /krɪˈsænθəməm/ *c.n* (*pl* **-s**) kind of garden plant with large flowers which have many petals.

chubby /ˈtʃʌbɪ/ *adj* (**-ier**, **-iest**) (of a body, face etc) fat and round: *The baby had chubby hands.*

ˈchubbiness *u.n.*

chuck¹ /tʃʌk/ *tr.v* (*informal*) throw (s.t) a short way: *Chuck the ball to him.* **chuck s.t away/off** get rid of s.t which one no longer wants: *You can chuck all that rubbish away.* **chuck s.t in/ up** stop doing s.t: *He chucked in his job.* **chuck s.o off** (**s.t**) make s.o leave (s.t), esp a vehicle: *He was chucked off (the bus) for not paying for a ticket.* **chuck s.o out** (**of s.w**) make s.o leave (a place), usu because he/she is not wanted, has been annoying etc: *Terry was chucked out of the cinema for making a noise.* **chuck s.t up** ⇒ chuck s.t in/up.

chuck² /tʃʌk/ *c.n* (*technical*) **1** part of a lathe that holds the piece of metal, wood etc which is being worked on. **2** part of a drill(1) that holds the bit¹(2).

chuckle /ˈtʃʌkl/ *c.n* **1** gentle quiet laugh, usu repeated: *He gave several little chuckles while watching the film.*

▷ *intr.v* **2** laugh with a chuckle(1).

chug /tʃʌg/ *c.n* **1** repeated sound of an engine working slowly: *He heard the chug of an old car passing his house.*

▷ *intr.v* (**-gg-**) **2** (usu — *along/down* (s.w), *away* etc) (of an engine, vehicle etc) make this sound, esp when moving (s.w): *The train chugged up the hill.*

chum /tʃʌm/ *c.n* (*informal old use*) close friend.

ˈchummy *adj* (**-ier**, **-iest**) (usu *pred*) (*informal*) very friendly: *I've got quite chummy with Mary over the last few weeks.*

chump /tʃʌmp/ *c.n* **1** (also **ˈchump ˌchop**) thick slice of meat, usu with a bone in it. **2** (*informal*) foolish but kind person.

chunk /tʃʌŋk/ *c.n* (often — *of* s.t) (*informal*) thick solid piece (of food, wood, metal etc): *He cut off a chunk of cheese to eat.*

ˈchunky *adj* (**-ier**, **-iest**) thick and solid.

church /tʃɜːtʃ/ *n* **1** *c.n* building where Christian(1) religious services are held and where people go to pray. **2** *def.n* organization and profession of Christians(3), their priests etc as a group: *He left the church because he no longer believed in it.*

3 *c/def.n* (often with capital **C**) one of a number of Christian(1) groups holding certain beliefs or organized in a certain way. ⇒ Church of England, Roman Catholic Church. **go to church** go to a church(1) in order to take part in a religious service.

'**church,goer** *c.n* person who goes to church regularly.

,**Church of 'England** *def.n* official Church(3) set up in England in the 16th century.

'**church,yard** *c.n* area round a church(1), often where people are buried.

churlish /'tʃɜːlɪʃ/ *adj* (*derog*; *formal*) rude and having bad manners.

'**churlishly** *adv.* '**churlishness** *u.n.*

churn /tʃɜːn/ *c.n* **1** machine for making butter from milk by beating it. **2** large round container for milk, used to carry it from a farm to the place where it is put in bottles etc.

▷ *v* **3** *tr.v* beat (milk) in order to make (it) into butter. **4** *tr.v* (often — *s.t up*) (cause (s.t, esp water, air) to) move about violently: *The aircraft's blades churned the air as it started up.* **5** *intr.v* be, become, disturbed: *My stomach churned at the sight of all the rich food.* **churn s.t out** (*informal*; often *derog*) produce s.t continually, esp s.t requiring not much thought or effort: *The machine churns out millions of nails a day.*

chute /ʃuːt/ *c.n* **1** sloping channel(1) down which things slide: *a rubbish chute.* **2** (*informal*) parachute(1).

chutney /'tʃʌtnɪ/ *u.n* kind of thick sauce with a strong taste, made from fruit or vegetables and spices(1) and eaten with meat, cheese etc: mango *chutney.*

CI *written abbr* Channel Islands (a group of islands in the sea between England and France).

CIA /,si: ,aɪ 'eɪ/ *def.n abbr* Central Intelligence Agency.

CID /,si: ,aɪ 'di:/ *def.n abbr* Criminal Investigation Department.

cider /'saɪdə/ *u.n* kind of alcoholic(1) drink made from apples.

cigar /sɪ'gɑː/ *c.n* number of dried tobacco leaves rolled together into a long fat or thin brown shape for smoking.

cigarette /,sɪgə'ret/ *c.n* (also *attrib*) long thin usu white paper tube containing small cut pieces of dried tobacco leaves for smoking: *a cigarette smoker*; *a packet of cigarettes.*

,**ciga'rette ,lighter** *c.n* device holding petrol or gas, used to light a cigarette.

,**ciga'rette ,paper** *c.n* (one of a number of) thin white papers sold in packets and used to roll dried pieces of tobacco in to make cigarettes.

C-in-C /,si: ɪn 'i:/ *written abbr* Commander-in-Chief.

cinch /sɪntʃ/ *c.n* **be a cinch** (*informal*) (**a**) be s.t that one does easily: *The driving test was a cinch and I had no trouble passing it.* (**b**) (in the opinion of the speaker) be s.t that is certain to happen: *If you lend me the money, it's a cinch that I'll make you rich.*

cinder /'sɪndə/ *c.n* piece of burnt coal, wood etc sometimes still hot: *A cinder fell out of the fire and burnt a hole in the carpet.*

cine-camera /'sɪnɪ ,kæmrə/ *c.n* special kind of camera used for making films.

cinema /'sɪnɪmə/ *n* (also *attrib*) **1** *c.n* building or hall where films are shown on a large screen in front of an audience. **2** *def.n* whole industry or art of making such films: *The cinema is losing its audiences to television.* **go to the cinema** go to a cinema(1) in order to see a film.

cinematography /,sɪnɪmə'tɒgrəfɪ/ *u.n* (*formal*) art or act of making moving pictures.

cinnamon /'sɪnəmən/ *u.n* (also *attrib*) **1** (powder made from the) bark of a tree found in Asia, used to flavour food: *cinnamon cakes.* **2** red-brown colour.

cipher /'saɪfə/ *n* (also '**cypher**) **1** *c.n* (*mathematics*) symbol '0'. **2** *c.n* (*mathematics*) any of the numbers 1 to 9. **3** *c/u.n* secret writing; code(3): *The message was in cipher to prevent it being understood by the enemy.*

circa /'sɜːkə/ *prep* (*written abbr* c or ca) (*Latin*) (of a date) at about; within a few years of: *The city was destroyed circa 1100 BC.*

circle /'sɜːkl/ *n* **1** *c.n* (*geometry*) perfect round shape like an 'O' in which every point on the round line is the same distance from a central point. **2** *c.n* line around this shape. **3** *c.n* something like this shape: *a circle of stones.* **4** *def.n* group of seats on a balcony(2) in a theatre: *The only seats left are in the circle.* **a circle of friends** *etc* a group of friends etc who see each other socially because of common interests etc. **come full circle** return to the point at which one began an activity. **move in the best, highest** etc **circles** work, live socially among a group of important etc people. **vicious circle** ⇒ vice².

▷ *tr.v* **5** draw or make a circle around (s.t): *Harry circled the report in the newspaper with a red pencil.* **6** *tr/intr.v* (often — (a)round *s.o/s.t*) move in a circle ((a)round *s.o/s.t*); form a circle ((a)round *s.o/s.t*): *The aircraft circled the airport several times before landing.*

circular /'sɜːkjʊlə/ *adj* **1** round; (being in the form of a circle: *a circular shape.* **2** moving in a circle: *He made a circular movement with his hand.* **3** (of a thought, idea, argument etc) not getting anywhere; coming back to the point where it first started: *This discussion is becoming circular so let's stop and decide what to do.*

▷ *c.n* **4** printed letter, notice, advertisement etc sent to many people: *I get so many circulars in the post trying to sell me something.*

circularize, -ise /'sɜːkjʊlə,raɪz/ *tr.v* send a circular(4) to (s.o): *We circularized the people concerned about the date of the meeting.*

circulate /'sɜːkjʊ,leɪt/ *v* **1** *tr/intr.v* (cause (s.t) to) move in a path from one point to others and back to the first point (and continue doing this): *The action of the heart circulates blood through the body.* **2** *tr/intr.v* (cause (information, a printed notice etc) to) move from one place to others: *News was circulating that the ship had been sunk.* **3** *intr.v* (of a person) move around a group of people, talking to them etc, esp at a party: *He circulated among his guests.*

circulation /,sɜːkjʊ'leɪʃən/ *n* **1** *c/u.n* (act of) blood moving around the body; ability of blood to do this: *The circulation of the blood was first discovered in the 17th century.* **2** *c.n* number of copies of a newspaper, magazine etc sold each day, week etc: *The new magazine claims a circulation of 100 000 copies.* **be (back) in circulation** (**a**) (of money, information etc) be moving (after not being available) from one place to others, from one person to others: *People did not like the new pound coins from the first day they were in circulation.* (b) (of a person) be meeting or visiting people socially (after an absence): *Andrew was back in circulation after a short holiday.*

circulatory /ˌsɜːkjʊˈleɪtərɪ/ *adj* of circulation, esp the movement of blood in the body: *the circulatory system; a circulatory disease.*

circuit /ˈsɜːkɪt/ *c.n* 1 (course of the) movement from one place around a circle and back to the beginning again: *the circuit of the planet around the sun; the circuit of a race track.* 2 (*law*) (number of) places or courts visited regularly by a judge in the course of her/his duties. 3 (*sport*) places sportsmen and women visit regularly and play matches at: *the tennis circuit.* 4 complete path of an electric current: *There was a fault in the circuit and the lights went out.* ⇒ integrated circuit.

circuitous /səˈkjuːɪtəs/ *adj* (*formal*) going a long way round; not going direct (to a place): *a circuitous route*(1).

circumcise /ˈsɜːkəmˌsaɪz/ *tr.v* remove the skin from the end of the penis for religious or health reasons.

circumcision /ˌsɜːkəmˈsɪʒən/ *c/u.n.*

circumference /səˈkʌmfərəns/ *c.n* (often *the — of s.t*) (length of the) line forming the edge of a circular shape: *the circumference of a circle.*

circumflex (accent) /ˈsɜːkəmˌfleks/ *c.n* (also *attrib*) special mark ˆ used in writing over certain vowels in some languages, but not in English, e.g château.

circumnavigate /ˌsɜːkəmˈnævɪˌgeɪt/ *tr.v* (*formal*) sail around (the world etc) and return to the place one started from.

circumnavigation /ˌsɜːkəmˌnævɪˈgeɪʃən/ *c/u.n.*

circumspect /ˈsɜːkəmˌspekt/ *adj* (*formal*) (of a person, action etc) behaving or doing s.t in a cautious way, after a lot of thought etc.

circumspection /ˌsɜːkəmˈspekʃən/ *u.n.* **circum-spectly** *adv.*

circumstance /ˈsɜːkəmstəns/ *c.n* 1 (usu *pl*; often *the — s of s.t*) fact or event that has an effect on other facts or events: *Do you know the circumstances of his leaving his job?* 2 (usu *pl*) (bad) state of one's own affairs: *Her poor circumstances after the death of her husband forced her to take a job.* **in/under the**, **these** etc **circumstances** because of the facts, conditions etc (of the matter): *In such circumstances I advise you to go to the police.* **under no**, **not under any**, **circumstances** never: *Under no circumstances should you talk to him.*

circumstantial /ˌsɜːkəmˈstænʃəl/ *adj* of or referring to one or more facts or events.

circum,stantial 'evidence *u.n* (*law*) information about a crime that has some value or truth in it but that does not (completely) prove that the crime has taken place.

circumvent /ˌsɜːkəmˈvent/ *tr.v* (*formal*) (try to) find a way to defeat or avoid (a law, tax etc): *Colin's very good at advising companies how to circumvent new taxes.*

circumvention /ˌsɜːkəmˈvenʃən/ *u.n.*

circus /ˈsɜːkəs/ *n* (*pl -es*) 1 *c.n* public show with performing animals, acrobats, clowns(1) etc that

usu takes place in a large round tent. 2 *def.n* performance of this show: *Let's go to the circus tonight.* 3 *unique n* (with capital **C** in names) (round) area in a town where a number of streets meet: *Oxford/Piccadilly Circus (in London).*

cirrhosis /sɪˈrəʊsɪs/ *u.n* (*medical*) (esp — *of the liver*) disease that attacks cells(4) (in the liver(1)), causes hard tissue(1) to grow and very often results in death.

cissy /ˈsɪsɪ/ *c.n* (*pl -ies*) = sissy(2).

cistern /ˈsɪstən/ *c.n* tank of water with pipes to and from it that is connected to a lavatory or that provides water for a building, garden etc.

citadel /ˈsɪtədl/ *c.n* strong building or tower (either on its own or part of a fortress in a town) to which an army and people can go when attacked.

cite /saɪt/ *tr.v* 1 (*law*) tell, call, (s.o) to be present at a court of law, e.g to answer a charge; mention, give (the name of s.o) in a case of law, esp divorce(1): *He was cited as* co-respondent. 2 (*formal*) mention, use, (a section from a book, the name of a writer etc) as part of an argument, to help one's own case etc; quote(3) (s.o/s.t): *He cited several passages from the book in defence of his own position.* 3 (*military*) mention (the name of s.o) in an official report because of her/his bravery: *He was cited for bravery in action.*

citation /saɪˈteɪʃən/ *c/u.n* (act of) citing s.o/s.t.

citizen /ˈsɪtɪzn/ *c.n* 1 person who lives in a town or city: *the citizens of London.* 2 person who is a member of a country either by birth or by naturalization(1) and who therefore has certain rights and duties there: *British citizens expect their country to protect them when they are abroad.*

'citizen,ship *u.n* fact or state of being a citizen(2); rights and duties of a citizen(2): *Eva wants to apply for American citizenship.*

citric acid /ˌsɪtrɪk ˈæsɪd/ *u.n* kind of acid found in certain fruits, e.g oranges, lemons(3), limes²(3).

citrus /ˈsɪtrəs/ *c.n* (*pl -es*) (also *attrib*) (one of the kinds of) tree found usu in hot countries and grown for its fruit, e.g oranges, lemons(3), limes²(3): *citrus fruits.*

city /ˈsɪtɪ/ *n* (*pl -ies*) 1 *c.n* (also *attrib*) area of buildings which is bigger and more important than a town(1): *city populations.* 2 *def/def.pl.n* all the people who live in a particular city(1): *The city voted against the idea.*

civic /ˈsɪvɪk/ *attrib.adj* 1 of or referring to the official work of a city or town: *A mayor has many civic duties to perform.* 2 of or referring to the rights and duties of a citizen: *It is a civic duty to vote in local elections.*

,civic 'centre *c.n* area in a city or town where the local government offices and sometimes other offices and shops are.

'civics *u.n* science and study of the way government works, the rights and duties of citizens etc.

civil /ˈsɪvl/ *adj* 1 of or referring to the duties and rights of a citizen: *Every citizen has certain civil rights.* 2 of or referring to ordinary people (as compared with military or religious people): *There are more civil marriages than religious ones.* ⇒ civilian. 3 (*law*) of or referring to cases and quarrels between people, not crimes against the state: *She brought a civil action against him for* *not keeping his garden fence repaired.* **4** (often — *to s.o*) (trying to be) polite and not rude (to s.o, even though it is difficult): *You could at least be civil to her since she was trying to help.* Opposite uncivil.

,**civil de'fence** *u.n* (organization of ordinary people for the) defending of one's country against attack by an enemy.

,**civil ,engi'neering** *u.n* science and practice of building of roads, railways, airports, buildings etc for the use of the public.

civilian /sɪ'vɪlɪən/ *c.n* (also *attrib*) person who is not a member of the armed forces: *Many civilians were killed in the fighting. The soldier found it hard to return to civilian life.*

civility /sɪ'vɪlɪtɪ/ *u.n* fact or act of showing politeness; act of being civil(4) to s.o: *You could show some civility when all he was trying to do was to help.* Opposite incivility.

civilization, -isation /,sɪvɪlaɪ'zeɪʃən/ *n* **1** *u.n* state reached after being civilized (⇒ civilize). **2** *u.n* level reached in the process of civilizing, or of being civilized (⇒ civilize): *We think we have an advanced civilization in our country.* **3** *c.n* (people who live in a) country that has developed an advanced (high) level of civilization(2): *Many people admire the ancient civilizations of Greece and Rome.*

'**civi,lize, -ise** *tr.v* (cause (s.o, a community) to) become educated and have advanced cultural, legal(2) and political organizations and activities: *The word 'civilize' is mostly to do with* ignorance *of other people's* culture(3).

'**civi,lized, -ised** *adj.* Opposite uncivilized.

,**civil 'liberties/'rights** *pl.n* freedom of a citizen to enjoy certain rights (⇒ right¹) (e.g to vote, give her/his opinion etc).

'**civilly** *adv* in a civil(4) way.

,**civil 'servant** *c.n* person who works for the civil service.

,**civil 'service** *def.n* (often with capitals **C** and **S**) (people who work in the) government departments concerned with the running of the country (apart from the law, the Church and the armed forces).

,**civil 'war** *c/u.n* (act, example of) fighting between people who belong to the same country.

cl written *abbr* centilitre(s).

clad /klæd/ *pred.adj* (often in combinations) (*literary*; *formal*) clothed or covered (in s.t): *a fur-clad hunter*; *hills clad in snow.*

claim /kleɪm/ *c.n* **1** statement (that what one is saying is true): *His claim is that he was not near the scene of the accident.* **2** (often — *for s.t*) request or demand (for s.t one considers one has a right to): *He put in a claim for the holiday due to him.* **3** (often — *for s.t*) request or demand (for money etc, esp that due to one under an insurance policy(2)): *The company had to meet many claims for houses damaged by the storm.* ⇒ no claims bonus. **4** area of land worked by a miner trying to find or collecting minerals, esp gold. *lay claim to s.t* (*formal*) make a demand for s.t one considers to be one's own right: *He laid claim to the* throne(2). *make, put in, a claim for s.t* make a (formal) request for s.t. *no claim(s) bonus* ⇒ bonus.

▷ *tr.v* **5** state (s.t as being true): *He claims no knowledge of what happened.* **6** make a request or demand for (s.t one considers one has a right to): *He claimed ownership of the house.* **claim against s.o/s.t** make a claim(2,3), esp for money, against s.o/s.t: *He claimed against his insurance for the damage to his car.* **claim damages (against s.o)** (*for s.t*) ⇒ damage(*n*).

claimant /'kleɪmənt/ *c.n* **1** person who makes a claim(2): *There were many claimants to the* throne(2). **2** person who makes a claim(3): *The number of claimants for unemployment benefit(2) has increased in the last month.*

clairvoyant /kleə'vɔɪənt/ *adj* **1** (of a person) (claiming to be) able to see or say what will happen in the future.

▷ *c.n* **2** person who is clairvoyant.

clair'voyance *u.n.*

clam /klæm/ *c.n* (also *attrib*) **1** kind of shellfish with two round shells, eaten as food: *clam soup.*

▷ *intr.v* (-mm-) **2** *clam up* (*informal*) suddenly become silent, refuse to speak, (after having spoken about s.t): *William clammed up when he realized he might have given away some secrets.*

clamber /'klæmbə/ *intr.v* (often — *around/over/ up* etc s.t) climb using one's hands and feet (around etc s.t): *They clambered over the rocks.*

clammy /'klæmɪ/ *adj* (-ier, -iest) damp or wet (and sometimes cold) when touched: *His hands were clammy. There was a clammy mist*(1).

'**clamminess** *u.n.*

clamour /'klæmə/ *c/u.n* (US '**clamor**) (*formal*) **1** (act of making a) loud shout or noise by a group of people (to attract attention, make a complaint etc): *There was a clamour at the back of the hall from people.* **2** (often — *for s.t*) (act of making a) public request or demand (for s.t to be done etc): *There was a clamour for a public inquiry into the new road plans.*

▷ *intr.v* **3** (usu — *for s.t*) make loud shouts or demands (for s.t): *The crowd outside the hall was clamouring for action.*

clamp /klæmp/ *c.n* **1** mechanical device consisting of two pieces of metal or wood that hold an object between them by means of a screw that can be tightened, esp so that the object can be worked on, e.g in a factory, workshop. **2** (UK) device used by the police to fit onto the wheel of a car to stop it being moved (because it is illegally parked).

▷ *tr.v* **3** put (an object) into a clamp(1); tie (two or more objects) together: *He clamped the two pieces of wood together to strengthen them.* **4** (UK) put a clamp(2) on (a car): *When he got back to the car he found the police had clamped* it. *clamp down (on s.o/s.t)* put pressure on s.t, control the activity of s.o, so that he/she stops doing s.t: *The government is clamping down on people who try to avoid paying parking fines.*

'**clamp,down** *c.n* (usu — *on s.o/s.t*) act of clamping down (on s.o/s.t).

clan /klæn/ *c.n* **1** (esp in Scotland) group of families descended from one family, usu with a chief and having the same surname. **2** (*informal*) large family group; group having the same interests: *the Kennedy clan* (i.e the family of the late US President John F Kennedy).

'**clannish** *adj* (of a group of people) sticking closely together and not allowing people from outside to join them.

'clansman *c.n* (*pl -men*) man who belongs to a clan(1).

'clans,woman *c.n* (*pl -,women*) woman who belongs to a clan(1).

clandestine /klæn'destɪn/ *adj* (*formal*) (of s.t done in) secret or private, esp because it is wrong or dangerous: *a clandestine marriage. They took part in clandestine operations against the enemy.*

clang /klæŋ/ *c.n* **1** loud sharp ringing noise, esp when two pieces of metal hit together: *the clang of* alarm(2) *bells.*

▷ *tr/intr.v* **2** (cause (s.t) to) make a noise of a clang(1): *He clanged the bell. The doors clanged shut.* Compare clank.

clanger /'klæŋə/ *c.n* (*informal*) unfortunate remark that shows lack of tact. **drop a clanger** make a mistake in this way: *She dropped a clanger by asking after his wife who had just died.*

clank /klæŋk/ *c.n* **1** loud dull noise, esp when two or more pieces of metal hit together: *He heard the clank of chains as the bridge was raised.*

▷ *intr.v* **2** make the noise of a clank(1): *The chains around the prisoner's feet clanked as he moved.* Compare clang.

clannish, clansman, clanswoman ⇒ clan.

clap /klæp/ *c.n* **1** loud sound made by hitting one's hands together, esp to show approval, draw attention to s.t, mark the time of a piece of music etc: *There were loud claps from someone in the audience when he appeared.* **2** (hard or gentle) hit with one's hand on s.o's body: *He felt a clap on his shoulder and turned around to see who it was.* **clap of thunder** very sudden loud noise made by thunder. ⇒ thunder-clap. **give s.o a clap on the back** (*fig*) praise s.o for s.t he/she has done well.

▷ *tr/intr.v* (-pp-) **3** hit (one's hands) together and so make a noise, esp to show approval of (s.o/s.t); applaud (s.o/s.t): *The audience clapped (him) for five minutes.* **clap s.o in jail/prison** quickly put s.o into a prison: *As soon as he was caught he was clapped in prison.* **clap s.o on the back** etc hit s.o on her/his back etc with one's hand, esp to draw attention, to show friendship etc: *He clapped him on the back and told him to cheer up.* **have not clapped eyes on s.o** ⇒ eye(*n*).

'clapping *u.n* (sound made by) many hands being hit together to show approval; applause.

claret /'klærət/ *n* (also *attrib*) **1** *c/u.n* (kind of) red wine made in the Bordeaux region of France. **2** *u.n* deep red colour.

clarify /'klærɪ,faɪ/ *tr/intr.v* (-ies, -ied) (*formal*) (cause (s.t) to) become clearer, be explained in more detail: *Could you please clarify that last statement as I did not understand it.*

clarification /,klærɪfɪ'keɪʃən/ *u.n.*

clarinet /,klærɪ'net/ *c.n* (also *attrib*) kind of musical instrument having a long wooden tube with holes and keys over them which are pressed by the fingers to give different sounds when one blows air through the tube: *a clarinet player.* **play the clarinet** (be able to) play this instrument, esp as one's job.

,clari'netist *c.n* (also **,clari'nettist**) person who plays the clarinet.

clarity /'klærɪtɪ/ *u.n* (*formal*) (often *the — of s.t*) **1** clearness (of s.t) so that one can see through it: *The clarity of the water allowed him to see right to the bottom.* **2** clearness (of s.o's thought,

argument etc): *the clarity of her argument. There was great clarity in the way he argued his case.*

clash /klæʃ/ *c.n* **1** loud noise made when two or more things hit together: *a clash of metal on metal.* **2** fight or battle (between two groups, armies etc): *a clash between the police and* strikers(1). **3** (often *— of s.t*) difference or disagreement between two people, groups etc (about opinions etc): *At the meeting there was a clash of views with neither side prepared to agree.* **4** strong, striking or unpleasant difference, esp between two or more colours: *a clash of colours.* **5** (of two or more events) interference with each other because they happen at the same time: *The clash in dates meant I could only attend one of the meetings.*

▷ *v* **6** *tr/intr.v* (cause (two or more things) to) hit together and make a loud noise: *Their swords clashed.* **7** *intr.v* (often *— with s.o*) (of two groups, armies etc) meet together and fight: *The police clashed with the* strikers(1). **8** *intr.v* (often *— with s.o/s.t* (*over s.t*)) (of two people, opinions etc) differ or disagree (with one another) (about s.t): *He clashed with him over what to do.* **9** *intr.v* (often *— with s.t*) (of colours etc) differ in a strong, striking or unpleasant way: *Her red blouse clashed with her green skirt.* **10** *intr.v* (often *— with s.t*) (of two or more events) interfere (with one another) because they happen at the same time: *The two meetings clashed (with each other).*

clasp /klɑːsp/ *c.n* **1** kind of fastener, usu made of metal, to hold two objects or the ends of one object together: *a clasp on a necklace.* **2** firm hold with a hand or the fingers: *He felt a clasp on his arm.*

▷ *tr.v* **3** join (two objects or the ends of one object) together using a clasp(1): *She asked Bernard to clasp the necklace round her neck.* **4** hold (s.o/s.t) firmly (in one's hands, between one's arms etc); embrace(2) (s.o): *He clasped her in his arms.*

class /klɑːs/ *n* **1** *c.n* (often *— of s.o/s.t*) (division into a) group (of people, animals or things) of the same kind or having some things in common: *There are several classes of dogs from which to choose.* **2** *u.n* (existence of a) system in which people are grouped according to their position or level in society: *Britain is a society ruled by class.* **3** *c.n* one of these groups in society: *the lower/middle/upper class(es); the working class(es); the ruling class(es).* **4** *c.n* (group of pupils or students taught together in a) lesson at school or college: *He's in the class above me at school. I've got a history class at 10 o'clock.* **5** *c.n* standard of s.t, e.g travel, hotels, shops etc. ⇒ club(1)/economy(1)/first/second(2)/third(1) class. **6** *c.n* (usu *the — of 1986* etc) (US) group of students who finish their college or university education in the same year: *the class of '82.* **be in a different class (from s.o/s.t)** (*fig*) be much better, of greater value etc (than s.o/s.t else). **have/show (a certain** etc) **class** (*informal*) have a good or noticeable style(3) (in one's dress, in what one does etc): *Ruth's got great class; I doubt if many women could wear that dress and get away with it.*

▷ *tr.v* **7** (often *— s.o/s.t as s.o/s.t*) say, think, (s.o/s.t) to be of a certain kind, type etc: *I would class him as a fool.*

,**class-'conscious** *adj* (being too) aware of one's own or others' (higher or lower) position in society.

,**class-'consciousness** *u.n.*

'**class,mate** *c.n* pupil or student in the same class(4) as oneself.

'**class,room** *c.n* room in a school in which a class(4) takes place.

,**class 'struggle/'war(fare)** *u.n* struggle between opposing classes(3) in society, esp between workers and those in power.

'**classy** *adj* (-*ier*, -*iest*) (*informal*) (of a person, clothes, behaviour etc) showing a good style(1).

classic /'klæsɪk/ *adj* (usu *attrib*) **1** of the best or highest quality: *He wrote the classic book on the subject.* **2** of or referring to an accepted or known (good) set of standards: *a classic building.* **3** being or showing a good example of s.t mentioned: *It was a classic case of love at first sight.*

▷ *c.n* **4** book, work of art etc that has become well known and is regarded as very important: *He wrote one of the classics of English literature.* Compare classics(2). **5** very good example of s.t: *His performance was a classic — the audience laughed and laughed.*

'**classical** *adj* **1** of or referring to the (study of) Greek and Roman civilizations, and esp their literature, works of art: *a classical education.* **2** (of music, acting etc) composed, done etc in a traditional way; accepted to be of the highest quality (as compared to more popular forms): *He plays only classical music.*

classicist /'klæsɪ,sɪst/ *c.n* student of classics.

'**classics** *n* **1** *u.n* (with a sing verb) the study of the Greek and Roman(1) civilizations: *He read classics at university.* **2** *def.pl.n* the whole literature of the Greek and Roman(1) civilizations.

classify /'klæsɪ,faɪ/ *tr.v* (-*ies*, -*ied*) **1** put (s.t) into a group or class(1): *The books in the library are classified according to their subjects.* **2** (often — *s.t as s.t*; — *s.t to be s.t*) (*formal*) describe or regard (s.t) to be of a certain, stated, kind: *He could only classify his attempt as a failure.*

classification /,klæsɪfɪ'keɪʃən/ *c/u.n* (example of the) act of classifying s.t.

'**classi,fied** *adj* **1** arranged in a certain group or class(1). **2** (of information) secret; not allowed to be spoken or written about: *I cannot tell you anything about the plan as it is classified.*

,**classi,fied ad'vertisement** *c.n* (also ,**classi,fied 'ad**) advertisement in a newspaper arranged according to its subject, e.g 'personal', 'for sale'.

classmate, classroom, classy ⇨ class.

clatter /'klætə/ *u.n* **1** number of short sharp noises made by things knocking together, things falling down etc: *There was a clatter of feet on the stairs.*

▷ *tr/intr.v* **2** (cause (s.t) to) make this noise.

clause /klɔːz/ *c.n* **1** (*grammar*) group of words containing a subject[1](4) and a predicate and forming part of a sentence: *In the sentence 'When I looked up, she was gone', the main clause is 'she was gone'.* **2** (*law*) separate section, usu numbered, in a written agreement, contract(1), will etc: *Clause 6 states that payments will be made on the first of the month.*

claustrophobia /,klɔːstrə'fəʊbɪə/ *u.n* (*medical*) fear of being in a small closed space: *I*

suffer from claustrophobia and can't ride in lifts. Compare agoraphobia.

,**claustro'phobic** *adj.*

clavicle /'klævɪkl/ *c.n* (*medical*) collarbone.

claw /klɔː/ *c.n* **1** one of the curved nails on the feet of birds, some animals and on the ends of the legs of some shellfish. **2** whole foot with claws(1). **3** mechanical device shaped like a claw(1), used for holding or lifting things.

▷ *tr.v* **4** (of an animal, bird) scratch (s.o/s.t) with a claw(1): *The cat clawed me because it was frightened.* **5** (of a person) scratch (s.o/s.t) with the nails of one's hand(s): *She clawed her husband's face in the fight.* **claw at s.o/s.t** (try to) scratch s.o/s.t; (try to) get hold of s.o/s.t with one's hands: *He clawed at the rocks to stop himself falling.*

clay /kleɪ/ *u.n* (also *attrib*) kind of thick sticky earth, often light brown or grey, that becomes hard when baked, used for making bricks, pots, china(2) etc.

,**clay 'court** *c.n* (,**clay-'court** when *attrib*) tennis court with a hard surface. Compare grass court, hard court.

clean /kliːn/ *adj* Opposite dirty. **1** (washed or wiped) free from dirt, dust etc: *His hands were clean. He wore a clean shirt.* **2** not yet used: *I need a clean sheet of paper to write on.* **3** (of a person, an animal etc) neat and tidy in her/his/its habits: *Monkeys are not very clean animals.* **4** honest; pure; free from crime: *He has led a clean life.* **5** (of language, jokes etc) not indecent(1); not obscene: *Keep your language clean in front of the children, please.* ⇨ unclean(1). **6** without rough edges; smooth: *The saw made a clean cut through the wood. The new aircraft has very clean lines.* (**get, give s.o) a clean bill of health** (get etc) a statement that one's/s.o has (now) no illness or disease, usu after having been ill. **make a clean breast of s.t** ⇨ breast. (**make**) **a clean sweep** (**of s.t**) ⇨ sweep. (**start with) a clean sheet/slate** ⇨ slate[1](*n*).

▷ *adv* **7** all the way (through s.t): *The axe went clean through the wood.* **8** completely: *I'm sorry, I clean forgot the appointment.* ⇨ clear(11). **be clean out of s.t** (*informal*) not have any of s.t that one normally has, e.g because it has been used or sold: *The shop was clean out of soap because of the strike.* **come clean** (*informal*) tell the truth, esp about s.t one has tried to keep secret: *He only came clean and told them where the money was when they threatened him.*

▷ *sing.n* **9** (often *give s.t a* (*good* etc) —) (complete etc) freeing from dirt, e.g by washing, wiping, brushing: *Could you give the room a clean as we have visitors tomorrow?*

▷ *v* **10** *tr.v* make (s.t) free from dirt by washing etc: *He cleaned his hands.* **11** *intr.v* (usu — *easily, well* etc) (of a surface, a material etc) be able to be cleaned(10) (easily etc): *This new frying pan cleans easily.* **clean s.t down** make s.t clean(1) by washing or wiping it. **clean s.o out** (*informal*) steal or win all of s.o's money, possessions etc: *I got cleaned out in the card game.* **clean s.t out** (**a**) remove all the dirt etc from (s.t, e.g a room, a cupboard). (**b**) steal all the things from (a place): *The shop was cleaned out by the thieves.* ⇨ clean-out. **clean (s.t) up** (**a**) make (s.t) clean(1) or tidy, esp after s.t has happened: *They had a big job* *cleaning up after the storm.* (**b**) get rid of (crime, criminals etc) from a place: *The government is trying to clean up the city.* (**c**) (*informal*) win, get, a lot (of money etc): *He cleaned up thousands of pounds on his first deal.*

'**cleaner** *c.n* **1** person who cleans offices, things etc. **2** device, substance etc that cleans things.

'**cleaners** *def.pl.n* shop that cleans clothes etc: *Could you take my suit to the cleaners?*

'**cleaning** *u.n* clothes etc which need to be or have been cleaned: *Could you collect the cleaning from the shop?*

'**cleaning ,lady** *c.n* (*pl -ies*) (also '**cleaning ,woman** (*pl ,women*)) woman whose job is to clean offices, houses etc.

cleanliness /'klenlınıs/ *u.n* fact or state of being clean(1).

'**cleanly** /'klenlı/ *adj* (*old use*) = clean(1).

▷ *adv* /'kli:nlı/ neatly and tidily, without rough edges: *The saw cut cleanly through the wood.*

'**clean-,out** *sing.n* **1** act of making a place clean. ⇒ clean s.t out(a). **2** act of stealing everything in a place. ⇒ clean s.t out(b).

cleanse /klenz/ *tr.v* (often — *s.t* of *s.t*) (*formal*) make (s.t) clean(1) (by removing s.t); wash, wipe, (the dirt from s.t): *He cleansed the wound before putting on a bandage.*

cleanser /'klenzə/ *c.n* **1** substance, e.g a liquid, powder, that cleans(10) a surface: *He used a powerful cleanser to get rid of the stains on the carpet.* **2** cream or oil used to clean the face.

clean-shaven /,kli:n 'ʃeɪvn/ *adj* (of a man's face) not having a beard or moustache.

'**clean-,up** *u.n* (also *attrib*) **1** act of making (a place) clean: *This room needs a good clean-up.* **2** act of getting rid of crime, criminals etc: *The police led the clean-up operations in the city.*

clear /klıə/ *adj* **1** not having anything in the way so that one can see through, beyond, into etc (s.t); free from clouds, marks, dust, dirt etc: *clear glass*; *a clear sky.* ⇒ unclear(1). **2** not having anything in the way so that one can move freely: *a clear road.* **3** easy to see, hear or understand: *clear details in a picture; a clear speaker.* Opposite unclear(1). **4** (of one's mind, thoughts etc) free from guilt, not worried: *My conscience is clear; I was not responsible for the accident.* **5** (*pred*) (often be — about s.t; be — that . . .) understanding well, certain, (about s.t, that . . . etc): *He's quite clear that he will not take the job.* Opposite unclear(3). **6** (*pred*) (often be — (to s.o) that . . .) plain; showing no doubt (in s.o's mind): *It's quite clear to me that he's lying.* **7** (*pred*) (usu be — of s.t) not touching (s.t); having moved away (from s.t): *When the ship was clear of the harbour, it began to move faster.* **8** (*pred*) (usu be — of s.t) free (from s.t); no longer affected (by s.t): *If only I was clear of debt, I could buy a horse.* **9** (esp of length of time) complete and without interruption: *I need three clear days* (or *three days clear*) *to do the job.* **10** (of profit etc) complete, after all expenses have been paid: *He made a clear (profit of) £5000 on the deal.* **get s.t clear** (*informal*) make s.t plain or obvious, esp by stating it or having it stated firmly: *Get this clear – I don't like it.* **make it/ oneself/s.t clear** state s.t firmly, explain s.t, so that there is no misunderstanding: *I must make it clear that I cannot permit you to do this.*

▷ *adv* **11** completely: *The thieves got clear away with*

the jewellery. ⇒ clean(8). **12** (often — of s.o/s.t) out of the way (of s.o/s.t); (moving so as to be) no longer touching s.o/s.t: *He only just managed to jump clear of the car.* (**say s.t**) **loud and clear** ⇒ loud(1). **stand clear of the doors** etc (request in a station, a lift etc to) move so that the doors, gates etc that are opening or closing do not hit one (and the train, the lift etc can move).

▷ *def.n* **13 be in the clear** (*informal*) be free from blame or guilt: *This time he was in the clear because he could prove he was with friends when the crime was committed.* ⇒ all-clear (⇒ all).

▷ *v* **14** *intr.v* become easy to see through, beyond, into etc; become calmer after being worried etc: *The sky cleared after the storm. Her face cleared when she heard the news.* **15** *tr/intr.v* (often — (s.t) away (from s.t/s.w)) take (s.t) away from s.t/s.w so that the surface is free, one can move etc: *Could you clear (the table), please. The road was cleared of all people and cars so that the president could drive down it.* **16** *tr.v* (often — s.o of s.t) show, state, that (s.o) is free (from blame), not guilty (of a crime): *He was cleared of all responsibility for the accident.* **17** *tr.v* move above, over, beyond, (s.t) so that one does not touch it: *They cleared the trees with only a few inches to spare.* **18** *tr.v* make or get (an amount of money) as profit: *He cleared £5000 on the deal.* **19** *tr.v* allow (s.t, e.g goods) to go through after examining them: *The customs men cleared the goods after some delay.*

clear the air ⇒ air(*n*).

clear (s.t) away (from s.t/s.w) ⇒ clear(15).

clear s.o/s.t of s.t ⇒ clear(15,16).

clear off (*informal*) go away, esp in a hurry, so as not to be caught etc: *Clear off before I call the police!*

clear out (*informal*) go away, leave a place: *I wish you'd clear out and leave me alone.* **clear s.t out** (**a**) get rid of s.t one does not want: *He had to clear out all the rubbish.* (**b**) make (a place) empty, clean etc by taking out everything: *He cleared out the room and burnt all the old furniture.* ⇒ clear-out.

clear one's throat ⇒ throat.

clear up (of weather) become brighter, esp after rain, a storm, clouds etc. **clear (s.t) up** (**a**) make (s.t) tidy and clean; finish (s.t): *He cleared up (the broken glass) before he left. Pat promised she would clear up the work by the end of the month.* (**b**) make (s.t) plain; discover the truth (of s.t): *The mystery was cleared up when he admitted he had been there all the time.*

clear s.t (with s.o) get the approval or permission of s.o for (s.t one wants to do etc): *I'll just clear this with my boss and let you know.*

'**clearance** *n* **1** *u.n* (*formal*) act of taking s.t away, tidying s.t, esp so that a space is free: *The clearance of the room allowed them to decorate it more easily.* **2** *c/u.n* amount of space, distance between two things, esp of one thing that is moving over, under or near another: *There was only just enough clearance under the bridge for the bus.* **3** *c/u.n* (official) permission for s.t to happen, esp for goods to move, ships to sail etc after examination etc: *Baggage clearance at airports seems to take longer and longer.*

'**clear-,cut** *attrib.adj* (,clear 'cut when *pred*) clear(6); plain and definite: *It was a clear-cut* decision and there could be no arguing about it.

clear-'headed adj having or showing sense; thinking well: *He was very clear-headed and always got to the centre of any problem.*

clear-'headedness u.n.

'clearing c.n open area (in a wood or forest) where trees do not grow or have been cut down.

'clearly adv 1 easily seen, heard or understood: *I could see Diana clearly. He spoke very clearly.* 2 without any doubt: *Clearly, he did not understand me.*

'clearness u.n. ⇒ clarity.

'clear-,out u.n act of throwing away things no longer wanted so that a place is empty, tidy etc.⇒ clear s.t out.

,clear'sighted adj able to think and understand well: *Matthew has a very clearsighted view of what he will train for.*

,clear'sightedness u.n.

'clear,way c.n (UK) section of a road where cars etc are not allowed to stop or park.

cleavage /'kliːvɪdʒ/ n 1 c.n split or division in s.t: *There was a cleavage in the rock.* 2 c/u.n (informal) space between a woman's breasts(1), the two sides of one's bottom(3) etc.

cleave /kliːv/ tr/intr.v (p.t cleaved, cleft /kleft/ or clove² /kləʊv/, p.p cleft /kleft/ or cloven /'kləʊvn/) (formal; old use) 1 cut through (s.t) with a blow of a sharp instrument, e.g an axe: *He clove the branch in two with his axe.* 2 force (one's way) through s.w: *They had to cleave their way through the forest.* **be in a cleft stick** (fig) not be able to decide which of two things to do.

,cleft 'palate c.n division in the roof of the mouth.

,cloven 'hoof c.n (pl -s, hooves /huːvz/) foot of some animals (e.g cows, sheep) with a split in it.

cleaver /'kliːvə/ c.n kind of knife with a big blade, used esp for cutting meat, wood etc.

clef /klef/ c.n (music) sign (either 𝄢 or 𝄞) at the beginning of a line of music to show the pitch¹(4) of the notes(5,6).

cleft /kleft/ p.t,p.p of cleave.

cleft palate ⇒ cleave.

clement /'klemənt/ adj (formal) 1 showing mercy, esp to s.o who has done s.t wrong: *The judge was clement when sentencing the prisoner.* 2 (of weather) mild and pleasant.

'clemency u.n.

clench /klentʃ/ tr.v bring (one's hands, one's teeth etc) together tightly and firmly: *He clenched his teeth against the pain.*

clergy /'klɜːdʒɪ/ def/pl.n Christian(1) priests as a group.

'clergyman c.n (pl -men) Christian(1) priest.

cleric /'klerɪk/ c.n Christian(1) priest. ⇒ clerk(3).

'clerical adj 1 of or referring to a Christian(1) priest: *He wore a clerical collar.* 2 of or referring to the work of a clerk(1): *There's a lot of ordinary clerical work in an office.*

,clerical 'error c.n mistake made in office work, e.g in typing, doing accounts etc.

clerk /klɑːk/ c.n 1 person who works in an office, bank etc and deals with letters, accounts etc: *a bank clerk.* ⇒ clerical(⇒ cleric). 2 official in charge of the business of a local town council:

the town clerk. 3 official in a parish who is not a priest. ⇒ cleric.

clever /'klevə/ adj 1 having or showing a good mind; able to think clearly, understand things: *Neal's a very clever child and will be very successful.* 2 having or showing good ability to do or make things: *He's very clever with his hands and makes all his own furniture.* 3 (of ideas, things done or made) showing ability or skill: *His plan was very clever.* 4 showing ability to trick(8) officials, people. **be clever at s.t** do or know how to do s.t well: *Harry's very clever at pretending he doesn't know anything.* **too clever by half** (expression used to describe s.o who thinks he/she is more clever(4) than he/she really is).

'cleverly adv. **'cleverness** u.n.

cliché /'kliːʃeɪ/ c.n (derog) expression, saying, idea etc that has been used too often and so loses its value: *His speech was full of clichés.*

click /klɪk/ c.n 1 (often — of s.t) small short sound made when s.t hard hits another thing, when s.t is turned or pressed etc: *He heard the click of the key in the lock. There was a click of cameras as she appeared on the steps.*

▷ v 2 tr/intr.v (cause (s.t) to) make a click(1): *The soldier clicked his heels together.* 3 (often — with s.o) (informal) (esp of s.t s.o has said that was not immediately clear) be understood: *It suddenly clicked with me what he was trying to explain.* 4 intr.v (often — with s.o) (informal) become a success; be liked (by s.o): *The television programme really clicked with viewers all over the country.* 5 intr.v (informal) (of two people) become very friendly, enjoy one another's company: *At their first meeting the two of them clicked immediately.* **click shut** (of a door, gate etc) close with the catch or lock making a noise: *The gate clicked shut after him.*

client /'klaɪənt/ c.n 1 person who uses (and pays for) the services of a professional person, such as a lawyer, accountant etc. 2 (formal) regular customer in a shop or place providing a service, e.g a hairdresser(2): *He had a large number of clients.*

clientèle /ˌkliːɒn'tel/ u.n (formal) group of clients(2), usu served by one shop etc: *He had several film-stars among his clientèle.*

cliff /klɪf/ c.n (face of a) high steep rock on a coast: *He was cut off by the tide and the cliff was too steep for him to climb.*

'cliff,hanger c.n point in a story or situation where the action has stopped at a critical moment and one does not know what is going to happen next: *It was a real cliffhanger and everybody was going to have to watch the second part of the programme to find out what happened.*

climate /'klaɪmɪt/ c/u.n 1 general weather conditions in a certain area: *I prefer a warm climate to a cold one.* 2 general conditions in a country, esp in terms of its politics, what people think etc: *The climate of opinion was that the government should resign.*

climatic /klaɪ'mætɪk/ adj of or referring to climate(1): *climatic regions.*

cli'matically adv.

climatology /ˌklaɪmə'tɒlədʒɪ/ u.n science and study of climate(1).

climax /'klaɪmæks/ c.n (pl -es) **1** (often — of s.t) highest point or moment (in a number of events); most important point (in a story, book etc): *The climax of his* career(2) *was when he was made Prime Minister. The climax of the book was the discovery of the jewels.* **2** orgasm.
▷ intr.v **3** have or reach a climax.

climb /klaɪm/ c.n **1** act or result of climbing (⇨ climb(3–6)): *He enjoys a good climb in the mountains. The aircraft went into a steep climb.* **2** steep place (to be climbed(3)): *We have quite a climb in front of us.*
▷ v **3** tr/intr.v go up (s.t) from a lower position to a higher one or to the top of (s.t), often using both one's hands and one's feet, a rope etc: *He climbed the ladder/tree. They were the first people to climb the mountain. He climbed higher until he could see over the house.* **4** tr/intr.v go up or down (a mountain, ladder etc), over (a wall etc), esp using one's hands and feet: *I've climbed in the Alps very often. We climbed down carefully.* **5** intr.v (of an aircraft, a road etc) go higher: *The aircraft had to climb steeply to avoid the houses.* **6** intr.v move higher in one's social position, career(1) etc: *He quickly climbed to the top of his profession.* **climb down** (a) ⇨ climb(4). (b) (fig; informal) admit that one is wrong; stop being against s.o/s.t: *After all his arguments he suddenly climbed down and said we were right after all.* ⇨ climb-down.
'climb-,down c.n admission that one was wrong. ⇨ climb down(b).
'climber c.n **1** person who climbs(3) mountains etc. **2** plant that climbs(4) a wall etc. **social climber** ⇨ social.
'climbing u.n art and practice of climbing (⇨ climb(3)) mountains. **go climbing** climb(3) as an activity or sport.

clinch /klɪntʃ/ c.n **1** (often be in, go into, a —) (of two people) tight hold of one another with the arms, esp in a fight, when in love etc: *The lovers went into a clinch.*
▷ v **2** tr/intr.v hold (one another) in a clinch(1): *The* boxers(1) *clinched in the middle of the ring.* **3** tr.v (informal) make (an agreement); settle (a business matter): *The deal was clinched in two hours.*
'clincher c.n (informal) final point, argument etc that settles or decides s.t: *The real clincher was his offer to pay immediately.*

cling /klɪŋ/ intr.v (p.t,p.p clung /klʌŋ/) (usu — (on)to s.o/s.t; — together) **1** hold tightly ((on)to s.o/s.t, each other) and not let go: *She clung onto him in the water because she could not swim.* **2** (fig) be very dependent (on s.o/s.t) and not want to leave (her/him) or to stop (doing s.t): *He clings to his mother even though he's now an adult.*
'cling-,film u.n kind of clear plastic film(1), used to wrap things, esp food, and stop air getting in.
'clinging adj (derog) very dependent; showing too much need: *She's very clinging and never lets her son go out on his own.*

clinic /'klɪnɪk/ c.n (part of a) hospital or other building where special medical services are provided, examinations are carried out etc: *I've got an appointment at an eye clinic next week.*
'clinical adj **1** of or referring to a clinic. **2** (attrib) of or referring to the examination of patients, esp as a method of teaching and learning: *clinical*

medicine. **3** (looking at s.t) without much feeling; (being) calm and not affected: *George has a rather clinical* attitude(2) *to his friends.*

clink /klɪŋk/ sing.n **1** short ringing sound made by things, e.g coins, glasses, hitting together. **be in (the) clink** (informal) be in (a) prison. **get out of (the) clink** leave (a) prison.
▷ tr/intr.v **2** (cause (s.t) to) make the sound of a clink(1): *They clinked their glasses together. The coins clinked in his pocket as he moved.*

clip /klɪp/ c.n **1** small piece of bent wire, plastic etc used for holding or fastening things together: *He used a clip to keep the sheets of paper together.* ⇨ hair-grip, paper-clip. **2** brooch: *She wore a gold clip on her dress.* **3** act or result of cutting hair, grass etc with scissors, shears(2) etc: *He gave the* hedge(1) *a short clip.* **4** (informal) short sharp blow with the hand: *I'll give you a good clip around the ear if you don't stop that noise!*
▷ v (-pp-) **5** tr.v fasten (s.t) (to s.t else) using a clip(1) or s.t like it: *He clipped the sheets of paper together so that he wouldn't lose them. Clip this cheque to your application.* **6** tr/intr.v fasten or fix (s.t, e.g a brooch, pin etc) on(to s.t else, e.g a dress): *She clipped her diamond pin (on) to her dress. Her new brooch just clips on.* **7** tr.v cut off (s.t, esp hair, wool etc from an animal, leaves from a hedge(1) etc) with scissors, shears(2) etc: *Some dogs have their hair clipped into peculiar shapes.* ⇨ clipping(2). **8** tr.v (often — s.t from s.t; — s.t out (of s.t)) take (s.t, esp an article) (from a newspaper) by cutting it out with scissors: *He clipped the photograph of himself out of the newspaper.* ⇨ clipping(3). **9** tr.v take a small piece out of (a ticket) with a clipper(2) to show that it has been used: *The guard was coming along the train clipping tickets.* **10** tr.v (informal) give (s.o) a short sharp blow: *I'll clip you if you don't keep quiet!*
'clipper c.n **1** kind of fast sailing ship with many sails. **2** (usu pl) instrument or tool for cutting things: *a nail clipper; hedge(1) clippers.*
'clipping n **1** u.n act of cutting with scissors, shears(2) etc: *They are bringing in the sheep for their yearly clipping.* **2** c.n piece(s) cut from s.t: *He swept up the* hedge(1) *clippings.* **3** c.n article etc cut from a newspaper etc: *She has a whole book of clippings about her favourite film-star.*

clique /kli:k/ c.n (usu derog) small group of people with special interests who act together and do not let other people join them.
'cliquish adj.

clitoris /'klɪtərɪs/ c.n (pl -es) part of the female sex organ that is very sensitive and becomes hard and larger during sexual intercourse.

cloak /kləʊk/ n **1** c.n kind of long loose coat without sleeves(1) that is worn over other clothes. **2** sing.n (often (under) a/the — of s.t) (formal) hidden or secret way: *They reached the village under the cloak of darkness.*
▷ tr.v **3** (formal) hide (s.t); keep (s.t) secret: *He cloaked his real intentions with a lot of talk about helping his neighbours.*
,cloak-and-'dagger attrib.adj (of stories, books etc) of or referring to crime, mystery, spies(1) etc.
'cloak,room c.n **1** room or place, usu in a public building, e.g a theatre or restaurant, where coats, bags etc can be left. **2** (polite word for a) room

with lavatories and basins, usu in a public building: *Where is the ladies' cloakroom, please?*

clock /klɒk/ *c.n* **1** instrument for measuring time in minutes, hours (and sometimes days, months and years). **2** (*informal*) instrument that looks like a clock(1), used for measuring other things, e.g speed, number of miles travelled etc: *The clock showed that the car had done 75 000 miles.* **alarm/digital clock** ⇨ alarm, digital. **against the clock** in order to get s.t done in or before a certain fixed time: *It was a race against the clock to get the sea wall repaired before the next tide.* **around the clock** = round the clock. **cuckoo clock** ⇨ cuckoo. **on the clock** (having a certain distance, time etc) showing on the clock(2). **put the clock back** (*fig*) stop progress in new or modern things, ideas etc and return to older, out-of-date ones: *The Government's action is likely to put the clock back 50 years.* **put the clock(s) back/forward** turn the time on clocks(1) back/forward by one hour because of the official changing of the time during the summer. **round the clock** (ˌround-the-ˈclock when *attrib*) for 24 hours, esp in order to complete s.t: *We worked round the clock to complete the order.* **watch the clock** (*informal*) be continually thinking of the time while one is working, esp looking forward to the moment one can officially stop work at the end of the day. ⇨ clockwatcher, clockwatching.
▷ *tr.v* **3** record (a certain amount of time, a speed etc) according to a clock(1,2), esp in a race, over a certain distance: *He clocked 9.6 seconds for the 100 metres. The racing car clocked 250 kilometres per hour on its first run.* **clock in/on** record the time on a special clock(2) when one arrives to start work in a factory, office etc. **clock off/out** record the time on a special clock(2) when one stops work in a factory, office etc. **clock s.t up** (*informal*) record a certain distance travelled, a certain number of points etc: *I've clocked up 25 000 miles in my car this year.*
ˈclock,face *c.n* front of a clock(1) showing the hours, minutes etc.
ˈclock,watcher *c.n* (*derog*) person who continually thinks of the moment when work stops. ⇨ watch the clock (⇨ clock(*n*)).
ˈclock,watching *u.n*.
ˈclock,wise *adj/adv* (moving around) in the same direction as the hands(4) of a clock (in a circular movement from left to right): *Turn the handle clockwise to open the tin.* Opposite anti-clockwise.
ˈclock,work *u.n* (also *attrib*) mechanism with gears(1) and springs³(1) that can be wound up, esp in toys, to produce movement: *a clockwork railway engine.* **(as) regularly as clockwork** regularly and never changing the time(s): *He arrives at 8 o'clock as regularly as clockwork.* **(go) like clockwork** (of a plan etc) (be done) very easily or exactly as planned: *The plan went like clockwork and we finished early.*
clod /klɒd/ *c.n* **1** (often — *of s.t*) thick sticky wet lump (of earth etc): *Clods of mud were sticking to his boots.* **2** (*derog; informal*) stupid or clumsy(1) person: *You stupid clod!*
ˈclod,hopper *c.n* (*derog; informal*) stupid or clumsy person.
clog¹ /klɒg/ *c.n* kind of shoe made of wood or with just the sole³(1) made of wood.

clog² /klɒg/ *tr/intr.v* (-gg-) (often — (*s.t*) (*up*) with *s.t*) (cause (s.t, esp a pipe, drain(1) etc) to) become blocked (with s.t, e.g earth, leaves, waste material etc): *The waste pipe is clogged (up) with mud and the water can't get through.*

cloister /ˈklɔɪstə/ *c.n* (usu *pl*) covered place with open arches¹(1) on one side and usu surrounding a courtyard or garden, forming part of a religious building such as a monastery or convent or part of a college.

close¹ /kləʊs/ *adj* **1** (often — *to s.o/s.t*) very near (to s.o/s.t) in space, distance, time etc: *The house is close to the sea. It was close to 10 o'clock when we arrived.* **2** (of family relations, friends) very near; very friendly: *He's a close relation of mine. They are close friends.* **3** (usu *attrib*) thorough; in great detail: *The report requires close examination. Pay close attention while I explain the background.* **4** (of a competition, race etc) with very little space or difference separating the people who win and the ones who lose: *It was a close game and the home side won by just one point.* **5** (*attrib*) with not much space in between; tight: *The dress was a close fit.* ⇨ close-fitting. **6** (usu *pred*) (of weather, the air one breathes) too warm and still, esp before a storm: *The weather was close and it felt as though a storm was coming.* **7** (*pred*) (often *be — about s.t*) (of a person) not saying very much; (be) very secretive (about oneself, one's past life etc): *He's very close; I never knew what he did when he worked for the government.* **a close call/shave/thing** (*informal*) a lucky escape by a very small margin(3): *That was a very close shave – we almost crashed into that other car.* **keep a close watch on s.o/s.t** watch s.o/s.t with great attention, usu for some time.
▷ *adv* **8** (often — *to s.o/s.t*) very near (to s.o/s.t): *We live close to the sea. We came closer to the coast.* **close at/to hand** ⇨ hand(*n*). **close by** /ˌkləʊs ˈbaɪ/ very near to s.t in space, distance: *There is a railway station close by.* **close on/to s.t** almost, very nearly s.t, esp a number, time etc: *Close to 10 000 people went on the march.* **close to/up** /ˌkləʊs ˈtuː/ˈʌp/ when seen from a very short distance after having been further away: *From a distance the town looked beautiful; close to, it was disappointing.* ⇨ close-up.
▷ *n* **9** *c.n* area and buildings round a cathedral. **10** *unique n* (with capital **C** in names) name for a street or road, often one that is closed at one end: *12 Ash Close, London.*
ˈclose-ˌfitting *attrib.adj* (of clothes) following the shape of the body; tight.
ˈclosely *adv* **1** thoroughly, in great detail: *Pam looked closely at the picture.* **2** very much; almost: *He resembles his father closely.*
ˈcloseness *u.n*.
ˈclose-ˌup *c.n* (also *attrib*) photograph or film taken from very near s.o/s.t so that he/she/it, esp a person's face, takes up the whole area of the picture. ⇨ close to/up.

close² /kləʊz/ *sing.n* **1** (often *at the — of s.t*) end or finish (of an activity, game, length of time etc): *At the close of the meeting they had only reached agreement on one point.* **bring s.t to a close** (*formal*) end s.t, esp a meeting or discussion, in a formal way. **(at) (the) close of play** (at) the time when a game, esp cricket¹, ends for the day: *Close of play today will be 7 pm. At the* close of play they had scored 250 runs. **come to a close** end: *The meeting came to a close without anything being decided.* **draw to a close** (*formal*) (of an activity, and sometimes a person's life) end in a gradual way: *His life is drawing peacefully to a close.*

▷ *tr/intr.v* **2** (cause (s.t) to) become shut, no longer open, e.g by moving s.t into the way: *Close your eyes and I'll give you a present. His eyes closed and he fell asleep. Close the gate when you leave. The door closed behind her.* **3** (cause (s.t) to) stop, be no longer in operation, either for a short time or for ever: *He usually closes the shop* (or *The shop usually closes*) *at 5.30 pm. They've closed the factory* (or *The factory has closed*) *and now 600 people are out of work.* ⇨ close (s.t) down, close (s.t) up. **4** (cause (s.t, e.g an activity, meeting, discussion) to) end, usu formally: *He closed the meeting* (or *The meeting closed*) *with a vote of thanks to the chair* (3). **close (s.t) down** (a) (cause s.t, esp a business, a factory to) shut for a long time, often for ever: *The factory closed down with the loss of 600 jobs.* (b) (of a radio or television broadcast) (cause (s.t) to) stop broadcasting at the end of the day: *And now we're closing down but we'll be back on the air at 5 am tomorrow.* ⇨ closedown (2). **close one's eyes to s.t** ⇨ eye (*n*). **close the gap** ⇨ gap. **close in** (of days) become much shorter because it is autumn and there are fewer hours of daylight: *The days are closing in and it's usually dark by 5 o'clock.* **close in** (**on s.o/s.t**) come very much nearer (to s.o/s.t), surround (s.o/s.t): *The army was closing in on the town.* **close one's mind to s.t** ⇨ mind¹. **close s.t off** put barriers (1) across s.t, esp a road, to stop people using it etc: *The police have closed off the road after the accident.* **close (s.t) up** (a) shut (s.t) completely so that it is not open for use etc: *He closed up* (*the shop*) *for the holidays.* (b) (cause (a space between two people, things etc) to) become smaller: *Would you please close up so that people behind you can get in.*

closed *adj* (of a shop, building etc) not open to the public: *The shop is closed on Wednesday afternoons.* (**be**) **a closed book** (**to s.o**) ⇨ book (*n*). **have a closed mind** (**about s.t**) ⇨ mind¹.

‚closed-‚circuit 'tele‚vision *u.n* system of television broadcasting that is not sent out to the public but kept for viewing in different places in a building or in several buildings: *The college has closed-circuit television so that students can watch lectures outside if the lecture room is full.*

'close‚down *u.n* **1** act of a business, theatre etc shutting for ever: *The factory closedown led to the loss of 600 jobs.* **2** ending of a radio or television broadcast at the end of the day. ⇨ close (s.t) down.

‚closed 'shop *c.n* (existence or practice of an agreement in a) factory, office etc where only workers belonging to a certain trade union are employed.

'closing *u.n* closure: *The closing of the factory led to the loss of 600 jobs.*

'closing ‚time *c/unique n* time of day or night when a place serving the public, esp a pub, shuts.

closure /'kləʊʒə/ *c/u.n* (often — *of s.t*) (example of the) act of shutting or stopping s.t: *Competition led to the closure of many factories.*

closet /'klɒzɪt/ *c.n* **1** (US) cupboard or small room for storing things. **2** (*old use*) = water closet.

'closeted *adj* (often — *with s.o*) in a place away from other people, e.g so that one can have a private or secret conversation (with s.o).

clot /klɒt/ *c.n* **1** lump of matter, esp blood, that is mainly liquid but has some solids in it: *A blood clot formed in her brain and she had to be operated on.* **2** (*derog; informal*) silly person.

▷ *tr/intr.v* (-tt-) **3** (cause (a liquid, esp blood) to) form into a lump: *The blood around the wound had clotted.*

‚clotted 'cream *u.n* very thick cream made by beating it.

cloth /klɒθ/ *n* (*pl* cloths /klɒθs/) **1** *u.n* (one of many kinds of) woven material, made from wool, cotton, nylon etc, used for making clothes. **2** *c.n* piece of this material. **3** *c.n* piece of this material used esp for cleaning, wiping or drying things: *Give me a cloth so I can wipe up this water.* ⇨ dishcloth, facecloth, floorcloth, tablecloth.

clothe /kləʊð/ *tr.v* (*formal*) provide (s.o) with, buy (s.o), clothes to wear: *Many people are finding it very difficult to feed and clothe their children.* **clothe s.o in s.t** (often passive) (*formal*) put s.o into certain kinds of clothes or certain kinds of material: *She was clothed in silk.* **clothe s.t in s.t** (often passive) (*formal*) cover or coat s.t, esp a place, with s.t, e.g snow, trees: *The fields were clothed in snow.*

clothes /kləʊðz/ *pl.n* (all the different kinds of) things made of material that one wears to cover one's body: *His clothes always looked as though he had slept in them.* ⇨ bedclothes.

'clothes-‚hanger *c.n* = coat-hanger.

'clothes-‚horse *c.n* frame with bars on which to hang wet clothes in order to dry them.

'clothes-‚line *c.n* = washing line.

'clothes-‚peg *c.n* wood or plastic device for fixing wet clothes to a clothes-line.

clothing /'kləʊðɪŋ/ *u.n* clothes: *The shop sells various articles of clothing. You need warm clothing in winter.* ⇨ underclothing.

clotted cream ⇨ clot.

cloud /klaʊd/ *n* **1** *u.n* (large amounts of) drops of water in the sky that form into a white, grey or black mass: *The mountain was covered in cloud.* **2** *c.n* one of these masses: *There were threatening black clouds in the distance bringing the promise of heavy rain.* **3** *c.n* large mass of s.t shaped like a cloud (2): *Clouds of smoke rose from the burning house.* **4** *c.n* large group of small things, esp insects, moving together: *There was a cloud of flies around the dead animal.* **5** *c.n* (*formal* or *literary*) thing that is threatening or causing fear: *The clouds of war are gathering.* **have one's head in the clouds** ⇨ head (*n*). **under a cloud** (of a person) regarded with suspicion because of s.t wrong one may or may not have done but which has not been proved: *Henry left under a cloud though no one actually accused him of cheating in the examinations.*

▷ *v* **6** *tr.v* cause (s.t) to become not clear, blocked: *Tears clouded her eyes.* **7** *tr.v* cause (s.t, esp one's ability to do s.t) to become affected, less efficient: *His love for her clouded his judgement.* **8** *intr.v* (often — *with s.t*) become not clear (because of

s.t): *Her eyes clouded with tears.* **cloud over** (of the sky) become grey and full of clouds.
'**cloud,burst** *c.n* sudden heavy fall of rain.
'**cloudiness** *u.n* state of being cloudy.
'**cloudless** *adj* (usu *attrib*) (of the sky) with no clouds in it; bright and blue.
'**cloudy** *adj* (*-ier, -iest*) **1** (of the sky) full of clouds. **2** (of a liquid) not clear; not able to be seen through: *This water is cloudy and I don't think we should drink it.*
clout /klaʊt/ *c.n* **1** (*informal*) blow or hit with one's hand: *I'll give you a clout if you don't stop that noise!* **have a lot of, some** etc **clout (with s.o)** (*informal*) have a great deal of, some etc influence or power (in connection with s.o): *He has a lot of clout with the government so it will pay you to be nice to him.*
▷ *tr.v* **2** hit or strike (s.o) with one's hand: *She clouted him over the ear.*
clove[1] /kləʊv/ *c.n* (also *attrib*) **1** kind of tree found in warm climates with a flower bud(1) that, when dried, is used as a spice(1). **2** dried bud of this tree. **3** (usu — *of s.t*) section of a bulb(1) of certain plants: *a clove of garlic.*
clove[2] /kləʊv/ *p.t* of cleave.
cloven /'kləʊvn/ *p.p* of cleave.
clover /'kləʊvə/ *u.n* kind of small green plant, usu with three leaves and white, pink or purple flowers, often found in grass and used as food for cattle. **(be) in clover** (*fig*; *informal*) (be) in great comfort and wealth (because of s.t one has done or sometimes because of luck etc): *If she marries Paul, she'll be in clover for the rest of her life.*
clown /klaʊn/ *c.n* **1** person, usu working in a circus, who dresses in funny clothes and tries to make people laugh by her/his actions, jokes etc. **2** person who behaves in a funny way or who looks silly to other people.
▷ *intr.v* **3** (often — *about/around*) act in a funny or silly way.
'**clownish** *adj* (acting) in a funny or silly way.
'**clownishly** *adv.* '**clownishness** *u.n.*
club[1] /klʌb/ *c.n* **1** group of people who come or meet together for a reason, esp an activity, e.g to play games, amuse themselves, take part in s.t special: *Jane belongs to the local sports/youth club.* **2** building or place where such people meet: *He goes to the club every Thursday evening to play squash*[2].
▷ *intr.v* (*-bb-*) **3 club together (to do s.t)** (of a group of people) join together and each give a certain amount of money (so that s.t can be bought for s.o, the whole amount can be given to s.o): *They all clubbed together to buy him a leaving present.*
'**club ,class** *u.n* class(5) of travel by air for business people, between first class and economy class.
club[2] /klʌb/ *c.n* **1** heavy stick, usu made of wood and often thicker at one end, used to hit s.o/s.t with. **2** = golf club(1).
▷ *tr.v* (*-bb-*) **3** (often — *s.o to death*) hit (s.o) with a club[2](1) or similar heavy object (and kill her/him): *They clubbed him as he came out of the shop.*
club[3] /klʌb/ *c.n* one of a set of playing cards with one or more black shapes on it that look like this ♣: *the five of clubs.*

cluck /klʌk/ *c.n* **1** sound (like one) made by a hen.
▷ *intr.v* **2** make the sound of a cluck(1).
clue /kluː/ *c.n* **1** fact, information, knowledge, object etc that helps to find the answer to a question or a mystery, esp one that helps to solve a crime, find a criminal etc: *The police could find no clues as to who had murdered him.* **2** written statement that helps to solve a problem or crossword: *I could only do six clues in the crossword.* **not have a clue (about s.t)** (*informal*) know nothing (about s.t): *Peter tries to pretend he knows all about modern art but really he hasn't a clue.*
▷ *tr.v* **3 clue s.o in (on s.t)** (*informal*) give s.o information about s.t: *He clued him in on the latest developments.* **4 be (all) clued up (about s.t)** (*informal*) know a lot (about a subject): *He's very clued up about modern painting.*
'**clueless** *adj* (*derog*; *informal*) (of a person) knowing nothing; stupid.
clump /klʌmp/ *c.n* (often — *of s.t*) **1** group (of trees, bushes, grass etc) growing together. **2** mass (of earth etc): *There were several clumps of mud on his boots.* **3** noise (made by heavy footsteps, boots etc): *the clump of heavy boots on the stairs.*
▷ *intr.v* **4** (often — *about/around* etc) make a clump(3): *He clumped across the wooden floor.*
clumsy /'klʌmzɪ/ *adj* (*-ier, -iest*) (*derog*) **1** (of a person) awkward; not able to do things well or neatly, to move easily etc: *He's so clumsy and he's always breaking plates when he does the washing-up.* **2** (of objects) awkwardly made, difficult in shape etc: *The design*[3] *of the cupboard is a bit clumsy.* **3** (of s.t one says) not very well thought out or said; likely to hurt s.o: *His clumsy remark made her blush(2).*
'**clumsily** *adv.* '**clumsiness** *u.n.*
clung /klʌŋ/ *p.t,p.p* of cling.
cluster /'klʌstə/ *c.n* **1** (often — *of s.o/s.t*) number of people or things grouped very closely together: *There was a cluster of people around the accident. He picked several clusters of grapes.*
▷ *intr.v* **2** (usu — (*together*) (a)*round s.o/s.t*) form into a group (around s.o/s.t): *They clustered around the noticeboard to read the statement.*
clutch /klʌtʃ/ *c.n* **1** (often — *on s.o/s.t*) very tight hold with a hand or hands (on s.o/s.t): *He felt his clutch on the rope slipping and he started to slide backwards.* **2** device in a car etc that can make the engine drive the wheels or stop it from doing so. **3** (also '**clutch-,pedal**) pedal(1) that works a clutch(2). ⇒ let in/out the clutch. **4** number (of baby birds) born at the same time. **5** number (of eggs) produced by a female bird, esp at the same time. **be in, fall into, s.o's clutches** be in, come into, s.o's power or control: *We fell into the clutches of a band of robbers.* **let in/out the clutch** push down, let out, the clutch(3) of a car etc with one's foot so that the engine can drive, stops driving, the wheels.
▷ *tr.v* **6** hold (s.o/s.t) very tightly: *She clutched her handbag to stop the thieves stealing it.* **clutch at s.o/s.t** try very hard to get hold of s.o/s.t: *She clutched at the branch of the tree to stop herself falling.* **clutch at straws** ⇒ straw.
clutter /'klʌtə/ *u.n* **1** (number of) things lying

about in an untidy way: *My son's room is always full of clutter.*
▷ *tr.v* **2** (often — *s.t* (**up**) **with** s.t) make (a place, a room etc) untidy (with a number of things): *His desk is always cluttered with papers.*

cm *written abbr* centimetre(s).

Cmdr *written abbr* Commander(1).

CO /ˌsiːˈəʊ/ *abbr* **1** Commanding officer. **2** *written abbr* conscientious objector.

Co /kəʊ/ **1** *abbr* company (used in business titles): *Green & Co.* **2** *written abbr* county: *Co Down.*

c/o *written abbr* care of, used in an address to show that the person who is named should give the letter etc to the person whom it is intended for: *Miss M Smith, c/o Mrs L Miller, 5 Park St, London.*

coach /kəʊtʃ/ *c.n* **1** (also *attrib*) bus used for travelling a long distance or for carrying private groups of people: *We went in a coach party from Manchester to London.* **2** carriage on a railway train that carries passengers. **3** person who trains people in a sport: *a tennis coach.* **4** (*old use*) carriage pulled by horses in which people ride. **by coach** using a coach(1,4): *travel by coach.*
▷ *tr.v* **5** train (s.o) in a sport; teach (s.o) s.t: *I coached him for the Olympic Games. My teacher is coaching me for the university* interviews(1).

'coach-ˌtour *c.n* holiday in a coach(1) that visits several places or countries.

coagulate /kəʊˈægjʊˌleɪt/ *tr/intr.v* (cause (s.t, esp a liquid such as blood) to) become thick: *The blood around the wound had coagulated.*

coagulant /kəʊˈægjʊlənt/ *c/u.n* (*technical*) substance that helps to make s.t else coagulate.

coagulation /kəʊˌægjʊˈleɪʃən/ *u.n.*

coal /kəʊl/ *n* **1** *u.n* kind of hard black mineral found under the ground and burnt to give heat, electricity etc. **2** *c.n* piece of this mineral: *live* (= burning) *coals.* **haul s.o over the coals** (*informal*) speak to s.o in a critical way, usu about s.t he/she has done wrong.

'coal-ˌcellar *c.n* place under a house where coal is stored.

'coalˌfield, **'coal-ˌmine**, **'coal-ˌpit** *c.n* places where coal is found and dug from under the ground.

'coal-ˌscuttle *c.n* ⇨ scuttle¹.

'coal ˌseam *c.n* long thick area of coal under the ground.

coarse /kɔːs/ *adj* **1** rough when touched: *a coarse cloth.* **2** made of large grains or pieces: *coarse sand.* Opposite fine¹(5). **3** (*derog*) not pleasant or attractive: *a coarse face/* complexion(1). **4** (*derog*) not polite; rude: *coarse language/behaviour.*

'coarsen *tr/intr.v* (cause (s.o/s.t) to) become coarse.

'coarsely *adv* in a coarse(4) way. **'coarseness** *u.n.*

coast /kəʊst/ *c.n* **1** (usu the —) land near the sea: *the coast of England; visit the coast.* **on the coast** near the sea.
▷ *intr.v* **2** move, usu downhill and without the use of power: *I put the car into* neutral(5) *and it coasted down the hill.* **coast along** (also *fig*) move or do s.t, esp work, without much effort or interest: *We coasted along, enjoying the view. He just coasts along without ever really trying to do a job well.*

'coastal *adj* of, referring to, the coast.

'coaster *c.n* kind of small ship that travels around the coast.

'coastˌguard *c/def.n* person or organization who/that rescues people from difficulties at sea or who/that tries to stop smuggling.

coat /kəʊt/ *c.n* **1** article of clothing worn out of doors over other clothes to protect oneself from the weather. ⇨ raincoat. **2** jacket(1), usu as part of a complete outfit(1): *She was wearing a coat and skirt.* **3** natural covering of fur or hairs of an animal: *The dog has a thick coat that needs regular brushing.* **4** (also **'coating**) (often — of s.t) covering of a surface of s.t (with s.t): *a coat of paint; a thin coat of dust.* ⇨ undercoat.
▷ *tr.v* **5** (often — s.t with s.t) cover (a surface) (with s.t): *The metal was coated with a rubber solution to protect it from rust.*

'coat-ˌhanger *c.n* (also **'hanger**) piece of wood, plastic etc with a hook, used for hanging one's coat or other clothes.

'coating *c.n* ⇨ coat(4).

ˌcoat of ˈarms *c.n* special sign, often in the shape of a shield with shapes, drawings of animals etc on it, that is given to s.o to show that he/she is of a noble or gentleman's family, or to a public organization such as a university or town.

coax /kəʊks/ *tr.v* **1** (often — s.o to do s.t; — s.o into, out of, (doing) s.t) make (s.o) do s.t by gentle and continual persuasion: *She tried to coax him to agree to let her go. Can you coax him out of his bad temper?* **2** (often — s.t from s.o) get (s.t) (from s.o) by persuasion: *I finally coaxed a decision from him.* **take some** etc **coaxing** be rather etc difficult to persuade: *It took very little coaxing to get him to agree.*

cob /kɒb/ *c.n* **1** main yellow part of the maize plant that one can eat. ⇨ corn-cob. **2** male swan(1). **3** horse that is used for riding.

cobalt /ˈkəʊbɔːlt/ *u.n* hard grey element(1) (a metal) that is often added to other metals to make an alloy and which is also used as a blue colouring material, *chem.symb* Co.

cobble /ˈkɒbl/ *c.n* **1** (also **'cobble-ˌstone**) square or shaped piece of stone formerly used to make a surface for roads, paths etc.
▷ *tr.v* **2** cover (a road, path etc) with cobbles(1). **3** (*old use*) mend (shoes).

'cobbler *c.n* (*old use*) person who mends shoes. **(be) a load of old cobblers** (*slang*) (be) nonsense.

'cobble-ˌstone *c.n* ⇨ cobble(1).

cobra /ˈkəʊbrə/ *c.n* kind of poisonous snake with a large flat head, found in Asia and Africa.

cobweb /ˈkɒbweb/ *c.n* network of thin threads made by a spider in order to catch insects.

Coca-Cola /ˌkəʊkə ˈkəʊlə/ *n* (*t.n*) (*informal* **Coke**; also without capitals) **1** *unique n* kind of sweet, brown-coloured drink with gas in it. **2** *c.n* bottle, cup or glass of this drink.

cocaine /kəˈkeɪn/ *u.n* (also **coˈcain**) kind of medicine used to stop pain and also used as a drug(2) to give a feeling of well-being.

cock /kɒk/ *n* **1** (also *attrib*) adult male bird, usu of the chicken family but also of other kinds: *a cock pheasant.* ⇨ hen(2). **2** *c.n* tap or valve that controls the flow of s.t. ⇨ stopcock. **3** *c/u.n* position of a lever(3) in a gun as it is ready to fire. **4** (*slang; do not use!*) *c.n. male sex organ.*
▷ *tr.v* **5** move a lever(3) in (a gun) so that it is ready

to fire: *I cocked my gun when I saw the rabbit.*
cock one's ears (up) ⇨ ear. **cock s.t up** (*slang*; do not use!) do s.t badly; make a mess of s.t: *The weather really cocked our holiday up.*

'cock-,up *c.n* (*slang*; do not use!) thing that is done badly; complete mess (2).

cockatoo /,kɒkə'tu:/ *c.n* kind of brightly-coloured parrot.

cockerel /'kɒkrəl/ *c.n* young cock.

cocker spaniel /,kɒkə 'spænɪəl/ *c.n* kind of dog with long ears and long smooth hair.

cock-eyed /'kɒk ,aɪd/ *adj* (*informal*) **1** not straight or level: *Her hat was a bit cock-eyed.* **2** not very well planned or properly thought about: *Most of his ideas are cock-eyed and I wouldn't trust him.*

cockily, cockiness ⇨ cocky.

cockney /'kɒknɪ/ *c.n* (also *attrib*) (often with capital **C**) person who was born in (esp the central city area of) London: *She's got a real cockney sense of humour (1).*

cockpit /'kɒk,pɪt/ *c.n* **1** place in an aeroplane where the pilot sits. **2** place in a racing car where the driver sits.

cockroach /'kɒk,rəʊtʃ/ *c.n* kind of large brown or black insect, found in dirty kitchens etc.

cocktail /'kɒk,teɪl/ *c.n* **1** drink with a mixture of various kinds of alcohol and sometimes fruit or fruit juices in it. **2** mixture of fruit, seafood etc, eaten cold as a starter (5).

'cock,tail ,party *c.n* (*pl -ies*) party in the early evening when cocktails are drunk.

cocky /'kɒkɪ/ *adj* (*-ier, -iest*) (*derog*; *informal*) too confident or sure of oneself: *He's a bit too cocky and one day he's going to make a mistake.*

'cockily *adv.* **'cockiness** *u.n.*

cocoa /'kəʊkəʊ/ *n* (also *attrib*) **1** *u.n* seeds from a plant (cacao (2)) that are crushed to make chocolate. **2** *c/u.n* drink made from such seeds.

coconut /'kəʊkə,nʌt/ *n* (also *attrib*) **1** *c.n* large brown nut, grown on a kind of palm², with a hard white substance inside it that one can eat and a kind of milk that one can drink. **2** *u.n* hard white part inside a coconut (1).

,coconut 'ice *u.n* kind of sweet made from sugar and coconut (2).

,coconut 'matting *u.n* material made from the hairy outer part of coconuts (1), used for covering floors.

'coconut ,palm *c.n* tree on which coconuts (1) grow.

cocoon /kə'ku:n/ *c.n* **1** silky cover that is made around itself by a caterpillar (1) during its stage as a chrysalis.
▷ *tr/reflex.v* **2** wrap (itself, s.t) in a cocoon (1). **3** (*fig*) protect (oneself, s.t) from difficulties, danger etc.

COD /,si: ,əʊ 'di:/ *abbr* cash on delivery (1).

cod /kɒd/ *n* (*pl* cod) **1** *c.n* (also **'cod,fish** (*pl* codfish)) large kind of fish found mainly in the Atlantic ocean. **2** *u.n* (also *attrib*) flesh of this fish as food: *cod* pie.

code /kəʊd/ *n* **1** *c.n* group of laws or rules: *the* legal (2) *code.* **2** *c.n* set of general rules that people accept and live by: *a moral code; a code of honour.* **3** *c/u.n* secret writings, symbols etc used in messages etc in order to prevent s.o, esp an enemy, from understanding

it/them: *The enemy was unable to understand our codes as we were using a new system.* **4** *c/u.n* (system of) instructions etc used to make computers work. **break a code** learn how to read a code (3,4) and understand it. **in code** (of a message etc) using a code (3,4). ⇨ binary code, genetic code, Morse code.
▷ *tr.v* **5** put (a message etc) into code (3,4): *The instructions have been coded into the computer.* ⇨ decode, encode.

codicil /'kɒdɪsɪl/ *c.n* (*law*) statement added to an agreement, will² (1) etc that changes s.t in it.

codify /'kəʊdɪ,faɪ/ *tr.v* (*-ies, -ied*) make (laws) into a code (1).

codification /,kəʊdɪfɪ'keɪʃən/ *u.n.*

co-driver /,kəʊ 'draɪvə/ *c.n* person who shares the driving of a car by taking turns with another driver, e.g in a car race.

co-ed /,kəʊ'ed/ *adj* (*informal*) *abbr* co-educational.

co-education /,kəʊ ,edjʊ'keɪʃən/ *u.n* teaching of boys and girls together in the same school.

,co-,edu'cational *adj.*

coerce /kəʊ'ɜ:s/ *tr.v* **coerce s.o into (doing) s.t** make s.o do s.t against her/his will by using threats, force etc: *The army officers coerced the population into accepting them by threatening to shoot anybody who resisted.*

coercion /kəʊ'ɜ:ʃən/ *u.n.*

coercive /kəʊ'ɜ:sɪv/ *adj* using coercion.

co-exist /,kəʊɪg'zɪst/ *intr.v* (often — with s.o/s.t) live at the same time as s.o/s.t else, usu in peace, without fighting etc: *The two religions co-existed happily (with each other).*

,co-ex'istence *u.n* state of living together in peace: *Politicians are always talking about peaceful co-existence but then spend most of their country's money on weapons.*

C of E /,si: əv 'i:/ *abbr* Church of England.

coffee /'kɒfɪ/ *n* (also *attrib*) **1** *u.n* brown beans from a kind of plant that grows in hot countries which are crushed to make a hot drink or a flavouring: *coffee beans.* **2** *u.n* these beans after they have been crushed: instant (2) coffee. **3** *c/u.n* drink made from these beans. **black coffee** ⇨ black (2). **white coffee** ⇨ white (3).

'coffee ,bar *c.n* place where one can buy and drink coffee (3).

'coffee ,mill *c.n* device that crushes or grinds coffee (1) beans.

'coffee ,perco,lator ⇨ percolate (*v*).

'coffee-,pot *c.n* container for hot coffee (3).

'coffee ,shop *c.n* (*esp US*) restaurant that serves coffee (3) and food.

'coffee ,table *c.n* low table in a living-room on which one can put magazines etc.

coffin /'kɒfɪn/ *c.n* long box in which a dead body is put and then buried.

cog /kɒg/ *c.n* one of a number of teeth on the edge of a wheel that meet other teeth on another wheel usu of a different size so that when the wheels turn, the speed of one of them is greater/less than that of the other. **a cog in the wheel** (*derog*; *informal*) a person with a small job in a large organization.

'cog,wheel *c.n* wheel with cogs.

cogent /'kəʊdʒənt/ *adj* (*formal*) (of a person, argument etc) showing or having an ability to prove s.t or to argue s.t well; strong and full of force: *He was very cogent in his reasoning.*

There are cogent arguments for accepting the offer.
'**cogency** *u.n.* '**cogently** *adv.*
cogitate /'kɒdʒɪˌteɪt/ *intr.v* (often — *about/* (*up*)*on s.t*) (*formal*) think long and deeply (about etc s.t): *He cogitated about what to do.*
cogitation /ˌkɒdʒɪ'teɪʃən/ *u.n.*
cognac /'kɒnjæk/ *n* (also *attrib*) **1** *u.n* (*French*) kind of brandy(1) that is made in the Cognac area of France. **2** *c.n* bottle or glass of cognac(1).
cognizance /'kɒgnɪzəns/ *u.n.* (*formal*) **take cognizance of s.t** consider s.t: *The Minister replied that his Department would take cognizance of all the information supplied to it.*
'**cognizant** *adj* (usu — *of s.t*) (*formal*) knowing (about s.t): *I am cognizant of the facts of the case.*
cogwheel ⇒ cog.
cohabit /kəʊ'hæbɪt/ *intr.v* (often — *with s.o*) (*formal*) live together (with s.o) as though married: *Gloria has cohabited with Frank* (or *They have cohabited*) *for five years.*
cohabitation /kəʊˌhæbɪ'teɪʃən/ *u.n.*
cohere /kəʊ'hɪə/ *intr.v* (*formal*) **1** join or stick together: *The handle will cohere to the cup if the glue is almost dry.* **2** (*fig*) (of ideas etc) connect with each other: *Do the points in her report cohere well?*
co'herence, co'herency *u.n* **1** state of being joined together. **2** agreement; consistency(1).
co'herent *adj* (of ideas, s.o's speech etc) (speaking, writing, in a way that is) well thought out; agreeing with one another: *At least his version of events was coherent even if it did not agree with other people's. He was hardly coherent after the accident.* Opposite incoherent.
co'herently *adv.*
cohesion /kəʊ'hiːʒən/ *u.n* (*formal*) state of being joined together; act of joining together: *The cohesion of the molecules was examined.*
cohesive /kəʊ'hiːsɪv/ *adj* joining together or being able to do so.
coiffeur /kwɑː'fɜː/ *c.n* (*French*) person who cuts and arranges s.o's hair; hairdresser(1).
coiffure /kwɑː'fjʊə/ (*French*) person's hair that has been arranged in a certain way; hairstyle.
coil /kɔɪl/ *n* **1** *c.n* (often — *of s.t*) thing formed into the shape of a circle or a number of joined circles: *a coil of rope; a coil of hair.* **2** *c.n* piece of wire arranged in a number of circles and used to carry electricity. **3** *c/def.n* object worn inside the womb and used by women to stop them having babies.
▷ *v* **4** *tr.v* (often — *s.t up*) arrange (s.t) in a round shape: *coil a rope* (*up*); *coil one's hair round one's fingers.* **5** *intr/reflex.v* (often — *around/ round/up*) go round (oneself); curl: *The snake coiled* (*itself*) *around the tree.*
coin /kɔɪn/ *n* **1** *c.n* piece of metal money: *I got three £1 coins in my change.* **2** *u.n* metal money, esp when compared to paper money: *silver coin.* **toss/flip a coin** choose by throwing up a coin and deciding according to which side of the coin lands upwards. **the other side of the coin** (*fig*) the opposite point of view. **pay s.o in her/his own coin** (*fig*) do to s.o exactly what she/he has done to oneself or s.o else.
▷ *tr.v* **3** make (metal money). **4** invent (a new word, phrase etc): *Scientists are fond of coining new*

words. **be coining money**; **be coining it** (*in*) (*informal*) get/earn a lot of money, usu in a very short time: *He started manufacturing cheap computers and soon he was coining it in.* **to coin a phrase** to pretend jokingly that an expression one is using is new when it is not: *'That method is as old as the hills, to coin a phrase!' he said.*
coinage /'kɔɪnɪdʒ/ *n* **1** *u.n* act of making coins(1). **2** *u.n* coins(1) that are made, esp in a country: *Britain introduced* decimal(1) *coinage in 1971.* **3** *c/u.n* (*formal*) (example of the) making of new words, phrases etc: *Space technology has led to the coinage of many new words.*
coincide /ˌkəʊɪn'saɪd/ *intr.v* (often — *with s.t*) **1** happen at the same time (as s.t else): *His birthday coincided with hers* (or *Their birthdays coincided*). **2** (esp of opinions, ideas) agree; be the same as each other: *Their views coincided.*
coincidence /kəʊ'ɪnsɪdəns/ *n* **1** *c.n* thing that happens at the same time as s.t else, esp by chance or luck: *Through a number of coincidences, they found themselves together in the same hotel.* **2** *u.n* state or act of happening by chance at the same time: *It was just coincidence that they met in London.*
coincidental /kəʊˌɪnsɪ'dentl/ *adj* happening by chance at the same time.
co,inci'dentally *adv.*
coke /kəʊk/ *n* (also *attrib*) **1** *u.n* kind of coal which is made by removing the gas from it. **2** *c.n* (*t.n*) (*informal*) Coca-Cola(1). **3** *u.n* (*slang*) cocaine (as a drug(2)).
Col *written abbr* Colonel.
col *written abbr* column.
colander /'kɒləndə/ *c.n* (also '**cullender**) kind of bowl with holes in it to let water drain(5) from vegetables etc.
cold /kəʊld/ *adj* **1** being at a low temperature; not warm, esp of weather, one's body or things that are usu at a higher temperature: *a cold day; cold hands; a cold room.* Opposite hot(1). **2** (of a person, action etc) having or showing no warm or friendly feeling: *I thought he was cold in the way he treated his relatives. You'll get a cold welcome in that house.* Opposite warm. Compare cool(2). (**break out**) **in a cold sweat** ⇒ sweat(*n*). **freezing cold** ⇒ freezing. **get, give s.o the cold shoulder** (*fig*) be treated, treat s.o, in a way that is not friendly, esp by being ignored(1), or ignoring her/him. ⇒ cold-shoulder. **get/have cold feet** ⇒ foot(*n*). **in cold blood** ⇒ blood. ⇒ cold-blooded(ly/ness).
▷ *n* **3** *u/def.n* low temperature of the weather, esp in winter: *Old people do not like the cold.* Opposite heat(3). **4** *c.n* illness in the nose, the throat and sometimes the chest that shows itself by a watery substance (mucus) that blocks the nose: *She suffered from colds all through the winter. I've got a cold on my chest.* **be left out in the cold** (*fig*) not be paid attention to, be neglected, e.g during a discussion, when jobs are given etc. **catch/get/ have a cold** get etc a cold(4). **the common cold** colds(4) as a general illness, esp ones that are easy to get from other people: *Nobody has yet found a cure for the common cold.*
,**cold-'blooded** *adj* **1** having blood that is cold when the outside temperature is cold: *Snakes and fish are cold-blooded animals.* Compare warm-blooded. **2** (*fig*) who/that shows no pity:

a cold-blooded murder. ⇨ in cold blood (⇨ blood).

‚cold-'bloodedly *adv* in a cold-blooded(2) way.

‚cold-'bloodedness *u.n.*

'cold ‚comfort *u.n* remark, advice etc of not much use or value, esp for s.o who needs help or sympathy.

'cold ‚cream *u.n* kind of white cream used on the face or hands to clean or protect it/them.

‚cold 'fish *c.n* (*derog*) unfriendly person who does not show much feeling etc.

'cold ‚frame ⇨ frame(4).

‚cold 'front *c.n* cold(1) air that is passing behind and below an area of warm air. Compare warm front.

'coldly *adv* in a cold(2) way: *She treated him very coldly and refused to see him.*

'cold ‚meat *u.n* meat that has been cooked and then allowed to get cold(1).

'coldness *u.n* fact or state of being cold(1,2).

‚cold 'snap *c.n* short period of very cold(1) weather.

‚cold 'shoulder *u.n* ⇨ cold(*adj*).

‚cold-'shoulder *tr.v* treat (s.o) in an unfriendly way; ignore (s.o).

'cold ‚sore *c.n* kind of sore, usu on the lips, that comes when one has a cold(4).

‚cold 'storage *u.n* act of storing food etc in a room or building that is kept very cold(1). **put s.t in cold storage** (*fig*) decide not to do s.t now but leave it until a better time.

'cold ‚store *c.n* large room or building where food etc is kept at a very low temperature.

‚cold 'turkey ⇨ turkey.

‚cold 'war *c/def.n* actions by countries that do not like each other and that do everything against each other except actually fighting.

coleslaw /'kəʊl‚slɔː/ *u.n* kind of salad(1) containing sliced raw cabbage and mayonnaise.

colic /'kɒlɪk/ *u.n* (*medical*) pain in the stomach and bowels(1).

collaborate /kə'læbə‚reɪt/ *intr.v* (often — (*with s.o*) *on/over s.t*) **1** work together (with s.o) (on some job): *He collaborated with her* (or *They collaborated*) *on the writing of the book.* **2** work with an enemy (esp when the enemy is inside one's own country): *The mayor was hanged for collaborating with the enemy during the war.*

collaboration /kə‚læbə'reɪʃən/ *u.n.*

col'labo‚rator *c.n* person who collaborates.

collage /kɒ'lɑːʒ/ *n* **1** *c.n* painting or picture made by sticking pieces of paper, cloth, metal and/or other material on a surface. **2** *u.n* act of making collages(1) as a kind of art.

collapse /kə'læps/ *n* **1** *u.n* sudden act of falling down or breaking into pieces: *The collapse of the chimney was due to the sudden storm.* **2** *c/u.n* sudden failure of one's body or mind: *She had a nervous collapse from working too hard.* **3** *c/u.n* sudden stopping of an activity, e.g because s.o is against it, there is no money: *The bank failure led to the collapse of many small companies.*

▷ *v* **4** *intr.v* fall down suddenly: *The* barriers(1) *collapsed under the weight of people.* **5** *intr.v* fall suddenly in one's body or mind: *She collapsed in the street and died on the way to hospital.* **6** *intr.v* fail suddenly: become much lower than before, esp because of lack of confidence or support: *All our hopes collapsed when we heard the bad*

news. **7** *tr.v* (*formal*) fold (s.t); make (s.t) flatter or smaller: *The bed can be collapsed by lifting it up and bending it in the middle.*

col'lapsible *adj* that can be collapsed(7): *a collapsible chair.*

collar /'kɒlə/ *c.n* **1** part of a shirt, dress, coat, jacket(1) etc which goes around the neck and that can usu lie flat or be turned up: *Her coat had a fur collar.* **2** piece of leather, plastic(3), metal etc that goes around the neck of an animal: *a dog('s) collar; a horse collar.* (**be/get**) **hot under the collar** (*fig*) (be/become) very angry.

▷ *tr.v* (*informal*) **3** seize, take hold of, (s.o), esp by the neck or body: *I collared him as he was trying to escape.* **4** take (s.t) without permission: *Somebody collared his box of tools while he wasn't looking.*

'collar‚bone *c.n* bone that goes across the shoulder.

'collar-‚stud *c.n* kind of button that fixes a separate collar(1) to a shirt.

colleague /'kɒliːg/ *c.n* person with whom one works as part of a group: *Bob criticized his colleagues for not working as hard as he did.*

collect¹ /'kɒlekt/ *c.n* prayer that is read in Christian(1) churches during some services.

collect² /kə'lekt/ *v* **1** *tr.v* (often — *s.t together/up*) bring (a number of things) together in one place, group etc; take (a number of things) from a group of people: *He went around the room collecting* (*up*) *all the empty glasses.* **2** *tr.v* take (s.t, esp money) from a group of people who want to or have to give it: *There was a man with a box collecting money for the poor.* **3** *tr.v* buy or get (a number of things, e.g stamps, coins) over a length of time because one is interested in them: *My son collects stamps.* **4** *tr.v* go and bring (s.o) from s.w: *It was my turn to collect the children from school.* **5** *intr.v* (often — *together*) come together in a group: *The teachers collected together in the staffroom. A crowd quickly collected around the scene of the accident.* **collect oneself, one's thoughts** etc stop and think about s.t one is going to say or do before saying and doing it: *I hardly had time to collect my thoughts before I was asked to speak.*

▷ *adv* **6 call collect** (US) make a telephone call in which the cost is paid by the person answering the call.

col'lect ‚call *c.n* (US) telephone call paid by the person answering it. ⇨ reverse charge(s) call.

col'lected *adj* calm and in control of one's feelings etc: *He remained calm and collected during all the arguments.*

collection /kə'lekʃən/ *n* **1** *c/u.n* (example of the) act of collecting²(1) things: *There are now only two collections on Saturday from the postbox in our street.* **2** *c.n* money etc collected²(2) from people at a meeting etc: *During the conference, a collection was made that raised £250 for the poor.* **3** *c.n* (number of) things that s.o has collected²(3): *He has the finest collection of British paintings in the country.*

col'lective *adj* **1** (usu *attrib*) as or in a group; taken as a whole in working as a group: *Government ministers have to take collective responsibility for their actions.*

▷ *c.n* (also *attrib*) **2** = collective noun. **3** group of people who work together, esp in communist(1) or socialist countries: *Workers' collectives were set up by the* socialists. *He was sent to work on a collective farm.*

col,lective 'bargaining *u.n* negotiations between employers and employees, trade unions etc about wages, conditions of work etc.

col'lectively *adv* in a collective(1) way.

col'lective ,noun *c.n* (*grammar*) singular noun that describes a group of people, animals, things etc: *The collective noun for 'a group' of fish is 'a school'.*

col'lector *c.n* person who collects²(3) things: *a stamp collector.* **ticket collector** ⇒ ticket.

college /'kɒlɪdʒ/ *n* (also *attrib*) (with capital **C** in names) **1** *c.n* school for higher education that is sometimes part of a university: *Balliol College is part of the University of Oxford. My daughter went to a college of education to train to be a teacher. She's a college student.* ⇒ CFE. **2** *u.n* place for higher education: *I'm going to college after leaving school.* **3** *c/def.n* group of people who have special interests, knowledge or training: *the College of Physicians.*

collegiate /kə'liːdʒət/ *attrib.adj* of or referring to a college(1): *collegiate life.*

collide /kə'laɪd/ *intr.v* (often — *with s.o/s.t*) **1** meet together in a sudden and violent way; crash together: *The car collided with the bicycle* (or *The car and the bicycle collided*). ⇒ head-on(1). **2** (of opinions, views etc) disagree (with each other) strongly; be the opposite (of each other): *His and my views on the matter collided and we could not agree.*

collision /kə'lɪʒən/ *c/u.n* (example of the) act or state of colliding with s.o/s.t: *There were a number of collisions during the thick fog. He tried hard to avoid a collision with his parents over what he wanted to do.* **be in, come into, collision (with s.t) (a)** have met, meet, (s.t) in a collision: *The van came into collision with a bus as it turned the corner.*.**(b)** (*fig*) be, become, opposed to s.t: *The students came into collision with the college* authorities(2) *over the number of lectures they had to attend.* **(be) on a collision course (with s.o/s.t) (a)** (be) going in a direction where s.t else is in the way: *The two ships were on a collision course and only a last-minute change by one of them prevented a* disaster(1). **(b)** (*fig*) (be) intending to do s.t that is the opposite of what s.o else wants to do: *The unions are on a collision course with the government over the next round of wage claims.*

collie /'kɒlɪ/ *c.n* kind of sheepdog with a long nose and long hair.

collier /'kɒlɪə/ *c.n* **1** (*old use*) person who digs coal out of the ground. **2** ship that carries coal from one place to another.

colliery /'kɒlɪərɪ/ *c.n* (*pl -ies*) = coal-mine.

collision ⇒ collide.

colloquial /kə'ləʊkwɪəl/ *adj* (of language) informal in the words or phrases which one uses, esp in speech; not literary: *The tourists had difficulty in understanding what their guide said as he used many colloquial expressions.*

col'loquia,lism *c.n* informal word or phrase.

colloquy /'kɒləkwɪ/ *c.n* (*pl -ies*) (*formal*) **1** formal conversation or discussion. **2** kind of meeting or conference at which people discuss special subjects.

collusion /kə'luːʒən/ *u.n* (often *act/be in* — *with s.o*) (*formal*) secret agreement (with s.o) to act in a way that is intended to deceive or harm others: *He was accused of acting in collusion with another employee to rob the company.*

cologne ⇒ eau de cologne.

colon /'kəʊlən/ *c.n* **1** mark **:** used in writing and printing to draw attention to what follows, usu a list or an example. **2** lowest part of the intestine into which food goes.

colonel /'kɜːnl/ *c.n* (*written abbr Col*) (*military*) officer in the army or the Royal Marines below a brigadier and above a lieutenant-colonel.

colonnade /,kɒlə'neɪd/ *c.n* long row of columns that hold up a roof.

colony /'kɒlənɪ/ *c.n* (*pl -ies*) **1** country or area settled by people from another country and controlled by them: *In the fifth century BC the Greeks had many colonies around the Mediterranean.* **2** group of people who live in or near a place and who share common interests, the same nationality etc: *a nudist colony; the British colony in Hollywood.* **3** (often — *of s.t*) group (of animals, insects etc) that live together: *a colony of ants.*

colonial /kə'ləʊnɪəl/ *adj* **1** (usu *attrib*) of, referring to, belonging to, a colony(1): *The people fought against colonial rule for many years before they finally won independence.*
▷ *c.n* **2** person who is a member of a colony(1).

co'lonial,ism *c.n* political act or state of having and keeping a colony(1).

co'lonia,list *c.n* person who believes in having colonies(1).

colonization, -isation /,kɒlənaɪ'zeɪʃən/ *u.n* act of setting up a colony(1).

'colo,nize, -ise *tr.v* send people to (a country) in order to make a colony(1): *The Spanish and the Portuguese were the first to colonize large parts of South and Central America.*

'colo,nizer, -iser *c.n* person or country who/ that colonizes a country.

color ⇒ colour.

colossal /kə'lɒsl/ *adj* very big: *It was a colossal house.*

colossus /kə'lɒsəs/ *c.n* (*pl -es, colossi* /kə'lɒsaɪ/) **1** very big statue. **2** (*fig*) person who is very important: *Charles Dickens was a colossus of literature.*

colour /'kʌlə/ *attrib.adj* (US **'color**) **1** having, using, colours(2,3): *colour television; colour magazines.*
▷ *n* (US **'color**) **2** *u.n* quality (e.g blue or yellow) that one can see in the surface of an object when light shines on it: *the colour of her eyes.* **3** *c.n* example of this quality: *I prefer bright colours like red and green.* **4** *c.n* paint or dye(1) that provides this quality: *He mixed several colours together in order to get the dark green he wanted.* **5** *u.n* presence or absence of red on one's face, esp when this shows one's health or lack of it: *She lost a lot of colour during her illness.* **6** *c/u.n* type of skin one has because of one's* race²(2): *People of all colours and beliefs joined in the religious service.* **7** *u.n* quality of reality or feeling about a place; realistic(2) description of s.t: *He managed to introduce lots of colour into his description of the battle.* **be/feel/look off colour** not be/feel/ look very well. **change colour (a)** become/look

different in colour(2): *Some animals change colour as they move from place to place.* (**b**) (of the face) become paler or redder, usu because of some feeling: *His face changed colour when he heard the bad news.* **in colour** using colours(2), esp in painting, printing, a film etc, as compared to black and white. **lose colour** (of the face) become pale.

▷ *v* **8** *tr.v* (often — *s.t blue*, *red* etc) put colour(1) on (s.t) or change the colour(3) of (s.t) (to s.t): *We shall colour the walls pink.* **9** *intr.v* (often — *up*) become red in the face (because of s.t that s.o has said, done etc); blush(2): *She coloured (up) when his name was mentioned.* **10** *tr.v* give a special emphasis(1), usu one that is not true, to (what one says or writes): *He always colours his stories with adventures that could not possibly have happened.* **11** *tr.v* influence or affect (s.o/ s.t), usu for the worse: *His whole attitude was coloured by his hatred of his parents.*

'colour-,blind *adj* unable to recognize some colours(3) because one's eyes do not work properly.

'colour-,blindness *u.n.*

'coloured *adj* **1** of a certain colour(2): *She wore a grey coloured dress.* **2** having additional (perhaps untrue) details to make it more interesting etc. Opposite uncoloured(2).

▷ *c.n* **3** (also *attrib*) (often with capital **C**) (*derog*; do not use!) person who is of mixed race²(2), esp in South Africa.

'colour ,film *c/u.n* photographic film that uses colour(2,3) (and is not black and white).

'colourful *adj* **1** that has many bright colours(3): *a colourful scene.* **2** (*fig*) exciting and full of interest or detail: *He has led a very colourful life.*

'colouring *u.n.* **1** substance used to make a colour(3): *Food companies use colouring to make their products look better.* **2** colour(5) on one's face: *His natural colouring shows the effects of a very healthy life.*

'colourless *adj* **1** without (much or any) colour(2); pale: *a colourless liquid.* **2** (*derog*) (of a person, way of living etc) who/that has not much character or interest: *He's rather colourless and I find it difficult to talk to him.*

'colours *pl.n* **1** special badge, cap, shirt etc worn to show that one has reached a certain level, that one plays for a certain team etc in a sport: *He got his England colours when he was only 18.* **2** shirt and cap with patterns worn by some riders to show who owns the horses they ride: *The rider was wearing the Queen's colours.* **3** (*military*) flag of a warship; special flag of a regiment(1). **show one's true colours** (*fig*) show what one is really like, esp after having hidden one's real, usu bad, character. **with flying colours** (*fig*) very successfully: *He passed his examination with flying colours.*

'colour ,scheme *c.n* set of colours(3) used for clothes, furniture, rooms etc that are intended to go well together.

'colour ,supplement *c.n* special magazine printed in colour(1) that is provided separately with some newspapers, esp ones sold on Sundays.

colt /kəʊlt/ *c.n* **1** young male horse. **2** young person who plays in a sports team that is

lower in rank than others. **3** (*t.n*) (US) kind of gun.

columbine /'kɒləm,baɪn/ *c.n* kind of plant with bright, colourful flowers that hang down.

column /'kɒləm/ *c.n* **1** vertical piece (of stone, wood, metal etc) that supports a roof, floor etc above it: *The road was carried across the river on a number of large columns.* **2** (usu — *of s.t*) thing like a column(1): *A column of smoke rose above the town.* **3** (often — *of s.o/s.t*) long line (of people, things one after the other): *a column of trucks.* **4** arrangement of lines of type, list of numbers etc in a vertical block on a page: *This dictionary has two columns. Will you please add up this column of figures for me?* **5** article in a newspaper, magazine etc written regularly by s.o: *His column on politics is always amusing.* **a/the fifth column** people in a country who work with an outside enemy to help the enemy conquer it. **personal column** ⇨ personal. **spinal column** ⇨ spinal.

columnist /'kɒləm,nɪst/ *c.n* person who writes a column(5).

coma /'kəʊmə/ *c.n* very deep sleep as a result of a severe injury or illness. **be in**, **go into**, **come out of**, **a coma** be, become, stop being, ill in this way.

comatose /'kəʊmə,təʊs/ *adj* (*formal*) sleeping in this way.

comb /kəʊm/ *n* **1** *c.n* piece of plastic(3), metal, bone etc made with a row of teeth, used to arrange and tidy one's hair or the hair of an animal. **2** *sing.n* action of arranging the hair with a comb(1): *Her hair needed a good comb* (i.e was not tidy). **3** piece of machinery with teeth, used for arranging or straightening s.t, esp cotton, wool etc. ⇨ card(8). **4** red flesh that sticks out on top of the head of a cock(1).

▷ *tr.v* **5** use a comb(1) on (s.o/s.t): *She combed her hair before she went out.* **6** search, look in, (a place) for s.t very carefully: *I combed my room for the missing sock.* ⇨ honeycomb.

combat /'kɒmbæt/ (*formal*) *n* **1** *u.n* fight; struggle: *He led the combat against crime.* **2** *c.n* act of fighting s.o/s.t. **(un)armed combat** fight (without) with weapons (and not with one's hands). **(meet) in combat** (start) fighting each other. **mortal combat** fight leading to death.

▷ *v* **3** *tr.v* fight (s.o/s.t); use all one's powers to stop (s.t): *Every attempt was made to combat the disease.* **4** *intr.v* (often — *against/with s.t*) (*formal*) fight or struggle (against s.t): *In crossing the Atlantic alone, he had to combat with terrible weather conditions.*

combatant /'kɒmbətənt/ *c.n* (also *attrib*) person who fights, esp as a member of the armed forces: *Several combatants and non-combatants were killed in the bombing raid.*

combative /'kɒmbətɪv/ *adj* (*formal*) eager to fight or argue: *He's too combative so don't argue with him.*

combine /'kɒmbaɪn/ *c.n* **1** group of companies either owned by one company or joined together to decide prices, fight competition etc: *He works for a large industrial combine.* **2** *c.n* = combine harvester.

▷ *v* /kəm'baɪn/ **3** *tr.v* (often — *s.t with s.t*) join (s.t and s.t) together; have or do (s.t) at the same time as s.t else: *If you combine oxygen with* hydrogen *you get water. He found it difficult to combine his ordinary work with writing.* **4** *intr.v* (often — *against/with s.o/s.t*) (*formal*) happen at the same time (to s.o's disadvantage/advantage): *Events combined against him and prevented him from completing the job on time.*

combination /ˌkɒmbɪˈneɪʃən/ *n* **1** *u.n* act or state of joining or happening together: *A combination of accidental events led to their meeting.* **2** *c.n* people, events etc who/that act together to do s.t: *Combinations of certain drugs with alcohol can lead to fatal results.* **3** *c.n* set of numbers that opens special kinds of locks: *Only the bank manager knows the combination for the safe.*

com,bined 'exer,cises/'forces/,ope'rations *pl.n* (*military*) the army, the airforce and the navy acting together as a group.

,combine 'harvester *c.n* machine that cuts wheat etc, separates the corn from the stems and makes bundles of hay.

combustible /kəmˈbʌstɪbl/ *adj* (*technical*) that is easily able to burn or be burnt: *Combustible materials must not be used in furniture.*

com'bustibles *pl.n* things that can burn easily, e.g paper, wood.

combustion /kəmˈbʌstʃən/ *u.n* act of burning or of being burnt.

come /kʌm/ *intr.v* (*p.t* came /keɪm/, *p.p* come) **1** move towards the speaker or writer; arrive; move from one place to another: *Come here! The postman comes twice a day.* **2** happen, take place, esp as a regular event: *Christmas is coming. The rains came.* **3** be in a certain fixed position, e.g of time, importance: *Easter comes early this year. My work comes before my hobbies.* **4** happen (as a result of s.t): *Real happiness can only come through hard work.* **5** (usu — *doing s.t*) move towards a place in the way shown by the verb after 'come': *He came running towards me.* **6** become (the condition etc mentioned): *The screw came loose. The plan will come clear as you study it.* **7** (*slang; do not use!*) have an orgasm.

come aboard (**s.t**) arrive on a ship or a plane either as a member of the crew or as a passenger: *A new crew came aboard (the plane) at New York.*

come about (**a**) happen; take place: *So you lost your job; how did that come about?* (**b**) (of a sailing ship) turn, change direction, by moving the sail(s): *The boat came about and passed very close to us.* **come about s.t** arrive s.w in order to ask about or to do s.t: *I've come about your burst water pipe (i.e to look at or repair it).*

come across (of a person, an idea etc) get the result that one intends: *His problem is that what he wants to say seldom comes across clearly.* **come across s.o/s.t** find, discover, s.o/s.t by accident or chance: *I first came across him in a small village.* **come across as s.o** appear to be a certain kind of person: *On television she comes across as a kind woman but in reality she's not friendly.*

come after s.o attack s.o; run towards s.o in a threatening way: *The crowd came after him with sticks and stones.* **come after s.o/s.t** be in a position or order later than s.o/s.t else: *M comes after L in the* alphabet.

come again (**a**) return, esp after one visit: *You must come again as we so enjoyed having you.* (**b**) (usu — *again?*) (*informal*) what did you say/ mean?: *Come again? I didn't hear you.*

come along (**a**) appear: *The right leader often comes along in times of danger.* (**b**) = come on(a). (**c**) improve, make progress; grow; get better in health: *After a bad start at the new school, he has now settled down and is coming along very well.* (**d**) follow later: *I must finish this work, so you go now and I'll come along later.* **come along** (**with s.o**) (**to s.w**) move (in the company of s.o) (to a place): *Why don't you come along with me to the show?*

come and go (**a**) (of people) arrive and leave, esp in a crowded place; move about freely: *The station was full of people coming and going.* (**b**) (of people, events etc) happen, have a result or influence, and then be finished: *Illnesses come and go; you just have to be careful at your age.*

come apart break; become separated into parts: *The toy clock just came apart in my hands.* **come apart at the seams** ⇒ seam.

come (a)round (**to s.t**) agree (with s.t), usu after disagreeing at the beginning: *It took some time but he finally came around to my way of thinking.* **come (a)round** (**to s.w**) visit s.o (in a place), usu not very far from one's own house: *Why don't you come around for drinks tonight?*

come at s.o move towards s.o, esp in order to attack her/him: *The thief came at her with a knife.* **come at s.t** discover s.t, esp the truth, a fact etc: *It is difficult to come at the true facts of the case as he tells so many lies.*

come away (**from s.t**) break or fall (from s.t to which it was fixed); separate (from s.t): *I tried to open the door but the handle came away.* **come away** (**from s.w**) leave (a place), esp before the end of s.t or because one is disappointed etc: *We came away from the play feeling we had wasted our money.* **come away** (**from s.w**) **with s.t** leave (a place) having learned or discovered s.t: *He came away with the clear idea that he was going to get the job.*

come back become fashionable again: *Short skirts are coming back this year.* **come back** (**at s.o**) (**with s.t**) continue an argument by trying to answer (s.o) (with an argument of one's own): *I thought I had stopped him but he came back at me with yet another criticism.* ⇒ comeback(2). **come back** (**to s.o**) be remembered (by s.o): *I've forgotten her name but it'll come back (to me) in a minute.* **come back** (**to s.w**) return (to a place) at another time: *I've got to go now but I'll come back later.*

come before s.o/s.t (**a**) be in a position earlier than s.o/s.t: *Queen Victoria came before King Edward VII.* (**b**) be present, in front of, in, be dealt with by, a judge, a court of law: *He came before the judge last week.* (**c**) be more important than s.o/s.t: *If there is a strike, my family comes before everything else.*

come between s.o/s.t (**and s.o/s.t**) (**a**) be in a position that separates (groups of) people, things etc on either side: *A crowd of tourists came between me and the girl and I lost sight of her.* (**b**) cause trouble by interfering with the lives of two (groups of) people: *When they married they said that they would never let anybody or anything come between them.* (**c**) prevent s.o's enjoyment of s.t: *He never allows anything to* *come between him and his Saturday afternoon football.*

come by (s.o/s.t) pass, move close to, (s.o/s.t): *A truck came by (me) just as I was turning the corner.* **come by s.t** (a) get s.t, usu by work or effort: *When you are out of work, a new job is difficult to come by.* (b) get s.t, usu by accident or chance: *How did you come by that cut on your cheek?*

come clean ⇨ clean(*adv*).

Come, come! (way of expressing mild criticism): *Come, come! You don't really mean that, do you?*

come a cropper ⇨ cropper (⇨ crop).

come down (a) fall, usu quickly or heavily or without being expected: *The rain was coming down as we left. The aircraft came down in the sea.* (b) become less (in price): *Fruit is coming down (in price) now that it is summer.* (c) leave a (big) city and come to stay in a (smaller) place: *He comes down regularly to see his aunt.* (d) become less important, less respected, esp because of s.t that one has done: *She's come down in my view ever since she admitted to stealing.* ⇨ comedown.

come down (from s.w) finish a course of study at a university, esp Oxford or Cambridge. **come down in favour of, on the side of, s.o/s.t** finally decide to support (s.o/s.t), usu after listening to all the arguments etc: *The government has finally come down in favour of more spending.* **come down in the world** ⇨ world. **come down on s.o/ s.t** (a) criticize s.o/s.t severely: *Our boss used to come down on us heavily if we made the slightest mistake.* (b) demand s.t, esp money, from s.o, an organization etc: *My bank came down on me as soon as it heard I had got some money.* **come down (to s.t)** (a) reach a certain point from one that is higher: *Her coat came down to her ankles.* (b) have a meaning that can be reduced to something simple (from s.t more complicated): *His story comes down to this; he was nowhere near the scene of the crime.* **come down (to doing s.t)** become lower in social etc position (and so forced to do s.t that one would not normally do): *After losing all his money, he had to come down to asking favours of his friends.* **come down to s.o/s.t (from s.o/s.t)** (of history etc) pass (from one person etc) to another and so reach the present: *The story of King Arthur has come down to us from ancient times.* **come down to earth** ⇨ earth(*n*). **come down with s.t** begin to suffer an illness: *She came down with a bad cold over Christmas.*

come for s.o/s.t arrive in order to take or collect s.o/s.t: *The car is coming for us at 7 pm.*

come forward (a) arrive in order to do s.t: *Witnesses to the accident came forward and told the police what they had seen.* (b) (of a business matter) be dealt with, discussed, at a later date: *This matter will come forward at our next meeting.*

come from s.w be born at a place; be s.t that is grown or made at a place: *She comes from Glasgow. These oranges come from Spain.* **come from/of s.o** be a descendant of s.o: *Charles comes from a poor family.* **come from/of doing s.t** be, act as, a result of s.t: *This is what comes from/of trying to interfere with nature — you get even more diseases.*

come full circle ⇨ circle(*n*).

come home to s.o ⇨ home(*adv*).

come in (a) enter a room etc: *'Come in!' she said when I knocked on the door.* ⇨ come into s.w.

(b) (of the sea, the tide) move towards the shore. (c) become fashionable: *Short hair is coming in this year.* (d) be ready to buy: *Strawberries won't come in until next month.* (e) (of money) be paid to one: *I have no money coming in until next month.* (f) finish (in a certain position) in a race: *He almost fell over at the last bend and came in last.* (g) (of a government) be elected: *When the new government came in, they had only six more seats than the other party.* (h) (of news, a report etc, esp on the radio or television) be received: *News is just coming in of a train crash at Paddington.* (i) have a part in s.t that is going to be done: *It's a good plan but where do I come in?* **come in for s.t** (a) get, receive, s.t that is due to one: *The book came in for a lot of praise when it was published.* (b) get, receive, blame or criticism: *Their actions came in for a good deal of criticism.* **come in handy/useful** ⇨ handy, useful. **come in (on s.t) (with s.o)** take a part, join, (s.o), (in some course of action by helping her/him, giving money etc, usu in order to get a profit): *If you come in on his deal you'll earn a fortune.*

come into s.t (a) receive money, goods etc as a result of an inheritance: *He came into several thousand pounds on the death of his uncle.* ⇨ come into s.o's hands (⇨ hand(*n*)) (b) begin to happen in the way that is described by the noun: *come into action, fashion* (see the noun). **come into s.o's head** ⇨ head(*n*). **come into s.w** move in to a place: *She turned as I came into the room. The train came into the station just as I arrived.* ⇨ come in(a).

come of age ⇨ age(*n*). **come of doing s.t** ⇨ come from/of doing s.t. **come of s.o** ⇨ come from/ of s.o.

come off (a) (*informal*) (of an event etc) happen; take place: *The whole show came off very smoothly and there was no violence.* (b) (*informal*) (of s.t which one wants to do) be successful: *Though the robbery was carefully planned, it didn't come off.* (c) manage or succeed or fail in relation to s.o/s.t else: *He came off badly in the struggle for the leadership of the Party.* (d) (of a play, musical etc) be no longer performed, usu because it is not successful: *The play came off after Christmas as ticket sales were so poor.* **come off it!** (*informal*) stop saying s.t that is not true; stop being silly: *Come off it! I don't believe a word you say!* **come off (s.t)** (a) fall (from s.t): *The boy came off (his bicycle) at the corner.* (b) become separated (from s.t): *The handle came off (the car door) as soon as I tried to open it.* (c) stop doing s.t; be finished with s.t: *The detective came off the murder case as he was not getting very far.*

come on (a) move, think etc more quickly: *Come on or we'll be late! Come on — you know the answer!* (b) = come along(c). (c) = come along(d). (d) (of electricity, machines etc) start to work: *If you put this switch on, the central heating will come on.* (e) (of seasons, the weather, the night etc) begin: *Winter is coming on. The snow came on just before we got indoors.* (f) (of an illness) begin: *I've got a cold coming on.* (g) appear, take part, (in a play or in a game of football etc): *Everybody applauded when the famous actress came on. He came on in the second half and scored the only goal.* (h) (of a play, film etc) be performed or shown: *The new James Bond film is coming on next week.* (i) (of a case in a court of law) be considered: *The murder* *case is coming on next week.* **come on s.o** ⇒ come (up)on s.o. **come on s.o/s.t** ⇒ come (up)on s.o/s.t. **come on the scene** ⇒ scene.

come out (**a**) (of the sun, the moon, the stars) appear; be seen: *The moon came out from behind a cloud.* (**b**) (of flowers etc) grow; blossom(3): *The roses have come out late this year.* (**c**) (of a photograph) be developed well: *Only half the photographs I took on my summer holidays have come out.* (**d**) be seen clearly or in detail: *The expression on her face in the painting comes out very well.* (**e**) be produced; become known: *A report on local government has just come out.* (**f**) gain (a certain position) in an examination: *I came out top in my class in the examinations.* **come out against s.t** decide not to do or agree with s.t: *The government has come out against any increase in taxes.* **come out** (**at s.t**) reach a total; have a certain result, in mathematics etc: *What does the whole cost come out at? come out for s.t* leave where one lives in order to do s.t: *Why don't you come out for a bite to eat tonight? come out in s.t* develop signs of an illness on one's body: *He came out in spots and his mother thought he had got measles.* **come out** (**of s.t**) (**a**) leave (a place): *I was just coming out (of the room) when she came in.* (**b**) become separated (from s.t): *The nail came out (of the wall) easily once I used a bit of pressure.* (**c**) (of a stain, mark etc) disappear (from s.t) as a result of washing or cleaning: *However much he tried, the grease marks just would not come out (of his coat).* **come out** (**on strike**) (of employees) stop work; go on strike: *The men came out (on strike) over the question of shorter working hours.* **come out to s.t** = come out for s.t: *Come out to dinner with me tonight.* **come out with s.t** (**a**) (*informal*) say s.t, either after some delay or suddenly in a way that is not expected: *He came out with the statement that he believed in* fairies(2). (**b**) publish(1) s.t: *The government has come out with a report criticizing the recent violence.*

come over (**a**) settle in a place having moved from s.w else: *His* ancestors *came over to America a hundred years ago.* **come over s.o** affect, trouble, s.o; happen to s.o: *What has come over him? He used to be so happy and now he spends his time complaining.* **come over ill** etc (*informal*) become ill etc, usu suddenly: *As he left the house, he came over all* dizzy(1). **come it** etc **over s.o** (*informal*) act towards s.o in an interfering, nasty or superior(3) way (or in the way that is stated): *Stop trying to come it over me with your silly opinions.* **come over** (**to s.o**) leave the side one is on and cross to another one: *When it saw it was beaten, the army came over to us.* **come over** (**to s.o/s.w**) (**a**) move towards (s.o/s.w): *As soon as he saw I was alone, he came over to me.* (**b**) visit (s.o/s.w) for a short time, esp from across the sea: *My cousin is coming over (to London) for a holiday.* **come round** (**a**) become conscious again after fainting etc: *The blow knocked him out and it took several minutes for him to come round.* (**b**) happen at a regular, expected time: *Christmas is coming round again and I haven't bought any presents yet.* (**c**) become calm after a disagreement, quarrel etc; change for the better: *It took him a long time to come round after the fierce argument.* **come round to s.t** decide to do s.t after a delay: *I finally came round to answering the pile of letters.*

come through (of s.t one is expecting) be declared; happen: *The results of his examination haven't come through yet.* **come through** (s.t) live or become better (after an illness, an operation etc): *The operation lasted six hours but she came through (it) well.* **come through** (**on s.t**) (of a message, news etc) be received (on a radio, telephone etc): *News was just coming through on the radio of an attempt to kill the President.* **come through** (**with s.t**) (*informal*) provide s.t, esp money, in an expected way: *My father came through with the loan just as I was becoming desperate.*

come to (**a**) become conscious again after fainting, sleeping etc: *He must have fainted; when he came to, he didn't know where he was.* (**b**) (of a boat, ship) stop in the sea: *The ship came to and waited for the pilot to come on board.* **come to s.o** (**a**) be received by s.o: *You have a pleasant surprise coming to you this Christmas.* (**b**) be remembered by s.o: *If you just give me a minute, her name will come to me.* ⇒ come back (to s.o). **come to s.t** (**a**) (of money, an amount) reach the total that is stated: *The bill for dinner came to £75.* (**b**) concern, be to do with, s.t: *When it comes to acting, she's the best.* (**c**) happen in the way that is described by the noun: *come to an* agreement(1); *come to his* attention. **come to a head** ⇒ head(n). **come to do s.t** (**a**) come(1) in order to do s.t. (**b**) begin to do s.t: *I soon came to realize what had happened.* (**c**) reach, be in a position to do, s.t: *How did you come to discover the truth? come to no harm* ⇒ harm(n). **come to oneself** become conscious again; return to one's usual state: *I came to myself with a sudden start; I must have dropped off to sleep.* **come to one's senses (again)** ⇒ senses. **come to s.w** (**a**) reach, arrive at, a place (from the point of view of the speaker): *He came to the front door when I rang the bell.* (**b**) ⇒ come (up) to s.w.

come together meet, often in order to discuss s.t; be united again, esp after a disagreement: *The two parties in the strike came together around the table.*

come under s.t (**a**) receive, be subjected to, s.t: *The army came under heavy fire as it neared the town.* (**b**) be controlled, influenced, by s.t: *He made an official request for the new section to come under the control of his department. While at university he came under the influence of* left-wing(1) *groups.* (**c**) be found in a certain place, esp as a smaller part in a larger list or classification: *'Apples' comes under 'fruit trees' in my gardening book.*

come up (**a**) (of flowers etc) grow; appear above the ground: *The roses were coming up in the garden.* (**b**) (of the sun, moon) rise; appear above the horizon: *The sun was coming up as I left the house.* (**c**) rise in position in society etc: *He came up through the ranks* (i.e of the army) *and became a captain at the age of twenty-five.* (**d**) be mentioned or discussed: *Your name came up when we were discussing the new appointment at the meeting.* (**e**) be present at, be dealt with by, a court of law: *His case comes up at the next sitting.* (**f**) happen; take place: *Something has come up which needs my attention, so I won't be able to leave the office yet.* (**g**) (of a number) be successful (in a raffle(1) etc): *My number came up in the draw and I won a bottle of wine.* **come up against s.o/s.t** find that one is fighting against, or having difficulties or problems with, s.o/s.t: *I have come up against him several times and have always failed to persuade him to change his views.* **come up in the world** ⇒ world. **come up (to s.o)** move near (to s.o): *She came up (to me) and asked the way to the market.* **come up (to s.w)** (a) move up the stairs (as far as s.w): *Come up (to my room) and I'll show you my paintings.* (b) visit a bigger town from a smaller one: *You must come up (to London) and stay with me.* (c) join a university, esp Oxford or Cambridge, for a course of study: *He came up (to Oxford) last year and is reading English.* **come (up) to s.w** reach a certain point, usu from one that is lower: *The level of water was rising and soon it came to my waist.* ⇒ come to s.w. **come up to s.t** reach a certain level, esp in work, results etc: *Her examination results did not come up to her parents' expectations.* **come up with s.o/s.t** move next to, become level with, s.o/s.t: *The bus came up with the procession and tried to go past it.* **come up with s.t** find, think of, s.t, esp as an answer to a problem: *You can always trust him to come up with a solution to any difficult problem.*

come (up)on s.o attack s.o; happen to s.o when he/she is not expecting it: *The soldiers came upon us as we were sleeping. The blow came on the family at the worst possible time.* **come (up)on s.o/s.t** meet, find, by accident or chance: *I came upon an old man sitting on a park bench.*

come within s.t be a part of s.t; be s.t that concerns s.t: *I'm afraid this matter doesn't come within my responsibility; you'll have to go to the police.* **come within range** ⇒ range. **come within sight (of s.t)** ⇒ sight.

How come ...? (*informal*) In what way ...?; For what reason ...?: *How come you never told me the real truth?*

in the days/years etc **to come** in future times: *You will regret what you said in the years to come.*

two etc **years** etc **come Monday** etc two etc years etc ago when Monday etc arrives: *It will be three years come May since my wife died.*

'come,back *c.n* **1** (usu *make/stage a* —) (successful) return to one's former profession: *After several years' absence, she made a comeback and appeared in several films.* **2** reply in an argument: *He couldn't think of a comeback while she was criticizing him.* ⇒ come back (at s.o) (with s.t). **3** ability or right to make sure that s.t can be changed or corrected: *If you sign the agreement without reading the small print, you may find that you have no comeback when things go wrong.*

'come,down *c.n* (*informal*) loss of importance; disappointment: *The new job was a bit of a comedown for him after he had managed his own firm for so long.* ⇒ come down(d).

-comer *c.n* person who arrives in the way stated in the first part of the word: *latecomers* (e.g at the theatre); *newcomers* (e.g people who have only recently arrived).

come-uppance /ˌkʌmˈʌpəns/ *c.n* **get**, **give s.o**, **her/his come-uppance** (*informal*) receive, give s.o, punishment that is well deserved.

'coming *attrib.adj* soon to arrive or happen: *The coming attraction at the cinema is a new James Bond film.*

,comings and 'goings *pl.n* movements of people in and out of s.w, esp in a busy or secret manner: *There were so many comings*

and goings at the house that we began to wonder what was happening. ⇒ come and go(a).

comedian /kəˈmiːdɪən/ *c.n* **1** actor who tells jokes, does funny things etc in a play, on television etc. **2** (*informal*) person who acts in a funny way.

comedienne /kəˌmiːdɪˈen/ *c.n* female comedian(1).

comedy /ˈkɒmɪdɪ/ *n* (*pl -ies*) **1** *c.n* play in a theatre, on television etc that is amusing and funny. Compare tragedy(1). **2** *u.n* this type of play etc as a form of art: *I don't like comedy.* **3** *u.n* funny or amusing action, situation etc: *There was a certain amount of comedy in watching him trying to swim.*

comely /ˈkʌmlɪ/ *adj* (*-ier, -iest*) (*formal*) (of a person) attractive; pleasant to look at. **'comeliness** *u.n.*

-comer ⇒ come.

comet /ˈkɒmɪt/ *c.n* large body or mass, looking like a star with a tail of gas etc, moving around the sun in outer space.

come-uppance ⇒ come.

comfort /ˈkʌmfət/ *n* **1** *u.n* state of having all one wants, being free of anxiety etc: *She provided for his comfort in his old age. He saved enough money to live in comfort when he retired.* **2** *u.n* (words that show) help or kindness to s.o: *All he could do was offer her a few words of comfort.* **3** *sing.n* (often *be a* — *to s.o*) person or thing who/that helps s.o when he/she is unhappy, ill etc: *She was a great comfort to me during my troubles.* **4** *c.n* thing, e.g a television, that makes s.o's life easier: *He likes his modern comforts.*

▷ *tr.v* **5** give help, encouragement etc to (s.o): *She comforted the baby when it started crying.*

comfortable /ˈkʌmftəbl/ *adj* **1** feeling well, free from anxiety; having all one wants etc: *He has a very comfortable life because his father pays for everything.* **2** that brings physical well-being: *The bed was not very comfortable.* Opposite uncomfortable.

'comfortably *adv.*

'comforter *c.n* **1** person who comforts(5) s.o. **2** baby's dummy(3) or teat(2).

'comforting *adj* that brings comfort(2): *Her words were very comforting.*

comfy /ˈkʌmfɪ/ *adj* (*-ier, -iest*) (*informal*) = comfortable(1).

comic /ˈkɒmɪk/ *adj* **1** of, referring to, causing, amusement: *She looks so comic in that hat. The event had a comic ending. The situation was comic to say the least.* ⇒ comical. **2** (*attrib*) of or referring to comedy: *a comic actor; a comic play.* **3** of or referring to comics(4): *a comic book.*

▷ *c.n* **4** magazine with stories told using a set of pictures with written speech. **5** person who tells jokes, funny stories etc, esp as a job.

'comical *adj* causing amusement: *He looked comical in the red coat.*

'comic ,strip *c.n* set of pictures with written speech used to tell a joke or story.

comma /ˈkɒmə/ *c.n* mark **,** used in writing to show a pause in a sentence etc. ⇒ inverted commas.

command /kəˈmɑːnd/ *n* **1** *c.n* order, demand, (for s.t to be done), esp by s.o with the power to do s.t, e.g in the armed forces: *The officer's* *commands must be carried out.* **2** *u.n* (often *be in/-have — of/over s.o/s.t*) full power or control (over s.o/s.t): *He is in command of the whole army.* **3** *sing.n* (often *have a good* etc *— of s.t*) ability to do (s.t) well: *He has quite a good command of spoken English.* **be, put s.o./s.t, under s.o's command** (*military*) be, become, subject to the power and control of s.o/s.t.

▷ *tr.v* **4** (often *— s.o to do s.t; — that . . .*) order (s.o to do s.t, that . . .): *I command you to obey my orders. He commanded that the army should move forward.* **5** (*military*) have power or control over (s.o/s.t): *He commands all the armed forces.* **6** have/get (s.t) that is due to one (because of one's position, ability etc): *He commands respect because of his work among the poor.* **7** (of a place) be higher than (another place) and so look down on (it) (and sometimes act as a control for it): *The fort commands the* approaches(2) *to the town.*

commandant /ˌkɒmənˈdænt/ *c.n* (*military*) officer in the armed forces in charge of a place or part of an army.

commandeer /ˌkɒmɪnˈdɪə/ *tr.v* (usu *military*) take (private goods, food etc or private houses etc) for military use during war or fighting.

com'mander *c.n* **1** (with capital **C** in names; *abbr Cmdr*) officer in the navy below the rank of captain and above the rank of lieutenant-commander. **2** (usu *— of s.o/s.t*) person in charge (of s.o/s.t): *He became commander of the group.*

com,mander-in-'chief *c.n* (with capital **C**s in names; *abbr C-in-C*) highest officer in charge of all the armed forces.

com'manding *adj* (*formal*) **1** (of a person, a voice, physical(1) appearance etc) demanding (and getting) respect and attention: *His commanding presence made everybody look at him.* **2** (*attrib*) (of a place) that commands(7) s.t: *The house has a commanding view of the sea.*

com,manding 'officer *c.n* (*abbr CO*) officer in charge of a group of men.

com'mandment *c.n* one of the ten laws said to be given by God to the Jews, according to the Bible(1).

com'mand ,module *c.n* section of a spacecraft used by the crew and used to return to Earth.

commando /kəˈmɑːndəʊ/ *c.n* (*pl -(e)s*) (also *attrib*) (one of a) group of specially trained soldiers who make sudden attacks on an enemy, do special jobs etc.

commemorate /kəˈmeməˌreɪt/ *tr.v* honour, keep alive, the memory of (s.o dead, s.t that happened in the past): *Every year they commemorate those who died in the war.*

commemoration /kəˌmeməˈreɪʃən/ *c/u.n* (also *attrib*) (often *do s.t in — of s.o/s.t*) (ceremony for) honouring s.o's death, a brave act etc: *a commemoration ceremony. It was built in commemoration of the soldiers who died in the war.*

commemorative /kəˈmemərətɪv/ *adj* that commemorates s.t: *a commemorative stamp.*

commence /kəˈmens/ *tr/intr.v* (*formal*) (cause (s.t) to) begin; start: *The meeting commenced with a speech by the chairman.*

com'mencement *c/u.n.*

commend /kəˈmend/ *tr.v* (*formal*) **1** (usu *— s.o for s.t*) praise (s.o) (for s.t he/she has done): *He was commended for bravery.* **2** (usu *— s.o/s.t to* s.o) suggest, propose, that (s.o/s.t) should be looked after, taken care of (by s.o): *I commend him to your care after my death.*

com'mendable *adj* worthy of praise: *His actions were highly commendable.*

commendation /ˌkɒmənˈdeɪʃən/ *n* **1** *u.n* act of commending(1) (s.o). **2** *c.n* official honour for s.t one has done: *He has received several commendations for bravery.*

commensurate /kəˈmenʃərɪt/ *adj* (*formal*) (usu *— with s.t*) equal (to s.t s.o has done or is doing); having the same value (as s.t): *The reward was not commensurate with the effort he put in.*

comment /ˈkɒment/ *c/u.n* **1** (often *— about/(up)on s.t*) spoken or written remark(s) or observation(s) (on s.t said or written by s.o else) as an explanation or in praise or criticism: *I have no comment to make on what she said except to say that I don't agree. He made several critical comments about her dress.*

▷ *tr/intr.v* **2** (often *— (up)on s.t; — that...*) remark (on s.t, that . . .); give an opinion (on s.t): *He commented that he knew nothing about it. He refused to comment on the strike.*

commentary /ˈkɒməntərɪ/ *c.n* (*pl -ies*) **1** (also **,running 'commentary**) continuous spoken description of an event, esp a sports game, on the radio or tele · vision: *I don't like the commentaries on football matches.* **2** (usu *— on s.t*) written collection of notes, explanations etc (esp on a book): *a commentary on the* Bible(1). **a running commentary ((up)on s.t)** **(a)** ⇒ commentary(1). **(b)** a continuous description of s.t that is happening, esp when this is not necessary: *I do wish you would stop giving a running commentary on what is happening; we can all see for ourselves.*

commentate /ˈkɒmənˌteɪt/ *intr.v* (often *— (up)on s.t*) give a commentary(1) (on s.t).

'commen,tator *c.n* person who gives a commentary(1), esp on radio or television.

commerce /ˈkɒmɜːs/ *u.n* act, business, of trading goods between countries, organizations, people etc. ⇒ chamber of commerce.

commercial /kəˈmɜːʃəl/ *adj* **1** of or referring to commerce: *commercial laws.* **2** making (or likely to make) a profit: *Gold has been found in commercial quantities as a result of the new exploration.* Opposite uncommercial.

▷ *c.n* **3** advertisement on radio or television.

com'mercia,lism *u.n* (*derog*) state of being too concerned with making profits to the disadvantage of other things: *I dislike the heavy commercialism of the big companies.*

commercialization, -isation /kəˌmɜːʃəlaɪ-ˈzeɪʃən/ *u.n* (often *— of s.t*) act or fact of commercializing (s.t).

com'mercia,lize, -ise *tr.v* (*derog*) make (s.t, e.g a time of celebration) a subject of profit (and so ruin it): *Even Easter is becoming commercialized nowadays.*

com'mercially *adv.*

com,mercial 'radio/'tele,vision *c/u.n* radio/ television station(s) accepting advertisements in order to pay for programmes.

com,mercial 'traveller *c.n* salesperson who travels around an area selling goods.

com,mercial 'vehicle *c.n* van, lorry etc used for carrying goods (and not for private use).

commie /'kɒmɪ/ *adj, c.n* (*derog*; *informal*) communist(1,2).

commiserate /kə'mɪzəˌreɪt/ *intr.v* (usu — *with s.o* (*about/over s.t*)) (*formal*) express sympathy (with s.o) (about s.t that has happened to her/ him): *I commiserated with her over the loss of her jewels.*
commiseration /kəˌmɪzə'reɪʃən/ *c/u.n* (*formal*) (act of) expressing such sympathy.

commission /kə'mɪʃən/ *n* **1** *c.n* official order given to s.o to do s.t, esp to design(5) or build s.t, to paint a picture etc, usu for money: *He received a commission to* design(5) *the new hospital.* **2** *c.n* group of people appointed officially to look into and report on s.t, esp for a government: *The government has appointed a royal commission on the state of prisons.* **3** *c.n* (*military*) (official paper giving the) appointment of s.o to an officer's rank in the armed forces: *He received his commission as second* lieutenant. Compare warrant(1). **4** *c/u.n* (extra) money paid to a salesperson, agent etc for selling goods, acting for s.o else etc often in addition to a salary: *He gets £10 000 a year* plus(5) *commission.* **High Commission** ⇒ high. **in commission** (esp of a machine, warship etc) working, being used, esp after having been tested. **on commission** (of a salesperson etc) working and receiving commission(4) on sales. **out of commission** (esp of a machine etc) not working and so unable to be used.
▷ *tr.v* **5** (often — *s.o to do s.t*) give (s.o) a commission(1) (to do): *She was commissioned to do a painting of the Queen.* **6** (*military*) give (s.o) a commission(3): *He was commissioned in 1984.*

commissionaire /kəˌmɪʃə'neə/ *c.n* person who wears a uniform and stands at the entrance to a hotel, theatre, cinema, office etc in order to direct visitors, guard the entrance etc.

com,missioned 'officer *c.n* (*military*) officer who has been given a commission(3). ⇒ non-commissioned.

com'missioner *c.n* official in charge of a government department or with special responsibilities or rank: *a police commissioner; a commissioner of* oaths(1).

commit /kə'mɪt/ *tr.v* (-*tt*-) carry out, do, (s.t wrong, a crime etc): *They were accused of committing several murders.* **commit s.o to s.w** (*formal*) officially send s.o to a place where he/ she will not harm anybody, where he/she has to wait until a court appearance etc: *She was committed to prison for causing a disturbance.* **commit oneself (to doing s.t)** decide, promise, (to do s.t); make up one's mind (to do s.t): *She has committed herself to working for the poor. He wouldn't commit himself to agreeing to the proposal.* **commit s.t to memory** ⇒ memory.

com'mitment *c.n* (often *pl*) thing one has to do or has already promised to do (so that one is not free to do other things): *We can't take a holiday this year because we have so many other commitments.*

committal /kə'mɪtl/ *c/u.n* (*law*) (act of) committing s.o to s.w. **start committal proceedings (against s.o)** go to a court of law and ask for s.o to be put in prison or a mental hospital.

com'mitted *adj* determined; strong in one's belief, in what one does in one's job etc: *She's a very committed teacher.* Opposite uncommitted.

committee /kə'mɪtɪ/ *c.n* (also *attrib*) group of people chosen from a larger group to do s.t special, e.g to look after the larger group's affairs, to deal with money, to examine s.t: *They appointed a small committee to run the sports club. Are you a committee member?* **be/serve on a committee** take part in the activities of a committee: *He's on several committees.*

commodity /kə'mɒdɪtɪ/ *c.n* (*pl -ies*) (often *pl*) **1** (*formal*) useful thing, esp as a group for buying and selling: *The shop sells different kinds of household commodities.* **2** (*commerce*) article of trade, esp a natural product such as food, a mineral etc: *He deals in commodities.*

commodore /'kɒmədɔː/ *c.n* (with capital **C** in names) (UK; *military*) officer in the navy with a rank above a captain and below a rear-admiral.

common /'kɒmən/ *adj* **1** found in large numbers; happening often; usual: *Cats are common pets in England. It is quite common for him to talk in his sleep.* Opposite uncommon. **2** being shared (among a group), belonging equally (to two or more people): *We have a common purpose in fighting crime. Our common language is English.* **3** belonging to the people as a whole; not private: *The village* green(6) *is common land.* ⇒ common(6). **4** (in society) of ordinary rank or position: *The common people have to be protected against those in power.* **5** (*derog*) (thought to be) not polite, low in social class, behaviour etc: *He's really very common and doesn't even know how to eat properly.* **be common knowledge (that . . .)** be s.t that many people know, have found out etc: *It was common knowledge that the government wanted to raise taxes.* **be on common ground** have the same beliefs about s.t (though possibly disagreeing about others): *We are on common ground when it comes to politics.*
▷ *c.n* **6** piece of land for everybody to use, not privately owned: *the village common.* **have nothing, s.t etc in common (with s.o)** have no, some etc interests, beliefs etc that are equally shared (by s.o else): *He has very little in common with his wife; for example, he likes to stay at home and she likes to go out and enjoy herself.* **have/own s.t in common** have/own s.t equally: *They own the house in common.*

,common 'cold *def.n* ⇒ cold(*n*).

'commoner *c.n* person who is not of royal or noble rank: *The Prince married a commoner.*

,common 'law *u.n* (UK) group of laws that are not written, not made by Parliament, that have become accepted by custom, as a result of court cases etc.

,common-,law 'husband/'wife *c.n* man/ woman who, though not married according to the law, has lived with a woman/man for three or more years and so has certain rights.

'commonly *adv* **1** in a common(1) way. Opposite uncommonly. **2** in a common(5) way.

,Common 'Market *def.n* (popular name for the) European Economic Community.

'commonness *u.n* state of being common(1,5).

,common 'noun *c.n* (*grammar*) ordinary noun, not one describing a particular person, place etc (and written or printed with a small letter at the beginning and not a capital, except at the beginning of a sentence). Compare proper noun.

'common,place *adj* happening often (and so rather ordinary and uninteresting): Strikes(1) *were becoming commonplace events.*

'common,room *c.n* room in a school, college etc, used for relaxation by a certain group, e.g teachers: *the staff commonroom.*

'commons *def.n* ⇨ House of Commons.

,common 'sense *u.n* (also *attrib*) ordinary practical intelligence, esp that based on people's experience: *She showed great common sense in her handling of the situation.*

'common,wealth *n* (with capital **C** in names) **1** *c.n* (*formal*) (all the people belonging to a) state or country. **2** *def.n* (usu *the — of s.t*) official name for certain countries: *The Commonwealth of Australia.* **3** *def.n* (formerly ,**British** ,**Common,wealth** (**of** '**Nations**)) group of countries, formerly parts of the British empire, that trade together, keep on friendly terms with each other etc.

commotion /kə'məʊʃən/ *c/u.n* noisy and confused movement of people, esp because they are disturbed about s.t: *There was a/some commotion outside the hall as people tried to get in.*

commune /'kɒmjuːn/ *c.n* **1** group of people who live (and possibly work) together, share their property among themselves etc. **2** (with capital **C** in names) (in some countries, e.g France, Italy) small district that runs its own affairs.

▷ *intr.v*/kə'mjuːn/ **3** (usu — *with s.o/s.t*) (*formal*) feel in sympathy (with s.o/s.t); talk or be silently in contact (with s.o/s.t): *He goes for long walks in order to commune with nature.*

communal /'kɒmjʊnl/ *adj* (usu *attrib*) **1** of or referring to a commune or a community: *She enjoys communal life.* **2** jointly shared between two or more people: *We have a communal entrance¹ with our neighbours.*

communicate /kə'mjuːnɪ,keɪt/ *v* (*formal*) **1** *tr.v* (usu — *s.t to s.o*) (be able to) make (information, an idea, what one wants to say etc) understood (by s.o): *He communicated the news to me.* **2** *intr.v* (usu — *with s.o*) be in touch (with s.o), share information (with s.o), esp over some distance by writing, telephoning etc: *He hardly ever communicates with me since he left the country.* **3** *intr.v* (esp of rooms) be joined together by a door or opening so that one can go directly from one to another: *The two bedrooms communicate.*

com'municable *adj* (esp of a disease, an illness) easily able to be passed on from one person to another. Opposite non-communicable.

com'municant *c.n* person who receives Communion(3).

communication /kə,mjuːnɪ'keɪʃən/ *n* (*formal*) **1** *u.n* act of making s.t known or understood (between one person or group of people and another or others); sending of information between one place and another: *There is very little communication between them even though they have been married for ten years.* **2** *c.n* written, spoken or telephoned message: *There have been several communications from the enemy about arranging peace talks.*

communicative /kə'mjuːnɪkətɪv/ *adj* very willing to talk about s.t, to give information etc: *He's very communicative and will tell you all about his work even though it's meant to be secret.* Opposite uncommunicative.

communion /kə'mjuːnɪən/ *n* **1** *u.n* (often *be in — with s.o/s.t*) (*formal*) state of sharing s.t, esp one's thoughts (with s.o/s.t): *He is in communion with nature.* **2** *c/def.n* group of people who share the same religious beliefs: *the* Anglican *communion.* **3** *unique n* (also *attrib*) (often with capital **C**; also ,**Holy Com'munion**) service in the Christian(1) Church in which the Eucharist is given to people: *I go to communion every Sunday. She's at a communion service.*

communiqué /kə'mjuːnɪ,keɪ/ *c.n* (*French*) special statement made, usu by a government, to the press or the public: *An official communiqué is expected from the government on the strike.*

communism /'kɒmjʊ,nɪzəm/ *n* **1** *u.n* political and social system in which all the goods produced by the people of a country are owned equally by them and in which all the people are (intended to be) equal in social rank. **2** *unique n* (with capital **C**) this system as practised by members of the Communist Party and countries controlled by it.

'commu,nist *adj* **1** of or referring to communism(1,2).

▷ *c.n* **2** person who believes in (and practises) Communism(2); member of the Communist Party.

'Commu,nist ,Party *def.n* political party that believes in (and practises) Communism(2).

community /kə'mjuːnɪtɪ/ *c.n* (*pl* -ies) (also *attrib*) **1** people living in a particular place or with a similar origin: *the London community; the black communities; community affairs.* **2** citizens as a whole: *The community wants better schools.*

com'munity ,centre *c.n* building for social and sporting activities.

commute /kə'mjuːt/ *v* **1** *tr.v* (usu — *s.t (from s.t) to s.t*) (*law*) change (a sentence for a crime) to a less severe one: *The judge commuted his sentence from ten to five years.* **2** *intr.v* (often — (*from s.w*) *to s.w*) travel some distance (from one's home, usu in the country or in the suburbs) (to one's (place of) work in a town every day by public transport): *He commutes to work from Cambridge.*

com'muter *c.n* person who commutes(2).

com'muter ,belt *c.n* area(s) outside a town with houses from which people commute(2).

compact¹ /kəm'pækt/ *adj* **1** closely joined or pressed together so as to form a mass: *The trees and plants formed a compact group at the end of the garden.* **2** neatly or tidily arranged so as to fit a small space: *My brother's new kitchen is very compact.*

▷ *tr.v* **3** (usu passive) make or press (s.t) into a solid mass: *The snow was compacted together by all the people walking on it.*

'compact ,disc /'kɒmpækt/ *c.n* (*abbr CD*) small record¹(1) played using a laser beam instead of a needle.

com'pactly *adv.* **com'pactness** *u.n.*

compact² /'kɒmpækt/ *c.n* **1** (*formal*) agreement (between two or more people, governments etc): *They made a compact not to discuss the matter again.* **2** small container with a lid, used for holding powder for the face.

companion /kəm'pænɪən/ *c.n* **1** person, animal or thing who/that goes with one regularly as a

friend, or met on a journey, as s.t that helps or amuses one etc: *He and his companions travel a lot together. Wherever he goes, he takes a book to be his companion.* **2** person with whom one is friendly: *He's a very amusing companion.* **3** person, esp a woman paid to stay with and help another person: *She has a paid companion to help her round the house.* **4** (also *attrib*) (often — *to s.t*) thing similar to, going together with, another thing, sometimes forming one of a pair or group: *This painting is a companion to the one in the local art collection. It's a companion* volume(2). **5** (with capital **C** in names) book intended to give advice on a subject: *A Companion to London.* **boon companion** ⇨ boon.
com'panionable *adj* very friendly.
Com,panion of 'Honour *unique n* (*written abbr* CH) (UK) title given to a person as a reward for her/his services.
com'panionship *u.n* state of being very friendly, of going with s.o, esp on journeys etc: *I enjoyed the companionship of several people on my travels.*
com'panion,way *c.n* staircase or ladder going through a ship and joining several decks etc.
company /'kʌmpəni/ *n* (*pl* -ies) **1** *c.n* (*abbr* Co) (name for a) group of people working together as a business, usu formed according to certain laws and rules: *Jones and Company/Co. I work for a large oil company.* **2** *c.n* group of people working together, esp in the theatre: *He joined a travelling theatre company.* **3** *c.n* (*military*) group of (about 120) soldiers in the army. **4** *u.n* act of being with s.o, spending time with s.o, sharing a friendship with s.o etc: *I enjoyed his company when I travelled around.* **5** *u.n* number of visitors or guests: *We're having company tonight, so we can't join you.* **be good etc company** be s.o whom people enjoy etc being with: *She's very good company and is always telling jokes and amusing people.* **in company** when other people are present, esp as guests: *He always makes a fool of himself in company.* **in company with s.o** going, travelling, with s.o: *She came in company with several people I didn't know.* **keep s.o company** be with s.o, travel with s.o, so that he/she is not alone: *I kept him company on the first part of his journey.* **part company (with s.o)** (*formal*) (**a**) leave (s.o) after having travelled or been with her/him for some time: *I parted company with him at the station. They parted company after several years of living together.* (**b**) (*fig*) disagree (with s.o): *I part company with him on the subject of hanging.*
comparable /'kɒmprəbl/ *adj* (*formal*) (often — *to/with s.o/s.t*) equal in some way (to s.o/s.t): *His victory is comparable to those won by great generals of the past.* Opposite incomparable.
comparative /kəm'pærətɪv/ *adj* **1** being of a certain (reasonable) standard when compared to s.t else (that is not usu stated): *They live in comparative comfort and I know a lot of people worse off than them.* **2** being or making a comparison (between two or more things): *the study of comparative religion.* **3** (*grammar*) (of (the forms of) adjectives and adverbs) showing an increase in quantity etc from the usual state: *'Happier' is the comparative form of 'happy'.* ⇨ superlative(2).

▷ *c.n* **4** (*grammar*) comparative(3) adjective or adverb: *'Better' and 'worse' are comparatives of 'good' and 'bad'.* ⇨ superlative(2).
com'paratively *adv.*
compare /kəm'peə/ *u.n* **1** (**be**) **beyond/past/without compare** (*formal*) (be s.o/s.t) who/that has no equal, who/which is much better than s.o/s.t else: *She is beyond compare.*
▷ *v* **2** *tr.v* (usu — *s.o/s.t to/with s.o/s.t*) look at, examine, (s.o/s.t) and see if he/she/it is like or unlike (s.o/s.t else): *If you compare his work with hers* (or *If you compare their work*), *you will see that they are very different.* **3** *tr.v* (usu — *s.o/s.t to/with s.o/s.t*) say or write that (s.o/s.t) is very like (s.o/s.t else): *He compared their actions to those of criminals.* **4** *intr.v* (usu (*not*) — *with s.o/s.t*) be as good (as s.o/s.t); be worthy of comparison (with s.o/s.t): *As a writer, he can't compare with his father.*
comparison /kəm'pærɪsn/ *n* **1** *u.n* (usu — *between/of s.o/s.t* (*and s.o/s.t*)) act or fact of comparing (two people or things): *There is no comparison possible between his performance and hers. The* clue involves(1) *comparison of the two shapes.* **2** *c.n* example or result of comparing: *He made several comparisons between what was happening now and what happened five years ago.* **3** *u.n* (*grammar*) making of the comparative(3) forms of adjectives and adverbs. **by/in comparison (to/with s.o/s.t)** when/if one compares (s.o/s.t else): *In comparison with other places, the town is very quiet.* **be no comparison with s.o/s.t; not stand comparison with s.o/s.t** not be as good as s.o/s.t; not be equal to s.o/s.t: *The new play does not stand comparison with his earlier work.*
compartment /kəm'pɑːtmənt/ *c.n* **1** one of the separate sections in a train in which passengers sit, goods are carried etc: *That bicycle will have to go into the luggage compartment.* **2** separate section of a cupboard, box etc in which certain things are kept: *There is a special compartment in the tool box for holding nails and screws.*
compartmentalize, -ise /,kɒmpɑː't'mentə,laɪz/ *tr.v* (*formal*) **1** put (things) into a compartment(2) or compartments. **2** divide (things, ideas, thoughts etc) into separate groups: *He had great difficulty compartmentalizing his thoughts.*
compass /'kʌmpəs/ *n* (*pl* -es) **1** *c.n* device with a magnetic(1) needle that points to the magnetic north and so helps one to find one's way when travelling: *Luckily he had a compass with him and was able to work out where the town was with the help of his map.* **2** *c.n* (often *a pair of* —es) device with two arms and a hinge(1) at the top, used for drawing circles, working out distances or areas on a map etc. **3** *u.n* (*music*) range(7) or extent of s.o's voice: *Her voice had an unusually wide compass.* (**not be**) **within s.o's compass** (*formal*) (not be) s.o's responsibility or job; (not be) s.t s.o is able to do: *I'm sorry, that's not within my compass; you'll have to talk to someone else about it.*
'compass ,point *c.n* (also **point of the compass**) one of the number of divisions into north, south, east or west or parts of these shown on a compass(1): *N, NE and NNE are compass points.*
compassion /kəm'pæʃən/ *u.n* (often — *for s.o*) (showing of) pity or sympathy towards s.o who

is suffering or has suffered: *He showed no compassion for the prisoners.*

compassionate /kəmˈpæʃənɪt/ *adj* having or showing pity or sympathy.

com,passionate 'leave *u.n* time one is allowed to take off from one's job, the armed forces etc because of death, illness etc in one's family.

compatible /kəmˈpætəbl/ *adj* (usu — *with s.o/ s.t*) Opposite incompatible. **1** (of people, ideas etc) able to exist alongside (s.o/s.t); being in (general) agreement (with s.o/s.t): *Their marriage broke up because they were not compatible.* **2** (of a machine etc) able to work, fit in (with another machine): *This new computer is not compatible with others on the market.*

compatibility /kəmˌpætəˈbɪlɪtɪ/ *u.n.* **com'patibly** *adv.*

compatriot /kəmˈpætrɪət/ *c.n* (*formal*) person who is a citizen by birth or naturalization of the same country (as s.o else): *I discovered we were compatriots when he told me where he was born.*

compel /kəmˈpel/ *tr.v* (*-ll-*) **1** (usu — *s.o to do s.t*) force (s.o to do s.t), usu against her/his will: *I was compelled to listen to him for two hours.* **2** (*formal*) (of an action etc) be s.t that draws (one's attention, admiration etc) often against one's will: *The way she works must compel our admiration.* ⇒ compulsion.

com'pelling *adj* (usu *attrib*) **1** forcing or demanding (a reason, an action etc): *Have you any compelling reason for leaving now?* **2** attracting attention, one's interest etc: *a compelling book; a compelling stare.*

compensate /ˈkɒmpənˌseɪt/ *v* **1** *tr.v* (usu — *s.o for s.t*) give (s.o) s.t (esp money) in order to make up for, replace s.t s.o has lost, some harm s.o has suffered etc: *The employer was forced to compensate his workers for their loss of earnings.* **2** *tr/intr.v* (usu — (*s.o*) *for s.t*) be equal to, make up for or replace, (s.t one has lost): *Nothing will compensate (me) for the death of my son.*

compensation /ˌkɒmpənˈseɪʃən/ *c/u.n* (often *as/in — for s.t*) (amount of s.t, esp money, given as an) act of making up for, replacing, (s.t): *He was given £10 000 in compensation for the loss of his sight.*

compere, compère /ˈkɒmpeə/ *c.n* **1** person whose job is to introduce different acts in a theatre, on a radio or television show.

▷ *tr.v* **2** act as a compere(1) (of a show) as a job: *He was asked to compere the programme.*

compete /kəmˈpiːt/ *intr.v* (usu — *against/with s.o (for s.t) (in s.t)*) try (by fighting against s.o in order to beat her/him) to win, get (s.t), esp in a race, game, business deal etc: *The local sports team is competing in the games for a chance to win the gold cup. The new company will have to compete with many others for orders.*

competition /ˌkɒmpəˈtɪʃən/ *n* **1** *u.n* act or acts of competing: *There was a lot of competition to get the order.* **2** *c.n* example of competing; race, game etc in which people compete: *There was a competition to find the best dressed man.* **3** *def.n* people, business(es) etc against whom/which one competes: *Our group beat the competition and got the order.*

competitive /kəmˈpetɪtɪv/ *adj* **1** (of a person)

having or showing a desire to compete: *He's very competitive.* Opposite non-competitive. **2** (of a price etc) fixed so as to be better than others.

com'petitively *adv.* **com'petitiveness** *u.n.*

competitor /kəmˈpetɪtə/ *c.n* person, company, product etc who/that competes with others: *Our company was one of the main competitors for building the factory.*

competent /ˈkɒmpɪtənt/ *adj* **1** (often — *in s.t/ to do s.t*) having or showing ability or skill (in a job/to do s.t): *She's very competent in what she does.* **2** that is done well: *It was a very competent piece of work.* Opposite incompetent(1).

'competence *u.n.* **'competently** *adv.*

compile /kəmˈpaɪl/ *tr.v* (*formal*) make (a list, an account, reference book etc) from other information, books etc one has examined: *He compiled an account of the accident by talking to people who had seen it.*

compilation /ˌkɒmpɪˈleɪʃən/ *n* **1** *u.n.* act of compiling s.t. **2** *c.n.* list, account, dictionary etc made as a result of compiling.

com'piler *c.n* person who compiles s.t: *a dictionary compiler.*

complacent /kəmˈpleɪsnt/ *adj* (often *derog; formal*) having or showing (too great a) feeling of satisfaction about oneself, what one has done etc: *The government has become far too complacent about its record.*

com'placence, com'placency *u.n.* **com'placently** *adv.*

complain /kəmˈpleɪn/ *intr.v* **1** (usu — *that . . .*) say (that) one is annoyed, dissatisfied (that s.t has (not) happened, that s.o has (not) done s.t etc): *He complained that the dinner had not been cooked properly.* **2** (usu — *to s.o (about s.o/s.t)*) state one's annoyance, dissatisfaction (to s.o) (about s.o else who has not done s.t, who has done s.t wrong etc, or about s.t that has happened, that has gone wrong etc): *He complained to the town council about the state of the roads.* **complain of s.t** say that one is suffering from s.t, esp a pain etc: *He complained of an ache in his back.*

com'plainant *c.n* person who complains(2), esp in a court of law.

com'plaint *n* **1** *u.n* (often — *against s.o/s.t*) act or cause for complaining: *I have no complaint against the police.* **2** *c.n* (statement of an) example of, reason for, complaining: *There have been several complaints about his behaviour.* **3** *c.n* thing one suffers from, esp a pain, an illness etc: *He has a chest complaint.* **have cause for complaint** (*formal*) have a reason why one complains or should complain.

complaisant /kəmˈpleɪznt/ *adj* (*formal*) having or showing (too great) a desire or willingness to please others, to do what they want etc: *He's far too complaisant about his family's behaviour.*

com'plaisance *u.n.* **com'plaisantly** *adv.*

complement /ˈkɒmplɪmənt/ *c.n* **1** person, thing who/that makes s.t complete or who/that, when included, makes s.t better: *White wine is a good complement to fish.* **2** all the persons or things who/that are needed to make s.t complete: *The ship now has its full complement.* **3** (*grammar*) word or words forming the predicate of certain verbs such as 'be'.

▷ *tr.v* **4** make (s.t) complete or better: *The furniture complements the room very well.*

complementary /ˌkɒmplɪˈmentərɪ/ *adj* that makes s.t complete or better.

complete /kəmˈpliːt/ *adj* **1** without anything missing; having all the necessary parts (of s.t): *He has a complete set of the writer's books.* **2** (of work etc) finished, done: *The report is not yet complete.* **3** (of an event, happening etc) thorough; total: *It was a complete* disaster (2).
▷ *tr.v* **4** finish (s.t); add to (s.t) and so make it whole: *They completed the job in time. He was looking for one more painting to complete his collection.*
com'pletely *adv.* **com'pleteness** *u.n.*
completion /kəmˈpliːʃən/ *u.n* (often the — of s.t) state or act of having finished or done s.t: *The completion of the work brought great satisfaction.* **on completion (of s.t) (a)** when or if s.t has been finished. **(b)** (*law*) when or if a contract(1) of sale has been signed: *You can move into the house on completion.*

complex /ˈkɒmpleks/ *adj* **1** (of a machine etc) having many different parts joined or working together: *This part has a complex* structure(1). ⇒ simple(2). **2** (of a plan, action etc) difficult to understand: *I'm afraid his argument is too complex for me.*
▷ *c.n* **3** group of things, esp a number of buildings or parts of one, joined together: *They have just built a new shopping complex in our town.* **4** disturbed state of one's mind showing esp in one's behaviour and usu without one knowing it: *He has a complex about the way he looks.* ⇒ inferiority complex, superiority complex.
complexity /kəmˈpleksɪtɪ/ *c/u.n* (*pl* -ies) (often the — of s.t) fact or state of s.t being complex(1,2).

complexion /kəmˈplekʃən/ *c.n* **1** (ordinary) colouring of one's skin and esp one's face: *a fair complexion.* **2** general look or appearance (of s.t); way s.t is composed or changed: *After the election, the government has a new complexion.*

compliance, compliant ⇒ comply.

complicate /ˈkɒmplɪˌkeɪt/ *tr.v* (of a person, thing, action etc) make (s.t) more difficult (than it should be): *He has complicated the problem by his refusal to agree.*
'compli,cated *adj* (of a machine, thought, action etc) very difficult to understand: *The rules are very complicated and I doubt if many people can understand them.* Opposite uncomplicated.
complication /ˌkɒmplɪˈkeɪʃən/ *c.n* **1** thing added that makes s.t more difficult to understand or do: *We have enough trouble as it is without you adding further complications.* **2** added illness coming as a result, or on top, of the main one: *He died of complications following the operation.*

complicity /kəmˈplɪsɪtɪ/ *u.n* (usu — in s.t) (*formal*) act of taking part, being concerned, (in s.t wrong, e.g a crime) with s.o else: *He was accused of complicity in the murder.*

compliment /ˈkɒmplɪmənt/ *c.n* **1** statement of praise or admiration: *He received many compliments on his performance.* **pay s.o a compliment** praise s.o.
▷ *tr.v* /ˈkɒmplɪˌment/ **2** (usu — s.o on s.t) praise (s.o) (for s.t he/she owns or has done): *I must compliment you on the beautiful flower arrangement.*
complimentary /ˌkɒmplɪˈmentərɪ/ *adj* (usu attrib) **1** (of a remark etc) that is intended as a compliment(1): *She got many complimentary remarks on her dress.* **2** (of a ticket etc) given free, esp as a favour: *I've got two complimentary tickets for the show.*
compliments /ˈkɒmplɪmənts/ *pl.n* (often — to s.o) (*formal*) expression of one's regards (to s.o): *Would you present my compliments to your father and say that I'm sorry that I cannot see him.* **fish for compliments** try to get s.o to praise one.

comply /kəmˈplaɪ/ *intr.v* (-ies, -ied) (usu — with s.t) (*formal*) obey (s.o's wishes, order etc): *He refused to comply with the order of the court.*
compliance /kəmˈplaɪəns/ *u.n* (often in — with s.t) (*formal*) act of complying (with s.t): *In compliance with your orders, I have told the soldiers to stop fighting.*
com'pliant *adj* (*formal*) showing (great) obedience.

component /kəmˈpəʊnənt/ *c.n* (also attrib) one of a number of parts that goes to make a whole, esp in an engine, a machine: *A new shop has just opened that sells components for cars.*

compose /kəmˈpəʊz/ *v* **1** *tr/intr.v* write, be the author(1) of, (music, words, a speech): *He didn't start to compose (music) until he was thirty.* **2** *tr.v* (usu passive) (*formal*) make (a group or a whole): *The party is composed of several people with different interests.* **3** *tr.v* (*printing*) typeset (words etc) for printing. **compose oneself** bring oneself, one's feelings, under control, esp after having been disturbed: *It took him a long time to compose himself after hearing the bad news.*
com'posed *adj* calm and in control of oneself or one's feelings. **be composed of s.o/s.t** ⇒ compose(2).
com'poser *c.n* **1** person who writes music. **2** person who composes(1) poems etc.
composite /ˈkɒmpəzɪt/ *adj* **1** (*formal*) made up from different things, parts etc: *a composite picture with photographs and drawings.*
▷ *c.n* **2** (*technical*) composite(1) material, esp one made with different metals, plastics(3) etc: *The blades of the aircraft engine were manufactured from a composite.*
composition /ˌkɒmpəˈzɪʃən/ *n* **1** *c/u.n* (example of the) art or act of composing(1) s.t: *She is studying composition at the college of music. He has written several compositions for the piano.* **2** *c.n* piece of writing (to be) done as an exercise: *The teacher gave us a composition to write for tomorrow.* **3** *u.n* (often the — of s.t) group of things, people etc arranged in a certain way: *the composition of a metal; the composition of the government.*
composure /kəmˈpəʊʒə/ *u.n* (*formal*) calmness and control of oneself.
compos mentis /ˌkɒmpɒs ˈmentɪs/ *adj* (*Latin*) in full control of one's mind; fully conscious. ⇒ non compos mentis.
compost /ˈkɒmpɒst/ *u.n* mixture of dead or rotting plants from a garden, unused food etc, used as a fertilizer for soil.
'compost ,heap *c.n* rotting pile of compost in a garden.
compound /ˈkɒmpaʊnd/ *c.n* **1** (also attrib) (*science*) substance consisting of or containing two or more things mixed together: *a chemical compound.* **2** (also attrib) (*grammar*) word made up from two or more other words joined together: *'Bathroom' is a noun compound (or a compound*

noun). **3** area with a wall or fence and/or buildings in or around it: *a prison compound*.

▷ *v* /kəm'paʊnd/ **4** *tr.v* (*technical*) mix (two or more things) together: *The two chemicals were compounded together in a specially* constructed *machine*. **5** *tr.v* (*formal*) make (s.t) more difficult; add to (an already bad situation, a crime etc): *He compounded our problem by not arriving in time. They compounded the crime by beating him up before they left*. **6** *intr.v* (usu — *with* s.o) (*commerce*) come to an arrangement, esp over matters of money, (with s.o): *He compounded with those to whom he owed money on the basis that he would pay them a certain amount each month*.

,**compound 'fracture** *c.n* fracture(1) in which a broken bone pushes through the skin. ⇨ simple fracture.

,**compound 'interest** *u.n* interest(4) calculated on both the whole amount of money borrowed or lent, and the actual interest(4). Compare simple interest (⇨ simple).

,**compound 'noun** *c.n* ⇨ compound(2).

comprehend /,kɒmprɪ'hend/ *tr.v* (*formal*) **1** understand (s.o/s.t): *It is difficult to comprehend the reason for their failure.* **2** consist of (s.t); cover or include (s.t): *Science can be said to comprehend all the known facts about the world we live in.*

comprehensibility /,kɒmprɪ,hensə'bɪlɪtɪ/ *u.n* ability to be understood easily.

comprehensible /,kɒmprɪ'hensəbl/ *adj* (*formal*) (of s.t said, an action etc) able to be understood easily: *His behaviour is comprehensible if you think of the pressure he has been under.* Opposite incomprehensible.

comprehension /,kɒmprɪ'henʃən/ *u.n* ability to understand (s.t); act of doing this: *He has a very good comprehension of the business.* Opposite incomprehension. **be beyond s.o's comprehension** be s.t that s.o does not understand (the reason for): *It's beyond my comprehension why he took the job at all.*

comprehensive /,kɒmprɪ'hensɪv/ *adj* **1** (*formal*) very complete; taking into account many things: *There was a very comprehensive report on the matter.* **2** (UK) (of a system of school education) covering a large number of students of different abilities and offering a wide variety of subjects: *comprehensive education.*

▷ *c.n* **3** = comprehensive school.

,**compre'hensive ,school** *c/u.n* (UK) secondary school that uses the comprehensive(2) system.

compress /'kɒmpres/ *c.n* **1** (folded) piece of cloth etc put on a wound to stop bleeding, or on a swelling to make it go down: *a cold compress.*

▷ *tr.v* /kəm'pres/ (*formal*) **2** force (s.t) into a smaller space (than it usually takes): *The soil had become compressed by the people walking over it.* **3** make (s.t, esp a speech, an argument) shorter by using fewer words: *He had the ability to compress his ideas into a few short sentences.*

com,pressed 'air *u.n* air forced into a small space, e.g in a container used for swimming under water, in a machine to drive it in some way.

compression /kəm'preʃən/ *u.n* act of compressing(2,3) s.t; state of being compressed(2,3).

com'pressor *c.n* device for compressing(2) a substance, e.g air, petrol, into a small space in order to drive an engine etc.

comprise /kəm'praɪz/ *tr.v* (*formal*) have, consist of, (two or more people, things etc): *Our household comprises five people, two dogs and six cats.*

compromise /'kɒmprə,maɪz/ *c/u.n* **1** (example of the) act of reaching an agreement by accepting that one has to give up (part of) s.t that one previously required: *He suggested a compromise that would suit both of them. The only way we'll agree is by some form of compromise.*

▷ *v* **2** *intr.v* (offer to) make a compromise(1): *He compromised by offering to take her out the next night if she would stay in that night.* ⇨ uncompromising. **3** *tr.v* put (s.o, s.o's position etc) into danger or dishonour by one's words or actions: *The secret service agent's position was compromised by a leak in the government.*

compulsion /kəm'pʌlʃən/ *c/u.n* (*formal*) (example of a) necessity, driving force, strong desire, that makes one do s.t: *It is on these occasions that Peter has a compulsion to shock everyone. Keeping fit has become a compulsion with Chris. There is no compulsion to come to the meetings.* (**be** etc) **under compulsion** (**to do s.t**) (be etc) forced (by other people to do s.t): *You are under no compulsion to do what he says.* ⇨ compel(1).

compulsive /kəm'pʌlsɪv/ *adj* acting as if one is forced to be or to do s.t though this may not be the case: *He is a compulsive drinker/eater. Jean is so compulsive about the things she does.*

com'pulsively *adv*. **com'pulsiveness** *u.n*.

compulsory /kəm'pʌlsərɪ/ *adj* that one must do; that one cannot avoid: *Attendance at these lectures is compulsory.*

com'pulsorily *adv*. **com'pulsoriness** *u.n*.

compunction /kəm'pʌŋkʃən/ *u.n* (often *have/ show little/no* — (*towards* s.o, *about* (*doing*) s.t)) (*formal*) feeling of regret or worry (about (doing) s.t): *I was so angry with her that I had no compunction about leaving her to find her own way home. You can use his car without compunction — after all he used yours when he needed to!*

computer /kəm'pju:tə/ *c.n* (also *attrib*) kind of machine that can store information, produce it in different forms when needed and make calculations when certain programs(1) are used. *home/personal computer* ⇨ home, personal.

computerization, -isation /kəm,pju:təraɪ'zeɪʃən/ *u.n* act or fact of computerizing s.t: *Many manufacturing processes benefit(5) from computerization.*

com'pute,rize, -ise *tr.v* introduce a computer or computers into (a place of work, one's job etc); use a computer to store (information etc): *The whole of this dictionary has been computerized.*

comrade /'kɒmreɪd/ *c.n* **1** (*formal*) friend, esp one with whom one does things: *We were comrades during the war.* **2** (word used for a) member of the same, usu socialist or communist(1), political party or of the same trade union as oneself: *It is up to us, comrades, to defeat this government.*

'comradely *adv* showing friendship.

'comradeship *u.n* state or fact of being friendly (with s.o).

con /kɒn/ *c.n* **1** (also **'con-,trick**) (*informal*) deceitful trick, esp by a criminal in order to get money etc from s.o: *The whole thing was a con as he lent them over £10 000 and never got a penny of it back*.

▷ *tr.v* (-nn-) **2** (often — s.o out of s.t) (*informal*) deceive, cheat, (s.o) (by getting money etc from her/him): *He conned the old lady out of all her savings. We've been conned because the travel agency that sold us our tickets doesn't exist any more*.

'con-,man/woman *c.n* (also **'confidence ,trickster**) a person who cons(2) people.

'con-,trick *c.n* (also **'confidence ,trick**) ⇒ con(1).

concave /'kɒnkeɪv/ *adj* having a curve that goes inwards, like the inside shape of a spoon: *a concave mirror*. Compare convex.

conceal /kən'siːl/ *tr.v* (*formal*) **1** hide (s.o/s.t), put (s.o/s.t) in a place, to stop other people seeing or finding her/him/it: *He concealed the jewels behind the cupboard*. **2** not allow (s.t esp one's thoughts) to become known: *She concealed her fear from the younger members of the group*.

con'cealment *u.n* act or fact of concealing s.t or of being concealed.

concede /kən'siːd/ *tr.v* (often — s.t to s.o) (*formal*) **1** give way on (s.t), admit that s.o may be right about s.t, usu without wanting to: *He conceded that point in the argument in order to get his way on the others*. **2** give (s.t, esp ownership of land etc, a right) (to s.o): *The country was forced to concede land on its borders to the enemy after the war*. **concede defeat** say, recognize, that one has been defeated: *The opposition party conceded defeat when it became clear that they had lost the election*. ⇒ cede.

concession /kən'seʃən/ *n* **1** *u.n* act of conceding(1) s.t: *The concession by the employers was greeted as a victory by the workers*. **2** *c.n* thing that has been conceded(1): *We won several concessions over working conditions*. **3** *c.n* (often — on s.t) reduction in the price (of a cost, ticket etc): *Do you give concessions to students? Students get concessions on bus fares(1)*. **4** *c.n* (*formal*) right given by s.o to s.o else to do s.t, esp to take minerals, oil etc from a place, to sell s.t etc: *a fishing/mining concession*.

concessionary /kən'seʃənəri/ *adj* (*formal*) given or allowed as a concession(3): *He has a concessionary ticket to use the swimming pool*.

conceit /kən'siːt/ *u.n* too great a feeling of one's own importance, value etc: *He has too much conceit for his own good and he should learn some humility*. **full of conceit** having, showing, this feeling: *Jane's so full of conceit about being accepted into Oxford University*.

con'ceited *adj* (*derog*) (of a person) having, showing, too great a feeling of one's own importance, value: *Don't be so conceited; we all have our weaknesses, even you*.

con'ceitedly *adv*. **con'ceitedness** *u.n*.

conceive /kən'siːv/ *v* (not used in the continuous tenses[2]) (*formal*) **1** *tr.v* think of, have, (a new idea, plan etc) in one's mind: *He conceived the idea of changing the course of the river to prevent flooding*. **2** *intr.v* imagine (s.t) being possible, happening: *I can't conceive how you can expect to win*. ⇒ concept, conception. **3** *tr/intr.v* (of a woman) become pregnant: *It was not until she*

was thirty-five that she conceived for the first time.

con'ceivable *adj* (often *not*, *scarcely* etc — (*that*) . . .) able to be believed or imagined: *It is hardly conceivable that you allowed him to do it. I can think of no conceivable reason why Lynne left her job*. Opposite inconceivable.

con'ceivably *adv* possibly; perhaps; if one thinks about it: *Conceivably, the situation could change*.

concentrate /'kɒnsən,treɪt/ *c/u.n* **1** substance made stronger, esp by removing unnecessary or extra liquid, e.g water: *orange concentrate. You need to use only a very little of this dishwashing concentrate to get your dishes clean*.

▷ *v* **2** *tr.v* make (a substance, esp a liquid) stronger by removing unnecessary, extra substances, esp water: *The juice was concentrated by boiling to get rid of excess water*. **3** *tr/intr.v* (often — (one's mind, attention etc) on s.o/(doing) s.t) make (one's mind etc) think hard, clearly, about s.o/s.t; direct (all one's attention etc) (towards s.o/(doing) s.t): *He concentrated all his efforts on winning the race. I can't concentrate (on my work) with you making all that noise*. **4** *tr.v* bring/put (s.t) in one place: *All the shops are concentrated in a small area in the middle of the town*.

'concen,trated *adj* **1** (of a substance) made by concentrating(2) s.t: *Add one part of the concentrated orange juice to three parts of water*. **2** (usu *attrib*) with all one's attention or strength: *They made a concentrated effort to defeat the government*.

concentration /,kɒnsən'treɪʃən/ *n* **1** *u.n* great attention of one's mind (on s.t): *It needed a lot of concentration to understand his lecture*. **2** *c.n* putting, existence, of a large number (of people, things etc) in one place: *There are concentrations of manufacturers in the north of the country*.

,concen'tration ,camp *c.n* place with fences and buildings where political or military(1) prisoners are kept (esp during a war).

concentric /kən'sentrɪk/ *adj* (of two or more circles) having the same centre as each other. Compare eccentric(2).

concept /'kɒnsept/ *c.n* idea, thought, plan, (that one has (formed) in one's mind about s.t): *Freedom is a concept that means different things to different people. The concept of colour is almost impossible to explain to a blind person*.

conception /kən'sepʃən/ *n* **1** *u.n* act of making or thinking of an idea, plan etc: *We have a falling apple to thank for the conception of gravity[2]*. **2** *c/u.n* idea, plan in one's mind about s.t, how s.t will happen etc: *The committee considered several conceptions for the city centre. You have no conception how hard I tried*. ⇒ conceive(2). **3** *u.n* act, fact, moment, of conceiving(3).

conceptual /kən'septjʊəl/ *adj* of or referring to a concept: *He is very good at conceptual thinking*.

concern /kən'sɜːn/ *n* **1** *c.n* thing that is of interest; matter of importance (to s.o): *My concern is that you should be happy*. **2** *u.n* (often — about/for s.o/s.t) feeling of worry, anxiety etc (about etc s.o/s.t): *Concern is being expressed for the safety of the children*. Opposite unconcern. **3** *sing.n* thing that is s.o's responsibility, duty or that concerns(8) one: *It's no concern of mine*.

Education is the concern of every parent. It's his concern if he goes to work late every day. There is growing concern about the shortage of housing in the city. **4** *c.n* (*formal*) business company; business interest: *He has several business concerns in America.* **a going/paying concern** a business that is already in existence and making profits: *He bought the company as a going concern.* (**be** etc) **a/no cause for concern** (be etc) (not) something that worries one: *Their disappearance is a cause for concern. There's no cause for concern yet.* **none of her, his** etc **concern** that does not involve her, him etc; that is none of her/his business(6): *This argument is none of your concern so go away.* **of concern (to s.o)** interesting, important, (to s.o); worrying (for s.o): *These are matters of concern to all teachers. The next part of the meeting is of no concern to our visitors so perhaps they'd like to take an early tea break.*
▷ *tr.v* **5** be of interest to, be important to, (s.o): *What you say or do doesn't concern me.* **6** cause (s.o) to feel worried, anxious, (about s.o/s.t): *What concerns me is that he's not eating at all. Sally is concerning us all because she seems so miserable all the time.* **7** (of an event, story etc) be about, deal with, (s.o/s.t): *What I have to say concerns a person you know.* **8** affect, involve(2), (s.o); be the responsibility of (s.o): *The matter of nuclear*(2) *arms concerns all of us, not just politicians.* **concern oneself about/in/with s.o/ s.t (a)** take an active interest in (s.o/s.t) (often in an anxious way): *You shouldn't concern yourself with men at your age; you'll have plenty of time when you're older.* (**b**) be worried about (s.o/s.t): *Don't concern yourself about him, he'll be okay.*
con'cerned *adj* Opposite unconcerned. **1** (often — about s.o/(doing) s.t) anxious or worried (about s.o/s.t): *Simon is very concerned about not finishing the work on time. I'm very concerned that she won't live through the operation.* **2** (usu — with s.t) taking part, involved(1), (in (doing) s.t): *She's not concerned with the everyday running of the business.* **as/so far as s.o/s.t is concerned** ⇒ far(*adv*). **the people** etc **concerned** those mentioned who are taking part in s.t, who are affected by s.t: *Will all those not concerned in this matter please leave the room.*
con'cerning *prep* (*formal*) of, referring to, about, (s.o/s.t): *I have little to say concerning your remarks about his character.*
concert /ˈkɒnsət/ *c.n* performance by one or more musicians and/or singers in front of an audience. **in concert (with s.o)** (acting) at the same time (as, together with, s.o): *The government acted in concert with other governments in trying to stop the trade in animal skins.*
concerted /kənˈsɜːtɪd/ *adj* (often (make) a — effort (to do s.t)) with everybody helping or doing their best, everything planned etc: *The government promised to make a concerted effort to raise living standards for the poor and old.*
concertina /ˌkɒnsəˈtiːnə/ *n* **1** *c.n* kind of musical instrument, like an accordion, played by squeezing(5) it between the hands and pressing keys at the ends.
▷ *intr.v* **2** become squashed[1](4), pressed into folds, like a concertina(1), esp as a result of a crash:

The carriages of the train concertinaed when the engine ran into them.
concerto /kənˈtʃeətəʊ/ *c.n* (*pl* -s) piece of music written for one or more musical instruments and an orchestra: *piano concertos.*
concession(ary) ⇒ concede.
conciliate /kənˈsɪlɪeɪt/ *tr.v* (*formal*) win the friendship of (s.o who was against one, angry with one etc); calm (s.o): *My attempts to conciliate him after our argument failed.*
conciliation /kənˌsɪlɪˈeɪʃən/ *c/u.n* act of conciliating, esp in a disagreement between employers and workers: *The government attempted conciliation but the talks broke down.*
conciliatory /kənˈsɪlɪətərɪ/ *adj* (*formal*) who/ that attempts to conciliate, offers conciliation: *After the disagreement, he became very conciliatory.*
concise /kənˈsaɪs/ *adj* (of a person, s.t said or written etc) very clear and brief[1] in what one says, writes etc: *You must try to make your reports more concise.*
con'cisely *adv.* **con'ciseness** *u.n.*
conclude /kənˈkluːd/ *v* (*formal*) **1** *tr/intr.v* (cause (a meeting, s.t being said etc) to) come to an end: *The meeting (was) concluded with a few words of thanks to the guest speaker. He concluded (his speech) by suggesting that further work on the subject was needed. The meeting concluded at 6 o'clock.* **2** *intr.v* (often — (from s.t) that . . .) reach an opinion, decide, (from what s.o has said, done etc) (that . . .): *He concluded from her remarks that she was interested in the job.*
conclusion /kənˈkluːʒən/ *c.n* **1** (*formal*) end: *At the conclusion of the meeting he thanked them all for their help.* **2** (often come to/reach a —) opinion, decision or judgement arrived at after some thought: *He came to the conclusion that she didn't want to see him again.* **a foregone conclusion** ⇒ foregone(1). **in conclusion** in the end, esp as the last of a number of remarks: *In conclusion I would like to thank everybody who helped.* **jump to conclusions; jump to the conclusion that . . .** form an opinion too quickly before one knows all the facts: *You're always jumping to conclusions and never let me finish what I want to say.*
conclusive /kənˈkluːsɪv/ *adj* (of facts etc) proving s.t is true, removing any doubt: *There is conclusive proof that the government was lying.*
con'clusively *adv.* **con'clusiveness** *u.n.*
concoct /kənˈkɒkt/ *tr.v* **1** make (s.t, esp a new dish, drink etc) by mixing different things together: *He concocted a drink from various fruit juices.* **2** invent, make up, (a story, reason etc, esp an untrue one): *He had to concoct a reason why he hadn't been able to go to the party.*
concoction /kənˈkɒkʃən/ *c/u.n* (example of the) act of concocting; thing that has been concocted.
concord /ˈkɒnkɔːd/ *u.n* (*formal*) (feeling of) friendliness or peace (between two or more people, countries etc): *There was not much concord when the two governments tried to settle their differences.* (**live** etc) **in concord (with s.o)** (live etc) peacefully, in agreement, (with s.o).
concordat /kɒnˈkɔːdæt/ *c.n* signed agreement

between two countries etc about their relations with each other.

concourse /'kɒnkɔːs/ *c.n* large space, either covered or open, in a railway station, shopping centre etc where people gather, meet etc: *The airport concourse was crowded with travellers.*

concrete /'kɒnkriːt/ *adj* **1** made of concrete(4): *a concrete path/floor.* **2** (of plans, ideas etc) very firm and real: *The police did not want to arrest the suspect until they found concrete proof of his guilt. We need concrete proposals about how to deal with the problem.* **3** (*formal*) (of objects, things etc) existing, solid, real, (that one can see, touch etc): *Wood in all its forms is a concrete substance.* Opposite abstract[1](1).

▷ *u.n* **4** kind of very hard substance made by mixing cement(1), sand, small stones and water together, used in building, roads, paths etc: *The builders are laying the concrete for the new floor today.*

▷ *tr.v* **5** use concrete(4) in the making of (s.t), for covering the surface of (s.t): *He concreted the front drive to his house.*

'concrete ,mixer *c.n* machine with an engine and a round drum that turns and mixes concrete(4) in it.

,concrete 'noun *c.n* (*grammar*) noun describing objects or real things: *'Chair' is a concrete noun.* Opposite abstract noun.

concubine /'kɒŋkjuːbaɪn/ *c.n* **1** (*old use*) woman living with a man and having a sexual relationship with him but not married to him: *The king had several concubines.* **2** (in some countries) second or less important wife.

concur /kən'kɜː/ *intr.v* (*-rr-*) (*formal*) **1** (usu — with s.o (on s.t)) agree (with s.o (about s.t)): *I concur with him on the proposed solution. We argued for hours but at last I concurred and said I'd go with him.* **2** (of events etc) happen at the same time: *Everything concurred to make our plans much easier.*

concurrence /kən'kʌrəns/ *c/u.n* (*formal*) (example of) agreement: *It took some time but at last there was concurrence (of opinion).*

concurrent /kən'kʌrənt/ *adj* (*formal*) **1** happening at the same time (as each other): *The two sentences for the crimes he had done were made concurrent.* Compare consecutive. **2** agreeing (with each other): *concurrent views on the subject.*

con'currently *adv* at the same time: *I've been given permission to study law and English concurrently.*

concuss /kən'kʌs/ *tr.v* (often passive) injure(1) or damage (s.o) by a hard blow on the head which affects the brain (and often leads to unconsciousness): *He was concussed for two hours after he fell down the stairs.*

concussion /kən'kʌʃən/ *u.n* act or state of confusion or unconsciousness caused by a blow on the head.

condemn /kən'dem/ *tr.v* **1** (often — s.o/s.t for s.t) criticize, disapprove of, (s.o/s.t) strongly (for s.t he/she has done wrong): *Neighbours condemned him for his ill-treatment of his wife. I condemn violence of any kind.* **2** (*law*) (usu — s.o to s.t (for s.t)) sentence (s.o) (to a certain punishment) (for a crime): *He was condemned to five years in prison for his part in the murder.* **3** (often — s.o to (do) s.t) (of a circumstance(1), accident etc) force (s.o) (to do, have, s.t he/she

would otherwise not have done/had): *Poverty had condemned him to a life of misery.* **4** say that (s.t, esp food, a building etc) is not safe, should not be used, lived in etc: *The building was condemned even though people still lived in it.*

con,demned 'cell *def.n* room in a prison in which a person condemned(2) to death stays.

condemnation /,kɒndem'neɪʃən/ *c/u.n* (example of the) act of condemning(1) (s.o/s.t): *The letter was a condemnation of the way the police handled the riots(1).*

condense /kən'dens/ *v* **1** *tr.v* make (an account, story etc) shorter (in length, time) by removing (less important) parts: *He was asked to condense his report into one page. The meeting had to be condensed into one hour.* **2** *tr/intr.v* (cause (a liquid) to) become thicker and stronger, concentrated(1), by removing some of the water. ⇒ condensed milk. **3** *intr.v* (esp of water present in the air) become liquid, esp when cooled: *As the temperature dropped, water condensed on the windows of his car.*

condensation /,kɒnden'seɪʃən/ *c/u.n* (example of the) act of condensing(3): *Small drops of condensation collected on the leaves during the evening.*

con'densed *adj* **1** made thicker, more solid and concentrated(2). **2** (of an account etc) made shorter but with all the important parts kept: *a condensed report; a condensed version of the play.*

con,densed 'milk *c.n* kind of milk made thicker and more concentrated(2) by heating, cooling and the addition of sugar.

condescend /,kɒndɪ'send/ *intr.v* **1** (often — to do s.t) (*formal*) agree kindly, gracefully or formally (to do s.t) though one's high position does not demand it: *The mayor has condescended to open the fair.* **2** (often — to s.o) (*derog*) act in a way (towards s.o) that shows that one thinks oneself to be more important socially: *I dislike the way she condescends to her neighbours.*

,conde'scending *adj* (*derog*) thinking/acting in a way that shows one thinks oneself more important socially: *his condescending attitude.*

,conde'scendingly *adv*.

condescension /,kɒndɪ'senʃən/ *u.n* (*formal*) fact or state of condescending: *There was no sign of condescension in his voice when he spoke to his farm workers.*

condiment /'kɒndɪmənt/ *c.n* (often *pl*) (*formal*) substance, such as salt or pepper, used to give flavour or seasoning to food.

condition /kən'dɪʃən/ *n* **1** *u.n* state in which s.t is or exists, esp when it is not as good as it should be: *Look at the condition of your bicycle; you don't look after it at all. What condition is the old stove in?* **2** *u.n* state of one's health or body, esp when it is not good: *His condition is causing concern and the doctors say he may not last the night.* **3** *c.n* action, promise etc that has to be agreed to or done (before s.t else follows): *He made two conditions before he accepted the job.* **be in no condition to do s.t** be unable to do s.t, esp because of one's bad health: *You're in no condition to be out of bed.* **in bad, good** *etc* **condition** (of an object, machine etc) (not) working well etc; (not) damaged in any way: *That tyre is in bad condition, you'd better get*

a new one. **in**, **out of**, **condition** (of a person, animal) fit, not fit: *Bob's very out of condition because he doesn't take any exercise. The horse will be in top condition for the race*. (**do s.t**) **on condition that...**; (**do s.t**) **on one** etc **condition**, (**which is**) **that . . .** (do s.t) if one thing or more is agreed, accepted, which is that . . . : *He said he would go on condition that the others would come with him. I'll lend you my bicycle on one condition, that you always leave it locked*. ⇒ on/ under certain conditions (⇒ conditions).
▷ *tr.v* **4** (often passive) influence or control (s.o, her/ his actions, way of life etc): *The way they lived was conditioned by their lack of money*. **5** (often — s.o to do s.t; — s.o into doing s.t) force s.o (to behave, think in a certain way), esp by continuous pressure: *Your ideas are conditioned by your background. I've conditioned myself to get up* (or *into getting up*) *early in the morning*.
conditional /kən'dɪʃənl/ *adj* **1** (often — (*up*)*on* s.t) if a certain condition(3) or conditions (which is/are s.t) is/are agreed: *I have a conditional offer of a job; it all depends on whether I'm prepared to go to London three times a week. The offer was conditional on them accepting by the end of the week*. ⇒ unconditional.
▷ *c.n* **2** = conditional clause/sentence.
con'ditional ,clause/,sentence *u.n* (*grammar*) clause/sentence that has a condition(3) in it, usu shown by 'if' or 'unless', e.g 'if there's time' in 'I'll come if there's time'.
con'ditionally *adv*.
con'ditioned *adj* forced to behave, think, in a certain way: *She shows every sign of conditioned thinking*. **a conditioned reflex** ⇒ reflex[1].
-conditioned *adj* put into the state shown by the first part of the word: *a well-conditioned engine*. ⇒ air-conditioned.
con'ditioner *c.n* substance or product that improves the quality of s.t, e.g one's hair, skin or another substance: *a hair conditioner; a* fabric(1) *conditioner*.
con'ditioning *u.n* (often *derog*) way in which one was brought up from childhood; influence of one's experiences: *It's your conditioning that makes you believe things like that*.
con'ditions *pl.n* (often bad) state of things; what one has around one which affects one: *His living conditions were terrible. Driving conditions were bad because of the weather*. **on/under certain** etc **conditions** if certain things are agreed to or accepted first: *He said he would only help on certain conditions*. ⇒ do (s.t) on condition that . . .; on one etc condition, (which is) that . . . (condition).
condole /kən'dəʊl/ *tr/intr.v* (usu — (*with*) s.o ((*up*)*on* s.t)) (*formal*) say that one sympathizes with (s.o) (about s.t, esp a death): *They condoled with her on the death of her husband*.
condolence /kən'dəʊləns/ *n* **1** *u.n* expression of sympathy: *He sent her a letter of condolence*. **2** *c.n* (often *pl*) expression of sympathy: *He sent her his condolences*.
condom /'kɒndɒm/ *c.n* thin rubber covering worn over the penis during the sexual act to stop sperm(2) and protect against disease; male contraceptive(2).
condone /kən'dəʊn/ *tr.v* (*formal*) forgive (s.o for s.t wrong he/she has done); overlook (s.t

wrong that s.o has done): *I find it difficult to condone her behaviour. This government will not condone violence*.
condonation /,kɒndəʊ'neɪʃən/ *u.n* (*formal*) act of condoning.
conducive /kən'djuːsɪv/ *adj* (often — *to* s.t) (*formal*) likely to produce s.t, leading towards s.t: *The quiet of the country is conducive to rest*.
conduct /'kɒndʌkt/ *u.n* **1** way, good or bad, in which a person behaves: *The teacher gave him marks for good conduct*. **2** way in which s.t is done, carried out: *Her conduct of the meeting made certain members angry*.
▷ *v* /kən'dʌkt/ **3** *tr.v* (*formal*) lead or guide (s.o): *The waiter conducted us to our seats*. **4** *tr.v* (*formal*) organize, manage or control (s.t, esp a business, one's affairs etc): *He conducts his affairs as though he had all the money in the world. We are conducting a* survey(1) *for the* BBC *so please would you answer a few questions?* **5** *tr/intr.v* direct (a performance of a musical work) (by a group of musicians and/ or singers) by standing in front (of them) and giving (them) signs with one's hands, a baton(2); do this as a job: *André Previn is conducting the New World Symphony, the London Symphony Orchestra, this week. He conducts very well*. **6** *tr.v* (*technical*) (of a substance or a passage) act as a path for (electricity, water, heat etc): *This wire conducts electricity. These pipes conduct hot water throughout the building*. **7** *reflex.v* (*formal*) behave (well etc): *He conducted himself very well during the ceremony*.
con,ducted 'tour *c.n* (also ,**guided 'tour**) visit to a place or places by s.o, a group of people, with a guide to explain it/them: *He went on a conducted tour of London*.
conduction /kən'dʌkʃən/ *u.n* (*technical*) act or fact of conducting(6) electricity through a substance, water, heat etc along a path or passage.
conductivity /,kɒndʌk'tɪvɪtɪ/ *u.n* (*technical*) (measurement of the) ability of things, e.g metals, to conduct(6) electricity etc.
conductor /kən'dʌktə/ *c.n* **1** (*technical*) thing, e.g a metal, that conducts(6) electricity etc: *Most metals are good conductors of heat*. **2** person who conducts(5) a group of musicians etc. **3** (also '**bus/'tram con,ductor**) person who collects money and gives out tickets on a bus/tram. **4** (US) guard(4) on a train.
conductress /kən'dʌktrɪs/ *c.n* (also '**bus/'tram con,ductress**) female conductor(3).
conduit /'kɒndɪt/ *c.n* (*technical*) pipe or channel(1) carrying water, electric cables etc.
cone /kəʊn/ *c.n* **1** (*geometry*) solid shape that is round at the bottom and comes to a point at the top. **2** = fir/pine[1](1) cone. **3** shape like this but hollow, in which s.t is put: *an ice-cream cone*. **4** shape like this, usu made of plastic(3) and brightly coloured, used on roads to stop traffic from going on certain sections, e.g because of repairs, accidents etc.
▷ *tr.v* **5 cone s.t off** put cones(4) on a section of a road, motorway etc to stop traffic using it: *Because of repairs, two* lanes(3) *of the* motorway *have been coned off*.
conic /'kɒnɪk/ *adj* (also '**conical**) shaped like a cone(1): *a conic shell; conical-shaped flowers*.
confectionery /kən'fekʃənərɪ/ *n* (*pl* -*ies*) **1** *u.n*

sweets, cakes etc: *They sell all kinds of confec-tionery.* **2** *c.n* shop for sweets, cakes etc or place where they are made.
confectioner /kən'fekʃənə/ *c.n* **1** (*formal*) person who makes or sells sweets, cakes etc. **2** (also **con'fectioner's**) *c.n* shop where sweets, cakes etc are sold.
confederacy /kən'fedərəsɪ/ *n* (*pl* -*ies*) **1** *c.n* group of states, esp in one country, joined together politically. **2** *def.n* (with capital **C**) (US) group of eleven states in the southern USA which broke away from the others in 1861 and so started the American Civil War.
confederate¹ /kən'fedərɪt/ *adj* **1** joined in a confederacy(1): *a confederate state.*
▷ *c.n* /kən'fedərɪt/ **2** (*derog*; *formal*) person who joins others in doing s.t, esp carrying out a crime: *He and his confederates were arrested by the police.* **3** (US) (also *attrib*) person who belonged to or supported the Confederacy(2): *a confederate soldier.*
▷ *tr/intr.v* /kən'fedəˌreɪt/ **4** (cause (s.t) to) become (part of) a confederacy(1).
confederation /kənˌfedə'reɪʃən/ *n* **1** *u.n* act of confederating or being confederated. **2** *c.n* group of states, organizations etc joined together for some purpose: *He formed a confederation of small shopkeepers.*
confer /kən'fɜː/ *v* (-*rr*-) (*formal*) **1** *intr.v* (often — *with* s.o) discuss, talk together, (with s.o): *He conferred with other members of the committee before reaching a decision.* **2** *tr.v* (usu — s.t (up)on s.o) give (an honour to s.o) in a formal ceremony: *Glasgow University conferred an honorary(2) degree on the politician.*
conference /'kɒnfərəns/ *c.n* meeting of a group of people in a place or room to discuss a particular subject for a short time or for a number of days: *He attended a conference on teaching languages.* **be in conference** be at a (business) meeting (and so unable to see visitors): *The manager is in conference, so could you call back later?*
confess /kən'fes/ *v* **1** *tr.v* (often — s.t to s.o; — that . . .) say, admit, (to s.o) that one has done s.t wrong: *He confessed his crime to the police. She confessed that she had taken the money.* **2** *intr.v* (often — *to* s.t) admit (to having done s.t wrong): *Under pressure from the police, he finally confessed.* **3** *tr/intr.v* (often — *to* s.t; — *that* . . .) (*formal*) say, express, (s.t); be honest about s.t: *I must confess to a certain surprise at his statement. I confess (that) I was very unhappy about your decision.* **4** *tr/intr.v* (in the Christian(1) religion) tell (one's sins(1)) to a priest: *He confessed (his sins) just before he died.*
confession /kən'feʃən/ *c/u.n* **1** (example of the) act of confessing(1,2): *The police got confessions from all of them.* **2** (example of the) act of confessing(4): *Confession is held at the church every Saturday evening.* **go to confession** go to a church and confess to a priest.
confessional /kən'feʃənl/ *c.n* place in a church where confessions(2) are heard by a priest.
con'fessor *c.n* priest to whom one makes a confession(2).
confetti /kən'fetɪ/ *u.n* very small pieces of coloured paper (to be) thrown at the bride and bridegroom at a wedding.

confide /kən'faɪd/ *v* **1** *intr.v* (usu — *in* s.o) share one's private thoughts (with s.o), tell a secret (to s.o), esp in the belief that he/she will not talk to others about it/them: *There was no one he could confide in.* **2** *tr.v* (often — s.t to s.o) tell (s.t secret or not known) (to s.o): *He confided his most secret thoughts to his best friend.*
confidant /'kɒnfɪˌdænt/ *c.n* person to whom one tells one's secrets etc.
confidante /'kɒnfɪˌdænt/ *c.n* female confidant.
confidence /'kɒnfɪdəns/ *n* **1** *u.n* (often — *in* oneself/s.o/s.t) belief or faith in one's own or others' ability: *He shows great confidence in his handling of people. They have no confidence in the government.* ⇒ self-confidence. **2** *c.n* something told as a secret to s.o who is not supposed to tell others: *They told each other confidences about their boyfriends.* **lose confidence (in s.o/s.t)** no longer have confidence (in s.o/s.t). **take s.o into one's confidence** tell s.o s.t secret: *She took her sister into her confidence because she knew she could trust her.* (**tell s.o s.t) in (strict) confidence** (tell s.o a secret etc) expecting her/him not to tell anybody else: *I'm telling you this in strictest confidence so you mustn't breathe a word of it to anyone.*
'confidence ˌman/'trickster *c.n* ⇒ con-man (⇒ con).
'confidence-ˌtrick *c.n* ⇒ con-trick (⇒ con(1)).
confident /'kɒnfɪdənt/ *adj* (often — *about/of* s.t; — *that* . . .) very sure and certain (about how s.t will happen, of one's ability to do s.t etc): *He's confident that he will win (or of winning). I don't feel confident about speaking in front of so many people.*
confidential /ˌkɒnfɪ'denʃəl/ *adj* **1** (of s.t said, written etc) secret, not to be told or shown to others: *The report was confidential but somebody sent a copy to the newspapers.* **2** (of a person) trusted to keep secrets: *He is advertising for a confidential secretary.*
confidentiality /ˌkɒnfɪˌdenʃɪ'ælɪtɪ/ *u.n* **1** fact or state of being secret: *I hope you understand the need for confidentiality in this matter.* **2** ability to keep s.t secret: *You can trust her confidentiality.*
ˌconfi'dentially *adv* in secret: *Confidentially, I don't trust him.*
confiding /kən'faɪdɪŋ/ *adj* (*formal*) (of a person) (too) trusting, esp in telling other people private things: *She has a too confiding nature and one day is going to get hurt.*
con'fidingly *adv.*
confine /kən'faɪn/ *tr.v* **1** (usu — s.o/s.t to s.t) keep (s.o/s.t) to within certain limits, esp in a conversation, talk, etc: *Could you confine your remarks to the subject in question, please?* **2** stop (s.t) spreading: *The firemen managed to confine the fire to the building.* **3** (usu — s.o, an animal, in/to s.w) (*formal*) keep (s.o, an animal) shut in a place, e.g as a prisoner or because he/she/it is ill: *He was confined in his prison cell. She was confined to bed because of a cold.*
con'fined *adj* (of a space) small, narrow and closed: *I hate being in a confined space.*
confinement /kən'faɪnmənt/ *c/u.n* **1** (act of) being imprisoned. ⇒ solitary confinement. **2** (*formal*) (act of) going to bed in order to give birth to a child.
confines /'kɒnfaɪnz/ *pl.n* (*formal*) limits or

borders (of a place, of knowledge etc). **beyond/within the confines of s.w/s.t** outside/inside such limits: *Because of the guards, he was not able to go beyond the confines of the garden. Could you please keep within the confines of the present subject during this meeting?*

confirm /kən'fɜːm/ *tr.v* **1** make (s.t) completely certain, often by putting it in writing, checking etc: *Phone me on Friday to confirm the arrangements. Could you please confirm your order for these goods in writing. Have you confirmed your flight?* **2** (in the Christian(1) religion) accept (s.o) into full membership of the church by a special ceremony. Compare baptize. **confirm (s.o in) s.t** make s.o believe s.t more strongly than before: *His remarks confirmed (me in) my opinion that he was a fool.*

confirmation /ˌkɒnfə'meɪʃən/ *c/u.n* (example of the) act of confirming: *This coupon(1) is your hotel confirmation. Have you received confirmation of our booking?*

con'firmed *adj* **1** very settled (in a way of life, a belief etc) and not likely to change: *He's a confirmed bachelor.* **2** (of reports etc) found to be true (by people who were there etc): *The government is waiting for a confirmed report of the event before taking action.* Opposite unconfirmed.

confiscate /'kɒnfɪˌskeɪt/ *tr.v* (of a person who has the power) take away (s.t s.o has or owns) without paying for it, esp because he/she should not have it, should not be using it at that time etc: *The teacher confiscated the magazine the boy had been reading in class.*

confiscation /ˌkɒnfɪ'skeɪʃən/ *u.n.*

conflict /'kɒnflɪkt/ *n* (formal) **1** *c/u.n* (example of a) disagreement or fight over an important matter: *There was a great deal of conflict between them before everything was settled.* **2** *c/u.n* (example — between s.t and s.t) (of feelings etc) (example of a) division (in which two things are opposed to each other): *suffer a conflict of loyalty between one's friends and family.* **3** *c.n* fight, war: *Thousands died in the conflict.* **be in conflict (with s.o/s.t)** be fighting or opposing (s.o/s.t): *The government is in conflict with the teachers over salaries.* **bring (s.o), come into, conflict with s.o/s.t** (cause (s.o) to) oppose, argue with, s.o/s.t: *His comments(1) brought him into conflict with his employers.*

▷ *intr.v* /kən'flɪkt/ (usu — with s.t) **4** (of a statement, report) disagree with, not be the same as, another statement etc: *The two reports conflict but I prefer to accept the second one.* **5** (of an activity) happen at the same time as s.t else and therefore make it necessary to choose: *The meeting conflicts with a dental appointment so I can't come this time.*

con'flicting *adj* (of activities, opinions, statements) disagreeing with one another; happening at the same time as one another: *Our lunch hours are at conflicting times today so we won't be able to meet.*

conform /kən'fɔːm/ *intr.v* (often — to s.t) follow, obey, the rules and normal behaviour of society (and so not be different from other people): *As a young person he refused to conform (to the social rules) but now he's a typical young businessman.* **conform to/with s.t** be of the quality, standard etc required by the law etc: *The building does not conform with the safety requirements.*

con'formist *adj* **1** (of a person, s.o's behaviour) who/that conforms.

▷ *c.n* **2** person who conforms. **3** person who obeys the rules of the Church of England. Opposite nonconformist.

con'formity *u.n* act of conforming, esp in one's behaviour. **(do s.t) in conformity with s.t** (formal) (do s.t) following or obeying rules, s.o's wishes etc: *In conformity with your instructions, I have paid him £500.*

confound /kən'faʊnd/ *tr.v* (formal) **1** surprise (s.o) to such an extent that he/she does not know what to do: *Her refusal completely confounded me.* **2** (usu — s.t with s.t) confuse (s.t with s.t else); mistake (s.t for s.t else): *He often confounds the two things because he doesn't think clearly.* **Confound it!** *interj* = Damn! Blast!

con'founded *attrib.adj* (formal) very annoying: *It's a confounded nuisance!*

confront /kən'frʌnt/ *tr.v* **1** (formal) face or oppose (an enemy etc) in order to stop her/his progress: *The police confronted the strikers(1) and stopped them from coming any closer.* **2** (often — s.o with s.o/s.t) force (s.o) to handle a problem, deal with s.o who is accusing her/him with s.t she/he has done wrong etc: *When he was confronted with the accusation he confessed. The only way to find out the truth is to confront him.*

confrontation /ˌkɒnfrʌn'teɪʃən/ *c/u.n.* (example of an) act of confronting s.o (with s.t): *The confrontation between the government and the unions led to a strike(1).*

confuse /kən'fjuːz/ *tr.v* **1** make (s.o) not understand s.t; mix (s.t) up in one's mind: *All the changes completely confused me so I didn't know what was happening.* **2** (usu — s.o/s.t with s.o/s.t) not be able to tell the difference (between s.o/s.t and s.o/s.t else): *He's always confusing the two brothers because they look so alike.*

con'fused *adj* (of a person, report etc) not at all clear (in one's mind); mixed up: *He's very confused and doesn't know who to believe.*

con'fusing *adj* (of a situation, account of s.t) not at all clear: *Her story is so confusing and I don't know who's telling the truth.*

confusion /kən'fjuːʒən/ *u.n* state of confusing s.o/s.t or of being confused: *The confusion was caused by selling more tickets than the number of seats.* **in confusion (a)** puzzled, not knowing what to do or think: *Ian was in some confusion as to what to do.* **(b)** (making s.o or becoming) surprised or embarrassed: *Peter was covered in confusion when he realized his mistake.* **throw s.o/s.t into confusion** make s.o, a situation, not at all clear.

congeal /kən'dʒiːl/ *tr/intr.v* (of blood, fatty liquids etc) (cause (s.t) to) become solid or dried: *The blood had congealed around the wound.*

congenial /kən'dʒiːnɪəl/ *adj* (formal) **1** (often — to s.o) (of a person) having the same interests (as oneself), showing warmth and friendliness (to one) and so pleasant to be with: *He was very congenial and I always enjoyed his company.* **2** (of a thing, activity, job etc) pleasant and easy: *congenial surroundings. The climate was congenial and her health improved.*

congenital /kən'dʒenɪtl/ *adj* (medical) (of a disease, of s.t wrong with one's body or mind) existing before, or at the time of, birth: *He suffers from a congenital disease of the brain.*

congested /kən'dʒestɪd/ *adj* **1** (of a place, esp a town, street etc) too full of traffic and people (and so not easy to move about in): *The centre of town becomes very congested with cars on Saturdays.* **2** (*medical*) (of a part of the body) having become too full of liquid: *His lungs were congested* (*with blood*).

congestion /kən'dʒestʃən/ *u.n* state of being congested: *congestion of the lungs.*

conglomerate /kən'glɒmərɪt/ *c.n* **1** (also *attrib*) (*technical*) (of rock) mass of small round stones stuck together: *a conglomerate rock. The rock was a conglomerate.* **2** (*commerce*) large company made up from several smaller ones: *He worked for a large conglomerate which had interests in oil,* transport(2) *and food.* **3** anything that consists of too many different kinds of things and therefore has no unity: *Your work is a conglomerate of disorganized thoughts.*
▷ *tr/intr.v* /kən'glɒmə,reɪt/ **4** (*formal; technical*) (cause (s.t) to) come together in a mass.

conglomeration /kən,glɒmə'reɪʃən/ *n* **1** *u.n* act of conglomerating(4) or state of being conglomerated. **2** *c.n* group of many different things joined together in a mass (often without much order): *The book is a conglomeration of other people's opinions.*

congratulate /kən'grætjʊ,leɪt/ *tr.v* (often — *s.o* (*up*)on *s.t*) (*formal*) say (to s.o) that one is pleased or happy (about s.t good which has happened to him/her): *I'd like to be the first to congratulate you on your success.* **congratulate oneself** be, say that one is, proud of oneself: *It's early to congratulate ourselves because we haven't won yet.*

congratulation /kən,grætjʊ'leɪʃən/ *u.n* (or *attrib*) act of congratulating: *Suzanna received many cards of congratulation* (or *congratulation cards*) *when she had her baby.*

con,gratu'lations *pl.n,interj* (also *attrib*) (word used when one wants to state one's) pleasure or happiness (to s.o) for s.t good which has happened to her/him: *Congratulations on your success!*

congratulatory /kən'grætjʊ,leɪtərɪ/ *adj* showing or offering congratulations: *We must send them a congratulatory telegram.*

congregate /'kɒngrɪ,geɪt/ *intr.v* (*formal*) come together in a group: *A crowd congregated round the speaker.*

congregation /,kɒngrɪ'geɪʃən/ *c.n* the whole number of people who gather together in a church for a religious service (except the priest and choir): *The priest led the congregation in prayers.*

congress /'kɒŋgres/ *n* **1** *c.n* formal meeting of people with the same jobs or interests, or representatives of countries etc, to discuss matters concerning them, usu for a number of days: *There was a dentists' congress on in town and I couldn't get into a hotel.* **2** *unique n* (with capital **C**) (US and other countries) the elected group of people who make the laws of the country. **3** *unique n* (with capital **C**) (in India) one of the political parties.

congressional /,kən'greʃənl/ *adj* of or referring to Congress(2): *a congressional committee/hearing.*

'Congressman *c.n* (*pl -men*) man who is a member of Congress(2).

'Congress,woman *c.n* (*pl -,women*) woman who is a member of Congress(2).

conic(al) ⇒ cone.

conifer /'kəʊnɪfə/ *c.n* (*technical*) kind of tree that produces fir cones or pine cones and stays green in winter.

coniferous /kə'nɪfərəs/ *adj* of, containing, this kind of tree: *coniferous forests.*

conj *written abbr* conjunction(1).

conjecture /kən'dʒektʃə/ *c/u.n* (*formal*) **1** (example of an) opinion or guess about s.t, esp when one does not know all the facts: *I can make no conjectures about his future actions. You don't actually know he murdered her; it's just conjecture on your part.* **be pure conjecture** (of a statement etc) be only what one thinks about s.t, not what one knows.
▷ *tr/intr.v* **2** (often — *that . . .*) form or make a conjecture(1) (about s.t): *He conjectured that the government would change its mind. One can only conjecture since we have no facts.*

conjectural /kən'dʒektʃərəl/ *adj* (of a thought, statement etc) based on conjecture(1).

conjugal /'kɒndʒʊgl/ *adj* (*formal*) of or referring to the relations and rights of a husband and a wife (esp in matters of sex, property etc): *conjugal happiness; conjugal rights.*

conjugate /'kɒndʒʊ,geɪt/ *tr.v* (*grammar*) state the different forms, e.g number, person and tense², of, (of a verb): *Have you learned how to conjugate verbs in Latin yet?*

conjugation /,kɒndʒʊ'geɪʃən/ *n* **1** *c/u.n* (example of the) act of conjugating verbs. **2** *c.n* group of verbs having the same kind of tenses², endings etc as each other: *Latin has four conjugations.*

conjunction /kən'dʒʌŋkʃən/ *n* **1** *c.n* (*written abbr conj*) (*grammar*) word that joins two words or clauses(1) together: *In the sentence, 'Mary and John love each other but John loves Mary more than she loves him',* 'and', 'but(2)' *and* 'than' *are conjunctions.* **2** *u.n* (*formal*) (of actions, events etc) joining or coming together: *The conjunction of her ability and his knowledge made them successful partners.* **in conjunction** (**with s.o/s.t**) together (with s.o/s.t): *The two governments worked in conjunction* (*with each other*) *to stop the trade in arms.*

conjure /'kʌndʒə/ *tr/intr.v* perform a trick by making (s.t) (seem to) appear, disappear etc: *He conjured a whole set of playing cards from his ear.* **conjure s.t up** (**a**) (by a description) form a picture of s.t in the mind: *Her words conjured up for me the beauty of the city.* (**b**) (*formal*) (by means of magic(3), spells²(1) etc) (appear to) make spirits (⇒ spirit(11)), dead people etc come into one's presence, come back to life etc: *He claimed he could conjure up the Devil(1).* (**c**) put together, cook, a meal, etc, esp in a hurry, without much warning etc: *David was very good at conjuring up an interesting meal from almost nothing.*

'conjurer *c.n* (also **'conjuror**) person who conjures, performs tricks, esp as a job.

'conjuring ,trick *c.n* trick in which s.t appears, disappears etc (as if) by magic(3).

conk /kɒŋk/ *c.n* **1** (*slang*) nose: *He's got a big red conk.*

▷ *tr.v* **2** (*slang*) hit (s.o) hard with the hand or with a hard object: *I conked him on the head with a chair*. **conk out** (**a**) (of a vehicle, machine etc) break down; stop working: *The old car conked out as I was driving to London*. (**b**) (of a person) stop doing everything and rest because of being very tired: *I'm so tired when I get home from work that I conk out on my bed for a few hours*.

conker /ˈkɒŋkə/ *c.n* (child's word for a) horse-chestnut.

'conkers *u.n* game played by children in which two horse-chestnuts, each on a string, are hit against each other until one breaks.

con-man = confidence man (⇨ confide).

connect /kəˈnekt/ *v* **1** *tr.v* (often — *s.t* up (*to/with s.t*)) join (s.t) (to another): *He connected* (*up*) *the two wires. The new bridge connects the surrounding villages with the town*. **2** *intr.v* (often — *up* (*with s.t*)) join, be joined, in some way (with s.t): *This wire connects up with that one to produce an electric current. When the two wires connect they produce electricity*. **3** *tr.v* (often — *s.t* (*up*) *to an electricity, gas etc supply*) join (s.t) to the supply of electricity etc that will make it work: *Can you come to connect up our stove today?* (i.e to the gas or electricity supply). *I've bought my new hi-fi system but it's not connected yet*. **4** *tr.v* (usu — *s.o to/with s.o*) (of a telephone operator(2)) use a telephone line, lines, to let (s.o) talk (to s.o else): *Just a moment, I'll connect you to the manager*. **5** *intr.v* (usu — *with s.t*) (of a train, boat, bus or aircraft) arrive at a station, port or airport at a time that allows one to catch another train etc going s.w else: *This flight connects with one leaving London for Manchester an hour later*. ⇨ **connecting flight**. **6** *tr.v* (usu — *s.o/s.t with s.o/s.t*) think of (s.o/s.t), have (s.o/s.t) in one's mind, in relation to (s.o/s.t else): *'Oh, he's your son? I didn't connect you two at all!' I always connect him with my schooldays*. ⇨ **connected**.

con'nected *adj* (often — *with s.t*) having some kind of relation (with s.t): *I'm sure his behaviour and her sickness are connected in some way*. Opposite **unconnected**. **be connected to/with s.o** be some kind of relation (esp a family one) with s.o: *She's connected with royalty on both her mother's and her father's sides*. ⇨ **well-connected**. **be connected with s.t** have some degree of association with an activity etc, (be considered to) be concerned in s.t: *The police think he's connected with the recent robberies. Do you think the two crimes are connected?*

con'necting *adj* (usu *attrib*) joining or being joined together in some way: *The hotel gave us connecting rooms*.

con'necting ,flight *c.n* flight that leaves a place soon after another arrives, giving passengers time to move to that plane and continue their journey: *If you go via(1) Paris you can catch the connecting flight to London*.

connection /kəˈnekʃən/ *n* (also, less usu, **con'nexion**) **1** *c.n* thing that joins s.t with s.t else or is made to join s.t else: *The connection between the two wires was loose*. **2** *c.n* (in telephoning) line joining a place with the whole telephone system; line joining two people who want to talk to each other: *We had a very bad connection and I couldn't hear what he was saying*. **3** *c.n* (often *catch/miss a* —) bus, boat etc

that connects(5) with another one: *Because the train was late I missed my connection*. **4** *c/u.n* (example of the) state of being joined, having a relation, with s.o, esp in a family or business sense; person one knows well and can therefore use: *He has connections with many important people. What connection do you have with that company?* **5** *c/u.n* (often *make a* — (*between s.t and s.t*)) (example of the) act of thinking that one thing has a relation (with s.t else): *It took me a long time to make the connection between his disappearance and hers*. **in connection with s.t** (*formal*) about, referring to, s.t: *I'm writing to you in connection with your letter of 25 April*. **in this** etc **connection** of or referring to the matter being considered: *That is all I can say in that connection*.

con'nective *adj* that connects(1) two or more things: *connective tissue in the body*.

con'nector *c.n* thing that connects(1,3) electrical equipment(2), wires etc.

connive /kəˈnaɪv/ *intr.v* (*formal*) **1 connive at s.t** allow s.t bad or wrong to be done without helping actively but also without trying to prevent it: *I will not connive at your lies*. **2 connive with s.o** (*in, over, to do, s.t*) act in secret with (s.o) (about doing s.t wrong): *He connived with her in the robbery*.

connivance /kəˈnaɪvəns/ *u.n* (*formal*) **1 connivance at s.t** act of conniving at s.t. **2 in connivance with s.o; with the connivance of s.o** (acting) so as to connive with s.o in s.t wrong.

connoisseur /ˌkɒnəˈsɜː/ *c.n* (often — *of s.t*) person who has a lot of knowledge of, and a liking for, (s.t, esp art, food etc): *She's a connoisseur of fine wine*.

connote /kəˈnəʊt/ *tr.v* (*formal*) (of a word or expression) have a special or extra meaning (in addition to the ordinary one): *To me the word 'politician' connotes ambition and power*. Compare **denote**.

connotation /ˌkɒnəˈteɪʃən/ *c.n* special or extra meaning of a word. Compare **denotation**.

conquer /ˈkɒŋkə/ *v* **1** *tr/intr.v* defeat or overcome (an enemy), win a victory, by fighting: *After a number of battles the king succeeded in conquering his enemies*. **2** *tr.v* gain control of (a country etc) by force: *He conquered England in 1066AD*. **3** *tr.v* succeed in controlling (an emotion(1), esp fear etc), not allow (s.t) to affect one: *He had to learn to conquer his dislike of crowds*.

'conqueror *c.n* (with capital **C** in names) person who conquers(1,2) an enemy, country etc: *William the Conqueror*.

conquest /ˈkɒnkwest/ *n* **1** *u.n* act of winning a victory (over s.o, a country etc): *the conquest of England*. **2** *c.n* land, country etc one has conquered(2): *The emperor made several conquests in Asia*. **3** *u.n* (*formal*) success in controlling s.t (esp an emotion, a disease etc): *A lot of effort is going into the conquest of this disease*. **4** *u.n* success in being able to do s.t, win control over s.t: *The conquest of space is still many years away*. **5** *c.n* person whom one succeeds in attracting to oneself, who becomes one's lover etc: *Her latest conquest is a young man in his twenties*. **make a conquest of s.o** succeed in attracting s.o to become one's boyfriend or girlfriend.

cons ⇨ pros and cons.

conscience /ˈkɒnʃəns/ c/u.n (example of a) feeling or sense in one's mind about what is good or bad, right or wrong etc: *Her conscience told her that she was doing wrong. Their consciences were moved by the sight of such poverty.* **be**, **have s.o/s.t**, **on one's conscience** think about s.o/ s.t in a guilty way: *He's been on my conscience for the last month and I still haven't phoned him.* **have a (bad/guilty) conscience (about s.o/s.t)** feel guilty in one's mind (about s.o/s.t): *I don't see why I should have a bad conscience about not writing to her since she never writes to me.* **have a clear conscience (about s.o/s.t)** feel in one's mind that one has not done anything wrong, has behaved well etc (with regard to s.o/s.t). **prisoner of conscience** ⇨ prison(n).

conscientious /ˌkɒnʃɪˈenʃəs/ adj (of a person, her/his work etc) done with great care and as well as one can: *She's very conscientious and never neglects her duties.*

conscientious objector c.n (written abbr CO) person who refuses to fight, esp in a war, because he/she believes it is morally(2) wrong.

conscientiously adv. **conscientiousness** u.n.

conscious /ˈkɒnʃəs/ adj Opposite unconscious. 1 awake, having some or all of one's senses working, esp after having been unconscious(1), e.g after a blow, an accident etc: *When he became conscious again he realized he must have hit his head against the table.* 2 (of an action etc) done with full knowledge or after careful thought: *He made a conscious decision not to go to university.* ⇨ subconscious. **be conscious of s.o/s.t** be thinking, know, about s.o/s.t; have a knowledge in one's mind about s.o/s.t: *I wasn't conscious of anyone watching me.* **be conscious that** . . . know or realize that . . .: *I'm conscious that she dislikes me.*

consciously adv.

consciousness u.n 1 state of being awake, conscious(1). Opposite unconsciousness. 2 knowledge in one's mind about what one should do; thoughts or feelings about s.t: *In his own mind there was the consciousness that to say or do nothing would be* morally(2) *wrong.* **lose consciousness** become unconscious(1). **recover/regain consciousness** become awake, conscious(1) again, after having been unconscious(1).

conscript /ˈkɒnskrɪpt/ c.n (also attrib) 1 person forced by law to serve in the armed forces (usu for a certain period of time): *The army has to rely on conscripts (or conscript soldiers) to keep to its full strength.*

▷ tr.v /kənˈskrɪpt/ 2 (usu — s.o into s.t) make (s.o) a member (of the armed forces etc) by law: *He was conscripted into the army at the age of eighteen.*

conscription /kənˈskrɪpʃən/ u.n act or fact of conscripting(2) s.o: *The government introduced conscription when it saw that it could not avoid war.*

consecrate /ˈkɒnsɪˌkreɪt/ tr.v (in Christianity) make (a place, building etc) holy in a special religious ceremony: *The church was consecrated by the* bishop(1) *last Sunday.*

consecration /ˌkɒnsɪˈkreɪʃən/ c/u.n (example of the) act of consecrating or being consecrated.

consecutive /kənˈsekjʊtɪv/ adj (of a number of things, dates, times etc) that follow one another with no break in between: *He won five consecutive games in the first set of the tennis match.* Compare concurrent(1).

consecutively adv (for) one following another: *I've been there two years consecutively for my holiday.*

consensus /kənˈsensəs/ sing/u.n (formal) agreement by a number of people (esp after discussion or a disagreement): *The general consensus was that the plan should be dropped.* **consensus of opinion** general agreement about s.t. **achieve/reach a consensus** (of a number of people) succeed in getting or coming to an agreement.

consent /kənˈsent/ u.n (often — to (do) s.t) (formal) 1 permission or agreement by s.o (about s.t that can/should be done etc): *He gave his consent to their marriage.*

▷ intr.v (formal) 2 permit (s.t), agree (to (do) s.t): *He consented to their marriage. He'll never consent to such a plan.* **age of consent** ⇨ age(n). **by general consent** with most people agreeing.

consequence /ˈkɒnsɪkwəns/ c.n thing that happens as a result or effect of s.t else: *You know the consequences of not studying hard enough!* **be (a matter) of little**, **no** etc **consequence** (formal) be s.t that is hardly/not important. **in consequence (of s.t)** (formal) as a result (of s.t); therefore: *The mine was forced to close; in consequence, 2000 people lost their jobs.* **suffer/take the consequences** accept the bad results of what one has done: *Mike sat in the sun all day and is now suffering the consequences.*

consequent adj (often — (up)on s.t) (formal) following, as a result of, s.t: *The refusal of the government to discuss a pay rise and the consequent teacher* strikes(1) *led to further* disruption *in the schools.*

consequently adv as a result; therefore: *I lost my job and consequently have very little money.*

conservation, conservatism, conservative(ly/ness) ⇨ conserve.

conservatory /kənˈsɜːvətrɪ/ c.n (pl -ies) 1 room with glass walls and roof, usu fixed to the side of a house or building, in which plants are grown at controlled temperatures. 2 (with capital **C** in names) kind of school where music, art or acting is taught at an advanced level: *He's going to the conservatory of music next year.*

conserve /kənˈsɜːv/ u.n 1 (formal) jam; fruit preserved in sugar: *mixed fruit conserve.*

▷ tr.v (formal) 2 look after, protect, (s.t, esp land, buildings etc so that they are not damaged or changed): *Many organizations help to conserve the countryside.* 3 tr.v use very carefully or not use too much of (s.t that cannot be replaced easily): *We have to learn to conserve our mineral wealth, our energies.* 4 tr.v (old use) make (fruit) into jam etc. ⇨ preserve(5).

conservation /ˌkɒnsəˈveɪʃən/ u.n act of conserving(2,3) or being conserved(2,3): *the conservation of old buildings in the town.*

conservatism /kənˈsɜːvəˌtɪzəm/ u.n (belief in the) desire to keep things, life etc as they are or were; dislike of change.

conservative adj 1 (of a person) wanting to keep things as they are or were; disliking change.

2 (of a quantity, guess about s.t etc) not as large as might be stated; fairly cautious: *These sales figures are conservative but I'd rather work on lower expectations than ones that are too high.*
▷ *c.n* **3** (with capital **C**; also *attrib*) (also **Tory**) member, supporter, of the Conservative Party.
con'servatively *adv* in a conservative(2) way: *Conservatively, at least 200 people were at the meeting.*
con'servativeness *u.n.*
Con'servative ,Party *def.n* (also **'Tory ,Party**) (UK) one of the main political parties representing right-wing(2) opinions.
consider /kən'sıdə/ *v* **1** *tr.v* think (carefully) about (s.t): *Please consider the matter fully before you act.* **2** *intr.v* (stop and) think carefully (esp before doing s.t): *You need to consider before you act.* **3** *tr.v* allow for, not forget, (s.o/s.t, esp the feelings etc of others): *She hardly ever considers other points of view when coming to a decision. Don't forget to consider your brother when you plan your holiday.* **all things considered** (used to introduce a judgement) after having examined all the facts: *All things considered, I think we should go ahead with our plans.* **consider s.o (to be) s.t** think that s.o is of a certain kind: *I consider him (to be) very selfish.*
considerable /kən'sıdərəbl/ *adj* large (in number); great (in quality or importance): *A considerable number of people came to the meeting. The new car is a considerable improvement on the old one.*
con'siderably *adv.*
considerate /kən'sıdərıt/ *adj* (often — *of s.o* (*to do s.t*)) (of a person) kind and thoughtful (about other people): *It was very considerate of you to remember my family's problems.* Opposite inconsiderate.
consideration /kən,sıdə'reıʃən/ *n* **1** *u.n* act or fact of thinking carefully (about s.t): *He promised to give the proposal his full consideration.* **2** *u.n* (often *have* (*some, no* etc) — *for s.o/s.t*) thought or allowance (esp for the feelings of others): *He has very little consideration for what other people may think or feel.* **3** *c.n* thing that must be thought about, taken into account, (when deciding or doing s.t): *Our main considerations are the cost of the job and the time it will take.* **4** *c.n* (usu *do s.t for a* (*small*) —) (*formal*) payment in money: *I'm afraid I'll have to ask for a small consideration if you want me to do the job in my free time.* (**do s.t**) **out of consideration for s.o/s.t** (do s.t) because one respects or pays attention to s.o, s.o's feelings etc: *He decided to keep quiet about the matter out of consideration for her husband.* **in consideration of s.t** when thinking (carefully) about s.t; when making allowance for s.t: *They gave her a box of chocolates in consideration of her help.* **take s.t into consideration** make allowance for (s.t), esp when deciding s.t else: *You have to take his past record into consideration when you decide whether to offer him the new job.*
con'sidered *attrib.adj* (of an opinion etc) carefully thought about; reached after a lot of thought: *My considered view is that we should go ahead.*
considering /kən'sıdərıŋ/ *adv* **1** (used at the end of a statement that says s.t is surprisingly successful, s.o surprisingly well) taking into account

all the problems, difficulties: *I think we did really well, considering.*
▷ *conj* **2** when one thinks about (what s.o has done, what has happened etc): *He has come a long way, considering he started from nothing.*
▷ *prep* **3** when one thinks about (s.t); with regard to (s.t): *She doesn't manage too badly, considering her problems.*
consign /kən'saın/ *tr.v* **1** (usu — *s.t to s.o/s.w*) (*commerce*) send (goods etc that have been ordered) (to s.o/s.w, esp so that they can be sold): *We have consigned the books to you by road.* **2** (usu — *s.o/s.t to s.o/s.t*) (*formal*) put or place (s.o/s.t in the care of s.o); get rid of (s.t, e.g by throwing it away): *His body was consigned to the sea. The old bed was consigned to the fire.*
con'signment *n* **1** *u.n* (*formal*) act of consigning(1) s.t. **2** *c.n* thing consigned(1): *A new consignment of books has just arrived.*
consist /kən'sıst/ *intr.v* **1 consist of s.o/s.t** (not used in continuous tenses) (of a whole thing, group of people, things etc) have a number of different parts; be made up from a number of people, things etc: *The touring party consists of players and officials.* **2 consist in s.t** (*formal*) have s.t as its most important or only part/point: *The meeting consisted only in her making decisions.*
con'sistence, con'sistency *n* (*pl* -ies) **1** *u.n* sense or state of having the same views or opinions over a period of time without changing them/it: *He lacks consistency and one never knows what he'll do next.* Opposite inconsistency. **2** *c/u.n* (of a liquid etc) amount or degree of thickness, esp when or after mixing with s.t else: *When making pastry, make sure you mix the flour and water to the right consistency. The consistency of the paint is too thick.*
con'sistent *adj* Opposite inconsistent. **1** (of a person, belief etc) not changing in one's views; who/that is/are the same over a length of time: *I have to admit that he's consistent as he still believes in the same things as he did ten years ago.* **2** (of a statement etc) (often — *with s.t*) in agreement (with s.t else); not differing to any great extent (from s.t else): *The two statements are not consistent with each other so one of them must be wrong.*
con'sistently *adv* often and very regularly: *He has consistently refused to take my advice.*
console[1] /'kɒnsəʊl/ *c.n* board with switches, buttons, dials etc for controlling the operation of a machine or electrical device: *The engineer sat at the console and controlled the recording.*
console[2] /kən'səʊl/ *tr.v* (*formal*) express one's sympathy, try to comfort, (s.o): *He was unable to console her over the loss of her child.* **console oneself with s.t** (after a disappointment) try to think of s.t that makes the situation better: *He consoled himself with the thought that he would pass the examination next time.*
consolable /kən'səʊləbl/ *adj* who can be consoled[2]. Opposite inconsolable.
consolation /,kɒnsə'leıʃən/ *n* **1** *u.n* act of consoling[2] (s.o) or fact of being consoled[2]. **2** *c.n* person or thing who/that provides comfort: *She was a great consolation to me when I was in trouble.*
,conso'lation ,prize *c.n* prize given to s.o

who did not win or get a (main) prize in a competition.

consolatory /kən'sɒlətərɪ/ *adj* offering consolation(1): *He wrote her a consolatory letter*.

consolidate /kən'sɒlɪˌdeɪt/ *v* **1** *tr.v* make (s.t, esp one's position, influence etc) strong(er): *The company consolidated its hold in the market by keeping its prices low*. **2** *intr.v* become strong(er), (better) organized: *The company needs to consolidate before it can grow any further*. **3** *tr.v* (often — *s.t into s.t*) bring (two or more things) together (into one unit): *The two companies were consolidated into one to improve efficiency*.

consolidation /kənˌsɒlɪ'deɪʃən/ *c/u.n* act or example of consolidating: *We need to work on the consolidation of our position before we try to expand further*.

consommé /kən'sɒmeɪ/ *u.n* (*French*) clear soup, usu made from meat and served either hot or cold.

consonant /'kɒnsənənt/ *adj* **1** (usu *be — with s.t*) (*formal*) in agreement (with s.t); matching (s.t): *Your views are not consonant with those held by most people*.

▷ *c.n* (*grammar*) **2** any of the printed letters, such as b, c, d, f etc which are not vowels (i.e not a, e, i, o, u and sometimes y). **3** *c.n* sound representing a consonant(2).

consort /'kɒnsɔːt/ *c.n* **1** (with capital **C** in a title) (*formal*) husband of a princess/queen or wife of a prince/king: *Prince Albert was the Prince Consort of Queen Victoria*. **2** naval ship that sails with other ships, esp to protect them. *in consort with s.o* together with s.o: *It's time the prince became king or at least ruled in consort with his mother*.

▷ *intr.v* /kən'sɔːt/ **3** *consort with s.o* (*formal*) be in the company of s.o; do things together with s.o, esp s.o bad: *He consorts with the worst kind of people*.

consortium /kən'sɔːtɪəm/ *c.n* (*pl* -s or, less usu, **consortia** /-tɪə/) (*commerce*) group of companies, banks etc that come together to do business: *A consortium of building companies are hoping to get the* contract(1) *for the new hospital*.

conspicuous /kən'spɪkjuəs/ *adj* (of a person, thing etc) very easily seen; who/that catches or attracts one's attention: *His height made him very conspicuous in a crowd*. Opposite inconspicuous. **con'spicuously** *adv*. **con'spicuousness** *u.n*.

conspire /kən'spaɪə/ *intr.v* (*formal*) **1** (usu — (*with s.o*) *to do s.t*) make secret plans (with s.o) (to do s.t, usu bad): *The generals conspired with the enemy to get rid of the government*. **2** (usu — *to do s.t*) (of events) happen together (and so lead to a result): *Events conspired to make him change his mind*.

conspiracy /kən'spɪrəsɪ/ *n* (*pl* -ies) **1** *u.n* act or fact of conspiring(1). **2** *c.n* secret plan (to do s.t bad): *The police discovered a conspiracy to rob a bank*.

conspirator /kən'spɪrɪtə/ *c.n* person who secretly plans to do s.t bad (with others).

constable /'kɒnstəbl/ *c.n* (also **po'lice ˌconstable**; *abbr* PC) police officer of the lowest rank: *The constable on duty at the police station took my message*.

constabulary /kən'stæbjʊlərɪ/ *c.n* (*pl* -ies) whole police force of an area.

constant /'kɒnstənt/ *adj* **1** (usu *attrib*) happening again and again; never stopping: *He was annoyed by the constant* dripping(1) *of water from the tap*. **2** (of a substance etc) not changing: *The temperature must be kept constant at all times*. **3** (often — *to s.o/s.t*) (*formal*) (of a person) very faithful (to s.o, an agreement) and not changing; staying with s.o: *He remained constant to her in spite of her rudeness. He was her constant companion*.

▷ *c.n* **4** (*mathematics*) number or figure that remains the same (in a calculation etc).

'constancy *u.n* (*formal*) fact or state of being faithful and not changing (in one's beliefs, feelings for s.o etc): *Her constancy of purpose was admired by everybody*.

'constantly *adv* very often or regularly: *He was constantly reminded of her by her photograph. We are constantly telling Paul to tidy his room*.

constellation /ˌkɒnstə'leɪʃən/ *c.n* (name for a) group of stars: *You can see several constellations in the sky with the* naked(2) *eye*.

consternation /ˌkɒnstə'neɪʃən/ *u.n* feeling of dismay, fear etc: *There was great consternation among the people when the government announced its plans*. **fill s.o with consternation** (of an event etc) make s.o very afraid, confused, surprised, unsure of what to do: *The child's desperate crying filled us with consternation*.

constipate /'kɒnstɪˌpeɪt/ *tr/intr.v* (cause (a person, animal) to) have difficulty in emptying the bowels(1): *I find that meat constipates (me)*.

'constiˌpated *adj* (having become) unable to empty one's bowels(1) easily or normally.

constipation /ˌkɒnstɪ'peɪʃən/ *u.n* fact or state of being constipated: *If you've got constipation, you should eat more fruit and vegetables*.

constituent /kən'stɪtjʊənt/ *attrib.adj* (*formal*) **1** (of an organization) having the right or power to make laws: *A constituent* assembly(3) *is one formed to pass laws*. **2** (of a part) that forms part of a whole: *The constituent parts of the substance were examined*.

▷ *c.n* **3** person who can vote in a constituency: *There was a meeting of constituents to complain about the MP's behaviour*. **4** (*formal*) one of the parts which make up a whole: *The constituents of the substance can be seen under a microscope*.

con'stituency *c.n* (*pl* -ies) (area in which there is a) group of voters who elect a member of parliament: *She lives in a* Tory *constituency*.

constitute /'kɒnstɪˌtjuːt/ *tr.v* (*formal*) **1** (of a quantity) make ((part of) the whole unit): *Twenty-four hours constitutes one day. What you've just eaten constitutes half of our food for the whole trip*. **2** be s.t that forms, makes up, leads to, (s.t): *The whole affair constitutes a serious attack on our liberties*.

constitution /ˌkɒnstɪ'tjuːʃən/ *n* **1** *c.n* (often with capital **C**) (written) laws, rights and rules of a country by which it is governed: *Britain has no formal written constitution*. **2** *u.n* act of forming or making up s.t, esp (a set of laws or rules for) an organization, its members etc: *The constitution of the* Board[3] *was such that the chairperson had very little power*. **3** *c.n* (good or bad) condition of a person's body or mind: *She has a very weak constitution and is often sick*.

constitutional /ˌkɒnstɪ'tjuːʃənl/ *adj* **1** of or

referring to a constitution(1); legal(1) according to its laws etc: *The judges decided that the earlier judgement was not constitutional.* Opposite unconstitutional. **2** (usu *attrib*) (of a king etc) not having real power but controlled by a constitution(1): *a constitutional* monarch. **3** (usu *attrib*) (*formal*) of or referring to a person's nature, constitution(3): *He suffers from a constitutional weakness of the heart.*
▷ *c.n* **4** (often *go for, take, a —*) (*old use*) regular walk for the sake of one's health: *I'm just going for my morning constitutional.*
͵consti'tutionally *adv* **1** in a way that is legal(1) or that follows the laws of a constitution(1): *Constitutionally, you are not forced to answer that question.* Opposite unconstitutionally. **2** (*formal*) referring to one's health: *She's constitutionally much stronger than she looks.*

constrain /kən'streɪn/ *tr.v* (often passive) (*formal*) **1** force (s.o) to act in a particular way: *He was constrained to agree to their demands.* **2** prevent (s.t) from developing, happening freely: *Her parents constrained her natural curiosity.*
con'strained *adj* (*formal*) forced and so a little awkward; not free and easy: *From his constrained conversation I gathered that there must be something wrong.* **constrained by s.o/ s.t** limited, controlled, (by s.o/s.t); prevented from being free, the way one would like to be, by s.o/s.t: *He felt constrained by other people's expectations of him.*
con'straint *n* **1** *u.n* fact or state of feeling that one cannot do what one wants, that one must behave carefully: *He showed some constraint when faced with all those people.* **2** *c.n* limit (in law etc) which controls what one does, how one should behave etc: *There are a number of constraints on press freedom. Our two big constraints are money and time.* **under constraint** because one is forced to: *He claimed that he had acted under constraint and was therefore not responsible for the crime.*

constrict /kən'strɪkt/ *tr.v* (*formal*) **1** hold (s.t) tightly; make (s.t) become narrower: *The bandage constricted the flow of blood and made his fingers swell.* **2** not allow (s.o) to feel free, able to move freely etc: *The place and the people made him feel constricted. The rope constricted his movements.*
con'stricting *adj* that causes one to feel limited, controlled: *Wearing a tie is very constricting. He found living at home too constricting.*
constriction /kən'strɪkʃən/ *n* **1** *c/u.n* (*formal*) (feeling of) lack of freedom of movement; tightness: *He felt a constriction in his chest. Chris did not find any constriction in living at home with his parents.* **2** *u.n* act of holding (s.o/s.t) very tightly: *The snake kills by constriction not poison.*
con'strictor *c.n* = boa constrictor.

construct /kən'strʌkt/ *tr.v* **1** build or make (s.t, esp a house, road etc) using various materials: *A new airport is being constructed twenty miles from the city. Peter constructed a garden shed from old bits of wood.* **2** make or form (a whole thing, e.g a sentence, idea etc) using different parts: *a well-constructed theory(2).*
construction /kən'strʌkʃən/ *n* **1** *u.n* (also *attrib*) (business of) building or making s.t: *They have started on the construction of the*

new *office block. He works in the construction industry.* **2** *c.n* thing built or made: *It was a very odd construction made out of bits of wire, metal sheets and so on.* **3** *u.n* act of forming or making a whole from different parts: *English sentence construction is easy once you know the rules.* **4** *c.n* (*formal*) meaning or one's understanding (of an event, what s.o said etc): *The statement he made is open to different constructions.* **be under construction** (of a building etc) be still being built and not finished. **put a different, wrong** etc **construction on s.t** understand the meaning of s.t done or said in a different, wrong etc way.
constructional /kən'strʌkʃənl/ *adj* of or referring to the construction(1) of s.t: *They gave him a constructional toy for his birthday.*
con'structive *adj* (of advice, a suggestion, criticism etc) very helpful; helping to make rather than destroy s.t: *I hope you will find my comments constructive rather than destructive. If you don't have anything constructive to say, it's better to keep quiet.* Opposite unconstructive. ⇨ destructive(3).
con'structively *adv*.

construe /kən'struː/ *tr.v* (*formal*) put a particular meaning on (s.o's words, actions etc), understand (them) in a certain way: *His anger at losing was construed as bad sportsmanship.*

consul /'kɒnsl/ *c.n* **1** official person who looks after the (interests of) people from her/his country in a foreign country or town. **2** (in Roman(1) history) one of the two chief officials of the state.
consular /'kɒnsjʊlə/ *adj* of or referring to (the position or duties of) a consul(1): *a consular official.*
consulate /'kɒnsjʊlɪt/ *c.n* **1** official work of a consul(1); time during which one is a consul(1). **2** building in which a consul(1) works.

consult /kən'sʌlt/ *tr.v* **1** (often *— s.o about s.t*) ask for advice from (s.o, esp a professional person) (about s.t that concerns one): *I advise you to consult your solicitor about making a will.* **2** (try to) find information from (a book, map etc): *Consult your dictionary if you do not know the meaning of a word.* **consult with s.o** (*about s.t*) (*formal*) ask s.o's advice (about s.t).
consultancy /kən'sʌltənsɪ/ (*pl -ies*) *c.n* (also *attrib*) office or job of a consultant: *a consultancy job to advise about books on medicine.*
consultant /kən'sʌltənt/ *c.n* **1** person who gives professional advice to people: *The company called in management consultants to help them.* **2** senior doctor in a hospital, usu an expert in a particular kind of medicine: *He works as a consultant on diseases of the nervous system.*
consultation /͵kɒnsl'teɪʃən/ *c/u.n* act or fact of consulting(1): *They held consultations with their members before accepting the proposal.* **do s.t in consultation** (*with s.o*) act together (with s.o who gives advice etc) in doing s.t: *We worked out the plan in consultation with our members.*
consultative /kən'sʌltətɪv/ *adj* (of an organization, report etc) having the power to offer advice only (and not action): *His job is purely consultative.*
con'sulting ͵room *c.n* room where a doctor examines patients.

consume /kən'sjuːm/ *tr.v* (*formal*) **1** eat and/

or drink (food etc), esp in terms of quantity: *We watched him consume large amounts of meat and potatoes.* **2** use up (an amount of food, energy(2) etc): *This fire consumes too much coal.* **3** (of a fire) burn and so destroy (s.t): *The house was consumed by the flames.* **4** (of a job, task etc) take up (an amount of time, one's energy(1) etc): *The new job consumed all his time.* **be consumed with s.t** be totally controlled by an emotion(1), e.g jealousy, anger etc, forgetting everything else: *He was consumed with jealousy when all his friends went to university.*

con'sumer *c.n* person who buys food, goods etc, uses services etc (esp when considered as one of the group of such people): *The consumer is not protected enough against the power of big companies.*

con'sumer ˌgoods *pl.n* things a person buys and uses in everyday life, such as food, clothing, household goods etc (as compared to machines etc needed for making things).

con'suming *adj* taking up all or most of one's time, interest etc: *His consuming interest is building model railways.* ⇨ all-consuming, time-consuming.

consumption /kənˈsʌmpʃən/ *u.n* **1** (*formal*) act or fact of consuming(1) food etc: *Consumption of wine has increased over the last two years.* **2** amount of food etc consumed(1): *Total consumption was calculated at two million tonnes.* **3** (*old use*) disease (tuberculosis) of the lungs.

consumptive /kənˈsʌmptɪv/ *adj* (*old use*) suffering from consumption(3).

consummate /ˈkɒnsʌmɪt/ *attrib.adj* (*formal*) **1** having/showing a very great amount of (ease, skill, ability etc): *She performed the task with consummate ease.*

▷ *tr.v* /ˈkɒnsəˌmeɪt/ (*formal*) **2** make (a marriage) complete by performing the sexual act for the first time: *Their marriage was never consummated.*

consummation /ˌkɒnsəˈmeɪʃən/ *n* **1** *u.n* act of consummating(2) a marriage. **2** *sing.n* (*formal*) final end or completion (of s.t): *The appointment was a consummation of all his efforts over the years.*

cont *written abbr* continued(2).

contact /ˈkɒntækt/ *n* **1** *u.n* act of touching or of being near s.o/s.t so as to touch her/him/it: *She felt the contact of someone's hand on her arm.* **2** *u.n* act of giving and receiving information between people: *I have very little contact with my neighbours.* **3** *c.n* person one knows and who can be useful to one (esp in business): *He has many contacts in the government.* **4** *c.n* part of an electrical circuit(4) which, when moved, causes the current to flow or stop. **5** *c.n* person who has been near s.o with a disease: *It's important that we find all the contacts of the person with the disease.* **be in contact (with s.o)** (see and) talk or write (to s.o) (regularly): *Are you still in contact with your sister in America?* **be in contact (with s.t)** be touching (s.t) all the time: *One foot must always be in contact with the floor.* **be out of contact (with s.o/s.t)** not (be able to) see or talk (together, to s.o): *We've been out of contact since she went to Africa.* **bring s.o/s.t into contact (with s.o/s.t)** bring two people or things together. **come/get**

into contact (with s.o/s.t) (a) touch or hit (s.o/s.t): *When the two wires came into contact there was a bright flash.* **(b)** meet, see, (s.o): *Since I changed my job, I don't come into contact with him any more.* **get in contact with s.o** find s.o in order to meet, talk, do business etc: *Do you know how I can get in contact with a good builder?* **keep in, lose, contact (with s.o/s.t) (a)** continue to, fail to, have or get regular information (from s.o/s.t), esp by radio etc: *We've lost contact with the aircraft.* **(b)** continue to, not, know, see, (s.o) any more, esp after having known her/him for some time: *We lost contact with them after we moved.* **make contact (with s.o)** find s.o in order to continue, start a friendship etc (with s.o): *I'd like to make contact with her again because we used to share a lot of interests.* **make contact (with s.t)** find a ship, plane etc in order to get information: *They tried to make contact with the plane that had called for help but they got no answer.*

▷ *tr.v* **6** find, communicate(2) with, (s.o) by writing, talking, telephoning etc in order to get/give information: *She said she would contact me when she arrived.*

'contact ˌlens *c.n* (*pl* -es) one of a pair of small pieces of clear plastic(3) fitted over the eyeballs to improve sight (used instead of glasses).

contagion /kənˈteɪdʒən/ *n* (*formal*) **1** *u.n* spreading of a disease from one person to another or others by touch or by being near: *Is there any possibility of contagion in this case?* **2** *c.n* disease spread in this way. **3** *u.n* spreading of a feeling, idea etc from one person to another or others: *The contagion of fear swept through the crowd.*

contagious /kənˈteɪdʒəs/ *adj* **1** (of a disease) that can be given by one person to another or others: *Measles is a contagious disease.* **2** (of a person) having a disease that can be given to s.o else: *She will be contagious for the first week.* **3** (of a feeling, idea etc) that can spread to, affect, s.o else: *The fear was contagious and soon everybody was trying to escape.*

con'tagiousness *u.n.*

contain /kənˈteɪn/ *tr.v* **1** (not used with continuous tenses) (of a hollow shape, box, bottle etc) have or hold (a certain quantity of s.t): *The case contained a dozen bottles of wine.* ⇨ content²(1), contents. **2** (not used with continuous tenses) (of a substance, liquid etc) have (s.t) as a part of the whole: *These chemicals contain poisons and should be handled with great caution.* **3** (*formal*) control (s.t, esp a feeling, disease etc) and not let it spread or become too strong or serious: *He could hardly contain his impatience at her stupidity. The doctors fought hard to contain the disease.* **4** (*formal*) keep (s.t) inside a boundary: *A dam(1) was built to contain the river and prevent flooding.* **contain oneself** control one's feelings: *Philip was so excited he could hardly contain himself.*

con'tainer *c.n* **1** hollow shape, box, bottle etc for holding s.t: *I need a plastic container for my sandwiches.* **2** (also *attrib*) very large metal box, used for putting goods into for carrying by lorries, ships or aircraft: *a container ship.*

con'tainer ˌport *c.n* port built to handle container ships.

con'tainer ,ship *c.n* ship built specially to carry containers(2).

containerization,-isation /kən,teɪnəraɪ'zeɪʃən/ *u.n.*

con'taine,rize, -ise *tr.v* **1** put (goods) into containers(2). **2** organize (the sending of goods by lorries, ships or aircraft) using containers(2): *The shipping of machinery has been containerized.*

contaminate /kən'tæmɪ,neɪt/ *tr.v* **1** make (food, water etc) impure (and therefore dangerous if eaten or drunk) by adding s.t harmful: *The water supply has become contaminated by factory waste.* **2** (of a person, idea etc) affect or influence (s.o, s.o's ideas etc) for the worse: *He has contaminated her mind with ideas of having freedom and no responsibilities or possessions.*

contamination /kən,tæmɪ'neɪʃən/ *u.n.*

contd *written abbr* continued(2).

contemplate /'kɒntəm,pleɪt/ *tr.v* (*formal*) **1** look at (s.o/s.t) in a serious or quiet way, often for some time: *He sat in the grass contemplating the mountains around him.* **2** think seriously, for some time etc, about (s.t one should do, what has happened etc): *She contemplated the idea of going* overseas(2) *but decided not to in the end.*

contemplation /,kɒntəm'pleɪʃən/ *u.n* (often *in* — (*of s.t*)) (*formal*) act of thinking seriously, for some time etc (about s.t): *He spent hours in deep contemplation of the problem. She was lost in contemplation when I came in and she didn't hear me.*

contemplative /kən'templətɪv/ *adj* (*formal*) (of a person, one's nature etc) serious, quiet, thoughtful: *a contemplative* mood[1](1).

contemporary /kən'tempərərɪ/ *adj* **1** living, happening, at the same time (as s.o/s.t else); belonging to the same time: *Contemporary accounts of the situation gave a different picture from those written by later* authors(1). **2** *adj* modern; (done) in the present time: *I must admit I don't like much contemporary music.*

▷ *c.n* (*pl -ies*) **3** person who lives or lived at the same time, or is/was the same age (as s.o else): *Most of my contemporaries were brought up to believe in obedience to their parents.*

contempt /kən'tempt/ *u.n* **1** (showing of one's) dislike, low opinion, lack of respect, (of s.o/s.t): *He showed his contempt for their actions by walking out of the meeting.* **2** (also **con,tempt of 'court**) (*law*) lack of respect towards a judge; ignoring of the rules (of behaviour etc) in a court: *The judge charged the prisoner with contempt when he swore at the witness.* **beneath** (**one's**) **contempt** so bad or unimportant that one does not want to give her/him/it any time, thought or value at all: *Your behaviour towards your mother is beneath* (*my*) *contempt and makes me wish I didn't know you!* **hold s.o in contempt** have a very low opinion of s.o: *She holds me in contempt because I never had her education.*

con'temptible *adj* (of a person, act etc) (thought to be) deserving of contempt(1): *His behaviour is absolutely contemptible.*

contemptuous /kən'temptjʊəs/ *adj* (often — about/of s.o/s.t) showing contempt(1) (towards s.o/s.t): *Greg is very contemptuous of other people's opinions.*

con'temptuously *adv.* **con'temptuousness** *u.n.*

contend /kən'tend/ *v* (*formal*) **1** *intr.v* (usu — *for s.t*) take part in a competition (for s.t, esp a prize): *He is contending for a place in the team.* **2** *intr.v* (usu — *against/with s.o/s.t*) deal (with a difficult person, problem); fight, struggle, (with s.o, against a difficulty): *He had a number of political enemies to contend with. I've got enough problems without having to contend with yours too.* **3** *tr.v* (usu — *that...*) argue, state strongly, (that...): *He's always contended that he was not guilty.*

con'tender *c.n* (often — *for s.t*) person who is competing against others (to win a title or prize in a sport, to be appointed to a position etc): *He's a contender for the leadership of the Party.*

contention /kən'tenʃən/ *n* (*formal*) **1** *c.n* strong argument or defence put forward by s.o: *It was his contention that the business would begin to lose money within a year.* **2** *u.n* disagreement and argument (among a group of people): *There was a lot of contention between them as to who was right and who was wrong.* **a bone of contention** reason for arguing; thing that people are arguing about.

contentious /kən'tenʃəs/ *adj* (*formal*) **1** (*derog*) (of a person) wanting to argue or disagree a lot: *He's very contentious, so don't get into an argument with him.* **2** (of a subject, matter etc) causing, likely to cause, argument or disagreement: *Arms control is proving to be a very contentious subject.*

content¹ /kən'tent/ *pred.adj* **1** (often — *to do, with, s.t*) happy and satisfied, usu in a quiet way (to do, with, s.t): *I'm quite content to stay home tonight because there are many things I'd like to do. Are you content to sit there and do nothing about this problem?*

▷ *u.n* **2** (usu *with* (*great etc*) —) happiness and pleasure: *He settled back into the chair with great content.* (**do s.t**) **to one's heart's content** ⇒ heart(*1*).

▷ *reflex.v* **3** (usu — *oneself with s.t*) allow (oneself) the pleasure or satisfaction (of s.t): *He contented himself with the thought that he could stay in bed late the next day.*

con'tented *adj* happy and satisfied in a quiet way: *a contented child. It's difficult to find many people who are completely contented with their lives.* Opposite discontented.

con'tentedly *adv* in a happy and satisfied way: *She smiled contentedly.*

con'tentment *u.n* feeling of happiness and satisfaction: *He sighed with contentment. She has a look of contentment.* Opposite discontentment.

content² /'kɒntent/ *u.n* **1** amount of a substance contained or present in another substance: *There's a very high water content in these vegetables.* ⇒ contain(1,2). **2** actual ideas or subject matter in a book, s.t one says etc: *This book has very little content and it's mostly just pictures.*

'contents *pl.n* (often *the* — *of s.t*) **1** what s.t, e.g a bottle, box, room, etc holds or contains: *The customs officials were examining the contents of his suitcase.* ⇒ contain(1). **2** printed list of subjects, chapters etc (with references to pages) placed at the front of a book: *The page of contents was missing from my copy of the book.*

contention, contentious ⇒ contend.

contest /'kɒntest/ *c.n* **1** (often — *for s.t*) competition or fight (for a prize, to win some advantage etc): *There was a contest for the leadership of the Party. Many people believe that beauty contests treat women like animals on show.*
▷ *tr.v* /kən'test/ **2** (esp in politics) put oneself forward as a candidate(1) for (a seat in an election, position in government etc): *He will be contesting the seat in the next* general election. **3** (*formal*) (esp in law or a matter of disagreement) fight against, bring arguments against, (s.t said, a decision etc): *We shall be contesting your claim to ownership of the property. We must contest this decision at the next meeting.*

contestant /kən'testənt/ *c.n* person taking part in a (sports etc) competition: *The oldest of the contestants in the race was seventy.*

context /'kɒntekst/ *n* **1** *c.n* words, phrases(1) or sentences which appear around a word or phrase(1) and help to explain its meaning: *You can often guess the meaning of words from their contexts.* **2** *u.n* things that happen around a particular event: *If you want to understand his failure, you have to look at the context within which he worked.* (**see**, **understand** etc **s.t**) **in context** (look at etc s.t) together with all the facts that affect it: *One has to examine the problems we are facing in context.* **out of context** alone and without the other things said at the same time which give the true meaning: *You deliberately took my words out of context and you know that's not what I meant!* **put s.t into context** understand s.t in relation to other important facts: *The figures alone don't look good but comparing them to last year's profits puts them into context.*

contextual /kən'tekstjʊəl/ *adj* of or referring to a particular context(1): *contextual meaning.*

continent /'kɒntɪnənt/ *n* **1** *c.n* one of the main large areas of land in the world: *the continent of Asia.* **2** *def.n* (with capital **C**) all Europe without the British Isles: *Many thousands of people visit the Continent every year.*

continental /ˌkɒntɪ'nentl/ *adj* **1** of or referring to a continent(1) or continents: *continental land masses.* **2** of or referring to the Continent(2): *The city is quite continental in its appearance.*

conti,nental 'breakfast *c.n* light breakfast, usu with rolls and coffee.

conti,nental 'quilt *c.n* covering for a bed that is filled with feathers, foam rubber etc.

contingency /kən'tɪndʒənsɪ/ *c.n* (*pl* *-ies*) (*formal*) thing that may happen to spoil or ruin a plan etc (and that one must therefore try to prepare for, stop happening): *Though he had prepared for a number of contingencies, he hadn't taken into account the possibility of bad weather.*

con'tingency ,plan *c.n* plan made to replace another plan in case s.t goes wrong with the first one.

con'tingent *adj* **1** (usu be — (*up*)*on s.t*) (*formal*) dependent ((up)on s.t else happening): *Success was contingent upon him raising enough money.*
▷ *c.n* **2** group of people (esp soldiers) or things who/that form part of a larger group: *The new contingent joined the main army just before the battle.*

continue /kən'tɪnju:/ *v* **1** *intr.v* (often — *to do s.t*; — *doing s.t*) keep on (doing s.t); not stop

(doing s.t): *They continued to talk* (or *talking*) *even though I told them to keep quiet.* **2** *intr.v* keep on happening (for a length of time, in a certain way etc): *The battle in the streets continued fiercely for some time.* **3** *intr.v* (of a place, road etc) extend, go on, (for a certain distance): *The road continues for another mile before it ends.* **4** *intr.v* (usu — *along s.t/s.w*) go, travel, (along a road etc): *If you continue along this street, you'll come to the shop.* **5** *tr/intr.v* (cause (s.t) to) start again after a pause, interruption etc: *They continued their conversation after he left the room. The story continues on page 3.*

continual /kən'tɪnjʊəl/ *adj* (usu of s.t bad or annoying) happening again and again; repeated: *There were continual complaints about the bad service.* Compare continuous.

con'tinually *adv* again and again: *He continually interrupted the speaker.*

continuance /kən'tɪnjʊəns/ *u.n* (often *the* — *of s.t*) (*formal*) fact of s.t continuing, not stopping: *The continuance of this state of affairs was heavily criticized.*

continuation /kənˌtɪnjʊ'eɪʃən/ *n* **1** *u.n* act of continuing (s.t), esp after a pause, interruption etc: *I hope there will be no continuation of this behaviour.* **2** *c.n* thing, e.g a story, action, place etc, that goes further on (from s.t else): *There is a continuation of the story on page 30.*

con'tinued *adj* **1** without interruption; always active or present: *He has shown a continued interest in local activities.* **2** (*written abbr* cont(d)) (of a story, account etc in a book, magazine etc) the next part will be found (on a certain page, in the next issue(2) etc): *continued on page 30.*

continuity /ˌkɒntɪ'nju:ɪtɪ/ *u.n* **1** fact or state of being connected together (in one whole, in a relationship, in time etc): *In times of trouble, continuity of government is a necessity.* **2** (in the making of television programmes, films etc) way in which the details in a scene match those of other scenes: *She was in charge of continuity on the new film.* **3** short programmes of music etc that help one main programme to move smoothly to the next on the radio, television etc.

continuous /kən'tɪnjʊəs/ *adj* (usu *attrib*) that goes on without stopping or interruption: *They worked all through the night in order to keep continuous production going. The rain has been continuous all week.* Compare continual.

con'tinuously *adv* without stopping: *It rained continuously for three days.*

con'tinuous ,tense *def.n* (also **pro'gressive ,tense**) (*grammar*) verb form used to show action that continues(2) or continued(2) for a length of time, e.g 'They *are playing* outside', 'We *were waiting* for you'.

contort /kən'tɔ:t/ *tr/intr.v* (cause (s.t, esp s.o's body, face etc) to) twist in an unusual way, esp because of pain: *Her face contorted with the pain.*

contortion /kən'tɔ:ʃən/ *c/u.n* (act or fact of) twisting out of shape: *I don't know how he manages such contortions.*

con'tortionist *c.n* person who entertains people by twisting her/his body into difficult positions.

contour /'kɒntɔː/ *c.n* **1** shape or outline (of a body, land etc): *He could just see the contours of a body underneath the blankets.* **2** (also **'contour ,line**) one of the lines on a map joining places with the same height above or below sea level.

contraband /'kɒntrə,bænd/ *u.n* (also *attrib*) goods that go into or out of a country illegally, esp to avoid paying tax: *He deals in contraband (radios and television sets).*

contraception /,kɒntrə'sepʃən/ *u.n* (act or method of) stopping a baby from being conceived(3) (usu by artificial means).
,contra'ceptive *adj* **1** of or referring to contraception: *contraceptive pills(1).*
▷ *c.n* **2** device or chemical pill(1) intended to stop conception(3).

contract /'kɒntrækt/ *c.n* **1** (usu written) legal agreement between two or more people, companies, states etc for s.t to be done, for the supply of services, goods etc: *The company has won a contract to build a new university. I've got a two-year contract with the government to teach in Zimbabwe.* **breach of contract** ⇒ breach(*n*). **enter into**, **make**, **sign**, **a contract** (**with s.o**) (**for s.t**) make a legal agreement (with s.o) (to do s.t). **exchange contracts** (**with s.o**) (esp when buying or selling a house, flat etc) (of the buyer and seller) sign two or more copies of a contract and give them to each other at the same time: *We exchanged contracts on Monday and moved into the house the next day.*
▷ *v* /kən'trækt/ **2** *tr/intr.v* (usu — (with s.o) to do s.t) make a legal(1), usu written, agreement (with s.o) (to do s.t): *We have contracted with a builder to mend the roof. The manufacturers contracted to supply the company with parts for its new machines.* **3** *tr.v* (*formal*) legally(1) agree to have (a marriage, a formal agreement etc): *The two countries contracted an alliance(2) against their enemies.* **4** *tr/intr.v* (cause (s.t) to) become smaller: *The metal contracted in the cold weather. Business has contracted this month.* Opposite **expand. 5** *tr.v* (*grammar*) cause (a word etc to become shorter by removing certain letters and using an apostrophe(1), as happens when speaking: *We usually contract 'I have' to 'I've' in speech.* **6** *tr.v* (*formal*) get, catch, (an illness or disease): *He contracted cholera on his travels.*

contraction /kən'trækʃən/ *n* **1** *c/u.n* (example of the) state of becoming smaller, shorter etc: *He felt a painful contraction in the muscle(1) of his leg. The contraction of industry in this country is causing unemployment.* **2** *c.n* (often *pl*) (in a pregnant woman) sharp pain before and during childbirth: *When did your contractions begin?* **3** *c.n* (*grammar*) shortened form of a word, esp as in speech: *'I've' is a contraction of 'I have'.*

contractor /kən'træktə/ *c.n* person or company supplying goods, services etc at an agreed price, esp in building or construction: *We used a building contractor to repair the house.*

contractual /kən'træktjʊəl/ *adj* of or referring to a contract: *He failed to meet his contractual obligations(2).*
con'tractually *adv.*

contradict /,kɒntrə'dɪkt/ *v* **1** *tr.v* (in a discussion or argument) say the opposite of (what s.o has said); argue with, try to correct, (s.o, s.t he/ she said): *Don't contradict me when you know*

nothing about the matter! Why do you always contradict what I say? **2** *reflex.v* (of a speaker, statement, opinion etc) not agree with (oneself, another statement, opinion etc): *The several reports of the affair all contradict each other.*

contradiction /,kɒntrə'dɪkʃən/ *n* **1** *u.n* state or act of disagreeing or disagreement: *I see very little contradiction between my views and yours.* **2** *c.n* example of s.t that does not agree with s.t else: *There are several contradictions in his account of what happened.* **a contradiction in terms** a statement that has, appears to have, a contradiction(2) in it: *I may be wrong but a happily married man seems to be a contradiction in terms nowadays.*

contradictory /,kɒntrə'dɪktərɪ/ *adj* (of statements, opinions etc) not agreeing; not the same: *All the reports are contradictory and it will take time to arrive at the truth. What you have just said is contradictory to what you told me yesterday.*

contraflow /'kɒntrə,fləʊ/ *c.n* (on a dual carriageway or motorway) use of one side of the road to take cars etc going in opposite directions when there are repairs or a block on the other side: *Contraflows are in operation on the motorway.*

contralto /kən'træltəʊ/ *c.n* (*pl* -s) (also *attrib*) **1** women's lowest singing voice. **2** woman with such a singing voice. Compare alto, bass¹.
▷ *adj/adv* **3** having the musical range of a contralto(1): *She sings contralto.*

contrary¹ /'kɒntrərɪ/ *adj* **1** (usu — to s.t) completely opposite (to s.t), different (from s.t): *Everything he has done is contrary to what he said he would do. Contrary to public opinion, he is actually quite a pleasant person.*
▷ *def.n* **2** (usu the — of s.t) complete opposite (of s.t): *The government says it will win the next election but most people believe the contrary. The contrary of 'cold' is 'hot'.* **on the contrary** (stating) the opposite (of s.t said): *'You don't look well.' 'On the contrary, I've never felt better.'* **to the contrary** (of s.t said or done) suggesting something different or the opposite: *If you don't hear to the contrary, expect to see me tomorrow night.*

contrary² /kən'treərɪ/ *adj* (of a person, behaviour etc) difficult to deal with because of changing her/his mind or doing, wanting to do, differently from everyone else: *Why do you always have to be so contrary? She's so contrary that nobody likes doing things with her.*
con'trarily *adv.* **con'trariness** *u.n.*

contrast /'kɒntrɑːst/ *n* **1** *c/u.n* (often — between s.o/s.t and s.o/s.t) (example of a) difference there is or seems to be (when one compares s.o/s.t with s.o/s.t else): *He is a complete contrast to his father. There is such a contrast between the work he does and what he's really able to do.* **2** *u.n* change or difference in the amount of light, colour, shade etc, esp in a painting, photograph etc: *He makes very good use of contrast in his compositions.* **by contrast** (**with s.t**) when one compares difference(s) (of s.t): *She is always happy and cheerful; he, by contrast, always seems miserable.* **in** (**marked/sharp**) **contrast to s.o/s.t** being or showing the (complete) opposite to s.o/s.t: *Their actions were in sharp contrast to their words.*
▷ *v* /kən'trɑːst/ **3** *tr.v* (usu — s.t and/with s.t) compare (two things) in order to see, show, their differences: *If you contrast their ways of working,*

you'll have to admit that she is more efficient than he is. The article contrasts our education system with others in different parts of the world. **4** *intr.v* (usu — *with s.t*) (of a person's actions etc) show some or great difference(s) (from s.t else): *His behaviour contrasts badly with that of his friend.* **5** *tr/intr.v* (often — (*s.t*) *with s.t*) (in painting, writing etc) (use (colour, different ways of saying, describing s.t etc) to) emphasize(1) differences: *The writer contrasts his style when describing the two characters. The blue here contrasts with the dark shadows there.*

con'trasting *adj* (that show the) difference(s): *contrasting colours/ideas.* Opposite matching.

contravene /ˌkɒntrəˈviːn/ *tr.v* (formal; law) break (a law or rule): *He was arrested for contravening the import*(1) *regulations*(1).

contravention /ˌkɒntrəˈvenʃən/ *c/u.n* (example of an) act of breaking a law or rule: *He was arrested for contravention of the law. That's a contravention of the law for the protection of animals.*

contretemps /ˈkɒntrətɑːn/ *c.n* (*pl contretemps*) (*French*) awkward thing that happens and that causes embarrassment(1) or annoyance to s.o: *There was a contretemps when he invited himself to the party.*

contribute /kənˈtrɪbjuːt/ *v* **1** *tr/intr.v* (usu — (*s.t*) *to/towards s.t*) give, offer, (money, help, information etc) together with other people (for some purpose etc): *Maggie contributed £10 to the collection for the repair* (or *towards the repair*) *of the church. Everyone contributed* (*something*) *including ideas, money,* energy(1), *and so the job got done. He hardly ever contributes to our discussions.* **2** *tr/intr.v* (usu — (*s.t*) *to s.t*) write (articles) for a magazine, newspaper etc: *He contributes regularly* (or *contributes regular articles*) *to the local newspaper.* **3** *intr.v* (usu — *to s.t*) (*formal*) (of an action, state etc) be one among a number of things which helps to cause (s.t, usu bad): *His own stupidity contributed to his arrest by the police.*

con'tributor *c.n* **1** person who gives money, help etc. **2** person who writes articles etc for a newspaper etc.

contribution /ˌkɒntrɪˈbjuːʃən/ *n* **1** *u.n* (formal) act or fact of contributing(1,2). **2** *c.n* thing, esp money, that is contributed(1,2): *All contributions are welcome.*

con'tributory /kənˈtrɪbjuːtəri/ *attrib.adj* (formal) **1** (of an action etc) that helps to bring about s.t (usu s.t bad): *The mistake in judgement was a contributory cause of the failure.* **2** to or for which one gives money regularly: *Our company has a contributory pension scheme.*

con,tributory 'negligence *u.n* (law) failure to do s.t so that an accident happens.

con-trick ⇒ con(1).

contrite /kənˈtraɪt/ *adj* (formal) very sorry (for s.t bad one has done): *She appeared very contrite about her bad behaviour.*

con'tritely *adv.*

contrition /kənˈtrɪʃən/ *u.n* (also, less usu, **con'triteness**) (formal) sorrow (for s.t bad one has done): *She's full of contrition for her behaviour last night. You could see his contriteness.*

contrive /kənˈtraɪv/ *tr.v* (formal) manage to do

or find (s.t), usu after some difficulty, in spite of s.o/s.t etc: *They contrived a way of getting out of the country without the police knowing.* **contrive to do s.t** succeed in doing s.t: *I contrived to get her attention by upsetting the jug.*

contrivance /kənˈtraɪvəns/ *n* **1** *u.n* act or fact of contriving. **2** *c.n* (formal) plan, s.t one invents as an excuse etc: *I could see that it was just a contrivance to get me out of the way.* **3** *c.n* (often joking) thing, esp a machine or device that has been constructed for some purpose: *There was a contrivance for controlling the flow of water.*

con'trived *adj* (*derog*) not natural; made, planned or produced awkwardly: *The whole story was a bit contrived and I did not believe it.*

control /kənˈtrəʊl/ *n* **1** *u.n* (often — *of/over s.o/ s.t*) power or right to do s.t, to make other people do s.t etc: *Who has control in this office? I have no control over my wife! Jane exercises very little control over her children. I'll lose control if I sell the business. If you can't manage it I'll have to take control* (*of the sale*). **2** *u.n* (often keep/lose — *of oneself*) stop one's emotions from getting too strong, allow one's emotions to get too strong: *She has very little control and cries easily. You must try to keep control of yourself* (or *your temper*). *He completely lost control of himself and started screaming at his children.* **3** *u.n* way s.t is organized or made to work smoothly: *It takes some time to learn control of an aircraft. Traffic control is necessary in a large city.* ⇒ controls. **4** *c.n* way or means of managing s.t in the way one wants, of keeping s.t in order or at a certain level etc: *The government has introduced price controls.* **5** *c/u.n* (place where there is) power or right to look at things, stop people etc so as to decide whether they can enter (a country, place etc): *He had to go through passport control.* **6** *c.n* (also *attrib*) (esp in experiments) group of people, animals or things who/that can be compared with other groups because s.t different is done with those: *One group of people were given the new medicine while the control group continued with the old one.* **beyond (s.o's) control** who/that cannot be managed, that s.o cannot do anything about or keep in order etc: *The fire is beyond control and will soon destroy the whole building. The children are beyond my control now.* **be in control** (**of s.o/ s.t**) have or exercise power (over s.o/s.t); be able to manage (s.o/s.t): *Now that Peter's in control, things should get better. They are in control of the situation.* (**get**) **out of control** who/that s.o cannot manage, keep in order etc: *Things are* (or *The crowd is*) *getting out of control. Our garden is completely out of control.* **under control** able to be managed, kept in order, working well, successfully (esp after he/she/it has been out of control): *Don't worry, everything's under control. They managed to bring the fire under control. He brought the aircraft under control and landed safely.* **under s.o's control** who/that is managed, controlled(7) by s.o: *The sales department came under his control when he accepted the new job.*

▷ *tr.v* (*-ll-*) **7** have power or rights over (s.o/s.t); manage (s.t): *He controlled a large empire. You can't control such a huge dog.* **8** make (s.t) work or move well, in a certain way etc: *How do you* *control this machine? He controlled the car on the wet road.* **9** keep (s.t, esp amounts, quantities etc) at a certain level: *Demand for a product usually controls its price. Who controls teachers' salaries?* **control oneself**, **one's temper** prevent oneself from being, becoming, too emotional(2); stop one's feelings from getting too strong: *You must learn to control yourself in political discussions.*

con'trollable *adj* who/that can be controlled(7). Opposite uncontrollable.

con'troller *c.n* person, esp an official, who manages s.t, e.g the movement of goods, aircraft, etc or the organization of a department: *an air traffic controller.*

con'trols *def.pl.n* set of instruments, wheels, buttons(2) etc in a vehicle, ship, aircraft, machine etc by which it can be started, moved, stopped etc: *The controls of a modern aircraft are very complicated.* **be at the controls** be driving etc the vehicle, plane etc.

con'trol ˌtower *c.n* tower or building from which the movement of aircraft landing or taking off is directed.

controversy /'kɒntrəˌvɜːsɪ, kənˈtrɒvəsɪ/ *c/u.n* (*pl -ies*) (*formal*) (example of an) argument or disagreement between people who take opposing views: *There was a good deal of controversy about the proposed law.*

controversial /ˌkɒntrəˈvɜːʃəl/ *adj* causing, leading to, argument or disagreement: *The decision to go ahead with the new road was very controversial.*

ˌcontro'versially *adv.*

contusion /kənˈtjuːʒən/ *c.n* (*medical*) bruise on the skin (but without the skin breaking).

conundrum /kəˈnʌndrəm/ *c.n* (*pl -s*) **1** kind of puzzle, esp one using words. **2** thing that is puzzling, difficult to understand: *I don't know exactly what happened; it's all a bit of a conundrum.*

conurbation /ˌkɒnɜːˈbeɪʃən/ *c.n* (*formal*) whole area of a very large town or city with its buildings, roads etc and its suburbs: *Birmingham is an example of a large conurbation.*

convalesce /ˌkɒnvəˈles/ *intr.v* have a restful and peaceful time without working etc in order to become well and healthy after an illness or operation: *She will have to convalesce for a couple of months after her operation.*

convalescence /ˌkɒnvəˈlesns/ *u.n* (length of time needed for) resting and getting better after an illness or operation.

ˌconva'lescent *adj* **1** (of, for, a person) resting and getting better after an operation or illness.
▷ *c.n* **2** person who is convalescing.

convection /kənˈvekʃən/ *u.n* (also *attrib*) (*technical*) process by which heat moves through air, a liquid etc: *convection currents. The heating system in this house works by convection.*

convector /kənˈvektə/ *c.n* (also **con'vector ˌheater**) heating device (for a house, room etc) which works in this way.

convene /kənˈviːn/ *v* (*formal*) **1** *tr.v* ask or arrange for (a group of people) to meet together, (a meeting) to take place, to discuss s.t: *A meeting of the board of governors has been convened for next Monday.* **2** *intr.v* have such a meeting: *We will convene at the same time next week.* ⇨ convention(2).

con'venor *c.n* person who arranges a meeting.

convenient /kənˈviːnɪənt/ *adj* **1** (often — *for s.o* (*to do s.t*)) suitable, easy, causing no trouble, (for s.o) (to do s.t): *I'm afraid it won't be convenient for me to see you tomorrow. Come whenever it's convenient (for you). That's not a very convenient time.* Opposite inconvenient. **2** (of a house, machine, device etc) easy and helpful (to use etc): *a convenient-sized garden. The food mixer is very convenient to use.* **3** (of a place etc) being near one and so easy to get to: *The shopping centre is very convenient for us at weekends.*

con'venience *n* **1** *u.n* state of being suitable, of making one's life, work etc easier and less trouble etc: *There is some convenience in being able to choose the hours one wants to work.* **2** *c.n* thing, esp a machine, device etc that helps to make life, work etc easier: *The house has all the modern conveniences.* **3** *c.n* ▷ public convenience. **at one's/your (earliest) convenience** (*formal*) as soon as possible; when, as soon as, it is convenient(1) for you: *Could you please call on us at your earliest convenience.* **for (the sake of) convenience** in order to make s.t easier or of more help: *They decided to meet at her house for convenience.*

con'veniently *adv* in a way that helps one/s.o: *It rained very conveniently just after we came in.*

convent /'kɒnvənt/ *c.n* house, building(s) etc in which nuns live. **enter**, **go into**, **a convent** join a group of nuns in a convent in order to become a nun oneself. Compare monastery, nunnery.

'convent ˌschool *c.n* school, usu for girls, run by nuns.

convention /kənˈvenʃən/ *n* **1** *c/u.n* (example of a) way of behaving that has become accepted as the right way over a period of time: *Many young people ignore social conventions. Jane doesn't behave according to convention.* **2** *c.n* (mainly US) formal meeting of a political party (esp to choose a candidate(1) for the presidency(2)), of a group of people, with a special interest or in a certain profession etc: *The Republican Party's Convention was held in San Francisco. There was a dentists' convention in town and all the hotels were full.*

conventional /kənˈvenʃənl/ *adj* **1** according to custom, the usual way of dressing, behaving etc: *He's very conventional in his dress. He has very conventional parents.* **2** (of an object, work of art etc) ordinary, done in the usual way (and so not very exciting, modern etc): *conventional ideas. It was a very conventional play and not worth going to see.* Opposite unconventional.

con'ventionally *adv.*

converge /kənˈvɜːdʒ/ *intr.v* (*formal*) **1** (of two or more things, people etc) move towards each other, one another, and meet at a certain point: *The lines appeared to converge in the distance.* **2** (of two or more beliefs, opinions etc) become the same, agree with each other: *After a long discussion, our thoughts began to converge.* **converge on s.o/s.t** (of a group or groups of people) move towards s.o/s.t so as to meet near him/her/it: *Crowds of people converged on the pop³ stars.*

convergence /kənˈvɜːdʒəns/ *c/u.n.*

con'vergent *adj.*

conversant /kənˈvɜːsənt/ *adj* (usu — *with s.t*) (*formal*) knowing a lot (about s.t): *He's* *not very conversant with the rules of the game.*

converse¹ /kən'vɜːs/ *intr.v* (usu — *with s.o* (*about s.t*)) (*formal*) talk, have a conversation, (with s.o about s.t): *He was conversing happily with his friend when I arrived.*

conversation /ˌkɒnvə'seɪʃən/ *c/u.n* (example of) talking between people (usu about matters that interest them) in which they exchange information etc: *There were several conversations going on around him and he found it difficult to hear what she was saying.* **fall into conversation** (**with s.o**) to begin to have an informal conversation without planning it.

conversational /ˌkɒnvə'seɪʃənl/ *adj* **1** (*formal*) (of a person) fond of talking: *He's not very conversational and I never know what to say to him.* **2** (usu *attrib*) (of a use of language) showing or using the informal words of ordinary speech: *My conversational French is not very good.*

converse² /'kɒnvɜːs/ *def.n* (also *attrib*) (often *the* — *of s.t*) (*formal*) opposite (of s.t): *Mine is a converse opinion. You say there is no hope but I would argue the converse.*

con'versely *adv* (used to introduce a statement that is opposite to the one just mentioned): *You could get up early and do it before work or conversely you could do it before you go to sleep.*

convert /'kɒnvɜːt/ *c.n* (often — (*from s.t*) *to s.t*) **1** person who has changed (from one religion) (to another religion); person who adopts a religion after not having one: *He was a convert to* Islam. **2** (*fig*) person who has accepted a new idea, a new way of doing s.t etc: *I'm a convert to health foods* (or *a health food convert*).

▷ *tr.v* /kən'vɜːt/ **3** (usu — *s.t* (*from s.t*) (*in*)*to s.t*) change (s.t) (from one thing, use etc) ((in)to another): *The heating unit converts water into steam. We are converting one of the bedrooms into a large bathroom.* **4** (usu — *s.o* (*from s.t*) *to s.t*) persuade (s.o) to change (from one religion) (to another religion), to adopt a religion after not having one): *He tried to convert him to* Christianity *but failed.* **5** (usu — *s.o to s.t*) (*fig*) persuade (s.o) to accept a new idea, do s.t different etc): *I've been completely converted to his way of thinking.* **6** (in rugby) complete (a try(2)) by making a conversion(3). **convert** (from s.t) into s.t (of an object, piece of furniture etc) be able to be changed (from one form) into another: *We bought a chair that converts into a bed.*

conversion /kən'vɜːʃən/ *n* **1** *c/u.n* (often — *of s.t* (*from s.t*) ((*in*)*to s.t*)) (example of an) act of changing or converting(3) (s.t) (from one thing, use etc) ((in)to another): *a house conversion; a roof conversion to a small room. He applied for planning permission for the conversion of the house into flats.* **2** *c/u.n* (often — *of s.o* (*from s.t*) (*to s.t*)) (example of an) act of changing or converting(4) (from one religion) (to another religion): *He was responsible for the conversion of thousands of people to* Christianity. **3** *c.n* (in rugby) completion of a try(2) by kicking the ball over the bar between the two uprights (so scoring two extra points).

convertibility /kən,vɜːtə'bɪlɪtɪ/ *u.n* (*formal*) ability of s.t to convert (from s.t) into s.t or to be converted(3).

convertible /kən'vɜːtəbl/ *adj* **1** (of furniture, a room etc) that can be converted(3): *The chair is convertible* — *it* converts(3) *into a bed when we need it.* **2** (of money, notes etc) that can be changed (into other kinds, coins etc): *I am afraid this* currency(1) *is not convertible.*

▷ *c.n* **3** car with a top that can be taken off or folded back. ⇨ estate car, hatchback, sedan, saloon(3), station wagon.

convex /'kɒnveks/ *adj* having a curve that goes outwards like the outside shape of a spoon: *a convex mirror/lens*(1). Compare concave.

convey /kən'veɪ/ *tr.v* **1** (usu — *s.t* (*from s.w*) *to s.w*) (*formal*) take or carry (s.t, e.g goods (from one place) to another): *The boxes are conveyed to the factory along this belt.* **2** (usu — *s.t to s.o*) (*formal*) make (one's ideas, feelings etc) known (to s.o): *Please convey my best wishes to your wife.* **3** (usu — *s.t to s.o*) (*formal*) (of an object, work of art etc) give, suggest, (an idea, a feeling etc) (to s.o): *The film conveys a powerful picture of what it must be like to be deaf.* **4** (usu — *s.t to s.o*) (*law*) give, transfer(5), the ownership of (property, a house etc) (to s.o) by means of a legal(2) document(1): *The house was conveyed to him by his mother.*

conveyance /kən'veɪəns/ *n* **1** *u.n* (*formal*) act or fact of conveying(1) s.t, e.g goods. **2** *c.n* (*formal*) vehicle, esp one used by the public: *Public conveyances are there to be used.* **3** *u.n* (*law*) act of conveying(4) (a property etc): *How long does the conveyance usually take?*

con'veyancing *u.n* (*law*) act or profession of conveying(4) (a property or properties): *A lot of their* legal(2) *work is conveyancing.*

conveyor /kən'veɪə/ *c.n* (*formal*) person or thing who/that takes or carries s.t.

con'veyor ,belt *c.n* endless belt made of rubber, metal etc, used for moving goods from one place to another, sometimes while work is being done on them: *As the apples moved along the conveyor belt they were sorted according to size.*

convict /'kɒnvɪkt/ *c.n* **1** person who is kept in a prison because he/she has been found guilty of a crime: *A convict escaped from prison last night.*

▷ *tr.v* /kən'vɪkt/ **2** (often — *s.o* (*of s.t*)) (*law*) find (s.o) guilty (of a crime) in a court of law: *He was convicted of robbery with violence and sent to prison for five years.* Opposite acquit.

conviction /kən'vɪkʃən/ *n* **1** *c.n* example of finding s.o, of being found, guilty (of a crime): *He has several convictions for robbery.* Opposite acquittal. **2** *c/u.n* (example of a) very strong belief, esp one that one is not likely to change: *He has strong convictions about what is right and wrong. Her conviction is to be admired.* **have the courage of one's convictions** ⇨ courage. **not carry** (**much**) **conviction** (of a person, s.t said etc) not have much persuasion, force etc (in it): *His explanation didn't carry much conviction.* (**do s.t**) **with** (**great** *etc*) **conviction** (do s.t) in a way that (almost etc) persuades or convinces s.o: *He spoke with complete conviction.*

convince /kən'vɪns/ *tr.v* (often — *s.o of s.t;* — *s.o that*...) persuade (s.o) (of the truth of s.t, that s.t is true): *It took a long time for me to convince him that I was right. She tried to convince me that she was happy but I didn't believe her.*

con'vinced *adj* (often *be* — *of s.t; be* — *that* ...) very certain, sure, (of the truth of s.t, that s.t is true etc): *I'm convinced of his honesty. Paul is convinced that that is the best way of doing it.*

con'vincing *adj* (of a person, argument etc) who/that persuades s.o, makes s.o believe s.t to be true: *The actor was so convincing that he had the whole audience in tears. Molly's argument is very convincing.* Opposite unconvincing.
con'vincingly *adv.*

convivial /kən'vıvıəl/ *adj* (*formal*) (of a person, special occasion etc) very pleasant and friendly, esp providing good food, drink, conversation etc: *He's very convivial and I enjoy his company.*
conviviality /kən,vıvı'ælıtı/ *u.n.*

convoke /kən'vəuk/ *tr.v* (*formal*) call, arrange, (a formal meeting, esp of a parliament).

convocation /,kɒnvə'keıʃən/ *n* 1 *c/u.n* (example of the) act of calling a meeting, esp in the Christian(1) Church or in a university, to make laws, rules etc. 2 *c/unique n* group of people who meet in this way.

convoluted /'kɒnvə,lu:tıd/ *adj* (*formal*) 1 (of an object, s.t made etc) twisted, out of shape, complicated; not straight: *a long convoluted journey.* 2 (of thoughts, speech etc) not very clearly or well expressed; complicated: *I couldn't follow his very convoluted argument.*
convolution /,kɒnvə'lu:ʃən/ *c.n* twisted shape.

convoy /'kɒnvɔı/ *c.n* 1 group of ships or vehicles travelling together (often for protection against attack): *A convoy of ships was moving through the canal.* 2 ships, vehicles etc that protect others: *He was given a police convoy to the airport.* **sail/travel in/under convoy** move together in this way: *We decided to travel in convoy in case one of the cars got stuck.*

convulse /kən'vʌls/ *tr.v* (*formal*) (often be —d by/with s.t) make (s.o) shake, esp with laughter: *His jokes convulsed the audience. We all convulsed with laughter.*

convulsion /kən'vʌlʃən/ *c.n* (often *pl*) sudden shaking of the body because the muscles become stiff etc: *It was frightening to watch the child's convulsions.* **in convulsions** (of a person) laughing so much that one's body shakes: *We were all in convulsions at his jokes.*
convulsive /kən'vʌlsıv/ *adj* having or producing convulsions.
con'vulsively *adv.*

coo /ku:/ *c.n* (*pl* -s) 1 soft gentle sound made by a dove(1) or pigeon(1), or by a person imitating this sound.
▷ *intr.v* 2 make a coo(1): *The doves(1) were cooing in the trees.* **coo at/over s.o** (of a person) make pleasant sounds to a baby, esp to make it happy or to show one likes it: *The old women were cooing over the new baby.*

cook /kuk/ *c.n* 1 person who prepares food in an oven, on a stove, fire etc for eating, often as a job or as a skill: *He's a cook in a small restaurant. Mike's not a very good cook but he does try.*
▷ *v* 2 *tr.v* prepare (food, a meal) (in an oven, on a stove, fire etc) by heating it: *He cooked us a wonderful meal.* 3 *intr.v* (of food) heat and become prepared, ready for eating: *Eggs cook very quickly but rice takes longer. Your dinner's cooking so don't be late back.* **cook the books** ⇒ books (⇒ book). **cook s.t up** (*informal*) (a) invent, make up, a false story, account etc in order to hide the truth, escape blame etc: *She just*

cooked up that story about being robbed so that you wouldn't ask where the money went. (b) plan s.t in secret: *What are those two cooking up?*
'cook,book *c.n* (US) = cookery-book.

'cooker *c.n* 1 kind of stove using gas, electricity, coal etc, with rings(3), an oven and sometimes a grill(2): *We bought a new cooker with gas rings and an electric oven.* 2 fruit, esp apple, which is used for cooking rather than eating raw: *Our apple tree produces excellent cookers.*

'cookery *u.n* (also *attrib*) art and practice of preparing food: *cookery lessons. Cookery was one of our subjects at school.*

'cookery-,book *c.n* book that has recipes to show one how to cook different kinds of food.

cookie /'kukı/ *c.n* (*pl* -ies) (US) = biscuit.

'cooking *u.n* art and practice of preparing food: *I love Chinese cooking.* **s.t etc is cooking** (*fig*; *informal*) s.t etc is happening which one does not know about: *'What's cooking?' 'Is there anything cooking tonight?'*

'cooking ,salt *u.n* salt in grains for adding to food especially during cooking. ⇒ table salt.

cool /ku:l/ *adj* 1 slightly (but usu pleasantly) cold; not warm: *Cool air came in from the sea. The weather was cool for the time of year.* Opposite warm(1). 2 (of a person) calm and not easily disturbed: *I don't know how she manages to stay so cool in a crisis(1).* ⇒ have/keep a cool head, keep cool. 3 (often — to/towards s.o/s.t) not very friendly to, interested in, concerned about, s.o/s.t: *He gave her a cool look. Sam was cool to her after her criticism of him.* 4 (*informal*) (of a person, action etc) bold and annoying: *It's just cool of him to walk into our house as though he owned it!* 5 (*slang*) very good; to be admired (for what one does, the way one looks, dresses etc): *You look really cool in that hat.* 6 (*informal*) (of an amount of money etc) at least, about, esp in order to draw attention to the size of the amount: *He's worth a cool million pounds.* (**have/keep) a cool head** = head(n). ⇒ cool-headed. **keep cool** (*fig*) stay calm and not get excited: *Just keep cool because it won't help to get angry with him.* ⇒ cool(2).
▷ *adv* 7 **play it cool** (*informal*) handle s.t, esp a difficult situation, without getting excited, annoyed, nervous or showing what one feels: *Just play it cool and no one will know that you shouldn't really be here.*
▷ *def.n* 8 (the — of s.t) slightly cold air or temperature (of s.t): *He looked forward to the cool of the evening.* **keep one's cool** (*informal*) stay calm even when the situation is difficult: *Please try to keep your cool when we have the discussion tonight.* **lose one's cool** (*informal*) become angry, annoyed: *He really lost his cool when I told him I wasn't going to stay and help him.*
▷ *v* 9 *tr/intr.v* (often — (s.o/s.t) down) (cause (s.t that was warm or hot) to) become less warm or hot: *He cooled his soup by blowing on it. A swim will cool us down. He waited for his soup to cool.* 10 *intr.v* (often — to/towards s.o/s.t) become less interested (in s.o/s.t), less friendly (to/towards s.o): *Since we last spoke he has cooled towards the idea of joining us.* **cool (s.o) down** (a) ⇒ cool(9). (b) (make s.o) become calmer, less excited, esp after being annoyed or angry: *It took some time to cool him down after their argument.* **cool one's**

heels ⇒ heel(n). **Cool it!** (slang) Stop doing it! Stop being excited or noisy! **cool (s.o) off** (make s.o) become less warm: *I'm going to cool (myself) off in a cold shower.* **cool off** become less interested in s.o, less friendly: *After the row their relations cooled off considerably.*

'cooler n 1 c.n device in which things, esp food, are cooled. 2 def.n (slang) = gaol(1).

,cool-'headed adj (of a person) who can keep calm and does not easily become excited, nervous, anxious, esp in a difficult situation.

,cooling-'off ,period c.n 1 length of time for s.o to calm down after being very angry. 2 time allowed for employers and workers to consider their positions in a dispute(1).

coolly /'ku:llɪ/ adv in a cool(2–4) way: *Coolly, he demanded that they pay him £50 000.*

'coolness u.n 1 state or fact of being cool(1) in temperature: *in the coolness of the evening.* 2 state of being calm or cool(2,4). 3 state or act of being cool(3) (to/towards s.o).

coop /ku:p/ c.n 1 cage for small animals, esp hens, chickens etc.
▷ tr.v 2 **coop s.o/s.t up** keep s.o/s.t, esp an animal, (as if) in a cage and so unable to escape: *I felt cooped up in the office and had to get out into the fresh air.*

co-op /'kəʊ ,ɒp/ c.n (informal) cooperative(4).

cooperate /kəʊ'ɒpə,reɪt/ intr.v (often — with s.o (in/on/over s.t)) act or work together (with s.o) (in order to get s.t done): *They agreed to cooperate with the government in the fight against crime.*

cooperation /kəʊ,ɒpə'reɪʃən/ u.n 1 (often in — with s.o) act of working together (with, helping, s.o): *This programme is presented in cooperation with the city council.* 2 (willingness to give) help for s.o/s.t: *I'd like your cooperation in this matter.*

cooperative /kəʊ'ɒprətɪv/ adj 1 (showing oneself to be) helpful or willing: *He's very cooperative if you handle him properly.* Opposite uncooperative. 2 of a group of people who work together, esp on a farm or to produce goods and sell them with the profit shared between everybody: *a cooperative farm.*
▷ n 3 c.n organization of people who work together to produce and/or sell goods and who share all the duties, responsibilities, costs, profits etc: *The health food shop is run by a cooperative.* 4 def.n (usu with capital C; informal Co-op) organization, and esp one of its shops, for the buying and selling of goods, food etc in which members share the profits.

co-opt /kəʊ'ɒpt/ tr.v (often — s.o onto s.t) (formal) choose (s.o) to become a member (of a committee etc): *Because of his experience they co-opted him onto the committee of inquiry.*

coordinate¹ /kəʊ'ɔ:dɪnɪt/ c.n 1 (geography) one of a number of fixed points or numbers on a printed map by which a place, area etc can be found: *Maps have a grid(2) system which provides a set of two coordinates for every place.*
▷ v/kəʊ'ɔ:dɪ,neɪt/ 2 tr.v make (s.t, esp a set of actions or activities) work smoothly together: *He was put in charge of coordinating the various groups.* 3 intr.v (often — with s.o) act together (with s.o): *You must coordinate with them if you want to succeed.*

co'ordinate ,clause c.n (grammar) one of two or more clauses(1) in a sentence with the same importance and joined by a coordinating conjunction. Compare subordinate clause.

coordinated /kəʊ'ɔ:dɪ,neɪtɪd/ adj 1 having, showing, actions which are smooth, well done: *He's a very well-coordinated child and is good at most sports.* 2 going well with each other: *coordinated colours in a design(2).*

co'ordinating con,junction c.n (grammar) conjunction(1) used to join coordinate clauses, e.g *and, but.* Compare subordinating conjunction.

coordination /kəʊ,ɔ:dɪ'neɪʃən/ u.n act of coordinating(2,3): *That child has poor physical coordination. There needs to be greater coordination between the different groups.*

coordinator /kəʊ'ɔ:dɪ,neɪtə/ c.n person who organizes people, groups etc who are working together, esp to make sure everything runs smoothly, works well together.

coot /ku:t/ c.n kind of bird with black or grey feathers which swims and dives. **as bald as a coot** (slang) very bald.

cop /kɒp/ c.n (slang) 1 (also **'copper**) police officer. **not much cop** (of a person, action etc) not very good or useful: *Don't get him to do it, he's not much cop.*
▷ tr.v (-pp-) (slang) 2 (usu — hold of s.t) catch, hold, (s.t): *Cop (hold of) this tool while I look at the engine.* **cop it** suffer; be punished: *You'll really cop it when he finds out what you've done.* **cop out (of s.t)** stop doing s.t; refuse to do, be part of, take responsibility for, s.t: *I know you, you'll cop out at the last moment and leave us to do all the dirty work.*

'cop-,out c.n (slang) example of the act of copping out (of s.t).

cope /kəʊp/ intr.v (usu — with s.o/s.t) (be able to) deal with (s.o/s.t), manage (s.o/s.t), successfully (sometimes even though one is busy with other things): *I can hardly cope with the work I've got so I can't take on anything else.*

copier ⇒ copy.

co-pilot /'kəʊ ,paɪlət/ c.n person who helps the pilot of an aircraft to fly it.

copious /'kəʊpɪəs/ adj (usu attrib) (formal) lots of; plentiful: *There was a copious supply of coffee. I've taken copious notes on the subject and now I must organize them.*

'copiously adv. **'copiousness** u.n.

copper /'kɒpə/ n 1 u.n (also attrib) kind of red-brown metal substance or element(1), used to make water pipes, electrical wires etc, chem.symb Cu. 2 u.n (also attrib) red-brown colour: *Her hair was almost copper in colour.* ⇒ copper-coloured. 3 c.n (informal) coin of a number of British coins made of this metal or of a similar mixture (with a value of one or two pence). 4 c.n = cop(1). 5 c.n (old use) large bowl or container made of copper(1) or another metal, used for boiling water, cleaning clothes etc.

'copper-,coloured adj red-brown like copper(1,2).

coppice /'kɒpɪs/ c.n ⇒ copse.

copra /'kɒprə/ u.n dried white substance inside a coconut(1), used to make oil for soap.

copse /kɒps/ c.n (also **'coppice**) small group of trees and shrubs.

copulate /'kɒpjʊ,leɪt/ intr.v (usu — with s.o/s.t)

(*formal* of animals; *derog* of people) have sex (with s.o/s.t).

copulation /ˌkɒpjuˈleɪʃən/ *u.n.*

copy /ˈkɒpɪ/ *n* (*pl -ies*) **1** *c.n* thing made to look like an original thing: *I'm afraid this painting is only a copy of the artist's original work.* **2** *c.n* thing that is copied(7) by a machine and is therefore exactly like the original: *Could you make me two copies of this letter, please?* **3** *c.n* one of a number of printed books, newspapers etc: *I tried to get hold of a copy of his first book but couldn't find one anywhere.* **4** *u.n* (also *attrib*) text(1) written to be printed as an article for a newspaper, to be included in an advertisement etc: *I need some copy for this space; do you have any ideas?* **a fair, neat, rough** etc **copy (of s.t)** thing written or copied from s.t else and done carefully etc: *I've done a rough copy of the work but I still have to write it out neatly.*

▷ *v* (*-ies, -ied*) **5** *tr.v* (often — *s.t out*) write (s.t) in one's own hand in a book, on paper etc, following what has been written or printed by s.o else: *Your work is very untidy so why don't you copy it out before you show it to your teacher? Copy out this passage for your homework.* **6** *tr.v* make s.t look exactly like (an original thing): *These dresses have been copied from an original* design(1). **7** *tr.v* use a machine to make an exact example of an original: *Could you copy this report for Mr Turner, please?* ⇒ photocopy. **8** *tr/intr.v* cheat in an examination by looking at (s.o else's work): *The teacher caught him copying (Peter's work).* **9** *tr.v* do the same (thing) as s.o else; imitate (s.o, an action etc): *You're always copying what she does.*

copier /ˈkɒpɪə/ *c.n* **1** person who makes a copy(1) of s.t. **2** machine for making copies(2) of written, printed pages etc. ⇒ photocopier.

ˈcopy,book ⇒ blot(*v*).

ˈcopy,cat *c.n* (*derog; informal*) (often used by children) person who imitates other people, what they do etc.

ˈcopy,right *u.n* **1** (also *attrib*) (*law*) (ownership of) right by an author(1) or producer to publish or make s.t, e.g a book, film, broadcast, music etc, which is held for a certain number of years: *Copyright in a book is usually shown by the symbol © printed on the back of the title page.*

▷ *tr.v* **2** protect (one's work) with a copyright(1).

ˈcopy,writer *c.n* person who writes copy(4), esp for an advertisement.

coral /ˈkɒrəl/ *u.n* **1** kind of, usu red, pink or white, hard substance found on the bed of the sea and made of the bodies of small sea animals. **2** (also *attrib*) deep pink colour: *She bought a coral lipstick.*

ˌcoral ˈisland *c.n* island made from coral(1) or with coral-reefs around it.

ˌcoral-ˈreef *c.n* reef(1) made from coral(1).

cord /kɔːd/ *n* **1** *c/u.n* (piece or length of) thick string: *He tied the parcel up with cord.* **2** *c/u.n* (piece or length of) electrical wire with a covering used to join an electrical device to a supply of electricity: *We need a longer cord for the lamp so it can reach the table.* **3** *c.n* (*old use* **chord**) long length of s.t like a cord(1) in the body: *the* spinal cord; *the* vocal cords. **4** *u.n* (*informal*) corduroy.

ˈcordless *adj* not having or needing a cord(2).

cordial /ˈkɔːdɪəl/ *adj* **1** (*formal*) warm and friendly: *They received a very cordial welcome.*

▷ *u.n* **2** kind of drink made from fruit juice with water added.

cordiality /ˌkɔːdɪˈælɪtɪ/ *u.n* (showing of) warmth and friendliness.

ˈcordially *adv.*

cordon /ˈkɔːdn/ *c.n* **1** line(s) of rope, soldiers, police, vehicles etc put across s.w or around s.w for protection, to stop people etc: *The crowd broke through the police cordon and entered the building.*

▷ *tr.v* **2** (usu — *s.t off*) protect (a place), stop people from entering (a place), by having a cordon(1) around it: *The street was cordoned off after the explosion.*

cords /kɔːdz/ *pl.n* (*informal*) corduroys.

corduroy /ˈkɔːdərɔɪ/ *u.n* (also *attrib*) (*informal* **cord**) kind of (cotton) cloth with raised lines on it, used for clothing: *a corduroy shirt.*

ˈcorduroys *pl.n* (*informal* **cords**) trousers made of this cloth: *a pair of black corduroys.*

core /kɔː/ *n* **1** *c.n* inner central part of s.t, esp fruit, the earth, a machine etc: *She threw away the apple core. It is extremely hot at the core of an atomic reactor(1).* **2** *def.n* (usu *the — of s.t*) main or most important part of s.t, esp a problem: *The core of the matter is that we don't know what to do.* **be rotten** etc **to the core** be completely or thoroughly rotten etc: *He's British to the core.* **get to the core of s.t** fix one's attention on the main part of s.t, esp a problem, and leave the less important details alone.

▷ *tr.v* **3** remove the core(1) of (a fruit): *Would you core these apples please?*

co-respondent /ˌkəʊ rɪˈspɒndənt/ *c.n* (*law*) person stated (in a couple's divorce(1) case) to have had sexual intercourse with the husband/wife (the respondent) of the person who wants a divorce(1).

corgi /ˈkɔːgɪ/ *c.n* (*pl -s*) kind of small dog with thick brown hair and short legs.

cork /kɔːk/ *n* **1** *u.n* (also *attrib*) bark of the cork oak, which is light in weight, used for floors, notice boards etc: *We are going to put cork* tiles(2) *on the kitchen floor. Cork is so light that it floats on water.* **2** *c.n* short round piece of this bark put in the top part of a bottle, esp of wine, to stop liquid from coming out.

▷ *tr.v* **3** put a cork(2) in (a bottle): *Would you cork the wine please or else it will spoil?*

ˈcork ˌoak *c.n* kind of tree found in southern Europe, north Africa etc which produces cork(1).

corked *adj* (of wine) spoilt because of a bad cork in the bottle.

ˈcork,screw *c.n* device with a handle and a short length of metal twisted into a spiral(1) shape, used for taking a cork(2) out of a bottle.

ˈcork-,tipped *adj* (of cigarettes) having a filter(1) made of cork or a similar substance at one end. Compare filter-tipped.

corn /kɔːn/ *n* **1** *u.n* (seed(s) of various kinds of) grain plants, e.g rye(1), maize etc, and esp wheat: *The price of corn has dropped.* **2** *c.n* one seed of this. ⇒ peppercorn. **3** *u.n* = sweetcorn. **4** *c.n* swelling of hard skin on the foot which is often painful: *She suffers from corns.* **5** *u.n* (*informal*) dull and uninteresting play, performance etc, esp because it has been done too often before, because it is too ordinary etc: *The song is pure corn but I suppose some people will like it.*

'corn,cob *c.n* central ear on which the seeds of maize grow.

,corned 'beef *u.n* pressed and salted beef¹(1).

'corn,field *c.n* field in which corn(1) is growing.

'corn,flakes *pl.n* small pieces of crushed and toasted¹(2) corn(1), usu eaten at breakfast with milk and sugar.

'corn,flour *u.n* kind of flour made from maize.

,corn-on-the-'cob *u.n* maize which is still fixed to the ear and is often eaten, cooked in this form.

'corny *adj* (*-ier*, *-iest*) (*informal*) dull, uninteresting, silly; full of corn(5): *That was a really corny joke.*

cornea /'kɔːnɪə/ *c.n* (*pl* -s) (*technical*) transparent covering over the eye which protects it.

corneal /'kɔːnɪəl/ *adj* (*technical*) of or referring to the cornea: *a corneal operation.*

corner /'kɔːnə/ *c.n* 1 point or place where two lines, edges, surfaces etc meet: *the corner of a box*; *the corner of a room.* 2 place where two roads, streets etc meet (and cross): *We'll meet at the corner of Oxford Street and Duke Street at 2 o'clock.* 3 (in football) free kick given and taken at one of the four corners of the football field. 4 (often *make a — in s.t*) (*commerce*) controlling position (in some produce, goods etc) by buying so much/many that others are forced to buy from one: *The company has made a corner in gold.* **be in a** (**tight**) **corner** (*informal*) be in a difficult situation from which it is not easy to escape: *Could you lend me some money as I'm in a bit of a tight corner at the moment?* **cut a corner** (in driving a car, riding a bicycle etc) go too close to a corner when going round it and so go over the pavement. **cut corners** (*fig*) do s.t by not following the normal rules or by not doing what one should do: *John cut a number of corners and offended a lot of people in his attempt to get control of the business.* **from/to all corners of the world**; **from/to the four corners of the earth** (coming) from, (going) to, all or many places in the world: *They're coming from all corners of the world to hear him speak.* **round the corner** very near in space or time. **turn the corner** (*fig*) get better (after a serious illness, a time of great difficulty etc): *After a year of bad trading, I am glad to say the company has now turned the corner.*

▷ *v* 5 *tr.v* force (a person, an animal) into a position from which he/she/it cannot escape easily: *They cornered the mad dog in the wood. He cornered me at the party and told me all about himself.* 6 *intr.v* (of a vehicle, bicycle, s.o driving) go round a corner of a road etc: *corner very fast.* **corner the market** ⇒ market(*n*).

'cornered *adj* (of a person, animal) trapped; unable to escape: *He fought like a cornered animal. I felt cornered and couldn't think of an excuse to get away.*

-cornered *adj* having the number of corners shown in the first part of the word: *a three-cornered hat.*

'corner ,shop *c.n* small general store (often on a corner) near homes.

'corner,stone *c.n* 1 stone placed at the bottom

corner of a building, often in a special ceremony. 2 (*fig*) thing that forms the basis, the most important part, (of s.t): *The cornerstone of our freedom is respect for the law.*

cornet /'kɔːnɪt/ *c.n* 1 kind of brass musical instrument like a small trumpet. 2 piece of biscuit rolled into the shape of a cone(3) into which ice-cream is put and the whole is eaten.

cornfield, cornflakes, cornflour ⇒ corn.

cornice /'kɔːnɪs/ *c.n* 1 decorated border, usu made of plaster(1), which runs around the ceiling or the tops of the walls of a room. 2 line or edge of stone which sticks out on the outside or top of a building.

corny ⇒ corn.

corollary /kə'rɒlərɪ/ *c.n* (*pl* -ies) (*formal*) thing, esp a statement, that follows on from another fact, statement: *If you believe him, the corollary is that she is the guilty party.*

coronary /'kɒrənərɪ/ *adj* 1 (*technical*) of or referring to the heart or the arteries(1) that take blood to and from the heart: *She has coronary problems.*

▷ *c.n* 2 (*informal*) = coronary thrombosis.

,coronary throm'bosis *c.n* (*pl* thromboses /'bəʊsiːz/) (heart attack caused by the) blocking of an artery(1) with a clot(1) of blood.

coronation /,kɒrə'neɪʃən/ *c.n* act, ceremony, of crowning a king or queen: *The last British coronation was in 1953.*

coroner /'kɒrənə/ *c.n* government official who examines the causes of the death of s.o when the circumstances are or may be suspicious.

coronet /'kɒrənɪt/ *c.n* 1 small crown worn by some classes of nobles. 2 ornamental crown made of jewellery, flowers etc, worn by a woman.

corp /kɔːp/ *abbr* 1 corporal(2). 2 (*written abbr*) corporation(1).

corpora ⇒ corpus.

corporal /'kɔːprəl/ *adj* 1 (*formal; technical*) of or referring to the human body.

▷ *c.n* 2 (*abbr* Corp or Cpl) rank in the British Army below a sergeant(1). ⇒ lance corporal.

,corporal 'punishment *c.n* (*formal*) hitting of the body, esp the hands, bottom, with a cane(3), stick, whip etc, in order to punish s.o for s.t he/she has done wrong.

corporate /'kɔːpərɪt/ *adj* 1 shared among, done by, a group of people working together as a whole: *No one person was responsible for our success; it was a corporate effort.* 2 of or referring to a corporation(1): *a corporate body.*

corporation /,kɔːpə'reɪʃən/ *c.n* (with capital **C** in names) 1 (*written abbr* Corp) large business organization run by a group of people: *He's just joined a large American corporation.* 2 official group of people who run a town: *The Corporation has cut the bus services.*

corps /kɔː/ *c.n* (*pl* corps /kɔːz/) (with capital **C** in names) 1 (*military*) special group in the army: *the Armoured Corps*; *the medical corps.* 2 (*military*) large group of soldiers etc in the army, consisting of two divisions. 3 (*formal*) group of people organized or trained for a particular purpose, job: *the diplomatic(1) corps*; *the press corps* (i.e all the representatives of the newspapers, radio, television etc working in a country, on a particular news item).

corps de ballet /ˌkɔː də ˈbæleɪ/ c.n (pl corps de ballet) (French) group of dancers (not the main dancers) in a ballet(1).

Corps Diplomatique /ˌkɔː ˌdɪpləʊmæˈtiːk/ def.n (abbr CD) (French) (also **the ˌdiplo-ˈmatic ˌcorps**) all the officials representing foreign countries who are stationed in one country.

corpse /kɔːps/ c.n dead body, usu of a human being: After the battle, the corpses were buried in mass graves.

corpulence /ˈkɔːpjʊləns/ u.n (formal) fatness of the human body: He's tending to corpulence in his middle age.

ˈcorpulent adj (formal) (of a person) fat.

corpus /ˈkɔːpəs/ c.n (pl -es /ˈkɔːpəsɪz/ or, less usu, corpora /ˈkɔːpərə/) (Latin) **1** (complete) collection of all the written work of an author: the Shakespeare corpus. **2** collection of written work for a particular subject: Who will provide the science corpus for the dictionary?

corpuscle /ˈkɔːpʌsl/ c.n (technical) one of the red or white cells(4) in blood.

corral /kəˈrɑːl/ c.n **1** (esp US) area surrounded by fences in which horses, cows etc are kept for a certain time.
▷ tr.v (-ll-) **2** (esp US) put (animals etc) into a corral(1).

correct /kəˈrekt/ adj Opposite incorrect. **1** (usu pred) without any mistakes: His homework was all correct. **2** right; not wrong (in what one says etc): Am I correct in believing that you are going to buy the house? **3** (of a person, behaviour, dress etc) proper according to normal social customs: He was very correct in his behaviour towards her.
▷ tr.v **4** mark, remove the mistake(s) in, (s.t): The teacher was correcting their homework. There are several printing mistakes that have to be corrected. **5** say that (s.t) is wrong and give the right form: He's always correcting my pronunciation.

correction /kəˈrekʃən/ n **1** u.n act of correcting(4,5) s.t. **2** c.n example of this, esp a mark made against s.t wrong and the addition of the right thing.

corrective /kəˈrektɪv/ adj (usu attrib) (formal) **1** helping to change s.t into s.t better: Corrective measures are needed if business is to improve.
▷ c.n **2** action or thing that is corrective(1).

corˈrectly adv. **corˈrectness** u.n.

correlate /ˈkɒrɪleɪt/ tr.v (often — s.t with s.t) (formal) show how (one thing) has a relation (with another): It is impossible to correlate these new results with the earlier experiments.

correlation /ˌkɒrɪˈleɪʃən/ c/u.n (often — between s.t and s.t; — of s.t with s.t) (formal) (example of the) act of doing this: What is the correlation between IQ and ability?

correspond /ˌkɒrɪˈspɒnd/ intr.v **1** (often — with s.o) (formal) write letters (to s.o) and receive letters (from her/him) regularly: They have been corresponding (with each other) for many years. **2** (often — to s.t) be (almost) the same in some way (as s.t): Our high schools correspond to your secondary schools. **3** (often — with s.t) match (s.t): Your letter does not correspond with the points we agreed in our discussion.

correspondence /ˌkɒrɪˈspɒndəns/ u.n (formal) **1** act or fact of writing and receiving letters: They had a lengthy correspondence before they reached an agreement. **2** (number of) letters: I've got a pile of correspondence to get through. **3** (often — between s.t and s.t) sameness; agreement (of/between two things): I can't find much correspondence between this set of results and that one. **be in correspondence with s.o** correspond(1) regularly with s.o.

ˌcorreˈspondence ˌcourse c.n set of lessons (in a subject) sent regularly by post to s.o's home: I'm doing a business correspondence course through the Open University.

ˌcorreˈspondent c.n **1** (formal) person who writes and receives letters: He's a very bad correspondent. **2** person who writes regularly for a newspaper (often reporting from a distance): He is a foreign correspondent for an American newspaper.

ˌcorreˈsponding adj matching or agreeing, esp when compared with s.t: In the corresponding month last year we sold 10 000 fewer cars.

ˌcorreˈspondingly adv.

corridor /ˈkɒrɪdɔː/ c.n enclosed passage in a building which joins several rooms, offices etc: Take the first corridor on the right and his office is the second door.

corroborate /kəˈrɒbəˌreɪt/ tr.v (formal) support or strengthen (the truth of s.t, what s.o has stated etc), esp by providing extra information or proof: His statement was corroborated by several people. This information corroborates what Mr Hunter said.

corroboration /kəˌrɒbəˈreɪʃən/ u.n.

corroborative /kəˈrɒbərətɪv/ adj that corroborates s.t: corroborative evidence(1).

corrode /kəˈrəʊd/ v **1** tr.v (of the action of oxygen in the air, acid etc) wear away, destroy, (the surface of s.t, esp a metal): The supports of the bridge had become corroded over the years. Sea air badly corrodes cars. **2** intr.v (of metal) become, be able to be, worn away by this action: A hard plastic substance is replacing certain metal parts on cars because it doesn't corrode easily. **3** (fig) tr.v slowly damage, destroy, (s.t, esp social behaviour, morals etc): Our society is being gradually corroded from within.

corrosion /kəˈrəʊʒən/ u.n.

corrosive /kəˈrəʊsɪv/ adj **1** having the power to corrode(1,2) (s.t): a corrosive acid.
▷ c.n **2** substance that corrodes(1,2) (s.t).

corˈrosiveness u.n.

corrugated /ˈkɒrʊˌgeɪtɪd/ adj (usu attrib) (of sheets of metal, paper etc) folded to form a series of curved waves that give extra strength: The walls of the hut were made of corrugated iron. The books were packed in corrugated cardboard.

corrupt /kəˈrʌpt/ adj **1** (derog) (of a person, action, system etc) dishonest, immoral, (esp because of bribery): The government is very corrupt. **2** (of a language) not correct; differing from the original form: The people on the island speak a corrupt form of English.
▷ tr.v **3** make (s.o) dishonest, immoral: They managed to corrupt the officials with offers of money. **4** tr.v change (the original form of a language) to s.t less correct: Their speech has become corrupted over the years.

corruptibility /kəˌrʌptəˈbɪlɪti/ u.n ability to be corrupted(3).

corruptible /kə'rʌptəbl/ *adj* (of a person) able to be corrupted(3). Opposite incorruptible.

corruption /kə'rʌpʃən/, **cor'ruptness** *u.n.*

corset /'kɔːsɪt/ *c.n* kind of tight underclothing with strong supports in it, worn either to improve the shape of one's body around the stomach, waist and hips¹ or to protect and support a weak/ damaged part of the body.

cortege, cortège /kɔː'teɪʒ/ *c.n* (French; *formal*) procession of people at a funeral that follows the coffin.

cortex /'kɔːteks/ *c.n* (*pl* cortices /'kɔːtɪsiːz/) (*technical*) **1** outer grey matter in the brain. **2** outer layer or bark of a woody(1) plant or tree.

cos¹ /kɒs/ *c.n* (also **'cos ,lettuce**) kind of lettuce with long leaves.

cos² *written abbr* cosine.

cosh /kɒʃ/ *c.n* (*informal*) **1** heavy short length of pipe, metal, rubber etc, used to hit s.o with: *They were armed with coshes and were prepared to use them if anybody got in their way.*
▷ *tr.v* **2** hit (s.o) with a cosh(1): *He was coshed over the head and robbed of his money.*

cosily, cosiness ⇨ cosy.

cosine /'kəʊ,saɪn/ *c.n* (*written abbr* cos) (often *the — of s.t*) (*mathematics*) value or ratio for an angle in a right-angled triangle produced by dividing the length of the side near to the right angle by the length of the side opposite the right angle. Compare sine, tangent(2).

cosmetic /kɒz'metɪk/ *adj* **1** (of a substance, medical operation etc) helping to improve one's beauty and good looks: *He had cosmetic* surgery(1) *to make him look younger.* **2** (*derog*) improving, dealing only with, the outward appearance and not the real substance, problem etc: *The government's recommendations are cosmetic and do not get to the heart of the problem.*
▷ *c.n* (usu *pl*) **3** substance, e.g cream, colouring, lipstick, used to make s.o's face etc look more beautiful.

cosmic /'kɒzmɪk/ *adj* of or referring to the whole universe (stars, space etc).

cosmonaut /'kɒzmənɔːt/ *c.n* (Russian word for a) person who travels in space; astronaut.

cosmos /'kɒzmɒs/ *def.n* whole universe.

cosmopolitan /,kɒzmə'pɒlɪtən/ *adj* **1** (of a place) having, containing, people from many parts of the world (and therefore interesting): *New York is a very cosmopolitan city.* **2** (of a person, opinion etc) showing little prejudice(1,2) because of a wide knowledge of other people, countries etc: *He has a very cosmopolitan outlook.*
▷ *c.n* **3** person who acts like this.

cosset /'kɒsɪt/ *tr.v* care for (s.o), look after (s.o), with great attention, providing everything he/she wants: *I was cosseted by my husband during the whole of my illness.*

cost /kɒst/ *n* **1** *u.n* amount of money, price, one pays or has to pay (for s.t) in order to own it, get s.t done etc: *The cost of car repairs is going up all the time. You need a holiday so don't think about the cost!* **2** *c.n* (*commerce*) amount of money one spends or has to spend in order to make s.t (onto which is added one's profit in order to arrive at a selling price): *Manufacturing costs have risen five*

per cent *in the last six months and this is sure to affect prices.* **3** *u.n* (often *the — in s.t*) what is or has to be used up, destroyed etc (in order to get a result, victory etc): *The cost in time and money is not worth the result. The war was won but the cost in human lives was high.* **at a cost of s.t** for a certain stated amount of money: *He bought it at a cost of £350.* (**not**) **at any cost** no matter what the price or what one has to do (to prevent it): *You are not to allow anyone to leave the house at any cost.* **at cost** (**price**) for the amount of money spent in manufacturing it (and not the normal selling price): *The manufacturers are selling kitchen units at cost in order to clear stock.* **at great, high** etc **cost** (**in s.t**) (**to s.o**) with the result of great etc suffering or loss (of s.t) (by s.o etc) while doing it: *She's a great star but only at a high cost to her family and friends.* **at the cost of** (**doing**) **s.t** (**a**) while suffering or losing s.t oneself: *He saved the child from drowning but at the cost of (losing) his own life.* (**b**) (*fig*) even though it may result in s.t: *At the cost of appearing stupid, I have to say that I still don't understand what you mean.* **cost of living** all the amounts of money one spends on food, clothes, heating, travel, services etc in normal everyday life. **count the cost** (**of s.t**) (*fig*) (be made to) realize what one may suffer, lose, (in doing s.t): *Before we decide whether to buy the business we should count the cost and make sure it's what we all want.* **to one's cost** to one's disadvantage; having learnt by painful (personal) experience: *It is not worth arguing with him as I have learnt to my cost.*
▷ *tr.v* (*p.t,p.p* cost except 6 below) **4** be the amount one has to pay or pays (for a product, service etc): *The coat cost her £60 in the sales. How much will it cost to put a window in this wall?* **5** (often *— s.o s.t*) (of an action) be (s.t) s.o suffers or loses: *His continual lateness cost him his job.* **6** (*p.t,p.p* costed) (*commerce*) work out the probable or likely cost(2) of (s.t): *The production people have costed the work at £1.50 per unit.* **cost (s.o) money, a fortune, a lot** etc be, prove to be, (very) expensive (for s.o): *It will cost you a lot of money to set up in business on your own.* **cost the earth** ⇨ earth. **cost a packet** ⇨ packet(*n*).

'costliness *u.n* (*formal*) fact of being costly: *The costliness of war. The costliness of her clothes was immediately clear.*

'costly *adj* (-ier, -iest) (*formal*) **1** expensive to buy or do: *It was a very costly reception.* **2** leading to, requiring, suffering, a loss of s.t: *The victory was a very costly one.*

costs *pl.n* (*law*) amount of money one has to pay for a court action (often paid by the side that loses): *She lost the case and had to pay costs of £30 000.* **at all costs** whatever, without regard to what, the amount of money, the loss or suffering may be: *We must win the* contract(1) *at all costs. Try to avoid that road at all costs.*

co-star /'kəʊ ,stɑː/ *c.n* **1** actor or actress who takes one of the two main parts in a play, film etc with s.o else: *His co-star was an unknown actress.*
▷ *intr.v* (-rr-) **2** (usu *— (with s.o) in s.t*) take one of the two main parts (with s.o) (in a play, film etc): *Ginger Rogers co-starred with Fred Astaire in 'Top Hat'.*

costliness, costly ⇒ cost.

costume /'kɒstjuːm/ c/u.n (example of a) thing one wears, esp a complete set of clothes of a certain style or historical time: *historical costumes. They had to dress in 16th century costume for the play.* ⇒ swimming costume.

cosy /'kəʊzɪ/ adj (-ier, -iest) (of a person, object, place etc) warm and well arranged for comfort: *I remember cosy evenings in front of the fire. Are you cosy now or do you want another cushion?* **egg cosy** ⇒ egg(n). **tea cosy** ⇒ tea. **'cosily** adv. **'cosiness** u.n.

cot /kɒt/ c.n child's small bed with high sides to stop her/him from falling or getting out: *Our baby's cot has one side that can be moved up or down.*

cottage /'kɒtɪdʒ/ c.n small house of one or two storeys, usu but not always found in the country: *He lived in one of a row of cottages off the main road.*

,cottage 'cheese u.n kind of white cheese with soft pieces, made from sour milk.

,cottage 'industry c.n work done by a group of people on a small scale, esp in their own homes: *The scent they make started as a cottage industry but they now have a factory employing a hundred people.*

cotton /'kɒtn/ u.n 1 (also *attrib*) kind of soft white substance found round the seed of a cotton plant, used for making material etc: *cotton pickers. She was wearing a white cotton dress.* 2 u.n thread of this material, used for sewing: *Have you any white cotton for me to sew this button on?*

▷ intr.v 3 **cotton on (to s.t)** (*informal*) (begin to) realize or understand what is being said, done etc: *It took me some time to cotton on to what was happening.*

'cotton ,plant c.n plant that produces cotton(1).

'cotton-,reel c.n small round piece of wood or plastic around which cotton(2) is wound.

,cotton-'wool u.n very clean cotton(1), used medically for cleaning wounds, putting over scratches etc.

couch /kaʊtʃ/ c.n 1 long padded seat, sometimes with a back and arms, on which one can sit or lie; sofa: *We bought a large comfortable couch for the living-room. There was a couch in the doctor's room on which he examined patients.* **studio couch** ⇒ studio.

▷ tr.v 2 (usu — s.t in s.t) (*formal*) state, express, (s.t, esp one's words, a reply etc) (in a certain way): *He couched his reasons for not publishing(1) her book in encouraging terms because he recognized her talent(1).*

couchette /kuːˈʃet/ c.n (*French*) one of a number of narrow beds in a railway compartment(1) on which one can sleep (and often which folds up to form a seat during the daytime).

cougar /'kuːgə/ c.n kind of large brown wild animal of the cat family found in north and south America; panther, puma.

cough /kɒf/ c.n (also *attrib*) 1 sound made by pushing air from the lungs and out of the mouth (because there is s.t, e.g phlegm or mucus, blocking the way as in a cold, because one wants to draw s.o's attention etc): *I heard a gentle cough behind me and turned to see someone making a sign to me.* 2 (usu *have/get a —*) illness of the throat or lungs which makes one cough(3): *You*

sound as though you've got a very bad cough. You need some cough mixture.

▷ intr.v 3 push air from the lungs and out of the mouth with a (loud) sound: *He coughed to clear his throat.* **cough s.t up** get rid of s.t from the lungs and throat by coughing(3): *He started coughing up a lot of blood.* **cough (s.t) up** (*fig; informal*) give, hand over, (money, information etc) when one doesn't want to: *With a bit of persuasion he'll cough up (a few pounds) for a good cause.*

'cough-,drop c.n kind of boiled sweet used to help stop a cough(2), make a sore throat better.

could p.t can¹.

couldn't /'kʊdnt/ = could not. ⇒ can¹.

could've /'kʊdəv/ = could have. ⇒ can¹.

council /'kaʊnsəl/ c.n (with capital **C** in names) 1 (official) group of people chosen or appointed to give advice or help on certain matters: *a sports council.* 2 group of people elected or appointed to run the affairs of a town, city or county: *the Oxford City Council.*

'council e,state c.n group of houses and/or flats owned by the local council(2) and rented to people.

'council ,house c.n house owned by the local council(2) and rented to s.o.

councillor /'kaʊnsələ/ c.n (with capital **C** in names) official elected to a council(2).

counsel¹ /'kaʊnsəl/ n 1 u.n (*formal; literary*) advice or suggestion(s) given to help s.o: *The counsel he gave us was to work towards a settlement.* 2 c.n (pl counsel) (*law*) lawyer(s) who defend(s) or prosecute(s) in a court of law: *Counsel for the defence argued that the witnesses were lying.* **King's/Queen's Counsel** ⇒ king, queen.

▷ tr.v (-ll-, US -l-) 1 (often — (s.o to do) s.t) (*formal*) offer advice to (s.o, on what to do) about (s.t): *I would counsel you to accept his offer. I counsel caution in your dealings with him.* 2 (often — s.o about/on s.t) give (s.o) advice about a problem (as part of one's job): *She counsels a lot of couples(3) on their marriage problems.*

'counselling u.n (US **'counseling**) (also *attrib*) act of giving people advice and help with problems, esp as part of one's job: *a counselling service. We give counselling to a lot of people who are having marriage problems.*

counsellor /'kaʊnsələ/ c.n (US **'counselor**) 1 c.n person who gives advice: *a marriage guidance counsellor.* 2 (US) lawyer.

count¹ /kaʊnt/ c.n 1 act of finding out the numbers of people, things etc present: *Let's do a count of the boxes in the shed to see if any are missing.* 2 total number of people, things etc found in this way: *The count of those attending the meeting came to fifty-five.* 3 (*boxing*) (often *a — of s.t*) one of the numbers between 1 and 10 spoken by the referee(2) from the time one of the boxers has been knocked to the floor till he gets up again: *He took a count of 8 in the fourth round but was knocked out in the fifth.* ⇒ be out for the count(a), count s.o out(a). 4 (*law*) one of a number of legal(2) charges brought against s.o: *He was found guilty on two counts of robbery with violence and not guilty on the other charges.* **at/on the count of s.t** as soon as a certain number has been counted: *On the count of ten open your eyes.*

be counted out ⇨ count s.o out(a), count(3). **be out for the count** (a) (*boxing*) be still knocked out or lying on the floor when a count(3) of 10 has been made. (b) (*informal*) be sleeping deeply, esp after being very tired: *Sharon came home from the trip so tired and she's still out for the count.* **keep/lose count (of s.o/s.t)** be able to, be unable to, note the total numbers (of people, things etc): *They kept count of the number of people crossing the border. I'm sorry, I've lost count; I'll have to start adding up again.*

▷ *v* **5** *tr.v* say, note in one's mind, the numbers one by one of (people or things) and so reach a total: *I've counted all the boxes and there are 150.* ⇨ count s.t up. **6** *intr.v* (be able to, know how to) say, note in one's mind, numbers one by one: *He's only five and can't count properly yet. He has to use his fingers to count.* ⇨ count (from s.t) (up) to s.t. **7** *intr.v* (of a person, what s.o does) be of value or importance: *Forget about him; his opinions don't count. What counts is what you really believe.* **8** *tr.v* (usu — oneself/ s.o (to be) s.o/s.t) think, consider, (oneself/s.o) (to be) of a certain kind: *I count him one of my closest friends.* **9** *tr.v* (often *if you — s.o/s.t*; (*not*) *counting s.o/s.t*) include (or not include) (s.o/s.t) in a total, group etc (to get the total number): *Not counting the officials, there were fifty-six people at the meeting.*

count (s.t) against s.o be, consider (s.t), to s.o's disadvantage: *His lack of work during the term will count against him when the examinations come.*

count for little, **nothing** etc (of an action etc) be of little, no etc importance or value: *Don't worry about him; his opinions count for very little.*

count from s.t (up) to s.t ⇨ count (from s.t) (up) to s.t.

count s.o in (*informal*) include s.o, esp as being ready to take part in s.t: *If you're going out to dinner, you can count me in.* Opposite count s.o out(b).

count s.o/s.t off (on s.t) say the numbers of people, things (by noting them on a list etc): *He counted off the points he was making on his fingers one by one.*

count on s.o/s.t (to do s.t, doing s.t) ⇨ count (up)on s.o/s.t (to do s.t, doing s.t).

count s.o out (a) (*boxing*) (of a referee(2)) declare that s.o has lost a fight by saying all the numbers from 1 to 10 before he gets up from the floor. (b) (*informal*) not include s.o (in some activity because he/she does not want to, cannot, take part): *I'm sorry, I haven't time so you'll have to count me out this time.* Opposite count s.o in.

count s.t out say the numbers, amount of s.t, esp coins (which one is going to give to s.o, e.g in change) up to a total: *He counted out £5.50 in change.*

count (from s.t) (up) to s.t (be able to, know how to) say, note in one's mind, numbers (from a lower number, usu 1) (up) to a certain higher number: *I'll count from one (up) to a hundred and then I'm coming to find you.*

count towards s.t (of a mark etc) be considered, recognized, included, when trying to decide s.t: *Your work during the term will count towards your final mark.*

count s.t up say, note, the numbers of s.t and so reach a total: *He counted up the boxes and found there were five missing.*

count (up) on s.o/s.t (to do s.t, doing s.t) expect, rely on, s.o/s.t (to do s.t): *I'm counting on you to help me next week.*

'countable *adj* **1** (of numbers) that can be counted: *Very large numbers are probably only easily countable on a* computer. **2** ⇨ count noun.

'countable ,noun *c.n* ⇨ count noun.

'count,down *c.n* (act of) saying or noting numbers (representing time) backwards from a point to zero, e.g when coming near to a special event etc: *The countdown to Christmas has started.*

'counter *c.n* **1** small flat round coloured piece of plastic(3), used in some (esp board'(4)) games to show one's progress, to keep count of one's score etc. **2** *c.n* device for measuring s.t (esp speed) or for counting the numbers of s.t produced: *If you want to make a lot of photocopies, you have to set the counter to the right number first.*

'countless *adj* (almost) too many to be counted: *I've told you countless times not to do that!*

'count ,noun *c.n* (also **'countable ,noun**) (*grammar*) noun that can have a plural and have 'a/an/the', numerals etc in front of it (marked *c.n* in this dictionary). Compare uncountable.

count² /kaunt/ *c.n* (used with capital **C** in names) (title of a) nobleman in some countries (but not UK where the title is earl). ⇨ countess.

countess /'kauntıs/ *c.n* wife of an earl (in Britain) or count² (in other countries); noblewoman who herself has that rank.

countenance /'kauntınəns/ *n* (*formal*) **1** *c.n* person's face (and what it looks like, what it shows etc): *He had a cruel countenance.* **2** *u.n* (usu *give — to s.o/s.t*) (give) approval, support, (to s.o/s.t, for s.t. to happen): *You should give no countenance to these proposals.*

▷ *tr.v* **3** (*formal*) approve, allow, (s.t): *I will not countenance bad behaviour in my class.*

counter¹ ⇨ count¹.

counter² /'kauntə/ *c.n* flat surface in a shop or other place (e.g a bank) on which to lay products that are being sold, from which customers can be served etc: *She's at the cheese counter.* **under the counter** (*fig*) (esp of buying or selling s.t) in a secret and dishonest way: *The deal was arranged under the counter so that other people couldn't profit from it.*

counter³ /'kauntə/ *pred.adj* **1** (usu — *to s.t*) (*formal*) opposite (to what was intended or expected): *The Party's win at the elections was counter to all the* forecasts(2).

▷ *adv* **2** (usu *act/run — to s.t*) (*formal*) in an opposite way, in opposition, (to s.t): *He acted counter to everyone's advice on the matter. What is happening runs counter to what was expected.*

▷ *tr/intr.v* (usu — (*s.t*) *with s.t*) **3** meet (an attack, blow, hit made by s.o) (with an attack, blow or hit of one's own): *She countered (his accusations) with a hit in the face.* **4** oppose (a proposal, offer etc made by s.o) (with a proposal, offer etc of one's own): *She countered with an offer to buy the whole company.*

counter- /kauntə-/ *adj* **1** (working) in the opposite direction to s.t: *counter-clockwise.* **2** (doing s.t) in opposition to s.t mentioned in the second part of the word: *a counter-attack*; *a* counter-offer. **3** equal to s.o/s.t, having the same position as s.o/s.t mentioned in the second part of the word: *counterbalance/ counterpart.*

counteract /ˌkaʊntəˈrækt/ *tr.v* (of a person, thing) act in a way that is intended to prevent (s.o doing s.t, s.t happening): *All their attempts . to counteract the growth of unemployment have failed.*

counteraction /ˌkaʊntəˈrækʃən/ *c/u.n.*

counter-attack /ˈkaʊntər əˌtæk/ *c.n* **1** (*military*) attack made in reply to an enemy's attack: *A counter-attack was made on the enemy's positions.* **2** speech, proposal etc made in reply to and usu opposing s.o else's speech, proposal etc: *A counter-attack on the government's criticism of the* Opposition(1) *is being planned.*
▷ *tr/intr.v* **3** make a counter-attack (against (s.o/s.t)). **go on the counter-attack** start a counter-attack after being attacked, opposed etc.

counter-attraction /ˈkaʊntər əˈtrækʃən/ *c.n* thing offered as an amusement, entertainment etc to compete against other attractions: *At the seaside there are several counter-attractions to sitting at home and watching television.*

counterbalance¹ /ˈkaʊntəˌbæləns/ *c.n* **1** weight, esp in a clock or mechanical device, which acts as an equal force to another weight (and so maintains equilibrium(1)). **2** (often — *to s.t*) force or check that acts to cancel out(b) another force or check: *As a counterbalance to the power of the workers the government is introducing a law to control their activities.*
▷ *tr.v* /ˌkaʊntəˈbæləns/ **3** act as a counterbalance to (s.t).

countercharge /ˈkaʊntəˌtʃɑːdʒ/ *c.n* **1** charge, accusation, made by s.o in answer to s.o else's charge, accusation.
▷ *intr.v* **2** make a countercharge(1).

counterclaim /ˈkaʊntəˌkleɪm/ = countercharge.

counter-clockwise /ˌkaʊntə ˈklɒkwaɪz/ *adj/ adv* (US) = anti-clockwise.

counter-espionage /ˌkaʊntər ˈespɪəˌnɑːʒ/ *u.n* spying(2) done by one country against the spying done by another country. ⇨ counter-intelligence.

counterfeit /ˈkaʊntəfɪt/ *adj* **1** (esp of money) copied to look like the real thing (with the intention of deceiving people): *There are a lot of counterfeit £20 notes around.* **2** (of a feeling etc) not real; pretended: *His expressions of sympathy are totally counterfeit.*
▷ *tr.v* **3** make, produce, a counterfeit(1) copy of (s.t): *They were counterfeiting old coins in a garden shed.* **4** (*formal*) pretend (a feeling etc): *He counterfeited pleasure at the news of her success.*
ˈcounterˌfeiter *c.n* person who makes counterfeit(1) money.

counterfoil /ˈkaʊntəˌfɔɪl/ *c.n* part of a cheque, money or postal order, ticket etc which one keeps as a record after the main part has been detached and given or sent to s.o.

counter-intelligence /ˌkaʊntər ɪnˈtelɪdʒəns/ *u.n* act of preventing an enemy from getting secret information about one's country; organization that does this. ⇨ counter-espionage.

countermand /ˌkaʊntəˈmɑːnd/ *tr.v* cancel(1), replace, (an order given by s.o or oneself)

with another order, usu one having an opposite effect: *The general has countermanded the orders already given.*

counter-measure /ˈkaʊntə ˌmeʒə/ *c.n* thing done or proposed in order to stop s.t or to reduce the effect of s.t: *New counter-measures are being planned against the rise in crime.*

counter-offer /ˈkaʊntər ˌɒfə/ *c.n* offer, proposal etc made in reply to another offer, proposal etc: *After much bargaining, the counter-offer was accepted.*

counterpane /ˈkaʊntəˌpeɪn/ *c.n* (*old use*) bedspread.

counterpart /ˈkaʊntəˌpɑːt/ *c.n* (*formal*) person or thing who/that is nearly the same, has the same position, value etc, as s.o/s.t else: *My counterpart in the other company earns nearly twice as much as I do.*

counter-revolution /ˌkaʊntə ˌrəvəˈluːʃən/ *c/ u.n* (example of a) political movement opposing a revolution in a country.
ˌcounter-ˌrevoˈlutionary *adj* **1** of or referring to a counter-revolution.
▷ *c.n* (*pl -ies*) **2** person who takes part in a counter-revolution.

countersign /ˈkaʊntəˌsaɪn/ *tr.v* write one's signature on (s.t, e.g a cheque, official document(1) etc), esp in order to give it extra authority(4): *Could you please countersign this cheque on the back?*

countess ⇨ count².

countless ⇨ count¹.

country /ˈkʌntrɪ/ *n* (*pl -ies*) **1** *c.n* state or nation including all the land and people it controls: *I like travelling to foreign countries.* **2** *c.n* (usu the —) all the people belonging to a state or nation: *The country will support the government in this matter.* **3** *u.n* area of land, esp of a certain stated kind or nature: *There is mountainous country to the north.* **4** *def.n* (also *attrib*) area of land with fields, woods etc and few houses etc (as opposed to towns or cities with many buildings): *country life; country dances; country roads. I enjoy a quiet day in the country now and again.* **difficult, new** etc **country** (*fig*) thing difficult, new etc that one has to deal with, that one has no experience of etc: *The experiment is a whole new country for me as I have never done anything like it before.*
ˌcountry-and-ˈwestern *u.n* (also *attrib*) music or songs in the style of folk music from the southern states of America for guitar, banjo etc and voices.
ˈcountry ˌclub *c.n* place in the country(4) where one can do many kinds of sports.
ˈcountryman, ˈcountryˌwoman *c.n* (*pl -men, -ˌwomen*) **1** man/woman who lives in the country(4). **2** (often *fellow* —) man/woman who belongs to the same country(1) as oneself: *There were several fellow countrymen staying at the hotel.*
ˌcountry ˈseat *c.n* large house in the country(4) owned by s.o who also has a home in a town.
ˈcountryˌside *u.n* (usu the —) country(4), esp as a place for enjoyment, a place of beauty etc: *The countryside was looking beautiful in the autumn sun.*

county /ˈkaʊntɪ/ *c.n* (*pl -ies*) (also *attrib*) (with capital **C** in names) **1** (UK) one of the large areas of land (each with its own name) into which the

UK is divided for purposes of local government: *the County of Avon.* **2** (US) one of the areas of land within a State with its own local government. **home counties** ⇨ home.

county 'council *c.n* (with capital **C** in names) group of people elected or appointed to run the affairs of a county(1): *Surrey County Council.*

coup /kuː/ *c.n* (*pl* -s /kuːz/) **1** success in getting s.t, esp a result in business (because of one's own efforts, against opposition etc): *It was quite a coup when he won the* contract(1) *to build the hospital.* **2** = coup d'état.

coup d'état /ˌkuː deɪ ˈtɑː/ (*pl coups d'état* /ˌkuːz deɪ ˈtɑː/) (*French*) violent and sudden change in the government of a country, esp one done by a group of people, the armed forces etc: *There have been several attempted coups d'état but so far they have all failed.*

coupé /ˈkuːpeɪ/ *c.n* (*pl* -s) kind of car with two doors and usu a sloping back.

couple /ˈkʌpl/ *c.n* **1** (usu *a — of s.t*) two of the same kind (of things): *We'll need a couple of bottles of milk for the weekend. Could I borrow a couple of chairs from your office?* ⇨ pair(1), brace³. **2** (usu *a — of s.o/s.t*) (*informal*) a few, not many (perhaps two or more): *There were only a couple of people around when I came out of the house.* **3** *c.n* two people together, e.g because they are married, going out together etc: *a married couple; courting couples.*

▷ *v* **4** *tr.v* (usu *— s.t together; — s.t with s.t*) join (two things) together by some mechanical means: *The railway carriages were coupled together and the train then left.* **5** *tr.v* (usu *— s.o/s.t together; — s.o/s.t with s.o/s.t*) think, make an association in one's mind, of (two people, things) together: *Her name has been coupled with his and most people believe they will get married.* **6** *intr.v* (usu of animals; *derog* of people) have sex together.

coupling /ˈkʌplɪŋ/ *n* **1** *c.n* mechanical device, chain etc joining a railway carriage, truck etc to another. **2** *u.n* (usu of animals; *derog* of people) act of having sex together.

couplet /ˈkʌplɪt/ *c.n* two lines of verse, one after the other, which rhyme.

coupon /ˈkuːpɒn/ *c.n* **1** printed piece of paper which allows the person having or receiving it to exchange it for s.t of the stated value, e.g money, goods etc: *The soap powder packet had a coupon on it worth 20p towards the next packet I bought.* **2** printed form in a newspaper, magazine etc which one fills in with one's name and address, cuts out and sends (sometimes with money) in order to enter a competition, get goods or services: *Fill in this coupon and send it to us for your free copy.* **football coupon** ⇨ football.

courage /ˈkʌrɪdʒ/ *u.n* quality of mind or strength of purpose that a person has to help face or handle fear, danger, pain etc; bravery: *He showed great courage during his illness.* **have the courage of one's convictions** think or do what one believes to be right (even though other people disagree, try to stop one etc). **have the courage to do s.t** not be afraid to do s.t: *I was surprised he had the courage to talk to her like that.* **lose courage** become afraid; not want to continue (doing s.t). **pluck up (the) courage (to do s.t)** ⇨ pluck². **take courage (from s.t)** become less afraid, become braver, (as a result of s.t): *He*

can take courage from the fact that others have succeeded even if with difficulty.

courageous /kəˈreɪdʒəs/ *adj* showing courage; brave: *The child was rewarded for her courageous attempt to save a friend from drowning.* **cou'rageously** *adv.*

courgette /kʊəˈʒet/ *c.n* kind of green vegetable like a small marrow(2).

courier /ˈkʊərɪə/ *c.n* **1** person who goes with people who are travelling on holiday and looks after them. **2** official who carries (secret) government papers from place to place, esp from one country to another: *a diplomatic(1) courier.* **3** person, e.g on a motorbike, who carries messages from one business to another. **by courier** using a courier(2,3): *send it by courier.*

course /kɔːs/ *n* **1** *u.n* (often the *— of s.t*) direction or movement (of s.t) from one place to another: *If you follow the course of the river, you'll soon get to the sea. The course of the aircraft was being followed on the radar screen.* **2** *c.n* (also **course of 'action**) direction one can take, thing that one can do, esp over a length of time: *There are several courses open to you but the best one is to get a new job.* **3** *c.n* (also *attrib*) one of the numbered or named sections into which a meal is divided: *a four-course dinner; a first course; a fish course; the main course.* **4** *c.n* set of lessons, talks etc one takes over a length of time: *a course in mathematics.* ⇨ correspondence course. **5** *c.n* set of treatments, medicines etc one takes over a length of time: *They're trying a new course of treatment.* **6** *c.n* place where certain kinds of races or sports take place (often ones which start in one place and come back to it at the end): *The course was marked out for the runners with white tape.* ⇨ golfcourse, racecourse. **(as) a matter of course** ⇨ matter(*n*). **change course (a)** change the direction in which one is travelling: *We had to change course to avoid the storm.* **(b)** (*fig*) change one's regular, usual or expected way of behaving. **course of action** ⇨ course(2). **during/in the course of s.t** while s.t is, was etc happening: *During the course of our talk he suddenly mentioned that he was married.* **in due course** when it can be expected; at a (normal) point of time in the future: *You will hear from us in due course.* **in the course of events** ⇨ event. **in the course of time** during a length of time: *In the course of time the child grew up into a beautiful young woman.* **(let s.t) follow/run/take its course** (let s.t, esp an illness, s.t that cannot be avoided) be completed in a natural way: *The disease must run its course and there's nothing we can do.* **of course (a)** certainly, definitely(2): *'You will tell me about it, won't you?' 'Of course I will.'* **(b)** naturally; in a way that must be expected: *Of course, I can't tell you everything as some of this has to remain secret.* **off/on course** (of a ship, aircraft etc) in the wrong/right direction. **stay the course** ⇨ stay¹(*v*).

▷ *intr.v* **7** (*formal; literary*) hunt rabbits etc with dogs. ⇨ coursing. **course down s.t** (*formal*) (esp of tears) go, pour, down s.t, esp one's face: *Tears were coursing down his cheeks.* **course through s.t** (*formal*) (esp of blood) move quickly (through one's veins(1) etc), esp because of a violent movement, excitement etc:

He felt the blood coursing through his body as he increased speed.

'**coursing** *u.n* (*formal*) (act of) hunting of rabbits etc with dogs.

court /kɔːt/ *n* **1** *c.n* building, room, in which legal cases are heard before a judge or magistrate: *I'm going to the court tomorrow to* observe(1) *the case.* ⇨ court of law, law court. **2** *c.n* (usu *the —*) all the people present in a court(1): *The court will rise when the judge enters.* **3** *c.n* area of ground marked out for certain kinds of games, esp tennis, squash², badminton: *There are several tennis courts in the local park.* ⇨ be on court. **4** *c.n* (usu with capital **C**) name for a block of flats, usu surrounding an area of ground on three sides: *He bought a flat in Sutton Court.* **5** *u.n* (with capital **C**) name for a palace(1) belonging to a king or queen: *Hampton Court.* **6** *def.n* (with capital **C**) the king/queen together with his/her family and all the officials and people who look after them: *The Court has moved to Windsor for two weeks.* **be on court** be playing, ready to play, a game of tennis, squash² etc: *The players are due on court at 2 o'clock.* **go to court (over s.t)** (*law*) have one's case (on some matter) presented in a court(1). **high court** ⇨ high. **hold court** (*fig*; often *derog*) act as though one is a king or queen by allowing people to come and speak to one as a favour: *He was holding court in a corner of the room and was surrounded by a group of admiring ladies.* **settle (s.t) in court** decide (a legal problem) in a court of law. **settle (s.t) out of court** decide (a legal problem) without going to court by agreeing to a sum of money. **take (s.o/s.t) to court** arrange for s.o/s.t to be tried(6) in a court of law to settle a dispute(1) etc.
▷ *v* **7** *tr.v* pay a lot of attention to (s.o), try to get (s.o's favour), in order to win some advantage: *He's been courting the boss for months now as he wants that job.* **8** *tr.v* (*old use*) (of a man) spend a lot of time with (a woman), esp to try to win her love in order to marry her: *He's been courting her for two years but there's no sign of them getting married yet.* **9** *intr.v* (*old use*) (of a man and woman) be spending a lot of time together with a view to marriage: *They've been courting for two years.* ⇨ courting couple. **court danger**, **disaster** etc (*fig*) run the risk of suffering s.t, esp by being too bold, foolish etc: *He's courting defeat if he goes on in that way.*

'**court ,card** *c.n* playing card with the picture of a King, Queen or Jack(2) on it.

courtier /'kɔːtɪə/ *c.n* (*old use*) person who attends the Court(6).

,**courting 'couple** *c.n* man and woman who are in love and go around together: *The park was full of courting couples.*

'**courtliness** *u.n* (*formal*) very polite behaviour.

'**courtly** *adj* (*-ier, -iest*) showing this polite behaviour.

court-martial /ˌkɔːt 'mɑːʃəl/ *c.n* (*pl* courts-martial) (*military*) **1** special court(1) in which a case against a member of the armed forces is heard. **2** an actual trial in this court.
▷ *tr.v* (*-ll-*, US *-l-*) **3** (*military*) bring (a member of the armed forces) before a court-martial(1) for trial.

,**court of in'quiry** *c.n* special court(1) that looks

into s.t, esp s.t that has gone wrong: *There will be a court of inquiry into the train crash.*

,**court of 'law** *c.n* = law court.

'**courtship** *c/u.n* (time taken for) courting(8) s.o or of being courted(8) by s.o.

'**court,yard** *c.n* area of ground, often paved or concreted(5), near to a building or surrounded by buildings: *There was a small courtyard which you could drive into through an arch.*

courteous /'kɜːtɪəs/ *adj* (*formal*) polite and friendly in one's manners: *He was always very courteous and got up from his seat whenever a woman entered the room.* Opposite discourteous.

'**courteously** *adv*. '**courteousness** *u.n.*

courtesy /'kɜːtɪsɪ/ *c/u.n* (*pl -ies*) (*formal*) (example of the) showing of politeness and good manners: *She welcomed the small courtesies he showed towards her.* Opposite discourtesy.

cousin /'kʌzn/ *c.n* **1** son or daughter of one's uncle or aunt: *I have three cousins on my aunt's side of the family.* **2** (more generally) son or daughter of any of the descendants of one's uncle or aunt, or of the uncle or aunt of one's mother or father: *Our family is so large I've lost track of how many cousins I have.* **first cousin** ⇨ first. **second cousin** ⇨ second.

cove /kəʊv/ *c.n* small bay²: *a rocky cove.*

covenant /'kʌvənənt/ *c.n* (*law*) **1** formal or written agreement between two or more people. **2** formal agreement to pay s.o regular amounts of money (often with tax advantages for that person): *I've arranged a covenant to pay for my grandson's university education.*
▷ *tr/intr.v* **3** (*formal*; *law*) make, sign, a covenant to do, give, (s.t): *William covenanted £250 a year for five years to his church.*

cover /'kʌvə/ *n* **1** *c.n* thing that goes over, on the top of, s.t, e.g as a protection: *There was a cover on the bed to make it look tidy.* **2** *c.n* front and/or back outer part(s) of a book, magazine etc: *The front cover had a picture of the author(1) on it.* **3** *u.n* thing, e.g tree, a hollow etc, that gives protection to animals and people from the sun etc: *There is very little cover so we'd better walk only in the early morning or in the evening or it'll be too hot.* ⇨ break cover, take cover. **4** *u.n* (often *— against s.t*) (amount of) insurance (against s.t bad happening to oneself, one's property etc): *Have you got enough cover against fire?* **5** *u.n* (*military*) protection provided by aircraft, guns etc when soldiers are attacking, when ships are landing troops etc: *Bad weather made it impossible for the air force to provide full cover to the soldiers as they retired.* ⇨ covering fire. **6** *c.n* (usu *be a — for s.t*) thing that hides one's real purpose, what one is actually doing etc: *His job was just a cover for his intelligence activities.* **7** *u.n* reporting of an event by a reporter, newspaper, radio, television etc: *There was hardly any cover of the strike by the newspapers.* **break cover** leave one's cover(3) and come out into the open. (**read s.t**) **from cover to cover** (read a book, newspaper) all the way through, not missing out anything. (**send s.t**) **under separate cover** (post s.t) in a separate envelope, parcel etc, writing that one is doing so in the main letter: *We are sending you the book you ordered under separate cover.* **take cover** hide oneself in a protected place (e.g a building, a wood etc) so that one cannot be seen, hit, hurt etc by s.o: *Take cover, they're shooting at us!* **under cover of s.t** while being protected by s.t or not seen because of s.t: *The escaped prisoners travelled under cover of darkness.*

▷ *tr.v* **8** (often — s.o/s.t (*up*) *with s.t*) protect, hide, (s.o/s.t), by putting s.t e.g material, all over her/him/it: *They covered the dead body with a sheet.* ⇨ cover s.o/s.t over, covering, cover-up. **9** (of things) lie all over the surface of (s.t): *Dust covered all the furniture. Snow covered the fields.* ⇨ be covered in/with s.t, covering. **10** hide (one's feelings etc) by doing s.t else: *He tried to change the conversation in order to cover his mistake.* **11** travel (a certain distance, esp in a certain length of time): *We covered 150 kilometres through the desert in one day.* **12** (of s.t written, a speech etc) deal with, include, (a certain number of things): *The book covers a wide variety of subjects. We have tried to cover all the main points.* **13** (often be —ed against s.t) protect oneself, one's property etc (against s.t bad happening) by means of insurance: *Are you covered against theft?* **14** (of guns, a fort etc) be in a position to attack, hit, (s.t): *The enemy's guns covered the roads to the town.* ⇨ covering fire. **15** (often have s.o —ed) (*informal*) point a gun or guns, at (s.o) (to stop her/him from doing s.t, from moving): *You're covered, so don't move!* **16** (of a reporter, newspaper, radio, television etc) deal with, report, (an event etc): *All the newspapers covered the murder trial in detail.* **17** (of money) be (just) enough to pay for (s.t): *Here's £20 to cover your expenses.* **be covered in/ with s.t** (a) (of an object etc) have a large amount or number of s.t on it: *The roads were covered with snow. Where've you been — you're covered in mud.* (b) (of a person) be completely affected by a feeling etc: *She was covered in confusion when he proposed to her.* **cover a lot of etc ground** ⇨ ground(n). **cover for s.o** take over s.o's work, job etc while he/she is away or cannot do it: *Teachers are complaining about having to cover for absent teachers.* **cover s.o/s.t over** put a cover(1) on s.o/ s.t so as to protect or hide her/him/it. **cover up (for s.o/s.t)** hide s.t (which s.o has done or not done): *It's no use covering up for him because the truth will come out in the end.* ⇨ cover-up. **cover s.o/s.t up (with s.t)** hide s.t. ⇨ cover(8).

coverage /ˈkʌvərɪdʒ/ *u.n* amount of cover(7) given by a reporter, newspaper etc to an event: *There was very wide coverage of the strike by the newspapers.*

'cover ,charge *c.n* fixed amount added to a bill in a restaurant for service.

'covering *c.n* thing that covers(8,9) s.t: *There was a light covering of ice over the pond.*

'covering ,fire *u.n* (*military*) shooting of guns etc to protect the movement of troops etc.

,covering 'letter *c.n* letter sent to explain other things included in the same envelope, packet etc: *I received a parcel of books but there was no covering letter to say who had sent it.*

coverlet /ˈkʌvəlɪt/ *c.n* (*old use*) bedspread.

'cover-,up *c.n* (*pl* -s) (also *attrib*) attempt to hide the truth about s.t. esp a crime or mistake: *a cover-up operation. Your story was just a cover-up to protect Tim.*

covert /ˈkʌvət/ *adj* (*formal*) **1** (of a look etc)

secret, trying not to be noticed: *The covert look she gave him from under her eyebrows worried him.* **2** (of s.t one does) secret and not to be revealed: *The intelligence service has several covert operations against foreign powers.*

covet /ˈkʌvɪt/ *tr.v* (*formal*) want very much to have or own s.t, esp s.t that belongs to s.o else: *I really covet that clock you've got.*

covetous /ˈkʌvɪtəs/ *adj* (often — of s.t) (*formal*) anxious to have or own s.t: *Stop giving my new ring such covetous looks.*

'covetously *adv.* **'covetousness** *u.n.*

cow¹ /kaʊ/ *c.n* **1** full-grown female of the ox family, kept for the milk it gives and the young it produces: *The farmer keeps a hundred cows and a couple of bulls*(1). **2** (also *attrib*) full-grown female of some other kinds of animals: *a cow elephant.* **3** (*slang*; do not use!) form of abuse¹ to or about a woman; (**do s.t**) **till/until the cows come home** (*fig*; *informal*) (do s.t) for a long time: *They look as though they are going to go on drinking till the cows come home.* **sacred cow** ⇨ sacred.

'cow,boy, 'cow,girl *c.n* man/woman on horseback who looks after cattle(1) on a ranch(1).

'cow,hand, 'cow,herd *c.n* person who looks after cattle(1) on a ranch(1) or farm.

'cow,hide *u.n* (also *attrib*) skin of a cow¹(1) used to make leather objects: *a coat made of cowhide.*

cow² /kaʊ/ *tr.v* (often — s.o into doing s.t) make (s.o) so frightened that he/she will do what one wants: *The people were cowed into submission*(1) *by the presence of the army.*

coward /ˈkaʊəd/ *c.n* (*derog*) person who shows great fear in a shameful way: *Those cowards ran away as soon as there was a sign of trouble.*

cowardice /ˈkaʊədɪs/ *u.n* (act of) showing this fear: *He was accused of cowardice in the face of the enemy.*

'cowardliness *u.n* fact or state of being cowardly.

'cowardly *adj* showing this fear: *cowardly behaviour.*

cowboy ⇨ cow¹.

cower /ˈkaʊə/ *intr.v* (often — away, down etc) (of a person, animal) try to make one's/its body smaller; bend down, move away etc (because of fear (of a blow etc)): *He found the family cowering in a corner away from the firing outside.*

cowgirl, cowhand, cowherd, cowhide ⇨ cow¹.

cowl /kaʊl/ *c.n* **1** kind of loose covering for the head, usu fixed to a cloak(1) and worn, esp, by monks. **2** cover for a chimney, often one that turns with the wind and so improves the flow of air. **3** = cowling.

cowling /ˈkaʊlɪŋ/ *c.n* (*technical*) metal cover for an engine, esp in an aircraft.

cox /kɒks/ *c.n* **1** person who steers¹ a rowing-boat, esp in a race. **2** (also **coxswain** /ˈkɒksən/) person in charge of an ordinary boat and its crew¹(1): *He's the coxswain of the local lifeboat.*

▷ *tr/intr.v* **3** be a cox(1) for (a boat): *He coxed the university boat.*

coy /kɔɪ/ *adj* **1** (of a child, woman, look etc) (pretending to be) shy: *The child gave her uncle a coy smile.* **2** unwilling to give information about

s.t: *Don't be coy with me — I know you saw who took my book.*
'coyly *adv.* **'coyness** *u.n.*

CP /ˌsiː ˈpiː/ *def.n abbr* Communist party.

Cpl *written abbr* Corporal.

cps /ˌsiː ˌpiː ˈes/ *abbr* cycles(2) per second.

CPU /ˌsiː ˌpiː ˈjuː/ *abbr* Central Processing Unit.

cr *written abbr* credit(2).

crab /kræb/ *n* **1** *c.n* kind of (almost) round shell-fish with ten legs, two of which have claws(1) on the ends. **2** *u.n* (also *attrib*) flesh of this shellfish as food: *crab soup.*
'crab ˌapple *c.n* (also *attrib*) kind of small wild apple with a bitter taste: *crab apple* jelly(2).

crack /kræk/ *attrib.adj* **1** (of a person) very skilled at s.t, esp a sport, firing a gun etc: *He's a crack* shot¹.
▷ *c.n* **2** line or break in the surface of s.t to a certain depth (but not so that the thing is completely broken): *This cup has a crack in it.* **3** narrow open gap between s.t and s.t, e.g a door and its frame, parts of a fence etc: *He could just see her through a crack in the wall.* **4** short sharp loud sound, esp one made by a gun, whip etc: *The lions in the circus obeyed commands given by cracks of the whip.* **5** short sharp hard blow, given by s.o or by hitting oneself unexpectedly against s.t: *I'll give you a crack on the jaw if you don't shut up!* **6** (often — *about s.o/s.t*) (*informal*) unpleasant joke (about s.o/s.t): *After several cracks about the clothes she was wearing he then started criticizing her looks.* **7** (*fig*) certain amount of loss of control (in one's behaviour, defence against s.o/ s.t etc): *Some cracks were beginning to be seen in the government's handling of the strike.* (**at**) **the crack of dawn** ⇨ dawn(*n*). **have a crack at s.t** (*informal*) try to do s.t one has not done before: *I'd like to have a crack at the world record as soon as I'm fit again.*
▷ *v* **8** *tr/intr.v* (cause (s.t) to) get a crack(2) or cracks in it: *The cup cracked when it knocked against a plate in the sink. Jill cracked a bone in her leg when she fell.* **9** *tr/intr.v* (cause (s.t) to) break into separate pieces: *He was so strong he could crack nuts between his fingers.* ⇨ nutcracker. **10** *tr/ intr.v* (cause (s.t) to) make a crack(4): *He gave a jump when a gun suddenly cracked near him.* **11** *tr.v* accidentally give (a part of one's body) a sudden crack(5): *She cracked her head against the low door frame.* **12** *tr.v* solve, find, (a hidden secret, esp a code(3)): *They finally succeeded in cracking the enemy's codes.* **13** *tr.v* (*informal*) (of a thief or burglar) break (s.t, esp a safe) open: *It took them several hours to crack the bank's safe.* **14** *intr.v* (usu — *up*) (*informal*) (of a person) become ill, lose control, esp because of pressure of work, circumstances(1,2) etc: *The problems of bringing up a large family on very little money were beginning to make her crack up.* ⇨ crackup. **crack a joke** ⇨ joke(*n*). Compare crack(6). **crack down** (**on s.o/s.t**) (of a person with power) act very strongly to stop (s.o doing s.t, s.t happening): *The police are cracking down on known criminals.* ⇨ crackdown. **crack up** ⇨ crack(14). **get cracking** (*informal*) start moving more quickly; hurry (with s.t): *You'll have to get cracking if you want to catch that train. You'd better get cracking with that job if you want to have it ready on time.* **not all he/she/it is cracked up**

to be (*informal*) not as good as people say he/ she/it is: *The new sports car is not all it's cracked up to be.*
'crack ˌdown *c.n* act or fact of cracking down (on s.o/s.t).
'cracker *c.n* **1** (also **'Christmas ˌcracker**) tube with coloured paper and decorations around it that is pulled apart at parties to get the paper hat and small gift inside: *When we pulled the cracker a blue paper hat and toy ring fell out.* **2** (also **ˌChinese 'cracker**) kind of small firework that makes a number of bangs(2). **3** thin dry biscuit (often eaten with cheese).
'crackers *pred.adj* (*derog*; *informal*) mad: *You must be crackers to believe that.*
'crack ˌpot *c.n* (also *attrib*) (*derog*; *informal*) person who is a little mad or who has strange ideas: *He's a bit of a crackpot so don't take his ideas too seriously.*
'cracksman *c.n* (*pl* -**men**) person who can crack(13) a safe.
'crack ˌup *c.n* act of becoming ill and no longer able to cope because of too much worry, hard work etc. ⇨ crack(14).

crackle /ˈkrækl/ *u.n* **1** (continuous) short little sound(s) made by s.t: *the crackle of logs burning on the fire.*
▷ *intr.v* **2** make the sound of a crackle(1).
'crackling *u.n* **1** sound of s.t crackling (⇨ crackle(2)): *The crackling of dry leaves made him realize somebody was following him.* **2** cooked hard skin or fat of roast pork.

cradle /ˈkreɪdl/ *c.n* **1** bed for a small baby, esp one with a curved base so that it can be rocked. **2** wooden, metal etc device that can hold s.o/ s.t or keep s.t in position while it is being made, repaired etc: *The new ship was resting in its cradle before being* launched(5). **from the cradle to the grave** from the time when one is born until the time when one dies: *From the cradle to the grave he had a protected and* privileged *life.* **the cradle of civilization** etc the country or place considered to be where s.t important, e.g a civilization began: *Greece has a very good claim to being the cradle of western civilization.*
▷ *tr.v* **3** (often — *s.o/s.t in s.t*) hold s.o/s.t closely (in one's arms etc), esp in order to protect her/him/ it: *She cradled the baby in her arms.*

craft /krɑːft/ *n* **1** *c.n* (*pl* craft) boat or ship, usu of a small kind with sails or engines: *a sailing craft.* **2** *c.n* (*pl* -s) particular skill or ability one learns or has learned, esp using one's hands and tools: *the craft of making clay pots.* ⇨ -craft(2). **3** *u.n* skill in deceiving s.o: *He used a lot of craft in stealing thousands of pounds from the company.*
'craftily *adv* in a crafty way.
'craftiness *u.n* show of craft(3).
'craftsman *c.n* (*pl* -**men**) person who is skilled at a craft(2).
'craftsman ˌship *u.n* ability, quality, in the making of s.t.
'crafty *adj* (-**ier**, -**iest**) (*derog*) showing (a lot of) craft(3): *It was very crafty of you to organize the party without my finding out about it.*
-craft *n* **1** vehicle of the kind mentioned in the first part of the word. ⇨ aircraft, spacecraft. **2** of a skill or craft(2) described in the first part of the word. ⇨ handicraft, needlecraft, woodcraft.

crag /kræg/ *c.n* (with capital **C** in names) (part

of a) hill or mountain with sharp steep rocks sticking out: *They had to climb a steep crag before they got to the top.*

'**cragginess** *u.n* fact or state of being craggy.

'**craggy** *adj* (*-ier, -iest*) having crags.

cram /kræm/ *v* (*-mm-*) **1** *tr.v* (often — *s.t into s.t*) use force to push (s.t) without any order (into s.t): *He crammed all his clothes into his bag.* **2** *tr.v* (often — *s.t with s.o/s.t*) fill (all the available space of s.t) (with people or things): *The train was crammed with passengers. He crammed his mouth with food.* **3** *tr.v* (usu — *one's head/ mind with s.t*) (*fig*) fill (one's mind) with (too much) information, (too many) facts etc: *His head was crammed with useless facts.* **4** *tr/intr.v* (often — (*s.o*) *for s.t*) (cause (s.o) to) get ready for an examination by studying hard, esp to be accepted by a university etc: *They are cramming him for Oxford.*

cramp /kræmp/ *n* **1** *c/u.n* (example of a) sudden painful tightening of the muscles(1), esp when swimming, running etc: *The player got cramp and had to leave the field.* **2** *c.n* mechanical device for holding s.t, e.g wood, metal etc, tight while it is being worked on. **writer's cramp** ⇨ write.

▷ *tr.v* **3** stop/limit the progress of (s.o/s.t): *All our efforts were cramped by his failure to help us.* **cramp s.o's style** (*informal*) not allow s.o's natural progress or development to take place: *'Can't you go out tonight?' Joe asked his father, 'Meg will be here and you'll cramp my style.'*

cramped *adj* (of a person, room etc) not having enough space to move around in: *We were very cramped in that small flat. The house was very cramped and there wasn't really enough space for our furniture.*

crampon /'kræmpɒn/ *c.n* metal plate with spikes(1) on it, fixed to a boot or shoe when climbing over s.t, esp ice.

cranberry /'krænbərɪ/ *c.n* (*pl -ies*) (also *attrib*) kind of small red sour berry used as a flavouring or made into a jelly(2) or sauce and often eaten with meat.

crane /kreɪn/ *c.n* **1** kind of tall bird with long thin legs which lives on or near water and eats fish. **2** mechanical device with a tall vertical tower and a long moving horizontal arm for lifting heavy objects and moving them from one place to another.

▷ *tr.v* **3** (usu — *one's neck to see s.o/s.t*) stretch, change the position of, (one's neck) (in order to see s.o/s.t): *He craned his neck to see what was happening in front of the crowd.* **4** *intr.v* (usu — *forward*) lean one's neck, head or body forward (in order to see s.o/s.t): *They craned forward to get a better view.*

'**crane,fly** *c.n* (*pl -ies*) kind of fly with long legs and long narrow wings.

cranium /'kreɪnɪəm/ *c.n* (*pl -s* or, less usu, *crania* /'kreɪnɪə/) (*technical*) skull.

cranial /'kreɪnɪəl/ *adj* of or referring to the cranium: *cranial surgery(1).*

crank /kræŋk/ *c.n* **1** piece of metal, usu shaped like an 'L' with a handle, used to start an engine, turn a mechanical device etc. **2** (*derog; informal*) person with strange ideas that he/she firmly believes in: *He's a crank — you should hear him on the subject of modern medicine.*

▷ *tr.v* **3** (often — *s.t up*) start (an engine); turn (s.t), by

using a crank(1): *In the old days you had to crank the engine up before the car would start.*

'**crankiness** *u.n* fact or state of being cranky.

'**crank,shaft** *c.n* shaft(4) or rod in an engine which is moved by a crank(1).

'**cranky** *adj* (*-ier, -iest*) (*derog*) (of a person) who is (like) a crank(2).

cranny /'krænɪ/ *c.n* (*pl -ies*) small gap or opening, esp in a wall. **nook and cranny** ⇨ nook.

crap /kræp/ *n* (*slang*; do not use!) **1** *u.n* (*derog*) (in the opinion of the speaker or writer) useless things; rubbish: *You'll have to clear out all this crap before I'll move in here.* **2** *u.n* (*derog*) stupid useless ideas, words etc; nonsense(2): *You're talking crap.* **3** *sing/u.n* (usu *have a —*) solid waste material from the body; the act of getting rid of solid waste material from the body. **be a load of crap** (*slang*) be stupid, worthless, useless etc. **cut the crap** stop talking rubbish; stop wasting time.

▷ *intr.v* (*-pp-*) **4** (*slang*; do not use!) get rid of solid waste material from the body; defecate.

'**crappy** *adj* (*-ier, -iest*) (*slang*; do not use!) (of an idea, s.t said etc) stupid, worthless: *That's the crappiest suggestion I've heard in a long time!*

crash /kræʃ/ *attrib.adj* **1** (of a special course in s.t) done in a very short time and with the greatest amount of effort and attention: *I'm taking a crash course in German.*

▷ *c.n* **2** violent, damaging and often accidental hitting of one or more cars, buses, trains etc together or against s.t; damage or destruction of an aircraft hitting the ground: *Several people were killed in the train crash.* **3** sound made by s.t falling, breaking or hitting s.t: *I heard a crash of breaking china(2).* **4** (*commerce*) very sudden fall in (the value of) trade, shares(3), business etc: *Some people are frightened that there will be a financial crash.*

▷ *v* **5** *tr/intr.v* (cause (s.t) to) have a crash(2): *He crashed his car the day after passing his driving test. The plane crashed on landing.* ⇨ crash-land. **crash-landing. 6** *tr/intr.v* (cause (s.t) to) fall onto, hit, the ground or a surface (and often break) with a loud noise: *The tray with all the glasses on it crashed to the floor.* **7** *intr.v* (*commerce*) suddenly fail in one's business; (of shares(3) etc) suddenly fall heavily in value: *The firm crashed leaving millions of pounds of debt and several hundred people out of jobs.* **8** *intr.v* (of a program(1) in a computer while in use) fail suddenly and without any obvious reason (often causing one to lose the information put into the computer or the work done). **9** *intr.v* (often — *about, around* etc) move violently and noisily (around, through (s.t) etc): *I could hear him crashing around in the next room.* **crash into s.o/s.t** (of a person, vehicle etc) hit s.o/s.t violently and noisily, usu by accident (and often hurt oneself and/or s.o, damage the vehicle etc): *His car crashed into a wall.* **crash a party** etc (*informal*) go to a party to which one was not invited. ⇨ gatecrash, gatecrasher.

'**crash ,barrier** *c.n* strong, usu metal, fence, used to stop vehicles going off the side of a road, crossing to the opposite lane of a motorway etc.

'**crash-,helmet** *c.n* hard metal or plastic covering for the head, worn by a rider on a motorbike, a driver of a racing-car etc.

,crash-'land *tr/intr.v* (cause (an aircraft) to) land, usu in an emergency when the wheels or undercarriage do not work, an engine or engines fail(s) etc: *The pilot managed to crash-land the aircraft safely.*

,crash-'landing *c.n* act of landing an aircraft, of an aircraft landing, in this way.

crass /kræs/ *adj* (usu *attrib*) (*derog*) (of behaviour, s.t said or done etc) showing very great stupidity, foolishness: *It was a really crass mistake on his part. Don't be so crass!* **'crassly** *adv*. **'crassness** *u.n*.

crate /kreɪt/ *c.n* **1** kind of box, usu made of (pieces of) wood or plastic(3), which is used for carrying or storing things, e.g fruit, food, bottles, goods etc: *a milk crate; a crate of wine.*
▷ *tr.v* **2** (often — *s.t up*) put (s.t) in a crate(1): *When we sold our house we had to have all the furniture crated up and stored.*

crater /'kreɪtə/ *c.n* **1** round opening on the top of a volcano. **2** shape like this made in the ground by s.t (esp a bomb, mechanical device etc): *The gas explosion left large craters in the ground.*

cravat /krə'væt/ *c.n* kind of scarf(1) worn around the neck instead of a tie(1) (usu by a man).

crave /kreɪv/ *v* **1** *tr/intr.v* (often — *after/for s.t*) have a very strong desire or need (for) (s.t): *What I'm really craving (for) is a glass of water. Do you ever crave (after) cigarettes any more?* **2** *tr.v* (*formal; literary*) ask, beg for, (s.t, esp forgiveness): *He craved forgiveness for interrupting her.*
'craving *c.n* (usu *have a — for s.t*) very strong desire or need (for s.t): *I have this craving for sweet things which I can't control. When Sally was pregnant she had such strange cravings.*

craven /'kreɪvn/ *attrib.adj* (*formal; literary*) very cowardly: *He's nothing but a craven bully(1).*
'cravenly *adv*. **'cravenness** *u.n*.

crawfish ⇒ crayfish.

crawl /krɔːl/ *n* **1** *sing.n* (often *at a —*) (esp of vehicles) very slow movement or speed: *The traffic was moving at a crawl during the rush hour.* **2** *sing/u.n* (example, act of) style of swimming in which one lies in the water on one's front and brings each arm over one's head in turn to push back the water while moving one's legs up and down: *Peter does/swims the crawl very well. Jane is good at crawl.* ⇒ breaststroke, freestyle. **reduced to a crawl** (of vehicles) forced to move very slowly (because of heavy traffic etc).
▷ *intr.v* **3** (of a person, esp a baby) move slowly on one's hands and knees along the ground: *Our baby is just learning to crawl.* **4** (usu — *across, along, into, out of* etc *s.t*) (of a person, animal, insect etc) move slowly (and in a low position) (across etc s.t) using one's/its arms, legs etc: *He crawled through the gap in the fence. There was an insect crawling up his leg.* **5** (often — *to s.o*) (*informal*) act in a very or too humble or flattering way (to s.o) in order to get her/his approval: *The way he crawls to the manager is so disgusting.* **crawl along** (of vehicles) move along very slowly (because of heavy traffic etc): *We could only crawl along at 10 miles an hour.* **crawl with s.o/s.t** (usu in continuous tenses) (of a place, surface etc) be very crowded (with people, insects etc): *The town is crawling with visitors at the weekend. The meat had been left out and was crawling with flies when we returned.*

'crawler *c.n* (*derog*) person who crawls(5).
'crawlers *pl.n* single piece of clothing covering a baby's body and legs and worn when crawling(3).

crayfish /'kreɪˌfɪʃ/ *n* (*pl* **crayfish**) (US **'craw,fish** /'krɔːˌfɪʃ/) **1** *c.n* kind of shellfish like a small lobster which lives in rivers or streams. **2** *u.n* flesh of crayfish(1) as food.

crayon /'kreɪən/ *c.n* **1** long round piece of coloured wax or chalk, used for drawing pictures.
▷ *tr/intr.v* **2** (use a crayon(1) to) draw or colour pictures (of s.t): *The child crayoned a picture for her mother's birthday.*

craze /kreɪz/ *c.n* **1** (often — *for s.t*) very sudden popular demand or fashion (for s.t), which usu only lasts for a short time: *There was a craze for this game a short while ago but now you hardly ever see anyone playing it.* **be (all) the craze** (*informal*) be s.t that is (very) popular, fashionable at the time: *I have to wear my hair like that, Mum, it's the craze.*
▷ *tr.v* **2** (usu only in *p.p*) make (s.o) mad, excited etc: *He wore a crazed expression on his face.*
'crazily *adv* in a crazy way.
'craziness *u.n* fact or state of being crazy.
'crazy *adj* (*-ier, -iest*) (*derog; informal*) stupid; silly: *You really would be crazy to take that job. That's the craziest idea I've heard of.* **crazy about s.o/s.t** very much in love with s.o; very excited about s.t: *She's just crazy about him and won't let him out of her sight.* **like crazy** ⇒ like¹ (*prep*).
,crazy 'paving *c.n* (path or area made up with) paving stones of different shapes fitted together.

creak /kriːk/ *c.n* **1** small sound like a squeak(1) made by the hinge(1) of a door that needs oiling, by wooden furniture, stairs etc that fit(s) badly.
▷ *intr.v* **2** make the sound of a creak(1) or one like it: *The stairs creaked as I went up them.*
'creakily *adv* in a creaky way.
'creakiness *u.n* fact or state of being creaky.
'creaky *adj* (*-ier, -iest*) (of a door, wood etc) making a sound of a creak(1).

cream /kriːm/ *attrib.adj* **1** having or using cream(3) in it: *a cream cake; cream cheese.* **2** pale yellow: *cream paint/walls.*
▷ *n* **3** *u.n* (also *attrib*) thick yellow-white fatty substance found on the top of milk, used for making butter, cheese etc: *Would you like cream or milk in your coffee?* ⇒ clotted cream, ice-cream. **4** *c/u.n* (example of a) substance made from vegetable oils, mineral oils etc and used esp on the face, hands etc to protect them: *Put some cream on your hands.* ⇒ cold cream, vanishing cream. **5** *u.n* (also *attrib*) pale yellow colour: *Do you call this yellow or cream?* **cream of tomato, vegetable** etc **soup** thick creamy soup of the stated flavour. **single/double cream** ⇒ single, double.
▷ *tr.v* **6** make (s.t) into a substance or mixture that is or looks creamy(1), esp in preparing food: *Cream the sugar and butter and then add the eggs.* **cream s.o off** take the best from among a group of people (for some purpose) and leave the rest: *The Civil Service used to be able to cream off the brightest people leaving university but now more of them are going into business.*
,cream 'sherry *c/u.n* very sweet dark sherry(1).
'creamery *c.n* (*pl* *-ies*) place, factory, where cream(3) is separated from milk and made into butter or cheese.

'creaminess *u.n* fact or state of being creamy.

'creamy *adj* (*-ier*, *-iest*) having a lot of cream(3,4) in it: *The milk was very creamy. I need something creamy for my dry skin.*

crease /kriːs/ *c.n* **1** sharp line from a fold purposely made in the material of an article of clothing etc to make it look tidy and smart'(1): *The creases in his trousers were as sharp as a knife.* **2** similar line or mark (accidentally made) in clothing etc that has not yet been ironed or because of sitting on it etc: *She had packed her clothes so badly that they were full of creases. You had better iron that dress, it's got creases in it.* **3** (in some games, esp cricket') white line in front of the wicket(1) used to mark the position of the batsman or bowler(1).
▷ *tr/intr.v* **4** (cause (s.t, e.g clothing, paper etc) to) have or get a crease(1) in it: *Silk dresses crease too easily.*

create /kriːˈeɪt/ *v* **1** *tr.v* bring (s.t new) into existence: *Do you believe that God created the world in six days? A new committee is being created to study the problem and make recommendations. The government has promised to create a million jobs.* **2** *tr.v* cause (s.t e.g a feeling of excitement, a disturbance etc) to happen: *His arrival created quite a stir in the normally quiet village. She created a fuss(1) when the manager refused to see her.* **3** *tr.v* (usu — s.o s.t) give (s.o) (a title): *He was created a knight(3) in 1985.* **4** *intr.v* (*informal*) make a disturbance: *Stop creating all over the place, it won't get you anywhere.*

creation /kriːˈeɪʃən/ *n* **1** *u.n* (often the — of s.t) act or fact of creating(1) s.t: *The government is working on plans for the creation of new industries in the town.* **2** *c.n* thing created(1) or made, esp s.t that has needed skill, art etc: *He held a fashion show for his latest creations* (i.e dresses etc). **3** *unique/def.n* (often with capital **C**) the universe, esp as thought to have been made by God.

cre'ative *adj* having or showing an ability to create(1) s.t: *He's a very creative writer.*

cre'atively *adv*. **cre'ativeness**, **creativity** /ˌkriːeɪˈtɪvɪtɪ/ *u.n*.

cre'ator *n* **1** *c.n* person who creates(1) s.t. **2** *def.n* (with capital **C**) God, esp as thought to have made the universe.

creature /ˈkriːtʃə/ *c.n* **1** living animal, insect etc (without stating which particular kind): *There were creatures crawling all over the meat.* **2** (*derog*) animal, person considered to be in a dirty, poor etc state: *I don't want that creature in my house.* **creature of habit** ⇒ habit.

crèche /kreʃ/ *c.n* (*French*) nursery provided for young babies, used esp by parents who go to work: *Our office has a crèche for the children of people who work here.*

credentials /krɪˈdenʃəlz/ *pl.n* written papers or documents(1) showing or proving that one has the power or authority(3) to do s.t: *You should always ask to see a stranger's credentials before you let her/him into the house.*

credible /ˈkredəbl/ *adj* that can be believed: *What made his story more credible was that it was supported by several other people who were there at the time.* Opposite incredible.

credibility /ˌkredəˈbɪlɪtɪ/ *u.n.* **'credibly** *adv*.

credit /ˈkredɪt/ *n* **1** *u.n* (permission for) payment at a later date for s.t one buys; length of time, amount of money, fixed for this purpose: *I am afraid we do not give credit and you will have to pay* cash(1). *They gave me three months' credit.* **2** *c.n* (also *attrib*) (*abbr* cr) (*commerce*) amount of money received in payment for s.t (and recorded in an account book): *Please enter the amount as a credit in the books.* Compare debit(1). **3** *u.n* amount of money one has in a bank account: *Your credit stood at £259 at the close of the day.* **4** *u.n* money lent by a bank etc to a customer: *The bank has refused to give me any more credit.* **5** *u.n* belief that s.o is able to pay (for goods, services etc): *Your credit is good with us and we are prepared to advance you the money you need.* **6** *u.n* (very) favourable reputation or trustworthiness: *He has shown himself to be a man of the highest possible credit.* Opposite discredit(1). **be a credit to s.o** (of a person) be s.o who brings honour to s.o (esp because of the education, training etc that the second person has given the first): *Your son is a real credit to you.* **be in credit** (**with s.o**) have an amount of money (with a bank, in one's account etc): *I have so many expenses that my account is hardly ever in credit.* (**buy s.t**) **on credit** (buy s.t) using credit(1), not cash(1). **do s.o credit** (of a person) = be a credit to s.o. **gain/lose credit** (of a story, account etc) be starting to be believed, not believed: *The story that is gaining credit is that he will resign.* **get/take the credit** (**for s.t**) be given, take for oneself, the honour or praise (for having done s.t): *He took all the credit for the idea though we worked on it together.* **give s.o the credit** (**for s.t**) say that s.o should have all the honour or praise (for having done s.t). **letter of credit** (*commerce*) document(1) from a bank that allows one to take money from the bank up to a stated amount. **to one's/s.o's credit** (**a**) in s.o's favour (even though there may be other things that are not): *It is to their everlasting credit that they did not give up in spite of the pressures placed on them.* (**b**) that is one's own, that one has succeeded in doing: *He already has a number of successful plays to his credit.*
▷ *tr.v* **7** (usu — s.t to s.o('s account); — s.o('s account) with s.t) put, record, (a sum of money) in s.o's (bank etc) account: *Your account has been credited with £200.* Opposite debit(2). **8** (often *hardly/not* — s.t) believe (s.t, esp s.t that is difficult to believe): *I could hardly credit what he said.* **credit s.o with s.t** (**a**) ⇒ credit(7). (**b**) accept that s.o has a certain ability, knowledge, common sense etc: *I hope you will credit me with more sense than to accept his offer.*

'credit ac,count *c.n* account with a shop etc which one uses for buying things using credit(1).

'credit ,card *c.n* plastic card provided by a bank or similar organization which one can use to buy goods and services using credit(1).

'credit ,column/,side *def.n* (in written accounts) right-hand column/side in which earnings are recorded. ⇒ debit column/side.

'credit ,limit *c.n* total amount of money fixed by a bank etc that one can have in order to buy goods and services using credit(1): *The bank has just increased my credit limit to £800.*

'credit ,note *c.n* written statement showing that

s.o has a credit(2) with s.o (often made when goods etc have not been supplied, have got lost or damaged etc, though they have already been paid for).

'credit ,rating c.n largest amount of money that a person, business company is able to borrow.

'credit ,squeeze c.n action by a government to control or reduce the amount or length of credit(1) that can be given.

'credit ,transfer c/u.n sending of money (by a bank etc) from one account, place or country to another: We are arranging for you to receive £5000 by credit transfer.

'creditable adj that can be considered worthy(1), honourable etc: They made a very creditable attempt to persuade him.

'creditor c.n person, business company etc to whom one owes money. Opposite debtor.

'credits pl.n (also 'credit ,titles) list of names of the people who acted in, directed, produced etc a film.

'credit,worthiness u.n fact or state of being creditworthy.

'credit,worthy adj (-ier, -iest) considered to be s.o, a business company etc to whom one can give credit(1).

credulous /'kredjʊləs/ adj (often derog; formal) (of a person) believing too much or too easily in s.t: She's not so credulous that she'll believe that story. Opposite incredulous.

credulity /krɪ'dju:lɪtɪ/, 'credulousness u.n.

creed /kri:d/ n 1 c.n (statement or system of a) person's beliefs, esp religious ones. 2 c.n person's general belief(s), way(s), of acting etc: His only creed is to make money. 3 def.n (with capital C) statement of the main beliefs of the Christian(1) religion.

creek /kri:k/ c.n small stream of water either at the edge of the sea or going into a river. be up the creek (without a paddle) (fig; informal) be in a very difficult position (and not be able to do much about it).

creep /kri:p/ n 1 c.n (derog; informal) unpleasant person, esp one whom one dislikes a lot: He is a little creep who always tries to get your attention. give s.o the creeps (informal) make s.o feel disgusted, uncomfortable: I like snails but slugs¹ give me the creeps. He gives me the creeps and I try to avoid him whenever possible.

▷ intr.v (p.t,p.p crept /krept/) 2 (often — along, into, out of, towards etc s.t) move as slowly and silently as possible (along etc s.t) (trying not to be noticed etc): He saw someone creeping down the passage but couldn't see who it was. 3 (often — along (s.t) etc) move very slowly (because one cannot do anything else): Traffic was creeping along. 4 intr.v (of plants etc) grow and spread (over the ground, a wall etc): There were climbing plants creeping all over the walls of the house. ⇨ creeper. creep in begin to happen: I notice a lot of mistakes are creeping in. creep into s.t begin to happen in (s.t one is doing): Mistakes are creeping into his work. creep up (on s.o, an animal) (a) = creep(2) silently (towards s.o, an animal). (b) gradually happen (to s.o), esp without her/him realizing it: Old age has crept up on him but he still acts as though he was a young man. make s.o's flesh creep ⇨ flesh(n).

'creeper c.n (one of a variety of a) kind of plant that grows and spreads over the ground, a wall etc.

'creepily adv in a creepy way.

'creepiness u.n fact or state of being creepy.

'creepy adj (-ier, -iest) causing or having a feeling of fear or fright: The house is very creepy at night.

cremate /krɪ'meɪt/ tr.v burn the body of (a dead person): He was cremated and his ashes were scattered over the fields.

cremation /krɪ'meɪʃən/ c/u.n (example of the) act or fact of cremating s.o.

crematorium /ˌkremə'tɔ:rɪəm/ c.n (pl -s or, less usu, crematoria /ˌkremə'tɔ:rɪə/) building in which dead people are cremated.

creosote /'krɪːəˌsəʊt/ u.n 1 kind of brown oily liquid made from coal, used to protect wood that is outside, e.g in fences etc.

▷ tr.v 2 put creosote(1) on (wood etc): He creosoted the fence in preparation for winter.

crepe, crêpe /kreɪp/ u.n kind of thin material like silk with wrinkles(1) in it.

,crepe 'paper, ,crêpe 'paper u.n kind of thin, often coloured, paper like crepe, used for decoration, wrapping presents etc.

,crepe 'rubber, ,crêpe 'rubber u.n rubber with wrinkles(1) in it, often used on the bottom of shoes.

crept /krept/ p.t,p.p of creep(2–4).

Cres(c) written abbr Crescent(3).

crescendo /krɪ'ʃendəʊ/ c.n (pl -s) 1 gradual increase in the amount of sound in a piece of music: There is a crescendo near the end of the music when all the instruments play together. 2 (often reach, grow to, a —) highest level of loudness: The shouts of the crowd reached a crescendo when he appeared.

crescent /'kresnt/ c.n 1 (also attrib) curved shape like/of the moon in its first and last quarters: a crescent moon. We made bread rolls in the shape of crescents. 2 c.n row of houses and the street they are in shaped like this: There was a crescent of houses surrounding the park. 3 (with capital C in names; written abbr Cres(c)) name for a street shaped like a crescent(1): My address is 5 Queen's Crescent.

cress /kres/ u.n kind of small plant(s) grown in water or damp places, eaten in salads(1), sandwiches etc when very young. ⇨ watercress. mustard and cress ⇨ mustard.

crest /krest/ c.n 1 set of feathers or a comb(4) on the top of the head of some birds. 2 decoration like a crest(1) on the top of the hat etc of a uniform. 3 decorated design on the top of a coat of arms; (more generally) the whole coat of arms: Their notepaper was printed with the family crest. 4 top part of s.t (long and) high, esp a hill, mountain or wave. be/ride on the crest of a wave (fig) be at a high point in one's fortunes, success etc (even if only for a short time): At the moment he's on the crest of a wave and is doing extremely well in his job.

▷ tr.v 5 (literary) get to, over, the top of (a hill, mountain, wave etc): The tall ship crested the wave.

'crested adj 1 (of a bird) having a crest(1). 2 having a crest(3) printed on it: crested notepaper.

'crest,fallen adj (showing an expression of) being disappointed: He was very crestfallen *when he learned that he didn't get the job.*

cretin /ˈkretɪn/ *c.n* **1** (*old use*) person whose brain (and sometimes body) is damaged and who is therefore mentally ill. **2** (*derog; informal*) stupid person.

crevasse /krɪˈvæs/ *c.n* deep split or gap in the ice on a mountain, esp a glacier.

crevice /ˈkrevɪs/ *c.n* narrow crack or opening in a rock.

crew[1] /kruː/ *c.n* **1** all the people who work on a boat, ship, aircraft etc (as compared to the passengers): *When we left Singapore, we had a completely new crew.* **2** all the people who work together on s.t, esp doing technical(1) jobs: *a film crew* (including people dealing with cameras, lighting, sound etc). **3** (*informal*; often *derog*) group of people often seen with s.o in particular: *Boris and his crew.*
▷ *intr.v* **4** (often — *for s.o*) act as (one of) a crew (on a boat, esp one with sails) (for s.o): *Will you crew for me in tomorrow's race?*

crew[2] /kruː/ *p.t,p.p* of crow(3).

crib /krɪb/ *c.n* **1** kind of baby's cot. **2** framework of wood with gaps in it, used for putting hay etc in for animals such as cows and horses. **3** (*informal*) book that contains a translation or set of notes, that helps one to understand a book in a foreign language, to pass examinations etc. **4** (*derog; informal*) person who copies s.t from s.o's work; thing copied by s.o: *She's a crib. Your work is full of cribs from a book I know well.*
▷ *tr/intr.v* (*-bb-*) **5** copy (the answers to an exercise, examination) from s.o else, esp dishonestly: *It is quite clear that you cribbed the answers from your friend.*

crick /krɪk/ *c.n* (often — *in the neck/back*) painful stiffness in the muscles(1) (in one's neck or back): *I got a crick in the neck from watching the people working on the tower.*

cricket[1] /ˈkrɪkɪt/ *u.n* kind of game with 11 players in each team that is played on a grass pitch(1) with a batsman trying to score runs(8) by hitting the ball while the bowler(1) and fielders from the other side try to get them out. *It/That etc is not cricket* (*fig*) It etc is not right or fair: *It's not cricket for you to talk about something you were told as a secret.*

cricket[2] /ˈkrɪkɪt/ *c.n* kind of small insect like a grasshopper; the male makes a chirping(2) noise by rubbing its wings together.

cried /kraɪd/ *p.t,p.p* of cry[2].

crier ⇒ town crier.

cries /kraɪz/ **1** *pl* of cry[1]. **2** *3rd person pres.t* of cry[2].

crime /kraɪm/ *c/u.n* (example of an) act of doing s.t wrong which is punished by law: *He was arrested for a crime he did not commit. There has been an increase in crime in the last six months.* *be a crime* (*against s.t*) (*fig*) be s.t that is not against the law but seems wrong (and goes against some standard of behaviour etc): *It really is a crime that he should do so well without doing any work!*

'crime ˌwave *c.n* period when many crimes are committed (⇒ commit).

criminal /ˈkrɪmɪnl/ *adj* **1** of or referring to (a) crime. **2** of or referring to s.t that seems wrong: *a criminal waste of his ability.*
▷ *c.n* **3** person who commits a crime.

ˌCriminal Inˌvestiˈgation Deˌpartment *def/ unique n* (*abbr CID*) (the UK detective department of the police).

criminologist /ˌkrɪmɪˈnɒlədʒɪst/ *c.n* person who studies crime.

criminology /ˌkrɪmɪˈnɒlədʒɪ/ *u.n* scientific study of crime.

crimson /ˈkrɪmzən/ *u.n* (also *attrib*) very strong red colour.

cringe /krɪndʒ/ *intr.v* (often — *away* (*from s.o/ s.t*)) (of a person, animal) move one's/its body lower and away (from s.o/s.t) because of fear (of being hit etc): *His wife cringed* (*away from him*) *when she thought he was going to hit her.*

crinkle /ˈkrɪŋkl/ *c.n* **1** wavy shape made when paper, material etc creases(4), squashes[1](4), wrinkles(1) etc.
▷ *tr/intr.v* **2** (cause(s.t) to) crease(4); have crinkles(1): *Her whole face crinkles when she laughs.*

'crinkly *adj* (*-ier, -iest*) having crinkles(1).

cripple /ˈkrɪpl/ *c.n* **1** (*old use*) person who is lame(1).
▷ *tr.v* **2** make (s.o) lame(1) in this way: *He was crippled by the accident.* **3** (of s.t that happens) very seriously affect, damage, destroy, (s.t, esp an activity, the ability of s.o to do s.t etc): *High taxes are crippling the country.*

'crippling *adj* (usu *attrib*) very seriously affecting, damaging or destroying: *a crippling blow to his hopes; crippling debts.*

crisis /ˈkraɪsɪs/ *c.n* (*pl crises* /ˈkraɪsiːz/) (also *attrib*) **1** (time of) very great danger (which may get worse or better): *The government is facing a crisis in its handling of the* strike(1). *Sally reaches for a cigarette at any* hint(1) *of a crisis.* **2** highest point in an illness when a patient may die or start to get better: *If he manages to get through the crisis he'll be fine. The crisis point was reached and then he got better.* ⇒ critical(3).

crisp /krɪsp/ *adj* **1** (of various kinds of vegetables, biscuits etc) fresh and firm: *These lettuces are nice and crisp.* **2** (of weather) cold, clear and fresh: *a crisp winter morning.* **3** (of s.t said, written etc) clear and well presented (often in a short, precise(2) form): *His report was crisp and to the point.*
▷ *c.n* **4** = potato crisp.

'crispiness *u.n* fact or state of being crispy.

'crisply *adv.* **'crispness** *u.n.*

'crispy *adj* (*-ier, -iest*) (of food that has been fried) crunchy and hard (and tasty and enjoyable to eat): *crispy chicken.*

crisscross /ˈkrɪsˌkrɒs/ *adj/adv* **1** having, being in, a pattern of straight lines or marks that cross each other: *The marks of people's feet had made a crisscross pattern in the snow.*
▷ *tr/intr.v* **2** (of such lines or marks) make a crisscross(1) pattern (on (a surface)): *The tracks the animals made crisscrossed* (*the field*) *and we couldn't follow them further.*

criterion /kraɪˈtɪərɪən/ *c.n* (*pl -s* or *criteria* /kraɪˈtɪərɪə/) standard that has been established(4) and can be used to judge s.t before coming to a decision or opinion: *He has very few criteria for judging the value of the people who work for him.*

critic /ˈkrɪtɪk/ *c.n* **1** person who comments(2) on works of art, books, plays etc and gives the public her/his opinion on whether they are good or not: *He works as a theatre critic on a London newspaper.* **2** (often — *of s.o/s.t*) person who is able, is in a position, to criticize s.o/s.t most effectively: *My wife is my best critic.*

critical /'krɪtɪkl/ *adj* **1** (usu *attrib*) of or referring to criticism(1) or the work of a critic(1): *He has just published(2) a collection of his critical articles.* **2** (often — *about/of s.o/s.t*) (of a person) having an unfavourable opinion (about s.o/s.t): *He is very critical of the government's handling of the situation.* Opposite uncritical. **3** (of an illness, state of health etc) having reached a point of crisis(2); very dangerous: *The patient was in a critical condition for several hours after the operation.* **4** (of a situation, state of affairs etc) very important, dangerous: *You came in at the critical moment just when I needed you most. Help arrived at the critical moment.* Compare uncritical.
'critically *adv*.

criticism /'krɪtɪ,sɪzəm/ *c/u.n* **1** (example of the) work of a critic(1): *He writes criticisms for the local newspaper.* **2** (often — *about/of s.o/s.t*) (example of an) unfavourable opinion (about s.o/s.t): *The government is facing a lot of criticism about the unemployment situation.*

criticize, -ise /'krɪtɪ,saɪz/ *v* **1** *tr/intr.v* give, state, an unfavourable opinion (about s.o/s.t): *You're always criticizing (me).* **2** *tr.v* examine (s.t) and state what is good and what is bad about (it): *I'd like you to criticize what I've written so far.*

croak /krəʊk/ *c.n* **1** harsh(3) low sound made in the throat (by a person, esp when her/his throat is sore), an animal, esp a frog, toad and also crows(1) etc.
▷ *v* **2** *intr.v* make this sound: *Listen to the frogs croaking.* **3** *tr.v* (of a person) say (s.t) with a croak(1) in one's voice: *He croaked that he was not feeling well.* **4** *intr.v* (slang) (of a person) die.

crochet /'krəʊʃeɪ/ *u.n* **1** (also *attrib*) kind of knitting done using one needle with a hook on the end (called a *crochet hook*).
▷ *tr/intr.v* (*-t-*) **2** knit (s.t) using a crochet(1) hook: *She was crocheting a scarf(1) for her daughter.*

crock /krɒk/ *c.n* (becoming *old use*) pot or jar, usu made of clay: *a crock of honey.* **old crock** ⇒ old.

'crockery *u.n* (also *attrib*) plates, cups, saucers, bowls, dishes etc made of china(1) and/or pottery(2): *a crockery cupboard. Put all the crockery in the dishwasher.*

crocodile /'krɒkə,daɪl/ *n* (*pl* -(s)) **1** *c.n* kind of large reptile with a long body and tail and a long mouth, found in rivers in Asia and Africa. Compare alligator. **2** *u.n* (also *attrib*) skin of this animal: *a crocodile handbag.*
'croco,dile ,tears *pl.n* sorrow that is pretended and not real: *He weeps crocodile tears at your misfortune but secretly he's glad.*

crocus /'krəʊkəs/ *c.n* (*pl* -es) kind of short flowering plant which flowers early in the spring.

croissant /'krwʌsɒŋ/ *c.n* (French) piece of light bread shaped like a crescent(1), usu eaten at breakfast.

croft /krɒft/ *c.n* small farm and the house on it, usu found in the highlands of Scotland.
'crofter *c.n* person who owns, works on, a croft.

crone /krəʊn/ *c.n* (often *old* —) (*derog*) old, useless and ugly person (usu a woman).

crony /'krəʊnɪ/ *c.n* (*pl* -ies) (usu *derog; informal*) friend one has known for a long time: *Eric spends all his time with his old cronies and never sees his family.*

crook /krʊk/ *n* **1** *c.n* (*informal*) thief; criminal: *I wouldn't trust him with your money; he's a crook.* **2** *c.n* long stick with a bent hook at the top, used for walking or as a sign of one's position or office: *a shepherd's(1) crook.* **3** *def.n* (usu *in the* — *of s.t*) shape or hollow made by having one's arm, finger etc bent: *She was carrying the baby in the crook of her arm.*
▷ *tr.v* **4** (usu — *one's finger (at s.o)*) bend (one's finger), esp in order to get s.o to come towards one or to do what one wants etc: *She has only to crook her little finger and he'll come to her.*
crooked /'krʊkɪd/ *adj* **1** (of a line, an object etc) not straight; not in a correct or straight horizontal or vertical position: *Your tie is crooked.* **2** (*derog; informal*) (of a person, activity) not honest: *The whole deal was crooked and they lost all their money.*
'crookedly *adv*. **'crookedness** *u.n*.

croon /kruːn/ *tr/intr.v* **1** sing (a song, words etc) in a low gentle voice: *She crooned a little song while she rocked the baby.* **2** sing (a romantic(1) song or songs) in a low voice: *When he comes on stage and starts crooning all the old ladies sigh.*
'crooner *c.n* person who croons(2).

crop /krɒp/ *n* **1** *c.n* (often — *of s.t*) mass of plants of one kind grown on a farm for use as food, e.g wheat, vegetables etc: *a crop of potatoes.* **2** *c.n* (often — *of s.t*) amount of such things that have been grown: *We had a very good crop (of wheat) this year.* **3** *c.n* (usu *sing*) (often — *of s.o/s.t*) (*fig*) (new or fresh) group (of people, things) who/that have to be dealt with: *The new crop of students are not nearly as good as last year's. We are facing a new crop of problems.* **4** *c.n* (also **'riding ,crop**) kind of short whip used when riding a horse. **5** *c.n* (very) short hair on a person's head or on an animal: *The dog had been given a close crop.*
▷ *tr.v* (*-pp-*) **6** (of animals such as cows, horses etc) eat (grass growing in a field): *The sheep were cropping the grass.* **7** *tr.v* cut (the hair of a person, an animal) short: *She had her hair cropped.*
crop up (*informal*) appear or happen suddenly, accidentally or unexpectedly: *His name cropped up in our conversation. I'm sorry I can't see you today; something's cropped up.*

'cropper *c.n* **come a cropper** (*informal*) (of a person) fall down; suffer a misfortune: *He'll come a cropper one of these days if he doesn't watch out.*

'crop ro,tation *u.n* planting of a different kind of crop in a field each year so that one that takes a lot out of the soil is followed by one that puts things back into it.

croquet /'krəʊkeɪ/ *u.n* (also *attrib*) kind of game played on a lawn¹ in which players with mallets hit balls through a number of hoops(3): *croquet players.*

crosier, crozier /'krəʊʒə/ *c.n* bishop(1)'s crook(2).

cross /krɒs/ *adj* **1** (of a person) having a bad temper: *He's always cross and nasty.* **2** (often — *with s.o (about s.t)*) angry or annoyed (with s.o) (about s.t) when s.t bad or wrong happens: *I was very cross about missing the train. She got very cross with him for staying out so late.*

▷ *n* **3** *c.n* sign or mark in which two lines go across each other, e.g + or ×, often made to show where s.t is: *He put a cross on the map to show where his house was.* **4** *c.n* wooden post with another one going across it near the top on which a criminal used to be hung, esp in Roman(1) times, until he/she was dead. **5** *def.n* (with capital **C**) cross(4) on which Jesus died. **6** *c.n* ornament shaped like the Cross(5), often worn on a chain: *He had a small gold cross on a chain round his neck.* **7** *def.n* (with capital **C** in names) stone monument shaped like the Cross(5) and often found where roads meet, e.g in the centre of a town: *St Margaret's Cross.* **8** *def.n* (with capital **C** in names) (name for a) medal(1) shaped like a cross(3) and given for bravery in war etc: *the Victoria Cross, the Iron Cross.* **be a cross between s.t and s.t** (a) (of a plant or animal) be a mixture of one kind of plant or animal and another: *The dog looked as though it was a cross between a* collie *and a* terrier. (b) be s.t made or produced that looks like one thing and another but is really neither: *The new vehicle looks like a cross between a bicycle and a car.* **have a cross to bear** (*fig*) have some kind of suffering in one's life that one cannot avoid and has to accept: *We all have our crosses to bear and yours seems to be your husband!* (**make the**) **sign of the Cross** (make the) movement of the (usu right) hand touching one's forehead, one's chest and one's shoulders in turn in the shape of the Cross(5), as a religious act.

▷ *v* **9** *tr/intr.v* move from one side (of s.t, e.g a road, a stretch of land, the sea) to another or the other side: *We crossed the river in a small boat. We can cross now as the traffic lights are green.* **10** *tr/intr.v* (of two people, things etc) move towards (each other), meet and then go past: *Our paths* (i.e two people walking) *crossed yesterday. Your letter crossed mine so you will have had my opinion already.* **11** *tr/intr.v* (of two roads etc) meet and pass (each other): *The two paths cross near the wood.* **12** *tr.v* (often — *s.t and/with s.t*) breed(2) or mix (one plant or animal) (with another) in order to produce a different one: *He crossed this rose with that one and got a new rose with a different colour.* **13** *tr.v* (of a person) try to stop or block (s.o doing s.t): *All she does is cross me at every opportunity.*

cross a cheque, postal order etc (*commerce*) put two parallel(1) lines across a cheque, postal order etc so that it can only be paid into s.o's (bank) account and not be exchanged for cash: *a crossed cheque.*

cross one's fingers ⇨ finger(*n*).

cross one's heart ⇨ heart.

cross one's legs (when one is sitting down) move one leg over and on top of the other. ⇨ cross-legged. Opposite uncross.

cross oneself make the sign of the Cross as a religious act, to prevent s.t bad happening etc: *She crossed herself as she came out of the church.*

cross s.o/s.t off draw a line through s.o's name or an item(1) in a list (either as a means of checking or because one does not want her/him/it in the list any more).

cross s.o's mind ⇨ mind[1].

cross s.t out draw a line or a cross(3) through s.t (because it is wrong, not needed etc).

'cross,bar *c.n* **1** metal tube that joins the front and back parts of a bicycle frame from just below the handlebars to just below the saddle. **2** (in football, rugby etc) wooden bar joining the two vertical posts or uprights(4) together: *The ball hit the crossbar and went out of play.*

'cross,bow *c.n* kind of bow[3](1) with a device that fires arrows or metal darts(2) (used in old days in war and now as a sport).

'cross,bred *adj* (of a plant or animal) made or produced by crossing(12) one kind of plant or animal with another.

'cross,breed *c.n* plant or animal that is produced by crossing(12).

,cross'check *c.n* **1** act of comparing s.t with s.t else or of using different ways of calculating s.t, to see if s.t is true, correct etc: *I'll have to do a crosscheck of these figures before I'm satisfied.*

▷ *tr/intr.v* **2** (often — (s.t) with s.t) use crosschecks(1) for checking (s.t): *I'd just like to crosscheck with my own records.*

,cross'country *adj/adv* (going) across fields etc in the countryside: *a crosscountry race; travelling crosscountry.*

'cross,current *c.n* **1** movement or flow of water in a different direction from normal, e.g because of rocks etc: *There are dangerous crosscurrents in the river here so don't take your boat near.* **2** (*fig*) thought or opinion that is different from, disagrees with, another or others: *There are various crosscurrents at work which make things very difficult.*

,cross-ex'amine *tr/intr.v* (*law*) (of a lawyer) question (a witness, defendant (who is on the opposite side) in a case) closely in order to find out if what he/she says is true or not: *Counsel(2) for the defence spent two hours cross-examining the witness.*

,cross-ex,ami'nation *c/u.n* (example of the) act or fact of cross-examining.

'cross-,eyed *adj* having one's eyes looking towards one's nose, either permanently or because one is looking too closely at s.t.

'cross,fire *u.n* the firing of guns or rifles from two positions so that the bullets or shells cross each other. (**be**) **caught in the crossfire** have guns or rifles firing from two positions at one and so not be able to move safely, or be in danger of being hit.

'crossing *n* **1** *c.n* place where a road, river, railway etc may be crossed(9) easily or safely: *You should use the crossing when the traffic is heavy.* ⇨ level crossing, pedestrian crossing, pelican crossing. **2** *c.n* journey from one land to another across a sea: *They made the Atlantic crossing in record time.* **3** *u.n* act of going across s.t, esp a road: *Crossing at this point is difficult when the traffic is heavy.*

,cross-'legged *adv* (sitting in a position) with one leg over and on top of the other. ⇨ cross one's legs.

'crossly *adv* in a cross(2) way: *She spoke crossly to the children.*

'crossness *u.n* fact or state of being cross(2).

'cross,over *c.n* place where s.o, an animal, road etc crosses over.

,cross-'purposes *pl.n* (usu *be/talk at* —) way that shows that neither or none of two or more people understands what the other person(s) is/are really saying: *We really were at cross-purposes; I thought he wanted one thing and he thought I wanted something completely different.*

,cross-re'fer *tr/intr.v* (-rr-) (cause (s.o) to) look from one place, esp in a book, to another (to check or find s.t etc): *You will have to cross-refer to the* index(1) *in the library to find the correct title.*

,cross-'reference *c.n* example of cross-referring.

'cross,road *c.n* road that crosses(11) another.

'cross,roads *c.n* (*pl* crossroads) place where two or more roads cross(11). **be at, come to, the crossroads (in s.t)** (*fig*) be at, arrive at, a point when a decision to do one or more things has to be made: *We are at the crossroads; what we do now will affect us for many years to come.*

'cross-,section *c.n* **1** (*technical*) (drawing of an) object, animal etc (as though it has been) cut through the middle, along its length etc: *If you take a cross-section of this plant leaf, you will see the* veins(1) *and* cells(4) *clearly under a microscope.* **2** number of people chosen from a larger group to be representative of it (and to be questioned or examined for some purpose): *They questioned a cross-section of the people in the town to see if they were in favour of the new road.*

'cross,word *c.n* (also **'cross,word ,puzzle**) printed puzzle, usu in the shape of a box, with black and white squares in it in which (the letters of) words are put as answers to a separate numbered list of clues(2).

crotch /krɒtʃ/ *c.n* **1** place in the front of the human body where the two legs join. **2** join like this in shape, esp in a pair of trousers, the branches of a tree etc.

crotchet /'krɒtʃit/ *c.n* (*music*) note of a length between a minim and a quaver² shown by the printed signs '♩ ♪'.

crotchety /'krɒtʃiti/ *adj* (*derog*) (of a person) having a bad temper; difficult to deal with: *She's got very crotchety in her old age.*

crouch /krautʃ/ *c.n* **1** (of a person or animal) position in which the body is near to the ground with the legs folded (and with arms touching the ground), often in order to jump s.w, to hide or because s.o/it is afraid.
▷ *intr.v* **2** (often — *down*) be in, go into, this position: *The tiger was crouching in the tall grass getting ready to jump on the deer.*

croupier /'kru:piə/ *c.n* person who collects or gives out money that is lost or won at a table where games of gambling are played.

crouton /'kru:tɒn/ *c.n* very small piece of fried bread, eaten with soup etc.

crow /krəu/ *c.n* **1** kind of large black bird with shiny feathers. **2** high loud cry of a cock(1). **as the crow flies** (of a distance from one place to another) in the shortest possible way; in a straight or direct line: *The village is only five miles away as the crow flies but with the hills and the river and the roads you have to take it's actually about ten miles.*
▷ *intr.v* **3** (*p.t* crew /kru:/ or crowed; *p.p* crowed) (of a cock(1)) make the sound(s) of a crow(2): *The cock crew at daylight.* **4** (*p.t,p.p* -ed) (often — *with delight/happiness* etc) make soft, gentle noises (because of happiness etc): *She was crowing with pleasure at the thought of her daughter winning the race.* **5** (*p.t,p.p* -ed) (usu — *about s.t; — over s.o/s.t*) (*informal*) speak in a boastful and annoying way (about s.t one has succeeded in doing, about s.o who has not succeeded as well as oneself or who has had a misfortune etc): *I wish he would stop crowing about how well he has done. There's nothing she likes better than crowing over people she's beaten at tennis.*

'crow's ,feet *pl.n* lines or wrinkles(1) in the skin under and by the sides of the eyes (showing that one is getting old(er)).

'crow's ,nest *c.n* place at the top of a mast on a ship where s.o can look out over the sea (to see land, other ships etc).

crowbar /'krəu,bɑ:/ *c.n* strong metal bar, usu with a hook at one end, for putting under heavy objects to lift them, for breaking and opening things, e.g boxes, cases.

crowd /kraud/ *n* **1** *c.n* large number or group of people in one place, without any order and often for some purpose: *A large crowd had gathered at the scene of the accident. I had to fight my way through crowds of people doing their* Christmas *shopping.* **2** *c.n* large number of animals, insects, things etc: *There was a crowd of flies on the meat.* **3** *sing.n* (*informal*; often *derog*) group of people who go around together, have common interests etc: *I advise you to keep away from Michael and his crowd because they spend all their time drinking.*
▷ *v* **4** *tr.v* (of people) move into and fill (a space, place): *People crowded the square in order to hear him speak.* **5** *tr.v* (of a number of people) come too close around (s.o) so that he/she cannot move, see, breathe etc easily: *Don't crowd him, please; could you all move back so he can get through.* **6** *intr.v* (often — *in*(to s.t), through etc (s.t)) move as a crowd(1) (in(to a place), through (a place) etc): *They all crowded in* (or *into the hall*) *to hear him speak.* **crowd round (s.o/s.t)** form a crowd(1) in a circle (round s.o/s.t): *They were crowding around* (him) *so that he couldn't get away.* **crowd together** come close together in a large group: *The people crowded together to shelter from the rain.* **crowd s.t with s.o** fill (all) the space in s.t with people: *They crowded the hall with their own friends.*

crowded /'kraudid/ *adj* (often — *with s.o/s.t*) very full (of people, things) (so that there is very little or no space for more): *a crowded shopping centre; a train crowded with passengers; shelves crowded with books.* ⇒ overcrowded.

crown /kraun/ *n* **1** *c.n* round, closed or open ornament for the head, often made of gold or other precious metals, and with jewels in it, worn by a king, queen, prince, princess etc as a sign of his/her position. **2** *def.n* (usu with capital **C**) (UK) position, office or power of a king or queen: *The Crown has very little power nowadays.* **3** *c.n* ornament like a crown(1) that a person gets as the winner of a competition, race etc; first prize: *She won the crown in the beauty competition.* **4** *c.n* top part of the head of a person: *He hit the crown of his head on the* *low door.* **5** *c.n* (often *the — of s.t*) top part (of a hill or mountain): *When they reached the crown of the hill they could see the whole valley below them.* **6** *c.n* (often *the — of s.t*) top part (of a hat, building etc): *The crown of his hat had a dent(1) in it.* **7** *c.n* top of a tooth outside the gum²; artificial replacement(2) for this part when it has broken or decayed: *The dentist said he would have to put crowns on two of her teeth.* **8** *def.n* (often *the — of s.t*) final and best thing (of all that s.o has done): *The crown of his* achievements(2) *was the honour shown to him by the people.* **9** *c.n* (UK; until 1971) (coin with a value of) five shillings(1) or sixty (old) pence (= twenty-five (new) pence); (in some countries) (coin of a) certain value: *Swedish/Danish crowns.*

▷ *tr.v* **10** (often *— s.o s.t (of s.w)*) put a crown(1) on (s.o) in an official ceremony and so make her/him a queen or king (of a country): *She was crowned (Queen of Great Britain and Northern Ireland) in 1953.* **11** (often *— s.o s.t*) put a crown(3) on s.o for winning a competition, race etc: *She was crowned Miss World 1989.* **12** (*informal*) hit (s.o) on the (top of the) head: *If you don't shut up, I'll crown you!* **13** (often *— s.t in/with s.t*) surround or cover the top of (s.t) (with s.t): *The mountain top was crowned in snow.* **14** put a replacement(2) crown(7) on (a tooth): *He had his front teeth crowned so that he would look better in his films.* **15** be the final and best thing of (all that one has done): *Success finally crowned his efforts.* **16** (often *— s.t by doing s.t*) mark the successful completion of (s.t) (by doing s.t): *Let's crown our success by holding a party.*

,crown 'court *c/u.n* court of law with a judge appointed by the Crown(2).

,crown 'jewels *def.n* all the crowns(1) and other precious objects belonging to the monarchy.

,crown 'prince/prin'cess *c.n* prince/princess who will become king/queen when the king/queen dies.

,crown 'witness *c.n* witness who appears for the prosecution(2) in a court case.

'crowned ,heads *def.pl.n* (usu *the — of s.w*) all the kings and queens (of a number of countries): *the crowned heads of Europe.*

'crowning *adj* being the top or most important or best (thing): *Her crowning glory was her red hair. The crowning* irony(2) *was that he lost the election when everybody thought he'd win.*

crow's feet, crow's nest ⇒ crow.

crozier ⇒ crosier.

crucial /'kruːʃəl/ *adj* (of a meeting, decision, moment of time etc) of the highest or greatest importance (when things could change for better or worse); critical(4): *The crucial point is whether we should agree to the plan or not.* ⇒ crux.

'crucially *adv.*

crucifix /'kruːsɪfɪks/ *c.n* (*pl -es*) Christian(1) religious object shaped like the Cross(5) on which Jesus died (sometimes with a representation(2) of his body fixed to it).

crucifixion /ˌkruːsɪ'fɪkʃən/ *n* **1** *c/u.n* (in history) (example of the) act of fixing s.o to a (wooden) cross with nails or ropes as a punishment, and killing her/him in this way. **2** *def.n* (with capital C) death of Jesus in this way.

crucify /'kruːsɪˌfaɪ/ *tr.v* (*-ies, -ied*) **1** punish and kill (s.o) by crucifixion(1). **2** (*fig*) destroy (s.o)

by attacking or ruining her/his reputation: *The newspapers crucified him when they got hold of the story of his affair with his secretary.*

crud /krʌd/ *c.n* (*derog; slang*) horrid person.

crude /kruːd/ *adj* **1** (of s.t found under the ground, s.t that is grown etc) being in a natural state before being treated, refined(1) etc: *crude oil; crude* ore(1); *crude sugar.* **2** (*derog*) (of objects) not very well made: *crude furniture.* **3** (*derog*) (of a person, idea, behaviour etc) not polite; not well thought out; rough: *His plan is a bit crude but then he's crude himself.* **4** (*derog*) (of a person, s.t said or written) nasty and vulgar(1): *Don't be so crude and especially not in front of the children!*

▷ *c/u.n* **5** (*technical*) crude(1) oil.

'crudely *adv.* 'crudeness, 'crudity *u.n.*

cruel /'kruːəl/ *adj* **1** (often *— to s.o/s.t*) (of a person) causing, or liking to cause, pain or hurt (to s.o, an animal etc): *He was very cruel to his children and used to beat them and then lock them in their bedrooms.* **2** (of s.t that happens) causing pain or distress(1): *It was a cruel blow when she lost her job.*

'cruelly *adv.* 'cruelness *u.n* = cruelty.

'cruelty *c/u.n* (*pl -ies*) (often *— to/towards s.o*) (example of the) act or fact of being cruel(1): *I can't stand cruelty to animals.*

cruet /'kruːɪt/ *c.n* small container, usu made of glass, metal etc, for salt, pepper, vinegar etc which is put on the table at mealtimes.

cruise /kruːz/ *c.n* **1** (often *go on a —*) voyage by boat or ship for pleasure, sometimes stopping at places on the way: *This summer we went on a cruise of the French canals.*

▷ *intr.v* **2** travel about for pleasure in a boat or ship: *We're planning to cruise around the islands this year.* **3** (usu *— at a certain speed*) (of a car, plane etc) go (at a certain, usu normal, speed) neither very fast nor very slow: *The aircraft was cruising at 500 miles an hour at a height of 30 000 feet.* **4** (usu *— through s.t*) (*informal*) (of a person) do only what is necessary without trying very hard (in one's work etc): *He just cruises through his work and always leaves exactly at 5.30.*

'cruise ,missile *c.n* kind of missile(1) that flies a long way at a low speed, sometimes not very far from the ground (in order to avoid radar).

'cruise ,ship *c.n* kind of (large) ship for people going on a cruise(1).

'cruiser *c.n* **1** kind of (small) boat that has beds in it and in which one can cruise(2). ⇒ cabin-cruiser. **2** kind of large warship, smaller than a battleship but bigger than a destroyer(1).

'cruising *u.n* act of being or going on a cruise(1).

go cruising = cruise(2).

crumb /krʌm/ *c.n* **1** very small piece (broken off) from bread, cake, biscuit etc: *He was dropping crumbs from his plate onto the carpet.* ⇒ breadcrumb. **2** (often *— of s.t*) (*fig*) very small piece (of information, advice, help, comfort etc): *There are very few crumbs of information to be gained from the government's statement.*

crumble /'krʌmbl/ *u.n* **1** pie with fruit inside and a covering of small pieces of pastry and sugar: *apple crumble.*

▷ *v* **2** *tr/intr.v* (cause (s.t) to) break into crumbs(1): *She crumbled the biscuits.* **3** *intr.v* (of a building etc) fall into pieces, be destroyed, esp over a length of time, because it has not been looked after etc: *The walls of the castle were crumbling.* **4** *intr.v* (*fig*) (of s.o's plans, hopes etc) (start to) fail: *With this new information he knew that his hopes were crumbling.*

'**crumbly** *adj* (*-ier, -iest*) easy to break into crumbs(1) or to crumble(2).

crummy /'krʌmɪ/ *adj* (*-ier, -iest*) (*derog*; *slang*) very low in value; poor in quality: *a crummy hotel; a really crummy job.*

crumpet /'krʌmpɪt/ *c.n* kind of small round soft cake which is toasted and spread with butter, jam etc, usu eaten hot at teatime.

crumple /'krʌmpl/ *v* **1** *tr/intr.v* (often — (s.t) up) (cause (material, paper, metal etc) to) have marks, lines, creases(2) or damage in it: *He had crumpled up the note and threw it into the* bin(1). *His* suit(1) *was crumpled from sitting in the car. The front of the car crumpled in the accident.* **2** *intr.v* (often — up) (of a person, expression) lose control of oneself, of the muscles(1) of one's face etc: *Her whole face crumpled when she was told of the accident.*

crunch /krʌntʃ/ *c.n* **1** (often — of s.t) heavy or hard sound made by s.t hitting s.t or by s.t putting pressure on s.t: *The crunch of footsteps on the snow told him someone was coming.* **if/when it comes to the crunch** if/when it is the most serious moment or decision: *When it comes to the crunch you will find that I am there to help you.*
▷ *tr/intr.v* **2** (cause (s.t) to) make a crunch(1), esp when moving: *He crunched through the deep snow.* **3** bite or chew (s.t) with one's teeth and make a noise while doing so: *I hate listening to him crunching his breakfast* cereal(3).

'**crunchiness** *u.n* fact or state of being crunchy.

'**crunchy** *adj* (*-ier, -iest*) (of food) being good to crunch(3); that one can crunch(3); crisp(1) and hard: *These nuts are lovely and crunchy.*

crusade /kruːˈseɪd/ *n* **1** *c.n* (often — against/for s.t) attack, struggle or movement (against s.t one considers bad or for s.t one wants or considers good): *He was one of the leaders of the crusade for civil rights.*
▷ *intr.v* **2** (often — against/for s.t) lead or take part in a crusade(1) (against/for s.t).

cru'sader *c.n* **1** (often — against/for s.t) person who leads or takes part in a crusade(1). **2** (usu with capital **C**) person who took part in the Crusades.

Cru'sades *def.n* attempts by Christian(1) armies to win the Holy Land from the Muslims(2) during the 11–13th centuries.

crush /krʌʃ/ *n* **1** *sing.n* large number of people packed together in one place: *There was such a crush at the bar that I wasn't able to get a drink.* **2** *u.n* drink made by crushing(3) fruit and adding sugar, water etc: *lemon/orange crush.* **have a crush on s.o** (*informal*) (usu of a young person) be attracted to, be in love with, s.o (usu for a short time).
▷ *v* **3** *tr.v* press (s.t) hard so as to get s.t from it or to break it into pieces: *The fruit is crushed in this machine to draw out the juice.* **4** *tr.v* hit or press (s.o/s.t) so hard that he/she/it is hurt or damaged: *His foot got crushed in the door and had to be operated on.* **5** *tr/intr.v* (cause (a material) to) get lines, marks or creases(2)

in it by pressure: *She found that the silk dress she had bought crushed very easily.* **6** *tr.v* (*fig*) severely damage or destroy (s.o who opposes(1) one, the reputation of s.o etc): *The army crushed the rising in two weeks. She crushed him with just a couple of remarks on his character.* **crush (s.o/ s.t) into s.t** try and get (as many people or things as possible) into s.t, e.g a place, container: *He was crushing his clothes into the* suitcase. *A large crowd was trying to crush into the hall.*

'**crush ˌbarrier** *c.n* barrier(1) put up in, at, places in a crowded area to prevent people being crushed(4).

'**crushing** *adj* (of s.t said) intended to destroy or crush(6) s.o, her/his reputation etc: *Her crushing remarks left him with nothing to say.* **a crushing defeat** a defeat that is total and complete.

crust /krʌst/ *c/u.n* **1** (piece of the) outer hard brown surface of bread: *I don't like crust so could you cut it off, please?* **2** (piece of the) outer (hard) pastry on a pie. **3** (*geology*) outer hard surface of the earth: *The earth's crust is broken in several places by* volcanos. **4** hard covering that forms on s.t, e.g ice, snow etc: *He had to break through the crust of ice to get to the water below.* **the upper crust** (*informal*) the upper class.

'**crustily** *adv* in a crusty(2) way.

'**crustiness** *u.n* fact or state of being crusty.

'**crusty** *adj* (*-ier, -iest*) **1** (of bread etc) having a thick, hard crust(1): *I like crusty bread.* **2** (*derog*) (of a person) not friendly; difficult to get on with: *He's got very crusty in his old age.*

crustacean /krʌˈsteɪʃən/ *c.n* (also *attrib*) (*technical*) any one of the different varieties of shellfish.

crutch /krʌtʃ/ *c.n* **1** stick with a support on the top which one puts under one's arm to help one walk when injured(1), e.g in the legs. **2** (*fig*) person or thing one uses to help one deal with problems etc: *She used him as her crutch when life became too difficult to manage.* **on crutches** having to use (two) crutches(1) to support oneself when walking etc because of an illness or injury.

crux /krʌks/ *def.n* (usu the — of the matter) the main or most important point (of s.t): *The crux of the matter is that we are going to lose.* ⇨ crucial.

cry /kraɪ/ *c.n* (*pl* cries) **1** (length of time when there are) tears coming from the eyes, because one is sad, hurt etc: *She was having a little cry in the corner because her mother was angry with her.* **2** (usu — of s.t) loud shout (expressing a feeling of pain, fear, joy etc): *He gave a cry of anger when he saw what the children were doing to his flowers.* **3** (usu — for s.t) loud call or shout (trying to get s.t, e.g help, attention): *They could hear cries for help coming from the bombed building.* **4** (often — of s.t) shouting (of certain words): *There was a cry (of), 'Throw him out' coming from the back of the hall.* **5** (often the — of s.t) ordinary natural sound (made by some animals and birds): *the cry of an eagle.* **6** shouting (of words) by soldiers, tribes etc as they attack an enemy (in order to make themselves braver or to frighten the enemy): *a battle/war cry.* **be a far cry (from s.t)** be not nearly like (s.t); be very different (from what one would like s.t to be): *This job is a far cry from what I am accustomed to.* **be in full cry (after s.o/s.t)** be running or pursuing(1) (after s.o/s.t, e.g a person, animal etc) with loud shouts.

▷ v (-ies, -ied) **7** intr.v make,have,tearscomingfrom one's eyes, because one is sad, hurt etc: *David, can't you stop the baby crying?* **8** intr.v (usu — (out) with s.t) give a loud shout (expressing a feeling of pain etc): *He cried out with pain as the doctor felt his broken leg.* **9** intr.v (usu — (out) for s.t) give a (loud) shout (trying to get s.t, e.g help): *The wounded were crying for attention.* **10** tr.v (often — s.t out; — that...) shout, call out loudly, (s.t, e.g certain words): *He cried 'Help!' He cried that he needed help.* **11** intr.v (of some animals) make its ordinary natural sound. **cry off** (*informal*) (say that one will) not be able to do s.t, go s.w etc: *She said she'd have dinner with him but cried off at the last moment.* **cry out (against s.t)** say strongly that one does not like or approve of s.t. **cry (out) for s.t (a)** ⇨ cry(9). **(b)** (*fig*) need s.t very much: *The whole house is crying out for a coat of paint.* **cry one's eyes/ heart out** ⇨ heart. **cry over spilt milk** ⇨ milk(n). **cry oneself to sleep** (go to bed and) cry(7) until one is so tired that one falls asleep.

'**crier** c.n ⇨ town crier.

'**cry,baby** c.n (*pl* -ies) (*derog*) person, esp a child, who cries too easily (when hurt etc): *Don't be such a crybaby, it's only a little cut and there's hardly any blood.*

'**crying** attrib.adj **1 a crying need** ⇨ need(n). **2 a crying shame** ⇨ shame(n).

▷ u.n **3** act or state of having tears: *Crying will not help you so you might as well stop.*

crypt /krɪpt/ c.n room or chapel(2) underneath the floor of a church (often where people are buried).

cryptic /'krɪptɪk/ adj having a hidden or secret meaning (either on purpose or because one cannot understand): *I like crosswords with cryptic clues(2) but not those that ask you for words with the same meanings. The message is a bit cryptic but I think it means you should fly to London immediately.*

crystal /'krɪstl/ adj **1** made of crystal(4): *a crystal earring. Is the vase crystal?*

▷ n **2** c.n (also *attrib*) shape that some substances have naturally when they are solid: *snow/ice crystals; crystal shapes.* **3** u.n kind of natural mineral substance found in the ground in rocks etc that is transparent, sometimes used as an ornament. **4** u.n kind of special glass that is very clear and reflects light, esp when it is cut in certain ways, often used for bowls, glasses etc: *wine glasses made of crystal* (*glass*).

crystallization, -isation /,krɪstəlaɪ'zeɪʃən/ u.n act of crystallizing(1).

'**crystal,lize, -ise** tr/intr.v **1** (cause (s.t) to) form into crystal(s)(2,3). **2** (*fig*) (cause (an idea, plan etc) to) take shape, become clearer etc: *We really must crystallize our thoughts if we are ever going to succeed.*

CS *written abbr* Civil Service.

CS gas /,si: ,es 'gæs/ u.n kind of gas that irritates(2) the eyes, skin and lungs; sometimes used by the police, army etc against people who take part in riots(1) etc.

cu *written abbr* cubic(2).

cub /kʌb/ c.n young of certain wild animals, e.g fox(1), bear, lion, tiger: *a tiger cub.*

▷ intr.v (-bb-) **2** give birth to a cub(1).

cubby-hole /'kʌbɪ ,həʊl/ c.n very small room or cupboard: *There is a cubby-hole under the stairs where we put all the cleaning things.*

cube /kju:b/ c.n **1** (*geometry*) solid shape with six equal sides. **2** solid shape like this but not necessarily regular: *a sugar cube.* **3** (*mathematics*) number got by multiplying a number by itself three times: *The cube of 5 is 125* (i.e $5 \times 5 \times 5 = 125$).

▷ tr.v **4** cut (s.t, esp food) into cubes(2): *Cube the meat before putting it into the pan.* **5** (*mathematics*) multiply (a number) by itself three times: *If you cube 5 the answer will be 125.*

cubed adj/adv (*mathematics*) (of a number, when it is) multiplied by itself three times: *5 cubed is 125* ($5^3 = 125$).

,**cube 'root** c.n (*mathematics*) number that, when divided by itself three times, produces a certain number: *The cube root of 27 is 3.*

cubic /'kju:bɪk/ adj **1** having the shape of a cube(1). **2** (*written abbr cu*) (of a measurement, quantity) being a shape, having or containing an amount, measured by multiplying its length, height and width: *a cubic centimetre* (i.e a shape that is one centimetre long × one centimetre high × one centimetre wide); *a cubic tonne of earth.*

,**cubic ca'pacity** c.n (*pl* -ies) (*written abbr cc*) (*technical*) measure of the size or power of an engine, esp of a car.

cubicle /'kju:bɪkl/ c.n small room (often part of a larger room), an area with a door and partitions(1), into which one can go to do s.t, e.g change one's clothes: *The shop had cubicles for people to try on their clothes in.*

cuckoo /'kuku:/ c.n (*pl* -s) kind of grey bird found in Europe which has a call sounding like its name: *Cuckoos often lay eggs in the nests of other birds.*

'**cuckoo ,clock** c.n kind of clock with a little house on top shaped like a chalet(1) with doors that open every hour when a toy cuckoo etc comes out and sounds the hours.

cucumber /'kju:,kʌmbə/ n **1** c.n long thin vegetable with a dark green skin and light green flesh inside. **2** u.n (also *attrib*) this vegetable as food, often used in salads: *cucumber sandwiches.* **as cool as a cucumber** being or keeping calm and not getting excited: *He walked into the shop and, as cool as a cucumber, walked out with a coat he hadn't paid for.*

cud /kʌd/ u.n food that has been partly digested(3) and is brought back into the mouth (by a cow etc) to be chewed again. **chew the cud** (*fig*) think about s.t.

cuddle /'kʌdl/ c.n **1** (often give s.o a —; have a — (with s.o)) hold or embrace(2) (s.o) as a sign of love, to get warm etc: *She gave the child a little cuddle.*

▷ tr.v **2** give (s.o) a cuddle(1): *She cuddled the baby in her arms.* **cuddle up (to s.o/s.t)** get as close together (or to s.o/s.t) as possible: *The dog cuddled up to his master.* **cuddle (up) together** get as close together as possible, esp for warmth, protection etc: *The children were cuddled up together under the blankets.*

'**cuddliness** u.n fact of being cuddly.

'**cuddly** adj (-ier, -iest) being or looking soft, round and pleasant enough to make one want to cuddle(2) her/him/it: *a cuddly toy. He's a round cuddly man.*

cudgel /'kʌdʒəl/ *c.n* **1** short heavy stick or club used for hitting s.o. **take up the cudgels on behalf of s.o/s.t** (*fig*) start to support or defend s.o/s.t: *They have taken up the cudgels on behalf of the people who lost their jobs.*

▷ *tr.v* **2** (*-ll-*, US *-l-*) hit (s.o) with a cudgel(1): *The thieves cudgelled him to the ground.*

cue /kju:/ *c.n* **1** (in acting a play) word(s), sign(s) or action(s) by s.o else that shows/show when one has to say or do s.t oneself: *When he opens the door, that is your cue to say 'Who's there?'* **2** (thing done or said by s.o else that acts as a) suggestion or hint(1) for what one should say or do oneself: *On a cue from the chairman, he started producing figures for the new factory.* **3** long stick that gets thinner towards one end, used to hit balls in the games of billiards, snooker(1) and pool³.

▷ *tr.v* **4** (*pres.p cueing, p.t,p.p cued*) give (s.o) her/ his cue(1). **5** (in snooker(1) etc) hit (a ball) with a cue(3): *He cued the yellow (ball) but failed to pocket it.* **miss one's cue** (in a play) fail to say or do s.t at the right time. **take one's cue from s.o** follow the cue(2) given by s.o in deciding what one should say or do oneself.

cuff /kʌf/ *c.n* **1** end part of the sleeve(1) of a shirt, coat etc around the wrist: *The cuffs of your shirt are dirty; go and change it.* **2** light blow (around the head or shoulder) given with the open hand. **off the cuff** (saying s.t, speaking) without having prepared in advance, without having given the matter deep thought: *Off the cuff, I'd guess we have sold six thousand copies.*

▷ *tr.v* **3** give (s.o) a cuff(2).

'cuff ‚link *c.n* (also **link**) (often *a pair of* —s) ornamental object like a button with chain or bar, used for joining cuffs(1) with holes in them.

cuffs *pl.n* (*informal*) = handcuffs(1).

cuisine /kwɪ'zi:n/ *c/u.n* (*French*; *formal*) (particular kind or style(4) of) cooking: *This restaurant has one of the best cuisines in the country.*

cul-de-sac /'kʌl də ‚sæk/ *c.n* (*pl* -s) (*French*) (short) street that is closed at one end (so traffic cannot get through). Compare dead end(1).

culinary /'kʌlɪnərɪ/ *adj* (*formal*) of or referring to (the art of) cooking or things used in cooking: *You will find pots and pans in the culinary department of the store.*

cull /kʌl/ *c.n* **1** act of killing a certain number of animals in order to reduce their population, e.g because they are damaging crops, eating too much food: *a deer cull.*

▷ *tr.v* **2** kill (animals) in a cull(1): *The government is continuing to cull seals'(1) in spite of protests(1).* **3** (often — *s.t from s.t*) (*formal*) get or gather (knowledge, information etc) (from books etc): *He's culled a large amount of information about the subject (from his reading).*

cullender /'kʌlɪndə/ *c.n* ⇒ colander.

culminate /'kʌlmɪ‚neɪt/ *intr.v* **culminate in s.t** (*formal*) end with some final thing happening; reach the highest or most important point in s.t: *The celebrations went on all night culminating in a procession around the streets.*

culmination /‚kʌlmɪ'neɪʃən/ *c.n* act or fact of culminating in s.t: *The culmination was that he lost his job.*

culpable /'kʌlpəbl/ *adj* **1** (*law*) deserving or needing punishment (because s.t was deliberately done): *culpable murder.* **2** (*formal*) guilty; deserving blame or criticism (because of s.t one has done): *I hold him culpable for what happened.*

culpability /‚kʌlpə'bɪlɪtɪ/ *u.n.* **'culpably** *adv.*

culprit /'kʌlprɪt/ *c.n* person who has done s.t wrong, damaged s.t etc, usu s.t not very important, not a crime: *I intend to find the culprits before tonight.*

cult /kʌlt/ *c.n* **1** system of religious beliefs (often part of or separate from a larger system): *a tribal cult.* **2** people who belong to or practise a cult(1): *They are a very peculiar cult who believe the world will end in 2000 AD.* **3** person or thing who/that has become fashionable or important (for a certain time, with some people): *This kind of art is a cult among some people.* (**have**) **a cult following** (of a person, thing etc) be s.o/s.t who/that some people regard as fashionable, important etc: *His paintings have a cult following.*

'cult ‚figure *c.n* person who is (considered to be) a cult(3).

cultivate /'kʌltɪ‚veɪt/ *tr.v* **1** make (land, a field etc) ready for growing crops on: *They are trying to cultivate the waste land just outside the town.* **2** grow (a crop etc) on a piece of land, a field etc: *He's taken to cultivating vegetables at the bottom of his garden.* **3** try to win the friendship of (s.o), often so as to get some advantage for oneself: *He spends his time cultivating the boss in the hope of getting a better job.*

'culti‚vated *adj* **1** (of land etc) made ready, used, for the growing of crops. Opposite uncultivated. **2** (of plants etc) specially prepared for growing in gardens; not wild: *These flowers are of the cultivated variety.* **3** (of a person) educated, having good taste; knowing a lot about s.t: *She is very cultivated so I find her conversation very interesting.*

cultivation /‚kʌltɪ'veɪʃən/ *u.n* act or fact of cultivating(1,2) s.t or of being cultivated. **under cultivation** (of land etc) having crops etc planted or growing on it.

'culti‚vator *c.n* kind of machine with blades that break up the ground, destroy weeds etc so that things can be planted.

culture /'kʌltʃə/ *n* **1** *u.n* development and improvement of s.o (either in the mind or body): *physical*(1) *and mental*(1) *culture.* **2** *u.n* (often *of high*, *low* etc —) level of development of one's mind: *She was a woman of immense*(1) *culture.* **3** *c/u.n* (example of the) set of customs, beliefs, achievements(2) in art, science etc developed and shown by a nation, race, group etc: *French culture.* **4** *u.n* (*formal*) (careful) growing of plants; raising of some living things for what they produce: *plant culture*; *bee culture.* **5** *c/u.n* (*technical*) (example of the) growing of cells(4), bacteria etc in a laboratory for study, for use in some way etc: *The new cell culture looked as though it might show the cause of the disease.*

cultural /'kʌltʃərəl/ *adj* of or referring to (a) culture(1–3): *a cultural exchange*(1) *between the two countries* (i.e when each sends people and/or examples of their culture to the other).

'cultured *adj* (of a person) having been highly

educated; having good manners, taste etc. Opposite uncultured.

,cultured 'pearl *c.n* kind of pearl made to grow by s.o's effort and not found naturally.

'culture ,shock *c/u.n* (example of the) feeling of being different, of being out of place, etc when suddenly living in a culture(3) that is not one's own.

cumbersome /'kʌmbəsəm/ *adj* (of a thing) large, heavy, difficult to handle etc: *This piano is cumbersome; can you help me move it?*

cummerbund /'kʌmə,bʌnd/ *c.n* wide piece of cloth worn round the waist with a dinner suit.

cumulative /'kju:mjʊlətɪv/ *adj* (of s.t being done) gradually increasing in strength, effect etc: *This medicine has a cumulative effect so do not take more than the recommended* dose(1).

cunning /'kʌnɪŋ/ *adj* 1 (often *derog*) (of a person, action) very clever (often in a hidden or deceitful way): *He's a bit too cunning for his own good.* 2 able to do s.t in a clever way: *He has this cunning little* gadget *that does practically everything.* **as cunning as a fox** ⇨ fox(*n*).
▷ *u.n* 3 act or state of being cunning(1): *She showed great cunning in her handling of him.*

'cunningly *adv.* **'cunningness** *u.n.*

cunt /kʌnt/ *c.n* (*derog, slang*; do not use!) 1 female sex organs. 2 (strongest form of abuse¹(1) to or about a) woman. 3 nasty person.

cup /kʌp/ *n* 1 *c.n* small round container made of china(1) etc, open at the top and with a handle, used for drinking liquids, e.g tea, coffee, milk: *a cup and saucer; a teacup; a coffee cup.* Compare mug¹(1). 2 *c.n* (also **'cupful**) as much as a cup(1) holds: *I drank two cups of tea.* 3 *c/def.n* (often with capital **C**) ornamental vase made of silver, gold etc, often with handles, given as a prize in a competition, race etc: *win a cup for the best roses.* 4 *def.n* (often with capital **C**) competition for which a cup(3) is given: *They got to the third round of the Cup last year.* 5 *c.n* shape, or thing shaped, like a cup(1): *in the cup of one's hands; the cup of a tulip.* ⇨ egg cup. **(s.t is) not my cup of tea** (*fig; informal*) (s.t is) not s.t I like (doing) or really understand: *This modern kind of music is not really my cup of tea.*
▷ *tr.v* 6 (-pp-) make (s.t, esp one's hands) into a shape like a cup(1): *He cupped his hands in order to get a drink of water from the tap. She cupped her chin in her hands and looked at me closely.*

'cup,cake *c.n* kind of small cake baked in a shape like a cup(1).

'cup ,final *c/def.n* last match in a competition (usu of football) in which the two teams who have won the earlier matches play each other for the cup(3).

'cupful *c.n* ⇨ cup(2).

cuppa /'kʌpə/ *c.n* (*slang*) cup(2) of tea: *What you want is a nice cuppa to cheer you up!*

'cup ,tie *c.n* one of the (football) matches in a competition for a cup(3).

cupboard /'kʌbəd/ *c.n* (small or large) structure(2) made of wood etc with doors and shelves inside, used for storing things in a building: *a clothes cupboard; a kitchen cupboard.*

'cupboard ,love *u.n* (showing of) love or affection that is not sincere, but only because one wants s.t.

cupidity /kju:'pɪdɪtɪ/ *u.n* (*formal*) unpleasant desire, esp for money, possessions etc; greed.

cuppa ⇨ cup.

cur /kɜ:/ *c.n* (*derog*) 1 (savage(2) kind of) dog (usu of mixed breed(1)). 2 (*old use*) nasty and unpleasant man.

curability, curable ⇨ cure.

curate /'kjʊərɪt/ *c.n* priest in the Christian(1) church who helps (and is lower in rank than) the priest, vicar or rector(1) of a parish.

curative ⇨ cure.

curator /kjʊə'reɪtə/ *c.n* (title for a) person who is in charge of looking after precious things, e.g in a museum, library, art gallery(1) etc.

curb /kɜ:b/ *c.n* 1 leather strap(1) put around a horse's mouth or head to control it. 2 (often put/keep a — on s.t) check or control (on s.t, e.g a feeling, what one wants to say or do): *I advise you to keep a curb on your temper if you want him to like you.* 3 *c.n* (US) kerb.
▷ *tr.v* 4 check or control (a feeling, what one wants to say etc): *You should learn to curb your anger. Curb your tongue and don't speak to me like that!*

curd /kɜ:d/ *c/u.n* (often *pl*) thick creamy substance that forms from milk when it goes sour, used in the making of cheese. **curds and whey** this substance and the thin watery milk that is left. ⇨ lemon curd.

curdle /'kɜ:dl/ *tr/intr.v* (cause (milk) to) turn sour and so make curds: *The milk had curdled in the hot sun.* **make one's blood curdle** (*fig*) (of s.t terrible that happens) make one very frightened: *The account of the murders was enough to make my blood curdle.* ⇨ blood-curdling.

cure /kjʊə/ *n* 1 *c.n* (usu — for s.t) thing, e.g a medicine or a course of treatment, that gets rid of a disease: *There is still no cure for many cancers(1).* 2 *c.n* return to good health after taking medicine, a course of treatment etc: *He claimed he could effect(3) cures just by laying his hands on sufferers.* 3 *c.n* (usu — for s.t) course of action that gets rid of, reduces the effect of, s.t bad: *They claimed that the only cure for unemployment was more public spending.* **rest cure** ⇨ rest².
▷ *tr.v* 4 get rid of (a disease, illness etc): *Physiotherapy cured my back trouble.* 5 (often — s.o of s.t) bring (s.o) back to good health after a disease, illness etc: *This new* drug(1) *has cured thousands of people.* 6 get rid of, reduce the effect of, (s.t bad): *They claimed that they would cure unemployment in two years.* 7 (often — s.o of s.t) stop (s.o) from doing s.t that is a bad habit: *Who can cure me of smoking?* 8 treat (certain kinds of food, tobacco etc) by putting them/it in rooms etc full of smoke for some time (and sometimes putting salt on them/it) and so preserve them/it: *They built a special shed for curing the* bacon.

curability /,kjʊərə'bɪlɪtɪ/ *u.n* state or fact of being curable.

curable /'kjʊərəbl/ *adj* of (a disease etc) that can be cured(4). Opposite incurable.

curative /'kjʊərətɪv/ *adj* leading to, helping towards, a cure(2): *curative medicine.*

'cure-,all *c.n* (*informal*) thing considered able to cure(4) all diseases etc.

cured *adj* 1 (of a person) brought back to good health. 2 (of food, tobacco etc) preserved by smoking: *home cured* ham(2). Opposite uncured.

curfew /'kɜːfjuː/ c.n **1** (official order by a government etc stating a) length of time when ordinary people should stay indoors, usu at night, in order to prevent disturbances, e.g during a war: *A curfew has been* imposed(1) *between 8 pm and 5 am. The army has lifted* (= ended) *the curfew.* **2** (*old use*) ringing of a bell to mark the end of work in a day.

curio /'kjʊərɪˌəʊ/ c.n (pl -s) object or thing that is interesting because it is old, rare, strange etc: *He had a shop selling curios.*

curious /'kjʊərɪəs/ adj **1** (of a thing, s.t that happens etc) strange; difficult to explain or understand: *There's a curious smell in this room. Something very curious happened to me last night.* **2** (usu — about s.o/s.t; — to know/learn (s.t)) (of a person) very or too interested (about s.o/s.t); expressing a desire to find out about s.o/s.t: *The neighbours are getting a bit too curious about us. I'm curious to know why you took the job after telling me you wouldn't.*
curiosity /ˌkjʊərɪ'ɒsɪtɪ/ n (pl -ies) **1** u.n state or fact of being curious(2). **2** c.n curious(1) object, esp one that is old or rare; curious(1) event, custom etc: *One of the curiosities of life is that the more one earns the more one wants.*
'curiously adv.

curl /kɜːl/ n **1** c/u.n (example of the) natural or artificial(1) curved shape of hair: *Her hair was a mass of curls. Her hair has very little natural curl in it.* **2** c.n thing shaped like a curl(1): *a curl of smoke from a chimney.*
▷ tr/intr.v **3** (cause (s.o's hair) to) form curls(1): *I'm having my hair curled next week.* **4** intr.v (often — up) (of things) bend into a position like a curl(2): *When he put the paper on the fire it immediately curled (up) and burst into flames.* Opposite uncurl. **curl (itself) (a)round s.t** of a plant, animal etc) twist or wind (itself) (a)round s.t: *The snake curled itself round the tree.* **curl (oneself/itself) up** get (one's/its body) into a position like a curl(2) or curve, usu when sitting or lying down: *She curled (herself) up in the armchair.* ⇒ curl(4). **curl (s.o) up** (*informal*) (cause (s.o) to) become or feel almost ill or disturbed (because of s.t stupid or annoying that s.o else has said or done): *It makes me curl up to see the way she treats him.* **make s.o's hair curl** ⇒ hair.
'curler c.n round device used to make one's hair curl(3).
'curliness u.n fact or state of being curly.
'curly adj (-ier, -iest) having curls(1): *She has very curly hair.*

currant /'kʌrənt/ c.n (also attrib) **1** kind of small dried grape without seeds, used in some kinds of cakes, bread, puddings(1) etc. Compare raisin, sultana. **2** small red, black or white fruit with juice in it which grows on bushes: *We are going to pick currants on the farm next week.* ⇒ blackcurrant, redcurrant(1).
ˌcurrant 'bun c.n small bun(1) with currants(1) in it.

currency /'kʌrənsɪ/ n (pl -ies) **1** c/u.n (different kind(s) of) money, including coins and notes, used in a country or countries: *As I'm going abroad next week remind me to get some foreign currency from the bank.* ⇒ decimal currency, hard currency. **2** u.n (formal) time during which s.t

happens, is in force, is accepted etc: *Several changes in the approach to talks have taken place during the currency of this President.* **gain/lose currency** (esp of a report, rumour etc) come to be thought true/untrue; become more/less known to people: *Reports of a deal over the* strike(1) *are gaining currency.* ⇒ current(2).

current /'kʌrənt/ adj **1** of, referring to, happening at, the present time: *the current month*; *current events.* **2** (*formal*) (of a report etc) known or accepted by many people: *There's a story current at the moment that he will soon resign. This word is old-fashioned and no longer current.* ⇒ gain/lose currency.
▷ n **3** c.n flow or movement of a liquid, air, gas etc (in a certain direction): *There was a strong current in the river which made it difficult to manage the boat. She felt a current of air coming from the open window.* ⇒ undercurrent(1). **4** c/u.n supply or flow of electricity through wires to devices etc: *Switch off the current when you replace a light bulb.* ⇒ alternating current, direct current.
'current ac,count c.n (bank) account that one has for ordinary expenses and payments using cheques. Compare deposit account, savings account.
ˌcurrent af'fairs u/pl.n (study of) all the things that are happening in the public, political, social life of a country at the present time: *Current affairs was popular as a subject in schools.*
'currently adv (doing s.t) at the present time: *Currently, he's only a director but he hopes to become chairman soon.*

curriculum /kə'rɪkjʊləm/ c.n (pl -s, or less usu, curricula /kə'rɪkjʊlə/) course in one or more subjects studied at, offered by, a school, college etc: *the science curriculum. The school offers a wide curriculum to suit different abilities.*
cur,riculum 'vitae /'viːtaɪ/ c.n (abbr **CV**) (*Latin*) written statement about one's education, qualifications, jobs one has had, one's interests etc which one uses when applying for a job.

curry /'kʌrɪ/ c/u.n (pl -ies) (also attrib) **1** (example of) food prepared and cooked with (hot) spices(1) etc: *vegetable curry*; *chicken curry. I like my curries very hot.*
▷ tr.v (-ies, -ied) **2** prepare and cook (food) in this way. **3** clean, rub down and comb the coat of (a horse). **curry favour (with s.o)** (*derog*) try to gain a favour (by flattering(1) s.o): *He's always trying to curry favour with the boss by agreeing with everything he says.*
'curry ,powder u.n (hot) spices(1) that have been ground(1) together into a powder, used in making a curry(1).

curse /kɜːs/ n **1** c.n (*formal*) word or words expressing one's anger, annoyance; (act of) swearing: *He dropped the hot iron with a curse.* **2** c.n word(s) spoken or used to bring evil or harm to s.o, e.g by saying that God or other supernatural(1) forces will do s.t: *Though he didn't really believe in it, he still felt frightened by the old woman's curse.* **3** c.n person or thing who/that causes harm, annoyance: *These flies are an absolute curse. She's the curse of his life, always interfering at every opportunity.* **4** def.n (*informal*) (time of) menstruation. **under a curse** the object of a curse(2).
▷ tr/intr.v **5** (often — at s.o/s.t) (*formal*) use words

expressing anger, annoyance etc (towards s.o, because of s.t): *He cursed (and swore at) her for her stupidity.* **6** say that s.t evil or harmful will happen to (s.o): *The old woman cursed him saying that he would never have children.*
cursed /kɜːst/ *adj* **1** being under a curse: *This house is cursed.* **2** /also 'kɜːsɪd/ *(old use)* very annoying: *It's a cursed nuisance but I have to go to London tomorrow.* **be cursed with s.o/s.t** suffer from having s.o/s.t; not be able to escape from s.o/s.t: *Her problem, actually, is that she is cursed with a lazy son.*
cursory /'kɜːsərɪ/ *adj* (of a look, s.t one does, says etc) quick and not detailed or thorough: *He gave the room only a cursory* glance(1). *He made a few cursory remarks about how pleased he was to be there before going on to the main subject.*
'cursorily *adv.* **'cursoriness** *u.n.*
curt /kɜːt/ *adj* (*derog*) (of s.t said, a person) impolite or rude because one says too little, does not explain oneself etc: *His reply was very curt and offended her.*
'curtly *adv.* **'curtness** *u.n.*
curtail /kɜːˈteɪl/ *tr.v* (*formal*) cut short, reduce, (s.t, esp the length of time one wanted to spend on s.t, the power that s.o has etc): *He was forced to curtail his tour and return to London. The new law has severely curtailed the unions' power.*
cur'tailment *c/u.n* (often — *of* s.t) (example of the) act or result of curtailing s.t.
curtain /'kɜːtn/ *n* **1** *c.n* piece of cloth or other material, hanging from a rail on hooks, which can be pulled across a window or windows. **2** *c.n* piece of cloth or other material (often one of two) in front of a stage in a theatre or cinema which either goes up and down, or moves sideways, (at the beginning or end of a play, film): *When the curtain came down at the end, the whole audience applauded.* ⇨ safety curtain. **3** *c.n* (*fig*) thing like a curtain(1) that gets in the way, prevents s.o seeing s.t etc: *a curtain of fog.*
▷ *tr.v* **4** make or provide curtains(1) for (a room etc): *When we move into the new house we shall have to curtain the bedroom first.* **curtain s.t off** provide curtains(1) so as to separate a part of a room (esp to hide s.t): *There were no cupboards in the room so the shelves for their clothes were curtained off.* **draw the curtain(s)** pull the curtain(s)(1) in a room, either opening or closing them. **ring down the curtain (on s.t) (a)** lower the curtain(2) in a theatre (after a performance). **(b)** (*fig*) bring an end to (a period of activity, discussion etc).
'curtains *pl.n* **be curtains (for s.o)** (*slang*) be the complete end of s.t, sometimes actual death, (for s.o): *It'll be curtains (for him) if he goes on like that.*
curtly, curtness ⇨ curt.
curtsy, curtsey /'kɜːtsɪ/ *c.n* (*pl* -ies, -eys) **1** (often *make a* — (*to* s.o)) (of a woman or girl) act of bending one's knee(s) (and crossing one's feet) as a sign of respect, esp to a king or queen: *The small girl made a curtsy (to the queen) and gave her a bunch of flowers.*
▷ *intr.v* (-ies, -ied; -eys, -eyed) **2** (often — *to* s.o) make a curtsy(1) (to s.o).
curve /kɜːv/ *c.n* **1** line that is not straight at any point but bends round smoothly like part of a circle. **2** thing shaped like this: *a curve in the road; the curves of her body.*

▷ *tr/intr.v* **3** (cause (s.t) to) have a curve: *At this point the road curves to go round the hill.*
curvature /'kɜːvətʃə/ *u.n* (usu — *of* s.t) (*formal*) state of having a curve or being curved in some way: *He suffers from permanent curvature of the spine(1). The curvature of the earth's surface can really only be seen clearly from space.*
curved *adj* having a curve: *a curved road.*
cushion /'kʊʃən/ *c.n* **1** kind of bag filled with soft material, e.g feathers, foam rubber, on which one can sit or lie comfortably or against which one can rest one's back, head etc. **2** thing that is soft or that supports s.t: *a cushion of air.* **3** soft lining on the inside edges of a billiard, snooker(1) or pool³ table against which balls can be hit. **4** (often — *against* s.t) (*fig*) protection (against s.t bad happening in the future): *The money he had saved would act as a cushion against rising prices.*
▷ *tr.v* **5** reduce the force of (s.t, esp a fall, blow etc): *The soft ground cushioned his fall.* **cushion s.o against s.t** (often passive) (*fig*) reduce the effect of s.t bad for s.o; act as a cushion(4) against s.t: *At least our money cushions us against the worst effects of the increase in taxes.* **cushion the blow (a)** = cushion(5). **(b)** (*fig*) reduce the effect of s.t bad: *A large* redundancy *payment cushioned the blow when he lost his job.*
cushy /'kʊʃɪ/ *adj* (-ier, -iest) (*informal*) (of a job, way of living etc) very easy, not demanding much effort: *He has a very cushy life and never gets up before 10 o'clock.* ⇨ jammy.
'cushily *adv.* **'cushiness** *u.n.*
custard /'kʌstəd/ *c/u.n* (also *attrib*) kind of sweet yellow sauce made by cooking a mixture of eggs (or custard-powder), milk and sugar together, usu eaten with fruit, puddings(1) etc.
'custard-,powder *u.n* cornflour with a flavouring, e.g vanilla(2), that is mixed with milk etc to make custard.
custody /'kʌstədɪ/ *u.n* (*formal; law*) **1** (often *be given, have,* — (*to* s.o/s.t)) right or duty to look after or care for (s.o/s.t): *The mother was given custody of the children.* **2** (often *be in* —; *take s.o into* —) guarding in a prison or other place controlled by the police while waiting for a trial etc: *He was taken into custody by the police during their inquiries.* **remand s.o in custody** ⇨ remand(*v*).
custodian /kʌˈstəʊdɪən/ *c.n* (often — *of* s.t) (*formal*) person appointed to look after s.t: *the custodian of a museum.*
custom /'kʌstəm/ *n* **1** *u.n* usual or accepted way of behaving in a social group: *It is a matter of custom to take off one's hat inside a house if one is a man.* **2** *c.n* one of the number of things that a social group, people of a country etc, do regularly as part of a way of living: *It is a custom in that country to feed the children first.* **3** *u.n* (*formal*) regular buying of goods etc from one shop by certain customers: *He gradually lost most of his custom to the bigger and more modern shops.*
customarily /'kʌstəmərɪlɪ/ *adj* (*formal*) usually, habitually.
customary /'kʌstəmərɪ/ *adj* (*formal*) done regularly; usual and done according to (a) custom(1,2): *It is customary here to give people a present when they leave a job.*

,**custom-**'**built** adj built or constructed according to what a customer wants, not ready-made: *custom-built furniture.* ⇨ custom-made.

customer /'kʌstəmə/ c.n person who buys goods, services etc from a shop, business etc: *The customer is always right.*

,**custom-**'**made** adj (usu of things made by hand) made according to what a customer wants, not ready-made: *a custom-made suit.* ⇨ custom-built.

'**customs** pl.n 1 (also '**customs** ,**duty**) tax one has to pay on certain goods when they come into a country. 2 (with capital **C**; also ,**Customs and** '**Excise**) government department that collects this tax. 3 (with capital **C**) place at a seaport, airport, on a road that crosses a border etc, where officers of the Customs(2) inspect(1) goods coming into a country. **go through customs** be allowed to enter a country (sometimes after having one's suitcase(s), goods etc checked by customs(2)).

'**customs** ,**duty** u.n ⇨ customs(1).

cut /kʌt/ c.n 1 result of making an opening in s.t, of dividing s.t, of breaking the surface of s.t, e.g skin, usu with s.t sharp: *He made a small cut in the material with his scissors. Paul got a cut on his thumb when slicing the vegetables.* 2 piece of s.t sliced or taken from a larger piece: *a choice cut of meat.* ⇨ undercut¹. 3 act of reducing or shortening the length of s.t with s.t sharp: *He gave the grass a good cut. Your hair needs a cut.* ⇨ haircut. 4 (often — *in* s.t) act of taking out or taking away a part of s.t, esp in a film, book etc (in order to shorten it, not to offend people etc): *They had to make several cuts in the film before it could be shown.* 5 (often — *in* s.t) reduction (in the size, quality etc of s.t, and esp in the amount of money one can have, spend etc): *a cut in salary; cuts in the health service.* ⇨ power cut. 6 (*informal*) share of money, profits etc one asks for or is given for having done s.t: *As we made £10 000 profit and my cut is 25%, you owe me £2500.* 7 act of dividing a pack of playing cards into two piles at the beginning of a game before they are dealt(4) etc.

(**be**) **a cut above s.o** (of a person) (be) higher in social standing, ability etc than s.o else or other people: *She's a cut above the ordinary type of student we get.* **cut and thrust** (**of s.t**) strong fierce competition (of business, companies etc): *He enjoyed the cut and thrust of big business.*

▷ v (-*tt-*, *p.t,p.p* cut) 8 tr.v make a cut(1) in (s.t): *He cut the material in two. He cut his thumb.* 9 tr.v (often — s.t *in* s.t) make (an opening, space etc) (in s.t) by using s.t sharp: *He cut a hole in the material.* 10 tr.v divide (s.t) into pieces or slices with a knife etc: *Will you cut the meat, please?* 11 intr.v (of a sharp instrument) be able to cut(8–10) things: *These scissors don't cut at all, they need sharpening.* 12 intr.v (of a substance etc) be able to be cut(8–10): *This wood is wet and won't cut easily.* 13 tr.v reduce or shorten (s.t) with s.t sharp: *He cut the grass. He had his hair cut.* 14 tr.v make a cut(4) in (a film, book etc): *They had to cut several passages from the book because of the bad language.* 15 intr.v (usu a command by a director) (say that the shooting of a film should) stop immediately (because the scene is completed, s.o has done s.t wrong etc):

When the actor moved at the wrong time, the producer shouted 'Cut!'. 16 tr.v make a cut(5) in (the size, quantity, amount of money one can have, spend etc): *The airline has cut the number of its flights to America. The government has announced* plans to cut public expenditure(1). 17 tr/intr.v (cause (a pack of playing cards) to) be divided into two piles before they are dealt(4) etc: *It's your turn to cut.* ⇨ cut for partners/trumps. 18 tr.v (*geometry*) (of a line etc) meet and cross (s.t): *The line DE cuts the line BC at an angle of 45°.* 19 tr/intr.v (cause (s.t, e.g an engine) to) stop working: *I was driving along when the engine cut for no reason that I could think of.* 20 tr.v (*informal*) not go to (s.t, e.g a class, meeting) that one should go to: *He started cutting lectures and spending his time playing football.* 21 tr.v (often — s.o *dead*) (*informal*) purposely and rudely not recognize the presence of, speak to, (s.o): ignore (her/him): *After their row, every time she saw him in the street she cut him (dead).* 22 tr.v (often — s.t *out*) (*informal*) (ask s.o to) stop doing (s.t that is getting no result) (and then get on with s.t more important): *OK, let's cut (out) all this polite chat(1) and get down to the real business.*

cut across s.t (**a**) be in, move in, a direction that goes across s.t: *The path cut across the field. He cut across the field to save time.* ⇨ short cut. (**b**) (*fig*) (of a new idea, grouping of people etc) be different from what has happened before (and sometimes unite people in some way): *His proposals are an attempt to cut across the usual political divisions on the subject.*

cut and run (*informal*) stop doing s.t and escape quickly: *When they heard the police coming they decided to cut and run.*

cut back (**on s.t**) reduce the production, quantity etc (of s.t) esp in order to save money, because people are not buying etc: *We have cut back on car production because of falling sales.* ⇨ cutback. **cut s.t back** (shoots, growths on a plant etc) to a point near the ground, e.g to improve growth next year.

cut both/two ways (of s.t said, a proposal, argument etc) be able to be applied to both sides, to favour one side or the other, depending on one's point of view.

cut a corner; cut corners ⇨ corner (n).

cut a dash/figure (*old use*) have a smart appearance, clothes etc and so get noticed. ⇨ figure.

cut s.o dead ⇨ cut(21).

cut a disc, record etc (*informal*) make a recording of music etc: *The group has just cut a new track.*

cut down (**on s.t**) reduce the amount (of s.t one eats, drinks, smokes, spends etc): *You're smoking far too much; can't you cut down or stop altogether?* **cut s.o down** knock s.o down to the ground (and sometimes kill her/him) with a bullet from a gun etc: *Fire from the hidden guns cut them down as they charged.* **cut s.t down** make s.t fall to the ground by cutting it: *They cut the tree down to get a better view.* **cut s.o down to size** ⇨ size¹ (n).

cut it/s.t fine ⇨ fine (adv).

cut for partners/trumps divide a pack of cards into a group or groups to decide who should play with whom (i.e by the value of the card(s)), what trumps(1) should be (i.e by turning up the card that is at the top of one of the groups etc).

cut oneself/s.o/s.t free/loose (from s.t) free (oneself etc) (from s.t one is tied to) by cutting with s.t sharp.

cut the ground from under s.o's feet ⇨ ground³ (*n*).

cut in (front of s.o/s.t; on s.o/s.t) move in a direction that goes in front of s.o/s.t moving in the same direction: *The car passed me and then suddenly cut in on me.* **cut in (on s.t) (with s.t)** interrupt (a conversation) (with a remark of one's own): *Do you mind not cutting in on our conversation with your stupid remarks?* **cut s.o in (on s.t)** (*informal*) allow s.o to have a cut (of s.t): *If you promise not to say a word to anyone, I'll cut you in on the deal.* **cut s.t in s.t** ⇨ cut (9).

cut into s.t (a) make a cut (1,2) in s.t: *She cut into the cake and made a birthday wish.* **(b)** reduce the amount, value etc of s.t: *The hospital expenses were cutting into his savings.*

cut no ice (with s.o) ⇨ ice (*n*).

cut one's losses ⇨ loss.

cut (oneself) off (from s.o) (often passive) not be or feel part of a group, have few friends etc: *I feel very cut off from the rest of the world in this small village.* **cut s.o off (a)** break or interrupt a telephone conversation between two people: *I'm sorry we got cut off; what were you saying before?* **(b)** stop supplying s.t to s.o: *We've been cut off because we didn't pay our electricity bill.* **cut s.o/s.t off (from s.o/s.t)** make s.o/s.t become separated (from the main group of people, the main part of s.t): *The village was cut off from the rest of the country by the snow.* **cut s.t off ((from) s.t) (a)** cut (10) a piece or slice from s.t with s.t sharp: *He cut a branch off (the tree) with a saw.* **(b)** stop the supply of s.t (from s.w): *The water has been cut off from the mains because of the burst pipe.* **cut s.o off (without a penny)** not give any money or possessions to s.o (usu a close relative) in one's will² (1).

cut s.t open (with s.t) (a) open s.t (using s.t sharp): *He cut the packet open with a knife.* **(b)** cause a cut (1) in s.t, usu accidentally: *He cut his leg open when he fell off the wall.*

cut out (of an engine, machine etc) stop working; cut (19) (sometimes because there is a device (⇨ cutout) to do this for reasons of safety): *When the temperature gets too high, the motor will cut out automatically.* **cut it, that (s.t), out** (usu a command) (*informal*) stop doing s.t annoying etc: *Come on, cut it (or that noise) out!* ⇨ cut (22). **cut s.t out (from/of s.t)** take s.t (from s.t) by using s.t sharp: *She cut the picture out of the newspaper. She cut out a dress from the piece of material.* **(not) cut out for, to do, s.t** (usu negative) (not) good enough to do s.t or suited to doing (s.t): *I'm really not cut out for this kind of job (or to be a teacher).* **have one's work cut out (for one)** ⇨ work (*n*).

cut s.o/s.t short ⇨ short (*adv*).

cut one's teeth; cut one's teeth on s.t ⇨ tooth.

cut through s.t (a) move or make a passage through s.t in one's way by cutting etc: *They cut a road through the forest.* **(b)** move in a direction through s.t, e.g as the shortest way: *He cut through the traffic at high speed.* **(c)** (*fig*) get rid of s.t that is in one's way (in order to get to the main point etc): *We need to cut through all this red tape if we are to get anything done.*

cut to pieces/ribbons (*fig*) (of an army etc) completely defeated: *The whole army was cut to ribbons by the enemy's fire.*

cut s.o to the quick (*formal*) (of s.t s.o says etc) hurt or injure s.o's feelings very much: *His criticism of her cut her to the quick.*

cut up (passive) (*informal*) very disturbed, very worried, (by s.t bad that has happened): *He was very cut up when his wife died.* **cut s.t up** cut (10) s.t into (smaller) pieces etc (to make it more usable etc): *Can you cut up that meat so the baby can eat it? They cut the wood up for the fire.* **cut up rough** ⇨ rough (*adv*).

ˌcut-and-ˈdried *adj* (of an opinion, argument etc) already decided and fixed and not likely to be changed by s.o: *You won't be able to persuade him as he'll stick to his cut-and-dried ideas.*

ˈcutˌback *c.n* reduction in the amount, quality, money that can be spent etc. ⇨ cut back (on s.t), cut s.t back (b).

ˌcut ˈglass *u.n* glass objects (e.g glasses, bowls, dishes etc) that are not smooth but have different angles or facets (1) in them where they have been cut ornamentally.

cutlet /ˈkʌtlɪt/ *c.n* small piece of meat, usu including a bone, ready for cooking and eating: *lamb (2) cutlets.*

ˈcut-ˌoff ˌpoint *c.n* (point at which there is a) division or change from one thing or state to another: *There is a cut-off point at this level of income; above it you start paying more tax.*

ˈcutˌout *c.n* device for the stopping of a machine, engine etc: *This cutout works when the temperature reaches 250°.*

ˌcut-ˈprice, ˌcut-ˈrate *adj* offered or sold at less than the normal price or rate.

ˈcutter *c.n* **1** person or thing who/that cuts s.t: *He's a tailor's cutter. Use this glass cutter.* **2** kind of small sailing ship.

ˈcutters *pl.n* = wirecutters.

ˈcut-ˌthroat *adj* (usu *attrib*) (*informal*) (of competition, business etc) very fierce: *This is a cut-throat business and only the fittest and strongest win.*

ˈcutting *adj* **1** (*derog*) (of a person, remark etc) rude, unpleasant: *He was very cutting about her.* **2** (of the wind) blowing very hard and coldly. ▷ *c.n* **3** article, picture etc cut out from a newspaper, magazine etc: *She had an album of cuttings about her days as an actress.* **4** piece (usu a stem) cut from a growing plant and used to make another plant when it is put in the earth. **5** deep cut (1) made through a hill (and open at the top) for a railway line etc.

cute /kjuːt/ *adj* **1** (mainly US) (usu of children or women) pretty and attractive; sweet (6): *What a cute little girl you have!* **2** (often *derog*) (of a person, an action etc, thought to be) (too) clever or cunning (1): *That was a cute little trick you played on him. I think she's too cute for her own good.*

ˈcutely *adv*. **ˈcuteness** *u.n*.

cuticle /ˈkjuːtɪkl/ *c.n* hard dead skin on the inner edge of a fingernail or toenail.

cutlass /ˈkʌtləs/ *c.n* kind of wide sword with a curved blade.

cutlery /ˈkʌtlərɪ/ *u.n* knives, forks and spoons.

cutlet, cut-off, cutout, cut-price, cut-rate, cutter, cut-throat, cutting ⇨ cut.

CV /ˌsiː ˈviː/ *abbr* curriculum vitae.

cwt *written abbr* hundredweight.

cyan /'saɪæn/ *u.n* (also *attrib*) strong green-blue colour; it is one of the three main colours used in printing. ⇨ magenta, yellow.

cyanide /'saɪəˌnaɪd/ *u.n* kind of very strong poison.

cybernetics /ˌsaɪbə'netɪks/ *u.n* science concerned with the way the human brain and some kinds of machines work and communicate(1).

cycle /'saɪkl/ *c.n* **1** number of things, events etc that happen regularly one after another and are then repeated: *Life followed its usual cycle: birth, youth, old age and death.* ⇨ life-cycle. **2** (*technical*) one of a regular number of completed pulses¹(2) in a form of energy such as radio waves, electrical current etc: *This device operates at 75 cycles per second* (*abbr* cps). ⇨ hertz. **3** complete group of poems, plays, musical pieces etc that are connected in some way: *a song cycle.* **4** (also *attrib*) bicycle: *a cycle path/shop.*
▷ *intr.v* **5** (usu — *to s.w*) ride, use, a bicycle (to go s.w): *Many people now cycle to work to save money and keep healthy.*

cyclic /'saɪklɪk, 'sɪklɪk/ *adj* (also '**cyclical**) (*formal*; *technical*) **1** happening in cycles(1). **2** (moving) in a circular way: *the cyclical movement of a* planet.
'**cyclically** *adv.*

'**cycling** *u.n* act of riding, using, a bicycle: *Cycling is good for your health.* **go cycling** go for a ride on a bicycle: *I'm going cycling this weekend if the weather is good.*

'**cyclist** *c.n* person who rides or is riding a bicycle: *You should watch out for cyclists when driving your car.*

cyclone /'saɪkloʊn/ *c.n* **1** very fierce and violent wind that moves in a circle around a centre where there is no wind. Compare hurricane, typhoon. **2** area where air pressure is low, often producing rain. Opposite anticyclone.

cyclonic /saɪ'klɒnɪk/ *adj* of or referring to a cyclone; having a force or strength like a cyclone(1): *The storm hit the house with almost cyclonic force.*

cygnet /'sɪgnɪt/ *c.n* young swan(1).

cylinder /'sɪlɪndə/ *c.n* **1** (*geometry*) long solid or hollow shape that is round throughout(4) its length and has straight sides. **2** (also *attrib*) hollow tube, usu made of metal, in an engine (e.g of a car) or similar device in which a piston moves up and down and so makes s.t move, happen etc: *a four-cylinder engine; brake cylinders.* **3** strong metal container, shaped like a cylinder(1), used to hold gas etc.

cylindrical /sɪ'lɪndrɪkl/ *adj* having the shape of a cylinder(1).

cymbal /'sɪmbl/ *c.n* one of two round brass objects shaped like large plates, used as a musical instrument by hitting them together to make a loud clashing(6) or clanging(2) sound.

cynic /'sɪnɪk/ *c.n* (usu *derog*) person who believes or thinks that most people and things are bad and will not get better, and who shows this in the way he/she treats people, life etc: *Peter's a real cynic and so he never has a kind word to say about anybody or anything.*

cynical /'sɪnɪkl/ *adj* **1** (usu *derog*) (often — *about s.o/s.t*) being or acting like a cynic: *He's so cynical about her chances of success that it's no*
wonder she feels discouraged(1). **2** (of a remark, action etc) said, done etc in a very unpleasant and harmful way (and without caring for the opinions of others): *The arrest of these people shows the government's cynical* disregard(1) *of public opinion.*
'**cynically** *adv.* **cynicism** /'sɪnɪˌsɪzəm/ *u.n.*

cypher ⇨ cipher.

cypress /'saɪprəs/ *n* (also *attrib*) **1** kind of tree like a pine¹(1) with dark green leaves and hard wood: *cypress forests.* **2** *u.n* wood from this tree.

cyst /sɪst/ *c.n* growth inside one's body or under the skin that is filled with liquid.

czar, czarina ⇨ tsar, tsarina.

Dd

D, d /diː/ *c/unique n* **1** 4th letter of the English alphabet.
▷ *written abbr* **2** date¹(1,2). **3** died. **4** (**D**) Director. **5** (**D**) Duchess; Duke.
▷ *symb* **6** (**d**)(UK) penny (before 1971). ⇨ p(8). **7** (**D**) Roman numeral for 500.

'd /d/ **1** = had: *He'd left before I got there.* **2** = would: *I'd write a letter if I were you. She'd have done it if you had asked her.*

dab¹ /dæb/ *adj* **a dab hand at** (**doing**) **s.t** (*informal*) a person who is very good (at (making/ doing) s.t): *He's a dab hand at making his own clothes.*

dab² /dæb/ *c.n* **1** soft gentle touch on the surface of s.t: *She gave the wound a few dabs with wet cotton wool.* **2** small quantity (of s.t): *She put a dab of cream onto each slice of cake.*
▷ *tr/intr.v* (-bb-) **3** touch (s.t) gently or lightly with small dabs(1): *The child cried as his mother dabbed his cut.*

dabble /'dæbl/ *v* **1** *tr/intr.v* (often — (s.t) *in s.t*) put (one's hands, feet etc) in water etc in a gentle way: *The children were dabbling* (*their toes*) *in the stream.* **2** *intr.v* (usu — *in s.t*) (*fig*; often *derog*) do s.t regularly but not in a very serious way: *He dabbles in painting but he's not very good at it.*
'**dabbler** *c.n* (sometimes *derog*) person who dabbles(2).

dachshund /'dækshʊnd/ *c.n* kind of small dog with a long body and very short legs.

dad /dæd/ *c/unique n* (also '**daddy**) (person's name for her/his) father: *Dad, can you lend me £57?* Compare mum¹, mummy¹.

daddy /'dædɪ/ *c.n* (*pl* -ies) ⇨ dad.
,**daddy-'long-,legs** *c.n* (child's name for a) kind of flying insect with long legs; crane-fly.

daffodil /'dæfədɪl/ *n* **1** *c.n* kind of plant that grows from a bulb(1), with long green leaves and a (usu yellow) flower in spring. **2** *u.n* (also *attrib*) yellow colour: *daffodil paint.*

daft /dɑːft/ *adj* (*derog*; *informal*) (of a person, idea etc) silly, stupid: *Don't be so daft! No one could write a dictionary in three weeks!* **'daftly** *adv.* **'daftness** *u.n.*

dagger /'dægə/ *c.n* kind of short knife with two sharp edges. **cloak-and-dagger** ⇨ cloak.

dahlia /'deɪlɪə/ *c.n* kind of plant with large flowers of various colours.

daily ⇨ day.

dainty /'deɪntɪ/ *adj* (*-ier, -iest*) **1** (of a person, thing etc) small, pretty and delicate; that looks as if he/she/it might easily be broken: *a dainty dancer; dainty cups and saucers.* ▷ *c.n* (*pl -ies*) **2** (*usu pl*) (*formal*) special, interesting, thing to eat: *What kinds of dainties can we make for the party?* **'daintily** *adv* in a delicate careful way: *She picked her cup up daintily.* **'daintiness** *u.n.*

dairy /'deərɪ/ *c.n* (*pl -ies*) **1** place, building, often on a farm, where milk is kept and products from it such as butter and cheese are made. **2** shop that sells milk, butter, cream and other products made from these, e.g cheese. **'dairy ,farm** *c.n* farm that has cows for their milk (and not for their meat). **'dairy,maid/man** *c.n* (*pl -,maids, -men*) woman/man who works on a dairy farm. Compare milkmaid, milkman.

dais /'deɪɪs/ *c.n* (*usu sing*) raised platform(1), usu in a hall or at a ceremony, from which speakers can talk to an audience.

daisy /'deɪzɪ/ *c.n* (*pl -ies*) kind of plant with small white flowers with a yellow centre that often grows wild in grass. (**feel**) **fresh as a daisy** ⇨ fresh. **push up the daisies** be dead and buried.

dal /dɑːl/ ⇨ dhal.

dale /deɪl/ *c.n* (with capital **D** in names) (name for a) valley, esp one found in northern England: *the Yorkshire Dales.*

dally /'dælɪ/ *intr.v* (*-ies, -ied*) (*old use*) **1** (often — *about/over s.t*) be slow or lazy (about doing s.t): *Stop dallying (about) or we'll miss our train.* **2** (often — *with s.t*) do, think about, s.t idly and without much effort: *I'm dallying with the idea of going abroad for a few months.* ⇨ dilly-dally.

dam¹ /dæm/ *c.n* **1** bank of earth, concrete(4) etc, built to contain water from a river etc, esp for irrigation or for a hydroelectric power station: *This whole valley will be flooded when the new dam is built.* **2** water contained in a dam(1): *Let's have a picnic by the dam.* ▷ *tr.v* (*-mm-*) **3** (often — *s.t up*) make or build a dam on or across (a river etc): *They dammed (up) the river to prevent further flooding.* **4** (often — *s.t up*) (*formal*) (of a person) control (one's feelings etc): *She managed to dam up her anger until she got home.*

dam² /dæm/ *c.n* mother of an animal, usu a horse. ⇨ sire(1).

damage /'dæmɪdʒ/ *u.n* **1** harm or destruction done to s.o/s.t: *The fire caused a lot of damage.* ⇨ damages. **2** (*informal; joking*) amount of money s.t costs: *Let's have a good lunch and I'll pay the damage.* ▷ *tr.v* **3** spoil, cause damage(1) to, (s.o/s.t): *The back of the car was damaged in the crash. The long war has damaged the country's trade.* **'damages** *pl.n* (*law*) money for some loss,

harm etc caused by s.o: *The judge awarded(4) her £3000 damages.*

dame /deɪm/ *c.n* **1** (usu with capital **D**) title given to a woman who has been awarded a high rank of the Order of the British Empire: *Dame Janet Vaughan.* Compare knight(3). **2** (US *slang*) woman.

damn /dæm/ *attrib.adj* **1** (also **damned**) (*informal*) (used to give extra emphasis(1) to a noun) great: *It's a damn shame you didn't get the job.* ▷ *adv* **2** (also **damned**) (*informal*) (used to give extra emphasis(1) to what follows, usu an adj/adv) very: *Don't be so damned stupid! You'll have to run damn quickly if you want to catch him.* **damn well** (*informal*) (used to give extra emphasis(1) to the verb) certainly; clearly: *You know damn well I didn't agree to that. He'd damn well better be on time tonight or I'm leaving without him.* ▷ *interj* **3** (*informal*) (often — *her, him, it* etc) (expression used to show (great) annoyance, esp about s.t one/s.o has (not) done): *Damn! I've left my keys in the car. Damn you/it!* ▷ *c.n* **4** (only in the following phrases) thing that is not important or has no value. **not care/give a damn** (*informal*) not be at all concerned or bothered: *I don't give a damn whether you stay or leave.* **not worth a damn** (*informal*) not worth anything: *He knows nothing about the subject so his opinions are not worth a damn.* ▷ *tr.v* **5** criticize (s.o/s.t) as being very bad: *All the reviews damned the new play.* **6** (of s.t s.o says or does) cause (s.o/s.t) to be criticized, condemned(1): *His first remarks damned him in the eyes of his audience.* **7** (*religion; formal*) (of God) condemn(3) (s.o, her/his soul) to hell(1).

damnable /'dæmnəbl/ *adj* (*formal*) **1** that deserves to be criticized, condemned(1): *damnable behaviour.* **2** (very) bad: *What a damnable situation!*

damnation /dæm'neɪʃən/ *interj* **1** = damn(3): *Damnation! I've lost my keys.* ▷ *u.n* (*formal*) **2** fact or state of damning(7) s.o or of being damned: *suffer eternal(1) damnation.*

damned /dæmd/ *adj/adv* **1** = damn(1,2). **be damned if I, you** etc **do s.t** etc (*informal*) I, you etc most certainly will not do s.t etc: *I'll be damned if I listen to any more of this nonsense!* ▷ *def.pl.n* **2** (all the) people or souls who have been damned(7).

damnedest /'dæmdɪst/ *u.n* **do/try one's damnedest (to do s.t)** (*informal*) do/try the very best one can (to do s.t): *I promise to do my damnedest to leave the meeting early.*

damp /dæmp/ *adj* **1** slightly wet; having some moisture (in/on it) (e.g from the air): *Don't wear damp socks.* ▷ *def/u.n* **2** fact or state of being damp(1): *There were signs of damp on the walls. You'll get ill if you sit in the damp like that.* ▷ *tr.v* **3** make (s.t) damp(1) for a purpose: *Some clothes iron better if you damp them first.* **4** make (s.o's interest etc) become less strong: *It takes a lot to damp her spirits.* **damp s.t down** (**a**) = damp(4) s.t. (**b**) make a fire burn less strongly, e.g by letting less air into it or by putting s.t that burns more slowly on it. **'dampen** *tr.v* (usu — *s.t down*) = damp(3,4). **'damper** *c.n* **1** device that controls the heat or temperature of a wood stove by the amount of air that is allowed through to the fire. **2** (usu *cast/ put a — on s.t*) (*fig*) action etc that reduces one's interest or enjoyment: *His puzzling behaviour cast a damper on the evening.*

'**dampish** *adj* a little damp(1): *It's still dampish so you can't wear it.*

'**damp,course** *c.n* (also '**damp-,proof ,course**) line of material, e.g slate¹(1), placed in a wall near the ground to prevent damp(2) rising and damaging the wall.

'**dampness** *u.n.*

'**damp-,proof** *adj* (of material) **1** that does not allow damp(2) to pass through.

▷ *tr.v* **2** lay a line of material in (a wall) to prevent damp(2) from rising and damaging it.

damsel /'dæmzl/ *c.n* (*old use*; *literary*) young, usu unmarried, woman.

damson /'dæmzn/ *n* (also *attrib*) **1** *c.n* (kind of tree that bears) small purple fruit of the plum¹(2) family: *Is that a damson (tree)?* **2** *u.n* dark purple colour.

dance /dɑːns/ *n* **1** *c/u.n* (also *attrib*) (example of the art of) moving one's feet and body in a particular way that suits a certain kind of music, often with a partner: *Do you know how to do that new dance? May I have the next dance with you? I've got a new dance partner.* **2** (also *attrib*) party mainly for dancing(3): *Have you decided what you're wearing to the dance tomorrow night? The meeting is in the dance hall.*

· ▷ *v* **3** *tr/intr.v* perform a dance(1): move to suit the beat of the music of (a particular kind of dance(1)): *Can you dance the 'twist'? 'Shall we dance?'* **4** *intr.v* (usu — *about*; — *around s.t/s.o*) move around a place quickly: *He danced around the room trying to tidy it before his guests arrived.* **5** *intr.v* (*fig*) (of an object) move in a way that is like a dance(1): *The leaves on the trees were dancing in the breeze.*

'**dancer** *c.n* person who is skilled in (a particular kind of) dancing: *He's a dancer with the Royal Ballet Company.*

'**dancing** *u.n* (also *attrib* and in combinations) act, art, of dancing(3): *You can't go dancing in those shoes. He's very good at dancing. She spent many years learning ballet(1) dancing. Where are your dancing shoes?*

dandelion /'dændɪ,laɪən/ *c.n* (also *attrib*) kind of wild plant with yellow flowers: *dandelion wine.*

dandruff /'dæn,drʌf/ *u.n* (also *attrib*) small pieces of dry skin that come off one's head under the hair: *Use a dandruff shampoo(1).*

danger /'deɪndʒə/ **1** *c.n* person, thing, situation etc who/that causes, or is likely to cause, harm or injury (to s.o/s.t): *They faced many dangers in their travels. Peter Smith is a danger to society and should be locked up.* **2** *u.n* (warning of the) fact or state of being likely to cause harm or injury to s.o./ s.t: *Danger! Road under repair. He is a man who likes danger and loves driving fast cars.* **in danger (of (doing) s.t)** in a situation where there is danger(2) (of s.t happening, s.o doing s.t etc): *Having lost all his food and warm clothes he knew he was in great danger. Tom is in danger of losing his job if he continues to come late.* **be little**, **no danger of (s.o doing) s.t** (s.o is) unlikely (to do s.t); s.t is unlikely (to happen): *There is very little danger of him trying to stop you now. There's no*

danger of that so don't worry. **out of danger** no longer in a situation of danger(2): *We'll be out of danger if we can cross that river. The doctors say she is now out of danger following the successful operation.*

'**dangerous** *adj* who/that causes, is likely to cause, danger(1): *a dangerous man*; *dangerous weather conditions for being on the sea. The roads are dangerous so drive carefully.*

'**dangerously** *adv* in a way that is likely to cause harm, difficulty: *Don't drive so dangerously. He came dangerously close to losing.*

'**danger ,zone** *c.n* place in which it is dangerous to be.

dangle /'dæŋgl/ *tr/intr.v* (cause (s.t) to) hang and swing about loosely or gently: *The children sat on the bridge dangling their feet in the water.* **dangle s.t before**, **in front of**, **s.o** (*fig*) offer s.o a future opportunity that one hopes will attract her/him: *His boss dangled in front of him the chance of more travelling and a bigger salary.*

dank /dæŋk/ *adj* (*derog*) (of a place, house etc) unpleasant because of being wet and lacking fresh air and light: *The empty house had a dank smell.*

'**dankness** *u.n.*

dapper /'dæpə/ *adj* (often *derog*) (of a person) (too) neat and tidy and well dressed: *He looked very dapper in his smart new suit.*

dappled /'dæpld/ *adj* **1** (of a horse) that is (usu) grey in colour with darker spots. **2** (*literary*) (of light and shade) with some parts lighter and other parts darker, e.g from the rays of the sun coming through trees, leaves etc in a wood: *They rested in a forest clearing dappled with sunlight.*

dare /deə/ *c.n* **1** risk; challenge(1). **do s.t for a dare** do s.t because s.o has dared(2) one to do it or because one likes the risk or challenge(3): *He climbed to the top of the tree for a dare.*

▷ *aux.v* (*3rd pers pres.t* dare; negative dare not or daren't /'deənt/) (often — *do s.t*) have the courage (to do s.t): *I daren't be late again. How dare you criticize me when you are just as much to blame! Dare we take another chocolate?*

▷ *v* **3** *tr.v* (often — *s.o to do s.t*) try to persuade or challenge(4) (s.o to do s.t), esp in a way that suggests he/she is a coward if he/she does not do it: *Go on! I dare you to ask her. I had to do it; she dared me!* **4** *intr.v* (often — *to do s.t*) be courageous enough (to do s.t): *He didn't dare to say what he thought.* **5** *tr.v* (*formal*) be ready to risk (s.t): *Will you dare his temper and ask permission to leave?* **I dare say**, **daresay**, **(that . . .)** I suppose (so or that. . .); I agree (that . . .): *I dare say (that) you may be right. 'She was right, wasn't she?' 'Oh, I daresay, but she needn't have gone on talking about it.'*

'**dare-,devil** *c.n* person who likes to take risks or do dangerous things.

'**daring** *adj* **1** (of a person, act etc) bold or risky: *a daring robbery/escape/rescue. That was a daring thing to do. That was daring of you.*

▷ *u.n* **2** boldness in doing s.t: *deeds of daring.*

'**daringly** *adv.*

dark /dɑːk/ *adj* **1** that has little or no natural or artificial light: *It was a dark night. The room was dark and I could hardly see anything. It's getting dark; I must get home.* **2** (of a colour; sometimes as the first part of a word) that seems to have more black than white in it: *dark green/red*; *dark-blue paint*. Opposite light¹(2). **3** (of skin, hair etc) (of a colour) nearer to brown or black than white or yellow; not fair or light: *dark (brown) hair*; *a dark complexion*(1). **4** (*formal*) (of s.t done etc) bad or evil: *These are dark days*. **keep it/s.t dark** (*informal*) (request s.o to) keep s.t secret, not say anything about s.t: *Keep it dark but I've just heard that the manager is going to resign*. **(not) look on the dark side (of s.t)** (not) think about the bad parts (of s.t); (not) become saddened, worried, (about s.t): *Don't look on the dark side; remember that at least you're alive*. Compare look on the bright side (of s.t) (⇒ bright).

▷ *def/u.n* **5** state of there being little or no natural or artificial light: *We drove home in the dark. The lights failed and we were left sitting in the dark*. **after/before dark** after/before it has become dark(1): *I'd like to get home before dark*. **be**, **keep/leave s.o, in the dark** (**a**) be etc in the dark(5). (**b**) (*fig*) be etc without any information or knowledge about s.t: *He kept us all in the dark about his problems*.

'**Dark ,Ages** *def.pl.n* time (after the fall of the Roman Empire) between about the 6th and 12th centuries AD when it is thought that there was not much civilization in Europe.

'**darken** *tr/intr.v* (cause (s.t) to) become dark(*adj*): *Clouds darkened the sky. We need to darken the paint a little*.

,**dark 'horse** *c.n* (*fig*) person about whom not much is known: *Helen is a bit of a dark horse but she certainly works hard*.

'**darkly** *adv* (*formal*) (saying s.t) in a secret and gloomy(2) way: *He suggested darkly that we would soon discover the real truth*.

'**dark ,meat** *u.n* meat from the legs of poultry. Compare white meat(1).

'**darkness** *u.n* fact or state of being dark(1): *We came to see you but everything was in darkness so we supposed you were out*.

'**dark,room** *c.n* room that is kept dark(1) for developing photographs in.

,**dark 'secret** *c.n* thing that is kept secret or hidden, esp because it is bad, evil: *What dark secrets does this old house hide behind its doors?*

darling /'dɑːlɪŋ/ *attrib.adj* **1** (of a person, thing etc) very attractive; much loved: *What a darling little girl/house! My darling husband/wife* (e.g when talking or writing to her/him).

▷ *c.n* **2** (often used to talk to the) person whom one loves or likes a lot: *Darling, can you help me for a moment? Our baby is a real darling, isn't she!*

darn¹ /dɑːn/ *c.n* **1** place (usu in s.t that one wears) where a hole has been repaired: *There were several darns in his socks*.

▷ *tr.v* **2** use thread, wool etc to repair (a hole, sock etc) by sewing: *Can you darn (the holes in) my socks?*

'**darning** *u.n* things that need to be darned(2): *He had piles of darning to do*.

'**darning-,needle** *c.n* large needle used to darn(2) things.

darn² /dɑːn/ *adj/adv/interj* (also **darned**) (*informal*) (a weaker form of) damn(1–3): *Those darned chickens have got out of their cage again. Darn it, I've missed the bus*.

darned /dɑːnd/ ⇒ darn².

dart /dɑːt/ *c.n* **1** (used in darts) small arrow with a sharp point and usually feathers at the end: *Her first dart scored double twenty*. **2** small arrow with a sharp point that is fired from a gun etc: *They used* tranquillizing *darts to* capture(3) *the lions*. **3** (often make a — across, around, into etc s.t) sudden quick movement or run (across etc s.t): *The prisoner made a sudden dart away from the guards and disappeared into the bushes*.

▷ **4** *intr.v* (usu — across, around, into s.t etc) move, run, very quickly (across etc (s.t)): *The rabbit darted from one side of the road to the other*. **dart a glance, look etc at s.o** give s.o a quick sudden glance(1)/look etc: *When he started his story, she darted a glance at him to stop*.

'**dart,board** *c.n* (used in the game of darts) round board that is divided into sections with numbers from 1 to 20.

darts *pl.n* game in which two or more players throw darts(1) at a dartboard: *Can you play darts?*

dash /dæʃ/ *n* **1** *c.n* (often make a — for s.o/s.t) sudden quick movement or run (towards s.o/s.t, in order to escape, reach s.w, quickly etc): *When the store opened its doors everybody made a dash for the best sales bargains*. **2** *c.n* small quantity of s.t (often added to s.t else): *Would you like a dash of lemon in your tea? This room needs a dash of colour to brighten it up*. **3** *c.n* quick or violent movement of water, waves etc against s.t: *The dash of waves against the rocks made it difficult for him to swim clear*. **4** *c.n* punctuation mark — used in a sentence to show a break, a list of things that follow etc: *I had to do it — she made me*. Compare hyphen. **5** *c.n* short fast running race: *the 60 metres dash*. **6** *u.n* (*formal*) lively spirit and sometimes brave behaviour: *He has a great deal of dash but he can't keep a job*.

▷ *v* **7** *intr.v* move, run, very quickly: *She dashed across the road. I'm afraid I must dash or I'll miss the plane. Susan dashed around the room emptying the ashtrays before her parents came home.* ⇒ dash off. **8** *tr/intr.v* (often — (s.t) against s.t) (cause (s.t) to) hit violently (against s.t): *She dashed the glass against the wall and it broke into small pieces. Waves were dashing (the boat) against the rocks*. **dash off** leave very quickly, esp in a hurry: *She dashed off because she was late for work*. **dash s.t off (to s.o)** write s.t, esp a letter, (to s.o), do a piece of work, quickly and hurriedly: *He dashed off a letter to her just before he left the country. Could you dash this job off before this evening?* **dash s.o's hopes (of doing s.t)** ⇒ hope(*n*).

'**dash,board** *c.n* (in the front of a road vehicle) board with instruments that tell the driver the speed the vehicle is travelling, the amount of petrol in the vehicle, the time etc.

'**dashing** *adj* (of a person) brave and lively; having dash(6): *a dashing young man/woman*.

data /'deɪtə/ *pl/u.n* (also *attrib*) known information or facts that can be used to find further information or facts, esp when fed into and analyzed(2) by a computer: *His report is based on* insufficient *data*.

'**data ,bank/,base** *c.n* (large amount of) information held in a computer that can be used for various purposes: *The police are building a data bank of information about all known criminals*.

'**data ,processing** *u.n* (*abbr* DP) action of

storing data in a computer and using/analyzing(2) it for various purposes.

date¹ /deɪt/ *c.n* **1** (statement of) time shown by giving the day, month and year or one of these: *The date on the letter was 5 August 1992. What's the date today (or What's today's date)?* **2** date(1) when s.t happened or is going to happen or (*pl*) between which s.t happened or is going to happen: *I never remember dates. Please fill in the date of your birth. Shakespeare's dates* (i.e when he was born and when he died) *are 1564 to 1616.* **3** arrangement for a certain time (and place) in the future: *I can't see you tomorrow, I have a date with my sister. We made a date to meet at his office the following Monday. Let's arrange a date to play tennis next week. That's a date then — tomorrow at 5.* Compare rendezvous(1). **4** (*informal*) social arrangement, meeting, (esp with s.o of the opposite sex): *He asked her for a date to go to a film but she refused. If you haven't got a date on Saturday come and watch television with me.* ⇨ blind date. **5** (*informal*) person with whom one has a date(4): *She introduced her date to her friends.* **out of date** ('**out-of-**,**date** when *attrib*) (**a**) (considered to be) not modern any longer; not fashionable: *out-of-date ideas. These methods are very out of date,* ⇨ dated, outdated. Opposite up to date. (**b**) that cannot be used any longer because it is not valid: *Paul's passport is out of date so he can't travel with us. This is an out-of-date ticket so you can't use it.* **to date** up to now, this time or moment: *We have received only five applications for the job to date.* **up to date** (**a**) ('**up-to-**,**date** when *attrib*) very modern; with all the latest and newest facts, ideas, fashions etc: *Our office has very up-to-date equipment(2). Her clothes are not very up to date.* (**b**) (*pred*) having finished all one's work, studies etc up to now: *Is your work up to date? Are you up to date with your studies?* **bring/keep oneself/ s.o up to date** get/give s.o (regularly) all the latest information about s.t: *Let's have dinner together so that you can bring me up to date with all that's been happening while I was away.* **bring/ keep s.t up to date** (**a**) cause s.t to (always) have the latest details or information: *We need to bring our records up to date. Have you been keeping our expenses up to date?* (**b**) complete a piece of work: *It'll take a week to bring the accounts up to date.* **get up to date** (**with s.t**) (**a**) complete the work or tasks (concerning a job etc): *How long will it take to get up to date with your work?* (**b**) (make sure to always) have the latest facts, information (about s.t): *Chris listens to the news every night to get up to date with events in the world.* ⇨ update.

▷ *v* **6** *tr.v* have, put, a date(1) on (s.t): *The cheque isn't dated. You forgot to date the cheque.* **7** *tr.v* decide the date(2) of (s.t old), e.g from evidence(1), examination: *They dated the painting at around 1650.* **8** *tr/intr.v* (*informal*) meet regularly for a date(4) (with s.o): *Mary is dating Mark. I don't like the idea of my daughter dating when she's so young.* **9** *tr/intr.v* (cause (s.o/s.t) to) (seem to) be no longer modern or fashionable because of belonging to another period in time: *Using expressions like 'Great, man!' dates you. Though he was writing 50 years ago, the views he expressed have not dated.* **date from. . .**; **date back to. . .** (of

s.t that happens, of a building etc) has been in existence since (a particular time): *Our friendship dates from our meeting in Greece last year. The church dates back to the twelfth century.*
'**dated** *adj* old-fashioned: *His views are dated.* Compare date(9).
'**date,line** *unique n* **1** (also ,**Inter,national 'Date,line**) line near or on the 180 degree meridian to the east of which the date is one day earlier than the date to the west of it. **2** (in a newspaper report etc) date, place etc when or where an article was written.

date² /deɪt/ *c.n* (also *attrib*) (kind of palm²(1) tree with) small brown sticky fruit with a stone inside.

daub /dɔːb/ *c.n* **1** (usu — of s.t) splash (of paint, mud etc): *He used daubs of paint to write rude words on the wall.* **wattle and daub** ⇨ wattle¹.
▷ *v* **2** *tr/intr.v* (often *derog*)paint(s.t),write(s.t)using paint, in a careless and unskilled way: *The child daubed different coloured paints on the floor. She can't paint — she just daubs. They were caught daubing slogans on the wall* (or *daubing the wall with slogans*).

daughter /'dɔːtə/ *c.n* **1** one's/s.o's female child: *My daughter is six years old. Their daughter is going to university this year.* Compare son(1). **2** (usu *pl*) female descendant.
'**daughter-in-,law** *c.n* (*pl* daughters-in-law) wife of one's/s.o's son. ⇨ son-in-law.

daunt /dɔːnt/ *tr.v* (*formal*) make (s.o) feel worried or less confident: *It's not the kind of work that daunts me, it's the amount of work. You may feel daunted by the new job at the beginning but you'll get used to it.* **nothing daunted** (*formal*) not worried, frightened, discouraged(1), by s.t (and so ready to do s.t): *We had been refused three times but nothing daunted we asked again.* ⇨ dauntless, undaunted.
'**daunting** *adj* (esp of work, a job etc) that is or seems difficult (often because of the amount to do): *After the party there was the daunting job of tidying up.* ⇨ undaunted.
'**dauntless** *adj* (*formal*) (of a person, behaviour) very brave, not easily discouraged(1).
'**dauntlessly** *adv.* '**dauntlessness** *u.n.*

dawdle /'dɔːdl/ *intr.v* do s.t, move, very slowly in a way that wastes time: *Stop dawdling or you'll be late for school.* **dawdle** (**the time**, **one's life** etc) **away** waste time etc in a lazy way: *She dawdled the time away by reading a magazine.*

dawn /dɔːn/ *c/u.n* **1** (example of the time when there is the) first light in the sky at the beginning of the day (just before the sun rises): *Some people have to get up at/before dawn to go to work.* **2** (usu the — of s.t) (*fig*) beginning (of s.t new): *the dawn of a new age in* technology. (**at**) **the break/crack of dawn** when dawn(1) is just starting.
▷ *intr.v* **3** (of (the first signs of) a day) start (to appear): *The day was just dawning as he got out of bed.* **4** (*fig*) (of s.t new) begin to happen: *A new age has dawned.* **dawn** (**up**)**on s.o** (**that. . .**) become clear to s.o, realize, (that. . .): *While I was listening to the radio, it dawned on me that the programme was about my family.*

day /deɪ/ *n* **1** *c.n* length of time of 24 hours from midnight to midnight: *There are seven days in a week. 'What day is it today?' We'll be away for 3 days.* **2** *c/u.n* length of time in a day(1) when there is light: *You should be out in the garden on a day like this. I'll be out all day so please take any messages.* **4** *c.n* (also *attrib*) length of time in a day(1) when one is doing s.t in particular, e.g one's job: *She works a ten-hour day. It'll be a long day tomorrow because there's so much work to finish.* **4** *c.n* (often *pl*) (*formal*) time (in the past or future) when s.o/s.t was, will be, important, when s.o lived, s.t existed, happened etc: *In those days it usually took three months to get to Australia.* ⇒ days. **all in a/the day's work** ⇒ work(*n*). **at the end of the day** (a) when the day(2) is finished. (b) (*fig*) when everything has been said, done etc; after one's efforts etc: *At the end of the day it won't matter who gets the job as long as he/she does it well.* **by day** during the day(2) when there is light: *We travelled by day and camped by night.* **call it a day** (*fig*; *informal*) decide to end, stop doing, s.t: *It was getting late so we called it a day and went home.* **lose the day** (*formal*) be the cause of defeat. **carry/win the day** (*formal*) be the cause of success: *Peace will win the day in the end. Determination carried the day for our team.* **day after day** continuously; for many days(2): *Day after day there were reports of violence in the streets.* **day and night; night and day** continuously; all the time: *To prevent him escaping he was guarded night and day.* **day by day** ('day-by-,day when *attrib*) a little every day(1,2); gradually: *We noticed a day-by-day improvement. The garden is improving day by day.* **day in day out** continuously for many days; day after day: *It rained day in day out for the whole of last week.* **day to day** ('day-to-,day when *attrib*) (a) (for) one day(3) at a time: *I'm employed on a day-to-day basis. I only work day to day.* (b) (only *attrib*) of things that happen every day, regularly: *She's in charge of our day-to-day accounts.* **from day to day** (used to describe uncertainty about each new day) for only one day(1,3) at a time: *For years we lived from day to day never knowing where our next meal would come from.* **from one day to the next** (used to describe uncertainty or continuous change during a length of time): *We never knew from one day to the next what he was going to do.* **have had one's/its day** be no longer successful, useful, popular: *Our old car has had its day and we'll have to sell it.* ⇒ day(4), days. **in one's/s.o's day** in the past when one/s.o was a certain age: *In my day it was easy to get into university.* ⇒ day(4). **in this day and age** (esp of s.t that happens that doesn't fit present conditions, social behaviour etc) at this present time: *In this day and age there are still people who can't read and write in this country.* (**it's**) **all in a day's work** (it's) s.t that one/s.o can, is prepared to, or had to, do as (part of) one's/her/his work: *For him, it was all in a day's work to look after the children, do the cooking and cleaning and run a sports shop.* **make s.o's day** (*informal*) (of s.t that s.o else does or that happens) make s.o very pleased: *Go and tell your parents the good news — it'll make their day.* **one day** (a) at some unstated time in the future: *One day we'll have a house of our own.* (b) (esp at the beginning of a story) at some unstated time in the past: *One day while we were swimming we heard someone shouting for help.* (c) on a particular day in the past or

future: *We met one day last week for a drink. I'll be in London one day next week.* **pass the time of day with s.o** talk to s.o for a certain amount of time, esp because one has not got anything else, important, to do: *I passed the time of day with a family from Brazil while waiting for the train.* **some day** at some unstated time in the future: *I suppose we'll meet again some day.* **That'll be the day** (*fig*; *informal*) It will be very surprising if that/s.t ever happens: *'He thinks he'll get the job.' 'That'll be the day!'* **the day after** (**tomorrow/s.t**) the day following (tomorrow/s.t): *The day after tomorrow is a holiday. He died the day after (the accident).* **the day before** (**yesterday/s.t**) the day coming immediately before (yesterday/s.t): *I saw him the day before yesterday. He was happy and cheerful the day before (he died).* (**the**) **next day** the day following (the) one already known or mentioned in the past: *We arrived on Friday and the next day we went to the beach. I saw him (the) next day and it was as though nothing had happened.* **the other day** a day(2) in the fairly recent past (but without being exact): *I saw him only the other day as I was crossing the street.* **the present day** ('present-,day when *attrib*) the times we are now living in: *The present day is full of violence. Present-day youth has no idea of what war is like.* **this day week** in exactly one week from today: *So it's agreed that we'll meet here again this day week at the same time.* **to the day** (exactly) on the day that was expected or agreed: *Nobody thought he could manage it but he made the final payment exactly to the day.* **to this day** until (and including) the present time (esp of s.t that happened in the past that has not been explained): *To this day no one knows where the money went.*

daily /'deɪlɪ/ *adj/adv* **1** (that is done, happens, appears) every day or every weekday (i.e not on Saturdays or Sundays): *Would you like to be paid on a daily or weekly basis? I can't miss my daily swim. She writes articles for the daily newspapers. He travels to work daily by train. We get the newspapers delivered daily.*
▷ *c.n* (*pl -ies*) **2** daily(1) newspaper: *She writes articles for the dailies.* **3** (also ,**daily 'help**) person, usu a woman, who is paid to do one's housework every day or on certain days of the week.

'**day,break** *unique n* (often *at —*) the time when light begins to appear at the beginning of the day(2).

day-by-day *attrib.adj* ⇒ day by day.

'**day,dream** *c.n* **1** state of appearing to dream while awake, esp about things one would like: *He's been walking around in a daydream the whole morning probably thinking about how he's going to spend his prize money.*
▷ *intr.v* **2** seem to dream in this way: *Stop daydreaming and get on with your work.*

'**day,light** *u.n* (also *attrib*) light at the beginning of or during the day(2): *We will have to get up before daylight to get to the airport on time. We walked fast in order to make the most of the daylight (or the daylight hours).* **daylight robbery** ⇒ robbery.

'**day ,nursery** *c.n* (*pl -ies*) nursery where children are looked after during the day while their parent(s) is/are at work.

,day re'turn *c.n* (also *attrib* **'day-re,turn**) bus/ train ticket for a journey to a place and back again on the same day: *a day-return ticket*.

days *pl.n* (length of s.o's/s.t's) life or work. ⇨ day(4). **end one's days** (**in s.t, s.w**) come to the end of one's life (doing s.t): *He ended his days peacefully in a small cottage near the sea.* **s.o's days are numbered** (*fig*) s.o is going to die, fail, lose her/his job etc, some time (very) soon: *He knew that when the accounts were checked his days would be numbered.* **have seen better days** (of a person, thing) be no longer as good as he/ she/it once was: *That coat has seen better days; you really should throw it away.* **in those days** ⇨ day(4). **it is early days** it is (still) too soon to know (what will happen, what the result will be etc): *I haven't heard about my job application yet but it's still early days.* **one of these days** (*informal*) at a time in the future: *One of these days I'll really tell him what I think of him.* **one of those days** (*informal*) a time, day(2), (like some others) when nothing goes right: *It was one of those days when you know everything is going to fail from the moment you wake up.* **these days** (*informal*) at the present time, esp when compared to the past: *It's not safe to be out on the streets late at night these days.* **Those were the days!** Life was more interesting and exciting then!

'day,school *c.n* school, esp a private one, that students go to during the day only and return home in the evening. Compare boarding school.

'day ,shift *c.n* ⇨ shift(3).

'day,time *u/def.n* time of day when it is (still) light: *I never sleep in the daytime.* ⇨ nighttime.

,day-to-'day *attrib.adj* ⇨ day to day.

'day ,trip *c.n* journey to a place and back home made in one day: *We took a day trip to France.*

'day ,tripper *c.n* person who takes a day trip.

daze /deɪz/ *c.n* **1** (usu *be*, *go around*, *in a —*) (of a person) state of confusion; state of not quite knowing what one is doing or what is happening, esp as a result of s.t: *He's been walking around in a daze since he heard he won £10 000.*

▷ *tr.v* **2** (often passive) make (s.o) confused, not quite know what he/she is doing etc, esp as a result of a blow or of s.t unexpected that happens: *He was dazed for a moment when he hit his head on the rock. She was dazed by the news that she had been chosen to play for England.*

dazzle /'dæzl/ *sing.n* **1** very bright light(s) that shine(s) into one's eyes (so one is unable to see properly): *The dazzle of the headlights from the cars coming towards him almost made him crash.* **2** (*fig*) brightness or charm: *the dazzle of her smile.*

▷ *tr.v* **3** (of a bright light) shine into s.o's eyes and make (her/him) unable to see properly: *Don't drive with full headlights on a busy road or you'll dazzle other drivers.* **4** (*fig*) (use charm, fame, to) influence (s.o): *His charm dazzled her. He was dazzled by the success of his first book.*

'dazzling *adj* shining very brightly or charmingly: *dazzling clothes/teeth; a dazzling smile.*

'dazzlingly *adv*.

db /,di: 'bi:/ *symb* decibel(s).

DC /,di: 'si:/ *abbr* direct current.

DD /,di: 'di:/ *abbr* Doctor of Divinity.

DDT /,di: ,di: 'ti:/ *u.n abbr* dichlorodiphenyl-trichloroethane (a chemical product used to kill insects).

deacon /'di:kən/ *c.n* official in some Christian churches, below a priest in rank.

'deaconess *c.n* woman deacon.

dead /ded/ *adj* **1** (of a person, animal, plant) no longer having any life in her/him/it: *She was found dead in her bed the next morning. Dead fish were floating on the surface of the water.* **2** in a state that is like death; having no feeling of life: *She was in a dead sleep. My arm felt dead after the injection.* **3** (of a machine etc) not working, esp because there is no power (left) in it: *The car battery seems to be dead. There's something wrong with the telephone — the line's dead.* **4** no longer active; no longer in use: *The love she had had for him was now quite dead. What's the use of studying dead languages like Latin?* **5** (usu *pred*) (of s.t that was burning or hot) no longer burning; not able to be used again: *The fire's dead so can you light it again? All he found in the box were dead matches.* **6** (*attrib*) complete (and often sudden): *We sat in dead silence for some time before anyone said a word. The car came to a dead stop.* **7** (of a ball in some games, e.g rugby) out of play. **dead as a dodo** ⇨ dodo. **dead as a doornail** ⇨ doornail. **dead to s.t** (*fig; formal*) not showing any sympathy or feeling towards s.t: *He remained dead to all our pleas(1) for help.* **dead to the world** (*fig; informal*) completely or fast asleep. **would not be seen dead in/at s.t** (*informal*) refuse totally to wear s.t or to be present at s.t: *I wouldn't be seen dead in the kind of clothes she wears. She wouldn't be seen dead at one of those parties.*

▷ *adv* **8** (of a direction, line etc) completely, exactly, (in front etc): *There is a road block dead ahead. Please hang the pictures dead straight.* **9** (*informal*) completely or very: *I'm dead tired. He's dead drunk. Are you dead certain? The answer's dead easy.* **cut s.o dead** (*fig*) deliberately not talk to s.o when seeing or meeting her/him; ignore s.o: *People I've known for years cut me dead since that newspaper article about our family.* **dead on**; **dead right** (*informal*) exactly right: *You were dead on when you said he would refuse to listen to me.* ⇨ dead(9). **dead on time, 1 o'clock** etc at exactly the right time, 1 o'clock etc: *He arrived dead on time.* **drop dead** ⇨ drop(v). **go dead** (of a machine etc) stop working, esp because there is no power: *We were in the middle of a conversation when the (telephone) line went dead.* ⇨ dead(3). **stop dead** stop completely (and suddenly): *The car in front stopped dead and I almost crashed into it.* ⇨ dead(6).

▷ *n* **10** *def.n* **in the dead of night, winter** etc during the time when night is at its darkest, winter is at its coldest etc. **11** *def.pl.n* dead(1) people: *The dead were buried in a common grave. The number of dead after the earthquake was over 5000.* ⇨ death, die.

,dead 'beat *adj* ⇨ beat(1). ⇨ dead(9).

'dead ,beat *c.n* (*derog; slang*) lazy and/or useless person.

,dead 'centre *adv/def.n* (at/on) the exact centre: *He hit the dead centre of the target(1) (or He hit (the) target(1)) dead centre).*

'deaden *tr.v* **1** make (a sound etc) less strong or

less able to be heard: *A thick carpet on the stairs will deaden the noise of children running up and down.* **2** make (pain, feeling etc) less strong: *The injection will deaden the pain.*

,dead 'end *c.n* (**'dead-,end** when *attrib*) **1** road or street that is closed at one end: *There's a dead-end sign on that road so we couldn't get through there.* **2** point, position etc, esp in work, where there is no (possibility of) further progress: *Our inquiries had reached a dead end. He knew he was in a dead-end job. Compare* cul de sac.

,dead 'heat *c.n* (in a race) situation when two or more people, horses etc cross the finishing line at exactly the same time: *There was a dead heat for second place.*

'dead,line *c.n* last possible date or time by which s.t must be done, finished etc: *Newspaper reporters have to write to very tight deadlines. What's your deadline for finishing the report?*

'deadliness *u.n* fact or state of being deadly.

'dead,lock *c/unique n* (often *end in, reach* (a), —) state in which no agreement is possible: *The talks with the union have reached* (a) *deadlock.*

,dead 'loss *c.n* (*derog; informal*) ⇒ loss.

'deadly *adj* (*-ier, -iest*) **1** extremely dangerous; that can cause (quick, instant) death or destruction: *Be careful, that's a deadly snake. That knife looks deadly.* **2** looking as though s.o is dead: *There was a deadly whiteness in her face.* **3** (*fig*) (of a person, remark etc) full of hate; attacking s.o in a way that hurts her/him: *deadly enemies; a deadly insult. Her deadly remarks silenced him.* **4** very great: *He spoke to her with deadly seriousness.* **5** (*informal*) very dull and without interest: *Her parties are deadly.*

▷ *adv* **6** (as if) like death: *She grew deadly pale at the news.* **7** very or extremely: *I'm deadly serious.*

'dead,pan *adj* (of a face, s.t funny etc) showing, or said, done etc with, no change of expression: *He told the joke with a deadpan expression.*

'dead ,weight *c.n* person or thing who/that is very/too heavy to lift: *His unconscious body was a dead weight in my arms.*

,dead 'wood *u.n* **1** wood that is dead(1) and needs to be cut off, removed etc. **2** (*derog; fig*) person(s) who no longer work(s) well and need(s) to be removed: *We must start from the top and cut out all the dead wood if we want an efficient organization.*

deaf /def/ *adj* **1** (of a person) unable to hear, either completely or to some extent: *He was born deaf. The explosion made me deaf for several minutes.* **deaf to s.t** (*informal*) refusing to listen to or pay attention to a request, advice etc: *He remained deaf to all her requests for help.* **fall on deaf ears; turn a deaf ear to s.t** ⇒ ear.

▷ *def.pl.n* **2** deaf(1) people: *He goes to a school for the deaf.*

'deaf-,aid *c.n* (*old use*) = hearing-aid.

'deafen *tr.v* (of a loud noise) make (s.o) deaf(1) for a short time: *We were deafened by the loud music and could hardly hear ourselves speak.*

'deafening *adj* **1** (of a loud noise) so loud as to make hearing difficult or impossible: *The noise from the road drill was so deafening I couldn't hear what she said.* **2** (of a period of silence) very obvious: *There was a deafening silence.*

'deafness *u.n*.

deal /diːl/ *n* **1** *c.n* arrangement or agreement, esp in business, between two or more people or organizations: *There's a meeting to discuss the new business deal between the companies concerned. The best deal would be to share expenses and profits.* **2** *c.n* (in card games) act of giving cards to each player: *It's your deal. Whose deal is it?* **3** *c.n* cards that a player gets in the deal(2): *What a terrible deal!* **big deal** (*informal*) (usu said sarcastically) thing, event etc that s.o considers important but others do not: *What's the big deal? You paid for the stamp. Big deal!* **do/make a deal (with s.o/s.t)** come to an arrangement (with s.o, an organization) that gives advantages to both sides: *I'll make a deal with you; you help me wash the dishes and I'll sew your trousers.* **a good, great** etc **deal (of s.t)** a large amount or degree (of s.t): *This is going to cost you a good deal of money. We all laughed a good deal and enjoyed ourselves.* **a good, great** etc **deal better, quicker** etc in a way that is very much better, quicker etc: *You'll have to work a good deal harder if you want to keep your job.* **it's a deal** (*informal*) the matter, business deal(1) etc is settled or agreed: *OK, it's a deal — we'll divide the cost.* **a raw deal** (*informal*) bad/unfair treatment or a bad/unfair agreement: *She got/ had a very raw deal when she sold her house.*

▷ *v* (*p,p,p.t* dealt/delt/) **4** *tr/intr.v* (often *— s.t* (*out*) (*to s.o*)) give (out) (cards) in a card game (to each player): *Whose turn is it to deal? He dealt the cards* (*out*) *to everybody.* **5** *tr.v* (often *— s.t out* (*to s.o*)) give (s.t) as a share (to each person): *He counted the £10 notes and then dealt them out equally to everybody present.* **deal s.o/s.t a blow** (*formal*) (**a**) hit s.o, a part of s.o's body, hard: *She threatened to deal him a blow* (*with her spade*) *if he didn't go away.* (**b**) (*fig*) harm or damage s.o, s.o's hopes etc badly: *His chances were dealt a blow when his application for a loan was refused.* **deal in s.t** do business by buying and/or selling s.t: *He deals in used cars. Our company deals mainly in oil and oil products.* **deal with s.o/ s.t** (**a**) do business with s.o, an organization: *I've dealt with him* (*or Jones & Co*) *for many years.* (**b**) handle s.o/s.t; organize, arrange, be responsible for, s.o/s.t: *The police were called to deal with the noisy crowd. Can you deal with this matter while I'm away? Who deals with your tax affairs?* (**c**) (of a person, book, subject etc) talk or write about, discuss, s.o/s.t: *His speech dealt with the problem of unemployment. The book deals with diseases in hot countries.* **wheeling and dealing** ⇒ wheel.

'dealer *c.n* **1** person who deals(4) cards. **2** (often *— in s.t*) person who buys and/or sells (s.t): *a furniture dealer; a dealer in stocks and shares.* **3** (often *— in s.t*) (*informal*) person who sells harmful drugs(2). ⇒ wheeler dealer.

'dealing *u.n* (example of the) fact or state of doing business, working with s.o, an organization, buying and/or selling things: *There has been very little dealing in these shares(3) over the past few months.*

'dealings *pl.n* **1** = dealing: *Our dealings have always been open and honest.* **2** (often *have — with s.o/s.t*) business work, contact, (with s.o/an organization): *Do you have many dealings with him* (*or that company*)*?* ⇒ wheeling and dealing.

dean /diːn/ *c.n* **1** (in some Christian(1) churches) important official in a cathedral or in charge of a group of parishes. **2** (in some universities) important official in charge of a department or some part of university life.

'**deanery** *c.n* (*pl* -ies) house or office of a dean(1).

dear /dɪə/ *adj* **1** (usu *pred*) expensive; high in price: *Most fruit is dear at this time of year.* Opposite cheap(1), inexpensive. **2** (often — *to s.o/s.t*) (of a person, s.t one is interested in) much loved or liked (by s.o): *He's a very dear friend. She is very dear to me. This subject is dear to my heart.* **3** (of a person, thing etc) very attractive, lovable: *What a dear little girl/house!* **4** (usu with capital **D**) (used to address s.o by a title or name at the beginning of a letter): *Dear Madam/Sir; Dear Mr/Mrs Jones; My dear John/Jane.* **near and dear** (**to s.o**) ⇒ near(*adj*).

▷ *adv* **5** at a (very) high price: *He succeeded in business by buying cheap and selling dear.* Opposite cheap(1). **cost s.o dear** (*fig; formal*) have a result that is more harmful than s.o wants or expects: *He gained fame but it cost him dear; his wife left him and he lost most of his friends.*

▷ *interj* **6 Dear, dear! Dear me! Oh dear!** (used to show surprise, worry, disapproval etc).

▷ *n* **7** unique *n* (used to address s.o one is fond of, esp s.o to whom one is married): *I've got some good news, dear. Hello, dear, come in.* **8** *c.n* person whom one likes a lot; lovable person: *Be a dear and fetch my glasses from upstairs.* **nearest and dearest** ⇒ near.

'**dearly** *adv* **1** with (very) great love and affection: *She loved him dearly.* **2** at a (very) high cost, esp in terms of people, effort etc: *The government paid dearly for its mistakes.* Compare dear(5). **would dearly like/love to do s.t** would like etc very greatly to do s.t: *I'd dearly love to see his face when you tell him the news.*

'**dearness** *u.n* (*formal*) high cost: *She was surprised by the dearness of houses in the area.*

dearth /dɜːθ/ *c.n* (usu — of s.t) (*formal*) lack or shortage (of people, things, ability etc): *There is a dearth of trained engineers in this country.*

death /deθ/ *n* **1** *c/u.n* (example of the) ending of life (of a person, animal, plant) either naturally or because of an accident etc: *He died a natural death. Are you afraid of death? Several deaths have been reported since the bad weather began. Deaths from the explosion have risen to over 100.* **2** *u.n* state of being dead: *In death his face looked calm.* **3** *def.n* (usu the — of s.t) (*fig*) complete end or finish (of s.t): *Is this the death of civilization as we know it? Failure would mean the death of all his hopes and dreams.* **at death's door** (usu *informal*) (of a person) dying and almost dead: *What happened? You looked like you were at death's door when you came in!* **be in at the death** (**of s.o/s.t**) (**a**) be present when s.o, an animal that is being hunted, dies. (**b**) be present at, taking part in, the last part of s.t, esp a competition: *Only three of the eight companies were in at the death.* **be the death of s.o** (**a**) be the cause of s.o's death(1): *Smoking/Drinking will be the death of him.* (**b**) (*fig; informal*) (be s.o/s.t who/that will) be the cause of too much anxiety or excitement to s.o: *That child will be the death of me!* **bleed, burn** etc **to death** bleed

etc until one is dead. **bore s.o to death** (of a person, work, a book etc) be so uninteresting and dull as to make s.o tired: *He bores me to death. I was bored to death at the party.* **catch one's death** (**of cold**) (*fig*) get a very bad cold: *Don't play in the rain or you'll catch your death (of cold).* **do s.t to death** do s.t so often that it becomes boring: *That joke has been done to death.* (**be/suffer**) **a fate worse than death** ⇒ fate(*n*). **flog s.t to death** ⇒ flog. (**hang on**) **like grim death** in a determined way; very strongly: *She held on to the rock like grim death.* **put s.o to death** cause s.o to be killed, sometimes as a punishment: *In some countries criminals are put to death.* **sentence s.o to death** (of a judge etc) state officially that s.o must die for a crime. ⇒ death penalty, death sentence. **sick to death of s.o/s.t** (*fig; informal*) very angry and tired because of s.o/s.t: *I'm sick to death of him and his complaints.* **the jaws of death** ⇒ jaw(*n*). **trample s.o, an animal, to death** ⇒ trample. **worried to death** (**about s.o/s.t**) (*fig*) extremely worried (about s.o/s.t): *Where have you been? I've been worried to death about you.*

'**death,bed** *c.n* (usu on one's —) (stage when one is in the) bed in which one dies or is going to die: *On his deathbed he asked everybody to forgive him if he had done them any wrong.*

'**death,blow** *c.n* (usu *fig*) thing, event etc that causes the death(1) of s.o or the complete end of s.t: *The final deathblow came when permission to use the hall for the meeting was refused.*

'**death cer,tificate** *c.n* official form signed by a doctor stating how s.o died.

'**death ,duty** *c/u.n* (*pl* -ies) (often *pl*) tax that has to be paid to the government on (part of) the estate(3) of a dead person.

'**deathly** *adj* (-ier, -iest) **1** that is like death(1): *There was a deathly silence.*

▷ *adv* **2** in a way that is like death(1): *It was deathly still and silent.* Compare deadly.

'**death ,penalty** *c/def.n* punishment of certain crimes by death(1): *Some politicians are arguing for a return of the death penalty for very serious crimes.*

'**death,rate** *u/def.n* number of deaths in a country, usu shown as a number for every 1000 of the population. Compare birthrate.

'**death ,roll** *c/def.n* (also '**death ,toll**) (list of the) number of people who have been killed, e.g in a war or an accident: *The death toll for the hotel fire is now over 500.*

'**death ,sentence** *c/def.n* official order from a judge for s.o, usu a criminal, to be killed for a crime.

'**death-,trap** *c.n* place, building etc from which it would be very difficult to escape if there was a fire etc.

'**death ,warrant** *c.n* official document(1) stating that s.o is to be killed, e.g for a crime.

deb /deb/ *c.n abbr* debutante.

débâcle /deɪˈbɑːkl/ *c.n* (*French*) complete failure, defeat: *After this débâcle, the government has very little chance of winning the next election.*

debar /dɪˈbɑː/ *tr.v* (-rr-) (usu — s.o from (doing) s.t) (*formal*) not allow (s.o) (to do s.t), usu officially: *Colin is debarred from voting as he is not a citizen.*

debase /dɪˈbeɪs/ *tr.v* (*formal*) make (s.t) worth-

less: *Money has been heavily debased in the last ten years. Ideas such as peace and freedom have become debased in recent years.*
de'basement *c/u.n.*

debate /dɪ'beɪt/ *c/u.n* **1** discussion, esp a formal one at a meeting, in a parliament or, more generally, between two or more people when there is some disagreement: *After some debate about where they wanted to go, the whole family decided to go on holiday together.*
▷ *v* **2** *tr/intr.v* discuss (s.t) formally: *Parliament debated (the Bill) until the early hours of the morning.* **3** *tr.v* (often — *what to do, whether, when etc to do s.t*) discuss (what to do etc) in order to make a decision: *We debated whether to go on holiday to Greece or France.*
de'batable *adj* (of a statement, point of view etc) that can be argued about, esp because it may not be true: *It's debatable* (*or a debatable subject*) *whether students should have the right to choose what they study at school.*
de'bater *c.n* person who debates(2) s.t.

debauched /dɪ'bɔːtʃt/ *adj* (*derog*) (of a person, behaviour) immoral because of too much drinking of alcohol, sexual pleasure etc.
de'bauchery *c/u.n* (*pl -ies*) (example of the) fact or state of taking part in excessive drinking and/or immoral acts: *a life of debauchery.*

debilitate /dɪ'bɪlɪˌteɪt/ *tr.v* (*formal*) cause (s.o) to become weak, e.g through illness or lack of food: *His illness debilitated him for months.*
de'bili,tating *adj* that causes weakness: *a debilitating disease.*
de'bility *u.n* weakness in the body, esp from illness: *His general debility made it difficult for him to walk very far.*

debit /'debɪt/ *c.n* (*commerce*; written *abbr dr*) **1** (also *attrib*) (record of an) amount of money that has been spent or that is owed to s.o: *His bank statement showed two debits that he didn't know anything about. I had a debit balance.* Opposite credit(2). **be in debit** (of a bank account) be in a position of having spent more money than is in one's account. Compare overdraft.
▷ *tr.v* **2** record the cost of (s.t on s.o's account); charge the cost of (s.t to s.o, s.o's account): *Shall we debit your account with our fee or would you prefer to pay now? Please debit (the cost to) my account. Who shall we debit for the repairs?* Opposite credit(7).
'debit ,column/,side *def.n* (in written accounts) left-hand column/side in which debits(1) are recorded. ⇨ credit column/side.

debrief /diː'briːf/ *tr.v* ask (a soldier, government official etc) questions about what he/she has done, seen etc in order to get the necessary information.
de'briefing *c/u.n* (example of the) act of reporting information gathered while on official business.

debris, **débris** /'deɪbrɪ/ *u.n* **1** broken pieces that remain after buildings etc have been destroyed: *They searched through the debris after the explosion to see if they could discover the cause.* **2** bits and pieces of rubbish etc: *He spent an hour clearing up the debris from the party the night before.*

debt /det/ *c.n* **1** (*commerce*) amount (of money) that one owes to s.o: *He has debts of over £5000.* **2** (*fig*) feeling (of being grateful), obligation(1) that one has towards s.o, for s.t he/she has done: *We owe him a debt of gratitude for the help he gave us when we first came to this country.* **bad debt** debt(1) that is unlikely ever to be paid. **be in debt** be in a state of having a debt(1) or debts(1). **be in s.o's debt** be in a state of owing a debt(2) to s.o: *I shall always be in your debt for saving my child's life.* ⇨ indebted.
'debtor *c.n* person who owes a debt(1) or debts(1). Opposite creditor.

debug /diː'bʌg/ *tr.v* (*-gg-*) **1** get rid of mistakes, things that do not work properly in (a computer, computer program(1)). **2** get rid of (secret) listening devices, e.g microphones, from (a room etc). Opposite bug(5).

debunk /diː'bʌŋk/ *tr.v* (*informal*) show (s.o/ s.o's ideas, opinions etc) to be false, not true: *The article debunked the government's plans to improve employment.*

debut /'deɪbjuː/ *c.n* (usu make one's — (as s.o/ s.t)) first public appearance (as a performer etc): *She made her debut as a pianist at the Royal Festival Hall playing Beethoven.*
debutante /'debjuˌtɑːnt/ *c.n* (*abbr deb*) (also *attrib*) young woman who is making her first formal appearance(s) in (upper-class(1)) society, e.g by attending social activities such as dances: *a debutantes' ball.*

Dec written *abbr* December.

decade /'dekeɪd/ *c.n* ten years as a unit of time: *The last decade of the eighteenth century* (i.e 1790–99) *was a time of great social change.*
'decades *pl.n* (*informal*) a very long time: *I feel like we've known each other for decades.*

decadent /'dekədənt/ *adj* (*derog*) (of a person, behaviour, artistic activity, the times in which one lives etc) who/that is or has become lower in (moral) standards, worth etc: *Adults usually believe that young people are more decadent than they were in their youth.*
'decadence *u.n* fact or state of being decadent.

decant /dɪ'kænt/ *tr.v* pour (wine etc) from a bottle into another container, e.g a decanter, esp in order to leave behind any sediment(1).
de'canter *c.n* (decorated) glass container, used for serving wine etc.

decapitate /dɪ'kæpɪˌteɪt/ *tr.v* **1** cut off (s.o's head), e.g in an accident. ⇨ guillotine(4). **2** cut off (the top of s.t, e.g a flower): *He was idly decapitating the weeds with a stick.*
decapitation /dɪˌkæpɪ'teɪʃən/ *c/u.n.*

decathlon /dɪ'kæθlɒn/ *def/c.n* athletic(1) competition for men which consists of ten different events; 100m running, long jump, shot put, high jump, 400m running, hurdles, discus, pole vault(1), javelin, 1500m running. Compare heptathlon, pentathlon, triathlon.

decay /dɪ'keɪ/ *u.n* **1** fact or state of becoming bad or rotten: *Tooth decay is often the result of eating too many sweets.* **2** (usu *in* (*a state of*) —) very bad state, condition: *When they bought the hotel it was in a state of decay.* **fall into decay** (of buildings etc) become broken and in need of repair.
▷ *v* **3** *tr/intr.v* (cause (s.t) to) become bad or rotten: *Too many soft drinks will decay your teeth.* **4** *intr.v* (of a state, condition) become bad,

worse: *The country has decayed over the last ten years.*

decease /dɪˈsiːs/ *u.n* (*law* or *formal*) death (of s.o): *On his decease his son will become a very rich young man.*

de'ceased *adj* (*law*) **1** having died: *his deceased parents.*

▷ *def/def.pl.n* (*law*) **2** person who has died; dead person/people who is/are being referred to: *The deceased left all his money to his daughter. All the deceased died in the same way.*

deceit /dɪˈsiːt/ *c/u.n* (usu *sing*) (example of the) act or state of saying or doing s.t dishonest or of lying: *He is so full of deceit that no one can believe a word he says. It's a deceit to say that you will do something when you know you have no intention of doing it.*

de'ceitful *adj* (*derog*) (of a person, s.t said or done) showing, full of, deceit: *a deceitful young man; a deceitful answer.*

de'ceitfully *adv.* **de'ceitfulness** *u.n.*

deceive /dɪˈsiːv/ *tr/intr.v* (of a person) lie (to s.o); make (s.o) think that s.t is true when it is not: *He deceived her with kind words and promises. Don't be deceived by appearances!* **deceive oneself/s.o** (**into believing**, **thinking** etc **s.t**, **that. . .**) cause (oneself/s.o) to believe, think etc that s.t is true, likely etc when it is not: *You are deceiving yourself if you think I'll help you. The room was arranged to deceive people into thinking it was larger than it was.*

de'ceiver *c.n* person who deceives.

deception /dɪˈsepʃən/ *c/u.n* (example of the) act or state of deceiving s.o: *He used deception to get his way. We were all tricked by his deceptions.*

deceptive /dɪˈseptɪv/ *adj* (esp of s.t one sees or looks at) that is, is likely to be, not quite true or right; misleading: *That mountain is deceptive – it's much steeper than it looks. Appearances can be deceptive* (i.e what a person etc looks like on the surface may not be what he/she etc is really like).

de'ceptively *adv.* **de'ceptiveness** *u.n.*

decelerate /diːˈseləˌreɪt/ *tr/intr.v* (cause (a car, plane etc) to) go slower: *The plane decelerated as it came in to land.* Opposite accelerate(1).

deceleration /diːˌseləˈreɪʃən/ *u.n.*

December /dɪˈsembə/ *c/unique n* (also *attrib*) (*written abbr* Dec) 12th month of the year: *There are thirty-one days in December. We always go on holiday in December. We leave on 6 December* (say 'the sixth of December' or 'December the sixth'). *It was a cold December day.*

decent /ˈdiːsnt/ *adj* **1** who/that shows politeness or respect; accepted in polite society: *She comes from a decent family.* **2** (usu *pred*) (of dress, language, behaviour) not likely to offend, esp in sexual matters: *Are you decent?* (i.e have you got clothes on so that I can come in etc?) *Please keep your language decent while my parents are here.* Opposite indecent(1). **3** reasonably good, enough, in quality, quantity etc: *He earns a decent wage. We had a very few decent days last summer.* **4** reasonably right or proper; suitable: *He let a decent amount of time pass before he phoned her again. That was the only decent thing I could do in the situation.* Opposite indecent(2). **5** (often — of s.o (to do s.t)) (*formal*) kind, helpful, nice (of

s.o) (to do s.t): *It's very decent of you to drive me to the station. Everyone's been very decent to us since the accident.*

'decency *u.n* fact or state of being decent. **have the decency to do s.t** be honourable enough to do s.t: *At least have the decency to admit that you were wrong. She didn't even have the decency to say thank you.*

'decently *adv* in a decent(2,3,5) way: *They treated me decently while I worked there.*

deception, deceptively ⇒ deceit.

decibel /ˈdesɪˌbel/ *c.n* (*abbr* db) unit for measuring the loudness of sound.

decide /dɪˈsaɪd/ *v* **1** *tr/intr.v* (cause (s.o) to) make up her/his mind, make a choice: *We've decided* (*not*) *to go on holiday this year. He decided* (*that*) *he would go to the party. What decided you to leave your job?* ⇒ undecided(1). **2** *tr/intr.v* (often — (s.t) *against, for, in favour of, s.o/s.t*) (*law*) (of a judge etc) make a judgement on (a case) against, for etc (s.o/s.t): *Has a judge been appointed to decide the case? The* jury(1) *decided in favour of the* defendant. **3** *tr.v* cause (a particular result): *It will be fitness that decides the winner of this game.* ⇒ undecided(2). **decide (s.o) against s.o/s.t** (**a**) (cause s.o to) decide(1) not to have, use etc s.o/s.t: *We decided against* (*employing*) *him. What decided you against buying that house?* (**b**) ⇒ decide(2). **decide between s.o/s.t and s.o/s.t** make a choice between s.o/s.t and s.o/s.t: *I can't decide between these two materials for new curtains.* **decide on s.o/s.t** make a (firm) choice of s.o/s.t: *Have you decided on what dress to wear? We've decided on Greece rather than France for our holiday this year.*

de'cided *adj* **1** (of a person, opinion etc) very fixed and determined: *She has very decided opinions on almost everything.* Compare undecided(1). **2** (*attrib*) (of a difference, advantage etc) very clear, easy to be seen: *There's been a decided improvement since I was last here. Knowing the language makes a decided difference when visiting a foreign country.*

de'cidedly *adv* in a very definite and clear way: *She is decidedly right in this case.*

decision /dɪˈsɪʒən/ *n* **1** *c/u.n* (example of the) act or state of deciding(1) s.t: *Was it your decision to employ him? Hurried decisions are likely to be bad ones.* **2** *c.n* act of deciding(2) a case (against, for etc s.o), esp in a case of law, in a competition etc: *The* umpire's(1) *decision is final. The decision went against him.* **3** *u.n* (*formal*) ability to decide(1) s.t (and esp to act with determination): *She showed great decision in her handling of the problem.* Opposite indecision. **arrive at, come to, reach, a decision** decide(1,2) s.t, esp after discussion, argument etc: *It took them a long time to reach a decision* (*about what to do*). *Has the* jury(1) *arrived at a decision yet?* **be s.o's decision** be the person, group responsible for deciding(1,2): *I can offer an opinion about it but it's not my decision. Whose decision is it?* **make, take** etc **a decision** (**to do s.t**) decide(1) to do s.t: *Have they made a decision about my salary yet?*

decisive /dɪˈsaɪsɪv/ *adj* **1** (of a person, act etc) who/that shows great decision(3): *She was very decisive in her handling of the problem.* Opposite indecisive(1). **2** (of a competition, result etc) that decides(3) s.t: *a decisive goal. The decisive* point in his getting the job is that he speaks Greek.

de'cisively *adv.* **de'cisiveness** *u.n.*

deciduous /dɪˈsɪdjʊəs/ *adj* (*technical*) (of trees) that lose their leaves each year, usu in autumn. Compare coniferous, evergreen(1).

decimal /ˈdesɪml/ *adj* **1** of, referring to, a system of calculation based on the number 10 and using a point . to show numbers less than 1: *the decimal system*; *a decimal* fraction(2) (e.g 0.563).

▷ *c.n* **2** decimal(1) number or fraction(2): *1/5th expressed as a decimal is 0.2.*

,decimal 'currency *c/u.n* (*pl* -*ies*) system of money using 10 or 100 as its base: *Britain has a decimal currency in which 100 pence equals £1.*

,decimal 'fraction *c.n* fraction(2) written as a decimal(2), e.g 1.75.

,decimal 'point *c.n* point . used to show numbers less than 1: *5.56 divided by 10 is 0.556.*

decimalization, -isation /ˌdesɪməlaɪˈzeɪʃən/ *u.n.*

'decima,lize, -ise *tr/intr.v* (of a country) change (one's system of money) to a decimal(1) one: *Britain decimalized* (*its* currency(1)) *in 1971.*

decimate /ˈdesɪmeɪt/ *tr.v* (*formal*) kill or destroy a very great number of (people, animals): *The local* birdlife *has been decimated by farmers using* insecticides.

decimation /ˌdesɪˈmeɪʃən/ *u.n.*

decimetre /ˈdesɪˌmiːtə/ *c.n* (US **'deci,meter**) tenth part of a metre, *symb* dm.

decipher /dɪˈsaɪfə/ *tr.v* **1** find the meaning of (a secret message, code(3)): *I can't decipher this message without a* code(3) *book.* **2** (often negative or in questions) be able to read or understand (s.t esp bad handwriting etc): *I can't decipher your writing. Can you decipher this signature?*

de'cipherable *adj* (*formal*) that can be deciphered. Opposite indecipherable.

decision, decisive(ly), decisiveness ⇒ decide.

deck¹ /dek/ *c.n* **1** main floor of a ship or any one of the floors above or below it: *The restaurant is on deck 4.* **2** floor or part of one in some planes: *Some* jumbo(2) *jets have an upper deck with a bar and seats for* first-class(2) *passengers. Our young son was invited to see the flight deck* (i.e where the pilot flies the plane). **3** floor in a bus: *Standing is not allowed on the top/upper deck of the bus.* ⇒ -decker(1,2). **4** (also **'record ,deck**) base that supports the turntable and pickup(1) arm of a record player. ⇒ tape deck. **5** (often — *of cards*) complete set of playing cards; pack(2). **below decks** below the main deck(1) in a ship: *When the storm came we were ordered* (*to go*) *below deck.* **clear the decks** (*fig*; *informal*) remove things that are in the way, finish small jobs etc (so that one is free to do s.t): *I'll need a little time to clear the decks so that I'll be ready for the meeting this afternoon. Clear the decks — I want to serve the dinner.* **on deck** on(to) the top deck(1) of a ship: *Let's go on deck now the weather's better.*

'deck,chair *c.n* kind of chair for sitting outdoors that folds flat.

-decker *c.n* **1** ⇒ double-decker, single-decker. **2** having one or more layer(s) in the thing mentioned: *a triple(1)-decker sandwich.*

'deck,hand *c.n* seaman who works on the decks(1) of a ship.

deck² /dek/ *tr.v* **deck oneself/s.o/s.t** (**out**) **in/ with s.t** dress or decorate o.s/s.o/s.t with s.t: *She decked herself out in her best clothes for the occasion. The streets were decked with flags.*

declaim /dɪˈkleɪm/ *tr/intr.v* (often — *against s.o/ s.t*) (*formal*) make (a speech), speak, strongly and with great feeling (against s.o/s.t): *He declaimed against the government's action in using the police to break the strike.*

declamation /ˌdekləˈmeɪʃən/ *c/u.n.*

declamatory /dɪˈklæmətərɪ/ *adj* (speech, style of speaking) that declaims.

declare /dɪˈkleə/ *v* **1** *tr.v* make (s.t) known; state (s.t) officially or publicly: *The government has declared its intention to reduce taxes. After looking at the photograph of the finish, the judges declared Smith the winner*(1). **2** *tr/intr.v* speak, say, (s.t) strongly: *He declared that he would never agree. 'I didn't say that at all!' she declared.* **3** *tr.v* make a formal statement, e.g to a customs or tax official, about (goods, payments etc on which import(1) duty(4) or tax may be payable): *The customs official at the airport asked them if they had anything to declare. We shall have to declare the plants we're bringing into the country.* **4** *tr/intr.v* (in cricket¹) stop batting²(2), end (an innings(1)), before losing all the players in one's team, because of the belief that the other team will not score as many runs: *India declared* (*its* innings(1)) *at 540 for 6.*

declaration /ˌdekləˈreɪʃən/ *c/u.n* (example of the) act or state of declaring s.t or of being declared: *a declaration of love.*

de'clared *attrib.adj* (of an intention etc) that has been declared(1): *It was their declared opinion that the government would lose the election.*

declassify /diːˈklæsɪˌfaɪ/ *tr.v* (-*ies*, -*ied*) allow (an official document(1) that has been) treated as secret to be seen and read by the public: *Some government papers are declassified after 30 years.* ⇒ classified(2).

declassification /diːˌklæsɪfɪˈkeɪʃən/ *u.n.*

declension ⇒ decline².

decline¹ /dɪˈklaɪn/ **1** (often — *in s.t*) slow decrease in (numbers, health, power, quality etc): *a slow decline in the price of petrol*; *a decline in* (*the*) *population*; *a decline in his health*; *the decline in popularity of the leader.* **2** (of a mountain; also *fig*) downward slope: *The path took us down a sharp decline into a valley below. The decline of his business began when the new* supermarket *opened.* **in decline**; **on the decline** gradually decreasing, getting worse etc: *Some people think religion is in decline. His health was on the decline.*

▷ *v* **3** *intr.v* (of numbers, strength, power, health etc) become less, worse etc: *The population has declined. His influence has declined this year. Her health declined after the operation.* Opposite increase(1). **4** *intr.v* (of a mountain; also *fig*) slope, move, downwards: *At this point the path declines sharply. Business always declines at this time of year.* **5** *tr/intr.v* (*formal*) state that one cannot accept (an invitation etc), usu in a polite way: *I'm sorry, I'm not free that evening so I must decline* (*your invitation*). Opposite accept(1).

decline² /dɪˈklaɪn/ *tr/intr.v* (*grammar*) give (the correct forms of endings of pronouns etc). Compare decline¹ (*v*).

declension /dɪˈklenʃən/ *c/u.n* (*grammar*) (example of the) changing of (the endings of) nouns, pronouns and adjectives because of their relation to other words in the sentence, e.g 'us' is the *objective* form of 'we' ('we' is the *subjective* form). Compare conjugation.

decode /diːˈkəʊd/ *tr.v* change (s.t written in a code(3,4)) into plain language. Compare encode.

decompose /ˌdiːkəmˈpəʊz/ *tr/intr.v* **1** (cause (s.t, e.g food) to) become bad or rotten: *The dead bodies were decomposing in the heat.* Bacteria *in the soil help to decompose dead plants.* **2** (cause (a substance) to) separate into its parts: *The experiment shows how the chemical decomposes under certain conditions.*

decomposition /ˌdiːkɒmpəˈzɪʃən/ *u.n.*

decompress /ˌdiːkəmˈpres/ *tr/intr.v* (*technical*) **1** (gradually) reduce the air pressure to normal (for (s.o)): *It's important to decompress slowly if you have been very deep under water where the pressure is higher than normal.* **2** (cause (s.t) to) lose air pressure very quickly, esp as a result of an accident etc: *When the explosion happened, the* cabin(3) *decompressed and three people were sucked out of the hole.*

decompression /ˌdiːkəmˈpreʃən/ *u.n.*

decontaminate /ˌdiːkənˈtæmɪˌneɪt/ *tr.v* remove a harmful substance, e.g poison, gas, radioactivity from (an area, a building etc) in order to make it safe: *The whole area will have to be decontaminated after the leak of radioactive waste.* Compare contaminate(1).

decontamination /ˌdiːkənˌtæmɪˈneɪʃən/ *u.n.*

decor, **décor** /ˈdeɪkɔː/ *c/u.n* (example of the) way a room, house etc is decorated, furnished etc: *The decor in the restaurant is very successful.*

decorate /ˈdekəˌreɪt/ *v* **1** *tr.v* (often — *s.t with s.t*) make (s.t) more beautiful or attractive (by putting extra (pretty) things in/on it): *Would you help me decorate the hall (with flowers) for the party? She is very good at decorating cakes.* **2** *tr/intr.v* paint, wallpaper(2) etc, (a room in a) house): *Are you still decorating (your house)?* **3** *tr.v* (often — *s.o for s.t*) (*formal*) give (s.o) a medal(1) etc as a sign of honour (for s.t brave he/she has done): *He was decorated by the Queen for his services to the country.*

decoration /dekəˈreɪʃən/ *n* **1** *u.n* act or state of decorating(1,2) s.t: *The decoration of the hall was done by the students. The clock doesn't work; it's just for decoration.* **2** *c.n* thing used for decorating(1) s.t: *Who put up all the decorations for the party?* **3** *c.n* medal(1) etc given to decorate(3) s.o. **4** *u.n* (*fig*) thing added to make s.t seem more attractive than it really is: *This red stamp is decoration and does not make the contract more official.*

decorative /ˈdekrətɪv/ *adj* who/that looks attractive or pleasing but is usually not useful: *a decorative flower* arrangement(1).

ˈdecoratively *adv.*

decorator /ˈdekəˌreɪtə/ *c.n* person whose job is decorating(2).

decorous /ˈdekərəs/ *adj* (*formal*) (of a person, behaviour etc) who/that shows correctness, politeness, according to the rules of society: *She is decorous only in the company of older people.*

decorum /dɪˈkɔːrəm/ *u.n* (*formal*) correct behaviour: *You don't have to act with too much decorum when you meet my parents.*

decoy /ˈdiːkɔɪ/ *c.n* **1** person, animal (or an imitation of one), who/that is intended to trap or mislead s.o, an animal: *She acted as a decoy to catch the* rapist. *Wooden ducks are used as decoys in hunting.*

▷ *tr.v* /dɪˈkɔɪ/ **2** trap, mislead, (s.o, an animal etc), esp by sending her/him/it somewhere else: *They decoyed the guard (away from the room) by telling him there was a telephone call for him.*

decrease /ˈdiːkriːs/ *c/u.n* **1** (usu — *in/of s.o/s.t*) (amount of a) reduction (in size, number etc): *a decrease in population/expenditure; a 10 per cent decrease in profit; a decrease of over 10 000. Have you noticed any decrease in the number of applications?* **on the decrease** becoming less: *Crime is on the decrease.* Opposite increase(1).

▷ *tr/intr.v* /dɪˈkriːs/ **2** (cause (numbers, size etc) to) become less: *The government wants to decrease imports. Profits decreased by 10 per cent last year.* Opposite increase(2).

decree /dɪˈkriː/ *c.n* **1** official order, usu by a government or a ruler. **2** judgement by a court of law: *a decree of divorce(1).* **by decree** using a decree(1) or decrees: *The new government ruled the country by decree.*

▷ *tr.v* **3** (usu — *that . . .*) make a decree(1,2) (that s.t should happen etc): *The judge decreed that the defendant should pay the woman £20 000.*

deˌcree ˈabsoˌlute *c.n* (*law*) decree(2) for a divorce(1) without further delay.

deˌcree ˈnisi /ˈnaɪsaɪ/ *c.n* (*law*) decree(2) for a divorce(1) to be legal on a certain later date unless there is an objection.

decrepit /dɪˈkrepɪt/ *adj* (*formal*) **1** (of a person, an animal) weak and sick, esp from old age, hard work etc: *a decrepit old dog.* **2** (of s.t built, made) broken, worn out: *decrepit machinery.*

decrepitude /dɪˈkrepɪˌtjuːd/ *u.n.*

decry /dɪˈkraɪ/ *tr.v* (-ies, -ied) (*formal*) criticize, complain about, (s.t), esp in order to make it look useless or worse: *He decried all their promises to improve the situation.*

dedicate /ˈdedɪˌkeɪt/ *tr.v* **1** (usu — *oneself, one's life, to (doing) s.t*) give, devote, (all of one's time, life, efforts) (to (doing) s.t): *He decided to dedicate himself to (helping) the poor. All her spare time is dedicated to teaching her deaf son to speak.* **2** (usu — *s.t to s.o*) say, write, that (a book, poem, song etc) is in honour of s.o: *The book was dedicated to his wife. She dedicated the song to everyone struggling for freedom.* **3** (usu — *s.t to s.o/s.t*) (esp religion) build, provide, (s.t), often with a special ceremony, (in honour of s.o/s.t): *The new church was dedicated to St Francis.*

ˈdediˌcated *adj* **1** who has/shows great dedication(1) to s.t: *She's dedicated to her work. He is a dedicated football fan.* **2** who gives a lot of time, love, attention to s.o: *She's dedicated to her father. He's a dedicated father and husband.*

dedication /ˌdedɪˈkeɪʃən/ *n* **1** *u.n* (showing of) great firmness of purpose, of dedicating(1) oneself, one's life etc, to s.t: *Terry showed great dedication in his job.* **2** *c.n* words said or written that dedicate(2) a book, poem etc to s.o. **3** *u.n* act of dedicating(3) s.t or of s.t being dedicated: *A date has been set for the dedication of the new church.*

deduce /dɪ'djuːs/ *tr.v* (often — *s.t from s.t*; — *that . . .*) (*formal*) make (a judgement), form (an opinion), discover (s.t), (from known facts, information etc that . . .): *I deduce from what you say that you are not in favour of the plan.*
de'ducible *adj* (*formal*) that can be deduced.
deduction[1] /dɪ'dʌkʃən/ *c/u.n* (example of the) act of deducing s.t: *By a simple process of deduction she knew that he was lying. What deductions do you make from this evidence?* Compare deduction[2] (⇒ deduct).
deduct /dɪ'dʌkt/ *tr.v* (usu — *s.t from s.t*) take away (s.t, esp money) (from an amount etc): *I'm going to deduct the cost of the new window from your pocket money.*
de'ductible *adj* that can be, is allowed to be, deducted: *deductible expenses.*
deduction[2] /dɪ'dʌkʃən/ *c/u.n* (example of the) act of deducting s.t; amount of money taken away from s.t: *My deductions this month added up to nearly a quarter of my salary. What deduction will you give me if I pay cash(1)?* Compare deduction[1] (⇒ deduce).
deed /diːd/ *c.n* **1** (*formal; literary*) thing done by s.o: *a good deed; the deeds of famous men and women.* **2** (*law*) document(1) or agreement, esp about ownership of s.t: *We sign the deeds of our new house tomorrow.*
deejay /ˌdiː'dʒeɪ/ *c.n* (*informal*) = dj (disc jockey).
deem /diːm/ *tr.v* (often — *s.t (to be) s.t*) (*formal*) think, decide, (s.t to be s.t): *She deemed the whole idea (to be) a waste of time.* **deem it wise, necessary** etc **to do s.t** judge/think that it is wise etc to do s.t: *He deemed it important to tell her what was happening. Do you deem it wise to tell her the truth?*
deep /diːp/ *adj* **1** being a long way down (from a surface, the top of s.t): *a deep river/mine/wound. I can't touch the bottom of the swimming pool — it's too deep.* Opposite shallow(1). **2** (of an area, object etc) measured downwards, across, from front to back etc (by a certain amount): *a mine 1000 metres deep; a box 30 centimetres deep by 20 centimetres wide and 10 centimetres across; a deep drawer/cupboard.* **3** (of colour) strong: *deep red; a deep blue sky.* ⇒ dark(2), light[1](2), pale(1). **4** (of a voice, sound) having a low pitch[1](4): *She spoke in a very deep voice. A deep sound came from the cave.* **5** (of a breath etc) taking in a lot of air; coming from down inside one: *He took a deep breath and dived in. She gave a deep sigh.* **6** (of sleep) so great that it is difficult to wake (s.o) up: *I fell into a deep sleep.* Compare light[2](8). **7** (of s.t bad) so great that it is difficult to escape: *You'll be in deep trouble if you don't finish the job on time.* **8** (of (the expression of) a feeling) very great; strongly felt: *She showed her deep happiness. Her love for him is very deep. You have our deepest sympathies.* **9** (of a person, thought, event etc) very or too difficult to understand: *He's far too deep for me; I never understand a word he says. The whole thing's a deep mystery.* **deep in s.t** (a) a long way inside s.t: *There was a house deep in the woods.* ⇒ deep(10). (b) totally concerned in s.t (so that one does not notice anything else etc): *He was deep in thought. She was deep in a book* (i.e reading it) *and didn't hear me come in.* (c) very greatly or heavily in a difficulty, problem etc: *They're deep in debt.* ⇒ depth(2). **go off at the deep end** ⇒ end(*n*).
▷ *adv* **10** (often — *into s.t*) (going, continuing) far down or in(to) (s.t): *The deeper you go (into the woods) the darker it gets. The discussion continued deep into the night. You have to dig deep if you want to find water.* ⇒ deep in s.t(a). **deep down** (**inside**, **in**(**to**) **s.t**) (a) very far down (in(to) s.t): *They dived deep down into the sea to find the wreck.* (b) (esp of the way one thinks, what one feels etc) hidden or buried (inside oneself etc): *Deep down (inside) she knew she would have to leave him. He's not such a bad person deep down. Deep down in her heart she was sorry.*
▷ *def.n* **11** (*literary*) sea: *His body was consigned(2) to the deep.* **in the deep of the night**, **winter** etc in the middle of the night etc.
-deep *adj* being deep(2) by the amount shown by the first part of the word; covered to a certain height (on one's body etc): *a metre-deep hole. The water is only knee-deep.*
'deepen *tr/intr.v* (cause (s.t) to) become deep(er)(1–9): *Do I need to deepen the hole any further? The colour needs to be deepened. His voice is deepening. His troubles deepened when the bills began to arrive. The mystery deepened.*
'deep-'freeze *c.n* **1** special kind of refrigerator or compartment(2) in an ordinary one that freezes food quickly, esp for storing.
▷ *tr.v* **2** freeze (food) in a deep-freeze(1).
'deeply *adv* **1** in a deep(1) way: *The beach slopes deeply at this point.* **2** (of a feeling) felt very greatly; in a deep(8) way: *I'm deeply worried about her. The film affected him deeply.*
'deepness *u.n* fact or state of being deep(*adj*).
'deep-'rooted/-'seated *adj* (esp of a belief, opinion) very strong and so not likely to be changed: *That's a deep-seated difficulty we had to accept long ago. His problems are deep-rooted.*
'deep-,sea *attrib.adj* of, in, places where the sea is very deep: *deep-sea diving/divers.*
,deep 'water *u.n* (**'deep-,water** when *attrib*) water, esp the sea, where it is (very) deep: *deep-water exploration.* **be in**, **get into**, **deep water** (*fig*) be etc in a lot of difficulty: *You'll get into deep water if you aren't more careful with your money.*
deer /dɪə/ *c.n* (*pl* deer) kind of large animal that is graceful and can run fast; the male has antlers.
de-escalate /ˌdiː 'eskə,leɪt/ *tr/intr.v* (cause (a dangerous political situation) to) become less dangerous: *Both governments are trying to de-escalate the tension(4) on their borders.*
de-escalation /ˌdiː ˌeskə'leɪʃən/ *u.n*.
def written *abbr* definite (used in this dictionary to describe the definite article ('the') or (*def.n*) nouns that always have 'the' in front of them).
deface /dɪ'feɪs/ *tr.v* (*formal*) mark, spoil or damage (a building etc): *The war memorial had been defaced by a peace group.*
de'facement *u.n*.
defame /dɪ'feɪm/ *tr.v* (*formal*) say bad things about (s.o, s.o's reputation): *She accused him of defaming her (good name).*
defamation /ˌdefə'meɪʃən/ *u.n* (*formal*; *law*) act or fact of defaming s.o or of being defamed. **defamation of character** (*law*) (case of accusing s.o of an) attack on one's reputation.

defamatory /dɪˈfæmətərɪ/ adj (of a remark, s.t written etc) that is thought, is likely, to defame s.o: *He brought a case against the newspaper for certain defamatory remarks made in an article.*

default /dɪˈfɔːlt/ u.n (formal) **1** act of failing to do s.t that one has to do, e.g pay money, appear at a certain time, esp according to the law or a rule: *It was a clear case of default.* **by default** (esp in competitions) because one/s.o does not appear at the right time: *They won the match by default* (i.e because the other team did not appear). **in default of s.o/s.t** (formal) through the absence of s.o or the lack of s.t: *In default of payment you'll lose the car.*
▷ intr.v **2** (often — on s.t) (formal) fail to do s.t that one has to do, e.g pay money, appear at a certain time: *He defaulted on his* mortgage(1) *payments and lost the house.*

defeat /dɪˈfiːt/ c/unique n **1** (example of the) act of winning a victory over an enemy or over s.o who opposes one: *Our main aim must be the defeat of the government in the next election.* **2** (example of the) act of losing in a competition, battle etc against s.o, a team, army etc: *We must avoid another defeat. Our team has had three defeats in a row.* Opposite victory. **a crushing defeat** ⇒ crushing.
▷ tr.v **3** win a victory over (s.o/s.t): *Our team defeated theirs by four goals to two. The government was defeated by 50 votes and had to resign.*

de'featism u.n fact or state of thinking that one will be easily defeated (so that one does not try hard enough): *His defeatism affects the whole group.*

de'featist c.n (also attrib) person who shows defeatism: *He's such a defeatist he doesn't even try to do well.*

defecate /ˈdefɪˌkeɪt/ intr.v (technical; formal) (of a person, an animal) pass waste matter from the bowels(1) out through the anus: *He was arrested for defecating in a public place.*

defecation /ˌdefɪˈkeɪʃən/ u.n.

defect¹ /ˈdiːfekt/ c.n (formal) fault (in a machine, in a system, in s.o, s.o's character etc): *There is a defect in these plates so they are being sold cheaply. She has a speech defect.*

de'fective adj (of a machine, system etc) that has one or more defects: *The manufacturers will replace any defective parts. He has defective hearing/* vision(1). ⇒ deficient.

de'fectively adv. **de'fectiveness** u.n.

defect² /dɪˈfekt/ intr.v (often — (from s.t/s.w) to s.t/s.w) leave (one's country, political party) and go to live in another country or join another political party: *Another* spy(1) *defected to the East(4)/West(4).*

defection /dɪˈfekʃən/ c/u.n (example of the) act of defecting: *There were several defections when the new political party was formed.*

de'fector c.n person who defects.

defence ⇒ defend.

defend /dɪˈfend/ v **1** tr.v (often — oneself/s.o/ s.t against/from s.o/s.t) protect (oneself/s.o/s.t against s.o, an attack): *He defended himself as best he could. They defended the town against the enemy attack.* **2** tr.v (often — s.t against/from s.o/s.t) speak, argue etc for (one's opinions etc) (against s.o, an attack etc): *You must learn to defend your beliefs (against other opinions).* **3** tr.v

(law) (of a lawyer) argue for (an accused person in a case): *If I were a lawyer I'd find it difficult to defend a murderer.* Compare prosecute. **4** tr/ intr.v (in sport) protect (a goal, etc) against attack by the other side: *They defended (the goal area) very well.* Opposite attack.

defence /dɪˈfens/ n (US **de'fense**) **1** u.n (often — against s.o/s.t) act of fighting, protecting oneself, (against an attack by an enemy or s.o who wants to harm one): *There was very little defence when we attacked. He offered no defence against the robbers.* **2** c/u.n (also attrib) method, means, thing, used to protect oneself/s.t against attack: *The castle had very strong defences. Their defence in the match was very strong. Defence* expenditure(2) *is being increased.* **3** c/u.n (often have no etc — against s.o/s.t) ability to resist (s.o, s.o's persuasions, a disease etc): *He had very little defence against their arguments. Her body was so weak that it had no defence(s) against the disease.* **4** c/u.n (also attrib) (law) answer or argument used by an accused person or a lawyer against an accusation: *The judge will be hearing the case for the defence (or the defence case) tomorrow.* Compare prosecution(1). **5** def.n (also attrib) (law) (the lawyer(s) who argue(s) the) case for the defence(4): *The defence produced two new witnesses. The defence rests* (i.e has completed its evidence(2)). Compare prosecution(2). **6** def.n (in sport) players who protect a goal from attack by the other side: *Gary broke through the defence and scored.* **Counsel for the defence** (law) lawyer or barrister who represents an accused person. **Department of Defense** (US); **Ministry of Defence** (UK) (abbr MOD) government department responsible for the defence(1,2) of the country against military attack. **in defence (of s.o/s.t)** in order to defend(1,2) o.s/s.o against attack (for s.t): *Few people would speak in her defence. He fought for many years in defence of freedom.*

de'fenceless adj who/that has no defence(1–3) against attack.

de'fencelessly adv. **de'fencelessness** u.n.

de'fence ˌmechanism c.n **1** uncontrolled movement of a part of the body, e.g blinking(2), to protect (a part of) the body: *You must have very quick defence mechanisms to have managed to avoid that car!* **2** way of acting or behaving to protect o.s, esp against criticism: *Her anger is just a defence mechanism — she's always like that when she feels criticized.*

defendant /dɪˈfendənt/ c.n (law) accused person. Compare plaintiff.

de'fender c.n person who defends(1–4) s.o/s.t.

de'fensible adj that can be defended(1,2): *a defensible position; a defensible action.* Opposite indefensible.

de'fensive adj **1** who/that shows or offers (a) defence(1–3): *The soldiers took up defensive positions. We are developing new defensive weapons.* Opposite aggressive(2).
▷ def.n **2** **on the defensive** in a state of defending(1,2), ready to defend(1,2), oneself/s.o/ s.t: *After its recent losses, the army has gone on the defensive. She's not very sure of herself and seems always on the defensive.*

de'fensively adv. **de'fensiveness** u.n.

defer¹ /dɪˈfɜː/ tr.v (-rr-) (formal) delay, postpone,

(s.t, doing s.t) to a later time: *As no one could agree, the decision was deferred.*

defer² /dɪ'fɜː/ *intr.v* (*-rr-*) (usu — *to s.o/s.t*) (*formal*) show respect to, accept, s.o, s.o's opinions etc, usu because of her/his higher position etc: *I defer to your better judgement in these matters.*

  deference /'defərəns/ *u.n* (often show — *to s.o/ s.t*) (*formal*) willingness to consider the views, opinions, needs of others: *She treats her teachers with deference. You must always show deference to older people.* **in, out of, deference (to s.o/ s.t)** showing willingness to defer² to s.o/s.t: *In deference to your mother's wishes, I will pay for your university education.*

  deferential /ˌdefə'renʃəl/ *adj* (of a person, behaviour) who/that shows deference.
  ˌdefe'rentially *adv.*

defiance, defiant ⇒ defy.

deficient /dɪ'fɪʃənt/ *adj* (often — *in s.t*) (*formal*) lacking (s.t), not having enough (of s.t), esp s.t that is important: *His skills for this job are deficient. Their bad eating habits meant that their bodies were deficient in the* vitamins *they needed.* ⇒ defect¹, defective.

  de'ficiency *c/u.n* (*pl -ies*) (example of the) fact or state of being deficient: *His deficiencies for the job are only too clear. There is still a deficiency of £5000. She has a* vitamin *deficiency.* Compare defect¹.

  de'ficiently *adv.*

deficit /'defɪsɪt/ *c.n* amount, esp of money, by which an actual amount is less than that needed to make payments: *We need only one thousand pounds to make up the deficit in our account. The country has a deficit on its balance of payments* (i.e more money is going out of the country to pay for goods, services etc than is coming in for goods, services etc it has sold).

defile /dɪ'faɪl/ *tr.v* (*formal*) **1** make (s.t that was clean) dirty: *Dog owners will be fined if their dogs defile the* grass (1). **2** make (s.o, s.o's mind) evil or impure: *He was accused of defiling the minds of the young.*

  de'filement *u.n.*

define /dɪ'faɪn/ *tr.v* **1** give the meaning of (a word): *Who can define (the word) 'punish'? Some dictionaries not only define words but also show the user how to use them.* **2** set or show the limits of (s.t, esp s.o's power): *His responsibilities were defined for him in his job description.* **3** (often passive) show the shape or outline of (s.o/s.t): *The moving figures were clearly defined against the blue sky.*

  de'finable *adj* that can be defined. Opposite indefinable.

  definition /ˌdefɪ'nɪʃən/ *n* **1** *c.n* (explanation of the) meaning of a word: *This dictionary gives the definitions of many words and* phrases (1). **2** *u.n* clearness, sharpness, of a shape, object, photograph etc: *The whole photograph lacks definition.*

definite /'defɪnɪt/ *adj* (of a person, statement, action etc) very certain: *She has such definite opinions. Is he definite about leaving his job? I can't decide; I'll give you a definite answer tomorrow. That's definite then, we'll meet at 5 o'clock. The whole thing was a definite failure/ success.* Opposite indefinite.

ˌdefinite 'article *c/def.n* (*grammar*) 'the'. Compare indefinite article.

'definitely *adv* **1** in a definite, clear way: *He is definitely right/wrong. Are you definitely going to the party?* **2** (in answer to a question) certainly; without doubt: *'Are you going?' 'Definitely (not)!'*

ˌdefinite 'noun *c.n* (*grammar*) noun that always has 'the' in front of it (marked *def.n* in this dictionary), e.g 'the North'.

ˌdefinite 'plural ˌnoun *c.n* (*grammar*) noun that can only be used with 'the' and that takes a plural verb (marked *def.pl.n* in this dictionary), e.g 'the poor'.

definitive /dɪ'fɪnɪtɪv/ *adj* (of a statement, book etc) that provides all that is known (about s.o/s.t) and is so complete that nothing else needs to be written or stated: *a definitive history of England.*

deflate /dɪ'fleɪt/ *v* (*formal*) **1** *tr/intr.v* (cause (a tyre, balloon etc) to) lose air or pressure so that it becomes smaller: *They deflated the hot air balloon in order to lose height.* **2** *tr/intr.v* (*fig*) (cause (s.o) to) lose one's enthusiasm, excitement, feelings, for s.t: *We worked so hard to prepare for the event I felt completely deflated afterwards.* **3** *tr.v* make (s.o) feel less important; reduce (a person's high opinion of herself/himself): *My remarks were intended to deflate him* (or his ego (2)). **4** *tr/intr.v* (*commerce*) reduce the amount of money that is available for spending in (a country's economy (4)) in order to reduce prices, incomes etc: *One of the ways a government may try to deflate the economy is by making it expensive to borrow money.* Compare inflate (2).

  deflation /dɪ'fleɪʃən/ *u.n.*

deflect /dɪ'flekt/ *v* **1** *tr/intr.v* (often — (s.t) *off s.o/s.t*) (cause (s.t, esp a moving object) to) turn, move, in a different direction (as a result of hitting s.o/s.t): *The ball deflected off the* goalkeeper's *boot and went over the goal.* **2** *tr.v* (often — *s.o from s.t*) (*formal*) turn (s.o, s.o's attention etc) away (from s.t he/she wants to do): *He tried to deflect her from her purpose but with no success.*

  deflection /dɪ'flekʃən/ *c/u.n.*

defoliate /diː'fəʊlɪeɪt/ *tr.v* (*technical*) remove the leaves from (a plant, tree etc), esp by the use of chemicals: *Pollution in rain is defoliating many forests in Europe.*

  defoliation /diːˌfəʊlɪ'eɪʃən/ *u.n.*

deforest /diː'fɒrɪst/ *tr.v* (*formal*) remove, cut down, trees from (an area): *Large areas have been deforested and the animals are dying.*

  deforestation /diːˌfɒrɪ'steɪʃən/ *u.n.*

deform /dɪ'fɔːm/ *tr.v* (*formal*) cause (s.t) to lose its shape; spoil the shape of (s.t): *His missing tooth deformed his smile.*

  deformation /ˌdiːfɔː'meɪʃən/ *c/u.n.*

  de'formed *adj* (esp of a person, part of the body) not having a natural shape; twisted, badly shaped: *a deformed back/shoulder.*

  deformity /dɪ'fɔːmɪtɪ/ *c/u.n* (*pl -ies*) (example of the) fact or state of being deformed: *She's walked here in spite of the deformity of her leg.*

defraud /dɪ'frɔːd/ *tr.v* (often — *s.o of s.t*) cheat (s.o) by getting and keeping s.t, esp money, that belongs to her/him: *He defrauded the old lady of all her savings by pretending to* invest (1) *them for her.* ⇒ fraud.

defray /dɪ'freɪ/ tr.v (formal) pay (the cost, expenses) for s.o/s.t: *He offered to defray her hospital bills provided she paid him back later.*

defrost /diː'frɒst/ v 1 tr.v (cause (a refrigerator) to) become free of ice: *You need to defrost the refrigerator regularly.* 2 tr/intr.v (cause (frozen food) to) become no longer frozen: *Let the meat defrost before cooking it. I've defrosted a chicken for dinner tonight.*

deft /deft/ adj (formal) (of a person, the way one handles s.t) neat and skilled: *His deft control(3) of the ball enabled him to score many goals. The government is very deft in dealing with awkward questions.*
'deftly adv. **'deftness** u.n.

defunct /dɪ'fʌŋkt/ adj (law; formal) no longer in force; no longer active or working; dead: *These laws have been defunct for some time now. These machines are defunct and you can't even get spare parts for them any more.*

defuse /diː'fjuːz/ tr.v 1 (technical) remove the fuse(1) from (a bomb etc) so that it will not explode. 2 remove or reduce the danger from (a bad situation): *Her anger was defused by the joke.*

defy /dɪ'faɪ/ tr.v (-ies, -ied) 1 refuse to obey (s.o, s.o's order etc): *He defied his parents and stayed out all night.* 2 (formal) avoid (s.o/s.t): *We managed to defy the danger by hiding during the day and moving only after dark.* 3 (usu — s.o to do s.t) ask, dare, (s.o to do s.t, explain s.t etc), esp because one thinks he/she cannot do it, explain it etc: *I defy you to give me a good reason for what he has done.* **defy description, solution** etc be impossible to describe, solve etc: *His behaviour defies belief.*

defiance /dɪ'faɪəns/ u.n fact or act of being defiant.

defiant /dɪ'faɪənt/ adj (derog) (of a person, behaviour) who/that opposes s.o/s.t, refuses to obey, accept orders etc: *a defiant young man. He remained defiant.*
de'fiantly adv.

degenerate /dɪ'dʒenərɪt/ adj 1 (derog) (of a person, behaviour etc) who/that is no longer moral, responsible etc: *As a student he led a degenerate life.*
▷ c.n /dɪ'dʒenərɪt/ 2 (derog) degenerate(1) person.
▷ intr.v /dɪ'dʒenəˌreɪt/ 3 (start to) become degenerate(1): *You have only to look around you to see that society is degenerating.* 4 (often — (from s.t) into s.t) change (from a normal state) to a much worse one: *The quarrel quickly degenerated into a fight.*
degeneracy /dɪ'dʒenərəsɪ/, **degeneration** /dɪˌdʒenə'reɪʃən/ u.n.
degenerative /dɪ'dʒenərətɪv/ adj that becomes gradually worse: *a degenerative disease.*

degrade /dɪ'greɪd/ tr.v (often — oneself/s.o by doing s.t) make (oneself/s.o) lose self-respect (by doing s.t that causes disgust with oneself, others etc): *She would not degrade herself by begging for help.*
degradation /ˌdegrə'deɪʃən/ c/u.n (formal) (example of) fact or state of degrading oneself/s.o or of being degraded.
de'grading adj that degrades oneself/s.o: *a degrading job.*

degree /dɪ'griː/ n 1 c.n unit of measurement of temperature shown by the sign °: *minus 20 degrees* (−20°); *15 degrees* Fahrenheit/Celsius/Centigrade (15°F, 15°C). 2 c.n unit of measurement of an angle shown by the sign °: *an angle of 45 degrees* (45°). *There are 360 degrees in a full circle.* 3 c/u.n (often — of s.t) certain amount on a general scale or measurement (of ability, skill etc): *Some degree of experience is needed for this job. The work demands a degree of skill. The school has students with different degrees of ability.* 4 c.n (also attrib) (often — in s.t) title given to s.o by a university, usu for having passed an examination (in a subject): *a degree in mathematics from Leeds University; a degree course; an* honorary(2) *degree* (i.e one given to s.o as a sign of respect). **by degrees** gradually; slowly: *She felt her game improving by degrees.* **first-degree** ⇒ first. **(not in) the least/ slightest degree (amused, interested** etc) (not) at all (amused etc): *He showed not the slightest degree of interest in her. Are you in the least degree interested in what I am saying?* **of high, low** etc **degree** (formal; old use) (of a person) having a high, low etc position in society. **third degree** ⇒ three. **to a degree** (formal) to a very great extent: *He is efficient to a degree.* **to a, some** etc **degree** to a certain (small etc) extent: *To some degree you are right but I don't think you have considered the whole problem.*

dehydrate /ˌdiː'haɪdreɪt/ tr/intr.v (cause (a body, substance, food etc) to) lose (its natural) water: *Many vegetables are dehydrated in order to preserve them. It's important to drink a lot when one is sweating so as not to dehydrate.*
ˌde'hydrated adj (esp of foods) dried by removing the natural water: *dehydrated* peas(1).

de-ice /ˌdiː 'aɪs/ tr.v remove the ice from (the outside surface of an aircraft, window of a car etc).
ˌde-'icer c.n device or chemical that de-ices s.t.

deify /'diːɪˌfaɪ/ tr.v (-ies, -ied) make (s.o) a god; treat (s.o/s.t) as a god.

deign /deɪn/ intr.v (formal) (usu not — to do s.t) be willing to lower one's high opinion of oneself, one's importance etc (enough to do s.t): *John thinks he is so important now that he doesn't deign to speak to us ordinary people.*

deity /'diːɪtɪ/ n 1 c.n (pl -ies) god or goddess. 2 def.n (with capital **D**) God.

dejected /dɪ'dʒektɪd/ adj (of a person, look etc) sad, miserable; in low spirits: *She was very dejected after losing the match.*
de'jectedly adv. **dejection** /dɪ'dʒekʃən/ u.n.

delay /dɪ'leɪ/ c/u.n 1 (example of the) act or state of having to wait for s.t (to happen), of s.t happening later than expected etc: *Because of the bad weather there have been flight delays at the airport. They announced a ten-minute delay. After some delay we finally got started.* **without delay** immediately: *They arrived to repair the gas leak without delay.*
▷ v 2 tr/intr.v (cause (s.o/s.t) to) be, arrive, happen etc later than expected: *The chairperson delayed the meeting until we arrived. I was delayed by the heavy traffic. Our flight was delayed.* 3 tr.v postpone ((doing) s.t that one has planned) to a later date: *The government has delayed the introduction of tax cuts.*

delectable /dɪ'lektəbl/ adj (formal) (of a person, food etc) extremely beautiful, pleasant, attractive etc: *The tables were full of the most delectable food you could imagine. She looked delectable in her wedding dress.*

delectation /ˌdi:lek'teɪʃən/ u.n.

delegate /'delɪgɪt/ c.n **1** person chosen or elected to represent a country, group of people etc at a meeting, conference etc: *a United Nations delegate; the miners' delegates in the pay negotiations.*
▷ v/'delɪˌgeɪt/ **2** tr.v (often — s.o to (do) s.t) (formal) choose (s.o) as a delegate(1) etc (to a meeting, to do s.t): *The union delegated her to attend the party conference. Why is it always me who's delegated to look after the children?* **3** tr/intr.v (often — (s.t) to s.o) give (power, responsibility, work etc) (to s.o else, esp s.o in a lower position): *She delegates a lot of the work to her staff. A good boss is one who can delegate.*

delegation /ˌdelɪ'geɪʃən/ n **1** u.n (often — of s.t (to s.o)) act of delegating(3) (s.t to s.o): *Who is responsible for the delegation of work in this office?* **2** c.n group of delegates(1): *the American delegation at the United Nations.*

delete /dɪ'li:t/ tr.v (often — s.t from s.t) remove, cross out, rub out etc (a word, sentence, name etc) (from a piece of writing, list etc): *This whole paragraph(1) should be deleted from your speech. Why has her name been deleted from the list?*

deletion /dɪ'li:ʃən/ c/u.n.

deliberate /dɪ'lɪbərɪt/ adj **1** (of s.t said, done etc) fully intended and not by chance: *a deliberate lie; a deliberate attempt to make her late.* **2** (of a person, way of moving, speaking etc) careful and slow in order to be sure: *He is very deliberate in everything he says and does.*
▷ v /dɪ'lɪbəˌreɪt/ **3** tr/intr.v (often — about/(up)on s.t) (formal) think, discuss, consider (s.t, about s.t etc) very carefully, for some time etc: *The committee deliberated (on the matter) for over an hour but reached no decision. We're still deliberating whether or not to go.*

de'liberately adv in a deliberate(1,2) way: *You deliberately hit her! He gave his speech slowly and deliberately.*

deliberation /dɪˌlɪbə'reɪʃən/ n **1** u.n fact or state of being deliberate(2): *speak with deliberation.* **2** c/u.n (example of) the act of deliberating(3) (s.t, about s.t etc): *After due deliberation he gave his views. The deliberations of the committee must remain secret.*

delicate /'delɪkɪt/ adj **1** easily broken and so needing to be held, moved etc carefully: *delicate cups/flowers.* **2** easily made ill, tired etc: *a delicate child; feel delicate after a long journey.* **3** using thin, pretty lines: *a delicate pattern on the wallpaper(1).* **4** pleasant and not strong: *a delicate taste/colour/smell; the delicate sound of very small bells.* **5** thin, light and soft: *delicate silk.* **6** easily affected by small changes and so able to do fine work: *delicate scientific instruments.* **7** likely to become unpleasant, bad etc and so needing careful treatment: *a delicate situation. I have to be very delicate with my son when discussing politics because he soon becomes angry.* Compare **indelicate**(2).

'delicacy n **1** c.n special (usu expensive) item of food that is particularly nice to eat: *Smoked*

salmon *is a delicacy in Britain.* **2** u.n (formal) fact of being delicate: *the delicacy of the flowers; the delicacy of the problem.*

delicatessen /ˌdelɪkə'tesn/ c.n ((department in a) shop selling) cooked meat, cheese, spices, foreign food etc. ⇨ delicacy(1).

delicious /dɪ'lɪʃəs/ adj **1** having a very pleasant taste: *That was a delicious meal.* **2** very pleasant (when tasted, smelled etc): *a delicious smell; the delicious taste of French bread.*

de'liciously adv. **de'liciousness** u.n.

delight /dɪ'laɪt/ c/u.n **1** (thing producing) pleasure or satisfaction: *It was such a delight to meet you. Seeing him win the medal(1) filled me with delight. We enjoy the delights of Paris in the spring.* **take delight in (doing) s.t** = delight in (doing s.t).
▷ v **2** tr.v please (s.o) very much: *He delighted the audience by singing another song. I'm delighted to see you here. We'd be delighted to come to your party.* **delight in (doing) s.t** (formal) get much pleasure from (doing) s.t: *She delights in walking in the mountains.*

de'lightful adj giving much pleasure: *Thank you for a delightful evening.*

de'lightfully adv.

delimit /di:'lɪmɪt/ tr.v (formal) (decide and) fix the limitations(1) of (s.t): *His power is delimited by the authority of the senior managers.*

delimitation /di:ˌlɪmɪ'teɪʃən/ c/u.n.

delineate /dɪ'lɪnɪˌeɪt/ tr.v (formal) give an idea of (s.t) by drawing it or by writing a description and giving small details: *The manager delineated her plans for a new sales effort in Europe.*

delineation /dɪˌlɪnɪ'eɪʃən/ u.n.

delinquent /dɪ'lɪŋkwənt/ adj (usu attrib) **1** (of a young person) who has done s.t that is unlawful, very bad etc: *a delinquent teenager.* **2** (of behaviour, actions) unlawful or very bad.
▷ c.n **3** young person who has done s.t unlawful or very bad, esp one who does this often: *juvenile delinquent.*

de'linquency c/u.n (pl -ies) (example of) unlawful behaviour, esp by young people.

delirious /dɪ'lɪərɪəs/ adj **1** not able to think or speak in an organized or controlled way, e.g because of a serious illness, a knock on the head etc. **2** (often — with s.t) (fig) wildly excited (because of s.t): *He was delirious with happiness when she said she would marry him.*

de'liriously adv: *deliriously happy.*

delirium /dɪ'lɪərɪəm/ u.n (formal) fact or state of being delirious.

de,lirium 'tremens /'tri:menz/ u.n (usu the dt's) state of extreme fear, excitement and uncontrolled shaking etc because of drinking too much alcohol.

deliver /dɪ'lɪvə/ tr.v **1** (often — s.o/s.t to s.o/s.t) (take and) give (s.o/s.t) over (to s.o/a place etc): *My post is delivered very early in the morning. This letter was delivered to the wrong address. Your children will be delivered to your homes by 6 o'clock.* **2** help a woman or girl to give birth to (a child): *My son was delivered in hospital.* **3** (formal) help (a woman) to give birth: *She will deliver you safely in your own home.* **4** (formal) say (s.t), esp to an audience: *deliver a speech/ lecture.* **5** (formal) give or do (s.t): *I delivered a kick to his left knee and he fell to the floor.* **6** (usu

— *s.o from s.t*) (*old use*) set (s.o) free (from prison, from a duty or a promise etc). **deliver the goods** ⇨ goods.

de'liverance *u.n* (usu — *from s.t*) (*old use*) fact of being delivered(6) (from prison etc).

de'livery *n* (*pl -ies*) **1** *c/u.n* (often — *to s.o/s.t*) (example of the) fact or act of delivering(1) s.o/s.t (to s.o/s.t): *postal deliveries to distant places.* **2** *c.n* act of giving birth: *It was an easy/difficult delivery.* **3** *c.n* act or way of speaking to an audience: *The speech was good but her delivery was poor.* **4** *c.n* act of throwing a ball, esp in cricket': *an overarm delivery.*

dell /del/ *c.n* (*poetry*) small valley with trees.

delouse /diː'laʊs/ *tr.v* take lice (⇨ louse(1)) from (s.o, s.o's hair, an animal etc).

delphinium /del'fɪnɪəm/ *c.n* **1** kind of garden flower with tall, usu blue, flowers on long stems. **2** (also *attrib*) its light blue colour.

delta /'deltə/ *n* **1** *c/unique n* 4th letter of the Greek alphabet (Δ, δ). **2** *c.n* area of land where a river joins the sea or a lake that is like a Greek Δ in shape, usu with one or more branches: *the Nile delta.*

'delta,wing *c.n* (also *attrib*) (plane with a) wing shaped like a Greek Δ.

delude /dɪ'luːd/ *tr.v* (often — *o.s/s.o into doing s.t; — o.s/s.o with s.t*) (*formal*) deceive (o.s/s.o) by giving wrong information, emphasis(1) on facts etc: *He deluded her into thinking he would give her the job. I was deluded with a description that left out several important details.*

delusion /dɪ'luːʒən/ *n* **1** *u.n* act or fact of being deluded. **2** *c.n* (usu *be under the — that . . .*) belief that is wrong: *She was under the delusion that he would give her the job.* **3** (often *pl*) uncontrolled false belief, esp because of mental(3) illness, severe anxiety etc: *He's suffering from delusions* (or *from the delusion*) *that everyone hates him.* **a snare and a delusion** ⇨ snare(2).

delusory /dɪ'luːsərɪ/ *adj.*

deluge /'deljuːdʒ/ *c.n* (*formal*) **1** large amount of water falling or flooding s.t; period(1) of heavy rain. **2** (*fig*) large amount of s.t coming at one time: *a deluge of replies to our request for an assistant(2).*

▷ *tr.v* **3** (usu passive) (often — *s.o with s.t*) (*fig*) send s.t in large amounts to (s.o): *The singer was deluged with requests for her autograph(1).*

delusion, delusory ⇨ delude.

de luxe /də 'lʌks/ *attrib.adj* (*French*) of the best quality (and so costing a lot or much more than the usual quality): *a de luxe edition(1) of a book.*

delve /delv/ *intr.v* (often — *among/in(to) s.t*) search thoroughly (among things, in furniture, into facts etc) in order to find s.t or solve a problem: *He was delving among his papers* (or *in a drawer*) *trying to find the missing pen.*

demagogue /'deməɡɒɡ/ *c.n* (*derog*) person, esp a political leader, who gets or keeps control of other people by exciting their feelings or prejudices and not using reasonable arguments.

demagogic /ˌdeməˈɡɒɡɪk/ *adj.*

demagogically /ˌdeməˈɡɒkɪklɪ/ *adv.*

demand /dɪ'mɑːnd/ *n* **1** *c.n* (often — *for s.t*) (act of making a) strong request: *students' demands for bigger grants(1).* **2** *c.n* (often *make a — on s.t*) (act of making a) claim (on s.t one feels one has a right to): *Some people make too many demands on their doctor's time.* **3** *u.n* (often — *for s.o/s.t*) wish or willingness to buy or get s.o/ s.t: *There is some/no demand for green shoes.* **be in** (**great**) **demand** be wanted or needed (very much): *Computer engineers are in great demand.* **on demand** when it is asked (for): *She expects me to stop work and do things for her on demand. You must pay on demand or your telephone will be removed.* **supply and demand** ⇨ supply.

▷ *tr.v* **4** ask for, claim, (s.o/s.t) in a determined way: *I demand to see the manager. She demands an answer to her question.* **5** (*formal*) need (a particular response(1)): *His request demands serious thought.*

de'manding *adj* needing much effort, attention or thought: *Teaching is very demanding work.* Opposite undemanding.

demarcate /'diːmɑːˌkeɪt/ *tr.v* (*formal*) set the limits of (an area, job etc).

demarcation /ˌdiːmɑːˈkeɪʃən/ *n* (*formal*) **1** *c.n* thing that sets or shows a limit: *This line is a demarcation showing where the other team must stay while the ball is kicked.* **2** *u.n* (also *attrib*) art of showing where one worker's job or responsibility ends and another's begins, where one trade union can have members and where another union can etc: *They are on strike because of a demarcation dispute(1).*

demean /dɪ'miːn/ *reflex.v* (*formal*) lower s.o's opinion about (o.s) (by doing s.t): *By refusing to speak the truth you have demeaned yourself in this community.*

demeanour /dɪ'miːnə/ *u.n* (US **de'meanor**) (*formal*) outward(1) appearance or behaviour: *Her demeanour showed that she was well educated.*

demented /dɪ'mentɪd/ *adj* (often — *with s.t*) **1** in a state of having lost one's mental(3) control (because of pain, suffering). **2** extremely concerned or affected (because of great worry etc): *She's demented with anxiety because of the news of the train crash.*

demerara /ˌdeməˈreərə/ *u.n* (also ˌ**deme'rera** ˌ**sugar**) kind of soft brown sugar.

demigod /'demɪˌɡɒd/ *c.n* **1** (in classical(1) stories) person considered to be like a god because he is so powerful, good etc. **2** (usu *derog*) person who considers himself to be as powerful, good etc as a god.

'demi,goddess *c.n* female demigod.

demijohn /'demɪˌdʒɒn/ *c.n* very large bottle, usu inside a basket, holding more than five litres: *a demijohn of wine.*

demilitarized, -ised /diːˈmɪlɪtəˌraɪzd/ *adj* (usu *attrib*) (*military*) (esp of an area near the border with another country) with armies and weapons removed and not allowed: *This is a demilitarized zone.*

demilitarization, -isation /diːˌmɪlɪtəraɪ'zeɪʃən/ *u.n.*

demise /dɪ'maɪz/ *u.n* **1** (*law* or *formal*) death: *after her painful demise.* **2** (*fig*; *formal*) ending (of a business, political power etc): *the demise of manufacturing in Europe.*

demist /diː'mɪst/ *tr.v* remove mist(2) from (a windscreen, the windows of a car etc).

de'mister *c.n* device/chemical that demists (s.t).

demo /'deməʊ/ *c.n* (*informal*) demonstration(3).

democracy /dɪ'mɒkrəsɪ/ n (pl -ies) **1** u.n form of government in which there are (free) elections and everyone can vote for political representatives and sometimes for policies[1]: Can you have true democracy in a one party state? **2** c.n country with democracy(1): Is your country a democracy? **3** u.n control by the members of a group: Is there enough democracy in the way trade unions are organized?

democrat /'demə,kræt/ c.n **1** person who supports democracy(1). **2** (with capital **D**) (US) person who supports the Democratic Party. Compare Republican(5). **3** (with capital **D**) (UK) person who supports the Social Liberal Democratic Party.

demo'cratic adj **1** of, belonging to, like, a democracy(1): a democratic form of government; a democratic state. **2** supporting or using a policy of equal opportunities for everyone: a democratic manager; a democratic way of solving a problem in which everyone had a chance to express their opinion. Opposite undemocratic.

demo'cratically adv.

Demo'cratic ,Party def.n one of the two main US political parties. ⇒ Republican Party.

demography /dɪ'mɒgrəfɪ/ u.n scientific study of population numbers, rate of increase etc.

de'mographer c.n person who studies, or is skilled in, demography.

demographic /,demə'græfɪk/ adj.

demolish /dɪ'mɒlɪʃ/ tr.v **1** destroy, pull down, (a building etc). **2** (joking) eat all of (a meal, the food) quickly: The boys soon demolished the chocolate cake.

demolition /,demə'lɪʃən/ u.n (also attrib) act or fact of demolishing(1) a building etc: a demolition team.

demon /'di:mən/ c.n **1** evil spirit(11). **2** (usu little —) child who causes much trouble or anxiety. **3** (usu — for work) (informal) person who does things with much energy(1) and determination.

demonic /dɪ'mɒnɪk/ adj of, like, a demon(1).

demonstrate /'demən,streɪt/ v **1** tr/intr.v (often — how, what to do, where etc to do s.t) show and explain (what s.t looks like, how s.t works etc): Let me demonstrate how this machine works. Allow me to demonstrate (it). **2** tr.v show, prove etc (s.t) by producing evidence, reasons etc: The meal demonstrated her lack of experience as a cook (or that she had no experience). **3** intr.v (often — against s.t) express one's political etc opinion in public by joining others at a meeting, walking with others in a group in the street etc often with placards: We joined a march(2) in London to demonstrate against the new Education policy(1).

demonstrable /dɪ'mɒnstrəbl/ adj (formal) able to be shown clearly or proved: Her lack of experience is demonstrable.

demonstration /,demən'streɪʃən/ n **1** c/u.n (also attrib) (often — of s.t) act of showing or explaining how s.t works etc: a demonstration of a new sewing machine; a demonstration model of a car. **2** c/u.n (often — of s.t) act that shows one's feelings, proves one's ability etc: I did not like that child's demonstration (of temper) when his balloon burst. ⇒ demonstrative. **3** c.n public show expressing people's political etc opinion: a demonstration against the government.

demonstrative /dɪ'mɒnstrətɪv/ adj (formal) (often) showing one's feelings or wishes: He's a demonstrative child. Opposite undemonstrative.

de'monstrative ,pronoun c.n (grammar) 'that', 'this', 'those', 'these' showing who/what is referred to.

'demon,strator c.n **1** person who takes part in a demonstration(3). **2** person who demonstrates(1) s.t, esp one who helps a teacher or lecturer in a science laboratory.

demoralize, -ise /dɪ'mɒrə,laɪz/ tr.v destroy (s.o's) confidence; make (s.o) feel not able, suitable etc: We were demoralized when we lost the football match.

demoralization, -isation /dɪ,mɒrəlaɪ'zeɪʃən/ u.n.

demote /dɪ'məʊt/ tr.v (often — s.o/s.t to s.t) (formal) put (s.o, a football team, part of a business etc) in a lower position, rank etc.

demotion /dɪ'məʊʃən/ u.n (often — of s.o/s.t (to s.t)) act or fact of demoting or being demoted: the demotion of the team to the second division.

demur /dɪ'mɜ:/ u.n **1** (formal) objection(1): He paid the whole bill for repairs without demur.
▷ intr.v (-rr-) **2** (usu — at s.t) (formal) express one's (mild) objection(1) (to s.t): He demurred at the need to pay all the expenses.

demure /dɪ'mjʊə/ adj modest and quiet; shy: a demure young woman; a demure expression on the boy's face.

de'murely adv. **de'mureness** u.n.

den /den/ c.n **1** home of certain wild animals: a lion's den. **2** small room in a house used as a study or a place for one's hobby. **3** place where bad people gather or where immoral things happen: a den of thieves; a den of vice[2](1)/iniquity.

denial ⇒ deny.

denier /'denɪ,eɪ/ u.n (technical) unit of weight of certain fine cloth, e.g silk, nylon: My tights(1) are 15 denier.

denigrate /'denɪ,greɪt/ tr.v (formal) try to destroy (s.o's good reputation etc) by using severe criticism: Don't denigrate him (or his ability) — he'll prove how wrong you are.

denigration /,denɪ'greɪʃən/ u.n.

denim /'denɪm/ adj **1** made of denim(2): a denim jacket(1). These trousers are denim.
▷ u.n **2** kind of (usu blue) strong cotton cloth, used to make jeans etc.

denims pl.n jeans made of denim(2).

denomination /dɪ,nɒmɪ'neɪʃən/ c.n **1** (of a stamp, bank note etc) value: The parcel had stamps of various denominations. **2** group having the same religious beliefs and (usu) attending the same kind of church: This prayer is used by every denomination.

de,nomi'national adj.

de'nomi,nator c.n (mathematics) lower number in a fraction(2), e.g 4 in $\frac{1}{4}$.

denote /dɪ'nəʊt/ tr.v (formal) be a sign or symbol of (s.t): What does a shake of one's head denote in Greece?

denotation /,di:nəʊ'teɪʃən/ u.n.

dénouement /deɪ'nu:mɒn/ c.n (French; formal) end part of a story, drama(1) etc when the last events or conversations happen that explain or decide the remaining matters.

denounce /dɪ'naʊns/ tr.v (often — s.o as s.o)

(*formal*) say things against (s.o, s.o's character etc) publicly: *She denounced him as a thief.*

de'nouncement,denunciation /dɪˌnʌnsɪ'eɪʃən/ *u.n.*

dense /dens/ *adj* **1** so thick that it is difficult to see or pass through: *a dense fog; a dense forest.* **2** (*derog; informal*) (of a person) not intelligent: *Are you dense or were you not listening to me?*

'densely *adv* very thickly; very close together: *densely packed buses after the factories and offices have closed.*

'denseness *u.n.*

'density *c/u.n* (*pl -ies*) (often *the — of s.t*) **1** (example of the) number (of people, animals, things) in a given area, esp when compared with that in other places: *the density of the population in our big cities. We are comparing population densities in different parts of the world.* **2** (*science*) amount (of matter) in a substance: *The density of a gas is lower than that of a solid.*

dent /dent/ *c.n* (often *— in s.t*) **1** part of a surface made into a hollow by a hit or a hard push: *You have made a dent in the door of my car.* **2** (*fig*) effect that causes a fall (in an amount, in one's confidence etc): *The holiday made a large dent in our savings.*

▷ *tr.v* **3** make a dent(1) in (s.t): *You have dented my car door.* **4** (*fig*) make a dent(2) in (s.t): *dent one's savings/pride.*

dentist /'dentɪst/ *c.n* **1** person who looks after and repairs teeth. **2** (also **'dentist's**) place where a dentist(1) works: *She's at the dentist this morning.*

'dental *attrib.adj* of or referring to the teeth: *dental treatment.*

,dental 'floss *u.n* strong thread like silk used to clean between the teeth.

,dental 'plate *c.n* = plate(4).

,dental 'surgeon *c.n* = dentist(1).

dentifrice /'dentɪfrɪs/ *u.n* (*formal*) toothpaste; tooth powder.

'dentistry *u.n* (*formal*) work of a dentist(1); repair of one's teeth: *You'll need less dentistry if you don't eat sugar.*

denture /'dentʃə/ *c.n* (usu *pl* except when *attrib*) (*formal*) plate(4) with artificial teeth.

denude /dɪ'njuːd/ *tr.v* (*formal*) remove the covering or top layer of (land etc): *Pollution is denuding the forests of trees.*

denunciation ⇒ denounce.

deny /dɪ'naɪ/ *tr.v* (*-ies, -ied*) **1** (often *— doing s.t; — that . . .*) say or write that (s.t) is not true: *She denied breaking the plate* (or *that she had broken the plate*). **2** refuse to give (one's permission or agreement to s.t): *She has been denied access(1) to the information she needs.* **3** refuse to give s.t to (o.s/s.o): *She denies her children nothing. You must not deny yourself food when you are ill.* **there is no denying (the fact) that . . .** it is impossible to disagree (with the fact) that . . .

de'nial *n* **1** *c/u.n* (example of the) act or fact of denying s.t. **2** *c.n* (public) statement saying that s.t is not true: *He demanded a denial from the newspaper.* ⇒ self-denial. ⇒ also undeniable.

deodorant /diː'əʊdərənt/ *c/u.n* (also *attrib*) substance used to hide unpleasant smells, esp body smells.

dep *written abbr* **1** (in bus, train etc time-tables) departs; departure. **2** (*commerce*) deposit. **3** (often with capital **D**) deputy.

depart /dɪ'pɑːt/ *intr.v* (usu *— from s.w*) (*formal*) **1** (of a bus, train, group of tourists etc) leave (a station, place etc): *The train will depart from platform(2) nine at 6 o'clock.* **2** (of a person etc) leave a building etc: *As soon as he had departed, I telephoned James.* **3** change from a right, usual or expected way of acting or behaving: *depart from the truth; depart from the agreed method.* **depart this life** (*literary*) die.

de'parted *def/def.pl.n* (*literary* or *formal*) person/people who is/are dead.

de'parture *c.n* (also *attrib*) act of departing: *departure lounge; train departures; departure from the plan.*

department /dɪ'pɑːtmənt/ *c.n* (with capital **D** in names of particular ones) section of a government, business, shop, college etc: *the Department of Education; the sales department; the men's department on the first floor of the shop; the department of foreign languages.*

departmental /ˌdiːpɑːt'mentl/ *attrib.adj* of, referring to, a department: *a departmental meeting/boss.*

de'partment ,store *c.n* large shop with several departments selling different kinds of goods.

depend /dɪ'pend/ *intr.v* **1** **depend (up)on s.o/ s.t (for s.t)** (**a**) trust s.o/s.t (to do s.t etc): *Can I depend upon you to help us next week? You can depend on us to vote for you. I'm depending on you to come.* (**b**) rely upon s.o/s.t to provide what is necessary: *Children depend on their parents for food and clothes. She depends on us to give her the correct information.* **2** **depend (up)on s.o/s.t** be determined by s.o/s.t: *Where we go depends upon the weather. The house we buy will depend upon how much money it costs.* **it (all) depends; that depends** I am not yet certain because it depends(2) on certain facts: *I may come to the meeting and I may not — it all depends.*

de'pendable *adj* (of a person) who can be trusted: *Catherine'll arrive on time; she's always dependable.*

de'pendant *c.n* (US **de'pendent**) person, esp a child, who is given money, food etc by another: *'How many dependants do you have?' 'I have my mother, my wife and two children.'*

de'pendence *u.n* (usu *— (up)on s.o/s.t*) **1** fact or state of being dependent(1) on s.o for help or for money, clothes etc. **2** (often *place/put — on s.o/s.t*) (*formal*) trust and confidence: *You can't put any dependence on his account of the events.*

dependency *n* (*pl -ies*) **1** *u.n* (usu *— (up)on s.o/s.t*) (*old use*) = dependence. **2** *c.n* country controlled by another more powerful one.

de'pendent *adj* (often *— (up)on s.o/s.t*) **1** (of a person) who relies upon s.o, a government, bank etc to provide what is necessary: *a dependent daughter; a shop that is dependent on the bank for support.* ⇒ independent(1). **2** (*pred*) (of a situation, action, decision etc) determined by s.o/s.t: *Our success is dependent upon your help.*

de'pendent ,clause *c.n* (*grammar*) = subordinate clause.

depict /dɪ'pɪkt/ *tr.v* (*formal*) **1** draw, paint etc (s.o/s.t): *The painter depicted the garden when* the roses were flowering. I prefer to depict her in a blue dress. **2** describe (s.o/s.t) in writing or in a speech: *His account depicted a very sad meeting in which the committee was severely criticized.*

depiction /dɪˈpɪkʃən/ *c/u.n.*

depilatory /dɪˈpɪlɪtərɪ/ *c.n* (*pl -ies*) (also *attrib*) (*technical*) substance used to remove unwanted hair growing on one's body: *depilatory cream.*

deplete /dɪˈpliːt/ *tr.v* (*formal*) cause (an amount of money, an audience, supplies etc) to get smaller: *The cost of buying a car has seriously depleted my savings.*

depletion /dɪˈpliːʃən/ *u.n.*

deplore /dɪˈplɔː/ *tr.v* (*formal*) feel or express one's strong disapproval of (s.t): *I deplore the fact that some criminals are given light punishments.*

de'plorable *adj* (*formal*) very bad; that one strongly disapproves of: *deplorable weather/ behaviour.*

de'plorably *adv.*

deploy /dɪˈplɔɪ/ *tr.v* **1** (*military*) send (soldiers etc) into an area (as preparation for a battle). **2** (*fig*) use or send (workers) to do a particular job: *Even if we deploy all our staff we will not be able to finish the job on time.*

de'ployment *u.n.*

depopulate /diːˈpɒpjʊˌleɪt/ *tr.v* (*formal*) cause (an area, town etc) to have fewer people.

de'populated *adj* (*usu attrib*) having fewer people than before: *depopulated villages.*

depopulation /diːˌpɒpjʊˈleɪʃən/ *u.n.*

deport /dɪˈpɔːt/ *tr.v* send (s.o) away from a country officially, e.g because he/she is not allowed to be there, has done s.t wrong etc.

deportation /ˌdiːpɔːˈteɪʃən/ *c/u.n* (also *attrib*) act of deporting: *a deportation order.*

deportee /ˌdiːpɔːˈtiː/ *c.n* person who is deported.

deportment /dɪˈpɔːtmənt/ *u.n.* way one stands, sits, esp to give a particular idea, e.g of fitness, pride etc: *a dancer's/soldier's deportment*; *a lazy deportment.*

depose /dɪˈpəʊz/ *tr.v* remove (a ruler, senior official etc) from a high position, esp because of disapproval: *The army deposed the president and took control of the country.*

deposit /dɪˈpɒzɪt/ *c.n* **1** act or example of putting money (in a bank, savings account etc): *We made three deposits last month.* **2** money put in a bank, savings account etc: *a deposit of £100* (or *a £100 deposit*) *in a building society.* **3** act of paying money as part of a payment for s.t, the rest of which has to be paid later: *After making, putting down, paying, a deposit, you can reserve(8) the carpet.* **4** money paid as a deposit(3): *We paid* (or *put down*) *a deposit of £2000 on the house. The deposit cannot be returned if you decide not to buy it.* **5** (amount of a) substance that collects at the bottom of a liquid or is left by a river etc: *sand deposits at the mouth of the river.* **6** (amount of a) substance, e.g oil, coal, gold, in rock.
▷ *tr.v* **7** put (money, valuables) (in a bank, savings account etc). **8** (usu — *s.t with s.o*) (*formal*) give (money, valuables) (to s.o) in order to have them kept safely: *I've deposited my jewels with my parents while I'm on holiday.* **9** put (a substance) down on a surface: *The river deposits sand at the edge of the sea.* **10** (*formal*) put (s.o/s.t) in the place shown: *We deposited all his tools on the*

floor. *She deposits the children with her parents while she does the shopping.* **deposit oneself s.w** (*formal*) sit down s.w: *He deposited himself at the front of the audience.*

de'posit ac,count *c.n* bank account for one's savings that pays interest(4) and from which money can be taken only after advance warning.

de'positor *c.n* person who deposits(7) money, e.g in a bank.

depository /dɪˈpɒzɪtrɪ/ *c.n* (*pl -ies*) (*formal*) place, e.g a warehouse, where goods are put.

depot /ˈdepəʊ/ *c.n* **1** building(s) where buses, trains etc are kept, cleaned, repaired etc: *This bus is returning to the depot.* **2** (*military*) place for stores; place where soldiers are trained etc.

deprave /dɪˈpreɪv/ *tr.v* (*formal*) cause (s.o, esp a child or s.o's mind) to become evil or immoral: *Do some films on television deprave children?*

de'praved *adj* made evil or immoral.

depravity /dɪˈprævɪtɪ/ *c/u.n* (*pl -ies*) (*formal*) (example of a) very wicked action or state.

deprecate /ˈdeprɪˌkeɪt/ *tr.v* (*formal*) express strong disapproval of (a condition, action, s.o's character etc).

deprecation /ˌdeprɪˈkeɪʃən/ *u.n.*

depreciate /dɪˈpriːʃɪˌeɪt/ *intr.v* decrease in value: *A car depreciates (in value) very quickly after the first two years.* Opposite appreciate(3).

depreciation /dɪˌpriːʃɪˈeɪʃən/ *u.n.*

depress /dɪˈpres/ *tr.v* **1** cause (s.o) to feel sad, miserable: *It depressed me to learn that he had failed again to pass the examination.* **2** (*formal*) push or press (s.t) down: *depress a switch.* **3** (*formal*) (of a drug(1) etc) cause (s.t) to be less active, have less energy(1) etc: *This medicine will depress your heartbeat.* **4** (*formal*) cause (trade, demand for goods etc) to be less active: *Bad weather depressed the demand for ice-cream.* Opposite stimulate.

de'pressant *c.n* medicine etc that depresses(3) s.t. Compare stimulant.

de'pressed *adj* **1** (of a person) sad; miserable. **2** (of trade etc) less or not active. **3** (of a place) without opportunity for commercial activity, employment etc. **4** (*formal*) (of a switch) pushed or pressed down.

de'pressing *adj* causing s.o to feel depressed(1): *depressing news.*

depression /dɪˈpreʃən/ *n* **1** *u.n.* state of feeling sad or miserable: *suffer from depression.* **2** *c/ u.n.* state of low activity in trade or commerce, high unemployment etc: *a time of economic(1) depression.* **3** *c.n* wide area of land etc which is lower than the surrounding area. **4** *c.n* = cyclone(2). **5** *def.n* (with capital **D**) period in the 1930s when there was a depression(2) in the USA and then in all parts of the world.

deprive /dɪˈpraɪv/ *tr.v* (often — *s.o/s.t of s.o/s.t*) take s.o/s.t away from (s.o/s.t); prevent (s.o, a business, place etc) from having s.t that he/she/it needs: *He was deprived of food and drink. That country is deprived of money to build factories.*

deprivation /ˌdeprɪˈveɪʃən/ *n* **1** *u.n.* act or state of being or feeling deprived: *deprivation in the Third World.* **2** *c.n* (often — *of s.t*) example of the act of depriving s.o (of s.t); lack (of s.t needed): *deprivations suffered by poor children.*

de'prived *adj* (of a person, place etc) suffering from deprivation(1).

depth /depθ/ *u.n* (often the — of s.t.) **1** distance, measurement, downwards or inwards: *the depth of the sea*; *the depth of a cupboard. This fish is found at a depth of 300 metres. The knife went into a depth of 5 centimetres.* **2** quality or fact of being deep: *depth of colour*; *the depth of her voice*/ *sigh*/ *knowledge*; *the depth of his love for her.* **beyond, out of, one's depth** (a) in water etc that is too deep for one to stand in and breathe. (b) (*fig*) in a situation that is outside one's level of ability, experience or knowledge. **in depth** (a) deep: *It is 2 metres in depth.* (b) ('**in-,depth** when *attrib*) thoroughly: *study a subject in depth.*

'depths *def.n* (usu the — of s.t.) **1** deepest part (of s.t.): *the depths of the sea.* **2** most severe or central part (of s.t.): *the depths of winter.* **3** very low mental or moral state: *the depths of despair*; *sink to the depths as a murderer.*

depute /dɪ'pju:t/ *tr.v* (*formal*) **1** (usu — s.o to do s.t) give (s.o) a job or responsibility, esp one that is usually one's own: *I have deputed Jenny to check the accounts while I am on holiday.* **2** (usu — s.t to s.o) give (a job, responsibility, esp one that is usually one's own) (to s.o): *He deputed the task of collecting the money to Polly.*

deputation /,depju'teɪʃən/ *n* **1** *u.n* act of deputing. **2** *c.n* group of people selected to act or speak on behalf of a larger group: *Let us send a deputation to discuss the problem with the Council.*

deputize, -ise /'depju,taɪz/ *intr.v* (*formal*) (usu — for s.o) act as a deputy(2) (for s.o): *My son will deputize for me at the meeting.*

deputy /'depjutɪ/ *attrib.adj* **1** acting as a deputy(2): *the deputy manager.*
▷ *c.n* (*pl -ies*) **2** person selected to represent another person in a job, meeting etc, e.g while he/she is absent or ill. **3** (often with capital **D**) member of the lower house in a legislative assembly in some countries, e.g France. Compare member of parliament.

derail /di:'reɪl/ *tr.v* (usu passive) cause (a train) to leave the rails, usu in an accident.
de'railment *c/u.n*.

deranged /dɪ'reɪndʒd/ *adj* insane; mad, e.g because of great anxiety, a high fever(1) etc.
derangement /dɪ'reɪndʒmənt/ *u.n* state of being deranged.

derelict /'derɪlɪkt/ *adj* deserted(1) and in a bad condition, in need of repair etc: *a derelict house.*
dereliction /,derɪ'lɪkʃən/ *u.n* state of being derelict. **dereliction of duty** (*formal*) deliberate neglect of one's responsibilities.

deride /dɪ'raɪd/ *tr.v* (*formal*) speak or write about, laugh at, (s.o, s.o's efforts etc) in a mocking way: *She (or Her writing) was derided in the newspapers.*

derision /dɪ'rɪʒən/ *u.n* act or fact of deriding s.o/s.t.

derisive /dɪ'raɪsɪv/ *adj* (also **de'risory**) **1** showing derision; mocking: *derisive comments.* **2** worthy of being mocked(2), esp because too small: *The price they offered was derisive.*
derisory /dɪ'raɪsərɪ/ *adj* = derisive.

derive /dɪ'raɪv/ *v* (often — (s.t) from s.t) (*formal*) **1** *intr.v* come (from s.t as a source or origin):

The word 'café' derives from the French word for 'coffee'. **2** *tr.v* get (s.t) (from s.t as a source or origin): *We derived great pleasure from your visit.*

derivation /,derɪ'veɪʃən/ *n* **1** *c.n* origin (of a word etc). **2** *u.n* fact or process of deriving. **3** = derivative(2).

derivative /dɪ'rɪvətɪv/ *adj* **1** (usu *derog*) (of a piece of music, writing etc) not original because taken from another person's work: *a derivative plot in a play.*
▷ *c.n* **2** word (or idea, substance etc) formed from another one: *'Descendant' is a derivative of 'descend'.*

dermatitis /,dɜ:mə'taɪtɪs/ *u.n* disease of the skin which produces a rash.

dermatologist /,dɜ:mə'tɒlədʒɪst/ *c.n* person who studies, or is skilled in, dermatology.

dermatology /,dɜ:mə'tɒlədʒɪ/ *u.n* science of skin diseases.

derogatory /dɪ'rɒgətərɪ/ *adj* (written abbr **derog** used in this dictionary) (*formal*) that makes s.o/s.t appear poor in quality, bad, unimportant etc: *'Fool' is a derogatory word.*

derrick /'derɪk/ *c.n* device like a simple crane(2), used for lifting heavy objects, e.g into or off ships.

derv /dɜ:v/ *acronym* (*t.n*) (**d**iesel **e**ngine **r**oad **v**ehicle) = diesel oil used for road vehicles.

DES /,di: ,i: 'es/ *def.n abbr* Department of Education and Science (government department in the UK).

descant /'deskænt/ *c/u.n* (person who sings or plays a) part of a song or piece of music that is usu above the basic(1) tune.

descend /dɪ'send/ *v* (*formal*) **1** *tr/intr.v* walk, climb etc down (a mountain, the stairs etc) to a lower level. Opposite ascend. **2** *intr.v* (often — to s.t) (of land) slope down to a lower level: *The fields descend sharply to the valley below.* **3** (of the sun or moon) move down, i.e towards the horizon: *The sun descended over the city.* **descend from s.o** have s.o as one's ancestor: *Our family are descended from Russian stock(5).* **descend (up)on s.o/s.t** (a) attack s.o, a place etc suddenly: *The army descended on the village during the night.* (b) (*fig*) visit s.o, one's home, a place (often without warning): *My mother and father descended on us last weekend. Thousands of tourists descend on Cambridge during the summer.* **descend to s.t** (a) ⇒ descend(2). (b) (*fig*) go down to a lower standard of behaviour: *Would you ever descend to cheating in an examination?*

de'scendant *c.n* person who has descended or will descend from s.o: *My descendants will have a comfortable house and a successful business.*

de'scent *n* (often — of s.o/s.t) (*formal*) **1** *c.n* act of going down to a lower level. Opposite ascent(1). **2** *c.n* slope: *a gradual descent to the sea.* Opposite ascent(2). **3** *u.n* family origin: *I'm of Russian descent.* **descent (up)on s.o/ s.t** act of descending (up)on s.o/s.t. **of British etc descent** having British etc people as one's ancestors.

describe /dɪ'skraɪb/ *tr.v* **1** (often — s.o/s.t as s.o/s.t) use words to tell or show what s.o/s.t is like: *Can you describe the man who stole your bag? I described the party as a long boring experience. I'd describe myself as a shy person.*

2 (*formal*) draw (a shape or figure): *He described a circle in the sand.*

description /dɪˈskrɪpʃən/ *n* (often — of s.o/s.t) **1** *c.n* use of words to describe(1) s.o/s.t: *I've sent her a description of my holiday.* **2** *c/u.n* (example of the) act of describing(1) s.o/s.t. **3** *c.n* (usu *sing*) (often of *every/some/any* —) (*informal*) kind or type: *We saw flowers of every description. She was driving a car of some description.*

descriptive /dɪˈskrɪptɪv/ *adj* that describes s.o/ s.t, esp well: *a descriptive account of what happened.* Compare indescribable.

desecrate /ˈdesɪˌkreɪt/ *tr.v* (*formal*) treat (an object, building etc that is holy) in a bad, immoral or evil way.

desecration /ˌdesɪˈkreɪʃən/ *u.n*.

desegregate /diːˈsegrɪˌgeɪt/ *tr.v* put an end to (racial(1) or sexual) segregation, e.g in a school, classroom.

desegregation /diːˌsegrɪˈgeɪʃən/ *u.n*.

desert¹ /ˈdezət/ *c.n* **1** (also *attrib*) (with capital **D** in names) sandy area with (almost) no plants because there is (almost) no rain: *The Sahara Desert; desert regions/flowers.* **2** (*fig*) place with (almost) no interesting or desirable(2) qualities: *Our village is a cultural desert.*

desert² /dɪˈzɜːt/ *v* **1** *tr.v* leave (s.o, a place, job etc) without intending to return: *He deserted his wife and children.* **2** *tr.v* (of courage, skill etc) suddenly not be present in (s.o), esp when needed urgently. **3** *tr/intr.v* (often — one's post) (*military*) (of a soldier etc) leave (one's duty, the army etc) without intending to return.

de'serted *adj* **1** (usu *pred*) without people: *The beaches were deserted because of the rain.* **2** (*attrib*) who has been left without help or support: *deserted children.*

de'serter *c.n* **1** soldier etc who deserts(3). **2** person who deserts(1).

desertion /dɪˈzɜːʃən/ *c/u.n*. (example of the) act of deserting(1,3): *She won the right to keep her children because of his desertion.*

deserve /dɪˈzɜːv/ *tr.v* be worthy of (s.o/s.t) because one has earned the right to it: *She deserves a medal(1). She is so bad-tempered that she deserves him as a husband because he is always quarrelling. It's a pity he lost because he deserves to succeed.*

de'serts *pl.n* **one's (just) deserts** punishment that one deserves: *That bully(1) will receive/get her just deserts one day.*

de'serving *adj* (*attrib*) that is worthy(1) of one's support or praise: *Giving money to sick children is a deserving cause/charity(3). Those hardworking people are a deserving family.* **deserving of s.t** (*formal*) worthy(1) of one's support, praise etc: *They are deserving of our support.*

deservedly /dɪˈzɜːvɪdlɪ/ *adv* rightly; justly: *Margaret was deservedly rewarded for her efforts.*

desiccated /ˈdesɪˌkeɪtɪd/ *attrib.adj* that has had all the water taken out in order to preserve it: *desiccated coconut(2).*

desiderata /dɪˌzɪdəˈrɑːtə/ *pl.n* (*formal*) things needed for s.o/s.t to be successful etc: *health, happiness and other desiderata.*

design /dɪˈzaɪn/ *n* **1** *c.n* plan, drawing etc used to show how s.t is to be made: *a new design for a coat.* **2** *c.n* pattern made by arranging shapes, colours etc: *a cloth with a pretty design on it.* **3** *u.n* (often

of good, poor etc —) way parts are put together to make a machine, instrument, organized method etc: *This engine/computer/building is of poor design.* **4** *c.n* idea; plan in the mind; scheme: *I have a clear design of how the goods should be arranged on the shelf.* **by design** intentionally; on purpose: *Were you out of the house when she called by design or did you forget that she was coming?* Compare by accident. **have designs on s.o/s.t** (*informal*) want, try to get, s.o who is with s.o else or s.t belonging to s.o else.

▷ *tr.v* **5** make and produce a design(1) for (s.t): *design a dress.* **6** (*formal*) intend (s.t) (for a certain purpose): *This punishment is designed to teach you the seriousness of your crime. This dictionary is designed for foreign learners of English.*

de'signer *c.n* person skilled in making designs(1) (of clothes, furniture, books etc).

de'signing *adj* (usu *attrib*) (*derog*) using deceit to be successful at getting or doing s.t: *He's a designing person who is only kind when it is to his advantage.*

designate /ˈdezɪgnɪt/ *adj* **1** (after the noun) appointed but not yet given control or power: *the head teacher designate.*

▷ *v* /ˈdezɪgˌneɪt/ (*formal*) **2** *tr.v* (often — s.t as s.t) decide and give (s.t) a description or name: *This land has been designated (as) an area of outstanding natural beauty.* **3** choose s.t to mean or be (s.t): *In this dictionary, the sign ▷ designates a change of the part of speech in an entry(4).* **designate s.o/s.t to do s.t** choose or appoint s.o/s.t to do s.t: *We have designated Mrs Jones to be our representative.*

designation /ˌdezɪgˈneɪʃən/ *c.n* (*formal*) official title: *Her designation is now 'assistant manager' and not 'department head'.*

designer, designing ⇒ design.

desire /dɪˈzaɪə/ *n* (often — for s.o/s.t, to do s.t) **1** *c.n* strong wish: *I've had a desire to meet you for a long time. He mentioned his desire for a meeting with you.* **2** *u.n* attraction or interest (often sexual): *My desire for you will never fade. The story is about Napoleon's desire for Josephine.* Compare lust(2). **3** *c.n* (usu *sing*) person, animal, thing who/that is wanted very much: *My one desire is to visit China.*

desirability /dɪˌzaɪərəˈbɪlɪtɪ/ *u.n* fact of (s.t) being desirable.

desirable /dɪˈzaɪərəbl/ *adj* Opposite undesirable. **1** attractive (esp sexually); pleasant: *a desirable woman.* **2** (usu *attrib*) that one would like to use or own: *a desirable house in the centre of the city.* **3** that one wants, would like to have etc: *a desirable job.*

▷ *c.n* **4** person who is desirable(1).

de'sirably *adv*.

desirous /dɪˈzaɪərəs/ *pred.adj* **desirous of s.t**; **desirous that ...** (*formal*) wishing very much (to have, get etc s.t, that ...): *He was always desirous of a quick way to become rich. The ambassador is desirous that the money should be given to a charity(3).*

desist /dɪˈzɪst/ *intr.v* (often — from (doing) s.t) (*formal*) not do (s.t) one has been doing; stop (doing s.t): *Please desist from smoking in here.*

desk /desk/ *c.n* (also *attrib*) **1** table with drawers and often a sloping top, used for writing, reading etc: *an office desk; a desk top; desk work.* **2** flat surface like a table at which people are given information, business is done etc; counter²: *the reception desk in a hotel; the information desk; a desk clerk; a desk job.*

desolate /'desəlɪt/ *adj* **1** (of land) without strong plants, trees etc: *a desolate hillside.* **2** (of a house, area) without people or activity: *desolate areas in the poorer parts of the country.* **3** (of a person) very lonely and sad: *feeling desolate.*

▷ *v* /'desəleɪt/ (*formal*) **4** *tr.v* make (land, a house etc) desolate(1,2). **5** make (a person) desolate(3).

desolated /'desəleɪtɪd/ *adj* (*formal*) **1** that is or has been made desolate(1, 2): *desolated places where the motorways cross each other.* **2** (usu *pred*) shocked and very sad: *He was desolated by the news of her death* (or *to hear that she had died*).

desolation /,desə'leɪʃən/ *u.n.*

despair /dɪ'speə/ *n* **1** *u.n* lack of hope: *Imagine my despair when I heard that his plane had crashed.* **2** *def.n* (usu the — *of s.o*) person or thing causing s.o to feel despair(1): *That boy has been the despair of his parents since he was very young.* **in despair** feeling despair(1): *I left the hospital in despair.* ⇨ desperate(2).

despairing *attrib.adj* having or showing despair(1): *speaking in a despairing voice.*

de'spairingly *adv.*

despatch ⇨ dispatch.

desperado /,despə'rɑːdəʊ/ *c.n* (*pl* -(e)s) (*literary* or *old use*) desperate(1) criminal.

desperate /'despərɪt/ *adj* **1** (of a person) willing to do anything including violence because he/she lacks any hope of success: *a desperate criminal.* **2** (of a person) needing s.t so much that he/she will do anything: *I'm desperate for money/news. I'd steal if I could, I'm so desperate.* **3** (of a situation) very bad or difficult; hopeless. **4** (of an action) showing despair(1) (and so often reckless): *She made one last desperate attempt/appeal(1). Desperate methods are needed to stop the spread of the disease.*

desperately *adv* **1** in a desperate way: *trying desperately to swim to the beach.* **2** (*informal*) very much: *I need you desperately.*

desperation /,despə'reɪʃən/ *u.n* (often *in* —) fact or state of being desperate(1,2): *We shouted in desperation but no one heard us.*

despise /dɪ'spaɪz/ *tr.v* **1** consider (s.o/s.t) to be very bad, worthless: *I despise parents who hit children.* **2** (*formal*) refuse to take, own, (s.t) because one disapproves strongly: *I despise fur coats when the animals are killed so cruelly.*

despicable /dɪ'spɪkəbl/ *adj* worthy of being despised(1): *despicable behaviour/people.*

de'spicably *adv: behave despicably.*

despite /dɪ'spaɪt/ *prep* (*formal*) in spite of (⇨ spite): *Despite all her efforts she failed. We went despite the rain and cold.*

despoil /dɪ'spoɪl/ *tr.v* (*formal*) take valuable things from (s.o, a place) by using force: *The bandits despoiled the villages/villagers.*

despondent /dɪ'spɒndənt/ *adj* **1** without any hope of an improvement or success: *I felt so despondent after speaking to the doctor about his illness.* **2** very miserable after lack of success: *He was despondent when he heard that he had failed the examination.*

de'spondency *u.n* fact or state of being despondent.

de'spondently *adv.*

despot /'despɒt/ *c.n* (*derog*) person in control of a country, business, government etc who uses her/his power in a cruel and unfair way; tyrant.

despotic /dɪs'pɒtɪk/ *adj.*

des'potically *adv.*

despotism /'despə,tɪzəm/ *u.n* (*derog*) (kind of) rule by a despot.

dessert /dɪ'zɜːt/ *n* (also *attrib*) **1** *u.n* sweet course (to be) eaten at the end of a meal: *What are we having for dessert? She hasn't prepared a dessert course.* **2** *c.n* fruit or other sweet food eaten at the end of a meal: *a dessert of* jelly(1) *and ice-cream.*

de'ssert,spoon *c.n* **1** fairly large spoon used to eat food. **2** (often — *of s.t*) as much as a dessertspoon(1) holds: *a dessertspoon of flour.*

de'ssert,spoonful *c.n* (*pl* dessertspoonfuls or dessertspoonful) = dessertspoon(2).

destination /,destɪ'neɪʃən/ *c.n* place where s.o/s.t is going to: *We are on a trip round Europe and our final destination is Finland. You should arrive at your destination before 6 o'clock.*

destined /'destɪnd/ *pred.adj* **1** (usu — *for s.o/s.t*) intended (for a certain use, purpose, person etc): *This tool is destined for use by photographers.* **2** (usu — *for s.w*) being sent (to s.w): *This plane is destined for South America.* **3** (usu passive, *be — for,* to do, *s.t*) arranged and certain (to be/do s.t, for s.t) because decided (esp by fate, God): *She was destined* (*by fate*) *to become a great actress* (or *for the stage*). ⇨ destiny(2).

destiny /'destɪnɪ/ *n* (*pl* -ies) **1** *u.n* power which seems to, is believed to, control future events; fate(1): *He wanted to become famous but destiny decided against it.* **2** *c.n* kind of future that is destined(3) for s.o; fate(2): *Her destiny was to live and work in Africa.*

destitute /'destɪ,tjuːt/ *adj* without even the basic necessities, e.g food, a home, clothes: *a destitute person. He ran away and left his wife and children destitute.* **destitute of s.t** (*formal*) completely without (information, ideas, sympathy etc): *This report is destitute of ideas for solving the problem.*

destitution /,destɪ'tjuːʃən/ *u.n* (*formal*) fact of being destitute.

destroy /dɪ'strɔɪ/ *tr.v* (-ys, -yed) **1** cause (s.t) to become a ruin, be ended etc: *The house was destroyed in the storm. Who destroyed my book? Was it the increase in immorality that destroyed the Roman Empire?* **2** (*informal*) kill (an animal that is very sick, old or a nuisance): *The dog that bit the child will have to be destroyed.*

de'stroyer *c.n* **1** kind of small fast warship. **2** person who destroys s.t.

destruction /dɪ'strʌkʃən/ *u.n* fact, state or process of destroying(1) or being destroyed(1): *The destruction of the forests is a threat to the lives of thousands of animals.*

destructive /dɪ'strʌktɪv/ *adj* **1** causing s.t to be destroyed(1): *a destructive fire.* **2** (of a person) causing s.t to be destroyed(1), esp when enjoying doing it: *destructive children.* **3** describing the faults (in a report, performance, piece of work, method etc) but without giving ideas for improvement. Opposite constructive.

de'structively *adv.* **de'structiveness** *u.n.*

desultory /'desəltərɪ/ *adj* (*formal*) without any organized method or plan: *a desultory account*; *thinking in a desultory way*.

detach /dɪ'tætʃ/ *tr.v* (often — *s.t from s.t*) remove (s.t), esp by unfastening it (from s.t) or taking it off (s.t larger): *I detached the key from the ring and gave it to Paul. Please detach the coupon(2) and send it with your money to the following address.* Compare attach(1).

de'tachable *adj* that can be detached (⇒ detach): *a detachable hood(1) on a coat*.

de'tached *adj* 1 built as a separate building or structure(1): *a detached house/garage.* ⇒ semi-detached; terrace(4). 2 not having or showing any personal opinion, prejudice or involvement: *Can you be detached when the teachers discuss your future? I can't take a detached position about that.* ⇒ undetached.

de'tachedly *adv* in a detached(2) way.

de'tachment *n* 1 *u.n* (state of being detached(2): *She showed detachment when dealing with the needs of the prisoners.* 2 *u.n* (*formal*) act of detaching s.t. 3 *c.n* (often — *of s.t*) (*military*) group (of soldiers) chosen from a larger group for a particular duty.

detail /'di:teɪl/ *n* 1 *c.n* separate item(1) or particular small part: *Can you describe the details of the accident?* 2 *u.n* (treatment of) all the details(1) as a whole: *There was too much detail in the report.* **go into detail** (**about s.o/s.t**); **go into details** give or include many details(1) (about s.o/s.t). **in detail** including (all) the details(1): *I wrote in detail about the causes of our failure.*

▷ *tr.v* (*formal*) 3 give all the details(1) about (s.t): *She detailed her reasons for resigning.* 4 (often passive) give (s.o) a certain job to do: *I have been detailed to visit the factory and discuss problems with the workers.*

'detailed *adj* including details(1): *a detailed report/plan/painting*.

detain /dɪ'teɪn/ *tr.v* 1 keep (s.o) in a place so that he/she is delayed: *I was detained in the office writing an urgent report. I won't detain you long.* 2 (of the police etc) keep (s.o) in a police station etc: *He has been detained for questioning.*

detainee /ˌdi:teɪ'ni:/ *c.n* person detained(2) by the police, esp for political reasons: *a political detainee*.

detention /dɪ'tenʃən/ *n* 1 *u.n* fact of being detained(1,2). 2 *c/u.n* (example of a) punishment at school etc by being forced to stay for an extra period(3) at the end of the day: *I was given detention for arriving late.* **in detention** in a prison etc: *He is in detention until his trial because he is so dangerous.*

detect /dɪ'tekt/ *tr.v* (*formal*) 1 notice (s.t): *I detected a certain amount of doubt in her voice.* 2 look for and find (s.o/s.t): *He couldn't detect the source of the electrical failure.*

detection /dɪ'tekʃən/ *u.n* act or process of detecting s.o/s.t.

de'tective *c.n* (also *attrib*) police officer whose job is to solve crimes and find criminals: *detective novels*. **private detective** ⇒ private.

de'tector *c.n* (also *attrib*) (usu as the second part of a word) machine that detects(2) s.t: *a metal detector; a detector van that finds people using a television without having bought a licence.*

detente /deɪ'tɑ:nt/ *c/u.n* act or fact of being

more friendly, willing to cooperate etc, esp between two or more countries.

detention ⇒ detain.

deter /dɪ'tɜː/ *tr.v* (-rr-) (often — *s.o from doing s.t*) make (s.o) unwilling (to do s.t), e.g by using fear: *We refused to be deterred by the bad weather from going to the meeting.*

deterrent /dɪ'terənt/ *adj* (*formal*) intended or likely to deter (s.o/s.t).

▷ *c.n* thing that deters s.o/s.t: *I am sending you to prison for five years as a deterrent to others who may think of such a crime. Do you agree that nuclear(2) weapons are a deterrent against another world war?*

detergent /dɪ'tɜːdʒənt/ *c/u.n* (also *attrib*) (example of a) substance that includes a chemical instead of soap, used to clean clothes, in shampoos(1) etc: *This is a powerful detergent for stubborn(2) stains. Which detergent powder do you use?*

deteriorate /dɪ'tɪərɪəreɪt/ *tr/intr.v* (cause (s.o/s.t) to) become worse: *Your health will deteriorate if you work so hard.*

deterioration /dɪˌtɪərɪə'reɪʃən/ *u.n.*

determine /dɪ'tɜːmɪn/ *tr.v* (*formal*) 1 (usu — *to do s.t*) decide (what to do, think etc) after considering the facts: *She determined to ask her parents to lend her the money. I've determined my position on this matter.* 2 influence or cause (s.t): *What determines success in life? What we do tomorrow will be determined by the weather.* ⇒ indeterminate. 3 find out (s.t): *The police are trying to determine the cause of the accident.* 4 fix (s.t): *These high mountains determine the natural boundary between the two countries.*

determination /dɪˌtɜːmɪ'neɪʃən/ *u.n* (*formal*) 1 (often — *to do s.t*) fact of being determined: *His determination was the main reason for his success. It was her determination to win that brought victory.* 2 act of determining s.t: *the determination of what to do* (or *of the cause, the boundary*).

de'termined *adj* (showing that one is) not willing to change one's decision: *a determined expression. I'm so determined to have it that nothing will change my mind.*

de'terminer *c.n* (*grammar*) word that limits the use of a following noun (phrase(1)), e.g. 'a', 'the', 'every', 'each', 'any' etc. ⇒ predeterminer.

deterrent ⇒ deter.

detest /dɪ'test/ *tr.v* hate (s.o/s.t) very much: *I detest violence.*

de'testable *adj* (*formal*) deserving to be detested: *a detestable person/act.*

detestably *adv*: *behave detestably.*

detestation /ˌdi:te'steɪʃən/ *u.n* (often — *of s.o/s.t*) (*formal*) great hatred; abhorrence.

dethrone /dɪ'θrəʊn/ *tr.v* 1 (*formal*) take authority(1) and position from (a king or queen). 2 (*fig*) force (s.o) to give up a top position or a position of power or influence: *Will the tennis champion(3) be dethroned by this brilliant young player?*

de'thronement *c/u.n.*

detonate /'detəneɪt/ *tr/intr.v* (*technical*) (cause (a mine(3), bomb, device etc) to) explode.

detonation /ˌdetə'neɪʃən/ *c/u.n* act or sound of exploding.

'detonator *c.n* device causing s.t to detonate.

detour /'di:tʊə/ c.n **1** (often *make a — (across/ round, through* etc (s.t))) route(1) that is not the usual (often shorter) one.
▷ *intr.v* **2** make a detour(1): *The new route detours across the farm to the other main road.*
detract /dɪ'trækt/ *intr.v* (usu — *from* s.t) *(formal)* take away or lessen the value etc (of s.t): *Those ugly buildings detract from the beauty of this village.*
detraction /dɪ'trækʃən/ *u.n.*
detriment /'detrɪmənt/ *u.n* (often — *to* s.o/ s.t) *(formal)* harm; disadvantage: *You cannot gamble(3) without detriment to your wife and children.* **to the detriment of s.o/s.t** with the result that there is harm or disadvantage to s.o/ s.t: *She studied until very late each night to the obvious detriment of her health.*
detrimental /ˌdetrɪ'mentl/ *adj* (often — *to* s.o/ s.t) causing harm: *Staying up late will be detrimental to your health.*
deuce¹ /dju:s/ c/u.n **1** (in tennis etc) situation in which 40 points have been gained by each player or pair of players. **2** throw of 2 on a dice(1).
deuce² /dju:s/ *def.n/interj (old use)* devil: *What the deuce are you doing in my room?*
devalue /di:'vælju:/ *tr.v* **1** cause the exchange value of (a currency) to be reduced: *The government has devalued the dollar.* Opposite **revalue**. **2** cause the worth of (s.t) to be reduced: *I don't want to devalue his efforts but this work is not very good.*
devaluation /di:ˌvælju'eɪʃən/ *u.n.*
devastate /'devəˌsteɪt/ *tr.v (formal)* **1** destroy (a place); cause a lot of damage to (s.t): *The storm devastated the valley.* **2** (usu passive) cause (s.o) to lose all hope or happiness: *I was devastated when I learned that all my books had been burned in the fire.*
'deva,stating *adj* that devastates s.o/s.t: *a devastating fire; devastating news.*
'deva,statingly *adv.*
devastation /ˌdevə'steɪʃən/ *u.n* act or result of devastating (⇒ devastate) s.o/s.t.
develop /dɪ'veləp/ *v* (-p-) **1** *tr/intr.v* (often — *(from* s.t) *into* s.o/s.t) (cause (s.o/s.t) to) change or grow bigger or grow into a particular or more advanced state, esp gradually: *He has developed into a very responsible young man. The caterpillar(1) develops into a butterfly. The plant developed from one thin stem into a beautiful bush.* **2** *intr.v* grow stronger: *A pain was developing in my knee. The business is developing well.* **3** *intr.v* come into existence, show details, gradually: *A black mark has developed on the wall. I think he's developing measles. A new idea was developing in her mind.* **4** *tr.v* get (s.t) gradually: *He has developed the habit of getting up late every day.* **5** *tr.v* use (a place) to build homes, factories etc. **6** *tr.v* use chemical substances to make (a photograph) from (a film): *He can develop his own films. Can you develop a photograph from this broken negative(5)?*
de'veloper c.n **1** chemical substance used to develop(6) film. **2** person who develops(5) a place: *a property developer.*
de'veloping *attrib.adj* growing bigger, stronger, esp economically: *a developing country/state.* ⇒ underdeveloped.

de,veloping 'world *def.n* poor countries that are trying to improve their economies(3).
de'velopment *n* **1** *u.n* (often — *of* s.o/s.t) act or process of developing (⇒ develop): *the development of children, children's education, a new language course, a business, a country's economy(3).* **2** c.n result of a search, academic study etc, esp one that produces change: *There have been several new developments in the search for a cure.*
developmental /dɪˌveləp'mentl/ *adj.*
de,velop'mentally *adv.*
deviate /'di:vɪˌeɪt/ *intr.v* (often — *from* s.t) *(formal)* change (from a usual or good standard of action, thought, belief etc): *deviate from one's expected good behaviour; deviate from the agreed plan.*
deviation /ˌdi:vɪ'eɪʃən/ c/u.n (often — *from* s.t) (example of the) act or fact of deviating (from s.t).
deviationist /ˌdi:vɪ'eɪʃəˌnɪst/ c.n person who deviates (from a religion, political belief or from accepted (sexual) behaviour).
device /dɪ'vaɪs/ c.n **1** tool or apparatus made for a particular purpose, e.g a tin-opener or screwdriver. **2** plan or way of doing s.t for a particular purpose: *I'll have to think of a device to avoid going to their wedding.* ⇒ devices. **3** *(formal)* design(2) representing s.t: *a medal(1) with a royal device round the edge.*
de'vices *pl.n* (usu *leave s.o to her/his own —*) ways of doing s.t or behaving in order to get a particular result.
devil /'devl/ *n* **1** *def.n* (often with capital **D**) chief spirit that produces or causes evil; ruler of hell(1); Satan. **2** c.n evil or very cruel person. **3** c.n (usu *a — with* s.o/s.t) person who does things considered daring, that show ability, are (slightly) bad etc: *She's a devil with a tennis racket¹ in her hand. He's a devil with women. I'm a devil when I drive on motorways.* ⇒ dare-devil. *a devil of a s.t (informal)* a very good example of s.t: *She's a devil of a good driver. between the devil and the deep blue sea* between two very bad alternatives(2). *devil's advocate* person who puts forward an unpopular opinion often to keep an argument going. *go to the devil* (usu imperative) (used to express one's anger with s.o or one's angry refusal). *have the devil to pay* have great difficulties, usu as the result of one's actions. *like the devil* with great speed, effort, determination etc. *poor devil* unfortunate person: *Look at that poor devil sitting by the road. speak/talk of the devil* (said when s.o one has been talking about suddenly appears). *the devil's own s.t* a very difficult thing: *I'm having the devil's own problem finding the money to pay. what, where, who etc the devil . . .?* (used to express anger, surprise etc): *What the devil are you doing? How the devil did you get in here?*
▷ *tr.v* (-ll-) **4** cook (food) using hot or strong spices(1): *devilled kidneys(2).*
'devilish *adj* **1** behaving very badly; wicked: *devilish behaviour.* **2** *(informal)* very great: *a devilish good meal/book/play.*
,devil-may-'care *attrib.adj* not caring at all about what might happen: *a devil-may-care attitude(2).*
'devilment *u.n (formal)* wicked behaviour.

'devilry n (pl -ies) (formal) **1** u.n = devilment. **2** c.n wicked act. **3** u.n = black magic.

devious /'di:vɪəs/ adj **1** (derog) not sincere, honest or frank'; using deceit: use devious methods to gain an advantage; devious thoughts. **2** (formal) not using a usual or direct way: take a devious route(1) round the city. **'deviously** adv. **'deviousness** u.n.

devise /dɪ'vaɪz/ tr.v plan or create(1) (s.t) in one's mind: devise a new way of growing carrots.

devoid /dɪ'vɔɪd/ pred.adj devoid of s.t (formal) lacking or without s.t: She's devoid of pity. The story is devoid of interest.

devolve /dɪ'vɒlv/ tr/intr.v (often — (up)on s.o; — s.t to s.o/s.t) (formal) (cause (s.t) to) become the duty of s.o: The responsibility devolved on the rest of the committee. The judge devolved the property to the wife of the deceased(2).

devolution /ˌdiːvə'luːʃən/ u.n (also attrib) act or fact of devolving, esp power or responsibility, to another person, group, government: a devolution of power from central to regional government.

devote /dɪ'vəʊt/ tr.v (usu — o.s/s.t to s.t) give o.s, all one's efforts, time etc (to a cause, course of action etc): She devoted herself/her energy/her life to helping poor children.

de'voted adj (often — to s.o/s.t) **1** very fond of and loyal to s.o, one's country, one's work etc: I'm devoted to my husband. She's a devoted friend (i.e very fond of me, loyal to me). Their devoted (i.e very loyal and committed) workers. **2** serious and sincere: a devoted student/Christian(3). ⇒ devout.

devotee /ˌdevə'tiː/ c.n (often — of s.o/s.t) keen supporter: a devotee of tennis.

devotion /dɪ'vəʊʃən/ u.n (formal) **1** (often — for s.o/s.t) deep love and respect: feel devotion for one's family/country. **2** (often — to s.t) act or fact of devoting oneself/s.t (to s.t): devotion to duty.

de'votional adj (formal) of, referring to, showing, devotion.

de'votions pl.n (formal) prayers.

devour /dɪ'vaʊə/ tr.v (formal) **1** eat (s.t) quickly and greedily: The dog soon devoured the bone. **2** (fig) read (s.t) with energy(1): He devoured all the information he could find. **3** (fig) destroy (s.t) quickly: The fire devoured the hay within a minute.

devout /dɪ'vaʊt/ adj **1** (very) religious: a devout Catholic. **2** (attrib) serious and sincere: devout thanks/gratitude. ⇒ devoted(2). **de'voutly** adv. **de'voutness** u.n.

dew /djuː/ u.n small drops of water that form on plants etc as the air cools, esp during the night: early morning dew. **'dew ˌdrop** c.n drop of dew. **'dewiness** u.n. **'dewy** adj (-ier, -iest) (esp literary) (as if) covered with dew: dewy leaves.

dexterity /dek'sterɪtɪ/ u.n (formal) ability or skill, esp when using one's hands. **dexterous** /'dekstrəs/ adj (also **'dextrous**) (formal) having or showing dexterity. ⇒ ambidextrous.

dextrose /'dekstrəʊz/ u.n kind of sugar (or glucose) found in fruit, honey etc and also in animal tissue(1). **dextrous** ⇒ dexterity. **DG** /ˌdiː 'dʒiː/ abbr director general.

dhal /dɑːl/ u.n (also **dal**) kind of food made by boiling lentils or beans and adding spices(1) etc. **DH** /ˌdiː 'eɪtʃ/ abbr/def.n Department of Health (a UK government department).

diabetes /ˌdaɪə'biːtɪs/ u.n kind of disease with too much sugar in one's blood, caused by lack of insulin. **diabetic** /ˌdaɪə'betɪk/ adj **1** suffering from diabetes: a diabetic child. **2** prepared for a person suffering from diabetes: diabetic chocolate. ▷ c.n **3** person suffering from diabetes: she is a diabetic.

diabolical /ˌdaɪə'bɒlɪkl/ adj (also **dia'bolic**) **1** very evil or wicked; devilish(1): That was diabolical behaviour. **2** (informal) very bad: diabolical weather. **dia'bolically** adv.

diadem /'daɪəˌdem/ c.n small royal crown with many jewels in it.

diag written abbr diagram.

diagnose /'daɪəgˌnəʊz/ tr.v **1** examine and find out (the cause of s.o being ill): diagnose a disease; diagnose the cause of a pain. **2** (fig) examine and find out (the cause of a problem or difficulty): diagnose a broken part in the engine.

diagnosis /ˌdaɪəg'nəʊsɪs/ n (pl diagnoses /ˌdaɪəg'nəʊsiːz/) **1** u.n act or fact of diagnosing s.t. **2** c.n result of diagnosing s.t: He arrived at a diagnosis of diabetes.

diagnostic /ˌdaɪəg'nɒstɪk/ attrib.adj of, referring to, used for, diagnosis(1): diagnostic instruments.

diagonal /daɪ'ægənəl/ adj **1** (often — to s.t) along or on a diagonal(2): a diagonal line. The path is diagonal to the edge of the field. ▷ c.n **2** line or route going across a four-sided figure or space to the opposite corner. **di'agonally** adv.

diagram /'daɪəˌgræm/ c.n (often — of s.t) plan, drawing etc made to explain or show s.t: a diagram of the inside of the heart. Compare map(1).

diagrammatic /ˌdaɪəgrə'mætɪk/ adj (usu attrib) of, referring to, using or like a diagram: diagrammatic information. **ˌdiagram'matically** adv.

dial /'daɪəl/ c.n **1** (front) part of a clock, radio, meter'(1) or similar instrument with the numbers, hands etc: a dial on a watch. ⇒ sundial. **2** round part (on a telephone) with holes and numbers which is moved when using it: a telephone dial. ▷ tr/intr.v (-ll-) **3** use a telephone by turning a dial(2) or pressing a particular set of numbers; make a telephone call to (a particular number, person, business, place etc): dial 515735/home/Australia. I dialled but no one answered. Pick up the receiver(1) and dial the number you want. **'dialling ˌtone** def.n special sound heard on the telephone showing that it is ready for s.o to dial(3) a number. Compare engaged(2) tone(1).

dialect /'daɪəˌlekt/ c.n way of speaking a language used in a certain region: the Welsh dialect; using a northern dialect. **dialectal** /ˌdaɪə'lektl/ adj (technical) of or referring to dialects.

dialogue /'daɪəˌlɒg/ c/u.n (US **'diaˌlog**) (example of) talk between two or more people: I heard an angry dialogue in the manager's office. The novel[1] *is interesting but the dialogue sounds very artificial.*

diameter /daɪˈæmɪtə/ *c.n* (measure of a) straight line from the side (of a circle) through the centre to the side opposite. **in diameter** along the diameter: *The circle is 10 centimetres in diameter.*

diametrically /ˌdaɪəˈmetrɪklɪ/ *adv* (usu — opposed (to s.t)) completely (opposite): *Their opinions are diametrically opposed (to mine).*

diamond /ˈdaɪəmənd/ *n* (also *attrib*) **1** *c/u.n* usu colourless[1], very valuable gem(1) that sparkles(1) a lot: *It's made of diamonds. It's a diamond ring. Diamond is one of the hardest natural substances on earth.* **2** *c.n* figure with 4 equal sides which stands on one of its points: *a diamond shape.* **3** *c.n* one of four suits(2) in a set of playing cards with one or more red shapes on it that look like this ◆: *I played a diamond.* **a rough diamond** (*informal*) a person who has no fine manners but is kind and likeable.

ˌdiamond ˈjubilee/ˈwedding *c.n* 60th year after an important event, e.g a wedding, a coronation. Compare golden jubilee/wedding, silver jubilee/wedding.

ˈdiamonds *pl.n* **1** jewellery containing diamonds(1): *I won't wear my diamonds tonight.* **2** suit(2) of cards(5) with diamonds(3): *Diamonds are trumps. I played the queen of diamonds.*

diaper /ˈdaɪəpə/ *c.n* (US) nappy.

diaphragm /ˈdaɪəˌfræm/ *c.n* **1** (*anatomy*) thin layer of muscle(1) under the lungs and between the chest and the stomach. **2** thin layer or piece of skin etc used to produce sound: *the diaphragm in a telephone transmits(2) sound to the ear.* **3** contraceptive(2) device.

diarist ⇒ diary.

diarrhoea /ˌdaɪəˈrɪə/ *u.n* (also, esp US, **ˌdiaˈrhea**) illness that produces too much liquid in one's solid waste matter, esp one that makes one empty one's bowels(1) too often: *I have diarrhoea and I don't think I can come for a walk.*

diary /ˈdaɪərɪ/ *c.n* (*pl -ies*) (book with a) record of past daily events, future appointments: *I'd love to come tomorrow but I will have to look at my diary and see if I am free.* **keep a diary** write a (usu daily) record of what happens during one's life.

ˈdiarist *c.n* person who keeps a diary.

diatribe /ˈdaɪəˌtraɪb/ *c.n* (often — against s.o/s.t) (*formal*) very strong attack in writing or speech: *write a diatribe against the government.*

dice /daɪs/ *c.n. pl.* (*sing.* die) **1** cube(1) with numbers on the sides, used in some board games etc and in gambling: *a throw of the dice.*
▷ *v* **2** *tr.v* cut (vegetables etc) into cubes. **3** *intr.v* gamble(3) using dice(1). **dice with death** (*fig*) do s.t dangerous and difficult.

dicey *adj* (*informal*) of or from which success is not certain; risky: *a dicey situation.*

dichotomy /daɪˈkɒtəmɪ/ *c.n* (*pl -ies*) (often — between s.t and s.t) (*formal*) division into two different or opposite groups: *the dichotomy between marriage and staying single.*

dickens /ˈdɪkɪnz/ *def.n* (usu what, who etc the — . . .?) used to show how strongly one feels about a situation: *What the dickens are you doing? Who the dickens are you?* ⇒ what, where, who etc the devil . . .? (⇒ devil).

dicky /ˈdɪkɪ/ *attrib.adj* (*informal*) likely to go wrong; weak: *a dicky heart.*

dickybird /ˈdɪkɪˌbɜːd/ *c.n* (used by or to children) bird. **do not, will not, say a dickybird** keep silent about s.t secret and important.

dictate /dɪkˈteɪt/ *v* (often — (s.t) to s.o) **1** *tr/intr.v* say (words, a message) (to s.o) that he/she must write down: *I've dictated a letter to my secretary. He was dictating when the telephone rang.* **2** *tr.v* state the details of (s.t) officially: *She dictated the rules of the competition to the players.* **3** *intr.v* give orders (to s.o) using one's authority(1) in an unpleasantly arrogant way: *I refuse to be dictated to by such a pompous man.* **4** *intr.v* (of a situation etc) provide the cause of s.t: *The holiday will be organized as the weather dictates.*

dictates /ˈdɪkteɪts/ *pl.n* (usu the — of s.t) orders, influences, that must be obeyed: *The dictates of tradition make such clothes necessary.*

dictation /dɪkˈteɪʃən/ *n* **1** *u.n* act of dictating(1). **2** *c.n* thing read when dictating(1), or written while being dictated(1) to. **take dictation** write down s.t that is dictated(1).

dictator /dɪkˈteɪtə/ *c.n* (*derog*) ruler who uses force to get and keep power and authority(1).

dictatorial /ˌdɪktəˈtɔːrɪəl/ *adj* (*derog*) like, of, a dictator: *Don't speak to me in that dictatorial manner.*

ˌdictaˈtorially *adv.*

dicˈtatorˌship *n* **1** *c.n* country ruled by a dictator. **2** *u.n* (way of getting) authority(1) as a dictator.

diction /ˈdɪkʃən/ *u.n* (*formal*) way of speaking: *perfect diction; lessons in diction.*

dictionary /ˈdɪkʃənrɪ/ *c.n* (*pl -ies*) (also *attrib*) (often — of s.t) **1** book listing words in alphabetical order and explaining them: *a dictionary of English; an English dictionary; a dictionary entry(4).* **2** book listing certain information in an alphabetical order: *a dictionary of scientific terms; a science dictionary.* **walking dictionary** ⇒ walk.

did /dɪd/ *p.t* of do.

didactic /daɪˈdæktɪk/ *adj* (*formal*) educational, esp morally: *a didactic speech about truth.*

diˈdactically *adv.*

diddle /ˈdɪdl/ *tr.v* (often — s.o out of s.t) (*informal*) get money etc from (s.o) by using deceit: *I was diddled out of my share of the profits.*

didn't /ˈdɪdnt/ = did not ⇒ do.

didst /dɪdst/ (*old use*) did used with 'thou': *Thou didst not come.*

die¹ /daɪ/ *c.n* **1** device with a raised design(2) on it, used to stamp the design on paper etc. **The die is cast** (*fig*) decision made which makes what will happen unavoidable. **2** ⇒ dice(1).

die² /daɪ/ *v* (*pres.p* dying; *p.t,p.p* died) **1** *intr.v* stop being alive: *The roses are dying. My dog has died. If you eat that, you will die.* **2** *tr.v* stop being alive in (a certain way): *They died a horrible death.* **3** *intr.v* (of things that do not have life) stop existing: *My love for you will never die. The day was dying as we reached the station. The fire is dying.* Compare undying. ⇒ dead.

be dying for, to do, s.t (*informal*) want (to do) s.t very much: *I'm dying for a cup of coffee. I'm dying to meet her.*

die away gradually stop being seen or heard: *The music died away as we closed the doors.*

die down (a) lose strength gradually: *The storm*

is dying down now. (b) (of a plant) stop being alive above the ground, e.g during the winter, after which it grows again from the roots.

die hard die(3) with difficulty: *Old habits die hard.* ⇨ diehard.

die of s.t die(1) because of s.t: *He died of cancer*(1).

die off die(1) in large numbers: *The animals are dying off because of the destruction of the forests.*

die out die(1) until there is/are none left: *Tigers have almost died out in India.*

die without issue ⇨ issue(*n*).

'die,hard *c.n* (also *attrib*) person who refuses to change her/his opinions: *a diehard socialist.*

diesel /'di:zl/ *u.n* (also *attrib*) kind of heavy fuel produced from petroleum, used to drive heavy engines in lorries etc: *diesel fuel/oil; a diesel engine.* ⇨ derv.

diet /'daɪət/ *c.n* **1** (also *attrib*) selection(3) of food for changing one's weight, improving one's health etc: *a slimming diet; a health diet; a diet of eggs and fruit; a diet sheet.* **on a diet** eating a special diet(1), usu to lose weight.

▷ *intr.v* **2** follow a diet(1): *I'm dieting because I am too fat.*

'dietary *adj* of or referring to a diet(1) or dieting(2).

dietitian /ˌdaɪə'tɪʃən/ *c.n* (also **die'tician**) (*technical*) person skilled in organizing or preparing special diets(1).

differ /'dɪfə/ *intr.v* (often — *from* s.o/s.t) not be like s.o/s.t: *We differ in the way we work. Her method differs from mine.* **agree to differ** accept that we/they have different opinions and stop arguing: *Let's agree to differ.* **differ with s.o** (*about/over s.t*) disagree with s.o (about/over s.t). ⇨ difference(4).

difference /'dɪfrəns/ *n* **1** *c.n* (often — *between* s.o/s.t *and* s.o/s.t) thing that makes one person or thing not like another: *What's the difference between a butterfly and a moth? The differences are obvious when you look at them.* **2** *def.n* (often the — *in* s.t) amount by which s.t is greater than s.t else: *The difference in price is about £10.* **3** *c.n* (often — *in* s.o/s.t) amount of change (in s.o/ s.t): *After the holiday, the difference in him was very clear. I noticed a difference in his behaviour.* **4** *c.n* (often *pl*) disagreement: *I've had a difference with my boss about working methods.* **difference of opinion** disagreement. **know the difference between right and wrong** ⇨ right(12). **make a, some** etc **difference (to s.o/s.t)** cause s.o/s.t to be different: *It will make a great difference to your health if you lose weight.* **make a world of difference (to s.o/s.t)** ⇨ world. **make no difference (to s.o)**; **not make any difference (to s.o)** not be important (to s.o); not matter: *It makes no difference to me whether you come or not.* **make up the difference** provide the rest of the amount (usu of money) needed: *You give her half the cost and I'll make up the difference.* **settle one's differences** agree and end a quarrel. **split the difference (a)** pay equal parts of the rest of an amount of money needed. **(b)** (*fig*) settle an argument by each side giving up the same number of demands.

'different *adj* (often — *from* s.o/s.t, but — *to* s.o/ s.t is now used although many people consider

this incorrect) not the same, either completely or partly: *It's a different colour/shape/size. I'll wear a different dress from the one I wore to Mike's party. It looks different in some way.*

differential /ˌdɪfə'renʃəl/ *c.n v.* (also *attrib*) (*formal*) difference(2), esp in wages or salaries: *Have we maintained the differential between workers' and managers' pay?*

differentiate /ˌdɪfə'renʃɪˌeɪt/ *v* (often — *between* s.o/s.t *and* s.o/s.t; — s.o/s.t *from* s.o/s.t) (*formal*) **1** *tr/intr.v* see, show, state etc a difference(1,3): *Can you differentiate between an apple tree and a pear tree? I couldn't differentiate a sick student from a lazy one who was not being honest.* **2** *tr.v* cause (s.o/s.t) to be different: *Using a large number of books in the library differentiates a first class student from others.*

differentiation /ˌdɪfərenʃɪ'eɪʃən/ *u.n.*

difficult /'dɪfɪkəlt/ *adj* **1** not easy to do or understand; hard(2): *Is English a difficult language to learn? This problem is too difficult for me to solve. I can't do it — it's very difficult. It's difficult to decide between them.* Opposite easy(1). **2** having, producing, many problems, troubles etc: *A difficult period*(1) *lies ahead. This is a difficult time for young people without a skill or training.* **3** not easy to deal with etc because causing problems or troubles, e.g by refusing: *a difficult child. Don't be difficult — please give it back to me.*

'difficulty *n* (*pl -ies*) **1** *u.n* (often — *in doing, with*, s.t) fact or state of being difficult(1): *I'm having a lot of difficulty in doing it (or with this work).* **2** *c.n* problem, task etc that is not easy: *There were many difficulties but we managed to finish the job.* **3** *c.n* thing that stops progress or makes success difficult(1): *Her age shouldn't be a difficulty since she has the greatest experience.* **4** *c.n* (usu *pl*) difficult(1) situation; trouble: *Coming when your former wife may be here could cause difficulties.* **in difficulty/difficulties** having problems, esp about money: *That new shop is in difficulties.* **make difficulties** cause problems by being stubborn(1), pessimistic etc. **with difficulty** lacking freedom from pain, trouble etc: *walk with difficulty; manage with difficulty to open the door.* Opposite with ease(1).

diffident /'dɪfɪdənt/ *adj* (*formal*) lacking confidence; shy: *a diffident speaker; be diffident about one's success as a singer.*

'diffidence *u.n.* **'diffidently** *adv.*

diffuse /dɪ'fju:s/ *adj* (*formal*) **1** spread out: *diffuse lighting used in a dance hall.* **2** (*derog*) (of writing) using too many (difficult) words: *The style of the book is too diffuse.*

▷ *tr/intr.v* /dɪ'fju:z/ **3** (*formal*) (cause (s.t) to) spread (into or through s.t): *The light was diffused through the trees.*

dif'fuseness /dɪ'fju:snəs/ *u.n* quality of being diffuse(1).

diffusion /dɪ'fju:ʒən/ *u.n* (*formal*) **1** act of diffusing(3) or fact of being diffused: *diffusion of light.* **2** quality of being diffuse(2): *diffusion in her writing style.*

dig /dɪg/ *c.n* **1** push (with s.t long and narrow): *a dig in the ribs with a stick/finger.* **2** act of digging(5): *a long dig in the garden.* **3** (usu a — *at* s.o/s.t) (*informal*) slight criticism, usu for fun: *His remark was a dig at me.* **4** (*informal*) (place where there is a) dig(2) to find things of interest to archaeologists: *She has joined an* archaeological *dig.*

▷ *v* (*-gg-*, *p.t,p.p* dug /dʌg/) **5** *tr/intr.v* (use a tool such as a spade to) turn over (land) in (a place): *digging soil to prepare for vegetables; dig the front garden. She's been digging for hours.* **6** *tr.v* make (s.t) by digging(5): *dig a hole for a tree; dig a tunnel.* **7** produce (s.t) out of the ground by digging(5): *dig* carrots. ⇨ dig s.t up(a). **8** *tr.v* (usu — s.o/s.t *in* s.t; — s.t *into* s.o/s.t) push (s.o, an animal) using (s.t long and narrow): *I dug her in the* ribs(1) *with my umbrella. He dug a knife into the chicken.* **9** *tr.v* (*slang*) like or enjoy (s.o/s.t) very much: *I dig his music/ sister.* **dig in** (a) (*fig; informal*) begin to eat, esp hungrily: *Don't wait to be asked, dig in!* **(b)** (*informal*) become determined about one's opinion and refuse to agree during an argument. **(c)** (*military*; also *fig*) make one's defensive(1) position strong, esp because it will be used for a long time. **dig oneself in** (*informal*) **(a)** = dig in(b). **(b)** make one's position fixed and secure in a job or place, on a committee etc. **dig s.t in** put s.t into soil etc by digging(5): *dig in weeds.* **dig in one's heels** = heel(*n*). **dig into s.t** (*fig*) begin to eat (a meal, food), esp hungrily. **dig s.o out (of s.t)** **(a)** get s.o out (of a destroyed building etc) by digging(5). **(b)** (*fig*) find s.o (in a large building, forest etc) after a search. **dig s.t out (of s.t)** (*fig; informal*) find s.t (in a desk, file³(1–3), book etc) after a search: *Can you dig out the information before Friday?* **dig s.t up** (a) get s.t by digging(5): *dig up potatoes.* **(b)** (*fig*) find s.t: *I dug up her diary when I emptied her desk.*

'digger *c.n* **1** machine used for digging(5): *a mechanical digger for collecting potatoes.* **2** person who digs(5): *My son's a slow digger.*

'digging *c.n* place where there is or was a mine¹(1).

'diggings *pl.n* (*formal*; *old use*) = digs.

digs *pl.n* (*informal*) rented room(s) in s.o's house; lodgings: *I live in digs near the station.*

digest /'daɪdʒest/ *c.n* **1** (often — *of s.t*) (*formal*) account that is an organized summary(3) (of information): *a digest of the day's news.* **2** magazine etc with news summaries(3), law reports etc.

▷ *tr.v* /daɪ'dʒest/ **3** change (food) in the stomach by chemical processes so that the body can absorb(3) it: *Give your food time to digest before you swim.* **4** (*fig*) take (information) into one's mind and think until one understands it: *Her reasons for leaving her job are difficult to digest.*

digestible /dɪ'dzestɪbl/ *adj* that can be digested(3): *digestible food.* Opposite indigestible.

digestion /dɪ'dʒestʃən/ *n* **1** *u.n* act or process of digesting(3) food. **2** *u.n* act of digesting(4) facts etc. **3** *c.n* individual power to digest(3) food: *He has a poor digestion and often feels sick after eating.* ⇨ indigestion.

digestif /ˌdɪʒe'stiːf/ *c.n* (*French*) drink, salad(2) etc taken during or after a meal to help digestion(1). Compare aperitif.

digestive /dɪ'dʒestɪv/ *adj* (usu *attrib*) used for, helping, digestion(1): *The digestive system includes the stomach and the intestines.*

di'gestive ˌbiscuit *c.n* sweet biscuit made of wholemeal flour.

digger, digging(s) ⇨ dig.

digit /'dɪdʒɪt/ *c.n* **1** (also *attrib*) figure from 0 to 9: *26 730 is a five digit number* (or *has five digits*). **2** finger; toe.

digital *attrib.adj* showing or using digits(1): *a digital watch.*

dignified /'dɪgnɪˌfaɪd/ *adj* showing dignity(1) in style or behaviour, clothes etc: *dress/speak in a dignified way; make a dignified exit(2) from a room where there is a quarrel.* Opposite undignified.

dignitary /'dɪgnɪtərɪ/ *c.n* (*pl -ies*) (*formal*) important person, esp in a high position in public life: *a dinner party for local dignitaries.*

dignity /'dɪgnɪtɪ/ *n* (*pl -ies*) **1** *u.n* (often *do s.t with* —) way of behaving, speaking, dressing etc that shows one has good manners, is serious, formal etc: *She walked up the stairs with great dignity.* **2** *u.n* (often *the* — *of s.t*) serious importance (of an occasion, situation). Compare indignity. **3** *c.n* (*formal*) important position or rank. **be on one's dignity** = stand on one's dignity. **beneath one's dignity** beneath one's personal standard of good social behaviour: *It's beneath my dignity to swear.* **stand on one's dignity** show that one expects to be treated with respect (esp in situations that easily make one upset).

digress /daɪ'gres/ *intr.v* (often — *from s.t*) (*formal*) move away from the main subject or point when speaking or writing: *I'd like to digress for a moment and describe the house.*

digression /daɪ'greʃən/ *c/u.n* (often — *from s.t*) (*formal*) (example of the) act or fact of digressing: *digressions from the main subject of the report.*

digs ⇨ dig.

dike /daɪk/ *c.n* = dyke¹, ².

dilapidated /dɪ'læpɪˌdeɪtɪd/ *adj* in a bad condition and needing repair: *a dilapidated house.*

dilapidation /dɪˌlæpɪ'deɪʃən/ *u.n.* process of becoming, or state of being, dilapidated.

dilate /daɪ'leɪt/ *tr/intr.v* (*technical*) (cause (an opening, esp in the centre of the eyes, to)) become larger: *Fear often makes the pupils² of the eyes dilate.* Opposite contract(4).

dilation /daɪ'leɪʃən/ *u.n.*

dilatory /'dɪlətərɪ/ *adj* (*derog; formal*) tending to cause delay by being slow: *dilatory workers/ behaviour.*

'dilatoriness *u.n.*

dilemma /daɪ'lemə/ *c.n* situation providing a choice between two (usu unpleasant) ways of acting: *I'm in a dilemma about whether to stay at home and be bored or join the others for a walk in the rain.* **on the horns of a dilemma** faced with a choice between equally bad alternatives(2).

dilettante /ˌdɪlɪ'tɑːntɪ/ *c.n* (*derog; formal*) person with only a slight interest in, or knowledge of, skill in, (usu artistic) things.

diligent /'dɪlɪdʒənt/ *adj* serious, careful and making or using much effort: *a diligent worker.* **'diligence** *u.n.* **'diligently** *adv.*

dill /dɪl/ *u.n* kind of herb with a strong smell, used in cooking, esp fish.

dilly-dally /'dɪlɪ ˌdælɪ/ *intr.v* (*informal*) (stop often while doing s.t and so) waste time: *Go straight to the shops and don't dilly-dally on the way.* ⇨ dally(1).

dilute /daɪ'luːt/ *attrib.adj* **1** that has been diluted(2): *dilute acid.*

▷ *tr.v* **2** (often — *s.t with s.t*) make (a liquid substance) less strong (by adding water etc): *dilute orange juice with cold water.* **3** (*fig*) make (a report, criticism etc) less strong by choosing words carefully, leaving details out etc.
dilution /daɪˈluːʃən/ *u.n.*

dim /dɪm/ *adj* (*-mm-*) **1** not bright, clear, strong etc: *a dim light/sound/colour.* **2** (of a place) badly lit: *a dim corner/staircase.* **3** (*fig*) slight; weak: *I have a dim recollection*(2) *of her.* **4** (*derog*; *informal*) (of a person) not clever or intelligent; not able to think quickly. **take a dim view of s.o/ s.t** have an unfavourable opinion of s.o/s.o's behaviour etc.
▷ *tr/intr.v* (*-mm-*) **5** (cause (s.t) to) become dim (1, 2): *Please dim the lights. The tree by the window dimmed the room.* **6** (US) dip (8).
'dimly *adv.* **'dimness** *u.n.*

dime /daɪm/ *c.n* US coin worth 10 cents. **be a dime a dozen** (*fig*) **(a)** be very cheap to buy. **(b)** have (almost) no value because very common.

dimension /dɪˈmenʃən/ *n* **1** *c.n* (often *pl, the —s of s.t*) measurement of length, width, height etc (of an object, space): *What are the dimensions of this carpet?* **2** *c.n* way s.t is considered, etc: *The discovery of DNA introduced a* major(1) *new dimension into science.*
dimensional /dɪˈmenʃənl/ *adj* (usu used in combinations) having the number of dimensions(1) shown by the first part of the word: *a two-dimensional drawing* (i.e with length and width); *a three-dimensional figure* (i.e with length, width and height). ⇒ three-dimensional.
di'mensions *pl.n* (usu *of great* etc —) size: *a task/problem/garden/tree of huge dimensions.*

diminish /dɪˈmɪnɪʃ/ *tr/intr.v* (cause (s.t) to) become less: *Her hopes diminished as the days passed. Making a fire every evening will diminish our supply of wood quickly.* Opposite increase.
diminished *adj* made less or smaller: *The man* pleaded(2) *diminished responsibility for his crime because he was suffering from a serious illness at the time.* Compare undiminished.

diminuendo /dɪˌmɪnjuˈendəʊ/ *c.n* (*pl -s*) (*music*) gradual reduction in the level of sound. Opposite crescendo(1).
diminution /ˌdɪmɪˈnjuːʃən/ *c/u.n* (usu — *of/in s.t*) (*formal*) act of reducing the level or amount (of s.t): *a diminution of our* savings (or *in the need for qualified typists*).
diminutive /dɪˈmɪnjʊtɪv/ *adj* **1** (*formal*) very small: *We saw the diminutive figure of a young child far below us in the valley.*
▷ *c.n* **2** (*technical*) word (made from another one and) used to express smallness, e.g one with '-let' at the end, such as 'droplet', 'hamlet', 'piglet'.

dimple /ˈdɪmpl/ *c.n* **1** round hollow, esp on the skin: *have a dimple on one's chin; a glass with dimples in it.*
▷ *tr/intr.v* **2** (cause (s.t) to) have a dimple(1): *Her smile dimpled her cheeks.*

din /dɪn/ *c.n* **1** long unpleasant noise: *My son makes such a loud din when he plays his drums.* **kick up a din** (*informal*) **(a)** make a very loud noise. **(b)** express one's disapproval or objection very strongly.
▷ *intr.v* (*-nn-*) **2** (*informal*) make a din(1). **din s.t**

into s.o (*informal*) make s.o learn and remember s.t by repeating it very often: *The only way he could learn the* equations(2) *was by having them dinned into him every afternoon.*

dine /daɪn/ *intr.v* (*formal*) have or eat dinner: *We're dining with the neighbours tonight.* **dine out** have one's dinner in a restaurant or in a friend's house. **dine (up)on s.t** (*formal*) eat s.t for dinner: *We dined on grilled fish and new potatoes.* **wine and dine (s.o)** ⇒ wine(*v*).
'diner *c.n* **1** (*formal*) person who eats a meal, esp in a restaurant. **2** (esp US) dining car.
'dining ,car *c.n* (also **'restaurant ,car**) carriage(2) on a train in which meals are served at tables.
'dining ,room *c.n* room in a house, hotel etc where meals are eaten.
'dining ,table *c.n* table used for eating meals.

dingdong /ˈdɪŋˌdɒŋ/ *attrib.adj* **1** (*informal*) (of a fight or quarrel) that has a repeated exchange of strong hits or words: *a dingdong battle between the two politicians.*
▷ *c.n* (*informal*) **2** sound of a bell. **3** (usu *have a —*) serious quarrel or fight.

dinghy /ˈdɪŋɪ/ *c.n* (*pl -ies*) small boat with or without an engine, often carried on a larger boat and used to reach the shore: *a sailing/rowing dinghy.*

dingy /ˈdɪndʒɪ/ *adj* (*-ier, -iest*) dark, dirty and with faded colours: *a dingy hotel; dingy paintwork.*
'dinginess *u.n.*

dinner /ˈdɪnə/ *c/u.n* **1** (also *attrib*) one of the main meals of the day, usu eaten in the evening: *What's for dinner? I love a dinner of roast meat and vegetables. Do you like the dinners in your college? Would you like to come to dinner with my parents? We're having a dinner party on Friday.* Compare lunch(1), supper. **2** formal dinner(1) for a special reason or occasion: *They are giving a dinner for the winners of the competition. I shall wear my long dress to the dinner.* ⇒ dine.
'dinner ,bell *c.n* bell used to call people to a meal, e.g in a hotel.
'dinner ,jacket *c.n* jacket(1) used for formal occasions in the evening.
'dinner ,service *c.n* set of plates etc used during a dinner(1,2).
'dinner ,suit *c.n* style of, usu black, jacket(1) and trousers worn for formal occasions in the evening.
'dinner ,table *c.n* table prepared for eating a dinner(1).
'dinner ,time *u.n* time when dinner(1) is eaten: *It's nearly dinner time.*

dinosaur /ˈdaɪnəˌsɔː/ *c.n* **1** (very) large reptile that became extinct about 100 million years ago. **2** (*derog; fig*) person with old-fashioned ideas who refuses to change (and so will probably be unsuccessful).

dint /dɪnt/ *c.n* (*old use*) dent(1,2). **by dint of s.t** (*formal*) by using, by means of, s.t: *He was successful by dint of determination and energy.*

diocese /ˈdaɪəsɪs/ *c.n* district which a bishop(1) controls.
diocesan /daɪˈɒsɪsn/ *adj* (*formal*) of or referring to a diocese.

dioxide /daɪˈɒksaɪd/ *c.n* (*chemistry*) oxide with 2 oxygen atoms(1), e.g carbon dioxide.

dip /dɪp/ *c.n* **1** part of the surface of the ground that is lower: *a dip in a road*; *a dip in the hillside with trees in it.* **2** (often *go for a —*) short swim. **3** semiliquid food into which one dips(4) raw vegetables, biscuits etc just before one eats them: *a cheese dip.*

▷ *v* (*-pp-*) **4** *tr.v* put (s.t) into a liquid, e.g to wet it or cover it: *He dipped the brush into the paint.* **5** *tr/ intr.v* put (one's hand, a container etc) into s.t in order to take s.t out: *She dipped (her hand) into her bag and pulled out her* purse'(1). **6** *intr.v* (of land) slope downwards: *The fields dip towards the river.* **7** *intr.v* (of the sun, moon) go down: *The sun dipped behind the hill.* **8** *tr.v* turn (front lights of a vehicle) so that the light is towards the ground. ⇒ dim(6). **9** *tr.v* put (a flag) into a lower position. **dip into s.t** (*informal*) **(a)** ⇒ dip(5). **(b)** read parts of a book, magazine etc without much attention. **(c)** use parts of a supply of s.t: *We'll have to dip into our savings to pay for the holiday.*

'dip,stick *c.n* metal rod with marks on it, used to measure the amount of oil in an engine.

diphtheria /dɪp'θɪərɪə/ *u.n* serious disease of the throat with high fever and difficult breathing.

diphthong /'dɪfθɒŋ/ *c.n* (*technical*) two vowels spoken as one syllable, e.g /aɪ/, /aʊ/, /eə/, /ɪə/, /ɔɪ/, /əʊ/, /ʊə/ as in 'line', 'down', 'pair', 'fear', 'coin', 'bone', 'sure'.

diploma /dɪ'pləʊmə/ *c.n* (also *attrib*) (often *a — in s.t*) written proof that s.o has successfully completed a course of training or education (in a certain subject): *a diploma course*; *a diploma in photography.* Compare degree(4).

diplomacy /dɪ'pləʊməsɪ/ *u.n* **1** business concerning the political relations and peaceful activities between one country and another: *international diplomacy.* **2** skill in working with people and persuading them to accept one's ideas or decisions: *It will need all your diplomacy to get them to agree.*

diplomat /'dɪpləˌmæt/ *c.n* **1** official whose work is in the field of diplomacy(1): *diplomats in the British* Embassy(1) *in Paris.* **2** person with great diplomacy(2): *As a manager you'll need to be a diplomat when dealing with the problems of angry workers.*

diplomatic /ˌdɪpləˈmætɪk/ *adj* **1** of or referring to diplomacy(1): *diplomatic affairs.* **2** showing, using, diplomacy(2): *She showed great diplomatic skill as* chairperson *during the argument.* Opposite undiplomatic.

ˌdiploˈmatically *adv.*

ˌdiploˈmatic ˌcorps *def.n* ⇒ corps diplomatique.

ˌdiploˌmatic imˈmunity *u.n* (often *claim —*) freedom from arrest for a crime or having to pay taxes because one is a diplomat(1).

ˌDiploˈmatic ˌService *def.n* (UK) part of the Civil Service that deals with diplomacy.

diplomatist /dɪ'pləʊməˌtɪst/ *c.n* (*old use*) diplomat.

dipsomania /ˌdɪpsəʊˈmeɪnɪə/ *u.n* desire to drink alcohol that cannot be controlled and makes one very ill.

dipsomaniac /ˌdɪpsəʊˈmeɪnɪˌæk/ *adj* **1** of, suffering from, dipsomania.

▷ *c.n* **2** person suffering from dipsomania.

dire /daɪə/ *adj* (usu *attrib*) causing disaster: *dire results if the government wins the election.*

direct /dɪ'rekt/ *adj* Opposite indirect. **1** (usu *attrib*) straight; shortest: *We took a direct* route(1) *across the fields to the road.* **2** (*attrib*) without change or interruption; not needing a link(2) on the way: *a direct telephone call to New Zealand*; *be a direct* descendant *of the artist.* **3** honest and frank¹: *give a direct answer. I'll be direct with you and say what I really think.* **4** complete; exact: *the direct opposite.* **5** (*attrib*) without any other causes, facts being involved (⇒ involve(1)): *Her failure was a direct result of her illness. It was the direct cause of her leaving the college.* **6** (*grammar*) ⇒ direct object, direct speech, indirect(5).

▷ *adv* **7** straight: *We drove direct to the station.*

▷ *v* **8** *tr.v* control, manage or organize (s.t): *direct the affairs of a committee/business*; *direct traffic in the city.* **9** *tr/intr.v* (*formal*) (often *— s.o to do s.t*) give orders to (s.o) (to do s.t): *I've been directed to leave the building.* **10** *tr/intr.v* organize and help (actors etc) in (a play, film, television programme etc): *Who directed the film? I prefer directing to acting.* **11** *tr.v* (often *— s.o to s.w*) (*formal*) show (s.o) how to get to a place: *Can you direct me to the post office, please?* **12** *tr.v* (often *— s.t at/ towards s.o/s.t*) aim, point, (s.t, one's attention) (towards s.o/s.t): *Don't direct that* hose¹(1) *at me, direct it towards those plants. Please direct your remarks to the* chair(3).

diˌrect ˈaction *u.n* form of demonstration(3) against an employer, the government etc, that includes a strike(1), go-slow, sit-in etc.

diˌrect ˈcurrent *c/u.n* (written *abbr* DC) (*electricity*) current(4) flowing in one direction. Compare alternating current.

direction /dɪ'rekʃən/ *n* **1** *c/u.n* (often *in s.o's/ s.t's —*; *in the — of s.o/s.t*) course along which s.o/s.t moves, points, looks etc: *I was looking in the opposite direction at the time. Which direction did the bus take? He drove in the direction of the sea. There's a storm coming in our direction.* **2** *c.n* (usu *pl*) (often *follow the —s (in/on s.t)*) instruction(3) about where to go, how to do s.t: *Follow the directions on the packet (or in the book). I gave her directions of how to get there (or for finding the shop).* **3** *u.n* (*formal*) act of directing(8,10,12) s.o/s.t: *the direction of a business/play/gun.* **a** (*good, poor* etc) **sense of direction** (good, poor etc) skill at finding one's way to a place, point etc. **under s.o's/s.t's direction**; **under the direction of s.o/s.t** **(a)** being controlled, managed, by s.o/ s.t: *The department is under the direction of* Ms *Plant.* **(b)** being ordered by s.o/s.t: *Under the direction of the government, you must pay these taxes immediately.*

diˈrectional *adj* of or referring to direction(1) in space: *A directional* microphone *picks up sounds from certain* directions(1) *only.*

diˈrective *c.n* (*formal*) official order, e.g from the government, a main office, senior official.

diˈrectly *adv* **1** taking the shortest route and without stopping: *Go directly to the docks.* **2** exactly: *It's directly opposite the garage.* **3** (*formal*) at once; as soon as possible: *She'll be back directly.*

direct object /dɪ'rekt ˈɒbdʒɪkt/ *c.n* (*grammar*) noun (phrase(1))/pronoun in a sentence with a transitive verb that represents s.o/s.t to which the action of the verb is directed, e.g 'him'

in 'I love him', 'her head' in 'She shook her head'
and 'a letter' in 'I'll write you a letter'. Compare
indirect object.

di'rector *c.n* **1** person who directs(8) a business,
senior department. **2** person who directs(10) a
film, play etc.

directorate /dɪ'rektərɪt/ *c.n* (*formal*) **1** position of a director(1). **2** group or board(3) of
directors(1) of a business, institution etc.

di'rector,ship *c.n* position, work, of a direc-
tor(1): *I've been given a directorship in the
business.*

directory /dɪ'rektərɪ/ *c.n* (*pl* **-ies**) book containing a list of names and addresses: *a
telephone/business directory.*

direct speech /dɪ'rekt 'spiːtʃ/ *u.n* (*grammar*)
act of reporting what s.o has said by giving
her/his exact words, e.g *'I'm hungry' she said*.
Compare indirect speech.

di,rect 'tax/ta'xation *u.n* taxes on people's earnings or property. Compare indirect
tax(ation).

dirge /dɜːdʒ/ *c.n* (*formal*) sad hymn or song (as)
used during a funeral.

dirt /dɜːt/ *u.n* **1** unclean substance, e.g mud,
dust etc; substance such as oil, paint, food that
makes s.o/s.t unclean because it is in a place
where it ought not to be: *She had dirt on her
shoes.* **2** immoral writing or speech. **dirt cheap**
(*informal*) having a very low price: *It was dirt
cheap. I bought it dirt cheap.* **treat s.o like dirt**
(*informal*) treat s.o in a way that shows one has
a very low opinion of her/him.

'dirtiness *u.n* fact or quality of being dirty(1,2).

'dirty *adj* (**-ier, -iest**) **1** not clean; covered with
dirt: *dirty hands/shoes.* **2** immoral; very rude:
dirty jokes/films/magazines. **3** very bad and
unfair: *Taking that old woman's money was a
dirty thing to do.*

▷ *tr/intr.v* (**-ies, -ied**) **4** (cause (s.o/s.t) to)
become dirty: *You dirtied my floor with your
muddy boots! His white shirts dirty so quickly.*

,dirty 'word *c.n* **1** word considered to be dirty(2) ;
swear word. **2** word representing an idea, way
of behaving etc that is considered wrong:
*'Ambition' seems to be a dirty word these
days.*

,dirty 'work *u.n* **do his, your** etc (**own**) **dirty
work** do s.t unpleasant but necessary to himself/
yourself: *I'm not going to sack²(2) her — do your
own dirty work.*

disable /dɪs'eɪbl/ *tr.v* cause (s.o) to lose her/his
mental or physical ability completely or partly:
*As a child he had an accident which disabled him
and left him blind.*

disability /ˌdɪsə'bɪlɪtɪ/ *c.n* (also *attrib*) (*formal*)
thing that prevents one from doing s.t (well,
properly): *a disability grant(1). Is it a disability
not having your own car when there's such a good
bus service?*

dis'abled *adj* **1** (of a person) who has lost her/
his mental or physical ability completely or
partly: *She goes to a special school for disabled
children.*

▷ *def.pl.n* **2** people who are disabled(1) in some
way: *She teaches at a special school for the
disabled.*

dis'ablement *u.n* (*formal*) act of disabling s.o/
s.t; fact, state, of being disabled: *His disablement*

was a terrible shock but he soon learned to cope
with it.

disabuse /ˌdɪsə'bjuːz/ *tr.v* (*formal*) free (s.o)
from a false idea: *If you're hoping I'll help you
let me disabuse you immediately.*

disadvantage /ˌdɪsəd'vɑːntɪdʒ/ *c.n* thing that
makes it hard for one to succeed; condition or
fact that is unfavourable: *The one disadvantage
of living there is the lack of a good bus service.* **at
a disadvantage** in an unfavourable position: *The
weather put us at a disadvantage but we managed
to finish the course.* **to s.o's disadvantage** thing
that puts s.o in an unfavourable position: *It will
be to your disadvantage if you arrive at the inter-
view(1) late.* Opposite advantage.

,disad'vantaged *attrib.adj* (*formal*) **1** suffering
from a lack of money, opportunities etc: *This
government does little to help disadvantaged
people.*

▷ *def.pl.n* **2** people who are disadvantaged in
some way: *Both political parties promise to
improve conditions for the disadvantaged.*

disadvantageous /ˌdɪsædvɑːn'teɪdʒəs/ *adj* (*formal*) that has disadvantages; unfavourable: *a disadvantageous agreement. It's disadvantageous to
us but not you.* Opposite advantageous.

disaffected /ˌdɪsə'fektɪd/ *adj* (*formal*) no
longer loyal or satisfied: *Many people are
beginning to feel disaffected towards the present
government.*

disaffection /ˌdɪsə'fekʃən/ *u.n* (usu — to(wards)
s.o/s.t) (*formal*) state of being disaffected: *The
members showed their disaffection to the chairperson by shouting 'Boo' when she stood up.*

disaffiliate /ˌdɪsə'fɪlɪˌeɪt/ *tr/intr.v* (*formal*)
(cause (s.o/s.t) to) stop being a member,
part, of a group, an organization etc; stop
being affiliated (to s.o/s.t): *After the argument
several members disaffiliated (themselves) from
the union.*

disagree /ˌdɪsə'griː/ *intr.v* (often — with s.o/s.t)
1 (of a person) have a different opinion (from
s.o); feel differently (from s.o else) about s.t;
not agree(1) (with s.o/s.t): *We often disagree but
not usually about important things. He disagrees
about the way I treated her. I disagree with you in
that matter.* **2** not agree(2) with, match, (s.t): *Your
account of what happened disagrees with what
I heard yesterday.* **3** (of food) cause problems
(to s.o, s.o's body): *Something I ate last night
disagreed with me because I was sick all night.*

,disa'greeable *adj* (*derog; formal*) (of a person,
job etc) who/that is unpleasant, not agreeable(1):
What's made you so disagreeable this morning?
,disa'greeably *adv.*

,disa'greement *n* **1** *u.n* fact or state of
disagreeing (with s.o/s.t): *We'll need to check
the facts because of the disagreement between
the two accounts of what happened.* **2** *c.n* act
of not agreeing: *I haven't seen him since the last
disagreement we had.* **in disagreement (with s.o/
s.t)** in a state of disagreeing (with s.o/s.t): *I'm in
complete disagreement with him over the issue(3)
of private education.*

disallow /ˌdɪsə'laʊ/ *tr.v* (*formal*) refuse to allow
(s.t) to count, be included: *The referee(2) disallowed the goal because of a foul(5). The new
information was disallowed by the judge.*

disappear /ˌdɪsə'pɪə/ *intr.v* **1** leave s.w in such a way that no one knows where one/it is; no longer to be found anywhere: *Where did you disappear to? The car keys have disappeared.* **2** no longer be visible(1), able to be seen: *The little animal disappeared behind a rock.* Opposite appear(1). **3** gradually stop existing: *Steam engines are disappearing.* Opposite appear(3).

disappearance /ˌdɪsə'pɪərəns/ *c/u.n* act of disappearing; state of having disappeared: *The child's disappearance is causing so much anxiety. The police have linked the two disappearances from the area.*

disappoint /ˌdɪsə'pɔɪnt/ *tr.v* **1** cause (s.o) to be unhappy or sorry by showing her/his hopes etc not to be possible: *He disappointed his daughter when he had to change their plan to go to a film together.* **2** *(formal)* cause (a plan etc) to fail: *All our hopes and expectations were disappointed by his failure to arrive.*

,**disap'pointed** *adj* **1** (of a person) unhappy, sorry, because one's plans etc have failed or are not possible: *I was very disappointed that you weren't able to come. Were they disappointed about the results? She bought the disappointed children an ice-cream each to cheer them up.* **2** *(formal)* (of hopes etc) failed: *our disappointed expectations.* **be disappointed in/with s.o/s.t** be sorry about the performance of s.o/s.t; be unhappy because one's expectations of s.o/s.t have failed: *My parents are very disappointed with my examination results. I'm disappointed in you; you behaved very badly.*

,**disap'pointing** *adj* that disappoints(1) (s.o): *a disappointing party. Our holiday was disappointing because the weather was terrible.*

,**disap'pointingly** *adv* in a way that disappoints(1): *The results were disappointingly bad.*

,**disap'pointment** *n* **1** *c/u.n* (example of the) fact or state of being disappointed(1): *She couldn't hide her disappointment.* **2** *c.n* person or thing who/that disappoints(1): *I was a great disappointment to my parents because they had such hopes for me!* **to s.o's disappointment** thing that causes s.o to be disappointed(1): *To everyone's disappointment, the party was* cancelled(1).

disapprobation /ˌdɪsæprəʊ'beɪʃən/ *u.n* *(formal)* disagreement and lack of approval: *They did not try to hide their complete disapprobation at our shameful behaviour.*

disapprove /ˌdɪsə'pruːv/ *intr.v* (often — of s.o/s.t (doing s.t)) strongly disagree with, dislike, s.o/s.t; not approve of s.o/s.t): *I disapprove of the way you talk to him. He strongly disapproved of his daughter staying out late at night.*

,**disap'proval** *u.n* (often — of s.o/s.t) fact or state of disapproving: *disapproval of her behaviour.* **to s.o's disapproval** thing that causes s.o to disapprove: *She married the person she loved to her whole family's disapproval.* Opposite approval.

,**disap'proving** *adj* that shows disapproval: *He gave his daughter a disapproving look when she criticized one of his guests.* Opposite approving.

,**disap'provingly** *adv* in a way that shows disapproval: *He watched the man disapprovingly.*

disarm /dɪs'ɑːm/ *v* **1** *tr.v* take away a weapon from (s.o): *He cut himself while disarming the man with a knife.* Opposite arm²(2). **2** *intr.v* (usu of a country at war) give up one's weapons

etc; make one's armed forces smaller and/or weaker. Opposite arm²(2). **3** *tr.v* *(formal)* cause (s.o) to be less suspicious, guarded: *I was about to say I was angry but she disarmed me with her apology.*

disarmament /dɪs'ɑːməmənt/ *u.n* act or fact of giving up weapons of war: *We are working for nuclear disarmament.*

dis'arming *adj* that makes s.o less cautious, suspicious: *a disarming greeting. Her welcome was so disarming that I didn't know what to say for a few minutes.* Compare disarm(3).

dis'armingly *adv.*

disarrange /ˌdɪsə'reɪndʒ/ *tr.v* *(formal)* cause (s.t) to lose its order, (agreed) arrangement: *When the fire bell rang panic(1) disarranged all plans to leave the building in an ordered way.*

,**disar'rangement** *u.n.*

disarray /ˌdɪsə'reɪ/ *u.n* (usu *in —*) *(formal)* fact or state of lacking order: *The thieves left the house in disarray.*

disassociate /ˌdɪsə'səʊʃɪ,eɪt/ = dissociate.

disaster /dɪ'zɑːstə/ *n* **1** *c/u.n* (also *attrib*) (event that causes a) state of great damage and unhappiness: *Many countries sent help to the disaster area. Regular reports were made from the scene of the air disaster. The company suffered financial disaster when they lost a big account.* **2** *c.n* *(fig)* event, occasion, that is a complete failure: *The party was a disaster — there wasn't enough food, there was a big argument between a few of the men and many things were broken.*

disastrous /dɪ'zɑːstrəs/ *adj* that causes, is, a disaster: *a disastrous journey/mistake. It would be disastrous to lend him money.*

di'sastrously *adv.*

disband /dɪs'bænd/ *tr/intr.v* (cause (a group etc) to) stop acting as a group: *The committee was disbanded when it had completed its work.*

dis'bandment *u.n.*

disbar /dɪs'bɑː/ *tr.v* (-rr-) (often passive, be —d from s.t) *(law)* remove, take away, the rights of (a barrister) to practise in the courts because he/she has done s.t seriously wrong: *He was disbarred from practising (or from the profession) because he accepted a bribe.*

dis'barment *u.n.*

disbelieve /ˌdɪsbɪ'liːv/ *tr.v* (not in continuous tenses) *(formal)* **1** not believe (s.o/s.t): *I don't disbelieve you but I think you've made a mistake.* **2** (usu — *in* s.o/s.t) not have faith (in God, a religion etc).

,**disbe'lief** *u.n* (often *in —*) *(formal)* state of not being able to believe (s.o/s.t): *He looked at her in total disbelief when she told him she was going to have a baby. I had to laugh at his look of disbelief when I told him I'd won the competition.*

,**disbe'liever** *c.n* person who does not believe or have any faith, esp in God or important aspects of religion. Opposite believer.

disbursement /dɪs'bɜːsmənt/ *c/u.n* *(formal)* (example of an) act of paying out (a small amount of) money: *She made several small disbursements from the petty cash tin.*

disc /dɪsk/ *c.n* (also, esp US, **disk**) **1** round object that is thin and flat: *You'll need to buy some parking discs for the machine. Our dog wears a disc with her name and our address on it.* ⇒ disk(1). **2** *(informal)* record¹(1). **3** flat round

structure in the body, e.g. between two vertebrae.
a slipped disc (slight) movement of a disc(3) in
the spine(1) so that it is out of position and causes
pain.

'disc ‚jockey *c.n* (abbr *DJ, dj*) person who
introduces the pieces in a programme of pop³(1)
music on the radio.

discard /'dɪskɑːd/ *c.n* **1** (in a card game) playing
card that one puts down and that is not a trump(1)
or of the suit(2) that is being played.
▷ *v*/dɪs'kɑːd/ **2** *tr.v* throw away (s.t that one has no
(more) use for): *He had to discard a number of*
items(1) *because they wouldn't fit into his suitcase.*
3 *tr/intr.v* play (a discard(1)).

discern /dɪ'sɜːn/ *tr.v* (not in continuous tenses)
(*formal*) see, judge, realize, (s.t) with difficulty:
I could just discern his figure in the distance. It's
not going to be easy to discern who is telling the
truth. We discerned nothing from his expression.
di'scernible *adj* (*formal*) that can be noticed,
seen, with difficulty: *A shape was discernible in*
the dark. There are no discernible differences.
di'scernibly *adv.*
dis'cerning *adj* **1** (of a person) who has the ability or power to notice the differences between
things, recognize the quality of things etc: *A*
discerning person will realize why this shirt is
more expensive than that one.
▷ *def.pl.n* **2** people who are discerning(1).
dis'cernment *u.n.*

discharge /dɪs'tʃɑːdʒ/ *n* **1** *u.n* (also *attrib*) act of
giving s.o permission to leave the army, hospital
etc: *I got my discharge* (*papers*) *today.* **2** *u.n*
(*formal*) act of discharging(5–10) s.o/s.t: *Please*
arrange the discharge of your debts before you
leave. The factory has been condemned(1) *for*
the discharge of waste into the river. **3** *c.n* thing
that is discharged(6–10): *The discharges from the*
chemical plant(2) *are dangerous.*
▷ *v* **4** *tr.v* give permission for (s.o) to leave a place:
When will you be discharged from hospital? **5** *tr.v*
send (s.o) away: *He had to discharge all his staff*
because he could no longer afford to pay them.
6 *tr/intr.v* get rid of (s.t); (cause (s.t) to) pass,
pour, out: *The factory discharges its wastes into*
the sea. The rivers discharge into the lake. **7** *tr.v*
(*formal*) pay (a debt): *Please discharge all your*
debts before you go on holiday. **8** *tr.v* (*formal*)
complete (s.t that one has to do): *He promised to*
try to discharge all his obligations *before he left the*
job. **9** *tr/intr.v* (cause (a ship) to) unload: *The ship*
discharged (*most of its* cargo) *and left.* **10** *tr/intr.v*
(of a wound) (cause (infected liquid) to) form and
come out: *A nasty yellow liquid was discharging*
from the wound.

disciple /dɪ'saɪpl/ *c.n* person who believes or
follows the particular teaching of s.o, esp in
religion: *Are you a disciple of Marx or Keynes?*
Part of the Bible(1) *describes the life of* Jesus *and*
his twelve disciples.

discipline /'dɪsɪplɪn/ *n* **1** *u.n* order, good behaviour, that is gained by strong control: *The teacher*
is worried about her ability to keep discipline in
her classes. Opposite indiscipline. **2** *u.n* control of
the mind and body that is gained by training: *You*
need a lot of discipline to be a top sportsperson.
3 *u.n* form of punishment: *That child will need*
a lot of discipline. **4** *c.n* (*formal*) area of study
(at a university etc).

▷ *tr.v* **5** train (o.s/s.t) to have control of (s.t): *You*
have to discipline yourself to work harder. He still
has to learn to discipline his temper. **6** punish
(s.o): *He'll have to be disciplined for lying.*

disciplinarian /‚dɪsɪplɪ'neərɪən/ *adj* **1** (*formal*)
(of the methods that are) used to discipline(5)
s.o: *He gets good results but only through his*
disciplinarian methods.
▷ *c.n* **2** person who uses disciplinarian(1) methods
to gain control.

disciplinary /‚dɪsɪ'plɪnərɪ/ *adj* (*formal*) of,
referring to, to get, discipline(1): *The police have*
taken disciplinary action against them.

disclaim /dɪs'kleɪm/ *tr.v* (*formal*) say that one
is not part of (s.t), knows nothing about (s.t);
deny(1) s.t: *He disclaimed all knowledge of the*
matter. Opposite claim(5).
dis'claimer *c.n* (*formal*) statement that dis-
claims s.t: *The newspaper printed the politician's*
disclaimer of his involvement in the scandal(1).

disclose /dɪs'kləʊz/ *tr.v* (*formal*) cause (s.t) to
be known, seen: *New information disclosed the*
real thief.
disclosure /dɪs'kləʊʒə/ *c/u.n* (*formal*) (example of the) act or fact of disclosing s.t: *The*
disclosure of the truth will hurt a lot of people.

disco /'dɪskəʊ/ *c.n* (*informal*) discotheque.

discolour /dɪs'kʌlə/ *tr/intr.v* (US **dis'color**)
(cause (s.t) to) lose its colour, or (to) change to
a less pleasant colour: *Smoking discolours your*
fingers and teeth.
discolouration /dɪs‚kʌlə'reɪʃən/ *n* (US **dis-
‚colo'ration**) **1** *u.n* act or fact of discolouring or
of being discoloured. **2** mark where s.t has been
discoloured.

discomfort /dɪs'kʌmfət/ *c/u.n* (example of s.t
that causes a) state of being uncomfortable: *the*
discomforts of travelling far by bus. She couldn't
hide the discomfort she felt at being in a room full
of people she didn't know. Opposite comfort(1).

disconcert /‚dɪskən'sɜːt/ *tr.v* (*formal*) cause
(s.o) to feel less confident, sure, about what to
do, think etc: *The pianist's* mistake *disconcerted*
the singer for a while but she soon gained control
again.
‚discon'certed *adj* (*formal*) who/that is uncertain, shows anxiety: *He was clearly disconcerted*
by the angry crowd.
‚discon'certing *adj* (*formal*) that causes one
to feel anxious, less confident: *I just heard rather*
disconcerting news.
‚discon'certingly *adv.*

disconnect /‚dɪskə'nekt/ *tr.v* cause (s.t) no
longer to be connected to s.t else, esp s.t that
makes it work, e.g electricity: *The telephone*
was disconnected while we were away. Opposite
connect.
‚discon'nected *adj* **1** that is no longer connected: *I found the fault — it was a disconnected*
wire! **2** (of ideas, thoughts, sentences) that are
not connected, joined together, well; that do not
follow one another in a sensible way: *His speech*
consisted of a lot of disconnected ideas. Compare
unconnected.
‚discon'nectedly *adv.*
disconnection /‚dɪskə'nekʃən/ *c/u.n.*

disconsolate /dɪs'kɒnsələt/ *adj* (often —
about/at s.t) (*formal*) unhappy, esp about s.t
over which one is helpless and unwilling to be

consoled[2]: *She was disconsolate at the loss of her dog.*

dis'consolately *adv.*

discontent /ˌdɪskən'tent/ *u.n* (also ˌ**discon-'tentment**) (often — *with s.t*) fact, state, of not being happy, content[1](1), satisfied: *Her discontent with her job is making her parents very unhappy.*

ˌ**discon'tented** *adj* (often — *with s.o/s.t*) not satisfied, contented, happy, (with s.o/s.t): *You seem discontented with your job. It always seems that he has such a discontented look on his face.*

ˌ**discon'tentedly** *adv.*

ˌ**discon'tentment** *u.n* ⇒ discontent.

discontinue /ˌdɪskən'tɪnjuː/ *tr/intr.v* (*formal*) (cause (s.t) to) stop, end: *Classes have been discontinued because of the bad weather.* Opposite continue.

discontinuation /ˌdɪskənˌtɪnjʊ'eɪʃən/ *u.n* (*formal*) act of discontinuing s.t; state of having been discontinued.

discontinuity /ˌdɪskɒntɪ'njuːɪtɪ/ *c/u.n* (*formal*) (example of the) fact, state of not being continuous: *The discontinuity in Paul's education was due to illness.* Opposite continuity(1).

discontinuous /ˌdɪskən'tɪnjuəs/ *adj* (*formal*) not continuous (in time or space).

ˌ**discon'tinuously** *adv.* Opposite continuous.

discord /'dɪskɔːd/ *n* (also **dis'cordance**) **1** *c/ u.n* (*formal*) (example of the) lack of agreement between people: *Discord in the meeting caused it to break up before any decisions could be made.* **2** *c.n* (*music*) unpleasant sound that is caused by notes which do not sound right when played together.

discordance /dɪs'kɔːdəns/ *n* ⇒ discord.

dis'cordant *adj* (*formal*) who/that do not fit, go, well together: *discordant notes.*

discordantly *adv.*

discotheque /'dɪskəˌtek/ *c.n* (*informal disco*) **1** place where people can dance to recorded pop[3](1) music. **2** business that provides the music and equipment and operates it at a party etc: *We've hired a disco to do the music for the dance.*

discount /'dɪskaʊnt/ *c.n* **1** amount of money, or percentage of the price, that is taken off the cost of s.t: *a £10 discount on all articles of furniture. I was given a 10% (or 10 per cent) discount because the dress was slightly dirty.*

▷ *tr.v* /dɪs'kaʊnt/ (*formal*) **2** consider (a fact, story etc) as not possible, likely, important: *New information discounted the possibility of his being guilty.*

'discount ˌstore *c.n* shop where goods are sold more cheaply than at most other shops.

discourage /dɪs'kʌrɪdʒ/ *tr.v* **1** reduce the confidence, hope, of (s.o): *She was discouraged by losing so many of her tennis matches.* **2** try to prevent (s.t) by showing it to be bad, dangerous, unwise etc: *His parents discouraged his interest in becoming a musician.* **discourage s.o from** (**doing**) **s.t** try to stop s.o from (doing) s.t that one disagrees with: *Nothing will discourage him from his determination to take part (or from taking part) in the London Marathon(1).* Opposite encourage(1,2).

dis'couragement *n* **1** *u.n* act of discouraging s.o/s.t: *His parents' discouragement was not enough to keep him at home.* **2** *c.n* thing

that discourages s.o/s.t: *He had many discouragements but he kept trying and in the end he found a suitable job.* Opposite encouragement.

dis'couraging *adj* that discourages: *His results were discouraging but he promised to try to do better next time.* Opposite encouraging.

dis'couragingly *adv.*

discourse /'dɪskɔːs/ *c.n* **1** (often — *on s.t*) (*formal*) serious speech, conversation, piece of writing: *a discourse on freedom of the press.*

▷ *intr.v* /dɪs'kɔːs/ **2** (*formal*) (usu — (up)on *s.t*) make a serious speech, talk seriously, (about s.t).

discourteous /dɪs'kɜːtɪəs/ *adj* (*formal*) (of a person, behaviour) not courteous, not polite: *a discourteous young man. It was discourteous of him to leave without saying goodbye.* Opposite courtesy.

dis'courteously *adv.* **dis'courteousness** *u.n.*

discourtesy /dɪs'kɜːtɪsɪ/ *c/u.n* (*pl -ies*) (*formal*) (example of the) act or fact of being discourteous: *He admitted that he had acted with discourtesy (towards her) and asked her forgiveness.*

discover /dɪs'kʌvə/ *tr.v* **1** find (s.t that was not known before): *Who discovered penicillin? America was discovered in the fifteenth century.* Compare invent(1). **2** find out (information, an answer etc): *We must try to discover the reason for her behaviour. I never did discover who broke the window.*

dis'coverer *c.n* person who discovers(1) s.t/s.w: *Christopher Columbus was a discoverer.*

dis'covery *n* (*pl -ies*) **1** *c/def.n* (example of the) act or fact of discovering s.t: *Scientists have made important discoveries in the field of medicine.* **2** *c.n* example of s.t that is discovered: *a book of great discoveries. Penicillin was an important discovery.*

discredit /dɪs'kredɪt/ *n* **1** *sing/u.n* (often — *to* s.o/s.t*) (*formal*) (example of s.t that causes) loss of trust, honour, (to s.o/s.t): *Your behaviour at the dance is a discredit to the school. His lying brought discredit to his family.* Opposite credit(6). **to s.o's discredit** a thing that affects s.o's reputation badly: *It was to his discredit that he didn't tell the truth at the time.*

▷ *tr.v* (*formal*) **2** know, show, (s.t) to be untrue: *His statement was publicly discredited at the meeting.* **3** cause (s.o/s.t) to lose honour: *She's been discredited by the scandal.*

dis'creditable *adj* (*formal*) that/who brings loss of honour, good reputation: *His discreditable action affected his whole family.* Opposite creditable.

dis'creditably *adv.*

discreet /dɪ'skriːt/ *adj* (of a person, behaviour) who/that shows care and good judgement, esp about what is said and not said: *I need to discuss something with you but you'll have to promise to be discreet about it.* Opposite indiscreet.

di'screetly *adv.* **di'screetness** *u.n.*

discretion /dɪ'skreʃən/ *u.n* **1** fact of being discreet: *You can trust her discretion.* **2** good judgement: *Use your discretion when deciding who should represent us at the meeting. I'll leave the arrangements to your discretion.* **at s.o's/s.t's discretion**; **at the discretion of s.o/ s.t** according to the decision, judgement, of s.o/ s.t: *Regular inspection of the house will be made at the discretion of the owner.* **Discretion is the**

better part of valour (*proverb*) It is always better to be careful about what one says or does than to risk danger by being a hero(1), too brave.

di'scretionary *adj* (*formal*) that makes it possible to use s.o's own good judgement, decision, about s.t: *a priest's discretionary powers.*

discrepancy /dɪ'skrepənsɪ/ *c/u.n* (often — between s.t and s.t) (*formal*) (fact, amount of) difference, disagreement, (between two or more things): *Can you explain the discrepancies between my figures and the* accountant's *? I found a discrepancy of £5 in my accounts.*

discrete /dɪ'skriːt/ *adj* (*formal*) that are not joined in any way: *discrete lines in the pattern.*
di'scretely *adv.* **di'screteness** *u.n.*

discretion ⇒ discreet.

discriminate /dɪ'skrɪmɪˌneɪt/ *v* 1 *intr.v* (often — between s.o/s.t and s.o/s.t) treat people, things differently from one another; see, notice, differences (between two or more people, things): *The law does not allow employers to discriminate between men and women who do the same jobs.* 2 *tr.v* (often — s.t from s.t) separate (one thing from another) in order to discover or show the differences: *He can't discriminate fact from* fiction(2). **discriminate against s.o** treat (a person, group) unfairly as compared with other people or groups: *It is against the law in most countries to discriminate against a person because of her/ his race.*

di'scrimiˌnating *adj* (*formal*) 1 (of a person) able to make good judgements by noticing small differences that make one thing better than another: *He's very discriminating about the films he goes to see.* 2 (*attrib*) that shows how s.t is different from s.t else: *One discriminating* feature(2) *is the male bird's brighter colours.* 3 who/that treats different people in different ways and esp treats some people unfairly: *They were criticized for their discriminating employment practices.*

discrimination /dɪˌskrɪmɪ'neɪʃən/ *n* 1 ability to be discriminating(1): *I trust his discrimination; he always chooses good places to eat.* 2 (often — against s.o) (*derog*) act of discriminating (⇒ discriminate against s.o) (against a person because of her/his race, sex etc): *He promised to* investigate *the complaints of discrimination against members of the staff.*

discriminatory /dɪˌskrɪmɪ'neɪtərɪ/ *adj* that shows discrimination(2); that discriminates against some people: *discriminatory practices.*

discursive /dɪ'skɜːsɪv/ *adj* (*formal*) (of speaking, writing) that seems to have no main point and moves from one idea to another without a plan: *A scientific piece of writing should not be discursive.*
di'scursively *adv.* **di'scursiveness** *u.n.*

discus /'dɪskəs/ *c.n* (also *attrib*) heavy disc(1) which is thrown as a sport: *He won a* medal(1) *in the discus. She is a discus thrower.*

discuss /dɪ'skʌs/ *tr.v* (often — s.t with s.o) talk seriously, in detail, about (s.t) (to s.o): *Come and discuss your ideas with me. The whole family sat around the table to discuss the holiday plans.*

discussion /dɪ'skʌʃən/ *c/u.n* (act of) discussing s.t: *There's a discussion tonight about the 'role of women in modern society'.* **under discussion** being discussed: *The matter is under discussion*

and you should get an answer by the end of the week.

disdain /dɪs'deɪn/ *u.n* 1 (*formal*) fact or quality of being too proud and showing no respect; scorn: *Her look of disdain shows that she thinks our ideas are worthless.*
▷ *tr.v* 2 (*formal*) show no respect for (s.t); scorn (s.t): *They disdain our help.* **disdain doing s.t**; **disdain to do s.t** be too proud, full of one's own importance, (to do s.t): *Pam disdains to attend one of our meetings.*
dis'dainful *adj* (often — of/towards s.o/s.t) (*formal*) who/that shows lack of respect (for s.o/s.t); scornful: *a disdainful look.*

disease /dɪ'ziːz/ *n* 1 *c/u.n* (example of an) illness or disorder that is caused by bacteria etc and not by an accident: *She's got a blood disease. The disease is spread by flies.* 2 *c.n* (*fig*) moral disorder, or disorder in the mind: *Greed is not a modern disease.*
di'seased *adj* that has a disease, is not healthy: *This plant is diseased.*

disembark /ˌdɪsɪm'bɑːk/ *tr/intr.v* (*formal*) (cause (a person, baggage etc) to) leave a ship: *At what time are we disembarking? All the passengers and their baggage have been disembarked.* Opposite embark.
disembarkation /ˌdɪsembɑː'keɪʃən/ *u.n.*

disembodied /ˌdɪsɪm'bɒdɪd/ *attrib.adj* (*formal*) (that seems to be) without a body: *Could those sounds be the disembodied cries of* ghosts(1)?

disembowel /ˌdɪsɪm'baʊəl/ *tr.v* (-*ll*-) (*formal*) remove the insides of (an animal).

disenchant /ˌdɪsɪn'tʃɑːnt/ *tr.v* (*formal*) cause (s.o) to lose faith in s.o/s.t, or stop admiring, believing in, s.o/s.t: *His actions have disenchanted the whole office.*
ˌdisen'chanted *adj.* **ˌdisen'chantment** *u.n.*

disenfranchise /ˌdɪsɪn'fræntʃaɪz/ *tr.v* = disfranchise.

disengage /ˌdɪsɪn'ɡeɪdʒ/ *tr/intr.v* (*formal*) (cause (s.t, esp one of the parts of a machine etc) to) become loose, free from an active position: *Don't disengage (the* gears(1)) *until you stop the car. He disengaged the* clutch(2) *and let the car roll down the hill.*
ˌdisen'gagement *u.n.*

disentangle /ˌdɪsɪn'tæŋɡl/ *tr.v* (*formal*) 1 separate (different pieces of s.t) that have become tangled(1), knotted, mixed together: *The cats made such a mess of the wool that it took hours to disentangle it.* 2 (*fig*) free (oneself/s.t) from a bad or difficult situation: *He tried to disentangle himself (from the agreement) because he knew it was wrong to go.*
ˌdisen'tanglement *u.n.*

disfavour /dɪs'feɪvə/ *u.n* (US **dis'favor**) (*formal*) 1 state of being disliked: *If I'm late again I'll really be in disfavour.* 2 (often *with* —) lack of respect and pleasure: *He regarded his son with disfavour because of his continuous lying.* **fall into disfavour** become unpopular; no longer be liked.

disfigure /dɪs'fɪɡə/ *tr.v* (*formal*) spoil the beauty of (s.o, s.t): *The new road will disfigure the* countryside.
dis'figurement *u.n.*

disfranchise /dɪs'fræntʃaɪz/ *tr.v* (also **disen'franchise**) take away (s.o's) rights as a citizen(2), esp the right to vote. Opposite enfranchise.

dis'franchisement *u.n* (also **disen'franchisement**).

disgorge /dɪsˈgɔːdʒ/ *tr.v* (*formal*) cause (s.t) to come out violently; vomit(3) (s.t): *The factory's chimneys disgorged clouds of thick black smoke. The cat disgorged lumps of fur.*

disgrace /dɪsˈgreɪs/ *n* **1** *u.n* state of shame: *The terrible event brought disgrace to the whole family.* **2** *sing.n* (often *a — to s.o/s.t*) (*derog; informal*) person who has behaved very badly; thing that causes shame (to s.o/s.t): *I am ashamed of your behaviour; you're a disgrace (to your family). Those shoes are a disgrace — take them off and throw them away.* **be in disgrace (with s.o)** be regarded with displeasure (by s.o) because of bad behaviour etc: *She's in disgrace with her parents because she came home so late.*
▷ *tr.v* **3** cause shame to (oneself/s.o): *Did I disgrace myself last night? How could you disgrace me by talking to me so rudely in front of visitors?* **4** (*formal*) dishonour (s.o): *He was publicly disgraced and forced out of his job.*

dis'graceful *adj* (*derog*) extremely bad; that is likely to cause shame: *That was a disgraceful thing to do.*

dis'gracefully *adv.*

disgruntled /dɪsˈgrʌntld/ *adj* (often — *about, at, with s.o/s.t*) not satisfied: *He's very disgruntled about conditions at work.*

disguise /dɪsˈgaɪz/ *n* **1** *c.n* set of clothes etc worn to hide one's true identity(2) or to pretend that one is s.o else: *The man dressed up as an old woman as a disguise to help him escape.* **2** *c/ u.n* (example of a) state of pretending to be/feel s.o/s.t else in order to hide one's true identity(2), feelings, beliefs: *Don't be fooled by that smile; it's a disguise to hide his true intentions.* **a blessing in disguise** ⇒ blessing.
▷ *tr.v* **3** use a disguise on (s.t.): *She disguised her voice so that her friend wouldn't know who was really speaking.* **4** hide (one's true feelings, beliefs, intentions etc): *Alan couldn't disguise his anger.*

disgust /dɪsˈgʌst/ *u.n* **1** state or quality of extreme dislike and bad feeling: *She looked up in disgust at his bad language.*
▷ *tr.v* **2** (not usu used with continuous tenses) cause (s.o) to feel great dislike, discomfort of the mind: *His behaviour disgusted her. He was disgusted at the way she spoke to the waiter. I'm disgusted with you — go away!* **3** (*fig*) cause (s.o) to hate s.t, feel sick: *They were disgusted by the dirt and smells in his room.*

dis'gusting *adj* (*informal*) who/that causes one to feel disgust: *What a disgusting way to live! I'm not eating this disgusting food!*

dis'gustingly *adv.*

dish /dɪʃ/ *c.n* **1** container for serving and cooking food, often with a lid: *an oven dish; a small glass dish for the beans.* **2** food cooked according to a particular recipe: *We ordered five different dishes and shared them.*
▷ *v* **3 dish s.t out** give, serve, (s.t) to a person/ people *Who's going to dish out the food? Would you dish out the forms to everyone, please?* **4 dish (s.t) up** put (food that is to be eaten) onto plates: *Please come to the table, I'm dishing up (the supper).*

'dish,cloth *c.n* cloth for drying dishes that have been washed.

'dishes *pl.n* plates etc that have been used to prepare, and eat from, during a meal: *Whose turn is it to do the dishes tonight?* **do the dishes** wash up.

'dishful *c.n* amount of food that fits on a dish: *a dishful of beans.*

'dish,washer *c.n* person/machine who/that washes dishes, cups, knives, forks, glasses etc.

'dish,water *u.n* **1** water used for washing dishes etc. **2** (*derog; informal*) soup etc that has very little taste: *This soup is like dishwater!*

'dishy *adj* (*-ier, -iest*) (*informal*) (of a person) charming, handsome: *He looks so dishy in that coat!*

disharmony /dɪsˈhɑːmənɪ/ *u.n* (*formal*) lack of agreement, harmony(2): *There's been disharmony in their family ever since their father remarried.*

disharmonious /ˌdɪshɑːˈməʊnɪəs/ *adj.*

dishcloth ⇒ dish.

dishearten /dɪsˈhɑːtn/ *tr.v* (*formal*) reduce the hope, courage, of (s.o): *He felt disheartened by his poor results.*

dis'heartening *adj* (*formal*) that makes a person lose hope, courage: *The results were disheartening after all their hard work.*

dis'hearteningly *adv.*

dishevel /dɪˈʃevl/ *tr.v* (*-ll-*) (*formal*) make (s.t) untidy: *The wind soon dishevelled her hair.*

di'shevelled *adj* (usu *pred*) untidy: *You're not coming anywhere with me looking so dishevelled.*

dishful ⇒ dish.

dishonest /dɪsˈɒnɪst/ *adj* (of a person, behaviour) not honest(1): *I wouldn't trust him — he seems dishonest. It was dishonest of you to let him believe that the car is in perfect condition.*

dis'honestly *adv.* **dis'honesty** *u.n.*

dishonour /dɪsˈɒnə/ *sing/u.n* (US **dis'honor**) **1** (*formal*) (person/thing. who/that causes a) state of shame, loss of honour: *You are a dishonour to your country. His spying brought dishonour on his family.*
▷ *tr.v* **2** (*formal*) bring shame to (s.o/s.t): *She dishonoured her family by marrying a thief.*

dishonourable /dɪsˈɒnrəbl/ *adj* (US **dis'honorable**) person/action who/that lacks honour(2); shameful: *It is dishonourable of you to allow him to believe that you'll marry him when that's not possible.*

dis'honourably *adv* (US **dis'honorably**).

dishwater, dishy ⇒ dish.

disillusion /ˌdɪsɪˈluːʒən/ *tr/v* (*formal*) cause (s.o) to know the truth about a bad situation that he/she believed was perfect: *Everyone thought their marriage had no problems but they were soon disillusioned.*

disil'lusioned *adj* (often — *at/with s.o/s.t*) sad, disappointed, as a result of discovering that s.o/ s.t is not as good as one had thought: *Robert is disillusioned with his friends because at the critical moment none of them helped him.*

disil'lusionment *u.n.*

disincentive /ˌdɪsɪnˈsentɪv/ *c.n* (*formal*) (often — *to* (*doing*) *s.t*) action that is intended to persuade s.o not to do s.t: *The government offered farmers money as a disincentive to producing too much milk.* Opposite incentive.

disinclination /ˌdɪsɪnklɪˈneɪʃən/ *sing/u.n* (*formal*) (usu — *for* (*doing*) *s.t*; — *to do s.t*) lack of desire, interest, willingness, (for (doing) s.t, to do s.t): *He has a strong disinclination for (doing) anything active.*

disinclined /ˌdɪsɪnˈklaɪnd/ *pred.adj* (often — *to do s.t*) (*formal*) not willing (to do s.t): *I'm disinclined to make a decision at this moment.*

disinfect /ˌdɪsɪnˈfekt/ *tr.v* destroy the germs(1) etc in (s.t): *They had to disinfect the soil before a new crop could be planted.*

disinˈfectant *c/u.n* (example of a) substance that can destroy germs(1) etc: *Put disinfectant into the water when you clean the kitchen floor.*

disinˈfection *u.n.*

disinfest /ˌdɪsɪnˈfest/ *tr.v* (*technical*) (often — *s.t of s.t*) destroy all small insects, rats etc in (s.t): *We had to call in the Health Department to disinfest the house of cockroaches.*

disinfestation /ˌdɪsɪnfeˈsteɪʃən/ *u.n.*

disingenuous /ˌdɪsɪnˈdʒenjʊəs/ *adj* (*formal*) not sincere.

disinherit /ˌdɪsɪnˈherɪt/ *tr.v* stop (s.o, esp one's child) from inheriting(1), getting money etc from one's estate(3): *He threatened to disinherit his son unless his behaviour improved.*

disintegrate /dɪsˈɪntɪˌɡreɪt/ *v* (*formal*) **1** *tr/ intr.v* (cause (s.t) to) break into small pieces and become useless: *The children watched the waves disintegrate their sand castle. The box disintegrated as it hit the ground.* **2** *intr.v* (*fig*) fall apart; become loose and without structure: *The idea of the family is disintegrating and the* divorce(1) *rate has increased.*

disintegration /dɪsˌɪntɪˈɡreɪʃən/ *u.n.* (also *fig*) act or fact of falling apart or being completely broken: *The article discussed the disintegration of moral values in society.*

disinter /ˌdɪsɪnˈtɜː/ *tr.v* (*-rr-*) (*formal*) take out (a body) from its grave. Opposite inter.

disinterested /dɪsˈɪntrɪstɪd/ *adj* **1** (the result of being) able to judge fairly because of not being concerned directly: *He was able to give a disinterested opinion as he didn't know any of us well.* Compare uninterested.

disjointed /dɪsˈdʒɔɪntɪd/ *adj* (of ideas, sentences) not following in a sensible order; not joined together well: *His story was so disjointed that we didn't really understand what happened.*

disˈjointedly *adv.* **disˈjointedness** *u.n.*

disjunctive /dɪsˈdʒʌŋktɪv/ *adj* (*technical*) (of a conjunction(1)) that expresses a choice or contrast(1) between two facts, ideas etc, e.g 'or', 'but'.

disk /dɪsk/ *c.n* **1** ⇒ disc. **2** round flat object used in computers to store information, programs(1) etc.

dislike /dɪsˈlaɪk/ *n* **1** *c.n* thing that one does not like: *One of his strongest dislikes is walking.* **2** *c/ u.n* (often a — *for/of s.o/s.t*) feeling of not liking s.o/s.t: *She has a dislike of chocolate. He took his children camping in spite of his own dislike of it.* **likes and dislikes** ⇒ likes (⇒ like¹). **take a dislike to s.o/s.t** begin not to like s.o/s.t: *I took an immediate dislike to him because of the way he treated his children.*

▷ *tr.v* (not usu used with continuous tenses) **3** not like (s.o/s.t); feel that (s.o/s.t) is not pleasant: *He disliked the idea of visiting my parents.*

dislocate /ˈdɪsləˌkeɪt/ *tr.v* (*formal*) cause (a bone) to come out of its position: *She dislocated her shoulder playing tennis.*

dislocation /ˌdɪsləˈkeɪʃən/ *c/u.n.*

dislodge /dɪsˈlɒdʒ/ *tr.v* (*formal*) cause (s.t) to move out of its position: *His bicycle fell and dislodged a few bricks from the wall.*

disloyal /dɪsˈlɔɪəl/ *adj* (*derog*) (of a person) not loyal: *I don't want to be disloyal to my brother but it's important to tell the truth.*

disˈloyalty *u.n.* state, quality, of being disloyal: *His disloyalty to his old political party was widely criticized.*

dismal /ˈdɪzməl/ *adj* who/that looks, is, very grey, unhappy, hopeless: *The weather's been dismal. What a dismal (-looking) group of people you are.*

ˈdismally *adv.*

dismantle /dɪsˈmæntl/ *tr.v* (*formal*) take (s.t) apart; put (s.t) into its separate pieces: *The machine had to be completely dismantled to discover what was wrong with it.*

disˈmantlement *u.n.*

dismay /dɪsˈmeɪ/ *u.n* **1** (often *in/with* —) state of surprise and fear: *We listened to the unexpected results in/with dismay. They stood in dismay unable to do anything to stop the attack on the old man.* **fill s.o with dismay** cause s.o to feel dismay(1) (about s.t): *The news filled us with dismay.* **to s.o's dismay** with the result that s.o feels dismay(1): *To our dismay, they left without us and we had no way of getting back.*

▷ *tr.v* **2** cause (s.o) to be surprised and afraid (because of s.t): *We were dismayed to find that everyone had gone home and we were alone in the building. They were dismayed by the results.*

dismember /dɪsˈmembə/ *tr.v* (*formal*) break (s.t) into pieces; pull (the arms, legs etc) off the body: *The lion had soon dismembered the young animal.*

disˈmemberment *u.n.*

dismiss /dɪsˈmɪs/ *tr.v* **1** (often — *s.o from a job*) end the employment of (s.o) (in a job): *She was dismissed (from her job) for criticizing the boss.* ⇒ sack²(1). **2** allow (s.o) to leave: *The whole school was dismissed late today because the head teacher gave us a lecture about manners.* **3** (also *fig*) take no notice of (s.o/s.t), esp because one does not believe her/him/it, or does not think her/him/it important: *Don't just dismiss the old man, his warnings, without checking what he said.* **4** (*law*) end (a court case): *Case dismissed!* **5** (often — *a team for 100 etc runs*) defeat (a team) after they have made only a small number of runs: *England was dismissed for 97 runs.*

dismissal /dɪsˈmɪsl/ *c/u.n* (example of the) act or fact of dismissing or of being dismissed: *We tried to prevent her dismissal by signing a petition(1). For the size of the company, the number of dismissals every year is very high.*

dismount /dɪsˈmaʊnt/ *tr/intr.v* (cause (s.o) to) get off a horse, bicycle etc: *The horse dismounted its rider who was being too strict with it. He helped her dismount (from her horse) and then led the animal away.*

disobey /ˌdɪsəˈbeɪ/ *tr/intr.v* refuse to obey (s.o); fail to do what has been ordered, requested, by (s.o): *Would you disobey your parents if you believed they were wrong?*

disobedience /ˌdɪsəˈbiːdɪəns/ *u.n* act or fact of disobeying: *You will be punished for your disobedience.* Opposite obedience.

disobedient /ˌdɪsəˈbiːdɪənt/ *adj* (of a person, behaviour) who/that fails, refuses, to do what has been ordered, requested: *He was a disobedient little boy. Don't be disobedient to your grand-mother.* Opposite obedient.
,**diso'bediently** *adv.*

disoblige /ˌdɪsəˈblaɪdʒ/ *tr.v* (*formal*) refuse to be helpful to (s.o): *We all expected him to help us prepare the room but he disobliged us.*
,**diso'bliging** *adj.* ,**diso'bligingly** *adv.*

disorder /dɪsˈɔːdə/ *n* **1** *u.n* (*formal*) lack of order(4); state of confusion: *We came home to total disorder; the cats had chased each other round the room and knocked everything over.* **2** *c/u.n* (act of) strong and often violent public disapproval: *The new laws led to scenes of dis-order throughout the country.* **3** *c.n* (*technical*) slight illness: *He wasn't at work because he has a stomach disorder.* **in disorder** in a state of confusion and lack of order: *She left her desk in disorder when she went home early.*

dis'orderly *adj* (*formal*) **1** not neat and tidy: *He arrived at work looking disorderly and tired.* **2** (of a person) who is behaving badly in a public place: *The police officer took him away for being drunk and disorderly.*

disorganize, -ise /dɪsˈɔːgənaɪz/ *tr.v* cause (an arrangement, plan etc) to lose, have no, order: *The children disorganized all the clothes in my cupboard.*
disorganization, -isation /dɪsˌɔːgənaɪˈzeɪʃən/ *u.n* state of being disorganized: *I can't work in such disorganization.*
dis'orga,nized, -ised *adj* not organized(1); hav-ing no order: *I'm still so disorganized and I'll need another week to get things ready.*

disorientate /dɪsˈɔːrɪənˌteɪt/ *tr.v* (US **dis'orient**) (usu passive) **1** cause (s.o) to not know where he/she is: *The dark dis-orientated him (or He was disorientated by the dark) and he walked in circles for hours.* **2** (*fig*) cause (s.o) to lose her/his certainty about things: *The accident so disorientated him that he hasn't been able to do anything for months.* Opposite orientate(1).
disorientation /dɪsˌɔːrɪənˈteɪʃən/ *u.n.*

disown /dɪsˈəʊn/ *tr.v* (*formal*) refuse to accept that (s.o/s.t) belongs to one: *She disowned her grandchild after he tried to steal money from her.*

disparage /dɪsˈpærɪdʒ/ *tr* (*formal*) speak of (s.o/s.t) as having no value: *Don't disparage her efforts because she did very well.*
dis'paragement *u.n* (*formal*) act of dispar-aging: *He spoke about the play with such disparagement.*
dis'paraging *adj* (*derog*; *formal*) (of a person, remark) that shows no respect for s.o/s.t; criti-cal: *Don't make disparaging remarks about your brother when he tried so hard.*
dis'paragingly *adv.*

disparate /ˈdɪspərət/ *adj* (*formal*) (of two or more things) that are completely different (and therefore should not be compared): *They enjoy such disparate hobbies that their friendship can't last long.*

disparity /dɪsˈpærɪtɪ/ *c/u.n* (*formal*) (size, amount etc of a) difference: *What's the disparity in their ages?*

dispassionate /dɪsˈpæʃənɪt/ *adj* (*formal*) fair; that does not show any particular preference: *a dispassionate judge/report.*
dis'passionately *adv.* **dis'passion** *u.n.*

dispatch /dɪsˈpætʃ/ *n* (*formal*) **1** *c.n* official written message or report: *He has to send an important dispatch to his newspaper.* **2** *c.n* act of sending s.t: *I'm responsible for the dispatch of food parcels to poor people in different parts of the world.* **3** *u.n* (often *with* —) (*formal*) quickness and efficiency: *He was praised for the dispatch with which he completed the work.* **4** *def.n* (with capital **D**) (used in the names of newspapers): *The Daily Dispatch.*
▷ *tr.v* (*formal*) **5** send (s.o/s.t): *Has the letter to the mayor been dispatched?* **6** finish (s.t) quickly and efficiently: *He dispatched several important matters before he left the office.*
dis'patch ,box *c.n* box that holds official papers, messages etc.
dis'patches *pl.n* (*formal*) official papers or reports.

dispel /dɪˈspel/ *tr.v* (-ll-) (*formal*) get rid of (fears etc): *His kindness dispelled her anxiety.*

dispense /dɪˈspens/ *tr.v* (*formal*) **1** (often — *s.t to s.o*) give a share of (s.t) (to s.o): *There are machines that dispense food and hot drinks twenty-four hours a day.* **2** prepare and give (the required medicine): *Doctors don't usually dispense medicine; you have to go to a chem-ist(2).* **3** (*law*) carry out (the law); give (a fair judgement) according to the law: *dispense justice.*
dispense with s.o/s.t (make it possible to) man-age without s.o/s.t: *The computer has dispensed with the need for a lot of filing space.*
di'spensable *adj* (of a person, service, thing) who/that is not necessary and one can manage without: *Mr White makes all his staff feel dispen-sable so they are afraid to complain.* Opposite indispensable.
dispensary /dɪˈspensərɪ/ *c.n* (*pl* -ies) place in a building, esp a hospital, where medicines are prepared and given out.
dispensation /ˌdɪspenˈseɪʃən/ *c/u.n* (*formal*) (certificate(1) that gives) permission to do s.t that is normally against the law, esp of the church: *He asked his church for dispensation to remarry.*
di'spenser *c.n* **1** person who dispenses(2) medicines. **2** machine that dispenses(1) food etc: *Dispensers in offices have taken jobs from women who used to prepare the tea and coffee.*
di'spensing ,chemist *c.n* (UK) **1** person who is trained to dispense and sell medicines. **2** (also ,**dispensing 'chemist's**) shop of a dispensing chemist.

disperse /dɪˈspɜːs/ *(formal)* **1** *tr/intr.v* (cause (s.o/s.t) to) spread widely, in many different directions: *Seeds are dispersed by means of animals, water and wind.* **2** *tr/intr.v* (cause (s.o/s.t) to) leave a place, move away, in different directions: *The police dispersed the crowds gathering around the accident. After the theatre the crowds dispersed.* **3** *tr.v* put/send (small groups of people, things) into positions a (short) distance from one another: *The police* were *dispersed throughout the town.* Compare distribute, scatter.

dispersal /dɪ'spɜːsl/ *u.n* (*formal*) act or fact of dispersing or being dispersed: *Seed dispersal is an important subject in biology.*

dispersion /dɪ'spɜːʃən/ *u.n* (*formal*) act or fact of scattering or causing people or things to move in different directions: *the dispersion of people in search of work.*

dispirit /dɪ'spɪrɪt/ *tr.v* (*formal*) cause (s.o) to lose her/his courage, enthusiasm: *Failure dispirits even confident people.*

di'spirited *adj* (*formal*) very disappointed; lacking hope and courage: *They came home looking very tired and dispirited.*

displace /dɪs'pleɪs/ *tr.v* (*formal*) **1** cause (s.o/s.t) to move out of its usual place, position: *A lot of things on her desk had been displaced but nothing seemed to be missing.* **2** cause (s.o/s.t) to be replaced: *Many workers are being displaced by machines.*

dis,placed 'person *c.n* person living in a country that is not her/his own because of being forced to leave the one where he/she was born.

dis'placement *n* **1** *u.n* (*formal*) act or fact of displacing or of being displaced: *The displacement of so many workers caused problems for the new manager.* **2** *sing/u.n* (*technical*) weight of water etc that is moved aside by an object (often a ship) in it: *a displacement of 1000 tonnes.*

display /dɪ'spleɪ/ *n* **1** *c/u.n* (example of an) act of showing the ability, beauty etc of s.o/s.t: *a gymnastic display. We used to walk through town in the evenings to look at the shops' window displays.* **on display** being shown in an exhibition(1).
▷ *tr.v* **2** arrange (s.o/s.t) in a way that shows it: *The older furniture is being displayed in a big hall.* **3** (*formal*) show (s.t): *They displayed great skill in the game.*

displease /dɪs'pliːz/ *tr.v* (*formal*) cause (s.o) to be angry, annoyed, not pleased: *Fred's unkind behaviour towards his younger brother displeased his mother.*

dis'pleased *adj* (*formal*) (often — *with* s.o/s.t) dissatisfied; annoyed; not pleased: *Your teachers are displeased with your lack of progress this year.*

dis'pleasing *adj* (*formal*) that causes one to be dissatisfied, annoyed, not pleased: *a displeasing result/end.*

displeasure /dɪs'pleʒə/ *u.n* (*formal*) lack of approval or satisfaction: *She did not try to hide her displeasure at his rude behaviour.*

dispose /dɪ'spəʊz/ *tr.v* (*formal*) **1** (usu passive) cause (s.o) to be willing (to do s.t): *This weather disposes me to spend more time at home.* **2** settle, finalize, (s.t): *I cannot leave the country before disposing certain important matters.* **dispose of s.o/s.t** get rid of (s.o/s.t): *If you don't throw away those old shoes I'll dispose of them for you.*

di'sposable *adj* that can be thrown away after use: *We used disposable cups and plates at the party because we were afraid of things being broken.*

di,sposable 'income *u.n* amount of money that one has left to spend after all regular costs, e.g rent, taxes etc, have been paid.

di'sposal *u.n* (*formal*) act of getting rid of s.t:

The disposal of our garden rubbish is always a problem. **at s.o's disposal** able to be used by s.o: *Do you have a car at your disposal?*

di'sposed *pred.adj* (often — *to do* s.t) (*formal*) willing: *You can come if you're disposed to.* Opposite indisposed. ⇨ ill-disposed, well-disposed.

disposition /ˌdɪspə'zɪʃən/ *n* **1** *c.n* (usu *sing*) natural way of being, behaviour; nature(3): *She always had a very happy disposition as a child.* **2** *c/u.n* (*formal*) organization or management of e.g soldiers during a battle, things at an exhibition(1) etc.

dispossess /ˌdɪspə'zes/ *tr.v* (often — s.o *of* s.t) (*formal*) take away the possession (esp of property) from (s.o): *They have been dispossessed of their land.*

dispossession /ˌdɪspə'zeʃən/ *u.n.*

disproportion /ˌdɪsprə'pɔːʃən/ *c/u.n* (usu — *between* s.t *and* s.t) (*formal*) (example that shows the) lack of equality (between two or more things): *The opposition(4) party criticized the government for the disproportion between money spent on defence and education.*

,dispro'portionate *adj* (usu — *to* s.t) (*formal*) that shows lack of proportion(1) or equality between two or more things: *The amount of time he spent on that job is disproportionate to the money he'll earn from it.*

disproportionately *adv.*

disprove /dɪs'pruːv/ *tr.v* (*formal*) prove that (s.t) is not true, is not correct: *He disproved the claims against him.*

dispute /dɪ'spjuːt/ *c/u.n* **1** discussion during which neither side will agree with what the other says; unpleasant argument: *The dispute about pay will develop into strike action. Can we settle this matter without dispute?* **beyond/past (all) dispute** that cannot be doubted: *His greatness is beyond dispute.* **in dispute (with s.o)** in a state of not being able to agree (with s.o): *The two companies are in dispute (with one another) over how to share responsibility.* **in/under dispute** being argued about, disputed(3): *The question of ownership is still under dispute and a settlement is not expected for some time.* **without dispute** (*formal*) without doubt: *He was declared champion(3) without dispute.*
▷ *v* **2** *tr.v* disagree with (s.t); argue against (s.t): *She disputed her uncle's claim to a share of her land.* **3** *tr/intr.v* (often — *about* s.t) argue, disagree, (about s.t): *They have been disputing (about the boundaries of their farms) for years.*

di'sputable *adj* (*formal*) that can be argued about; not necessarily correct or true: *It's disputable whether or not the holiday is a good idea.* Opposite indisputable.

disputation /ˌdɪspjuː'teɪʃən/ *c/u.n* (*formal*) (example of the) act of arguing about s.t.

disputatious /ˌdɪspjuː'teɪʃəs/ *adj* (*formal*) who enjoys, encourages, a dispute(1).

disqualify /dɪs'kwɒlɪfaɪ/ *tr.v* (*-ies*, *-ied*) (often — s.o *for/from* (*doing*) s.t) cause (s.o) to be unable, unsuitable (to do s.t): *His age disqualifies him from the competition (or for the job). Anyone who works for the company is disqualified from entering the competition.*

disqualification /dɪsˌkwɒlɪfɪ'keɪʃən/ *c/u.n* (reason for the) act or fact of being disqualified.

disquiet /dɪsˈkwaɪət/ *u.n* **1** (*formal*) lack of calm or satisfaction.
▷ *tr.v* **2** (*formal*) cause (s.o) to feel worried, anxious: *She became disquieted after her son failed to come home for dinner.*
dis'quieting *adj* (*formal*) that causes s.o to worry, become anxious: *disquieting silence.*
disregard /ˌdɪsrɪˈgɑːd/ *u.n* (*formal*) **1** (usu — *for/of s.o/s.t*) act or fact of ignoring, neglecting or of being ignored, neglected: *His disregard for her feelings led her to realize she could never marry him.*
▷ *tr.v* (*formal*) **2** ignore, neglect, (s.o/s.t); refuse to pay attention to (s.o/s.t): *If you continue to disregard all advice, you'll have no one to ask any more.*
disrepair /ˌdɪsrɪˈpeə/ *u.n* (often *be in, fall into,* —) (*formal*) state of needing attention, repair: *They didn't have the money to look after the large house and it soon fell into disrepair.*
disrepute /ˌdɪsrɪˈpjuːt/ *u.n* (often *be in, bring s.t into, fall into* —) (*formal*) state of having lost the good opinion of others: *After the new management took over, the restaurant fell into disrepute.*
disreputable /dɪsˈrepjʊtəbl/ *adj* (*derog*) (of a person, behaviour, appearance) who/that has or shows a low reputation, deserves no respect: *a disreputable character.* Opposite reputable.
dis'reputableness *u.n.* **dis'reputably** *adv.*
disrespect /ˌdɪsrɪˈspekt/ *u.n* lack of respect: *How can you treat her with such disrespect?*
ˌdisre'spectful *adj* (*formal*) (often — *of s.o/ s.t*) who/that shows no respect; rude: *If you continue to be so disrespectful (of my family) you can expect no help from me.*
ˌdisre'spectfully *adv.*
disrobe /dɪsˈrəʊb/ *v* (*formal*) **1** *intr.v* take off one's outer clothes: *She disrobed and dived into the swimming pool.* **2** *tr.v* take off (s.o)'s outer clothes.
disrupt /dɪsˈrʌpt/ *tr.v* break, disturb, interrupt, the usual order or pattern of (s.t): *The performance was disrupted by a noise in the audience. I don't want it to disrupt my work.*
disruption /dɪsˈrʌpʃən/ *c/u.n* (example of a) state or fact of disrupting or being disrupted: *The accident caused disruption on the motorway.*
dis'ruptive *adj* (of a person, behaviour, an event) who/that disturbs or interrupts the usual or expected pattern, order: *If you continue to be disruptive, I'll send you out of my classes.*
dissatisfy /dɪsˈsætɪsˌfaɪ/ *tr.v* (*-ies, -ied*) fail to please, satisfy, (s.o).
dissatisfaction /dɪˌsætɪsˈfækʃən/ *u.n* lack of satisfaction: *He made his dissatisfaction known at the meeting by criticizing the committee.*
dis'satis,fied *adj* (of a person) who is not pleased, satisfied: *a dissatisfied customer. She's dissatisfied with the way this office is run.*
dissect /dɪˈsekt/ *tr.v* **1** (*technical*) cut (a body, plant) into parts for close study: *We had to dissect a worm in our biology examination.* **2** (*fig; formal*) study each detail about (s.o/s.t): *The team watched a video(1) of the match and dissected every move to learn from their mistakes.*
dissection /dɪˈsekʃən/ *c/u.n* (example of an) act of dissecting(1) s.t or state of being dissected: *a longitudinal/horizontal(1) dissection of a stem.*

dissemble /dɪˈsembl/ *tr/intr.v* (*formal*) hide, lie about, (one's real feelings about s.o/s.t): *She dissembled her dislike of him and he believed her.*
dis'sembler *c.n* (*derog*) person who dissembles.
disseminate /dɪˈsemɪˌneɪt/ *tr.v* (*formal*) spread (information etc) widely.
dissemination /dɪˌsemɪˈneɪʃən/ *u.n.*
dissent /dɪˈsent/ *u.n* **1** (*formal*) act or fact of disagreeing and arguing: *The political party was criticized for the dissent among its members.*
▷ *intr.v* (*formal*) **2** (often — *from s.t*) disagree (with the accepted opinion or idea of s.t); have a different opinion (from the accepted idea etc): *She dissents from the view that people should pay for spectacles.* **3** state one's disagreement, opposition(2), to s.t: *There was a large group who still dissented at the end of the meeting.*
dissension /dɪˈsenʃən/ *u.n* (*formal*) fact or state of disagreement and argument: *Dissension has reduced the popularity of that political party.*
dis'senter *c.n* person who dissents, esp from a law or belief of a particular church.
dis'senting *attrib.adj* (of a person, opinion) who/that refuses to agree with the accepted opinion: *a dissenting viewpoint.*
dissertation /ˌdɪsəˈteɪʃən/ *c.n* long piece of formal writing on a particular subject, esp as part of a higher university degree: *What are you writing your dissertation on?* Compare thesis(2).
disservice /dɪˈsɜːvɪs/ *sing/u.n* (usu *do s.o* (*a*) —) (*formal*) harm, damage; unfair treatment (of s.o): *You do your parents great disservice by criticizing them after all they have done for you.*
dissident /ˈdɪsɪdənt/ *attrib.adj/c.n* (of a) person who strongly opposes/criticizes the government etc: *a political dissident; dissident opinion.*
'dissidence *u.n* opposition to the government etc; expressing opposing views: *They were thrown into jail for dissidence.*
dissimilar /dɪˈsɪmɪlə/ *adj* (esp in the negative) (*formal*) different; not similar(1): *The ideas they expressed were not dissimilar; they were simply described in different ways.*
dissimilarity /ˌdɪsɪmɪˈlærɪtɪ/ *c/u.n* (*formal*) (example of a) lack of similarity(1) (between two or more things): *Is there any dissimilarity between these two products?*
dissimulate /dɪˈsɪmjʊˌleɪt/ *tr/intr.v* (*formal*) hide, lie about, (one's true actions, beliefs, feelings etc): *They managed to bring things into the country illegally by dissimulating (the truth).*
dissimulation /dɪˌsɪmjʊˈleɪʃən/ *u.n.*
dissipate /ˈdɪsɪˌpeɪt/ *v* **1** *tr/intr.v* (*formal*) (also *fig*) (cause (s.t) to) scatter and/or disappear completely: *He sent flowers to dissipate her anger after their quarrel. After the rainstorm, the clouds quickly dissipated.* **2** *tr.v* use, waste, (time, money etc) foolishly: *You'll dissipate your inheritance very quickly if you spend money so readily.*
'dissi,pated *adj* (*derog; formal*) (of a person, way of living) who/that wastes money and time on alcohol and other pleasures: *He led a dissipated life at university.* Compare dissolute.
dissipation /ˌdɪsɪˈpeɪʃən/ *u.n* (*formal*) **1** act or fact of disappearing or causing (s.t) to disappear: *His kindness led to the dissipation of her anxiety.* **2** act or fact of wasting time, money etc: *There's*

a discussion this evening on ways of preventing the dissipation of natural resources(1). **3** state of living a dissipated life or of ruining one's health by drinking too much alcohol etc: *You'll die young if you continue with such dissipation.*

dissociate /dɪˈsəʊʃɪˌeɪt/ *v* (also **disas'sociate**) (*formal*) **1** *reflex.v* (usu — *oneself from s.o/s.t*) take away one's support (from s.o/s.t); show that one is not, or is no longer, connected to, part of, s.o/s.t: *The political group dissociated itself from the violence.* **2** *tr.v* (usu — *s.o/s.t* (*from* (*s.o/s.t*))) separate (one person, thing) (from another); see (two or more people, things) as separate: *I can't dissociate the person from his opinions and ideas.*

dissociation /dɪˌsəʊʃɪˈeɪʃən/ *u.n* (*formal*) act or fact of separating (s.o/s.t) from (s.o/s.t).

dissolute /ˈdɪsəˌluːt/ *adj* (*derog*; *formal*) (of a person, behaviour) immoral: *a dissolute son*; *dissolute behaviour.* Compare dissipated.

'disso,luteness *u.n.*

dissolve /dɪˈzɒlv/ *v* **1** *tr/intr.v* (often — *s.t in s.t*) (cause (s.t) to) lose its own form and become part of (the liquid into which it is put): *Dissolve the sugar in hot water. Will the tablet dissolve in water?* **2** *tr.v* (*formal*) cause (a formal group, marriage etc) to end: *Parliament was dissolved and the election date was set.* **3** *tr/intr.v* (*fig*) (cause (pain, fear etc) to) disappear: *All her fears dissolved when she saw him.* **dissolve into laughter/tears** lose control because of a strong feeling of happiness/sadness etc and therefore laugh/cry: *We all dissolved into laughter when he walked into the room dressed as a baby.*

dissolubility /dɪˌsɒljʊˈbɪlɪtɪ/ *u.n* fact, quality, of being able to be dissolved.

dissoluble /dɪˈsɒljʊbl/ *adj* that can be dissolved. Opposite indissoluble.

dissolution /ˌdɪsəˈluːʃən/ *u.n* (*formal*) act or fact of dissolving(2) s.t.

dissonance /ˈdɪsənəns/ *n* **1** *c/u.n* (*music*) (sound made by the) combining of two or more musical notes that do not sound right together: *He uses dissonance very effectively in his music.* **2** *u.n* (*formal*) lack of agreement: *The dissonance between what he says and does reduces the value of his ideals.*

'dissonant *adj* (usu *attrib*) lacking in harmony, agreement.

'dissonantly *adv.*

dissuade /dɪˈsweɪd/ *tr.v* (often — *s.o from doing s.t*) (*formal*) persuade (s.o) not to (do s.t): *You must dissuade him from leaving school without taking the examination.* Compare persuade(1).

dissuasion /dɪˈsweɪʒən/ *u.n.*

dist *written abbr* **1** district. **2** distance.

distance /ˈdɪstəns/ *n* **1** *c/u.n* (amount of) space between two points: *It's a distance of about ten miles. Do you have a big distance to travel to work every day? What's the distance from here to London?* **2** *sing.n* point that is far away: *We saw a light in the distance. We began to see signs of the fire from a long distance away.* **3** *c/u.n* (*fig*; *formal*) lack of friendliness: *We used to be good friends but our last argument has produced a distance between us.* ⇨ distance(4). **at a distance** from a point that is far away: *It looks fine . . . at a distance!* (**at**) **a safe distance** (**from s.o/s.t**) (in) a place that is far enough away (from s.o/s.t) to

be safe: *While taking photographs of the lions, she made sure she was always (at) a safe distance from them.* **keep one's, a safe, distance (from s.o/s.t)** stay far away (from s.o/s.t): *Keep your distance from the edge. When he's that angry I prefer to keep a safe distance!* **keep s.o at a distance** not allow s.o to get too physically close or too friendly: *I have to keep him at a distance because he wants to be more than just friends and that's not possible.* **within walking** etc **distance** near enough to be able to walk etc there: *It's not really within walking distance but it's only a ten-minute bus ride.* ⇨ hail(*v*).

▷ *reflex.v* **4** (often — *oneself from s.o/s.t*) make o.s less friendly (towards s.o/s.t), less involved(2) (with s.o/s.t): *I can't distance myself from the production enough to judge it fairly.*

distant /ˈdɪstənt/ *adj* **1** (of a place, time) far away: *Tibet is a distant land full of mystery and beauty. That's a name out of the distant past.* **2** (*attrib*) (of a relative) not close: *She's a distant relation of mine but we've never met.* **3** (*derog*; *fig*) not friendly: *She's been very distant since I got the job she wanted.* **4** seeming to be thinking of s.o/s.t else: *She seemed tired and distant.* **in the distant future, in the not too distant future** ⇨ future(*n*).

'distantly *adv* **1** (from) far away: *We could distantly hear the traffic far below us.* **2** not closely: *We are distantly related(1).* **3** in a manner that is not friendly: *He greeted me rather distantly.* **4** as if thinking of s.o/s.t else: *He looked at me distantly.*

distaste /dɪsˈteɪst/ *sing/u.n* (often — *for s.o/s.t*) (*formal*) lack of pleasure (in s.o/s.t): *Her distaste for the business led her to retire early.*

dis'tasteful *adj* that causes displeasure, disgust: *She finds the job of collecting the snails from her garden distasteful.*

dis'tastefully *adv.* **dis'tastefulness** *u.n.*

distemper[1] /dɪsˈtempə/ *u.n* kind of dangerous disease, esp affecting dogs and rabbits.

distemper[2] /dɪsˈtempə/ *u.n* **1** kind of paint that is mixed with water, not oil, and used for painting walls etc.

▷ *tr.v* **2** paint (a room) with distemper(1).

distend /dɪsˈtend/ *tr/intr.v* (*formal*) (cause (s.t) to) swell: *Something that I ate has distended my stomach.*

distension /dɪsˈtenʃən/ *u.n.*

distil /dɪsˈtɪl/ *tr.v* (US **di'still**) (-ll-) **1** heat (a liquid) to form a gas and then cool it again to get a pure form of the liquid: *Use only distilled water in a steam iron.* **2** make (alcoholic(1) drinks) by distilling(1): *How do you distil gin*[1]*?*

distillation /ˌdɪstɪˈleɪʃən/ *u.n.*

di'stiller *c.n* person or company that distils.

di'stillery *c.n* (*pl* -*ies*) place for distilling alcoholic(1) drinks.

distinct /dɪsˈtɪŋkt/ *adj* **1** clear; easy to see, hear, understand: *He left distinct instructions as to what we had to do. He has a very distinct way of walking.* Opposite indistinct. **2** (often — *from s.t*) different, separate: *Those plants are from the same family but they are quite distinct from one another.* **as distinct from s.t** in contrast(1) to s.t: *These stones were collected on our various trips abroad as distinct from these that we've found in the garden.*

distinction /dɪ'stɪŋkʃən/ n 1 c/u.n (often — between s.t and s.t) (feature(2) that shows the) difference (between s.t and s.t): *What are the distinctions between the male and female of this bird? Examples in the dictionary make a fine(8) distinction between one meaning and another.* 2 u.n quality of excellence: *an actor of high distinction. He got his degree with distinction.* 3 c.n mark, sign, of honour: *She got a distinction in her* ballet(3) *examination. He was given the distinction of sitting at the main table.*

di'stinctive adj that can be easily identified: *I'd know her voice anywhere because she has a very distinctive way of talking.*

di'stinctively adv. **di'stinctiveness** u.n.

di'stinctly adv 1 in a way that is very clear and easy to understand: *He described where you live very distinctly.* 2 definitely; very clearly: *I distinctly told you to lock the office when you left.*

distinguish /dɪ'stɪŋgwɪʃ/ v 1 tr.v (often — s.t from s.t) make or mark s.t as different (from s.t else): *Our house is distinguished from others in the street by its large windows.* 2 tr.v recognize, identify, (s.o/s.t): *You'll be able to distinguish the real stones because they're colder than plastic ones.* 3 intr.v (often — between s.o/s.t and s.o/ s.t) be able to notice, recognize, the difference(s) (between two or more people or things): *Can you distinguish between butter and* margarine? 4 reflex.v do s.t so well that other people notice (one): *She distinguished herself as a climber and a leader when she led a small group of women to the top of Everest.*

di'stinguishable adj that makes it possible to distinguish s.o/s.t: *His painting is distinguishable by the bright colours he uses.* Opposite indistinguishable.

di'stinguished adj 1 (of a person, her/his work etc) who/that is very successful because of her/ his/its excellence: *a distinguished writer/singer.* 2 (of a person, appearance) dignified; noble: *He looked very distinguished in a suit.*

di'stinguishing attrib.adj that distinguishes(1) s.o/s.t from s.o/s.t: *We were asked to list the distinguishing* features(2) *of the male bird of the species.*

distort /dɪ'stɔːt/ v 1 tr/intr.v (cause (s.t) to) change its shape: *His face was distorted with anger. The plastic bowl distorted in the heat.* 2 tr.v *(fig)* change the meaning of (a story etc): *He has a way of distorting the truth. Time has distorted the facts of his crime.* 3 tr/intr.v (cause (a sound) to) be unclear: *The electric wires distort the music on the radio.*

distortion /dɪ'stɔːʃən/ n 1 c.n result of distorting s.t; sound, story etc that has been distorted: *That's a distortion of the facts; that's not the way it actually happened.* 2 u.n act or fact of distorting s.t, state of being distorted: *I can't watch the television when there's so much distortion to the picture.*

distract /dɪ'strækt/ tr.v cause (a person, one's attention) to move away from what one is doing etc: *Don't distract me while I'm working. What's distracting you today — your mind seems to be somewhere else?*

di'stracted adj not giving one's complete attention to s.o/s.t because of worry or because one

is thinking about s.o/s.t else: *My daughter is very distracted at the moment because of her examinations. He waited until her attention was distracted and then took her money.*

di'stracting adj that takes one's attention from what one is doing or thinking: *There are too many distracting noises here.*

distraction /dɪ'strækʃən/ n 1 u.n act or fact of distracting; state of being distracted: *I need three hours without distraction to finish my work.* 2 c.n activity etc that takes one's attention away from problems, serious matters etc: *I can't work at home because there are too many distractions.* **drive s.o to distraction** annoy s.o greatly; make s.o very angry: *Tony's drumming drives his parents to distraction.*

distraught /dɪ'strɔːt/ adj *(formal)* (often — with s.t) extremely anxious, frightened, worried, (because of s.t): *The mother was distraught with worry about her missing child.*

distress /dɪ'stres/ u.n *(formal)* 1 (also attrib) state of great worry, sadness, trouble: *It is natural that you should feel distress after such a frightening experience. We have had a signal from a ship in distress. It sent a distress signal.*
▷ tr.v *(formal)* 2 make (s.o) very worried, unhappy: *She was very distressed when she lost her job.*

di'stressing adj *(formal)* that causes one to feel very worried, unhappy: *He found his wife's illness very distressing.*

di'stressingly adv.

distribute /dɪ'strɪbjuːt/ tr.v 1 give a share of s.t) (to s.o): *Please distribute the cake among the members of staff. Wealth is not evenly distributed in our society.* 2 deliver (s.t) widely; spread (s.t) over a wide area: *We need people to help distribute* leaflets *in several parts of the city.*

distribution /ˌdɪstrɪ'bjuːʃən/ u.n (also attrib) act or fact of distributing s.t: *Have you organized the distribution of the* leaflets? *He criticized the unfair distribution of wealth.*

distributor /dɪ'strɪbjuːtə/ c.n 1 person/company who/that supplies certain kinds of goods to shops in the area. 2 (also attrib) part of an engine, e.g in a car, that sends electricity to the spark plugs: *a distributor cap.*

district /'dɪstrɪkt/ c.n (also attrib) (with capital **D** in names) 1 area in a town or in the country: *We often go to the Lake District for walking holidays. They live in a very old district of the city.* 2 official areas with boundaries decided for administrative purposes.

district 'nurse c.n nurse paid for by the government who visits people's homes when they are ill and need medical attention.

distrust /dɪs'trʌst/ u.n *(formal)* 1 (often — of s.o/s.t) lack of trust in s.o/s.t): *She has a distrust of all politicians. He views the whole subject with deep distrust.*
▷ tr.v 2 be suspicious of (s.o/s.t) and not trust her/ him/it: *Why do you distrust politicians?*

dis'trusted adj *(derog; formal)* (of a person) who is not trusted: *a distrusted member of our staff at work.*

dis'trustful adj (usu — of s.o, s.o's behaviour) having no trust (in s.o, s.o's behaviour).

dis'trustfully adv. **dis'trustfulness** u.n.

disturb /dɪ'stɜːb/ tr.v 1 interrupt (s.o/s.t): *Sorry to disturb you but can you tell me the time? I*

wouldn't disturb her unless it was very important.
2 cause (s.o) to worry or become upset: *She was very disturbed by the recent violence in her home town.* **3** cause (the arrangement, order etc of s.t) to be changed, spoiled, slightly: *The room was exactly as she'd left it and nothing had been disturbed.* **disturb the peace** (*law*) annoy people by making too much noise or behaving badly in public.

di'sturbance *n* **1** *c.n* interruption: *How can I finish my work with so many disturbances?* **2** *c.n* event that is noisy and sometimes violent: *There was a disturbance in town today and some people were injured*(1). **3** *u.n* act of disturbing: *He was charged*(10) *with disturbance of the peace.*

dis'turbed *adj* **1** very anxious, worried: *He seemed disturbed about something but didn't talk about it.* **2** (of a person) who is anxious and unhappy and in some cases violent for no clear reason and needs medical help: *a mentally/emotionally disturbed person.*

di'sturbing *adj* that causes one to feel anxious, worried: *disturbing news.*
dis'turbingly *adv.*

disunite /ˌdɪsjuˈnaɪt/ *tr/intr.v* (*formal*) (cause (a group) to) divide, lose its unity, agreement etc.
ˌdisu'nited *adj* divided; lacking unity, agreement: *The group is disunited over the question of nuclear*(2) *arms.*

disunion /dɪsˈjuːnɪən/ *u.n* = disunity.

disunity /dɪsˈjuːnɪtɪ/ *u.n* (*formal*) lack of unity: *The subject of education always causes disunity in our family.*

disuse /dɪsˈjuːs/ *u.n* (often *fall into* —) state of no longer being used: *They couldn't afford to spend money looking after the old building and it soon fell into disuse.*

disused /ˌdɪsˈjuːzd/ *adj* that is no longer used: *Their home was a disused school.*

ditch /dɪtʃ/ *c.n* **1** long channel cut in the ground, esp to take away water. **last ditch** (also *attrib*) (*fig*) final place or position of defence: *make a last ditch stand against being dismissed.*
▷ *tr.v* **2** (*informal*) throw (s.t) away; abandon(1) (s.t): *Bob ditched the bag so that he could run faster.* **3** (*slang*) abandon(1) (a boyfriend or girlfriend).

ˈditch,water *u.n* (**as**) **dull as ditchwater** (*derog*; *informal*) (of a person, speech etc) very boring.

dither /ˈdɪðə/ *c.n* **1** **all of a dither**; **in a dither** very nervous or excited (so not able to make a decision).
▷ *intr.v* **2** (often — *about s.t*) be uncertain, unable to decide, (often because nervous or excited): *She has been dithering all week about whether to accept the offer or not.*

ditto /ˈdɪtəʊ/ *pron* (*written abbr* do. or *"*) (used to avoid repeating s.t) the same (person(s), thing(s)): *I need 30 tickets for Friday, ditto for Saturday.*

ditty /ˈdɪtɪ/ *c.n* (*pl -ies*) short simple song.

div *written abbr* **1** dividend. **2** division. **3** divorced.

divan /dɪˈvæn/ *c.n* sofa without a back, usu placed next to a wall.
di,van 'bed *c.n* bed without a board, rails etc at the top or bottom.

dive /daɪv/ *c.n* **1** act of diving, esp a formal one in a particular style as for a competition. **2** (*slang*) cheap, often dirty, place for drinking

alcohol: *He's drinking in one of the dives near the harbour.*
▷ *intr.v* (*p.t,p.p -d*, US **dove** /dəʊv/) **3** (often — *into s.t*) jump up, turn one's head down and go head first into water: *Mary dived into the sea from the rocks.* **4** go under the water wearing special apparatus in order to be able to breathe.
⇨ **skindive.** **5** = nosedive(3). **dive down s.t** go quickly along a road, path etc, esp to escape: *The thief dived down the side street and disappeared.*
dive for s.t dive(3) in order to find s.t: *They have been diving for crabs*(1) *all afternoon.*

ˈdiver *c.n* person who dives.

ˈdiving *u.n* (also *attrib*) act or sport of diving (⇨ dive(3,4)): *a diving instructor.*

ˈdiving-,board *c.n* long piece of wood etc from which s.o can dive(3).

ˈdiving ,suit *c.n* rubber etc suit worn by s.o who dives(4).

diverge /daɪˈvɜːdʒ/ *intr.v* **1** (of a road etc) separate and go in two or more different directions. **2** (often — *from s.t*) (*formal*) (of one's opinion etc) be different (from another): *Our view of the cause of the accident diverges from theirs.*
di'vergence *u.n.*
di'vergent *adj* (*formal*) not the same: *divergent interests/opinions.*

divers /ˈdaɪvəz/ *det/pron* various (types): *He owns divers business companies. Divers of them are in Scotland.*

diverse /daɪˈvɜːs/ *adj* (*formal*) made up of different kinds: *She has diverse interests.*
di'versely *adv.* **di'verseness** *u.n.*

diversify /daɪˈvɜːsɪˌfaɪ/ *tr/intr.v* (*-ies, -ied*) (cause (a person, company etc) to) begin having more than one interest, activity etc: *The factory must diversify if it is to become profitable.*

diversity /daɪˈvɜːsɪtɪ/ *u.n* (often — *of s.t*) variety (of s.t): *They sell a wide diversity of camping equipment*(2).

divert /daɪˈvɜːt/ *tr.v* **1** cause (traffic, people, animals etc) to change direction: *They diverted the crowds away from the town centre.* **2** (often — *s.o/s.t from s.t*) cause (a person, s.o's attention, look etc) to change (away from s.t important, secret, unpleasant etc): *She pointed to the left to divert the child's attention while she hid the cake. Playing tennis is diverting your attention from your examinations.* **3** (*formal*) amuse (s.o): *What can we do to divert the children on a cold, wet day?*

diversion /daɪˈvɜːʃən/ *n* **1** *c.n* change of a route(1) for traffic, e.g because of repairs to the road. **2** *c/u.n* (example of the) act of diverting(1,2). **3** *c/u.n* (*formal*) (example of a) form of amusement: *He has too many diversions and does not study enough.*

diversionary /daɪˈvɜːʃənərɪ/ *adj* (usu *attrib*) causing s.o's attention etc to be diverted(2): *diversionary tactics*(2) *while hiding the cake.*

divest /daɪˈvest/ *tr.v* (usu — *s.o/s.t of s.t*) (*formal*) take away from (s.o/s.t) her/his property, awards(1) or titles, power or authority etc, esp because of having done wrong: *When they discovered that she had cheated, she was divested of all her medals*(1). **divest o.s of s.t** give s.t away: *She divested herself of her money.*

divide /dɪˈvaɪd/ *c.n* **1** (esp *a great* —) (*formal*) difference; division(6): *There is a great divide* *between opportunities in the north and the south of the country.*

▷ *v* **2** *tr/intr.v* (cause (a group, object, area etc) to) separate into two or more parts or groups: *The children were divided according to age. The road divides at the bottom of the hill. They divided the money into six equal amounts.* **3** *tr.v* (often — *s.t among/between s.o/s.t*) share (s.t) (among/between s.o/s.t): *They divided the food among the children. We divided the orange between us.* **4** *tr.v* cause (people) to become different, be enemies, disagree etc: *Their education divides them.* **5** *tr/intr.v* (*mathematics*) find out the number of times one amount/number is contained in a (larger) amount/number: *8 divided by 2 equals/is 4* $(8 \div 2 = 4)$. ⇒ division sign. **be divided** (of two or more people) have different opinions: *The managers are divided and no one knows what will be decided about the future of the factory.* ⇒ undivided.

dividend /'dɪvɪˌdend/ *c.n* **1** money paid out to the shareholders of a company, usu once or twice a year. **2** part of this money paid to one shareholder, or on each share. **3** (*mathematics*) number or amount to be divided(5). ⇒ divisor.

di'viding *attrib.adj* making a division(3): *a dividing wall between the two gardens.*

di'viders *pl.n* (*mathematics*) instrument with two pointed pieces connected by a hinge(1), used to measure lines or to divide a line into parts.

divisibility /dɪˌvɪzɪ'bɪlɪtɪ/ *u.n.*

divisible /dɪ'vɪzəbl/ *pred.adj* (*mathematics*) (of a number, amount) that can be divided(5): *12 is divisible by 2, 3, 4 and 6.* Opposite indivisible.

division /dɪ'vɪʒən/ *n* **1** *c/u.n* (often — (of s.t) *into s.t*) (example of the) act of dividing(2) groups, things (into parts or groups): *the division of the money into six equal amounts.* **2** *c/u.n* (often — (of s.t) *among/between s.o/s.t*) (example of the) act of dividing(3) things. **3** *c.n* thing that is or acts as a barrier: *The division between the houses is marked by a low wall.* **4** *c.n* separate section or group: *a division in the army; the sales division of a business company.* **5** *c.n* separation or sharing (of duties etc). **6** *c/u.n* separation, esp according to wealth, opportunity, education etc: *Divisions between rich and poor countries are increasing.* **7** *u.n* lack of agreement, often with hatred or lack of respect: *divisions between members of the committee.* **8** *u.n* (*mathematics*) act of dividing(5): *I'm not very good at division.* **long division** ⇒ long¹.

divisional /dɪ'vɪʒənl/ *attrib.adj* of or referring to a division(4): *the divisional head office.*

divisive /dɪ'vaɪsɪv/ *adj* causing division(7): *Giving special attention to some members and not others can be divisive.*

di'visively *adv.* **divisiveness** *u.n.*

divisor /dɪ'vaɪzə/ *c.n* (*mathematics*) number or amount divided(5) into another. ⇒ dividend(3).

divine /dɪ'vaɪn/ *adj* **1** of or referring to God or the worship of God: *divine prayer; divine happiness in heaven.* **2** (*fig*) very good, beautiful: *divine weather. You look divine in that dress. This cake tastes divine.*

▷ *tr.v* **3** (*formal; old use*) find out (s.t hidden), guess (s.t that will happen), esp using intelligent thought or intuition: *Paul was able to divine the cause by suddenly realizing the effect*

of the sun on the metal roof. **4** find (water, metal objects) using special instruments (e.g a divining-rod).

divination /ˌdɪvɪ'neɪʃən/ *u.n* (*formal*) act or fact of divining(3,4) s.t.

di'viner *c.n* (esp) person who (claims that he/she) has a special skill at divining(4) water or metal.

di,vine 'worship *u.n* religious service(s).

di'vining-,rod *c.n* stick of wood with a divided end, used to divine(4) water or metal.

divinity /dɪ'vɪnɪtɪ/ *n* (*pl -ies*) **1** *u.n* study of God, religion or religions. **2** *u.n* state of being divine(1). **3** *def.n* (with capital **D**) God. **4** *c.n* god: *ancient Greek divinities.*

diving, diving-board/-suit ⇒ dive.

divisibility, divisible, division, divisional, divisive, divisor ⇒ divide.

divorce /dɪ'vɔːs/ *n* **1** *c/u.n* (often *get a —*) (example of the) ending of a marriage in a court of law. **2** *c.n* (*formal*) total separation or difference: *a divorce from the usual way of deciding who will lead the political party.*

▷ *v* **3** *tr/intr.v* (cause (a married couple) to) get a divorce(1): *They divorced after ten years of marriage. I'm divorcing him on the grounds(2) of adultery.* **4** *tr.v* (often — *oneself/s.o/s.t from s.o/s.t*) (*formal*) separate completely (oneself/s.o/s.t) from another, esp in one's thoughts: *She could not divorce her idea of him from his behaviour at the party.* **get divorced** get a divorce(1).

di'vorced *adj* having got a divorce(1): *divorced parents.* **divorced from s.t** (*formal*) separated completely from the truth, what is or should be expected etc.

divorcee, divorcée /ˌdɪvɔː'siː/ *c.n* person who has obtained a divorce(1).

divulge /daɪ'vʌldʒ/ *tr.v* (often — *s.t to s.o*) (*formal*) let (s.t) become known: *divulge a secret; divulge one's feelings of failure (to s.o).*

di'vulgence *u.n.*

DIY /ˌdiː aɪ 'waɪ/ *abbr* do it yourself (⇒ yourself).

dizzy /'dɪzɪ/ *adj* (*-ier, -iest*) **1** feeling confused, esp after turning round many times; giddy(1). **2** (*attrib*) causing one to feel dizzy(1): *look down from a dizzy height.*

'dizzily *adv.* **'dizziness** *u.n.*

DJ /ˌdiː 'dʒeɪ/ *abbr* **1** dinner jacket. **2** (also *dj*) disc jockey.

dk *written abbr* **1** dark(2): *dk blue.* **2** deck¹(1).

D Litt /ˌdiː 'lɪt/ *abbr* (also **D.Lit**) Doctor(2) of Literature.

dm *written abbr* decimetre.

D Mus *written abbr* Doctor(2) of Music.

DNA /ˌdiː en 'eɪ/ *def.n abbr* deoxyribonucleic acid (the molecule that is the main part of all chromosomes and produces the characteristics that are inherited(2)).

D-notice /'diː ˌnəʊtɪs/ *c.n* (UK) government refusal to allow newspapers, radio and television to give (a piece of) information that may affect national safety.

do /duː/ *c.n* (*pl dos, do's*) **1** occasion for ceremony or celebration, e.g a formal dinner, dance, party, wedding etc. **dos and don'ts** (*informal*) advice or rules about what to do and what not to do on a particular occasion, in order to succeed at s.t etc.

▷ *aux.v* (strong form /duː/, weak forms /dʊ, də/)

(*3rd pers pres.t* **does** (strong form /dʌz/, weak form /dəz/); *pres.p* **doing** /'duːɪŋ/; *p.t* **did** /dɪd/, *p.p* **done** /dʌn/; negative forms **do not** or **don't** /dəʊnt/, **does not** or **doesn't** /'dʌznt/, **did not** or **didn't** /'dɪdnt/; 'do you' can be *d'you* /dju:/; 'do' is followed by the infinitive of a verb without *to*). **2** (used with other verbs to make questions): *Do you like her? Didn't they buy it? Why did he come? How does it work? Where do you come from?* **3** (used to make the negative): *I don't want it. He doesn't care about it. You didn't even try.* **4** (used with other verbs to give an invitation in the form of a polite order): *Do come to my party!* **5** (used with other verbs to give a negative order): *Don't go near the edge!* **6** (used to avoid repeating an earlier verb (phrase(1))): *She said I would win and I did! 'Do you like beer?' 'No, I don't.'* **7** (used to make a statement stronger): *I do think you ought to apologize.* **8** (*formal*) (used in a special word order after 'rarely', 'seldom' etc meaning the same as the usual word order): *Rarely did I see him* (= I saw him rarely) *without a hat on. Seldom do we* (= We seldom) *find* eagles(1) *in Britain.*

▷ *v* (verb forms are the same as aux.v but pronunciations are as strong forms only) **9** *tr.v* act in such a way as to complete (s.t): *Have you done your work? What shall I do when I've finished? It's your turn to do the* washing-up. **10** *tr.v* clean or tidy (s.t): *do the floors/garden; do one's hair.* **11** *tr.v* (of a restaurant, shop etc) provide (s.t): *Does that café do hot breakfasts? Our local shop does an excellent cooked* ham(1). **12** *tr.v* solve (a puzzle etc): *do the* crossword. **13** *tr.v* cover (a certain distance, area); drive etc at (a certain speed etc): *We did a hundred miles in less than two hours. You must have done more than seventy miles an hour on the motorway. When you've done the walls you can start on the ceiling.* **14** *tr.v* cause (an effect) (to s.o/s.t): *Your remark did (me) harm. The water did some damage to the floors. A holiday will do you good.* Compare undo(2). **15** *tr.v* study, work at, (a subject etc): *I'm doing* science research(1) *at university.* **16** *tr.v* act (a play): *Our school is doing 'The Birthday Party' in the summer.* **17** *tr/intr.v* be enough (for (s.o/s.t)): *£10 will have to do (you) until I go to the bank. That chicken won't do all the family! It will have to do.* **18** *tr/intr.v* be suitable (for (s.o)): *This old bicycle will have to do for now — I'll get the car repaired tomorrow. A red pen will do (me) if you haven't got a green one. I'd like it by Friday but Saturday will do if you are busy.* **19** *tr.v* produce (a certain good or bad public effect) for s.o/s.t: *You've done the school* credit(6). *She did us a great honour by visiting the college.* ⇒ do oneself/s.o down. **20** *intr.v* manage; live; get on: *She's doing well/badly at college. How is your family/business doing in Spain? Alex has done very well since he left school.* **21** *intr.v* behave: *Do as I tell you! He did well during the* crisis(1). *You can do as you like, I don't care any more.* **22** *tr.v* (*informal*) visit (s.t, a place): *We did Europe in ten days.* **23** cheat (s.o): *He did me when he sold me that car. You were done!* **24** *tr.v* (*slang*) steal from (a place, business etc): *The same four boys did several homes/cars last night.*

do away with oneself kill oneself. **do away with s.o/s.t** (*informal*) (**a**) abandon(1) or abolish an official form of dress, behaviour etc: *Mary's school has done away with* uniform(2). (**b**) kill a person, animal.

do oneself/s.o down (*informal*) make oneself/s.o appear inferior(1), by one's behaviour or by criticizing oneself/s.o.

do for s.o (*informal*) clean s.o's home regularly as a job. **be done for** (*informal*) have no chance of avoiding ruin or death: *The radio is broken and the nearest ship is a hundred miles away so we're done for.*

do s.o good ⇒ good(5). ⇒ do-gooder.

do s.t by halves ⇒ half.

do s.o in (*informal*) kill s.o. **be**, **look** etc **done in** be, look etc exhausted.

do it yourself ⇒ yourself.

do one's (own) thing (*informal*) do(9) whatever one likes or prefers (and ignore criticism).

do or die use every effort to try to succeed.

do s.t out clean a room, cupboard etc thoroughly. **do s.o out of s.t** cheat s.o so that he/she does not get money, property etc: *He did me out of my share of the profits.*

do s.o over (*slang*) hit s.o often and with hard blows. **do s.t over** (*informal*) paint, wallpaper(2) etc a room: *We're having the kitchen done over.*

do s.t to death (*fig*) sing s.t, act a play, say a joke etc so often that it loses all value, attraction etc: *That old story has been done to death—I've heard it a hundred times before.*

do up be fastened (in a certain way): *This dress does up down the back.* **do s.t up** (**a**) fasten a bag, clothing etc using buttons, a zip-fastener etc: *Do up your coat — it's cold outside.* Opposite undo(1). (**b**) repair and paint etc a house, room etc. (**c**) wrap and tie a parcel, packet etc.

do well by s.o; **do well out of s.o/s.t**; **do well to do s.t**; **doing well** ⇒ well¹(*adv*).

do with s.o/s.t (**a**) (esp *can/could* —) need s.t very much: *She could do with a bath!* (**b**) (*informal*) (esp *can't/couldn't* —) bear, tolerate, s.t: *I can't be doing with* jazz(1). **be/have done with s.t** have finished with s.t: *When will you be/have done with that book?* **be/have to do with s.t** be connected to, concerned with, caused by, etc s.t: *It has to do with the way she speaks.* **have (anything, nothing** etc) **to do with s.o** (not) be the responsibility, cause, concern, of s.o: *Her problems have nothing to do with me. Has her disappointment anything to do with you?* **have anything, something** etc **to do with s.t** be responsible for s.t: *Does your wife have anything to do with your sadness? He had something to do with her failure.* **not know what to do with oneself** not know how to pass the time, survive(1) a pain etc: *He didn't know what to do with himself when he lost his job. My tooth hurt so much that I didn't know what to do with myself.* **over and done with** ⇒ over(1). **what to do with s.o/s.t** (in questions) do(9), behave, decide etc concerning s.o/s.t: *What did you do with the keys? What shall we do with the rubbish? What are you doing with* (= why are you using) *that old bicycle?*

do without (s.t) manage, succeed, without (the use of) s.t: *I haven't any money so we'll have to do without (dinner).* ⇒ go without (s.t).

how do you do? ⇒ how.

make s.t do; **make do (with s.t)** ⇒ make(*v*).

nothing doing ⇒ nothing(*pron*).

That does it! That's done it! (used to express one's angry decision not to do s.t): *That does it! I refuse to help her if she's so rude about my work.*

doer /'duːə/ *c.n* **1** person who acts (and does not only promise or think): *We need doers, not planners.* **2** (used in combinations) person who acts in the way shown by the first part of the word: *an evil-doer.*

'doings *pl.n* (*informal*) things s.o does, esp during a particular period(1): *Write and tell me all your doings in London.*

done /dʌn/ *pred.adj* **1** (of food) cooked. ⇨ overdone, underdone. **2** (*informal*) acceptable behaviour: *It's not done to put a knife in one's mouth.* **the done thing** ⇨ thing.

▷ *v* **3** *p.p* of do. **easier said than done**; **no sooner said than done** ⇨ say(*v*).

ˌdo-'gooder *c.n* (*informal*; often *derog*) person who is (too) willing to help others, esp one with ideas etc that are not possible.

do. *written abbr* ditto.

doc¹ /dɒk/ *c.n* (*informal*) doctor(1).

doc² *written abbr* document(1).

docile /'dəʊsaɪl/ *adj* (of a person, animal) easy to control, teach; obeying orders readily: *a docile child/dog.*

'docilely *adv.* **docility** /dəʊ'sɪlɪtɪ/ *u.n.*

dock¹ /dɒk/ *n* **1** *c/u.n* place in a harbour where ships stop for passengers, goods etc. **2** *c.n* place in a court of law for s.o accused of s.t. **in dock** (of a ship) at a dock(1) (and not travelling).

▷ *tr/intr.v* **3** (cause (a ship etc) to) enter a harbour and stop at a dock(1).

'docker *c.n* person who works in the docks.

docks *def.pl.n* (buildings in the) area round docks¹ in a harbour.

'dockˌyard *c.n* docks for the navy where ships are loaded, repaired etc.

dock² /dɒk/ *tr.v* **1** cut (a tail etc) short(er). **2** take a part away from (wages etc): *Her salary was docked after she damaged the car.*

docket /'dɒkɪt/ *c.n* **1** (*commerce*) label listing the contents of a container, parcel etc.

▷ *tr.v* **2** (*commerce*) put a docket(1) on (s.t).

doctor /'dɒktə/ *c.n* (with capital **D** in names; *abbr* **Dr**) **1** person qualified to treat sick or injured(1) people: *If he gets any worse, please call the doctor.* **2** (person with a) high university degree (in any subject): *a doctor of* philosophy(1). **be under the doctor (for s.t)** be being treated by a doctor (for an illness etc). **be (just) what the doctor ordered** (*fig*) be s.t that one needs very much in order to succeed or survive(1): *This hot weather is just what the doctor ordered for the tennis competition.*

▷ *v* (*informal*) **3** *intr.v* be a doctor(1): *She's been doctoring in Botswana for many years.* **4** *tr.v* (order s.o to) take s.t in order to cure (an illness etc): *There are many ways to doctor a cold.* **5** *tr.v* change, interfere with, (s.t) for one's own advantage or in order to deceive: *doctor the accounts.*

doctorate /'dɒktərɪt/ *c.n* degree of doctor(2).

'doctored *adj* **1** interfered with: *a doctored report/drink.* ⇨ doctor(5). **2** (*informal*) (of an animal) having been made unable to produce young.

doctrine /'dɒktrɪn/ *c/u.n* belief(s) of a religious, political etc group. ⇨ indoctrinate.

doctrinaire /ˌdɒktrɪ'neə/ *adj* (often *derog*) stubborn(1) in stressing the details of a doctrine even when this may not be suitable, possible etc.

doctrinal /dɒk'traɪnl/ *attrib.adj* of or referring to a doctrine: *doctrinal teachings from the* Bible(1).

document /'dɒkjʊmənt/ *c.n* **1** paper(s) with a formal written statement for official or legal(2) use: *Have you got your driving documents with you?*

▷ *tr.v* /'dɒkjʊment/ **2** make a detailed record of (s.t), e.g in a newspaper: *The murder trial has been fully documented.* **3** give details of sources, facts etc for (one's ideas etc) in a book, lecture etc.

documentary /ˌdɒkjʊ'mentərɪ/ *attrib.adj* **1** of, using, written sources¹ or proof: *documentary* evidence(1).

▷ *c.n* (*pl* -ies) **2** (also *attrib*) film or television programme concerning a particular subject and including many facts and detailed evidence(1): *a documentary on life in India*; *documentary films.*

documentation /ˌdɒkjʊmen'teɪʃən/ *u.n* **1** act of using, supplying, detailed evidence(1) (from written sources(1)). **2** material produced by documentation(1).

'docuˌmented *adj* **1** reported in detail: *a documented story in a magazine.* **2** supported with detailed evidence(1): *a well-documented* theory(1).

dodder /'dɒdə/ *intr.v* (*informal*) stand or walk in a shaky manner, e.g because old or ill.

'dodderer *c.n* (*informal*) person who dodders.

'doddery *adj* (-ier, -iest) tending to shake when on one's feet: *a doddery old woman.*

dodge /dɒdʒ/ *c.n* **1** act of dodging(3) s.o/s.t: *a dodge to avoid a passing car.* **2** (*fig*; *informal*) trick; clever way of behaving to avoid trouble or extra work for oneself: *She's worked in this factory for many years and knows all the dodges.*

▷ *v* **3** *tr/intr.v* move suddenly to avoid (s.o/s.t): *She dodged across the road avoiding the traffic.* **4** *tr.v* avoid (doing) (s.t one does not enjoy, want to do): *Harry leaves work late in order to dodge the traffic. Don't try to dodge cleaning the bathroom; it's your turn.* **5** *tr.v* avoid (a subject of conversation etc): *He dodged the question and talked about something completely different.*

'dodger *c.n* person who avoids work, difficult questions, being caught etc, esp by using clever means.

'dodgy *adj* (-ier, -iest) (*informal*) **1** difficult; dangerous: *Leaving ourselves with only three minutes to get to the station is a bit dodgy. That's a dodgy old car.* **2** involving deceit, tricks etc: *a dodgy business selling insurance.*

dodgem /'dɒdʒəm/ *c.n* (*t.n*) (also **'dodgem ˌcar**) electrical vehicle made to be driven in a small space at a funfair where one can crash into other similar(1) cars for fun.

dodo /'dəʊdəʊ/ *c.n* (*pl* -(e)s) large bird that could not fly and lived on the island of Mauritius; it is now extinct(1). **(as) dead as the dodo** (a) no longer living. (b) very old-fashioned.

doe /dəʊ/ *c.n* female deer, rabbit etc.

doer ⇨ do.

does (strong form /dʌz/, weak form /dəz/) *3rd pers pres.t* of do.

doesn't /'dʌznt/ = does not ⇨ do.

doff /dɒf/ *tr.v* **doff one's cap/hat** take off one's cap etc as a polite greeting to a woman etc.

dog /dɒg/ *c.n* **1** (also *attrib*) one of many different kinds of animal that bark and are kept as pets, to guard property, hunt etc: *a large dog*; *dog meat*. **2** (*informal*) fellow: *You lucky dog, Peter!* **3** (also *attrib*) male of the family of animals including dogs, foxes(1), wolves(1). **a dog's chance** (*informal*) any chance at all: *I didn't have a dog's chance against the* champion(3). **a dog's breakfast/dinner** (*informal*) a mess¹(2); s.t badly made. **a dog's life** (*informal*) a very difficult and poor way of living. **dog eat dog** competition in which both sides will do anything to win however cruel or bad. **cannot teach an old dog new tricks** not able to make an older or experienced person change her/his methods. **dog in the manger** ⇨ manger. **let sleeping dogs lie** not try to change a situation in case this makes it worse. ⇨ dogs.
▷ *tr.v* (**-gg-**) **4** follow (s.o) closely like a dog(1): *He dogged her across southern Europe.* **be dogged by s.t** continually suffer ill health, bad luck etc.

'dog ‚collar *c.n* **1** collar for the neck of a dog. **2** (*informal*) (usu white) ring of usu stiff cloth worn round the neck by a clergyman.

'dog-‚eared *adj* with the corners (of the pages) turned down: *a dog-eared book/page.*

'dog-‚fight *c.n* **1** battle between two small military(1) planes in the sky. **2** rough fight by a small group.

dogged /'dɒgɪd/ *adj* (*formal*) determined and serious: *a dogged approach to one's studies.*
'doggedly *adv*. **'doggedness** *u.n*.

'doggish *adj* like a dog(1).
'doggishly *adv*. **'doggishness** *u.n*.

'doggy, 'doggie *c.n* (*pl* **-ies**) (also *attrib*) (esp child's word for a) dog: *My doggy's called 'Spot'. Have some doggy biscuits.*

'doggy-‚bag *c.n* paper etc bag given in a restaurant etc for meat etc that is left over to be taken home.

'dog ‚handler *c.n* police officer, soldier etc who works with a specially trained dog.

'dog‚house *def.n* **in the doghouse** (*informal*) not liked or favoured; in disgrace(1).

'dog ‚kennel *c.n* = kennel.

'dog ‚paddle *def.n* **1** (often **do the —**) way of swimming with short, fast movements of the arms and legs up and down like a dog, esp as a first stage in learning to swim.
▷ *intr.v* **2** swim the dog paddle(1).

'dog ‚rose *c.n* kind of wild rose with a small white or pink flower.

dogs *def.n* racing with greyhounds. **go to the dogs** (of a person, business) be (financially) ruined.

'dogs‚body *c.n* (*pl* **-ies**) (often *derog*) person who does small (often unpleasant) jobs for other people: *Who's the dogsbody in your office?*

'dog-‚tired *adj* extremely tired.

'dog‚tooth *c.n* (*pl* **-‚teeth**) = canine tooth.

dog-eared, dogfight, dogged ⇨ dog.

doggerel /'dɒgərəl/ *u.n* (also *attrib*) poetically bad verse: *doggerel verses.*

doggish(ly), doggishness, doggy(-bag), doghandler, doghouse ⇨ dog.

dogma /'dɒgmə/ *u.n* belief, opinion, decided by an authority(2), esp officials of the church.

dogmatic /dɒg'mætɪk/ *adj* (*derog*; *formal*) forcing, or trying to force, others to accept one's own opinions or beliefs.
dog'matically *adv*.
'dogma‚tism *u.n* (*formal*) fact of being dogmatic.
'dogma‚tist *c.n* (*formal*) person who is dogmatic.

do-gooder ⇨ do.

dog rose, dogsbody, dog-tired, dog-tooth ⇨ dog.

dolly /'dɒlɪ/ *c.n* (*pl* **-ies**) mat (usu of paper) with patterns made by cutting many small holes in it, as used under cakes etc.

doing(s) ⇨ do.

do it yourself ⇨ yourself.

doldrums /'dɒldrəmz/ *def.n* (usu **in(to) the —**) **1** state of feeling sad or bored: *She's been in the doldrums since she lost the race.* **2** (*technical*) area of the sea near the equator where there is no wind.

dole /dəʊl/ *def.n* **1** (usu **on the —**) government payment given to a person who is unemployed: *How long has Kim been on the dole?*
▷ *tr.v* **dole s.t out** (*informal*) **2** share s.t out: *He doled out the ice-cream.* **3** spend money on s.t: *I've been doling out money on this old car for years.*

doleful /'dəʊlfʊl/ *adj* (*formal*) sad: *with a doleful look.*
'dolefully *adv*. **'dolefulness** *u.n*.

doll /dɒl/ *c.n* **1** toy that is a small model of a baby or sometimes a soldier, young woman etc.
▷ *tr.v* **2** (usu **— oneself/s.o up** (**in s.t**)) (*informal*) dress oneself/s.o (in expensive or showy clothes). **be all dolled up** (**in s.t**) (*slang*) be dressed in very showy clothes.

'dolly *c.n* (*pl* **-ies**) (child's word for a) doll(1).

dollar /'dɒlə/ *c.n* unit of decimal currency in many countries, including the US, Canada, Singapore, Australia, *symb* $. **in dollars** using dollars as payment: *Can I pay in dollars?*

dollop /'dɒləp/ *c.n* **1** (often **— of s.t**) (*informal*) small lump or portion (of food, e.g ice-cream, mashed potato, jam, cream).
▷ *tr.v* **2** (often **— s.t out**) (*informal*) give (s.t) out in dollops(1): *She dolloped the ice-cream onto my plate.*

dolly ⇨ doll.

dolorous /'dɒlərəs/ *adj* (*formal*) causing or showing pain or sadness: *a dolorous expression.*
'dolorously *adv*. **'dolorousness** *u.n*.

dolphin /'dɒlfɪn/ *c.n* kind of large sea animal with a long pointed face that can be trained to do tricks; it is dark blue above, and white below. Compare porpoise.
dolphinarium /ˌdɒlfɪ'neərɪəm/ *c.n* place where trained dolphins do tricks for a paying audience.

dolt /dəʊlt/ *c.n* (*derog*) stupid person.
'doltish *adj* (*derog*) stupid.

domain /də'meɪn/ *c.n* **1** (*formal* or *old use*) land or region of a ruler, government or rich owner: *They took us for a drive round their domains.* **2** (often **be/fall within/outside one's —**) (*fig*) area of authority(6), interest, knowledge etc: *This problem is outside my domain.*

dome /dəʊm/ *c.n* **1** round roof like half a ball. **2** (*slang*) person's head, esp when bald(1).
domed *adj* shaped like a dome(1).

domestic /dəˈmestɪk/ adj 1 (attrib) of, referring to, for, a person or home: for domestic use only; domestic appliances such as a vacuum cleaner and a washing machine. 2 concerning one's private life (and not one's work etc): domestic quarrels; live in domestic bliss. 3 of or referring to the internal(2) affairs of a country; not foreign. 4 (informal) good at, willing to do, cooking, cleaning etc at home: He's quite domestic. 5 (of animals) living at home with people (as pets or to do work).
▷ c.n 6 person paid to clean s.o's home.
doˈmestically adv.
domesticate /dəˈmestɪˌkeɪt/ tr.v 1 train (an animal) to be a pet. 2 cause (s.o) to become good at cooking, willing to clean, at home: He couldn't fry an egg before they got married but Jackie has domesticated him.
doˈmestiˌcated adj: domesticated animals.
domestication /dəˌmestɪˈkeɪʃən/ u.n state, ability or process of being, becoming, domesticated.
domesticity /ˌdəʊmeˈstɪsɪtɪ/ u.n ability to organize or help with life at home.
doˌmestic ˈhelp c.n = domestic(6).
doˌmestic ˈscience u.n training (at school or college) in cooking, running a home etc.
domicile /ˈdɒmɪˌsaɪl/ c.n 1 (formal; law) place where one lives or is considered by the law to have one's home.
▷ tr/intr.v 2 (formal; law) be living, (cause (s.o) to) have her/his legal home, in a particular place: Are you domiciled in Britain or are you a visitor?
dominant /ˈdɒmɪnənt/ adj 1 having or showing greatest authority(1), control, power etc: the dominant group in the party; a dominant personality(1). 2 main; most important; most influential: the dominant points in the report. 3 (science) existing in larger numbers than others in an area: a dominant plant/insect. 4 (science) (of a gene) able or likely to produce the same features in an offspring, e.g brown eyes and hair. ⇒ recessive(2).
ˈdominance u.n. **ˈdominantly** adv.
dominate /ˈdɒmɪˌneɪt/ tr/intr.v 1 (formal) control, have authority(1) over, (s.o/s.t): The taller boys dominated the smaller ones in the playground. 2 (fig) be most obvious (in a place, area of study, group of effects(1) etc): The large old tree dominates the horizon(1). Her novels' dominate all her literature of the early part of this century. ⇒ predominate.
domination /ˌdɒmɪˈneɪʃən/ u.n.
domineer /ˌdɒmɪˈnɪə/ intr.v (usu — over s.o/ s.t) (often derog; formal) act, behave, with (too) strong authority(1) (over s.o/s.t).
ˌdomiˈneering adj (derog) too fond of giving orders, using one's authority(1): a domineering husband/ personality(1).
dominion /dəˈmɪnɪən/ u.n 1 (often — over s.o/ s.t) (formal) rule; powerful authority(1) (over s.o/s.t): He was too fond of his dominion over the workers on his estates(1). 2 (with capital D) official title for some countries, e.g Canada and New Zealand, that had been British colonies(1).
domino /ˈdɒmɪˌnəʊ/ c.n (pl -es) one of a set of oblong pieces with different numbers shown by

spots; each must be joined to similar ones in the game of dominoes.
ˈdomino efˌfect def.n (also **ˈdomino ˌtheory**) idea that if one lets one's country be invaded and/or taken over by, e.g communism, its neighbours will soon fall in the same way, and then their neighbours too etc.
ˈdominoes u.n game in which one has to join each domino to another.
don¹ /dɒn/ c.n university teacher (at Cambridge or Oxford).
don² /dɒn/ tr.v (-nn-) (old use) put on (clothing): She donned her coat and hat and went outside.
donate /dəʊˈneɪt/ tr.v (often — s.t to s.o/s.t) (formal) 1 give (money) (to a charity(3) etc): The school has donated £100 to the local church. 2 (fig) give (one's time, effort etc) (to a task): She donated all her energies(1) to finishing the job.
donation /dəʊˈneɪʃən/ c.n 1 thing, esp money, given to a collection or fund(1): make a donation of clothes for the flood victims. 2 thing given, esp free of charge, to be used in a report, collection etc; contribution(2): donations of poems to be used in a book.
donor /ˈdəʊnə/ c.n 1 person who gives money etc to a charity(3), fund etc. 2 person who gives part of her/his body for medical use: a kidney(1) donor; a blood donor.
done /dʌn/ p.p of do.
donkey /ˈdɒŋkɪ/ c.n 1 animal like a small horse but with long ears, used for carrying people or things. 2 (derog; fig) silly person. Compare mule.
ˈdonkey ˌjacket c.n kind of straight jacket(1) of thick material with large pockets, worn by builders, miners etc.
ˈdonkey's ˌyears pl.n (often for —) (informal) a very long time: I've waited donkey's years for this opportunity.
ˈdonkey-ˌwork def/u.n (informal) regular and dull work as a necessary part of a system: He gets the exciting jobs and I'm left with (or left to do) the donkey-work.
donor ⇒ donate.
don't /dəʊnt/ = do not. ⇒ do.
doodle /ˈduːdl/ c.n 1 complicated mark or shape made with a pen, pencil etc while not noticing what one is doing and that has no meaning or purpose.
▷ intr.v 2 make doodles: You have doodled all over the cover of this book.
ˈdoodler c.n person who doodles(2).
doom /duːm/ u.n 1 (state giving a feeling of a) terrible fate or death: The family was filled with doom when the news came that the money was not available. She'll go to her doom with the secret rather than tell you.
▷ tr.v 2 (usu passive, be —ed to (do) s.t) cause (s.o/s.t) to fail, be harmed, have a terrible fate etc: He has worked so little that he is doomed to fail/failure.
doomed adj: a doomed future/plan/explorer.
doomsday /ˈduːmzˌdeɪ/ u.n till/until doomsday (often with capital D) for a very long time; for ever: I'll wait for you till doomsday if necessary.
door /dɔː/ c/def.n 1 flat board etc on hinges(1), used to open and close a space in a wall, cupboard etc: the back/front door of a house. 2 doorway: He stood in the door and refused to let me pass. 3 (fig) opening that gives a chance

of escape, success etc: *A university degree opens all kinds of doors.* **answer the door** go to the door of a house because a visitor has rung or knocked. **be at death's door** be about to die. **close/shut the door on/to s.o/s.t** (*fig*) stop allowing s.o/ s.t to be successful or to try to succeed. **lay s.t at s.o's door** (*fig*) say or show that s.o is responsible for s.t bad or unpleasant. **next door** ⇒ next. **out of doors** outside a building; in the open air. **show s.o the door** order s.o to leave one's house because one is angry etc. **show s.o to the door** take s.o to the exit of a building, set of offices etc. **shut the door on/to s.o/s.t** = close the door on/to s.o/s.t.

'**door-** *n* thing shown by the second part of the word that is for use on or near a door(1): *a* doorbell, doorhandle, door knob, door knocker.

'**door,frame** *c.n* wood etc frame round the edges of a doorway.

'**door,keeper** *c.n* person whose job is to guard an entrance to a building.

'**doorman** *c.n* (*pl* -men) = doorkeeper.

'**door,mat** *c.n* **1** small mat by a door for people to wipe their shoes on before going into a building. **2** (*derog*; *fig*) weak person who is treated badly by others and who does not complain.

'**door,nail** *c.n* (**as**) **dead as a doornail** (*informal*) completely dead and without any possibility of doubt about it.

'**door,step** *c/def.n* step in front of a door outside a building. **on one's doorstep** (*fig*) very near to where one lives: *We prefer to live with the mountains on our doorstep because we love climbing.*

,**door-to-'door** *attrib.adj* going from one house to the next: *a door-to-door salesman.*

'**door,way** *c/def.n* (space near an) opening in a wall for a door: *Don't put chairs in the doorway in case there is a fire.*

dope /dəʊp/ *n* (*informal*) **1** *c.n* (*derog*) stupid person. **2** *u.n* (also *attrib*) illegal drug(s)(2) (esp cannabis): *a dope user.* **3** *def/u.n* information: *Have you any dope on how the machine works?*
▷ *tr.v* **4** (often— oneself/s.o/s.t up) use dope(2) on (oneself, s.o, a horse etc). Compare dose oneself/ s.o/s.t up.

'**dopey** *adj* (*informal*) **1** (*derog*) stupid: *a dopey child.* **2** affected by dope(2). **3** (usu *pred*) very tired or sleepy: *I'm always dopey after a long journey.*

dorm /dɔːm/ *c.n* (*informal*) dormitory(2).

dormant /'dɔːmənt/ *adj* (*technical*) not active: *a dormant volcano.* **lie dormant** be in a dormant state: *Many seeds lie dormant during the cold weather.*

dormer /'dɔːmə/ *c.n* (also '**dormer-,window**) pointed window that stands out from a roof.

dormitory /'dɔːmɪtərɪ/ *attrib.adj* **1** of or referring to a part of a town, area etc from where people go into the city or town to work: *a dormitory section/town.*
▷ *c.n* (*pl* -ies) **2** room in a school, camp etc with several beds.

dormouse /'dɔː,maʊs/ *c.n* (*pl* -mice /-,maɪs/) kind of small brown animal that is like s.t between a mouse and a squirrel.

dorsal /'dɔːsl/ *attrib.adj* (*technical*) of or referring to the back (part): *a dorsal bone/*fin(1).

dose /dəʊs/ *c.n* (usu — of s.t) **1** portion (of medicine). ⇒ overdose. **2** (*informal*) unpleasant

experience (of s.t): *She is suffering from a dose of flu. He's had a full dose of her bad temper.*
▷ *tr.v* **3** (often — s.o with s.t) give (s.o) a dose(1) (of a certain medicine): *His mother dosed him with aspirin.* **dose oneself/s.o/s.t up** take, give s.o/an animal, a lot of medicine in order to cure oneself/ s.o/s.t quickly.

dosage /'dəʊsɪdʒ/ *c/u.n* (act of giving a) quantity of medicine: *What is the correct dosage for children?*

doss /dɒs/ *c.n* (*slang*) **1** period of sleep in a cheap place.
▷ *tr/intr.v* **2** (often — (s.o) down) (*slang*) (organize (s.o) to) sleep in a very cheap or temporary place: *We dossed (the children) down on the floor.*

'**doss-,house** *c.n* (*slang*) very cheap place to sleep.

dot /dɒt/ *c.n* **1** small round spot: *a line of dots.* **on the dot** (*informal*) at the exact time mentioned or agreed: *Be here at 6 o'clock on the dot.* **the year dot** ⇒ year.
▷ *tr.v* (-tt-) **2** make small marks or spots on (s.t): *You have dotted my skirt with paint.* **3** cover or fill (s.t) with things that make shapes: *fields dotted with trees.*

'**dotted** *attrib.adj* **1** made using dots(1) ⇒ dotted line. **2** covered with dots(1): *a dotted skirt.*

,**dotted 'line** *c/def.n* line[1](2) made of dots(1): *Sign on the dotted line.*

dote /dəʊt/ *tr.v* **dote** (**up**)**on s.o/s.t** like or love (s.o/s.t) very much (esp foolishly): *She dotes on her children.*

'**doting** *attrib.adj*: *doting parents.*

dotty /'dɒtɪ/ *adj* (-ier, -iest) (*derog*; *informal*) stupid: *a dotty idea/person.* **a bit dotty** a little mad.

double /'dʌbl/ *attrib.adj* **1** of two of the same kind (joined) together: *a double window; double inverted commas; a double fault in tennis.* **2** of two different kinds, possibilities etc together: *a phrase(1) with a double meaning; lead a double life.* **3** having two times the standard amount, size etc: *a double gin; a double portion(2) of potatoes.* **4** for two people: *a double bed; a double room in a hotel; a double sheet.* Compare single(2).
▷ *adv* **5** twice; two times: *The job took double the time expected.* **6** two together: *After the hit on the head I was seeing double.* **7** (in order) to make two (joined) parts: *fold the sheets double. He was bent double with age.*
▷ *n* **8** *u.n* twice the amount: *He won £5 but I won double.* **9** *c.n* person who looks the same as s.o else: *She's your sister's double.* **10** *c.n* double(4) room. Compare single(4). **11** portion(2) of drink that is twice the standard amount. Compare double(3). **12** *c.n* person who acts instead of s.o else in a play or film when there is s.t dangerous or needing special skill to do. **13** *c.n* call in bridge[2] that s.o will lose (or win) two times the score if he/she loses (or wins) the tricks(7) he/she said he/she can win. **at/on the double** (**a**) immediately: *Come here on the double.* (**b**) (*military*) at twice the usual marching speed: *The soldiers came/marched at the double.*
▷ *v* **14** *tr/intr.v* (cause (s.t) to) become twice as large or much: *Prices have doubled. I can double my salary if I join the police force.* **15** *intr.v* (usu — as s.o/s.t) have two uses, jobs etc (the other being s.t): *This chair doubles as a bed when we*

have visitors. He doubles in the play (as a servant and a visitor). **16** *tr/intr.v* (usu — (s.o/s.t) over/ up) (cause (s.o/s.t) to) fold or bend: *She doubled her arms across her chest. He's doubled over/up with pain.* **17** *tr/intr.v* call a double(13) to (s.o).

double as s.o/s.t ⇨ double(15). **double back** return to or towards the place one has come from: *We doubled back over the fields.* **Double for s.o** act as a double(12) for another actor. **double or quits/nothing** (said as a bet(1) when one has won all the money so far) *You must pay double what I have won from you if you lose or you do not need to pay me anything if you win.* **double (s.o/s.t) over/up** ⇨ double(16). **double time** ⇨ time(*n*).

¡double 'agent *c.n* spy(1) who works for both sides.

¡double 'bass *c.n* largest stringed musical instrument with the deepest sound.

¡double 'bed *c.n* large bed for two people. ⇨ double(4). Compare twin bed.

¡double-'breasted *c.n* (of a jacket(1) or coat) having two rows of buttons with the front parts overlapping(2). Compare single-breasted.

¡double 'check *intr.v* check information etc again.

¡double 'chin *c.n* chin with a fold of skin under it.

¡double 'cream *u.n* thick cream(3) that can be whipped(9) to become semi-solid.

¡double-'cross *tr.v* (*informal*) deceive (two different people or groups by pretending to each that one supports their side).

¡double-'crosser *c.n* (*informal*) person who double-crosses (s.o).

¡double 'decker *c.n* (**'double-,decker** when *attrib*) **1** with stairs: *a double-decker bus.* **2** with two layers: *a double-decker sandwich.*

¡double 'Dutch *u.n* talk that seems to have no meaning or that cannot be understood.

double entendre /¡duːbl ɑːnˈtɑːndrə/ *c.n* (*French*) statement with two possible meanings.

¡double 'figures *pl.n* (often *in*(to) —) numbers between 10 and 99: *Your debts were well into double figures.*

¡double 'first *c.n* (UK) bachelor's degree with first-class honours in two subjects.

¡double 'glazing *u.n* system with two pieces of glass in a window to keep out cold and noise.

¡double 'Gloucester /-ˈɡlɒstə/ *u.n* kind of mild cheese of an orange colour.

¡double 'negative *c.n* statement etc using two negatives, e.g *'I don't never want to see you again'.*

¡double-'parked *adj* with cars parked in two rows by the side of the road.

¡double-'quick *adj/adv* very quick(ly).

doubles *pl.n* game of tennis etc with two players on each side. **mixed doubles** with a man and woman on each side. Compare singles(1).

¡double 'spacing *u.n* ⇨ spacing (⇨ space).

¡double 'take *sing.n* (often *do a* —) (*informal*) slightly delayed and sudden response(2) to s.t said, esp for an amusing effect.

'double-,talk *u.n* talk that is impossible to understand because it is a mixture of sense and nonsense.

'doubly *adv* (esp) twice as strongly or much;

very: *Make doubly sure you are right before you accuse him.*

doublet /ˈdʌblɪt/ *c.n* (usu — *and hose*) short tight jacket(1) worn by men about 400 years ago.

doubt /daʊt/ *c/u.n* **1** (example of the) feeling that one is not certain: *I have strong doubts about his honesty.* **be in doubt** be uncertain: *His ability is not in doubt but will he work hard?* **beyond a shadow of a doubt** without any doubt(1) at all. **give s.o the benefit of the doubt** ⇨ benefit(*n*). **have a/no doubt, (no) doubts, about s.o/s.t** have a/no reason to be uncertain about s.o/s.t: *I have no doubts about your honesty.* **no doubt** probably: *No doubt you'll phone me when you get there. She'll be back, no doubt.* **room for doubt** ⇨ room(*n*). **without doubt** certainly: *I'll be there by 6 o'clock without doubt.*

▷ *tr/intr.v* **2** (often — *if/whether . . .; — that . . .*) not feel certain about (a fact, that something exists or happened etc): *I have never doubted the existence of God. I doubt if/whether you'll believe what I'm going to say. Many doubted that you would tell her the truth.*

'doubter *c.n* person who doubts(2), esp the existence of God.

'doubtful *adj* **1** (*pred*) (often — *about s.o/s.t*) feeling doubt(1) (about s.o/s.t): *I'm doubtful about the weather; I think it will rain.* **2** causing doubt(1): *a doubtful story/excuse* ⇨ indubitable, undoubted. **3** (*attrib*) causing suspicion; looking dishonest: *There's a doubtful person near the school gates.* ⇨ dubious. **'doubtfully** *adv.* **'doubtfulness** *u.n.*

'doubtless *adv* (*formal*) very probably: *Doubtless you'll agree with me if I show you the weapon.*

douche /duːʃ/ *c.n* **1** water poured or forced out onto (part of) the body to clean it. **2** (*medical*) instrument like a large syringe(1) used to force water into/onto part of s.o.

▷ *tr/intr.v* **3** (*medical*) use a douche(2) (on (s.o/ s.t)).

dough /dəʊ/ *u.n* **1** flour, fat, eggs etc mixed together into a mass but not yet cooked. **2** (*slang*) money: *I haven't the dough for another holiday.*

'dough,nut *c.n* small kind of cake, usu with a hole in the middle, which is fried and rolled in sugar: *a jam doughnut.*

'doughy *adj* (*-ier, -iest*) soft and semi-solid.

doughty /ˈdaʊtɪ/ *adj* (*-ier, -iest*) (*formal*) determined and strong: *doughty officers in the army.* **'doughtily** *adv.* **'doughtiness** *u.n.*

dour /dʊə/ *adj* severe and never showing pleasure: *a dour old man.* **'dourly** *adv.* **'dourness** *u.n.*

douse /daʊs/ *tr.v* (also **dowse**) cause (oneself/ s.o/s.t) to be put into water etc; put water on (s.t): *I doused myself (or my clothes) with water before I ran through the fire. What can I use to douse the fire?*

dove¹ /dʌv/ *c.n* **1** one of various kinds of pigeon. **2** (*informal*) person who is not in favour of war or dangerous weapons. Compare hawk(2).

dovecote /ˈdʌvkɒt/ *c.n* (also **'dovecot**) building with many small compartments inside for pigeons.

'dove,tail *c.n* **1** (also *attrib*) (*technical*) joint for wood shaped like a wedge(1) that fits closely into another.

▷ *tr/intr.v* **2** (*technical*) join (wood etc) using dovetail(1) joints. **3** (*fig*) arrange (things) so that one fits exactly with another according to time, ideas etc: *Their arrangements dovetail beautifully. I hope you can dovetail your plans to fit mine.*

dove² /dəʊv/ US *p.t/p.p* of dive.

dowager /ˈdaʊədʒə/ *c.n* **1** (also *attrib*) widow of a peer'(1): *the dowager* duchess. **2** rich old lady who looks important.

dowdy /ˈdaʊdɪ/ *adj* (*-ier, -iest*) (*derog*) **1** (of a woman's or girl's clothing) dull, old-fashioned and not attractive. **2** (usu of a woman/girl) wearing dowdy(1) clothes.

'**dowdily** *adv*. '**dowdiness** *u.n*.

down¹ /daʊn/ *attrib.adj* **1** going, taking its contents, towards a lower position or level: *the down stripes in a pattern*; *a down pipe.*

▷ *adv* **2** from a higher to a lower position: *Sharon dived down into the water. He got out of the window, climbed down and ran across the garden. Has Philip come down* (= downstairs) *yet?* Opposite up(1). Compare down(7). **3** from a (more) vertical position to a (more) horizontal one; on(to) or towards the ground: *I lay down on the warm sand. The pole has fallen down. Put down that stick! Sit down! They've taken down their tents.* Compare up(2). **4** in or towards a position or direction that is lower: *I looked down from the top of the hill. The sun goes down in the west. We live two floors down.* Opposite up(4). **5** (and those) having a lower position or less authority(1): *Everyone came to the meeting from the managing director down.* **6** to or towards a place lower on a slope, nearer a river, the sea etc: *Let's walk down to the café by the sea.* Compare along(1), down'(18), up(6). **7** from a place considered more active or important to one considered less active or important: *I've just come down from London. They've gone down to the country* (i.e from a city) *for the weekend.* Compare up(7). **8** in or towards the south: *Jean lives down south. I live down in Devon.* Compare up(8). **9** in or towards a place or position nearer the mouth of a river: *We sailed down to the sea. This is Westminster Bridge and London Bridge is about a mile further down.* Opposite up(9). Compare down'(19). **10** from a higher rank, grade etc to a lower one: *Charles has been moved down to the third group.* Opposite up(10). **11** lower in amount, degree etc: *The temperature/cost/price/fare has been put down. The level is down by nearly a metre.* Opposite up(11). **12** from an earlier time to a later one: *This* tradition(3) *has come down* (or *has been handed down*) *from our* ancestors. **13** so as to be fastened, closed, covered etc: *I nailed down the lid. Screw it down tightly.* Compare up(14). **14** in written form: *Write/Put it down in your book. It's down* (or *I have it down*) *already.* **15** worse than a competitor or previous performance: *We were a goal down at half time. We are £100 down on last week's profits.* Opposite up(19). For verb + 'down', e.g get down, put s.o down, take s.t down, ⇒ the verb. **it is down to s.o** (**to do s.t**) (*informal*) s.o is the last possibility, hope, to get s.t done: *It's down to you to find out what happened.* Compare up to s.o (⇒ up(*adv*)). **down to the ground** ⇒

ground(*n*). **down under** (in) Australia or New Zealand. **down with s.o/s.t** (imperative) I do not support, am not in favour of, (s.o/s.t): *Down with school* uniform(2)! Opposite up with s.t. **up and down** ⇒ up(*adv*). **upside down** ⇒ up.

▷ *sing.n* **16** (*informal*) sad, disappointed, mood'(1): *She's been on a down ever since he left.* **be**, **have a**, **down on s.o** (*informal*) not like s.o, wish s.o bad fortune etc. **ups and downs** ⇒ up(20).

▷ *prep* **17** at or to a lower position or level in, on, (s.o/s.t): *He climbed down the ladder.* Opposite up(21). Compare down'(2). **18** along (a road, river etc): *We drove down the street.* Compare down'(6), up(22). **19** at or towards a place nearer the mouth of (a river): *He sailed down the river until he reached the sea.* Opposite up(23). Compare down'(9). **down river** ⇒ river(*n*).

▷ *tr.v* **20** hit, knock, (s.o) so that he/she falls: *I downed him with one blow.* **21** (*informal*) drink(s.t) very quickly or with one swallow: *We downed our coffees and ran to the bus stop.* **down tools** ⇒ tool(*n*).

down-and-'out *adj* **1** (*informal*) extremely poor and without work or a home: *a down-and-out old man.*

▷ *c.n* (*pl -s*) **2** (*informal*) person who is down-and-out.

down-at-'heel *adj* (*informal*) poor, dirty, in need of repair etc: *The house was very down-at-heel when we bought it. Old Bill is looking very down-at-heel.*

'**down,cast** *adj* **1** (of s.o's eyes) looking down(4). **2** (of a person) sad, disappointed.

'**downer** *c.n* (*slang*) drug(2) used to make s.o less excited, anxious etc. Compare upper(5).

'**down,fall** *c.n* **1** sudden heavy fall of snow or rain. **2** sudden failure or ruin (of a person, company etc): *Your bad temper will be* (= cause) *your downfall.*

down'grade *tr.v* put (a person, job etc) on a lower level of importance, authority(1), value etc. ⇒ upgrade.

down'hearted *adj* sad, disappointed, esp because of (thoughts of) failure: *She was so downhearted when she didn't get the job.*

down'hill *attrib.adj* **1** towards a lower level: *Our profits are on a downhill path.* ⇒ uphill.

▷ *adv* **2** towards a lower level: *I prefer to cycle downhill.* **go downhill** (*fig*) (of a person, company etc) become worse: *His behaviour has gone downhill since he joined that school.*

'**down 'payment** *c.n* deposit(3) paid for s.t, e.g a house, car, the rest of the money for which has to be paid later.

'**down,pour** *c.n* sudden and heavy fall of rain.

'**down,right** *attrib.adj/adv* complete(ly); extreme(ly): *You're a downright liar. You were downright rude.*

Downs *def.n* area of low chalk hills in south-east England.

'**down'stage** *adj/adv* at or towards the front of a stage. Opposite upstage(1).

'**down,stairs** *adj* **1** who/that is, works etc downstairs(2): *a downstairs* cleaner(1)/*bathroom.* Opposite upstairs(1).

▷ /ˌdaʊnˈsteəz/ *adv* **2** to a lower floor: *The children came downstairs.* Opposite upstairs(2).

▷ *c/def.n* **3** floor at ground level or one that is lower. Compare upstairs(3).

,down'stream *adj/adv* (that is) towards or nearer the mouth of a river: *swim downstream.* Opposite upstream.

,down-to-'earth *adj* (*informal*) sensible; interested in what it is possible to do and not in ideals etc: *a down-to-earth way of dealing with difficulties.*

'down,town *attrib.adj* **1** (*informal*) (area) with large shops, offices etc: *We own a restaurant in the downtown area of London.*
▷ *adv* **2** /,daʊn'taʊn/ in, to, the most active, important area of a city: *We live downtown. Let's eat downtown.*

'down-,trodden *adj* (*fig*) treated badly by others: *I feel so downtrodden when my boss shouts at me.*

'downward *adj* going down(4): *a downward slope.* Opposite upward.

'downwards *adv* (US **downward**) towards a lower position or level: *The profits are moving downwards.* Opposite upwards.

,down'wind *adj/adv* in the opposite direction to the one from which the wind is blowing: *sail downwind. Opposite* upwind.

down² /daʊn/ *u.n* (also *attrib*) soft feathers as on a young bird, used to fill cushions etc.

'downy *adj* (-ier, -iest) **1** covered with down². **2** very soft: *cloth with a downy feel.*

Downs ⇒ down¹.

dowry /'daʊərɪ/ *c.n* (*pl* -ies) money, things etc, given by a woman or her family to the man she marries.

dowse /daʊs/ *tr.v* ⇒ douse.

doz *written abbr* dozen.

doze /dəʊz/ *c.n* **1** short sleep, e.g in a chair.
▷ *intr.v* **2** sleep for a short time: *dozing in the sun.*
doze off fall asleep, e.g while reading, watching television.

'dozer *c.n* person who dozes(2).

'dozily *adv* in a dozy way.

'doziness *u.n* fact or state of being dozy.

'dozy *adj* (-ier, -iest) **1** tired; sleepy. **2** sleepy because of drugs(1), a knock on the head etc. **3** (*derog*) stupid.

dozen /'dʌzn/ *det/c.n* (*pl* dozen except in phrases(1) as shown) (*written abbr* doz, dz) 12; group containing twelve: *Can I have a dozen eggs, please? I need two dozen more.* **by the dozen** in sets of a dozen: *sell eggs by the dozen.* **dozens** (of s.o/s.t) many: *Dozens (of us) refused to go. I have been there dozens of times.* **half-a-dozen** six. **in dozens** in groups of twelve: *packed in dozens.* **talk nineteen to the dozen** ⇒ nineteen.

D Phil /,diː 'fɪl/ *abbr* Doctor(2) of Philosophy.

dpt *written abbr* department.

dr *written abbr* **1** debit. **2** dram.

Dr *written abbr* Doctor.

drab /dræb/ *adj* **1** dull to look at: *drab colours.* **2** boring; not interesting: *a drab evening with one's neighbours.*

'drably *adv.* **'drabness** *u.n.*

drabs /dræbz/ *pl.n* **in dribs and drabs** ⇒ drib.

draconian /dreɪ'kəʊnɪən/ *adj* (*formal*) very harsh(1): *draconian rules.*

draft /drɑːft/ *n* **1** *c.n* rough drawing; rough plan (for a speech, piece of writing etc). **2** *c.n =* bankdraft. **3** *c.n* (*military*) group of soldiers (to be) for a special duty. **4** *def.n* (esp US) conscription. **5** *c/u.n* (US) draught. **in draft (form)** in the form of a rough plan: *My book is only in draft at the moment.*
▷ *tr.v* **6** produce a draft(1) of (s.t): *Please draft a letter to the lawyers.* **7** (*military*) choose (soldiers) for a draft(3): *You've been drafted to work in the kitchens.* **8** (esp US) take (s.o) into military service; conscript(2) (s.o).

'draftsman *c.n* (US) draughtsman.

'drafty *adj* (US) draughty.

drag /dræg/ *n* **1** *c/u.n* act or state of pulling s.t heavy or with difficulty. **2** *c/u.n* thing that stops s.t moving or progressing easily: *This mud causes a drag on the wheels. The* design(3) *of the aircraft reduces drag.* **3** *c.n* (*slang*) act of breathing in air from a cigarette. **4** *sing.n* (*slang*) annoying or boring person, activity, event etc: *Ironing sheets is a drag.* **5** *u.n* (also *attrib*) (*slang*) (esp in —) (of a man or boy) act of wearing women's clothes: *He appeared in drag as the* fairy(2) *queen in the play. He's a well known drag artist* (performs on the stage wearing women's clothes).
▷ *v* (-gg-) **6** pull (s.o/s.t) that is heavy or difficult to move: *He dragged the chain through the mud. I tried to drag her out of the water. I had to drag the box because I couldn't lift it.* **7** *tr/intr.v* (cause (s.t) to) move along the floor or through s.t: *Sheep often drag their tails through bushes. Your belt has been dragged along behind you.* **8** *tr.v* search (a river, lake etc) by pulling a net or line through the water: *The police dragged the river looking for the missing girl.* **9** *reflx.v* move (oneself) (away, out, to a place etc) with difficulty: *I had to drag myself out of bed two hours later. I felt ill but I dragged myself to work.* **10** *tr.v* (*fig*) take (s.o who does not want to go) with one (to an event, place etc): *My parents had to drag me to the dentist when I was a child.* **11** *intr.v* (often — on) (*fig*) (of an event, period of time etc) seem to happen or pass slowly because one is bored, has no interest in what is happening etc: *Time dragged until we met again. The lecture dragged on and on.*

cannot, could not, drag oneself away cannot, could not, make oneself go away from an exciting or interesting event, place etc.

drag s.o down make s.o feel sad, lose hope etc.

drag one's feet ⇒ foot(n).

drag s.o/s.t in(to s.t) mention s.o, a name, subject etc without any obvious reason or right: *Why drag my sister into the conversation?*

drag s.o's name in the mud try to destroy s.o's good reputation.

drag s.t out make a story, report etc long(er) in order to waste time. **drag s.t out of s.o** make s.o tell s.t that he/she did not want to.

drag s.t up (*informal*) mention s.t unpleasant that others did not want mentioned: *Do you have to drag up that old story about the quarrel again?*

dragon /'drægən/ *c.n* **1** (in stories) animal that is like a very large lizard with wings and that breathes out fire. **2** (*derog; informal*) bad-tempered, fierce, person: *My boss is a dragon.*

dragonfly /'drægən,flaɪ/ *c.n* (*pl* -ies) kind of insect with a long body and two pairs of long wings.

dragoon /drə'guːn/ *n* (*old use*) **1** *c.n* heavily armed soldier on a horse. **2** *def.pl.n* (often with capital **D**) one of the branches of the army that used to ride horses: *The Royal Dragoons.*

▷ *tr.v* **3** (often — *s.o into doing s.t*) force (s.o) to do s.t, e.g by using threats: *Peter was dragooned into helping us by his father.*

drain /dreɪn/ *c.n* **1** pipe, covered place in the road etc, that carries away water, dirty liquid etc. **2** (usu *a — on s.t*) thing that takes supplies, energy(1) etc away (from s.t): *Working so hard has been a constant drain on his health/strength.* **3** (*medical*) device put into a wound etc to take away unwanted liquid, e.g pus. **go down the drain** (*fig*) be foolishly wasted: *All his money went down the drain when he bought that old house.* **brain drain** ⇒ brain(*n*). **laugh like a drain** (*informal*) laugh loudly in a bad-mannered way.

▷ *v* **4** *tr/intr.v* (cause (water etc) to) flow (away from or into s.o): *The rainwater drains into this pipe.* **5** *tr/intr.v* cause, allow, water etc to flow away from (s.t): *Shall I drain the beans? Leave the plates to drain by the sink.* ⇒ draining-board. **6** *tr.v* make water leave (land) using channels(1), rivers, pipes etc: *This whole area will need draining before we can plant seeds.* **7** *intr.v* leave or disappear slowly: *The blood drained from his face. My energy(1) drained as I climbed up the mountain.* **8** *tr.v* (*formal*) drink all the contents of (s.t): *She drained her cup and then asked for more.* **9** *tr.v* (*fig*) use all of (s.t): *The work on the house has drained our energy(1)/health/savings.*

drainage /ˈdreɪnɪdʒ/ *u.n* (also *attrib*) fact, process or system of carrying away water etc: *a drainage system.*

ˈdrainer *c.n* (*informal*) draining-board.

ˈdraining-ˌboard *c.n* flat area built on the side of a sink to drain(5) plates, pots etc that have been washed.

ˈdrainˌpipe *c.n* pipe on a building for carrying away rainwater.

drake /dreɪk/ *c.n* male duck.

dram /dræm/ *c.n* (written *abbr* dr) measurement of weight: *1 dram equals 0.18 grams. 16 drams equal 1 ounce*(1).

drama /ˈdrɑːmə/ *n* (also *attrib*) **1** *c.n* (*formal*) play to be performed on a stage, television etc. **2** *u.n* (activity of writing) plays in general: *I'm studying drama* (or *am a drama student*). **3** *c/u.n* (example of) exciting, emotional(1) or very sad events: *I don't want too much drama in my life. That is one of life's many dramas. Don't make a drama out of such a small problem.*

dramatic /drəˈmætɪk/ *adj* **1** (*attrib*) of or referring to drama(2): *a dramatic performance.* **2** that is easy to notice, esp because so great: *a dramatic improvement; a dramatic fall in prices.* **3** very showy or emotional(2): *She made a dramatic exit*(2). **4** (*derog*) (of a person) showing too much emotion(2): *Don't be so dramatic — the stone didn't even touch you.*

draˈmatically *adv.*

draˈmatics *u/pl.n* **1** art of performing or producing plays: amateur(1) *dramatics.* **2** behaviour that is too emotional(2).

dramatis personae /ˌdræmətɪs pəˈsəʊnaɪ/ *pl.n* (*Latin*) list of the characters in a play (and the actors who perform them).

dramatist /ˈdræmətɪst/ *c.n* person who writes plays.

dramatization, -isation /ˌdræmətaɪˈzeɪʃən/ *n* **1** *c.n* act of changing a story etc into a play. **2** *u.n* act or fact of dramatizing(2) s.t.

ˈdramaˌtize, -ise *v* **1** *tr.v* change (a story etc) into a play. **2** *tr/intr.v* deal with, express etc s.t in a dramatic(4) way: *Don't dramatize your difficulties — they are bad enough already!*

drank /dræŋk/ *p.t* of drink.

drape /dreɪp/ *tr.v* **1** hang or spread (clothing, cloth, oneself) (on furniture etc): *She draped her coat on the back of the chair. He was draped over the piano fast asleep. The table was draped with a red cloth.* **2** (often — *s.o/s.t in/with s.t*) cover (s.o/s.t) (with folds of cloth etc): *The statue is still draped in the national flag. The whole room was draped with gold cloth.*

ˈdraper *c.n* (*old use*) **1** person who sells cloth, clothes. **2** (also **ˈdraper's**) shop of a draper(1).

ˈdrapery *n* (*pl -ies*) (*old use*) **1** *c.n* = draper(2). **2** *u.n* cloth.

drapes *pl.n* (US) curtains.

drastic /ˈdræstɪk/ *adj* serious and extreme; severe; sudden and strong: *We must make drastic changes if we hope to win.*

ˈdrastically *adv.*

draught /drɑːft/ *n* (US **draft**) **1** *c.n* (usu unpleasant) movement of air in a room etc: *Close the window; I can feel a draught.* **2** *c.n* amount of a drink taken without stopping: *a draught of medicine; a long draught of beer.* **3** *u.n* (also *attrib*) beer, wine etc kept in large barrels etc, not in bottles: *draught beer.* **4** *c.n* one of the 12 pieces used by each player in a game of draughts. **5** *u.n* (*technical*) amount of water needed to float a ship. **on draught** in a barrel etc, not in bottles: *beer on draught.* Compare draught(3).

ˈdraughtˌboard *c.n* square board for playing draughts on.

ˈdraughtiness *u.n* (US **ˈdraftiness**) fact or state of being draughty.

draughts *u.n* (US **ˈcheckers**) game played on a board by two players using 12 draughts(4) each.

ˈdraughtsman *c.n* (*pl -men*) (US **ˈdraftsman**) **1** person who draws pictures, plans etc, or whose job it is to do these things, e.g for building s.t. **2** = draught(4).

ˈdraughty *adj* (*-ier, -iest*) (US **ˈdrafty**) (of a room etc) having or causing draughts(1).

draw /drɔː/ *c.n* **1** act of drawing(5) s.t: *a quick draw with a pencil.* **2** (fact of a) game or competition ending with both sides having the same score: *The football match was a* (or *ended in a*) *draw.* **3** act of choosing winners(1) of prizes, e.g by taking tickets out of a hat etc. **4** thing that attracts people's attention or interest: *Offering two tickets for the price of one was a real draw.* **be quick on the draw** (*fig*) act, understand s.t, respond(1) to s.t etc, quickly: *You'll have to be quick on the draw and buy the car as soon as it arrives.*

▷ *v* (*p.t* drew /druː/, *p.p* drawn /drɔːn/) **5** *tr/intr.v* produce (a picture, map etc) using a pen, pencil etc: *I can't draw* (*people*). *Don't draw on walls.* **6** *tr.v* cause (s.o/s.t) to move (in the direction mentioned) by pulling: *He drew the cupboard away from the wall. She drew the child towards her.* **7** *tr.v* open or close (curtains, a blind² etc) by pulling. **8** *tr.v* take out (s.t) (as if) from a container: *He drew his hands out of his pockets. She drew a card from the pack. A dentist draws teeth. He drew his gun and shot the thief.* **9** *intr.v* (of a person, event etc) come or move: *A crowd*

drew near/round as the speaker came in. Evening is drawing near. ⇒ draw away, draw in, draw out, draw up. **10** *tr/intr.v* take part in a game, competition etc at the end of which both sides have the same score: *Liverpool and Chelsea drew, 2-2.* Compare draw(2). **11** *tr.v* (often — *s.t out*) take out (money) from a bank, savings account etc. ⇒ overdrawn. **12** *tr.v* take (a regular sum of money) from a special account: *draw one's salary.* **13** *tr.v* gain or earn (s.t): *an account that draws interest.* **14** *tr.v* attract (a crowd, attention etc): *She drew the respect of us all.* Compare draw(4). **15** *tr.v* (think about s.t and then) produce or describe (the result): *draw a comparison between the eye and a camera*; *draw a* conclusion(2) *from the* evidence(1). **16** *intr.v* (of a chimney etc) take up air, smoke etc (esp in the way mentioned): *This chimney draws well.* **17** *tr/intr.v* (often — *for s.t*) choose (tickets etc) in a draw(3) (to see who will win): *Let's draw for it.* **18** *tr.v* cause (blood, pus etc) to flow.
draw (s.o/s.t) apart (cause two or more people, things to) separate.
draw s.o aside take s.o a short distance away, esp to speak to her/him in private.
draw (s.t) away (from s.t) (of a driver) move (a vehicle) away (from the kerb etc).
draw (s.o/s.t) back (from s.o/s.t) (cause s.o/s.t to) move away (from s.o/s.t): *The crowd drew back from the flames.*
draw a blank ⇒ blank.
draw the line at s.t ⇒ line¹ (*n*).
draw lots ⇒ lots¹.
draw in (**a**) (of a vehicle) (come near and) stop by the side of the road: *Please draw in, I want to check the wheels.* (**b**) (of evening, night) arrive because darkness is increasing.
draw on (*literary*) = draw in(b). **draw s.t on** pull clothing on: *He drew on a jumper.* **draw on s.t (to do s.t)** use (information, experience etc) (to do s.t): *She had to draw on all her experience in order to win the game.*
draw out (of a vehicle) leave the side of a road; leave a small road and enter a larger one etc. **draw s.o out** help s.o to talk more, show pleasure etc. **draw s.t out** (**a**) ⇒ draw(11). (**b**) make an event etc longer than necessary: *Her speech was drawn out by her many stops to drink water.* ⇒ long-drawn-out (⇒ long¹).
draw up (of a vehicle) (come near and) stop: *The bus drew up behind us at the traffic lights.* **draw oneself up** stand up straight: *John drew himself up to his full height.* **draw s.t up** (**a**) put together a list, line of people, things: *Let's draw up a list of those people we shall invite. The children were drawn up into rows.* (**b**) put together a contract(1) etc.
'draw,back *c.n* thing that hinders, makes success less likely etc: *Your plan has several drawbacks.*
'draw,bridge *c.n* bridge (e.g over a canal or at the entrance to a castle) that can be pulled up to let boats pass or to stop people coming in.
drawer¹ /'drɔːə/ *c.n* person who draws(5).
drawer² /drɔː/ *c.n* part of a piece of furniture, like a box with a handle, that moves in and out. ⇒ chest of drawers.
'drawing *n* **1** *u.n* (also *attrib*) art or practice of making pictures, maps etc using a

pen, pencil etc. **2** *c.n* picture made by drawing(5).
'drawing ,board *c.n* flat board for drawing(5) plans etc on. **go back to the drawing board** (*fig*) begin to plan s.t again and in a new way.
'drawing-,pin *c.n* pin with a flat head for fastening paper etc on a wooden, cork(1) etc surface.
'drawing-,room *c.n* (becoming *old use*) living-room.
drawn *adj* **1** (of curtains, blinds² etc) pulled together or down. **2** (of a game, competition) with both sides having the same score. **3** (of a person) looking tired and ill.
▷ *v* **4** *p.p* of draw.
'draw,string *c.n* long piece of string etc put through holes in a bag, jacket(1) etc and pulled to close it.
drawers /drɔːz/ *pl.n* (*old use*) panties.
dread /dred/ *sing/u.n* **1** extreme fear: *Kate has a dread of spiders. I was filled with dread as I listened to the* footsteps. *We lived in dread of being discovered.*
▷ *tr.v* **2** fear (s.t) extremely: *I dreaded the thought of being killed.*
'dreadful *adj* **1** extremely bad: *dreadful behaviour/weather*; *a dreadful piece of writing.* **2** causing great suffering: *a dreadful accident/war.*
'dreadfully *adv* **1** very badly: *behave dreadfully.* **2** (*informal*) very: *I'm dreadfully sorry.*
dream /driːm/ *n* **1** *c.n* pictures in one's mind and thoughts, usu in the form of a story which one sees during sleep. ⇒ nightmare(1). **2** *sing.n* thing considered to be very good or beautiful: *Her new car is a dream.* **3** *c.n* strong ambition: *Janet's dream is to be a world* champion(3). **in a dream** completely lost in one's own thoughts (and so not aware(1) of where one is, what one is doing): *He went about all day in a dream thinking about the money he had won.* ⇒ daydream.
▷ *v* (*p.t,p.p* dreamed, dreamt /dremt/) **4** *tr/intr.v* (often — *of s.o/s.t*; — *that* . . .) experience a dream(1) or dreams (about s.t): *Do you often dream? I dreamt (that) I was a dancer. He dreamt of her all night.* **5** *intr.v* (usu in continuous tenses²) have ideas, thoughts etc that are not likely or practical: *He's always dreaming and never succeeds in anything.* **6** *intr.v* = daydream(2). **dream s.t up** invent (an excuse, a way of solving a problem etc). **would not dream of (doing) s.t** refuse to consider even the possibility of doing s.t bad, unpleasant, unwanted etc.
'dreamer *c.n* **1** person who dreams(4–6). **2** person who has unlikely dreams(3): *Don't just be a dreamer — do something.*
'dreamily *adv* in a dreamy way.
'dreaming *u.n* act or fact of having dreams(1).
'dream,land *unique n* ideal world in one's mind.
'dreamless *attrib.adj* (deep and) without dreams(1): *a dreamless sleep.*
'dream,like *adj* as if dreaming(4–6).
'dreamy *adj* (*-ier, -iest*) **1** (as if) having just woken up: *a dreamy smile.* **2** not likely or practical: *dreamy ideas/ambitions.*
dreary /'drɪərɪ/ *adj* very dull: *dreary weather/ clothes/people.*
'drearily *adv*. **'dreariness** *u.n*.
dredge /dredʒ/ *c.n* **1** mechanical device for

dredging(3) a river etc. **2** device with small holes, used for dredging(4) food.
▷ *tr/intr.v* **3** take away ((dirty) substances) from the bottom of a river, canal etc by dragging or sucking it up. **4** put or sprinkle(2) flour, sugar etc on (cakes, pies etc) using a device like a tin with holes in the lid. **dredge s.t up** (*fig*; *informal*) make oneself remember (a name, address etc) from a long time ago.
'dredger *c.n* boat with a dredge(1) fitted on it.
dregs /dregz/ *def.pl.n* **1** small bits of unwanted material that settle at the bottom of tea, wine etc in a bottle, pot, glass etc. **2** (usu the — of society) (*derog*; *slang*) worst or least useful people.
drench /drentʃ/ *tr.v* (often — *s.o/s.t with s.t*) make (s.o/s.t) very wet (by pouring s.t on her/him/it): *We were drenched in the storm.* ⇒ sun-drenched.
dress /dres/ *attrib.adj* **1** of, referring to, for, dresses(3): *a dress designer; a dress shop.* **2** suitable for formal occasions: *a dress shirt.*
▷ *n* **3** *c.n* piece of clothing for a woman or girl that covers the body from the shoulders to the knees or ankles. **4** *u.n* clothing (of the kind mentioned): *informal/formal dress.*
▷ *v* **5** *tr/intr.v* put clothing on (s.o): *Have you dressed the baby? Dress quickly — you're late!* ⇒ dress (s.o) in s.t, dress (s.o) up (in s.t). Opposite undress(*v*). **6** *intr.v* (often — *up*) *for dinner, meals* etc) put on formal clothes (for a particular occasion). ⇒ evening-dress(2), overdress. **7** *tr.v* put ointment, a bandage etc on (a wound or injury). **8** *tr.v* put a sauce etc on (a salad(1) etc). ⇒ dressing(1). **9** *tr.v* decorate (food) with colourful pieces of food: *dress sandwiches with cress.* **10** *tr.v* arrange items(1) for sale in (a shop window, display(1) in a shop etc). **dress s.o down** scold s.o. ⇒ dressing-down. **dress (s.o) in s.t** put clothes of the kind, colour etc mentioned on (s.o): *She was dressed in black. I always dress the baby in pure cotton.* **dressed to kill** (*fig*; *informal*) in very beautiful clothes that will attract attention, particularly from the opposite sex. **dress (s.o) up (in s.t)** (a) = dress(6). (b) = dress (s.o) in s.t. (c) put very formal, expensive, attractive, amusing etc clothes of the kind, colour etc mentioned on (s.o): *The children got dressed up in their parent's clothes.* **dress s.t up** (*informal*) make an excuse, account of an event etc seem more acceptable, interesting etc by adding (often untrue) details.
'dress ˌcircle *c/def.n* area of seats above the ground floor of a theatre etc.
'dresser *c.n* **1** person who dresses(5) in the way mentioned: *a good dresser.* **2** (also **'kitchen ˌdresser**) piece of furniture with drawers and shelves, for storing plates, knives, forks etc.
'dressing *n* **1** *c/u.n* = salad dressing. **2** *c.n* bandage etc for a wound or injury. **3** *c.n* (also **'top ˌdressing**) (often — *of s.t*) layer(1) (of s.t that provides goodness or protects) put on soil etc: *a (top) dressing of* manure(1).
ˌdressing-'down *sing.n* (usu *give s.o a —*) (*informal*) scolding.
'dressing-ˌgown *c.n* piece of clothing like a coat or dress that opens all the way down the front and is worn over pyjamas usu before going to bed or after getting up.
'dressing ˌtable *c.n* piece of furniture like a

table with a mirror fixed to it, used in a bedroom for doing one's hair, putting on make-up(1) etc.
'dressˌmaker *c.n* person who makes clothes for women and children.
'dress reˌhearsal *c.n* final and complete rehearsal of a play etc for which the actors wear their costumes.
dressage /'dresɑːʒ/ *u.n* (method of training a horse to perform) formal movements made in response to the rider's signals.
drew /druː/ *p.t* of draw.
dribble /'drɪbl/ *c/u.n* **1** very small stream of liquid, esp from the mouth: *a dribble (of water) from a tap.*
▷ *tr/intr.v* **2** allow a dribble(1) (of saliva etc) to fall, esp from the mouth: *Babies often dribble.* **3** move (a football, hockey ball etc) along the ground using one's feet, a stick etc.
'dribbler *c.n* person who dribbles(2,3).
'driblet *c.n* very small dribble(1).
dribs *pl.n* **in dribs and drabs** in very small amounts or numbers: *The customers came in dribs and drabs all day today.*
dried *p.t,p.p* of dry(*v*).
drier, driest ⇒ dry(*adj*).
drier *n* ⇒ dry.
drift /drɪft/ *n* **1** *c.n* (also **'snowˌdrift**) heap (of snow) made by the wind. **2** *def/u.n* (often the — of s.t) real or actual meaning or purpose (of s.o's statement): *I can't follow the drift of his argument. Do you get my drift?* **3** *def.n* (often the — of s.t) general direction in which an activity, group of people etc is progressing: *the drift (of society) towards war.*
▷ *v* **4** *tr/intr.v* (cause (s.t) to) blow or be blown in the direction mentioned: *The little boat drifted towards the rocks. The wind drifted the snow against the wall.* **5** *intr.v* (of a person) go from place to place, changing one's job and/or home often. **drift in (to s.w, to do s.t)** enter a town, building etc in a casual(2) way, without warning or without a purpose: *Look who has drifted in (to town)* (or *drifted in to see us*)!
'drifter *c.n* **1** person who drifts(5). **2** boat with a net for fishing near the surface of the sea.
'driftˌwood *u.n* pieces of broken branches, wooden beams etc that are carried onto beaches etc by the movement of the sea or rivers.
drill[1] /drɪl/ *c.n* **1** tool with a long piece that turns to make holes in s.t: *an electric drill; a dentist's drill.* **2** *u.n* (military) form of marching to orders as exercises for soldiers. **3** *u.n* (esp *know, explain* etc the —) (*informal*) usual or accepted method or routine(2) when doing s.t, e.g greeting people formally, making a speech etc: *Tell me the drill for addressing a* bishop(1).
▷ *v* **4** *tr/intr.v* use a drill(1) to make (a hole) in (s.t): *He drilled (a hole in) my tooth.* **5** *tr/intr.v* train (soldiers), be trained, using drill(2). **6** *tr.v* (often — *s.o in s.t*) show (s.o) the drill(3) (for a particular method, event etc).
drill[2] /drɪl/ *c.n* long channel(1) made in the ground for sowing seeds.
drily ⇒ dry.
drink /drɪŋk/ *n* **1** *c.n* liquid that can be taken into the mouth and swallowed: *cold/hot drinks.* **2** *c.n* act of drinking(5): *a drink of water/milk.* **3** *c/u.n* (glass etc of) alcoholic(1) liquid: *I need a drink. Too much drink is very bad for one's* liver(1).

▷ **def**.*n* **4** (*informal*) sea.

▷ *v* (*p.t* drank /dræŋk/, *p.p* drunk /drʌŋk/) **5** *tr/ intr.v* swallow (any drink(1)): *I drank a whole bottle of milk. Do you drink coffee at night? I never drink after 9 o'clock.* **6** *tr/intr.v* swallow drink(3): *You drink too much. I don't drink beer.* **drink s.t in** (*fig*) take in, feel, eagerly the excitement, beauty etc of an event, sight etc. **drink to s.o, s.t, s.o's health** state one's good wishes concerning s.o, s.t, s.o's health, and then drink(6). **drink s.o under the table** drink(6) with s.o until he/she cannot continue because he/she is too drunk(1). **drink (s.t) up** drink(5,6) what is in one's cup, glass etc: *Drink up your milk. Drink up, please, because we must close the bar.*

'drinkable *adj* fit for drinking(5,6): *This water/ wine is not drinkable.* Opposite undrinkable.

'drinker *c.n* person who drinks(6) (usu in the way mentioned): *a heavy drinker* (i.e who drinks(6) a lot and often).

'drinking ˌwater *u.n* water that is clean and fit for drinking(5).

drunk /drʌŋk/ *adj* **1** affected by having had too much drink(3): *You're drunk. A drunk man was lying in the road.* **drunk with s.t** (*fig*) very happy or excited because of success, power etc.

▷ *c.n* **2** person who is (often) drunk(1): *He's an old drunk.*

▷ *v* **3** *p.p* of drink.

drunkard /'drʌŋkəd/ *c.n* = drunk(2).

'drunken *attrib.adj* (caused by) being drunk(1): *a drunken sailor; be in a drunken sleep.*

'drunkenly *adv.* **'drunkenness** *u.n.*

drip /drɪp/ *c.n* **1** (noise made by) water falling (usu slowly) in small drops: *a drip from a tap.* **2** (*medical*) device for allowing a liquid to enter the body slowly through the skin. **3** (*derog; informal*) person with a weak character: *He's a real drip and always cries when he is hurt.*

▷ *tr/intr.v* **4** (often — *down*) (cause (a liquid) to) fall in drips(1): *The paint dripped (down) onto the floor.* **drip with s.t** produce, be covered with, drips(1) of the kind mentioned: *He was dripping with blood/sweat.*

ˌdrip-'dry *adj* **1** (usu *attrib*) (of clothing, sheets etc) not needing to be ironed if hung up carefully when drying: *drip-dry shirts.*

▷ *tr/intr.v* (-ies, -ied) **2** (allow (clothing etc) to) be hung up to dry and so not need to be ironed.

'dripping *u.n* **1** drips(1): *I could hear dripping next door.* **2** fat that falls from meat while it is being roasted.

ˌdripping-'wet *adj* very wet.

drive /draɪv/ *n* **1** *c.n* (esp *go for a* —) activity of travelling in a car, esp for pleasure: *We had a nice drive this afternoon. How was your drive to the airport?* **2** *c.n* (also **'drive,way**) way for cars from a road through a person's property to her/his house. **3** *c.n* (with capital **D** in names) small street: *I live at 10 King's Drive.* **4** *c/u.n* (also *attrib*) (*technical*) part of a machine or engine that produces movement: *a car with front/ rear¹(1) wheel drive; a drive belt in a machine.* **5** *c.n* strong forward movement with a bat²(1), stick etc in sports. **6** *u.n* enthusiasm, determination and energy(1): *Robert has a lot of drive and will be successful.* **7** *c.n* effort with drive(6): *He has begun a new drive to increase sales*

in Europe. It is a new kind of sales drive. **8** *u.n* natural interest in s.t that makes s.o act: *our sex drive; his drive to survive(1) imprisonment.* **9** *c.n* (often — *on* s.t) (*military*) strong attack (against the enemy, a place etc).

▷ *v* (*p.t* drove /drəʊv/, *p.p* driven /drɪvn/) **10** *tr/ intr.v* control the engine and movement of (a car etc) as it goes along: *Can you drive? I drove my father's car into a tree. He drove out of the gates.* Compare ride(3). **11** *tr.v* (often — *s.o* to s.t) take (s.o) in a car etc (to a place, event): *Who will drive me to the station? I was driven to the wedding in a big black car.* **12** *tr.v* cause (s.t, esp a ball in sport) to move quickly through the air by hitting it. **13** *tr.v* (often — *s.t in(to* s.t)) force (s.t) into s.t by hitting it: *He drove a nail into the wall.* **14** *tr.v* cause (s.t) to make (a hole etc): *Your bicycle has driven a hole in my car!* **15** *tr.v* (often passive) cause (a machine etc) to work: *This wheel drives that one. The machine is driven by electricity.* **16** *tr.v* encourage, urge, force, (s.o, animals) to do s.t: *The dog drove the sheep into a corner. What drove you to say that?* **be driving at s.t** (usu in questions or negative) be trying to explain or suggest s.t: *I don't know what you're driving at. What is he driving at?* **drive a hard bargain** ⇒ bargain. **drive s.t home (to s.o)** ⇒ home(*adv*). **drive off** (**a**) drive(10) away from s.w. (**b**) (in golf) hit the ball hard as the first stroke towards a hole. **drive s.o/s.t off** (try to) force s.o, an animal to go away. **drive on** continue driving(10): *Let's drive on to the next town.* **drive s.o/s.t on** encourage or force s.o, an animal to continue doing something: *Only the thought of failure drove her on.* **drive up** arrive at a place, position etc in a car etc: *He drove up and stopped opposite my house.*

'drive-ˌin *c.n* (also *attrib*) (esp US) outdoor cinema, restaurant etc for people sitting in their cars: *a drive-in cinema.*

'driver *c.n* person who drives(10): *a car driver. Who was the driver of the car?*

'drive,way *c.n* ⇒ drive(2).

'driving *u.n* (also *attrib*) act or fact of driving(10): *Driving while you are tired is dangerous. May I see your driving licence?*

'driving-ˌwheel *c.n* = steering-wheel.

drivel /drɪvl/ *u.n* **1** nonsense.

▷ *intr.v* (-ll-) **2** (often — *on* (*about* s.o/s.t)) talk nonsense (about s.t) (for a long time).

'driveller *c.n* (*derog*) person who drivels(2).

drizzle /drɪzl/ *u.n* **1** (period of) light rain.

▷ *intr.v* **2** (of rain) fall in light drops: *It's drizzling.*

'drizzly *adj* (-ier, -iest).

droll /drəʊl/ *adj* (*old use*) strange and amusing: *a droll sense of humour(1).*

'drolly *adv.* **'drollness** *u.n.*

dromedary /'drɒmədərɪ/ *c.n* (*pl* -ies) kind of camel with one hump.

drone /drəʊn/ *n* **1** *c.n* male bee. **2** *u.n* long deep sound: *the drone of distant traffic.* **3** *c.n* (*derog; informal*) lazy person who does not help.

▷ *intr.v* **4** (of a bee, aircraft, traffic etc) make a long deep sound. **drone on** (*fig*) (of a person) give a long, boring talk: *The speaker droned on and on and everyone fell asleep.*

drool /druːl/ *intr.v* **1** allow saliva etc to fall from the mouth; dribble(2). **2** (usu — *about/over* s.o/s.t) show one's excitement or pleasure when seeing s.o/s.t, thinking about future success etc: *We were drooling over the idea of a trip to China.*

droop /druːp/ *sing.n* **1** act or fact of drooping: *a droop of his shoulders as he heard he had failed.*
▷ *v* **2** *tr/intr.v* (cause (branches of a tree, one's arms etc) to) hang down. **3** *tr.v* drop (one's shoulders), esp when hearing bad or sad news or when very tired. **4** *intr.v* (of a person) become weak, e.g because very tired or sad.

drop /drɒp/ *n* (often — *s.t*) **1** *c.n* small round amount of a liquid: *drops of paint/rain/sweat.* **2** *sing.n* small amount: *There isn't a drop of milk in the house. Is there a drop left in that bottle?* **3** *c.n* thing shaped like a drop(1): *My favourite sweets are pear drops.* **4** act or example of s.t falling in amount, degree etc: *a drop in prices/temperature/speed.* **5** distance that s.o/ s.t falls: *a drop of 10 metres to the bottom.* **6** act of sending down (goods, soldiers) using a parachute(1). **a drop in the ocean** (*fig*) a thing that is very small, not at all important etc. (**do s.t**) **at the drop of a hat** (*fig*) at once, without any delay: *I telephoned and he came at the drop of a hat.*
▷ *v* (**-pp-**) **7** *tr.v* allow (s.o/s.t) to fall, esp by accident: *I've dropped my keys somewhere. We dropped the sick man at the side of the road and rested for a few minutes.* **8** *intr.v* jump down: *I dropped onto the ground from the wall.* **9** *intr.v* (of s.t) fall (usu into or through s.t): *I heard the coin drop (into the box).* **10** *intr.v* (of a person) fall, sit etc because of being tired, ill, wounded etc: *She dropped into a chair. I was almost dropping towards the end of the race.* **11** *tr.v* (often — *s.o off*) (of a bus, train, taxi etc) put (s.o) down: *Please drop me (off) at the gates.* **12** *tr.v* send (s.o/s.t) down using a parachute(1): *drop supplies.* **13** *tr.v* (of an animal) give birth to (young ones). **14** *intr.v* (of a level, price, temperature, speed, wind etc) become less or lower. **15** *tr.v* stop seeing (s.o), doing (s.t): *I've dropped studying science. Why has Alan dropped me?* **16** *tr.v* stop using, employing, (s.o/s.t): *I've dropped my lawyer. The captain has dropped me from the team.* **17** *tr.v* write and send (s.o) (a short letter, note etc): *I'll drop you a note about it. Drop me a postcard if you have time. I'll drop a letter to Mary about it.* **18** *tr.v* say (s.t) quickly and often without thinking: *She dropped a remark about his clothes. He dropped the fact that he had no money left.*
drop a brick/clanger (*fig; informal*) make an unsuitable remark that causes embarrassment(1).
drop by visit (s.o) for a short time: *I'll drop by later with the money I owe you.*
drop dead (**a**) fall down dead. (**b**) (*slang*) (imperative) (used to express one's extreme dislike of s.o).
drop in (**on s.o**) = drop by.
drop off (**a**) fall off. (**b**) fall asleep. **drop s.o/s.t off** (**a**) ⇨ drop(11). (**b**) visit s.o/s.w and leave s.o/ s.t there: *I'll drop off your coat at the cleaners.*
drop one's h's ⇨ H, h.
drop out (**of s.t**) (**a**) leave a course of study before finishing it. (**b**) refuse to act according to the accepted social ways: *drop out of society.* ⇨ drop-out.
‚drop 'goal *c.n* (in rugby) goal scored with a drop-kick.
'drop‚kick *c.n* (in rugby) kick made by dropping

the ball on the ground and kicking it as it bounces(3) up again.
'droplet *c.n* very small drop(1).
'drop-‚out *c.n* person who has dropped out(a,b).
'dropper *c.n* instrument used to make liquid (e.g medicine) fall in drops(1). ⇨ drops.
'droppings *pl.n* solid waste matter from animals; dung.
drops *u.n* liquid medicine to be applied using a dropper: *eye/nose drops.*
dross /drɒs/ *u.n* **1** useless material that comes to the top when metal is melted. **2** (*derog*) useless people: *the dross of the community.*
drought /draʊt/ *c/u.n* (example of a) long time with no rain: *The wheat was killed by the drought.*
drove /drəʊv/ *c.n* **1** group or number of moving farm animals: *a drove of* cattle(1); *a* cattle(1) *drove.* **2** (*fig*) large group moving in a place: *droves of tourists.*
▷ *v* **3** *p.t* of drive.
'drover *c.n* person who controls moving farm animals.
drown /draʊn/ *v* **1** *tr/intr.v* (cause (s.o, an animal) to) go under water and die because not able to breathe. **2** *tr.v* flood (s.t, a place): *The heavy rain has drowned the fields.* **3** *tr.v* (often — *s.t in/ with s.t*) (*fig*) cover (food) (with too much liquid): *The meat was drowning in grease.* **4** *tr.v* (often — *s.o/s.t out*) cause (s.o who is speaking, a sound) to be not heard (because of a louder sound): *The students drowned out the speaker. The singer was drowned (out) by the music.* **drown one's sorrows** make oneself forget s.t unpleasant by drinking alcohol.
drowsy /'draʊzɪ/ *adj* (**-ier, -iest**) **1** tired; sleepy: *feeling drowsy.* **2** that causes s.o to feel drowsy(1): *drowsy weather/music.*
'drowsily *adv.* **'drowsiness** *u.n.*
drubbing /'drʌbɪŋ/ *sing.n* (*informal*) (usu *get, give* s.o, a —) complete defeat, esp in a sports contest: *Our team suffered a drubbing.*
drudge /drʌdʒ/ *c.n* **1** person who does hard boring work.
▷ *intr.v* **2** do hard boring (usu physical) work.
drug /drʌg/ *c.n* (also *attrib*) **1** chemical or similar substance used as a medicine: *What drug did they give you for the pain?* **2** drug(1) used in order to feel very excited etc; narcotic: *a drug dealer.* **on drugs** taking drugs(1,2).
▷ *tr.v* (**-gg-**) **3** (often — *oneself/s.o/s.t up*) give (oneself/s.o/an animal) a drug(1,2): *She drugged herself (up) with* aspirin *in order to stop the pain.*
'drug ‚addict *c.n* person who must have drugs(2) and cannot stop taking them.
'drug ad‚diction *u.n* fact or state of being a drug addict.
'druggist *c.n* (US) = chemist(2).
'drug ‚pusher *c.n* person selling (illegal) drugs(2), esp in public places.
'drug‚store *c.n* (US) shop selling drugs(1) as well as fruit drinks, sweets, newspapers etc.
drum /drʌm/ *c.n* **1** (also *attrib*) musical instrument played by hitting the skin stretched across its body. **2** sound made (as if) by a drum. **3** thing shaped like a tall drum: *an oil drum.*
▷ *v* (**-mm-**) **4** *intr.v* play on a drum(1). **5** *tr/intr.v* (often — *on s.t*) make a sound of a drum(1)

on (a surface), e.g with one's fingers: *The rain drummed on the window.* **drum s.t into s.o** make s.o remember facts, a warning etc by repeating it/them often. **drum s.t out (on s.t)** produce a tune, sound of a drum(1) etc (on a drum(1), hard surface etc). **drum s.t up** get support, extra sales etc by asking many people and working hard.

'**drum ,beat** *c.n* (sound of a) hit on a drum(1).

'**drummer** *c.n* person who plays a drum(1).

'**drum ,stick** *c.n* **1** one of a pair of sticks used to play a drum(1). **2** cooked lower part of the leg of a chicken, turkey(1) etc.

drunk, drunkard, drunken ⇒ drink.

dry /draɪ/ *adj* (-ier, -iest) **1** with little or no water in or on it: *dry ground/clothes/eyes.* Opposite wet(1). **2** without rain: *dry weather.* Opposite wet(2). **3** (of food) needing more liquid or juice: *This meat is a little dry.* **4** without butter etc: *dry toast/bread.* **5** (of wine etc) not sweet: *a dry sherry*(1). **6** without interest: *a dry story.* **7** (of humour(1), wit(2)) quiet, clever and not showing personal feelings. **8** without extra details: *He gave me only the dry facts.* **dry as a bone** ⇒ bone. **high and dry** ⇒ high. **run (s.t) dry** (cause (a river etc) to) lose all of its water.

▷ *tr/intr.v* (-ies, -ied) **9** (cause (s.o/s.t) to) become dry(1): *The clothes are outside drying in the sun. The sun dried the clothes quickly.* **dry (oneself/ s.o) off** dry(9) oneself/s.o usu with a towel: *Dry off quickly after your swim.* **dry (oneself/s.o) out** (*informal*) cure oneself/s.o of being an alcoholic(3): *She's gone to a* clinic *to dry out.* **dry (s.t) out** (cause (s.t) to) become dry: *The sheets are drying out on the line.* **dry up** (**a**) (of a liquid or a place that produces water) stop producing water completely. (**b**) (of an actor) forget one's words during a performance. (**c**) (of a source for supplies of s.t) stop providing s.t. **dry (s.t) up** make pools of water, dishes etc being washed etc dry(1,2).

'**drier, ,dryer** *c.n* (often used as the second part of a word) machine that dries(9) (in the way, or the things, mentioned): *a spin-drier*; *a clothes-drier*; *a hair-drier.*

'**drily, 'dryly** *adv* in a dry(7) way.

,**dry-'clean** *tr.v* clean (clothes etc) in a machine that uses chemicals and not water.

,**dry-'cleaner's** *c/def.n* shop where clothes etc may be dry-cleaned.

,**dry-'cleaning** *n* **1** *def.n* clothes etc (to be) dry-cleaned. **2** *u.n* process used to dry-clean.

'**dryer** *c.n* ⇒ drier.

,**dry-'eyed** *adj* without tears; not crying.

'**dryness** *u.n.*

,**dry 'rot** *u.n* condition with drying and rotting of wood caused by fungi.

,**dry 'run** *c.n* = dummy run.

DSS /ˌdiː ˌes 'es/ *def.n abbr* Department of Social Security (UK government department).

DTI /ˌdiː ˌtiː 'aɪ/ *def.n abbr* Department of Trade and Industry (UK government department).

dt's /ˌdiː 'tiːz/ *def.pl.n abbr* delirium tremens.

dual /'djuːəl/ *attrib.adj* having two parts, members etc: *a dual interest as wife and mother*; *have dual roles in a play*; *dual* nationality(1).

,**dual 'carriage,way** *c.n* wide road divided by a barrier(1), on each side of which traffic passes in one direction.

,**dual-'purpose** *attrib.adj* having, used for,

two purposes: *a dual-purpose* knob(2) *on a* radio.

dub¹ /dʌb/ *v* (-bb-) (often — s.t into s.t) give (a film etc) sound using a different language: *The film has been dubbed into French.*

'**dubbing** *u.n* process of dubbing (⇒ dub¹).

dub² /dʌb/ *v* (-bb-) **1** (*formal*) give a title to (s.o *e.g.* make s.o a knight by touching her/his shoulder with a sword). **2** give (s.o) an amusing or special name; nickname(2) (s.o) s.t: *She was dubbed 'Superwoman'.*

dubious /'djuːbɪəs/ *adj* **1** (*pred*) (often — about s.o/s.t) causing doubt: *I'm a little dubious about his excuse.* **2** (*derog*) likely to be untrue, dishonest: *a dubious account of what happened.*

dubiety /djuː'baɪɪtɪ/ *u.n* fact of s.o/s.t being dubious(1,2).

'**dubiously** *adv.* '**dubiousness** *u.n.*

ducal ⇒ duke.

duchess /'dʌtʃɪs/ *c.n* (with capital **D** in names; often the *Duchess of s.w*) **1** wife of a duke. **2** woman with the rank of a duke.

duchy ⇒ duke.

duck¹ /dʌk/ *n* (*pl* -(s)) **1** *c.n* kind of bird that lives on water and has webbed feet and short legs. **2** *u.n* (also *attrib*) duck(1) eaten as food: *roast duck*; duck stew(1). **3** *c.n* (in cricket) score of 0: *He was out for a duck.* **like water off a duck's back** (of a threat, anger etc) without any effect. **a sitting duck** (*fig*) easy target(2). **take to s.t like a duck to water** become able to do or like s.t quickly and easily.

'**duckling** *c.n* very young duck(1). **ugly duckling** ⇒ ugly.

duck² /dʌk/ *c.n* **1** act or example of ducking²(2,3).

▷ *v* **2** *intr.v* lower one's head (as if) to avoid being hit on the head. **3** *tr/intr.v* (cause (s.o, an animal etc) to) go, be sent, under water: *The children ducked each other in the swimming pool.* **duck out of s.t** (*informal*) avoid doing one's duty, s.t one has promised to do etc. **duck under s.t** duck(2) and avoid s.t above one's head.

ducky /'dʌkɪ/ *c.n* (*slang*) name for s.o one likes.

duct /dʌkt/ *c.n* (*technical*) **1** tube in the body for liquid: *a tear duct.* **2** tube, channel(1) etc for electricity, gas etc. **3** place where air flows in a ventilator etc.

ductile /'dʌktaɪl/ *adj* (*technical*) (of a substance) able to be pulled or pressed so that it becomes a thread or wire without having to be heated.

dud /dʌd/ *adj* **1** (*informal*) worthless; no longer working: *a dud cheque/watch/torch.*

▷ *c.n* **2** (*informal*) dud(1) person or thing: *This battery is a dud.*

dudgeon /'dʌdʒən/ *u.n* **in high dudgeon** (*formal*) (of a person) very angry or annoyed.

due /djuː/ *adj* **1** (*pred*) that should be paid (now): *Payment is due.* **2** (*pred*) expected (now): *The train is due, so hurry. It's due in the next five minutes.* ⇒ overdue. **3** (*attrib*) suitable; correct: *Please take due care of my piano. I paid the due amount and now I own the house.* **due to s.o/s.t** (**a**) caused by s.o/s.t: *Your problems are all due to your bad temper.* (**b**) because of s.o/s.t: *Due to the rain, we can't go for a walk.*

▷ *c.n* **4** amount that is owed to s.o: *He asks only for his due — you can keep the rest.* ⇒ dues. **to give s.o her/his due . . .** if one wants to be fair about s.o: *To give him his due, your father did offer to lend us the car.*

dues *pl.n* fees(1), esp taxes: *What dues must we pay at customs(2)?*

'duly *adv* as agreed or expected: *The train duly arrived.*

duel /'dju:əl/ *c.n* (often — *between* s.o *and* s.o) **1** (in history) fight with swords etc between two men caused by a personal quarrel. **2** (*fig*) struggle, e.g between two teams, companies etc.
▷ *intr.v* (-*ll*-, US -*l*-) **3** (often — *with* s.o) fight a duel(1) (with s.o).

'duelling *u.n* activity of fighting a duel(1).

'duellist *c.n* person who duels(3).

duet /dju:'et/ *c.n* song, piece of music etc for two people.

duffel coat /'dʌfl ˌkəʊt/ *c.n* kind of thick coat with hooks and pegs(1) instead of buttons.

dug /dʌg/ *p.t,p.p* of dig.

duke /dju:k/ *c.n* (with capital **D** in names; often *the Duke of* s.w) man who is a noble(3) of the highest rank.

ducal /'dju:kl/ *adj* (*formal*) of or referring to dukes.

duchess ⇨ separate entry.

duchy /'dʌtʃɪ/ *c.n* (*pl* -*ies*) (*formal*) area (formerly) ruled by a duke.

'dukedom *c.n* rank, title, area ruled by, a duke.

dulcet /'dʌlsɪt/ *attrib.adj* (*literary*) pleasant to listen to: *the dulcet tones of the violin.*

dull /dʌl/ *adj* **1** not bright, not clear, not shining etc: *a dull sky; dull weather; dull wood; a dull grey colour.* **2** (*derog*) not able to understand or learn quickly: *dull students.* **3** not interesting: *a dull story/party.* **4** (*formal*) not sharp: *the dull edge of an old knife.* (**as**) **dull as ditchwater** ⇨ ditchwater (⇨ ditch).
▷ *tr.v* **5** make (s.t) less sharp: *dull a knife by trying to cut stone.* **6** make (a pain, feeling etc) less strong: *I took an aspirin to dull the ache.*

dully /'dʌllɪ/ *adv.* **'dullness** *u.n.*

duly ⇨ due.

dumb /dʌm/ *adj* **1** not able to speak: *be born dumb.* **2** (*derog; informal*) stupid: *He's so dumb that he didn't realize he was in danger.* **be struck dumb** (*fig*) be unable to say anything because one is so surprised, shocked etc.

ˌdumbˈfound *tr.v* unable to say anything because he/she is so surprised, shocked etc: *I was dumbfounded when I heard the news.*

'dumbly *adv* without saying or doing anything (against an order, idea etc): *They dumbly accepted the leader's suggestion.*

'dumbness *u.n.*

dummy /'dʌmɪ/ *c.n* (*pl* -*ies*) (also *attrib*) **1** thing that is made to look real but is not: *dummy soldiers in the trees.* **2** model of a person as used in shop windows. **3** rubber or plastic(3) copy of a woman's nipple(1) used to comfort a baby. **4** (*slang*) stupid person: *Don't be a dummy!*

ˌdummy ˈrun *c.n* practice that will test an idea, one's ability, a new process etc before it is done seriously. Compare dry run.

dump /dʌmp/ *c.n* **1** place where rubbish is put or left. **2** (*derog*) dirty cheap place to live: *I refuse to live in that dump.*
▷ *tr.v* **3** put or leave (rubbish, unwanted things): *They dumped the old car in a ditch.* **4** (*informal*) put (s.t heavy) down quickly: *We dumped our cases*

on the floor and sat down. **5** (*informal*) put or leave (s.o): *The driver dumped us at the side of the road and drove off.*

dumpiness ⇨ dumpy.

dumpling /'dʌmplɪŋ/ *c.n* (also *attrib*) ball of dough(1) (to be) cooked in gravy(2) etc: *dumpling stew*(1).

dumps /dʌmps/ *def.pl.n* (**down**) **in the dumps** feeling very sad and disappointed.

dumpy /'dʌmpɪ/ *adj* (-*ier*, -*iest*) short and thick: *dumpy fingers.*

'dumpiness *u.n.*

dun /dʌn/ *attrib.adj* pale yellow or brown: *a dun cow.*

dunce /dʌns/ *c.n* (*derog*) person who cannot understand or learn quickly.

dunderhead /'dʌndəˌhed/ *c.n* (*derog; old use*) stupid person.

dune /dju:n/ *c.n* (also **'sand,dune**) low hill or pile of sand, e.g at the edge of a beach.

dung /dʌŋ/ *u.n* solid waste matter from animals such as cows, used as manure(1) or in some countries dried and used as fuel for cooking etc. Compare faeces.

dungarees /ˌdʌŋgə'ri:z/ *pl.n* trousers made of strong cotton cloth with a flap(2) at the top to cover the chest, and straps(1) for the shoulders.

dungeon /'dʌndʒən/ *c.n* damp and dark prison, usu under the ground.

dunk /dʌŋk/ *tr.v* put (a biscuit etc) into a drink.

duodenum /ˌdju:ə'di:nəm/ *c/def.n* (*technical*) first part of the intestines after the stomach.

ˌduoˈdenal *adj* of, referring to, in, the duodenum: *a duodenal ulcer.*

duologue /'dju:əˌlɒg/ *c.n* (*technical*) conversation (in a play etc) between two people. Compare dialogue, monologue.

dupe /dju:p/ *c.n* **1** person who has been deceived, esp easily.
▷ *tr.v* **2** (often — s.o *into doing* s.t) deceive (s.o) (so that he/she does s.t): *I was duped into believing I would get the job.*

duplicate /'dju:plɪkɪt/ *attrib.adj* **1** exact; exactly the same: *a duplicate copy/key.*
▷ *c.n* /'dju:plɪkɪt/ **2** thing that is exactly the same: *This key is a duplicate of that one. I've made a duplicate of my letter.* **in duplicate** in two exact copies; two times: *We need your application in duplicate.* ⇨ triplicate.
▷ *tr.v* /'dju:plɪˌkeɪt/ **3** make a duplicate(2) of (a letter, key etc). **4** do the same (piece of work) that s.o has done or is doing: *Joy realized that she was duplicating my work.*

duplication /ˌdju:plɪ'keɪʃən/ *u.n.*

'dupli,cator *c.n* machine using ink and pressure to make an exact copy of a letter, drawing etc. Compare copier(2).

duplicity /dju:'plɪsɪtɪ/ *u.n* (*formal*) deception: *She was accused of duplicity.*

durable /'djʊərəbl/ *adj* **1** able to last a long time: *I hope this is a durable agreement.* **2** (able to be used for a long time): *durable clothes.*

'durables *pl.n* (*commerce*) goods, e.g tinned or bottled food, that can be kept on shelves etc for a long time.

durability /ˌdjʊərə'bɪlɪtɪ/ *u.n.*

duration /djʊ'reɪʃən/ *u.n* (*formal*) period(1) of time that s.t lasts: *We'll stay by the sea for the duration of the summer.*

duress /dju're̅s/ *u.n* **under duress** while suffering threats, forced to stay s.w or do s.t: *I only agreed to sign it under duress.*

durex /'djuəreks/ *c.n* (*t.n*) (also with capital **D**) ⇒ condom.

during /'djuərɪŋ/ *prep* **1** at or in the same time as: *I live there during the winter. She slept during the journey/play.* **2** within the time mentioned: *I work during the day but I am free in the evening.* **3** at a particular time or date in: *She died during the night. They came here during 1989.*

dusk /dʌsk/ *u.n* period(1) when the sun has gone down and it is getting dark: *The dusk is short in the* tropics. *We met at dusk.*

'duskiness *u.n* fact or quality of being dusky.

'dusky *adj* (-*ier*, -*iest*) dark in colour: *a dusky brown.*

dust /dʌst/ *u.n* **1** very small pieces of dirt: *The furniture was covered with dust.* **2** (often in combinations) very small pieces of the metal etc mentioned: *gold dust.* ⇒ sawdust. **bite the dust** (*fig*; *informal*) (**a**) be completely defeated. (**b**) die. **kick up**, **raise**, **a dust** (*fig*; *informal*) make a fuss(1).

▷ *tr.v* **3** make (s.t) dirty with dust(1). **4** take dust(1) off s.t by wiping its surface. ⇒ duster. **5** shake flour, sugar etc onto (food). **dust s.t down** brush or wipe (s.t) to take away dust(1).

'dust,bin *c.n* (US **'garbage ,can**, **'trash ,can**) (also *attrib*) container for rubbish from a house, flat etc: *Put all those bottles in the dustbin. Where's the dustbin lid?*

'dust,cart *c.n* large vehicle used to collect refuse(*n*) from buildings.

'duster *c.n* cloth, or bunch of feathers on a handle, for wiping dust(1) off things.

'dustiness *u.n* fact or state of being dusty.

'dust-,jacket *c.n* loose paper cover put round a book.

'dustman *c.n* (*pl* -*men*) person who collects refuse(*n*).

'dust,pan *c.n* small flat container used for dirt and dust that is brushed or swept into it.

'dust-,sheet *c.n* large sheet or cloth (to be) put over furniture, carpets etc, e.g while being stored, while (s.o is) painting walls etc.

'dust-,up *c.n* (*informal*) quarrel, often with fighting.

'dusty *adj* (-*ier*, -*iest*) filled or covered with dust(1): *dusty curtains/rooms/furniture.*

Dutch /dʌtʃ/ *u.n* **go Dutch** (of two people eating in a restaurant, going to the cinema etc) share the cost. ⇒ double-dutch (⇒ double), Netherlands (in the appendices).

'dutch ,cap *c.n* (also **cap**) device like a thin rubber disc, used by women as a contraceptive(2).

duty /'dju:tɪ/ *n* (*pl* -*ies*) **1** *c.n* job, piece of work etc that needs to be done, that one has agreed or promised to do, that is one's responsibility etc: *Your job will include the following duties. Whose duty was it to lock the door?* **2** *u.n* (often do one's —) (thing that one must do because of) moral responsibility, the law etc: *It's your duty as a parent to send your child to school. You should do your duty and tell the police.* ⇒ duty-bound. **3** *u.n* (often *one's* — *as* s.o/*towards* s.o) fact of obeying or respecting one's parents, teachers, old people etc: *my duty towards my parents; his duty as a husband.* **4** *c.n* government tax, esp on

goods brought into a country. (**off**)**on duty** (not) at work; (not) working. **go on/off duty** begin/stop working.

'dutiable *adj* on which duty(4) must be paid.

'dutiful *adj* obeying orders; obeying a person in authority, one's parents, the law etc: *a dutiful son.*

,duty-'bound *adj* (*formal*) obliged to obey or do s.t because it is her/his duty(2).

,duty-'free *adj* with no duty(4) to be paid: *duty-free goods.*

duvet /'dju:veɪ/ *c.n* (also *attrib*) continental quilt: *a duvet cover.*

dwarf /dwɔ:f/ *c.n* (*pl* -s) **1** (also *attrib*) animal, person or plant that is smaller than usual: *dwarf rose trees.* **2** (in stories) very small man, usu with a long beard, who has magical(1) powers.

▷ *tr.v* (often passive) **3** make (s.o/s.t) appear small(er) by being close and much bigger: *These houses have been dwarfed by that new office building.* **4** cause (a plant, tree etc) to grow slowly: *These trees have been dwarfed by the shade from that wall.*

dwell /dwel/ *intr.v* (*p.p,p.t* dwelled, dwelt /dwelt/) (*literary*) live (in a place): *We dwelt in the south of England until I was 11 years old.* **dwell on s.t** think, speak or write about (s.t) for a long time: *Don't dwell on your bad luck.*

-dweller *c.n* person living in the place shown by the first part of the word: *city-dwellers; town-dwellers.*

'dwelling *c.n* (*formal*; *law*) house, flat etc where s.o lives; home: *The council has built twenty new dwellings.*

dwindle /dwɪndl/ *intr.v* (often — *away*) become less in size, strength, power etc: *Her savings have dwindled away. The crowds are dwindling. His* authority(1) *is dwindling (away).*

dye /daɪ/ *c/u.n* **1** (kind, colour of a) substance used to dye(2) s.t: *a green dye. Can I use dye on nylon?*

▷ *tr.v* **2** (*pres.p* dyeing; *p.t,p.p* dyed) (usu — *s.t red* etc) put a colour in (cloth, hair, wool etc): *I washed my shirt with his jeans and the jeans dyed my shirt blue.*

,dyed-in-the-'wool *adj* (*informal*) (of a person) with strong, firm opinions: *a dyed-in-the-wool socialist.*

dying ⇒ die.

dyke[1] /daɪk/ *c.n* (also **dike**) **1** wall or bank of soil built to stop floods. **2** channel built to carry water to or from flat land.

dyke[2] /daɪk/ *c.n* (also **dike**) (*slang*) lesbian.

dynamic /daɪ'næmɪk/ *adj* **1** (*technical*) of, referring to, a force that produces motion. Compare static(3). **2** (of a person) full of energy(1), enthusiasm, determination: *Sally has a dynamic* personality(1). *He's a dynamic manager.* Compare static(2).

dy'namically *adv.*

dy'namics *n* **1** *u.n* (*science*) study of forces that produce or change motion. Compare statics. **2** *pl.n* facts affecting the size or energy(2) of a situation, task etc.

'dyna,mism *u.n* energy(1) and determination: *Keith's full of dynamism.*

dynamite /'daɪnə,maɪt/ *u.n* **1** kind of powerful explosive. **2** (*fig*) thing that causes a strong, bad effect: *To tell her the bad news when she's angry would be dynamite.*

▷ *tr.v* **3** use dynamite(1) to (try to) break or destroy (s.t): *the building was destroyed completely when it was dynamited.*

dynamo /ˈdaɪnəˌməʊ/ *c.n* (*technical*) device that changes mechanical energy(2) into electrical energy, e.g used to light the lights on a bicycle.

dynasty /ˈdɪnəstɪ/ *c.n* (*pl -ies*) series(1) of (generations(2) of) members of the same family, esp with reference to rulers, rich or powerful families etc: *the Churchill dynasty.*
   dynastic /dɪˈnæstɪk/ *adj.* **dyˈnastically** *adv.*

d'you /dju:/ = do you. ⇨ do.

dysentery /ˈdɪsəntrɪ/ *u.n* disease of the intestine causing solid waste from the body to become liquid.

dyslexia /dɪsˈleksɪə/ *u.n* (*technical*) condition, not concerned with one's intelligence, causing difficulty in reading and writing.
   dysˈlexic *adj* **1** suffering from dyslexia.
   ▷ *c.n* **2** person who is dyslexic(1).

dyspepsia /dɪsˈpepsɪə/ *u.n* indigestion.
   dysˈpeptic *adj.*

dystrophy ⇨ muscular dystrophy.

dz *written abbr* dozen.

Ee

E, e /iː/ *c*/*unique n* **1** 5th letter of the English alphabet.
   ▷ *symb* (**E**) **2** east. **3** earth(4). **4** English.

each /iːtʃ/ *adv* **1** for or to every one: *He gave us a tape each.*
   ▷ *det* **2** (of a person or thing in a group of two or more) every one considered separately: *Each student should listen to the tape. There are trees on each side of the river.* **each other** (only after a verb or preposition) (referring to) both (or all) of the persons mentioned in turn: *The three children liked each other.*
   ▷ *pron* **3** every one (in a group of two or more) considered separately: *Each of us* (or *We each*) *listened to the tape.*

eager /ˈiːgə/ *adj* full of a strong desire, interest or keenness: *be very eager; eager faces.* **be eager for, to do,** *s.t* be very anxious to get, do, s.t: *He's eager for success* (or *to succeed*).
   ˌeager ˈbeaver *c.n* (*informal*) person who is willing to do more work than is necessary or who is too eager to do s.t.
   ˈeagerly *adv.* **ˈeagerness** *u.n.*

eagle /ˈiːgl/ *c.n* **1** kind of large bird of prey. **2** (in golf) score for a hole that is two less than a good player is expected to get. Compare birdie(2), bogey(2), par(2).
   ˌeagle-ˈeyed *adj* **1** having very good sight. **2** noticing every small detail: *The eagle-eyed examiner marked every mistake.*

eaglet /ˈiːglɪt/ *c.n* young eagle(1).

ear /ɪə/ *n* **1** *c.n* organ of hearing found on each side of the head (of a person or animal). **2** *sing.n* ability to distinguish between sounds: *He has a good ear for languages.* **3** *c.n* part with seeds inside at the top of a corn, wheat or barley plant. **be all ears** listen attentively. **be music to one's ears** ⇨ music. **be out on one's ear** (*informal*) lose one's job suddenly, usu for bad behaviour. **(be) up to one's ears in s.t** (a) (be) very busy doing s.t, esp work, a job etc, and so not free to do anything else. **(b)** (be) deeply involved (⇨ involve(2)) in s.t, esp s.t bad: *He's up to his ears in debt.* **(be) wet behind the ears** (*derog; informal*) (be) lacking in experience. **cock one's ears up** = prick up one's ears. **fall on deaf ears** be heard but not answered: *His plea(1) for mercy fell on deaf ears.* **give/lend an ear (to s.o/s.t)** (*formal*) listen (to s.o/s.t). **go in (at) one ear and out (at) the other** (*informal*) (of news, instructions(2) etc) be heard but not understood or remembered. **grin from ear to ear** ⇨ grin(*v*). **have/keep an/one's ear to the ground** keep oneself informed about what is being said or planned, esp in secret. **play s.t by ear** (a) play an instrument or piece of music from memory, without any printed music. **(b)** (*fig*) do s.t which may be difficult without any preparation: *You can't prepare for the interview — you'll have to play it by ear.* **prick up one's ears** (of an animal, a person) suddenly start paying attention to s.t that can be heard or to what is being said. **turn a deaf ear (to s.o/s.t)** refuse to listen (to s.o/s.t). **walls have ears** ⇨ wall(*n*).

   ˈearˌache *u.n* pain inside the ear.

   ˈearˌdrum *c.n* layer of thin skin inside the ear which moves when sound waves hit it.

   ˈearˌlobe *c.n* small piece of skin and flesh that forms the bottom of the ear.

   ˈearˌmark *c.n* **1** mark put on a sheep's ear to show who owns it.
   ▷ *tr.v* **2** (usu — s.o/s.t for s.t) (*fig*) plan to use (s.o, a certain time, amount of money etc) (for a particular purpose): *This area is earmarked for development.*

   ˈearˌphone *c.n* part of a telephone or thing like it which one puts close to the ear to hear what is being said.

   ˈearˌplug *c.n* piece of soft rubber or wax put into the ear to keep out noise, wind or water.

   ˈearˌring *c.n* ornament worn on the ear.

   ˈearˌshot *u.n* (**be/move**) **out of earshot** (be/move) too far away to be heard. (**be/come**) **within earshot** (be/come) close enough to be heard.

   ˈearˌsplitting *attrib.adj* (of a sound) so loud and high that it hurts the ear: *an earsplitting shriek*(1).

earl /ɜːl/ *c.n* British nobleman who is higher in rank than a marquess, but lower than a viscount.
   earldom /ˈɜːldəm/ *c.n* rank or title of an earl or the land owned by an earl.

early /ˈɜːlɪ/ *adj* (*-ier, -iest*) **1** coming before the agreed, correct, usual etc time: *You're early!* Opposite late(1). **2** happening in or belonging to the first part of a particular length of time: *early evening.* Opposite late(2). (**it is**) **early days (yet)** (*informal*) (it is) too soon to be able to say what is going to happen.

▷ *adv* **3** near the beginning of a particular length of time: *early in the year.* ⇒ late(5). **4** before the agreed, correct, usual etc time: *Jenny always gets up early and goes to bed late.* **early on** near the beginning of a particular length of time or particular event: *She realized he was lying early on in their conversation.* ⇒ later on.

'**earliest** *def.n* time that is as early as possible: *The earliest I can come is 8 o'clock.* **at the earliest** (often after a negative) at the earliest time: *I can't come until 8 o'clock at the earliest.* Compare at the latest (⇒ latest).

'**earliness** *u.n.*

'**early ,bird** *c.n.* person who gets out of bed early and is ready to begin her/his day before most people.

,**early 'closing** (,**day**) *c.n* (UK) day on which shops close for the afternoon.

,**early 'warning ,system** *c.n* radar system that warns when enemy aircraft etc are coming.

earmark ⇒ ear.

earn /ɜːn/ *tr.v* **1** get (money, one's living etc) in return for one's work: *She earns a high salary as a doctor.* **2** gain (s.t) as a reward for what one has done: *He has earned everyone's respect.* **3** (of s.o's work, deeds etc) cause (s.o) to get (s.t): *His cooking has earned him fame and fortune.*

'**earner** *c.n* person who earns(1) money.

-earner *c.n* referring to s.o who earns(1) money in the way shown by the first part of the word: *a wage-earner.*

'**earnings** *pl.n* money that is earned.

earnest /ˈɜːnɪst/ *adj* **1** serious and determined: *a very earnest young man; an earnest face.* **2** showing sincere feelings and intentions: *an earnest attempt; an earnest desire.*

▷ *u.n* **3 in** (**deadly**) **earnest** sincere(ly); not joking: *Believe me, I am in deadly earnest. She spoke in earnest.* **4** (**do s.t**) **in earnest** (do s.t) in a determined and serious way: *The students got down to work in earnest a month before the examination.*

'**earnestly** *adv.* '**earnestness** *u.n.*

earnings ⇒ earn.

earphone, earplug, earring, earshot, earsplitting ⇒ ear.

earth /ɜːθ/ *n* **1** *def/unique n* (often with capital **E**) planet on which we all live: *There's been life on earth for millions of years.* **2** *u.n* surface of the land, ground: *The dead bird dropped to earth like a stone.* **3** *u.n* soil: *Put some* moist *earth round the plant's roots.* **4** *c.n* (technical) (symb E) (means of) contact(4) with the ground which completes an electric circuit(4). **5** *c.n* hole in the ground in which animals such as foxes(1) and badgers' live. **cost the earth** (informal) be very expensive. **come back/down to earth** (fig) stop day-dreaming(2); come back to reality. **down to earth** (,**down-to-'earth** when attrib) honest, practical: *a very down-to-earth person.* **from/to the four corners of the earth** ⇒ corner(n). (**go to**) **the ends of the earth** (to do s.t) ⇒ end (n). **move heaven and earth** (to do s.t **(for s.o)**) ⇒ heaven. **how/what on earth . . .?** (informal) (used for emphasis(1) or to show great surprise in questions): *How on earth did you get here? What on earth is he wearing?*

▷ *tr.v* **6** connect (an electrical machine etc) to an earth(4): *Is the iron earthed properly?* **earth s.t**

up cover the roots of a plant with soil: *Earth up the rose bushes.*

'**earthiness** *u.n.* state or quality of being earthy.

'**earthly** *adj* **1** of or belonging to this world. Compare unearthly(1). (**be**) (**of**) **no earthly use** ⇒ use(n).

▷ *c.n* **2 not have an earthly** (**chance of doing s.t**) (informal) not have any likelihood of succeeding (in doing s.t).

earthquake /ˈɜːθ₁kweɪk/ *c.n* violent movement of the earth's surface.

earthshaking /ˈɜːθ₁ʃeɪkɪŋ/ *adj* (fig) astonishing; sensational.

'**earth ,tremor** *c.n* small earthquake.

earthward /ˈɜːθwəd/ *adj* moving towards the earth.

'**earthwards** *adv* towards the earth.

'**earth,worm** *c.n* kind of worm that lives in the soil.

'**earthy** *adj* (-ier, -iest) **1** of or referring to soil. **2** coarse: *earthy humour*(1).

earwig /ˈɪə₁wɪg/ *c.n* kind of small insect that has pincers(1) on its tail.

ease /iːz/ *u.n* **1** freedom from work, trouble, difficulty or worry: *a life of ease.* (**be/feel**) **at ease** (be/feel) comfortable and not worried or nervous. Compare unease. (**be/feel**) **ill at ease** (be/feel) uncomfortable, worried or nervous. **put s.o at** (**her/his**) **ease** make s.o feel comfortable and not worried or nervous. (**stand**) **at ease** (military) (of soldiers) (stand) with legs apart and hands behind their backs. Compare (stand at) attention. **with ease** easily: *She won the match with ease.*

▷ *v* **2** *tr.v* reduce (pain, difficulty, trouble etc) or make (it) easier to bear: *The hot bath eased the pain in his back.* **3** *intr.v* (of pain, fears, trouble etc) become less. **4** *tr.v* make (s.t) less tight: *ease the elastic in a skirt so that it is not so tight around the waist.* **ease** (**s.o/s.t**) **away/in(to s.t)/off/open/through** (**s.t**) move (s.o/s.t) away etc by using gentle force: *It's too painful to ease the plaster off; just pull it. She eased the door open.* **ease s.o's mind** ⇒ mind'. **ease off/up** (**a**) (of rain, floods, wind etc) gradually become less strong or stop. (**b**) (of a person) do s.t with less effort: *In the last part of the race he eased off (his speed) a little.*

easel /ˈiːzl/ *c.n* kind of tall support for a painting etc: *The artist left the painting on the easel to dry.*

easily, easiness ⇒ easy.

east /iːst/ *adj* **1** in or coming from the direction in which the sun rises, *symb* E: *an east wind.*

▷ *adv* **2** towards an east(1) direction: *They sailed east.* **out east** (informal) in/towards an east(1) direction. Opposite out west (⇒ west(adv)).

▷ *n* (often with capital **E**) **3** *def/unique n* direction that is east(1). **4** *def.n* part of a country or of the world that is further east(1) than the rest of it: *The East has often seemed mysterious to people from the West.* **in the east** (**a**) in the direction that is east(1): *The sun rises in the east.* (**b**) in that part of a country or the world that is further east(1) than the rest: *Living in the East has its attractions.* **in the east of s.t** inside the eastern part of s.t. **the Far East** ⇒ far. **the Middle East** ⇒ middle. (**to the**) **east of s.t** further east(1) than s.t: *Moscow is to the east of Leningrad.*

'east,bound adj going towards the east(3): east-bound traffic.

,East 'End def.n eastern part of London.

'easterly adj 1 from, in, towards the east(3): an easterly wind.
▷ c.n 2 wind from the east(3).

'eastern adj (often with capital **E**) of, belonging to, the east(3) of a place: Eastern Europe.

'Easterner c.n person who lives in or comes from the eastern part of the world or a region.

,Eastern 'Hemisphere def.n ⇨ hemisphere.

'eastern,most adj that is furthest to the east(3).

'east,facing adj that looks towards, faces, the east(3): an eastfacing garden.

eastward /'i:stwəd/ adj towards the east(3).

'eastwards adv (US **'eastward**) towards the east(3).

Easter /'i:stə/ c/unique n (also attrib) (in Christianity) yearly religious celebration in March or April of the return of Jesus after his death two days earlier on Good Friday: Easter Sunday.

'Easter ,egg c.n painted egg or one made of chocolate etc, given as a present at Easter.

easy /'i:zı/ adj (-ier, -iest) **1** (often — to do (s.t)) not difficult, simple, (to do (s.t)): The students found the examination easy. The questions were easy to answer (or It was easy to answer the questions). **2** (usu attrib) not troubled, worried or nervous: an easy manner; an easy conscience.
▷ adv **3** (used as a command) move s.t gently: Easy now! Put the cupboard down gently. **(be/go) easy on s.o** (be) not strict with s.o: You're too easy on her; she'll never learn that way. **easier said than done** easier to say one will do s.t than actually to do it. **Easy does it!** Be slow and careful: Easy does it! He's broken his leg so lift him gently. **go easy on/with s.t** (informal) be careful or moderate in one's use of s.t: Go easy on the milk — that's all that's left. **I'm easy** (informal) I do not mind what you decide.

'easily adv **1** without difficulty: We won easily. **2 easily the** . . . without doubt the . . .; certainly the . . .: This is easily the best book she has written.

'easiness u.n.

'easy-,going adj (of a person, behaviour etc) not strict; easy to get on with; tolerant: an easy-going manner.

,easy 'touch c.n (informal) person from whom it is easy to get money.

eat /i:t/ v (p.t ate /et/, p.p eaten /'i:tn/) **1** tr/intr.v take in (food) through the mouth, chew (it) and swallow (it): He fell asleep after eating his dinner. **2** intr.v have a meal: Have you eaten yet? ⇨ overeat.

eat s.t away destroy s.t gradually: The river is eating away the banks.

eat one's heart out ⇨ heart(n).

eat into s.t begin and continue to destroy s.t gradually: Acids can eat into metals.

eat out of s.o's hand ⇨ hand(n).

eat through (s.t) make a hole (in s.t) as if by biting it: The moths have eaten through the curtains.

eat (s.t) up eat all (of s.t): Come on, eat up (your dinner). **eaten up with s.t** feeling jealousy, envy, disappointment etc very strongly and painfully: She was eaten up with jealousy when her friends went to university.

eat one's words ⇨ word(n).

eatable /'i:təbl/ adj (of food) in a good enough condition to be eaten; not spoiled: His cooking's so bad the food's barely eatable. Opposite uneatable. Compare edible.

'eater c.n (usu a big, small etc —) person who eats (a lot, a little etc).

'eating ,apple c.n apple that can be eaten raw.

eats pl.n (informal; becoming old use) food.

eau de cologne /,əʊ də kə'ləʊn/ u.n (also **co'logne**) (French) kind of scent(2).

eaves /i:vz/ pl.n lower part of a sloping roof that sticks further out than the wall below: Birds often nest under the eaves of houses.

eavesdrop /'i:vz,drɒp/ intr.v (-pp-) (usu — on s.o/s.t) listen secretly (to s.o talking, a private conversation) on purpose: He likes to eavesdrop on his friends.

'eaves,dropper c.n person who eavesdrops.

ebb /eb/ u.n **1** movement of the tide away from the land. **be at a low ebb** (fig) in a weak or poor state: Bob's at rather a low ebb; he needs cheering up. My finances(2) are at a low ebb.
▷ intr.v **2** (of the tide) flow back from the land. **3** (often — away) (fig) get less; become weaker; fade (away): The colour ebbed from his face. His courage was slowly ebbing away. **ebb and flow (a)** (of the tide) flow away from the land and back towards the land. **(b)** (fig) change from good to bad, then back to good etc: His fortunes ebb and flow.

,ebb 'tide c.n tide that is flowing away from the land. Opposite flood tide.

ebony /'ebənɪ/ u.n (also attrib) **1** kind of hard black wood: ebony furniture. **2** blackness: His hair was the colour of ebony (or He had ebony hair).

ebullient /ı'bʌlıənt/ adj (formal) having or showing happiness, high spirits, enthusiasm: He became ebullient when he heard the good news.
e'bullience u.n. **e'bulliently** adv.

eccentric /ık'sentrık/ adj **1** not behaving in the normal way; not conventional(1); slightly mad: an eccentric professor; an eccentric idea. **2** (of two or more circles that overlap) not having the same centre. Compare concentric. **3** (of an orbit(1)) not circular or regular: Some planets travel in eccentric orbits.
▷ c.n **4** eccentric(1) person.

ec'centrically adv.

eccentricity /,eksen'trısıtı/ n (pl -ies) **1** u.n state or quality of being eccentric. **2** c.n example of eccentric(1) behaviour.

ecclesiastic /ı,kli:zı'æstık/ c.n Christian(1) priest, bishop or clergyman.

e,cclesi'astical adj of the Christian(1) Church or clergy.

e,cclesi'astically adv.

echo /'ekəʊ/ c.n (pl -es) **1** second sound heard after the first sound has bounced(3) off a surface such as a rock face: We shouted to each other inside the tunnel so that we could hear our echoes.
▷ v **2** intr.v (of a sound) be repeated by echoes(1): Her voice echoed in the empty church. **3** tr.v imitate, repeat, (the words, feelings etc of s.o else): Her words echoed what I was thinking. **echo**

back be sent back as an echo(1): *The sound of thunder was echoing back from the mountains.*

éclair /ɪˈkleə/ *c.n* (*French*) kind of cake made of soft pastry which is usu shaped like a finger filled with cream and with chocolate on top.

eclipse /ɪˈklɪps/ *c.n* **1** total or partial(1) loss of light from the sun or moon: *An eclipse of the sun is caused when the moon passes between it and the earth, and an eclipse of the moon when the earth passes between it and the sun.* **2** (*fig*) loss of power, fame, reputation etc. **in eclipse** (*fig*) in a state of having lost power, fame, reputation etc: *The artist's fame has been in eclipse for many years.*

▷ *tr.v* **3** (of the moon or earth) cause an eclipse(1) of (the sun or moon) by blocking its light. **4** (*fig*) reduce the attraction or fame of (s.o/s.t) by being much better: *His fame was eclipsed by his brother's great success.*

ecology /ɪˈkɒlədʒɪ/ *n* **1** *u.n* study of the relations of all living things to each other and to where they live (i.e their environment). **2** *c.n* example of this: *the different ecologies of the world.*

Ec'ology ,Party *def.n* political party in some countries with a policy[1] for protecting the environment etc. ⇨ Green Party.

ecological /ˌiːkəˈlɒdʒɪkl/ *adj* of or referring to ecology(1).

ecologist /ɪˈkɒlədʒɪst/ *c.n* person who studies, or is skilled in, ecology(1).

economy /ɪˈkɒnəmɪ/ *attrib.adj* **1** (of s.t for sale etc) that shows a saving in price etc: *an economy pack of soap.* ⇨ economy class.

▷ *n* **2** *c/u.n* (example of the) careful use of money, time, effort etc so as to avoid wasting it: *We must make economies in the amount of petrol we use.* **3** *u.n* (state of the) management of the money, goods etc belonging to a country or a home: *household economy*; *The British economy is improving.* **4** *c.n* system for controlling the trade, industry and money in a country: *The Soviet Union has a socialist economy.*

economic /ˌiːkəˈnɒmɪk/ *adj* **1** (*attrib*) of or referring to (the system for controlling) trade, industry or business: *We are studying economic history this term. The government has a good economic policy.* **2** that produces, shows, a profit when all the costs are met: *an economic rent.*

,eco'nomical *adj* careful in the use of money, time, effort etc; not wasteful: *An economical car does not use much petrol.*

,eco'nomically *adv* **1** in an economical way. **2** in a way that concerns the economy(3,4).

,eco'nomics *u.n* scientific study of the production, sharing out and use of wealth etc.

economist /ɪˈkɒnəmɪst/ *c.n* person who studies, or is skilled in, economics.

economize, -ise /ɪˈkɒnəˌmaɪz/ *intr.v* (often — on s.t) spend less money than before (on s.t): *We must economize if we want to go abroad next year. We are trying to economize on electricity.*

e'conomy ,class *adj/adv* (**e'conomy-,class** when *attrib*) of or by the cheapest class of (air etc) travel: *an economy-class air ticket. We always travel economy class.*

e'conomy-,size *adj* large and usu good value for money: *an economy-size tube of toothpaste.*

ecstasy /ˈekstəsɪ/ *c/u.n* (*pl -ies*) (example of

the) feeling of great joy and happiness. **in ecstasies** very happy: *He was in ecstasies when she agreed to marry him.* **go into ecstasies** (**over s.t**) become very happy (because of s.t).

ecstatic /ɪkˈstætɪk/ *adj* showing ecstasy.

ec'statically *adv*.

ecumenical /ˌiːkjuˈmenɪkl/ *adj* **1** of or representing the whole Christian(1) Church. **2** trying to bring about Christian(1) unity: *the ecumenical movement.*

eczema /ˈeksɪmə/ *u.n* kind of skin disease that causes the skin to become red and itchy.

eddy /ˈedɪ/ *c.n* (*pl -ies*) **1** circular movement of dust, fog, mist, smoke, wind or water.

▷ *intr.v* (*-ies, -ied*) **2** (of water etc) move in small circles: *The water eddied wherever there were rocks at the bottom.*

edge /edʒ/ *n* **1** *c.n* sharp cutting side of a knife, an axe, scissors etc. **2** *c.n* outer limit, border etc: *He fell off the edge of the cliff into the sea.* **3** *sing.n* (of a voice or feeling) (showing of a) certain amount of annoyance or anger: *There was an edge in his voice when he answered my criticism.* (**be**) **on edge** (be) anxious or nervous. **have an/the edge on/over s.o/s.t** have an advantage over s.o/s.t. **set s.o's teeth on edge** ⇨ tooth. **take the edge off s.t** (**a**) weaken, dull, s.t: *The bad news took the edge off my appetite.* (**b**) make s.t seem less exciting or important.

▷ *v* **4** *tr.v* give a border to (s.t): *The bottom of her skirt was edged with lace.* **5** *tr/intr.v* (often — s.o/s.t) along, forward, into s.t etc) (cause (s.o/s.t) to) move along etc cautiously: *They edged along the slippery path. The long queue edged slowly into the cinema.* **edge one's way forward, through, in**(**to s.t**) ⇨ way(*n*).

'edge,ways *adv* (also **'edge,wise**) with the edge outwards or in front; sideways. **not/hardly get a word in edgeways** (*informal*) find it impossible or difficult to say s.t because another person will not stop speaking.

'edgily *adv* in an edgy way.

'edginess *u.n* state of being edgy.

'edging *c.n* narrow border, esp on a piece of clothing: *Lace makes a pretty edging for tablecloths.*

'edgy *adj* (*-ier, -iest*) anxious, nervous or irritable.

edible /ˈedɪbl/ *adj* that is of a kind that can be used as food; not rotten or poisonous: *edible berries.* Opposite inedible. Compare eatable.

edibility /ˌedɪˈbɪlɪtɪ/ *u.n*.

edict /ˈiːdɪkt/ *c.n* (*formal* or *old use*) official statement or order, e.g given by a government.

edify /ˈedɪˌfaɪ/ *tr.v* (*-ies, -ied*) (*formal*) improve (the mind) in a moral or spiritual(1) way.

edification /ˌedɪfɪˈkeɪʃən/ *u.n*.

edifice /ˈedɪfɪs/ *c.n* (*formal*) large building.

edit /ˈedɪt/ *tr.v* **1** prepare (a book, newspaper, article etc written by s.o else) for publication(1). **2** direct the production of (a newspaper or magazine). **3** prepare (a cinema film or tape recording) by arranging parts that have previously been filmed or recorded into a suitable order. **4** (*technical*) arrange (data) for use in a computer. **edit s.t out** remove s.t from a piece of writing, a film, a recording etc.

edition /ɪˈdɪʃən/ *c.n* **1** form in which a book, newspaper etc is published or one copy of this:

A paperback *edition is cheaper than the* hardback. **2** total number of copies of a book, newspaper etc published(1) at one time: *The magazine was so popular that the whole edition sold out in one day.*

editor /'edɪtə/ *c.n* **1** person who edits a book, newspaper, radio programme etc. **2** person who is in charge of the preparation of a particular part of a newspaper: *a news editor.*

editorial /ˌedɪ'tɔːrɪəl/ *attrib.adj* **1** of an editor or editing: *editorial work*; *an editorial decision.*
▷ *c.n* **2** article in a newspaper usu written by the chief editor and often expressing her/his own opinion.

educate /'edjuˌkeɪt/ *tr.v* train or teach (s.o): *She was educated at the best school in the country.*

,**edu**,**cated** '**guess** *n* (usu *sing*) guess based on the knowledge one already has about s.t.

educative /'edjukətɪv/ *adj* (*formal*) that is likely to give s.o knowledge or experience: *It will be an educative experience for him to work among the poor for a while.*

education /ˌedju'keɪʃən/ *n* **1** *u.n* system of training and teaching, esp of young people in schools and colleges etc: *Britain has both private and state education.* **2** *sing/u.n* knowledge etc received as a result of being educated.

,**edu**'**cational** *adj.*

,**edu**'**cationalist** *c.n* (also ,**edu**'**cationist**) person who is skilled in educational methods or systems.

EEC /ˌiː ˌiː 'siː/ *def.n abbr* European Economic Community.

eel /iːl/ *c.n* kind of fish shaped like a snake. **as slippery as an eel** (a) very difficult to hold. (b) (*derog*; *fig*) (of a person) difficult to manage; not to be trusted.

eerie /'ɪərɪ/ *adj* (*-ier, -iest*) (of a place, building etc) strange and mysterious: *The old house looked eerie in the moonlight.*

'**eerily** *adv.* '**eeriness** *u.n.*

efface /ɪ'feɪs/ *tr.v* (*formal*) **1** rub (s.t) out. **2** (*fig*) remove (s.t) as if by rubbing it out: *Nothing will ever efface the memory of my first train journey.*
⇒ self-effacing.

effect /ɪ'fekt/ *c/u.n* (often — *on s.o/s.t*) **1** (example of the) result of s.t that has happened: *What effects are the price rises having (on poor people)?* **2** (example of the) impression(1) made by s.o/s.t on s.o: *His entry onto the stage had a great effect on the audience.* **bring/carry/put s.t into effect** cause s.t to work or happen etc. **come into effect** become operative(2); come into force: *The new laws will come into effect next year.* **for effect** in order to make an impression(1) on s.o: *She cried for effect, not because she was really upset.* **give effect to s.t** make s.t happen or have a result. **in effect** in fact; really: *What he was trying to say in effect was that there was no money left.* **take effect** (a) happen; come into force: *The new law takes effect from midnight tonight.* (b) have the result that is wanted: *The medicine took effect immediately.* **to the effect that . . .** stating that . . ., with the meaning that . . .: *He made an announcement to the effect that there would not be an examination.*
▷ *tr.v* **3** (*formal*) cause, succeed in causing, (s.t) to happen: *The prisoner effected his escape with little difficulty.*

effective /ɪ'fektɪv/ *adj* **1** that produces or can produce the desired result(s): *We have to have effective plans if we are to deal with serious flooding.* Opposite ineffective. Compare effectual. **2** producing a strong impression(1); striking: *an effective description.* **3** (*attrib*) really existing; actual: *The effective leadership of the country is now in the hands of the army.* Compare theoretical. **4** (*pred*) (often — *from s.t*) starting, in force, (from a certain time or date): *The increase in pay agreed by the union will be effective from next month.*

ef'**fectively** *adv.* ef'**fectiveness** *u.n.*

e'**ffects** *pl.n* goods; property: *He kept all his valuable personal effects in a safe.*

effectual /ɪ'fektjuəl/ *adj* (of a plan, a method etc) that can produce the desired results. Opposite ineffectual(2). Compare effective(1).

ef'**fectually** *adv* **1** in an effectual way. **2** actually; in fact: *The new law effectually banned unions.*

ef'**fectualness** *u.n.*

effeminate /ɪ'femɪnət/ *adj* (*derog*) (of a man or boy, his behaviour) too much like a woman or the way women are thought to behave.

effervesce /ˌefə'ves/ *intr.v* **1** give off gas in the form of a mass of bubbles(2); fizz(2). **2** (*fig*) (of a person) show great happiness and excitement; be in high spirits.

,**effer**'**vescence** *u.n.* ,**effer**'**vescent** *adj.*

efficacious /ˌefɪ'keɪʃəs/ *adj* (*formal*) (of a plan, medicine etc) producing the desired result.

,**effi**'**caciously** *adv.* **efficacy** /'efɪkəsɪ/ *u.n.*

efficient /ɪ'fɪʃənt/ *adj* who/that works well or can produce the desired result with the least possible effort or expense: *an efficient secretary*; *an efficient machine.* Opposite inefficient.

ef'**ficiency** *u.n.* ef'**ficiently** *adv.*

effigy /'efɪdʒɪ/ *c.n.* (*pl -ies*) model or representation(2) of a person made out of wood or stone etc. **in effigy** in the form of an effigy: *The people hated the president so much that they burnt him in effigy.*

effluent /'efluənt/ *n* **1** *c.n* stream flowing out of a river or lake. **2** *u.n* waste liquid etc from a factory etc that flows into a river or the sea.

'**effluence** *u.n.* act or process of flowing out.

effort /'efət/ *n* **1** *u.n* use of all of one's strength when one is trying hard to do s.t: *He put a lot of effort into learning to swim.* **2** *c.n* result of s.t that one has tried hard to do: *The sick man was so weak that even breathing was an effort for him.* **3** *c.n* strong attempt: *His effort to run the mile in four minutes succeeded.* (**be**) **an effort** (**to do s.t**) (be) very difficult (to do s.t). **make an effort** (**to do s.t**) try hard (to do s.t): *Please make an effort not to be late.*

'**effortless** *adj* showing no effort; without effort.

'**effortlessly** *adv.* '**effortlessness** *u.n.*

effrontery /ɪ'frʌntərɪ/ *u.n* (*formal*) shameless boldness. **have the effrontery to do s.t** be cheeky enough to do s.t: *Gary had the effrontery to ask me to lend him my new car.*

effusive /ɪ'fjuːsɪv/ *adj* (often *derog*) (of a person, a person's speech) showing one's feelings too freely; excessive: *effusive thanks.*

ef'**fusively** *adv.* ef'**fusiveness** *u.n.*

e g /ˌiː 'dʒiː/ *abbr* (also **e.g.**, **e g**) for example (from the Latin 'exempli gratia').

egalitarian /ɪˌgælɪˈteərɪən/ adj **1** believing in equal social and political rights for all people: *an egalitarian society.*
▷ c.n **2** egalitarian(1) person.
e.gali'taria,nism u.n.

egg /eg/ n **1** c.n oval(1) object in a shell produced by female birds and some other animals from which young birds or animals are born. *Hens' eggs and ducks' eggs are used as food.* **2** c.n object inside jelly(4) etc produced by some female animals and insects from which young animals or insects are born. **3** u.n substance inside the shell of an egg(1) used as food: *You've got some egg on your shirt.* **have egg all over one's face**(fig) (be seen to) be in an embarrassing situation because of s.t wrong one has done. **put all one's eggs in(to) one basket** (fig) risk everything by limiting one's efforts to one course of action only. **teach one's grandmother to suck eggs** (fig) try to tell s.o with more experience than oneself how to do s.t etc.
▷ tr.v **4 egg s.o on** (**to do s.t**) encourage or urge s.o (to do s.t, esp s.t bad or dangerous).
'egg ,cosy c.n (pl -ies) cover put over a boiled egg to keep it hot.
'egg ,cup c.n small cup used to hold a boiled egg(1).
'egg,head c.n (informal; often derog) highly educated person who spends (too) much time studying and thinking.
'egg-,plant c.n large oval(1) vegetable with thin purple skin; aubergine.
'egg,shell n **1** c.n shell of an egg(1). **2** c/u.n (also ,egg,shell 'paint) very fine oil paint.
,egg,shell 'china u.n very thin fine china(1).

ego /ˈiːgəʊ/ n **1** c/def.n person's inner self and her/his feelings about herself/himself. **2** c.n one's good opinion of oneself: *His failure in the examination damaged his ego.*
egocentric /ˌegəʊˈsentrɪk/ adj selfish, self-centred.
,ego'centrically adv. **egocentricity** /ˌiːgəʊˌsenˈtrɪsɪtɪ/ u.n.
egoism /ˈiːgəʊˌɪzəm/ u.n **1** state of thinking only of oneself. **2** feeling that causes all one's behaviour to be in one's own interests.
egoist /ˈiːgəʊɪst/ c.n (usu derog) person who believes in or shows egoism.
,ego'istic(al) adj. **,ego'istically** adv.
egotism /ˈiːgəˌtɪzəm/ u.n **1** state of talking about oneself too much or too often. **2** state of thinking one is more important or special than one really is.
egotist /ˈiːgətɪst/ c.n (derog) person who shows egotism.
,ego'tistic(al) adj. **,ego'tistically** adv.
'ego ,trip c.n (informal) activity etc for one's own interest or pleasure: *His party was a complete ego trip for him.*

eh /eɪ/ interj (expression of surprise, inquiry or doubt): *Eh! What did you say?*

eiderdown /ˈaɪdəˌdaʊn/ c.n thick covering for a bed filled with soft feathers.

eight /eɪt/ det/pron/c.n **1** (cardinal number) number 8 (between 7 and 9): *Eight of us will be there. It's 8 (o'clock). Eight people came.* **have one over the eight** (informal) drink too much alcohol.
▷ c.n **2** crew of eight in a rowing-boat for racing.

eighteen /eɪˈtiːn/ det/pron/c.n (cardinal number) number 18 (between 17 and 19).
eighteenth /eɪˈtiːnθ/ det/pron **1** (ordinal number) (person or thing) following 17 in order; 18th.
▷ c.n **2** one of eighteen equal parts; $\frac{1}{18}$.
eighth /eɪtθ/ det/pron **1** (ordinal number) (person or thing) following 7 in order; 8th.
▷ c.n **2** one of eight equal parts; $\frac{1}{8}$.
eightieth /ˈeɪtɪəθ/ det/pron **1** (ordinal number) (person or thing) following 79 in order; 80th.
▷ c.n **2** one of eighty equal parts; $\frac{1}{80}$.
eighty /ˈeɪtɪ/ det/pron/c.n (cardinal number) number 80 (between 79 and 81): *My mother is nearly eighty-five (years old).* **in one's eighties** between 80 and 89 years of age. (**in/into**) **the eighties** (or **the 80(')s**) (**a**) (speed, temperature, marks etc) between 80 and 89: *The temperature today is in the eighties.* (**b**) (years) between '80 and '89 in a century.

either /ˈaɪðə, ˈiːðə/ adv **1** (used after negative statements) also: *I haven't read this book and he hasn't either.* **2** (used after negative phrases(1) in fact; moreover: *She used to be able to run a mile in four minutes and that wasn't so long ago either.* ⇒ neither(adv).
▷ conj **3 either . . . or . . .** (used to introduce the first of two possibilities): *You can go to London either by bus or by train. You can either stay here or come with us.* ⇒ neither(3).
▷ det **4** (of a person or thing in a group of two) one or other: *Either book would be interesting to read.* **5** (of a person or thing in a group of two) each: *There are houses on either side of the street.* ⇒ neither(4).
▷ pron **6** one or the other of two: *You can borrow either of these books.* ⇒ neither(5).

ejaculate /ɪˈdʒækjʊˌleɪt/ tr/intr.v send out (sperm(2)) from the penis.
ejaculation /ɪˌdʒækjʊˈleɪʃən/ c/u.n act of sending out semen from the penis.

eject /ɪˈdʒekt/ v **1** tr.v (usu — s.o/s.t from s.w) (formal) force (s.o/s.t) to leave (s.w): *He was ejected from the restaurant because he was not dressed properly.* **2** intr.v (often — from s.t) leave an aircraft by parachute(1) in an emergency: *The pilot ejected safely from the burning plane.*
ejection /ɪˈdʒekʃən/ u.n.
e'jector ,seat c.n aircraft seat with a parachute(1) fixed to it which is shot out of an aircraft in an emergency with the pilot etc fixed to it.

eke /iːk/ tr.v **eke s.t out** make s.t last or be enough by using it carefully or adding s.t else to it: *She managed to eke out the soup by adding water to it.* **eke out a living** manage to live by getting just enough money for food etc.

elaborate /ɪˈlæbərɪt/ adj **1** complicated; very detailed: *Her skirt was decorated with elaborate embroidery(1). He made elaborate plans for his daughter's wedding.*
▷ v /ɪˈlæbəˌreɪt/ **2** tr.v talk about or work on (s.t) in detail: *He elaborated his plans for the business.* **3** intr.v (often — on s.t) (formal) talk in detail (about s.t): *I need not elaborate further (on what I said).*
elaborately /ɪˈlæbrɪtlɪ/ adv. **e'laborateness** u.n.
elaboration /ɪˌlæbəˈreɪʃən/ n **1** u.n act of

elaborating(*v*) (on) s.t or of being elaborated. **2** *c.n* thing added to give greater detail.

elapse /ɪˈlæps/ *intr.v* (*formal*) (of time) pass: *Three weeks elapsed before I heard from my sister again.*

elastic /ɪˈlæstɪk/ *adj* **1** (of a thing or a substance) able to go back to its original shape or size after being stretched or squashed¹(4). **2** (*fig*) not fixed; easily changed; flexible(2): *The rules of this game are elastic.*
▷ *u.n* **3** narrow band of material with rubber in it that can be stretched easily: *a metre of elastic.*
eˈlastically *adv.*
e,lastic ˈband *c.n* very thin strap of rubber made into a ring: *Elastic bands are put round papers to keep them together.*
elasticity /ˌiːlæˈstɪsɪtɪ/ *u.n* quality of being elastic(*adj*).

elate /ɪˈleɪt/ *tr.v* (*formal*) make (s.o) excited and very happy: *The news of his daughter's first baby elated him.*
eˈlated *adj* (often — at/by s.t) excited and very happy (because of s.t): *He was elated at the news.*
elation /ɪˈleɪʃən/ *u.n.*

elbow /ˈelbəʊ/ *c.n* **1** joint between the upper arm and lower arm. **2** (also *attrib*) object shaped like an elbow(1): *an elbow joint in the pipe.* **at s.o's elbow** close or near s.o.
▷ *tr.v* **3 elbow one's way through (s.t)** force one's way through (a group of people etc) by pushing with one's elbow(s): *He elbowed his way through the crowd.* **4 elbow (s.o) out of the way** push (s.o) out of the way with one's elbow(s).
ˈelbow ˌgrease *u.n* (*fig*; *informal*) hard work, esp with the hands: *We'll need a lot of elbow grease if we're going to get this room clean.*

elder¹ /ˈeldə/ *attrib.adj* **1** (of one of two closely related people) older; senior(2): *His elder brother was the head of the family business.* Opposite younger(1).
▷ *n* **2** *c.n* official in certain Christian(1) Churches. **3** *def.n* (usu *s.o the* —) older of two in the same family or group: *Winston Churchill the younger became a politician like his grandfather, Winston Churchill the elder.* Compare senior(4).
ˈelderly *adj* **1** (of people) old.
▷ *def.pl.n* **2** old people: *Our society does not provide enough for the elderly.*
ˈelders *pl.n* people older than oneself: *We were taught to respect our elders.* **one's elders and betters** people who are older and wiser than oneself.
ˌelder ˈstatesman *c.n* (*pl* -men) old, usu retired, politician who is still asked to give advice because of her/his great experience.
ˈeldest *attrib.adj* **1** (of members of the same family) oldest still living: *The eldest daughter took over the family business when her father died.* Compare elder(1).
▷ *def/def.pl.n* **2** person(s) who is/are oldest.

elder² /ˈeldə/ *c.n* (also **ˈelder ˌtree**) kind of small tree with white flowers and black berries.
ˈelderberry /ˈeldəˌberɪ/ *c.n* (*pl* -ies) (also *attrib*) fruit of the elder tree: *elderberry wine.*

elect /ɪˈlekt/ *adj* (after the noun it qualifies) chosen for a special job or position: *He was mayor elect for a year before taking up the position.*
▷ *tr.v* **2** (often — s.o/oneself s.t) choose (s.o to be

one's member of parliament etc) by voting: *He was elected president for the second time.* **elect s.o to s.t** choose s.o to be a member of s.t by voting: *She was elected to* Parliament *with a majority of 10 000.* **elect to do s.t** decide or choose to do s.t (from various possibilities): *We elected to go to town by bus rather than take the car.*
election /ɪˈlekʃən/ *c/u.n* (example of the) act or fact of electing(2) s.o or of being elected: *In Britain there is a* Parliamentary *election every five years.* **stand for election** be a candidate(1) in an election. ⇨ general election, local election.
electioneer /ɪˌlekʃəˈnɪə/ *intr.v* try to get votes in an election by giving speeches, talking to people etc.
eˈlector *c.n* person who has the right to vote in an election.
electoral /ɪˈlektərəl/ *attrib.adj* of electors: *an electoral roll/* register(1).
electorate /ɪˈlektərət/ *c/def.n* all the people who have the right to vote in an election.

electric /ɪˈlektrɪk/ *adj* **1** of electricity: *electric current.* **2** worked by electricity: *electric lights; an electric cooker.* **3** that makes electricity: *an electric generator.* **4** (*fig*) very excited: *The atmosphere(2) was electric when the Queen arrived.*
eˈlectrical *adj* of, using, electricity: *A lot of electrical work was needed to make the old house safe.*
e,lectrical ,engiˈneering *u.n* science and practice of using electricity in machines and engines.
e,lectric ˈchair *def.n* (US) chair in which a person is executed(1) by being electrocuted.
eˈlectric ,cooker *c.n* stove with rings(3) used for cooking by electricity. Compare gas cooker.
e,lectric ˈfence *c.n* fence charged with electricity, usu to keep animals in a particular area.
electrician /ɪˌlekˈtrɪʃən/ *c.n* person skilled in setting up and repairing electrical machines, systems etc.
electricity /ɪˌlekˈtrɪsɪtɪ/ *u.n* kind of energy(2) that can be produced, e.g by a battery in a car or by a generator in a power station, and that is carried along wires to produce light, heat etc and to drive machines.
e,lectric ˈlight ,bulb *c.n* = light bulb.
e,lectric ˈshock *c.n* unpleasant or dangerous sensation caused by an electric current passing through (part of) one's body.
e,lectric ˈstorm *c.n* storm in which there is lightning(2).
electrification /ɪˌlektrɪfɪˈkeɪʃən/ *u.n* **1** act of electrifying(1) s.t: *The electrification of the entire railway network will take many years to complete.* **2** state of electrifying(2) s.o or being electrified.
electrify /ɪˈlektrɪˌfaɪ/ *tr.v* (-ies, -ied) **1** cause (s.t) to be worked by electric power. **2** (*fig*) surprise and excite (s.o): *The audience was electrified by the actor's performance.*
electrocardiogram /ɪˌlektrəʊˈkɑːdɪəʊˌgræm/ *c.n* (*medical*) record of a patient's heartbeats drawn by an electrocardiograph.
electrocardiograph /ɪˌlektrəʊˈkɑːdɪəʊˌgrɑːf/ *c.n* (*medical*) machine that draws lines on paper to show a patient's heartbeats.
electrocute /ɪˈlektrəˌkjuːt/ *tr.v* kill (s.o, an animal) by electricity: *The horse was electrocuted when it bit through the electric wire.*

electrocution /ɪˌlektrəˈkjuːʃən/ c/u.n.

electrode /ɪˈlektrəud/ c.n (technical) rod, plate or wire taking electricity into or out of a liquid, gas etc.

electrolysis /ˌɪlekˈtrɒlɪsɪs/ u.n 1 (technical) chemical division of a substance into its separate parts by passing an electric current through it: The electrolysis of water produces oxygen and hydrogen. 2 use of electricity to get rid of unwanted hair on a person's body.

electromagnet /ɪˌlektrəuˈmægnɪt/ c.n (technical) magnet(1) in the form of a metal rod with wire wound around it through which an electric current is passed.

electron /ɪˈlektrɒn/ c.n (science) negative(4) electric charge that forms part of an atom(1).

electronic /ˌɪlekˈtrɒnɪk/ adj 1 (science) of or referring to electrons. 2 of or referring to electronics; worked or produced by the methods etc of electronics: electronic music; an electronic typewriter.
ˌelecˈtronically adv.
ˌelecˈtronics u.n study of electrons and their use in machines such as radios, televisions, computers etc.

elegant /ˈelɪgənt/ adj 1 (of a person, dress, manners, style etc) graceful; attractive in style: She looked very elegant in her new suit. Opposite inelegant. 2 skilfully simple and effective: an elegant solution to the problem.
ˈelegance u.n. **ˈelegantly** adv.

elegy /ˈelɪdʒɪ/ c.n (pl -ies) poem or song of sadness, esp for s.o who has died.

element /ˈelɪmənt/ c.n 1 (science) substance that cannot be split up into simpler substances by ordinary means: All pure metals are elements. 2 small part: There is an element of truth in what she said. 3 necessary part: Timing was an important element in the success of the advertising. 4 wire or bar in an electric heater or fire that gets hot when the current is switched on. in, out of, one's element in, out of, one's favourite or usual surroundings; doing, not doing, a thing one is used to (and therefore enjoys and is good at): She's in her element when she's in the mountains.

elemental /ˌelɪˈmentl/ adj strong, simple and natural: elemental passions.

elementary /ˌelɪˈmentərɪ/ adj 1 simple; dealing with the first stages: an elementary course in English. Opposite advanced(2). 2 not fully developed: elementary wings on a young bird.

ˈelements def.pl.n 1 forces of nature, e.g wind, rain etc. 2 (often the — of s.t) beginnings (of a subject); the parts to be learnt first: You must master the elements of arithmetic before you can do complicated calculations.

elephant /ˈelɪfənt/ c.n kind of large grey land animal with a long nose (trunk(3)) that is found in Africa and southern Asia. **white elephant** ⇒ white.

elephantine /ˌelɪˈfæntaɪn/ adj 1 of or like an elephant. 2 (informal) huge and awkward: He had elephantine feet.

elevate /ˈelɪveɪt/ tr.v (formal) 1 raise, lift up, (s.o/s.t). 2 (often — s.o to s.t) move (s.o) up (to a higher rank or title): He was elevated to the rank of general before he was forty. 3 improve the mind and/or morals of (s.o).

ˈeleˌvating adj that improves a person's mind or morals: an elevating book/experience.

elevation /ˌelɪˈveɪʃən/ n 1 c/u.n (formal) state or action of elevating(2) s.o or of being elevated: They were proud of their father's elevation to the peerage(2). 2 c.n height, esp above sea-level; hill or high place: From that elevation, you can see for many kilometres. 3 c.n angle in relation to the horizon. 4 c.n plan of one side of a building: The builder looked at the elevation frequently to check that the work was being done correctly.

elevator /ˈelɪveɪtə/ c.n 1 machine for raising or lifting people, things, e.g grain, to a higher place. 2 place for storing grain. 3 (US) = lift(1).

eleven /ɪˈlevn/ det/pron/c.n 1 (cardinal number) number 11 (between 10 and 12): Eleven people came. I'm eleven (years old). There'll be eleven for dinner.
▷ c.n 2 team of 11 players, esp in football, hockey etc: I'm in the first eleven.

elevenses /ɪˈlevnzɪz/ pl.n (informal) light refreshments, e.g coffee or tea and biscuits, taken in the middle of the morning.

eleventh /ɪˈlevnθ/ det/pron 1 (ordinal number) (person or thing) following 10 in order; 11th. (at) **the eleventh hour** (at) the latest possible time to do s.t: Help came at the eleventh hour when they got a loan from their parents.
▷ c.n 2 one of eleven equal parts; $\frac{1}{11}$.

elf /elf/ c.n (pl elves /elvz/) small fairy(1); mischievous(1) little creature.

elfin /ˈelfɪn/ adj of or like an elf, usu in a charming way: She has an elfin face.

elfish /ˈelfɪʃ/ adj (also **elvish** /ˈelvɪʃ/) (of a person) of or like an elf; fond of playing tricks on people.

elicit /ɪˈlɪsɪt/ tr.v (often — s.t from s.o) (formal) draw out (an answer, information etc) (from s.o): The question elicited the correct response from the pupil.

eligible /ˈelɪdʒəbl/ adj (often — for, to do, s.t) (of a person) qualified to be chosen; fit, suitable, (for, to do, s.t): They were looking for eligible young people to do the job. She is now eligible to vote. Opposite ineligible.
eligibility /ˌelɪdʒɪˈbɪlɪtɪ/ u.n.

eliminate /ɪˈlɪmɪneɪt/ tr.v 1 get rid of, remove, (s.o/s.t): Ten people applied for the job and we have already eliminated six of them. David was in France at the time of the murder so the police have eliminated him from their inquiries. 2 make (s.o, a team etc) leave a competition etc by beating her/ him/it: Bristol were eliminated when they lost to Cambridge United.
elimination /ˌɪlɪmɪˈneɪʃən/ u.n.

élite /ɪˈliːt/ c/def.n (French) social group that considers itself to be better than others because of the power, wealth, abilities etc of its members: Many countries are ruled by educated élites.

élitism /ɪˈliːtɪzəm/ u.n (often derog) 1 belief that society etc should be ruled by an élite. 2 belief that education should aim to produce an élite. 3 feeling that one is a member of an élite.

éˈlitist adj 1 showing élitism: an élitist approach.
▷ c.n 2 person who believes in élitism.

elk /elk/ c.n ⇒ moose.

ellipse /ɪˈlɪps/ c.n regular oval(2) that is shaped like an egg.

elliptical /ɪˈlɪptɪkl/ *adj* (also **el'liptic**) shaped like an ellipse.

elm /elm/ *n* 1 *c.n* (also **'elm ,tree**) kind of large tree that grows very high. 2 *u.n* (also *attrib*) wood of this tree: *chairs made of elm; an elm table.*

elocution /ˌeləˈkjuːʃən/ *u.n* (*formal*) (also *attrib*) skill of speaking clearly with good pronunciation: *elocution lessons. She teaches elocution.*

elongate /ˈiːlɒŋˌgeɪt/ *tr.v* (*formal*) make (s.t) longer: *The snake elongated itself and slid away into the bushes.*

elongated /ˈiːlɒŋˌgeɪtɪd/ *attrib.adj* long and narrow; (as if) stretched: *an elongated garden.*

elongation /ˌiːlɒŋˈgeɪʃən/ *u.n.*

elope /ɪˈləʊp/ *intr.v* (often — *with* s.o) (of a person or two people) run away secretly (with s.o one loves) in order to get married: *He eloped with his girlfriend because her parents didn't want them to get married.*

e'lopement *c/u.n.*

eloquent /ˈeləkwənt/ *adj* having or showing ability and skill in speech or writing: *an eloquent letter/speech; an eloquent preacher.*

'eloquence *u.n.* **'eloquently** *adv.*

else /els/ *adv* 1 in addition; besides: *What else shall I do before I go? We didn't go anywhere else. Who else wants to come? Someone else has it. Is anyone else coming? I have nothing else to say.* 2 (often *or else*) if not; otherwise: *Hurry (or) else you'll be late.* (**be**) **anyone/someone, no one** *etc* **else's** belonging to anyone etc other than oneself: *It must be someone else's towel; I've got mine.* **little else** not much more: *There was little else to do so we left.* **how else** in what other way: *I wish you'd told us. How else could we have known you needed help?* **or else** (**a**) ⇨ else(2). (**b**) (as a threat) if s.t is not done there will be trouble: *Come inside this minute, Tommy, or else!* **who/ what else but s.o/s.t** which other person or thing except her/him/it: *Who else but him would make such a remark?* (i.e only he would make such a remark).

elsewhere /ˌelsˈweə/ *adv* in/to another place: *If you can't find your pen here, look elsewhere.*

elucidate /ɪˈluːsɪˌdeɪt/ *tr.v* (*formal*) make the meaning of (s.t) clear; explain (s.t): *The manager elucidated her sales plan at the meeting.*

elucidation /ɪˌluːsɪˈdeɪʃən/ *u.n.*

elude /ɪˈluːd/ *tr.v* (*formal*) 1 avoid (s.t); escape being caught by (s.o), esp by a trick: *The robber eluded the police by hiding behind a wall.* 2 fail to be remembered by (s.o): *His name eludes me for the moment.*

elusive /ɪˈluːsɪv/ *adj* 1 difficult to catch or find: *She's so elusive; I can never find her at home.* 2 difficult to understand or remember: *She found dates in history very elusive at school.*

e'lusively *adv.* **e'lusiveness** *u.n.*

elves, elvish ⇨ elf.

emaciated /ɪˈmeɪsɪˌeɪtɪd/ *adj* (*formal*) (of a person) very thin and very weak through illness or lack of food: *emaciated bodies/children.*

emaciation /ɪˌmeɪsɪˈeɪʃən/ *u.n.*

emanate /ˈeməˌneɪt/ *intr.v* **emanate from s.o/ s.t/s.w** (*formal*) (of smell, gas, light, idea, opinion etc) come from (s.o etc): *Delicious smells emanated from the kitchen. This harmful rumour emanates from someone inside the government.*

emanation /ˌeməˈneɪʃən/ *c/u.n.*

emancipate /ɪˈmænsɪˌpeɪt/ *tr.v* (often — *s.o from s.t*) free (s.o) (from moral, social or legal(1) controls): *The suffragettes worked to emancipate women. Education emancipates people from boring lives.*

emancipation /ɪˌmænsɪˈpeɪʃən/ *u.n.*

embalm /ɪmˈbɑːm/ *tr.v* preserve (a dead body) from decay by treating it with chemicals etc.

em'balmer *c.n* person who embalms bodies.

embankment /ɪmˈbæŋkmənt/ *c.n* bank, wall of earth, stone etc that holds back a river or canal, carries a road, railway etc.

embargo /ɪmˈbɑːgəʊ/ *c.n* (*pl* **-es**) 1 order forbidding trade with, or the movement of ships etc to or from, a country. 2 prohibition(1). **lay/ place/put an embargo on s.t** stop or prohibit(1) s.t. **lift/raise/remove an embargo from s.t** allow s.t to move or happen freely again. **under (an) embargo** prohibited(1).

▷ *tr.v* (**-es, -ed**) 3 place an embargo on (s.t): *These goods have been embargoed while the trade dispute continues.*

embark /ɪmˈbɑːk/ *tr/intr.v* go, put (s.o/s.t), on board a ship at the beginning of a journey: *All passengers were asked to embark an hour before the ship left.* **embark on s.t** begin (a new activity); begin to take part in s.t: *At the age of 40 he embarked on a new* career(1) *as a teacher.*

embarkation /ˌembɑːˈkeɪʃən/ *c/u.n* (example of the) act of embarking: *The bad weather delayed his embarkation for Britain.*

embarrass /ɪmˈbærəs/ *tr.v* 1 make (s.o) feel awkward or ashamed: *The children's bad behaviour embarrassed their mother.* 2 cause difficulty to (s.o): *Emma was embarrassed by money problems.*

em'barrassed *adj* feeling awkward or ashamed: *an embarrassed look/silence.*

em'barrassing *adj* awkward, difficult; causing embarrassment(1): *an embarrassing moment/ situation. He's so embarrassing when he's drunk.*

em'barrassment *n* 1 *c/u.n* (example of the) act of embarrassing s.o or of being embarrassed: *She couldn't hide her embarrassment.* 2 *c.n* person or thing who/that embarrasses(1) s.o: *He's such an embarrassment to his wife when he gets drunk.*

embassy /ˈembəsɪ/ *n* (*pl* **-ies**) 1 *c.n* (also *attrib*) official building in which an ambassador and her/ his staff work: *the British Embassy in Rome; embassy business.* 2 *c.n* duty of an ambassador. 3 *c/def.pl.n* ambassador and her/his staff.

embed /ɪmˈbed/ *tr.v* (**-dd-**) (often — *s.t in(to) s.t*) 1 fix (s.t) firmly and deeply (into surrounding material): *The poles were embedded firmly into the ground.* 2 (*fig*) fix (s.t) firmly, esp in one's mind, memory etc: *That terrible day will always stay embedded in my mind.*

embellish /ɪmˈbelɪʃ/ *tr.v* (often — *s.t with, by doing, s.t*) 1 decorate (s.t), make (s.t) beautiful, (with s.t extra): *She embellished the cake with pink* icing(1). 2 (*fig*) improve (s.t) by adding details: *Joanna embellished her story by adding a few imaginative details to it.*

em'bellishment *n* 1 *u.n* act of embellishing s.t or of being embellished. 2 *c.n* thing that embellishes s.t.

ember /ˈembə/ *c.n* (usu *pl*) small piece of

coal, wood or other material that is hot and red in a fire.

embezzle /ɪmˈbezl/ *tr.v* use (money etc that has been put into one's care) dishonestly for one's own gain or purposes: *The bank manager embezzled all the old lady's money.*
em'bezzlement *u.n.*
em'bezzler *c.n* person who embezzles money.

embitter /ɪmˈbɪtə/ *tr.v* (*formal*) cause (s.o) to feel bitter: *His failure embittered him.*
em'bittered *adj* feeling bitter or annoyed.
em'bitterment *u.n.*

emblem /ˈembləm/ *c.n* sign or symbol representing s.t: *A drawing of a red heart is often an emblem of love.*

emblematic /ˌembləˈmætɪk/ *adj* (often — *of s.t*) (*formal*) of or used as an emblem: *A dove*(1) *is emblematic of peace.*

embody /ɪmˈbɒdɪ/ *tr.v* (*-ies, -ied*) (*formal*) be an expression of (s.t); represent (s.t): *Her latest book embodies all her new ideas on education.*
em'bodiment *c.n* (usu *an/the* — *of s.t*) thing that embodies (s.t) or is embodied (by s.t); perfect example (of s.t): *The little boy was the embodiment of good behaviour.*

embolden /ɪmˈbəʊldən/ *tr.v* (often — *s.o to do s.t*) (*formal*) make (s.o) bold (enough to do s.t): *His first attempt was successful and this emboldened him to make a second.*

emboss /ɪmˈbɒs/ *tr.v* decorate (s.t) with raised patterns etc that stand out from the surface: *His writing-paper is embossed with his address.*
em'bossed *adj* decorated with a pattern etc that stands out from the surface: *embossed writing-paper.*

embrace /ɪmˈbreɪs/ *c.n* (*formal*) 1 act of holding s.o tightly in one's arms; hug(1).
▷ *v* (*formal*) 2 *tr.v* hold (s.o) tightly in one's arms, usu as a sign of affection; hug(2) (s.o). 3 *intr.v* (of two people) hold, hug(2), each other: *The sisters embraced when they met.* 4 *tr.v* accept (s.t) eagerly; make use of (s.t): *He embraced every opportunity that life offered him.* 5 *tr.v* include (s.t): *His knowledge embraced languages, literature and science.*

embroider /ɪmˈbrɔɪdə/ *v* 1 *tr/intr.v* (often — *s.t with s.t*) decorate (cloth etc) (with needlework, a pattern etc): *She embroidered the cloth with flowers. He embroidered flowers on the cloth.* 2 *tr.v* (*fig*) add details that are not true to (a story etc) to make it more interesting or exciting: *He embroidered the story when he told it to his friends.* **embroider s.t in s.t** embroider(1) s.t using a particular colour, type of thread etc: *The dress was embroidered in red silk.*
em'broidery *u.n* 1 skill or art of embroidering(1) s.t; example of this; piece of this work: *She's good at embroidery.* 2 (*fig*) additions to a story that are not true but make it more interesting: *His story contains more embroidery than fact.*

embroil /ɪmˈbrɔɪl/ *tr.v* (often — *s.o in s.t*) cause (s.o) to be involved (⇒ involve(2)) (in a quarrel or trouble etc): *Why do you always have to get embroiled in other people's arguments?*

embryo /ˈembrɪˌəʊ/ *c.n* (*pl -s*) 1 young animal, plant etc before birth or before coming out of an egg or seed. 2 human during its first eight weeks in the womb: *the human embryo.* 3 (*fig*) thing that is still developing: *the embryo of an idea.* **in**

embryo (*fig*) not yet developed; still developing: *Her plans for her next book are still in embryo.*

embryonic /ˌembrɪˈɒnɪk/ *adj* 1 of or like an embryo(1,2). 2 (*fig*) not yet developed: *an embryonic idea.*

emend /ɪˈmend/ *tr.v* make changes, correct errors etc, in a (book, piece of writing etc): *She emended her article before it was printed.* Compare amend.
emendation /ˌiːmenˈdeɪʃən/ *c/u.n.*

emerald /ˈemərəld/ *n* (also *attrib*) 1 *c.n* bright green precious stone: *a ring with five emeralds; an emerald ring.* 2 *u.n* bright green colour: *emerald fields; emerald green.*

emerge /ɪˈmɜːdʒ/ *intr.v* 1 (often — *from s.t/s.w*) come into view, appear (from s.w hidden): *A man emerged suddenly from the shadows.* 2 (of facts, ideas, opinions etc) become known: *New ideas began to emerge after the discussion. It later emerged that he was responsible for the crime.*
e'mergence *u.n.*
e'mergent *adj* (*formal*) 1 emerging. 2 (of a nation) developing; newly independent: *Africa has many emergent nations.*

emergency /ɪˈmɜːdʒənsɪ/ *c/u.n* (*pl -ies*) (also *attrib*) suddenly dangerous or very serious situation needing immediate action: *There was an emergency when the river flooded the town. A state of emergency was declared when the forest caught fire. The thieves used the emergency exit to escape.* **in an emergency; in case of emergency** if there is an emergency: *In an emergency you can always ring me for help.*

emery /ˈeməri/ *u.n* (also *attrib*) powder made from hard metal, used for polishing or making s.t smooth: *emery paper.*
'emery ,board *c.n* strip of cardboard coated with emery and used for smoothing or filing (⇒ file¹(2)) fingernails.

emetic /ɪˈmetɪk/ *adj* 1 (*medical*) causing vomiting (⇒ vomit(*v*)).
▷ *u.n* 2 (*medical*) medicine used to cause vomiting (⇒ vomit(*v*)): *The child was given an emetic after it swallowed the cleaning liquid.*

emigrate /ˈemɪˌɡreɪt/ *intr.v* (usu — (*from s.w*) *to s.w*) leave one's own country in order to go and settle in another one: *Many people have emigrated from Europe to Australia.* Compare immigrate.
emigrant /ˈemɪɡrənt/ *c.n* person who emigrates.
emigration /ˌemɪˈɡreɪʃən/ *c/u.n.*

eminent /ˈemɪnənt/ *adj* (usu *attrib*) 1 (of a person) distinguished, famous: *an eminent politician.* 2 (*formal*) (of a quality) of a very high level/degree; remarkable: *She showed eminent common sense.*
eminence /ˈemɪnəns/ *n* 1 *u.n* state of being famous, distinguished, important or in high office: *He rapidly gained eminence as a writer.* 2 *c.n* (*formal*) piece of high ground: *From an eminence just outside the town we could look down on the castle.* **His/Your Eminence** title given to a Cardinal(2).
'eminently *adv* in an eminent(2) way; remarkably; in the highest degree: *Jill is eminently suitable for the job because she speaks three languages.*

emir /eˈmɪə/ *c.n* (often with capital **E** in names)

1 title of an independent Muslim(1) ruler. **2** title of a male descendant of Mohammed.

emirate /e'mɪərɪt/ *c.n* (with capital **E** in names) rank and title, lands etc of an emir(1): *the United Arab Emirates.*

emissary /'emɪsərɪ/ *c.n* (*pl -ies*) (*formal*) messenger, esp one sent to deliver unpleasant or secret news.

emit /ɪ'mɪt/ *tr.v* (*-tt-*) (*formal*) send out, give out, (heat, light, sound, a stream of s.t etc): *The chimney emitted clouds of smoke.*

emission /ɪ'mɪʃən/ *n* (*formal*) **1** *c.n* thing emitted. **2** *c/u.n* (example of the) act of emitting s.t: *Many countries are introducing controls on car* exhaust(2) *emissions.*

emolument /ɪ'mɒljʊmənt/ *c.n* (usu *pl*) (*formal*) payment (in money or another form such as free use of a car) for work done.

emotion /ɪ'məʊʃən/ *n* **1** *c/u.n* (example of a) (strong) feeling: *Love and hate are opposite emotions.* **2** *u.n* excitement of the mind or feelings: *She heard the terrible news without showing any emotion.*

e'motional *adj* **1** of or filled with emotion: *He made an emotional speech on behalf of the prisoner.* **2** likely to show too much emotion(2): *He is very emotional and is likely to burst into tears when upset.*

e'motiona₁lism *u.n* (tendency towards the) show of too much emotion(2): *The politician's speech was full of emotionalism.*

e'motionally *adv.*

e'motionless *adj* not feeling or showing any emotion.

e'motionlessly *adv.*

emotive /ɪ'məʊtɪv/ *adj* tending to work on, play with, people's emotions(1): *Emotive speeches can start a revolution.*

empathy /'empəθɪ/ *u.n* **1** power to understand and share another person's feelings etc because of having had the same experience. **2** power to share in and understand the feeling created(2) by a place, a work of art etc. *in empathy with s.o/ s.t* able to share and understand s.o's feelings or what s.t means. Compare sympathy.

emperor ⇒ empire.

emphasis /'emfəsɪs/ *c/u.n* (*pl emphases* /'emfəsiːz/) **1** special importance given to an idea or fact etc: *The emphasis in our classes is on speaking English as often as possible.* **2** stress(2) put on a syllable, word or words to show its/ their importance compared to other syllables or words. *lay/place/put* (the) *emphasis on s.t* emphasize s.t.

emphasize, -ise /'emfə₁saɪz/ *tr.v* **1** bring out the importance of (one thing) in relation to others: *The teacher emphasized the need for students to use English when talking to each other.* **2** stress(4) (a syllable, word or words) to show its/their importance in relation to other syllables or words.

emphatic /ɪm'fætɪk/ *adj* **1** having, showing or using emphasis(1): *We got an emphatic 'no' to our request.* **2** expressing s.t with emphasis(1) and force: *He was quite emphatic about not wanting to go to college.*

em'phatically *adv.*

empire /'empaɪə/ *c.n* **1** (with capital **E** in names) group of countries ruled by one

country or government: *the Roman Empire*; *the British Empire.* **2** group of businesses controlled by one person or family. *She runs a jewellery empire.*

emperor /'empərə/ *c.n* (with capital **E** in names) man who rules an empire.

'empire ₁builder *c.n* person who gains power by forming empires(2).

empress /'emprɪs/ *c.n* (with capital **E** in names) **1** woman who rules an empire. **2** wife of an emperor.

empirical /ɪm'pɪrɪkl/ *adj* (also, less usu. **em'piric**) (*formal*) based on the results of direct observation or experiment, not on theory(2): *empirical tests/* methods(1).

em'pirically *adv.*

empiricism /ɪm'pɪrɪ₁sɪzəm/ *u.n* (*formal*) **1** belief that experience is the only way of gaining knowledge. **2** empirical practice.

employ /ɪm'plɔɪ/ *tr.v* **1** (often — *s.o as/in, to do*, *s.t*) pay (s.o) to work for one (in a particular job): *The farmer employed five new workers. He's been employed as the manager's secretary.* **2** (*formal*) make use of (s.t): *She employs several different* techniques *in her painting.* **3** (*formal*) spend or use (time): *How do you employ your free time?*

employee /₁emplɔɪ'iː/ *c.n* person who is employed(1) and paid a salary.

em'ployer *c.n* **1** person who employs(1) one or more other people and pays them a salary. **2** (often *an — of s.t*) (*formal*) person who makes use of s.t (esp to make things).

em'ployment *u.n* **1** act of employing(1) s.o: *What would be the cost of the employment of another ten people?* **2** state of being employed: *I'm in full-time employment.* Opposite unemployment. **3** paid work: *The new factory will provide employment for a hundred people. be in employment* have a job. *be in s.o's employment* be employed(1) by s.o.

em'ployment ₁agency *c.n* business that is paid to find jobs for people.

empower /ɪm'paʊə/ *tr.v* (usu — *s.o/s.t to do s.t*) (*formal*) give power or rights to (s.o/s.t) (to do s.t).

empress ⇒ empire.

empty /'emptɪ/ *adj* (*-ier, -iest*) **1** containing nothing; lacking its usual contents: *an empty box*; *an empty room.* Opposite full(1). **2** (usu *attrib*) (*fig*) without meaning or worth: *empty promises*; *empty threats. be/feel empty* (a) feel hungry. (b) feel sad. (*do s.t*) *on an empty stomach* ⇒ stomach.

▷ *c.n* (*pl -ies*) **3** (usu *pl*) (*informal*) empty bottle etc: *Take the empties back to the shop.*

▷ *v* (*-ies, -ied*) **4** *tr.v* remove the contents of (a container) or put (the contents of) s.t (into s.t else): *The cat emptied the rubbish bin on to the floor.* **5** *intr.v* become empty: *After the play, the theatre quickly emptied. empty s.t out* (*of s.t*) pour, take, out the contents (of s.t): *She emptied her money out of her purse to find the right change.*

'emptily *adv* in an empty(2) way.

'emptiness *u.n* state of being empty(1,2).

₁empty-'handed *adj* (usu *pred*) **1** bringing nothing: *She arrived empty-handed.* **2** taking nothing away: *Although he came to ask his father for money, he left empty-handed.*

‚empty-'headed *adj* (*derog*) silly or stupid; lacking common sense: *an empty-headed boy.*

emu /'iːmjuː/ *c.n* kind of large Australian bird that cannot fly but can run very fast.

emulate /'emjʊˌleɪt/ *tr.v* (*formal*) **1** try to equal or do better than (s.o); rival (s.o). **2** eagerly imitate (s.o/s.t): *You should emulate your brother's good example.*

emulation /ˌemjʊˈleɪʃən/ *u.n.*

emulsion /ɪˈmʌlʃən/ *n* **1** *c/u.n* creamy liquid containing two or more liquids mixed together so that they cannot be separated. **2** *u.n* (also **e'mulsion ‚paint**) creamy paint containing water, used for painting walls and ceilings.

enable /ɪˈneɪbl/ *tr.v* (usu – *s.o/s.t to do s.t*) make (s.o/s.t) able (to do s.t); make it possible (for s.o/s.t to do s.t): *The scholarship enabled her to go to university.*

enact /ɪˈnækt/ *tr.v* **1** (*law*) make (a law) official: *The government has enacted several new laws.* **2** act (a part), perform (a scene or a play), on stage.

e'nactment *n* **1** *u.n* act of enacting s.t or of being enacted. **2** *c.n* law.

enamel /ɪˈnæml/ *u.n* **1** (also *attrib*) substance like melted glass used to form a hard shiny covering for metal, china etc in order to decorate or protect it: *an enamel bowl.* **2** (also **e'namel ‚paint**) hard paint that gives a smooth shining surface, esp for wood and metal. **3** hard shining outer covering of teeth.

▷ *tr.v* (*-ll-*, US *-l-*) **4** (often – *s.t in s.t*) coat or decorate (s.t) with enamel(1) (usu in bright colours): *The bowl had been enamelled (in red).*

enamoured /ɪˈnæməd/ *adj* (usu *pred*; – *of s.o/s.t*) (*formal or joking*) in love with (s.o/s.t); fond of (s.o/s.t): *He doesn't seem too enamoured of his new job.*

encampment /ɪnˈkæmpmənt/ *c.n* (*military*) place where soldiers etc are camping.

encase /ɪnˈkeɪs/ *tr.v* (*formal*) **1** put (s.o/s.t) in a container such as a case. **2** surround (s.o/s.t) completely as if in a case: *He was encased from head to toe in mud.*

enchant /ɪnˈtʃɑːnt/ *tr.v* (*formal*) **1** charm, delight, (s.o): *The little girl was enchanted with her new dress.* **2** use magic(3) on (s.o/s.t); place (s.o/s.t) under a spell²(1).

en'chanted *adj* **1** delighted: *I was enchanted by the child's gift.* **2** under a spell²(1): *an enchanted forest.*

en'chanter *c.n* person who enchants s.o/s.t.

en'chanting *adj* delightful; charming: *an enchanting smile.*

en'chantingly *adv.*

en'chantment *n* **1** *u.n* state of enchanting (⇨ enchant) s.o/s.t or of being enchanted. **2** *c.n* thing that enchants s.o/s.t. **3** *c.n* delight, charm, attraction.

en'chantress *c.n* woman who enchants s.o/s.t.

encircle /ɪnˈsɜːkl/ *tr.v* form a circle round (s.o/s.t): *A beautiful garden encircled the house* (or *The house was encircled with a beautiful garden*).

en'circlement *u.n.*

enclave /'enkleɪv/ *c.n* (*formal*) area of land belonging to one country but completely within the boundaries of another country: *West Berlin is an enclave in East Germany.*

enclose /ɪnˈkləʊz/ *tr.v* (often – *s.t in s.t*) **1** put (s.t) in the same envelope as s.t else: *I'm enclosing a few photographs with my letter.* **2** surround (s.t) with a fence, wall etc: *The old town was enclosed by a high wall.*

en'closed *adj* that is put in the same envelope as s.t else, e.g the letter that mentions it: *Please see the enclosed copy of the agreement.* Compare attached.

enclosure /ɪnˈkləʊʒə/ *n* **1** *c.n* (*commerce*) thing enclosed, esp with a letter in an envelope etc. **2** *c.n* piece of ground that has been fenced off: *The sheep were kept in an enclosure during the bad winter weather.* **3** *c/u.n* (example of the) act of enclosing(2) s.t.

encode /enˈkəʊd/ *tr.v* write (a message etc) in code(3): *He encoded the secret message in a new code.* Compare decode.

encompass /ɪnˈkʌmpəs/ *tr.v* (*formal*) **1** surround (s.o/s.t); encircle (s.o/s.t). **2** consist of, contain, (s.t): *Our mathematics course encompassed arithmetic, algebra and geometry.*

encore /ˈɒŋkɔː/ *c.n* (*French*) **1** request by an audience for a repeat or an extra (musical) performance. **2** repeated or extra performance given at an audience's request: *The singer was called back to give three encores.*

▷ *interj* **3** (used by an audience esp after a musical performance) Again! Once more! Repeat!

encounter /ɪnˈkaʊntə/ *c.n* **1** meeting, often one that is not expected: *a mysterious encounter with a stranger. I liked her on our first encounter* (when we first met). **2** meeting with an enemy in battle.

▷ *tr.v* (*formal*) **3** meet (s.o), esp by chance. **4** meet, experience, (danger, difficulty etc): *We encountered many problems while we were climbing the mountain.* **5** meet (an enemy) in battle.

encourage /ɪnˈkʌrɪdʒ/ *tr.v* **1** (often – *s.o/s.t in, to do, s.t*) give courage, confidence, support or hope to (s.o, an animal) (to do s.t etc); urge (s.o, an animal) to do better: *His success encouraged him to make even greater efforts.* **2** help (s.t) to develop or spread: *The government encouraged the campaign(2) against smoking.* Compare discourage.

en'couragement *n* **1** *u.n* act of encouraging(1) s.o: *She needs a lot of encouragement.* **2** *c.n* thing that encourages(1) s.o: *Her early success was a great encouragement to her.* Opposite discouragement.

en'couraging *adj* giving courage, support or confidence: *an encouraging smile; an encouraging start.* Opposite discouraging.

en'couragingly *adv.*

encroach /ɪnˈkrəʊtʃ/ *intr.v* (usu – *on s.o/s.t*) **1** go beyond one's rights (into s.o else's); go beyond what is normal or suitable: *She felt that she was encroaching on her friend's privacy and so she did not ask any more questions.* **2** gradually spread or come (onto s.t): *The flooded river had encroached on the fields and they were now covered with water.*

en'croachment *n* **1** *c/u.n* (example of the) act of encroaching. **2** *c.n* thing gained by encroaching.

encumber /ɪnˈkʌmbə/ *tr.v* (*formal*; usu passive) **1** get in the way of (s.o); hamper² (s.o): *We were encumbered with a lot of luggage when we went* *away on holiday.* **2** fill up (a place etc) in a harmful or useless way: *The library was encumbered with a lot of old newspapers that no one ever read.*

encumbrance /ɪnˈkʌmbrəns/ *c.n* (*formal*) person or thing who/that encumbers one: *The children are an encumbrance when I'm shopping.*

encyclopaedia /enˌsaɪkləˈpiːdɪə/ *c.n* (also **en,cyclo'pedia**) book or set of books containing information on several different subjects or different kinds of information on one particular subject.

encyclopaedic /enˌsaɪkləˈpiːdɪk/ *adj* (also **en,cyclo'pedic**) **1** of or like an encyclopaedia. **2** having/containing a wide range of knowledge on many subjects: *She has an encyclopaedic mind.*

end /end/ *c.n* **1** last part; farthest/furthest limit: *Tie the ends of the rope together. Soon the path came to an end. The house at the end of the street was sold last week.* **2** (often — *of s.t*) finish, final part, (of s.t): *The children were happy to go to bed at the end of a tiring day.* **3** small piece (of s.t) that remains: *a cigarette end.* **4** death: *His end was peaceful as he died in his sleep.* **5** (often *pl*) aim; thing one is trying to get: *He will do almost anything to reach his ends.* **at an end** finished; going no further: *Our friendship is at an end and I do not want to see you again.* **at a loose end** (*informal*) without having anything or very much to do or occupy oneself with. **bring s.t to an end** finish, stop, s.t: *As there was no further business he brought the meeting to an end.* **end on** (**a**) with the ends (of two things) meeting: *The cars hit each other end on.* (**b**) with the end of s.t nearest to one: *He looked at the piece of wood end on to see if it was straight along its length.* **end to end** with the ends (of two or more things) touching. **for days, weeks** etc **on end** continuing, lasting, for days, weeks etc: *It rains for days on end in April.* **get (hold of) the wrong end of the stick** ⇒ stick (*n*). **go off at the deep end** (*fig*) become angry very suddenly. (**go to**) **the ends of the earth** (**to do s.t**) (go) anywhere, however far away or difficult to reach (to do s.t): *He was willing to go to the ends of the earth to find his sister.* **in the end** finally; at last: *In the end I told him what he had been wanting to know.* **make (both) ends meet** (*fig; informal*) manage to live within one's income or means. **a means to an end** ⇒ means. **no end of s.t** (*informal*) very much/many of s.t: *We have had no end of problems since we bought the house.* **on (its) end** standing on one end: *Put the ladder on (its) end against the wall.* **put an end to s.t** finish s.t; get rid of s.t: *He put an end to his own life. We need to put an end to all this quarrelling.* **the (absolute) end** (*informal*) beyond the limit of what one can accept or put up with: *The children have been the absolute end today; they've been so naughty.* **the end justifies the means** ⇒ means. **to that/ this end** for that/this purpose: *Success was his aim and to that end he worked fifteen hours a day.* **to/until the bitter end** (**a**) until death or until all hope has ended: *She fought to the bitter end for her life.* (**b**) until s.t is completely finished: *We stayed until the bitter end.* **without end** never stopping or finishing:

The song seemed to go on without end. ⇒ unending.

▷ *v* **6** *tr.v* finish, complete, (s.t); cause (s.t) to finish; spend the last part of (a period of time etc): *We ended the meal with coffee.* **7** *intr.v* stop; come to or reach an end(2): *The story ended happily.* **end in s.t** have s.t as a result: *The day ended in disaster(2).* **end it (all)** (*informal*) kill oneself. **end off (s.t)** (**with s.t** or **by doing s.t**) finish (s.t) (by having or doing s.t): *We ended off (the party) by all of us singing songs.* **end up at s.w** arrive at a place finally after visiting other places: *We ended up at Mary's house after our day in London.* **end up with s.t** (or (**by**) **doing s.t**) finish by having (or doing) s.t: *After all the arguments we ended up going to the cinema.*

'ending *c.n* last part of a story, a play, a word etc; finish: *The film had a happy ending.*

'endless *adj* **1** without end; not stopping: *The speech was so boring that it seemed endless to the audience.* **2** (*attrib*) (*informal*) very many: *The children asked endless questions.*

'endlessly *adv.* **'endlessness** *u.n.*

'end,ways *adv* (also **'end,wise**) with an end facing s.o who is looking at it; with its end forward; end on(b): *If you hold it endways, we might be able to get it through the door.*

endanger /ɪnˈdeɪndʒə/ *tr.v* cause danger to (s.o/ s.t); put (s.o/s.t) in danger: *The storm endangered many lives.*

endear /ɪnˈdɪə/ *tr/reflex.v* (usu — oneself/s.o/ s.t to s.o) (*formal*) cause (oneself/s.o/s.t) to be loved or liked by s.o: *The pretty child endeared himself to everyone.*

en'dearing *adj* (*formal*) attractive; likeable; lovable: *an endearing smile; endearing ways.*

en'dearment *c/u.n* act/word(s) of liking or love: *'Darling' is a term of endearment. He whispered many endearments in her ear.*

endeavour /ɪnˈdevə/ *c/u.n* **1** strong attempt or effort: *He made every endeavour to pass his examinations.*

▷ *intr.v* **2** (usu — *to do s.t*) try hard (to do s.t): *She endeavoured to win their respect.*

endemic /enˈdemɪk/ *adj* (esp of a disease) often occurring in a particular area or among a particular group of people: *Malaria is endemic in many hot countries. Violence is becoming endemic in our cities.* Compare epidemic.

ending ⇒ end.

endive /ˈendaɪv/ *c.n* kind of vegetable with curly leaves, used in salads(1).

endless(ly/ness) ⇒ end.

endorse /ɪnˈdɔːs/ *tr.v* **1** write one's signature on the back of (a cheque etc) (so that it can be put into an account etc). **2** write remarks etc in, on the back of, (a document(1)): *If you are found guilty of driving too fast, your licence(1) will be endorsed.* **3** approve of, support, (s.o/s.t): *I endorse everything he said in his speech.*

en'dorsement *c/u.n* (example of the) act of endorsing s.o/s.t, e.g a driving licence(1).

endow /ɪnˈdaʊ/ *tr.v* (often — s.o/s.t *with* s.t) give money or property to (a person, an institution etc) for her/his/its permanent use: *He endowed his old college with a large sum of money.* **be endowed with s.t** (*formal*) be born with s.t; have s.t naturally: *She is endowed with great musical ability.*

en'dowment *n* **1** *c/u.n* (example of the) act of endowing s.t. **2** *c.n* sum of money etc given to a person or institution.

endure /ɪn'djuə/ *v* (*formal*) **1** *tr.v* bear, put up with, (s.t): *I cannot endure seeing small children fighting.* **2** *tr.v* suffer (pain, difficulties etc): *She endured her long illness with great courage.* **3** *intr.v* last, continue, stand firm: *The poet's work will endure for ever.*

en'durable *adj* that can be endured(1,2); bearable: *The hot sticky weather was only just endurable.*

en'durance *u.n* **1** power to endure(1,2) s.t; continuing strength: *You will need great endurance to climb that mountain.* **2** act or state of enduring(1,2) s.t. **beyond/past endurance** at/to a point where s.t can no longer be endured(1,2).

en'durance ,test *c.n* **1** test to see or show how long s.o/s.t can endure(1,2) s.t. **2** (*fig*) very difficult thing: *Swimming in rough seas is an endurance test for even the strongest swimmer.*

en'during *attrib.adj* lasting a long time; lasting for ever: *There was an enduring agreement between the two countries over fishing rights.*

en'duringly *adv.*

endways, endwise ⇒ end.

enema /'enɪmə/ *c.n* (*medical*) **1** injection of liquid into the rectum through the anus in order to clean the body's (digestive) system. **2** device for injecting the liquid.

enemy /'enəmɪ/ *n* (*pl* -ies) **1** *c.n* person who shows hatred for s.o/s.t or who tries, wishes, to attack or harm s.o/s.t: *I had one enemy at school who was always getting me into trouble.* **2** *c.n* (often — to s.o/s.t) thing that harms s.o/s.t: *Very cold weather is an enemy to the poor and the old.* **3** *def.n* the armed forces of a nation or nations that is/are at war with one's own country; member of such a force: *We must defeat the enemy and end the war.*

energy /'enədʒɪ/ *n* (*pl* -ies) **1** *c/u.n* power, force or ability to do work: *At the beginning of term most students are full of energy.* **2** *u.n* (*science*) ability of a substance or heat to do work: *solar energy.*

energetic /ˌenə'dʒetɪk/ *adj* full of energy(1); very active: *Why is it that children become very energetic at bedtime?*

,ener'getically *adv.*

enervate /'enəˌveɪt/ *tr.v* (*formal*) cause (s.o) to lose strength or feel weak: *He's always enervated by hot weather.*

enforce /ɪn'fɔːs/ *tr.v* **1** make s.o obey (s.t): *The police enforce the law.* **2** give force or strength to (an argument, a point etc): *Roger enforced his argument by showing the manager the new sales figures.* **enforce s.t (up)on s.o** force s.o to do/be s.t: *The captain enforced discipline on his team.*

en'forceable *adj* that can be enforced(1): *This law is not enforceable.*

en'forcement *u.n.*

enfranchise /ɪn'fræntʃaɪz/ *tr.v* (*formal*) give political rights to (s.o), esp the right to vote in government elections: *In Britain in 1918 women over the age of 30 were enfranchised for the first time.*

en'franchisement *u.n.*

engage /ɪn'geɪdʒ/ *v* **1** *tr.v* (*formal*) take (s.o)

into one's employment: *She engaged a new secretary when the old one left.* **2** *tr.v* (*formal*) hire (s.t); arrange to have the use of (s.t): *We engaged a taxi to take us to the station.* **3** *intr.v* (of parts of a machine etc) lock/fit together: *The teeth of the two wheels had to engage before the machine would work.* **4** *tr.v* attack, begin fighting with, (an enemy etc): *The officer ordered his men to engage the enemy at dawn(1).* **be engaged (by s.t)** (of s.o's attention etc) be occupied(4); be held (by s.t): *At the zoo the children's attention was engaged by the games the monkeys were playing.* **engage s.o as s.t** employ s.o to do a particular job: *He was engaged as a secretary last year.* **(be) engaged in (doing) s.t** (be) busy doing s.t. **engage s.o in conversation** (start and) carry on a conversation with s.o. **be engaged (to s.o)** have promised to marry (s.o).

en'gaged *adj* **1** promised in marriage to s.o, one another: *an engaged couple.* **2** already in use: *The telephone line is engaged. The toilet is engaged.*

en'gagement *c.n* **1** promise, esp a formal one made in writing. **2** (also *attrib*) agreement, promise, to marry s.o: *an engagement ring.* **3** arrangement to go s.w, meet s.o, do s.t, at a fixed time: *She had so many engagements to keep that she didn't have time for any lunch.* **4** (*formal*) battle: *a naval engagement.*

en'gaging *adj* (*formal*) attractive; delightful: *That child has an engaging smile.*

engine /'endʒɪn/ *c.n* **1** machine that changes energy into power or movement: *Most car engines use petrol to make them go.* **2** = railway engine.

'engine ,driver *c.n* person who drives a railway engine.

engineer /ˌendʒɪ'nɪə/ *c.n* **1** person whose profession is engineering, esp one who builds or makes plans for engines, machines, roads, bridges, railways etc. **2** person trained and skilled in the control of an engine or engines, esp a ship's engine. **3** (US) = engine driver. ▷ *tr.v* **4** arrange, organize, (s.t) skilfully for one's own advantage or s.o else's: *He engineered a meeting between his son and the rich young woman.*

engineering /ˌendʒɪ'nɪərɪŋ/ *u.n* practical use of scientific knowledge in the planning and making of engines, machines etc; work, profession, of an engineer(1). **civil/electrical/mechanical engineering** ⇒ civil, electrical, mechanical.

English /'ɪŋglɪʃ/ *adj* **1** of or belonging to England. **2** written or spoken in the language that many people in the UK, US and the Commonwealth speak: *English books.* ▷ *n* **3** *u.n* language spoken by many people in the UK, US and the Commonwealth. **4** *def.pl.n* people of England.

'Englishman *c.n* (*pl* -men) man who comes from England.

'English,woman *c.n* (*pl* -,women) woman who comes from England.

engrained /ɪn'greɪnd/ *adj* = ingrained.

engrave /ɪn'greɪv/ *tr.v* cut (lines, letters, patterns etc) on a hard surface for decoration or making plates(3) for use in printing. **engrave s.t (up)on s.t** (a) decorate (s.t) by cutting lines, letters etc on it. (b) (often passive) (*fig*) put (s.t) deeply into the memory or mind: *The terrible accident will* *always be engraved upon his memory.* **engrave s.t with s.t** decorate s.t by cutting s.t into it: *The watch was engraved with his name.*

en'graver *c.n* person whose job is to engrave s.t.

en'graving *n* **1** *c.n* copy of a picture printed from an engraved metal plate(3) etc. **2** *u.n* art or skill of engraving (⇨ engrave).

engross /ɪnˈɡrəʊs/ *tr.v* (*formal*) take the whole attention of (s.o); occupy (s.o) totally: *The film engrossed the children and they forgot that they were supposed to be home for tea.* **be engrossed in (doing) s.t** be completely absorbed by s.t interesting: *Sally was so engrossed in (reading) her book she did not hear the phone ring.*

en'grossing *adj* (*formal*) so interesting that it takes up one's whole attention: *an engrossing book.*

engulf /ɪnˈɡʌlf/ *tr.v* swallow up (s.o/s.t): *During the storm the boat was engulfed by huge waves.*

enhance /ɪnˈhɑːns/ *tr.v* make (s.o/s.t) more attractive, valuable, powerful etc; increase (the value, attraction, power etc of s.t): *His smart clothes enhanced his appearance. The artist's fame enhanced the value of her pictures.*
en'hancement *u.n.*

enigma /ɪˈnɪɡmə/ *c.n* **1** mystery; puzzle. **2** person or situation who/that is hard to explain, understand: *My brother is a complete enigma to me; he earns a lot of money but always wears old clothes.*

enigmatic /ˌenɪɡˈmætɪk/ *adj* (*formal*) mysterious, puzzling; hard to explain, understand: *an enigmatic smile.*
,enig'matically *adv.*

enjoy /ɪnˈdʒɔɪ/ *tr.v* **1** take pleasure in (s.t): *I always enjoy good food.* **2** have the use of (s.t); possess (s.t that is an advantage): *He's always enjoyed good health.* **enjoy oneself** feel pleasure, delight etc because of what one is doing or where one is: *The children really enjoyed themselves at the seaside.*

en'joyable *adj* giving, able to give, pleasure, delight etc: *an enjoyable film.* Opposite unenjoyable.

en'joyment *n* **1** *u.n* pleasure; act or state of enjoying(1) s.t. **2** *u.n* use, possession of, s.t that is an advantage: *His enjoyment of the money he had stolen was short-lived.* **3** *c.n* thing that causes pleasure: *The afternoon drives were her one enjoyment in life.*

enlarge /ɪnˈlɑːdʒ/ *v* **1** *tr.v* make (s.t) larger: *I want this photograph enlarged.* **2** *intr.v* become larger. **enlarge (up)on s.t** (*formal*) speak/write (more) fully about s.t; explain s.t in greater detail: *He enlarged upon his plans for their holiday.*
en'largement *n* **1** *u.n* act of making s.t larger. **2** *c.n* copy of a photograph that is larger than the original. Opposite reduction(2).

enlighten /ɪnˈlaɪtn/ *tr.v* give (s.o) information or knowledge which he/she does not already have but ought to have: *He didn't know he had to pay his rent in advance until I enlightened him.*
en'lightened *adj* free from false or old-fashioned ideas: *a very enlightened teacher.*
en'lightenment *u.n.*

enlist /ɪnˈlɪst/ *v* **1** *tr/intr.v* (cause (s.o) to) become a member of the armed forces: *People hurried to enlist when the war started.* **2** *tr.v* (*formal*) get (s.t)

as help or support: *He enlisted a lot of sympathy when he broke his leg.*
en'listment *c/u.n* (example of the) act or state of enlisting s.o/s.t or of being enlisted.

enliven /ɪnˈlaɪvn/ *tr.v* (*formal*) make (s.t) (more) lively(1) or cheerful: *The teacher's jokes enlivened the lesson.*

enmesh /ɪnˈmeʃ/ *tr.v* (also **in'mesh**) involve (s.o/s.t) in an embarrassing situation, public scandal(1) etc.

enmity /ˈenmɪtɪ/ *n* (*pl -ies*) **1** *c.n* feeling of hatred. **2** *u.n* state of being an enemy; hatred: *There was enmity between the two countries but war had not actually been declared.*

enormous /ɪˈnɔːməs/ *adj* very large; huge: *enormous feet; an enormous amount of money.*

enormity /ɪˈnɔːmɪtɪ/ *n* (*pl -ies*) **1** *u.n* very great size or importance: *The enormity of his responsibilities frightened him.* **2** *c/u.n* (example of) very great wickedness or crime: *Do you realize the enormity of what you have just done?*

e'normously *adv* very much; to a great extent: *I enjoyed the film enormously.*
e'normousness *u.n* huge or great size.

enough /ɪˈnʌf/ *adv* **1** to the correct or necessary amount or degree: *The paint has not been stirred enough yet.* **2** (used after an adj/ adv) to the necessary degree: *Can she swim well enough to take the test? His work is not good enough.* **(be) fool/foolish enough to do s.t** (be) so foolish as to do s.t: *Only he would be fool enough to believe that story.* **curiously/ oddly/funnily/strangely enough** in a way that is curious/odd(4)/strange: *'I'm sorry to hear Peter's so ill.' 'Oddly enough, I was thinking of him only this morning.'* **fair enough** ⇨ fair[1] (*adv*). **just enough** ⇨ just[2]. **right enough** ⇨ right[1] (*adv*). **sure enough** ⇨ sure (*adv*).

▷ *det* **3** as much, as many, as necessary; not too little, nor too few, nor too much, nor too many: *Have we got enough money to buy that car?* **more than enough (s.t)** too much (of s.t); enough and with some left over: *Let's ask some friends round for dinner; we've more than enough food for us all.*

▷ *pron* **4** quantity (of s.t) that is as much as is wanted or needed: *I haven't got enough left to pay the bill so can you pay?* **have had (more than) enough of s.o/s.t** have more of s.o/s.t than one can stand: *I've had more than enough of the children quarrelling. I'm going out!*

enquire(r), enquiring(ly), enquiry ⇨ inquire.

enrage /ɪnˈreɪdʒ/ *tr.v* make (s.o, an animal) very angry: *The behaviour of other drivers on the road always enraged him.* **(be) enraged at s.o/s.t** be made very angry because of s.o/s.t.
en'raged *adj* very angry: *The enraged bull[1](1) chased the children across the field.*

enrapture /ɪnˈræptʃə/ *tr.v* (*formal*) fill (s.o) with great delight: *I was enraptured by the beautiful sunset.*

enrich /ɪnˈrɪtʃ/ *tr.v* (*formal*) make (s.o/s.t) rich; make (s.t) more splendid; improve (s.o/s.t) in quality: *Reading enriches the mind.*
en'richment *c/u.n.*

enrol /ɪnˈrəʊl/ *tr/intr.v* (*-ll-*) (also **en'roll**) (often — (s.o) for/in s.t) (cause (one's or s.o's name) to) be written down in a list, to show that one is going to do s.t, become a member of s.t etc: *He enrolled* *me at the tennis club. She enrolled for a course in mathematics. All the new students were enrolled last week.*

en'rolment *n* (also **en'rollment**) **1** *u.n* act or state of enrolling s.o or of being enrolled. **2** *c.n* number of people enrolled: *The school enrolment this term is two hundred and fifty.*

en route /ɒn 'ruːt/ *adv* (*French*) (often — *for s.w*) on the way (to s.w): *We left early in the morning en route for Paris.*

ensconce /ɪn'skɒns/ *tr/reflex.v* (often — *one-self/s.o in s.t*) (*formal*) place (oneself/s.o) comfortably or safely (in a place, chair etc): *He ensconced himself in the armchair by the fire.*

ensemble /ɒn'sɒmbl/ *c.n* (*French*) **1** thing made up of parts but considered as a whole thing; total effect(2): *The green of the scenery and the blue dresses of the dancers made a very effective ensemble.* **2** (*music*) piece of music in which all the instruments come together; group of musicians (smaller than an orchestra) who play together: *a string ensemble.* **3** (*formal*) jacket(1) and matching skirt, hat etc worn together: *She wore a blue ensemble consisting of a coat, dress and matching hat and shoes.*

enshrine /ɪn'ʃraɪn/ *tr.v* (*formal*) **1** put/keep (s.t) in a shrine(1). **2** (*fig*) keep (s.t precious) as if in a shrine(2): *The happy memories were enshrined in his heart.*

enshroud /ɪn'ʃraʊd/ *tr.v* (*formal*) **1** cover (s.o/ s.t) with a shroud(1). **2** (usu — *s.t in s.t*) (*fig*) cover (s.o/s.t) completely (in s.t): *The top of the mountain was enshrouded in mist. The strange events were enshrouded in mystery.*

ensign /'ensaɪn/ *c.n* **1** (esp of a navy) flag: *The white ensign is used by the* Royal Navy *and the red ensign by the* Merchant Navy. **2** (US) officer of the lowest rank in the US navy.

enslave /ɪn'sleɪv/ *tr.v* **1** make a slave(1) of (s.o). **2** (*formal*) control (s.o) completely: *Many people are still enslaved by strict government controls.*

en'slavement *u.n.*

ensnare /ɪn'sneə/ *tr.v* **1** catch (an animal etc) in a trap: *The farmer ensnared many rabbits because they were damaging his crops.* **2** (*fig*) trap, get control of, (s.o) by tricking her/him or by playing on a weakness: *He was ensnared by his greed for money.*

ensue /ɪn'sjuː/ *intr.v* (*formal*) follow, happen, as a result: *Trouble ensued because the student had forgotten to bring his book.*

en'suing *attrib.adj* following or resulting: *After such a good lecture, the ensuing discussion seemed disappointing.*

ensure /ɪn'ʃʊə/ *tr.v* **1** make (s.t) sure: *Can you ensure that you will arrive on time every day?* **2** (*old use* and US) insure. **ensure s.o s.t** make sure that s.o will get s.t: *The extra lessons ensured him a good pass in the examinations.*

entail /ɪn'teɪl/ *tr.v* **1** make (s.t) necessary; have (s.t) as a necessary result: *Our holiday will entail a long flight.* **2** (*law*) leave (land etc) to a line of direct descendants so that none of them can sell it or give it away.

entangle /ɪn'tæŋgl/ *tr.v* Opposite disentangle. **1** cause (s.t) to be twisted together so that it is difficult to separate. **2** get (s.o) into a bad

situation from which it is difficult to escape; trap (s.o): *He was entangled by his greed.* **become/get entangled in/with s.t** become/get so twisted in/ with s.t that it is difficult to get free: *Her long hair got entangled in the machine.* **entangle oneself/ s.o among/in s.t** get oneself/s.o into s.t from which it is difficult to escape: *He entangled himself in the activities of a group of criminals.*

en'tanglement *n* (*formal*) **1** *u.n* act or state of entangling s.o/s.t or of being entangled. **2** *c.n* difficult situation. **3** *c.n* relationship that is likely to put one into a difficult situation: *He decided to try to avoid all* emotional(1) *entanglements for a while.*

enter /'entə/ *v* **1** *tr/intr.v* come, go, in(to s.w): *They all stood up when she entered (the room).* **2** *tr.v* become a member of (a group, profession etc): *Ann decided to enter the medical profession.* **3** *tr.v* (say that one will) take part in (a competition, a race etc): *She entered the competition at the last minute.* **4** *tr.v* (often — *s.t(up) in s.t*) write (s.t) down in a list, book etc: *He entered (up) what he had done that day in his diary.* **enter (s.o) for s.t** put one's own (or s.o else's) name down for a competition, a race etc: *I entered my sister for the competition because I didn't want to enter for it myself.* **enter into s.t** form part of s.t: *Thoughts of danger did not enter into our plans for the expedition.* **enter into s.t (with s.o)** begin, take part in, s.t (with s.o): *On the train I entered into a long conversation with the person sitting opposite me.* **enter (up)on s.t** (*formal*) begin s.t; make a start on s.t: *He entered on a new life when he became a teacher.*

entrance¹ /'entrəns/ *n* **1** *c.n* door, gate, passage, opening etc through which one enters: *The entrance to the garage is at the back of the house.* **2** *c.n* act of entering s.w: *a grand entrance.* **3** *u.n* (also *attrib*) right to enter or be admitted: *They were refused entrance to the club because they were too young. What is the entrance fee?*

entrant /'entrənt/ *c.n* person who enters a competition, profession etc: *All the entrants for the race were very nervous. Last year there were fewer entrants to the university.*

entry /'entri/ *n* (*pl -ies*) **1** *c.n* example of the act of coming or going in(to s.w): *He made a noisy entry into the classroom.* **2** *c/u.n* way in, entrance: *The sign on the gate said 'No entry' so they had to turn back.* **3** *c.n* narrow passage between buildings: *a long dark entry.* **4** *c.n* thing noted down (in a diary, register(1) etc): *I try to keep my diary up to date by making regular entries.* **5** *c.n* number, list, of people etc entering for a competition: *The entry for the* Olympic Games *last year was the biggest ever.* **make an entry (in(to) s.t)** put s.t down in writing (in a diary, register(1) etc).

'entry ,permit/,visa *c.n* official paper giving permission to enter a particular country.

enterprise /'entəpraɪz/ *n* **1** *c.n* thing that is difficult or risky and needs courage: *His new business enterprise was a great success.* **2** *u.n* courage and willingness to do s.t new or different; initiative(2): *They only succeeded because of their enterprise.* **private/state enterprise** (example of the) control of businesses etc by private companies or by the state.

'enter,prising *adj* having or showing courage

and imagination; having a spirit of adventure; resourceful: *The explorers had to be enterprising in order to stay alive.* Opposite unenterprising.

entertain /ˌentəˈteɪn/ v 1 *tr/intr.v* receive (s.o) as a guest: *She enjoys cooking and often entertains (friends).* 2 *tr.v* amuse (s.o); interest (s.o) pleasantly: *At the party the children were entertained by a* conjurer. 3 *tr.v* (*formal*) consider (s.t); bear (s.t) in mind: *I found it impossible to entertain any suspicions about him.*

enterˈtainer *c.n* person who entertains(2) audiences professionally: *There are some very good entertainers on television.*

enterˈtaining *adj* (*formal*) amusing, interesting: *We thought that the new play was most entertaining.* Opposite unentertaining.

enterˈtainment *n* 1 *c.n* musical, theatrical etc performance whose purpose is to entertain(2) people. 2 *u.n* act of entertaining(2) s.o; state of being entertained: *The monkeys at the zoo provided the children with a lot of entertainment.*

enthral /ɪnˈθrɔːl/ *tr.v* (*-ll-*) (US also **enˈthrall**) (*formal*) hold the attention or interest of (s.o); please (s.o) very much: *The football match enthralled the crowd.*

enˈthralled *adj* greatly interested in and pleased by s.t; spellbound (⇒ spell²): *As soon as I started reading the book, I became enthralled and could not put it down.*

enˈthralling *adj* so greatly interesting that one can think of, look at, nothing else; spellbinding (⇒ spell²): *What an enthralling play!*

enthrone /ɪnˈθrəʊn/ *tr.v* 1 put (a king, queen, bishop) on a throne(1) in a special ceremony. 2 (*formal* or *literary*) give (s.o) a high place in one's feelings: *Their leader was enthroned in the hearts of the people.*

enthuse /ɪnˈθjuːz/ v (*formal*) 1 *intr.v* (often — about/over s.t) become enthusiastic, express enthusiasm, (about/over s.t): *He enthused over his new car to all his friends.* 2 *tr.v* make (s.o) enthusiastic: *She enthused us all with her plans for the holiday.*

enthusiasm /ɪnˈθjuːzɪˌæzəm/ *c/u.n* (often — about/for/over s.o/s.t) (example of a) great admiration, eagerness or interest (about etc s.o/s.t): *The audience showed great enthusiasm for the young actress.*

enthusiast /ɪnˈθjuːzɪˌæst/ *c.n* person who is filled with great admiration for, interest in, s.t: *He was a sports car enthusiast and liked driving fast.*

enthusiastic /ɪnˌθjuːzɪˈæstɪk/ *adj* (often — about/over s.t) filled with great enthusiasm, eagerness or interest (because of s.t): *We were very enthusiastic about going abroad for our holiday.* Opposite unenthusiastic.

en,thusiˈastically *adv.*

entice /ɪnˈtaɪs/ *tr.v* attract, persuade or tempt (s.o, an animal): *The thief enticed the dog with a piece of meat when he broke into the house.* **entice s.o/s.t away from s.o/s.t** tempt a person, an animal, into leaving s.o/s.t. **entice s.o/s.t into (doing) s.t** tempt a person/an animal into moving to s.w (or doing s.t).

enˈticement *n* (*formal*) 1 *u.n* act of enticing s.o; state of being enticed. 2 *c.n* thing that entices s.o: *The enticement of a large reward made all the children look for the lost dog.*

enˈticing *adj* attractive; tempting: *The food on the table looked very enticing.*

entire /ɪnˈtaɪə/ *attrib.adj* whole; complete: *The entire family went on holiday together.*

enˈtirely *adv.*

entirety /ɪnˈtaɪərɪtɪ/ *u.n* state of being complete or whole. **in its entirety** as a whole; in its complete form: *We must look at the problem in its entirety in case we overlook something.*

entitle /ɪnˈtaɪtl/ *tr.v* 1 give a title to (a book, person etc): *The book was entitled 'Gardening For You'.* 2 (usu — s.o to (do) s.t) give a right etc to (s.o) (to have, do, s.t): *You are entitled to extra money for working late.*

enˈtitlement *n* (*formal*) 1 *u.n* right; rightful claim. 2 *c.n* thing to which one is entitled(2): *Under the terms of the will, his entitlement was £1000.*

entity /ˈentɪtɪ/ *c.n* (*pl -ies*) thing that has real existence as an independent unit: *England, Scotland and Wales are all parts of Great Britain but each is also a separate entity.*

entomology /ˌentəˈmɒlədʒɪ/ *u.n* scientific study of insects.

entomological /ˌentəməˈlɒdʒɪkl/ *adj* of or referring to entomology: *an entomological study.*

entomologist /ˌentəˈmɒləˌdʒɪst/ *c.n* person who studies insects.

entourage /ˌɒntʊˈrɑːʒ/ *c.n* (*French*) all the people who go with and attend an important person: *The film-star was rarely seen in public without her entourage.*

entrails /ˈentreɪlz/ *pl.n* organs inside the body, esp of an animal.

entrance¹ /ˈentrəns/ *n* ⇒ enter.

entrance² /ɪnˈtrɑːns/ *tr.v* (*formal*) fill (s.o) with great delight and wonder: *I am always entranced by this particular piece of music.*

enˈtranced *adj* (usu *pred*) (often — at/by/with s.o/s.t) filled with feelings of great delight and wonder (because of s.o/s.t): *He stood entranced at the sight of the mountain.*

enˈtrancing *adj* (*formal*) very delightful: *an entrancing smile; an entrancing piece of music.*

entrant ⇒ enter.

entreat /ɪnˈtriːt/ *tr.v* (often — s.o to do s.t) (*formal*) ask (s.o) earnestly (to do s.t): *She entreated the judge to free her son.*

enˈtreaty *c/u.n* (*pl -ies*) (example of the) act of requesting s.t from s.o earnestly: *The cruel ruler would not listen to their entreaties and had them all killed.*

entrée /ˈɒntreɪ/ *n* (*French*) 1 *c.n* light part of a formal meal, usu served between the fish and meat courses. 2 *c/u.n* right of admission or entry, esp into a particular social group: *Can you get me an entrée to that party?*

entrench /ɪnˈtrentʃ/ *tr/intr.v* dig a trench(1) for protection against attack; put (s.o) into a trench(1) to protect her/him from attack: *The enemy were well entrenched at the foot of the hill.* **(be) entrenched in one's ideas, opinions** etc (be) fixed in one's ideas, opinions etc and not willing to change.

enˈtrenched *adj* (usu *attrib*) 1 protected by a trench(1) or trenches: *entrenched soldiers; an entrenched position.* 2 (*fig*) (of an opinion, a belief etc) fixed: *She had entrenched ideas.*

enˈtrenchment *n* 1 *c.n* trench(1) or trenches for

protection against attack. **2** *u.n* act of entrenching; state of being entrenched.

entrepreneur /ˌɒntrəprəˈnɜː/ *c.n* (*French*) person who organizes and manages commercial organizations, often taking risks to do so and usu very successfully: *We borrowed money for our new business from an entrepreneur who liked our idea.*

entrust /ɪnˈtrʌst/ *tr.v* **entrust s.o/s.t to s.o** give s.o/s.t into a person's care: *Before he died he entrusted his family to his brother.* **entrust s.o with s.t** give s.o the care of s.t: *She entrusted him with her money.*

entry ⇨ enter.

entwine /ɪnˈtwaɪn/ *tr.v* (often — *s.t with/round s.t*) twist (s.t) together; curl (one thing) (with/round another): *The weeds were entwined round the old garden seat.*

enumerate /ɪˈnjuːməˌreɪt/ *tr.v* (*formal*) count (s.t); go through (a list) naming the items one by one (often in order): *The teacher enumerated the subjects that would be dealt with during the term.* **enumeration** /ɪˌnjuːməˈreɪʃən/ *n* (*formal*) **1** *u.n* act of counting. **2** *c.n* detailed account; list: *George made an enumeration of all the jobs that needed to be done.*

enunciate /ɪˈnʌnsɪˌeɪt/ *v* (*formal*) **1** *tr/intr.v* speak, pronounce (words), clearly: *The teacher always enunciates clearly so that her students can understand.* **2** *tr.v* state (s.t) formally or carefully: *He enunciated his opinions very clearly.* **enunciation** /ɪˌnʌnsɪˈeɪʃən/ *n* (*formal*) **1** *u.n* way of pronouncing words: *Her enunciation is very clear.* **2** *c/u.n* clear statement of one's views, ideas etc.

envelop /ɪnˈveləp/ *tr.v* (*formal*) surround, cover, (s.o/s.t) completely: *A thick fog enveloped the town.* **be enveloped in s.t** be covered, surrounded, completely by s.t: *He was enveloped in a thick cloak* (1). **en'velopment** *u.n*.

envelope /ˈenvəˌləʊp/ *c.n* cover or wrapper in which a letter is put: *Make sure you address the envelope before you send the letter.*

enviable, envious(ly/ness) ⇨ envy.

environment /ɪnˈvaɪrənmənt/ *c/def.n* surroundings or conditions in which s.o, an animal or a plant lives: *Children should have a secure and happy environment. Paul formed a group to protect the local environment.* **environmental** /ɪnˌvaɪrənˈmentl/ *adj* (usu *attrib*) of or belonging to the environment: *Environmental pollution is a great problem.* **environmentalist** /ɪnˌvaɪrənˈmentəˌlɪst/ *c.n* **1** person who wants to protect the environment from damage or pollution. **2** person who studies the environment. **3** person who believes that the environment is the chief influence on animal or human development.

environs /ɪnˈvaɪrənz/ *pl.n* (*formal*) surrounding areas (of a town etc): *We visited London and its environs.*

envisage /ɪnˈvɪzɪdʒ/ *tr.v* (*formal*) imagine (s.o/ s.t) as a reality: *Try to envisage how the house will look after the changes.*

envoy /ˈenvɔɪ/ *c.n* **1** official representative (for a government, large company etc) sent on special business. **2** official in an

embassy (1) next in rank below an ambassador.

envy /ˈenvɪ/ *u.n* **1** (cause of a) feeling of jealousy caused by s.o's qualities or possessions: *I could see envy in their faces as I described my holiday.* **(be) green with envy** ⇨ green (*adj*). **envy at s.t** strong desire to possess qualities or possessions that s.o has: *He was filled with envy at her success.* **envy of s.o** cause of a strong desire to possess qualities or possessions that s.o has: *My new car is the envy of all my neighbours.* ▷ *tr.v* (**-ies, -ied**) **2** (often — *s.o* (*doing*) *s.t*) feel envy (1) about (s.o/s.t): *I envy your success but I'm very pleased for you. I don't envy you waiting in the rain.* **enviable** /ˈenvɪəbl/ *adj* causing envy (1): *an enviable opportunity.* Opposite unenviable. **envious** /ˈenvɪəs/ *adj* (often — *of s.o/s.t*) feeling or showing envy (1) (of s.o/s.t): *He stared at his friend with envious eyes.* **'enviously** *adv.* **'enviousness** *u.n*.

enzyme /ˈenzaɪm/ *c.n* (*science*) chemical produced by living cells (4) that causes particular chemical changes without being changed itself: *Yeast produces enzymes that change sugar into alcohol.*

epaulette /ˈepəˌlet/ *c.n* (US **'epau,let**) ornament or decoration on the shoulder of a uniform (2), usu to show the rank and group to which s.o (a soldier, sailor etc) belongs.

ephemeral /ɪˈfemərəl/ *adj* (*formal*) lasting for a short time only: *The beauty of apple blossom* (2) *in spring is ephemeral.*

epic /ˈepɪk/ *adj* (usu *attrib*) **1** describing the adventures, deeds, of one or more heroes (1) or the important events in the history of a nation: *Do you know about Hannibal's epic journey with elephants over the Alps?* **2** (*informal*) full of adventure or excitement: *an epic struggle.* ▷ *c.n* **3** (*literature*) long poem about the adventures, deeds, of one or more heroes (1) or the important events of a nation's history. **4** (*informal*) long film, story etc that contains many adventures.

epicentre /ˈepɪˌsentə/ *c.n* (*technical*) area of land over the place where an earthquake starts.

epidemic /ˌepɪˈdemɪk/ *c.n* (also *attrib*) disease that spreads quickly and suddenly among many people in one area but does not usually last for very long: *Many old people died during the flu epidemic last winter. The disease reached epidemic proportions.* Compare endemic.

epidermis /ˌepɪˈdɜːmɪs/ *c/u.n* (*technical*) outside layer (1) of the skin, a leaf.

epidiascope /ˌepɪˈdaɪəˌskəʊp/ *c.n* projector for producing a picture from a solid object, e.g a page of a book, or a transparency (2), e.g a piece of film, on a screen.

epiglottis /ˌepɪˈɡlɒtɪs/ *c.n* (usu *sing*) (*technical*) small thing like a lid at the entrance of the throat which prevents food etc from entering the lungs.

epigram /ˈepɪˌɡræm/ *c.n* short poem or saying that expresses an idea in a clever (and often amusing) way: *'Better late than never but better never late' is an epigram.* **epigrammatic** /ˌepɪɡrəˈmætɪk/ *adj*.

epilepsy /ˈepɪˌlepsɪ/ *u.n* brain disease causing attacks of violent movements that cannot be controlled and often leading to unconsciousness.

epileptic /ˌepɪˈleptɪk/ adj **1** of or referring to epilepsy: an epileptic attack; an epileptic fit[2](1).
▷ c.n **2** person who suffers from epilepsy.

epilogue /ˈepɪˌlɒg/ c.n (US **ˈepiˌlog**) **1** short speech with a special message spoken to an audience at the end of a play. **2** short programme containing a religious message before a radio or television station closes for the night.

Epiphany /ɪˈpɪfənɪ/ unique n Christian(1) religious day (6 January) for Western churches in memory of the visit of the three wise men to Jesus, and for Eastern churches in memory of the baptism of Jesus.

episcopacy /ɪˈpɪskəpəsɪ/ n (pl -ies) **1** c.n system of government of the Christian(1) Church by bishops(1). **2** u.n period of time a bishop(1) is a member of this governing body.
episcopal /ɪˈpɪskəpəl/ adj.

episode /ˈepɪˌsəʊd/ c.n one of a group of events from a book or a particular length of time, e.g a holiday, a life etc: The television production of 'Bleak House' was produced in ten episodes. The most exciting episode of my holiday was winning the fishing competition.

episodic /ˌepɪˈsɒdɪk/ adj (formal) **1** consisting of separate parts. **2** (often derog) (of a story etc) so loosely joined that the events do not form a strong continuous story.
ˌepiˈsodically adv.

epistle /ɪˈpɪsl/ n **1** c.n (old use) letter. **2** c.n (joking) very long letter. **3** def.n (often pl; usu with capital **E**) one of the letters in the New Testament of the Bible(1) written by the early followers of Jesus: The Epistle to the Romans.

epitaph /ˈepɪˌtɑːf/ c.n words, usu on a gravestone, in memory of a dead person.

epithet /ˈepɪˌθet/ c.n adjective or name used to describe s.o/s.t: 'Great' in Catherine the Great of Russia is an epithet.

epitome /ɪˈpɪtəmɪ/ def.n **the epitome of s.o/s.t** (usu sing) (formal) person or thing who/that represents in a short, small form the character of s.o/s.t much larger: She is the epitome of her father. He is the epitome of good manners.
epitomize, -ise /ɪˈpɪtəˌmaɪz/ tr.v be an example of (s.o/s.t): You epitomize everything that is wrong with the students at this school.

epoch /ˈiːpɒk/ c.n length of time (in history, life etc) that is important because of an event or discovery during it which changes the way of life, understanding etc: The invention of the steam engine marked a new epoch in industry.
ˈepoch-ˌmaking adj (esp of an event or discovery) very important: The wheel was an epoch-making discovery.

eponymous /ɪˈpɒnɪməs/ adj who gives her/ his name to a group, place, story etc: The eponymous discoverer of Tasmania was the explorer Tasman.

equable /ˈekwəbl/ adj (esp of temperature, personality(1)) without extreme changes; steady and regular: This equable climate makes it possible to grow crops all the year round. He remained equable in spite of all the criticism.
equability /ˌekwəˈbɪlɪtɪ/ u.n. **ˈequably** adv.

equal /ˈiːkwəl/ adj the same in amount, degree, force, number, quality, size, value etc: Women had to fight for equal opportunities and equal pay. They swam equal distances but in different times. Are both sides equal? The land was divided into four equal parts. Opposite unequal. **all things being equal** unless s.t happens to change the situation before the event: All things being equal we'll arrive in Rome at 6 o'clock this evening. **(be/ feel) equal to s.t** able and strong enough to deal with s.t: After her illness she didn't feel equal to the long journey. He prepared everything to make sure that he was equal to the occasion. **equal to s.o in s.t** (formal) as good as s.o in s.t: Are you equal to her in mathematics? **on equal terms (with s.o)** ⇒ terms.
▷ c.n **2** (often s.o's — in s.t) person with the same ability, age, rank etc (as s.o else): He was my equal in all sports at school.
▷ tr.v **3** be the same in size, number etc as (s.t): £4 and £2 equals £6. These three boxes equal that large one in mass. We promise to equal the lowest price in the market. **4** (often — s.o/s.t in s.t) be the same as (s.o/s.t) (in ability etc): This car equals any other (car) of its size in comfort.

equality /iːˈkwɒlɪtɪ/ u.n. state of being equal(1): equality between the sexes; fight for equality. Opposite inequality.

equalization, -isation /ˌiːkwəˌlaɪˈzeɪʃən/ u.n state of equalizing(1) s.t or of being equalized.

equalize, -ise /ˈiːkwəˌlaɪz/ v **1** tr.v make (s.t) equal(1) in amount, size, quality etc: equalize conditions of work throughout the factory. **2** intr.v (sport) get the same score as the opposing team: Jones equalized by putting the ball neatly through the basket.
ˈequaˌlizer, -iser c.n goal etc that equalizes(2): Tom scored the equalizer.

ˈequally adv **1** in equal(1) parts: The children divided the cake equally. Opposite unequally. **2** to an equal(1) degree: They are all equally efficient. **3** (when making another point in a speech or giving another reason for s.t) in addition; also: Equally, we must use some of our money to build a sports centre. **4** in the same way: I will try to understand you, but equally, you must think of my needs.

equanimity /ˌekwəˈnɪmɪtɪ/ u.n. (formal) balance of mind; state of feeling calm: He accepted the newspaper's criticism with surprising equanimity.

equate /ɪˈkweɪt/ tr.v **equate s.o/s.t with s.o/s.t** (formal) treat or think of (two or more people, things) as equal: Do you equate such results with hard work?

equation /ɪˈkweɪʒən/ n **1** c.n (mathematics) statement of equality shown by the = sign: The equation is $x + y = 12$. **2** c.n (chemistry) statement using the = sign and symbols to show a chemical reaction(1): The equation $4Ag + O_2 = 2Ag_2O$ represents the reaction of silver and oxygen to form silver oxide. **3** u.n act of making or treating s.o/s.t as equal: the equation of terrorists with freedom fighters.

equator /ɪˈkweɪtə/ def.n (often with capital **E**) imaginary circle drawn round the earth an equal distance between the north and south poles[2](1).
equatorial /ˌekwəˈtɔːrɪəl/ adj about, in or near the equator (i.e in areas that are usually very hot and wet): equatorial forests.

equestrian /ɪˈkwestrɪən/ adj **1** of or referring to horses or the riding of horses: The jumping competition demands great equestrian skill.

▷ *c.n* **2** (*formal*) person who rides, or is skilled in riding, horses.

equidistant /ˌiːkwɪ'dɪstənt/ *adj* (often — *from s.t*) at equal distances (from s.t/s.w): *The two places are equidistant* (*from our house*).

equilateral /ˌiːkwɪ'lætərəl/ *adj* (geometry) having sides with the same length: *A square is an equilateral figure with four equal sides.*

equilibrium /ˌiːkwɪ'lɪbrɪəm/ *u.n* **1** state of balance where no force is stronger than any other force: *The scale is held in equilibrium when the weights on either side are the same.* **2** sense of balance of the body or mind: *As the stone hit his head, he lost his equilibrium and fell. Ever since his son's death, David's equilibrium has been disturbed.*

equine /'ekwaɪn/ *adj* (*technical*) of or like horses: *He has spent years studying equine habits. She has an equine face.*

equinox /'iːkwɪˌnɒks/ *c/def.n* one of two times in the year when day and night are of equal length. **the autumnal equinox** September 23rd. **the vernal equinox** March 21st. Compare solstice.

equip /ɪ'kwɪp/ *tr.v* (-*pp-*) **1** (often — *s.o/s.t for s.t*) provide (a person, vehicle etc) with everything necessary (for a particular purpose): *Is this car equipped for long distance driving? What do you need to equip yourself for your trip?* **2** (often — *s.o/s.t with s.t*) provide (s.o/s.t with s.t): *Each member of the rescue party was equipped with food and bandages for the survivors.*

e'quipped *adj* having what is necessary for a particular purpose. ⇒ ill-equipped, well-equipped.

e'quipment *u.n* **1** act of providing everything necessary for a particular purpose: *The equipment of this factory with the most modern machinery will begin soon.* **2** collection of things needed for a particular purpose: video(2) *equipment. We checked all our equipment before we started to climb the mountain.*

equitable /'ekwɪtəbl/ *adj* (*formal*) giving fair and equal attention to each person (when deciding or agreeing s.t): *They made an equitable arrangement for looking after the children. Everyone agreed that it was the most equitable solution.* Opposite inequitable.

'equitably *adv.*

equity /'ekwɪtɪ/ *u.n* (*formal*) fair and equal dealing or treatment, esp in matters of law: *He complained that there had been no equity in the decision.* Opposite inequity.

'equities *pl.n* (*commerce*) kind of investment(1) (in a company) that does not give a fixed interest.

equivalent /ɪ'kwɪvələnt/ *adj* **1** (often — *to s.o/ s.t*) the same (as s.o/s.t); equal in meaning, amount, value, (to s.t): *If you have no butter, use the equivalent amount of margarine. Five miles is equivalent to about eight kilometres. He is equivalent in rank to a professor.*

▷ *c.n* **2** person, thing, word etc who/that is equivalent(1): *The American equivalent for the 'boot' of a car is the 'trunk'.*

equivocal /ɪ'kwɪvəkl/ *adj* (*formal*) Opposite unequivocal. **1** (of meaning) misleading; often having more than one possible meaning: *His reply to my question was equivocal.* **2** (of a situation, behaviour) uncertain; suspicious: *She found herself in the equivocal position of having*

(*to admit that she'd*) *forgotten to pay for her shopping.*

era /'ɪərə/ *c.n* length of time that starts with a particular event or gets its name from an important event: *The industrial era started with the invention of the steam engine. This is the era of the* computer. Compare age(3), epoch.

eradicate /ɪ'rædɪˌkeɪt/ *tr.v* destroy, get rid of, (s.o/s.t) completely: *The police force has been increased to eradicate violence from the streets.*

eradication /ɪˌrædɪ'keɪʃən/ *u.n* act or state of eradicating s.t or of being eradicated: *the eradication of* smallpox/*crime.*

erase /ɪ'reɪz/ *tr.v* (*formal*) rub out, remove, (marks, sounds etc, esp a mistake or s.t no longer wanted): *I erased all the pencil notes I'd made in the book before returning it to the library. You don't have to erase the* cassette(1) *before you record something else.*

e'raser *c.n* thing made of rubber etc that erases written marks from paper etc: *I need an eraser as my drawing is wrong!* ⇒ rubber(3).

erasure /ɪ'reɪʒə/ *n* (*formal*) **1** *c.n* work that has been erased or has marks left by erasing s.t: *All these erasures show you didn't plan your work carefully before you began writing.* **2** *u.n* act of erasing s.t.

ere /eə/ *conj/prep* (*old use* or *literary*) before: *ere dawn.*

erect /ɪ'rekt/ *adj* **1** (of walking, standing, sitting) straight; upright: *The prisoner held her head erect when the judge spoke to her.*

▷ *tr.v* **2** build (s.t); put up (a bridge, block of flats, monument etc): *A modern office block will be erected here. Try to erect your tent before it rains.*

erection /ɪ'rekʃən/ *n* **1** *u.n* act of putting up or building s.t large: *The erection of such an ugly hotel on the mountain will be very unpopular.* **2** *c.n* (usu *derog*) (large) structure(2) that has been erected(2): *Those ugly erections are the new science laboratories.* **3** *c/u.n* (example of the) state of the penis when it is stiff and enlarged(1).

e'rectly *adv.* **e'rectness** *u.n.*

erg /ɜːg/ *c.n* (*science*) unit for measuring energy(2) or work in the metric system.

ergonomics /ˌɜːgə'nɒmɪks/ *u.n* study of the conditions in factories that help people work most efficiently.

ermine /'ɜːmɪn/ *n* (*pl* -(*s*)) **1** *c.n* small animal with brown fur in summer (then called a stoat) and white fur in winter. **2** *u.n* (also *attrib*) its white fur or clothing made from this fur: *a coat with a collar made of ermine; an ermine collar.*

erode /ɪ'rəʊd/ *v* **1** *tr/intr.v* (often — (s.t) *away*) (of water, rain, ice, wind etc) (cause (s.t) to) be gradually removed, destroyed etc by continuous action or rubbing against it: *These cliffs have been eroded* (*away*) *by the sea. The banks of the river are eroding away.* **2** *tr/intr.v* (cause (a relationship, friendship etc) to) break down: *This silly jealousy will erode our friendship.*

erosion /ɪ'rəʊʒən/ *u.n* **1** state of being worn away: *soil erosion.* **2** action of wearing away: *A large wall has been built to stop the erosion of the cliffs by the sea.*

erosive /ɪ'rəʊsɪv/ *adj* that causes erosion(2): *Some erosive forces are rain, wind and rivers.*

e'rosiveness *u.n* quality of being erosive.

erogenous /ɪˈrɒdʒɪnəs/ *adj* (esp of parts of the (human) body) capable of producing a sexual feeling when touched etc.

e,rogenous 'zone *c.n* particular part of the body that is erogenous.

erotic /ɪˈrɒtɪk/ *adj* describing sexual desire or love: *an erotic film/book.*

e'rotically *adv.*

eroticism /ɪˈrɒtɪ,sɪzəm/ *u.n* state or quality of sexual excitement, desire etc.

err /ɜː/ *intr.v* (*old use*) be or go wrong; make a mistake. **err on the side of s.t** (*formal*) follow a course of action that avoids s.t bad by being more careful or safe than necessary: *It's better to err on the side of caution* (*than to risk an accident*).

errand /ˈerənd/ *c.n* small job that requires a short journey, usu for s.o else: *My mother sent me on an errand to buy some milk.* **do**, **run**, **go on**, **errands** (**for s.o**) take messages, go shopping etc (for s.o): *I can't play tennis this afternoon as I've promised to run some errands for my grandmother.*

errant /ˈerənt/ *attrib.adj* (*formal*) (of a person, s.o's action) who/that has moved away from accepted behaviour: *Their errant son has been arrested again. If you don't give up your errant ways, I won't leave you any money in my will.*

erratic /ɪˈrætɪk/ *adj* (of behaviour, a movement, a performance etc) that is irregular and uncertain: *She is a very erratic tennis player. The quality of his work is erratic.*

e'rratically *adv.*

erratum /eˈrɑːtəm/ *c.n* (*pl* errata/eˈrɑːtə/) (*Latin*) mistake, esp in a printed book, magazine, programme etc.

er'ratum ,slip *c.n* list of errata and their corrections, usu placed at the front of a book etc.

erroneous /ɪˈrəʊnɪəs/ *adj* (*formal*) (of a fact, belief etc) not correct: *His argument is based on erroneous information.*

error /ˈerə/ *n* **1** *c.n* thing that is done wrong; mistake: *There are too many spelling errors in your work — please do it again. The driver made an error of judgement and turned the corner too fast.* **2** *u.n* state of not being correct in behaviour or action: *It will be too late when he realizes the error of his ways.* **in error** by mistake: *I took the wrong bag in error.* **trial and error** ⇒ trial.

erudite /ˈeruˌdaɪt/ *adj* (*formal*) having or showing great knowledge and learning: *Her answers were very erudite.*

'eru,ditely *adv.* **erudition** /ˌeruˈdɪʃən/ *u.n.*

erupt /ɪˈrʌpt/ *intr.v* **1** (of a volcano) send lava, rocks etc into the air: *The volcano erupted without warning and caused a lot of damage to the surrounding area.* **2** (of angry, violent behaviour) begin suddenly: *There has been continued fighting since violence erupted two days ago.*

eruption /ɪˈrʌpʃən/ *n* **1** *c/u.n* (of a volcano) (example of the) action of erupting(1): *People were warned of the possible eruption of Mount St Helen.* **2** *c.n* (*fig*) sudden violent beginning of fighting, disease etc): *There have been eruptions of typhoid in several places in the north of the country.* **3** *c.n* (*medical*) (sudden appearance of a) boil, rash, on the skin.

escalate /ˈeskəˌleɪt/ *tr/intr.v* (*formal*) (cause (a war, problem etc) to) increase, spread and become more serious: *The recent development will escalate their dissatisfaction. The disagreement between the two countries escalated into war. Unemployment has escalated in the last few years.*

escalation /ˌeskəˈleɪʃən/ *u.n.*

escalator /ˈeskəˌleɪtə/ *c.n* moving staircase for carrying people up/down to, and between, floors or different levels in a building: *Most underground railways have escalators.*

escapade /ˈeskəˌpeɪd/ *c.n* wild activity full of adventure that may be dangerous and often causes annoyance or trouble: *The teacher was not amused by the escapades of the students.*

escape /ɪˈskeɪp/ *n* (often — *from s.o/s.t*) **1** *c/u.n* (also *attrib*) (example of) getting free (from s.o/s.t) or finding a way out (from s.t); fact of having got free: *No one noticed my escape as I slipped out of the crowded room. Escape from this prison is considered to be impossible. Any escape of gas* (*from the pipe*) *could be dangerous. He worked out an escape* route(1). **2** *c.n* (also *attrib*) means of getting out or avoiding danger: *There is an escape for the stream through this pipe. The device has an escape pipe.* **3** *u.n* thing, esp music, reading, sleeping etc, that gives relief from reality or everyday activities: *At the end of the day, my escape is listening to good music.* **fire escape** ⇒ fire. **a narrow escape** an avoidance of a dangerous situation with difficulty and only just in time: *The two boys had a narrow escape when they were cut off by the tide and rescued only minutes before being washed away.*

▷ *v* **4** *intr.v* (usu — *from s.o/s.t*; — *out of s.t*) get free/ away (from s.o/s.t); find a way out (of s.t): *Not all the prisoners managed to escape when the prison gate was broken down. Poisonous gas escaped from the barrels when they fell off the truck.* **5** *tr.v* (— (*doing*) *s.t*) avoid, get away from, ((doing) s.t): *He narrowly escaped death in a car accident. He escaped paying the bill by going to the lavatory and then leaving the restaurant.* **6** *tr/intr.v* (often — (*from*) *s.t*) get away or find relief (from reality or dull everyday activities): *I go camping in order to escape* (*from*) *the pressures of work. Every weekend I escape* (*from the city*) *into the country.* **7** *tr.v* be forgotten or not noticed by (s.o): *The name of the film escapes me. Your absence will not escape the notice of the* chairperson.

e'scaped *attrib.adj* having got free or escaped(4): *an escaped lion.*

escapee /ˌeskeɪˈpiː/ *c.n* person who escapes(4) or has escaped, e.g from prison.

escapism /ɪˈskeɪpɪzəm/ *u.n* desire to avoid, habit of avoiding, unpleasant realities, situations etc by escaping(6) into a nicer or safer world (often imagined): *Her need to study so hard is a kind of escapism.*

e'scapist *adj* **1** (usu *attrib*) (of an activity) helping a person to escape(6) from reality: *Escapist literature* (e.g love stories) *is very popular in a world full of problems.*

▷ *c.n* **2** person who prefers a world of escapism.

escarpment /ɪˈskɑːpmənt/ *c.n* long steep, usu rocky, side of a hill or mountain.

eschew /ɪsˈtʃuː/ *tr.v* (*formal*) keep away from, avoid, (s.t that is thought to be bad): *eschew alcohol/drugs*(2).

escort /'eskɔːt/ n 1 c.n person or group of people (often in ships, aircraft or armoured cars) who go with another/others to protect or honour her/him/it/them: *The Queen always has an escort on ceremonial occasions. There was an armed escort when the gold was moved from one bank to another.* 2 u.n (usu *under* —) guards, protection: *The prisoner was taken to court under heavy police escort.* 3 c.n person who goes with another, or takes another, to a social event, e.g a party, film: *I don't need an escort; I can go to the party alone.*
▷ tr.v /ɪ'skɔːt/ 4 go with (s.o/s.t) as an escort: *I'd be happy to escort you around the house when you visit. Do you need to be escorted home?*
'escort ,agency c.n agency or organization that people pay to find them an escort(3).
esophagus ⇒ oesophagus.
esoteric /,esə'terɪk/ adj (formal) understood by, having meaning for, only the speaker/writer and a small group of people: *His lecture was so esoteric that few students understood the real meaning of what he said.*
,eso'terically adv.
esp written abbr especially.
especial /ɪ'speʃəl/ adj (formal) particular; special.
especially /ɪ'speʃəlɪ/ adv (also **'specially**) for the particular, special, purposes of; more than usual; more than anything else: *I came early especially to see you. I came especially early because I wanted to see you alone. I am especially fond of tennis.*
espionage /,espɪə'nɑːʒ/ u.n activity of spying (⇒ spy(2)) or collecting secret information for the purpose of giving/selling it to an enemy country or a rival business company; use of spies(1) to find out the secret information of an enemy country or a rival business company: *He's been arrested for espionage. There is a lot of industrial espionage in the fashion industry.*
esplanade /,esplə'neɪd/ c.n long stretch of land, usu by the sea, that has been levelled and often paved for walking for pleasure.
espouse /ɪ'spaʊz/ tr.v (formal) support, speak, act, in favour of (a cause, an aim etc): *He stood up and said that he espoused the cause of state education.*
espousal /ɪ'spaʊzl/ c/u.n (often — of s.t) (formal) support in favour of (a cause, an aim etc): *I cannot understand your espousal of further tax cuts.*
espresso /e'spresəʊ/ c/u.n (also attrib) (Italian) (cup of) strong coffee made by forcing boiling water or steam through ground coffee beans: *an espresso (coffee).*
Esquire /ɪ'skwaɪə/ unique n (written abbr Esq) (formal) (used instead of Mr and written after the name): *J P Smith Esq/Esquire.*
essay /'eseɪ/ c.n 1 story; short piece of writing (not in verse) on a particular subject: *The students gave their history essays to their teacher for marking.* 2 (also /e'seɪ/) (often — at (doing) s.t) (formal) attempt (at (doing) s.t): *My first essays at drawing were not very good.*
▷ tr.v /e'seɪ/ 3 (formal) attempt to do (s.t): *He essayed the jump.*
essayist /'eseɪ,ɪst/ c.n person who writes literary essays(1).

essence /'esəns/ c/u.n 1 strong concentrate(1) made by reducing the quantity/mass of a substance without changing its quality, e.g of flavour, taste: *strawberry/meat essence.* 2 thing that makes s.t, e.g an idea, what it is or that gives s.t its character, identity; most important quality of s.t: *Thinking of other people is the essence of good manners.* **in essence** as a summary(3): *And that in essence is all I have to say.* **of the essence** (formal) the most important thing: *One's health is of the essence in life.*
essential /ɪ'senʃəl/ adj 1 of or referring to an essence(1): *essential oils.* 2 very important; necessary: *It is essential to eat regularly for good health. It is essential that you practise if you want to be really good. There is only space for essential articles of clothing.* Opposite inessential. 3 (attrib) of or belonging to the essence(2) of s.t; that is fundamental(1) (to the understanding, identity(1) etc of s.t): *The essential point of his argument is that every effort be made to find a peaceful settlement.*
▷ c.n (usu pl) 4 thing that is necessary or very important: *We put all the essentials for our holiday into our luggage.* 5 thing that is central, fundamental(1), (to the understanding, identity(1) etc of s.t): *I am going on a five-day course to learn the essentials of bricklaying.*
es'sentially adv 1 in an essential(3) way; basically; fundamentally: *You are all essentially very lazy.* 2 in reality: *Essentially, this is the last day of term since tomorrow is sports day.*
Est written abbr (of a business etc) (having been) established (⇒ establish(1)) (on a certain date): *Est 1978.*
establish /ɪ'stæblɪʃ/ tr.v 1 set up (s.t); give a firm and permanent basis to (a rule, a business, a government etc): *Early in our friendship we established the rule that we each pay for ourselves. He established a successful business when he was a young man.* 2 (often — s.o as s.o/s.t, in s.t) place, settle, gain recognition for, (oneself or another in a position/place): *We are now established in our new jobs. My father helped to establish me in the trade. She has established herself as a world authority(6) on seabirds.* 3 prove the truth of (a belief, claim etc): *Columbus established the fact that the earth is round. The workers believed that their strike action would establish the seriousness of their position.* 4 make (a Church, religion, system of government etc) official or the most important in a country: *A one-party state will soon be established.*
e'stablished attrib.adj 1 describing s.t, e.g a business company, belief, custom, that has been fixed or present for some time: *an established business; a well-established peace.* 2 recognized; admired: *an established reputation.* 3 proved or shown to be true: *an (or a well-)established fact/solution/method.* 4 accepted; official: *the established Church/religion.*
e'stablishment n 1 u.n act of setting up or establishing(1) s.t: *The establishment of jobs should be a government's chief aim.* 2 c.n building and staff of a large (business) organization: *The staff in that establishment are very efficient.* 3 u.n (often the — of s.t) act of proving or showing the truth (of s.t): *the establishment of his guilt by the police.* 4 def.n (with capital **E**)

(UK) people, groups, with the main power and influence.

estate /ɪ'steɪt/ *c.n* **1** large piece of property, esp in the country, that consists of land and a very big house, usually owned by one family: *We spent the summer holidays fishing on his estate in Scotland.* **2** land used for a particular kind of building development: *a new council/housing/industrial estate.* **3** (*law*) all of s.o's possessions including property and money, esp after her/his death: *After his death, his estate was divided among his three children.* **real estate** ⇨ real.

e'state ˌagent *c.n* **1** person in the real estate business who buys and sells houses, land, property for others. **2** (also **e'state ˌagent's**) place where an estate agent works.

e'state ˌcar *c.n* (US **'station ˌwagon**) car with a large section behind the back seats for carrying a lot of luggage etc.

e'state ˌduty *c.n* (*pl -ies*) tax that is paid on a person's estate(3) after her/his death.

esteem /ɪ'stiːm/ *u.n* (*formal*) **1** strong feeling of respect; good opinion: *His lies have lowered him in her esteem.* **hold s.o/s.t in great/high esteem** have a high opinion of s.o/s.t; have great respect for s.o/s.t: *The priest is held in great esteem by the people of this village.*
▷ *tr.v* (*formal*) **2** respect, value, (s.o/s.t); have a high opinion of (s.o/s.t): *The students esteem their professor (or his knowledge) highly.* **3** (often — *it to be s.t*) consider, believe, (s.t) (to be s.t) (usu good): *He esteemed it an honour to be invited. I would esteem it a favour if you'd help me tonight.*

esthetic(s), esthetically ⇨ aesthetic.

estimate /'estɪmət/ *c.n* **1** calculation of the probable amount, cost, size etc of s.t (before one does it): *I asked the garage for an estimate before I had my car repaired.* ⇨ overestimate(1), underestimate(1). (**at**) **a rough estimate** a calculation that is not based on exact figures: *At a rough estimate, I'd say the job will take two weeks.*
▷ *tr.v* /'estɪmeɪt/ **2** work out, calculate, (the probable amount, cost, size, time etc); form an opinion about (s.t): *The builders estimate the total cost of the job at (or to be) about £1000. We estimate that we can cycle eighty miles in a day.*
estimation /ˌestɪ'meɪʃən/ *u.n* opinion; judgement. **in s.o's estimation** according to s.o's opinion: *In the teacher's estimation she was the cleverest student in the class.*

estrange /ɪ'streɪndʒ/ *tr.v* (*formal*) cause a loss of friendly (or loving) feeling in (s.o): *The government's new laws will estrange a lot of its voters.* **be/become estranged (from s.o)** (esp in a marriage or family relationship) be/become separated (from s.o), esp because one no longer loves or likes her/him/them: *They became estranged (from each other) because of his continual affairs.*
e'stranged *attrib.adj* (of a husband, wife) separated: *He hardly ever sees his estranged wife.*
e'strangement *c/u.n.*

estuary /'estjʊərɪ/ *c.n* (*pl -ies*) wider part at the mouth of a river where the tide comes in: *a river estuary.*

et al /ˌet 'æl/ *adv* (*Latin*) (of people) and all the

others: *He recommended that we read the book by Jones, Smith et al.*

etc *written abbr* et cetera.

et cetera /et 'setrə/ *adv* (*written abbr* etc) (*Latin*) and others (like those already mentioned); and the rest: *We'll need a lot of things for the party — drinks, nuts et cetera. I saw Peter, Joe, Mary et cetera yesterday.*

etch /etʃ/ *tr/intr.v* **1** make (a picture) by cutting shapes with a needle and acid on a metal plate that is then used to make prints. **2** (often *passive*) (*fig*) (cause (an event) to) be, become fixed, clear (in one's mind, memory etc): *The accident will remain etched in my mind.*
etching /'etʃɪŋ/ *n* **1** *u.n* art or skill of etching (⇨ etch(1)) s.t. **2** *c.n* print that is made from an etched(1) plate: *I bought a lovely etching at the art show.*

eternal /ɪ'tɜːnl/ *adj* **1** having no beginning and no end; that goes on for ever without change: *Do you believe in eternal life?* **2** (*attrib*) (*formal*) never stopping; (happening) too often: *Please stop this eternal noise. Your eternal complaining will make her leave home.*
e'ternally *adv* for ever; always: *I shall be eternally grateful for your help.*
eternity /ɪ'tɜːnɪtɪ/ *n* (*pl -ies*) **1** *u.n* state of being eternal(1), esp after death. **2** *c.n* (usu *sing*; often (*for*) *an* —) length of time that seems to have no end: *We waited for (what seemed) an eternity.*

ether /'iːθə/ *u.n* liquid made from alcohol that has no colour and burns easily, *chem.form* $C_4H_{10}O$: *Ether used to be used to make patients unconscious for an operation.*

ethereal /ɪ'θɪərɪəl/ *adj* (*formal*) like s.t too delicate and light to belong to this world: *She has an ethereal beauty that makes you want to touch her to make sure she's real.*

ethic /'eθɪk/ *c.n* system of moral values; set of rules for correct behaviour: *We all need an ethic by which to lead our lives.*
'ethical *adj* **1** that concerns an ethic or ethics: *an ethical matter.* **2** (of a person or her/his behaviour) right or correct in moral terms: *Do you think his behaviour was entirely ethical?*
e'thically *adv.*
'ethics *n* **1** *u.n* (also *attrib*) scientific study of systems of moral values: *In ethics classes we studied the ideas of Plato.* **2** *pl.n* rules that govern behaviour: *I understand the ethics of your political struggle but you may be sent to prison.*

ethnic /'eθnɪk/ *adj* **1** of or referring to a particular national, religious, racial(1) group. **2** (*informal*) of or referring to art, clothing, patterns etc from particular racial(1) groups: *She always wears ethnic dresses from India.*
ˌethnic mi'nority *c.n* (*pl -ies*) racial(1) group that forms a small part of a larger population.

ethnography /eθ'nɒɡrəfɪ/ *u.n* scientific description of different groups of people.
eth'nographer *c.n* person who is a student of, or is skilled in, ethnography.
ethnographic /ˌeθnə'ɡræfɪk/ *adj.*

ethnology /eθ'nɒlədʒɪ/ *u.n* scientific study of different groups of people.
ethnological /ˌeθnə'lɒdʒɪkl/ *adj.*
ethnologist /eθ'nɒlədʒɪst/ *c.n* person who is a student of, or is skilled in, ethnology.

ethos /ˈiːθɒs/ *sing.n* set of values by which a person or particular group of people behaves or lives.

ethyl /ˈeθaɪl/ *u.n* (*technical*) liquid made from the chemical combination of two atoms(1) of carbon(1) and five atoms(1) of hydrogen, *chem.form* C_2H_5.

ethyl ˈalcoˌhol *u.n* (*technical*) **1** base of alcoholic(1) drinks, *chem.form* C_2H_5OH. **2** liquid added to petrol to make a car engine less noisy.

etiquette /ˈetɪˌket/ *u.n* rules of polite behaviour among people in a formal professional or social situation.

etymology /ˌetɪˈmɒlədʒɪ/ *n* (*pl -ies*) **1** *u.n* science, study, of the origin, history and development of words. **2** *c.n* description of the origin, history and development of a word.
etymological /ˌetɪməˈlɒdʒɪkl/ *adj.*
etymologist /ˌetɪˈmɒləˌdʒɪst/ *c.n* person who is a student of, or is skilled in, etymology(1).

eucalyptus /ˌjuːkəˈlɪptəs/ *c/u.n* (*pl -es*, or, less usu, *eucalypti* /ˌjuːkəˈlɪptaɪ/) (also *attrib*) one of many types of tall trees originally from Australia, e.g a gum tree, with strong-smelling leaves that produce an oil (ˌeucaˈlyptus ˌoil) used as a medicine.

Eucharist /ˈjuːkəˌrɪst/ *def/unique n* part of the Christian(1) religious service when the bread and wine is consecrated. ⇒ communion(3).

eulogy /ˈjuːlədʒɪ/ *c/u.n* (*pl -ies*) (*formal*) (speech, piece of writing, containing) very high praise of a person or her/his qualities.
eulogistic /ˌjuːləˈdʒɪstɪk/ *adj.*
eulogize, -ise /ˈjuːləˌdʒaɪz/ *tr.v* (*formal*) praise (s.o) very highly in a speech or in writing: *Her performance in 'Romeo and Juliet' was eulogized by the newspaper critics.*

euphemism /ˈjuːfəˌmɪzəm/ *c/u.n* (example of the) use of a mild, pleasant word or phrase instead of the actual word(s) that one prefers not to use, e.g because of politeness, fear: *'Put an animal down' is a euphemism for 'kill an animal'.*
euphemistic /ˌjuːfəˈmɪstɪk/ *adj*: *The doctor was being euphemistic when he said that my father was seriously ill — he was dying.*
ˌeupheˈmistically *adv.*

euphoria /juːˈfɔːrɪə/ *u.n* state of feeling very well and very pleasantly excited.
euphoric /juːˈfɒrɪk/ *adj* full of euphoria: *She was euphoric at the birth of her first grandchild.*
ˌeuˈphorically *adv.*

Europe /ˈjʊərəp/ *unique n* one of the continents(1) that includes the countries Germany, France, Spain, Britain etc.
European /ˌjʊərəˈpiːən/ *adj* **1** of, from or belonging to Europe; known, happening throughout Europe: *the European Cup Final.*
▷ *c.n* **2** person from Europe.
ˌEuroˌpean ˌEcoˌnomic Comˈmunity *def.n* (*abbr EEC*) group of European(1) countries that have agreed to act together in economic(1) matters for the good of the members; the Common Market.

euthanasia /ˌjuːθəˈneɪzɪə/ *u.n* (causing of a) merciful and painless death (usu at the request) of a person, e.g because he/she is suffering from a disease that cannot be cured.

evacuate /ɪˈvækjʊˌeɪt/ *tr.v* (cause (people, soldiers etc) to) leave a dangerous place: *the villagers evacuated their homes when they heard noises coming from the volcano.*

evacuation /ɪˌvækjʊˈeɪʃən/ *c/u.n* (example of the) act of evacuating people or of being evacuated from a dangerous area: *The police ordered the evacuation of the church so that they could search for a bomb.*

evacuee /ɪˌvækjʊˈiː/ *c.n* person who has been removed from a dangerous area, esp in time of war.

evade /ɪˈveɪd/ *tr.v* **1** escape, keep out of the way of, (s.o/s.t): *They managed to evade the danger by tying everyone together when they crossed the flooded river.* **2** avoid, find a way of not doing, (s.t): *evade the law; evade paying income tax.* **3** avoid giving a complete or truthful answer: *Somehow Bill has managed to evade every question put to him tonight.*

evasion /ɪˈveɪʒən/ *n* **1** *u.n* act of evading s.o/s.t: *The official managed to avoid problems by the skilful evasion of every accusation. Income tax evasion can get you into serious trouble.* **2** *c.n* excuse, action, used to avoid telling the truth: *Her speech was full of evasions.*

evasive /ɪˈveɪsɪv/ *adj* (often *derog*) (of a person, s.t said or done etc) who/that evades(3) or tries to evade s.t; not fully honest: *I never know what she really wants or thinks, she's always so evasive.*
take evasive action act in order to avoid, get out of the way of, danger, trouble: *If the drivers had not taken evasive action, there would have been a bad accident.*
eˈvasively *adv.* **eˈvasiveness** *u.n.*

evaluate /ɪˈvæljʊˌeɪt/ *tr.v* **1** calculate, find out the value or importance of, (s.o/s.t): *Can you evaluate the suitability of this book for my students?* **2** (*mathematics*) calculate the numerical value of (symbols in algebra): *Evaluate $3x^2 + 2y$ if $x=1$ and $y=2$.*
evaluation /ɪˌvæljʊˈeɪʃən/ *c/u.n.*

evangelical /ˌiːvænˈdʒelɪkl/ *adj* (*religion*) **1** of, according to, found in, the teachings of Jesus as written in the Gospels(1). **2** (usu with capital **E**) of the beliefs of Protestants(2) who believe in faith and religious teaching.

evangelist /ɪˈvændʒəˌlɪst/ *c.n* **1** Christian(1) person who travels and holds meetings (often in large halls or open spaces) where he/she preaches the Gospels to people who wish to hear his/her message. **2** *def.n* (usu with capital **E**) (in Christianity) one of the four writers (Matthew, Mark, Luke and John) of the Gospels(1).

evaporate /ɪˈvæpəˌreɪt/ *v* **1** *tr/intr.v* (cause (s.t) to) change into steam: *The sun evaporates the sea to form clouds. Petrol is a liquid that evaporates quickly.* **2** *tr.v* remove liquid from (a substance), esp by heating: *Continue to evaporate this sea water and you will soon be left with solid salt. Evaporated milk is thick because the water has been evaporated from it.* **3** *intr.v* (*fig*) disappear: *Any chance of her getting into university evaporated when she failed her examinations.*

evaporation /ɪˌvæpəˈreɪʃən/ *u.n* act of evaporating(1,2) (s.t); state of being evaporated: *Evaporation takes place from the surface of a liquid.*

eve /iːv/ *def/unique n* (often with capital **E**)

evening; day before an important event or festival: *Christmas Eve is 24 December and New Year's Eve is 31 December.* **on the eve (of s.t)** on the day/night just before (s.t): *On the eve of her wedding she was so nervous that she almost changed her mind.*

even /'i:vn/ *adj* **1** (of numbers) that can be exactly divided by two, e.g 2, 4, 6 etc: *All the houses on the left side of the street have even numbers.* Compare odd(1); uneven(3). **2** flat, smooth; regular: *Find a piece of even ground to put up your tent.* Opposite uneven(1). **3** (of amounts, lengths, quantities, sizes, values) equal; the same: *Cut even lengths of wood for the shelves. At half-time the score was even but during the second half our team scored all the goals.* **4** equal; equally balanced: *We all had an even chance of passing our examinations. It was a very good game; the two teams were very even and everyone played well.* Opposite uneven(2). **5** steady: *She made even progress in all her studies.* Opposite uneven(4). **6** (of temper) calm; not easily annoyed or worried. **be/get even (with s.o)** do s.t (bad) (to s.o) because of s.t (bad) that he/she has done; have revenge (on s.o): *Now we're even! I'll get even with you for causing so much trouble.* **break even** end (some kind of business) without gaining but also without losing money: *I don't expect to make a profit at the beginning but I'll be very happy if I break even.*

▷ *adv* **7** (used to state s.t more strongly): *'Are you ready?' 'No, I'm not even dressed yet!' She didn't even telephone to tell us she wasn't coming. Even a child could do that! I felt hurt, angry (even (or even angry), when I heard what she had said about me.* **8** (used with a comparative(3) to make it stronger): *She was even more beautiful than I'd imagined. She's very dirty but I'm even dirtier (than her).* **even as** (*formal*) at the same time as: *Even as I went out it was beginning to rain.* **even if/though** in spite of the fact that, although, (that may mean (s.t not so good)): *I promise to come even if I have to miss a day's work. She went to the concert even though she had a bad cold.* **even now/then** in spite of what has/had happened: *Even now he won't agree to come with us. I told her how sorry I was but even then she wouldn't forgive me.* **even so** although that is true; in spite of that: *It is an old car but even so it still goes very well.*

▷ *v* **9** *tr.v* make (a score) equal: *The last point evened the score.* **even (s.t) out (a)** (cause s.t to) be or become regular, smooth, level: *She evened out the soil before planting the seeds. After a while his breathing evened out and he became calmer.* **(b)** make (s.t) equal: *Joe went to play for the weaker team in order to even out the teams.* **even (s.t) up** make (s.t) equal: *I owe you £5 so if I pay for both our meals that will even things up between us.* **even with s.o** (*informal*) tell s.o the truth: *OK, I'll even with you as you deserve to know what happened.*

,**even-'handed** *adj* fair; treating (two or more people) equally fairly: *She was always even-handed in the way she treated her children.*

'**evenly** *adv* in an even(2–5) way.

'**evenness** *u.n.*

,**even-'tempered** *adj* not easily annoyed.

evening /'i:vnɪŋ/ *c/unique n* (also *attrib*) time of day between sunset or late afternoon and total darkness: *this/tomorrow evening; the evening newspaper/meal/news. It will soon be evening.*

'**evening ,class** *c.n* lesson held in the evenings for adults(1,2) at college(2).

'**evening ,dress** *n* **1** *c.n* (also '**evening ,gown**) dress worn by a woman at a formal occasion in the evening. **2** *u.n* (often *in* —) very formal clothes, e.g a black suit for a man, worn at important evening occasions.

'**evening ,gown** *c.n* ⇒ evening dress(1).

'**evening ,prayer** *u.n* = evensong.

,**evening 'star** *def.n* the planet Venus when it appears in the sky soon after sunset. ⇒ morning star.

'**evening ,wear** *u.n* formal clothes worn in the evening for parties etc.

evensong /'i:vnˌsɒŋ/ *u.n* church service held in the evening in the Church of England.

event /ɪ'vent/ *c.n* **1** thing, esp s.t important, that happens: *It will not be easy to forget the events of this month.* ⇒ non-event. **2** one of the games, races etc in a sports competition: *My son is in three events at the sports day.* **at all events** whatever else happens/happened; in any case: *It's been a bad year but at all events it can't get worse.* **in any event** whatever may happen: *I expect I'll see you at the meeting but in any event let's meet for lunch afterwards.* **in either event** whichever of two things happens: *It may or may not rain but in either event I'll be waiting for you at the station.* **in that event** if that happens, is true: *It may rain but in that event I'll have my umbrella.* **in the event** in fact; as it happens/happened: *I was very nervous but in the event everything went very well.* **in the event of s.t** if s.t happens: *It is always a good idea to take an umbrella in the event of rain. In the event of an accident please take care of my cats.* **in the natural/normal/usual course of events** in the way that things happen naturally/normally/usually: *The news will become known in the normal course of events.* **the turn of events** ⇒ turn(*n*). **wise after the event** ready to say what s.o/one ought to have done when s.t bad has happened.

e'ventful *adj* full of happenings which are usu easily remembered: *I had a most eventful last term at university.* Opposite uneventful.

e'ventfulness *u.n.*

eventual /ɪ'ventʃʊəl/ *attrib.adj* happening finally (as a result of s.t); in the end: *His bad management caused the eventual failure of his business.*

eventuality /ɪˌventʃʊ'ælɪtɪ/ *c.n* (*pl -ies*) (*formal*) result that may possibly occur: *We must consider every eventuality (or all eventualities) before we make a decision.*

e'ventually *adv* finally; in the end: *We eventually arrived home after a long and tiring journey.*

ever /'evə/ *adv* **1** (used in negative statements and questions) at any time: *No one ever comes to see me. Have you ever been to Paris? Has anyone ever told you about it? I have never ever been to America.* Compare never. **2** (used after a comp or superl) up to this time: *You must work harder than ever if you want to pass your examinations. This is the best restaurant I've ever been to.* **ever after** (*old use* or *literary*) for ever (after an event already described): *They lived happily ever after.* **ever since (s.t)** ⇒ since(3,4), since(*prep*). **ever so . . .** (used with an adj or adv) (*informal*) very . . .: *The film was ever so long.* **ever such an . . .** (used with an adjective and a noun) (*informal*) a very . . .: *She's ever such a nice person.* **for ever** , **forever** , (**and ever**) always, without any end: *I'd like to stay young for ever (and ever).* **hardly ever** ⇨ hardly. ⇨ however, whatever, whenever, wherever, whichever, whoever. **Yours ever** ; **As ever** (expressions used to end an informal letter).

'ever,green *adj* **1** (of a tree, plant) that does not lose its leaves during winter.
▷ *c.n* **2** evergreen(1) tree, plant.

,ever'lasting *adj* **1** lasting for a very long time; lasting for ever: *These are everlasting flowers that are dried in a particular way so that they last almost for ever.* **2** (*attrib*) (*derog*) lasting too long or repeated too often (so as to be annoying): *I'm tired of your everlasting arguments.*
,ever'lastingly *adv.*

,ever'more *adv* (usu for —) (*formal*) for ever; always: *She said she would stay with him (for) evermore.*

every /'evrɪ/ *det* **1** each one of (a number which is more than 2): *Every orange in the basket is bad. I have seen every film in town. Not every member voted for her. I loved every moment of our holiday. We used to meet every day for lunch.* **2** the most possible; as much (chance, hope, opportunity, reason etc) as possible: *There is every chance that you will be successful. They gave me every assistance when looking for my brother. You have every reason to be proud of yourself.* **3** (used with numbers, 'other' and 'few' to show an action that is repeated at regular distances, moments, lengths of time) once (in) each: *I go for a run every morning. Every third book on his shelf is about sex. Service your car every 10 000 km.* **every bit as good** etc **as s.o/s.t** ⇨ bit¹. **every few days** , **hours** etc again and again with gaps of a number of days, hours etc: *We had to stop the car every few hours to check the water because it was so hot.* **every** (**last/single**) **one** , **thing** etc (**of s.o/s.t**) that includes each one (of a group of people or things) without exception: *Every one of our teachers is good this year. He ate every last chocolate. She took every single record when she left.* **every other . . .** (**a**) all the remaining (people, things etc): *Every other person has finished except you.* (**b**) the second of each pair in a series(1): *She comes every other Saturday.* **every now and again/then** ; **every so often** occasionally; sometimes: *We go camping every now and again. We still see each other every so often.* **every single s.o/s.t** all the people, animals, days etc: *He took every single apple on the tree.* **every time** always: *It works every time.* **every time (that) . . .** each time (that) s.t happens: *Every time I go into the country I get hayfever.* (**in**) **every way** (in) all possible ways: *My new school is better than the old one in every way. Every way you look at it she made the right decision.*

everybody /'evrɪ,bɒdɪ/ *pron* (also **'every,one**) each or every person: *I'm going to invite everybody I can think of to my party.*

,every'day *attrib.adj* that happens daily; usual: *Eating and sleeping are everyday events.*

everyone /'evrɪ,wʌn/ *pron* = everybody.

everything /'evrɪ,θɪŋ/ *pron* **1** all (the) things: *Everything is in a mess so please tidy it all up. I'll*

tell you everything when I get back from holiday. **2** (*informal*) the most important thing: *That job means everything to him. You are everything to me.*

everywhere /'evrɪ,weə/ *adv* at, in, to, all places: *I've searched everywhere but I can't find it!*

evict /ɪ'vɪkt/ *tr.v* put out (s.o) from a rented house or land (with the help of the law): *He was evicted from his flat for not paying the rent.*
eviction /ɪ'vɪkʃən/ *c/u.n.*
e'viction ,order *c.n* order to s.o (from a judge in a court of law) to move out of a rented house or land by a stated date.

evidence /'evɪdəns/ *n* **1** *u.n* (esp *law*, *science*) action(s), object(s), word(s) etc that give(s) a reason for believing s.t or provide(s) proof or clearer information about s.t: *I need evidence that you will be able to pay me back before I lend you the money. What evidence do you have to support your theory(1)? We have enough evidence to arrest him.* **2** *u.n* (*law*) written or spoken statement, usu on oath: *I shall have to appear in court to give evidence about the accident I witnessed. Most of the witnesses gave evidence for the accused but one or two gave evidence against her.* **3** *u.n* (also used in the *pl*) (usu — of s.t) mark(s), sign(s) that show(s) s.t: *When the police searched the house, they found evidence(s) of a struggle. His attempted escape is evidence of his guilt.* **be in evidence** be easily noticed, clearly seen: *The police were very much in evidence in the ruined village.* **on the evidence of s.t** based on information from s.t: *My book was accepted on the evidence of some articles I wrote in the newspapers.* **turn King's/Queen's evidence** (US **turn State's evidence**) (of a criminal) give evidence(2) against another criminal or other criminals in order to get a less severe punishment or none at all oneself.
▷ *tr.v* **4** (*formal*) show (clear) signs of (s.t): *She evidenced all the signs of guilt.*

'evident *adj* (usu *pred*) containing/showing the signs that make s.t clear: *It is quite evident that you are not satisfied with our results.*

'evidently *adv* **1** in a way that shows clearly: *They were evidently excited at the idea of a holiday by the sea. Evidently, you don't understand me at all.* **2** (in answer to a question or comment) so it seems: *'He wants to go to university next year.' 'Evidently.'*

evil /'iːvl/ *adj* **1** (*derog*) very bad; harmful; wicked: *an evil person* ; *evil thoughts. If you don't change your evil ways, you will end up in prison.*
▷ *n* **2** *u.n* wickedness: *He was punished for the evil that he had done.* **3** *c.n* bad/wicked thing: *War is an evil that mankind has made for itself.* **be/choose the lesser of two evils** be/choose the less unpleasant of two difficult, unpleasant things: *I don't know which is the lesser of two evils, to go to the party and suffer or to lie and say I'm ill.*

,evil-'doer *c.n* person who does evil(2).

'evilly *adv* in an evil(1), wicked way: *He moved evilly towards her.*

,evil-'minded *adj* (*derog*) (of s.o) with cruel or wicked thoughts and desires: *He was an evil-minded child whose only thoughts were ways of hurting others and causing trouble.*

,evil-'mindedness *u.n.*

,evil-'tempered adj (derog) (of s.o, an animal) who/that has a very bad, sometimes dangerous, temper.

evince /ɪ'vɪns/ tr.v (formal) show (a particular feeling, interest etc): The student evinced great interest in computers at his interview.

evoke /ɪ'vəʊk/ tr.v (formal) 1 cause, produce, (an expression of admiration, excitement, feeling etc): The appearance of the home team on the field evoked cheers from the crowds. 2 bring (memories from the past) into the mind: The sea always evokes (memories of) my childhood.

evocation /ˌevə'keɪʃən/ c/u.n.

evocative /ɪ'vɒkətɪv/ adj (often — of s.t) (formal) that produces strong feelings, memories etc (of s.t): That music is evocative of my few years in Africa.

evolve /ɪ'vɒlv/ tr/intr.v 1 (cause (an idea, plan, system etc) to) develop gradually and naturally: The engineer evolved a plan to supply the town with water and electricity. Her ideas have evolved over many years. 2 (technical) (cause (s.o/s.t) to) develop from a simpler, lower form to a higher form of life: Millions of years ago, certain water creatures gradually evolved into land creatures. **evolve (s.t) out of s.t** develop (s.t) from s.t slowly: This system evolved out of years of experimenting.

evolution /ˌiːvə'luːʃən/ u.n 1 act of gradual development and change: The evolution of modern farming practices has taken many years. 2 (technical) (scientific description of the) development of more complicated, organized forms of life from simpler forms over a long time: Darwin produced a book in which he describes his ideas on the evolution of plants and animals.

evolutionary /ˌiːvə'luːʃənərɪ/ adj of, by, evolution: I am in favour of evolutionary rather than revolutionary(1) change.

ewe /juː/ c.n female sheep.

ewer /'juːə/ c.n large water jug: There was no running water in the bedroom but a ewer of hot water was brought to the room every morning.

ex /eks/ c.n (informal) former boyfriend, girlfriend, husband or wife: I'm seeing my ex tonight.

exacerbate /ek'sæsəˌbeɪt/ tr.v (formal) make (a disease or a dangerous situation) worse: The child's poor health was exacerbated by not having enough food to eat.

exacerbation /ekˌsæsə'beɪʃən/ u.n.

exact /ɪg'zækt/ adj Opposite inexact. 1 absolutely correct; containing no mistakes: Give me the exact measurements of the window and I'll buy some glass for it. Can you tell me the exact time, please? 2 (able to be) very accurate in small details: The information in the tax form must be exact. Mathematics is an exact science.
▷ tr.v (often — s.t from s.o) (formal) 3 demand, force, (payment) (from s.o): The government exacts taxes from everyone who earns money or owns property. 4 demand and get (s.t) by force (from s.o): The manager exacts respect from his workers.

ex'acting adj 1 (usu attrib) (of a person) who demands hard work and high standards (from others): He's an exacting manager but we all respect him. 2 (of work, a job) that demands extra effort and attention: That job was exacting but I'm proud of the result.

exaction /ɪg'zækʃən/ u.n (usu the — of s.t from s.o) act of exacting(3) taxes etc (from s.o).

exactitude /ɪg'zæktɪˌtjuːd/ u.n (formal) state of being correct or accurate in every way: She answered our questions with the exactitude we expected of her.

ex'actly adv 1 (used to add force to a statement) right in all ways: You are exactly the person I've been looking for. That's exactly what I wanted — thank you very much. 2 in an exact(1) way: We arrived at exactly 6 o'clock. That's exactly £2.50 please. Where exactly did you drop it? 3 (used to show agreement or to reply strongly) that's, you're, absolutely right!: 'We don't have any food in the house so we'll have to go out anyway.' 'Exactly!' **not exactly** not quite; not completely; not really: That's not exactly what I wanted but it will do. 'Isn't that what you said, Peter?' 'Not exactly.'

ex'actness u.n quality, state, of being exact(1): The teacher praised the student for the exactness of her work.

exaggerate /ɪg'zædʒəˌreɪt/ tr/intr.v represent (s.t) as, make (s.t) seem, greater, worse, more important etc than it really is: Don't exaggerate the danger because if we walk carefully, we'll be fine. Those tight trousers exaggerate his thin legs. I'm not exaggerating; their captain is about 7 feet tall! How can anyone believe anything you say if you are always exaggerating (everything)?

ex'agge,rated adj more than it really is; overdone: You have an exaggerated idea of your own importance. Her sadness is rather exaggerated.

exaggeration /ɪgˌzædʒə'reɪʃən/ c/u.n (example of) exaggerating: 'We walked 50 kilometres today.' 'What (an) exaggeration!' 'Well, it is a bit of an exaggeration but we did walk far!'

exalt /ɪg'zɔːlt/ tr.v (formal) 1 raise (s.o) to a higher rank; give (s.o) greater power: The officer was exalted to the rank of general after his astonishing victory. 2 praise (s.o) highly: The musicians were exalted for their excellent performance.

exaltation /ˌegzɔː'teɪʃən/ u.n (formal) 1 act of exalting s.o; state of being exalted. 2 state of great happiness and excitement: There was great exaltation in the town when their team returned with the victory cup.

exalted /ɪg'zɔːltɪd/ adj (formal) 1 high in rank: She received respect because of her exalted position in society. 2 full of great happiness and excitement, usu because of success: The students' exalted celebrations continued all through the night.

exam /ɪg'zæm/ c.n (informal) examination(3).

examine /ɪg'zæmɪn/ tr.v 1 look at, study, (s.t) carefully or thoroughly: All baggage is examined before it is allowed onto a plane. 2 (of a doctor) check, study, (s.o/s.o's body) thoroughly (to make sure nothing is wrong or to find out what is wrong). 3 test (s.o/s.o's ability, knowledge) by asking questions: You will be examined on this term's work and I expect you all to do well. 4 (law) ask (a witness) questions in court. **need one's head examined** ⇒ head(n).

examination /ɪgˌzæmɪ'neɪʃən/ n 1 c/u.n (often

example 284 except

on —) careful study (of s.t): *After a long examination of the car engine, he found the fault. On closer examination, it is clear that this is only a copy of the original painting.* **2** *c/u.n* (often *on* —) (of a doctor) thorough check of the body: *a medical examination. On examination, it was found that my blood pressure was rather high.* **3** *c.n* (informal *exam*) testing of ability or knowledge by asking (written, spoken) questions: *I'm worried about my chemistry examination.* **4** *c/u.n* (*law*) questioning of a witness in court: *After (the) examination by the lawyer, the witness was allowed to return to her chair.* **under examination** **(a)** being questioned: *While the witness is under examination, no reporters will be allowed in court.* **(b)** (still) being considered and no decision has yet been made: *'Has the committee reached a decision about my request?' 'I'm afraid it's still under examination.'*

ex'aminer *c.n* **1** person who prepares and marks examination papers. **2** person who examines s.t.

example /ɪɡ'zɑːmpl/ *c.n* **1** person, animal or thing who/that is one of, or that represents, a group of other things of the same kind: *Some animals have learnt to live happily with people. The cat is an example.* **2** thing that shows the quality of others in the same group: *This picture is a good example of Turner's painting.* **3** one of many other things that supports a fact: *Such swearing is another example of your rudeness.* **4** person or thing who/that is (good enough) to be copied, imitated: *Your helpfulness is an example to us all.* **5** warning; sign of what will happen (if the same behaviour is repeated): *He was sent to prison as an example to others causing trouble at football matches.* **6** (in a textbook) exercise; problem: *Do examples 6–10 in Exercise 1 for homework.* **follow s.o's example** do the same as s.o; copy s.o's (good, bad etc) behaviour: *I think I'll follow my sister's example and work for a year before I decide what to study.* **for example** (*abbr* e.g., e g or eg) one or some of that kind (is/are . . .); as an example: *I've read many of Doris Lessing's books, for example 'The Grass is Singing' and 'The Golden Notebook'.* **make an example of s.o** punish s.o as a warning to others: *I know you are not the only one responsible but I'm going to make an example of you and report you to the police.* **set a good, bad** etc **example (to/for s.o)** behave in a way that is good, bad etc (for s.o) to copy: *Set a good example for your younger brother and go to bed quietly.* **without example** never before equalled; unique.

exasperate /ɪɡ'zæspəˌreɪt/ *tr.v* annoy (s.o) very much; make (s.o) very angry: *She was exasperated at/by their total lack of interest in anything.*

ex'aspe,rating *adj* very annoying; that causes great anger and frustration: *I spent an exasperating four hours waiting for the train.*

exasperation /ɪɡ,zæspə'reɪʃən/ *u.n* (usu *in* —) state of great anger, annoyance, frustration: *She swore at him in exasperation.*

excavate /'ekskəˌveɪt/ *tr.v* **1** form (a hole etc) by digging; dig (s.t) out: *They have begun excavating the land where the new shopping centre will be built. Why are they excavating that old mine?* **2** uncover (an old place, building etc) that is covered with earth, other

buildings etc: *This ancient village was excavated last year.*

excavation /ˌekskə'veɪʃən/ *n* **1** *u.n* act of excavating(2) s.t: *The excavation of that ancient village took many years.* **2** *c.n* place discovered by digging; area being excavated(2) (by archaeologists): *The excavations are on top of that hill.*

'exca,vator *c.n* **1** person, esp an archaeologist, who excavates(2) s.t. **2** machine used for excavating(1) s.t.

exceed /ɪk'siːd/ *tr.v* **1** be greater than (s.t stated, expected): *The book must not exceed 200 pages. The result exceeded our greatest hopes.* **2** be greater than, go beyond, (what is allowed, necessary): *I received a heavy fine for exceeding the speed limit.*

ex'ceedingly *adv* very; extremely: *It has been an exceedingly cold winter. It was exceedingly kind of you to lend me your car.*

excel /ɪk'sel/ *tr/intr.v* (*-ll-*) (often — (s.o/s.t) as s.o.; — at/in s.t) be, do better, (than s.o/s.t) (in some activity etc); be very good (at s.t), do very well (in s.t): *He excels us all at/in cooking. His work far excels all the other paintings shown here. She excels as a businesswoman.*

excellence /'eksələns/ *u.n* quality of being extremely/very good: *He praised her for the excellence of the meal.*

Excellency /'eksələnsɪ/ *c.n* (*pl* -ies) title of honour given to a very important official (a governor etc) and her/his husband/wife: *Her/His/Your Excellency; Their/Your Excellencies.*

excellent /'eksələnt/ *adj* of great value, quality etc; the best quality possible: *I got an excellent reference from my last employer. Excellent food, excellent music and an excellent partner to share it all!*

'excellently *adv*.

except /ɪk'sept/ *prep* **1** (— *for* at the beginning of a sentence or if 'except' is not immediately followed by a noun or pronoun; — (*for*) when followed by a noun or pronoun anywhere in the sentence; do not use 'for' when 'except' is followed by a verb) apart from; besides; but (not); not including: *Except for a headache, I feel fine now. I like all sports except (for) swimming. I go every day except (for) Sunday. Everyone passed the test except (for) me. The room was empty except for an old table in the corner. I could do nothing except sit and wait.* **except for s.o/s.t** if it weren't for s.o/s.t: *I would leave the country tomorrow except for my parents* (i.e but I wouldn't because they are still here). *Except for the money I would leave this job.* **except that . . .** apart from the fact that . . .: *I know nothing about the other students except that there are twelve of them.*

▷ *tr.v* **2** leave out, not include, (s.o/s.t): *I will except only Ben from punishment because he has admitted his guilt.*

ex'cepted *adj* (placed immediately after the noun(s)) except for; not included: *Everyone has gone to bed — present company excepted* (i.e not including those of us still here). **not excepted** (placed immediately after the noun(s)) also included: *You will all go to bed now — Joe and David not excepted.*

ex'cepting *prep* not including, except for, (s.o/s.t); leaving out (s.o/s.t): *Everyone excepting two young girls was killed in the plane crash.* **always**

excepting s.o/s.t except for s.o/s.t (who/that does not usu form part of that group anyway): *Everyone was willing to try, always excepting Peter.* **not excepting s.o/s.t** including s.o/s.t also; not leaving out s.o/s.t: *Will you all please stay to tidy up after the party – not excepting you, Harry.*

exception /ɪkˈsepʃən/ *n* **1** *c/u.n* (example of the) act of leaving s.o/s.t out: *You will all attend the meeting — there can be no exceptions.* **2** *c.n* person or thing who/that is not included: *Most of us enjoyed ourselves tonight; the few exceptions were Peter, Jane and Mary.* **3** *c.n* thing that does not follow the rule: *I usually play tennis on Saturdays but today's an exception. His books are usually very good but this one is certainly an exception.* **exception to the rule** thing that does not follow the usual order, way etc: *The trouble with English grammar is that there are too many exceptions to the rules.* **make an exception for s.o/s.t** allow s.o/s.t not to be included or considered: *Anyone who arrives late will not be allowed inside — we can make no exception for anyone.* **take exception (to s.o/ s.t)** be offended (by s.o/s.t); be angered by (s.o/ s.o's behaviour): *She took the greatest exception to her son's rudeness.* **without exception** with no exceptions; leaving out no one, nothing: *Answer all the questions without exception.*

exˈceptional *adj* very unusual; special: *exceptional beauty/intelligence/greed. She's an exceptional dancer. It is quite exceptional to have rain at this time of year.*

exˈceptionally *adv* to an unusual degree; particularly: *It's exceptionally hot for this time of year. Well done! You did exceptionally well.*

excerpt /ˈeksɜːpt/ *c.n* passage that is chosen from a book, film, play etc: *She read some excerpts from her latest book to the audience.*

excess /ˈekses/ *attrib.adj* **1** extra; more than the amount allowed, necessary etc: *You'll have to pay for your excess luggage.*

▷ *n* /ɪkˈses/ **2** *u.n* state of having more than is usual, necessary: *Excess and poverty often exist in the same city.* **3** *c.n* (often *an — of s.t*) amount (of s.t) that is extra or more than necessary: *We have an excess of milk this morning.* **4** *c.n* (often *an — of s.t*) amount (of s.t) that is too much, goes beyond (acceptable, usual) limits: *I've had an excess of wine and food this week.* **5** *u.n* fixed amount of money agreed and stated in an insurance policy[2] that must be paid by an insured person towards the cost of a claim: *The excess on my car insurance is £50.* **in excess of s.t** more than s.t: *That price is far in excess of what we can afford.* **to excess** beyond acceptable or usual limits: *It is not healthy to eat and drink to excess.*

exˈcesses *pl.n* acts that go beyond what is acceptable, healthy, wise etc: *You will die young if you continue with all these excesses.*

excessive /ɪkˈsesɪv/ *adj* too great; too much; not reasonable: *Their prices are excessive.*

exˈcessively *adv.* **exˈcessiveness** *u.n.*

exchange /ɪksˈtʃeɪndʒ/ *n* **1** *c/u.n* (act of) giving or doing s.t in order to get s.t else: *When I was at school, I went on an exchange to France (and a French girl came to our school) for a year. At the meeting there was an open exchange of feelings on the subject.* **2** *c.n* argument: *There*

was an angry exchange (*of words*) between the two drivers. **3** *u.n* giving and receiving money of one country for that of another of the same value: *the exchange of French francs for American dollars.* ⇨ rate of exchange (⇨ rate). **4** *c.n* place where particular things are bought and sold: *foreign exchanges* (i.e where money and shares are sold). **bill of exchange** ⇨ bill[1]. **in exchange (for s.t)** in return (for s.t); in order to get (s.t): *I gave her some vegetables in exchange for helping me in the garden. If I give you these stamps, what will you give me in exchange?* **rate of exchange** ⇨ exchange rate. **stock exchange** ⇨ stock. **telephone exchange** ⇨ telephone(*n*).

▷ *tr.v* **5** (often *— s.t for s.t*) change (one thing for another); give (s.t) in order to get s.t else: *Dad, will you exchange seats with me — I can't see? Can you exchange this £5 note for five pound coins?* **6** give and receive (one thing for another): *They all exchanged addresses before they parted.* **exchange blows** fight: *The two boys exchanged a few blows before someone was able to stop them.* **exchange contracts (with s.o)** ⇨ contract(*n*).

exˈchangeable *pred.adj* that can be given back in order to get s.t else: *Are these shoes exchangeable — I need a bigger size?*

exˈchange ˌrate *c/def.n* (also ˌrate of exˈchange) rate(3) at which money is exchanged(3): *The rate of exchange has gone down.*

Exchequer /ɪksˈtʃekə/ *def.n* (UK) government department that controls the country's money matters. **Chancellor of the Exchequer** ⇨ chancellor.

excise[1] /ˈeksaɪz/ *c.n* tax on particular articles produced, sold or used in a country: *It is the excise on beer and tobacco that makes those things so expensive in this country.* **Customs and Excise** ⇨ customs(2).

excise[2] /ekˈsaɪz/ *tr.v* (formal) cut out, cut away, cut off, (s.t, esp from the body): *The doctor excised a painful swelling from his leg.*

excision /ekˈsɪʒən/ *u.n* (formal) act of removing s.t from the body: *I was asleep during the excision of my tooth.*

excite /ɪkˈsaɪt/ *tr.v* **1** cause strong feelings, esp of happiness, in (s.o, an animal): *We are very excited about our holiday. They were excited by the news from abroad.* **2** cause, bring about, (an emotion(1), event etc): *Her speech excited their admiration.* **3** cause (a part of the body) to become active: *Don't excite your heart too much.*

exˈcited *adj* (of a person) full of strong, usu happy, feelings: *The excited crowd waited for the Queen to drive past.*

exˈcitedly *adv.*

exˈcitement *n* **1** *u.n* state of being excited: *The crowd cheered and shouted with excitement when their team scored a goal.* **2** *u.n* quality of being exciting: *I love the excitement of learning new things.* **3** *c.n* thing that excites(1) s.o: *I'm going to bed; that's been enough excitement for one day.*

exˈciting *adj* who/that excites(1) s.o: *What an exciting football game that was!*

exclaim /ɪkˈskleɪm/ *tr/intr.v* say (s.t) loudly or suddenly because of anger, fear, surprise etc: *'Don't go there!' she exclaimed. He exclaimed in surprise that he hadn't known about her illness.* **exclaim against s.o/s.t** (formal) criticize s.o/

s.t strongly: *The speaker exclaimed against the bad treatment of political prisoners.* **exclaim at s.t** (*formal*) speak in a surprised way because of s.t that is not expected: *She exclaimed in astonishment at the size of her telephone account.*

exclamation /ˌeksklə'meɪʃən/ *n* (*formal*) **1** *u.n* act of saying s.t loudly or suddenly: *He washed the dishes with much exclamation at the unfairness* (*of his having to do it*). **2** *c.n* short cry, shout that expresses anger, fear, surprise etc: *'Be careful!', 'Look out!', 'Oh no!' are exclamations.*

excla'mation ˌmark *c.n* (*technical*) mark **!** printed or written after an exclamation(2).

exclamatory /ek'sklæmətərɪ/ *adj* (*formal*) of, like, using, an exclamation(2): *The exclamatory remarks made by people at the political meeting interrupted the speaker.*

exclude /ɪk'sklu:d/ *tr.v* **1** (often — *s.o from s.t*) keep (s.o) out (of s.t); prevent, stop, (s.o) (from joining, becoming part of, s.t): *Children are excluded* (*from becoming full members*). **2** not include (s.o/s.t) with others: *We can't exclude the Smiths if we're inviting the Browns.* **3** consider (the chance of s.t happening) as impossible: *We can't exclude the possibility that there's been an accident.*

ex'cluding *prep* except for; not including: *This is your total bill, excluding any telephone calls you make today.*

exclusion /ɪk'sklu:ʒən/ *u.n* **1** act of excluding(1) s.o: *I refused to join the club because of their exclusion of female members.* **2** state of being excluded(1,2): *He was very sad about his exclusion from the party.* **to the exclusion of s.o/s.t** in a way that excludes(2) s.o/s.t: *She spends all her time with Peter to the exclusion of all her other friends.*

exclusive /ɪk'sklu:sɪv/ *adj* **1** (of a person, group) admitting only people of the same education, social position etc to join, esp in order to keep out people thought to be unsuitable: *She has an exclusive circle of friends and they are always seen together. That club is very exclusive — only artists and writers are given membership.* **2** for the use of only one particular person, group: *The newspaper had exclusive rights to print the story. This car is for your exclusive use.* **3** belonging to, following, a particular fashion and therefore usually expensive: *an exclusive club/restaurant/shop.* **4** taking up all one's time: *My exclusive job is looking after the children.* **exclusive of s.o/s.t** not including s.o/s.t: *The rate is £24 exclusive of food and drink.* Compare inclusive. **exclusive to s.o/s.t** belonging to, able to be sold by, only one person, shop etc: *This style is exclusive to Grey's Fashion Stores.*

ex'clusively *adv* only; particularly; for one reason, group only: *We came exclusively to see the baby. This meeting is exclusively for women.*

ex'clusiveness *u.n* state, quality, of being exclusive(1): *The exclusiveness of that club makes it difficult for ordinary people to join.*

excommunicate /ˌekskə'mju:nɪˌkeɪt/ *tr.v* formally remove (s.o) from membership of the Christian(1), esp the Roman Catholic, Church as a punishment: *He was no longer allowed to be married in church after he had been excommunicated.*

excommunication /ˌekskəˌmju:nɪ'keɪʃən/ *c/u.n.*

excrement /'ekskrɪmənt/ *u.n* (*formal*) solid waste matter removed from the body through the bowels(1). ⇒ **excreta.**

excrete /ek'skri:t/ *tr.v* (*formal*) (of a person, an animal, a plant) get rid of waste matter from the system: *When we get very hot, our bodies excrete sweat.*

excreta /ek'skri:tə/ *pl.n* (*technical*) waste matter from the body, e.g excrement, sweat etc.

excretion /ek'skri:ʃən/ *n* (*formal*) **1** *u.n* act of excreting s.t. **2** *c.n* sweat, excrement etc that is excreted.

excruciating /ɪk'skru:ʃɪˌeɪtɪŋ/ *adj* causing extreme pain (to the body or mind): *I've got an excruciating headache. That continual loud noise is excruciating.*

excursion /ɪk'skɜ:ʃən/ *c.n* **1** short trip or journey made for pleasure, often with a group of people: *We're going on an excursion into the countryside tomorrow.* **2** (*fig; formal*) movement away from the main subject, e.g in a speech.

ex'cursioˌnist *c.n* person who makes a short trip, journey for pleasure.

excuse /ɪk'skju:s/ *c.n* **1** (true or not true) reason used to explain one's actions, behaviour: *I've heard a thousand different excuses for your being late.* **make one's excuses (to s.o)** explain why one cannot do s.t and apologize (to s.o) (for not doing it): *Please make my excuses to Mr Jones and tell him I'll see him tomorrow.*

▷ *tr.v* /ɪk'skju:z/ **2** accept (s.o's reasons), forgive (s.o), for a mistake or for not doing s.t: *The teacher excused the student for arriving late. Please excuse my voice — I've got a cold.* **3** (often — *s.o* (*from doing s.t*)) free (s.o from a duty etc) for a good reason: *May I be excused* (*from*) *homework today as I have a football match?* **4** be a reasonable excuse(1) for (s.t): *His own unhappy childhood does not excuse the way he treats his wife and children.* **be excused** (*informal*) (polite request to) be allowed to go to the lavatory: *Please may I be excused?* **excuse me** (**a**) (polite way to attract s.o's attention, interrupt s.o, introduce disagreement etc): *Excuse me, may I take this chair? Excuse me, but I think you are quite wrong.* (**b**) polite way to approach a stranger and ask for s.t: *Excuse me, could you tell me how to get to the station?* (**c**) apology after an interruption, e.g coughing.

excusable /ɪk'skju:zəbl/ *adj* that can be excused(2), pardoned: *His wild behaviour is excusable today considering he has just received such excellent results for his examinations.* Opposite inexcusable.

ex-directory /ˌeks dɪ'rektərɪ/ *adj* (of a person, telephone number) not listed in the telephone directory (and so remaining private): *He is ex-directory as he's so famous.*

execute /'eksɪˌkju:t/ *tr.v* **1** punish (s.o) by death: *The electric chair is still used to execute criminals in America.* **2** carry out, do, perform, (an order, plan, job etc): *The team practised their plan of attack and during the match they executed it perfectly.* **3** perform (s.t difficult, e.g a movement, piece of music): *The diver stood on the edge of the high board and prepared to execute a difficult dive.* **4** (*law*) carry out what has been requested (in a will): *The lawyers executed my grandfather's will faithfully.* **5** (*law*) cause (s.t) to be lawful by signing, witnessing and delivering (an important or official paper).

executant /ɪgˈzekjʊtənt/ *c.n* (*law* or *formal*) person who executes(4,5) s.t.

execution /ˌeksɪˈkjuːʃən/ *n* 1 *c/u.n* (example of the) punishment (of s.o) by death: *The execution was delayed when a new witness for the defence was found.* 2 *u.n* act, way, of doing a job, plan etc: *The execution of the plan failed because of a lack of preparation.* 3 *u.n* skill in the performance (of a difficult movement, piece of music etc): *The audience applauded her execution of the difficult piece of music on the piano.* 4 *u.n* (*law*) carrying out of a sentence(2); carrying out of requests (in a will). **stay of execution** ⇨ stay¹(2).

ˌexeˈcutioner *c.n* person who carries out the order to execute(1) s.o.

executive /ɪgˈzekjʊtɪv/ *adj* (usu *attrib*) 1 of, referring to, concerned with, managing decisions etc: *She did well in the firm because of her executive abilities.* 2 having power to carry out decisions, laws etc: *The plans were put to the executive council for their agreement.* 3 of or referring to important business people, officials etc: *I was invited to lunch in the executive dining room.*

▷ *n* 4 *c/def.n* person, group, in a business with the power of direction and management: *All the important decisions are made by the company's executive(s).* 5 *def.n* (often with capital **E**) section of the government that carries out the laws made by another section of the government.

executor /ɪgˈzekjʊtə/ *c.n* (*law*) person appointed to execute(4) s.o's will.

executrix /ɪgˈzekjʊˌtrɪks/ *c.n* (*law*) woman appointed to execute(4) s.o's will.

exemplary /ɪgˈzemplərɪ/ *adj* (*formal*) 1 (of a person, thing) who/that deserves praise, serves as a model: *The child was praised for her exemplary behaviour.* 2 that serves as an example and esp a warning: *an exemplary punishment.*

exemplify /ɪgˈzemplɪˌfaɪ/ *tr.v* (*-ies, -ied*) serve as an example of (s.t); show (s.t) by example(s): *This picture exemplifies the artist at her best.*

exemplification /ɪgˌzemplɪfɪˈkeɪʃən/ *n* 1 *u.n* act of exemplifying s.t. 2 *c.n* person or thing who/that exemplifies s.t: *My children are an exemplification of good manners.*

exempt /ɪgˈzempt/ *adj* (usu *pred*) 1 (often — *from* s.t) free (from a tax, duty etc): *Clothing is usually taxed, only children's clothes are exempt. Milk is exempt from taxation.*

▷ *tr.v* 2 (often — *s.o/s.t from* s.t) free (s.o/s.t from s.t that others must do): *I was exempted (from the army) because of my flat feet.*

exemption /ɪgˈzempʃən/ *c/u.n* (example of the) act or state of exempting(2) s.o/s.t or of being exempted: *I don't have to do the examination as I've got an exemption. Exemption of tax on the main foods is necessary to help poor people.*

exercise /ˈeksəˌsaɪz/ *n* 1 *u.n* act, practice, of using the body (or mind) in a way that will strengthen it, improve performance etc: *Walking and swimming are excellent forms of exercise.* 2 *c.n* activity for practising s.t and intended for improvement: *Please do the addition exercises on page 40. These exercises will strengthen your fingers.* 3 *c.n* activity or set of activities for training soldiers: *The soldiers went on a training exercise*

for a week. **get/take exercise** improve health, strength etc by running, swimming, walking etc: *It is important to get some exercise every day.*

▷ *v* 4 *tr/intr.v* give exercise to (s.o/s.t); practise; train (s.o/s.t): *I exercise my fingers every day to strengthen them for playing the piano. He's fat because he eats a lot and doesn't exercise enough.* 5 *tr.v* (*formal*) make use of (a right, a skill etc): *Please exercise some judgement before you choose a new car. I intend to exercise my right to complain at the next meeting.* 6 *tr.v* cause anxiety to (s.o/s.o's mind): *The problem has been exercising us (or our minds) for several days.*

exercises *pl.n* (often *do* (one's) —) body movements to improve one's health, strength etc: *I do my exercises every morning before I get dressed.*

exert /ɪgˈzɜːt/ *tr.v* use (a lot of energy, skill etc): *I had to exert all my strength to move the tree out of the way. He exerted his influence to get his daughter a place in university.* **exert oneself** make an effort; try very hard: *We'll have to exert ourselves to finish this job on time.*

exertion /ɪgˈzɜːʃən/ *n* (*formal*) 1 *u.n* use (of energy(1), influence etc): *It was only by the exertion of pressure that they managed to get what they wanted.* 2 *c/u.n* (example of the) act of great effort: *Our exertions left us completely worn out.*

exeunt /ˈeksɪˌʌnt/ *intr.v* (*Latin*) (used as a stage direction) they leave (the stage): *All exeunt left.* ⇨ exit(3).

exhale /eksˈheɪl/ *tr/intr.v* (*formal*) breathe out (air): *He breathed in deeply, dived into the water and exhaled slowly while he swam underwater.* Opposite inhale.

exhalation /ˌekshəˈleɪʃən/ *c/u.n*.

exhaust /ɪgˈzɔːst/ *n* 1 *c.n* (also *attrib*) (also **exˈhaust ˌpipe/ˌsystem**) pipe/system through which waste gas, steam etc is passed when it leaves an engine: *The car made a terrible noise when the exhaust (pipe) fell off.* 2 *u.n* (also *attrib*) waste gas, steam from an engine, machine etc: *It is dangerous to breathe in the exhaust fumes(1) from a car.* ⇨ manifold(2).

▷ *tr.v* 3 use up (s.t) completely: *After climbing the mountain my strength was exhausted. We will soon have exhausted our water supplies. You have exhausted my patience.* 4 finish, use up, the valuable part of (s.t): *Your land will soon be exhausted because you grow only one crop year after year and do not feed the soil.* 5 make (s.o) very tired: *The journey exhausted me.* 6 examine, deal with, every part of (a subject): *The police have exhausted all possibilities in their inquiries into the crime.*

exˈhausted *adj* very tired (because of having worked hard etc).

exˈhaustible *adj* (of a quantity or a quality such as patience etc) that is not enough to prevent it from being used up. Opposite inexhaustible.

exˈhausting *adj* that makes one very tired: *What an exhausting journey!*

exhaustion /ɪgˈzɔːstʃən/ *u.n* 1 act of exhausting (⇨ exhaust(*v*)) s.t or of being exhausted: *The exhaustion of our food means that we'll have to return earlier than we'd planned.* 2 state of being very tired: *Your son is suffering from exhaustion — after a few days' rest, he'll be fine again.*

exˈhaust ˌpipe *c.n* ⇨ exhaust(1).

exhibit 288 exorbitant

ex'haustive *adj* complete; thorough: *The doctor did exhaustive tests on the patient to find out what was wrong. Although their inquiries seemed exhaustive, they got no results.*

ex'haust ,system *c.n* ⇨ exhaust(1).

exhibit /ɪgˈzɪbɪt/ *c.n* **1** object or collection of objects, shown in a public place: *There were many interesting exhibits at the art centre.* **2** (*law*) object, written statement, that is produced in a law court to help discover the truth: *The lawyer held up exhibit 4, a knife, and asked if the man had seen it before.*
▷ *tr.v* **3** show (works of art, objects for sale etc) in a public place for people to look at: *I have been given a whole room to exhibit my latest photographs.* **4** (*formal*) show signs of (a quality): *He exhibited signs of greatness while still young.* **5** (*formal*) express, show signs of, (interest etc): *She exhibited great interest in his work.*

exhibition /ˌeksɪˈbɪʃən/ *c.n* **1** collection of objects of art, industry etc that are shown in public for a limited time, for the purposes of advertisement, competition, interest, sale etc. **2** (*formal*) act of showing (a quality): *That'll be an opportunity for the exhibition of your knowledge of wild flowers.* **3** (*UK*) money that is given to a student by a school, college etc for one or more years so that he/she can study there. Compare award(3), bursary(2), scholarship(2). **make an exhibition of oneself** make a fool of oneself; behave badly or foolishly in a public place: *Stop behaving so stupidly, you're making an exhibition of yourself.* **on exhibition** being shown in public: *The picture will be on exhibition for a month.*

,exhi'bitio,nism *u.n* **1** (*derog*) behaviour that is intended to attract attention to oneself: *His continued exhibitionism annoys his friends.* **2** illness of the mind that causes a person to show in public part(s) of the body normally clothed.

,exhi'bitio,nist *c.n* person who enjoys exhibitionism(1): *Everyone considered her an exhibitionist because of the strange hats she wore.*

ex'hibitor *c.n* person, company etc who/that exhibits(3) s.t.

exhilarate /ɪgˈzɪləˌreɪt/ *tr.v* make (s.o) feel happy and full of joy, excitement etc: *The children were exhilarated by their visit to the fun fair.*

ex'hila,rating *adj* that makes a person feel happy, excited, full of joy etc: *We went for an exhilarating walk along the mountain path.*

exhilaration /ɪgˌzɪləˈreɪʃən/ *u.n.*

exhort /ɪgˈzɔːt/ *tr.v* (usu — *s.o* to do s.t) (*formal*) encourage (s.o) (esp to do s.t good): *She exhorted her husband to stop drinking alcohol.*

exhortation /ˌegzɔːˈteɪʃən/ *c/u.n.*

exhume /eksˈhjuːm/ *tr.v* (*formal*) dig up, remove, (a dead body) from the earth: *The body was exhumed from the grave near the place where he died and taken to his home town.*

exhumation /ˌekshjuːˈmeɪʃən/ *c/u.n.*

exigent /ˈeksɪdʒənt/ *adj* (*formal*) that causes difficulty and needs urgent attention: *Certain exigent problems must be solved before we leave.*

'exigency *c.n* (*pl -ies*) (also **'exigence**) (often *pl*) (*formal*) problem that makes immediate action necessary: *The exigencies of the situation left them no choice but to leave immediately.*

exile /ˈeksaɪl/ *n* **1** *c.n* person who is sent away from her/his country, esp as a punishment; person who lives outside her/his country for her/his own, usu political, reasons: *Many exiles live in neighbouring countries.* **2** *u.n* act or fact of sending s.o, or of being sent, to a place that is not one's country (often as a punishment): *He faced exile for his political activities.* (**be/live) in exile** (be etc) an exile(1) from one's country. **be sent**, **go**, **into exile** be forced to leave, leave, one's country and become an exile(1).
▷ *tr.v* **3** send (s.o) away from her/his own country, esp as a punishment or for political reasons: *He was exiled for his political activities and went to live in England.*

exist /ɪgˈzɪst/ *intr.v* **1** be (s.t) real; live: *The idea that you will win the £50 000 exists only in your mind.* **2** (usu — *on* s.t) keep living, continue to live, (by using or having s.t): *The prisoners had to exist on bread and water alone. I can't exist without love.* **3** be found, live, (s.w): *These animals exist only in high mountain areas.*

ex'istence *u.n* state of being (real): *They discovered the existence of some very unusual birds on the island. Many people question the existence of God.* **in existence** that exists(1) now: *This church has been in existence for centuries.* **come into existence** become real; begin to operate: *A new law comes into existence tomorrow.*

ex'istent *adj* that exists(1), is in existence: *This law has been existent for several years now.* Opposite non-existent.

existential /ˌegzɪˈstenʃəl/ *adj* (*formal*) of, having, existence; of, belonging to, existentialism.

existentialism /ˌegzɪˈstenʃəˌlɪzəm/ *u.n* system of thought that believes that there is no god, that people are free to make their own decisions, choices etc and that they alone are responsible for their lives.

,exi'stentia,list *c.n* person who believes in existentialism.

ex'isting *adj* **1** that is in existence: *I'd like copies of all the existing material he's written.* **2** (*attrib*) that is real, true, now: *The existing conditions are unlikely to change for some time.*

exit /ˈeksɪt/ *c.n* Opposite entrance. **1** (often printed above the door that is the) way out (of a building, esp a cinema, theatre etc): *We always use the fire exit because it takes us to the road where we park our car.* **2** act of leaving, e.g of an actor leaving the stage during a play: *At that moment, the thief made a quick exit.*
▷ *intr.v* **3** (used as a stage direction) he/she goes out, leaves the stage: *Exit Hamlet.* ⇨ exeunt. Opposite enter.

'exit ,visa *c.n* official stamp in a passport that allows s.o to leave a country. Compare entry permit/visa (⇨ enter).

exodus /ˈeksədəs/ *c.n* (usu *sing*) leaving of many people together: *There was a sudden exodus when fire broke out in the building.* **exodus (of s.o) (from s.w) (to s.w)** leaving (of people) (from one place) (to go to another): *the exodus of people from the country to the cities.*

exonerate /ɪgˈzɒnəˌreɪt/ *tr.v* free (s.o) from blame, guilt etc: *The prisoner was exonerated when the real criminal was found.*

exoneration /ɪgˌzɒnəˈreɪʃən/ *u.n.*

exorbitant /ɪgˈzɔːbɪtənt/ *adj* (of a price, demand

etc) that is too great, high: *Their prices are exorbitant. His job makes exorbitant demands on his life.*

ex'orbitance *u.n* quality of being too great in price, demands etc.

exorcize, -ise /ˈeksɔːˌsaɪz/ *tr.v* drive away, get rid of, (s.t evil); remove an evil spirit from (s.o): *A priest was called in to exorcize the evil spirits from the house.*

exorcism /ˈeksɔːˌsɪzəm/ *c/u.n* (example of the) act of exorcizing s.o/s.t.

exorcist /ˈeksɔːˌsɪst/ *c.n* person who exorcizes s.o/s.t.

exotic /ɪgˈzɒtɪk/ *adj* **1** bright, colourful, unusual and exciting: *I love exotic clothes and travelling to exotic places.* **2** whose origin is another distant country: *exotic birds/plants.*

ex'otically *adv.*

expand /ɪkˈspænd/ *v* **1** *tr/intr.v* (cause (s.t) to) become bigger, larger: *When you blow up a balloon it expands. He has expanded the business in the year he's been here. Rocks expand in the hot sun.* **2** *tr/intr.v* spread (s.t) (out); broaden (s.t): *We have expanded our programme to provide activities for children as well. The water expanded over the fields when the river flooded.* **3** *tr/intr.v* (often — on s.t) develop (a story, idea, plan etc): *I like some of your ideas but you need to expand (on) them.*

expanse /ɪkˈspæns/ *c.n* wide open unbroken area or surface: *From the cliff, the wide expanse of the sea stretched in front of us.*

expansion /ɪkˈspænʃən/ *u.n* act of increasing in size, making s.t larger: *The expansion of the factory will mean over a hundred new jobs. Don't forget to leave space for expansion in hot weather.*

ex'pansive *adj* (*formal*) **1** that affects a wide area or group: *The new government planned expansive changes.* **2** (*fig*) (of a person, behaviour) friendly and generous: *You're in a very expansive mood*[1](1) *tonight, taking us all out for dinner.*

ex'pansively *adv.* **ex'pansiveness** *u.n.*

expatiate /ekˈspeɪʃɪˌeɪt/ *intr.v.* **expatiate on s.t** (*formal*) speak, write, in great detail about s.t: *In his speech he expatiated on the need for careful management.*

expatriate /eksˈpætrɪət/ *c.n* (also *attrib*) person who lives in a country that is not her/his own: *There are many expatriates living in Britain.*

expect /ɪkˈspekt/ *tr.v* **1** be waiting for (s.o/s.t to arrive etc, s.t to happen): *I'm expecting her any minute. Is any news about her expected?* **2** think (s.t) likely; believe (s.t) is probable: *I expect to see her tomorrow. I'm expecting her to telephone. I expect (that) it will rain. 'He failed the examination.' 'What did you expect when he didn't do any work?'* ⇒ unexpected. **3** suppose, think, (that (s.t) is probably true): *'Who left the door open?' 'I expect it was Mary.' I expect you're tired after your long journey.* **4** (often — s.o to do s.t) demand, require, (s.o to do s.t): *I expect you all (to be) back here in five minutes.* **be expecting (a baby)** be pregnant: *Mrs Jones is expecting her sixth child.* **expect s.t of s.o** demand, require, s.t from s.o: *You expect too much of Peter — he's only 10 years old. With parents like that, what can you expect of the child?* **expect so** ⇒ so(*pron*).

to be expected (what one knows) will happen as a result: *It's to be expected that he won't believe you because you tell so many lies.*

ex'pectancy *u.n* (*formal*) state of believing that s.t is going to happen: *The boy watched with a look of expectancy as his mother cut the cake.* **life expectancy** ⇒ life.

ex'pectant *adj* (*formal*) (of a person) waiting eagerly; full of hope: *The expectant faces of the audience changed to cheers when the pop*[3](1) *star came on stage.*

ex,pectant 'mother *c.n* woman waiting for her baby to be born; pregnant woman.

expectation /ˌekspekˈteɪʃən/ *n* (*formal*) **1** *u.n* state of expecting s.t: *There is every expectation that England will win.* **2** *c.n* (often *pl*) thing that is expected: *What are your expectations for the future?* **against all expectation(s)** in a way that is/was the opposite of what is/was expected: *Against all expectation(s) she won a place in the university of her choice.* **beyond (all) expectation(s)** in a way that is/was better, greater, than expected or hoped: *We knew we'd won a prize but winning first prize was beyond all our expectations.* **contrary to (all) expectation(s)** = against all expectation(s). **fall short of, not come up to, not meet, one's expectations** be not as good, successful, as one expected: *Our holiday did not come up to our expectations; the weather wasn't good and nor was our hotel.* **in (the) expectation of s.t** expecting s.t to happen soon: *He bought a cottage in the country in (the) expectation of his retirement.*

,expec'tations *pl.n* (*formal*) things one expects, hopes for, in the future: *I have great expectations of you; I think you'll be very successful.* ⇒ expectation (2).

expedient /ɪkˈspiːdɪənt/ *adj* (*usu pred*) **1** (of an action) convenient; useful for a particular purpose (though it may not be morally right): *In some situations it is better to do what is expedient than what you believe to be best.* Opposite inexpedient.

▷ *c.n* **2** (*formal*) action, plan, way, that is the right or necessary thing to do or get s.t: *The only expedient left was to go to the police.*

ex'pediency *u.n* (also **ex'pedience**) (*formal*) **1** (*derog*) consideration of one's own advantage only: *He does everything out of expediency rather than for the good of the group.* **2** convenience: *Sarah took a taxi for expedience and not because there were no buses.*

expedite /ˈekspɪˌdaɪt/ *tr.v* (*formal*) make (s.t, a job) move, work, faster, more efficiently: *His job was to expedite customers' orders.*

expedition[1] /ˌekspɪˈdɪʃən/ *u.n* (*formal*) speed: *We were asked to complete and return the forms with all expedition.* Compare expedition[2].

expeditious /ˌekspɪˈdɪʃəs/ *adj* (*formal*) quick, efficient: *My enquiry received an expeditious reply.*

,expe'ditiously *adv.*

expedition[1] ⇒ expedite.

expedition[2] /ˌekspɪˈdɪʃən/ *c.n* (all the people who take part in a) long and usu difficult journey, esp for exploration, climbing mountains etc: *We planned a large expedition to the Himalayas.*

expel /ɪkˈspel/ *tr.v* (-ll-) **1** (usu — s.o from s.t/s.w) force (a student, member, foreigner etc) to leave permanently (a school, group, country etc), usu as a punishment: *The boy was expelled from school for stealing.* **2** (usu — *s.t from s.t*) get rid of, force out, (air etc from the lungs, a room etc): *Modern kitchens usually have a fan to expel stale air and cooking smells.* ⇒ extractor.

expulsion /ɪkˈspʌlʃən/ *c/u.n* (also *attrib*) (example of the) act of expelling s.o/s.t or of being expelled: *an expulsion order.*

expend /ɪkˈspend/ *tr.v* (often — *s.t on s.t*) (*formal*) spend, use up, all of (one's money, strength, time etc on (doing) s.t): *We are expending too much time on this subject.*

ex'pendable *adj* who/that can be got rid of, used up, without serious loss, esp for some cause, gain; that can be replaced: *Many employers treat their staff as (if they are) expendable.*

expenditure /ɪkˈspendɪtʃə/ *n* (*formal*) **1** *u.n* (often — *of s.t (on s.t)*) act of spending, using up, money etc (on s.t): *expenditure on food and clothing in preparation for the journey.* **2** *c/u.n* amount (of money) spent: *That's an added expenditure we can't afford at the moment.*

expense /ɪkˈspens/ *n* **1** *u.n* cost, price, that is paid: *He always gives his children the best — no matter what the expense.* **2** *c.n* cost; thing that costs a lot: *We've had so many expenses this month.* **at great, no** etc **expense** having to spend a lot, nothing etc: *They allowed him to eat in their restaurant at no expense.* **at s.o's expense** (a) with s.o (else) paying: *We stayed in the hotel at the firm's expense.* (b) in such a way that s.o else loses, suffers: *His jokes are always at somebody else's expense.* **at the expense of s.t** causing the sacrifice of s.t: *He was a rich man by 30 but at the expense of his health.* **go to the expense of doing, a lot of** etc **to do, s.t** spend money, time etc doing, to do, s.t for some particular purpose: *I went to a lot of expense to get this information for you.* **put s.o to a lot of** etc **expense, to the expense of s.t** cause s.o to spend money, time etc on s.t: *You put me to a lot of expense and you don't even say thank you.* **spare no expense** spend as much money as necessary: *He spared no expense for his only daughter's wedding.*

ex'pense ac,count *c.n* (account for) money spent in connection with work, including the cost of food, hotels, travel etc, that is paid by a business company.

ex'penses *pl.n* money needed or used while doing s.t: *Her employer paid all her travel expenses and gave her a clothes allowance.*

expensive /ɪkˈspensɪv/ *adj* costing a lot of money: *She likes expensive jewellery. It's expensive to travel.* Opposite inexpensive.

experience /ɪkˈspɪərɪəns/ *n* **1** *u.n* (practice in an activity that provides) knowledge, skill: *I haven't had enough experience to apply for that job.* Opposite inexperience. **2** *c.n* activity, event, set of activities, events, during a length of time that adds to one's knowledge, understanding or affects one in some way: *My time in Africa was the most important experience of my life. They wrote about their experiences in China.* **by/ from/through/with experience** as a result of experience(1): *I learnt by experience not to trust him. With experience you will know what to do.*
▷ *tr.v* **3** (*formal*) feel, have knowledge of, (s.t): *Did you experience any difficulty finding your way here?*

ex'perienced *adj* (of a person) who has gained knowledge, skill, from experience(1): *an experienced driver; experienced in dealing with marriage problems.* Opposite inexperienced.

experiment /ɪkˈsperɪmənt/ *c/u.n* **1** (example of) testing in order to observe or study the result, to gain (new) facts, knowledge: *Many people are against performing scientific experiments on animals. Great discoveries have been made by careful scientific experiment.*
▷ *intr.v* /ɪkˈsperɪˌment/ **2** (often — *on/with s.o/s.t*) use different tests (in order to learn, discover, s.t): *She loves experimenting when cooking. She experiments on her friends first. He experimented with many materials before he found a suitable one.*

experimental /ɪkˌsperɪˈmentl/ *adj* (usu *attrib*) as, of, an experiment(1); not yet completely proved, tested: *We are only in the experimental stages — we won't know for some time whether the machine will work properly.*

experimentation /ɪkˌsperɪmenˈteɪʃən/ *u.n* (*formal*) act of experimenting(2): *Through experimentation we learnt several new facts about the metal.*

expert /ˈekspɜːt/ *adj* **1** (often — *at/in s.t*) (of a person) who has a particular knowledge; highly skilled (in s.t): *She went to her doctor for an expert opinion. She's an expert cook. He's expert at cards.* Opposite inexpert.
▷ *c.n* **2** (often — *in/on s.t*) person with great knowledge (of s.t) or who is highly skilled (in s.t in particular) and is often known for her/his knowledge, skill: *He's an expert in old musical instruments.* **3** (often — *at (doing) s.t*) person who has a lot of experience, usu in doing s.t bad: *He's an expert at getting out of his responsibilities.*

expertise /ˌekspɜːˈtiːz/ *u.n* special knowledge, training, skill: *Joanna's well known for her expertise in cooking.*

'expertly *adv.* **'expertness** *u.n.*

expiate /ˈekspɪˌeɪt/ *tr.v* (*formal*) do s.t as punishment for (s.t wrong that one has done): *He expiated his crime by going to prison.*

expiation /ˌekspɪˈeɪʃən/ *u.n.*

expire /ɪkˈspaɪə/ *intr.v* **1** (of a length of time) end: *What time does the parking meter expire?* **2** (of an official document etc) no longer be able to be used; be no longer valid(2): *My passport expires soon so I need to apply for a new one.*

expiration /ˌekspɪˈreɪʃən/ *u.n.*

ex'piry *u.n* (also *attrib*) ending of a length of time, agreement etc: *Check the date of expiry (or the expiry date) on your passport.*

explain /ɪkˈspleɪn/ *v* **1** *tr/intr.v* (often — (*s.t*) to *s.o*; — *what, how* etc . . .) show the meaning (of s.t to s.o); make clear (what happens, how s.t works etc): *He explained the rules to me. 'Can you explain how the machine works?' Please explain what happened last night.* **2** *tr.v* be or give (a reason for s.t happening): *The trouble at home probably explains his disappearance. Please explain why you are so late.* **explain oneself** (a) make one's meaning easier to understand: *I still don't understand. Will you explain yourself again?* (b) give good reasons for one's behaviour: *Late home again! Please explain yourself!* **explain s.t away** make a problem, mistake etc seem less important; make an excuse for s.t or show why one should not be blamed for an accident, problem etc: *She tried to explain away her bad behaviour by saying she had been tired.*

explanation /ˌeksplə'neɪʃən/ *n* **1** *u.n* act of explaining: *What explanation did she give?* **2** *c.n* fact, description, that makes s.t easy to understand: *Did she give any explanation for not coming?* **in explanation** (**of s.t**) (*formal*) in order to explain (s.t): *What do you have to say in explanation of your behaviour?* **without explanation** not giving a reason for s.t: *She left the room without explanation.*

explanatory /ɪk'splænətərɪ/ *adj* (usu *attrib*) that gives or tries to give an explanation: *I'll give you some explanatory notes to help you understand the poem.*

explicable /ɪk'splɪkəbl/ *adj* able to be explained: *I can see no explicable reason for Wendy's resignation — unless she's found a better job.* Opposite inexplicable.

explicit /ɪk'splɪsɪt/ *adj* **1** stated very clearly, giving all the necessary information: *She left explicit instructions about where to find everything and what you should do. He described the accident in explicit detail so we could almost see it.* **2** (usu *pred*) showing or describing personal things, esp those related to sex, in great detail: *The film was too explicit for my taste.*

ex'plicitly *adv.* **ex'plicitness** *u.n.*

explode /ɪk'spləʊd/ *v* **1** *tr/intr.v* (cause (s.t) to) burst violently and with a loud noise: *The bomb exploded when it hit the ground and destroyed many houses.* **2** *tr.v* make (a drawing, photograph etc) larger using magnifying(1) equipment. **3** *intr.v* (often — *into/with s.t*) suddenly show strong feelings: *Everyone exploded into laughter when they saw the colour I'd done my hair. He exploded (with anger) when he saw the damage to his new car.* **4** *tr.v* (*fig*) show (an idea, an opinion) to be false: *That idea was exploded ages ago.*

explosion /ɪk'spləʊʒən/ *n* **1** *c.n* (loud noise caused by) sudden and violent bursting: *The explosion could be heard for miles.* **2** *u.n* act of exploding(1). **3** *c.n* burst (of anger, laughter etc): *There was an explosion of laughter from the audience.* **4** *c.n* sudden large increase in size: *a population explosion.*

explosive /ɪk'spləʊsɪv/ *adj* (usu *attrib*) **1** likely to explode(1,3): *All explosive substances must be handled with care. My father has an explosive temper. The situation between the two countries is explosive and war could break out at any time.* ▷ *c/u.n* **2** (often *pl*) substance that can explode(1), esp if fired, lit, struck: *The road builders used explosives to cut into the rock.* ⇒ high explosive(s).

exploit /'eksplɔɪt/ *c.n* **1** (brave) act, adventure, deed: *Their brave exploits in the war were highly praised.* ▷ *tr.v* /ɪk'splɔɪt/ **2** develop, make full use of, (a situation, natural supply of s.t): *The large waterfall was exploited to make electricity.* **3** (*derog*) use (s.o) selfishly or unfairly, esp for one's own gain: *He exploits women by giving them part-time work for low wages.*

exploitation /ˌeksplɔɪ'teɪʃən/ *u.n.*

ex'ploiter *c.n* person who exploits(v) s.o/s.t: *an exploiter of good opportunities.*

explore /ɪk'splɔː/ *v* **1** *tr/intr.v* travel (a place, space etc) in order to find, learn about, s.t/s.w: *explore other planets for signs of life.* **2** *tr/intr.v* search (a place) in order to find (s.t interesting): *explore (a wreck) for treasure.* **3** *tr.v* examine (a situation) carefully in order to understand it, find out about it: *We explored all the possibilities before coming to a decision.*

exploration /ˌeksplə'reɪʃən/ *c/u.n* **1** (example of) travelling s.w, esp to learn, discover, s.t: *Early sailors went on many voyages of exploration.* **2** (example of) looking, searching, for s.t: *I suggest the exploration of all possibilities before we decide. The oil company is carrying out explorations just off the coast.*

explorative /ek'splɒrətɪv/ *adj* = exploratory.

exploratory /ek'splɒrətərɪ/ *adj* for the purpose of gaining further information: *The politicians held exploratory discussions before coming to any decision. The operation on his stomach is purely exploratory — when we know what is happening, we can decide what to do.*

ex'plorer *c.n* person who explores(1).

ex'ploring *u.n* (often go —) exploration.

explosion, explosive ⇒ explode.

Expo /'ekspəʊ/ *c.n* (*informal*) exposition(2).

exponent /ek'spəʊnənt/ *c.n* (often — *of s.t*) (*formal*) **1** person who is skilled in a particular art: *She is a skilful exponent of classical(2) acting.* **2** person who supports and often describes a known belief etc: *He is a well known exponent of existentialism.* **3** (*mathematics*) number, symbol, that shows the power of a quantity: *In x^2, 2 is the exponent of x.*

export /'ekspɔːt/ *n* **1** *u.n* act, business, of sending goods abroad for trade: *The best fruit is kept for export.* **2** *c.n* article, goods, sent abroad for trade: *Fruit is one of their main exports.* ▷ *tr.v* /ek'spɔːt/ **3** send (goods etc) abroad for purposes of trade: *This country exports cars all over the world.* **4** (*fig*) allow, send, (ideas, methods, systems etc) to be used or developed abroad.

ex'portable *adj* that can be exported(3).

exportation /ˌekspɔː'teɪʃən/ *u.n.*

ex'porter *c.n* person, business company, country etc who/that exports(3) things: *Canada is one of the world's leading grain exporters.*

expose /ɪk'spəʊz/ *tr.v* **1** (often — *s.t to s.t*) leave (s.t) without cover, protection etc (against s.t): *The floods washed away the soil, exposing the rocks beneath. His back was badly burnt because he exposed it to the sun for too long.* **2** make (the truth) known; tell the truth about (s.o/ s.t): *The newspaper exposed the activities of the secret organization. When we discovered the truth we exposed him as a liar.* **3** allow light to act on (a camera film etc). **4** (often — *oneself*) uncover (oneself, the sexual parts of one's body) in public: *He was sent to prison for exposing himself to women in the park.* **expose oneself/s.o to criticism, danger** etc put oneself/ s.o in a position that makes it possible for others to criticize, that leads to danger etc: *If you admit our plans now you will expose us to a lot of criticism.*

exposure /ɪk'spəʊʒə/ *c/u.n* (example of the) act of exposing s.t or of being exposed: *He suffered from exposure after being on the mountain all night. The photographer worked out the* *necessary exposure for the effect he wanted in his picture.*

exposition /ˌekspəˈzɪʃən/ n **1** c/u.n (formal) (example of the) act of explaining s.t: *His exposition of the facts left us in no doubt about how the accident had happened.* **2** c.n (informal Expo) international show of manufactured goods etc.

expostulate /ɪkˈspɒstjʊˌleɪt/ intr.v (often — (with s.o) about/on s.t) (formal) argue, complain loudly, ((to s.o) about s.t): *She expostulated with her son about his not washing the dishes.*
expostulation /ɪkˌspɒstjʊˈleɪʃən/ c/u.n.

exposure ⇒ expose.

expound /ɪkˈspaʊnd/ tr.v (formal) explain (an idea, belief etc) in detail: *She expounded her ideas to the crowds.*

express /ɪkˈspres/ attrib.adj **1** that is stated very clearly: *It was his express wish that the house should never be sold.* **2** that is sent, travels, very fast: *Please send this letter by express delivery. If you catch the express train, it will take you under an hour to get to London.*
▷ adv **3** by the fastest form of delivery: *I'd like this parcel to go express, please.*
▷ n **4** c.n very fast train which stops at a few main stations only. **5** u.n (usu by —) fastest delivery service offered by the post office, railways etc: *I sent the papers by express so I'm sure they'll reach you in time.*
▷ tr.v **6** explain (s.t, one's meaning): *Could you try to express that in another way as I don't quite understand what you mean?* **7** show (one's feelings etc) by an action, look, words etc: *Joan expressed her thanks by sending them a bunch of flowers.* **8** send (a letter, parcel etc) by the quickest form of delivery: *Please express the goods because I need them urgently.* **9** (formal) press out (juice, liquid etc): *We expressed the juice from the fruit to make wine.* **express oneself** explain/show one's feelings, meaning etc (by doing s.t): *You have expressed yourself very clearly.*

expression /ɪkˈspreʃən/ n **1** c/u.n (example of the) act of showing one's feelings etc by actions, looks, words: *Her smile was an expression of her pleasure.* **2** c.n look on s.o's face that shows what he/she is feeling, thinking: *I could tell by the expression on her face that Sue had got the job she'd applied for.* **3** u.n show of feeling when reading, singing, playing music: *Put some expression in your voice when you're reading.* **4** c.n word(s) with a particular meaning, usually spoken for a particular effect: *'Get lost!' is an expression that tells someone to go away.* **5** c.n (mathematics) group of numbers and signs that show a quantity, e.g $2ab^3$. **beyond/past expression** that is too beautiful, pleasing to be described: *Her beauty is beyond expression.* **find expression in s.t** be able to express oneself/s.t through an action, activity: *Her artistic interest found expression in painting with watercolours.* **give expression to s.t** show one's feelings by doing s.t: *She gave expression to her anger by throwing the glass at the wall.*

expressionism /ɪkˈspreʃəˌnɪzəm/ u.n (in painting, music etc) tendency to express oneself/s.t by using (personal) symbols rather than by trying to imitate reality. Compare impressionism.

ex'pressio̱nist adj **1** of or referring to expressionism: *an expressionist painting.*

▷ c.n **2** person who practises expressionism: *Kandinsky was a Russian expressionist.* Compare impressionist.

ex'pressionless adj (of a face, voice etc) without showing what one is thinking, feeling etc: *Her expressionless voice gave no signs of her anger.*

ex'pressive adj showing a feeling, meaning, clearly: *She has a very expressive face.* **expressive of s.t** that shows a particular feeling: *expressive of guilt/hunger/fear.*
ex'pressively adv. **ex'pressiveness** u.n.

ex'pressly adv plainly; particularly: *You were expressly told not to play with matches! These boots are made expressly for rock climbing.*

expropriate /eksˈprəʊprɪˌeɪt/ tr.v (formal) take away (land, property etc), sometimes without payment: *The government has expropriated a large piece of my land for the new highway.*
expropriation /eksˌprəʊprɪˈeɪʃən/ u.n.
ex'propri̱ator c.n person or government who/ that expropriates s.t.

expulsion ⇒ expel.

expunge /ekˈspʌndʒ/ tr.v (formal) get rid of, remove, (a sign, word etc) so that there is nothing left: *All information about his past life has been expunged from the records.*

expurgate /ˈekspəːˌgeɪt/ tr.v remove (s.t, esp s.t likely to cause offence) from a book, film etc: *Several passages in the book had to be expurgated before it could be printed.*
'expuṟgated adj (of a book etc) that has had rude, offensive parts taken out: *We were allowed to read only the expurgated copy of 'Lady Chatterley's Lover' when we were young.* Opposite unexpurgated.
expurgation /ˌekspəːˈgeɪʃən/ c/u.n.

exquisite /ɪkˈskwɪzɪt/ adj **1** very beautiful; done, made, played, with great skill: *an exquisite piece of jewellery; an exquisite work.* **2** (of an action, feeling) that gives very great pleasure: *It was exquisite to dive into the cool water after a long day walking in the sun.*
ex'quisitely adv. **ex'quisiteness** u.n.

ex-service /ˌeks ˈsɜːvɪs/ adj (of a person, thing) formerly belonging to the armed forces: *My son only buys ex-service clothes.*
ˌex-'serviceman c.n (pl -men) man who has been in the armed forces.
ˌex-'service̱woman c.n (pl -ˌwomen) woman who has been in the armed forces.

extant /ekˈstænt/ adj (formal) still in existence: *This is the only known extant copy of the missing painting.*

extempore /ɪkˈstempərɪ/ adj/adv (done, said) without earlier thought or preparation: *He made an extempore speech on the workers' expectations.*
extemporaneous /ɪkˌstempəˈreɪnɪəs/ adj without earlier thought or preparation.
ex̱tempo'raneously adv. **ex̱tempo'raneousness** u.n.
extemporization, **-isation** /ɪkˌstempəraɪˈzeɪʃən/ c/u.n act or fact of extemporizing.
extemporize, **-ise** /ɪkˈstempəˌraɪz/ tr/intr.v (formal) do (s.t), speak, without the help of earlier preparation: *I had no time to prepare my speech so I had to extemporize (it).*

extend /ɪkˈstend/ v **1** tr.v make (s.t) longer, larger, esp to reach a stated point: *We extended* *the path down to the river. They extended their holiday for another week.* **2** *tr/intr.v* (cause (s.t) to) continue (to a certain point, for a certain period): *Our garden extends to that line of trees. The film has been extended for another few days. The washing line was extended between two trees.* **3** *tr.v* (*formal*) stretch (one's body, legs etc): *The little boy extended his arm as far as he could but he still couldn't reach the door handle.* **4** *tr.v* (often — *s.t* to *s.o*) give, offer, (help etc to s.o): *Building societies only extend loans* (2) *when they are sure they can be repaid. They always extend a warm welcome to their friends.* **5** *tr.v* (often — *oneself*) force (oneself) to use one's full power, strength: *I was fully extended in the race but I still came last.*

extension /ɪkˈstenʃən/ *n* **1** *u.n* (often the — of s.t) act of extending s.t or of being extended: *The extension of our holiday gave us another week in the sun.* **2** *c.n* (also *attrib*) extra part, time; part that has been added: *We're drawing up the plans for an extension to our house. We applied for an extension for* (paying) *this month's rent as our money hadn't arrived yet. The bank gave us an extension period* (1) *of one month.* **3** *c.n* extra telephone connected to the main telephone system in a house, an office etc: *Ask for extension 135 when you telephone my office.*

extensive /ɪkˈstensɪv/ *adj* reaching, spreading, far; covering a large area: *The newspaper reported extensive damage from the fire. Her knowledge of ancient Greek history is extensive.*

exˈtensively *adv.*

exˈtensiveness *u.n* (*formal*) quality, state, of being extensive: *I didn't realize the extensiveness of the desert until I began to travel through it.*

exˈtent *c/u.n* (usu *sing*) amount that s.t reaches, stretches over/to s.t; area, length, size etc: *How long is a snake at its full extent? By this evening we will know the full extent of the damage. The extent of his influence was very great. To what extent can I use this information in my speech?* **to a certain/ limited extent**; **to some extent** to a limited amount only: *I can use his help to a certain extent. You are right to some extent.* **to a large extent** mostly but not completely: *I agree to a large extent.* **to such an extent that . . .** so much that . . .; to such a degree that . . .: *They argued to such an extent that it was best to keep them apart.*

extenuate /ɪkˈstenjʊˌeɪt/ *tr.v* (*formal*) make (a crime, bad behaviour) appear less serious: *Is there anything to extenuate such a terrible crime?*

exˌtenuˌating ˈcircumˌstances *pl.n* facts, information (esp in a law court) that make a person's actions, crime, seem less serious: *The judge did not send the woman to prison because of the extenuating circumstances.* ⇨ mitigating circumstances.

extenuation /ɪkˌstenjʊˈeɪʃən/ *c/u.n* (often in — of s.t) (*formal*) thing that partly excuses s.t; act of offering an excuse for a crime, one's behaviour etc: *Do you have anything to say in extenuation of your crime?*

exterior /ɪkˈstɪərɪə/ *adj* (usu *attrib*) **1** on, from, the outside: *Use this paint on all exterior walls.* ▷ *c.n* **2** outer part, surface or appearance: *The exterior of the building is very ugly but it's lovely inside.*

He presents a very tough exterior but actually he's a very frightened little boy.

exterminate /ɪkˈstɜːmɪˌneɪt/ *tr.v* completely destroy (all members of a particular group); put an end to (a disease, idea etc): *They had to exterminate the rabbits because they were destroying the crops.*

extermination /ɪkˌstɜːmɪˈneɪʃən/ *u.n* act or state of exterminating s.o/s.t or of being exterminated: *The extermination of mosquitoes in many parts of the world has reduced disease in those areas. Certain animals such as crocodiles have to be protected against extermination.*

external /ɪkˈstɜːnl/ *adj* (usu *attrib*) for, from, of, on, the outside: *The external wall needs painting. This medicine is for external use only. External pressures* (from other countries) *force changes within a country.* Opposite internal.

exˌternal exˌamiˈnation *c.n* **1** examination given by an organization outside the college, school etc where one studies. **2** (*medical*) examination of the outside parts of the body.

exˌternal exˈaminer *c.n* person who carries out or marks an external examination (1).

exˌternal ˈstudent *c.n* person who studies a course at a college etc but is not a member of that college etc.

exˈternally *adv* (about, on, the) outside: *The doctor examined her externally.*

extinct /ɪkˈstɪŋkt/ *adj* **1** no longer in existence: *Many birds and animals are in danger of becoming extinct.* **2** no longer active or burning: *It's an extinct volcano.*

extinction /ɪkˈstɪŋkʃən/ *u.n* **1** act or state of becoming, being, making s.t, extinct: *We must try to prevent the extinction of threatened animals.* **2** (*formal*) act of putting out a fire etc: *The extinction of the fire was helped by the rain.*

extinguish /ɪkˈstɪŋgwɪʃ/ *tr.v* (*formal*) **1** put out (a fire, light): *The forest fire was extinguished before it could cause too much damage. Please extinguish your cigarettes and prepare for the plane to land.* ⇨ extinction (2). **2** destroy (hope, love, feelings etc): *All our hopes of a holiday were extinguished after an accident ruined our car.*

exˈtinguisher *c.n* person or thing who/that extinguishes (1) s.t: *a fire extinguisher.*

extol /ɪkˈstəʊl/ *tr.v* (-ll-) (US **exˈtoll**) (*formal*) praise (s.o) highly: *Simon was extolled for the bravery of his attempt to save a child from drowning.*

extort /ɪkˈstɔːt/ *tr.v* (often — s.t from s.o) get (money, information) by force or threats (from s.o): *The landlord extorted high rents from the people who lived in his house.*

extortion /ɪkˈstɔːʃən/ *c/u.n* **1** (example of the) act of gaining (s.t) by force or threats (from s.o): *He gained the information by extortion.* **2** (example of the) act of charging prices that are too high: *Your extortions have gone too far and I will not pay another penny. That's extortion! I wouldn't pay that price!*

extortionate /ɪkˈstɔːʃənɪt/ *adj* (*formal*) (of an amount, demand, price etc) that is too much, excessive: *That's an extortionate price for such an old horse!*

exˈtortioˌnist *c.n* person who extorts s.t.

extra /ˈekstrə/ *adj* **1** beyond the usual amount, number etc; additional: *We shall need extra chairs* *tonight because more people are expected. The teachers are asking for an extra 10 per cent* (i.e on their salaries). *Our rate is £12 per night and meals are extra.*

▷ *adv* **2** more than usually; additionally: *He needs an extra strong bed because he's so heavy. You'll have to work extra hard this year.* **3** more; in addition: *You don't have to pay extra for meals on a plane journey.*

▷ *c.n* **4** thing that is in addition, is more than needed: *They took two tents on holiday, one for themselves and an extra for friends who might visit.* **5** thing for which more money is charged: *The price includes all your food but coffee is an extra.* **6** (in films etc) person with a very small part, e.g in crowd scenes. **7** special edition(1) of a newspaper printed for important late news.

extract /'ekstrækt/ *n* **1** *c.n* passage chosen from a book, play, poem, newspaper article etc: *The author chose three extracts from her new book to read to her audience.* **2** *u.n* substance obtained by extracting(5) s.t: *meat extract*; *extract of chicken.*

▷ *tr.v* /ık'strækt/ **3** pull/take out (s.t) using care and some strength: *I have to have two teeth extracted.* **4** get (s.t) by using persuasion: *I'll ask if she's got the results, but extracting information from her is usually impossible.* **5** get (juice, oil etc) by boiling, crushing etc: *extract oil from nuts.* **6** (*formal*) choose a short part from (a book, film, play etc): *Lucy extracted the important parts of the speech for her report.*

extraction /ık'strækʃən/ *n* **1** *c/u.n* (example of the) act of taking out (a tooth): *I've had eight extractions altogether. The extraction of a tooth can be very painful.* **2** *u.n* act of extracting(5) s.t: *The extraction of oil from the earth costs a lot of money.* **3** *u.n* place of origin: *My family is of French extraction.*

ex'tractor *c.n* (also **ex'tractor ,fan**) device that removes bad or stale air from a building, room etc, e.g in a kitchen.

extracurricular /,ekstrəkə'rıkjulə/ *adj* outside the requirements of study at a school, college etc: *Our school offers many extracurricular activities such as the* drama(2) *society, swimming, tennis.*

extradite /'ekstrə,daıt/ *tr.v* (*formal*) **1** send (s.o) out of the country where he/she is living to a country where he/she is wanted by the police for a crime done. **2** get (s.o) sent from one country to one's own country to be tried(6) for a crime etc: *Britain has applied to extradite him.*

'extra,ditable *adj* (of a crime) for which a person can or may be extradited: *Murder is an extraditable offence in most countries.*

extradition /,ekstrə'dıʃən/ *u.n* (also *attrib*) act of extraditing s.o: *Britain has asked France for the extradition of a person suspected of murder. Britain and Spain have now signed an extradition agreement.*

extramarital /,ekstrə'mærıtl/ *adj* (*law or formal*) (esp of sexual relations) outside the marriage agreement: *an extramarital affair.*

extramural /,ekstrə'mjuərəl/ *adj* (usu *attrib*) **1** outside the usual activities of an organization etc: *Our company offers extramural sporting activities for the members of staff.* **2** separate from one's studies: *extramural activities such as sports.*

extraneous /ık'streınıəs/ *adj* (often — *to* s.t) (*formal*) not belonging (to the subject being considered or the object to which it is joined): *Your remarks are quite extraneous to the main discussion.*

extraordinary /ık'strɔːdənrı/ *adj* beyond what is common or ordinary; unusual, strange: *What extraordinary weather for this time of year! His general knowledge is extraordinary.*

extraordinarily /ık'strɔːdınərılı/ *adv* in an extraordinary way; to an extraordinary extent: *You've been extraordinarily kind to me. He's extraordinarily bright.*

extrapolate /ık'stræpə,leıt/ *tr/intr.v* (often — (s.t) *from* s.t) **1** (*formal*) work out (what is not yet known or what will probably happen in the future) (from s.t that is already known): *Since we don't know what will happen, we can only extrapolate (from the information we have).* **2** (*mathematics*) use known facts, numbers etc to work out (the unknown values in a group): *From the number pattern 16, 25, 36, we can extrapolate 1, 4, 9 before and 49, 64, 81 after the pattern* (i.e because the known numbers are each squares too: $1 \times 1 = 1; 2 \times 2 = 4$ etc).

extrapolation /ık,stræpə'leıʃən/ *u.n.*

extrasensory /,ekstrə'sensərı/ *adj* beyond the known or normal use of the senses: *Extrasensory* perception *is an ability to learn about events without the help of the usual senses.*

extraterrestrial /,ekstrətə'restrıəl/ *adj* (from) outside the earth: *People have wondered for centuries whether there is any extraterrestrial life.*

extraterritorial /,ekstrə,terı'tɔːrıəl/ *adj* free from the laws of the country in which one lives: Diplomats(1) *have extraterritorial rights in the countries where they are serving their governments.*

extravagant /ık'strævəgənt/ *adj* **1** spending, using, too much; wasteful: *He was poor because of his son's extravagant ways. Don't be so extravagant with the wine.* **2** (of behaviour, expression of feelings, opinions etc) going beyond reasonable limits; excessive: *The critics were extravagant in their praise of the young author's first play.*

ex'travagance *n* **1** *u.n* act or state of being extravagant: *Your extravagance will ruin you.* **2** *c.n* thing that is very expensive or beyond what is necessary: *We can no longer afford all your extravagances. I know you were tired but sleeping for 18 hours is an extravagance.*

ex'travagantly *adv.*

extravaganza /ık,strævə'gænzə/ *c.n* (*theatre*) expensive and spectacular(1) entertainment.

extreme /ık'striːm/ *adj* (usu *attrib*) **1** furthest (away) possible; in, to, the outer limits: *Walk down to the extreme end of the field and then follow the path to the river. I'm reaching the extreme end of my patience.* **2** very great; of the highest degree: *The nurse showed extreme kindness to her patients. The heat was too extreme for the firemen to get close enough to beat out the flames.* **3** (esp of ideas, opinions) going very far in one direction or another; away from the centre; not moderate: *He always takes an extreme viewpoint in our discussions. They are members of the extreme left.* **4** most severe: *The extreme punishment for a crime in this country is life imprisonment. The police were forced to take extreme measures to*

prevent further violence at football matches. ⇨
extremities (2).

▷ *c.n* **5** furthest limit; greatest degree: *It's impossible to live there because of the extremes of temperature.* **6** (often *pl*) quality that is as different from another as possible: *Love and hate are two extremes.* **be driven**, **go**, **take s.t**, **to extremes** (be forced to) act in a way that is more than reasonable: *Don't you think locking the door is taking your anger to extremes?* **go from one extreme to another**; **go to the opposite/other extreme** move from one extreme (2,3) state (of mind etc) to one that is the opposite one: *One minute I feel very hot, the next I feel icy cold — I go from one extreme to another. From being an excellent student you have gone to the other extreme and become very lazy.* **in the extreme** in, to, the highest degree: *This is worrying in the extreme.* **to the extreme** to the furthest possible limit: *Your behaviour is testing my patience to the extreme.*

ex'tremely *adv* to a very high degree; very: *She always works extremely hard. I'm extremely tired so I'm going to bed.*

ex'tremism *u.n* state of holding extreme (3) ideas, esp about politics, religion etc.

ex'tremist *adj* **1** (of s.o's opinions) extreme (3). ▷ *c.n* **2** person with extreme (3) ideas, opinions etc.

extremities /ɪk'stremɪtɪz/ *pl.n* (formal) **1** hands and feet: *My extremities suffer during the cold weather.* **2** severe measures taken to punish s.o: *Surely you can get justice without going to such extremities.*

extremity /ɪk'stremɪtɪ/ *n* (*pl -ies*) (formal) **1** *c.n* furthest point: *We went to the extremity of the cliff to look at the sea below.* **2** *c/u.n* highest degree, esp of misfortune: *She suffered an extremity of pain before she died.*

extricate /'ekstrɪ,keɪt/ *tr.v* (often — oneself/ s.o *from* s.t) free (oneself/s.o) (from danger, difficulty etc): *She had to find a good excuse to extricate herself from trouble.*

extrication /,ekstrɪ'keɪʃən/ *u.n.*

extrinsic /ek'strɪnsɪk/ *adj* (often — *to* s.t) (formal) (of a quality, value etc) that is not essential or not an important part (of s.t): *That matter is extrinsic to our main consideration and we can discuss it another time.* Compare intrinsic.

extrovert /'ekstrə,vɜːt/ *adj* **1** (of a person) who is more interested in other people and things around her/him than in her/his own thoughts and feelings. **2** (of a person) who enjoys being the centre of attraction: *His extrovert behaviour makes him fun to be with.* Opposite introvert. ▷ *c.n* **3** extrovert (1,2) person: *She's such an extrovert that she soon has everyone watching her.* Opposite introvert.

exuberant /ɪg'zjuːbərənt/ *adj* (formal) **1** very excited, happy; in high spirits: *They're exuberant about their cycling holiday.* **2** (of plants) growing strongly: *These plants have an exuberant growth in this warm, wet weather.*

ex'uberance *u.n.* **ex'uberantly** *adv.*

exude /ɪg'zjuːd/ *v* (formal) **1** *tr/intr.v* (cause (s.t) to) come out slowly in large quantities: *He was so nervous that sweat was exuding from his skin.* **2** *tr.v* show large quantities of (a feeling etc): *After the race she exuded*

excitement. She's so in love she simply exudes happiness.

exult /ɪg'zʌlt/ *intr.v* (formal) **1** (usu — *at/in* s.t) rejoice greatly (for a particular reason): *She exulted at her success in getting the job she wanted.* **2** (usu — *over* s.o) behave boastfully (towards s.o): *It is bad manners to exult over a person one has beaten in a race.*

ex'ultant *adj* very happy; victorious (perhaps too much so): *There were exultant shouts after he had won the race and broken the world record.*

exultation /,egzʌl'teɪʃən/ *u.n* (usu — *at* s.t) great happiness and lively rejoicing (about s.t): *There was exultation at the birth of the prince.*

eye /aɪ/ *c.n* **1** one of the two organs of sight: *After his accident he could only see out of one eye. She has beautiful brown eyes.* **2** hole in a needle for thread: *I can't put the cotton through the eye (of the needle).* **3** part (on a branch or tuber) where a new plant grows: *the eye of a potato.* **4** part for the hook to hold when joining two sides, things: *Please do up the hook and eye on my dress — I can't reach them.* **an eye for an eye** a punishment that matches the pain suffered. **as far as the eye can reach/see** as far as one can see, usu to the horizon. **be all eyes** watch with great interest: *The children were all eyes as their father opened the huge box.* **be in the public eye** be noticed because of often being brought to the public's attention, e.g by newspapers, television etc. **be up to one's/the eyes** (**in** s.t) (a) have a great deal of work to do. (b) be surrounded (by s.t, e.g dirt, problems etc): *He is up to his eyes in debt.* **before one's** (**very**) **eyes** right in front of one, usu with no attempt to hide what is being done: *They took the jewels before her very eyes and she did nothing to stop them.* **cannot believe one's eyes** be unable to believe what one sees: *I could not believe my eyes when I saw her picture in the newspaper!* **cannot take one's eyes off** s.o/s.t be unable to stop looking at s.o/s.t: *She was so lovely I couldn't take my eyes off her.* **cast an eye over** s.t written to check it. **catch s.o's eye** cause s.o to notice, look at, one: *She waved her hat in an effort to catch her friend's eye.* **close/shut one's eyes to** s.t (usu *fig*) take no notice of s.t: *We should wear ties to school but most of us don't and the teachers usually close their eyes to it.* **cry one's eyes out** (*fig*) cry a lot for a long time. **eye of a storm** calm part in the middle (of a hurricane or cyclone). **fasten/fix one's eyes** (**up**)**on** s.o/s.t (formal) watch s.o/s.t very carefully: *Her eyes were fastened on the dark stranger in the corner.* **feast one's eyes** (**up**)**on** s.o/s.t ⇨ feast (*v*). **get/keep one's eye/hand in** learn/know by practice to judge the movement of the ball in a ball game (e.g cricket¹, football etc). **get**, **give s.o**, **a black eye** ⇨ black eye. **have an eye for** s.t be a good judge of beauty, colours, quality etc. (**have/with**) **an eye to** s.t (have/ with) s.t as one's main object: *She had an eye to winning the race for the third time.* **have a good eye** have the ability to see detail clearly. **have eyes for** s.o be interested in one particular person, e.g as a boyfriend or girlfriend. **have one's eye on** s.o/s.t (a) be interested in s.o/s.t or have s.o/s.t as one's goal: *I've got my eye on a coat in Marks and Spencer.* (b) be watching s.o/ s.t: *You'd better behave because I've got my* *eye on you.* **(have/with an eye to)** *the main chance* ⇒ main chance. **have eyes in the back of one's head** (*fig*) be able to sense everything happening around one. **have not clapped/ laid/set eyes on s.o** have not seen or noticed s.o at all or for some time: *Since that day in London a year ago I've not clapped eyes on him.* **in a twinkling; in the twinkling of an eye** ⇒ twinkle(*n*). **in one's/the mind's eye** in one's imagination. **in the eye(s) of s.o/the law** in s.o's/ the law's opinion: *I can do nothing right in the eyes of my parents. In the eyes of the law you are only an adult when you reach 18.* **keep an eye on s.o/s.t** look after, watch, s.o/s.t: *Keep an eye on my bags for a moment, please.* **keep an eye open/out for s.o/s.t** try to notice, watch for, s.o/s.t: *I kept an eye out for my friend's arrival.* **keep one's eye(s) on s.o/s.t** watch s.o/s.t carefully: *Keep your eye on the ball!* **keep one's eyes open/fixed/peeled** watch very carefully. **lay eyes on s.o/s.t** meet s.o, see s.t, during one's usual or ordinary activities. **look s.o in the eye** look directly at s.o's eyes: *He looked the judge in the eye and promised he was telling the truth.* **make eyes at s.o** look at s.o with sexual interest. **more in/to s.t than meets the eye** (a) s.t is more difficult, complicated, than one thinks at first sight: *There's more in playing the piano well than meets the eye.* (b) s.t more is hidden and does not appear on the surface: *There's more to this problem than meets the eye.* **My eye!** (*informal*) (used to express a degree of disbelief or surprise). **open s.o's eyes (to s.t)** cause s.o to realize, understand, the truth (about s.t). **roll one's eyes (at s.o)** look at s.o and then look up to show one's disapproval, that one expected such a bad result etc. **see eye to eye (with s.o) (about s.t)** agree (with s.o) (about s.t); have the same opinion (as s.o) (about s.t): *Those two never see eye to eye about anything.* **shut one's eyes to s.t** ⇒ close one's eyes to s.t. **turn a blind eye (to s.t)** pretend not to notice s.t: *I'll turn a blind eye to it this time but don't do it again.* **(see s.t with) the naked eye** (see s.t with) only the eye and no help from a magnifying glass, a microscope etc: *Germs(1) are too small to see with the naked eye.* **a sight for sore eyes** ⇒ sight(*n*). **take one's eyes off s.o/s.t** stop looking at s.o/s.t: *Take your eyes off that cake — it's mine! She's so beautiful that I can't take my eyes off her.* **under one's very eyes** right in front of one and without any attempt to hide it: *I told you not to do that and here you are taking apples from under my very eyes.* **up to one's eyes in s.t** very busy doing (work etc). **weather eye** ⇒ weather. **with an eye to s.t.** ⇒ (have/with) an eye to s.t. **with half an eye** without looking (too) carefully: *You only need to look with half an eye to know that they're not very happy together.* **with one's eyes open** understanding the situation perfectly: *If you do take the job, at least you'll be doing it with your eyes open since everyone's told you how difficult it is.*

▷ *tr.v* **6** observe, watch, (s.o/s.t) carefully: *The cat was eyeing the birds in the tree.*

'**eye,ball** *c.n* whole round body of the eye. **eyeball to eyeball** (*fig; informal*) face to face (with s.o/s.t); very close to s.o/s.t.

'**eye,brow** *c.n* arch of hair growing just above the eye. **raise one's eyebrows** (*fig*) show doubt,

surprise: *Her explanation caused a few eyebrows to be raised.* **up to one's eyebrows** (*in s.t*) (*fig; informal*) very busy (with s.t).

'**eye,brow ,pencil** *c.n* pencil for colouring eyebrows.

'**eye-,catching** *adj* very noticeable; attractive.

-eyed *adj* (with the kind of eye(s) mentioned in the first part of the word): *a brown-eyed man.* **s.o's blue-eyed boy/girl** s.o's favourite man/ woman who can do no wrong in s.o's opinion.

'**eyeful** *c.n* (*informal*) (usu *have/get an —*) as much as one is able to look at or deal with: *I can't look at any more pictures — I've had an eyeful.*

'**eye,glass** *c.n* piece of shaped glass used to improve the sight of one eye that may be weaker than the other or to examine s.t closely: *The jeweller used an eyeglass to look at the inside of the broken watch.*

'**eye,glasses** *pl.n* (*formal*) = spectacles.

'**eye,lash** *c.n* one of the hairs that grow from the edge of the eyelids.

eyelet /'aɪlɪt/ *c.n* small hole, usu with a metal ring around it, for rope, shoelaces etc, to go through.

'**eye,lid** *c.n* one of the upper or lower pieces of skin that open and close and cover the eye: *She put blue eye shadow on her upper eyelids.* **not bat an eyelid** ⇒ bat³.

'**eye,liner** *c/u.n* dark colour used for drawing a line along the edge of the eyelids in order to make the eyes appear more beautiful.

'**eye-,opener** *c.n* thing that causes one to understand, believe, s.t unexpected: *I thought I knew a lot about Cuba but visiting it was a real eye-opener.*

'**eye,piece** *c.n* lens(1) in a microscope, telescope etc for looking through.

'**eye,shade** *u.n* kind of flap(2) worn above the eyes to protect them from the glare(2).

'**eye ,shadow** *u.n* coloured powder or cream for the eyelids to make the eyes appear more beautiful.

'**eye,sight** *u.n* power/quality of seeing: *I have to wear glasses for driving because my eyesight is not good.*

'**eye,sore** *c.n* (*derog*) thing that is very unpleasant to look at, esp because it does not fit into its surroundings: *Rubbish left in the streets is always an eyesore.*

'**eye,strain** *u.n* tired state of the eyes usually caused by reading a lot, esp books with small print or without enough light: *She suffered from eyestrain after working in the library all day.*

'**eye,tooth** *c.n* (*pl* eyeteeth) one of the two pointed teeth in the top jaw.

'**eye,wash** *u.n* **1** liquid for bathing the eyes. **2** (*fig; informal*) thing done, said, in order to mislead s.o: *Don't give me that eyewash! You didn't miss the bus — you got up late.*

'**eye,witness** *c.n* (also *attrib*) person who has seen a particular event happen and is able to describe it or the people in it, esp in a court case: *I have to appear in court today because I was an eyewitness to an accident. She gave an eyewitness account of the event.*

eyrie /'ɪərɪ/ *c.n* nest, esp of eagles(1), birds of prey etc, usually built high up in mountains etc.

Ff

F, f /ef/ c/*unique* n **1** 6th letter of the English alphabet.
▷ *written abbr* **2** fathom(s). **3** female; feminine(4). **4** folio(1). ⇒ ff(3). **5** (used after a number) following (a certain page number): *See page 20f.* ⇒ ff(2).
▷ *symb* **6** frequency(3). **7** (**F**) Fahrenheit. **8** (**F**) Fellow(4). **9** forte¹.

fab /fæb/ *adj abbr* (*informal*) fabulous(1).

fable /'feɪbl/ n **1** c.n short story (esp one in which the main characters are animals or objects) which has a moral lesson: *Aesop's fables.* **2** c/u.n (one of a) group of stories about imaginary people. **3** c/u.n story, account that is not true: *I don't know whether her story is fact or fable.*
'fabled *adj* made famous by fables(2). ⇒ fabulous(3).

fabric /'fæbrɪk/ n **1** c/u.n (kind of) cloth or material that is made of threads that are knitted, woven etc: *I'm using a green fabric for the curtains.* **2** u.n (often the — of s.t) framework; system: *She's studying the fabric of modern French society.* **3** u.n structure(1), esp of the outside part of a building etc: *It's expensive to keep the fabric of old stone buildings in good repair.*

fabricate /'fæbrɪˌkeɪt/ tr.v (*formal*) **1** make up, invent, (an excuse, story that is not true): *She fabricated the whole thing — not a word she said is true.* **2** make a copy of (a document(1), will etc) in order to deceive. **3** build, manufacture, (s.t): *This house is fabricated out of wood.*
fabrication /ˌfæbrɪ'keɪʃən/ n (*formal*) **1** u.n act of inventing (a story, account that is not true). **2** c.n false story or account; lie: *Your story is a complete fabrication.* **3** c.n copy of a document(1), will etc that deceives.

fabulous /'fæbjʊləs/ adj **1** (abbr (*informal*) fab) wonderful; very good: *You look fabulous tonight. What a fabulous view!* **2** (esp of money) difficult to believe the truth of (usu because it's so much): *They bought that house for some fabulous amount.* **3** (*formal*) from, described in, fables(1): *The unicorn is a fabulous creature.* ⇒ fabled.
'fabulously *adv* very; in a wonderful or unbelievable way: *fabulously wealthy/beautiful.*

facade, façade /fə'sɑːd/ c.n **1** (outside surface of the) front of a building facing a street, open area etc: *Our house has a stone facade.* **2** (*fig*) outside appearance, esp one that is false, different from what is (felt) inside: *Although she was sad, Emma put on a cheerful facade.*

face /feɪs/ c.n **1** front part of the head including the forehead, eyes, nose, mouth, cheeks, chin: *The children washed their faces.* **2** c.n expression, look: *I was met by a row of smiling faces.* **3** (often — of s.t) surface, esp a front surface, (of a mountain, clock, building etc). **4** = typeface. **5** (*mining*) surface of rock where miners are working: *a rock/coal face.* **face to face (with s.o/ s.t)** (a) (of people) together; with everyone or everything present: *At last they agreed to discuss their differences face to face.* (b) (often *bring s.o, come, —*) (cause (s.o) to) become very close to s.t (so as to learn s.t about it): *His illness brought him face to face with death.* **fly in the face of s.t** do s.t that opposes(2) what is usually accepted, considered right, natural etc: *fly in the face of nature/tradition(1).* **have egg all over one's face** ⇒ egg(n). **have the face (to do s.t)** have enough courage (esp when it needs some cheek(2)) (to do s.t): *I don't have the face to see her again after last night.* **in one's face** (a) directly into, straight onto, one's face: *The wind blew in our faces.* (b) in front of one, without hiding anything: *They laughed in our faces.* **in the face of s.t** in the presence of s.t, esp s.t that opposes(2); in spite of s.t: *You will have to be brave in the face of great danger.* **keep a straight face** avoid showing one's amusement by not smiling etc: *When you saw her hat how did you manage to keep a straight face?* **laugh in s.o's face** show one's lack of respect for s.o openly. **laugh on the other side of one's face** show one's disappointment after being confident. **look s.o in the face** look directly at s.o (esp without showing shame, guilt etc): *Can you look me in the face after what you've done?* **lose face** (*fig*) lose the respect of others: *You'll have to admit your mistake if you don't want to lose face.* ⇒ save face. **make/pull a face; make/pull faces** give one's face a funny, rude, mocking, disapproving etc expression: *Don't pull faces (or pull a face) when I tell you to do something.* **make s.o's face fall; s.o's face fell** (make s.o's) expression change to sadness, disappointment, nervousness etc: *The news that the singer had been delayed made everyone's face fall. Her face fell when she saw me with him.* **on the face of it** (*fig*) on the surface: *The plan seems good on the face of it but once you start you'll find it too difficult.* **pull faces** ⇒ make/pull a face, faces. **put on a bold, good** etc **face** pretend to be bold, brave, in spite of difficulties, fears etc: *She put on a bold face in spite of her serious illness.* **save face** (*fig*) avoid losing respect or being ashamed: *The only way to save face in this situation is to admit your mistake and apologize.* ⇒ lose face. ⇒ face-saver, face-saving. **show one's face (s.w)** appear (s.w); (have the confidence to) go, be, (s.w): *Don't you dare show your face here again.* **stare s.o in the face** (a) look very hard at s.o's face: *I saw her taking the money but she stared me in the face, daring me to tell someone.* (b) (of danger, death, a fact etc) be very close to s.o: *At every stage in the long journey across the desert, danger stared them in the face.* (c) be so clear, easy to understand, that one should see it: *The answer is staring you in the face.* **take s.o/s.t at face value** treat, judge, s.o/s.t as he/she/it appears on the surface: *Don't take anything he says at face value.* **till/until s.o is blue in the face** ⇒ blue(n). **to s.o's face** openly; while s.o is present: *I dare you to say that to his face.* Compare behind s.o's back. **(wear a) long face** (have a) sad, disappointed, unhappy look: *You've been wearing that long face for long enough now — stop feeling sorry for yourself.*
▷ *tr.v* **6** look at (s.o/s.t); stand so as to be, or have one's face, towards (a particular direction): *We faced one another but neither of us could speak.*

The theatre faces the river. Our garden faces south. **7** deal confidently with (s.o/s.t); have the courage, energy(1) to meet (s.o/s.t): *We had to face many difficulties. I just can't face another meeting.* **8** (cause (s.o) to) accept or recognize (the truth, reality, fact of s.t): *We had to face Harry with the truth that it was his son who had stolen from him. When will you face the reality that we are not as rich as we used to be?* **9** present itself to (s.o); need to be dealt with by (s.o): *The problem that faces us now is getting the food to the people.* **10** (often — s.t with s.t) cover the surface of (s.t) (with a different material): *We'll have to face these walls with plaster before we paint.* **face facts**; **face it** (*informal*) accept s.t unpleasant, unpleasant facts: *Let's face it; our marriage is finished. Face facts, you're too old to play as well as you did twenty years ago.* **face s.t out** deal bravely with a problem etc until the end: *We faced out the storm for several hours.* **face the music** ⇒ music. **face up to s.t** accept unpleasant facts, reality etc; recognize, treat, s.t bravely or honestly: *It's time you faced up to your responsibilities and found a job.*

'face,cloth *c.n* small square piece of cloth like a towel, used for washing the body, esp the face.

-faced *adj* with a face of the kind mentioned in the first part of the word: *red-faced*; *round-faced.*

'faceless *adj* **1** (*derog*) having no clear character: *You're faceless — you have no opinions, you show no feelings.* **2** unknown to the general public: *There are many faceless people in government.*

'face,lift *c.n* operation to lift loose old skin in order to make one look younger.

'face,pack *c.n* cream or paste spread over the face and left to dry in order to clean and freshen the skin: *The white of an egg when beaten stiff is a very good facepack.*

'face ,powder *u.n* powder, usu with a slight colour, put on the face to improve one's appearance.

'face-,saver *c.n* (*informal*) act, event, that prevents one being shamed or losing respect. ⇒ save face (⇒ face(n)).

'face-,saving *adj* (*informal*) done or made to prevent one being shamed or losing respect: *Chelsea won today's match in a face-saving game that has brought new respect from the team's fans.* ⇒ save face (⇒ face(n)).

,face-to-'face *adj/adv* (standing) opposite one another: *The management and workers had a face-to-face discussion about their problems.*

,face 'value *n* **1** *c/u.n* value shown on a coin, bank note, stamp etc. **2** *u.n* (usu at —) judging the value or importance of s.t by outside appearances: *At face value I doubt that the car is worth much.*

facial /'feɪʃəl/ *adj* (usu *attrib*) of or referring to the face(1): *facial expressions.*

'facing *attrib.adj* **1** opposite: *the facing page.*
▷ *adv* **2** with the front side towards (each other): *stand facing each other.* ⇒ back to back (⇒ back(n)).
▷ *c/u.n* **3** (material for making a) surface or outer covering on a wall, collar etc. ⇒ lining (⇒ line²).

'facings *pl.n* pieces of material, esp of a different colour, on the collar, cuffs(1) etc of a uniform(2) etc.

facet /'fæsɪt/ *c.n* (often — *of s.t*) **1** one of the small surfaces (of a cut stone, jewel etc): *The facets of the diamond shone in the sunlight.* **2** (*formal*) view (of a difficulty, problem etc): *We will need to consider all the facets of this matter before we decide.*

-faceted *adj* having the number of sides or parts shown in the first part of the word: *a multi-faceted diamond*; *a many-faceted problem.*

facetious /fə'siːʃəs/ *adj* of (making) jokes or remarks that are not suitable: *How can you be so facetious about such a serious matter?*
fa'cetiously *adv.* **fa'cetiousness** *u.n.*

facia ⇒ fascia.

facile /'fæsaɪl/ *adj* (*formal*) **1** done, said, obtained, too easily or quickly (without thought or preparation) to have any importance: *Such facile answers won't get you anywhere.* **2** (*derog*) (of behaviour) that is without thought: *Don't be so facile — think about how sad you make her.*
'facilely *adv.* **'facileness** *u.n.*

facilitate /fə'sɪlɪˌteɪt/ *tr.v* (*formal*) make (s.t) easy or easier: *The invention of the aircraft has greatly facilitated travel between countries.*

facility /fə'sɪlɪtɪ/ *n* (*pl* -ies) (*formal*) **1** *u.n* ease (when doing s.t): *Her facility with foreign languages is wonderful.* **2** *c.n* (often have/show a — for/in doing s.t) ability to do s.t with ease: *How is it that you have such a facility for knowing what I'm thinking?* **3** *c.n* (usu *pl*) thing that makes an activity possible: *The university has excellent sports facilities.*

facsimile /fæk'sɪmɪlɪ/ *attrib.adj* **1** that is a facsimile(2): *a facsimile picture of an original Van Gogh.*
▷ *c.n* **2** exact copy (of a picture, writing etc): *a facsimile of a famous painting.*

fact /fækt/ *n* **1** *c.n* thing or event that is known to exist or to have happened: *The police gathered all the facts about the crime.* **2** *c.n* information that is (accepted as) real or true: *What facts does the writer give us about his childhood? Who first stated the fact that the earth is round?* **3** *u.n* reality; truth: *The fact is that we have very little food and water left. You can't tell the difference between fact and fiction(2).* **an accessory after/before the fact** ⇒ accessory. **as a matter of fact** ⇒ matter(n). **face facts** ⇒ face(v). **for a fact** = for certain (⇒ certain(adj)). **in (actual) fact** (used to state one's opinion more strongly) actually; really: *I'm sure I saw her yesterday; in fact, I know I did.* **in (point of) fact** (used to state a fact with more force) actually; really: *They promised to finish two weeks ago but in point of fact they only finished yesterday.* **the fact of the matter is** the truth, the main point of a difficulty, is: *You make an excuse for not visiting me but the fact of the matter is that you don't love me, isn't it?*

'fact-,finder *c.n* (*informal*) (small) book that provides facts about a particular subject or place.

'fact-,finding *attrib.adj* that is set up to discover facts: *a fact-finding committee.*

,fact of 'life *c.n* (*pl* facts of life) (often *pl*) thing that we must accept because it is a necessary part of our life or because it is something that happens: *Poverty is a fact of life. Sickness and death are facts of life.* Compare facts of life(1) below.

,facts and 'figures *pl.n* all the details (about a matter): *I want all the facts and figures on my desk in the morning.*

,facts of 'life *pl.n* **1** (*informal*) knowledge of human sexual behaviour; details about sex and having babies: *You don't have to give me a lecture on the facts of life, dad; I know it all already!* **2** ⇨ fact of life.

factual /'fæktʃʊəl/ *adj* of, referring to, containing, facts: *She gave the police a factual account of what she had seen. Is this account factual?* **'factually** *adv.*

faction /'fækʃən/ *n* (also *attrib*) **1** *c.n* small group (within a larger group) which has different opinions from the main group: *The political party split up into rival factions.* **2** *u.n* argument or fighting among different small groups within a group, political party etc: *There is so much faction* (or *faction fighting*) *in their group that it's impossible to agree on any important matter.*

factor /'fæktə/ *c.n* **1** (*mathematics*) number (except 1) by which a larger number can be divided exactly: *2 and 5 are factors of 10.* **2** fact, force, condition, which helps to bring about a result: *A major*(1) *factor in our decision to leave the country was my daughter's education.* **highest common factor** (*abbr hcf*) highest number that is a factor(1) of a group of numbers. ⇨ lowest common multiple.

factorize /'fæktə,raɪz/ , **-ise** *tr.v* divide (a number) into factors(1): *factorize the following numbers.*

factory /'fæktərɪ/ *c.n* (*pl -ies*) (also *attrib*) building or workshop in which goods are manufactured in large quantities: *I own a small furniture factory. Bob's a factory worker.* **'factory-,made** *adj* made in a factory using machines: *factory-made shoes.* Compare handmade, machine-made.

faculty /'fækəltɪ/ *c.n* (*pl -ies*) **1** (often — *for* (*doing*) s.t) particular ability, skill, (to do s.t): *He has a wonderful faculty for* (*learning*) *languages.* **2** (often — *of* s.t) natural power or ability (of the body's sense organs, the mind etc): *Many people believe that the faculty of hearing is more important than the faculty of sight. She's over 90 but she still has all her faculties.* **3** (often with capital **F**) (also *attrib*) department, group of connected departments and the staff, in a university: *The Faculty of Law. I teach in the law faculty.*

fad /fæd/ *c.n* (*informal*) fashion, interest, preference, that does not last a long time: *She won't remain a* vegetarian(3) *for long — it's just a fad.* **'faddish** *adj* **1** having likes and dislikes that are not reasonable: *faddish tastes in food.* **2** (of interests) that do not last a long time: *I'm tired of wasting money on your faddish hobbies.*

fade /feɪd/ *v* **1** *tr/intr.v* (cause (s.t) to) lose colour, freshness, strength: *The sun has faded the chairs near the window. These flowers were lovely but they are fading now. Hopes of finding the climbers alive are fading.* **2** *intr.v* (often — *away* (*from* s.t)) disappear (slowly) (from hearing, memory, view): *The music gradually faded* (*away*) *into the distance. The name has faded from our minds.* **fade away** (**a**) ⇨ fade(2). (**b**) lose strength and die: *After a long illness, she faded away.* (**c**) (*fig*)

get very much thinner than before: *What have you done to yourself, you're fading away.* **fade (s.t) in(to s.t)/out** (in filming, broadcasting, recording) (cause (sound, light) to) become less clear and disappear (into s.t else): *One record faded into the next one.*

faeces /'fiːsiːz/ *pl.n* (*technical*) solid waste material that comes out of the bowels(1).

fag /fæg/ *n* (*slang*) **1** *sing.n* job, piece of work, that is tiring and uninteresting: *I don't want to wash the dishes; it's too much of a fag.* **2** *c.n* cigarette: *Have you got any fags?*
▷ *v* (*-gg-*) (*informal*) **3** *intr.v* (often — *away* at s.t) do tiring and uninteresting work: *You've been fagging away at that floor for hours.* **4** *tr.v* (often — *s.o* out) (of work) make (s.o) very tired: *Sawing wood all day must really fag you* (*out*).
'fag-,end *c.n* (*slang*) **1** small end part of a cigarette left after it has been smoked. **2** (usu the — *of* s.t) last part (of s.t), esp the less valuable or useful end: *I only heard the fag-end of their argument so I don't really know who started it.*

faggot /'fægət/ *c.n* **1** number of small sticks tied together and used for burning. **2** meat ball (esp one made of liver(2)) for frying.

Fahrenheit /'færən,haɪt/ *unique n* (also *attrib*) scale of temperature in which the freezing-point of water is taken as 32° (degrees) and its boiling-point as 212° (degrees), *symb* F: *Bake the cake at 350°F. Is that a Fahrenheit thermometer?*

fail /feɪl/ *unique n* **1 without fail** for certain; no matter what the difficulties are: *Don't worry, I'll be there without fail.*
▷ *v* **2** *tr.v* decide, judge, that (s.o/s.t) is not good enough to pass (an examination, test etc): *The examiner failed me the first time I took my driving test.* **3** *tr/intr.v* (often — *in* s.t; — *to do* s.t) be unsuccessful (in trying (to do) (s.t)): *I failed my driver's test. We failed* (*in our efforts*) *to rescue our boat before it sank.* **4** *intr.v* come to an end or stop working when still expected or needed: *If our brakes fail now we'll have no chance!* **5** *intr.v* (of health, hearing, sight etc) become weak; lose strength: *Our eyesight often fails as we get older.* **6** *tr.v* disappoint, not be useful to, (s.o/s.t): *I hope I haven't failed you as a parent.* Compare unfailing. **7** *intr.v* become bankrupt(1): *Even big businesses are known to fail in bad times like these.* **words fail me** ⇨ word(*n*).
'failing *c.n* **1** fault; weakness: *The fat woman's greatest failing is her love of cakes.*
▷ *prep* **2** in the absence of; if (s.t) fails or is not present: *Failing a reply to my letter, I shall have to get advice from my lawyer.*

'fail-,safe *adj* made so that a failure in any part of the machine, system etc causes the whole of it to stop working so that damage is avoided.

failure /'feɪljə/ *n* **1** *c.n* (*derog*) person or thing who/that fails, is unsuccessful: *She was a complete failure as a politician. Our plan is a failure.* **2** *u.n* act, state, of being unsuccessful, failing: *Everything she attempts ends in failure.* **3** *c/u.n* (example of a) thing that stops before expected or normal, or when it is still needed: *The failure of the crops left many people hungry. He nearly died from heart failure.* **4** *c/u.n* (often — *to do* s.t) fact of neglecting, or being unable, (to do s.t): *Her repeated failure to arrive on time annoyed her friends.* **5** *intr.v* (often *the* — *of* s.t) inability (of a business) to continue to operate because of lack of money: *The failure of old and successful businesses should tell you that this is not the time to start a new one.*

faint /feɪnt/ *adj* **1** (of a sound, light, smell etc) weak; lacking strength or brightness: *The music is very faint. There's a faint smell of cigarettes in this room.* **2** (often *the* —*est s.t*) (of a chance, idea etc) slight or small: *Is there at least a faint chance that he'll get better? Do you have the faintest idea what I'm talking about?* **3** (of the action of parts of the body) weak; lacking strength: *His* heartbeats *are faint.* **4** (usu *pred*) weak; close to losing consciousness: *I feel faint when I see blood.* **5** (usu *pred*) (often — *with s.t*) (of a person) tired, weak, (because of s.t): *The children were faint with hunger.* **6** (usu *attrib*) (of action, efforts etc) weak, unlikely to succeed: *He made a faint attempt to stop her from leaving.*
▷ *sing.n* **7** state of unconsciousness for a limited time: *He felt a faint coming on.*
▷ *intr.v* (often — *from s.t*) **8** lose consciousness (because of s.t): *She fainted from shock.* **9** (*informal*) become weak: *He was fainting from hunger.*
‚faint-'hearted *adj* (*derog*) lacking courage: *He made a faint-hearted attempt to rescue the cat.*
‚faint-'heartedly *adv.*
‚faint-'heartedness *u.n.*
'faintly *adv* **1** in a faint way: *The lights shone faintly in the distance. She speaks so faintly I can hardly hear her.* **2** slightly: *I faintly remember it.*
'faintness *u.n.*
fair¹ /feə/ *adj* **1** not showing preference to either/ any person, side etc; acting in an honest way, according to the rules (of a game etc): *That's not fair; her piece is bigger than mine. He's a very fair judge.* Opposite unfair. **2** (of size, quality etc) average: *It's a fair attempt but I'm sure you could do better. 'Are you a good player?' 'I'm fair'.* **3** (of weather) good; dry and sunny: *We're hoping for fair weather for the game tomorrow.* **4** (of hair, skin) light coloured: *She has fair hair but a dark skin.* **5** (*attrib*) (*informal*) (of size, distance etc) quite large: *We did a fair amount of work this weekend.* **6** (*old use; literary*) beautiful. **be fair game** ⇒ game(*n*). **fair to middling** of average standard, quality etc. **give s.o, get, a fair hearing** ⇒ hearing(3). **by fair means or foul** ⇒ means.
▷ *adv* **7** in a just way; according to the rules: *play/ act fair.* **fair and square (a)** honestly: *We won fair and square.* **(b)** directly: *She hit him fair and square in the middle of the stomach.* **fair enough** (*informal*) (used to express agreement or to admit that s.o has acted or spoken reasonably) agreed, all right: *Fair enough — I'll take my car and you pay for the petrol.*
'fairly *adv* **1** justly; in a fair¹(1) way: *The competition was judged fairly.* **2** (of degree) quite; moderately: *I found your house fairly easily. It's fairly heavy. It was fairly successful.*
‚fair-'minded *adj* (of s.o) fair(1); just, not favouring or supporting one side only: *a fair-minded judge.*
‚fair 'play *u.n* equal conditions and treatment for all: *We invited observers from both sides to make sure of fair play.*
'fair ‚sex *def.n* (also **'gentle ‚sex**) women.
'fair‚way *c.n* **1** water passage that is safe for ships. **2** large open area prepared for golf(1).

‚fair-'weather *attrib.adj* only while there are no difficulties: *my fair-weather friend.*
fair² /feə/ *c.n* **1** (cattle, sheep) market held in a particular place at certain times of the year: *We're expecting some good prizes for our bulls¹(1) at this year's fair.* **2** = funfair: *Let's go to the fair.* **3** (with capital **F** in names) show of manufactured goods, usu of many different kinds and from many different countries: *a trade fair*; *the World Fair.* **4** sale of goods in order to raise money (for a particular cause): *a charity(2) fair.*
'fair‚ground *c.n* open space where fairs²(1–3) are held.
fairy /'feərɪ/ *attrib.adj* **1** of or referring to fairies(2): *fairy tales.*
▷ *c.n* (*pl* -ies) **2** small imaginary person who has wings and can do magic.
'fairy‚land *n* **1** *unique n* country/home of fairies(2). **2** *c.n* beautiful place: *The forest was a fairyland after the first* snowfall(1).
'fairy ‚light *c.n* small coloured electric light, used mainly for decoration: *We decorated the Christmas tree with fairy lights.*
'fairy ‚story *c.n* (*pl* -ies) **1** story about fairies(2) and/or other imaginary creatures. **2** untrue account of s.t, esp by a child: *I don't want to hear any more fairy stories about your brother.*
'fairy ‚tale *c.n* = fairy story(1).
fait accompli /ˌfeɪt ə'kɒmpli/ (*pl* faits accomplis /ˌfeɪt ə'kɒmpliːz/) *c.n* (*French*) thing that has already been completed and therefore can no longer be changed: *How can you ask my advice now when it's clearly a fait accompli?*
faith /feɪθ/ *n* **1** *u.n* (often *have* — *in s.o/s.t*) strong belief, trust, (in s.o/s.t) that one does not question: *You'll only get better if you have faith in your doctor.* **2** *c/u.n* religious belief: *Nothing will make him lose his faith.* **break faith with s.o** ⇒ keep/break faith with s.o. **in (all) good faith** sincerely; with good intentions: *Her offer of help was made in good faith.* **in bad faith** with bad intentions: *Their agreement was made in bad faith since they clearly had no intention of doing what they promised.* **keep/break faith with s.o** be loyal/disloyal to s.o; (not) do what one has promised s.o: *Francis kept faith with me right through my troubles.*
'faithful *adj* **1** (often — *to s.o/s.t*) loyal, true, (to s.o/s.t): *If he said he would help, I'm sure he'll be faithful to his promise.* Opposite unfaithful. **2** accurate; true to the facts: *a faithful description of the events.*
▷ *def.pl.n* **3** true believers, esp in Christianity, Islam etc.
'faithfully *adv* **1** sincerely: *He promised faithfully that he would come.* **2** in an accurate way; exactly: *She copied the whole story down faithfully.* **3** regularly: *She comes to see me faithfully at least twice a week.* **Yours faithfully** formal way of ending a letter that starts 'Dear Madam/Sir'. Compare Yours sincerely, Yours truly.
'faithfulness *u.n.*
'faith ‚healer *c.n* person who treats diseases, illness by prayer instead of medicine.
'faith ‚healing *u.n* act or practice of treating disease, illness by prayer instead of medicine.
'faithless *adj* **1** having no religious faith. **2** not loyal or faithful; not to be trusted: *a faithless friend.*

'faithlessly *adv.* **'faithlessness** *u.n.*

fake /feɪk/ *adj* **1** made in imitation of s.t, usu s.t valuable: *Are these diamonds real or fake?* **2** (*attrib*) pretending to be what one is not: *a fake policeman.*
▷ *c.n* **3** imitation of s.t, usu s.t valuable: *The painting was a fake but I thought it was an original.* **4** person who pretends to be s.o he/she is not.
▷ *v* **5** *tr.v* make an imitation of (a picture, jewellery etc) (usu to deceive others or for safety): *A lot of modern furniture is faked to look old.* **6** *intr.v* pretend (to be ill, sad, happy etc): *I thought she was ill but she was faking.*
'faker *c.n* person who fakes(*v*).

falcon /'fɔːlkən/ *c.n* kind of small bird that hunts and kills other small birds and animals, and which can be trained by people to hunt.
'falconer *c.n* person who keeps, trains, hunts with, falcons.
'falconry *u.n.* **1** art of training falcons. **2** sport of hunting with falcons.

fall /fɔːl/ *n* **1** *c.n* act of falling (⇨ fall(7)), usu from a height: *She hurt herself in a fall from her horse. Pat's had a bad fall.* **2** *c.n* (often — in s.t) decrease, reduction, (in price, quantity, temperature, value etc): *There was a fall in the price of oil last month. We expect a sharp fall in temperature tonight.* **3** *c.n* (often — of s.t) (amount of a) thing, e.g snow, rocks or rain, that has fallen: *a heavy fall of snow*; *rock falls.* ⇨ rainfall. **4** *c.n* (often — of s.t) drop, distance, (of an amount) between one height and another: *There was a fall of several hundred metres on either side.* **5** *c.n* (often the — of s.o) defeat (of an army, country etc): *the rise and fall of the Roman Empire.* **6** *def/unique n* (US) autumn.
▷ *intr.v* (*p.t* fell /fel/, *p.p* fallen /'fɔːlən/) **7** come/ go down freely or naturally from a higher to a lower position (e.g by force of weight): *Snow fell all night. During the autumn the leaves fall off the trees. The ball fell into the water.* **8** *intr.v* (often — down/off/over (s.t)) come down, drop to the ground, esp suddenly and without intention: *Many buildings fell down during the earthquake. While I was riding, my horse tripped and I fell off. He fell over (a stone).* **9** become less or lower: *The value of gold has fallen. The temperature fell sharply during the night. The wind has fallen.* **10** become: *She fell ill suddenly and died. I'm falling asleep. He fell in love with the girl who lived next door.* **11** (of one's face) become sad, disappointed etc: *Her face fell when she heard the bad news.* **12** hang: *The material for curtains should fall very nicely.* **13** happen; occur(1): *Easter falls very early this year.* ⇨ fall (up)on s.t. **14** (often — to s.o/s.t) (*formal*) be taken, defeated, (by the enemy): *After a long battle, the city finally fell (to the enemy).* **15** (*literary*) die in battle: *Many soldiers fell in the battle.* **16** slope down: *The hillside falls gently to the valley.* **17** (*formal*) be spoken: *She promised not to let a word of her friend's secret fall (from her lips).* **18** (*old use*) give in to temptation and do s.t immoral.
fall about (**laughing**, **with laughter**) (*informal*) laugh without any control.
fall among s.o become friendly with (people outside the law): *After he ran out of money he fell among a group of thieves.*
fall apart (**a**) (of a machine, instrument) break

into pieces: *This old bicycle is practically falling apart.* (**b**) (*informal*) (of a marriage, partnership) break up. (**c**) (*fig; informal*) lose control of oneself; be unable to behave in an organized way: *You're falling apart; you're always dirty and untidy, and now you're rude to people.*
fall away (**a**) decrease; slowly become less in number or importance: *The crowds began to fall away after the game had ended.* (**b**) slope down steeply: *The garden falls away to the river.*
fall back move or turn back: *She shouted at us to fall back when she saw the danger ahead.* **fall back on s.o/s.t** have s.o/s.t that will help support one in difficult times: *He fell back on his family when he needed extra money.*
fall behind (s.o/s.t) fail to stay (with the group); be slower (than the rest): *Please don't fall behind the others. You'll have to work very hard if you don't want to fall behind in mathematics.* **fall behind with s.t** fail to do s.t at the right time; be late with s.t: *Don't fall behind with your payments or you'll be in trouble.*
fall down hang down: *Her hair falls down to her waist.* **fall down** (**on s.t**) (*informal*) fail (in s.t); (cause the result of s.t to) be below standard: *You fell down on questions 2 and 4.*
fall flat (**a**) (usu — on one's back/behind/face) (of a person) fall to the ground (so that one is lying on one's back, behind, face): *He tripped and fell flat on his back.* (**b**) fail completely; produce no result: *His joke fell flat — no one found it at all funny. Our plans for the weekend fell flat when the only driver got sick.*
fall for s.o (*informal*) become very fond of s.o; begin to like s.o very much: *I knew you'd fall for her because she's very much your type of person.* **fall for s.t** (*informal*) be deceived by a lie, trick etc: *How could you fall for such an unbelievable story?*
fall ill ⇨ ill(*adj*).
fall in (**a**) (of a roof, high covering) break and fall down: *The roof of the old factory fell in during the fire.* (**b**) (*military*) (of soldiers) get into a line or lines: *The officer ordered the soldiers to fall in.* ⇨ fall out(b).
fall in love (**with s.o**) find that one is in love (with s.o): *John fell in love (with Maria) while he was travelling in France.* **fall in with s.o** meet s.o by chance: *At the party we fell in with friends we hadn't seen for years.* **fall in with s.t** agree to s.t: *Everyone fell in with her suggestion.*
fall into s.t be naturally divided into s.t: *The year falls into four seasons.* **fall into conversation** (**with s.o**) ⇨ conversation. **fall into s.o's hands** ⇨ hand(*n*). **fall into line** (**with s.o/s.t**) ⇨ line¹(*n*). **fall into place** ⇨ place(*n*).
fall off (**a**) ⇨ fall(8). (**b**) become less; decrease: *The number of newspapers sold every day has begun to fall off.*
fall on deaf ears ⇨ ear. **fall on one's feet** ⇨ foot(*n*). **fall (up)on s.o/s.t** (**a**) attack s.o/s.t: *The wild dogs fell (up)on the young deer.* (**b**) descend on s.o/s.t: *Darkness fell on the city.* **fall (up)on s.o** (**to do s.t**) (*formal*) be the duty of s.o (to do s.t): *It fell (up)on the police officer to tell the woman's husband about her fatal accident.* **fall (up)on s.t** happen on a certain day: *Christmas Day falls on a Sunday this year.* Compare fall(13).
fall out (**of s.t**) (**a**) give (s.t) up: *Many students*

fell out of the course because it was too difficult.
⇒ fall-out(2). Compare drop out. (**b**) (*military*) (of soldiers) leave one's place in line. ⇒ fall in(b). **fall out of the habit** (**of doing st**) ⇒ habit. **fall out with s.o** (**over s.o/s.t**) (*informal*) quarrel with s.o (about s.o/s.t): *He fell out with his father over his girlfriend.* ⇒ fall-out(4).

fall over ⇒ fall(8). **fall over oneself** (**to do s.t**) be very eager (to do s.t, esp to please s.o or to gain, win s.t): *The manager of the store fell over himself to satisfy the angry customer.* **fall over backwards** (**to do s.t**) (*fig*) try very hard, make a great effort, (esp to please s.o): *They all fell over backwards to make me feel welcome.*

fall short (**of s.t**) ⇒ short(*adv*).

fall through (of plans etc) fail; be unsuccessful: *My plan fell through because I couldn't raise enough money.*

fall to (*old use*) eagerly begin doing s.t (esp eating): *When the food arrived the children fell to hungrily.* **fall to s.o/s.t** ⇒ fall(14). **fall to s.o to do s.t** (*formal*) be s.o's duty to do s.t: *It falls to you to welcome everyone this week.* **fall to doing s.t** (*formal*) begin to do s.t: *I fell to considering the problem.* **fall to the ground** ⇒ ground³(*n*).

fall under s.t be divided into s.t; be classified under s.t: *My examination of the problem falls under four main headings.*

fall upon s.o/s.t ⇒ fall (up)on s.o/s.t.

'fallen *attrib.adj* **1** (of s.t) that has fallen: *Please pick up the fallen apples.* **2** (*fig*) (of s.o) who has fallen (⇒ fall(18)): *a fallen priest; a fallen woman.*

▷ *def.pl.n* **3** (*literary*) soldiers who have been killed in battle.

‚falling 'star *c.n* = meteor.

'fall-‚out *attrib.adj* **1** of or referring to fall-out(3): *fall-out dust.* **2** concerning people who fall out (of s.t(a)): *the fall-out rate at universities.*

▷ *u.n* **3** (also **‚nuclear 'fall-‚out**) radioactive dust in the air caused by a nuclear(2) explosion.

falls *pl.n* (with capital **F** in names) place where a wide river suddenly drops (over a cliff etc): *the Victoria Falls in Zimbabwe.*

fallacy /'fæləsɪ/ *n* (*pl -ies*) (*formal*) **1** *c.n* mistaken or wrong belief, opinion, esp one believed by many to be true: *One of the great fallacies of the past was the belief that the world was flat.* **2** *u.n* false reasoning: *Your whole argument is based on fallacy.*

fallacious /fə'leɪʃəs/ *adj* (*formal*) mistaken; caused by false reasoning: *The results of your experiment are fallacious since you have not considered all the effects.*

fal'laciously *adv.* **fal'laciousness** *u.n.*

fallible /'fælɪbl/ *adj* (usu *pred*) able, likely, to be wrong, make mistakes: *We are all fallible in certain ways.* Opposite infallible.

fallibility /‚fælə'bɪlɪtɪ/ *u.n* Opposite infallibility.

Fallopian tube /fə‚ləʊpɪən 'tjuːb/ *c.n* tube that carries the eggs of female mammals from the ovary to the womb.

fallow /'fæləʊ/ *adj* (of land) ploughed but not planted (usu to allow the land to rest after a time of heavy cultivation): *fallow fields.* (**let s.t**) **lie fallow** (allow an area to) remain not cultivated: *The farmer lets a field lie fallow every third year.*

fallow deer /'fæləʊ ‚dɪə/ *c.n* (*pl fallow deer*)

kind of small deer with a red-yellow coat that has white spots on it in summer.

false /fɔːls/ *adj* **1** not right or true; mistaken: *Say whether the following statements are true or false.* **2** misleading; lying: *The criminal made a false statement when he was arrested by the police. The accusation is false.* **3** artificial; not real: *a false tooth.* **4** (*formal*) not loyal: *a false friend.* **bear/give false witness** ⇒ witness(*n*).

▷ *adv* **5** (esp *play s.o —*) cheat, deceive, (s.o): *He played his partner false by selling information to competing companies.* **ring false** ⇒ ring².

‚false a'larm *c.n* warning of danger that does not exist or happen; warning that proves to be unnecessary: *The firemen were angry because the call they answered was a false alarm.*

'false‚hood *c/u.n* (*formal*) (practice of telling a) lie: *You must stop these falsehoods or no one will ever believe anything you say.*

'falsely *adv.* **'falseness** *c.n.*

‚false pre'tences *pl.n* acts etc that deceive. (**do, get** *etc* **s.t**) **by/on/under false pretences** (do, get etc s.t) by lying, by using dishonest means: *He got money from his father on false pretences. You came here under false pretences because you never really cared about me.*

‚false 'start *c.n* early start in a race (i.e before the signal to start has been given).

‚false 'teeth *pl.n* artificial teeth used in place of ones that have been lost.

falsification /‚fɔːlsɪfɪ'keɪʃən/ *c/u.n* (act of) falsifying s.t.

falsify /'fɔːlsɪ‚faɪ/ *tr.v* (*-ies, -ied*) **1** make (s.t) false: *He falsified the accounts to hide the fact that he had stolen money.* **2** represent (s.t) wrongly: *She falsified the facts to her own advantage.*

'falsity *n* (*pl -ies*) (*formal*) **1** *u.n* quality of being false: *We discovered the falsity of his stories.* **2** *c.n* lie: *He is guilty of several falsities.*

falter /'fɔːltə/ *v* **1** *intr.v* act/move with hesitation because of nervousness, illness etc: *He faltered before knocking at the manager's door.* **2** *intr.v* speak with hesitation because of nervousness, illness etc: *She said the speech without faltering.* ⇒ unfaltering.

'falteringly *adv.*

fame /feɪm/ *u.n* fact or state of being widely known or talked about (esp favourably): *Bob's effort to raise money for the desperate and hungry people of Africa brought him worldwide fame.*

famed *adj* (usu *attrib*) (*formal*) (often *— for s.t*) well-known; celebrated (because of s.t): *famed for his bravery.*

famous /'feɪməs/ *adj* (often *— for s.t*) having fame; well-known (because of s.t): *This city is famous for its beauty. David Hockney is a famous painter.* Compare infamous.

'famously *adv* (esp *get on — (with s.o)*) (*informal*) excellently; very well: *He's getting on famously at his new school.*

familiar /fə'mɪlɪə/ *adj* **1** seen or heard before; known: *It won't be long before you become a familiar name in the literary world.* Opposite unfamiliar. **2** (*attrib*) personal; friendly: *We're on familiar terms — I know her quite well.* **3** (*derog*) unsuitably, too, friendly: *He was being familiar with my younger sister.* ⇒ familiarity(2). **familiar to s.o** well known to s.o: *This piece of music is not familiar to me.* **familiar with s.o/**

s.t knowing about, having knowledge of, s.o/s.t: *Are you familiar with this part of the city?*

familiarity /fə,mɪlɪˈærɪtɪ/ *n* (*pl* -*ies*) **1** *u.n* fact or state of being familiar with s.t: *His familiarity with the subject was astonishing.* **2** *u.n* familiar(3) behaviour: *How dare you treat my wife with such familiarity.* **3** *c.n* (usu *pl*) (often *derog*) act that is considered to be too friendly: *He dislikes the familiarities of his staff, especially when they call him by his first name.*

familiarize, -ise /fəˈmɪlɪə,raɪz/ *tr.v* (*formal*) **1** (often — *oneself*/s.o/s.t with s.o/s.t) make (oneself/s.o/s.t) familiar with, cause (oneself/s.o/s.t) to know about, s.o/s.t: *Television familiarizes us with distant parts of the world.* **2** make (s.t) known: *The newspapers have familiarized his ideas.*

fa'miliarly *adv* in a (too) friendly manner: *I don't think he treats you too familiarly.*

family /ˈfæmlɪ/ *attrib.adj* **1** of/for a family: *We had a very good family life.* **in the family way** (*slang*) (of a woman) expecting a baby.

▷ *n* **2** *u.n* group of people consisting of the parents and children: *My family lives in London. The members of her family work in Oxford.* **3** *c.n* group of people consisting of uncles, aunts, grandparents, cousins, brothers, sisters etc: *You'd never believe that he comes from a poor family.* **4** *c/u.n* children of the same parents: *We can't afford to have a large family so we'll probably only have two children.* **5** *c.n* group of living animals, plants, languages etc that have common origins or are like each other in certain ways: *Lions and tigers are members of the cat family.* **a family man** (a) a man who is fond of his home life with his wife and children. (b) a man who has a wife and child(ren). **nuclear family** ⇒ nuclear. **raise a family** give birth to children and look after them until they become adults. **run in my, the etc family** (of an appearance, characteristic etc) be s.t that appears again and again through different generations(2) (of a family): *Red hair runs in our family.* **start a family** begin to have children.

,**family 'circle** *c.n* close relatives: *We're only inviting the family circle.*

,**family 'doctor** *c.n* general practitioner.

'**family ,name** *c.n* = surname. ⇒ married name.

,**family 'planning** *u.n* (also *attrib*) planning of the number of children in a family and the time between their births (using birth control): *a family planning* clinic.

,**family 'tree** *c.n* (plan showing a) person's ancestors: *I know my family tree up to my great-grandparents* (⇒ great-).

famine /ˈfæmɪn/ *c/u.n* (also *attrib*) (occasion of) great lack of food in an area: *This has been a famine area for many years.*

famished /ˈfæmɪʃt/ *pred.adj* (*informal*) very hungry: *I'm famished after that ride.*

famous(ly) ⇒ fame.

fan /fæn/ *c.n* **1** (hand or electrical) device used to make air flow faster, esp to cool s.o/s.t: *The woman opened her fan and waved it in front of her face. During the hot weather I often leave the fan on all night.* **2** thing that is or can be spread out, e.g a peacock's fan. **3** (often — *of* s.o/s.t) supporter, great admirer (of s.o/s.t): *a football fan. She's become a great fan of yours.*

▷ *tr.v* (-*nn*-) **4** cool (oneself/s.o/s.t) with (s.t used as)

a fan: *I fanned myself with my programme because it was so warm in the theatre.* **5** (*formal*) (of air, wind etc) blow gently on (s.o/s.t). **6** (*fig*) cause (esp feelings) to become stronger; stir up (anger): *The union leader's speech fanned the workers' anger and they threatened to go on strike.* **fan (s.t) out** open, spread, (s.t) out: *The police fanned out across the field to search the area thoroughly. Instead of playing he fanned his cards out on the table to show everyone that he couldn't be beaten.* **fan the flames (of s.t)** ⇒ flame(*n*).

'**fan ,belt** *c.n* circular rubber belt which turns the cooling fan of an engine (e.g in a car).

'**fan ,club** *c.n* association of people who are fans(3) of a particular actor, team etc.

'**fan ,mail** *u.n* letters written to a (famous, well-known) person or team by people who admire her/him/it.

fanatic /fəˈnætɪk/ *c.n* person who is filled with great (often excessive) eagerness for s.o/s.t: *a health/religious fanatic. He's a fanatic about motorcycle racing.*

fa'natical *adj* (often *derog*) filled with great (often excessive) eagerness for s.o/s.t: *He's fanatical about the food he eats. She's a fanatical* jogger.

fa'natically *adv*.

fanaticism /fəˈnætɪ,sɪzəm/ *u.n* (often *derog*) behaviour, ideas, of a fanatic, which are not reasonable: *It's impossible to have a discussion with him about religion because of his fanaticism.*

fancy /ˈfænsɪ/ *adj* (-*ier*, -*iest*) **1** brightly coloured or decorated: *The shop sells cheap fancy goods to tourists.* **2** not plain or ordinary (and therefore often expensive) and highly decorated: *The material is too fancy.* **3** based on unrealistic ideas; not reasonable and so impossible: *She had some fancy ideas about educating her children.*

▷ *n* (*pl* -*ies*) **4** *c.n* thing that is imagined: *Did I hear the door bell or was it just a fancy?* **5** *u.n* imagination; power of forming pictures in the mind (which often seem real): *Children often live in a world of fancy.* **6** *sing.n* (often — *for* s.t) unusual fondness or liking for s.t which does not last long: *I have a sudden fancy for eating out (in a restaurant) tonight.* **a passing fancy** a thing that one is attracted to for a short time only: *I'm sure his decision to become an actor is just a passing fancy.* **catch/take s.o's fancy** attract/please s.o: *The new Honda car has really caught my fancy.* **footloose and fancy free** ⇒ footloose (⇒ foot). **take a fancy to s.o/s.t** become fond of s.o/s.t: *My cat seems to have taken a fancy to you.*

▷ *tr.v* (-*ies*, -*ied*) **7** (*informal*) like the idea of having, doing, (s.t): *Do you fancy (seeing) a* video(3) *tonight?* **8** (*formal*) imagine (s.t); form a picture of (s.t) in one's mind: *Can you fancy my son as a doctor?* **9** (often — *that...*) (*formal*) suppose (s.t); believe (s.t), think but without any real reason to be sure, (that . . .): *I fancy (that) they'll come home for the weekend.* **10** (*informal*) be attracted to (s.o); like, be interested in, (s.o): *I really fancied her when we were younger.* **11** (introducing an expression or statement of surprise): *Fancy that! Fancy saying such a thing in front of all those people!* **fancy oneself** (*derog*) have an excessively high opinion of oneself: *He's done very well but he really fancies himself.* **fancy oneself as s.o** like the idea of being, becoming, s.o important, successful etc: *I've always fancied myself as a writer.*

-fancier *c.n* person with a special knowledge of, interest in, liking for, animals, birds etc shown by the first part of the word: *She's been a dog-fancier most of her life.*

'fanciful *adj* (*formal*) **1** (of people) having ideas based in the imagination rather than reality: *a fanciful writer/painter.* **2** (of an idea, thought) unreal: *Their idea of the way we live is rather fanciful.* **3** (of objects) strange; full of unusual things; highly decorated: *The artist is well known for his fanciful paintings.*

'fancifully *adv.*

,fancy 'dress *u.n* (also *attrib*) clothes (from history, characters in a book, film etc) worn for a special occasion, esp a party: *a fancy dress party. Everyone must come in fancy dress tonight.*

,fancy-'free *adj* able to live freely because not bound by any duty etc: *I'm tired of this fancy-free life and I want to settle down and get married.*

fanfare /'fænˌfeə/ *c.n* short piece of music played loudly by bugles, trumpets etc, e.g to announce the arrival of an important person.

fang /fæŋ/ *c.n long sharp tooth* (*of dogs etc*); *tooth of a snake.*

fanlight /'fænˌlaɪt/ *c.n* semicircular window above a door.

fantasia /fæn'teɪzɪə/ *c.n* **1** (*music*) free musical composition not limited by any particular form. **2** selection of (parts of) well-known tunes loosely put together for a purpose, e.g music for a dance, film etc.

fantasy /'fæntəsɪ/ *c/u.n* (*pl -ies*) (also *attrib*) (idea, situation, story that is the result of) strong, unrealistic thoughts: *I had wonderful fantasies about winning a holiday in Honolulu. She lives in a world of fantasy* (or *a fantasy world*). Compare dream(1). ⇨ fancy(4).

fantastic /fæn'tæstɪk/ *adj* **1** (usu *attrib*) impossible to believe, do etc because too unrealistic: *How can you expect anyone to believe such a fantastic story?* **2** (*informal*) large: *I still have a fantastic amount of work to do.* **3** (*informal*) wonderful; excellent: *What a fantastic film! You look fantastic!*

fan'tastically *adv.*

far /fɑː/ *adj* (*comp* farther, further; *superl* farthest, furthest) **1** (*literary*) who/that is a long way away: *He lives in a far country.* **2** (*attrib*) (usu of s.t that has two parts, sides) (of the part, side that is the) longer way away: *His house is on the far side of the river.* **be a far cry (from s.t)** ⇨ cry(n).

▷ *adv* (*comp* farther, further; *superl* farthest, furthest) **3** (esp in negative statements and questions) describing distance, progress: *Do you live far from here? Is it far to town? No, it's not far. Did you get far with your work? Yes, I got quite far.* **4** (with an adverb or preposition) at or to a long way (away), a long time (ahead, back etc): *He's gone far away. It rose far above the clouds. They sailed far out to sea. They could see far into the distance. He remembered as far back as 1963. His ideas are far in advance of his time. Why are you preparing the meal so far in advance?* **5** to a great degree; very much: *You'll have to work far harder if you want to go to university. He's far more intelligent than the rest of his friends. He's done far more than he needs to.* **as far as (a)** to

(the place stated): *I'll come with you as far as the gate.* **(b)** (also when with negatives **so far as**) the same distance as: *I'm not walking as far as you.* **(c)** (also **so far as**) to the extent that, as much as (possible): *As far as I know, they still live in the same house.* **as/so far as s.o/s.t is concerned** in s.o's opinion; with regard to s.o/s.t: *As far as I'm concerned, he's a good tennis player. As far as money is concerned, I'm willing to pay half the expenses.* ⇨ in as/so far as . . . **as far as it/that goes** within the limits that s.t is useful, satisfactory etc. **by far** by a large amount: *She is by far the best chairperson we've ever had. It's the biggest by far.* **carry (s.t)/things too far** ⇨ carry. **far and away** (usu with superl) (*formal*) by a very large amount: *She's far and away the best tennis player I've ever seen.* **far and near/wide** = near and far (⇨ near(*adv*)). **far be it from me (to say s.t)** I'm (possibly) not the person who should (tell you what to do): *Far be it from me to offer you any advice.* **far from (being/doing) s.t (a)** instead of (doing) s.t: *Far from enjoying the play, I left in the middle because it was so bad.* **(b)** not at all s.t; a long way from (being) s.t: *This is far from good enough/being suitable.* **(be) far gone** ⇨ gone. **few and far between** ⇨ few(*pron*). **go far (a)** (think that s.o will) succeed in her/his work, life etc: *David's very clever and most people think he will go far.* **(b)** (often with a negative verb) (of money) (not) buy a lot of things: *What little he earns doesn't go far with prices rising all the time.* **go too far** do or say s.t that is not liked or accepted: *You've gone too far in accusing him of dishonesty. That joke is going too far.* **in as/so far as** ⇨ in². **(just) so far (and no farther/further)** (esp) up to a certain point (but no further): *I can agree with you so far and no further.* **so/thus far** until now; until this point: *So far we've been lucky but there are still 10 kilometres to go. I can get so far without that information but I can't finish the job.* **so far as** ⇨ as far as(b,c). **so far, so good** up till this point everything has gone well, is all right.

,Far 'East *def.n* countries in the eastern part of Asia including China, Japan etc.

'fara,way *attrib.adj* **1** a long way away; distant: *faraway countries.* **2** dreamy; thinking of s.t else: *You had such a faraway look in your eyes.*

,far'fetched *adj* unlikely; difficult to believe (because unlikely): *a farfetched excuse.*

,far-'flung *adj* distant and spread over a large area: *My business connections are far-flung. I have worked in far-flung areas.*

,far-'off *attrib.adj* distant: *The far-off mountains look blue from here.*

,far-'out *adj* **1** a long way in the distance: *a far-out island.* **2** (*slang*) very good; excellent: *That music is far-out.* ⇨ far(4).

,far-'reaching *adj* extensive; likely to affect many things: *These changes will cause far-reaching results. The effects of increasing interest rates will be far-reaching.*

,far'sighted *adj* **1** (also **,long'sighted**) able to see distant objects more clearly than near ones. Opposite shortsighted. **2** (*fig*) (showing the quality of) being able to judge future needs and prepare for them: *It was very farsighted of you to buy the tickets so early because the performances are sold out.*

,far'sightedness u.n.

farther /'fɑːðə/ adj (comp of far) **1** more distant (part, esp of a place, direction with two parts): *She crossed to the farther side of the road.*

▷ adv (comp of far) **2** at, to, a great distance: *The children were too tired to walk any farther.* Compare further.

'farthest adj (superl of far) **1** most distant (part of s.t/s.w): *The farthest side of the field.*

▷ adv (superl of far) **2** at, to, the greatest distance: *She can throw farthest.* Compare furthest.

further /'fɜːðə/ adj (comp of far) **1** more; additional: *I need further information. Have you had any further news? No further progress is possible today.* **2** more distant; farther(1): *The village was further than I remembered.*

▷ adv (comp of far) **3** (preferred to farther(2)) at, to a greater degree, distance, extent: *We can't go further today because it's too dark. I can't help you any further.* **4** (also **,further'more**) in addition (to s.t already said, written); also: *She said she'd done everything possible and, further, it would be a waste of time and money to try anything else.* **further to s.t** (esp in formal letters, speeches etc) in addition to information already provided: *Further to my letter of 2 May, I now enclose a copy of our new price list.*

▷ tr.v **5** (formal) help (s.t) to progress, move forward, succeed: *How can I help you to further your cause of peace?*

,further ,edu'cation u.n (also attrib) education that is continued after school at a college or university: *a further education college.* ⇒ CFE.

furtherance /'fɜːðərəns/ u.n (formal) (often the — of s.t) act of furthering(5) (s.t): *She got a job in a hotel for the furtherance of her ambition to buy a small inn in the country.* **in furtherance of s.t** in order to further(5) s.t: *They held discussions in furtherance of a peace settlement.*

,further'more adv = further(4).

'further,most adj (formal) most distant: *We sat at the furthermost table.*

'furthest adj.adv (superl of far) most distant, furthest away, (from s.t); at, to, the greatest distance or degree: *That's the furthest I've ever walked.* Compare farthest.

farce /fɑːs/ n **1** c/u.n (type of) play in the theatre, on television etc in which the characters and situations are amusingly silly. **2** c.n (fig) (serious) event, situation, that is a waste of time, useless, silly etc: *It's a farce for him to apply for a job in which he's had no experience.*

'farcical adj (of s.t that causes laughter or scorn because it is) silly, useless etc: *It's farcical to try to cross the desert in that little car.*

fare /feə/ n **1** c.n price of a journey by bus, train etc: *bus fares. What is the (plane) fare from London to Los Angeles?* **2** c.n passenger who pays to travel by bus, taxi etc: *Some taxi drivers wait at railway and bus stations hoping to pick up a fare.* **3** u.n (old use) food served at the table: *simple fare.*

▷ intr.v **4** (formal) make progress; do (badly, well): *How did we fare in the elections? We're faring very badly this year.*

farewell /ˌfeə'wel/ interj **1** (literary; old use) goodbye: *'Farewell, my friend!'*

▷ c.n (also attrib) **2** (of the) act of saying goodbye: *Tonight is my last opportunity to say all my farewells. He's giving a farewell party.*

farm /fɑːm/ c.n **1** (also attrib) area of land including fields, buildings etc, used for growing crops, keeping animals, producing milk etc. **2** (also **'farm,house**) main house on a farm(1). **3** place for breeding(2) a particular kind of animal, bird, fish etc for a particular purpose: *At a chicken farm chickens are bred(2) for eggs or for eating. Cows are bred(2) for milk on a dairy farm.*

▷ tr/intr.v **4** grow crops, keep animals, produce milk etc on (land etc): *What do you farm? I farm in the Lake District.* **farm s.o/s.t out (to s.o)** (a) arrange for (a child etc) to be cared for (by others): *The child was farmed out to some neighbours while his mother was in hospital.* (b) arrange for (work) to be done (by others): *If we want to get this job finished on time we'll have to farm out a lot of the work to other companies.*

'farmer c.n person who farms(4): *a sheep farmer.*

'farm,hand c.n worker on a farm(1): *We employed an extra six farmhands to help us harvest our wheat.*

'farm,house c.n main house on a farm(1). ⇒ farm(2).

'farming u.n business of farming (⇒ farm(4)).

'farm,yard c.n (also attrib) open area between, in front of etc, farm(1) buildings: *There are always a few chickens and ducks in the farmyard. We also have farmyard animals such as chickens and ducks.*

far-off, far-out, farsighted(ness) ⇒ far.

fart /fɑːt/ c.n (slang; do not use!) **1** air that escapes (sometimes noisily) from the anus. **2** (derog; do not use!) stupid person.

▷ intr.v **3** (slang; do not use!) send out air, allow air to escape, through the anus: *Who farted?*

farther, farthest ⇒ far.

farthing /'fɑːðɪŋ/ n **1** c.n (UK) coin with a value of a quarter of an old penny (until 1961). **2** sing.n (fig) (even a) small value: *Your advice isn't worth a farthing.*

fascia /'feɪʃɪə/ c.n (also **'facia**) (technical) **1** part (of a car etc) that is in front of the driver and has the instruments and gauges(3) etc on it. **2** front part (of a building).

fascinate /'fæsɪneɪt/ tr.v charm, interest, (s.o) greatly: *China fascinates me. I am fascinated by ancient history.*

'fasci,nating adj having great attraction, charm or interest: *a fascinating book. What a fascinating life you've had. He's fascinating.*

fascination /ˌfæsɪ'neɪʃən/ n (often have a — for s.o) **1** sing/u.n act of fascinating (⇒ fascinate); state of being fascinated: *She has a fascination for different kinds of cooking.* **2** c/u.n power to fascinate: *History has a fascination for many people.*

fascism /'fæʃɪzəm/ u.n (also with capital **F**) political system (with a dictator) in which only one party is allowed, and which is strongly nationalistic and against communism(1).

'fascist adj **1** of, referring to, supporting, fascism: *a fascist government.*

▷ c.n **2** person who supports fascism. **3** (derog) person with extreme rightwing opinions, esp one who is cruel: *She's a real fascist.*

fashion /'fæʃən/ n **1** c/u.n (also attrib) style of

clothing: *I always wear the same kind of clothes no matter what the fashion is. What colour is in fashion this season? She loves fashion magazines.* **2** *c.n* popular custom, taste etc: *It was the fashion among rich families to send their children abroad to be educated.* **3** *c.n* (*formal*) way of doing s.t: *She walks in the strangest fashion.* **after/in a fashion** in some way but not very satisfactorily: *He can ride after a fashion.* **after/in the fashion of s.o** in imitation of s.o: *She paints in the fashion of many of the great 19th century artists.* **be all the fashion** be very popular: *Tight trousers are all the fashion again.* **be in, out of, fashion** (esp of dress, behaviour etc) be, not be, popular or fashionable: *What shape is in fashion this year?* **come into fashion** become popular: *Don't throw that* jacket(1) *away; it'll come back into fashion in a few years' time.* **follow the fashion** do/ wear what others do/wear etc: *Students follow their own form of fashion.* **go out of fashion** no longer be popular: *I often wear clothes that have gone out of fashion.* **set a/the fashion** start a new fashion by being, giving, the example: *She set a new fashion by wearing black clothes.*
▷ *tr.v* **4** (*formal*) (often — *s.t into, out of, s.t*) form, make, shape, (s.t) (into, out of, s.t): *She fashioned the piece of clay into a beautiful vase* (or *fashioned a vase out of a piece of clay*).
ˈfashionable *adj* Opposite unfashionable. **1** following the latest fashion(1,2): *fashionable clothes. It is fashionable to have leather chairs.* **2** used, visited, by many (esp rich) people: *The 'Randolph' is the most fashionable hotel in town.*

fast¹ /fɑːst/ *adj* Opposite slow. **1** quick; moving quickly: *The train to London travels very fast.* **2** (*pred*) (of a clock, watch) showing a time later than the actual time. **3** (of a surface) allowing quick movement: *The racecourse is faster when it's dry than when it's wet.* **4** (of photographic film) needing to be exposed(3) to light for a short time only: *I bought a fast film in order to take photographs of the racing cars.* **5** (becoming *old use*) fond of spending too much time and money on pleasure: *His studies began to suffer because of his fast living.* **fast and furious** active; wild; very fast(1): *He was talking at a rate that was fast and furious.* **play a fast one (on s.o)** (*informal*) trick (s.o): *He played a fast one on me when he told me he owned the shop.*
▷ *adv* **6** quickly: *Please don't drive so fast! He can run faster than I can.* Opposite slowly. **fast and furiously** wildly; very quickly: *They worked fast and furiously to get the job done in time.* **play fast and loose (with s.o/s.t)** behave (towards s.o/s.t) in a way that is not responsible: *If you continue to play fast and loose with women, they will never take you seriously.*

fast² /fɑːst/ *adj* **1** (of colours) that do not fade: *I thought the colour was fast but all my clothes are now a pale shade of green.* **2** (usu *pred*) (*formal*) tight; firm; unlikely to move: *Make sure the rope is fast. The car was stuck fast in the mud.* **3** (*attrib*) (*old use*) close; loyal: *Ron and Maggie have been fast friends for many years.* **hard and fast** ⇒ hard(*adj*). **make s.t fast** fix, tie, (s.t) firmly: *Make the rope fast, please.*
▷ *adv* **4** firmly; tightly: *Hold the rope fast.* **be/fall fast asleep** ⇒ asleep. **stand fast** ⇒ stand(*v*).

fasten /ˈfɑːsn/ *tr/intr.v* fix, join, tie, (s.t) firmly: *Please fasten your safety belt.* Opposite unfasten. **fasten s.t down** close, fix, s.t firmly: *She fastened down the lid of the biscuit tin.* **fasten one's eyes (up)on s.o/s.t** ⇒ eye(*n*). **fasten s.t together** fix, join, s.t together: *Fasten all the pages together with a pin.* **fasten s.t up** join s.t together; make s.t tight/firm: *Can you fasten up my buttons at the back?*
ˈfastener *c.n* device for fastening, holding, s.t together: *A paper fastener holds pieces of paper together. Can you do up the fasteners on my dress, please?* ⇒ zip fastener.
ˈfastening *c.n* thing that holds s.t closed: *He used a belt around his case because the fastenings were broken.*
ˈfastness *u.n* (of a colour) quality of being fast²(1): *Are you sure about the fastness of this red?*

fast³ /fɑːst/ *c.n* **1** (time of) going without food (esp as a religious duty).
▷ *intr.v* **2** go without (certain) food (esp as a religious duty): *Next week people will fast for one day and give the money they would have spent on the food to the 'Beat Hunger' campaign(2).*

fastidious /fæˈstɪdɪəs/ *adj* (*formal*) critical; not willing to accept anything that is not completely clean etc; difficult to please: *Lucy has always been fastidious about the way she dresses.*
faˈstidiously *adv*. **faˈstidiousness** *u.n*.

fat /fæt/ *adj* (*-tt-*) **1** (of a person or animal) having much mass around the body: *a fat child/cow. That kind of food will make you even fatter.* Opposite thin, slim, slender. **2** (of meat) containing a lot of fat(5). Opposite lean¹(2) **3** (usu *attrib*) thick; full: *That's a fat book you're reading.* **4** (*attrib*) (*informal*) (of an amount of money) large: *I got a fat cheque for my birthday.* **a fat lot** (*informal*) not much; very little: *A fat lot that will help* (= it won't help at all). **a fat lot of good** (*informal*) not at all useful; of very little use: *A fat lot of good he/that will be now.*
▷ *n* **5** *u.n* white or yellow substance found between the skin and flesh in human or animal bodies: *I don't like meat with too much fat on it.* Opposite lean¹(4). **6** *u.n* substance like fat(5) found in some plant seeds. **7** *c/u.n* animal/plant fat(5,6) made into a form that can be used for cooking: *I prefer not to use animal fats when I cook.* **live off the fat of the land** have the best of everything. **The fat is in the fire** (*fig*) The trouble is really about to begin (now).
ˈfat,free *adj* having no fat(5,6): *fatfree milk.*
ˈfat,head *c.n* (*derog*; *slang*) stupid person.
ˈfatless *adj* having no fat(5,6): *fatless meat.*
ˈfatness *u.n* quality or state of being fat(1): *Such excessive fatness must be the result of illness.*
ˈfatted *attrib.adj* (of an animal) made fat(1): *They killed a fatted pig to cook during the celebrations.* **kill the fatted calf** (*fig*) hold a great celebration, esp to welcome s.o important.
ˈfatten *tr.v* (often — *s.o/s.t up*) make (s.o, an animal) fatter (⇒ fat(1)), esp an animal that will be killed for food: *We are fattening* (*up*) *a goose(1) for Mary's wedding. You're looking very pale and thin; you need fattening up a bit.*
ˈfattiness *u.n* quality or state of being fatty.
ˈfattish *adj* rather fat(1): *She has a fattish face.*

'fatty adj (-ier, -iest) **1** containing a lot of fat: Fatty foods are not healthy.
▷ c.n **2** (derog) (name for a fat person).

fate /feɪt/ n **1** u.n power that is believed to determine future events and to be unable to be changed; destiny(1): They believe that it was fate that brought them together. **2** c.n future, result, that cannot be avoided; destiny(2): It is not my fate to spend my life taking orders from a man like him. **3** c.n death; end: She met her fate after a horse-riding accident. **as sure as fate** certainly: If you don't get out of bed now you'll be late for work as sure as fate. ⇨ quirk. **(be/suffer) a fate worse than death** (be/experience) s.t terrible, very bad: He believed that to lose his job would be a fate worse than death. **quirk of fate** ⇨ quirk.

fatal /'feɪtl/ adj **1** causing death: He died in a fatal accident. The disease was fatal. **2** (fig) causing ruin, disaster(1): He made a fatal mistake.

'fata,lism u.n belief that all events are caused or controlled by fate(1).

'fata,list c.n **1** person who believes in fatalism. **2** person who accepts her/his fate(2): She's a complete fatalist and never plans for the future.

,fata'listic adj (of a person) who accepts her/his fate(2): a fatalistic person.

fatality /fə'tælɪtɪ/ c.n (formal) death (caused by an accident, war etc): There were thousands of fatalities caused by the earthquake.

'fatally adv so as to cause death: He was fatally hurt in a car accident.

'fated pred.adj (often be — to do s.t) caused by fate(1): We were fated never to meet again. ⇨ ill-fated.

'fateful adj (usu attrib) showing the influence, strength, power of fate(1) and very important in its later results: I remember that fateful day when the police arrested your brother.

father /'fɑːðə/ n **1** c.n male parent: What kind of work does your father do? **2** c.n (usu with capital **F**) (written abbr Fr) priest, esp in the Roman Catholic Church: I'll ask Father Jones for his advice. **3** c.n (often the — of s.t) person who is the leader or is very important in the beginnings of (s.t): He is the father of modern medicine. **4** (fig) person who protects s.o: He was the father of the poor in the village. **5** unique n (with capital **F**) God.
▷ tr.v (formal) **6** be the father of (a child). **7** act as a father to (s.o): Don't you think I'm a bit old to still be fathered by my older brother? Compare mother(4). **8** be the one to start work on, suggest, (an idea, plan etc): Who fathered the idea of a national health service?

,Father 'Christmas unique n (also **'Santa ,Claus**) imaginary man who brings children presents at Christmas.

'father ,figure c.n older man who one loves and trusts as if he was one's own father.

'father,hood u.n state of being a father(1).

'father-in-,law c.n (pl fathers-in-law) father(1) of one's husband/wife.

'fatherliness u.n quality of being, acting like, a father(1).

'fatherly adj having, showing, the qualities of a father(1): He took a fatherly interest in everything his nephew did.

'fathers pl.n = forefathers.

,father-to-'be c.n (pl fathers-to-be) man who is soon to become a father(1).

fathom /'fæðəm/ c.n **1** (technical; written abbr f) unit of measurement of the depth of water (1.8 metres): The shallowest part of the harbour is only 3 fathoms deep.
▷ tr.v **2** (technical) measure the depth of (water). **3** (often — s.o/s.t out) (fig) understand (s.o/s.t mysterious): I simply can't fathom her out. I just can't fathom (out) why she's so angry.

'fathomless adj **1** very deep. **2** (fig) impossible to work out or understand. Compare unfathomable(2).

fatigue /fə'tiːg/ n **1** u.n (formal) fact or state of being very tired (esp because of great effort): They were suffering from fatigue after walking in the heat. **2** u.n (also **'metal fa,tigue**) (technical) weakness in metals caused by excessive use: Metal fatigue is the reason given for several recent plane crashes. **3** c.n (often pl) (military) (tiring) work done by a soldier which is not of a military nature and is often given as a punishment, e.g cleaning: They are all doing fatigues for coming back to camp late.
▷ **4** tr.v (formal) cause (s.o) to feel very tired: I found the work very fatiguing. It was fatiguing work.

fa'tigue ,party c.n (pl -ies) (military) group of soldiers doing fatigues(3).

fatuous /'fætjʊəs/ adj (derog; formal) foolish: Your fatuous remarks insult my intelligence.

fatuity /fə'tjuːɪtɪ/ c/u.n (pl -ies) (formal) (example of) fatuous behaviour or words: I expect such fatuity only from a young child.

'fatuously adv. **'fatuousness** u.n.

faucet /'fɔːsɪt/ c.n (US) tap¹(1).

fault /fɔːlt/ c.n **1** (usu sing) (be s.o's —) responsibility for a mistake, thing that is (done) wrong: It's not my fault if you fail. It's your own fault. **2** (wrong) behaviour that makes s.o not perfect: We all have our faults. **3** (often — in s.t) mistake (in the making or building of s.t)): There's a fault in this material. **4** (technical) break in the earth's surface. **at fault** in the wrong: I admit I was at fault when I borrowed your car without asking. **find fault with s.o/s.t** complain about, criticize, s.o/s.t: He always finds fault with the work I do for him. **the fault lies with s.o/s.t** the blame, responsibility, belongs to s.o/s.t; s.o/s.t is to blame for it: The fault lies with the driver, not the car. **to a fault** excessively: She's honest to a fault.
▷ tr.v **5** (usu with negatives) (formal) = find fault with (s.o/s.t) (⇨ fault(n)): I couldn't fault their performance. No one could fault his behaviour tonight.

'fault,finder c.n (derog) person who frequently finds s.t to criticize, complain about.

'fault,finding u.n act of (frequently) looking for s.t to criticize, complain about.

'faultless adj perfect; containing no mistakes, faults(2,3): a faultless performance.

'faultlessly adv. **'faultlessness** u.n.

'faulty adj (-ier, -iest) having a fault or faults: It's dangerous to touch faulty electrical machines.

faun /fɔːn/ c.n (in Roman mythology(1)) one of a group of gods with horns, a tail, goat's feet and pointed ears.

fauna /'fɔːnə/ c/u.n (science) all the animal life in a particular area. ⇨ flora.

faux pas /ˌfəʊ ˈpɑː/ c.n (pl **faux pas** /ˌfəʊ ˈpɑːz/) (French) silly or embarrassing mistake: I made such a faux pas I could feel my face turn red.

favour /ˈfeɪvə/ n (US **favor**) 1 c.n act of kindness: It was the little favours she did that made me realize how much I needed her. 2 u.n (usu with —) (formal) approval, willingness, sympathy: The committee considered her requests with favour. 3 u.n treatment that gives or shows preference (sometimes unfairly) to/for s.o/s.t: She did not want any special favour when she started the job. **curry favour** (**with s.o**) ⇒ curry(v). **find favour** (**with s.o**) get support, respect etc (from s.o) ⇒ lose favour with s.o. **in favour** (**of s.o**, **of** (**doing**) s.t) in support (of s.o, of (doing) s.t), in agreement (with s.o, with (doing) s.t): We voted/ were in favour of Mary as chairperson. Everyone's in favour (of a picnic). ⇒ against(1,3). **in s.o's favour** (**a**) to s.o's advantage: We should plan our holiday now while the exchange rate is in our favour. (**b**) helping, supporting, s.o: The wind is in our favour. The decision went in his favour. (**be**) **in favour with s.o**; (**be**) **in s.o's favour** have s.o's support, help, friendship: He has been in his boss's favour (or He has been in favour with his boss) ever since he helped the business to win a large account. **do** (**s.o**) **a favour** (**a**) (usu in questions) do a favour(1) (for s.o): Would you do me a favour and post these letters on your way to town? (**b**) (informal) (expression of irritation(1), disagreement): Do me a favour and don't talk such nonsense (2)! **lose favour in s.o's eyes, with s.o** (cause s.o to) lose the support, respect etc of s.o: His criticism of the newspapers has caused him to lose favour with many journalists. **out of favour** (**with s.o**) (without support, respect, help, (from s.o)): Don't be seen around with him because he's out of favour. If you don't change your behaviour, you'll find yourself out of favour (with the whole group). **return a favour** do a favour(1) for s.o who has done one a favour(1).
▷ tr.v 4 approve of, support, (a particular action, plan, person etc): I favour equal opportunities for everyone. 5 support, like, (s.o/s.t) more than others; show a preference for (s.o/s.t): My father has always favoured my youngest sister. 6 (formal) tend to make (s.t) possible or easy: The good weather favoured the harvesting of their crop.

ˈfavourable adj (US **ˈfavorable**) (often — for/ to s.t) helpful; giving, showing approval or advantage, (for s.t): The weather is favourable for a good day's sailing. I'm waiting for a favourable opportunity to ask. Opposite unfavourable.

ˈfavourably adv (US **ˈfavorably**) in a favourable way: She spoke very favourably of you (expressed her approval). **be favourably impressed** (**by s.o/ s.t**) have, gain, a good opinion (of s.o/s.t): I was favourably impressed by the way she addressed the crowd.

ˈfavoured adj (US **ˈfavored**) 1 (usu — with s.t) (formal) fortunate (to have s.t); having an advantage (in having s.t): She was favoured with a wonderful skin. 2 (attrib) (formal) receiving, having, the most advantages; favourite: She was his favoured niece.

favourite /ˈfeɪvrɪt/ attrib.adj (US **ˈfavorite**) 1 (liked) best; preferred above all others: Who's your favourite singer? It's my favourite food.
▷ c.n 2 person or thing who/that is preferred above all others: His youngest grandchild was his favourite. 3 competitor (e.g in a horse race) that most people expect to win: The favourite only came third in the race. 4 person who is given unfair advantages (because he/she is in favour): The leader gave his favourite an important position in his new government.

ˈfavouriˌtism u.n (US **ˈfavoriˌtism**) (often — to(wards) s.o) practice of giving unfair advantages (to s.o who is preferred): I must not show any favouritism towards my son.

fawn¹ /fɔːn/ adj/u.n 1 (of a) pale yellow-brown colour.
▷ c.n 2 deer that is less than a year old. **in fawn** (of a deer) carrying a baby deer that will soon be born.
▷ tr/intr.v 3 (of a deer) give birth (to (a baby deer)).

fawn² /fɔːn/ intr.v 1 (often — on s.o) (of dogs) show love and pleasure (to s.o) by licking, moving the tail etc. 2 (usu — (up)on s.o) (of a person) try to gain (s.o)'s favour by flattery(1) etc: I watched him fawning on his rich grandfather.

FBI /ˌef ˌbiː ˈaɪ/ def.n abbr (US) Federal Bureau of Investigation.

fear /fɪə/ n (often — of s.o/s.t) 1 c/u.n (example of an) unpleasant feeling when danger is close; feeling of being afraid: She has a terrible fear of the dark. They were shaking with fear. 2 u.n feeling of anxiety (caused by the thought or possibility of s.t unfavourable happening): Fear of dismissal does not usually make people work harder. 3 u.n risk, chance, (of s.t unfavourable happening): There's little fear of his business failing. There's not much fear of her losing the race. 4 c/u.n respect (mixed with fear(2)): Fear of God made her live a strict Christian(1) life. **for fear of s.o/s.t** because of anxiety, worry, about, s.o/s.t: At midnight we made the music softer for fear of complaints (or of the neighbours complaining). **for fear that s.o may do s.t bad, that s.t bad should happen** in case s.o may do s.t bad, s.t bad should happen: We locked the doors at night for fear that a thief might try to get into the house. **in fear** (**of s.o/s.t**) in a state of fear(1,2) (caused by s.o/s.t); afraid (of s.o/ s.t): We hid in fear (of thieves) when we heard the noise. **in fear of one's life** afraid of being killed: Since he told the police about his friends' crimes he has been in fear of his life. **No fear!** (informal) Certainly not! **put the fear of God into s.o** make s.o very frightened: The doctor put the fear of God into his patient by telling her about the dangers of smoking. **strike fear into s.o** make s.o suddenly feel very afraid (of one).
▷ v 5 tr/intr.v (formal) be frightened (of (s.o/s.t), about (s.t)): She feared her husband when he was drunk. He feared what his father would say about the damage to his car. 6 tr.v respect (s.o), esp when also a little afraid of that person: He always feared his father when he was a child. 7 tr.v (often — that...; — not/so) (used esp when giving bad news) regret (that)...; be sorry to have to say (that..., s.t is (not) true): I fear (that) we'll miss the bus. 'Are we late?' 'I fear so.' 'Is there no way of getting home tonight?' 'I fear not.' **Never fear!** (used to calm s.o) Don't worry!

fearful adj (formal) 1 (often — about/of s.t; — that...) afraid; frightened; anxious; worried: We were fearful of getting lost. I'm fearful that we have missed the start of the play. He gave his father a *fearful look*. **2** frightening; terrible: *We saw a fearful accident on the way here*. **3** (*informal*) very great; very bad: *I have a fearful headache*.

'fearfully *adv* **1** anxiously; in a frightened way: *They looked around fearfully*. **2** (*informal*) very; extremely: *I'm fearfully sorry. It's fearfully hot.*

'fearfulness *u.n.*

'fearless *adj* (*formal*) brave; having, showing, no fear: *He's fearless about rock climbing.*

'fearlessly *adv*. **'fearlessness** *u.n.*

fearsome /'fɪəsəm/ *adj* (esp of appearance) causing fear: *The angry mother gave her children a fearsome look.*

feasible /'fi:zɪbl/ *adj* **1** able to be done; possible: *I like your idea but I don't think it's feasible.* **2** likely; probable; that can be believed: *It is feasible that they may have tried to escape.* **3** that is convenient, possible, able to be managed: *Is it feasible for you to come an hour earlier?*

feasibility /ˌfiːzə'bɪlɪtɪ/ *u.n.* (also *attrib*) possibility of s.t being done: *They carefully considered the feasibility of their plans. We'll do a feasibility study before we make any decisions.*

feast /fiːst/ *c.n* **1** large and often expensive meal with plenty to eat and drink: *They held a feast in the village every year at harvest time.* **2** (also **'feast ,day, re'ligious ,feast**) religious period or day for rejoicing, e.g Christmas, Easter. **3** (usu *a* — *of s.t*) (*fig*) thing that gives pleasure or delight (because of s.t): *Our garden is a feast of colour in spring.* **a movable feast** (a) a religious celebration the date of which varies every year: *Easter is a movable feast but Christmas is not.* (b) (*fig*) a celebration that happens every year but the date for which does not have to be the same: *The office party is a movable feast but I hope we can have it in September.*

▷ *v* **4** *intr.v* (usu — *on s.t*) have a feast(1) (of s.t); eat a lot of very good food: *We feasted on the fish we'd caught.* **5** *tr.v* feed (s.o) very well: *He feasted us like royalty.* **feast one's eyes** (**up**)**on s.o/s.t** take pleasure in, enjoy looking at, s.o/s.t: *We feasted our eyes on the beautiful valley.* **feast** (**oneself/s.o**) (**up**)**on s.t** give (s.o), have, a feast(1) (by eating s.t): *We feasted ourselves on strawberries*(1).

'feast ,day *c.n* feast(2).

feat /fiːt/ *c.n* (often — *of s.t*) (*formal*) difficult or great act (of bravery, skill, strength etc): *It was a feat of courage to rescue the drowning man.*

feather /'feðə/ *c.n* **1** one of various parts of a bird's covering which grow from the skin and together cover and protect the body. *a feather in one's cap* (*fig*) thing that one can be proud of: *Breaking the school record is quite a feather in your cap.* **as light as a feather** having a very small weight; very light: *I'll take my new camera on our walk because it's as light as a feather.* **birds of a feather** ⇒ bird. **smooth s.o's ruffled feathers** (*fig*) make s.o less angry etc.

▷ *tr.v* **2** (*formal*) supply (a nest, arrow, fish hook etc) with feathers: *Our duck is feathering its nest for its eggs.* **3** turn the blade of a rowing oar, propeller) so that it goes through the water or the air flat and offers no resistance(3). **feather one's nest** (*fig*) make oneself comfortable, rich, (esp at s.o else's expense): *We agreed to take equal shares from the profits but he has been quietly feathering his own nest all along.*

,feather 'bed *c.n* **1** kind of mattress filled with feathers. **2** (*fig*) easy comfortable situation.

'feather,brained *adj* (*derog*) very stupid; unable to behave responsibly.

'feather,weight *c.n* (also *attrib*) boxer who weighs between 53.5 and 57 kg.

'feathery *adj* (*-ier, -iest*) **1** covered with feathers: *a feathery hat.* **2** looking like feathers: *feathery clouds.*

feature /'fiːtʃə/ *c.n* **1** (often *pl*) part of the face: *His nose is his most noticeable feature.* **2** part by which s.t is known or recognized: *The desert is the feature that brings most tourists to Namibia.* **3** main or special article in a newspaper, programme on the radio or television etc: *The weekend magazine is doing a feature on China over the next three weeks.* **4** (also *attrib*) main film at a cinema: *What time does the feature begin? What's the feature film this week?*

▷ *tr/intr.v* **5** (cause (s.o/s.t) to) be a main or special part: *Who featured most at the meeting? She'll see any film that features Paul Newman.* **feature in s.t** have a (large) part in a report, film etc.

'featureless *adj* (*derog*) dull; lacking anything interesting: *The view was featureless.*

February /'februərɪ/ *unique n* (also *attrib*) 2nd month of the year: *There are usually twenty-eight days in February. We arrived on February 8* (say 'February the eighth' or 'the eighth of February'). *It was a cold February morning.*

feckless /'feklɪs/ *adj* (*derog*; *formal*) (of a person) aimless; not responsible: *She's a feckless student and prefers having fun to studying.*

'fecklessly *adv*. **'fecklessness** *u.n.*

fecund /'fekənd/ *adj* (*formal*) **1** fertile(1): *a fecund apple tree.* **2** (*fig*) very productive: *a fecund artist.*

fecundity /fɪ'kʌndɪtɪ/ *u.n.* (*formal*) ability to give birth to many young ones: *The fecundity of rabbits often has to be controlled.*

fed *p.t,p.p* of feed(*v*).

federal /'fedrəl/ *attrib.adj* **1** (with capital **F** in names) (of a group of countries, states) joined together, ruled as one: *the Federal Republic of Germany.* **2** (esp US) of central government rather than that of the separate states: *Although many states disagreed, a federal decision was taken over the* boycott(1) *of the* Olympic Games.

,Federal ,Bureau of In,vesti'gation *def.n* (also *attrib*) (*abbr FBI*) US department of the central government which is responsible for matters concerning the safety of the whole country.

'federa,lism *u.n.* belief in, idea of, federation(2).

'federa,list *adj* **1** of or referring to federation(2).

▷ *c.n* **2** person who believes in and supports a federation(2).

federate /'fedə,reɪt/ *tr/intr.v* combine, unite, (organizations, societies, states etc) for a common purpose: *Several trade unions have federated to form one union.*

federation /ˌfedə'reɪʃən/ *n* (with capital **F** in names) **1** *u.n.* act or fact of federating. **2** *c.n* (example of a) political system in which a group of countries or states join together to form a central government, esp for purposes of defence and trade. **3** society or organization with a common purpose: *the Federation of International Tennis Players.*

fee /fiː/ *c.n* **1** charge or price for professional service: *Fortunately the lawyer's fees were paid by the other driver.* **2** cost for attending a course, school etc: *My grant(1) pays for my university fees and books but not my living expenses.* **3** price for entering a club, examination, taking part in a competition etc: *The membership fee is £50 a year.*

'fee-,paying *adj* for which, or from whom, a charge or payment is expected: *fee-paying schools; fee-paying parents.*

feeble /'fiːbl/ *adj* **1** weak: *My grandfather has become feeble since his bad fall. She made a feeble excuse for arriving late.* **2** faint; having no force; not clear: *a feeble cry.*

,feeble-'minded *adj* (*derog*) **1** of lower than normal intelligence. **2** unable to make a decision or act decisively: *Don't be so feeble-minded; say what you think.*

'feebleness *u.n.* **'feebly** *adv.*

feed /fiːd/ *n* **1** *c.n* meal (esp for babies and animals): *The mother prepared her baby's 6 o'clock feed.* **2** *u.n* food for animals: *chicken feed.* **3** *sing.n* (*informal*) large amount of food; big meal: *They gave us such a feed that I couldn't eat for a week.* **4** *c.n* (also *attrib*) part of a machine, esp a pipe, carrying gas, petrol etc to the engine: *The car wouldn't start because the petrol feed was blocked.*

▷ *v* (*p.p.p.t* fed /fed/) **5** *tr.v* give food to (s.o/s.t): *Have you fed the cats yet? I must feed the children before I go out.* ⇨ feed s.o/s.t on s.t. **6** *tr/intr.v* give milk to (a baby); breast-feed: *My mother is still feeding (the baby).* **7** *intr.v* (esp of animals) eat: *The sheep are feeding in the hills.* Compare feed on s.t. **8** *tr.v* supply (material to make a fire burn, fuel to make a machine work etc): *Petrol is fed to the car engine by this pipe.* **9** (*fig*) encourage (a feeling etc): *Don't feed her pride; she already thinks she's better than most of us.* **10** *tr.v* (often — s.t into s.t) provide (information) (for a computer etc): *Her job is to feed data into the computer.* **feed off/on s.t** eat s.t; take s.t as food: *Young babies feed mainly on milk.* **feed s.o/s.t on s.t** give s.t as food to s.o/s.t: *We feed our dog on tinned food and biscuits.* **feed s.t to s.o/s.t** provide, give, s.t as food for s.o/s.t: *We usually feed corn to the chickens.* **feed s.o/s.t up** fatten s.o/s.t; give s.o/s.t extra food, esp to build up energy(1). **be fed up (with s.o/s.t) (about s.o/s.t)** (*informal*) be tired (of s.o/s.t) in one's mind (because of s.o/s.t); be annoyed (with s.o/s.t) (about s.t.): *I'm fed up about his refusal to help. We're all fed up with this wet weather.*

'feed,back *u.n* information about a product, sales etc that is sent to a manufacturer, producer etc so that the business can be improved: *Feedback from users of the new car caused the manufacturers to make some changes to it.*

'feeder *c.n* **1** person, animal or plant who/that feeds(7): *Some plants are heavy feeders.* **2** baby's feeding bottle or bib. **3** (also *attrib*) less important railway line, river, road etc that leads to a main one: *a feeder canal. These are all feeders leading to the motorway.*

'feeding ,bottle *c.n* bottle from which a baby is fed milk, orange juice etc.

feel /fiːl/ *sing.n* **1** sensation produced when one touches s.t or is touched by s.t: *I don't like the feel of this material. You can tell by the feel of it that it's plastic(1). Compare touch(4).* **2** act of touching and becoming aware of the sensation it gives: *It looks so soft — can I have a feel?* **get the feel of s.t** (*fig*) learn to understand, get used to, s.t; become accustomed to s.t, esp s.t new: *Once you get the feel of the car you'll love it.* **a feel for s.t** an inner understanding of s.t; an ability to do s.t naturally, easily: *She's got a feel for drawing.*

▷ *v* (*p.t,p.p* felt/felt/) **3** *tr.v* use the hand(s) (or sometimes another part of the body) to discover the condition, presence, shape, size, temperature, texture etc of (s.t): *The doctor felt my leg to see if any bones were broken. Feel how soft the cat's fur is.* **4** *tr.v* (often — s.o/s.t do s.t) become aware(1) of (s.o/s.t) (doing s.t) by touching or being touched: *As she picked up the frightened child she could feel her trembling.* **5** *tr.v* be aware(1) of, experience, (a sensation, feeling) through the nervous system and not by touch: *She felt her anger building up inside her. As he hit the ground he felt a sharp pain in his right shoulder.* **6** *intr.v* (often — good etc about s.o/s.t; — sure etc (that) . . .) be in a particular mental(1) or physical(1) condition (which is good etc): *feel angry/happy/sad/frightened (about what happened); feel hungry/sick/better/thirsty/tired. I feel sure you'll win/get the job.* **7** *tr.v* be able to experience (a sensation) (by touch or through the nervous system): *I was so cold that I couldn't feel a thing. He's such a hard person he feels nothing.* **8** *intr.v* seem to oneself to be (s.t): *I felt so stupid/silly/proud. I feel good in these clothes. It feels wrong to be here.* ⇨ feel as if/though . . ., feel like s.o/s.t. **9** *tr.v* (not used in continuous tenses) (often — that . . .) believe, consider, (that) (s.t): *He felt (that) if he didn't go abroad soon he probably never would.* **10** *tr.v* agree with and understand (s.o/s.t) deeply: *We all feel the truth of her words.*

feel about/around (s.t) (for s.o/s.t) (a) search, usu with one's hands, (for s.o/s.t) without being able to see: *She felt around for the light switch. She was feeling around the floor for her glasses.* (b) (*fig*) examine a situation, look everywhere, (for s.t): *I'll have to feel about to try to find the solution to our problem. I'll have to feel about for an answer.* ⇨ feel for s.o/s.t.

feel as if/though . . . seem, have the idea, that . . .: *It feels as if it's going to rain. I feel as though I'm going to be lucky today.*

feel equal to s.t ⇨ equal(*adj*).

feel for s.o/s.t (a) have sympathy for s.o/s.t: *I really felt for him when he lost his job.* (b) search for s.o/s.t, e.g with one's hands, without being able to see: *I felt for some sweets in my pocket.*

feel free (to do s.t) ⇨ free(*adj*).

feel funny (about s.t) ⇨ funny.

feel (s.t) in one's bones ⇨ bone(*n*).

feel like s.o/s.t (a) have the same feel(1) as s.o/s.t, esp when guessing what it is: *It feels like leather but I don't know what it is.* (b) have the feelings(4) that one might have if one were s.o/s.t: *I felt like a clown(1) in that hat.* (c) have a desire to do s.t; want to do s.t: *I don't feel like eating tonight. I feel like a beer.*

feel s.o out carefully find out s.o's opinion about s.t: *Can you feel your father out about our holiday plans?*

feel small ⇨ small (*adj*).

feel up to *s.t* feel well enough, able, to do s.t: *He has been very ill and doesn't feel up to (going to) parties yet.*

feel one's way ⇨ way(*n*).

how/what does *s.o* **feel about** *s.o/s.t* what is s.o's opinion, idea about s.o/s.t: *How do you feel about a holiday in France? What do you feel about the present government?*

'feeler *c.n* **1** (in certain animals, insects) organ of touch (usu one of two, e.g on a snail's, butterfly's or grasshopper's head. **2** (*fig*) (usu *put out a —, —s, (about s.t)*) effort (or efforts) to find out, test, the opinion (of s.o) (about s.t): *We'd be wise to put out (some) feelers about our new model before we make the final decisions.*

'feeling *attrib.adj* **1** (*formal*) expressing or having strong emotion(1); sensitive: *a feeling speech.* Compare unfeeling.

▷ *n* **2** *u.n* act or fact of touching; sense of touch: *You can only tell the difference between them by feeling.* **3** *u.n* ability, power, to feel(7): *The dentist's injection left him with no feeling in his jaw for several hours.* **4** *c.n* (usu *— of s.t*) sensation in the body or mind: *a feeling of hunger/pain/weakness*; *feelings of anger/guilt/happiness/love.* Compare feel(6). **5** *c.n* emotion(1); sensation that a person gets from feeling(6) rather than by thinking: *How can you behave like that; don't you have any feelings?* ⇨ feelings. **6** *u.n* emotion(2); sensitive understanding: *He played the piano with great feeling.* **7** *c.n* (often have a — (that) . . .) belief, idea, usu about s.t one expects to happen: *I had a feeling you'd be here. I have a feeling that we've met before.* **8** *u.n* (often have — for s.o/s.t*) affection; love: *I no longer have any feeling for him.* **9** *u.n* (often have — for s.o/s.t*) concern, sympathy, understanding, (for s.o/s.t): *You have no feeling for the misery of some people's lives.* **10** *c.n* (usu have a — for s.t*) natural ability (to do, learn s.t): *He has a feeling for mathematics.* **11** *c.n* (usu *sing*) (general) opinion: *The feeling in our group was that she has too much power.* **12** *c/u.n* state of excitement and strong opinion (esp caused by anger, dissatisfaction, strong emotion etc): *Feeling among the workers over the closing of the mine was very strong.* **bad/ill feeling(s)** anger; bitterness: *There's a lot of ill feeling between the brothers over the running of the family business. There were no ill feelings between us after that argument.*

'feelings *pl.n* emotional(1) or sensitive part of a person's character: *I'm so confused that I don't know my own feelings.* **have mixed feelings (about** *s.o/s.t*) have conflicting emotions (about s.o/s.t). **hurt** *s.o's* **feelings** cause emotional(1) pain to s.o: *I didn't mean to hurt your feelings when I told you that you're getting fat.* **have mixed feelings (about** *s.o/s.t*) be uncertain (about s.o/s.t): *I've mixed feelings (about going away) as I don't want to leave my mother alone.* **no hard feelings** (expression of (asking for) forgiveness and no further anger about s.t, e.g from s.o one has cancelled(1) an arrangement with): *'No hard feelings?' 'No, of course not, no hard feelings (at all).'*

feet /fiːt/ *pl* of foot(1).

feign /feɪn/ *tr.v* (*formal*) pretend (s.t) in order to deceive: *She feigned illness because she didn't want to go to school.*

feint¹ /feɪnt/ *adj* (usu *attrib*) (printing) not dark; light: *feint lines*.

feint² /feɪnt/ *c.n* **1** (*formal*) action, movement, intended to deceive; pretence.

▷ *intr.v* **2** (usu *— at/against s.o/s.t*) (*formal*) pretend (s.t) in order to deceive: *They confused the enemy by feinting at them from the right and coming in force from the left.*

feldspar /'feldspɑː/ *u.n* (also **'felspar**) (*technical*) one of a group of mineral rocks used in making glass and pottery(2).

felicity /fə'lɪsɪtɪ/ *u.n* (*formal*) happiness.

felicitate /fə'lɪsɪˌteɪt/ *tr.v* (often — *s.o* (*up*)*on s.t*) (*formal*) congratulate (s.o) ((up)on a special occasion).

felicitations /fəˌlɪsɪ'teɪʃənz/ *pl.n* (often — (*up*)*on s.t*) (*formal*) congratulations ((up)on s.t, e.g an important occasion): *We offered our felicitations on their marriage.*

felicitous /fə'lɪsɪtəs/ *adj* (*formal*) apt(1): *a felicitous remark.*

feline /'fiːlaɪn/ *adj* **1** of, like, a cat.

▷ *c.n* **2** (*technical*) member of the cat family: *Lions, tigers and wild cats are all felines.*

fell¹ /fel/ *p.t* of fall(*v*).

fell² /fel/ *tr.v* **1** cut down (trees): *They had to fell many trees to make a road through the forest.* **2** (*formal*) wound or kill (s.o); cause (s.o) to fall to the ground: *He felled several of the enemy before he was killed.*

fell³ /fel/ *n* (also attrib) **1** *c.n* rocky or bare hill: *The fell is only good for sheep in the summer.* **2** unique *n* (with capital **F** in names) rocky height (esp in northern England): *Bow Fell is one of the fells in the Lake District.*

fells *def/unique n* (also with capital **F**) group of fells(2) in the Lake District of England.

fell⁴ /fel/ *adj* **at one fell swoop** ⇨ swoop(*n*).

fellow /'feləʊ/ *attrib.adj* **1** belonging to the same group; in the same situation: *I enjoy meeting my fellow countrymen(2) when I go abroad. James is a fellow teacher.* **one's fellow man** all people as a group.

▷ *c.n* **2** (*old use*; *informal*) man: *He's a pleasant/ strange fellow.* **3** (usu *pl*) companion: *We were all school fellows.* **4** (with capital **F**) member (of a learned or professional society): *Fellows of the Royal Academy(2) of Sciences.* **5** member of a governing body of a college or university. **6** person who is paid to do research(1) at a university: *a research fellow in chemistry.* **7** (*formal*) one of a pair: *Here's one black sock but where's its fellow?*

fellow 'feeling *sing.n* (often *a — for/with s.o*) shared understanding, sympathy, (for s.o): *I have a fellow feeling for her because I know what it is like to lose one's job.*

fellow 'traveller *c.n* companion during a journey.

'fellowˌship *n* **1** *c.n* club, society, group of people who spend a lot of time and energy(1) doing things together for a common or shared aim: *She was pleased to have been accepted into the fellowship by the other members.* **2** *c.n* position of a fellow(4–6): *She's got a fellowship to do research(1) at Sussex University.* **3** *u.n* (*old use*) companionship; friendly association (with s.o): *I enjoyed her fellowship on the long journey.*

felon /'felən/ c.n (law) person who is guilty of serious crime; criminal.

felonious /fɪ'ləʊnɪəs/ adj criminal; done with criminal intention.

'**felony** c/u.n (pl -ies) serious crime: He's been found guilty of felony. Murder is a felony.

felspar /'felspɑ:/ u.n ⇒ feldspar.

felt[1] /felt/ p.t.p.p of feel.

felt[2] /felt/ u.n (also attrib) kind of thick cloth made from fur, hair or wool which has been pressed together tightly (not woven): a felt hat.

'**felt ,tip** c.n ('felt-,tip when attrib) pen that has a felt[2] writing point instead of a nib: Felt-tip pens are made with many different coloured inks.

'**felt-,tipped** adj (of a pen) having a felt[2] writing point.

fem written abbr female, feminine.

female /'fi:meɪl/ adj 1 (written abbr f, fem) (of a person, animal) of the sex that produces eggs, gives birth to young: a female cat. The form asks you to say whether you are male or female. 2 (of plants) of the parts that help produce seeds: The stigma, style and ovary are the female parts of a flower. 3 of or referring to girls or women: female rights; female workers. 4 (of machines) hollow part into which another part fits: The electric socket is the female part and the plug(3) is the male part.
▷ c.n 5 female animal or person: The male and female take turns to look after the eggs. 6 woman. ⇒ all-female.

feminine /'femɪnɪn/ adj 1 (usu attrib) of girls or women: feminine beauty. 2 suitable for, like, a girl or woman: She dresses her daughters in very feminine clothes. 3 having the essential qualities of a girl or woman: One of his daughters is very feminine and the other is a tomboy. 4 (grammar) of the female form (of s.o/s.t): Feminine nouns and pronouns include 'actress', 'her', 'she'. Compare masculine.
▷ def.n 5 (written abbr f, fem) (grammar) female form: The feminine of 'boy' is 'girl'.

femininity /,femɪ'nɪnɪtɪ/ u.n quality of being feminine(3): He was particularly attracted by her femininity.

'**femi,nism** u.n belief, set of beliefs, that women should have the same (legal(1), financial, political, social) rights and (social(1) as men.

'**femi,nist** c.n (also attrib) person who believes in and practises feminism.

femme fatale /,fæm fə'tɑ:l/ c.n (pl femmes fatales /,fæm fə'tɑ:lz/) (French) woman who can cause great problems or danger to anyone (usu a man) who associates with her.

femur /'fi:mə/ c.n (medical) thigh bone.

fen /fen/ c.n (esp in east England) low marshy land (often covered with water).
Fens def.pl.n flat area near the coast in east England: Have you been to the Fens?

fence[1] /fens/ c.n 1 barrier(1); structure(2) made of iron, wooden posts and wooden or wire railings which surrounds or divides an area of land (esp to keep animals in or out). **be/sit on the fence** (fig) refuse to take a particular side in an argument, discussion etc, esp in order to wait until it is clear which side offers the greatest advantage: He always sits on the fence in the most important debates(1).
▷ tr.v 2 (often — s.t in/off) divide, protect, surround,

(s.t) with a fence(1): We'll have to fence (off) the field if we want to prevent the cows from wandering in. **fence s.o in** (fig) prevent s.o from doing what he/she wants to do: I feel too fenced in at home.

'**fence-,sitting** u.n (informal) practice of refusing to give an opinion until it is known where the best advantage lies. ⇒ be/sit on the fence.

'**fencing**[1] u.n (material for making) a fence(1): How much fencing will we need? ⇒ fencing[2] (⇒ fence[2]).

fence[2] /fens/ intr.v (usu — with s.o) 1 practise the art or skill of fighting with a sword, esp as a sport (against s.o). 2 (fig) avoid an argument (with s.o); avoid giving a direct answer (to s.o): You've been fencing with me for two hours and I still don't know what you really believe.
'**fencer** c.n person who fences[2](1).
'**fencing**[2] u.n art, skill of fighting with a sword, esp as a sport. ⇒ fencing[1] (⇒ fence[1]).

fence[3] /fens/ c.n 1 (slang) person who receives stolen goods.
▷ intr.v 2 (slang) receive stolen goods.

fend /fend/ v 1 **fend for oneself** look after, support, oneself: After his parents died he had to fend for himself. 2 **fend s.o/s.t off** defend or protect oneself from s.o/s.t: She used a stick to fend off the wild dogs.

fender /'fendə/ c.n 1 thing, e.g heavy rope or a tyre, used to protect the sides of a boat, ship, esp in a harbour. 2 metal guard placed in front of an open fireplace to protect things in the room from the burning coals etc. 3 (US) = bumper(2).

fennel /'fenl/ u.n kind of plant with yellow flowers and a strong smell and taste, used in cooking.

ferment /'fɜ:mənt/ u.n 1 substance, e.g yeast, that causes other substances to ferment(2). **be in a (state of) ferment** (fig) be in a state of excited (usu political) activity: The country was in a ferment during the elections.
▷ tr/intr.v /fə'ment/ 2 (cause (s.t) to) go through chemical changes that change the taste, smell or form of a substance: After a few days in a warm place, fruit juice will begin to ferment. 3 (fig) (formal) cause, excite, (strong feelings, trouble etc): Reducing their salaries is just the kind of action to ferment further trouble. ⇒ foment.
fermentation /,fɜ:mən'teɪʃən/ u.n.

fern /fɜ:n/ c.n (also attrib) kind of plant with leaves like feathers and no flowers: fern plants.

ferocious /fə'rəʊʃəs/ adj (derog) cruel; fierce; very dangerous: That dog looks ferocious but it won't bite you. George has a ferocious temper.
fe'rociously adv. **fe'rociousness** u.n. **ferocity** /fə'rɒsɪtɪ/ u.n.

ferret /'ferɪt/ c.n 1 kind of small animal with a pointed nose and sharp teeth, kept for forcing rabbits out of their holes, for killing mice, rats etc.
▷ intr.v 2 hunt with ferrets(1). 3 (usu — about/around (for s.t)) (fig) search thoroughly (in s.t; for s.t; among s.t etc): If you ferret about among those papers, you'll find her letter. **ferret s.o/s.t out** (informal) discover s.o/s.t by searching: He is determined to ferret out the truth.

ferrous /'ferəs/ adj (technical) of, containing, iron: ferrous sulphate.

ferroconcrete /,ferəʊ'kɒŋkri:t/ u.n concrete(4)

made stronger with rods of steel or iron, esp used for building.

ferry /'ferɪ/ *c.n* (*pl -ies*) **1** (place where there is a) ship, aeroplane, regular service etc for taking people, cars, goods etc across a river etc: *We'll take the 6 o'clock ferry to the island.* **by ferry** in a ferry(1): *go/travel by ferry.*
▷ *tr.v* (*-ies, -ied*) **2** take (people, cars, goods) from one side (usu of a river) to another: *The farmer ferried the sheep across the river in a large boat.* **ferry s.o/s.t (a)round** take s.o/things around: *I've been ferrying the children around all day.*
'ferry,boat *c.n* boat or ship for carrying passengers, goods, cars etc across a river, narrow strip of water etc.
'ferryman *c.n* (*pl -men*) person who operates a ferry(1).

fertile /'fɜ:taɪl/ *adj* Opposite infertile. **1** producing, able to produce, a large healthy crop: *fertile fields/soil.* **2** (of a person's mind) very active, esp in forming plans, ideas: *She has a fertile imagination.* **3** able to produce children, young, seeds, fruit: *fertile trees.* **4** able to grow and develop: *fertile eggs/seeds.*
fertility /fə'tɪlɪtɪ/ *u.n* **1** state, quality, of being fertile. **2** (also *attrib*) thing that makes s.o/s.t fertile(3): *fertility* drugs(1).
fertilization, -isation /,fɜ:tɪlaɪ'zeɪʃən/ *u.n* act of fertilizing s.o/s.t or making s.o/s.t fertile; state of being fertilized: *The fertilization of frogs' eggs happens after the eggs have been laid.*
'ferti,lize, -ise *tr.v* **1** make (soil) productive by putting fertilizers on/into it. **2** make (eggs etc) fertile(3).
'ferti,lizer, -iser *c/u.n* (chemical or natural) substance added to the soil to make it (more) fertile(1).

fervent /'fɜ:vənt/ *adj* (*formal*) eager; showing strong true feelings: *fervent supporters.*
'fervency *u.n.* **'fervently** *adv.*

fervid /'fɜ:vɪd/ *adj* (usu *attrib*) (*formal*) eager; very strong: *Colin has a fervid desire to see the world.*

fervour /'fɜ:və/ *u.n* (*formal*) eagerness and strength of feeling: *religious fervour.*

festal /'festl/ *adj* = festive.

fester /'festə/ *intr.v* **1** (of a cut, wound etc) become full of a poisonous substance (called pus) because of infection: *After a few days the dirty wound began to fester.* **2** (*fig*) (of anger, worry etc) become greater, worse as time passes: *Her anger festered in her mind for many years.*

festival /'festɪvl/ *c.n* **1** day(s) for public celebration: *During the festival everyone danced in the streets.* **2** (with capital **F** in names) (title for a) group of music, drama(2), dance performances etc during a particular time, often held once a year: *the Edinburgh Festival.*

festive /'festɪv/ *adj* (also **'festal**) (*formal*) joyful, merry, (often for some special occasion or reason): *We were in a very festive mood*[1] *just before Christmas.*

festivity /fe'stɪvɪtɪ/ *n* (*pl -ies*) **1** *u.n* enjoyment; celebration: *The village is full of festivity at this time of year.* **2** *c.n* (often *pl*) celebration; joyful occasion: *Everyone enjoyed the wedding festivities.*

festoon /fe'stu:n/ *c.n* **1** (usu *pl*) (*formal*) chain of flowers, leaves, ribbons etc hung between two points as a decoration. *Festoons decorated the hall.*
▷ *tr.v* **2** (usu — s.o/s.t with s.t) (*formal*) decorate (s.o/s.t) (with a chain of flowers, leaves, ribbons etc): *The shops were festooned with decorations for Christmas.*

fetal ⇨ foetus.

fetch /fetʃ/ *tr.v* **1** go to get (s.o/s.t) (and bring her/him/it back to s.w): *Can you fetch me for the meeting tonight? Fetch my bag please.* **2** (*informal*) be sold for (an amount of money): *That old car won't fetch much money.* **fetch and carry (s.o/s.t) (for s.o) (a)** take (s.o/s.t) to and from different places (for s.o): *I've been fetching and carrying the children all afternoon.* **(b)** do (many) small duties, (esp moving, taking things from one place to another) (for s.o): *I need someone to fetch and carry for me this afternoon.*
'fetching *adj* (*old use*) attractive: *That's a fetching dress. You look very fetching in it.*
'fetchingly *adv.*

fete, fête /feɪt/ *c.n* **1** (*formal*) (*French*) organized games, competitions, entertainment, usu held outdoors to raise money for a particular cause, charity(3) etc: *The school fete raised £400 for the sports hall.*
▷ *tr.v* **2** (*formal*) honour (s.o) by entertaining well: *I'm always feted by my relatives when I visit them.*

fetid /'fetɪd/ *adj* (*formal*) having a bad or rotten smell: *These eggs have a fetid smell.*

fetish /'fetɪʃ/ *c.n* **1** object worshipped or feared by some people because of its supposed magical(1) powers. **2** (*fig*) thing given too much attention, love, respect etc: *He has a fetish about his hair and he's always combing it.* **make s.t a fetish; make a fetish of s.t** be too interested in s.t; pay too much attention to s.t: *It's a good idea to eat natural foods but don't make a fetish of it.*
fetishism /'fetɪ,ʃɪzəm/ *u.n* **1** practice of having, worshipping, a fetish(1) as a religion. **2** (*fig*) excessive interest in s.o/s.t.

fetlock /'fetlɒk/ *c.n* part of a horse's leg above the hoof.

fetter /'fetə/ *c.n* **1** (usu *pl*) (*formal*) chain around the leg(s) of a prisoner or animal to prevent escape: *We'll have to put the horse in fetters until we've repaired the fence.* **2** (*fig*) thing that hinders progress or freedom: *He wants to free himself from the fetters of a nine to five job.*
▷ *tr.v* **3** tie (s.o, an animal) with chains, rope etc to prevent escape: *The prisoner was fettered to a wall.* **4** (*fig*) hinder, prevent, (s.o, s.o's/s.t's progress, improvement etc): *We are fettered by the manager's inefficiency.*

fettle /'fetl/ *u.n* **in fine/good fettle** very healthy; in good condition: *It was a difficult journey but we were all in fine fettle.*

fetus ⇨ foetus.

feud /fju:d/ *c.n* **1** long and bitter quarrel between two people, families, groups: *There has been a feud between those families for a hundred years.*
▷ *intr.v* **2** (often — over s.t) have, continue, a long quarrel (with s.o): *They are feuding over the ownership of their father's home.*

feudal /'fju:dl/ *adj* of or referring to the way of using land and giving loyalty and service to the owner, esp during the Middle Ages in Europe: *the feudal system/laws.*

'feuda,lism *u.n.*

feudalistic /ˌfjuːdəˈlɪstɪk/ *adj* **1** of, like, the feudal system. **2** (of practices or opinions concerning organizations etc) very old-fashioned.

fever /ˈfiːvə/ *c/u.n* **1** (example of a) condition of the body when the temperature is higher and the heartbeat is faster than normal (often because of illness): *You've got a fever so you'd better get into bed.* ⇨ have/run a temperature. **2** (*formal*) excited state of mind: *There was a fever of nervousness as the students waited for their results.*

'fevered *attrib.adj* (*formal*) **1** affected by fever(1): *She put a cool towel on his fevered face.* **2** showing or having fever(2): *He has a fevered imagination.*

'feverish *adj* **1** showing signs of a fever(1): *I feel feverish so I think I'll try and sleep for an hour.* **2** (*fig*) excited; nervous: *She was in a feverish state as she opened the telegram.*

'fever ,pitch *u.n.* (often *be at, reach, —*) high level of excitement: *Excitement was at fever pitch when the first goal was scored.*

few /fjuː/ *det* (used with pl nouns) **1** (used without 'a' to show a small number) not many (and usu not enough): *Few people have seen his work. There are very few opportunities like this one.* Compare few(4), little(3). **2** (used with 'a' to show that it is not a large number) some (and usu enough): *We have a few eggs left (so I won't get any more yet). I've lived here for a few years.* Compare few(5), a little s.t. **a good few (s.o/s.t)** ⇨ good(17). **every few days , hours** etc ⇨ every. **no fewer than a thousand** etc as many as a thousand etc: *There were no fewer than 500 people at the meeting.* **quite a few s.o/s.t** many, but not very many, (people, things). Compare many(1).

▷ *def.n* **3** small group of people: *The few who came to class yesterday needn't do the extra work.*

▷ *pron* (of pl nouns) **4** (used without 'a' to show a small number) not many (usu not enough): *We invited a lot of people but few were able to come. Fewer came this year than last year.* Compare few(1), little(8), many(2). **5** (used with 'a' to show that although it's not a large amount or number it is some at least) some (and usu enough): *There are a few in this bag. I've got a few.* Compare few(2), little(8). **few and far between** very rare: *Good restaurants are few and far between.* **quite a few** many, but not very many.

ff *written abbr* **1** (*music*) fortissimo (= very loud). Compare f(9). **2** and the following pages etc: *See pages 56ff.* Compare f(5). **3** folios. Compare f(4).

fiancé /fɪˈɒnseɪ/ *c.n* man whom one is going to marry: *Have you met my fiancé?*

fiancée /fɪˈɒnseɪ/ *c.n* woman whom one is going to marry.

fiasco /fɪˈæskəʊ/ *c.n* (*pl -s*) (often *end in —*) complete failure: *The party was a fiasco. The match ended in fiasco when heavy rain fell.*

fib /fɪb/ *c.n* **1** (*informal*) lie that is harmless or not important: *You're telling fibs.*

▷ *intr.v* (*-bb-*) **2** (often *— about s.t*) tell a fib(1) (about s.t): *I'm sure she's fibbing about her age.*

'fibber *c.n* person who tells fibs(1).

fibre /ˈfaɪbə/ *n* (US **'fiber**) **1** *c.n* one of many thin threads that form certain plant products: *cotton/wool/wood fibres. This cloth contains only natural fibres.* **2** *c.n* one of many thin threads that form an organ in a person, animal:

muscle(1)/nerve(1) *fibres.* **3** *u.n* material made of fibres(1): *This is made of natural fibre.* **4** *u.n* (*fig*) character, strength: *We need a leader who is a person of strong moral fibre.*

'fibre,glass *u.n* material made of glass fibres(1) mixed with chemical substances and used for many purposes, e.g insulation(2).

fibrous /ˈfaɪbrəs/ *adj* (*technical*) made of, like, fibres(1,2): *The seed has a strong fibrous covering.*

fibrositis /ˌfaɪbrəʊˈsaɪtɪs/ *u.n* (*medical*) kind of illness that often affects the muscles(1).

fibula /ˈfɪbjʊlə/ *c.n* (*technical*) outer bone between the ankle and knee.

fiche /fiːʃ/ *c.n* (*informal*) microfiche.

fickle /ˈfɪkl/ *adj* (of weather, s.o's character etc) often changing and therefore not to be trusted: *He's very fickle and often changes his mind.*

'fickleness *u.n.*

fiction /ˈfɪkʃən/ *n* **1** *u.n* (also *attrib*) literary work that describes imaginary people, events etc: *Most people prefer reading fiction to true stories. She's a fiction writer.* ⇨ non-fiction. **2** *c/u.n* (usu *sing*) (example of a) statement, story etc that is invented, not true: *It was (a) pure fiction from beginning to end.*

'fictional *adj* (of a story, description) invented, imagined: *It's a fictional story about a child.*

fictitious /fɪkˈtɪʃəs/ *adj* **1** (*formal*) not true: *What he told you is completely fictitious.* **2** not real: *All the people in my story are fictitious.*

fiddle /ˈfɪdl/ *c.n* (*informal*) **1** instrument belonging to the violin family. **2** (*slang*) dishonest business operation; dishonest act: *He did a fiddle to get extra tickets.* ⇨ fiddle(5). (**as**) **fit as a fiddle** ⇨ fit¹(*adj*). **on the fiddle** (*slang*) behaving dishonestly, esp in business: *I knew he was on the fiddle when he offered to sell me the goods so cheaply.* **play second fiddle (to s.o/ s.t)** (*informal*) take a less important part, place, (than s.o/s.t): *All my life I had to play second fiddle to my brother.*

▷ *v* **3** *intr.v* (*informal*) play a violin. **4** *intr.v* (often *— about/around with s.t*) play aimlessly (usu with s.t between one's fingers): *Stop fiddling about (with that piece of paper)! You've been fiddling (around) with that clock for hours but can you mend it?* **5** *tr.v* (*slang*) buy or sell (s.t) dishonestly or unlawfully; manage (business accounts) dishonestly: *He's been fiddling our accounts.*

'fiddler *c.n* (*informal*) **1** person who plays the fiddle(1). **2** (*slang; derog*) person who cheats in business.

'fiddling *attrib.adj* (*informal*) small and unimportant: *fiddling little jobs.*

'fiddly *adj* (*-ier, -iest*) (*informal*) (of a job) demanding careful or detailed attention: *It's a fiddly job because there are so many little parts to fix.*

fidelity /fɪˈdelɪtɪ/ *u.n* (*formal*) **1** act or state of being faithful or loyal (esp in a marriage): *She never questioned her husband's fidelity.* Opposite infidelity. **2** (often *— to s.t*) care taken to be accurate and truthful in all details: *Her report showed great fidelity to historical fact.* **3** accurate and high quality in the reproduction(1) of sound, colours etc: *Modern recording methods produce a high quality of fidelity.* ⇨ high fidelity.

fidget /ˈfɪdʒɪt/ *c.n* **1** (*informal*) person who

moves her/his body around nervously. **get/have the fidgets** (*informal*) (start to) be full of nervous energy: *Children often get the fidgets when they have to sit still for a long time.*

▷ *intr.v* **2** move about nervously or impatiently: *The children started fidgeting after we'd been waiting for an hour.*

'fidgety *adv* (*informal*) nervous; restless: *I get fidgety on long journeys.*

field /fiːld/ *n* **1** *c.n* area of land inside hedges(1), fences etc, used for growing crops or keeping animals: *Every year he plants two fields and keeps his cows on the third field.* **2** *c.n* area of land which produces s.t, e.g coal, minerals etc: *a coal field*; *an oil field*. **3** *c.n* wide open area used for a particular purpose or where s.t, e.g a sport, takes place: *an ice field*; *a cricket/football field*; *a battle-field*. **4** *c.n* area, department of activity, study, knowledge, observation: *'What field are you in?' 'I'm in politics'. She's very well known in her field.* **5** *c.n* particular area that is affected or in which forces can be felt, observed: *a magnetic(1) field*. **6** *def.n* place (in the open air) where conditions are natural (not planned or studied): *I prefer working in the field to working in an office.* **7** *def/ def.pl.n* (in cricket¹, baseball etc) team that is not batting. ⇨ bat². Compare field(9), fielder. **8** *c.n* (*sport*) all the people, animals etc taking part in an event (esp a horse race): *There's a field of ten horses in the race.*

▷ *tr/intr.v* **9** (esp in cricket¹, baseball etc) be the field(7); catch and return (the ball).

'field ,day *c.n* (*military*) day on which army operations are practised. **have a field day** (*fig*) have a time of great activity, celebrations, success: *We had a field day at the sales in town.*

'fielder *c.n* person who fields(9).

'field e,vent *c.n* kind of athletic(1) event, e.g high or long jump, throwing the javelin or discus etc, which is not one of the running or track events.

'field ,glasses *pl.n* special glasses that make it possible to see animals etc clearly from a distance; binoculars.

'field ,hockey *u.n* = hockey(1).

'field ,hospital *c.n* (*military*) hospital set up for a short time at or near the scene of fighting.

'field ,marshal *c.n* (*written abbr* FM) (title of an) officer of the highest rank in the army.

'field,mouse *c.n* (*pl* -,mice) kind of small mouse.

'field ,officer *c.n* (*written abbr* FO) (title of an) army officer higher than a captain but lower than a brigadier.

,field of 'vision *c.n* area that one is able to see: *That ugly building spoils my field of vision.*

'field ,sports *pl.n* sports(3) played on a field(3), e.g football.

'field ,test *c.n* (*science*) observation, examination, trial, of s.t in the field(6), under natural conditions and not in a laboratory.

'field-,test *tr.v* (*science*) observe, examine, test, (s.t) in the field(6), under natural conditions and not in a laboratory: *Have any of these methods been field-tested?*

'field ,trip *c.n* (usu school) activity outdoors studying nature etc.

'field,work *u.n* scientific observation, study, done outside the laboratory, in the field(6).

fiend /fiːnd/ *c.n* **1** devil; evil spirit. **2** (*derog*) very

cruel or wicked person: *He's been such a fiend to his old mother.* **3** (*informal*) person who is excessively fond of s.t: *a health food fiend*.

'fiendish *adj* **1** (usu *attrib*) very cruel; wicked: *He has a fiendish temper.* **2** (*informal*) very clever: *a fiendish device.*

'fiendishly *adv*. **'fiendishness** *u.n.*

fierce /fiəs/ *adj* **1** very angry, violent: *He looks fierce but he won't bite you.* **2** very strong: *The wind was so fierce that it made progress difficult. There is fierce competition between those two businesses.*

'fiercely *adv*. **'fierceness** *u.n.*

fiery /'faiəri/ *adj* (-ier, -iest) **1** like, containing, fire: *The sky is bright and fiery this evening.* **2** (usu *attrib*) (*fig*) (easily or quickly made) angry: *Be careful of her fiery temper.* **3** excessively eager; full of energy(1) and enthusiasm: *That horse is too fiery for me to ride.*

fiesta /fi'estə/ *c.n* **1** (*religious*) holiday (esp in Italy and Spanish countries). **2** festival(1); celebration.

fifteen(th), fifth, fiftieth, fifty ⇨ five.

fig¹ /fig/ *n* (also *attrib*) (kind of tree with broad leaves which bears) soft sweet green or purple fruit full of small seeds: *fig jam*; *dried figs*. **not care/give a fig (for s.o/s.t)** consider s.o/s.t to be of no value, importance: *I don't give a fig for your opinion.*

'fig ,leaf *c.n* way of covering male sex organs in old pictures, on old statues etc by using a design(1) like a fig leaf.

fig² *written abbr* figure(3).

fight /fait/ *n* **1** *c.n* violent act of physical force between animals, people, countries: *You look as if you've been in a fight. My dog was hurt in a fight.* **2** *c.n* (usu — against/for s.t) struggle; use of great effort (to stop or get s.t): *the fight against unemployment*; *the fight for freedom.* **3** *u.n* will or ability to continue (s.t): *There's still a lot of fight in that old lady.* **4** *c.n* boxing or wrestling match: *Let's go to the fight tonight.* **a fight to the finish** a fight until one side is defeated. **put up a good, poor etc fight** try, not try, very hard to protect oneself, to succeed (in s.t): *She lost the match but she put up a good fight.*

▷ *v* (*p.t,p.p* fought /fɔːt/) **5** *tr/intr.v* use weapons or physical(1) force (against (s.o/s.t)): *Why are those two boys fighting? Everyone helped fight the fire until the firemen arrived.* **6** *tr/intr.v* (often — for/ against s.o/s.t) struggle; use great effort to stop ((s.t) from happening), prevent (s.o from doing, losing s.t): *The miners will fight (against) the decision to close the mine. The little girl is fighting for her life after the road accident.* **7** *intr.v* argue; quarrel: *What are you two fighting about now?* ⇨ infighting.

fight back defend oneself against s.o who attacks one (in an argument etc): *It doesn't matter what he does to her, she never fights back.* **fight s.t back** control anger, tears etc: *She fought back the tears when she heard the bad news.*

fight s.o/s.t off struggle successfully against s.o/ s.t: *The old lady bravely fought off the thieves. She's trying to fight off a cold.*

fight on continue fighting: *They fought on even when they knew they had lost everything.*

fight s.t out (between s.o (and s.o)) continue

fighting, arguing, (with each other) until a decision is reached: *I can't decide so you fight it out between yourselves.*

fight over s.o/s.t have a fight(1) or argument because of a person, place etc: *It's no good you two fighting over me because I'm not interested in either of you.*

fight one's way s.w (also *fig*) use effort to reach s.w, succeed: *She fought her way through the thick bushes. He started as a clerk and fought his way to the top.*

'fighter *c.n* **1** person who fights in a boxing or wrestling match. **2** person who fights(6), struggles, for/against s.t: *She's well known as a fighter for human rights.* **3** (also **'fighter ,plane**) military aircraft for attacking other aircraft in war.

'fighter ,pilot *c.n* person who flies a fighter(3).
'fighter ,plane *c.n* = fighter(3).
,fighting 'chance *sing.n* good possibility of success (esp with effort).
'fighting ,spirit *u.n* will, ability or strength to struggle (for s.t), continue (in s.t): *You can do better than that — where's your fighting spirit?*

figment /'fɪgmənt/ *sing.n* (usu a — of one's imagination) idea that is imagined: *Her success is a figment of her imagination.*

figure /'fɪgə/ *c.n* **1** shape, size, form, of the (human) body; drawing or picture of this: *She still has a lovely figure. I could see two figures in the dark. She drew two figures sitting under a tree.* **2** important person: *She's a well-known figure in politics.* **3** (written abbr **fig**) drawing etc to explain or show s.t: *Figure 2 (or Fig 2) shows the results of the experiment.* **4** (mathematics) (drawing of a) shape: *We had to copy a square, a triangle and other figures into our books.* **5** number: *The teacher wrote some figures on the board and told us to add them together. My salary has reached five figures (= is (over) £10 000).* ⇒ figures. **6** (informal) price: *Did they state a figure for the job?* **facts and figures** ⇒ fact. **in round figures** ⇒ round (adj).
▷ *v* (informal) **7** *intr.v* (usu — (in s.t) (as s.t)) have a part, appear, (in s.t) (as s.t): *You will figure in my book as the most important influence on my life.*
figure on (s.o) doing s.t expect (s.o) to do s.t: *I didn't figure on you arriving so early. I figure on spending £20 in all.* **figure s.o out** understand s.o's character: *I can't figure her out.* **figure s.o out** calculate, understand, s.t: *It took a long time to figure out the answer to the problem.* **figure (that) . . .** (esp US) think, consider (that . . .): *I figured (that) you'd be late. I figure it'll cost £100.* **in round figures** ⇒ round(adj). **That figures!** (informal) That makes sense, explains things.
figurative /'fɪgjʊrətɪv/ adj (written abbr **fig** in this dictionary) (of words, phrases etc) used in an imaginative way rather than with the ordinary meaning: *In 'She has a heart of gold', 'gold' is used in its figurative sense.* ⇒ figure of speech. Opposite literal(2).
'figuratively adv.
,figure of 'eight *c.n* pattern or movement in the shape of 8.
,figure of 'speech *c.n* expression (esp a simile) that has extra force or meaning because the words are used in an imaginative sense rather than with their ordinary meaning, as in 'The meat is as tough as old boots'. ⇒ figurative.

'figure,head *c.n* person who has an important position but no real power.

'figures *pl.n* numbers; counting; arithmetic: *I'm not very good at figures. I don't have a head for figures.* ⇒ figure(5).

figurine /,fɪgjʊ'riːn/ *c.n* (formal) small statue of a person, used as an ornament.

filament /'fɪləmənt/ *c.n* thin (wire) thread, esp inside a light bulb.

filch /fɪltʃ/ *tr.v* (informal) steal (esp s.t of little value): *He's been filching paper from school.*

file¹ /faɪl/ *c.n* **1** kind of metal tool with a rough surface for smoothing, cutting metal, wood etc or making it thinner, narrower etc. ⇒ nail-file.
▷ *tr.v* **2** (often — s.t away/down) smooth, cut, reduce (a piece of wood, metal etc) with a file(1): *File away the rough edges. You'll have to file it (down) here so that it'll fit.*
'filings *pl.n* small bits of metal (often those removed by a file(1)): *We often use iron filings in chemistry experiments.*

file² /faɪl/ *c.n* **1** (esp in single —) line of people (esp soldiers, children etc) one behind another: *The children entered the room in single file.* **the rank and file** ⇒ rank².
▷ *intr.v* **2** (often — past/through s.o/s.t) walk, march, in file²(1) (past etc s.o/s.t): *The passengers filed past the ticket collector.*

file³ /faɪl/ *c.n* **1** box, folder etc for keeping or storing papers together: *Alan has one file for each subject.* **2** collection of papers on one particular subject that is kept for reference: *The police must have a thick file on all his crimes.* **3** information recorded on a computer. **on file** recorded for future reference: *We don't need this information now but we'll keep/store it on file.*
▷ *v* **4** *tr.v* (often — s.t away) place (letters, papers etc) in the correct file³(2); put (information) on file for future reference: *Please file these papers for me. On which computer disk did you file the sales figures?*
'filing *u.n* work of placing information, papers etc in the correct file³(1,2): *Christine does the filing on Fridays.*
'filing ,cabinet *c.n* cupboard or set of drawers for storing files³(1,2) etc safely.
'filing ,clerk *c.n* person whose job is to file³(4) things.

filial /'fɪlɪəl/ adj (formal) of or referring to a daughter or son: *It's your filial duty to respect your parents' wishes.*

filibuster /'fɪlɪˌbʌstə/ *c.n* **1** (person who makes a) very long speech, esp in order to delay a decision, a new (government) law etc.
▷ *intr.v* **2** make such a speech.

filigree /'fɪlɪˌgriː/ *u.n* (also attrib) delicate ornamental work in fine metal (esp gold, silver etc) threads: *filigree earrings; earrings of silver filigree.*

fill /fɪl/ *u.n* (usu one's — of s.o/s.t) **1** as much as is needed or wanted (of s.t): *I've had my fill and I couldn't eat another thing.* **2** (informal) as much as one can bear (of s.o/s.t): *I've had my fill of you and your nonsense.* ⇒ full.
▷ *v* **3** *tr/intr.v* (often — (s.o/s.t) up (with s.t)) make (s.o/s.t) become full (of s.t): *Please fill up the car with petrol. The news filled her with fear. The theatre is filling up slowly.* **4** *tr.v* put s.o in, take, (a position that is vacant(2)): *Has the position*

advertised in the newspaper been filled yet? A part-time teacher will fill your place while you're sick. **5** *tr.v* (often — *s.t with s.t*) put s.t in (a hole, e.g in a tooth) to block it (using s.t): *I have to go to the dentist to have a tooth filled.* **6** *tr.v* (often — *s.t with s.t*) occupy(3) (one's time etc) completely (by doing s.t): *My day is filled with meetings.* **7** *tr.v* (not used with continuous tenses²) satisfy (a condition, need): *Your qualifications do not fill our needs.*

fill the bill ⇨ bill¹ (*n*).

fill the gap ⇨ gap.

fill in for s.o do s.o's job while he/she is sick, on holiday etc: *I'm filling in for your driver for a few days.* **fill s.o in (on s.t)** (*informal*) give s.o details (about s.t): *I had to fill Jane in on what had been discussed at the meeting.* **fill s.t in (a)** add what is needed to complete (s.t): *Read the passage and fill in the spaces.* (**b**) (also **fill s.t out**) provide information requested in an application form etc: *Fill in/out the form and return it to me.* (**c**) use spare time; do s.t while waiting for a period of time to pass: *I have a few hours to fill in until I have to meet my wife.*

fill (s.o) out (cause s.o to) become larger/fatter: *She was so thin from her illness but she's beginning to fill out a bit now.* **fill s.t out** = fill s.t in(b).

fill (s.t) up (with s.t) (cause s.t to) become completely full (with s.t): *They're waiting for the theatre to fill up before they start. You can fill up with petrol on your way home.*

'fill-,in *c.n* person or thing who/that acts in place of s.o/s.t for a limited time: *You'll have to find a fill-in for me because I'm away next week.*

'filling *c/u.n* thing used to fill(5) s.t: *Would you like a cream filling or a lemon filling in the cake? How many of your teeth have got fillings?*

'filling ,station *c.n* = petrol station.

fillet /'fɪlɪt/ *c.n.* (also *attrib*) long piece of meat or fish without bones: *fillet steak; fillet of plaice(2).*

fillip /'fɪlɪp/ *c.n.* (usu *sing*) (often *a* — *to s.t*) (*informal*) encouragement; person or thing who/that increases interest in s.t: *Your help has been a fillip to his studies.*

filly /'fɪlɪ/ *c.n* (*pl* -ies) young female horse. Compare colt(1), foal(1).

film /fɪlm/ *n* **1** *c.n* (often — of s.t (on s.t)) fine thin covering (of s.t): *a film of oil on the surface of the water.* **2** *c.n* story shown in moving pictures in a cinema, on television etc: *Have you seen the latest 'Superman' film?* **3** *c/u.n* (roll or strip of) thin material that has been treated chemically for photography: *Have you got a colour film or a black and white film in your camera?*

▷ *tr/intr.v* **4** (usu — (s.t) over (with s.t)) (cause (s.t) to) become covered with a fine, thin covering (of s.t): *The window in the bathroom filmed over with steam.* **5** make, produce, (a film(2)): *They are filming 'Nicholas Nickleby' for television. When do you start filming?*

'film-,star *c.n* very successful or famous actor/actress who appears in films.

'film-,strip *c.n* strip of film with a number of separate pictures on it, shown one after the other by using a projector: *The teacher showed some film-strips of science experiments.*

'filmy *adj* (-ier, -iest) cloudy; having a thin covering: *Her eyes became filmy as they filled with tears.*

filter /'fɪltə/ *c.n* **1** (also *attrib*) instrument for separating solid substances from a liquid or gas: *They got clean water by passing a mixture of sand and water through a filter. We need some more filter papers for our coffee filter.* **2** (*chemistry*) kind of apparatus for making air or water pure. **3** (also *attrib*) arrow at a traffic light which allows one line of cars etc to move: *You can go because the left filter is on.*

▷ *v* **4** *tr/intr.v* (cause (a liquid mixture) to) pass through a filter(1): *We had to filter the wine several times before it was clear.* **5** *intr.v* (usu — *into, out* (of), *through*, (s.t)) flow or pass slowly (into etc s.t); gradually come in/out, become known: *The audience filtered out of the cinema after the film had ended. Light filtered through the curtains. The news of her death slowly filtered through the crowds.* **6** *intr.v* (of traffic) be allowed by a filter(3) light to move while the rest of the traffic is stopped by the traffic lights.

'filter ,paper *c/u.n* (example of a) kind of paper used as a filter(1), e.g in chemistry experiments.

'filter ,tip *c.n* (cigarette with a) filter(1) at the mouth end to filter(4) the smoke.

'filter-,tipped *adj* (of a cigarette) with a filter(1) at the mouth end.

filth /fɪlθ/ *u.n* **1** dirt that is very unpleasant: *How can you live in such filth!* **2** (*fig*) (thing that contains) shocking, immoral references, esp to sexual matters: *I don't know how you can read such filth!*

'filthily *adv.* **'filthiness** *u.n.*

'filthy *adj* (-ier, -iest) **1** very dirty: *The children were filthy after playing in the mud.* **2** (of language, ideas etc) immoral, shocking, esp because of references to sexual matters: *filthy language.* **3** (*fig*) mean; very unpleasant: *That was a filthy trick. You're a filthy liar!*

▷ *adv* **4** (*slang*) very: *filthy rich.*

fin /fɪn/ *c.n* **1** thin movable(1) part of a fish that sticks out of the body and is used to help it balance, swim, turn, stop. **2** thing shaped or used like a fin(1): *the tail-fin of an aircraft.*

final /'faɪnl/ *adj* **1** (*attrib*) last; coming at the end: *We are now in the final stage of our journey.* **2** (of a decision etc) that cannot, will not, be changed: *What is your final decision? You can't go out and that's final.*

▷ *c.n* **3** (often *pl*) last (and usually decisive) one of a group of games, races, examinations etc: *Have you worked hard for your finals* (= last examinations at university)*? He was very pleased when he reached the finals of the tennis* tournament.

finale /fɪ'nɑːlɪ/ *c.n* (often the — of s.t) last part (of a concert, opera(1), play etc): *All the actors came on to the stage for the finale.*

'fina,list *c.n* competitor in a final(3).

finality /faɪ'nælɪtɪ/ *u.n* (*formal*) quality or state of being final(2): *We realized it was useless to argue because of the finality in his voice.*

finalize, -ise /'faɪnə,laɪz/ *tr.v* put (arrangements, dates, plans etc) into final(2) form: *Have you finalized the dates of your holiday?*

'finally *adv* **1** in the end; after a long time: *We finally arrived after a long journey.* **2** lastly: *First we went to the museums, then to the art gallery(1) and finally we went to the theatre.* **3** decisively; in a way that is final(2): *We must settle this question finally.*

finance /'faɪnæns, fɪ'næns/ *n* **1** *u.n* (science of the) managing of money: *She's got a top job in finance in a large business.* **2** (usu *pl*) money for a business, nation, person: *I'm worried about our finances.*

▷ *tr.v* **3** provide money (for s.o/s.t): *My parents financed me at university. How can we finance a trip to the Himalayas?*

financial /faɪ'nænʃəl, fɪ'nænʃəl/ *adj* of or referring to money matters: *financial problems.*

fi,nancial 'year *c.n* period(1) (12 months e.g from April to March) for which accounts are calculated: *Our records show a very good profit for this financial year.*

financier /faɪ'nænsɪə, fɪ'nænsɪə/ *c.n* **1** person who provides money for business. **2** person who is skilled in raising and managing money.

finch /fɪntʃ/ *c.n* one of various kinds of small birds, e.g a goldfinch.

find /faɪnd/ *c.n* **1** thing that is found or discovered, esp s.t useful or interesting: *That little restaurant is a real find because the food is excellent and it's not expensive.*

▷ *tr.v* (p.p,p.t found /faʊnd/) **2** get back (s.o/s.t who/that was lost) after a search; discover where (s.o/s.t) is: *Have they found her yet? Did you find the bag (that) you lost?* Opposite lose(1). **3** discover (s.t) by effort, study, search etc: *They still haven't found the reasons for his death. Have you found a solution to the problem?* **4** (often — s.t out; — out (that) . . ., where etc . . .) learn (s.t) by inquiry: *He found (out) that there were several buses to London every day.* **5** experience (s.t) as (good, bad etc); have an opinion of (s.t) as, consider (s.t) to be, (good, bad etc) after experience, testing etc: *We found the people there very friendly. How are you finding university? Did you find the work difficult?* **6** provide, supply, get, (time, money, courage etc) (to do, for, (s.t)): *Are you finding time to see everyone you wanted to see? How will you find the money? Where did you find the courage to ask her?* **7** discover (s.o/ s.t) by chance (without looking or searching for her/him/it): *I found it while I was digging in the garden. You'll find a lot to do there.* **8** reach (s.w) naturally or without effort: *Water finds its own level.*

all found including everything (esp all costs): *The holiday cost £200 all found.*

find expression in s.t ⇒ expression.

find fault with s.o/s.t ⇒ fault(*n*).

find favour (with s.o) ⇒ favour(*n*).

(find s.o) (not) guilty (of s.t) ⇒ guilty.

find it in one's heart (to do s.t) ⇒ heart(*n*).

find oneself discover who one is and what etc one's abilities are: *She really found herself when she went to live in Africa.* **find oneself in s.t** discover that one is in a particular place, situation: *After walking for two hours we found ourselves in a beautiful valley. I found myself in the middle of an argument.*

find one's feet ⇒ foot(*n*).

find one's place ⇒ place(*n*).

find one's tongue/voice be able to say s.t (usu with difficulty because of shyness, fear etc): *Why don't you say something — can't you find your tongue?*

find one's/the way (about, (to) s.w) ⇒ way(*n*).

find s.o/s.t wanting (in s.t) discover, realize, that (s.t) is needed to make (s.o/s.t) satisfactory: *I found Peggy wanting in manners.*

find (s.o) out discover the truth (about s.o) (usu about s.t he/she has done wrong): *He had been lying to his wife for years until she found (him) out.* **find (s.t) out; find out that, where, how** etc . . . learn about, discover, (s.t) by inquiry, study, calculation: *Please find out what time the train arrives. 'What happened?' 'I don't know but I'm going to try to find out.' We found out that he'd moved to Paris.*

take s.o/s.t as one finds her/him/it accept a person, situation as he/she/it is, without criticism: *If you want to marry me, you'll have to take me as you find me and not try to change me.*

'finder *c.n* person who finds s.t that is lost: *Will the finder of my umbrella please return it to me?*

-finder *c.n* person or thing who/that finds, provides information or something one is looking for: *a* fact-finder; *a* view-finder.

'finding *c.n* (usu *pl*) **1** thing that is learnt by an inquiry: *The committee's findings will be printed in the newspaper.* **2** (*law*) result of an inquiry, court case etc: *The judge sent the man to prison after the court's findings.*

fine¹ /faɪn/ *adj* **1** excellent; of good quality; skilfully made: *He's a fine painter. You'll get a fine view of the whole valley from the top of the hill.* **2** (of weather) bright and clear; not raining. **3** (usu *pred*) healthy; well: *You'll feel fine after a holiday.* **4** delicate; carefully made (and usu easily damaged): *fine china; a fine* lace(2) *handkerchief.* **5** made of very small grains or pieces: *The wind blew the fine sand into our eyes.* Opposite coarse(2). **6** (usu *attrib*) sharp; thin: *a pencil with a fine point.* **7** (of metals) pure: *fine gold.* **8** noticeable only with effort or difficulty: *There is such a fine difference between the two that it doesn't matter which you choose.* **9** (*informal*) (*pred*) good enough; satisfactory: *Don't worry about what he says; your work is fine!* **10** (*ironic*) good; wonderful: *Thanks for leaving my home in such a fine state! This is a fine time to tell me you can't come!* **a fine figure of a man , woman , child** etc a very good or handsome example of a man etc. **not to put too fine a point on it**; **the finer points of s.t** ⇒ point(*n*).

▷ *adv* **11** (*informal*) very well: *'Shall we meet on Friday?' 'That'll suit me fine.'* **cut it/s.t fine** (*informal*) leave the least possible amount of time that is necessary: *I had cut it so fine that I almost missed the train.*

▷ *interj* **12** agreed: *'See you next week.' 'Fine!'* **13** that's good; well done: *'Finished already? Fine!'*

fine- *adj* **1** as a very good example of the thing mentioned: *fine-sounding words; a fine-looking baby.* **2** being a delicate kind of the thing mentioned: *a fine-featured face.* **3** carefully made example (of s.t); of good quality (because closely woven etc): *fine-spun cloth.*

,fine 'art *u.n* art in the form of painting, drawing etc: *I want to study fine art at university.*

,fine 'arts *def.pl/pl.n* arts in the form of painting, music, sculpture(1) etc rather than aiming mainly to produce useful things.

'finely *adv.* **'fineness** *u.n.*

finery /'faɪnərɪ/ *u.n* (usu her, your etc —) best

clothes (and jewellery), appearance: *Go to the dance in all your finery.*

,fine-'tooth ,comb comb with the teeth close together. **go over/through s.t with a fine-tooth comb** (*fig*) examine (s.t) carefully or thoroughly: *I've been through my cupboard with a fine-tooth comb but I can't find it.*

fine² /faɪn/ *c.n* **1** amount of money that is (to be) paid for breaking a law, rule: *I had to pay a £20 fine for parking on a yellow line.*
▷ *tr.v* **2** punish (s.o) by a fine²(1): *I was fined for speeding.*

finesse /fɪ'nes/ *u.n* (*formal*) clever or skilful way of treating a (difficult) situation: *She showed great finesse in dealing with that difficult customer.*

finger /'fɪŋgə/ *c.n* **1** one of the five parts at the end of a hand or glove. **2** one of the four fingers(1) not including the thumb: *I hurt my little finger.* **3** thing shaped like a finger(1): *I cut the bread into fingers to dip into my egg.* **be all (fingers and) thumbs** be awkward, clumsy(1), with one's hands: *He was all fingers and thumbs when he tried to put the little parts together.* **burn one's fingers; get one's fingers burnt** (*fig*) suffer, get hurt, because of interfering with s.o/s.t or doing s.t foolish. **have a finger in every pie** (*fig*) have a part in, be concerned with, everything that's happening: *He's not satisfied unless he has a finger in every pie.* **have green fingers** ⇨ green (*adj*). **index finger** ⇨ index. **keep one's fingers crossed** hope that s.o/s.t will be successful or good, or that nothing bad will happen: *Keep your fingers crossed for me today.* **(not) lay a finger on s.o** (*fig*) (not) harm, touch s.o: *If you lay a finger on me, I'll* scream(3). **lay/put one's finger on s.t** discover, describe, explain, show, exactly what is wrong with s.o/s.t or the cause of s.t: *You've put your finger on it; that's exactly why he's so unhappy.* **(not) lift a finger (to do s.t)** (*fig*) (not) do anything (to do s.t): *She didn't lift a finger (to help) all weekend.* **little finger** ⇨ little. **pull one's finger out** (*fig*; *slang*) start doing (s.t); start working harder: *If you want to finish tonight you'll have to pull your finger out.* **ring finger** ⇨ ring. **(let s.o/s.t) slip through one's fingers** (*fig*) (allow s.o/s.t to) get lost, escape: *Don't let this opportunity slip through your fingers.* **snap one's fingers** make a sound by sliding one's second finger across one's thumb quickly. **snap one's fingers at s.o/s.t** (*fig*) treat s.o/s.t with no respect. **twist s.o round one's little finger** (*fig*) control, influence, s.o very easily: *She can twist her father round her little finger.* **work one's fingers to the bone** (*fig*) work very hard.
▷ *tr.v* **4** touch (s.t) with one's fingers: *She fingered the material to test its quality.*

'finger,board *c.n* long part of a guitar, violin etc where the player presses the strings to get particular sounds.

'finger ,bowl *c.n* small bowl (of water) placed on a table for washing one's fingers, esp during or after a meal that one eats with one's fingers.

'fingering *u.n* actions of the fingers, esp when playing a musical instrument, e.g a violin.

'finger,mark *c.n* dirty mark caused by s.o's finger(s).

'finger,nail *c.n* nail at the top of a finger.

'finger,print *c.n* mark made by the pattern of the skin on the tip of a finger: *The police*

use fingerprints to identify *criminals.* **take s.o's fingerprints** cover the ends of (s.o's) fingers with ink and make a print of them by pushing them onto paper.

'finger,tip *c.n* end of a finger. **have s.t at one's fingertips** (*fig*) know s.t thoroughly: *By Monday you must have all the facts at your fingertips.*

finicky /'fɪnɪkɪ/ *adj* (*derog*) **1** (often — about s.t) too particular (about dress, food etc): *She's so finicky about her food.* **2** concerned with, containing, too much detail: *That picture is too finicky.*

finish /'fɪnɪʃ/ *n* **1** *sing.n* (also *attrib*) end; last part (of a race, game, film etc): *We didn't see the finish because we left early.* **2** (paint, polish, hard work) that makes (a piece of) work complete, perfect: *This polish gives wooden furniture a lovely finish.* **a fight to a/the finish** ⇨ fight(*n*).
▷ *v* **3** *tr/intr.v* complete (s.t); (cause (s.t) to) come to an end: *When do you finish work? Have you finished reading? You're too late; we've finished.* **4** *tr/intr.v* drink, eat, use etc the last (of (s.t)): *Who finished the milk? We'll go when you've finished (your meal).* **5** *tr.v* make (s.t) complete or perfect: *They finished the old chairs beautifully.* **finish s.o/s.t off** put an end to, kill, destroy, (s.o/s.t): *This cold weather will finish off the last flowers in the garden.* **finish (s.t) off/up (a)** drink, eat, use, all (of s.t): *Finish up all your food before you leave the table.* **(b)** complete, stop, what one is doing: *You'll have to finish off/up now.* **finish up with s.t** have s.t at the end (of s.t): *She finished up with a cold after she'd been in the rain all day.* **finish with s.o/s.t (a)** no longer need s.o/s.t: *Have you finished with my pen?* **(b)** no longer enjoy or like s.o/s.t; end an association with s.o: *She finished with her boyfriend after six months. I used to like smoking and drinking but I'm finished with all that now.* **put the finishing touches to s.t** ⇨ touch(*n*).

'finished *adj* **1** completed: *He looked at the finished picture with pride.* Opposite unfinished. **2** (*pred*) ended: *The television programme is finished so you missed it.* **3** (*pred*) all used (with nothing left): *The cake is finished.* **4** (of a piece of work, performance, performer) perfect; polished(1): *His work is beautifully finished. The musician gave a finished performance.*

finite /'faɪnaɪt/ *adj* **1** having an end or limit: *Human knowledge is finite.* Opposite infinite(1). **2** (*grammar*) (of part of a verb) agreeing in number and person with the subject¹(4): *'Am', 'are', 'is', 'was' and 'were' are the finite forms of the verb 'to be'; 'be', 'being', 'been' are the non-finite forms.* ⇨ infinitive.

fiord /fjɔː d/ *c.n* (also **fjord**) part of the coastline (esp in Norway) where the force of the sea has made deep cuts into steep cliffs.

fir /fɜː/ *c/u.n* (also *attrib*) (wood from) one of a group of trees that is evergreen(1) and has leaves like needles: *a fir tree.* ⇨ conifer.

fire /faɪə/ *n* **1** *c.n* act, process, of burning coal, wood, gas, oil etc for cooking, heating etc: *I love an open fire on a cold winter evening.* **2** *c.n* instrument for heating a room etc; heater: *a gas/ electric fire.* **3** *c.n* burning that causes destruction: *Many animals are killed in forest and bush fires.* **4** *u.n* chemical action that has heat, light and flame; condition of burning: *Fire produces heat.*

⇨ fiery(1). **5** *u.n* (*fig*) angry, excited or strong feeling: *She looked at him with fire in her eyes.* ⇨ fiery(2). **catch fire** begin to burn: *Paper catches fire quickly.* **cease fire** (*military*) (order to) stop shooting (guns). **come under fire (a)** (*military*) begin to be shot at. **(b)** (*fig*) begin to be criticized. **go through fire and water** (*fig*; *joking*) suffer great dangers: *I'd go through fire and water to please you.* **hang fire** (*informal*) delay, wait, (before making a decision or continuing with s.t): *We were told to hang fire until a final decision had been reached.* **make a fire** prepare materials for burning (and put a flame to them). **make up a/the fire** put, add, (more) wood, coal etc to a fire that is not burning strongly enough. **on fire** burning: *The table is on fire.* **open fire** start shooting (guns). **play with fire (a)** burn things as a game without a purpose: *It's dangerous to play with fire.* **(b)** (*fig*) take foolish risks; do s.t dangerous: *You must enjoy playing with fire if you argue with him!* **set fire to s.t**; **set s.t on fire** cause s.t to begin to burn: *The candle fell over and set fire to the curtains.* ⇨ set(6). **the fat is in the fire** ⇨ fat(*n*). **there's no smoke without fire** ⇨ smoke(*n*). **under fire (a)** (*military*) being shot at (by an enemy's gun or guns). **(b)** (*fig*) being strongly criticized: *Their plan was under fire at the meeting.*

▷ *v* **6** *tr.v* heat, bake, (s.t made of clay) in an oven (called a kiln) in order to harden, strengthen it: *All these* (*clay*) *pots are ready to be fired.* **7** *tr/intr.v* (often — *at/on s.o/s.t*) shoot, operate, (a gun) (against s.o/s.t); cause (a bullet etc) to be shot from a gun: *She fired* (*her gun*) *at the wild dog. He fired two bullets above their heads to chase them away.* **8** *tr.v* (often — *s.o from s.t*) dismiss (s.o who is employed) (from a job, position): *She was fired because she was always late.* **9** *tr.v* (*fig*) say (s.t) very quickly: *She fired a stream of angry words at the naughty children.* **10** *tr.v* (often passive) (*fig*) cause (s.o) to become excited, eager etc: *The audience was fired by her performance.* **fire away (a)** (often — *away at s.o/s.t*) continue shooting (guns). **(b)** (*informal*) start: *'Fire away!' she said when she was ready to answer questions.*

'fire a,larm *c.n* signal (bell etc) that gives a warning if there is a fire.

'fire-,arm *c.n* (often *pl*) gun, e.g a pistol, revolver or rifle.

'fire bri,gade *c.n* team of people who are trained to put out fires.

'fire ,cracker *c.n* small firework that explodes with a noise.

'fire ,drill *c/u.n* organized practice of what must be done if a fire begins.

'fire ,engine *c.n* vehicle with pumps, ladders etc for dealing with fires.

'fire ,escape *c.n* means of escape from a building if there is a fire, e.g a metal staircase on the outside of the building.

'fire ex,tinguisher *c.n* kind of container full of chemicals for putting out a small fire.

'fire ,fighter *c.n* person who helps to put out bush, forest, mountain etc fires.

'fire,fly *c.n* (*pl* -ies) kind of small insect with wings and a tail that shines in the dark.

'fire,guard *c.n* metal frame or screen put in front of a fireplace to stop burning coals etc from escaping and causing damage.

'fire ,hydrant *c.n* pipe (esp in a street) from which water is taken to put out a fire.

'fire ,irons *pl.n* instruments that are used for tending a fire in a fireplace, e.g a poker etc.

'fire,light *u.n* light that comes from a fire in a fireplace, at a campsite etc.

'fire,lighter *c.n* (piece of a) substance that burns easily and is used to start a fire in a fireplace, barbecue etc.

'fireman *c.n* (*pl* -men) member of a fire brigade.

'fire,place *c.n* place in a room for a fire to heat the room or building.

'fire,proof *adj* **1** made of s.t that does not burn and that resists heat or direct flame: *Firemen wear fireproof clothing.*
▷ *tr.v* **2** make (material etc) fireproof.

'fire ,risk *c.n* place or thing that is dangerous because it can burn easily and quickly: *That old wooden house is a fire risk.* ⇨ fire trap.

'fire,side *n* (also *attrib*) **1** *def.n* place near the fire in a fireplace or campsite: *a fireside rug.* **2** (*fig*) home: *How I'd love to be at my own fireside instead of in this hotel.*

'fire ,station *c.n* building for fire engines etc.

'fire ,trap *c.n* place that is dangerous because it will burn easily and will be difficult to escape from if there is a fire. ⇨ fire risk.

'fire,watcher *c.n* person whose job is to watch a forest area for fires.

'fire,watching *u.n*.

'fire,wood *u.n* wood cut into pieces for burning in a fireplace, barbecue(1), campfire etc.

'fire,work *c.n* (often *pl*) (also *attrib*) small container with chemicals, explosive materials etc that burn with beautiful coloured lights and patterns and sometimes also make a loud noise: *We watched the firework display(1).*

'fire,works *pl.n* (*fig*) show of great anger: *There were fireworks at home when his mother discovered he'd broken the window.*

firm¹ /fɜːm/ *adj* **1** having, allowing, little movement; steady: *Put the ladder on firm ground.* **2** (*fig*) decided; fixed in purpose and not easily changed or influenced: *Be firm with the children. She was quite firm about not coming.* **3** severe; strong: *She gave him a firm warning.*
▷ *adv* **4** **stand firm** not allow oneself to be influenced: *They tried hard to change her mind but she stood firm.*
▷ *tr/intr.v* **5** (usu — (*s.t*) *up*) (cause (s.t) to) become firmer: *I do exercises every morning to firm up my stomach muscles(1).*

'firmly *adv*. **'firmness** *u.n*.

firm² /fɜːm/ *c.n* business company: *I've worked for the same firm for over twenty years.*

firmament /'fɜːməmənt/ *def.n* (*literary*; *formal*) sky including the moon, stars, sun etc.

first /fɜːst/ *adv* **1** before anyone/anything else: *We arrived at the party first. Who came first? What must I add first, the eggs or the milk?* **2** before all other times: *We first met when we were children.* **3** before another (named) time: *I can't come now; I have to do my homework first.* **4** (*informal*) in preference: *She said she'd never admit she was wrong — she'd leave her job first.* **first and foremost** before anything else; first and most importantly: *First and foremost I'd like to thank you all for your help.* **first of all (a)** before (one does) anything else: *First of all you must* *apologize.* (**b**) (the) first (reason etc) being: *I don't agree with you, first of all because it's too expensive and secondly because the food's not so good.* **First things first** The most important things must be done, dealt with, first. ⇒ first thing.

▷ *det/pron* **5** (*ordinal number*) earliest in order, time; 1st: *We must pay before the first (day) of the month. I've loved her since the first time I saw her.* **6** chief; highest in rank or quality: *Who's the first lady?* **at first sight** when one first sees s.o/ s.t: *It was love at first sight.* **in the first place** ⇒ place(*n*). **not know the first thing about s.t** ⇒ thing.

▷ *n* **7** *def.n* person, thing, time, who/that is first: *We were the first to arrive.* ⇒ last(7). **8** *c.n* highest grade(3) in a British university examination: *I want to get a first in French.* **at first** in the beginning: *I wasn't happy there at first but I love it now.* ⇒ at (long) last. **First come first served** Those who arrive first will be served first: *We can't reserve a place for you because it's first come first served.* **from the (very) first** from the (absolute) beginning: *I knew we would win from the (very) first.*

,**first** '**aid** *u.n* treatment given to s.o who is hurt or sick until a doctor arrives.
'**first,born** *c.n* (also *attrib*) first child born to s.o: *a firstborn child. He's my firstborn.*
,**first** '**class** *u.n* (,**first-**'**class** when *attrib*) **1** (of the) best quality: *It was a first-class hotel.* **2** (also *adv*) (of travel) (by the) best class: *We only travel first class.* **3** (also *adv*) (of the British postal services) (by the) fastest and most expensive class. **4** best; excellent: *a first-class meal.*
,**first** '**cousin** *c.n* child of one's aunt or uncle.
,**first-de**'**gree** *attrib.adj* **1** of the lowest level of seriousness: *first-degree burns.* **2** of the highest level of seriousness: *first-degree murder.* ⇒ second-degree, third-degree burn.
,**first** '**floor** *def.n* (also *attrib*) (US ,**second floor**) floor in a building which is directly above the ground floor.
,**first-**'**hand** *adj/adv* (obtained) directly: *a first-hand account of what happened. I heard it first-hand from someone who saw the accident.* ⇒ second-hand(2).
'**firstly** *adv* as a beginning; in the first place: *Firstly, I'd like to thank you all for coming.*
'**first ,name** *c.n* person's name that is not her/ his family name: *My first name is Julie.* **be on first name terms (with s.o)** know one another (or s.o) well enough to use her/his first name when speaking or writing to her/him: *I know her well and we're on first name terms.*
,**first** '**night** *c.n* (evening of the) first public performance of a play etc.
,**first of**'**fender** *c.n* (*law*) person found guilty of a crime for the first time.
,**first** '**person** *def.n* (*grammar*) (form used with the) pronouns 'I', 'me', 'we', 'us'.
'**first,principles** *pl.n* basic(1) principles(2) needed to understand or do s.t.
,**first-**'**rate** *adj* of the very best: *a first-rate performance.*
,**first** '**thing** *adv* at the earliest possible moment; before doing anything else: *I must post the letter first thing in the morning.* ⇒ first things first (⇒ first(*adv*)). **not know the first thing about s.t** (⇒ thing).

fiscal /'fɪskl/ *adj* (*technical*) of or referring to public money: *the government's fiscal policy*[1].
fish /fɪʃ/ *n* (*pl* -(es)) (also *attrib*) **1** *c.n* animal that has cold blood, lives only in water, breathes through gills[1] and swims with fins(1): *Did you catch any fish today?* **2** *u.n* flesh of such animals used as food: *fish soup. Can we have fried fish for lunch?* **drink like a fish** (*fig*) drink alcohol excessively. **a pretty kettle of fish** ⇒ kettle. (**like**) **a fish out of water** (feeling) awkward, uncomfortable, because one is in strange, unsuitable surroundings.

▷ *v* **3** *intr.v* try to catch fish: *fish in the sea.* **4** *intr.v* (*fig*) (usu — *for* s.t) try to get (information) by using indirect ways: *She's fishing to find out who the new chairman is.* **fish for compliments** ⇒ compliments. **fish s.t (out) (from/of s.t)** bring (s.t) out (of a deep, awkward place): *She fished (out) the missing sock from the bottom of the drawer.* **fish s.t up** (**a**) pull s.t out of water: *We fished up an old shoe.* (**b**) (*fig*) bring back, remind s.o of, s.t that has been forgotten, hidden: *Where did you fish up that old dress?*
'**fish,cake** *c/u.n* (example of a) small round and flat piece of fish, potato, egg etc covered with breadcrumbs and fried.
'**fish ,eagle** *c.n* (also '**fish ,hawk**) = osprey.
'**fisheries** *pl.n* **1** part of the sea where fishing is done for business purposes. **2** businesses etc dealing with fishing.
'**fisherman** *c.n* (*pl* -**men**) person who catches fish.
,**fish** '**finger** *c.n* long piece of fish covered with egg and breadcrumbs and then fried.
'**fish ,hook** *c.n* hook tied to the end of a fishing-line to catch fish.
'**fishiness** *u.n* fact or state of being fishy.
'**fishing** *n* **1** *u.n* (action, sport, of) catching fish: *Do you enjoy fishing?* **2** *def.n* possibility of catching fish: *I know a place where the fishing is excellent.* **go fishing** fish(3) as a sport, business or activity.
'**fishing-,boat** *c.n* boat for fishing.
'**fishing-,line** *c/u.n* length of strong nylon etc thread (usu used with a rod) to which a hook is fixed for catching fish.
'**fishing-,net** *c.n* large net put into the sea, a lake etc to trap fish.
fishmonger /'fɪʃ,mʌŋə/ *c.n* **1** person whose business is selling fish. **2** (also '**fish,monger's**) shop where fish is sold.
'**fishing-,rod** *c.n* long thin rod which is used with a fishing-line and hooks to catch fish.
'**fishing ,smack** *c.n* ⇒ smack[3].
'**fishing ,tackle** *u.n* hooks, lines, rods etc needed for fishing(1).
'**fish,wife** *c.n* (*pl* -,**wives**) (*derog*) coarse rude (old) woman: *She shouts like a fishwife.*
'**fishy** *adj* (-**ier**, -**iest**) **1** (smelling or tasting) like a fish: *There's a fishy smell in here.* **2** (*informal*) causing doubt, suspicion: *There's something fishy about that man.*
fission /'fɪʃən/ *u.n* (*technical*) breaking into parts; division: *nuclear(2) fission.* ⇒ fusion.
fissure /'fɪʃə/ *c.n* (*technical*) crack: *They studied the fissures in the rocks after the earthquake.*
fist /fɪst/ *c.n* hand when the fingers are closed together tightly in a ball: *He hit him with his fist.* **hand over fist** ⇒ hand(*n*). **shake one's fist(s)**

(at s.o) make one's hand(s) into a fist or fists and shake it/them to show one's anger (with s.o). ⇨ tight-fisted.

fit¹ /fɪt/ *adj* (*-tt-*) (often — *for, to do, s.t*) Opposite unfit. **1** in good health, condition, (for, to do, s.t): *If you don't have a rest, you won't be fit for the rest of the journey.* **2** strong and healthy (enough for, to do, s.t): *I'm trying to get fit for the* marathon(1). *How do you manage to stay so fit?* ⇨ keep fit. **3** right, suited, (for, to do, s.t): *You're not fit to sit with us* (*because of your behaviour*). *We received a welcome fit for any famous person.* **4** good enough (for, to do, s.t): *That milk is not fit to drink.* **(as) fit as a fiddle** (*informal*) in very good health: *I'll feel as fit as a fiddle after I've had an hour's sleep.* **fit to burst, drop, explode** *etc* ready to burst from eating so much food, drop because of tiredness, explode with anger etc. **keep fit** (**,keep-'fit** when *attrib*) (do exercises etc to) remain strong and in good health: *I swim to keep fit. She's in my keep-fit class.* **see/think fit** consider what is right and proper: *Don't expect me to tell you what to do — do as you think fit.*

▷ *sing.n* **5** way in which an article of clothing matches the size and shape of a person: *These trousers are a good/tight/poor fit.*

▷ *v* (*-tt-*) **6** *tr/intr.v* be the correct size and shape (for (s.o/s.t)): *You must wear shoes that fit* (*you*) *properly. The cupboard won't fit* (= will not go) *through the door.* **7** *tr.v* make (an article of clothing, esp one that is not yet finished) the right size and shape: *I have to go to the tailor to have my new suit fitted.* **8** *tr.v* (rarely used in continuous tenses²) (often — *s.o/s.t for s.t*) (make (s.o/s.t)) be suitable for (s.t): *Her qualifications fit her well for the job. We must have a celebration to fit the occasion.* **9** *tr.v* put (s.t) in position or in place: *They're coming out to fit a new piece of glass in the window.* **10** *tr.v* supply (s.t) that is needed: *We're having new tyres fitted on the car.* **fit (s.o) like a glove** ⇨ glove. **fit the bill (for s.t)** ⇨ bill¹. **fit s.o/s.t in** make or find time for s.o/s.t: *I'm very busy but I'll try and fit it in this afternoon.* **fit in** (**with s.o/s.t**) (**a**) be able to join in the activities, and share the ideas etc of other people in a particular group: *I never liked girls of my own age when I was young because I never seemed to fit in.* (**b**) make any necessary changes (to s.t) (in order to suit s.o/s.t): *I hope you can fit in with our plans for a holiday this year.* **fit s.o/s.t out** (**with s.t**) supply s.o/s.t (with everything that is necessary or needed): *We've had the car fitted out so that we can sleep in it.* **fit s.o/s.t up** (**with s.t**) supply s.o/s.t (with s.t) that is needed, esp for a new purpose or for improvement: *We're trying to fit up the rooms in time for the holiday season.*

'fitment *c.n* (*formal*) **1** (also **'fitting**) (often *pl*) piece of furniture which is fixed and forms part of a larger unit, e.g the cupboards, working surfaces etc in a kitchen. **2** extra part for a machine that enables it to do additional jobs etc: *If you buy this electric drill you can choose two fitments free.*

'fitness *u.n* **1** (often — *for s.t*) state or quality of being suitable (for s.t): *I am in no doubt about his fitness for the job.* **2** (also *attrib*) state of being fit¹(1,2): *You can improve your general fitness by walking more. You'll have to have a fitness test.*

'fitted *adj* **1** (usu *attrib*) made to the correct size and shape and fixed in place: *Does your new house have fitted carpets?* **2** (usu *pred*, — *with s.t*) supplied (with s.t): *The car door was fitted with a safety lock.*

'fitter *c.n* **1** person, e.g a tailor, who fits¹(6) clothes. **2** person who cuts and fits¹(8) a carpet, cupboard etc. **3** person who puts the parts of a machine together.

'fitting *adj* **1** right and proper; suitable: *Have you found a fitting moment to tell Peter the bad news?*

▷ *c.n* **2** act of fitting (⇨ fit¹(6)) s.t: *I have to go for a final fitting for my dress tomorrow.* **3** ⇨ fitment(1).

fit² /fɪt/ *c.n* **1** (often — *of s.t*) sudden sharp attack (of coughing, laughing, sneezing etc). **2** (sudden attack of an) illness that causes violent uncontrolled movements and often unconsciousness: *suffer from fits.* **3** (often *a* — *of s.t*) sudden burst (of emotion(1), activity): *a fit of anger.* **by/in fits and starts** from time to time and without regularity: *It took Fred a long time to paint the house because he only did it in fits and starts.* **give s.o a fit** (*fig; informal*) do s.t that frightens s.o: *You gave me a fit when you appeared at the window!* **have/throw a fit** (*informal*) be/become very angry, annoyed, worried: *My wife will have a fit when she sees what I've done to the new car!*

'fitful *adj* (*formal*) irregular: *He fell into a fitful sleep.*

'fitfully *adv.* **'fitfulness** *u.n.*

five /faɪv/ *det/pron/c.n* (*cardinal number*) number 5 (between 4 and 6): *The cloth cost me five pounds. Five of us arrived early. She's five* (*years old*). *Come at 5* (*o'clock*).

fifteen /fɪf'tiːn/ *det/pron/c.n* **1** (*cardinal number*) number 15 (between 14 and 16).

▷ *c.n* **2** group of (15) players forming a rugby team: *I play for the first fifteen* (the top rugby team).

fifteenth /fɪf'tiːnθ/ *det/pron* **1** (*ordinal number*) (person or thing) following 14 in order; 15th.

▷ *c.n* **2** one of fifteen equal parts; ¹⁄₁₅.

fifth /fɪfθ/ *det/pron* **1** (*ordinal number*) (person or thing) following 4 in order; 5th.

▷ *c.n* **2** one of five equal parts; ⅕.

'fifthly *adv* as the fifth(1) point, item etc.

fiftieth /'fɪftɪəθ/ *det/pron* **1** (*ordinal number*) (person or thing) following 49 in order; 50th.

▷ *c.n* **2** one of fifty equal parts; ¹⁄₅₀.

fifty /'fɪftɪ/ *det/pron/c.n* (*pl -ies*) (*cardinal number*) number 50 (between 49 and 51): *It weighs fifty pounds. Fifty-three of them passed the examination.* **in one's fifties** between 50 and 59 years old. **(in/into) the fifties** (or **the 50s**) (**a**) (speed, temperature, marks etc) between 50 and 59: *The temperature is in* (or *rose into*) *the fifties.* (**b**) (years) between '50 and '59 in a century.

,fifty-'fifty *adj* **1** equal: *We have a fifty-fifty chance of winning.*

▷ *adv* **2** equally: *We always share everything fifty-fifty.* **go fifty-fifty** (**with s.o**) share costs etc equally (with s.o).

,five-a-'side *u.n* (also *attrib*) indoor football game with five players in each team: *a five-a-side football team.*

'fiver *c.n* (UK *informal*) five pound bank note; £5.

fix /fɪks/ *c.n* **1** (often *be in*, *get* (s.o) *into*, (*a bit of*) *a* —) (*informal*) awkward or difficult situation: *I'm in (a bit of) a fix; I seem to have two arrangements for tonight. You've really got me into a fix now.* **2** position of s.t found by comparing it with the position of the sun, stars etc. **3** (*slang*) injection of a drug(2), esp for an addict.

▷ *tr.v* **4** (often — *s.t to s.t*) join, fasten, (s.t) firmly (to s.t): *He fixed a handle to the cupboard door.* **5** attract and hold, direct, (one's look, attention) (towards s.t): *The view of the mountain fixed her attention. She fixed her eyes on a suspicious man in the corner of the room.* **6** (*informal*) mend (s.t): *Can you fix my radio?* **7** (*informal*) decide (s.t): *We've fixed a date for our next meeting.* ⇒ fix s.t up (for s.o). **8** (*informal*) arrange, prepare, (s.t) (for s.o): *Can I fix you something to eat? She's fixing a dinner for me.* **9** make (a colour, image(2), in a photograph) permanent with certain chemicals. **10** (*slang*) arrange (s.t) in a dishonest, improper way: *Can you fix it so that I get the job?* **11** (*slang*) get one's revenge on (s.o): *I'll fix him for lying about me!* **fix (up)on s.o/s.t** decide, choose, s.o/ s.t; settle one's choice on s.o/s.t: *Have you fixed on a date for your move? They fixed upon living in the country.* **fix one's eyes (up)on s.o/s.t** ⇒ eye(*n*). **fix s.t up (for s.o)** (*informal*) arrange, organize, s.t (for s.o): *Have you fixed up a place to live? My father has fixed up a job for me in his business.* **fix s.o up (with s.o)** provide a partner for s.o; arrange for s.o to meet s.o, esp for romantic(1), social reasons: *Can't you fix me up with one of your friends?* **fix s.o up (with s.t)** provide s.o with s.t: *Can you fix me up with a job? If you want to go on holiday I'll fix you up* (i.e provide you with the money). **fix s.o with s.t** look at s.o with a particular look: *He fixed me with cold eyes/with a stare.* **get (o.s/s.o) into a fix** ⇒ fix(1).

fixated /fɪkˈseɪtɪd/ *pred.adj* (usu — *by/with* s.o/s.t) (*informal*) too concerned emotionally (about s.o/s.t): *She is fixated by/with her father.*

fixation /fɪkˈseɪʃən/ *c/u.n* (often — *on/with* s.o/ s.t) (example of) being fixated.

fixative /ˈfɪksətɪv/ *c.n* **1** substance that fixes(9) s.t. **2** sticky substance for keeping false teeth, hair etc in position. **3** (*science*) substance that preserves(3) cells(4) etc for study.

fixed *adj* **1** firmly fastened; not able to be moved: *The chairs are fixed.* Opposite movable(1). **2** not able to be changed: *fixed prices. She has very fixed ideas.*

fixedly /ˈfɪksɪdlɪ/ *adv* (*formal*) in a steady, unchanging way. **stare fixedly at s.o/s.t** look with long and steady attention at s.o/s.t.

fixture /ˈfɪkstʃə/ *c.n* **1** (often *pl*) thing permanently fastened to s.t: *The price of the house includes the fixtures.* ⇒ fitment(1). **2** fixed(2) date for a sporting event: *A list of fixtures has been put on the club noticeboard.* **3** (*fig*) person or thing that is not likely to go away from a place: *Mrs White is a permanent fixture in our office.*

fizz /fɪz/ *n* **1** *c.n* noise made when gas escapes from a liquid, e.g when one opens a bottle of lemonade after it has been shaken. **2** *u.n* carbon dioxide in water or other liquid: *Someone left the top off the lemonade and it's lost its fizz.* **3** *u.n* (*informal*) champagne.

▷ *intr.v* **4** make bubbles(1) as gas escapes from a liquid, e.g lemonade: *The beer fizzed when David took the cap off.*

fizzle /ˈfɪzl/ *intr.v* fizz(4) slightly. **fizzle out** (*fig*) fail; end slowly: *The group started well but after a month it began to fizzle out.*

'fizzy *adj* (*-ier*, *-iest*) (of cold drinks) containing gas bubbles(1), esp carbon dioxide: *fizzy drinks.*

fjord ⇒ fiord.

flabbergasted /ˈflæbəˌɡɑːstɪd/ *pred.adj* (often — *at/by* s.t) astonished (at/by s.t): *I am flabbergasted (at the price of petrol here)!*

flabby /ˈflæbɪ/ *adj* (*-ier*, *-iest*) **1** (of muscles(1), skin) soft and loose: *She's become very flabby since she stopped dancing.* **2** (*fig*; *derog*) (of s.o, s.o's character) weak; having no moral strength.

flaccid /ˈflæksɪd/ *adj* (*formal*) weak and soft: *Her cheeks were flaccid after her long illness.*

flaccidity /flækˈsɪdɪtɪ/ *u.n*.

flag[1] /flæɡ/ *c.n* **1** piece of cloth with the colours, design(2) etc of a particular country, association etc. **2** = flagstone. **3** kind of plant with long pointed leaves and blue, white or yellow flowers; iris². **4** sign used by a taxi to show if it is hired or free for hire. **show the flag** (*fig*; *informal*) (appear s.w in order to) show one's support for s.t. **white flag** ⇒ white. (**do s.t**) **under the flag of s.o/s.t** (do s.t) representing a particular group, country, business etc.

▷ *tr.v* (*-gg-*) **5** decorate (s.t) with flags: *The streets were flagged for the ceremony.* **6** (usu — *s.o/s.t down*) signal (a driver, car, train etc) with one's arm etc to stop: *We flagged down a car and asked the driver to get some help.*

'flag ,day *c.n* day on which money is collected for charity(2) by selling small paper flags(1).

'flag,pole *c.n* (also **'flag,staff**) high post on which a flag is hung.

'flag,ship *c.n* **1** main ship of a group of warships etc. **2** (*fig*) main hotel, office etc of a group: *Grosvenor House is the flagship of the Forte hotels.*

'flag,stone *c.n* flat square stone used to make a path etc.

flag[2] /flæɡ/ *intr.v* become or grow weak: *The flowers began to flag in the hot weather.* ⇒ unflagging.

flagon /ˈflæɡən/ *c.n* (*old use*) large, usu glass, container in which liquids are sold or served: *Let's order a flagon of wine with our meal.*

flagrant /ˈfleɪɡrənt/ *adj* (usu *attrib*) (of a crime or unfair deed) openly wicked: *She was told to leave the group because of her flagrant lies.* **'flagrancy** *u.n*. **'flagrantly** *adv*.

flair /fleə/ *sing/u.n* (often *a* — *for* s.t) natural ability (to do s.t well): *She has a flair for cooking. He dances with flair.*

flake /fleɪk/ *c.n* **1** very small light piece of (s.t): *flakes of skin.* ⇒ snowflake, soapflakes.

▷ *intr.v* **2** (usu — *off* (s.t)) come off (s.t) in flakes(1): *The paint is flaking (off the wood).* **flake out** (*informal*) fall asleep; stop all activity in order to rest completely: *When she got home after a hard day at work she flaked out (in front of the television).*

'flakiness *u.n* fact or state of being flaky.

'flaky *adj* (*-ier*, *-iest*) like, in the form of, flakes(1): *My skin goes flaky if I sit in the sun. It's very difficult to make flaky pastry.*

flamboyant /flæm'bɔɪənt/ adj intended to attract attention; showy: *flamboyant clothes*.
flam'boyance u.n. **flam'boyantly** adv.

flame /fleɪm/ n 1 c/u.n very hot burning gas that comes from s.t that is burning. 2 u.n (also *attrib*) bright orange-red light or colour: *The clouds turned to flame (or flame red) above the setting sun*. 3 c.n (*literary*) very strong feeling: *Her eyes were flames of anger*. **burst into flame(s)** (suddenly) start burning with many flames(1): *There was an explosion and the car burst into flames*. **fan the flames (of s.t)** (*fig*) increase anger, excitement etc. **go up in flames** start to burn fiercely and be destroyed. **in flame(s)** burning; on fire: *The plane was in flames as it crashed*. **old flame** (*informal*) person who has been one's boyfriend/girlfriend.
▷ *intr.v* 4 burn with flames(1): *The coal is flaming nicely now*. 5 (often — with s.t) show great anger, excitement etc (because of s.t): *Her eyes flamed with anger during their argument*.
'flaming *attrib.adj* 1 burning with flames: *We could see the flaming ship in the distance*. 2 (also *adv*) very hot: *The sun was flaming hot at midday. It has been a flaming June*. 3 brightly coloured (esp orange-red): *She wore a flaming red ribbon in her hair*. 4 very strong (feelings): *She has a flaming temper when she's really angry*. 5 (*slang*) big; great: *Don't be such a flaming idiot!*
flammable /'flæməbl/ adj (also **in'flammable**) likely to burst into flames and burn easily. Opposite non-(in)flammable.

flamingo /flə'mɪŋgəʊ/ c.n (*pl* -(e)s) kind of large water bird with a long neck and legs and pink feathers.

flan /flæn/ c/u.n round open tart'(1) filled with fruit, cheese etc.

flange /flændʒ/ c.n (*technical*) flat edge of a wheel, pipe etc which is shaped to keep it in position, e.g the flanges on the wheel of a railway engine so that it stays on the railway line.

flank /flæŋk/ c.n 1 side of (an animal, mountain, group): *The cow's flank is very fleshy. The path goes over the left flank of the mountain*.
▷ *tr.v* 2 be at the side of (s.o/s.t): *The streets were flanked with crowds during the procession*. 3 go round the side of (an army, mountain etc). Compare outflank(1).

flannel /'flænl/ n 1 u.n (also *attrib*) woollen material that is loosely woven: *flannel trousers*. 2 c.n = facecloth.
flanne'lette u.n (also *attrib*) kind of cotton material made to look like flannel(1): *sheets made of flannelette; flannelette pyjamas*.
'flannels *pl.n* sports trousers made of white flannel(1).

flap /flæp/ c.n 1 (sound of an) action of moving up and down or from side to side quickly: *the flap of the sails in the wind*. 2 piece of material which hangs, esp to cover an opening: *We tied up the tent flaps during the day*. 3 part of a table top which can be raised or lowered. 4 part of an aircraft wing which can be raised or lowered to control its up and down movement or speed. 5 (often be in, get into, a —) (*informal*) state of nervousness, confusion or excitement: *Don't get into such a flap; everything will be fine*.
▷ *v* (-pp-) 6 *tr/intr.v* (cause (s.t) to) move up and down or from side to side, sometimes with a slight noise: *The bird flapped its wings and flew up into the tree. I can't sleep with that sheet flapping (about) in the wind*. 7 (usu — s.t off (s.t)) use one's hand, a piece of paper etc to push (s.t) off (s.t): *She flapped the insect off (her arm)*. 8 *intr.v* (often — about (s.t)) (*informal*) become nervous, confused, excited, (about s.t): *What are you flapping about? Stop flapping!* ⇒ unflappable.

flapjack /'flæpˌdʒæk/ c.n kind of sweet thin cake made from oats.

flare /fleə/ n 1 c.n bright light that shines suddenly and only for a' short time: *the flare of a match being lit in the dark*. 2 c.n object that burns brightly and is used as a signal etc: *We fired a flare so that the rescue party would know our position*. 3 u.n gradual widening at one end: *These trousers have too much flare for Ben*.
▷ *intr.v* 4 burn brightly but unsteadily, often for only a short time: *The match flared in the darkness*. 5 spread; become wider at one end: *The fashion then was to wear trousers that flared at the bottom*. **flare up (a)** burn with bright flames: *The curtains flared up as they caught fire*. **(b)** (*fig*) become suddenly very strong, angry: *Violence flared up again today. She often flares up in arguments*. ⇒ flare-up.
flared adj wider at one end, usu the bottom: *I prefer flared skirts to straight ones*.
'flare-ˌup c.n sudden burst of flame, anger, violence etc.

flash /flæʃ/ c.n 1 sudden short burst of light: *a flash of lightning*. 2 (also **'flash, light**) instrument used with a camera to produce bright light when taking photographs in poor light. 3 (often a — of s.t) (*fig*) sudden short burst or sign (of feeling, understanding): *I noticed a flash of understanding on her face as she realized who I was*. 4 sign worn on a uniform(2) to show the person's group etc. **(as) quick as a flash** very quickly; as fast as possible: *I'll be as quick as a flash so wait for me*. **a flash in the pan** (*fig*) thing that begins well but soon fails. **in a flash** suddenly; very quickly: *I'll be with you in a flash*.
▷ *v* 5 *tr/intr.v* (cause (a light) to) shine brightly: *Flash the torch into that corner*. 6 *tr/intr.v* (often — (s.t) at s.o/s.t) (also *fig*) signal (to s.o/s.t) by shining (a light), giving (a smile etc), for an instant only: *The driver flashed his lights at the car in front of him. She flashed a smile of encouragement at her friend*. 7 *intr.v* (usu — by/past) go past quickly: *Many cars flashed past us before one stopped to give us a lift. Our holiday flashed by. His life flashed before him as he fell*. 8 *tr.v* send (a message), usu by radio: *The news of the president's death was flashed around the world*. ⇒ newsflash. 9 *tr.v* (often — s.t about/around) show (s.t) in a flashy way: *He flashes his money (around) to show how rich he is*. 10 *tr.v* show (s.t) for an instant: *He flashed his pass and was allowed to enter*. 11 *intr.v* (usu — through one's mind etc) pass suddenly (through one's mind etc): *The idea that she'd been there before flashed through her thoughts*. **flash back (to s.t)** (of thoughts) go back quickly to an earlier time: *Her thoughts flashed back to her childhood*.
'flash,back c/u.n part of a story, one's life, which occurred earlier than the main story or

present time. **in flashback** (told, shown) using the technique of flashback.

'flash,bulb *c.n* light bulb in a flash(2) which gives a short bright light when a photograph is taken in poor light.

'flasher *c.n person who* flashes(10) his sexual organs in public.

,flash 'flood *c.n* sudden short but violent flood after a rainstorm: *Flash floods are common in desert areas after heavy rainfall.*

'flashiness *u.n* fact or state of being flashy.

'flash,light *c.n* **1** light that goes on and off, e.g in a lighthouse. **2** small electric torch. **3** ⇒ flash(2).

'flashy *adj* (*-ier, -iest*) **1** (usu *derog*) large, bright and often looking expensive, but in reality cheap and of poor quality: *flashy jewellery; flashy clothes.* **2** excessively showy: *a flashy car.*

flask /flɑːsk/ *c.n* (often — *of s.t*) **1** (also **'thermos/'vacuum ,flask**) (amount contained in a) container for keeping hot or cold liquids at the same temperature: *She takes a flask of tea to work every day.* **2** (also **'hip ,flask**) small flat bottle for carrying alcoholic(1) drinks in one's pocket: *He always took a flask of* brandy(1) *with him on his walks.* **3** glass bottle with a narrow neck, used for oil, wine etc and also in chemistry experiments.

flat /flæt/ *adj* (*-tt-*) **1** level; having an even surface: *We need a large flat surface to lay the papers on.* **2** having a wide level surface and little depth: *My cake didn't rise enough and it's rather flat.* **3** (of a tyre) with little or no air in it: *I'm sorry I'm late but I had a flat tyre.* **4** (of a battery) without an electrical charge: *We couldn't start the car because the battery was flat.* **5** (of liquids, esp fizzy cold drinks) no longer fizzy: *This* coke(2) *is flat.* **6** (*music*) (of a note) lower in tone(1) than the natural(3) note: *C flat (C♭*). (Notice that 'flat' comes after the name of the note.) ⇒ sharp(12). **7** (*music*) below the correct note(5): *Oh dear, that was a flat note.* ⇒ sharp(13). **8** (usu *pred*) dull; without interest: *The party was flat at first but it improved after about 10 o'clock.* **9** (*attrib*) direct; complete: *a flat refusal. She gave a flat 'no' to my request.* **as flat as a pancake** very flat(1,3): *The countryside was as flat as a pancake.* **fall flat** ⇒ fall(*v*). **go flat** become flat(3–8): *My tyre has gone flat. The battery's gone flat. This coke has gone flat. You've (your playing, singing etc has) gone flat. The party went flat after they left.* **(and) that's flat!** (*informal*) (and) I won't change my decision: *You're not going out tonight and that's flat.* ⇒ flat(11).

▷ *adv* **10** stretched horizontally (on the ground): *Lie flat on your back. He fell flat on his face.* (*informal*) directly; completely; absolutely: *He was told flat that he could not leave early.* **12** (*music*) in a flat(7) way: *He plays (the violin) flat.* **flat broke** ⇒ broke(*adj*). **flat out** (*informal*) as fast as possible; with all one's effort, strength etc: *I ran flat out but I still missed the bus. He worked flat out all week and rested over the weekend.*

▷ *n* **13** *c.n* (also, esp US, **a'partment**) group of rooms including a kitchen, bedroom(s), bathroom, living-room etc, usu on the same level in a building: *Many of the large old houses have been divided into flats.* **14** *c.n* tyre with little or no air in it: *We've got a flat so we'll have to change the tyre.* **15** *c.n* (*music*) note that is half

a tone(1) lower than a natural(3) note. ⇒ flat(6). ⇒ sharp(17). **16** (usu *pl*) area of low flat(1) land, esp near water: *mud flats.* **17** *def.n* = flat racing. **the flat of s.t** flat side, part, (of s.t): *He hit the boy with the flat of his hand.* **on the flat** on level ground: *I'll park my car on the flat because I'm not sure about the brakes.*

,flat-'bottomed *adj* having a flat(1) bottom: *a flat-bottomed boat.*

'flat,fish *c.n* (*pl* flatfish) one of many kinds of fish having a wide flat(2) body, e.g a plaice(1).

,flat-'footed *adj* **1** (of one's feet) having flat(1) soles³(1) with a low or no arch¹(3). **2** (*derog; informal*) awkward; clumsy(3): *a flat-footed remark.*

'flatly *adv* absolutely; completely; directly; plainly: *She flatly refused to go to the wedding.*

'flatness *u.n.*

'flat ,race *c.n* horse race over level ground and with no fences to jump over.

'flat ,racing *u.n* (also **the Flat**) racing of this kind.

'flat ,rate *c.n* price that is the fixed one for each kind of service etc: *We agreed to do the work for a flat rate.*

,flat 'spin *c.n* (usu be in, get into, a —) (*informal*) state of great nervousness, confusion etc: *We were all in a flat spin trying to get things ready.*

'flatten *v* **1** *tr/intr.v* (cause(s.t) to) become flat(1): *The road flattens after the next hill. She flattened herself against the wall as the car sped past.* **2** *tr.v* (*fig*) make (s.o) become far less confident: *She flattened me with her remarks.*

flatter /'flætə/ *tr.v* **1** give (s.o) too much praise; try to please (s.o) with praise that is not (totally) sincere: *You're flattering me because you want something from me.* **2** give (s.o) a feeling of pleasure: *She was flattered by everyone's kind remarks.* **3** (esp of pictures) show (s.o/s.t) as better than he/she/it really is: *That photograph doesn't flatter you at all.* **flatter oneself (that . . .)** be pleased to be able to say (sometimes wrongly) (that one can do s.t etc): *I flatter myself that I could speak six languages by the time I was twelve years old.*

'flatterer *c.n* person who flatters(1,2) s.o.

'flattering *adj* that flatters s.o/s.t: *That photograph is not very flattering.*

'flattery *n* (*pl-ies*) **1** *u.n* act or fact of flattering(1, 2) s.o: *Flattery will get you nowhere* (You will gain nothing by flattering(1,2) me). **2** *c.n* example of praise that is not sincere.

flatulence /'flætjʊləns/ *u.n* (*formal*) gas in the stomach and discomfort caused by this: *He suffers from flatulence if he eats too quickly.*

flaunt /flɔːnt/ *tr.v* attract attention to oneself/ s.t by showing (oneself/s.t) in an excessive way: *We're tired of the way you flaunt your success.*

flautist /'flɔːtɪst/ *c.n* person who plays the flute.

flavour /'fleɪvə/ *n* (US **'flavor**) **1** *c/u.n* (particular kind of) taste: *What flavour of ice-cream would you like? Her food is always full of flavour.* **2** *sing.n* (often a — *of s.t*) suggestion (of s.t): *There was a flavour of hatred in her voice.*

▷ *tr.v* (often — *s.t with s.t*) **3** give flavour(1) to (s.t esp food) (by using s.t): *She flavoured the meat with wine and* herbs. **4** (*fig*) give special character, quality, to (s.t): *She flavoured her story with interesting bits of information.*

'flavouring *u.n* (US **'flavoring**) substance used for adding (a particular kind of) flavour to food: *chocolate/lemon flavouring.*

'flavourless *adj* (US **'flavorless**) without flavour(1): *That meal was flavourless.*

flaw /flɔː/ *c.n* **1** fault; thing that reduces the beauty, perfection or value (of s.t): *This jacket has a slight flaw in the material. There must be a flaw in her character as no one is perfect. The flaw in that argument is easy to see.*
▷ *tr.v* **2** reduce the perfection, quality, of (s.t): *He flawed his argument by using out-of-date facts.*

flawed *adj* having a flaw(1): *flawed cloth/ beauty.*

'flawless *adj* perfect; having no flaws(1): *a flawless diamond; a flawless performance.*

flax /flæks/ *u.n* plant whose seeds produce linseed oil and whose fibres are used to weave cloth.

'flaxen *adj* (of hair) of, like, flax; pale yellow.

flay /fleɪ/ *tr.v* **1** take, strip, the skin off (an animal). **2** (*fig*) beat (s.o) severely. **3** (*fig*) criticize (s.o) very strongly.

flea /fliː/ *c.n* kind of small insect with no wings and a powerful jump; it sucks blood: *Her cat has fleas.*

'flea,bite *c.n* **1** bite from a flea which causes discomfort or irritation(1). **2** (*fig*) small irritation(1) or annoyance: *This test is a mere fleabite compared to the examinations next year.*

'flea ,market *c.n* market where one can buy cheap or second-hand goods.

fleck /flek/ *c.n* **1** very small spot or bit: *Can you see the flecks of dust in the light?*
▷ *tr.v* **2** mark (s.o/s.t) with flecks(1): *The bird's back was flecked with small red feathers.*

fled /fled/ *p.t,p.p* of flee.

fledged /fledʒd/ *adj* (completely) developed (esp of a young bird's feathers so that it can fly). ⇒ fully-fledged (⇒ full).

'fledgling *c.n* **1** young bird that is learning to fly. **2** (*fig*) young person who does not have much experience yet.

flee /fliː/ *tr/intr.v* (*p.t,p.p* fled /fled/) (often — *from* s.w) (*formal*) run away, escape, ((from) s.o/ s.t/s.w): *They fled the country to escape their debts. Thousands of people are fleeing from the danger of the leaking poisonous gas. They collected their valuables and fled.* ⇒ flight².

fleece /fliːs/ *c/u.n* **1** sheep's coat of wool.
▷ *tr.v* **2** cut wool from (a sheep). **3** (*fig; informal*) rob (s.o) (esp of money): *I was fleeced (of all my money) at tonight's card game.*

'fleecy *adj* (*-ier, -iest*) made of, soft like, fleece: *a fleecy coat.*

fleet¹ /fliːt/ *adj* **fleet of foot** (also ,**fleet-'footed**) (*literary*) able to move quickly.

'fleeting *attrib.adj* that passes quickly: *a fleeting glimpse(1); a fleeting visit.*

fleet² /fliːt/ *c.n* **1** number of warships under one command; all the warships of a country (their navy): *the American fleet.* **2** number of buses, ships, taxis etc under single ownership.

flesh /fleʃ/ *n* **1** *u.n* soft substance, meat, that covers the bones of animal bodies: *Chicken flesh is lighter than that of other animals.* **2** *u.n* soft part of fruit and vegetables. **3** *def.n* (*literary*) body (as compared with mind), esp sexual desire: *the weaknesses of the flesh.* **flesh and blood**

(a) family, relative(s): *I can't refuse her because she's my own flesh and blood.* (b) human nature: *It's more than flesh and blood can bear.* **in the flesh** actually there; in person: *I've seen pictures of her but I've never seen her in the flesh.* **make s.o's flesh creep** make s.o feel very frightened or disgusted.
▷ *tr.v* **4 flesh s.t out** make s.t, e.g a report, more complete by adding details etc: *You need to flesh out your ideas and make the characters more real.*

'flesh-,eating *adj* (usu *attrib*) that eats meat: *Lions are flesh-eating animals but cows only eat grass.*

'fleshiness *u.n* fact or state of being fleshy.

'flesh ,wound *c.n* wound that is not deep.

'fleshy *adj* (*-ier, -iest*) like flesh(1); fat; juicy: *I love fleshy fruits like peaches(2).*

flew /fluː/ *p.t* of fly².

flex¹ /fleks/ *c/u.n* (*pl* -es) (piece of) covered (insulated(1)) wire that carries electric current.

flex² /fleks/ *tr.v* bend and stretch (an arm, muscle(1) etc) esp in order to test it: *Flex your leg and see if it hurts.*

flexibility /ˌfleksəˈbɪlɪtɪ/ *u.n* **1** ability to bend easily (without breaking): *There's not much flexibility in these shoes.* **2** (*fig*) ability to change according to particular situations or conditions: *The flexibility of our programme will enable people to do different things at different times.*

'flexible *adj* Opposite inflexible. **1** able to be bent easily (without breaking): *a flexible material that will not break easily.* **2** (*fig*) able to change according to particular situations, conditions: *flexible working hours.*

flick /flɪk/ *c.n* **1** quick light movement, e.g with the tip of a finger: *With a flick of the finger she told him to leave.* **2** short sharp sudden and often twisting movement: *A flick of the wrist sent the stone jumping over the water.*
▷ *v* **3** *tr.v* touch (s.o/s.t) with a quick light movement: *Flick the switch to turn the light on or off.* **4** *tr.v* (often — *s.t at* s.o/s.t; — *s.t away, off s.t* etc) move, remove, (s.t) by hitting it with a flick(2) (in the direction of s.o etc): *She flicked her cigarette ash into the ashtray. He flicked the insect off her arm.* **flick through s.t** turn the pages of a book etc quickly: *She flicked through the magazine and decided not to buy it.*

'flick-,knife *c.n* (*pl* -,knives) kind of knife with a blade that springs out of the handle when a button is pressed.

flicker /ˈflɪkə/ *c.n* **1** unsteady light, flame or movement: *We watched the flicker of sunlight on the leaves.* **2** (*fig*) (usu *a — of s.t*) thing that lasts for only a short time (and that shows s.t): *There was a flicker of a smile and then he was serious again.*
▷ *intr.v* **3** (of light) burn or shine unsteadily: *We watched the city lights flickering in the distance.* **4** (*fig*) be present, move, unsteadily: *Hope still flickered in her heart.*

flier ⇒ flyer.

flies /flaɪz/ **1** *pl* of fly¹. **2** *3rd person pres.t* of fly².

flight¹ /flaɪt/ *c/u.n* (act of) escaping, fleeing (⇒ flee) or running away, esp from danger: *It's the story of their flight from a country at war.*

flight² ⇒ fly².

flimsy /'flɪmzɪ/ adj (-ier, -iest) **1** thin; light: flimsy cloth. **2** weak; easily broken: That envelope is too flimsy for a heavy object. **3** (fig) weak: Surely you don't expect me to believe such a flimsy excuse! **'flimsily** adv. **'flimsiness** u.n.

flinch /flɪntʃ/ intr.v move away, move back, suddenly because of fear, pain: He flinched when he put his toe into the icy water. **flinch from (doing) s.t** avoid (doing) s.t unpleasant: She always flinched from punishing her children.

fling /flɪŋ/ c.n **1** sudden sharp throw: He threw the rope over the right branch in one fling. **2** (usu have a —) (informal) short length of time of uncontrolled pleasure: He had a fling on the last day of his holiday.

▷ v (p.t,p.p flung /flʌŋ/) **3** tr.v (often — s.t away, at s.o, etc) throw (s.o/s.t) quickly, with force (at s.o etc): They flung their hats into the air. **4** reflx/tr.v move (oneself, one's arms etc) angrily, quickly, violently etc: She flung herself onto her bed. He flung his arms in the air and shouted angrily. **fling s.t away** ⇒ fling(3). **fling s.t off** (a) take (s.t) off very quickly: She flung off her school uniform(2) and put on her jeans. (b) get rid of (s.t): She managed to fling off her cold by staying in bed for two days. **fling out (of s.w)** leave (s.w) angrily: She flung out of the room in tears. **fling s.o/s.t out (of s.w)** remove s.o/s.t with (great) force or speed (from s.w): His mother flung him out of the house. **fling oneself into s.t** (fig) begin doing s.t with great eagerness: She flung herself into her painting lessons. **fling s.o/s.t into s.t** throw s.o/ s.t into s.t: They flung the drunk into prison. He flung a few clothes into a bag and left hurriedly.

flint /flɪnt/ n **1** u.n kind of very hard stone. **2** c.n piece of this stone used to produce a spark(1) by hitting it against steel.

flip /flɪp/ c.n **1** quick light movement (of the fingers, body etc), esp to turn s.t over: He turned the card over with a flip of his finger.

▷ tr.v (-pp-) **2** cause (s.t) to turn over by a quick light movement, esp of the fingers: I flipped the pages of the magazine. **flip a coin** ⇒ coin(n). **flip (s.t) over** turn (s.t) over by a quick light movement of the fingers: Flip the record over; I'd like to hear the other side. **flip through s.t** turn the pages of a book etc quickly without reading thoroughly: I'll flip through the newspaper to see what the headlines(1) are.

'flip-,flop c.n (informal) one of a pair of open shoes with a strap(1) between the toes.

'flip ,side c/def.n side of a record¹(1) which is considered to be less popular.

flippant /'flɪpənt/ adj (derog) not serious or showing respect: How can you be so flippant about something so serious? **'flippancy** u.n. **'flippantly** adv.

flipper /'flɪpə/ c.n **1** flat broad part, like a wing, on the side of a whale, penguin etc, used for swimming. **2** object like a flipper(1), usu made of rubber or plastic, worn on one's foot to increase one's speed or power when swimming.

flirt /flɜ:t/ c.n **1** (derog) person who tries to attract s.o.'s attention in a sexual way but without serious intentions.

▷ intr.v **2** (often — with s.o) behave as or like a flirt(1) (with s.o): He flirts with every woman he meets. **3** (often — with s.t) think about doing s.t but usu not in a serious way: She flirted with the idea of becoming a nurse.

flirtation /flɜ:'teɪʃən/ c/u.n the act or fact of flirting(2).

flirtatious /flɜ:'teɪʃəs/ adj (derog; formal) (of a person, her/his behaviour) fond of flirting(2). **flir'tatiously** adv. **flir'tatiousness** u.n.

flit /flɪt/ c.n **1** (esp do a (moonlight) —) (informal) secret move from one place to another (at night), esp to avoid paying s.t, e.g rent.

▷ intr.v (-tt-) **2** move quickly and quietly from one place to another: The butterfly flitted from one flower to the next. **3** (informal) move secretly from one house to another, esp to avoid paying the rent etc. **flit through one's mind** pass quickly through one's mind: A strange thought flitted through her mind.

float /fləʊt/ c.n **1** piece of cork(1) (or other light material) fastened to a fishing-line which moves when a fish has been hooked. **2** one of the pieces of cork etc fixed round the edge of a fishing-net to support it in the water. **3** hollow ball that controls the level of water in a tank. Compare ballcock. **4** vehicle, esp one with an open back, which is decorated for use in a procession. **5** (informal) amount of money needed at the start of trading in order to give change, pay small bills etc: a petty cash float.

▷ v **6** tr/intr.v (cause (s.t) to) be supported in air or on the surface of a liquid: The children floated the boats they'd built on the pond. Cork(1) floats on water. **7** tr.v start (a new business): We managed to raise enough money to float our own business. **8** tr.v allow the rate (at which the money of one country) is exchanged for foreign money) to vary: The government tried to improve trade by floating the pound. **float about/around (s.t)** (a) move about on the surface of (s.t esp a liquid) or in air. (b) (fig) move around with no particular purpose: You've been floating around for over six months now and you must look for a job.

'floating adj (usu attrib) **1** that floats(6): a floating bridge. **2** (fig) that changes or varies: Most university towns have a large floating population because of the students who come and go.

,floating 'vote c.n vote of a person or persons who does/do not support any political party (and is/are not sure which party to vote for).

,floating 'voter c.n person who does not support any political party.

flock¹ /flɒk/ n **1** c/def.pl.n (usu — of s.t) large number (of birds, animals) kept together or moving and feeding together: a flock of sheep/geese (⇒ goose(1)). **2** c.n (fig) large group or crowd of people: Tourists come in flocks to see the colleges of our university. **3** c.n group of Christians(3) who go to the same church.

▷ intr.v **4** come or go together in large numbers: People flocked to see the new film. **flock in(to s.t)** come/go in(to s.t) in great numbers: Supporters are flocking in(to) the meeting. **Birds of a feather (flock together)** ⇒ bird.

flock² /flɒk/ n **1** c.n small bunch of wool or hair. **2** u.n small pieces of wool or cotton waste, used to stuff soft furniture, toys etc.

flog /flɒg/ tr.v (-gg-) **1** beat, whip, (s.o/s.t) severely: The cruel man flogged his horse for refusing to jump the fence. **2** (slang) sell (s.t): I'm going to flog all my old records. **flog a**

dead horse ⇨ horse(*n*). **flog s.t to death** (*fig*; *informal*) repeat (an idea etc) so often that all interest in it is lost.

'flogging *c/u.n* (punishment by) beating with a stick or whip. **get, give s.o, a (good) flogging** receive, give s.o, a (severe) beating (as a punishment).

flood /flʌd/ *n* **1** *c/u.n* large amount of water flowing over land: *Heavy rain caused floods in the north of the country.* **2** *def.n* (with capital **F**) (in the Bible) time when the whole world was covered with water. **3** *c.n* (often — *of s.t*) great amount (of s.t): *A flood of light entered the room as she opened the curtains. Brian burst into floods of tears when his toy broke.* **in flood** in a state of flooding(4): *The river is dangerous when it's in flood.*

▷ *tr/intr.v* **4** (cause (s.t) to) overflow with water: *The river has flooded its banks.* **5** (*fig*) (often — *s.t with s.t*) put an excessive amount of (s.t) (into s.w): *The market is being flooded with cheap toys from abroad.* **flood in(to s.t)** (*fig*) come in(to s.t) in large numbers, quantities, amounts: *Replies to our advertisement are flooding in.* **flood out (of s.t)** come out (of s.t) in large numbers, quantities, amounts. **flood s.o/s.t out (of s.t)** force s.o/s.t to leave (s.t) because of a flood(1): *Thousands of people were flooded out (of their homes).* **flood s.o/s.t out with s.t** (*fig*) send s.o/s.t a very large amount or number of s.t: *We were flooded out with applications for the job.*

'flood ,gate *c.n* (often *pl*) gate that can be opened or closed to control the flow of flood water. **open the flood gates (to s.o/s.t)** (*fig*) allow free action (to s.o/s.t); allow ideas to be expressed freely: *If you listen to one person's complaints you'll open the flood gates to everyone to complain.*

'flood,light *c/u.n* **1** (beam from a) powerful artificial light: *The grounds can be lit up with floodlights. We're playing tennis under floodlights.*

▷ *tr.v* (*p.t,p.p* floodlit /-ˌlɪt/) **2** light (s.t) with powerful artificial lights: *During the summer the mountain is floodlit at night. It's a floodlit tennis court.*

floor /flɔː/ *c.n* **1** lower surface of a room on which one walks: *the bedroom floor.* ⇨ underfloor. **2** surface at the bottom of the sea, a cave etc. **3** all the rooms, passages on the same level of a building; horizontal division of a building: *My office is on the tenth floor of that building.* ⇨ first floor, ground floor. **4** main area of a hall: *When the band started playing, people went onto the floor to dance.* The chairperson *allowed three questions from the floor* (i.e from the audience in the hall). **5** (also *attrib*) (*commerce*) lower limit (of prices). Compare ceiling(4). **get/have the floor** (*fig*) have an opportunity to express one's opinion to the rest of the people at the meeting etc. **open the discussion** etc **to the floor** allow questions, remarks etc from the audience. **take the floor** (**a**) (*fig*) rise to speak in a debate(1), discussion etc. (**b**) (*informal*) begin to dance: *Find your partners and take the floor for the next dance.* **wipe the floor with s.o** (*fig*; *informal*) completely defeat s.o in an argument, fight etc.

▷ *tr.v* **6** put a floor in (a room, building etc): *I'd like*

to floor the whole house in wood. **7** (*informal*) knock (s.o) to the ground: *He floored the thief with one blow.* **8** (*fig*; *informal*) defeat, confuse, (s.o): *The last question floored me completely.*

'floor,board *c.n* one of the lengths of wood used to make a wooden floor.

'floor,cloth *c.n* piece of cloth used to clean a floor.

'flooring *u.n* material for making or covering a floor: *That shop sells all kinds of flooring.*

'floor,show *c.n* entertainment in a nightclub.

flop /flɒp/ *n* **1** *c/u.n* (example of a) movement (or noise of moving, sitting etc) in a tired or heavy way: *He sat down with a flop.* **2** *c.n* (*informal*) complete failure: *The play was a flop.*

▷ *v* (*-pp-*) **3** *intr.v* (often — *about/around*) move (about/around) in a tired or heavy way: *flopping about in the kitchen.* **4** *tr/intr.v* (cause (s.t) to) fall on, into, s.t in a tired or heavy way: *She flopped her book down on the table. He was so tired when he got home that he flopped into the chair.* **5** *intr.v* (*informal*) fail; be unsuccessful: *Our plans flopped and we had to think of new ideas.*

'floppiness *u.n* state or fact of being floppy.

'floppy *adj* (*-ier, -iest*) hanging down loosely: *She likes wearing floppy hats.*

flora /'flɔːrə/ *c/u.n* (*technical*) all the plants in a particular area. Compare fauna.

'floral *adj* (usu *attrib*) of, covered with, flowers: *a floral display; a floral pattern.*

florid /'flɒrɪd/ *adj* (*formal*) **1** excessively decorated: *a florid way of writing.* **2** (of s.o's face) naturally red.

florin /'flɒrɪn/ *c.n* British coin (until 1971) worth two shillings(1).

florist /'flɒrɪst/ *c.n* **1** person who grows or sells flowers. **2** (also **'florist's**) shop where flowers are sold.

floss /flɒs/ *u.n* (silk thread from the) rough threads spun by a silkworm. ⇨ dental floss.

flotilla /flə'tɪlə/ *c.n* (*pl -s*) group of small boats: *A flotilla was in the harbour to welcome the winning boat.*

flotsam /'flɒtsəm/ *u.n* (usu — *and jetsam*) parts of a wrecked ship and the goods it was carrying found floating on the sea. ⇨ jetsam.

flounce /flaʊns/ *c.n* **1** sudden impatient movement: *She went out of the room with an angry flounce of her head.* **2** ornamental strip of cloth sewn around the edge of a skirt, tablecloth etc.

▷ *intr.v* **3** (usu — *off, away, out* etc (*of s.w*)) move away etc with a sudden angry and impatient movement: *He flounced out of the room.*

flounder¹ /'flaʊndə/ *c/u.n* kind of small flatfish used as food.

flounder² /'flaʊndə/ *intr.v* **1** (often — *about*) struggle awkwardly, esp to get out of s.t: *The bird floundered helplessly but the oil on its wings prevented it from flying. We floundered about in the deep snow.* **2** be, become, confused: *She floundered with embarrassment(1) when he spoke to her.*

flour /'flaʊə/ *u.n* **1** white or light brown powder made by grinding (wheat) grain, used for making bread, cakes etc. ⇨ wholemeal.

▷ *tr.v* **2** cover (s.t, e.g s.t one is going to cook) with flour.

'flouriness *u.n* fact or state of being floury.

'flour ,mill *c.n* mill(1) where grain is ground into flour.

'floury *adj* (-ier, -iest) **1** of or like flour: *I don't like floury apples.* **2** covered with flour: *She made her hands floury before she shaped the bread.*

flourish /'flʌrɪʃ/ *c.n* (often — *of s.t*) **1** sweeping movement, esp with (s.t in) the hand: *She sent everyone out of the room with a flourish of her hand.* **2** decoration in one's handwriting (made by the sweep of one's pen). **3** short exciting piece of loud music: *a flourish of trumpets.*

▷ *v* **4** *intr.v* be healthy; grow or develop well: *Our garden is flourishing in this weather. His new business flourished for the first year.* **5** *intr.v* (of ideas, people) be active, well, successful, (at the time mentioned): *Learning began to flourish in Europe in the 14th century.* **6** *tr.v* (formal) wave (s.t) about: *The children flourished their flags as the procession passed by.*

flout /flaʊt/ *tr.v* deliberately go against (s.t); insult (s.o) by refusing to obey her/him: *You can't expect me to help you if you flout my wishes.*

flow /fləʊ/ *c/u.n* **1** (often the — *of s.t*) (also *fig*) act or state of moving forward/back etc in a steady stream or way: *the flow of the river along the valley. Something ahead has stopped the flow of traffic.* **2** (also *fig*) quantity, amount, (of s.t) that is directed toward s.o/s.w: *We'll need a strong flow of water. We received a steady flow of enquiries.* ⇒ overflow.

▷ *intr.v* **3** move along smoothly or continuously: *The river flows to the sea. The traffic is flowing again. Orders are flowing in.* ⇒ inflow. **4** (often — *down*, *along* etc) hang (down) loosely and gracefully: *Her hair flowed down her back. Her long veil flowed behind her.* **5** (often — *from s.t*) be the result (of s.t): *Knowledge flows from learning.* **ebb and flow** ⇒ ebb(*v*).

'flow ,chart *c.n* plan of how s.t moves through various stages from start to finish.

flower /'flaʊə/ *c/n* **1** part of a plant that is white or coloured and often has a smell: *My garden is full of flowers this year.* **in flower** in the state, time, of bearing flowers: *There is a lovely smell in the garden when the roses are in flower.* (**in**) **the flower of s.t** (*fig*) (in) the best or finest part or time of s.t: *She is in the flower of her youth.*

▷ *intr.v* **2** (of plants) produce flowers: *Roses flower in spring.* **3** (*fig*) reach the best state of development: *Kate's artistic ability flowered when she was in her forties.*

'flower ,bed *c.n* (small) piece of earth, e.g in a garden, for growing flowers.

'flower ,garden *c.n* garden where only flowers are grown (and not vegetables).

'floweriness *u.n* fact or state of being flowery.

'flowering *adj* that bears flowers: *A fern is not a flowering plant.* Opposite non-flowering.

'flowerless *adj* not having flowers: *Most plants are flowerless in winter.*

'flower ,pot *c.n* container for growing plants.

'flowery *adj* **1** (usu *attrib*) decorated with flowers; having or like flowers: *a flowery pattern; a flowery river bank.* Compare floral. **2** (*fig*) (of language) containing fancy or poetic words etc: *a flowery speech of thanks.*

flown /fləʊn/ *p.p* of fly[2].

flu /fluː/ *def/u.n* (*informal*) influenza.

fluctuate /'flʌktjʊˌeɪt/ *intr.v* change or vary often in number, price, level etc: *The price of vegetables fluctuates during the year. Her feelings for him fluctuate daily.*

'fluctu,ating *attrib.adj* that varies often: *fluctuating prices.*

fluctuation /ˌflʌktjʊ'eɪʃən/ *n* **1** *c/u.n* (often — *in s.t*) (example of the) act or fact of fluctuating: *fluctuations in house prices; fluctuations in the weather.* **2** *c.n* degree of fluctuating: *The value of the pound showed a fluctuation of 2 cents against the dollar.*

flue /fluː/ *c.n* pipe for hot air or smoke from a stove etc; small chimney.

fluent /'fluːənt/ *adj* (often — *in s.t*) able to speak (a language) easily and well: *She is fluent in French and English. My German is not fluent but I can express myself fairly well.*

'fluency *u.n.* **'fluently** *adv.*

fluff /flʌf/ *u.n* **1** small bit or thread of light woolly(1) material: *There were bits of fluff in the washing machine after she'd washed the blankets.* **make a fluff** (*informal*) make a small mistake: *He made a bit of a fluff when he forgot his words but the audience didn't notice.* ⇒ fluff(3).

▷ *tr.v* **2** (often — *s.t out/up*) shake (s.t) to make it fluffy: *The duck fluffed out its feathers to shake the water off. She fluffed (up) the pillows when she was making the bed.* **3** (*slang*) make a mistake in (s.t): *She fluffed her speech.*

'fluffiness *u.n* state of being fluffy.

'fluffy *adj* (-ier, -iest) **1** soft; woolly(1): *a fluffy toy.* **2** light and full of air: *fluffy clouds; fluffy pastry.*

fluid /'fluːɪd/ *adj* **1** able to flow: *a fluid substance.* **2** (usu *pred*) (*fig*) not fixed; able to be changed: *Our plans have to be fluid because of the uncertainty of the weather.*

▷ *c/u.n* **3** liquid: *You must drink lots of fluids.*

fluidity /fluː'ɪdɪtɪ/ *u.n* quality or state of being fluid (*adj*).

,fluid 'ounce *c.n* measure of an amount of fluid(3), equal to 2.841 centilitres.

fluke /fluːk/ *c.n* (*informal*) piece of unexpected good luck: *It was a fluke that she won that game.*

flummox /'flʌməks/ *tr.v* (*informal*) confuse (s.o): *It was the last question that flummoxed me.*

flung /flʌŋ/ *p.t,p.p* of fling.

flunk /flʌŋk/ *tr.v* (*informal*) (cause (s.o) to) fail (an examination etc).

fluorescent /fluə'resnt/ *adj* (of a substance) having the quality of changing energy(2) to bright white light: *All our offices have fluorescent lights.*

fluo'rescence *u.n.*

fluoride /'fluəˌraɪd/ *u.n* (*chemistry*) substance containing fluorine: *Some toothpastes contain fluoride which helps to prevent tooth decay.*

fluoridate /'fluərɪˌdeɪt/ *tr.v* add fluoride to (water etc).

fluoridation /ˌfluərɪ'deɪʃən/ *u.n.*

fluorine /'fluəˌriːn/ *u.n* kind of poisonous yellow gas, *chem.symb* F.

flurry /'flʌrɪ/ *c.n* (*pl -ies*) (often — *of s.t*) **1** sudden short rush (of wind), fall (of snow) etc. **2** (*fig*) quick, sometimes confused, movement (of s.t): *There was a flurry of activity when they arrived.* **in(to) a flurry** in(to) a state of confusion and anxiety: *There's no need to be in a flurry* (or *get into a flurry*), *they'll understand if we're a bit late.*

▷ *tr.v* (*-ies, -ied*) **3** cause (s.o) to become nervous, confused or feel rushed: *She's flurried by all the excitement and she'll be calmer in a few minutes.*

flush /flʌʃ/ *adj* (often — *with s.t*) **1** forming one continuous surface (with s.t): *The builder made sure the window frame was flush with the wall.* **2** (*informal*) having plenty (of s.t, esp money): *I'm feeling flush* (*with money*) *today so I'll buy you dinner.*

▷ *adv* **3** (often *fit* (*s.t*) — *into/with s.t*) on the same level (as s.t): *The door fits flush into the wall.*

▷ *n* **4** *c.n* sudden rush of water, esp to clear s.t (that is blocked etc): *Give the toilet an extra flush.* **5** *c.n* (heat and redness caused by a) rush of blood to the face: *She felt a hot flush as she was telling the lie.* (**in**) **the first flush of s.t** (*fig*) (in) the first stages of growth, development, an event, esp when (one is at one's) strongest, fittest, most effective: *She was most successful in the first flush of her youth.*

▷ **6** *tr.v* (often — *s.t out*) clean (s.t) by a rush of water: *flush the lavatory*; *flush out the pipes.* **7** *intr.v* (also — *with s.t*) become red with a rush of blood to the face (because of s.t): *The children's faces flushed with excitement.* **8** *tr.v* (usu — *s.o/s.t from, out of, s.w*) cause (s.o/s.t) to leave a place of shelter suddenly: *The escaped prisoner was flushed from* (or *out of*) *his hiding place by the police.*

flushed *adj* (usu *pred*, often — *with s.t*) made red in the face (because of s.t): *I become very flushed after hard exercise. Their faces were flushed with excitement.*

fluster /ˈflʌstə/ *u.n* **1** (esp *be in, get into, a* —) state of nervous confusion: *She was in* (or *She got into*) *a fluster when she couldn't find her bus ticket.*

▷ *tr.v* **2** cause (s.o) to become confused or nervous: *Stop flustering me.*

'flustered *adj* in a state of nervous confusion: *He gets so flustered when he has to make a decision.*

flute /fluːt/ *c.n* musical instrument in the shape of a pipe with holes on the top, played by blowing across a hole with the flute held sideways: *Can you play the flute?* ⇒ flautist.

flutter /ˈflʌtə/ *n* **1** *c.n* (usu *sing*) quick irregular movement (esp of wings) or sound (in a record player etc). **2** *sing.n* (usu *in a* —) state of nervous excitement: *She's in such a flutter about their holiday.* **3** *c.n* (usu *sing*) (often (*have*) *a* — (*on s.t.*))(*informal*) bet or gamble(1) (esp on horse races).

▷ *v* **4** *tr/intr.v* (cause (s.t, esp wings) to) move quickly and irregularly (usu without flying): *The bird fluttered its wings to frighten the cat away. She said I was fluttering my eyelashes at her husband!* **5** *intr.v* fly, move back and forth, with no particular pattern: *The flag fluttered in the wind.* **6** *intr.v* (esp of a heartbeat) make a quick irregular movement: *Her heart fluttered a few times before she finally died.*

flux /flʌks/ *u.n* (usu *in a state of* —) continuous change or movement: *We shall be in a state of flux until a final decision is taken.*

fly¹ /flaɪ/ *c.n* (*pl* -ies) **1** one of many kinds of small insect with wings: *Get those flies off the food.*

2 imitation of a fly¹(1) which is fastened onto a fish hook to catch fish (esp trout(1)). **3** (usu *pl*) opening at the front of trousers with a zip fastener or buttons. **4** = flysheet. **a fly in the ointment** (*fig*) thing that prevents pleasure from being perfect. (**there are**) **no flies on s.o** (*fig*) s.o is not a fool and cannot easily be tricked. **s.o would not harm a fly** s.o could not, would not, cause the slightest pain, hurt to anyone or anything.

'fly,catcher *c.n* **1** kind of small bird that catches insects while flying. **2** kind of plant that catches flies.

'fly-,fishing *u.n* fishing with a fly¹(2).

'fly,paper *u.n* sticky poisonous paper, used to trap flies.

'fly,swatter *c.n* object for hitting and killing flies.

'fly,trap *c.n* kind of plant that traps and eats insects.

'fly,weight *c.n* (also *attrib*) boxer(1) who weighs less than about 51 kg.

fly² /flaɪ/ *v* (*pres.p* flies, *p.t* flew /fluː/, *p.p* flown /fləʊn/) **1** *tr/intr.v* (cause (s.o/s.t) to) move or travel through the air (like an aeroplane, bird): *The children are in the garden flying their kites.* **2** *tr.v* send (goods, passengers) in an aeroplane: *We flew more than a million people to France this summer.* **3** *tr/intr.v* control (an aeroplane) in the air: *The pilot flew* (*us/the plane*) *over the Alps.* **4** *tr.v* use (a particular airline): *I always fly British Airways.* **5** *intr.v* go or pass quickly; become: *You'll have to fly if you want to catch the next train. The windows flew open. Time flies when one is having fun.* **6** *tr/intr.v* raise (a flag); (cause (a flag) to) wave in the air: *All the flags were flying.* **7** *tr/intr.v* escape or run away (from (s.w)): *They've flown* (*the country*).

as the crow flies ⇒ crow(*n*).

fly at s.o/s.t attack s.o/s.t suddenly.

fly in the face of s.t ⇒ face(*n*).

fly into a rage, temper etc become suddenly and violently angry: *He flew into a rage(1) when he heard that his son had damaged his car.*

fly off the handle ⇒ handle(*n*).

I, we etc **must fly** (*informal*) I etc must leave immediately or in a hurry.

let (*s.t*) **fly** (*at s.o/s.t*) send, throw s.t rather violently (at s.o/s.t): *John let fly* (*a list of rude words*) *at the referee*(2).

'flier ⇒ flyer.

flight² /flaɪt/ *n* **1** *c/u.n* act or fact of flying: *a bird's power of flight.* **2** *c.n* journey in a plane: *What time is your flight to London?* ⇒ maiden flight. **3** *c.n* (often — *of s.t*) number, group, (of birds) flying together: *a flight of ducks.* **4** = flight of stairs/steps. **5** *u.n* (often the — *of s.t*) (*fig*) movement (of s.t) through air: *the flight of a ball.*

in flight flying: *Come and watch the pelicans in flight.*

'flightiness *u.n* fact or state of being flighty.

,flight of 'stairs/'steps *c.n* set (of stairs/steps): *There are two flights of stairs between each floor of the building.*

'flighty *adj* (-*ier*, -*iest*) (*derog*) having ideas that change easily, quickly: *She's very flighty and one never knows what she's going to do next.*

,fly-by-'night *c.n* (*pl* -s) (also *attrib*) business set up for a short time only to make a profit and not to be trusted; person who is not to be trusted.

'flyer, **'flier** *c.n* person who flies²(3) (a plane, kite etc).

'flying *attrib.adj* **1** that moves very quickly: *He took a flying jump over the stream.* **a flying visit** a very short visit, usu made when passing through s.w. **get off to a flying start** (*fig*) have a very good beginning; start (s.t) extremely well: *The sales this year have got off to a flying start.* **knock/send s.o/ s.t flying** hit/knock s.o/s.t so that he/she/it falls violently (in all directions): *The boy ran into a woman and sent all her shopping flying.*
▷ *u.n* **2** act of travelling by air: *He prefers flying to travelling by ship.*

,flying 'colours *pl.n* flags which are flown to show victory. **pass s.t with flying colours** make a great success of s.t: *She passed all her examinations with flying colours.*

,flying 'doctor *c.n* doctor who uses an aeroplane to reach patients because of the large distances, esp in Australia and Africa.

,flying 'fish *c.n* kind of fish that can jump out of the water and fly a short distance.

,flying 'saucer *c.n* bright object shaped like a saucer (thought to be from outer space) which people claim to see flying at high speed across the sky. ⇒ UFO.

'fly,leaf *c.n* (*pl* -,*leaves*) page at the beginning or end of a book which has nothing printed on it.

'fly,over *c.n* road that is built over another road or railway: *The traffic problem in the city was reduced when the flyover was completed.*

'fly,past *c.n* ceremonial flight of aeroplanes low over a particular place where people are watching, e.g for the Queen's birthday.

'fly,sheet *c.n* material put over a tent and fastened to the ground.

'fly,wheel *c.n* (*technical*) heavy wheel that keeps the speed of a machine regular.

FM /ˌef 'em/ *abbr* **1** frequency(3) modulation. **2** *written abbr* Field Marshal.

FO /ˌef 'əʊ/ *abbr* **1** *def.n abbr* Foreign Office. **2** *written abbr* Field Officer.

foal /fəʊl/ *c.n* **1** young horse or donkey. **in/with foal** (of a female horse or donkey) pregnant.
▷ *intr.v* **2** give birth to a foal(1).

foam /fəʊm/ *u.n* **1** (also *attrib*) mass of small bubbles(1) that form on the surface of a liquid: *I like a good head of foam on my beer. I have a foam bath every night.*
▷ *intr.v* **2** form, produce, foam(1): *The soap foamed in the bowl of water.* **foam at the mouth; be foaming (with anger)** (*fig*) be very angry.

'foaminess *u.n* fact or state of being foamy.

,foam 'rubber *u.n* kind of soft rubber which contains very small bubbles of air, used to fill cushions, make mattresses etc.

'foamy *adj* (-ier, -iest) like foam(1); full of foam(1): *Beat the eggs till they are foamy.*

fob¹ /fɒb/ *c.n* (*old use*) **1** small pocket in a waistcoat for a watch. **2** (also **'fob ,chain**) chain for fastening a watch to clothing.

fob² /fɒb/ *tr.v* (-bb-) **fob s.o/s.t off** refuse to listen to (s.o, advice etc). **fob s.o off (with s.t)** trick s.o into accepting s.t worthless: *He had to fob her off with lies.* **fob s.t off (on(to) s.o)** trick s.o into accepting, taking, s.t worthless: *He tried to fob his broken furniture off onto me.*

FOB /ˌef ˌəʊ 'biː/ *abbr* free on board.

focus /'fəʊkəs/ *c.n* (*pl* -es or, less usu, *foci* /'fəʊsaɪ/) **1** (*technical*) point at which rays of light, heat etc meet. **2** point at which the sharpest outline of an object is seen through a camera, telescope(1). ⇒ in/out of focus. **3** (often *the — of s.t*) (*fig*) person, object or activity who/that is the centre (s.t) or who/that draws s.o's attention: *You'll be the focus of everyone's attention at the party.* **bring/get s.t into focus** (*fig*) make s.t clear, exact: *You must get all your ideas into focus before you meet the journalists.* **in , out of , focus** (of a photograph) made when the camera was set to give, not give, the clearest, sharpest outline of an object: *That picture is out of focus.*
▷ *v* (-s- or -ss-) **4** *tr/intr.v* set (a camera etc) to get a clear sharp outline of an object: *Have you focused (the camera) properly?* **5** *tr.v* (often — s.t on s.o/s.t*) direct (attention etc) (on s.o/s.t): *The workers are striking to focus public attention on the injustice of their situation.* **6** *intr.v* (*informal*) think clearly: *I'm so tired that I'm not focusing very well.*

'focal *attrib.adj* (*technical*) of, at, a focus(1).

,focal 'length *c.n* distance from the centre of a lens(1) to its focus(1).

'focal ,point *c.n* (often *the — of s.t*) (*fig*) centre of activity, interest (of s.t): *The sports club is the focal point of our town.*

fodder /'fɒdə/ *u.n* dried food, e.g hay, for farm animals.

foe /fəʊ/ *c.n* (*old use; literary*) enemy.

foetus /'fiːtəs/ *c.n* (*pl* -es) (US **'fetus**) (*technical*) young person, animal, bird etc developing inside an egg or womb.

'foetal *attrib.adj* (US **'fetal**) (*technical*) of or like a foetus: *She sleeps in a foetal position.*

fog /fɒg/ *n* **1** *c/u.n* thick mass of very small water drops in the air, esp near the surface of land, water etc, which is very difficult to see through: *Fog at sea can be very dangerous. Turn on your lights if you have to drive in (a) fog.* Compare mist(1). **2** *sing.n* (often *in a —*) state of confusion: *The mathematics lesson put me in a fog.*
▷ *v* (-gg-) **3** *tr/intr.v* (often — (s.t) up*) (cause (s.t) to) be covered or surrounded with fog or made cloudy, unclear: *The steam from my coffee has fogged (up) my glasses. The car windows are fogging up.* Compare mist(4). **4** *tr.v* (usu passive) (*fig*) confuse (s.o): *He was completely fogged by her refusal.*

'fog,bank *c.n* thick mass of fog(1) resting on the sea.

'fog,bound *adj* prevented from travelling because of fog(1): *fogbound passengers.*

'fogginess *u.n* fact or state of being foggy.

'foggy *adj* (-ier, -iest) **1** full of fog(1); not clear because of fog(1): *foggy weather.* **2** (*fig*) confused; unclear: *I have only a foggy idea of what you're trying to explain.* **3** (of negatives(8) or prints in photography) cloudy, not clear: *This part of the negative looks foggy.* **not have the foggiest (idea)** (*informal*) have no knowledge of s.t at all: *'What time does the train arrive?' 'I haven't the foggiest (idea)!'*

'fog,horn *c.n* kind of instrument that makes a loud noise, used for warning ships in fog(1).

'fog,lamp *c.n* (also **'fog,light**) lamp on a car etc which gives a yellow beam of light, for use in foggy weather.

fogy /'fəʊgɪ/ c.n (pl -ies) (also **'fogey**) (derog; informal) older person, usu considered by young people to be old-fashioned in ideas, dress etc.

foible /'fɔɪbl/ c.n unimportant, slight, weakness in a person's character, or unusual habit that a person enjoys which has become part of her/his character.

foil[1] /fɔɪl/ n 1 u.n very thin sheet of metal, used esp in cooking or to keep food fresh: aluminium/silver/tin foil. 2 c.n (usu sing) person or thing who/that makes s.o/s.t else seem much better: His brother's old car is a foil to his new one.

foil[2] /fɔɪl/ c.n kind of blunt sword with a button on its point, used in the sport of fencing[2].

foil[3] /fɔɪl/ tr.v prevent (s.o) from doing s.t planned; cause (a plan etc) to become useless: He was foiled in his plan to leave before they returned.

foist /fɔɪst/ tr.v (usu — s.t (off) on(to) s.o) pass (s.t worthless, useless) (on(to) s.o): He tried to foist a stolen television set on to us. They foisted all their old furniture (off) on us.

fold[1] /fəʊld/ c.n 1 mark or place where one part of a piece of paper etc has been bent over another part: He likes his trousers ironed with folds down the legs. 2 hollow part inside s.t that has bent over: Jill put the comic(4) inside the fold of another book so that no one would know she was reading it. 3 bend in a valley or hill and the hollow between the bends. **in folds** in such a way as to form a set of folds[1](1,2): The curtain hung in loose folds.
▷ v 4 tr/intr.v (cause (s.t) to) bend back so that one part of it is over another part: Fold the paper in half. 5 intr.v be able to be bent over or back: The bed folds and can be put away when it's not in use. Do the chairs fold flat? ⇨ unfold(1). 6 tr.v bend and hold (s.t) close to the body: She folded her arms. 7 tr.v (often — s.o/s.t in s.t) cover, wrap, (s.o/s.t) (in s.t): She folded the baby in her arm. 8 tr.v (usu — s.t in(to) s.t) (in cooking) mix (one ingredient) (into another) by turning them with a spoon: Slowly fold in the flour. 9 intr.v (usu — up) (informal) begin to laugh a lot: She folded (up) when she saw his blue hair. 10 tr/intr.v (often — (s.t) up) (cause (s.t) to) come to an end: The business folded during the strike. We'll have to fold up the shop if we don't increase the profits. **fold up** ⇨ fold(9). **fold (s.t) up (a)** (cause (s.t) to) fold(4,5) into two or more parts: Fold up the newspapers and put them outside. **(b)** ⇨ fold(10).

'fold,away attrib.adj (also **'fold-,up**) that folds(5), esp for storing: a foldaway/fold-up chair.

'folder c.n piece of folded(4) cardboard, used for keeping loose papers in.

'folding attrib.adj that folds(5): a folding bed.

fold[2] /fəʊld/ c.n 1 enclosure (for sheep): a sheep fold. 2 (fig) number of people who attend the same church. **return to the fold** return to the place where one originally came from, to the beliefs, religion etc one once held.

foliage /'fəʊlɪdʒ/ u.n (formal) leaves of a tree or plant.

folio /'fəʊlɪəʊ/ n (pl -s) 1 c.n (abbr f, pl ff) sheet of paper which has writing and a number on the front or on one side only; number of a page: How many folios is your manuscript? 2 c.n (formal) book made of large sheets of paper folded once with writing and a number on one side of the paper only. **in folio** in the form of folios(2): a few copies printed in folio.

folk /fəʊk/ attrib.adj 1 of the ordinary people, esp of things not learnt formally but through tradition: folk dancing; folk music.
▷ n 2 pl.n people in general: We didn't meet many folk on our holiday. 3 pl.n (also informal **folks**) family, esp parents: Do your folk(s) still live there? 4 u.n (informal) folk(1) music.

'folk ,dance c.n traditional popular dance.

'folk,lore u.n (formal) (study of) traditional belief, customs, stories etc of a people, which have been learnt through their stories, songs etc.

folks pl.n ⇨ folk(3).

'folk,tale c.n popular traditional story told to children.

follicle /'fɒlɪkl/ c.n (technical) place on the skin from which a hair grows.

follow /'fɒləʊ/ v 1 tr/intr.v be, come, go, happen, after (s.o/s.t); be etc next: They followed her into the room. He went first and we all followed (him). What followed was totally unexpected. 2 tr.v go in the same direction as (s.o, a road, river etc): If you follow this road you'll arrive at the station. She follows her brother wherever he goes. 3 tr/intr.v understand (s.o/s.t) clearly: The students found it difficult to follow the teacher/lecture. 4 tr.v act according to (s.o's advice, example etc): You should follow his advice. 5 intr.v (usu it —s that . . .) happen, be true, as a result (of s.t): Just because he was born in London, it doesn't follow that he knows everyone from there. 6 tr.v listen to, watch, study, (s.t) carefully and with interest: They followed every minute of the football match.

as follows in such a way as is about to be explained, stated: Do the job as follows: first clean the surface, then. . . .

follow s.o about/around follow s.o wherever he/she goes.

follow in s.o's footsteps do the same as s.o else has done before: Will you follow in your father's footsteps and become a lawyer?

follow on (informal) come a short while later: You go now and I'll follow on later.

follow s.t out do all of, complete, s.t, e.g a job, instructions: Did they follow out my instructions?

follow (s.t) through (a) (in sport) complete a stroke by continuing to move the bat[2](1), racket[1] etc after hitting the ball, esp in the direction one wants to send the ball. ⇨ follow-through. **(b)** provide everything that has been promised; complete the job: Many businesses promise after-sale service but not many follow (their promise) through.

follow (s.t) up (a) continue one's interest in s.t: The doctor followed up her patient's progress. **(b)** find out more (about s.o/s.t): I followed up that advertisement you showed me and they've got exactly what I want. ⇨ follow-up.

follow suit ⇨ suit(n).

to follow (coming) afterwards, later: We'll have soup, duck and cheese to follow. The rest of the books you ordered are to follow (in two weeks' time).

'follower c.n person who follows(1,4,6) or supports (s.o/s.t): Barbara's a follower — she'll never be a leader. Eric has many followers.

'following *attrib.adj* **1** that comes next: *I can't play this Thursday but I can the following Thursday. They met again (on) the following day.* **2** that is about to be mentioned: *The following example should help you.*
▷ *c.n* **3** group of supporters: *She has a large following.*
▷ *prep* **4** after: *We'll go to the theatre following dinner.*
▷ (*pron*) **5** one or more people or things about to be mentioned: *Will the following stay after the meeting: Peter, Mary . . . .*
'following ,wind *c.n* wind blowing in the same direction as a person, ship is moving. Opposite headwind.
,follow-'through *c.n* **1** (*sport*) act of following through (a) (a stroke). **2** act of following through (b) (a promise etc): *A company without follow-through will soon lose its customers.*
'follow-,up *c/u.n* (also *attrib*) second or later stage of an action or effort: *You'll need several follow-up visits after the operation. Did you get any follow-up to your newspaper advertisement?*
folly /'folɪ/ *c/u.n* (*pl* -ies) (*formal*) (often *the* — *of s.o/s.t*) (act of) foolishness (of s.o/s.t): *He reminded her of her follies as a young girl. He realized the folly of his behaviour and apologized.*
foment /fə'ment/ *tr.v* to encourage or cause (trouble etc). ⇨ ferment.
fond /fond/ *attrib.adj* loving: *She gave her husband a fond smile.* **be fond of s.o, (doing) s.t** like s.o/s.t, enjoy (doing) s.t: *I was fond of collecting stamps as a child. He's very fond of you.*
'fondly *adv.*
'fondness *c/u.n* (*c.n* usu *sing*) (often *a* — *for s.o/s.t*) liking (for s.o/s.t): *Her fondness for cream cakes is making her fat.*
fondle /'fondl/ *tr.v* touch (s.o/s.t) gently or lovingly: *She loves fondling her little dog.*
fondue /'fondjuː/ *c/u.n* food cooked at the table by dipping meat etc into hot boiling water, bread into hot cheese etc: *I love cheese fondue(s).*
font¹ /font/ *c.n* big container in a church, usu made of stone, which has water put in it to baptize babies with.
font² ⇨ fount².
food /fuːd/ *n* **1** *u.n* thing eaten by plants, animals and people which provides energy (1) for growth and movement etc: *Do you like Chinese food? This mixture is excellent food for indoor plants.* **2** *c.n* kind of food (1): *Do you buy frozen foods?* **food for thought** thing that makes one think about s.t: *Her ideas certainly gave us food for thought.*
'food-,mixer *c.n* electric machine that mixes (4) different kinds of food.
'food,stuff *c/u.n* (*formal*) (substance used as) food, esp in large quantities: *Do you have enough foodstuffs for the winter?*
fool /fuːl/ *c.n* **1** person who has no sense or whose behaviour is considered to be silly, stupid: *I was a fool to believe her. How could you be such a silly fool? Only a fool would behave like that.* ⇨ folly. **make a fool of oneself/s.o** do s.t that makes oneself/s.o appear a fool (1). **be no fool** be clever, sensible, and not easily tricked: *He's no fool when it comes to money.* **be nobody's** etc **fool** be a person who cannot be deceived, tricked:

She was not going to be anybody's fool and refused to pay such a price for the dress. **play the fool (with s.o)** behave in a silly joking way (with s.o): *He loves playing the fool with his grandchildren.*
▷ *v* **2** *intr.v* (esp — *about/around* (with s.o/s.t)) behave in a silly or stupid way (with s.o/s.t): *Stop fooling (about) with that knife or you'll hurt someone.* **3** *tr.v* cheat, deceive, (s.o): *She fooled us with her fancy talk. You can't/don't fool us.* **4** *intr.v* (often — *about/around* (with s.o/s.t)) be playful or not serious (with s.o/s.t): *I was only fooling (with you) and I don't really think you're ugly. He likes fooling around (with his friends) during the weekends.*
'foolery *c/u.n* (*pl* -ies) foolish act(s) or behaviour: *The children were sent to bed early because of their foolery.*
'fool,hardiness *u.n* fact of being foolhardy.
'fool,hardy *adj* (-ier, -iest) (usu — (*of s.o*) *to do s.t*) taking silly, unnecessary risks: *It is foolhardy of you to plan such a trip in this weather.*
'foolish *adj* **1** lacking good judgement, reason, sense: *It was foolish to drive so fast. He's a foolish young man.* ⇨ folly. **2** silly; stupid: *I felt so foolish in that hat.*
'fool,proof *adj* that can be easily understood, used and does not fail: *a foolproof plan.*
,fool's 'paradise *sing.n* (esp *live in a* —) state of happiness which is based on deceiving oneself and cannot last.
foot /fut/ *c.n* (*pl* feet /fiːt/) **1** end part of a leg on which s.o/s.t stands: *His feet ached from standing all day. Take one foot of the table and help me lift it.* ⇨ underfoot. **2** bottom; lower part: *We started our climb from the foot of the mountain. The cat usually slept at the foot of the bed.* **3** part of a sock etc which covers the foot (1). **4** (*pl* foot or feet; written abbr ft) measurement of length: *12 inches*(1) *equals one foot. A metre is a little more than 3 feet. Pam's only 5 foot 1 inch (5′ 1″) tall. Ben's six feet (tall).* ⇨ -footer. **5** (*technical*) division in a line of poetry which consists of one strong stress and one or more weak stresses as in 'U'nited/ we 'stand/ di'vided/ we 'fall' in which there are 4 feet. **6** (*literary*) step: *light of foot* (i.e able to walk softly). ⇨ fleet-footed. **be caught on the wrong foot** not be ready or prepared. **be on one's feet (a)** be standing: *I've been on my feet all day and I'm very tired.* **(b)** move into a standing position in order to speak: *He was on his feet immediately to answer the accusations against him.* ⇨ get to one's feet. **(c)** (*fig*) healthy again after an illness: *She's on her feet at last after a long attack of flu.* **bind/tie s.o hand and foot (a)** tie s.o up so tightly around the hands and feet that he/she cannot move or leave. **(b)** (*fig*) (esp passive) make s.o not able to give help because of rules, other promises etc. **drag one's feet** (*fig*) delay (s.t) by acting slowly. **fall on one's feet** (*fig*; *informal*) be fortunate, lucky, esp after a bad experience: *She always manages to fall on her feet.* **find one's feet** (*fig*) learn to manage alone: *Don't worry if you don't understand immediately; you'll soon find your feet.* **get/have cold feet** (*fig*) decide not to do s.t because of fear, anxiety: *She was going to go walking with them but at the last moment she got cold feet and decided to stay at home.* **get off on the right/wrong foot (with s.o)** begin a friendship, conversation etc

well/badly. **get s.o back on her/his feet** get s.o healthy again, confident again etc. **get to one's feet** stand up: *Everyone got to their feet when the judge entered the court.* **have a foot in both camps** (*fig*) be on, take, both sides (in an argument, discussion). **have/keep a foot in the door** (*fig*) be partly accepted; begin to be known; take the first step towards a final goal: *She knew she had a foot in the door when she was asked to attend the next meeting.* **have/keep both (one's) feet on the ground** (*fig*) be very practical, sensible and unlikely to do foolish things. **have/with one foot in the grave** (*fig*) be close to dying, esp because of old age. **land on one's feet** (*fig*) be fortunate, esp when it is not expected. **my foot!** (*informal*) (used to express disbelief) nonsense! **on foot** by walking: *We missed the bus and had to go home on foot.* **put a foot wrong** (*fig*) make a mistake; say, do, the wrong thing: *She hasn't put a foot wrong since she started the job.* **put one's best foot forward** (**a**) walk as fast as possible. (**b**) (*fig*) try as hard as possible: *You'll have to put your best foot forward if you want her to change her mind about you.* **put one's feet up** (often *fig*; *informal*) rest; relax(1): *I don't mind working really hard as long as I can put my feet up at the end of the day.* **put one's foot down** (*fig*; *informal*) be determined, firm: *I've allowed Sam to do most things he wants to but I'll have to put my foot down after so many late nights.* **put one's foot in it** (*fig*; *informal*) do or say the wrong thing: *I really put my foot in it when I asked how his wife was.* **run/rush s.o off her/his feet** (usu passive) (*fig*) be extremely busy. **set foot in/on s.t** (often negative) enter s.t: *She was so angry she promised never to set foot in their house again.* **stand on one's own (two) feet** (*fig*) support oneself; no longer need help from s.o else. **sweep s.o off her/his feet** (*fig*) fill s.o with strong feelings of love: *The young man has swept her off her feet.* **wait on s.o hand and foot** ⇒ hand(*n*). **walk s.o off her/his feet** cause s.o to walk so much that she/he is very tired.

▷ *tr.v* **7 foot the bill** (*informal*) pay the bill: *It's our turn to foot the bill for a meal at the Chinese restaurant.* **foot it** (*informal*) go on foot; walk: *Since we don't have any money we'll have to foot it.*

footage /ˈfʊtɪdʒ/ *u.n* length of film.

foot-and-ˈmouth diˌsease *u.n* very serious disease that affects cattle so that they have to be destroyed to stop the disease from spreading.

ˈ**foot,ball** *c/u.n* (also *attrib*) (leather or plastic(1) ball filled with air that is used in a) game played by two teams of eleven (or five (⇒ five-a-side)) players who kick a ball and try to score a goal: *a football match/player.* ⇒ Association football, rugby.

ˈ**football ,coupon** *c.n* coupon(2) used to enter the football pools.

ˈ**foot,baller** *c.n* person who plays football.

ˈ**football ,pools** *pl.def.n* organized betting (⇒ bet(2)) on the results of football matches.

ˈ**foot,brake** *c.n* brake in a car etc that is operated by the foot. Compare handbrake.

ˈ**foot,bridge** *c.n* bridge for people walking (not cars).

-**footed** *adj* having the number or kind of feet

shown by the first part of the word: *a four-footed animal. She's very sure-footed on the rocks.*

-**footer** *c.n* person who is as tall as the number of feet shown in the first part of the word: *He was a six-footer when he was sixteen years old.*

ˈ**foot,fault** *c.n* (in tennis) service which is not allowed because the player's foot was over the serving line.

ˈ**foot,hold** *c.n* **1** safe place or position, esp for a climber's foot while climbing: *The climber found a good foothold and rested for a short while.* **2** (often *gain/get a* — (*in s.t*)) small position in order to start (in s.t): *We have now gained a foothold in that market.*

ˈ**footing** *n* **1** *c/u.n* firm/safe place or surface for the feet: *He lost his footing and fell off the ladder.* **2** *sing.n* organized, settled, state (of affairs, business etc): *I'll help you until the business is on a good footing.* **gain/get a footing** (*in s.t*) (**a**) get a footing(1). (**b**) (*fig*) find a way of becoming accepted (into s.w, by s.o): *They have large parties in an effort to gain a footing in the community*(1).

ˈ**foot,lights** *pl.n* row of lights in front of a stage in a theatre.

ˈ**foot,loose** *pred.adj* **footloose and fancy free** independent and without cares or responsibilities.

ˈ**foot,note** *c.n* note, usu at the bottom of a page, which gives an explanation of s.t mentioned in a book, report etc.

ˈ**foot,path** *c.n* path for people walking in the country, mountains etc.

ˈ**foot,print** *c.n* mark made by a foot.

ˈ**foot,sore** *adj* having painful feet, esp after walking a long distance: *They were hungry and footsore after their adventure.*

ˈ**foot,step** *c.n* (sound of a) step of s.o walking: *I can hear footsteps downstairs.* **follow in s.o's footsteps** (*fig*) do as s.o else has done before: *She intends to follow in her mother's footsteps and become a doctor.*

ˈ**foot,stool** *c.n* low stool¹ for a person who is sitting to rest her/his feet on.

ˈ**foot,wear** *u.n* (*commerce*) boots, shoes etc.

ˈ**foot,work** *u.n* skilful use of the feet in dancing, sport etc.

for (strong form /fɔː/, weak form /fə/) *prep* **1** (showing extent in amount, distance, time): *We drove for a long time and then we walked for about eight miles.* **2** (showing movement, progress, towards): *The next train for Oxford leaves at 6 o'clock. They set out for home.* **3** intended to be received, taken etc by (s.o): *Are there any letters for me? There's someone on the telephone for you.* **4** (in buying and selling) in exchange for: *How much did you get for your car? You can buy a television for about £200 now.* **5** in order to get or have: *I would never ask my parents for money. Let's go out for a drink. Let's hope for good weather on Saturday.* **6** because of (the purpose shown): *I have to go to London for a doctor's appointment.* **7** (introducing s.o/s.t who/that one's thoughts or feelings are directed to): *He has no love for hard work. I'm very sorry for you. She has no respect for me.* **8** having the mentioned purpose or function(1) of s.t: *A thermometer is for measuring temperature. I need another shelf for my books.* **9** (used to introduce an explanation or a reason): *She gave several reasons for her anger. She's angry with me for coming home late.* **10** concerning: *Who is responsible for her safety? We were worried for you. I'm very pleased/happy/sad for you.* **11** showing intention in connection with (s.t): *We must buy some food for the picnic. Are you ready for school tomorrow?* **12** (used to show suitability and introducing the person or thing s.o/s.t is suitable for): *That's the perfect colour for her. Smoking is not good for you.* **13** with regard to (s.t): *have a good ear for music; have an understanding for science.* **14** instead of (s.o); in place of (s.o): *Will you do something for me? She went to the meeting for her father because he couldn't go. 'GB' stands for Great Britain.* **15** representing: *Who is the Member of Parliament for Oxford East?* **16** in favour of: *Who did you vote for? Who's for a swim? 'Are you for or against this plan?' 'I'm all for it.'* **17** considering (the conditions etc): *She's small for her age. There's a lot of rain for this time of year.* **18** as being: *He mistook my sister for me.* **19** in spite of: *For all his money, he was never very happy.* **20** (introducing one of the sides of a comparison): *I'll do two miles for each one of yours.* **21** (enough, too much etc (s.t) for s.o/s.t; too big, difficult etc for s.o/s.t) (showing connection with s.o/s.t): *Is there enough food for all of us (or for the weekend)? That's too heavy for you to carry.* **22** (in 'noun 'for' noun', e.g *man for man*, *weight for weight* etc) when one compares one man, weight etc with another man, weight etc: *Man for man the two teams have about the same amount of experience.* **23** (in 'be adj 'for' s.o/s.t to do s.t', e.g *be necessary for him to go* etc) **(a)** (expressing importance) that s.o/s.t should do s.t: *There's no need for you to go. It's essential for them to sign now.* **(b)** (expressing frequency): *It's not usual for him to be late.* **as for s.o/s.t** (used to draw attention to (s.o/s.t) in particular): *As for her I don't care if I never see her again. George loves tennis but as for football he doesn't like that very much.* **be (all) for s.t** ⇒ for(16). **be (in) for it** (*informal*) be likely to be punished: *You've broken the window — now we're (in) for it.* **but for s.o/s.t** ⇒ but(*prep*). **for all I, you** etc **care/know** (used to show that s.o does not care/know at all): *Tessa may not like him at all for all we know.* **for all that** ⇒ that(*pron*). **for a fact** ⇒ certain (*adj*), fact, sure(*adv*). **for ever** ⇒ ever, forever. **for example** ⇒ example. **for good (and all)** ⇒ good(*n*). **for instance** ⇒ instance. **for once** ⇒ once(*adv*). **I for one** I and perhaps other people: *I for one do not agree with her.* **Oh for s.t!** I wish I had (s.t): *Oh for some quiet!* **once and for all** ⇒ once(*adv*). For other phrases with 'for', e.g *for hire/rent/sale, for one thing, get on for s.t, take s.o/s.t for granted*, ⇒ the noun or verb.

forage /ˈfɒrɪdʒ/ *u.n* **1** food for cows, horses etc.

▷ *intr.v* **2** (often — *about (for s.t)*) search (in order to find, esp food): *They foraged (about) in the grass but couldn't find their ball.*

foray /ˈfɒreɪ/ *c.n* (often *go, be sent, on a* —) short attack/search, esp to get food, catch animals etc.

forbad, forbade *p.t* of forbid.

forbear¹ /fɔːˈbeə/ *intr.v* (*p.t* forbore /fɔːˈbɔː/, *p.p* forborne /fɔːˈbɔːn/) (usu — *from doing s.t*) (*formal*) stop oneself (from doing s.t):

I must forbear from saying anything to her yet.

for'bearance *u.n* (*formal*) patience: *Show some forbearance while her mother is ill.*

for'bearing *adj* (*formal*) patient: *a forbearing mother.*

forbear² ⇒ forebear.

forbid /fəˈbɪd/ *tr.v* (*p.t* forbade /fəˈbeɪd/ or forbad /fəˈbæd/, *p.p* forbidden /fəˈbɪdn/) (often — *s.o to do s.t*) order (s.o) not to do s.t; refuse to allow (s.t): *Should smoking be forbidden in public places?* **God forbid (that . . .)** I/we hope very much that (s.t will not happen): *God forbid that you should lose your job.*

for'bidden *adj* (usu *pred*) not permitted: *It is forbidden to drive without a licence.*

for'bidding *adj* unfriendly or threatening (⇒ threaten(2)) in appearance: *I don't like going to that place; there's something forbidding about it.*

force /fɔːs/ *n* **1** *u.n* (often *the* — of s.t) power, strength, (of s.t): *The force of the storm caused great damage. The force of her character gained her much respect.* **2** *c.n* person or thing with the power to cause change: *He was a powerful force in the Peace Movement.* **3** *c.n* organized group of police, soldiers etc trained for armed or military action: *the police force. The armed forces consist of the army, navy and airforce together.* **4** *c/u.n* (*science*) (strength, measurement, of) pressure etc at a point which affects the state of movement or rest: *Force is measured in newtons.* **brute force** ⇒ brute. **by force** using strength to make s.o do s.t against her/his will: *If you don't eat anything, you'll be made to eat by force.* **by force of numbers** because of having more people. **in force (a)** in large numbers: *The police were at the football match in force.* **(b)** (of a law, rule) in operation, applying: *A law is in force to make people wear seat belts when travelling in a car.* **bring, put (a law), come, into force** (cause (a law) to) begin operating: *When was this law brought into force?* **force of habit** (because of) having done s.t often before: *I still get up at six o'clock out of force of habit.* **join forces (with s.o)** unite (with s.o) in order to have greater power, strength.

▷ *tr.v* **5** use force to get or do (s.t): *We had to force our way through the crowds.* **6** (often — *oneself/s.o to do s.t*) cause or make (oneself/s.o) do s.t, usu against one's/her/his will: *She forced herself to eat though she wasn't really hungry. Don't force her to eat if she doesn't want to.* **7** cause (s.t) to open, esp by breaking or using strength: *I couldn't find my key so we had to force the door.* **8** cause (a plant etc) to develop more quickly than normal by using artificial means. **force s.o's hand** ⇒ hand(*n*). **force s.o from s.w** (use force to) make s.o leave a place. **force s.t from s.o/s.t** use one's strength, influence to get s.t from s.o/s.t: *She forced the key from the child's hand.* **force s.o into s.t** make s.o do s.t that he/she doesn't necessarily want to do: *I don't want to go but I'm being forced into it.* **force s.t into s.t** use force to make s.t fit into s.t: *Don't force the key into the lock.* **force s.o/s.t out of s.t/s.w** use force to make s.o/s.t leave, explain, s.t: *We were forced out of the meeting. The police forced the information out of the men they were questioning.* **force s.t (up)on s.o** make s.o accept s.t that he/

she does not necessarily want: *The responsibility was forced upon her; she didn't want the job. She became annoyed when he continued to force his attentions on her.* **force the issue** ⇒ issue(*n*).

forced *adj* **1** done or made with great difficulty and not naturally or freely: *a forced smile.* **2** artificially produced: *Forced fruit has no taste.*

'force-,feed *tr.v* (*p.t,p.p* force-fed /-,fed/) make (an animal, person) eat (and drink) esp when he/she/it cannot or refuses to.

'forceful *adj* powerful; strong: *a forceful speech.* **'forcefully** *adv.* **'forcefulness** *u.n.*

'forcible *adj* (*formal*) **1** (*attrib*) done by force: *The police made a forcible entry into a building.* **2** very strong: *a forcible argument to prove one's point.*

'forcibly *adv.*

forceps /'fɔːseps/ *pl.n* (*medical*) instrument used by a dentist, doctor etc for holding s.t tightly: *The dentist used forceps to pull out the tooth.*

'forceps de,livery *c.n* way of aiding the birth of a baby by using forceps.

ford /fɔːd/ *c.n* **1** shallow part of a river where it is possible to cross easily.

▷ *tr.v* **2** cross (a river etc) by walking or driving through a place where the water is shallow.

'fordable *adj* able to be crossed by walking or driving: *a fordable river.*

fore /fɔː/ *adj* **1** (*formal*) situated towards the front (part esp of a boat, train etc): *Our carriage is in the fore part of the train.*

▷ *adv* **2** (*formal*) at, in, towards, the front part, esp of a boat. Opposite aft. **fore and aft** from end to end of a ship; at the back and front of a ship.

▷ *c.n* **3** front part of a boat. **to the fore** clearly present and ready to be useful. **come to the fore** become well known, important: *She came to the fore as a journalist after her articles on the dangers of* nuclear(2) *power.*

forearm *c.n* /'fɔːrɑːm/ **1** part of the arm between the hand and elbow(1).

▷ *tr.v* /ˌfɔːr'ɑːm/ **2** (*formal*) prepare (oneself/s.o) in advance, esp to protect oneself/s.o: *I'm giving you some tips so you can forearm yourself.* Forewarned *is forearmed.*

forebear /'fɔːˌbeə/ *c.n* (also **'for,bear**) (usu *pl*) person from whom one is descended: *Our forebears have lived in this valley for hundreds of years.*

forebode /fɔː'bəud/ *tr.v* (*formal*) **1** be a warning of (s.t) that is going to happen: *The sudden stillness of the sea forebode a storm.* **2** sense (s.t, e.g that trouble is coming): *She forebode a death in the family.*

fore'boding *c/u.n* feeling of s.t bad about to happen: *He had a horrible foreboding about their trip.*

forecast /'fɔːˌkɑːst/ *c.n* **1** statement about what is likely to happen in the future: *Did you listen to the weather forecast this morning?*

▷ *tr.v* (*p.t,p.p* forecast or -ed) **2** say that (s.t) is likely to happen (at a particular time) in the future: *Rain is forecast for tonight.* Experts(2) *are forecasting a heavy fall in shares.*

'fore,caster *c.n* person who forecasts(2) s.t.

foreclose /fɔː'kləuz/ *tr/intr.v* (often — on s.o/s.t) (*law*) use the right to gain possession of

property etc (from (s.o)) when money has not been paid: *The bank is threatening to foreclose (on our loan).*

foreclosure /fɔː'kləuʒə/ *u.n.*

forecourt /'fɔːˌkɔːt/ *c.n* enclosed area in front of a building.

forefather /'fɔːˌfɑːðə/ *c.n* (usu *pl*) person from whom one is descended.

forefinger /'fɔːˌfɪŋgə/ *c.n* (also **'index ,finger**) finger next to the thumb, usu used for pointing.

forefront /'fɔːˌfrʌnt/ *def.n* (esp *in the — of s.t*) front; very important part (of s.t): *My holiday has been in the forefront of my mind for weeks.*

forego ⇒ /fɔː'gəu/ *tr.v.* to go before/in front of, precede, in place or time: *Experience must forego understanding.*

foregoing /'fɔːˌgəuɪŋ/ *adj/u.n* (usu *the — (s.t)*) already mentioned: *Remember the foregoing (reasons) and use them to explain your answer.*

foregone *attrib.adj* /'fɔːˌgɒn/ **1 a foregone conclusion** an ending that can easily be seen coming before it happens: *It was a foregone conclusion that she would get the job.*

▷ *v* /fɔː'gɒn/ **2** *p.p* of forgo.

foreground /'fɔːˌgraund/ *def.n* what can be seen in the front of s.t; view etc that is in the nearest part of a picture: *There were several animals in the foreground of the painting.* **in the foreground (of s.t) (a)** ⇒ foreground. **(b)** in the most noticeable position (in s.t): *In order to become known he had to remain in the foreground during the time before the elections.* Opposite background(1).

forehand /'fɔːˌhænd/ *c.n* (also *attrib*) tennis, squash² etc stroke made with the front of the hand facing forward. Opposite backhand.

forehead /'fɒrɪd/ *c.n* front part of the head between the eyes and hair.

foreign /'fɒrɪn/ *adj* **1** from, in, of, a country that is not one's own: *Are you good at learning foreign languages? There are a lot of foreign students at the university.* **2** not naturally to be found in a particular place: *There's a foreign object in my soup.* **foreign to s.o/s.t** strange to s.o/s.t; not natural to s.o/s.t: *Eating with* chopsticks *is foreign to her.*

,foreign 'aid *u.n* help given by rich countries in the form of money, education, advice etc to developing countries.

'foreigner *c.n* person from another country: *There are a lot of foreigners in Oxford in summer.*

'Foreign ,Office *def.n* (*abbr* FO) government department that deals with the country's foreign affairs.

foreknowledge /fɔː'nɒlɪdʒ/ *u.n* (*formal*) knowledge of s.t before it actually happens: *Do you have any foreknowledge of the arrangements for next year?*

foreleg /'fɔːˌleg/ *c.n* one of the front legs of an animal that has four legs.

forelock /'fɔːˌlɒk/ *c.n* (esp of horses) piece of hair that grows over the forehead.

foreman /'fɔːmən/ *c.n* (*pl* -men /-mən/) **1** experienced or skilled workman who is in charge of other workers. **2** (*law*) leader and person who speaks for a jury(1). ⇒ forewoman.

foremost /'fɔːˌməust/ *attrib.adj* **1** most well known, important: *He is one of the foremost writers of this century.*

▷ *adv* **2 first and foremost** ⇨ first(*adv*).

forename /ˈfɔːˌneɪm/ *c.n* one's first name, or one of one's first names, i.e before one's family name: *Write your forename here and your family name on the next line.* Compare Christian name, surname.

forensic /fəˈrensɪk/ *attrib.adj* (*formal*) of or referring to (courts of) law.

fo,rensic 'medicine *u.n* medical knowledge that is applied to legal matters: *A doctor skilled in forensic medicine was asked to give her opinion about the cause of death.*

fo,rensic 'science *u.n* science that deals with crime and criminals.

foreplay /ˈfɔːˌpleɪ/ *u.n* sexual behaviour, action, to prepare one's partner for sexual intercourse.

forequarters /ˈfɔːˌkwɔːtəz/ *pl.n* front parts of an animal including its front legs.

forerunner /ˈfɔːˌrʌnə/ *c.n* (often — *of s.t*) person or thing who/that is a sign of what is to come: *Autumn leaves are a forerunner of winter.*

foresee /fɔːˈsiː/ *tr.v* (*p.t* foresaw /fɔːˈsɔː/, *p.p* foreseen /fɔːˈsiːn/) know, sense, (s.t) before it happens: *How could anyone have foreseen what would happen?* Compare unforeseen.

fore'seeable *adj* that can be known, sensed in advance: *There is no foreseeable chance of our going to America.* Opposite unforeseeable. **for/ in the foreseeable future** within a fairly short space of time.

'fore,sight *u.n* (often *have the — to do s.t*) ability to sense future needs in advance and make the right preparations: *Fortunately, my brother had the foresight to book a hotel room otherwise we'd have had nowhere to sleep.*

foreshadow /fɔːˈʃædəʊ/ *tr.v* (*formal*) be, give, a sign in advance of (s.t unpleasant or unwanted that is going to happen): *The dark sky foreshadowed rain.*

foreshore /ˈfɔːˌʃɔː/ *c/def.n* **1** part of the shore that is without water when the tide goes out. **2** part of the shore between the sea and buildings, fields etc.

foreshorten /fɔːˈʃɔːtn/ *tr.v* (in drawings) draw (an object) with some lines shorter in order to show distance etc.

foresight ⇨ foresee.

foreskin /ˈfɔːˌskɪn/ *c.n* piece of skin which covers the end of the penis.

forest /ˈforɪst/ *n* **1** *c/u.n* (also *attrib*) large area of land covered with trees. Compare wood(2). **2** *c.n* (*fig*) thing that looks like a forest: *When you look out of his flat window, you see a forest of television aerials(2).* **under forest** covered with forest(1): *A large part of the land is under forest.*

▷ *tr.v* **3** plant trees on (s.t) to grow into a forest(1): *They intend to forest the hills.* ⇨ re(af)forest.

'forester *c.n* **1** official in charge of a forest. **2** person who works in a forest.

'forestry *u.n* scientific study and care of forests.

forestall /fɔːˈstɔːl/ *tr.v* (*formal*) do s.t first and so make it unnecessary or impossible for (s.o else) to do it or for (s.t else) to be done: *I wanted to go to Joan Armatrading's concert but was forestalled because all the tickets were sold early.*

foretaste /ˈfɔːˌteɪst/ *c.n* (usu *a* — *of s.t*) slight experience (of s.t) in advance: *Let's hope that this warm spring is a foretaste of a good summer and a mild winter.*

foretell /fɔːˈtel/ *tr.v* (*p.t,p.p* foretold /fɔːˈtəʊld/) say (what will happen) before it happens: *Some people claim they can foretell the future.*

forethought /ˈfɔːˌθɔːt/ *u.n* (*formal*) careful or kind consideration, thought or preparation for s.t in the future: *Her forethought made the occasion a great success.*

forever /fəˈrevə/ *adv* (also **for 'ever**) (for) always; without end: *She told him that this time he was leaving forever. Let's stay together forever.* ⇨ for ever (⇨ ever).

forewarn /fɔːˈwɔːn/ *tr.v* (*formal*) warn (s.o) in advance: *If you'd forewarned me I'd have been able to prepare something.* ⇨ forearm(2).

forewent /fɔːˈwent/ *p.t* of forego.

forewoman /ˈfɔːˌwʊmən/ *c.n* (*pl* -,women) female foreman.

foreword /ˈfɔːˌwɜːd/ *c.n* introduction at the front of a book which describes the writer etc.

forfeit /ˈfɔːfɪt/ *pred.adj* **1** (*formal*) taken (by law) as a punishment: *The extra wine you take into the country will be forfeit if you're discovered.*

▷ *c.n* **2** (esp in games) thing that must be given up, done, because one has done s.t wrong: *If you can't answer a question you have to sing a song as a forfeit.* **3** thing that suffers or is lost because one does s.t (wrong): *Your family is becoming the forfeit for working so hard.*

▷ *tr.v* **4** lose (s.t) as a result of s.t: *He forfeited his family life for his* career(1). *He forfeited his claim to the prize by throwing away his completed card.*

forfeiture /ˈfɔːfɪtʃə/ *u.n* (*formal*) act of losing s.t as a result of s.t: *The forfeiture of your right to vote is a result of not filling in your form.*

forgave /fəˈgeɪv/ *p.t* of forgive.

forge¹ /fɔːdʒ/ *c.n* **1** blacksmith's(1) workshop: *The farmer took his plough to the forge to be mended.* **2** furnace in which metal is softened before it is shaped.

▷ *tr.v* **3** shape (metal) by heating until soft and then pressing and hammering. **4** (*fig*) form (s.t, e.g a friendship, connection): *A strong friendship was forged between us over the months.* **forge ahead** make good progress (by working very hard): *They're forging ahead with the preparations.*

forge² /fɔːdʒ/ *tr/intr.v* make an exact copy of (s.t) in order to deceive: *He was sent to jail for forging* (bank notes).

'forger *c.n* person who forges² s.t.

'forgery *c/u.n* (*pl* -ies) (example of an) act, crime, of forging²; thing that has been forged: *That's not my signature on the cheque; it's a forgery.*

forget /fəˈget/ *v* (-tt-, *p.t* forgot /fəˈgɒt/, *p.p* forgotten /fəˈgɒtn/) **1** *tr/intr.v* fail to remember (s.o/s.t): *Surely you haven't forgotten my name! Please don't forget — the meeting's on Tuesday.* ⇨ unforgettable. **2** *tr.v* (often — *to do s.t*) fail (to do s.t) accidentally: *I forgot (to pay the telephone bill).* **3** *tr.v* leave (s.t) accidentally: *You forgot your bag in the restaurant.* **4** *tr/intr.v* lose the memory of (s.t once learned): *I used to be able to speak French as a child but I've forgotten it now.* **5** *reflex.v* (**a**) behave in a way that is not normal to one's character or situation: *In her anger she completely forgot herself and said some terrible things.* (**b**) behave in an unselfish way: *He forgot himself when he saw the child fall into the river and dived in to save her.* **not forgetting s.o/s.t**

(used to show that an invitation etc is also) including s.o/s.t: *You must all come to tea on Sunday, not forgetting the children.*

for'getful *adj* (*derog*) (of a person) who forgets easily: *It was very forgetful of you not to remember our appointment.*

for'getfulness *u.n.*

forget-me-not /fə'get mɪ ˌnɒt/ *c.n* kind of small plant with light blue flowers.

forgive /fə'gɪv/ *v* (*p.t* forgave /fə'geɪv/, *p.p* forgiven /fə'gɪvn/) **1** *tr/intr.v* (often — s.o for doing s.t) excuse, pardon, (s.o who has done s.t wrong): *Will you forgive me for lying to you? It's important to be able to forgive and forget.* **2** *tr.v* excuse (s.t); no longer be angry about (s.t): *Please forgive my foolishness.*

for'givable *adj* that can be forgiven: *Is a little lie forgivable?* Opposite unforgivable.

for'giveness *u.n* **1** act or fact of forgiving s.o or of being forgiven: *You will have to ask (for) forgiveness.* **2** ability or willingness to forgive: *Forgiveness is an important quality in a person's character.*

for'giving *adj* willing to forgive: *He's not a for-giving person.* Opposite unforgiving.

forgo /fɔː'gəʊ/ *tr.v* (also **fore'go**) (*p.t* for(e)went /fɔː'went/, *p.p* for(e)gone /fɔː'gɒn/) give up (s.t); manage without (s.t): *We'll have to forgo our holiday this year because we don't have enough money.*

foregone /fɔː'gɒn/ *adj* **1 a foregone conclusion** ⇒ conclusion.
▷ *v* **2** p.p of forgo.

forgot, forgotten ⇒ forget.

fork /fɔːk/ *c.n* **1** instrument that has two or more points, used for lifting food to the mouth when eating. **2** garden or farm tool with two or more points, used for turning or breaking up the soil, lifting hay etc. **3** place where a road, river, tree etc divides into two or more parts or directions; one of these directions: *Drive until you reach a fork in the road and then take the left one.* **4** part of a bicycle frame in which the wheel is fixed: *the front fork.*
▷ *v* **5** *tr.v* lift (s.t), dig (the soil), with a fork(2): *Then I forked the soil lightly to prepare for planting.* **6** *tr/intr.v* (of roads, rivers etc) divide into branches: *The road forks after the bridge.* **7** *intr.v* (of people etc) follow one of the forks(3) where a road divides: *We have to fork left at the bottom of the hill.* **fork (s.t) out (for s.t)** (*informal*) provide (money) (for s.t), pay (for s.t), (esp when one is unwilling): *You haven't forked out any money on this trip. Who'll fork out for my meal?* **fork up (for s.t)** (*informal*) pay (for s.t): *You owe me £5 so come on, fork up!*

forked *adj* having two or more divisions: *A snake has a forked tongue.*

ˌforked 'lightning *u.n* lightning(2) that has several branches.

'fork,lift *c.n* (also **ˌfork'lift ,truck**) vehicle with a platform on the front, used for lifting and loading large, heavy loads.

forlorn /fə'lɔːn/ *adj* (*literary*) unhappy.

for'lornly *adv.* **for'lornness** *u.n.*

form¹ /fɔːm/ *n* **1** *c.n* printed paper (with spaces for information requested to be written in): *You'll need to fill in this (application) form if you want a new passport.* **2** *c.n* class in some high

schools, esp when referring to a set of classes for children of about the same age: *'What form is Stuart in?' 'He's in the fifth form.'* **3** *c/u.n* (*grammar*) (example of the) way a word is written when it is doing a job in a sentence: *What is the plural form of 'person'? 'People' is a plural form of 'person'.* **4** *c.n* (often *a* — of s.t) particular kind, variety, structure(1), (of s.t): *These flowers are a form of the pea(1) family.* **5** *c.n* shape, outline, of s.t: *In the dull light we could see the form of a person sitting in a chair.* **6** *u.n* (often — of s.t) general arrangement, structure(1) that affects the result, shape, (of s.t): *I wrote it in the form of a letter. What form does this illness take?* **7** *c/u.n* (socially correct) way of behaving, speaking, writing: *It is bad form to interrupt someone who is talking. What form of address must I use, doctor or mister(1)?* **8** *u.n* (often in good etc —) state of fitness, training, (esp of people in sport, horses etc): *What form is the England team in? They're in excellent/good/bad/fine form.* **9** *u.n* (esp in/on —) (*informal*) performing (well, badly): *He's in fine form tonight and he's making everyone laugh. I wasn't on form so I played very badly.* **application form** ⇒ application. **be/feel on top form** be/feel very well, fit, confident etc. **take form/shape** = take shape (⇒ shape(*n*)).
▷ *v* **10** *tr.v* make (s.t) into the shape of s.t: *The children formed figures out of clay. They formed clay into figures.* **11** *tr/intr.v* (cause (s.t) to) become a certain shape: *Just before water boils, little bubbles(2) begin to form around the pot.* **12** *tr/intr.v* (cause (s.t, e.g ideas) to) develop, take shape: *It's too early to form an opinion about it. Our characters are formed from an early age.* **13** *tr/intr.v* organize, arrange, (oneself/s.o/s.t) in a certain way: *We formed ourselves into a working group. Join hands and form a circle.* **14** *tr.v* act as (s.t); be (s.t): *This area of study forms the first part of your course.*

formation /fɔː'meɪʃən/ *n* **1** *u.n* (often the — of s.t) act of forming or shaping (s.t): *We had a meeting to discuss the formation of a new committee.* **2** *c.n* thing that is formed or made: *These rock formations are the result of waves and rain.* **3** *c/u.n* arrangement of s.t in a particular shape: *Look at those lovely cloud formations.*

formative /'fɔːmətɪv/ *adj* (*formal*) causing s.o/s.t to develop, form, in a certain way: *Which are the formative years in a child's life?*

'formless *adj* **1** without a regular shape or form. **2** (*derog*) lacking order or structure(1): *a formless piece of writing.*

'formlessness *u.n.*

form² /fɔːm/ *c.n* long wooden seat, usu without a back.

formal /'fɔːml/ *adj* Opposite informal. **1** done, organized, according to strict rules: *You'll have to send them a formal invitation otherwise they won't come. It's a formal dinner/dance.* **2** suitable for a formal(1) occasion: *We have to wear formal clothes. Don't be so formal — call me Jack.* **3** (of behaviour) stiff in manner, not friendly: *He's very formal and he doesn't smile or relax(1).* **4** (of language) written, spoken using unusual words, exact grammar etc and not the natural ways of everyday conversation: *She speaks a very formal English.*

formality /fɔː'mælɪtɪ/ *n* (*pl* -ies) **1** *u.n* strict attention to rules etc: *I don't like the formality but that's the way she always organizes her dinner parties.* **2** *c.n* (often *pl*) action(s) required by habit, rule, custom etc: *There are so many* legal(2) *formalities connected with starting a new business.* **a mere formality** a thing one is expected or required to do but which has no real use or meaning: *Their marriage is a mere formality as they've been living together for five years already.*

formalization, -isation /ˌfɔːməlaɪˈzeɪʃən/ *u.n* act or fact of formalizing s.t.

'forma,lize, -ise *tr.v* **1** make (a plan, idea, agreement) formal(1) (esp by writing it down and by signing it). **2** make (an occasion) formal(1), e.g by requiring people to wear formal(2) clothes and behave formally. **'formally** *adv.*

formalin /ˈfɔːməlɪn/ *u.n* (*chemistry*) particular solution used as a disinfectant and to preserve (parts of) dead bodies.

format /ˈfɔːmæt/ *c.n* **1** (esp of books etc) shape, size: *This kind of book requires a large format.* **2** structure(1); arrangement: *It was decided that future meetings would have a different format.*

former /ˈfɔːmə/ *attrib.adj* **1** from, in, an earlier time: *Who was the former captain? They were very happy in former times.* **2** of or referring to the first of two that have been mentioned: *The former idea is better than this one.* Opposite latter(1).

▷ *def.n* **3** first of two that have been mentioned: *I like London and New York but the former is safer to walk about in.* Opposite latter(2).

'formerly *adv* in earlier or past times: *Formerly, this lake was a beautiful green valley. She formerly worked in an office.* ⇒ latterly.

Formica /fɔːˈmaɪkə/ *u.n* (also *attrib*) (*t.n*) material which resists heat and is used for surfaces, esp in kitchens.

formidable /ˈfɔːmɪdəbl/ *adj* (*formal*) **1** frightening: *The climb looked formidable.* **2** (*fig*) difficult to handle, manage, overcome: *The difficulties we shall have to face are formidable.*

formula /ˈfɔːmjʊlə/ *attrib.adj* **1** (of racing cars) of the stated class: *Formula 1.*

▷ *c.n* (*pl* -s, formulae /ˈfɔːmjʊliː/) **2** short statement in signs or numbers of a law or rule (esp in science or mathematics etc): *Einstein's theory(1) is shown by the formula* $E = m \times C^2$ *where* E = energy(2), m = mass and C = the speed of light. **3** (*chemistry*) set of figures and numbers which shows what a substance consists of: *The* (*chemical*) *formula for water is* H_2O. **4** (set of) directions for making or doing s.t: *Is there a formula for success? We have found a new formula for making your teeth whiter.*

formulate /ˈfɔːmjʊleɪt/ *tr.v* (*formal*) **1** give (one's) thoughts, arguments a clear, fixed form: *The best way to formulate one's ideas is usually to write them down.* **2** express (s.t) in a formula(2).

formulation /ˌfɔːmjʊˈleɪʃən/ *n* **1** *u.n* act of formulating s.t. **2** *c.n* clear statement.

fornicate /ˈfɔːnɪkeɪt/ *intr.v* have sexual intercourse with s.o to whom one is not married. **'forni,cator** *c.n* (*derog*) person who fornicates. **fornication** /ˌfɔːnɪˈkeɪʃən/ *u.n.*

forsake /fəˈseɪk/ *tr.v* (*p.t* forsook /fəˈsʊk/, *p.p* forsaken /fəˈseɪkən/) (*formal*) give up, leave,

(s.o/s.t): *He has forsaken his* career(1) *for his family.*

forswear /fɔːˈsweə/ *tr.v* (also **fore'swear**) (*p.t* for(e)swore /fɔːˈswɔː/, *p.p* for(e)sworn /fɔːˈswɔːn/) (*formal*) give up (doing or using s.t): *He has forsworn smoking since the doctor's warning.*

forsythia /fɔːˈsaɪθɪə/ *c/u.n* kind of small bush with bright yellow flowers.

fort /fɔːt/ *c.n* building(s) strong enough to provide a defence against an enemy. ⇒ fortify(1), fortress. **hold the fort** look after a place, shop etc for a short time.

forte¹ /ˈfɔːteɪ/ *adj/adv* (*written abbr f*) (*music*) (played) loud(ly). ⇒ fortissimo.

forte² /ˈfɔːteɪ/ *c.n* thing that one can do well: *Baking is not my forte.*

forth /fɔːθ/ *adv* **1** (esp *back and* —) forwards: *I've been going back and forth between our two houses all day.* Compare backwards and forwards. **2** (*formal*) onwards: *I never saw him again from that day forth.* **and so forth/on** ⇒ so¹(*adv*). **go/ set forth** ⇒ go(*v*), set²(*v*). **hold forth** ⇒ hold(*v*).

forthcoming /ˌfɔːθˈkʌmɪŋ/ *adj* **1** appearing, coming, happening, soon: *Do you have a list of forthcoming films/books?* **2** provided; available: *The bank manager warned that no more money would be forthcoming.* **3** (usu *pred*) (of a person) willing to talk, give information (about s.t): *She's not very forthcoming about the new job.* Opposite unforthcoming.

forthright /ˈfɔːθraɪt/ *adj* honest and direct: *They're a forthright group of students.* **'forth,rightness** *u.n.*

forthwith /ˌfɔːθˈwɪθ/ *adv* (*formal*) immediately: *He was ordered to leave the room forthwith.*

fortieth ⇒ four.

fortify /ˈfɔːtɪfaɪ/ *tr.v* (-ies, -ied) (*formal*) **1** make (oneself/s.o/s.t) strong and able to be defended, protected: *That shop has had so many robberies that it has now been fortified with extra locks and bars.* Take vitamins *to fortify yourself against sickness.* **2** make (food) richer or healthier by adding vitamins etc. **3** make (wine) stronger by adding grape brandy(1), alcohol.

fortification /ˌfɔːtɪfɪˈkeɪʃən/ *n* **1** *u.n* act of fortifying (s.t). **2** *c.n* (usu *pl*) walls, locks, bars etc for protection. ⇒ fort, fortress.

'forti,fied *adj* (usu *attrib*) (esp of wine) that has been made strong (by adding alcohol): Port³(2) and sherry(1) *are fortified wines.*

fortissimo /fɔːˈtɪsɪməʊ/ *adj/adv* (*written abbr ff*) (*music*) (played) very loud(ly).

fortitude /ˈfɔːtɪˌtjuːd/ *u.n* (often *with* —) (*formal*) courage and strength, esp during a long and painful or dangerous time: *She bore her long illness with fortitude.*

fortnight /ˈfɔːtnaɪt/ *c.n* two weeks: *I'll see you in a fortnight. We're taking a fortnight's holiday.* **a fortnight tomorrow, yesterday, today** etc two weeks after tomorrow etc. **on Monday** etc **fortnight** on the second Monday etc after next Monday etc. **'fort,nightly** *adj/adv* once every two weeks: *I have fortnightly appointments. Are you paid weekly or fortnightly?*

fortress /ˈfɔːtrɪs/ *c.n* group of buildings that are well fortified or strengthened for defence against an enemy or attack. ⇒ fort, fortification(2).

fortuitous /fɔː'tjuːɪtəs/ *adj* (*formal*) that happens by chance and not by planning: *a fortuitous meeting with an old friend.*
for'tuitously *adv.* **for'tuitousness** *u.n.*
fortune /'fɔːtʃuːn/ *n* 1 *c.n* large amount of money; wealth: *He made his fortune in the shipping industry. Our car cost a fortune but it's worth every penny.* 2 *u.n* chance; luck: *It was good fortune that brought us together. We met by good fortune.* Opposite misfortune. 3 *c.n* (usu *tell s.o's* —) things that will happen in the future: *She can tell your fortune by examining your hands.*
a small fortune a lot of money: *A car costs a small fortune to keep on the road.* **come into a fortune** inherit(1) a lot of money. **make a fortune out of (doing) s.t** (*informal*) get or earn a lot of money (by (doing) s.t): *He made a fortune out of selling used cars.* **seek one's fortune** attempt to gain success, wealth: *He went to the city to seek his fortune.*
fortunate /'fɔːtjənɪt/ *adj* lucky; caused by good fortune: *It was fortunate that the bus was a little late, otherwise we would have missed it. You're very fortunate to have such understanding parents.* Opposite unfortunate(1,2).
fortunately *adv* luckily: *Fortunately no one was seriously hurt in the accident.* Opposite unfortunately.
fortune ,hunter *c.n* person who wants to get rich quickly, esp by marrying s.o who is rich.
fortune ,teller *c.n* person who (says he/she) is able to tell one's fortune(3).
fortieth, forty ⇨ four.
forum /'fɔːrəm/ *c.n* (place for a) public meeting, discussion: *Our school is providing the forum for a discussion on the new examination system.*
forward /'fɔːwəd/ *adj* 1 (usu *attrib*) at, in, near, the front: *The forward part of the bus is a 'no smoking' area.* ⇨ rear¹(*adj*). 2 (usu *attrib*) towards the front; making, in order to make, progress: *There's no forward movement to report. How many forward gears(1) does your car have?* Opposite reverse(1). 3 (*pred*) (esp of plants) ahead; developing faster than usual: *Your beans are forward for this time of year.* Opposite backward(3), late(1). 4 (often *derog*) (too) eager or ready to help: *It was forward of you to ask her for the money.* 5 very modern: *He has very forward ideas about the treatment of criminals.*
▷ *adv* (also **forwards**) 6 towards the front: *She stepped forward to shake his hand. Has anyone come forward with some new ideas?* Opposite back(6). 7 for all future times: *From this time forward you'll have to pay at the beginning of each month.* 8 (esp **bring s.t** —) to an earlier time than originally agreed: *We'll have to bring the meeting forward if we're going to meet the deadline.* Opposite back(13). 9 (of clocks, watches) so as to show a later time: *We'll have to put our watches forward an hour.* Opposite back(11). 10 to the front; to an important position: *I'll bring that proposal forward at the next meeting. Please have your ideas ready to put forward at the meeting.* **backwards and forwards** ⇨ backwards. **put one's best foot forward** ⇨ foot(*n*).
▷ *c.n* 11 (in sport) player in the front line in football, hockey etc. ⇨ defender, midfield, striker.
▷ *tr.v* 12 (often — *s.t to s.o/s.t*) send (s.t) (to s.o/ s.t): *The firm promised to forward my order as*

soon as my money was received. 13 (often — *s.t to s.o/s.t*) send (letters, parcels etc) on to a stated address: *I've organized my post to be forwarded to my new address.* 14 (*formal*) help make (s.o/s.t) successful: *Your good results will forward your chances of getting into university.*
forwarding ad,dress *c.n* new address to which one's post should be sent: *I've left a forwarding address with the people who bought my house.*
forwarding ,agent *c.n* person or company who/that forwards(12) goods.
forward-,looking *adj* thinking of the future; modern: *We need to employ some young people with forward-looking ideas.* Opposite backward-looking.
forwardness *u.n* 1 state of being well advanced, forward(3). 2 state of being forward(4): *She was disliked by teachers because of her forwardness.*
forwards *adv* ⇨ forward (adv).
for(e)went /fɔː'went/ *p.t* of forgo.
fossil /'fɒsl/ *c.n* 1 (also *attrib*) (remains of) animals, plants dead for thousands of years and preserved as stone in rocks: *We found fossils of sea animals high in the Himalayas which proved that the area had been covered by the sea.* 2 (also ,old 'fossil) (*fig*; *derog*) person who cannot accept new or modern ideas: *She called her grandfather an old fossil because he didn't like pop(1) music.*
fossilization, -isation /ˌfɒsɪlaɪ'zeɪʃən/ *u.n.* state or fact of being fossilized; action of fossilizing.
fossi,lize, -ise *tr/intr.v* (cause (s.t) to) become a fossil.
fossi,lized, -ised *adj* changed into a fossil(1): *We visited an area full of fossilized trees.*
foster /'fɒstə/ *tr.v* 1 care for (another person's child) for a limited amount of time only: *We fostered a little boy until a permanent home could be found for him.* Compare adopt(1). 2 help (ideas etc) to develop: *He helped to foster good relations between the managers and workers.*
foster- *n* person who is fostered(1) by s.o or fosters(1) s.o: *a foster-child; a foster-father/mother. My foster-parents' family were always good to me.*
fought /fɔːt/ *p.t, p.p* fight(*v*).
foul /faʊl/ *adj* 1 (esp of smell, taste) very unpleasant; disgusting: *Let's open the windows and get rid of this foul smell.* 2 (of language) full of bad or rude words. 3 (of weather) very bad; stormy: *I'm not going sailing in this foul weather.* 4 extremely bad or mean: *Your room is in a foul mess. Your behaviour to your parents has been foul.* **by fair means or foul** ⇨ means. **fall foul of s.o/s.t** (*fig*) lose s.o's respect; get into trouble with s.o/s.t: *She fell foul of her boss because she was coming to work late every day.*
▷ *c.n* 5 (in sport) action that is against the rules, esp because it could hurt a player: *The player was warned that another foul would result in his being sent off the field.*
▷ *v* 6 *tr/intr.v* (in sport) play unfairly against (s.o), esp in a way that breaks the rules of the game: *He fouled the player as he was trying to score a goal.* 7 *tr.v* make (s.t) dirty, esp with faeces: *Do not allow your dog to foul the pavement.* 8 *tr.v*

(esp — s.t up) (*informal*) spoil (s.t); do (s.t) badly: *You've really fouled up our weekend plans.*

,foul-'mouthed *adj* (*derog*) in the habit of using foul(2) language.

'foulness *u.n*.

,foul 'play *u.n* **1** (in sport) act of making a foul(5). **2** crime, esp with violence: *Police stated that foul play was not suspected in the case of his death.*

foully /ˈfaʊlɪ/ *adv*: *behave foully*.

found¹ /faʊnd/ *p.t.p.p* of find(v).

found² /faʊnd/ *tr.v* start (s.t), often by providing money for it: *This company was founded over a hundred years ago. A new sports club has been founded by the local council.* **found s.t (up)on s.t** (esp passive) base s.t (up)on s.t: *Most of his knowledge is founded on experience rather than learning.*

foundation /faʊnˈdeɪʃən/ *n* **1** *u.n* act of founding²(1) (a school, sports club, society, university etc). **2** *c.n* thing that has been founded². **3** *c.n* (with capital **F** in names) organization (and a sum of money needed for it) provided for a particular purpose: *a foundation for the encouragement of the arts; the Ford Foundation.* **4** *c.n* (usu *pl*) prepared base, esp below ground level, on which a building is built: *Have they finished digging the foundations yet?* **5** *c/u.n* (*fig*) base on which beliefs, ideas, opinions etc are formed: *What he said is a lie and it has no foundation in fact.*

foun'dation ,cream *u.n* kind of cream applied to the face before make-up(1) is put on it.

foun'dation ,stone *c.n* stone with a written message laid by s.o important, esp in a ceremony, during the early stages of building a new building.

'founder¹ *c.n* person who founds² s.t.

,founder 'member *c.n* person who helps to found² s.t.

founder² /ˈfaʊndə/ *intr.v* **1** (*formal*) (of ships) fill with water and sink: *The ship foundered on the rocks during the storm.* **2** (of horses) fall, slip: *The horse foundered in the mud.* **3** (*fig*) fail: *Their plans foundered after attempts to raise money failed.*

foundling /ˈfaʊndlɪŋ/ *c.n* (*old use*) child that has been found after being abandoned by its parents.

foundry /ˈfaʊndrɪ/ *c.n* (*pl* -**ies**) factory where glass or metal is melted and shaped: *She works in an iron foundry.*

fount¹ /faʊnt/ *c.n* **1** (*literary*) place where natural water appears out of the surface of the ground. **2** (*fig*) = fountain(2).

fount² /faʊnt/ *c.n* (also **font** /fɒnt/) complete set of a particular kind and size of printing type: *How many different founts does the printer have?*

fountain /ˈfaʊntɪn/ *c.n* **1** (water coming from a) (stone) structure(2) for water to be forced up, over etc in an attractive way. **2** (*fig*) origin; place where s.t starts: *Nature is the fountain of beauty and knowledge.*

'fountain ,pen *c.n* kind of pen that has a place for storing liquid ink and that can be filled when the ink is finished: *My fountain pen leaks.*

four /fɔː/ *det/pron/c.n* (cardinal number) number 4 (between 3 and 5): *Four and four are eight* (4 + 4 = 8). *Alex scored four goals. Only four of you can come. He's four* (years

old). **from/to the four corners of the earth** ⇒ corner(*n*). **on all fours** on one's hands and knees: *We had to crawl through the tunnel on all fours.*

fortieth /ˈfɔːtɪəθ/ *det/pron* **1** (*ordinal number*) (person or thing) following 39 in order; 40th: *I came fortieth in the race.*

▷ *c.n* **2** one of forty equal parts; $\frac{1}{40}$.

forty /ˈfɔːtɪ/ *det/pron/c.n* (*pl* -**ies**) (*cardinal number*) number 40 (between 39 and 41): *She died forty years ago. Forty-two of us decided to go.* **in one's forties** between 40 and 49 years old. **in/into the forties** (or **the 40s**) (**a**) (of speed, temperature, marks etc) between 40 and 49: *The temperature is only in the forties.* (**b**) from '40 to '49 in a century: *It was built in the 40s* (or *the 1840s*).

,forty 'winks *pl.n* (*informal*) short sleep, e.g in a chair.

'four-,legged *adj* (of an animal) having four legs.

,four-'poster *c.n* (also *attrib*) bed with posts at each corner that support a frame of curtains: *a four-poster bed.*

'four ,score *c.n/det* (*old use*) (four times twenty) eighty: *He's been dead four score years or more.*

fourteen /ˌfɔːˈtiːn/ *det/pron/c.n* (*cardinal number*) number 14 (between 13 and 15): *There are fourteen* (*tickets*) *left. Fourteen of them refused. Are you fourteen* (*years old*)?

fourteenth /ˌfɔːˈtiːnθ/ *det/pron* **1** (*ordinal number*) (person or thing) following 13 in order; 14th.

▷ *c.n* **2** one of fourteen equal parts; $\frac{1}{14}$.

fourth /fɔːθ/ *det/pron* **1** (*ordinal number*) (person or thing) following 3 in order; 4th.

▷ *c.n* **2** one of four equal parts; quarter(2); $\frac{1}{4}$.

,fourth di'mension *def.n* time(1).

'fourthly *adv* as the fourth(1) point, item etc.

fowl /faʊl/ *n* (*pl* -(**s**)) **1** *c.n* (*old use*) bird. **2** *c.n* chicken kept for its eggs or meat. **3** *u.n* (also *attrib*) meat of a chicken or other bird.

fox /fɒks/ *c.n* **1** kind of wild animal with red fur and a bushy tail which belongs to the dog family: *A family of foxes lives on the railway line.* ⇒ vixen(1). **2** (usu an old —) (*fig*) person who tricks others. **as cunning as a fox** very clever, able to trick others easily.

▷ *tr.v* **3** confuse or trick (s.o): *That'll fox them. I was completely foxed by the last question.* ⇒ outfox.

'fox,glove *c.n* kind of tall wild plant with white, pink or purple flowers.

'fox,hound *c.n* kind of dog trained and used for hunting foxes(1).

'fox,hunt *c.n* **1** sport of hunting foxes(1) by riders on horses and foxhounds.

▷ *intr.v* **2** chase foxes(1) as a sport.

'fox,hunter *c.n* **1** person who chases foxes(1) as a sport. **2** horse trained and used for chasing foxes(1) as a sport.

'fox,hunting *u.n* sport of chasing foxes(1) with riders on horses and foxhounds.

'foxiness *u.n* fact or state of being foxy.

,fox 'terrier *c.n* kind of small dog with short hair kept as a pet or used to force foxes(1) out of their holes.

'fox,trot *def/c.n* **1** (music for a) kind of dance with quick and slow steps.

▷ *intr.v* (-*tt*-) **2** dance the foxtrot(1).

'foxy *adj* (*-ier, -iest*) who/that is or looks clever in a way that tricks s.o.

foyer /ˈfɔɪeɪ/ *c.n* (often *the — of s.t*) entrance hall (of a theatre, cinema, hotel etc): *I'll meet you in the foyer at 8 o'clock.*

fr *written abbr* franc.

Fr *written abbr* **1** French. **2** Father(2).

fracas /ˈfrækɑː/ *c.n* (*pl* fracas) noisy argument, quarrel: *There's a terrible fracas outside.*

fraction /ˈfrækʃən/ *c.n* **1** very small part, amount: *Can you move along a fraction so that I can also sit down? It's a fraction of the amount I thought we'd have to pay.* **2** (*mathematics*) number that is not a whole number, e.g 1/2, 3/4; 0.5, 1.75 etc.
decimal fraction ⇒ decimal. **improper fraction** ⇒ improper. **proper fraction** ⇒ proper. **vulgar fraction** ⇒ vulgar.

fractional /ˈfrækʃənl/ *adj* **1** of, in, fractions(2). **2** so small as to be unimportant: *The difference in price is fractional.*
'fractionally *adv* by a very short distance, time, amount: *We arrived fractionally before the others.*

fractious /ˈfrækʃəs/ *adj* (*formal*) bad-tempered: *a fractious old man. Don't be so fractious.*
'fractiously *adv.* **'fractiousness** *u.n.*

fracture /ˈfræktʃə/ *c/u.n* **1** (example of the) act or fact of breaking or cracking (esp a bone), or the fact or state of being broken, cracked: *Did you find any fracture? It looks like a fracture of the hip bone.* **compound fracture** ⇒ compound. **simple fracture** ⇒ simple.
▷ *tr/intr.v* **2** break, crack, (s.t): *He fractured both legs in the car crash. The pipe fractured because of the cold.*

fragile /ˈfrædʒaɪl/ *adj* **1** easily broken, hurt, destroyed: *fragile glass.* **2** (*fig*) weak; ill: *Be kind to her because she's feeling a little fragile today.*
fragility /frəˈdʒɪlɪtɪ/ *u.n.*

fragment /ˈfrægmənt/ *c.n* (often *—s of s.t*) **1** piece broken off (s.t): *I collected the fragments of the broken cup and tried to stick them together.* **2** part (of s.t) and not the whole thing: *I only heard fragments (of their conversation).*
▷ *tr/intr.v* /fræɡˈment/ **3** (*formal*) (cause (s.t) to) break into pieces: *If you put a rubber floor in the kitchen, things won't always fragment when dropped.*

fragmentary /ˈfrægməntrɪ/ *adj* not complete; consisting of pieces that don't fit together well: *a fragmentary account of what happened.*
fragmentation /ˌfrægmənˈteɪʃən/ *c/u.n.*

fragrant /ˈfreɪɡrənt/ *adj* (often *— with s.t*) having a sweet, pleasant smell (of s.t): *She left the air fragrant with her perfume(2).*
'fragrance *c/u.n* sweet smell: *These flowers have a lovely fragrance.*

frail /freɪl/ *adj* weak, esp in health: *She's still very frail since her operation.*
'frailness *u.n.*
'frailty *c/u.n* (*pl* -ies) weakness (of body and mind): *We watched his frailty increase.*

frame /freɪm/ *c.n* **1** plastic(1), wooden, steel etc border or edge that surrounds a picture, door etc: *I want a very simple frame for this picture. I have to change the lenses(1) of my glasses but I can use the same frame. The window frames are in but we still have to put in the glass.* **2** structure(2) that forms the shape and provides support for

s.t being built: *Before you put up the tent you must put the frame together.* **3** form, shape of an animal; person's body: *He has a large frame but he's not fat.* **4** (also **'cold ,frame**) structure(2), mostly made of glass, which protects (young) plants from the cold: *We have to grow melons in a frame because we don't have enough sun.* **5** one of a series(1) of pictures that make up the complete (roll of) film. **6** one round in a game of billiards or snooker(1). (**in a**) **good, bad** etc **frame of mind** (*formal*) (in a) good, bad etc state of mind at a particular time: *Is she in a strong enough frame of mind to make such an important decision?* **frame of reference** (*formal*) order, system, to which one can refer.
▷ *tr.v* **7** surround (s.t) with a frame(1): *Have you had your new pictures framed yet?* **8** (*formal*) form, develop, (s.t): *Together they framed a plan which they hoped would work.* **9** (*informal*) cause (s.o) to appear guilty of a crime when he/she is not: *The man kept saying that he had been framed and was not guilty.*
'frame-,up *c.n* (*informal*) plan to cause s.o to appear guilty of s.t that he/she has not done: *The police soon realized that it was a frame-up.*
'frame,work *c.n* **1** part of a structure(2) which contains or supports s.t: *The building needs a steel framework.* **2** (*fig*) (often *the — of s.t*) plan, organization, (of s.t): *She wrote the framework of her argument from facts she'd observed.*

franc /fræŋk/ *c.n* (*written abbr* fr) unit of money in Belgium, France, Switzerland etc.

franchise /ˈfræntʃaɪz/ *n* (*formal*) **1** def.n right to vote (in an election etc): *There are still places in the world where part of the population is fighting for the franchise.* ⇒ enfranchise. **2** *c.n* right given to a person by a company etc to do s.t: *We applied for a franchise to sell ice-cream on the beach during the summer.*
▷ *tr.v* **3** (*formal*) give (s.o) a franchise(2).

frank¹ /fræŋk/ *adj* expressing one's thoughts, feelings, honestly: *To be frank I don't like the picture at all. She's a frank person who will always say what she thinks.*
'frankly *adv.* **'frankness** *u.n.*

frank² /fræŋk/ *tr.v* stamp (a mark on a letter, parcel etc) to show that postage has been paid.
'franking ma,chine *c.n* machine used to frank² letters etc.

frankfurter /ˈfræŋkˌfɜːtə/ *c.n* kind of sausage that has been smoked and flavoured.

frankincense /ˈfræŋkɪnˌsens/ *u.n* sticky substance from trees used for the sweet smell it produces when burnt.

frantic /ˈfræntɪk/ *adj* **1** extremely worried or upset: *She became frantic after her child failed to return home from school. We heard frantic cries for help.* **2** extremely active or excited: *She found life in the city too frantic.*
'frantically *adv.*

fraternal /frəˈtɜːnl/ *attrib.adj* (*formal*) of, like, a brother: *There is no fraternal love between those two boys.*
fra'ternally *adv.*
fra'ternity *n* (*pl* -ies) **1** *u.n* quality of brotherly love or feeling. **2** *c.n* group of professional people joined together by common interest: *the legal(2) fraternity.* **3** *c.n* (US) society of students in a college or university. Compare sorority.

fraternization, -isation /ˌfrætənaɪˈzeɪʃən/ u.n act or fact of fraternizing.

'frater‚nize, -ise intr.v (often — with s.o) act, behave, in a friendly way (towards s.o): No one in the village would talk to her after she had fraternized with an enemy soldier.

fraud /frɔːd/ n 1 u.n (law) criminal dishonesty, esp in matters of money: She was sent to prison for fraud. 2 c.n person or thing who/that deceives, often for criminal purposes: That man is a fraud so don't believe a word he says. Their offer was a fraud and we didn't get any of the things we'd been promised.

fraudulence /ˈfrɔːdjʊləns/ u.n (formal; law) quality of being fraudulent.

fraudulent /ˈfrɔːdjʊlənt/ adj (formal; law) operating or acting with, gained by, fraud(1): That's a fraudulent way of earning your living.

'fraudulently adv.

fraught /frɔːt/ adj (formal) 1 very worried, anxious: The longer we waited the more fraught we all became. 2 (pred) causing worry, anxiety: The economic(1) situation is becoming more fraught as each day passes. **fraught with s.t** full of s.t, esp s.t that causes worry, anxiety etc: Our journey was fraught with dangers.

fray¹ /freɪ/ tr/intr.v 1 (cause (material, rope etc) to) wear, become worn, from rubbing that causes the threads to loosen: His shirt has frayed around the collar. 2 (fig) (cause (one's temper, nerves(2)) to) become worn; make (s.o) irritable and nervous: The slow traffic frayed everyone's nerves(2).

fray² /freɪ/ def.n (old use) fight: Everyone was caught in the fray.

frazzle /ˈfræzl/ u.n **burnt/worn to a frazzle** (informal) completely burnt/worn: We were burnt to a frazzle after spending the day on the beach in the sun. We were worn to a frazzle after the long day's work.

freak /friːk/ c.n 1 (also attrib) very unusual act, event: That wave was a freak. We're having a freak summer. 2 person or thing who/that is unusual, not normal, in form or behaviour: You look like a freak with that hairstyle. 3 (informal) person who is very interested in, eager about, s.t: She's a music freak.
▷ intr.v 4 (esp — out) (informal) behave with extreme emotion, e.g anger: She'll freak (out) when you tell her what you've done! ⇒ freak-out.

'freakish adj unusual; extraordinary: She's rather freakish but I like her.

'freakishly adv. **'freakishness** u.n.

‚freak of 'nature c.n (pl freaks of nature) 1 animal, person or plant who/that is not normal in form, shape: It is a freak of nature to have six toes on your foot. 2 weather etc that is not normal: That storm was a freak of nature.

'freak-‚out c.n 1 (informal) act of freaking(4): She had a total freak-out when she heard the news. 2 (slang) state caused by drugs(2) in which a person feels separated from reality.

'freaky adj (-ier, -iest) (informal) strange; odd.

freckle /ˈfrekl/ c.n 1 one of the (often many) small brown spots on the skin: She has a lot of freckles on her face.
▷ tr/intr.v 2 (cause (s.o/s.t) to) become covered with freckles(1): I freckle very easily.

free /friː/ adj 1 (esp of people, animals etc; also fig) not controlled by another person, people,

rulers; not in prison; not tied or fixed; not prevented from doing what one wants to do: After five years in prison he was a free man. What are you going to do now that you are free? 2 (esp of a country and its citizens) having a system of government which allows personal rights and political freedom: This is a free country and you can say and write whatever you want. 3 which costs nothing; without payment: I've got two free tickets for tonight's game. 4 not being used: If you have a free hand could you hold this for me for a moment. 5 not busy; not working: Are you free sometime this week because I need to talk to you? 6 (often — with s.t) generous: There is always a free supply of water from this spring. She's very free with her money/suggestions/advice. 7 (usu pred) open; not controlled: I feel quite free in your company. **feel free (to do s.t)** (informal) do what one wants: Please feel free to use my house as your own. **free from/of s.o/s.t** away from, without, no longer having, (s.o/s.t who/that was unpleasant): Put a bandage on the wound to keep it free from dirt. Are you pleased to be free of her? This proves that he is free of guilt. **for free** (informal) without paying: We tried to get in for free but we had to pay. ⇒ free(8). **give s.o, have, a free hand (in/ with s.t)** allow s.o to do, arrange, organize, s.t in her/his own way: I was given a free hand to reorganize my department. **set s.o/s.t free** give s.o/s.t her/his/its freedom: She set the bird free after its wing had mended.
▷ adv 8 without any payment or cost: I got it free. Can my son travel free on the train? 9 so as to be free(1); freely(1): The rope hung free. **free of charge** without having to pay: We were allowed in free of charge. **work (s.t) free** (cause (s.t) to) become loose, e.g after a lot of use: The screws have worked free.
▷ tr.v 10 release (s.o/s.t); let (s.o/s.t) go: Will you free the bird when its wing is mended? **free oneself/ s.o/s.t from/of s.o/s.t** (unpleasant) to be removed (from one/s.o/s.t): How can I free myself from these feelings of guilt? Please will you free me from my duties today so that I can visit my father in hospital?

‚free 'agent c.n person who acts on her/his own behalf and takes full responsibility for her/ his actions.

freedom /ˈfriːdəm/ n 1 u.n state or fact of being free(1): Is there freedom of the press in your country? She won her freedom after two years because of good behaviour. 2 c/u.n particular kind of freedom(1): We have fought for our freedoms and must defend them. **freedom from s.t** condition or state of being away from or without s.t unpleasant: They've never known freedom from hunger. **freedom of s.t** state of being free(1) to have s.t: freedom of speech. **freedom of the town/city** full rights given to s.o by a town/city as an honour.

‚free 'enter‚prise u.n business or trade that is not controlled by the State.

‚free-'fall c/u.n (example of) falling from an aeroplane as a sport and opening one's parachute(1) only at the last possible moment that it is safe to do so.

'free-for-‚all c.n argument or fight in which everyone is allowed to join in, express themselves etc.

‚free 'hand sing.n (often give s.o, have, a — (in/

with s.t)) (give s.o. have. an) opportunity to do s.t in a free way.

'free,hold *adj* **1** (*law*) that is owned without limit of time: *The college would not sell any of its freehold property.* Compare leasehold.

▷ *c/u.n* **2** (*law*) ownership of land, buildings etc without limit of time: *I bought the freehold when I bought the house.* Compare leasehold.

'free,holder *c.n* person who owns a freehold(2).

'free ,house *c.n* (UK) pub that is not controlled by a brewery and is therefore free to buy its beer from any company.

,free 'kick *c.n* (*football*) kick that is given after a foul(5) and that may not be interfered with by any player from the offending team.

'free,lance *adj/adv* **1** of, by, an independent artist, writer etc who does not work for only one company: *She's a freelance journalist. I prefer working freelance.*

▷ *c.n* **2** = freelancer.

▷ *intr.v* **3** earn money by selling one's work on a freelance(1) basis: *I'm freelancing now so that I can make my own decisions.*

'free,lancer *c.n* (also **'free,lance**) person who freelances(3).

'free,load *intr.v* (*derog*; *informal*) accept food, lodging etc from other people without paying anything.

'free,loader *c.n* (*derog*; *informal*) person who freeloads.

'freely *adv* **1** in a free way (and without being limited): *The animals can move about freely here. Let the rope hang freely.* **2** openly and without hiding anything: *You can speak freely; we're all friends.* **3** willingly: *He freely admitted that he'd taken the car without permission.* **4** in large quantities; generously: *Please give (money) freely.*

'Free,mason *c.n* member of a secret society for men only.

'free,masonry *u.n* organization and practices of Freemasons.

,free on 'board *adj/adv* (*abbr FOB*) (*commerce*) using the arrangement by which the seller (and not the buyer) pays all the transport costs to deliver the goods to the ship.

'free,post *u.n* system by which a company will pay the postal charges on all orders etc sent to it.

,free'range *adj* **1** (of chickens) allowed to move freely: *We only buy eggs from freerange chickens.* **2** (of eggs) produced from freerange(1) chickens. Compare battery(3).

,free 'speech *u.n* right to express one's opinions freely.

'free,standing *adj* not supported by anything or fixed to anything: *It's a freestanding bookcase.*

'free,style *c/u.n* (also *attrib*) (race using a) style chosen by the swimmer, usu the crawl(2).

,free 'trade *u.n* trade with foreign countries without having to pay duties, taxes etc.

'free,way *c.n* (US) = motorway.

,free'wheel *intr.v* travel, move, (in a car, on a bicycle etc) (esp downhill) without using the engine, pedals(1) etc: *It's dangerous to freewheel because you easily lose control.*

,free 'will *u.n* use of one's power or right to do or choose what one thinks: *I did it of my own free will.*

freesia /ˈfriːzɪə/ *c.n* kind of brightly coloured flower with a strong sweet smell.

freestanding, **freestyle**, **freeway**, **freewheel** ⇒ free.

freeze /friːz/ *n* **1** *sing.n* time of icy weather: *Our water pipes burst after the freeze.* **2** *c.n* forced control of s.t, e.g prices, wages etc: *The government put a freeze on all wage increases for six months. There was a price freeze on all milk products.* ⇒ deep-freeze.

▷ *v* (*p.t* froze /frəʊz/, *p.p* frozen /ˈfrəʊzən/) **3** *intr.v* (of weather) be extremely cold, icy: *It's freezing outside so dress up warmly. Put the plants inside in case it freezes tonight.* **4** *tr/intr.v* (cause (water etc) to) become ice because of cold: *If this icy weather continues it will soon freeze the river.* **5** *tr/intr.v* (cause (s.o/s.t) to) be or feel very cold: *The cold wind is freezing.* **6** *tr.v* make (food) very hard with cold in order to preserve it: *We froze the beans from the garden.* **7** *tr.v* stop (trade). keep (prices, wages etc) at a certain level, (for a length of time): *The government is threatening to freeze wages.* **8** *tr/intr.v* (*fig*) cause (s.o/s.t) to) be still or unable to move: *My blood froze when I heard the scream. She froze when she saw the snake.* **freeze s.t in** prevent a ship etc from moving because of being surrounded by ice. **freeze s.o out** (*fig*; *informal*) keep s.o out of a conversation, society etc by behaving in an unfriendly way towards her/him. **freeze s.t out** prevent s.t from happening by being too cold, icy: *Our football match was frozen out on Saturday.* **freeze (s.t) over** (cause (s.t) to) become covered with ice: *The lake froze over during the very cold winter.* **freeze (s.t) up** (a) (cause (s.t) to) become solid, hard, because of ice: *The water pipes have frozen up.* (b) (*fig*) (cause (s.o) to) be unable to continue or move: *She was so nervous that she froze up when she sat in front of her piano.* **frozen to the bone** ⇒ bone(*n*).

,freeze-'dry *attrib.adj* **1** preserved by freeze-drying: *We only take freeze-dry products when we go camping.*

▷ *tr.v* (*-ies*, *-ied*) **2** dry (food) by freezing it and removing the frozen water in order to preserve it: *It's not possible to freeze-dry all kinds of food.*

,freeze-'drying *u.n.*

'freezer *c.n* kind of refrigerator (sometimes as big as a room in some businesses) used to freeze food and store frozen foods.

'freezing *adj* (also **,freezing 'cold**) (of a person, weather) very cold: *My feet are freezing! It's freezing cold so let's go inside.*

'freezing-,point *c/unique n* temperature at which a liquid freezes(4) or becomes solid: *Temperatures will be below freezing-point tonight.* Compare boiling-point, melting-point.

freight /freɪt/ *u.n* (*commerce*) **1** (also *attrib*) goods being taken by train, lorry etc from one place to another: *All freight must be loaded before 3 o'clock. The goods will be delivered by freight train.* **2** (also *attrib*) (cost of the) carriage, transport(1), of goods: *What is the freight charge?* **3** transport(1), carriage, of goods: *I'll send the goods as freight.* ⇒ airfreight.

▷ *tr.v* **4** pack and send (goods): *Your order has been freighted.* ⇒ airfreight(*v*). **5** (often — *s.t with goods*) load (a ship, train etc with goods): *The ship was freighted with grain.*

ˈfreight ˌcar *c.n* (US) railway carriage for goods.

ˈfreighter *c.n* aeroplane or ship that carries (mostly) goods.

ˈfreight ˌtrain *c.n* (esp US) goods train.

French bean /ˌfrentʃ 'biːn/ *c.n* kind of long green bean eaten as a vegetable.

French bread /ˌfrentʃ 'bred/ *u.n* (piece of a) kind of long loaf of white bread.

French door /ˌfrentʃ 'dɔː/ *c.n* = French window.

French dressing /ˌfrentʃ 'dresɪŋ/ *u.n* kind of sauce made of oil, vinegar etc, used for salad(1).

French fry /ˌfrentʃ 'fraɪ/ *c.n* (*pl* French fries) (usu *pl*) small narrow fried potato chip.

French horn /ˌfrentʃ 'hɔːn/ *c.n* kind of musical instrument made of brass which is played by blowing into a mouthpiece(2).

Frenchman /'frentʃmən/ *c.n* (*pl* -men /-mən/) man from France.

ˌFrench 'polish *u.n* kind of liquid put on furniture to make it shine for a long time.

French-ˈpolish *v.t* put French polish on (s.t).

ˈFrench window /ˌfrentʃ 'wɪndəu/ *c.n* long window that serves as a door and a window.

Frenchwoman /'frentʃˌwumən/ *c.n* (*pl* -women /-ˌwɪmɪn/) *c.n* woman from France.

frenetic /frɪ'netɪk/ *adj* very eager, excited: *As he was preparing for his exams, he became more and more frenetic.*

freˈnetically *adv.*

frenzy /'frenzɪ/ *sing.n* (often *in*(to) a — (*of* s.t)) state of great, wild, uncontrolled excitement, fear etc (because of s.t): *You're getting yourself into a frenzy. The audience listened to the music in a frenzy of excitement.*

ˈfrenzied *attrib.adj* mad; wildly excited or worried: *She had a frenzied look on her face as she searched for the missing ring.*

ˈfrenziedly *adv.*

frequent /'friːkwənt/ *adj* **1** who/that comes, that happens or is done often: *We are frequent visitors to that part of the country.* Opposite infrequent.

▷ *tr.v* /frɪ'kwent/ **2** go to, visit, (s.w) often: *They used to frequent a little French restaurant.* ⇒ unfrequented.

frequency /'friːkwənsɪ/ *n* (*pl* -ies) (often — of s.t) **1** *u.n* fact or condition of (s.t) happening often. *The frequency of rain in this area produces many beautiful lakes.* **2** *c.n* (*technical*) number of times that s.t, e.g a radio wave, happens in a stated length of time: *Have you noted the frequency of the pains?* **3** *c.n* particular wavelength on which a radio station broadcasts, *symb* f.

ˈfrequently *adv* (*formal*) often: *She frequently takes a walk at this time of day.*

fresco /'freskəu/ *c.n* (*pl* -(e)s) (method of making a) picture painted onto a wet plaster surface: *You can see many fine frescoes in Rome.*

fresh /freʃ/ *adj* **1** (often — *from* s.t) recently collected, made, produced, arrived (from s.w): *She's fresh from school/the country. Do you have any fresh eggs? The bread is fresh from the oven. The vegetables don't look very fresh.* **2** (of food) not artificially preserved: *fresh fruit.* **3** (of water) not salty: *You can get some fresh water from that spring.* ⇒ freshwater. **4** (of air, wind etc) cool and clean: *The air is so fresh after the rain.* **5** (*attrib*) another; not yet used, known, started: *The secretary put a fresh piece of paper*

in her typewriter. *Is there any fresh news about the accident?* **6** healthy; bright; not tired: *You look fresh after that swim. You'll need a fresh horse for the rest of the journey.* **7** (often *get* — (*with* s.o)) (*fig*; *informal*; *derog*) behaving in a too familiar way, esp to s.o of the opposite sex: *I wouldn't try to get fresh with her; you'll make her very angry.* (**feel**) **fresh as a daisy** (feel) extremely well, healthy, rested.

ˈfreshen *tr/intr.v* (often — (*oneself/s.o*) *up*) (cause (oneself/s.o) to) become brighter, less tired: *A shower will freshen you up. I must freshen myself up before we go out.*

ˈfresher *c.n* (*informal*) student in her/his first year at university.

ˈfreshly *adv* (used with *p.p*) newly; a short time before: *The flowers are freshly picked. I have some freshly ground coffee.*

ˈfreshness *u.n.*

ˈfreshˌwater *attrib.adj* of, living in, fresh(3) water: *freshwater fish.*

fret¹ /fret/ *c.n* (*technical*) **1** wood that is decorated by cutting/sawing fine patterns. **2** one of the wooden or metal strips on the fingerboard of a musical instrument, e.g a guitar.

▷ *tr.v* (-tt-) **3** (*technical*) decorate (wood) by cutting, sawing fine patterns.

ˈfretˌsaw *c.n* kind of narrow saw with fine teeth for doing fretwork.

ˈfretˌwork *u.n* decorative patterns cut into thin wood.

fret² /fret/ *sing/u.n* **1** anxious state of mind: *Don't get into a fret.*

▷ *v* (-tt-) **2** *intr.v* (often — *about* s.o/s.t) feel anxiety, worry (about s.o/s.t): *There's no need to fret. She's fretting about her examination results.* **3** *tr/intr.v* cause (s.t) to become worn by rubbing etc: *The rubbing is fretting the rope.*

ˈfretful *adj* anxious, worried; unhappy: *She's feeling a little fretful today because she hasn't been sleeping well.*

ˈfretfully *adv.* **ˈfretfulness** *u.n.*

friar /'fraɪə/ *c.n* (with capital **F** in names) man who is a member of a particular Christian(1) religious order, esp one who lives without owning things.

friary /'fraɪərɪ/ *c.n* (*pl* -ies) place where friars live, pray etc.

friction /'frɪkʃən/ *u.n* **1** act of rubbing one thing against another: *Friction produces heat.* **2** (*technical*) force that offers resistance when one surface passes very closely over another one: *We put chains on the wheels to give the car friction as we drove through the snow.* **3** (*fig*) bad relations between people caused by differences in opinion etc: *There was some friction between the players after a disagreement about the score.*

Friday /'fraɪdɪ/ *c/unique n* (also *attrib*) sixth day of the week in Christian(1) (and some other) countries; day after Thursday and before Saturday. **last Friday** the last Friday before today. **next Friday** the first Friday after today. **on a Friday** on a day of one week that is/was a Friday. **on Friday** on the nearest Friday before/after today or on the Friday of the week being referred to: *We arrived on Friday.* **on Fridays** every Friday: *I am paid on Fridays.* **Friday after next** the second Friday after today. **Friday before last** the Friday before last Friday. **Friday afternoon**,

morning *etc* the afternoon, morning etc of last, next, Friday.

fridge /frɪdʒ/ *c.n abbr* refrigerator.

fried /fraɪd/ *p.t,p.p* of fry.

friend /frend/ *c.n* **1** (often *a* — *of s.o*) person who one/s.o knows and likes: *Mary has been my friend for years.* **2** person who helps or supports s.o/s.t: *Don't worry, you're among friends here.* **3** (*fig*) helpful or useful quality, thing: *Her radio was a good friend while she was living alone.* **4** person or animal that is one's companion: *Hello Joe, who's your young friend?* **5** (usu *pl*) person one is addressing, esp in a speech: *Friends, I have come here tonight to give you some good news!* **6** (often *derog*) person whose name one does not know or want to use: *Our friend from next door is listening to his music again.* **7** *c.n* (with capital **F**) member of the Society of Quakers. *a friend of mine, yours etc* one of my etc friends: *He's no friend of mine. I'm a friend of Bill's.* **my learned friend** (in law courts) (form of addressing one of one's colleagues).

ˈfriendless *adj* having no friends(1,2); being without friends(1,2).

friendliness *u.n* fact or state of being friendly.

ˈfriendly *adj* (*-ier, -iest*) **1** (often — *to/with s.o*) (willing to behave) like a friend(1) (to one (another)): *friendly countries. Are your neighbours friendly? His family has been very friendly to me. Are you friendly with other people in your class?* Opposite unfriendly. **2** (*attrib*) without any serious anger: *It was just a friendly argument.* **3** (*attrib*) (esp of sports, games) not part of a competition: *We should arrange a few friendly games for practice.* ▷ *c.n* (*pl -ies*) **4** (*informal*) friendly(3) game.

friends *pl.n* **1** *pl* of friend. **2** friends(1) of each other: *We've been friends for years.* **be friends with s.o** be s.o's friend(1): *Are you friends with your neighbour?* **make friends (again)** become friends(2) after an argument or quarrel. **make friends (with s.o)** become s.o's friend(1): *Have you made friends with your neighbours yet?*

ˈfriendship *c/u.n* (example of the) state of being friends: *Their friendship lasted for forty years.*

frieze /friːz/ *c.n* **1** narrow painted or decorated area just below the ceiling of a room. **2** carving(s) or patterns on the top part of a wall of a building.

frigate /ˈfrɪgət/ *c.n* **1** kind of small fast warship, often used to guard other ships. **2** (*old use*) warship of this kind with sails.

fright /fraɪt/ *n* **1** *c/u.n* (example of) fear caused by s.t sudden and unexpected: *I didn't hear you come in and I had such a fright!* **2** *c.n* (*informal*) person or thing who/that looks silly, terrible: *She looks a fright in those clothes.* **die of fright** (*fig; informal*) be very surprised and afraid: *I nearly died of fright when the dog ran in front of my car.* **give s.o a fright** frighten s.o: *I didn't hear you come; you gave me such a fright!* **take fright** become (suddenly) frightened: *The boys took fright when they saw the police and ran off.*

ˈfrighten *tr.v* cause (s.o, an animal) to be afraid: *The storm is frightening her.* **frighten s.o/s.t away/off** cause s.o/an animal to run away in fear: *We frightened them off with our cries.* **frighten s.o out of s.t** cause s.o not to do s.t through fear: *If you keep talking like that you'll*

frighten him out of going with you. **frighten s.o out of her/his wits** ⇒ wit(*n*).

ˈfrightened *adj* (often *be* — *about/of s.o/s.t*) afraid (about/of s.o/s.t): *Are you frightened of the dark? There's nothing to be frightened about/of.*

frightening /ˈfraɪtnɪŋ/ *adj* that causes fear: *Being in that crowd was very frightening.*

ˈfrightful *adj* **1** (usu *attrib*) terrible: *There's been a frightful car accident.* **2** (*informal*) very unpleasant: *That meal was frightful.* **3** (usu *attrib*) (*informal*) very large: *I've still got a frightful amount of work to do.*

ˈfrightfully *adv* (*informal*) very: *I'm frightfully sorry. She's frightfully worried.*

frigid /ˈfrɪdʒɪd/ *adj* (*formal*) **1** very cold: *The north and south poles are frigid zones.* **2** very unfriendly: *We got a frigid welcome when we arrived at the party uninvited.* **3** lacking normal sexual desire.

frigidity /frɪˈdʒɪdɪtɪ/ *u.n.*

ˈfrigidly *adv* in a frigid(2,3) way.

frill /frɪl/ *c.n* narrow strip of cloth which is gathered on one side and often sewn on to the edge of an article of clothing as a decoration: *Chris won't wear anything that has frills on it.*

ˈfrilliness *u.n.*

frills *pl.n* (*informal*) **1** unnecessary additions to speech, writing etc: *She can't describe anything without a lot of frills.* **2** extra benefits: *The frills that go with the job include money for suitable clothes and travelling expenses.*

ˈfrilly *adj* (*-ier, -iest*) having frills: *a frilly blouse.*

fringe /frɪndʒ/ *c.n* **1** hair (usu cut short) on the forehead. **2** loose threads around the edge of a rug etc. **3** (often *the* — *of s.t*) outer edge (of a city, desert etc): *They planted trees around the fringes of the town.* **4** (usu *the* — *of s.t*) (*fig*) edge just inside (a certain usu bad) condition): *They're living on the fringe of poverty.* **5** (also *attrib*) outside area (of an activity): *Many actors start in fringe theatre.* ▷ *tr.v* **6** (often — *s.t with s.t*) provide (s.t) with a decorative border: *The avenue was fringed with large trees.*

ˈfringe ˌbenefit *c.n* extra advantage, payment etc: *What are the fringe benefits that go with this job? One fringe benefit is a car.*

frisk /frɪsk/ *v* **1** *intr.v* jump, run, about while playing: *The young horses were frisking in the morning sunshine.* **2** *tr.v* (*informal*) search (s.o) (esp for weapons) by passing one's hands up and down her/his body: *The police frisked the man for weapons before they arrested him.*

ˈfriskily *adv* in a frisky way.

ˈfriskiness *u.n* fact or state of being frisky.

ˈfrisky *adj* (*-ier, -iest*) lively and ready to run about and play: *Your horse is frisky this morning.*

fritter /ˈfrɪtə/ *c.n* **1** slice (of fruit, potato etc) that has been dipped in an egg mixture and fried: *potato fritters.* ▷ *tr.v* **2** **fritter s.t away** (*informal*) waste time, money etc: *The children frittered their money away on sweets.*

frivolous /ˈfrɪvələs/ *adj* (*derog*) (of people, behaviour etc) not serious; doing things, done, for pleasure or fun: *Stop being so frivolous; can't you take anything seriously? She answered* her friend's request for advice with a *frivolous remark.*

frivolity /frɪ'vɒlɪtɪ/ *c/u.n* (*pl -ies*) (example of) silly, frivolous, behaviour: *After my examinations I'll have lots of time for frivolities.*

'frivolously *adv.* **'frivolousness** *u.n.*

frizz /frɪz/ *sing.n* **1** very curly state of one's hair; very curly hair: *Her hair went into a frizz after the rain.*

▷ *tr/intr.v* **2** (cause (hair) to) form very tight curls: *My hair frizzes in the rain.*

'frizziness *u.n* fact or state of being frizzy.

'frizzy *adj* (*-ier, -iest*) (of hair) in tight curls.

frizzle /'frɪzl/ *tr/intr.v* **1** (cause (s.t) to) fry until it burns: *I like bacon to be frizzled.* **2** (*fig*) burn (one's body) in the sun: *We lay frizzling in the sun all day.* **frizzle** (**s.t**) **up** (cause (s.t) to) burn completely: *The leaves frizzled up in the fire.*

'frizzled *adj* burnt: *We came off the beach feeling frizzled.*

fro /frəʊ/ *adv* **to and fro** ⇒ to(*adv*).

frock /frɒk/ *c.n* **1** (*old use*) dress. **2** long loose article of clothing worn by a monk.

frog /frɒg/ *c.n* kind of small animal with cold blood which lives on land and in water and has no tail when it is fully grown. Compare toad. **have a frog in one's throat** (*fig*; *informal*) have s.t that blocks one's throat for a short time, making it difficult (and sometimes painful) to speak.

'frogman *c.n* (*pl -men*) person who swims underwater with the help of flippers(2) and a container for air.

'frog,march *tr.v* **1** force (s.o) to walk by holding her/his arms together firmly and pushing her/him from behind. **2** carry (s.o) away using two or more people and each holding an arm or a leg.

'frog,spawn *u.n* mass of frogs' eggs in a jelly(4) substance in water.

frolic /'frɒlɪk/ *c.n* **1** time of fun and play: *We went to the beach for a frolic in the evening.*

▷ *intr.v* (*-ck-*) **2** play in a lighthearted, lively(1) way: *The children frolicked in the park while their parents talked among themselves.*

'frolicsome *adj* (*formal*) lively(1); merry: *The children were very frolicsome during the party.*

from (strong form /frɒm/, weak form /frəm/) *prep* **1** (used to introduce the place, point, time where s.o/s.t begins): *They'll be coming from the north. Where does she come from? I'm from India. She travels by train from home to work every day.* **2** (used to introduce the person or thing that gives, sends, s.t): *The letter is from my parents. Who are all these cards from?* **3** (used to introduce distance): *We're five miles from the nearest telephone. They live about ten minutes* (*away*) *from the beach.* **4** (often — *s.t* to *s.t*) (used to introduce the lower limit of s.t): *They take children from the age of 6 on their courses. Prices are from £100 (to about £400).* **5** (used to introduce the thing from which s.t comes, is taken, chosen, or from which it hangs, sticks out etc): *I got the book from the library. Most of my ideas come from that book. It was translated from French. Big rings hung from her ears.* **6** (used to introduce the thing used to make s.t) using: *The table is made from wood/metal.* Compare out(26), of(7). **7** according to; as a result of: *From the look on her face we all knew that*

she was guilty. *From what he says he didn't know anything about it.* **8** (often away — *s.o/s.t*) (used to indicate separation, absence etc): *How long has she been away from school? Take those matches* (*away*) *from that child before he causes an accident. Why was he sent home from school?* **9** (after words showing difference, and introducing the second thing compared): *He can't tell one cat from another. You don't know your left from your right.* **10** (used to introduce a cause, reason): *You're fat from eating too much.* **11** (usu — *s.t* to *s.t*) (used to introduce a state of change): *The patient's condition suddenly went from bad to worse. He changed from being a good student to a very lazy one.* **as from/of s.t** ⇒ as(*conj*). **aside from s.o/s.t** ⇒ aside(*adv*). **far from** (**being/doing**) **s.t** ⇒ far(*adv*). **from day, week** etc **to day, week** etc (**a**) more and more each day etc: *Their love grew from day to day.* (**b**) each day etc: *We used to see her from month to month.* **from end to end** starting at one end and going right to the other. **from s.t to s.t** (**a**) ⇒ from(4,11). (**b**) from one place to another, the other: *He went from room to room trying to find small jobs to do.* **from now/then on** starting now/then and continuing: *He promised to try harder from then on. From now on you can do everything on your own.* **from side to side** first to one side, then to the other, (then to the first one again etc). **from time to time** ⇒ time(*n*).

frond /frɒnd/ *c.n* large leaf of a fern etc.

front /frʌnt/ *n* (also *attrib*) **1** *c.n* (usu the — (*of s.t*)) part (of s.t) which is nearest the direction in which one is facing, usu faces, or in which s.t is moving: *Are there any seats near the front* (*of the theatre*)? *Turn round and face the front, please. Who wants to sit in the front row? I'd prefer a front seat.* ⇒ back(1,18). **2** *c.n* (usu the — (*of s.t*)) part (of s.t) which faces outwards esp the part which one sees and which is often the most important part: *You only need to polish the front of the cupboard. It has a green front and a yellow back.* ⇒ back(18). **3** *c.n* (usu the — (*of s.t*)) face, side, (of a building): *The south front of the hotel was damaged by the storm.* **4** *def.n* part of a town along the side of the sea: *We have a house on the beach front. Let's go for a walk along the sea front.* **5** *def.n* (in war) place where there is the main fighting: *My son's been sent to the front.* **6** *sing. n* (usu a bold/brave —) (*fig*) appearance that hides a different feeling: *His loudness is only a front to hide his shyness. He put on a brave front so no one would realize how frightened he really was.* **7** *sing.n* (usu a — for s.t) (*slang*) thing that hides, or serves as a cover for, (unlawful activities): *Their restaurant is a front* (*for their* gambling *tables at the back*). **8** *c.n* boundary between cold and warm air masses: *The warm front coming from the south will bring better weather.* **9** *c.n* (with capital **F** in names) (political) movement that unites various groups, purposes: *The Popular Front is united for freedom. They formed a united front in an attempt to defeat the government.* **at the front** (**of s.t**) in the front part (of s.t): *There are still a few seats left at the front* (*of the cinema*). ⇒ back(18). **in front** (**of s.o/s.t**) (**a**) ahead of (s.o/s.t): *The French team is still in front.* ⇒ behind(4). (**b**) in or towards the place where the front(1) of s.o/s.t is (moving): *The* *dog ran in front of the car. Do you want to sit in front of me?* ⇒ behind(6,9). **in front of s.o** in a position where one can be seen or heard (by s.o/s.t): *Please don't talk like that in front of the children.* **on all fronts** (**a**) (in war) wherever there is fighting. (**b**) in every situation (where there is activity): *We're winning on all fronts.* **out front** among the audience in a theatre: *Is your family out front tonight?* **up front** (**a**) ahead; in a leading position: *Who's that up front?* (**b**) in the most forward part (of a sports field): *We put two of our stronger players up front.*

▷ *tr.v* **10** (often — *on s.t*) face (s.t); stand opposite (s.t): *Our hotel fronts (onto) the sea.*

frontage /'frʌntɪdʒ/ *c.n* front end or edge of a building or piece of land: *The nicest part of the house was its river frontage.*

'frontal *adj* of, on, from, to, the front: *a frontal attack/view.*

,front 'bench *def.n* (usu *pl*) (also attrib **'front-,bench**) important Members of Parliament who sit in the front(1) seats: *She's a front-bench MP.* Compare back bench.

,front'bencher *c.n* front-bench Member of Parliament. Compare backbencher.

,front 'door *c.n* main door which is (usu) at the front of a house. ⇒ back door.

,front 'line *def.n* **1** (in war) position nearest the enemy during war and where the fighting takes place. **2** (often *the — of s.t*) (*fig*) position which is the most important, advanced, (of s.t): *Teachers should be in the front line of educational progress.*

,front-'line *attrib.adj* of, in, the front line: *front-line action/doctors.*

frontier /'frʌntɪə/ *c.n* **1** (also attrib) (*formal*) (area near the) border between two countries: *frontier* disputes(1). **2** *def.n* (US history) furthest land settled and worked by early American settlers. **3** (often *—s of s.t*) (*fig*) extreme limit, border, (esp of knowledge and discovery): *The frontiers of medicine are moving all the time.*

frontispiece /'frʌntɪs,piːs/ *c.n* picture at the front of a book, esp on the page next to the one with the title of the book.

frost /frɒst/ *n* **1** *c/u.n* (occasion of) weather when the air temperature is below that at which water freezes: *If you don't cover your plants tonight, the frost will kill them.* **2** *u.n* white powdery substance that covers the ground, roofs etc when the air temperature falls below the freezing-point of water: *The frost is still on the grass.*

▷ *v* **3** *intr.v* (usu — *over/up*) become covered with frost(2): *The car windows have frosted up and I can't see anything.* **4** *tr.v* cover (a cake) with a powder of fine white sugar.

'frost ,bite *u.n* damage to the body, esp the ends of fingers and toes, caused by severe cold.

'frost,bitten *adj* damaged by frostbite.

'frosted *adj* (esp of glass) having a rough surface that is not clear so that it cannot be seen through.

'frostily *adv* in a frosty(3) way.

'frostiness *u.n* fact or state of being frosty.

'frosting *u.n* **1** roughness on glass which makes it difficult to see through. **2** white powder of fine sugar which is put on cakes.

'frosty *adj* (-*ier*, -*iest*) **1** cold as a result of frost(1): *It's rather frosty outside.* **2** covered with

frost(2): *The grass is still frosty.* **3** (*fig*) very unfriendly: *She gave him a frosty look when he arrived late.*

froth /frɒθ/ *u.n* **1** mass of very small bubbles(2) that form on top of a liquid that contains gas: *froth on beer.*

▷ *intr.v* **2** (often — *at the mouth*) (**a**) have/produce froth: *The horse was frothing (at the mouth) after a long hard ride.* (**b**) (*fig*) be/become very angry: *He started frothing at the mouth when his daughter disobeyed him again.*

'frothiness *u.n* fact or state of being frothy.

'frothy *adj* (-*ier*, -*iest*) of, covered with, froth(1): *She likes her coffee with frothy milk on top.*

frown /fraʊn/ *c.n* **1** look of anger, displeasure, deep thought etc produced by drawing the eyebrows together and causing lines on the forehead.

▷ *intr.v* **2** (sometimes — *about/at s.o/s.t*) produce a frown(1) because of anger, displeasure or deep thought (about s.o/s.t): *Why are you frowning? What are you frowning at/about?* **frown (up)on s.o/s.t** (*fig*) disapprove of s.o/s.t; not like s.o/s.t: *My father frowns on our wild parties.*

froze, frozen /frəʊz, 'frəʊzn/ ⇒ freeze.

FRS /,ef ,ɑːr 'es/ *abbr* Fellow(4) of the Royal Society.

frugal /'fruːgl/ *adj* (*formal*) **1** not spending or costing a lot: *We only had time for a frugal meal before we had to leave.* **2** careful not to waste anything or spend too much money; economical: *We'll have to be frugal for the next few months if we want to save for a holiday.*

frugality /fruː'gælɪtɪ/ *u.n.* **'frugally** *adv.*

fruit /fruːt/ *n* (*pl* -(s)) **1** *c/u.n* (also attrib) part of a plant or tree which contains the seeds and which is often eaten: *Take her some fruit; she loves apples and oranges. We only plant fruit trees in our garden.* **2** (often *pl, the —s of s.t*) (*fig*) gain, reward, (that comes from s.t): *After we've finished, we'll be able to enjoy the fruits of our hard work for many years.* **bear fruit** (*fig*) produce success: *Has all your hard work borne fruit?*

▷ *intr.v* **3** (of trees etc) produce fruit: *When does this tree fruit?*

'fruit,cake *c/u.n* kind of rich cake containing different kinds of dried fruit: *Would you like some fruitcake?* **as nutty as a fruitcake** (*informal*) mad; likely to behave strangely.

'fruiterer *c.n* **1** person who sells fruit. **2** (also **'fruiterer's**) shop selling fruit.

'fruitful *adj* (*fig*) producing (good) results: *That telephone conversation was very fruitful.* Opposite fruitless.

'fruitfully *adv.* **'fruitfulness** *u.n.*

'fruitiness *u.n* fact or state of being fruity.

fruition /fruː'ɪʃən/ *u.n* **1 bring s.t, come, to fruition** (cause s.t to) be completed successfully: *When will these ideas be brought to fruition?* **2 the fruition of s.t** the success of what one has hoped or worked for: *After months of work I'll see the fruition of my plans.*

'fruitless *adj* (*fig*) producing no results, rewards: *It's fruitless to try to save the plants.* Opposite fruitful.

'fruitlessly *adv.* **'fruitlessness** *u.n.*

'fruit ma,chine *c.n* kind of machine into which one puts coins for gambling(3).

,fruit 'salad *c/u.n* different kinds of fruit cut up and mixed in a bowl.

'fruity *adj* (*-ier, -iest*) of or like fruit, esp having the smell or taste of fruit: *This drink has a lovely fruity taste.*

frump /frʌmp/ *c.n* (*derog*) person (usu a woman) who is dressed in old-fashioned or plain clothes.

'frumpish *adj*.

frustrate /frʌ'streɪt/ *tr.v* **1** prevent (s.t) happening, (s.o) from doing s.t: *Our plans to go camping have been frustrated by the rain.* **2** make (s.o) angry, disappointed, dissatisfied, by not allowing her/him to do s.t which he/she wants to do: *Nothing frustrates me more than waiting for someone who is late.*

fru'strated *adj* **1** feeling disappointed, angry and dissatisfied because of failure to get or do what one wants: *She's a frustrated musician because she never had time to practise enough while her children were young.* **2** not sexually satisfied.

fru'strating *adj* (of a person, thing that happens etc) who/that frustrates s.o/s.t: *It's been a very frustrating day with nothing going right.*

frustration /frʌ'streɪʃən/ *c/u.n* (example of) feeling, being, frustrated: *Their frustration grew as they struggled to score a goal.*

fry[1] /fraɪ/ *tr/intr.v* (*-ies, -ied*) cook (s.t) in hot oil: *Have you fried the eggs yet? The tomatoes are frying nicely.*

'frying ,pan *c.n* shallow pan with a long handle, used for frying food. **out of the frying pan (and) into the fire** (*fig*) (going) from one difficult or dangerous situation to a worse one.

'fry-,up *c.n* (*informal*) mixture of fried foods: *a fry-up of sausages, eggs and bacon.*

fry[2] /fraɪ/ *u/pl.n* **small fry** ⇨ **small**.

ft *written abbr* foot, feet.

fuchsia /'fjuː.ʃə/ *c.n* kind of small bush with pink, white, red or purple flowers that hang down.

fuck /fʌk/ *c.n* (*slang*; do not use!) **1** act of sexual intercourse. **not care/give a fuck (for s.o/s.t)** be not at all worried or concerned about s.o/s.t.

▷ *interj* (*slang*; do not use!) **2** (also — *it*) (used to express great anger, annoyance etc).

▷ *tr/intr.v* (*slang*; do not use!) **3** have sexual intercourse (with (s.o)). **fuck about/around** act, play, aimlessly. **Fuck off!** Go away! **fuck s.t up** spoil s.t; do s.t badly. ⇨ **fuck-up.**

'fucking *attrib adj/adv* (*slang*; do not use!) (used to add force to statement of anger, annoyance etc): *It's fucking painful. You're a fucking idiot.*

'fuck-,up *c.n* (*slang*; do not use!) thing that is spoilt, not managed well or badly done.

fuddyduddy /'fʌdɪˌdʌdɪ/ *c.n* (*pl -ies*) (*informal*) old-fashioned person.

fudge /fʌdʒ/ *u.n* **1** kind of soft creamy sweet made from milk, sugar etc.

▷ *tr.v* **2** (*informal*) put (s.t) together, prepare (s.t), without care or attention.

fuel /fjuːl/ *c/u.n* **1** substance used to produce energy(2) by burning, esp to make an engine work: *Oil and petrol are fuels.* **add fuel to the fire/flames** (*fig*) make s.o's anger, feelings etc stronger: *Your criticisms will only add fuel to the fire so it's better to leave the matter alone.*

▷ *v* (*-ll-*) **2** *tr/intr.v* (also — (s.t) *up*) fill (s.t) with fuel(1): *The plane was fuelled before we left.*

3 *tr.v* (usu passive) use a particular kind of fuel(1) in (s.t): *The boat is fuelled by diesel.* **4** *tr.v* increase (s.o's anger, feelings etc): *He fuelled the crowd's anger by telling them how badly they were treated.*

fugitive /'fjuːdʒɪtɪv/ *c.n* (also *attrib*) person running away from danger, police etc: *The church gave the fugitive children a place to live.*

fugue /fjuːg/ *c.n* (*music*) composition in which one or two tunes are repeated by different voices or parts of the orchestra in such ways as to form patterns.

fulcrum /'fʊlkrəm/ *c.n* (*technical*) point about which a lever(1) turns or moves: *A children's seesaw(1) moves on a fulcrum.*

fulfil /fʊl'fɪl/ *tr.v* (*-ll-*) (US **ful'fill**) (*formal*) make (s.o) happy, satisfied, complete; do all that is required, expected, in (a duty, promise etc): *Does your job fulfil you? She promised to do everything possible to fulfil her duties as a leader of the group.* **fulfil a task** (*fig*) be suitable for s.t.

,ful'filled *adj* (of a person) feeling satisfied because of having done the thing(s) that one has aimed at or having received the things one wanted. Opposite **unfulfilled.**

ful'filment *u.n* (US **ful'fillment**) act of fulfilling; thing that fulfils: *His greatest fulfilment would be to have a piece of land he could call his own.*

full /fʊl/ *adj* **1** containing all that s.t can hold: *Take the next bus because this one is full. Don't make the cup too full otherwise he'll spill his tea. We couldn't see the film because the cinema was full.* Opposite **empty(1).** **2** (*attrib*) including all the information; complete: *Can you give me a full description of the thief?* **3** (*attrib*) of the total extent, length, time etc: *Even at full speed the boat can only go 30 mph. The garden is beautiful when the trees are in full flower. He kept me waiting a full week before he gave me his decision.* **4** having a round fat shape: *He looks a lot like his sister but he has a fuller face than she has.* **5** (of clothes) loose and made of a lot of material: *Are full or tight skirts in fashion?* **6** (usu *pred*) (*informal*) having eaten enough: *I'm so full I can't eat another thing!* **7** (of a taste, smell, flavour etc) rich, strong: *Time gives many wines their full flavour.* **full of beans** ⇨ **bean. full marks (for (doing) s.t)** ⇨ **mark(n).** **full of oneself** (*informal*) having a strong opinion of one's own abilities etc. **full of s.t** containing, having, a lot of s.t: *In summer Oxford is full of tourists. Her parents were full of joy/pride when they learned of her success.*

▷ *adv* **8** completely: *fill the box full;* **full well** clearly and well: *You knew full well what time the film was starting.* **9** (often — *on(to) s.t*) exactly, directly, (on s.t): *The light shone full on his face.*

▷ *n* **10 at/to the full** at/to the greatest possible degree, extent etc: *The moon will be at its full tonight. She lived her life to the full.* **in full** without omitting anything: *Please write your name and address in full.*

'full-,back *c.n* player at the back of the field whose main purpose is to defend the goal area. Compare **goalkeeper.**

,full 'blast *adv/u.n* (usu *at* —) as loudly as s.t can be: *They played their music (at) full blast until midnight.*

,full 'board *u.n* (also *attrib* **'full-,board**) (often *with* —) all meals included in the price: *The price* *for the room is with full board.* Compare half board (⇨ half).

,full-'grown *adj* having finished growing: *Is it a full-grown horse?*

,full 'house *c.n* (esp of a cinema, theatre etc) occasion when all the seats have been sold, are occupied: *We should buy our tickets for the film early because they've had a full house all week.*

,full-'length *adj* (usu *attrib*) **1** of the length of the whole body: *a full-length coat/dress/photograph.* **2** of the usual or general length: *a full-length film/play.*

,full 'moon *c.n.* ⇨ moon.

'fullness *u.n* state of being complete. **in the fullness of time** when the correct amount of time has passed: *Your turn will come in the fullness of time.*

'full-,page *attrib.adj* that fills a whole page: *a full-page article on her adventure.*

'full-,scale *attrib.adj* **1** total; using everyone and everything: *a full-scale rescue/attempt.* **2** (of a drawing, map, plan etc) of the same size as the actual object: *He made his model aeroplane from a full-scale drawing.*

,full 'speed *adv/u.n* (often *at —*) greatest possible speed: *The whole boat shakes when we travel at full speed. We went full speed ahead.*

,full 'stop *c.n* punctuation mark . which shows the end of a sentence and is sometimes used in or after abbreviations such as 'i.e', 'etc.'.

,full 'time *u.n* end of a game (e.g of football). Compare half time.

'full-,time *attrib.adj* for all the normal working hours: *I'm looking for a full-time job.* ⇨ full time (⇨ time(*n*)). Compare part-time.

'fully *adv* **1** completely: *Are you fully clear about what you're expected to do? How big will it be when it's fully grown?* **2** at least: *It takes fully five hours to get to London from here.*

,fully-'fledged *attrib.adj* (*fig*) completely trained: *It took her three years to become a fully-fledged teacher.*

fumble /'fʌmbl/ *v* **1** *intr.v* feel with, use, one's hands in an uncertain way: *She fumbled in the dark for the light switch. He fumbled with the ball but he didn't drop it. He fumbled about in the drawer looking for the other sock.* **2** *tr.v* manage to find (s.t) with difficulty: *He fumbled his way through his speech.*

fume /fjuːm/ *c.n* **1** (usu *pl*) gas or smoke with a strong smell: *petrol fumes.*

▷ *intr.v* **2** give off fumes(1): *This acid fumes when you remove the top from its bottle.* **3** (often *— about/over s.o./s.t*) (*informal*) be extremely angry (about s.o./s.t): *My father is fuming about what we did to his car.*

fumigate /'fjuːmɪˌgeɪt/ *tr.v* remove dangerous germs, insects etc from (s.t) by using a particular kind of smoke: *We're having the whole house fumigated to get rid of the fleas.*

fumigation /ˌfjuːmɪ'geɪʃən/ *u.n.*

fun /fʌn/ *u.n* (also *attrib*) (thing that causes) amusement, pleasure, enjoyment: *The holiday was great fun. I enjoy being with them as they're such fun.* **for fun** for pleasure or enjoyment and not for any serious or particular reason: *Let's ride into town for fun.* **for the fun of it** for no other reason than enjoyment: *I swim one mile a day partly to keep fit and partly for the fun of it.*

have fun enjoy oneself: *Did you have fun at the picnic?* **in fun** as a joke and not for any serious reason: *They only did it in fun; they didn't mean to make him cry.* **make fun of, poke fun at, s.o/s.t** cause others to laugh at s.o/s.t: *He's always making fun of people but he gets very angry when someone makes fun of him. Stop poking fun at me!*

'fun,fair *c.n* (also **fair**) many kinds of entertainments together in a place where people pay to enjoy themselves.

'funnily *adv* in a funny or strange way: *He speaks funnily.* **funnily enough** ⇨ enough(*adv*).

'funniness *u.n.*

'funny *adj* (*-ier, -iest*) **1** who/that makes one laugh: *He's very funny when he's got an audience. She told us such funny stories about their holiday. That's not funny; why are you laughing?* **2** strange; unusual: *The child couldn't help staring at the funny way in which the man walked. She has such funny ideas about education.* **3** mysterious: *That's funny; I thought I had paid that account.* **feel funny (about s.t)** feel uncomfortable (about s.t) because it seems wrong or one can't agree with it: *I feel funny about accepting money from her.* **try anything/something funny** (*informal*) try to trick or deceive s.o: *I'll let you go if you promise not to try anything funny.*

'funny ,bone *c.n* (*informal*) very sensitive part of the elbow(1).

'funny ,business *u.n* (*informal*) strange events, esp ones that are not quite legal(1): *He's involved* (⇨ involve(2)) *in some funny business and I hope he doesn't get into trouble.*

function /'fʌŋkʃən/ *c.n* **1** (usu *the — of s.o/s.t*) natural or special duty, activity, purpose, (of s.o/s.t): *The main function of a doctor is to try to make sick people well again. What is the function of this handle?* **2** large social occasion: *As mayor you will have to attend all the important functions in the town.*

▷ *intr.v* **3** (*formal*) operate; work(6): *This machine is not functioning and I don't know what's wrong with it.*

'functional *adj* (*formal*) practical; able to carry out its functions(1): *I prefer functional clothes to fashions. Their house may be ugly but it's very functional.*

fund /fʌnd/ *c.n* **1** amount of money used for a particular purpose: *They've set up a fund for students who don't have enough money for their books.* **2** (usu *a — of s.t*) large supply (of s.t): *She has a fund of stories and she loves telling them.*

▷ *tr.v* **3** provide (s.o/s.t) with money: *Our trip is being funded by several manufacturers of climbing equipment(2).*

funds *pl.n* (*informal*) money: *I can't write out another cheque until I have more funds in my account.*

fundamental /ˌfʌndə'mentl/ *adj* **1** (often *— to s.t*) very important (for s.t); forming the basis (for s.t): *There will have to be fundamental changes in his working habits before he will be accepted by any university. Understanding the rules of the game is fundamental to playing well.*

▷ *c.n* **2** (usu *a — of s.t or —s*) essential part (of s.t): *Having a knowledge of mathematics is a fundamental of all scientific study. You must know the fundamentals if you want to pass the examination.*

funda'mentally *adv* in the most important way: *Although William is being unkind, he is fundamentally a good person.*

funeral /ˈfjuːnərəl/ *c/u.n* (also *attrib*) ceremony for burying or burning a dead body: *They read his favourite poem during his funeral. The funeral director visited the family to discuss the kind of funeral they wanted.* Compare cremation.

funereal /fjuːˈnɪərɪəl/ *adj* sad; of, like, a funeral: *That music is rather funereal.*

funfair ⇒ fun.

fungus /ˈfʌŋgəs/ *c/u.n* (*pl* fungi /ˈfʌŋgaɪ/, -*es*) plant without leaves, flowers or chlorophyll which lives on other plants or in warm, damp places: *Some fungi are poisonous but we can eat many kinds of fungi, especially* mushrooms(1).

fungicide /ˈfʌŋgɪˌsaɪd/ *c/u.n* kind of substance used to destroy fungi that spoil crops.

fungoid /ˈfʌŋgɔɪd/ *adj* of, like, a fungus: *a fungoid growth on the young plant.*

fungous /ˈfʌŋgəs/ *adj* of, like or caused by a fungus: *a fungous disease attacking our tomato plants.*

funk /fʌŋk/ *u.n* 1 (*derog*; *informal*) state of being afraid.

▷ *tr.v* 2 avoid doing (s.t) because of fear: *At the last moment she funked her turn to jump.*

funky /ˈfʌŋkɪ/ *adj* (-*ier*, -*iest*) (*slang*) (of music) having a rough strong rhythm.

funnel /ˈfʌnl/ *c.n* 1 vessel shaped like a Y, through which liquid etc can be poured into a container with a narrow opening: *You'll need a funnel to get the petrol into the petrol tank.* 2 metal chimney on a ship or (steam etc) railway engine through which smoke escapes.

▷ *tr/intr.v* (-*ll*-) 3 (cause (s.o/s.t) to) move (as if) through a funnel(1): *Funnel some of this liquid into a bottle for me. The crowd was funnelled out of the burning building.*

funnily, funniness, funny ⇒ fun.

fur /fɜː/ *n* 1 *u.n* soft hair covering certain kinds of animals, e.g cats. Compare hair(1). 2 *c/u.n* (also *attrib*) (of the) skin of animals that have fur which is used as clothing or to make, decorate, clothes: *It's nearly cold enough to wear my fur (coat).* 3 *u.n* hard white substance formed inside pipes, kettles(1) etc when the water supply is hard(7): *This piece of metal is supposed to prevent fur from collecting in the kettle.* 4 *u.n* white substance that covers a person's tongue when he/she is ill.

▷ *tr/intr.v* (-*rr*-) 5 (often — (s.t) up) (cause (a pipe, kettle(1), .tongue etc) to) become covered with fur(3,4): *Kettles*(1) *and pipes fur (up) quickly because of the* hard(7) *water in this area.*

furrier /ˈfʌrɪə/ *c.n* person who prepares and/or sells furs(2).

furry /ˈfɜːrɪ/ *adj* (-*ier*, -*iest*) covered with, like, of, fur(1): *a furry kitten; a furry carpet.*

furious /ˈfjʊərɪəs/ *adj* 1 (often — with s.o) extremely angry (with s.o): *She's furious with you for forgetting to telephone. He's in a furious temper over losing the* contract(1). 2 wild, violent and without control: *They had a furious argument. The sea was looking furious.* **fast and furious** ⇒ fast(*adj*).

'furiously *adv*. **'furiousness** *u.n*.

fury /ˈfjʊərɪ/ *n* (*pl* -*ies*) 1 *c/u.n* (usu *sing*) wild, violent anger or excitement: *He could hardly control his fury. He was filled with fury when* she refused to listen to him. 2 *c.n* person who is (often) in a fury(1). **like fury** (*informal*) extremely fast, hard: *They worked like fury to finish the job on time.*

furl /fɜːl/ *v* 1 *tr.v* roll up (flags, sails, umbrellas etc); curl: *The wind dropped so they furled the sails and used the motor.* Opposite unfurl. 2 *intr.v* be able to be furled (⇒ furl(1)): *This umbrella furls into a small shape.*

furled *adj* (usu *attrib*) curled; rolled up: *Furled flags lay on the ground.*

furlong /ˈfɜːlɒŋ/ *c.n* length measuring 220 yards or one eighth of a mile.

furlough /ˈfɜːləʊ/ *c/u.n* (*formal*) permission to be away from one's duty, esp as a soldier or official working overseas: *She was given one week's furlough to attend her brother's wedding.* Compare holiday(*n*), leave[1](2), vacation(1). **on furlough** (while) having a furlough: *He was able to come home on furlough every two years.*

furnace /ˈfɜːnɪs/ *c.n* place (in a factory etc) in which great heat can be produced by fire for melting metals etc or for making steam to heat buildings.

furnish /ˈfɜːnɪʃ/ *tr.v* 1 provide, supply, (a house etc) with furniture: *Is your flat furnished? It'll cost us a lot of money to furnish our new house but we'll do it slowly.* 2 (*formal*) provide, supply, (s.o) (with things that are necessary): *Each child will be furnished with the necessary books.*

'furnished *adj* containing furniture etc: *A furnished house will cost more to rent.* Opposite unfurnished.

'furnishings *pl.n* things needed to furnish(1) a room, e.g furniture, carpets, curtains.

furniture /ˈfɜːnɪtʃə/ *u.n* (also *attrib*) things needed in a house, office, room, e.g chairs, tables, beds, desks, cupboards: *Together we've got enough furniture to fill a huge house. There's a very good furniture shop in town.* **piece of furniture** single article of furniture, e.g a chair, table.

furore /fjʊˈrɔːrɪ/ *sing.n* (usu *a — over s.t*) general wild excitement, interest, admiration, anger etc (about s.t): *There was a furore over the new laws.*

furrier ⇒ fur.

furrow /ˈfʌrəʊ/ *c.n* 1 long narrow cut in the soil, made by a plough for planting. 2 (*fig*) line in the skin of the face, esp the forehead.

▷ *tr.v* 3 make furrows(*n*) in (the soil, skin): *The farmer furrows his fields in spring.*

'furrowed *adj* (usu *attrib*) having furrows(*n*): *Her face was furrowed with age.*

furry ⇒ fur.

further, furtherance, furthermore, furthermost ⇒ far.

furtive /ˈfɜːtɪv/ *adj* (*formal*) (suspicious because) acting secretly and without anyone knowing or noticing, esp so as to deceive: *His furtive behaviour made the police suspicious.*

'furtively *adv*. **'furtiveness** *u.n*.

fury ⇒ furious.

fuse¹ /fjuːz/ *c.n* 1 short piece of wire used in an electric circuit(4) because it melts and breaks if the electric current which passes through it is too strong: *This plug(3) uses a 5 amp fuse. If the lamp isn't working check the fuse.* 2 (*informal*) break in an electric current caused by a fuse[1](1) melting: *The lights went out because of a fuse.*

▷ *v* **3** *tr/intr.v* (cause (an electric circuit(4)) to) break because a fuse(1) melts and makes the electrical instruments stop working: *The lights fused because they were all on at the same time.* **4** *tr/intr.v* (often — (s.t) together) (*technical*) melt (s.t), become melted, through great heat, esp in order to join two or more substances: *Zinc and copper fuse (together) to make brass.*

fusion /'fju:ʒən/ *c/u.n* (often *a* — *of s.t*) (*formal*) mixing of different things together; mixture of things: *The population of this city is a fusion of people of many different races[2](3) and* cultures(3).

fuse² /fju:z/ *c.n* piece of material or string, electrical device, that causes a bomb to explode: *He lit the fuse but it went out and the bomb didn't explode.*

fuselage /'fju:zɪˌlɑːʒ/ *c.n* body (of an aircraft) to which the wings etc are fastened.

fusillade /ˌfju:zɪ'leɪd/ *c.n* **1** (*military*) continuous shooting of guns: *The soldiers let off a fusillade.* **2** (*fig*) large quantity of s.t, e.g questions, aimed at s.o: *The leader of the government had to face a fusillade of accusations.*

fusion ⇒ fuse[1].

fuss /fʌs/ *c/u.n* **1** (usu *sing*; often *a* — *about s.o/ s.t*) excessive concern, worry or activity, (about s.o/s.t that is not important): *They made so much fuss that the manager gave them the room they wanted. What's all the fuss about?* **kick up a fuss (about s.o/s.t)** (*informal*); **make a fuss (about s.o/s.t)** complain angrily; be excessively concerned or worried (about s.o/s.t that is often not very important). **make a fuss of s.o/s.t** pay a great or excessive amount of attention to s.o/ s.t: *Don't make such a fuss of it; it's not important. Jean enjoys being made a fuss of.*

▷ *intr.v* **2** (often — *about/over s.o/s.t*) be excessively concerned, anxious, (about/over s.o/s.t): *I wish you'd stop fussing. She's always fussing about something. The way he fusses over his children makes them angry.*

'fussily *adv* in a fussy way.

'fussiness *u.n* state or fact of being fussy.

'fuss,pot *c.n* (*derog*; *informal*) person who always fusses (⇒ fuss(2)).

'fussy *adj* (-*ier*, -*iest*) **1** (of a person, behaviour) who/that fusses(2); that shows fussiness: *a fussy old man. She has a fussy way of cleaning everything before she uses it.* **2** too concerned with detail, esp that satisfies one's tastes or standards: *He's a fussy eater. I'm not fussy and I don't mind where we stay.* **3** having too much decoration, esp details etc that are not important: *I don't like fussy clothes.*

fusty /'fʌstɪ/ *adj* (-*ier*, -*iest*) (that smells) old and damp: *It smells very fusty in here.*

futile /'fju:taɪl/ *adj* (*formal*) useless; having no possible result: *It's futile to dream of buying such an expensive car.*

futilely /'fju:taɪllɪ/ *adv.*

futility /fju:'tɪlɪtɪ/ *c/u.n* (often *the* — *of s.t*) (example of a) state, (or of the) fact, of (s.t) being useless: *the futility of war. She soon realized the futility of her efforts to save the sick bird.*

future /'fju:tʃə/ *adj* **1** that will be or happen later, in time still to come: *She met her future husband at a party.* **2** (*grammar*) expressing an action, time that is still to happen: *Use future tenses[2] to describe what you want to do when you leave college.*

▷ *n* **3** *c/def/u.n* (often *the* — *of s.o/s.t*) time, events, life, still to come: *He has a great future as a musician. We want to share our future together. The future of this company is in doubt.* **4** *def.n* (*grammar*) = future tense. **in (the) future** from this time onwards: *You'll have to pay your rent on the first of each month in future.* **in the future** at some time later: *I hope we'll meet again in the future.* **in the distant/near future** at a future(1) time which is far from/near to the present. **in the not too distant future** not immediately but quite soon. ⇒ foreseeable.

future 'perfect (ˌtense) *def.n* (*grammar*) verb form used to show action that will have finished by a certain time in the future, e.g 'We *will have seen* it', 'They*'ll have arrived* by Friday'.

future 'tense *def.n* (*grammar*) verb form showing action, time, that is still to be, come, happen, e.g 'He *will come* tomorrow'.

futuristic /ˌfju:tʃə'rɪstɪk/ *adj* (*informal*) very modern and strange.

fuzz /fʌz/ *n* **1** *u.n* mass of soft short hair that stands up: *I don't like the fuzz on peaches(2).* **2** *def.pl.n* (*slang*) police.

'fuzzily *adv* in a fuzzy way.

'fuzziness *u.n* fact or state of being fuzzy.

'fuzzy *adj* (-*ier*, -*iest*) **1** not clear: *The television picture is fuzzy. Your ideas are still rather fuzzy; you need to think about the plan a little more.* **2** (usu *attrib*) covered with, like, fuzz(1): *I still have my old fuzzy toys.*

fwd *written abbr* forward.

Gg

G, g /dʒi:/ *c/unique n* **1** 7th letter of the English alphabet.

▷ *symb* **2** (**g**) gallon(s). **3** (**g**) gram(s). **4** (**G**) good. ⇒ VG. **5** (US *slang*) grand(6).

gab /gæb/ *u.n* (*informal*) (a lot of) talking: *Let's cut out all this gab and get on with the job.* (**have**) **the gift of the gab** (often *derog*) (have) the ability to talk easily and well (often on any subject).

gabardine /ˌgæbə'di:n/ *n* (also ˌgaber'dine) **1** *u.n* (also *attrib*) kind of cotton or silk material: *a gabardine raincoat.* **2** *c.n* (rain)coat made of this material: *He was wearing a gabardine.*

gabble /'gæbl/ *u.n* **1** quick speech, or the sound of several people talking, that is difficult to understand: *The gabble of voices in the background made it difficult for me to hear her.*

▷ *tr/intr.v* **2** speak (words) quickly and in a way that is difficult to understand. **gabble away/on** (**about s.t**) (*informal*) continue to gabble(2) (about s.t):

Bob was gabbling on about how good he was but I wasn't listening. **gabble s.t out** say s.t quickly and in a way that is difficult to understand. Compare babble.

gable /'geɪbl/ *c.n* top part of the outside wall of a house shaped like a triangle(1) and supporting sloping roofs.

'gabled *adj* (of a house or roof) having a gable.

gad /gæd/ *intr.v* (-dd-) **gad about/around (s.w)** (*informal; derog*) go, wander, about (a place or places) without any real purpose except pleasure: *William gads around town going to parties and never does any work.*

gadabout /'gædə,baʊt/ *c.n* (*derog*) person who does this.

gadfly /'gæd,flaɪ/ *c.n* (*pl -ies*) kind of fly with a sharp sting that suck the blood of animals such as horses and cows.

gadget /'gædʒɪt/ *c.n* (*informal*) (small) mechanical, electrical etc device that does s.t (that may be useful or not): *The car has so many gadgets that I never know what button to press.*

gadgetry /'gædʒɪtrɪ/ *u.n* (number of) gadgets: *a house full of the latest gadgetry.*

gaff /gæf/ *c.n* long stick with a hook on one end used to pull a large fish from a river or stream usu when it has been caught on a fishing line. **blow the gaff** (*fig; informal*) talk about, reveal, s.t that should have been kept secret.

gaffe /gæf/ *c.n* (usu **make a —**) thing that was not intended to be rude but was: *That was a real gaffe you made praising his first wife when his second was standing next to him.*

gag /gæg/ *c.n* **1** thing, e.g a piece of material, put into s.o's mouth or tied around s.o's face and covering the mouth so that he/she cannot speak. **2** funny joke, amusing trick etc, told or done by s.o, esp as part of a performance: *The actors did a number of gags that made us laugh loudly.*
▷ *v* (-gg-) **3** *tr.v* put a gag(1) on (s.o). **4** *tr.v* (*fig*) stop (s.o) from speaking or writing freely: *The government has managed to gag the press by threatening to close any newspaper that writes anything against it.* **5** *intr.v* (of an actor etc) say or use a gag(2): *He gagged for ten minutes before the main act started.* **6** *intr.v* (usu **— on** s.t) feel or be (almost) sick (because of swallowing s.t bad, because of s.t bad one has seen etc): *She gagged on the bone she had accidentally swallowed. At the sight of the dead body he almost gagged.*

gage ⇨ gauge.

gaggle /'gægl/ *c.n* **1** (collective name for a) flock¹(1) of geese (⇨ goose(1)). **2** (*informal*) group of men/women/children, esp ones doing s.t noisily: *There was a gaggle of women enjoying themselves in the corner.*

gaiety, gaily ⇨ gay.

gain /geɪn/ *c/u.n* **1** (example of an) amount of money one gets as a profit: *He's only in the business for gain. When he sold his house he made a gain of £10 000.* ⇨ capital gains (tax), ill-gotten gains. **2** (often **a — of, in,** s.t (**over** s.o/ s.t)) (example of an) increase (e.g in weight, distance etc): *He ate so much that one could almost see his gain in weight. Joe ran faster and soon had made a gain of ten metres over his rivals.* Opposite loss(1).
▷ *v* **3** *tr/intr.v* make a profit (of (so much)) on s.t:

Did you gain (anything) when you sold the car? Opposite lose(6). **4** *tr.v* have an increase of (s.t) (in weight etc), sometimes wanted, sometimes not: *Ann gained a kilo after she stopped the diet(1).* Opposite lose(6). **5** *tr.v* get (more of) (s.t, esp knowledge, experience etc): *He gained a lot of information just by listening to them.* **6** *tr/ intr.v* (of a clock/watch etc) go too fast (by (a certain amount)): *My watch gains (two minutes) every day.* Opposite lose(5). **7** *tr.v* (*formal*) arrive at, reach, (s.w) esp after an effort: *We gained the top of the hill just as darkness fell.* **gain currency** ⇨ currency. **gain ground** ⇨ ground³(*n*). **gain power** ⇨ power(*n*). **gain speed** ⇨ speed(*n*). **gain (s.t) (up)on s.o/s.t (a)** begin to get nearer (by a certain amount) to s.o/s.t in front of one: *She had gained (five metres) on the runners in front of her.* **(b)** begin to get further away (by a certain amount) from s.o/s.t behind one: *The other car was faster and had soon gained on the one following.* **gain the upper hand (over s.o)** ⇨ upper hand. **gain time** ⇨ time (*n*).

'gainful *adj* (*formal*) earning money or profit: *gainful employment.*

'gainfully *adv* (*formal*): *gainfully employed.*

gainsay /geɪn'seɪ/ *tr.v* (*3rd pers sing, pres.t -says* /-'sez/, *p.t,p.p -said* /-'sed/) (*formal*) say that (s.t) does not exist; deny(1) (s.t): *It is difficult to gainsay Kevin's skill at cards.*

,gain'saying *u.n* (often **there is no — (the fact) that . . .**) act of denying(1) s.t: *There is no gainsaying the fact that the country is in a bad state.*

gait /geɪt/ *c.n* (*formal*) way of walking or running: *He has a rather awkward gait as a result of an accident to his leg.*

gal(l) *written abbr* gallon(s).

gala /'gɑːlə/ *c.n* (also *attrib*) special occasion when there are celebrations, gatherings of people, sports activities, competitions etc: *a miners' gala; a swimming gala; a gala ball.*

'gala per,formance *c.n* special performance of a play, showing of a film etc, attended by famous people and usu in aid of charity(2).

galaxy /'gæləksɪ/ *c.n* (*pl -ies*) **1** one of the large groups of stars in the universe. **2** (usu **a — of** s.o/ s.t) (*fig*) (a) large number of (famous) people, of (good) things (to choose from) etc: *There was a whole galaxy of well-known faces at the opening of the new theatre.*

galactic /gə'læktɪk/ *adj* of or referring to a galaxy(1).

gale /geɪl/ *c.n* very strong wind: *Gales have struck the country and destroyed a lot of property.*

'gale ,force *u.n* (**'gale-,force** when *attrib*) (having reached the) strength of a gale: *Winds reaching gale force (or Gale-force winds) are forecast(2) over much of the country.*

,gale of 'laughter *c.n* (*pl gales of laughter*) (usu *pl*) sudden burst of noisy laughter.

gall /gɔːl/ *n* **1** *u.n* bitter yellow liquid produced by the liver(1). ⇨ bile. **2** *u.n* (*literary; formal*) bitter feeling. **3** *u.n* (usu **have the — to do/say** s.t) (*informal*) (show a great deal of) rudeness, cheek(2) or impudence (by saying/doing s.t): *She had the gall to accuse me of being lazy when she herself stays in bed as long as she can!* **4** *c.n* painful swelling on an animal, esp a horse, caused by rubbing. **5** *c.n* growth, like a swelling, on a tree made by one or more insects.

▷ *tr.v* **6** greatly annoy or hurt the feelings of (s.o): *Her behaviour really galls me when I think of what I have done for her.*

'**gall-,bladder** *c.n* kind of bag connected to the liver (1) which contains gall (1).

'**galling** *adj* very annoying or hurtful: *It was galling to realize that he had lost the job through his own stupidity.*

'**gall,stone** *c.n* hard object like a stone sometimes found in the gall-bladder and sometimes harmful.

gallant /'gælənt/ *adj* (*old use*) **1** brave: *a gallant deed; a gallant soldier.* **2** (also /gə'lænt/) (of a man) showing special attention or respect towards women: *He was always very gallant in the presence of women.*

▷ *c.n* (also /gə'lænt/) **3** (*old use*) man of fashion who is very gallant (2).

'**gallantly** *adj* bravely.

gallantry /'gæləntrɪ/ *u.n* **1** bravery (esp in war): *He was awarded a* medal (1) *for gallantry in action.* **2** (*old use*) special attention or respect towards women.

galleon /'gælɪən/ *c.n* kind of large sailing ship, usu armed, esp one used by Spain in the 15th to the 17th centuries.

gallery /'gælərɪ/ (*pl* -*ies*) **1** *c.n* (room in a) building in which works of art are shown (sometimes for sale): *There are many art galleries in central London.* **2** *c.n* upper floor fixed to the inside of the wall of a building, hall etc and open in the front, from which one can look down and watch what is happening in the main part: *There was a gallery running around the back and sides of the church.* **3** *c.n* highest floor in a theatre in which are the cheapest seats. **4** *def.pl.n* all the audience in a gallery (3): *The gallery cheered when she made her first appearance.* **5** *c.n* long narrow passage covered on top but open along one side. **6** *c.n* long narrow room used for shooting practice, testing of guns etc: *a shooting gallery.* **7** *c.n* horizontal tunnel or passage in an underground mine. **play to the gallery** (*fig; informal*) try to win the approval of ordinary people by saying or doing things that they will like.

galley /'gælɪ/ *c.n* (*pl* -*s*) **1** (in history) kind of long ship with sails and rows of oars, usu pulled by slaves (1). **2** kitchen on a ship.

galling ⇒ gall.

gallivant /ˌgælɪ'vænt/ *intr.v* **gallivant about/around** (**s.w**) (*derog; informal*) = gad about/around (s.w).

gallon /'gælən/ *c.n* (*written abbr* gal(l)) liquid measure equal to 8 pints or 4 quarts (in the UK it is equal to 4.54 litres, in the US to 3.78 litres). **gallons** (**of s.t**) large amount or quantity (of s.t liquid): *He's ordered gallons of wine for the party.*

gallop /'gæləp/ *c.n* **1** (of a horse or other animals with four feet) fastest speed, in which all four feet are off the ground at the same time during each movement or stride (1) forward. **at a gallop** (moving) at this speed: *They rode across the field at a gallop.* **break into a gallop** start to move at this speed. Compare canter (1); trot (1).

▷ *v* **2** *tr/intr.v* (cause (a horse) to) move at this speed: *They galloped* (*their horses*) *across the fields.* **3** *intr.v* (*joking*) (of a person) run: *He galloped down the road after her.* **gallop through s.t** (*fig;*

informal) do or say s.t very quickly (esp in order to finish it and do s.t else): *He galloped through his speech because he had a train to catch.*

'**galloping** *attrib.adj* (*fig*) increasing at a very fast rate: *galloping inflation* (2).

gallows /'gæləuz/ *pl.n* (usu with sing v) kind of wooden frame, used for putting criminals to death by hanging. **send s.o to the gallows** order s.o to be hanged in this way.

gallstone ⇒ gall.

Gallup poll /'gæləp ˌpəul/ *c.n* (*t.n*) method of discovering public opinion about s.t, esp before an election on how people expect to vote, by asking questions of a (small) group of people who are chosen by chance.

galore /gə'lɔː/ *adj* (usu *s.t* (*and s.t*) —) in large amounts or quantities: *We had food and drink galore at the party.*

galoshes /gə'lɒʃɪz/ *pl.n* (often *a pair of*—) kind of rubber shoes worn over ordinary shoes to protect them in wet weather. ⇒ overshoe.

galvanize, -ise /'gælvəˌnaɪz/ *tr.v* **1** put a thin coat of zinc on (a metal such as iron or steel) to protect it from rust. **2** (often — *s.o into doing s.t*) (*fig*) force or compel (1) (s.o) (to do s.t, become very active etc, as a result of s.t that has happened): *He was galvanized into action when he realized he might lose a lot of money.*

gambit /'gæmbɪt/ *c.n* **1** (in chess) one of the different moves of one's pieces, esp to start a game. **2** (often *an opening* —) (*fig*) thing one says, does etc at the beginning of a discussion etc in order to get some (future) advantage: *His opening gambit was to say that the prices they charge are too high.*

gamble /'gæmbl/ *c.n* **1** (often — *on s.o/s.t*) act of betting (4) (on (on s.o/s.t): *I like a gamble on the horses now and then.* **2** attempt etc that is uncertain, has a lot of risk or chance in it, but may bring profit or an advantage: *It's a gamble whether that company will succeed or not and my advice is not to lend it any money.* **have a gamble** (**on s.t**) = gamble (3) once (on s.t). **take a gamble** (**on s.t**) = gamble (4) (on s.t).

▷ *tr/intr.v* **3** (often — (*s.t*) *on s.t*) bet (4) or risk (one's money) on horses, games of chance etc: *He gambled £5000 on a horse that came in last. She spent all her money gambling on cards.* **4** take a chance/risk (on a fact, that s.t will happen etc): *I'm gambling* (*on the fact*) *that they don't know as much as I do about the state of the company.* **gamble s.t away** lose s.t by gambling (3): *Maurice gambled away all his money.*

'**gambler** *c.n* person who gambles (3,4).

'**gambling** *u.n* (also *attrib*) act of betting (4) money.

gambol /'gæmbl/ *c.n* **1** quick light playful jumping about, esp of lambs (1) or children.

▷ *intr.v* (-*ll*-, US -*l*-) **2** (often — *about/around* (*s.t*)) jump in this way: *The lambs were gambolling in the field.*

game /geɪm/ *adj* **1** (often — *to do s.t;* — *for s.t*) ready and eager (to do s.t, for s.t); brave: *He was always game to try anything for the first time.* **2** = gammy.

▷ *n* **3** *c.n* (often *play a*—; *play* —*s*) one of a number of activities, usu with rules, which people, esp children, take part in to amuse themselves: *The children were in the garden playing a game of* 'hide-and-seek'. **4** *c.n* (often (*play*) *a — of s.t*) organized form of play with (written) rules in which a person or team is in competition with another one: *a football game*; *a game of tennis*; *a card game*; *a board game*. **5** *c.n* (in some sports, e.g tennis) single round or part of a complete game(4): *She won the first* set¹(5) *six games to one (6–1)*. **6** *c.n* all the objects, cards etc and usu a printed board needed to play certain kinds of indoor games(4): *a game of* ludo. **7** *u.n* (also *attrib*) wild animal(s), bird(s) etc hunted (and shot) for sport or food: *game birds. Every autumn he goes shooting for game*. **8** *c.n* (often s.o's (*little* —)) (*informal*) plan or trick made by s.o in order to deceive s.o: *'She's pretending to be ill.' 'So that's her little game, is it?'* **be fair game** (*fig*) be a person or thing who/that can be attacked or criticized: *His failure to do the job properly made him fair game for all the people who disliked him*. **big game** ⇨ big. **give the game/show away** (*informal*) let s.t secret become known, usu by accident: *It was supposed to be a surprise party but he gave the game away by telling her all about it*. **off one's game** not playing a game(4) as well as one usually can. **play a game** (or **games**) (**with s.o**) (**a**) ⇨ game(3,4). (**b**) act in a teasing(2) or dishonest way (with s.o): *I wish you would stop playing these games with me and tell me the truth for once*. **play s.o's game** help s.o's plan, join in her/his activities, even if unwillingly or without realizing that one is doing so: *If you do what he wants, you do understand, I hope, that you will just be playing his game*. **play the game** (**a**) keep to the rules of a game(4). (**b**) (*fig*) act in a fair and honest way: *At least he played the game and told me what he was planning to do*. **the game is up** (*fig*; *informal*) the plan etc has been discovered and so has failed. **two can play at that game** ⇨ two.

'**game,keeper** *c.n* person whose job is to look after game(7).

'**gamely** *adv* in a game(1) way: *He bore his illness gamely*.

,**game 'point** *c.n* (in tennis etc) last point needed to win the game(5).

games *n* **1** *def.pl.n* (usu with capital **G**) (name for a) number of sports competitions played during a particular time, at a particular place etc: *the Olympic/Commonwealth Games*. **2** *u.n* (UK) games(4) as a subject to be taught in school: *We have games every Wednesday afternoon*.

'**gamesman,ship** *u.n* skill at winning games(4) mainly by damaging the confidence of one's competitor(s).

'**gaming** *u.n* (*old use*) = gambling.

gamma /'gæmə/ *c.n* 3rd letter of the Greek alphabet (Γ γ).

'**gamma ,rays** *pl.n* (also '**gamma ,radi,ation** *u.n*) (form of) powerful, usu harmful, rays given off by radioactive substances.

gammon /'gæmən/ *u.n* (also *attrib*) ham(1) or bacon that has been smoked or cured(8): *gammon rashers*.

gammy /'gæmɪ/ *adj* (*informal*) (esp of a leg) lame; crippled(2): *She could hardly climb the stairs because of her gammy leg*. = game(2).

gamut /'gæmət/ *c.n* **1** (*music*) whole and complete range of sounds a voice or an instrument can make. **2** whole range, scale or extent of s.t,

esp feelings. (**run**) **the** (**whole**) **gamut of s.t** (experience) the (whole) range of s.t: *Her face went through the whole gamut of emotions(1) — first, joy that he was alive, followed by fear that he was hurt and then anger that he had done something so stupid*.

gander /'gændə/ *c.n* male goose(1). **have/take a gander** (**at s.o/s.t**) (*slang*) have a (quick) look (at s.o/s.t); make a (quick) examination (of s.o/ s.t): *Could you have a gander at the engine?*

gang /gæŋ/ *c.n* **1** group of criminals who work together: *The gang robbed the bank and got away with £20 000*. **2** group of workmen, esp those employed in building work, making or repairing roads etc: *There was a gang of workmen digging up the road*. **3** group of (young) people who go about together (often doing s.t wrong and fighting against other groups): *The police were called because a fight broke out between the two rival gangs*.

▷ *intr.v* **4 gang together** form into a group (esp in order to get s.t done, to fight s.t etc): *Instead of quarrelling among ourselves why don't we gang together and fight the Council's plans as a group?* **5 gang up against/on s.o** come together as a group, join a group, in order to act against s.o else: *The other children all ganged up against him in the playground because he was the teacher's pet*. **6 gang up with s.o** join s.o or a group (and go around together for some purpose): *He ganged up with a crowd of* teenagers *who spent their time riding around on* motorbikes.

ganger /'gæŋə/ *c.n* person in charge of a gang(2).

gangster /'gæŋstə/ *c.n* criminal who is a member of an armed gang(1).

gangling /'gæŋglɪŋ/ *adj* (also **gangly** /'gæŋglɪ/ (*-ier, -iest*)) (of a person) tall, thin and looking awkward or moving awkwardly.

gangplank /'gæŋ,plæŋk/ *c.n* board placed between a ship or boat and the land, or another ship or boat, on which one can walk onto or off the ship or boat.

gangrene /'gæŋgriːn/ *u.n* decay and death of a part of the body caused by the blood supply having been stopped by a wound, the cold etc: *His leg had to be* amputated *because it was affected by* gangrene.

gangrenous /'gæŋgrɪnəs/ *adj* (of a part of the body) affected by gangrene.

gangster ⇨ gang.

gangway /'gæŋ,weɪ/ *c.n* **1** kind of (covered) bridge between an opening in the side of a ship and the land along which one can walk onto or off the ship. **2** passage or space between groups of rows of seats in a theatre, cinema etc.

▷ *interj* **3** (*informal*) Please make a space so that s.o can get through: *Gangway, please! This woman's ill and she needs to get out into the fresh air*.

gannet /'gænɪt/ *c.n* kind of large bird that lives mostly on or beside the sea and eats fish.

gantry /'gæntrɪ/ *c.n* (*pl -ies*) steel framework that supports a crane(2), carries heavy loads, carries railway signals above and over a number of railway tracks etc.

gaol /dʒeɪl/ *n* (US **jail**) **1** *c.n* prison building: *Britain's gaols are overflowing with prisoners*. **2** *u.n* state or act of being held in (a) prison: *The judge ordered gaol for the prisoner*. **be in**

gaol be kept in (a) prison. **send s.o to gaol** order s.o to go to and stay in (a) prison, e.g for a crime or to wait for a trial.

▷ *tr.v* (US **jail**) **3** put (s.o) in (a) prison: *He was gaoled for life.*

'gaol,bird *c.n* (US **'jail,bird**) (*informal*) prisoner, esp one who is often sent to (a) prison.

'gaoler *c.n* (US **'jailer**, **'jailor**) person who is in charge of a gaol(1) or the prisoners in it. Compare warder.

gap /gæp/ *c.n* **1** opening, break, empty space, in s.t, between two things etc: *She climbed through the gap in the fence.* **2** (with capital **G** in names) (name for a) pass or space between mountains: *the Cumberland Gap.* **3** length of time in which s.t does not happen, when there is silence etc (for a certain length of time): *After a gap of several hours the train service started again. There was a gap in the conversation when no one could think of anything to say.* **4** difference (of opinion, views etc) between two groups of people: *The gap between the teachers' demands and what the government is prepared to offer is very wide.* **5** (often *a — in* s.t) thing that is missing (from s.t), that one has not learnt (about s.t) etc: *He decided to go to night classes to fill in the gaps in his education.* **bridge a gap** ⇒ bridge(7). **close the gap** make the difference between two amounts smaller. **fill a gap** provide s.t needed that is not present. ⇒ generation gap, stop gap, trade gap.

gape /geɪp/ *c.n* **1** kind of stare(1) with the mouth wide open, showing e.g surprise: *a gape of astonishment.*

▷ *intr.v* **2** (often *— in s.t*) open one's mouth widely (esp because of surprise): *He just stood and gaped in amazement as the tree crashed to the ground.* **3** be or become open wide: *The ground shook and suddenly a hole gaped in front of him.* **gape at s.o/ s.t** (**a**) look in surprise or astonishment at s.o/s.t: *He stood there gaping at her when she told him her news.* (**b**) look in a foolish or uneducated manner at s.o/s.t, because one has not seen her/him/it before, is not used to the sight etc: *The place was full of foreign tourists gaping at the sights.* **gape open** gape(3) (very) widely.

'gaping *adj* (very) wide: *a gaping hole in the ground.*

garage /'gærɑːʒ, 'gærɪdʒ/ *c.n* **1** building at the side of a house, or that is part of it or completely separate, in which a car or cars is/are kept. **2** building or area near a road where one can get petrol, have one's car repaired or serviced etc.

▷ *tr.v* **3** put (a car or cars) in a garage(1): *I won't be a moment, I'm just going to garage the car.*

garb /gɑːb/ *u.n* **1** (*literary* or *formal*) clothing; (certain kind of) things one wears: *He was wearing the garb of a priest.*

▷ *tr.v* (*literary* or *formal*) **2** clothe or dress (s.o) (in a certain way): *He garbed himself as a priest.* **be garbed in s.t** be wearing a certain kind of clothing: *She was garbed from head to toe in a long black* cloak(1).

garbage /'gɑːbɪdʒ/ *n* **1** *u.n* (mainly US) waste material from a house etc (e.g bits of food, waste paper); rubbish(2). **2** *u.n* (*informal*) worthless thing; statement of no value: *The whole of his speech was complete garbage from beginning to end.*

'garbage ,can *c.n* (US) dustbin, rubbish bin.
'garbage col,lector *c.n* (US) dustman, rubbish collector.
'garbage ,truck *c.n* (US) dustcart.

garble /'gɑːbl/ *tr.v* make (a statement, message etc) confused or mixed up: *She garbled the message that had been given to her over the phone so that I couldn't understand it.*

garden /'gɑːdn/ *c.n* **1** (also *attrib*) area of ground or land used for growing flowers, grass, vegetables, trees etc: *a small garden*; *garden flowers*; *a garden path.* ⇒ gardens. **lead s.o up the garden path** (*fig*; *informal*) deceive or mislead s.o. **market-garden(er/ing)** ⇒ market.

▷ *intr.v* **2** work in a garden, planting and making things grow, removing weeds etc: *He's gardening at the moment; do you want to speak to him?*

'garden ,centre *c.n* large shop with grounds around it where one can buy flowers, plants, tools etc for the garden.
,garden 'city/'suburb *c.n* town/suburb arranged and laid out with a lot of (public) gardens, trees and open spaces.
'garden ,party *c.n* (*pl* **-ies**) (official or private) social occasion held out of doors in a garden: *The Queen holds a number of garden parties in the grounds of Buckingham Palace.*

gardener /'gɑːdnə/ *c.n* **1** person who likes to garden: *Jackie's a* keen(1) *gardener.* **2** person whose job is to work in a garden.

gardening /'gɑːdnɪŋ/ *u.n* (also *attrib*) act of working in a garden: *I don't like gardening much. He keeps the gardening tools in a shed.*

'gardens *pl.n* (with capital **G** in names) **1** (name for a) public park, usu with flower beds etc or with special things such as animals, rare flowers, trees etc: *the* botanical/zoological *gardens.* **2** (*written abbr* **Gdns**) (name for a) road or street (sometimes with public gardens near it): *He lives at 21 Queen's Gardens.*

gardenia /gɑːˈdiːnɪə/ *c.n* kind of plant with white or yellow flowers, found in hot damp countries.

gargantuan /gɑːˈgæntjuən/ *adj* (esp of a meal) very large: *It took me some time to* recover(1) *from such a gargantuan meal.*

gargle /'gɑːgl/ *c.n* **1** act of cleaning or washing the throat or mouth with a liquid by mixing it with air from the lungs. **2** bubbling(7) noise made while doing this. **3** special liquid used for this purpose.

▷ *intr.v* **4** clean or wash one's throat or mouth in this way: *The dentist advised me to gargle after every meal.*

gargoyle /'gɑːgɔɪl/ *c.n* stone or metal figure, made in the shape of an (ugly) animal or human face or body, that sticks out from the roof of a building and carries rainwater that then pours out without touching the wall(s).

garish /'geərɪʃ/ *adj* (*derog*) (of colours, clothes etc) too bright; not going well together: *She wore garish clothes to attract attention.*
'garishly *adv.* **'garishness** *u.n.*

garland /'gɑːlənd/ *c.n* **1** circle of flowers and/ or leaves used as a decoration, an ornament or a prize for victory etc.

▷ *tr.v* **2** (often *— s.o/s.t with s.t*) decorate (s.o/s.t) with a garland(1): *As the passengers came off the ship they were garlanded with flowers.*

garlic /'gɑːlɪk/ *u.n* kind of plant like an onion that has a strong taste and smell, used in cooking.

garment /'gɑːmənt/ *c.n* (*formal*) article of clothing.

garnet /'gɑːnɪt/ *c.n* kind of dark red transparent stone, used in jewellery.

garnish /'gɑːnɪʃ/ *c.n* **1** thing, e.g leaves, small pieces of s.t, used to decorate a dish of food for the table.
▷ *tr.v* **2** (often — *s.t with s.t*) decorate (food, a dish etc) (with s.t): *He garnished the dish with slices of lemon.*

garret /'gærət/ *c.n* room at the top of a house under the roof, esp a small dark one: *He lived in a garret because he couldn't afford anything else.*

garrison /'gærɪsən/ *c.n* **1** (*military*) group of soldiers stationed in or near a town or in a fort in order to guard it.
▷ *tr.v* **2** (*military*) put or have soldiers in (a town or fort) for its defence.

garrulous /'gærʊləs/ *adj* (*formal*) (of a person) (fond of) talking too much (often about things that are not important): *a garrulous old woman.*
'garrulously *adv.* **garrulity** /gæ'ruːlɪtɪ/, **'garrulousness** *u.n*.

garter /'gɑːtə/ *c.n* band, usu made of elastic, worn around the thigh to hold a stocking up, or below the knee to hold a sock up. **(the Order of) the Garter** (badge belonging to) the highest rank of knighthood in the UK.

gas /gæs/ *n* **1** *c/u.n* (one of a) variety of substances like air, consisting of atoms(1) and molecules that move freely in space and that will fill all the space available to them: *Oxygen and nitrogen are gases.* **2** *u.n* (also *attrib*) gas(1) made from coal (coal gas) or oil, or found in a natural form (natural gas) under the ground, used for cooking, heating, lighting etc: *a gas cooker.* **3** *u.n* special gas(1) used esp by dentists to put patients to sleep when drilling or removing teeth. **4** *u.n* poisonous gas(1) used in war. ⇨ teargas (⇨ tear¹). **5** *u.n* (US *informal*) gasoline ((UK) = petrol). **by gas** using gas(2): *cook by gas.*
▷ *v* **6** *tr.v* poison, kill or overcome (s.o, oneself, an animal) with gas (2,4): *He gassed himself by putting his head in the oven.* **7** *intr.v* (often — *on* (about s.o/s.t)) (*slang*; *derog*) talk too much or too long, usu not saying anything very important (about s.o/s.t): *He was gassing on about how clever she was.*

'gas,bag *c.n* (*derog*; *slang*) person who talks too much.

'gas ,boiler *c.n* boiler in a central heating system using gas(2) to heat water.

'gas ,chamber *c.n* room in which people (and sometimes animals) are killed by poisonous gas(4): *Some States in the USA have used gas chambers for putting murderers to death.*

'gas ,cooker *c.n* stove with gas rings, an oven etc, used for cooking by gas(2). Compare electric cooker.

gaseous /'gæsɪəs/ *adj* of or referring to gas(1,2); having gas(1,2) in it: *gaseous substances.*

'gas ,fitter *c.n* person whose job is to put in pipes for a gas supply to a building, house etc, to connect up gas cookers, gas fires etc.

'gas,holder *c.n* very large tank used for storing gas(2).

'gas,lamp *c/u.n* (also **'gas,light**) (light or lamp giving) light by means of burning gas(2).

'gas,man *c.n* (*pl* -,men) person who works in the gas industry, esp one who is a gas fitter or who reads gas meters: *The gasman's coming to fix our boiler tomorrow.*

'gas ,mask *c.n* device worn over the face to stop one breathing poisonous gas(4).

'gas ,meter *c.n* device in a building, house etc for measuring how much gas(2) one uses (and therefore has to pay for).

gasoline /'gæsə,liːn/ *u.n* (also **'gaso,lene**) (US) petrol.

gasometer /gæ'sɒmətə/ *c.n* = gasholder.

'gas ,ring *c.n* ring(3) on a gas cooker with small holes in it through which gas(2) comes out which is then lit and heats things for cooking.

'gassiness *u.n* fact or state of being gassy.

'gassy *adj* (-ier, -iest) (esp of liquids) having a lot of gas(1) (that forms into bubbles(1)).

'gas ,station *c.n* (US) petrol station.

'gas ,stove *c.n* = gas cooker.

'gas,works *c.n* (*pl* gasworks) place, building(s), etc where gas(2) is made, usu from coal or oil.

gash /gæʃ/ *c.n* **1** long deep cut or open wound: *He has a nasty gash on his head.*
▷ *tr.v* **2** get a gash(1) on (one's body); cut (s.t) deeply: *She gashed her knee when she fell on the rocks.*

gasket /'gæskɪt/ *c.n* flat piece of material placed between two parts of a machine etc that are to be joined together so as to prevent a liquid or gas from getting out.

gaslamp, gaslight, gasman, gasoline, gasometer ⇨ gas.

gasp /gɑːsp/ *c.n* **1** (sound made by a) sudden act of breathing in air, because one is surprised, frightened, in pain etc: *We could hear the gasps of the children as they watched the circus performer.* **at one's last gasp** (*informal*) (**a**) having reached the limit of one's strength. (**b**) being near to death.
▷ *v* **2** *intr.v* make this sound; breathe with difficulty, esp because one is running, doing s.t too hard etc: *She gasped when she saw how badly he had been hurt. The old man was gasping as he struggled up the hill.* **3** *tr.v* (often — *s.t out*) say (s.t) while gasping(2): *After all the running he was only able to gasp out a few words at a time. 'Help me!' she gasped.* **be gasping for s.t** (*fig*; *informal*) be wanting to have s.t very much; be longing for s.t: *After this walk I'm gasping for a long cool drink.* **gasp for air/breath** gasp(2) in order to try to get air into one's lungs. **gasp with s.t** gasp(2) because of s.t one feels: *She gasped with anger when she heard what they had done.*

gassiness, gassy ⇨ gas.

gastric /'gæstrɪk/ *adj* of or referring to the stomach: *gastric juices; a gastric ulcer.*

gastritis /gæ'straɪtɪs/ *u.n* (*medical*) inflammation of the stomach.

gastroenteritis /ˌgæstrəʊˌentə'raɪtɪs/ *u.n* (*medical*) inflammation of the stomach and intestines.

gastronomy /gæ'strɒnəmɪ/ *u.n* art and science of good cooking; liking for good food.

gastronomic /ˌgæstrə'nɒmɪk/ *adj* of or referring to gastronomy.
ˌgastro'nomically *adv*.

gasworks ⇨ gas.

gate /geɪt/ *c.n* **1** framework of wooden or metal

bars that goes across an opening in a wall, fence, hedge(1), at the entrance to a park etc and can be opened or closed: *a garden gate. Always remember to close the farm gate properly so that the animals can't get out.* **2** (name for an) opening in the walls of a city or town with strong gates(1): *West Gate. The city gates were closed every night at 10 o'clock.* **3** number of people (or the amount of money they pay for) attending a sports event: *Gates for most of the football clubs have been low this season.*

▷ *tr.v* **4** punish (s.o, esp a student at a university) by not allowing her/him to go out (esp in the evening): *He was gated for the rest of the term because he had damaged college property.*

'gate,crash *tr/intr.v* (*informal*) go to (a party etc) to which one has not been invited.

'gate,crasher *c.n* person who gatecrashes.

'gate,house *c.n* building by or over a gate(1,2).

'gate,keeper *c.n* person in charge of opening and closing a gate(1,2) or gates, esp in a public place, e.g a park.

'gate ,money *c.n* = gate(3).

'gate,post *c.n* one of the two wooden or metal posts at the sides of a gate(1). **between you, me and the gatepost** (expression used for warning s.o that what one is going to say should be) treated as a secret: *Between you, me and the gatepost, I don't think he is to be trusted.*

'gate,way *c.n* **1** opening in a wall, a building etc that has a gate(1,2) in it. **2** (usu — *to s.t*) (*fig*) place that acts as a starting point (for getting s.w); thing that acts as an opportunity (to get s.t): *Bombay has been described as the gateway to India. He hoped that the classes he was going to at night would be his gateway to success.*

gâteau /'gætəʊ/ *c/u.n* (pl **gâteaux** /'gætəʊz/) (*French*) kind of very rich cake with cream etc.

gather /'gæðə/ *v* **1** *tr.v* pick or collect (flowers, fruit etc): *The children were gathering flowers in the garden.* **2** *tr.v* collect or bring together (a number of things): *They were gathering the leaves to burn them. He gathered his notes and put them in the desk drawer.* **3** *tr/intr.v* (cause (a number of people) to) come together, meet etc in one place: *He soon gathered a large crowd. A large crowd gathered in front of the building.* **4** *tr.v* (often — (*from s.o/s.t*) *that . . .*) understand, arrive at a conclusion(2) about s.t, (from what s.o says etc) that . . .: *I gather* (*from what he said*) *that he'll be leaving some time next week.* **5** *tr.v* make one or more small folds in (a cloth material) by pulling it together with a thread: *She wore a dress which had been gathered at the waist.*

gather s.t in (a) collect (a number of) things together: *They were gathering in the harvest.* (b) make s.t (e.g cloth) narrower by gathering(5) it: *She made the dress fit better by gathering it in at the waist.*

gather momentum ⇨ momentum.

gather (s.o) round (s.o) (cause (a group of people) to) come close together round (s.o): *She gathered the children round her. Gather round and I'll tell you a story.*

gather speed ⇨ speed(*n*).

gather (s.o/s.t) together (cause (a number of people/things) to) come together in one place; gather(1–3) (s.o/s.t).

gather one's thoughts etc (**together**) collect and

arrange one's thoughts etc in an orderly way: *I'll need to gather my thoughts together and write them down if you're to make any sense of them.*

gather s.o/s.t up collect or bring a number of people or things together, esp by taking them from a place or places: *He gathered up as many people as he could find to go to the meeting. Bob gathered his papers up from the desk.*

'gathering *c.n* (act of) people coming (or who have come) together; meeting (or people who have met) in one place: *There was a large gathering outside the town hall. We always have a family gathering at Christmas.*

gauche /gəʊʃ/ *adj* (*French*) (of a person) awkward in social matters (sometimes because of inexperience, youth etc): *He's a bit gauche in mixed company.*

'gauchely *adv.* **gaucherie** /,gəʊʃə'ri:/ *c/u.n.*

gaudy /'gɔːdɪ/ *adj* (*derog*) (*-ier*, *-iest*) (of colours, clothes etc) too bright or showy (sometimes considered not to be in good taste): *She wore gaudy clothes to attract attention to herself.*

'gaudily *adv.* **'gaudiness** *u.n.*

gauge /geɪdʒ/ *c.n* (US also **gage**) **1** (measurement of a) width or thickness of s.t, e.g a tube, sheet of metal, bullet: *What gauge is this wire?* **2** instrument for measuring a width or the thickness of s.t. **3** instrument or device for measuring a quantity of s.t, e.g force or pressure: *a wind gauge; a rain gauge; a petrol gauge.* **4** (measurement of the) distance between the inside of the rails of a railway track or between the left and right wheels of a railway carriage etc: *a narrow gauge railway.* **5** (*fig*) way of measuring or judging s.t, esp s.o's character, value etc: *As a gauge of his worth to us, last year he sold £100 000 of our products.*

▷ *tr.v* **6** measure (s.t) accurately using a gauge(2,3): *They had a long glass tube marked in millimetres to gauge the rainfall.* **7** (*fig*) try to guess (the measure of s.t); judge (the value of s.t, what will happen etc): *He gauged the length as about 5 metres. It's very difficult to gauge his opinion.*

gaunt /gɔːnt/ *adj* **1** (of a person, a face etc) very thin (e.g because one does not eat enough, is in ill health etc). **2** (of a place, building etc) bare and unpleasant; lonely: *a gaunt ruined castle.*

'gauntness *u.n.*

gauntlet /'gɔːntlɪt/ *c.n* **1** (in history) kind of glove covered with metal plates, worn by soldiers. **2** long glove, usu of leather, covering the hand, wrist and part of the lower arm: *The man on the motorbike pulled off his gauntlet and told me the time.* **pick/take up the gauntlet** (*fig*) accept the challenge(1) to do s.t, esp to fight. **run the gauntlet (of s.t)** (*fig*) have to suffer, be the subject of, criticism etc: *Their handling of the situation had to run the gauntlet of a wave of criticism.* **throw down the gauntlet** (*fig*) make a challenge(1), esp to a fight.

gauze /gɔːz/ *u.n* (also *attrib*) **1** kind of thin cotton material like a net, used for curtains, bandages etc: *a gauze curtain; a gauze bandage.* **2** thin net of wire used to keep flies, insects away (e.g from food): *The food cupboard had gauze* (*wire*) *on the doors to let air in but keep the flies out.*

gave /geɪv/ *p.t* of give.

gavel /'gævl/ *c.n* small wooden hammer that an

auctioneer(1) hits on a desk etc to announce that s.t is sold, that a chairperson hits on a table to attract attention etc.

gawk /gɔːk/ *intr.v* = gawp.

gawky /ˈgɔːkɪ/ *adj* (*-ier, -iest*) (*derog*) (of a person) awkward in the way one stands or moves.

'**gawkily** *adv.* '**gawkiness** *u.n.*

gawp /gɔːp/ *intr.v* (also **gawk**) (often — *at s.o/ s.t*) (*informal*) look or stare(2) (at s.o/s.t) in a silly way: *The crowd was gawping at the man lying in the road.*

gay /geɪ/ *adj* **1** (*formal*; becoming *old use*) happy, light and cheerful: *the gay sound of children playing.* **2** (of colours, clothes, music etc) bright and attractive: *She liked gay dresses.* **3** (*informal*) of or referring to a homosexual(2) or homosexual activity: *He's gay. He supports gay rights.*
▷ *c.n* **4** (*informal*) homosexual(1) person: *Gays complained that the police attacked them.*

gaiety /ˈgeɪətɪ/ *n* (*pl -ies*) (*formal*) **1** *c/u.n* (example of a) happy and cheerful time, occasion etc: *I try and avoid the forced gaieties of Christmas.* **2** *u.n* state of being gay(1,2): *The gaiety of the music and dancing soon had everybody applauding.*

'**gaily** *adv* **1** in a gay(1,2) way: *gaily coloured clothes.* **2** (of a person doing or saying s.t) without care; without thinking of the effects: *She gaily declared that she wasn't going to university after all.*

'**gayness** *u.n* state of being gay(1,2).

gaze /geɪz/ *c.n* (usu *sing*) **1** long steady or fixed way of looking: *He became very nervous under the gaze of all these people.* **fasten/fix one's gaze on s.o/s.t** (start to) look long and steadily at s.o/ s.t.
▷ *intr.v* **2** (often — *at s.o/s.t*) look long and steadily or fixedly (at s.o/s.t) often showing some feeling: *She gazed at him in some surprise. He was sitting there gazing out of the window.* **gaze (up)on s.o/ s.t** (*formal*) look at s.o/s.t; fix one's eyes on s.o/ s.t: *When we reached the top we were able to gaze down upon a most beautiful valley.*

gazebo /gəˈziːbəʊ/ *c.n* small building, e.g in a garden, or balcony(1) with windows from which one has a pleasant view.

gazelle /gəˈzel/ *c.n* (*pl -(s)*) kind of small antelope.

gazette /gəˈzet/ *n* (with capital **G** in names) **1** *c.n* official newspaper or publication(1) giving details of public appointments, government notices etc. **2** *def.n* name or title for a newspaper: *The Evening Gazette.*
▷ *tr.v* **3** put (s.t or the name of s.o, esp a member of the armed forces) in a gazette(1) to show a change in rank, a transfer(1) to another regiment(1) etc: *He has been gazetted to a new regiment.*

gazetteer /ˌgæzəˈtɪə/ *c.n* alphabetical list or index(1) of geographical names in an atlas.

gazump /gəˈzʌmp/ *tr/intr.v* (*derog*; *informal*) break one's agreement to sell a house to (s.o) at a certain price by asking a higher price: *We've been gazumped because the owner's accepted an offer of £2000 more.*

GB /ˌdʒiː ˈbiː/ *abbr* Great Britain.

GBH /ˌdʒiː biː ˈeɪtʃ/ *informal abbr* grievous bodily harm (⇒ grief).

GCSE /ˌdʒiː siː ˌes ˈiː/ *abbr* General Certificate of Secondary Education (⇒ general).

Gdns *written abbr* Gardens(2).

gear /gɪə/ *n* **1** *c/u.n* (one of a) set of wheels of different sizes with teeth in them that join up to an axle or other moving part in an engine, esp in a car, truck etc, and so make the car etc go faster, slower or backwards, or to give it more/less power for hills etc: *Most cars have four forward gears.* **2** *u.n* mechanical device or system for making s.t work: *an aircraft's landing gear* (i.e the wheels and the machinery that raises or lowers them). **3** *u.n* all the things, e.g equipment(2), clothes etc, that one needs or uses for some particular purpose: *We should check all our gear before we go climbing tomorrow. Have you got your swimming gear with you?* **4** *u.n* (*informal*) (fashionable) clothes: *She dressed in the latest gear.* **change (down/up) into third** etc **gear** use the gear-lever to go from a higher/lower gear(1) (to a lower/higher one). **change gear(s)** (use the gear-lever to) go from one gear(1) to another: *He changed gear as he came to the corner.* ⇒ gear change. (**in**) **bottom/top gear** (travelling or moving in) the lowest/highest gear(1) (and so going at the lowest/fastest speed). (**in**) **first, second** etc **gear** (travelling or moving in) the first etc gear(1). **in gear** having a gear(1) of a car etc connected so that the car etc can move: *Check that the car is in gear before you release(9) the brake.* (**in**) **high/low gear** (moving or being in a) gear(1) that makes a car etc go quickly/ slowly or that gives it less/more power: *You should always go down hills in low gear.* (**in**) **reverse gear** (moving or being in the) gear(1) that makes a car etc go backwards. **put a car into gear** (use the gear-lever to) connect one of the gears(1) of a car etc so that the car etc can move: *No wonder it's not moving, you haven't put it into gear!*
▷ *tr.v* **5** (usu — *s.t to s.t*) (often passive) arrange (s.t) in a way that makes it suitable (for a certain purpose, need etc): *He tried to gear his talks to the abilities of his students.*

'**gear,box** *c.n* metal box in a car etc that encloses all the gears(1).

'**gear ,change** *c.n* act of changing from one gear(1) to another.

geared *adj* **geared up** (**for s.t, to do s.t**) (*fig*) (having got oneself) ready, prepared (for s.t etc), in a state of excitement (for s.t etc): *The players were all geared up for the big match.*

'**gear-,lever/-,shift/-,stick** *c.n* short metal stick connected to the gearbox and gears(1) of a car etc that one pushes into a certain position in order to put the car etc into a gear(1).

geese /giːs/ *pl* of goose(1).

Geiger counter /ˈgaɪgə ˌkaʊntə/ *c.n* instrument used for discovering the presence, or measuring the amount, of radioactivity.

gel /dʒel/ *c/u.n* **1** substance like (a) jelly(4) made from water and gelatine and used to make things stay in a certain shape: *She uses a (hair) gel to make her hair stand up.*
▷ *intr.v* (*-ll-*) **2** set into (a) jelly(1): *The pudding hasn't gelled properly.* **3** (*informal*) (of an idea, plan etc) take full shape; become complete: *Her ideas took several weeks to gel.* ⇒ jell(2).

gelatine /ˈdʒeləˌtiːn/ *u.n* substance made from

boiled bones and skin that, when it is mixed with hot water and then cooled, forms into (a) jelly(1).

gelatinous /dʒɪ'lætɪnəs/ *adj* of or like gelatine or jelly.

geld /geld/ *tr.v* castrate (a horse).
'**gelding** *c.n* horse that has been gelded.

gelignite /'dʒelɪgˌnaɪt/ *u.n* highly explosive form of dynamite(1): *They used gelignite to blow open the bank's safe.*

gem /dʒem/ *c.n* **1** jewel; precious stone that has been cut and polished. **2** (*fig*) thing or person considered to be very (or the most) important, valuable etc: *The gem of his collection was a painting by Constable. She's a gem, she'll do anything you ask her.* **an absolute gem** (*informal*) a person of the highest value.

Gemini /'dʒemɪˌnaɪ/ *n* **1** *unique n* one of the 12 signs of the zodiac. **2** *c.n* person born under this sign.

gen /dʒen/ *def.n* (*informal*) **1** all the (correct) information one has or needs to have: *Can you give me the gen on this proposed deal so that I can decide what to do?*
▷ *tr/intr.v* (*-nn-*) **2 gen (s.o) up (on s.o/s.t)** (cause (s.o) to) get all the (correct) information (about s.o/s.t): *Can you gen me up on this proposed deal?*
ˌ**genned-'up** *adj* (usu — *about s.o/s.t*) (*informal*) having got all the necessary or correct information (about s.o/s.t).
Gen *written abbr* General(s)(4,5).

gender /'dʒendə/ *unique n* **1** (*grammar*) (act of) grouping of words into classes according to whether they are masculine(2), feminine(4) or neuter(1). **2** *c.n* one of these classes: *Some European languages have all three genders.* **3** *u.n* (male or female) sex (of an animal etc): *I don't know what gender the cat is without examining it more closely.*

gene /dʒiːn/ *c.n* unit in the nucleus(1) of a cell(4) that controls a characteristic(1) feature inherited(2) from a parent: *His blue eyes are the result of a particular set of genes.*

genetic /dʒɪ'netɪk/ *adj* of or referring to genes or genetics.
ge,netic 'code *c.n* way chromosomes in a cell(4) are arranged and by which inherited(2) characteristics(2) are passed on.
ge,netic ,engi'neering *u.n* changes made by scientists in a genetic code in plants or animals in order to produce different qualities.
ge'netically *adv*.
geneticist /dʒə'netɪˌsɪst/ *c.n* person skilled in (the study of) genetics.
ge'netics *u.n* scientific study of the way inherited(2) characteristics(2) are passed on (or can be improved) to the young of humans, animals and plants.

genealogy /ˌdʒiːnɪ'ælədʒɪ/ *n* (*pl -ies*) **1** *c/u.n* (list or plan showing the) history of a family or families in terms of births, marriages and deaths over a long time: *the genealogy of the Royal Family.* **2** *u.n* study or science of the development of animals, plants etc from earlier forms.
genealogical /ˌdʒiːnɪə'lɒdʒɪkl/ *adj* of or referring to (a) genealogy(1,2).
ˌgenea,logical 'tree *c.n* list or plan, shaped like

the branches of a tree, showing a genealogy(1). Compare family tree.

genealogist /ˌdʒiːnɪ'ælədʒɪst/ *c.n* person who studies or produces (a) genealogy.

genera /'dʒenərə/ *pl* of genus.

general /'dʒenərəl/ *adj* **1** not limited to one section or part of a whole; not in detail: *I have a very general idea of how a car works.* **2** of, referring to, affecting, (almost) all people: *I think this book will be of great general interest.* **3** common or usual; widespread: *Icy roads are a general danger in this part of the world.* **4** (with capital **G** in titles) (sometimes put after the noun it describes) (title for a) chief person in an organization: *the General Secretary of a trade union*; *an inspector*(1) *general.* (**as**) **a general rule** ⇒ rule(*n*). **in the general interest** ⇒ interest(*n*). **on general release** ⇒ release(*n*).
▷ *c.n* **5** (*written abbr* Gen) (*military*) (title for an) officer next in rank below a Field Marshal in the British army and Royal Marines or in the air force of some other countries. **in general** as applies in most cases, on most occasions, with most people etc; usually or normally: *In general, people don't like extremes in politics.*
ˌGeneral Cerˌtificate of ˌSecondary ˌEdu'cation *c.n* (*abbr* GCSE) public examination in school subjects for children of about 16 years of age.
ˌgeneral e'lection *c.n* (UK) election of Members of Parliament by the whole country at one time. Compare by-election. ⇒ local election.
ˌGeneral 'Headˌquarters *pl.n* (*abbr* GHQ) main headquarters of an army group.

generality /ˌdʒenə'rælɪtɪ/ *n* (*pl -ies*) (*formal*) **1** *c.n* general(1) rule or statement; remark etc that is not detailed enough to be useful: *When her mother asked her what she had done at school, her daughter only replied with generalities.* **2** *c/u.n* quality of being general(2,3), of applying in most cases etc: *His observations have an almost universal generality.* **3** *u/def.pl.n* (usu *the* — of s.o/s.t) the greater part or number (of s.o/s.t): *The generality of drivers are careful and full of consideration for others.*

generalization, -isation /ˌdʒenərəlaɪ'zeɪʃən/ *c/u.n* (example of the) act or fact of generalizing.
'**genera,lize, -ise** *intr.v* **1** talk in a very general(1) way about s.t without giving enough detail or information: *He always generalizes and never gives you any hard facts.* **2** (often — *about s.t*; — *from s.t*) form a general(1) opinion (about s.t or on the basis of particular facts etc): *We can only generalize about the future from our knowledge of the present.*
ˌgeneral 'knowledge *u.n* **1** (also *attrib*) knowledge of a wide variety of subjects: *a general knowledge test.* **2** thing or things known by (almost) everybody: *It is general knowledge that John has been in prison twice.*

generally /'dʒenrəlɪ/ *adv* **1** (as happens) in most cases or on most occasions; usually: *He generally takes the dog for a walk at 10 o'clock.* **2** without going into (too) much detail: *Generally speaking, your suggestions look good.* **3** (as applies) to most people, for the most part: *The plans for the shopping centre have been generally welcomed.*
ˌGeneral 'Manager *c.n* (usu *the* —) manager

with authority(1) over other managers in a company.

'general ,officer *c.n* (*military*) officer with the rank of a general(5), lieutenant-general or major-general.

,general ,officer co'mmanding *c.n* (*abbr* GOC) (*military*) general officer in command of s.t, e.g an army.

,general 'practice *c/u.n* (UK) (example of the) work of a general practitioner: *He has a general practice* (or *He's in general practice*) *in a small town in the country.*

,general prac'titioner *c.n* (*abbr* GP) (UK) medical doctor who looks after a number of patients in her/his office and/or in their homes but not in a hospital.

,general 'public *def.pl.n* (almost) all the ordinary people: *The general public has no high opinion of politicians.*

,general 'staff *c/def./def.pl./n* (*military*) group of officers at the headquarters of a commanding officer who act as her/his personal staff.

,general 'strike *c.n* strike by (nearly) all the workers (esp those belonging to trade unions) in a country.

generate /'dʒenə,reɪt/ *tr.v* 1 (often — *s.t from s.t*) (*technical*) produce (s.t, esp a form of power) (from s.t else): *This machine will generate quite a lot of electricity from the power of the wind.* 2 (*formal*) cause (s.t) to happen: *His arrival generated a lot of excitement in the town.*

'gene,rating ,station *c.n* power station that produces electricity.

generation /,dʒenə'reɪʃən/ *n* 1 *u.n* (usu *the* — *of s.t*) act or process of generating(1) s.t, esp power: *Various types of power stations are used for the generation of electricity.* 2 *c.n* one stage or step, represented by each group of children, parents, grandparents etc, in a line of a family descent: *I can trace(4) my family back six generations.* 3 *c.n* length of time, usu considered to be about 25 or 30 years, in which children grow up, marry and have children of their own: *He's a generation older than I am.* 4 *c.n* all the people as a group who are born and grow up at the same time: *Older generations often do not understand the needs of the young.* **the rising generation** (all) the young people who are now growing up.

,gene'ration ,gap *c/def.n* (the time and the) differences in beliefs, opinions, ways of behaving etc that occur between one generation(4) and another.

'gene,rator *c.n* machine or device that generates(1) s.t: *a generator in a power station; a wind generator.*

generic, generically ⇒ genus.

generous /'dʒenərəs/ *adj* Opposite ungenerous. 1 ready or willing to give s.t, esp money, help etc, freely; (of money, help etc) given freely: *He was never very generous with his money. That was a generous gift.* ⇒ overgenerous. 2 noble in one's nature, esp by being kind, showing forgiveness etc: *You should try to be more generous in what you say about him; he hasn't had your advantages.* 3 large and plentiful (perhaps too much so): *She gave him a very generous helping of pudding.*

generosity /,dʒenə'rɒsɪtɪ/ *c/u.n* (*pl* -ies) (example of the) act or quality of being generous.

'generously *adv.*

genesis /'dʒenɪsɪs/ *n* 1 *c.n* (*pl geneses* /'dʒenɪ,siːz/) (often *the* — *of s.t*) beginning, start or origin (of s.t new): *the genesis of civilization; the genesis of a new idea.* 2 *unique n* (with capital G) first book of the Old Testament of the Bible(1) describing the creation(1) of the world etc.

genetic(s), genetically, geneticist ⇒ gene.

genial /'dʒiːnɪəl/ *adj* 1 (*formal*) (of a person, s.o's nature etc) kind, friendly and cheerful: *He has a genial personality(1) and likes to have friends around him.* 2 (of the weather, climate etc) pleasant and warm and without extremes: *In this genial climate it's quite easy to grow most things.*

geniality /,dʒiːnɪ'ælɪtɪ/ *u.n.* **'genially** *adv.*

genital /'dʒenɪtl/ *adj* of or referring to the sexual organs of humans and animals: *the genital organs; genital diseases.*

genitalia /,dʒenɪ'teɪlɪə/ *pl.n* (*Latin*) (*technical*) genitals.

'genitals *pl.n* those parts of the sexual organs of humans and animals that can be seen from the outside.

genitive /'dʒenɪtɪv/ *adj* 1 (*grammar*) of or referring to a genitive(2): *the genitive case.*
▷ *c/def.n* 2 (*grammar*) (example of the) form (of a noun, pronoun etc) used to show possession or origin (of s.t): *In the sentence 'That's John's book', 'John's' is a genitive* (or *is in the genitive*).

genius /'dʒiːnɪəs/ *n* (*pl* -es) 1 *u.n* very great cleverness or ability, esp in one's mind: *His early work in mathematics showed great genius.* 2 *c.n* person having or showing genius(1): *He proved to be a genius when it came to playing the piano.* **have a genius for (doing) s.t** have a natural ability for, or in respect of, s.t one does (sometimes for doing s.t wrongly or without thought): *He has a genius for saying the wrong things at the wrong time.*

genned-up ⇒ gen.

genocide /'dʒenəʊ,saɪd/ *u.n* murder of (almost) a whole race, nation or religious group.

gent, Gents ⇒ gentleman.

genteel /dʒen'tiːl/ *adj* (often *derog*) (of a person, manners etc) having or showing (too) much attention to correct or polite behaviour: *She tries to be very genteel when she has guests in the house.*

genteelly /dʒen'tiːllɪ/ *adv.* **gen'teelness** *u.n.*

gentility /dʒen'tɪlɪtɪ/ *u.n* 1 = genteelness. 2 noble birth; state of being a member of the upper class(2): *Her claims to gentility are not supported by the facts of her birth.*

gentile /'dʒentaɪl/ *adj* 1 (of a person, race) (considered by Jews as) not belonging to or being a member of the Jewish race.
▷ 2 *c.n* gentile(1) person.

gentle /'dʒentl/ *adj* 1 (of a person) friendly, pleasant or quiet in one's manner: *She was a gentle person and never shouted or screamed.* 2 (of a person) acting in a careful way without being rough or violent: *He was very gentle when he moved the injured man.* 3 (of a surface, slope of a hill etc) going up or down very gradually: *There was a gentle slope in front of us which would be easy to walk up.* 4 (of a temperature, weather etc) very mild or moderate: *Use only a* *gentle heat when cooking these vegetables. There was a gentle* breeze *blowing.*

'gentleness *adj* state of being gentle(1–4).

'gently *adv* in a gentle(2–4) manner or way: *He picked her up very gently. The hill sloped gently down to the sea.*

gentleman /'dʒentlmən/ *c.n* (*pl* **-men** /-mən/) (*formal*) **1** man who shows good manners towards others: *It was the mark of a gentleman to stand when a lady entered the room.* **2** (polite way of describing, or word used for, a) man of any kind: *There's a gentleman to see you. Shall I show him in?* **3** (*old use*) man belonging to the upper classes(2) or a high social group, esp one connected to a royal court or a noble household. **a gentleman's/gentlemen's agreement** agreement (to do s.t) that is not formal or written down and has no force in law but that is usually carried out as a matter of honour between people: *They came to a gentleman's agreement not to take the matter to law.* **ladies and gentlemen** ⇒ lady.

gent /dʒent/ *c.n abbr* (*slang*) gentleman(1): *I can't bear these city gents who think they know everything. Thanks, you're a real gent.*

'gentlemanliness *u.n* act or state of being gentlemanly.

'gentlemanly *adj* behaving like a gentleman(1): *gentlemanly behaviour.*

gentry /'dʒentrɪ/ *def.n* people of high social standing: *the landed gentry* (i.e those owning a lot of land).

Gents *c/def/def.pl.n* public lavatory for men and boys: *Is there a Gents near here? The Gents is over there.* Compare Ladies.

gentlewoman /'dʒentl,wumən/ *c.n* (*pl* **-women** /-,wɪmɪn/) (*old use*) woman of high social standing but not usu of noble birth.

gently ⇒ gentle.

gentry, Gents ⇒ gentleman.

genuflect /'dʒenju,flekt/ *intr.v* bend one's knee, esp as a sign of respect, in an act of Christian(1) worship etc.

genuflection /,dʒenju'flekʃən/ *c.n* act of doing this.

genuine /'dʒenjuɪn/ *adj* **1** (of an object etc) real, not false; not copied: *This is a genuine painting by Turner.* **2** (of a person, action etc) sincere or honest: *I don't think he's very genuine when he says he loves her. She made a genuine attempt to be friendly with her.*

'genuinely *adv* in a genuine(2) way.

'genuineness *u.n.*

genus /'dʒiːnəs/ *c.n* (*pl* **genera** /'dʒenərə/) (classification of a) group of animals, plants etc that are part of a family or species, are all like each other etc: *The genus 'Felis' includes lions, tigers and cats.*

generic /dʒɪ'nerɪk/ *adj* of or referring to a genus or a general class of s.t: *The generic name for cats, tigers etc is 'Felis'.*

ge'nerically *adv.*

geography /dʒɪ'ɒɡrəfɪ/ *u.n* (also *attrib*) science or study of the earth's surface, climate, things produced etc: *the geography of Asia; a geography lesson/book.*

ge'ographer *c.n* person who studies geography.

geographic /,dʒɪə'ɡræfɪk/ *adj* (also **geo-**graphical**).

,geo'graphically *adv.*

geology /dʒɪ'ɒlədʒɪ/ *u.n* (also *attrib*) (*science*) study of the earth's crust(3), its rocks, the way rocks were formed etc: *the geology of the area; a geology course.*

geological /,dʒɪə'lɒdʒɪkl/ *adj* of or referring to geology: *a geological fault* (i.e a crack etc in the earth's surface).

geo'logically *adv.*

,ge'olo,gist *c.n* person who studies geology.

geometry /dʒɪ'ɒmɪtrɪ/ *u.n* (also *attrib*) (*mathematics*) science or study of lines, surfaces, shapes etc and their relationship to each other: *the geometry of plane surfaces; a geometry lesson/book.*

geometric /,dʒɪə'metrɪk/ *adj* (also **geo-**'metrical**) **1** of or referring to geometry. **2** (of lines, shapes etc) regular; repeated in a regular way: *The tiles on the floor were arranged in a geometric pattern.*

geo,metric pro'gression *c.n* (*mathematics*) (set of numbers having a) regular or fixed relation to the one(s) before or after it/them: *2, 4, 8, 16, 32 is a geometric progression in which each number is double the number before it.*

,geo'metrically *adv.*

geophysics /,dʒiː əʊ'fɪzɪks/ *u.n* science or study of the nature of the earth, esp with regard to its magnetism(1), density(2) or natural events such as earthquakes etc.

,geo'physical *adj* of or referring to geophysics.

,geo'physically *adv.*

geophysicist /,dʒiː əʊ'fɪzɪ,sɪst/ *c.n* person who studies geophysics.

geopolitics /,dʒiː əʊ'pɒlɪtɪks/ *u.n* study of the ways a nation/nations acts/act in political terms because of its/their geographical position in relation to other nations.

geopolitical /,dʒiː əʊpə'lɪtɪkl/ *adj*. **,geo-po'litically** *adv.*

geranium /dʒɪ'reɪnɪəm/ *c.n* (*pl* **-s**) kind of plant with round leaves and white or red or pink flowers.

geriatric /,dʒerɪ'ætrɪk/ *adj* **1** (of a person, her/his medical(2) state) very old (and usu ill): *He is a geriatric case.*

,geri'atric ,ward *c.n* ward(1) in a hospital for geriatric(1) patients.

▷ *c.n* **2** (often *joking*) person who is very old: *He goes round as though he's a geriatric.*

geriatrician /,dʒerɪə'trɪʃən/ *c.n* doctor or person who studies geriatrics.

,geri'atrics *u.n* medical study of the diseases and illnesses of old age.

germ /dʒɜːm/ *c.n* **1** very small living thing that lives and grows on other living things or food etc and can cause disease: *Use your handkerchief when you've got a cold as I don't want to catch your germs.* **2** (usu — of s.t) (*fig*) very small beginning or start of s.t, esp an original idea or thought: *From this small germ of an idea he built an industry covering the world.* Compare bacillus, bacteria, virus.

germicide /'dʒɜː.mɪ,saɪd/ *c/u.n* (example of a) chemical substance used to kill germs(1).

,germ 'warfare *u.n* use of germs(1) to spread disease or kill people in war.

German measles /,dʒɜːmən 'miːzəlz/ *c.n* (also **ru'bella**) disease that causes red spots on the skin and that can be given to or caught by other people.

germane /dʒɜː'meɪn/ *adj* (usu — to s.t) (*formal*) (of a point in an argument, discussion etc) useful or relevant (to s.t): *The points he made are germane to my argument.*

germinate /'dʒɜːmɪˌneɪt/ *tr/intr.v* (cause (a seed, plant etc) to) start growing and showing a shoot(1), leaves etc: *These delicate plants will only germinate in a greenhouse.*
germination /ˌdʒɜːmɪ'neɪʃən/ *u.n.*

gerund /'dʒerənd/ *c.n* (*grammar*) noun formed from a verb by adding '-ing' (and sometimes with other changes): *'Swimming' and 'diving' are gerunds of the verbs 'swim' and 'dive'.* ⇒ verbal noun.

gestation /dʒe'steɪʃən/ *u.n* (*technical; formal*) act of carrying a child or young animal in the mother's body before birth.

ge'station ˌperiod *c.n* length of time from conception(3) to birth: *The normal gestation period for babies is nine months.*

gesticulate /dʒe'stɪkjʊˌleɪt/ *intr.v* (*formal*) move or wave one's hands and arms about in order to attract attention, to emphasize s.t while speaking etc: *I could see him gesticulating in the distance but for what reason I couldn't find out.*
gesticulation /dʒeˌstɪkjʊ'leɪʃən/ *c/u.n.*

gesture /'dʒestʃə/ *c.n* **1** movement or waving of one's hand(s) and arm(s) in order to emphasize s.t, express a feeling etc: *When he speaks he always uses a lot of gestures.* **2** action or behaviour intended to show a certain feeling, esp of friendship: *You must make a gesture and invite them around to dinner.*
▷ *intr.v* **3** make a gesture(1): *He gestured to me and so I went over to talk to him.*

get /get/ *v* (*pres.p* getting, *p.t, p.p* got /gɒt/; US *p.p* gotten /'gɒtn/) (⇒ has/have got to do s.t (⇒ have (*aux.v*), have(2–5).) **1** *tr.v* receive (s.t): *I got his letter this morning. I can get foreign programmes on my television set.* **2** *tr.v* (often — s.o s.t; — s.t for s.o) (go to a place and) collect, buy or take away s.t (for s.o): *When you go shopping would you get (me) some potatoes.* **3** *tr.v* make a (telephone) connection to (s.o/s.w): *Could you get me our London office, please.* **4** *tr.v* earn (an amount of money): *She gets £6 an hour as a typist.* **5** *tr.v* catch (an illness, disease etc): *He got a cold from walking in the rain.* **6** *tr/intr.v* (cause (s.o/s.t) to) become the state described or act as described: *She's getting old. I'll get angry if you do that. He's not getting any better. Get well soon! Can you get this job done quickly? Get your things ready.* **7** *intr.v* (usu — across, in, out, through etc) move (successfully) (across etc): *We managed to get across the river. Get off that wall! I got on a bus.* **8** *tr.v* prepare (s.t, esp food, a meal etc): *She was just getting dinner when the bell rang.* **9** *tr.v* receive (a punishment etc): *He got five years (i.e in prison) for robbery.* **10** *tr.v* find, catch or arrest (s.o): *The police finally got the murderer after a long hunt.* **11** *tr.v* (often — s.t in s.t) become affected or hurt by (s.t) (in a part of one's body): *He got sand in his eye.* ⇒ get into s.t(b). **12** *tr.v* (often — s.o between, in, on etc s.t) hit (s.o) (on a part of her/his body): *The blow got him right between the eyes.* **13** *tr.v* have (s.t) as a result (of s.t else): *Divide 80 by 5 and*

you get 16. If you boil water you get steam. **14** *tr.v* (*informal*) (want to) harm, destroy or kill (s.o): *When I come out of prison I'll get you for what you did to me. They were determined to get the enemy.* **15** *tr.v* (*informal*) annoy (s.o): *It really gets me the way he's always talking about how much he earns.* **16** *tr.v* (*informal*) deeply affect or move (s.o) in a pleasant way: *The sunset really got me.* ⇒ get to(g). **17** *tr.v* (often negative or in questions) (*informal*) understand (s.o, what he/she has said etc): *I don't get it so could you tell me the joke again? Get it?* ⇒ get s.t done, get s.o to do s.t, get to do s.t.

get about/around (a) (be able to) move, walk, drive etc about/around, sometimes with some difficulty, e.g after an accident: *He's getting about a bit more after his long illness.* (b) travel (a lot, regularly etc): *He's getting around quite a lot in his new job.* (c) (of news etc) spread, become more widely known: *There's a report getting around that she is going to resign.*

get above oneself (be thought by others to) consider oneself more important, in a higher social position etc, than one really is: *He's getting a bit above himself with his talk of friendships with members of the royal family.*

get (s.o/s.t) across/over (s.t) (cause s.o/s.t to) move, be carried etc, across/over (s.t) (often with some difficulty): *The river was deep but we got the animals across (it) without losing any.* **get s.t across/over (to s.o)** make s.t be understood (by s.o): *It took a long time to get across/over to them the way the system worked.*

get after s.o/s.t (start to) follow, run towards, s.o/s.t so as to catch her/him/it: *Get after him! He's escaping!*

get ahead (of s.o) become more successful (than s.o else): *Brains and hard work have enabled him to get ahead of his competitors.*

get along/on (with s.t) make progress (in some task, job etc); start or continue (s.t): *How are you getting along (with that report)? Well, get on with it, we haven't got all day!* **get along/on (badly, well etc) (with s.o)** have a (bad, good etc) relationship, esp in social or work terms (with s.o): *He gets on badly with the people in his office.* **get along/on (well etc) without s.o/s.t** manage to live, work etc without s.o/s.t to help one: *She found she got along quite well without him in the house.* **get along/away/on with you!** (*informal* expression used to show surprise, disbelief etc at what s.o has said, done etc): *Get along with you! I don't believe a word of it!*

get around ⇒ get about/around. **get (a)round s.o** gain the confidence of s.o, manage to persuade s.o to agree to s.t or to do s.t, esp when he/she does not want to: *She gets round her father by acting like a little girl.* **get (a)round/over s.t** manage to make progress by not having to deal with s.t that has been preventing progress: *We can get round this problem by asking the government to help.* **get (a)round to (doing) s.t** (find time to) start (doing) s.t: *After several telephone calls, the Council finally got around to clearing the rubbish away.*

get at s.o (a) (*informal*) criticize, find fault with, s.o: *She was always getting at the children for being so untidy.* ⇒ get back at s.o. (b) influence s.o, esp in an improper way, e.g by threats or bribery: *I* *think the officials holding the inquiry have been got at by the other side.* **get at s.t (a)** (be able to) reach, touch, s.t, often with some difficulty: *I can't get at the box, there are too many things in front of it.* ⇒ get-at-able. **(b)** start to do s.t, esp a job, task etc: *He was anxious to get at the problem immediately.* **(c)** succeed in finding or discovering s.t, esp the truth of s.t: *In this complex situation, it's difficult to get at the real reason why things went wrong.* **(d)** (often *what s.o is —ting at*) mean, suggest or imply s.t by what one says (esp of s.t that has not been put clearly): *Though he tried to explain, I just couldn't understand what he was getting at.*

get (s.o/s.t) away (from s.o/s.t/s.w) (cause s.o/ s.t to) leave or be removed (from s.o/s.t/s.w): *She got the child away from the edge of the cliff. We need to get away (from here) by six if we're going to catch the train.* **get away from it all** (*informal*) leave one's job, home etc and move s.w else to do s.t new, esp in order to have a less demanding time, a holiday etc: *I'd like to get away from it all and go and live on a desert island.* **get away with s.t (a)** steal s.t from a place and escape without getting caught: *The thieves got away with several thousand pounds' worth of jewellery.* ⇒ getaway. **(b)** not receive punishment for s.t wrong one has done, even though deserving it: *Even though he had actually broken the vase he got away with it by saying his sister was to blame.* **(c)** receive only a small or slight punishment for s.t wrong one has done: *He got away with only three months in prison.* **get away with murder** ⇒ murder(*n*). **get away with you!** ⇒ get along/away/on with you.

get back (from s.w) (a) move (from the position one is in) to one further back: *Get back and let these people come through.* **(b)** return to one's original place, home etc after having been s.w else: *When he got back from the office he was very tired.* **get back ((in) to s.t) (a)** return (to one's original place, position etc): *Will you please get back into bed at once.* **(b)** start (doing s.t, esp a job) again after an absence: *He was dying to get back (into his old job) after his illness.* **(c)** (of a political party) become the government, return (to power), again after an election: *The* Labour Party *got back (into power) with an increased* majority(3). **get back at s.o** (*informal*) criticize, attack s.o, esp after having been criticized, attacked by her/him: *She got back at me by saying I had no right to tell her how to look after her children.* **get s.o/s.t back** have s.o/s.t returned to one after losing her/him/ it etc: *He got his old job back when he joined the company again.* **get s.o back on her/his feet** ⇒ foot.

get s.o's back up ⇒ back(*n*).

get behind (with s.t) not be able to manage or finish (s.t one should do) because there is too much, one is not working hard enough etc: *He's getting behind with his work because he has all these long lunch hours.*

get the best etc **out of s.o** succeed in encouraging or getting s.o to do s.t to the best of her/his ability: *He always gets the best out of people by making them believe in themselves.*

get the better of s.o/s.t ⇒ better(4).

get busy ⇒ busy.

get by (in/with s.t) manage, succeed, be accepted (in s.t one has or wears, with what (little) one has got, does etc): *He gets by with only working two*

days a week. **get by (on s.t)** be able to live, pay for necessary things, (using only a small amount of money etc): *She gets by on what she earns doing cleaning.*

get s.t clear ⇒ clear.

get cold feet ⇒ foot.

get cracking/moving ⇒ crack.

get down (s.t) (manage to) descend s.t (e.g a mountain, high place etc): *We got down the hill by sliding on our behinds.* **get down (from s.t/ s.w) (a)** (of a child, ask to) be allowed to leave (one's chair at a table) after a meal: *I've finished my dinner now, can I get down (from the table)?* **(b)** remove oneself (from a higher position, from the back of a horse etc) to a lower position, to the ground etc: *Get down from that tree or you'll fall.* **get s.o down** (*informal*) (of work etc) make s.o feel unable to manage s.t, feel depressed(1) etc: *His debts and the trouble at home are really getting him down.* **get s.o/s.t down** cause s.o/s.t to fall or be moved from a higher place to a lower one: *Can you get that jar down from the shelf?* **get s.t down (a)** (be able to) swallow s.t, esp food, medicine etc: *He's one of those nervous people who just can't get tablets down.* **(b)** (be able to) write s.t (that s.o is saying) on paper: *Could you speak more slowly so that I can get it all down?* **get down on one's hands and knees (to s.o, to do s.t)** ⇒ hand(*n*). **get down to s.t** start doing s.t with all one's attention, after an absence etc: *I've got to get down to all this work I've been neglecting.* ⇒ get down to brass tacks (⇒ tack¹).

get even (with s.o) ⇒ even.

get one's eye in ⇒ eye.

get s.o's goat ⇒ goat.

get (s.o/s.t) going (cause (s.o/s.t) to) start moving, doing s.t etc: *She got the car going by pushing it. All right, let's get going if we want to catch the bus. He got him going on his favourite subject with just a few admiring remarks.*

get a grip on oneself ⇒ grip(*n*).

get one's hand in ⇒ hand(*n*).

get one's hands on s.o/s.t ⇒ hand(*n*).

get the hang of s.t ⇒ hang(*n*).

get hold of s.t ⇒ hold(*n*). **get hold of the wrong end of the stick** ⇒ stick¹.

get home; **get (s.t) home (to s.o)** ⇒ home(*adv*).

get the idea (that . . .) ⇒ idea.

get in ⇒ get in (to s.t/s.w). **get s.o in** ask s.o to visit one's house, office etc in order to do s.t, esp repairs: *We'll have to get an electrician in to repair the cooker.* **get s.t in (a)** go outside a house etc, collect s.t and bring it inside: *Would you get the washing in; it's going to rain.* **(b)** (manage to) do s.t, e.g work, in a certain amount of time: *If you woke up earlier you could get in a couple of hours' work before breakfast.* **get in on s.t** take part in s.t, esp s.t that is to one's advantage, that others do not know about, are not allowed to join etc: *If you want to get in on this deal I can help you provided you've got £20 000 to spare.* **get in on the act** ⇒ act. **get in on the ground floor** ⇒ ground floor. **get in with s.o** join a small group of people (e.g who have a certain social position, who do certain, usu not very good, things etc): *Their son was getting in with a* gang(3) *that wandered around the streets frightening old ladies.* **get in first** etc **(with s.t)** say or do s.t (first etc, before others) and so gain an advantage: *He got in first with a remark about how well she was*

looking. **get in contact (with s.o)** ⇒ contact(*n*).
get in touch (with s.o) ⇒ touch(*n*).
get into s.t (a) put on (a set of) clothes: *Get into your swimming costumes before you go near the water.* **(b)** (of an object etc) enter s.t, usu by mistake: *Sand got into her eyes. Water had got into the engine.* ⇒get(11). **(c)** cause oneself to be in a difficult position, esp by one's own actions: *He got into difficulties while swimming. They got into a lot of trouble. He got into debt.* **(d)** reach a certain state, feeling etc: *He gets into a temper whenever you try to tell him what to do.* **get in(to s.t/s.w) (a)** (be able to) enter (a place) (often with some difficulty): *We can't get in(to) the house as I haven't got a key.* **(b)** (of a bus, train etc) arrive (at a destination): *What time does your train get in (to Ayr) ?* **(c)** (of a political candidate(1), party) be elected (to a parliament); be elected (to form a government): *He got into Parliament with a majority*(3) *of only 300 votes.* **get (oneself/s.o) into a fix** ⇒fix(*n*). **get into a/the habit (of doing s.t)** ⇒ habit(*n*). **get s.t into one's/s.o's head** ⇒ head(*n*). **get into a rut** ⇒ rut. **get into deep water(s)** ⇒ water(*n*). **get into hot water** ⇒ water(*n*).
get a kick out of s.t ⇒ kick(*n*).
get lost ⇒ lost.
get the message ⇒ message(*n*).
get one's money's worth ⇒ money.
get a move on ⇒ move(*n*). **get moving** ⇒ get cracking.
get (s.o) nowhere, somewhere etc (*informal*) (of s.t s.o does, says etc) (not) be of (any) help or use (to s.o) towards what he/she wants: *That stupid talk will get you nowhere. We're not getting anywhere arguing all the time.*
get off (s.t) remove oneself (from s.t, esp a bus, train, horse etc, from a higher place to a lower one or to the ground): *You need to get off* (i.e the underground train) *at Oxford Circus and change to the Victoria Line. Get off that wall!* **get s.t off (s.t)** remove s.t, e.g clothes, paint, an object etc, (from s.t, e.g one's body, a surface): *The doctor asked the patient to get his shirt off. I can't get this mark off* (*the wall*). **get (s.o/s.t) off (to s.w)** (cause (s.o/s.t) to) leave a place (and be taken to s.w else): *He had to get the children off to school at 8 o'clock. Can you get this parcel off to them at once? We need to get off early to catch the train.* **get (off) to sleep** ⇒ sleep. **get off to a good start** ⇒ start. **get (s.o) off (with s.t)** (cause s.o to) suffer (no, or a small, punishment, e.g in a court of law): *The lawyer got his client*(1) *off with a fine. He got off scot-free.* **get s.t off one's chest** ⇒ chest. **get off on the right/wrong foot (with s.o)** ⇒ foot. **get off with s.o** (*informal*) succeed in attracting a member of the opposite sex, in developing a friendship with her/him (sometimes in order to have sex together): *She had to stand and watch her boyfriend getting off with another girl at the party.* **get off with s.t** suffer only a small damage, injury etc: *They got off with only a few bruises in the car crash.*
get on (a) ⇒ get (s.o/s.t) on(to s.t). **(b)** (of time) become late (in the day etc), pass (more quickly than one realized): *Time* (*or It*) *is getting on and it will soon be too dark to see.* **(c)** (often *be getting on* (*in years*)) (of a person) become older, esp towards the end of one's life: *She's getting on* (*in years*) *and can't move about very much.* Compare get on for

s.t(b). **get on one's feet** ⇒ foot. **get on s.o's nerves** ⇒ nerves. **get on the wrong side of s.o** ⇒ side(*n*).
get on s.o's wick ⇒ wick. **get on for s.t (a)** (of time) nearly reach a point, e.g hour of the day, time when s.t happens: *It's getting on for lunch, so let's stop now.* **(b)** (of a person) nearly reach a certain (old) age: *She's getting on for fifty.* **get on (in s.t)** manage one's life, affairs (well, badly etc); succeed (in s.t one does): *I asked him how he was getting on and he replied that things were terrible. I didn't get on very well in the examination.* **get on (well** etc) **(with s.o)** ⇒ get along(b). **get on with s.t** start or continue to do s.t: *Get on with your homework while I'm away.* **Get on with you!** ⇒ get along/away/on with you! **get on (well** etc) **without s.o/s.t** ⇒ get along/on (well etc) without s.o/s.t.
get (s.o/s.t) on(to s.t) (cause s.o/s.t to) enter (a bus, train etc), mount (a horse), be carried (on s.t) etc: *They got him onto the train at the last moment. I got on the horse and rode off.* **get onto s.o/s.w** telephone s.o/s.w: *Would you get onto New York and give them the news.* **get onto s.o/s.t (a)** be on the point or finding, manage to find, s.o/s.t: *The police are getting onto the* trail(1) *of the thieves.* **(b)** be (almost) ready to deal with the next person/ thing: *I'll be getting onto you in a minute after I've talked to this patient.*
get out (a) ⇒ get (s.o/s.t) out (of s.t/s.w). **(b)** (of news etc) become known: *A report is just getting out that the government is going to resign.* **get s.o out** (in cricket[1]) make s.o who is batting[2](2) finish his innings by hitting his wicket(1), catching a ball hit by him etc. **get s.t out (a)** say s.t, usu with difficulty, e.g because one has no breath, is dying etc: *He managed to get a few words out describing what had happened before he died.* **(b)** find an answer (to a calculation etc): *It took him several attempts to get out the right answer.* **get out (of s.t)** escape, be accidentally released(6), (from s.t): *The tiger had somehow got out (of its cage).* **get (s.o/s.t) out (of s.t/s.w)** (cause s.o/s.t to) leave (s.t/s.w), be pulled out (of s.t/s.w), often with difficulty: *Let's get out of here, it's too crowded. The fireman got her out of the burning building. I can't get this nail out (of the wood).* **get out of (doing) s.t** manage not to do what one should or had promised to do: *How did you get out of taking the children to the zoo?* **get s.t out of s.o/s.t (a)** gain s.t, e.g an advantage, from s.o/s.t: *I can't see what you will get out of this deal.* **(b)** take or find s.t, e.g information, from s.o/s.t, often with some difficulty: *How did you get the secret plans out of the man?* **get out of bed (on) the wrong side** ⇒ bed. **get out of control** ⇒ control. **get out of the habit (of doing s.t)** ⇒ habit. **get out of hand** ⇒ hand(*n*).
get over s.t (a) ⇒ get (a)round/over s.t. **(b)** manage to recover from s.t (e.g a disappointment): *The next time I saw him he had got over his anger.* **(c)** (usu negative) (not) really accept, believe or understand s.t, esp s.t s.o has said, done etc: *I can't get over the way he treated them.* **get (s.o/ s.t) over (s.t)** ⇒ get (s.o/s.t) across/over (s.t). **get s.t over (to s.o)** ⇒ get s.t across/over (to s.o). **get s.t over (and done) with** finish s.t completely, esp s.t that is necessary, that one did not want to do, so that one does not have to concern oneself with it any more: *Now we've got that over and done with, we can go on to other things.*

get one's own back (**on s.o**) (**for s.t**) ⇒ own.
get one's own way ⇒ way.
get s.o/s.t right ⇒ right[1].
get round s.o ⇒ get (a)round s.o. **get round s.t**
(**a**) ⇒ get (a)round/over s.t. (**b**) (manage to) avoid
the effects of s.t, esp a rule or law: *He was
accused of getting round the law by not declaring
certain payments.* **get round s.t.** (**in s.t**) (*sport*)
make a complete circle of a race track (in a certain
time): *The runners got round in 61 seconds.* **get
round to** (**doing**) **s.t** ⇒ get (a)round to (doing) s.t.
get the sack ⇒ sack[2].
get one's skates on ⇒ skate[1].
get (**s.o**) **somewhere** ⇒ get (s.o) nowhere,
somewhere etc.
get s.t straight ⇒ straight(*adv*).
get stuffed ⇒ stuff(*v*).
get one's teeth into s.t ⇒ tooth.
get there (**in the end** *etc*) ⇒ there[1].
get through s.t (**a**) (manage to) force one's
body through a narrow space (often with some
difficulty): *He got through the gap in the fence.*
(**b**) eat, drink, use etc (a lot of) s.t: *They got through
a dozen bottles of wine during the meal.* (**c**) manage
to complete doing s.t, e.g reading a book: *Alice gets
through a dozen books a week.* **get** (**s.o**) **through
s.t** (help s.o to) pass an examination, test etc: *His
teacher spent many extra hours trying to get him
through the examinations.* **get** (**s.t**) **through** (**s.t**)
(cause a law or bill to) be passed, approved (by
parliament): *The bill got through* (*parliament*) *on
its third reading.* **get** (**s.o**) **through to s.t** (in
sport, a competition etc) (help s.o to) win a race,
competition etc so that he/she can go on to the
next stage: *Just one goal got the team through to
the Final.* **get** (**s.o/s.t**) **through** (**to s.w**) (cause
s.o/s.t to) arrive, be carried to (s.w) (often with
some difficulty): *We got supplies through to the
town in spite of the enemy.* **get** (**s.t**) **through to
s.o** (**a**) (cause a message etc to) reach s.o, esp
by telephone: *Get the report through to Jones in
London. Can you get through to Jones as I want to
talk to him?* (**b**) make s.o understand (s.t): *I can't
get* (*it*) *through to him that I don't want to see him
again.* **get through with s.o** (*informal*) (make
and) finish one's attack (in actions or words)
on s.o: *When the thieves had got through with
him he was a mass of bruises. When I get
through with her, she'll realize how stupid she
has been.* **get through with s.t** finish or complete
doing s.t: *When they had got through with the
introductions they settled down to business.*
get to s.o (*informal*) affect s.o deeply: *His kind
of music really gets to me.* ⇒ get(16). **get to s.t**
reach, arrive at, a certain point in s.t: *When he
got to the end of his speech, we applauded.* **get**
(**s.o/s.t**) **to s.w** (cause s.o/s.t to) reach, arrive
at, a place: *When they got* (*them*) *to the station,
the train had left.* **get to be s.t** become or reach
a certain state: *He soon got to be very powerful.*
get to doing s.t start doing s.t: *When he got to
thinking about what had happened he realized she
had deceived him.* **get to know** *etc* **s.o/s.t/that...**
reach a state of knowing etc s.o/s.t/that...: *She
soon got to realize that he had no intention of
marrying her.* **get to the bottom of s.t** ⇒ bottom.
get to grips with s.t ⇒ grip. **get to the top** ⇒
top[1](4). **get to work** (**on s.t**) ⇒ work(*n*).
get (**s.o**) **together** (**with s.o**) (cause s.o, some

people to) join in a group (with s.o, other people),
usu for some purpose: *He got the children all
together with their parents and told them the bad
news.* ⇒ get-together. **get oneself**, **it**, **one's act** *etc*
together (*informal*) (try to) organize, so that
one does it well or better (often with the idea
that one is not organized properly): *He needs to
get his act together if he is to succeed.*
get too big for one's boots ⇒ boot.
get tough (**with s.o**) ⇒ tough(*adj*).
get under s.t make one's body pass underneath s.t
(and sometimes come out on the other side): *He
got under the bed to hide. They got under the wire
fence and into the garden.* **get under s.o's skin** ⇒
skin.
get up (**a**) ⇒ get (s.o) up. (**b**) (of the wind, a storm
etc) start to happen, become fiercer: *There's a
storm getting up so close the windows.* (**c**) ⇒ get
(s.o) up (on s.t). **get** (**s.o**) **up** (**a**) (make s.o) rise in the
morning, leave their bed: *Would you get the chil-
dren up or they'll be late for school. I got up late
this morning.* (**b**) (help s.o to) stand after sitting,
lying, falling etc: *He got the old lady up on her feet.
They all got up when she came into the room.* **get**
(**s.o**) **up** (**on s.t**) (help s.o to) climb or mount s.t,
e.g a horse, wall etc: *Here, let me get you up on the
horse. Get up* (*on that wall*) *and tell me what you
can see.* **get** (**s.o/s.t**) **up s.t** (help s.o or cause s.t
to) climb, be carried, to the top of s.t: *They got
their tents up the mountain with difficulty.* **get s.t
up** cause s.t to happen, organize s.t: *We got up a
party to celebrate.* **get up speed** ⇒ speed(*n*). **get
up steam** ⇒ steam(*n*). **get oneself/s.o up in s.t**
dress oneself/s.o in (a set of) clothes, often of a
special or strange kind: *She had got herself up
in a long dress for the party.* ⇒ get-up. **get up
to s.t** (**a**) reach a certain (high) standard: *I'll
never get up to his level.* (**b**) (be thought to)
be doing s.t bad, but without others knowing
exactly what: *The children must be getting up to
something; it's too quiet upstairs.* **get up to s.w**
reach a certain level, place: *The water had got
up to his neck before he was rescued.* **get up to
date** (**with s.t**) ⇒ up to date (⇒ date[1](*n*)).
get the upper hand (**over s.o**) ⇒ upper hand.
get one's own way ⇒ way.
get what's coming to one (*informal*) suffer, be
punished in a way that is to be expected, for s.t
wrong that one has done etc: *If you ask me,
he got what was coming to him because he
shouldn't have treated her like that.*
get wind of s.t; **get the wind up** ⇒ wind[1](*n*).
get wise to s.o/s.t ⇒ wise[1](*adj*).
get s.o/s.t wrong ⇒ wrong.
have got s.t; **have got to do s.t** ⇒ have.
tell s.o where to get off (or **where he/she gets
off**) (*informal*) tell s.o that he/she should not
interfere, should go away etc: *When he started
criticizing me I told him where to get off.*
get-at-able /ˌget ˈæt əbl/ *adj* (of an object etc,
esp one that is in a difficult or awkward place) that
can be reached, touched, got at (⇒ get at s.t(a)):
*The cave is not get-at-able from below; you have
to climb up above it and get in through a hole.*
'geta,way *c.n* (usu *sing*; also *attrib*) (often make
one's —) escape, usu from the scene of a crime,
using a car or cars: *The gang(1) made their getaway in a stolen car. The getaway car was
found a mile away.* ⇒ get away with s.t(a).

'get-to,gether *c.n* (*informal*) gathering of people, kind of party, usu for some purpose: *He usually attends the yearly get-together held by his old school friends.* ⇨ get (s.o) together (with s.o).

'get-,up *u.n* (*informal*) (special or strange kind of) clothes that one/s.o is wearing: *You can't go to the party in that get-up!* ⇨ get oneself/s.o up in s.t.

,go-'getter *c.n* ⇨ go.

geyser /'giːzə/ *c.n* **1** underground spring that sends hot water or mud to the surface and, in some cases, forces the water high into the air. **2** tank of water heated by gas and used in kitchens, bathrooms etc in the home.

ghastly /'gaːstlɪ/ *adj* (*-ier*, *-iest*) **1** very bad or frightening: *a ghastly accident*; *a ghastly scream* (*1*). **2** (of an object etc) very badly made, very unpleasant to look at; very ugly: *a ghastly dress*; *a ghastly piece of furniture.* **3** (of s.t one or s.o has done) (*informal*) very bad (and that one/s.o now regrets doing): *It was all a ghastly mistake and I didn't mean to hurt him.* **4** (*informal*) (of s.t that one is present at, takes part in etc) very upsetting and unpleasant: *We had an absolutely ghastly holiday — there were too many people around and it rained all the time.* **5** (of the way s.o looks, feels etc) pale and ill: *I felt ghastly after staying up all night.*
'ghastliness *u.n.*

gherkin /'gɜːkɪn/ *c.n* kind of small green cucumber (1) that is pickled (3) and then eaten.

ghetto /'getəʊ/ *c.n* (*pl -s*) **1** (usu poor) part of a city in which groups of people of the same race or religion (are forced to) live because they do not have the same advantages etc as richer people. **2** (*old use*) place like this in a city in which Jews used to live.

ghost /gəʊst/ *n* **1** *c.n* form of dead person, esp one that (some people believe) appears to living people: *The house is said to be* haunted (1) *by the ghost of one of its former owners.* **2** *sing.n* (usu a/ the *— of s.t*) very small indication or suggestion (of s.t): *A ghost of a smile crossed her face.* **give up the ghost** (*formal*) die. **not have/stand the ghost of a chance** (**of doing s.t**) (*fig*) not have a chance at all (of doing s.t): *He hasn't a ghost of a chance of getting into university.*
▷ *tr.v* **3** = ghostwrite.
'ghostliness *u.n* state of being ghostly.
'ghostly *adj* (*-ier*, *-iest*) **1** of, looking like, a ghost (1). **2** (of an object, light etc) very faint or pale and hard to see: *A ghostly shape could just be seen in the dark.*
'ghost ,town *c.n* town built to serve an industry, e.g goldmining, but now (almost) completely empty because the industry has stopped.
'ghost,write *tr/intr.v* (*p.t -,wrote*, *p.p -,written*) write (a book, article etc) for another person who can then claim he/she is the author.
'ghost,writer *c.n* person who ghostwrites.

ghoul /guːl/ *c.n* **1** (*old use*) spirit that was believed by some people to eat dead bodies. **2** person who shows an unhealthy interest in death, disasters (1), accidents etc.
'ghoulish *adj* being or acting like a ghoul (2): *He takes a ghoulish interest in murder trials.*
'ghoulishly *adv.* **'ghoulishness** *u.n.*

GHQ /,dʒiː ,eɪtʃ 'kjuː/ *abbr* General Headquarters.

GI /,dʒiː 'aɪ/ (*pl GIs, GI's*) (*informal*) soldier in the US Army.

giant /'dʒaɪənt/ *attrib.adj* **1** (of an object etc) much larger than is normal or usual: *a giant plant*; *a giant packet of soap powder.*
▷ *c.n* **2** (in stories) man who is very much bigger than normal people. **3** person who is very big, tall strong etc: *There was an absolute giant (of a man) guarding the door.* **4** person who has outstanding ability and importance: *He's one of the giants of English literature.*
giantess /'dʒaɪəntɪs/ *c.n* female giant (2).
,giant 'panda ⇨ panda (*n*).

gibber /'dʒɪbə/ *intr.v* (of an animal, person) make sounds that cannot be understood, are nonsense etc: *The monkeys were gibbering away in the trees. He was gibbering with fear.*
gibberish /'dʒɪbərɪʃ/ *u.n* talk, words, writing etc that cannot be understood or is/are nonsense: *This story you wrote is complete gibberish.*

gibbet /'dʒɪbɪt/ *c.n* (*old use*) kind of gallows on which criminals were put after they were dead.

gibbon /'gɪbən/ *c.n* kind of ape (1) with very long arms and no tail that is found in Asia.

gibe /dʒaɪb/ *c.n* (also **jibe**) **1** (usu *— about/at s.o/ s.t*) remark intended to hurt s.o, make fun of s.o/ s.t: *I've had enough of your cheap gibes about my work.*
▷ *intr.v* (also **jibe**) **2** (usu *— at s.o/s.t*) make gibes (1) (about s.o/s.t).

giblets /'dʒɪblɪts/ *pl.n* inside parts, e.g the heart, liver (1), of a bird such as a chicken, goose (1), turkey (1) etc which are removed before cooking.

giddy /'gɪdɪ/ *adj* (*-ier*, *-iest*) **1** feeling faint and unsteady, as though one, or everything around one, is spinning: *I feel rather giddy — can I sit down for a moment?* **2** (becoming *old use*) behaving in a silly, not very sensible way: *She's a giddy young thing, always going to parties and staying out all night.*
'giddily *adv.* **'giddiness** *u.n.*

gift /gɪft/ *c.n* **1** thing that is given to one or s.o freely and without having to be paid for: *The book was a gift from my aunt. He made several gifts to the poor in his will.* Compare present[2]. **2** (usu *have a — for (doing) s.t*) natural ability, esp for s.t artistic or sometimes for doing s.t wrong: *She has a gift for languages. He just has this gift for annoying people.* **3** (usu *be a —*) (*informal*) thing that is very easily done, that costs very little etc: *The examination was a complete gift.* (**have**) **the gift of the gab** ⇨ gab. **a gift from the gods** a thing that is entirely unexpected and that helps one a lot.
▷ *tr.v* **4** (*formal*) give (s.t) as a gift (1) (to s.o): *He gifted the house to the National Trust.*
'gifted *adj* (of a person) having a special gift (2): *Gifted children need special teaching.*
'gift-,horse *c.n* (usu *(not) look a — in the mouth*) thing that comes unexpectedly but that is exactly what one wants, needs etc: *So, he offered you money just when you need it; why look a gift-horse in the mouth?*
'gift ,voucher *c.n* voucher (1) that one buys from a shop etc with a stamp or stamps in it representing a certain amount of money; one gives it to s.o as a gift (1) so that he/she can go to the shop and buy what he/she wants: *a £20 gift voucher.*

gig¹ /gɪg/ *c.n* **1** (*old use*) carriage with two wheels pulled by a horse. **2** small boat belonging to a larger ship.

gig² /gɪg/ *c.n* (*informal*) performance of music, esp jazz(1) and popular music, by a musician or group of musicians in a place: *We are doing a gig at the local hall next week.*

gigantic /dʒaɪˈgæntɪk/ *adj* extremely large in size: *a gigantic plant.*
giˈgantically *adv.*

giggle /ˈgɪgl/ *c.n* **1** silly laugh, e.g because one is nervous. **be a giggle** (*informal*) be s.t very easy or amusing to do: *It's a giggle, all you have to do is fill in the form and send the money.* **do s.t for a giggle** do s.t because it is amusing. **have the giggles** be unable to stop giggling(2).
▷ *intr.v* **2** (often — *at/over s.o/s.t*) laugh in a silly, perhaps nervous, way (at s.o, what s.o says, does etc): *I tried to be serious but all he could do was giggle at me* (or *at what I said*).
ˈgiggly *adj* (*-ier, iest*) giggling(2) a lot; behaving in a silly way: *giggly schoolchildren.*

gild¹ /gɪld/ *tr.v* (*p.t gilded, p.p gilded* or *gilt*/gɪlt/) cover or paint (a surface) with a very thin coat of gold or gold paint as a decoration. **gild the lily** ⇒ lily.
ˈgilding *u.n* (act of putting) gold or gold paint on a surface: *a wooden ceiling with gilding on it.*

gilt /gɪlt/ *u.n* (also *attrib*) gold, gold paint or s.t shiny like gold, used as a decoration: *The cup had an edge of gilt* (or *a gilt edge*). **take the gilt off the gingerbread** (*fig*) (of s.t bad that happens) make s.t that one thought was good become not so good, become bad etc: *Though I got an increase in pay the extra tax took some of the gilt off the gingerbread.*
ˌgilt-ˈedged *adj* (*commerce*) (of stocks(10), shares(3) etc) very secure and/or financially rewarding (in terms of interest etc): *a gilt-edged investment(1).*

gild² /gɪld/ *c.n* ⇒ guild.

gill¹ /gɪl/ *c.n* one of the two openings on each side of the body of a fish through which it breathes.

gill² /dʒɪl/ *c.n* (becoming *old use*) liquid measure equal to one quarter of a pint (0.142 litres).

gilt ⇒ gild¹.

gimlet /ˈgɪmlɪt/ *c.n* small tool (a metal rod with a screw shape at the end), used for making holes in wood, e.g for screws.

gimmick /ˈgɪmɪk/ *c.n* (*informal*) object, idea etc used to interest people, to make s.o/s.t seem more attractive than (than he/she/it really is): *The advertisement is just a gimmick to make people buy their products.*
ˈgimmicky *adj.*

gin¹ /dʒɪn/ *c/u.n* (glass of) kind of alcoholic(1) drink made from grain and juniper berries that looks like water: *I'll have a gin and orange please.*

gin² /dʒɪn/ *c.n* trap or snare(1) for catching (wild) animals.

ginger /ˈdʒɪndʒə/ *u.n* (also *attrib*) **1** hot-tasting brown root of a plant (or sometimes its stem) used in cooking. **2** (esp of hair) brown-red colour: *a wall painted in ginger; a ginger moustache.*
▷ *tr.v* **3 ginger s.o/s.t up** make s.o more active; make s.t more interesting etc: *The business needs gingering up if it is to succeed.*

ˌginger-ˈale/ˈbeer *c/u.n* (glass of) kind of non-alcoholic drink made with ginger(1).
ˈginger,bread *u.n* kind of cake or biscuit flavoured with ginger(1). ⇒ gilt.
ˈginger ,group *c.n* small group of people, esp in a government or political party, who try to make others do s.t, become more active etc.
ˈgingerly *adj* **1** very careful, e.g so as not to break or damage s.t, because one does not know what to expect etc: *gingerly steps along the wall.*
▷ *adv* **2** in a very gingerly(1) way: *He picked up the animal gingerly, afraid that it was going to bite him.*

gipsy /ˈdʒɪpsɪ/ *c.n* (*pl -ies*) (also **ˈgypsy**) person belonging to a race that came from Asia and that now travels around a country or countries without settling down, often living in caravans(2).

giraffe /dʒɪˈrɑːf/ *c.n* (*pl -(s)*) kind of animal found in Africa with four very long legs and a tall neck.

girder /ˈgɜːdə/ *c.n* large beam of wood, metal etc used to hold up s.t, e.g a roof, building, bridge: *The bridge was supported by steel girders.*

girdle /ˈgɜːdl/ *c.n* **1** kind of woman's corset. **2** kind of wide belt worn around the waist.
▷ *tr.v* **3** (*formal*) go completely around (s.t); surround or encircle (s.t): *The village was girdled by a forest.*

girl /gɜːl/ *c.n* **1** baby or child of the female sex: *Their first child was a girl and the second a boy.* **2** young woman: *He spends his time looking at girls as they go past in the street.* **3** daughter of any age: *We have two girls and a boy in our family.* **4** (*old use*) woman doing a certain kind of work: *a shop girl.*
ˈgirl,friend *c.n* **1** girl or woman with whom a boy or a man is friendly, with whom he goes out etc. Compare boyfriend. **2** girl or woman with whom another woman is friendly etc.
ˌGirl ˈGuide *c.n* (*old use*) = Guide(5).
ˈgirl,hood *u.n* (*formal*) length of time when one is a girl.
ˈgirlish *adj* of or like a girl; acting or looking like a girl, esp when one is an older woman or when one is a male: *girlish laughter; a girlish dress.*
ˈgirlishly *adv.* **ˈgirlishness** *u.n.*

giro /ˈdʒaɪrəʊ/ *def/unique n* system of banking in some countries in which a payment can be made directly from one bank account to another. **the National Giro** (UK) this system run by the Government. **by giro** using this system: *pay (an account) by giro.*

girth /gɜːθ/ *n* **1** *c/u.n* (example of the) measurement of a round object, e.g the trunk(2) of a tree, a person's waist. ⇒ circumference. **2** *c.n* strap, usu made of leather, that goes under the stomach of a horse and holds a saddle in place.

gist /dʒɪst/ *def.n* (usu the — *of s.t*) (a summary(1) of) the main points (of s.t said, written etc): *Don't read it all to me, just tell me the gist of his argument.*

git /gɪt/ *c.n* (*derog; slang;* do not use!) useless stupid person: *You silly git! Why didn't you do what I told you?*

give /gɪv/ *u.n* **1** (of a substance, object etc) ability or amount by which s.t bends, changes shape etc under a force or pressure without breaking: *This new plastic(3) has a lot of give in it.* ⇒ give(11).
▷ *v* (*pres.p giving, p.t gave* /geɪv/, *p.p given*

/ˈgɪvn/) **2** *tr.v* (usu — *s.o s.t*; — *s.t to s.o*) cause (s.o) to receive (s.t) by handing it to them: *Could you give me that book that's beside you? Give that toy to me!* **3** *tr.v* (usu — *s.o s.t*; — *s.t to s.o*) cause (s.o) to receive (s.t) as a present or gift: *He gave her £50 on her birthday.* **4** *tr.v* (usu — (s.o) *s.t for s.t*) cause (s.o) to receive (an amount of money, s.t in order to own, in exchange for, s.t else): *He gave him £500 for the car. I gave my most valuable coin for his stamps.* **5** *tr.v* (often — *s.o s.t*; — *s.t to s.o*) cause (s.o) to suffer (the same thing, e.g an illness) as oneself: *He gave her his cold.* **6** *tr.v* (usu — (s.o/s.t) *a s.t*) perform (an action as described by the noun) (aimed at s.o/s.t): *He gave (her) a smile. Would you give him a ring* (i.e telephone him)? **7** *tr.v* (often — *oneself/s.o time etc* (*to do s.t*)) allow (oneself/s.o) (a certain amount of time to do, say or finish s.t): *I gave myself plenty of time to catch the train. I'm sorry, I'm rather busy, I can only give you ten minutes.* **8** *tr.v* organize, hold, deliver, (s.t, e.g a party, a talk): *He gave a large party on his birthday. He gave a lecture on gardening.* **9** *tr.v* (often — (s.o) *s.t*) produce (s.t for the benefit(1) of people), esp as a natural product: *Bees give (us) honey.* **10** *tr.v* (*mathematics*) have (an answer) as a result: *75 divided by 5 gives 15.* **11** *intr.v* (of a substance, object etc) bend, move, break or change shape (as a result of a force or pressure): *Feel the way this new* plastic(3) *gives when you press it. The fence gave under the weight of all the people trying to get out.* ⇒ give way.

give as good as one gets (in a fight, an argument etc) fight or defend oneself as well as the person who is attacking one: *It was a fierce argument, but he gave as good as he got.*

give s.o away (a) (in a marriage ceremony) formally give a woman as a bride to her future husband: *The bride was given away by her father.* (b) (of an expression, way of saying s.t etc) show s.o to be of a certain kind or type: *His foreign* accent(1) *gave him away and he was arrested as a* spy(1). ⇒ give-away(2). (c) let s.o/others know about s.o, esp s.o who is trying to hide, disguise(3) herself/himself etc: *Will you promise not to give me away if I tell you my new name?*

give s.t away (esp in a sport or competition) do s.t, often accidentally, that allows s.o else to win: *In the last ten minutes they gave away the game by letting the other side get two easy goals.* Compare give the game/show away (⇒ game). **give s.t away** (**to s.o/s.t**) (a) hand, present, s.t as a gift (to s.o/s.t): *He gave all his money away to* charity(2). ⇒ give-away(1). (b) allow s.t, e.g one's plans, to become known (to s.o), either accidentally or on purpose: *He gave away the place where the* gang(1) *was hiding to the police.*

give (s.o) back s.t; **give s.t back** (**to s.o**) return s.t that one has had, borrowed etc (to its owner): *If I let you read the book, do you promise to give it back to me* (or *to give me it back*)? **give s.o back s.t** restore(2) to s.o the use of s.t that he/ she has lost through illness, accident etc: *Though he had several operations nothing could give him back his sight.*

give birth (**to s.o/s.t**) ⇒ birth.
give chase ⇒ chase(n).
give ground (**to s.o/s.t**) ⇒ ground²(n).
give in (a) admit that one does not know s.t, the

answer etc: *I give in! What's the answer?* Compare give up (doing s.t). (b) say that one wants to stop fighting etc: *I give in! Stop* tickling(2) *me!*
give in (**to s.o/s.t**) (say that one wants to) stop fighting, arguing etc (against s.o/s.t): *They were forced to give in to the greater forces of the enemy.*
give s.t in (**to s.o**) hand or present s.t (to s.o) when one has finished with it etc: *Examination papers should be given in* (*to the teacher*) *at the end of the two hours.*
give it to s.o straight ⇒ straight(adv).
give one's life for s.t ⇒ life.
give off s.t (of a substance, process etc) produce s.t (as a result of s.t): *When you mix the chemical with water it gives off a* horrible(3) *smell.*
give or take s.t allowing for a certain difference in quantity or amount either way: *It must weigh fifty kilos, give or take a kilo or two.*
give out be all used, finished so that there is nothing more: *His money gave out after a week on holiday and he had to return home.* **give out** (**on s.o**) (of a machine, car etc) stop working (as one is using, driving it): *The car gave out (on me) half a mile down the road.* **give out s.t** (a) = hand out s.t. (b) produce s.t, esp as a result of s.t: *The fire was giving out a lot of heat.* **give s.o out** (of an umpire(1) in cricket¹ etc) make a batsman leave the pitch¹(1) because he/she has been bowled out etc. **give s.t out** (**to s.o**) (a) hand or present s.t (to s.o, a number of people etc), esp a gift, prize etc: *They were giving out food parcels to the poor.* (b) let s.t, e.g news, information, be known (to s.o): *News of the defeat was given out on the radio.*
give over (*informal*) stop (doing s.t): *Give over! You're hurting me!* **give s.o/s.t over** (**to s.o**) hand or present s.o/s.t (to s.o) usu in a formal way: *The prisoners were given over to the police.* ⇒ given (over) to s.t.
give place to s.o/s.t ⇒ place(n).
give rise to s.t ⇒ rise(n).
give s.t etc to know what etc . . . want very anxiously to know what etc . . .: *I'd give a great deal to know why he left his job so suddenly.*
give s.o to understand (**that**) . . . (try to) tell s.o, perhaps in not quite a clear or direct way, (that) . . .: *You gave me to understand (that) I would get the job and now you say I won't.*
give up (**doing s.t**) say that one does not know s.t, the answer etc: *I give up! What's the answer? He gave up trying to find out what had happened.* Compare give in(a). **give s.o up** = give up on s.o.
give s.o up as/for dead/lost no longer look for s.o who is lost because one thinks he/she is dead, has been killed. **give s.o/s.t up as a bad job** ⇒ job. **give up on s.o** stop trying to see, find, wait for etc s.o: *After waiting for an hour he gave up on her.* **give oneself up** (**to s.o**) (come out of hiding and) surrender(2) oneself (to s.o in authority(1)): *The escaped prisoner gave himself up to the police.*
give s.t up (**to s.o**) allow s.t to be used or taken (by s.o): *Children should give up their seats* (e.g in a bus) *to old people.*
give way bend and break as a result of a force or pressure: *The floor gave way under the weight of all the people.* ⇒ give(11). **give way** (**to s.o/s.t**):
give way to s.t ⇒ way.
give s.o what for ⇒ what(pron).
give one's word (**to s.o**) ⇒ word(n).
I/I'll give you that, **but . . .** I agree with what you

say about that, but (not about other things etc): *All right, I'll give you that, but you're wrong about everything else.*

What gives? (*informal*) What is happening, what are you doing etc?: *Have you talked to her? Come on, tell me, what gives?*

,**give-and-'take** *u.n* willingness to accept s.t from s.o whom one disagrees with in return for her/him accepting s.t from oneself: *You must allow for some give-and-take if you want to settle the matter.*

'**give-a,way** *c.n* (also *attrib*) **1** thing sold at a very low price; small thing given free: *The washing machines are give-aways at that price* (or *are being sold at give-away prices*). ⇒ give s.t away (to s.o/s.t). **2** thing, e.g one's voice, action, that shows s.t about one, esp s.t one is trying to hide etc: *Though he tried to remain calm, the expression on his face was a complete give-away.* ⇒ give s.o away (b).

given /'gɪvn/ *adj* **1** of or referring to s.t that is (to be) stated or decided: *You'll have to get the job done in the given time.* **2** (often — *that* . . .) if or accepting (that s.t is so, true etc, then s.t else follows): *Given that you're right, we won't be able to do anything about it.* **given** (**over**) **to s.t** continually (in the habit of) doing s.t: *He's given to making far too quick judgements.*

'**giver** *c.n* person who gives or has given s.t as a gift.

glacial /'gleɪsɪəl/ *adj* **1** of or referring to the existence or forming of ice, e.g in a glacier: *the glacial* era. **2** very cold: *a glacial wind.* **3** (*fig*) (of a feeling, look etc) showing a complete lack of warmth or interest: *a glacial smile.*

glacier /'gleɪsɪə/ *c.n* large amount of ice formed from snow on mountains that moves gradually down towards a lower level.

glad /glæd/ *adj* (-**dd**-) **1** (*pred*) (often — *about* s.t; — (*to know* etc) *that* . . .) pleased and happy (about s.t that has happened, is going to happen etc): *Aren't you glad about the news that the strike is over? I was very glad* (*to hear*) *that you'll be moving to London.* **2** (*pred*) (usu — *of* s.t) pleased and satisfied (because of s.t one has got, s.t s.o has done etc): *I was glad of your help when I was ill.* **3** (*pred*) (usu — *to do* s.t) willing and eager (to do s.t): *I'd be very glad to help you when you move.* **4** (*attrib*) (*formal*) (of news etc) bringing pleasure: *He brought the glad news that the fighting was over.*

gladden /'glædn/ *tr.v* (*formal*) make (s.o) happy: *The news gladdened him.* **gladden s.o's heart** make s.o feel happy.

'**gladly** *adv.* '**gladness** *u.n.*

glade /gleɪd/ *c.n* (*old use*) open space or clearing in a wood or forest.

gladiator /'glædɪ,eɪtə/ *c.n* (in ancient Rome) man trained to fight animals or other people as a public sport.

gladiolus /,glædɪ'əʊləs/ *c.n* (*pl* **gladioli** /,glædɪ'əʊlaɪ/, **-es**) tall plant with long green stems[1](1), wide leaves and brightly-coloured flowers.

gladly, gladness ⇒ glad.

glamour /'glæmə/ *u.n* (US '**glamor**) (appearance of) attraction and beauty (of s.o/s.t) that may be real or may be only on the surface, e.g because of beautiful clothes, make-up(1) etc:

She brought a touch of glamour to the occasion by wearing her jewels. He was attracted by the glamour of New York.

glamorization, -isation /,glæməraɪ'zeɪʃn/ *u.n.*

'**glamo,rize, -ise** *tr.v* make (s.t appear to be) attractive and glamorous: *He tried to glamorize the job by saying it meant doing lots of travelling.*

glamorous /'glæmərəs/ *adj* having or showing (a lot of) glamour: *a glamorous woman*; *a glamorous job.*

glance /glɑːns/ *c.n* **1** (often — *at* s.o/s.t; *give* s.o/s.t *a* —) quick short look (at s.o/s.t, e.g while really looking at s.o/s.t else or because one has not got time to study s.t in detail): *After* (*taking*) *a quick glance at her to see if she was all right, he turned away. He gave the newspaper a glance and saw nothing of interest.* **at a glance** (just by) looking quickly: *I could see at a glance that things were not going well.*

▷ *intr.v* **2** (usu — *at* s.o/s.t) take a glance(1) (at s.o/s.t): *He glanced at her slyly.* **glance away/back/round** etc (turn one's head and) look quickly away/back/round etc. **glance down** (**s.t**) look quickly down (towards the ground, to see s.t or move one's eyes over a list of s.t etc): *He glanced down and saw the sea below him. He glanced down the list of names to see if his was there.* **glance off s.o/s.t** (of a blow, moving object etc) hit s.o/s.t and move or bounce(1) off, to one side etc, usu without seriously harming her/him/it: *The bricks and stones just glanced off the policemen's shields.* **glance over/through s.t** look quickly over/through s.t (in order to get some idea of the contents): *He glanced through the report and found nothing of interest.* ⇒ glance-over, glance-through.

'**glance-,over,** '**glance-,through** *c.n* (usu *give* s.t *a* —) quick, not very thorough look (e.g through a report).

'**glancing** *attrib.adj* (of a blow) that only just hits s.o/s.t and then moves or slides to one side: *He received a glancing blow from one of the falling rocks.* ⇒ glance off s.o/s.t.

gland /glænd/ *c.n* one of the organs in the body that produce substances from blood that are used for various purposes: *sweat glands.*

glandular /'glændjʊlə/ *adj* of or referring to a gland: *glandular fever.*

glare /gleə/ *n* **1** (very) fierce angry look: *He got angry glares from people when he stood up to leave in the middle of the film.* **2** *u.n* very hard bright unpleasant light (that is difficult to look at): *the glare of the sun.* (**in**) **the** (**full**) **glare of s.t** (*fig*) with (all) the public's attention etc directed towards s.o/s.t: *The wedding was performed in the full glare of publicity(2).*

▷ *intr.v* **3** (usu — *at* s.o/s.t) look fiercely and angrily (at s.o/s.t): *They glared at each other as they got ready to fight.* **4** (usu — *down*) (of the sun, a hard bright light etc) shine very brightly and hotly (downwards) (and painfully to the eyes): *The sun glared down and she wished she had remembered to bring her hat.*

'**glaring** *adj* **1** (of the sun, light etc) shining very hard and brightly: *When he came into the glaring light he had to shade his eyes.* **2** (of colours) far too bright and unpleasant: *The walls were painted* *in glaring colours.* **3** (*fig*) (of a mistake, s.t wrong that has been done etc) very easy to be seen; very obvious: *There were several glaring mistakes in her answers. A glaring injustice has been done to those too poor to help themselves.*

glass /glɑːs/ *n* **1** *u.n* (also *attrib*) hard transparent substance made into sheets, shapes etc, e.g for windows, bottles etc: *a sheet of glass; broken glass; a glass bottle/jug.* **2** *c.n* container with a round shape, made of glass(1), used for holding liquids: *Can you wash the glasses, please?* ⇒ wineglass. **3** *c.n* (also **'glassful**) (often — *of s.t*) amount a glass(2) can hold: *a glass of orange/wine.* **4** *c.n* mirror: *Sue checked her appearance in the glass by the front door.* **5** *u.n* (collection of) a number of objects, e.g bowls, dishes, glasses(2), made of glass(1): *He collects old glass and china(2).* **6** *c.n* barometer(1) showing the rise or fall in air pressure: *The glass is rising.*
▷ *tr.v* **7** put (a sheet or sheets of) glass(1) on or in (s.t, esp a window); glaze(6) (s.t). **glass s.t in/over etc** put glass(1) in/over etc an area to protect it.
'glasses *pl.n* (often *a pair of* —) two pieces of glass(1) in a metal, plastic(3) etc frame worn in front of the eyes to improve one's sight: *Mary has to wear glasses because her eyesight is failing.*
'glassful *c.n* = glass(3).
'glass,house *n* **1** *c.n* small building made mostly of glass(1) and used for growing plants, flowers etc; greenhouse. **2** *def.n* (often *be* (*put*) *in the* —) (*slang*) army prison.
'glassily *adv* in a glassy(1) way.
'glassiness *u.n* state of being glassy.
'glassy *adj* (*-ier, -iest*) **1** (of a person's face or expression) very fixed or empty of feeling: *His glassy stare(1) made me think he was dead.* **2** (of a surface, esp water) smooth, still and shining like glass(1): *The sea was glassy as though a storm was coming up.*

glaze /gleɪz/ *n* **1** *c/u.n* (example of a) thin shiny covering of clay put on a pot, piece of china(2) etc, in liquid form and then hardened by heating in an oven to make it more attractive, to protect it etc. **2** *c/u.n* (example of a) thin shiny covering of melted sugar etc put on fruit, a cooked dish etc: *The apples had a glaze over them.* **3** *c.n* fixed or empty expression in one's eyes etc: *A glaze came over him as she went on talking.* Compare glassy(1).
▷ *v* **4** *tr.v* put a glaze(1) on (a pot etc). **5** *tr.v* put a glaze(2) on (fruit etc). **6** *tr.v* put (a sheet or sheets of) glass(1) into (a frame of a window): *The front windows had been glazed in diamond patterns.* **7** *intr.v* (often — *over*) (of the eyes, an expression) become fixed or empty of feeling; become glassy(1): *His eyes glazed over and suddenly he was dead.*
glazier /'gleɪzɪə/ *c.n* person whose job is to glaze(6) windows.
'glazing *u.n* glass(1) used for windows. **double glazing** ⇒ double.

gleam /gliːm/ *c.n* (usu — *of s.t*) **1** bright shining light (from/of s.t), esp one that is seen for a short or long time or at a distance, that reflects on s.t etc: *He could see the gleam of a fire down in the valley.* **2** very small amount (of a feeling or expression of interest, hope etc): *When he mentioned the money he would pay her, she allowed a gleam of interest to cross her face.*

▷ *intr.v* **3** give out a gleam(1): *The silver gleamed after the polishing he gave it.* Compare glimmer(1).
glean /gliːn/ *v* **1** *tr.v* (often — *s.t from s.o/s.t*) (manage to) get a small amount of (information) (from s.o/s.t): *What did you glean from your conversation with him?* **2** *tr/intr.v* (*old use*) pick up (the remaining pieces of grain) left in a field after the main part has been harvested: *It used to be a common sight to see women gleaning in fields.*
'gleaner *c.n* person who gleans(2).
'gleanings *pl.n* **1** (often — *of s.t*) small amounts (of information). **2** (*old use*) grain that has been gleaned(2).
glee /gliː/ *u.n* (expression of) happy pleasure, esp by laughing, because of s.t that has happened either to one's advantage or to s.o else's disadvantage: *Colin showed great glee when he heard of their bad luck.*
'gleeful *adj* showing, being full of, glee.
'gleefully *adv.* **'gleefulness** *u.n.*
glen /glen/ *c.n* (with capital **G** in names) (name for a) long valley, esp in Scotland: *Glen Lomond.*
glib /glɪb/ *adj* (*-bb-*) (*derog*) (of a person, what s.o says etc) able to talk easily, said easily, but without much thought or while offering explanations that seem true but usu are not: *He's very glib* (*with his excuses*) *but I don't believe anything he says.*
'glibly *adv.* **'glibness** *u.n.*
glide /glaɪd/ *c.n* **1** continuous smooth (almost silent) movement (of s.o/s.t), esp over a smooth surface, e.g ice, or through the air: *The bird came nearer to the nest in one long glide.*
▷ *intr.v* **2** (usu — *across, by, over, past* etc (*s.t*)) move in this way (across etc (s.t)): *They glided across the ice.* **3** (of an aircraft or a glider) fly in a smooth continuous movement using currents of air and esp without engines: *The aircraft came gliding in to land.* **glide by (a)** ⇒ glide(2). **(b)** (*literary*) (of time) pass smoothly and quickly almost without one noticing it: *The hours glided by.*
'glider *c.n* kind of aeroplane that has no engine(s) and uses currents of air to fly: *Gliders pulled by aircraft were used to carry troops in the last war.*
'gliding *u.n* (often *go* —) sport or activity using gliders: *He goes gliding every weekend.*
glimmer /'glɪmə/ *c.n* (usu — *of s.t*) **1** very faint light (from/of s.t), esp one seen at a distance: *A glimmer of light came from the window.* **2** very small amount (of s.t, esp hope, interest etc): *There was at least one glimmer of hope that everything would come right in the end.*
▷ *intr.v* **3** give or show a faint light: *Lights glimmered down in the valley.* Compare gleam.
glimpse /glɪmps/ *c.n* **1** (often — *catch/get a — at/of s.o/s.t*) very quick look (at s.o/s.t); quick, not very clear, view (of s.o/s.t) before he/she/it disappears, is taken away etc: *I just caught a glimpse of him before he went round the corner.*
▷ *tr.v* **2** see (s.o/s.t) in this way: *I glimpsed him through the fog.*
glint /glɪnt/ *c.n* **1** (often — *of s.t*) bright shining light, or reflection of light, often one seen for a short moment or from a shiny surface, e.g a metal: *There were glints of light coming from between the curtains.* **2** (often — *of s.t; a — in s.o's eyes*) slight

or quick expression (of a feeling or of interest) shown by a change or hardening of one's face or eyes: *There was a glint of anger on her face when she realized she would not get her own way. When you see that glint in his eyes you know that Richard's planning something.*

▷ *intr.v* **3** shine with a glint(1): *The gold glinted in the sunlight.* **4** (often — *with s.t*) (of s.o's eyes, face) express (a feeling): *His eyes glinted (with greed) when he saw the treasure.*

glisten /'glɪsn/ *intr.v* **1** (of a surface etc) shine, reflect light, as if from a wet surface: *The snow glistened in the light of the moon.* **2** (often — *with s.t*) (esp of s.t wet, e.g tears in s.o's eyes) catch or reflect light: *Her eyes glistened with tears.*

glister /'glɪstə/ *intr.v* (*old use*) = glitter(3).

glitter /'glɪtə/ *u/def.n* (often *the* — *of s.t*) **1** state or quality of (s.t) shining brightly with a light that comes and goes: *the glitter of lights; the glitter of jewellery.* **2** beautiful or attractive appearance (of s.t): *She was attracted by all the glitter of the ball.*

▷ *intr.v* **3** (often — *with s.t*) shine brightly with a light that comes and goes often reflecting light from s.t: *She was glittering with jewels (i.e seemed to be shining with all the jewels she was wearing). All that glitters (or glisters) is not gold* ⇒ gold.

'glittering *adj* **1** shining brightly with a light that comes and goes: *glittering lights.* **2** (of s.t one does or gains) very successful, showing a very high quality or ability: *a glittering performance* (e.g of a piece of music); *a glittering prize.*

gloat /gləʊt/ *c.n* **1** (usu *sing*) (often *have a — over s.o/s.t*) selfish and satisfied feeling (when thinking about s.o, her/his misfortune etc, when looking at s.t valuable one has got etc): *I don't like the way John has a gloat over their troubles. Pauline takes the jewels out every now and then and has a little gloat over them.*

▷ *intr.v* **2** (usu — *over s.t*) look (at s.t) or think (about s.t) in this way: *He gloated over all his valuable things. She gloated over his misfortune.*

'gloatingly *adv.*

globe /gləʊb/ *n* **1** *def.n* the whole world; the earth: *People from all parts of the globe attended the celebrations.* **2** *c.n* large round ball that is fixed to a stand with a map of the world painted on it. **3** *c.n* round glass bowl used to hold things, e.g chemicals, or to act as a cover or shade, e.g for a lamp.

global /'gləʊbl/ *adj* **1** of or referring to the globe(1): *global politics; global war.* **2** (often *a — view of s.t*) in as general a way as possible; taking into account as many things as possible: *Don't concern yourself with the details but try and take a more global view of the business.*

'globally *adv.*

'globe ,artichoke *c.n* ⇒ artichoke(1).

'globe-,trotter *c.n* person who spends a lot of time travelling around the world, for pleasure or on business.

'globe-,trotting *u.n* act of doing this.

globule /'glɒbjuːl/ *c.n* (*formal; technical*) small round drop from a liquid or s.t that has melted: *a globule of water; globules of wax.*

globular /'glɒbjʊlə/ *adj* of, shaped like, a globe(3) or a globule.

gloom /gluːm/ *n* **1** *def.n* (often *in the* —) darkness that is not quite complete but has some light left,

e.g in the late evening: *He could just see a shadowy figure in the gloom.* **2** *sing/u.n* feeling of great sadness or despair because of s.t bad that has happened: *The news caused great gloom among the citizens.* **cast a gloom over s.o/s.t** (of bad news etc) (*formal*) cause great sadness to s.o; make s.t, e.g an event, sadder etc: *The news of his sudden death cast a gloom over the celebrations.* **fill s.o with gloom** (of bad news etc) cause s.o to become very sad or despairing.

'gloomily *adv* in a gloomy(2) way.

'gloominess *u.n* state of being gloomy.

'gloomy *adj* (-*ier*, -*iest*) **1** (of a place, house etc) dark (and so not very attractive or pleasant): *The whole house was gloomy and I certainly didn't want to live in it.* **2** (of a person) very sad, not at all cheerful; (of s.t that has happened etc) causing great sadness or despair: *Why are you always so gloomy? The news George brought was very gloomy.*

glory /'glɔːrɪ/ *n* (*pl -ies*) **1** *u.n* (often *gain/win* —; *cover oneself in* —) great honour or praise (for s.t one has done): *They won great glory by their defeat of the enemy.* **2** *u.n* state or quality of being very beautiful: *The glory of the scene overcame them.* **3** *c.n* (often *pl*) thing, e.g a building, that is famous because of its beauty: *The church was one of the glories of the city.* **4** *u.n* (word used in a prayer to show) praise and respect (to God): *Glory to God in the highest.* **for the glory of s.t** in order to bring glory(1) to s.t: *He fought for the greater glory of his country.* **in (all its) glory** (being seen) with (all) its beauty present: *In summer you will see the garden in all its glory* (i.e with all the colourful flowers etc out).

▷ *intr.v* (-*ies*, -*ied*) **5** **glory in s.t** take (too) much pleasure in s.t that one does, that happens to other people etc: *He gloried in the destruction of his enemies.*

glorification /,glɔːrɪfɪ'keɪʃən/ *u.n.*

glorified /'glɔːrɪ,faɪd/ *attrib.adj* (of an object, building etc) made to look better than it actually is (and, in the opinion of the speaker, still remaining what it was originally): *He calls it his 'summer-house' but really it's nothing but a glorified shed.*

glorify /'glɔːrɪ,faɪ/ *tr.v* (-*ies*, -*ied*) **1** make (s.t) appear to be more attractive or pleasant than it really is: *His speech tried to glorify war but didn't succeed.* **2** praise and honour (God): *Now let us glorify God and thank him for our victory.*

'glorious *adj* **1** bringing or gaining glory(1): *It was a glorious victory.* **2** very good, beautiful: *glorious flowers/weather.* ⇒ inglorious.

'gloriously *adv.* **'gloriousness** *u.n.*

gloss /glɒs/ *n* **1** *c/u.n* (example of a) smooth shining brightness, esp on the surface of s.t or as a reflection: *Her hair had a pleasant gloss. Don't put that hot cup down on the table, you'll damage the gloss.* **2** *u.n* (also **'gloss ,paint**) kind of paint with a hard shiny surface when it dries that is used mainly on wood. Compare emulsion(2). **3** *c.n* note in a book, an article etc, usu at the bottom of a page, explaining a difficult word, phrase etc.

▷ *tr.v* **4** write, make a gloss(3) about, (a word, phrase etc). **gloss over s.t** (try to) make s.t look better than it really is; (try to) hide a mistake, fault etc: *In his speech he glossed* over the fact that the Government had spent too much.

glossary /'glɒsərɪ/ *c.n* (*pl -ies*) book or list containing glosses(3).

'glossiness *u.n* state of being glossy.

'glossy *adj* (*-ier, -iest*) smooth, shiny and bright: *glossy hair.*

ˌglossy ˌmaga'zine *c.n* magazine printed on shiny paper with articles and photographs about e.g fashion, famous people etc.

glove /glʌv/ *c.n* (often *a pair of —s*) one of the two coverings made of wool, leather etc worn over the hands with separate parts to put one's fingers and thumbs in. Compare mitten. **(be) hand in glove (with s.o)** ⇨ hand(*n*). **fit (s.o) like a glove** be exactly the right size and shape (for s.o): *That dress fits (you) like a glove.* **handle (s.o/s.t) with kid gloves** ⇨ kid(*n*). **The gloves are off** (*fig*) All pretence of being polite is finished and now one intends to try to get one's way, to fight etc without mercy.

'glove-comˌpartment *c.n* shelf with a cover on it in the dashboard of a car, in which maps etc are put.

'glove ˌpuppet *c.n* ⇨ puppet(1).

glow /gləʊ/ *c.n* (usu *sing* only) (often *— of s.t*) **1** soft light given out by a fire (but without actual flames), a lamp etc: *He could just see their faces in the glow of the camp fire.* **2** warm bright colour or light (coming from s.t): *The red glow of the sunset.* **3** signs of feelings of physical(1) well-being, happiness, interest etc in the way one appears or seems to appear: *She felt a warm glow through her body after the swim.*

▷ *intr.v* **4** (of s.t burning or heated) give out light without flames: *The fire was still glowing so I put some more coal on it.* **5** show warm bright colours or light: *The sun glowed with an orange light as it sank in the west.* **glow with s.t** show signs or feelings of physical(1) well-being, happiness etc, esp in the face: *She was glowing with (good) health. The child was glowing with happiness.*

'glowing *attrib.adj* **1** (of a colour etc) warm and bright: *a glowing sunset.* **2** (of s.t said etc) (*fig*) full of praise or enthusiasm: *a glowing account/ description.*

'glowingly *adv* in a glowing(2) way.

'glow-ˌworm *c.n* kind of insect (of the firefly family), the female of which gives out a bright green light in the dark.

glower /'glaʊə/ *c.n* **1** angry staring(1) expression: *She had to face the glowers of her children when she refused to take them to the cinema.*

▷ *intr.v* **2** (often *— at s.o/s.t*) look, stare(2), (at s.o/ s.t) with a glower(1): *Stop glowering at me; it wasn't my fault, it was yours.*

'glowering *adj* (of a look) very angry.

'gloweringly *adv*.

glucose /'gluːkəʊs/ *u.n* form of sugar found naturally in plants and esp fruit; it is one of the main sources of energy(1) and growth, *chem.form* $C_6H_{12}O_6$.

glue /gluː/ *c/u.n* **1** (example of a) sticky substance made from natural products or chemically, used for sticking or joining things together: *Use glue to join the two parts* (or *Join the two parts with glue*).

▷ *tr.v* (*pres.p glu(e)ing*) **2** (usu *— s.t to s.t; — s.t together*) join (one thing to another) using

glue(1): *Next glue each ear to the head.* **sniff glue** (*informal*) breathe in the vapour given off by some kinds of glue as s.t pleasurable (but dangerous) to do. ⇨glue-sniffing.

glued *pred.adj* **be glued to s.t** (*fig*) have one's whole attention fixed on s.t, esp s.t one is watching or listening to, and not want or be able to turn away: *Every night he's glued to the television and if you say anything he never hears you.*

'glue-ˌsniffing *u.n* act of breathing in the vapour from glue.

gluey /'gluːɪ/ *adj* (of a substance) sticky; like glue(1): *very gluey mud.*

glum /glʌm/ *adj* (*-mm-*) (of a person, one's expression etc) sad; gloomy(2): *Paul always looks so glum.*

'glumly *adv*. **'glumness** *u.n*.

glut /glʌt/ *c.n* (usu *sing*) (often *a — of s.t*) **1** too great a quantity (of s.t, such as food, having been produced) and unable to be sold, used etc: *This summer there's been a glut of fresh fruit.*

▷ *tr.v* (*-tt-*) **2** supply (a market, shops etc) with too great a quantity of s.t: *The market has been glutted with apples and prices have fallen very low.* Compare shortage.

glutinous /'gluːtɪnəs/ *adj* (of a substance) (having become) sticky or stuck together: *The rice had cooked too long and had become one glutinous mass.*

glutton /'glʌtn/ *c.n* person who regularly eats too much. **a glutton for s.t** (*fig*) a person who is very eager to do s.t, who does or accepts a lot of s.t: *a glutton for work; a glutton for punishment* (i.e often putting oneself in positions where one gets hurt physically or mentally or where one gets more than one's fair share of work etc).

'gluttony *u.n* habit or state of being very greedy.

glycerin /'glɪsəˌrɪn/ *u.n* (also ˌglyce'rine /-'riːn/) kind of sweet liquid substance used in the making of soap, medicine etc, *chem.symb* $C_3H_8O_3$.

GM /ˌdʒiː 'em/ *abbr* **1** General Manager. **2** (UK) George Medal (given for bravery).

GMT /ˌdʒiː ˌem 'tiː/ *abbr* Greenwich Mean Time.

gnarled /nɑːld/ *adj* (*formal*) **1** (of wood, trees etc) twisted into odd shapes etc: *a gnarled old tree.* **2** (of s.o's skin, hands etc) having bumps etc as a sign of old age: *His gnarled fingers couldn't untie the knot.*

gnash /næʃ/ *tr.v* **1 gnash one's teeth** make one's top teeth hit against one's bottom teeth and so make a noise: *Stop gnashing your teeth like that.* **2 gnash one's teeth (at s.o/s.t)** (*fig*) show that one is angry (at s.o, about s.t) by (almost) doing this: *He gnashed his teeth when he heard what had happened.* ⇨ grind(4).

gnat /næt/ *c.n* kind of very small insect that flies around stinging people and sucking their blood.

gnaw /nɔː/ *c.n* **1** (often *have a — at s.t*) series of small bites (at s.t): *The dog was having a good gnaw at the bone.*

▷ *v* **2** *tr.v* bite (s.t hard, e.g a bone) using many small bites (in order to get meat etc off, break it etc): *He was gnawing the bone as though he was a dog.* **3** *tr/intr.v* (often *— s.t in/through s.t; — s.t away*) use its/one's teeth to make (a hole in/through s.t), to remove s.t: *The rats had gnawed a hole* through the wood (or *had gnawed through the wood*). **gnaw (away) at s.t** (try to) gnaw(1) s.t. **gnaw at s.o/s.t** (*fig*) hurt, worry or concern s.o, one's mind etc, either physically or mentally: *Something worrying was gnawing at my mind but what it was I couldn't say.*

'gnawing *attrib.adj* causing pain or worry often in a way that one cannot explain: *a gnawing pain in one's stomach*; *a gnawing doubt.*

gnome /nəʊm/ *c.n* (in stories) small ugly man with a beard.

GNP /ˌdʒiːˌenˈpiː/ *abbr* Gross National Product.

gns *written abbr* guineas(1).

gnu /nuː/ *c.n* (*pl* -(s)) kind of antelope found in some parts of Africa.

go /gəʊ/ *n* (*pl* goes) **1** *c.n* (often have a — on s.t) opportunity, chance or turn (to do s.t, to ride on s.t, to play in a game etc): *Can I have a go on the roundabout? Come on, it's your go now so choose two cards.* **2** *c.n* (often *have a — at* (*doing*) *s.t*) attempt or try (at doing s.t, esp s.t that may be difficult): *He had several goes at (solving) the problem but failed each time.* **3** *u.n* (often *be full of —*; *have a lot of —*) energy(1) or drive(6): *He's so full of go that it makes me quite tired watching him in action.* **from the word go** (*informal*) from the very beginning (of s.t): *He hasn't liked me from the word go.* **It's all go** (*informal*) There is a lot of work being done or needing to be done without any time to stop, rest etc. **no go; no-go area** ⇒ no. **on the go** (*informal*) (of a person) very active, energetic(1) etc: *He's always on the go and never stops working for a moment.*

▷ *v* (*3rd pers. pres.t goes, pres.p going, p.t went* /went/, *p.p gone* /gɒn/) **4** *intr.v* leave the presence of s.o (and move to s.w else): *I'm sorry, I must go now or I'll be late. Where are you going? I didn't say you could leave.* ⇒ go away, go to s.w. Compare come(1). **5** *intr.v* (often a command) (start to) move, run etc, esp in a race: *Go on, go! One, two, three, go! On your marks, get set, go!* **6** *intr.v* (of time) pass (in a certain way, e.g quickly, slowly): *Doesn't time go quickly when you're enjoying yourself! The hours went slowly as he waited for news.* ⇒ go by. **7** *intr.v* (of a machine etc) work, move, in the correct way: *The car won't go; there must be something wrong with the battery.* **8** *intr.v* (of a course of action, s.t one does etc) happen in a certain way, e.g well or badly; show a certain amount of progress; have a certain result: *'How are things going at the moment?' 'Not very well, I'm afraid.' 'How did the meeting go?'* **9** *intr.v* (often *has/have gone*) be lost, stolen, used up etc: *My bag's gone! If you continue to spend your money like that, it will soon go* (or *be gone*). **10** *intr.v* (of a person) be removed (from a position, job etc); (of a thing) be sold, destroyed etc: *I'm afraid you'll have to go at the end of this month as there is no more work. The car will have to go as it's too expensive to run.* **11** *intr.v* fail to work properly; become broken: *His sight is going. I was driving the car down the hill when the brakes suddenly went.* **12** *intr.v* **go mad**, **deaf** etc reach, get into, a condition or state as described by the adj: *He's going blind. This food's gone bad.* **13** *intr.v* **go hungry** etc be, remain, in a condition or state as described by the adj: *While half the world goes hungry, the other half eats too much.* **14** *intr.v*

go unnoticed etc be, remain, in the condition or state described by the negative adj, often with the idea that it should not have been so: *Many criminals go unpunished.* **15** *intr.v* (of an expression, saying, words in a song etc) have a particular form, contain certain words etc (that one knows, remembers etc): *'Least said, soonest mended', as the saying goes. 'How does the song go?'* **16** *tr.v* **go bang**, **pop** etc make a sound or noise as described by the noun: *The bell went ding-dong(2). 'Baa(2)' went the sheep.* **17** *tr.v* (in boxing) last (a number of rounds): *Joe went ten rounds against the Frenchman before he was knocked out.* **18** *intr.v* (*informal*) be s.t that s.o has to accept, that operates in certain circumstances(1) etc: *What he says goes and you'd be foolish not to obey him. There are no rules in this competition; in fact anything goes.* **19** *intr.v* die: *He's going fast. I'm sorry, she's gone.* For 'go' followed by an adjective or a noun, e.g *go mad*, *go places*, *go right/wrong*, *go straight*, *go the whole hog*, ⇒ the adjective or noun.

a long etc **way to go** (a) a long etc way to travel: *There is some way to go before we arrive at the house.* (b) a lot etc to do (before one can complete s.t): *There's a long way to go before the problem is finally solved.*

as far as it/that goes (of s.t stated etc earlier, be true, be complete etc but) only to that or the stated extent: *The report is correct as far as it goes but it doesn't mention a number of important points.* Compare (far) gone, go far, go too far.

as people/things etc **go** if/when one considers people/things etc as a group or as having a certain character, esp when comparing them to a particular person/thing: *As typists go she's not bad.*

be going to do s.t (a) (of a person) have the intention of doing s.t soon or in the future: *We're going to go abroad for our holidays this year.* (b) (of a person) be on the point of doing s.t: *If you're not careful, you're going to drop it.* (c) (of an event etc) be about or almost certain to happen soon: *It looks as though it's going to snow.*

far gone ⇒ gone.

Here goes! ⇒ here(*adv*).

go about/(a)round (of a story, news etc) be spread among people, become known: *There's a story going about that the Government will resign.* **go about s.t** (start to) deal with s.t, esp a problem: *He went about the whole matter in a very thorough way.* **go about/(a)round doing s.t** move from person to person, place to place etc doing s.t: *He went about saying that I had treated him badly.* **go about (s.w) in/on s.t** move, travel, from place to place having, wearing or using s.t: *I like nothing better than going about in my old clothes. He goes about everywhere on his motorbike.* **go about/(a)round with s.o** spend one's time with s.o, esp as a friend or lover: *He's going around with a very unsuitable girl.*

go across s.t (to s.w) move from one side of s.t to another side (in order to arrive at, reach, s.w): *You can go across this field to the church.*

go after s.o/s.t move towards s.o/s.t (who/which is moving or has moved away from one) in order to catch or stop her/him/it: *He's just left so if you want to give him the news you'd better*

go after him. go after s.t (**a**) try to get or win s.t: *Are you going after that job that was advertised?* (**b**) (of s.t arranged in an order or a list) follow, be placed after, s.t: *'Go' goes after 'gnu' in this dictionary.*

go against s.o (**a**) (of a law case, decision etc) have a result that is unfavourable to s.o: *The decision of the judge went against him.* (**b**) (of circumstances(1), luck etc) be generally unfavourable to s.o: *When he lost the game he complained that luck had gone against him.* **go against s.t** (of an action etc) be contrary¹(1) to s.t that one believes, has been taught etc: *This new proposal goes against all the* principles(1) *that I hold dear.*

go ahead (**of s.o/s.t**) move, travel, in a certain direction, in advance (of s.o/s.t) or earlier (than s.o/s.t): *The guides went ahead of the main party. If you go straight ahead you'll come to the river.* **go ahead** (**with s.t**) start (to do s.t); continue (s.t): *They went ahead with their plans for the new factory. Though I warned him, he just went ahead and did what he wanted.* ⇒ go-ahead.

go along (**to s.w**) (**with s.o**) (*informal*) move from s.w (to s.w else, esp to a meeting, a party etc) (in the company of s.o): *Are you going along to the meeting? It starts in a couple of minutes. I'll go along with you as far as the bridge.* **go along with s.o/s.t** (**on s.t**) (*informal*) accept or agree with s.o, what he/she says etc (about s.t): *I can go along with you on that point but not on the others.* **go along with s.t** be a (necessary) part of s.t: *You know, don't you, that a car goes along with the job?* **Go along/on with you!** (*informal* expression used to show one's surprise at, lack of belief in, s.t s.o has said): *Go along with you! I don't believe a word of what you say!* Compare get along.

go and do s.t (**a**) move (to s.w) in order to do s.t: *I must go and see what the children are doing.* (**b**) (*informal*) do s.t, esp s.t stupid, wrong etc: *Now you've gone and done it; she'll never speak to you again. I just don't understand why you go and say these silly things in front of everybody.*

go (a)round ⇒ go about.

go astray ⇒ astray.

go at s.o attack s.o (with blows, words etc): *It was a real fight — the two of them were going at each other* tooth and nail. *She went at him at the top of her voice so that the neighbours heard every word.* **go at s.t** (**with s.t**) deal with, tackle²(7), a problem, a job etc (with a lot of attention, will etc): *He went at the* task *of cleaning the house with a will.*

go away (**a**) (be asked by the speaker to) leave her/his presence (because she/he is busy, does not want one there etc): *Would you please go away! Can't you see I'm busy? He went away but came back ten minutes later.* (**b**) (usu negative) (of a problem etc) be no longer important, disappear: *This matter won't just simply go away if you don't do something about it.* **go away in s.t** (of a bride after a wedding) leave for one's honeymoon(1) dressed in certain clothes: *The bride went away in a blue silk dress.* ⇒ going-away.

go back (of a clock) have its time changed to an earlier one, e.g by one hour, at the end of summer time: *Remember that the clocks go back one hour on Sunday morning.* **go back** (**to s.t**) (**a**) return (to an earlier point in what one was saying, to an earlier time, e.g when things were different): *Just to go back to what I was saying earlier, we do need to make a decision as soon as possible. What is done is done and there can be no going back.* (**b**) (of a family descent) be shown to have a number of generations(2) that can be traced(4) (to some point in the past): *Our family goes back to the sixteenth century.* **go back** (**to s.w**) (**a**) leave s.w and return (to s.w else): *I'll have to go back to the house as I've forgotten something.* (**b**) return (to s.w) after an absence: *When do you go back (i.e. to school) after Christmas?* **go back on s.t** not do, change one's mind about doing, s.t that one has said one would do: *He went back on his word/promise and said he wouldn't lend us any money after all.* **go back to doing s.t** start doing s.t again that one had stopped doing: *It's very bad; he's gone back to drinking.*

go before (**s.t**) (of an event etc) happen at an earlier time (than s.t): *I have no certain knowledge of what went before (this extraordinary occasion).* **go before s.o** (of an accused person) appear in a court of law in front of a judge: *The prisoner went before the judge the next day to have his case heard.*

go behind s.o/s.t move behind s.o/s.t, esp so that one is hidden: *He went behind a bush so that he couldn't be seen from the road.* **go behind s.o's back** ⇒ back(n).

go between s.t and s.t be placed, fit or take a space between s.t and s.t: *This cupboard should go between the two windows.* ⇒ go-between.

go beyond s.t be much greater than s.t, esp s.t that one expects: *I had hoped to get good marks in the examinations but the results went beyond my wildest dreams.* **go beyond a joke** ⇒ joke(n).

go by (**a**) (of time) pass: *As the hours went by their hopes of a rescue faded.* (**b**) (of an opportunity, chance etc) pass without being used, taken advantage of: *It's your own fault that you let this one chance of earning a lot of money go by without doing anything about it.* **go by** (**s.o/s.t**) move past (s.o/s.t): *As the procession went by (them) they all cheered.* **go by s.t** (**a**) be guided by, be steered¹ by, s.t, e.g a compass(1), the stars, in order to know where one is, where to move to etc: *He had only a very rough map of the area to go by.* (**b**) accept, be guided by, what s.o believes, says, does etc: *His opinions are nothing to go by, as he's always wrong.* **go by the book** ⇒ book(n). **go by the name of s.o/s.t** ⇒ name(n). **go by the rules** ⇒ rule(n).

go down (**a**) (of the sun, stars etc) disappear below the horizon: *As the sun went down it got cooler.* (**b**) (of a ship) sink: *The ship went down with the loss of all hands.* (**c**) (of temperature, a price, a quantity etc) reduce, become less: *His temperature has gone down since last night. Prices of vegetables are going down. Stocks of butter are going down.* Opposite go up(a). (**d**) (of a person or thing) fall to the ground, e.g because of being hit, attacked: *Many soldiers went down in the face of the enemy fire.* (**e**) (of food etc) be swallowed in one's throat: *The medicine went down the wrong way and he almost* choked(3). (**f**) leave a university at the end of a term or year or on the completion of a course of study: *When I finally* *go down I'm going to have a year of travelling before getting a job.* **go down** (**in s.t**) be written or recorded in a notebook etc): *Every word he said went down in the reporter's book.* **go down** (**in the world**) (of a person or place) lose one's/ its social position, become less fashionable or desirable: *He's been going down in the world ever since he lost all his money.* **go down on one's hands and knees** (**to s.o, to do s.t**) ⇒ hand(*n*). **go down to s.o/s.t** (in sport etc) be defeated by s.o or the action of s.o: *The young* boxer(1) *went down to the* champion(3) *in the fifth round.* **go down to s.t** (of an account, history etc) reach as far as s.t (e.g a time, an event etc): *This book goes down to the 15th century and then stops.* **go down to s.w** (a) move, travel, to s.w, esp from a more important place to one that is less important: *I'm going down to my house in the country for the weekend.* (b) (of an area, a path etc) reach as far as s.w; lead to s.w: *This field/path goes down to the river.* **go down** (**badly, well** etc) (**with s.o**) be (badly, well etc) received (by s.o): *His rude jokes didn't go down very well with my aunt.* **go down with s.t** become ill with s.t *Several people have gone down with flu in the last week.*

go easy on/with s.t ⇒ easy.

go far ⇒ far(*adv*). Compare go too far.

go for s.o (a) attack s.o: *She went for him with a knife.* (b) (of s.t said, ordered etc) apply to s.o also; be intended also for s.o: *Stop that noise! And that goes for you over in that corner also!* (c) (*informal*) like s.o a lot: *I really go for him, he's so handsome.* **go for s.t** (a) leave a place and do s.t, e.g have a walk etc: *I'm just going for a short walk.* (b) leave a place in order to get or fetch s.t: *I'm just going for the papers; I'll be back soon.* (c) be sold at a certain price: *The house went for £50 000.* **go for a song** ⇒ song.

go forth leave; start a journey.

go forward (a) move to the front of s.o: *As the soldiers went forward the enemy retired.* (b) (of a clock) have its time changed to a later one, e.g by one hour, at the end of winter time. **go forward** (**on/with s.t**) (start to) make progress (on/with s.t): *They are going forward with their plans to introduce higher taxes.*

go from s.w to s.w move, travel, from one place to another: *He went from Edinburgh to London in five hours.* **go from bad to worse** (of a situation etc) be already bad and become even worse as time passes: *The situation went from bad to worse and we finally had to sell the house.*

go home ⇒ home(*adv*).

go in (a) enter a house, one's home: *Let's go in; it's getting cold.* ⇒ go into s.w(a). (b) (of the sun etc) disappear behind a cloud: *The sun has gone in and I don't think it will get any warmer today.* (c) (in cricket¹) start to bat²(2): *He went in when the score was 90 for 6 and scored 120 runs.* (d) (of s.t that has been said, of information etc; usu negative) (not) be understood: *The news of his wife's death just didn't go in immediately but when it finally did he fainted.* **go in** (**s.t**) be put or placed in (s.t), fit in (s.t), esp as a normal or usual thing: *'Where does this go?' 'Oh, it goes in that cupboard over there.' I'm afraid these extra clothes won't go in the* suitcase; *there's not enough room.* ⇒ go into s.t(b). **go in for s.t** (a) offer oneself as a candidate(2) for an examination; choose s.t

as a career(1) or profession (and study for it): *She hopes to go in for law.* ⇒ go into s.t (c). (b) do s.t regularly as a sport, hobby etc: *He goes in for collecting stamps.*

go into s.t (a) hit, strike, s.t violently: *The car went into a tree when he lost control.* (b) be placed inside s.t, fit into s.t: *The knives go into that drawer. The screw won't go into the hole.* ⇒ go in (s.t). (c) choose s.t as a career(1) or profession: *I'm hoping to go into television when I leave university.* ⇒ go in for s.t(a). (d) (start to) behave in a certain, often unexpected way; reach a certain state (in one's mind or body): *He went into fits of laughter when he heard the news.* ⇒ go off into s.t. *He went into a coma and died five days later.* (e) examine or discuss s.t (in a detailed way): *They went into the whole plan very thoroughly.* (f) (*mathematics*) (of a number) be able to divide a number without having a fraction(2) etc: *10 goes into 20. 7 doesn't go into 13.* **go into s.w** (a) enter a place, a room etc: *She went into the house when it rained.* ⇒ go in(a). (b) be admitted into a hospital etc: *She will be going into a nursing home soon as she cannot look after herself.* **go into action** ⇒ action.

go off (a) (of a gun, an alarm(3) in a clock etc) suddenly fire, make a sound etc: *The gun went off with a loud* bang(2). (b) (of food etc) become bad, not fit to eat etc: *This milk has gone off.* (c) (of a supply of electricity, water etc) stop being supplied suddenly: *Just as we were cooking dinner, the power went off.* **go off s.o/s.t** (*informal*) no longer like s.o/s.t: *I've gone off him since he changed his views on politics. I'm going off all these competitions they have on television.* **go off badly, well** etc (of an event etc) have a bad, good etc result: *I thought the party went off quite well, didn't you?* **go off one's head** ⇒ head(*n*). **go off the rails** ⇒ rails. **go off one's rocker** ⇒ rocker (⇒ rock²). **go off into s.t** start to do s.t unexpectedly: *He went off into fits of laughter.* ⇒ go into s.t(d). **go off** (**to s.w**) be sent, e.g by post, (to s.w): *This package needs to go off (to New York) by this evening.* **go off to do s.t, to s.w** leave a place in order to do s.t or to move to s.w else: *I'm going off to get tickets for the show. I'm going off to New York next week.* **go off with s.o/s.t** leave a place in the company of s.o, having taken s.t etc, often in a secret or wrong way: *I'm just going off with a friend for a drink. Peter went off with his neighbour's wife. Alexander went off with all her money.*

go on (a) continue a journey, esp after a stop, pause etc: *We had a short rest and then went on.* (b) continue speaking, esp after a stop, pause etc: *'Go on,' he said, 'what were you saying?' 'Well,' she went on, 'I was just saying how cold it was.'* (c) (of a light etc) be switched on: *The lights suddenly went on so we knew power had been* restored(3). (d) (of time) pass, be used up: *As time went on their hopes faded.* (e) (of an event etc, esp of s.t that one does not know about) happen, take place: *I wish somebody would tell me what's going on.* **go on** (**at s.o**) (**about s.o/s.t**) continue complaining (to s.o) (about s.o/s.t): *It's no use your going on at me about her behaviour; she's not my responsibility.* **go on** (**doing s.t**) continue (doing s.t): *He went on practising on the drums though his mother had asked him to stop.* **go on**

s.o/s.t (of money) be spent on s.o/s.t: *all their spare money goes on their children/holidays.* **go on s.t** (a) mount s.t, e.g for a ride, for pleasure, in order to get to a place: *We're going on a train for the last part of the journey.* (b) leave a place in order to do s.t: *We're going on our holidays next week.* (c) be guided by s.t: *I hope you're not going on his advice because he knows nothing.* **go on the dole** ⇒ dole(1). **go on (for an hour** etc) last (as long as an hour etc); speak (for an hour etc): *'How long does this play go on for?' He went on for two hours about how badly the government was doing.* **be going on for 15** etc have nearly reached the age of 15 etc: *He's going on for 60 but you wouldn't think so.* **go on to be, do** etc **s.t** become, do etc s.t new (after being, doing etc s.t else): *After two years in films he went on to be a writer.* **go on(to) s.t** have, take, a special course of s.t, e.g treatment, to improve one's health: *I need to go onto a diet*(1) *as I'm getting fat. Some women are afraid to go on the pill*(2) *because they think it's dangerous.* **go on (to s.t)** (having dealt with one matter, subject etc) start to deal with (the next etc): *Time is short so can we go on (to the next* item(1)*), please.* **go on with s.t** continue doing s.t: *Don't let me disturb you; just go on with what you were doing before I came.* **Go on with you!** ⇒ Go along/on with you!

go out (a) leave one's house, a place etc: *Harry went out about half an hour ago but didn't tell me when he would be back.* ⇒ go out (to s.w). (b) leave one's house and attend a party, visit a theatre, have a meal etc (often as a regular thing): *They go out every night.* (c) (of the tide) move away from the beach etc: *When the tide's gone out we can play on the sands.* (d) (of a fire, a light etc) stop burning or giving light: *Put some more wood on the fire to stop it going out. The lights went out suddenly and left us in complete darkness.* **go out for s.t** = go for s.t(a,b). **go (all) out (for, to get, s.t)** try very hard to win or get s.t, esp in business: *If you want orders for your new machines, you'll have to go all out to get them.* **go out like a light** ⇒ light(*n*). **go out (of s.t)** be no longer able to take part in s.t, esp a competition, because one has lost a match, a game etc: *Our team went out in the third round.* **go out of s.t** (of a (strong) feeling etc) disappear from s.t, e.g a discussion, an argument: *The heat had gone out of the discussion by the time I arrived.* **go out of business** ⇒ business. **go out of fashion** ⇒ fashion(*n*). **go out of one's mind (with s.t)** ⇒ mind¹. **go out of s.o's mind** ⇒ mind¹. **go out to s.o** (*informal*) (of a feeling, e.g of sympathy) be shown, offered, to s.o: *Our hearts go out to all those who have lost sons in the war.* **go out (to s.w)** (a) leave one's house etc (and visit s.w): *I'm just going out to the shops.* (b) leave one's country (and travel to another one, sometimes to settle in it permanently): *Several members of my family went out to Australia at the beginning of this century.* **go out with s.o** be seen in public regularly, usu with s.o of the opposite sex: *Helen's been going out with the boy next door for the last year.*

go over s.t (a) examine, check, s.t, usu thoroughly: *He went over the account in detail. The garage went over the car thoroughly but couldn't find anything wrong.* ⇒ going-over(1). (b) clean s.t, e.g a room: *Could you go over the furniture with a duster, please.* ⇒ going-over(2). (c) check, test, one's knowledge of s.t, esp in order to improve it, learn it properly etc: *I want to go over my part in the play again as I'm afraid I'll forget my lines tonight.* (d) consider, examine, s.t, e.g facts, arguments, in detail (and often more than once): *I refuse to go over all that we discussed again; you'll just have to accept my decision.* **go over s.o's head** ⇒ head(*n*). **go over (to s.w)** cross an area of water, sea etc (to get s.w): *A boat goes over (to the mainland) once a week.* **go over badly, well** etc **(with s.o)** (of a person, of s.t said, done etc) be (badly, well etc) received (by s.o): *The new film didn't go over at all well with the critics but the public loved it.* **go over to s.o/s.t** (a) decide to join s.o, become part of a group etc, leaving s.o or another group to whom/which one belonged: *Some soldiers went over to the enemy when they saw the battle was lost.* (b) (in a radio or television broadcast etc) move one's broadcast (from the place one is in) to s.o who is s.w else or to another place, e.g so that a report can be made: *We're now going over to (our man in) New York for the latest report on the situation.*

go overboard ⇒ overboard.

go past (s.w) ⇒ past(*adv/prep*).

go places ⇒ place(*n*).

go round (a) move, turn, in circles: *The record was going round and round but there was no sound.* (b) (of a person, one's head, a room etc) (appear to) spin, move, become dizzy(1) etc, e.g because one is ill, fainting, drunk: *The room seemed to go round and round and then I lost consciousness.* **go round (s.o)** (of food etc) be enough (for a number of people to eat or drink): *Have you got enough wine to go round everybody? Because of the bad harvest there was hardly enough rice to go round.* ⇒ go about/around doing s.t, with s.o.

go slow (of workers etc) work much more slowly than usual, usu as part of an industrial dispute(1): *The car workers are going slow to force the management to make an improved offer on pay.* ⇒ go-slow.

go through (of a plan or proposal, a bill(3) in parliament etc) be accepted, approved, completed etc: *The new Bill on local government organization went through on its third reading. As soon as my* divorce(1) *goes through, I plan to marry again.* **go through s.t** (a) enter into s.t and come out on the other side: *He went through the doorway into the next room. The bullet went through his leg.* (b) search or examine the contents of) s.t: *She went through all his pockets to find some money. I need to go through the figures he has provided to make sure that they are right.* (c) use all of s.t so that there is nothing left: *In six months he had gone through all the money that had been left to him.* (d) perform, take part in, s.t, esp a formal ceremony, e.g of marriage: *They went through a* civil(3) *marriage ceremony but there was no church wedding.* (e) suffer, endure(2), s.t: *You just don't know what I had to go through, bringing up three children on my own.* **go through (the) proper channels** ⇒ channel(*n*). **go through the motions (of s.t)** ⇒ motion(*n*). **go through with s.t** (decide to) do or complete s.t: *Once you have* *started something it's better to go through with it and not stop halfway.*

go to s.o (of a prize, an inheritance etc) be given to s.o: *The first prize for the best vegetables goes to Mr Smith. Under the terms of his will, the house will go to his daughter.* **go to s.t** ⇨ go (up) to s.t.

go to a lot of etc **expense/trouble** (**to do s.t**) spend a lot of money, work very hard (in order to do s.t well): *I went to a lot of trouble to get you that job and now you say you don't like it!*

go to s.w (a) leave a place and move, travel, to s.w: *I'm going to the shops as we need quite a lot of things. We're going to France for our holidays this year.* (b) visit or attend a place (often regularly): *When are you going to university?* **go to**(**wards**) (**doing**) **s.t** (of s.t given etc) be of help to(wards) (doing) s.t: *The money they saved went towards repairing the roof.* For 'go to' + noun, e.g go to bed, go to extremes, go to hell, go to town, go to the wall, go to war, ⇨ the noun.

go together (usu of a man and woman) be (seen) in each other's company, have friendly, sometimes sexual, relations with each other: *They've been going together for the last year and expect to marry soon.* **go** (**badly, well** etc) **together** (of two or more things, clothes, colours etc) match, fit, look badly, well etc (when worn, seen etc with each other): *That tie and shirt don't go very well together.*

go too far ⇨ far(*adv*).

go towards (**doing**) **s.t** ⇨ go to(wards) doing s.t.

go under (a) (of a person, boat etc) sink: *Another wave came and she went under.* (b) (of a person, business etc) fail, stop operating, become bankrupt(1): *He was not very good at business and his company went under after a year.* **go under s.t** move or pass below s.t: *The train went under the bridge.* **go under the name** etc **of s.o/s.t** have the name of s.o/s.t, be known as s.o/s.t, esp in order to hide oneself, deceive others etc: *When he was in England he went under the name of Jones to avoid discovery by the police.*

go up (a) (of temperature, a price, a quantity etc) become greater, higher etc: *Prices of houses are going up all the time.* Opposite go down(c). (b) (of a building etc) be built: *A new factory is going up in the field behind our house.* (c) (of a building etc) be destroyed, break into pieces, e.g because of an explosion: *The ship received a direct hit and went up with a terrible explosion.* (d) (of a curtain in a theatre etc) be lifted or moved to show the stage: *The curtain went up and the play started.* (e) (of lights in a theatre etc) be switched on, usu at the end of a performance: *As the lights went up, the audience started to leave their seats.* **go up** (**s.t**) move from a lower position to a higher one (on s.t): *As I went up* (*the hill*) *I could see more of the town below me.* **go up in flames/ smoke** be burnt, destroyed, by fire: *A paint drum caught fire and the factory went up in flames.* ⇨ go up(c). **go up to s.o** approach(5), get or go near to s.o: *He went up to her and asked her for a dance.* **go** (**up**) **to s.t** (be ready to) spend up to a certain amount of money in order to buy s.t: *I'll go* (*up*) *to £40 000 for the painting but not a penny more.* **go up** (**to s.w**) (a) move from a less important place or one that is further south (to a more important one or one that is further north): *I'm going up* (*to London*) *tomorrow for some*

shopping. *I'm planning to go up to Manchester next week.* (b) start to attend (a university): *When are you going up* (*to Oxford*)?

go with s.o (a) move/travel with, in the company of, s.o: *I'll go with you as far as the station.* (b) be (seen) in the company of s.o of the opposite sex, esp with a view to marriage: *She's been going with him for the last six months.* **go with s.t** be a part of s.t, be included with s.t, esp when sold: *Disease often goes with poverty. All the furniture goes with the house.* **go** (**badly, well** etc) **with s.t** (of clothes, colour etc) match, fit, look, (badly, well etc) with s.t: *Those green curtains don't go very well with the red carpet.*

go without (**s.t**) not be able to have or use (s.t); lack (s.t): *There's no more tea left so you'll have to go without* (*it*) *until I get some more.* **it goes without saying** (**that . . .**) ⇨ say(*v*).

it (**all**) **goes to show s.t/that . . .** ⇨ show(*v*).

keep going ⇨ keep.

let oneself go; **let** (**s.o/s.t**) **go**; **let go of s.t** ⇨ let¹.

make s.t go; **make s.t go round** ⇨ make(*v*).

one (**more**) **day, thing** etc **to go** one more day left, one more thing etc that needs to be done: *There are five days to go before Christmas. Just two more jobs to go and then we're finished.*

'go-a,head *adj* **1** (of a person, organization) having a lot of (new) ideas in order to be successful: *Jane's a very go-ahead woman and has changed the company into a very rich one.*

▷ *def.n* **2** (usu get/have, give s.o, the — (to do s.t)) approval or permission (to do s.t): *If you give us the go-ahead we should finish in two weeks.*

'go-be,tween *c.n* person who carries messages, esp between two people who are in love or who do not want to talk to each other: *I'm tired of being the go-between for you two; why don't you settle your quarrel yourselves?*

'goer *c.n* (*informal*) person or animal who/that runs fast; person who is very active, e.g in social life: *The horse is a bit of a goer and should win the race easily. He's a great goer and is out every night at parties.*

-,goer *c.n* person who attends or visits a place as described by the first noun, often regularly: *church-goers; theatre-goers.* ⇨ -going.

,go-'getter *c.n* (*informal*; often *derog*) person who gets, or tries to get, what he/she wants, who succeeds or tries to succeed: *He's something of a go-getter and will let nothing stand in his way.*

'going *adj* **1** (usu *attrib*) of or referring to s.t, a price, that applies at the present time: *the going price/rate for a job.* **2** (usu *pred*) of or referring to s.t that one can have, that is ready for eating, drinking etc: *Is there any food going?* **a going concern** ⇨ concern(*n*). **going, going, gone** (esp in an auction(1) or sale) (expression used to show that) s.t is ready to be sold to a bidder, and is now sold.

▷ *u.n* **3** act of leaving a place, job etc: *We had a party for his going.* **4** (often *hard, heavy* etc —) (be/ become a very (difficult) situation, esp because of the conditions, the difficulties etc: *The going was very tough in such weather conditions. It was very heavy going talking to him as he had nothing interesting to say.* **make heavy going of s.t** ⇨ heavy(*adj*).

-going *u.n* (also *attrib*) act of attending or visiting a place as described by the noun: *Theatre-going is decreasing because of television.* ⇨ -goer.

,going-a'way *attrib.adj* (esp of a dress, clothes etc) that is/are worn when a woman leaves for her honeymoon(1): *Her going-away* outfit(1) *was a pink suit with matching shoes.*

,going-'over *c.n* (*pl* goings-over) **1** (often *give s.t a good* etc —) examination: *He gave the car a good going-over but found nothing wrong.* ⇨ go over s.t.(a). **2** (often *give s.t a good* etc —) complete clean: *She gave the room a thorough going-over before the guests arrived.* ⇨ go over s.t(b). **3** (often *give s.o a* —) (*informal*) beating or punishment: *They gave him a hard going-over and left him bruised and bleeding.*

'goings *pl.n* comings and goings ⇨ comings.

,goings-'on *pl.n* things that happen or have happened, often ones that are difficult to explain or understand: *There are some very strange goings-on in that house.*

gokart /'gəʊˌkɑ:t/ *c.n* kind of very small car with an engine, used for racing, esp by children.

gone /gɒn/ *p.p* of go. **(be) far gone** (*informal*) (be) very drunk, unconscious etc. **(be) gone on s.o** (*informal*) (be) very much in love with s.o: *She's really gone on him and won't look at anybody else.* **(have) gone and done s.t** ⇨ go and do s.t(b). ⇨ bygone.

goner /'gɒnə/ *c.n* (*informal*) person who is or will be dead or killed: *If he tries to fly that aircraft in his condition he'll be a goner.*

gonna /'gɒnə/ (esp US *slang*) (way of saying he/she/it etc will be) going to: *We're gonna kill you.*

,go-'slow *c.n* act of going slow (⇨ go slow): *There was a go-slow on the railway and I got to the office late.*

goad /gəʊd/ *c.n* **1** person or thing that makes one want to do s.t: *She was the goad he needed to make a success of his job.* **2** stick with a point at the end used for driving cattle(1) etc.

▷ *tr.v* **3** (often — *s.o into* (*doing*) *s.t*) drive, force, (s.o to do s.t, or to act in a certain way) usu by constant pressure, complaints etc: *Bob was finally goaded into action by their remarks about his laziness.* **goad s.o/s.t on** (**a**) make a person or an animal move faster: *Emma goaded them on to reach the top of the mountain before night fell.* (**b**) urge or drive s.o to work faster.

goal /gəʊl/ *c.n* **1** (in football, rugby, hockey etc) two upright posts (goalposts) with a bar across them (crossbar(2)) (and often with a net at the back) at each end of a pitch¹(1) between which (or, in rugby, over the bar of which) a player tries to kick or hit a ball etc in order to get a goal(2), score points etc. **2** act of kicking or hitting the ball etc between these posts (and so the points or score gained for one's side): *Scotland won by three goals to two.* **3** what one wants to do or succeed in; purpose; aim: *Their goal was to break the land speed record.* **one's/s.o's goal in life** one's/s.o's main or only purpose during (the whole of) one's/her/his life: *Her one goal in life is to become a famous film-star.* **score a goal** kick the ball etc between the goalposts and so gain a point or points: *Liverpool scored the only goal of the game in the last minute.*

'goal,keeper *c.n* player who defends the goal(1).

'goal ,kick *c.n* (*football*) kick taken in front of the goal(1), usu by the goalkeeper, after the ball has been kicked over the goal line by an opposing player. Compare corner(3).

'goal ,line *def.n* line marked in white at each end of a pitch¹(1) where the goal(1) is.

'goal,mouth *def.n* space between the posts and the bar across them.

'goal,post *c.n* one of the two upright posts forming part of the goal(1).

goat /gəʊt/ *c.n* kind of animal with four feet, long hair, two horns and usu a beard; its hair is sometimes used to make wool. ⇨ billy goat, kid(2), nanny goat. **act/play the (giddy) goat** (*fig*; *informal*) behave in a silly or stupid way (to attract attention etc): *He's always acting the giddy goat when he has friends around.* **get s.o's goat** (*fig*; *informal*) (of a person, her/his action etc) annoy or irritate(1) s.o a lot: *What really gets my goat is that he's always telling me what I should do.*

goatherd /'gəʊtˌhɜ:d/ *c.n* person who looks after a herd(1) of goats.

'goat,skin *c/u.n* (also *attrib*) (piece of the) skin of a goat used for clothing etc: *a coat made of goatskin; a goatskin coat.*

gob /gɒb/ *c.n* (*slang*; do not use!) mouth: *Go on, hit him in the gob!* **Shut your gob!** (very impolite way of saying) Stop talking!

gobble /'gɒbl/ **1** *tr/intr.v* (often — *s.t down/up*) eat (food, a meal etc) very, or far too, quickly: *The children gobbled* (*up*) *their dinner and rushed out to play.* **2** *tr.v* (usu — *s.t up*) (*fig*) use a lot of (s.t); (of a country, business company etc) take control over (other countries, businesses etc): *The new* computer *gobbles up paper at a great rate. The company has been gobbling up its competitors.* **3** *intr.v* (of a male turkey(1)) make a (continuous) noise in its throat on a low note.

gobbledegook /'gɒbldiˌgu:k/ *u.n* (also 'gobbledy,gook) (*informal*) thing said or written that is, or appears to be, nonsense; thing one cannot understand etc (because too difficult words have been used etc): *His speech was complete gobbledegook to me.*

go-between ⇨ go.

goblet /'gɒblɪt/ *c.n* kind of cup made of glass, metal etc with a long stem, used for drinking wine etc: *a wine goblet.*

goblin /'gɒblɪn/ *c.n* (also 'hob,goblin) (in stories) evil ugly creature like a dwarf(2) that plays tricks on people.

GOC /ˌdʒi:ˌəʊ'si:/ *abbr* General Officer Commanding (⇨ general).

god /gɒd/ **1** *c.n* (in some (ancient) religions) one of a number of supernatural(1) male beings thought to have made the world, people etc, to have some (special) control over parts of it etc: *They worshipped many gods.* ⇨ goddess. **2** *unique n* (with capital **G**) (in some religions) supernatural(1) being who created(1) everything and whom people worship: *Do you believe in* (*the existence of*) *God?* **3** *c.n* (*fig*) thing one regards as the most important thing (in one's life, work etc): *His gods are wealth and position.* **for God's sake** (*informal*) (**a**) (used to increase the force of a request): *For God's sake help me!* (**b**) (used to show one's extreme annoyance etc): *For God's sake, that's the fifth time you've asked me for money.* **God (alone) knows (. . .)** (*informal*) no one knows, no one can say, e.g what has happened, what s.o has done, where s.o has gone: *God alone knows what he meant by that remark.* **God forbid (that . . .)** (*formal*) I very much hope (that s.t will not happen etc): *God forbid that we should ever have another World War!* **God Save the King/Queen** title of the British national anthem; expression used to honour the British King/Queen: *Forty years ago everybody stood up when God Save the King was played.* **God willing** (*formal*) if everything goes well; if there are no misfortunes: *God willing, we should be able to reach the coast in a couple of hours' time.* **Good God!** ⇨ good(*adj*). **My God!**; **Oh God!**; **Oh my God!** (used to show great surprise, worry, fear, annoyance etc): *Oh my God! The house is on fire! Oh God! Not you back again!* **Thank God (. . .)** I am very glad (that s.t has or has not happened etc): *Thank God you've arrived! I thought you might have had an accident.*

'god,awful *attrib.adj* (*slang*) extremely bad: *What a godawful mess you've made of everything!*

'god,child *c.n* (*pl* **'god,children**) child whom a godparent promises, during the act of baptism, to bring up in the Christian(1) religion.

goddamn /'gɒdæm/ *adj/adv* (also **'god-damned**) (do not use!) (used to show great annoyance etc): *He's a goddamn nuisance!*

'god,daughter *c.n* female godchild.

goddess /'gɒdɪs/ *c.n* female god(1).

'god,father *c.n* male godparent.

'god,fearing *adj* (*formal*) (of a person) very religious; observing Christian(1) beliefs and customs: *He's a godfearing man and always goes to church on Sunday.*

'godfor,saken *adj* (esp of a place) wild, not at all beautiful or attractive: *He lives in some godforsaken place miles from anywhere.*

'god,head *u.n* state or quality of being a god(1) or God(2).

'godless *adj* (*formal*) (of a person) not being religious (and so considered to be wicked): *They are a godless lot, never go to church and spend all their time in pubs.*

'godlessness *u.n.*

'god,like *adj* looking, behaving, like a god(1) or God(2): *He has a godlike beauty.*

'godly *adj* (*-ier, -iest*) (*formal*) (of a person, behaviour etc) acting in a religious way (and so considered to be good); saintly: *He was a godly man whom all people admired.*

'godliness *u.n.*

'god,mother *c.n* female godparent.

'god,parent *c.n* person who promises, during the act of baptism, to (help) bring up a child (her/his godchild, goddaughter, godson) in a Christian(1) religion.

gods *def pl.n* (*informal*) (all the people in) the top (cheapest) rows of seats (the balcony(2)) in a theatre, furthest away from the stage.

'god,send *sing.n* thing that happens, arrives etc that one did not expect but is very welcome: *The money was a godsend and at last she was able to buy the children some proper clothes.*

'god,son *c.n* male godchild.

goer, -goer, go-getter ⇨ go.

goggle /'gɒgl/ *intr.v* (often — at s.o/s.t) look

with wide eyes, with very great surprise, (at s.o/s.t): *What are you goggling at?*

,goggle-'eyed *adj* (usu *pred*) (looking) with wide fixed eyes: *She watched goggle-eyed as he did his tricks.*

'goggles *pl.n* (often *a pair of* —) special kind of glasses worn over the eyes and with a close-fitting (⇨ close¹) edge to stop water, dust etc from getting in; they are worn when riding a motorbike, swimming under water, working in factories etc.

going, -going, going-over, goings, goings-on, gokart ⇨ go.

gold /gəʊld/ *n* (also *attrib*) **1** *u.n* kind of precious yellow metal found in rocks, sand etc and used for making coins, jewellery etc, *chem.symb* Au: *a bar of gold; a gold coin/watch.* **2** *u.n* deep yellow colour like gold(1): *He painted the walls in gold.* **3** *c.n* = gold medal. *All that glitters/glistens is not gold* (*proverb*) Something that looks valuable or seems attractive on the surface often proves to be of no or little value or worth. *as good as gold* (esp of a child) very well behaved: *The children were as good as gold while you were away.* (**have**) *a heart of gold* (*fig*) (be) very kind and helpful: *Charlotte has a heart of gold and will do anything you ask.* *worth one's weight in gold* (*fig*) extremely helpful and useful, often with the idea that he/she is worth much more than one pays for his/her services: *The electrician I use is worth his weight in gold because he always arrives on time, does the job properly and never charges too much.*

golden /'gəʊldən/ *adj* (*literary*; *formal*) made of gold(1); having the colour of gold(2): *a golden sword; golden hair.*

,golden 'age *c/def.n* (long) period of time when things (life, art etc) are or were (considered to be) better than at any other time: *This was the golden age of English literature.*

,golden 'hand,shake *c.n* large amount of money when one/s.o retires from, or is asked or forced to leave, an important job.

,golden ,jubi'lee/'wedding *c.n* 50th year after an important event, a wedding, usu celebrated in some way. Compare diamond jubilee/wedding, silver jubilee/wedding.

,golden ,oppor'tunity *c.n* time, opportunity etc that offers s.o a very great advantage: *The job is your golden opportunity to see the world.*

,golden 'rule *c/def.n* rule that one follows or observes very carefully etc (and does not break): *My golden rule is never to lend money.*

,golden 'wedding *c.n* ⇨ golden jubilee.

'gold,field *c.n* area where gold(1) is found, dug out of the ground etc.

'gold,finch *c.n* kind of small yellow bird the male of which has a red and white face, found in Europe. ⇨ finch.

'gold,fish *c.n* (*pl* goldfish) (also *attrib*) kind of small fish, usu yellow-red in colour, often kept in a pond or as a pet in a bowl: *a goldfish bowl.*

,gold 'medal *c.n* medal given for winning a race or contest.

'gold,mine *c.n* **1** mine from which gold(1) is dug. **2** (*fig*) thing, e.g a business, piece of information, that is, or can be, very profitable(1): *We had a friend in the government who proved to be a goldmine of information.* *be sitting on* *a* **goldmine** (*fig*) have or know s.t that is or will be very valuable.

'gold-,rush *c.n* movement of a large number of people to a place where gold(1) has been found.

'gold,smith *c.n* person who makes precious objects, jewellery etc in gold(1).

'gold ,standard *def.n* (*commerce*) system in which the value of a country's ordinary money is based on, and can be changed into, gold(1).

golf /gɒlf/ *u.n* **1** kind of open-air game in which players hit a golfball with a golf club(1), usu over some distance, into holes (there are usu 18 holes in a golf course); the object is to do this with the least number of hits.

▷ *intr.v* **2** (know how to) play this game as a regular thing: *I'm afraid I don't golf.*

'golf,ball *c.n* **1** small hard white ball used to play golf(1). **2** round metal ball with letters, numbers etc on it, used in some kinds of typewriters.

'golf ,club *c.n* **1** one of a number of long sticks with differently shaped pieces of metal or wood at one end, used to hit a golfball(1). **2** (building for) members of a group of people who play golf(1).

'golf ,course *c.n* place where golf(1) is played.

'golfer *c.n* person who plays golf(1).

'golf ,links *c.n* (*pl golf links*) = golf course.

goliath /gə'laɪəθ/ *c.n* (*formal*) man who is very strong: *He's a real goliath and can lift up a car.*

gondola /'gɒndələ/ *c.n* **1** kind of long narrow boat with high ends, used in the canals of Venice (Italy). **2** kind of cabin(3) under a hot-air balloon etc.

gondolier /,gɒndə'lɪə/ *c.n* person who rows a gondola(1).

gone, goner ⇨ go.

gong /gɒŋ/ *c.n* round piece of metal hanging from a frame; when it is hit with a hammer or stick it makes a deep echoing sound and is used to tell people when meals are ready etc.

gonna ⇨ go.

gonorrhoea /,gɒnə'rɪə/ *u.n* (US **,gonor'rhea**) kind of venereal disease.

good /gʊd/ *adj* (*comp* **better**, *superl* **best**) **1** (of a person, or thing done, written or performed) of a high quality, having reached a reasonable standard (in the opinion of s.o): *a good actor/ doctor; a good book/film; a good performance/ job; good food* (i.e well chosen, prepared and cooked); *good English.* **2** (of a person) living one's life according to high moral standards: *a good man; a good* Christian(2). **3** (of a person, esp a child) behaving in a reasonable or polite way; not being naughty: *If you promise to be a good boy, I'll take you to the cinema.* **4** (of a person's behaviour) polite and according to the rules of society: *Sue's manners are very good.* **5** (often — *to s.o; — of s.o to do s.t*) (of a person, an action) showing kindness or helpfulness (to s.o in what one does etc): *a good deed. He was very good to me when I was ill. It was good of you to come so quickly.* **6** (usu — *at s.t; — with s.o/s.t*) (of a person) showing skill or ability (in one's job, in handling or dealing with s.o/s.t): *He's very good at his job. Ben's very good with children. She's very good with her hands* (i.e can make things, use tools etc well). **7** (of a person's face, body etc) attractive, beautiful, handsome: *She's got very good looks. She looks very good in that dress.* ⇨

good-looker, good-looking. **8** (of a person, one's feelings towards s.o etc) showing friendship, kindly feelings: *We're very good friends. He's in a very good* mood¹(1) *today.* **9** (of a state of the body, a device etc) working or performing in the way it should, not having any faults: *His health is quite good for his age. The engine's very good but the body's a bit rusty.* **10** (often — *for s.o/s.t*) (of a medicine, s.t one uses etc) helping (s.o, to make s.o better etc); proving useful (for s.t, to make s.t work etc): *Exercise is good for you. Is that medicine any good (for colds)?* **11** (of the weather, time spent etc) pleasant and enjoyable: *The weather has been good all week. We had a very good time at the seaside. It was a good day for swimming.* **12** (of a course of action, circumstances(1) etc) favourable, bringing, or likely to bring, a pleasing result: *We received some good news last night. There's a good chance she will win. I wish you good luck.* **13** (of an action) complete; thorough (and so leading to s.t being done well or to s.t that one wants): *You need a good rest. Take a good look at the picture and tell me if you see anything strange. The room needs a good clean.* **14** (of s.o's social position, the way s.o is thought of) having a certain amount of importance or respect: *He's from a very good family.* **15** (of s.t one owns, wears etc) of high quality and kept for use on special occasions (and so almost in its original condition): *He was wearing his good suit.* **16** (of a thought, argument etc) sensible: *It was a good idea of yours to leave early. Can you give me one good reason why I should lend you money?* **17** (of size, quantity, length, time etc) quite or rather (large/small, a lot/few, long/short etc): *The shirt was a good deal too small. The town was a good ten kilometres away. A good few (people) were present. We had to wait a good five hours before our flight was called.* (**all**) **in good time** ⇨ time(*n*). **as good as gold** ⇨ gold. **as good as new** ⇨ new(*adj*). **as good as one's word** ⇨ word(*n*). **be a good thing** be s.t that is useful, suitable, acceptable etc: *It will be a good thing if it doesn't rain during the football match.* **be in s.o's good books** ⇨ books. **be in good hands** ⇨ hand(*n*). **be onto a good thing** (*informal*) be in a position where one can get a profit or advantage from s.t: *You'll be onto a good thing if you buy this land now.* **good and proper** ⇨ proper(*adv*). **good and ready** etc (*informal*) very ready etc: *When the time came to fight, they were good and ready.* **good at s.t** ⇨ good(6). **good for s.o/s.t** ⇨ good(10). **good for a laugh** likely or certain to make one laugh: *The stories he tells are always good for a laugh.* **good for another 10 years** etc (of machines, buildings etc) likely or certain to last 10 more years etc: *The car is good for another 5 years if you look after it.* **good for £10** etc (of a person) having, able to pay or lend, £10 etc: *He's good for a few hundred pounds so why don't you try to borrow from him?* **Good for you** etc (*informal*) (expression used to show approval of what s.o has done). **Good God/ gracious/heavens!** (expression used to show (great) surprise, worry etc). ⇨ Goodness(3). **one's/s.o's/s.t's good name** ⇨ name(*n*). **good of s.o to do s.t** ⇨ good(5). **good old Joe** etc (*informal*) (expression used to show that one likes or approves of Joe etc, what he/she has done etc): *Good old Jim — he's always there when you need him.* **good riddance!** ⇨ riddance. **good to s.o** ⇨ good(5). **have a good mind to do s.t** ⇨ mind¹. **have a good time**; **in good time (for s.t)** ⇨ time(*n*). **It's a good thing (that)** . . . (*informal*) I am glad (that) . . .; It has proved to be important (that) . . . (esp about s.t one did not know that might have caused one to do s.t wrong): *It's a good thing you told me about the broken stair; I nearly put my foot on it.* **keep good time** ⇨ time(*n*). **make good** (of a person) become successful: *He left England and is now making good in Canada.* **make good s.t** (a) repair the damage to s.t so that it is back to its original condition: *He was asked to make good the damage done to the flat during the party.* (b) show or prove s.t, esp s.t one claims to be true etc: *He was unable to make good his claim that he was nowhere near the scene of the crime.* **Be good enough to do s.t** (*formal*) (polite way of saying) Would you please do s.t. **make good time** ⇨ time(*n*). **not have a good word (to say) for s.o/ s.t** ⇨ word(*n*). **put in a good word for s.o (with s.o)** ⇨ word(*n*). **so far, so good** ⇨ far(*adv*). **take (good etc) care of s.o/s.t** ⇨ care(*n*).

▷ *n* **18** *u.n* (state or existence of) s.t that is morally right or correct (in the way one lives, acts etc): *The lecture was all about good and evil in the world.* Opposite evil. **19** *u/def.n* (often *the, some* etc — *in* s.o) good(2) virtues or feelings (that s.o has): *There is some good in him but it's difficult to find it sometimes.* **20** *def.n* (often *the* — of s.o/s.t) thing that will be of help or advantage (to s.o/s.t): *He always has the good of society in mind.* **be no good**; **(not) be any good** (of a machine, device etc) not be working at all (or properly); (not) be at all useful: *This typewriter's no good now. Will this screwdriver be any good for what you want to do?* ⇨ it's no good/use (. . . ing) (⇨ no(*det*)). **come to no good** (of a person) end in a bad way (because of the wrong things one has done): *He'll come to no good if he continues behaving in that way.* **do good**; **do-gooder** ⇨ do. **do s.o (no) good (to do s.t)** be of (no) help or advantage to s.o (to do s.t): *This medicine will do you good. Crying will do you no good.* **(do s.t) for the good of s.o/s.t** (do s.t) with the intention of helping or improving s.o/s.t: *He has spent his whole life working for the good of mankind.* ⇨ good(20). **for good (and all)** for ever; for the rest of one's life; permanently: *He won't be back again; he's gone for good.* **for s.o's own good** in order to help s.o, improve s.o, e.g by correcting a fault: *I'm punishing you for your own good.* **give as good as one gets** ⇨ give. **up to no good** (*informal*) doing s.t wrong, harmful, naughty etc: *When he gets that expression on his face you can be sure he's up to no good.* **What's the good of** (or **What good is it**) (**your** etc) **doing s.t?** In what way will (your etc) doing s.t help or improve s.o/s.t?, esp with the suggestion that it will not help: *What's the good of (your) complaining? The government won't listen to you.*

▷ *interj* **21** (expression showing approval, pleasure, agreement etc): *'I've done my homework.' 'Very good! Now you can do the washing-up!'*

‚**good ,after'noon** *interj/c.n* (expression used when one meets (or (*formal*) leaves) s.o during the afternoon).

goodbye /‚gʊd'baɪ/ *interj/c.n* (expression used when one leaves s.o or when s.o leaves one). **wave (s.o) goodbye**; **wave goodbye to s.o** wave(7) one's hand instead of saying 'goodbye'.

‚**good 'evening** *interj/c.n* (expression used when one meets (or (*formal*) leaves) s.o during the evening).

‚**Good 'Friday** *unique n* (in the Christian(1) religion) the Friday before Easter (Sunday) when Jesus was crucified(1).

‚**good-'humoured** *adj* (of a person, expression etc) friendly: *The conversation was very good-humoured.*

goodish /'gʊdɪʃ/ *adj* **1** good to a certain extent but not completely: *He's goodish but you have to watch him.* **2** (of size, quantity, length, time etc) rather (large, a lot, long etc): *We had to walk a goodish number of kilometres to get to the town.*

‚**good-'looker** *c.n* (*informal*) person who is (thought to be) beautiful, attractive, handsome: *Ann's a real good-looker and always attracts attention at parties.* ⇨ good(7).

‚**good-'looking** *adj* (*informal*) (of a person) beautiful, attractive, handsome: *He's very good-looking but he's not very intelligent.*

‚**good 'morning** *interj/c.n* (expression used when one meets (or (*formal*) leaves) s.o during the morning).

‚**good-'natured** *adj* (of a person, an act etc) showing kindness, helpfulness etc: *Stephen's very good-natured and always ready to help.*

'**goodness** *n* **1** *u.n* state of being morally good(2) or acting in a good(5) way: *His goodness to other people was praised.* **2** *u/def.n* thing that is the main or best part of s.t, esp food: *If you boil the vegetables too long you'll lose all the/their goodness.*

▷ *interj* **3** (also — gracious!; — me!; My —!) (*formal*) (expression used to show (great) surprise): *Goodness! I didn't expect to see you here!* ⇨ Good God/gracious/heavens! **for goodness' sake . . .!** ⇨ sake(4). **Thank goodness (. . .)!** (expression used to show that one is glad, relieved (about s.t)): *Thank goodness you're safe!*

‚**good'night** *interj/c.n* (expression used when one leaves s.o or when s.o leaves one during the evening or night): *Goodnight, I'll see you tomorrow.*

goods *pl.n* manufactured articles that can be moved, bought and sold etc: *This shop sells all kinds of household goods.* **deliver the goods** (*fig; informal*) do or complete s.t one has promised or said one can do: *He made the boast that he could sell that quantity; now it's up to him to deliver the goods.* **goods and chattels** all the things that one owns. **worldly goods** ⇨ worldly.

'**goods ,train**/,**wagon** *c.n* train/wagon(2) used for carrying goods (and not passengers).

‚**good'will** *u.n* **1** (also *attrib*) (often — *towards* s.o) friendliness shown (to s.o); attempt to improve relations (between people, nations etc): *He acted out of goodwill towards her. He paid a goodwill visit to the country.* **2** (*commerce*) (value of the) reputation that a company or business has in relation to its customers etc: *He bought the business for £100 000 including the goodwill.*

'**goody** *c.n* (*pl* -ies) (*informal*) **1** (usu *pl*) pleasant thing, esp s.t to eat: *We've got lots of goodies for the party.* **2** (often *pl*) person who is morally good(2), who does the correct, right things etc, esp in a play, film etc: *The goodies always won in the old films.* Opposite baddy.

▷ *interj* **3** (also **,Goody 'goody!**) (*informal*) (expression used by a child or jokingly to show pleasure, one's thanks etc): *'I'll take you out to a restaurant for lunch.' 'Goody!'*

'goody-,goody *c.n* (*pl -ies*) (also *attrib*) (*informal*) person, child etc thought by others to be rather too full of virtue, goodness etc to be really liked: *He's a real little goody-goody and he never plays with rough boys.* Compare Goody goody! (⇒ goody(3)).

gooey /'guːɪ/ *adj* (*-ier, -iest*) (*informal*) (of food) sticky and usu sweet: *a gooey cake.*

goof /guːf/ *c.n* (*informal*) **1** stupid mistake.

▷ *intr.v* **2** make a goof(1): *I really goofed when I asked the chairman of my own company what he did for a living.*

'goofiness *u.n* state of being goofy.

'goofy *adj* (*-ier, -iest*) (of a person) stupid or silly.

goon /guːn/ *c.n* (*slang*) **1** person who acts in a silly, humorous or stupid way: *He's a bit of a goon, always trying to be funny.* **2** (mainly US) (*derog*) person who uses violence, who is ready to fight etc in order to get his way, protect s.o etc: *The gangster had his goons around him ready to beat up anybody who opposed him.*

goose /guːs/ *n* (*pl geese* /giːs/) **1** *c.n* kind of large bird, often with white feathers, found in the wild and also kept on farms etc for food, its eggs etc. ⇒ gander, gosling. **2** *u.n* flesh of this bird as food: *We often have goose at Christmas time.* **3** *c.n* (also *interj*; often (**you**) *silly* —!) (*informal*) person who is (or has done s.t) stupid or silly: *You* (*silly*) *goose! You shouldn't have told him that.* **can't say boo to a goose** (*fig*) (of a person) is so afraid or timid that he/she cannot say or do s.t. **cook s.o's goose** (*fig*; *informal*) stop s.o from doing s.t, carrying out a plan etc: *That's properly cooked his goose; he won't be able to make any profit now.* (**kill**) **the goose that lays the golden egg(s)** (*fig*) (stop or destroy) s.t from which one has gained a lot of advantages, money etc.

'goose,flesh *u.n* (feeling of having) lots of little bumps on one's skin because of the cold or through being afraid.

'goose ,pimples *pl.n* = gooseflesh.

'goose ,step *def.n* **1** way of marching, esp by soldiers, in which each leg is kept straight and lifted quite high at each step.

▷ *intr.v* (*-pp-*) **2** march in this way.

gooseberry /'guːzbərɪ/ *c.n* (*pl -ies*) (also *attrib*) **1** plant on which grows small round green fruit: *a gooseberry bush.* **2** fruit of this plant as food: *a gooseberry* pie; *gooseberry* jam(1). **be a gooseberry**; **play gooseberry** (*fig*) (of a person) be present when a man and a woman who are in love with each other want to be alone.

gore /gɔː/ *u.n* **1** (*literary*; *formal*) large amount of blood coming from a wound: *His body was covered in gore after the fight.*

▷ *tr.v* **2** (of an animal) wound (another animal or a person) with its horn(s) or tusk(s): *The bull*'(1) *attacked and gored the boy as he crossed the field.*

'gory *adj* (*-ier, -iest*) (of a fight, story etc) having, producing, a lot of blood through

wounds, killing etc: *a very gory battle*; *a gory film.*

gorge /gɔːdʒ/ *n* **1** *c/unique n* (with capital **G** in names) (name for a) deep narrow valley (often with a stream or river) with high cliffs on either side: *Cheddar Gorge.* **2** *c.n* (*old use*) inside of one's throat. **make s.o's gorge rise** make s.o feel ill or disgusted, usu because of s.t unpleasant: *The sight of all that blood made my gorge rise.* **s.o's gorge rises** s.o feels this way: *My gorge rose when I saw all that blood.*

▷ *tr/intr.v* **3** (often — (*oneself*) *on/with s.t*) eat food very greedily, push a lot of food into one's mouth: *The sight of them gorging* (*themselves*) *on all that food made him feel sick.*

gorgeous /'gɔːdʒəs/ *adj* **1** very beautiful, attractive; brightly coloured: *a gorgeous woman*; *gorgeous flowers.* **2** (*informal*) extremely pleasant and enjoyable: *a gorgeous day*; *a really gorgeous meal.*

'gorgeously *adv.* **'gorgeousness** *u.n.*

gorilla /gə'rɪlə/ *c.n* (*pl gorilla(s)*) **1** largest kind of African ape(1) with a big heavy body. **2** (*informal*) strong ugly man, esp one who uses his strength against other people: *He's a gorilla and I wouldn't want to get into a fight with him.*

gormless /'gɔːmlɪs/ *adj* (*derog*; *informal*) (of a person) very stupid.

gorse /gɔːs/ *u.n* (also *attrib*) kind of bush with evergreen(1) leaves, thorns and yellow flowers that grows in the wild: *He fell into a gorse bush.*

gory ⇒ gore.

gosh /gɒʃ/ *interj* (*informal*) (expression used to show mild or gentle surprise): *Gosh! I never knew you were so clever!*

gosling /'gɒzlɪŋ/ *c.n* young goose(1).

go-slow ⇒ go.

gospel /'gɒspl/ *n* **1** *def.n* (usu with capital **G**) stories of Jesus's life and teachings contained in the first four books of the New Testament. **2** *unique n* (also **the ,gospel 'truth**) thing said that is, or should be accepted as being, completely true: *What I'm telling is gospel* (or *the gospel truth*) *as I got it from somebody who really knows what happened.* **the Gospel according to St Matthew** etc one of the first four books of the Gospel(1), written by Saint(1) Matthew etc.

gossamer /'gɒsəmə/ *u.n* **1** fine threads made into webs(1) by spiders. **2** (also *attrib*) kind of very thin light cloth: *a dress made of gossamer*; *a gossamer dress.*

gossip /'gɒsɪp/ *n* **1** *u.n* talking by people about other people, their lives etc, esp about things they (are thought to) have done wrong etc: *There was a lot of gossip in the village about their affair.* **2** *c.n* (often *have a* — (*with s.o*)) friendly conversation between (a group of) people (or with s.o): *We had a friendly gossip and a drink.* **3** *c.n* person who spends her/his time in gossip(1): *He's a nasty little gossip.*

▷ *intr.v* **4** (often — (*with s.o*) *about s.o/s.t*) talk gossip(1), have a gossip(2), (with s.o, about s.o/ s.t): *She spends her time gossiping about what her neighbours are doing.*

'gossip ,column *c.n* section in a newspaper or magazine with stories about the (private) lives of famous people.

'gossipy *adj* (*-ier, -iest*) (of a person) fond of

gossip(1) or a gossip(2): *She's the gossipiest old woman I know.*

got /gɒt/ *p.t,p.p* of get. ⇨ have/has got to do s.t, have (2–5).

gotta ⇨ get.

gotten /ˈgɒtn/ (US) *p.p* of get. ⇨ ill-gotten.

gouge /gaʊdʒ/ *c.n* **1** kind of chisel(1) with a sharp rounded edge, used for making a groove(1) in wood. **2** groove or shape made (as if) by a gouge(1): *There was a great gouge in the wood.*
▷ *tr.v* (often — *s.t out*) **3** make (a groove(1) or hole) using a gouge(1). **4** cut or force (s.t) out of, or from, s.t: *The sharp edge caught him and gouged a piece of flesh from his arm.*

goulash /ˈguːlæʃ/ *c/u.n* stew(1) of meat, vegetables and spices(1), esp paprika.

gourd /gʊəd/ *c.n* **1** kind of large fruit with a soft fleshy inside and a hard shell. **2** empty shell of this fruit used for drinking from, as a cup etc.

gourmand /ˈgʊəmənd/ *c.n* (*French*) person who is very fond of food. Compare gourmet.

gourmet /ˈgʊəmeɪ/ *c.n* (*French*) person who takes great pleasure in eating good food, who knows a lot about food etc. Compare gourmand.

gout /gaʊt/ *u.n* kind of disease that causes painful swelling in the joints of bones, esp in the toes or knees: *In his old age, Arthur suffered from gout.*
ˈgouty *adj* (-ier, -iest).

gov *written abbr* government(3).

govern /ˈgʌvn/ *v* **1** *tr/intr.v* rule or control (a country, state etc); have political power (over a country etc): *They had governed (the country) so badly that they lost the election.* **2** *tr.v* (*formal*) control (s.t, esp one's feelings): *You must learn to govern your temper.* ⇨ ungovernable. **3** *tr.v* (often *be* —*ed by s.t*) (of a person, an outside influence etc) act as a control on, as a strong guide to, (s.o, what he/she does): *It is hard to say what governs his behaviour. We have been governed by a number of* factors(2) *in coming to our decision.*

ˈgoverness *c.n* (becoming *old use*) woman employed to teach young children in their own home. Compare tutor(1).

ˈgoverning *attrib.adj* of or referring to s.t that governs(3) s.o: *The governing reason for his decision to resign was the low salary.*

ˌgoverning ˈbody *c.n* (*pl* -ies) group of people who govern(1) or control an organization, esp a school, university etc.

government /ˈgʌvnmənt/ *n* **1** *u.n* act of ruling or governing(1) a country, state etc: *I believe in strong government.* **2** *u.n* (*political*) method or way of governing(1) a country, state etc: democratic(1) *government.* **3** *c/def.n* (also *attrib*) (sometimes with capital **G**; *written abbr* gov(t)) all the people, usu those who have been elected, who rule or govern(1) a country, state etc: *foreign governments; form a government* (i.e choose the ministers who will control departments etc); *the French Government; government* policy¹.

governmental /ˌgʌvənˈmentl/ *adj* of or referring to a government(3): *governmental decisions.*

governor /ˈgʌvənə/ *c.n* (with capital **G** in titles) **1** (title of a) person who is in charge of an organization, esp a school, college etc: *the governors of the school; the hospital governors; the Governor of the Bank of England.* **2** (esp US)

official who is elected to govern(1) a state: *the Governor of California.* **3** (*informal* **guv** /gʌv/, **guv'nor** /ˈgʌvnə/) boss; manager: *I must tell the governor what's gone wrong.*

ˌGovernor-ˈGeneral *c.n* (*pl* Governors-General) official who represents the British Queen/King in some countries belonging to the (British) Commonwealth.

govt *written abbr* government(3).

gown /gaʊn/ *c.n* **1** (becoming *old use*) formal dress worn by a woman. ⇨ evening gown. **2** = dressing gown. **3** kind of (usu black) robe worn by officials, e.g judges, teachers at universities, and by students at colleges and universities, esp on official occasions.

GP /ˌdʒiː ˈpiː/ *abbr* general practitioner.

Gp Capt *written abbr* Group Captain.

grab /græb/ *c.n* **1** (often make a — at/for s.o/s.t) attempt to get hold of s.o/s.t quickly or suddenly: *They made a grab for him but he managed to run away.* **be up for grabs** (*informal*) be s.t that one can get, take or buy: *The business is up for grabs if you have the money.*
▷ *v* (-bb-) **2** *tr/intr.v* get hold of (s.o/s.t) in a sudden, rough and usu rude way: *He grabbed her by the arm. When I was young I was taught it was rude to grab (food) at* mealtimes. **3** *tr.v* (*informal*) find and take (s.t) quickly or in a hurry, esp in order to do s.t else: *You've just got time to grab a bite* (or *something*) *to eat before we leave.* **grab at s.t** (*fig*) try to make full use of s.t, esp a chance, opportunity etc: *You should grab at any chance to travel.* **smash-and-grab** (**raid**) ⇨ smash.

grace /greɪs/ *n* **1** *c/u.n* (example of a) pleasing beauty, esp in a person's body, movement etc: *She walked down the stairs with a certain grace.* **2** *u.n* quality of behaving well, doing the right thing etc (often after doing s.t wrong): *There was a certain grace in the way he admitted that she had been right all along.* **3** *u.n* (often have, give s.o, a day's etc —) more time in which to do s.t, esp to pay money that is owed: *They were given a week's grace to pay the final amount.* **4** *u.n* (*formal*) favour and mercy (of God): *May the grace of God help us in our time of need.* **5** *c/u.n* (often say —) short Christian(1) prayer said before or after meals: *Will you say grace or shall I?* **by the grace of God** (*formal*) because of the grace(4) that God has shown, esp in helping or saving s.o from harm etc: *It was only by the grace of God that we were rescued.* **have the grace to do s.t** show grace(2) when one does s.t, admits that one is wrong, has done s.t bad etc: *Well, at least he had the grace to apologize after his behaviour.* **in s.o's good graces** thought favourably of by s.o; welcome to s.o: *I'm not in her good graces after what I said about her at the party.* **s.o's (one) saving grace** the one good thing that s.o has or shows, though everything else is bad: *Ted's one saving grace is that he is kind to animals.* **with (a) good/bad grace** in a willing/unwilling, polite/impolite, way: *Colin accepted his defeat with very bad grace.* **Your/Her/His Grace** (*pl* Your/Their Graces) title used when talking to or about a duke, a duchess or an archbishop.
▷ *tr.v* **6** (often — *s.t with one's presence*) (*formal*) add honour to (an occasion, esp by one's presence at it): *The ball was graced with the presence of the King and Queen.*

'graceful adj **1** showing grace(1): a graceful dance. **2** (formal) showing grace(2): a graceful apology.

'gracefully adv. **'gracefulness** u.n.

'graceless adj **1** showing a lack of grace(1): a graceless movement. **2** (formal) showing a lack of grace(2): a graceless remark.

'gracelessly adv. **'gracelessness** u.n.

gracious /ˈɡreɪʃəs/ adj (of a person, what s.o says or does etc) polite and kind (often to s.o who is lower in a social scale): It was very gracious of her to agree to see us. Opposite ungracious. **Good gracious!**; **Goodness gracious!**; **Gracious!** ⇒ good(adj), goodness(3).

'graciously adv. **'graciousness** u.n.

grade /ɡreɪd/ c.n **1** one of a group or set into which things (or people) are divided according to rank, size, quality, colour etc: He has reached the highest grade in his particular job. Eggs marked 'Grade I' are supposed to be the biggest size and the best quality. ⇒ graduate(6). **2** (US) one of a number of levels in a school; class(4): He's in the fifth grade. **3** mark(s) given for work at school etc: You'll need to get good grades if you want to stay. **4** (US) = gradient. **make the grade** (informal) succeed in what one attempts, esp in an examination, one's job etc: You'll never make the grade if you don't work.

▷ v **5** tr.v (often — s.t into s.t) separate (a number of things) (into groups) according to rank, size, quality etc: The machine can grade peas(1) into different groups according to their size. ⇒ graduation(3). **6** tr.v make (a slope) smoother or more level, e.g for a road. **7** intr.v (often — (from s.t) into s.t) (esp of colours) change gradually or in stages (from one colour into another): As the sun set, the colour of the sky graded from yellow into orange and then red.

gradation /ɡrəˈdeɪʃən/ c/u.n (example of a) set of gradual changes from one stage or state to another or others: It is difficult to see any real gradation of colour in these pictures.

gradient /ˈɡreɪdɪənt/ c.n amount of slope, esp on a road or railway track: Because of the steep gradient two engines were needed to pull the train. **a gradient of 1 in 5** etc a measurement of slope in a road etc in which the road rises or falls 1 metre for every 5 etc metres that it goes forward (now usu given as a percentage(1), e.g 20% = 1 in 5).

'gradu.ate¹ tr.v ⇒ graduate²(6).

,gradu'ation¹ c.n ⇒ graduate² (esp graduation²(3)).

gradual /ˈɡrædjʊəl/ adj (of a change of some kind, e.g in size, temperature etc) happening, increasing or decreasing, slowly or gently: The change in the weather was so gradual we hardly noticed it. There has been a gradual increase in the number of people out of work.

'gradually adv in a gradual way: Gradually, he took more and more control over the company.

'gradualness u.n.

graduate² /ˈɡrædjʊət/ adj **1** of or referring to s.o who has a (first) university degree (and who is studying a postgraduate course); of a course of study or an institution of this kind: a graduate student; a graduate course.

▷ c.n /ˈɡrædjʊət/ **2** (usu a — in s.t; a — of/from s.w) person who has got a (first) university degree (in a subject, from a university): She's a graduate

in chemistry. He's an Oxford graduate (or a graduate of/from Oxford). **3** (US) person who has got a degree or diploma from an educational institution: a high school graduate. Compare postgraduate, undergraduate.

▷ v /ˈɡrædjʊˌeɪt/ **4** intr.v (often — in s.t (at/from s.w)) get, be given a (first) university degree (in a subject from a university): He graduated in mathematics from Cambridge in 1980. **5** intr.v (US) get a (university) degree or a diploma (from an educational institution): She graduated from the local High School in 1988. **6** tr.v mark or divide (s.t) into a set of grades(1), e.g of temperature, size, value etc: The weighing scale was graduated in grams and kilos. ⇒ graduated.

'gradu.ated adj (of a scale or set of things) marked or divided into sets or groups: a graduated thermometer; a graduated salary scale (i.e one divided according to the amount one can earn at each level).

graduation² /ˌɡrædjʊˈeɪʃən/ n **1** u.n act or state of getting, being given, having, a (first) university degree or (US) a diploma: After graduation, Paul got a job on a newspaper. **2** c.n (also attrib) ceremony in which a degree etc is given: a graduation ceremony. **3** c.n (one of the marks showing a) division of s.t according to grades(1): the graduations on a (weighing) scale.

graffiti /ɡrəˈfiːtɪ/ pl.n (with sing or pl v) words, messages, jokes, pictures etc written or drawn on a wall or other surface, esp those done without permission.

graft¹ /ɡrɑːft/ c.n **1** piece cut from a branch of a tree or plant that is fixed to another tree or plant to make a new growth. **2** piece of skin or bone taken from one part of a body and put on or in another part that has been damaged.

▷ tr.v (often — s.t on(to) s.t) **3** fix, put (a graft¹(1)) on another tree or plant: He developed a new variety of rose by grafting different types onto older ones. **4** put (a graft¹(2)) on or in a place in the body: In the operation new skin was grafted on the places where he had been burned.

graft² /ɡrɑːft/ u.n **1** gaining of profit, advantage etc for oneself by illegal means, esp by bribery or by doing favours for s.o: He was accused of having got the job by graft. **2** (informal) continuous hard work: He got to his position as manager by hard graft.

grain /ɡreɪn/ n **1** u.n (general name for the) seeds of various wheat, rice etc plants: bags of grain. **2** c.n (usu a — of s.t) single example (of such seeds): grains of rice. **3** c.n (usu a — of s.t) single very small hard piece (of a substance): grains of sand; sugar grains. **4** c.n (usu (not) a — of s.t) (fig) (not being or having a) very small amount (of mental ability, truth etc): If he had the slightest grain of intelligence/sense he would have known he wouldn't have succeeded. There is not a grain of truth in what he said. **5** def.n arrangement or pattern of lines that are present in some substances such as wood, rock, cloth etc: If you hit the rock hard enough it will split along the grain. **6** c.n smallest unit of weight in the avoirdupois system or in weighing medicines, gold etc (= 0.0648 grams). **go against the grain** (for s.o to do s.t) (fig) be s.t that s.o does not want to do: It goes against the grain for me to agree with him but on this occasion *he is right.* **take s.t with a grain/pinch of salt** ⇒salt(*n*).

gram¹ ⇒ gramme.

gram² *written abbr* grammar, grammatical.

grammar /ˈgræmə/ *n* **1** *u.n* (science or study of) rules for the ways words, phrases(1) etc are formed and used in making sentences etc in various languages: *French/Greek grammar.* **2** *c.n* (also **ˈgrammar ˌbook**) (book with a) description of the rules of grammar(1): *a Japanese grammar.* **3** *u.n* (good or bad) way a person speaks or writes a language: *He needs a lot of practice in grammar. That sentence is bad grammar.*

grammarian /grəˈmeərɪən/ *c.n* person who studies, or is an expert in, grammar(1).

ˈgrammar ˌschool *c/u.n* (UK) type of secondary(2) school which is intended to train pupils for universities. Compare comprehensive(2) school, public school.

grammatical /grəˈmætɪkl/ *adj* **1** of or referring to grammar(1): *a grammatical rule.* **2** showing good grammar(3); correct in terms of grammar(1): *That sentence is not grammatical.* Opposite ungrammatical.

gramme /græm/ *c.n* (also **gram**) (*written abbr* g) unit of weight in the metric system (1000 grams = 1 kilogram).

gramophone /ˈgræməˌfəʊn/ *c.n* (also *attrib*) (becoming *old use*) = record player(⇒ record¹). **ˈgramoˌphone ˌrecord** *c.n* ⇒ record¹(1).

gran /græn/ *c.n* (*informal*) grandmother.

granary /ˈgrænərɪ/ *c.n* (*pl -ies*) place or building in which grain, e.g wheat, is stored.

ˈgranary ˌbread/ˌloaf *c/u.n* (loaf of) bread made from whole grains of wheat. ⇒ wholemeal.

grand /grænd/ *adj* **1** (of a sight, view etc) splendid: *The procession was a grand sight. The view from the top of the hill was very grand.* **2** (of a person) (looking) splendid or important: *You look very grand dressed up like that. She tries to pretend she's grand and important but I know better.* **3** (*informal*) (of s.t one does) very enjoyable and pleasant: *We had a grand time at the races.* **4** (of an event) most important or final (part): *a grand opening* (e.g of a new building, a play etc); *the grand finale* (i.e the final and most important event in a number of events). **5** (with capital **G** in titles) (esp in a title) chief or most important (person in an organization, some orders of knighthood etc): *a grand master* (i.e a champion(3) at chess).
▷ *c.n* (*informal*) **6** (*pl grand*) (US) 1000 dollars or pounds: *Did you know, he paid over two hundred grand for that house?* **7** = grand piano.

granddad /ˈgrænˌdæd/ *c.n* (also **ˈgranˌdad**) (*informal*) grandfather.

grandchild /ˈgrænˌtʃaɪld/ *c.n* (*pl* **ˈgrandˌchildren**) daughter or son of s.o's daughter or son.

granddaughter /ˈgrænˌdɔːtə/ *c.n* (also **ˈgranˌdaughter**) daughter of s.o's daughter or son.

grandeur /ˈgrændʒə/ *u.n* (*formal*) (often *the — of s.t*) very great beauty or importance (of s.t): *the grandeur of Rome.* **have delusions of grandeur** (of a person) think or act in a way that tries to make oneself seem more important than one really is. *He suffers from delusions of grandeur.*

grandfather /ˈgrænˌfɑːðə/ *c.n* father of s.o's father or mother.

ˈgrandˌfather ˌclock *c.n* tall clock in usu a wooden case that stands by itself on the floor.

grandiose /ˈgrændɪˌəʊs/ *adj* (often *derog*) intended to be or look very great, splendid or important: *a grandiose building*; *grandiose plans* (i.e to do s.t important but unlikely to succeed).

ˈgrandly *adv* in a grand(2) manner: *She grandly allowed me to kiss her hand.*

grandma /ˈgrænˌmɑː/ *c.n* (*informal*) = grandmother.

grandmother /ˈgrænˌmʌðə/ *c.n* mother of s.o's father or mother. **teach one's grandmother to suck eggs** ⇒ egg(*n*).

ˈgrandness *u.n* very great beauty or importance; grandeur: *the grandness of the occasion.*

ˌgrand ˈopera *u.n* kind of opera(1) in which all the words are sung.

grandpa /ˈgrænˌpɑː/ *c.n* (*informal*) = grandfather.

grandparent /ˈgrænˌpeərənt/ *c.n* father or mother of s.o's father or mother.

ˌgrand piˈano *c.n* large piano in which the strings are horizontal. Compare upright piano.

Grand Prix /ˌgrɒn ˈpriː/ *c.n* (*pl Grands Prix* /ˈgrɒn ˌpriː/) (*French*) one of a number of races held around the world for racing cars.

grandson /ˈgrænˌsʌn/ *c.n* son of s.o's daughter or son.

grandstand /ˈgrænˌstænd/ *c.n* large building, usu with a roof, that has seats for people to watch a sport, e.g football, horse racing.

ˌgrand ˈtotal *c.n* final or complete total or amount added up from other totals or amounts: *The grand total after adding all the columns up comes to £5100.*

granny /ˈgrænɪ/ *c.n* (also **ˈgrannie**) (*pl -ies*) (*informal*) grandmother.

granite /ˈgrænɪt/ *u.n* kind of very hard grey rock, used on the outside of buildings.

grant /grɑːnt/ *c.n* **1** amount of money given by s.o, esp a government or organization, to (help) pay for s.t that s.o needs to do: *student grants* (i.e to pay for university courses, accommodation etc); *a grant to repair a house.*
▷ *tr.v* **2** (often *— s.o s.t*; *— s.t to s.o*) (*formal*) agree to allow (s.t that s.o has asked for): *He granted her request on certain conditions. He granted her permission to go.* **3** (often *— s.o s.t*; *— (s.o) that . . .*) admit (s.t to s.o); agree (with s.o) (about s.t, that s.t is true etc): *I'll grant (you) that point but what about the others I mentioned?*

granted *p.p/adv* (expression used to say) yes, I agree about one point, but . . .: *'I was right, wasn't I?' 'Granted, but you got the rest wrong.'* **granted (that . . .)** even if (that is true etc): *Granted you were right about that, you were still wrong about the rest.* **take it for granted (that . . .)** think, believe, (that s.t has happened or will happen though it may or may not be true): *I took it for granted that you would come.* **take s.o/s.t for granted** pay very little attention to s.o/s.t, because one expects he/she/it always to be present, do what is wanted etc: *I'm tired of being taken for granted all the time; why don't you do some work as well?*

ˈgranting *conj* (*formal*) (expression used to say) yes, I agree or (if) I accept (s.t/that . . .):

Granting your main argument, does it follow that the government is wrong?

granule /'grænjuːl/ *c.n* very small piece (of a substance); grain(2): *sugar granules.*

granular /'grænjulə/ *adj* consisting of granules.

granulate /'grænjuˌleɪt/ *tr/intr.v* (cause (s.t) to) form into granules.

ˌgranuˌlated 'sugar *u.n* sugar made into granules or crystals(2).

grape /greɪp/ *c.n* (also *attrib*) kind of small round green, yellow or black fruit with a skin that grows in bunches on vines; it is eaten raw or made into wine: *a bunch of grapes; grape juice.* **(be) sour grapes** (*fig*) (be s.t that one says or does in a) pretence (that is actually full of envy) that one does not want s.t that s.o else has got or has succeeded in: *He says Mary's impossible to work with but that's just sour grapes because she's more successful than he is.*

'grape,vine *c.n* vine that produces grapes. **hear s.t on/through the grapevine** (*fig*) hear about s.t unofficially as a result of gossip(1) etc: *I've heard on the grapevine that she's going to resign.*

grapefruit /'greɪpˌfruːt/ *c/u.n* (pl grapefruit(s)) (also *attrib*) (juicy inside of a) large yellow fruit with a thick skin like an orange: *half a grapefruit; a tin of grapefruit; grapefruit juice.*

graph /grɑːf/ *c.n* line or lines drawn on paper to show changes in s.t or comparisons between things, e.g temperatures, sales of goods etc, esp over a length of time: *The graph Tom prepared showed how sales had dropped over the last six months.*

graphic /'græfɪk/ *adj* **1** of or referring to s.t written, drawn or designed(5): *graphic design* (e.g of letters, type etc); *the graphic arts.* **2** (of an account, description etc, done) in a very detailed and dramatic(3) way: *David gave a very graphic account of the fight.*

'graphically *adv* **1** by using graphs; by writing letters, designs etc. **2** in a graphic(2) way.

'graph ,paper *u.n* sheet(s) of paper printed with small squares on which graphs can be drawn.

'graphics *u.n* (art of) writing, drawing or designing(1) letters, type etc; arrangement of such things in a book, magazine etc.

graphite /'græfaɪt/ *u.n* (also *attrib*) kind of black or grey carbon(1) used in lead pencils.

grapnel /'græpnəl/ *c.n* **1** piece of steel with a hook or hooks on the end and fixed to a rope, used in climbing etc by being thrown to catch on to ledges(2) etc. **2** (*old use*) object like this used in fights at sea to hold an enemy ship close to one's own ship.

grapple /'græpl/ *intr.v* **1 grapple with s.o** get hold of and fight with s.o: *He grappled with the thief.* **2 grapple with s.t** (*fig*) (try to) deal with s.t difficult: *The government is grappling with the problem of unemployment.*

grasp /grɑːsp/ *c.n* (usu *sing*) **1** firm hold or grip(1) using one's hand(s) or arm(s): *He held her body in a tight grasp. Get a good grasp on the rope before you start climbing.* **2** (often *be in the — of s.o*) control, power or grip(2) (of s.o): *The grasp of the country's rulers has tightened in the last few months. She was in the grasp of the very person she hated.* **3** (often *have a good, poor etc — of s.t*) knowledge or understanding (of some subject): *His grasp of the language is not*

very good. **beyond/within s.o's grasp** (**a**) that s.o may (not) succeed in getting or doing: *Success was now within his grasp.* (**b**) that s.o does (not) understand: *The whole lecture was beyond my grasp.*

▷ *tr.v* **4** take (and keep) a firm hold on (s.o/s.t) with one's hand(s) or arm(s); grip(5) (s.o/s.t): *He grasped her firmly by the hand.* **5** make (the best) use of (s.t, esp a chance, an opportunity etc): *He grasped the chance that was offered to him.* **6** understand (s.t, esp s.t said, a meaning etc): *It took me a little time to grasp what he meant.* **grasp at s.o/s.t** try to grasp(4) or get hold of s.o/s.t. **grasp at s.t** try to grasp(5) or use s.t, esp in order to help oneself: *He would grasp at any opportunity to leave home.*

'grasping *adj* (*derog*) (of a person) greedy (for money, possessions etc): *He's very grasping and will cheat you if you're not careful.*

grass /grɑːs/ *n* **1** *u.n* (also *attrib*) kind of plant with many thin green leaves that covers the earth in fields, gardens, wild places etc: *grass seed. Cows eat grass. The grass needs cutting.* **2** *c.n* one of a number of different kinds of grass(1): *He is experimenting with a variety of grasses in his fields.* **3** *c.n* (*slang*) person who tells the police or authorities about s.o who has committed a crime but has not been caught. **4** *u.n* (*informal*) = marijuana. **not let the grass grow under one's feet** (*fig*) not waste time, but be very active; not miss an opportunity to do s.t.

▷ *tr.v* **5** cover (a place) with grass(1): *He grassed the field after it had been ploughed.* **grass on s.o** (*slang*) (usu of a criminal) tell the police or authorities about s.o one knows who has committed a crime: *He grassed on the people who had robbed the bank with him in order to get a lighter sentence himself.* **grass s.t over** grow, put, grass(1) on a place that did not have any before.

ˌgrass 'court *c.n* (**'grass-ˌcourt** when *attrib*) tennis court with a thin layer of grass on the surface. Compare concrete court, clay court.

grasshopper /'grɑːsˌhɒpə/ *c.n* kind of insect that jumps about and makes a clicking(2) noise by rubbing its wings together.

'grass,land *u.n* stretch of land covered with grass(1) and usu without any trees.

ˌgrass 'roots *pl.n* (**'grass-ˌroots** when *attrib*) all the ordinary people in a country or organization in contrast(1) to/with those who have political or other forms of power: *He decided to find out what the opinion was at the grass roots* (or *what the grass-roots opinion was*).

ˌgrass 'widow/'widower *c.n* wife whose husband, husband whose wife, has gone away, e.g abroad, for a length of time (but who will return).

'grassy *adj* (*-ier, -iest*) covered with grass(1): *a grassy spot.*

grate¹ /greɪt/ *c.n* kind of metal framework for holding coal, wood etc in a fireplace or oven.

'grating¹ *c.n* open metal framework of bars placed over a window (to stop people getting in), over a hole in a pavement etc. Compare grating² (⇒ grate²).

grate² /greɪt/ *v* **1** *tr.v* break or cut (cheese, vegetables etc) into small pieces or slices by rubbing it/them against a grater: *Grate the* carrots(1) *and put them in the bowl.* **2** *tr.v* make a grinding(4) (unpleasant) noise by rubbing (one's teeth) together: *He grates his teeth in his sleep.* **grate against/on s.t** (of an object) make a grinding(4) unpleasant noise by rubbing against s.t: *The gate grated on its hinges(1) as they had not been oiled for some time.* **grate on s.o/s.t** (of an unpleasant noise) irritate, be unpleasant to, s.o, her/his senses etc: *His high voice grated on me. The sound of the drill grated on my ears/nerves.*

'grater *c.n* metal object with a rough surface or surfaces with holes in it/them used in the kitchen for breaking or cutting hard food, e.g cheese, vegetables, into small pieces or slices by rubbing.

'grating² *adj* (of a noise) grinding(4) and unpleasant to hear: *That grating noise is driving me mad!* Compare grating¹ (⇨ grate¹).

grateful /'greɪtfəl/ *adj* (often — (to s.o) for s.t) being, or showing oneself to be, full of thanks (to s.o, for s.t he/she has done): *I'm most grateful (to you) for all your help.* Opposite ungrateful.

'gratefully *adv.* **'gratefulness** *u.n.*

gratitude /'grætɪˌtjuːd/ *u.n* (often show one's — to/towards s.o (for s.t)) (*formal*) state of being grateful (to s.o for s.t he/she has done): *It is almost impossible for me to express my gratitude for all you have done.* Opposite ingratitude.

gratify /'grætɪˌfaɪ/ *tr.v* (-ies, -ied) (*formal*) **1** please, give pleasure to, (s.o): *It gratifies me to know that she is now a success. They were very gratified to learn they had been successful.* **2** satisfy, make complete, (s.t s.o wants to do, know etc): *I can gratify your curiosity by telling you exactly what happened.*

gratification /ˌgrætɪfɪˈkeɪʃən/ *n* (*formal*) **1** *c/ u.n* (example of the) state or act of giving pleasure (to s.o), of being pleased (about s.t): *There is some gratification in knowing that I have been able to help a little.* **2** *u.n* (often the — of s.t) act of satisfying (one's/s.o's desires, wants etc): *All he is concerned with is the gratification of his own selfish interests.*

'grati,fying *adj* (of an event, a result etc) causing pleasant satisfaction: *The result was very gratifying (or It was a very gratifying result).*

grating ⇨ grate¹, grate².

gratis /'greɪtɪs, 'grɑːtɪs/ *adj/adv* free(ly); without any charge or payment: *This book is a gratis copy. We had gratis tickets for the concert. I'll do the job for you gratis.*

gratitude ⇨ grateful.

gratuity /grəˈtjuːɪtɪ/ *c.n* (pl -ies) **1** (*formal*) money given to s.o, e.g a waiter or waitress, as a tip or reward for good service: *Staff in this hotel are not allowed to accept gratuities.* **2** amount of money given to s.o, esp a member of the armed forces, when he/she leaves or retires: *He has to live on his pension(1) and a small gratuity.*

gra'tuitous *adj* (*formal*) **1** (of help, advice etc) given freely or without payment (sometimes without it being asked for or wanted): *Thank you for that piece of gratuitous advice but I know what I want to do.* **2** (of a remark) given without any good reason and so causing offence: *That was a gratuitous insult and I must ask you to apologize.*

gra'tuitously *adv.* **gra'tuitousness** *u.n.*

grave¹ /greɪv/ *adj* **1** (of a situation, state etc)

causing great concern or worry; very bad: *The news from the hospital is that his condition is very grave and he will probably die.* **2** (of a person, an expression on s.o's face) very serious or solemn, esp because one is worried: *His face was grave when he gave us the news.* **3** (of s.t that one has to do etc) serious and important: *The government has a grave responsibility to prevent a war.*

'gravely *adv* in a grave(2) way.

'graveness *u.n* state of being grave(1-3).

gravity¹ /'grævɪtɪ/ *u.n* (usu the — of s.t) state of being grave(1-3); graveness (of s.t): *The gravity of the situation was very worrying.* Compare gravity².

grave² /greɪv/ *c.n* hole in which a dead person is buried; place where this has happened: *They lowered the coffin into the grave.* **dig one's own grave** (*fig*) do s.t, get into a situation, from which there is no escape (and usu suffer a misfortune) through one's own fault: *He's digging his own grave by always arguing against the company chairman.* **from the cradle to the grave** ⇨ cradle(n). **have/with one foot in the grave** ⇨ foot(n). **(make s.o) turn in her/his grave** (*fig*) (do s.t bad that would cause s.o who is now dead to) feel very annoyed if she/he was still alive: *Your mother would turn in her grave if she could see the way you live now.*

'grave,stone *c.n* (also **'head,stone**) stone with the name of the person who is buried and with other details written on it put on a grave.

'grave,yard *c.n* place, e.g around a church, where dead people are buried. ⇨ cemetery.

grave³ /grɑːv/ *c.n* (**'grave ac,cent**) mark put on some vowels in some languages usu to show pronunciation: *In the French word 'mère' there is a grave on the first e.* Compare acute accent, circumflex (accent).

gravel /'grævl/ *u.n* (also *attrib*) **1** small stones, sometimes mixed with sand, used for making paths, concrete(4) etc.

▷ *tr.v* (-ll-, US -l-) **2** put, use, gravel(1) on (a path, road etc).

'gravelled *adj* (US **'graveled**) (of a path etc) having gravel(1) on it: *a gravelled drive.*

gravitate /'grævɪˌteɪt/ *intr.v* **gravitate to/towards s.o/s.t** (*formal*) move towards s.o/s.t as though attracted by some special force: *People gravitate to the places where jobs can be found easily.*

gravitation /ˌgrævɪˈteɪʃən/ *u.n.*

gravity¹ ⇨ grave¹.

gravity² /'grævɪtɪ/ *u.n* (*science*) force by which objects are attracted to each other by their electrical nature, esp the way a heavier object, e.g the Earth, pulls smaller lighter objects to it causing them to fall to the ground: *Sir Isaac Newton is said to have discovered gravity when he watched an apple fall to the ground.*

gravy /'greɪvɪ/ *u.n* **1** liquid that comes from meat while it is being cooked or roasted. **2** this liquid mixed with flour etc to make a sauce that is served with meat. ⇨ sauce(1).

gray ⇨ grey.

graze¹ /greɪz/ *c.n* **1** scrape or number of scratches breaking the skin on one's body, e.g when one falls and hits s.t: *He had a graze on his knee from falling over on the pavement.*

▷ *tr.v* **2** damage (a part of one's body) in this way: *He* grazed his knee when he fell over. **3** touch and slightly damage or scrape (s.t), usu while going past it: *His car grazed mine as it passed by.*

graze² /greɪz/ *intr.v* (of some animals) eat grass: *The cows were grazing in the field.*

'grazing *u.n* (also *attrib*) (fields, land etc intended for the) act of eating grass: *The farm has many fields for grazing. It's good grazing land.*

grease /griːs/ *u.n* **1** fat that comes from an animal, esp when melted in cooking: *The top of the cooker was covered in grease from frying.* **2** thick substance like oil made from chemicals and used esp to protect metal from rust, make moving parts, e.g of an engine, move easily etc: *Put grease on the joints to make them work more smoothly.* **elbow grease** ⇨ elbow(*n*).
▷ *tr.v* **3** put grease(1) or a substance like it on/over (s.t), esp to prevent burning or sticking in cooking: *First grease the pan lightly with butter before putting in the cake mixture.* **4** put grease(2) on/over (s.t) to protect it etc: *Grease the joints carefully.*

'grease ˌgun *c.n* device used for forcing grease(2) onto/into a mechanical part by pressure.

'greasiness *u.n* state of being greasy.

'greaseˌpaint *u.n* kind of make-up(1) used by actors and actresses in the theatre.

ˌgreaseˌproof 'paper *u.n* specially coated paper that stops grease(1,2) from getting through it, used esp in wrapping greasy(1,2) things.

'greasy *adj* (*-ier, -iest*) **1** having a lot of grease(1): *This meat is very greasy.* **2** covered in grease(1,2): *I got my hands very greasy from trying to repair the engine.* **3** (of a surface) slippery (as though) from oil or grease(2): *The road was very greasy after the rain.*

great /greɪt/ *adj* **1** (of a person) showing or having very high qualities or abilities: *He was a truly great man.* **2** (of a thing, event etc) of very high quality or importance: *one of the great cities of the world; a great occasion for celebrating.* **3** very big: *a great crowd; a great explosion.* **4** (often *a — big, many* etc (s.o/s.t)) (*informal*) (used to give more emphasis(2)) very (big, many etc): *a great big crowd; a great big explosion; a great many people.* **5** (of a person) being in a certain (close) relationship (with s.o): *He's my greatest friend/enemy.* **6** (of a person) being very active (in s.t one does): *He's a great reader.* **7** to a very high degree or extent: *He was in a great deal of pain* (or *in great pain*). *You must take great care when crossing the road.* **8** (*informal*) (of s.t that happens or of a person) very good (in some way): *That was a great party. 'Did you have a good time at the party?' 'It was great!'* (or *'Great!'*) *'Do you like Mike?' 'Oh, he's great!'* **9** (with capital **G**, usu . . . *the Great*) (used after a name to show how important s.o was historically): *Catherine the Great; Alexander the Great.*

great- (used to show a family relation one generation(3) away from the relation mentioned in the second part of the word): *a great-aunt/-uncle* (the sister/brother of one's grandfather/grandmother); *a great-niece/-nephew* (the granddaughter/grandson of one's brother/sister); *a great-grandfather/-grandmother* (the father/mother of one's grandfather/grandmother); *a*

great-granddaughter/-grandson (the daughter/son of one's granddaughter/grandson).

Great Britain /ˌgreɪt 'brɪtn/ *unique n* (*abbr GB*) (name for the countries of) England, Scotland and Wales (but not including Northern Ireland). Compare United Kingdom.

'greatˌcoat *c.n* kind of thick heavy coat, esp as worn by soldiers.

'greatly *adv* to a great(7) degree or extent: *I was greatly surprised by his actions.*

'greatness *u.n* state/quality of being great(1–3).

ˌGreat 'War *def.n* = World War I (1914–18).

greed /griːd/ *u.n* **1** too great a desire for food: *It is greed that makes you eat like that.* **2** (often — *for s.t*) too great a desire (for money, power etc): *In his greed for money he stole from his mother.*

'greedily *adv.* **'greediness** *u.n.*

'greedy *adj* (*-ier, -iest*) (*derog*) **1** showing, full of, greed(1): *Don't be so greedy; give one of the cakes to Sally.* **2** (often — *for s.t*) showing, full of, greed(2) (for s.t): *Dennis is greedy for power and will not let anyone stop him.*

green /griːn/ *adj* **1** having the colour of grass: *a green dress; green peas*(1); *green fields* (i.e ones where grass is growing, where wheat etc is not yet ripe etc). **2** (of fruit, vegetables etc) not yet ripe or ready to eat: *The apples are still green so don't pick them yet.* **3** (*fig; informal*) (of a person) not having very much experience or knowledge and so likely to do s.t wrong or be cheated: *He's so green he'll believe anything you say.* **4** (often *be/turn* —) (of a person, s.o's face) pale (as though) from sickness: *The movement up and down in the boat made us turn green.* (**be**) **green with envy** (*fig*) (be) very jealous: *She was green with envy when she heard they had won all that money.* **get, give s.o, the green light (to do s.t)** ⇨ light¹ (*n*). **have green fingers** (*fig*) be very good at gardening, growing flowers, plants etc.
▷ *n* **5** *c/u.n* green(1) colour. **6** *c.n* area of grass, esp in a village, that is used by all the people: *They danced on the village green.* ⇨ common(6). **7** *c.n* (in golf(1)) one of nine or eighteen flat areas of grass with a hole in each one into which a player has to hit her/his ball. Compare rough(15). **8** *c.n* flat area of grass on which the game of bowls (⇨ bowl²) is played: *a bowling green.* **in green** having green clothes on: *dressed in green.*

'green ˌbelt *c.n* ring of land without buildings that is round a city; it has open farmland, parks etc.

'greenery *u.n* mass of green leaves, plants etc, esp when seen as a whole, used as decoration etc.

ˌgreen-'fingered *adj* very good at growing plants.

'greenˌfly *c.n* (*pl* greenfly, -ies) kind of small green insect that attacks and eats some flowers and plants.

greengage /'griːnˌgeɪdʒ/ *c.n* kind of plum¹(2) with a green-yellow skin and flesh.

'greenˌgrocer *c.n* **1** person who sells fruit and vegetables. **2** (also **'greenˌgrocer's**) shop where fruit and vegetables are sold: *I'll go to the greengrocer's and get some carrots.* ⇨ grocer.

'greenˌhouse *c.n* building, usu on a farm or in a garden, in which plants are grown, esp those needing protection from the weather.

'greenish *adj* rather green.

'greenness *u.n.*

'Green ,Party *def.n* political party that is in favour of protecting the environment, controlling the use of natural resources(1) etc.

greens *n* **1** *pl.n* kinds of vegetables with green leaves, e.g lettuce, spinach, broccoli, esp when cooked and eaten: *Come on, eat your greens.* **2** *def.pl.n* (with capital **G**) (*informal*) Green Party.

,green 'salad *c.n* salad(1) made with green vegetables.

Greenwich Mean Time /,ɡrɪnɪdʒ 'miːn ,taɪm/ *unique n* (*abbr* **GMT**) time measured from the imaginary line of longitude that is near Greenwich (in south London); this line divides the world into east and west, and time in different parts of the world is linked to it: *When it is 11am GMT in London it is 6am in New York.*

greet /ɡriːt/ *tr.v* **1** (often — *s.o with s.t*) meet and say words of welcome to (s.o); welcome (s.o) (in a certain way): *He arrived to find a large crowd ready to greet him. She greeted him with a kiss at the doorway.* **2** (of s.t one sees, hears etc) come to the attention of (s.o); be seen, heard etc by (s.o): *When he opened the door a terrible noise greeted him.* **3** (often — *s.t with s.t*) receive, show what one feels about, (s.t, e.g an idea) (a proposal, in a certain way): *They greeted his speech with cries of approval.*

'greeting *c.n* words used to welcome s.o: *He gave her a friendly greeting when they met.*

'greetings *pl.n* friendly words written or spoken to s.o, esp on a special occasion: *Christmas greetings.*

'greetings ,card *c.n* (general name for a) special card sent with a message at certain times, e.g Christmas or birthdays .

gregarious /ɡrɪ'ɡeərɪəs/ *adj* (of a person, animal etc) (*formal*) fond of being with others; not liking to be alone: *He's very gregarious and likes to have friends around him all the time.*

gre'gariously *adv.* **gre'gariousness** *u.n.*

gremlin /'ɡremlɪn/ *c.n* kind of goblin that is thought to make engines, machines etc not work properly: *I think there's a gremlin in this car; it's always stopping when I least expect it.*

grenade /ɡrɪ'neɪd/ *c.n* kind of small bomb usu thrown by the hand (a **'hand gre,nade**) or fired from a gun.

grew /ɡruː/ *p.t* of grow.

grey /ɡreɪ/ *adj* (US **gray**) **1** having the colour of clouds in the sky on a rainy day: *a grey dress/suit; a grey sky.* **2** (often go/turn —) grey(1), esp as one gets older: *In spite of her age she has very few grey hairs. She turned grey before she was forty.* **3** (often go/turn —) (of one's face, expression etc) pale, esp because of s.t bad that has happened: *When she heard the news of the accident her face turned grey.* **4** (of the weather, a time in one's life etc) dull and not interesting: *It was a grey day and he didn't feel like doing anything.*

▷ *n* **5** *c/u.n* grey(1) colour. **6** *u.n.* (of weather etc) dullness; grey(1) light: *In the grey of the morning he could hardly see anything.* **in grey** having grey(1) clothes on: *dressed in grey.*

▷ *tr/intr.v* **7** (cause (s.t, esp one's hair) to) become grey(1,2): *He noticed that his hair was greying.*

greyhound /'ɡreɪ,haʊnd/ *c.n* kind of dog with long legs and a thin body that can run very fast, often trained for racing.

'greyish *adj* rather grey.

'grey ,matter *u.n* (*informal*) a person's brain: *Use your grey matter to solve the problem — that is if you have any!*

'greyness *u.n.*

grid /ɡrɪd/ *c.n* **1** set of parallel(1), usu metal, bars over a space: *He drove over a cattle(1) grid* (i.e one that stops cows etc from getting onto a road, out of a field etc because they are afraid of putting their feet through the gaps). ⇨ **grating'** (⇨ **grate'**). **2** (also *attrib*) system of numbered squares printed on a map to enable one to find an exact place, where one is etc: *You'll need a grid reference/number to find the right place.* **3** system of cables(2) and wires that carry electricity from power stations to places where electricity is used: *the national grid* (i.e the system covering the whole country).

griddle /'ɡrɪdl/ *c.n* flat, often round, piece of iron on which things, e.g cakes, can be cooked on top of an oven or over a fire.

gridiron /'ɡrɪd,aɪən/ *c.n* set of iron bars placed over a fire for cooking things on.

grief /ɡriːf/ *c/u.n* (usu *sing*) (*formal*) (thing, event or person that/who causes) great sorrow or unhappiness: *His death caused great grief in the family. He was a great grief to his mother.* **come to grief** (of a person, plan etc) not be successful, suffer a misfortune: *He came to grief because his ideas were too ambitious.* **Good grief!** (expression used to show some surprise or worry): *Good grief! Why did you sell the house!*

grief-stricken /'ɡriːf ,strɪkn/ *adj* (often — *at/by s.t*) overcome with grief (at/by s.t that has happened): *She was grief-stricken at the news of her son's death.*

grievance /'ɡriːvns/ *c.n* reason for complaining about s.t, esp in matters of work etc: *The workers had several grievances which management would not listen to.* **have/nurse a grievance (against s.o/s.t)** have some reason for feeling annoyed or bitter (about s.o, or about s.t that has happened): *He nursed a grievance against his boss for not giving him a better job.*

grieve /ɡriːv/ *v* **1** *tr.v* (*formal*) cause great sorrow or unhappiness to (s.o): *His behaviour grieved his mother.* **2** *intr.v* (often — *for s.o/s.t; — over s.t*) feel great sorrow or unhappiness (for s.o who is dead or has gone away, for/over s.t that has happened etc): *The dog grieved for its dead owner. Stop grieving over him — he's gone.*

grievous /'ɡriːvəs/ *adj* (usu *attrib*) (*formal*) causing (a lot of) pain or suffering; very severe: *He suffered grievous wounds.*

,grievous ,bodily 'harm *u.n* (*informal abbr* **GBH**) (*law*) (act, crime or accusation of causing) great physical hurt or injuries (to s.o).

'grievously *adv.*

grill /ɡrɪl/ *c.n* **1** set of metal bars on which food is cooked by direct heat, e.g in an oven or over an open fire. **2** section in a cooker(1) in which food is cooked on a grill(1): *Our oven has a separate grill.* **3** food cooked in this way. ⇨ **mixed grill.** **4** = **grille.**

▷ *v* **5** *tr/intr.v* (cause (food) to) become cooked using a grill(1,2): *The meat's grilling nicely.* **6** *tr/intr.v* (cause (oneself) to) become very hot or burnt by lying out in the sun: *The beach was crowded with people grilling* (*themselves*) *in the hot sun.* **7** *tr.v* (*informal*) (of an official, esp a police officer) question (s.o) hard and for a long time in order to find out about s.t, e.g a crime he/she may have committed (⇒ commit(*v*)) etc: *They grilled the* suspect *for ten hours but he still admitted nothing.*

grille /grɪl/ *c.n* (also **grill**) set of metal bars fixed over a window, opening etc to protect it or the person(s) behind it from s.t, e.g an attack, robbery: *The police advised them to put grilles over their windows to prevent further burglaries*(2).

grim /grɪm/ *adj* (*-mm-*) **1** (of s.t that has happened, has to be done etc) very unpleasant, causing sorrow or pain: *It was a grim business counting all the dead bodies.* **2** (of an expression on s.o's face) severe and hard, e.g because he/she is angry, determined or worried: *His face was grim when he told them the sad news. With a grim smile he said he could do nothing more.* **3** (*attrib*) (of s.t one does or wants to do) using all one's power or energies(1) without stopping: *Only grim determination/necessity kept him going.* **like grim death** ⇒ death(*n*).

'grimly *adv.* **'grimness** *u.n.*

grimace /'grɪməs/ *c.n* **1** twisted expression on s.o's face, e.g because he/she is in pain, s.t bad has happened or he/she wants to make s.o laugh: *She made a grimace of pain when he touched her swollen ankle.*

▷ *intr.v* **2** (often — **with** s.t) make a grimace(1) (because of pain, annoyance etc): *She grimaced* (*with pain*) *when he touched her swollen ankle.*

grime /graɪm/ *u.n* (covering or coating of) greasy dirt, dust etc: *The area around the oven was covered in grime. His face was covered in grime after he had crawled through the tunnel.*

'griminess *u.n* state of being grimy.

'grimy *adj* (*-ier, -iest*) covered in grime: *Go and wash those grimy hands!*

grim(ly/ness) ⇒ grim.

grin /grɪn/ *c.n* **1** wide smiling expression on a person's face, usu with the lips stretched and sometimes with the teeth showing: *There was a big grin on his face when he gave her the good news.* *Take that grin off your face!* Stop being amused or pleased about s.t (because I am not amused, you should be more serious etc). *wipe the grin off s.o's face* (*fig*) stop s.o being pleased about s.t (because of some bad news or by forcing her/him to think about or do s.t more unpleasant etc): *I'll soon wipe the grin off his face when I tell him I know he lied.*

▷ *v* (*-nn-*) **2** *intr.v* (often — *at s.o/s.t* (*with s.t*)) make/have a grin(1) on one's face (when looking at s.o/s.t and showing one's pleasure, amusement etc): *She grinned at him* (*with delight*) *when he arrived.* **3** *tr.v* show or express (one's pleasure, satisfaction etc) with a grin(1): *He grinned his approval of the plan.* *grin and bear it* (*fig*) (be forced to) continue doing s.t one does not like: *I know you hate the work but you'll just have to grin and bear it for the next few months.* *grin from ear to ear* (*fig*) have a very wide grin(1) on one's face.

grind /graɪnd/ *sing.n* **1** hard dull uninteresting work, esp over a length of time: *I find studying* (*a bit of*) *a grind.*

▷ *v* (*p.t,p.f* ground /graʊnd/) **2** *tr/intr.v* (often — *s.t up*) (esp of a machine) (cause (s.t) to) break or be crushed into small pieces or powder: *I prefer to grind my own coffee. The coffee's grinding.* **3** *tr.v* make (a knife, blade etc) sharp on a grindstone. **4** *tr/intr.v* make a sharp unpleasant noise by (accidentally) rubbing (things) together: *He ground his teeth* (or *His teeth were grinding*) *in annoyance.* **5** *tr.v* press or push (s.t) hard (in(to) s.t): *He ground his cigarette in the ashtray* (or *under his foot*). *grind away* (*at s.t*) (*fig*; *informal*) continue to work very hard (at s.t): *With the examinations coming up he was grinding away until late at night.* *grind s.o down* (*fig*) force s.o, a group of people etc, to be or remain poor by making her/him/them work without any opportunity to improve themselves: *The rulers ground them down with ever higher taxes.* *grind s.t down* (*to s.t*) grind(2) s.t (until it is in small pieces or a powder). *grind s.t out* (*fig*) (esp of a musician, writer, record player etc) produce music, writing etc, usu of a bad quality, continuously: *The band was grinding out tired old songs.* *grind to a halt* (of s.t that is moving, e.g traffic, a system of production) gradually slow down and then stop (because there is s.t in the way, s.t has gone wrong etc): *The traffic ground to a halt in the morning rush.* *have an axe to grind* ⇒ axe(*n*).

'grinder *c.n* **1** machine that grinds(2) things: *a coffee-grinder.* **2** person who grinds(3) things: *a knife-grinder.*

'grind,stone *c.n* thick flat round piece of stone like a wheel which, when made to go round, grinds(3) knives, blades etc. (*get etc*) *back to the grindstone* (*fig*; *informal*) (stop enjoying oneself and) start working again: *I'll just finish this drink and then it's back to the grindstone.* *keep one's/s.o's nose to the grindstone* (*fig*; *informal*) keep oneself/s.o working very hard without stopping for any length of time: *If you want to pass your examination you must keep your nose to the grindstone.*

ground¹ /graʊnd/ *adj* of or referring to s.t that has been ground(⇒ grind(2)): *I like my coffee freshly ground* (or *I like freshly ground coffee*).

grounds¹ *pl.n* small solid pieces of coffee etc left in a cup etc after it has been drunk. Compare grounds² (⇒ ground²).

grip /grɪp/ *n* **1** *c/u.n* (usu *sing*) firm tight hold with one's hand(s) and/or arm(s), legs etc or of a tool etc: *He held her in a very tight grip. This* spanner *hasn't got much grip.* **2** *c.n* (often *keep a — on/over s.o/s.t*) very close control (over s.o/s.t): *She keeps a firm grip on her children. We need to keep a firmer grip over* expenditure(2). **3** *c.n* (often *have a* (*good*) *— of s.t*) knowledge or understanding (of s.t): *He's shown by his results that he has a good grip of the subject.* **4** *c.n* (*old use*) kind of small bag used by travellers. ⇒ hairgrip. *come/get to grips with s.t* (*fig*) (start to) deal properly with s.t, e.g a problem: *We need to get to grips with what is going wrong or we'll never be successful.* *get a grip on oneself* make oneself act more calmly, esp after some loss of control: *Get a grip on yourself! Crying like that is useless.* *lose one's grip* not be able to do s.t as well as one once could: *He makes so many mistakes now that I'm beginning to think he's losing his grip.*

▷ *v* (-pp-) **5** *tr/intr.v* take (and keep) a firm hold (on (s.o/s.t)) with one's hand(s) and/or arms, legs etc: *He gripped her round the waist to stop her falling. You must grip (the rope) more tightly.* **6** *tr/intr.v* (of a moving object) keep close to the surface (of s.t): *These new tyres grip (the road) much better than the old ones.* **7** *tr.v* of a performance, speech etc) attract and keep the attention of (s.o, an audience etc): *His fine acting gripped the audience for two hours.*
'gripping *adj* that keeps or grips(7) the attention: *The play was very gripping.*

gripe /graɪp/ *c.n* **1** (*informal*) complaint, esp of dissatisfaction: *My main gripe is that he never listens to what I say.*
▷ *intr.v* **2** (often — about/at s.t) (*informal*) complain (about s.t): *What are you griping about? Don't you know how lucky you are?*

grisly /'grɪzlɪ/ *adj* (-ier, -iest) terrible, nasty, unpleasant, (to look at, hear or read about): *a grisly murder/story.*

grist /grɪst/ *u.n* **all** etc **is grist to s.o's mill** (*proverb*) everything, even the smallest things that one does, brings or will bring some advantage or profit to s.o: *Buying and selling old clothes, furniture, tools, even cars — it's all grist to his mill.*

gristle /'grɪsl/ *u.n* hard tough kind of tissue(1) found near the bones in meat and too difficult to eat: *Don't buy that meat; it's full of gristle.*
'gristly *adj* (-ier, -iest) (of meat) having (a lot of) gristle in it.

grit /grɪt/ *u.n* **1** small hard piece(s) of dirt or stone: *I've got a piece of grit in my eye. Lorries were spreading grit on the icy roads.* **2** (*informal*) strength of purpose; determination: *She's full of grit and will never accept defeat.*
▷ *tr.v* (-tt-) **3** put, spread, grit(1) on (a surface, esp a road) when weather conditions are bad, to prevent sliding or skidding(1): *There were complaints that the local council had failed to grit the roads after the snow fell.* **grit one's teeth** (**a**) close one's teeth tightly together to control oneself, stop oneself from crying out etc: *He gritted his teeth when he felt the pain coming back.* (**b**) (*fig*) show great determination, esp when things are going wrong: *In spite of all the problems you'll just have to grit your teeth and keep going.*
'gritty *adj* (-ier, -iest) **1** having (a lot of) grit(1): *I've got something gritty in my eye.* **2** (*informal*) having or showing a lot of grit(2): *Julia's a very gritty person.*
'grittiness *u.n.*

grizzle /'grɪzl/ *intr.v* (often — about s.t) (esp of a child) cry quietly (and continuously) (about s.t): *Stop grizzling about your broken toy.*

grizzled /'grɪzəld/ *adj* (of a person) having grey hair or a grey beard: *a grizzled old man.*

grizzly /'grɪzlɪ/ *c.n* (*pl* -ies) (also **,grizzly 'bear**) large fierce bear found in north America.

groan /grəʊn/ *c.n* **1** low deep sound made in a person's throat because of pain, despair, disappointment etc: *He gave a groan when they tried to move him from the crashed car. There were groans all round when he started telling his terrible jokes.* **2** (of an object) low deep sound made when weight or pressure is put on it: *The table gave a groan when he stood on it.*
▷ *v* **3** *intr.v* (often — with s.t) make a groan(1) or

groans(1) (because of pain etc): *He groaned (with pain) when they moved him. The crowd groaned with disappointment when the result was given.* **4** *tr.v* say (s.t) with a groan(1) in one's voice: 'Not again!' he groaned. **5** *intr.v* (of an object) make a groan(2): *The table groaned when he stood on it.* **groan under s.t** (*fig*) (of people) suffer a lot because of the things done to them, esp by bad rulers etc: *The country groaned under the heavy burden(2) of taxes.* **groan with s.t** (esp of a table) (*fig*) have (too) many things, esp food, put on it: *The tables at the party were groaning with food.*

grocer /'grəʊsə/ *c.n* **1** person who sells most kinds of food and goods for use in the household. **2** (also **'grocer's**) shop where these things are sold. Compare greengrocer.
'groceries *pl.n* food, household goods etc bought or sold by a grocer: *Would you put the groceries in the cupboard, please.*
'grocery *u.n* (often *attrib*) (the trade of, business of a) grocer's shop: *a grocery store. My son is going into grocery* (or *the grocery business*).

groggy /'grɒgɪ/ *adj* (usu *pred*) (-ier, -iest) (*informal*) feeling weak and unsteady, e.g after an illness, after being hurt in some way, after having too much to drink: *I felt very groggy when I woke up after the party.*
'groggily *adv.* **'grogginess** *u.n.*

groin /grɔɪn/ *c/def.n* (usu *sing*) place or area on the front of the body where the legs join in it: *He got hit in the groin by a ball.*

groom /gru:m/ *c.n* **1** person whose job is to look after, take care of, horses. **2** = bridegroom.
▷ *tr.v* **3** look after (a horse) by brushing, cleaning it etc. **groom s.o** (**as s.t**) **for s.t** prepare and train s.o (as s.t) for s.t new, more important, special etc, (e.g a better job, acting a part): *She is being groomed (as a star) for the new television programme.* ⇒ well-groomed.

groove /gru:v/ *c.n* **1** long narrow channel(4) cut into wood, metal etc into which s.t fits or along which s.t can move: *The frame of the cupboard had a groove in it for the sliding doors.* **2** channel(4) cut into a record or disc(2) along which the needle moves. (**be**) **in the groove** (*slang*) (**a**) (be) playing jazz(1) music well. (**b**) (be) very up-to-date, fashionable etc. (**be**) **stuck in a groove** (*informal*) (be) in a position, e.g at work, that one finds dull but that one cannot, or does not want to, change: *He's stuck in a groove in his present job but he's too lazy to make a change.*
▷ *tr.v* **3** cut, make, a groove(1) in (s.t): *This machine grooves both wood and metal.*
'groovy *adj* (-ier, -iest) (*slang*) very up-to-date and fashionable: *This is groovy music!*

grope /grəʊp/ *c.n* **1** (often **have a — around** (s.t/ s.w) (for s.t)) action of using one's hands to feel (around s.t/s.w) or to touch (s.t), esp when one cannot see properly: *He put his hand into the hole and had a grope around.*
▷ *v* **2** *intr.v* (often — about, around etc (for s.t)) use one's hands to feel (about/around for s.t), esp when one cannot see properly: *He was groping (about) in the dark for the way out.* **3** *tr.v* (often — one's way into, out of etc s.w) try to find (one's way) using one's hands in the dark because one cannot see (in order to get into/out of etc s.w): *He groped his way to a seat in the cinema.* **4** *intr.v*

(often — *after/for* s.t) (*fig*) try to find (a solution to a problem, a word that one has forgotten etc): *I left him groping for an answer but I knew he wouldn't find one.*

gross¹ /grəʊs/ *adj* **1** (of a person) very or too fat (and so unpleasant): *He's got really gross over the last few years.* **2** (often *attrib*) (of s.o's behaviour, manners) very nasty, unpleasant, rude: *There is no need for you to use such gross language when talking to me.* **3** (usu *attrib*) very great (and bad); that cannot be excused: *It was a gross error*(1). *He was arrested for gross indecency* (⇨ indecent(1)).
'grossly *adv* **1** (behaving) in a gross(2) way: *He behaved grossly towards all the women before he got thrown out.* **2** in a gross(3) way: *We grossly underestimated*(2) *the demand for the new product.*
'grossness *u.n.*

gross² /grəʊs/ *adj* **1** (of an amount, weight etc) total or whole before any deductions² (⇨ deduct) are made; including the contents, the packaging etc: *My gross salary is £20 000 but after paying tax and various contributions*(2) *I'm lucky if I'm left with £12 000. The gross weight of the parcel comes to 10 kilos.* Compare net²(1).
▷ *n* **2** *u.n* the total amount or weight of s.t when everything is added together: *The gross comes to £50 000 but from that we have to deduct costs to arrive at the profit.* **3** *c.n* (becoming *old use*) (of things sold, in quantities of) twelve dozen (= 144): *You can still find some things sold in shops in dozens and grosses.*
▷ *tr.v* **4** earn, receive, (a total amount of money) before costs, expenses are deducted: *The business grossed £10 million but net profit was only £700 000.*
,Gross ,National 'Product *c/def.n* (*abbr* GNP) total amount and value of all the goods and services that a country produces in any one year.

grotesque /grəʊ'tesk/ *adj* (*derog*) very strange, odd or ugly: *grotesque behaviour.*
gro'tesquely *adv.* **gro'tesqueness** *u.n.*

grotto /'grɒtəʊ/ *c.n* (*pl* -(e)s) kind of cave made naturally, e.g by the action of the sea, or made specially for a garden.

grotty /'grɒtɪ/ *adj* (-ier, -iest) (*slang*) (of appearance, clothes, a place, room etc) not very clean; dirty, unpleasant etc: *She was living in a grotty little flat.*
'grottily *adv.* **'grottiness** *u.n.*

grouch /graʊtʃ/ *c.n* **1** (often — *about/against* s.o/s.t) (*informal*) bitter complaint or grumble(1) (about/against s.o/s.t): *His main grouch (about the conditions) is that no one will do anything.* **2** person who complains or grumbles.
▷ *intr.v* **3** (often — *about* s.o/s.t) complain bitterly (about s.o/s.t): *He's always grouching about his lack of money.*
'grouchily *adv.* in a grouchy way. **'grouchiness** *u.n* fact or state of being grouchy.
'grouchy *adj* (-ier, -iest) (of a person) full of grouches(1): *He's a grouchy old man.*

ground¹ /graʊnd/ *adj* ⇨ grind.
ground² /graʊnd/ *p.t,p.p* of grind.
ground³ /graʊnd/ *adj* **1** of or referring to the surface of the earth: *a ground frost*(2). Compare underground(1). **2** (of a building etc) of or referring to the part resting on, or level with, the

ground¹(3): *The house had two rooms on the first floor and three at ground level.* ⇨ ground floor.
▷ *n* **3** *def.n* surface of the earth on which we walk: *He was lying on the ground. The aircraft hit the ground and exploded.* ⇨ underground(3). **4** *def/u.n* soil or area of the earth in which things grow: *Prepare the ground well before you plant the seeds.* **5** *c.n* area of ground¹(4) with grass etc and buildings used for certain sports or activities: *a sports ground; a football ground.* ⇨ playground. **6** *c.n* (*old use*) background: *The plate was decorated with blue patterns on a yellow ground.* **7** *u.n* cause or reason for believing or saying s.t: *Have you any ground for this complaint?* ⇨ grounds²(2). **be on dangerous ground** (*fig*) be in a position, esp in an argument, that cannot be easily defended, proved etc and so may cause one trouble: *You're on dangerous ground if you accuse him of stealing when you have no proof.* **break fresh/new ground** (*fig*) do s.t new, s.t that has not been done before: *He is breaking new ground with these experiments.* **cover a lot of ground** (a) travel a long way, esp in a certain length of time: *By walking fast we managed to cover a lot of ground during the day.* (b) (*fig*) manage to deal with a (large) number of things: *They covered a good deal of new ground at the meeting.* **cut the ground from under s.o's feet** make s.o feel less sure or lack confidence by criticizing an important part of her/his argument, by doing s.t before she/he can etc. **down to the ground** completely: *That coat suits you down to the ground.* **fall to the ground** (a) fall to the surface of the earth. (b) (*fig*) (of an argument, belief etc) not succeed, not be true, esp because of s.t else: *The whole of his argument falls to the ground because he forgot one important point.* **gain (a lot of etc) ground (on s.o/s.t)** (a) make progress (against s.o/s.t in a race, competition etc): *The new political party gained a lot of ground in the local elections.* (b) (*fig*) become more widely known: *The rumour that the minister will resign is gaining ground.* **get (s.t) off the ground** (*fig*) start working (on s.t, e.g a plan, proposal etc): *We'll all have to work hard to get these ideas off the ground.* **give ground (to s.o/s.t)** (be forced to) retire, go back, (in the face of an enemy, attack etc). **go over the same (old) ground** (*fig*) discuss, argue about, s.t that has been discussed, argued about (several times) before. **have/keep both (one's) feet on the ground** ⇨ foot(*n*). **have/keep an/one's ear to the ground** ⇨ ear. **hold/stand one's ground (against s.o/s.t)** (a) stay in the same position, not retire, (in the face of an enemy, attack etc). (b) (*fig*) defend one's views, opinions etc (against s.o, an attack by s.o): *In spite of all the criticisms, he stood his ground and refused to change anything.* **lose ground (to s.o/s.t)** (a) (be forced to) retire, move back, from one's position (in the face of an enemy, attack etc). (b) (*fig*) suffer some disadvantage or loss, esp in a competition etc: *The ruling party lost ground to the other parties in the election.* **shift one's ground** (*fig*) change one's opinions, arguments, esp as a result of an attack. **suit s.o down to the ground** (*fig*) be exactly what s.o wants, likes etc: *The change in plans suited George down to the ground as he could now have his holiday.* **thin on the ground**

⇒ thin(*adj*). **worship the ground s.o walks on** love s.o very much.

▷ *v* **8** *tr.v* cause (a pilot of a plane, a plane) to stay on the ground and not fly, e.g because of s.t wrong, weather conditions: *All planes of this type have been grounded because of mechanical* defects[1]. **9** *intr.v* (usu — *on s.t*) (of a boat) hit and stay (on the bed of the sea (where the water is shallow) or on the shore): *The boat grounded (on the beach) and we jumped out.* ⇒ aground. **10** *tr.v* (usu passive, s.o *is —ed in s.t*) teach (s.o) the knowledge or facts (of a subject): *He is well-grounded in advanced mathematics.* **11** *tr.v* (usu passive, s.t *is —ed on s.t*) base (an argument, opinion etc on some fact etc): *His whole case is grounded on a mistaken belief.*

'**ground** ,**crew** *c/u.n* the people who repair etc an aircraft when it is on the ground.

,**ground** '**floor** (US **first floor**) *c.n* floor in a building or house that rests on, or is level with, the ground. **be/come/get in on the ground floor** (*fig*; *informal*) be/get in a favourable position at the beginning of s.t, e.g a business deal, that will prove to be profitable.

'**grounding** *c.n* (usu *sing*) (often *get/have a (good) — in s.t*) basic knowledge (of a subject): *You need a good grounding in the* basic(1) structure(1) *of the language.*

'**groundless** *adj* (of a feeling, esp of fear) not having a basis in reason: *Your worries are groundless because she's safe.*

'**groundlessly** *adv.* '**groundlessness** *u.n.*
'**ground,nut** *c.n* = peanut.

'**ground** ,**rule** *c.n* basic rule or principle(1) according to which s.o acts, a competition is organized, a business is run etc.

grounds[2] *pl.n* **1** (large) area of land, gardens etc around a house, building etc: *After visiting the castle we went for a walk in the grounds.* **2** (often *have (good etc) — for (believing etc) s.t*) reason or reasons, (for believing etc s.t): *Have you any grounds for thinking she is guilty?* **on these** etc **grounds** for this etc reason, these etc reasons: *On what grounds do you believe him to be guilty?* Compare grounds[1] (⇒ grind).

'**ground,sheet** *c.n* waterproof sheet placed on the ground, e.g in a tent when camping.

'**groundsman** *c.n* (*pl -men*) person whose job is to look after a ground[3](5) for a sports activity.

'**ground** ,**staff** *pl.n* = groundsmen.

'**ground,work** *u.n* work at the beginning of s.t which forms the basis for the work or result that follows: *Careful preparation and groundwork are needed before you can expect to be successful in selling your goods.*

group /gruːp/ *c.n* **1** number (of people, things etc) who/which is/are together in some way, has/have a connection of some kind: *a group of children*; *a group of plants*; *a family group*; *an age group*; *a language group* (i.e similar languages having a common root). **2** number of people who play and sing, usu popular, music together or who act in plays together etc: *a rock group*; *a theatre group.*

▷ *v* **3** *tr/intr.v* (often — *(s.o/s.t) into s.t, together, around etc (s.o/s.t)*) (cause (a number of people, things etc) to) form a group (or into a group or groups): *They all grouped together for the photograph.* **4** *tr.v* (often — *s.o/s.t with s.o/s.t*)

put, join, connect, (s.o/s.t with s.o/s.t of a similar kind): *For riding we group the boys with the girls, but not for other sports.*

,**group** '**captain** *c.n* (*written abbr* Gp Capt) (title for an) officer in the British Royal Air Force higher in rank than a Wing Commander.

'**groupie** *c.n* (*slang*) young person who follows pop[3](1) music groups(2) around.

'**grouping** *c.n* arrangement (of people, things etc) into a group or groups: *The new political groupings will mean trouble for the government.*

,**group** '**practice** *c/u.n* (way of organizing the) work of a group of doctors (general practitioners) serving a local community.

grouse[1] /graʊs/ *c.n* **1** (often *have a — about s.o/ s.t*) (*informal*) complaint, complaining words, (about s.o/s.t): *He's always full of grouses about his job.*

▷ *intr.v* **2** (often — *about s.o/s.t*) (*informal*) complain (about s.o/s.t): *He's grousing about his job again.*

grouse[2] /graʊs/ *c.n* (*pl grouse*) kind of bird with a fat body and often brown-red feathers that is shot for sport and food.

grove /grəʊv/ *n* **1** *c.n* (*literary*) small group of trees. **2** *unique n* (with capital **G**) (name for a) street or road: *He lives at 133 The Grove.*

grovel /'grɒvl/ *intr.v* (*-ll-*, US *-l-*) **1** (of a person, an animal) lower one's/its body (almost) to the ground, esp in fear, in order to show respect etc: *The dog grovelled in front of its owner.* **2** (often — *to s.o*) (of a person) act in too humble a way, esp towards one's superiors, in order to get a favour etc: *He's always grovelling to the boss in the hope of getting noticed.*

'**groveller** *c.n* (*derog*) person who grovels(2).

grow /grəʊ/ *v* (*p.t* grew /gruː/, *p.p* grown /grəʊn/) **1** *tr/intr.v* (cause (s.t, esp a seed, young plant etc) to) develop naturally or by artificial means in soil etc: *He grows vegetables in his garden. Some delicate plants grow better in a* greenhouse. **2** *intr.v* (of a child, young person) become taller as he/she gets older: *Your son has grown a lot since I last saw him.* **3** *tr/intr.v* (cause (s.t, esp hair, a beard) to) become longer naturally: *She's letting her hair grow longer.* **4** *intr.v* become bigger, greater in number etc: *The swelling grew (and grew) until it burst. The crowd grew as the evening went on.* **5** *intr.v* (usu — *big, more confident* etc) get to, reach a state as described by the adj: *He's growing older. He grew rather fat from lack of exercise. It was growing dark as we reached the village. The crowd grew bigger and bigger.* Compare become(1). **6** *intr.v* (of a friendship, influence etc) develop, become more important: *As time went on, their friendship grew. His power has grown since he was elected to* parliament.

grow away from s.o (esp of a member of a family, a friend) become less close to s.o (in the family, a friend) as one grows older.

grow (s.t) from s.t (cause (a plant etc) to) develop from a seed etc: *I grew these roses from cuttings.*

grow into s.o/s.t (of a person, animal or plant) develop to a certain (final) stage as he/she/it grows: *She's growing into a nice person.* Caterpillars(1) *grow into butterflies.* ⇒ grow to be s.t.

grow on s.o slowly become liked by s.o or a habit

for s.o: *I didn't like his paintings at first but they grew on me after a while.*

grow out of s.t (**a**) (of a person) become too big for one's clothes etc as one grows: *He grows out of his shoes a few months after I buy him a new pair.* ⇨ outgrow(1). (**b**) (of a situation, feeling etc) develop from, or because of, s.t: *The new movement grew out of the failure of the government to honour its promises.*

grow (**s.t**) **over s.t** (cause (a plant etc) to) cover, spread all over an area, place etc: *The climbing plants have grown all over the wall.* ⇨ overgrown.

grow to be s.t reach a certain state as one grows: *She grew to be very beautiful.* **grow to hate, like** etc **s.o/s.t** slowly reach a state where one hates, likes etc s.o/s.t: *The more I've seen of them the more I've grown to like them.*

grow up (**a**) (of a young person) become older, more adult, more mature(1); (of an adult person) stop behaving in a childish way and act as an adult should: *He grew up in a poor neighbourhood. It's time you grew up and faced your responsibilities.* ⇨ grown-up. (**b**) (of a situation, feeling etc) (start to) develop, become greater: *A friendship had grown up between them.* **grow up into s.o/s.t** = grow into s.o/s.t.

'grower *c.n* person who grows things, esp as a business: *a fruit grower.*

'growing *attrib.adj* **1** of or referring to a child or young person who is getting bigger and older: *He's a growing boy.* **2** of or referring to s.t that is developing, becoming greater or more important: *The club has a growing membership. There is a growing feeling in the country that a change in the government is necessary.* ⇨ ingrowing.

grown *attrib.adj* (of a person) having reached adulthood (and so (should be) able to act sensibly etc): *He's a grown man and knows what will happen if he leaves his wife.*

'grown-₁up *attrib.adj* **1** having reached adulthood, maturity: *She has two grown-up sons.*
▷ *c.n* (*pl* grown-ups) **2** adult: *When I was a child, grown-ups were always telling me what to do and what not to do.*

growth /grəʊθ/ *n* **1** *u.n* (of a plant, animal etc) state of development, act of growing bigger: *The growth of the plant is slow in the first year. Our cat has almost reached its full growth.* **2** *c/u.n* (often — *of, in, s.t*) (example of an) increase in size, number, amount etc (of s.t): *The growth of world trade has slowed in the last year. The growth in the number of unemployed.* **3** *c.n* living thing that has grown, esp s.t that is not wanted, needs to be removed etc: *He shaved off a four-day growth of beard.* **4** *c.n* thing growing as a disease either inside the body or as a swelling on the body: *They had to operate on him to remove a growth.*

growl /graʊl/ *c.n* **1** very deep low sound made in the back of the throat, usu by a dog but sometimes by a person, as a threat, to show fierceness, anger etc: *There was an angry growl from the crowd when the gates were shut against them.*
▷ *v* **2** *intr.v* (often — *at s.o/s.t*) make a growl(1) as a threat etc (to/against s.o, because of s.t): *The dog growled at the stranger.* **3** *tr.v* (often — *s.t at s.o/s.t*) say (s.t) using a growling voice (to/against s.o/s.t, because of

s.t): *The crowd growled its* displeasure *at the news.*

grub¹ /grʌb/ *n* **1** *c.n* (stage of an) insect after it has come out of an egg; larva. **2** *u.n* (*informal*) food; things to eat: *Mum, is there any grub?*

grub² /grʌb/ *v* (-bb-) **1** *intr.v* (often — *about, around* etc (*for s.t*)) (of an animal) use its nose, mouth, feet etc to turn over things (in order to find food etc): *The pigs were grubbing about for scraps of food.* **2** *intr.v* (often — *about, around* etc (*for s.t*)) (of a person) search about etc using one's hands (in order to find s.t): *An old man was grubbing about in the dustbin for food.*

grubby /'grʌbɪ/ *adj* (*-ier, -iest*) dirty; not very clean: *Your face is grubby, go and wash it.*
'grubbiness *u.n.*

grudge /grʌdʒ/ *c.n* **1** (often *have/bear a — against s.o; bear s.o a — for s.t*) feeling of envy (against s.o, usu because he/she had, or is thought to have, done s.t wrong to one): *He's had this grudge against me ever since I refused to lend him some money. I bear him no grudge for what he did to me.*
▷ *tr.v* **2** (also **be'grudge**) (often — *s.o s.t*) have a grudge(1) against (s.o, for s.t he/she has done, has succeeded in doing, esp s.t that one wanted oneself): *I can't say I really grudge him his success since he worked so hard.* **3** (often — *doing s.t*) not be willing to do (s.t); do (s.t) unwillingly: *I grudge spending any time away from my studies.*
'grudging *adj* (said, done) without much willingness; without much praise or generosity: *They could get only grudging support for their plans. He's rather grudging in his praise.*
'grudgingly *adv.*

gruel /grʊəl/ *u.n* (*old use*) watery mixture of oats etc boiled in water or milk.

gruelling /'grʊəlɪŋ/ *adj* (US **'grueling**) (of an activity, work etc) very hard and exhausting: *It was gruelling work lifting the heavy boxes all day.*

gruesome /'gruːsəm/ *adj* very terrible and frightening: *a gruesome murder.*
'gruesomely *adv.* **'gruesomeness** *u.n.*

gruff /grʌf/ *adj* **1** (of a person's voice) deep and rough sounding: *Michael spoke in a gruff voice.* **2** (of a person, behaviour) unfriendly(1) and rough, or seeming to be so: *He's a bit awkward and gruff with people.*
'gruffly *adv.* **'gruffness** *u.n.*

grumble /'grʌmbl/ *c.n* **1** complaint, feeling of dissatisfaction: *I wish you'd stop your grumbles and get on with the job.* **2** low noise, esp as made by thunder at a distance; rumble(1).
▷ *intr.v* **3** (often — *about/at/over s.o/s.t*) complain in a dissatisfied way (about s.o/s.t): *He's always grumbling about having too much work.* **4** (of thunder etc) make a low noise; rumble(2): *The thunder was grumbling over the hills.*
'grumbler *c.n* (*derog*) person who grumbles(3).

grumpy /'grʌmpɪ/ *adj* (*-ier, -iest*) (of a person) having a bad temper and not very friendly; cross or annoyed (for some reason): *He's a grumpy old man. Why are you so grumpy today, is something wrong?*
'grumpily *adv.* **'grumpiness** *u.n.*

grunt /grʌnt/ *c.n* **1** short low sound made in the throat by some animals, esp pigs. **2** similar sound made by a person to show displeasure or

annoyance, but also sometimes approval of s.t: *He gave a grunt of approval.*
▷ *v* **3** *intr.v* (of a pig etc) make grunts(1): *There was an animal of some kind grunting in the bushes.* **4** *tr/intr.v* (often — (*s.t*) *at* s.o/s.t) (of a person) do, say, (s.t) with a grunt(2) (because of s.t or to s.o): *He grunted with pain when they moved him. He grunted some words at me.*

guarantee /ˌgærən'tiː/ *c.n* (also *formal* or *law* ,**guaran'ty** in senses (1,2,4)) **1** (*law*) (written or printed) statement by a manufacturer of goods that the goods will be repaired or replaced if anything is wrong with them within a certain time: *My television has a year's guarantee.* ⇨ be under guarantee/guaranty. **2** (*law*) agreement or promise to pay money to s.o if s.o else who has promised to pay it to that person does not do so: *I gave my guarantee to the bank for £500 when my son wanted to borrow the money.* **3** (also ,**guar-an'tor**) (often *act as* —) (*law*) person who gives a guarantee(2): *I acted as guarantee/guarantor for my son's loan(2).* **4** (*law*) thing of value, e.g money, document(1) of ownership, given to s.o which that person can keep if one does not carry out one's promise: *We shall need some kind of guarantee from you, say £5000, before we can start the work.* **5** (often *a* — *of s.t*; *a* — *against s.t*) thing that offers, seems to offer, a promise (of s.t else happening, that s.t else will not happen etc): *Have you any guarantee of success* (or *that you will succeed*)? *Hard work is some guarantee against failure.* **be under guarantee/guaranty** (of s.t manufactured) (still) have a guarantee(1) for a certain length of time: *My car is still under guarantee so I can get it fixed free of charge.*
▷ *tr.v* **6** (usu — *s.t for 1 year* etc; — *s.t against s.t*) (*law*) (of a manufacturer) give a guarantee(1) on (s.t manufactured) for 1 year etc, that s.t will not go wrong etc): *The video is guaranteed for six months. The car is guaranteed against ordinary mechanical defects*[1]. **7** (often — *s.o s.t*; — *that*...) (*law*) give a guarantee(2) (to s.o, about s.t, that s.t will happen etc): *I guaranteed my son's loan(2)* (or *that I would pay my son's loan*). **8** (often — *s.o s.t*; — *that*. . .) promise (s.o s.t); state firmly (that s.t will happen): *I can guarantee you a good time if you'll join our holiday.*
,**guaran'tor** *c.n* = guarantee(3).
'**guaranty** *c.n* (*pl -ies*) = guarantee(1,2,4).
guard /gɑːd/ *n* **1** *u.n* (often *keep/stand* —) state of readiness or watchfulness in order to protect s.o/s.t against attack: *There were soldiers keeping guard all round the camp.* ⇨ on guard(a). **2** *u.n* (in sports, e.g boxing) position of the body in order to defend oneself. ⇨ (be) off/on one's guard, on guard(b), s.o's guard is down/up(a). **3** *c.n* person, or group of people, esp a soldier or soldiers or an official or officials, who protects/protect s.o/s.t or stops/stop s.o from escaping: *There was a guard* (or *There were guards*) *all round the camp.* **4** *c.n* official who is in charge of a train and who usu travels at the back of it (US = conductor(4)). **5** *c.n* object that protects one against injury, danger etc: *There was a guard in front of the fire.* ⇨ fireguard, mudguard. **be off/on one's guard** (*against* s.o/s.t) be in a position where one is unready/ready to defend oneself (against s.o, an attack etc): *I was off my guard when he hit me. You should be on your guard against people*

who try to borrow money. **catch s.o off** (**her/his**) **guard** attack s.o (with a blow, with s.t surprising etc) when she/he is not expecting an attack, is not ready for it etc: *Her criticism caught him off guard and he was unable to think of anything to say in reply.* **keep a** (**close** etc) **guard on s.o/s.t** watch, protect, s.o/s.t (very) carefully: *A close guard was kept on the prisoner to prevent him escaping.* **on guard** (**a**) (be) keeping guard(1): *There were soldiers on guard all around the camp.* (**b**) (be) in a position of defence, e.g in boxing: *On guard!* (i.e a command at the beginning of a fencing match to get ready for an attack). **s.o's guard is down/up** (**a**) s.o has her/his guard(2) unready/ready for s.t, e.g a surprise attack: *His guard was down and he got hit on the chin.* (**b**) (*fig*) s.o is unready/ready to meet an attack, criticism: *He knew they would be difficult to deal with so his guard was up when he began to speak.* **under** (**armed**) **guard** watched or protected by a guard(3) or guards (who is/are armed with guns etc).
▷ *tr.v* **6** (often — *s.o/s.t against/from* s.o/s.t) (of a soldier etc) protect (s.o/s.t) (from attack), stop (s.o) from escaping: *Soldiers were guarding the camp against an attack. They guarded the prisoners day and night.* ⇨ unguarded(1). **guard against s.t** (try to take special care in order to) stop s.t happening: *The only way to guard against this ever happening again is to check everything thoroughly.*
'**guarded** *adj* (of s.t said) cautious, not saying or admitting much: *He gave a guarded reply* (or *His reply was guarded*). Opposite unguarded(2).
'**guardedly** *adv.* '**guardedness** *u.n.*
'**guard,house**, '**guard,room** *c.n* building, room, in which guards(3) stay.
guardian /'gɑːdɪən/ *c.n* **1** (*law*) person who has the right or duty of looking after and protecting a child or a young person, esp one whose parents are dead or who are not able to look after her/him for some reason. **2** person who looks after s.t, who (thinks he/she) is responsible for s.t etc: *They appointed him guardian of the enemy property. He has made himself guardian of the morals of the country.*
,**guardian 'angel** *c.n* **1** (in the Christian(1) religion) angel(1) who is thought to look after a person. **2** (*fig*) person who helps s.o, esp in times of difficulty: *A guardian angel gave me £1000 to pay my debts.*
'**guardian,ship** *u.n* state or act of being a guardian(1,2).
,**guard of 'honour** *c.n* special guard(3), e.g of soldiers, who line up to show respect or honour to an important person, at a special occasion etc.
'**guard,rail** *c.n* rail on a path, road, bridge etc put there to stop people from falling off the edge.
'**guard,room** *c.n* ⇨ guardhouse.
'**guard's ,van** *c.n* van at the end of a railway train in which a guard(4) stays and also in which luggage etc is put.
Guards *def.pl.n* (title for a) regiment(1) or unit of an army: *the Horse Guards; the Irish Guards.*
'**guardsman** *c.n* (*pl -men*) soldier in one of the Guards regiments.
guava /'gwɑːvə/ *c.n* (*pl -s*) **1** kind of tree found in hot countries that has a yellow round-shaped

fruit with seeds in it. **2** (also *attrib*) fruit of this tree.

guerrilla /gə'rɪlə/ *c.n* (also *attrib*) (also **gue'rilla**) person who fights against regular soldiers, a government etc in a country, usu for political reasons: *It is dangerous to go outside the main cities as there are guerrillas everywhere.* **guer,rilla 'warfare** *u.n* (also **gue'rilla-**) fighting by guerrillas against a government etc.

guess /ges/ *c.n* **1** (often *have/make a* —) opinion, judgement, that may be right or wrong because one does not have or know (all) the facts, one does not consider (all) the information etc: *How much do you think I weigh? Go on, have a guess. When he's not sure of his facts, he makes wild guesses.* **at a guess** making a guess(1); stating what one thinks may be about right though one is not sure: *At a guess, I'd say the painting was worth £5000.* **be anyone's guess** anyone can have an opinion about it but no one really knows the truth: *What happened to him after the war is anyone's guess.* **your guess is as good as mine** (expression used to state that) you and I can make guesses(1) but we don't really know the truth.

▷ *v* **2** *tr/intr.v* make a guess(1) (about (s.t)): *You have to guess the weight of the cake to win it as a prize. Don't believe what he says, he's just guessing.* **3** *tr.v* arrive at the truth of (s.t) by a clever guess(1): *The enemy forces guessed our intentions and so were able to defend themselves.* **4** *tr.v* (often — (*that*)...) (*informal*, esp US) state, think, suppose, (that...): *I guess I'd better go now.* **guess at s.t** make an attempt to guess(2) s.t: *She guessed at his age and got it nearly right.* **guess what** ⇒ what(*pron*). **keep s.o guessing** not let s.o know the truth, what is happening etc, by hiding information, confusing her/him by what one says etc: *She keeps changing her mind about getting married but I think she just likes to keep him guessing.*

'guess,work *u.n* acts of guessing(2): *He arrived at the right answer by sheer*[1](2) *guesswork.*

guest /gest/ *c.n* **1** person who comes to s.o's house for a short time, e.g for a meal, to stay one or more nights etc: *We have guests tonight so we won't be able to come to your party.* **2** person one invites out to do s.t, e.g go to a restaurant, theatre etc: *We were guests of the Lord Mayor at the reception.* **3** person who stays in a hotel etc and pays for doing so: *hotel guests.* **Be my guest!** (*informal*) (polite expression used to say) You can do, have etc what you asked for: *'Can I use the telephone?' 'Be my guest!'* **paying guest** ⇒ pay.

'guest ,artist *c.n* actor, singer etc who makes a special appearance in s.o else's show, esp on television.

'guest,house *c.n* kind of small hotel or private house that has guests(3).

'guest ,room *c.n* (also **'guest ,bedroom**) room in a house kept specially for any guests(1) who come to stay.

guffaw /gʌ'fɔ:/ *c.n* **1** loud noisy laugh (usu considered rude): *There were several guffaws from the audience when he fell over.*

▷ *intr.v* **2** (often — at s.t) make a guffaw(1) (at s.t one sees or considers funny etc): *He guffawed loudly at her jokes.*

guide /gaɪd/ *c.n* **1** person who shows s.o, a group of people etc, the way around a place, city, museum etc, who knows the way to get s.w etc: *If you don't take a guide with you, you'll get lost in these mountains.* **2** = guidebook. **3** (with capital **G** in titles) (title for a) book that describes s.t, shows how to do s.t etc: *A Guide to Flower Arrangement.* **4** person or thing who/that acts as an influence or model for s.o's behaviour etc: *You should let your own conscience be your guide.* **5** (usu with capital **G**) member of an organization for girls that is similar to the Scouts(1).

▷ *tr.v* **6** act as a guide(1) to (s.o): *She has a job guiding people around Bath.* **7** (often — s.o across, to etc s.t) show (s.o) the way (across, to etc a place, how to do s.t etc): *He guided the blind man across the road. She taught him to write letters by guiding his hand as he wrote.* **8** (often — s.o/s.t through s.t) control and direct (s.o/s.t) (through a problem, difficulties etc): *He guided the country through all its difficulties.* **be guided by s.o/s.t** be influenced by s.o/s.t; accept what s.o says: *I will be guided by your opinion.*

'guidance *u.n* act of giving help or advice: *We need guidance on this matter or we'll get it wrong.* **under the guidance of s.o** with the help and advice (and control) of s.o: *Under his guidance we managed to solve our problems.*

'guide,book *c.n* (also **guide**) book intended to help travellers, tourists etc to find their way around a country, city, museum etc and having information, maps etc in it: *He bought a guide(book) for his visit to London.*

,guided 'missile *c.n* kind of rocket(2) that can be directed towards its target(1) after being fired, usu by radio or electronic(2) means.

,guided 'tour *c.n* = conducted tour.

'guide,lines *pl.n* general points or rules that act as guides(4) on what to do but that do not contain details: *The Government has published new guidelines on claiming unemployment benefit(2).*

guild /gɪld/ *c.n* (with capital **G** in names) (also (*old use*) **gild**) (title for an) organization, dating from the Middle Ages, of a group of people who have a particular skill or profession: *the Guild of Artists.*

,guild'hall *n* **1** *c.n* building with a hall in which a guild meets. **2** *def.n* (with capital **G**) town hall of the City of London.

guile /gaɪl/ *u.n* clever deceit, esp by hiding one's true intentions; cunning(1): *He used a lot of guile to get their agreement to his proposals.*

'guileful *adj* full of guile.

'guilefully *adv.* **'guilefulness** *u.n.*

'guileless *adj* showing, or appearing to show, a lack of guile: *The look he gave her was guileless but she felt that he was hiding something.*

'guilelessly *adv.* **'guilelessness** *u.n.*

guillotine /ˌgɪlə'ti:n/ *n* **1** *c/def.n* device once used in France for executing(1) criminals by cutting off their heads; a sharp blade fixed between two wooden posts falls onto the person's neck. **2** *c.n* machine with a blade used in a factory, an office etc for trimming (⇒ trim(3)) the edges of books, cutting paper etc. **3** *c/def.n* (in the British Parliament) way of getting a Bill approved by not letting it be discussed for too long a time (and so 'talked out' (⇒ talk s.t out)) and fixing a time for a vote to be taken on it: *The Government used the guillotine on the* debate(1) *and managed to get the Bill approved.* **send s.o to the guillotine** sentence s.o to be guillotined(4): *He was sent to the guillotine for the murder.*

▷ *tr.v* **4** execute (s.o) by using a guillotine(1): *He was guillotined for his part in the murder.* **5** trim(3) (the edges of a book), cut (paper etc), using a guillotine(2). **6** (in the British Parliament) shorten the time for (a discussion, debate(1) etc on a Bill[1](3)) by using a/the guillotine(3).

guilt /gɪlt/ *u.n* **1** (*law*) state or fact of s.o having broken the law, having committed a crime: *It is going to be difficult to prove her guilt as we haven't got enough* evidence(1). **2** blame or responsibility for having done s.t wrong: *They must take some of the guilt for the mistake as they were in charge.* **3** sense, feeling or showing of shame because one has done s.t wrong: *There was guilt all over his face when his mother asked about the broken vase.* Compare innocence.

'guiltily *adv* in a guilty(3) way.

'guiltiness *u.n.*

'guiltless *adj* (often — *of s.t*) not responsible for s.t wrong that has been done; innocent(1) (of any wrong-doing): *The government is not entirely guiltless in the matter.*

'guiltlessness *u.n.*

'guilty *adj* (-ier, -iest) **1** (often find s.o — (of s.t)) (*law*) (in a court of law, declare s.o as) having broken the law, having committed a crime: *He was found guilty of murder.* **2** (often — *of s.t*) responsible for having done (s.t) wrong: *He was guilty of not taking proper care of the children in his charge.* **3** having a sense or feeling of guilt(3): *I feel a bit guilty about not letting you know earlier.* (**find s.o**) (**not**) **guilty (of s.t)** (*law*) ((decide and) declare that one/s.o is) innocent(1)/guilty(1) (of a crime): *'How do you find the defendant?' 'Not guilty, My Lord.'*

guinea /'gɪnɪ/ *c.n* **1** (*written abbr pl* gns) (mainly *old use*) sum of money equal to one pound and one shilling (before 1971) or one pound five pence (after 1971); it was/is used for stating some prices for valuable objects, horses: *The horse cost him twenty thousand guineas.* **2** gold coin of this value.

'guinea ˌpig *c.n* **1** kind of animal like a small rat with usu golden or brown hair that is kept as a pet or sometimes used in scientific experiments. **2** person used in an experiment, to test certain new ideas etc: *My children are being used as guinea pigs for the government's educational plans.*

guise /gaɪz/ *c.n* (*formal*) **1** (often in/under the — of s.o) clothes, outward appearance (of s.o), esp in order to deceive: *He got into the military base in the guise of a general.* Compare disguise(1). **2** (often under a/the — of s.t) pretence (of saying, doing s.t etc): *Under the guise of being friendly, he managed to find out all he wanted to know.*

guitar /gɪ'tɑː/ *c.n* kind of musical instrument with a long neck and a hollow body with six or more strings stretched along it; it is played by plucking²(4) the strings, usu with one's fingers.

gulf /gʌlf/ *c.n* **1** (with capital **G** in names) (name for a) large area of sea, bigger than a bay², that is almost surrounded by land: *the Gulf of Mexico.* **2** very deep hollow space or gap, e.g in the earth:

When the earthquake came, it opened deep gulfs in the earth. **3** (often a wide etc — between s.o and s.o) (*fig*) very wide division(s) of opinion, feeling etc (between people): *There is a very wide gulf between their demands and what the employers are prepared to pay.*

gull¹ /gʌl/ *c.n* (also **'sea,gull**) kind of seabird with either black and white or grey and white feathers and webbed feet.

gull² /gʌl/ *tr.v* (often — s.o into, out of, s.t) cheat or deceive (s.o) (into doing s.t, by taking away s.t of value from her/him): *He was gulled into taking part in the robbery.*

ˌgulli'bility *u.n* state of being able or likely to be cheated or deceived: *He got most of his money by working on the gullibility of old people.*

'gullible *adj* showing gullibility.

'gullibly *adv.*

gullet /'gʌlɪt/ *c.n* tube that carries food from the mouth to the stomach: *He nearly* choked(4) *to death when a bone got stuck in his gullet.* **s.t sticks in s.o's gullet** (*fig; informal*) s.t that has happened, that s.o else has done etc, really annoys or angers s.o: *It sticks in my gullet that he's more successful than I am.*

gully /'gʌlɪ/ *c.n* (*pl* -ies) **1** small narrow channel(1) formed by rainwater flowing down a hill or mountain. **2** small narrow channel(1) specially made for carrying water, e.g from a building or a road.

gulp /gʌlp/ *c.n* **1** quick swallowing movement, or breathing in, made in the mouth and throat, e.g to get air, to take in food or drink, because one is afraid etc: *He gave a quick gulp when she appeared suddenly in front of him.* **2** (often — of s.t) amount or quantity (of s.t) that one swallows or breathes in quickly: *He took a gulp of air before he dived under the water again.* **at/in one gulp** (eating or drinking s.t) with only one swallowing movement: *He drank the coffee in one gulp.*

▷ *v* **3** *tr.v* (often — s.t down) swallow (s.t) quickly, with a gulp(1): *She gulped (down) her coffee and left.* **4** *intr.v* make a quick swallowing movement, esp through surprise, fear etc: *He gulped when he saw how much it would cost.*

gum¹ /gʌm/ *n* **1** *c/u.n* (example of a) kind of sticky substance that comes from the trunks of trees, stems of some plants etc. **2** *u.n* this substance, or one like it made from chemicals etc, used as a glue for sticking things, esp paper, together. **3** *c.n* (also **'gum,drop**) kind of hard or chewy(2) sweet: *fruit gums.* **4** *u.n* = chewing-gum.

▷ *tr.v* (-mm-) **5** (often — s.t to s.t; — s.t and s.t together) use gum¹(2) or glue to stick (s.t to s.t, two things together): *He followed the instructions and gummed one edge of the model castle to the other.* **gum s.t down/up** close s.t, e.g an envelope, a packet, by using gum¹(2). **gum up the works** (*fig; informal*) (**a**) make a machine fail to work because s.t has gone wrong, has blocked it: *A tiny piece of metal had gummed up the whole works.* (**b**) make a system or method of working or doing s.t not work or perform properly or at all, because of s.t one has done etc: *He's really gummed up the works with all his stupid ideas for improvements.*

'gum,boot *c.n* (often a pair of —s) kind of heavy rubber or plastic boot worn in wet weather, for walking on muddy ground etc; wellington boot.

'gum,drop *c.n* ⇒ gum¹(3).

'gumminess *u.n* fact or state of being gummy.

'gum-,tree *c.n* tree from which gum¹(1) can be got. **(be) up a gum-tree** (*fig*; *informal*) (be) in difficulties from which one cannot (see any way to) escape: *No job, no wife, no house — he's really up a gum-tree!*

'gummy *adj* (-ier, -iest) sticky; having gum¹(2) on it: *a gummy label.*

gum² /gʌm/ *c.n* (often *pl*; also *attrib*) the pink flesh in which teeth grow: *My gums are sore. I think I've got some kind of gum disease.*

'gum,boil *c.n* painful swelling or boil on the gum²(s).

gun /gʌn/ *c.n* **1** one of a number of different kinds of weapons (from which fire bullets or shells ⇒ grease. **jump the gun** (*fig*) do s.t before it is the right or correct time to do it or before anybody else can do it: *He jumped the gun and mentioned the meeting before it was official.* **stick to one's guns** (*fig*) not change one's opinions, statements etc (in spite of pressure to do so): *Through all the argument he stuck to his guns and refused to change his mind.*
▷ *tr.v* (-nn-) **2 gun s.o down** shoot s.o with a gun so that he/she falls to the ground: *The police officer was gunned down by the robbers.* **be gunning for s.o** (*fig*; *informal*) (be wanting to) attack, harm, get rid of, s.o, esp s.o who is in one's way, who has done s.t one does not like etc: *He's made so many mistakes that it's not surprising that the boss is gunning for him.*

'gun,boat *c.n* kind of small warship with a number of guns on it.

'gun ,carriage *c.n* carriage with two or more wheels on which a large gun is fixed.

'gun,fire *u.n* (sound made by the) firing of a gun or guns: *I could hear gunfire coming from across the valley.*

'gunman *c.n* (*pl* -men) criminal who carries and uses a gun.

'gunner *c.n* (*military*) **1** soldier or officer in an artillery(2) regiment(1). **2** lowest rank in an artillery(2) regiment(1), equal to a private in some other regiments.

'gunnery *u.n* (also *attrib*) science and practice of firing guns accurately: *gunnery practice.*

'gun,point *unique n* (**hold s.o, rob s.o** etc) **at gunpoint** (hold s.o, rob s.o etc) by pointing a gun at her/him and threatening to kill her/him if she/he does not do what she/he is told.

'gun,powder *u.n* kind of explosive(2) in the form of a powder.

'gun,runner *c.n* person who brings guns secretly into a country, esp to arm people who want to attack a government.

'gun,running *u.n* act of doing this.

'gun,shot *c.n* (also *attrib*) sound or act of firing a gun: *I heard gunshots and then two men ran past me. He was suffering from gunshot wounds.* **out of**, **within**, **gunshot** not in, within, the range(5) of a gun when it is fired.

'gun,smith *c.n* person whose job is to make or repair guns.

gunwale /'gʌnl/ *c.n* upper part of the side of a small boat or ship.

gurgle /'gɜːgl/ *c.n* **1** low bubbling(7) sound made

by a liquid, esp water, as it moves: *the gurgle of a stream flowing over rocks; the gurgle of water in the pipes.* **2** sound like this made by a person or baby, esp when he/she/it is happy: *a gurgle of laughter.*
▷ *intr.v* **3** make a gurgle(1): *The chemical gurgled as it was heated.* **4** (often — *with s.t*) (of a person or baby) make a gurgle(2), because of happiness etc: *The baby gurgled with pleasure.*

guru /'guːruː/ *c.n* (*pl* -s) **1** religious teacher in the Hindu(1) religion. **2** person who acts as a teacher or guide and whom people respect, esp in some subject or matter: *He's one of the leading gurus of modern political thought.*

gush /gʌʃ/ *c.n* (often — *of s.t*) **1** sudden quick flow (of a liquid, from s.t/s.w): *a gush of water; a gush of blood from a wound.* **2** sudden quick flow (of words); high degree (of interest, enthusiasm etc) but only for a short time: *He was unable to say anything when faced with her gush of words.*
▷ *intr.v* **3** (often — *from s.t*; — *out (of s.t)*) (of a liquid) flow in a gush(1) (from s.t or out (of s.t)): *Blood was gushing from the wound. When his axe hit the pipe, water gushed out (of it).* **4** (often — *about/ over s.o/s.t*) (*derog*) speak (about s.o/s.t), praise (s.o/s.t), with too much enthusiasm, in a way that is not sincere etc: *She's always gushing over our house and about how beautiful it is but then tells her friends how nasty it is.*

'gushily *adv* in a gushy way.

'gushiness *u.n* state or act of being gushy.

'gushing *adj* **1** (of water) flowing quickly and freely: *a gushing spring.* **2** (*derog*) (of a person, s.t one says) showing too much praise and in an insincere way: *I can't stand her gushing compliments(1).*

'gushy *adj* (-ier, -iest) (*derog*) (of a person) talking in too praising and insincere a way.

gust /gʌst/ *c.n* **1** (often — *of s.t*) sudden quick hard blow or rush (of wind, smoke etc): *A gust of smoke from the fire got in my eyes.*
▷ *intr.v* **2** (often — *to 40 kph etc*) (of a wind) suddenly blow hard and quickly for a short time: *The boat was caught in winds that were gusting to over 50 kilometres per hour.*

'gustiness *u.n* state of being gusty.

'gusty *adj* (-ier, -iest) (of a wind) blowing suddenly and quickly.

gusto /'gʌstəʊ/ *u.n* (often (**do s.t**) **with** (**great** etc) —) amount of energy(1), enthusiasm etc: *He started painting the house with great gusto but soon he was working more slowly.*

gut /gʌt/ *n* **1** *c.n* pipe or tube in the lower part of the body that carries food. **2** *u.n* thread like string made from the gut(1) of an animal and (sometimes) used as the strings of a violin, tennis racket etc. ⇒ catgut. **a gut feeling**, **reaction** etc (*informal*) a feeling/reaction(1) etc that one has as an instinct almost as though one's body feels, reacts etc: *I know you want to take part in the plan but my gut feeling is to have nothing to do with it.*
▷ *tr.v* (-tt-) **3** remove the guts(1) and other unwanted parts from (the body of an animal, a fish etc). **4** (esp of a fire) almost completely destroy (a house, building etc) so that only a part, e.g the walls, remain: *Fire completely gutted the factory.*

'gutless *adj* (*derog*; *informal*) (of a person, behaviour etc) not having, showing, any guts(3).

'gutlessness *u.n.*

guts *pl.n* **1** inside organs in the lower part of the body (gut(1), liver(1), kidneys(1), intestine etc). **2** (often *the* — *of s.t*) (*informal*) main or central part(s) (of s.t, e.g an engine, a problem): *You have to lift off this cover before you can get to the guts of the machine. We need to get to the guts of the problem before we can solve it.* **3** (often *have/show* (*a lot of* etc) —) (*informal*) courage and firmness, esp in the face of danger, harm to oneself etc: *I must admit he's got plenty of guts when it comes to a fight even if he almost always loses.* **hate s.o's guts** (*fig; informal*) hate s.o very much.

gutter /'gʌtə/ *n* **1** *c.n* open channel(1) or pipe at the bottom edge of a roof that collects and takes away rainwater. **2** *c.n* channel(1) at the side of a road or street where it meets the pavement or kerb and along which rainwater flows to the drains(1). **3** *def.n* (also *attrib*) poorest social conditions, parts of a city etc in which people live; unpleasant way of behaving or speaking in such conditions: *He came from the gutter though you wouldn't know it now. I would be grateful if you would stop using the language of the gutter* (or *gutter language*).

,gutter 'press *def.n* (*derog*) newspapers that have stories and articles about people's personal lives, esp the nastier parts of them.

guttersnipe /'gʌtəˌsnaɪp/ *c.n* (*derog*) poorly dressed, badly behaved etc child.

guttural /'gʌtərəl/ *adj* **1** (of a sound) formed in and produced from the throat. **2** (of a way of speaking) harsh(1) and unpleasant: *He spoke with a very guttural* accent(1).
▷ *c.n* **3** guttural(1) sound.

guv'nor /'gʌvnə/ *c.n abbr* (also **guv** /gʌv/) (*informal*) governor(3).

guy¹ /gaɪ/ *c.n* **1** (*informal*) man: *He's a great guy.* **2** (*informal*) person: *Could you guys help me with this box?* **3** figure of a man dressed in old clothes and burnt on Guy Fawkes Night. **wise guy** ⇒ wise.
▷ *tr.v* **4** imitate (s.o), esp in an attempt to make her/him look silly: *He walked behind the soldier, guying his every movement.*

Guy Fawkes Night /'gaɪ ˌfɔːks ˌnaɪt/ *unique n* (UK) night of 5 November when a guy¹(3) is burnt and fireworks are let off; it celebrates the occasion when Guy Fawkes and others failed to blow up the Houses of Parliament on 5 November 1605.

guy² /gaɪ/ *c.n* (also **'guy ˌrope**) one of the ropes that hold up a tent and its sides.

guzzle /'gʌzl/ *tr/intr.v* (*informal*) eat and/or drink (food, liquids) in a very greedy way: *Stop guzzling* (*your food*).

'guzzler *c.n* (*derog*) person who guzzles.

gym /dʒɪm/ *n* **1** *c.n* = gymnasium. **2** *u.n* (also *attrib*) school subject of physical(1) education or training: *We've got gym this afternoon. When's the next gym lesson?*

'gym ˌshoe *c.n* kind of light cloth shoe with rubber or plastic soles³(2), used in a gymnasium, for certain sports etc.

gymkhana /dʒɪm'kɑːnə/ *c.n* (*pl* -s) public sports competition, usu with horse riding, jumping etc.

gymnasium /dʒɪm'neɪzɪəm/ *c.n* (*pl* -s, **gymnasia** /dʒɪm'neɪzɪə/) (*abbr* gym) building or hall with different kinds of equipment(2) (ropes for climbing, wooden bars on the walls, vaulting horses etc) for learning or practising physical(1) exercises.

gymnast /'dʒɪmnæst/ *c.n* person who does, is skilled in, gymnastics.

,gym'nastic *adj* of or referring to gymnastics: *gymnastic exercises.*

,gym'nastically *adv.*

,gym'nastics *u.n* (also *attrib*) (different kinds of) physical(1) exercises for which one trains one's body, often as a sport, for competitions etc: *She won a gold medal in gymnastics* (or *in the gymnastics competition*).

gynaecology /ˌgaɪnɪ'kɒlədʒɪ/ *u.n* (US **,gyne'cology**) section of medicine that deals with the health of women, bearing of children etc.

gynaecological /ˌgaɪnɪkə'lɒdʒɪkl/ *adj* (US **,gyneco'logical**) of or referring to gynaecology: *a gynaecological operation.*

,gynaeco'logically *adv* (US **,gyneco-'logically**).

gynaecologist /ˌgaɪnɪ'kɒləˌdʒɪst/ *c.n* (US **,gyne'colo,gist**) doctor who specializes in gynaecology.

gypsy ⇒ gipsy.

gyrate /dʒaɪ'reɪt/ *intr.v* turn round and round (as though fixed) at/on one central point: *The spinning* (⇒ spin(8)) *object was gyrating on its* axis(1).

gyration /dʒaɪ'reɪʃən/ *c/u.n.*

gyroscope /'dʒaɪrəˌskəʊp/ *c.n* **1** device with a heavy wheel inside it that spins round and keeps the rest of the device steady in one position (used to keep a compass(1), instruments on an aircraft, a ship etc, steady). **2** child's toy like this, used for spinning.

gyroscopic /ˌdʒaɪrə'skɒpɪk/ *adj* of or referring to a gyroscope(1): *a gyroscopic* compass(1).

Hh

H, h /eɪtʃ/ *c/unique n* **1** 8th letter of the English alphabet. **drop one's h's** not pronounce the letter 'h' where it should be pronounced: *He's always dropping his h's like saying "at' instead of 'hat'.*
▷ *written abbr* **2** height. **3** hour.
▷ *symb* **4** (**H**) hardness of lead¹(3): *a 2H pencil.* ⇒ HB.

ha¹ /hɑː/ *interj* sound used to show that one has discovered s.t, that one has caught s.o doing s.t etc: *Ha! So that's where you are!*

,ha 'ha *interj* **1** sound used to show laughter: *Ha ha! That was a good joke!* **2** = ha¹.

ha² *written abbr* hectare(s).

habeas corpus /ˌheɪbɪəs 'kɔːpəs/ *u.n* (*Latin; law*) (often *a writ of* —) order for a person who is in prison to appear in a court of law, esp to decide whether he/she should be kept there.

haberdasher /'hæbə,dæʃə/ c.n **1** person who sells small articles such as pins, cotton, buttons etc used in making clothes etc. **2** (also **'haber-,dasher's**) shop in which such articles are sold. **'haber,dashery** u.n (also attrib) articles sold in a haberdasher's(2): She works in the haberdashery department of a large store.

habit /'hæbɪt/ n **1** c/u.n (example of) thing one does normally or regularly (and often cannot change easily): It was his habit to go for a walk every morning. Biting your nails is a very bad habit. It's just that habit that makes me get up early in the morning. **2** c.n set of clothes worn by a particular group of people, e.g monks and nuns or for a particular purpose, e.g for horse riding: a riding habit. **be in**, **fall/get into**, **the habit of doing s.t** be/get used to a (regular) way of doing s.t: I've got into the habit of catching the 9 o'clock train every day. Are you in the habit of taking things that don't belong to you? **creature of habit** (often derog) a person who cannot easily change the way he/she does things: He's a creature of habit and always has his lunch at exactly the same table in the restaurant he always goes to. **break a/the habit (of doing s.t)** stop doing s.t that has been a habit(1): Even on holiday I find it difficult to break the habit of getting up early. ⇒ kick a/the habit. **fall/get out of the habit (of doing s.t)** stop doing s.t that has been a habit(1): She's fallen out of the habit of visiting us when she's in town. **force of habit** ⇒ force(n). **have**, **fall/get into**, **bad habits** have, get, habits(1) that are not good for one: All this drinking and staying out late – you're getting into some really bad habits. **kick a/the habit** (informal) stop doing s.t that has become a (bad) habit: I can't kick the habit (of smoking). **make a habit of (doing) s.t** do s.t regularly: I make a habit of visiting her to see if she is all right.

'habit-,forming adj (esp of medicine, a drug(2) etc) that can become impossible to stop taking because one's body begins to need it (and is then very dangerous): These tablets can become habit-forming so don't take them for too long.

habitual /hə'bɪtjʊəl/ adj (usu attrib) **1** being s.o who does s.t (often s.t bad) as a habit(1): He's a habitual liar/smoker. **2** that is done regularly: He went for his habitual walk. **ha'bitually** adv.

habituate /hə'bɪtjʊ,eɪt/ tr.v (usu — oneself/s.o to (doing) s.t) (formal) cause (oneself/s.o) to get used to (doing) s.t: It is difficult to habituate them to the idea that work brings its own rewards.

habitué /hə'bɪtjʊ,eɪ/ c.n (often — of s.t) (French) person who regularly visits or goes to a place, e.g a restaurant, theatre etc: Habitués of this restaurant will know how good the food is.

habitable /'hæbɪtəbl/ adj (formal) (of a house or building) that can be lived in, is fit for living in: We can make the house habitable but only if we spend a lot of money. Opposite uninhabitable.

habitat /'hæbɪ,tæt/ c.n place and the surrounding conditions of nature, climate etc in which plants, animals etc normally live and develop: That plant's natural habitat is shady forest.

habitation /,hæbɪ'teɪʃən/ n **1** (formal) u.n act or state of living in a house, building etc: The houses are not suitable for habitation. **2** c.n (literary) house or building in which people are living: There were no habitations for miles around. **fit/unfit for human habitation** (of a house etc) suitable, not suitable, for people to live there.

hack¹ /hæk/ c.n **1** (often make a — in s.t; take a — at s.t) rough cut (in s.t, esp with a knife, axe etc): He made two hacks in the tree as a sign that it was ready to be cut down. **2** kick or cut on the leg (often done intentionally, e.g in a game like football): He got a hack on his leg when he was tackled²(3).

▷ v **3** tr.v cut (s.t) roughly (often into separate pieces): Stop hacking the meat like that; use a sharper knife. He hacked the branches into several smaller pieces. **4** tr/intr.v kick (s.o, s.o's leg) (often intentionally, e.g in a game): As the forward passed him he hacked him on the shin(1). **hack (away) at s.t** try (continually) to cut s.t with a knife, axe etc: He's been hacking away at those bushes for hours. **hack s.t down** cut s.t, e.g a tree, with an axe etc until it falls to the ground. **hack s.t off (s.t)** cut a piece of s.t roughly with a knife, axe etc from s.t: He hacked the branch off the tree. He hacked off a slice of meat. **hack one's way through s.t**; **hack a path through s.t** cut a path etc through s.t, e.g a forest, bushes etc. **hack s.o to death/pieces** kill s.o by stabbing (⇒ stab(v)), chopping (⇒ chop(v)), cutting etc her/his body several times: The man had been hacked to death. **hack s.t to bits/pieces** (a) cut s.t roughly into small bits/pieces. (b) (fig) severely criticize s.o's art, writing etc.

,hacking 'cough c.n rough cough that hurts one's throat.

'hack,saw c.n kind of saw for cutting metal.

hack² /hæk/ attrib.adj **1** dull and uninteresting: Why do I always get the hack jobs?

▷ c.n **2** (also attrib) (derog) person who works as a writer doing dull and uninteresting work often for very little pay: He's just a hack (writer) who will write anything you ask him to. **3** (often derog) horse that can be hired for riding and is often not very good.

hackles /'hæklz/ pl.n **1** short hairs on a dog's neck. **2** short feathers on a bird's, e.g a cock's, neck. **get/have one's hackles up** (a) (of a dog, bird) show that it is angry by having its hackles standing up. (b) (of a person) become angry/annoyed. **(make) its/s.o's hackles rise** (a) (make) the hackles (of a dog, bird etc stand up (because it is angry, afraid etc): The dog's hackles rose when it saw the stranger. (b) (fig) make s.o angry, annoyed: I dislike him so much that it makes my hackles rise if he comes anywhere near me.

hackney /'hæknɪ/ c.n (old use) carriage, pulled by a horse or horses, which can be hired.

'hackney ,cab/,carriage c.n **1** (old use) = hackney. **2** (formal name for a) taxi: This hackney carriage is licensed to carry six passengers.

hackneyed /'hæknɪd/ adj (of an expression, saying) too common, used too much, (and so having lost any real meaning or value): 'It's better late than never' is one of those hackneyed sayings you're always using.

hacksaw ⇒ hack¹.

had (strong form /hæd/, weak forms /həd/) p.t,p.p of have.

haddock /'hædək/ n (pl haddock(s)) **1** c.n kind

of fish found in the sea. **2** *u.n* flesh of this fish as food: *boiled haddock.*

hadn't /'hædnt/ = had not. ⇒ have.

haemoglobin /ˌhiːmə'gləubɪn/ *u.n* (US **ˌhemo'globin**) (*technical*) substance in blood that gives it its red colour.

haemophilia /ˌhiːməu'fɪlɪə/ *u.n* (US **ˌhemo-'philia**) (*medical*) inherited(2) disease found in a male person in which blood does not clot(3) or coagulate properly so that when such a person cuts himself he bleeds for a long time.

ˌhaemo'philiac *adj* (US **ˌhemo'philiac**) (*medical*) **1** of or referring to haemophilia.

▷ *c.n* **2** person who has haemophilia.

haemorrhage /'hemərɪdʒ/ *c/u.n* (US **'hemorrhage**) (*medical*) **1** (example of) bleeding a lot, esp from broken blood vessels.

▷ *intr.v* **2** bleed in this way: *Alexander started haemorrhaging after the operation.*

haemorrhoids /'heməˌrɔɪdz/ *pl.n* (US **'hemorˌrhoids**) (*medical*) (illness caused by) swollen veins in a person's bottom around the anus. ⇒ piles.

haft /hɑːft/ *c.n* (*formal*) wooden, steel etc handle of an axe, dagger etc. Compare shaft(2).

hag /hæg/ *c.n* (*derog*) ugly (old) woman who is usu also thought to be unpleasant: *She's an old hag who never has a kind word for anyone.*

haggard /'hægəd/ *adj* (of a person, s.o's appearance) showing signs of worry, tiredness etc, e.g with lines on the face, grey colour, red eyes: *You look a bit haggard; aren't you getting enough sleep?*

haggis /'hægɪs/ *c/u.n* (*pl* haggis(es)) (in Scotland) (example of a) kind of food made from the insides of a sheep (its heart, lung, liver(2)) and oatmeal and cooked in the skin of the sheep's stomach.

haggle /'hægl/ *intr.v* (often — (with s.o) about/ over s.t) argue (with s.o) about the contents of a contract(1) etc or the price of s.t one is selling or buying in order to get a better arrangement/ deal: *I haggled with him over (the price of) the carpet and finally I got it for £10 less.* Compare bargain(*v*).

ha ha ⇒ ha¹.

hail¹ /heɪl/ *n* **1** *u.n* drops of rain that become frozen and fall as small balls of ice: *the sound of hail hitting the iron roof.* **2** *c.n* (usu a — of s.t) (also *fig*) large number (of things) being thrown at or hitting s.o/s.t; large amount (of s.t) attacking s.o/s.t: *a hail of stones; a hail of abuse¹(1).*

▷ *v* **3** *intr.v* come down or fall from the sky as hail(1): *It was starting to hail as I left the house. It's hailing.* **4** *tr/intr.v* (often — (s.t) (down) on s.o; — s.t as s.o/ s.t)) (also *fig*) (cause (a number of things) to be thrown (at s.o/s.t): *They hailed stones down on us* (or *Stones hailed down on us*) *as we climbed. He hailed* abuse¹(1) *at me when I tried to calm him down.*

'hail,stone *c.n* single piece of hail(1).

'hail,storm *c.n* storm with hail(1).

hail² /heɪl/ *c.n* **1** (often *give s.o/s.t a —*) shout or call in order to attract s.o's/s.t's attention: *They gave the boat a hail but nobody on board took any notice.* **within hail** (*of s.o/s.t*) (being) close enough (to s.o/s.t) for a shout to be heard.

▷ *v* **2** *tr.v* shout or call to (s.o/s.t) to attract her/his/ its attention: *He hailed him from across the street.*

They hailed the boat but there was no answer. **hail a cab/taxi** (try to) get a cab(1)/taxi to stop for one in the street so that one can ride in it. **hail from s.w** (*formal*) be from a place (because one was born there, lives there or has travelled from there): *He hails from Manchester.* **hail s.o/ s.t as s.o/s.t** (*formal*) praise or recognize (s.o/ s.t) as being s.o/s.t very good: *They hailed him as the* saviour(1) *of their country. His discoveries were hailed as a great medical advance.* **within hailing distance** (**of s.o/s.t**) = within hail (of s.o/ s.t).

hair /heə/ *n* **1** *u.n* (all of the) very thin short or long pieces like thread that grow from the skin of people and some animals, esp the mass of these on the top of a person's head: *He has short dark hair. The hair on his chest was turning grey. She shaves the hair on her legs once a month. Our dog's hair needs regular brushing as it is so long.* Compare fur(1). **2** *c.n* single example of this: *There were hairs all over the bed from where the cat had been lying.* **cut, dry, wash etc one's/s.o's hair** cut etc the hair on the top of one's/s.o's head to make it look better, tidier, cleaner etc. **get in s.o's hair** (*fig; informal*) annoy s.o, esp by being present and demanding attention: *When he's home for a day he really gets in my hair asking me to do this and that when I've got a lot of my own work to do.* **have one's hair cut, dyed, permed etc** go to the hairdresser(2) who then cuts etc one's hair(1). **have one's hair done** go to a hairdresser(2) who washes and gives one's hair(1) a style: *I can't meet you till after lunch because I'm having my hair done in the morning.* **keep your hair on** (*fig; informal*) (request to) not lose one's temper, get annoyed etc: *Keep your hair on! There's no need to shout at me like that.* **let one's hair down** (*fig; informal*) behave in a free and easy way, talk freely about things esp after having had to behave more correctly, not having been able to talk freely. **lock of hair** ⇒ lock². **make s.o's hair curl** (*fig; informal*) (of s.t said, done etc) frighten or disturb s.o: *The story he told of how very wrong everything had gone was enough to make my hair curl.* **make s.o's hair stand on end** (*fig*) (of s.t seen, heard etc) frighten s.o greatly: *The dark shadows and the odd noises in the old house made their hair stand on end.* (**miss s.o**) **by a hair** = hair's breadth. **not harm a hair on s.o's head** (*fig*) not harm or hurt s.o in any way at all: *Though he's often a rough man he loves his daughter so much that he would never harm a hair on her head.* **not turn a hair** (*fig; informal*) show no fear or surprise at all (when s.t bad happens, when s.t is difficult etc): *She didn't turn a hair when he said they would have to climb up the cliff.* **split hairs** (*fig; derog*) (in a discussion etc) make very small unnecessary divisions about s.t; concern oneself with very unimportant differences between things: *You're always splitting hairs and making life difficult for yourself.* ⇒ hair-splitting. **tear one's hair** (**out**) (*fig; informal*) get very annoyed, upset etc (because of s.t wrong, a delay etc): *By the time I got there two hours later, he was tearing his hair* (out) *and swearing at everybody.*

'hair,brush *c.n* brush used to make hair tidy, smooth etc.

'hair,cut *c.n* act or style of cutting s.o's hair: *I need a haircut. Have you seen a haircut that you'd like?* **get/have a haircut** have s.o, usu a hairdresser, cut, style etc one's hair. **give s.o a haircut** cut or style s.o's hair.

'hair,do *c.n* (*pl* hairdos or hairdo's) (*informal*) (esp of a woman's hair) act or fact of having one's hair arranged in a particular style or way: *I like your new hairdo; where did you get it done?*

'hair,dresser *c.n* **1** person whose job is to cut, arrange, colour etc a person's, esp a woman's, hair. **2** (also **'hair,dresser's**) place where this is done. Compare barber.

'hair,dressing *u.n* art or profession of cutting, arranging etc people's hair.

'hair-,drier, **'hair-,dryer** *c.n* electrical device that dries wet hair by blowing hot air on and through it. ⇨ drier, dryer (⇨ dry).

-haired *adj* having hair of the colour, length etc shown by the first part of the word: *dark-haired*; *long-haired*; *curly-haired*.

'hair-,grip *c.n* (also **'hair-,clip**) thin metal clip(1) used to hold (a piece of) long hair in place.

'hairiness *u.n* fact or state of being hairy.

'hairless *adj* having no hair (on one's head, body etc).

'hair,line *attrib.adj* **1** very fine, thin, narrow: *The X-ray showed a hairline fracture(1) of the knee. Hairline cracks were beginning to form in the houses near the railway line.*

▷ *c.n* **2** line along the top of the forehead where one's hair starts.

'hair,piece *c.n* piece of false or natural hair put on a (man's) head to cover bald(1) parts etc.

'hair,pin *c.n* **1** thin piece of wire bent into a U shape and used to hold (a woman's) hair in place. **2** (also **,hairpin 'bend**) very sharp bend like a U in a road (esp on hills or mountains).

'hair-,raising *adj* (*fig*) (of s.t said, done etc) very frightening: *He told us a hair-raising story about his escape from the earthquake.*

'hair's-,breadth *c.n* (often *miss* (s.o/s.t) *by a* —) (of s.t thrown, falling, moving etc) very small or narrow amount in distance: *He threw a brick at me and it only missed* (*me*) *by a hair's-breadth.*

'hair-,slide *c.n* decorated hair-grip used for keeping hair in place.

'hair-,splitting *u.n* act or state of splitting hairs (⇨ hair).

'hair,style *c.n* way one's hair is cut, arranged etc: *Do you like my new hairstyle?*

'hairy *adj* (-ier, -iest) **1** (of a person or animal) having a lot of hair on one's/its body or face (but not referring to the hair on a person's head): *He has very hairy arms.* **2** (*informal*) very frightening; hair-raising: *The journey down the river was even hairier than the journey up.*

hake /heɪk/ *n* **1** *c.n* (*pl* hake(s)) kind of fish found in the sea. **2** *u.n* flesh of this fish as food.

halcyon days /ˌhælsɪən 'deɪz/ *pl.n* (*formal*) length of time when everything is/was pleasant, calm etc, esp when remembered afterwards: *He keeps talking about the halcyon days of his youth when things, he says, were much better than now.*

hale /heɪl/ *adj* **hale and hearty** (of an older person) fit and healthy: *For all his age he's very hale and hearty.*

half /hɑːf/ *attrib.adj* **1** that is (equal to) one of two equal parts that make the whole: *a half bottle of wine* (i.e a bottle that is half(3) the size of an ordinary one); *a half mile/hour/dozen. We were given a half chicken each.* Compare half(3). **2** not quite; not complete: *There was a half smile on his face. I'm tired of your half answers.* **3** (usu — a/ *the s.t*) (equal to only) one of two (almost) equal parts (of s.t): *half a bottle of wine* (i.e. a bottle that contains only one half(6) of the normal quantity); *half a mile; half an hour; half the cost; half the audience. I can only eat half that amount. Jack finished in half the time allowed. The work won't take more than half a day.* (Notice 'half' is called a predeterminer when it is placed before a determiner such as 'a', 'the', 'his' etc, e.g *half an apple.*) Compare half(1). (**be**) **half the battle** ⇨ battle(*n*). **one, two** etc **and a half** one, two etc wholes and one half(6) of a whole: *one and a half cups; six and a half bottles; an hour and a half wait* (= 90 minutes). ⇨ half(8).

▷ *adv* **4** being, having, containing, only one half(6): *The swimming-pool was half empty/full. He's half Irish and half English.* **5** to a certain extent but not completely; partly: *This meat is only half cooked; put it back in the oven. Peter was half dead when he came home from his tennis match. I had been half expecting him not to come to the party.* **half and half** having two equal parts of two different things; divided into two equal parts or shares: *When making this drink, use orange and lemon – about half and half. Can we go half and half on the bill?* (i.e each of us pays one half(6) of the cost). ⇨ go halves (⇨ half(*n*)). **half past one, two** etc (**a**) (the act of) dividing 2 etc into two equal parts: *Half 6 is 3.* (**b**) (*informal*) (the time is) half past two (2.30) etc: *See you at half seven then.* **Not half!** (*informal*) Very much (so)!: *'Do you like it?' 'Not half!'* **not half as bad, ill** etc **as** (expected etc) not bad, ill etc by very much. **not half bad** ⇨ bad(*adj*). **not half s.t** (*informal*) (used to add force to the way s.o feels or does s.t) very greatly s.t; in a very determined way: *He wasn't half angry with her when she didn't come. She didn't half complain when things went wrong.*

▷ *c.n* (*pl* halves /hɑːvz/, halfs) **6** one or other of the two equal parts that make a whole or into which s.t can be divided equally: *two kilos and a half* (2½ kg); *a year and a half; a mile and a half; one half of the audience; join two halves together to make a whole. Half of it was gone by the time I arrived.* **7** (in certain games, e.g football) one of the two equal lengths of time into which a match is divided with a break in the middle for a rest and to change ends: *Arsenal scored two goals in the first half.* **8** ticket that is half(1,3) the value or cost of an ordinary ticket, e.g on a bus or train for a child below a certain age: *One and two halves to Victoria, please.* ⇨ half-fare. **9** thing that is half(1,3) the size, amount, quantity etc (of a normal or usual size etc): *Two halves of beer, please* (i.e two glasses with half(3) a pint of beer in each). **10** = half-back. **one's/s.o's better/other half** (*informal*; *joking*) one's/s.o's husband, wife. (**do s.t**) **by halves** (do s.t) not very well, in an incomplete way: *You'll never succeed if you always do things by halves.* **go halves** (**in/ on s.t**) (**with s.o**) share (the work, cost etc of s.t) equally (with s.o): *Let's go halves on the bill.*

⇒ half and half (⇒ half(*adv*)). **in(to)** *half/halves* (of s.t cut or divided) in(to) two equal parts or shares: *He cut the lemon into halves and gave her one.* **too clever by half** ⇒ clever.

half- *adj* **1** being or having one of the two equal parts: *a half-kilo/*pint(2)*/pound.* **2** being only partly or incompletely: half-hearted. **3** (also *adv*) (happening) at every half-(hour etc): *Boats leave for the island half-hourly. We have half-weekly meetings to discuss any problems.*

'half-₁back *c.n* (in some games) player whose position is between the forwards(*n*) and the backs(19).

₁half 'baked *adj* (of a person, belief, idea etc) not very sensible; rather stupid: *Most of his ideas are half-baked so don't pay any attention to them.*

₁half 'board *u.n* (also *attrib* **'half-₁board**) price of staying in a hotel etc that includes breakfast and one other meal. Compare full board (⇒ full).

'half-₁brother *c.n* brother who has only one parent the same as his brother(s) and/or sister(s), e.g because one parent has married again. Compare stepbrother.

'half-₁caste *c.n* (do not use!) person whose parents are of different races (esp in the colour of their skin).

₁half-'cock *u.n* **go off (at)** *half-cock* (*informal*) (of a plan etc) not do very well, not succeed, usu because it is not properly prepared: *Most of his ideas go off at half-cock simply because he doesn't plan them well enough.*

'half-₁day *c.n* (also *attrib*) job when one works for only half a day, i.e in the morning or in the afternoon: *a half-day job* (a job that one has for mornings or afternoons only and not a full-time job): *I have a half-day on Wednesday so I could come for tea then.* ⇒ half(3).

₁half-'dozen *c.n* (*pl* half-dozens) (also **₁half a 'dozen**)(*cardinal number*) six: *a half-dozen eggs* (or *half a dozen eggs*).

₁half-'fare *adj/c.n* (also *attrib*) (travelling with a) ticket that is half(1,3) the cost of a normal ticket, esp for a student or a child below a certain age: *My children still go half-fare on the buses. The railway company is offering half-fare concessions(3) to senior citizens.* ⇒ half(8).

₁half-'hearted *adj* (of s.t one does) not showing or having great interest, will etc: *His attempts to get work were a bit half-hearted.*

₁half-'heartedly *adv.* **₁half-'heartedness** *u.n.*

₁half-'holiday *c.n* part of a day, usu in the afternoon, when one does not work or go to school: *I took a half-holiday to go and see my aunt.* ⇒ half-day.

₁half-'hourly ⇒ half(3).

₁half-'mast *u.n* (usu *at* —) (of a flag) position in the middle of a flagpole usu because s.o important has died: *All flags were (flying) at half-mast as a sign of respect on the death of the King.*

₁half 'measures *pl.n* acts or attempts to do s.t that are not strong enough or are incomplete: *In this situation half measures will not work so you will have to arrest all those who took part and not just the leaders.*

₁half-'monthly ⇒ half(3).

₁half 'moon ⇒ moon¹.

'halfpence ⇒ halfpenny.

halfpenny /'heɪpnɪ/ *c.n* (*pl* -ies /'heɪpnɪz/,

halfpence /'heɪpəns/) (also **a half p** or **half a p**) (UK until 1985) (coin with a) value of one half of one penny (½p): *three halfpenny coins; ten and a halfpence* (10½p).

₁half-'price *adj/adv* (costing or sold for) one half(6) of the price.

'half-₁sister *c.n* sister who has only one parent the same as her sister(s) and/or brother(s), e.g because one parent has married again. Compare stepsister.

₁half 'term *c.n* (**'half-₁term** when *attrib*) holiday of a few days or a week in the middle of a school term: *I've got a lot of homework to do during the half-term holidays.*

₁half 'time *u.n* (**'half-₁time** when *attrib*) short length of time in the middle of a game or match when players have a rest: *When half time came there was still no score. The half-time whistle blew just when he thought he was going to score.* ⇒ half(7).

₁half-'truth *c.n* something said that is partly true but not completely (often because s.o wants to hide s.t).

₁half'way *adv/adj* (happening) at a point that is exactly/nearly at the middle of the distance or time etc between two points: *They met at a halfway point in their travels. He was halfway through the job when he was told to stop.* **meet s.o halfway** (*fig*) (in trying to reach an agreement) accept things from s.o in return for her/him accepting some things from oneself: *I'm prepared to meet you halfway because that's the only way we'll settle this matter.*

₁half-'weekly ⇒ half-(3).

'half₁wit *c.n* (*derog*) person who behaves stupidly.

₁half'witted *adj* (of s.o, s.o's behaviour) stupid.

₁half-'yearly ⇒ half-(3).

halve /hɑːv/ *tr.v* **1** divide or cut (s.t) into two equal parts: *She halved the apple and gave him one piece.* **2** make (s.t) smaller by (about) a half(6): *The company has halved the number of its workers. We must find ways of halving our costs.*

halves *pl* of half(*n*).

halibut /'hælɪbət/ *n* (*pl* halibut(s)) **1** *c.n* kind of large flatfish found in the sea. **2** *u.n* flesh of this fish as food.

halitosis /₁hælɪ'təʊsɪs/ *u.n* fact or state of having bad breath.

hall /hɔːl/ *c.n* **1** passage or area behind the front door of a house or flat with doors to rooms and sometimes a staircase to other floors etc. **2** (large room in a) building in which public or private meetings can be held: *a church hall; the town/village hall.* **3** (UK) (with capital **H** in names) (name for a) large house in the country: *He has just bought Batty Hall.*

₁hall of 'residence *c.n* building with rooms in it in which students at a university etc live.

'hall₁way *c.n* = hall(1).

hallelujah /₁hælɪ'luːjə/ ⇒ alleluia.

hallmark /'hɔːl₁mɑːk/ *c.n* **1** special mark put on gold and silver objects to show the quality of the gold or silver used, where the object is made etc. **the hallmark of s.o/s.t** (*fig*) thing that shows the value or quality of s.o/s.t: *One hallmark of a good politician is his ability to influence people. The robbery had the hallmarks of a well-planned job.*

▷ *tr.v* **2** put a hallmark(1) on (s.t): *The silver vase had been hallmarked at Birmingham.*

hallo /hæˈləʊ/ *c.n* (also **helˈlo, hulˈlo**) (*pl* -s) **1** (use of this word as a) greeting: *After we had said our hallos we had a long talk.*

▷ *interj* **2** (word spoken as a greeting when meeting s.o, to attract s.o's attention etc): *'Hallo! I haven't seen you around for some time.' 'Hallo! You there! Could you help me with this suitcase?'*

hallow /ˈhæləʊ/ *tr.v* (*formal*) make (s.t) holy.
ˈhallowed *adj* that has been made holy or very special: *hallowed ground* (e.g around a church); *hallowed memories.*

Halloweˈen /ˌhæləʊˈiːn/ *unique n* (also *attrib*) night of 31 October when ghosts(1) and witches(1) are said to appear so children dress in funny clothes, play tricks on people, ask for sweets etc.

hallucinate /həˈluːsɪˌneɪt/ *intr.v* see things that are not actually there (because one's mind is disturbed, because one has taken drugs(2) etc).
hallucination /həˌluːsɪˈneɪʃən/ *c/u.n* (example of the) act of doing this.
hallucinatory /həˈluːsɪnətrɪ/ *adj* being in, producing, this state: *hallucinatory drugs(2).*

hallway ⇒ hall.

halo /ˈheɪləʊ/ *c.n* (*pl* -(e)s) **1** circle of light painted around the head of a person in a religious picture to show that he/she is very holy, a saint(1) etc. **2** circle of light sometimes seen around the sun or moon.

halt /hɔːlt/ *c.n* (*formal*) **1** complete stop after moving, walking etc: *There was a halt in the march because of the crowds.* **2** (name of a) very small railway station (usu in the country). **call a halt (to s.t)** (agree to) stop ((doing) (s.t): *We need to call a halt to the arms race.* **come to a halt** stop (often suddenly or unexpectedly): *The train came to a halt just outside the station.* **grind to a halt** ⇒ grind(*v*).

▷ *tr/intr.v* **3** (cause (s.o/s.t) to) stop: *The strike has halted car production. The train halted outside the station.*
ˈhalting *attrib.adj* (of s.o's speech) showing hesitation: *He spoke in a halting voice.*

halter /ˈhɔːltə/ *c.n* rope put around the head of a horse etc and used to lead or guide it.
ˈhalterˌneck *adj* **1** (of a dress etc) having a piece of material that goes around the neck holding the dress up and leaving the shoulders and back bare: *a halterneck blouse.*

▷ *c.n* **2** style of a dress, blouse etc that allows the shoulder and back to be bare because it is held up by a piece of material that goes around the neck: *My new evening dress has a halterneck.*

halve(s) ⇒ half.

ham /hæm/ *n* **1** *c.n* top part of a pig's leg that has been salted, smoked and dried for food. **2** *u.n* (also *attrib*) piece or slice of this as food: *a slice of ham; a ham sandwich.* **3** *c.n* (*informal*) actor/ actress who is not very good, esp because he/ she acts in an exaggerated way. **4** *c.n* (also **ˈradio ˌham**) (*informal*) person who operates a radio in her/his own home as a hobby to send and receive messages.

▷ *tr/intr.v* (-mm-) **5** (often — (s.t) *up*; — *it up*) act (a part in a play etc) badly, in an exaggerated way: *Whoever played Hamlet really hammed it* (*up*).

ˌham-ˈfisted/-ˈhanded *adj* awkward and clumsy(1) when using one's hands: *He's so ham-fisted that he makes a mess of every job.*

hamburger /ˈhæmˌbɜːgə/ *c.n* flat round piece of minced meat that is fried or grilled and often eaten in a bread roll.

hamlet /ˈhæmlɪt/ *c.n* very small village with only a few houses and no church.

hammer /ˈhæmə/ *c.n* **1** tool with a handle and a metal head used for hitting nails into wood, breaking things etc. Compare mallet. **2** piece of metal in a gun that hits the cap of a bullet etc and makes it explode. **3** piece of wood or metal in a piano that hits a string and so makes a musical note. **4** (*sport*) heavy metal ball at the end of a wire that is swung round and round and then thrown as far as possible. **5** wooden mallet used by an auctioneer(1) when selling things. **be/ come under the hammer** (*fig*) (of an object) be/ become ready to be sold in an auction(1). **hammer and tongs** (*fig*) very fiercely: *The two men were still going at it, fighting, hammer and tongs when the police arrived.*

▷ *v* **6** *tr.v* (often — s.t *in*(to s.t)) hit (a nail etc) in(to wood etc) with a hammer(1) or s.t like it: *It took just a couple of blows to hammer the nail in* (*to the wood*). ⇒ hammer s.t into s.t, s.o's head. **7** *intr.v* (often — *at* s.t) hit s.t with one's fist, a stick etc (to attract attention, to break it etc): *Tom had been hammering at the door for five minutes before anybody heard him.* **8** *tr.v* (*fig; informal*) beat (s.o) in a fight or a game: *Our team was hammered by the other side (and we lost)* 7–0.
hammer away at s.t (*fig*) continue trying to work on, solve, s.t (e.g a problem): *Shelley hammered away at her father until he agreed to pay for her studies.* **hammer s.t home (to s.o)** (*fig*) (try continually to) make s.o understand or realize the importance of s.t: *How do we hammer home* (*to them*) *the message that they will fail if they do not work harder for these examinations.* **hammer s.t into s.o, s.o's head** (*fig*) (try to) make s.o learn s.t by continual pressure or repetition(⇒ repeat(2)): *His mother spent hours hammering the French verbs into him* (or *his head*). **hammer s.t out** (*fig*) reach a decision or agreement about s.t after a lot of discussion and argument: *The new arrangements were hammered out between the management and the workers during several meetings.*

hammock /ˈhæmək/ *c.n* long piece of canvas(1) or net that is hung between two trees or uprights for sleeping/resting on (esp in a ship or garden).

hamper¹ /ˈhæmpə/ *c.n* large basket with a lid used for food, esp for a picnic(1): *a hamper of different kinds of special food and fruit.*

hamper² /ˈhæmpə/ *tr.v* make difficulties for (s.o, her/his free movement); block or get in the way of (s.o/s.t): *The police were hampered by the large crowds in their attempt to catch the thief.*

hamster /ˈhæmstə/ *c.n* kind of small animal like a rat, often kept as a pet.

hamstring /ˈhæmˌstrɪŋ/ *c.n* **1** kind of muscle (tendon) at the back of the leg: *The person who was expected to win the marathon(1) strained¹(6) a hamstring and had to stop running.*

▷ *tr.v* (*p.t,p.p* hamstrung /ˈhamˌstrʌŋ/) **2** (*fig*) make (s.o) unable to do s.t properly: *The new government rules have hamstrung our business so we'll have to close down.*

hand /hænd/ *n* **1** *c.n* part of the body at the end of the arm including the palm¹(1), fingers and thumb: *He writes with his left hand.* **2** *sing.n* (*fig*) applause: *He asked for a hand to welcome the singer.* ⇒ give s.o a (big) hand (⇒ hand(*n*)). **3** *c.n* person who does certain kinds of work with her/his hands esp in a factory, on a ship etc: *a factory hand. The farm needs extra hands at this time of year to help with planting. All hands on deck!* (i.e an order for all the people who work in a ship to go up on deck). **4** *c.n* pointer on a clock, watch etc that moves round to show the time: *the second/minute/hour hand.* **5** *c.n* (set of playing cards dealt to s.o in one) round of a card game: *I didn't have one good hand all night. Let's have one more hand before we stop.* **6** *c.n* unit for the measurement of the height of a horse from the ground to the top of its shoulder (1 hand = 4 inches(1) (about 10 cm)): *a horse of 15 hands.* **7** *c.n* help or assistance asked for from s.o or given to s.o: *Do you need a hand to move the cupboard?* ⇒ give/lend (s.o) a (helping) hand. **a dab hand at (doing) s.t** ⇒ dab(*adj*). **ask for s.o's hand (in marriage)** (*old use*) ask permission to marry s.o: *The young man asked him for his daughter's hand.* **at second, third** etc **hand** (of information) passed on by, received from, two or more people in turn. Compare second-hand. **at s.o's hands** from or by the actions of s.o (when one is in her/his power): *She suffered a lot at the hands of the soldiers who arrested her.* **a bad, good** etc **hand at (doing) s.t** person who is bad, good etc at (doing or making) s.t: *He's a great hand at decorating the house.* **bare hands** ⇒ with bare hands. **(be, become, get** etc**) out of hand** (be etc) not controlled, without order etc: *The crowd got out of hand and started burning cars and breaking shop windows.* Compare out of hand(b). **be in good hands** (of a person, a job etc) be the responsibility of s.o who is very good at doing s.t, looking after s.o/s.t: *If you send your children to this school, you will know that they will be in good hands.* **be in s.o's hands** be s.o's responsibility: *The matter is not in my hands so I can't do anything to help you.* ⇒ be out of s.o's hands. **(be) off s.o's hands** (esp of a daughter, son etc) (be) no longer s.o's responsibility (because he/she is an adult, has left home etc): *We can enjoy ourselves now that the children are off our hands. I'll be glad to get them off my hands for a couple of weeks.* **be out of s.o's hands** be no longer s.o's responsibility: *I'm afraid the matter is out of my hands and you will have to talk to my boss about it.* ⇒ be in s.o's hands. **bind/tie s.o hand and foot** (a) tie s.o with ropes etc around the arms, hands, legs and feet so that he/she cannot move. **(b)** (*fig*) (usu passive) make s.o not able to give help because of rules, other promises etc. **by hand** (a) using one's hand(s): *This device operates by hand.* **(b)** in handwriting, not typed or printed: *He writes his stories by hand first and then gets them typed.* **(c)** (of a letter, parcel etc) sent or delivered by a person directly (and not in the post etc): *This letter must go to their office by hand.* **change**

hands (of an object, house etc) move from the ownership of one person to that of another: *This painting has changed hands many times over the last fifty years.* **(close/near) at/to hand** (a) near (the position of the speaker or writer): *There are some quite good shops close at hand.* **(b)** (esp of help) soon to come; present and of use: *Help was near at hand in the form of a mountain rescue team. I'll be close to hand in case you need me.* **come/fall into s.o's hands** be caught or found by s.o: *He fell into the hands of his enemies. The secret plans came into their hands by accident.* **eat out of s.o's hand** (*fig*) do whatever s.o tells one to do because one wants to please her/him, because he/she has control over one etc: *Now that I know all about his past I'll have him eating out of my hand.* **force s.o's hand** make s.o do s.t that he/she does not want to do or is delaying doing: *The best way to force their hands is to stop lending them any more money.* **gain/get/have the upper hand (over s.o)** ⇒ upper hand (⇒ up). **get/go down on one's hands and knees (to s.o, to do s.t)** (a) kneel in order to work, look for s.t, on the floor: *We all got down on our hands and knees to look for her earring.* **(b)** (*fig*) beg (s.o) (for s.t): *He went down on his hands and knees to his brother for the money he needed to pay his debt.* **get one's hands on s.o** (*informal*) (try to) find (and attack) s.o, esp s.o who has done s.t wrong: *If I ever get my hands on him, he won't know what has hit him.* **get one's hands on s.t** (want to) have and use s.t: *I'd like to get my hands on that new computer but it's expensive.* ⇒ hands-on. **get/keep one's hand in** learn/practise a skill/ability in order to do s.t, esp a sport or game, well: *Golf(1) is a difficult game and you need to keep your hand in to play well.* **(get) out of hand** ⇒ (be, become, get etc) out of hand(a). **give/lend (s.o) a (helping) hand** help (s.o): *You can rely on Anne; she's always around to lend a helping hand.* ⇒ hand(7). **give s.o a (big) hand** (*informal*) applaud, clap(3) for, s.o: *Wasn't that a great act? Let's give them a big hand.* ⇒ hand(2). **give s.o, have, a free hand (in/with s.t)** ⇒ free(*adj*). **hand in glove with s.o** (*fig*) very closely with s.o: *The city council is working hand in glove with employers who are willing to train young people in a job.* **hand in hand** (a) (of two people walking, moving etc) with one person holding the hand of the other in her/his hand: *They walked down the street hand in hand.* **(b)** (*fig*) (of two things) happening, acting, being connected, with each other: *Poverty and crime are often thought to go hand in hand.* ⇒ (work) hand in hand (with s.o). **hand over fist** (*fig*) (get money, wealth etc) in large quantities (and often very quickly): *His books sell so well that he must be making money hand over fist.* **Hands off!** ⇒ (keep/take one's) hands off (s.o/s.t). **Hands up!** ⇒ (put one's) hands up. **have a hand in s.t** (*fig*) be one of a number of people who are doing or have done s.t: *Did you have a hand in getting the decision changed?* **have one's hands full** (*fig*) be very busy, have many things to do: *She had her hands full, what with doing her job, running the house and looking after the children.* **have s.t in hand** (a) be dealing with s.t: *I have the matter well in hand and will give you my decision shortly.* **(b)** have s.t extra (that one is saving or still has after using some of it): *We still have a few supplies in hand so we won't run short yet. Manchester United has the same number of points as Liverpool but it has a game in hand.* **have s.o/s.t on one's hands** have s.o/s.t for whom/which one is responsible. **join hands (with s.o)** hold s.o's hand or hands. **(keep/take one's) hands off (s.o/s.t)** (order to) not touch (s.o/s.t): *Keep your hands off me or I'll call the police. Hands off (the food)!* **lay one's hands on s.o** = get one's hands on s.o. **lay one's hands on s.t** (often negative) (be able to) find or discover s.t: *I know I put the papers somewhere but I can't lay my hands on them just at the moment.* **lend (s.o) a hand (with s.t)** = give/ lend (s.o) a (helping) hand. **an old hand (at s.t)** ⇒ old hand (⇒ old). **on hand** available, ready to be used or to do s.t if needed: *I always keep a few tins on hand in case we have guests suddenly for dinner. I'll be on hand in case you need me.* **(on the one hand) . . . (and/but) on the other (hand)** (expression used to present) first one point of view or argument and then another one that is opposite or different: *(On the one hand) if we go abroad for our holidays we'll have good weather but on the other hand it will be much more expensive than staying at home.* **out of hand (a)** ⇒ (be, become, get etc) out of hand. **(b)** immediately and without waiting or getting permission: *At that time anyone found in town after dark was arrested out of hand.* **play into s.o's hands** (do s.t that will) let s.o gain an advantage over one: *He played right into their hands when he started selling shares in the company.* **(put one's) hands up** (order to) put one's hands in the air. **rub one's hands (a)** keep one's hands warm by rubbing them together. **(b)** (*fig*) show that one is happy, satisfied. **shake hands (with s.o)**; **shake s.o's hand**; **shake s.o by the hand** take hold of s.o's (right) hand with one's own (right) hand and move them up and down, usu as a greeting, when leaving or as a sign of agreement, congratulation, friendship etc: *Though I had never seen him before, he came up and shook me by the hand and told me he agreed with everything I had said. Now that you've settled your quarrel, why don't you shake hands and forget about it?* **show one's hand** (*fig*) make known what one intends to do (after having kept it hidden): *He kept us guessing for some time before he showed his hand and told us he was buying the company.* **a show of hands** ⇒ show(*n*). **stay one's hand** (*formal*) not do what one was intending to do. **take s.o/s.t in hand** (*fig*) look after, control and/or train s.o, an animal: *This young horse needs to be taken in hand now if you want to teach it to jump properly.* **take s.o's life in one's hands** ⇒ life. **throw in one's hand** (*fig*) decide not to continue doing s.t, fighting against s.o etc: *He saw he was losing the fight so he decided to throw in his hand.* **to hand** (*formal*) near to one; present: *I don't have the papers to hand at the moment so could you come back later?* **try one's hand (at s.t)** attempt to do s.t, esp for the first time: *Would you like to try your hand at fishing?* **turn one's hand to s.t** start to do s.t, esp s.t that needs skill or practice: *He's very skilled and can turn his hand to any job that needs to be done around the house.* **wait (up)on s.o**

(hand and foot) ⇒ wait(*v*). **wash one's hands of s.o/s.t** no longer wish to be responsible for s.o/ s.t: *When he started going around in bad company his parents washed their hands of him.* **win (s.t) hands down** win (a race, game etc) completely, very easily: *The other players were not very good so he won hands down.* **with bare hands** without the help of a weapon, tool: *He killed the snake with his bare hands.* **(work) hand in hand (with s.o)** (work) very closely together (with s.o).

▷ *tr.v* **8** (usu — *s.o.s.t*; — *s.t to s.o*) have or take (s.t) in one's hand(1) and give it (to s.o): *Hand me that book next to you. I handed her the parcel. Could you hand this to that man over there?*

hand s.t (a)round (to s.o) go (a)round (a group of people) and give s.t to each person in turn: *Your job at the party is to hand round the drinks (to everyone).*

hand s.o back to s.o/s.w (a) send or give s.o back to s.o or the place where he/she came from. **(b)** (*fig*) (in a radio or television broadcast) (after making a report in one place) return the listeners or viewers(1) back to the original person or place: *That completes my report on Belfast and I'm now handing you back to London.* **hand s.t back to s.o** return s.t to the person who had it before.

hand s.t down (to s.o) (*fig*) give s.t as a kind of inheritance (to one's children etc): *This painting has been handed down from father to son for the past two hundred years.*

hand s.t in (to s.o) carry s.t in one's hands, take it and give it (to s.o): *Your case has been found and handed in to the police. When the bell goes you must immediately stop writing and hand your examination papers in.*

hand s.t on (to s.o) pass s.t one has, or has been given, (to another person who in her/his turn may/will pass it to s.o else): *When you've read the report please hand it on to the next person.*

hand s.t out (to s.o) give or distribute (1) a number of things free (to a group of people): *The rescue workers were handing out food and clothing to the people who had lost their homes. They were handing out leaflets to people in the street.* ⇒ handout.

hand s.o/s.t over (to s.o) give or send s.o/s.t (to s.o so that he/she will look after her/him/it, take responsibility for her/him/it etc): *The thief was handed over to the police. Hand over the money or I'll shoot.*

hand s.t round (to s.o) = hand s.t out (to s.o).

(have to, must) hand it to s.o (*informal*) (have to) say or admit that s.o has done well, is good at doing s.t etc: *You must hand it to him, he didn't look as though he would succeed but he did in the end.*

'hand,bag *c.n* small bag that is carried in the hand (usu by a woman).

'hand ,baggage *u.n* (also **'hand ,luggage**) (small) bag(s) that can be carried in the hand (and so taken with one into a plane etc).

'hand,ball *u.n* game in which a ball is hit by players with their hands.

'hand,bill *c.n* (*old use*) small printed sheet of paper announcing s.t (and often given to people in the street etc). ⇒ handout.

'hand,book *c.n* (title for a short or small) book giving information about a subject, place etc: *A Handbook to the British Isles.*

'hand,brake *c.n* brake in a car etc that is operated by hand. Compare footbrake.

'hand,cart *c.n* small cart, usu with two wheels and two handles, pushed with the hands.

'hand,clap *c.n* act of clapping(⇒ clap(3)) with one's hands (usu to applaud s.o/s.t). **get, give s.o, a slow handclap** be given, give s.o, a slow regular handclap usu as a sign of displeasure from the audience.

'hand,cuff *c.n* **1** (usu *a pair of —s*) one of two metal rings joined by a chain that are fastened with a lock around the wrist(s) of s.o, esp a criminal to stop her/him escaping.
▷ *tr.v* **2** (often *— oneself/s.o/s.t to s.o/s.t*) put handcuffs(1) on oneself/s.o/s.t (and on s.o/s.t else to join the two together): *As a* protest(1) *she handcuffed herself to the railings outside the town hall.*

'handful *c.n* **1** (usu *— of s.t*) number or amount (of s.t) that can be held in one hand: *He took a handful of sweets and shared them among his friends.* **2** (usu *a — of people*) (*fig*) only a small number (of people): *They were expecting a large crowd but only a handful actually came to the meeting.* **be** (**quite, a bit of**) **a handful** (*fig*) (of one or more people or animals) be very lively(1) and so difficult to control: *Your children are a bit of a handful. I just don't know how you manage!*

'hand ,grenade *c.n* ⇒ grenade.

,hand'made *adj* made using one's hands or with tools in one's hands and not made by machines: *handmade shoes.* Compare machine-made, factory-made, ready-made(2).

'hand,out *c.n* **1** (sometimes *derog*) thing, e.g food, clothing or money, given free to s.o, esp s.o in need of it: *They were so poor they had to live on handouts from the local church.* **2** printed sheet or leaflet with information about s.t given to people free. ⇒ hand s.t out (to s.o).

,hand-'pick *tr.v* choose (s.o, a small number of people etc) very carefully from a larger group: *I must be allowed to hand-pick the people I need for this job.*

,hand-'picked *adj* (of a person, a number of people) chosen very carefully, e.g because he/she/they has/have certain skills.

'hand,rail *c.n* rail in a steep or dangerous place, e.g a staircase, path, bridge, that one can hold on to with one's hand to stop oneself falling etc.

'hand,shake *c.n* **1** act of shaking s.o by the hand. ⇒ shake hands (with s.o) at hand. **2** strength of this act: *a* limp(1)*/strong handshake.* **golden handshake** ⇒ gold.

'hands-,on *adj* (usu *— experience*) practical knowledge of s.t instead of knowing it/them only in theory(2): *There is nothing like hands-on experience to remove the mystery that surrounds computers in many people's minds.*

'hand,stand *c.n* (usu *do a —*) act of balancing on one's hands and lifting one's body up into the air with the feet straight up.

,hand-to-'hand *adv/adj* (often *— fighting*) with one's body close to s.o else's (and using only one's hands or weapons held in one's hands).

,hand-to-'mouth *adv/adj* (often *— existence*) very poor(ly) and without much money, which has all to be spent on simple necessities: *They*

live hand-to-mouth and never know whether they will have enough money to feed their children.

'hand,work *u.n* work done using one's hands and not machines. Compare handiwork.

'hand,writing *sing/u.n* (example of) writing with a pen, pencil etc: *I teach handwriting. Her handwriting is very clear.*

,hand'written *adj* (of a letter etc) written with a pen, pencil etc and not typed or printed: *The message was handwritten.*

handicap /'hændɪˌkæp/ *c.n* **1** thing that acts as a disadvantage to s.o or that prevents s.o from doing s.t: *His handicap is that he doesn't know how to manage people.* **2** disability in one's body or mind: *He has a slight* physical(1) *handicap in that one leg is shorter than the other. Her child was born with a* mental(1) *handicap.* **3** (in some sports, esp horse racing) disadvantage of some kind, e.g extra weight to carry, a longer distance to run, given to a stronger animal or person to make the competition more equal.
▷ *tr.v* (*-pp-*) **4** be/become a handicap(1) to (s.o): *He was handicapped by his lack of imagination.* **5** (in some sports etc) put a handicap(3) on (a horse or person): *Because it had already won two times, the horse was handicapped with extra weight.*

'handi,capped *adj* **1** (of a person) having a handicap(2): *He is* mentally/physically *handicapped.*
▷ *def.pl.n* **2** handicapped(1) people as a group: *a home for the* mentally *handicapped.*

handicraft, handiwork ⇒ handy.

handkerchief /'hæŋkətʃɪf/ *c.n* (also **hanky, hankie**) square or oblong piece of cloth used for blowing one's nose, drying one's eyes etc. Compare tissue(3).

handle /'hændl/ *c.n* **1** part of s.t that enables one to pick it up, hold it etc, in one's hand: *the handle of a cup; the handle of a frying pan.* **2** part of s.t that enables one to open/close, operate, it etc, with one's hand: *a door handle. Pull this handle to start the machine.* **fly off the handle** (*fig*) lose one's temper.
▷ *tr.v* **3** take and hold (s.o/s.t) in one's hands: *If I give you the baby will you promise to handle him carefully? Handle the box with care because it contains glasses.* **4** deal with, treat, manage, (s.o/s.t) (in a certain way): *He is not very good at handling people. He handled the situation very well.* **5** manage (a certain kind of business); sell and/or buy (certain kinds of things): *I need somebody to help me handle my accounts. He only handles modern paintings.* (**handle s.o/s.t**) **with kid gloves** ⇒ kid(*n*).

'handle,bars *pl.n* bar fixed above the front wheel of a bicycle or motorbike which the rider holds in her/his hands and uses for steering etc.

'handler *c.n* person who trains and looks after an animal, esp a dog: *The handler of a police dog.*

'handling *u.n* way s.t is dealt with or handled (⇒ handle(4)): *His handling of the situation was much admired.*

handmade, handout, handpick, hand-rail, handshake ⇒ hand.

handsome /'hænsəm/ *adj* **1** (usu of a man) attractive to look at, good-looking. **2** (*formal*) (of s.t done, given etc) generous: *a handsome* *gift. It was very handsome of him to forgive them.*

'handsomely *adv* in a handsome(2) way.

'handsomeness *u.n* fact or state of being handsome.

hands-on, handstand, hand-to-hand, hand-to-mouth, handwork, handwriting, handwritten ⇒ hand.

handy /'hændɪ/ *adj* (*-ier, -iest*) **1** (of an object, tool, machine etc) easy to use; useful for some purpose: *This is a very handy tool for various jobs around the house. Don't throw those boxes away because they will be very handy for storing things.* **2** (of a person) clever with her/his hands (in making or repairing things): *She's very handy and has done all the decorating in her house.* **3** (*pred*) (often *— for s.t*) (of an object, place etc) near and convenient (for s.t, some purpose): *The station is quite handy (or Our house is quite handy for the station*). **come in handy** be (likely to be) useful: *Those boxes will come in handy to store things in.* **have/keep s.t handy** have/keep s.t close and easy to use when needed: *We always had our raincoats handy when we went walking. I keep a number of reference books handy in case I want to check something in them.*

'handi,craft *c/u.n* (example of) work done using the hands and not a machine, e.g the making of small objects in wood, clay etc: *Wendy is skilled in many kinds of handicraft. The shop sold handicrafts made by local people.*

'handily *adv* in a handy(2,3) way.

'handiness *u.n* fact or state of being handy.

'handi,work *u.n* **1** work done using one's hands: *There was an exhibition(1) of the local children's handiwork in the village hall.* **2** (usu bad) thing done by s.o which is recognized as being typical of her/him: *This robbery looks like the Jones brothers' handiwork.*

'handy,man *c.n* (*pl -,men*) person who does small jobs, esp repairs, around the house either for pay or for herself/himself.

hang /hæŋ/ *def.n* **1** way in which s.t, esp material, a dress etc, falls naturally or hangs(3): *The hang of those curtains is not quite right; did you put them up properly?* **get/have the hang of s.t** (*informal*) (**a**) learn or begin to know how to use s.t: *I haven't got the hang of this computer at all!* (**b**) understand (the meaning of) s.t: *It was difficult to get the hang of what he was saying as he didn't express himself clearly.*

▷ *v* (*p.t,p.p* hung /hʌŋ/ except for (5)) **2** *tr.v* put (s.t) in a position above the floor or ground on a hook, rail etc: *Hang your coat in the cupboard. He hung the painting in the hall.* **3** *intr.v* (often *— from/on s.t*) be fixed (to s.t) above the floor or ground, sometimes with the lower part moving freely: *A rope was hanging from the wooden beam. This skirt doesn't hang very well — the hem(1) is not straight.* **4** *tr.v* fix (wallpaper(1)) to a wall with paste: *You haven't hung that paper straight.* **5** *tr/intr.v* (*p.t,p.p -ed*) kill (oneself/ s.o) or be killed, esp for having committed a crime, by having a rope put around one's neck and one's body dropped: *In Britain people used to hang (or used to be hanged) for murder. He used a rope to hang himself.*

be/get hung over (*fig; informal*) be suffering, suffer, a headache as a result of drinking too much alcohol: *I was very hung over when I woke up the next morning.* ⇒ hangover(1).

be/get hung up (**about/on s.t**) (*fig; informal*) be/become very concerned (and perhaps worried) (about s.t): *He's very hung up about money, or rather, his lack of it.* ⇒ hang-up .

hang about/around (*fig; informal*) wait or delay (when one should be doing s.t, hurrying etc): *If we hang about much longer we're going to miss the beginning of the film.* **hang about/around** (**s.o/ s.w**) (*fig; informal*) stay near (to s.o/s.w) in an idle way or because one wants to see s.o: *There was a group of youths hanging about (the town square) with nothing to do. I don't like the idea of him hanging about my daughter.*

hang back (**from (doing) s.t**) (*fig*) be unwilling or reluctant (to do s.t, move forward etc): *The fire was so hot that we all hung back (from it).*

hang behind (*fig*) stay, wait or delay, esp when others have moved forward or have left: *James hung behind after the others had gone in order to speak to his teacher in private.*

hang (s.t) by s.t hang(3) (s.t) using s.t as a support or having s.t by which it is fixed: *The climber was hanging by her fingers. Hang the door by its hinges(1).* **hang by a (single) thread** (*fig*) (of a person's life, a situation etc) be in a critical state: *His life was hanging by a single thread and even the doctors were starting to give up hope.*

hang down (from s.t) fall naturally (from a fixed point); be suspended(1) (from s.t): *Her hair was hanging down around her shoulders. Cobwebs hung down from the ceiling.* ⇒ hang(3).

hang fire ⇒ fire(*n*).

hang one's head (in shame) ⇒ head(*n*).

hang in the balance ⇒ balance(*n*).

Hang it all! (*fig; informal*) (expression used to show annoyance, displeasure etc about s.o/s.t): *Why is he interfering? Hang it all, I can finish the job without his help.*

hang off s.t have some part falling from s.t that is attached: *The door is hanging off its hinges(1).*

hang on (*fig; informal*) (**a**) wait (for s.o to do s.t); wait (to speak to s.o on a telephone): *Hang on a moment — I just want to get a stone out of my shoe. I'm afraid Mr Lewis is on the other phone. Do you want to hang on?* (**b**) (expression used to ask s.o to) stop for a moment while one considers what he/she has said or because one wants to correct her/him: *Hang on, that wasn't what I agreed to at all!* **hang on (in/with s.t)** (*fig; informal*) continue doing s.t, often without much interest or determination: *You'll just have to hang on in your present job as there aren't any others around.* **hang on s.t** (*fig*) (of a result) be dependent on s.t else happening: *The success of the peace talks hangs on agreement on a few important points.* **hang on (to s.o/s.t)** hold or grip(5) (s.o/s.t) tightly in order to stop oneself falling etc: *Hang onto me and I'll try and pull you up. Hang on tight as we go around the corner.*

hang onto s.t (**a**) ⇒ hang on(to s.o/s.t). (**b**) (*fig*) keep ownership or possession of s.t (and not sell it): *You should hang onto your shares in the company as they are certain to increase in value.*

hang out s.w (*fig; informal*) live s.w; visit s.w regularly: *'Where does he hang out now?' A lot of young people hang out at that café.* ⇒ hang-out.

hang out (of s.t/s.w) (**a**) be outside one's/its

normal position; be sticking out(⇒ stick (s.t) out (from/of s.t)): *You look so untidy with your shirt hanging out* (i.e the bottom part is not inside the trousers). *The dog's tongue was hanging out (of its mouth) because the weather was so hot.* (**b**) put (part of) one's body outside (a window etc): *People were hanging out of the windows to watch the procession.* **hang s.t out** put s.t in the open air, esp wet clothes etc on a washing line so that they can dry: *It's stopped raining so I'll just hang out the washing. They hung flags out to welcome him home.* **let it all hang out** (*fig*; *slang*) (expression used to tell s.o that he/she should) do what he/she wants, e.g cry, and not control her/his feelings etc: *Just let it all hang out — you'll feel a lot better.*

hang over s.o/s.t (*fig*) (**a**) = hang over one's head (⇒ head(*n*)). (**b**) (of a sad, gloomy(2) feeling etc) affect s.o/s.t completely: *A feeling of despair hung over them as they realized that they might not be rescued in time.* **hang (s.t) (all) over s.t** put/fix s.t, be fixed, in a position (all) over a surface, an object etc: *There were pictures hanging all over the walls in the front room. She hung a sheet over the cage.* ⇒ be/get hung over, hangover.

hang together (*fig*) (**a**) (of a group of people) stay with each other, not get separated from each other: *We must all hang together or we'll get lost in this fog.* (**b**) (of things s.o says, of points in an argument etc) be in agreement with each other; be organized to fit/match one another sensibly: *You've only got to examine his views in detail to see that they just don't hang together.*

hang up (on s.o) stop speaking (to s.o) on the telephone and put the receiver back on its rest: *She hung up on me just as I was trying to explain what had gone wrong. Don't hang up; I'll get the address for you.* **hang s.t up (on s.t)** put/fix/hang(2) s.t in a position (on s.t) so that it is above the floor or ground: *Hang your coat up on that hook.* ⇒ be/get hung up (about/on s.t), hang-up.

hang (up)on s.o's every word, s.o's lips (often *derog*) listen very closely to what s.o is saying because one admires her/him, wants to understand everything he/she says etc: *He was surrounded by a crowd of adoring fans who hung on his every word as though he was God.*

I'll be hanged(!) (*informal*) (expression used to show surprise, annoyance etc): *I'll be hanged! They've decided to get married after all!* **I'll be hanged if I'll . . .!** I completely refuse to do s.t: *I'll be hanged if I'll listen to your complaints any longer!*

'**hanger** ⇒ coat-hanger.

,**hanger-'on** *c.n* (*pl* hangers-on) (*derog*) person who stays close to s.o and tries to be friendly with her/him, usu to get some advantage: *The band was surrounded by hangers-on who were always offering to help so they could stay near.*

'**hang-,glider** *c.n* kind of glider with a large sail made of nylon etc below which is a metal framework for a person to hold on to, rest her/his body on etc.

'**hang-,gliding** *u.n* sport or activity of flying with a hang-glider: *Have you ever tried hang-gliding?*

'**hangings** *pl.n* kinds of material that are hung(2) across windows, on walls etc: *The wall hangings showed scenes from the Bible(1).*

'**hangman** *c.n* (*pl -men*) person whose job is to hang(5) criminals.

'**hang-,out** *c.n* (*informal*) place where one lives or to which one goes regularly: *His usual hangout is a small club in Soho.* ⇒ hang out s.w.

'**hang,over** *c.n* **1** (usu *have a —*) headache or ill feeling from drinking too much alcohol: *I had a terrible hangover after last night's party.* ⇒ be/get hung over. **2** (often *be a — (from s.t)*) result, usu small, that is left (after s.t else has happened); all that remains (from s.t): *His habit of folding his clothes so neatly is a hangover from his army days.*

'**hang-,up** *c.n* (often *have a — about s.o/s.t*) (*informal*) worried state of mind about s.t that makes one unable to act or think clearly about her/him/it: *He has so many hang-ups about women that I doubt if he'll ever get married.* ⇒ be/get hung up (about/on s.t).

hangar /'hæŋə/ *c.n* large building or shed for aircraft.

hanker /'hæŋkə/ *intr.v* **hanker after/for s.t** (*informal*) want, long(2) for, s.t (esp s.t that one has not got or cannot get easily): *She hankers for a bit of warmth and friendship from home but he's unlikely to give her any.*

'**hankering** *c.n* **have a hankering after/for s.t** (have a) need/longing² for s.t: *I've a hankering for something salty to eat.*

hanky /'hæŋkɪ/ *c.n* (*pl -ies*) (also '**hankie**) (*informal*) handkerchief.

hanky-panky /,hæŋkɪ 'pæŋkɪ/ *u.n* (*informal*) naughty behaviour; bad or wrong thing(s) that s.o does, has done (and often tries to hide): *Now, don't you two children get up to any hanky-panky while I'm out.*

hansom /'hænsəm/ (also **hansom ,cab**) *c.n* (*old use*) kind of carriage with two wheels that was pulled by a horse and could be hired for a short journey in a town.

haphazard /hæp'hæzəd/ *adj/adv* (that happens) in a way that is not organized/planned very well: *Their plans to develop the business seemed a bit haphazard to me.*

hap'hazardly *adv.*

happen /'hæpn/ *intr.v* **1** (of an event, accident etc) take place, occur(1), often by chance: *I was there when the accident happened.* **2** (usu *— to s.o/s.t*) be s.t that is done (to s.o/s.t), that affects or changes (s.o/s.t): *A strange thing happened to me last night.* **3** (usu *— to be/do s.t*) (of a person) be/do s.t either by chance or because of certain circumstances(1): *I happen to be one of the few people who know the full story.* **as it (so) happens/happened, . . .** as an actual fact (although perhaps surprisingly) . . .: *As it happened, I was able to show them where you live. I know him quite well as it happens.* **happen (up)on s.o/s.t** (*formal*) find s.o/s.t by chance: *I happened on him in India of all places. He happened upon the answer to the main problem when he was working on something else.* **it so happens/happened (that)** . . . it is an actual fact, though perhaps as a matter of chance, (that) . . .: *It so happened that I was there when she fell, otherwise it might have been days before anybody found her.*

'**happening** *c.n* (often *pl*) (strange) thing that happens(1): *Nobody could explain the strange happenings of that night.*

happy /'hæpɪ/ *adj* (*-ier, -iest*) **1** having or showing

a feeling of content/pleasure: *She had a happy smile on her face. He's happiest when he's playing with his model trains. I was very happy to hear that you had passed your exami.. tions.* Opposite sad(1), unhappy(1). **2** (*pred*, usu — *to do s.t*) willing or eager (to do s.t, to help s.o etc): *I'd be very happy to help you decorate your room.* **3** (*pred*, usu — *with s.o/s.t*) pleased or satisfied (with s.o/ s.t): *I can't say I'm happy with the way he's been doing his job.* **4** (*attrib*) (of an expression, idea etc) well chosen, right for a particular occasion: *That was hardly a happy choice of words when you know her husband is dying.* Opposite unhappy(2). **5** (*attrib*) (*formal*) (of s.t happening by chance) lucky: *By a happy coincidence*(1) *they met in the hotel bar.* **a happy medium** ⇒ medium.
'happily *adv* **1** in a happy(1,2) way: *She smiled happily. I'll happily help you when I've got the time.* **2** luckily, fortunately: *Happily, they were all rescued in time.*
'happiness *u.n* state of being happy(1,2).
,Happy 'Birthday, 'Christmas, ,New 'Year etc *interj* (expression used to greet s.o and wish her/him a happy(1) time on her/his birthday, at Christmas etc).
,happy-go-'lucky *adj* (of a person, her/his nature etc) cheerful and without any worry about things that happen or might happen: *He's got a very happy-go-lucky nature and always seems to be without a care in the world.*
'happy ,hour *c.n* time (usu an hour only in the evening) when alcoholic drinks are sold at a cheaper price in a pub, bar etc.
harangue /hə'ræŋ/ *c.n* **1** strong speech, usu addressed to a group of people, that tries to persuade them or criticize them for s.t: *I don't want to listen to any more of his harangues about how we should all work harder.*
▷ *tr.v* **2** make such a speech to (s.o): *The speaker harangued the workers against accepting the deal offered by the management.*
harass /'hærəs/ *tr.v* worry or annoy (s.o), esp by following her/him around all the time, making her/him do too many things etc: *He complained that the local officials were harassing him and not allowing him to run his business.*
'harassed *adj* worried because of having too much to do: *I felt so harassed trying to finish all my work at the office before going on holiday.*
'harassing *adj* causing one to feel harassed: *I've had such a harassing day at the office.*
'harassment *u.n.*
harbinger /'hɑːbɪndʒə/ *c.n* (usu — *of s.t*) (*formal*) sign or indication (of s.t in the future): *The arrival of some birds on these shores is a harbinger of summer.*
harbour /'hɑːbə/ *c.n* (US **'harbor**) **1** place on the coast where ships are protected from storms, where they can stop or tie up and land people, goods etc: *This bay is a natural harbour. They are building a new modern harbour for private yachts.* Compare haven(2), marina, port¹. **2** (often — *a safe —*) place where one can hide, feel safe and protected (from other people etc): *This country is becoming known as a safe harbour for criminals of all kinds.* ⇒ haven(1).
▷ *tr.v* (*formal*) **3** give (s.o) a harbour(2): *She harboured him for several months after his escape from prison.* **4** (often — *a grudge, thoughts of*

revenge etc (*against s.o*)) have (bad feelings etc) for a long time in one's mind (against s.o): *He harboured a feeling of* resentment *against her for leaving him.*
'harbour ,master *c.n* official in charge of a harbour(1).
hard /hɑːd/ *adj* **1** (of a substance) very solid and firm, not easy to break: *She broke a tooth on a hard sweet. The ground is as hard as rock.* Opposite soft(1). **2** (of a sum, language, problem etc) difficult to do, understand, solve etc: *It was a very hard examination paper. Chinese is very hard* (or *a very hard language*) (*to learn properly*). Opposite easy(1). **3** (of s.o's life, experiences etc) having or causing many problems; being difficult to bear and without much happiness: *She has had a very hard life. Stephen had a very hard time when he first went to the new school. These are hard times we live in.* Opposite easy(2). **4** (usu *attrib*) (of weather) very severe, cold etc: *a hard frost*(1)/ *winter.* Opposite mild(3). **5** (of a person, what he/she does etc) using or needing a lot of effort or energy(1): *He is a very hard worker. Give the door a hard push. It was hard work moving the furniture.* ⇒ hardworking. **6** (often — *on s.o/ s.t*) (of a person, expression on s.o's face etc) not showing much or any sympathy, pity etc (towards s.o/s.t); not allowing s.o to relax(1) or enjoy herself/himself: *Aren't you being hard on your children making them study so much?* ⇒ lenient. **7** (of water) containing many chemicals or salts that make it difficult for soap to form bubbles(1) (and so not very good for washing etc): *The water in our area is very hard and the pipes get blocked with* lime¹(1). Opposite soft(9). **8** (of the sound of the letters 'c' and 'g') pronounced as /k/ and /g/ (in certain words): *The 'c' in 'coat' is hard.* Opposite soft(10). **9** strong and therefore more dangerous: *hard drink/* drugs(2). ⇒ hard pornography. Opposite soft(11). (**do s.t**) **the hard way** (do s.t) in what is the most difficult way when there are easier ways in which to do it: *I'd rather do it the hard way than ask him for help. Why do you always choose the hard way to do things when there's such a simple way?* (**do it/s.t, learn (s.t)**) **the hard way** (do it etc) by having to experience the difficulty of actually doing it: *If you want to succeed in this work you'll have to do it the hard way and start at the bottom.* **drive a hard bargain** ⇒ bargain(*n*). **hard and fast** that cannot be changed or ignored: *a hard and fast rule.* **hard by (s.o/s.t)** (*formal*) very close or near (to s.o/ s.t): *There's a small path hard by the side of our house.* **hard of hearing** ⇒ hearing. **hard on s.o/ s.t** ⇒ hard(6). **hard times** ⇒ time(*n*). **hard up (for s.t)** (*informal*) not having very much money (for buying things): *I'm very hard up at the moment so I mustn't do anything that's going to cost a lot.* **hard (up)on s.t** (*formal*) following (almost) immediately after s.t that has happened: *Hard upon the news of the earthquake came a report that there were heavy floods.* **make hard work of s.t** ⇒ work(*n*). **play hard to get** (*informal*) (of a person) behave in a way that makes one seem unwilling to be friendly, agree to s.t s.o wants etc (though this may not be completely true): *She was playing hard to get; sometimes she accepted my invitations to dinner and sometimes she just*

said no. **take a (long) hard look (at oneself/s.o/ s.t)** ⇒ look(*n*), hard(14).

▷ *adv* **10** with a lot of effort or energy(1): *He works very hard. Push the door hard. You must try harder if you want to succeed.* ⇒ hard(5), hard-working. **11** (of a success, victory etc) (gained) with great difficulty: *Our victory was hard-earned.* ⇒ hard-earned. **12** (of rain, snow etc) coming down with/in large amounts, heavily: *It was hailing/ raining/snowing hard when I left the house.* **13** (of a blow etc) done with great force: *He hit me hard on the chin.* **14** (of a look etc) showing a lot of attention or concentration(1) (towards s.o/s.t): *He was staring* (⇒ stare(2)) *hard at me but didn't recognize me.* **15** going (in a different/new direction) to the fullest extent possible: *Turn the wheel hard right.* **be hard at it** (*informal*) be working very hard(10) on s.t: *When I came into the office he was already hard at it.* **be/feel hard done by** be or feel badly or unfairly treated: *Though he was rewarded for his efforts he still feels he was hard done by as other people got more than him.* **hard on s.o's heels** ⇒ heel(*n*). **be hard put (to it) (to do s.t)** find it very difficult (to do s.t): *Joe was hard put (to it) to control his feelings when he got the news.* **die hard, diehard** ⇒ die². **go hard with s.o** (*formal*) (of s.t that has happened or will happen) affect s.o badly: *It will go hard with him if he loses his job.* **hit s.o hard** (often passive) (*fig*) (of a loss, damage etc) affect or upset s.o badly: *The death of his wife has hit him hard. The town was hard hit by the closing of the factory.* **take s.t hard** be greatly or badly affected by s.t: *He took the loss of his wife very hard.*

'hard,back *c.n* (also *attrib*) book that has stiff covers made of cardboard, usu with cloth on them: *Hardbacks (or hardback books) are so expensive these days.* ⇒ paperback.

,hard-'bitten *adj* (of a person) having become tough and perhaps unpleasant through hard(3) experiences: *Life has made him hard-bitten so don't expect much kindness from him.*

'hard,board *u.n* sheet(s) of wood made by pressing small pieces of wood together with glue.

,hard-'boiled *adj* **1** (of an egg) boiled in water so that the white part and the yolk are hard(1). ⇒ soft-boiled. **2** (*fig*) (of a person) tough and unpleasant: *He's a really hard-boiled character and has been to prison several times.*

,hard 'case *c.n* person, often a criminal, whom it is difficult or impossible to change from her/ his (bad) ways: *He's a really hard case and no amount of punishment has any effect.*

,hard 'cash *u.n* (often (pay s.o) *in —*) bank notes and/or coins but not a cheque etc: *Mr Grey wants payment in hard cash so he doesn't have to declare it to the tax office.*

,hard 'core *u.n* (**'hard-,core** when *attrib*) (small) group of people within an organization who have the strongest views, the most influence etc (and who sometimes resist change): *None of these recommendations will be accepted unless we can interest the hard core in the business.*

,hard 'court *c.n* (**'hard-,court** when *attrib*) tennis court with a hard, usu concrete(1), surface: *hard-court tennis. I prefer to play on a hard court.* Compare clay court, grass court.

,hard 'currency *c/u.n* (example of the) money of a country that keeps its value and is therefore used in international trading.

,hard 'drinker *c.n* person who drinks a lot of, too many, alcoholic drinks.

,hard 'drinking *u.n* act or fact of drinking a lot of alcoholic drinks: *There was a lot of hard drinking at last night's party.*

'hard ,drug ⇒ hard(9).

,hard-'earned *adj* gained with great difficulty or effort (and so well deserved): *He is now enjoying his hard-earned wealth.* ⇒ hard(11).

harden /'hɑːdn/ *v* **1** *tr/intr.v* (cause (a substance) to) become hard(1): *The steel is then hardened by the addition of certain alloys. The chocolate will harden again when it is cold.* Opposite melt(1). **2** *tr/intr.v* (cause (oneself, s.o, one's expression etc) to) become hard(6): *He hardened himself not to show any pity towards them.* **3** *intr.v* (of evidence(1) etc) become stronger (against s.o): *The case against them has hardened with the discovery of new evidence.* **harden one's heart (against/to s.o/ s.t)** = harden(2) oneself (against/to s.o/s.t).

'hardened *adj* (often *a — criminal*) who is not likely to change her/his ways.

,hard 'fact *def/c.n* (often *pl*) fact that is true and cannot be avoided: *The hard facts are that our costs are too high and sales have fallen!*

,hard 'feelings *pl.n* (often *no —*) feelings of anger or annoyance (against s.o, about s.t etc): *There are no hard feelings between them though they both tried for the same job.*

,hard-'headed *adj* (of a person) very tough and practical and not easily influenced, esp in matters of business: *He's very hard-headed so you won't find it easy to get the price you want.*

,hard-'hearted *adj* (*derog*) (of a person) having or showing little or no sympathy or pity; being hard(6): *Don't be so hard-hearted! Can't you see she wants to be friends again?* ⇒ soft-hearted.

,hard-'heartedness *u.n*.

'hardiness *u.n* state of being hardy.

,hard 'labour *u.n* (punishment given to a criminal consisting of) work with one's hands such as digging, breaking stones etc: *He was sentenced to six months' hard labour.*

,hard 'line *c.n* (**'hard-,line** when *attrib*) (often take a *— (against s.o/s.t)*) (opposing s.o/s.t) position, point of view, that one is determined not to change in spite of pressure etc: *a hard-line approach(4). The government is taking a hard line against the strikers(1) and is refusing to negotiate(1).*

,hard-'liner *c.n* person who has fixed ideas or ways of doing things.

,hard 'lines *interj/pl.n* (*informal*) hard luck.

,hard 'liquor *u.n* drink that contains a high level of alcohol. Compare soft drink, long drink.

,hard 'luck *interj/u.n* (expression used to show sympathy towards s.o because of her/his) misfortune: *Hard luck! I'm sure you'll win next time. It was just hard luck that he didn't win.*

'hardness *u.n* state of being hard(1–3,6,7).

,hard of 'hearing ⇒ hearing.

,hard por'nography *u.n* (*informal,* **hard 'porn**) pornography that is very explicit(2); having or showing very detailed sexual acts. ⇒ soft porn(ography).

,hard 'sell *def.n* (**'hard-,sell** when *attrib*) way of selling goods or services using a lot of persuasion or pressure: *He believes in the hard sell* (or *the hard-sell* approach(4)) *and doesn't easily take no from his* customers. ⇨ soft sell.

'hardship *c/u.n* (example of) suffering or difficulties that one has in one's life, way of living etc: *She suffered many hardships in bringing up her children on her own.*

,hard 'shoulder *c.n* strip with a concrete(1) or tarred(⇨ tar(2)) surface beside a motorway or dual carriageway that is wide enough for a vehicle to stop on in an emergency (but not intended for driving along or parking): *A number of drivers were fined for parking on the hard shoulder.*

'hard,top *c.n* car that has a fixed metal roof. ⇨ soft top.

'hard,ware *u.n* (also *attrib*) **1** things such as pots, pans, tools etc used in the home: *the hardware department in a store.* **2** (all the) machines and equipment of a computer: *Good hardware can be useless if you haven't got the right programs.* ⇨ software.

,hard-'wearing *adj* (esp of clothes) that (will) last a long time without wearing out(⇨ wear (s.t) out): *These shoes are very hard-wearing; in fact I've had them for five years.*

'hard,wood *c/u.n* (example of) very solid heavy wood that comes from certain trees, e.g oak(2), teak(2). Compare softwood.

,hard'working *adj* (of a person) who works very hard(10).

'hardy *adj* (-ier, -iest) **1** (of a person or animal) strong and able to bear or endure(1) a lot of work, extremes of cold etc: *You must be very hardy to come dressed in such light clothes in this weather.* **2** (of a plant) strong, able to endure(1) extremes of cold, difficult growing conditions etc: *This is a hardy plant and doesn't need very good soil.*

,hardy 'annual *c.n* plant or flower that is able to survive(1) winter conditions.

hardly /'hɑːdlɪ/ *adv* **1** only to a very small extent; only a very little; only with difficulty: *I hardly knew him as we had only met a couple of times. I could hardly talk my throat was so sore.* ⇨ barely(1), scarcely. **2** not very (likely, probable etc): *It's hardly likely that he would lie to you.* **had hardly done, finished** etc **s.t before/when . . .; hardly had I** etc **(done s.t) when . . .** had only just, not quite completely, done etc s.t before/ when (s.t else happened): *I had hardly finished my breakfast when they arrived. Hardly had we arrived at the station when our train was called.* ⇨ barely(2), scarcely. **hardly anyone, anything** etc almost no one, nothing etc; only a very few people/things etc: *Hardly anybody agrees with you. There are hardly any biscuits left, so who ate them all? Hardly any people came.* **hardly ever** almost never; on almost no occasion: *He hardly ever goes out any more. We hardly ever see them these days.*

hare /heə/ *c.n* **1** wild animal like a rabbit but with a bigger body and longer ears. **(as) mad as a March hare** ⇨ mad. ⊳ *intr.v* **2** (often — *away, back, off* etc) run/go (away etc) very fast: *The children hared off as soon as I came near. Cars hared past us and none stopped to offer us a lift.*

'hare,brained *adj* (of a person, plan etc) very foolish; not thinking, not thought out, at all well:

He has some harebrained idea about starting a business when he knows nothing about it.

'hare,lip *c.n* top lip of a person that is divided into two parts because it did not form properly before birth.

'hare,lipped *adj* having a harelip.

harem /'hɑːriːm/ *c.n* (in Muslim countries) (all the women who live in a) special part of a house for the women/wives of the household.

haricot /'hærɪkəʊ/ (also **,haricot 'bean**) *c.n* yellow or white bean, often dried or boiled.

hark /hɑːk/ *intr.v* **1** (often — *at* s.t) (*formal*; *literary*) listen (to the sound of s.t): *Hark at the rain!* **2** (usu — *at* s.o) (*informal*) listen (to s.o, what he/she is saying), often with the idea that he/she is wrong, stupid etc: *Hark at her — she's always complaining but is the first to take advantage of anything.* **hark back (to s.t)** return in one's conversation, thoughts etc (to an earlier point in the discussion, in time etc): *Harking back to what you said earlier, I'm not sure that I agree.*

harlequin /'hɑːlɪkwɪn/ *c.n* comic(1) character dressed in clothes of different colours, who appears in traditional theatre plays, esp in Italy.

harlot /'hɑːlət/ *c.n* (*old use*) prostitute.

harm /hɑːm/ *u.n* (often *do* s.o/s.t —) injury, damage or distress(1) (to s.o/s.t): *A lot of harm was done to his reputation by the* rumours. *It won't do you any harm to visit your grandmother now and again.* ⇨ harm(3). **be no harm (in doing s.t)** cause no problem, be worthwhile (doing s.t): *There's no harm in asking if you can use her car as she can only say 'no'.* **come to no harm** not suffer anything: *The children will come to no harm while she's looking after them.* **mean no harm (to s.o/ s.t)** not intend/want to cause harm(1) (to s.o/s.t): *I know he felt he had to tell the truth about you but he meant you no harm personally.* **out of harm's way** (removed to, put in, a place) where s.o/s.t is or will be safe: *Those medicines need to be out of harm's way when there are children about.* ⊳ *tr.v* **2** cause harm(1) to (s.o/s.t): *Don't be frightened of the dog — it won't harm you.* **3** (usu *will not — s.o* to *do* s.t) affect (s.o) very badly (if he/she does it): *It wouldn't harm you to do the washing-up once in a while.* ⇨ harm(1).

'harmful *adj* causing (a lot of) harm(1): *This medicine is harmful if taken in large quantities.*

'harmfully *adv.*

'harmless *adj* **1** causing no harm(1). **2** (of a person) weak; not likely to hurt anyone or cause trouble: *They attack harmless women and rob them. I can't see why you're so frightened of Ben; he seems harmless enough to me.*

'harmlessly *adv.* **'harmlessness** *u.n.*

harmonic ⇨ harmony.

harmonica /hɑː'mɒnɪkə/ *c.n* (*pl* -s) kind of musical instrument that one holds in or near the mouth and blows into; mouth organ[2].

harmonious(ly), harmoniousness ⇨ harmony.

harmonium /hɑː'məʊnɪəm/ *c.n* (*pl* -s) kind of musical instrument like a small organ[2].

harmony /'hɑːmənɪ/ *n* (*pl* -ies) (often *in* (*perfect* —) **1** *c/u.n* (example of the) arrangement of different sounds in music, colours in a pattern etc to form a pleasant whole: *They sang in perfect harmony. The composition has some attractive* *harmonies.* **2** *u.n* (often *live in* — (*with s.o*)) (state of) agreement and sympathy (with s.o) and without any fights or trouble: *The two races have so far lived together in perfect harmony.*

harmonic /hɑː'mɒnɪk/ *adj/c.n* (of or referring to a) piece of harmony(1).

harmonious /hɑː'məʊnɪəs/ *adj* **1** having or showing harmony. **2** (of colours, an arrangement of s.t etc) matching pleasantly, fitting well together: *The room was painted in a harmonious colour scheme* (⇒ colour). **har'moniously** *adv.* **har'moniousness** *u.n.*

harmonization, -isation /ˌhɑː'mənaɪ'zeɪʃən/ *c/u.n* (example of) harmonizing.

harmonize, -ise /'hɑː'məˌnaɪz/ *v* **1** *intr.v* (often — *with s.o/s.t*) sing or play a piece of music in harmony(1) (often *with s.o/s.t*): *The singers harmonized very well with each other.* **2** *tr.v* add (notes) to (a piece of music) to make a harmony(1) or harmonies. **3** *tr/intr.v* (often — (*s.t*) *with s.t*) (cause (s.t) to) be or become harmonious(2) (with s.t else); (in trade) (cause (s.t) to) be or become the same as, equal to, (s.t else), esp in a group of countries: *These colours harmonize very well* (*with each other*). *The European Commission*(2) *spends a lot of time trying to harmonize the production of steel in the member countries.*

harness /'hɑːnɪs/ *c/u.n* **1** (example of the) leather straps and bands put on a horse and tied to a cart so that the horse can pull it. **2** (example of the) straps and bands that hold s.t, often on a person's body: *a baby harness* (i.e one that allows one to carry a baby or control it when it is in a pram, learning to walk etc); *a parachute*(1) *harness.*
▷ *tr.v* **3** (usu — *s.t to s.t*) put a harness(1) on (s.t) (to connect it to s.t): *He harnessed the horse to the cart.* **4** use or control (the power of s.t in nature) to produce s.t, e.g a form of power such as electricity: *Scientists are developing more efficient solar panels to harness the sun's* energy(2).

harp¹ /hɑːp/ *c.n* kind of musical instrument with strings in a large frame shaped like a triangle: *The woman sat at her harp and* plucked²(4) *the strings to produce beautiful sounds like running water.* **'harpist** *c.n* person who plays a harp¹.

harp² /hɑːp/ *intr.v* **harp on** (*about s.t*) keep talking or complaining (about s.t, esp s.t one thinks is wrong): *I wish you would stop harping on about how ill you are!*

harpoon /hɑː'puːn/ *c.n* **1** spear with a long rope tied to it that is used to catch whales, or other large animals or fish in the sea.
▷ *tr.v* **2** use a harpoon(1) to catch (a whale etc).

harpsichord /'hɑːpsɪˌkɔːd/ *c.n* kind of musical instrument like a piano that was used especially in earlier times.

harrow /'hærəʊ/ *c.n* **1** device with short spikes(1) pulled behind a tractor to break large lumps of earth into small pieces.
▷ *tr/intr.v* **2** use a harrow(1) (on a field etc) to break large lumps of earth: *The farmer was harrowing* (*the field*) *to prepare for planting.* **'harrowing** *adj* (of s.t that happens, a story etc) that causes great distress(1): *It was a harrowing experience to see her child knocked over by the car.*

harry /'hærɪ/ *tr.v* (*-ies, -ied*) (*formal*) **1** (often — *s.o for/over s.t*) worry or annoy (s.o) continually

(in order to get s.t from her/him): *The bank is harrying me over my debts.* **2** (*military*) attack (s.o) continually in small groups but without fighting a proper battle.

harsh /hɑːʃ/ *adj* **1** (often — *to*(*wards*)/*with s.o*) (of a person, what s.o does etc) too tough, strict or cruel (to s.o): *He is a very harsh parent. Don't be so harsh with her, it wasn't her fault.* **2** (of a condition, the weather etc) very severe: *a harsh winter.* **3** (of a voice, sound, colour, taste etc) not at all pleasant; rough: *Her harsh voice got on my* nerves(2). *The colours used in the room were too harsh.* **'harshly** *adv* in a harsh(1) way: *He was treated very harshly when he was in prison.* **'harshness** *u.n.*

harvest /'hɑːvɪst/ *n* **1** *c/def.n* (time in the year for the) collecting of ripe crops, esp corn, from the fields. **2** *c.n* amount of crops collected in this way: *We're expecting a good harvest this year.* **reap the harvest of s.t** (*fig; formal*) get the advantage, or suffer the loss, from s.t one has done: *He is now reaping the harvest of all his hard work* (or *of his mistakes*).
▷ *tr/intr.v* **3** (cause (crops etc) to) be collected: *We were harvesting* (*the corn*) *until late in the evening.* **'harvester** *c.n* **1** person who harvests(3). **2** = combine harvester.

harvest 'festival *c.n* special occasion, often held in a church, to celebrate the end of harvesting(⇒ harvest(3)).

has (strong form /hæz/, weak form /həz/) *3rd pers sing pres.t* have.

has-been ⇒ have.

hash /hæʃ/ *n* **1** *c/u.n* (example of a) cooked dish made from vegetables, meat etc mixed together. **2** *u.n* (*slang*) = hashish. **make a hash of s.t** (*fig*) make a mess of s.t(b).
▷ *tr.v* **3 hash s.t out** (*informal*) decide/settle s.t, esp after a lot of discussion: *The deal was hashed out over a number of secret meetings.* **4 hash s.t up** (*informal*) do s.t very badly; mess s.t up(a): *Tom said he really hashed up his science examination.*

hashish /'hæʃɪʃ/ *u.n* (also **'hasheesh**) drug(2) made from the dried leaves, juice etc of a variety of the hemp(1) plant and smoked, chewed and sometimes eaten for its calming effect, the feelings of well-being etc it produces; cannabis.

hasn't /'hæznt/ = has not. ⇒ have.

hasp /hɑːsp/ *c.n* metal fastener with a hole in it that fits over a staple²(2) on a door, box etc and through which a padlock(1) is put and locked.

hassle /'hæsl/ *c/u.n* (usu *sing*) (*informal*) **1** (example of) trouble, annoyance; argument or fight: *It's always a bit of a hassle getting the children ready for school in the morning.*
▷ *tr.v* **2** (*informal*) annoy (s.o), esp by continually asking her/him to do s.t: *Stop hassling me!* **hassle about/over s.t** argue or fight about s.t: *They're always hassling over who should pay.*

hassock /'hæsək/ *c.n* cushion used for kneeling on in a church when praying.

hast /hæst/ (*old use*) form of have used with thou.

haste /heɪst/ *u.n* (*formal*) hurry or speed (in going s.w, doing s.t, sometimes too quickly): *There was great haste to get there before any of the others. This work was carelessly done and showed* *signs of haste.* **in haste** in a hurry, without having much time to spare: *I'm writing this letter in haste as I want to catch the post.* **make haste** (*formal*) hurry (to go s.w): *Make haste or you will miss the procession.* **More haste, less speed** (*proverb*) The more one hurries, the more likely it is that one will make mistakes and so not actually succeed.

hasten /'heɪsn/ *tr/intr.v* (*formal*) **1** (cause (one's movement, steps) to) become faster (in order to get s.w): *They hastened their march. He hastened away to tell her the news.* **2** *tr.v* make (s.t, e.g a process(1)) happen more quickly: *This new chemical will hasten the development process. Nothing you can do will hasten the day* (i.e. make it come more quickly).

'hastily *adv* in a hasty way.

'hastiness *u.n* fact or state of being hasty.

'hasty *adj* (*-ier, -iest*) **1** done in a quick or hurried way: *I just had time to make a hasty telephone call to her before I left.* **2** (*derog*) acting or doing s.t too quickly, without thinking properly: *Don't be so hasty in forming a judgement till you have all the facts.*

hat /hæt/ *c.n* covering for the head (sometimes with a brim(2)), worn esp when out of doors. Compare cap(1). ⇨ bowler (hat) (⇨ bowl[2]). **a bad hat** (*fig; informal*) a bad person, esp a criminal. **(do s.t) at the drop of a hat** ⇨ drop(*n*). **hat in hand** ⇨ cap/hat in hand (⇨ cap(*n*)). **keep s.t under one's hat** (*fig; informal*) keep s.t secret: *Keep it under your hat but I'm leaving my job next month.* **old hat** (*fig; informal*) (of s.t said) thing that is already very well known; useless, worthless information: *That's old hat! I've known about it for years.* **pass/send the hat round** (*fig; informal*) (try to) collect money from a group of people in an informal way (usu for a good or charitable) purpose): *They passed the hat round in the office to buy flowers for her when she was in hospital.* **raise one's hat (to s.o)** greet s.o by raising one's hat. **take one's hat off to s.o** (*fig; informal*) (said to show that one admires or praises s.o for s.t he/she has done): *I have to take off my hat to her for the way she handled him.* **talk through one's hat** (*fig; informal*) talk nonsense, esp about s.t one does not know or understand: *Peter is talking through his hat. He knows nothing about what I want.*

'hat,band *c.n* band of material that goes round the bottom of the crown(6) of a hat.

'hat,pin *c.n* pin used by a woman to hold a hat on her head.

'hat,stand *c.n* upright pole' with hooks or pegs(1) on it on which to hang hats, coats etc.

'hatter *c.n* person whose job is to make and/or sell hats. **(as) mad as a hatter** ⇨ mad.

'hat,trick *c.n* (often *get/score a* —) **1** (in cricket') act of bowling[2](3) three batsmen out in three balls one after each other. **2** (in football etc) act by one player of getting three goals in a match.

hatch[1] /hætʃ/ *c.n* **1** (cover for an) opening in a ship or plane, esp over a cargo hold etc. **2** opening, sometimes with a small door or doors, in a wall between two rooms through which food, dishes etc is/are passed.

'hatch,back *c.n* (shape or style of a) car with a (sloping) back that opens for storing luggage etc. ⇨ convertible(3), estate car, saloon(3), station wagon.

'hatch,way *c.n* opening for a hatch.

hatch[2] /hætʃ/ *v* **1** *tr/intr.v* (cause (eggs) to) break open and let out the baby birds etc: *The hen has hatched half a dozen baby* chicks. *The eggs are hatching. The baby* crocodile(1) *hatches out of its egg and moves towards water.* **2** *tr.v* (often — *s.t up*) plan (s.t) esp in secret: *What are you two hatching up between you?*

hatchet /'hætʃɪt/ *c.n* kind of small axe. **bury the hatchet** (*fig; informal*) (agree to) stop quarrelling: *After being enemies for several years they met and decided to bury the hatchet and become friends again.*

hate /heɪt/ *n* **1** *u.n* feeling of very great dislike (of s.o/s.t): *There was hate in his eyes when he looked at her.* Opposite love(1,2). **2** *c.n* (often *have a* — *of doing s.t*) no or very little enjoyment (from doing s.t): *He has a hate of offending people.* **s.o's pet hate** ⇨ pet(1).

▷ *tr.v* (not often used in continuous tenses[2]) **3** (often — *s.o/s.t for s.t*) dislike (s.o/s.t) very greatly (for some reason): *He hated his parents for the way they treated him when he was young. I hate crowded trains.* **4** (often — (*doing s.t*), (*having*) *to do/say s.t*) not enjoy (doing/saying s.t, having to do/say s.t) although one may have to: *I hate speaking in public. I hate to tell you this but I can't take you out to dinner tonight.*

'hateful *adj* done with, causing, hate(1): *It was hateful of you to try to destroy my friendship with her.*

'hatefully *adv.* **'hatefulness** *u.n.*

hatred /'heɪtrɪd/ *sing/u.n* (often *have a* — *of/for* s.o/s.t) feeling of very great dislike (of s.o/s.t): *He gave her a look of hatred. I have a hatred of snakes. There was hatred in her eyes.*

hatpin, hatstand, hatter ⇨ hat.

haughty /'hɔːtɪ/ *adj* (*-ier, -iest*) (*derog*) (of a person, expression, behaviour) showing too much pride or superiority towards other people: *She was very haughty to me when I tried to talk to her, perhaps because we hadn't been properly introduced.*

'haughtily *adv.* **'haughtiness** *u.n.*

haul /hɔːl/ *c.n* **1** (often *give s.t a* —; *give a* — *on s.t*) strong hard pull (on s.t): *He gave several hauls on the rope but it wouldn't come free.* **2** quantity or amount of fish caught, esp in a net at one time. **3** quantity of things taken or stolen: *The thieves got away with a large haul of jewellery.* **a long haul** (**a**) a long distance (to go or travel): *It was a long haul driving to the South of France.* (**b**) a long time (that s.t difficult takes to do etc): *It will be a long haul before the job is completed. Sally has a long haul before she'll be back to health.*

▷ *v* **4** *tr.v* (often — *s.o/s.t across, down, through, up* etc) pull (s.o/s.t heavy or difficult) (across etc) with some force or effort: *He hauled her over the mountain. Can you haul that box down from the shelf?* **5** *intr.v* (often — (*away*) *at/on s.t*) (try to) pull (at/on s.t, esp a rope): *Everyone haul away on the rope; let's bring the boat to the shore. We were all hauling away when the rope broke.* **haul s.o over the coals** ⇨ coal.

haulage /'hɔːlɪdʒ/ *u.n* (also *attrib*) (cost of the) sending or carrying of goods, usu by road: *haulage charges.*

'haulier *c.n* person or company who/that carries goods in trucks.

haunch /hɔːntʃ/ *c.n* **1** part of the body of a person or animal from below the waist or ribs(1) to above the knees: *He was sitting on his haunches* (i.e with his legs folded under him). **2** this part of the body, esp of a deer, as food: *a haunch of venison.*

haunt /hɔːnt/ *c.n* **1** (often — *of s.o*) place that is regularly visited (by s.o): *This part of the country is one of my favourite haunts. Don't go into that area as it is a criminals' haunt.*

▷ *tr.v* **2** regularly visit (a place); follow (s.o) around (so that he/she cannot get away from one): *He haunts the streets around her house hoping to see her.* **3** (of a ghost(1)) (be thought to) appear, be present, in (a house, place etc) regularly: *The ghost of a horseman haunts the grounds of the castle.* **4** (often passive) (of s.t one has done, a memory etc) return very often to (s.o, one's mind) in a disturbing way: *He was haunted by the memory of that day when he almost killed her.*

'haunted *adj* **1** (of a place that is thought to be) lived in by a ghost(1) or ghosts: *a haunted house.* **2** (of a person, expression etc) very worried or disturbed (by some memory etc): *He has a haunted look on his face.*

'haunting *adj* (of a memory, of s.t said, done etc) remaining in one's mind for a long time: *a haunting* melody(1).

have (strong form /hæv/, weak form /həv/) *aux.v* (*3rd pers sing pres.t has* (strong form /hæz/, weak form /həz/); *pres.p having*; *p.t,p.p had* (strong form /hæd/, weak form /həd/); negative forms *have not* or *haven't* /'hævnt/, *has not* or *hasn't* /'hæznt/, *had not* or *hadn't* /'hædnt/; 'I have' can be *I've* /aɪv/, 'you have' can be *you've* /juːv/, 'he/she has' can be *he's/she's* /hiːz, ʃiːz/, 'it has' can be *it's* /ɪts/, 'we have' can be *we've* /wiːv/, 'they have' can be *they've* /ðeɪv/, 'I had' can be *I'd* /aɪd/, 'you had' can be *you'd* /juːd/, 'he/she had' can be *he'd/she'd* /hiːd, ʃiːd/, 'it had' can be *it'd* /'ɪtəd/, 'we had' can be *we'd* /wiːd/, 'they had' can be *they'd* /ðeɪd/) **1** (used with other verbs to form tenses[2]) **(a)** (perfect tenses): *She has* (or *She's*) *passed her examination. Has he painted the room yet? They haven't done their homework. Christina had just finished her dinner when he arrived. She may have finished the dress by the time you need it. They have not eaten yet.* **(b)** (continuous tenses): *I have* (or *I've*) *been waiting two hours for you. They haven't been waiting long. Have you been waiting long? I had* (or *I'd*) *been waiting two hours for her before she arrived.* **(c)** (conditional tense): *Sharon would have* (or *would've*) *finished the dress if you had given her more time* (but she didn't finish it because you didn't give her more time). *He would not* (or *wouldn't*) *have gone if he had known you were coming.* **had s.o/s.t done s.t, (then)** . . . if s.o/s.t had done s.t (but he/she/it did not do it), (then s.t else would have happened): *Had you told me you were coming, I would have met you at the station.* **have/has got something** (*informal*) **(a)** possess a certain quality that one cannot quite describe: *She's got* (*a certain*) *something that makes her very attractive.* **(b)** have said s.t that seems true, right etc though perhaps not completely so: *She's got something there — let's examine what she said a bit more closely.* ⇨ have(8). **have/has (got) to do s.t (a)** be necessary for s.o to do s.t; be

forced to do s.t: *I've got to* (or *I have to*) *get a job. Have you got to* (or *Do you have to*) *leave now? I'm glad I haven't got to* (or *I don't have to*) *go to work today.* **(b)** (with main stress on 'have/has') (used as a way of criticizing s.o or s.t some one does): *Did you have to swear at him like that?* (i.e I think you were wrong to do so.) Compare must. **have/has had it** (*informal*) **(a)** (of a person, animal, machine etc) be no longer useful (because he/she/it is too old, is damaged or broken etc): *I'm afraid he's had it; nobody will employ him at his age. The car's had it; the engine's worn out.* **(b)** (of a person) be dead or on the point of dying: *He's had it and the doctors don't expect him to last the night.* **(c)** have missed an opportunity (to get or do s.t): *You've had it! You won't get another chance to enter the competition.* **(d)** (*informal*) (expression used to say that a person is in trouble because of s.t he/she has done): *Now you've had it! I told you, you'd break the window.* **I've got it!** (*informal*) I have discovered the answer, truth, real reason etc: *'So, who did murder her?' 'I've got it! It was the neighbour, wasn't it?'* **You've got me there!** (*informal*) I don't know what to say or what the answer is (in reply to s.t that s.o has said or asked): *You've really got me there; I don't think there is a solution to the problem.* **you** etc **had best/better do s.t** (*informal*) (you etc are) strongly recommended to do s.t: *You'd best forget all about it. She'd better hurry if she still wants to eat before we leave.*

▷ *tr.v* (usu (esp UK) *have/has got s.o/s.t*(2–5)) **2** possess (a natural characteristic(2), quality): *He has* (or *He's got*) *brown hair and blue eyes. She has a happy nature. Has he got brown hair? She hasn't got blue eyes, she's got brown eyes.* (Compare US use of 'do' for questions and negative forms: *Does he have brown hair? She doesn't have blue eyes.*) **3** own (s.t); hold or possess (s.t belonging to s.o else) for a certain length of time: *I've* (*got*) *quite a large collection of stamps. Who's got* (or *Who has*) *my pen? You can have my electric drill for as long as you need it.* **4** be connected in terms of family, friendship etc to (s.o): *They haven't* (*got*) *any children. She has* (*got*) (or *She's got*) *lots of friends.* **5** (of a whole thing, device, object etc) contain (s.t) as part of the whole; possess (s.t) in connection with s.t: *The house has a large garden. The boat has* (or *The boat's got*) *a powerful engine.* **6** receive (s.t, esp information, news etc); eat, drink (s.t): *I've just had a letter from my sister in Australia. Won't you have something* (*to eat*) *before you go?* **7** (usu — *s.t done, repaired etc*) (arrange to) get (s.t) done: *have the house painted; have your hair cut; have a new dress made.* **8** (usu — *a s.t*) do (s.t shown by the noun): *Let's have a walk. I had a talk with Richard about his work.* **9** (usu — *a/the idea, feeling etc* (*that*) . . .) (used to express a thought, idea etc): *I had a feeling I might see you here. Ann has the idea that you are leaving the country.* **10** experience (s.t, either good or bad): *What terrible weather we're having! We all had a very good time* (or *A good time was had by all*) *on our holiday. Have a nice day!* **11** (suddenly) produce or form (s.t, esp a new idea in one's mind etc): *I've just had a thought; why don't we start our own business?* **12** give birth to (a baby etc): *She* *told him she was going to have a baby. The cat's had three kittens.*

have a/no doubt, **(no) doubts**, **about s.o/s.t** ⇒ doubt(*n*). **have s.t about one** (*formal*) hold or possess s.t on one's person, e.g in a pocket etc: *I have some matches about me; now, where did I put them?* ⇒ have's.t on one. **have a/this thing about s.o/s.t** (*informal*) experience a certain strong feeling, e.g of attraction or fear, with regard to s.o/s.t: *Tom has a thing about Jean and won't leave her alone. I have this thing about chocolate — I just can't resist it.* **have one's wits about one** ⇒ wit(*n*).

have (got) something, **nothing**, **not anything**, **against s.o/s.t** ⇒ against(*prep*).

have s.o (a)round/over (for s.t) invite s.o to visit one's house (for some purpose); entertain s.o in one's house (by providing food, holding a party etc): *We're having a few people around for drinks tomorrow evening. We must have the Hodges over some time (for a meal).*

have it away/off (with s.o) (*slang*; do not use!) perform the sexual act (with s.o), usu regularly and in secret.

have (got) it made be in a situation in life when one has all one wants. ⇒ have(8).

have s.o/s.t back get s.o/s.t returned to one, e.g after an absence or after being borrowed: *She was the one who left home and I'm not having her back under any circumstances. Can I have my electric drill back?*

have it/s.t coming to one (*informal*) be (almost) certain to suffer s.t bad: *I believe Harry's been dismissed; well, he had it coming to him, always arriving late and doing no work!*

have s.o do s.t arrange for, ask, s.o to do s.t: *Would you have him come and see me tomorrow.*

have done (with s.o/s.t) be finished, no longer concern oneself, (with s.o/s.t): *I've done with her for good after that last row. 'Have you done (i.e stopped talking/complaining)? Now, can I say a word or two?'*

have (got) s.t for s.o hold or possess s.t that one intends to give to s.o or that is intended for s.o: *I've got a present for you. I have a message for you to phone your wife.* **have (got) s.t for s.t** own or possess s.t that will be useful for s.t: *I've got just the thing for your cold — here, try this medicine. Robert has got some extra paper for the machine.* For other phrases including a noun, e.g *have an eye/ear/nose for s.t, have a flair/gift for s.t, have no time/use for s.o/s.t,* ⇒ the noun.

have it/s.t from s.o learn or receive s.t, esp information, from s.o: *I have it from the highest authority*(1) *that there will be no tax cuts this year.*

have a go (at/on s.t) try (s.t): *Can I have a go on your new bicycle?*

have a hand in s.t ⇒ hand(*n*).

have a heart; **(not) have one's heart in s.t**; **have one's heart in one's mouth**; **have one's heart in the right place**; **have one's heart set on s.t** ⇒ heart(*n*).

have (got) it in for s.o (*informal*) want to cause trouble for s.o (often because one is annoyed by s.t he/she has done): *He has had it in for her ever since she refused to go out with him.*

have it in mind to do s.t; **have (got) s.o/s.t in**

mind ⇒ mind[1]. **have it in one(self) to do s.t** possess the ability to do s.t (though perhaps this ability is not realized or developed): *He has it in him to become one of the world's best tennis players.* **have (got) a say/voice in s.t** ⇒ say(2), voice(*n*). **have (got) s.o in** have (a builder, s.o doing repairs etc) working in one's house: *The house is in a terrible state! We've got the painters in to paint the kitchen.* **have (got) a stake in s.t** ⇒ stake[2](1). **have (got) s.t in (stock)** have s.t in one's shop ready for sale: *We have a new wine in (stock) this week.*

have it off (with s.o) ⇒ have it away/off (with s.o).

have s.t off get s.t, esp clothes, removed (from one's body): *Let's have those wet clothes off before you catch a cold.*

have s.o on (*informal*) deceive or trick s.o, esp by saying s.t untrue, misleading etc. **have (got) s.t on (a)** be wearing (certain kinds of) clothes: *She had her new dress on when I met her.* **(b)** be busy with s.t; occupy one's time with s.t, e.g a meeting: *If you haven't got anything on this evening let's go out for a meal.* **have one's mind on s.o/ s.t** ⇒ mind(*n*). **have s.t on one's/the brain** ⇒ brain(*n*). **have s.t on one** carry s.t in a pocket, bag etc: *Have you got a match on you?* **have (got) s.t on s.o** possess knowledge, information etc about s.o (usu about s.t wrong that he/she has done): *The police have got nothing on us, so don't get so worried.* For 'have' + noun + 'on', e.g *have pity on s.o, have a crush on s.o, have a down on s.o, have one eye on s.t* ⇒ the noun.

have it out (with s.o) (*informal*) discuss s.t, settle an argument (that has been going on for some time) freely and openly (with s.o): *This quarrel has been going on too long; I'm going to have it out with him this evening.* **have s.t out** get s.t, esp a tooth, an appendix(2), removed.

have s.o over (for s.t) ⇒ have s.o (a)round/over (for s.t). **have control over s.o/s.t** ⇒ control(1). **have an/the edge on/over s.o** ⇒ edge(*n*). **have a hold over s.o** ⇒ hold(5).

have a part in s.t ⇒ part(*n*).

have s.o round (for s.t) ⇒ have s.o (a)round/over (for s.t).

have a stab/try (at s.t) = have a go (at/on s.t).

have s.o up (for s.t) make s.o appear in a court of law (for s.t wrong he/she has done): *He was had up for robbery.* **have the wind up** ⇒ wind[1] (*n*).

have a bearing (up)on s.t ⇒ bearing(2). **have an effect/impact (up)on s.o/s.t** ⇒ effect(1), impact(2).

have what it takes (*informal*) possess certain qualities, e.g bravery, strength of mind, to be able to do s.t successfully: *You've got to admit that she has what it takes and deserves her position in the company.*

have an affair (with s.o) ⇒ affair(3). **have dealings with s.o/s.t** ⇒ dealings(2). **have no truck with s.o/s.t** ⇒ truck[2]. **have sex (with s.o)** ⇒ sex(3). **have (got) (s.t) to do with s.o/s.t** be (s.t that is) connected in some way with, that concerns, s.o/s.t: *Does what you are saying have anything to do with what happened last night? What's that got to do with me? It's got nothing to do with you.* **have a way with one** ⇒ way(*n*). **have a word with s.o (about s.o/s.t)**; **have words (with s.o)** ⇒ word(*n*).

let s.o have it (*informal*) attack s.o (with blows

or words): *I was so angry that I really let him have it.*

not have s.o do/doing s.t not (be prepared to) allow s.o to do s.t: *I just won't have the children running all over the house like that!*

not have s.t not (be prepared to) allow s.t (to happen): *I'm not having any more of your complaining; if you don't like it here, then leave.*

will have s.o (for s.t) (*informal*) (be determined to) make s.o suffer (for s.t he/she has done against one): *I'll have him for the way he treated me if it's the last thing I do.*

'**has-,been** *c.n* person who is no longer important, fashionable etc: *He may have sold millions of records once but now he's a has-been.*

haves (and ,have-'nots) *def.pl.n* people or countries considered as two groups, one that is wealthy (and one that is not): *Our society is becoming more and more divided into the haves and have-nots.*

haven /'heɪvn/ *c.n* (*formal* or *literary*) **1** place of safety: *The house is a haven for battered wives.* **2** harbour or bay: *a sheltered haven for ships.*

haven't /'hævnt/ = have not. ⇨ have.

haversack /'hævə,sæk/ *c.n* bag with straps(1), usu carried on one's back, esp when going for long walks etc. ⇨ backpack, knapsack, rucksack.

haves (and have-nots) ⇨ have.

havoc /'hævək/ *u.n* (often *cause* —) great confusion, damage or destruction: *The earthquake* created(2) *havoc.* **make havoc of s.t**; **play havoc with s.t** cause confusion or disturbance to s.t, e.g a plan; upset s.t that has been arranged: *The late arrival of the plane played havoc with my timetable.* **wreak havoc (on s.o/s.t)** cause great harm or damage (to s.o/s.t): *The storm wreaked havoc on the crops* (or *over a wide area*).

haw ⇨ hum and ha/haw (⇨ hum).

hawk¹ /hɔːk/ *c.n* **1** kind of fierce bird that hunts other birds or small animals. **2** person, usu in government, who is in favour of a strong military force and (the threat of) its use against enemies. Compare dove(2).

'**hawk-,eyed** *adj* (usu of a person) having very good eyesight, like a hawk(1).

'**hawkish** *adj* being or acting like a hawk(2).

'**hawkishness** *u.n.*

hawk² /hɔːk/ *tr.v* carry (goods) from house to house trying to sell them: *He spent some time in his youth hawking household goods from door to door.* **hawk s.t about/around** (*fig*) try to get s.t, e.g an idea or plan, accepted or known among a number of people: *He's been hawking his invention around for some time but nobody is interested.*

'**hawker** *c.n* person who hawks² goods.

hawk³ /hɔːk/ *c.n* = mortar board.

hawser /'hɔːzə/ *c.n* strong thick rope made of fibre(1) or steel, used for pulling or lifting heavy things.

hawthorn /'hɔː,θɔːn/ *n* (also *attrib*) **1** *c.n* kind of (example of a) bush or tree with thorns, white or red flowers and (in the autumn) red berries. **2** *u.n* wood from this tree.

hay /heɪ/ *u.n* long grass that has been cut and dried, esp to be used as food for horses, cows etc. **hit the hay** (*fig*) go to bed. **make hay while the sun shines** (*proverb*) take advantage of a good, the right, time in order to get s.t done.

'**hay-,fever** *u.n* allergy, illness like a cold, caused by grass, pollen in the air, dust etc.

'**hay,stack** *c.n* big pile of (packed or pressed) hay that is being stored. ⇨ rick¹.

'**hay,wire** *adj* (usu *be/go* —) (*informal*) **1** (of a machine etc) not working properly: *My computer's gone haywire and I've lost all the programs*(1) *I put into it.* **2** (of a person) mad or out of control: *He's (gone) totally haywire and is shouting at people in the streets.*

hazard /'hæzəd/ *c.n* **1** thing that is likely to cause harm; risk: *Drinking and smoking are health hazards.*

▷ *tr.v* **2** (*formal*) risk (s.t, one's life etc) by doing s.t dangerous: *Men in lifeboats hazard their lives trying to save people at sea.*

'**hazardous** *adj* causing, likely to cause, a hazard(1).

'**hazardously** *adv.* '**hazardousness** *u.n.*

haze /heɪz/ *c/u.n* (usu *sing*) **1** (often — of s.t) thin light mist(1) as a result (of smoke etc): *The fields were covered in haze. I could only just see him through the haze of smoke.* **be in a haze** (of a person) be rather confused; be hazy(2).

▷ *intr.v* **2** (usu — *over*) have a haze(1) forming (over s.t): *The sky was starting to haze over after being clear all day.*

'**hazily** *adv* in a hazy way.

'**haziness** *u.n* fact or state of being hazy.

'**hazy** *adj* (*-ier, -iest*) **1** being or becoming misty(1) or cloudy: *It's very hazy in the mornings but it begins to clear by midday.* **2** (of a person, her/his thoughts, memories etc) not very clear or certain: *Peggy's a bit hazy about what actually happened. I've only a hazy idea of how a car engine works.*

hazel /'heɪzl/ *adj* **1** (esp of the eyes) having a colour between light brown and light green.

▷ *n* (also *attrib*) **2** kind of small tree that has small round nuts growing on it. **3** *u.n* wood from this tree.

'**hazel-,nut** *c.n* round nut from this tree.

HB *symb* medium hardness of lead¹(3): *an HB pencil.* ⇨ B, H.

H-bomb /'eɪtʃ ,bɒm/ *c.n* (*informal*) hydrogen bomb.

hcf /,eɪtʃ ,siː 'ef/ *abbr* highest common factor (⇨ factor).

HE *written abbr* **1** high explosive. **2** Her/His Excellency. **3** His Eminence.

he /hiː/ *c.n* **1** male: *Is your cat a he or a she?*

▷ *pron* (strong form /hiː/, weak form /hɪ/) **2** (as the subject of a verb or (*formal*) a subjective(3) complement(3)) male person or animal (or thing thought of as male) who/that has been recently mentioned or is clear from the context(1): *Do you see that boy? He's in my class. 'Whose horse is that?' 'He belongs to the farmer.' Look, it is he — the man I was telling you about!* Compare him. ⇨ she, it, him, his.

'**he-** *adj* male of the animal shown in the second part of the word: *a he-goat.* ⇨ he-man.

head /hed/ *adj* **1** of or referring to the head(3): *He suffered severe head injuries.* **2** chief or most important (person or place in a group, organization etc): *the head cook/waiter; the head office.* ⇨ head(9).

▷ *c.n* **3** (top) part of the body of a person, animal etc containing the brain, eyes, ears, nose, mouth etc:

He got hit on the head. Cut the head of the fish off before you serve it. **4** (usu *sing*) height or length of a head(3) as a measure: *He's a head taller than his brother. The horse lost/won by a head.* **5** person's mind or brain, esp as a centre of thought or intelligence: *It was in my head* (i.e I intended) *to tell him exactly what I thought of him. I'd like to know what's going on in* (side) *his head* (i.e what he is thinking). *Jennifer's got a good head* (i.e she's intelligent). **6** top part of s.t, esp of s.t that one hits or uses for hitting: *the head of a hammer/nail/pin.* **7** top (flowering) part of s.t growing: *You should cut off all the dead heads of the roses. The cabbage had a good head on it.* **8** (often *at the* — *of s.t*) top or most important position (in/of s.t): *the head of a bed; at the head of the table; an address at the head of a letter; at the head of a procession.* **9** (often — *of s.t*) chief or most important person (in a group, organization etc): *the head of a department; heads of government/state* (i.e the prime ministers, presidents etc of countries). **10** (often with capital **H**) (*informal*) = head teacher: *I shall report you to the Head if your behaviour doesn't improve.* **11** place where a river or lake starts: *the head of the River Nile.* **12** (usu *a* — *of steam/water*) quantity (of steam or water) that produces force or pressure, e.g to drive s.t: *After the dam(1) was built they had to wait for a head of water to build up before the power station could operate. There was a good head of steam in the engine.* **13** (also **mag,netic 'head**) point of contact(1) in a tape recorder, video(3) etc where the sound etc from the tape is transferred(6): *You should clean the heads on your cassette player regularly.* **14** (*pl head*) (usu *pl*) number of animals, esp when counting: *He has 200 head of* cattle(1). **15** = heading: *I have divided the subject of my speech today under five heads.* **16** (with capital **H** in names) (name for a) headland: *Beachy Head; St David's Head.* **17** amount of foam(1) on top of a glass of beer etc: *I like my beer with a good head on it.* **a/per head** (calculating or dividing the cost of s.t) for each person (who is present, takes part etc): *There will be 20 people at the dinner and at £10 per head the total cost will be £200.* **at the head of s.t** ⇨ head(8). **(be/go) (way) above/over s.o's head** (be/become) (much) too difficult for s.o to understand: *This new mathematics is way above my head.* **(be/go) off one's head** (*informal*) (be/become) mad: *He's gone right off his head.* **bite s.o's head off** (*fig; informal*) show one's annoyance, e.g by shouting at s.o, esp because one is upset or s.o has done s.t wrong etc: *There's no need to bite my head off just because I laughed at you.* **bring s.t, come, to a head** (esp of a problem) (make s.t) reach a (difficult) point where s.t happens, has to be done, decided etc: *The government's action has brought to a head the problem of its relations with the unions.* **bury one's head in the sand** (*fig*) not look at a problem one is facing; try to avoid dealing with s.o/s.t. **come into s.o's head** (of a thought, idea etc) (suddenly) appear, be thought: *The idea of starting a bakery came into my head while I was making bread this morning.* **come to a head** ⇨ bring s.t, come, to a head. **do s.t standing on one's head** (*fig*) do s.t very easily: *This is the kind of job Sarah can do standing on*

her head. **eat**, **laugh**, **shout**, **talk** etc **one's head off** (*informal*) eat etc a lot or too much. **enter one's head/mind** ⇨ (not) enter one's head/mind (to do s.t). **(fall) head over heels** ⇨ head over heels. **get/have a swollen head** (*fig*) become/be too full of pride. ⇨ swollenheaded. **get s.t into one's/s.o's head** (*that . . .*) (make s.o) have an idea in one's/her/his mind (that . . .): *He's got it into his head that nobody loves him.* **give s.o her/his head** allow s.o to do what she/he wants in a free way: *I'm going to give you your head in this department but I expect to see results quickly.* **go off one's head** ⇨ (be/go) off one's head. **go over s.o's head (to s.o)** ignore s.o less important (and deal with s.o more important, with more influence): *The only way to get some things done is to go over the heads of the ordinary officials and talk to the manager.* **go to s.o's head (a)** (of an alcoholic drink etc) make s.o dizzy(1) or a bit drunk: *This wine is going to my head.* **(b)** (of success etc) make s.o too proud: *Her victory in the competition has gone to her head and now she thinks she can win anything.* **hammer s.t into s.o's head** ⇨ hammer(*v*). **hang one's head (in shame)** have one's head down when one is ashamed of s.t. **hang over one's head**, **have s.t hanging over one's head** (*fig*) be/have s.t bad that is likely to happen to one and that one may not be able to avoid: *They had the threat of losing their home hanging over them* (or *their heads*). **have a good**, **no**, **poor** etc **head for s.t** have a good etc ability to do s.t: *He has a remarkable head for figures* (i.e he is good at adding etc numbers). **(have/keep) a cool head** (of a person) (be/stay) calm, not easily excited: *Try to keep a cool head when you speak to the man who crashed into our car.* ⇨ cool-headed. **have one's head in the clouds** (*fig*) not be thinking or acting according to the ordinary demands of life: *He goes around with his head in the clouds and hardly notices what is happening around him.* **have s.t in one's head** be thinking of s.t. **head and shoulders above s.o** (*fig*) much more able or intelligent etc than s.o else: *He stood/was head and shoulders above the other competitors.* **head over heels** with one's head going right down and one's feet going up into the air (like in a somersault(1)): *He slipped and fell head over heels down the slope.* **(fall) head over heels in love (with s.o)** (suddenly) be/become) completely and deeply in love (with s.o): *When he first saw her he fell head over heels in love with her.* **heads (or tails)** (call made when throwing a coin up in the air and trying to guess whether it will land on the ground, one's hand etc with the) side that has the picture of the head (of a king, queen etc) on top (or the other side, when trying to decide who gets the choice to do s.t). **hold one's head high** act proudly, esp because of s.t good one has done. **keep one's head** keep calm in a difficult situation: *We shall need to keep our heads if we're to escape alive.* ⇨ lose one's head. **keep one's head above water (a)** (in swimming etc) not sink, esp when it is difficult not to do so: *He managed to keep his head above water for three hours.* **(b)** (*fig*) manage to live or survive(1) on just enough money etc: *It's difficult to keep one's head above water with all these taxes.* **knock s.o's and s.o's heads**

together (*fig*) (try to) make two people who are quarrelling act more reasonably towards each other: *I'd like to knock their heads together when they behave so stupidly.* **knock s.t on the head** (*fig*; *informal*) stop s.t from happening: *Their refusal to lend us any money has certainly knocked our plans on the head.* **lose one's head** (*fig*) act in a wild way or without any control: *He completely lost his head and started shouting and crying.* ⇒ keep one's head. **make s.t up out of one's head** invent s.t by oneself without anyone else helping (sometimes with the intention of deceiving s.o): *The whole story was made up out of his head and there was not a word of truth in it.* ⇒ made-up(1) (⇒ make). **need one's head examined** (*fig*; *informal*) (behave in a foolish way so as to seem) mad enough to need a doctor: *How can you ignore this opportunity? You need your head examined!* (**not be able to**) **make head or/nor tail of s.t** (*informal*) (not be able to) understand s.t at all or discover what is the truth of s.t: *I can't make head or tail of what he is saying.* (**not**) **enter s.o's head/mind** (**to do s.t**) (not) think of (doing) s.t: *It doesn't enter his head to apologize when he's done something wrong.* **off one's head** mad. **on one's own head be it** one must accept the result or consequence of what one has decided to do: *All I can say is that if you marry her on your own head be it.* **put our** etc **heads together** discuss s.t with each other etc (in order to reach a decision etc): *We need to put our heads together if we're going to solve the problem.* **put s.t into s.o's head** make s.o think (about) s.t (by suggesting it etc): *Who or what put that silly idea into your head?* **shake one's head** (**at s.o/s.t**) (make a side-to-side movement of the head to) show disagreement, disapproval (of s.o/s.t): *Joanna shook her head at her son's bad behaviour.* **snap s.o's head off** (*fig*; *informal*) = bite s.o's head off. **take it into one's head to do s.t** decide to do s.t (often s.t foolish or not well considered): *He's suddenly taken it into his head to go round the world on a bicycle.* **turn s.o's head** (*fig*) make s.o become too proud: *Success has turned his head and now he won't speak to us.*

▷ *tr.v* **18** lead, be at the front or top of, (a procession, column, list etc): *The mayor headed the procession. When the examination results were published(2), his name headed the list.* **19** move towards (a particular direction, place etc): *They're heading north. It's time to head home, back.* ⇒ head for s.o/s.t/s.w. **20** be the chief person in, be in charge of, (a group of people, an organization etc): *He was appointed to head the new department.* **21** (usu — s.t.s) (often passive) give (a report, article etc) a certain title or heading: *He headed his paper on eating habits 'Food for Thought'.* **22** (in football) hit (the ball) with one's head (sometimes scoring a goal in this way): *He headed the ball into the net.* ⇒ header(1). **head** (**back**) **s.w** (begin to) move (or return) to s.w: *I must start heading (back) home or I'll be late.* **head for disaster**, **trouble** etc be doing s.t that is certain or likely to end in disaster(2) etc: *If he does that, he'll be heading for trouble.* **head for s.o/s.t/s.w** move towards s.o/s.t/s.w: *When they got to the party he headed straight for the food. It's time to head for home.* **head s.o/s.t off**

move to meet s.o/s.t and stop her/him/it from continuing: *The police formed a roadblock to head off the thieves' escape.*

head- *n* **1** thing for, of, about, the head(3) that is shown by the second part of the word: headache; headphones. **2** thing at the front of s.t: headland; headlight. **3** person or thing who/that is chief or most important: head teacher; headquarters.

'head,ache *c.n* (often *have a* —) pain in one's head: *I had a headache after working so hard.*

-headed *adj* **1** having the type of head or hair shown by the first part of the word: square-headed; curly-headed. **2** having the number of heads shown by the first part of the word: *a two-headed* monster(2). **3** showing the mental(1) state or (lack of) ability shown by the first part of the word: big-headed; empty-headed.

'header *c.n* (*informal*) **1** (in football) act of heading(⇒ head(22)) the ball: *Arsenal scored their first goal with a* brilliant(1) *header.* **2** dive made with the head going first: *He took a header into the wave.* **3** = heading.

,head'first *adv* (moving) with one's head(3) in front of the rest of one's body: *He fell headfirst into the river.*

'head,hunt *tr.v* (often passive) try to persuade (s.o, usu in an important position) to leave her/his present job and join another company etc: *Because he had been so successful he found himself being headhunted by several of his competitors.*

'head,hunter *c.n* (*fig*) person whose job is to headhunt people.

'head,hunting *u.n.*

'headily *adv* in a heady(1) way.

'headiness *u.n* fact or state of being heady.

'heading *c.n* words or title written at the top of (each section of) a piece of writing: *You must organize your report under a number of headings.*

'head,lamp *c.n* (becoming *old use*) = headlight.

headland /'hedlənd/ *c.n* part of the land, often with a high cliff, that sticks out into the sea.

'head,light *c.n* strong main light, or one of these, on the front of a car, motorbike, train etc, used to show the way in the dark etc. Compare sidelight(1).

'head,line *c.n* (usu *pl*) **1** words in large type at the top of a newspaper article, esp the ones on the front page. **2** main point(s) or summary(3) of the news in a radio or television broadcast. **banner headline** ⇒ banner. **hit the headlines** (of a person, action) be part of the main news in a newspaper, on television etc because of being so important, interesting etc: *The story of the politician's accident hit the headlines of the big newspapers.*

'head,long *adj/adv* **1** (moving) with one's head in front of the rest of one's body: *They made a headlong rush* (or *They rushed headlong*) *into the water.* **2** (doing s.t) too quickly, without thinking carefully: *There's no need to rush headlong into setting up your own business.*

,head'master *c.n* male head teacher.

,head'mistress *c.n* female head teacher.

,head-'on *adj/adv* **1** (esp of a collision between cars, trains, ships etc) (meeting and crashing) with the front of one vehicle hitting the front of the other: *There was a head-on collision between*

the two cars. The two cars crashed head-on.
2 (facing or dealing with s.o/s.t) in a direct and forceful way: *Joan is the type of person who handles difficulties head-on.*

'**head,phones** *pl.n* pair of electronic(2) receivers(1) that fit over or into each ear allowing one to listen to a radio, tape recorder etc without other people hearing it.

,**head'quarters** *c.n* (*pl headquarters*) (*abbr HQ*)
1 place from which the chief officers of an army etc direct operations. ⇨ General Headquarters.
2 chief office of a company, organization etc: *Our headquarters are in London.*

'**head,rest** *c.n* kind of cushion fixed on top of a seat in a car, plane etc that supports the back of the head(3).

'**head,room** *u.n* **1** amount of space above one's head(3) to the top of a room, to the roof of a car etc. **2** amount of space above the top of a vehicle to the lowest point of a bridge, tunnel etc: *There was not enough headroom for the bus to go under the bridge.*

'**head,scarf** *c.n* kind of scarf(2) worn by women around the head(3).

'**head,set** *c.n* set of headphones.

'**head ,start** *c.n* (often *have a — on/over s.o/s.t*) advantage, esp at the beginning of a race or a competition (over s.o): *He had a head start over his competitors because of his knowledge of the market.*

'**head,stone** *c.n* = gravestone.

'**head,strong** *adj* (*derog*) (of a person) very determined and unwilling to listen to the advice of other people.

,**head 'teacher** *c.n* person in charge of the staff and children of a school.

'**head,way** *u.n* **make headway** (**against s.t**) **1** (of a ship etc) move forward (against the tide etc): *The boat could make very little headway when the wind died.* **2** progress (in the face of a difficulty, opposition(3) etc): *We are not making very much headway against our competitors.*

'**head,wind** *c.n* wind blowing directly from the direction in which a person, ship etc is trying to go: *Strong headwinds forced the boat to change course.* Opposite following wind.

'**head,word** *c.n* main word at the beginning of an entry in a dictionary.

'**heady** *adj* (*-ier, -iest*) **1** (of an alcoholic drink) causing a feeling of giddiness or drunkenness.
2 (of a feeling) exciting or excited, e.g because of a success etc: *It was a heady feeling to know that he had won.*

heal /hi:l/ *tr/intr.v* (often *— (s.t) over/up*) **1** (cause (a cut, wound etc) to) mend, become healthy: *This cream will soon heal those cuts you've got. It took some time for the wound to heal over/up properly.* **2** (*fig*) (cause (a disagreement, division etc) to) become settled, no longer a problem etc: *Party officials are trying to heal over the splits in the members' ranks.* ⇨ faith-healing.

'**healer** *c.n* **1** person who tries to heal(1) people, esp through her/his mental(1) powers (and not usu through surgery(1)). ⇨ faith healer. **2** (*fig*) thing that heals(2): *Time is known as the great healer.*

health /helθ/ *n* **1** *u.n* (of the body and mind) state of being in a good condition and free from any illnesses: *What is the point of having*

money without health? Opposite sickness(1).
2 *u.n* (often *be in good, bad etc —*) condition of one's body: *He's been in poor health ever since last winter.* **3** *u.n* (of a nation, organization etc) fact or state of working well, earning money etc: *The health of our economy(3) must be our main concern.* **4** *c.n/interj* (often *Your —!; drink (to) s.o's —*) (way of honouring s.o by an) act of drinking a toast²(1) (to her/him): *Your very good health! After the speeches they drank to the health of all the visitors.* **National Health Service** ⇨ national. **World Health Organization** ⇨ WHO.

'**health ,centre** *c.n* place where a group of doctors, general practitioners etc work and provide medical services to local people.

'**health ,farm** *c.n* (*informal*) kind of clinic, usu in the country, where people go to improve their health(2) by special diets(1), exercises etc.

'**health ,food** *c/u.n* (also *attrib*) special kind of food that is (thought to be) very healthy(2), esp because it is natural or grown naturally without artificial(1) fertilizers and has few or no preservatives in it: *Health food shops are now very popular.*

'**healthily** *adv* in a healthy(2) way: *He lived healthily.*

'**healthiness** *u.n* state of being healthy.

'**healthy** *adj* (*-ier, -iest*) Opposite unhealthy.
1 having health(1); being in good health(2): *He's one of the healthiest people I know. Chris keeps healthy by swimming every day.* Compare sick(1).
2 causing or likely to cause health(1): *I think it's healthier to live in the country.* **3** (*fig*) having or showing health(2) are very healthy: *My finances(2) are very healthy* (i.e I have a lot of money). **4** (of a feeling, way of thinking about s.o/s.t) showing good sense: *He showed a healthy dislike of politicians, lawyers and estate agents.*

heap /hi:p/ *c.n* **1** large amount of s.t, large quantity of things, placed or arranged in a pile: *heaps of earth; a heap of dirty washing.* **in a heap** in a pile: *She left her clothes in a heap on the floor.*
▷ *tr.v* **2** (often *— s.t up*) put a large amount of (s.t) a quantity of (things), in a pile: *He heaped (up) the earth around the plants.* **3** (often *— s.t with s.t; — s.t (up)on s.t*) cover (s.t) with a large pile of s.t; put (a large pile of s.t) on s.t: *He heaped his plate with food. He heaped food on his plate.* **heap s.t (up)on s.o/s.t** (**a**) ⇨ heap(3). (**b**) (*fig; formal*) use bad words against s.o/s.t: *She heaped abuse¹(1) on her neighbour.*

'**heaps** *u.n* (often *— of s.t*) large amount of s.t: *There is heaps (of food) left from the party.*

hear /hɪə/ *v* (*p.t,p.p* heard /hɜ:d/) (not usu in the continuous tense except in (5,6)) **1** *tr/intr.v* be able to receive (and understand) speech or sounds (from s.o/s.t) using one's ears: *Could you speak a little louder as I can't hear (you) very well? Did you hear what I said?* **2** *tr.v* (often *— s.o/s.t do/doing s.t*) receive (the sound of a noise, of s.o doing or saying s.t) through one's ears: *I heard a loud explosion in the distance. I could hear two people arguing in the room next to me. I heard him say he wanted to leave his job.* ⇨ overhear. **3** *tr.v* (often *— that . . .*) be told or informed (s.t, that . . .): *I hear you are leaving your job. I heard that you'd been sick.* **4** *tr.v* (often *— what s.o has to say*) listen with attention to (what s.o is saying): *He heard her* (or *what she had to* *say*) *in complete silence and then walked away.* ⇒ unheard. **5** *tr.v* (*law*) (esp of a judge) attend to and listen to (a case) in a court of law: *The complaint against the police was heard by a special committee.* **6** *tr.v* attend (a religious service); (of a priest) listen to (confession): *I hear* Mass(1) *every Sunday. The priest is hearing her confession.*

Hear! Hear! (expression used to show one's approval of what s.o has just said): *His speech was greeted with cries of 'Hear! Hear!'*

hear (s.t) about s.o/s.t be told (s.t) about s.o/s.t: *What's this I hear about you getting a new job!*

hear from s.o receive news, a letter etc, from s.o: *I've just heard from my sister that she's coming to London next week.*

hear of s.o/s.t (often negative) have some/any knowledge about s.o/s.t: *I've never heard of him so he can't be as famous as he says he is.* Compare will/would not hear of s.t.

hear s.o out listen to the whole of what s.o says without interrupting: *She heard him out patiently but then said she wouldn't be able to help him.*

will/would not hear of s.t will/would not allow s.t (to happen): *She wouldn't hear of him paying for the meal.* Compare listen (to s.o/s.t).

'hearer *c.n* person who is present when s.o is talking, giving a speech etc: *His hearers applauded almost every word he said.* Compare listener.

'hearing *n* **1** *u.n* ability to hear(1): *Can you speak a bit louder as my hearing's not very good.* ⇒ hard of hearing. **2** *u.n* (often *in* s.o's —; *out of* —; *within* —) distance in which s.o can hear(2) s.t or in which s.o/s.t can be heard (⇒ hear(2)): *Did you realize he was within hearing when you were complaining about him?* ⇒ earshot. **3** *c.n* (often *give* s.o, *get*, *a fair/sympathetic* etc —) act of listening with attention to what s.o says: *The boss gave them a fair hearing and promised to deal with their complaints.* **4** *c.n* (*law*) act of listening to a case in a court of law: *The hearing (of his case) is fixed for Monday next.* (**the**) **hard of hearing** (*pl* when a *n*) (people who are) not able to hear(1) very well: *He's a bit hard of hearing, so speak louder. The hard of hearing want help, not sympathy.*

'hearing ,aid *c.n* device, usu placed inside an ear, that increases the volume of sound received through it so that s.o who does not hear(1) very well can hear(1) things better.

'hear,say *u.n* thing(s) said that may or may not be true because one has no means of checking it/ them: *All the accusations against him are merely hearsay; what we need is actual proof.*

hearken /'hɑːkən/ *intr.v* (often — *to* s.o/s.t) (*literary*) listen attentively (to s.o/s.t): *Hearken to him — you'd think he knew everything from the way he talks!* (i.e one really shouldn't pay much attention to him).

hearse /hɜːs/ *c.n* special kind of car or carriage pulled by horses, for carrying a coffin to a church, burial ground etc.

heart /hɑːt/ *n* **1** *c.n* (also *attrib*) organ in the body of a person or animal that controls the flow of blood to other parts by pumping it around the body: *I could feel his heart beating slowly. He's training to be a heart specialist* (i.e a doctor who deals with *heart diseases* etc). **2** *sing/u.n* (expression of one's good or bad) feelings or emotion(1): *She has a kind heart and will help you*

if you are in trouble. He has no heart at all so don't expect any sympathy from him. **3** *u/def.n* (often (*not*) *have the* — (*to do* s.t)) courage or enthusiasm (to do s.t): *I hadn't the heart to tell him the bad news. They had no heart for the job they were asked to do.* ⇒ lose heart. **4** *c.n* central or main part of s.t growing: *I need a* lettuce *with a good heart.* ⇒ heart(8). **5** *c.n* (usu *the* — *of* s.t) central part of (a place): *We went deeper into the heart of the wood/forest.* **6** *c.n* one of a set of playing cards with one or more solid red shapes drawn on it that look like this ♥: *He had only a king and a three of hearts left in his hand.* **7** *c.n* shape ♥ supposed to represent a heart(1), esp as a sign of love: *He drew a heart with their names in it on the wall.* ⇒ sweetheart. **at heart** (**a**) really or essentially: *He's a kind man at heart though he often doesn't seem so.* (**b**) showing attention or concern, esp for s.o's interests: *I am giving you this advice because I have your own best interests at heart.* **be s.o after one's own heart** be a person of the kind one likes a lot: *You're a man after my own heart.* **break s.o's heart** cause s.o a lot of sorrow: *It nearly broke my heart to see the way the town had been destroyed.* **cross my heart (and hope to die)** (said esp by a child and often while making the sign of a cross over her/his heart, to show that what he/she has said is really true). **eat one's heart out** (*fig*) suffer a lot, esp because of s.t one cannot get, do etc: *Charles is eating his heart out because his wife will not come back to him.* **find it in one's heart (to do s.t)** have/ feel enough pity or kindness (to forgive etc). **from (the bottom of) one's heart** with a very sincere and warm feeling: *I would like to thank you from the bottom of my heart for all you have done for me.* **gladden s.o's heart** ⇒ gladden. **have a change of heart** ⇒ change(*n*). **Have a heart!** (*informal*) Be reasonable; Show some pity!: *Have a heart! You know I can't pay you now.* **have a heart of gold** ⇒ gold(*n*). **have one's heart in one's mouth** (*fig*) be very frightened: *He had his heart in his mouth as he watched her being rescued.* (**not**) **have one's heart in s.t** (not) work very hard at doing s.t because one is really (not) interested in it: *He had his whole heart in his job and had very little time for anything else.* ⇒ s.o's heart is not in s.t. **have one's heart**, or **one's heart is**, **in the right place** be really or essentially very kind. **have one's heart set on s.t; set one's heart on s.t** be very determined to have or do s.t: *Sarah has set her heart on going to Bristol University.* **heart and soul** completely and fully: *He worked heart and soul to relieve the suffering of the poor.* **s.o's heart bleeds for s.o** s.o feels very anxious about, sorry for, s.o: *My heart bleeds for him in his present troubles.* **s.o's heart is not in s.t** s.o is not very or at all enthusiastic about s.t: *My heart was just not in the job I had to do.* ⇒ (not) have one's heart in s.t. **the heart of the matter**, **problem** etc the main point of s.t: *We need to get to the heart of the matter if we want to make progress.* **in one's heart (of hearts)** really and truly: *He didn't like to admit it but in his heart of hearts he knew she didn't really love him.* **know**, **learn** etc s.t (**off**) **by heart** know etc a fact, a poem, a piece of literature etc, so well that one can repeat or recite it from memory. **lose heart** become discouraged(1): *So many problems faced* *her that she began to lose heart.* **lose one's heart to s.o/s.t** (*formal*) become very attracted to s.o/s.t; fall in love with s.o/s.t: *Sam lost his heart to a girl he met in Venice.* **not have the heart to do s.t** ⇨ heart(3). **set one's heart on s.t** ⇨ have one's heart set on s.t. **sick at heart** very troubled or disturbed: *He was sick at heart when he thought of all the killing that had taken place.* **take heart** become encouraged: *She took heart from the fact that her troubles would soon be over.* **take s.o to one's heart** show great affection for s.o: *He looked so sad and lost that she immediately took him to her heart.* **take s.t to heart** (a) pay great attention to s.t (because it affects one and one should do s.t about it): *He took her remarks to heart and promised he'd try harder.* (b) be disturbed by s.t s.o has said etc: *Don't take what she said to heart; she didn't really mean it.* **tear s.o's heart out** (*fig*) make s.o very unhappy. **to one's heart's content** as much as one wants (to have of s.t, to do s.t etc): *Soon it will be your school holidays and then you can listen to your music to your heart's content but now you must study.* **wear one's heart on one's sleeve** (*fig*) not (try to) hide one's feelings about a person: *He wears his heart on his sleeve when he's near Jane.* **with all one's heart** completely and very sincerely: *I wish you success with all my heart.* **young at heart** (of an old(er) person) feeling youthful(2).

▷ *intr.v* **8** (often — *up*) form a heart(4): *The lettuces are beginning to heart* (*up*).

'heart,ache *u.n* feeling of unhappiness, esp in matters of love.

'heart at,tack *c.n* sudden stopping or irregular action of the heart(1), often leading to death.

'heart,beat *c/u.n* (usu regular sound of the) movement of a heart(1) as it pushes blood around the body.

'heart,breaking *adj* causing very great unhappiness or sorrow: *It was heartbreaking work trying to bring relief to all the people dying in the famine.*

'heart,broken *adj* (*,broken-'hearted* when *attrib*) (of a person) full of unhappiness or sorrow, esp in matters of love.

'heart,burn *u.n* feeling of pain in one's chest, usu because of s.t one has eaten that has given one indigestion.

'heart di,sease *c/u.n* illness in the heart(1).

-hearted *adj* having a feeling as shown by the first part of the word; *big-hearted*; *broken-hearted*; *hard-hearted*; *kind-hearted*.

'hearten *tr.v* (*formal*) encourage(s.o); strengthen (s.o's intentions etc): *We were greatly heartened by our first success.*

'heartening *adj* encouraging: *heartening news.* Opposite disheartening.

'heart ,failure *u.n* stopping of the action of the heart(1), often leading to death.

'heart,felt *adj* very sincere: *You have my heartfelt thanks for all you have done for me.*

'heartily *adv* in a hearty way: *eat heartily.*

'heartiness *u.n* state or fact of being hearty.

'heartless *adj* (*derog*) showing no pity; being very cruel: *His treatment of her during her illness was particularly heartless.*

'heartlessly *adv*. **'heartlessness** *u.n*.

heart-rending /'hɑːt ,rendɪŋ/ *adj* causing very great pity or distress(1): *There were heart-rending cries coming from people trapped in the building.*

'heart-,searching *u.n* deep examination of one's conscience, e.g because one has done s.t wrong: *After a good deal of heart-searching she had to admit his criticism of her had some truth.*

'heart,strings *pl.n* **pull/tug at s.o's heartstrings** attract, have a great effect on, s.o's feelings or emotions(1): *The sight of her suffering tugged at his heartstrings.*

'heart,throb *c.n* (*informal*) person such as a film-star who is admired a lot because he/she is very attractive.

,heart-to-'heart *c.n* (also *attrib*) very full and frank discussion with s.o (usu in private): *I had a real heart-to-heart* (*talk*) *with him about his problems.*

'heart ,transplant *c.n* ⇨ transplant(2).

'heart-,warming *adj* causing great pleasure: *It was heart-warming to see their happy expressions when they received their gifts.*

'hearty *adj* (*-ier*, *-iest*) **1** showing great friendliness and warmth: *Let's give a hearty welcome to our visitors from abroad.* **2** (of a person) very or too cheerful or noisy: *He's one of those hearty types who is always slapping(3) you on the back and offering you a drink.* **3** (of an action) rather strong, big: *He gave the bell a hearty pull.* **hale and hearty** ⇨ hale. **a hearty appetite, meal** etc a big appetite etc: *He has a very hearty appetite and eats three full meals a day.*

hearth /hɑːθ/ *c.n* area of floor in front of and around a fireplace.

'hearth,rug *c.n* small rug placed in front of a hearth.

heat /hiːt/ *n* **1** *u.n* degree of being hot: *What heat do you want the oven?* **2** *u.n* (amount or degree of) hotness (of s.t), esp as s.t that can be felt: *The heat from the fire soon warmed him. The heat of the sun caused the metal to bend.* **3** *u.n* hot weather: *I can't stand this heat; let's go into the shade.* **4** *c.n* (*sports*) one of a number of races, competitions etc that people take part in, the winners or best ones of which go on to (other races until they reach) the final race etc: *Because there were so many runners there were six heats and two* semifinals *before the final.* **in/on heat** (of a female animal, esp a dog) in a state of sexual readiness for mating(⇨ mate(7)). **in the heat of the moment, argument, debate** etc when feelings of excitement, anger etc are at their highest because of an argument etc: *He said things in the heat of the moment which he regretted afterwards.*

▷ *tr/intr.v* **5** (often — (s.t) *up*) (cause(s.t) to) become hot: *Can you heat* (*up*) *a pan of water for the vegetables? It didn't take long for the water to heat up. Shall I heat the chicken or would you prefer to eat it cold?* Compare warm(9). ⇨ overheat.

'heated *adj* **1** having or been made hot or warm: *It is best to keep the* greenhouse *heated during the winter.* **2** having or showing feelings of excitement, anger etc: *There was a heated argument about who should pay for the damage.*

'heatedly *adv* in a heated(2) way: *He spoke very heatedly about the wrongs she had done him.*

'heatedness *u.n*.

'heater *c.n* device for making s.t, e.g water, a room etc, hot: *an electric/oil/gas heater* (i.e one that uses electricity, oil, gas to heat a room).

'heating *u.n* (also *attrib*) system of boilers, water pipes etc for making a house, office etc warm: *We don't normally have the heating on during the day as we both go out to work.* ⇒ central heating.

'heat,proof *adj* that will not break when heated: *heatproof glass.*

'heat-re,sistant *adj* (of a material) designed(6), made, to protect s.o/s.t against very hot temperatures.

'heat,stroke *u.n* feeling of illness, fainting etc from having too much heat(2,3). Compare sunstroke.

'heat ,wave *c.n* length of time when the weather is very hot.

heath /hi:θ/ *c/u.n* stretch of open land that is wild and usu has small plants such as heather growing on it.

heathen /'hi:ðən/ *c.n* **1** (becoming *old use*) person who does not belong to an organized religion (and so is considered by members of one to be in need of conversion(2) etc). **2** (*derog*; *informal*) young person who is considered to be badly behaved: *That boy's a little heathen.*

heather /'heðə/ *c/u.n* (example of a) short plant with usu purple flowers and woody stems that grows on heaths, moors¹ etc.

heave /hi:v/ *c.n* **1** (often *give* (s.t) *a* —) act of pulling, pushing or lifting (s.t) with a lot of effort: *He gave the rope a heave* (or *He gave a heave on the rope*) *and managed to pull the boat further up the shore.*

▷ *v* **2** *tr.v* (often — *s.o/s.t down/up*) pull, push or lift (s.o/s.t) with a lot of effort: *I need a couple of strong men to help heave the trunk down from the bedroom.* **3** *intr.v* (often — *at/on s.t*) try to pull, push or lift (s.t heavy): *Several men were heaving on the rope trying to get the boat to the shore.* **4** *tr.v* (often — *s.t at/through s.t*) (*informal*) throw (s.t heavy) (at/through s.t): *He heaved a brick through the shop window.* **5** *intr.v* (of waves, the earth, a person's chest etc) move up and down slowly and with difficulty: *His chest was heaving after that long run.* **heave a sigh** (**of relief**) ⇒ sigh(*n*). **heave to** (*p.t,p.p* hove /həʊv/) (of a ship) stop moving: *The ship hove to outside the harbour.*

heaven /'hevn/ *n* **1** *c/unique n* (often with capital **H**) place where God or the gods is/are thought to live and to which good people (or their souls) are thought to go when they die: *She believed she would go to heaven when she died.* Compare hell(1). **2** *unique n* (usu with capital **H**) God or some divine(1) being: *Heaven will help you in your present troubles.* **3** *unique n* the sky above one: *If you look up to heaven on a clear night you can see thousands of stars.* ⇒ heavens(1). **4** *u.n* (*informal*) state of great happiness or pleasure: *It was absolute heaven to get home to a warm fire after a day out in the rain.* Compare hell(2). **heaven help you** (**if . . .**) (expression used to show that s.o will be in great trouble or difficulty (if he/she does s.t etc): *Heaven help him if I find out that he's been lying.* **heaven knows** (**if/what** *etc* . . .) (expression used to show that one does not know (if/what etc)): *Heaven knows what I would have done without him.* **heaven knows**

(**why** (**. . .**)) (expression used to show surprise about s.t that happens): *Heaven knows why he goes there every day!* **move heaven and earth** (**to do s.t** (**for s.o**)) try everything that one can (to do s.t (for s.o)). **thank heaven!** ⇒ thank.

'heavenliness *u.n* fact or state of being heavenly.

'heavenly *adj* **1** of or referring to heaven(1,2). **2** (*informal*) very pleasing or pleasant: *heavenly weather*; *a heavenly dress.*

,heavenly 'body *c.n* the sun, moon or a star.

'heavens *def.pl.n* **1** = heaven(3): *The rain came so suddenly; it was as if the heavens had opened up.*

▷ *interj* **2** (also **,heavens a'bove!**) (expression of surprise, anger etc): *Heavens! Is that the time? I must go!* **good heavens** ⇒ good(*adj*). **thank heaven(s)** (**that . . .**) ⇒ thank.

'heaven,sent *adj* (usu *a* — *opportunity*) that comes at exactly the right time (usu when one is not expecting it).

heavy /'hevɪ/ *adj* (*-ier, -iest*) **1** who/that has a great weight that makes her/him/it difficult to carry, lift etc: *The child was so heavy that I could only just lift him. The box is too heavy for him to carry alone.* Opposite light²(1). **2** who/that has a certain weight: *How heavy are you?* **3** falling, happening, in large amounts: *There was a heavy fall of snow during the night. Irena is a very heavy smoker/drinker. The traffic was very heavy as I drove out of town. I have had some rather heavy expenses this month.* ⇒ light²(2,4). **4** of more than average weight: *a heavy coat*; *a heavy metal.* ⇒ light²(3). **5** (of food) solid and difficult to eat or digest(3): *a heavy meal.* ⇒ light²(5). **6** (of work etc) difficult to do, occupying much time and energy(1): *After a heavy day at the office all I want to do is stay at home.* ⇒ light²(6). **7** (of soil) solid and without much air in it, so often wet. ⇒ light²(7). **8** (of sleep) deep and so not easily woken, disturbed: *a heavy sleeper.* ⇒ light²(8). **be heavy on s.t** (*informal*) use a lot, too much, of s.t: *My car's rather heavy on petrol. He was a bit heavy on the drink last night, don't you think?* **heavy going** ⇒ going(4). **make heavy going/weather of s.t** make s.t seem more difficult/complicated than it really is: *Jack is learning to drive but he is making heavy weather of it.* **9** being or coming with great force: *As he came in the door he received a heavy blow on his head.* ⇒ light²(9). **10** (of a book, music etc) (too) serious and so difficult to read or understand: *The play was very heavy and I left before it finished.* ⇒ light²(10). **11** (*pred*) (of a person, movement) slow and difficult: *He's a bit heavy in his movements.* ⇒ light²(11). **12** (of a sound etc) rather loud or deep: *heavy breathing*; *heavy footsteps.* ⇒ light²(12). **13** (*derog*; *informal*) (of a person) not easy to deal with (in her/his character): *I find him a bit heavy.* **14** (of waves, seas) stormy: *They almost drowned in the heavy seas.* ⇒ light²(13). **15** (of weather) rather hot and still, e.g before a storm.

▷ *adv* **16** (usu *hang/lie* — *on s.o/s.t*) (*formal*) in a heavy(3) way: *Time hangs heavy on my hands* (i.e I have not got much to do). *The murder was lying heavy on his conscience.*

▷ *c.n* (*pl -ies*) **17** (*slang*) strong person, often a criminal, who protects s.o: *The gangster always* *went around with a couple of heavies following him.*

'heavily *adv.* **'heaviness** *u.n.*

,heavy-'duty *adj* (of clothes, objects etc) strongly made and able to be used in hard conditions, to do hard work etc: *heavy-duty tyres.*

,heavy-'handed *adj* (*derog*) not doing s.t well, not done well, usu because not enough skill or care has been used: *The newspaper article criticized the government for their heavy-handed treatment of the* riots(1).

,heavy-'handedly *adv.* **,heavy-'handedness** *u.n.*

,heavy-'hearted *adj* (*formal*; *literary*) feeling sad.

,heavy 'industry *u.n* group of industries that use big machines to produce or manufacture things, e.g coal, steel, ships, cars etc. Compare light industry.

,heavy-'laden *adj* (of a vehicle etc) carrying a heavy weight of goods: *The ship was heavy-laden.*

'heavy,weight *c.n* (also *attrib*) boxer(1)(⇒ box²), wrestler etc who weighs more than 175 pounds/79 kilogrammes and belongs to the heavy class of boxers etc: *the heavyweight* championships(2): *He was the heavyweight* champion(3) *of the world for five years.*

Hebrew /'hi:bru:/ *u.n* (also *attrib*) language of the Jewish people.

heck /hek/ *c.n* (*slang*) **a heck of a lot** (**of s.t**) a lot (of s.t): *Leave me alone — I've got a heck of a lot of work to do.* (**have**) **a heck of a cheek/ nerve** (have) too great a rudeness: *You've got a heck of a nerve asking for my help after the way you talked to me yesterday.* **What the heck (. . .)!** (**a**) (expression used to show great annoyance or surprise (at what s.o is doing, has done etc)): *What the heck do you mean by using my car without asking?* (**b**) (expression used to show that s.t does not matter, that one does not care etc): *Oh well, what the heck (does it matter)? We lost that game but we should win the next.*

heckle /'hekl/ *tr/intr.v* interrupt (s.o while he/ she is speaking in public), e.g by asking awkward questions, shouting etc, esp to annoy, confuse or upset the speaker, meeting etc: *Several people were heckling (the speaker) from the back of the crowd.*

'heckler *c.n* person who heckles.

hectare /'hekta:/ *c.n* (*written abbr* ha) metric measurement of an area of land (= 10 000 square metres or 2.471 acres).

hectic /'hektik/ *adj* very or too busy; having (too) much to do; rushing about a lot: *We had such a hectic day at the office.*

'hectically *adv.*

he'd (strong form /hi:d/, weak form /hid/) **1** = he had. ⇒ have. **2** = he would. ⇒ will¹, would.

hedge /hedʒ/ *c.n* **1** line or row of bushes or plants growing in a mass (and often cut or shaped) to form an edge or barrier(1) like a wall in a garden, field, road etc. **a hedge against s.t** (*fig*) a thing one does, buys etc in order to protect oneself against s.t bad happening in the future: *He bought a lot of gold coins as a hedge against* inflation(2).

▷ *v* **2** *tr.v* (often — *s.t around*, *in*, *off* etc) put or

grow a hedge(1) round (a garden etc): *They decided to hedge in the rose garden.* **3** *intr.v* not give a full or proper answer to a question: *Stop hedging and tell me what you really think.* **hedge one's bets** (*fig*) try to protect oneself by doing more than one thing (and so spreading the risk of s.t going wrong): *I'm not certain about which job I'll get so I'll hedge my bets and apply for both.*

'hedge,hog *c.n* kind of small brown animal with short spines(3) on its back which can roll itself into a ball to protect itself.

'hedge,row *c.n* row of bushes etc, esp one at the edge of a field, road etc.

hedonism /'hi:dəˌnizəm/ *u.n* belief that the most important thing in life is pleasure.

'hedo,nist *c.n* person who believes in hedonism.

,hedo'nistic *adj.*

,hedo'nistically *adv.*

heed /hi:d/ *u.n* **1** (usu *give/pay — to s.o/s.t*; *take — of s.o/s.t*) (*formal*) attention (to s.o, what he/ she says etc); notice (of s.o/s.t)): *She paid no heed to his warning so has only herself to blame.*

▷ *tr.v* **2** (*formal*) pay attention to (s.o, what he/ she says etc): *If you had heeded my words you wouldn't be in the trouble you're now in.*

'heedful *adj* (usu — *of s.o/s.t*) (*formal*) paying attention (to s.o/s.t): *You ought to be heedful of your mother's advice.*

'heedfully *adv.* **'heedfulness** *u.n.*

'heedless *adj* (usu — *of s.o/s.t*) (*formal*) not paying attention (to s.o/s.t): *Heedless of the crowd of people watching her, Pam completed the daring act.*

'heedlessly *adv.* **'heedlessness** *u.n.*

heel /hi:l/ *c.n* **1** back part of the foot. **2** part of a sock, stocking etc covering a heel(1): *I have a hole in the heel of my sock.* **3** part of a shoe, boot etc that supports a heel(1): *High heels are coming back into fashion.* **4** (*derog*; *slang*) person who behaves badly, esp a man with regard to women: *He's a bit of a heel leaving her like that after his promise to marry her.* **at/on s.o's heels** (following, chasing etc) close behind s.o: *He ran off with the dog (close) on his heels.* **bring s.o to heel** make s.o obey, stop doing s.t: *The threat of punishment soon brought the children to heel.* **come to heel** stop being disobedient: *He thought his son would come to heel if he threatened not to give him any more money.* **cool/kick one's heels** (*fig*; *informal*) (be forced to) wait, waste one's time waiting, (while s.t is happening): *I was left kicking my heels in the waiting room as the doctor was busy with another patient.* **dig in one's heels** become determined and refuse to agree during an argument. **down-at-heel** ⇒ down¹. **head over heels**; (*fall*) **head over heels in love (with s.o)** ⇒ head(*n*). **hard on s.o's heels** following s.o very closely: *The thief ran away with the police hard on his heels.* **Heel!** (command to a dog to return to the side of its owner). **hot on s.o's/s.t's heels** following or chasing s.o/s.t (and nearly at the point of catching/finding her/him/it). **hot on s.t's heels** happening very soon after s.t else: *Hot on the heels of the news that he'd escaped came a report that he'd been seen in France.* **kick one's heels** ⇒ cool one's heels. **take to one's heels** (*fig*) (start to) run away, esp to escape s.o/s.t. **tread on s.o's heels** (**a**) (often *fig*) follow very or too close behind s.o. **(b)** (*fig*) do s.t that is the same as, or interferes with, what s.o else is doing: *He'll accuse you of treading on his heels if you take up the same cause.* **turn on one's heel** turn (quickly) and face in a different direction, usu in order to leave s.w: *He turned on his heel and walked away.* **under s.o.'s heel** (*fig*) under s.o's control (often that of s.o who is cruel): *With that final victory the whole country was now under the heel of the enemy.*

▷ *v* **5** *tr.v* put, repair, a heel(3) on (a shoe): *My shoes need heeling.* ⇒ reheel. **6** *tr/intr.v* (in football, rugby) (cause (the ball) to) move backwards by using one's heel(1). **7** *intr.v* (often — *over*) (of a ship) lean (over) to one side, e.g because of the wind or waves: *The boat heeled over as the wind caught it.*

-heeled *adj* **1** having the kind of heel(s)(3) on one's shoes shown by the first part of the word: *high/low-heeled shoes.* **2** (*informal*) having an amount of wealth shown by the first part of the word: *well-heeled.*

hefty /'heftɪ/ *adj* (*-ier*, *-iest*) **1** (of a person, her/his body) big and solid: *He's got hefty shoulders from all the lifting he does.* **2** (usu *attrib*) (of a blow etc) having great force or power: *He gave him a hefty kick on the* shin(1). **3** (usu *attrib*) large: *a hefty fine for breaking the speed limit*; *a hefty increase in one's salary.*
'heftily *adv.* **'heftiness** *u.n.*

heifer /'hefə/ *c.n* young cow that has not yet given birth.

height /haɪt/ *n* **1** *c/u.n* (written *abbr* ht) (usu s.o's —; *the* — *of* s.t) measurement (from the bottom to the top) of how tall s.o is, how high s.t is: *What's your height? What is the height of that wall? What height can you jump? According to the map, the height of the mountain is 8848 metres (above sea level).* **2** *c.n* (high) point (on s.t); high place: *From that height he could see all the country around for miles.* **3** *c/u.n* (often *the* — *of* s.t) greatest or most important point (of s.t) that one reaches or can reach: *The height of his* career(2) *was when he was made manager of the branch. It was the height of stupidity to say that.* **in the height of fashion** wearing the most fashionable clothes, doing the most fashionable things. ⇒ high.

heighten *v* **1** *tr.v* make (s.t) higher: *We need to heighten the fence to stop the neighbours looking over at us.* **2** *tr/intr.v* (cause (s.t, esp an effect) to) become greater, more noticeable: Tension(1) *heightened as the day of the examination results came closer.*

heinous /'heɪnəs/ *adj* (*formal*) (esp of a crime) very serious or bad.
'heinously *adv.* **'heinousness** *u.n.*

heir /eə/ *c.n* (often *be/fall* — *to* s.t) person who, according to law, will receive (part of) the wealth, property etc of s.o, or who will have a noble title etc, after s.o dies: *Under his aunt's will, he was* sole'(1) *heir to her considerable fortune. The king had no children so his brother was heir to the throne.*

heiress /'eərɪs/ *c.n* female heir, esp one who will receive a lot of money etc when s.o dies.

'heir,loom *c.n* valuable object that has been passed down from one generation(2) to another in a family.

held /held/ *p.t,p.p* of hold.

helicopter /'helɪ,kɒptə/ *c.n* aircraft with one or more large propellers above the main body which rotate(1) horizontally and allow it to take off and land vertically, and to stay in one position in the air.

'heli,port *c.n* small airport for helicopters.

helium /'hi:lɪəm/ *u.n* element that is a very light gas found in the air and that does not burn, *chem.symb* He.

hell /hel/ *n* **1** *u/unique n* (often with capital **H**) place where the Devil or devils is/are thought to live and to which bad people (or their souls) are thought to go as a punishment when they die: *Do you really believe in the existence of hell?* Compare heaven(1,2). **2** *c.n* (cause of) great suffering: *He made her life an absolute hell on earth.* Compare heaven(4). **a hell of a s.t** (*slang*) a great (amount/number of) s.t: *a hell of a lot of food/people. That was a hell of a job you did! You've got a hell of a* nerve(3) *telling me what I should do!* **be/have hell to pay** (*informal*) be/have very bad consequences (because of s.t that has (not) been done): *There'll be hell to pay if you don't finish the report on time.* **come hell or high water** whatever (difficult) things may happen or in spite of them: *I intend to fight for my rights, come hell or high water.* **for the hell of it** (*informal*) for no special reason, simply because one wants to (do s.t): *When asked why they had stolen the car the boys said that it was just for the hell of it.* **give s.o hell** (*informal*) shout at, criticize, attack, s.o very strongly: *He gave her hell when he heard what she had done.* **go through hell** suffer a great deal (either in one's mind or body): *He went through hell during those three days when his daughter was missing.* **go to hell** (*slang*; often *interj*) go away, stop annoying me etc; do what he/she likes (as I/we am/are not interested): *He can go to hell as far as I'm concerned if that's the way he treats me after all I've done for him.* **like hell** (*slang*) **(a)** (doing s.t) with great effort: *We worked like hell to finish in time.* **(b)** = the hell you will, won't etc. **play hell with s.t** affect s.t badly: *The delay of my flight played hell with my* schedules(1). **the hell you will, won't** etc (*slang*) you most certainly will (not) (do s.t, esp if I/we have anything to do with it): *'I won't take orders from you!' 'The hell you won't' (or 'Like hell you won't')!*

▷ *interj* **3** (often *Oh* —!) (*slang*) (expression used to show annoyance, anger, pain etc): *Hell! I've forgotten to bring my books! 'Oh hell! Have I got to listen to all your complaints yet again?'*

'hellish *adj* causing (great) suffering: *We had a hellish journey; the train was packed and we had to stand all the way.*

'hellishly *adv* **1** in a hellish way. **2** (becoming *old use*) very (greatly): *The puzzle was hellishly difficult.*

he'll (strong form /hi:l/, weak form /hɪl/) = he shall/will ⇒ will.

hello ⇒ hallo.

helm /helm/ *c.n* (usu *sing*) wheel, handle or tiller that controls the rudder and so helps steer a ship, boat etc: *Could you take the helm while I lower the sails, please?* **at the helm (of s.t)** (*fig*; *formal*) in charge (of s.t), controlling (a business etc): *It is important to choose the right person to be at the helm (of the company) during this difficult time.*

'helmsman *c.n* (*pl* -*men*) person who operates a helm.

helmet /'helmɪt/ *c.n* strong covering made of metal, plastic, leather etc for the top and sometimes also the sides of the head, worn as a protection by motorcyclists etc: *It is illegal to ride a* motorbike *without a helmet.* ⇒ crash-helmet.

help /help/ *n* **1** *u.n* act of aiding(2) or assisting s.o (who is in some kind of difficulty) to do s.t: *I need help to move this box. Can I give you any help?* **2** *sing.n* (often *be a* (*great* etc) — (*to s.o*)) person or thing who/that is (very) useful (to s.o): *She was a great help to my family during my illness. Thank you for lending me the ladder — it was a big help.* **3** *c.n* person employed to do certain kinds of usu manual(1) work: *a farm help.* ⇒ home help.

be beyond help (of a person or thing) be in a situation where there is nothing that one can do to save her/him/it (from s.t bad happening, death etc): *The doctors say he is beyond help and will probably die during the night.* **be of help** (**with s.t**) (*formal*) help(6) (with s.t): *Can I be of help with those suitcases?* **there's no help for it** there is no way that it/s.t can be avoided, stopped etc: *The matter was decided long ago and there's no help for it now.*

▷ *interj* **4** (shout or cry to attract s.o's attention because one is in difficulty or danger): *'Help! We're trapped!'* **5** (mild expression of surprise, need for help(1) because of a problem etc): *'Help! That meal is far too big for me!'*

▷ *tr/intr.v* **6** (often — *s.o with/over s.t*; — *s.o* (*to*) *do s.t*) do s.t (for/with s.o) that he/she cannot do (easily) alone; give (s.o) assistance or aid(1) (to do s.t): *Can you help* (*me*) *with these suitcases* (i.e Can you carry one etc for me)? *He helped her to paint the house. It would help* (*me*) *if you would give him a lift home.* **7** (cause (s.o/s.t) to) become better, less ill etc: *I need something to help my* headache. *It would help to cheer her up if she could just express her feelings for once. That sort of behaviour doesn't help* (*us*), *you know.* **8** do s.t useful that will lead (s.o) to success (in s.t): *The government is doing all it can to help. He helped them find a successful* remedy(1). **9** serve (a customer) in a shop: *Can I help you?*

can/can't/couldn't help it (**if . . .**) be s.t that one is unable to stop, avoid etc; be s.t that one does (not) consider to be one's responsibility, fault etc: *I know I get angry very easily but I just can't help it. Can I help it if you think everything I say is wrong?* **can't/couldn't help doing** , **but do** , **s.t** be unable to stop doing s.t: *She couldn't help laughing when she saw them dressed up like that. I can't help but think that she doesn't really know what she's doing.* **can't/couldn't help oneself** (**doing s.t**) be unable to stop oneself (doing s.t): *She just couldn't help herself; she started laughing the moment she saw them.*

help s.o down/up (**s.t**) (**with s.t**) help(6) s.o to stand up, climb down/up (s.t) (or to move s.t down/up): *Can you help me down* (*the cliff*)? *Joe helped his son up by letting him stand on his shoulders. Can you help me up the stairs with this table?*

help (**s.o**) **out** do s.t (for s.o) that is of help(1), usu for a short time: *During the holidays he helped* (*his mother*) *out in the shop. Can you help me out with this puzzle?*

help oneself/s.o (**to s.t**) take (food, drink etc) for oneself; give s.o (food, drink etc): *He helped himself to a large slice of cake. Can I help you to some more* (*food*)? *'Could I have a drink?' 'Yes, of course. Help yourself.'* **help oneself to s.t** take or steal s.t that doesn't belong to one: *The thieves broke the shop window and then helped themselves to the jewels.*

It can't/couldn't be helped It is/was s.t that can't/couldn't be changed, stopped etc: *It can't be helped — what's done is done.*

not do more than one can help do only the smallest amount of s.t, e.g work, that is necessary: *He's very lazy and never does more work than he can help.*

'helper *c.n* person who helps(6–9).

'helpful *adj* (of a person or thing) who/that gives help or is useful: *He was very helpful when I was ill. I think you'll find this book the most helpful for that particular question.*

'helpfully *adv.* **'helpfulness** *u.n.*

'helping *c.n* (often — *of s.t*) amount (of food) (put) on one's plate: *He took a large helping of vegetables.*

,helping 'hand ⇒ give/lend (s.o) a (helping) hand (⇒ hand(*n*)).

'helpless *adj* unable to do s.t or to help s.o, e.g because one is old, does not know how etc: *He's become old and helpless. I felt helpless and unable to give her the support she needed.*

'helplessly *adv.* **'helplessness** *u.n.*

helter-skelter /ˌheltə 'skeltə/ *adj/adv* **1** (doing s.t) in a very hurried and confused way: *Sam threw his clothes helter-skelter into the suitcase and ran for the bus.*

▷ *c.n* **2** tall structure in an amusement park that has a slide going from the top around and down the outside to the bottom.

hem /hem/ *c.n* **1** edge on a piece of cloth, a dress etc that has been folded up and sewn. **take a hem down/up** make (a dress, skirt etc) longer or shorter by changing the hem(1).

▷ *tr.v* (-mm-) **2** put/sew a hem(1) on (a dress etc): *The trousers are almost finished; I only have to hem them.* **hem s.o/s.t in** (**a**) surround a person or thing so that it is difficult to escape: *Mike had to chase the chicken round the garden until he managed to hem it in near the fence.* (**b**) (*fig*) make s.o (feel) unable to act freely: *I feel hemmed in working in such a small office.*

'hem,line *c.n* bottom edge of a dress or skirt: *The fashion is for shorter hemlines this year.* **lower/raise a hemline** make a hemline lower/ higher.

he-man /'hiː ˌmæn/ *c.n* (*pl* 'he-ˌmen) very strong or manly man.

hemisphere /'hemɪˌsfɪə/ *c.n* half of a sphere(1). **the northern/southern hemisphere** (also with capital **N/S** and **H**) the top/bottom half of the Earth: *Australia is in the Southern Hemisphere.* **the eastern/western hemisphere** (also with capital **E/W** and **H**) the east/west half of the Earth: *Russia is in the eastern hemisphere.*

hemoglobin, **hemophilia,** **hemophiliac,** **hemorrhage, hemorrhoid** ⇒ haemoglobin etc.

hemp /hemp/ *u.n* **1** (kind of plant that has) fibres(1) used to make rope and cloth. **2** = hashish.

hen /hen/ *c.n* **1** adult female bird of the chicken family. **2** (also *attrib*) (name for a) female bird of other families: *a hen pheasant.* ⇨ cock(1).

'hen,house *c.n* building for keeping hens(1) in.

'hen ,party *c.n* (*informal*) party for women only. Compare stag party (⇨ stag(1)).

'hen,pecked *adj* (*derog; informal*) (of a husband) who always does what his wife tells him to do.

hence /hens/ *adv* (*formal*) **1** for that/this reason, because of that/this: *We are offering a high salary and hence we expect to get someone good.* **2** (often *one etc day, month etc —*) after this present time: *Payment will have to be made one year hence.*

,hence'forth, ,hence'forward *adv* (*formal*) from the present time into the future: *Henceforward, you will be responsible for this department.*

henchman /'hentʃmən/ *c.n* (*pl -men*) (*derog*) person used by s.o to protect her/him, to do what he/she says without question and often to attack other people: *He was surrounded by his henchmen, some of whom appeared to be carrying guns.*

henna /'henə/ *u.n* **1** kind of small plant with white/red flowers from Asia and North Africa. **2** red-brown dye(1) made from its leaves and used esp on the hair.

▷ *tr.v* (*hennaes, hennaed, hennaing*) **3** use this dye(1) on (hair): *Have you ever hennaed your hair?*

henpecked ⇨ hen.

hepatitis /,hepə'taɪtɪs/ *c.n* (*medical*) painful swelling of the liver(1).

heptagon /'heptəgən/ *c.n* flat shape with seven (usu equal) sides.

heptagonal /hep'tægənəl/ *adj* having the shape of a heptagon.

heptathlon /hep'tæθlɒn/ *def/c.n* athletic(1) competition for women which consists of seven different events; hurdles, high jump, shot put, 200 m running, long jump, javelin, 800 m running. Compare decathlon.

her (strong form /hɜː/, weak form /hə/) *possessive pron* **1** belonging to, for, her(2): *Jane said that she would lend him her book. Her parents are still in Kenya. Our cat is fond of her kittens. The ship and all her crew*¹(1) *were lost. France is proud of her heritage.* Compare his(1).

▷ *pron* **2** (form of 'she' used as the object of verbs and prepositions and as the objective complement in informal English) female person, animal etc or thing, country etc that is considered to be female or that has already been mentioned or known: *There she is — go and talk to her. Go on, stroke her. God bless this ship and all who sail in her. Though our country is not powerful, that is no reason why we shouldn't still be proud of her. Yes, it's her — the woman I saw with him.*

hers /hɜːz/ *possessive 'pron* the one/ones belonging to, for, a female person, animal etc already mentioned or known: *This book is mine not hers. Which room is hers? This hat is hers — yours is on the table.* Compare his(2). **of hers** of, belonging to, her(2): *He's a friend of hers.* ⇨ she, her.

herself (strong form /hɜː'self/, weak form /hə'self/) *pron* **1** (*reflex.pron*) (used as the object of a verb or preposition referring to the female person, animal etc that is the subject): *She hurt herself. She washed herself and her clothes in the river. She looked at herself in the mirror.* **2** (used to emphasize(2) the female person, animal etc who/that is the subject or object of a verb) the female person, animal etc in particular: *She (or The woman) herself knew nothing about what had happened. We want to see the girl herself.* **3** without help: *She did it herself — no one helped her.* (**all**) **by herself** (**a**) without help: *She can't carry it (all) by herself — it's too heavy.* (**b**) alone: *Why is she sitting there all by herself?* **be herself; keep s.t to herself** ⇨ oneself.

herald /'herəld/ *c.n* **1** (*old use*) person who carries messages, esp from a king or queen and delivers or reads them to other people. **2** (often with capital **H**) one of a group of people who deal with coats of arms (⇨ coat) and other makers of heraldry: *the College of Heralds.* **3** (name for a) newspaper: *The Glasgow Herald.* **4** (usu *a — of s.t*) (*formal*) thing or sign that shows that s.t is coming: *Daffodils*(1) *are a herald of spring.*

▷ *tr.v* **5** (*formal*) be or act as a sign of (s.t that is coming): *The new law heralds the end of our freedom.*

heraldic /he'rældɪk/ *adj* of or referring to heraldry: *a heraldic shield.*

'heraldry *u.n* study and use of coats of arms (⇨ coat), and esp the history of the families that are allowed to use them.

herb /hɜːb/ *c.n* (also *attrib*) one of many different kinds of small plants used to give flavour to food etc or as medicine: *Chives and parsley are good herbs to use with potatoes. He drinks some kind of herb tea.*

'herbal *adj* of or referring to herbs: *herbal medicine.*

herbaceous /hɜː'beɪʃəs/ *adj* (of a plant) that has soft, not woody(1), stems and continues to grow and flower year after year.

her,baceous 'border *c.n* stretch of a garden with herbaceous plants.

herbivore /'hɜːbɪ,vɔː/ *c.n* (*technical*) animal that eats only grass, leaves, plants etc (and not flesh). Compare carnivore, omnivore.

herbivorous /hɜː'bɪvərəs/ *adj* (of an animal) that eats grass, plants etc (and not flesh). Compare carnivorous, omnivorous.

herculean /,hɜːkjʊ'liːən/ *adj* (*formal*) (of work, a task etc) done with, needing, very great effort: *It was a herculean task to clear up after the explosion.*

herd /hɜːd/ *c.n* **1** (often *— of s.t*) group of the same kind (of animals), either ones kept on a farm or ones that keep together in the wild: *a herd of cows/sheep; herds of elephants.* **2** (*derog*) group of people that act together and not as individuals(3), esp when unsure(2) or frightened about s.t: *Just look at that herd following everything he says or does.* **follow the herd** (*fig; derog*) say or do exactly what other people say or do.

▷ *tr/intr.v* **3** (cause (a group of animals or people) to) come in(to a place) or together (as if) in a herd(1): *The farmer herded the cows into the shed. We all herded together waiting for our flight to be called.*

'herdsman *c.n* (*pl -men*) man who looks after a herd(1) of animals, esp cows. ⇨ goatherd, shepherd(1).

here /hɪə/ adv **1** at, in or to this place (near the speaker or writer): *I'm here. It's here. Could you come here, please.* **2** (used with verbs 'is/was/come(s)' when s.o/s.t is close to one or coming towards one; the main stress(2) is on 'here') **(a)** if the subject is a pronoun, the order is 'here' + subject + verb): *Here it is! Here I am. Here we come!* **(b)** (if the subject is a noun (phrase), the order is 'here' + verb + subject[1](4)): *Here comes the bus! Here come the others!* Compare there[1](2). **3** (used to emphasize the person or thing) near (to the speaker or writer): *My friend here will help you. This tool here is what you need.* ⇒ there[1](3). **4** at this point (in time, in a discussion etc): *Here is when I must leave you. Here I must disagree with you.* ⇒ there[1](4). **be neither here nor there** (*informal*) be of very little value or importance: *What you say is neither here nor there.* **here and there** at, in, to, a number of different places, occasions etc: *We've tried here and there to find an old desk and we haven't found anything yet.* **Here goes!** (*informal*) I/we am/are going to start (doing s.t): *'I've never dived before. Well, here goes!'* **Here is/are . . .** This is/are (the person(s), thing(s) etc that you want, are looking for etc): *Here are your letters.* **Here s.o/s.t is/are** s.o/s.t has/have arrived, been found etc: *Here they are at last!* **Here's to s.o/s.t!** (expression used when drinking a toast[2](1) to s.o/s.t): *Here's to the happy couple(3)!* **here, there and everywhere** at, in, to, a large number of different places. **here today (and) gone tomorrow** (of a person, fashion, opinion etc) important for only a short time and then disappearing (and so not worth much): *I have no intention of spending so much money on something that is here today and gone tomorrow.* **Here you are** this/these is/are the thing(s) that you want, are looking for, that I/we am/are giving you etc: *You asked for £20? Well, here you are.* **Look/see here!** (expression used to draw attention to s.t, esp s.t one does not like or wants to criticize): *Look here! You just can't behave like that!* Compare there[1].

'herea,bouts adv at, in, near, this place: *I lost it hereabouts.* Compare thereabouts.

,here'after adv **1** (*formal*; *law*) after this time: *The New Kitchen Company, hereafter called 'The Company' . . .* Compare thereafter.
▷ c/def.n **2** (*formal*) life (that is thought to exist) after death: *Who knows what waits for us in the great hereafter.*

'here,by adv (*formal*; *law*) by means of this statement etc: *I hereby agree to observe all these conditions.* Compare thereby.

,here'in adv (*formal*; *law*) enclosed with, coming with, included in (this letter, statement etc): *Please sign the copy of this letter enclosed herein and return it to us.* Compare therein.

,herein'after adv (*formal*; *law*) = hereafter.

,here'on adv (*formal*) = hereupon.

,here'to adv (*formal*) **1** to this place, matter, thing etc. ⇒ thereto. **2** = hitherto.

'hereu,pon adv (*formal*) as a result of, following, this: *'You are fools,' he said. Hereupon, everybody started shouting at him.* ⇒ thereupon(2).

,here'with adv (*formal*) enclosed or sent with this letter etc: *Herewith is our statement of expenses.*

heredity /hɪ'redɪtɪ/ u.n passing on, receiving, of

(good or bad) qualities from a parent to a child (and from this child to her/his children etc): *He claimed that his life of crime was all due to heredity.*

hereditary /hɪ'redɪtərɪ/ adj **1** of s.t that has been passed on by heredity: *hereditary diseases.* **2** of s.t that one has, is or owns because of one's (high social) birth and family descent: *hereditary privileges(1)/peers[1](1).*

herein, hereinafter ⇒ here.

heresy /'herɪsɪ/ c/u.n (pl -ies) **1** (example of having a) belief or opinion about a religious matter that is regarded as wrong by people in an established(1) religion. **2** (*fig*) (example of having an) opinion that is not accepted by most people, esp those who have official positions: *He preached the heresy that full employment and state spending would solve the country's difficulties.*

heretic /'herɪtɪk/ c.n person who has heretical opinions etc.

heretical /hɪ'retɪkl/ adj of or referring to heresy.
he'retically adv.

hereto, hereupon, herewith ⇒ here.

heritage /'herɪtɪdʒ/ sing.n all the most important things, e.g buildings, art, literature, that were made in the past and exist today, esp those belonging to a family or country: *He was proud of his family's heritage. The government must spend more money on preserving our national heritage.*

hermetic /hɜː'metɪk/ adj (*technical*) (being) very tightly closed; airtight: *Do not break the hermetic seal[2](5) on this jar until you are ready to use the contents.*
her'metically adv (usu — *sealed*) (closed) with a hermetic seal.

hermit /'hɜːmɪt/ c.n person who lives alone, usu in a deserted place, and usu in order to pray or think.

hernia /'hɜːnɪə/ c/u.n (*medical*) (example of an) illness in which an organ in the body, e.g the bowel, pushes through a weak part of the wall surrounding it. ⇒ rupture.

hero /'hɪərəʊ/ c.n (pl -es) **1** person who has done s.t brave or honourable (and who is remembered or praised for it): *the hero in the rescue attempt.* **2** most important person in a work of fiction(1), e.g a book, play: *The hero, after many adventures, finally married the princess.*

heroic /hɪ'rəʊɪk/ adj of or referring to a hero(1)/heroine(1) or s.t that was done bravely: *He was given a medal(1) for his heroic efforts to rescue the children.*
he'roically adv.
he'roics pl.n talk or acts that one wants to be or seem more important than they actually are: *Stop those heroics! You're a coward and you know it.*

heroine /'herəʊɪn/ c.n female hero.

heroism /'herəʊ,ɪzəm/ u.n very great bravery: *The young fireman was praised for his heroism.*

'hero-,worship u.n **1** (too) great admiration for s.o (esp s.o famous or in a position of authority).
▷ tr.v (-pp-) **2** show hero-worship(1) to (s.o): *He hero-worshipped his father.*

heroin /'herəʊɪn/ u.n (also *attrib*) kind of powerful drug(2) made from morphia that is taken for pleasure, to reduce pain etc but if taken often can cause addiction and sometimes death: *The number of heroin addicts is increasing.*

heroine, heroism ⇨ hero.

heron /ˈherən/ *c.n* kind of bird with long legs and a long neck which lives near water and catches and eats fish.

herpes /ˈhɜːpiːz/ *u.n* kind of disease of the skin in which blisters(1) or sores form, usu around the mouth or the sex organs.

herring /ˈherɪŋ/ *n* (*pl* herring(s)) **1** *c.n* kind of silver fish found in the sea. **2** *u.n* (also *attrib*) flesh of this fish as food: *a herring* pie. **a red herring** (*fig*) s.t said to take s.o away from the main point in an argument or discussion (usu intentionally): *Talking about what you want to do in the holidays is just a red herring; we should be talking about your preparations for your examinations.*

hers, herself ⇨ her.

hertz /hɜːts/ *c.n* (*pl* hertz) (*written abbr* Hz) (*technical*) unit of measurement of the frequency(2) of esp radio waves equal to 1 cycle(2) per second. ⇨ kilohertz, megahertz.

he's (strong form /hiːz/, weak form /hɪz/) *abbr* **1** he is. ⇨ be. **2** he has. ⇨ have.

hesitate /ˈhezɪˌteɪt/ *intr.v* **1** (often — *about/over* s.t; — *before doing* s.t) stop for a short time (about/over s.t or before doing s.t) because one is not certain (what to do, say etc): *He was hesitating about what course of action he should take. Jean hesitated for a moment before giving her opinion.* **2** (often (*do not*) — *to do* s.t) be doubtful (about doing or saying s.t) because one might offend s.o: *Don't hesitate to phone if you need my help.*

hesitance /ˈhezɪtəns/ *u.n* (also **'hesitancy**) fact or state of showing hesitation.

hesitation /ˌhezɪˈteɪʃən/ *c/u.n* (example of) hesitating(1): *After a moment's hesitation he replied that he could not come. I have no hesitation in recommending her for the job.*

hessian /ˈhesɪən/ *u.n* (also *attrib*) kind of material made from hemp(1) or jute: *hessian* wallpaper(1).

het /het/ **be/get** (**all**) **het up** (**about** s.t) (*informal*) be/get very worried or annoyed (about s.t): *What are you getting so het up about?*

heterogeneous /ˌhetərəʊˈdʒiːnɪəs/ *adj* (of people, things etc) having many different kinds in a group: *a heterogeneous population* (i.e with many different races etc). Compare homogeneous.

heterogeneity /ˌhetərəʊdʒɪˈniːəti/ *u.n*.

heterosexual /ˌhetərəʊˈseksjʊəl/ *adj* **1** who is attracted to a person of the opposite sex. Compare homosexual.

▷ *c.n* **2** heterosexual(1) person. Compare homosexual.

heterosexuality /ˌhetərəʊˌseksjʊˈæliti/ *u.n*. **hetero'sexually** *adv*.

hew /hjuː/ *v* (*p.t* hewed, *p.p* hewed, hewn /hjuːn/) (*formal*) **1** *tr.v* (often — s.t *down*; — s.t *out* (of s.t)) cut (s.t down or out (of s.t)) using an axe or a sharp tool: *He hewed down the tree. They hewed a path through the forest.* **2** *intr.v* (often — (*away*) at s.t) try to cut s.t using an axe etc: *She hewed (away) at the bushes but without much effect.*

hexagon /ˈheksəgən/ *c.n* flat shape with six (usu equal) sides.

hexagonal /hekˈsægənəl/ *adj* having the shape of a hexagon.

hey /heɪ/ *interj* (cry or shout used to attract attention, show surprise etc): *Hey! What do you think you're doing throwing that rubbish there?*

heyday /ˈheɪˌdeɪ/ *sing.n* (often *the* — of s.t; *in* one's/s.t's —) time when s.o/s.t was important, famous, fashionable etc (but no longer is): *I was born just after the heyday of swing music. In her heyday she earned thousands of pounds as an actress.*

HF /ˌeɪtʃ ˈef/ *abbr* high frequency.

HH *written abbr* Her/His Holiness. ⇨ holy.

hi /haɪ/ *interj* (*informal*) **1** hallo: *Hi! How're you doing?* **2** (cry or shout to attract attention etc): *Hi! Can you help me?*

hiatus /haɪˈeɪtəs/ *c.n* (*pl* -es) (*formal*) **1** gap (in s.t, e.g s.t written) where s.t is missing. **2** pause or break in s.t: *There was a short hiatus in the conversation as we moved from the dining-room.*

hibernate /ˈhaɪbəˌneɪt/ *intr.v* (of some animals) go into, be in, a state that is like sleep during the winter.

hibernation /ˌhaɪbəˈneɪʃən/ *u.n*.

hibiscus /hɪˈbɪskəs/ *c.n* kind of plant or bush with large red, white or brightly coloured flowers, usu found in hot countries.

hiccough /ˈhɪkʌp/ *c.n* (also **'hiccup**) **1** (often *pl*) (sound(s) made by a) sudden quick stop in one's breathing, often repeated a number of times and caused by drinking or eating s.t too quickly, by laughing etc: *If the baby gets hiccups, pat(4) him on the back. I've got (the) hiccups* (i.e an attack of hiccups(1))*!* **2** (*fig*) sudden stop or difficulty, esp in the manufacturing of s.t: *We've had a few hiccups which have slowed us down but production is going smoothly now.*

▷ *intr.v* **3** (*p.t,p.p* hiccoughed, hiccup(p)ed) make hiccoughs/hiccups(1).

hickory /ˈhɪkəri/ *c/u.n* (*pl* -ies) (also *attrib*) (kind of tree with) hard wood and nuts that can be eaten, found in North America.

hide¹ /haɪd/ *c.n* **1** small hut or place from which one can watch wild animals or birds without being seen oneself.

▷ *v* (*p.t* hid /hɪd/, *p.p* hidden /ˈhɪdn/) **2** *tr/intr.v* (cause (oneself/s.o/s.t) to) be (put) in a position behind, under etc s.t where one/s.o/it cannot be seen or easily found: *He hid (himself) behind the cupboard. Joe found Julia hiding under the table. He had to hide her present so that she wouldn't see it before her birthday.* **3** *tr.v* not admit, show, reveal, (s.t, esp one's feelings): *He hid his true feelings about her.*

'hidden *adj* (of a thing, meaning etc) not easy to be seen, recognized etc: *a hidden entrance*; *a hidden* clue(1).

'hide-and-ˌseek *u.n* (usu *play* —) children's game in which children hide and have to be found.

'hideaˌway *c.n* (also **'hideˌout**) place where one hides oneself in the hope of not being found (esp by officials, the police etc).

'hiding *unique n* **be in**, **go into**, **hiding** hide¹(2), be hiding(⇨ hide¹(2)), from the police, officials etc: *She had to go into hiding because of her criticism of the rulers.* Compare hiding²(⇨ hide²).

'hiding-ˌplace *c.n* place where one hides oneself or s.t: *He found a good hiding-place for his gold.*

hide² /haɪd/ *c/u.n* (also *attrib*) (example of the)

skin of certain animals, esp one used to make clothes, bags etc: *He deals in animal hides. I bought a hide bag.* **tan s.o's hide** ⇨ tan².

'hide,bound *adj* (*derog*) (of a person, her/his beliefs etc) very fixed and unable to change, esp from old ideas to new ones.

hiding² *c.n* (often **get**, **give s.o**, **a** —) (*informal*) hard beating, often on the bottom: *Your son needs a good hiding.* Compare hiding¹.

hideous /'hɪdɪəs/ *adj* **1** very ugly or unpleasant to look at: *She looked hideous in her new dress. How could they paint their house such a hideous colour?* **2** very severe; causing (great) distress(1); extremely unpleasant: *It was a hideous accident. Stop that hideous noise!*

'hideously *adv.* **'hideousness** *u.n.*

hierarchy /'haɪərɑːkɪ/ *c/u.n* (*pl -ies*) (example of the) order or organization of a group of people or things from the lowest to the highest in importance, e.g in a business, classification system etc: *He knew he would never be able to move up the hierarchy in his office.*

hierarchical /ˌhaɪəˈrɑːkɪkl/ *adj* of or referring to a hierarchy.

ˌhieˈrarchically *adv.*

hieroglyph /ˈhaɪərəˈglɪf/ *c.n* one of a number of signs, pictures or symbols used as writing in old times, e.g by Egyptians.

hieroglyphic /ˌhaɪərəˈglɪfɪk/ *adj* of or referring to such writing.

ˌhieroˈglyphics *pl.n* (examples of) such a system of writing.

hi-fi /ˈhaɪ ˌfaɪ/ *adj* **1** (*informal*) high fidelity.

▷ *c/u.n* **2** (example of a) hi-fi sound system: *This is an expensive hi-fi.*

high /haɪ/ *adj* Opposite low (except 2,4,7,8) **1** (of a thing, building, mountain etc) being at, reaching to, a certain (usu great) distance from the ground: *How high do you think that hill is? I don't like high buildings. I prefer rooms with high ceilings. The window was too high above the ground for me to see through it.* **2** (usu 2 etc *feet*, *metres* etc —) (of a measurement) that is a certain measured distance above the ground or another fixed point: *The wall was about 3 metres high. He's only about 5 feet high.* Compare tall(2). **3** more than is usual or expected: *Your charges are too high so I'm giving the job to someone else. The battle was won but at a very high price* (i.e many soldiers died). *He had a high temperature so his mother put him to bed. I have high hopes of getting the job.* Opposite low¹(2). **4** (of a wind, the sea) being much stronger than usual; blowing, moving, with great force: *There are warnings on the radio of high winds expected at sea.* **5** (of a note of music, a sound of a voice) at/near the top end of the range(7): *She could reach high notes easily when she sang.* **6** (usu *attrib*) very noble; important (in value etc): *Serious crimes are heard in the High Court. He has always lived by certain high ideals. We were invited to eat at high table with the senior staff of our college. She has a high opinion of herself.* Compare low¹(3). **7** (of meat, food etc) (going) bad: *Throw that meat away it's high.* **8** (of a person) (often *be/get — on s.t*) (*informal*) drunk (from alcoholic drinks); influenced or affected (by certain kinds of drugs(2)): *Everyone got high during the office party. He was high on pot(3) and I couldn't get*

any sense out of him. **9** (of a number, a playing card etc) having a value greater than the others: *When I have to work out high numbers I use my* calculator(1). *Aces(1) are high* (i.e are more important than all the other cards). **10** used for fast speeds: *a high gear*(1). ⇨ low¹(9). **hold one's head high** ⇨ head(*n*).

▷ *adv* **11** at or towards a (great) distance above the ground: *I could see several aircraft high above the clouds. The bird flew high into the sky.* **12** (often *aim/rise —*) at/to a high(6) level of importance or power: *You should aim high if you really want to succeed.* (**feelings**) **run high** (feelings among a group of people) become excited, angry etc: *Feelings were running very high over the plan for the new road.* (**leave s.o** etc) **high and dry** (go away leaving s.o etc) without any help, money, support etc: *All his money was stolen and he was left high and dry in a country where he knew nobody.* **high and mighty** arrogant. **hunt**, **look**, **search**, **high and low** (**for s.o/s.t**) look etc in all the possible places one can think of (for s.o/s.t): *I searched high and low (for the necklace) but I couldn't find it anywhere.*

▷ *c.n* **13** (of a price, cost etc) (too) great value; high(3) point in a scale: *Shares(3) in the Stock Exchange*(1) *reached a new high today.* Opposite low¹(*n*). ⇨ height. **be on a high** (*informal*) be feeling very happy or pleased (because of s.t good that has happened to one). **from** (**on**) **high** (**a**) (as if) from Heaven. (**b**) (coming) from the most important person(s) at the top of an organization: *The message from on high is that there will be no salary increases this year.*

-high *adj* at a height shown by the first part of the word: *knee-high; waist-high; sky-high.*

ˌhigh ˈaltar *c.n* main altar(1) in a church.

ˌhigh and ˈmighty *adj/adv* (*informal*) in a way that is full of feeling of one's own importance or without consideration for others: *Ever since he got that job, he's become so high and mighty that he's not interested in any of his old friends.*

'high-ˌbrow *adj* **1** (often *derog*) (of a person, literature etc) showing or needing a (too) great degree of knowledge or intelligence (to understand etc). Compare low-brow, middle-brow.

▷ *c.n* **2** person who knows about, is interested in and enjoys high-brow literature etc.

'high,chair *c.n* kind of chair with long legs for a baby or young child to sit in and eat its meals.

'high-ˌclass *adj* of extremely good quality: *a high-class grocer's*(2); *a high-class performance.*

ˌHigh Comˈmission *c.n* (building for the) office of an official, like an ambassador, who represents her/his government in certain countries of the British(1) Commonwealth(3).

ˌHigh Comˈmissioner *c.n* highest official in a High Commission.

ˌHigh ˈCourt *c/def.n* (UK) most important court of justice.

ˌhigher ˌeduˈcation *u.n* education at a college or university (after secondary(2) education).

ˌhigh exˈplosive(s) *u/pl.n* (*abbr* HE) very powerful explosive(s)(2).

ˌhigh fiˈdelity *adj* (*informal* **'hi-ˌfi**) (of a record, sound system) having or producing a very good quality of sound: *a high fidelity recording* (⇨ record¹).

ˌhigh-ˈflier *c.n* (also **ˌhigh-ˈflyer**) (*informal*)

person who is likely to succeed, reach an important position etc.

'high-,flown adj (derog) (esp of s.t said or written) sounding rather important but not actually so: Such high-flown ideas are all very well but let's be practical.

,high 'frequency c/u.n (abbr HF) (technical) frequency(2) of radio waves between 3 and 30 megahertz. ⇒ very high frequency (VHF).

,high-'handed adj (derog; informal) (acting) in a way that (shows one's power but) does not consider the feelings or opinions of others: It was very high-handed of him to take such a decision without asking us.

,high-'handedly adv. ,high-'handedness u.n. ,high 'horse sing.n be/get on one's high horse ⇒ horse(n).

'high,jack, 'high,jacker, 'high,jacking ⇒ hijack, hijacker, hijacking.

'high ,jump def.n sport in which people try to jump over a bar that is moved higher after each successful attempt. be for the high jump (fig; informal) be about to be punished, forced to leave one's job etc (for s.t wrong one has done).

highland /'haɪlənd/ attrib.adj 1 having high hills and mountains. Opposite lowland.
▷ def.n (usu pl) 2 highland(1) areas of a country.
'highlander c.n person who lives in the highlands(2). ⇒ lowlander.
'Highlands def/pl.n area of high hills and mountains, esp in Scotland.

'high-,level attrib.adj of or referring to people who are in very important positions (and their discussions etc): high-level talks between two governments.

'high,light c.n 1 (often — of s.t) most important part or thing that one remembers most, in a number of events, a play, broadcast etc: The highlight of our holiday was a visit to the caves. They will be showing highlights of the football match on television tonight. 2 (often pl) special light colouring put onto parts of one's hair: He decided that he wanted to have pink highlights in his hair. 3 lighter colouring or tone(6) in a painting, photograph etc, in contrast(2) to the darker areas.
▷ tr.v 4 put special attention or emphasis(1) on (s.t): This report highlights the problems facing the poorest members of the community(2). 5 put highlights(2) into (hair).

'highly adv to a very great degree or extent: I was highly amused by his remarks. Workers in this industry are very highly paid. speak, think etc highly of s.o speak etc with great praise or approval of s.o.

,highly-'strung adj (derog) (of a person) likely to become or very easily, excited or nervous: She was so highly-strung that the slightest criticism would make her burst into tears.

,high 'mass c.n (in the Roman Catholic religion) complete mass²(1), usu with music, a choir(1) etc.

,high-'minded adj (formal) thinking or showing high(6) ideals, beliefs etc: His high-minded approach to life was much praised. Compare low-minded.

,high-'mindedly adv. ,high-'mindedness u.n.
'highness c.n state of being high(3,5): The highness of these costs will make it impossible for us to sell the goods. The highness of his voice annoyed me. Compare height. Her, His, Your etc (Royal) Highness (abbr HRH) (title of a) prince or princess: I have great pleasure in welcoming Their Royal Highnesses to our country.

,high 'noon unique n 12 o'clock in the morning.
'high-,pitched adj (of a sound, voice etc) at the top end of the range; high(5): There was a high-pitched noise coming from the radio.

'high ,point/,spot c.n (usu — in/of s.t) most important thing, memory etc (of s.t one has done etc): The high point in our holiday was a journey we made to a small island.

'high-,powered adj 1 (of an engine etc) having a lot of power in it: He likes driving high-powered motorbikes. 2 (of a person, s.t he/she does etc) full of drive, force etc (perhaps too much so); important, influential: a very high-powered businessman. There was a high-powered meeting to discuss what to do (i.e a meeting of important people in the organization).

'high-,pressure attrib.adj 1 (of a machine etc) that works with or under a great deal of pressure or force: They used high-pressure hoses(1) to put out the fire. 2 (of an action) using a great deal of pressure or persuasion (perhaps too much so): They decided to start a high-pressure sales drive to beat their competitors.

,high 'priest c.n (in some religions) chief priest.
'high-,ranking attrib.adj (of an official) very important; having a high rank (and so able to make decisions etc): high-ranking government officials.
'high-,rise attrib.adj (usu of a block of flats(13)) having many storeys: She had an apartment on the thirtieth floor of a high-rise block. Opposite low-rise.

'high,road c.n main road, esp between towns.
'high ,school c.n 1 (UK) secondary(2) school: She goes to Putney High School. 2 (US) school for students over the age of 14.

,high 'seas pl.n all the area of the seas (beyond the parts near to a country's coast) that are not controlled by any country. be on, sail, the high seas travel in a ship in this area, away from the land.

'high ,season def.n (also attrib) part of the year when the weather is good and things are at their best, and therefore holidays, fruit etc are expensive. ⇒ low season.

'High ,Sheriff ⇒ sheriff(1).
'high-,speed attrib.adj 1 travelling or working very fast: The police finally caught the thieves after a high-speed car chase(1) through the town. 2 (esp of photographic film) able to record pictures with a very short exposure time.

,high 'speed c.n very fast speed: He kept up a very high speed in order not to lose time.

,high-'spirited adj lively(1); being in, having, highspirits: Flash is a high-spirited young horse who needs a good rider. Opposite low-spirited.

,high 'spirits pl.n (often be in —) (feeling of a) great deal of fun and liveliness. ⇒ low spirits.

,high 'stakes pl.n (often play for —) 1 a lot of money bet(4) on horse-racing, playing cards etc: Don't play cards with him as he always plays for high stakes. 2 a great deal of money (in business etc): They were offering high stakes to get the contract(1). ⇒ stakes²(1).

'high ,street *c.n* main street in a town which has the most important shops etc.

,high 'tea *c/u.n* (UK) main early evening meal, usu with cooked food instead of a later dinner or supper: *We usually have (a) high tea at about 6 o'clock and then just a small snack before bed.*

,high tech'nology *u.n* very sophisticated(2) electronic devices, methods, systems etc.

'high-,tension *attrib.adj* (*technical*) (of an electric cable(2)) able to carry high-voltage electricity.

,high 'tide *c/u.n* (often *at* —) (time of the) position of the sea at its highest point on a coast: *It is almost impossible to swim in this bay at high tide.* Opposite low tide.

,high 'time *u.n* (usu *be* — (*that*) . . .) now the time (that one/s.o should do s.t, that s.t should happen etc, often with the idea that one/s.o should have done it etc much earlier): *It is high time you realized that the world does not owe you a living.*

,high 'treason *u.n* = treason.

'high-,up *c.n* (*informal*) person (above oneself, one's own position) with an important position or job: *I don't think the high-ups know very much about how we less important people do our jobs.*

,high 'water *u.n* time/state when the tide, esp in a river, is at or reaches its highest point. **come hell or high water** ⇒ hell(*n*).

,high-'water ,mark *c.n* mark left on a bank of a river etc by the water when it is at its highest level.

'high,way *c.n* (also *attrib*) (general name, esp in law, for a) main road, esp between or in towns: *The local council was responsible for the repair of the highways in its area.*

,Highway 'Code *def.n* (UK) (booklet with all the) rules and laws for people who use the roads, esp car, lorry etc drivers.

'high,wayman *c.n* (*pl -men*) (*old use*) man, often on horseback, who stopped travellers, esp in coaches(4) and robbed them.

hijack /'haɪˌdʒæk/ *c.n* (also **'high,jack**) (usu — *of s.t*) 1 act of taking control (of an aircraft etc) and forcing the pilot to fly to s.w other than its normal destination, often as a form of political protest(1) etc. 2 act of stopping a truck etc and stealing the goods in it etc.

▷ *tr.v* 3 take control of (esp an aircraft) and force the pilot to fly s.w: *The plane was hijacked over Greece, flown to the Lebanon and then blown up.* 4 stop (a lorry etc) and steal (the goods) from it: *They hijacked the van just outside the town.*

'hi,jacker *c.n* (also **'high,jacker**) person who hijacks s.t.

'hi,jacking *c/u.n* (also **'high,jacking**) (example of the) act of hijacking (⇒ hijack(*v*)) an aircraft etc.

hike /haɪk/ *c.n* 1 (usu *go for a* —) long walk in the country for enjoyment, often wearing special clothes and carrying a rucksack etc.

▷ *intr.v* 2 walk for enjoyment in the country, mountains etc, usu a long way: *We hiked for thirty kilometres yesterday. It's a five day hike.*

'hiker *c.n* person who hikes(2).

'hiking *u.n* (often *go* —) activity of walking long distances for enjoyment: *I enjoy hiking as long as I don't have to walk too far.*

hilarious /hɪ'leərɪəs/ *adj* very funny and amusing: *There was a hilarious play on television last night. She looked hilarious dressed up like that.*

hi'lariously *adv.* **hi'lariousness** *u.n.*

hilarity /hɪ'lærɪtɪ/ *u.n* (*formal*) great amusement or much laughter: *There was a great deal of hilarity in the office when he told his joke.*

hill /hɪl/ *c.n* piece of land that rises above the level ground to form a high place, smaller than a mountain: *We could see a range(1) of low hills in the distance. The car had to climb a steep hill before reaching the main road.*

'hilliness *u.n* fact or state of being hilly.

'hill,side *c.n* side or slope of a hill.

'hill-,top *c.n* highest point of a hill.

'hilly *adj* (-*ier*, -*iest*) (of an area of land) having many hills.

hilt /hɪlt/ *c.n* handle (of a sword or knife). (**up**) **to the hilt** (*fig*) completely; to the greatest extent possible: *He said he would support her to the hilt.*

him /hɪm/ *pron* (form of 'he' used as the object of verbs and prepositions and as the objective complement in informal English) male person, animal etc or thing that is considered to be male or that has already been mentioned or is known: '*Do you know where Charles is?* '*No, I haven't seen him for some time.*' *That* bull(1) *is dangerous, so don't go anywhere near him. Is that him — the man you were telling me about yesterday?*

himself /hɪm'self/ *pron* 1 (*reflex.pron*) (used as the object of a verb or preposition referring to the male person, animal etc that is the subject): *He hurt himself. He washed himself and his clothes in the river. He looked at himself in the mirror.* 2 (used to emphasize(2) the male person, animal etc who/that is the subject or object of the verb) the male person, animal etc in particular: *He (or The man) himself knew nothing about what had happened. We want to see the boy himself.* 3 without help: *He did it himself — no one helped him.* (**all**) **by himself** (**a**) without help: *He can't carry it all by himself — he's too small.* (**b**) alone: *Why is he sitting there all by himself?* **be himself**; **keep s.t to himself** ⇒ oneself.

hind¹ /haɪnd/ *adj* (usu of an animal) at, belonging to, the back part of the body: *the hind legs of a donkey.*

'hind,most *adj* (*formal*) last or furthest away towards the back (of s.t): *The people at the hindmost end of the procession knew nothing of what was happening.*

'hind,quarters *pl.n* back parts of an animal including its back legs.

'hind,sight *u.n* (usu *with* —) ability to realize why s.t happened, went wrong etc after the event is over: *With hindsight it's easy to see where I went wrong.*

hind² /haɪnd/ *c.n* female (red) deer.

hinder /'hɪndə/ *tr.v* (often — *s.o from* (*doing*) *s.t*; — *s.t from happening*) delay, stop, prevent, (s.o from (doing) s.t or s.t from happening); get in the way of (s.t, s.o who is trying to do s.t): *My work was hindered by continual interruptions.*

hindrance /'hɪndrəns/ *c.n* (often *a* — *to s.o/s.t*) person or thing who/that hinders s.o/s.t: *He was a real hindrance when I was trying to get the job done.*

hindmost, hindquarters, hindsight ⇒ hind¹.

Hindu /'hɪndu:/ *adj* 1 of a person who believes in Hinduism and follows the laws and teachings of this religion.

▷ *c.n* **2** Hindu(1) person.

'Hindu,ism *u.n* kind of Indian religion that worships gods and believes in life after death.

hinge /hɪndʒ/ *c.n* **1** kind of metal (or plastic) device or joint made to hold two parts together in a way that allows one piece, e.g a door, to swing, be moved etc freely: *The hinge on the lid needs mending. Please oil the gate hinges.*
▷ *tr.v* **2** put a hinge(1) on (s.t). ⇨ unhinge(1). *hinge* **(up)on s.t** depend on s.t: *Everything hinges on the successful conclusion(1) of the talks.*

hint /hɪnt/ *c.n* **1** thing said that suggests s.t in a general but not direct way: *I had several hints from friends that my breath smelled bad.* **2** piece of helpful advice, esp on how to do s.t; clue(1): *The television programme gave useful hints on decorating a house. Give me a hint where you hid it.* **3** small amount (of s.t): *There was only a hint of onion in the soup.* **a broad hint** ⇨ broad. **drop a hint** (**in s.o's ear**, **to s.o**) give a hint(1) (privately to s.o): *He dropped a number of hints in my ear about what had been happening in the office while I was away.* (**be able to**) **take a/the hint** (be able to) understand a/s.o's hint(1) and do s.t about it: *I can take a hint; you clearly don't want me here so I'll go.*
▷ *tr.v* **4** (often — (*to s.o*) *that . . .*) suggest (s.t) in a general but not direct way; give a hint(1) (to s.o) about (s.t): *What are you hinting? She hinted (to me) that the neighbours were complaining about the noise.* **hint at s.t** suggest that s.t has happened or will happen in a general but not direct way: *He hinted at the problems he was facing but would not go into any detail.*

hinterland /'hɪntə,lænd/ *c/u.n* (*formal*) land beyond the coast or the banks of a river: *The explorers were planning to travel into the hinterland.*

hip¹ /hɪp/ *c.n* (also *attrib*) either of the two sides of the body above the legs and below the waist: *She stood there with her hands on her hips. Can we take your hip measurement to see whether your dress will fit?*

hip² /hɪp/ *interj* **Hip**, **hip**, **hurrah/hooray/ hurray!** ⇨ hurrah.

hip³ /hɪp/ *c.n* kind of red berry or fruit that grows on wild roses after the flowers have died.

hippie /'hɪpɪ/ *c.n* (also **'hippy**) (*pl -ies*) (also *attrib*) (*informal*) person, esp in the 1960s, who rejects(3) many of the rules of society, often wears strange clothes, has long hair and believes strongly in peace and love.

hippo /'hɪpəʊ/ *c.n* (*pl -s*) hippopotamus.

hippopotamus /,hɪpə'pɒtəməs/ *c.n* (*pl -es*, or less usu, *hippopotami* /,hɪpə'pɒtə,maɪ/) (*informal* **'hippo**) large heavy animal with a thick skin and a broad flat head found living in and near rivers in Africa.

hippy ⇨ hippie.

hire /haɪə/ *u.n* **1** (amount of money paid for the) use of s.t, services of s.o, for a short time: *Car hire is a growing business. The charge for the hire of this bicycle is £1 a day.* (**be**) **for hire** (be) available for use for a (usu short) time on payment of money: (notice) *Bicycles for hire.* (**be**) **on hire** (be) being used for a (usu short) time on payment of money: *I have this car on hire for the whole of the week.*
▷ *tr.v* **2** (often — *s.t from s.o/s.t*) get the use of (s.t)

(from s.o, a business) for a (usu short) time on payment of money: *He hired a car to drive to the airport.* **3** (often — *s.o to do s.t*) employ (s.o), usu for a short time (to do s.t): *They hired several extra workers for the busy holiday season.* **hire s.t out** (**to s.o**) let s.o have the use of s.t, usu for a short time, in return for payment: *We hire out wedding suits.* Compare rent².

'hire ,car *c.n* car one has hired(2) to drive oneself.

,hire 'purchase *u.n* (*abbr HP*) (also *attrib*) (often (*buy s.t*) *on —*) agreement to make regular small payments over a stated length of time which allows one to use the thing while one is paying for it and to keep it when all the payments have been made: *I bought the radio on hire purchase. He failed to keep up the hire purchase payments and so the shop came and took the television away.*

his /hɪz/ *possessive pron* **1** belonging to, for, him: *He claims that it is his painting. His parents are in France.* Compare her(1). **of his** of, belonging to, him: *Is she a friend of his?* ⇨ he, him.
▷ *pron* **2** the one/ones belonging to, for, the male person, animal etc already mentioned or known: *He claimed that the painting was his. Which coat is his?* Compare hers. ⇨ him, himself.

hiss /hɪs/ *c.n* **1** sound like a long 's' made by some animals, e.g snakes, cats, esp when they are disturbed, angry etc and also by steam when it escapes from an engine. **2** sound like this made by a person to show displeasure about s.o/s.t: *The hisses of the audience did not stop him from finishing his act.*
▷ *tr/intr.v* (often — (*at*) *s.o/s.t*) **3** (of a snake, etc) make a hiss(1) (towards (s.o/s.t)): *The cat hissed (at me) when I tried to stroke it.* **4** make a hiss(2) to show one's displeasure (at (s.o/ s.t)): *The audience* booed(2) *and hissed (at) the speaker when he tried to continue.* **hiss s.o off s.t** hiss(4) s.o so much that he/she cannot continue talking, performing etc and has to leave the stage, platform(1) etc.

hissing /'hɪsɪŋ/ *attrib.adj* **1** that sounds like a hiss(1): *What's that hissing noise?*
▷ *u.n* **2** act of making hissing(1) sounds; sound of a hiss(*n*): *The hissing began the moment he started his speech.*

history /'hɪstərɪ/ *n* (*pl -ies*) **1** *u.n* (science or study of) past events, esp of a country, its rulers, people etc: *I'm studying history for my examinations.* **2** *c.n* (also *attrib*) (often — of s.o/ s.t) (written) account (of s.o/s.t in the past): *He is writing a new history of France. You won't find any mention of this event in the history books.* **3** *c.n* (all the) things that have happened in the past to a person, esp in medical or social terms, or in connection with s.t: *He has a long history of illness. He was studying their case* histories *to see if there was any common cause for the disease. The development of the new product has a long history.* **ancient history** ⇨ ancient. **make history** do s.t, esp s.t for the first time, that is very important and will be remembered: *The scientists made history when they first split the* atom(1). **medieval history** ⇨ medieval(1). **modern history** ⇨ modern. **natural history** ⇨ natural. **s.o's/s.t's past history** events in the life or history(3) of s.o/s.t: *His past history is full of illnesses.*

historian /hɪˈstɔːrɪən/ *c.n* person who studies history(1), writes histories(2) etc.

historic /hɪˈstɒrɪk/ *adj* (likely to become) famous or important in history(1): *A historic battle was fought here. It was a historic meeting.*

historical /hɪˈstɒrɪkl/ *adj* **1** of or referring to history(1): *a historical account of the war*; *historical* research(1); *a historical* novel¹ (i.e one that has history(2) in it). **2** who/what actually existed in history(1): *There is some doubt whether King Arthur was a historical figure.*

hiˈstorically *adv* in a historical way: *The book is historically accurate.*

histrionic /ˌhɪstrɪˈɒnɪk/ *adj* (*derog*) (of a person's behaviour etc) very false and exaggerated; showing too much emotion, esp feelings that are not sincere: *histrionic behaviour.*

ˌhistriˈonically *adv.*

ˌhistriˈonics *u/pl.n* histrionic behaviour: *I'm getting really tired of his histrionics whenever things don't go his way.*

hit /hɪt/ *c.n* **1** blow or strike: *He received a hit on the head from a flying stone.* **2** point scored by hitting(8) a target(1): *In the competition he scored three hits and one miss.* **3** (also *attrib*) play, performance, song etc that proves to be very successful: *a hit record. The new play was a hit and it was very difficult to get tickets for it.* **a smash hit** (*informal*) a very successful hit(3). **be a hit at s.o** be a criticism aimed at s.o: *I suppose that remark is a hit at me because you don't like what I'm doing.* **be/make a hit with s.o** (*informal*) (of a person) be/become liked by s.o, esp when one first meets her/him: *You certainly made a hit with her; she talks of nothing else.*

▷ *v* (*-tt-*, *p.t,p.p* **hit**) **4** *tr.v* give a blow or strike to (s.o/s.t), usu with some force: *A stone hit him on the head* (or *He was hit on the head by a stone*). *Dave doesn't believe in hitting his children when they're naughty. Try hitting the nail with a stone.* **5** *tr/intr.v* (cause (two or more things) to) meet or crash together violently: *Her head hit a low beam. Their boat hit ours with a terrible crash. The cars hit (each other) head on. Tom hit the pavement and fell off his bicycle.* **6** *intr.v* (know how to, be able to) strike a blow, e.g in boxing: *When he gets going, he hits hard.* **7** *tr.v* (in sports) strike (a ball); make (a score): *Ben hits the ball very hard in tennis. Ian hit 50 runs in twenty minutes.* **8** *tr.v* succeed in reaching or getting (a target(1)), e.g in a shooting competition: *He only managed to hit the outer circle once.* **9** *tr.v* reach or find (a place), sometimes by chance: *If we go straight ahead we should hit the river in about a kilometre, according to the map.* **10** *tr.v* reach, get to, (a certain state, new high/low level etc): Shares(3) *on the* Stock Exchange(1) *hit a new high today.* **11** *tr.v* (often passive) (often — *s.o hard*) affect (s.o) badly; cause (s.o) to suffer: *Poorer people were hit hard* (or *hard hit*) *by the rise in prices.*

hit at s.o/s.t try to hit(4) s.o/s.t.

hit back (at s.o) (**a**) hit(4) s.o after he/she has hit one: *He struck me on the face so I hit him back.* (**b**) criticize or attack s.o after he/she has criticized or attacked one: *He hit back at his critics by saying they had got their facts wrong.*

hit (s.o) below the belt ⇒ belt(*n*).

hit the bottle ⇒ bottle(*n*).

hit the ceiling ⇒ ceiling.

hit the hay/sack ⇒ hay.

hit the headlines ⇒ headline.

hit home ⇒ home(*adv*).

hit it off (with s.o) (*informal*) succeed in becoming friends (with s.o): *We hit it off (with each other) from the very first meeting.*

hit the mark ⇒ mark(*n*).

hit the nail on the head ⇒ nail(*n*).

hit out against/at s.o/s.t (**a**) try to hit(4) s.o/ s.t, perhaps a little wildly. (**b**) (*fig*) criticize or attack s.o/s.t: *She hit out against the people who complained but did nothing to help change the system.*

hit the road ⇒ road.

hit the roof ⇒ roof(*n*).

hit (up)on s.t (*fig*) find or discover an answer, solution etc to a problem, often by chance: *I've just hit on a way out of our difficulties; let's sell the house and move to the country.*

hit town ⇒ town.

ˌhit-and-ˈrun *attrib.adj* **1** (of a driver) who causes an accident to s.o by knocking her/him down and then does not stop: *She was killed by a hit-and-run driver.* **2** (of an accident) caused in this way.

ˌhit and/or ˈmiss *adj* (ˌhit-and/or-ˈmiss when *attrib*) (of s.t s.o does) that may or may not succeed, often because it is not properly planned or controlled: *It was a very hit-and-miss business and no one really knew what was happening.*

ˈhit paˌrade *def.n* (becoming *old use*) list of popular songs or records that have sold the most (in a week or a month) ⇒ top twenty(⇒ top¹(1)).

ˈhit ˌsong *c.n* popular song that has become a hit(3).

ˈhitter *c.n* (in cricket¹, baseball etc) person who hits(7) or who is good at hitting(7), a ball: *He was one of the biggest hitters of his time* (i.e he could hit the ball a long way).

hitch /hɪtʃ/ *c.n* **1** (often *give s.t a* —) quick or short pull or tug(1), e.g to lift s.t up, straighten s.t etc: *He gave his trousers a hitch and tightened his belt.* **2** problem or difficulty that causes a delay or causes s.t to stop: *There's some hitch about our luggage; they want the keys to check inside the bags.* **3** (often *get, give s.o, a* —) free lift or ride in a car etc for a certain distance. ⇒ hitchhike. **4** kind of knot: *Tie the rope to the branch with a round turn and two (half-)hitches.* (**go (off)**) **without a hitch** (succeed, happen) without any difficulty or problem: *The first flight of the new aircraft went off without a hitch.* **a technical hitch** (problem or delay caused by) a fault in a device, system etc: *Because of a technical hitch we are unable to show the advertised programme.*

▷ *v* **5** *tr.v* (usu — *s.t up*) lift or pull (s.t) up: *He hitched up his trousers.* **6** *tr.v* (often — *s.t (up) to s.t*) fasten or connect (s.t) (to s.t else): *She hitched the* hosepipe *to the tap. Is the power hitched up yet?* **7** *tr/intr.v* get (a free lift or ride) in a car etc; hitchhike; be given a hitch(3): *As we haven't got any money, let's see if we can hitch (a lift) to Manchester.* **be/ get hitched** (*informal*) be/become married.

ˈhitchˌhike *intr.v* travel (to s.w) by getting one or more free lifts in s.o's car etc: *He hitchhiked all the way across Europe.*

'hitch,hiker *c.n* person who hitchhikes.
'hitch,hiking *u.n.*

hither /'hɪðə/ *adv* (*old use*; *literary*) to here; to this place. **hither and thither** (*old use*; *literary*) in different directions: *People were running hither and thither.*

,hither'to *adv* (*formal*) until now; up until this point: *Hitherto, I have done everything you have told me to do but from now on I shall do what I want.*

HIV /,eɪtʃ ,aɪ 'viː/ *abbr* (*medical*) Human Immunodeficiency Virus: *I am HIV positive* (I am infected(1) with the virus).

hive /haɪv/ *c.n* **1** (also **'bee,hive**) small hut or box made for bees to live and produce honey in. **2** all the bees that live in a hive(1): *Be careful! The hive is* swarming(2)! *a hive of activity/industry* a place, e.g an office, factory etc where a lot of work is going on, that is very busy etc: *With the election coming the local party office was a hive of activity.*

▷ *tr/intr.v* **3** hive **(s.t)** off **(from s.t)** (cause (s.t) to) become separate, work separately, (from the main or larger part of an organization etc): *Any work that they could not manage was hived off to one of their* subsidiary(1) *companies. The engineering division hived off from the parent company to give themselves greater freedom.*

hm /həm/ *interj* (way of writing the sound made to show (mild) surprise, criticism, uncertainty etc): *Hm! I just don't believe you! Hm! I'm not sure about that — I don't think I agree with you.*

HM *written abbr* Her/His Majesty.

HMS /,eɪtʃ ,em 'es/ *abbr* (UK) Her/His Majesty's Ship (title used for a ship in the British Royal Navy): *HMS Dreadnought.*

HMSO /,eɪtʃ ,em ,es 'əʊ/ *abbr* Her/His Majesty's Stationery(1) Office (organization that prints and publishes(1) official government documents(1), books etc).

HNC /,eɪtʃ ,en 'siː/ *abbr* (UK) Higher National Certificate(1) (examination or qualification(1) in one of a number of technical(1) subjects).

ho /həʊ/ *interj* (usu *literary* or *joking*) (expression used to show surprise, amusement, laughter etc): *Ho! What are you doing? Ho! Ho! That was a good joke!*

hoard /hɔːd/ *c.n* **1** collection or store of things, e.g food, money, gold that one has saved (and often hidden in secret) for later use: *When he was digging in his garden he found a hoard of gold coins. He had a secret hoard of tinned food in case there was a war.*

▷ *tr/intr.v* **2** collect and store a quantity of (s.t) (often in secret) for later use: *He hoarded gold as he didn't trust paper money.*

'hoarder *c.n* (*derog*) person who hoards(2): *Sheila is such a hoarder so she can never throw anything away.*

'hoarding¹ *u.n* act of doing this: *The Government has warned people against hoarding.*

hoarding² /'hɔːdɪŋ/ *c.n* **1** high fence, usu put up for a short time, around a place where a building is being knocked down or built, or to keep people away from a dangerous place etc. **2** large flat, usu wooden, board in a public place on which advertisements are put.

hoarfrost /'hɔː,frɒst/ *u.n* light frost(2) that forms on grass, leaves etc.

hoarse /hɔːs/ *adj* (often — *from s.t*) (of a person, her/his voice) sounding rough or harsh (from shouting, having a sore throat etc): *He was hoarse from shouting at the football match.* **shout oneself hoarse** shout so much that one's voice becomes hoarse.

'hoarsely *adv.* **'hoarseness** *u.n.*

hoary /'hɔːrɪ/ *adj* (-ier, -iest) **1** (*formal*; *literary*) (of a person, her/his hair) white or grey because of age: *His hoary head was bowed with sorrow.* **2** (*literary*; *formal*) being or looking ancient: *hoary ruins; a hoary old joke.*

'hoarily *adv.* **'hoariness** *u.n.*

hoax /həʊks/ *c.n* (also *attrib*) **1** trick in which one makes s.o believe s.t (bad) has happened or is going to happen when really it has not happened or will not happen: *They received a telephone call that there was a bomb in the cinema but it turned out to be a hoax. I'm not sure if that was a hoax call but let's not take any chances.* **play a hoax (on s.o)** carry out such a trick (but usu not a very bad one) (on s.o): *Let's play a hoax on him and tell him that he's won £10 000.*

▷ *tr.v* **2** play a hoax(1) on (s.o) (usu not very seriously): *He was hoaxed into believing he had won a big prize.*

'hoaxer *c.n* person who hoaxes(2).

hob /hɒb/ *c.n* **1** flat part on top of a cooker (or a separate unit) that has gas or electric rings¹(3), hot plates etc on which to cook or heat things in pans etc: *an electric hob.* **2** (*old use*) shelf next to a fireplace on which pans etc can be placed for cooking or heating.

hobble /'hɒbl/ *c.n* **1** (often *walk with a* —) slow halting or stumbling(2) way of moving, esp because one's foot/feet hurts/hurt, one's feet are tied etc: *He had injured his ankle and could only walk with a hobble.*

▷ *v* **2** *intr.v* walk in this way: *Though the thieves had tied him up, he managed to hobble to the door and shout for help.* **3** *tr.v* tie two legs of (a horse etc) to stop it from moving too far away.

hobby /'hɒbɪ/ *c.n* (pl -ies) something one does as a pleasant activity, usu in one's spare time: *His main hobby is building model aeroplanes.*

'hobby,horse *c.n* **1** (often *derog*) matter or subject that one talks about a lot (and often in an annoying way): *Don't get him on his hobbyhorse of what's wrong with the government or we'll be here all day!* **2** wooden horse's head on a stick, used as a child's toy.

hobgoblin /,hɒb'gɒblɪn/ *c.n* = goblin.

hobnail /'hɒb,neɪl/ *c.n* kind of nail with a flat or pointed head, fixed to the sole³(2) of a boot or shoe to give better grip(1) or wear.

,hob,nail(ed) *boots pl.n* boots with hobnails.

hobnob /'hɒb,nɒb/ *intr.v* (-bb-) (usu — *with s.o*; — *together*) meet and be friendly (with s.o. together), esp on social occasions (and often with s.o whom one wants to know because he/she is more important than oneself): *She spends all her time hobnobbing with her rich neighbours.*

hobo /'həʊ,bəʊ/ *c.n* (pl -(e)s) (mainly US) (*informal*) person who wanders from place to place, usu without having any (regular) work; tramp(1).

hock¹ /hɒk/ *c.n* kind of white wine from the Rhine area of West Germany.

hock² /hɒk/ *u.n* **1** in hock (*informal*) (of s.t

one owns) pawned(3) or in a pawnshop: *My camera's in hock as I needed the money.* **be in hock** (**to s.o/s.t**) (**for s.t**) owe (s.o) money (of a certain amount): *I'm in hock to my brothers for thousands of pounds.*

▷ *tr.v* 2 pawn(3) (s.t); put (s.t) in a pawnshop: *I've had to hock my camera.*

hock³ /hɒk/ *c.n* joint on the back (hind) leg of a horse etc.

hockey /'hɒkɪ/ *u.n* 1 (also **'field ,hockey**) (also *attrib*) kind of game played by eleven players with a small hard ball and sticks that are bent at the bottom: *Our hockey team won by four goals to two.* 2 = ice hockey.
'hockey-,stick *c.n* stick used in hockey.

hocus-pocus /,həʊkəs 'pəʊkəs/ *u.n* trick (using words or actions) intended to deceive or distract s.o (esp while one is doing s.t else): *The whole thing is a lot of hocus-pocus that sounds all right but just doesn't mean anything if you look at it closely.*

hoe /həʊ/ *c.n* 1 kind of instrument (either a tool with a blade and a long handle or one fixed to a tractor) used for breaking up earth, removing weeds etc.

▷ *tr/intr.v* 2 use a hoe(1) to break up earth, remove weeds etc (on/around s.t): *Jeff hoes his vegetables regularly. I could see the farmer hoeing (his field).*

hog /hɒg/ *c.n* 1 (esp US) pig; male pig that has been castrated. 2 (*derog*) person who is very greedy and often dirty: *You greedy hog — you didn't leave any pudding for us!* **go the whole hog** (*informal*) not do only part of s.t but do it completely: *Why don't we go the whole hog and fly all the way around the world?* **a road hog** ⇒ road.

▷ *tr.v* (**-gg-**) (*derog; slang*) 3 use (s.t), take (s.t, e.g food), greedily so that nobody else has much or any: *He's hogged the whole cake!* **hog the limelight** get the attention of everybody so that others will not get noticed. **hog the road** (of a driver) take too much space on a road so that other cars cannot pass etc.
'hoggish *adj* (*derog*) being or acting like a hog(2).

Hogmanay /,hɒgmə'neɪ/ *unique n* celebration in Scotland held on the evening of 31 December (New Year's Eve) when there are parties and people visit each other etc.

hoist /hɔɪst/ *c.n* 1 kind of device like a crane(2) or lift for lifting heavy objects, e.g in a factory. 2 push or lift up (over s.t, so that he/she/it is higher etc): *Give the dog a hoist up.*

▷ *tr.v* 3 use a hoist(1) to lift (s.t): *The engine had to be hoisted out of the boat to be repaired.* 4 (often — *s.o/s.t up*) give (s.o/s.t) a hoist(2). **hoist a flag** make a flag go to the top of a mast or flagpole, using a rope or ropes. **hoist sail** lift the sails up on a mast or masts on a boat using a rope or ropes. **be hoist on/with one's own petard** suffer the results of one's own plans against s.o else; have one's schemes turned against one.

hoity-toity /,hɔɪtɪ 'tɔɪtɪ/ *adj* (*derog*; becoming *old use*) (being) too proud; thinking oneself to be socially superior(1): *She's very hoity-toity and won't talk to her neighbours.*

hold /həʊld/ *c.n* 1 (usu *sing*) act or way of having, taking, s.o/s.t in one's hand(s), arm(s), between

one's knees, teeth etc (so that one does not lose her/him/it); grip(1): *When you've got a firm hold of the rope, pull yourself up on it. The dog's hold* (i.e with its teeth) *on the stick could not be broken.* 2 (in wrestling, judo etc) method of gripping(5) s.o with one's hands, arms, knees or legs: *He couldn't get out of her hold.* 3 (esp when climbing s.t) place where one can put one's feet, object, e.g a rock, branch etc that one can take in one's hand(s), to help lift oneself up: *The cliff had a number of holds which made the climbing easier.* 4 large area below the deck(s) of a ship or in a plane, in which cargo is put. 5 (often *have a — over s.o*) (*fig*) power or influence, often in a bad way (over s.o): *She has had too much hold over her children — she should let them decide for themselves. He's got some sort of hold over her as she will do whatever he wants.* **catch/ lay/take hold of s.o/s.t** catch etc s.o/s.t in a (firm) grip(1). **get hold of s.o/s.t** (**a**) take s.o/ s.t in a (firm) grip(1). (**b**) manage to find s.o/s.t (in order to talk to her/him, to use, read, it etc): *Could you get hold of Jones on the telephone as I want to tell him the good news? I've just got hold of a copy of that secret report.* **keep/lose hold of s.o/s.t** (not) keep one's hold(1) or grip(1) on s.o/s.t: *He lost hold of the rope and fell to his death.* **lose one's hold over s.o/s.t** not be able to keep one's control, influence over s.o/s.t. **no holds barred** (**a**) (esp in fighting, wrestling etc) without any kind of hold(2) being illegal. (**b**) (*fig*) without any rules (when competing for s.t). **on hold** (**a**) (of an aircraft) having to continue flying and not (allowed to) land. (**b**) (of s.t that needs to be done) not to be acted upon or decided for the present: *A final decision has been put on hold until the manager gets back.*

▷ *v* (*p.t,p.p* **held** /held/) 6 *tr.v* take or have (s.o/ s.t) in one's hand(s), arm(s), one's lap¹, between one's knees, teeth etc: *She held the baby in her arms. Can you hold this tray for a moment? This part of the machine holds the wood while you are shaping it.* 7 *tr.v* keep (s.o/s.t) in a certain (fixed) position/state or at a certain level, usu for some time: *Hold him like that while I take the photograph. Can't you hold your head straight while I'm cutting your hair? Can you hold that note* (i.e of music) *for two bars? We intend to hold our prices for the next month.* ⇒ hold(20), hold still. 8 *tr.v* be able to support or carry ((the weight of) s.o/s.t): *You're too heavy so that branch won't hold your weight. Don't be frightened — the rope will hold you.* 9 *intr.v* be able to take a weight or force and not break under the pressure: *The knot held for a few moments and then came apart. In spite of the very heavy floods, the dam(1) held.* 10 *tr.v* (be able to) contain, have, (an amount or quantity) inside: *The tank can hold 70 litres. Will that cupboard hold all your clothes?* 11 *tr.v* defend (a place, position) against attack: *The enemy held the town for three days before being forced to retire(4).* 12 *intr.v* defend one's position against attack: *We can't hold for much longer without reinforcements.* 13 *tr.v* keep (s.o) under one's control; not allow (s.o) to leave, escape etc: *A man is being held by police in connection with the robbery. The hostages were held captive(adj) for two months.* 14 *tr.v* keep (s.t) in one's possession or control, usu for a short time, while s.o (who owns it) is away etc: *Do you want me to hold your seat for you until you come?* **15** *tr.v* have or possess (s.t, esp shares in a company): *He holds the controlling interest in quite a large engineering company.* ⇒ holding. **16** *tr.v* have or cause (s.t, e.g a meeting) to happen: *We're going to hold an election for president of the society. He held a party at his house for fifty people.* **17** *tr.v* have or keep (a certain position in an organization etc): *She holds the office of* chairperson *for the present year.* ⇒ hold office. **18** *tr.v* (often — (*the position, view* etc) *that...*) (*formal*) believe strongly in (the position, view etc that...): *I hold (the view) that it is wrong to speak ill of one's neighbours.* ⇒ hold by s.t, hold to s.t. **19** *tr.v* attract and keep (the interest/attention of (s.o)): *He held his audience* (or *their attention*) *with an entertaining speech lasting over an hour.* **20** *intr.v* (of the weather, a condition, offer of s.t etc) remain in the same state and not change, be withdrawn (⇒ withdraw(2)) etc: *I hope this warm weather will hold for our holiday. In spite of your criticism, my argument still holds.* **21** *intr.v* stay on the telephone (and not put the receiver(1) down): *Mr Green is on the other line at the moment. Do you want to hold or would you like to phone back later?* ⇒ hold on(c), hold the line.

hold s.t against s.o continue to be angry with s.o, blame s.o, because of s.t that he/she has done or s.t that has happened: *I've always held it against him that he was unkind to me in our youth. I really won't hold it against you if you decide not to come.*

hold s.o/s.t at bay ⇒ bay⁵(*n*).

hold back ((*from doing*) *s.t*) **(a)** show unwillingness or hesitation (about (doing) s.t): *Because of the uncertain state of the market buyers are holding back (from buying* shares(3)). **(b)** stop s.t from happening: *She couldn't hold back her laughter for another moment so she quickly left the room.* **hold s.o back** not allow s.o to improve, get a better position etc: *I'm afraid his lack of training is holding him back in the company.* **hold s.o back (from s.o/s.t)** not allow s.o to move forward (towards s.o/s.t): *The police held the crowd back from the princess.* **hold s.t back (from s.o)** keep s.t, e.g knowledge, information etc, secret (from s.o): *He hasn't told us the whole truth; I'm sure he's holding something back (from us).*

hold one's breath ⇒ breath.

hold by s.t (*formal*) believe or hold(18) s.t strongly: *I hold by the view that arming the police is wrong.* ⇒ hold to s.t.

not hold a candle to s.o/s.t ⇒ candle.

hold court ⇒ court (*n*).

hold s.o down keep s.o, esp a group of people, a population etc, under one's control and not allow them to be free: *The ruler held the people down by using the army against them.* ⇒ hold s.o under.

hold s.o/s.t down not let s.o/s.t get, fly etc, up (from the ground): *He was held down by two men sitting on top of him. The balloon was held down by ropes.* **hold s.t down** not let s.t, e.g costs, prices etc increase; hold(7) s.t: *It is going to be difficult to hold our costs down when prices for materials are increasing.* **hold a job down** succeed in doing the job one is employed to do: *He'll never be able to hold down that job; he's too lazy.*

hold good/true for s.o/s.t continue to be right, true, as arranged or promised.

hold no fears for s.o ⇒ fear(*n*).

hold the fort ⇒ fort.

hold forth (**about/on s.o/s.t**) (*formal* or *joking*; often *derog*) speak at great length and often in an annoying way (about s.o/s.t one thinks one knows a lot about): *He started holding forth about how he would run the* economy(3) *so I left.*

hold one's ground ⇒ hold/stand one's ground (against s.o/s.t) (⇒ ground³).

hold s.t in (a) keep s.t in a fixed position close or closer to one's body etc: *Hold your chest in while I take your measurements. I have to hold my stomach in when I wear my* swimming costume. **(b)** not allow s.t, e.g a feeling, to be expressed or shown: *She had great difficulty holding in her laughter while he was talking.*

hold oneself in readiness (for s.t) ⇒ readiness.

hold s.o/s.t in check ⇒ check(*n*). **hold s.o/s.t in high/low regard** ⇒ regard(*n*).

Hold it! (expression used to ask s.o to stop or not start doing s.t): *Hold it! We can't go in yet as I can't find my keys.*

hold the line ⇒ hold(21), line(*n*). ⇒ hold on(c).

hold off (of bad weather, rain etc) not arrive or happen (though likely to do so): *The rain is holding off for the moment so we should be all right.* **hold off (from (doing) s.t)** not do s.t; delay (doing s.t): *Peter asked the shop to hold off from calling the police until he'd had a chance to talk to the man who was causing trouble.* **hold s.o off** stop s.o (who is attacking one): *He held his attacker off while his wife shouted for help.*

hold office ⇒ office(5).

hold on (a) manage to stay in or keep one's position in spite of difficulties etc: *We've got enough food and water so we should be able to hold on for another week or so.* **(b)** (often a request to) wait or stop for a moment: *Can you hold on for a moment while I have a word with her?* **(c)** remain connected on the telephone; hold(21): *Do you want to hold on while I try and find him?* **hold s.t on** keep s.t in a fixed position (on s.t else): *These two screws hold this part of the machine on. What's holding this piece on?*

hold on(to s.o/s.t) take or have a grip(1) on (s.o/ s.t): *Hold onto me and I'll pull you up. He couldn't hold on(to the rope) any longer and had to let himself fall.* **hold onto s.t** keep one's position, one's ownership or possession of s.t: *His horse held onto the lead for most of the race. I advise you to hold onto those* shares(3) *as they are bound to (⇒ bound¹) increase in value.*

hold out (a) manage to continue living, surviving(1) (for a certain length of time, until s.t happens etc): *The boy who was lost in the cave managed to hold out for four days until rescue came.* **(b)** (of food, stocks etc) last: *If we are careful, our supplies should hold out for the next two weeks.* **hold out for s.t** ask for or demand s.t (and not intend changing one's position until one has got it): *The workers are holding out for a big increase in their wages.* **hold out (on s.o)** (*informal*) refuse to give information (to s.o); refuse to deal (with s.o): *Something's not quite right about his story; I think he's holding out on us.* **hold s.t out (to s.o) (a)** move s.t away from a position, e.g away from one's body (and towards s.o): *Hold out your hand and I'll give you some sweets. Chris held out her hand to her little girl.* **(b)** offer s.t, e.g a hope, a prospect(1), (to s.o): *The doctors don't hold out much hope of his living more than a few months.*

hold s.t over s.o threaten s.o with s.t: *How can I work with the threat of losing my job being held over me?* **hold s.t over** delay s.t; postpone considering or doing s.t about s.t (to another date etc): *Discussion of the proposal was held over until the next meeting.* **hold s.t over (for a week** etc) continue s.t (for a certain time): *The play is so popular that it's going to be held over for another week.*

hold one's own (with s.o) ⇨ own(*pron*).

hold oneself/s.o responsible (for s.t) ⇨ responsible.

hold the road ⇨ road.

hold still ⇨ still² (*adj*).

hold to s.t (*formal*) not change one's opinion, belief etc about s.t: *I still hold to the view that I was right and he was wrong.* ⇨ hold(18), hold by s.t. **hold s.o to s.t** make s.o keep a promise, do what he/she has agreed etc: *Thanks for your offer — I'll certainly be holding you to that!*

hold (s.o/s.t) together (a) (cause (s.o/s.t) to) remain joined or united: *The two parts are held together by this screw. Their friendship held them together. We must hold together if we are to succeed.* **(b)** (of an argument etc) be complete, well worked out, coherent etc: *The whole thing just doesn't seem to hold together when you start examining it in detail.*

hold one's tongue ⇨ tongue.

hold s.o under (*formal*) keep s.o, e.g a group of people, a population etc, under one's control and not allow them to be free: *The people were held under by the unjust laws of the ruler.* ⇨ hold s.o down. **hold s.o/s.t under (s.t)** put or keep s.o/ s.t under or below (s.t): *Hold your finger under the tap until the blood has stopped running.*

hold s.o/s.t up (a) lift s.o/s.t high(er) (so that he/ she/it can see or be seen etc): *Hold up your hands if you have finished.* **(b)** delay s.o/s.t; cause s.o/ s.t to go slower: *I got held up by the traffic and so missed my flight. The work has been held up by the lack of staff.* ⇨ hold-up(1). **(c)** (stop and) rob s.o/s.t (often using guns etc to do so): *The armed* gang(1) *held up the van and got away with £20 000 in wages.* ⇨ hold-up(2). **hold s.o/s.t up as an example, model** etc use or point to s.o/s.t as a (good/bad) example or model(5) (that others should (not) follow): *The manager held her work up as an example of how things should be done.*

hold s.o/s.t up to ridicule, scorn ⇨ ridicule(*n*).

hold water ⇨ water(*n*).

(not) hold with s.o/s.t (*formal*) (not) like or approve of s.o/s.t: *Do you really hold with taking the law into their own hands?*

hold your horses! ⇨ horse(*n*).

There is/was etc **no holding her/him** etc It is/ was etc impossible to stop s.o from doing s.t or to control s.o: *There'll be no holding her once her foot is better. Once she'd started talking there was no holding her.*

'hold,all *c.n* bag for carrying everything one needs including clothes etc, esp when travelling for a short time.

'holder *c.n* **1** person who holds(17) a position.

office etc: *Holders of this office have to attend meetings four times a year.* **2** person who possesses or has s.t: *Only holders of blue tickets may park here.*

-holder *n* **1** person who possesses or has s.t shown by the first part of the word: *ticket-holders.* ⇨ householder, shareholder. **2** thing that holds(1) s.t shown by the first part of the word: *a cigarette-holder; a pen-holder.*

'holding *c.n* (usu (have) *a — in* s.t) ownership or possession (of s.t, esp land, shares in a company etc): *He has quite a large holding in this company.* ⇨ smallholding, shareholding.

'hold-,up *c.n* **1** (thing that causes a) delay or stop: *There's been a hold-up in production because of the lack of raw materials.* ⇨ hold s.o/s.t up(b). **2** act of (stopping s.o and) carrying out a robbery: *In the bank hold-up one of the staff was shot.* ⇨ hold s.o/s.t up(c).

hole /həʊl/ *c.n* **1** empty or hollow space in s.t, usu open at the top, bottom or side but with the other sides solid: *He dug a hole in the ground to bury the rubbish.* **2** (often — *in* s.t) opening or gap (in s.t) (often one that should not be there and is caused by an accident etc): *George had a hole in his sock. This is the hole in the fence through which the prisoners escaped.* **3** hollow space in the ground in which some kinds of animals live: *a rabbit hole.* **4** (in golf) one of nine or eighteen small holes(1) in the ground into which one tries to hit a golfball: *They played only nine holes.* **5** (in golf) point scored by hitting a golfball into a hole(4) using fewer strokes than one's opponent(1): *He won by four holes.* **6** (*derog; informal*) unpleasant place, e.g one that is not nice to live or work in: *The town's a bit of a hole and there's nothing to do there but I've got a good job.* **burn a hole in one's pocket** (*fig*) (of money) be in one's pocket, handbag etc so that one feels keen to spend it. **in holes** having many holes(2) in it: *When he got the shirt back from the* laundry(3) *it was in holes.* **make a hole in s.t** (*fig*) use a great deal of s.t and so not have much left: *The repairs made a large hole in our savings.* **pick holes in s.o/s.t** (*fig*) (try to) criticize s.o/s.t; find small unimportant things wrong about s.o/s.t in an annoying way: *The teacher picked holes in Pam's* essay(1) *because he had nothing* constructive *to say about it.*

▷ *tr.v* **7** cause or make a hole(2) in (s.t): *The ship was holed badly when it hit the rocks.* **8** (in golf) hit (one's golfball) into a hole(4): *She holed the ball in four* (i.e four strokes). **hole up s.w** (go and) hide s.w so that one cannot be found, to escape from other people, the law etc: *The robbers holed up in a lonely farm until the hunt for them was over.*

,hole-and-'corner *adj* (*derog*) (of s.t s.o does) that is very secret, usu because it is bad: *They were having a hole-and-corner affair because he was married.*

holiday /'hɒlɪdɪ/ *c.n* **1** day when one does not work, either because one has decided not to or because it is an official day of rest: *I took two days' holiday because I wanted to decorate my bedroom. Christmas Day is a holiday in Britain.* ⇨ bank holiday. **2** (often *pl*) number of days or weeks when one does not work and usu goes s.w to enjoy oneself and rest: *the school/summer* holidays; *a holiday in Spain*. **be/go on holiday** be having, start to have, one's holidays(2). Compare leave¹(2), vacation.

▷ *intr.v* **3** have a holiday(2): *We holidayed in Spain this year.*
'holiday-,maker *c.n* person who is having a holiday(2).
'holiday-,making *u.n*.
holiness ⇨ holy.
holler /'hɒlə/ *v* (*informal*) **1** *intr.v* (often — at/ to s.o) shout loudly (at/to s.o): *The man hollered at the boys to get out of his garden.* **2** *tr/intr.v* (often — (s.t) out) say (s.t) in a very loud voice: *He hollered out something but I was too far away to hear it.* **holler about s.t** (*fig*) complain (loudly) about s.t: *What are you hollering about?*
'hollering *u.n* (*informal*) act of crying or complaining: *Stop that hollering or I will really give you something to cry about!*
hollow /'hɒləʊ/ *adj* **1** (of an object etc) having an empty space in it: *This tree trunk is hollow.* Opposite solid(2). **2** (of a shape etc) having a curve that goes inwards: *She had hollow cheeks from not eating enough.* ⇨ concave. **3** that sounds as if it is made in, comes from, s.t that is hollow(1): *a hollow* echo(1)/groan(1). **4** (*fig*) (of a promise etc) not real or sincere; not proving to have any value: *I've had enough of the government's hollow promises. It turned out to be a hollow victory* (i.e one that was not really a victory at all). **beat s.o hollow** (*informal*) beat s.o completely (in a game, competition etc). **ring hollow** sound untrue or not sincere: *Her promise rang hollow after all the lies she'd told us.*
▷ *c.n* **5** area, esp in the ground, that is lower than the rest: *The house had been built in a hollow to protect it from the fierce winds.*
▷ *tr.v* **6** **hollow s.t out of** (s.t) take out the contents of s.t in order to make it hollow(1,2): *They hollowed out a tree trunk to make a boat* (or *They hollowed a boat out of a tree trunk*).
'hollowly *adv* in a hollow(3,4) way.
'hollowness *u.n*.
holly /'hɒlɪ/ *u.n* (also *attrib*) kind of tree or shrub with evergreen prickly(1) leaves and bright red berries used at Christmas as a decoration.
hollyhock /'hɒlɪ,hɒk/ *c.n* kind of flower with a tall stem and white, red, purple etc flowers on the top of it.
holocaust /'hɒlə,kɔːst/ *c.n* (*formal*) great destruction with many deaths, esp in a fire, war etc: *Many people are afraid that they will die in a* nuclear(3) *holocaust.*
hologram /'hɒləʊ,græm/ *c.n* photograph that uses certain kinds of light, e.g a laser beam, to make the picture appear solid or three-dimensional.
holster /'həʊlstə/ *c.n* case for holding a hand gun (usu worn on a belt around the waist or over the shoulder).
holy /'həʊlɪ/ *adj* (-ier, -iest) Opposite unholy. **1** (of a thing or things) connected with religion and the worship of God: *Mecca*(1) *is a holy city. The* Bible(1) *is a holy book.* **2** (of a person, s.o's life etc) very good and pure because of the practice of religion: *She had led a very holy life.*
'holiness *u.n* fact or state of being holy.
His, Your etc **Holiness** (title of) the Pope.
,Holy 'Bible *def.n* ⇨ bible(1).

,Holy Com'munion *u.n* ⇨ communion(3).
,Holy 'Father *def.n* Pope.
,Holy 'Ghost/'Spirit *def.n* (in Christianity) third person in the Trinity.
'Holy ,Land *def/unique n* Palestine; area where the Jewish and Christian(1) religions began.
,holy 'orders *pl.n* ⇨ order(*n*).
,Holy 'Trinity *def/unique n* ⇨ trinity(3).
'Holy ,Week *unique n* (in Christianity) week before Easter.
homage /'hɒmɪdʒ/ *u.n* (usu do/pay — to s.o/ s.t) great respect (to s.o/s.t): *They came to pay homage to their new king.*
home /həʊm/ *attrib.adj* **1** of or referring to the place where one lives: *one's home town*; *home life*; *home comforts*; *home cooking*. **2** of or referring to one's own country (as opposed to others): *home industries*; *the home market* (i.e for goods etc). **3** (of a football etc team, game etc) (playing or played) at its own ground (and not at another's): *The home team scored first.* ⇨ away(3).
▷ *adv* **4** in, at, to or from, the place (house, town or country) where one lives: *He stayed home because he had a cold. I left home early to catch the train. If you're home tonight I'll come and see you. I'm going home.* **5** (often drive/hit s.t —) to or into the place or position that it should have: *He hit the nail home with two blows. His first blow went home* (i.e hit the person/thing). **bring s.t home to s.o** (*fig*) make s.o realize or become aware(1) of (s.t): *Her remarks brought home to me the fact that she never really understood what was going on.* **come home to s.o** (*fig*) be realized or understood by s.o: *It has just come home to me what he was really trying to explain.* **drive/press s.t home (to s.o)** (*fig*) force s.o to realize or understand s.t: *He tried to drive home (to them) the points he was making by repeating them often.* **get home (a)** arrive back at one's house. **(b)** (in a race etc) reach the end, winning post etc (usu first in front of others). **get s.t home (to s.o)** cause s.t to be understood, realized (by s.o): *How can I get it home to you that I love you?* **go/hit home** (*fig*) make s.o realize s.t; affect s.o rather a lot: *His remarks about her behaviour certainly hit/went home and she was forced to apologize.* **hammer s.t home (to s.o)** ⇨ hammer(*v*). **nothing to write home about** (*fig*; *informal*) thing that one considers to be not very important or interesting (though others may think so): *He kept talking about his holiday but from what I could gather it really wasn't anything to write home about.*
▷ *n* **6** *c/u.n* place (house, flat, town, country etc) where one (and/or one's family) usu lives/live: *My home is in Bristol but I work in Exeter. The police asked the spectators to return to their homes and not block the road. The council is building new homes on the land it has bought.* **7** *c.n* house or building for groups of people who have no homes(6) of their own, who are ill, old etc: *a children's home* (e.g for children who have no parents); *an old people's home*. **8** *c.n* house or building for people doing certain jobs to live in: *a nurses' home*. **9** *def.n* (usu the — of s.o/s.t) place, esp a country, where a person, animal etc normally lives, where he/she/it originated; place where s.t started, had its origins; place that is famous for s.t: *India is the home of tigers.*

Nashville is the home of country-and-western music. **at home (a)** (present) in one's own house, flat etc: *There was nobody at home when I called so I left her a note.* **(b)** (of a football etc team) on one's own ground, in one's own town etc: *Fulham is playing at home this Saturday.* ⇨ home(3). ⇨ away(3). **be/feel at home (in/with s.t) (a)** be/feel comfortable and relaxed (as if one was in one's own home): *She didn't feel at home in such a large and empty house.* **(b)** be/feel able to manage (s.t) successfully: *I felt really at home with the new* computer. **find a home for s.t** find a place where s.t can be put, fitted in etc: *Can you find another home for all those plates?* **make one's home s.w** settle s.w (after moving from s.w else): *He made his home in the south of France because of the climate.* **make oneself at home** make oneself comfortable (as if one was in one's own home): *Make yourself at home — there are drinks in that cupboard and plenty of books to read.*

▷ *intr.v* **10 home in on s.o/s.t (a)** (of a missile(1) etc) (be aimed so as to) move towards and hit s.o/s.t: *The guns homed in on the enemy.* **(b)** direct one's attention towards s.o/s.t: *We need to home in on the main problem and deal with that first.*
'home,coming *c.n* return to, arrival at, one's home (house, flat, town, country etc), usu after some time away: *The street was decorated with flags for his homecoming.*
,home com'puter *c.n* = personal computer.
,Home 'Counties *def.pl.n* counties around London.
,home ,eco'nomics *u/pl.n* (science and study of) matters connected with the running of a home, e.g food, cooking, care of children, money.
'home-,grown *adj* (esp of food) grown by oneself in one's own garden or grown in one's own country (compared to being grown abroad and imported(2)): *Home-grown vegetables always taste nicer than bought ones.*
,home 'help *c.n* person who does work in s.o's house for pay, esp one who is employed by a local council to look after old or sick people.
homeland /'həʊm,lænd/ *c.n* (formal) person's own country or native land: *He longed to return to his homeland.*
'homeless *adj* **1** having no home.
▷ *def.pl.n* **2** people (as a group) who are homeless: *It is the responsibility of the local council to house the homeless.*
'homelessness *u.n.*
'homeliness *u.n* fact or state of being homely.
'homely *adj* (-ier, -iest) **1** (of a person, s.o's looks) not very beautiful but pleasant and friendly: *She was a homely sort of person who always made you feel extremely welcome.* **2** (of a thing, place etc) pleasant and comfortable: *The old inn had a very homely feeling about it. The new chairs made the room feel much homelier.*
,home-'made *adj* (of food, furniture etc) prepared or made in one's/s.o's own home (and not prepared or made by factories): *They sold their home-made jam and cakes at the village fair.*
'Home ,Office *def/unique n* (UK) government department concerned with matters of law and order, immigration etc inside England and Wales.
,home 'rule *u.n* government of a country by its

own people with its own parliament etc, esp after being governed by another country: *Many people are in favour of home rule for Scotland.*
,Home 'Secretary *def/unique n* government minister in charge of the Home Office.
'home,sick *adj* (of a person) sad because one misses, wants to go back to, one's own home when one is away: *My son was homesick for the first few days of his holiday.*
'homesickness *u.n.*
,home 'truth *c.n* thing one says or wants to say to s.o, esp about her/his behaviour, that contains a truth that may be unpleasant for her/him to hear: *It's about time that she learnt a few home truths about herself and that she can't continue to treat people so badly.*
homeward /'həʊmwəd/ *attrib.adj* that goes to(wards) one's home: *Our homeward journey was delayed by a railway accident.*
homeward(s) /'həʊmwəd(z)/ *adj/adv* towards one's home: *Our journey homeward (or homeward journey) was delayed. We start going homewards tomorrow.*
'home,work *u.n* work or study done in one's home, esp when one is a school pupil or student: *They complained that the teacher had given them too much homework.*
'homing *attrib.adj* **1** (of a torpedo(1), missile(1) etc) having a device in it that enables it to find and hit a target(1). **2** (of an animal's instinct) that makes it possible, likely, that it will return to the same place, esp for breeding (⇨ breed(2)).
'homing ,pigeon *c.n* pigeon that is trained to find its way back home when it is set free a long way from it, esp in a race against other pigeons.
homeopath /'həʊmɪə,pæθ/ *c.n* (also **'homeoo-,path**) doctor who practises homeopathy.
homeopathic /,həʊmɪə'pæθɪk/ *adj* (also **,homeoo'pathic**) of or referring to homeopathy and esp the treatment or medicine used in it.
,homeo'pathically *adv.* (also **homeoo-'pathically**).
homeopathy /,həʊmɪ'ɒpəθɪ/ *u.n* (also **,homoe'opathy**) (medical) treatment of an illness or disease by using very small doses(1) of a drug(1) etc that is like the illness or disease.
homicide /'hɒmɪ,saɪd/ *n* (law; formal) **1** c/u.n (example of the) (unlawful) killing of a person by another: *He was found guilty of homicide. There have been three homicides in this street.* ⇨ murder(1). **2** c.n person who has killed another: *Several convicted homicides have been moved to a new prison.* ⇨ murderer.
homicidal /,hɒmɪ'saɪdl/ *adj* (formal or joking) (showing signs of) wanting to kill s.o: *homicidal tendencies. He drives (his car) like a homicidal maniac(3).* ⇨ murderous.
homily /'hɒmɪlɪ/ *c.n* (pl -ies) (formal) **1** (old use) sermon(1). **2** serious talk (often rather boring) intended to improve s.o's behaviour, correct her/his faults etc: *He delivered a short homily on the subject of their rudeness.*
homogeneous /,həʊmə'dʒiːnɪəs/ *adj* (formal) being of, forming, a group of the same kind (as one another): *a homogeneous group of students (e.g of the same nationality or age).* Compare heterogeneous.

homogeneity /ˌhɒmə'dʒe'niːəɪtɪ/ *u.n.* **,homo-
'geneously** *adv.*

homogenize, -ise /hɒ'mɒdʒɪˌnaɪz/ *tr.v* treat
(milk) through heating it so that the fat or cream
is mixed up with the rest and does not become
separate.

ho'moge,nized ,milk *u.n* milk treated in this
way.

homograph /'hɒməˌgrɑːf/ *c.n* (*technical*) one
of two or more words that are spelt the same
but have different meanings; they may be pronounced the same or differently: *'Tear' meaning
'to rip(3) something' and 'tear' meaning 'a drop of
liquid from the eyes' are homographs.* Compare
homonym, homophone.

homonym /'hɒməˌnɪm/ *c.n* (*technical*) one of
two or more words that are spelt (and usu pronounced) the same but have different meanings:
*'Cow' meaning 'a female animal of certain spe-
cies' and 'cow' meaning 'to frighten someone' are
homonyms.* Compare homograph, homophone.

homophone /'hɒməˌfəʊn/ *c.n* (*technical*) one
of two or more words pronounced the same but
different in spelling, meaning etc: *'Beer' meaning
'an alcoholic(1) drink' and 'bier' meaning 'a thing
on which one carries or puts a dead person' are
homophones.* Compare homograph, homonym.

homo sapiens /ˌhəʊməʊ 'sæpɪˌenz/ *unique n*
(name used to describe) human beings as a group
having intelligence etc (esp when compared to
other animals).

homosexual /ˌhəʊmə'seksjʊəl/ *adj* **1** who is
attracted to a person of the same sex. ⇨ gay(3),
heterosexual, lesbian.
▷ *c.n* **2** homosexual(1) person.

homosexuality /ˌhəʊməˌseksjʊ'ælɪtɪ/ *u.n.*
,homo'sexually *adv.*

hon, Hon *written abbr* **1** honorary. **2** Honour-
able(2).

hone /həʊn/ *c.n* **1** hard stone used for sharpening
knives, tools etc.
▷ *tr.v* **2** sharpen (a knife, tool etc) using a hone(1).
3 (often passive) (*fig*) improve, prepare, (s.o/
s.t) for a particular purpose: *Navratilova uses a
computer to hone her tennis (shots).*

honest /'ɒnɪst/ *adj* Opposite dishonest. **1** (of a
person, s.o.'s behaviour etc) acting in a good and
fair way, not telling lies, not cheating or stealing
etc: *He's an honest man. We run an honest business and don't try to cheat our customers.* **2** (of an
opinion etc) said or stated without trying to lie or
hide the truth, what one thinks etc: *In my honest
opinion* (or *To be perfectly honest*) *I think that
picture you want to buy is terrible.* **3** (of a person's
face, looks etc) appearing to be honest(1): *He has
an honest look about him.* **earn/make an honest
living** earn (enough) money to live (reasonably)
without trying to get more by cheating etc. **make
an honest man/woman of s.o** (say that one will)
marry a man, woman after having lived with him/
her as if he/she was one's husband/wife: *After all
these years Sally has agreed to make an honest
man of me and we're getting married.*
▷ *adv/interj* **4** (*informal*) (way of saying that one is
not lying or cheating): *Honest! I didn't take the
money.*

'honestly *adv* **1** in an honest(1) way: *Peter
behaved very honestly towards Di.* **2** (way of
showing that what one says is what one believes);

really and truly: *I honestly don't know what's
wrong with him.*
▷ *interj* (*informal*) **3** = honest(4): *Honestly! I had
nothing to do with it.* **4** (way of showing anger,
annoyance etc): *Honestly! Do you really expect
me to believe that?*

'honesty *u.n* fact, state or quality of being hon-
est(1). **in all honesty** in my etc honest(2) opinion;
if I etc want to be truthful: *We must in all honesty
admit that we were partly to blame.*

honey /'hʌnɪ/ *n* **1** *u.n* (also *attrib*) thick sweet
yellow substance made by bees from the nectar
in flowers, often eaten like jam or used as a
flavouring: *honey cake.* **2** *c.n* (usu *sing*) (esp US)
(informal word used when talking to s.o one likes
or loves, e.g one's husband/wife) dear, darling(2):
*Honey, you shouldn't work so hard. Be a honey
and bring me a drink.*

'honey,bee *c.n* bee that makes honey(1).

'honey,comb *c.n* **1** group of hollow six-sided
cells(5) made of wax in which bees lay eggs and
store honey(1). **2** (also *attrib*) place, shape, area
etc that looks like a honeycomb(1): *There was
a honeycomb of passages in the underground
mine.*

'honey,combed *adj* (usu — with s.t) having a
honeycomb(2) shape or pattern (consisting of s.t):
The old mine was honeycombed with passages.

'honey,moon *c.n* **1** special holiday that newly
married people have after their wedding.
▷ *intr.v* **2** (usu — *in*) (s.w) have, go on, a honey-
moon(1) (s.w): *They honeymooned in Bermuda.*

'honey,mooner *c.n* (usu *pl*) one of the two
newly married people on their honeymoon(1):
The hotel was full of honeymooners.

honeysuckle /'hʌnɪˌsʌkl/ *c/u.n* kind of climbing plant with yellow, white or purple flowers
that have a sweet smell.

honk /hɒŋk/ *c.n* **1** sound made by the horn of a
vehicle, esp as a warning etc. **2** (sound made by
the) cry of a goose(1).
▷ *v* **3** *tr/intr.v* (usu — (*one's horn*) *at s.o/s.t*) (cause
(one's car etc horn) to) make a honk(1) (esp to
warn s.o or to show one's annoyance at s.o/s.t):
*He came out of the side road without looking
carefully and a lorry driver honked loudly at him.*
4 *intr.v* (often — *at s.o/s.t*) (of a goose(1)) make
a honk(2) (to warn, frighten s.o/s.t etc): *When I
got near to her young the goose honked at me.*

'honking *u.n* continuous honks(*n*): *The air was
filled with the honking of cars in the traffic jam.*

honour /'ɒnə/ *n* (US **'honor**) **1** *u.n* (sign of)
great (public) respect, good opinion etc shown
to s.o: *She won great honour in her fight against
poverty. He is held in great honour in his own
country.* Opposite dishonour(1). **2** *u.n* good character or reputation (of a person, organization,
country etc): *He is a man of honour.* Opposite
dishonour(1). **3** *c.n* (usu *sing*) person or thing
who/that causes great pride: *He was an honour
to the school. It was an honour to know him.*
4 *u.n* (often *have the — of (doing)* s.t, *to do*
s.t) (*formal*) (polite way of making a request
or statement (about s.t), introducing s.o etc)
pleasure, pride: *The Mayor requests the honour
of your company at lunch on Friday. I have* (or
was given) *the honour of introducing Mr Tony
Brand, President of the largest car manufacturers
in the country.* **be a point of honour (with s.o)**

be a matter that affects the honour(2) (of s.o): *It was a point of honour with him to pay his bills promptly*. **Companion of Honour** ⇨ companion. **(put s.o, be) on her/his/one's honour** (put s.o, be) in a state or position where her/his (or one's) honour(2) may be damaged, e.g if she/he/(or one) does not do s.t: *I'm putting you on your honour not to tell anybody about this. On my honour, I had nothing to do with it*. **roll of honour** ⇨ roll(*n*).

▷ *tr.v* **5** show great respect or honour(1) to (s.o/ s.t): *A service was held to honour the dead*. **6** (*formal*) make (s.o) feel great pride: *Are you going to honour us with your presence at dinner tonight?* **7** give (s.o) a title, award(1) etc for her/ his achievements(2): *He was honoured by many countries for his work for peace*. **8** (say that one will) do (s.t to which one has agreed), pay (money that one owes or has promised etc): *Of course we will honour the agreement we signed. The bank has refused to honour his last cheque.*

honorary /'ɒnrərɪ/ *adj* (often with capital **H**; written abbr Hon) **1** (having a position) that brings honour(1) but no payment or salary: *He is honorary secretary/chairman of the local sports club*. **2** (of a university degree etc) given as a sign of honour(1) (without the person having had to do a course of study): *Many universities give honorary degrees to famous people.*

honourable /'ɒnrəbl/ *adj* (US **'honorable**) **1** having or showing honour(2): *an honourable man; honourable behaviour*. Opposite dishonourable. **2** (with capital **H**; written abbr Hon) (UK) **(a)** title used of or to a judge or other official, or to the daughter/son of a hereditary peer¹(1) below the rank of Marquess: *the Honourable Justice Green; the Hon Miss Susan Brown*. **(b)** polite title used when talking to or about a Member of Parliament in parliament itself: *Can the Honourable Member for Paddington North please answer the question properly?* ⇨ Right Honourable (⇨ right(10)).

'honours *pl.n* (US **'honors**) **1** special titles or awards(1) given to s.o for her/his achievements(2): *He received many honours for his work*. **2** (also *attrib*) (often written with capital **H**; written abbr Hons) (UK) (title of the) highest first degree course (or the (grade of) degree given) in a university (in a subject): *I'm doing an honours degree in History. She got First Class Honours in German. Charles Smith, BA (Hons)*. **do the honours** (*informal* or *joking*) act as if one is in charge(6), e.g in looking after a guest: *Who's going to do the honours and serve the pudding?* **with full (military) honours** with all ceremony as a sign of respect (esp when burying one or more soldiers): *He was buried with full military honours.*

hood /hʊd/ *c.n* **1** covering for the head that has an opening in the front, is closed on the sides and is often fixed to the back of a coat etc: *I pulled the hood of my* anorak *up when it started to rain*. **2** cloth, plastic etc covering for the seat area of a car, the end of a pram which can be folded down or removed: *He liked driving his sports car with the hood down*. **3** (US) bonnet(2). **4** metal device with an opening placed over a fire, a stove etc to take smoke, the smell of cooking etc away from a room: *In a small kitchen you need an* extractor *hood to get rid of the smells*. **5** covering

for the head, like a hood(1), worn round the neck and down the back on special occasions by graduates(2). **6** (*informal*) hoodlum(1): *These boys behave like young hoods.*

'hooded *adj* **1** wearing a covering over the head and face: *The robbers were all hooded to avoid recognition*. **2** having a shape or covering (like that of a hood(1)): *hooded eyes.*

-hood /-ˌhʊd/ *n* used as the second part of a noun to show a state or condition described by the first part of the word: *boyhood; childhood.*

hoodlum /'huːdləm/ *c.n* **1** violent person who causes damage to property and/or people: *They are introducing laws to prevent hoodlums from getting into football matches*. ⇨ hooligan. **2** (US) criminal.

hoodwink /'hʊdˌwɪŋk/ *tr.v* trick or deceive (s.o), esp by pretending (to be) s.t: *The old lady was hoodwinked into giving him all her savings.*

hoof /huːf/ *c.n* (pl hooves /huːvz/, hoofs) hard part on the bottom of the foot of some animals, e.g horses, deer. ⇨ cloven hoof (⇨ cleave).

hook /hʊk/ *c.n* **1** small piece of metal, wood, plastic etc with a curve in it on which to hang things: *Put your coat on the hook* (or *on the coat-hook*) *behind the door*. ⇨ leave/take the telephone off the hook. **2** piece of metal with a curve at the bottom end, used for catching things: *a fish-hook; a boat-hook*. **3** piece of metal, plastic etc with a curve in it which goes into a loop(1) (called an eye(4)) to fasten clothes: *Can you do up the hook above the* zip *fastener for me, as I can't reach it?* **4** sharp tool with a curve in it, used for cutting grass, hay, branches etc: *a* reaping (⇨ reap(1)) *hook*. **5** (in boxing) short sharp blow with the fist made with the elbow bent: *a left/ right hook*. **6** (*sport*) act of hitting/kicking a ball so that it twists up and over, to the side. Compare slice(3). **be/get, let s.o, off the hook** (*fig; informal*) be allowed, allow s.o, to escape from a difficult situation or from punishment: *I'll let you off the hook this time if you promise never to do it again*. **by hook or by crook** (*fig; informal*) using every means possible (some of which may be dishonest): *I intend to get that job by hook or by crook*. **leave/take the telephone off the hook** leave/take the telephone off the place where it normally rests (by mistake or because one does not want it to ring). **(swallow, fall for, s.t) hook, line and sinker** (*fig; informal*) (believe s.t s.o says, often s.t that it is not true or because one is not clever enough) totally and completely: *I told him that I was poor and he swallowed it hook, line and sinker and lent me £500!*

▷ *v* **7** catch (a fish etc) using a hook(2). **8** *tr.v* catch s.t by using a stick etc like a hook(2): *Sarah hooked the keys through the window with a stick*. ⇨ unhook(2). **9** *tr/intr.v* (often — s.t up) (cause (esp clothes) to) be joined with a hook(3) or hooks: *The skirt hooks up* (or *is hooked up*) *at the side*. ⇨ unhook(1). **10** *tr/intr.v* (usu — (s.t) up to s.t) join or connect (one thing to another): *This device hooks up to that one with this* cable(2). *The television broadcast will be international and will hook up several stations around the world*. **11** *tr.v* (*sport*) hit or kick (a ball) with a hook(6): *He hooked the* golfball *and it landed in the river*. **hook s.t (a)round/on/onto s.t** put s.t, e.g one's arm or leg, round etc s.t in such a way that it holds or catches it like a hook(2): *Colin hooked his foot around the leg of the chair and pulled it towards him.* **hook onto s.t** become joined to s.t (as if) with a hook(2): *He hooked (his boat) onto the boat next to him.* **hook (s.t (and s.t)) together** (cause s.t (and s.t)) to become joined together (as if) with a hook(2) or hooks: *We hooked the boats together so that they could be pulled into the harbour.*

hooked *adj* shaped like a hook(1); having a bend in it: *He had a hooked nose.* **be/get hooked (on s.t)** (*informal*) be/become addicted or very fond of s.t: *He's hooked on drugs(2). I didn't like the new television series at first but now I'm completely hooked (on it).*

'hooker *c.n* 1 (in rugby) player in the middle of the front row of the scrum(1) who tries to hook(11) the ball when it is thrown into it. 2 (US) (*derog*; *slang*) prostitute.

'hook-,up *c.n* (device for the) joining up, connecting or hooking(10) up of two or more things, esp of radio or television broadcasts between places, countries etc: *The World Games are being broadcast live all over the world through an international hook-up.*

hooligan /'hu:lɪɡən/ *c.n* violent destructive (usu young) person: *young hooligans who destroy public property.*

'hooliga,nism *u.n* way(s) in which a hooligan behaves.

hoop /hu:p/ *c.n* 1 metal band fixed around a wooden barrel to hold it together. 2 open round circle of metal, plastic(3) or wood used as a toy to roll along or, e.g in a circus, for a person or animal to jump through. 3 U-shaped piece of metal etc with the ends in a surface so that it forms a hole.

hooray /hu:'reɪ/ *interj* ⇒ hurrah.

hoot /hu:t/ *c.n* 1 sound made by the horn of a vehicle, the siren(1) on a ship etc: *He gave three hoots on his horn to tell her he had arrived.* 2 sound or call made by an owl. 3 (often *pl*, *a* —, *hoots, of laughter, disapproval* etc) sound(s) expressing one's feelings of amusement, disapproval etc: *There were hoots of laughter after he told his joke.* 4 (often *be a* —) (*informal*) person, event etc who/that is extremely funny: *What a hoot! She's such a hoot!* **not care a hoot, two hoots, (about s.t)** (*informal*) not care at all (about s.t that has happened or might happen): *I don't care two hoots if he leaves or stays.*

▷ *tr/intr.v* 5 (often — *at s.o/s.t*) (cause (the horn of a vehicle, a ship's siren etc) to) make hoots(1) (at s.o/s.t): *I hooted at the other car to get out of my way.* 6 *intr.v* (of an owl) make a hoot(2). 7 *tr.v* (usu — *s.o down*; — *s.t off (s.t)*) shout so loudly at (s.o who is speaking, acting etc) that he/she cannot continue (and has to leave the platform(1), stage etc): *The singer was so bad that the audience hooted him off the stage.* 8 *intr.v* (often — *with laughter, disapproval* etc (*at s.o/s.t*)) shout or cry out (with laughter etc at s.o/s.t): *The crowd hooted (with disapproval) when the politician started speaking.*

'hooter *c.n* 1 kind of device like a horn in a car, on a motorbike etc that makes a noise to warn other vehicles, people etc on the road. 2 siren(1) that makes a hooting(⇒ hoots(5)) noise, esp one in a factory, used at the beginning and/or ending

of work. 3 (*derog*; *slang*) large nose: *He's got a big red hooter.*

hoover /'hu:və/ *c.n* (*t.n*) 1 kind of vacuum cleaner.

▷ *tr/intr.v* 2 clean (a room, carpet etc) with a hoover(1): *Don't get in my way now as I've got to hoover (the carpets).* **hoover s.t up** use a hoover(1) to suck up dust etc: *Can you hoover up all that mess'(3) around the fireplace.*

hooves ⇒ hoof.

hop¹ /hɒp/ *c.n* 1 action of jumping forwards, backwards etc on one foot or two feet together (by people, birds, some animals, e.g frogs, and insects, e.g grasshoppers). 2 (*informal*) distance or travel between two places by an aircraft: *Our plane made the journey in three hops* (i.e it landed twice before reaching its destination). **catch s.o on the hop** (*fig*; *informal*) do s.t that finds s.o not prepared or ready to deal with it: *They came earlier than I expected and caught me on the hop with no food ready yet.* **hop, skip/step and jump** = triple jump. **keep s.o on the hop** (*fig*; *informal*) do s.t that makes s.o keep busy, pay attention, esp because he/she does not know what things one will ask her/him to do: *His continual demands for us to do this and that kept us all on the hop.*

▷ *intr.v* (-pp-) 3 (often — *about*, *around* etc) (of a person, bird, animal, insect etc) jump (about, around etc) using one foot or two feet together: *Though his feet were tied he managed to hop to the door and escape. The frog hopped across the road.* **hop in(to s.t)**, **on(to) s.t**, **out (of s.t)** (*informal*) get in, on, out of, a vehicle: *Hop in and I'll give you a lift to the station. Let's hop onto that bus.* **Hop it!** (*slang*) go away (because one is not wanted etc)!: *Go on, hop it before I call the police!* **hop over to s.w** make a quick, usu short visit/journey to s.w: *He hopped over to Amsterdam for the weekend.* **hopping mad** ⇒ mad.

'hop,scotch *u.n* game played by children in which they hop¹(3) in different ways (sometimes on one foot, sometimes on two) on a number of squares drawn on the ground, on a pavement etc.

hop² /hɒp/ *c.n* 1 kind of climbing plant the seeds of which are used in the brewing(3) of beer. 2 (usu *pl*) seed from this plant.

'hop-,picker *c.n* person who picks hops²(2).

'hop-,picking *u.n* (usu *go* —) act of picking hops²(2).

hope /həʊp/ *n* 1 *c/u.n* (often — *of (doing) s.t*, *that s.t will happen* etc) (reason for) feeling that s.t one wants will, can or may happen: *Have you any hope of passing your exams? He has high hopes of becoming a doctor. There was little hope of rescue as the area was deserted. Hopes that the talks will succeed are fading as neither side will agree.* 2 *c.n* person or thing who/that may be of help: *The bank was my last hope but it refused to lend me the money.* **(be) beyond/past hope** (be) without any chance of improving, getting better etc: *The doctors say he is beyond hope and will die soon.* **dash s.o's hopes (of (doing) s.t)** destroy s.o's hopes (of (doing) s.t): *Her hopes of getting into university were dashed by her examination results.* **give up hope (of (doing) s.t)** stop hoping (for s.t, to do s.t). **hold out some, little, no** etc **hope (of (doing) s.t)**

say or state that there may be (some etc) hope(1) (of s.t happening etc): *I'm afraid I can hold out very little hope of finding her alive.* **in the hope of (doing) s.t, that...** having a hope(1) or expectation of (doing) s.t, that ...: *I came here in the hope of meeting you* (or *in the hope that I'd meet you*). **live in hope(s) (of (doing) s.t)** continue to have a hope(1) or hopes (of (doing) s.t): *She lives in hopes of inheriting(1) a lot of money from her rich relatives.* **lose (all) hope (of (doing) s.t)** stop believing or hoping(3) (that s.t will happen etc): *After three weeks they were beginning to lose (all) hope (of being rescued).* **pin one's hopes on s.o/s.t** rely on s.o/s.t for a successful result. **raise s.o's hopes** make s.o think or believe s.t he/she wants will happen (often however leading to disappointment): *Our hopes were raised when we saw the aircraft but it flew on without seeing us.*

▷ *tr/intr.v* **3** (often — *that...*; — *to do s.t*; — *so/not*) expect or wish (that ..., to do s.t) with the feeling that it will, can or may happen: *I hope (that) you can come to the party. I hope to see her soon. 'Is he coming to the party?' 'I hope so* (i.e I hope he is).' *'Do you think it's going to rain?' 'I hope not* (i.e I hope it is not).' ⇨ unhoped-for. **hope against hope (that...)** continue to hope (that...) though it is very unlikely: *We hoped against hope that she would get better but three weeks after the operation she died.* **hope for s.t** expect, wish for, s.t: *I'm hoping for a big increase in salary this year.* **hope for the best** continue to wish that what one wants will happen although there are reasons for uncertainty: *It is difficult to know whether we will succeed or not but we're all hoping for the best.*

'hopeful *adj* **1** (often — *of (doing) s.t*) being full of hope(1) (about (doing) s.t): *I'm hopeful of a successful conclusion(1) to our talks.* **2** that gives one hope(1): *We should know tomorrow whether we've got the contract(1) but the signs definitely look hopeful.*

▷ *c.n* **3** person who wants or expects to succeed (in a competition, in getting a job etc): *There was a queue of young hopefuls waiting to be auditioned(2) for a part in the play.*

'hopefully *adv* **1** in a hopeful(1) way: *She waited hopefully for him to arrive.* **2** (*informal*) I, we etc hope(3) that (s.t will happen): *Hopefully, everything will work out well in the end.*

'hopefulness *u.n.*

'hopeless *adj* **1** offering no hope(1); not going to, not likely to, succeed: *The situation is hopeless and there's nothing more we can do about it. It is hopeless to attempt to escape.* **2** (of a medical condition etc) not going to, or likely to, improve (so one should give up hope(1)): *The doctor said his case was hopeless and gave him three months to live.* **3** (often — *at s.t*) (of a person) not at all good (at doing s.t): *I'm hopeless at mathematics. He's hopeless; I could have done the job better myself.*

'hopelessly *adv.* **'hopelessness** *u.n.*

hop-picker, hop-picking ⇨ hop².

hopscotch ⇨ hop¹.

horde /hɔːd/ *c.n* (often — *s of s.o/s.t*) large number (of people, insects etc) in a group: *Hordes of tourists go to Greece in the summer.*

horizon /həˈraɪzn/ *n* **1** *def.n* line seen from a distance, where the sky and earth seem to meet. **2** *c.n* (often *pl*) limit or extent of a person's knowledge,

experience: *New horizons were opening up to her with her new job.* **above/below/beyond/on the horizon** in a position above etc the horizon(1), esp so that it can, cannot, be seen etc: *I could see a figure on the horizon. The sun sank below the horizon.*

horizontal /ˌhɒrɪˈzɒntl/ *adj* (usu *attrib*) **1** that is flat, lying in a position that is level with the horizon(1) or in relation to the ground: *Draw three horizontal lines one above the other.* ⇨ vertical.
▷ *c.n* **2** horizontal(1) line, object etc: *First, draw a horizontal 3 cm long and then a vertical half way along it.*

ˌhoriˈzontally *adv.*

hormone /ˈhɔːməʊn/ *c.n* (also *attrib*) kind of chemical substance produced in certain organs of the body (and in plants) that controls growth, changes etc: *She was suffering from a hormone deficiency that left her very weak. Use hormone powder on the end of a* cutting(4) *to encourage growth.*

hormonal /hɔːˈməʊnəl/ *adj.*

horn /hɔːn/ *n* **1** *c/u.n* (also *attrib*) long hard growth (usu one of two) found on top of the head of some animals, e.g cattle(1), sheep, goats; this growth removed and used to make objects etc: *a deer horn; a horn spoon; a knife handle made of horn.* ⇨ shoehorn. **2** *c.n* thing shaped like a horn(1): *the horns of a snail.* **3** *c.n* (also **'motor ˌhorn**) device in a car etc that produces a sound intended to warn other drivers etc; hooter(1): *He blew/sounded his horn as he came to the sharp bend.* ⇨ foghorn. **4** *c/def.n* (also *attrib*) one of a number of different kinds of musical instruments that are made of a brass tube bent into shape; sounds are produced when the player blows into one end (and presses the valves(1)): *a French horn. Jonathan plays the horn* (or *is a horn player*) *in the local* orchestra. **on the horns of a dilemma** ⇨ dilemma. **draw in one's horns** (*fig*) (decide to) protect one's position or state by not doing s.t that would be risky, e.g by not spending (too much) money: *We've spent rather a lot of money these last few months and it's now time that we drew in our horns.* **take the bull by the horns** ⇨ bull¹.

▷ *intr.v* **5 horn in (on s.o/s.t)** (*informal*) join in (a conversation, s.o's activities, work etc) in a rough or rude way and without waiting to be asked: *We must keep the deal secret or we'll find our competitors trying to horn in on it.*

horned *adj* having, shaped like, a horn(1) or horns: *The* rhinoceros *is a horned animal.*

-horned *adj* having a horn(1) or horns of a shape, length, number etc as described by the first part of the word: *long-horned* cattle(1).

'horn-ˌrimmed *adj* (esp of glasses) having edges around the pieces of glass that are made of horn(1) or a plastic material that looks like it: *He was wearing heavy horn-rimmed glasses.*

'horny *adj* (-*ier*, -*iest*) **1** of or like horn(1): *a horny substance.* **2** (esp of one's hands, feet) hard and rough, esp from hard physical work or walking without shoes. **3** (*slang*; do not use!) (of a person) very excited in a sexual way.

hornet /ˈhɔːnɪt/ *c.n* kind of large wasp with a painful sting. **stir up a hornet's nest** (*fig*) cause a great deal of angry feeling to be expressed (because of s.t (wrong) one has done): *You really* *stirred up a hornet's nest when you criticized the leadership.*

hornpipe /ˈhɔːnˌpaɪp/ *c/def.n* (music for a) kind of lively dance formerly done by sailors.

horoscope /ˈhɒrəˌskəʊp/ *c.n* (account of a) person's future life that is predicted from the position of the stars and planets at a certain time, e.g at her/his birth: *Newspapers and magazines have regular horoscopes but I don't believe a word of them.* ⇨ zodiac. **read s.o's horoscope** make such an account by asking s.o questions about the date of her/his birth, past activities etc.

horror /ˈhɒrə/ *n* **1** *c/u.n* (usu *sing*) feeling of very great fear, shock or disgust: *The newspapers were full of the horror of the murders.* **2** *c.n* (*derog*; *informal*) person, often a child, who behaves very badly or unpleasantly: *That boy is a real little horror and he's always breaking things.* **be filled with horror** be very frightened, shocked etc: *I was filled with horror when I saw the destruction caused by the explosion.* (**cry out**, **watch** etc) **in horror** (cry out etc) with great fear, shock etc: *The audience looked on in horror as the acrobat fell to his death.* **have a horror of s.t** dislike s.t very greatly, esp in a way that one cannot control: *I have an absolute horror of spiders.*

horrendous /həˈrendəs/ *adj* **1** very shocking, frightening: *a horrendous accident/crash.* **2** (*informal*) very large, unpleasant: *The price of meat is horrendous.*

hor'rendously *adv.* **hor'rendousness** *u.n.*

horrible /ˈhɒrəbl/ *adj* **1** causing horror(1): *a horrible accident.* **2** (*derog*) (of a person, s.o's actions) very, rather, nasty and unpleasant: *He's a horrible man who never has a kind word to say about anybody. That was a horrible thing to do/say.* **3** (of s.t that happens) not at all pleasant or enjoyable: *We had a horrible time on our holiday. The weather was horrible!* **be horrible of s.o** (**to do s.t**) be a horrible(2) thing for s.o to do: *It was really horrible of you to treat her in that way.*

'horribleness *u.n.* **'horribly** *adv.*

horrid /ˈhɒrɪd/ *adj* = horrible.

'horridly *adv.* **'horridness** *u.n.*

horrific /həˈrɪfɪk/ *adj* very frightening or terrible: *a horrific accident. It was horrific driving in the dark along that dangerous mountain road.*

hor'rifically *adv.*

horrify /ˈhɒrɪfaɪ/ *tr.v* (*-ies*, *-ied*) frighten or shock (s.o) very greatly: *Her story of how she had been attacked horrified me.* **be horrified by/at s.t**, **to discover** etc **s.t** be shocked by/at, to discover, s.t: *I was horrified to learn how she had been treated. Tessa was horrified at the state of her sister who had become so thin.*

'horri,fying *adj* causing horror(1): *a horrifying accident. What a horrifying thought — another five years with her in charge!*

'horri,fyingly *adv.*

'horror ˌcomic/ˌfilm/ˌstory *c.n* comic(4) etc that has monsters(1), murders etc in it that are intended to make people very frightened.

'horrors *pl.n* things, events etc that cause horror(1): *The horrors of war have to be seen to be believed.*

'horror-ˌstricken *adj* (also **'horror-ˌstruck**) (usu *pred*, *— at/by s.t*) very frightened or shocked (by s.t): *She was horror-stricken by* (or *to hear*) *what had happened.*

hors d'oeuvre /ɔː ˈdɜːvr/ *c.n* (*pl hors d'oeuvre(s)* /ɔː ˈdɜːvr/) (*French*) dish or dishes of (small pieces of) food served as appetizers at the beginning of a meal.

horse /hɔːs/ *n* **1** *c.n* kind of large animal with four legs and a head with a mane on its long neck, used for riding, racing, pulling carts etc. ⇨ carthorse, colt(1), filly, foal(1), gelding, mare, stallion. **2** *u.n* flesh of this animal as meat; horseflesh; horsemeat. **3** *c.n* = rocking horse. **4** *c/def.n* (also **'vaulting ˌhorse**) high box in a gymnasium for jumping etc over. **5** *c.n* = clothes-horse. **back the wrong horse** (*fig*) choose s.o/s.t (instead of s.o/s.t else) who/that does not succeed, turns out to be the wrong person, thing etc: *If you think the new political party will win the next election you'll be backing the wrong horse.* **be/get on one's high horse** (*fig*) be/become very offended, cross because of s.t s.o has done: *There's no need to get on your high horse just because I said you ought to be kinder to Jack.* **a dark horse** ⇨ dark. **eat like a horse** eat a great deal of (or too much) food, either continually or at one time. **flog a dead horse** (*fig*) continue to try to say/do s.t when the opportunity has gone, when it is no longer possible for s.t to happen etc: *You're flogging a dead horse if you think you can make him change his mind.* **Hold your horses!** (*fig*) Stop; do not decide, do, s.t so quickly: *Hold your horses! I haven't said that I'll give you the money yet!* (**not**) **look a gift-horse in the mouth** ⇨ gift-horse. **put the cart before the horse** ⇨ cart(*n*). (**straight**) **from the horse's mouth** (*fig*) direct from the original person, source(1) etc: *It must be true because I got the tip about the changes in the government straight from the horse's mouth.* **a willing horse** (*fig*) a person who works, will work, very hard (for s.o, on s.t etc). **work like a horse** work very hard.

▷ *intr.v* **6 horse about/around** (*informal*) (of a person) act in a silly, usu rough and noisy, way: *Will you two stop horsing around and get on with your work.* ⇨ horseplay.

'horse,back *u.n* (on —) on a horse.

'horse,box *c.n* closed box on wheels (pulled by another vehicle) in which a horse or horses is/are taken from place to place.

ˌhorse 'chestnut *c.n* ⇨ chestnut(1).

'horse,flesh *u.n* flesh of a horse as meat. ⇨ horse(2).

'horse,fly *c.n* (*pl -ies*) kind of large insect that drinks the blood of horses and some other animals.

'horse,hair *u.n* (also *attrib*) hair from the mane or tail of a horse, esp used as a filling for mattresses etc.

'horseman *c.n.* (*pl -men*) man riding, skilled in riding, a horse. ⇨ horsewoman.

'horseman,ship *u.n* art or skill of riding horses.

'horse,meat *u.n* = horseflesh.

'horse,play *u.n* silly rough noisy play, sometimes including fighting but not in a serious way: *Stop that horseplay at once and go to bed!* ⇨ horse(6).

'horse,power *c.n* (*pl horsepower*) (*abbr HP, hp*) (also *attrib*) (becoming *old use*) measurement of the power of an engine: *His old car had a twelve horsepower engine.* ⇨ cubic capacity.

'horse ,race *c.n* race between horses with riders, jockeys(1) often for money, a prize. ⇒ racehorse.

'horse ,racing *u.n* sport in which horses are raced against each other.

'horse,radish *c/u.n* (also *attrib*) kind of plant with a root that has a sharp bitter taste which is used as a flavouring, esp with cooked beef¹(1): *horseradish sauce*.

'horse ,riding *u.n* (also *attrib*) skill or act of riding horses: *horse riding lessons*.

'horse ,sense *u.n* (*informal*) common sense.

'horse,shoe *c.n* **1** piece of metal shaped like a U that is nailed into the hard part of a horse's foot to protect it. **2** shape like this as a sign of good luck: *He got a birthday card with a horseshoe on it*.

'horse,woman *c.n* (*pl* -,women) woman riding, or skilled at riding, a horse. ⇒ horseman.

'horsiness *u.n* fact or state of being horsy.

'horsy *adj* (*-ier, -iest*) (usu *derog*) **1** very or too interested in horses: *She's one of those horsy people who can't talk about anything else*. **2** (of a person, her/his appearance, face etc) looking (long and thin) like a horse: *a horsy face*.

horticulture /'hɔːtɪˌkʌltʃə/ *u.n* (science or practice of the) growing of flowers, vegetables etc.

horticultural /ˌhɔːtɪˈkʌltʃərəl/ *adj* of or referring to horticulture: *Our village has a horticultural show every year* (i.e when prizes are given for the best flowers etc).

,horti'cultura,list *c.n* person who practises horticulture.

hose¹ /həʊz/ *c.n* **1** (also **'hose,pipe**) long hollow tube made of plastic(3), rubber, canvas(1) etc through which water or other liquids can flow: *a fire hose. A garden hose often has a nozzle on one end to help spray(4) water over the flowers*. **2** (often *give s.t a* —) quantity of water for cleaning or wetting (s.t) using a hose¹(1) attached to a tap: *The car's very dirty; could you give it a hose?*

▷ *tr.v* **3** (often — *s.o/s.t down*) put water on, wash, (s.t) using a hose¹(1): *hose down the car. During dry weather it is important to hose the garden regularly*.

'hose,pipe *c.n* = hose¹(1).

hose² /həʊz/ *u.n* **1** (*commerce*) socks, tights(1) etc. **2** (in history) single piece of clothing worn by a man and covering the lower part of the body from the feet to the waist (the top half is called a doublet). ⇒ pantyhose.

hosier /'həʊzɪə/ *c.n* person who makes or sells hose²(1).

'hosiery *u.n* (also *attrib*) (*commerce*) socks, stockings, underclothing etc: *the hosiery department in a store*.

hospice /'hɒspɪs/ *c.n* **1** kind of hospital for people who are dying. **2** (*old use*) house where travellers can stay.

hospitable /hɒs'pɪtəbl/ *adj* showing friendship and kindness to people, esp by/when having them as guests in one's home: *Henry was very hospitable to us when we visited him*. Opposite inhospitable.

hos,pitably *adv*.

hospitality /ˌhɒspɪ'tælɪtɪ/ *u.n* (act of) showing of hospitable feelings, e.g by giving s.o food, drink, a place to sleep etc: *We greatly enjoyed your hospitality on our last visit to you*.

hospital /'hɒspɪtl/ *c/unique.n* (also *attrib*) building(s) for the treatment of people who are sick, injured(1) etc: *a hospital for tropical diseases; a children's hospital; hospital parking; hospital staff. I went to the hospital to see him after the accident. When is Ian coming out of hospital? My uncle is in hospital for a small operation*.

hospitalization, -isation /ˌhɒspɪtəlaɪ'zeɪʃən/ *c/u.n* (example of) being hospitalized.

'hospita,lize, -ise *tr.v* put (s.o) in a hospital for treatment: *Your mother will have to be hospitalized for a week*.

host¹ /həʊst/ *n* **1** *c/unique.n* person who receives and looks after guests, often in his own home: *Our host kept asking us if we had enough to eat and drink. He was (or acted as) host to a group of visitors from abroad*. ⇒ hostess. **2** *c.n* (*technical*) animal or plant on which a parasite(1) lives.

▷ *tr.v* **3** (*formal*) act as a host(1) or hostess (to (s.o)) by holding (a party, meeting etc): *Who's hosting the (party for the) visitors from Japan tonight?*

,host 'city/'country/'nation *c.n* country etc that acts as a host(1) for people coming from other countries, esp for a special event: *The host country did all it could to make the Olympics a success*.

'hostess *c.n* female host(1). ⇒ air hostess.

hostage /'hɒstɪdʒ/ *c.n* person who is made a prisoner by s.o or a group of people who threaten to harm, kill her/him unless certain conditions are met by s.o else or another group. **hold/take s.o hostage** have/capture s.o and keep her/him as hostage: *Several women and children were among the hostages taken during the hijack(1)*.

hostel /'hɒstl/ *c.n* place where people stay when they are living or working away from their home: *a students' hostel; a working men's hostel*. **youth hostel** ⇒ youth.

'hostelry *c.n* (*pl* -*ies*) (*old use*) inn or hotel.

hostile /'hɒstaɪl/ *adj* **1** ready and wanting to fight or attack s.o: *The tribes in the hills were very hostile*. **2** (usu *attrib*) of or referring to an enemy: *a hostile army on one's borders*. **3** (often — *to/towards s.o/s.t*) (of a person, attitude(2)) showing a great amount of dislike, unfriendly feeling, (to/towards s.o/s.t): *His speech met with a hostile reception(1). You can't blame Jane for being so hostile towards you after the way you treated her*.

hostilities /hɒ'stɪlɪtɪz/ *pl.n* acts of fighting between armies, esp at the beginning of a war: *Hostilities have begun (or have broken out) between the two countries*.

hostility /hɒ'stɪlɪtɪ/ *u.n* state of being hostile: *Why do you treat Brian with such hostility?*

hot /hɒt/ *adj* (*-tt-*) **1** that has a high temperature, a lot of heat; very warm: *hot food/water/weather; feel hot. I'm so hot I must get into the shade*. Opposite cold(1). Compare warm(1). **2** (of certain kinds of food) having a burning taste, esp because of a spice(1): *I like really hot curries(1)*. Opposite mild(1). **3** (of a person's temper) easily becoming angry: *She has a hot temper so don't ever argue with her*. **4** (*informal*) (of news) very new or recent: *This news is hot (or This is hot news) and no other newspaper knows about it yet*. **5** (*informal*) good: *The first part of the book is excellent* *but the second half is not so hot.* **6** (*slang*) (of things, objects) stolen (and so difficult to sell or get rid of): *I wouldn't handle those jewels if I were you — I'm sure they're hot.* (**be in**) **the hot seat** (*fig*; *informal*) (be in the) most important position or job where difficult decisions have to be made, where one can be criticized for doing things wrongly etc. **be in, get into, hot water** (*fig*) be in, get into, a lot of trouble (for s.t one has (not) done): *You'll be in hot water with your father if you don't tidy your room.* **drop s.o like a hot potato** ⇨ potato. (**be/get**) **hot under the collar** ⇨ collar(*n*). (**go/sell**) **like hot cakes** ⇨ cake(*n*). **hot and bothered** angry, worried and concerned (about s.t): *There's no need to get so hot and bothered just because things didn't work out right this time.* **hot off the press** ⇨ press(*n*). ⇨ hot(4). **hot on s.t** (**a**) (*fig*; *informal*) good at, knowing a lot about, s.t: *I'm not so hot on Shakespeare.* (**b**) following or chasing s.o very closely: *The police are hot on the thieves' track/trail(1). The dogs are hot on the* fox*'s scent.* **hot on s.o's/s.t's heels** ⇨ heel(*n*). **in hot pursuit** ⇨ pursuit. **make it/things (too) hot for s.o** (*fig*; *informal*) cause (too many) difficulties for s.o; make s.o feel very disturbed: *I'll make things so hot for him that he'll wish he had not come.* **not so hot** (*fig*) (**a**) (of a person) not (feeling) very well: *I'm not feeling so hot today; I think I've caught a cold.* (**b**) (of a state, activity etc) not (proving to be) very good: *'How's work going?' 'Oh, not so hot because I've been having problems with the boss.'* ⇨ hot(5).

▷ *v* **hot** (**s.t**) **up 7** *tr/intr.v* (*informal*) (cause (food etc) to) become hot(1): *Would you like me to hot up some soup for you? The soup is hotting up on the stove.* ⇨ heat(5). **8** *intr.v* (*fig*) (of an event, activity etc) become greater in degree, more intense(2) etc: *Five minutes before the end of the game things really began hotting up and the* referee(2) *had to warn several players not to* foul(5). **9** *tr.v* make ((the engine of) a car etc) more powerful: *He spends his free time hotting up old cars.* ⇨ soup s.t up (⇨ soup(*v*)).

hot 'air *u.n* (*fig*; *informal*) things said, promised etc that are of no worth or value, will not be carried out etc: *All his talk of becoming rich is a lot of hot air.*

hot,bed *c.n* (usu *a* — of s.t) place, organization etc that acts as a centre for the development (of usu bad things): *Don't go near that part of the city — it's a hotbed of crime.*

hot'blooded *adj* (of a person) having, easily able to show, very strong feelings (of anger, sexual passion etc). Compare coldblooded.

hot ,cross 'bun *c.n* sweet bun with a white cross on the top, usu eaten on Good Friday.

hot 'dog *c.n* hot sausage, often with onions and a sauce, in a long bread roll.

hot'foot *adv* **1** (moving, arriving, coming, after s.o/s.t) in a very great hurry, very close behind: *She came hotfoot after us.*

▷ *tr.v* **2 hotfoot it s.w** (*informal*) move, run, in a very great hurry s.w: *They hotfooted it from the scene before anyone could stop them.*

hot,head *c.n* (*derog*) person who acts too quickly and without control, thinking: *The police moved in and started arresting the young hotheads who were* demonstrating(3) *outside the* Embassy(1).

hot'headed *adj* (*derog*) acting, likely to act, like a hothead: *a very hotheaded young man/woman.* **hot'headedly** *adv.*

hot,house *c.n* kind of greenhouse in which the temperature is kept high, esp to grow tropical flowers, plants etc.

hot ,line *c/def.n* special direct telephone line connecting important people, e.g leaders of countries so that they can talk to each other, esp during a crisis(1) etc: *The President of the United States can get on the hot line to Moscow whenever a* crisis(1) *arises.*

hotly *adv* (doing s.t) with very strong feelings (of anger etc): *She hotly denied that she had ever said anything of the kind.* **hotly pursued by s.o/s.t** pursued, chased after, very closely and eagerly by s.o/s.t: *He ran down the road hotly pursued by the dog.* ⇨ in hot pursuit.

hotness *u.n* degree or state of being hot(1,2).

hot,plate *c.n* **1** flat top part of a cooker or stove or a section of this on which dishes, pans etc can be heated or kept hot. **2** metal tray which can be heated with a candle etc beneath, for putting on a table to keep dishes of food etc warm.

hot ,pot *c.n* = casserole(2).

hot 'spring *c.n* natural spring where the water comes out very hot because it is near a volcano etc.

hot 'tempered *adj* (,hot-'tempered when *attrib*) having a hot(3) temper.

hot-'water ,bottle *c.n* kind of flat rubber container into which very hot water is put, used to warm a bed and the person in it.

hotchpotch /'hɒtʃ,pɒtʃ/ *c.n* (usu *a* — of s.t) (*informal*) mixed-up, confused mass (of things, ideas etc): *His book is just a hotchpotch of thoughts and ideas.*

hotel /həʊ'tel/ *c.n* (also *attrib*) building with bedrooms, bathrooms and sometimes a restaurant, where people who are travelling can stay for a time in return for payment: *hotel guests.* Compare guesthouse, inn.

hotelier /həʊ'teliei/ *c.n* person who owns and/or runs a hotel.

hound /haʊnd/ *c.n* **1** dog used for hunting and/or as a pet: *an Afghan hound; hounds trained to hunt* foxes(1). ⇨ fox hound.

▷ *tr.v* **2** (often passive) disturb (s.o) by continually following, questioning etc her/him: *Sally is being hounded by reporters who want her story.* **3** (often — s.o *down*) chase or pursue (s.o) very hard (until one catches her/him): *The police hounded the escaped criminal down and finally caught him in a wood.* **4** (often — s.o *out of, from, s.t/ s.w*) force (s.o) to leave a job, place etc by continual pressure: *He was hounded from the office by continual accusations from his enemies. They were hounded out of town.*

hour /aʊə/ *c.n* (also *attrib*) (*written abbr* h, hr(s)) **1** sixty minutes; one of the 24 equal lengths of time into which a whole day (including the night) is divided: *There are sixty minutes in one hour. It took him three hours to get home. She'll be back in half an hour. I waited a quarter of an hour and then left. She often works a twelve-hour day. Let's take a half-hour/quarter-hour break and start again at 2 pm. Some people find it difficult to understand 24-hour timetables.* **2** (length of) time set aside for doing s.t: *the lunch hour; an hour of* meditation. *What are the working hours here?* ⇨ hours(1). **at the eleventh hour** ⇨ eleventh(*det*). (**every hour**) **on the hour** (happening) (at intervals of an hour and) exactly when a new hour starts: *Trains leave for Edinburgh every hour on the hour.* **in my**, **her** etc **hour of need** (*formal*) at the time when I/she etc really needed help: *Since you didn't do anything in my hour of need, please don't expect me to help you now.* **small hours** ⇨ small. **zero hour** ⇨ zero.

'hour ,hand *c/def.n* shorter of the two main pointers on some kinds of watches, clocks etc that moves round and shows the time in hours. ⇨ minute/second hand, hand(4).

'hourly *adj* **1** that happens once every hour: *an hourly train service.* **2** likely to happen at any time: *He lived in hourly fear of being found out.*
▷ *adv* **3** doing s.t, happening, at/for every hour: *For this part-time job you will be paid hourly.*

hours *pl.n* **1** (exact) length of time, number of hours, during which s.t is done: *Our hours of work are 9.30 to 5.30 five days a week. Opening and closing hours* (i.e for a shop etc) *are 9am and 6pm every day except Wednesdays when they are 9am and 1pm. You can find me on this telephone number during business/office hours* (i.e during the day when the office is normally open). **2** (often *00.30*, *01.00* etc —) (in a time system using a 24-hour clock) (at exactly the) hour or part of it stated: *The plane leaves at 17.30 hours* (say 'seventeen thirty hours'): *Be at the airport at 05.00* (say 'oh five hundred hours') (= 5am). **3** (long) period of time (which may or may not be an actual number of hours) in which one does s.t: *It took hours to complete the job. I've been waiting for hours.* ⇨ (for) hours (and hours). **after hours** after the normal time when a shop, business etc is closed: *You can get me at this telephone number after hours.* (**at**) **all hours** (**of the day and night**) very frequently, at any time, during the whole night and day: *In our area there are one or two shops open all hours.* (**for**) **hours** (**and hours**) (for) a very long time: *We spent hours over the meal. We spoke for hours* (*and hours*) *on the telephone.* (**in/into**) **the small hours** (during/including) the hours in the night after midnight: *He worked into the small hours trying to finish the report.* **keep good hours** arrive regularly at one's place of work at the right time. **keep late hours** stay up, away from one's home etc, until late in the night. **visiting hours** ⇨ visit.

house /haʊs/ *c.n* (*pl* **-s** /'haʊzɪz/) (also *attrib*) **1** building, often with two or more storeys, in which s.o and/or a family lives/live: *Our house is number 95, Garden Street. The house has been divided up into four flats.* **2** building used for a definite purpose: *an elephant house* (i.e in a zoo); *a country/town house* (i.e one that one can live in when one is in the country or a town) ⇨ -house. **3** (with capital **H** in names) business company (often owned by one family or owning other companies): *work for a large publishing/trading house*; *the House of Fraser.* **4** (size of an) audience in a theatre, cinema etc: *I'm sorry, the house is full tonight and there are no tickets left. They* (i.e the actors) *were playing to empty/full/packed houses every night.* **5** (in some schools) (division of students of all ages into a) group: *The school has six houses named*

after famous people. (**as**) **safe as houses** ⇨ safe(*adj*). **be**, **put s.o**, **under house arrest** be, have s.o, forced to stay in one's/her/his house (often guarded by the police, army etc) as a form of punishment etc. **bring the house down** (*fig*) (in a theatre etc) make an audience laugh a lot. **eat s.o out of house and home** (*informal*) eat such a large amount of food that it becomes very/too expensive for the person(s) paying for it: *Paul has a huge appetite and he's eating us out of house and home.* **get on** (**with s.o**) **like a house on fire** (**a**) become very or extremely friendly (with s.o), esp at a first meeting. (**b**) do s.t very well, successfully: *Joe is getting on like a house on fire; he's learning the job very quickly.* **keep house** (**for s.o**) look after a house, provide food etc (for s.o): *I'm keeping house while they're away on holiday.* Compare housekeeping. **move house** ⇨ move(6). **on the house** (esp of drinks, food) provided free by the owner or manager (of a restaurant, public house etc): *Since you come here so often the first round of drinks is on the house.* **put/set one's/ s.o's house in order** arrange or organize all one's/s.o's (own) affairs so that they are in good order: *You should set your own house in order before you criticize the way I run my business.*
▷ *tr.v* /haʊz/ **6** provide a house/shelter or houses/shelters for (s.o, people, who has/have not got one of her/his/their own): *When the explosion destroyed their homes, they were housed in tents.* **7** provide a (protected) place for (s.t): *That building houses the main generators for the power station.*

-house *n* building used for the purpose described by the first part of the word: henhouse; warehouse.

'house ,agent *c.n* = estate agent.

'house,boat *c.n* boat with a flat bottom that has bedrooms, a living-room, kitchen etc on it so that one can live on it; it is usu kept tied up in the same place on a river, lake etc.

'house,bound *adj* forced to stay in one's house and not able to leave it because one is ill, old etc.

'house,breaker *c.n* person who breaks into a house in order to steal things.

'house,breaking *u.n.*

'house,hold *c.n* all the people, esp a whole family, who live in one house.

'house,holder *c.n* person who owns or looks after a house.

,house,hold 'name/'word *c.n* person/thing who/that is famous and known to very many people: *This product is a household name. He is a household name from his many appearances on television.*

'house,keeper *c.n* (female) servant who looks after, has the management of, a (large) house as a paid job.

'house,keeping *u.n* **1** act of looking after, running, a house: *Who does most of the housekeeping in your family?* **2** (also **'house,keeping ,money**) money needed to run a house (including paying for all the food etc for the people in it): *As we both have jobs we contribute(1) equally to the housekeeping.*

'house,maid *c.n* (*old use*) servant who works in a house.

'house ,martin *c.n* small bird (martin) with

white and blue-black feathers which lives near buildings.

'house,master c.n male teacher in charge of a house(5) in a school.

'house,mistress c.n female teacher in charge of a house(5) in a school.

,House of 'Commons def.n (UK) (building for the) elected Members of Parliament (who sit there, discuss and pass laws etc).

'house ,officer c.n junior(1) doctor in a hospital.

,House of 'Lords def.n (UK) (building for the) nobles, bishops(1) etc who are not elected but who can give their opinions about laws passed by the House of Commons and sometimes get them changed.

,Houses of 'Parliament def.pl.n (UK) (buildings for the) House of Commons and House of Lords.

,House of ,Repre'sentatives def.n (US) (building for the) elected members of Congress(2) (who sit there, pass laws etc).

'house-,proud adj having, wanting to have, one's house very clean and tidy and spending a lot of time doing this.

'house,room u.n not give s.t houseroom not allow or want s.t to be in one's house, esp because it is ugly: I wouldn't give houseroom to such an old chair.

,house-to-'house attrib.adj visiting a number or row of houses one after the other to search for s.t or sell s.t etc: a house-to-house salesman. The police were conducting(4) a house-to- house search for the escaped criminal.

'house-,trained adj (of an animal kept as a pet) trained not to empty its bowels(1) or bladder(1) anywhere in the house but to do it outdoors or in a special tray.

'house,warming c.n (also attrib) party held when one has moved into a (new) house one has just bought: a housewarming party.

'house,wife c.n (pl -,wives) woman/wife who looks after a house and her family and usu does not have a full-time job outside the home.

'house,work u.n all the work done, needing to be done, to keep a house clean and tidy.

housing /'haʊzɪŋ/ n 1 u.n (act of providing) houses or places for people to live in: The government has cut back its expenditure on housing for the poor. 2 c.n (technical) metal etc covering to protect an engine, machine etc: One of the housings fell off the aircraft as it took off.

'housing as,soci,ation c.n group of people who join together to buy and/or improve houses, flats etc for themselves and others to live in.

'housing e,state c.n area of land on which a group of houses has been built for sale or renting, e.g by a local council.

hove /haʊv/ hove to p.t,p.p of heave to. ⇒ heave(v).

hovel /'hɒvl/ c.n (derog) small dirty house, esp one in which poor people (are forced to) live: hovels on the edges of the city.

hover /'hɒvə/ intr.v 1 (of a bird, aircraft) stay in the air in one place (by using its wings, rotors(2) etc): I could see an eagle(1) hovering high in the sky above me. 2 (often — about/around/over (s.o/ s.t)) move around close (to s.o/s.t) often in an annoying way: What are you children hovering

(around) for? hover between s.t and s.t (a) be unable to make up one's mind, choose between doing one thing and another: He hovered between accepting the new job and staying where he was. (b) (esp of s.o who is very ill) be in a critical(3) state where one might live or die: She is hovering between life and death.

'hover,craft c.n (pl -(s)) kind of vehicle that is able to travel over both land and water supported by a cushion of air underneath it. by hovercraft in this vehicle: go/travel by hovercraft.

how /haʊ/ adv 1 (esp in a question) in what way?; by what means?: How do you do this sum? Do you know how to cook? How do you know about it? How do you get to the station from here? Show me how you got that answer. 2 (esp in a question) in what state or condition?: How's your work getting on? How are your parents? 3 (esp in a question, used with an adj or adv of quantity, size, distance, length etc) (to) what amount, extent, size etc?: How many children have you got? He used his hands to show her how big it was. Can you tell me how far/near the station is? How long is it? How much does it cost? How old is he? 4 (in an exclamation, emphasizing a feeling, action etc) to a very great extent: How they laughed when they saw him fall over! How horrible of you to say that! How kind of you! And how! (informal) (esp in answer to s.t s.o has said) most certainly, to a very great degree!: 'Isn't this a great party?' 'And how!' How about (doing) s.t? What do you think of my suggestion that we should do s.t?: How about (going to) the cinema tonight? How about her, him, it etc? What does she/he etc think? In what way does it affect her, him, it etc?: I rather like him. How about you? (i.e Do you like him?) How are you? (polite expression used to ask) What is your state of health (usu only in a general way and not expecting a detailed answer)? How 'can/'could you (do s.t)? (expression used as emphasis(2)) What makes/made you do s.t so bad etc?: How could you (talk to her like that) when you knew she was not well? How come(. . .)? (informal) Why(. . .)?: How come I wasn't told about this? How do you do? (formal) (polite expression used when meeting s.o for the first time, when being introduced etc): 'How do you do? My name's Isabel Green.' 'I'd like you to meet my father.' 'How do you do?' How ever . . .? ⇒ however(3).

▷ conj 5 the fact that (s.t happened, s.o did s.t etc): Do you remember how we used to enjoy a game of football after school? You know how she can fall asleep wherever she is.

,howso'ever adv/conj (old use) any way, in whatever way.

however /haʊ'evə/ adj 1 in spite of this/that (already stated or done): 'You may be right. However, I still intend to do what I planned.' 'We stayed until quite late. Our friends, however, left early as they wanted to catch a train.' 2 (used with an adj of quantity, size etc) to whatever amount, size etc (that is or seems necessary); it does not matter how(3): I'm going to get this job finished, however long it takes. 3 (also ,how 'ever) (informal) (in a question or exclamation showing surprise) how(1), in what way, (is/was etc it possible that) . . .?: How ever did you find me?

▷ *conj* **4** in whatever way or manner (one does, says s.t etc): *However you look at it, it just doesn't seem possible that we can finish it in time.* **5** but: *She'd like to come; however she has promised to work late.*

howl /haʊl/ *c.n* (often — *of s.t*) **1** loud cry made by some animals, esp wolves (⇨ wolf(1)), dogs etc: *the howls of wild dogs in the distance.* **2** cry like this made by a person (esp a baby or because of pain etc): *a howl of pain; howls of laughter.*
▷ *v* **3** *intr.v* (of a wolf(1), dog etc) give a howl(1) or howls: *We could hear the wolves howling in the forest.* **4** *intr.v* (often — *in/with s.t*) (of a person) give a howl(2) or howls (expressing pain etc): *Can't you stop that baby howling? He howled in anger when he heard they had escaped.* **5** *intr.v* (often — *through* etc *s.t*) (of a strong wind) make a noise like a howl(1) as it moves (through etc s.t): *The wind howled through the trees (or howled around us).* **6** *tr/intr.v* (usu — (*s.t*) *out, at s.o*) shout (s.t) in a very loud voice (at s.o): *He had to howl out his message over the noise of the storm. 'What do you think you're doing?' he howled (at them).*
howl s.o down (of a group of people) prevent s.o from talking, being able to be heard, by shouting very loudly: *The speaker was howled down by the audience and had to leave the* platform(1).
ˈhowler *c.n* (*informal*) very bad (often amusing) mistake (esp in written work): *Examiners sometimes publish examples of the howlers they find in examination papers.*
hoy /hɔɪ/ *interj* (word used to get s.o's attention, often when he/she is doing s.t one does not like): *Hoy! What are you doing with my car?*
HP, hp /ˌeɪtʃ ˈpiː/ *abbr* **1** hire purchase. **2** horsepower.
HQ, hq /ˌeɪtʃ ˈkjuː/ *abbr* headquarters.
HRH *written abbr* Her/His Royal Highness ⇨ high.
hr(s) *written abbr* hour(s).
ht *written abbr* height(1).
hub /hʌb/ *c.n* **1** central part of the wheel of a vehicle. **2** (often *a* — *of s.t*) (*fig*) central point or place where there is a lot of activity, s.t important happens: *This area has become a hub of industry.*
ˈhub,cap *c.n* metal cover for the hub(1).
hubbub /ˈhʌbʌb/ *sing.n* **1** confused mixture of noises and sounds, esp of people talking: *He had to shout to make himself heard above the hubbub of voices in the room.* **2** (often *cause a* —) great confusion, anger: *The speaker's rude comments(1) caused an angry hubbub in the hall.*
huddle /ˈhʌdl/ *c.n* **1** number (of people or things) brought or grouped closely together, usu without any order: *He had to fight his way through the huddle of people around the entrance. We all sat in a huddle to keep warm.* **go into a huddle** (of people) form into a close group, esp to discuss or do s.t secretly: *The trades union members went into a huddle at the end of the room to discuss the company's new offer.*
▷ *v* **2** *tr/intr.v* (often — (*s.o/s.t*) *together*; — (*s.o/ s.t*) *into s.t*) (cause (a group of people, animals etc) to) group or crowd (together, into a place): *The dogs huddled all the sheep together. When the snow came they huddled together to keep warm.* **3** *intr. v* (often — *up* (*against/to s.o/s.t*)) move very close (to s.o/s.t), esp in order to keep

warm, feel protected etc: *The kittens huddled up against their mother in the basket.*
hue¹ /hjuː/ *c.n* (*formal*) (shade of a) colour: *The pullover was knitted using many different hues of wool. The wall had been painted in a light yellow hue.*
hue² /hjuː/ *sing.n* **hue and cry** noisy public complaint or protest(1) (about/against s.o/s.t): *There was a great hue and cry when the government announced its cuts in spending.*
huff /hʌf/ *c.n* (usu *in/into a* —) state of annoyance because s.o has offended one (and showing this by not talking to her/him): *He walked off in a huff when she laughed at him. There's no need to get into a huff just because I can't go to the party.*
▷ *intr.v* **2** (often — *and puff*) breathe very heavily, usu because of some hard activity: *He was huffing and puffing by the time he got to the top of the hill.*
ˈhuffily *adv* in a huffy way.
ˈhuffiness *u.n* fact or state of being huffy.
ˈhuffy *adj* (*-ier, -iest*) (*derog; informal*) (of a person) who is in a huff(1); easily offended: *What is he so huffy about?*
hug /hʌɡ/ *c.n* **1** (often *give s.o/s.t a* —) close and tight hold with one's arms around s.o's body, esp to show affection: *The child gave the dog a hug.*
▷ *tr.v* (*-gg-*) **2** give (s.o/s.t) a hug(1): *She hugged and kissed him just as he was leaving. The child went to sleep hugging her new toy.* **3** (esp of a ship) follow a course that keeps close to (s.t, e.g the shore, coast): *The sailing boat hugged the shore during the storm. The new car handles very well and really hugs the road.*
huge /hjuːdʒ/ *adj* **1** very big (often in an exaggerated way): *That house is huge; it has over twenty rooms. We've had to spend a huge amount of money on repairs this month.* **2** very great: *The new film was a huge success.*
ˈhugely *adv* in a very great way: *That car is hugely expensive; it's much more than we can spend. Life has changed hugely since I met Chris.*
ˈhugeness *u.n.*
huh /hə/ *interj* (expression used to show surprise, lack of belief in s.t, annoyance etc): *Huh! You're the kind of person who'll believe anything!*
hulk /hʌlk/ *c.n* **1** main body (or hull) of a ship, from which the most important things, e.g masts, engine(s) etc have been removed so that it is no longer any use. **2** (usu *derog*) person or thing who/that is large and awkward: *He was a big hulk of a man.*
ˈhulking *attrib.adj* (often — *great s.o/s.t*) (*informal*) very large and awkward (person or thing): *You hulking great brute(2) — you're standing on my foot!*
hull /hʌl/ *c.n* main body or frame (of a ship).
hullabaloo /ˌhʌləbəˈluː/ *c.n* (usu *sing*) **1** great deal of noise, esp of people talking: *No one could hear him talking because of the hullabaloo.* **2** noisy public complaint: *There was a great hullabaloo when the government increased taxes.*
hum /hʌm/ *sing.n* **1** (often *a* — *of s.t*) low, often quiet, continuous noise, like a buzz(1) (of people talking, of bees, insects, machines working etc): *A hum of conversation followed the end of his speech.*

▷ *v* (*-mm-*) **2** *tr/intr.v* (of a person) make a musical sound (of (a song etc)) like a long 'm' in one's mouth and throat with one's lips closed: *He hummed quietly to the song on the radio as he was working. I don't know the words so you sing and I'll hum* (*the tune*). **3** *intr.v* (of bees, insects, machines etc) make a (quiet) buzzing(2) sound: *He could hear bees humming among the flowers.* **4** *intr.v* (often — *with s.t*) (of work etc) be, look, very busy (with a lot of activity etc): *Things have started humming* (*with activity*) *since the new boss arrived.*

,**hum and 'ha** /'hɑː/ *intr.v* (also ,**hum and 'haw** /'hɔː/) not be able to make up one's mind (and show this by expressions of doubt, hesitation etc): *When I asked for a decision he just hummed and haed/hawed and said he'd like to wait and see.*

'**humming** *c.n* (usu *sing*) (also *attrib*) = hum(1): *There was a humming* (*noise*) *coming from my record player.*

'**humming-,bird** *c.n* kind of very small bird, found in south America, that makes a humming sound through the action of its wings.

human /'hjuːmən/ *adj* **1** of or referring to a person or people in general, esp as a living being, living beings, in this world when compared to animals, birds etc: *the study of human behaviour patterns ; study the human body. Some animals seem almost human in the way they act.* **2** having or showing the (good) qualities of being human(1): *What are you afraid of? He's only human! I know she's a bit hard to deal with but she can be quite human at times.* Compare inhuman.

▷ *c.n* **3** (also ,**human 'being**) person: *He's written a story about the future when humans first meet creatures from outer space.*

,**human 'being** *c.n* ⇒ human(3).

humane /hjuː'meɪn/ *adj* showing, acting in a way that shows, human(2), esp kind, qualities in one's dealings with people, animals etc: *Their treatment of the prisoners was very humane. There are arguments about the most humane ways of killing animals.* Opposite inhumane.

hu'**manely** *adv.* hu'**maneness** *u.n.*

,**human 'error** *u.n* mistake made by a person (and not the result of a fault in a machine etc): *The plane crash was due to human error and not engine failure as was first thought.*

,**human 'interest** *u.n* subject or matter about a person/people and her/his/their life/lives that is likely to interest other people: *His reports on television were full of human interest and attracted large audiences.*

'**huma,nism** *u.n* (belief in a) system of thought based on the thoughts and actions of people and not relying on other outside principles(1) such as belief in God.

'**huma,nist** *c.n* (also *attrib*) person who believes in or practises humanism.

,**huma'nistic** *adj.*

,**huma'nistically** *adv.*

humanitarian /ˌhjuː mænɪ'teərɪən/ *adj* **1** (of a person, action) showing respect for human(2)

values; trying to improve people's welfare(1) etc: *His motives for suggesting reforms*(1) *were entirely humanitarian.*

▷ *c.n* **2** humanitarian(1) person.

,**humani'taria,nism** *u.n.*

hu'**manities** *def.pl.n* (often with capital **H**) courses of study, esp at a university, concerned with languages, literature, history etc (as compared to the sciences and technology): *I hope to study the Humanities when I go to university.*

humanity /hjuː'mænɪtɪ/ *u.n* **1** people as a whole: *The deaths of so many people in the war was described as a crime against humanity.* **2** state or quality of being humane: *All his life he showed great humanity in his dealings with other people.*

humanize, -ise /'hjuːmə,naɪz/ *tr.v* make (s.o/ s.t) become (more) human(2) or humane: *I've tried but failed to humanize him and his behaviour.*

,**human'kind** *u.n* (*formal*) humanity(1).

'**humanly** *adv* **humanly possible** within the abilities or power of a person: *If humanly possible I'll get the job done on time. It's not humanly possible for me to be in two places at once!*

,**human 'nature** *u.n* (ordinary good or bad) qualities and/or actions of people: *It's human nature to complain when things go wrong.*

,**human 'race** *def.n* people as a whole; humanity(1); humankind.

,**human 'rights** *pl.n* freedom of a person to enjoy rights(⇒ right¹) (e.g justice, opportunities to live and work): *He campaigned*(*v*) *many years for human rights.*

humble /'hʌmbl/ *adj* **1** not having a high opinion of oneself; not acting in a proud way: *He's quite a humble man in spite of all he's* achieved(1). *In my humble opinion you've got it all wrong.* **2** (*formal*) (of a person, position etc) low in (social) rank; not very important: *His origins are quite humble. He was forced to take a humble job in a factory since he could find no other work.* ⇒ humility.

▷ *tr.v* **3** (*formal*) make (oneself/s.o) humble(1): *Last year's top team was humbled when they were beaten by a team of* amateurs(3).

'**humbly** *adv* (acting, doing s.t) in a humble(1) way: *I must humbly ask for your forgiveness.*

'**humbleness, humility** /hjuː'mɪlɪtɪ/ *u.n* state or quality of being humble(1): *He had the humility to admit his own weaknesses.*

humbug /'hʌm,bʌg/ *n* (*informal*) **1** *u.n* nonsense; stupid ideas, talk etc: *You're talking a load of old humbug!* **2** *sing.n* trick intended to deceive s.o: *He told us there was going to be a big party but it turned out to be just a humbug.* **3** *c.n* (*derog*; *old use*) person who thinks/pretends he/ she is important, knows a lot etc but who is not: *He's a humbug the way he talks about all these famous people as if they're his best friends!* **4** *c.n* hard boiled sweet, often with peppermint(1) in it.

▷ *tr.v* (*-gg-*) **5** deceive or trick (s.o): *Stop trying to humbug me with all that talk of how much money we're going to make.*

humdrum /'hʌm,drʌm/ *adj* (of a person, s.o's life etc) rather dull and ordinary: *He was getting tired of his humdrum existence with nothing exciting ever happening.*

humerus /'hjuːmərəs/ *c.n* (*pl humeri*

/ˈhjuːməˌraɪ/) (*technical*) bone in the upper part of a person's arm.

humid /ˈhjuː mɪd/ *adj* (of the weather, air etc) damp; containing a lot of water in it: *I prefer a dry climate to a humid one. It feels very humid today; I think there's going to be a storm.*

humidifier /hjuːˈmɪdɪˌfaɪə/ *c.n* kind of device for adding humidity to the air in a room or building so that the air is not too dry.

humidify /hjuːˈmɪdɪˌfaɪ/ *tr.v* (*-ies, -ied*) make (air in a room or building) damp(er).

humidity /hjuːˈmɪdɪtɪ/ *u.n* (measurement of the amount of) dampness in the air, weather etc: *The weather forecast(1) says that the humidity will reach a new high today.*

humiliate /hjuːˈmɪlɪˌeɪt/ *tr.v* make (s.o) feel ashamed, hurt (s.o) by making her/him look foolish, esp in the presence of other people: *You deliberately tried to humiliate me in front of all those people.*

huˈmiliˌating *adj* causing humiliation (to s.o): *It was humiliating to have to stand there while he criticized my work in front of everyone.*

humiliation /hjuːˌmɪlɪˈeɪʃən/ *c/u.n* (example of the) act or fact of humiliating(⇒ humiliate) s.o or of being humiliated.

humility ⇒ humble.

hummed *p.t,p.p* of hum.

humming, humming-bird ⇒ hum.

humour /ˈhjuː mə/ *u.n* (US **ˈhumor**) **1** ability to amuse s.o or be amused by s.o/s.t: *Lynne has a great sense of humour (or is full of humour) and always has some funny story to tell.* **2** state of being amusing; thing that is amusing: *You may laugh but I don't see any humour in the situation.*

▷ *tr.v* **3** (try to) keep (s.o) happy, calm etc by agreeing with her/him, doing what he/she wants etc (even though it may be stupid, seem unnecessary etc): *You've got to humour him when he gets into these* moods¹(2) *and not try to argue with him.*

ˈhumoˌrist *c.n* person who tells or writes funny jokes or stories.

ˈhumorous *adj* funny and amusing; causing humour(1): *a humorous film/remark/story.*

ˈhumorously *adv.* **ˈhumorousness** *u.n.*

-humoured *adj* having the (good or bad) quality or sense shown by the first part of the word: *good-humoured; bad-humoured; ill-humoured.*

hump /hʌmp/ *c.n* **1** round lump on the back of some animals (esp a camel): *Some camels have two humps.* **2** raised round lump sticking above a flat surface, e.g of a road: *The car bounced up and down as it went over the humps in the road.* **over the hump** (*informal*) having the main or worst part of s.t, e.g a job, done and completed: *Once you've dug the garden you'll be over the hump and the rest will be fun!*

▷ *tr.v* **3** cause (s.t, e.g one's back) to form into an arch: *The cat humped its back when it saw the dog.* **4** (*informal*) lift and carry (s.t heavy): *Can you help me hump this chair upstairs?*

ˈhumpˌback *c.n* = hunchback.

ˈhumpˌbacked *adj* **1** (esp of a bridge) having a hump(2) or arch in it: *You should approach a humpbacked bridge with care as you can't see over to the other side.* **2** (of a person) = hunchbacked.

humus /ˈhjuː məs/ *u.n* (*technical*) soil or earth made from leaves, plants etc that have rotted.

hunch¹ /hʌntʃ/ *c.n* (often *have a — that . . .*)

(*informal*) idea or feeling that is something of a guess and not based on complete evidence (that s.t will happen etc): *I have a hunch that things are going to get better soon. I had a hunch you'd be here.* **play one's hunch(es)** (*informal*) act according to one's hunch(es), esp to gain some advantage: *He played his hunches and made a lot of money selling his* shares *at the right time.*

hunch² /hʌntʃ/ *tr/intr.v* (often *— (s.t) up*) (cause (s.t, esp one's body) to) form into an arch or a rounded shape: *He hunched up in the* armchair.

ˈhunchˌback *c.n* person who has a large round lump on her/his back (as a deformity): *The Hunchback of Notre Dame* (title of a book).

ˈhunchˌbacked *adj* (of a person) having a large round lump on one's back.

hundred /ˈhʌndrəd/ *det/pron/c.n* (*cardinal number*) (used with 'a' (*a hundred*) unless there is another det, e.g *one hundred*, *the first hundred*; *pl* hundred after another number, e.g *six hundred*, otherwise hundreds, e.g *hundreds of people*) 100; number between ninety-nine and one hundred and one: *One hundred and twenty* (120) *people came. I was born in 1968* (say 'nineteen sixty-eight' or 'nineteen hundred and sixty-eight'). **a hundred and one** (*informal*) very many: *I've got a hundred and one things to do today.* **one hundred etc hours** (01.00) ⇒ hours(2).

ˈhundreds *pl.n* (often *— of s.o/s.t*) **1** several hundred (people, things etc) (usu more than 200/300 but less than 1000): *He spent hundreds of pounds on buying old stamps.* **2** (*informal*) quite a lot (of people, things etc) but probably less than a thousand: *There were hundreds (of people) on the march.* Compare thousands(2), millions(2).

hundredth /ˈhʌndrədθ/ *det/pron* (*ordinal number*) **1** (person or thing) following 99 in order; 100th.

▷ *c.n* **2** one of a hundred equal parts; 1/100

ˈhundredˌweight *c.n* (*pl* -(s)) (*written abbr cwt*) (in the avoirdupois system of weight) **1** (UK) 112 pounds (= 50.8 kilograms); one-twentieth of a (long) ton. **2** (US) 100 pounds (= 45.4 kilograms); one-twentieth of a (short) ton.

hung /hʌŋ/ *p.t,p.p* of hang.

hunger /ˈhʌŋgə/ *n* **1** *u.n* desire or need for food: *One way to satisfy your children's hunger is to feed them lots of potatoes.* **2** *u.n* state of not having but needing food in order to stay alive: *People are dying of hunger in many parts of the world.* **3** *sing.n* (usu *— for s.t*) (*formal*) very strong desire (for knowledge, information etc): *His hunger for adventure took him to many strange places.*

▷ *intr.v* **4 hunger after/for s.t** (*formal*) want, desire, s.t very much: *He hungered for the sight of her.*

ˈhunger ˌstrike *c.n* (usu *be/go on a —*) strike when one refuses to eat or drink anything as a form of protest(1) or to get s.o to agree to what one wants, esp when in prison.

ˈhunger ˌstriker *c.n* person who is/goes on hunger strike.

ˈhungrily *adv* in a hungry way.

ˈhungriness *u.n* fact or state of being hungry.

ˈhungry *adj* (*-ier, -iest*) feeling hunger(1): *I'm hungry; is there anything to eat?* **go hungry** not eat anything; remain without any food: *If I don't find a job today I'll have to go hungry for the rest* *of the week.* **hungry for s.t** (*formal*) wanting or desiring s.t, e.g knowledge etc very much: *He was hungry for news of what she was doing.*

hunk /hʌŋk/ *c.n* (usu — *of* s.t) large rough piece (cut or broken from a bigger piece): *hunks of meat. He tore off a hunk (of bread) from the loaf.*

hunt /hʌnt/ *c.n* **1** act of following after, catching and sometimes killing, wild animals: *an elephant/ tiger hunt.* **2** (also **'fox,hunt**) group of people who regularly hunt(5) foxes(1). **3** (usu *a — for s.o/s.t*) careful search (for s.o/s.t who/that is missing): *The police have started a hunt for the man who escaped from prison last week.*
▷ *v* **4** *tr/intr.v* follow after, catch and sometimes kill, (wild animals): *You are not allowed to hunt (animals) in this part of the forest.* **5** *intr.v* be one of a group of people who regularly chase(3) foxes(1) in order to kill them: *She hunts with the local foxhunt* (⇒ hunt(2)). **6** *intr.v* (usu — (*through* s.t/ s.w*) for s.o/s.t*) search carefully (through s.t/s.w) (in order to find s.o/s.t, esp who/that is missing): *I've hunted through all the drawers but I still can't find the other sock.* **hunt high and low (for s.o/ s.t)** ⇒ high(*adv*). **hunt s.o/s.t down** follow after s.o/s.t until one finds and catches her/him/it: *The angry villagers hunted down the wild dog that was killing their chickens.* **hunt s.o/s.t out/ up** search, look, for s.o/s.t until one finds her/ him/it: *When he got to the town he decided to hunt up some old friends. I'll have to hunt out the information you want in our old files³(2).*
'hunter *c.n* **1** person who hunts(4). **2** horse that is used for hunting(5). ⇒ fortune hunter.
'hunting *u.n* (also *attrib*) (often *go* —) activity of following after (and killing) animals: *I don't like hunting as I think it is cruel.*
'huntsman *c.n* (*pl* -men) man who hunts(5).

hurdle /'hɜːdl/ *c.n* **1** one of a number of low frames that a hurdler has to jump in races. **2** (*fig*) difficulty or problem that is in one's way and that one has to solve before going further: *Our main hurdle is finding the money.*
▷ *intr.v* **3** (*sport*) run a certain distance with a number of hurdles(1) to jump in between: *Can you hurdle? He hurdles for England.*
'hurdler *c.n* person who hurdles(3).
'hurdle-,race *c.n* = hurdles.
'hurdles *def.n* race over hurdles: *The men's hurdles is the last event on the programme.*
'hurdling *u.n* sport of jumping hurdles(1): *Jill's good at hurdling.*

hurl /hɜːl/ *tr.v* **1** (usu — *s.t at* s.o/s.t, *through* s.t etc) throw(s.t) with great force (at s.o/s.t, through s.t etc): *The boys hurled stones at the window.* **2** (usu — *abuse, words* (*at* s.o)) (*fig*) shout (words of abuse(1) etc) (at s.o) in an argument etc: *They stood there hurling insults at each other.*

hurly-burly /,hɜːlɪ 'bɜːlɪ/ *c/u.n* (*pl* -ies) (example of the) noisy activity of many people, things etc: *the hurly-burly of modern living.*

hurrah /hʊ'rɑː/ *c.n/interj* (also **hoo'ray, hur'ray** /hʊ'reɪ/) (word expressing) joy, pleasure, enthusiasm etc: *Hurrahs were shouted as he entered the hall. Hurrah! We've succeeded at last!* **Hip, hip, hurrah/hooray/hurray!** (used to show appreciation(1) of s.o, s.o's actions).

hurricane /'hʌrɪkən/ *c.n* big storm with very

strong violent winds which is sometimes given a name: *Hurricane Diana.*
'hurricane ,lamp *c.n* kind of oil or gas lamp with glass around the light to stop the wind from blowing it out.

hurry /'hʌrɪ/ *u.n* **1** act or fact of doing s.t quickly; haste: *In his hurry to finish his work he made many mistakes.* **2** need to do s.t quickly: *Is there any hurry over this job or can I take my time?* **in a hurry (a)** wanting to act or move (too) fast: *Don't be in so much of a hurry, we'll get there in time. Sorry, I can't stop but I'm in a hurry — I'm late for work.* **(b)** easily or (too) soon: *I won't forget what you said in a hurry.* **in a/no hurry (to do s.t)** anxious, not at all anxious, (to do s.t, get s.t done): *I'm in no hurry (or I'm not in any hurry) to agree to the terms he proposed.*
▷ *v* (-*ies*, -*ied*) **3** *tr/intr.v* (often — (*s.o/s.t*) *up*) (cause (s.o) to) move or act more quickly: *Can you hurry him (up)? There's no need to hurry as we've plenty of time. Hurry up!* **4** *tr.v* move, bring or send (s.o/s.t) as quickly as possible: *He was hurried to the hospital after his stroke. They hurried supplies to the famine areas.*
'hurried *adj* (of a person, job etc) working or done too quickly (and so often making, or with, mistakes etc): *a hurried job. I can't do a good job if I feel hurried.* Opposite unhurried.
'hurriedly *adv.* **'hurriedness** *u.n.*

hurt /hɜːt/ *adj* **1** injured(1), wounded or harmed in some way: *The badly hurt people were taken to hospital.* **2** (often — *at/by* s.t) being or feeling upset or disturbed (because of s.t): *I was very hurt by your refusal to talk to me. Marion looked so hurt when you offered everyone except her a lift to the party.*
▷ *n* **3** *sing/u.n* (example of an) injury, wound: *It was only a little hurt and his mother soon made it better.* **4** *u.n* (often negative) (feeling of) harm or upset: *It will do you no hurt to meet her and talk the matter over.*
▷ *v* (*p.t,p.p* hurt) **5** *tr/intr.v* (cause (s.o, a part of the body) to) feel pain, suffer an injury: *He hurt himself, hurt his knee, when he fell over. My back hurts. I must have hurt it when I tried to lift that heavy box.* **6** *tr.v* upset or worry (s.o, s.o's feelings etc): *You really hurt me* (or *my feelings*) *when you said I was selfish.* **7** *tr/intr.v* (often (*not*) — (s.o) to do s.t) (not) be a matter that will affect s.o badly (if he/she does s.t): *It really won't hurt (you) to wait a little while I fetch my things.*
'hurtful *adj* (*derog*) causing hurt(4): *a hurtful remark.*
'hurtfully *adv.* **'hurtfulness** *u.n.*

hurtle /'hɜːtl/ *tr/intr.v* (usu — (s.t) *across, down, towards* etc *s.w*) (cause (s.t) to) rush or move, throw (s.t), with great speed or force (across etc s.w): *The cars hurtled down the motorway. The huge wave hurtled him onto the beach.*

husband /'hʌzbənd/ *c.n* **1** man to whom a woman is married. ⇒ wife.
▷ *tr.v* **2** (*formal*) use as little as possible of (s.t, e.g food, one's strength) so that it is not wasted, lasts a long time etc: *We must husband all the world's resources(1) if we are to survive(1).*
'husbandry *u.n* (*formal*) **1** farming; farm management: *animal husbandry.* **2** (careful) management of the things one needs and uses to live: *With good husbandry a family*

should be able to live quite comfortably on this income.

hush /hʌʃ/ *interj* **1** be quiet, silent: *Hush! You'll wake your father.*

▷ *sing/u.n* **2** (moment or length of) silence: *A hush came over* (or *descended on*) *the audience when the singer appeared on the stage. In the hush of the early evening he could hear a bird singing.*

▷ *tr/intr.v* **3** (often — (s.o) *up*) (ask, cause (s.o) to) become silent: *The people around him hushed him when he tried to speak. Would you please hush (up) for a moment so I can listen to the news.* **hush s.t up** stop s.t from becoming public knowledge, usu because it would be damaging to s.o if it was made known: *His affair with his secretary was hushed up to prevent any embarrassment(1) to the government.*

ˌhush-ˈhush *adj* (usu *pred*) (*informal*) very secret: *The deal between the two companies is very hush-hush.*

ˈhush ˌmoney *u.n* (*informal*) money given to s.o in return for not talking about s.t, not revealing s.t bad etc.

husk /hʌsk/ *c.n* **1** outer covering of some kinds of seeds, grains and fruits.

▷ *tr.v* **2** remove the husks(1) from (seeds etc).

husky¹ /ˈhʌskɪ/ *adj* (-*ier*, -*iest*) (of a person, voice) sounding low and hoarse and full of breath (either as a natural state or as a result of a cold, from shouting etc): *Some people find a husky voice very attractive. He was husky from shouting at the crowd.*
ˈhuskily *adv.* **ˈhuskiness** *u.n.*

husky² /ˈhʌskɪ/ *c.n* (*pl* -*ies*) kind of dog with a thick coat, found in North America and used by Eskimos etc to pull sledges(1) over snow etc.

hussar /hʊˈzɑ:/ *c.n* (with capital **H** in names) (title for a) soldier who belongs to (in former times) a cavalry regiment(2) or (in present times) a regiment(2) of tanks or armoured cars.

hussy /ˈhʌsɪ/ *c.n* (*pl* -*ies*) (*derog*) **1** (often *a brazen, shameless* —) prostitute. **2** girl who is very naughty, cheeky: *Come back here you little hussy!*

hustle /ˈhʌsl/ *u.n* **1** (often — *and bustle* (of s.o/ s.t)) noisy quick activity (of a group of people, a place etc): *He got caught in the hustle and bustle of the crowds doing their shopping.*

▷ *v* **2** *tr.v* (often — s.o *across, into, out of* etc s.t/ s.w) make (s.o) move fast (across etc s.t/s.w); push (s.o) with some force (across etc s.t): *Every morning she had to hustle him out of the house to catch the train. The kidnappers hustled the boy into the car and drove off at high speed.* **3** *tr.v* (often — s.o *into doing s.t*) try to force (s.o to do s.t), usu without giving her/him time to think, or when he/she is unwilling: *Stop hustling me (into making a decision)! I'll make up my mind in my own good time.*

ˈhustler *c.n* (*derog*) person who is willing to use any method(1) even illegal ones, to gain money or advantage.

hut /hʌt/ *c.n* small building, usu made of wood, used for storing things, sheltering or living in for a short time: *a mountain hut.* Compare shed¹.

hutch /hʌtʃ/ *c.n* small box or cage, usu with an open wire front, used for keeping rabbits etc in.

hyacinth /ˈhaɪəˌsɪnθ/ *c.n* kind of plant that grows

from a bulb(1) and has pink, red, purple or blue etc flowers in a bunch.

hyaena ⇒ hyena.

hybrid /ˈhaɪbrɪd/ *c.n* (also *attrib*) (*technical*) **1** animal, plant, seed etc that is produced or formed by breeding(1) or crossing(⇒ cross(12)) two different animals etc: *a hybrid rose.* Mules *are hybrids of horses and donkeys.* **2** word formed from (parts of) words from different languages: *'Monorail' is a hybrid word as 'mono-' is Greek and 'rail' is English.*

hydrangea /haɪˈdreɪndʒə/ *c.n* kind of plant or bush with white, pink or blue flowers in a bunch.

hydrant /ˈhaɪdrənt/ *c.n* pipe in a street (either below the ground or above it) that comes from a water main and provides a source of water.

hydraulic /haɪˈdrɔ:lɪk/ *adj* (*technical*) of or referring to a system of tubes or cylinders(2) filled with a liquid such as water or oil that acts under pressure to make (part of) a device or machine work: *hydraulic brakes; a hydraulic lifting system for a bridge.*

hyˈdraulically *adv* using a hydraulic system: *a hydraulically operated system.*

hyˈdraulics *u.n* science or study of the use of liquids in hydraulic systems.

hydroelectric /ˌhaɪdrəʊɪˈlektrɪk/ *adj* (*technical*) of or referring to the production of electricity by using turbines driven by water: *a hydroelectric power station.*

ˌhydroeˈlectrically *adv.* **ˈhydroˌelecˈtricity** *u.n.*

hydrogen /ˈhaɪdrədʒən/ *u.n* element(1) that is a very light gas without colour or smell and is present in the air; it burns very easily and when combined with oxygen forms water, *chem. symb* **H**.

ˈhydrogen ˌbomb *c.n* (*informal H-bomb*) very powerful kind of atom(ic) bomb in which the explosion is caused by the fusion of hydrogen nuclei to produce helium nuclei(⇒ nucleus(2)). ⇒ fusion, thermonuclear.

ˌhydrogen perˈoxide ⇒ peroxide(n).

hydrophobia /ˌhaɪdrəʊˈfəʊbɪə/ *u.n* **1** fear of water, shown esp as an illness and an inability to drink water without being ill. **2** = rabies.

hyena /haɪˈi:nə/ *c.n* (also **hyˈaena**) (*pl* —(s)) kind of wild animal like a dog, found in Africa and parts of Asia, that is yellow with darker spots or stripes, eats dead animals and has a cry that sounds like a laugh.

hygiene /ˈhaɪdʒi:n/ *u.n* (science or study of) good physical health and cleanliness, esp by keeping rules with regard to the preparation of food, the washing of one's body etc.

hygienic /haɪˈdʒi:nɪk/ *adj* **1** of or referring to hygiene: *the hygienic preparation of food.* **2** (very) clean: *The conditions in the restaurant's kitchen were not very hygienic.* Opposite unhygienic.

hyˈgienically *adv.*

hymen /ˈhaɪmen/ *c.n* (*technical*) thin skin or membrane that partly closes the vagina in a woman who is a virgin(3).

hymn /hɪm/ *c.n* (also *attrib*) (religious) song of praise, esp one sung in Christian(1) churches: *a hymn book.*

hype /haɪp/ *c.n* **1** (*informal*) attempt to make s.t more important, more noticed, than it actually is (worth), esp by means of extra publicity(1): *The campaign*(2) *to sell the new book is just a hype.*

▷ *tr.v* **2** (often — *s.o/s.t.up*) (*informal*) use extra publicity(1) to make (s.o/s.t) appear more important than he/she/it actually is: *The new film has been so hyped up that it was a great disappointment when we actually saw it.*

hyperbole /haɪˈpɜːbəlɪ/ *c/u.n* (*technical*) (example of the) use of an expression in speech or writing that is very exaggerated and intended to produce a certain effect: *'His eyes were as big as saucers' is a hyperbole.*

hyperbolic /ˌhaɪpəˈbɒlɪk/ *adj* showing hyperbole.

hypercritical /ˌhaɪpəˈkrɪtɪkl/ *adj* (*derog; formal*) (of a person) (being) too critical.

hypermarket /ˈhaɪpəˌmɑːkɪt/ *c.n* very large supermarket, usu outside, or on the edges of, a town or city.

hypersensitive /ˌhaɪpəˈsensɪtɪv/ *adj* (often *derog*) very or too sensitive.

ˌhyperˈsensiˈtivity *u.n.*

hyphen /ˈhaɪfən/ *c.n* short mark - used to join two or more words, parts of a word, together, e.g in house-to-house, co-opt.

ˈhypheˌnate *tr/intr.v* use or put a hyphen or hyphens (in a word or words): *You must learn to hyphenate* (*words*) *properly.*

hyphenation /ˌhaɪfəˈneɪʃən/ *u.n.*

hypnosis /hɪpˈnəʊsɪs/ *u.n* state like a deep sleep that is produced artificially in a person and during which he/she can be controlled or told what to do by another person.

hypnotic /hɪpˈnɒtɪk/ *adj* **1** of or referring to hypnosis: *a hypnotic state.* **2** that seems to produce hypnosis; that produces sleep: *a hypnotic stare*(1); *a hypnotic drug*(2).

▷ *c.n* **3** hypnotic(2) drug(2). **4** person who is or can be easily hypnotized(1).

hypˈnotically *adv.*

hypnotism /ˈhɪpnəˌtɪzəm/ *u.n* (practice or act of) producing hypnosis.

ˈhypnoˌtist *c.n* person skilled in hypnotism.

hypnotize, -ise /ˈhɪpnəˌtaɪz/ *tr.v* **1** put (s.o) into a hypnotic(1) state. **2** attract or fascinate (s.o), so that he/she does not notice other things/people: *He was hypnotized by the repeated action of the windscreen wipers. Her beauty and charm hypnotized him.*

hypochondria /ˌhaɪpəʊˈkɒndrɪə/ *u.n* state of being (always) concerned, worried about one's health, although there is (usu) nothing wrong.

hypochondriac /ˌhaɪpəʊˈkɒndrɪˌæk/ *adj* **1** (of a person, s.o's behaviour) suffering from hypochondria: *hypochondriac complaints.*

▷ *c.n* **2** person who suffers from hypochondria.

hypocrisy /hɪˈpɒkrəsɪ/ *c/u.n* (*pl -ies*) (example of the) state or practice of pretending to be better than one actually is, to believe or do things that one does not actually believe or do: *It was sheer*[1](2) *hypocrisy for him to say that he worked harder than anyone else when he was never in the office until 10 o'clock.*

hypocrite /ˈhɪpəˌkrɪt/ *c.n* (*derog*) person who shows hypocrisy: *Alex is such a hypocrite telling us to improve our eating habits when he smokes.*

hypocritical /ˌhɪpəˈkrɪtɪkl/ *adj* of or referring to hypocrisy or a hypocrite: *It's hypocritical of Joe to refuse to eat meat when he has ham in his pizza.*

ˌhypoˈcritically *adv.*

hypodermic /ˌhaɪpəˈdɜːmɪk/ *adj* **1** of or referring to the way of putting a drug into the body with a needle etc that goes under the skin and into a vein: *a hypodermic needle/injection.*

▷ *c.n* **2** needle or syringe(1) that does this.

ˌhypoˈdermically *adv.*

hypotenuse /haɪˈpɒtɪˌnjuːz/ *c.n* (*mathematics*) longest side of a right-angled triangle(1), which is opposite the right angle.

hypothermia /ˌhaɪpəˈθɜːmɪə/ *u.n* (*medical*) state when the temperature of the body drops below the normal level from being in severe cold for a long time.

hypothesis /haɪˈpɒθɪsɪs/ *c.n* (*pl hypotheses* /haɪˈpɒθɪˌsiːz/) thing stated or thought which one thinks may be true and uses as a basis for stating other things: *Our hypothesis, based on present* evidence(1), *is that employment will increase by 2 per cent next year.*

hypothetical /ˌhaɪpəˈθetɪkl/ *adj* (also **ˌhypoˈthetic**) of or referring to a hypothesis (and therefore not necessarily true or accurate).

ˌhypoˈthetically *adv.*

hysterectomy /ˌhɪstəˈrektəmɪ/ *c.n* (*pl -ies*) (*medical*) operation in which a woman's womb is removed.

hysteria /hɪˈstɪərɪə/ *u.n* **1** (mental(1)) state or condition of extreme excitement and nervousness in a person, shown by frequent rapid changes of mood[1](1) between laughing and crying etc. **2** very great excitement, esp one created(2) among a large group of people. *mass hysteria* ⇨ mass[1].

hysteric /hɪˈsterɪk/ *c.n* person who suffers from hysteria(1).

hyˈsterical *adj* **1** of, referring to, suffering from, hysteria(1): *She gets hysterical at the sight of blood.* **2** (*informal*) causing great amusement: *It was hysterical, the way he kept falling over and getting up again.*

hyˈsterically *adv.*

hyˈsterics *pl.n* (usu *go into, have, —*) fit(s) of hysteria(1). *be in hysterics* be laughing a lot (in an uncontrolled way): *The story was so funny, we were all in hysterics* (or *he had us all in hysterics*).

Hz *written abbr* hertz.

I i

I[1]**, i** /aɪ/ *c/unique n* **1** 9th letter of the English alphabet.

▷ *written abbr* (with capital **I**) **2** independent. **3** Institute. **4** Island. **5** International.

▷ *symb* **6** Roman number for 1 etc: *iii* (= 3); *iv* (= 4); *ix* (= 9); *MCMXXI* (= 1921).

I[2] /aɪ/ *pron* (as the subject of a verb or (*formal*) a subjective(3) complement(3)) person who is speaking or writing: *I saw her yesterday. It was I who gave the order. I'll be busy this evening.* Compare me, mine, my, myself.

i/c *written abbr* **1** (*military*) (of an officer etc who controls a military group, a place etc) in command. **2** (of a person or official who runs (part of) an organization) in charge.

ice /aɪs/ *n* **1** *u.n* water that has become frozen to a solid state: *Drive carefully, there's ice on the roads.* **2** *c.n* = ice-cream. **break the ice** (*fig*) do s.t that helps people who do not know each other well to become friendly etc. ⇒ icebreaker(2). **cut no ice** (**with s.o**) fail to be believed; fail to seem important. **keep s.t on ice** (*fig*) postpone s.t until a better time. **skate on thin ice** (*fig*) do or say s.t that could cause offence, harm, danger etc: *You'll be skating on thin ice if you try to offer her advice.*
▷ *tr.v* **3** put icing(1) on (a cake etc): *I'll have to wait till the cake cools before I ice it.* **ice over/up** (of a river etc) form a surface of, become, ice(1): *Has the river iced over? The water pipes iced up in the cold weather.*

iceberg /'aɪsˌbɜːg/ *c.n* very large mass of ice(1) that floats in the sea with most of it underneath the surface.

'ice,breaker *c.n* **1** ship with a specially strengthened hull and bow so that it can cut through ice(1). **2** event or activity that makes it possible for people to get used to a new situation, group of friends etc.

,ice-'cream *c/u.n* (example of a) kind of sweet made from cream(3) etc and frozen: *Do you want an ice-cream? What's your favourite ice-cream?*

,ice-,cream 'soda *c/u.n* (ice-cream mixed with soda water to make a) kind of thick drink.

'ice ,hockey *u.n* (also **'hockey**) kind of game like hockey(1) but played on an iced surface with a flat round disc(1) (called a puck) instead of a ball.

,ice 'lolly ⇒ lolly(1).

'ice ,rink ⇒ rink(1).

'ice-,skate ⇒ skate¹.

'ice-,skater *c.n* (also **'skater**) person who skates¹(3).

'ice-,skating *u.n* (also **'skating**) (also *attrib*) sport or activity of going round on skates¹(2): *an ice-skating champion(3). Let's go (ice-)skating.*

icicle /'aɪsɪkl/ *c.n* long thin piece of ice(1) formed when dripping water freezes: *Huge icicles formed in the waterfall.*

'icily *adv* in an icy(3) way: *She looked at him icily.*

'iciness *u.n* state of being icy.

'icing *u.n* **1** mixture of sugar, butter, flavouring etc used to cover, decorate, cakes etc: *chocolate icing.* **2** act or fact of ice forming on the surface of a ship, aircraft etc in very cold weather: *The accident was a result of icing on the wings of the plane.*

'icy *adj* (-ier, -iest) **1** covered in ice(1) (and so often very slippery): *icy roads.* **2** extremely cold (and likely to make ice(1) form): *an icy wind. The weather is icy.* **3** (*fig*) very unfriendly(1): *She gave him an icy look.*

icon /'aɪkɒn/ *c.n* (also **'ikon**) religious painting of Jesus or a saint(1), found esp in Eastern or Orthodox(2) churches.

iconoclasm /aɪ'kɒnəˌklæzəm/ *u.n* attack on,

attempt to destroy, traditional customs of religious beliefs.

i'cono,clast *c.n* person who practises(3) iconoclasm.

iconoclastic /aɪˌkɒnə'klæstɪk/ *adj.* **i,cono-'clastically** *adv.*

icy ⇒ ice.

I'd /aɪd/ **1** I had. ⇒ have. **2** I would. ⇒ will¹, would.

ID /ˌaɪ 'diː/ (also ˌI'D ,card) *c.n* (*informal*) identity card.

idea /aɪ'dɪə/ *c.n* **1** thought or picture in one's mind (about s.t): *This book will give you an idea of how people lived then. I had an idea that you might be here.* **2** plan or suggestion: *He has several ideas on how to improve production. We need some ideas about where to go on holiday.* **3** opinion, belief: *Paul has very fixed ideas.* **4** knowledge or general opinion: *Have you any idea (of) how much it costs?* **get the idea** (**of s.t, that . . .**) begin to understand, realize (that . . .): *I get the idea that you don't really like your job much. I didn't understand it at all when I started but I'm beginning to get the idea of it now.* **have big ideas** have great or important plans, schemes etc. **have no idea (of) how, what** etc . . . not be able to imagine or understand how, what etc . . .: *I had no idea what he was talking about. You've no idea how worried we were.* **put ideas into s.o's head** allow s.o to imagine that s.t may be possible when this is not likely: *You know we can't afford that — who's putting ideas into your head?* **don't run away with the idea etc that . . .** ⇒ run away.

ideal /aɪ'dɪəl/ *adj* **1** (thought to be) perfect, exactly right: *ideal weather; the ideal person for the job.*
▷ *c.n* **2** person or thing etc who/that is ideal(1): *He was her ideal of the perfect husband.* **3** (*often pl*) (belief in the) correct, perfect, way of behaving, doing things: *a politician with high ideals.*

i'dea,lism *u.n* **1** state of believing that ideals(3) are possible. **2** (in art, literature) act of representing things in an ideal(1) or perfect way instead of as they really are. Opposite realism(2). **3** (in philosophy(1)) belief that only one's mind is real and everything that is outside it is an idea. Opposite realism(3).

i'dea,list *c.n* person who has high standards for the way people should act, behave etc.

idealistic /aɪˌdɪə'lɪstɪk/ *adj.* **i,dea'listically** *adv.*

idealization, -isation /aɪˌdɪəlaɪ'zeɪʃən/ *u.n* act or state of idealizing s.o/s.t.

i'dea,lize, -ise *tr.v* believe/consider (s.o/s.t) to be perfect: *She idealizes her husband/childhood.*

i'deally *adv* **1** (thought to be) perfectly (suitable, right etc): *The house is ideally situated for schools.* **2** (if it could happen) in an ideal(1) way: *Ideally, we need three people to help.*

identical /aɪ'dentɪkl/ *adj* **1** (often — *to/with s.o/ s.t*) exactly the same (as s.o/s.t); exactly like (s.o/ s.t): *His views were identical to mine. Are they identical twins? The houses are identical. That chair is identical with the one I have at home.* **2** the very same (thing etc): *That's the identical way I was tricked. I ordered the identical meal that I had when I was last here.*

i'dentically *adv.*

identify /aɪˈdentɪˌfaɪ/ tr.v (-ies, -ied) say, claim, prove, that (s.o/s.t) is a certain person, thing etc or belongs to s.o: *She identified the man who attacked her. He was unable to identify his suitcase as they all looked the same.* ⇒ unidentified.
identify oneself with s.o/s.t show oneself to be of the same mind, opinion, belief etc as s.o else: *He refused to identify himself with the right wing of the party.* **identify with s.o/s.t** think or feel in the same way as s.o/s.t: *I can identify with your problems as I've had them myself. Who did you identify with in the film?*
identification /aɪˌdentɪfɪˈkeɪʃən/ u.n 1 (often — of s.o/s.t) act of identifying s.o/s.t. 2 proof of who or what s.o/s.t really is: *Have you any (means of) identification on you?*
identikit /aɪˈdentɪˌkɪt/ c.n (also **iˌdentiˌkit ˈpicture**)(separate parts of a face that can be used to produce a) picture of s.o who is described to the police (to help them find, arrest, her/him): *An identikit of the thief was printed in all the newspapers.*
identity /aɪˈdentɪtɪ/ n (pl -ies) 1 c/u.n (often — of s.o/s.t) name (of s.o/s.t); who or what s.o/s.t is: *Do you know the identity of the man who attacked you? It was a case of mistaken identity.* 2 u.n (formal) state of being exactly the same (as s.t else).
iˈdentity ˌcard c.n (informal ID (card)) document with one's name, address etc and usu a photograph of oneself.
ideology /ˌaɪdɪˈɒdʒɪ/ c/u.n (pl -ies) (example of a) (strongly held) set of beliefs, esp of a political party: *Marxist(1) ideology. Her ideas do not match any known ideologies.*
ideological /ˌaɪdɪəˈlɒdʒɪkl/ adj 1 referring to, using, ideology: *an ideological explanation.* 2 (of a person) who uses strongly held beliefs to explain her/his actions although these may not be considered right, practical, realistic(2) etc.
ˌideoˈlogically adv.
ˌideˈoloˌgist c.n person who holds such beliefs.
idiocy ⇒ idiot.
idiom /ˈɪdɪəm/ n 1 c.n (grammar) expression, phrase(1) etc with a meaning that is different from the meanings of the individual words that make it up: *'Take a back seat' meaning 'not take an active part in s.t so that others can do it' is an idiom.* 2 u.n particular kind of language spoken or used in a country, area etc: *I couldn't understand the local idiom.* Compare dialect.
idiomatic /ˌɪdɪəˈmætɪk/ adj 1 of or referring to idioms(1): *an idiomatic expression.* 2 (of language) using many idioms(1) (and so speaking in the way a person does who learns it from childhood): *Maria speaks perfect English but it's not very idiomatic.*
ˌidioˈmatically adv.
idiosyncrasy /ˌɪdɪəˈsɪŋkrəsɪ/ c.n (pl -ies) way of behaving, esp one that is rather odd, that a particular person shows: *His one idiosyncrasy is to wear different coloured socks.*
ˌidiosynˈcratic adj, **ˌidiosynˈcratically** adv.
idiot /ˈɪdɪət/ c.n (derog) person whom one thinks is stupid or foolish: *You idiot! Why did you lend him money? Don't be an idiot!*
idiocy /ˈɪdɪəsɪ/ n 1 u.n stupid or foolish state. 2 c.n stupid or foolish action or behaviour.
idiotic /ˌɪdɪˈɒtɪk/ adj (often — of s.o (to do s.t))

(of a person, action) very stupid or foolish: *idiotic behaviour. It was idiotic of me to think he'd care what I did.*
ˌidiˈotically adv.
idle /ˈaɪdl/ adj 1 (of a person, machine etc) not working; not being used: *Whole factories were left idle when the power lines failed.* 2 (derog) (of a person) lazy, not willing or eager to work: *You're so idle — why don't you go out and find a job?* 3 (attrib) (of s.t s.o says etc) not having any real force or reason: *an idle threat; idle fears; idle gossip(1).* **bone-idle** ⇒ bone.
▷ intr.v 4 spend one's time not doing very much: *There was very little to do on the island so we just idled.* 5 (of a car engine etc) be turned on but without being in gear(1): *Keep the engine idling; I won't be long.* **idle away one's time** etc spend one's time in a lazy way: *Instead of idling away your time, you should be studying for your exams.*
ˈidler c.n (derog) person who is idle(2).
ˈidleness u.n. **ˈidly** adv.
idol /ˈaɪdl/ c.n 1 image(1), statue etc worshipped as a god or goddess. 2 (often the — of s.o) person who is greatly loved or admired (by s.o): *He's the idol of his mother;* teenage *idols* (e.g film-stars, pop stars³(1) etc).
idolatrous /aɪˈdɒlətrəs/ adj. **iˈdolatrously** adv.
idolatry /aɪˈdɒlətrɪ/ u.n worship of idols(1).
idolize, -ise /ˈaɪdəˌlaɪz/ tr.v love or admire (s.o/ s.t) very/too much: *He idolized his father.*
idyll /ˈɪdɪl/ c.n (also **ˈidyl**) description (sometimes a poem) of a pleasant scene or place, e.g in the country.
idyllic /ɪˈdɪlɪk/ adj perfect because of its peace and simplicity: *an idyllic scene.*
iˈdyllically adv.
i.e /ˌaɪ ˈiː/ abbr (Latin) id est (= that is to say or mean (s.t)): *He got into a huff(1), i.e he became annoyed.*
if /ɪf/ conj 1 in the (likely or unlikely) event that (s.o does or will do s.t, s.t will happen etc): *If he comes, let me know. If you had warned me, I might have been able to change my plans. I'll help you if you can't find someone else.* 2 when, whenever (often of a repeated action): *I always feel ill if someone is smoking near me.* 3 though, although: *He is quite handsome, if somewhat small in size.* 4 whether: *Do you know if he'll be there?* **even if** ⇒ even(adv). **If I were you ...** (expression used to offer advice to s.o): *If I were you, I'd get another job.* **If only ...** (exclamation used to say) I wish that ...: *If only I had known earlier, I would have helped.*
▷ c.n 5 **ifs and buts** (informal) excuses; things said to delay doing s.t: *He was full of ifs and buts so I told him just to do it.*
igloo /ˈɪgluː/ c.n (pl -s) kind of small, usu round, house made of blocks of hard snow or ice and lived in by Eskimos.
igneous /ˈɪgnɪəs/ adj (technical) of or referring to rocks formed from molten matter, e.g in a volcano. Compare sedimentary.
ignite /ɪgˈnaɪt/ tr/intr.v (formal) (cause (s.t) to) catch fire, burn: *A lighted match caused the petrol to ignite.*
ignition /ɪgˈnɪʃən/ n 1 u.n act of igniting or being ignited. 2 c.n (also attrib) mechanism in an engine, esp of a car, that ignites the petrol and

so turns the engine on: *the ignition key. Switch on the ignition and then press the* pedal(1).

ignoble /ɪgˈnəʊbl/ *adj* (*formal*) (of a person, act etc) dishonourable; shameful: *It was ignoble of you to treat her like that.*
igˈnobly *adv.*

ignominy /ˈɪgnəmɪnɪ/ *c/u.n* (*pl -ies*) (often — of *s.t*) (*formal*) (example of a) state or act of public shame or dishonour: *She had to suffer the ignominy of being searched by the police.*
ignominious /ˌɪgnəˈmɪnɪəs/ *adj* (*formal*) that causes shame or dishonour: *an ignominious defeat.*
ignoˈminiously *adv.* **ignoˈminiousness** *u.n.*

ignoramus /ˌɪgnəˈreɪməs/ *c.n* (*pl -es*) (*derog*) person who does not know very much (about a subject etc): *He's a complete ignoramus about women.*

ignorant /ˈɪgnərənt/ *adj* **1** (of a person) not having much knowledge (about a subject etc) and sometimes considered stupid as a result: *He's ignorant about politics. For someone who claims to have been to university, he's really rather ignorant.* **2** (often — of *s.t*) (of a person) not aware(1) (of *s.t*); not knowing (*s.t*): *He drove home ignorant of the fact that he was being followed.*
ignorance *u.n* lack of knowledge or information (about *s.t*): *That kind of remark shows your ignorance.*
ignorantly *adv.*

ignore /ɪgˈnɔː/ *tr.v* pay no attention to, take no notice of, (*s.o/s.t*): *She ignored me at work this morning. Ignore his insults — he can't hurt you.*

ikon ⇒ icon.

ill /ɪl/ *adj* (*comp worse, superl worst*) **1** sick; not well: *I was ill last week so I couldn't go to the meeting.* ⇒ ill health(2). **2** (*attrib*) (leading to *s.t*) bad or harmful: *Did last night's meal have any ill effects on you?* **3** (*attrib*) (*formal*) (of a feeling etc) unpleasant, nasty: *He was in a very ill temper/ mood when he got home.* ⇒ ill feeling, ill-tempered, ill will. **fall, be taken, ill** become ill(1). **(be/feel) ill at ease** ⇒ ease(*n*).
▷ *adv* **4** badly, not enough: *They ill feed the animals on that farm.* ⇒ afford (to do) *s.t.* **5** (usu *speak, think* etc — of *s.o/s.t*) in an unfavourable way: *One should not speak ill of the dead.* **ill afford (to do) s.t** not easily be able to afford (to do) *s.t* or waste time etc doing *s.t: I can ill afford the time to listen to your complaints.* Compare well(2).
▷ *n* **6** *u.n* (*formal*) harm or injury: *He means to do her ill.* **7** *c.n* (often *pl*) bad thing or trouble: *the ills of poverty.*

ill-adˈvised *adj* (of *s.t* one does or wants to do) not well thought out or planned; foolish: *You would be ill-advised to* invest(1) *in that company.*

ill-ˈbred *adj* (*derog*) (of a person, her/his behaviour etc) not showing good manners: *It was ill-bred of you to interrupt like that.*

ill-disˈposed *adj* (usu — to/towards *s.o/s.t*) (*formal*) not at all friendly (to/towards *s.o*); not approving (of *s.t*): *Are you ill-disposed towards all football* supporters?

ill-eˈquipped *adj* (often —for *s.t, to do s.t*) not having enough of the necessary things, e.g equipment(2), ability etc (to do *s.t* properly): *Our group was ill-equipped for the bad weather. He's very ill-equipped for the job.*

ill-ˈfated *adj* that ends in failure or disaster: *an ill-fated journey.*

ill feeling ⇒ feeling(*n*).

ill-ˈgotten *adj* **ill-gotten gains** (goods, money, profit) obtained in an illegal way.

ill-ˈmannered *adj* ⇒ -mannered.

ill-ˈnatured *adj* ⇒ -natured.

illness *c/u.n* (example of the) state of being ill(1): *There has been a lot of illness in our company recently. What serious illnesses have you had?*

ill-ˈtempered *adj* (*derog*) showing (one's) bad temper: *an ill-tempered old man.* ⇒ -tempered.

ill-ˈtimed *adj* that happens at the wrong or unsuitable time: *My arrival was clearly ill-timed.* ⇒ -timed.

ill-ˈtreat *tr.v* treat (*s.o*, an animal etc) badly: *Their children are ill-treated.*

ill-ˈtreatment *u.n.*

ill-ˈuse /ˈjuːz/ *tr.v* = ill-treat. **be/feel ill-used** be/ think that one has been treated badly.

ill will *u.n* feeling of hatred (towards *s.o*): *I bear him no ill will for what he has done.*

I'll /aɪl/ I will, I shall. ⇒ will[1].

illegal /ɪˈliːgl/ *adj* not legal(1); against the law: *They've had an illegal telephone in their house for years.*
illegality /ˌɪlɪˈgælɪtɪ/ *c/u.n* (example of a) state of being illegal.
ilˈlegally *adv.*

illegible /ɪˈledʒɪbl/ *adj* that cannot be read (at all or not very easily); not legible: *Our doctor has an illegible signature.*
illegibility /ɪˌledʒəˈbɪlɪtɪ/ *u.n.* **ilˈlegibly** *adv.*

illegitimate /ˌɪlɪˈdʒɪtɪmɪt/ *adj* **1** (of a person) whose parents were not married when one was born; not legitimate(1). **2** (of an action etc) not allowed, e.g by law or a rule; not legitimate(2): *He made illegitimate use of the money entrusted to him.*
illeˈgitimacy *u.n.* **illeˈgitimately** *adv.*

illicit /ɪˈlɪsɪt/ *adj* (usu *attrib*) not allowed by law: *illicit actions; illicit drugs*(2).
ilˈlicitly *adv.* **ilˈlicitness** *u.n.*

illiterate /ɪˈlɪtərɪt/ *adj* **1** (of a person) not able to read or write (at all or very well); not well educated or literate(2): *It is surprising to learn of the number of illiterate adults in such a rich country. Don't show how illiterate you are by talking about books you've never read!*
▷ *c.n* **2** illiterate(1) person.
ilˈliteracy *u.n* state of being illiterate(1): *adult illiteracy.*

illness ⇒ ill.

illogical /ɪˈlɒdʒɪkl/ *adj* (of a person, act etc) that does not show clear or proper thought; not logical(1): *illogical behaviour. It is illogical of you to say one thing and do another.*
illogicality /ɪˌlɒdʒɪˈkælɪtɪ/ *c/u.n.* **ilˈlogically** *adv.*

illuminate /ɪˈluːmɪˌneɪt/ *tr.v* (*formal*) **1** provide a light or lights for (a room, street etc) sometimes for special occasions: *Our street is poorly illuminated.* **2** make (*s.t* one says, writes etc) clearer, easier to understand, e.g by giving examples: *He illuminated his argument with many* quotations(2).
ilˈlumiˌnated *adj* (esp of old manuscripts) decorated with brightly coloured and ornamental writing etc.

il'lumi,nating *adj* (of s.t s.o says etc) that helps to make (s.t) clearer, easier to understand: *an illuminating description of life in ancient Egypt.*

illumination /ɪ,luːmɪˈneɪʃən/ *u.n* fact or state of illuminating (⇒ illuminate(*v*)) s.t.

il,lumi'nations *pl.n* decorative lights put on for special occasions: *the illuminations in London's main streets at Christmas time.*

illusion /ɪˈluːʒən/ *n* 1 *c.n* thing that one sees wrongly, esp because one is not looking properly or because something causes this: *The heat rising off the road causes the illusion that there is water ahead.* ⇒ optical illusion. 2 *c/u.n* (often *be under an/the — that . . .*) false idea or belief (that . . .): *He is under* (or *has*) *the illusion that it will be easy to find a job but he'll soon discover how wrong he is.* **have no illusions about s.o/s.t** not be deceived about s.o/s.t, understand s.o/s.t well, esp that he/she/it is not as perfect, easy etc as he/she/it seems. Compare delusion.

illusive /ɪˈluːsɪv/ *adj* (also **illusory** /ɪˈluːzərɪ/) not real.

il'lusively, il'lusorily *adv.*

illustrate /ˈɪləˌstreɪt/ *tr.v* 1 provide (a story, book etc) with pictures or photographs: *The book was illustrated with line drawings.* 2 make (s.t one says, does etc) clearer by providing pictures, examples etc: *He illustrated his talk with slides(6). The graph illustrates the fact clearly.* 3 show the meaning of (s.t), esp as an example of it: *His behaviour illustrates perfectly what is wrong with our society.*

'illu,strated *adj* having pictures or photographs in it: *an illustrated book.* **be illustrated in s.t** be illustrated (⇒ illustrate(1)) using s.t: *It's illustrated in full colour so it will be expensive.*

illustration /ˌɪləˈstreɪʃən/ *n* 1 *c.n* picture or photograph (in a book etc): *The book is full of illustrations.* 2 *c/u.n* (example of) s.t that illustrates(3) s.t: *Does this point need illustration?*

illustrative /ˈɪləstrətɪv/ *adj* (*formal*) that helps to illustrate(3) s.t.

'illustratively *adv.*

illustrator /ˈɪləˌstreɪtə/ *c.n* person who draws pictures (for a book etc).

illustrious /ɪˈlʌstrɪəs/ *adj* (*formal*) (of a person, action) famous; that has shown great ability: *illustrious ancestors/deeds.*

il'lustriously *adv.* **il'lustriousness** *u.n.*

I'm /aɪm/ = I am. ⇒ be.

image /ˈɪmɪdʒ/ *c.n* (often *— of s.o/s.t*) 1 picture, statue etc (of s.t), used esp in religion etc: *stone images of the Roman Emperors.* 2 reflection or picture (of s.o/s.t), e.g as seen in a mirror or a lens(1) of a camera: *The image in the mirror showed her she was looking tired and ill.* 3 (often *the* (*living, very*) *— of s.o*) (of a person) very close likeness (to s.o): *You're the image of your father.* 4 picture one has in one's mind (of s.o/s.t): *For a long time after he kept an image of that beautiful countryside in his mind. The image I have of her is of a very active little girl.* 5 (good) opinion (of oneself, s.t) that others have and that one wants to protect etc: *The company will have to improve its image* (or *the image it has of itself*) *if it is to succeed.* **the spitting image of s.o** the exact likeness of s.o else. ⇒ image(3).

'imagery *u.n* use of words, esp in writing, to create a certain feeling or image(4): *That poem is full of imagery that reminds one of the evils of war.*

imagine /ɪˈmædʒɪn/ *tr.v* 1 (often *— that, what etc . . .*) form a picture in one's mind of (s.o doing s.t, s.t happening etc): *I imagined him sitting there waiting for me. Imagine for a moment that you are living in the fifth century BC. Joe doing the ironing — I can't imagine it!* 2 (often *— that . . .*) believe or feel (s.t that is not true, that . . .): *You're just imagining things; there's no one there. She imagined (that) she'd seen someone at the window.* 3 (often *— that . . .*) think or suppose (that . . .): *I imagine (that) he'll be here any moment.*

i'maginable *adj* that can be thought of, imagined(1): *We've dealt with every imaginable possibility of failure.* Opposite unimaginable.

imaginary /ɪˈmædʒɪnərɪ/ *adj* not real or true; invented: *All the characters in this book are imaginary.*

imagination /ɪ,mædʒɪˈneɪʃən/ *n* 1 *sing/u.n* (example of the) ability of the mind to imagine(1) s.t: *You will need to use your imagination to picture the scene properly. She has a good imagination.* 2 *u.n* special power or ability of the mind: *He showed little imagination in his handling of the job.* 3 *u.n* fact or state of imagining(2) s.t: *It was all imagination — she doesn't have a younger brother at all. It's just your imagination — no one hates you.*

imaginative /ɪˈmædʒɪnətɪv/ *adj* showing or using (great) imagination(1): *a very imaginative story/child.* Opposite unimaginative.

i'maginatively *adv.*

imbalance /ɪmˈbæləns/ *c/u.n* 1 (*formal*) lack of proper balance(3) or equality in quality or quantity between two things: *There's a degree of imbalance between trained and untrained workers in this factory.* 2 (*commerce*) difference in amount between two things, totals etc, esp in trade: *the imbalance between* exports(2) *and* imports(1).

imbecile /ˈɪmbɪˌsiːl/ *adj* 1 (usu *attrib*) (*derog*) (of s.t said or done) foolish or stupid: *an imbecile remark.*
▷ *c.n* 2 (*derog*) stupid or foolish person.

imbecility /,ɪmbɪˈsɪlɪtɪ/ *c/u.n.*

imbibe /ɪmˈbaɪb/ *tr/intr.v* (*formal*) drink, take in, (s.t).

imbue /ɪmˈbjuː/ *tr.v* (usu *passive*) (*formal*) fill (s.o/s.t) or be filled (with a strong feeling etc): *He was imbued with the desire to please her.*

imitate /ˈɪmɪˌteɪt/ *tr.v* copy (s.o/s.t): *The boy walked behind her imitating the way she walked. He's very good at imitating bird calls.*

imitation /,ɪmɪˈteɪʃən/ *n* 1 *u.n* fact or state of imitating s.o/s.t: *Steve's very good at imitation.* 2 *c/u.n* (also *attrib*) copy of s.t, not the original/real thing: *imitation jewellery. This picture is only an imitation; the original is in a museum.*

imitative /ˈɪmɪtətɪv/ *adj* copying s.o/s.t: *His behaviour was very imitative.*

'imitativeness *u.n.*

'imi,tator *c.n* person who copies s.o/s.t, who models herself/himself on s.o: *The artist had several imitators but they weren't nearly as good.*

immaculate /ɪˈmækjʊlət/ *adj* (*formal*) 1 (of a person, room, clothes etc) very clean, perfect etc: *She kept the house immaculate only by*

spending several hours a day cleaning it. She always looks immaculate. **2** (*fig*) (of s.t· one says, does etc) perfect, without any faults: *an immaculate performance.*
im'maculately *adv.*

immaterial /ˌɪməˈtɪərɪəl/ *adj* not (at all) important or relevant: *Your objections are quite immaterial and will not alter our views. It's immaterial to me what you decide to do.*

immature /ˌɪməˈtjʊə/ *adj* **1** (often *derog*) (of a person, behaviour etc) not yet fully developed as an adult; childish: *That was rather immature behaviour for someone of your age. He's a very immature 17 year-old.* **2** (*formal*) (of a plant, fruit etc) not yet fully grown. Opposite mature(2).
ˌimma'turely *adv.* ˌimma'turity *u.n.*

immeasurable /ɪˈmeʒərəbl/ *adj* that cannot be measured; very great: *You've given us immeasurable pleasure. Having a car will make an immeasurable difference to your life.* Opposite measurable.
im'measurably *adv.*

immediate /ɪˈmiːdɪət/ *adj* **1** that is done, happens, (almost) at once, without any delay: *His response was immediate. We want immediate action on this proposal.* **2** (of position etc) nearest or next (to s.o/s.t): *My immediate neighbours are the Greens. Who's your immediate boss? Peter is on my immediate right and Jane is next to him.*
im'mediately *adv* **1** (almost) at once: *He came immediately. She promised to do the job immediately.* **immediately after, behind** etc (**s.o/s.t**) (following) nearest or next after etc (s.o/s.t): *Immediately in front of him was a church. Who lives immediately behind you?*
▷ *conj.* **2** as soon as: *He came immediately he heard the news.*
im'mediateness *u.n.*

immemorable /ɪˈmemrəbl/ *adj* not memorable.
im'memorably *adv.*

immemorial /ˌɪmɪˈmɔːrɪəl/ *adj* **from/since time immemorial** (*formal*) going back to a time in the far distant past: *There have been great travellers in my family since time immemorial.*

immense /ɪˈmens/ *adj* **1** very large (in size, space, quantity etc): *an immense distance.* **2** (of a feeling etc) very great: *Colin gets immense satisfaction from his job.*
im'mensely *adv* to a very great extent: *Sally's immensely popular. He's immensely proud of her. We enjoyed the performance immensely.*
im'mensity *c/u.n* (*pl -ies*) (often — *of s.t*) (*formal*) (example of the) fact or state of s.t being immense: *the immensity of the change in his home town; the immensity of his love for her.*

immerse /ɪˈmɜːs/ *tr.v* **1** (usu — *s.o/s.t in s.t*) (*formal*) put (s.o/s.t) under the surface of a liquid so that he/she/it is completely covered: *Immerse the pudding in a pan of boiling water. She immersed the burning pan in cold water.* **2** (often — *oneself in s.t; be —d in s.t*) give all one's attention to (s.t): *He was immersed in the job of getting the report ready in time.*
im'mersion /ɪˈmɜːʃən/ *c/u.n* (example of the) fact or state of immersing(1) s.t or being immersed.
im'mersion ˌheater *c.n* system using an electrical device immersed(1) in water, for heating water, esp in the home.

immigrant /ˈɪmɪɡrənt/ *c.n* (also *attrib*) person from one country who settles in another one: *immigrants from India; the immigrant population.* Compare emigrant.

immigrate /ˈɪmɪˌɡreɪt/ *intr.v* (often — (*from s.w*) *to s.w*) come (from one country) and settle (in another): *They immigrated to this country in the last century.* Compare emigrate.

immigration /ˌɪmɪˈɡreɪʃən/ *c/u.n* (also *attrib*) (example of the) act or fact of immigrating: *Immigration in the 1960s was very high. You'll have to speak to the immigration department/ office.* Compare emigration.

imminence /ˈɪmɪnəns/ *u.n* (often — *of s.t*) (*formal*) fact or state that (s.t) is going to happen very soon: *The imminence of his arrival stirred them into action.*
ˈimminent *adj* (esp of s.t bad) expected, likely, to happen very soon: *Storms are imminent in this area.* Compare impending.
ˈimminently *adv.*

immobile /ɪˈməʊbaɪl/ *adj* (*formal*) **1** unable to move, e.g because of an accident: *The accident left him immobile and he had to have a wheelchair.* Opposite mobile(1). **2** (*informal*) not having a vehicle to go about in. Without moving: *He remained immobile for several minutes hoping not to be seen.* Opposite mobile(2).
im'mobility /ˌɪməʊˈbɪlɪtɪ/ *u.n* (also *attrib*) fact or state of being immobile: *His immobility made him dependent on his family. He receives an immobility* pension(1). Compare mobility.
im'mobilize, -ise /ɪˈməʊbɪˌlaɪz/ *tr.v* (*formal*) make (s.o/s.t) unable to move: *We'll be immobilized while our car is in the garage. They were immobilized by their fear of heights.* Compare mobilize.

immoderate /ɪˈmɒdərɪt/ *adj* (*formal*) (of eating, drinking, behaviour etc) going beyond what is normal or accepted: *immoderate eating habits.* Compare moderate(1,2).
im'moderacy *u.n.* im'moderately *adv.*

immodest /ɪˈmɒdɪst/ *adj* (*derog*) **1** (*formal*) (of dress, behaviour etc) not decent(2) or modest; likely to shock people: *His behaviour was most immodest and offended all the women present.* **2** not showing modesty or humbleness: *It's a bit immodest of you to claim all the success when actually others helped.*
im'modestly *adv.* im'modesty *u.n.*

immoral /ɪˈmɒrəl/ *adj* (*derog*) (of a person, action etc) not right according to accepted standards (often in sexual matters); wicked; not moral(1): *It was immoral of him to cheat her in that way. He was arrested for immoral behaviour in a public place.*
im'morally *adv.* immorality /ˌɪməˈrælɪtɪ/ *u.n.*

immortal /ɪˈmɔːtl/ *adj* **1** who/that does not die; who/that lives for ever; not mortal(1): *Do you believe that the soul is immortal?* **2** (of fame, s.t good one has done etc) likely to be remembered for ever: *He won immortal fame for his bravery in battle.*
▷ *c.n* **3** (*formal*) person who is likely to be remembered for ever: *He is one of the immortals of English literature.* Compare mortal(4).
immortality /ˌɪmɔːˈtælɪtɪ/ *u.n* fact or state of being immortal(1,2): *the immortality of great artists because of their work.* Opposite mortality(1).

immortalize, -ise /ɪˈmɔːtəˌlaɪz/ *tr.v* make (s.o/ s.t) be remembered for ever: *He immortalized the small village where he was born in his poetry.*

immoveable /ɪˈmuːvəbl/ *adj* (also **im'movable**) **1** (of a person, thing etc) (also *fig*) who/that cannot be moved or changed (from a position, belief etc): *That cupboard is immovable — it's built into the wall. He's quite immovable on that subject.* **2** (*fig*) unable to feel, show pity etc for others: *That woman is immovable — she shows no pity for anyone.*
im'moveables *pl.n* (also **immovables**) property that belongs to a house, property etc because it is fixed in some way: *The immovables in the house we're buying include the carpets but not the curtains.* Compare moveables.

immune /ɪˈmjuːn/ *adj* **1** (often — *to s.t*) protected (against s.t, esp a disease) often because of a natural defence in one's body or through an injection etc: *The drug(1) made her immune to smallpox.* **2** (often — *to s.t*) (*fig*) not affected (by s.t, e.g criticism): *He remained immune to all attacks on his beliefs.* **3** (often — *from s.t*) protected (from s.t, e.g punishment), usu because of one's position, as a result of law etc: *Foreign diplomats(1) are immune from prosecution(1) under international law.*
im'munity *u.n* (often — *to/from s.t*) fact or state of being immune (to/from s.t): *People seem to develop a natural immunity to certain diseases around them. How did he win immunity from paying the fees?* ⇒ diplomatic immunity.
immunization, -isation /ˌɪmjʊnaɪˈzeɪʃən/ *c/ u.n* (often — *against s.t*) (example of the) act of immunizing s.o (against a disease).
'immu,nize, -ise *tr.v* (often — *s.o against s.t*) make (s.o) immune(1) (to a disease) by giving her/him an injection, usu of a small or weak form of the disease itself: *We were immunized against rabies.*

immutable /ɪˈmjuːtəbl/ *adj* (*formal*) that cannot be changed: *the immutable laws of physics.*
immutability /ˌɪmjuːtəˈbɪlɪtɪ/ *u.n.*

imp /ɪmp/ *c.n* **1** (in children's stories) small, naughty devil(1). **2** (*informal*) naughty child: *I just can't control him; he's a little imp.*
'impish *adj* behaving like an imp(2).
'impishly *adv.* **'impishness** *u.n.*

impact /ˈɪmpækt/ *c.n* **1** force or effect of one object hitting against another; collision: *When the two cars crashed, the impact threw him forward against the windscreen.* **2** (often *have/make an —* *on s.o/s.t*) (great) influence or effect (on s.o/s.t): *His speech made a great impact on his audience.*
on impact at the time of hitting s.t: *The seat belt will protect you from being thrown out of the car on impact.*
▷ *tr.v* /ɪmˈpækt/ **3** (*formal*) force or press (s.t, two or more things) closely together: *The path had been (or was) impacted by the thousands of visitors.* Compare compact¹(3).
im'pacted *adj* (of a tooth) unable to grow through the gums properly because of being stuck against another tooth: *My wisdom teeth are impacted so they will have to be cut out.*

impair /ɪmˈpeə/ *tr.v* (*formal*) harm or weaken (s.t, esp one's health, senses etc): *Smoking will impair your health.*
im'pairment *u.n.*

impale /ɪmˈpeɪl/ *tr.v* (often — *s.o/s.t on s.t*) (*formal*) force a hole through (s.o/s.t) using a sharp object such as a spear(1), stick etc: *His arm was impaled on the barbed wire.*
im'palement *u.n.*

impart /ɪmˈpɑːt/ *tr.v* (usu — *s.t to s.o*) (*formal*) tell or give (information, news etc) (to s.o): *I have some important news to impart to you.*

impartial /ɪmˈpɑːʃəl/ *adj* (of a person, opinion, decision etc) not favouring one side more than another: *an impartial judge/judgement. It will be impossible for me to be impartial because I know too much about her past.* Opposite partial(2).
impartiality /ˌɪmˌpɑːʃɪˈælɪtɪ/ *u.n.* **im'partially** *adv.*

impassable /ɪmˈpɑːsəbl/ *adj* (of a road, pass etc) that one cannot travel along, through etc: *The roads through the mountain are impassable because of heavy snow.* Opposite passable(1).

impasse /æmˈpɑːs/ *c.n* (often *reach an —*) (*formal*) situation where no (further) progress is possible, e.g because of a disagreement: *Talks between the employer and the union have reached an impasse and a strike looks likely.*

impassioned /ɪmˈpæʃənd/ *adj* (usu *attrib*) (*formal*) (of s.t one says, asks for etc) full of very strong feelings: *He made an impassioned speech on behalf of the miners.*

impassive /ɪmˈpæsɪv/ *adj* (*formal*) (of a person, expression on s.o's face) not showing any feeling: *William's face remained impassive even when she criticized him. It was impossible to know from her impassive expression what Martina was really thinking and feeling.*
im'passively *adv.* **impassivity** /ˌɪmpæˈsɪvɪtɪ/ *u.n.*

impatient /ɪmˈpeɪʃənt/ *adj* **1** (often — *for, to do, s.t*) not wanting to wait (for, to do, s.t): *The children are impatient for the show to start. She was impatient to get started on the work. Don't be so impatient, we'll soon be there.* Opposite patient(1). **2** (often — *with s.o*) (*derog*) not willing to overlook s.o's faults etc: *She got very impatient with his habit of always being late.*
im'patience *u.n* fact or state of not wanting to wait for s.o/s.t or of not being willing to overlook s.o's faults: *She waited with growing impatience for him to arrive.* Opposite patience(1).
im'patiently *adv.*

impeach /ɪmˈpiːtʃ/ *tr.v* (*law*) accuse (s.o, esp a member of a government) of a crime against the country.
im'peachment *c/u.n.*

impeccable /ɪmˈpekəbl/ *adj* (*formal*) **1** (of a person, clothes etc) perfect, very clean and tidy: *Linda always looks impeccable. She wore an impeccable outfit(1).* **2** (of behaviour etc) perfect, not (ever) doing or having done anything wrong: *an impeccable character.*
im'peccably *adv.*

impecunious /ˌɪmpɪˈkjuːnɪəs/ *adj* (*formal*) having very little or no money to spend: *They are too impecunious to buy anything but necessities.*
impe'cuniousness *u.n.*

impede /ɪmˈpiːd/ *tr.v* (*formal*) cause (s.o/s.t) to move very slowly; prevent the immediate progress of (s.o/s.t): *The large crowds impeded the movement of the procession. The rescue has been impeded by the weather.*

impediment /ɪmˈpedɪmənt/ *c.n* **1** (often *an — to s.t*) (*formal*) thing that delays or prevents the progress (of s.t): *His lack of experience was an impediment to further progress.* **2** (*technical*) small problem that affect's one's eyesight, speech etc: *a slight speech impediment. You have an impediment in your left eye but it can be corrected by wearing glasses.*

impel /ɪmˈpel/ *tr.v* (-ll-) (*formal*) **1** (often — *s.o/ s.t forwards, backwards* etc) push (s.o/s.t) with some force (forwards etc): *The pressure of the people behind impelled him to the front of the crowd.* **2** (usu — *s.o to do s.t*) force or drive (s.o to do s.t): *I felt impelled to defend her against such an unjust accusation.*

impending /ɪmˈpendɪŋ/ *adj* (often of s.t bad) that is going to happen very soon: *He had a feeling of impending disaster. With examinations impending, he became nervous* ⇨ imminent.

impenetrable /ɪmˈpenɪtrəbl/ *adj* (*formal*) **1** (of a place) impossible to get through, be entered, penetrated(1): *At this time of year that forest is impenetrable because of the thick undergrowth.* **2** (*fig*) impossible to see through: *impenetrable darkness.* **3** (*fig*) (of s.t mysterious etc) that cannot be understood: *an impenetrable mind/ mystery.*
impenetrability /ɪmˌpenɪtrəˈbɪlɪtɪ/ *u.n.* **impenetrably** *adv.*

impenitent /ɪmˈpenɪtənt/ *adj* (*formal*) unrepentant.

imperative /ɪmˈperətɪv/ *adj* **1** (usu *pred*) (*formal*) most urgent and necessary: *It is imperative that you have the plans ready by Monday.* **2** (usu the — *mood*) (*grammar*) of the mood² of a verb used to express a command, e.g 'Go away!'
▷ *c/def.n* **3** (*grammar*) mood² of a verb used to express a command: *'Stop!' and 'Go!' are imperatives.*

imperceptible /ˌɪmpəˈseptɪbl/ *adj* (*formal*) (of a difference, movement etc) too small to be noticed: *He gave an almost imperceptible shake of the head. The difference between the two offers is imperceptible.*
imperceptibility /ˌɪmpəˌseptəˈbɪlɪtɪ/ *u.n.* **imperceptibly** *adv.*

imperfect /ɪmˈpɜːfɪkt/ *adj* **1** having or showing a fault (in it); not perfect(1,2): *These plates are half-price because they are imperfect.* **2** (usu the — *tense*) (*grammar*) of the tense² of a verb which shows that an action/state began before that time and was still true, in progress, at that time.
▷ *def.n* **3** (*grammar*) imperfect tense.
im,perfect 'tense *def.n* (*grammar*) verb form used to show that an action/state began before that time and was still true, in progress, at that time: *In 'I was watching him', 'was watching' is in the imperfect tense.* ⇨ continuous tense.

imperfection /ˌɪmpəˈfekʃən/ *c/u.n* (example of) the fact or state of being imperfect(1): *His character shows imperfections under stress(1). My job is to find any imperfections in the material.*
im'perfectly *adv.*

imperial /ɪmˈpɪərɪəl/ *adj* (*attrib*) **1** of or referring to (the power of) an emperor, empress or empire: *imperial rule; an imperial command.* **2** (UK) of a standard system of weights and measures: *an imperial ounce(1).*

im,peria,lism *u.n* **1** (belief in the) political system of having power and control over other countries. ⇨ Empire(1). **2** (belief in the) political system of having economic(1) power and control over other countries.
im'peria,list *c.n* (also *attrib*) person who believes in imperialism.
im,peria'listic *adj.* **im,peria'listically** *adv.*
im'perially *adv* in an imperial(1) way: *Imperially, she ordered him to stand in front of her.*

imperil /ɪmˈperɪl/ *tr.v* (-ll-, US -l-) (*formal*) place or put (s.o/s.t) in (great) danger: *You have imperilled our plans by your stupidity.*

imperious /ɪmˈpɪərɪəs/ *adj* (*formal*) (often *derog*); (of a way of behaving, speaking) (too) proud and arrogant, and showing that one expects always to be obeyed: *I object to the imperious way he orders everybody about.*
im'periously *adv.* **im'periousness** *u.n.*

impermeable /ɪmˈpɜːmɪəbl/ *adj* (*technical*) (of a substance, e.g earth, rock) that does not allow water or other liquids to go through it/them; not permeable: *an impermeable layer(1) of rock.*

impermissible /ˌɪmpəˈmɪsɪbl/ *adj* (*formal*) that cannot be allowed; not permissible: *impermissible conduct.*

impersonal /ɪmˈpɜːsənl/ *adj* **1** not having, showing, one's personal feelings or attitudes(2); not allowing personal feelings to affect s.t: *Anne wrote us a very impersonal letter of thanks. You must try to be impersonal when reviewing staff salaries.* **2** (*attrib*) (often — *pronoun/verb*) (*grammar*) that is/has a subject that is not, and does not refer to, a person or thing: *In 'It is raining', 'It' is an impersonal pronoun.*
im'personally *adv.*

impersonate /ɪmˈpɜːsəˌneɪt/ *tr.v* **1** copy the way (s.o) talks, behaves etc to amuse other people: *He's very good at impersonating many of the famous sports people.* **2** pretend to be (s.o) in order to deceive: *He impersonated the commander and got past the guards.*
impersonation /ɪmˌpɜːsəˈneɪʃən/ *c/u.n.*
im'perso,nator *c.n* person who impersonates s.o, esp in order to amuse people.

impertinent /ɪmˈpɜːtɪnənt/ *adj* (*formal*) rude; showing no respect: *Don't be so impertinent to your mother! She's such an impertinent little girl.*
im'pertinence *c/u.n* (example of the) fact or state of being rude or showing no respect, esp to s.o older: *I've had enough of your impertinence!*
im'pertinently *adv.*

imperturbable /ˌɪmpəˈtɜːbəbl/ *adj* (*formal*) who/that shows great calm; not easily excited: *His imperturbable nature has got him out of many difficulties.*
imperturbability /ˌɪmpəˌtɜːbəˈbɪlɪtɪ/ *u.n.* **imper'turbably** *adv.*

impervious /ɪmˈpɜːvɪəs/ *adj* (often — *to s.t*) **1** (*formal*) (of a person) not (easily or at all) affected (by s.t, esp criticism, a threat etc): *She remained impervious to all attacks on her views.* **2** (*technical*) (of a substance, material etc) that does not let a liquid, gas etc pass through it: *This cement(1) is impervious to water.*
im'perviousness *u.n.*

impetuous /ɪmˈpetjʊəs/ *adj* (*derog*) acting too quickly or in a hasty way, without proper care or thought: *Don't be so impetuous — stop and think for a moment.*

impetuosity /ɪmˌpetjʊˈɒsɪtɪ/ *u.n.* **im'petuously** *adv.*

impetus /ˈɪmpɪtəs/ *c/u.n* (*pl* **-es**) **1** (usu *sing*) force with which s.t, e.g a body, moves: *It only needs a little impetus to get a ball rolling. On a slope it will move under its own impetus.* **2** (example of the) encouragement or extra force (given to s.t): *Government money has given (a) fresh impetus to efforts to improve* exports(2).

impinge /ɪmˈpɪndʒ/ *intr.v* (usu — (*up*)on *s.o/ s.t*) (*formal*) have an effect (on s.o/s.t); interfere (with s.o/s.t): *A horrible noise impinged on my ears. The new law will impinge on our liberty.* **im'pingement** *u.n.*

impious /ˈɪmpɪəs/ *adj* (*formal*) showing a lack of piety or of respect for religious beliefs etc. **impiety** /ɪmˈpaɪətɪ/ *c/u.n.*

impish, impishly, impishness ⇨ imp.

implacable /ɪmˈplækəbl/ *adj* (*formal*) (of a person, feeling etc) not at all able to be satisfied, improved, placated: *an implacable hatred. We've tried to calm her down but she's implacable.* **implacability** /ɪmˌplækəˈbɪlɪtɪ/ *u.n.* **im'placably** *adv.*

implant /ˈɪmplɑːnt/ *c.n* **1** thing, device etc that is implanted(3).

▷ *tr.v* /ɪmˈplɑːnt/ **2** (usu — *s.t in(to) s.t*) (*formal*) place (s.t, e.g an idea, thought) deeply (into s.t, e.g s.o's mind): *The idea that she hated him was firmly implanted in his mind.* **3** (usu — *s.t in(to) s.o/s.t*) (*medical*) place (s.t, e.g a tissue(1), mechanical device) in a body: *The surgeon implanted a heart pump (into his body) to help his* circulation(1). Compare transplant. **implantation** /ˌɪmplɑːnˈteɪʃən/ *c/u.n.*

implausible /ɪmˈplɔːzəbl/ *adj* (*formal*) (of a story etc) that is, seems, very unlikely, untrue; not plausible(1): *His account of his escape sounds totally implausible to me.* **implausibility** /ɪmˌplɔːzəˈbɪlɪtɪ/ *u.n.* **im'plausibly** *adv.*

implement¹ /ˈɪmplɪmənt/ *c.n* (general name for a) tool or instrument: *farm/garden implements.*

implement² /ˈɪmplɪment/ *tr.v* (*formal*) cause (a plan etc) to be put into action: *Your proposal will be implemented at the earliest opportunity. When will the new rules be implemented?* **implementation** /ˌɪmplɪmenˈteɪʃən/ *u.n.*

implicate /ˈɪmplɪˌkeɪt/ *tr.v* (usu — *s.o in s.t*) (*formal*) show or imply that (s.o) is (also) responsible for s.t, esp a crime: *He was implicated in the robbery because someone had seen him there.* **implication¹** /ˌɪmplɪˈkeɪʃən/ *u.n.* fact or state of implicating s.o or being implicated: *His implication in the* scandal(1) *has affected his whole family.* ⇨ implication² (⇨ imply).

implicit /ɪmˈplɪsɪt/ *adj* **1** (often — *in s.t*) (*formal*) (of s.t said etc) not fully or plainly stated (in s.t) but intended or meant to be understood: *an implicit statement/threat. Implicit in her words was a belief that everything would come right in the end.* Compare explicit(1). **2** fully trusting and without questioning: *He has an implicit belief in the skills of the medical profession.* **im'plicitly** *adv.* **im'plicitness** *u.n.*

implore /ɪmˈplɔː/ *tr.v* (often — *s.o to do s.t*) ask, beg, for (s.t, s.o to do s.t etc) in a very earnest way:

He implored her not to leave him. I implored his forgiveness.

imply /ɪmˈplaɪ/ *tr.v* (*-ies, -ied*) (often — *that ...*) suggest (s.t, that . . .) without fully or plainly stating it: *Are you implying (that) he knew about it all the time?*

implication² /ˌɪmplɪˈkeɪʃən/ *c/u.n.* (example of the) fact or state of implying s.t or of s.t being implied: *The implication is that they were all* involved(⇨ involve(2)). *What are the implications of changing the date of the meeting?* **by (way of) implication** by implying s.t: *Though he said very little, by implication it was clear that he was blaming them.* ⇨ implication¹(⇨ implicate).

impolite /ˌɪmpəˈlaɪt/ *adj* (often — *of s.o to do s.t*) rude, not polite, (of s.o who does s.t): *It was impolite of him to interrupt our conversation.* **ˌimpo'litely** *adv.* **ˌimpo'liteness** *u.n.*

imponderable /ɪmˈpɒndərəbl/ *adj* too difficult or complicated to be thought about and assessed.

import /ˈɪmpɔːt/ *c/u.n* **1** (also *attrib*) (example of, thing that is part of, the) act of bringing goods (usu for sale) into a country: *import* duty(4); *an import* licence(1). *Imports are at their highest level for several years.* Compare export(2).

▷ *tr/intr.v* /ɪmˈpɔːt/ **2** (often — (*s.t*) *from s.w* (*into s.w*)) (cause (s.t) to) be brought (from one country, into another country): *The country has to import most of its oil. A lot of fruit is imported throughout the year.* Compare export(3). **importation** /ˌɪmpɔːˈteɪʃən/ *c/u.n.* **im'porter** *c.n* person whose business is importing(2) things: *a wine importer.*

important /ɪmˈpɔːtənt/ *adj* Opposite unimportant. **1** (often — (*for s.o*) (*to do s.t*); — *that . . .*) having great value etc; being s.t that is necessary (for s.o to do etc): *There is a very important meeting tomorrow. It is important for you to realize (or that you realize) this is a serious matter.* **2** having a high (social etc) position, influence or importance(2): *He's quite an important man in the government now.* **im'portance** *u.n* Opposite unimportance. **1** (often — *of s.t*) fact or state of (s.t) having a certain (great) effect, value or significance(1): *I don't think he realizes the importance of the decision. It is a matter of little importance.* **2** (of a person) high (social etc) position or influence: *a person of great importance.*

importune /ɪmˈpɔːtjuːn/ *tr.v* (often — *s.o for, to do, s.t*) (*formal*) ask (s.o) again and again in an annoying way etc (for s.t etc): *He spent his time importuning his father for money.*

importunate /ɪmˈpɔːtjʊnɪt/ *adj* (*derog; formal*) (always) making demands (for s.t, e.g money, favours) that are annoying, not reasonable etc: *an importunate beggar/child.*

impose /ɪmˈpəʊz/ *v* **1** *tr.v* (often — *s.t on s.o/s.t*) place (a tax etc) (on s.o/s.t): *The government is planning to impose extra duty on a number of* imported(2) *goods.* **2** *tr.v* (often — *oneself, s.o/ s.t on s.o*) force (oneself, s.o, one's power etc) (on s.o): *If you are to run the office properly you need to impose your* authority(1) *on those who work for you. He imposed a certain* (unfair) advantage (of s.o, her/his kindness etc): *I don't want to impose (on you) but could I come and stay with you for a few days?*

im'posing *adj* that makes a strong impression, has a great effect on s.o, esp because of her/his/ its size, appearance etc: *an imposing figure of a man*; *an imposing house.* Opposite unimposing.

imposition /ˌɪmpə'zɪʃən/ *n* **1** *c/u.n* (example of the) act of imposing(1) a tax etc: *The imposition of a tax on books has made many people angry.* **2** *c.n* thing that imposes(3) on s.o: *It was a bit of an imposition, his coming and staying with us for so long.*

impossible /ɪm'pɒsəbl/ *adj* **1** (often — (for s.o) (to do s.t)) that one cannot do or that cannot be done; not possible: *That's impossible; it can't be that late. It is impossible (for me) to meet you tomorrow.* **2** who/that cannot be suffered or endured(1) because he/she/it is so difficult, annoying etc: *Really, that son of yours is impossible! His behaviour is making life impossible for me in the office.*

▷ *def/sing.n* **3** thing that is impossible(1) to do or accept: *You're asking (for) the impossible as I just don't have the money to lend you.*

impossibility /ɪmˌpɒsə'bɪlɪti/ *c/u.n* (example of a) thing that is impossible(1): *That's an impossibility; you couldn't have seen her because she's not in the country. She is finally beginning to understand the impossibility of her plans.*

im'possibly *adv* (only with an adj/adv): *It's impossibly complicated.*

impostor /ɪm'pɒstə/ *c.n* (US also **im'poster**) person who pretends to be s.o else in order to deceive or trick s.o: *He said he was a doctor but when they checked they found he was an impostor.*

imposture /ɪm'pɒstʃə/ *c/u.n* (example of) deceiving s.o by being an impostor.

impotent /'ɪmpətənt/ *adj* **1** *(formal)* (of a person etc) lacking power etc to do s.t or against s.o/s.t: *He felt impotent to prevent the thieves damaging his house. He stood in impotent anger as they removed everything from his suitcase.* **2** (of a man) unable to have sexual intercourse.

'impotence *u.n* **1** *(formal)* lack of power, ability or strength to do s.t: *The unions were forced to recognize their impotence in the face of the government's new laws.* **2** (of a man) lack of ability in sexual intercourse.

impound /ɪm'paʊnd/ *tr.v* (law; *formal*) (remove and) take possession of (s.t) because it is not legal(1), because money is owed on it etc: *All his goods were impounded by the court because he had not paid the fine.*

impoverish /ɪm'pɒvərɪʃ/ *tr.v (formal)* **1** make (s.o) very poor: *His gambling will impoverish his family.* **2** reduce the quality of (s.t, e.g land, soil): *Keeping too many cows on the land has gradually impoverished it.*

impracticable /ɪm'præktɪkəbl/ *adj* (of an idea, plan etc) that cannot be done, used etc in practice; not practicable: *Your drawings for the new building are totally impracticable.*

impracticability /ɪmˌpræktɪkə'bɪlɪti/ *u.n.* **im'practicably** *adv.*

impractical /ɪm'præktɪkl/ *adj* (of an idea, plan etc) not able to do s.t well, e.g with one's hands; that does not work in practice; not practical: *Phil's so impractical that he can't even put up a bookshelf. It sounded like a good idea but it was*

impractical. Opposite practical(2). Compare unpractical.

impracticality /ɪmˌpræktɪ'kælɪti/ *u.n.* **im'practically** *adv.*

imprecise /ˌɪmprɪ'saɪs/ *adj (formal)* (of a person, statement etc) not stating or being stated very clearly; not precise: *an imprecise account of the accident. I'll have to explain how to put up the tent because the description is imprecise.*

impre'cisely *adv.*

impre'ciseness, imprecision /ˌɪmprɪ'sɪʒən/ *u.n* state of not being at all clear: *She gave us directions with such imprecision that we knew we'd never find the place.*

impregnable /ɪm'pregnəbl/ *adj (formal)* (of a place, building, position etc) that cannot be captured(4) by force; that cannot be beaten, e.g in a competition: *He was now in an impregnable position with control over 60% of the company's shares(3).*

impregnability /ɪmˌpregnə'bɪlɪti/ *u.n.* **im'pregnably** *adv.*

impregnate /'ɪmpregˌneɪt/ *tr.v (formal)* **1** (usu — s.t with s.t) (make (s.t, e.g a substance)) become full (of s.t), mix (s.t) (with s.t, e.g a liquid): *The cloth was impregnated with some kind of insect repellent(2). The poison impregnated the water.* **2** cause (an animal, sometimes also a woman) to become pregnant.

impresario /ˌɪmprɪ'sɑːrɪˌəʊ/ *c.n* (pl -s) person whose job is to arrange and put on shows, plays etc in theatres, concert halls etc.

impress /'ɪmpres/ *c.n* **1** *(formal)* mark or dent(1) made or left in the surface of s.t by s.t: *the impress of a seal²(2) on a letter.*

▷ *tr.v* /ɪm'pres/ **2** (often passive, *be* —*ed by/with s.o/ s.t*) cause a feeling of admiration in (s.o) (because of s.t one has done well): *Her honesty impressed me. She impressed me with her honesty. I was impressed (by her honesty).* **3** (usu — s.t (up)on s.o) state or make clear (to s.o) the importance of (s.t): *I must impress upon you all the need to work hard if you want to pass the examinations.* **4** (usu — s.t into/on s.t) *(formal)* press (s.t) hard (into/on s.t else) in order to make a mark, shape, impress(1): *A pattern of flowers had been impressed into the cloth.* **5** (fig; *formal*) form an image(4) of (s.t) (in one's mind): *The memory of that day is impressed on my mind.*

impression /ɪm'preʃən/ *n* **1** *c/u.n* (often *leave/ make a bad, good* etc — (*on s.o*)) (cause a bad, good etc) feeling (in s.o) because of what one does, what one sees etc; (show the) good, bad etc points about s.o/s.t: *He made a very good impression in his interview. The performance left very little impression on the audience.* **2** *c/u.n* (often *be under, get/have the* — *that . . .*) idea that is not certain and may be mistaken: *I was under the impression that you had agreed to everything but I seem to be wrong. I had the impression that their marriage was at an end.* **3** *c.n* (often *do/give an* — *of s.o/s.t*) imitation (of s.o, what s.o does), esp in order to amuse people, e.g in a show: *He's good at impressions of politicians.* **4** *c.n* mark or shape made in the surface of s.t by force: *an impression of a footprint in the snow.* **5** *c.n* quantity of copies (of a book) printed at one time: *The book has gone through several impressions since it was first published(1).*

im'pressionable *adj* who is very easily impressed(2) or influenced.

impressionability /ɪmˌpreʃənəˈbɪlɪtɪ/ *u.n.*

im'pressio,nism *u.n* style of painting (and also of literature) developed, esp in France in the late 19th century, in which effects of light and colour etc are shown in greater detail than actual real forms. Compare expressionism.

im'pressionist *adj* **1** of or referring to impressionism.
▷ *c.n* **2** person, esp a painter, who practises impressionism. Compare expressionist.

im,pressio'nistic *adj* based on feelings or impressions(1).

im,pressio'nistically *adv.*

im'pressive *adj* causing a very good impression(1) (on s.o); that impresses(1) s.o: *an impressive performance by a young pianist. Your work has been most impressive in the last few months.*

im'pressively *adv.* **im'pressiveness** *u.n.*

imprint /ˈɪmprɪnt/ *c.n* **1** (usu — of s.t) mark or shape made by (the pressure of) s.t: *the imprint of a shoe in the snow.* **2** (often — of s.t (on s.o)) (*fig*) (sign of a) feeling or effect (of s.t on s.o) caused by pain, suffering etc: *Years of illness had left their imprint on his face.* **3** name of a publisher(2), printer etc printed in a book etc.
▷ *tr.v* /ɪmˈprɪnt/ **4** (usu — s.t on s.t) cause an event, an idea etc to become fixed (in one's mind, memory etc): *Those terrible events are forever imprinted on my memory.*

imprison /ɪmˈprɪzn/ *tr.v* put (s.o) into a prison; keep (s.o) locked up in a place (against her/his will).

im'prisonment *u.n.*

improbable /ɪmˈprɒbəbl/ *adj* not likely to happen or be true; not probable: *an improbable story. Rain is improbable this weekend.*

improbability /ɪmˌprɒbəˈbɪlɪtɪ/ *c/u.n.* **im'probably** *adv.*

impromptu /ɪmˈprɒmptjuː/ *adj/adv* (done, spoken etc) without any preparation: *an impromptu speech. He's good at speaking impromptu.*

improper /ɪmˈprɒpə/ *adj* (*derog*) **1** not (considered to be) suitable according to accepted standards of behaviour etc; not proper: *The way you talked to her was most improper considering you don't know her.* **2** causing offence, esp in sexual matters; indecent(1): *improper language; an improper remark/suggestion.* **3** (*formal*) not correct: *an improper use of the* idiom(1).

im,proper 'fraction *c.n* fraction(2) that has a larger number above the line than below it, e.g ¹⁰⁄₅. ⇨ proper fraction.

im'properly *adv* in an improper(1) way: *Bill was improperly dressed for the occasion.*

impropriety /ˌɪmprəˈpraɪɪtɪ/ *c/u.n* (*pl* -ies) (*formal*) behaviour etc that is considered to be unsuitable: *You should apologize for the impropriety of your actions. He was criticized for various improprieties.*

improve /ɪmˈpruːv/ *tr/intr.v* (cause (s.o/s.t) to) become better: *He has improved (his work) over the last month. His health is improving slowly. They've improved the performance of their cars.*
improve (up)on s.t produce s.t better, of a higher quality than s.t else: *I'm sure I can improve on my first efforts.*

im'provement *c/u.n* **1** (often — on s.t) (example of the) act or state of improving or being improved (in comparison with a previous state): *His work has shown great improvement in the last month. This is a great improvement on your last results.* **2** (example of a) thing done that improves s.t, adds to its value etc: *Home improvement is one way of increasing the value of your house.*

improvident /ɪmˈprɒvɪdənt/ *adj* (*formal*) (of a person, behaviour) who/that wastes one's time and money (and does not care about what may be needed in the future): *It's very improvident of you to spend all that money and not save any.*

im'providence *u.n* (*formal*) act or state of being improvident: *He regretted his improvidence as a young man which had caused the ruin of his business.*

im'providently *adv.*

improvise /ˈɪmprəˌvaɪz/ *tr/intr.v* **1** act, sing or perform (s.t) without preparation or because one has forgotten what one is supposed to do, say etc: *It was a bad performance because the actors were not well prepared and improvised badly.* **2** do or make (s.t) using whatever is available because of the lack of the usual material etc: *As we haven't got a tent we'll have to improvise (one) using branches and so on.*

improvisation /ˌɪmprəvaɪˈzeɪʃən/ *c/u.n.*

imprudent /ɪmˈpruːdənt/ *adj* (*formal*) who/that does not show wisdom or good sense; not prudent: *an imprudent person; an imprudent remark.*

im'prudence *u.n.* **im'prudently** *adv.*

impudent /ˈɪmpjʊdənt/ *adj* (of a person, behaviour etc) who/that shows no shame, respect for s.o: *It was impudent to speak to him like that.*

'impudence *u.n.* **'impudently** *adv.*

impulse /ˈɪmpʌls/ *c.n* **1** (also *attrib*) sudden urge or desire, often without thinking about the results etc: *I had this sudden impulse to give up my job. Shops put particular products near the tills to attract impulse buyers.* **2** push or extra effort: *The government's action was an impulse to industry. It gave me an impulse to work harder.* **3** (*technical*) driving force or movement, e.g of electricity along a wire etc: *electrical impulses.* (**do s.t**) **on impulse** (do s.t) quickly and without thinking too much about it: *He bought her a bunch of flowers on impulse.*

im'pulsive *adj* (usu *derog*) (of a person, behaviour etc) acting or being done suddenly or quickly without thinking etc: *Don't be impulsive — you need to think about this carefully.*

im'pulsively *adv.* **im'pulsiveness** *u.n.*

impunity /ɪmˈpjuːnɪtɪ/ *u.n* (usu *with* —) (acting with the thought or belief of having) freedom from punishment, esp in matters of law: *She stole from her company with impunity.*

impure /ɪmˈpjʊə/ *adj* **1** (of a substance etc) mixed with s.t else; not pure(1); dirty, not clean: *impure air/drugs(1,2).* **2** (*formal*) morally wrong, esp in sexual matters; not pure(3): *impure thoughts.*

im'purity *n* (*pl* -ies) (*formal*) **1** *u.n* act or state of being impure: *People have criticized the impurity of the water from the taps.* **2** *c.n* substance etc mixed or contained in s.t else that makes the whole thing impure(1): *The impurities in the water make it unsafe for drinking.*

impute /ɪmˈpjuːt/ *tr.v* (usu — s.t to s.o/s.t) (*formal*) say or consider (s.t usu bad) to be the fault (of s.o/s.t): *The failure of this business has been imputed to bad management.*

imputation /ˌɪmpjuːˈteɪʃən/ *c/u.n* (example of the) act of imputing s.t or of s.t being imputed: *He rejected the imputation that it was all his fault.*

in[1] *written abbr* inch(1).

in[2] /ɪn/ *adj* **1** (*attrib*) (showing the direction of movement into s.t/s.w): *Go through the in door and turn left and my office is the third one.* Opposite out(1). **2** (*attrib*) (showing s.t that is popular, fashionable etc): *That pub is the in place to go. Jogging was the in thing a few years ago.* ⇒ in(10). **3** (*pred*) having power: *Labour's in and the Conservatives are out(3).* ⇒ in(7).

▷ *adv* **4** (also *pred.adj*) present at one's home, office etc: *Let's stay in tonight. I'll be in late tonight.* ⇒ out(7). **5** coming to, arriving at, looking at a place from the outside (of s.t): *When does the next train come in? She walked in and sat down. She opened the door and looked in.* ⇒ out(9). **6** putting, placing, (s.t) so that it is inside, surrounded by, s.t: *First boil the water and then put the eggs in. Put the money in and then lift the receiver.* ⇒ out(10). **7** (of a political party) elected: *Will the Labour Party get in in these elections?* ⇒ in(3). **8** so as to include s.o/s.t: *Shall we count you in for the picnic on Sunday?* **9** so as to be present, seem: *Please write in your names.* ⇒ out(13). **10** (also *pred.adj*) (of styles of clothes etc) so as to be in fashion: *Bright colours are in this spring.* ⇒ in(2), out(14). **11** available for sale: *Is the new stock in yet? New potatoes aren't in yet.* Compare out(15). **12** not existing; not visible: *The stars have gone in.* ⇒ out(16). **13** (of members of a team in some sports, esp cricket[1] and baseball) present on the field and in the batting(⇒ bat[2](v)) position: *Surrey won the toss(1) and went in to bat[2]. Who's in?* Compare out(19). **14** (also *pred.adj*) (esp of a ball in some sports, e.g tennis, football) inside the boundary lines: *The ball bounced in. Was the ball in?* ⇒ out(20). **15** (also *pred.adj*) (in some ball games) so as to score a goal, point: *Jones has put in another one. And it's in! That makes the score 80–64!* **16** (also *pred.adj*) (of the tide) at, or going to, its highest point: *The tide has come in, is in.* ⇒ out(21). For verb, or a verb followed by a noun (phrase)/pron, followed by 'in', e.g *drive-in, sit-in, work-in,* ⇒ the verb. in-. **be/come/go in and out (of s.w)** be etc sometimes inside (s.w) and sometimes outside (s.w), esp of continuous movement: *During the holidays the children were in and out (of the house) all day.* **be in for it** (*informal*) be likely to be punished: *Stop that noise at once or you'll be in for it. Oh dear, the window's broken — now we're in for it!* **be in for s.t** (*informal*) be likely to have s.t, esp s.t bad: *From the look of those clouds we're in for a storm. You're in for trouble — the boss wants to see you.* **be/come/get in with s.o** (*informal*) be/become friendly with s.o: *I'm sure Anne will be able to help us because she's in with the organizers.* **day, month** etc **in day, month** etc **out** every day etc on a regular basis, without change: *We went there on holiday year in year out.* For verb, or a verb followed by a noun (phrase(1))/pron, followed by 'in', e.g *bring s.t in,* **take s.o in** etc, ⇒ the verb.

▷ *prep* **17** present at (a place); putting, placing,

(oneself/s.o/s.t) inside (s.t, an area etc): *She's in Oxford today and won't be back until tomorrow. We live in a small village. Is Denver in America? Put the plates in the cupboard. He's in the bath.* ⇒ out(23,24). **18** (without 'a', 'the') present (in a place), inside, a building etc, for the usual purpose: *She's in school today* (i.e studying, teaching there). *He's in hospital/prison.* Compare 'He's in the church', e.g looking at it but not for a religious service. **19** (moving) towards (a certain direction, point etc): *I saw him heading in the direction of the station. He shone the torch in my eyes.* **20** (of time) (at some time) during (a period of time): *I was still at school in 1980. We usually go walking in (the) summer. Will you be away in July? She's in her thirties. I woke up several times in the night.* **21** (of time) after the end of (a period of time) and usu not later than it: *He promised to come again in a month* (or *in a month's time*). *I'll be finished in a minute, so please wait.* **22** (of time) using or needing the whole of (a period of time): *He wrote the whole book in a month.* **23** (showing the amount or number of s.t as a relation, part or total of a whole): *There are sixty seconds in a minute. They were taxed at 50p in the pound. One in five of the population could not read* ⇒ out(31). **24** wearing (a certain kind of clothing, material etc): *She was in white for her wedding. He came in his* uniform(2). *She dressed herself in her mother's clothes.* **25** (showing one's job, the area of one's work, study etc): *He's in banking/politics. She's in the army. What's your degree in?* ⇒ out(25). **26** (showing the means, methods etc of doing s.t or what one uses to do s.t): *Let's try to speak in English. He paints mostly in oils* (i.e using oil paint). ⇒ out(26). **27** (showing s.o/s.t to be part of, to take part in, s.t): *What was the name of the play you were in? Who's that in the picture? I found myself in a group of tourists.* **28** (showing the fact or state of s.t etc, the way or condition in which s.t happens): *They met in public/secret. They're madly in love. Don't you realize you're in danger? She was in tears. Sorry I can't stop, I'm in a hurry.* ⇒ out(28). **29** (showing how s.o/s.t is arranged, has or is given a certain order etc): *They stood around me in a circle. Could you put these books in alphabetical* order, *please? We usually work in twos/threes/pairs.* ⇒ out(29). **30** having: *be in profit; be in debt.* ⇒ out(30). **31** (showing how s.o/s.t is affected with reference to s.t): *The cat was blind in its left eye. He's getting better in every way.* **32** with reference to (a particular person, as an example of a certain kind of ability etc): *In this young man you see all the faults of our present system of education.* **in all** ⇒ all(pron). **in as much as**; **inasmuch as** (*formal*) taking into account the (limited) fact that: *You have to take some of the blame inasmuch as you knew what was going on and could have stopped it.* **in itself** if one considers only this one thing: *Wine is not bad in itself provided you don't drink too much of it.* **in as/so far as**; **insofar as** (*formal*) to the degree or extent that: *I'll give you the facts insofar as I know them.* **in that . . .** (*formal*) for the (very) reason or cause that . . .: *Smoking in public places is harmful in that it damages the health of other people.*

in- *adj* **1** showing that s.t is used for things

coming in: *an in-tray*. Compare in²(1). Opposite out. **2** popular: *an in-group*. ⇨ in-joke, in-patient, in-service. Compare in²(2).

‚inas'much ‚as ⇨ in².

'in-‚depth *attrib.adj* thorough: *an in-depth survey(1)*.

'in-‚joke *c.n* joke about a person, situation etc which is amusing only to people who know the person, situation etc.

inmost /'ɪn‚məʊst/ ⇨ innermost.

'inner *attrib.adj* **1** (being placed) inside s.t: *an inner room*; *the inner ear*. **2** (also **'inner‚most**) (of thoughts, a feeling etc) that one keeps hidden, secret: *He's not the kind of person who shows his inner feelings*.

‚inner 'circle *c.n* group of people who are at the centre of an activity/organization, who have positions of power etc: *She's part of an inner circle who have all the authority(1)*.

innermost /'ɪnə‚məʊst/ *adj* (also **'in‚most**) **1** (being, placed) in the furthest position from the outside, from the surface of s.t: *The innermost rooms in the building have no direct sunlight*. **2** ⇨ inner(2).

'inner ‚tube *c.n* rubber tube that holds the air inside a tyre.

ins *def.pl.n* **the ins and outs (of s.t)** (*informal*) all the various different ways in which a system, business etc works: *It took him a long time to learn the ins and outs of his father's business*.

‚inso'far ‚as ⇨ in²(*prep*).

‚in-tray *c.n* tray that letters, papers etc are put in before they are dealt with. ⇨ out-tray.

inward /'ɪnwəd/ *attrib.adj* **1** of, on, towards, the inside (of s.t): *We followed the path until it made an inward bend then we left it and walked across the fields*. **2** inside (oneself, one's mind etc): *I noticed his inward smile as he watched his daughter with pride*. ⇨ outward.

'inwardly *adv* secretly, privately: *Inwardly he was very disappointed when he lost the match but he didn't show it too much*. ⇨ outwardly.

'inwardness *u.n*.

'inwards *adv* (US **'inward**) towards the inside or inner part (of s.t): *Her feet turn inwards when she walks. The road followed the coast and then bent inwards towards the town*.

inability /‚ɪnə'bɪlɪtɪ/ *u.n* (usu — *to do s.t*) lack of power or ability (to do s.t): *He expressed his inability to help us over our problems. I was surprised at her inability to be alone for any length of time*. ⇨ unable.

inaccessible /‚ɪnæk'sesəbl/ *adj* (often — *to s.o/s.t*) (*formal*) (usu of a place) that cannot be reached (by s.o/s.t); not accessible (to s.o/s.t): *The lack of proper roads made the village almost inaccessible to motor vehicles. The bad weather made the district inaccessible (by car) and supplies had to be flown in*.

inaccessibility /‚ɪnæk‚sesə'bɪlɪtɪ/ *u.n*.

inaccurate /ɪn'ækjʊrɪt/ *adj* who/that is not correct or accurate (i.e in what one says, writes etc): *That statement is completely inaccurate; you should check the facts before you speak*.

inaccuracy /ɪn'ækjʊrəsɪ/ *c/u.n* (*pl-ies*) (example of) fact or state of not being correct: *Your composition is full of inaccuracies. The inaccuracy of your sums shows that you did not check your answers*. Opposite accuracy.

in'accurately *adv*.

inactive /ɪn'æktɪv/ *adj* **1** (*formal*) not doing anything; not taking part in anything; not active: *She's been politically inactive for the last few months because she's been too busy studying*. **2** not doing much physical(1) exercise: *If I've been inactive for a few days I start to feel fat and uncomfortable*. **3** (of a volcano) no longer likely to explode and send out lava.

in'actively *adv*. **‚inac'tivity** *u.n*.

inaction /ɪn'ækʃən/ *u.n* (*formal*) fact or state of doing nothing, not moving, not being active: *By your inaction we have lost any chance of getting the work*.

inadequate /ɪn'ædɪkwɪt/ *adj* **1** not enough or sufficient (of s.t); not adequate(1): *The supplies were inadequate to keep us going for more than a few days*. **2** (of a person) (feeling) not able to manage or deal with s.t, e.g a problem, one's life, because of a lack of training, knowledge, one's own failures etc: *Her criticism of his behaviour left him feeling rather inadequate*.

inadequacy /ɪn'ædɪkwɪsɪ/ *c/u.n* (*pl-ies*) (often — *of s.o/s.t*) (example of) being or feeling inadequate: *The inadequacy of the staff causes all kinds of problems*. Opposite adequacy.

in'adequately *adv*.

inadmissible /‚ɪnəd'mɪsəbl/ *adj* (*law*) (of evidence(2)) that cannot be admitted or accepted (in a court of law): *The evidence was ruled inadmissible and the case was dismissed*. Opposite admissible.

inadmissibility /‚ɪnəd‚mɪsə'bɪlɪtɪ/ *u.n*.

inadvertent /‚ɪnəd'vɜːtənt/ *adj* (*formal*) (done or happening) by mistake, without proper attention: *His inadvertent remarks caused a row between them*.

‚inad'vertence *u.n*. **‚inad'vertently** *adv*.

inadvisable /‚ɪnəd'vaɪzəbl/ *adj* (*formal*) that is unwise, cannot be recommended; is not advisable: *It is inadvisable to go out at night alone in this city*.

inadvisability /‚ɪnəd‚vaɪzə'bɪlɪtɪ/ *u.n*.

inalienable /ɪn'eɪlɪənəbl/ *attrib.adj* (*formal*) (of a right) that cannot be given or taken away: *It is an inalienable right of the people to take wood from the common land near their homes*.

inane /ɪ'neɪn/ *adj* (*derog*) (of a person, remark, behaviour etc) stupid, foolish, boring: *I got tired of listening to his inane conversation and left*.

i'nanely *adv*. **inanity** /ɪ'nænɪtɪ/ *c/u.n*.

inanimate /ɪ'nænɪmɪt/ *adj* (*formal*) not having the quality of being alive (esp as compared to living things such as people, animals, plants); not animate: *inanimate objects such as stones and rocks*.

inanity ⇨ inane.

inapplicable /‚ɪnə'plɪkəbl/ *adj* (often — *to s.o/s.t*) (esp of a rule etc) that does not apply (to s.o/s.t); cannot be used (against s.o/s.t); not applicable: *The rules are inapplicable in such a situation*.

inapplicability /‚ɪnə‚plɪkə'bɪlɪtɪ/ *u.n*.

inappropriate /‚ɪnə'prəʊprɪət/ *adj* (often — *for, to (do), s.t*) not suitable or right (for an occasion etc); not appropriate¹: *It would be inappropriate to say anything about our plans at this stage. Is this hat inappropriate for/to the meeting?*

‚inap'propriately *adv.* **‚inap'propriateness** *u.n.*

inarticulate /‚ɪnɑː'tɪkjʊlɪt/ *adj* (*formal*) **1** (of a person) not able to express oneself clearly; not articulate(2): *He's rather shy and becomes almost inarticulate when you ask him a question.* **2** (of s.t said) not spoken clearly (so that it is difficult to hear or understand); not articulate(1): *He gave such an inarticulate speech that it was difficult to understand what he really felt about the subject.* **‚inar'ticulately** *adv.* **‚inar'ticulateness** *u.n.*

inasmuch as ⇨ in².

inattentive /‚ɪnə'tentɪv/ *adj* (often — *to s.t*) (*derog*) not listening carefully, not attentive , (to s.t): *The teacher had to deal with a lazy and inattentive class.*

inattention /‚ɪnə'tenʃən/ *u.n* (often — *to s.t*) fact or state of not being attentive (to s.t): *His inattention to detail led to many mistakes in the book.* Opposite attention. **‚inat'tentively** *adv.* **‚inat'tentiveness** *u.n.*

inaudible /ɪn'ɔːdəbl/ *adj* (*formal*) who/that cannot be heard at all or at all clearly; not audible: *She was almost inaudible and I had to lean forward to catch what she was saying.* **inaudibility** /ɪn‚ɔːdə'bɪlɪtɪ/ *u.n.* **in'audibly** *adv.*

inaugurate /ɪn'ɔːgjʊˌreɪt/ *tr.v* (*formal*) **1** hold a ceremony to introduce (s.o) to a high position or office: *The new American President was inaugurated in Washington yesterday.* **2** officially open (a new building, an exhibition etc): *The Health Minister inaugurated the new hospital.* **3** be the start or beginning of (s.t new): *The* launch(3) *of the* satellite(2) *inaugurated a whole new era of space exploration.*

inaugural /ɪn'ɔːgjʊrəl/ *attrib.adj* **1** of or referring to a speech etc made by a person starting a new job or at the opening of s.t: *an inaugural lecture/ceremony.* ▷ *c.n* **2** inaugural(1) speech, lecture or ceremony: *I'll never forget her inaugural when she first came to this university.*

inauguration /ɪn‚ɔːgjʊ'reɪʃən/ *c/u.n* (often — *of s.o/s.t*) (example of the) fact or state of inaugurating s.o/s.t or of being inaugurated: *Are you going to Professor Scott's inauguration?*

inauspicious /‚ɪnɔː'spɪʃəs/ *adj* (*formal*) (of s.t that happens) unlucky; starting badly (and so likely to lead to further bad things); not auspicious: *Missing the train proved to be an inauspicious start to our holiday.* **‚inau'spiciously** *adv.* **‚inau'spiciousness** *u.n.*

inboard /'ɪnbɔːd/ *adj* (esp of an engine in a boat) that is inside the hull: *an inboard motor.* Opposite outboard.

inborn /'ɪnbɔːn/ *adj* (of a personal characteristic(2)) (that appears to be) possessed by s.o from her/his birth: *an inborn* talent(1) *as a painter; an inborn love of music.* Compare inbred(1).

inbred /ɪn'bred/ *adj* **1** (usu of s.t in one's character) that one has had from an early age because of one's training etc: *He has an inbred politeness. Her opinions are inbred.* Compare inborn. **2** (of a person, group of people etc) having (come from generations(2) of) closely related ancestors (and often leading to mental or physical deformities: *Many people living in those distant islands are inbred* (or *have inbred* physical(1) *problems*).

inbreeding /ɪn'briːdɪŋ/ *u.n* fact or state of being inbred(2): *People in that area show signs of many years of inbreeding.*

Inc /ɪŋk/ *abbr* (US) incorporated: *World Tours Inc.*

incalculable /ɪn'kælkjʊləbl/ *adj* (*formal*) that cannot be counted, valued or measured (often because it is so great); not calculable: *a painting of incalculable value; an incalculable risk.*

incandescent /‚ɪnkæn'desnt/ *adj* (*technical*) that gives out light when heated: *an incandescent lamp.* **‚incan'descence** *u.n.*

incantation /‚ɪnkæn'teɪʃən/ *c/u.n* (*formal*) (example of the) using or saying of words in making a magic(1) spell.

incapable /ɪn'keɪpəbl/ *adj* (often — *of* (*doing*) *s.t*) **1** not able (to do s.t), usu because of one's nature; not capable(2): *He's incapable of doing a full day's work.* **2** not able to control oneself, manage s.t, e.g because one is drunk, mentally or physically(1) weak: *He was found drunk and incapable behind the wheel of his car. He was judged to be incapable of running his affairs.* **incapability** /ɪn‚keɪpə'bɪlɪtɪ/ *u.n.*

incapacitate /‚ɪnkə'pæsɪˌteɪt/ *tr.v* (*formal*) (of an accident etc) make (s.o) unable to do s.t, esp her/his usual work: *The accident incapacitated him and he had to give up his job. He was incapacitated by his fear of making a mistake.* **incapacitation** /‚ɪnkəˌpæsɪ'teɪʃən/, incapacity /‚ɪnkə'pæsɪtɪ/ *u.n.*

incarcerate /ɪn'kɑːsəˌreɪt/ *tr.v* (*formal*; *joking*) put (s.o) in prison; stop (s.o) from leaving a place: *The heavy snow meant that we were incarcerated in the house for days.* **incarceration** /ɪn‚kɑːsə'reɪʃən/ *u.n.*

incarnate /ɪn'kɑːnɪt/ *adj* **1** (placed after the noun) (*formal*) (being thought of as) having the physical body or shape represented by the noun: *He's a devil incarnate. She is evil incarnate.* ▷ *tr.v* /ɪn'kɑːˌneɪt/ **2** (*formal*) show or represent (s.o/s.t) in one's own physical form; be a living example of (s.o/s.t): *He incarnates all that is wrong with our society.*

incarnation /‚ɪnkɑː'neɪʃən/ *n* **1** *c/u.n* (usu — *of s.o/s.t*) (example of the) fact or state of being incarnate(1): *He's the incarnation of cruelty.* **2** *def.n* (usu with capital **I**) (in the Christian(1) religion) taking of bodily form by Jesus.

incautious /ɪn'kɔːʃəs/ *adj* (*formal*) (saying or doing s.t) without taking proper care, thinking clearly etc; not cautious: *an incautious remark.* **in'cautiously** *adv.* **in'cautiousness** *u.n.*

incendiary /ɪn'sendɪərɪ/ *adj* (usu *attrib*) **1** (of a device, bomb etc) that causes s.t, e.g a building, to burn: *incendiary bombs.* **2** (of a speech etc) that is intended to cause trouble, stir up feelings: *He gave an incendiary speech that soon had the audience shouting.* ⇨ inflammatory. ▷ *c.n* (*pl -ies*) **3** incendiary(1) bomb. **4** person who sets light to buildings etc unlawfully; arsonist.

incense¹ /'ɪnsens/ *u.n* substance burnt for its sweet smell, often in religious ceremonies.

incense² /ɪn'sens/ *tr.v* (*formal*) make (s.o) very angry: *His remark incensed me and I felt like hitting him. I was incensed by his rude behaviour.* **in'censed** *adj* (usu — *about/at s.t*) very angry (about/at s.t): *We were so incensed at the plans to close the market that we prepared a* petition(1).

incentive /ɪnˈsentɪv/ *c/u.n* (often — *to do s.t*) (example of) something that encourages one (to do s.t, e.g to work harder): *The employers were offering incentives to their workers to complete the job on time. There is little incentive to work in a job that is so* unsatisfying.

inception /ɪnˈsepʃən/ *c.n* (often *at/from/since its* —) (*formal*) beginning or start (of s.t): *The plan went wrong from the moment of its inception.*

incessant /ɪnˈsesnt/ *adj* without stopping; happening continuously without any break: *incessant noise/rain.* ⇒ intermittent.
inˈcessantly *adv.*

incest /ˈɪnsest/ *u.n* (unlawful) sexual intercourse between close members of the same family: *He was accused of* committing *incest with his sister.*
incestuous /ɪnˈsestjʊəs/ *adj* of or referring to incest: *an incestuous* relationship.
inˈcestuously *adv.* **inˈcestuousness** *u.n.*

inch /ɪntʃ/ *c.n* **1** (*written abbr in*) (UK, US) measurement of length (= about 2.54 centimetres): *There are twelve inches in a* foot(4). *Inches are not officially used or taught in England any more.* **2** very small amount: *We packed our suitcases until there wasn't an inch of space left.* **by inches** by a very small amount, distance etc: *The falling brick missed me by inches.* **every inch a s.o/s.t** completely and in every way an example of s.o/s.t: *She's every inch a lady.* **inch by inch** (moving) a very small distance at a time: *Inch by inch he climbed up the rock face.* **not budge/ give an inch** not give up any of one's position, advantage, e.g in an argument. **within an inch of doing s.t** very near to doing s.t: *We were within an inch of winning the match when the final whistle went.*
▷ *tr/intr.v* **3** move (one's body) very slowly and carefully and a little at a time (forward etc): *He inched* (*his way*) *carefully along the branch taking care not to fall.*

incident /ˈɪnsɪdənt/ *c.n* thing that happens; event: *In separate incidents yesterday a number of small bombs exploded in the centre of Belfast.*
ˈincidence *sing/u.n* (usu — *of s.t*) rate at which, extent that, s.t happens: *There is a high incidence of disease in the poorer parts of the country.*
incidental /ˌɪnsɪˈdentl/ *adj* that forms an unplanned or unimportant part of something: *an incidental advantage*; *incidental expenses*; *incidental music in a play. The fact that there wasn't an accident is incidental because you drove like a* maniac(2). ⇒ incidentals.
ˌinciˈdentally *adv* **1** that happens in an unplanned way: *He incidentally remarked that he was pleased with my work.* **2** by any (small) chance: *Incidentally, do you know where he lives?*
ˌinciˈdentals *pl.n* extra things, costs: *She gave me another £5 for incidentals.*

incinerate /ɪnˈsɪnəˌreɪt/ *tr.v* (*formal*) burn (s.t, e.g rubbish) completely so that only ashes are left: *Those papers must be incinerated.*
incineration /ɪnˌsɪnəˈreɪʃən/ *u.n.*
inˈcineˌrator *c.n* oven, furnace etc that burns rubbish etc: *The hospital has a large incinerator to burn everything that can no longer be used.*

incipient /ɪnˈsɪpɪənt/ *adj* (*formal*) that is starting to happen: *incipient disease*; *an incipient* rebellion.

inˈcipience *u.n.*

incise /ɪnˈsaɪz/ *tr.v* (usu — *s.t on/in(to) s.t*) (*technical*) cut (s.t, e.g a shape, pattern) (in(to) a surface, metal etc): *A flower pattern had been incised on the silver bowl.*
incision /ɪnˈsɪʒən/ *c/u.n* **1** act of incising s.t. **2** (*medical*) (example of the) act of cutting into a body in an operation by a surgeon: *He made a neat incision above the knee.*
incisive /ɪnˈsaɪsɪv/ *adj* (of a person, what s.o says etc) very clear and able to understand/show the most important points of s.t: *an incisive mind/ person/statement.*
inˈcisively *adv.* **inˈcisiveness** *u.n.*
incisor /ɪnˈsaɪzə/ *c.n* one of the four front teeth on the upper and lower jaws for cutting food etc.

incite /ɪnˈsaɪt/ *tr.v* (often — *s.o to* (*do*) *s.t*) (*formal*) encourage, urge, (s.o) (to (do) s.t, usu s.t bad): *He incited the crowd to attack the police. The speaker incited anger.*
inˈcitement *c/u.n* (often — *to* (*do*) *s.t*) (*formal*) (example of the) act or fact of inciting: *The mystery around the island was an incitement to them to visit it. Incitement of crowds is often dangerous.*

incivility /ˌɪnsɪˈvɪlɪtɪ/ *c/u.n* (*formal*) (example of) rudeness, not being civil(4): *He was ashamed of his incivility and apologized to his teacher.*

inclement /ɪnˈklemənt/ *adj* (*formal*) (of the) weather) bad and unpleasant; stormy: *What inclement weather for this time of year!*
inˈclemency *u.n.*

incline /ɪnˈklaɪn/ *c.n* **1** slope (upwards or downwards): *a steep incline*; *an incline of 1 in 3.*
▷ *v* (*formal*) **2** *tr.v* bend or bow (one's head, body): *He inclined his head to* acknowledge(3) *the cheers of the crowd.* **3** *tr/intr.v* (often — *s.o to do s.t*; — *to/towards s.t*) (cause (s.o) to) think or almost believe (that one should do s.t, that one should accept s.t): *The way he told the story inclines me to believe him. I must admit that I incline towards his view of the matter.* ⇒ inclined.
inclination /ˌɪnklɪˈneɪʃən/ *n* **1** *c/u.n* (*formal*) (example of the) act of inclining(⇒incline(2)) one's head etc: *They showed their respect with an inclination of their heads.* **2** *c/u.n* (often — *to do s.t*; — *to/towards s.t*) (example of the) fact or state of wanting or liking (to do, have, s.t etc): *I have very little inclination to go climbing mountains. In this matter you should follow your own inclinations and not listen to other people.* **3** *c.n* (*technical*) = incline(1).
inˈclined *adj* **1** (usu *be* — *to do s.t*) in a state of feeling (that one should do s.t): *I'm inclined to believe him.* **2** (usu *be* — *to be s.t*) likely, having a tendency, (to be s.t): *He's inclined to be rather* talkative.

inclose, inclosure ⇒ enclose.

include /ɪnˈkluːd/ *tr.v* (often — *s.o/s.t in s.t*) have, take or consider (s.o/s.t) as being part (of a group of people, things etc): *You must include her when you send out the invitations. Are you including me in your remarks* (i.e Are you referring to me also)*? The work includes travelling three months of the year.* Opposite exclude(2).
inˈcluded *adj* (placed after the noun) also, together, with the person, thing mentioned: *The house is for sale with the contents included.*
inˈcluding *prep* that also includes (s.o/s.t): *Now*

pay attention — including you James. It'll cost £5 each including coffee.

inclusion /ɪnˈkluːʒən/ *c/u.n* (often (*with*) *the — of s.o/s.t* (*in s.t*)) (example of the) act or state of including(⇒ include) s.o/s.t or being included (⇒ include) (in s.t): *Air letters may not have any inclusions. There will be ten of us all together with the inclusion of the staff.* Compare exclusion.

inclusive /ɪnˈkluːsɪv/ *adj* (often — *of s.t*) that includes (s.t mentioned); that is part of the whole of the total (thing, time etc): *He'll be away on holiday from 1 August to 10 September inclusive* (i.e including 1 August and 10 September in the time). *The price of the meal is inclusive of tax.* Compare exclusive. **all-inclusive** ⇒ all.

incognito /ˌɪnkɒɡˈniːtəʊ/ *pred.adj/adv* (doing s.t while) hiding one's identity(1), e.g by using a false name, in order not to be known or recognized: *The film-star usually travels incognito to escape her fans.*

incoherent /ˌɪnkəʊˈhɪərənt/ *adj* (often — *with s.t*) (of a person, s.t said etc) not able to express s.t clearly; not expressed clearly so that the ideas etc are confused (often because of a disease, anger etc); not coherent: *She gave me a long list of incoherent excuses for being so late. He became incoherent with rage(1) when he heard the news.*
,inco'**herence** *u.n.* ,inco'**herently** *adv.*

income /ˈɪŋkʌm/ *c/u.n* (example of the) amount of money received, usu by a person for her/ his work but also by a business company, government etc for goods, services etc: *He has a monthly income of £200 before tax. The new company found that its* expenditure(2) exceeded(1) *its income.*
'**income** ,**tax** *c/u.n* (example of the amount of) tax paid to a government on some or all of one's income.

incoming /ˈɪnˌkʌmɪŋ/ *attrib.adj* who/that is coming into (a place, position etc): *the incoming tide; an incoming telephone call; the incoming President* (i.e. who has just been elected but has not yet taken office). ⇒ outgoing(1).

incommunicado /ˌɪnkəˌmjuːnɪˈkɑːdəʊ/ *pred. adj/adv* in a place where one is not able to talk to or see other people: *They were held incommunicado for several hours while the police carried out their enquiries.*

incomparable /ɪnˈkɒmpərəbl/ *adj* (*formal*) (esp of a quality, amount of s.t) that cannot be compared to anything; that is greatly superior(1) to anything else: *incomparable beauty/wealth.*
incomparability /ɪnˌkɒmprəˈbɪlɪtɪ/ *u.n.* in-'**comparably** *adv.*

incompatible /ˌɪnkəmˈpætəbl/ *adj* (often — *with s.o/s.t*) who/that is not suited to, does not fit well with, (s.o/s.t else); not compatible (with s.o/s.t): *I was surprised when they got married as I would have thought they (or their* personalities(1)) *were incompatible.*
incompatibility /ˌɪnkəmˌpætəˈbɪlɪtɪ/ *c/u.n.*

incompetent /ɪnˈkɒmpɪtənt/ *adj* **1** (*derog*) (of a person) who is not able to do s.t, e.g a job, (at all) well; not competent(1): *Don't employ him as he's totally incompetent.*
▷ *c.n* **2** (*derog*) person who is incompetent(1): *He's a total incompetent.*
in'competence *u.n.* in'**competently** *adv.*

incomplete /ˌɪnkəmˈpliːt/ *adj* that has s.t missing; not finished; not complete: *an incomplete report. The builders stopped work and left the house incomplete.*
,**incom'pletely** *adv.* ,**incom'pleteness** *u.n.*

incomprehensible /ɪnˌkɒmprɪˈhensəbl/ *adj* (of a person, s.t said etc) who/that cannot be understood; not comprehensible: *He uses such long words in his speeches that he's almost incomprehensible. After all his support for us his present* attitude(2) *is totally incomprehensible.*
incomprehensibility /ɪnˌkɒmprɪˌhensəˈbɪlɪtɪ/ *u.n.* in,**compre'hensibly** *adv.*
incomprehension /ɪnˌkɒmprɪˈhenʃən/ *u.n* fact or state of not understanding s.o/s.t; lack of comprehension: *His angry speech was met with total incomprehension by his audience.*

inconceivable /ˌɪnkənˈsiːvəbl/ *adj* that cannot be imagined or believed; not conceivable: *The distances to the furthest stars seem inconceivable. It was inconceivable that he could be so cruel.*
inconceivability /ˌɪnkənˌsiːvəˈbɪlɪtɪ/ *u.n.* ,in-con'**ceivably** *adv.*

inconclusive /ˌɪnkənˈkluːsɪv/ *adj* (esp of s.t done, a result, evidence(1) etc) that is not complete or satisfactory (and so not able to be finished, not leading to a definite result etc); not conclusive: *The evidence against him was inconclusive and the case was dismissed.*
,**incon'clusively** *adv.* ,**incon'clusiveness** *u.n.*

incongruous /ɪnˈkɒŋɡrʊəs/ *adj* (usu of an object, building etc but also sometimes a person) who/that does not fit in with, does not match, her/his/its surroundings etc: *He looked rather incongruous dressed in* casual(3) *clothes at such a formal party. Such a modern building is incongruous in this ancient town.*
incongruity /ˌɪnkɒŋˈɡruːɪtɪ/ *c/u.n* (*pl -ies*) (example of the) fact or quality of being incongruous.
in'**congruously** *adv.* in'**congruousness** *u.n.*

inconsequent /ɪnˈkɒnsɪkwənt/ *adj* (*formal*) that has very little importance, esp because it does not fit in with or match s.t said or done before: *an inconsequent remark.*
in'**consequence** *u.n.* in'**consequently** *adv.*
inconsequential /ɪnˌkɒnsɪˈkwenʃəl/ *adj* inconsequent.
in,**conse'quentially** *adv.*

inconsiderable /ˌɪnkənˈsɪdərəbl/ *adj* (usu *not —*) (*formal*) that is of very little value, importance etc; not considerable: *He spent a not inconsiderable amount* (i.e a lot) *of money on* restoring(2) *the house.*

inconsiderate /ˌɪnkənˈsɪdərɪt/ *adj* (often *be — of s.o to do s.t*) (*derog*) (of a person, her/his behaviour etc) not showing (proper) respect or attention towards other people, their feelings etc; not considerate: *It was very inconsiderate of him to play his radio so loudly.*
,**incon'siderately** *adv.* ,**incon'siderateness**, **inconsideration** /ˌɪnkənˌsɪdəˈreɪʃən/ *u.n.*

inconsistent /ˌɪnkənˈsɪstənt/ *adj* (often — *with s.t*) (*derog*) (of a person, s.t said etc) who/that does not fit in, match, agree, (with s.t else that he/she has said, believes, that has happened etc); not consistent: *He is very inconsistent; one moment he supports the government, the next he's attacking it. Their two stories of* *what happened were inconsistent (with each other).*

incon'sistency *c/u.n* (*pl -ies*) (example of) being inconsistent.

incon'sistently *adv.*

inconsolable /ˌɪnkənˈsəʊləbl/ *adj* (*formal*) (of a person, grief etc) who/that cannot be comforted or made to feel happier; not consolable: *She was inconsolable when she heard that she had not got the job.*

inconsolability /ˌɪnkənˌsəʊləˈbɪlɪtɪ/, **incon'solableness** *u.n.* **incon'solably** *adv.*

inconspicuous /ˌɪnkənˈspɪkjʊəs/ *adj* who/that cannot be seen easily or at all; not conspicuous: *The colour of the animal's skin made it inconspicuous in the tall grass.*

incon'spicuously *adv.* **incon'spicuousness** *u.n.*

incontinent /ɪnˈkɒntɪnənt/ *adj* (*technical*) not able to control the emptying of one's bowels(1) and/or bladder(1): *He had become incontinent in his old age.*

in'continence *u.n.*

incontrovertible /ˌɪnkɒntrəˈvɜːtəbl/ *adj* (*formal*) (esp of evidence, facts etc) that cannot be shown to be wrong: *I have incontrovertible evidence of his part in the crime.*

incontro'vertibly *adv.*

inconvenient /ˌɪnkənˈviːnɪənt/ *adj* that causes inconvenience(1); not convenient(1): *It will be inconvenient for me to meet you then. His request for help came at an inconvenient time.*

incon'venience *c/u.n* **1** (example of the) fact or state of causing a problem or difficulty (to s.o): *I'm sorry if I caused any inconvenience by arriving late.*

▷ *tr.v* **2** (*formal*) cause inconvenience(1) to (s.o): *I hope it will not inconvenience you if I change the date of our meeting.*

incon'veniently *adv.*

incorporate /ɪnˈkɔːpəˌreɪt/ *tr.v* (often — *s.t in(to) s.t*) (*formal*) include (s.t) (in s.t larger) so that it forms a part of it; have (s.t) as a part (of s.t else): *They were unable to incorporate all his ideas in the new model of the car. The new housing development incorporates flats for old people.*

in'corpo,rated *adj* (often with capital **I**; *abbr Inc*) (US) (in the title of a business company) made a corporation(1) by law: *International Services, Inc.* ⇒ limited liability.

incorporation /ɪnˌkɔːpəˈreɪʃən/ *u.n* (often *the — of s.t into s.t*).

incorrect /ˌɪnkəˈrekt/ *adj* **1** wrong; not accurate; not correct(1,2): *The measurements were incorrect so the wood was too short.* **2** (*formal*) that is not (considered to be) right according to accepted standards of behaviour; not correct(3): *It was incorrect of him to go to a formal dinner dressed in a shirt with short sleeves.*

incor'rectly *adv.* **incor'rectness** *u.n.*

incorrigible /ɪnˈkɒrɪdʒəbl/ *adj* (*formal*) (of a person, behaviour etc) who/that is (continually) bad in some way and unlikely to change for the better: *Her son is an incorrigible liar.*

incorrigibility /ɪnˌkɒrɪdʒəˈbɪlɪtɪ/ *u.n.* **in'corrigibly** *adv.*

incorruptible /ˌɪnkəˈrʌptəbl/ *adj* (of a person) who cannot be bribed(2); not corruptible: *We expect the police to be incorruptible.*

incorruptibility /ˌɪnkəˌrʌptəˈbɪlɪtɪ/ *u.n.* **incor-'ruptibly** *adv.*

increase /ˈɪnkriːs/ *c/u.n* **1** (often — *in s.t*) (amount, quantity etc of the) fact or state of getting larger, greater etc: *There has been some increase in crime in the last year. He received an increase in his salary.* **be on the increase** be becoming larger, more frequent: *Crime is on the increase.* Opposite decrease(1).

▷ *tr/intr.v* /ɪnˈkriːs/ **2** (cause (s.t) to) become larger, greater etc (in amount, quantity etc): *Crime has increased in the last year. They increased her salary to £1000 a week.* Opposite decrease(2).

in'creasingly *adv* more and more: *It was becoming increasingly difficult to live on such low wages. Increasingly, young people today are prepared to question the opinions of their parents.*

incredible /ɪnˈkredəbl/ *adj* **1** that cannot (really) be believed; not credible: *His excuse was incredible and nobody believed him.* **2** (*informal*) (of a person, thing etc) who/that is very surprising (because he/she/it is so good, bad, wonderful etc): *It's incredible the way Jane can work twenty hours a day! She has an incredible amount of energy(1).*

incredibility /ɪnˌkredəˈbɪlɪtɪ/ *u.n.* **in'credibly** *adv.*

incredulous /ɪnˈkredjʊləs/ *adj* who/that shows a lack of belief (about s.t): *She gave him an incredulous look when he swore.* Compare credulous.

incredulity /ˌɪnkrɪˈdjuːlɪtɪ/ *u.n.* **in'credulously** *adv.*

increment /ˈɪnkrɪmənt/ *c/u.n* (*formal*) (example of an) increase in amount (esp in one's salary): *He received only a small increment at the beginning of the year.*

incriminate /ɪnˈkrɪmɪˌneɪt/ *tr.v* cause or show (s.o) to (seem to) have taken part in a crime: *Her evidence(1) incriminated him and he was arrested.*

in'crimi,nating *adj* (esp of evidence(1)) that incriminates s.o.

incrimination /ɪnˌkrɪmɪˈneɪʃən/ *u.n.*

incubate /ˈɪnkjʊˌbeɪt/ *tr/intr.v* keep (eggs) warm by sitting on them or putting them in an incubator(1) until young birds are born.

incubation /ˌɪnkjʊˈbeɪʃən/ *u.n* act, state or time of incubating an egg or eggs.

'incu,bator *c.n* **1** machine that incubates eggs. **2** (*medical*) machine like a box in a hospital used to keep alive babies who are born ill or prematurely(1).

inculcate /ˈɪnkʌlˌkeɪt/ *tr.v* (often — *s.o with s.t*; — *s.t in s.o*) (*formal*) cause (s.o) to have a certain standard of behaviour, a belief etc by one's own example, by often talking to her/him etc; fix (such a standard of behaviour etc) in s.o's mind: *He tried to inculcate his children with a respect for honesty (or to inculcate a respect for honesty in his children).*

inculcation /ˌɪnkʌlˈkeɪʃən/ *u.n.*

incumbent /ɪnˈkʌmbənt/ *adj* **1** (usu — (*up*)*on s.o to do s.t*) (*formal*) necessary or advisable (for s.o to do s.t), esp as a (moral) duty: *It is incumbent on you to support your husband during the trial.*

▷ *c.n* **2** (*formal*) person who holds an office or position (esp in a church, parish etc): *The* *present incumbent is leaving to go to a larger parish.*

incur /ɪnˈkɜː/ *tr.v* (*-rr-*) (*formal*) **1** cause (s.t bad or unpleasant) to happen to one, usu by one's own actions: *He incurred her displeasure by his remarks about her.* **2** become responsible for (a debt etc) because of spending or borrowing money: *He incurred heavy debts/expenses when he bought that big car.*

incurable /ɪnˈkjʊərəbl/ *adj* (of a person, disease) who/that cannot be cured: *The doctors told him that his disease was incurable.*
incurability /ɪnˌkjʊərəˈbɪlɪtɪ/ *u.n.*
in'curably *adv* in a way that cannot be changed or corrected: *He's incurably dishonest/ill.*

incursion /ɪnˈkɜːʃən/ *c.n* **1** (*formal*) (often — *into s.w*) attack/raid(1) (into s.w, crossing from one's own territory to s.o else's), usu without being at war: *The government has protested about the incursions of foreign troops across its northern borders.* **2** (usu — *on s.t*) thing that affects (s.t, esp one's time, privacy etc): *There were far too many incursions on his time and he was unable to work properly.*

indebted /ɪnˈdetɪd/ *pred.adj* (usu — *to s.o* (*for s.t*)) (*formal*) being or showing that one is grateful (to s.o for s.t he/she has done): *I am indebted to many people who have helped me in my work.*
in'debtedness *u.n.*

indecent /ɪnˈdiːsnt/ *adj* Opposite decent. **1** (of dress, behaviour, words etc) that is/are offensive(3), esp in matters of sex: *an indecent joke. He was accused of indecent behaviour in a public place.* **2** that is not (considered to be) acceptable according to usual moral standards: *It was indecent of you to behave so badly when your father is so worried about you.*
in'decency *c/u.n.* **in'decently** *adv.*

indecipherable /ˌɪndɪˈsaɪfərəbl/ *adj* (of s.t written badly, a code(3) etc) that cannot be read; not decipherable: *His handwriting is completely indecipherable.*
indecipherability /ˌɪndɪˌsaɪfrəˈbɪlɪtɪ/ *u.n.*

indecision /ˌɪndɪˈsɪʒən/ *u.n* fact or state of not being able to make up one's mind or decide about s.t; lack of decision: *Her indecision about whether to go led to her losing the chance of a ticket.*
indecisive /ˌɪndɪˈsaɪsɪv/ *adj* (*derog*) **1** (often — *about s.t*) showing indecision (about s.t): *He's so indecisive that you can never get him to give a firm opinion on anything.* **2** (of a battle, argument etc) that has no clear result or victory (for s.o).
ˌinde'cisively *adv.* **ˌinde'cisiveness** *u.n.*

indeed /ɪnˈdiːd/ *adv* **1** (esp *very happy, ill, fast* etc —) (used to emphasize (1) s.t): *The meal was very good indeed. She can run very fast indeed.*
▷ *interj* **2** (used to show surprise, lack of belief etc): *'I think you're wrong.' 'Oh indeed! And why?'*

indefatigable /ˌɪndɪˈfætɪgəbl/ *adj* (*formal*) (of a person) not (ever) getting tired; not wanting to give up (trying to do) s.t: *He's indefatigable in his attempts to buy that business.*
indefatigability /ˌɪndɪˌfætɪgəˈbɪlɪtɪ/ *u.n.* **inde'fatigably** *adv.*

indefensible /ˌɪndɪˈfensəbl/ *adj* **1** (of a point of view, argument, behaviour etc) that cannot be (reasonably) defended or maintained(4): *His cruel behaviour is indefensible. Her position in the argument was indefensible and they soon reached*

an agreement. **2** (of a place etc) that cannot be defended against attack: *Their forces were in an indefensible position and had to retreat(3).*

indefinable /ˌɪndɪˈfaɪnəbl/ *adj* (*formal*) that cannot be (easily) described; not definable: *He was surrounded by an indefinable air of mystery.*
ˌinde'finably *adv.*

indefinite /ɪnˈdefɪnɪt/ *adj* **1** (usu *attrib*) that has no clear or precise(1) limit, e.g in length of time, amount, area; not definite: *I'll be away for an indefinite period(1) and I don't know when I'll get back.* **2** who/that is not very clear; rather vague(1); not definite: *an indefinite answer; an indefinite subject.*
in,definite 'article *c.n* (*grammar*) either of the words 'a' or 'an'. Compare definite article.
in'definitely *adv.* **in'definiteness** *u.n.*

indelible /ɪnˈdelɪbl/ *adj* **1** (of a pencil, ink, mark etc) that cannot be rubbed out, washed off etc: *His name was written in indelible ink on all his clothes.* **2** (of a memory etc) that will never disappear, be forgotten etc: *The sight of the accident left an indelible impression(1) on his mind.*
in'delibly *adv.*

indelicate /ɪnˈdelɪkɪt/ *adj* (*derog*; *formal*) **1** (of a person, behaviour, s.t said etc) rude and slightly indecent(1); not delicate(7): *His indelicate remarks made her blush(2).* **2** not showing much thought or tact: *I thought it was rather indelicate of him to ask her such a personal question.*
in'delicacy *u.n.* **in'delicately** *adv.*

indemnify /ɪnˈdemnɪˌfaɪ/ *tr.v* (*-ies, -ied*) (often — *s.o against/for s.t*) (*law; commerce*) promise that one will pay (s.o) money (against/for any loss that he/she may suffer): *The insurance company agreed to indemnify him against damage to his tools.*
indemnification /ɪnˌdemnɪfɪˈkeɪʃən/ *c/u.n.*
indemnity /ɪnˈdemnɪtɪ/ *c/u.n* (payment etc giving s.o) protection against loss, damage etc.

indent /ˈɪndent/ *c.n* **1** (usu — *for s.t*) written order (for s.t, e.g equipment(2)), usu sent to a place that supplies such things: *We must send an indent for spare parts to the head office.* **2** (in writing, printing) act or fact of starting a line, e.g at the beginning of a paragraph(1), a little way in from the edge.
▷ *v* /ɪnˈdent/ **3** *intr.v* (usu — (*on s.o/s.t*) *for s.t*) make or place an indent(1) (on s.o/s.t for s.t, e.g equipment(2)): *You will have to indent (on the stores) for special clothing.* **4** *tr.v* start (a line) with an indent(2): *Do you indent the first line of a paragraph(1)?*
indentation /ˌɪndenˈteɪʃən/ *n* **1** *c.n* = indent(2). **2** *c/u.n.* mark or dent(1) made in the surface of s.t, e.g by pressure, cutting: *The indentation in the cushion showed that somebody had sat there recently.*

independent /ˌɪndɪˈpendənt/ *adj* **1** (often — *from/of s.o/s.t*) being free (from the control of another person, organization, country etc); not dependent(1): *She is very independent and will not accept help from anyone. The country became independent from Britain in 1961.* **2** acting or decided freely and without being influenced by others: *The United Nations has sent independent observers to watch the elections. I would value your independent advice.* **3** (often — *of s.t*) not connected or related in any way (to s.t else, each other etc): *The matters under discussion are quite independent of each other and should be dealt with separately.* Compare dependent(1).

▷ *c.n* **4** (with a capital **I**) politician who does not belong to any of the main political parties: *He is standing as an Independent in the local election.*

,inde'pendence *u.n* (often — *from s.o/s.t*) fact or state of being free (from the control of another person, organization, country etc) and so able to manage one's own life, affairs etc: *She showed considerable independence and refused to be supported by her family. The country gained its independence from Britain in 1963.* Opposite dependence(1).

,inde'pendently *adv* in an independent(2, 3) way.

,inde,pendent 'means *pl.n* (often *of* —) enough money etc to be independent(1): *Diana's (a woman) of independent means.*

indescribable /,ɪndɪ'skraɪbəbl/ *adj* that cannot be described because it is so bad/good etc: *The destruction was indescribable.*

,inde'scribably *adv*: *indescribably beautiful.*

indestructible /,ɪndɪ'strʌktəbl/ *adj* who/that cannot be destroyed or damaged: *In spite of all they have suffered, the will of the people remains indestructible.*

indestructibility /,ɪndɪ,strʌktə'bɪlɪtɪ/ *u.n.* **,inde'structibly** *adv.*

indeterminate /,ɪndɪ'tɜːmɪnɪt/ *adj* (*formal*) that is not fixed or decided; that cannot be judged clearly: *At this stage our plans are indeterminate as we do not have all the information we need.*

index /'ɪndeks/ *c.n* (*pl* -es, or (4) *indices* /'ɪndɪsiːz/) **1** list of names, subjects etc mentioned in a book, magazine etc and arranged in alphabetical order at the end of the book etc. ⇨ card index. **2** mark or pointer(2) on an instrument, e.g a scale. **3** scale showing or comparing the costs, prices, wages etc of things, often based on costs etc during an earlier period: *The price index has risen five points in the last three months.* ⇨ index-linked. **4** (*mathematics*) number written or printed above and next to a number or sign to show that it is the square(14), cube(3) etc of that number: *In* 6^2 *and* $^3\sqrt{9}$ *the numbers 2 and 3 are indices.* **5** (usu — *of s.t*) (*formal*) thing that shows or explains (s.t that is happening, e.g a change in public opinion): *The disturbances in the capital are an index of the public's lack of support for the government.*

▷ *tr.v* **6** make an index(1) for (a book etc); put (a name, subject etc) in an index(1): *This title has been indexed under 'sport'.*

'index ,finger *c/def.n* = forefinger.

,index-'linked *adj* (usu of savings, a pension(1), wage) that rises/falls when an index(3) rises/ falls.

india rubber /,ɪndɪə 'rʌbə/ *c/u.n* (*old use*) = rubber².

Indian ink /,ɪndɪən 'ɪŋk/ *u.n* very black ink used for writing, drawing etc.

Indian summer /,ɪndɪən 'sʌmə/ *c.n* **1** (unusual) time of warm sunny weather in the late autumn. **2** time in one's later life when one feels young again.

indicate /'ɪndɪ,keɪt/ *v* **1** *tr.v* point at/to (s.o/

s.t); draw attention to (s.o/s.t): *He indicated the direction they should go in. It would be helpful if you could indicate the ideas we should look for in her lecture.* **2** *tr.v* (often — *that . . .*) show (s.t) by a sign, movement etc: *He indicated a wish to leave* (or *that he wanted to leave*) *immediately.* **3** *tr.v* (esp *medical*) be a sign of (s.t); make (s.t, e.g an operation) necessary: *His red face indicates high blood pressure. In this case* surgery(1) *is indicated.* **4** *intr.v* (when driving a car etc) use an indicator(1) to show that one wants to turn left, right etc: *You should have indicated when you changed lanes*(3).

indication /,ɪndɪ'keɪʃən/ *c/u.n* (often — *of s.t*) thing or sign that shows that s.t exists or may happen: *There is every indication that things will improve soon.*

indicative /ɪn'dɪkətɪv/ *adj* **1** (*formal*) (often — of *s.t*) of or referring to an indication (of s.t): *The way he treats her is indicative of his whole approach*(4) *to women.* **2** (*grammar*) of or referring to the mood² of verbs used in statements or questions: *In the sentence 'John likes me', 'likes' is in the indicative mood.*

▷ *def.n* **3** (*grammar*) indicative(2) mood² of verbs: *In that sentence 'likes' is in the indicative.*

'indi,cator *c.n* **1** (also **'traffic ,indi,cator**) one of the lights on the front or back of a car etc that can be flashed to show one is turning left, right etc. **2** needle or pointer(2) on an instrument, dial(1) etc to show speed, quantity of s.t left etc: *The indicator showed that he was travelling at over 100 kilometres an hour.* **3** sign, board etc that shows information about trains, planes etc.

indices /'ɪndɪsiːz/ *pl* of index(4).

indict /ɪn'daɪt/ *tr.v* (often — *s.o for s.t*) (*law*) charge (s.o) in a formal way (for s.t wrong he/ she is accused of doing, having done): *He was indicted for murder.*

in'dictable *adj* (often *an* — *offence*) that one can be indicted for.

in'dictment *n* **1** *c/u.n* (*law*) (example of a) formal charge for an offence. **2** *c.n* (often — of *s.o/s.t*) (*formal*) (act of) criticism (directed towards s.o/s.t, for s.t he/she has done wrong): *The rise in unemployment is an indictment of the government's policies.*

indifferent /ɪn'dɪfrənt/ *adj* **1** (often — *to s.o/ s.t*) showing one's indifference (to s.o, about s.t): *He's completely indifferent to the sufferings of the poor.* **2** (*derog*) not very good or skilled, esp in some activity, sport etc: *He's an indifferent tennis player.*

in'difference *u.n* (often — *to/towards s.o/s.t*) (showing of a) lack of interest or sympathetic feeling (to/towards s.o/s.t): *The government has shown complete indifference to the requests of the workers for help.*

indigenous /ɪn'dɪdʒɪnəs/ *adj* (often — *to s.w*) (of people, animals, plants etc) coming originally from, belonging naturally to, (a country, area etc): *the indigenous population*; *plants indigenous to these mountains.*

indigestible /,ɪndɪ'dʒestəbl/ *adj* (of food) that cannot (easily) be absorbed (⇨ absorb(3)) in the stomach; not digestible: *The food they served us in the restaurant was almost indigestible.*

indigestibility /,ɪndɪ,dʒestə'bɪlɪtɪ/ *u.n.*

indigestion /,ɪndɪ'dʒestʃən/ *u.n* (pain or illness

caused by) difficulty in absorbing(3) food in the stomach: *Simon suffers from indigestion whenever he eats fatty meat.*

indignant /ɪnˈdɪgnənt/ *adj* showing or expressing one's anger or annoyance, esp because one is accused of s.t: *He became very indignant when I said he wasn't telling the whole truth.*
inˈdignantly *adv.* **indignation** /ˌɪndɪgˈneɪʃən/ *u.n.*

indignity /ɪnˈdɪgnɪtɪ/ *c/u.n* (*pl* **-ies**) (example of a, treatment that leads to a) sense of shame because s.t bad is done to one or happens to one, often in public: *He suffered the indignity of having eggs thrown at him when he got up to speak. The prisoners suffered many indignities at the hands of the soldiers.* Compare dignity(2).

indigo /ˈɪndɪˌgəʊ/ *u.n* (also *attrib*) **1** deep blue dye(1) made from a plant: *indigo cloth.* **2** deep blue colour: *an indigo sky.*

indirect /ˌɪndɪˈrekt/ *adj* **1** (usu *attrib*) (of a road, journey etc) not going straight to a place but using a longer way: *The car had to take a very indirect* route(1) *to the station because of flooding.* **2** (*attrib*) with change or interruption; needing to be linked(4): *an indirect descendant.* **3** not (completely) honest or frank': *an indirect answer.* **4** that happens as a result of s.t else though it may not be planned or intended: *The indirect cause of the accident was that someone had left his car parked badly.* **5** (*grammar*) ⇒ indirect object, indirect speech. Compare direct(6).
ˌindiˈrectly *adv.* **ˌindiˈrectness** *u.n.*
ˌindiˌrect ˈobject *c.n* (*grammar*) noun (phrase(1)) or pronoun in a sentence who/that receives etc the direct object, e.g 'you' in 'I'll write you a letter'. Compare direct object.
ˌindiˌrect ˈspeech *u.n* (also **reˈported ˌspeech**) (*grammar*) words spoken by s.o and reported, using verbs such as 'say', 'tell', 'ask' etc, e.g 'She said she was hungry'; the direct speech is, 'I am hungry'. Compare direct speech.
ˌindiˌrect ˈtax *c/u.n* (also **ˌinˌdirect taxˈation**) (form of) tax that is not paid directly by the taxpayer to the government but is put on the prices of goods, services etc. Compare direct tax.

indiscipline /ɪnˈdɪsɪplɪn/ *u.n* (*formal*) (bad behaviour because of a) refusal to obey s.o in a position of authority; lack of discipline: *The indiscipline in the school was a result of the failure of the teachers to control the students.*

indiscreet /ˌɪndɪˈskriːt/ *adj* (*derog*) (of a person, remark, behaviour etc) not careful in what one says or does or in what is said or done, and so saying, doing etc s.t one should not; not discreet: *They were so indiscreet about their affair that almost everyone in the office knew about it.*
ˌindiˈscreetly *adv.* **indiscretion** /ˌɪndɪˈskreʃən/ *c/u.n.*

indiscriminate /ˌɪndɪˈskrɪmɪnɪt/ *adj* (of an action) done without making any difference or distinction(1) between groups of people, things etc: *indiscriminate punishment because there was no way to find out those responsible for the broken window.*
ˌindiˈscriminately *adv*: *act indiscriminately.*

indispensable /ˌɪndɪˈspensəbl/ *adj* (of a person, thing etc) who/that one cannot do or

manage without; not dispensable: *She proved indispensable when the work became too much for him. A car is indispensable in this job.*
indispensability /ˌɪndɪˌspensəˈbɪlɪtɪ/ *u.n.* **ˌindiˈspensably** *adv.*

indisposable /ˌɪndɪˈspəʊzəbl/ *adj* not disposable.

indisposed /ˌɪndɪˈspəʊzd/ *adj* (*formal*) not feeling very well (and so unable to do s.t, work etc): *He phoned the office to say that he was indisposed and would not be coming in.* **indisposed to do s.t** (*formal*) not (at all) willing to do s.t: *He was indisposed to help them as he was too busy.* Compare disposed, ill-disposed.
indisposition /ˌɪndɪspəˈzɪʃən/ *c/u.n.*

indisputable /ˌɪndɪˈspjuːtəbl/ *adj* (*formal*) (of a fact, argument etc) that cannot be denied or disputed(3); not disputable: *He had indisputable evidence that she was guilty.*
ˌindiˈsputably *adv.*

indissoluble /ˌɪndɪˈsɒljʊbl/ *adj* **1** (*technical*) (of a substance) that cannot be made into a liquid or dissolved(1) when mixed with another substance; not soluble(1). **2** (*formal*) that cannot be broken, finished or dissolved(1): *Some people regard marriage as indissoluble.*
indissolubility /ˌɪndɪˌsɒljʊˈbɪlɪtɪ/ *u.n.* **ˌindisˈsolubly** *adv.*

indistinct /ˌɪndɪˈstɪŋkt/ *adj* that is not seen, heard, understood, remembered etc very clearly; not distinct(1): *From this distance, only an indistinct shape of the house could be seen. I have only an indistinct memory of what he said.*
ˌindiˈstinctly *adv.* **ˌindiˈstinctness** *u.n.*

indistinguishable /ˌɪndɪˈstɪŋgwɪʃəbl/ *adj* (often — *from s.o/s.t*) (of a person, thing, opinion etc) who/that cannot be (easily) shown to be different (from s.o/s.t else); not distinguishable: *The twins were indistinguishable unless you knew them well.*

individual /ˌɪndɪˈvɪdjʊəl/ *adj* **1** (*attrib*) of, for, referring to, one person, thing etc: *The children will need individual attention while they are learning to read. Each individual piece should be numbered before you put them in the box.* **2** (of a person, animal, what he/she/it does etc) special or peculiar to that person etc: *His humour(1) is quite individual.*
▷ *c.n* **3** single person, esp when compared to a group, society as a whole etc: *No individual should put her or his claims before those of society.* **4** person or animal who behaves etc in a peculiar way: *He's a bit of an individual and wears extraordinary clothes.* **5** (*informal*) person: *What an odd individual he is!*
ˌindiˈviduaˌlism *u.n* state or practice of showing that one is independent in one's beliefs, way of behaving etc.
ˌindiˈviduaˌlist *c.n* person who practises individualism.

individuality /ˌɪndɪˌvɪdjʊˈælɪtɪ/ *u.n* fact or state of being individual(2). *Her writing was greatly admired for its individuality.*
ˌindiˈvidually *adv* (considering/dealing with s.o/s.t, s.o/s.t considered etc as) one by one, on her/his/its own; separately: *I will see each of them individually. Individually, the paintings are quite pleasant but when you see them all together they look the same.*

indivisible /ˌɪndɪˈvɪzəbl/ adj (formal) that cannot be divided or separated; not divisible: *The bonds*(1,2) *that unite our two families are indivisible.*
indivisibility /ˌɪndɪvɪzəˈbɪlɪtɪ/ u.n. **indiˈvisibly** adv.

indoctrinate /ɪnˈdɒktrɪˌneɪt/ tr.v (often — s.o with s.t) (usu derog) get or force (s.o, s.o's mind) to believe or accept certain ideas, esp through a long period of education: *He has been indoctrinated with the idea that it is rude to ask questions.*
indoctrination /ɪnˌdɒktrɪˈneɪʃən/ u.n.

indolent /ˈɪndələnt/ adj (derog; formal) lazy or idle: *indolent students.*
ˈindolence u.n. **ˈindolently** adv.

indomitable /ɪnˈdɒmɪtəbl/ adj (formal) who/ that cannot (easily) be defeated: *His confidence is indomitable in spite of all the problems he has suffered.*
inˈdomitably adv.

indoor /ˈɪndɔː/ attrib.adj happening, used etc inside a house, building etc: *indoor activities/ games/sports.* Opposite outdoor.
inˈdoors adv inside/into/in a house, building etc: *When it rained we went indoors. We stayed indoors most of the day.* Opposite outdoors.

indubitable /ɪnˈdjuːbɪtəbl/ adj (formal) (of a fact etc) that cannot be doubted or questioned: *He has an indubitable right to the property.*
inˈdubitably adv.

induce /ɪnˈdjuːs/ tr.v (formal) 1 (often *nothing will* etc — s.o *to do* s.t) make or persuade (s.o) to do s.t, often against her/his will: *Nothing would induce me to go near her again.* 2 (often — s.t *in* s.o) get or bring about (a certain feeling etc) (in s.o): *Good food and wine induces in me a feeling of all being right with the world.* 3 (*medical*) make (a pregnant woman) give birth; make (a baby) be born, by using certain drugs, esp when the baby is overdue(1): *Two of my children had to be induced.*
inˈducement n 1 c/u.n (example of) something that induces(1) s.o to do s.t: *He required very little inducement to join the scheme.* 2 c.n (derog) money or help provided to s.o, esp as a bribe, to persuade her/him to do s.t: *He was accused of accepting inducements from the builders to give them the* contract(1).

induction¹ /ɪnˈdʌkʃən/ c/u.n (example of the) act or state of inducing s.o or being induced.
inductive /ɪnˈdʌktɪv/ adj of or referring to induction¹.

induct /ɪnˈdʌkt/ tr.v (usu — s.o *into* s.t) (formal) introduce (s.o) into a new job, organization etc (and train her/him for it): *Ian had a week's training to induct him into the sales operation.*
induction² /ɪnˈdʌkʃən/ n 1 u.n process of reasoning in which a conclusion is reached based mainly on experience or premises. Compare deduction¹. 2 u.n (*technical*) process by which electrical or magnetic(1) forces are moved from one place to another without physical(4) contact(1).
inˈduction ˌcoil c.n (*technical*) set of wires wound round a metal object such as iron that changes electricity from a low voltage to a higher one by induction²(2).
inˈduction ˌcourse c.n short course of study at the beginning of a larger course of study or in preparation for a job etc.

inductive² /ɪnˈdʌktɪv/ adj of or referring to induction².
inˈductively adv.

indulge /ɪnˈdʌldʒ/ tr.v 1 let (s.o) do or have what he/she wants, often too often: *He indulges his children by buying them expensive presents.* 2 let oneself or s.o do, have, (s.t he/she enjoys very much): *She indulges her interest in music by spending all her free money on* concert tickets.
indulge in s.t let oneself do, have, express etc s.t that may be wrong or unpopular but that one enjoys very much: *She indulges in telling the neighbours how badly they garden.*
indulgence /ɪnˈdʌldʒəns/ c/u.n (often — *in* s.t) (example of the) fact or state of indulging s.o or indulging in s.t: *Buying such expensive wine is (a) pure indulgence.*
inˈdulgent adj (often — *towards* s.o/s.t) showing indulgence (towards s.o/s.t).
inˈdulgently adv.

industry /ˈɪndəstrɪ/ n 1 c/u.n (pl -ies) (example of the) group of businesses/organizations that manufacture goods, provide raw materials etc (esp as compared to others that provide services etc): *the aircraft/oil industries;* investment(1) *in industry.* 2 u.n (formal) fact or state of working with great effort: *He* tackled²(7) *the job with great industry.* ⇨ industrious.

industrial /ɪnˈdʌstrɪəl/ adj of or referring to an industry(1) or industries: *industrial costs; an industrial area.* Compare industrious.
inˌdustrial ˈaction u.n. action such as a strike(1) or go-slow by workers in an industry about conditions of work, wages, etc.
inˌdustrial disˈpute c.n dispute by workers in an industry about conditions of work, wages etc.
inˌdustrial eˈstate c.n area of land kept specially for factories.
inˈdustriaˌlist c.n person who owns, has an important position in, an industry(1): *He is a big industrialist with interests in steel, coal and oil.*
industrialization,-isation /ɪnˌdʌstrɪəlaɪˈzeɪʃən/ u.n fact of industrializing.
inˈdustriaˌlize, -ise tr/intr.v (often passive) set up, introduce, industries(1) (in a place, country etc): *Over the last twenty years India has become heavily industrialized.*
inˌdustrial reˈlations pl.n (sometimes with sing verb) good/bad relationship between management and its workers, esp over conditions of work, wages etc.
inˌdustrial ˌrevoˈlution c/def.n change(s) made in society by the introduction of new ways of manufacturing etc things, esp those that took place in the 18th and 19th centuries when machines driven by steam etc were invented: *Computers have started a new industrial revolution.*
inˈdustrious adj showing (great) industry(2): *When the subject interests her she becomes a very industrious student.*
inˈdustriously adv. **inˈdustriousness** u.n.

inebriated /ɪnˈiːbrɪˌeɪtɪd/ adj (formal) drunk: *They left the party rather inebriated.*
inebriation /ɪnˌiːbrɪˈeɪʃən/ u.n.

inedible /ɪnˈedɪbl/ *adj* (of a plant, food etc) not good for eating; not edible: *Waiter, take this meat away — it's inedible.* Compare uneatable.
inedibility /ɪnˌedəˈbɪlɪtɪ/ *u.n.*

ineffective /ˌɪnɪˈfektɪv/ *adj* (*formal*) (of a person, plan etc) not able to produce the result that is wanted; not effective(1): *His attempt to settle matters was completely ineffective.*
ˌinefˈfectively *adv.* **ˌinefˈfectiveness** *u.n.*

ineffectual /ˌɪnɪˈfektjʊəl/ *adj* (*formal*) 1 (*derog*) (of a person) not sure of oneself, lacking confidence (and so not good at getting things done): *As a manager she's pretty ineffectual.* 2 (of a plan etc) not leading to a (good) result; not effectual: *His attempts to calm her were ineffectual.*
ˌinefˈfectually *adv.* **ˌinefˈfectualness** *u.n.*

inefficient /ˌɪnɪˈfɪʃnt/ *adj* (*derog*) (of a person, organization, machine etc) who/that does not work (at all) well or produce good results, e.g because he/she is badly organized, it wastes a lot of energy, material etc: *The method was very inefficient and the workers produced only half of what was hoped for.*
ˌinefˈficiency *u.n.* **ˌinefˈficiently** *adv.*

inelegant /ɪnˈelɪgənt/ *adj* (*derog*) awkward and lacking grace; not elegant(1): *Some birds look very inelegant when they are landing on the ground.*
inˈelegance *u.n.* **inˈelegantly** *adv.*

ineligible /ɪnˈelɪdʒəbl/ *adj* (often — *for*, *to do*, *s.t*) (of a person) not able to take part (in s.t), e.g by law or custom, because of one's position, age etc; not eligible: *He is ineligible to vote until he's eighteen.*
ineligibility /ɪnˌelɪdʒəˈbɪlɪtɪ/ *u.n.*

inept /ɪnˈept/ *adj* (*derog*) 1 (often — *at* (*doing*) *s.t*) (of a person) completely unable (to do s.t): *He's totally inept at his job.* 2 (of s.t said, done etc) stupid or foolish, esp because it comes at the wrong time, does not apply to the situation etc: *That is the most inept remark I've heard for a long time.*
inˈeptly *adv.* **ineptitude** /ɪnˈeptɪˌtjuːd/, **inˈeptness** *u.n.*

inequality /ˌɪnɪˈkwɒlɪtɪ/ *c/u.n* (*pl -ies*) (example of the) lack of equality, esp in matters of wealth, social position, justice etc: *Inequalities in society often lead to* revolution'(1). Compare unequal.

inequitable /ɪnˈekwɪtəbl/ *adj* (*formal*) not equitable.

inequity /ɪnˈekwɪtɪ/ *c/u.n* (*pl -ies*) (*formal*) (example of the) fact or state of a lack of justice or fairness; lack of equity.

inert /ɪnˈɜːt/ *adj* 1 (of matter, substance, gas etc) that does not move, grow, act etc, e.g when mixed with other things. 2 (of a person, animal) who/that does not move; slow or lazy: *The bird lay inert on the ground. I can't get him to do anything,he's so inert.*
inˈertly *adv* in an inert(2) way. **inˈertness** *u.n.*

inertia /ɪnˈɜːʃə/ *u.n* 1 fact or state of being inert(2): *You must end this inertia and get a job.* 2 (*technical*) state of being at rest and without movement (until a force or pressure is put on it): *It needed a very hard push to overcome the inertia of the machine and get it moving.*

inescapable /ˌɪnɪˈskeɪpəbl/ *adj* (*formal*) (esp of a conclusion(2), result etc) that cannot be rejected(2) or avoided, that one has to accept:

I have come to the inescapable conclusion that he was right after all.

inessential /ˌɪnɪˈsenʃəl/ *adj* 1 (*formal*) that is not needed or necessary; not essential: *We need to get rid of all the inessential details.*
▷ *c.n* 2 (often *pl*) (*formal*) thing(s) that is/are not needed or necessary: *Why waste all your money on such inessentials?* ⇒ essential(4), non-essential.

inestimable /ɪnˈestɪməbl/ *adj* (*formal*) (of a value, quality etc) that cannot be (easily) calculated; that is of very great worth or importance: *He was of inestimable help when we were in difficulties.*
inˈestimably *adv.*

inevitable /ɪnˈevɪtəbl/ *adj* 1 (of a result etc) that cannot be avoided, that must happen: *She wasn't looking where she was going, with the inevitable result that she crashed into him. It was inevitable that I would meet him sooner or later.* 2 (*informal*) that often happens or is expected; who/that often appears or is present: *The place was crowded with the inevitable tourists.*
inevitability /ɪnˌevɪtəˈbɪlɪtɪ/ *u.n.* **inˈevitably** *adv.*

inexact /ˌɪnɪgˈzækt/ *adj* (*formal*) not correct or true; not exact(1,2): *His report was inexact in many details.*
ˌinexˈactitude, **ˌinexˈactness** *u.n.*

inexcusable /ˌɪnɪkˈskjuːzəbl/ *adj* that cannot be forgiven or excused; not excusable: *His bad behaviour towards his family is inexcusable.*
ˌinexˈcusably *adv.*

inexhaustible /ˌɪnɪgˈzɔːstəbl/ *adj* (of a quantity or a quality such as patience etc) that is or seems so great, large etc that it cannot be (completely) used up; not exhaustible: *Dennis has an inexhaustible supply of jokes and will go on telling them all night if you let him. Jill warned the children that her patience was not inexhaustible.*
ˌinexˈhaustibly *adv.*

inexorable /ɪnˈeksərəbl/ *adj* (*formal*) (of a movement (forward), a demand, progress etc) that cannot be stopped or prevented: *Is there no way we can stop the inexorable destruction of the world's rain forests?*
inexorability /ɪnˌeksərəˈbɪlɪtɪ/ *u.n.* **inˈexorably** *adv.*

inexpedient /ˌɪnɪkˈspiːdɪənt/ *adj* (*formal*) (often — (*of s.o*) *to do s.t*) not right or suitable given the circumstances (for s.o to do s.t); not expedient(1): *It would be inexpedient (of me) to say what I think about him in the present company.* Opposite expedient.
ˌinexˈpedience, **ˌinexˈpediency** *u.n.*

inexpensive /ˌɪnɪkˈspensɪv/ *adj* that does not cost (very) much; cheap; not expensive: *an inexpensive watch.*
ˌinexˈpensively *adv.* **ˌinexˈpensiveness** *u.n.*

inexperience /ˌɪnɪkˈspɪərɪəns/ *u.n* lack of knowledge or skill gained from practice; lack of experience: *He's only been in the job two months and shows all the signs of inexperience.*
ˌinexˈperienced *adj* (of a person) having or showing a lack of experience: *an inexperienced driver.*

inexpert /ɪnˈekspɜːt/ *adj* (often — *at* (*doing*) *s.t*) (*formal*) lacking skill (at (doing) s.t); not expert(1): *I'm totally inexpert at cooking.*

in'expertly adv. **in'expertness** u.n.

inexplicable /ˌɪnɪkˈsplɪkəbl/ adj (of s.t that happens) that cannot be (properly) explained; not explicable: *His disappearance is totally inexplicable.*

inexplicability /ˌɪnɪkˌsplɪkəˈbɪlɪtɪ/ u.n. **inex'plicably** adv.

inexpressible /ˌɪnɪkˈspresəbl/ adj (formal) (of a feeling etc) that cannot be (easily) shown or expressed: *To their inexpressible joy, they won a trip abroad.*

ˌinex'pressibly adv.

inextricable /ˌɪneksˈtrɪkəbl/ adj (formal) (of a situation etc) that is or seems to be too difficult for one to escape from: *It was his own fault that he had got into such an inextricable mess.*

ˌinex'tricably adv (involved, joined) in a way from which there is no escape: *Our fates were inextricably combined from the moment we met.*

infallible /ɪnˈfæləbl/ adj 1 (of a person, judgement, decision etc) who/that is (thought to be) without any mistake or error(1); not fallible: *Kate has an infallible eye for a bargain.* 2 (esp of a cure etc) that is (almost) certain to work, that does not fail: *My doctor claims that he has an infallible remedy for stiff backs.*

infallibility /ɪnˌfæləˈbɪlɪtɪ/ u.n. **in'fallibly** adv.

infamous /ˈɪnfəməs/ adj (formal) (of a person, act, reputation etc) (known or thought to be) very bad or wicked: *an infamous man/deed/ remark.* (Notice that 'infamous' does not mean 'not famous'.)

infamy /ˈɪnfəmɪ/ c/u.n (pl -ies) (example of the) fact or state of being infamous.

infant /ˈɪnfənt/ attrib.adj 1 of or referring to a baby or babies, or a very young child or children: *infant diseases/mortality(2): an infant teacher.*

▷ c.n 2 baby or very young child, esp as one of a group up to about the age of 7: *She teaches infants.*

'infancy u.n (often in her, his, its etc —) 1 state or time of being a baby or a very young child: *He spent his infancy in a small village in the country.* 2 state or time when s.t new is just starting (to develop): *When I first started work, computer systems were in their infancy.*

infanticide /ɪnˈfæntɪˌsaɪd/ n (formal) 1 u.n unlawful killing of an infant(2). 2 c.n person who is guilty of infanticide(1).

infantile /ˈɪnfənˌtaɪl/ adj 1 of or referring to infants(2): *infantile diseases.* 2 (derog) (of a person, behaviour etc) foolish as if like a child; very childish: *His jokes are a bit infantile.*

ˌinfanˌtile pa'ralysis u.n (old name for) poliomyelitis.

'infant ˌschool c/u.n (also **'infants** def.pl.n) (part of a) primary school for children between about the ages of 5 and 7: *My daughter has just started infant school (or has just started in the infants).*

infantry /ˈɪnfəntrɪ/ u/def/def.pl.n (also attrib) (with sing or pl verb) (part of the army with) soldiers who fight on foot: *The infantry was/were ordered to follow up behind the tanks.*

infatuated /ɪnˈfætjʊˌeɪtɪd/ adj (usu — with s.o/ s.t) (derog) filled with too great, and usu too foolish, a feeling of love (for s.o/s.t): *He became infatuated with an older woman. Irena is infatuated with the idea of being rich and successful.*

infatuation /ɪnˌfætjʊˈeɪʃən/ c/u.n (usu — with s.o/s.t).

infect /ɪnˈfekt/ tr.v (often — s.o/s.t with s.t) 1 cause (s.o/s.t) to be affected (by a disease, germs etc): *She infected me with her cold. The wound became infected and he almost lost his leg.* 2 cause (s.o/s.t) to be affected (by a feeling etc): *She infected us all with her happiness. Her happiness infected us all. We were all infected by her happiness.*

in'fected adj affected by a disease, germs etc: *an infected cut.*

infection /ɪnˈfekʃən/ c/u.n (example of the) fact or state of infecting(1) s.o/s.t or being infected(1): *The only way to avoid infection is to stay at home. He has an ear infection.*

infectious /ɪnˈfekʃəs/ adj 1 that causes or is likely to cause infection(1): *infectious diseases.* 2 (of a feeling etc) that infects(2) s.o/s.t; that passes quickly to s.o: *Her happiness was infectious and soon we were all smiling and laughing.*

in'fectiously adv. **in'fectiousness** u.n.

infer /ɪnˈfɜː/ tr.v (-rr-) (often — s.t from s.t; — that . . .) (formal) decide (that s.t is true etc), form an opinion, (from s.t said, from facts, evidence(1) etc): *I infer from your remarks that you don't really believe her story.*

inference /ˈɪnfərəns/ c/u.n.

inferior /ɪnˈfɪərɪə/ adj 1 (often — to s.o/s.t (in s.t)) (of a person, thing etc) (considered to be) lower or poorer in social position, quality, value etc (than s.o/s.t else, in a certain way etc): *He tries to make me feel inferior (to him) with all his talk of success. This pen is inferior to that one in every way.* Opposite superior(1).

▷ c.n 2 (often derog) person who is (thought to be) inferior(1): *He treats all his neighbours as his inferiors.* Opposite superior(3).

inferiority /ɪnˌfɪərɪˈɒrɪtɪ/ u.n fact or state of being or feeling inferior. Opposite superiority.

inˌferiˈority ˌcomplex c.n feeling or belief that one is inferior(1) to other people (and the effect that this has on oneself): *He has an inferiority complex about people who are taller than himself.* Opposite superiority complex.

infernal /ɪnˈfɜːnl/ attrib.adj 1 (informal) (used to express a feeling) annoying because he/she/it is bad, noisy etc: *He's an infernal nuisance with all his demands for money.* 2 (formal) of or referring to hell(1): *the infernal regions.*

inferno /ɪnˈfɜːnəʊ/ c.n (pl -s) (often blazing —) building, place etc that is burning fiercely: *The plane crashed in a blazing inferno.*

infertile /ɪnˈfɜːtaɪl/ adj not fertile.

infertility /ˌɪnfəˈtɪlɪtɪ/ u.n.

infest /ɪnˈfest/ tr.v (often passive, be —ed with s.o/s.t) fill or be present in (a place etc) in large numbers (with s.o/s.t bad): *The whole building was infested with rats. The mountains were infested with bands of robbers who made them unsafe to travel through.*

infestation /ˌɪnfesˈteɪʃən/ c/u.n.

infidel /ˈɪnfɪdl/ c.n (derog) person who is thought by others to have no (acceptable) religious beliefs.

infidelity /ˌɪnfɪˈdelɪtɪ/ c/u.n (formal) (example of the) fact or state of not being faithful(1) to s.o, usu s.o to whom one is married: *She could no* longer ignore his *infidelities* and told him that she was divorcing(3) *him.* Compare fidelity(1).

infighting /'ɪn,faɪtɪŋ/ *u.n* quarrels and arguments between people who belong to the same group or organization with each trying to gain an advantage over others: *I'm sick of all this infighting when what we should be doing is working together to win the next election.*

infiltrate /'ɪnfɪl,treɪt/ *tr/intr.v* (usu — (s.o/s.t) in(to) s.t) (cause (soldiers, people etc) to) get into a place, organization etc gradually and without being noticed (so that they can attack, control etc it): *The student union was gradually infiltrated by right-wing students.*

infiltration /,ɪnfɪl'treɪʃən/ *c/u.n* (usu — of s.o/s.t in(to) s.t).

'infil,trator *c.n* person who infiltrates.

infinite /'ɪnfɪnɪt/ *adj* **1** that has no end or limit, esp of s.t that cannot be measured; not finite(1): *Space appears to be infinite.* **2** (*fig*) very great, often for a long time: *She showed me infinite kindness. Infinite harm could come from taking this course of action.*

'infinitely *adv* in an infinite(2) way: *I was infinitely grateful for his help.*

infinitesimal /,ɪnfɪnɪ'tesɪməl/ *adj* (*formal*) very small, esp in a way that will not be noticed, does not affect s.o/s.t very much etc: *The reduction in taxes is infinitesimal and I certainly won't be much richer.*

in'finity *u.n* **1** (of space, time, quantity etc) fact or state of being or seeming to be infinite(1): *the infinity of space; an horizon disappearing into infinity.* **2** (*mathematics*) number or quantity that is infinite(1), *symb* ∞.

infinitive /ɪn'fɪnɪtɪv/ *c/def.n* (*grammar*) simple form of a verb, with or without 'to', usu used after another verb to express a state or action: *In the sentence 'To be or not to be — that is the question', 'to be' is in the infinitive. In the sentences 'Why don't you leave him alone?' and 'I told him to leave him alone', 'leave' and 'to leave' are infinitives.*

infinity ⇒ infinite.

infirm /ɪn'fɜ:m/ *adj* **1** (*formal*) weak and ill in the body or mind, esp because of old age: *She is now too infirm to leave the house.*

▷ *def.pl.n* **2** (often the old and —) (*formal*) infirm(1) people as a group.

infirmary /ɪn'fɜ:məri/ *c.n* (*pl -ies*) **1** (with capital **I** in names) (title sometimes used for a) hospital: *The Manchester Royal Infirmary.* **2** room used for people who are ill, esp one in a school: *the school infirmary.*

in'firmity *c/u.n* (*pl -ies*) (example of a) weakness or illness: *He's always complaining about his infirmities.*

inflame /ɪn'fleɪm/ *tr.v* (often — s.o with s.t) (*formal*) cause (s.o) to become very excited, disturbed etc (with a feeling); cause (a feeling) to become stronger: *Her words inflamed him with anger* (or *inflamed his anger*).

in'flamed *adj* **1** having become sore and red, esp because of an infection: *The wound was inflamed because it had not been treated properly.* **2** (often — with s.t) (*formal*) (having become red and) excited and disturbed (by a feeling, e.g of anger): *His inflamed face warned me that he was very angry.*

inflammation /,ɪnflə'meɪʃən/ *c/u.n* (example of an) inflamed(1) state or condition of a part of the body: *inflammation of the eyes from smoke.*

inflammatory /ɪn'flæmətəri/ *adj* (esp of s.t said) intending or likely to inflame (the feelings of) people, and esp to lead them to do violent things: *He delivered an inflammatory speech urging the workers to walk out of the factory.*

inflammable /ɪn'flæməbl/ *adj* (of a substance) that can be easily set on fire: *Some kinds of furniture have proved in tests to be highly inflammable and should be removed from sale.* Compare non-flammable.

inflate /ɪn'fleɪt/ *v* **1** *tr/intr.v* (cause (a tyre, ball etc) to) become filled with air or gas by blowing it up, pumping it etc: *You must make sure that you inflate your tyres to the correct pressure. The balloon will inflate when you open this valve(1).* **2** *tr/intr.v* (*commerce*) (cause (an economy(3) etc) to) have or get more money in circulation(2) and so cause prices to rise: *The government has no intention of inflating the* economy(3) *at present.* **3** *tr.v* cause (a feeling of too great pride or importance) in s.o: *Every word of praise he received inflated his sense of importance.* Compare deflate.

in'flatable *adj* (esp of a boat made with hollow rubber rings) that can be inflated(1): *an inflatable life raft.*

in'flated *adj* (usu *attrib*) **1** that has been blown up, pumped up with air etc: *an inflated tyre.* **2** (*derog*) filled with too great pride or importance: *a man with an inflated opinion of himself.*

inflation /ɪn'fleɪʃən/ *u.n* **1** act or state of inflating(1) s.t or being inflated (⇒ inflate(1)). **2** fact or state of more money being in circulation(2) in a country and of prices etc rising: *The government has managed to keep inflation down to 2% (i.e prices etc have only risen by 2% when compared to an earlier period).* Opposite deflation.

inflationary /ɪn'fleɪʃənəri/ *adj* that causes, is likely to cause, inflation(2).

inflect /ɪn'flekt/ *v* **1** *tr/intr.v* (*grammar*) (cause (a word) to) have an ending that is different from its simple form, e.g when it is plural, is in the present or past tense: *Most nouns in English inflect by the addition of '-s' or '-es' to the base form.* **2** *tr.v* change the tone(5) or pitch(4) of (one's voice) as one speaks, sometimes to get a special effect or for emphasis(2): *When you are reading this poem you should inflect your voice more to get the full* dramatic(1) *effect.*

in'flected *adj* (*grammar*) (of a word, language etc) that inflects(1): *English is an inflected language.*

inflection /ɪn'flekʃən/ *c/u.n* (also, less usu, **in'flexion**) (*technical*) **1** (example of the) change in the ending of a word. **2** (example of the) change in tone(5) or pitch(4) of spoken words.

inflexible /ɪn'fleksəbl/ *adj* **1** (often *derog*) (of a person, her/his beliefs etc) not (at all) willing to change; not giving way to pressure from others; not flexible(2): *Once he has decided on a course of action, he becomes totally inflexible and nothing you say will make him change his mind.* **2** (*technical*) (of a substance, material etc) that does not bend under pressure; not flexible(1): *The new hardened* plastic(3) *is intended to remain inflexible under most conditions.*

inflexibility /ɪnˌfleksəˈbɪlɪtɪ/ *u.n.* **inˈflexibly** *adv.*

inflict /ɪnˈflɪkt/ *tr.v* **1** (usu — *s.t* (*up*)*on s.o/s.t*) deliver (a blow, s.t bad etc) (to s.o/s.t): *He inflicted a heavy blow on the man's head with a piece of wood. Our soldiers have inflicted heavy losses on the enemy.* **2** (usu — *s.o/s.t* (*up*)*on s.o*) (try to) force (s.o, one's presence, an idea etc) (on s.o who may not want to accept her/him/ it): *Don't try to inflict modern ideas on people like them — they will never accept them. He inflicts his company on people who don't want to talk to him at parties because he's so boring.* **inflliction** /ɪnˈflɪkʃən/ *c/u.n.*

inflow /ˈɪnfləʊ/ *c/u.n* (often *an/the* — of *s.t into s.t/s.w*) (example of the) fact or state of a thing or things flowing or coming (into s.t/s.w): *There has been an inflow of money into the country because of the high interest rates.* Opposite outflow.

influence /ˈɪnfluəns/ *n* **1** *u.n* power to persuade (s.o to do s.t) because of one's ability, important position etc: *He has very little influence over what she does. Could you use your influence with him to get me a job?* **2** *c.n* person or thing etc who/ that has influence(1) that is good, bad etc: *His friends at school are bad influences.* **3** *c/u.n* (often — of *s.t* (*up*)*on s.t*) thing that affects or changes (s.t): *Do you think our climate has an influence on our character?* **be an influence for good/evil** be a good/bad influence(2).
▷ *tr.v* **4** have an effect or influence(3) on (s.o/s.t); cause (s.o/s.t) to change, do s.t different etc as a result of pressure etc: *A full moon seems to influence him for the worse. Don't let what I say influence you* (or *your decision*)*; you must do what you think is right.*

influential /ˌɪnfluˈenʃəl/ *adj* (of a person, s.t said or done etc) having or showing a strong influence(1,3): *He's very influential and knows many important people. What you said was very influential when we came to make a decision.* **ˌinfluˈentially** *adv.*

influenza /ˌɪnfluˈenzə/ *u.n* (*informal* **flu, ˈflu**) infectious(1) illness that causes fever and aches in the body.

influx /ˈɪnflʌks/ *c.n* (usu *sing*) (often — of *s.o/s.t*) coming in (to a place etc), usu in large numbers or quantities (of people, things): *The city is getting ready for an influx of visitors during the summer season.*

info /ˈɪnfəʊ/ *u.n* (*informal*) information.

inform /ɪnˈfɔːm/ *tr.v* (often — *s.o about/of s.o/s.t; — s.o that. . .*) (*formal*) tell/give knowledge or information to (s.o) (about s.t, that . . .): *Have you informed the company of your wish to leave it* (or *that you wish to leave it*)*? I'm afraid you were wrongly informed about the matter.* **inform against/(up)on s.o** make an accusation against s.o by giving the police, people in authority(1) etc evidence(1) of what he/she may have done wrong, and so perhaps leading to his/her arrest.

inˈformant *c.n* person (esp one who one wants to keep secret) who gives one (special) information: *My informant tells me that there are plans to close the factory.*

information /ˌɪnfəˈmeɪʃən/ *u.n* (also *attrib*) knowledge of facts (about s.o/s.t): *Have you any information about what actually happened? His head is full of useless bits of information. Go to the information counter[2]/desk/office and ask about hotels.* **a mine of information** (**about s.o/ s.t**) ⇒ mine[1] (*n*).

ˌinforˌmation techˈnology *u.n* (*abbr IT*) development, use, of computers (in industry etc).

informative /ɪnˈfɔːmətɪv/ *adj* (of a person, book, s.t said etc) who/that gives much (good or useful) information: *Once he starts talking about his main interests he's very informative. The lecture on Egypt was most informative.* **inˈformatively** *adv.*

inˈformed *adj* (often *well, badly* etc — (*about s.t*)) (of a person) having (a lot of, little) information or knowledge (about s.t): *I'd like to be kept informed about his progress. He keeps in touch with the people in power and is therefore well informed about politics.* ⇒ well-informed, uninformed. **s.o's informed opinion** person's opinion based on good knowledge and information: *The bank manager should be able to give you his informed opinion about the state of your business.*

inˈformer *c.n* (often *derog*) person who informs against/(up)on s.o.

informal /ɪnˈfɔːməl/ *adj* **1** (of a person, dress, behaviour) friendly and relaxed(1); not being full of ceremony; not formal: *He's very informal in spite of his high position. It's only a small party so dress will be informal.* **2** (of words, language etc) (as) used in conversation, in letters to friends etc, as compared to speaking in public, writing official letters etc.

informality /ˌɪnfɔːˈmælɪtɪ/ *c/u.n* (example of) informal speech or behaviour. **inˈformally** *adv.*

infrared /ˌɪnfrəˈred/ *adj* (*technical*) (of rays etc) that are below the red light at one end of the spectrum(1): *Infrared rays give out heat and they cannot usually be seen because they have a longer wavelength than normal light.* Compare ultraviolet.

infrastructure /ˈɪnfrəˌstrʌktʃə/ *u.n* (*formal*) basic internal(2) structure(2) of an organization; all the things that form part of a system and help to make it work: *The government has plans to improve the country's infrastructure by spending more on roads, schools, hospitals and so on.*

infrequent /ɪnˈfriːkwənt/ *adj* (doing s.t, happening) not very often; only now and then; not frequent: *I saw him recently on one of his infrequent visits to London.* **inˈfrequency** *u.n.* **inˈfrequently** *adv.*

infringe /ɪnˈfrɪndʒ/ *tr.v* (*formal*) break (a rule, law etc): *They were taken to court for infringing the building regulations(1).* **infringe (up)on s.t** harm, interfere with, s.o's rights, liberty etc): *The power that the police have to stop and search anybody infringes on our freedom as citizens.* **inˈfringement** *c/u.n* (example of the) fact or state of infringing: *He had to pay £10 for a parking infringement. This is an infringement on my private life.*

infuriate /ɪnˈfjʊərɪˌeɪt/ *tr.v* cause (s.o) to become very angry and annoyed: *His remarks about my appearance infuriated me and I nearly hit him.* **inˈfuriˌated** *adj* having or showing great anger and annoyance: *I get infuriated by all these delays. He received an infuriated letter from a dissatisfied customer.*

in'furi,ating adj (derog) (of a person, behaviour etc) who/that causes or is likely to cause great anger and annoyance: He is very infuriating the way he can never make up his mind. The delays at airports are getting really infuriating.
in'furi,atingly adv.

infuse /ɪn'fju:z/ v (formal) **1** tr.v (often — s.o with s.t; — s.t into s.o) fill (s.o) (with a (good) feeling, e.g of enthusiasm, energy(1)): She tried to infuse her students with a love of language (or infuse a love of language into her students). They were infused with a desire to improve the world. **2** tr/intr.v pour hot or boiling water over (tea, herbs) in order to bring out its/their special flavour: Infuse the tea for about five minutes. Let the leaves infuse for a little while.
infusion /ɪn'fju:ʒən/ c/u.n.

ingenious /ɪn'dʒi:nɪəs/ adj **1** (of a person) clever at thinking about, inventing or making s.t: He's very ingenious with his hands. Amy's an ingenious inventor. ⇒ genius. **2** (of an idea, machine etc) showing great or too much cleverness; made or working with great skill: I must admit that your plan is ingenious but will it work? This ingenious robot(1) does the work of four people and does it better.
in'geniously adv. **ingenuity** /,ɪndʒɪ'nju:ɪtɪ/ u.n.
in'geniousness u.n.

ingenuous /ɪn'dʒenjʊəs/ adj (often — of s.o (to do s.t)) (formal; often derog) (of a person, expression on s.o's face, what s.o says, does etc) simple and frank, perhaps too much so, esp because one lacks experience, is too trusting or wants to hide s.t: That ingenuous look on her face makes people think that she's more innocent(2,4) than she really is. It's rather ingenuous of him to accept such a wild story. Compare disingenuous.
in'genuously adv. **in'genuousness** u.n.

inglorious /ɪn'glɔ:rɪəs/ adj (formal) shameful; lacking any (feeling of) honour: an inglorious defeat/retreat(1).
in'gloriously adv. **in'gloriousness** u.n.

ingoing /'ɪn,gəʊɪŋ/ attrib.adj (accepting and) starting in (a job, place etc): the ingoing tenant(1). Opposite outgoing(1).

ingot /'ɪŋgət/ c.n mass (of (pure) metal, esp of gold, silver) made into a shape like a brick.

ingrained /ɪn'greɪnd/ adj (also **en'grained**) **1** (of dirt, a stain) going deep into the surface of s.t. **2** (fig) (of a belief, feeling etc) very firmly fixed (in one's mind etc) and unlikely to be changed: an ingrained fear of people with loud voices.

ingratiate /ɪn'greɪʃɪ,eɪt/ reflex.v (often — oneself with s.o) (derog; formal) (try to) gain the favour of s.o; make oneself (too) pleasant and nice (to s.o so as to be liked by him/her): He has a habit of ingratiating himself with important people.
in'grati,ating attrib.adj (derog) (of a person, expression on s.o's face) showing that one wants to ingratiate oneself with s.o: an ingratiating look on the dog's face.
in'grati,atingly adv.

ingratitude /ɪn'grætɪ,tju:d/ u.n (often — (of s.o) to(wards) s.o) fact or state of not being grateful or thankful (to(wards) s.o); lack of gratitude: I was astonished at the ingratitude he showed to her after all her help. ⇒ grateful, ungrateful.

ingredient /ɪn'gri:dɪənt/ c.n (often — for s.t) **1** one of a number of substances that make up a mixture, esp in food, when cooking etc: Manufacturers must now list all the ingredients on packets of food. **2** (fig) thing that with other things helps to form a whole or to make s.t better: The two basic ingredients for success are confidence and hard work.

ingrowing /'ɪn,grəʊɪŋ/ adj (usu attrib) growing inwards or into the skin: ingrowing toenails.
'in,grown adj having grown into the skin.

inhabit /ɪn'hæbɪt/ tr.v (of people, animals) live in (a place, area, building etc), often over a length of time or as their natural place: The mountains are inhabited only by wild goats and sheep. The castle has not been inhabited for many years.
in'habitable adj (of a place, area, building) that can be inhabited: The house was no longer inhabitable after the fire. Opposite uninhabitable.
in'habitant c.n person or animal who/that lives in a place, area, building etc: The inhabitants of the block of flats were woken up by an explosion.

inhale /ɪn'heɪl/ tr/intr.v breathe (air, gas, smoke etc) into one's lungs: She inhaled a mouthful of gas which made her cough. Do you inhale when you smoke (i.e inhale the smoke from a cigarette etc)? Opposite exhale.
inhalation /,ɪnhə'leɪʃən/ c/u.n. Opposite exhalation.
inhaler /ɪn'heɪlə/ c.n kind of small device used to inhale medicine through one's nose or mouth to make breathing easier, clear one's lungs etc.

inherent /ɪn'hɪərənt/ adj (often — in s.o/s.t) (formal) (of a quality, feeling etc) that exists naturally (in s.o/s.t): His inherent good nature prevented him from complaining. One cannot avoid the dangers inherent in such risky activities.
in'herently adv.

inherit /ɪn'herɪt/ v (often — s.t from s.o) **1** tr/intr.v receive (property, money, a title etc) (from s.o who has died), e.g through a will² or because one is the closest relative: A distant cousin inherited (the title) when the duke died. **2** tr.v receive (a quality, feature(1) of the body etc) (from a parent or parents): He inherits his good looks from his mother.
in'heritance c/u.n.

inhibit /ɪn'hɪbɪt/ tr.v (often — s.o from (doing) s.t) make (s.o) (feel) unable (to do s.t), esp through fear of s.o/s.t, because of being shy etc: She is so firm and decisive in her opinions that her very presence inhibits me from opening my mouth.
in'hibited adj (of a person, character) unable to express oneself well or clearly or to act in a normal way because of being shy etc: He's so inhibited that he hardly dares talk to a woman. Opposite uninhibited.
inhibition /,ɪnhɪ'bɪʃən/ c/u.n (example of the) fact or state of inhibiting s.o or being inhibited (⇒ inhibit).
inhibitory /ɪn'hɪbɪtərɪ/ adj (formal) that inhibits s.o/s.t: an inhibitory factor(2).

inhospitable /,ɪnhɒ'spɪtəbl/ adj **1** (of a person, welcome etc) not showing kindness or friendliness to s.o, e.g when he/she visits one; not hospitable: It was inhospitable of you not to invite them in for a drink when they called. **2** (of a place, country etc) that is very difficult to live in because it is too cold or too hot, cannot support people,

crops etc: *As you travel further the land becomes* bleak(2) *and inhospitable.*
,inhos'pitably *adv.*

inhuman /ɪn'hjuːmən/ *adj* (*derog*) (of an act, treatment etc) very cruel and without proper human feeling: *The newspapers are full of reports of parents' inhuman treatment of their children.* Compare inhumane.
inhumanity /ˌɪnhjuː'mænɪtɪ/ *u.n.* **in'humanly** *adv.*

inhumane /ˌɪnhjuː'meɪn/ *adj* (*derog*) (of an act, treatment etc) cruel and unkind and without showing proper respect for human beings or animals; not humane: *I think it is inhumane to experiment on animals.* (Notice that inhumane is slightly different from 'inhuman' in meaning as it shows a lack of real kindness; inhuman is stronger as it shows a (complete) lack of human feelings.)
,inhu'manely *adv.*

inimical /ɪ'nɪmɪkl/ *pred.adj* (often — *to* s.o/s.t) (*formal*) (of a state, condition, act etc) not at all favourable (to s.o, to letting s.t happen); hostile: *The climate in this area is inimical to the proper development of crops.*

inimitable /ɪ'nɪmɪtəbl/ *adj* (of a person's quality, style(3) etc) that cannot be imitated by s.o else because it is so individual(2): *He told his jokes in his usual inimitable* style(1).
i'nimitably *adv.*

iniquitous /ɪ'nɪkwɪtəs/ *adj* (*derog*; *formal*) (of an act, treatment etc) very bad and wicked; unjust: *It is iniquitous for the rich to be treated more favourably than the poor.*
i'niquitously *adv.* **i'niquitousness** *u.n.*
i'niquity *c/u.n* (*pl* -ies) (example of the) fact or state of being iniquitous or being treated iniquitously: *a* den(3) *of iniquity.*

initial /ɪ'nɪʃəl/ *adj* **1** (usu *attrib*) (being or happening) at the beginning/front of s.t: *Initial letters should be in capitals. The initial work was done by a small group but more people took part in the later stages.*
▷ *c.n* **2** (usu *pl*) capital letter at the beginning of s.o's name, a sentence etc: *Would you please sign here with your initials.*
▷ *tr.v* (-ll-, US -l-) **3** sign (a letter, document(1) etc) using only one's initials(2): *He was asked to initial each page of the* contract(1).
i'nitially *adv* at the beginning of s.t: *Initially she was very nervous but she soon got over it.*

initiate /ɪ'nɪʃɪət/ *c.n* **1** (*formal*) person who has (just) become a member of an organization, society etc, esp one that is secret and has special ceremonies for new members: *All the initiates had to promise never to tell anyone what happened at the meetings.*
▷ *tr.v* /ɪ'nɪʃɪˌeɪt/ **2** (*formal*) start (s.t); be the person who makes (s.t) happen: *The government has initiated a new* scheme(2) *to help the unemployed.* **3** (usu — s.o *into* s.t) make (s.o) a member (of an organization, secret society etc): *I was initiated into the group nearly ten years ago.*
initiation /ɪˌnɪʃɪ'eɪʃən/ *c/u.n* **1** (example of the) fact or state of initiating(2) s.t or of s.t being initiated: *He was responsible for the initiation of the new plans.* **2** (also *attrib*) (often — (*of* s.o) *into* s.t) (example of the) fact or state of initiating(3) s.o or of being initiated: *an initiation ceremony.*

initiative /ɪ'nɪʃɪətɪv/ *n* **1** *c.n* (usu *sing*) (move or

act that is the) beginning or start of s.t new: *It was from her initiative that the present organization grew.* The United Nations *is trying to encourage peace initiatives* (i.e talks etc to stop a war). **2** *u.n* (often *lack/show* —) ability to decide things for oneself: *When it comes to making even the smallest decisions he shows a complete lack of initiative* (or *completely lacks initiative*). (*act/do* s.t) *on one's own initiative* (act etc) as one wants to without asking for help or advice from others. *gain/lose/take the initiative* gain etc an advantage, e.g by (not) making the first move or by defeating s.o else's moves.

inject /ɪn'dʒekt/ *tr.v* **1** (usu — s.o/s.t *with* s.t; — s.t *into* s.o/s.t) make (s.o, an animal etc) receive (a medicine, drug etc) in her/his/its body using a needle and a syringe(1): *He was injected with a painkiller at the scene of the accident. He was caught in the act of injecting* heroin *into his arm* (or *injecting himself with* heroin). **2** (*fig*) (often — s.t *into* s.t) (try to) create (a feeling, e.g of enthusiasm) (in s.o/s.t): *Mike always manages to inject a feeling of excitement into those around him.* **3** (usu — s.t *into* s.t) (*commerce*) put (more money etc) (into an organization): *The new owner is injecting money into the firm.*
injection /ɪn'dʒekʃən/ *n* (often — *of* s.t) **1** *c/u.n* (example of the) act of injecting(1) (s.o/s.t against a disease etc) or of being injected(1): *If you are travelling in that area you'll need injections against* cholera *and* typhoid. **2** *c.n* (*fig*) act of producing (enthusiasm etc): *an injection of new ideas/energy.* **3** *c.n* (*commerce*) new amount (of money, capital etc) given to s.t: *an injection of capital into the housing programme.*
by injection using the method of injecting(1).

in-joke ⇒ in-.

injudicious /ˌɪndʒuː'dɪʃəs/ *adj* (*formal*) (of s.t said, an act etc) not very wise, not showing good judgement; not judicious: *It was rather injudicious of you to mention the spot on his nose.*
,inju'diciously *adv.* ,inju'diciousness *u.n.*

injunction /ɪn'dʒʌŋkʃən/ *c.n* (often *take out an* — *against* s.o/s.t) (*law*) order in a court of law (against s.o, an organization etc) stopping her/him/it from doing s.t or making her/him/it do s.t: *The company took out an injunction against its rival selling cameras based on its own* design(1).

injure /'ɪndʒə/ *tr.v* **1** hurt, harm or wound (s.o, part of the body etc): *He injured his leg in the accident. He was very badly injured in the fire.* **2** harm or damage (s.o's feeling of pride, reputation etc); affect (s.o) badly: *Attacks from people like them are not likely to injure his reputation.*
'injured *adj* **1** (of a person) who has been hurt or wounded, esp in an accident: *The injured passengers were taken to hospital.* **2** (of a feeling, expression in one's voice etc) showing that one feels hurt or offended: *'Why do you hate me so much?' he asked in an injured voice.*
▷ *def.pl.n* **3** injured(1) people: *The injured were taken to hospital.*
injurious /ɪn'dʒʊərɪəs/ *adj* (often — *to* s.o/ s.t) (*formal*) causing harm, damage, (to s.o/s.t): *Smoking is injurious to your health.*
injury /'ɪndʒərɪ/ *c/u.n* (*pl* -ies) (example of the) fact or state of injuring s.o/s.t or of being injured(⇒ injure): *a leg/fatal injury*; *an injury to one's pride.* *add insult to injury* ⇒ insult(*n*). *do*

oneself/s.o an injury (*informal*) harm oneself/ s.o: *Don't play with that knife because you could do yourself a terrible injury.*

injustice /ɪnˈdʒʌstɪs/ *c/u.n* (example of the) fact or state of being unjust; lack of justice: *He accused the government of injustice in handling his complaint. The poor suffer many injustices at the hands of the rich.* **do oneself/s.o an injustice** (*formal*) not treat oneself/s.o fairly, esp by not considering her/his point of view or by thinking s.t bad about her/him: *You are doing her a great injustice if you think she could do such a cruel thing.*

ink /ɪŋk/ *u.n* **1** coloured liquid used for writing, esp with a pen. **in ink** using ink(1): *He drew a picture of the house in ink.*
▷ *tr.v* **2** (often — *s.t in*) put ink(1) on a drawing, picture etc, esp one that has first been drawn using a pencil: *He inked in the details.*

'ink ,bottle *c.n* bottle containing ink(1).

'inkiness *u.n* (*literary*) fact or state of being very black or dark like black ink(1): *In the inkiness of the cave he could hardly see his hands in front of his face.*

'ink,pot/,well *c.n* small pot for ink(1), esp one that is placed in a hole in a desk.

'inky *adj* (*-ier, -iest*) **1** having, covered with, (a lot of) ink(1): *inky fingers.* **2** (*literary*) very black or dark like black ink(1): *an inky darkness* (i.e at night etc).

inkling /ˈɪŋklɪŋ/ *c.n* (usu *have an, no, some etc* — (*of s.t, that . . .*)) small idea or suspicion (about s.t, that. . .): *I had no inkling* (or *I hadn't an inkling*) *that he was in trouble until I read about it in the newspapers.*

inky ⇨ ink.

inlaid ⇨ inlay.

inland /ˈɪnlənd/ *attrib.adj* **1** (in or at a place) away from the sea or coast: *inland towns/waterways.* **2** happening, done etc inside a country: *inland trade/taxes.*
▷ *adv* /ɪnˈlænd/ **3** (being or moving) in or towards the interior(3) of the country, away from the sea or coast: *They travelled inland towards the mountains.*

,Inland 'Revenue *def.n* (UK) government department responsible for collecting taxes inside the country.

in-laws /ˈɪnˌlɔːz/ *pl.n* (*informal*) parents and sometimes other members of the family of the person one has married: *Though he didn't like them, he invited his in-laws to stay for a week.* ⇨ brother/daughter/father/mother/son/sister-in-law.

inlay /ˈɪnˌleɪ/ *c/u.n* (example of a) piece of wood, metal etc, or the pattern it makes, that is placed level with the surface of another piece of wood, metal etc, esp in furniture: *The cupboard had inlays of different coloured woods on the doors.*

'in,laid *adj* (often — *with s.t*) having an inlay (using a (certain kind of) wood, metal etc): *a box inlaid with silver.*

inlet /ˈɪnˌlet/ *c.n* **1** small narrow stretch of water or small bay coming into the land from the sea, a river or lake. **2** (often — *for s.t*) (pipe etc that acts as an) opening allowing liquid etc to go in. Opposite outlet(1).

inmate /ˈɪnˌmeɪt/ *c.n* (often — *of s.t*) person who lives in a place, esp a prison or hospital: *Some*

of the inmates of the mental hospital *are being put in houses in the town.*

inmesh ⇨ enmesh.

inmost ⇨ in.

inn /ɪn/ *c.n* kind of pub that one can stay in, have meals at, as well as alcoholic(1) drinks etc.

'inn,keeper *c.n* person who owns or looks after an inn.

,Inns of 'Court *def.pl.n* (UK) buildings in London for the four law societies that provide training for the law and have the right of appointing people to the bar(10).

innards /ˈɪnədz/ *pl.n* (*informal*) **1** inside organs (of an animal or person): *Remove the innards from the chicken before cooking.* **2** (often *joking*) inner parts (of a machine etc): *You'll have to remove the covering to get at the innards.*

innate /ɪˈneɪt/ *adj* (*formal*) (of a (good) quality) that one has naturally as part of oneself: *an innate sense of justice; innate kindness.*

inner, innermost ⇨ in.

innings /ˈɪnɪŋz/ *c.n* (*pl innings*) **1** (in cricket[1]) one of the times when a player or team bats. **2** (often *have a good —*) (*informal*) length of time when one is able to do things, when one is active etc, during the course of one's life: *He said 'I've had a good innings and I'm not afraid to die.'*

innkeeper ⇨ inn.

innocent /ˈɪnəsənt/ *adj* **1** (often — *of s.t*) (of a person) not guilty (of a crime etc): *In English law a person is usually regarded as innocent* (*of a crime*) *until proved guilty.* **2** being pure, free from evil etc: *an innocent young child.* **3** being (too) trusting etc: *Are you so innocent as to believe her story?* **4** (of s.t said or done) not (intended to be) harmful; simple and straightforward(1): *Her innocent remarks about him led to a terrible row.*

'innocence *u.n* **1** fact or state of not being guilty: *He had several witnesses to prove his innocence.* **2** fact or state of being pure, free from evil, not knowing wickedness etc: *She has the innocence of a young child.* **3** (often *in her/his —*) state of being (too) trusting, believing things too easily: *In his innocence he believed her story although it was a lie from beginning to end.*

'innocently *adv* in an innocent(2–4) way.

innocuous /ɪˈnɒkjuəs/ *adj* (*formal*) **1** (of a substance etc) that has no bad effects; harmless: *This medicine is quite innocuous.* **2** (of a person, s.t said or done) who/that does not cause any harm: *He's an innocuous old man who wouldn't hurt a fly.* Compare noxious.

in'nocuously *adv.* **in'nocuousness** *u.n.*

innovation /ˌɪnəˈveɪʃən/ *c/u.n* (example of the) fact or state of inventing s.t new, introducing a new idea or method etc: *Peter introduced a number of innovations into the way the office was run.*

innovative /ˈɪnəvətɪv/ *adj* showing innovation.

'innovatively *adv.*

'inno,vator *c.n* person who shows innovation.

innuendo /ˌɪnjuˈendəʊ/ *c/u.n* (*pl -(e)s*) (example of the) saying of s.t that suggests s.t bad about s.o/s.t but without actually stating it: *His speech was full of innuendo about bribery in high places. Try and ignore his innuendoes about your behaviour.*

innumerable /ɪˈnjuːmərəbl/ *adj* (*formal*) that

are (almost) too many to be counted or described: *In spite of innumerable difficulties we finally managed to get them to agree.*

inoculate /ɪˈnɒkjʊˌleɪt/ *tr.v* (usu — *s.o/s.t* (*with s.t*) *against s.t*) give (s.o, an animal) an injection (of a small amount of a disease) so as to protect her/him/it (against the (full effects of) the) disease): *Have you been inoculated against cholera?*
inoculation /ɪˌnɒkjʊˈleɪʃən/ *c/u.n*: *They gave him an inoculation against diphtheria.*

inoffensive /ˌɪnəˈfensɪv/ *adj* (of a person, s.t said etc) who/that does not cause offence or harm; not offensive (2,3): *an inoffensive old man*; *inoffensive remarks.*
ˌinofˈfensively *adv.* **ˌinofˈfensiveness** *u.n.*

inoperable /ɪnˈɒprəbl/ *adj* (*medical*) (of a disease etc) that cannot be operated upon to successfully remove it or stop its progress: *inoperable cancer (1).*

inoperative /ɪnˈɒprətɪv/ *adj* (of a rule, law etc) that does not work (any longer); that has no effect; not operative: *As from 1 January these regulations (1) will be inoperative.*

inopportune /ɪnˈɒpəˌtjuːn/ *adj* (*formal*) (of s.t that happens, is said etc) that does not come at a suitable time; that is not suitable (for the occasion etc); not opportune: *He arrived at a most inopportune moment just as we were leaving the house.*
inˈoppor,tunely *adv.* **inˈoppor,tuneness** *u.n.*

inordinate /ɪnˈɔːdɪnɪt/ *adj* (*formal*) that is too great or large to be borne; excessive: *an inordinate delay*; *inordinate demands on my time.*
inˈordinately *adv.*

inorganic /ˌɪnɔːˈgænɪk/ *adj* (of a substance etc) that does not have a living structure (1) or organism of the kind that animals or plants have; not organic (3): *Rocks and metals are classified as being inorganic.*
ˌinorˌganic ˈchemistry *u.n* branch of chemistry concerned with the study of inorganic substances. Compare organic chemistry.
ˌinorˈganically *adv.*

in-patient /ˈɪn ˌpeɪʃənt/ *c.n* person being treated in a hospital and sleeping there. Compare outpatient.

input /ˈɪnˌpʊt/ *c/u.n* **1** (example of a) thing, e.g power, energy (2) etc that is put into a machine etc to make it work. Compare output (3). **2** (also *attrib*) (example of (the amount of)) information or data (to be) put into a computer for processing (3): *The new computer is capable of handling inputs from several terminals (5).* Compare output (4).
▷ *tr.v* (*-tt-*) **3** put (information or data) into a computer: *Data can be input using the special program (1).*

inquest /ˈɪnˌkwest/ *c.n* (often *hold/order an* — (*into s.t, on s.o*)) official inquiry (into the death (of s.o)), esp when the death is not natural or if there are suspicious circumstances.

inquire /ɪnˈkwaɪə/ *v* (also **enˈquire**) (*formal*) **1** *tr.v* ask (if, what etc. . .): *I inquired whether she wanted any help.* **2** *intr.v* (usu — *about/after s.o/s.t*) ask for information (about s.o/s.t): *She inquired about the times of flights to London. Sylvia inquired after his parents* (i.e to find out if they were well, what they were doing etc). **3** *intr.v* (usu — *after/for s.o/s.t*) ask to see s.o/s.t:

Somebody came into the office inquiring for you. **4** *intr.v* (usu — *into s.t*) try to find information/ facts about a matter; investigate s.t: *The police are inquiring into his sudden disappearance.*

inˈquirer *c.n* (also **enˈquirer**) (*formal*) person who inquires, esp one asking for information, wanting to see s.o/s.t: *Would you please tell all inquirers that I will make a statement tomorrow.*
inˈquiring *attrib.adj* (also **enˈquiring**) (of a person's mind, nature) having or showing a strong desire to learn or find out about things: *Young children have inquiring minds and are always asking questions.*
inˈquiringly *adv* (also **enˈquiringly**): *She looked at me inquiringly.*
inˈquiry *c/u.n* (also **enˈquiry**) (*pl -ies*) **1** (example of the) act or state of inquiring (⇒ inquire (2,4)) about etc s.o/s.t: *His inquiries led him nowhere.* **2** (often — *into s.t*) (official or a public) investigation (into s.t): *The government will be holding, have organized, a public inquiry into the causes of the accident.* **court of inquiry** ⇒ court.

inquisition /ˌɪnkwɪˈzɪʃən/ *c.n* (*formal*) investigation, often in an unfair way, about s.t wrong that s.o is considered, believed, to have done: *I really don't have to put up with this inquisition into my religious beliefs.*

inquisitive /ɪnˈkwɪzɪtɪv/ *adj* (often *derog*) (of a person) asking (too) many questions, showing (too) great an interest in s.o's affairs etc: *You're far too inquisitive about things that are the private matters of other people.*
inˈquisitively *adv.* **inˈquisitiveness** *u.n.*

inroads /ˈɪnrəʊdz/ *pl.n* **make inroads** (*into s.t*) (**a**) make sudden attacks (on a place, country etc). (**b**) manage to finish important or large parts (of a task): *She's made inroads into finishing the work.* (**c**) use up a large amount (of time, supplies): *The holiday made inroads into our savings.*

inrush /ˈɪnˌrʌʃ/ *c.n* (often — *of s.o/s.t* (*into s.t*)) sudden rushing in (of people, things, water etc) (into a place): *When the doors opened there was an inrush of people into the hall all wanting to get the best seats.*

insane /ɪnˈseɪn/ *adj* **1** (of a person) mad; not sane (1): *After examination by the doctors, he was found to be insane.* **2** (*informal*) (of a person, act etc) very stupid; not showing much or any sense: *He was insane to try to walk so far with such a weak heart.*
inˈsanely *adv.* **insanity** /ɪnˈsænɪtɪ/ *u.n.*

insanitary /ɪnˈsænɪtərɪ/ *adj* (of a state, condition of s.t) very unhealthy (3) and likely to cause disease; not sanitary (1): *The hospital kitchens were found to be insanitary.*

insatiable /ɪnˈseɪʃəbl/ *adj* (*formal*) (of a person, need, appetite etc) who/that cannot be satisfied: *He has an insatiable appetite for new experiences.*
insatiability /ɪnˌseɪʃɪəˈbɪlɪtɪ/ *u.n.* **inˈsatiably** *adv.*

inscribe /ɪnˈskraɪb/ *tr.v* (*formal*) write or carve (3) (words, a name etc) (in/on s.t); mark or cut (the surface of s.t) (with words, a name etc): *He had his name inscribed on the inside of the book. The stone above the fireplace is inscribed with a date.*

inscription /ɪn'skrɪpʃən/ *c.n* words inscribed in/ on s.t, esp in a book, on a coin etc.

inscrutable /ɪn'skruːtəbl/ *adj* (*formal*) (of a person, expression etc) who/that cannot be understood, esp because he/she/it remains secret: *He tried to find out what she was thinking but her expression remained inscrutable.*
inscrutability /ɪnˌskruːtə'bɪlɪtɪ/ *u.n.* **in'scrutably** *adv.*

insect /'ɪnsekt/ *c.n* (also *attrib*) (general name for) one of many different kinds of small creatures, with six legs and a body divided into sections(1), e.g a fly, ant: *an insect colony(3).*
insecticide /ɪn'sektɪˌsaɪd/ *c/u.n* (example of a) chemical substance used for killing insects.

insecure /ˌɪnsɪ'kjʊə/ *adj* **1** (of a person) not feeling sure of oneself, lacking confidence; not secure(2): *He always feels insecure in the presence of people he thinks are more intelligent than himself.* **2** (of a person, position etc) not (feeling) safe, not protected; not secure(2): *He felt very insecure climbing such a steep cliff. With so much unemployment even his own job was beginning to look insecure.* **3** (of an object, building etc) not properly fixed, not providing proper support; not secure(1): *Don't use that ladder because it's insecure.*
ˌinse'curely *adv.* **insecurity** /ˌɪnsɪ'kjʊərɪtɪ/ *u.n.*

inseminate /ɪn'semɪˌneɪt/ *tr.v* **1** (*technical*) put (semen) into (a woman). **2** (*formal*) put (ideas etc) into (s.o, s.o's mind): *The children were inseminated with political ideology.*
insemination /ɪnˌsemɪ'neɪʃən/ *u.n* ⇒ artificial insemination.

insensible /ɪn'sensəbl/ *adj* (usu *pred*) **1** (of a person) (having been made) unconscious, e.g as a result of a blow: *He was knocked insensible by a falling brick.* **2** (usu — of/to s.t) (*formal*) (of a person) not showing an understanding or recognition (of s.t): *He was insensible of/to the danger.*
insensibility /ɪnˌsensə'bɪlɪtɪ/ *u.n* (usu — to s.t) (example of the) fact or state of being insensible(2) (to s.t).
in'sensibly *adv.*

insensitive /ɪn'sensɪtɪv/ *adj* (often — to s.t) **1** (*derog*) (of a person, remark, act etc) who/ that does not show understanding or respect (towards the feelings etc of s.o); not sensitive(1): *It was rather insensitive of you to say that when her husband has just died.* **2** not feeling or able to feel (s.t, e.g pain, that one usually would feel): *The injection made him insensitive to pain while having his tooth taken out.*
in'sensitively *adv.*
insensitivity /ɪnˌsensɪ'tɪvɪtɪ/ *u.n.*

inseparable /ɪn'seprəbl/ *adj* (of two or more people, things etc) who/that cannot be separated (from each other); who/that are very closely connected (to each other): *The two boys are inseparable and always spend their time together. We have to find solutions for both these problems as they are inseparable.*
inseparability /ɪnˌseprə'bɪlɪtɪ/ *u.n.* **in'separably** *adv.*

insert /'ɪnsɜːt/ *c.n* **1** thing that has been placed inside s.t else: *Sunday magazines often have inserts for different products.*

▷ *tr.v* /ɪn'sɜːt/ **2** (usu — s.t in(to) s.t) (*formal*) put or place (s.t) (in(to) or inside s.t else): *Lift the telephone receiver, insert your money (in the slot(1)) and then dial(3) the number.*

insertion /ɪn'sɜːʃən/ *c/u.n* (often — (of s.t) in(to) s.t) (*formal*) (example of the) fact or state of inserting(2) s.t or of s.t being inserted(2) (in(to) s.t): *The insertion of a tube through the nose and throat into the lungs is necessary to help breathing.*

in-service /'ɪn ˌsɜːvɪs/ *attrib.adj* (often — training) that takes place during the time when one has a job, (as compared to learning, training etc before one gets a job): *an in-service course.*

inset /'ɪnˌset/ *c.n* map, photograph etc put inside a larger one.

inshore /'ɪnˌʃɔː/ *attrib.adj* **1** near the shore or coast: *inshore fishing boats.*
▷ *adv* **2** being at, moving towards, the shore or coast: *The boat was blown inshore by the storm.* Compare ashore, offshore, onshore.

inside /'ɪnˌsaɪd/ *adj* **1** in, leading to, the inner area of a building; having a position within: *an inside door; an inside market; the inside pages of the newspaper.* ⇒ outside(1). **2** (of information etc) coming from a central point, esp from s.o who knows s.t that should be secret: *Jim knew their plans in advance because he had inside information. We never did discover the inside story of what actually happened.*
▷ *adv* /ɪn'saɪd/ **3** within or into a place, space etc: *Did you find anything inside? They went inside when it started to rain.* Compare outside(6). **4** (*slang*) in(to) (a) prison: *He was put inside for three years.* Compare outside(9). **inside of a minute, week** etc within, or in less than, a minute etc: *I phoned for a taxi and it arrived inside ten minutes.* **inside out** (esp wearing clothes) with the inner side wrongly on the outside: *Did you know you've got your socks on inside out?* **know s.t inside out** (*fig*) know a subject very completely or thoroughly.
▷ *def.n* /ɪn'saɪd/ **5** (often the — of s.t) inner part, inner surface area, (of s.t): *The inside (of the box) was lined with cloth.* Compare outside(10).
▷ *prep* /ɪn'saɪd/ **6** being, moving, within (a place, space etc): *They went inside the house when it started to rain.* Compare outside(11).
ˌin'sider *c.n* person who belongs to a small group at the centre of power or influence and who therefore has a lot of secret information, power etc herself/himself. ⇒ inside(2). Compare outsider(1).
ˌinˌside 'job *c.n* (*informal*) crime, e.g a robbery, committed by s.o who lives or works in a place where it happens and/or who helps others outside to commit it.
ˌinˌside 'lane *c.n* lane on a motorway or on a road that is divided into separate lanes which is next to the edge (where traffic drives more slowly): *In Britain it is forbidden to overtake(1) on the inside lanes.*
ˌin'sides *pl.n* (*informal*) stomach and other organs inside the body: *I've got a pain in my insides.*

insidious /ɪn'sɪdɪəs/ *adj* (*formal*) (of s.t bad) that happens or grows slowly or gradually without really being noticed until too late: *an insidious disease; insidious revenge.*

in'sidiously *adv.* **in'sidiousness** *u.n.*

insight /'ɪn,saɪt/ *c/u.n* (often — *into s.t*) understanding (of s.t) through the use of one's mind, and esp through one's own ability: *His two years' stay in India gave him some insight into the way such a complicated society worked.*

insignia /ɪn'sɪgnɪə/ *pl.n* things such as a badge, crown, chain that s.o has or wears to show her/his official position: *the insignia of a mayor.*

insignificant /,ɪnsɪg'nɪfɪkənt/ *adj* (of a person or an amount, act etc) who/that is not very important or worth noticing; that is of very little value; not significant(1): *This event is insignificant compared to what happens next. Standing next to his tall brother he looked small and insignificant.*

,insig'nificance *u.n.* **,insig'nificantly** *adv.*

insincere /,ɪnsɪn'sɪə/ *adj* (derog) (of a person, s.t said or done) not showing one's feelings honestly; not sincere: *an insincere smile/apology.*

,insin'cerely *adv.* **insincerity** /,ɪnsɪn'serɪtɪ/ *u.n.* Opposite sincerity.

insinuate /ɪn'sɪnjʊ,eɪt/ *v* (derog) **1** *tr.v* (often — (*to s.o*) *that. . .*) suggest (to s.o) (s.t bad about her/him/s.o else or that there is s.t bad etc) but without stating it clearly or directly: *Are you insinuating that I am a coward?* **2** *reflx.v* (usu — *oneself into s.t*) (formal) gradually get oneself accepted (into s.o's favour etc) by pretending to be pleasant and helpful: *She insinuated herself into the old man's affections by listening to his complaints but what she really wanted was his money.*

insinuation /ɪn,sɪnjʊ'eɪʃən/ *c/u.n* (example of the) act of insinuating(1) s.t. **by insinuation** by saying s.t that insinuates(1) s.t: *He didn't attack them directly but by insinuation managed to show that his opinion of them was low.*

insipid /ɪn'sɪpɪd/ *adj* (derog) (of a person, remark, taste, food etc) not at all interesting; lacking excitement, flavour etc: *He's an insipid little man who has nothing important to say. It was an expensive restaurant but our meal was insipid.*

,insi'pidity *u.n* **in'sipidly** *adv.* **in'sipidness** *u.n.*

insist /ɪn'sɪst/ *v* **1** *tr.v* (usu — *that . . .*) state strongly and continuously (that s.t is true, one is right etc), esp when other people say s.t else: *He insisted that he had been right all along.* **2** *tr.v* (usu — *that. . .*) demand or urge strongly (that s.o should do s.t, s.t should happen etc): *He insisted that I should listen to what he had to say.* **3** *intr.v* (usu — (*up)on doing s.t*) decide, be very determined, (to do s.t) in spite of it not being necessary, in spite of objections etc: *He insisted upon helping me though I could have managed by myself. 'It's all right, you don't have to carry my bag.' 'No, I insist'.* **4** *intr.v* (usu — (*up)on (s.o doing) s.t*) demand or require(2) (s.t, that s.o should do s.t): *He insists on punctuality from all his staff (or on all his staff being punctual).* **5** *intr.v* (usu — (*up)on s.t*) (formal) make a very strong statement (about s.t that one believes to be true etc): *He insisted upon his innocence(1).*

in'sistence *u.n* (often — (*up)on s.t*) fact or state of insisting(3–5) (up)on s.t: *Her insistence on male staff wearing suits is not fair.* **at s.o's insistence** (formal) because s.o insists(2,3) that. . .

or (up)on s.t: *He took a week's holiday at his wife's insistence.*

in'sistent *adj* **1** (formal) (of an action etc) happening continuously and therefore demanding attention: *There were insistent requests for more help.* **2** (often — *that*; — (*up)on s.t*) (of a person) who insists very often (that...; (up)on s.t): *He was insistent that we listen to his complaints.*

in'sistently *adv.*

in so far as, insofar as ⇨ in(prep).

insolent /'ɪnsələnt/ *adj* (derog) (of a person, behaviour, an expression etc) who/that shows rudeness and a lack of respect: *Take that insolent look off your face at once!*

'insolence *u.n.* **'insolently** *adv.*

insoluble /ɪn'sɒljʊbl/ *adj* **1** (often — *in s.t*) (technical) (of a substance) that cannot be dissolved (in a liquid); not soluble(1). **2** (formal) (of a problem etc) that cannot be worked out or solved; that cannot have a satisfactory result: *The difficulties the country faced over its increasing debt appeared insoluble.*

insolubility /ɪn,sɒljʊ'bɪlɪtɪ/ *u.n.* Compare solvency.

insolvent /ɪn'sɒlvənt/ *adj* (commerce) (of a person) (having become or having been declared to be) unable to pay one's debts through lack of money; not solvent¹: *A lot of people lost money when he became insolvent.*

in'solvency *u.n.* Compare solvency.

insomnia /ɪn'sɒmnɪə/ *u.n* lack of ability to sleep, esp for several nights: *I was kept awake by insomnia.*

insomniac /ɪn'sɒmnɪæk/ *adj* **1** suffering from insomnia: *He's insomniac and spends most of his nights reading.*

▷ *c.n* **2** person who suffers from insomnia.

inspect /ɪn'spekt/ *tr.v* **1** look at, examine, (s.o/s.t) very carefully and in detail: *Before you buy anything secondhand, you should inspect it carefully.* **2** visit (a place, e.g a school, organization) in order to see that it is working properly: *When they inspected the restaurant's kitchen they found rats.* **3** officially review (soldiers etc): *The general inspected the troops before the battle.*

inspection /ɪn'spekʃən/ *c/u.n* (example of the) act of inspecting s.o/s.t or of being inspected. **on inspection** after, as a result of, inspecting(1) s.t: *On inspection, the engine proved to be faulty.*

in'spector *c.n* **1** official who inspects(2) a place: *a schools inspector; a health and safety inspector.* **2** (also with capital **I**) (title for a) police officer with a rank below a superintendent(2) and above a sergeant(2): *a Chief Inspector.*

inspectorate /ɪn'spektərɪt/ *c/def.n* group of inspectors(1).

inspire /ɪn'spaɪə/ *tr.v* **1** (often — *s.o to do s.t*) give (s.o) the desire or courage (to do s.t), esp by one's own example or encouragement(1): *It was your advice that inspired me to set up my own business. I was inspired by what Janet said.* **2** (often — *s.o with s.t*; — *s.t in s.o*) give (s.o a good feeling; cause (such a feeling in s.o): *He inspired her with confidence. His words inspired confidence in her.* **3** (formal) be the cause or origin of (s.t artistic): *The poem was inspired by the countryside.*

inspiration /,ɪnspɪ'reɪʃən/ *n* **1** *u.n* (thought or feeling that leads to the) causing or making of s.t artistic: *The inspiration for this poem was the* *countryside. At the moment I lack inspiration and can't continue writing.* **2** *c.n* person or thing who/ that inspires(1) s.o: *His courage is an inspiration to us all.* **3** *(informal or joking)* (good) idea, thought or plan: *Was it your inspiration to make us walk when we could have taken a bus?*

in'spired *adj* (of an idea, s.t said or done etc) very good because it seems to come unexpectedly and as though from an outside or unknown force: *That was an inspired guess.* Opposite uninspired.

in'spiring *adj* (of an idea, s.t said or done etc) that inspires(1) s.o: *His inspiring words gave me confidence.* Opposite uninspiring.

instability /ˌɪnstə'bɪlɪtɪ/ *u.n* lack of firmness, esp in one's character; lack of stability: *His failure to keep any job longer than six months shows his instability.* Compare stable[1](2), unstable.

install /ɪn'stɔːl/ *tr.v* (US **in'stal**) (*-ll-* US *-l-*) **1** (often — *s.t in s.t*) put or fix (s.t, e.g machinery) (in a place): *We've just installed central heating in our house.* **2** (often — *s.o in s.t*, as *s.o/s.t*) appoint (s.o) officially or using a ceremony (to a position, as *s.o/s.t*): *She was installed as president.*

installation /ˌɪnstə'leɪʃən/ *n* **1** *u.n* act of installing s.o/s.t or of being installed: *the installation of electricity in a house.* **2** *c.n* thing, e.g machinery, that has been installed(1): *Before you buy the factory you will need to check all the installations.*

instalment /ɪn'stɔːlmənt/ *c.n* (US **in'stallment**) **1** regular (weekly etc) amount of money: *You can pay for the television with twelve monthly instalments that also include the interest.* **2** one of a number of parts into which a story, radio or television programme etc, is divided and printed, broadcast or shown over a certain length of time: *Did you see the last instalment on television last night?* **by** (**monthly** etc) **instalments** using (monthly etc) instalments(1) as the method of payment: *We paid for it by weekly instalments.*

instance /'ɪnstəns/ *c.n* (often — *of s.t*) example (of s.t), esp when referring to a general state or condition: *There are far too many instances of lateness among the staff.* **for instance** as an example (used esp when giving an example of a general state or condition): *Consider, for instance, the government's plans for education.* **in the first instance** at the very beginning; as the first thing (that s.o should do or consider): *In the first instance, you're completely wrong. If you have a complaint you should write in the first instance to the local council.* **in that/this instance** in that/ this particular case: *You may be right about the other matters but in this instance you're wrong.*

instant /'ɪnstənt/ *adj* **1** happening (almost) at once, immediately: *The film was an instant success. He gave up smoking and the effect on his health was instant.* **2** *(attrib)* (of food, drink etc) prepared so as to be cooked, used etc quickly without (much) further preparation: *I hate instant coffee.*

▷ *c.n* **3** (exact) very short moment or point in time: *There was just an instant when he could not think who she was but then he remembered her.* **at/in that instant** at that exact moment: *He called out to warn her and at that instant she fell.* (**do s.t) the instant** (**that**)... (do s.t) immediately (that) one hears, knows, about s.t etc: *The instant (that) he got the good news he phoned up all his friends.* **for an instant** for a very brief[1] moment in time:

For an instant I didn't recognize her. **in an instant** very quickly or shortly; suddenly: *I'll be with you in an instant. In an instant the whole situation was changed.* **this instant** immediately, at once, esp in an order or demand: *Stop that noise this instant!*

instantaneous /ˌɪnstən'teɪnɪəs/ *adj* *(formal)* happening, done, immediately: *Death was instantaneous.*

ˌinstan'taneously *adv.* **ˌinstan'taneousness** *u.n.*

'instantly *adv* at once; immediately: *I phoned her and she came around to the house instantly.*

instead /ɪn'sted/ *adv* in place of, replacing, s.o/ s.t; as an alternative(2) to doing s.t else: *As she was not at home, I spoke to her brother instead. I don't want to go out tonight. Let's stay home instead and watch the television.* **instead of s.o/s.t**; **instead of doing s.t** replacing s.o/s.t; as an alternative(2) to doing s.t: *As I'm busy, could you go instead of me? Instead of just talking why don't you do something?*

instep /'ɪnˌstep/ *c.n* **1** upper curved part of the foot. **2** part of a shoe, boot etc that covers the instep(1).

instigate /'ɪnstɪˌɡeɪt/ *tr.v* *(formal)* start (s.t, usu bad, happening): *The disturbance was instigated by people opposed to the government.*

instigation /ˌɪnstɪ'ɡeɪʃən/ *u.n* (usu *at s.o's* —) suggestion or encouragement: *It was at your instigation that we employed him.*

'instiˌgator *c.n* person who instigates s.t.

instil /ɪn'stɪl/ *tr.v* (US **instill**) (*-ll-*) (usu — *s.t in(to)* s.o/s.t) *(formal)* put (an idea, feeling, virtue etc) (in(to) s.o, s.o's mind) by continuous effort, teaching etc: *From early childhood they had instilled (into them) the need for politeness.* **instillation** /ˌɪnstɪ'leɪʃən/ *u.n.*

instinct /'ɪnstɪŋkt/ *c/u.n* (example of the) natural feeling or power that makes s.o, an animal, do s.t without thinking, without having been trained or taught: *My instinct is to trust her whatever she says. In difficult situations like these you should follow/ trust your instincts.* **by instinct** using or following one's instinct: *Dogs seem to know by instinct if a person is friendly or not.*

in'stinctive *adj* coming from, as a result of, one's instinct: *My instinctive reaction(1) was to run away.*

in'stinctively *adj.*

institute /'ɪnstɪˌtjuːt/ *c.n* **1** (with capital **I** in names) (title for a) society, organization, school etc set up for a special purpose, e.g education, social activities; building used for this purpose: *He was studying science at the local institute. She runs the village's Women's Institute.*

▷ *tr.v* **2** *(formal)* set up, start, (a society, organization etc): *The Society was instituted in 1950.* **institute (legal) proceedings (against s.o)** *(law)* start an action in a law court (against s.o).

institution /ˌɪnstɪ'tjuːʃən/ *n* **1** *c.n* place, building, organization etc set up for a special purpose, esp for helping people, providing care or services etc: *In the old days children in need of care were put into an institution.* **2** *u.n* (often — *of s.t) (formal)* act of starting (s.t, e.g an official inquiry, a legal(2) action): *The institution of new taxes caused much anxiety.* **3** *c.n* thing that has become a habit or custom through long use:

Our monthly meetings have become something of an institution. **4** *c.n (joking)* person who has become well known, who has been present a long time: *Old Harry is a bit of an institution in the office because he's been here so long.*

insti'tutional *adj* (usu *attrib*) of or referring to an institution(1): *He hated the institutional life in the hospital.*

institutionalized, -ised /ˌɪnstɪ'tjuːʃənəˌlaɪzd/ *adj* affected by the regular pattern of life in an institution(1): *He was so institutionalized after a long period in prison that he could not* adapt(1) *to life outside it.*

instruct /ɪn'strʌkt/ *tr.v* **1** (often — *s.o in s.t*) *(formal)* teach, train, (s.o in a skill, subject etc): *He instructed them in the proper use of the new machinery. Can you instruct me (on) how to operate the washing machine?* **2** (usu — *s.o to do s.t*) order or officially request (s.o to do s.t): *I was instructed to come on Monday at 9 o'clock.*

instruction /ɪn'strʌkʃən/ *n* **1** *u.n (formal)* act or state of instructing(1) s.o or of being instructed(1): *He is receiving instruction in the use of the new machinery.* **2** *c.n* (often *pl*) order or official request: *Have you had any instructions from head office yet?* **3** *c.n* (often *pl*) written help or advice on how to make or use s.t, e.g a machine: *Follow the instruction carefully when you start gluing the pieces together.* **under instruction** receiving or getting instruction(1).

in'structional *adj* that gives practical instruction(1): *instructional books.*

in'structive *adj* that gives knowledge or information: *The book about management was very instructive.*

in'structively *adv.* **in'structiveness** *u.n.*

in'structor *c.n* person who instructs(1) s.o: *a driving instructor.*

instrument /'ɪnstrəmənt/ *c.n* **1** device or tool used for doing certain kinds of work, esp those of a delicate kind: *medical/scientific instruments.* **2** (also ˌmusical 'instruˌment) object, e.g a piano, violin, trumpet, that one plays to produce musical sounds: *He can play several instruments.*

instrumental /ˌɪnstrə'mentl/ *adj* **1** *(music)* of or referring to the use of instruments(2) and not voices, in playing music: *an instrumental piece/work.* **2** (usu — *in (doing) s.t*) (of a person) mainly responsible (for (doing) s.t, getting s.t done): *I was instrumental in getting him the job.*

ˌinstru'mentaˌlist *c.n* person who plays an instrument(2).

insubordinate /ˌɪnsə'bɔːdɪnɪt/ *adj* (often — *to s.o*) *(formal)* (of a person) not being obedient; not accepting orders, esp from s.o of a higher rank: *He was charged with being insubordinate to his* superior(1) *officer.*

insubordination /ˌɪnsəˌbɔːdɪ'neɪʃən/ *u.n* act or state of being insubordinate.

insubstantial /ˌɪnsəb'stænʃəl/ *adj (formal)* **1** not solid or satisfying; not substantial(1,2): *an insubstantial meal.* **2** that has no real proof: *The evidence against him was too insubstantial and the case was dismissed.*

insufferable /ɪn'sʌfərəbl/ *adj (derog)* (of a person, behaviour etc) too proud or too sure of one's own worth and so greatly disliked by

other people: *He really is insufferable in the way he tries to tell you what to do.*

in'sufferably *adv.*

insufficient /ˌɪnsə'fɪʃənt/ *adj* not enough (for s.o to use, for a purpose etc); not sufficient: *There was insufficient food to feed everybody. The case against him was dismissed because of insufficient* evidence(1).

ˌinsuf'ficiency *c/u.n.* **ˌinsuf'ficiently** *adv.*

insular /'ɪnsjulə/ *adj* **1** *(attrib)* of or referring to an island or islands, or people who live on an island: *insular life/customs.* **2** *(formal)* (of a person, point of view etc) narrow in one's beliefs and not accepting outside ideas or influences: *He is somewhat insular in his outlook on life.*

insularity /ˌɪnsju'lærɪtɪ/ *u.n* fact or state of being insular(2).

insulate /'ɪnsjuˌleɪt/ *tr.v* **1** cover (a surface, wire etc) with a material, e.g glass, glass fibre(3), plastic(3), to stop heat, electricity, sound etc from getting through: *We were spending so much on heating that we decided to have the roof of our house insulated.* **2** (usu — *s.o from s.t*) *(formal)* keep (s.o) away (from harm, harmful influences etc): *The parents tried to insulate their children from what they considered the harmful effects of modern life.*

'insuˌlating ˌtape *u.n* special tape used for wrapping round bare electric wires.

insulation /ˌɪnsju'leɪʃən/ *u.n* **1** (often — *against/ from s.t*) act or state of insulating(1) s.t or of being insulated(1) (against/from the loss of heat, electricity etc). **2** material used for insulating(1) s.t, esp to stop the loss of heat in a house, building etc.

'insuˌlator *c.n* material or device that stops electricity, heat etc from getting through.

insulin /'ɪnsjulɪn/ *u.n (medical)* hormone produced in the pancreas that controls the amount of glucose in one's blood.

insult /'ɪnsʌlt/ *c/u.n* **1** (example of the) act of saying or doing s.t rude, which offends or is intended to hurt s.o: *When faced with people he disliked, he uses insult(s).* **add insult to injury** say or do s.t that causes even more harm than the harm one has already caused: *Dick's behaviour had been bad enough but then, adding insult to injury, he refused to apologize.* **an insult to one's intelligence** something said, done etc by s.o that does not need to be said, done etc because one knows it already or is clever enough not to need it explained: *The talk he gave was so childish that it was an insult to our intelligence.*

▷ *tr.v* /ɪn'sʌlt/ **2** (often — *s.o by doing, saying etc s.t*) show rudeness to (s.o), offend (s.o) (by doing etc s.t): *He insulted her by making remarks about her appearance. He was insulted when Rose refused to talk to him.*

in'sulting *adj (derog)* (of a person, remark, behaviour etc) who/that is (an) insult(1): *Get out! I've had enough of your insulting remarks.*

insuperable /ɪn'sjuːpərəbl/ *adj (formal)* (of a difficulty etc) that cannot be dealt with successfully or defeated: *an insuperable problem.*

insure /ɪn'ʃuə/ *tr/intr.v* (often — (s.o/s.t) (for an amount of money) against s.t) make a formal agreement and pay money (to an insurance company) to protect (s.o, s.o's life, property etc) (against sickness, death, loss, damage etc): *He insured* the contents of the house for £15000. Have you insured (your boat) against theft, accidental damage? Compare ensure(2), assure(2).

insurance /ɪn'ʃʊərəns/ n (also attrib) **1** u.n (often — against s.t) (act of making an) agreement to pay a regular amount of money to an insurance company, to the state etc to protect oneself, one's life, property etc (against sickness, death, loss, damage etc): car/life/travel insurance. Have you taken out any insurance against loss of earnings while you are sick? **2** u.n amount of money paid to an insurance company or received from it when there is a loss etc: I have to pay nearly £300 a year insurance on my car (or car insurance). She received over £50 000 in insurance when her husband was killed. **3** u.n business of insurance(1) as a job: He works in insurance. She's an insurance agent. **4** sing.n (often as an — against s.o/ s.t) means of protection (against s.o/s.t, s.t else happening etc): They decided to have a second plan ready as an insurance against the first one failing. **National Insurance** ⇒ national.

in'surance ˌcompany c.n (pl -ies) company, business etc that deals in insurance(1).

in'surance ˌpolicy c.n (pl -ies) written agreement of insurance(1).

in'surance ˌpremium c.n (one) amount of money paid for insurance(1): Car insurance premiums have been increased following the increase in claims for accidents.

in'sured adj **1** (often — against s.t) having insurance(1): The building is insured against fire. Are you insured? ▷ def/def.pl.n **2** person(s) who has/have insurance(1).

in'surer c/def.n person or business company who/that insures s.o/s.t.

insurgent /ɪn'sɜːdʒənt/ adj **1** (usu attrib) (formal) rising up, fighting, against a government, people in power etc: The insurgent army has taken over the town. ⇒ insurrection. ▷ c.n **2** (formal) person who fights against a government etc; rebel(1).

in'surgency u.n.

insurmountable /ˌɪnsə'maʊntəbl/ adj (formal) (of a difficulty etc) that cannot be settled or defeated: They faced insurmountable problems in trying to deal with unemployment.

insurrection /ˌɪnsə'rekʃən/ c/u.n (formal) (example of the) rising up against a government, people in power etc: The government used the army to put down the insurrection. ⇒ insurgent.

intact /ɪn'tækt/ pred.adj **1** (of an object) whole and complete without having been damaged in any way: In spite of the rough handling it received, the parcel arrived intact. **2** (of a feeling, belief, course of action etc) remaining the same or not changed in spite of outside pressure etc: Few people believe that the government's economic(1) programme will remain intact.

in'tactness u.n.

intake /'ɪnˌteɪk/ sing.n **1** number of people allowed or admitted into a place, esp for a course of study: Universities are being forced to cut their annual(1) intake (i.e of students). **2** (technical) place, channel(1), tube etc where a liquid, gas etc enters a system: The air intake in a jet engine. **intake of air/breath** taking in of air/

breath into one's lungs, esp in surprise or fear. She gave a quick intake of breath when she saw the dangerous position he was in.

intangible /ɪn'tændʒɪbl/ adj (formal) **1** (of a feeling, sense etc) that cannot be described or shown clearly though it may be present, felt to some extent etc; not tangible(2): The government remains popular but there has been an intangible change in people's feeling towards it. **2** (of a substance, presence etc) that cannot be touched or held: The house was very old and we felt the intangible presence of its many dead owners.

intangibility /ɪnˌtændʒə'bɪlɪtɪ/ u.n. **in'tangibly** adv.

integer /'ɪntɪdʒə/ c.n (mathematics) whole number (not a fraction(2)).

integral /'ɪntɪɡrəl/ pred.adj (usu an — part of s.t) necessary and important (part of s.t) without which the whole thing would not be complete: Travel is an integral part of the job.

'integrally adv.

integrate /'ɪntɪˌɡreɪt/ tr/intr.v (often — (s.o/s.t) into/with s.t) (cause (s.o, a group of people, organizations etc) to) join and mix together (with s.o else, another group etc), esp in a social sense: The people who had just settled in the country found it difficult to integrate with the local population. Compare segregate, disintegrate.

'inteˌgrated ˌcircuit c.n (technical) very small circuit(4) made of a group of elements(1) in a material such as silicon.

integration /ˌɪntɪ'ɡreɪʃən/ u.n.

integrity /ɪn'teɡrɪtɪ/ u.n **1** (of a person) complete honesty and high moral virtue: a person of integrity. **2** (often the — of s.t) (formal) fact or state of being a complete whole from which nothing can or should be removed without damage: What you say does not affect the integrity of my main argument.

intellect /'ɪntɪˌlekt/ n **1** sing/u.n power and ability to use one's mind: a man of great/low intellect. He has a high intellect. **2** c.n person of very great intelligence: He was one of the leading intellects of his time.

intellectual /ˌɪntɪ'lektʃʊəl/ adj **1** (of a person, discussion etc) who/that uses the intellect(1) and not feelings or actions, often showing great intelligence when doing so: He is so intellectual that I find it difficult to understand him sometimes. The argument was becoming too intellectual for me. ▷ c.n **2** (sometimes derog) person who is (too) intellectual(1): He considers himself an intellectual but I've never seen him reading a book.

ˌintel'lectually adv.

intelligent /ɪn'telɪdʒənt/ adj (of a person, animal, s.t said, done etc) who/that has or shows good or great mental ability: intelligent students. It was very intelligent of you to realize what was wrong. Opposite unintelligent.

in'telligence u.n **1** (good/bad) ability to use one's mind to think, learn, understand etc: a person of great/low intelligence. The answer is quite simple if only you use your intelligence. **2** (collecting of) information, esp secretly, e.g about an enemy, its plans: We received intelligence of a large army moving up to the borders of the country. **3** (often with capital **I**) government department that collects intelligence(2): *He works for military intelligence.*

In**'telligence ,Quotient** *c.n* (*abbr IQ*) measure of the intelligence of a person shown as a number on a scale which is the result of a test or tests; the number is a person's mental age as shown by the test(s) divided by her/his actual age and multiplied by 100: *Arthur has an IQ of 140.*

in**'telligence ,test** *c.n* test or examination designed to show a person's intelligence(1).

in**'telligently** *adv.*

intelligible /ɪnˈtelɪdʒəbl/ *adj* (often negative) (of s.t said, written etc) that can be understood clearly: *His reply was barely/scarcely intelligible.* Opposite unintelligible.

intelligibility /ɪnˌtelɪdʒəˈbɪlɪti/ *u.n.* **in'telligibly** *adv.*

intend /ɪnˈtend/ *tr.v* **1** have or make a definite plan (for s.o) to do s.t etc: *I was intending to visit her. What do you intend doing about it?* **2** (often passive) mean (s.t to be understood, as being s.t): *My remarks were not intended to be taken so seriously.* **3** (often passive, be —ed for s.o/s.t) send or direct (s.o/s.t) (to s.o, for a particular purpose etc): *Was that bunch of flowers intended for me?*

in**'tended** *attrib.adj* planned: *My intended visit had to be postponed because of the weather.*

in**'tent** *adj* **1** (usu — (up)on (doing) s.t) very determined (to do s.t, about doing s.t); having fixed one's mind (on (doing) s.t): *She's intent on getting a good job. They were intent upon revenge.* **2** (often — (up)on s.t) paying very close attention (to s.t); (of a look, expression on one's face) fixed, not turning away (from what one is looking at): *They were so intent on what they were doing that they didn't see me come in. There was an intent look on his face when she started to speak.*

▷ *u.n* **3** (*formal*) purpose; plan: *My intent was to get there first. I think it is reasonable for me to ask what your true intent was when you took my bag.* **to all intents (and purposes)** almost completely; with regard to all the main or essential points: *Although he gave me a separate talk later on, it was to all intents and purposes exactly what he had said earlier.* **with intent to do s.t** (usu *law*) fully intending to do s.t, esp s.t bad: *He took the gun with intent to kill.*

intention /ɪnˈtenʃən/ *c/u.n* fixed desire or determination; plan or purpose: *What are your intentions in this matter? I have no intention of leaving until I get a satisfactory answer.* (**be full of**) **good intentions** (be meaning to do a lot of) good things for other people but usu not doing them.

intentional /ɪnˈtenʃənl/ *adj* (often negative) (of s.t said, done etc) that is/was intended(⇒ intend(1)); said, done etc on purpose and not by accident: *I'm sorry I hit you but it wasn't intentional.* Opposite unintentional.

in**'tentionally** *adv.*

-in'tentioned *adj* ⇒ well-intentioned.

in**'tently** *adv* in an intent(2) way.

in**'tentness** *u.n.*

intense /ɪnˈtens/ *adj* **1** (of cold, heat) very great in degree: *They were not able to get into the burning building because of the intense heat.* **2** (of an effort, argument, feeling etc) very great or deep: *an intense search; intense happiness/*

sorrow. **3** (*derog*) (of a person) showing too much feeling; being thought too strong in one's beliefs, opinions etc: *It's very difficult to have an ordinary conversation with Adrian because he's so intense about everything.*

in**'tensely** *adv.* in**'tenseness** *u.n.*

intensification /ɪnˌtensɪfɪˈkeɪʃən/ *u.n* fact or state of intensifying s.t or of becoming intensified.

intensify /ɪnˈtensɪˌfaɪ/ *tr/intr.v* (*-ies, -ied*) (cause (s.t) to) become greater, stronger or more intense(2): *The search for the missing child was intensified. Our efforts must intensify if we are to succeed.*

in**'tensity** *u.n* (often — of s.t) fact or state of being intense: *the intensity of the fire; the intensity of one's feelings; a woman of great intensity.*

in**'tensive** *adj* to a very great degree; showing a great amount of effort, care etc: *They carried out an intensive search of the building for bombs.* Compare extensive.

in**,tensive 'care** *u.n* (also *attrib*) (often *in —*) special room or section of a hospital where there is very great care of seriously ill patients using special machines: *The baby is in intensive care* (or *is in the intensive care unit*).

in**'tensively** *adv.* in**'tensiveness** *u.n.*

inter /ɪnˈtɜː/ *tr.v* (*-rr-*) (*formal*) bury (a dead person). Compare disinter.

in**'terment** *u.n* act of interring s.o or being interred.

interact /ˌɪntərˈækt/ *intr.v* (often — with s.o/s.t) (of two or more persons, things etc) act, have an effect, (on s.o/s.t, each other): *These two chemicals interact to form another one. The children are interacting well with each other.*

interaction /ˌɪntərˈækʃən/ *c/u.n.*

,inter'active *adj* that interacts or shows interaction.

intercede /ˌɪntəˈsiːd/ *intr.v* (*formal*) (try to) use one's influence (to persuade s.o (not) to do s.t about s.o/s.t else); act to bring peace, stop an argument etc (between two or more people etc): *Is there any chance of you interceding with John to get him to change his mind? He's been asked to intercede between those involved(2) in the quarrel.*

intercession /ˌɪntəˈseʃən/ *c/u.n.*

intercept /ˌɪntəˈsept/ *tr.v* catch or stop (s.o/s.t) before he/she/it gets to the person, place etc to whom/which he/she/it was going etc: *The police intercepted the criminals before they reached the town. The letter bomb was intercepted by the post office before it reached the minister.*

interception /ˌɪntəˈsepʃən/ *c/u.n.*

,inter'ceptor *c.n* **1** (*military*) fast aircraft used to intercept other aircraft before they can attack. **2** person who intercepts s.o/s.t.

intercession ⇒ intercede.

interchange /ˈɪntəˌtʃeɪndʒ/ *n* **1** *c/u.n* (often — of s.t) (*formal*) (example of the) act or state of giving and receiving in turn (s.t, e.g ideas): *There was a full interchange of views at the meeting.* Compare exchange(1). **2** *c.n* system of roads that join other roads (to each other), esp on a motorway: *If you want to go back along the way you've just been, you'll have to wait until you reach the next (motorway) interchange.*

▷ *tr/intr.v* /ˌɪntəˈtʃeɪndʒ/ **3** (often — (s.t) with s.o/s.t) (*formal*) (cause (s.t, e.g ideas) to) be given and received in turn (with s.o/s.t): *Their views were freely interchanged at the meeting.*

interchangeability /ˌɪntəˌtʃeɪndʒəˈbɪlɪtɪ/ *u.n* fact or state of being interchangeable.

interchangeable /ˌɪntəˈtʃeɪndʒəbl/ *adj* (often — *with s.t*) that can be interchanged; that can be used (instead of s.t else): *These two parts of the machine are interchangeable (with each other).*

intercom /ˈɪntəˌkɒm/ *c.n* kind of radio device or system with a microphone, loudspeakers etc that enables s.o to talk to another person in another place, e.g in an aircraft, office: *The captain of the aircraft welcomed the passengers over the intercom.*

intercommunicate /ˌɪntəkəˈmjuːnɪˌkeɪt/ *intr.v* communicate(3) with each other: *intercommunicating rooms in the hotel.*

intercontinental /ˌɪntəˌkɒntɪˈnentl/ *adj* (usu *attrib*) of or referring to the connections between different continents(1): *intercontinental trade.*

intercourse /ˈɪntəˌkɔːs/ *u.n* **1** = sexual intercourse. **2** (*formal*) social exchange of views, opinions etc between people; conversation(s), dealings, e.g in business: *There has been little intercourse between the two groups following the violent disagreements last year.*

interest /ˈɪntrɪst/ *n* **1** *c/u.n* (often — *in s.o/s.t*) desire or willingness to know or learn (about s.o/s.t), to give one's attention (to s.o/s.t): *I have very little interest in politics. It is often difficult to hold the interest of young pupils. She attracted great interest wherever she went. My interest was aroused(2) by the report in the newspapers.* **2** *u.n* (often *be of some, no etc* — (*to s.o*)) matter or subject that is of (some etc) concern (to s.o), that attracts the attention (of s.o): *What you do or say is of very little interest to me.* **3** *c.n* thing, activity etc that one does, often as a hobby or for pleasure, usu separate from one's work: *Bill's two main interests are gardening and music.* **4** *u.n* amount of money (to be) paid or received for borrowing or lending money, usu expressed as a percentage(1) per year of the amount borrowed or lent: Building societies *are now paying* 8·5% *interest to investors and charging* 11% *to* borrowers. ⇨ interest rate. **5** *c.n* (often — *in s.t*) share (in a business company etc): *He has a small interest in a building company.* **6** *c.n* (often *pl*) group of business companies etc of the same kind, esp when acting together to protect themselves etc: *The government has not been able to persuade the banking interests to support small firms.* **compound interest** ⇨ compound. **have an interest (in s.t)** have a particular reason for (wanting etc) s.t because it is of concern to oneself, to one's advantage etc: *He has an interest in the proposal and he'll make a lot of money if it succeeds.* ⇨ vested interest. **in s.o's (own) (best) interest(s)** to s.o's (own) (best) advantage: *It is in your own interest to keep in touch with him as he may offer you a job.* **in the general interest** in order to take account of the needs of most people. **in the interest(s) of s.t** in order to take account of, protect or help, s.t: *In the interests of public health, please wash your hands before leaving.* **lose interest (in s.t)** stop having any interest(1) in s.t: *As soon as he started talking I lost interest.* **rate of interest** = interest rate. **show (an) interest (in s.t)**; **take an interest in (s.o/s.t)**

(start to) be interested (in s.o/s.t). **simple interest** ⇨ simple. **vested interest** ⇨ vest².

▷ *tr.v* **7** attract the interest(1) of (s.o, an animal): *This subject doesn't interest me. The bone didn't interest the dog at all.* **interest s.o in (doing) s.t** make s.o do or consider (doing) s.t, e.g taking part in s.t, buying s.t: *I've tried to interest him in joining us but without success. Can I interest you in (buying) this fine piece of furniture?*

interested *adj* (often — *in (doing) s.t*; — *to do s.t*) (of a person) showing interest(1) (in (doing) s.t): *Could you please go away as I'm not interested (in talking to you). I'll be interested to learn what exactly went wrong.* Compare disinterested, uninterested.

interested 'party *c.n* (*pl -ies*) person or group of people who is/are concerned in some (business) matter, esp one over which there may be disagreement and whose opinions etc are important: *Can you persuade the interested parties to accept your terms?* ⇨ disinterested.

interesting *adj* who/that creates, holds etc s.o's interest(1): *He's always very interesting when he talks about his travels. It will be interesting to see what happens.* Opposite uninteresting.

interestingly *adv* **1** in an interesting way: *He talked very interestingly about his life.* **2** (often — *enough*) it is or may be a matter that I think you will find interesting: *Interestingly enough, I said exactly the same thing to him as you did.*

interest ,rate *c.n* (also **,rate of 'interest**) calculation of interest(4) usu expressed as a percentage(1): *Bank interest rate has increased by* 1%.

interface /ˈɪntəˌfeɪs/ *c/u.n* **1** (*formal*) point or place where two or more things, subjects, disciplines etc meet, have connections with or affect each other etc: *There is some degree of interface between the two subjects she is studying.* **2** (*technical*) (esp of a machine, e.g a computer) point or place where one (part of a) system or program(me) connects with another: *The new computer uses a standard interface to run the* word processor.

▷ *tr/intr.v/ˌɪntəˈfeɪs/* (often — (*s.t*) *with s.t*) (*formal*) **3** (cause (s.t, e.g a subject, discipline etc) to) meet, have a connection, (with s.t else): *If we are to get anywhere, we need to interface our work with what other people are doing.* **4** (cause (one part of a computer etc system or program(me)) to) connect (with another): *It is not possible to interface these two systems as they use different languages.*

interfere /ˌɪntəˈfɪə/ *intr.v* **1** (often — *between s.o/s.t and s.o/s.t*; — *in s.t*) (of a person) get in the way of (two people, things etc); try to help or stop (s.o, s.t happening), often when it is not necessary or wanted by s.o else: *I had to interfere between the two of them to prevent a fight. Would you please stop interfering (in my work) as I know exactly what to do.* **2** (often — *with s.t*) touch or examine (s.t, esp a machine) in a way that might damage it: *Don't interfere with the electrical connections as you don't know how they work.* **3** (usu — *with s.o*) touch etc s.o (usu a child) in an immoral way. **4** (often — *with s.t*) (of s.t that happens) prevent (s.t else happening): *All these interruptions are interfering with my work.*

interference /ˌɪntəˈfɪərəns/ *u.n* **1** fact or state

of interfering(⇨ interfere): *interference in s.o's method, with s.o's tools.* **2** (*technical*) noise on a radio, bad picture on a television etc, caused by other programmes, a storm, electrical machine etc: *What's causing the interference on my radio?*

,inter'fering *adj* (*derog*) (of a person) who interferes(1) too much: *an interfering old woman.*

interim /'ɪntərɪm/ *attrib.adj* **1** who/that is intended to be only for a short time, usu until s.o/s.t else replaces her/him/it: *an interim government/measure/report.*

▷ *def.n* **2** (often *in the* —) short length of time between two (main) things happening: *The new house isn't finished yet so in the interim we're borrowing a friend's flat.*

interior /ɪn'tɪərɪə/ *attrib.adj* **1** of or referring to the inside (of a house, building etc): *an interior wall.* Opposite exterior.

▷ *n* **2** *c.n* interior(1) part of a house, building etc: *The interiors of some houses I've seen are very badly designed(3).* **3** *def.n* place or area away from the coast of a country: *He travelled by boat into the interior.*

in,terior ,deco'ration *u.n* (work of) designing (⇨ design(5)), decorating, furnishing etc the interior(2) of a house, building etc.

in,terior 'deco,rator *c.n* person skilled in interior decoration.

interj *abbr* interjection.

interject /,ɪntə'dʒekt/ *tr/intr.v* (*formal*) say (s.t), speak, while interrupting what s.o else is saying; break into a conversation etc by saying s.t: *At this point he interjected* (*some remarks of his own*) *into the conversation. 'But,' he interjected, 'that is simply not true.'*

interjection /,ɪntə'dʒekʃən/ *n* **1** *c.n* (*written abbr* interj) (*grammar*) word, expression, sound or the word(s) representing a sound, spoken quickly or suddenly to show a feeling, e.g of surprise, pain, annoyance, pleasure (often followed by an exclamation mark (!) in writing): *'Oh!', 'Oh dear!', 'Great!', 'Ah!', 'Ouch!' are all interjections.* **2** *u.n* act or fact of interjecting.

interlock /,ɪntə'lɒk/ *tr/intr.v* (cause (s.t) to) lock together (with s.t else), fit (into s.t else), and so make the two things more complete, joined etc: *This piece of the machine interlocks with that one.*

interloper /'ɪntə,ləupə/ *c.n* **1** (*derog; formal*) person who goes, gets, into a place where he/she should not go, often to do s.t bad: *The police arrested an interloper in the women students' hall.* **2** person who joins, tries to join, a group of people who do not want or accept her/him: *Ken was regarded as an interloper by the other members of the club.*

intermarry /,ɪntə'mærɪ/ *intr.v* (*-ies*, *-ied*) (often — *with* s.o) marry s.o of a different religious group, race etc: *Families from different religions have been intermarrying* (*with each other*) *for the past 100 years in this country.*

intermarriage /,ɪntə'mærɪdʒ/ *u.n.*

intermediary /,ɪntə'miːdɪərɪ/ *c.n* (*pl -ies*) (often — *between* s.o/s.t *and* s.o/s.t) person, organization etc who/that comes, who acts as a messenger, (between two groups of people, organizations etc, esp those who are fighting against each other, disagree about s.t etc): *The*

government *has offered to act as an intermediary between the two countries in the quarrel over their borders.*

intermediate /,ɪntə'miːdɪət/ *adj* **1** that is at a stage, e.g of difficulty, development, between a lower stage and a higher one: *an intermediate language course*; *intermediate* technology (i.e one that is more advanced than the use of very basic tools but does not use the latest, most advanced machines etc). Compare elementary(1), advanced.

▷ *intr.v* /,ɪntə'miːdɪ,eɪt/ **2** = mediate.

interment ⇨ inter.

interminable /ɪn'tɜːmɪnəbl/ *adj* (of s.t said, done; of a delay etc) that seems as though it will never end and is therefore becoming very annoying: *After interminable delays our plane finally took off.*

in'terminably *adv.*

intermission /,ɪntə'mɪʃən/ *c/u.n* (example of the) short break or interval(1) or the time this lasts, usu between acts in a play, parts of a film or radio/television broadcast: *The film will continue after a short intermission. During the intermission we had a drink in the bar.* ⇨ interval(2).

intermittent /,ɪntə'mɪtənt/ *adj* that happens with stops or pauses in between: *intermittent rain/pain.* Compare incessant.

intern¹ /'ɪntɜːn/ *c.n* (also **'interne**) (US) young doctor who is still training and who lives and works in a hospital while doing so. Compare house officer.

intern² /ɪn'tɜːn/ *tr.v* (during a war) put (s.o, esp one who is of the same nationality(1) as the enemy or who is considered likely to help the enemy) into a special camp, building etc or prevent her/him from moving about freely.

internee /,ɪntɜː'niː/ *c.n* person who is interned².

in'ternment *c/u.n* (also *attrib*) (example of the) act or state of interning² s.o or of being interned²: *an internment camp.*

internal /ɪn'tɜːnl/ *adj* (usu *attrib*) **1** of or referring to the inside of the body: *the internal organs. He is suffering from internal injuries.* **2** of or referring to matters, things that happen etc, inside a country: *No country has the right to interfere in the internal affairs of another country.* Opposite external .

in,ternal com'bustion *u.n* (also *attrib*) (*technical*) burning of fuel(1) inside an engine, e.g of a car, to produce power: *an internal-combustion engine.*

international /,ɪntə'næʃənl/ *adj* **1** that refers to, is done between, two or more nations or countries; that refers to all nations: *an international football match*; *international law*; *international waters* (i.e seas not belonging to any country); *international airlines/trade.* Compare national(1).

▷ *c.n* **2** (player who takes part in a) match, sport etc that is international(1): *I watched the international between France and England on television.*

,inter,national 'date,line *unique n* = dateline.

,inter'nationalist *c.n* **1** = international(2). **2** person supporting close cooperation(1) between all nations.

,inter'nationally *adv.*

interne ⇨ intern¹.

internecine /ˌɪntəˈniːsaɪn/ adj (formal) (esp of war, fighting etc) that causes death and destruction to both sides; (of people fighting other members of their own group) that leads to death, destruction, great damage etc among them all: an internecine war/struggle/dispute(1).

internee, internment ⇨ intern².

interplay /ˈɪntəˌpleɪ/ u.n action, effect, of one thing on another: the interplay of light and shade, between the various colours.

interpose /ˌɪntəˈpəʊz/ tr/intr.v (formal) add (s.t) to (a discussion); say s.t, interrupt, make an objection, during s.t being said by s.o else: Can I interpose a few questions, please?
interposition /ˌɪntəpəˈzɪʃən/ c/u.n.

interpret /ɪnˈtɜːprɪt/ v 1 tr/intr.v translate (what s.o is saying) into another language, usu while the person is speaking, so that others can understand it: I will need someone to interpret for me when I meet the Chinese visitors. 2 tr.v (often — s.t as s.t) (formal) take or understand (s.t as meaning s.t); explain (s.t as meaning s.t): This passage in the book is rather difficult to interpret. Am I to interpret your remarks as a refusal? 3 tr.v play (a character in a play, a piece of music etc) in a certain way to bring out a special meaning: Larry interpreted the part of the king in an interesting way.
interpretation /ɪnˌtɜːprɪˈteɪʃən/ c/u.n (example of the) act or state of interpreting s.t. **put one's own interpretation on s.t**, give s.t a meaning, level of importance etc that suits one's own needs or opinion.
in'terpreter c.n person who interprets(1) s.t, for s.o etc: He had a job as interpreter at the United Nations.

interracial /ˌɪntəˈreɪʃəl/ adj of or referring to two or more races: interracial harmony(2).

interrogate /ɪnˈterəˌɡeɪt/ tr.v question (s.o, esp s.o who is suspected of having done s.t wrong or who has information one wants) very fully: They interrogated the captured soldiers in order to find out about the enemy's strength.
interrogation /ɪnˌterəˈɡeɪʃən/ c/u.n.
in'terrogator c.n person who interrogates s.o.
interrogative /ˌɪntəˈrɒɡətɪv/ adj 1 (grammar) of or referring to a question, questions, words used in questions etc: the interrogative form; an interrogative pronoun.
▷ c/def.n 2 word, sentence etc that is interrogative(1): Change these statements into the interrogative.

interrupt /ˌɪntəˈrʌpt/ v 1 tr/intr.v break into (the conversation of s.o); stop (s.o) from talking by talking oneself: His speech was interrupted by shouts from outside. Please do not interrupt (us) while we are talking. 2 tr.v cause (s.t) to stop, not continue etc for a short or long time: Supplies have been interrupted because of the strike. His arrival at my door interrupted the rest I was having. ⇨ uninterrupted.
interruption /ˌɪntəˈrʌpʃən/ c/u.n (example of the, length of time of the) act or state of interrupting s.o/s.t or of being interrupted: After a short interruption he went back to work.

intersect /ˌɪntəˈsekt/ tr/intr.v (of two or more lines, roads etc) cross (each other, another line, road etc) at a certain point: Line AB intersects line CD at E.

intersection /ˌɪntəˈsekʃən/ n 1 u.n (often the — of s.t and s.t) act or state of intersecting or being intersected. 2 c.n place where two or more lines, roads etc intersect.

intersperse /ˌɪntəˈspɜːs/ tr.v (often — s.t with s.t) (formal) interrupt, break up, (s.t, a speech) by putting in other things: His remarks were interspersed with attacks on the government.

intertwine /ˌɪntəˈtwaɪn/ tr/intr.v (cause (s.t, e.g ropes, climbing plants) to) twine(2) or twist together: Different climbing roses intertwined over the front door.

interval /ˈɪntəvəl/ c.n 1 (length of) time between two things happening: He started work again after a short interval. 2 (length of) time between acts of a play, radio or television programmes etc: There will be an interval of 15 minutes after the second act. ⇨ intermission. 3 (often at —s (of s.t); at 2 hour, metre etc —s) space(s) (of a certain length or time) between each pair of things: The seeds should be sown at intervals of about 3 centimetres. The bell rings at hourly intervals.

intervene /ˌɪntəˈviːn/ intr.v 1 (often — between s.o and s.o; — in s.t) (of a person) come (between s.o and s.o) so as to stop them fighting, quarrelling etc; interfere (in s.t) so as to stop it getting worse: If we don't intervene (between them) soon, there will be a serious quarrel. You must not intervene in quarrels between husband and wife. 2 (of s.t that happens) happen or come between now and another event: If nothing else intervenes I'll see you at 6 o'clock.
ˌinter'vening attrib.adj (of time etc) happening or coming between a certain moment and another event: In the intervening months before he went abroad, Sam occupied(3) his time learning German.
intervention /ˌɪntəˈvenʃən/ c/u.n.

interview /ˈɪntəˌvjuː/ c.n 1 formal meeting where s.o is asked questions about herself/himself/s.t, e.g because she/he wants a job: I've got an interview next week for a job as Sales Manager. 2 meeting where s.o gives information about herself/himself/s.t, is asked questions etc, e.g by a reporter for printing in a newspaper, broadcasting on radio or television: The footballer held an interview to explain why he was retiring.
▷ tr.v 3 have an interview with (s.o): I was interviewed for the job but didn't get it. The police are interviewing a number of people who saw the robbery.
'inter,viewer c.n person who interviews(3).

intestate /ɪnˈtesteɪt/ pred.adj (usu die —) (law) without having made a will²(1).

intestine /ɪnˈtestɪn/ c.n (usu pl) long coiled(1) tube forming part of the alimentary canal that carries waste food from the stomach to the anus: the large/small intestine (i.e different parts of this tube).
intestinal /ɪnˈtestɪnl/ adj (usu attrib) of or referring to the intestine(s): intestinal disorders(3).

intimate¹ /ˈɪntɪmɪt/ adj 1 (often — with s.o) very close and friendly (in one's relations with s.o), often in a sexual way: His wife accused him of having been intimate with their nextdoor neighbour. 2 (of a person's behaviour, life etc) very personal and private: She found it difficult to talk about the intimate details of her life. 3 (of knowledge etc) very detailed and complete: Her intimate knowledge of their customs comes from having lived among them for many years. **be intimate** (**with s.o**) have sexual intercourse (with s.o). **be on intimate terms** (**with s.o**) be intimate¹(1) (with s.o).

▷ *c.n* **4** (*formal*) very close friend.
intimacy /ˈɪntɪməsɪ/ *u.n.* **ˈintimately** *adv.*

intimate² /ˈɪntɪˌmeɪt/ *tr.v* (often — (to s.o) that . . .) (*formal*) make (s.t) known (to s.o); suggest (to s.o that. . .) without stating it clearly: *They intimated their approval of the plan. He seemed to be intimating that I'd get the job if I applied.*
intimation /ˌɪntɪˈmeɪʃən/ *c/u.n.*

intimidate /ɪnˈtɪmɪˌdeɪt/ *tr.v* make (s.o) frightened so that he/she does what one wants or does not do s.t: *He was accused of trying to intimidate the witnesses by getting his friends to threaten them with violence. Some children are so sensitive that they are easily intimidated by older and rougher children.*
inˈtimiˌdating *adj* who/that causes fear: *I find his presence rather intimidating.*
intimidation /ɪnˌtɪmɪˈdeɪʃən/ *u.n.*

into (strong form /ˈɪntuː/, weak form /ˈɪntə/) *prep* **1** (showing movement from outside a place etc to inside or within it): *Pam came into the room. The train went into the tunnel.* Compare in²(5,17). **2** (moving so that one/s.t is fully or partly covered by or enclosed within s.t): *She fell into the stream. Get into old clothes before you start painting the house.* Compare in²(6,17). **3** (hitting) against (s.o/s.t): *She ran into him and almost knocked him over.* **4** looking at, facing towards the direction of, (s.o/s.t): *You'll damage your eyesight if you look into the sun. Speak into the* microphone *if you want to be heard clearly.* **5** (showing a change (from one state) to a new state): *The liquid will turn into gas when heated. At the final stage the* chrysalis *turns into a butterfly.* **6** (showing the development of a new condition or state): *He plans to go into business on his own. You'll get into trouble if you do that. We all burst into laughter when we saw him.* **7** (*mathematics*) (showing one number divided by another): *10 into 100 goes 10 times (or equals 10).* **8** (often be/get — s.t) (*informal*) very interested (in s.t); used (to s.t): *He's getting into health foods in a big way. He's heavily into* drugs(2). For 'into' with verbs and nouns, e.g *back into s.t, get into s.w, get one's hooks into s.o, go into s.t, go into action, put into s.w, put ideas into s.o's head,* ⇒ the verb/noun.

intolerable /ɪnˈtɒlərəbl/ *adj* that cannot be borne; that is too much to put up with; not tolerable: *The pain was almost intolerable.*
inˈtolerably *adv.*

intolerant /ɪnˈtɒlərənt/ *adj* (often — of s.t) (of a person) who cannot accept (the ideas, beliefs etc of s.o else); esp when they are different from one's own; not tolerant: *Her views about other people's opinions show how intolerant she is. He is intolerant of other people's opinions.*
inˈtolerance *u.n.* **inˈtolerantly** *adv.*

intonation /ˌɪntəˈneɪʃən/ *c/u.n.* (example of the) rise and fall in the level of pitch¹(4) of the voice when speaking: *As he got angrier, his intonation grew more marked. Questions are often marked with a rising intonation at the end.*

intoxicate /ɪnˈtɒksɪˌkeɪt/ *tr.v* (*formal*) **1** (of

alcoholic(1) drink) make (s.o) drunk. **2** (of s.t that happens, that one sees etc) make (s.o) become pleased and very excited: *The beauty of the scene intoxicated her.*
intoxicant /ɪnˈtɒksɪkənt/ *c.n* (*formal*) alcoholic(1) drink.
inˈtoxiˌcated *adj* in a state of intoxication: *He was arrested for being intoxicated. I was intoxicated by my success.*
intoxication /ɪnˌtɒksɪˈkeɪʃən/ *u.n* fact or state of intoxicating s.o or of being intoxicated.

intr *written abbr* intransitive.

intractable /ɪnˈtræktəbl/ *adj* (*formal*) (of a person, s.o's temper, a difficulty, problem etc) who/ that cannot be (easily) controlled or managed: *He always was an intractable child and when he grew up he became even worse. The problems we face look intractable.*
intractability /ɪnˌtræktəˈbɪlɪtɪ/ *u.n.*

intransigent /ɪnˈtrænsɪdʒənt/ *adj* (*derog; formal*) (of a person, behaviour etc) who/that remains unwilling to change, give up s.t, e.g beliefs or opinions, in spite of pressure: *In spite of all we said against the scheme, he remains intransigent and says he will organize it.*
inˈtransigence *u.n.* **inˈtransigently** *adv.*

intransitive /ɪnˈtrænsɪtɪv/ *adj* **1** (*written abbr intr*) (*grammar*) (of a verb) that does not have a direct object, e.g 'knock' in 'I knocked on the door' or 'talked' in 'I talked to him'. Compare transitive(1).
▷ *c.n* **2** (*written abbr intr.v*) intransitive(1) verb.

intrauterine /ˌɪntrəˈjuːtərɪn/ *adj* inside the womb.
ˌintraˌuterine deˈvice *c.n* (*abbr IUD*) a kind of contraceptive like a plastic loop or ring placed in a woman's uterus.

intravenous /ˌɪntrəˈviːnəs/ *adj* (*medical*) inside, going into, a vein(1) or veins: *an intravenous injection.*
ˌintraˈvenously *adv.*

intrepid /ɪnˈtrepɪd/ *adj* (*formal*) (of a person, act etc) who/that shows no fear: *an intrepid explorer.*
intrepidity /ˌɪntreˈpɪdɪtɪ/ *u.n.* **inˈtrepidly** *adv.*

intricate /ˈɪntrɪkɪt/ *adj* (of (the details of) an object, machine, story etc) complicated and therefore difficult to understand: *You need to follow the instructions very closely as the knitting* pattern(2) *is very intricate. The story became so intricate that I lost interest.*
intricacy /ˈɪntrɪkəsɪ/ *n* (*pl -ies*) (often — of s.t) (*formal*) **1** *c.n* (often *pl*) thing that is intricate: *the intricacies of the* digestive *system.* **2** *u.n* fact or quality of being intricate: *the intricacy of the* plot.
ˈintricately *adv.*

intrigue /ˈɪntriːg/ *c/u.n* **1** (example of the) act or state of having or making secret plans or plots(1), esp against s.o, to get an advantage for oneself etc: *As a result of all the political intrigue(s), he lost his job as a government Minister.*
▷ *v* /ɪnˈtriːg/ **2** *intr.v* (often — (with s.o) against s.o) (*formal*) make secret plans or plots(1) (with s.o) (against s.o else): *He seems to spend most of his time intriguing against his boss so that he can get his job.* **3** *tr.v* (of a person, idea etc) catch the interest or attention of (s.o): *Her ideas for a change in society intrigued us.*

in'triguing *adj* who/that intrigues(3) s.o: *What an intriguing idea!*

intrinsic /ɪnˈtrɪnsɪk/ *adj* (of a quality, value etc) that belongs to the thing, object etc itself and not taking into account any other considerations: *The intrinsic value of the jewellery is very little but because it was owned by a film-star its actual value is very high.* Compare extrinsic.

in'trinsically *adv* (if one considers s.t) in an intrinsic way: *Intrinsically, I suppose you are right but you ought to look at the wider problems also.*

introduce /ˌɪntrəˈdjuːs/ *tr.v* **1** (often — *oneself/ s.o to s.o*) formally make (oneself/s.o) known by saying one's/s.o's name (to s.o and giving or asking the other person's name at the same time): *Can I introduce myself? My name's Chris Hodge. Mary, I'd like to introduce you to Stephen. I don't think we've been introduced. I will now introduce our guest speaker for tonight.* **2** (often — *s.t into s.t/s.w* (*from s.w*)) bring (s.t new) (into a place, country, organization etc) (from s.w else): *Coffee was introduced into Europe from America. We need to introduce new working practices if we are to become a profitable(1) business.* **3** propose, put forward, (s.t, e.g a subject for discussion): *Before we go on to other matters, I'd like to introduce a new item(1) for discussion.*

introduction /ˌɪntrəˈdʌkʃən/ *n* **1** *c.n* act of introducing(1) s.o: *I think I can arrange an introduction for you.* **2** *u.n* (often — of s.t (*into s.t/s.w*)) act or state of introducing(2) s.t (into/to s.t/s.w): *the introduction of new working practices into the factory.* **3** *u.n* act of introducing(3) s.t: *the introduction of a new Bill.* **4** *c.n* (short) explanation at the beginning of a book, article, speech etc that describes what follows etc: *In his introduction, Victor spoke about his early life.* **5** *c.n* (often with capital I) (title of a) book etc that gives simple information about a subject: *An Introduction to Mathematics.* **make the introductions** tell people in a group who each person is: *You make the introductions and I'll pour the drinks.*

introductory /ˌɪntrəˈdʌktərɪ/ *adj* (usu *attrib*) that is or acts as an/the introduction(2–4): *an introductory chapter/offer/remark.*

introspection /ˌɪntrəˈspekʃən/ *u.n* (*formal*) fact or state of considering one's own thoughts, feelings etc.

introspective /ˌɪntrəˈspektɪv/ *adj* (*formal*) who/that shows introspection: *He's very introspective and does not get on well with other people.*

introvert /ˈɪntrəvɜːt/ *c.n* person who is very concerned with her/his own thoughts, feelings etc and not with things outside her/him: *Introverts like Francis seldom have lasting friendships.* Opposite extrovert.

'intro,verted *adj* who is an introvert: *He's so introverted that he never pays any attention to other people's problems.*

introversion /ˌɪntrəˈvɜːʃən/ *u.n* (*formal*) fact or state of being introverted.

intrude /ɪnˈtruːd/ *v* **1** *intr.v* (often — (*up*)*on s.o/ s.t*) come (into s.o's company), take up s.o's time etc, esp when not wanted: *I hope I'm not intruding (on you) but could you spare me a moment?* **2** *tr.v* (often — *s.t into s.t*) (*formal*) bring (s.t, esp s.t not wanted), into s.t: *The*

thought of failure kept intruding itself into his mind.

in'truder *c.n* person who gets into a place, usu when not wanted, esp as a burglar: *Dogs were used in the grounds of the house to keep out intruders.*

intrusion /ɪnˈtruːʒən/ *c/u.n* (often — *on s.t*) (example of the) act or state of intruding(1) (on s.o's time, private life etc).

intrusive /ɪnˈtruːsɪv/ *adj* (*formal*) who/that intrudes(1) (on s.o/s.t): *He objected to the intrusive nature of their questions.*

in'trusiveness *u.n.*

intr.v written abbr intransitive verb.

intuition /ˌɪntjuˈɪʃən/ *c/u.n* (example of the) ability to understand or realize s.t without having to work it out or study it: *Intuition told me that something was wrong.*

intuitive /ɪnˈtjuːɪtɪv/ *adj* who/that shows intuition.

in'tuitively *adv.* **in'tuitiveness** *u.n.*

inundate /ˈɪnʌndeɪt/ *tr.v* (*formal*) **1** (often passive, *be* —*d with s.t*) give or send to (s.o) so much, so many things, (that he/she cannot manage): *We were inundated with offers of help. I'm inundated with work and won't be able to go on holiday.* **2** cover (a place) with a flood of water: *The countryside was inundated after the heavy rains.*

inundation /ˌɪnʌnˈdeɪʃən/ *c/u.n.*

inure /ɪˈnjʊə/ *tr.v* (usu passive, *be/become* —*d to s.t*) (*formal*) accustom (s.o to s.t difficult or bad, e.g pain, hardship) over a length of time: *Over twenty years of marriage she has become inured to his insults.*

invade /ɪnˈveɪd/ *v* **1** *tr/intr.v* (of an army etc) cross the borders of (a country) and attack so as to get control of it: *Julius Caesar invaded Britain in 55 BC.* **2** *tr.v* (of people) come in large numbers into (a place): *London is invaded by tourists in the summer.* **3** *tr.v* interfere with (s.o's private life, rights etc): *He accused the newspapers of invading his privacy.*

in'vader *c/def.n* person, army etc who/which invades(1).

invasion /ɪnˈveɪʒən/ *c/u.n* (example of the) act or state of invading a place, s.o's private life etc or of being invaded: *the invasion of France; an invasion of my rights.*

invalid¹ /ˈɪnvəlɪd/ *c.n* **1** (also *attrib*) person who is, has become, ill or unable to live or move properly because of illness: *He has been an invalid all his life.*

▷ *tr.v* **2 invalid s.o out** (**of s.t**) let/make s.o, esp a soldier, leave the army etc (because of illness, a wound etc): *He was invalided out of the service after being wounded in the leg.*

invalid² /ɪnˈvælɪd/ *adj* (usu *pred*) **1** (*law*) (of an agreement, document(1) etc) that is not legal(1), that is no longer in force; not valid(2): *His claim was rejected(2) as invalid. This passport is invalid because it is out of date.* **2** (of an argument etc) not correct because the reasoning behind it is wrong; not valid(1): *The whole of his argument is invalid because it is based on false information.*

invalidate /ɪnˈvælɪdeɪt/ *tr.v* (*formal*) make (s.t), show (s.t) to be, invalid²: *The agreement was invalidated when they did not pay their share of the money. Recent discoveries have invalidated that line of argument.* Opposite validate.

invalidation /ɪnˌvælɪ'deɪʃən/, **invalidity** /ˌɪnvə-'lɪdɪtɪ/ *u.n.*

invaluable /ɪn'væljʊəbl/ *adj* (of a person, help etc) who/that is of so great a value that he/she/it cannot be measured or done away with: *Thank you for your invaluable help. He was invaluable to her in getting the work done.* Compare valuable, valueless.

invariable /ɪn'veərɪəbl/ *adj* (of s.t that one does, a habit etc) that does not or cannot change; not variable: *My invariable practice is to get up early and work for two hours before breakfast.*

in'variably *adj* always, without ever changing: *The trains are invariably late so there's no need to hurry.*

invasion ⇨ invade.

invective /ɪn'vektɪv/ *u.n.* (*formal*) spoken or written words full of hate towards s.o or about s.t, often including swear words: *His speech was full of invective against the politician.*

invent /ɪn'vent/ *tr.v* **1** (be the first person to) make or think of (a new machine, method for doing s.t) for the first time: *Nobody knows who invented the wheel.* **2** think of, find, (a reason, excuse etc), esp in order (not) to do s.t: *Sally invented an excuse to avoid going to the party.*

invention /ɪn'venʃən/ *n* **1** *u.n.* (often — *of s.t*) act or fact of inventing(1) s.t: *the invention of television.* **2** *c.n* thing, method etc that has been invented(1): *He has earned a lot of money from his inventions.* **3** *u.n.* (*formal*) ability or power to think of ways of doing s.t: *She showed great invention when bringing up her large family on such a small salary.* **4** *u.n.* ability to invent(2) a reason or excuse for (not) doing s.t: *His story about being ill at the time was pure invention.*

in'ventive *adj* (of a person, s.o's mind) good at inventing.

in'ventiveness *u.n.*

in'ventor *c.n* person who invents(1) s.t.

inventory /'ɪnvəntrɪ/ *c.n* (*pl* -ies) (written) list of all the goods in a place, e.g furniture etc in a house, stock in a warehouse.

inverse /ɪn'vɜːs/ *adj* **1** (often — *to s.t*) (*formal*) opposite (to s.t): *The results were inverse to the amount of effort put in.* **in inverse proportion/ ratio/relation to s.t** (esp *mathematics*) having the opposite order or relationship to s.t: *The volume(3) is in inverse proportion to the pressure.*

▷ *c.n* **2** (often — *of s.t*) opposite (of s.t): *The inverse of ⅘ is ⅘. He argued that the inverse of the statement might equally be true.*

inversion /ɪn'vɜːʃən/ *c/u.n.* (example of the) act or state of s.t being inverse(1) or of inverting s.t.

invert /ɪn'vɜːt/ *tr.v* (*formal*) turn (s.t) upside down; change the order of (s.t): *Invert the bowl and shake it until everything falls out.*

in,verted 'comma(s) *c/pl.n* punctuation mark(s) ' ' or " " to show that the word(s), phrase(s)(1) or sentence(s) in between is/are in direct speech, e.g 'Oh dear!' she said. ⇨ quotation marks.

invertebrate /ɪn'vɜːtɪbrɪt/ *adj* **1** (*technical*) (of an animal, insect etc) that does not have a backbone: *worms are invertebrate.*

▷ *c.n* (*technical*) **2** invertebrate(1) animal etc.

invest /ɪn'vest/ *v* **1** *tr/intr.v* (usu — (*s.t*) *in s.t*) put (money) into a business, property etc, buy shares in a business company, in order to try to make a profit (in s.t): *Ian invested all his savings*

in a building society. If you invest with us you will earn 10%. **2** *tr.v* (often — *s.o with s.t*) (*formal*) place (s.o) in a position of power, often with special powers: *The governor was invested with full powers. By virtue of the powers invested in me I now pronounce that the court is in session.*

investiture /ɪn'vestɪtʃə/ *c/u.n* (ceremony for the) act of investing(2) s.o.

in'vestment *n* **1** *c/u.n* (often *pl*) (example of the, amount of money used for the) act of investing(1) (in s.t): *He has made several investments in oil.* **2** *c.n* thing, e.g a house, object, crop(1) etc that one buys or puts money into in order to try to get a profit: *Coffee is not a very good investment at the moment.*

in'vestor *c.n* person who invests(1) money in s.t.

investigate /ɪn'vestɪˌgeɪt/ *tr/intr.v* look into, examine, (s.o/s.t) very carefully in order to find out about her/him/it: *You should investigate him and his background before you employ him. The police are investigating (into) the causes of the accident.*

investigation /ɪnˌvestɪ'geɪʃən/ *c/u.n* (example of the) act or fact of investigating s.t.

in'vesti,gator *c.n* person, esp an official, who investigates s.o/s.t.

investiture, investment ⇨ invest.

inveterate /ɪn'vetərɪt/ *adj* (*formal*) (of a person, habit etc) very fixed in a bad habit: *He's an inveterate liar.*

invidious /ɪn'vɪdɪəs/ *adj* (usu *attrib*) (*formal*) (of s.t said, done etc) that causes or is likely to cause bad feelings in other people: *They had the invidious job of having to decide who was to stay and who had to leave.*

in'vidiously *adv.* **in'vidiousness** *u.n.*

invigilate /ɪn'vɪdʒɪˌleɪt/ *tr/intr.v* (*formal*) watch (students, an examination) in order to prevent cheating: *He was asked to invigilate during the final examination.*

invigilation /ɪnˌvɪdʒɪ'leɪʃən/ *u.n.*

in'vigi,lator *c.n* person who invigilates.

invigorate /ɪn'vɪgəˌreɪt/ *tr.v* (usu *passive*) (of an activity, exercise etc) give strength, extra energy to (s.o): *I was invigorated by my swim.*

in'vigo,rating *adj* that invigorates s.o: *an invigorating climate/walk.*

invincible /ɪn'vɪnsəbl/ *adj* (*formal*) (of a person, army, argument etc) who/that cannot be defeated: *Her invincible will to win was the main thing that kept her going.*

invincibility /ɪnˌvɪnsə'bɪlɪtɪ/ *u.n.* **in'vincibly** *adv.*

inviolable /ɪn'vaɪələbl/ *adj* (*formal*) (of a law, right etc) that cannot or should not be taken away or broken: *Freedom of speech is an inviolable right of every citizen.*

inviolability /ɪnˌvaɪələ'bɪlɪtɪ/ *u.n.* **in'violably** *adv.*

inviolate /ɪn'vaɪəlɪt/ *adj* (*formal*) (of an oath(1), promise etc) that is kept unchanged; not violated(1).

invisible /ɪn'vɪzəbl/ *adj* (often — *to s.o/s.t*) (of a person, thing etc) who/that cannot be seen (by s.o); not visible(1): *Have you ever seen the film 'The Invisible Man'? These creatures are invisible to the naked eye.*

invisibility /ɪnˌvɪzə'bɪlɪtɪ/ *u.n.* **invisibly** *adv.*

invite /ɪn'vaɪt/ tr.v 1 (often — s.o for/to s.t) ask (s.o) to come s.w (for a special event, e.g a meal, performance etc): *My boss has invited us to dinner next Tuesday.* 2 (often — s.t (from s.o); — s.o to do s.t) ask for (questions, remarks etc from s.o); ask (s.o) to do s.t: *The chairman invited* comments(1) *from the audience* (or *invited the audience to* comment(2)). 3 (be s.t that is likely to) cause or make (trouble, a problem for s.o): *The presence of so many police on the streets was inviting trouble.* **invite s.o along** invite(1) s.o to join a meeting, holiday, party etc. ⇨ uninvited.

invitation /ˌɪnvɪ'teɪʃən/ n 1 c.n (often an — (from s.o) to s.o/s.t)) written or spoken request (from s.o) for s.o to come or go s.w for a special event: *They sent out hundreds of invitations to the wedding.* 2 u.n (often by —; on the — of s.o) (as a result of the) act of inviting(1) s.o (made by s.o): *Attendance at the ceremony is by invitation only.* 3 c.n (often — to s.o/s.t) act that encourages s.o (to do s.t, usu bad), s.t (to happen): *Not locking your doors at night is an invitation to thieves.*

in'viting adj that is or seems attractive: *The offer of a holiday in the country was very inviting.* Opposite uninviting.

invocation ⇨ invoke.

invoice /'ɪnvɔɪs/ c.n 1 written or printed document(1) with details of goods, services etc and their prices, sent to a customer: *Would you remind them that they haven't paid the last invoice we sent them?*
▷ tr.v 2 (often — s.o for s.t) prepare and send an invoice(1) to (s.o) for (goods etc supplied): *Please invoice me for the books you sent on approval. Shall we invoice the spare parts to you or to your head office?*

invoke /ɪn'vəʊk/ tr.v (formal) 1 call upon (a higher power, e.g God, the law) to help one: *If you feel your rights are threatened you should be able to invoke the law to protect you.* 2 ask for (help etc) in order to defend oneself etc: *He invoked the support of his fellow members to get elected.* 3 call up (a spirit, feeling etc) (as if by magic): *He claimed he could invoke the spirits of the dead.*
invocation /ˌɪnvə'keɪʃən/ c/u.n.

involuntary /ɪn'vɒləntərɪ/ adj (of s.t said, done etc) happening or working without conscious control; not planned or intended: *When he saw the dead body he gave an involuntary gasp. The heart has involuntary* muscles(1). Compare voluntary(4).
in'voluntarily adv. **in'voluntariness** u.n.

involve /ɪn'vɒlv/ tr.v 1 (often — (s.o) doing s.t) include (s.t, e.g an activity) as a necessary part: *My job involves a lot of travelling. It also involves (me) meeting people.* 2 (often — s.o/s.t in s.t) cause (s.o/s.t) to become a part (of s.t, esp s.t that one does not want): *It's nothing to do with me so don't try to involve me (in your problems).*

in'volved adj 1 (of s.t said, done etc) complicated; not at all clear: *His argument was so involved that I couldn't follow it.* 2 (often — with s.o/s.t) having a very close relationship or connection(4) (with s.o/s.t): *He's got himself involved with another woman.*
in'volvement c/u.n.

invulnerable /ɪn'vʌlnərəbl/ adj (often — to s.t) (formal) (of a person, position etc) who/that cannot be attacked, harmed or wounded (by s.t); not vulnerable: *He is invulnerable to criticism. The enemy was so well dug in that their position looked invulnerable.*
invulnerability /ɪnˌvʌlnərə'bɪlɪtɪ/ u.n.

inward, inwards ⇨ in².

iodine /'aɪəˌdiːn/ u.n substance or element(1) that is blue-black in colour, used in medicine and photography, and also to make dyes(1), *chem.symb* I.

ion /'aɪən/ c.n (science) electrically charged atom(1) or group of atoms(1) formed when electrons are added or taken away.

ionization, -isation /ˌaɪənaɪ'zeɪʃən/ u.n (science) act or fact of ionizing.

'io,nize, -ise tr.v (science) make or change (s.t) into ions.

ionosphere /aɪ'ɒnəˌsfɪə/ def/unique n (science) area of the Earth's atmosphere(1) about 60 kilometres above the Earth and extending to about 1000 kilometres where there are many ions and electrons, used to reflect(1) radio waves.

iota /aɪ'əʊtə/ c.n 1 letter of the Greek alphabet, 'i'. 2 (usu not be an — of s.t (in s.t)) smallest bit of s.t, e.g truth (in s.t): *There's not an iota of truth in his accusation.*

IOU /ˌaɪ ˌəʊ 'juː/ abbr 'I owe you'.
▷ c.n (often — for £5 etc) written piece of paper promising to pay s.o (£5 etc) at a later date: *I haven't got any money on me at the moment so can I give you an IOU?*

IPA /ˌaɪ ˌpiː 'eɪ/ u.n abbr (also attrib) International Phonetic Alphabet (the phonetic (system of) symbols used in this dictionary).

IQ /ˌaɪ 'kjuː/ abbr Intelligence Quotient.

irascible /ɪ'ræsɪbl/ adj (derog; formal) (of a person) who tends to get angry or annoyed very easily: *Don't argue with him as he's very irascible.*
irascibility /ɪˌræsə'bɪlɪtɪ/ u.n. **i'rascibly** adv.

ire /aɪə/ u.n (formal; literary) great anger: *He was full of ire against those who* opposed(2) him.

irate /aɪ'reɪt/ adj (formal) (of a person) very angry: *He gets very irate when he reads about cruelty to animals.*
i'rately adv. **i'rateness** u.n.

iridescent /ˌɪrɪ'desnt/ adj (formal) shining with many different colours, (as if) like a rainbow, which seem to change as one watches: *The waters of the lake were iridescent in the sunlight.*
ˌiri'descence u.n.

iris¹ /'aɪrɪs/ c.n round coloured part of the eye surrounding the pupil².

iris² /'aɪrɪs/ c.n kind of tall flowering plant with broad green leaves and usu yellow or purple flowers.

irk /ɜːk/ tr.v (often — s.o to do s.t) (formal) cause (s.o) some annoyance (to be forced to do s.t): *It does, I admit, irk me to recognize that he is better than I am.*

'irksome adj (of a job, s.t one has to do) annoying, esp because one cannot avoid it, would rather do s.t else etc: *We had the irksome task of clearing up after the party.*

iron /'aɪən/ n 1 u.n (also attrib) very hard metal substance or element(1), used in the making of steel, tools, objects etc and also found in very small quantities in food, blood etc, *chem.symb* Fe: *This was the first bridge made almost entirely* *of iron. He used an iron bar to break the door down. Take these iron tablets to build up your strength.* **2** *c.n* device with a flat bottom and a handle that is heated and used to make clothes, sheets etc smooth: *an electric iron.* ⇨ steam iron. **3** *u.n* (also *attrib*) (too) great hardness or strength that does not change, esp in one's character or determination: *a man/woman of iron. He had a will of iron* (or *an iron will*). **4** *c.n* (often *a number two, three etc* —) one of a number of different kinds of golf-clubs with a metal head and different slopes on the hitting surface. **cast iron** ⇨ cast. **have several etc irons in the fire** (*fig*) have many things that one can do, be doing many things, esp so that if one thing fails one can do another or the others: *Richard has so many irons in the fire that he is bound¹ to succeed with some of them.* **rule (s.o/s.t) with a rod of iron, with an iron hand** (*fig*) rule or control (s.o/s.t) very severely and harshly: *He ruled his children with a rod of iron and they were never allowed any freedom.* **soldering iron** ⇨ solder. **strike while the iron is hot** (*fig*) do s.t when it is the right or best moment to do it: *Since he is being so nice to you, you should strike while the iron is hot and ask him for a salary raise.*

▷ *tr/intr.v* **5** use an iron(2) to make (clothes etc) smooth: *I need to iron my shirt if we're going out. I spent the whole evening ironing.* ⇨ non-iron. **iron s.t out (a)** use an iron(2) to get rid of creases(2) or wrinkles(1) in clothes etc: *Use a steam iron to iron out these creases.* **(b)** (*fig*) settle or remove (a problem, difficulty etc): *They held a meeting to iron out their differences.*

'Iron ,Age *def.n* period in the past, beginning about 1000 BC, in the Middle East when iron tools, weapons etc began to be used. Compare Bronze Age.

,Iron 'Curtain *def.n* barrier(1) that was said to exist between the USSR with its allies and other countries in Europe and the West and that interfered with trade, travel etc until 1989.

'iron ,foundry *c.n* (*pl -ies*) foundry where iron is melted and made into shapes, objects etc.

'ironing *u.n* **1** act or task of using an iron(2) to iron(5) s.t: *Can you do the ironing?* **2** thing(s) that need to be, have been, ironed(5): *Just look at the pile of ironing!*

'ironing ,board *c.n* flat board, usu with folding legs, on which one irons(5).

,iron 'lung *c.n* (*medical*) kind of machine in a hospital into which a person is put to help her/him breathe, esp when the lungs fail.

ironmonger /'aɪən,mʌŋgə/ *c.n* **1** person who has a shop that sells household goods, tools etc. **2** (also **'iron,monger's**) shop that sells these things.

'iron,mongery *u.n* things sold by, the business of, an ironmonger.

,iron 'rations *pl.n* basic food supplies for use in an emergency.

'irons *pl.n* **clap/put s.o in irons** (*old use*) put chains on s.o and keep her/him prisoner.

irony /'aɪrənɪ/ *n* (*pl -ies*) **1** *u.n* use of words in speech or writing where one intends the opposite effect or meaning to the effect or meaning of the actual words one uses: *Because everything started going wrong she said, with gentle irony, what a nice time she was having.* **2** *c/u.n* (example of

the) fact or state of a situation etc where there is a difference between what one wants and what one actually gets: *You can understand the irony of the situation with him having had to beg her when earlier she had had to beg him. It was one of life's little ironies that he died a month after winning the money.*

ironic /aɪ'rɒnɪk/ *adj* (also **i'ronical**) (of a remark, situation etc) that has or shows irony: *I get tired of his ironic way of looking at things. It is ironic to think we put these people in power and now we complain about them.*

i'ronically *adv*.

irradiate /ɪ'reɪdɪ,eɪt/ *tr.v.* throw light on (s.o/s.t) make (s.o/s.t) bright.

irrational /ɪ'ræʃnl/ *adj* (*derog*) (of a person, behaviour, feeling, e.g of fear etc) who/that is not reasonable; not rational: *He has a quite irrational belief that he will succeed where the others have failed.*

irrationality /ɪ,ræʃə'nælɪtɪ/ *u.n.* **ir'rationally** *adv*.

irreconcilable /ɪ'rekən,saɪləbl/ *adj* (often — **with s.o/s.t**) (of two or more people, opinions etc) who/that cannot (be made to) agree (with each other or with s.o/s.t); not reconcilable or able to be reconciled: *The peace talks failed because the parties were found to be irreconcilable (with each other).*

irreconcilability /ɪ,rekən,saɪlə'bɪlɪtɪ/ *u.n.* **ir're-con,cilably** *adv*.

irrecoverable /,ɪrɪ'kʌvərəbl/ *adj* not recoverable.

irrefutable /ɪ'refjʊtəbl/ *adj* (of an argument, evidence etc) that cannot be proved wrong; not refutable or able to be refuted: *The evidence he produced of her part in the crime was irrefutable.*

irrefutability /ɪ,refjʊtə'bɪlɪtɪ/ *u.n.* **ir'refutably** *adv*.

irregular /ɪ'regjʊlə/ *adj* Opposite regular(1–3,8) **1** (of a shape, surface etc) not even or level; not formed in a regular way: *The surface of the road was so irregular that we could not drive the car along it. Her irregular handwriting made it difficult to read the letter.* **2** not happening at equally spaced points; not at regular intervals(1): *Nobody could explain the irregular appearances of the newly discovered star.* **3** (usu *pred*) (of s.t said, done etc) not according to a rule or custom: *It was highly irregular of him to try to influence the Minister in that way.* **4** (*grammar*) (of a word) not having usual or regular forms, e.g in endings (plurals, past tenses² etc): *You have to learn English irregular verbs by heart.* **be irregular in s.t** do s.t in an irregular(2) way: *She was very irregular in her attendance at lessons.*

irregularity /ɪ,regjʊ'lærɪtɪ/ *c/u.n* (*pl -ies*) (example of the) fact or quality of being irregular.

ir'regularly *adv*.

irrelevant /ɪ'reləvənt/ *adj* (often — **to s.t**) (of a remark, statement etc) that has nothing to do with the main point of s.t; not relevant: *Your argument about the cost is irrelevant (to the discussion) as we have already agreed an amount of money.*

ir'relevance, ir'relevancy *c/u.n.* **ir'relevantly** *adv*.

irreligious /ˌɪrɪˈlɪdʒəs/ *adj* (of a person, behaviour etc) who/that is against, does not show any interest in, religion; not religious: *She's totally irreligious and never goes to church.*
irˈreligiously *adv*. **irˈreligiousness** *u.n.*

irreparable /ɪˈrepərəbl/ *adj* (*formal*) (of damage, loss etc) that cannot be repaired, replaced or restored(2): *They suffered irreparable losses in the fire.*
irˈreparably *adv*.

irreplaceable /ˌɪrɪˈpleɪsəbl/ *adj* who/that is so valuable, so loved etc that he/she/it cannot be replaced: *The paintings that were stolen were irreplaceable. My wife is irreplaceable.*

irrepressible /ˌɪrɪˈpresəbl/ *adj* (of a person, (good) feeling etc) who/that cannot be controlled, stopped in any way: *The boy's irrepressible pleasure when he saw the new bicycle infected(2) us all.*
irrepressibility /ˌɪrɪˌpresəˈbɪlɪtɪ/ *u.n.* **irreˈpressibly** *adv*.

irreproachable /ˌɪrɪˈprəʊtʃəbl/ *adj* (*formal*) (of a person, behaviour etc) who/that is entirely free from blame, criticism or fault: *Her behaviour during the whole of that difficult time was irreproachable.*

irresistible /ˌɪrɪˈzɪstəbl/ *adj* (of a person, argument etc) who/that is too strong, pleasing or tempting to be resisted(3): *She looked irresistible in her new dress. Those chocolates are irresistible though I really shouldn't have another one.*
irresistibility /ˌɪrɪˌzɪstəˈbɪlɪtɪ/ *u.n.* **irreˈsistibly** *adv*.

irresolute /ɪˈrezəˌluːt/ *adj* (*formal*) (of a person, behaviour etc) who/that is not strong enough in the making of decisions; hesitating or not resolute: *Wendy paused irresolute, not able to decide what was the best thing to do.*
irˈresoˌlutely *adv*. **irˈresoˌluteness**, **irresolution** /ɪˌrezəˈluːʃən/ *u.n.*

irrespective of s.t /ˌɪrɪˈspektɪv/ *adj* (*formal*) without considering or taking into account s.t: *These jobs are open to all, irrespective of age, sex or race.* Compare respective.

irresponsible /ˌɪrɪˈspɒnsəbl/ *adj* (*derog*) (of a person, behaviour etc) who/that cannot be trusted or relied upon; not responsible(2): *It was quite irresponsible of him to leave the work to be done by other people.*
irresponsibility /ˌɪrɪˌspɒnsəˈbɪlɪtɪ/ *u.n.* **irreˈsponsibly** *adv*.

irretrievable /ˌɪrɪˈtriːvəbl/ *adj* (of a mistake, loss etc) that cannot be corrected, replaced or retrieved(1): *The business failed because of irretrievable losses.*
irretrievability /ˌɪrɪˌtriːvəˈbɪlɪtɪ/ *u.n.* **irreˈtrievably** *adv*.

irreverent /ɪˈrevərənt/ *adj* (*derog*) (of a person, behaviour etc) who/that does not show proper respect, esp in religion, to important people etc; not reverent: *He was asked to leave the church because of his irreverent behaviour.*
irˈreverence *u.n.* **irˈreverently** *adv*.

irreversible /ˌɪrɪˈvɜːsəbl/ *adj* (of a change, decision etc) that cannot be changed or gone back on; not reversible: *After the operation she went into an irreversible decline*(1) (i.e gradually weakened until she died without anybody being able to stop it).

irreversibility /ˌɪrɪˌvɜːsəˈbɪlɪtɪ/ *u.n.* **irreˈversibly** *adv*.

irrevocable /ɪˈrevəkəbl/ *adj* (of a decision) that, having been once made, cannot now be changed or revoked: *Under the new law the Chief Justices' decisions are irrevocable so no* appeal(2) *against them is allowed.*
irrevocability /ɪˌrevəkəˈbɪlɪtɪ/ *u.n.* **irˈrevocably** *adv*.

irrigate /ˈɪrɪˌgeɪt/ *tr.v* supply or bring water to (land, crops etc) using canals or channels(1): *There is a plan to irrigate the desert and grow grass and trees on it.*
irrigation /ˌɪrɪˈgeɪʃən/ *u.n.* (also *attrib*): *a new irrigation scheme.*

irritate /ˈɪrɪteɪt/ *v* **1** *tr.v* make (s.o) annoyed or disturbed, esp by doing s.t he/she dislikes etc: *Her continual complaints were beginning to irritate him.* **2** *tr/intr.v* (of a substance, material etc) cause soreness (to s.o, s.o's body), e.g by touching or rubbing it: *The soap got into her eyes and irritated them. Some skin creams can irritate (sensitive skins) and should be avoided.*

irritable /ˈɪrɪtəbl/ *adj* (of a person, feeling etc) who/that shows or can show annoyance (too easily): *Everything's gone wrong today so I'm feeling very irritable.*
irritability /ˌɪrɪtəˈbɪlɪtɪ/, **irritableness** *u.n.* **irritably** *adv*.

irritant /ˈɪrɪtənt/ *adj* **1** (*technical*) (of a substance) that causes soreness or irritation(2).
▷ *c.n* **2** substance that causes soreness or irritation(2): *The new soap powder had a chemical in it that acted as an irritant to people with sensitive skins.*

ˈirriˌtated *adj* (of a person) in a state of irritation(1): *The irritated audience started shouting.*

ˈirriˌtating *adj* (of a person, habit, behaviour etc) who/that one finds annoying: *Don't be so irritating and tell me what actually happened. She has an irritating habit of not looking at you when she's talking to you.*

ˈirriˌtatingly *adv*.

irritation /ˌɪrɪˈteɪʃən/ *c/u.n* **1** (example of the) fact or state of irritating(⇒ irritate(1)) s.o or of being irritated(⇒ irritate(1)): *Boris considered every interruption to his work as a serious irritation.* **2** (example of the) fact or state of irritating(⇒ irritate(2)) (s.o, s.o's body) or of being irritated(⇒ irritate(2)): *Be careful how you use this* ointment *as it may cause some skin irritation.*

is /ɪz/ *3rd pers sing, pres.t of* be.

ISBN /ˌaɪ ˌes ˌbiː ˈen/ *c.n abbr* International(1) Standard Book Number (used by librarians etc. for ordering and identifying books).

Islam /ɪzˈlɑːm/ *unique n* (countries, people practising the) Muslim(1) religion founded by Muhammad.
Islamic /ɪzˈlæmɪk/ *adj* of or referring to Islam: *an Islamic* festival(1).

island /ˈaɪlənd/ *c.n* **1** (with capital **I** in names) (name for a) piece of land surrounded by the sea or by water, e.g of a river: *the* Channel(3) *Islands*; *a desert island* (i.e one with no people on it). **2** = traffic island ⇒ traffic(*n*). **3** place that is like an island(1) because it is separate or different from other places, what surrounds it etc: *The house and its grounds were an island of peace after the noise and crowds of the town.*

'islander *c.n* person who lives on an island(1).

isle /aɪl/ *c.n* (with capital **I** in names) (*literary* or name for an) island: *the British Isles*.

islet /'aɪlɪt/ *c.n* (very) small island.

isn't /'ɪznt/ = is not. ⇨ be.

isobar /'aɪsəʊˌbɑː/ *c.n* (*technical*) line on a weather chart(2) or map showing places where the pressure of the atmosphere(1) is the same at a certain time. Compare isotherm.

isolate /'aɪsəˌleɪt/ *tr.v* **1** (often — *s.o/s.t from s.o/ s.t*) make or keep (s.o/s.t) separate (from other people, things etc) or on her/his/its own: *The earthquake destroyed the mountain road and this isolated several villages. He was found to be suffering from a rare* infectious(1) *disease and had to be isolated from other patients. His views on defence have isolated him from the rest of the party.* **2** find (a new substance etc) by separating it from other substances by experiment, research(1) etc: *Scientists have isolated a new kind of* bacteria *that may protect against this disease.*

'iso,lated *adj* **1** (of a house, place etc) on its own; lonely and without other houses, places etc near it: *an isolated village.* **2** (of a person, life etc) on one's/its own; lonely and without friends: *He lives a rather isolated life.* **3** (*attrib*) (of s.t that happens) single and not like anything else (that happens): *There was only one isolated* violent incident.

isolation /ˌaɪsə'leɪʃən/ *u.n* **1** (often *in* (*complete*) — (*from s.o/s.t*)) state of isolating(1) s.o/s.t (from s.o/s.t else) or of being isolated: *The doctor said he should be kept in complete isolation for a week.* **2** act or fact of isolating(2) s.t or of being isolated(1,2). **in isolation** (a) ⇨ isolation(1). (b) (considered) on its own without reference to other things; in an isolated(3) way: *It is wrong to treat this disturbance in isolation as it must be seen as part of the increase in violence in our society.*

,iso'lation ,hospital/,ward *c.n* hospital/ward¹(1) where patients are kept separate from other patients because they have an infectious(1) disease.

isosceles triangle /aɪˌsɒsɪˌliːz 'traɪæŋgl/ *c.n* (*mathematics*) triangle(1) with two equal sides.

isotherm /'aɪsəʊˌθɜːm/ *c.n* (*technical*) line on a weather chart or map showing places where the (average) temperature is the same at a certain time. Compare isobar.

isotope /'aɪsəʊˌtəʊp/ *c.n* (*science*) one of two or more atoms(1) in an element(1) with the same atomic number but with different mass numbers.

issue /'ɪʃuː/ *n* **1** *u.n* act or state of sending or giving s.t out or of making it able to be obtained, sold etc: *I bought the magazine on its first issue. The change in the law led to the issue of new orders to government officials.* **2** *c.n* thing that has been made, printed etc and is able to be obtained, sold etc: *Have you seen the latest issue of the magazine?* **3** *c/u.n* (example of a) matter or subject that is or needs to be discussed or argued about: *All your talk of improved living standards for some people avoids the real issues that face this country.* **die without issue** (*law*) die without leaving any children. **force the issue** (try to) get a decision made: *I don't want to force the issue but we've been talking for two hours and haven't agreed anything.* **make an issue of s.t** argue or disagree about s.t (that s.o else has said or believes): *I don't*

think you're right but let's not make an issue of it. **(the point) at issue** (the point, matter) that is or needs to be discussed or argued about. **take issue with s.o/s.t** (**on s.t**) (*formal*) disagree with s.o/s.t (on a certain point): *I must take issue with you on what you said about their behaviour.*

▷ *v* **4** *tr.v* (often — *s.t to s.o; — s.o with s.t*) send/ give out (s.t to s.o), provide (s.o with s.t), esp in an official way, for the first time, for sale etc: *The government has issued a warning to the public that these toys are dangerous. The group has been* issued with new textbooks(2) (or *New* textbooks(2) have been issued to the group). *A new set of stamps has just been issued.* **5** *intr.v* (often — (forth) (from s.t/s.w)) (*formal*) come, flow, (out into the open) (from s.t/s.w): *The spring issues (forth) from a crack in the rocks. Blood was issuing from the wound.* **6** *intr.v* (often — *from s.t*) (*formal*) come (from s.t) be a result (of s.t): *Their problems issue from a misunderstanding of their position.*

isthmus /'ɪsməs/ *c.n* (with capital **I** in names) (*technical*) narrow length of land that joins two larger areas of land: *the Isthmus of Corinth.*

IT /ˌaɪ 'tiː/ *abbr* information technology.

it /ɪt/ *n* **1** *c.n* (usu *sing*) shape, animal etc that is neither male nor female or of which the sex is not known etc: *We talked of the baby as an it before he was born.* **2** *u.n* (*informal*) attraction to s.o: *He's tall and handsome and I think he's really got it.* **be it** (*informal*) (a) be the most important, serious, point, esp of disaster, death etc: *I turned the corner and a car came towards me. 'This is it,' I thought.* (b) be the person (in a child's game) who must run and try to catch the other players: *It's your turn to be it.* **be with it** (*informal*) (a) be very modern, esp referring to fashion. (b) know the right people in society, fashionable places etc: *She's very with it — she knows all the right people and where to go in London.*

▷ *pron* **3** (as the object/subject of a verb or object of a preposition) (a) thing, fact, animal or person, baby or child (where the sex is not known or is not important) already mentioned or known: *I can't find my watch; have you seen it? I'm sure you'll get the job but it* (i.e getting the job) *doesn't depend on me. Don't go near that dog because it often bites people. The phone rang. 'It's your mother,' he said. A child is often frightened when it first goes to school. Look at that baby — isn't it sweet!* (b) group, organization, business company, country etc already mentioned or known: *The government has made mistakes and it must do something to improve things. It is a country in southern Europe.* ⇨ its. **4** (usu *it is, was* etc . . .) (as the subject of a verb to introduce statements about distance, dates, time, the weather etc): *It's Friday. It's 6 o'clock. It's cold, raining, too late. It was five miles to the nearest town. It'll be a month before we finish. It'll soon be five years since we met.* **5** (as the object of a prep) situation, fact etc already mentioned or known: *This pain is so bad that I can't bear it. And the worst of it is that he then stole the key.* **6** (usu — verb (adj) *that . . .; —* verb (adj) *of s.o to do s.t*) (used to introduce a following statement): *It seems/ appears that they don't know what to do. It's been clear that he would not come. It was nice of you to say so.* (Notice, 'it' is called 'impersonal *it*' or 'notional subject'.) **7** (usu *—is, was* etc) (used to emphasize the person, thing etc mentioned, esp to distinguish her/him/it from s.o/s.t else): *I'm sure it was James (that) I saw. It was in the classroom that I really learned to teach. What is it that you want to know?* **8** (as the object of some verbs when describing certain kinds of (good/bad) experience, situations, activities etc): *'How's it going?' 'Oh, the job is fine.' I've decided to go it alone* (i.e work by/for myself). **be in for it** be in trouble: *You'll be in for it if you continue to be late.* For 'it' + verb, e.g *ask for it, cut it out, make it, rub it in,* ⇒ the verb.

itself /ɪtˈself/ *pron (pl themselves)* **1** (*reflex pron*) used as the object of a verb or preposition referring to a thing, animal that is the subject: *The cat has hurt itself. The dog looked at itself in the mirror.* **2** (used for emphasis(2)): *Even the date itself was wrong.* (**all**) **by itself** (**a**) alone: *The child was walking in the shop all by itself.* (**b**) without help: *The door opened by itself.* **in itself** ⇒ in².

italic /ɪˈtælɪk/ *u.n* (also *attrib*) (often *in —*) handwriting or print having thick and thin letter shapes that slope at an angle: *These examples are printed in italic. He uses a special pen for italic handwriting.* Compare roman, bold(4).

italicize, -ise /ɪˈtælɪˌsaɪz/ *tr/intr.v* write or print (words etc) in italic handwriting, print etc.

i'talics *u/pl.n* (often *in —*) italic handwriting, print etc.

itch /ɪtʃ/ *c.n* **1** (often *have an —*) feeling of soreness or irritation(2) on or under the skin that makes one want to scratch: *I've got an itch on my back that I can't reach; could you rub it for me?* **2** (*fig*) (often *have an — for, to do, s.t*) strong desire (for, to do, s.o): *I have an itch to see the world before I die.*
▷ *intr.v* **3** have an itch(1): *The cut above his eye itched. I'm itching all over.* **4** (often *— for s.t; — (for s.o) to do s.t*) have an itch(2) (for s.t, (for s.o) to do s.t): *He was itching for a chance to escape. She was itching to tell him exactly what she thought of him.*

¹itchiness *u.n.* **¹itching** *u.n.*

¹itchy *adj (-ier, -iest)* having or feeling an itch(1) or itches.

it'd /ˈɪtəd/ **1** = it had. ⇒ have. **2** = it would. ⇒ will¹.

item /ˈaɪtəm/ *c.n* **1** one of a number of things, objects, esp in a list or as a class or group: *Shops now give you a list of all the items you buy with their individual(1) prices and the total amount. The police found various items of clothing near the scene of the murder.* **2** (also **¹news ˌitem**) (small) piece of news reported in a newspaper, on the radio or television: *Did you see the item last night about the lion that escaped from the zoo?*

itemize, -ise /ˈaɪtəˌmaɪz/ *tr.v* make a (detailed) list of (all the items(1) in s.t, esp an account or a bill): *You must itemize your expenses before the accounts department will pay them.*

itinerant /aɪˈtɪnərənt/ *adj* (usu *attrib*) (*formal*) (of a person) who travels from place to place: *an itinerant judge/preacher.*

itinerary /aɪˈtɪnərəri/ *c.n (pl -ies)* plan or route(1) for a journey, esp one stopping at different places: *Our itinerary covers several countries in Europe.*

it'll /ˈɪtl/ = it will/shall. ⇒ will¹/shall.

its /ɪts/ *possessive pron* the one(s) belonging to it (the thing, object, animal etc already mentioned or known): *I held the pot by its handle. The cat had lost its tail.* Compare it's.

it's /ɪts/ **1** = it is. ⇒ be. **2** = it has. ⇒ have.

itself ⇒ it.

ITV /ˌaɪ tiː ˈviː/ *abbr* (UK) Independent(1) Television.

IUD /ˌaɪ juː ˈdiː/ *abbr* intrauterine device.

I've /aɪv/ = I have. ⇒ have.

ivory /ˈaɪvərɪ/ *u.n* (also *attrib*) **1** hard white substance from the tusks of an elephant, used for making carved(1) objects etc: *He bought a box made of ivory (or an ivory box).* **2** white or cream colour like ivory(1): *They painted the walls ivory. She wore an ivory dress for her wedding.*

ivy /ˈaɪvɪ/ *u.n* (also *attrib*) kind of evergreen(1) plant with shiny leaves that climbs up walls, trees etc: *ivy leaves.*

Jj

J, j /dʒeɪ/ *c/unique n* **1** 10th letter of the English alphabet.
▷ *symb* (**J**) **2** jack(2). **3** joule.

jab /dʒæb/ *c.n* **1** quick or sudden blow or push, esp with s.t pointed or sharp, e.g a finger, stick: *She gave me a jab in the back with her elbow.* **2** sudden sharp feeling, esp of pain: *He felt a jab (of pain) as he bent down.* **3** (*informal*) injection(1): *a jab against cholera.*
▷ *v (-bb-)* **4** *tr.v* (often *— s.o with s.t; — s.t into s.o/ s.t*) give (s.o) a jab(1) (with s.t pointed); push (s.t pointed) (into s.o/s.t): *He jabbed me with his elbow. He jabbed the knife into the wood.* **5** *intr.v* (often *— at s.t*) push or poke(2) (at s.t): *He jabbed at the leaves trying to pick them up with his stick.*

jabber /ˈdʒæbə/ *sing/u.n* **1** quick excited talk, often not very clear or easy to understand: *Children! Stop all this jabber!*
▷ *v* **2** *intr.v* (often *— (away) (at s.o, among one-selves* etc)) speak quickly and excitedly (to s.o etc): *The children were jabbering among themselves quite happily.* **3** *tr.v* (often *— s.t out*) say (s.t) quickly and excitedly that cannot be understood clearly: *He jabbered out an excuse but I didn't know what he meant.*

jack /dʒæk/ *c.n* **1** instrument for lifting s.t heavy, e.g a vehicle, so that one can look at the underneath, change a wheel etc. **2** (also **knave** (*old use*)) (often *the — of hearts, spades* etc) playing card between a ten and a queen with a picture of a young man on it, *symb* J.
▷ *tr.v* **3** **jack s.t in** (*informal*) stop doing s.t: *I've decided to jack the job in and go and live in the country.* **4** **jack s.t up** lift s.t heavy, e.g a

vehicle, using a jack(1): *You'll need to jack the car up before you change the wheel.*

jackal /'dʒækɔːl/ *c.n* (*pl* jackal(s)) kind of wild animal belonging to the dog family.

jackdaw /'dʒækˌdɔː/ *c.n* kind of bird belonging to the crow(1) family (known for stealing small bright shiny objects).

jacket /'dʒækɪt/ *c.n* **1** kind of short coat, usu with sleeves, reaching to the thighs. **2** (also *attrib*) skin, esp of a potato: *potatoes cooked in their jackets*; *jacket potatoes* (i.e ones cooked with their skins on). **3** = dust-jacket.

jack-in-the-box /'dʒæk ɪn ðə ˌbɒks/ *c.n* toy in which a figure fixed to a spring jumps up out of a box when it is opened.

jack-knife /'dʒæk ˌnaɪf/ *c.n* (*pl* -knives) **1** kind of pocket knife with a folding blade.
▷ *intr.v* **2** (esp of a lorry with a separate trailer(1)) slide or skid(1) so that the cab(2) and the trailer are at right angles to each other: *The articulated lorry went out of control and jack-knifed right across the road.*

jackpot /'dʒækˌpɒt/ *c.n* amount of money that increases until it is won in games of chance such as cards or in competitions. **hit the jackpot** (a) win the largest amount of money in a competition etc. (b) (*fig*) gain a great success, esp through luck.

jade /dʒeɪd/ *u.n* (also *attrib*) kind of very hard green stone, used to make objects, jewellery etc: *a horse carved in jade*; *a jade earring.*

jaded /'dʒeɪdɪd/ *adj* (of a person, feeling etc) very tired, esp because one has done too much of s.t: *Joe looks very jaded; he needs a holiday.*

jagged /'dʒægɪd/ *adj* having sharp or rough edges: *jagged rocks*; *a jagged hole in the fence.* **jaggedly** *adv.* **jaggedness** *u.n.*

jaguar /'dʒægjʊə/ *c.n* kind of large wild animal belonging to the cat family and found in America.

jail, jailbird, jailer, jailor ⇒ gaol.

jam¹ /dʒæm/ *c/u.n* (example of a) fruit boiled with sugar and spread on bread and butter etc: *strawberry*(1) *jam.*
jam-jar *c.n* (also **jam-pot**) container for jam. **jammy** *adj* (-ier, -iest) **1** covered in jam (and so sticky): *jammy fingers.* **2** (*fig*; *informal*) (esp of a job) very easy; not needing much effort or work: *He's got a jammy job that needs only a few hours' work a week.* ⇒ cushy.

jam² /dʒæm/ *c.n* **1** large number of people or things, e.g vehicles, crowded together so that they cannot move easily or at all: *There was a jam at the door and I couldn't get out. He got caught in a traffic jam.* **be in, get into, a jam** (*informal*) be in, get into, a difficult situation: *I'm in a bit of a jam and wonder if you could lend me £10.*
▷ *v* (-mm-) **2** *tr/intr.v* (often — (s.o/s.t) *into* s.t; — s.o/s.t *together*) (cause (a number of people, things) to) crowd or be crowded (into a space, close together): *He jammed his clothes into the suitcase. The hall was jammed with people.* **3** *tr/intr.v* (often — (s.t) *into* s.t) (cause (s.t) to) become fixed or stuck (in s.t) (and so be unable to move): *He jammed a piece of wood into the hole. The door's jammed and I can't open it.* **4** *tr.v* stop (a radio broadcast, station) from being heard by broadcasting noise, music etc on the same wavelength, usu for political or military(1)

reasons. **jam on the brake(s)** ⇒ brake(*n*).
jam s.t on(to) s.t push or force s.t firmly on(to s.t): *Jane jammed her hat on(to) her head and walked out.*

jam-packed *adj* (often — *with* s.o/s.t) very full or crowded (with people or things).

jamboree /ˌdʒæmbə'riː/ *c.n* **1** (*informal*) large, usu noisy, gathering of people, e.g for a party. **2** large gathering of Scouts.

jam-jar, jammy, jam-pot ⇒ jam¹.

jam-packed ⇒ jam².

Jan *written abbr* January.

jangle /'dʒæŋgl/ *c.n* **1** harsh, usu unpleasant, noise, often (like) that made by metal objects hitting together.
▷ *tr/intr.v* **2** make a harsh unpleasant noise: *He jangled his keys. The bells were jangling.* **3** (usu — (*on*) s.o's *nerves*) cause (s.o's nerves) to become irritated.

janitor /'dʒænɪtə/ *c.n* **1** = caretaker. **2** (mainly US) person who cleans and looks after the entrance, stairs etc of a building, esp a block of flats.

January /'dʒænjʊərɪ/ *c/unique n* (also *attrib*) (*written abbr* Jan) 1st month of the year: *There are thirty-one days in January. I was born on January 10* (say 'January the tenth' or 'the tenth of January'). *It was a cold January day.*

jar¹ /dʒɑː/ *c.n* **1** container made of glass, pottery(2) etc and often with a lid, used esp for holding food, e.g jam-jar. **2** (also **jarful**) as much as a jar(1) holds.
jarful *c.n* = jar(2).

jar² /dʒɑː/ *c.n* **1** harsh sound or sudden movement like a vibration(1): *The ship gave a jar as though it had hit something.* **2** sudden unpleasant feeling or shock: *All that noise was a jar on my nerves.*
▷ *v* (-rr-) **3** *tr.v* cause an unpleasant shock to (s.o/s.t): *It seemed as though I had jarred every bone in my body when I fell.* **4** *tr/intr.v* (often — (*on*) s.o, s.o's *nerves*) (of a harsh noise, s.o's voice etc) (cause (s.o, s.o's nerves) to) become irritated: *Her high voice jarred* (*on*) *my nerves.* **5** *intr.v* (usu — *with* s.t) (of a colour, clothes, opinions) not match, not go together well, (with s.t); clash(9) (with s.t): *His tie jarred with his suit.*

jargon /'dʒɑːgən/ *u.n* (often *derog*) (example of) language that is difficult for other people to understand because it has special words used by a group of people in a particular subject: *medical/scientific jargon.*

jasmine /'dʒæzmɪn/ *c/u.n* (example of a) kind of climbing plant or shrub with small white or yellow flowers.

jaundice /'dʒɔːndɪs/ *u.n* kind of disease that makes the skin and the whites of the eyes turn yellow.
jaundiced *adj* **1** (looking as if) suffering from jaundice. **2** (of a person, opinion etc) having feelings of jealousy and mistrust(1), esp because one has suffered badly: *He has a very jaundiced view of life.*

jaunt /dʒɔːnt/ *c.n* **1** short trip, esp in a car, to s.w, usu for pleasure: *We had a jaunt up to town to see the lights.*
▷ *intr.v* **2** (often — *about/around*) take a short trip, usu for pleasure.

jaunty /'dʒɔːntɪ/ *adj* (-ier, -iest) (of a person,

feeling etc) showing that one is pleased, happy or satisfied: *You seem very jaunty today.*

'jauntily *adv.* **'jauntiness** *u.n.*

javelin /'dʒævlɪn/ *c.n* kind of long light thin spear that is thrown over a distance (in old times used for fighting but now as a sport). **throw the javelin** do this as a sport.

jaw /dʒɔː/ *c.n* **1** one of the two bones in the face in which the teeth are set: *the lower/upper jaw*; *the jaws of a* shark(1). **2** (usu *pl*) part of a tool or machine that grips or holds s.t: *the jaws of a* vice¹. **the jaws of death** (*fig*) very dangerous situation in which one could die: *He was saved from the jaws of death by the arrival of the rescue party.*

▷ *v intr.v* **3** (often — on/away (at s.o) (about s.t)) (*derog; informal*) talk at great length and in a boring way (to s.o about s.t): *Pete was jawing on at her about the new car he had bought.*

'jaw,bone *c.n* lower jaw(1).

jay /dʒeɪ/ *c.n* kind of bird with brightly coloured feathers and a harsh cry.

jaywalk /'dʒeɪ,wɔːk/ *intr.v* walk in a careless way across streets etc not paying attention to traffic.

'jay,walker *c.n* person who jaywalks.

'jay,walking *u.n*: *He was fined for jaywalking.*

jazz /dʒæz/ *u.n* (also *attrib*) **1** kind of popular music that was originally played by black people in the US; it has a strong rhythm(2) and usu has a number of improvisations in it: *modern/ traditional jazz*; *a jazz player.*

▷ *intr.v* **2** play jazz(1): *We jazzed all night.* **3 jazz s.t up** (*informal*) make s.t more attractive or interesting: *You need to jazz the book up with some pictures.*

'jazz-,band *c.n* group of musicians who play jazz(1).

'jazzy *adj* (-ier, -iest) **1** of or like jazz(1): *jazzy music.* **2** (*informal*) brightly coloured; attractive, interesting: *He was wearing a very jazzy tie.*

JC /,dʒiː 'siː/ *abbr* Jesus Christ.

jealous /'dʒeləs/ *adj* **1** (often — of s.o/s.t) feeling dislike or envy of (s.o/s.t), usu because he/she has s.t one has not got, s.t better than s.t one has got etc: *She was jealous of her brother who got all her parents' attention.* **2** feeling or showing dislike of other people who may be attracted to s.o one loves: *a jealous husband.* **3** (usu — of s.t) (*formal*) wanting to keep or protect s.t one has or owns and not give it up: *He was very jealous of his rights.*

'jealously *adv.* **'jealousness** *u.n.*

'jealousy *c/u.n* (*pl* -ies) (example of the) state of being jealous(1,2): *You must try and avoid all the little jealousies that go on in the village.*

jeans /dʒiːnz/ *pl.n* trousers, often made of denim(2) and blue in colour, worn informally by men, women and children.

jeep /dʒiːp/ *c.n* kind of small strong vehicle used for travelling over rough ground. **by jeep** in a jeep: *go/travel by jeep.*

jeer /dʒɪə/ *c.n* **1** loud rude laugh or cry that shows disapproval of s.o/s.t: *There were jeers and boos when he started his speech.*

▷ *tr/intr.v* **2** (often — at s.o/s.t; — at s.o/s.t) make such a laugh or cry (at s.o, s.o's remarks etc): *The crowd jeered ((at) him, (at) his speech).*

'jeering *adj* **1** making jeers(1): *a jeering crowd.*

▷ *u.n* **2** act or state of making jeers(1): *His speech was met by jeering.*

'jeeringly *adv.*

jell /dʒel/ *intr.v* **1** (of a substance) become firm as if, or like, jelly(1): *Let the soup get cold and when it jells you can serve it.* **2** (*fig*) (of an idea etc) become clearer and more detailed: *A plan of action was beginning to jell in my mind.* ⇒ gel.

jelly /'dʒelɪ/ *n* (*pl* -ies) **1** *c/u.n* (example of a) kind of sweet pudding made by mixing fruit flavouring and gelatine with hot water that will cool and become a solid but wobbly shape. **2** *u.n* kind of jam made from only the juice of fruit and sugar: *apple jelly.* **3** *u.n* liquid from other foods that has become solid like jelly(1): *meat jelly.* **4** *c/u.n* substance that looks like jelly(1): *The frog's eggs were surrounded by jelly.* **like (a) jelly** (*fig*) unsure, not very firm, because of fear etc: *My knees felt like jelly when I went for my interview(1).*

'jelly,fish *c.n* (*pl* -(es)) kind of sea creature with a body that looks like jelly(1), usu with long thin tentacles.

jemmy /'dʒemɪ/ *c.n* (*pl* -ies) kind of iron bar, often with a hook at one end, used to break open s.t, e.g a box, door, esp when stealing s.t.

jeopardize, -ise /'dʒepə,daɪz/ *tr.v* put (a plan, a chance of success) in danger, at risk (because of s.t one does): *You'll jeopardize the whole plan if you tell her.*

jeopardy /'dʒepədɪ/ *u.n* (often be, put s.t, in —) state of danger or risk of not succeeding: *Through your stupidity the whole plan is in jeopardy.*

jerk /dʒɜːk/ *c.n* **1** (often give (s.t) a —; with a —) sudden short sharp movement or pull: *There was a violent jerk as the aircraft landed. He gave her elbow a jerk to get her out of the way. He woke up with a jerk.* **2** (*slang*) stupid person.

▷ *v* **3** *tr.v* pull or push (s.o/s.t) with a jerk(1): *He jerked her elbow.* **4** *intr.v* move with a jerk(1): *The car jerked forward and stopped.* **jerk at s.t** pull or push at s.t, e.g in order to pull it out. **jerk to a halt/stop** move or slow down with a number of jerks(1) and then stop: *The car jerked to a stop.*

'jerkily *adv.* in a jerky way. **'jerkiness** *u.n.* fact or state of being jerky.

'jerky *adj* (-ier, -iest) having or moving with jerks(1).

jerkin /'dʒɜːkɪn/ *c.n* kind of short coat, usu without sleeves.

jerry-build /'dʒerɪ,bɪld/ *tr/intr.v* (*p.t,p.p* jerry-built /-,bɪlt/) (*derog*) build (houses) using poor materials so that they do not last long.

'jerry-,builder *c.n* person who builds houses using poor materials.

'jerry-,built *adj.*

jersey /'dʒɜːzɪ/ *n* **1** *c.n* kind of clothing made of soft wool and worn over the upper part of the body. ⇒ pullover, sweater. **2** *u.n* (also **'jersey-,wool**) (also *attrib*) kind of soft material made from wool: *a jersey dress.* **3** (with capital **J**; also **Jersey 'cow**) kind of cow that originally came from **Jersey** (one of the Channel Islands).

Jerusalem /dʒə'ruːsələm/ **Jerusalem artichoke** ⇒ artichoke(2).

jest /dʒest/ *c.n* **1** (*formal*) kind of joke, often said without being serious: *He made several jests about her appearance.* **(speak) in jest** (speak) in

a joking, not serious, way: *I was only speaking in jest so there's no need to get so annoyed.*
▷ *intr.v* **2** (often — *about/at s.t*) make jests(1) (about s.t): *Don't jest about my age!*
'jester *c.n* (in history) man whose job was to amuse a king, queen, nobles etc by telling jokes etc.
Jesus /'dʒiːzəs/ *unique n* (also ,**Jesus 'Christ** /'kraɪst/) founder of the Christian(1) religion.
jet¹ /dʒet/ *c.n* **1** strong narrow flow of water, liquid, gas etc that is pushed out with some force through an opening, e.g in a pipe. **2** narrow opening in a pipe etc through which a jet¹(1) comes: *Light the gas jet to start the boiler.* **3** (also '**jet ,aero,plane/,air,craft**) plane that flies using jet engines. **by jet** in a jet¹(3): *go/travel by jet.*
▷ *tr/intr.v* (-*tt*-) **4** (usu — (*s.t*) *out of* (*of s.t*)) (cause (s.t) to) come, be forced, out (of s.t) in a jet¹(1): *Steam jetted out of the* radiator(1). **5** (often — (*s.o/s.t*) *into, over to* etc, *s.w*) (cause (s.o/s.t) to) fly, be carried, by a jet¹(3) (to, over to etc, s.w): *He jetted into London for the meeting.*
,**jet 'engine** *c.n* kind of engine used in aircraft that sucks in air in front, mixes and burns it with a form of paraffin and pushes it out at the back.
'**jet ,lag** *u.n* feeling of tiredness one gets after having flown quickly through one or more time zones by jet¹(3); one's mind and body think that one should be asleep or awake when the actual time for doing these is now different: *Paul suffered from jet lag for two days after his arrival in New York.*
'**jet-,lagged** *adj* suffering from jet lag.
'**jet-pro,pelled** *adj* (of an aircraft or some vehicles) using a jet engine to move: *A jet-propelled car recently broke the land speed record.*
,**jet pro'pulsion** *u.n* system or method of driving an aircraft etc using a jet engine.
'**jet ,set** *c/def.n* (usu *derog*) group of rich people who spend their time travelling around the world enjoying themselves: *He belongs to the jet set.*
jet² /dʒet/ *u.n* (also *attrib*) hard black mineral substance, often used as jewellery or in ornaments: *jet earrings.*
,**jet-'black** *adj* very black in colour: *jet-black hair.*
jetsam /'dʒetsəm/ *u.n* goods, things etc thrown out from a ship and washed up on the shore. ⇒ flotsam.
jetty /'dʒetɪ/ *c.n* (*pl -ies*) kind of solid wall or structure(2) with supports built out into a sea or river, esp for boats to tie up against or to protect the coast or a harbour.
Jew /dʒuː/ *c.n* member of a race or group of people who once lived in the old state of Israel. ⇒ Judaism.
Jewish /'dʒuːɪʃ/ *adj* of or belonging to this group of people or to their religion.
jewel /'dʒuːəl/ *c.n* **1** (general name for) one of a number of different kinds of precious stones. **2** (*fig*) person or thing that one has a very good opinion of: *My wife is a jewel. The jewel of his collection was a Picasso painting.*
'**jeweller** *c.n* **1** person who makes and/or sells jewellery and other precious objects. **2** (also '**jeweller's**) shop where jewellery is sold.
'**jewellery** /'dʒuːəlrɪ/ *u.n* (also (mainly US) '**jewelry**) articles made with jewels, gold etc and worn as decoration on the body.

jib¹ /dʒɪb/ *c.n* **1** small sail shaped like a triangle that is placed in front of the mainsail. **2** top part of a crane¹(1) or other lifting device that sticks out like an arm.
jib² /dʒɪb/ *intr.v* (-*bb*-) **jib at** (*doing*) *s.t* **1** (esp of a horse) refuse to move further or to jump over s.t: *My horse jibbed at the hedge and I had to take it through the gate.* **2** (of a person) be unwilling to do s.t: *Though he was rich, he jibbed at paying such a high price for the painting.*
jibe ⇒ gibe.
jiffy /'dʒɪfɪ/ *sing.n* (often *be/take a —; in a —*) (*informal*) very short time: *It will only take a jiffy for me to be ready (or I'll be ready in a jiffy).*
'**Jiffy ,bag** *c.n* (*t.n*) padded envelope or packet used for posting books, clothes etc.
jig /dʒɪg/ *c.n* **1** (music played for a) kind of lively dance: *a Scottish jig.*
▷ *intr.v* (-*gg*-) **2** (usu — *about/around*; — *up and down*) move one's body (about/around or up and down) with little jumps in a jerky fashion: *The children were jigging up and down on their chairs.*
jiggle /'dʒɪgl/ *c.n* **1** (often *give s.t a —*) quick short movement from side to side or up and down: *He gave the key a jiggle but it still wouldn't open the door.*
▷ *tr/intr.v* **2** (often — (*s.o/s.t*) *about*) (cause (s.o/s.t) to) move from side to side or up and down: *He jiggled the baby on his knees. Stop jiggling about for a moment while I take a photograph of you.*
jigsaw /'dʒɪgsɔː/ *c.n* (also '**jigsaw ,puzzle**) puzzle made of many pieces of wood or cardboard of different shapes that fit together to form a picture.
jilt /dʒɪlt/ *tr.v* refuse to see or have anything to do with (s.o with whom one has been in love or whom one had promised to marry): *After three years Kate suddenly jilted him for another man.*
jingle /'dʒɪŋgl/ *c.n* **1** small noise made by metal objects, e.g coins, bells, hitting together. **2** short simple rhyme or poem, sometimes with music: *Many advertisements on television have specially written jingles.*
▷ *tr/intr.v* **3** (often — (*s.t*) *about*) (cause (s.t) to) make a jingle(1): *He was jingling the money in his pocket.*
jinks /dʒɪŋks/ *pl.n* **high jinks** excited noisy play; high spirits: *Stop those high jinks at once!*
jinx /dʒɪŋks/ *c.n* (often *be, put, a — on s.o/s.t*) bad or evil influence (on s.o/s.t) so that s.t goes wrong: *There seemed to be a jinx on their plans as nothing went right.*
jitters /'dʒɪtəz/ *def.pl.n* (usu *get/have, give s.o, the — (about s.t)*) (*informal*) very nervous feeling (about s.t frightening that is happening or going to happen): *She gives me the jitters with her talk about the escaped prisoner.*
'**jittery** *adj* feeling very nervous or afraid.
jiujitsu /dʒuː'dʒɪtsuː/ *u.n* (also **ju'jitsu**) judo.
jive /dʒaɪv/ *c/u.n* **1** (example of a) kind of dance and its music, popular in the 1950's and 1960's, in which one moves one's body, feet and hands about a lot.
▷ *intr.v* **2** dance a jive(1).
Jnr *written abbr* Junior.
job /dʒɒb/ *c.n* **1** regular work or employment for which one is paid money; kind or type of work that one does regularly: *He has a job in a bank.*

Her job is to check all the payments before they go out. **2** single piece of work: *When you've finished that job you can clean the car.* **and a good job too!** I am pleased with that result, event etc: *The police have caught the thief, and a good job too!* **be a good job (that . . .)** (*informal*) be an event, happening etc that is satisfactory, has a good result etc: *It was a good job you told me what to do or I might have made a bad mistake.* **be/have a job to do** (or **doing**) **s.t** (*informal*) be/find s.t difficult to do or complete: *She had quite a job finding him in that large crowd.* **give s.o/s.t up as a bad job** (*informal*) decide not to continue with (trying to improve) s.o/s.t because he/she/ it cannot be improved, is hopeless etc. **job lot** ⇒ lot(*n*). **just the job** (*informal*) exactly right for doing or completing s.t: *This tool is just the job for pulling out those nails.* **make a bad/good** etc **job of s.t** do s.t badly/well etc. **make the best of a bad job** do as much or as well as is possible in a difficult situation. **odd jobs** small separate jobs(2) that s.o does: *He's not very fit and so all he can get are odd jobs here and there. She does a lot of odd jobs around the house.* **out of a job** not employed at the present time: *He's been out of a job for the last year.*

ˈjobless *adj* not having a job(1).

jockey /ˈdʒɒkɪ/ *c.n* **1** person whose job is to ride horses in a race. ⇒ disc jockey.
▷ *v* **2** *tr.v* (*usu* — *s.o into, out of, s.t*) force (s.o) (into, out of, s.t) often by deceit or pressure: *He was trying to jockey her into accepting the job.* **jockey for position** (*fig*) try to get into a favourable situation in order to have an advantage over other people.

jockstrap /ˈdʒɒkˌstræp/ *c.n* belt with a bag that is worn by male athletes to support the genitals.

jocose /dʒəˈkəʊs/ *adj* (*formal*) funny(1); humorous.
joˈcosely *adv.* **joˈcoseness, jocosity** /dʒəˈkɒsɪtɪ/ *u.n.*

jocular /ˈdʒɒkjʊlə/ *adj* (*formal*) funny(1); humorous.
jocularity /ˌdʒɒkjʊˈlærɪtɪ/ *c/u.n.* **ˈjocularly** *adv.*

jodhpurs /ˈdʒɒdpəz/ *pl.n* (*often a pair of* —) trousers that fit closely below the knee; they are worn for riding horses.

jog /dʒɒg/ *c.n* **1** (*often give s.o/s.t a* —) small push or shake: *He gave her a jog to wake her up.* **2** (*often go for a* —) slow run as a form of exercise.
▷ *v* (*-gg-*) **3** *tr.v* give (s.o/s.t) a jog(1): *He jogged her elbow as he passed her.* **4** *intr.v* go for a jog(2): *I jog every morning before breakfast.* **5** *intr.v* (*often* — *along*) travel slowly often with an up and down movement (to s.w): *The bus jogged along and I thought the journey would never end.* **jog s.o's memory** make s.o remember s.t: *I showed him a photograph of Mary to see if that would jog his memory.*
ˈjogging *u.n* (*often go* —) activity of going for a jog(2) regularly.
ˈjog ˌtrot *c.n* (*often at a* —) speed that is a little slower than running.

joggle /ˈdʒɒgl/ *c.n* **1** (*often give s.t a* —) gentle shake or movement from side to side and up and down: *He gave the handle a joggle but the door wouldn't open.*
▷ *tr/intr.v* **2** (*cause* (s.t) to) shake or move: *He*

joggled the telephone receiver up and down but he had already been cut off.

join /dʒɔɪn/ *c.n* **1** line or place where two things meet or are fixed together: *You can just see the join where he repaired the cup.*
▷ *v* **2** *tr/intr.v* (*cause* (two or more things) to) meet, be tied together, be connected(1) in some way: *Join this wire to that one* (or *Join the two wires together*). *The blade is joined onto the handle by a small screw. This road joins* (*up*) *with the main road at the next village.* **3** *tr.v* become a member of (an organization etc): *He joined the* Liberal Party. *He joined the army after leaving school.* ⇒ join up. **4** *tr.v* come or go into the presence of (s.o); take part (in s.t) with (s.o): *I'm busy at the moment but I'll join you as soon as I've finished. Will you join me for a drink?* **join forces (with s.o)** ⇒ force(*n*). **join hands (with s.o)** ⇒ hand(*n*). **join in (s.t) (with s.o/s.t)** (begin to) take part (in s.t) (with s.o/s.t): *Can I join in (with your game)?* **join on (to s.o/s.t)** add oneself (to a group): *As they were going the same way as us, we joined on.* **join up** join(3) the army. **join up (with s.o/ s.t) (a)** ⇒ join(2). **(b)** meet and go together (with s.o); form a group together (with s.o/s.t) in order to do s.t: *We'll join up with the others later. The two companies joined up to get a better share of the market.* ⇒ joint, junction.

joiner /ˈdʒɔɪnə/ *c.n* **1** person whose job is to make or put in wooden parts, e.g windows, doors, frames, inside a building. Compare carpenter. **2** (also **ˈjoiner's**) workshop of a joiner(1).
ˈjoinery *u.n* work done by a joiner(1).

joint /dʒɔɪnt/ *adj* (*usu attrib*) **1** done, shared, held etc by two or more people acting together: *joint action; joint efforts; joint responsibility.*
▷ *c.n* **2** line or place where two or more things meet or are joined together: *a joint in the water pipes.* **3** place where two bones meet in the body in such a way as to allow them to move: *finger joints.* **4** piece of meat with a bone in it for cooking: *a lamb(2) joint.* **5** (*often derog; informal*) place, e.g a club, café, usu of poor quality: *He spends his time hanging around cheap joints in town.* **6** (*slang*) cigarette with a drug, esp cannabis, in it. **put s.o's nose out of joint** ⇒ nose(*n*). **put s.t out of joint** (accidentally) dislocate a bone.
▷ *tr.v* **7** cut (the body of an animal) into pieces at the joints(3) as a preparation for cooking: *First joint the chicken and then fry the pieces.*
ˈjoint (ˌbank) acˌcount *c.n* bank account held by two or more people.
jointed /ˈdʒɔɪntɪd/ *adj* having one or more joints(2) in it, esp one(s) that moves/move: *a toy with jointed arms.*
ˈjointly *adv* in a joint(1) way: *jointly responsible.*

joist /dʒɔɪst/ *c.n* beam, usu of wood or steel, that supports the floor or ceiling of a building.

joke /dʒəʊk/ *c.n* **1** short story that is intended to be funny, to cause laughter: *He told several jokes to make the audience laugh.* **2** thing that one does or that happens that causes amusement: *As a joke he wore red socks to the office.* **3** (*informal*) person who is not thought to be good at doing s.t: *As a minister in the government he's a joke.* **be/go beyond a joke** be/become too serious a matter to be amusing: *The way she's acting has gone beyond a joke.* **can't take a joke** not be able to laugh at a funny story about oneself. **crack a**

joke tell a joke. **dirty joke** joke(1) that is about sex or is obscene. **It's no joke (doing s.t)** (*informal*) It is a serious matter (doing s.t): *It was no joke when the car broke down miles from a garage.* **not see the joke** not understand what is funny, the amusing point, in s.t. **play a joke (on s.o)** play a trick (on s.o): *We played a joke on him and took away all his clothes while he was asleep.*

▷ *intr.v* **4** (often — (*with s.o*) (*about s.t*)) talk in a funny or amusing way (with s.o) (about s.t): *They were joking about how silly he looked in that hat.* **5** say s.t that one intends to be amusing (though others may not think so): *There's no need to get so upset; I was only joking.*

'joker *c.n* **1** person who likes making jokes(1) or playing tricks. **2** (usu *the* —) playing card with a picture of a jester on it; it often has a value greater than other cards.

'jokingly *adv.*

jolly /'dʒɒlɪ/ *adj* (*-ier, -iest*) (becoming *old use*) **1** cheerful, happy, merry: *You're feeling very jolly today! Did you have a jolly time?*

▷ *adv* **2** (often — *bad, good* etc (*of s.o. to do s.t*) (*informal*) very (bad/good etc): *It was jolly good of you to meet me..*

▷ *tr.v* (*-ies, -ied*) **3** (usu — *s.o along*; — *s.o into* (*doing*) *s.t*) try to get the help of (s.o) (to do s.t) by being pleasant or nice to her/him: *You need to jolly him along as he won't do it willingly.*

'jolliness, 'jollity *u.n.*

jolt /dʒəʊlt/ *c.n* **1** sudden violent movement or bump: *There was a jolt and then the train started.* **2** sudden shock, e.g as caused by electricity: *I got a jolt when I touched the bare wire.* **3** sudden shock (to one's feelings): *It was a bit of a jolt when she heard he had died.*

▷ *v* **4** *tr/intr.v* (cause (s.o/s.t) to) move suddenly and violently: *The train jolted and then stopped.* **5** *tr.v* (usu — *s.o out of s.t*) give (s.o) a shock (so that he/she stops doing s.t): *Sally was jolted out of her sleep by a loud explosion.*

joss stick /'dʒɒs ˌstɪk/ *c.n* hard material on a stick that produces a pleasant smell when it is burning. ⇨ incense.

jostle /'dʒɒsl/ *tr/intr.v* (usu — (*against*) *s.o*) knock or push (against s.o, each other) rather roughly: *A group of youths jostled (against) us as we came out of the cinema.*

jot /dʒɒt/ *sing. n* **1** (often *not a* — *of s.t* (*in s.t*)) very small amount (of truth, feeling etc in s.t): *There's not a jot of truth in the story she's telling.* Compare iota(2).

▷ *tr.v* (*-tt-*) **2** (usu — *s.t down*) write (s.t), usu briefly and quickly, on a piece of paper: *He jotted down her telephone number.*

'jotter *c.n* notebook or pad for jotting(2) things down.

'jottings *pl.n* short notes that have been written down.

joule /dʒuːl/ *c.n* (*technical*) unit of energy equal to 1 watt per second, *symb* J. ⇨ kilojoule.

journal /'dʒɜːnəl/ *c.n* **1** (often with capital **J**) (part of the title of a) newspaper, magazine etc: *The Woman's Journal.* **2** daily record of events, business dealings etc; diary: *He kept a journal describing his work among the poor.*

journalese /ˌdʒɜːnəˈliːz/ *u.n* (often *derog*) style of (bad) writing used by some journalists.

'journaˌlism *u.n* profession or business of

running, working or writing for, a newspaper, magazine etc.

'journalist *c.n* person who works or writes for a newspaper, magazine etc.

journa'listic *adj* (often *derog*) of or referring to (a style of writing for) a newspaper, magazine etc: *an unpleasant journalistic style.*

journey /'dʒɜːnɪ/ *c.n* **1** (often (*go*) *on a* —; *make a* — (*to s.w*)) trip, usu a long one, (to s.w): *He went on a journey round the world.* **2** distance travelled (and the time taken) on a journey(1): *It was a long journey that took several weeks.* ⇨ trip, voyage. **break one's journey (at s.w)** stop (and rest s.w) during a journey(1).

▷ *intr.v* **3** (often — *around, to(wards)* etc *s.w*) (*formal*) travel (around/to(wards) s.w): *They journeyed the rest of the way to the town on foot.*

joust /dʒaʊst/ *c.n* **1** (in history) fight on horseback with lances(1) between knights(1), either in a battle or as a sport.

▷ *intr.v* (often — *with s.o*) **2** fight in this way (with s.o). **3** (*fig*) argue, compete, with s.o.

jovial /'dʒəʊvɪəl/ *adj* (*formal*) (of a person, a mood¹(1) etc) cheerful.

joviality /ˌdʒəʊvɪˈælɪtɪ/ *u.n.* **'jovially** *adv.*

jowl /dʒaʊl/ *c.n* (often *pl*) lower part of the side of the face around the jaws of a person and some animals, esp dogs; it often has loose flesh and skin hanging down: *a man with heavy jowls.*

joy /dʒɔɪ/ *u.n* **1** (*formal*) very great happiness: *Sue was filled with joy when she got the news. He found it difficult to express his joy at the results.* **2** *c.n* thing that causes or gives great happiness: *the joys of life.* **jump for joy** show one's excitement or pleasure (when s.t happens).

'joyful *adj* causing great joy(1); filled with joy(1): *joyful event/news.*

'joyfully *adv.* **'joyfulness** *u.n.*

'joyless *adj* not having or causing any joy(1); gloomy(2) or sad: *a joyless occasion.*

'joylessly *adv.* **'joylessness** *u.n.*

'joyous *adj* = joyful: *a joyous celebration.*

'joyously *adv.* **'joyousness** *u.n.*

'joyˌride *c.n* drive in a car, sometimes that one has stolen, esp for the excitement and thrill(1) of doing so.

'joyˌrider *c.n* person who goes for a joyride.

'joyˌriding *u.n.*

'joyˌstick *c.n* (*informal*) stick or handle that controls the movements of an aircraft, computer game.

JP /ˌdʒeɪ ˈpiː/ *abbr* Justice of the Peace.

Jr *written abbr* Junior.

jubilant /'dʒuːbɪlənt/ *adj* (often — *about s.t*) (*formal*) showing great joy or triumph(3) (about s.t): *The crowd was jubilant when they heard the good news.*

'jubilantly *adv.*

jubilation /ˌdʒuːbɪˈleɪʃən/ *c/u.n* (example of an) expression of great joy or triumph.

jubilee /'dʒuːbɪˌliː/ *c.n* (date for a) celebration of an event, e.g a marriage, that happened in the past, usu at an interval of 25, 50 or 60 years: *the Queen's jubilee* (i.e 25 etc years after she became queen). **diamond/golden/silver jubilee** ⇨ diamond, golden, silver.

Judaism /'dʒuːdeɪˌɪzəm/ *u.n* religion, beliefs, customs etc of the Jews.

judder /'dʒʌdə/ *c.n* **1** (of a vehicle, machine

etc) shaking movement, esp when not working properly: *The engine gave a judder and then stopped.*
▷ *intr.v* **2** make a judder(1).

judge /dʒʌdʒ/ *c.n* **1** (with capital **J** in names) (title of a) public official with power to decide cases in a court of law: *a High Court judge*; *Judge Green*. **2** person who decides who wins in a competition: *a judge in a beauty* contest(1). *The judges' decision is final* (i.e one cannot argue with it). Compare referee(2), umpire(1). **3** (often *a bad/ good* etc — *of s.o/s.t*) person (who is bad/good etc at) giving an opinion (about s.o, the value of s.t): *She is not a very good judge of people's characters.*
▷ *v* **4** *tr.v* act as a judge(1) in (a case in a court of law): *Do you know who is judging your case?* **5** *tr/intr.v* act as a judge(2) (in a competition etc): *She was chosen to judge (the* entries) *at the local flower show.* **6** *tr/intr.v* (often — *that . . .*) form an opinion (about s.o/s.t); make an estimate(1) (of a distance, size etc): *Because of your refusal I judged that you disagreed with me. From this distance it is difficult to judge how high the mountain is. Judging from your remarks I gather you don't like Dan.* **7** *tr.v* criticize (s.o), esp for s.t he/she has done wrong: *You've no right to judge her as you don't know all the facts.*
'judgement *n* (also US (and UK *law*) **'judgment**) **1** *u.n* (usu pass — *on s.o*; *sit in — on s.o/ s.t*) act of judging(4) s.t or of being judged(4): *He passed judgment on the prisoner and sent him to prison for five years.* **2** *c.n* decision given by a judge(1) or a court of law: *The judgment went against him* (i.e he lost his case). **3** *u.n* ability in judging(6) the value, worth, of s.o/s.t: *He showed good judgement in his choice of people. You must use your own judgement and do what you think is right.* **4** *c/u.n* (often in *one's/ s.o's* —) opinion or belief: *In his judgement, most politicians are dishonest.* **5** *c.n* (often *be a — on s.t*) (*literary* or *formal*) punishment or misfortune (that s.o suffers) (thought to have come) from God: *Some people thought the earthquake was a judgement on them for their wicked ways.*
'judgement ,day *unique n* (often with capital **J** and **D**) day when God will decide who goes to Heaven and who to Hell(1).

judicature /'dʒuːdɪkətʃə/ *u/def.n* (all the) judges and the system of judging in a country.

judicial /dʒuː'dɪʃəl/ *adj* of or referring to a court of law, a judge or judges or to a decision in a court of law: *a judicial* inquiry. Compare judicious.
ju'dicially *adv.*

judiciary /dʒuː'dɪʃərɪ/ *c/def.n* (*pl* -ies) (all the) judges in a country.

judicious /dʒuː'dɪʃəs/ *adj* (*formal*) having, showing, good sense or judgement; making a careful wise choice, esp in what one says: *a judicious opinion*; *a judicious choice of words.* Opposite injudicious.
ju'diciously *adv.* **ju'diciousness** *u.n.*

judo /'dʒuːdəʊ/ *u.n* (also **,jiu'jitsu**) (also *attrib*) kind of wrestling first developed in Japan.

jug /dʒʌg/ *c.n* **1** kind of container or pot, usu with a handle and a lip, used for liquids: *a milk jug.* **2** (often — *of s.t*) as much as a jug(1) holds: *a jug of wine.*
'jugful *c.n* = jug(2).

juggernaut /'dʒʌgəˌnɔːt/ *n* **1** *c.n* very large lorry, esp one thought to cause traffic problems: *There were complaints about the way juggernauts were keeping people awake at night with their noise.* **2** *c/def.n* (*formal*) thing or belief that people sacrifice themselves to (and which is difficult to stop): *the juggernaut of war.*

juggle /'dʒʌgl/ *tr/intr.v* (often — (*with*) *s.t*) **1** throw and keep (a number of objects) in the air, catching them one at a time and throwing them up again: *His circus act consisted of juggling (with) ten plates.* **2** (often *derog*) arrange, change, (figures, amounts etc) in such a way as to deceive people, make the figures look better than they are etc: *He was accused of juggling the company's accounts.*
'juggler *c.n* person who juggles(1).

jugular /'dʒʌgjʊlə/ *c/def.n* (also **'jugular ,vein**) one of the veins(1) in the neck: *The blade sliced through the jugular and he bled to death.*

juice /dʒuːs/ *n* **1** *c/u.n* (example of the) liquid part of fruit, vegetables, meat etc: *apple juice*; *fruit/meat juices.* **2** *c.n* liquid in the body, esp the stomach, that helps digestion(1): *gastric juices.* **3** *u.n* (*informal*) petrol, electricity etc that makes a machine, vehicle etc work: *I've run out of juice. There's no juice — did you switch the electricity on?* **stew in one's own juice** ⇒ stew(*v*).
▷ *tr.v* **4 juice s.t up** (*informal*) make s.t more lively or interesting: *You need to juice up the story if you want anyone to read it.*
'juiciness *u.n* fact or state of being juicy.
'juicy *adj* (-ier, -iest) **1** (of fruit etc) having (a lot of) juice in it: *a juicy orange.* **2** (*informal*) (of s.t said, done etc) providing interesting information to talk about, usu because it concerns s.o's bad or scandalous behaviour: *a bit of juicy* gossip(1); *the juicy details of his affair with her.*

jujitsu ⇒ jiujitsu, judo.

jukebox /'dʒuːkˌbɒks/ *c.n* machine in a public place, e.g a café, that plays records when one puts money into it.

July /dʒuː'laɪ/ *c/unique n* (also *attrib*) (*written abbr* Jul) 7th month of the year: *There are thirty-one days in July. She was born on July 2* (say 'July the second' or 'the second of July'). *It was a wet July morning.*

jumble /'dʒʌmbl/ *n* **1** *sing.n* (often *a — of s.t*) untidy collection or heap (of things): *Her clothes were all in a jumble on the floor.* **2** *u.n* unwanted things, esp those suitable for a jumble sale: *Can you spare us any jumble?*
▷ *tr.v* (often — *s.t* (*up*) (*together*)) **3** cause (things) to be mixed (up/together) in an untidy heap: *Her clothes were all jumbled up on the floor.* **4** have (one's thoughts, ideas etc) mixed (up) in one's mind: *Her memories of what happened were all jumbled up.*
'jumble ,sale *c.n* sale of things that are no longer wanted by their owners, esp for a charitable(2) cause.

jumbo /'dʒʌmbəʊ/ *attrib.adj* **1** very large (in quantity, size etc): *a jumbo packet of soap powder.* **2** (of an aircraft) very large: *a jumbo* jet¹(3).
▷ *c.n* **3** = jumbo(2) jet¹(3).

jump /dʒʌmp/ *c.n* **1** quick sudden movement, made by pushing with one's feet, legs etc from the ground up into the air (or) across, over, out of etc s.t; leap(1): *He got over the fence in one jump. The cat made a jump and landed on its legs.* **2** (often *give a —*) sudden movement of the body, esp in surprise or fear: *I gave a jump when the bell rang.* **3** height, length etc reached or (to be) attempted in one jump(1): *a jump of at least six metres.* **4** thing, e.g a fence, that a person or animal tries to jump(6) over in a race or competition: *The horse managed the first four jumps easily but then fell at the fifth.* **5** (usu — *in s.t*) sudden rise (in the quantity, value etc of s.t): *There has been a big jump in the number of unemployed.* **a/one jump ahead (of s.o/s.t)** (in) a position of advantage (against s.o, competition etc): *be/stay one jump ahead.* **the high/long/triple jump** ⇒ high, long, triple.

▷ *v* **6** *intr.v* make or take a jump(1) (in order to get across, over etc s.t); leap(3): *Come on, jump (across the stream)! He jumped out (of the car) just as we started moving. I jumped up to catch the ball.* **7** *tr.v* get across (s.t) with a jump(1): *He jumped the fence easily.* **8** *intr.v* (often *make s.o —*) give a jump(2): *You made me jump, coming into the room so quietly.* **9** *tr.v* make (a horse etc) go over a jump(4): *Dave jumped his horse over the fence.* **10** *intr.v* (of a quantity, price etc) suddenly increase: *The price of coffee has jumped in the last month.* **jump at s.t** (*fig*) want or accept s.t offered very eagerly: *I'd jump at the chance of travelling around the world.* **jump for joy** ⇒ joy. **jump the gun** ⇒ gun(*n*). **jump on s.o** (**a**) suddenly attack s.o, esp from a hiding place: *I was jumped on by two men as I was coming home.* (**b**) (*fig; informal*) criticize s.o very heavily: *Why are you always jumping on me? I don't make nearly as many mistakes as he does.* **jump the queue** ⇒ queue(*n*). **jump to conclusions; jump to the conclusion that . . .** ⇒ conclusion.

'jumped-,up *attrib.adj* (*derog*) (of a young man or woman) who has achieved success, an important position etc quickly and behaves in an arrogant way.

'jumpily *adv* in a jumpy way.

'jumpiness *u.n* state of being jumpy.

'jumping *u.n* = show jumping.

'jumpy *adj* (*-ier, -iest*) (of a person, animal, state of mind) nervous: *You're very jumpy tonight. Is anything wrong?*

jumper /'dʒʌmpə/ *c.n* kind of clothing, made of wool etc and often with sleeves, worn on the upper part of the body from the neck to the hips; sweater, pullover.

Jun *written abbr* **1** June. **2** Junior.

junction /'dʒʌŋkʃən/ *n* **1** *c.n* (name for a) place where two or more things, e.g a road, railway lines, meet (and cross): *Stop at the junction just ahead.* **2** *c/u.n* (*formal*) act of joining or coming together: *The junction of their two forces made them more powerful than the enemy.*

'junction ,box *c.n* (*technical*) metal or plastic box in which two or more electrical wires meet and are connected together.

juncture /'dʒʌŋktʃə/ *u.n* (often *at that/this —* (*in s.t*)) (*formal*) point in time (during s.t): *At this juncture I suggest we stop and have lunch.*

June /dʒuːn/ *c/unique n* (also *attrib*) (*written abbr* Jun) 6th month of the year: *There are thirty days in June. He arrived on June 8* (say 'June the eighth' or 'the eighth of June'). *It was a sunny June afternoon.*

jungle /'dʒʌŋgl/ *c/u.n* **1** (land covered with) thick forest, plants etc that are difficult to get through, esp as found in hot countries: *He had to cut his way through a jungle of weeds to reach the shed.* **2** (*fig*) place, situation etc with many difficulties and problems, with many people competing with each other: *Big business is a jungle where only the strong will survive(1).*

junior /'dʒuːnɪə/ *adj* (with capital **J** in names or titles) Opposite senior. **1** (often *— to s.o*) younger (than s.o); lower in rank, importance, (than s.o): *Lynne is junior to me. He is a Junior Secretary in the government.* **2** (*written abbr* Jnr, Jr, Jun) (esp US) (placed after the name) title given to s.o who has the same name as s.o, e.g a father, but who is younger: *Henry R Green Junior.*

▷ *c.n* **3** often *s.o's — (by 5 etc years)* person who is (five etc years) junior(1) (to s.o): *She is my junior by three years.*

juniper /'dʒuːnɪpə/ *c.n* (also **'juniper ,bush/,tree**) bush or tree with purple berries (which are used in the making of gin').

junk[1] /dʒʌŋk/ *u.n* (*informal*) **1** things that are old, no longer of any use or value: *He had to pay a man to clear all the junk out of the house.* **2** (of s.t said, performed etc) thing of no worth; nonsense: *That remark is a load of junk and you know it!*

▷ *tr.v* **3** get rid of (s.t) because it is no longer useful, working etc: *If I were you, I'd junk your car and get yourself a better one.*

'junk ,food *c/u.n* (*derog*) food, usu prepared, sold etc quickly, that is considered to have very little nutritional value.

'junk ,shop *c.n* shop that sells junk'(1).

junk[2] /dʒʌŋk/ *c.n* kind of sailing ship found in China and other parts of the Far East.

junkie /'dʒʌŋkɪ/ *c.n* (also **'junky**) (*pl -ies*) (*slang*) person who regularly takes drugs(2), esp heroin.

Jupiter /'dʒuːpɪtə/ *unique n* **1** (*astronomy*) fifth (and largest) planet away from the sun. **2** (in Roman mythology) chief god.

jurisdiction /,dʒʊərɪs'dɪkʃən/ *u.n* (often *fall outside/within s.o's/s.t's —*) power and authority(3) (of s.o who is an official, e.g in a court of law) to deal with, settle, a matter; area or place where such power is used: *The court ruled that the case fell outside/within its jurisdiction.*

jurisprudence /,dʒʊərɪs'pruːdəns/ *u.n* science of law.

jury /'dʒʊərɪ/ *c.n* (*pl -ies*) **1** group of men and women (in UK, usu 12 people) chosen from the electoral rolls to hear a case in a court of law and decide on the facts, e.g whether a person is or is not guilty. **2** group of people chosen to judge a competition, give their vote for s.o/s.t etc: *The jury from England gave their highest vote to the French singer.*

'jurist *c.n* person who is an expert in law.

'juror, 'juryman, 'jury,woman *c.n* (*pl -men, -,women*) person, man, woman, who is a member of a jury(1).

just[1] /dʒʌst/ *adj* Opposite unjust. **1** (of a person, decision etc) fair, right, acting or done without showing favour to one person, one side of an

argument etc: *a just and honourable man*; *a just verdict*(1). **2** being or getting what one deserves (good or bad) for what one has done: *It was a just reward/punishment.* **3** based on what is reasonable or what one may have a right to: *The court accepted that Jill had a just claim to ownership of the house.*
'**justly** *adv.* '**justness** *u.n.*

just² (strong form /dʒʌst/, weak form /dʒəst/) *adv* **1** (*has/had/have* — . . . (e)*d*) very recently, in the immediate past (have/had done s.t etc): *I have just arrived. I had just sat down when the bell rang.* **2** (— . . .*ing*) at this/that moment (be doing, be going to do, was/were doing, s.t etc): *I won't be a moment, I'm just finishing. I'm just going to go out for a breath of fresh air. I was just sitting down when the bell rang.* ⇒ just about to do s.t. **3** (usu *only*) — *do/did s.t*) with only a little time, effort etc to spare; barely: *We just caught/ missed the train. The box was so heavy, I could only just lift it.* **4** (usu — *cannot* . . . , *do not* . . . , *will not* . . . etc) (used to emphasize that one is not able to do s.t): *I just can't/don't understand what went wrong.* **5** (usu with imperatives) all that is necessary is (for you to (not) do s.t): *There's no need to write, just telephone. Don't just listen to me, talk to her also.* **6** (usu with imperatives) it is necessary (for you to do s.t); I suggest (that you do s.t): *You just listen to me and stop what you're doing! Just look at her dressed up like that!* **7** (used with an adj or (pro)noun) only; merely: *It's all right, I'm just (a little) tired. He's just a simple man at heart. We don't need all those things, just one or two of them.* **8** (used with an adj or adv) exactly: *That chair will be just right in our living room. Would you put it down just here/there?* **9** (often — (on) one (o'clock) etc) almost exactly ((at) one o'clock etc): *It's just 6 o'clock. I arrived just on ten (o'clock).* **10** (used with an adj) completely; absolutely: *I'm afraid that's just impossible. He was just splendid in the play.* **be just about** (**s.t**) be almost exactly (s.t): *That amount is just about right.* **be just about to do s.t.** be almost on the point of doing s.t: *I was just about to telephone you.* **be just as bad**, **good** etc (**as s.o/s.t**) be equally bad, good etc (as s.o/s.t else): *Why don't you buy this car? It's just as fast (as that one) and it's cheaper.* (**be**) **just as I thought** etc (be) exactly what I thought etc he/she/it would be: *The house was just as I pictured it.* **be just as well** (*informal*) be a good thing (in view of the circumstances(1)): *'I won't be able to meet you tomorrow.' 'That's just as well as I'll be busy.'* **be just the thing**; **be just what I want** etc be exactly right, what I want etc: *This tool is just the thing for the job.* **be not just s.t/that** . . . it is not simply or only s.t/that . . . (but there is s.t else etc): *It's not just his rudeness, it's his general attitude(2) I don't like.* **just after**, **before** etc (**s.t**, **s.o does s.t**) a very short time after, before etc: *'Was it you who telephoned at midnight?' 'No, it was just after (that).'* *Can you wait just until I've finished this letter?* **just as . . .**, **so** . . . (*formal*) (used in comparisons) in the same way as (s.t is true etc), so (s.t else is true etc): *Just as oil and water do not mix, so two people of such different characters cannot get on with each other.* **just as/when** . . . at exactly the same time as when (s.t happens): *The bell rang*

just as I was going to bed. **just as well** (as an answer to a statement) that is in fact quite a good thing; that is lucky: *That's just as well because there isn't room for him in the car.* **just because of s.t**; **just because s.o is s.t** simply or only because of s.t etc: *Ian lost his job just because of his laziness. Just because you are rich, it doesn't mean you can tell me what to do.* **just enough** (**s.t**) only or barely enough (of s.t): *There's just enough wood to light a fire.* **just in time** (**to do s.t**) at the last possible moment (before it is too late to do s.t): *We got to the station just in time (to catch the train).* **just a second/minute/moment** (*informal*) (could you please) wait a little time; (could you please) stop (while I think about what you said, have an opportunity to say s.t etc): *Just a second! I think I've forgotten my bag. Hey, just a minute, I didn't agree to all that!* **just now** (**a**) at this present time: *Come back later as I'm busy just now.* (**b**) at a very recent time in the past: *I telephoned him just now, but he wasn't in.* **just then** at the exact moment in the past: *Just then the bell rang.* **just what**, **who** etc (**exactly/precisely**) . . . (used in questions to give greater emphasis to s.t one is asking and esp to show surprise, anger etc): *Just what (exactly) do you think you are doing with my bag?* **s.o may/might just as well do s.t** ⇒ may. **not just yet** not at this/that moment (but probably later etc): *'Would you like coffee?' 'Not just yet; I want to finish this first.'*

justice /'dʒʌstɪs/ *n* **1** *u.n* quality of rightness or fairness (in the way people are treated etc): *He tried to be fair and deal with the two of them with equal justice. There is some justice in what you say.* Opposite **injustice**. **2** *def/unique n* (usu with capital **J**) (title of a) judge in a higher court: *Justice Roberts; the Lord Chief Justice.* **bring s.o to justice** (*formal*; *law*) bring s.o to a court of law to be sentenced for her/his wrongdoing. **do oneself/s.o/s.t justice** (**a**) treat oneself etc fairly: *I would not be doing him justice (or doing justice to him) if I didn't mention how brave he was.* (**b**) show oneself etc in the best possible way: *He didn't do himself justice by those remarks.* **miscarriage of justice** ⇒ miscarriage. **to do s.o justice** . . . if one is going to be fair about s.o . . . : *To do him justice, he did apologize in the end.*
'**Justice of the 'Peace** *c.n* (*abbr* JP) official in charge of a lower court.

justify /'dʒʌstɪˌfaɪ/ *tr.v* (*-ies*, *-ied*) **1** show, prove, (s.o/s.t) to be right, correct etc: *I must ask you to justify your request for more money.* **2** be a (good) reason or excuse for (s.t): *The fact that you were ill really doesn't justify such bad behaviour.*
justifiable /'dʒʌstɪˌfaɪəbl/ *adj* that one can justify or that can be justified: *justifiable homicide*(1). Opposite **unjustifiable**.
'**justi,fiably** *adv.*
justification /ˌdʒʌstɪfɪ'keɪʃən/ *u.n* (often — *for s.t*) (good) reason or excuse (for doing s.t): *There is very little justification for killing someone.*

justly, **justness** ⇒ just¹.

jut /dʒʌt/ *intr.v* (*-tt-*) **jut out** (**over s.t**) stick out (over s.t): *The platform jutted out over the river.*

jute /dʒuːt/ *u.n* (also *attrib*) fibre(1) of a kind of plant, used for making ropes, sacks etc.

juvenile /'dʒuːvɪˌnaɪl/ *adj* **1** of or referring to a child or young person: *juvenile literature*; *a juvenile court.* **2** (*derog*) (of an adult, an adult's behaviour etc) like a child: *Don't you think it's a bit juvenile to stamp your feet?*

▷ *c.n* **3** (*formal* or *law*) young person.

juve,nile de'linquency *u.n* (*law*) breaking of the law by a young person.

juve,nile de'linquent *c.n* young person who breaks the law.

juxtapose /ˌdʒʌkstəˈpəʊz/ *tr.v* (*formal*) place, arrange, (one or more things) next to each other or another: *If you juxtapose the two pictures, it will give a better effect.*

juxtaposition /ˌdʒʌkstəpəˈzɪʃən/ *u.n.*

Kk

K, k /keɪ/ *c/unique n* **1** 11th letter of the English alphabet.

▷ *symb* (**K**) **2** king(2); king(3). **3** one thousand (used esp in the amount of a salary): *a 20K salary* (i.e £20 000). **4** group of 1024 units (called bytes) in a computer.

kaftan /ˈkæftæn/ *c.n* ⇒ caftan.

kaleidoscope /kəˈlaɪdəˌskəʊp/ *c.n* **1** tube with pieces of coloured glass or plastic at one end which make patterns when viewed through mirrors; it is used as a toy. **2** (*fig*) any set of situations, events etc that often change.

kaleidoscopic /kəˌlaɪdəˈskɒpɪk/ *adj* **1** having lights or colours that often change. **2** (*fig*) often changing: *the kaleidoscopic life in a large city.*

kangaroo /ˌkæŋɡəˈruː/ *c.n* kind of animal found in Australia with very large back legs, the female having a kind of pocket on her front for carrying her young.

,kanga,roo 'court *c.n* illegal trial, e.g by political extremists(2).

kaolin /ˈkeɪəlɪn/ *u.n* kind of fine white clay, used to make china(2) or a kind of medicine.

karat /ˈkærət/ *c.n* ⇒ carat.

karate /kəˈrɑːtɪ/ *u.n* (also *attrib*) kind of fighting without weapons by using the arms and legs to hit and kick: *a karate expert.*

kayak /ˈkaɪæk/ *c.n* kind of small light canoe.

KC /ˌkeɪ ˈsiː/ *abbr* King's Counsel.

kc *symb* kilocycle.

kebab /kəˈbæb/ *c.n* small pieces of meat and vegetables on a stick, usu cooked over a fire.

keel /kiːl/ *c.n* **1** one of the pieces along the bottom of a ship on which the side pieces are fixed. **on an even keel** in a calm and balanced state of mind.

▷ *intr.v* **keel over 2** (of a boat) turn over; capsize. **3** (*informal*) (of a person) fall down suddenly because one faints, dies or is ill.

keen /kiːn/ *adj* **1** (often — *about* (*doing*) *s.t; — to do s.t*) eager (to do something, take part etc): *a keen swimmer/student. He's not all that keen about going to the party.* **2** (*attrib*) (of a wind etc)

very cold and sharp. **3** (of sight, smell etc) able to notice small or weak qualities: *My dog has a keen sense of smell. His hearing is keen.* **4** (of desire) very strong. **5** (of the edge of a knife etc) sharp. **6** (of a price) good for the buyer. **keen on s.o/ s.t** very fond of, interested in, s.o/s.t: *She's been keen on him for months. I'm not keen on football.* **as keen as mustard** ⇒ mustard.

'keenly *adv.* **'keenness** *u.n.*

keep /kiːp/ *n* **1** *u.n* (cost of) rent and food: *Chris will have to earn his keep if he stays with us.* **2** *u.n* care and control: *Leave the cat in our keep for the weekend.* **3** *c.n* main tower in a castle. **for keeps** (*informal*) for always: *Can I have the bicycle for keeps?*

▷ *v* (*p.t,p.p* kept /kept/) **4** *tr.v* have (s.t) for always or a long time: *I don't want my pen back, you can keep it. I'll keep the bicycle until you are old enough to ride it.* **5** *tr.v* have and look after, pay for, (s.o/s.t): *Are you allowed to keep animals in your flat? If you leave home, who will keep you?* **6** have and pay for or run (s.t): *Can you afford to keep a car as well as a motorbike? He keeps a small shop.* **7** *tr.v* have, make, (s.o/s.t) stay in a particular place or position: *Where do you keep your keys? Do you keep your car in a garage? My mother kept me at home yesterday.* **8** *tr.v* have a supply of (s.t) for sale: *We don't keep buttons — try the shop next door.* **9** *tr.v* have (s.t) to use if necessary: *We always keep candles in the bathroom.* **10** *tr/intr.v* (cause (s.o/s.t) to) be or stay in a particular condition: *Please keep calm. This tea will keep her warm. 'How are your parents keeping?' 'They are keeping well, thanks.'* ⇒ keep fit(⇒ fit(*adj*)), keep one's head. **11** *intr.v* (of food, drink) stay fresh: *Milk doesn't keep in hot weather.* **12** *intr.v* (of information) not need to be told or revealed at this moment, but perhaps later: *Your news can keep for another day.* **13** *tr.v* write (s.t) down as a record: *keep a record of expenses.* **14** *tr.v* do, treat, (s.t) as agreed or arranged: *keep a secret/promise/date.* **15** *intr.v* (often — (on) doing s.t) continue (doing s.t): *I kept (on) looking for you. He keeps (on) interrupting me.* **16** *tr.v* make (s.o) late, wait etc: *Don't keep her waiting. What kept you?*

keep s.o/s.t at bay ⇒ bay⁵. **keep (s.o) at it/s.t** (make s.o) continue to work hard at a job etc: *We were kept at it the whole of that day and the next without any rest. You'll only succeed if you keep at your studies.*

keep (s.o) away (from s.o/s.t) (cause (s.o) to) not go or get near (to s.o/s.t): *Keep away! That man is dangerous! They kept their children away from school because of the epidemic.*

keep (s.o) back (from s.o/s.t) (cause (s.o) to) stay where he/she is and not go or get near (to s.o/s.t): *Keep back from the edge! The police kept the crowd back from the princess.* **keep s.t (back) from s.o** refuse to give information (to s.o).

keep s.o company ⇒ company.

keep it/s.t dark ⇒ dark(*adj*).

keep a diary ⇒ diary.

keep one's distance ⇒ distance(*n*).

keep s.o down force s.o, esp a population, to stay in the same low (social or economic(1)) position.

keep s.t down (a) not allow food etc to come up from the stomach: *Now try and keep your medicine down this time.* **(b)** not allow prices, costs etc to increase: *We must keep our expenses down this month.* (**c**) not show one's feelings, e.g anger: *Ian was not very good at keeping his emotions down.* **keep (one's head** etc) **down** not let oneself (or one's head etc) be seen above s.t: *Keep down or else they'll see you!*

keep an eye on s.o/s.t; **keep an eye out for s.o/ s.t** ⇒ eye(*n*).

keep/break faith with s.o ⇒ faith.

keep fit ⇒ fit(*adj*). ⇒ keep-fit.

keep from doing s.t not allow oneself to do s.t: *I must ask you to keep from interrupting me.*

keep s.t from s.o ⇒ keep s.t (back) from s.o.

keep going continue to make an effort to move or do s.t although there are problems: *She kept going in spite of her sore feet.* **keep s.o going** make it possible for s.o to continue trying, working, living etc: *Here's £20 to keep you going until Friday.*

keep one's head; **keep one's head above water** ⇒ head(*n*).

keep hold of s.o/s.t ⇒ hold (*n*).

keep (s.o) in (cause (s.o) to) stay inside a house etc: *During the winter old people keep in in order to stay warm. We kept the children in during the bad weather.* **keep s.o in** not allow pupils to leave school at the end of lessons as a punishment: *Our teacher kept us in because we hadn't done our homework.* **keep s.t in** not show one's (true) feelings, tell a secret etc: *I can't keep it in any longer.* **keep s.o in s.t** provide s.o with (all) the things that he/she may want or need in order to live comfortably: *Do you think I earn all this money just to keep you in drink and cigarettes?* **keep one's hand in** ⇒ hand(*n*). **keep s.o/s.t in check** ⇒ check(*n*). **keep s.o in the dark** ⇒ dark(*n*). **keep in touch (with s.o/ s.t)** ⇒ touch(*n*). **keep in with s.o** continue to have good or friendly relations with s.o: *You must keep in with your teacher if you want her to recommend you.*

keep off (of rain etc) not start: *I hope the snow keeps off until we get home.* **keep off s.t** (**a**) not use or eat s.t: *The doctor told him to keep off drink for a month.* (**b**) not talk about a particular subject etc: *Try to keep off politics this evening.* **keep (s.o) off (s.t)** not (allow (s.o) to) walk (on s.t); not (allow (s.o) to) go or get near (to s.t): (*Notice*) *Keep off the grass! Keep the children off the swings as they are dangerous.* **keep one's hands off (s.o/s.t)** ⇒ hand(*n*).

keep on continue in a forward direction: *Keep on until you arrive at a garage.* **keep s.o on** continue to employ s.o: *Because of the fall in orders it was decided to keep on only half the workers.* **keep s.t on** not remove (part of) one's clothes: *As it's cold I'll keep my coat on.* **keep on about s.t** continue to talk about a matter that others do not want to hear about: *Don't keep on about that silly mistake.* **keep on at s.o** continue to complain to s.o, esp about her/his bad behaviour: *She's always keeping on at her son to brush his teeth.* **keep a check on s.o/s.t** ⇒ check(*n*). **keep (on) doing s.t** ⇒ keep(15). **keep your hair on** ⇒ hair. **keep your shirt on** ⇒ shirt. **keep a tab, tabs, on s.o** ⇒ tab(*n*).

keep (s.o/s.t) out (of s.t/s.w) (cause (s.o/s.t) to) stay outside (a place etc); not (let s.o/s.t) get in(to s.t): *Keep out or I'll scream! Keep that dog out of*

here! *The tent is not very good at keeping out the rain.*

keep the peace ⇒ peace.

keep to s.t stay, move, in one direction or along s.t without changing: *Please keep to the right. The farmer told them to keep to the paths and not walk across the fields.* **keep (s.o) to s.t** (**a**) (cause (s.o) to) do s.t that one/he/she has agreed to do: *You said you'd help me and I'm going to keep you to it.* (**b**) (often — (s.o) *to the point*) (cause (s.o) to) stay with a particular subject when talking: *There was a lot of shouting and he found it difficult to keep everybody to the point under discussion.* **keep oneself to oneself** avoid speaking to or visiting others. **keep s.t to oneself** not tell s.t that one wants to keep secret.

keep together do s.t, e.g row a boat, sing a song etc, at the same time as, in tune with, everybody else in the group: *The rowers couldn't keep together and the boat swung around.* **keep (s.o/s.t) together** not (allow a group of people, animals etc to) get separated: *We need to keep (everybody) together in this fog.*

keep s.o under continue to make s.o unconscious with drugs(1) etc. **keep (s.o) under (s.t)** (cause (s.o) to) stay below (a surface, e.g water): *He can keep under (water) for over 3 minutes.* **keep s.t under one's hat** ⇒ hat.

keep up (of weather etc) continue without change: *If this weather keeps up we should have a good holiday.* **keep it up** (usu as an order; *informal*) continue to work well: *You're doing fine; keep it up!* **keep s.o up** stop s.o from going to bed: *I hope the party didn't keep you up.* **keep s.o/s.t up** not allow s.o/s.t to sink or fall: *He kept her up* (i.e in the sea) *until rescue came.* **keep s.t up** continue to do s.t: *Why do you keep up this pretence that you're rich? Joe was arrested for failing to keep up his payments to his former wife.* ⇒ upkeep. **keep up (with s.o/s.t)** (**a**) make the same progress (as s.o/s.t): *He had to walk faster to keep up (with them).* (**b**) (work in order to) stay at the same level (as s.o, of knowledge etc): *I try my best to keep up with the latest developments in my subject.*

keep watch ⇒ watch[2].

'keeper *c.n* (often as the second part of a word) **1** person who looks after animals (in a zoo): *a zoo-keeper.* **2** person in charge of a particular place or responsibility: *a book-keeper, door-keeper, goalkeeper, housekeeper, shopkeeper.* **3** person in charge of a collection in an art gallery, a museum etc.

,keep-'fit *u.n* (also *attrib*) form of exercising to improve one's physical fitness: *keep-fit classes.*

'keeping *u.n* (often as the second part of a word) the act of putting s.t in order: *house-keeping; book-keeping.* **in s.o's (safe) keeping** with s.o having the care and responsibility: *The money is in the bank's safe keeping.* **in**, **out of**, **keeping (with s.t)** (*formal*) suitable, unsuitable, (for the situation etc): *She wears clothes in keeping with her high position.*

'keep,sake *c.n* small thing given to s.o to remind her/him of s.o/s.t.

keg /keg/ *c.n* container for liquid like a small barrel: *a keg of* sherry(1).

kennel /'kenl/ *c.n* (also **'dog ,kennel**) small hut for a dog.

'kennels *pl.n* place where a dog can be looked after for a short while, e.g while the owners are on holiday. Compare cattery.

kept /kept/ *p.t,p.p* of keep.

kerb /kɜːb/ *c.n* line of long stones etc at the edge of a pavement.

kernel /'kɜːnl/ *c.n* **1** (soft or hard) part inside the shell of a nut. **2** (often — *of s.t*) (*fig*) most important part (of an argument etc): *The boy's statement formed the kernel of the lawyer's argument. There is a kernel of truth in what he says.*

kerosene /'kerə,siːn/ *u.n* = paraffin.

kestrel /'kestrəl/ *c.n* kind of small European falcon.

ketch /ketʃ/ *c.n* kind of small sailing boat with two masts.

ketchup /'ketʃəp/ *u.n* kind of tasty sauce: *tomato ketchup.*

kettle /'ketl/ *c.n* **1** pot with a spout(1) and a lid, used for boiling water: *an electric kettle.* **2** amount of water a kettle(1) holds: *a kettle of water.* **a pretty kettle of fish** (*fig, informal*) a difficult or disorganized situation: *I've arrived late in the rain and I can't get into the house – what a pretty kettle of fish!* **put the kettle on** make the water in a kettle(1) begin to get hot, e.g by switching on the electricity: *Put the kettle on and we'll have tea.*

'kettle-,drum *c.n* kind of drum shaped like a bowl and covered with skin.

key /kiː/ *attrib.adj* **1** very important or useful: *Taxes will be a key issue(3) in the next election. Mr Brown is a key member of the teaching staff.*
▷ *c.n* **2** shaped metal device used to open or close a lock: *a door key.* **3** shaped device used for turning a part in a machine etc: *a key for winding a clock.* **4** button or knob that one presses to make an instrument or machine work: *piano keys; the keys of a typewriter.* **5** (usu — *to s.t*) thing that explains s.t or provides an answer or solution: *The weapon is the key to the murder. What is the key to lasting peace? There is a key on page 40 with answers to the exercises.* **6** (*music*) set of notes (called a scale¹(6)) connected with a particular note (called a keynote): *the key of C minor.* **7** style or tone: *The newspapers reported the event in a low key.*
▷ *tr.v* **8** type (s.t) on a machine, especially a typewriter or word-processor. **be** (**all**) **keyed up** (*informal*) feel (extremely) excited or tense¹(2): *I was all keyed up before the meeting but it went well.* **key s.t in** type or enter (figures, information) on a form, into a computer. **key s.t to s.t** make (s.t) balance (with s.t): *You must key your efforts to your desire to win.*

'key,board *c.n* **1** set of keys(4) on an instrument or machine: *a piano keyboard; a typewriter keyboard.*
▷ *tr.v* **2** use a keyboard(1) to put (information, instructions etc) into a computer.

'key,board ,ope,rator *c.n* person who operates the keyboard(1) of a computer or word-processor.

'key,hole *c.n* opening in a lock for a key(2).

'key,note *c.n* (*music*) ⇒ key(6).

'key,stone *c.n* **1** stone in the centre at the top of an arch. **2** (*fig*) most important part: *The keystone of his argument was that the shop had not allowed him to test the camera when he bought it.*

'key,stroke *c.n* one press of a key(4) on a computer or word-processor.

kg *symb* kilogram(me)(s).

KGB /,keɪ ,dʒiː 'biː/ *def/def.pl.n abbr* secret police department of the USSR.

khaki /'kɑːkɪ/ *u.n* (also *attrib*) **1** dull brown-yellow (colour): *a khaki shirt.* **2** kind of strong cloth of this colour, often used to make military(1) uniforms: *dressed in khaki; khaki trousers.*

kick /kɪk/ *c.n* **1** hit with the foot: *His kick sent the ball up into the trees.* **2** (*informal*) sudden excited and pleasant feeling: *Strong drink can give you a powerful kick. I get a kick each time we meet.* **3** (*informal*) short period of enthusiasm for s.t: *Her latest kick is learning to play the piano.* **do s.t for kicks** do s.t in order to feel a kick(2): *He drives cars very fast for kicks.* **get a kick out of** (**doing**) **s.t** (*informal*) feel a kick(2) when one does s.t. **a kick in the pants** (*slang*) a serious warning or telling off: *That lazy student needs a kick in the pants or he'll fail the examination.* **a kick in the teeth** (*slang*) an unexpectedly bad response to one's serious attempts or efforts: *It was such a kick in the teeth when her parents did not go to see her collect her prize.*
▷ *v* **4** *tr/intr.v* hit (s.o/s.t) with the foot: *Bob kicked the ball high into the sky. If you kick, I'll bite you! You've kicked a hole in the fence.* **5** *intr.v* move the legs as if kicking(4) s.t, e.g when swimming: *The baby lay kicking on the bed.* **6** *tr.v* score (a goal) by kicking(4) a ball: *Tom kicked a goal in the last minute of the game.* **7** *intr.v* (*informal*) suddenly run faster: *Coe kicked about 100 metres from the end of the race.* **8** *tr.v* (*informal*) stop (an unhealthy or illegal habit): *I'm trying to kick smoking/drugs(2). You'll never be able to kick the habit.*

alive and kicking ⇒ alive.

kick s.o about/around (*fig, informal*) treat s.o unfairly, esp by giving her/him orders. **kick s.t about/around** (*informal*) discuss suggestions etc freely and informally.

kick the bucket ⇒ bucket.

kick a/the habit ⇒ habit.

kick one's heels ⇒ heel(*n*).

kick s.t in break something by kicking it: *The police kicked the door in.*

kick off (**a**) (in football, rugby) start a game by kicking(4) the ball. ⇒ kick-off. (**b**) (*fig*) (of a meeting, discussion) start: *The meeting will kick off at 8 o'clock.* ⇒ kick-off.

kick s.o out (**of s.w**) (*informal*) force s.o to leave (a place, job etc): *He kicked his son out (of the house) because of his behaviour.*

kick up s.t cause trouble, a quarrel etc: *Penny kicked up such a fuss when I asked her to wash up. He'll kick up a row if he sees you.*

'kick,back *c.n* (*informal*) unlawful payment to s.o who has been responsible for one being successful in a business deal, getting a particular job etc.

'kicker *c.n* person who kicks(4) a ball etc: *He's a poor kicker.*

'kick-,off *c.n* start of a football or rugby game, or meeting: *The kick-off is at two o'clock.* ⇒ kick off.

for a kick-off (*informal*) (used when beginning an explanation etc): *For a kick-off I don't like the colour and also the wood is so thin.*

'kick-,start *c.n* **1** lever, e.g on a motorbike, used to start the engine by pressing it with the foot.
▷ *tr.v* **2** start (a motorbike etc) by pushing the kickstart(1).

kid /kɪd/ *n* **1** *c.n* (also *attrib*) (*informal*) young boy or girl: *Some kids stole apples from our garden. Pam's my kid* (younger) *sister.* **2** *c.n* young goat. **3** *u.n* (also *attrib*) skin of a young goat: *kid slippers.* (**handle s.o/s.t**) **with kid gloves** (*fig*) (deal with s.o/s.t), using carefully chosen words or actions in order not to cause anger or offence, to prevent s.t going wrong: *You must treat that man with kid gloves if you want him to help you.*
▷ *tr/intr.v* (-dd-) **4** deceive (s.o) for fun: *He kidded me that he was 18 years old. You're not 18 — you must be kidding!*

kidnap /'kɪdnæp/ *tr.v* (-pp-, US -p-) take away (s.o) by force, esp in order to get money for her/his safe return.
'kidnapper *c.n* person who kidnaps s.o.

kidney /'kɪdnɪ/ *c.n* **1** either of the parts of the body that clean the blood and produce urine. ⇒ renal. **2** *u.n* (also *attrib*) kidneys(1) of certain animals eaten as food: steak(3) *and kidney* pie.
'kidney-,bean *c.n* any bean shaped like a kidney(1), esp the red kind used in salads(1) and stews(1).
'kidney ma,chine *c.n* machine used to clean the blood of s.o with diseased kidneys(1).

kill /kɪl/ *c.n* **1** act of killing, esp after a hunt(1), bullfight etc. **2** animal killed in a hunt(1). **be in at the kill** (*fig*) be present for the most rewarding, exciting, important part of s.t: *I hope to be in at the kill when the prizes are given out.*
▷ *tr.v* **3** (often — *s.o/s.t off*) cause (s.o/s.t) to die: *The cold weather killed* (*off*) *the young plants. He killed the snake with a stone. It was loneliness that finally killed the old man off.* **4** cause (hope, interest etc) to end: *His bad temper killed any love she had felt for him.* **5** cause (s.o) to feel pain, very tired etc: *This work is killing me. My feet are killing me!* **Don't kill yourself** (*informal*) (**a**) (as a friendly warning) Don't work too hard. (**b**) (used to mean the opposite of what one is saying) you are being very lazy. **kill oneself doing s.t, with s.t** (used for emphasis to show the strength of one's happiness etc): *I nearly killed myself laughing* (or *with laughter*) *when I heard the news.* **kill time** ⇒ time(*n*).
'killer *c.n* **1** person who kills(3) s.o: *a child killer.* **2** (also *attrib*) thing that causes death: *This cold wind is a killer. It's a killer disease.* **3** (*fig; informal*) activity, job etc that is difficult or makes s.o very tired.
'killing *adj* (*informal*) **1** very tiring: *This walk is killing. We walked at a killing pace.* **2** (*attrib*) very funny: *a killing joke.*
▷ *c.n* **3 make a killing** make a large profit on a business deal.
'kill-joy *c.n* (*derog*) person who destroys s.o's pleasure or enjoyment.

kiln /kɪln/ *c.n* kind of oven used for baking clay pots or bricks.

kilo /'ki:ləʊ/ *abbr* kilogram(me).

kilocycle /'kɪləʊ,saɪkl/ *c.n* (*old use*) = kilohertz, *symb* kc.

kilogramme /'kɪləʊ,græm/ *c.n* (also **'kilo,gram**) (*technical*) 1000 gram(me)s, *symb* kg.

kilohertz /'kɪləʊ,hɜːtz/ *c.n* (*technical*) 1000 hertz, *symb* kHz.

kilojoule /'kɪlədʒuːl/ *c.n* (*technical*) 1000 joules, *symb* kJ.

kilolitre /'kɪləʊ,liːtə/ *c.n* (US **'kilo,liter**) (*technical*) 1000 litres, *symb* kl.

kilometre /'kɪləʊ,miːtə/ *c.n* (US **'kilo,meter**) (*technical*) 1000 metres, *symb* km.

kilowatt /'kɪləʊ,wɒt/ *c.n* (*technical*) 1000 watts, *symb* Kw, kw.

kilt /kɪlt/ *c.n* short skirt with folds, esp one worn by men in Scotland.

kimono /kɪ'məʊnəʊ/ *c.n* (*pl* -s) kind of loose robe, esp one worn by women in Japan.

kin /kɪn/ *pl.n* (*formal*) members of one's family. **next of kin** ⇒ next. **kith and kin** ⇒ kith.

kind¹ /kaɪnd/ *adj* (often — *to s.o*; — *of s.o to do s.t*) pleasant, helpful and friendly (towards s.o etc): *We have very kind neighbours. Joan's so kind to our children.* Opposite unkind.
,kind-'hearted *adj* showing a kind¹(1) personality: *a kind-hearted teacher.*
'kindly *attrib.adj* **1** (*formal*) showing a willingness to please or be friendly: *a kindly expression on her face; a kindly act.*
▷ *adv* **2** in a kind¹(1) way: *I smiled kindly but he still looked angry.* **3** please (often used when a little angry): *Would you kindly help me with this box. Kindly be quiet while I am thinking.*
'kindness *n* **1** *c.n* kind¹(1) act: *To give her something to stop the pain would be a kindness.* **2** *u.n* fact or quality of being kind¹(1): *Your kindness to me will always be remembered.* Opposite unkindness. *the milk of human kindness* ⇒ milk(*n*).

kind² /kaɪnd/ *c.n* (often — *of s.o/s.t*) example, type, (of a number of people, animals, things, who/that have certain qualities that are the same); sort(1): *Paul's the kind of man you can't trust. These kinds of machines are very easy to operate. An oak is a kind of tree.* **in kind** (**a**) by giving goods or services, not money, as payment: *He paid for the work in kind by giving them fruit and vegetables from his farm.* (**b**) (*fig*) in the same (bad) way as he/she has treated one/s.o: *If you harm her at all I'll pay you back in kind.* **kind of** (*informal*) rather; to some extent: *I kind of like her. She's kind of worried about it all.* **nothing of the kind** ⇒ nothing. **s.t of a kind** thing that is not quite like others of the same kind²: *I suppose you could call it a car of a kind but it certainly doesn't look like one.* **s.t of that/the kind** thing that is similar: *They called us 'noisy' or something of that kind.* **two etc of a kind** two or more people, things etc who/that are like each other: *They're all of a kind — lazy, selfish and stupid.*

kindergarten /'kɪndə,gɑːtn/ *c.n* (becoming *old use*) school for very young children. ⇒ nursery school, playschool.

kindle /'kɪndl/ *tr/intr.v* (cause (a fire) to) begin to burn: *Use this wood to kindle the fire. Dry wood kindles easily.*
'kindling *u.n* small pieces of dry wood used for beginning a fire.

kindred /'kɪndrɪd/ *attrib.adj* of the same kind: *kindred pleasures.*
,kindred 'spirits *pl.n* people with the same interests.

kinetic /kɪ'netɪk/ *attrib.adj* (*technical*) involving movement: *kinetic* energy(2).

king /kɪŋ/ c.n **1** (often with capital **K** in titles) man who rules a country as a monarchy: *King Edward I.* **2** (usu *the* — *of clubs*, *diamonds* etc) playing card between a queen(5) and an ace(1) with a picture of a king(1) on it, *symb* K. **3** most important piece in the game of chess, *symb* K. **4** (usu — *of s.t*) most important member (of s.t): *The lion is the king of the beasts/jungle*(1). Compare queen(3).

kingdom /'kɪŋdəm/ c.n (often with capital **K**) country ruled by a king(1) or queen: *the United Kingdom* (*of Great Britain and Northern Ireland*). **the animal/mineral/plant kingdom** ⇨ animal, mineral, plant. **kingdom come** (a) the end of life: *I'll wait for you until kingdom come.* (b) state of being unconscious: *He knocked the other man into kingdom come.*

'king,fisher c.n kind of brightly coloured bird that lives near rivers and eats fish.

'kingly adj (suitable) for a king(1): *kingly responsibilities; a kingly crown.*

'king,maker c.n (*informal*) person with power to give s.o a high position in government, a business etc.

'king,pin c.n (*informal*) most important person in a business, organization, committee etc.

,king 'prawn c.n kind of large prawn found in Australia.

,King's 'Counsel c.n (*abbr* KC) (UK) (title of a) barrister who is appointed to act for the Crown(2) when a king(1) is on the throne(2). Compare Queen's Counsel.

,king's 'evidence ⇨ evidence(n).

'king-,size attrib.adj (also **'king-,sized**) of a large size: *king-size cigarettes; a king-size bed.*

kink /kɪŋk/ c.n **1** short bend or twist in rope, wire etc. **2** (*informal*) example of odd (sexual) behaviour.

'kinky adj (-ier, -iest) (*informal*) (of a person, behaviour) having or showing a kink(2).

kiosk /'kiːɒsk/ c.n **1** small place with a public telephone: *a telephone kiosk.* **2** small shop with an open front where newspapers, cigarettes, sweets etc are sold.

kip /kɪp/ c.n **1** (often *have a* —) (*slang*) sleep. ▷ intr.v (-pp-) **2** (often — *down*) sleep (in a place): *Is there anywhere I can kip down for the night?*

kipper /'kɪpə/ c.n herring(1) that has been cut open and smoked: *Some people eat kippers for breakfast in England.*

kirk /kɜːk/ c.n (in Scotland) church.

kiss /kɪs/ c.n **1** act of touching s.o with one's lips on her/his lips, face, hand etc to show love or as a friendly act or sign of respect: *a kiss on the lips.* **the kiss of life** the method of helping s.o to breathe by breathing into her/his mouth: *She pulled the girl out of the water and gave her the kiss of life.*
▷ tr/intr.v **2** give (s.o/s.t) a kiss(1): *We kissed (each other) goodnight. She kissed the Pope's ring.*

kit /kɪt/ c.n **1** set of equipment(2), clothes etc for a particular purpose: *a repair kit for a bicycle; a kit for building a boat. Have you brought your swimming kit? My kit* (e.g for playing tennis) *is in my car.*
▷ tr.v (-tt-) **2** (usu — *s.o out/up*; — *s.o in s.t*) provide (s.o) with clothes or a special kit(1): *David was kitted out as though he was going to climb Mount Everest.*

'kit,bag c.n kind of strong bag for a soldier's or sportsperson's kit(1).

kitchen /'kɪtʃɪn/ c.n (also *attrib*) room or place where food is prepared: *the hospital kitchens; a kitchen cupboard.*

'kitchen ,dresser c.n = dresser(2).

,kitche'nette c.n small kitchen.

,kitchen 'sink c.n basin with taps, esp in a kitchen for washing dishes etc in. **everything but the kitchen sink** a lot of unnecessary things: *When she goes away for a weekend she takes a suitcase that has everything but the kitchen sink in it.*

'kitchen,ware u.n (*commerce*) pots, knives, bowls etc used in a kitchen.

kite /kaɪt/ c.n **1** light object on a string (to be) flown high in the air as a toy. **2** kind of hawk¹(1).

kith /kɪθ/ pl.n (**one's own**) **kith and kin** (one's) close friends and relations. ⇨ kin.

kitten /'kɪtn/ c.n young cat. **have kittens** (*fig*; *informal*) become very afraid or worried: *I was having kittens until I heard that she was safe.*

kitty /'kɪtɪ/ c.n (pl -ies) **1** (container with an) amount of money shared by a group for a purpose: *We had a kitty for the food during our holiday.* **2** (*informal*) (word used by a child or to show affection for a) kitten or cat.

kiwi /'kiːwiː/ c.n kind of large bird found in New Zealand that cannot fly.

klaxon /'klæksn/ c.n kind of horn that used to be on cars.

kleptomania /,kleptəʊ'meɪnɪə/ u.n uncontrollable wish to steal.

kleptomaniac /,kleptəʊ'meɪnɪˌæk/ c.n person suffering from kleptomania.

km *symb* kilometre(s).

knack /næk/ *sing/def.n* (*informal*) ability to do s.t: *I'd like to make bread but I haven't got the knack. Mary has a peculiar knack of making you feel uncomfortable.*

knackered /'nækəd/ pred.adj (*slang*) very tired: *After a hard day at work I'm completely knackered!*

knapsack /'næp,sæk/ c.n kind of small light haversack.

knave /neɪv/ c.n (*old use*) **1** = jack(2). **2** dishonest man.

'knavery u.n (*old use*) dishonest behaviour.

knead /niːd/ tr/intr.v **1** press and roll (dough(1)) with the hands when making bread etc. **2** press (muscles(1)) with the hands, e.g to reduce aches: *I kneaded my aching muscles.*

knee /niː/ c.n **1** (also *attrib*) part where the leg bends in the middle: *a knee joint. I was on my knees washing the floor when he arrived. She went down on one knee and picked up the book.* ⇨ knock-kneed. **2** part of clothes covering the knee(1): *He's torn the knee of his trousers.* **3** any part of s.t like a knee(1) in position or shape, e.g a bend in a pipe. **bring s.o/s.t to her/his/its knees** (*fig*) force s.o, a business, country etc to (accept defeat and) be in a difficult situation: *The strike brought the industry to its knees. Unemployment has brought his family to its knees.* **get/go down on one's hands and knees** (**to s.o**, **to do s.t**) ⇨ hand(n).
▷ tr.v **4** hit or push (s.o/s.t) with the knee(1): *He kneed her in the back.*

'**knee,cap** *c.n* flat bone on the front of the knee(1).

,**knee-'deep** *pred.adj* deep enough to reach the knee(1): *The water was knee-deep.* **knee-deep in s.t** (a) covered up to the knees(1) in s.t: *knee-deep in mud.* (b) (*fig*) very involved in s.t: *knee-deep in work/debt.*

,**knee-'high** *adj* tall enough to reach the knee: *I've known her since she was knee-high.*

kneel /ni:l/ *intr.v* (*p.t,p.p* knelt /nelt/) (often — *down*) be, move to, a position of supporting oneself on one or both knees(1), sometimes as a sign of respect: *He knelt down and picked up a stone. Pam was kneeling on the floor looking for her ring. He knelt in front of the king.*

knell /nel/ *c.n* (*formal* or *old use*) sound of a large bell, esp one warning or announcing a death.

knelt /nelt/ *p.t,p.p* of kneel.

knew /nju:/ *p.t* of know. ⇨ known.

knickers /'nɪkəz/ *pl.n* (*informal*) pants(1) for women or girls.

knick-knack /'nɪk ˌnæk/ *c.n* small cheap ornament.

knife /naɪf/ *c.n* (*pl* knives /naɪvz/) 1 instrument with a long sharp edge for cutting: *I need a sharp knife to cut this meat. This is a good carving-knife.* 2 instrument like a knife(1) used as a weapon: *The thief pulled out a knife.*

▷ *tr.v* 3 cut or kill (s.o) using a knife(2): *He knifed the man in the back.*

'**knife-,edge** *c.n* (often *on a* —) (*fig*) feeling of great anxiety before an important decision or result: *We were on a knife-edge waiting for the examination results.*

knight /naɪt/ *c.n* 1 (in history) person who dressed in armour(1) and acted as a soldier for a powerful and rich family. 2 (in history) person given an official title (Sir) by a ruler because of his services as a knight(1). Compare baronet. 3 (*written abbr* Kt, usu after a name) person given a high honorary title (with the word Sir before the name) for service to his country, profession etc: *Sir Isaac Newton.* 4 piece in chess with the head of a horse, *symb* Kt.

▷ *tr.v* 5 make (s.o) a knight(2,3): *He was knighted by the Queen for his work in Africa.*

'**knighthood** *c.n* rank or title of a knight(2,3): *He was given his knighthood by the Queen.*

knit /nɪt/ *v* (-tt-) 1 *tr/intr.v* use wool and knitting needles (or a machine) to make (cloth, a garment etc): *I can sew but I cannot knit. She's knitting me a sweater.* 2 *intr.v* (of bones, muscles(1) etc) join together after being damaged. 3 *tr.v* cause (people) to form a group: *Their religion knits them (together) in their determination to reach a peaceful settlement.* **knit one's brows** ⇨ brow.

'**knitter** *c.n* person who knits(1).

'**knitting** *u.n* 1 wool etc that is being knitted(1): *Where have I put my knitting?* 2 process of producing knitted(1) cloth.

'**knitting-ma,chine** *c.n* kind of machine used to knit(1) cloth from wool etc.

'**knitting-,needle** *c.n* long rod used with wool etc to knit(1).

knives /naɪvz/ *pl* of knife.

knob /nɒb/ *c.n* 1 round lump on the surface of s.t: *a chair with knobs on the arms; a glass with knobs on it.* 2 round handle on furniture, a door,

machine etc: *I pulled the knob and the lid opened. What is the red knob in your car for* (i.e what is its purpose)?

'**knobbly** *adj* (-ier, -iest) having knobs(1): *knobbly knees.*

knock /nɒk/ *c.n* 1 act of making a sound by hitting a surface with a closed hand, a stick etc, esp to get attention: *He gave a knock on the door.* 2 sound of a knock(1): *I heard a knock at the door.* 3 act of hitting or being hit: *That knock has left a large bruise on my leg.* 4 (*informal*) bad experience: *The old lady had suffered some hard knocks during her long life.*

▷ *v* 5 *intr.v* (often — *at/on s.t*) make a knock(1,2) (on s.t, esp a door) to get attention: *I knocked (at/on the door) but no one came.* 6 *tr.v* (usu — *s.t in s.t*) make (a hole, dent(1), etc (in s.t)): *The builder knocked a hole in our wall.* ⇨ knock s.t in(to s.t). 7 *tr/intr.v* (often — *against/into s.o/s.t*) hit (s.o/s.t) usu accidentally: *He knocked (into) the chair in the dark.* ⇨ knock s.o/s.t down, knock s.o/s.t off (s.t), knock s.o/s.t over. 8 *tr.v* make (s.o) unconscious etc by hitting her/him very hard: *I was knocked stupid, sideways, to the floor, by that fall.* ⇨ knock s.o out, knock s.o/s.t down. 9 *tr.v* (*informal*) say or write that (s.o, s.o's work) is bad: *Why are you always knocking me?* 10 *intr.v* (of an engine) make a sound like a number of knocks(1) because of a fault.

knock about/around (*informal*) move about a part of town etc without much purpose: *The youths were knocking about on street corners.* **knock about/around with s.o** (*informal*) go about with s.o, a group etc: *Liz has been knocking about with some older boys recently.* **knock s.o about/around** (*informal*), hit, kick s.o badly. **knock s.t about/around** (*fig*; *informal*) discuss s.t, e.g a suggestion, in a group.

knock against s.o/s.t ⇨ knock(7).

knock at s.t ⇨ knock(5).

knock s.o back s.t (*informal*) cost s.o a certain amount of money: *Our new car knocked us back a few thousand.* **knock s.t back** (*informal*) drink s.t, esp alcohol, quickly: *He knocked back his drink and left in a hurry.*

knock s.o/s.t down hit s.o/s.t either accidentally or on purpose (sometimes when driving a car) and make her/him/it fall. **knock s.t down** (a) destroy a building etc by hitting it. (b) reduce a price, fee(1) etc. ⇨ knock-down.

knock s.t in(to s.t) hit s.t with a hammer etc and force it into s.t: *He knocked the nail in(to the wood) with a couple of blows.* ⇨ knock(6).

knock (some) sense into s.o ⇨ sense(*n*).

knock into s.o/s.t (a) ⇨ knock(7). (b) (*informal*) meet s.o by chance. ⇨ run into s.o. **knock s.t into shape** ⇨ shape(*n*).

knock off (work) (**at 5.30 pm** etc) (*informal*) finish, stop (work) (at 5.30 pm etc): *I'm tired, let's knock off for lunch and finish the job later.* **Knock it off** (usu imperative) (*informal*) Stop doing that! (i.e s.t annoying). **knock s.o off** (*slang*) kill s.o. **knock s.t off** (a) (*slang*) steal s.t; steal from s.t: *She knocked a dress off while nobody was looking. They've knocked off the bank.* (b) (*informal*) complete a piece of work, esp writing or composing, quickly: *Rob knocked off a song in 10 minutes.* (c) drink (a lot of) s.t quickly: *They knocked off a whole bottle of wine*

between them. **knock s.o/s.t off** (s.t) hit s.o/
s.t and make her/him/it fall (from s.t): *The car
knocked the boy off his bicycle. The cat knocked
the bottle off the table.*

knock on (in rugby) knock(7) the ball forwards
with one's hands, which is not allowed. ⇨ knock-
on(2). **knock on s.t** ⇨ knock(5). **knock s.t on the
head** ⇨ head(*n*).

knock s.o out (a) make s.o unconscious by
hitting her/him, esp in a fight, boxing etc. ⇨
knock-out(3). (b) (of a drug(1) etc) make s.o
sleep deeply: *The tablets knocked me out for
10 hours.* ⇨ knock-out(1). (c) (*informal*) make
s.o very surprised and pleased: *Her new dress
really knocked me out.* ⇨ knock-out(4). **knock
s.o/s.t out (of s.t)** defeat s.o, a team etc so that
he/she/it must leave the competition: *Our team
was knocked out (of the Cup) in the third round.*
⇨ knock-out(2). **knock s.t out of s.o** (*fig*) cause
s.o to lose a quality, characteristic: *a punishment
to knock the rudeness out of his son.* **knock s.t
out (of s.t)** hit s.t and remove it (from s.t): *I had
a tooth knocked out in the fight. First we had to
knock the broken glass out (of the window).*

knock s.o/s.t over = knock s.o/s.t down.

knock s.o's and s.o's heads together ⇨
head(*n*). **knock s.t together** ⇨ knock s.t up(a).

knock s.o unconscious = knock s.o out(a): *The
man knocked the thief unconscious.*

knock up (with s.o) (in tennis, squash² etc) hit
the ball (with s.o) in order to warm oneself and
prepare for a game. **knock s.o up** make s.o wake
up by knocking(5) at the door etc: *Could you
knock me up at 6 o'clock?* **knock s.t up** (a) make,
prepare, s.t quickly: *Alan knocked up a meal in
10 minutes.* (b) (in cricket¹) score a number of
runs(8): *He knocked up a 100 in 55 minutes.*

'knock-,down *attrib.adj* (of a price) cheap;
reduced from what it was: *selling goods at
knock-down prices.* ⇨ knock s.t down(b).

'knocker *c.n* object on a door etc used for
knocking(5).

,knock-'kneed *adj* having legs that bend
inwards at the knees when standing.

,knock-'on *adj* **1** (of s.t that happens) having a
result that affects other things: *The rise in the
price of petrol will have a knock-on effect in other
industries.*
▷ *c.n* **2** (in rugby) act of knocking the ball on(⇨
knock on).

'knock-,out *attrib.adj* **1** (of a drug(1) etc) causing
deep sleep: *knock-out pills*(1). ⇨ knock s.o out(b).
2 (of a competition) in which players or teams
are out of a competition if they lose a game. ⇨
knock s.o/s.t out (of s.t).
▷ *c.n* **3** act of hitting s.o unconscious. ⇨ knock s.o
out(a). **4** (*informal*) person or thing who/that is
very attractive: *Her new book is a knock-out!* ⇨
knock s.o out(c).

knoll /nəʊl/ *c.n* small round hill.

knot /nɒt/ *c.n* **1** join or folded part in rope, wool,
hair etc: *I can't undo the knot in this string. I've
got knots in my hair.* **2** lump or dark place
in wood where a branch or stem joins the tree.
3 small crowd: *There was a knot of people round
the sports car.* **4** unit of measurement of speed
through water (about 1.85 km per hour); nautical
mile per hour.
▷ *tr.v* (-*tt*-) Opposite unknot. **5** tie the ends of (string,

wool etc) by folding them over each other and
pulling them tight: *He knotted the ropes together.*
6 cause (hair etc) to form into knots(1): *The wind
knotted her long hair.*

'knotty *adj* (-*ier*, -*iest*) **1** having knots(1): *knotty
string/hair/wool.* **2** (usu *attrib*) (*informal*) very
difficult: *a knotty problem.*

know /nəʊ/ *def.n* **1 be in the know** (*informal*) be
aware of s.t when most people are not: *Because I
live next door they think I am in the know about
his private life.*
▷ *tr.v* (*p.t* knew /njuː/, *p.p* known /nəʊn/)
2 (often — (that) . . .; — what, why etc . . .) be,
feel, certain about the truth of (s.t): *I know he's
not there because he did not answer the phone.
Do you know why she refused to come? I know
(that) she's a good cook.* **3** (often — how to do s.t)
have knowledge of and be able to remember (s.t):
*Do you know how to drive? I know Spanish but
I don't know Greek. She knows all the words to
the songs.* **4** have knowledge of the identity and
personality of (s.o): *We've known each other for
ten years. Knowing John* (or *If I know John*),
he'll refuse to do it. **5** understand (s.t): *Do you
know what I mean? I don't know what you are
talking about.* **6** (*literary*) have an experience of
(s.t): *Jeff has never known happiness.*

I know (what) . . . (*informal*) (expression used to
make a suggestion): *I know what, let's ask Susan
to do it.*

know (s.t) about s.o/s.t know(3) (s.t) about s.o/
s.t: *What do you know about him? I don't know
(much) about music but I do know about
painting.*

know s.t backwards (*informal*) know s.t, e.g a
job, words of a song, extremely well: *I know my
lines for the play backwards.*

know better (for s.o to) be experienced enough
not to do s.t unwise etc: *You should not be so rude
— you are old enough to know better.*

know s.o/s.t from s.o/s.t be able to tell the
difference, to distinguish, between s.o/s.t and
s.o/s.t: *Pete doesn't know his left from his right.*

know of s.o/s.t have (some) knowledge of
s.o/s.t: *'Do you know Dr Jones?' 'Well, I know
of him but I'm not his patient.' Do you know
of anywhere we could get a quiet drink?* **know
one's own mind** ⇨ mind¹.

you know (*informal*) (expression used to provide a short pause when speaking): *It helps, you
know, to warn people if you are going to be late.*

'know-,all *c.n* (*derog*; *informal*) person who
thinks he/she knows all the facts, esp more than
others.

'know-,how *u.n* (*informal*) practical ability to
do s.t: *She has a lot of know-how about
organizing parties.*

'knowing *attrib.adj* **1** showing one knows the
facts or understands: *a knowing look.*
▷ *u.n* **2 there is no knowing s.t** it is impossible
to decide and state (an opinion, usu about the
future): *There's no knowing what she'll do next.*

'knowingly *adv* in a knowing(1) way: *He looked
at me knowingly.* ⇨ unknowingly.

knowledge /'nɒlɪdʒ/ *n* **1** *sing/u.n* facts, experiences etc known or learned: *How much know-
ledge did you gain from the history lessons? Polly
has a good knowledge of French.* **2** *u.n* all that
can be learned about a subject: *Biology is an area*

of scientific knowledge. **3** *u.n* fact of knowing: *I had no knowledge of the meeting until you told me.* **carnal knowledge** ⇨ carnal. **come to s.o's knowledge** become known to s.o: *It has come to my knowledge that you used my bicycle without asking me.* **common knowledge** ⇨ common(*adj*). **general knowledge** ⇨ general. **to my knowledge** as far as I know: *To my knowledge, he hasn't come to work today.*

'knowledgeable *adj* (also **'knowledgable**) (often — *about s.t*) knowing many facts about s.t: *a knowledgeable teacher; teachers who are knowledgeable about their subject.*

known /nəʊn/ *attrib.adj* **1** easily identifiable as and agreed to be: *a known liar/expert.* ⇨ unknown, well-known.

▷ *v* **2** *p.p* of know.

knuckle /'nʌkl/ *n* **1** *c.n* joint in the finger: *He knocked on the door with his knuckles.* **2** *c/u.n* joint of the knee of a young cow or pig used as food.

▷ *intr.v* **3 knuckle down** (**to s.t**); **knuckle under** (*informal*) begin to work seriously (on s.t): *You must knuckle down to your studies if you want to do well.*

koala /kəʊ'ɑːlə/ *c.n* (also **ko'ala ,bear**) kind of small grey animal found in Australia that lives in trees.

Koran /kɔː'rɑːn/ *def.n* holy book of Muslims(2).

kowtow /ˌkaʊ'taʊ/ *intr.v* (often — *to s.o*) be too obedient, e.g because one is too afraid or is forced to do so: *Ben refused to kowtow to his boss and so he changed his job.*

Kt *written abbr/symb* knight(3,4).

kung fu /ˌkʌŋ 'fuː/ *u.n* (also *attrib*) kind of fighting from China using hits and kicks; it is a mixture of karate and judo.

kW, kw *symb* kilowatt(s).

Ll

L, l /el/ *c/unique n* **1** 12th letter of the English alphabet.

▷ *written abbr* **2** lake. **3** left. **4** length. **5** (**L**) Liberal.

▷ *symb* **6** litre(s). **7** (**L**) learner driver. **8** (**L**) large. **9** Roman numeral for 50.

lab /læb/ *c.n* (*informal*) laboratory.

Lab *written abbr* (UK) Labour Party.

label /'leɪbl/ *c.n* **1** small piece of paper or cord put on an object to state what it is, who owns it, where it is to be sent etc: *Please put labels on all your luggage. The label on the parcel has come off. The size of the shirt is on the label inside the collar.* **2** (*informal*) short description about a person, idea etc: *He was given the label 'Brains' by his friends. This food comes under the label 'Health Food'.*

▷ *tr.v* (*-ll-*, US *-l-*) **3** put a label(1) on (s.t): *We have labelled all the suitcases.* **4** give (s.o/s.t) a label(2): *She was labelled a thief by her friends. That period has been labelled as a time of fast economic(1) progress.*

laboratory /lə'bɒrətrɪ/ *c.n* (*pl -ies*) (*informal* **lab**) (also *attrib*) building, room etc with special equipment for practical scientific work: *a physics laboratory; laboratory equipment(2).* ⇨ language laboratory.

labour /'leɪbə/ *adj* (US **'labor**) **1** (with capital **L**) of or referring to the Labour Party: *the Labour vote; vote Labour in the election.* ⇨ labour(4).

▷ *n* (US **'labor**) **2** *c/u.n* physical work, esp to earn wages: *skilled(1)/unskilled(1) labour.* **3** *u.n* (also *attrib*) group in society who earn wages for their work in factories etc: *the labour vote; labour relations.* ⇨ Labour Party. **4** *u.n* (with capital **L**) Labour Party: *Will Labour get in? What is Labour's position in this matter?* **5** *u.n* (also *attrib*) effort and process of giving birth: *She's gone into labour. Her labour lasted several hours. Can you feel any labour pains?*

▷ *intr.v* (US **'labor**) **6** do physical work: *labour on a building site.* **labour under s.t** have difficulty, a disadvantage because of (s.t): *I have been labouring under a misunderstanding.*

laborious /lə'bɔːrɪəs/ *adj* **1** involving, needing, much effort, work etc: *Writing dictionaries is a laborious task.* **2** (*derog*) (of a speech, piece of writing) long, difficult to understand, not at all interesting.

la'boriously *adv*.

'laboured *adj* (of breathing) done with difficulty or effort.

'labourer *c.n* man who does physical work, esp on a building site.

,labour of 'love *c.n* (*informal*) work done for one's own pleasure or to please s.o: *Knitting him that sweater was a labour of love.*

'Labour ,Party *def.n* (*written abbr* Lab) (UK) political party supporting the interests of labour(2) and trade union members: *He is a member of the Labour Party* (or *is a Labour Party member*). ⇨ labour(1,4).

'labour-,saving *adj* designed to reduce the amount of physical work needed: *labour-saving equipment(2) in the kitchen.*

labrador /'læbrəˌdɔː/ *c.n* kind of large dog with short yellow-brown, brown or black hair.

labyrinth /'læbərɪnθ/ *c.n* system of many linked paths or tunnels in various directions that is difficult to follow.

labyrinthine /ˌlæbə'rɪnθaɪn/ *adj*.

lace /leɪs/ *n* **1** *c.n* piece of string etc used to fasten two edges: *shoelaces.* **2** *u.n* (also *attrib*) kind of cloth in which the threads produce open patterns: *a lace tablecloth.*

▷ *v* **3** *tr/intr.v* (often — (*s.t*) *up*) fasten two edges (of s.t) together, be fastened, using a lace(1): *Lace* (*up*) *your shoes. This dress laces down the back.* Opposite unlace. **4** *tr.v* add a small amount of alcoholic(1) drink to (another drink): *tea laced with rum.*

'lacy *adj* (*-ier, -iest*) made of, like, lace(2): *a lacy pattern.*

lacerate /'læsəˌreɪt/ *tr.v* (*formal*) tear (skin) roughly: *The nail lacerated his arm.*

laceration /ˌlæsə'reɪʃən/ *c/u.n* act or result of lacerating: *lacerations in his arm.*

lack /læk/ *sing/u.n* **1** (often — *of s.t*) need; condition of not having (s.t): *suffer through lack of food, money. There's a lack of good children's books in this library. We could prove nothing because of (a) lack of information.*
▷ *tr.v* **2** have need of (s.t); have none, not enough, of (s.t): *This city lacks a sports centre. Their children lacked warm clothes.* **be lacking** be not there, not available: *It's not her interest or effort that is lacking — it's jobs that are lacking.* **lack for s.t** need s.t: *His wife lacks for nothing.* **be lacking in s.t** have need of s.t: *The food is lacking in salt. She's lacking in experience.*

laconic /ləˈkɒnɪk/ *adj* (*formal*) (of s.o's way of speaking) using only a few words to say s.t. **la'conically** *adv.*

lacquer /ˈlækə/ *c/u.n* **1** (example of a) kind of colourless paint giving a hard, shiny surface to metal or wood. **2** substance put on hair to make it stay in a particular position: *hair lacquer.*
▷ *tr.v* **3** put lacquer(*n*) on (s.t).

lacy ⇨ lace.

lad /læd/ *c.n* (also **'laddie**) (*informal*) boy or young man. ⇨ lass.

ladder /ˈlædə/ *c.n* **1** kind of wooden or metal device with a row of steps between two long pieces, used to go up or down. ⇨ stepladder. **2** (*fig*) means of marking progress: *Her university degree has put her up the social ladder.* **3** long series of broken stitches, esp in stockings.
▷ *tr/intr.v* **4** (cause (a stocking etc) to) get/have a ladder(3): *I've laddered my tights. Stockings ladder easily.*

laddie /ˈlædɪ/ ⇨ lad.

laden /ˈleɪdn/ *adj* (usu — *with s.t*) carrying a large load: *a car laden with luggage; a heavily laden horse.*

lading /ˈleɪdɪŋ/ *u.n* (esp *bill of* —) (*commerce*) cargo: *A bill of lading is a list of a ship's cargo.*

ladle /ˈleɪdl/ *c.n* **1** large spoon with a deep round end, used for serving soups etc.
▷ *tr.v* **2** (often — *s.t out*) give out (food etc) using a ladle(1): *ladling (out) the soup.* **ladle s.t out** (a) ⇨ ladle(2). (b) (*fig*) give out large amounts of s.t: *ladling out work to the students.*

lady /ˈleɪdɪ/ *c.n* (*pl -ies*) **1** (also *attrib*) woman: *There's a lady at the door. I prefer a lady doctor.* ⇨ gentleman. **2** woman with good manners: *She's no lady swearing like that!* ⇨ gentleman. **3** woman of high social position. ⇨ gentleman. **4** (with capital **L**) title given to a woman who is a peer or wife/daughter of a peer or knight(2,3). ⇨ lord(3). **5** (with capital **L**) title given to a woman in a high official position: *the Lady Mayor(ess)/Chair.* ⇨ lord(4).
'Ladies *def.n* (*informal*) public lavatory for women. ⇨ Gents.
,ladies and 'gentlemen (form of address used to begin a public speech).
'lady,like *adj* like, suitable for, a lady(2): *ladylike behaviour.*
'lady,killer *c.n* (*informal*) man who women find attractive.
'ladyship *c.n* (often used with capital **L**) title used when speaking about/to a lady(4), woman judge etc: *Her/Your Ladyship.* ⇨ lordship.
ladybird /ˈleɪdɪˌbɜːd/ *c.n* (also *attrib*) kind of small beetle, usu red with black spots.

lag¹ /læg/ *n* **1** *u.n* act or state of being slower,

later. **2** *sing.n* amount of time of lag(1): *a lag of several minutes.* ⇨ time-lag.
▷ *intr.v* (*-gg-*) **3** (usu — *behind*) be/fall behind in time, development, progress etc: *The smallest child was lagging behind (the group).* **4** become less strong: *Effort needed to finish the job is lagging.*

lag² /læg/ *tr.v* (*-gg-*) cover (a pipe etc) with thick cloth etc to prevent loss of heat.

lag³ /læg/ *c.n* (esp *old* —) (*informal*) person who has often been sent to prison.

lager /ˈlɑːgə/ *c/u.n* (example or amount of a) kind of light beer: *a pint of lager; a German lager. Two lagers, please.*

lagoon /ləˈguːn/ *c.n* area of shallow sea water (almost) surrounded by a sandbank or coral-reef.

laid /leɪd/ *p.t,p.p* of lay².

lain /leɪn/ *p.p* of lie²(v).

lair /leə/ *c.n* place used as a home by a large wild animal: *The lion is in its lair.*

laity ⇨ lay¹.

lake /leɪk/ *c.n* large area of water surrounded by land.

lam /læm/ *intr.v* (*-mm-*) (usu — *into s.o*) (*informal*) criticize (s.o) severely.

lamb /læm/ *n* **1** *c.n* young of a sheep. **2** *u.n* (also *attrib*) flesh of a lamb(1) as food: *lamb stew; roast lamb.* **3** *c.n* (*informal*) quiet, gentle child.
▷ *intr.v* **4** (of pregnant sheep) (begin to) give birth.
'lamb,like *adj* quiet and gentle.
'lamb,skin *c/u.n* (also *attrib*) skin of a lamb(1) with the wool on, used to make clothing.
'lambs,wool *u.n* (also *attrib*) kind of soft wool from a lamb(1), used to make sweaters etc.

lame /leɪm/ *adj* **1** (esp of animals) not able to walk properly because of damage to the leg or foot: *a lame horse.* **2** not done with effort or enthusiasm: *a lame attempt.* **3** not believable: *a lame excuse.*
▷ *def.pl.n* **4** people who cannot walk correctly.
▷ *tr.v* **5** cause (an animal) to be lame(1): *The dog was lamed by the sharp wire.*
,lame 'duck *c.n* (*derog; informal*) person, business company, plan etc that is shown to be not efficient, useful etc.
'lamely *adv.* **'lameness** *u.n.*

lament /ləˈment/ *c.n* **1** (*formal*) expression of deep sorrow or regret.
▷ *tr/intr.v* **2** (*formal*) express deep sorrow or regret (about (s.t): *He lamented (over) his failure.*
lamentable /ˈlæməntəbl/ *adj* (*formal*) very bad, disappointing: *lamentable efforts to improve conditions at work.*
lamentation /ˌlæmənˈteɪʃən/ *c/u.n* lament(1).

laminated /ˈlæmɪˌneɪtɪd/ *adj* (*technical*) made by putting together several thin layers: *laminated wood.*
lamination /ˌlæmɪˈneɪʃən/ *c/u.n.*

lamp /læmp/ *c.n* kind of device designed to produce light: *a table lamp; a street lamp.*
'lamp,post *c.n* tall structure supporting a lamp in a street.
'lamp,shade *c.n* covering on a lamp or hanging light to direct or shade light from a light bulb.

lampoon /læmˈpuːn/ *c.n* **1** statement that attacks s.o or a written piece in an amusing way (trying to make her/him/it seem foolish).
▷ *tr.v* **2** produce a lampoon(1) about (s.o/s.t).

lance /lɑːns/ *c.n* **1** (in history) long pointed

weapon. **2** (also **'lancet**) (*medical*) very sharp, pointed knife used by a surgeon.
▷ *tr.v* **3** (*medical*) make a hole in (an infected spot etc) with a lance(2) to remove the poison.

lance corporal /ˌlɑːns 'kɔːprəl/ *c.n* (*written abbr* L/Cpl) non-commissioned officer of the lowest rank in the army.

lancet /'lɑːnsɪt/ *c.n* lance(2).

land /lænd/ *n* **1** *u.n* part of the surface area of the world that is not covered by water: *travel by land.* **2** *c.n* country: *This is the land where I was born. He's the best in the land.* **3** *u.n* (area of) ground: *The land on this farm is poor.* **4** *c/u.n* (often *pl*) area of ground owned by s.o: *She owns some land in the mountains. He* inspects(2) *his lands regularly. The house will be sold with the land.* **find out, see, how the land lies** ⇨ lie²(*v*). **live off the fat of the land** ⇨ fat(*n*). **no-man's land** ⇨ no.
▷ *v* **5** *tr/intr.v* (cause (an aircraft) to) come down to rest on a surface: *He landed the plane in a field. Their plane will land at 6 o'clock.* **6** *tr/intr.v* (cause (s.o/s.t) to) arrive from a ship, boat etc onto land: *We're landing at the main port tomorrow. They landed many tonnes of fish.* **7** *tr.v* (*informal*) be successful in getting(s.t): *I've landed a job with the government.* **8** *tr/intr.v* (esp — (s.o) (up) in s.t) (cause (s.o) to) finish (in an unpleasant or unwanted situation): *You'll land (up) in prison if you behave like that. He's landed me in a very embarrassing position. We landed up in hospital after the accident.* **land on one's feet** ⇨ foot(*n*).

'landed *adj* owning land(3): *the landed classes.*

'landing *c.n* **1** flat area between two flights of stairs (⇨ fly²). **2** (also *attrib*) act of landing(⇨ land(5,6)): *get landing approval; a* bumpy/*smooth landing.*

'land,lady *c.n* (*pl* -*ies*) woman who owns and rents a house etc to s.o.

'land,lord *c.n* man who owns and rents a house etc to s.o.

'land,mark *c.n* **1** part of an area of land that is easy to see or is well known: *That large tree is a landmark used by walkers in this valley.* **2** important discovery, event etc: *The invention of the wheel was a landmark in history.*

'land,owner *c.n* person who owns land(4).

landscape /'lænskeɪp/ *c.n* **1** (also *attrib*) view across an area of land: *a landscape painting.*
▷ *tr.v* **2** choose and arrange trees and plants on (an area of land): *Let's have the garden landscaped.*

,landscape 'gardening *u.n* (profession of) landscaping(2) gardens and parks.

,landscape 'gardener *c.n* person skilled in landscape gardening.

'land,slide *c.n* **1** (act of a) large mass of land moving down a hillside or mountain. **2** (also *attrib*) (*fig*) victory in an election by a very large number of votes: *a landslide victory.*

landward /'lændwəd/ *adj* (facing) towards the land. ⇨ seaward.

'landwards *adv* (US **'landward**) towards land. ⇨ seawards.

lane /leɪn/ *c.n* **1** narrow road in the country: *a lane through the fields to the house.* **2** (with capital **L** in names) narrow street in a town: *a market in Brick Lane.* **3** (also *attrib*) marked division along a wide road for use by one row of vehicles: *the inside/outside lane; two-lane traffic; lane* closures. **4** marked division along the length of a race-course, swimming pool etc for one competitor. **5** route(1) used regularly by ships in a long narrow area of the sea or by aircraft near airports.

language /'læŋgwɪdʒ/ *n* **1** *u.n* (also *attrib*) (power of) human communication(1) using words and sentences: *use of language between young children; language development.* **2** *c.n* (also *attrib*) example of language(1) used by a particular group: *the English/French language; learn a foreign language; language schools.* **3** *c.n* particular words used by a group: *medical/technical language.* **4** *c/u.n* system of communication(1) between people used like a language(2): *Deaf people use (a) sign language. Giving flowers is part of the language of love.* **5** *c.n* system of codes(4) used to put information into a computer. **mind one's language** control what one says and not swear.

'language la,boratory *c.n* (also **'language ,lab**) place with equipment for learning a foreign language by listening to tapes(3).

languid /'læŋgwɪd/ *adj* (*formal*) having or showing no energy(1) or enthusiasm: *a languid expression.*

'languidly *adv*.

languish /'læŋgwɪʃ/ *intr.v* (*formal*) lose energy(1), enthusiasm, strength etc: *The old man was languishing in hospital.*

languor /'læŋgə/ *u.n* (*formal*) lack of energy(1) or enthusiasm.

languorous /'læŋgərəs/ *adj*.

lank /læŋk/ *adj* **1** (of hair) long and straight. **2** (of a person) tall and thin. **3** (of arms, legs etc) long and thin.

'lanky *adj* (-*ier*, -*iest*) lank(2,3).

lantern /'læntən/ *c.n* light with a glass or metal case, esp one that can be carried.

lap¹ /læp/ *c.n* part of the body from the waist to the knees when sitting: *She had the baby on her lap.* **the lap of luxury** most favourable, rich state or situation: *After he won the competition he lived in the lap of luxury.*

lap² /læp/ *c.n* **1** complete journey round a race track.
▷ *tr.v* (-pp-) **2** pass (another competitor) so that one is one or more laps(1) ahead.

lap³ /læp/ *c.n* **1** act/sound of lapping(⇨ lap³(2,3)): *the lap of waves on the sand.*
▷ *tr/intr.v* (-pp-) **2** (of waves, water) hit (the land, a boat etc) with short tapping sounds: *The waves lapped against the rocks.* **3** (often — *s.t* up) (of an animal) use the tongue to take (small amounts of liquid) into the mouth with short tapping sounds. **lap s.t up** (*fig*) clearly enjoy the experience of s.t: *lap up praise. He told her she was beautiful and she lapped it up.*

lapel /lə'pel/ *c.n* front part below the collar of a coat etc that is folded back: *He had a flower in the lapel of his jacket.*

lapse /læps/ *c.n* **1** break in time between events, happenings etc: *After a lapse of four weeks we met again.* **2** small mistake: *a lapse in* concentration(1). **3** fall in good standards of behaviour, morals etc: *We'll forgive this one lapse in your behaviour.*
▷ *intr.v* **4** fall gradually in standards to a worse

state: *The quality of your work has lapsed.* **5** stop: *Their conversation lapsed during dinner.* **6** (of a claim, agreement etc) be no longer effective: *Our right to use this field lapses if we don't pay by the end of the week.* **lapse into s.t** gradually change to (another condition): *lapse into silence, sleep, deep thought.*

larceny /'lɑ:sənɪ/ *c/u.n* (*pl -ies*) (*law*) act or fact of stealing.

lard /lɑ:d/ *u.n* **1** fat from a pig, used to cook food.

▷ *tr.v* **2** use lard(1) on (s.t) when preparing food.

larder /'lɑ:də/ *c.n* cupboard/room for keeping food.

large /lɑ:dʒ/ *adj* **1** having a great size; able to hold many or much etc: *a large house/tree/hand/box/meal*; *a large number of children.*

▷ *adv* **2 by and large** ⇒ by(*adv*).

▷ *unique n* **3 at large** (**a**) (esp of a dangerous person, animal) free: *A wild dog is at large in the city.* (**b**) generally: *The people at large do not approve.*

,large in'testine *def/c.n* lower part of the alimentary canal from the colon(2) to the anus. ⇒ small intestine.

'largely *adv* (*formal*) to a great extent; mainly: *Their success was due largely to their hard work.*

'largeness *u.n.*

,large-'scale *attrib.adj* covering a wide area or much detail: *a large-scale map/inquiry.*

lark¹ /lɑ:k/ *c.n* kind of bird with an attractive song.

lark² /lɑ:k/ *c.n* **1** example of fun, esp when being a little naughty: *have larks in the classroom while the teacher is out.*

▷ *intr.v* **2 lark about/around** enjoy oneself by taking part in larks(1): *larking about in the swimming pool.*

larva /'lɑ:və/ *c.n* (*pl* larvae*-vi:/*) (*technical*) first stage of an insect's development, e.g a caterpillar(1), grub¹(1).

larynx /'lærɪŋks/ *c/def.n* (*technical*) top of the tube taking air to the lungs which encloses the part of the body which produces the voice.

laryngitis /,lærɪn'dʒaɪtɪs/ *u.n* illness with a sore condition of the larynx.

lascivious /lə'sɪvɪəs/ *adj* (*formal*) feeling or showing strong sexual desire: *a lascivious smile.*

la'sciviously *adv.*

laser /'leɪzə/ *c.n* (*technical*) (instrument producing a) very strong narrow beam of light, used for many purposes in industry.

lash /læʃ/ *c.n* **1** = eyelash. **2** (quick blow made with a) length of rope, leather etc. ⇒ lash(4). **3** strong blow made by s.t: *the lash of rain on the window.* ⇒ lash(5).

▷ *v* **4** *tr.v* hit (s.o/s.t) using a length of rope, leather etc: *The cruel boy lashed the animal with his belt.* ⇒ lash(2). **5** *tr/intr.v* (of water, rain etc) hit (a surface etc) with force: *The waves were lashing (against) the sides of the boat.* ⇒ lash(3). **6** *tr.v* (of an animal) move (the tail) like a lash(2): *The lion was lashing its tail.* **7** *tr.v* tie (s.t) together using a rope, length of leather etc: *They lashed the boat to the side of the ship.* **lash out (at s.o)** (usu *fig*) attack (s.o) using strong cruel words. **lash out (on s.t)** (*fig; informal*) spend money (on s.t) extravagantly: *I've lashed out on a new coat.*

'lashing *n* **1** *c.n* rope etc used to lash(7) s.t. **2** *c.n* act of lashing (⇒ lash(*v*)).

'lashings *pl.n* (usu — *of s.t*) (*informal*) very large amounts (of s.t): *lashings of ice-cream.*

lass /læs/ *c.n* (also **'lassie**) (*informal*) girl or young woman. ⇒ lad.

lassitude /'læsɪtju:d/ *u.n* (*formal*) lack of energy(1) or interest; laziness.

lasso /læ'su:/ *c.n* (*pl* -(e)s) **1** rope with a loop that can become small when the rope is pulled, used to catch animals etc.

▷ *tr.v* **2** catch (an animal etc) with a lasso(1).

last¹ /lɑ:st/ *adv* **1** after all others: *Who finished last? I don't want to come last in the examination.* **2** most recently: *We last met in Paris.* **last of all** (**a**) after (one does) everything else; finally: *Last of all I'll describe the scenery.* (**b**) (the) last (reason etc) being. ⇒ first of all (first(*adv*)).

▷ *det/pron* **3** coming, happening, after all other people, things etc: *the last person on the list*; *be last to arrive; on the last Sunday in July.* ⇒ first(5). **4** (*attrib*) coming, happening, immediately before this one: *last night/Saturday/year.* ⇒ next(2). **5** (*attrib*) only remaining: *This is my last pound coin.* **6** (*attrib*) most unsuitable, unlikely etc: *She was the last person you'd imagine could be a good teacher.* **last but not least** mentioned last(3) but still important: *And last but not least I'd like to thank my parents.* **last but one** next to last(3): *He was last but one to finish the race.* **last ditch** ⇒ ditch. **on her/his/its last legs** ⇒ leg. **have the last laugh/word** ⇒ laugh(*n*), word(*n*). **the last thing** ⇒ thing.

▷ *def.n* **7** person or thing who/that is last(1): *I was the last to arrive.* ⇒ first(7). **at (long) last** finally (after much effort, difficulty etc): *At (long) last we got to the top of the mountain.* ⇒ at first. **the last of s/o/s.t** the final appearance (of s.o/s.t): *We've seen the last of him now.*

'lastly *adv* finally (after others): *Lastly, we need someone to feed the animals.* ⇒ firstly.

,last-'minute *attrib.adj* done at the latest time possible: *a last-minute attempt. Last-minute things that must still be done before we leave.*

last² /lɑ:st/ *v* **1** *tr/intr.v* (often — (for) an hour, day etc) continue, exist: *The headache lasted (for) an hour.* **2** *tr/intr.v* (often — (out) until a date/time) be enough (for (s.o)): *The money will have to last (you) until Friday. Will their money last (out) until the end of their holiday?* **3** *tr/intr.v* keep in a good condition: *Those shoes have lasted (you) well (or for a long time).*

'lasting *adj* (usu *attrib*) continuing to exist: *lasting happiness.*

lat /læt/ *abbr* **1** latrine. **2** *written abbr* latitude(1). **3** (with capital **L**) *written abbr* Latin.

latch /lætʃ/ *c.n* **1** kind of device for fastening a door or gate which has a metal or wooden bar that is lifted into, out of, a slot(1).

▷ *tr.v* **2** fasten (a door etc) with a latch(1).

late /leɪt/ *adj* **1** (usu *pred*) coming after the agreed, correct, usual etc time: *You're late!* ⇒ early(1). **2** towards the end (of s.t): *in the late afternoon.* ⇒ early(2). **3** (*attrib*) having (recently) died: *my late father.* **4** (*attrib*) most recent: *the late owner of the shop.* **of late** during recent times; lately: *I haven't seen her of late.*

▷ *adv* **5** near the end of a particular length of time: *late in the afternoon.* ⇒ early(3). After the agreed, correct, usual etc time: *I finished work late. They married late.* ⇨ early(4). **later on** at/during a time afterwards: *We had a meal and later on we went to the* disco. ⇨ early on. **sooner or later** ⇨ soon.

¹**lately** *adv* during recent times: *We haven't met lately. Lately I've been too ill to get out.*

¹**late-,comer** *c.n* person who arrives late(5).

¹**latest** *def.n* time that is as late as possible: *The latest you can stay is 11 o'clock.* **at the latest** not later than the time, date, mentioned: *Come home by 11 o'clock at the latest.*

latish /ˈleɪtɪʃ/ *adj* a little late(1).

latent /ˈleɪtnt/ *adj* (*technical*) capable of existing but not (yet) developed etc: *latent* energy(1), *ability.*

lateral /ˈlætərəl/ *adj* at/from/to the side: *a lateral glance, position.*

¹**laterally** *adv.*

lathe /leɪð/ *c.n* (*technical*) machine that holds a piece of wood, metal etc so that it turns while it is being cut or shaped.

lather /ˈlɑː.ðə/ *sing/u.n* **1** mass of small bubbles as produced by soap in water.
▷ *intr.v* **2** form a lather(1): *Soap will not lather easily on greasy skin.*

Latin /ˈlætɪn/ *adj* **1** of Latin(n). **2** of a Latin(4): *a Latin sense of humour.*
▷ *n* **3** *unique n* language spoken by the ancient Romans. **4** *c.n* person of Italian, Spanish, Portuguese or South American origin.

latitude /ˈlætɪˌtjuːd/ *n* **1** *c.n* (*written abbr* lat) (*technical*) distance that a place is north or south of the equator. Compare longitude. **2** *u.n* (*fig*) (opportunity of) freedom to act etc: *My studies give me very little latitude for pleasure.*

latitudinal /ˌlætɪˈtjuːdɪnl/ *adj.*

latrine /ləˈtriːn/ *c.n* (*abbr* lat /læt/) temporary lavatory, e.g a hole in the ground, used when camping.

latter /ˈlætə/ *attrib.adj* **1** of the second of two parts, things (mentioned): *the latter part of the afternoon.* Opposite former(2).
▷ *def.n* **2** second of two things, parts (mentioned): *I prefer the latter.* Opposite former(3).

¹**latterly** *adv* (*formal*) recently: *Latterly he's been painting the outside of the house.* ⇨ formerly.

lattice /ˈlætɪs/ *c/u.n* (example of a) pattern of crossed bars, esp producing diamond shapes.

laudable /ˈlɔːdəbl/ *adj* (*formal*) deserving to be praised (although not successful): *It was a laudable attempt even though you didn't win.*

¹**laudably** *adv.*

laudatory /ˈlɔːdətrɪ/ *adj* (*formal*) expressing praise: *laudatory remarks.*

laugh /lɑːf/ *c.n* **1** particular act or sound of laughing: *child's laugh; hear a laugh in the crowd.* ⇨ laughter. **have the last laugh** (*fig*) win after a defeat.
▷ *intr.v* **2** express one's amusement, joy etc by making sounds and usu smiling: *The television show made us laugh. I laughed so much that my sides ached.* **be laughing** (*fig; informal*) be sure to succeed; be in a favourable situation: *His parents are rich so he's laughing.* **don't make me laugh** (*informal*) I don't believe you. **laugh at s.o/s.t** (a) laugh(2) because of s.o/s.t: *laugh at her, his clothes.* (b) laugh(2) in an unkind way that makes (s.o) feel foolish: *Don't laugh at someone who is*

in difficulty. **laugh in s.o's face** ⇨ face(n). **laugh like a drain** ⇨ drain(n). **laugh on the other side of one's face** ⇨ face(n). **laugh s.o/s.t to scorn** ⇨ scorn(n). **laugh up one's sleeve** ⇨ sleeve.

¹**laughable** *adj* (*derog*) very foolish, weak: *His effort was laughable.*

¹**laughing** *attrib.adj* expressing feelings of amusement: *laughing faces.* **burst out laughing** ⇨ burst out.

¹**laughing ,stock** *c.n* (*derog; informal*) person who people laugh at(a) because he/she appears foolish: *If you wear those shoes you'll be the laughing stock of the town.*

¹**laughingly** *adv.*

¹**laughter** *u.n* act or sound of a person or group laughing(⇨ laugh(2)): *children's laughter. They must be having fun because there's a lot of laughter coming from their room. We could hear (the sound of) laughter.* **gales of laughter** ⇨ gale(n).

launch /lɔːntʃ/ *c.n* **1** kind of boat with an engine, used on rivers or near the coast. **2** act of launching (⇨ launch(5)) a boat or ship. **3** act of launching (⇨ launch(6)) s.t. **4** act of launching(⇨ launch(7)) a new product etc: *When's the launch of your new book?*
▷ *tr.v* **5** move (a boat or ship) so that it goes into the water: *The boat was launched into the river.* **6** make (a rocket(3), missile(1) etc) go up into the air. **7** make (a new idea, plan etc) begin: *launch a new road scheme for the town's traffic; launch a new product onto the market.* **launch into s.t** begin to talk or write about (s.t) with enthusiasm: *launch into an explanation.* **launch oneself/s.o into s.t** (*informal*) begin to involve oneself/s.o in an activity with enthusiasm: *She launched herself into her studies.* **launch out** (*informal*) begin an activity, attack etc with enthusiasm.

¹**launching ,pad** *c.n* place where a spacecraft is launched(6).

launder /ˈlɔːndə/ *tr/intr.v* (*formal*) wash (clothes etc).

launderette /ˌlɔːndəˈret/ *c.n* place where the public can pay to use washing machines.

¹**laundry** *n* **1** *def.n* (also *attrib*) dirty clothes, sheets etc waiting to be washed: *the laundry basket. When are you doing the laundry; I need my shirt for Saturday?* **2** *def.n* (also *attrib*) washed (and dried) clothes etc: *Your new shirt is in the laundry, the laundry cupboard.* **3** *c.n* place where bedclothes etc can be sent for washing: *We send our sheets to the laundry.*

laurel /ˈlɒrəl/ *c.n* (also *attrib*) kind of small tree with shiny leaves: *a laurel tree/leaf.* One kind of *laurel produces leaves* (bay leaves) *used as a herb. Long ago a branch of laurel leaves was a symbol of victory.* **rest on one's laurels** (*fig*) make no effort to repeat or improve an earlier success.

lava /ˈlɑːvə/ *u.n* hot melted rock coming out of a volcano.

lavatory /ˈlævətrɪ/ *c.n* (*pl* -ies) (also *attrib*) (room with an) open bowl with a seat on top, used to receive waste matter from the body: *a lavatory seat/brush.* **go to the lavatory** urinate or defecate: *I need to go to the lavatory.*

lavender /ˈlævɪndə/ *adj* **1** light blue in colour: *lavender blue; a lavender bathroom.* **2** having a strong smell from the lavender(3) plant: *lavender tissues(3); lavender soap; lavender perfume.*

▷ *u.n* (also *attrib*) **3** kind of plant with stems of small light blue flowers that have a strong pleasant smell: *We bought a lavender (bush) to plant in our garden.* **4** light blue colour of these flowers.

lavish /'lævɪʃ/ *adj* **1** extravagant; too rich or elaborate(1): *lavish birthday presents*; *lavish decorations.* **2** too generous: *Don't be so lavish with my expensive chocolates.*

▷ *tr.v* **3** (usu — *s.t on s.o/s.t*) give (s.t) (too) generously (to s.o/s.t): *lavishing praise on her cooking*; *lavish one's love on a daughter.*
'lavishly *adv.* **'lavishness** *u.n.*

law /lɔː/ *n* **1** *c.n* official rule made by a parliament etc and saying what people are (not) allowed to do: *There ought to be a law against smoking in the street.* ⇒ by-law. **2** *def.n* all the laws(1) as a group: *obey/break the law.* **3** *def.n* (*informal*) police force: *hiding from the law.* **4** *u.n* (particular area of) law(2) as a subject for study: *read law at University*; *be qualified in international law.* **5** *c.n* (*science*) statement of a principle(2) in science, mathematics, philosophy, psychology etc: *the laws of magnetism/gravity/ethics.* **be against the law** be s.t that is considered a crime. **be a law unto oneself** ignore general rules and laws. **go to law** use the lawcourts to settle a disagreement. **keep on the right side of the law** not do anything illegal. **lay down the law** (*fig*) state one's opinion or give an order in a strong arrogant way: *She's always laying down the law about how we must behave.* **law and order** state of society generally obeying the law(2) and not causing trouble etc. **take the law into one's own hands** try to punish s.o, get revenge etc, without using the help of the police or the law courts.
'law-a,biding *adj* obeying the law(2): *law-abiding people.*
'law ,court *c.n* (also **,court of 'law**, *pl* courts of law) official place where it is decided, after questions etc, if a person has done wrong and if so how he/she should be punished.
'lawful *adj* allowed because obeying the law(2): *his lawful wife.* Opposite unlawful. ⇒ legal.
'lawfulness *u.n.*
'lawfully *adv*: *lawfully married. By tomorrow the house will be lawfully ours.*
'lawless *adj* without laws; ignoring the law(2): *a lawless group of young people.*
'lawlessly *adv.* **'lawlessness** *u.n.*
,law of 'nature *c.n* (also **,natural 'law**) law(5) in science.
'law ,school *c/u.n* place where students go to study law.
'law,suit *c.n* serious disagreement brought to a law court by s.o against another person: *She intends to bring a lawsuit against the newspaper because of what they said about her.*
lawyer /'lɔːjə/ *c.n* person who is qualified to advise s.o about the law(2), act for s.o in a law court etc: *If you refuse to pay my bill, I'll speak to my lawyer.*
lawn¹ /lɔːn/ *c.n* flat piece of land covered in short grass: *Let's sit on the lawn.*
'lawn,mower *c.n* machine that cuts grass on a lawn¹.
,lawn 'tennis *u.n* tennis played on grass.
lawn² /lɔːn/ *u.n* thin cotton cloth.
lawyer ⇒ law.
lax /læks/ *adj* (esp of behaviour) not being careful; careless: *be lax in one's work*; *have lax morals.*
'laxity *u.n.* **'laxly** *adv.* **'laxness** *u.n.*
laxative /'læksətɪv/ *adj* **1** that causes, helps, s.o to defecate more easily: *a laxative effect.*

▷ *c/u.n* **2** (example of a) substance that makes a person defecate more easily.
lay¹ /leɪ/ *attrib.adj* (of a person) not an official member of the clergy: *a lay preacher.*
laity /'leɪɪti/ *def.n* people who are not members of the clergy.
'layman *c.n* (*pl* -men) ordinary person, i.e s.o who is not (scientifically etc) trained: *Some words used by a scientist are difficult for a layman to understand.*
lay² /leɪ/ *v* (*p.t,p.p* laid /leɪd/) **1** *tr.v* put (s.o/s.t) in a particular place, on a surface etc: *He laid his coat over a chair. We're having a new carpet laid in the living-room. She laid the baby (down) on the bed.* ⇒ lay s.o/s.t down. **2** *tr.v* arrange (s.t) in a particular order for a purpose: *lay a trap*; *lay a water pipe to the bottom of the garden*; *lay a fire.* ⇒ lay the table(⇒ table(*n*)). **3** *tr/intr.v* (of a bird, insect etc) produce (eggs): *The frog has laid many eggs. The hens are laying well.* **4** *tr.v* make (a bet(1)): *I'll lay you £5 that I win.*
be laid low be made ill or very sad: *I was laid low by a bad cold.*
be laid up be ill in bed.
lay s.t aside (a) put s.t down near to one's side, esp for a short time: *She laid aside her knitting and had a short sleep.* (b) stop (doing) s.t; give s.t up: *Let's lay aside our differences and be friends again.*
lay s.t by save (money) for future needs: *I can lay by £10 each week to pay for my holiday.*
lay claim to s.t ⇒ claim(*n*).
lay s.o/s.t down (a) put s.o/s.t down on a surface: *He laid the child, his books, down on the carpet.* ⇒ lie down. (b) bet(3) money: *He laid down £5 on the brown horse.* **lay down one's arms** ⇒ arms.
lay down the law ⇒ law.
lay s.o/s.t flat knock s.o/s.t down: *The rain laid all the flowers flat.*
lay s.t in gather together supplies of s.t: *lay in wood for the winter.*
lay into s.o attack s.o with blows or words: *I only asked why he was late and he laid into me as if I was accusing him of something terrible.*
lay off s.o stop attacking s.o: *Lay off your brother — you're always teasing him.* **lay s.o off** send s.o away from a job in a factory etc because there is not enough work for her/him. ⇒ lay-off.
lay s.t on (a) supply electricity, water etc: *lay on water for a bath.* (b) provide s.t, esp in large, generous amounts: *lay on soup for the walkers.*
lay the blame (for s.t) on s.o ⇒ blame(1). **lay eyes on s.o/s.t** ⇒ eye(*n*). **(not) lay a finger on s.o** ⇒ finger(*n*). **(can't) lay one's hands on s.o/s.t** ⇒ hand(*n*). **lay it on thick** ⇒ thick(*adv*).
lay oneself/s.o open (to s.t) make oneself/s.o likely to be attacked, criticized etc: *You laid yourself wide open to her painful remarks.*
lay s.o out (a) (*informal*) make s.o unconscious by hitting her/him. (b) prepare a dead body for burial. **lay s.t out** (a) arrange things in order: *lay out one's clothes ready for packing.* (b) arrange parts of an area in a particular pattern: *lay out a garden, a new traffic system.* ⇒ lay-out.

lay s.o/s.t to rest ⇨ rest(*n*).
lay the table ⇨ table(*n*).
lay s.t up = lay s.t in. ⇨ be laid up.
lay s.t waste ⇨ waste.
'**lay-a,bout** *c.n* (*derog*) lazy person.
'**lay,by** *c.n* area at the side of a major road where people can park their cars and rest.
'**layer** *c.n* **1** (one) thickness of a (flat) substance, e.g paint: *The windows need two layers of paint. There are three layers of paper on the walls. The cake has two layers.* ⇨ -layered. **2** animal, esp a hen, that lays²(3) eggs.
▷ *tr.v* **3** cut, arrange, (s.t) in layers(1): *layer one's hair, a cake.*
-layered *adj* having the number or kind of layers(1) mentioned in the first word: *a three-layered cake.*
'**lay-,off** *c.n* act of laying s.o off.
'**lay-,out** *c.n* (drawing of the) arrangement of parts in a particular design: *the lay-out of (new trees in) a park; the page lay-out of a book.*
lay³ /leɪ/ *p.t* of lie²(*v*).
layby ⇨ lay².
layer ⇨ lay².
layette /leɪˈet/ *c.n* clothes for a newly born baby.
layman ⇨ lay¹.
layout ⇨ lay².
lazy /ˈleɪzɪ/ *adj* (-*ier*, -*iest*) **1** (*derog*) (of a person) not willing to work, make any effort etc: *lazy children; feel lazy.* **2** not encouraging people to work: *hot lazy summer days.*
laze /leɪz/ *intr.v* be lazy: *lazing in the hot sun.*
lazily /ˈleɪzɪlɪ/ *adv.* '**laziness** *u.n.*
'**lazy-,bones** *c.n* (*informal*) person who is lazy.
lb *written abbr* pound(s)¹(2).
lcm /ˌel ˌsiː ˈem/ *abbr* lowest common multiple(⇨ multiple(*n*)).
L/Cpl *written abbr* lance corporal.
lea /liː/ *c.n* (*literary*) field; meadow.
lead¹ /led/ *adj* **1** made of, containing, lead¹(2): *lead pipes; the lead content in petrol.*
▷ *n* **2** *u.n* soft heavy dull grey metal, used widely in industry and building, *chem. symb* Pb: *We must remove lead from petrol because it is poisonous.* **3** *c/u.n* (also *attrib*) (piece of a) dark grey substance (graphite) inside a pencil: *You'll need a hard lead pencil for the drawing.* **as heavy as lead** very heavy.
'**leaden** *adj* **1** like, made of, lead(2). **2** very heavy: *I'm so tired that my eyelids feel leaden.*
,**lead-'free** *adj* containing no lead(2): *lead-free petrol.*
lead² /liːd/ *n* **1** *def.n* (also *attrib*) first, most important, best, position: *Who is in the lead in the race? He has the lead position. She's the lead musician in the group.* **2** *c.n* (usu *sing*, a — (of s.t) over s.o/s.t) (amount/distance of the) condition of being first: *a lead of several metres over others in the race; have a lead over other business companies in this market.* **3** *u.n* (fact of being a) good example: *You ought to follow your brother's lead and work harder.* **4** *c.n* piece of information used as a guide or clue: *The owner has given us some useful leads about the thief's appearance.* **5** *c.n* act, right, of making the first move in certain games: *It's your lead.* **6** *c.n* (also *attrib*) most important part in a play, film etc: *I've got the lead! Who's the lead actor?* ⇨ leading(2).
7 *c.n* (also **leash**) long piece of leather, chain etc which is fixed to a dog's collar and used to control it: *All dogs must be kept on a lead in this park.*
▷ *v* (*p.t,p.p* led /led/) **8** *tr/intr.v* go ahead of (s.o, a group) and show the way: *He led us across the river. Joe led them to safety. It's my turn to lead. He led me up the stairs.* ⇨ follow(1). **9** *tr/intr.v* (usu — (s.o) to s.o/s.w) (of a map, road, sound etc) follow the direction, show the way, (to s.o/s.w): *This river leads to the sea. The noise led them to the children. Which wire leads to the plug(2)?* **10** *tr.v* (often — s.o to (do) s.t) cause (s.o) to think, feel, act, in the way mentioned: *You led me to believe that you loved me. He led me to a life of crime.* **11** *tr/intr.v* guide (s.o/s.t), be the first or most important one (in s.t): *lead a horse, an orchestra, expedition; lead a discussion.* **12** *tr/intr.v* be the first, best, (in (s.t)): *lead the other students in the class.* **13** *tr.v* live (the kind of life mentioned): *She's led a difficult, exciting life.* **14** *tr/intr.v* (usu — with s.t) have (s.t) as the first activity; make the first move in certain games or sports: *The first player led (with) the ace(1) of hearts. The band led with a slow tune. The television programme led with a short explanation. She led with a throw of 70 metres.* **Lead on** (as an order) Go first! **lead s.o on** try to make s.o think, feel, do, s.t by giving her/him false information: *He said I would get the job but he was only leading me on.* **lead s.o up the garden path** ⇨ garden. **lead up to s.t** be a preparation for, cause of, s.t: *Describe the events leading up to the fight. What is he leading up to* (i.e. preparing to state) *in his speech?* **lead the way** ⇨ way.
'**leader** *c.n* **1** person who leads(8,11,12): *the leader of an expedition, a political party.* **2** (also ,**leading 'article**) piece of writing in a newspaper giving the opinions of the editor.
'**leader,ship** *u.n* (qualities needed for the) position of leader(1): *She has great powers of leadership. Who won the leadership of the committee?*
'**leading** *attrib.adj* **1** first, most important: *the leading runner/car; the leading member of the group.* **2** of the lead(6): *a leading actor; the leading role.*
,**leading 'article** *c.n* = leader(2).
,**leading 'light** *c.n* (*fig*; *informal*) most important or useful member of a group or organization.
,**leading 'question** *c.n* question said in a way that shows that a particular answer is desired or expected, e.g 'What do you think about the total lack of sports equipment in our schools?'
leaf /liːf/ *n* (*pl* leaves /liːvz/) **1** *c.n* flat thin (usu green) part of a plant or tree growing singly or in groups from the stem or a branch: *Does this tree lose its leaves in winter?* **2** *c.n* one sheet of paper in a book. ⇨ overleaf. **3** *u.n* metal in the form of a very thin, flat piece: *gold leaf.* **4** *c.n* flat hinged(2) part of a piece of furniture that can increase the size of the surface: *the leaf of a table/desk.* **take a leaf out of s.o's book** (*fig*) decide to follow s.o's example, esp of behaviour. **turn over a new leaf** (*fig*) (decide to) improve one's behaviour.
▷ *intr.v* **5 leaf through s.t** turn the pages of a book (as if) looking for information, a particular page.

leaflet /'li:flɪt/ *c.n* printed and often folded piece of paper giving information.

'leafy *adj* (*-ier, -iest*) having many leaves(⇒ leaf(1)).

league /li:g/ *c.n* (often with capital **L**) (also *attrib*) group of teams, countries, businesses etc for a shared purpose: *the League of Nations*; *the Football League*; *League football.* **be in league with s.o** be planning or working with s.o, esp to do s.t wrong. **not be in the same league (as s.o)** be less capable, important, rich etc (than s.o).

leak /li:k/ *c.n* **1** small hole, broken area etc that allows liquid or air to enter or escape: *There's a leak in the boat/pipe.* **2** (*fig*) act or situation that allows secret information to become known: *a leak in the government committee.* **3** secret information that is leaked(6): *hear a leak about who will get the job.* **4** (*technical*) loss of electricity from a circuit(4) because of a fault. **spring a leak** develop, get a leak(1): *The new pipe has sprung a leak.*

▷ *tr/intr.v* **5** (allow/cause s.t to) have a leak(1) (of (s.t)): *This boat leaks (water).* **6** (often — *out*) (allow (secret information) to) become known intentionally or by mistake: *Facts about the new appointment have been leaked to the newspapers. Details will soon leak out.*

leakage /'li:kɪdʒ/ *c/u.n* (act of) leaking(*v*): *leakage of gas/information.*

'leaky *adj* (*-ier, -iest*) having leaks(1): *a leaky pipe.*

lean¹ /li:n/ *adj* **1** (of a person, animal) thin and not heavy: *a small lean woman/figure.* Opposite fat(1). **2** (of meat) without much fat(5): *lean beef.* **3** (*attrib*) not producing much; not earning, not getting, enough: *a lean harvest; a lean month for buying things; lean times during a war.*

▷ *u.n* **4** part of meat that is lean(2). Opposite fat(5).

leanness /'li:nnɪs/ *u.n.*

lean² /li:n/ *tr/intr.v* (*p.t,p.p* leant /lent/, *leaned*) **1** (usu — *against, on* etc s.o/s.t) (cause (s.o/s.t) to) rest against, on, (s.o/s.t) for support: *She leant against my shoulder, on my arm. Lean the ladder against the wall.* **2** (usu — *across, over* etc (s.t)) (cause (s.o/s.t) to) be, rest, in a sloping or bent position: *He leant out of the window, over the wall. After the storm a tree was leaning dangerously over the road.* **lean on s.o** (*fig*) **(a)** choose or use s.o for personal encouragement, support etc: *I'm glad I have you to lean on for advice.* **(b)** (*informal*) put personal pressure on s.o to make her/him do s.t: *You'll have to lean on him to pay what he owes.* **lean over backwards (to do s.t)** ⇒ backwards.

'leaning *c.n* (often — *towards* (doing) s.t) liking for, interest in, ((doing) s.t): *When she was young she showed a leaning towards becoming a doctor. He has leanings towards studying biology, joining the army.*

leant /lent/ *p.t,p.p* of lean².

leap /li:p/ *c.n* **1** (height of an) act of leaping(⇒ leap(*v*)): *a leap over a wall; a leap of two metres.* **2** (often *a* — *in* s.t) sudden increase, improvement etc that is easy to notice: *After the operation her health made a great leap forward. There was a leap of £50 in the price.* **by leaps and bounds** extremely quickly: *The bus service has improved by leaps and bounds.*

▷ *v* (*p.t,p.p* leapt /lept/, *leaped*) **3** *intr.v* jump or

move very quickly: *She leapt onto the stage, over the wall, into the river, off the edge.* **4** *tr.v* jump over (s.t): *He leapt the river/fence.* **5** *tr.v* cause a horse to jump over (s.t). **leap at s.t** (*fig*) accept, use, (an opportunity) with enthusiasm: *I leapt at the chance to go with them.* **leap up** stand up quickly.

'leap,frog *c.n* **1** child's game in which one person jumps over another person who is bending down by putting her/his hands on the other person's back.

▷ *tr.v* (*-gg-*) **2** play leapfrog(1). **3** (*fig*) go ahead of (another person, business organization etc) by a (fairly) large amount.

'leap ,year *c.n* year of 366 days happening every four years in which February has 29 days.

leapt /lept/ *p.t,p.p* of leap(*v*).

learn /lɜ:n/ *v* (*p.t,p.p* learnt /lɜ:nt/, *learned*) **1** *tr/intr.v* get knowledge (of (s.t)), skill (in (s.t)): *learn English; learn (how) to swim.* ⇒ unlearn. **2** *intr.v* (usu — *about/of* s.o/s.t, *that* . . .) get information (about s.o/s.t): *When did you learn about/of her illness (or that she was ill)? I've learned that friends are essential.*

learned /'lɜ:nɪd/ *adj* having much knowledge, esp after studying: *a learned scientist.* **my learned friend** ⇒ friend.

'learner *c.n* (also *attrib*) person who is learning (⇒ learn(1)) s.t: *a learner driver.*

'learning *u.n* **1** knowledge from studying: *full of learning.* **2** act of learning(⇒ learn(1)): *Learning is often not easy.*

learnt /lɜ:nt/ *p.t,p.p* of learn.

lease /li:s/ *c.n* **1** (written) agreement giving a building, room etc to s.o in exchange for rent: *take out a (two-year) lease on a flat.* **a new lease of life** (*fig*) opportunity to enjoy much better health, standard of living etc.

▷ *tr.v* **2** give a lease(1) to (s.o): *I'll lease you the shop for two years.* **3** take (a house etc) on a lease(1) from (s.o): *I've leased a house from them.*

'lease,hold *u.n* (also *attrib*) held under a lease(1): *leasehold property.* ⇒ freehold.

'lease,holder *c.n* person who has a lease(1) from s.o.

leash /li:ʃ/ *c.n* = lead²(7).

least /li:st/ *adv* **1** (used with adjectives and adverbs) to the smallest degree: *He's the least successful/interesting/qualified. That is least likely to happen. Which do you like least? I like all vegetables but I like cabbage least of all.* ⇒ less(2), little(3), most(*adv*).

▷ *det* **2** (often the — s.t) smallest possible amount, number, (of s.t): *Who earned (the) least money? The least amount of food was kept for the journey home.* ⇒ most(*det*).

▷ *pron* **3** (usu the — (of s.t)) smallest possible amount, number (of s.t): *Who learned the least? The least you could do is say you're sorry! Money is the least of his difficulties.* **at least (a)** apart from anything else: *You could at least apologize!* **(b)** as the smallest possible amount, number: *At least fifty people came.* **(c)** at any rate: *She's coming on Saturday, at least that's what she told me.* **not in the least** not at all: *I'm not in the least cold. 'Do you mind if I come?' 'Not in the least!'* Compare less(6), little(8), most(*pron*).

'least,ways *adv* (also **'least,wise**) (*informal*)

at any rate; at least: *He's very good at tennis, leastways he always beats me.*

leather /'leðə/ *u.n* (also *attrib*) material made from the skin of an animal: *a leather coat; shoes made of leather.*

'leathery *adj* **1** like leather: *a leathery feel.* **2** (*derog*) very tough and difficult to eat: *leathery meat.*

leave¹ /liːv/ *n* **1** *u.n* (*formal*) permission (to do s.t): *I was given leave to speak at the meeting.* **2** *c/u.n* permission to be away from work, e.g for a holiday: *I have four weeks' leave each year. I haven't taken leave for years.* (**away**) **on leave** away from work: *She's (away) on leave this week. When are you going on leave?* **take one's leave (of s.o)** (*formal*) say goodbye (to s.o). ⇨ leave-taking. **take leave of one's senses** ⇨ senses.

'leave-,taking *c.n* act of saying goodbye and going away.

leave² /liːv/ *v* (*p.t,p.p* **left** /left/) **1** *tr/intr.v* go away (from (s.o/s.t/s.w)) (without intending to return): *When did you leave school? I left him at the bus station. They left Rome on Saturday.* **2** *tr.v* (often — *s.o/s.t behind*) go away without taking (s.o/s.t) (often by mistake): *Did you leave this book in my house? Don't leave me behind!* **3** *tr.v* abandon(1) (s.o/s.t) stop living with (s.o); stop being a member of (s.t): *When did you leave the* Liberal *party? He's left his wife.* **4** *tr.v* cause (s.o/s.t) to be/stay in the condition mentioned; cause (s.t) as a result: *The walk left me very tired. I was left without a friend in the world. The accident left a large scar. The book left a deep impression*(1) *on me.* **5** *tr.v* put a task etc in (s.o else's) care: *I've left her in charge.* **6** *tr.v* allow (an amount) to remain afterwards: *When I've paid the rent I'll be left with £50 to spend. 20 from 35 leaves 15.* **7** *tr.v* have (s.o) still alive after one's death: *He left a wife and a son.* **8** *tr.v* (usu — *s.t to s.o*) give (s.t to s.o) in one's will²(1): *I'm leaving all my books to you.*

leave s.o/s.t alone (usu as an order) not touch, be in contact with, interfere with, s.o/s.t: *Leave that cake alone! Leave me alone!*

leave s.o/s.t behind ⇨ leave²(2).

leave s.o for s.o end a relationship or marriage with s.o and go to s.o else: *She's left her husband for a younger man.* ⇨ leave(3).

leave go (used as an order) (*informal*) = let go.

leave it at that do or say nothing more about a matter.

leave off (**a**) (usu as an order) (*informal*) stop doing that. (**b**) (of rain etc) stop. **leave s.t off** not wear the clothes mentioned: *You can leave your coat off.* ⇨ leave s.t on(a).

leave s.t on (**a**) not take off the clothes mentioned: *You must leave your shoes on.* ⇨ leave s.t off. (**b**) allow a light, tap etc to remain working: *Who left the cooker/fire/tap/light on?*

leave s.o/s.t out (of s.t) not include s.o/s.t; not consider s.o/s.t when deciding (s.t): *Don't leave me out! You left the cost of repairs out of your list.*

leave s.t over (usu passive) cause s.t to remain (after the largest or best part has been eaten or used): *So much food was left over.* ⇨ leftovers.

leave s.t to s.o (**a**) ⇨ leave(8). (**b**) allow s.o to manage, decide s.t: *I'll leave the responsibility/*

decision/work to you. Don't worry about telling him — leave it (all) to me.

leave s.t up to s.o allow an important matter to be decided by s.o: *You can go if you want to — I leave it entirely up to you.*

leave word with s.o ⇨ word(*n*).

'left,overs *pl.n* thing(s) remaining after an event, esp food after a meal.

leaven /'levn/ *u.n* (*old use*) substance, e.g yeast, that causes dough(1) to rise.

'leavened *attrib.adj* containing yeast: *leavened bread.* Opposite unleavened.

leaves /liːvz/ *pl* of leaf.

lecherous /'letʃərəs/ *adj* (*derog*) having or showing uncontrolled sexual desire: *a lecherous man.*

'lecherously *adv.* **'lechery** *u.n.*

lectern /'lektɜːn/ *c.n* tall desk used to stand at while reading, e.g in a church.

lecture /'lektʃə/ *c.n* **1** (often *give a/the — (to s.o) about/on s.t*) long serious public speech (to s.o) (on a particular subject): *a set of lectures on the origins of plants. Who's giving the lecture tonight?* **2** (esp *give s.o a —*) (*informal*) long (boring) talk, esp expressing one's disapproval, anger etc: *My father gave me a lecture about being nice to my younger brother.*

▷ *tr/intr.v* **3** (often —*s.o on s.t*) give/read a lecture(1) to (an audience) (on a subject): *lecture (to) students on electricity.* **4** (often — *in s.t*) lecture(3) as a job (usu to students) (on a particular subject): *Denise lectures (in) economics.* **5** give (s.o) a lecture(2).

'lecturer *c.n* person who lectures(3).

'lecture,ship *c.n* official position of s.o who lectures(4) at a university or college.

led /led/ *p.t,p.p* of lead²(*v*).

ledge /ledʒ/ *c.n* **1** narrow shelf on a wall, esp under a window. **2** thing shaped like a ledge(1), e.g an area of rock on a mountain.

ledger /'ledʒə/ *c.n* book in which a business company's financial accounts are recorded.

lee /liː/ *def.n* side of s.t that is sheltered from the wind.

leeward /'liːwəd/ *adj/adv* **1** towards which the wind blows. Opposite windward(1).

▷ *u.n* **2** (often *to —*) direction towards which the wind blows. Opposite windward(2).

leeway /'liːweɪ/ *u.n* space or opportunity for free movement or other activity: *I was given very little leeway to move the car. My wages leave me no leeway for buying more clothes.*

leech /liːtʃ/ *c.n* kind of worm which can suck blood.

leek /liːk/ *c.n* (also *attrib*) kind of vegetable like a long thin onion: *leek soup.*

leer /lɪə/ *c.n* **1** act of leering(⇨ leer(2)).

▷ *intr.v* **2** (often — *at s.o/s.t*) produce an unpleasant expression of sexual desire or self-satisfaction: *He leered at every girl who passed by.*

leeward, leeway ⇨ lee.

left¹ /left/ *p.t,p.p* of leave².

left² /left/ *adj* Opposite right. **1** (usu *attrib*) that is on or towards the same side of a person's body as the heart; of the side of s.o/s.t that is towards the west when one faces north: *In Britain people drive on the left side of the road.* **2** (*attrib*) worn on a left hand or foot: *a left shoe.* **3** (usu *attrib*) (often with a capital **L**) (in politics) of a political opinion or party favouring socialism: *the Left point of view*; *a Left supporter*.

▷ *adv* Opposite right. **4** in or towards a left(1,3) direction: *look/point/turn/vote left*.

▷ *n* Opposite right. **5** *def.n* left²(1) side, position or direction: *Keep to the left. Stand on the left. The window was to my left. Take the first turning to the left.* **6** *c/def.n* (blow with one's) left²(1) hand: *I gave him a hard left.* **7** *def/def.pl.n* (usu with a capital **L**) (in politics) Left²(3) political opinion, politics or political groups: *What is the Left's opinion? She's joined the Left.*

,left-'hand *attrib.adj* in or to a left(1) position: *a left-hand turn; it's in the left-hand cupboard.*

,left-'handed *adj* **1** (of/for s.o) able to do more things with the left hand than the right hand: *a left-handed writer; left-handed scissors.* **2** (*derog*; *informal*) (of a remark) not sincere: *a left-handed compliment.*

,left-'hander *c.n* **1** person who is left-handed(1). **2** blow using the left²(1) hand.

'leftist *adj* **1** supporting left²(3) opinion: *a leftist newspaper, politician.*

▷ *c.n* **2** (*informal*) = left-winger.

,left 'wing *n* (**'left-,wing** when *attrib*) **1** *c.n* (in football etc) (player who is in the) position on the extreme left²(5) of the front line of players. **2** *def/def.pl.n* (often with capital **L** and **W**) (extreme) left²(7): *Left-Wing opinions*; *support the Left Wing.*

,left-'winger *c.n* person holding left(3) views.

'lefty *c.n* (*pl* -ies) (*informal*) person holding (extreme) left(3) views.

leftovers ⇒ leave².

leg /leg/ *n* **1** *c.n* (also *attrib*) (in people and birds) either of the two long parts of the body between the hips and the feet: *Many birds stand on one leg. He suffered a leg injury.* **2** *c.n* (in animals and insects) one of the long parts which support the body and on which the animal etc walks. **3** *c.n* part of clothing that covers a leg: *a trouser leg.* **4** *c/u.n* part of an animal's leg used as food: *roast leg of* lamb(2). **5** *c.n* long vertical support of furniture: *a chair/table leg.* **6** *c.n* stage in a journey: *The first leg of our trip took us to America.* **7** *c.n* game, match etc as a stage in a competition: *We must win the next leg of the competition.* **not have a leg to stand on** (*fig*; *informal*) be unable to give an acceptable excuse, get support for s.o, one's opinion etc: *If you are right you won't have a leg to stand on in the law court.* **on her/his/its last legs** (*informal*) worn out; dying. **pull s.o's leg** (*fig*; *informal*) make fun of s.o. **stretch one's legs** stand up and walk around to exercise.

-legged /'legɪd/ *adj* having the number or kind of legs(1,2) mentioned in the first word: *four-legged*; *long-legged.*

'leggings *pl.n* clothes made from heavy strong material for covering the legs (usu worn on top of ordinary trousers to protect them): *put the child in leggings.*

'leggy *adj* (-ier, -iest) (*informal*) having long thin legs(1,2) or stems: *Those young plants will get very leggy if we don't plant them in the ground.*

legacy /'legəsɪ/ *c.n* (*pl* -ies) **1** money or property given to s.o in a will²(1). **2** (*fig*) thing left by a person who did the same job, lived in the same place, earlier: *This picture is a*

legacy from the student who lived here before me.

legal /'li:gl/ *adj* **1** allowed by law: *Parking here is legal.* Opposite illegal. **2** of, referring to, the law: *the legal profession.*

,legal 'aid *u.n* money given by the government to pay the costs when s.o without money gets legal(2) advice.

legality /lɪ'gælɪtɪ/ *u.n* state or fact of being legal(1): *What legality does this letter have?*

legalization, -isation /,li:gəlaɪ'zeɪʃən/ *u.n* act of legalizing s.t.

'lega,lize, -ise *tr.v* make (s.t) legal(1): *Should we legalize driving at 16 years old?*

'legally *adv.*

,legal 'tender *u.n* type of money that can legally be used to pay a debt.

legato /lɪ'gɑ:təʊ/ *adj/adv* (*music*) (of a way of playing music) with each note played softly and joined to the next one. Opposite staccato.

legend /'ledʒənd/ *c.n* **1** story about s.o/s.t passed from one generation to another (and probably not true): *Greek legends.* **2** (*technical*) short written explanation produced with an illustration.

legendary /'ledʒəndərɪ/ *adj* (*formal*) **1** of, described in, legends(1). **2** well known: *Her ability is legendary.*

leggings ⇒ legl.

legible /'ledʒɪbl/ *adj* able to be read easily: *This writing isn't legible.* Opposite illegible.

legibility /,ledʒɪ'bɪlɪtɪ/ *u.n.* **'legibly** *adv.*

legion /'li:dʒən/ *c.n* **1** large group of soldiers. **2** (*fig*) large number: *legions of people living in the cities.*

legislate /'ledʒɪs,leɪt/ *intr.v* (esp — against/for s.t) make, agree, laws (against, in favour of, s.t).

legislation /,ledʒɪs'leɪʃən/ *u.n* **1** act of legislating. **2** set of laws: *agree new legislation to make vehicles safer.*

legislative /'ledʒɪslətɪv/ *adj* of legislation; having the power to make laws: *a legislative assembly(3).*

legit /lə'dʒɪt/ *pred.adj* (*informal*) legitimate(3): *Is it legit to do that?*

legitimate /lə'dʒɪtɪmɪt/ *adj* **1** (of a child) born of parents who are married to each other. Opposite illegitimate. **2** according to the law: *the legitimate owner.* **3** (*informal* **le'git**) according to accepted and correct practice or reasoning: *a legitimate use of a word*; *a legitimate question/excuse.*

le'gitimate *u.n.* **le'gitimately** *adv.*

leisure /'leʒə/ *u.n* (also *attrib*) free time for pleasure and not as part of one's work or responsibility: *I go fishing for leisure. My leisure (time) is spent listening to music. We don't have enough leisure hours.* (**do s.t**) **at one's leisure** (do s.t) when one is willing and able to: *Please come at your leisure.*

'leisurely *adv* without hurrying and in a relaxed (way): *eat a leisurely meal.*

lemon /'lemən/ *adj* **1** (of the colour that is) bright yellow. **2** (*attrib*) tasting of lemons: *lemon juice.*

▷ *n* **3** *c/u.n* (also *attrib*) kind of oval fruit with a yellow leathery skin (when ripe) and a sour taste: *a lemon tree/drink.* **4** *u.n* bright yellow colour. **5** *c.n* (*informal*) foolish person: *I feel a lemon in this silly hat.*

,lemon'ade *c/u.n* (glass of) usu fizzy lemon drink.

,lemon 'curd *u.n* kind of jam made from lemons, sugar, eggs etc.

lemur /'li:mə/ *c.n* kind of animal with a long tail that lives in trees and is like a monkey.

lend /lend/ *tr.v* (*p.t,p.p lent* /lent/) **1** (often — *s.o s.t*; — *s.t to s.o*) allow (s.o) to have and use (s.t) that must be returned afterwards: *I'll lend you my pen but please give it back. He lent it to me yesterday. Can you lend me £5 until Friday?* ⇒ loan(1). Opposite borrow(1). **2** (*formal*) give (a particular quality) to s.t: *The new carpet lends beauty to this room.* **lend (s.o) an ear** ⇒ ear. **lend (s.o) a hand (with s.t)** ⇒ hand(*n*).

'lender *c.n* person who lends(1) s.t to s.o.

length /leŋθ/ *n* **1** *c/u.n* (amount of the) measurement from one end to the other end in space, a period of time etc: *What is the length of the room? The lessons are of short length. What length must the speech be? I swam the length of the lake.* ⇒ long, breadth, width. **2** *c.n* thing of a particular or known length: *a length of cloth, pipe, rope. The material comes in lengths of 2 metres.* **3** *c.n* length(1) of a particular object, animal, place etc: *I can swim 50 lengths of the pool. The first horse was a length ahead.* **at length** (**a**) eventually; after quite a long time: *At length we arrived at the station.* (**b**) for a long time and giving many details: *He spoke at length about his difficulties.* **go to any length(s)** (**to do s.t**) do anything however difficult, however long it takes etc, in order to be successful: *He'll go to any length(s) to persuade her to do the work for him.* **in length** when one measures its length(1): *The room is 10 metres in length. This book is 60 pages in length.*

lengthen /'leŋθən/ *tr/intr.v* (cause (s.t) to) become longer: *I must lengthen these trousers. The string lengthened when I pulled it.* ⇒ shorten.

'length,ways *adv* (also **'length,wise**) along the direction of the length: *Cut the cloth lengthways.*

'lengthy *adj* (*-ier, -iest*) having a large length(1): *a lengthy meeting; a lengthy piece of writing.*

lenient /'li:nɪənt/ *adj* behaving in a kind and forgiving way: *be lenient towards a boy who has done wrong.*

'leniency *u.n* fact or state of being lenient: *show leniency towards him.*

'leniently *adv*.

lens /lenz/ *c.n* (*pl -es*) **1** piece of glass or similar material used in spectacles, a camera or a telescope etc to make an image appear larger, nearer, clearer etc. ⇒ contact lens. **2** part of the eye that acts like a lens(1).

lent /lent/ *p.t,p.p* of lend.

Lent /lent/ *unique n* period before Easter during which Christians give up certain foods, pleasures etc: *I'm not going to smoke during Lent.*

lentil /'lentl/ *c.n* (also *attrib*) hard yellow or brown seed of a kind of bean plant used in cooking: *lentil soup.*

Leo /'li:əʊ/ *n* **1** *unique n* one of the 12 signs of the zodiac. **2** *c.n* person born under this sign.

leopard /'lepəd/ *c.n* (also *attrib*) kind of large wild animal of the cat family with black spots: *leopard skin.*

leotard /'li:ə,tɑ:d/ *c.n* kind of clothing which fits the body tightly from the shoulders to the top of the legs, worn by women for dancing, exercising etc.

leprosy /'leprəsɪ/ *u.n* kind of serious skin disease causing destruction of fingers, toes, the nose etc.

'leper *c.n* person suffering from leprosy.

leprous /'leprəs/ *adj*.

lesbian /'lezbɪən/ *c.n* (also *attrib*) woman who is sexually attracted to another woman: *a lesbian novel.*

'lesbia,nism *u.n*.

lesion /'li:ʒən/ *c.n* (*technical*) injury; wound.

less /les/ *adv* **1** (used to form the comparative of many adjs and advs, esp those with three or more syllables): *We did it less easily than you. He's much less interesting.* ⇒ more(1). **2** to a smaller amount or degree: *I eat less than I want to. You must work less.* ⇒ more(2). **less and less** (also *det*) (in a way that is becoming) smaller in degree, amount etc, all the time: *It's less safe to travel alone.* **more or less** ⇒ more(adv). **much/still less** (used to add force to a negative statement): *I wouldn't have it still less pay for it.*

▷ *det* (comparative of little(3)) **3** smaller amount, quantity: *Eat less meat. Drink less beer.* **4** (often — *s.t than . . .*) a smaller amount, quantity: *I've got less work to do than you. They've got less money than we have.* ⇒ fewer. **the less . . . the less/more** the amount of s.t that one does, gives, sees etc has a smaller/greater effect on what s.o does etc: *The less help you give them the more problems they have.* **the more . . . the more/less** ⇒ more(det).

▷ *prep* **5** taking away (an amount, length of time); minus: *The trip will take a month less a few days. It will cost £150 less the* deposit(4).

▷ *pron* **6** (often — *of s.t, than . . .*) a smaller amount, quantity etc: *I weigh less than you. Less of it was ruined than we had first thought. The less I see you the sadder I am.*

'lessen *tr/intr.v* (cause (s.t) to) become less(1): *The smell is lessening. His apology lessened my anger.*

'lesser *attrib.adj/adv* **1** not as large or important: *a lesser crime than murder; a lesser known poet.* **to a lesser/greater extent** ⇒ extent.

▷ *def.n* **2** **be/choose the lesser of two evils** ⇒ evil(*n*).

lesson /'lesn/ *c.n* **1** (time used for a) thing (to be) learned or taught: *a geography lesson; a lesson in good manners. Let that injury you suffered be a lesson to you!* **learn one's lesson** discover the danger, harmful result etc of s.t: *I learned my lesson when I was rude to her!* **2** part of the Bible used in a church service.

lest /lest/ *conj* (*old use*) to avoid the possibility that: *Write the message down lest you forget it.*

let¹ /let/ *tr.v* (*-tt-, p.t,p.p let*) (used with another verb without *to*) **1** allow (s.o) to (do s.t); give one's permission to (s.o) (to do s.t): *Please let me carry your bag. He won't let me pay. I'd love to come but my parents won't let me. I'll let you have some if you want.* **2** cause (s.o/s.t to be, go, happen): *You've let the cat out? He let the air out of my tyres. Let 'x' be the length and 'y' the height.* **3** (*formal*) (used as an order): *Let them eat cake if they have no bread! Let me go!* ⇒ let us. **4** (often — *s.t out*) allow s.o to use (a room, building, piece of equipment etc) in exchange for rent: *We're letting* (*out*) a room to a student next year. Do you have a room to let?

let alone s.o/s.t and I have not mentioned (s.o/s.t) yet: *The drive will take two days let alone the long boat trip across to the island.* **let s.o/s.t alone** = leave s.o/s.t alone.

let s.o down disappoint s.o by not carrying out a promise etc: *If you don't work harder you'll let all your teachers down.* ⇨ let-down. **let s.t down** (a) cause a tyre etc to lose air. (b) lower s.t: *let the curtains down.*

let go (of s.o/s.t); **let s.o/s.t go** (usu imperative) stop holding/hindering s.o/s.t: *Let go (of me, my arm, the rope)! Let me, my arm, go! You're hurting.* **let oneself go** = let one's hair down.

let one's hair down ⇨ hair.

let s.o know (s.t, where etc...) inform s.o (about s.t): *Let me know when you're ready to begin. Let Jane know where it is.*

let s.o in allow s.o to enter a room, house etc by opening the door. **let oneself/s.o in for s.t** include/involve oneself/s.o in an unpleasant or difficult activity: *When I offered to help I didn't realize what I'd let myself in for!* **let s.o in on s.t** (*informal*) tell s.o a secret; allow s.o to take part in a secret activity: *Who let Fred in on our arrangements?*

let s.o into s.t tell s.o a secret.

let s.o off (a) stop and allow s.o to leave a bus, car, ship etc: *Will you let me off at the next corner, please.* (b) allow s.o who has done s.t wrong to go without being punished: *I'll let you off this time but don't steal again.* ⇨ let-off. **let off steam** ⇨ steam(*n*).

let on (about s.o/s.t) (often negative) tell a secret: *Don't let on about our decision to sell the house.*

let s.t out (a) make s.t wider: *let out a skirt.* (b) cause (s.t) to be available for hire: *We let out our tools but they must be kept in good order.* ⇨ let(4). (c) cause (a secret) to become known (often suddenly and without wanting to): *She let out that he was very poor.*

let's = let us.

let up (a) stop making so much effort, trying so hard: *He'll never let up until you agree to see him.* (b) (of rain etc) stop. ⇨ let-up.

let us (also **let's**) (used to make a suggestion): *Let us know what you're going to do. Let's go to the cinema. Let's be friends. Let's go!*

let-down *c.n* (*informal*) disappointment: *After many let-downs he finally found someone he could trust.* ⇨ let s.o down.

let-off *c.n* (*informal*) example of being let off. ⇨ let s.o off(b).

let-up *c.n* (*informal*) stopping or gradual lessening of s.t: *There was no let-up in the rain last night.* ⇨ let up.

lethal /ˈliːθl/ *adj* able to cause death: *a lethal poison.*

lethargy /ˈleθədʒɪ/ *u.n* (*formal*) state of being without energy or enthusiasm.

lethargic /ləˈθɑːdʒɪk/ *adj* (*formal*) having no energy etc: *feeling lethargic.*

let's /lets/ = let us. ⇨ let.

letter /ˈletə/ *c.n* **1** sign or symbol used in writing to represent sounds: *The word 'English' has seven letters. What do the letters 'PhD' mean?* **2** piece of writing to s.o (to be) put in an envelope: *I've had*

a letter from my mother. I like writing letters. The bank has sent you a letter. **to the letter** following every detail exactly as written: *I've carried out your orders to the letter.*

letter bomb *c.n* small device inside an envelope that explodes when the envelope is opened.

letter box *c.n* **1** public box where people post their letters. **2** small long hole in a door etc where letters are delivered to a home, office etc.

letter-head *c.n* printed (name and) address on writing-paper.

lettering *u.n* **1** act, way or style of writing. **2** letters, esp used in an advertisement, sign for a shop, poster etc.

letter of credit *c.n* ⇨ credit(*n*).

lettuce /ˈletɪs/ *c/u.n* (also *attrib*) kind of plant with large green leaves, used in salads: *lettuce leaves. There are lots of lettuces in the garden.*

leukaemia /luːˈkiːmɪə/ *u.n* (US **leukemia**) very serious disease of the blood.

level /ˈlevl/ *adj* **1** horizontal: *Is the shelf level?* **2** (having a surface that is) flat and even: *The carpet must be completely level.* **3** (often — with s.o/s.t) at the same standard, distance, height, weight etc (as s.t else): *The water in the tube is level with the green line. The sugar must be level with the top of the spoon. Add a level spoonful of salt. The three runners are level at the moment. The black horse was level with the other one until the last few metres.* **4** not easily made angry; not showing any strong feeling; calm: *a level personality, voice.* ⇨ level-headed. **do one's level best** ⇨ best(*pron*).

▷ *c.n* **5** position, rank, height, compared to another or others: *What level are you at with your studies? The level of the water is too high. We're at the same level in the office. We reached 6000 metres above sea-level. He has a high level of understanding.* **6** one whole floor(3) in a building: *the ground floor level; at street level; the third level of the shopping centre.* ⇨ storey. **7** device used to find out whether a surface is horizontal: *a spirit level.* **8** (area with a) flat surface: *build a house on the level.* ⇨ split-level. **9** (*fig*) natural or correct position in society: *He'll find his own level when he goes to university.* **on the level** (*informal*) honest; sincere: *Were you on the level when you told her you would pay?* ⇨ level with s.o.

▷ *tr.v* (*-ll-*, US *-l-*) **10** (often — s.t off) make the surface of (s.t) flat: *level (off) land for building.* **11** cause (s.o/s.t) to be the same position, amount etc as s.o/s.t else: *My goal levelled the score.* **12** cause (a building, plants etc) to fall down: *The rain levelled the flowers.* **level s.t at s.o** aim criticism, a weapon etc at s.o: *Why has the criticism been levelled at me personally? He levelled the gun at me.* **level off/out** (a) become horizontal: *The plane levelled off above the city.* (b) become steady: *The price of petrol has levelled off after rising so quickly.* **level s.t off** ⇨ level(10). **level out** = level off. **level with s.o** tell s.o the truth; be honest (with s.o): *I'll let you borrow it if you level with me and explain why you want it.*

level crossing *c.n* place where a railway crosses a road using the same surface.

level-headed *adj* not easily made angry, annoyed or worried: *be level-headed when there is a difficulty.*

,level-'pegging *pred.adj* sharing the same score, standard etc: *The teams are level-pegging.*

lever /'li:və/ *c.n* **1** long bar used under s.t that is heavy in order to lift it: *We need a lever to move that heavy stone.* **2** device used to push s.t off or up: *Use this as a lever to get the lid off.* **3** bar pushed to make (part of) a machine work: *a gear lever; press that lever down to start the machine.* **4** (*fig*) method of using force or pressure to get s.t one wants: *use a famous relation as a lever to get the best jobs.*
▷ *tr.v* **5** (usu — *s.t off;* — *s.t into, out of, position* etc) move (s.t) using a lever(1,2): *lever off the lid.*

leverage /'li:vərɪdʒ/ *u.n* **1** (amount of the) action or power of a lever(1): *A short pole has only a small leverage.* **2** (*fig*) power to achieve s.t by using a lever(4): *She has strong leverage in the college.*

levitate /'levɪˌteɪt/ *tr/intr.v* (cause (s.o/s.t) to) rise up into the air without support and not fall down.

levitation /ˌlevɪ'teɪʃən/ *u.n.*

levity /'levɪtɪ/ *u.n* (*formal*) tendency to behave in a silly or amusing way about s.t that is serious: *Failing an examination is no occasion for levity.*

levy /'levɪ/ *c.n* (*pl -ies*) **1** (amount of money from the) act of collecting a tax, rate etc: *a levy of 10p for each pound spent.*
▷ *tr.v* (*-ies, -ied*) **2** collect (a tax, rate(4), fine etc): *How much tax is levied on petrol?*

lewd /lju:d/ *adj* disgusting, esp about sexual intercourse: *lewd humour; lewd jokes.*

'lewdly *adv.* **'lewdness** *u.n.*

lexical /'leksɪkl/ *adj* (*technical*) of or referring to words, vocabulary: *A lexical item(1) can be a word, phrasal verb, idiom etc.*

lexicon /'leksɪkən/ *c.n* (*technical*) dictionary, esp of an ancient language.

lexis /'leksɪs/ *u.n* (*technical*) vocabulary.

liable /'laɪəbl/ *adj* **1** (*pred,* — *to do s.t*) likely (to do s.t): *Please watch your baby brother; he's liable to swallow anything he picks up.* **2** (*pred,* — *to s.t*) (*formal*) likely (to have, get, suffer from, s.t): *This wood is liable to splitting and cracking.* **3** (usu *pred,* — *for* s.t) responsible by law (for s.t): *I'm not liable for your mistakes.*

liability /ˌlaɪə'bɪlɪtɪ/ *c.n* (*pl -ies*) **1** *u.n* (*formal*) state of being responsible by law: *They have accepted liability and promise to pay for the repairs.* **2** *c.n* (often *pl*) serious responsibility, duty, debt: *I've got too many liabilities and can't think about having a holiday.* **3** *c.n* (*informal*) thing that causes problems rather than gives pleasure: *Our country cottage is becoming a liability.*

liaison /lɪ'eɪzɒn/ *n* **1** *c/u.n* (also *attrib*) fact or state of working together, being closely connected: *We have a good liaison with our offices abroad. They have set up a liaison committee.* **2** *c.n* sexual relationship, esp in which the man or woman (or both) is married to s.o else: *I've known about their liaison for years.*

li'aise *intr.v* (often — *with s.o;* — *between s.o and s.o*) work closely (with s.o, between people): *My job is to liaise with teachers who are using our new courses.*

liar ⇒ lie[1].

libel /'laɪbl/ *c/u.n* **1** (*law*) written statement that harms s.o's reputation: *You can* sue *that newspaper for libel.* Compare slander(1).
▷ *tr.v* (*-ll-*, US *-l-*) **2** write/print s.t that harms (s.o)'s reputation. Compare slander(2).

'libellous *adj* (US **'libelous**) of a (printed) piece of writing that can harm s.o's reputation: *a libellous statement.*

'libellously *adv* (US **'libelously**).

liberal /'lɪbərəl/ *adj* **1** (*formal*) giving in large, generous amounts: *She's very liberal with her money but not her time.* **2** (of behaviour, opinions) accepting of other people's beliefs, different ways of living etc: *I have liberal parents and they don't mind the way I dress.* **3** (of education) that aims to give general information and ideas about many subjects rather than train students for a particular job or place in society. **4** (with capital **L**) of or referring to the Liberal Party: *She votes Liberal.*
▷ *c.n* **5** (with capital **L**) person who supports the Liberal Party: *When were the Liberals in power?*

liberalism /'lɪbrəˌlɪzəm/ *u.n* belief that accepts other people's right to their own opinions, religion, way of life etc.

liberality /ˌlɪbə'rælɪtɪ/ *c/u.n* (*pl -ies*) (*formal*) (example of) being liberal (1–3) (*adj*).

liberalization, -isation /ˌlɪbərəlaɪ'zeɪʃən/ *u.n* act or fact of liberalizing.

'libera,lize, -ise *tr.v* make (s.o/s.t) more accepting of other beliefs and ways of life.

'liberally *adv* in a free and generous way: *Thousands of people gave liberally to 'Food for Africa'.*

'Liberal ,Democrats *def.n* (also *attrib*) (UK) one of the political parties ⇒ Social Liberal Democratic Party.

liberate /'lɪbəˌreɪt/ *tr.v* (*formal*) cause (s.o) to be free: *He promised to liberate all the political prisoners when he became prime minister. It was a liberating experience for her to go on holiday without her family for the first time.*

,libe'ration /ˌlɪbə'reɪʃən/ *u.n* act of freeing s.o/ s.t or being freed: *Women's liberation became an important question in the late 19th century.*

'libe,rator *c.n* person who frees s.o/s.t.

liberty /'lɪbətɪ/ *n* (*pl -ies*) (*formal*) **1** *u.n* state of being free (from imprisonment): *The governor gave him his liberty after fifteen years in prison.* **2** *u.n* freedom to live or do as one chooses: *Don't you think you give your daughter too much liberty?* ⇒ liberties. **3** *c.n* too much freedom in s.t one says or does: *Taking my book without asking was a bit of a liberty but I don't really mind.* **at liberty** (of a person) free: *Please feel at liberty to use my library whenever you please.* **take liberties, a liberty, with s.o/s.t** behave too freely with s.o/s.t: *Don't take too many liberties with your father's trust.* **take the liberty of (doing)** s.t do s.t without asking permission: *I took the liberty of using your office while you were out.*

'liberties *pl.n* rights given by law: *The new powers of the government threaten to remove people's liberties.*

libido /lɪ'bi:dəʊ/ *c.n* (*pl -s*) desire for sexual satisfaction.

Libra /'li:brə/ *n* **1** *unique n* one of the 12 signs of the zodiac. **2** *c.n* person born under this sign.

library /'laɪbrərɪ/ *c.n* (also *attrib*) (place for a) collection of books (or records etc): *He's gone* to the public library to return some books he borrowed. Have you returned your library books? She belongs to a record library.

librarian /laɪˈbreərɪən/ c.n person who works in a library.

librarian,ship u.n profession of a librarian.

libretto /lɪˈbretəʊ/ c.n (pl -s, **libretti** /lɪˈbretiː/) words of an opera etc.

lice ⇒ louse.

licence /ˈlaɪsns/ n (US **'license**) **1** c/u.n (written/printed) permission by law to drive a car, own a television, fish in a river etc: When did you get your driving licence? Do you need a licence to fish in the canal? Your position does not give you licence to come and go as you please. **2** u.n (esp wrong use of) freedom to do what one wants: Are teenagers given too much licence today? ⇒ off-licence, poetic licence.

license /ˈlaɪsns/ tr.v give a licence(1) to (s.o), for (s.t): Are you licensed to sell alcohol?

licentious /laɪˈsenʃəs/ adj (formal) (of behaviour) immoral.

li'centiously adv. **li'centiousness** u.n.

lichee, lichi ⇒ lychee.

lichen /ˈlaɪkən/ c/u.n kind of small simple plant that grows on rocks and trees.

lick /lɪk/ c.n **1** act of licking (⇒ lick(2,3)): Give me a lick of your ice-cream.

▷ v **2** tr/intr.v move the tongue over (s.o/s.t) in order to eat, comfort, relieve pain etc: The cat licked its wounds. Lick your ice-cream quickly; it's melting. That dog doesn't stop licking. ⇒ lick s.t up. **3** tr.v (fig) (esp of flames) touch (s.t) lightly but in a way that destroys: The flames of the fire licked the wooden walls and climbed up them to the roof. **4** tr.v (slang) gain an easy victory over (s.o, a team): We licked them. ⇒ licking. **lick one's lips** ⇒ lip. **lick one's wounds** ⇒ wound¹ (n). **lick s.t up** use the tongue to eat or drink (s.t): I spilled the milk but the cat has already licked it all up.

'licking sing.n (slang) easy defeat: We got such a licking (i.e lost badly) yesterday. We gave them such a licking (i.e won easily).

licorice /ˈlɪkərɪs/ u.n (also **'liquorice**) (plant of which the root is used to make a) black sweet with a strong taste.

lid /lɪd/ c.n cover for a container etc: Where's the lid for this jar? ⇒ eyelid.

lie¹ /laɪ/ c.n **1** statement that is not true: I never believe anything he says because he's told me so many lies. That's a lie! I never said that! **white lie** ⇒ white. **a tissue of lies** ⇒ tissue.

▷ intr.v **2** (pres.p lying) make a statement that is not true: I've never lied to you. Stop lying — you know that's not true. He's lying; you don't think that he'd tell you the truth, do you?

liar /ˈlaɪə/ c.n (derog) person who makes, has made, a statement that is not true: He's such a liar!

lie² /laɪ/ def.sing.n (esp the — of the land) **1** what the land looks like: We'll have to study the lie of the land before we draw up the building plans. **2** (fig) what the situation is like: Before we make any changes in the company we've just bought we'll have to study the lie of the land.

▷ intr.v (pres.p lying, p.t lay /leɪ/, p.p lain /leɪn/) **3** (of a person) be in a flat position (esp in order to rest): They lay on the grass and talked. **4** (of a person or animal) put one's body in a flat

position: I'm so tired I think I'll go and lie on the bed for half an hour. ⇒ lie down. **5** (of things) be in a flat position: What's that lying on the floor? There were papers lying all over the room. Compare lay²(1). **6** be found/situated: The house lies just off the road. Their land lies along a huge river. The trouble lies in his family background. The problem lies in finding enough money. **7** stay in a particular state (for a fairly long time): That house has lain empty for years. Don't leave money lying in the bank without earning interest(4).

find out, see, how the land lies (fig) learn about a particular situation: Let's find out how the land lies before deciding.

lie ahead (of s.o) be, happen, in (s.o)'s future: If we'd known what lay ahead we may not have started out. Who knows what lies ahead of us.

lie back (a) lie flat on one's back or with one's back against a support. **(b)** (fig) stop working, making an effort: Why don't you just lie back and let everyone else do the work for a change?

lie before, in front of, s.o be (spread) in front of s.o/s.t: Your whole life lies before you. Compare lie ahead.

lie down be, put oneself, in a flat or resting position: You'll feel better after you've lain down for a while. She's got a headache so she's gone to lie down.

lie in stay in bed late: Sunday is my only day to lie in and read the newspapers. ⇒ lie-in. **lie in state** ⇒ state(n). **lie in wait (for s.o)** ⇒ wait(n).

lie heavy/well on s.o/s.t be difficult/easy to handle: His father's death lay heavy on the young man. Responsibility lies well on her shoulders.

lie low ⇒ low(adv).

(not) take s.t lying down (fig) (not) accept (criticism etc) without an effort to avoid, change, stop, it: Why can't you take such an insult lying down?

'lie-,in c.n extra time in bed in the morning: Why don't you have a lie-in this morning?

lieu /ljuː/ **in lieu (of s.t)** (formal) instead (of s.t): They offered me a car in lieu of a pay rise.

lieutenant /lefˈtenənt/ c.n (UK) (written abbr Lt, Lieut) **1** (in the army) officer below a captain. **2** (in the navy) junior officer.

lieu,tenant-'colonel c.n officer with the highest rank under colonel.

life /laɪf/ n (pl **lives** /laɪvz/) **1** unique n quality consisting of breathing, growth, movement etc that plants/animals/people have, that is not in earth, rocks etc: What is life and how did it begin? There was no sign of life in the old man. **2** u.n living things in general: We're studying plant life at school. There is no life as we know it on the Moon. **3** c/u.n (state of being a) living person: Thousands of lives were lost in the earthquake. Loss of life in a modern war would be huge. **4** c.n (also attrib) length of time between birth and death or from birth to the present time: I've had a very good life. Did you live there all your life? The judge gave him a life sentence in prison. **5** c.n length of time during which s.t continues, is active etc: My life with the circus went on for nearly 15 years. This washing machine should have a (working) life of at least 10 years. ⇒ life-span, life expectancy. **6** c.n story of s.o's life: Have you read the life of Martina Navratilova? **7** c/u.n way of living: How do you like married life? We don't have time for any social life. **8** u.n entertainment, activities: *What's the night life like here? 9 u.n* liveliness: *The* kittens *are full of life and play all day. There's still some life in the old man.* **as large as life** in person; real: *I didn't expect to see her but there she was as large as life.* **bring s.o/s.t to life (a)** cause s.o to recover: *That injection seems to have brought him back to life.* (**b**) make s.t interesting: *The photographs in the book have brought it to life.* **come to life** become lively, interesting: *The film never really came to life.* **early/late in life** when young/older: *She married late in life and had no children.* **for life** during the length of one's life(4); for ever. **give one's life for s.t** die for one's country, queen etc. **have the time of one's life** ⇒ time(*n*). **the life and soul of the party** person who is the most amusing, lively at a party. (**a matter of**) **life and/ or death** very serious situation (and sometimes one in which s.o could die). **make s.o's life a misery** ⇒ misery. **s.o's mission in life** ⇒ mission. **new lease of life** ⇒ lease(1). **not for the life of s.o** no matter how hard s.o tries, he, she etc cannot: *I can't for the life of me remember where I put the car keys!* **Not on your life!** Certainly not! **run for one's/dear life** run as fast as possible in order to escape s.t. **the simple life** a quiet life without problems. **take one's/s.o's life** kill (oneself/s.o): *She considered taking her life after two years without a job.* **take s.o's life in one's hands** take a very great risk: *He took everyone's lives in his hands when he allowed someone who had been drinking* alcohol *to drive.* **true to life** ⇒ true(4). **way of life** ⇒ way.

'**life,belt** *c.n* belt that contains air or is made of material that floats, worn to prevent a person from sinking in water.

'**life,blood** *u.n* (*fig*) thing that is necessary for s.o/s.t to live or work properly: *Your letters were my lifeblood during all those years away from home.*

'**life,boat** *c.n* (**a**) small boat carried on a ship in case of an accident. (**b**) boat for rescuing people at sea.

'**life,buoy** *c.n* thing made to float and support a person in the water: *Hold on to the lifebuoy until help comes.*

'**life-,cycle** *c.n* different stages of development that a plant or animal goes through until it becomes fully grown.

'**life ex,pectancy** *u.n* length of time that a person or animal is expected to live. ⇒ life-span.

'**life ,force** *u.n* energy(2) that is essential for life to continue.

'**life ,form** *c.n* living plant or animal of any kind: *The book is about life forms in the sea.*

'**life,guard** *n* **1** *c.n* strong swimmer on duty at a bathing place to guard swimmers. **2** *pl.n* (with capital **L**) soldier (on a horse) belonging to a regiment that attends the Queen at ceremonies.

'**life-,jacket** *c.n* jacket(1) without sleeves made of material that floats and worn for safety when near or on water.

'**lifeless** *adj* **1** having no life; dead: *The fish lay lifeless on the beach.* **2** (*derog*) dull; not interesting: *The party was lifeless so we left early.*

'**lifelessly** *adv.* '**lifelessness** *u.n.*

'**life,like** *adj* (usu *pred*) very much like real: *The painting was so lifelike that it made me feel uncomfortable.*

'**life,line** *c.n* **1** rope used in rescues or to protect people when they are climbing, diving etc. **2** (*fig*) very important form of contact(1): *The radio was my lifeline while I was lost in the desert.* **3** line on one's hand which is believed to show important events in one's life etc.

'**life,long** *adj* (usu *attrib*) continuing through one's life: *my lifelong friend.*

,**life 'peer/'peeress** *c.n* honour or title given to s.o for the length of his/her life.

,**life 'peerage** *c.n* peerage(1) for the length of one's life and not to be passed on to one's children.

'**life ,raft** *c.n* raft made of plastic(3) etc and ready for use in an emergency at sea.

'**life-,saver** *c.n* **1** person skilled in life-saving. **2** (*fig*) something that prevents personal disaster(2).

'**life-,saving** *u.n* (also *attrib*) (skill of) rescuing people from drowning.

'**life-,size** *adj* (also '**life-,sized**) having the same size as in real life: *He's making a life-size(d) model of his cat.*

'**life-,span** *c.n* length of time that a person, animal or plant is likely to live. ⇒ life expectancy.

'**life-,story** *c.n* (*pl* -ies) history of s.o's life.

'**life ,style** *c.n* way of living: *If you continue with such a wild life style, you'll die very young.*

'**life,time** *c.n* length of a person's life: *I doubt if we'll see any real changes in our lifetime.* **the chance of a lifetime** ⇒ chance(*n*).

lift /lɪft/ *c.n* **1** thing like a small room with doors that moves up and down in a building taking people, goods etc from one level to another. **2** ride in s.o's car etc: *Can you give me a lift to the office tomorrow?* **3** (also '**lift-,up**) act of raising something: *Can you give my little boy a lift(-up) so he can see what's happening?* **4** (*fig*) feeling of being happy, important etc: *What he said about my work really gave me a lift.*

▷ *v* **5** *tr.v* (often — *s.o/s.t up*) raise (s.o/s.t) to a higher level: *It's too heavy for me to lift alone. Will you help me lift this box up?* **6** *tr.v* pick (s.o/s.t) up and take her/him/it away: *I need someone to help me lift the box to my car.* **7** *intr.v* rise: *The balloon lifted into the sky.* **8** *intr.v* (of clouds etc) disappear; go away: *The storm seems to be lifting. The mist hasn't lifted yet. The pain is beginning to lift now.* **9** *tr.v* (often — (*one's voice*) *up*) make (one's voice) louder: *Lift (up) your voices so everyone can hear.* **10** *tr.v* steal (s.t); take (s.t) without permission: *He's been lifting sweets from the shop.* ⇒ shoplift. *The lazy student lifted his whole piece of work from a book.* **11** *tr.v* end (a ban etc); allow (s.t that was not allowed): *When will the water restrictions(2) be lifted?* (**not**) **lift a finger** (**to do s.t**) ⇒ finger(*n*). **lift off** (of a spacecraft) take off; leave the ground: *What time do you expect to lift off?* ⇒ lift-off. **lift one's/s.o's spirits** ⇒ spirits.

'**lift-,off** *c.n* act of a spacecraft taking off: *Millions of people watched the lift-off on television.*

'**lift-,up** *c.n* ⇒ lift(3).

ligament /'lɪɡəmənt/ *c.n* group of strong fibres(2) that hold two or more bones together: *She hurt a ligament while we were playing tennis.* **pull/strain/tear a ligament** damage a ligament by causing it to stretch or tear.

light¹ /laɪt/ *adj* Opposite dark. **1** having light(3):

What time does it get light in the mornings? The room is much lighter since we put in a window. **2** (of a colour) pale; less strong than the full colour: *light blue. Light colours show the dirt more.* **3** (of hair, skin etc) (of a colour) pale; nearer to white: *a light complexion* (1).

▷ *n* **4** *def/u.n* brightness caused by the sun, fire, an electric lamp etc which makes it possible to see things: *I prefer driving in the light. Open the curtains — let's have some sunlight.* **5** *c.n* thing that produces light(4), e.g by electricity etc: *Switch on the light please. Who turned on/off the lights? Leave a light on while you're out.* **6** *c.n* thing for providing a flame: *Do you have a light (for my cigarette)?* **7** effect, e.g in a painting, photograph etc caused by the light(4): *The light in the painting is beautiful.* **8** *c/u.n* brightness in one's smile or eyes that expresses happiness, excitement. **9** *c.n* person that other people are proud of: *My brother was the shining light of the school.* **10** *u.n* way of regarding/understanding s.t: *Fortunately our efforts were seen in a favourable light. If you look at our problem in the light of everything that has happened, it doesn't seem nearly so bad.* **bring s.t, come, to light** (cause s.t to) be, become, known or discovered: *More information has come to light since scientists have been able to use new technology to help study things from the past.* **give s.o/s.t, get, the green/red light** give s.o/s.t, get, a signal that one is (not) allowed to start s.t: *We are waiting for the green light so that we can start work. The plans haven't got the green light yet.* **(go) out like a light** fall asleep very quickly. **leading light** ⇒ leading. **in the light of s.t** considering s.t: *He will probably change his mind in the light of the latest information.* **see the light** realize the truth: *I'm sure she'll see the light if you explain things to her.* **set light to s.t** cause s.t to begin to burn. **shed/throw (new) light on s.o/s.t** provide (new) information to make s.t clearer, easier to understand. **strike a light** make a match² light up.

▷ *v* (*p.t,p.p lit* /lɪt/) **11** *tr.v* provide light(4) to see (s.t): *We used a torch to light our way.* **12** *tr/intr.v* (cause (s.t) to) begin burning: *Light me a cigarette. Who wants to light the fire? The sticks are wet; they won't light.* **light (s.t) up** **(a)** (cause s.t to) become full of light(4): *The fire lit up everything for miles around. Slowly all the windows lit up and people began to get ready for the day.* **(b)** (cause s.t to) begin to produce light(4): *Everything lights up at about 4 in the afternoon during winter.* **(c)** (*informal*) light a cigarette etc: *He sat down, took out a cigarette and lit up.* **(d)** (*fig*) (often — *up with s.t*) (cause s.o's face etc to) shine brightly, happily: *Her smile lit up the child's face. Her face lit up with pleasure when she saw her mother.*

light ˌbulb *c.n* (also ˌelectric **'light ˌbulb**) glass covering for an electric light.

'lighten¹ *tr/intr.v* (cause s.t to) become lighter (*adj*), brighter: *Can you lighten the colour a little because it's too dark. The extra window lightened the room. We'll leave as soon as it lightens.*

'lighter¹ *adj* **1** ⇒ light¹ (*adj*).

▷ *c.n* **2** instrument for lighting (⇒ light¹ (12)) (esp cigarettes etc).

'light ˌhouse *c.n* building with a strong flashing

light for warning ships of dangerous rocks etc in the sea.

'lighting *u/def.n* light(4) provided for something: *We couldn't see the photographs very well because the lighting in the hall was so bad.*

'light ˌyear *c.n* unit for measuring distance in space equal to about 9.5 million million kilometres (which is the distance light travels in one year).

light² /laɪt/ *adj* **1** not heavy; easy to carry, lift: *I can carry it — it's very light. Is it light enough for me to carry alone? I'll carry the lightest box.* Opposite heavy(1). **2** falling in small amounts; little in quantity: *We walked in a light rain all day.* Opposite heavy(3). **3** of less weight than average: *Take only light clothes because it's very hot at this time of year. Which metal is lighter — aluminium or tin?* ⇒ heavy(4). **4** (*pred*) less than usual; less than the correct amount, weight etc: *We received our order but it was eight kilos light.* **5** (of food) small in amount: *We'll have a light dinner tonight because we ate so much at lunch time.* ⇒ heavy(5). **6** (of work etc) easy to manage and not tiring etc: *After the operation she was allowed to do only light jobs around the house. The judge gave him a light (prison) sentence because it was his first offence.* ⇒ heavy(6). **7** (of soil) that contains a lot of air and allows water to pass through easily: *Carrots grow well in light sandy soil.* ⇒ heavy(7). **8** (of sleep) not deep and therefore easily woken: *She's a very light sleeper and wakes up if there's any noise.* ⇒ heavy(8). ⇒ deep(6). **9** soft, gentle: *She gave her sleeping child a light kiss on the cheek.* ⇒ heavy(9). **10** (of books, music etc) not serious or difficult to understand: *It's a very light book — you'll find it easy reading.* ⇒ heavy(10). **11** (*pred*) (of a way of moving) skilful and lively: *He's very light on his feet.* ⇒ heavy(11). ⇒ light-footed. **12** (of a sound) quiet and not deep: *light footsteps; light breathing.* ⇒ heavy(12). **13** (of waves, seas) calm. ⇒ heavy(14). **as light as a feather** ⇒ feather(n). **make light of s.t** treat s.t as if it is not important, serious: *He made light of his fall so that no one would worry about him.*

▷ *adv* **travel light** ⇒ travel(v).

'lighten² *v* **1** *tr/intr.v* (cause (s.t) to) become less heavy: *The bag will lighten after we've eaten the apples.* **2** *tr.v* (*fig*) cause (s.o, s.o's mind etc) to feel less serious etc: *I've got some news that will lighten your heart.* **3** *tr.v* make (work etc) easier to manage: *I need some help to lighten my work load.*

'lighter² *adj* less light² (*adj*).

ˌlight-'fingered *adj* good at stealing: *Watch your handbag — there are some light-fingered people in the streets.*

ˌlight-'footed *adj* skilled at moving easily on one's feet.

ˌlight-'headed *adj* feeling a little dizzy: *The wine is making me feel light-headed.*

ˌlight-'hearted *adj* happy; not serious: *The newspaper article made a light-hearted attack on his performance.*

ˌlight 'industry *u.n* group of industries that produce food, clothes, toys etc. Compare heavy industry.

'lightly *adv* **1** in a gentle, soft, way; not heavily, hard or in great quantities: *He kissed her lightly*

on the top of her head. It rained lightly last night.
2 (of sleep) not in a deep way and therefore easily disturbed: *She sleeps lightly so don't be noisy.* **let s.o off**, **get off**, **lightly** (allow s.o to) be given a small punishment: *I'm letting you off lightly this time but don't cause trouble again.*

'lightness *u.n.*

'light,weight *adj* **1** (usu *attrib*) thing that is not heavy in weight or thickness: *You only need a lightweight coat. I want to buy a lightweight camera.* ⇒ light²(1,3). **2** (*derog*) lacking in importance: *His speech was rather lightweight.* **3** (of a boxer) weighing between 57 and 61 kg.
▷ *c.n* **4** (esp *fig*; *derog*) person who is not very well known, important etc: *Don't accept his answer because he's a lightweight — go and see the manager.*

light³ /laɪt/ *tr.v* (*p.t,p.p* lit /lɪt/) **light** (**up**)**on s.t** (*literary*) find s.t unexpectedly.

lighter ⇒ light¹, light².

lights /laɪts/ *pl.n* animals' lungs used for food.

lightning /'laɪtnɪŋ/ *adj* **1** very quick or short: *a lightning visit.*
▷ *u.n* **2** flash of electricity produced during a storm between clouds or between a cloud and the earth, usu followed by thunder. **as fast/quick as lightning** very fast.

'lightning-con,ductor *c.n* metal rod on a building to protect it from lightning(2).

like¹ /laɪk/ *adj* **1** the same in certain ways; similar: *Like minds think alike. We're as like as sisters.* Opposite unlike. ⇒ alike. **like mother/father like daughter/son** as the one is, does etc so will the other be, do.
▷ *adv* **2** for example; such as: *countries like Norway and Sweden.* **as like as not** = as likely as not.
▷ *conj* **3** (in the same way) as: *Can you sing like your sister can? No one makes me feel happy like you do.*
▷ *n* **4** *c.n* person or thing who/that is similar, equal, to another: *We studied painting, drawing and the like. One doesn't often meet people of their like.* ⇒ likes.
▷ *prep* **5** (almost) the same as; similar to: *We were like brothers when we were growing up. He's like a wild animal when he's angry. Compare unlike.* **6** exactly what is expected of (s.o): *It's not like you to be so rude. Isn't it just like him to forget!* **7** in the same or a similar way as; to the same or a similar degree as: *She cooks like a professional. He worked like a slave to finish the job. How could you behave like that in front of all these people?* **don't be like that** don't behave, say s.t, in that unfriendly way. **feel like s.o/s.t** feel the same as one would expect to feel if one was s.o/s.t in particular: *I feel like a clown in these trousers. You make me feel like a child.* **feel like** (**doing**) **s.t** be in the mood¹(1) for (doing) s.t; want, to go, have etc: *I feel like a drink. Do you feel like going for a walk with me?* **like anything/crazy/mad** (*informal*) as fast, hard etc as possible: *I ran like anything but I missed the bus. We worked like crazy this afternoon and managed to finish everything.* **like hell** ⇒ hell. **like so** like this (using one's hands to show size, method etc). **like this** in this manner; using this method. **look like** (**a**) ⇒ like(5). (**b**) (used to show probability) be signs of: *It looks like there's going to be a storm. It looks like rain over there.* **nothing like**; **nothing like as**

bad, **good** etc (**as s.o/s.t**) ⇒ nothing. **something like . . .** ⇒ something(*pron*). **what s.o/s.t is like** (used to ask for a description of s.o/s.t): *What's your job like? What's your mother like? What's the weather like?*

'likeli,hood *u.n* (usu the — of s.t) probability: *What's the likelihood of your coming for the weekend?* Opposite unlikelihood.

'likely *adj* (-*ier*, -*iest*) Opposite unlikely. **1** probable: *The likeliest time to get him at home is between 6 and 7 in the evening. It is likely that she'll be chosen.* **2** (usu *attrib*) probably suitable: *I've found a likely person for the job.* **a likely story** ⇒ story. **be likely to do s.t** be probable that s.t will happen: *He is likely to refuse to talk to you. It is likely to explode if you do that.*
▷ *adv* **3** **most likely** very probably: *She'll most likely write to you herself.* **as likely as not** probably: *He will come as likely as not. He is as likely as not to forget.* **not likely** (used to emphasize one's refusal) certainly not.

,like-'minded *adj* having the same ideas etc.

'liken *tr.v* (usu — s.o/s.t to s.o/s.t) (*formal*) describe (s.o/s.t) as similar (to s.o/s.t): *He likened the journey to a ride on the back of a wild horse.*

'likeness *c/u.n* (example of) being similar: *Yes, I can see the likeness — you're Bob's son.* **a good**, **poor etc likeness of s.o** photograph, picture etc of s.o that looks, does not look, like that person: *The drawing is a very good likeness of you.*

likes *pl.n* **likes** (**and dislikes**) things that one likes (and things that one does not like): *We found that we were quite similar in our likes and dislikes.* **the likes of s.o/s.t** people or things of that kind: *I didn't expect to find the likes of him at this party.*

'like,wise *adv* **1** in (almost) the same way: *We watched him carefully and then did likewise.*
▷ *conj* **2** also: *You all managed to do well in the last test; likewise I'd like you to succeed in these.*

like² /laɪk/ *tr.v* **1** find (s.o/s.t) pleasing; tasty: *Do you like cabbage? I like my new science teacher. Would you like some cheese? Does he like his new job? She likes the changes we've made to our house.* Opposite dislike. **2** enjoy: *Do you like swimming? Would he like to come camping with us?* **3** prefer: *How do you like your steak? He likes his tea without sugar.*

'likeable *adj* (also **likable**) (of a person) easy to like²(1): *He's not a very likeable person — he's always complaining.* Opposite unlikeable.

'liking *n* **1** *u.n* (esp to one's —) the way one likes¹; satisfaction: *Since you're going to live in this room you can decorate it to your liking.* **2** *c.n* taste (for s.t): *She has a liking for fast cars and fun.* **take a liking to s.o/s.t** begin to enjoy, like²(1), s.o/s.t: *I could easily take a liking to this place.*

lilac /'laɪlək/ *adj* **1** pale pink-purple: *The women were all carrying lilac balloons.*
▷ *n* (also *attrib*) **2** *c.n* kind of small tree with white or purple flowers with a sweet smell. **3** *u.n* pale pink-purple colour: *Lilac is a good colour for the bedroom.*

lilt /lɪlt/ *c.n* (song etc with) strong up and down sounds or rhythm(1): *He has a lovely lilt to his voice when he speaks.*

'lilting *adj*: *a lilting voice.*

lily /'lɪlɪ/ *c.n* (*pl* -*ies*) kind of plant that grows in many varieties from a bulb(1) in the ground and produces tall flowers. ⇨ arum lily, water lily.

'lily-,white *adj* of a very bright white: *We bought lily-white paint for the walls.*

limb /lɪm/ *c.n* (*formal*) **1** arm or leg: *No limbs were broken in the accident.* **2** branch (of a tree). **out on a limb** (*fig*) in a lonely or dangerous position where there is no one to help: *I felt a bit out on a limb working in that little village. You'll be putting yourself out on a limb if you criticize them in public.*

-limbed *adj* having the legs and/or arms shown by the first word: *She is long-limbed so she'll be a good runner.*

limber /'lɪmbə/ *intr.v* **limber up** loosen one's muscles in preparation for sport, exercise etc: *It is important to limber up before any kind of active sport.*

limbo /'lɪmbəʊ/ *u.n* **in limbo** in a state in which nothing is being done about s.t: *Our plans to build on to the house are in limbo until we can raise the money.*

lime¹ /laɪm/ *u.n* **1** white powder from limestone, used esp in making cement and in fertilizers.

▷ *tr.v* **2** add lime(1) to (fields) to balance acid soils.

'lime,light *u.n* (esp *be in, get into, the* —) attention from the public: *She will do anything to get into the limelight.* ⇨ hog the limelight(⇨ hog(*v*)).

'lime,stone *u.n* kind of rock that contains lime¹(1).

lime² /laɪm/ *adj* **1** (also **'lime ,green**) of the pale green colour like a lime(3) fruit. **2** having the flavour of a lime(3) fruit: *Do you want a/some lime juice? I don't like lime sweets.*

▷ *n* **3** *c.n* (also *attrib*) (kind of tree with) pale green citrus fruit like a lemon: *Limes are more acid than lemons.* **4** *u.n* (also **,lime 'green**) pale green colour.

lime³ /laɪm/ *n* (also *attrib*) **1** *c.n* kind of tree with leaves shaped like hearts and yellow flowers with a sweet smell. **2** *u.n* wood from this tree.

limerick /'lɪmərɪk/ *c.n* amusing poem with five lines (which usu begins, 'There was an (old) man/woman from . . ., Who . . .').

limit /'lɪmɪt/ *c.n* **1** boundary; furthest possible line, point: *a 70 miles per hour speed limit; an age limit for a film. We must give ourselves a limit for the amount of money we're going to spend. Give yourself a time limit and then stick to it. There seems to be no limit to his lying.* **2** (often *to the* —) greatest or smallest degree: *That course tested us to the limit. You're pushing me to the limits of my patience.* **beyond the limit** going too far to be acceptable: *The test showed that he was beyond the limit for drinking and driving (i.e had drunk too much alcohol(1) to be allowed to drive). His behaviour was beyond the limit.* **within limits** to a reasonable degree: *Of course I'll help you — within limits of course.*

▷ *tr.v* (often — *s.o/s.t to s.t*) **3** set a limit(1) of (time, amount etc) on (s.o/s.t): *If we don't limit our time in each place we won't manage to see everything. Time was limited so we couldn't finish the job properly. We must limit you to three potatoes each.*

limitation /,lɪmɪ'teɪʃən/ *n* **1** *c/u.n* act of limiting(1); condition that limits(1): *Time and money are the usual limitations.* **2** *c.n* what

one is and is not able to do: *I know my limitations.*

'limited *adj* some but not very much: *I'm willing to give you a limited amount of help. Space is limited but we may be able to help you.* ⇨ unlimited.

,limited ,lia'bility (,**company**) *c.n* (*pl* -*ies*) (*written abbr* (Co) *Ltd*) business whose owners etc are responsible for any debts only to the amount of money they provided for the business. ⇨ public liability company.

'limitless *adj* having no limits(1) or boundaries: *When you're young time seems to be limitless.* Compare unlimited.

limousine /'lɪməˌziːn/ *c.n* large car as used to take important people on official duty or to carry rich people.

limp¹ /lɪmp/ *adj* **1** not firm or stiff: *a limp handshake. The flowers need some more water — they've gone limp.* **2** (*fig*) weak: *The heat made us feel limp.*

'limply *adv.* **'limpness** *u.n.*

limp² /lɪmp/ *c.n* **1** act of walking unevenly, esp as a result of an accident or illness: *Her leg has healed but she still has a limp.*

▷ *intr.v* **2** walk unevenly (because of a pain in one's leg or as a result of an accident, illness etc): *Why are you limping? Brian limped home after he'd fallen off his bicycle.* **3** (*fig*) move slowly because of some damage: *Our boat limped into the harbour after the heavy storm.*

limpet /'lɪmpɪt/ *c.n* kind of small shellfish that sticks to rocks in the sea.

limpid /'lɪmpɪd/ *adj* (*formal*) (of liquid, the eyes) clear: *large limpid eyes.*

linchpin /'lɪntʃpɪn/ *c.n* **1** (*technical*) iron rod through an axle that keeps a wheel in position. **2** (*fig*) very important person in an organization, business: *We can't manage without her — she's the linchpin in the business.*

line¹ /laɪn/ *n* **1** *c/u.n* (length of) rope, thread, wire etc, e.g for fishing etc: *Hang the clothes on the (washing-)line to dry.* **2** *c.n* long (continuous) mark: *Draw a straight line under the heading. He was so dirty that the water left a thick line of dirt round the edge of the bath.* **3** *u.n* (also *attrib*) use of lines(2), esp in art: *a line drawing. The drawing shows the artist's very effective use of line.* **4** *c.n* mark on the skin where it folds often: *He can read the lines on one's hand. Lines begin to appear on her face when she gets thin.* **5** *c.n* mark, usu drawn on a field etc, to show the boundary or special areas (esp in a game): *The ball was kicked over the line.* **6** *c.n* (often *pl*) outline that shows the shape of s.t: *That dress fits the line of her body beautifully.* **7** *c.n* row of people or things arranged next to one another or one behind the other: *They planted a line of trees along the path.* ⇨ stand in line. **8** *c.n* row of words on a page of writing or print: *He asked the child to read ten lines from the book.* ⇨ lines(1). **9** *c.n* railway; track for trains to run on: *Which line must I take for London? The bridge must be wide enough for a road and railway line.* **10** *c.n* (often — *of s.t*) direction/course (of s.t) which is followed: *We need to meet to discuss our line of action. Where is this line of questioning leading to?* **11** *c.n* people of one generation after the other who have the same skills, interests etc: *She comes*

from a long line of artists, actors, bank robbers.
12 *c.n* system (of pipes, telephone lines(1) etc)
that connect one place, person etc with another:
*The (telephone) lines to Australia are all busy. We
must get our lines of* communication(1) *working
well if this business is to succeed.* **13** *c.n* company
that provides a regular transport(1) service: *a bus
line; an airline.* **14** *c.n* (often *pl*) (*military*) area
where an army is camped during war: *He was
given a two-week holiday before being sent to the
front line. She had to go behind the enemy lines
to find the information she needed.* **15** *c.n* class
or type of goods: *I'm trying out some new lines
in my shop.* **16** *u.n* area or type of work, interest
etc: *What line of business are you in?* **be in line
with s.o/s.t** agree with s.o/s.t: *What she says is in
line with our company's new* policy¹. **bring s.o/
s.t into line** make s.o/s.t agree to, or with, what
other people want. **come/fall into line (with s.o/
s.t)** agree to take the action that other people
want: *I am willing to fall into line with the rest
of the team.* **dotted line** ⇨ dot(*v*). **draw the line
(at s.t)** refuse to go beyond (a certain limit): *I
don't mind you using my phone when you need
to but I draw the line at overseas calls.* **drop s.o
a line** (*informal*) write s.o a short letter: *I'll drop
you a line as soon as I know when I'll be arriving.*
(follow) the party line ⇨ party line. **hot line** ⇨
hot. **in line for s.t** likely to be given s.t: *She's in line
for a salary increase.* **out of line (a)** not behaving
as one ought to: *You're out of line there — you
have no right to talk to me like that.* **(b)** doing s.t
before one's turn. **(reach) the end of the line**
(*fig*) (arrive at) the end of s.t, esp accepting
failure: *We tried to make our marriage work but
we've reached the end of the line.* **read between
the lines** (*fig*) look for, find, information or
meaning in a letter etc which is not actually
written: *Her letter was full of the things she was
doing but reading between the lines I'm sure she's
unhappy.* **rod and line** ⇨ rod(*n*). **shoot (s.o) a
line** tell (s.o) an exaggerated and untrue story
in order to deceive. **stand in line (a)** form a
queue. **(b)** wait for one's turn for s.t. **step out
of line** ⇨ step(*v*). **take a strong/firm line (with
s.o) (about/over s.t)** deal firmly (with s.o) (about
a problem etc): *You'll have to take a stronger line
with your son over his drinking habits.* **(take) the
line of least resistance** ⇨ resistance. **toe the line**
(*fig*) do what one is told; behave in an acceptable
way: *If you don't toe the line, you'll be asked to
leave the college.*
▷ *tr.v* **17** mark (s.t) with lines(2,4): *Her face was lined
with age. I'd prefer lined paper if you've got it.*
18 form a line(7) along (a road etc): *The trees
lining the streets were in full flower. Thousands
of people lined the streets to see the procession.*
line (s.o/s.t) up (a) (cause s.o/s.t to) form a
line(7): *Everyone lined up behind Peter. Line
all the chairs and tables up against the wall.*
(b) organize (s.o/s.t) for a purpose: *I've lined
up several appointments for you. What's lined up
for tonight?* ⇨ line-up. **line up s.t with s.t** arrange
s.t so that it forms a straight line with s.t else: *Line
up all the tables with this one.*
'lineage /'lɪnɪɪdʒ/ *u.n* (*formal*) family line(11):
Do you know anything about your lineage?
'lineal /'lɪnɪəl/ *adj* (usu *attrib*) (*formal*) directly
descended, e.g from father to son: *He's not a*

lineal descendant of the composer but he is a
relative.
'lineally *adv*.
'linear /'lɪnɪə/ *adj* (usu *attrib*) **1** consisting
of, like, using, lines: *a linear arrangement.*
2 (of measuring) along a straight line: *a linear measurement.*
lined¹ /laɪnd/ *adj* with lines(2): *lined paper. The
paper isn't lined.* Opposite unlined. ⇨ lined²(⇨
line²).
'liner¹ *c.n* **1** ship belonging to a line(13): *I've never
travelled in a large liner before.* ⇨ airliner. **2** kind
of pencil etc used to draw lines(2): *an eye-liner.*
lines *pl.n* **1** words that an actor/actress learns to
say on stage or in a film: *The actor was so nervous
that he forgot his lines on stage.* **2** punishment that
consists of writing a sentence a stated number of
times: *The boy was given 100 lines by his teacher.*
hard lines! ⇨ hard.
'linesman *c.n* (*pl* -men) (*sport*) person who sits
or runs near a boundary(1) to judge if a ball touches
or goes over a line.
'line-,up *c.n* **1** group of people arranged in
a line(7). **2** group of players in a particular
arrangement: *Let's talk about the players in
tonight's line-up.* **3** things organized to happen in
a programme etc: *Tonight's line-up on television
includes top singers from all over the world.*
line² /laɪn/ *tr.v* cover the inside of (s.t) with paper,
material etc: *She lined the box with cotton-wool
and placed the eggs inside. We'll have to line the
curtains for extra protection.*
'lined² *adj* (of material) covered on the inside:
The curtains are not lined. Opposite unlined,
well-lined. ⇨ lined¹(⇨ line¹).
'liner² *c.n* thing used for covering the inside of
s.t: *We need to buy some* dustbin *liners.*
'lining *c/u.n* material (to be) on the inside of s.t:
*The handbag has a strong lining. Buy some lining
for the curtains.*
lineage, lineal, linear ⇨ line¹.
linen /'lɪnɪn/ *n* (also *attrib*) **1** *u.n* kind of strong
cloth made from flax: *a linen tablecloth.* **2** *u/def.n*
articles made from linen(1) including tablecloths,
sheets etc: *Put the sheets and the other linen in the
linen cupboard.*
liner ⇨ line¹, line².
linger /'lɪŋgə/ *intr.v* be slow in leaving a place:
*The smell of cooking lingered in the kitchen for a
long time.*
'lingering *attrib.adj* that stays for a long time:
*I still have lingering doubts about buying the
house.*
lingerie /'lænʒerɪ/ *u.n* (*French*) women's
underclothing.
lingo /'lɪŋgəʊ/ *c.n* (*pl* -es) (*informal*) language
used by a particular group of people and therefore not widely known: *I just can't understand the
lingo of today's teenagers.*
lingua franca /ˌlɪŋgwə 'fræŋkə/ *c.n* (*pl lingua
francas*) language used by people in a country
or situation where many different languages are
spoken: Pidgin *English is the lingua franca in
Papua New Guinea.*
linguist /'lɪŋgwɪst/ *c.n* person who studies or is
good at languages.
linguistic /lɪŋ'gwɪstɪk/ *adj* of (the study of)
languages.
lin'guistics *sing.n* science of language: *She's*

studying linguistics. **applied linguistics** practical application of linguistics, esp for teaching languages.

lining ⇒ line².

liniment /ˈlɪnɪmənt/ *c/u.n* oily substance for rubbing into the skin to ease aches and pains.

link /lɪŋk/ *c.n* **1** (one) ring of a chain. **2** person or thing who/that holds or connects other things: *My radio was the only link I had with the world. There is still a missing link in your argument.* **3** = cuff links. ⇒ golf links. **missing link** ⇒ miss².

▷ *tr.v* **4** join (s.t): *The road system links all the main cities. Everyone link arms for the next song.* **5** (often passive, *be —ed with s.t*) consider (s.o/s.t) to be connected (with s.t): *Steve has been linked to the murder.* **link (s.t) up (to/with s.t)** connect (s.t) (with s.t): *We're not linked up to the main water supply yet. We spent the day doing our own things and linked up with the group for the evening.*

links /lɪŋks/ *c/pl.n* = golf links.

lino /ˈlaɪnəʊ/ *c.n* (*informal*) linoleum.

linoleum /lɪˈnəʊlɪəm/ *u.n* (*informal* **'lino**) (*old use*) kind of strong waterproof floor covering.

linseed /ˈlɪnˌsiːd/ *u.n* seed of flax.

  ,linseed 'oil *u.n* oil made from flax seed, used to prevent wood from cracking, to make ink etc.

lint /lɪnt/ *u.n* soft material for putting on a wound, cut etc.

lintel /ˈlɪntl/ *c.n* flat piece of wood or stone placed at the top of a door or window.

lion /ˈlaɪən/ *c.n* large wild yellow animal of the cat family that hunts other animals for food and is found mostly in Africa. **the lion's share (of s.t)** the largest part (of s.t): *The oldest son was given the lion's share of his father's fortune.*

lioness /ˈlaɪənɪs/ *c.n* female lion.

lip /lɪp/ *n* **1** *c.n* either the top or bottom edge of the mouth: *He licked his dry lips.* **2** *c.n* edge of the opening of a bottle, cup etc: *Don't drink from the bottle — the lip may be dirty.* **3** *u.n* (*slang*) rudeness: *Don't give me any of your lip.* **bite one's lip** (*fig*) stop oneself from telling the truth, saying what one really thinks: *I was about to tell him but I bit my lip when I realized you probably didn't want him to know.* **keep a stiff upper lip** (*fig*) not complain or talk about one's pain, suffering etc. **lick one's lips** (*fig*) show that one is looking forward to s.t: *The smell from the kitchen is making us all lick our lips — when do we eat?*

  'lip-,read *intr.v* understand speech by watching lip movements: *Although she's deaf she knows what's happening in films because she lip-reads.*

  'lip-,reading *u.n* method taught to deaf people of understanding speech by watching lip movements.

  'lip-,service *u.n* **pay lip-service to s.t** behave as if one agrees but do nothing to show that one really does: *Up to now you've been paying lip-service to our new business but when are you going to put in your money?*

  'lip,stick *c/u.n* coloured stick used for colouring the lips.

liquefy ⇒ liquid.

liqueur /lɪˈkjʊə/ *c/u.n* alcoholic(1) drink with a strong flavour, usu drunk in small quantities after a main meal.

liquid /ˈlɪkwɪd/ *adj* **1** in a form that flows: *food in liquid form.* **2** (*fig*) clear and bright (as if wet): *liquid eyes.* **3** (*attrib*) easily exchanged for money: *Although he's very rich, he cannot lend you the money because he has no liquid assets(3).*

▷ *c/u.n* **4** substance like water that flows: *By the time we got the ice-cream home it had become liquid.* Compare gas, solid.

liquefy /ˈlɪkwɪˌfaɪ/ *tr/intr.v* (*-ies*, *-ied*) (cause (s.t) to) become a liquid(4): *The ice-cream liquefied in the sun.*

liquidate /ˈlɪkwɪˌdeɪt/ *tr.v* **1** end (an unsuccessful business) by selling all its property etc to pay its debts. **2** (*informal*) get rid of (s.o/s.t), esp by using extreme violence: *He threatened to liquidate all his enemies.*

liquidation /ˌlɪkwɪˈdeɪʃən/ *u.n* (esp *go into —*) act of closing a business and selling everything to pay its debts.

liquidator /ˈlɪkwɪˌdeɪtə/ *c.n* official whose job it is to close a business that cannot pay its debts.

'liqui,dize, -ise *tr.v* use a machine to make (food) into a liquid: *She boiled the vegetables and then liquidized them to make soup.*

'liqui,dizer, -iser *c.n* machine used to liquidize food.

liquor /ˈlɪkə/ *u.n* **1** (also *attrib*) strong alcoholic(1) drink: *a liquor cupboard.* **2** liquid with a strong flavour made by boiling s.t: *Use the liquor from the meat to make gravy.*

liquorice ⇒ licorice.

lisp /lɪsp/ *c.n* **1** act or fact of saying 'th' instead of 's' or 'z' in speech.

▷ *intr.v* **2** speak with a lisp(1) because of a problem in forming those sounds.

lissom /ˈlɪsəm/ *adj* (also **lissome**) (*formal*) (of movement) graceful.

list¹ /lɪst/ *c.n* **1** number of things written one below the other, esp to remind one of things to do, buy, remember etc: *We need to make a shopping list. Here is a list of names of people who want to come.*

▷ *tr.v* **2** put (s.t) on a list: *Please list all the things you want me to order.*

'list ,price *c.n* price of s.t as printed in a catalogue(1) or advertisement: *What is the list price of a new Honda car?*

list² /lɪst/ *c.n* **1** (of a ship etc) act of leaning over to one side; the amount that a boat leans to one side.

▷ *intr.v* **2** (often *— to port/starboard*) (of a ship etc) lean to one side (to the left/right).

listen /ˈlɪsn/ *intr.v* (often *— to s.o/s.t*) **1** pay attention (to s.o/s.t) in order to hear what is said: *Why don't you listen (to me) when I'm speaking to you? You're not listening. Listen to this song — it's beautiful.* **2** take s.o's advice: *If you'd listened (to my advice) none of this would have happened.* **listen in (on/to s.o/s.t)** (a) listen carefully (to s.o/s.t): *Come and listen in (on the meeting) tonight — you don't have to say anything.* (b) listen to s.t that is not meant for one to hear: *I didn't realize that he was listening in (on us, our conversation) last night.*

'listener *c.n* **1** person who listens rather than talks: *a good listener.* **2** person who listens to the radio. Compare hearer.

listless /'lɪstlɪs/ *adj* tired and without strength: *She's been listless for days and I don't know what's the matter with her.*
'listlessly *adv.* **'listlessness** *u.n.*

lit /lɪt/ *p.t,p.p* of light¹(*v*).

litany /'lɪtənɪ/ *c.n* (*pl -ies*) fixed group of prayers used in a church service.

litchi ⇨ lychee.

liter ⇨ litre.

literacy ⇨ literate.

literal /'lɪtərəl/ *adj* **1** matching word for word: *The literal translation is not always the correct one.* **2** (*usu attrib*) having, using, the exact meaning: *I didn't mean that in the literal sense of the word.* Opposite figurative. **3** (*formal*) (of a person) without imagination: *He has such a dull literal mind.*
'literally *adv* **1** in a literal(1) way: *You must not translate the French literally — think how we'd say that in English.* **2** according to the exact meaning of the words: *Don't take me so literally — of course you can finish your tea first!* **3** (*informal*) (used to add force to what one is saying): *We were literally dying of hunger by the time we got home.*

literate /'lɪtərət/ *adj* Opposite illiterate. **1** able to read and write. **2** (*formal*) educated and having read many books: *He's a very literate young man.*
'literacy /'lɪtərəsɪ/ *u.n* ability to read and write.

literature /'lɪtərɪtʃə/ *u.n* **1** written works of art such as poetry, plays, novels etc: *I studied English literature at University.* **2** something written on a particular subject: *When we first decided to go walking in Nepal we wrote to many different travel agents for their literature.*

literary /'lɪtərərɪ/ *adj* **1** of or referring to literature: *His books are of a high literary standard.* **2** (of a person) who knows about or writes books etc: *Ask John who wrote 'The Outsider' — he's very literary.*

lithe /laɪð/ *adj* (of a person's body) able to bend and move easily: *He's lithe and strong.*
'lithely *adv.* **'litheness** *u.n.*

litigation /ˌlɪtɪ'geɪʃn/ *u.n* (*law*) act of settling a problem in a law court: *The matter will have to be settled by litigation.*

litigant /'lɪtɪɡənt/ *c.n* (*law*) person concerned in a case which is to be settled in a law court.

litigate /'lɪtɪˌɡeɪt/ *tr/intr.v* (*law*) go to court to settle a problem.

litmus /'lɪtməs/ *u.n* (also *attrib*) (*technical*) substance that turns red when mixed with an acid and turns blue when mixed with an alkali: *litmus paper.*

litre /'liːtə/ *c.n* (US **'liter**) (also *attrib*) unit of measurement for capacity(1), esp of liquids, about 1.75 pints: *a litre of milk; a litre bottle.*

litter¹ /'lɪtə/ *n* **1** *u.n* rubbish of any kind: *Please don't leave any litter lying around after your picnic.* **2** *c.n* (esp of cats, dogs) group of animals born at one time of the same mother.
▷ *v* **3** *tr.v* cover (a place) with rubbish: *Don't litter the parks.* **4** *tr.v* cover (s.t/s.w) with papers etc in an untidy way: *Your desk is littered with papers.* **5** *intr.v* (*formal*) produce a litter¹(2): *Our dog has already littered twice and she's only three years old.*

litter² /'lɪtə/ *c.n* kind of bed with long poles, used to carry a sick or injured person.

little /'lɪtl/ *adj* **1** small (esp in comparison or to show some feeling): *The ring only fits my little finger. We hired a little cottage for the summer. What a horrible little boy you are!* **2** young: *May I bring my little sister?* **3** hardly any; not much at all: *He shows little interest in his children. I have little time for myself and my family these days.* ⇨ least(2), less(3). Compare few(1). **4** (*fig*; *attrib*) less/not important: *It's such a little thing — why are you so upset? The little pleasures in life count.* **a little s.t** (a) a short time, distance etc: *I need to rest for a little while; we still have a long way to go.* (b) a small amount of: *Do you have a little butter I could borrow? I need a little extra time to finish this.* Compare few(2).
▷ *adv* **5** not much; hardly ever: *We go out very little now that we have a baby. She arrived little more than five minutes before you.* Opposite a lot, much. **6** (esp with verbs like 'know', 'think', 'realize', 'give' etc) not at all: *Little did I guess what they were planning!* **7** to a small degree only: *That fact is little remembered these days. That's a little-known fact. She's little thought about now. I'm still a little hungry. You'll have to try a little harder next time.* **little by little** (a) in small amounts at a time: *Add the oil little by little.* (b) slowly: *You'll get used to things little by little.* **not a little** (*informal*) very: *He was not a little angry when I admitted what I'd done.*
▷ *pron* **8** (**a/the little** is positive; **little** is negative) a small amount; not much: *Keep me a little. We see little of them. You can share the little that I have.* Compare less(6), least(3). **after/for a little** after/for a short time: *Stay for a little.* **make little of s.t** (a) treat s.t as unimportant: *She made little of the trouble she was in and didn't ask for help.* (b) be able to understand very little of s.t: *I could make little of what he was saying.* **think little of s.o/s.t** have a low opinion of s.o/s.t: *She thinks very little of me because she blames me for what happened.*

liturgy /'lɪtədʒɪ/ *c.n* (*pl -ies*) usual form of a church service.
li'turgical /lɪ'tɜːdʒɪkl/ *adj.*

live¹ /laɪv/ *adj* **1** (*attrib*) alive; having life: *There's a live mouse in the kitchen.* Opposite dead. **2** performance seen or heard as it happens rather than a recording of it: *I went to a live performance by the Rolling Stones. Tonight we are presenting a live broadcast of the meeting between the two presidents.* **3** still active or burning and therefore dangerous: *A bird died when it landed on live wires. Don't put live cigarettes in the rubbish bin.* **4** (*fig*) still interesting, important: *The danger of smoking is a live issue(3).* ⇨ alive.
▷ *adv* **5** (esp of a radio or television broadcast) as the event is happening: *They are showing the football match live. Tonight live from New York — we bring you the famous Toddler Twins! I've seen the Beatles live.*
'liveliness *u.n* fact or state of being lively.
'lively *adj* (*-ier, -iest*) **1** full of life(9); cheerful: *They're a lively group of children. The party was very lively.* **2** active; interesting: *She takes a lively interest in her grandchildren. He gave a lively account of the holiday.*
'liven /'laɪvn/ *tr/intr.v* (often — (s.o/s.t) **up**)

(cause (s.o/s.t) to) become lively: *Things have livened up since you arrived. How can we liven (up) the party?*

'live,stock *u/def.n* farm animals, e.g cows, pigs, sheep etc.

,live 'wire *c.n* **1** ⇒ live¹(3). **2** (*fig*) person who is very active and lively(1): *You were a real live wire at the party.*

live² /lɪv/ *v* **1** *intr.v* be alive: *So many insects live in the forests.* **2** *intr.v* continue to be alive; have life(1): *He's not expected to live for longer than a year.* **3** *intr.v* make one's home: *I was born in Africa but I live in England now. We live near the station, by a river, on a farm.* **4** *tr/intr.v* pass one's life in a certain way: *They lived happily for the first few years. She lived a lie all her life. They live in poverty.* **5** *intr.v* have an exciting life: *I want to live and not be at home cooking and looking after children.*

live and let live accept what other people do, believe etc and hope or expect others will accept the way one does things etc.

live by (doing) s.t earn enough money by (doing) s.t: *He lives by working in other people's gardens.*

live s.t down try to continue living normally until s.t bad or foolish that was done is forgotten or forgiven: *How will I ever live this stupidity down?*

live in/out have one's home at, away from, the place where one works: *We are given the choice of living in or accepting a slight increase in pay.*

live off s.o take money from s.o without doing work: *She's been living off her brother for years.*

live off s.t earn one's living(3) from s.t: *Can you live off your painting or do you have to get other work?*

live on continue to live²(1,2), be alive: *Her memory will live on long after she's dead. That old man seems to live on and on — how old is he?*

live on s.o/s.t use s.o/s.t as a source of support esp money: *She is forced to live on the State because she can't find a job. He still lives on his parents.*

live on s.t.(a) eat only certain kinds of food: *I could live on bread and cheese.* **(b)** have/use a certain amount of money for all one's needs: *How much do you live on per month? Can you live on £20 a week?*

live out ⇒ live in/out.

live through s.t continue living after s.t dangerous or difficult happens: *It was a terrible storm but we lived through it and got back safely.*

live it up (*informal*) have a very good time: *Let's go out and live it up.*

live up to s.o/s.t behave, succeed, in a way that is expected because of s.t: *I find it very difficult to live up to my brother's expectations of me. I'll never be able to live up to those high standards.*

live with s.o/s.t (a) share a home with s.o (sometimes as a married couple(3)): *Who do you live with?* **(b)** accept a fact: *I don't like it but I'll have to learn to live with it.*

-lived *adj* of the kind, length etc mentioned in the first part of the word: *That was a short-lived romance(4).*

'living /'lɪvɪŋ/ *adj* **1** that is living (⇒ live²(1), has life(1)) at the time shown by the verb: *He's the greatest living writer in the world.* **2** active; still in use: *Why must I learn Latin when it's not a living*

language? in/within living memory ⇒ memory. **the living image of s.o** ⇒ image(3).

▷ *n* **3** *c.n* (usu *earn/make a —*) money for one's needs: *Does he earn a good living? She makes a living by writing.* **4** *u.n* (also *attrib*) (esp a high, low, poor etc standard of —) quality of life measured by the things one uses or buys in one's life, e.g food, entertainment: *They have a very high standard of living. The cost of living here is very high.*

'living-,room *c.n* room in one's home for relaxing, entertaining etc: *Let's take our coffee into the living-room and sit by the fire.*

'living ,standard *u.n* = standard of living(⇒ standard).

,living 'wage *c.n* salary that is enough for a person and her/his family to live on(b).

livelihood /'laɪvlɪ,hʊd/ *c.n* means of earning money: *The closing of mines affects the livelihood of thousands of families.*

livelong /'lɪv,lɒŋ/ *attrib.adj* (**all**) **the livelong day/night** the whole day/night.

lively ⇒ live¹.

liven ⇒ live¹.

liver /'lɪvə/ *n* (also *attrib*) **1** *c/def.n* large organ in the body used mainly for cleaning the blood. **2** *u.n* the same organ in an animal used as food: *liver paste.*

livery /'lɪvərɪ/ *c.n* (*pl* *-ies*) **1** (also **'livery ,stable**) place where horses live and are fed for payment. **2** (*formal*) special clothes worn by male servants.

'liveried *adj* wearing livery(2): *liveried servants.*

'livery,man *c.n* (*pl* *-,men*) **1** person who works in a livery stable. **2** one of a group of liveried servants.

lives /laɪvz/ *pl* of life.

livestock ⇒ live¹.

livid /'lɪvɪd/ *adj* (usu *pred*) (*informal*) very angry: *She'll be livid when she hears what's happened.*

living ⇒ live².

lizard /'lɪzəd/ *c.n* kind of small cold-blooded creature with four short legs and a long tail.

'll ⇒ shall, will².

llama /'lɑːmə/ *c.n* kind of animal from South America with woolly hair, used to carry things.

lo /ləʊ/ *interj* (*old use*) look.

load /ləʊd/ *c.n* **1** thing or amount (to be) carried: *a heavy load; a lorry load of wood.* **2** (often *— of s.t*) (*informal*) large amount (of s.t): *I've a load of (or loads of) work to do. I've been there loads of times.* **3** (*technical*) amount of power in a supply of electricity (measured in amperes). **a load of crap** ⇒ crap(*n*). **get a load of this, her, him** etc (*informal*) (suggesting surprise, particular interest etc) look at this, her etc. **a load on/off one's mind** a worry that is (no longer) in one's thoughts: *Finding the missing money is a load off my mind.*

▷ *v* Opposite unload. **4** *tr.v* (often *— s.t up*) put (things) on (s.t): *The men loaded the boxes onto the lorry. They loaded her with parcels. We've loaded up the car and there is no room for the dog.* ⇒ overload. **5** *intr.v* (of a vehicle etc) have things put in or on it: *The van was loading at a dangerous corner.* **6** *tr.v* put (a bullet etc) into a gun, (a film etc) into a camera, (a tape(3) etc) into a machine, (coded(5) information) into a computer etc. **load s.o down (with s.t)** give s.o heavy things to carry: *She was loaded down with shopping.* ⇨ laden, lading.

'loaded *adj* **1** carrying a load(1,2): *a loaded lorry*; *a loaded shopper.* **2** (of a gun, camera, machine etc) containing a bullet, film, tape(3) etc. ⇨ load(6). **3** (usu *pred*) (*informal*) very rich: *That man's loaded.* **4** trying to cause s.o to do or say s.t unwillingly: *a loaded question/ statement.*

loaf¹ /ləʊf/ *c.n* (*pl* loaves /ləʊvz/) kind of shaped piece of cooked bread: *a sliced loaf*; *three brown/ wholewheat* *loaves.* **use one's loaf** (*informal*) be sensible.

loaf² /ləʊf/ *intr.v* (often — *about/around*) stand or move about without any purpose: *loafing about/ around on street corners.*

'loafer *c.n* (*derog*) person who loafs²; lazy person.

loam /ləʊm/ *u.n* rich soil.

'loamy *adj* (-*ier*, -*iest*)

loan /ləʊn/ *c.n* **1** act or fact of lending. **2** thing that is lent, esp for interest(4): *a bank loan*; *a loan of £100.* **get/have the loan of** s.t (arrange to) be lent s.t. **on loan** (a) borrowed: *This car is on loan until my own has been repaired.* (b) lent to s.o usu for a long time: *My own dictionary is on loan to my friend so can I borrow yours?*

▷ *tr.v* **3** (usu — *s.t to s.o/s.t*) (*formal*) lend (usu s.t valuable) (to an organization etc) for a long time: *These paintings have been loaned to the* art gallery. **4** (esp US) lend (esp money): *Can you loan me £5 until Friday?*

'loan ,shark *c.n* person who lends money at a very high interest(4).

loath /ləʊθ/ *adj* (also **loth**) **loath to do s.t** unwilling to do s.t: *I'm loath to buy a present for a rude child.*

loathe /ləʊð/ *tr.v* (*formal*) feel a strong dislike for (s.o/s.t): *I loathe dishonest people, boiled fish, rudeness.*

'loathing *u.n* (usu *a* — *of/for s.o/s.t*) (*formal*) strong dislike (of s.o/s.t): *a loathing for violent films.*

'loathsome *adj* (*formal*) extremely unpleasant: *loathsome food/people.*

loaves /ləʊvz/ *pl* of loaf¹.

lob /lɒb/ *c.n* **1** hit or throw that goes high up into the air.

▷ *tr/intr.v* (-*bb-*) **2** hit or throw (a ball etc) high into the air.

lobby /'lɒbɪ/ *c.n* (*pl* -ies) **1** wide entrance to a hotel, group of offices etc. **2** group of people who meet politicians to try to persuade them to agree to s.t.

▷ *tr.v* (-*ies*, -*ied*) **3** try to persuade (politicians etc) as a lobby(2): *We lobbied the town council about the cost of using the swimming pool.*

'lobby,ist *c.n* member of a lobby(2).

lobe /ləʊb/ *c.n* **1** lower fleshy part of the outer ear. **2** round division of a lung, liver(1), brain etc.

lobed *adj* having a wavy edge that makes lobes(2).

lobster /'lɒbstə/ *c/u.n* (also *attrib*) (food from a) kind of shellfish with large claws: *lobster soup.* ⇨ crab, crayfish.

local /'ləʊkl/ *attrib.adj* **1** about, in, from, the place one lives in or is referring to: *local news*; *local*

government; *a local restaurant.* **2** of or affecting a limited or particular area of the body: *a local pain/* anaesthetic/ *injection.*

▷ *c.n* **3** (*informal*) person from a particular place: *If you want to know where the post office is, ask a local.* **4** (UK) nearest or nearby pub: *She's in her/the local having a drink.*

,local e'lection *c.n* election of officials for local government.

,local 'government *u.n* government of the affairs of a town, county etc by people elected in the same area.

lo'cale /ləʊˈkɑːl/ *c.n* (*formal*) particular place when referring to an event there.

lo'cality /ləʊˈkælɪtɪ/ *c.n* (*pl* -ies) (*formal*) particular area where s.t happens/is: *It was found within the locality of the school.*

localize, -ise /'ləʊkəˌlaɪz/ *tr.v* (*formal*) limit (a fire, bad effect, disease etc) to a particular area: *They managed to localize the fire by clearing a large area around it.*

'locally *adv* **1** inside this area: *He works locally. The weather locally is sunny but it's raining in other parts of the country.* **2** inside a particular area: *Those kinds of decisions are made locally.*

locate /ləʊˈkeɪt/ *tr.v* (*formal*) **1** find out the position, place, home etc of (s.o/s.t): *locate a friend in a city.* **2** (often passive) place or set (s.t) in a particular area: *The school is located near the main road.*

location /ləʊˈkeɪʃən/ *n* (*formal*) **1** *c.n* position: *a dangerous location for the school.* **2** *u.n* (often *the* — *of s.t*) act of finding out where s.o/s.t is: *the location of the cause of the pain.* **on location** (when making a film) in a place outside the film or television studios(2).

loch /lɒk/ *c.n* (in Scotland) lake.

lock¹ /lɒk/ *c.n* **1** device used with a key to fasten s.t: *You have left the key in the lock.* ⇨ padlock. **2** part of a canal with gates to control the flow of water and allow boats to pass. **3** amount by which the front wheels of a vehicle can turn: *Taxis have a good lock.* **4** part of a gun that makes it fire. **lock, stock and barrel** completely: *We've sold all the furniture lock, stock and barrel.* **pick a lock** open a lock(1) with something that is not a key.

▷ *tr/intr.v* Opposite unlock. **5** (cause (a door etc) to) become fastened using a lock and key, a bolt(1) etc: *Please lock that drawer. This cupboard doesn't lock.* **6** (cause (s.t) to) become fixed and unable to move: *The brush is locked inside the pipe. My bicycle wheel locked and I fell off.* **7** (often *be* —*ed in s.t*) hold, become involved with, s.o (in a fight, embrace(1) etc): *They were locked in battle, in each other's arms.* **lock s.o away** put s.o in prison. **lock s.t away** put s.t inside a locked place: *He locked his money away in a drawer.* **lock s.o in/out** prevent s.o from entering/leaving by locking the door. **lock s.o up** lock the doors etc of a building: *Let's lock s.o up and go home.* **lock s.o up** = lock s.o away. **lock s.t up** = lock s.t away.

'locker *c.n* small cupboard, e.g for clothes etc in a sports centre, school etc.

'locket *c.n* small ornament that opens to show a picture etc, worn on a chain.

'lock,jaw ⇨ tetanus(*n*).

'lock,out *c.n* act of preventing workers from entering a factory etc during a strike.

'lock,smith c.n person who makes and repairs locks(1).

lock² /lɒk/ c.n small division of curly hair.

loco /'ləʊkəʊ/ pred.adj (slang) mad.

locomotive /ˌləʊkə'məʊtɪv/ adj 1 (technical) about, using, movement from one place to another.
▷ c.n 2 railway engine.

locomotion /ˌləʊkə'məʊʃən/ u.n movement from one place to another.

locum /'ləʊkəm/ c.n doctor etc who does the work of another, e.g while he/she is on holiday.

locust /'ləʊkəst/ c.n kind of hopping and flying insect of Africa and Asia that eats food plants. ⇒ grasshopper.

lodge /lɒdʒ/ c.n 1 small house (near the gate) in the grounds of a larger house. 2 small house for hunters, climbers etc to use for the night.
▷ v 3 intr.v rent a room in s.o's home: I lodged with a nice family while I was a student. 4 tr.v (formal) leave (s.t) for safety (with s.o): I've lodged my will²(1) with the bank. 5 tr/intr.v (cause (s.t) to) become fixed and unable to be moved: The fish bone lodged in my throat. Opposite dislodge. 6 tr.v make an official statement about (a complaint, request etc): We've lodged a complaint about our neighbour with the police.

'lodger c.n person who rents a room in s.o's home.

'lodging c.n (price of a) place to stay: board and lodging £30 a week.

'lodgings pl.n rented room or rooms: a student's lodgings.

loft /lɒft/ c.n room inside the roof of a building.

lofty /'lɒftɪ/ attrib.adj (-ier, -iest) (formal) 1 very high: a lofty building. 2 of a high quality: such lofty feelings as pride and love.
'loftily adv. **'loftiness** u.n.

log /lɒg/ c.n 1 cut section of (a branch etc of) a tree: fire logs. 2 = registration book. 3 (mathematics; informal) logarithm. **sleep like a log** sleep very well.
▷ tr.v (-gg-) 4 write down (information) in a log(2).
'log,book c.n = log(2).

logarithm /'lɒgəˌrɪðəm/ c.n (also **log**) (mathematics) number of times a particular number can be multiplied by itself to make another number: The logarithm of 16 to the base 4 is 2 ($16 = 4 \times 4$ or 4^2).
ˌloga'rithmic adj. **ˌloga'rithmically** adv.

loggerheads /'lɒgəˌhedz/ pl.n **be at loggerheads (with s.o)** be quarrelling (with s.o): We are at loggerheads with them over the faulty repairs.

logic /'lɒdʒɪk/ u.n 1 reasonable way of thinking and deciding: What is the logic of your argument? There's no logic in doing that. 2 science of reasoning correctly: study logic at college.

logician /lə'dʒɪʃən/ c.n person who uses, is skilled at, logic(2).

logical /'lɒdʒɪkl/ adj 1 using or showing the use of logic(1): a logical decision. Opposite illogical. 2 obvious because sensible: He's the logical choice as manager.

lo'gistics /lə'dʒɪstɪks/ u.n (often the — of s.t) sensible arrangements for the movement, supply etc of soldiers, workers, equipment etc.

loin /lɔɪn/ c.n 1 (usu pl) part of the lower back and hips. 2 u.n (also attrib) meat from this part of an animal, eaten as food: loin chops(2).

'loin,cloth c.n short piece of cloth worn round the hips, e.g by very poor people, esp in hot countries.

loiter /'lɔɪtə/ intr.v (formal) stand or move about without any purpose: young people loitering outside the school gates.

loll /lɒl/ v 1 intr.v (often — about) lie or sit in a lazy way: loll in a chair; loll about on the bench. 2 tr/intr.v (often — out) (cause (the tongue) to) hang (out) loosely: The dog's tongue lolled out in the hot sun.

lollipop /'lɒlɪˌpɒp/ c.n = lolly(1).

lolly /'lɒlɪ/ n (pl -ies) 1 c.n piece of frozen flavoured ice or hard sweet on a stick: an ice lolly. 2 u.n (informal) money: I've earned lots of lolly this week.

lone /ləʊn/ attrib.adj (formal) without another person: a lone traveller. ⇒ alone.

'loneliness u.n 1 feeling of being lonely(1): Loneliness forced him to give up his job and go home. 2 state of being far from others: The loneliness of the place gave her the peace she needed to finish her work.

'lonely adj (-ier, -iest) 1 unhappy and needing a friend etc when alone: I feel lonely in this large house. 2 far from other people or places: a lonely farm/cottage.

'lonesome adj unhappy because alone; lonely(1): feeling lonesome.

long¹ /lɒŋ/ adj 1 having a large length; covering a big distance from one end to the other: a long piece of string; a long journey in a bus. Opposite short(1). 2 using up a large amount of time: a long holiday; a long time waiting for a bus; a long discussion. Opposite short(1). 3 having the stated length: My garden is 80 metres long. How long is that carpet? 4 using, needing, the stated amount of time: The film is 2 hours long. How long will the journey be? 5 (of a drink) that is usually drunk out of a tall glass, esp because it is mixed with water. ⇒ short(4). 6 (of the odds(3) for a bet(1)) not likely to win so favourable to the person who makes a bet(1). ⇒ short(5). 7 (technical) (of a syllable in a word, poem etc) stressed(4). Opposite short(6). 8 (attrib) feeling as if a large amount of time is/was used: It was a long day at work because I had very little to do. **a long shot** ⇒ shot(n). **at long last** ⇒ last(n). **be long** use a large amount of time: Will you be long with the scissors? Wait for me — I won't be long. **in the long run** ⇒ run(n). **in the long term** ⇒ term¹. **(not by) a long shot** ⇒ shot(n). **long in the tooth** ⇒ tooth.
▷ adv 9 (for) a large amount of time: She arrived long before me. Have you been sitting here long (= for a long time)? This won't take long. **as/so long as** (a) if; on condition that: You can borrow it as long as you return it tomorrow. (b) during the period that: As long as she's in control there will always be problems. **long ago** a long time ago: He lived here long ago. **long since** for a long time since then: I used to be afraid of flying but I've long since got used to it. **no longer** not now or in the future (although in the past): I no longer love you. **so long** (informal) goodbye.
▷ u.n 10 large amount of time. **before long** soon: You'll be sorry you did that before long. **for long** for a large amount of time: You haven't worked here for long, have you? **take (s.o) long** need,

use, a large amount of (s.o's) time: *This typing shouldn't take (Mollie) long.* **the long and the short of it is . . .** the important facts are. . . .

,long-'distance *attrib.adj* covering a large length: *a long-distance race, telephone call.*

,long di'vision *u.n* (*mathematics*) division(8) of large numbers using a long written method.

,long-,drawn-'out *adj* taking a lot of, too much, time: *a long-drawn-out conversation.*

'long ,drink *c.n* ⇨ long(5).

,long 'face *c.n* (often *pull a —*)(put an) unhappy, disappointed, expression on one's face: *Why has she got such a long face?*

'long,hand *u.n* handwriting with words written in full. ⇨ shorthand.

,long 'haul *c.n* **1** journey covering a large length. **2** job etc taking a long time: *Getting back to good health after the operation was a long haul.*

'long ,johns *pl.n* (*informal*) long thick under-clothing for the legs in cold weather.

'long ,jump *def.n* sport in which s.o jumps the longest distance possible. ⇨ high jump.

,long-,playing 'record *c.n* ⇨ LP.

,long-'range *attrib.adj* **1** covering a long (future) time: *a long-range weather forecast.* **2** over a long distance: *a long-range telescope.*

,long 'sighted *adj* **1** (usu *pred*) able to see things in the distance better than near things. Opposite short sighted. **2** = far sighted.

,long-'standing *attrib.adj* having existed for a long time: *a long-standing agreement/invitation.*

,long-'suffering *adj* bearing pain, trouble etc for a long time without complaining: *long-suffering parents.*

,long-'term *adj* (usu *attrib*) (of a plan, possibility etc) referring to a large amount of future time: *long-term plans; the long-term chances of success, effects of poverty.*

,long 'wave *c.n* (**'long-,wave** when *attrib*) radio wave(2) with a length of more than 1000 metres: *long-wave radio programmes.* ⇨ medium wave, short wave.

'long,ways/-,wise *adv* = lengthways.

,long-'winded *adj* (usu *pred*) (*derog*) (of a speaker, speech) dull and taking a long time.

long² /lɒŋ/ *intr.v* (usu *— for s.o/s.t; — to do s.t*) have a great desire (for s.o/s.t) (to do s.t): *I'm longing for my sister to arrive, for an ice-cream. I long to meet her. He's longing to stop working.*

'longing *attrib.adj* **1** showing great desire: *a longing look.*

▷ *c.n* **2** great desire: *a longing to meet her.*

'longingly *adv.*

longevity /lɒn'dʒevɪtɪ/ *u.n* (*formal*) long period of living.

longitude /'lɒndʒɪ,tjuːd, 'lɒŋgɪ,tjuːd/ *c.n* (*technical*) distance that s.w is east or west of a line drawn north to south on a map. Compare latitude(1).

longitudinal /,lɒndʒɪ'tjuːdɪnl, ,lɒŋgɪ'tjuːdɪnl/ *adj.* **,longi'tudinally** *adv.*

loo /luː/ *c/def.n* (UK *informal*) lavatory: *Who's in the loo?*

look /lʊk/ *c.n* **1** (esp *a — at s.o/s.t*) act of looking(3) (at s.o/s.t): *A look at the child's face was enough to tell he was ill.* **2** (sometimes *pl* with a *sing* meaning) appearance: *That boy has the look of a champion. I don't like the looks of that mark on your arm. She kept her good looks*

by eating carefully. **by the look(s) of her/him/ it** etc probably (after considering her/him/the facts etc): *By the looks of her she hasn't had a bath for a week. It'll be sunny this weekend by the looks of it.* **have/take a (quick) look (at s.o/s.t)** look(3) (at s.o/s.t) (for a short time): *Can I have a look at your photos?* **have a look round (s.t)** = look round (s.t). **take a (long) hard look (at oneself/s.o/s.t)** examine (oneself/s.o/s.t) very closely, esp when things are not going well, because one has not paid proper attention before etc.

▷ *v* **3** *intr.v* (often *— at/for s.o/s.t*) use the eyes to see or find s.o/s.t: *I've looked everywhere for my pen. Have you looked (for it) in the bathroom? Look in that cupboard. She looked round the room. Look at me when I'm speaking to you.* **4** *tr.v* look at (s.o) in a particular way: *He looked me up and down as I came in.* ⇨ look s.o/s.t over. **5** *intr.v* (esp *— as if . . .; — like . . .*) have the appearance of being . . .; seem likely to (be) . . .: *It looks wet outside. The film looks interesting. It looks as if it will rain. It looks like rain* (or *we'll have rain soon*). *She looks like her sister. He looks as if he's seen a* ghost(1). **6** *tr.v* have the appearance of (s.t): *She doesn't look her age.*

be not much to look at not be attractive: *He, the horse, isn't much to look at.*

look after s.o/s.t take care of s.o/s.t: *look after a sick parent. Who looks after the bills in your family?*

look ahead (to s.t) consider and make plans for the future; consider a future time: *We're looking ahead to next week and deciding when to meet again.*

look around (for s.o/s.t) search (for s.o/s.t).

look at s.o/s.t ⇨ look(3).

look back (to s.t) remember and consider the past (or a past time): *We looked back to last week and decided that sales must be improved.*

look down on s.o/s.t consider s.o/s.t to be of a lower standard than oneself or s.t one has done, made etc: *They look down on us because we live in a poor area of the city.* **look down one's nose at s.o/s.t** ⇨ nose(*n*).

look for s.o/s.t ⇨ look(3), unlooked-for.

look forward to s.t wait with excitement for s.t pleasant to happen: *I'm looking forward to your party, to meeting you.*

look here ⇨ here.

look in on s.o visit s.o for a short time: *I'll look in on your mother on my way to work.* ⇨ look-in.

look into s.t examine a situation, event, possibility etc: *We don't know the cause of the* riot(1) *but we are looking into it.*

look on watch a sport, contest etc and not take part. **look on s.o/s.t as s.o/s.t** consider s.o/s.t to be s.o/s.t: *I look on her as a future leader of the party.*

look onto s.t (of a building, room) have a view of s.t: *My bedroom looks onto the garden.*

look out (as a warning) be careful. **look out for s.o/s.t** look carefully in order to see s.o/s.t. **look s.o/s.t out** find s.o/s.t by searching: *I've looked out some old clothes for you. I'll look out my relatives when I go there. Look out for me, my car, at 6 o'clock.*

look s.o over (a) (by a doctor) check that s.o is healthy. **(b)** meet and talk to s.o to see whether he/she is suitable (for a job etc). **(c)** look at s.o carefully: *She looked me over and said I looked all right for my first day in the new job.* **look s.t over** examine a report, building etc carefully.

look round (s.t) look(3) at the various parts or areas of a place, room, shop etc.

look sharp ⇒ sharp(*adv*).

look through s.t examine accounts, a list, magazine etc usu briefly: *I've looked through your report but I have not had time to read it thoroughly.*

look to s.t give one's attention to s.t: *Look to the future and forget past failures.* **look to s.o/s.t (for s.t)** hope that s.o/s.t will provide s.t that one wants, needs etc: *You must look to your family for the money to go to college.*

look up improve: *My social life has been looking up lately.* **look s.o up** find and visit s.o: *I'll look up your sister while I'm in New York.* **look s.t up** search for s.t in a reference book: *look up an address in the phone book. I looked up the word in my dictionary but it isn't there.* **look s.o up and down** look at s.o very carefully esp to note her/his clothes, the shape of her/his body etc. **look up to s.o** show that one considers s.o to be more experienced, clever etc than oneself: *Should all children look up to their parents?*

,looker-'on *c.n* (*pl* lookers-on) person who watches but does not take part: *lookers-on during a fight in the street.* ⇒ onlooker.

'look-,in *c.n* (*informal*) **1** short visit: *a look-in by an old friend.* **2** chance to take part: *I wanted to play but I didn't get a look-in.*

'looking-,glass *c.n* (*old use*) mirror.

'look,out *c.n* (often *be on the — for s.o/s.t*) act of searching for s.o/s.t: *We're on the lookout for a cheap computer. Keep a lookout for her at the station.* **2** (also *attrib*) place where one watches: *a lookout for wild animals; a lookout post on a hill.* **3** (*informal*) cause for worry; responsibility: *It's your own lookout if she sees you leaving work early.*

'look-,see *c.n* (usu *have a —*) (*informal*) quick view or search: *Your camera is very nice — can I have a look-see?*

loom¹ /luːm/ *c.n* device or machine used to make cloth out of threads.

loom² /luːm/ *intr.v* (often *— up*) begin to appear, get nearer, (often causing worry or concern): *A strange shape loomed (up) in the darkness. The examination is looming and I've done no work.*

loony /'luːnɪ/ *c.n* (*pl -ies*) (*slang*) lunatic(2).

loop /luːp/ *c.n* **1** circle made when string etc is curved round so that the ends touch. **2** act or shape made when an aircraft flies in a circle by going up, round and then down again.

▷ *tr.v* **3** make (s.t) into a loop(1): *He looped the string (and tied it) round his finger.*

'loop,hole *c.n* way of escaping or avoiding s.t, esp in an agreement, rule, law etc: *He used a loophole in the law to avoid paying the money.*

loose /luːs/ *adj* Opposite tight for (2,3). **1** free and not kept inside: *A dangerous criminal is loose in the woods. They let the horses loose in the field.* ⇒ on the loose. **2** not fastened, tied or controlled: *a loose rope; with one leg loose and the other held down by a stone.* **3** not fitted or stretched: *a loose coat.* **4** not in a packet, box etc: *loose biscuits.* **5** not firmly fixed: *There's a loose button on your coat.* **6** not exact: *a loose explanation of what a*

word means; *a loose arrangement to telephone her during the week.* **7** (*attrib*) not caring about any bad effect: *loose conversation/talk about a neighbour.* **8** (*attrib*) (*derog*) immoral: *loose teenagers.* **9** (of faeces) semi-liquid. **be at a loose end** ⇒ end(*n*). **loose change** ⇒ change(*n*).

▷ *adv* **10** in a loose(2–5) way: *The rope hung loose. He wore a loose-fitting* jacket(1). **play fast and loose (with s.o/s.t)** ⇒ fast(*adv*).

▷ *def.n* **11 on the loose** (of a criminal, prisoner etc) free from police control, prison etc.

▷ *tr.v* **12** (*formal*) make (an animal etc) free from control: *We loosed some fish into the river.*

'loose,leaf *adj* (of a file³(1), notebook etc) having pages that can be removed or put in by opening a ring¹(1).

'loosely *adv.* **'looseness** *c.n.*

loosen /'luːsn/ *tr/intr.v* (cause (s.o/s.t) to) become not tied, fixed, firm, fastened etc: *He loosened his tie and opened his shirt. She loosened the lid with a spoon before she opened the bottle. Her hand loosened as the minutes passed and then she fell down the mountain.* Opposite tighten. ⇒ unloosen. **loosen up (a)** make one's muscles etc warm and relaxed: *The runner did some exercises to loosen up before the race.* **(b)** become less serious, strict etc when talking or working, doing things, with others.

loot /luːt/ *u.n* **1** things stolen from shops etc during a war or riot(1).

▷ *tr/intr.v* **2** take things from (homes, shops etc) during a time of violence: *The soldiers looted the village as they marched through.*

lop /lɒp/ *tr.v* (*-pp-*) (often *— s.t off*) (*informal*) cut (parts) from the top or end of (s.t): *He lopped off the branches with an axe.*

lope /ləʊp/ *intr.v* (of an animal) run quickly with long steps: *The rabbits loped across the field.*

lop-sided /,lɒp 'saɪdɪd/ *adj* leaning to one side because that side is heavier, bigger etc.

loquacious /lə'kweɪʃəs/ *adj* (*formal*) talking often and for a long time.

lo'quaciously *adv.* **lo'quaciousness** *u.n.*

loquat /'ləʊkwɒt/ *c.n* (also *attrib*) (kind of small tree with white flowers and a) yellow fruit having a bitter taste: *loquat jelly.*

lord /lɔːd/ *c.n* **1** man with power over others, e.g a ruler. **2** animal with power over other animals: *Which bird is the lord of the air?* **3** (with capital **L**) title given to a peer¹(1) or son of a peer¹(1): *Lord Snowdon.* ⇒ lady(4), House of Lords. **4** (with capital **L**) title given to a man in a high government position: *the Lord Mayor.* ⇒ lady(5). **5** (with capital **L**) God.

▷ *tr.v* **6 lord it over s.o** (*informal*) use one's authority unkindly to order s.o to do things.

,Lord 'Chancellor *c/def.n* (UK) official who is head of the jucidiary and also speaker(4) of the House of Lords.

'lordly *adj* (*-ier, -iest*) (proud) like a lord(3).

,Lord 'Mayor *c/def.n* mayor of a city or large/ important borough.

Lords *def.n* = House of Lords.

'lordship *c.n* (often with capital **L**) title used when speaking to a lord(3), judge, bishop etc: *His/Your Lordship.* ⇒ ladyship.

lore /lɔː/ *u.n* (*formal; old use*) traditional knowledge about a subject: *the lore of the countryside.* ⇒ folklore.

lorry /'lɒrɪ/ c.n (pl -ies) (also, esp US, **truck**) (also attrib) kind of large motor vehicle used for carrying heavy loads: a lorry driver. We sent the parcels by lorry.

lose /luːz/ v (p.t,p.p lost /lɒst/) 1 tr.v no longer have (s.o/s.t) because of forgetting where it is, theft, carelessness etc: I've lost my pen. My bicycle was lost outside the school. If you lose this watch I won't buy you another one. Opposite find(2). 2 tr.v no longer have (s.o/s.t) because of death, an accident, bad weather etc: I lost my father during the war. The plane was lost over the sea. 3 tr.v fail to keep (s.t): She's lost her right to vote. I've lost my job. They've lost interest in the lessons. They lost their balance and fell. You lost a good opportunity to win. 4 tr/intr.v not be able to win, gain, (s.t): He lost the match/game. They lost by 10 points. You'll lose the argument, your case, if you shout like that. You can't lose if you apologize now. Opposite win(2). 5 tr/intr.v (of a clock, watch) work too slowly (by a particular amount): My clock loses (10 minutes a day). Opposite gain(6). 6 tr/intr.v not have (an amount of) (money, weight etc) after doing s.t: He lost £10 betting on a horse race. We lost £1000 when we sold the house. You'll lose if you sell the car. We lost (several pounds in) weight during our travels. Compare make(9), gain(4). 7 tr.v not continue to hear, see, understand etc (s.t): I've lost the point of your speech. They lost each other in the crowds.

be lost in s.t have all one's attention on one's thoughts, a book etc: I was lost in my book and didn't hear the telephone ring.

be lost on s.o have no effect on s.o: His silly jokes are lost on me.

lose face ⇒ face(n).

lose ground ⇒ ground(n).

lose one's head ⇒ head(n).

lose heart; **lose one's heart to s.o/s.t** ⇒ heart(n).

lose hold of s.o/s.t; **lose one's hold over s.o/s.t** ⇒ hold(n).

lose oneself in s.t give all one's attention to a book, television programme, one's studies etc. ⇒ be lost in s.t.

lose one's memory ⇒ memory.

lose one's mind ⇒ mind¹.

lose out (on s.t) not be able to win, have an advantage etc (in s.t): We lost out on the chance to join them on holiday.

lose sight of s.o/s.t ⇒ sight(n).

lose one's temper ⇒ temper(n).

lose to s.o be defeated by another player, team: England lost to Scotland.

lose one's voice ⇒ voice(n).

lose one's way fail, not be able, to find which way to go: We lost our way in the fog.

'loser c.n person who does not win a game etc: She's a good/poor loser (= behaves well/badly when she is defeated). Opposite winner.

loss /lɒs/ n 1 c/u.n (often — of s.o/s.t) act or fact of losing s.o/s.t: the loss of one's pen, an opportunity, a friend in a crowd. 2 c.n thing or amount (of money, weight etc) lost: How many losses did you suffer in those two fires? There was a loss of £100 in the business deal. 3 c.n death: the loss of a friend; too many losses during the war. **at a loss** (a) in such a way that one loses(6) money: We had to sell our house at a loss. (b) unable to do

or say anything because of being upset, confused etc: I'm at a loss about what I can do to help. **cut one's losses** stop continuing to spend money on, give one's support to, work for, s.t that is losing money, being defeated etc. **a dead loss** (derog; slang) a useless person or thing.

lost /lɒst/ adj 1 not able to be found, seen etc: a lost book. My cat's lost. 2 (of a game etc) not won. 3 not used; not taken advantage of: a lost opportunity. The moment to speak was lost. 4 no longer used or done: Is writing letters a lost art? **get lost** (slang, usu imperative) go away. **lost cause** ⇒ cause(n).

lot¹ /lɒt/ n 1 c.n (— of s.o/s.t) group (of people, animals, things): a new lot of trousers in the shops; another lot of books to read; the next lot of people on the list. 2 sing.n (formal) fate: It was her lot to marry a thief. 3 c/u.n thing, e.g piece of paper with a number on it which is taken from among others to decide s.t. ⇒ lots, lottery. 4 thing, group of things, to be sold at an auction. **a bad lot** (derog; informal) unpleasant or evil person. **by lot** by drawing lots: We decided by lot who should go. **job lot** collection of (usu cheap) things sold as one lot(4).

lots¹ pl.n **draw lots** choose one or more lots (⇒ lot¹(3)) in order to decide s.t: We drew lots to decide who should go.

lot² /lɒt/ c.n (often — of s.o/s.t) a large number or amount (of s.o/s.t): a lot of people/dirt/money/ sunshine/unhappiness. **a fat lot**; **a fat lot of good** ⇒ fat(adj). **the (whole) lot (of s.o/s.t)** the whole number or amount (of it/them); all (of it/them): He ate the (whole) lot. We can get the lot of them into our car.

lots² pl.n (often — of s.o/s.t) a lot² (of s.o/s.t): lots of love/effort/students. **lots of times** ⇒ times.

loth ⇒ loath.

lotion /'ləʊʃən/ c/u.n kind of liquid used to clean or improve the skin, hair etc: body lotion.

lottery /'lɒtərɪ/ c.n (pl -ies) 1 way of winning prizes by buying a numbered piece of paper etc from among others. ⇒ lot¹(3). 2 gamble(2): Some people say that life is a lottery — some people are lucky and others are not.

lotus /'ləʊtəs/ c.n (also attrib) kind of beautiful flower growing in water in Asia: lotus flowers.

'lotus po,sition c.n position sitting with legs crossed, as used for meditation.

loud /laʊd/ adj 1 (of sound) large in amount, degree, having/producing a lot of noise; noisy: a loud voice/shout; loud music. Opposite quiet. 2 (of colours, decoration etc) too bright: a loud tie/pattern. Opposite quiet(5). 3 (derog) (of a person, behaviour) unpleasant because forcing attention from others.

▷ adv 4 in a loud(1) way: Your radio is playing too loud.

'loudly adv. **'loudness** u.n.

,loud'speaker c.n device used to make sound (from a voice, record player etc) louder.

lounge /laʊndʒ/ c.n 1 (formal) room in one's house where one sits and relaxes; living-room: Our television is in the lounge. 2 (also attrib) similar room in a hotel, pub etc: a coffee/television lounge; a lounge bar.

▷ intr.v 3 sit or lie in an informal lazy way: He's been lounging in that chair all evening. 4 (usu — about/ around) stand or move about in an informal lazy way: *lounging about at home*; *lounging around doing nothing all day.*

'lounge ,suit *c.n* man's suit worn for informal or ordinary occasions.

lour ⇒ lower².

louse /laʊs/ *c.n* (*pl lice* /laɪs/) **1** kind of very small insect without wings that sucks blood. **2** (*derog; slang*) bad and unpleasant person.

▷ *tr.v* **3** (usu — *s.t up*) (*informal*) spoil (s.t) by bad work, behaviour etc: *She loused up the interview for a job by arriving late.*

lousy /'laʊzɪ/ *adj* (*-ier, -iest*) **1** (*derog; informal*) very bad: *a lousy cold/driver.* **2** having many lice (⇒ louse(1)): *lousy hair.*

lout /laʊt/ *c.n* (*derog*) young man with bad manners.

'loutish *adj* (*derog*) having bad manners.

love /lʌv/ *n* **1** *sing/u.n* (often *a* — *of s.t*) very strong feeling of pleasure and enjoyment (from s.t): *a love of pop music, ice-cream, fast cars, watching football, brown eyes.* Opposite hate(*n*). **2** *u.n* (often — *for s.o*) strong feeling of liking or being fond (of s.o): *a mother's love for her children. Please give my fondest love to your parents.* **3** *u.n* (often — *for s.o*) very strong feeling of pleasure with sexual desire (for s.o): *My love for you is sincere. Love is a wonderful feeling.* **4** *c.n* activity or object that causes a strong feeling of pleasure: *My greatest love is having a good meal with my best friends.* **5** *c.n* person who causes a feeling of love(2,3): *Peter, my love, will you make me a cup of coffee?* **6** *c.n* (used when talking to a friend): *Well, love, it was nice to see you.* **7** *u.n* (in tennis) score of 0. Compare nil, zero. **for love** because of love(2,3): *I'll marry for love, not money. I did it for love, not profit.* **in love (with s.o)** feeling love(3) (for s.o): *I've been in love with you for months.* **fall in love (with s.o)** (suddenly) begin to feel love(3) (for s.o): *I fell in love (with her) at Bob's party.* **make love (to/with s.o)** have sexual intercourse (with s.o).

▷ *tr.v* **8** be very fond of (s.o/s.t); like (s.o/s.t) very much: *I love swimming, roasted chicken, men in colourful sweaters. I love my son even when he's annoying.* **9** be very fond of (s.o) and feel sexual desire for her/him: *I like you very much but I don't love you.*

'lovable *adj* (also **'loveable**) able to cause feelings of love(2,3): *a lovable child.* Opposite unlovable.

'love af,fair *c.n* = affair(3).

'loveliness *u.n* fact or state of being lovely(1).

'lovely *adj* (*-ier, -iest*) **1** causing feelings of pleasure, liking etc because beautiful: *a lovely dress/pattern/song/view.* **2** very pleasant: *lovely weather/food/wine.* Compare loving.

'love-,letter *c.n* letter written to s.o one loves(9).

'love-,making *u.n* sexual intercourse.

'love-,sick *adj* feeling sad and worried because feeling love(3).

'lover *c.n* **1** person who is having an affair(3) with s.o. **2** (often — *of s.t*) person who is very fond (of animals, art, music, sport etc): *a lover of modern music/painting; an art lover.*

'loving *adj* feeling or expressing love(2,3): *a loving husband, look in her eyes.* Compare lovely.

'lovingly *adv.*

low¹ /ləʊ/ *adj* Opposite high (except 4,7). **1** not

(reaching, rising) far above the ground, a surface etc: *a low ceiling/hill/cloud/bridge.* **2** small in amount, degree, force etc: *a low wage/price/cost; a low temperature/heat; speak in a low voice; a low supply of flour. Our (supply of) milk is getting low.* Compare high(3). **3** not rich and having an influence in society or profession: *come from a low class* ⇒ middle(2), upper(3). **4** rude or immoral: *low humour; jokes that are low in taste.* Compare high(6). **5** (of singing, music) deep: *the low note of a cello.* **6** ill or sad and unhappy: *feel low; be in low spirits.* **7** (*informal*) without enough money: *I'm a bit low until Friday.* **8** (of a number, a playing card etc) having a value smaller than the others. **9** used for slow speeds: *a low gear*(1). ⇒ high(10). **low on s.t** having only a small supply left of s.t: *We're low on milk/money.* ⇒ low(7).

▷ *adv* **10** in or to a low¹(1) position: *low-lying hills. The branches bent low over the river.* **11** using deep notes: *sing low.* **keep/lie low** stay hidden or quiet (until a good opportunity comes). **be laid low** ⇒ lay². **run low** have only a small supply left.

▷ *c.n* **12** position, amount, level etc that is low¹(2): *The price/Confidence, is at a new low.* Opposite high(*n*).

'low-,brow *adj/c.n* (of a) person with no knowledge of, interest in, serious books, music, art, philosophy etc. Compare high-brow, middle-brow.

'low-,down *attrib.adj* **1** (*derog*) cruel and dishonourable: *a nasty low-down trick/thief.*

▷ *def.n* **2** (often *the* — *on s.o/s.t*) (*informal*) information (esp to use against s.o/s.t): *We've got all the low-down on how you got that money.*

'lower¹ *adj* **1** comparative of low¹. **2** (*attrib*) being the bottom of two: *the lower shelf.* Opposite upper(1). **3** of or referring to the bottom part: *She has hurt her lower leg.*

▷ *v* **4** *tr/intr.v* (cause (s.t) to) become low(2): *lower one's voice, the television, the gas. The temperature has lowered since this morning.* Opposite raise(4), rise(5), turn s.t up. **5** *tr.v* cause (s.t) to go down to another level: *lower one's hands, a flag.* Opposite raise(2). **6** *reflex.v* (used with 'not', 'refuse' etc) cause (oneself) to have less worth: *David would not (or refused to) lower himself by quarrelling with his wife in public.*

,lower 'class *def.n* (often *pl*) = working class.

,Lower 'House *def.n* one of two parts of a legislative assembly, with members elected by the people. Compare Upper House.

,low-'key *adj* not meant to produce a strong result: *a low-key report/speech.*

lowland /'ləʊlənd/ *attrib.adj* **1** having low land generally: *lowland areas of Europe.* Opposite highland.

▷ *def.n* (usu *pl*) **2** lowland(1) areas of a country.

'lowlander *c.n* person who lives in the lowlands(2). ⇒ highlander.

'lowliness *u.n* lowly state.

'lowly *adj* (*-ier, -iest*) **1** having a low position or rank: *lowly workers.* **2** (*formal*) not proud: *a lowly way of behaving.*

,low-'lying *adj* **1** (of land) generally not much higher than the level of the sea. **2** (of a hill etc) not high.

,low-'minded *adj* (*derog*) rude and immoral: *low-minded humour.* Compare high-minded.

,low 'profile *c.n* (often *have/keep a* —) way

of behaving that avoids drawing attention to oneself.

,low-'rise *attrib.adj* (of a building) with only a few storeys: *low-rise office blocks.* Opposite high-rise.

'low ,season *def.n* (also *attrib*) part of the year when the weather is bad and food etc is not at its best, and therefore holidays, fruit etc are cheap. ⇒ high season.

,low-'spirited *adj* (*formal*) sad. Opposite high-spirited.

,low 'spirits *pl.n* (often *be in* —) tired and sad. ⇒ high spirits.

,low 'tide *c/u.n* (often *at* —) (time of the) position of the sea at its lowest level near the coast. Opposite high tide.

low² /ləʊ/ *intr.v* = moo.

lower¹ /'ləʊə/ ⇒ low¹.

lower² /'laʊə/ *intr.v* (also **'lour**) (*formal*) frown because angry.

loyal /'lɔɪəl/ *adj* (often — *to s.o/s.t*) having or showing willingness to be true to one's friends, employer, government, beliefs etc. Opposite disloyal.

'loyally *adv*.

'loya,list *c.n* person who is a loyal member of a political party or supports the government against opposition.

'loyalty *n* (*pl -ies*) **1** *u.n* fact or state of being loyal: *prove one's own loyalty by openly supporting the government.* **2** *c.n* (often *pl*) loyal feeling or act.

lozenge /'lɒzɪndʒ/ *c.n* kind of small flat sweet with a strong flavour.

LP /ˌel 'piː/ *c.n* (also *attrib*) long-playing record, usu with several songs, pieces of music etc on each side: *an LP* album. Compare single(11).

L-plate /ˌel ˌpleɪt/ *c.n* small notice with a large L on it on a car etc to show that the driver is a learner.

LSD /ˌel ˌes 'diː/ *u.n* kind of drug(2) often used illegally to cause very excited and strange feelings.

Lt *written abbr* lieutenant.

Ltd *written abbr* (used after names of business companies) limited liability (company). ⇒ plc.

lubricate /'luːbrɪˌkeɪt/ *tr.v* put oil etc into/on (a machine etc) to make the parts move easily.

'lubricant *c.n* oil or grease used to lubricate.

lucid /'luːsɪd/ *adj* (*formal*) **1** easy to understand: *a lucid way of speaking/writing.* **2** (esp between times of being confused, ill, insane(1)) able to think, speak etc clearly.

lu'cidity *u.n.* **'lucidly** *adv*.

luck /lʌk/ *u.n* **1** (state of) s.t (good or bad) happening by chance: *Luck is not always favourable. What luck to discover £5 in your pocket!* **2** good fortune: *I hope you have luck in your search. Wish me luck because I'll need it! Don't leave it to luck; work for the examination.* **a stroke of luck** ⇒ stroke(*n*). **bad luck** (used to express one's sympathy to s.o who has failed). **be down on one's luck** be failing, without success etc. **be in**, **out of**, **luck** have, not have, success. **push one's luck** (*informal*) try after an earlier success to gain another favour which one is not likely to get. **good luck** (used to express one's hope for s.o to have success): *Good luck for tomorrow* (or *with your examination*)! *He wished me good luck.* **no such luck** (*informal*) unfortunately I,

he, she, it etc was not successful: *'Did you find it?' 'No such luck!'* **worse luck** ⇒ worse.

'luckily *adv* it is, was etc lucky; s.o has, had etc the luck(2) that . . .: *Luckily, I didn't have to go.* Opposite unluckily.

'luckiness *u.n* state of being lucky.

'lucky *adj* (*-ier, -iest*) having or causing good fortune: *a lucky woman/number. This is your lucky day. It was lucky that you arrived after the fire.* Opposite unlucky.

lucrative /'luːkrətɪv/ *adj* (*formal*) producing good earnings or profits: *a lucrative job/business.*

'lucratively *adv*.

ludicrous /'luːdɪkrəs/ *adj* (*formal*) very foolish and absurd (esp causing laughter): *a ludicrous idea. It was ludicrous to think you would win.*

'ludicrously *adv*.

ludo /'luːdəʊ/ *u.n* game played on a board¹(4) with counters(1) that move along a path according to the number on a dice.

lug /lʌg/ *tr.v* (*-gg-*) pull (s.o/s.t) with difficulty, i.e because heavy or unwilling: *She lugged the box up the stairs, her child to the dentist.*

'luggage /'lʌgɪdʒ/ *u.n* (also *attrib*) cases, bags etc used by s.o during a journey: *a luggage van on a train.*

lugubrious /luː'guːbrɪəs/ *adj* (*formal*) very sad; full of sorrow: *lugubrious faces during a funeral.*

lu'gubriously *adv*. **lu'gubriousness** *u.n*.

lukewarm /ˌluːk'wɔːm/ *adj* **1** not very hot: *lukewarm soup.* **2** (*fig*) (of interest, support etc) not very strong: *There was only a lukewarm effort to find the missing ball.*

lull /lʌl/ *sing.n* **1** (often *a* — *in s.t*) period of calm (during a violent activity): *a lull in the storm.*

▷ *tr.v* (usu — *s.o to s.t*) **2** cause (s.o) to sleep, become calm etc: *The sound of the sea lulled her to sleep.*

lullaby /'lʌləˌbaɪ/ *c.n* (*pl -ies*) gentle song used to help a child to go to sleep.

lumbago /lʌm'beɪgəʊ/ *u.n* pain in the lower part of the back.

lumber¹ /'lʌmbə/ *u.n* **1** (esp large or heavy) useless object(s). **2** (*technical*) timber.

▷ *tr.v* **3** (often — *s.o with s.t*) (*informal*) give (s.o) an unpleasant responsibility: *I've been lumbered with* (*the job of*) *looking after the baby.*

'lumber,jack *c.n* person who cuts down trees.

lumber² /'lʌmbə/ *intr.v* (usu — *about/around s.w*) (of a heavy animal etc) move in a slow clumsy way.

luminary /'luːmɪnərɪ/ *c.n* (*pl -ies*) (*formal*) person who is famous and respected in some area of knowledge etc.

luminous /'luːmɪnəs/ *adj* giving or showing bright light (esp in the dark): *the luminous hands of a clock.*

'luminously *adv*.

lump /lʌmp/ *attrib.adj* **1** (*informal*) **lump sum** ⇒ sum(*n*).

▷ *c.n* **2** (often — *of s.t*) small mass (of s.t): *a lump of butter; lumps in the gravy.* **3** (usu — *of s.t*) small cube(2) (of s.t): *a lump of sugar.* **4** round and raised part of a surface: *I can feel a lump in my neck.* **5** (*derog; informal*) awkward and unattractive person. **feel a lump in one's throat** feel nervous, pity for s.o, ready to cry etc.

▷ *tr.v* (*informal*) (usu — *s.t together*; — *s.t with s.t*)

6 put (two or more things) together when doing something: *He lumped the expenses together on one list.* **7** treat (two or more things) in the same way or as similar: *He lumped low sales with poor profits in his report.* **lump it** (*informal*) put up with a thing, situation, decision etc without complaining: *If you don't like the red one, you can lump it.*

'lumpy *adj* (*-ier, -iest*) having lumps(2): *lumpy sauce.*

lunacy /'luːnəsɪ/ *u.n* (*formal*) very foolish behaviour, thought etc: *It would be lunacy to believe her.*

'lunatic *adj* **1** of, like, a lunatic(*n*): *lunatic behaviour.*
▷ *c.n* **2** (*derog*) person who behaves very foolishly. **3** (*rare*; *old use*) person who is insane(1).

lunar /'luːnə/ *attrib.adj* of, for, to, the moon: *a lunar eclipse/spacecraft.*

'lunar ˌmonth *c.n* length of time (28 days) taken by the moon to go round the earth.

lunch /lʌntʃ/ *c.n* **1** (also *attrib*) meal eaten in the middle of the day: *Will you have lunch with me? What's for lunch? This is the lunch menu. What shall we do in the lunch hour?*
▷ *intr.v* **2** eat lunch(1): *We lunched together yesterday.*

'luncheon /'lʌntʃən/ *u.n* (*formal*) lunch(1).

'lunch ˌtime *u.n* length of time (esp during working hours) when people have lunch.

lung /lʌŋ/ *c.n* one of the two organs in the chest, used for breathing.

lunge /lʌndʒ/ *c.n* **1** act of making a sudden and violent movement forward.
▷ *intr.v* **2** (often — *at s.o/s.t*) make a sudden and violent movement (towards s.o/s.t): *She lunged at me with a knife.*

lupin /'luːpɪn/ *c.n* kind of tall garden flower with a group of small round flowers on each stem.

lurch /lɜːtʃ/ *c.n* **1** sudden movement forward or to one side that cannot be controlled: *He came towards me with a lurch. The bus stopped with a lurch.* **leave s.o in the lurch** (*informal*) **(a)** leave s.o in a difficult or dangerous situation. **(b)** refuse to marry s.o after promising to do so.
▷ *intr.v* **2** move forward with steps that are not controlled: *The sick man lurched towards the door.*

lure /ljʊə/ *c/def.n* **1** (often the — *of s.t*) thing, idea etc that attracts: *the lure of the mountains, becoming rich quickly.* ⇨ allure.
▷ *tr.v* **2** tempt (s.o) (often falsely): *She was lured away from her job by a larger salary. He lured her into marriage by pretending to love her but he really wanted her money.*

lurid /'lʊərɪd/ *adj* (*derog*) **1** not attractive because too bright: *lurid colours/clothes.* **2** unpleasant and shocking: *lurid details of the murder.*

'luridly *adv.* **'luridness** *u.n.*

lurk /lɜːk/ *intr.v* wait hidden in order to do s.t wrong: *He was lurking in the bushes.*

luscious /'lʌʃəs/ *adj* (*formal*) very pleasant and sweet: *luscious fruit.*

'lusciously *adv.* **'lusciousness** *u.n.*

lush¹ /lʌʃ/ *adj* (usu *attrib*) (*formal*) (of plants) green and growing strongly: *lush grass.*

lush² /lʌʃ/ *c.n* (*derog*; *informal*) person who is often drunk.

lust /lʌst/ *c/u.n* (usu — *for s.o/s.t*) **1** strong desire (for power, money etc). **2** strong sexual desire (for s.o).
▷ *intr.v* **3** (usu — *after/for s.o/s.t*) have feelings of lust(*n*) (for s.o/s.t): *He lusted after power, her sister.*

'lustful *adj* (*formal*) feeling or showing strong (esp sexual) desire: *lustful looks.*

'lustfully *adv.* **'lustfulness** *u.n.*

'lustily *adv* in a lusty way.

'lustiness *u.n* state of being lusty.

'lusty *adj* (*-ier, -iest*) **1** very healthy and strong: *a lusty youth.* **2** strong and loud: *a lusty cry.*

lustre /'lʌstə/ *u.n* (US **'luster**) brightness (because shiny or polished): *The lustre of the jewels in her ring.*

'lustrous /'lʌstrəs/ *adj* (*formal*) bright and shining.

lusty ⇨ lust.

lute /luːt/ *c.n* musical instrument with strings and a round body with a long neck.

lutenist /'luːtənɪst/ *c.n* person who plays a lute.

luxuriant /lʌɡ'zjʊərɪənt/ *adj* (*formal*) (of plants) growing well and usu in large numbers: *luxuriant trees in* tropical *forests.*

lux'uriance *u.n.* **lux'uriantly** *adv.*

luxuriate /lʌɡ'zjʊərɪˌeɪt/ *intr.v* (often — *in s.t*) (*formal*) enjoy (s.t physical) very much without having to make any effort: *luxuriate in swimming naked in the sea, in a* bubble bath.

luxury /'lʌkʃərɪ/ *n* (*pl -ies*) **1** *u.n* (also *attrib*) great (and expensive) comfort: *live in luxury, in a luxury flat; a life of luxury.* **2** *c.n* thing that is expensive and enjoyable but not necessary: *Eating in restaurants is a luxury. I enjoy luxuries such as expensive soap and good wine.* **the lap of luxury** ⇨ lap¹.

luxurious /lʌɡ'zjʊərɪəs/ *adj* (*formal*) providing or having luxuries: *a luxurious hotel; lead a luxurious life.*

lux'uriously *adv.* **lux'uriousness** *u.n.*

lychee /'laɪtʃiː/ *c.n* (also **'lichee, 'lichi**) kind of Asian fruit with a hard rough skin and sweet white flesh round a brown stone.

lying /'laɪɪŋ/ *pres.p* of lie¹ (*v*) and lie² (*v*).

lynch /lɪntʃ/ *tr.v* attack and kill (s.o) for doing s.t wrong but without a legal trial.

lynx /lɪŋks/ *c.n* kind of wild animal of the cat family with long brown fur and upright ears with long hair on them.

lyre /laɪə/ *c.n* kind of ancient musical instrument with strings and a body shaped like the letter U.

lyric /'lɪrɪk/ *adj* **1** (of poetry) expressing personal feelings (and often written as a song).
▷ *c.n* **2** (usu *pl*) words of a song. **3** lyric(1) poem.

'lyrical *adj* expressing personal feelings.

'lyrically *adv.*

'lyriˌcist *c.n* person who writes words for songs.

Mm

M, m /em/ *c/unique n* **1** 13th letter of the English alphabet.

▷ *written abbr* **2** male; masculine. **3** married. **4** month. **5** (**M**) Member(2). **6** (**M**) Monday. **7** (**M**) mountain.

▷ *symb* **8** Roman numeral for 1000. **9** (**m**) metre(s). **10** (**m**) mile(s). **11** (**m**) million(s). **12** (**m**) minutes. **13** (**M**) Mach. **14** (**M**) (UK) (used with a number) Motorway: *the M40.* ⇒ A(11).

-'m /m/ *v* shortened form of *am* from the verb 'be' (used after I): *I'm coming.*

ma /mɑː/ *c.n* (*informal*) mama; mother (used by a daughter or son): *Ma, where are my shoes?*

MA /ˌem ˈeɪ/ *abbr* Master of Arts.

mac /mæk/ *c.n* (UK *informal*) mackintosh.

macabre /məˈkɑːbrə/ *adj* causing fear because very strange, esp connected with horrible(1) death: *It was a macabre television play, full of murder and* horror(1).

macaroni /ˌmækəˈrəʊnɪ/ *u.n* (also *attrib*) form of pasta in, usu, short pieces of hollow tubes: *Let's have macaroni cheese for dinner.*

mace¹ /meɪs/ *u.n* spice(1) from the dried skin of nutmeg.

mace² /meɪs/ *c.n* **1** ceremonial pole¹ that represents the order and power of a parliament, council etc, esp during important occasions. **2** (*old use*) weapon in the shape of a heavy metal club.

macedoine /ˌmæsɪˈdwɑːn/ *u.n* mixture of small pieces of vegetables in a sauce, sometimes eaten as a salad(1).

Mach /mæk/ *unique n* (also ¹**Mach** ˌ**number**) unit of measurement that compares the speed of an aircraft with the speed of sound, *symb* M: *A plane flying at Mach 3 is flying at three times the speed of sound.*

machete /məˈʃetɪ/ *c.n* large knife with a wide blade, used as a tool or weapon, esp in South America.

machinations /ˌmækɪˈneɪʃənz/ *pl.n* plan with the intention of causing harm.

machine /məˈʃiːn/ *attrib.adj* **1** made or produced by a machine(2): *a machine finish.*

▷ *c.n* **2** manufactured device, usu with many parts, that uses power to do a particular job: *a washing-machine; a sewing-machine.* Compare appliance, gadget, instrument(1), tool(1). **3** group of people who organize the activities of a political party: *The party machine is working very hard for the next election.* **4** (*fig*) person who does something without question or thought.

▷ *tr.v* **5** use a machine(1) to make, shape, polish etc (s.t): *This old sewing-machine cannot machine thick cloth. The shelves have been machined to a smooth finish.*

ma'chine-ˌgun *c.n* gun that continues to fire as long as the trigger(1) is being pulled.

maˌchine-'made *adj* made by a machine(2). Compare factory-made, handmade.

ma'chine-ˌtool *c.n* tool using electric power that machines(5) s.t.

machinery /məˈʃiːnərɪ/ *u.n* **1** different kinds of machines(2): *The machinery in the factory is very old.* **2** different parts in a machine(2): *The machinery is broken so the dishwasher doesn't work.*

machinist /məˈʃiːnɪst/ *c.n* person who works a machine(2) in a factory.

macho /ˈmætʃəʊ/ *adj* (*informal*) concerned too much with male pride and manly qualities.

mackerel /ˈmækrəl/ *n* (*pl* -(s)) **1** *c.n* dark grey sea fish with stripes which often lives in harbours and can be eaten. **2** *u.n* flesh of this fish as food: *smoked mackerel; mackerel pâté.*

mackintosh /ˈmækɪntɒʃ/ *c.n* (*informal* mac) (UK) kind of raincoat: *Bring a mac because it may rain.* ⇒ anorak, parka, raincoat.

mad /mæd/ *adj* (-dd-) **1** (often *become/go* —) suffering from illness of the mind shown by uncontrolled behaviour: *She went mad after her baby died.* **2** (often *make s.o* —) (*fig*) very angry or upset because of annoying behaviour, extreme pain, loud noise etc: *He makes me mad when he behaves like that.* **3** (*fig*) of behaviour that is a little careless and irresponsible but not dangerous: *We did the maddest things when we were students. Don't be mad — you can't go out dressed like that!* **4** (of a dog) affected by a disease (rabies) that causes dangerous uncontrolled behaviour. (**as**) **mad as a hatter**; **as mad as a March hare** behaving very foolishly. **be mad about s.o/ s.t** be very interested in, very fond of, s.o/s.t: *She's mad about Jonathan/cats.* **be mad about/ at s.o/s.t** feel angry because of s.o/s.t: *I'm so mad about/at missing that television programme. He's mad at me for being late.* **drive s.o mad** cause s.o to be very angry: *Her rudeness drives me mad!* **hopping mad** (*informal*) extremely angry. **like mad** (*informal*) with as much effort as possible: *She ran like mad but she didn't win.* **raving mad**; **stark staring mad** extremely mad(1).

madden /ˈmædn/ *tr.v* cause (s.o) to be angry: *She maddens me with all her lies.*

maddening /ˈmædnɪŋ/ *adj* (*informal*) very annoying: *maddening behaviour. This cold weather is maddening.*

¹madˌhouse *c.n* **1** (*old use*) hospital for mad(1) people. **2** (*informal*) noisy place with much activity: *The children have turned their room into a madhouse!*

¹madly *adv* **1** (*informal*) extremely: *We were all madly excited at the news.* **2** as if mad(1): *She shouted madly and then* collapsed.

¹madman, **¹madˌwoman** *c.n* (*pl* -men, -ˌwomen) *c.n* man, woman who is mad(1).

¹madness *u.n* **1** condition of being mad(1): *His madness has destroyed his mother's life.* **2** irresponsible behaviour: *It would be madness to try to climb a mountain without training.* **method in s.o's madness** ⇒ method.

madam /ˈmædəm/ *c.n* (usu *sing*) Compare sir. **1** (also with capital **M**) polite way of addressing a woman, esp when she is a customer in a shop or restaurant: *Good morning, madam, can I help you?* Compare miss¹. **2** (with capital **M**) written form of address in a formal letter to a woman whose name is not known: *Dear Madam.* **3** (*derog*) woman who is bossy and too confident: *What an annoying madam she is becoming.*

made /meɪd/ *p.t,p.p* of make.

ˌmade-'up *adj* ⇒ make(v).

made-to-measure, made-up ⇒ make.

Madonna /məˈdɒnə/ *def*/*unique n* (picture, figure of) Mary, mother of Christ in the Christian(1) religion.

madrigal /ˈmædrɪgəl/ *c.n* **1** song for several voices performed without music. **2** short poem about love or country life that can be sung.

maestro /ˈmaɪstrəʊ/ *c.n* (*pl -s*) great musician, esp a composer or conductor(2).

magazine /ˌmægəˈziːn/ *c.n* **1** (also *attrib*) (*informal abbr mag*) publication(2) produced once a week, month etc with articles, photographs and advertisements: *fashion magazines*; *magazine articles on health foods*. Compare journal. **2** place in a camera where the film is put. **3** place in some kinds of guns where the bullets or shells are put. **4** room for storing arms, explosives etc.

magenta /məˈdʒentə/ *u.n* (also *attrib*) red-purple colour; it is one of the three main colours used in printing. ⇒ cyan, yellow.

maggot /ˈmægət/ *c.n* small worm that comes out of certain insects' eggs (e.g a fly's), found on bad meat etc.

'maggoty *adj* (*-ier, -iest*) full of maggots.

magic /ˈmædʒɪk/ *adj* **1** used in, caused by, as if by, magic(3): *a magic charm*/*trick*; *using her magic touch to turn tasteless food into a wonderful meal.* **2** (*informal*) particularly beautiful, exciting, good etc: *Women are magic!*

▷ **n 3** *u.n* system of influencing or controlling people and events using secret methods that are supposed to get power from supernatural(1) forces: *Witches(1) used magic to change people into ugly animals.* ⇒ black magic, voodoo, witchcraft. **4** *u.n* ability to produce mysterious and unexpected results by deceiving an audience: *And now I shall use magic to make this table disappear.* **5** *sing.n* quality that demands attention: *She has a magic that attracts many people to her — is it the magic of her smile?* **as if by magic**; **like magic** in a way that is impossible to explain: *We needed rain for days and then as if by magic the clouds formed and the rain fell.*

'magical *adj* **1** of or using magic(3). **2** mysterious; exciting: *The atmosphere at the open-air concert was magical.*

'magically *adv.*

magician /məˈdʒɪʃən/ *c.n* person who is skilled in magic(3,4). ⇒ conjurer.

magistrate /ˈmædʒɪˌstreɪt/ *c.n* (**'magis,trates'** when *attrib*) person who acts as a judge of less serious crimes (in a *magistrates' court*): *The magistrate fined him £20 for parking on a yellow line.*

magisterial /ˌmædʒɪˈstɪərɪəl/ *adj* **1** of, controlled by, a magistrate: *a magisterial district.* **2** (behaving like a person) having complete control of an action, event, people etc: *a magisterial manner.*

ˌmagiˈsterially *adv.*

magnanimous /mægˈnænɪməs/ *adj* (often *— of s.o to do s.t*) very generous (of s.o to do s.t): *a magnanimous gift*/*person. It was magnanimous of you to lend her the money.*

magnanimity /ˌmægnəˈnɪmɪtɪ/ *u.n* more than usual generosity, esp when forgiving s.o/s.t: *He showed his magnanimity when he gave Bill the job after Bill had come out of prison.*

magˈnanimously *adv.*

magnate /ˈmægneɪt/ *c.n* person with much power and influence in business or industry: *oil magnates.*

magnesia /mægˈniːʃə/ *u.n* white powder used in liquid form (**ˌmilk of magˈnesia**) as a medicine for the stomach, esp to stop indigestion, *chem.form* MgO.

magnesium /mægˈniːzɪəm/ *u.n* silver-white metal that burns with a bright light, *chem.symb* Mg.

magnet /ˈmægnɪt/ *c.n* **1** object that can attract iron and some other metals because of a force produced by its natural properties or because an electric current is passed through it (⇒ electromagnet): *A magnet will easily separate pieces of iron from sand.* **2** (*fig*) person or thing who/that attracts attention: *The art exhibition was a magnet for crowds of tourists.*

magnetic /mægˈnetɪk/ *adj* **1** having the same qualities as a magnet(1) or worked by a magnet(1): *The cupboard doors are magnetic.* **2** (*fig*) attracting a lot of attention: *a magnetic smile.*

magˌnetic 'field *c.n* area round a magnet(1) where there is magnetic(1) force.

magˌnetic 'head *c.n* ⇒ head(13).

magˌnetic 'needle *c.n* thin piece of magnetic(1) metal used in a compass(1) to show directions.

magˌnetic 'north *unique n* (*technical*) direction in which a compass(1) needle always points.

magˌnetic 'pole *c.n* **1** one of two ends of a magnet(1) where magnetic(1) force is strongest. **2** area near the North or South Pole²(1) in which direction the needle of a compass(1) points.

magˌnetic 'tape *c.n* ⇒ tape(2).

magˈnetically *adv*: *magnetically operated.*

magnetism /ˈmægnəˌtɪzəm/ *u.n* **1** (science of) magnets(1) and their properties. **2** (*fig*) power to attract attention: *Her popularity is due to her personal magnetism.*

magnetize, -ise /ˈmægnəˌtaɪz/ *tr.v* **1** make (s.t esp a metal object) magnetic(1): *Most metals can be magnetized using electricity.* **2** (*fig*) attract the attention of (s.o): *The audience was magnetized by his performance.*

magnificent /mægˈnɪfɪsənt/ *adj* (of something that is well done or well made) extremely good; splendid; very beautiful: *a magnificent view*; *a magnificent show*; *a magnificent gold ring.*

magˈnificence *u.n.* **magˈnificently** *adv.*

magnify /ˈmægnɪˌfaɪ/ *tr.v* (*-ies, -ied*) **1** make (s.o/s.t) appear bigger than her/his/its actual size: *magnifying small insects in order to study them.* **2** (*fig*) make (s.t) appear more important, serious etc than it actually is: *She always magnifies her problems to get more sympathy.*

magnification /ˌmægnɪfɪˈkeɪʃən/ *n* **1** *c*/*u.n* power, strength, amount, of magnifying(1): *This photograph shows the fly with a magnification of ten times its actual size.* **2** *u.n* process of magnifying(1) s.t: *use magnification to study the blood sample.*

'magniˌfier *c.n* instrument that magnifies(1) (s.t).

'magniˌfying ˌglass *c.n* shaped piece of glass designed to magnify(1) s.t: *The old man uses a magnifying glass to read the newspaper.*

magniloquent /mægˈnɪləkwənt/ *adj* (*formal*) (of the way a person speaks) full of self-importance and exaggerated pride.

mag'niloquence *u.n.* **mag'niloquently** *adv.*

magnitude /'mægnɪ‚tjuːd/ *u.n* (*formal*) **1** very large size: *It is impossible to imagine the magnitude of the universe.* **2** very large importance and size: *A job of this magnitude will need a lot of expensive help.*

magnum /'mægnəm/ *c.n* bottle for wine etc that can hold as much as two ordinary bottles, i.e about 1.5 litres: *a magnum of* champagne.

‚**magnum** '**opus** *c.n* greatest work of an artist, writer, composer(1) etc.

magpie /'mæg‚paɪ/ *c.n* kind of large black and white bird that collects small shiny objects.

mahogany /mə'hɒgənɪ/ *n* (also *attrib*) **1** *c.n* kind of tree that has dark red wood. **2** *u.n* hard wood of this tree: *a mahogany table.*

maid /meɪd/ *c.n* **1** woman who cleans rooms, furniture etc in a hotel, house etc: *a hotel maid*; *a housemaid.* Compare nursemaid. **2** (*literary*) young unmarried woman. **an old maid** (*informal*) an older woman who is not married: *She'll probably die an old maid.*

‚**maid of** '**honour** *c.n* (*pl* maids of honour) **1** (usu married) woman who is the chief attendant of a bride. **2** unmarried woman who attends a queen or princess.

maiden /'meɪdn/ *c.n* **1** (*literary*) young unmarried woman. **2** (in cricket¹) over² in which no runs are scored: *Botham's bowling figures are five overs, two maidens, one for seventeen.*

‚**maiden** '**aunt** *c.n* unmarried aunt.

‚**maiden** '**flight** *c.n* first time an aircraft is used.

'**maiden‚hood** *u.n* (*formal*) length of time of being a young unmarried woman.

'**maidenly** *adj* behaving like a maiden(1): *maidenly modesty.*

'**maiden** ‚**name** *c.n* woman's family name before she marries.

‚**maiden** '**over** *c.n* (in cricket¹) = maiden(2).

‚**maiden** '**speech** *c.n* first official speech, e.g by a Member of Parliament.

‚**maiden** '**voyage** *c.n* first journey by a ship or boat.

mail¹ /meɪl/ *u.n* **1** system of collecting and delivering letters, parcels etc: *The British postal system is called the Royal Mail.* **2** *c/u.n* (esp US) things sent or delivered by mail¹(1): *Where's this morning's mail?* ⇨ post¹(1).

▷ *tr.v* **3** (esp US) send (a letter, parcel etc) by post. ⇨ post¹(2).

'**mail‚bag** *c.n* bag used to carry letters, parcels etc.

'**mail‚box** *c.n* (US) = postbox(1,2).

'**mailing** ‚**list** *c.n* list of names and addresses used by an organization to send information, advertisements etc by post: *We are on the mailing list for the National Theatre.*

‚**mail** '**order** *u.n* (**'mail-‚order** when *attrib*) system of buying from a catalogue(1) sent by post: *buy something by mail order*; *a mail-order* catalogue(1).

mail² /meɪl/ *u.n* (*old use*) kind of armour(1), usu in the form of steel rings, worn on the body. ⇨ chain mail.

maim /meɪm/ *tr.v* (often passive) damage (s.o, s.o's body) so badly that he/she cannot use it again: *She was maimed for life in the car accident.*

main /meɪn/ *attrib.adj* **1** most important in standard, size, seriousness, value etc: *We have our main meal of the day in the evening. You are my main reason for staying.*

▷ *def.n* **2** **in the main** most of the time; on most points: *I agree with you in the main.* **3** **by/with** (*all one's*) **might and main** ⇨ might².

‚**main** '**chance** *def.n* (usu have/with an eye to the —) best opportunity: *He married her with an eye to* (thinking about) *the main chance.*

‚**main** '**clause** *c.n* (*grammar*) clause(1) that can be used by itself without any others or with others. Compare dependent/subordinate clause.

mainland /'meɪnlənd/ *def.n* land area of a country or city without its islands: *I live on a small island but I do my shopping on the mainland.*

‚**main** '**line** *c.n* ('**main‚line** when *attrib*) the most important line(9) in a railway system: *a mainline train.*

'**mainly** *adv* more than anything else; for the most part: *The weather was mainly responsible for the accident.*

‚**main** '**road** *c.n* (usu the —) most important road in a town or city: *There is a chemist on the main road.*

mains /meɪnz/ *def.pl.n* pipe that carries water or gas, or wire that carries electricity, to a building: *You must turn off the electricity at the mains before you can touch the wire.*

'**main‚stay** *c.n* (usu the — of s.t) most important support or part (of s.t): *Tourism is the mainstay of the economy of Greece.*

'**main‚stream** *c.n* (also *attrib*) (usu the —) most usual opinion, thought, influence etc: *As a student she began to question the mainstream of politics.*

maintain /meɪn'teɪn/ *tr.v* **1** keep (s.t) the same as before: *I will leave you to maintain order while I am away. We have maintained our friendship through many years of difficulty.* **2** keep (a building, car, road etc) in good condition. **3** pay for (s.o's) food, clothes, education etc: *A man who marries a second time often has to maintain two families.* **4** (often — that ...) continue to believe and claim (that a fact, opinion, is true): *Eric maintains that he was not at the party but I'm sure I saw him.*

main'tainable *adj* that can be maintained(4).

maintenance /'meɪntənəns/ *u.n* **1** act of keeping a building, car, road etc in good condition: *Who is responsible for the maintenance of this road? I'm studying car maintenance at college.* **2** act of maintaining(3) s.o; money to be paid for maintaining(3) s.o: *She has to pay her husband maintenance because he is looking after the children.*

maisonette /‚meɪzə'net/ *c.n* (also ‚**maison-'nette**) flat(13) on two levels, often part of a larger building.

maize /meɪz/ *u.n* (also **corn**) (also *attrib*) kind of grain plant that has a large head covered with round yellow seeds. ⇨ corncob.

'**maize** ‚**flour** *u.n* powder made from crushed maize seeds, used as food.

Maj *written abbr* Major.

majesty /'mædʒɪstɪ/ *n* (*pl* -ies) **1** *u.n* greatness of a king or queen. **2** *u.n* greatness in appearance, character etc: *the majesty of the mountains.* **3** *c.n*

Her/His/Your Majesty; *Their Majesties* title used when speaking to or of a king and/or a queen.

majestic /məˈdʒestɪk/ *adj* showing greatness and power: *a majestic ceremony.*
maˈjestically *adv.*

Maj-Gen *written abbr* Major-General.

major /ˈmeɪdʒə/ *adj* (usu *attrib*) **1** more important than others: *It was a major medical discovery. The major roads on the map are red. My major interest is football.* Compare minor(1).
▷ *c.n* **2** (often with capital **M**; *written abbr* Maj) (title of an) officer in the army between a captain and a lieutenant-colonel. **3** (*law*) person who is an adult (over 18 in age). Compare minor(2). **4** (esp US) most important subject studied at university: *My majors were English and French.*
▷ *intr.v* **5 major in s.t** (esp US) study a particular subject at university and pass the examinations: *What did you major in at University?*

ˌmajor-ˈgeneral *c.n* (often with capital **M** and **G**; *written abbr* Maj-Gen) officer in the army immediately below a lieutenant-general.

majority /məˈdʒɒrɪtɪ/ *attrib.adj* **1** agreed by most of the members of a group: *a majority vote/verdict*(1). Compare minority(1).
▷ *n* (*pl -ies*) **2** *c.n* (usu *sing* with sing/pl.v) larger number, amount or part: *The majority of these tomatoes is/are bad. She spent the majority of her life in India. The majority is/are against the new law.* **3** *c.n* amount by which one group has more than another group: *He was elected by a majority of 550. Areas with the largest majorities* (*of votes*) *should be safe in the next election.* **4** *u.n* (often *reach one's —*) (*law*) age of becoming an adult: *You cannot marry without your parents' permission until you have reached your majority.*
be in the majority be in the group having the largest number (of people in favour etc): *This is one occasion when our representatives are in the majority.* Opposite minority(2).

make /meɪk/ *c.n* **1** product that is designed and produced by a particular manufacturer: *What make is your television set?* **be on the make** (*derog*) be looking for an easy way to make a personal profit: *Don't trust Peter — he's always on the make.*
▷ *v* (*pres.p* making; *p.t,p.p* made /meɪd/) **2** *tr.v* (often *— s.t from s.t*; *— s.t for s.o*; *— s.o s.t*) produce, shape, prepare, establish(1) etc (s.t) (for s.o): *I make all my clothes. Butter is made from milk. He's making a model boat for his son. What shall I make with this piece of cardboard? Please make me a cup of coffee. Stop making such a noise! The rules were made 100 years ago. He made four telephone calls* (telephoned four times). *We have come here to make peace* (agree conditions for peace). ⇒ maker. **3** *tr.v* (used with many nouns to produce a meaning that is the same as the verb from which the noun is formed): *make an agreement* (= agree); *make an application* (= apply); *make an attempt* (= attempt); *make a decision* (= decide); *make a success of s.t* (= succeed in s.t). For other examples ⇒ the noun, e.g *allowance, appearance, arrangement, bid, fuss, love, move, note, offer, promise, run, speech, suggestion, will.* **4** *tr.v* (usu *— (s.o) s.t*) cause (s.o) to be, become or seem (s.t): *The meal made her ill. The committee made Linda chairperson. You've made me very happy. What*

makes you so sure that you're right? **5** *tr.v* (usu *— s.t do s.t*) cause (s.t to happen): *Water makes iron rust. The photograph makes my nose look big. How do I make this radio work?* **6** *tr.v* (usu *— s.o do s.t*) force, persuade, (s.o to do s.t): *He made her come although she did not want to. Don't make me laugh!* **7** *tr.v* (usu *— s.t s.t*) calculate (s.t to be s.t); work out (an amount) as an answer: *What time do you make it? What do you make the time? What size do you make this room?* **8** *tr.v* add up to (s.t); equal (s.t): *That makes four biscuits he's eaten. 5 and 2 make 7. A hundred centimetres make a metre.* **9** *tr.v* earn, gain, (money): *I make £100 a week. We hope to make a profit next year but this year we made a loss.* **10** *tr.v* gain (a position, place, rank etc): *He made his place in the team by working hard. He made captain of the team. At last she's made her mark/name/reputation as a writer* (is considered to be a good writer). **11** *tr.v* have, provide, (the right qualities for) (s.o/s.t): *This box will make a useful container. Will he make a good husband? This book makes good reading.* **12** *tr.v* (*informal*) have a quality that produces a very good effect on (s.t): *Those curtains really make this room.* **13** *tr.v* arrive at, reach, (s.w): *They hope to make Paris by tonight. Can you make it for dinner tomorrow?* **14** *tr.v* (sport, esp cricket[1]) score (s.t): *I made 121 runs yesterday.*

have s.t made ⇒ have(8). **have (got) it made** ⇒ have(*tr.v*).

ˌmade to ˈmeasure ⇒ measure(*n*).

make after s.o/s.t run towards s.o/s.t and try to catch her/him/it: *She made after me with a knife.*

make as if to do s.t act as if one is going to do s.t: *She made as if to leave the room.*

make away/off with s.t steal s.t and run: *Someone has made off with my watch.*

make a/one's/the bed ⇒ bed(*n*), unmade.

make s.o's blood boil ⇒ blood.

make or break be either very successful or very unsuccessful.

make certain (of s.t, that . . .) ⇒ certain(*adj*).

make s.o's day ⇒ day.

make s.t do; make do (with s.t) manage by using s.t although it may not be enough, ideal etc: *Can you make this bread do until I've been shopping? She'll have to make do with these pens for the moment.*

make (both) ends meet ⇒ end(*n*).

make a face; make faces ⇒ face(*n*).

make for s.o move towards s.o in order to attack her/him: *The dog made for me as I opened the gate.* **make for s.t** (a) move towards s.t in order to escape: *The prisoners made for the open door.* (b) cause s.t to be possible: *Travelling makes for better international understanding.* **make for s.w** go/travel towards s.w: *They were making for Paris when their car broke down.*

make a fortune ⇒ fortune.

make s.t from s.t ⇒ make(2), make s.t (out) of s.t.

make fun of s.o/s.t ⇒ fun.

make a fuss (about s.o/s.t); make a fuss of s.o/s.t ⇒ fuss(*n*).

make s.t go cause s.t, e.g an engine, car, to start, work properly: *I can't make this toy go; it needs a new* battery[2].

make s.t go round cause s.t to be enough when sharing: *I've added more water to make the soup go round.*

make good; **make good s.t** ⇨ good(*adj*).

make the grade ⇨ grade(*n*).

make a habit of (doing) s.t ⇨ habit.

make s.o's hair stand on end ⇨ hair.

make s.o/s.t into s.o/s.t cause s.o/s.t to change and become s.o/s.t different: *Being poor has made him into a thief. We can easily make these curtains into cushions.*

make it (*informal*) (**a**) be successful: *If you work hard enough, you'll make it.* ⇨ have (got) it made (⇨ have). (**b**) manage to get to s.t: *The party starts at 8. Can you make it?*

make a killing (by) (doing s.t) ⇨ killing(*n*).

make a living (as s.o; at/by/out of s.t) ⇨ living(3).

make a man of s.o ⇨ man(*n*).

make a mess (of s.t) ⇨ mess(*n*).

make s.t of s.t consider s.t to be, to explain, s.t: *What do you make of these strange marks?* ⇨ make s.t (out) of s.t.

make off with s.t ⇨ make away/off with s.t.

make s.t on s.t earn, gain, money as a profit on s.t: *He made £100 on the sale of his car. I made £10 on that bet*(1).

make out (as s.o) (*informal*) be successful (as s.o): *How is Anne making out (as a doctor)?*

make s.o/s.t out (**a**) be able to see, identify s.o/s.t (in bad light etc): *I couldn't make him out from such a distance.* (**b**) be able to understand s.o/s.t: *He was such a quiet and reserved person that I couldn't make him out.* **make s.t (out) of s.t** produce s.t using s.t as material: *It's made of plastic. He made the chair out of an old box.* ⇨ make s.t from s.t. **make s.t out to be s.t** claim that s.t is true, exists etc: *Air travel is not as exciting as everyone makes it out to be.* **make (out) a case (against/for s.o/s.t)** ⇨ case¹.

make s.t over to s.o change money, property, to s.o else's ownership: *The house was made over to his daughter.*

make a packet ⇨ fortune.

make sense; **make sense (out) of s.t** ⇨ sense(*n*).

make sure (of s.t, that . . .) ⇨ sure(*adj*).

make (oneself/s.o/s.t) up (as s.o/s.t) use cosmetics to change or improve oneself's/s.o's appearance, face etc: *He made himself up as a clown*(1). *Have I time to make up before breakfast?* ⇨ made-up(2), make-up(1). **make s.t up** (**a**) invent a story, excuse etc: *John made up a story about his mother being an actress. Don't believe him as he has made it all up.* ⇨ made-up(1). (**b**) compose a piece of music: *He made the tune up out of his head.* (**c**) form the whole or part of s.t: *Foreign students make up most of the class* (or *The class is made up mostly of foreign students*). ⇨ make-up(2). (**d**) prepare a mixture: *The chemist made up a medicine for my cold.* (**e**) complete what is left, what remains: *If you save £10, I'll make up the rest. He had several metres to make up on the leaders of the race.* **make up a/the fire** ⇨ fire. **make up one's mind (about s.o/s.t, to do s.t)** ⇨ mind¹. **make up for s.t** be a suitable replacement for s.t: *Money cannot make up for having one's son killed in a car accident. How can I make up for my bad behaviour?* **make up (for) lost time** ⇨ time(*n*). **make s.t up into s.t** shape, reorganize, material into s.t: *I made up the cloth into a dress.* **make up to s.o** (*informal*) be pleasant to s.o in order to get s.t: *A man should not make up to his secretary.* **make it up (to s.o)** (*informal*) do s.t for s.o, give s.t to s.o, because of s.t he/she has suffered, lost etc: *I'm sorry I can't take you to Athens but I'll make it up to you soon.* **make (it) up (with s.o)** (*informal*) end a quarrel (with s.o): *Let's make (it) up and be friends again. Have you made it up with Emma?*

make with s.t (*slang*) (usu as an order) produce s.t: *Make with the food — we're starving!*

‚made-'up *adj* **1** (of an excuse etc) imagined or invented: *a made-up story.* ⇨ make s.t up(a). **2** (of a face) changed by using cosmetics: *The actor was well made-up.* ⇨ make (oneself/s.o/s.t) up (as s.o/s.t), make-up(1).

'make-be‚lieve *u.n* (also *attrib*) untrue or imagined excuse, idea etc: *Children's stories are full of make-believe. They live in a make-believe world of fairies*(1) *and gnomes.*

'maker *n* **1** *c.n* (often as the second part of a word) person who makes(2) s.t: *a Swiss maker of clocks; a watchmaker; a dressmaker.* **2** unique *n* (usu *with capital* **M**) God: *one's Maker.*

makeshift /'meɪkˌʃɪft/ *adj* used (esp in an emergency) to replace another thing like it for a short time: *We used the school as a makeshift hospital during the storm.*

'make-‚up *u.n* **1** (art, skill of using) cosmetics: *do* (or *put on*) *one's make-up. Which kinds of make-up do you use?* ⇨ made-up(2), make (oneself/s.o/s.t) up (as s.o/s.t). **2** way that the parts of s.t are arranged: *the make-up of a collection/committee.* ⇨ make s.t up(c). **3** physical and mental qualities: *Being a liar is not part of his make-up.*

'making *def.n* **1** *be s.o in the making* be on the way to becoming s.o: *She's a world-class athlete in the making.* **2** *be the making of s.o* cause s.o to be successful or to become more grown up: *Time spent on a physical training course could be the making of him.* **3** *have the makings of s.o* be capable of becoming s.o: *He has the makings of a first-class student.*

maladjusted /ˌmælə'dʒʌstɪd/ *adj* (of a person) behaving in an awkward or unreasonable way because unable to accept social life and its responsibilities: *a maladjusted teenager.*

malady /'mælədɪ/ *c.n* (*pl* **-ies**) (*formal*) disease or illness.

malaise /mæ'leɪz/ *c/u.n* (example of the) feeling of being ill or uneasy(2).

malaria /mə'leərɪə/ *u.n* disease with periods of sweating and high temperature, carried by a kind of mosquito: *suffer from/with malaria.*

male /meɪl/ *adj* **1** of the sex that cannot give birth: *a male fish/frog/bird.* **2** of, for, a man or men: *a male hairdresser; male clothes.*
⊳ *c.n* **3** animal, insect etc that cannot give birth: *My cat is a male.* **4** male person: *courses for males and females.* ⇨ all-male.

‚male 'chauvi‚nism *u.n* belief by men that men are better than women.

‚male 'chauvi‚nist *c.n* man who believes in male chauvinism.

‚male ‚chauvi‚nist 'pig *c.n* (*abbr* **MCP, mcp**) (*derog*) very great male chauvinist.

malediction /ˌmælɪˈdɪkʃən/ c.n (formal) statement that curses s.o or accuses s.o of doing s.t wrong.

malefactor /ˈmælɪˌfæktə/ c.n criminal(3).

malevolent /məˈlevələnt/ adj (formal; derog) wanting to do a lot of harm to s.o: a malevolent neighbour who tried to poison our cat. **maˈlevolence** u.n. **maˈlevolently** adv.

malformation /ˌmælfɔːˈmeɪʃən/ c/u.n (often — of s.t) (example of) being or having the wrong shape or form (of one's body): a malformation of the left foot.

malformed /mælˈfɔːmd/ adj wrongly shaped or formed: a malformed finger.

malfunction /mælˈfʌŋkʃən/ c.n 1 example of a machine, engine etc going wrong, not working properly.

▷ intr.v 2 (of a machine, an engine) work badly or wrongly: The computer is malfunctioning.

malice /ˈmælɪs/ u.n (formal) hate towards, and wish to harm, s.o: be full of malice. **bear malice (towards s.o)** wish to do (s.o) harm: George has borne malice towards his boss for many years. **malice aforethought** (law) harmful act planned in advance (to injure or kill s.o).

malicious /məˈlɪʃəs/ adj (of a person, an act, a thought etc) feeling or showing malice: a malicious old man; malicious gossip(1)/thoughts.

malign /məˈlaɪn/ tr.v say bad and harmful things about (s.o/s.t) to others: She was maligned by her teacher in his report.

malignancy /məˈlɪgnənsɪ/, **malignity** /məˈlɪgnɪtɪ/ u.n malignant condition.

malignant /məˈlɪgnənt/ adj (of a disease) very dangerous and uncontrollable: malignant cancer(1).

malinger /məˈlɪŋgə/ intr.v behave as if one is ill in order to avoid having to do s.t: malinger in bed to escape school sports day. **maˈlingerer** c.n person who malingers. **maˈlingering** u.n act of a malingerer: Stop all this malingering!

mall /mɔːl, mæl/ c.n 1 a street, often covered and between buildings, with large shops: a shopping mall. 2 wide avenue: Pall Mall /mæl/ (in London).

mallard /ˈmælɑːd/ c.n kind of wild duck.

malleable /ˈmælɪəbl/ adj 1 (of a substance, esp metal) able to be given a different shape by beating. 2 (fig) (of a person) able to change easily to new conditions: A malleable person can live and work anywhere. **malleability** /ˌmælɪəˈbɪlɪtɪ/ u.n.

mallet /ˈmælɪt/ c.n tool like a hammer but with a large, usu wooden, head.

malnutrition /ˌmælnjuːˈtrɪʃən/ u.n condition of having too little food or the wrong balance of food, causing ill health: Thousands of children die of malnutrition every year.

malpractice /mælˈpræktɪs/ c/u.n (law) (example of) doing s.t that is against the law.

malt /mɔːlt/ u.n kind of grain, usu barley, prepared for making beer or whisky.

maltreat /mælˈtriːt/ tr.v (formal) treat (s.o, an animal) badly. **malˈtreatment** u.n.

mama /məˈmɑː/ c.n (becoming old use) (child's word for) mother. ⇒ ma.

mammal /ˈmæməl/ c.n kind of animal of which the female can produce milk for its young: People, monkeys, cows, dogs and whales are all mammals.

mammary /ˈmæmərɪ/ adj of the female breast(1): A mammary gland produces and stores milk in female mammals.

mammoth /ˈmæməθ/ adj 1 very large or important: a mammoth shopping centre; a problem of mammoth importance.

▷ c.n 2 kind of hairy elephant that is no longer in existence.

man /mæn/ n (pl men /men/) 1 c.n grown-up male person: Men and women of all ages visited the exhibition(1). 2 c.n person, male or female: Men are the guardians(2) of life on earth. 3 c.n male person in the army, navy or airforce who is not an officer: the captain and his men. 4 c.n (informal) expression of friendship between males: Hi, man! 5 unique n every person; all people: Man is mortal(1). **as well as the next man** in a way that is as good as everybody else: I can cook a meal as well as the next man. **be a man** (usu as an order) behave as a man(1) should: Stop crying about your stolen bicycle and be a man. ⇒ manly. **a family man** ⇒ family. **one's fellow man** ⇒ fellow(1). **man and boy** from (one's) days as a child until the time one is an adult: Paul's been interested in trains for years, man and boy. **the (best, right, wrong etc) man for the job** the person who can do s.t (well etc): He's just the man for the job. **make a man of s.o** help a young male person to be a man: A month camping in the snow ought to make a man of you. **the man in the street** (general example of) an ordinary person: What is the man in the street's opinion of trade unions? **no-man's land** ⇒ no. **the odd man out** ⇒ odd. **a man of one's word** a person who carries out his promises. **may the best man win** (used before the start of a competition to show one has no particular interest in who wins): OK, let's begin the race — and may the best man win! **to a man** with the agreement of everybody: They voted to a man to accept the proposal. **to the last man** until every person is/was killed: We shall fight to the last man.

▷ tr.v (-nn-) 6 provide (s.t) with men(1,3): We must man the ship/defences. Do we have enough trained people to man all the machinery? 7 (take a position and) work (a machine): I've been manning this machine all week.

-man /-mən/ c.n (pl -men /-mən/) man(1) with the job etc shown by the first part of the word: a workman/policeman/sportsman.

ˌman-atˈarms c.n (old use) soldier.

ˈman-ˌeater c.n animal that eats human flesh: Some tigers and sharks are man-eaters.

ˈman-ˌeating adj (usu attrib): man-eating sharks(1).

ˌmanˈhandle tr.v 1 hold or push (s.o) roughly: Sometimes I do not like the way parents manhandle their children. 2 move (s.t) by pulling and/or pushing it with one's hands, usu when this is not the normal thing to do: We had to manhandle the car when it got stuck in the mud.

ˈman,hole c.n opening for a worker to get inside an underground passage.

ˈmanhood u.n 1 time or state of being a man(1) after one is no longer a child: reach manhood. 2 male qualities such as physical strength and courage: *Is manhood necessary in the modern army?* ⇨ womanhood.

'man,hour *c.n* work completed by one person in one hour: *How many manhours will it take to do the job?*

'man,hunt *c.n* organized hunt (for s.o, esp a criminal): *The police organized a large manhunt for the escaped murderer.*

man'kind *unique n* people in general. ⇨ womankind.

'manliness *u.n* manly qualities.

'manly *adj* (*-ier, -iest*) having male qualities such as physical strength and courage: *manly behaviour.* Compare mannish. Opposite unmanly.

,man'made *adj* **1** produced by men(2): *Manmade materials are now used to manufacture cars.* Plastics *are manmade.* **2** produced using people and not machines. Compare factory-made, handmade.

manned *adj* (usu of a spacecraft) with people on board: *a manned* capsule(2). Opposite unmanned. ⇨ overmanned, undermanned.

'mannish *adj* (of a woman) having an appearance or qualities like a man(1).

'mannishly *adv.* **'mannishness** *u.n.*

,man of the 'world *c.n* man with a lot of experience of life, business etc. ⇨ woman of the world.

'man,power *u.n* **1** physical strength provided by men(1): *use manpower to lift the car back onto the road.* **2** number of people ready to work, do a duty etc: *We need more manpower in the building industry.*

'man,servant *c.n* male servant.

'man,size *adj* (also **'man,sized**) **1** of a size suitable for a man(1): *a mansized meal/* tissue(3). **2** very big: *a mansize problem.*

'man,slaughter *u.n* (*law*) killing of s.o without planning or wanting to do so: *A person who kills a person in a car accident may be guilty of manslaughter.*

,man-to-'man *adj* (of a conversation) speaking openly about s.t without keeping anything back: *man-to-man talks between father and son.* ⇨ woman-to-woman.

manacle /'mænəkl/ *c.n* **1** (often *pl*) chain used to tie the hands or feet together.

▷ *tr.v* **2** put manacles on (s.o): *The prisoner was manacled as they led him to the police van.*

manage /'mænɪdʒ/ *v* **1** *tr.v* control, be in charge of, (s.o/s.t): *manage a business/shop/ football team. I use a computer to manage our household accounts.* **2** *tr/intr.v* (often — *to do* s.t) be able (to do s.t); be successful (at doing s.t): *We tried but we couldn't manage to get the table through the doorway. Even though Sue was getting old she managed a trip to Australia.* **3** *intr.v* continue to do s.t, esp to live, even though there is difficulty: *How can anyone manage on £50 a week? I can't manage without you.* **4** *tr.v* be able to attend (s.t): *Can you manage a meeting next week?* **5** *tr.v* (*informal*) be able to have, eat etc (s.t): *We can manage one more passenger only. Could you manage another potato?*

manageability /,mænɪdʒə'bɪlɪtɪ/ *u.n* fact or state of being manageable.

manageable /'mænɪdʒəbl/ *adj* Opposite unmanageable. **1** able to be controlled: *I'm not willing to take the dog with us until she is more* manageable. **2** able to be dealt with: *Such a large amount of work is not manageable by one person.*

management /'mænɪdʒmənt/ *n* **1** *c/def/ def.pl.n* (collective name for the) people in control of an organization, department, business etc: *We have a sympathetic management. The management has/have decided to increase our wages.* **2** *u.n* science, method of managing(1): *Management has changed a lot since the introduction of computers.* **be under new management** have new owners or new people in control. **under the management of s.o/s.t** managed(1) by s.o/ s.t.

'manager *c.n* **1** (*written abbr Mgr*) person in control of an organization, department, business etc. **2** person who looks after the financial affairs and organization of a professional athlete, singer, player, team etc: *a football team manager.* **3** person with responsibility for the general organization of s.t: *He's the best manager of household expenses that I know.*

manageress /,mænɪdʒə'res/ *c.n* woman who manages(1) a shop, restaurant, factory department etc.

managerial /,mænɪ'dʒɪərɪəl/ *attrib.adj* of or referring to a manager or the responsibilities, activities etc of a manager: *managerial power/ responsibility/* methods.

,managing di'rector *c.n* (*abbr MD*) chief person who manages a company, business etc.

mandarin /'mændərɪn/ *n* **1** *c.n* (also *attrib*) (tree with a) kind of fruit like a tangerine(1): *mandarin oranges.* **2** *c.n* official with power that is considered to be too great for political control: *the mandarins who control state industries.*

mandate /'mændeɪt/ *c.n* **1** official order or instruction: *They have a mandate to improve* productivity *in the factory.* **2** authority(3) or support given by voters to a political party, trade union etc to carry out its policies(1): *We have (been given) a mandate to improve education and increase employment.*

▷ *tr.v* **3** give a mandate(1,2) to (s.o): *They were mandated at the conference to accept the wage offer.* **4** give a country official rights to manage(1) (another country) (not done since 1966): *South West Africa was mandated to South Africa in 1920.*

mandatory /'mændətrɪ/ *adj* **1** having the official powers of a mandate(1,2): *mandatory authority.* **2** (of an order, decision etc) that must be carried out or accepted: *a mandatory decision by the union to strike. The use of* safety belts *in cars is mandatory.*

mandible /'mændɪbl/ *c.n* **1** lower jaw(1) in people and animals. **2** (usu *pl*) one of two parts of the head of insects etc used for biting and breaking food. **3** (usu *pl*) one of two parts of a bird's beak.

mandolin /,mændə'lɪn/ *c.n* kind of musical instrument with eight strings and a body like half a ball.

mane /meɪn/ *c.n* set of long hair on the neck of a horse or lion.

man-eater, man-eating ⇨ man.

maneuver ⇨ manoeuvre.

manganese /'mæŋɡə,niːz/ *u.n* hard, light grey metal used to make steel. *chem.symb* Mn.

mange /meɪndʒ/ *u.n* kind of skin disorder(3) that attacks animals, esp cats and dogs, causing itching and loss of hair.

mangy /'meɪndʒɪ/ *adj* (*-ier, -iest*) suffering from mange.

manger /'meɪndʒə/ *c.n* long box used to hold food for cattle or horses. **dog in the manger** (*derog*; *fig*) person who refuses to allow s.o to have or use s.t that is of no use to herself/ himself.

mangle /'mæŋgl/ *c.n* 1 machine with two rollers(1) used to press water out of clothes etc.
▷ *tr.v* 2 damage, destroy, (s.o/s.t) by pressing, tearing etc: *His arm was mangled in the machine.*

mango /'mæŋgəʊ/ *c/u.n* (*pl -es*) (also *attrib*) large tropical fruit with bright yellow-orange flesh round a large flat stone; it grows on a mango tree.

mangrove /'mæŋgrəʊv/ *c.n* (also *attrib*) tree growing in mud or shallow water along coasts(1) and large rivers in hot countries, with many long roots above the water: *mangrove* swamps(1).

manhandle, manhole, manhood, manhour, manhunt ⇒ man.

mania /'meɪnɪə/ *u.n* mental disorder producing violent behaviour and excitement. **have a mania for s.t** (*fig*) have an extreme liking, desire, for s.t: *I have a mania for chocolates.*

maniac /'meɪnɪˌæk/ *c.n* 1 person who is suffering from a form of mania(1). 2 (*informal*) person who has an extreme liking or desire for s.t: *He's a maniac for ice-cream.* 3 (*derog*; *informal*) person who behaves in a wild and uncontrolled way: *Don't try to persuade Fred — he's a maniac and will probably hit you.*

maniacal /mə'naɪəkl/ *adj* of a maniac or her/ his behaviour: *a maniacal temper.*

manic /'mænɪk/ *adj* 1 of, affected by, mania.
▷ *c.n* 2 person suffering from mania.

,manic-de'pression *u.n* mental disorder producing periods of extreme sadness and then ones of extreme excitement.

,manic-de'pressive *c.n* person suffering from manic-depression.

manicure /'mænɪˌkjʊə/ *c/u.n* 1 (example of) cutting, polishing and shaping the fingernails: *have a manicure.*
▷ *tr.v* 2 cut, polish and shape (fingernails).

manicurist /'mænɪˌkjʊərɪst/ *c.n* person whose job is to manicure (s.t).

manifest /'mænɪˌfest/ *adj* 1 (*formal*) (of the result or kind of behaviour) very clear: *a manifest lie. Their deceit was manifest.*
▷ *c.n* 2 (*commerce*) list of goods etc on a ship, aircraft, train etc: *Does this* item *appear on the ship's manifest?*
▷ *v* (*formal*) 3 *tr.v* show (s.t) very clearly: *He manifested his deep personal sadness. Her love for David was manifested in her smile.* 4 *intr.v* (of a ghost(1) etc) appear: *The dead woman manifested in the room.*

manifestation /ˌmænɪfe'steɪʃən/ *c/u.n.*

manifesto /ˌmænɪ'festəʊ/ *c.n* (*pl -(e)s*) written statement of aims, beliefs, policies(1) etc, esp of a political group.

manifold /'mænɪˌfəʊld/ *adj* 1 (*formal*) of many kinds, uses etc: *manifold abilities/ excuses.*
▷ *c.n* 2 (*technical*) pipe etc with many branches

used to collect and send a gas in many directions: *an* exhaust(1) *manifold of a car.*

manila /mə'nɪlə/ *u.n* (also *attrib*) (also **ma'nilla**) kind of strong brown paper used for envelopes and wrapping paper: *manila envelopes.*

manipulate /mə'nɪpjʊˌleɪt/ *tr.v* 1 control and use (s.t) with the hands: *manipulate an electric* drill(1). 2 (usu *derog*) use, influence or manage(1) (s.o/s.t) well, esp to one's own advantage: *manipulate a committee.*

manipulation /məˌnɪpjʊ'leɪʃən/ *u.n.*

manipulative /mə'nɪpjʊlətɪv/ *adj* (usu *derog*) (of a person, behaviour etc) able to manipulate(2) s.o/s.t well.

mankind, manliness, manly, manmade, manned ⇒ man.

mannequin /'mænɪkɪn/ *c.n* (also *attrib*) man, woman, employed to wear new clothes in order to show them to buyers etc.

manner /'mænə/ *n* 1 *c.n* way in which s.t is done or s.t happens: *Don't speak to me in that manner. I don't like his manner of doing things. Don't hold the records in that manner, please.* 2 *sing.n* way in which a person acts, behaves, speaks etc: *She has such a rude manner. It wasn't what he said that annoyed me, but his manner made me so angry.* Compare manners. 3 *c.n* style of writing, painting, building etc: *I learnt to weave in the manner of the ancient Arabs.* 4 *c.n* (*old use*) kind: *What manner of leader is she?* **all manner of s.t** many different kinds of s.t: *The hospital can deal with all manner of diseases.* **by no**, **not by any**, **manner of means** not at all; definitely not: *I am by no manner of means pleased with your work this year. 'Would you agree to becoming chairman?' — 'Not by any manner of means!'* Compare by no means (⇒ means). **in a manner of speaking** in a certain way; which can almost or just be described in that way: *'Are you a teacher, then?' — 'Well, in a manner of speaking, but I don't teach in a school.'* **mend one's manners** ⇒ mend (*v*).

'mannered *adj* (*derog*; *formal*) (of a way of speaking, behaving, etc) unnatural: *He speaks in a very mannered style.*

-mannered *adj* having the manners shown by the first part of the word: *a bad-/ill-/well-mannered child.*

'manne,rism *c.n* unusual habit in the way a person acts, speaks, moves etc: *She's a very nice person but she has the funniest mannerisms — she holds her nose when she's thinking!*

'manners *pl.n* set of rules for accepted polite social behaviour: *He has no/bad/good manners. He has excellent table manners.*

mannish(ly/ness) ⇒ man.

manoeuvre /mə'nuːvə/ *c.n* (US **ma'neuver**) 1 (often *pl*) (planned) movement or set of movements (often of an army and army vehicles) for training or any other purpose: *Don't worry about loud noises in the night; the army uses a field near here for its manoeuvres. I had to do some quite complicated manoeuvres during my driving test.* 2 act of using one's skill or ability, often secretly (in order to get s.t): *It took several manoeuvres on my part before I managed to get the job.*
▷ *tr/intr.v* 3 (cause (s.o/s.t) to) move (s.w) through complicated stages requiring effort, skill: *She manoeuvred the car slowly into the space.* 4 use

a manoeuvre(2) in order to get what one wants, to persuade (s.o into doing s.t): *He manoeuvred her into agreeing with his plan.* **manoeuvre (s.o/s.t, one's way) around**, **through (s.t)** move skilfully in order to avoid (s.t): *You'll have to manoeuvre (yourself/your way) around all the luggage, I'm afraid.*

ma'noeuvrable *adj* (US **ma'neuvrable**) able to be moved (around) easily.

manoeuvrability /mə,nu:vrə'bɪlɪtɪ/ *u.n* (US **ma,neuvra'bility**) condition of being able to be directed or moved about easily: *My new car has excellent manoeuvrability on narrow roads.*

manor /'mænə/ *c.n* **1** (also **'manor ,house**) large house, usu surrounded by a large area of land. **2** (in history) large area of land occupied by the workers who paid rent and taxes to the owner in the form of their services and part of their crop.

manorial /mə'nɔ:rɪəl/ *adj.*

manpower, manservant ⇒ man.

mansion /'mænʃən/ *c.n* very large house.

'mansions *pl.n* (with capital **M** in names) (name of a) block of flats: *She's moving into Grosvenor Mansions.*

mansize(d), manslaughter ⇒ man.

mantel /'mæntl/ *c.n* structure(2) round the opening of a fireplace.

'mantel,piece *c.n* part of a mantel that forms a shelf above the fireplace: *Every year we put our Christmas cards on the mantelpiece.*

mantis /'mæntɪs/ *c.n* ⇒ praying mantis.

mantle /'mæntl/ *c.n* **1** very thin net in a gas or oil lamp that shines and provides light when lit. **2** (*fig*) (often — of s.t) thing that covers s.t completely (and is made of s.t): *The fields were hidden under a mantle of fog.*

manual /'mænjʊəl/ *adj* **1** of or using the hands: *manual work*; *a manual worker.* **2** operated by hand: *Is your new car* automatic(1) *or manual?*

▷ *c.n* **3** book containing information on the way s.t works, how to do s.t etc: *a car manual*; *an* instruction *manual.* **4** car with manual(2) gears(1). Compare automatic(4).

'manually *adv.*

manufacture /,mænjʊ'fæktʃə/ *n* **1** *u.n* production of goods for sale, usu by machine: *They're building a new factory for the manufacture of radios and televisions.* **2** *c.n* (usu *pl*) thing that is produced, usu by machines: *The government must give money to encourage local manufactures.*

▷ *tr.v* **3** produce (goods) by machine in large quantities: *This factory manufactures furniture. Where was this manufactured?* **4** invent (an excuse, a reason or story that is not true): *He manufactured a story about having to visit a sick aunt so that he wouldn't have to go to the meeting.*

,manu'facturer *c.n* person, company etc who/ that manufactures(3) s.t: *a furniture manufacturer.*

manure /mə'njʊə/ *u.n* **1** waste products from animals sometimes mixed with hay and added to soil to make it richer and healthier: *horse manure. It is important to add manure to the soil at the end of each growing season.*

▷ *tr.v* **2** spread manure(1) over (soil) (and usu dig it into the soil): *We manure our fields twice a year.*

manuscript /'mænjʊ,skrɪpt/ *c.n* (abbr **ms**, *pl*

mss) written or typed material prepared for (the printing of) a book. Compare typescript.

many /'menɪ/ *det* **1** a large number of: *Many families live in this street. I've been there many times. Not many people believe him. Don't eat too many cakes.* Compare a lot of, much(5). **a good many (s.o/s.t)** ⇒ good(17). **a great many (s.o/ s.t)** a very large number (of s.t): *There are a great many jobs to be done.* **many a s.o/s.t** a large number of people, things, times, occasions etc: *Many a day I've wondered where you are.* **(not) in so many words** ⇒ word(*n*).

▷ *pron* **2** (often — of s.o/s.t) a large number (of people, things): *Many of us survived the train crash. He used to have a big collection but now there are not many left.* Compare a lot of, much(6). *How many have you got?* **one as many again** the same number again. **many's the time that/when . . .** ⇒ time(*n*). **one (s.t) too many**; **one too many (of s.t) (for s.o)** more than is acceptable, healthy etc: *He's had one (drink) too many. I've listened to one too many of your insults — I'm leaving.*

▷ *def.pl.n* **3** the largest number of people: *The many are ruled by the few.*

,many-'sided *adj* **1** having a large number of sides: *a many-sided shape.* **2** having a large number of different considerations, parts: *a many-sided discussion. The attitudes towards the bomb are many-sided.*

map /mæp/ *c.n* **1** picture representing the surface of the earth and showing particular information, e.g roads, railways, rivers, towns, height of the land above sea level: *Let's buy a map of Europe and plan a holiday. You'll need a street map to help you find your way around London. Can you find this road on the map?* **2** drawing representing the sky, e.g the moon, stars, planets etc. **off the map** (a) not local. (b) no longer important. **put s.t on the map** cause s.t to become known or important: *The success of our football team has really put our town on the map.*

▷ *tr.v* (-pp-) **3** make a map(1) of (s.w): *Many people have tried to map Central Africa but there are many difficulties.* **map s.t out** plan a route(1), events, activities etc: *We'll need to meet to map out the weekend's events.*

'map-,reader *c.n* person who can understand, or who has the job of understanding, maps.

'map-,reading *u.n* (usu *give/take a* —) place on a map that shows where one is.

maple /'meɪpl/ *n* **1** *c.n* kind of tree with hard wood used for furniture and producing a substance made into a sweet liquid. **2** *u.n* (also *attrib*) wood of this tree.

,maple 'sugar *u.n* sugar made from the juices of one kind of maple(1).

,maple 'syrup *u.n* sweet liquid made from the juices of one kind of maple(1).

mar /mɑ:/ *tr.v* (-rr-) spoil, damage, (the beauty, appearance, happiness etc of s.o/s.t): *The new road mars the view. It seemed as if nothing could mar their happiness.*

marathon /'mærəθən/ *n* **1** *c/def.n* running race of 42 km 195 m (26 miles 385 yards): *I'm training for the London marathon.* **2** *c.n* (also *attrib*) (*fig*) activity that continues for a long time and is usually very tiring: *The job turned out to be a real marathon. It was a marathon performance.*

maraud /mə'rɔ:d/ *tr/intr.v* move around and

attack (people, places) and steal from (them): *They have formed into small groups and are marauding villages and frightening the people off their land.*

ma'rauder *c.n* person or animal who/that marauds.

marble /'mɑːbl/ *n* **1** *u.n* (also *attrib*) kind of very hard stone, often with coloured patterns, used in building and sculpturing(3) because it polishes well: *a marble table/statue. We found an old piece of marble to use as a table top in the kitchen.* **2** *c.n* small glass ball with different colours inside used as a toy: *I've got more marbles than you.* **lose one's marbles** (*fig*; *informal*) become mad: *Jane has really lost her marbles!*

'marbled *adj* decorated with colours and patterns like marble(1): *marbled paper.*

March /mɑːtʃ/ *c/unique n* (also *attrib*) (*written abbr* Mar) 3rd month of the year: *There are thirty-one days in March. I saw him on March 1* (say 'March the first' or 'the first of March'). *It was a pleasant March evening.* (**as**) **mad as a March hare** ⇒ mad.

march /mɑːtʃ/ *n* **1** *c.n* act of walking with regular steps: *We're going on a 10 kilometre march tomorrow.* **2** *c.n* walk by a large number of people from one place to another in order to express an opinion about s.t: *Over 10 000 people took part in the march in support of more jobs.* **3** *def.n* (*formal*) regular movement forward: *the march of time.* **4** *c.n* piece of music with a regular beat suitable for marching(5): *The band played a march.* **on the march** (**a**) moving forward: *The armies are on the march.* (**b**) improving, progressing, quickly: *Technology is on the march.* **steal a march on s.o** do better than s.o by acting unexpectedly and quickly.

▷ *v* **5** *tr/intr.v* (cause (s.o) to) walk with regular steps like a soldier: *The soldiers marched past. After an argument with the attendant, he marched out angrily. She was marched off to the headmaster's office.* **6** *intr.v* move forward steadily: *Time marches on.* **Quick march!** command to soldiers to begin marching quickly.

'marcher *c.n* person who marches(5).

'marching ,orders *pl.n* (usu *get one's, give s.o their, —*) **1** official order to move from one place to another. **2** official order to leave one's job: *We gave him his marching orders and told him never to come back again.*

'march-,past *c.n* (usu *sing*) official march of soldiers past an important person or place.

marchioness /'mɑːʃənɪs/ *c.n* **1** woman who holds a position equal to a marquess. **2** woman who is a wife, widow of a marquess.

mare /meə/ *c.n* female horse or donkey.

margarine /ˌmɑːdʒə'riːn/ *u.n* food made from animal or vegetable fats used instead of butter: *Some people believe margarine is healthier than butter.*

marge /mɑːdʒ/ *u.n* (*informal*) margarine.

margin /'mɑːdʒɪn/ *c.n* **1** place along one or both edges of a page where there is no writing or printing. **2** (*formal*) edge or border around s.t: *Many different kinds of birds and animals live in the bushes that grow round the margin of the lake.* **3** amount (of time, money etc) that is extra, more than what is needed: *Give yourself a wide margin for error(2). Leave yourself a comfortable*

margin to work in so that you don't find yourself without money later. **4** (*commerce*) difference between the cost of buying and price of selling: *In some businesses the profit margin is very low on each article and sellers depend on quantities of sales for making money.* **5** score, amount etc that separates success from failure: *They won the match by a comfortable/narrow margin.*

marginal /'mɑːdʒɪnl/ *adj* **1** small and unimportant; hardly noticeable: *Improvement in your behaviour has been marginal — I expect you to try harder. There's been a marginal growth in our sales.* **2** where it is not clear which political party or candidate(1) is most popular: *The marginal seats will be decisive in the next election.*

'marginally *adv.*

marigold /'mærɪˌgəʊld/ *n* **1** *c.n* kind of golden or yellow garden flower. **2** *u.n* (also *attrib*) yellow colour.

marijuana /ˌmærɪ'wɑːnə/ *u.n* (also ˌmari-'huana) kind of plant dried and (usu) smoked in cigarettes to produce a pleasant feeling of excitement and happiness: *The sale of marijuana is illegal in many countries.*

marina /mə'riːnə/ *c.n* small harbour area for pleasure boats.

marinate /'mærɪˌneɪt/ *tr/intr.v* soak (food) in a marinade.

,mari'nade *c/u.n* sauce of spices, vinegar, wine etc in which meat etc is soaked before cooking.

marine /mə'riːn/ *attrib.adj* **1** of, by, in, from, the sea: *marine life.* **2** of ships, the navy etc: *marine law.*

▷ *n* **3** *u.n* shipping: *the merchant marine.* **4** *c.n* soldier on a ship: *My brother is a marine.*

mariner /'mærɪnə/ *c.n* sailor: *A master(1) mariner is, or has the right to be, a captain of a merchant ship.*

marionette /ˌmærɪə'net/ *c.n* kind of doll (puppet(1)) moved by strings.

marital /'mærɪtl/ *adj* of or referring to marriage: *Our marital problems began when my husband lost his job.*

maritime /'mærɪˌtaɪm/ *adj* (usu *attrib*) **1** of or referring to the sea, shipping etc: *maritime laws.* **2** having the sea very near and therefore concerned with activities of the sea: *Britain is no longer a great maritime nation.*

marjoram /'mɑːdʒərəm/ *u.n* kind of herb used in cooking and in herbal medicine: *Marjoram adds flavour to all meat dishes.*

mark /mɑːk/ *c.n* **1** spot, stain, tear etc that spoils the appearance of s.t: *Who made these dirty marks on my clean floor?* **2** spot on a person, animal, object, by which it can be recognized: *'Do you have any distinguishing marks?' 'I have a birthmark on my left leg.'* **3** sign that shows where a particular thing is or what a person must do at a particular place: *There's a mark on the map to show you where I live.* **4** sign that shows what a thing is and often the quality of the product: *My new washing machine has a wool mark so I can wash our jumpers in it.* **5** sign that shows what a thing has been used for, the way s.o feels, the quality of s.o's activities, intelligence, feelings, life etc: *He has the marks of suffering. This factory has the marks of good management. He bought her flowers as a mark of his love.* **6** number of points showing how well one has performed in an examination or test: *Who got the highest marks for mathematics?* **7** place that one is aiming for, e.g in sport: *You are a metre off the mark.* **8** (usu with a capital **M** and often with a number) name of a particular type of engine, car etc: *Have you seen the new Mark 10?* **be below**, **up to**, **the mark** be under/at the necessary standard: *Your work is not up to the mark.* **be quick/slow off the mark** (*fig*) understand or decide quickly/slowly: *You'll have to explain it again — he's rather slow off the mark. She's always ready with an amusing answer — she's quick off the mark.* (**fall**) **wide of the mark** (be) a long way from the truth, correct answer etc. (**get**, **give s.o**) **full marks** (**for** (**doing**) s.t) (**a**) (get etc) the highest possible number of points for an examination. (**b**) show one's admiration for an activity, effort, quality etc: *You certainly get full marks for trying.* **hit the mark** (*fig*) succeed in an attempt to do s.t etc: *I could see that my words had hit the mark as he went red.* **leave/make one's mark** (**as s.o**, **on s.t**) have a lasting effect (on s.t etc): *The earthquake will leave its mark on these people's lives. It's taken a long time but at last I'm beginning to make my mark as a journalist.* **miss the mark** (*fig*) not succeed in an attempt to do s.t: *I didn't think the play was very good — in fact I thought it missed the mark.* **On your marks** (**get set, go**)! (call from the starter(1) of a race that tells the runners to get into the starting position). **punctuation mark** ⇨ punctuation. **trademark** ⇨ trade. **up to the mark** good enough in quality of performance: *Your examination results are not quite up to the mark.*

▷ *v* **9** *tr/intr.v* (cause (s.t) to) become stained, spoilt: *The coffee you spilt has marked the cloth. This white carpet marks too easily.* **10** *tr.v* put a sign on (s.t) so that it can be recognized: *Please mark your name on your clothes.* **11** *tr.v* show (s.t) by putting a sign (at the place): *Please mark your choice with an X.* **12** *tr.v* show which answers are right and which wrong (in a piece of work) and give points, an alphabetical symbol etc, to show how well a student has done: *I've got two sets of school work to mark this weekend. He marked her essay(1) 9 out of 10.* **13** *tr.v* show, be a sign of, (s.o/s.t): *What are the qualities that mark a good captain? The invention of* plastic *marked the end of many uses for tin.* **14** *tr.v* have, show, an effect on (s.o/s.t): *This experience will mark Sally for the rest of her life.* **15** *tr.v* note (s.t) down; make a sign to help one remember (s.t): *Mark the date in your* diary. **16** *tr.v* (*sport*) keep close guard of (one member of the other team and her/his movements): *Please mark your opposite number closely.* **17** *tr.v* (*old use*) listen, pay attention, to (what s.o says): *Mark what I say. Mark my words — you'll fail the examination.*

mark s.t down reduce the price of s.t: *We are marking down all last year's stock for two weeks.* ⇨ markdown.

mark s.t off (**a**) put a sign next to a name etc for a particular reason, e.g to show s.t has been done: *Please mark off all the goods as they arrive so that we know what hasn't been sent.* (**b**) separate one thing from another: *Mark off the last week's work before you start today's.*

mark s.t out draw a line to show the boundary

of an area: *This weekend we'll mark out the area that needs digging.* **mark oneself/s.o out** (**for s.t**) show oneself able to succeed in, choose s.o for, (s.t in particular): *He was marked out for a career(1) on the stage from early in his life. She marked herself out for success.*

mark time ⇨ time(*n*).

mark s.t up increase the price of s.t: *Next year we'll mark up all our services.* ⇨ markup.

'**mark,down** *c.n* amount by which a price is reduced: *We will have a general markdown of 25% on all goods.*

marked *adj* **1** (usu *attrib*) clear; easily noticeable: *There has been a marked improvement in the weather. There has been a marked increase in prices over the last few years.* **2** (usu — by s.t) noticeable (because of s.t in particular): *His writing is marked by a certain* childishness.

markedly /'mɑːkɪdlɪ/ *adv* to a noticeable extent: *Their performance has improved markedly.*

ˌ**marked** '**man** *c.n* **1** person being hunted by an enemy: *If you tell the police what you have seen you will become a marked man and neither you nor your family will be safe.* **2** person whose reputation has been spoilt: *Ever since my political student years, I've been a marked man and I find it very difficult to be considered seriously for a job in government.*

'**marker** *c.n* **1** person or machine who/that keeps and reports the score in a game. **2** thing used to show the distance, position, of s.t: *You must drive from one marker to the next.* **3** person who marks(12) examination papers etc.

'**marking** *c.n* (often *pl*) pattern of colours, lines, spots etc on an animal, bird, car etc: *That bird has beautiful markings.*

'**marking** ˌ**ink** *u.n* ink used for putting one's name etc on cloth because it doesn't wash off easily.

'**marksman**, '**marks,woman** *c.n* (*pl* -**men**, -ˌ**women**) man, woman, skilled at aiming at a target with a gun, arrow etc.

'**marksman,ship** *u.n* quality of a person as a marksman or markswoman.

'**mark,up** *c.n* amount by which the price of s.t is increased, esp because of increased costs or to get extra profit.

market /'mɑːkɪt/ *n* **1** *c.n* public building or open place where people meet to buy and sell goods. **2** *c/unique n* (also *attrib*) occasion for people to meet to buy and sell goods, usu on a particular day in the week: *market day.* **3** *c/def.n* (condition of) trade, buying and selling of particular products as shown by the prices: *The market rose this morning and farmers were getting good prices for their potatoes.* **4** *c.n* (place where there is a) demand for particular goods: *Foreign markets will help us increase production. We have not yet tried all areas of the home market.* **corner the market** get enough of a commercial product, e.g materials, goods, to have control of the market(3) for it. **falling market** market(3) where the prices are dropping: *It's a good idea to buy in a falling market, but not to sell.* **in the market** (**for s.t**) ready to buy (s.t): *Are you in the market for old cookers?* **on the market** for sale: *Is the new model on the market yet?* **play the market** be in the business of buying and selling s.t, esp shares(3), to make profit. **price oneself/s.t out**

of the market ⇒ price(*v*). *rising market* market(3) where the prices are rising.

▷ *tr.v* **5** (try to) sell, find buyers for, (a product): *I travel all over the world to market our products.*

,**marketa'bility** *u.n* fact or state of being marketable.

'**marketable** *adj* wanted, needed by, the public; able to be sold: *It's no good producing something unless it's marketable.* Opposite unmarketable.

'**market ,day** *c.n* day of the week when there is a market(2).

'**marketer** *c.n* person or company who/that sells, finds markets(4) for, products.

,**market-'garden** *c.n* ground used for growing fruit and/or vegetables for sale.

,**market-'gardener** *c.n* person who grows fruit and/or vegetables for sale.

,**market-'gardening** *u.n* act, business, of growing fruit and/or vegetables for sale.

'**marketing** *u.n* (also *attrib*) (study of the) process, activities, that is/are important in successful selling: *new marketing methods. I used to be on the production side of the business but now find marketing more interesting.*

'**market ,place** *c.n* **1** (usu open) place in a town where a market(2) is held. **2** people who are likely to buy a product: *We must test our new product in the market place.*

'**market ,price** *c/def.n* price that people are willing to pay for s.t: *The market price of gold is very low at the moment.*

,**market re'search** *u.n* study of the reasons why people choose to buy certain products and not others.

,**market 'square** *c.n* open area in a town where a market(2) is held.

'**market ,town** *c.n* town that is or was a centre for farmers to bring their animals and products to sell or for a market(2).

,**market 'value** *c.n* price of s.t at a particular time: *Julia regularly checks the market value of her house although she does not want to sell it.*

marmalade /'mɑːmə,leɪd/ *u.n* kind of jam made from oranges, lemons or grapefruit.

marmoset /'mɑːmə,zet/ *c.n* one of many kinds of small monkey from South America which have thick hair and long tails.

marmot /'mɑːmət/ *c.n* kind of small animal of the squirrel family.

maroon[1] /mə'ruːn/ *adj* **1** having a dark brown-red colour.

▷ *c/u.n* **2** maroon[1](1) colour.

maroon[2] /mə'ruːn/ *tr.v* (usu passive) **1** leave (s.o) in a place without help: *I was marooned in London without a job and a place to live.* **2** put or leave (s.o) in a lonely place, esp an island, from which there is no escape: *We were marooned on an island for many months.*

marquee /mɑː'kiː/ *c.n* very large tent used for celebrations, particular occasions etc: *We hired a marquee for the party in the garden.*

marquess /'mɑːkwɪs/ *c.n* (with capital **M** in titles) **1** (UK) nobleman who is higher in rank than an earl but lower than a duke: *The Marquess of Salisbury.* **2** (also **marquis**) (outside UK) rank of a nobleman above a count(5). ⇒ marchioness.

marriage ⇒ marry.

marrow /'mærəʊ/ *n* **1** *u.n* (also *attrib*) soft substance in the hollow parts of bones: *bone*

marrow; *a marrow* transplant(2). **2** *c.n* (also ,**vegetable 'marrow**) large green vegetable with a thick skin and white flesh inside. **3** *u.n* (also *attrib*) this vegetable as food: *We're having marrow for dinner tonight.* **chilled to the marrow** extremely cold.

'**marrow,bone** *c.n* bone containing a lot of marrow(1), used for cooking.

'**marrow,fat** *c.n* (also ,**marrow,fat 'pea**) kind of extra large pea.

marry /'mærɪ/ *v* (-ies, -ied) **1** *tr.v* (of an official) unite (two people) as husband and wife in an official ceremony: *The priest who married us is an old friend of the family.* **2** *tr/intr.v* take (s.o) as a husband or wife: *She married someone she's only known for one month. When are you getting married?* **3** *tr.v* (often — *s.o* off) give a son as a husband, or daughter as a wife: *My mother wants to marry me (off) to a rich old man.*

marriage /'mærɪdʒ/ *n* **1** *c.n* (also *attrib*) official uniting of a man and woman by a legal and/or religious ceremony that makes them husband and wife: *a marriage ceremony. We decided not to have a church marriage.* **2** *c/u.n* (example of the) state of being united as husband and wife: *Our marriage didn't last very long.* **3** *c.n* close joining (of ideas etc): *Their partnership is a marriage of her originality and his practical ability.* **by marriage** because of a marriage: *She is a relation by marriage, not by blood.* **mixed marriage** (example of a) marriage(1) between two people of different races or religions.

marriageability /,mærɪdʒə'bɪlɪtɪ/ *u.n.*

marriageable /'mærɪdʒəbl/ *adj* ready or suitable for marriage, esp by being old enough: *She's not yet of marriageable age.*

'**marriage ,licence** *c.n* official paper stating that two people are legally married.

'**married** *adj* **1** having a husband or wife: *Are you married? Do you have any married children?* Opposite unmarried. **2** of marriage: *Our married life together was never happy.* Compare marital. **3** (*fig*) united to s.t as if it were a husband or wife: *She's married to the idea of becoming a doctor.*

'**married ,name** *c.n* woman's family name (her husband's family name) after she marries.

Mars /mɑːz/ *unique n* **1** fourth planet away from the sun. **2** (in Roman mythology) god of war.

Martian /'mɑːʃən/ *adj* **1** of or referring to Mars(1) or an imaginary person from Mars(1), as described in stories or science fiction: *the Martian climate.*

▷ *c.n* **2** Martian(1) person.

marsh /mɑːʃ/ *u.n* (area of) low wet land.

'**marshiness** *u.n* quality or state of being marshy.

'**marshy** *adj* (-ier, -iest) of, like a marsh; having many marshes: *Keep away from the area near the river because it's very marshy.*

marshal /'mɑːʃəl/ *c.n* (with capital **M** in names or titles) **1** officer in an army or airforce of the highest rank or one of the highest: Field Marshal; Air Marshal. **2** person who organizes or arranges ceremonies, people etc at a special event: *a marshal at a flower show*; *a traffic marshal at the scene of an accident.* **3** (UK) official in the royal household. **4** (US) head of a police or fire department.

▷ *tr.v* (-ll-, US -l-) **5** arrange, organize, (thoughts,

ideas, facts) into order: *I need time to marshal my thoughts on this matter.* **6** lead, show the way (to s.o), with ceremony: *He marshalled the winners in front of the president.*

'marshalling ,yard *c.n* place where railway carriages and/or goods trucks are cleaned, sorted and made up into trains.

marsupial /maː'sjuːpɪəl/ *c.n* (also *attrib*) one of a group of animals whose females have a pouch(2) to carry their young: *Most marsupials such as kangaroos and wombats are found in Australia.*

mart /maːt/ *c.n* place where particular things are sold: *a car mart.*

martial /maːʃəl/ *adj* (usu *attrib*) of or referring to fighting or war: *martial music.*

,martial 'arts *pl.n* group of kinds of self-defence learnt from Eastern countries and now practised as sports, e.g karate and judo.

,martial 'law *u.n* government by the army during wartime or when there are disturbances and ordinary laws are replaced: *The country was placed under martial law by the enemy.*

martin /ˈmaːtɪn/ *c.n* kind of bird of the swallow[1] family: *a house martin; a sand martin.*

martinet /ˌmaːtɪˈnet/ *c.n* (*derog; formal*) person who expects and demands strict discipline: *What that school needs is an understanding head teacher, not a martinet.*

martyr /ˈmaːtə/ *c.n* **1** person who dies or suffers greatly for her/his beliefs: *We learn about many martyrs in early* Christian(1) *history.* **be a martyr to s.t** suffer greatly and for a long time from a disease etc: *He's a martyr to pain.* **make a martyr of oneself/s.o** sacrifice oneself/s.o or one's/s.o's wishes in order to please others: *You're making a martyr of yourself — there's no need for you to paint the whole room.*
▷ *tr.v* **2** cause (s.o) to die or suffer because of her/his beliefs.

martyrdom /ˈmaːtədəm/ *u.n* death or suffering of a martyr(1).

marvel /ˈmaːvl/ *c.n* **1** thing that is astonishing, surprising, wonderful, (about s.t): *the marvels of nature/science/*technology. *How we escaped is still a marvel to me.* **2** person who is very good (at doing s.t) and deserves admiration: *He's a marvel in the kitchen. She's a marvel when it comes to mending things.* **3** (often — *of s.t*) perfect example (of s.t): *You're a marvel of good sense. Our new model will be a marvel of* technology. **do/work marvels** produce unusually good results: *The new medicine worked marvels.*
▷ *v* (-*ll-*, US -*l-*) **4** *intr.v* (often — *about/at s.o/s.t*) be very surprised and filled with wonder (about s.o/s.t): *She marvelled at his knowledge of literature.* **5** *tr.v* say (s.t) in a surprised way: *'How did you do it?' she marvelled.*

marvellous /ˈmaːvələs/ *adj* wonderful, esp when not expected: *We've had a marvellous day. What a marvellous view! It'll be marvellous to see you all again.*

'marvellously *adv.* ·

Marxism /ˈmaːksɪzəm/ *unique n* belief in and following of the economic(1) and political philosophy of Karl Marx, a German philosopher(1).

'Marxist *adj* **1** of the ideas of Karl Marx.
▷ *c.n* **2** person who believes in (and practises) Marxism.

marzipan /ˈmaːzɪˌpæn/ *u.n* mixture of sugar, eggs and almond powder, put round fruit cake, sweets etc.

masc *written abbr* masculine.

mascara /mæˈskaːrə/ *u.n* substance for colouring the eyelashes: *Do you use mascara?*

mascot /ˈmæskət/ *c.n* object, person or animal used to represent s.t, e.g a sports team, and considered to bring good luck: *That baby bear is the team mascot.*

masculine /ˈmæskjʊlɪn/ *adj* **1** (usu *attrib*) of boys and men: *masculine strength.* **2** suitable for, like, a boy or man: *masculine clothes.* **3** having the essential qualities of a boy or man. **4** (*grammar*) of the male form: *Masculine nouns and* pronouns include *'ox', 'his', 'he'.* Compare feminine.
▷ *def.n* **5** (written abbr *m*, *masc*) (*grammar*) male form: *The masculine of 'woman' is 'man'.*

masculinity /ˌmæskjʊˈlɪnɪtɪ/ *u.n* fact or state of being masculine(1).

maser /ˈmeɪzə/ *c.n* (*technical*) device used to produce microwaves(1) or make them larger. Compare laser.

mash /mæʃ/ *u.n* **1** cooked potatoes made into a soft mass: *sausages and mash.* **2** soft mixture of grain and water given to animals as food.
▷ *tr.v* **3** **mash s.t** (**up**) form potatoes etc into a mash: *mashed potato(es).*

mask /maːsk/ *c.n* **1** covering for the eyes or face, e.g at parties, to avoid being recognized etc and often showing another person's face or an animal. **2** covering for the mouth and nose, used by doctors etc to prevent the spread of diseases. **3** covering for the face, used to prevent s.o from breathing gas etc or from being injured. **4** ornament like a face: *an African mask.* **5** activity, expression, statement etc used to hide s.t: *Her tears were only a mask because she was pleased that he left her.* **6** = masque.
▷ *tr.v* **7** put a mask(1–3) on or over (one's face): *All the thieves were masked. Nurses are often masked in hospitals.* **8** hide (s.t, e.g a smell, one's feelings, an activity) with a different thing: *use scent to mask the bad smell; mask one's sadness with a brave smile.* ⇨ unmasked.

,masked 'ball *c.n* formal dance where guests wear masks(1).

'masking ,tape *u.n* sticky tape(1) used to cover a surface to protect it from dirt, light, paint etc.

masochism /ˈmæsəˌkɪzəm/ *u.n* abnormal condition of the mind in which s.o gets pleasure from feeling pain, being treated badly etc. Compare sadism.

'maso,chist *c.n* person suffering from masochism. Compare sadist.

,maso'chistically *adv.*

mason /ˈmeɪsn/ *c.n* **1** person whose job is to build with stone. **2** (often with capital **M**) = Freemason.

masonic /məˈsɒnɪk/ *adj* **1** of masons(1) or masonry. **2** of masons(2).

masonry /ˈmeɪsənrɪ/ *u.n* **1** job of a mason(1). **2** work, product, of a mason(1): *There is some excellent masonry in our church.*

masque /maːsk/ *c.n* (also **mask**) (music for a) dramatic entertainment with songs and dance in England about 400 years ago.

masquerade /ˌmæskəˈreɪd/ *c.n* **1** party or formal dance where guests wear masks(1) or strange clothes. **2** thing worn at a masquerade(1). **3** (*fig*) activity, expression, statement etc used to hide one's feelings, the truth etc: *His happiness was only a masquerade — privately he was very sad.*

▷ *intr.v* (often — *as s.o/s.t*) **4** take part in a masquerade(1) (as *s.o/s.t*). **5** deceive by using a masquerade(3): *He was masquerading as an explorer. She was masquerading under the name (of) Charlotte Bunn.*

,masque'rader *c.n* person who masquerades.

mass¹ /mæs/ *n* **1** *c.n* (large) amount of any substance without a particular shape: *a cloud mass*; *a mass of broken glass.* **2** *c.n* (also *attrib*) large number (of people/things in a group): *a mass of people/insects*; *a mass meeting*; *a mass outbreak of cholera.* **3** *u.n* (*technical*) amount of matter in s.t: *The mass of this ball is 2 kg.*

▷ *intr/tr.v* **4** form (s.o/s.t) into a mass¹(2): *They massed (their supporters) near the football ground.*

'masses *def.pl.n* ordinary people: *Does the government have the support of the masses?* **masses of s.o/s.t** (*informal*) large numbers/amounts of s.o/s.t: *He has masses of friends. We've masses of time before the film starts.*

,mass hy'steria *u.n* state in which a large number of people run, shout etc because of fear or excitement.

'massive *adj* extremely large: *a massive prison door*; *a massive amount of smoke*; *a massive increase in price.*

'massively *adv.* **'massiveness** *u.n.*

,mass 'media *def/def.pl.n* systems, e.g television, radio, newspapers, that can be used to give information to many people.

'mass ,noun *c.n* (*grammar*) word that names a mass¹(1) of a general substance: *'Land' is sometimes a mass noun but 'hill' is not.* ⇒ count(able)/ uncountable noun.

,mass-pro'duce *tr.v* make (a large number of the same object) using machines or organized workers.

,mass-pro'duction *u.n* (system of) mass-producing things.

mass² /mæs/ *n* (often with capital **M**) **1** *c/u.n* (in the Roman Catholic(1) Church) most important religious service: *go to mass*; *say mass. There are masses at 7, 8 and 10 o'clock on Sunday.* **2** *c.n* music and words used for (part of) a mass²(1): *Bach composed masses.* **high mass** ⇒ high.

massacre /'mæsəkə/ *c.n* **1** (example of a) cruel killing of a large number of people, animals etc: *The battle became a massacre.* **2** (*fig*) easy and complete defeat in a game or contest: *The result was a massacre for the English team.*

▷ *tr.v* **3** kill (a large number of people, animals): *The elephants were massacred by the hunters.* **4** (*fig*) defeat (s.o) easily and completely in a game or contest.

massage /'mæsɑːʒ/ *c/u.n* **1** (act of) rubbing parts of the body to exercise the muscles(1): *do massage*; *have/be given a massage*; *a face massage.*

▷ *tr.v* **2** perform a massage(1) on (s.o/s.t): *After massaging her back, my hands ached.*

masseur /mæ'sɜː/ *c.n* person whose job is to massage(2) s.o/s.t.

masseuse /mæ'sɜːz/ *c.n* woman whose job is to massage(2) s.o/s.t.

massive(ly/ness) ⇒ mass¹.

mast /mɑːst/ *c.n* upright pole¹ used to support the sails of a boat or a flag.

mastectomy /mæ'stektəmɪ/ *c/u.n* (*pl -ies*) (example of) cutting off a person's (usu woman's) breast(1) by a surgeon(1), or of removing (part of) what is inside it, because of disease.

master /'mɑːstə/ *c.n* **1** man who is in control of people, animals or things: *the master of a sailing ship. A dog must learn to obey its master.* ⇒ mistress(3). **2** man who teaches in a school: *the geography master.* ⇒ headmaster, mistress(1). **3** (often with capital **M**) person with a university degree that is higher than a Bachelor(2): *a Master of Surgery.* **4** (also *attrib*) skilled worker in a trade: *a master carpenter.* **5** artist, performer, object, of the highest standard: *an old master* (i.e an artist or picture from a long time ago of a very high standard); *a chess master* (i.e a player with a high international reputation). **6** man who is in control or gains control: *Who's the master in this family?* **7** (also *attrib*) original copy (of a letter, a report, a plan etc) from which others are made: *a master copy of an agreement.* **8** (often with capital **M**) title placed before the name of a boy. **be master of s.t** be in, keep control over, s.t: *be master of one's future.*

▷ *tr.v* **9** manage to avoid showing (one's feelings etc): *A child learns to master emotions(1).* **10** become able to do (s.t) by practising: *I have not mastered (the art of playing) the piano.*

'master ,bedroom *c/def.n* main bedroom, e.g for parents, in a house.

'master ,card *c.n* (*fig*) piece of information, way of acting etc that is one's best chance to win an argument, a contest etc: *At the point when it seemed he had failed, David played his master card and made a new offer that was impossible to refuse.*

'master ,craftsman *c.n* (*pl -men*) skilled worker at a craft(2).

'masterful *adj* **1** fond of acting as a master(1,6). **2** masterly.

'master ,key *c.n* key that is able to open many different locks.

'masterly *adj* showing great ability or skill: *a masterly demonstration(1) of how to cook.*

'master,mind *c.n* **1** person with great intelligence: *be a mastermind at/in mathematics.*

▷ *tr.v* **2** organize and control (an activity, esp a crime): *Who masterminded the train robbery?*

,Master of 'Arts *c.n* (*abbr MA*) (person with a) university degree in art subjects (languages, education, literature, history etc) that is higher than a Bachelor of Arts.

,master of 'ceremonies *c.n* (*pl masters of ceremonies*; *abbr MC*) person who manages a ceremony, formal dinner, entertainment.

,Master of 'Science *c.n* (*abbr MSc*) (person with a) university degree in science subjects (biology, chemistry, physics etc) that is higher than a Bachelor of Science.

'master,piece *n* **1** *c.n* excellent example of s.t: *This building/play is a masterpiece.* **2** *sing.n* most important or best work of an artist, architect(1), writer, actor etc: *This painting is his masterpiece.*

'master ,stroke *c.n* idea, act, during an argument, battle, discussion etc that is the reason for success: *Your suggestion that we ask to see the original calculations was a master stroke — he dropped his claim for more money.*

'mastery *u.n* **1** complete understanding (of s.t studied): *Irena has complete mastery of three European languages.* **2** complete control: *have mastery over many smaller businesses.*

masticate /'mæstɪˌkeɪt/ *tr/intr.v* (*formal*) break (food) into small pieces with the teeth; chew.

mastication /ˌmæstɪ'keɪʃən/ *u.n.*

mastiff /'mæstɪf/ *c.n* kind of large strong dog.

masturbate /'mæstəˌbeɪt/ *tr/intr.v* produce sexual excitement by rubbing (the sexual organs).

masturbation /ˌmæstə'beɪʃən/ *u.n.*

'masturˌbator *c.n* person who masturbates.

mat /mæt/ *c.n* **1** piece of thick material placed on the floor, e.g by a door or fireplace: *a door mat.* **2** piece of soft material placed on the floor in a sports centre to prevent injury when falling, jumping etc. **3** small piece of material placed on a table etc to prevent furniture burning or becoming damaged when s.t is placed on it: *a table mat.* **4** mass[1](1) piece, hair etc on a surface: *a mat of long grass near the river.*

matted /'mætɪd/ *adj* (of hair) in a thick untidy mass(1).

'matting *u.n* rough material for making mats.

matador /'mætəˌdɔː/ *c.n* chief fighter who kills the bull in a contest called bullfighting.

match¹ /mætʃ/ *n* **1** *c.n* sports competition between people or teams: *a football match*; *a tennis match between* (*teams from*) *France and Italy.* **2** *c.n* (often *a/no — for s.o*) person with/without the same strength, ability etc as another person: *I'm no match for her — she's a much better player.* ⇒ unmatched. **3** *sing.n* person or thing who/that suits another person or thing when together: *This carpet and these curtains are a good/bad match.* **4** *c.n* partnership, esp a marriage: *We talked about their love and hopes and we all agreed that it was a good match.* **5** *c.n* person considered to be suitable for marriage, esp because he/she is rich or successful: *When Anne was given her father's money she suddenly became an attractive match.* **find/meet one's match** discover s.o who is as strong (or stronger) or has as much (or more) ability as oneself: *He thought he would win the election easily but he met his match when Margaret* opposed(2) *him.* **a perfect match** an example of a very successful match(3,4).

▷ *v* **6** *intr./tr.v* (often *— s.o/s.t with s.o/s.t*) be suitable for (another person or thing) when together: *These colours do not match. I've been unable to match this coat with any of the dresses. It's difficult to match children from unhappy homes with a suitable* foster-mother. **7** *tr.v* find s.t to be a match(3) for (s.t): *I'm trying to match the yellow in this material.* **with s.t to match** with s.t as a match(3): *She wore a blue coat and shoes with gloves to match.* **match s.o/s.t against s.o/s.t** (**a**) put s.o/s.t together with s.o/s.t to see if they are suitable together: *I matched the curtain against the wallpaper but I did not like the result.* (**b**) put s.o together with s.o in a sports competition to see if they have the same strength, ability etc: *I was matched against a huge man.* **match s.o/s.t up** (**to s.o/ s.t**) put s.o/s.t (with another person or thing) to make a match(3): *You must match up the paint to the* wallpaper *before you choose the carpets.* (**not**) **match up to s.o/s.t** (not) reach the

same high standard as s.o/s.t: *He doesn't match up to his father in ability.*

'matching *attrib.adj* making a match(3): *matching shoes and gloves.*

'matchless *adj* without any example of the same high quality: *matchless beauty.*

'match,maker *c.n* **1** (*informal*) person who brings two people together hoping that they will marry each other. **2** person who arranges sports competitions.

,match 'point *c.n* (in tennis etc) last point needed to win the match(1).

match² /mætʃ/ *c.n* small piece of wood etc with a chemical substance on the end that lights easily when rubbed on a rough surface: *a box of matches*; *light the fire with a match.* ⇒ safety match. **put/set a match to s.t** light s.t so that it burns. **strike a match** rub a match against s.t to make it light up.

'match,box *c.n* box for matches².

'match,stick *c.n* small piece of wood used to make a match².

'match,wood *u.n* **1** kind of light wood used to make matches². **2** small pieces of wood, e.g after an explosion: *The house was reduced to matchwood.*

mate /meɪt/ *c.n* **1** (*informal*) fellow worker: *I had a drink with my mates after work.* **2** person who lives in the same room as oneself (a room mate), who is in the same class at school (a classmate) or is in the same sports team (a team mate). **3** young person who helps a skilled worker: *a builder's mate.* **4** officer in a merchant ship below a captain. **5** one of a pair of birds or animals used to produce young. **6** *u.n* (*informal*) = checkmate(1). **running mate** ⇒ run.

▷ *v* **7** *tr/intr.v* (of birds, animals) unite (one with another) to produce young: *We mated the blue bird with the yellow one.* **8** *tr.v* (*informal*) = checkmate(2).

'matey *adj* **1** (*informal*) friendly, esp in conversation: *We've been matey for years.*

'mating ,season *c.n* (usu the *—*) time of the year when birds or animals are ready to mate(7).

▷ *c.n* **2** (*informal*) friend: *Hallo, matey!*

material /mə'tɪərɪəl/ *adj* **1** of or referring to, made of, s.t one can see or touch: *Ann's more interested in having material things than being happy.* **2** of or referring to things that provide physical comfort: *She seems to ignore her material needs.* **3** (usu *— to s.o/s.t*) important (to s.o/s.t): *Is the offer of money material to people who lose their jobs?* Opposite immaterial.

▷ *n* **4** *c/u.n* (often *pl*) substance used to do or make s.t: *writing materials*; *building materials. What material will you use for the walls?* **5** *c/u.n* (example of) cloth: *dress material*; *cotton/* synthetic(2) *materials. How much material do I need to make a skirt?* **6** *u.n* pieces of information that can be used to prepare a book, report etc: *I do not have enough material for my account of the events.* **7** *u.n* person with qualities suited to doing s.t: *Is your son Ben university material?* **raw material** ⇒ raw.

ma,terial 'evidence *u.n* (*law*) important evidence(1) concerning the particular case being discussed.

materialism /mə'tɪərɪəˌlɪzəm/ *u.n* **1** opinion that material(1) substances are the only things that exist, and that feelings, thoughts etc are used to support their existence: *Materialism does not accept any religious or* spiritual(1) *account of the meaning of life.* **2** (*derog*) too much interest in owning expensive things: *Is it materialism in some parts of the world that causes other areas to be very poor?*

ma'teria,list *c.n* **1** person who believes in materialism(1). **2** (*derog*) person who is materialistic.

ma,teria'listic *adj* (*derog*) too interested in owning expensive things.

ma,teria'listically *adv.*

materialization, -isation /məˌtɪərɪəlaɪˈzeɪʃən/ *u.n* act or state of materializing.

'materia,lize, -ise *intr.v* **1** (of a spirit) become a form that one can see and touch. **2** (*informal*) become fact; come into existence: *A solution to the problem materialized after a long discussion. I thought I'd lost my bicycle but it materialized as if by magic outside the house.*

ma'terially *adv* to an important extent: *Will this new report affect our decision materially?*

ma,terial 'science *c/u.n* science of the qualities and uses of metals, plastics etc.

ma,terial 'witness *c.n* (*law*) witness(2) with important information concerning the particular case being discussed.

maternal /məˈtɜːnl/ *adj* **1** (usu *attrib*) of or referring to a mother: *maternal love.* **2** (*attrib*) of or referring to a relative on the mother's side of the family: *my maternal grandfather* (i.e my mother's father). Compare paternal.

maternity /məˈtɜːnɪtɪ/ *u.n* (also *attrib*) condition or process(2) of becoming a mother: *maternity clothes. During maternity it is dangerous for a woman to smoke.* Compare paternity.

ma'ternity ,dress *c.n* dress that is shaped for a woman who is having a baby.

ma'ternity ,hospital/,ward *c.n* place where a woman is given medical help while having a baby.

mathematics /ˌmæθəˈmætɪks/ *u.n* (*abbr* **maths**, US *math*) study of numbers and quantity: *Mathematics was my favourite subject at school.*

mathematical /ˌmæθəˈmætɪkl/ *adj* of or referring to mathematics: *mathematical problems.*

,mathe'matically *adv.*

mathematician /ˌmæθəməˈtɪʃən/ *c.n* person skilled in, or a student of, mathematics.

matinée /ˈmætɪˌneɪ/ *c.n* (also *attrib*) afternoon performance of a film, play etc: *Matinée tickets are often cheaper.*

matins /ˈmætɪnz/ *pl/unique n* (in some Christian(1) churches) a service held in the morning.

matriarch /ˈmeɪtrɪˌɑːk/ *c.n* woman who is head of a group of people, esp a woman with a strong character. Compare patriarch.

,matri'archal *adj* **1** of a matriarch: *matriarchal duties.* **2** with women in control or more important than men: *There are very few matriarchal societies in the world.*

'matri,archy *c.n* (*pl -ies*) society, system, with women in control.

matrices /ˈmeɪtrɪˌsiːz/ *pl* of matrix.

matricide /ˈmeɪtrɪˌsaɪd/ *c/u.n* (example of the) murder of one's mother. Compare patricide.

matriculate /məˈtrɪkjʊˌleɪt/ *tr/intr.v* (*old use*) **1** (allow (s.o) to) gain an academic(1) standard

that is needed to go to a college, university etc. **2** (allow (s.o) to) become a member of a college or university.

matriculation /məˌtrɪkjʊˈleɪʃən/ *c/u.n* (example of the) act of matriculating.

matrimony /ˈmætrɪmənɪ/ *u.n* (*formal*) (state of) marriage: *Matrimony is not as popular with young people as it used to be.*

matrimonial /ˌmætrɪˈməʊnɪəl/ *adj* of (the state of) marriage: *matrimonial happiness.*

matrix /ˈmeɪtrɪks/ *c.n* (*pl matrices* /ˈmeɪtrɪˌsiːz/, *-es*) **1** (*technical*) substance in which s.t is formed or developed: *Fossils*(1) *are often formed in a matrix of* limestone. **2** hollow mould'(1) in which a liquid substance is poured to make s.t: *Liquid* plastic *is poured into a matrix to make a* record'(1). **3** (*mathematics*) regular arrangement of lines, numbers etc in rows and columns. **4** (*biology*) substance round a cell(4). **5** (*anatomy*) substance at the bottom of a nail(1) out of which it grows.

matron /ˈmeɪtrən/ *c.n* **1** (often with capital **M**) (title of a) woman in charge of nurses in a hospital. **2** woman in charge of health arrangements in a school, children's home, old age home etc. **3** (*old use*) older married woman.

'matronly *adj* (of an older woman) **1** being a little fat. **2** behaving in a formal, polite and organized way: *My matronly aunt always wears a hat and walks with her head up and a straight back.*

,matron of 'honour *c.n* (*pl matrons of honour*) **1** married woman who helps a woman at her wedding. Compare bridesmaid. **2** married woman who helps a princess or queen, esp during public duties.

matt /mæt/ *adj* (also **matte**) having or producing a dull, not polished, surface: *We've used matt paint on the walls.* Compare gloss(2).

matted ⇒ mat.

matter /ˈmætə/ *n* **1** *u.n* substances that make up the physical world: *Do the earth and the moon share the same matter?* **2** *c/u.n* substance that s.t is made of and that can be seen or touched, not thoughts or feelings: *Some matters are heavier than others. She eats only vegetable matter.* **3** *c.n* particular thing to be done, considered etc: *I have many important matters to attend to before I can join you. This is a matter for the police.* **4** *def.n* cause of trouble, pain, difficulty etc: *We must solve the matter of the missing bicycle.* **5** *u.n* written contents (of a book etc), not the way in which s.t is written: *There is very little matter to interest readers in many magazines.* **6** *u.n* liquid that comes out of a cut etc on the skin: *poisonous matter.* Compare pus. **a matter of life and/or death** ⇒ life. **a matter of opinion** thing about which people can have different opinions: *Whether eating certain kinds of food is good for your health or not is a matter of opinion.* **a matter of s.t (a)** a (small) amount (of money, time etc): *It's only a matter of another £1000 and the house is yours.* **(b)** a (small) action, detail etc: *It's just a matter of an apology* (or *of apologizing*) *and then the argument will be over.* **a matter of taste** thing that some people like and others do not like: *Modern art is a matter of taste.* **(and) make matters worse** (and) causing an already bad situation to become worse: *The rain has* *made driving dangerous and to make matters worse there is now thick fog in the area.* **as a matter of course** as expected or usual: *I brush my teeth every night as a matter of course.* ⇨ matter-of-course. **as a matter of fact** (used to add force when giving more information) in fact: *I didn't go to the meeting; as a matter of fact I'm no longer a member.* ⇨ matter-of-fact. **be nothing, something** etc **the matter (with s.o/s.t)** be nothing, s.t etc wrong (with s.o/s.t): *There's nothing, something the matter with this clock. What's the matter with Peter?* **for that matter** (used when adding more information) with reference to what has just been said: *She doesn't believe you and for that matter neither do I.* **grey matter** ⇨ grey. **let the matter drop/rest** stop discussing, searching for, s.t: *I wish he would let the matter drop and accept that he'll never find the person who took his watch.* **mind over matter** ⇨ mind¹. **printed matter** ⇨ print. **reading matter** ⇨ read. **subject matter** ⇨ subject¹. **the fact of the matter** ⇨ fact. **the heart of the matter** ⇨ heart.

▷ *intr.v* **7** (often (*not*) — (to s.o) *if*, *whether* etc . . .) be important (to s.o if etc . .): *It does not matter when you come as long as you telephone first. You may think breaking my pen doesn't matter but it matters to me. She's so sad that nothing seems to matter to her anymore.*

matter-of-'course *attrib.adj* (of a person, s.t s.o does etc) thinking that situations, results etc (good or bad) cannot be changed: *He's a person with a matter-of-course attitude towards his studies.*

matter-of-'fact *attrib.adj* (of a person) without a strong imagination: *She always writes matter-of-fact accounts of her activities as a student.*

matting ⇨ mat.

mattress /'mætrɪs/ *c.n* thick layer of foam rubber, springs etc covered with material and placed on top of a bed for comfortable sleeping: *A hard mattress is better for your back than a soft one.*

mature /mə'tjʊə/ *adj* **1** (of people) having mental(1) or physical qualities that are fully developed; showing adult qualities: *Although she's only 14 she has very mature ideas about life. Young girls are often more mature than young boys.* Opposite immature(1). **2** (of plants) fully grown and developed; ready to produce fruit, seeds: *It takes most fruit trees about 7 years before they are mature enough to produce good fruit.* Opposite immature(2). **3** (of cheese, wine, that has been given time to become) ready to eat or drink: *If you leave that cheese to become any more mature it will be too smelly to eat!* **4** (of a bill¹(1), an investment(1) etc) due for payment: *By the time you retire(1), you should have enough mature life insurance policies(2) to help you.*

▷ *v* **5** *tr/intr.v* (cause (s.o/s.t) to) be, become, mature(1): *The fact of growing up in a very large family has matured her earlier than other girls at her age.* **6** *intr.v* be, become, mature(2–4): *How long will it take for this young apple tree to mature? This insurance policy(2) will mature when you're 60.*

ma'turely *adv* in an adult or mature(1) way: *You behaved very maturely at the dinner party.* Opposite immaturely.

maturity /mə'tjʊərɪtɪ/ *u.n* state of being

mature(1–4): *Your decision shows maturity. My policy(2) reaches maturity next year.*

maudlin /'mɔːdlɪn/ *adj* (*formal*) foolishly sad, esp from drinking too much alcohol(1): *They sat up all night drinking wine and telling one another maudlin stories about their youth.*

maul /mɔːl/ *tr.v* **1** (esp of an animal) hurt (s.o/ s.t) badly by tearing the skin etc: *The hunter died after being badly mauled by a lion.* **2** (often — s.o/s.t *about*) (*fig*) (of a person) handle (s.o/ s.t) in a rough unpleasant manner: *The young girl left the party because she didn't enjoy being mauled by strange men. I wrote a strong letter to the newspaper but after they'd mauled it about it didn't seem to say much.*

mausoleum /ˌmɔːzə'lɪəm/ *c.n* large stone structure(2) above the grave of an important person.

mauve /məʊv/ *adj* **1** having the colour that is a lighter shade of purple.

▷ *c/u.n* **2** mauve(1) colour.

maverick /'mævərɪk/ *c.n* (*derog*) (also *attrib*) person who thinks and acts independently and does not always follow the group, esp in a political party.

max *written abbr* maximum.

maxi /'mæksɪ/ *attrib.adj* full length to the ankles: *a maxi dress/skirt.* Compare midi, mini.

maxim /'mæksɪm/ *c.n* saying that expresses a sensible rule for behaviour in a short statement: *'Don't cross your bridges until you come to them' is a popular maxim.*

maximum /'mæksɪməm/ *attrib.adj* (*written abbr* **max**) **1** greatest, largest, (amount, size of s.t): *What's your maximum speed for the 100 metres? The maximum amount of time I can give you is 2 weeks. He's grown to his maximum size now.* Opposite minimum(1).

▷ *c.n* (*pl* -**s**, or much less usu, *maxima* /'mæksɪmə/) **2** greatest, largest, possible amount, extent etc: *The maximum I can work in a day is 7 hours. I drink a maximum of 8 cups of coffee a day.* Opposite minimum(2).

maximal /'mæksɪməl/ *adj* (*formal*) (in order to achieve, be) as much, great as possible: *To get maximal use of your machine, you must service it regularly.* ⇨ minimal.

maximization, -isation /ˌmæksɪmaɪ'zeɪʃən/ *u.n* act or fact of maximizing s.t.

'maxi,mize, -ise *tr.v* (*formal*) make (s.t) as great, large, as possible: *If we're going to maximize our profits this year, we must cut our costs over the next months.* Opposite minimize.

May /meɪ/ *unique n* 5th month of the year: *There are thirty-one days in May. He came on May 4 (say 'May the fourth' or 'the fourth of May'). It was a warm May morning.*

'May ,Day *unique n* (also *attrib*) May 1, in many countries a day when workers celebrate: *May Day celebrations.* Compare mayday.

'may,pole *c.n* upright pole¹(1), usu in villages, which people dance round to celebrate the start of spring.

'May ,Queen *c.n* girl chosen to lead the celebrations to mark the start of spring.

may /meɪ/ *aux. v* (no *pres.p, p.p* or *p.t* forms; *might* /maɪt/ is used after a *p.t*); negative forms *may not* or *mayn't* /'meɪnt/; 'may' is followed by the infinitive form of a verb without *to*). Compare might¹. **1** (used to express present or future possibility): *I may go to the cinema tomorrow but I'm not sure. He may not be able to come next week. She may be thinking of you at this exact moment. If Alan is made captain, who can tell what may happen!* **2** (used to express a possible result): *If you work hard you may pass the examination.* **3** (*formal*) (used to ask for or give permission): *May I borrow your pen? You may go out later if you have finished your work. My father says we may use his car.* Compare can[1](3). **4** (used to express official permission): *In England you may marry at sixteen.* **5** (used to express a wish): *May you both be happy always.* **be that as it may** regardless of the possible truth about what has been mentioned: *William can be very unpleasant, but be that as it may I still like him.* **come what may** whatever happens: *I'll be at the airport to meet you come what may.* **may have** + *p.p* (used to express an opinion or suggestion about the possibility of a past activity or situation having happened): *Ask Emma — she may have found your watch.* Compare might have + *p.p* (⇨ might[1]). **s.o may/might (just) as well do s.t** there is no strong reason for or against s.o doing s.t: *We may as well go to her party because there's nothing better to do.* **that's as may be (but . . .)** that is possibly true (but . . .): *'I've no money.' 'That's as may be, but you still owe me £15.'*

maybe /'meɪˌbiː/ *adv* possibly: *Maybe he'll decide to buy it. Maybe he will and maybe he won't. 'Will you forgive me if I promise never to do it again?' 'Maybe.'*

mayday /'meɪˌdeɪ/ *c.n* international radio signal used to ask for help. Compare May Day. ⇨ SOS(1).

mayhem /'meɪhem/ *u.n* (*formal*) great confusion; much fighting: *If we don't want complete mayhem we must at least listen to their demands.*

mayn't /'meɪnt/ = may not. ⇨ may.

mayonnaise /ˌmeɪəˈneɪz/ *u.n* sauce made from eggs, oil and vinegar: *Would you like some mayonnaise on your eggs?* **egg mayonnaise** hard-boiled eggs with mayonnaise on them.

mayor /meə/ *c.n* (title of the) most important official of a town etc. ⇨ Lord Mayor.

mayoral /'meərəl/ *adj* of a mayor.

mayoralty /'meərəltɪ/ *n* **1** *u.n* office of a mayor. **2** *c.n* length of time during which a mayor is in office.

mayoress /'meərɪs/ *c.n* **1** (title of a) female mayor. **2** (title of a) mayor's wife.

mayst /meɪst/ (*old use*) *2nd pers sing* of may.

maze /meɪz/ *c.n* **1** set of paths (often lined on both sides with hedges) many of which are blocked and one or some of which lead to the centre and back to the outside again. **2** (often — of *s.t*) (*fig*) confusing situation or set (of information, facts, streets etc): *I got lost in a maze of little streets and it took hours to find the hotel.*

MB /ˌem 'biː/ *abbr* Bachelor of Medicine.

MBE /ˌem ˌbiː 'iː/ *abbr* Member(2) of the Order of the British Empire (a British honorary title).

MC /ˌem 'siː/ *abbr* **1** Master of Ceremonies. **2** (UK) Military Cross (a medal for bravery in war). **3** (US) Member(2) of Congress(2).

MCC /ˌem ˌsiː 'siː/ *abbr* Marylebone Cricket Club (organization for the England cricket[1] team).

M.Ch *written abbr* Master(3) of Surgery (an academic qualification).

MCP, mcp /ˌem ˌsiː 'piː/ *abbr* (*informal*) male chauvinist pig.

MD /ˌem 'diː/ *abbr* **1** Doctor(2) of Medicine (an academic qualification). **2** Managing Director.

me (strong form /miː/, weak form /mɪ/) *pron* (form of 'I' used as the object of verbs and prepositions in formal speech and writing and also in informal speech as the subjective complement) *Did you bring me a drink? Mr Jones gave Peter and me a lift to town. Did he see me? Give that book to me — it's mine. 'Who said that?' 'Me'* (instead of 'I did'). ⇨ my, myself.

mead /miːd/ *u.n* alcoholic(1) drink made from honey and water.

meadow /'medəʊ/ *c.n* grassy field: *The meadows are covered with wild flowers at this time of year.*

meagre /'miːgə/ *adj* (US **meager**) (*formal*) **1** not enough: *How can anyone live on such a meagre salary?* **2** (of a part of the body) very thin, weak: *The newspapers are full of photographs of the meagre little bodies of starving(1) children.* **'meagrely** *adv.* **'meagreness** *u.n.*

meal[1] /miːl/ *c.n* (occasion of an) amount of food eaten at one time: *We usually have three meals a day. Let's go out for a meal — I don't feel like cooking.* **make a meal of s.t** (*fig*) spend an excessive amount of time, effort, on a job: *You don't have to make such a meal of it — I only wanted you to tidy up, not polish the whole room!* **meals on wheels** cooked meals delivered by car (to old or ill people).

'meal-ticket *c.n* **1** sign that money has been paid for a meal. **2** (*fig*) person or thing who/ that provides money, food etc.

'mealtime *u.n* agreed time for eating.

meal[2] /miːl/ *u.n* grain that is ground into powder form like flour: *Meal is often used to feed animals during winter.* ⇨ oatmeal.

'mealy *adj* (-ier, -iest) of, like, meal[2].

mealy-'mouthed *adj* (*derog*) not clear; not honest: *Our leaders are all mealy-mouthed — we'll never get the truth from them.*

mean[1] /miːn/ *adj* **1** (*derog*) not generous: *She's very mean and never shares her sweets. Alan's so mean with his money.* **2** (*derog*) extremely unkind: *Stealing money from a poor old woman was a mean thing to do. How mean of you to do that!* **3** poor: *wearing mean clothes.* **4** full of shame or guilt: *I felt so mean taking the last place on the bus and leaving the child standing in the cold.* **5** likely to cause injury or be violent: *My neighbour/dog has a mean temper. That's a mean-looking dog.* **6** humble: *She came from mean origins.* **no mean s.t** (**a**) s.t very difficult: *That was no mean achievement(2).* (**b**) s.t of a very good standard: *Pelé was no mean footballer.* **'meanly** *adv* in a mean[1](1-3) way: *behave meanly; meanly dressed.*

meanness /'miːnnɪs/ *u.n* state of being mean[1](1-6).

'meany *c.n* (*pl* -ies) (*informal*) mean(1) person.

mean[2] /miːn/ *attrib.adj* **1** (of measurement) average: *The mean temperature for London in October is 10°C.*

▷ *c/def.n* **2** middle point between two extremes, e.g of behaviour, quality: *They used the red material as the mean to decide standards of quality for the* *rest.* **3** average: *The mean of £14, £18 and £7 is £13.*

meantime /ˌmiːnˈtaɪm/ *adv* **1** during this length of time: *The next programme will begin in five minutes; meantime let's listen to some music.*
▷ *def.n* /ˈmiːnˌtaɪm/ **2 in the meantime** during this length of time: *I had to wait an extra hour so I wrote letters in the meantime.*

meanwhile /ˌmiːnˈwaɪl/ *adv* meantime(1): *The meal will be ready in half an hour; meanwhile let's have a drink.*

mean³ /miːn/ *tr.v* (*p.t, p.p* meant /ment/) **1** (of a word etc) have (a particular sense(2)), represent (s.t): *This dictionary tells you what words mean by giving explanations and examples of how they are used.* **2** (often — *that*. : .) (of a sign, symbol, abbreviation etc) show, represent (s.t): *'What does a black spot on a map mean?' 'It means that there is a station there.'* **3** (often — *that* . . .) be a sign (of s.t, that . . .): *Does general public anger mean that the government is not popular?* **4** cause (an effect(1) or result): *A shorter working week will mean more free time but lower wages.* **5** (often — *s.o s.t*; — *to do s.t*) have in mind (s.t) as an intention (towards s.o): *He didn't mean you any harm. I meant to tell you but I forgot.* **6** (often — *to do s.t*) be determined (to do s.t): *I promised to help her whatever the cost and I mean to do it. He said that he would report the boys to the police and he meant it.* **be meant for s.o/s.t** be intended, planned, for s.o/s.t: *The coffee was meant for you but I drank it by mistake. She was meant for international success after winning the national competition.* **be meant to do s.t** be intended, supposed, to do s.t: *You are meant to keep your ticket until you leave the station.* **mean a lot/everything/nothing/something to s.o** have a lot of/very great/no/some importance for s.o: *You mean a lot to me. His job means everything to him. Does failing examinations mean nothing to you?* **mean business** ⇒ business. **mean mischief** ⇒ mischief. **mean no harm (to s.o/s.t)** ⇒ harm(*n*). **mean well** have the intention of doing s.t helpful or kind (although the result may be the opposite): *Robert meant well when he offered to help even though his work was useless.* **mean what one says (about s.t)** be serious (about s.t one says): *The chairman meant what he said about dismissing members who make too much noise.* **take s.t as meaning**, **to mean**, s.t treat s.t as if it means s.t; believe that s.t means s.t.

'meaning *attrib.adj* **1** (often as the second part of the word) giving an idea of an intention, opinion etc: *a meaning look*; *a well-meaning thought/person.*
▷ *c.n* (often — *of s.t*) **2** what a word etc means³(1): *What is the meaning of 'sympathy' in English?* **3** true or useful idea (from a dream, experience, sign etc): *Do you know the meanings of dreams?* **4** idea or purpose (of an intention or action): *What is the meaning of all this noise when I'm trying to work?* **5** value or importance (in what it contains): *This law has no meaning for poor people. Her life lost all its meaning while the baby was ill.* (**do**, **say s.t) with meaning** (do, say s.t) seriously and showing its importance to oneself.

'meaningful *adj* **1** showing one is serious or that

s.t is important to one: *a meaningful expression.* **2** having a meaning(2) that can be known or explained: *a meaningful statement.*

'meaningfully *adv.* **'meaningfulness** *u.n.*

'meaningless *adj* having no meaning(2) that can be known or explained: *a meaningless act of violence.*

'meaninglessly *adv.* **'meaninglessness** *u.n.*

meander /mɪˈændə/ *c.n* **1** twist or turn (of the path of a river etc). **2** twisting and turning movement.
▷ *intr.v* **3** (of a river, road, railway line etc) follow a path that has many twists and turns. **4** (often — *about*) (of a person, train etc) move in a twisting path: *meander all over the place*; *meandering through the crowds.* **5** (of a person) speak about several things in a disorganized way, e.g when ill: *meander from one subject to another.*

me'anderings *pl.n* **1** twisting and turning path. **2** examples of meandering(5), e.g by a person who is ill or weak.

meanly, meanness ⇒ mean¹.

means /miːnz/ *n* (*pl* means) **1** *c.n* (often — *of s.t*) method (to get a result): *Television is a popular means of advertising. Use any means you like but you must bring her to me.* **2** *pl.n* (enough) money or wealth: *Do your parents have the means to send you to university? I'd like to help but I don't have the means.* **a man/woman of means** a person with a lot of money. **a means to an end** a method or process necessary to get a particular result: *The decision to visit the country would not solve the problem but was an important means to that end.* **by all means** (a) certainly: *If you consider that a visit would be useful, by all means go.* (b) (used as a reply to a request) yes, do: *'May I take this chair?' 'By all means.'* **by fair means or foul** using any method whether honest or not: *I'll find the person who took your jewels, by fair means or foul.* **by means of s.t** using s.t: *They escaped by means of a tunnel. Information is gathered by means of a computer.* **by no, not by any, manner of means** ⇒ manner. **by no, not by any, means** not at all: *It's by no means a certainty that you'll win the prize.* **independent means** ⇒ independent. (**live**) **beyond/within one's means** (live) using money that is more than, not more than, one has or earns: *If you live beyond your means, your debts will increase.* **means of support** money needed to pay for food, rent etc. **the end justifies the means** the method (to be) used is acceptable because the intended result is important or necessary: *Those people who use bombs in cities clearly believe that the end justifies the means.*

'means ˌtest *c.n* test of a person's wealth used to decide whether he/she must be given government money, e.g to pay for a university course.

meant /ment/ *p.t,p.p* of mean³.

meantime, meanwhile ⇒ mean².

meany ⇒ mean¹.

measles /ˈmiːzəlz/ *def/u.n* (*medical*) disease causing spots on the skin and a high temperature: *My son is suffering from (the) measles.* **German measles** ⇒ German.

measly /ˈmiːzlɪ/ *adj* (*-ier, -iest*) (*informal*) **1** small in quantity, value etc: *a measly payment for washing the car.* **2** (*derog*) (of a person) not at all generous: *a measly father.*

'measliness *u.n.*

measure /'meʒə/ *n* **1** *u.n* method, system, of finding the size, mass, quantity etc of s.t: *The metric measure is preferred because it is easier.* **2** *c.n* (unit of) size, mass, quantity etc of s.t as determined by measure(1): *The room has a measure of 25 sq m.* *A* degree(1) *is a (unit of) measure of temperature. The money collected is a measure of our popularity.* **3** *c.n* instrument for finding the size, mass, quantity etc of s.t: *The thermometer is a measure of temperature.* **4** *c.n* particular quantity used as a standard: *A measure of salt must be added to each bottle.* **5** *sing.n* quite large or great quantity: *He was given a measure of independence by his manager.* **beyond measure** too great to be calculated: *Your kindness is beyond measure. They gave wealth beyond measure to the flood victims.* **for good measure** in addition, esp as an extra way of avoiding defeat or failure: *We've decided to take another torch for good measure.* **give (s.o) full/short measure** give (s.o) as much, less than, the agreed quantity: *Be careful because some traders will try to give you short measure.* **in great/large measure** (*formal*) to a large degree: *Their success was in large measure due to Mary's qualities as a leader.* **in some measure** (*formal*) to a certain degree: *The weather was in some measure the cause of the accident.* **made to measure** (*attrib* **made-to-measure**) (of clothes) made in a particular size and shape for a particular person: *I always have my suits made to measure* (or *I only buy made-to-measure suits*). Compare ready-made. **tape measure** ⇨ tape.

▷ *v* **6** *tr/intr.v* find the size, mass, quantity of (s.t) using a system or an instrument: *I measured (the width of) the wall to find out how much wood I would need. I was measured for a new suit yesterday. Can you measure accurately with that cup?* **7** *tr.v* be, have, (a particular measure(2)): *The carpet measures 4 metres by 5 metres.* **8** *tr.v* (of an instrument) show (a particular measure(2)): *A thermometer measures temperature.* **measure s.t off** find a particular length and mark it: *The shop assistant took the roll of dress material and measured 3 metres off.* **measure s.t out** find a particular quantity of s.t: *The nurse measured out a* teaspoonful *of cough mixture.* **measure up (to s.o/s.t)** have, reach, the (same) quality or standard (as s.o/s.t else, or that is expected of one): *His work does not measure up to his teachers' expectations. We needed a determined new manager and wondered if Peter Jones would measure up.*

'measurable /'meʒrəbl/ *adj* able to be measured(6): *It's a measurable distance from here. He has made no measurable improvement.* Opposite immeasurable, measureless.

'measurably *adv.*

'measured *adj* **1** found by measuring(6): *a measured mile.* **2** carefully considered: *He gave a measured answer.* **3** (of movement) slow and careful: *She walked up the dark path with a measured step.*

'measureless *adj* not able to be measured(6) because it has no limit or end: *Distances in space are usually measureless.* Compare immeasurable.

'measurement *n* **1** *u.n* system/method used for measuring(6): metric *measurement.* **2** *c.n* (often

pl) particular size, degree etc: *What is the measurement of your garden? The measurements of the box are 1 cm by 2 cm by 1 cm.* **take s.o's measurements** find and record the size of particular parts of s.o's body, e.g for clothes.

'measures *pl.n* methods or actions intended to get a particular result: *The measures used to end the strike were not all fair.* **take measures (to do s.t, against s.o/s.t)** adopt plans (to do s.t, against s.o/s.t): *What new measures are being taken to prevent this kind of thing happening again?*

meat /mi:t/ *u.n* **1** (pieces of an) animal's dead body eaten as food (but not including fish): *I don't eat meat. Chicken meat is white or light brown in colour. The butcher sells fresh and cooked meat.* **2** other food, e.g from fish, seafood, that is like meat. **3** (*fig*) important or interesting parts, esp details: *There was not much meat in her argument.* **be meat and drink to s.o** (*fig*) be a cause of great pleasure to s.o: *Playing the piano was meat and drink to her.* **One man's meat is another man's poison** (*fig*) s.t liked or enjoyed by one person is not necessarily liked or enjoyed by everybody.

'meat,ball *c.n* ball of a mixture of small pieces of meat, breadcrumbs, onion etc.

'meatiness *u.n* fact, state, of being meaty(1,2).

'meaty *adj* (*-ier, -iest*) **1** having a lot of meat(1); like meat(1): *a meaty soup.* **2** (*fig*) having many important or interesting parts, esp details: *a meaty discussion.*

mecca /'mekə/ *n* **1** *unique n* (with capital **M**) holy city for Muslims in Saudi Arabia where Mohammed was born. **2** *c.n* (usu *a — for s.o*) (*fig*) place that attracts many (of one kind of) people: *Los Angeles is a mecca for film-stars.*

mechanic /mɪ'kænɪk/ *c.n* skilled worker who repairs machines: *a car mechanic.*

mechanical /mɪ'kænɪkl/ *adj* **1** made or operated by machines: *a mechanical* process(1) *for producing furniture.* **2** of or referring to machines: *mechanical engineering.* **3** (of an answer, a movement etc) done without thinking or feelings: *give a mechanical wave.*

me,chanical ,engi'neering *u.n* science and practice of the design(3), building and operation of machines.

mechanically /mɪ'kænɪklɪ/ *adv.*

me'chanics *u.n* **1** (usu *the — of s.t*) way a machine, process(1), system etc works: *I'll never understand the mechanics of writing short stories.* **2** (*technical*) science of the effects of force acting on any object or material. **3** = mechanical engineering.

mechanism /'mekə,nɪzəm/ *n* **1** *c.n* system or structure(1) of parts of a machine: *a watch with a delicate mechanism. Do you understand the mechanism of a car engine?* **2** *def.n* structure(1) of (parts of) a system: *the mechanism of the eye; the mechanism of British government.* **3** *def.n* method, process(1), for producing something: *the mechanism of writing successful textbooks.* **4** *c.n* kind of behaviour used for a particular effect(2): *Laughing was her defence mechanism when she was afraid.*

mechanistic /,mekə'nɪstɪk/ *adj* (usu *attrib*) of or referring to mechanics.

,mecha'nistically *adv.*

mechanization, -isation /,mekənaɪ'zeɪʃən/

u.n system, process, of putting machinery into a factory.

'mecha,nize, -ise *tr.v* **1** put machinery into (a factory etc). **2** make (a manufacturing process(1)) work (almost) completely by machines. **3** give (an army etc) machines, vehicles etc as part of a process(1) of modernizing: *The* infantry *is now being mechanized.*

med *written abbr* **1** medical. **2** medieval. **3** medium(1).

MEd /,em 'ed/ *abbr* Master(3) of Education.

medal /'medl/ *c.n* **1** flat round piece of metal with words and/or a picture on it, given to s.o as a reward for success in a sports competition, being brave during a battle, carrying out important duties for one's country etc: *A* gold medal *is given to the winner of an important sports event, a* silver medal *is given to the person who is second and a* bronze medal *to the person who is third.* **2** thing like this worn as a decoration, as part of one's religion etc: *Ian had a religious medal on a chain around his neck.*

medallion /mɪ'dælɪən/ *c.n* large medal(2).

medallist /'medəlɪst/ *c.n* (US **'medalist**) **1** person who is given a medal as a reward: *an* Olympic gold medallist. **2** person who designs(5) medals.

meddle /'medl/ *intr.v* **1** (often — *in s.t*) interfere (in s.t); make oneself part (of s.t that is not one's business): *Stop meddling in my private affairs.* **2** (often — *with s.o/s.t*) interfere.(with s.o/s.t) so that one annoys her/him, disturbs it etc: *Jane wished her brother would not meddle with her record collection.*

'meddler *c.n* person who meddles.

meddlesome /'medlsəm/ *adj* interfering: *My meddlesome uncle tried to persuade my parents to refuse me permission to go to the party.*

media /'miːdɪə/ *n* **1** *def/def.pl.n* (also *attrib*) (*informal*) methods of giving out information to many people, e.g television, radio, newspapers: *The media is/are very powerful and can persuade people to believe almost anything. Media jobs as in* journalism *are difficult to get.* **2** *pl* of medium.

mass media ⇨ mass[1].

mediaeval ⇨ medieval.

mediate /'miːdɪˌeɪt/ *tr/intr.v* (often — *between s.o;* — *in s.t*) try to produce agreement on (s.t), (between people who are arguing about it): *The chairman has been asked to mediate between the two members in finding a solution to their quarrel.*

mediation /ˌmiːdɪ'eɪʃən/ *u.n.*

mediator /'miːdɪˌeɪtə/ *c.n* person who mediates.

medic /'medɪk/ *c.n* (*informal*) doctor, esp in a hospital.

medical /'medɪkl/ *adj* **1** of or referring to the process(1) of treating people who are ill or keeping people in good health: *a medical degree*; *a medical student.* **2** using or needing medicine, not surgery(1), to get a cure: *Is there a medical solution to* deafness*? I was kept in the medical* ward[1](1) *of the hospital.*

▷ *c.n* **3** (*informal*) medical examination: *Children should have a medical once a year.*

'medical cer,tificate *c.n* paper giving information about s.o's health.

,medical e,xami'nation *c.n* examination of the body to report on s.o's physical condition.

'medically *adv* concerning s.o's health: *In order to become a soldier you must be medically fit.*

,medical 'officer *c.n* doctor with responsibility for public health in an area or part of a town.

,medical prac'titioner *c.n* (*formal*) doctor or surgeon(1). ⇨ general practitioner.

'medical ,school *c/u.n* place where doctors are trained.

medicament /mɪ'dɪkəmənt/ *c.n* (*formal*) medicine: *Years ago doctors used various strange medicaments to cure diseases.*

medicated /'medɪˌkeɪtɪd/ *adj* (of a liquid etc) having a medical(2) substance in it: *I use a medicated* shampoo(1) *to keep my hair healthy.*

medication /ˌmedɪ'keɪʃən/ *n* **1** *u.n* use of medicine to cure people who are ill. **2** *c.n* particular kind of medical(2) substance that is used on the body and not inside it: *Many young boys need a medication for spots on their faces.* Compare medicine(2).

medicine /'medsɪn/ *n* **1** *u.n* science or practice of trying to cure people who are ill, or of keeping people healthy: *I hope to study medicine when I leave school.* **2** *c/u.n* (also *attrib*) (example of a) substance containing s.t to cure a person of a disease, esp one that is swallowed and not one used on the outside of the body: *a cough* medicine; *a medicine bottle. He needs to take* medicine *every day.* **get, give s.o, a dose/taste of her/his own medicine** (*fig*) suffer, make s.o suffer, a similar unpleasant experience as one that one has suffered because of her/him: *She got a taste of her own medicine after getting rid of so many other* people. **preventive medicine** ⇨ preventive. **take one's medicine** (*fig*) suffer a punishment that one deserves: *Although I know I ought to be punished I will not take my medicine easily.*

'medicine ,cabinet/,chest *c.n* box, small cupboard, for medicines.

'medicine ,man *c.n* (*pl men*) person who uses particular substances to produce magic(3), esp in a developing country.

medicinal /me'dɪsɪnl/ *adj* acting as, like, medicine: *Medicinal plants are used in herbal cures.*

medieval /ˌmedɪ'iːvl/ *adj* (also ˌmedi'aeval) **1** of the period between about AD1000 and 1500: *medieval history.* **2** (*derog*) old-fashioned: *These practices are so medieval!*

mediocre /ˌmiːdɪ'əʊkə/ *adj* (usu *derog*) of ordinary standard, neither good nor bad (but usu suggesting that the standard is not good enough): *a mediocre student/programme.*

mediocrity /ˌmiːdɪ'ɒkrɪtɪ/ *u.n* condition of being mediocre: *Mediocrity is not good enough at a university.*

meditate /'medɪˌteɪt/ *intr.v* **1** (keep one's mind on a particular thought or object and) keep one's thoughts away from ordinary problems or subjects, either for religious reasons or to make oneself feel calm and peaceful: *I try to meditate for an hour each morning.* **2** (often — (up)on *s.t*) keep one's mind on a particular subject and think about it: *I have been meditating on the problem of my son's education but I have no solution as yet.*

meditation /ˌmedɪ'teɪʃən/ *c/u.n.*

medium /'miːdɪəm/ *attrib.adj* **1** in the middle

of two opposite limits: *of medium size/mass*; *a medium-priced ticket.*

▷ *c.n* (*pl -s* or, less usu, *media* /'miːdɪə/) **2** middle point, stage, condition etc: *Their price is the medium and we have decided to buy from them.* **3** (often *through the — of s.t*) method or way of giving information to many people: *Television is an important medium for advertising. The news became known through the medium of international radio programmes.* Compare media(1), mass media (⇒ mass¹). **4** substance for carrying or sending (the effect of) s.t: Copper(1) *is a good medium for electricity.* **5** substance or conditions in which living things exist: *In which medium do fish live?* **6** method of artistic expression: *Shakespeare wrote many poems but his most successful medium was* drama(2). **7** (*pl -s*) person considered able to send messages to dead people and receive messages from them. (**strike**) *a happy medium* (**between s.t and s.t**) (find) a middle point (between two things) that the people concerned (can) accept: *The agreement was a happy medium between their wishes and our ability to pay.*

'medium ,wave *c/def.n* (**'medium-,wave** when *attrib*; *abbr* MW)) (*technical*) radio signal using waves(2) that are a medium(1) distance apart (between about 100 and 1000 metres): *This programme can also be heard on 240 metres in the medium wave. This radio gives poor medium-wave reception.* ⇒ waveband (⇒ wave). Compare longwave, shortwave.

medley /'medlɪ/ *c.n* **1** (often *— of s.t*) piece of music using parts of other music: *We shall now play a medley of songs from her films.* **2** swimming race in which swimmers use a different way of swimming for each part of the race: *the men's 400 metres medley.* **3** (often *— of s.t*) mixture (of different kinds of things): *The report includes a medley of useful suggestions.*

meek /miːk/ *adj* **1** having a gentle patient character and quickly agreeing to accept another person's opinion or decision: *Being a salesman is not a job for a meek person.* **meek and mild** very meek.

▷ *def.pl.n* **2** meek people: *The meek shall* inherit(1) *the earth.*

'meekly *adv.* **'meekness** *u.n.*

meet¹ /miːt/ *v* (*p.t,p.p.p* met /met/) **1** *tr/intr.v* come towards (s.o) or together (from different directions) either by arrangement or accidentally: *Let's meet at the theatre at 6 o'clock. I met George in the post office and he was surprised to see me. Liverpool will meet Arsenal in the semi-finals.* **2** *tr/intr.v* come into contact (with s.o) or together and get to know (each other): *I first met my wife on holiday in Italy. It is difficult to meet new friends in a big city.* **3** *tr/intr.v* join (s.t): *There is a hotel where the two roads meet. Sand is built up where the river meets the sea.* **4** *tr/intr.v* make violent contact (with s.t or each other): *As the two trains met there was a loud explosion.* **5** *intr.v* (of a group of people) come together: *The committee meets once a month.* **6** *tr.v* experience (s.t bad): *He met his end in an air crash.* **7** *tr.v* satisfy (a demand, need, desire etc): *I cannot meet all your wishes but I can promise to help you find a job.* **8** *tr.v* manage to achieve(1) (s.t promised): *The date for finishing*

this work *is impossible to meet. If you can't meet your debts, you will lose your house and car.* **9** *tr.v* agree with (s.o about s.t): *If you can meet me on a price and a delivery date, I'll sign the order.* **make** (**both**) **ends meet** ⇒ end(*n*). **meet s.o halfway** ⇒ halfway. **meet one's Waterloo** be faced with a defeat, esp after some successes: *We'd managed to paint nearly all the house but when we began to paint the stairs we realized we'd met our Waterloo.* **meet up** (**with s.o**) (*informal*) meet¹(1) (s.o), esp again after a period of time: *We separated after arranging to meet up at the entrance in half an hour.* **meet with s.o** (*informal*) have a meeting with s.o: *The chairman is meeting with government officials to discuss unemployment.* **meet with s.t** experience, suffer, s.t: *They met with an accident on the* motorway. **meet s.t with s.t** respond(1) to an action, condition etc by doing s.t: *Their decision to close the factory was met with silence by the workers.* **more in/to s.t than meets the eye** ⇒ eye(*n*).

'meeting *n* **1** *c.n* act of coming together by arrangement or by accident: *Their meetings were kept secret for a long time.* **2** *c.n* gathering of two or more people to do s.t: *The meeting voted to support the management. We are looking forward to a meeting between the young tennis star and the* champion(2).

'meeting ,house *c.n* place where Quakers worship together.

'meeting-,place *c.n* place for a meeting(2).

meet² /miːt/ *adj* (*old use*) (of behaviour, an action) proper.

meet³ /miːt/ *c.n* gathering of people, horses and dogs in order to hunt foxes, deer etc.

megacycle /'megə,saɪkl/ *c.n* = megahertz.

megadeath /'megə,deθ/ *c.n* killing of one million people, e.g by using a nuclear bomb.

megahertz /'megə,hɜːts/ *c.n* unit of measurement of frequency of radio waves(2), equal to one million each second, *symb* MHz.

megalith /'megə,lɪθ/ *c.n* very large stone, esp as part of an ancient monument.

,mega'lithic *adj* **1** consisting of one or more megaliths. **2** very large.

megaphone /'megə,fəʊn/ *c.n* instrument shaped like a funnel used to make sound from the voice louder: *The speaker used a megaphone to speak to the crowds.*

megaton /'megə,tʌn/ *c.n* **1** one million tons. **2** explosive power, e.g of a bomb, equal to one million tons of a well-known explosive substance called TNT.

megavolt /'megə,vəʊlt/ *c.n* unit of measurement of electric force, equal to one million volts.

megawatt /'megə,wɒt/ *c.n* unit of measurement of electric power, equal to one million watts, *symb* MW.

melancholy /'melənkəlɪ/ *adj* **1** (*formal*) (of a person, situation etc) extremely sad: *She seems a melancholy child. Winter produces a melancholy feeling.*

▷ *u.n* **2** (*formal*) extreme sadness: *Her words were filled with melancholy.*

melancholia /,melən'kəʊlɪə/ *u.n* (*formal*) (mental illness causing) extreme sadness.

melancholic /,melən'kɒlɪk/ *adj* **1** (*formal*) (of a person) likely to be extremely sad often.

▷ *c.n* **2** (*formal*) melancholic person.

melee /'meleɪ/ *c.n* (also **mêlée**) noisy fight or quarrel by a crowd: *The police were called to stop the melee among the people in the stadium.*

mellifluous /mɪ'lɪfluəs/ *adj* (also **mellifluent** /me'lɪfluent/) (*formal*) (of a sound) pleasant, gentle and even: *singing with a mellifluous voice.*
mel'lifluously, mel'lifluently *adv.* **mel'lifluousness, mel'lifluence** *u.n.*

mellow /'meləʊ/ *adj* **1** (of a colour, sound) pleasant, soft and warm. **2** (of fruit and wine) full of pleasant flavour. **3** (of a person) kind, gentle and full of sympathetic understanding. **4** (of soil) soft and rich.
▷ *tr/intr.v* **5** (cause (s.o/s.t) to) become mellow(1–4): *Red wine mellows if you leave it for a few years. The man's opinions mellowed as he grew older.*
'mellowly *adv.* **'mellowness** *u.n.*

melodrama /'melə,drɑːmə/ *n* **1** *u.n* behaviour showing excessive feelings of excitement, sadness, worry, fear etc. **2** *c.n* play, film, television programme etc containing excessively emotional(1) scenes that prevent one from being seriously interested in the events.
melodramatic /,melədrə'mætɪk/ *adj* having or showing, excessive feelings of excitement, sadness, worry, fear etc: *melodramatic behaviour*; *a melodramatic play.*
,melodra'matically *adv.*

melody /'melədɪ/ *n* (*pl* -ies) **1** *c.n* simple pleasant tune: *playing melodies on the piano.* **2** *c/ u.n* musical arrangement like a tune, as part of a longer work: *Mozart's symphonies are full of melody.*
melodic /mɪ'lɒdɪk/ *adj* **1** of or referring to melody. **2** melodious.
melodious /mɪ'ləʊdɪəs/ *adj* (*formal*) pleasant to listen to: *She has a melodious voice.*
me'lodiously *adv.* **me'lodiousness** *u.n.*

melon /'melən/ *c/u.n* kind of large fruit with a hard skin and yellow or white flesh, and containing many seeds. ⇨ watermelon.

melt /melt/ *v* **1** *tr.v* make (s.t solid or hard) become liquid or very soft, esp by using heat: *Melt the butter in a saucepan. This special torch will melt steel.* ⇨ molten. Opposite harden(1). **2** *intr.v* (of s.t solid or hard) become liquid or very soft, esp as a result of heat: *As the sun became warmer, the ice began to melt.* **3** *intr.v* (of a person) become kind or willing to agree, esp after being angry or refusing to give permission: *When he saw the woman with her baby the man melted and gave her some money.* **melt away** (*fig*) gradually disappear: *The crowd began to melt away after the speakers had gone. Suddenly my fear melted away and I spoke bravely.* **melt s.t down** make s.t, e.g metal, become a liquid by using heat: *They are melting down old metal bars so that they can produce farm machinery.* **melt in the mouth** (of food) become pleasantly soft and almost liquid as one eats it: *My mother's biscuits melt in the mouth.*
'melting-,point *c/def.n* temperature at which s.t melts: *The melting-point of gold is higher than the melting-point of ice.* Compare freezing-point, boiling-point.
'melting ,pot *c.n* (*fig*) area, occasion, where different ideas, people etc come together and mix: *Let's use the meeting as a melting pot for the various opinions.* **in the melting pot** being discussed or changed.

member /'membə/ *c.n* **1** person who has joined a club, association or similar group: *Are you a member of the* Liberal Party? *I became a trade union member ten years ago.* **2** (often with capital **M**) person elected or invited to join an official group: *He's the* Member (of Parliament) *for North Devon. She was made a Member of the Order of the British Empire* (i.e given this title as an honour). **3** person belonging to a group: *She's the youngest member of our family. Zimbabwe is a member of the* Commonwealth. *A* mushroom(1) *is a member of the* fungi *group of plants.* **4** part of an animal's body, esp an arm or leg. ⇨ dismember. **5** part of a building, or s.t like it, that holds s.t up: *Many engineers questioned the strength of the wooden members below the bridge.* **6** (*mathematics*) unit that is a part of a set.
,Member of the ,House of 'Commons *c.n* (*abbr MP*) (used only to distinguish between this and the House of Lords) elected political representative in the House of Commons.
,Member of the ,House of 'Lords *c.n* (used only to distinguish between this and the House of Commons) person allowed to be a representative in the House of Lords.
,member of 'parliament *c.n* (often capital **M** and **P**; *abbr MP*) (title of an) elected political representative in the House of Commons.
'membership *n* **1** *u.n* (also *attrib*) state of being a member(1): *Membership of the unions is increasing. Please show your membership cards.* **2** *c/def/def.pl.n* members(1) as a group: *The membership has/have been asked its/their opinion about building a new sports centre.*
,member 'state *c.n* country that is a member(3) of an international(1) or political organization: *All the member states voted for the peace plan.*

membrane /'membreɪn/ *c.n* (*technical*) very thin layer of skin that covers (and often protects) a delicate part of the body or an instrument: *The membrane inside the nose prevents* germs(1) *in the air from entering the body.*
membranous /mem'breɪnəs/ *adj* (also **mem'braneous**).

memento /mɪ'mentəʊ/ *c.n* (*pl* -(e)s) (often — of s.o/s.t) thing collected or given to remind one (of a person, place, event etc): *She collects matchboxes as mementoes of the places she's been to.*

memo /'meməʊ/ *c.n* (*pl* -s) (also *attrib*) (*informal*) memorandum, a short note written to remind one/s.o of s.t (a date, meeting etc) or to inform other people in an organization about a particular matter: *He wrote a quick memo giving the time and date of their next meeting.*
'memo ,pad *c.n* blank(1) pad of paper on which one writes memos.

memoir /'memwɑː/ *c.n* (*French; formal*) piece of writing of historical interest by s.o who has studied the subject or has had personal experience of it: *a memoir of life in England in the 60s.*
'memoirs *pl.n* written description of one's own life: *You should write your memoirs because I'm sure they'd make very interesting reading.*

memorable /'memrəbl/ *adj* worthy of being

remembered: *That was a memorable occasion. The celebration was memorable for its simplicity.* Opposite **immemorable.**
'memorably *adv.*

memorandum /ˌmeməˈrændəm/ *c.n* (*pl* -s, or less usu, **memoranda** /ˌmeməˈrændə/). ⇒ memo.
ˌmemorˌandum of aˈgreement *c.n* (*law*) legal written form of an agreement.

memorial /mɪˈmɔːrɪəl/ *c.n* (also *attrib*) (often — to s.o/s.t) thing built, done, written, to remind people (of, or in honour of, a person, event etc): *There is a war memorial in every city in the world. There will be a memorial service for her in the church this afternoon. I planted a rose garden as a memorial to my dead child.*

memorize ⇒ memory.

memory /ˈmemərɪ/ *n* (*pl* -ies) **1** *c/u.n* ability, power, to store information in the mind and remember it when necessary: *I have a poor memory. She used to have an excellent memory for details but she's getting old now.* **2** *c.n* (also *attrib*) collection of information in the mind or in a computer: *After the car accident she lost her memory for several weeks. My new typewriter has a built-in memory.* **3** *c/u.n* thing that is remembered: *I have no memory of meeting her before. Ada described her memories of living in Kenya.* **commit s.t to memory** learn s.t in order to store it in one's memory(1). ⇒ memorize. **from memory** by remembering and without help from notes, books etc: *She played the whole piece from memory.* **have a short memory** fail to remember things. **in/within living memory** within the time that people alive now can still remember: *the most exciting discovery in living memory.* **in memory of s.o/s.t** as a reminder, in honour, of s.o/s.t: *I shall read the next poem in memory of my mother who loved it so much.* **jog s.o's memory** ⇒ jog(*v*). **lose one's memory** forget s.t. **refresh one's/s.o's memory** (**of s.o/s.t**) make one's/s.o remember (s.o/s.t). **slip s.o's memory/mind** be forgotten by s.o, usu for a short time: *His name slips my memory but I'll remember it in a minute.* **to the best of one's memory** as far as one can remember: *I've never been in this part of the town before to the best of my memory.*
'memoˌrize, -ise *tr.v* learn (s.t) and keep it in one's memory(1) until it is needed: *Jill memorized her speech so that she could speak to her audience without using notes.*

men /men/ *pl* of man.

-men /-mən/ *pl.n* men with the job etc shown by the first part of the word: *chairmen/workmen/ sportsmen.*

menace /ˈmenɪs/ *c/u.n* **1** (often be a — to s.o/s.t) person or thing who/that can cause damage, trouble, be a threat, (to s.o/s.t): *This drought is a menace to our struggling economy(3). He's a menace on the roads. He spoke with such menace in his eyes.*
▷ *tr.v* **2** (*formal*) threaten (s.o/s.t): *The world is menaced by poverty and greed.*
'menacing *adj* (*formal*) threatening to damage, harm, s.o/s.t: *a menacing look in his eyes; menacing clouds.*
'menacingly *adv.*

ménage /meɪˈnɑːʒ/ *c.n* (*French*) house and the people who live there.
ménage à trois /ˌmeˌnɑːʒ ɑː ˈtrwɑː/ *c.n* (*French*)

(*pl* **ménages à trois** /ˌmeˌnɑːʒ/) three people who live together as lovers.

menagerie /mɪˈnædʒərɪ/ *c.n* (place for keeping a) collection of different kinds of wild animals.

mend /mend/ *n* **1** *c.n* part repaired after being broken, damaged etc: *a mend in his sleeve.* (**be**) **on the mend** (be) improving in health: *She was very ill but she's on the mend now.*
▷ *v* **2** *tr.v* fix, repair, (s.t broken, damaged etc): *Is it possible to mend these shoes or will I have to buy a new pair?* **3** *intr.v* (of health, esp a broken bone) repair itself, get better, improve: *The doctor says my arm is mending nicely.* **mend one's manners/ ways** improve one's behaviour: *The judge told the young man to mend his ways or he'd find himself in prison.*
'mending *u.n* **1** act, work, of fixing or repairing s.t broken: *I'll do the mending of the chair if you paint it afterwards.* **2** articles, esp clothing, that need to be mended(2): *There is a lot of mending in that basket.*

mendacious /menˈdeɪʃəs/ *adj* (*formal*) false; lying: *a mendacious report about the activities of the* opposition(4) *party.*
menˈdaciously *adv.* **menˈdaciousness** *u.n.*
mendacity /menˈdæsɪtɪ/ *n* (*pl* -ies) (*formal*) **1** *c.n* lie; statement that is not true. **2** *u.n* act of lying; lying behaviour: *His mendacity makes me so angry.*

menfolk /ˈmenˌfəʊk/ *pl.n* men of a particular group or family: *The menfolk are out in the garden playing with the children.* Compare womenfolk.

menial /ˈmiːnɪəl/ *adj* **1** (of work) not interesting or requiring any skill; inferior: *She does all the menial jobs around the house.*
▷ *c.n* **2** (*derog*) servant, esp one who does housework.

meningitis /ˌmenɪnˈdʒaɪtɪs/ *u.n* serious illness (inflammation of the membrane round the brain or spinal cord) that affects the brain.

menopause /ˈmenəʊˌpɔːz/ *def.n* (*informal* ˌchange of ˈlife) length of time during which changes occur in a woman's body, e.g the ending of menstruation, so that she is no longer able to bear a child.
ˌmenoˈpausal *adj.*

menstruate /ˈmenstrʊˌeɪt/ *intr.v* (of a woman) produce blood etc from the uterus once a month: *Most girls begin to menstruate between the ages of 12 and 14.*
menses /ˈmensiːz/ *def.pl.n* (*technical*) blood etc that leave the uterus once a month. ⇒ menstrual period.
menstrual /ˈmenstrʊəl/ *adj* of or referring to the changes in a woman's body during one month that lead to the production and discharge(6) of the menses: *A menstrual cycle is usually 28 days.*
ˌmenstrual ˈperiod *c.n* = period(4).
menstruation /ˌmenstrʊˈeɪʃən/ *u.n* fact or state of menstruating.

mental /ˈmentl/ *adj* (usu *attrib*) **1** of the mind: *His mental development is ahead of most other children's in his class.* **2** by, in, the mind: *a mental exercise; mental arithmetic. I have a very clear mental picture of what happened.* **3** for, referring to, s.o suffering from an illness of the mind: *He has some kind of mental condition.* **4** (*informal*) appearing as if a little mad(1): *You* *must be mental — do you know what you're suggesting?*

'mental ,age *c.n* measurement of the development of a person's mind based on what a person can usually do at a certain age: *All the children in the hospital are over 12 but none has a mental age of more than 5.*

,mental a'rithmetic *u.n* act or fact of working with numbers in the mind.

,mental 'breakdown *u.n* (nervous) breakdown(2).

,mental de'ficiency *c/u.n* (suffering from a) lack of development of the mind.

'mental ,home/,hospital *c.n* place where people suffering from a mental illness are cared for.

,mental 'illness *c/u.n* (example of an) illness during which the mind loses its usual abilities, power etc.

mentality /men'tælɪtɪ/ *n* (*pl -ies*) **1** *c/u.n* (degree, level, of) mental ability or power: *have a childish mentality.* **2** *c.n* (person with a) particular way of thinking or attitude(2) of mind: *What kind of mentalities rob poor helpless old people?*

'mentally *adv.*

'mental ,patient *c.n* person being treated in a mental hospital.

menthol /'menθɒl/ *u.n* kind of white substance obtained from peppermint(1) oil and used in medicines, for flavour etc.

mentholated /'menθəˌleɪtɪd/ *adj* containing menthol: *mentholated cigarettes.*

mention /'menʃən/ *n* **1** *c/u.n* (often *make* (*no*) — *of s.o/s.t*) (example of the) act of saying, writing, s.t (about s.o/s.t) or (not) referring to s.o/s.t, esp briefly: *Our prize got a short mention in the newspaper. He made no mention of having seen you. Did they make any mention of the matter at the meeting?* **2** *c.n* short notice or report about s.t brave, important, successful etc that s.o does: *He was given a special mention in the newspaper report about the rescue.*

▷ *tr.v.* **3** refer to (s.o/s.t); say (the name of s.o/s.t): *Did Harry mention me when you spoke to him? If you mention my name I'm sure they'll help you. With reference to the matter mentioned by Mr Brown, a notice will be sent out giving you all the details.* **4** refer to (s.o/s.t) without giving any or much information or details: *I'll mention your idea* (*to her*) *when I see her. Diana mentioned something about going to town but I don't know where she went.* ⇒ unmentionable. **Don't mention it!** (used in conversation as a polite reply to s.o who thanks one for s.t): *'Thanks for your help.' 'Don't mention it!'* **not to mention (the fact) that** *.../s.t* (used to add force to an opinion, decision, remark by giving an extra fact) in addition: *I don't want to go to the cinema tonight — it's cold and raining, not to mention (the fact) that there's nothing I want to see.*

-mentioned (used with an adv, esp *above-/below-mentioned*) that was referred to earlier (above) or will be referred to later (below): *Please will the above-mentioned people meet me in my office at 2 o'clock.*

mentor /'mentɔː/ *c.n* (*formal*) wise and respected person who provides advice and help (about a particular subject) (esp to a student): *I studied history under her and*

she became my mentor and friend for nearly 20 years.

menu /'menjuː/ *c.n* **1** (list of) all the (different kinds of) food available at a restaurant or for a particular meal: *Could you bring me the menu please, waiter? Let's go to Mike's Kitchen — they've got an excellent menu. What's on the menu for dinner?* **2** list of things, subjects etc shown on the screen of a computer or in a program from which one can choose what one wants.

mercantile /'mɜːkənˌtaɪl/ *attrib.adj* (*formal*) of commerce, trade: *a mercantile ship.*

,mercan,tile 'law *c.n* set of laws concerning the business and trade of a particular country.

,mercan,tile ma'rine *u.n* people and boats concerned with a country's trade.

mercenary /'mɜːsɪnərɪ/ *adj* **1** (*derog*) influenced only by rewards of money or other forms of personal gain: *You wouldn't be so mercenary as to leave him without any money, would you?*

▷ *c.n* **2** (*pl -ies*) soldier paid to fight for the army of a country that is not his own.

merchandise /'mɜːtʃənˌdaɪz/ *u.n* **1** goods for sale: *Harrods has merchandise from all over the world.*

▷ *tr.v* (also **-ize**) **2** make (goods) known and available for sale: *We must make efforts to merchandize our new products thoroughly so that they are in all the shops before Christmas.*

merchant /'mɜːtʃənt/ *adj* **1** of trade and the carriage of goods by sea: *merchant ships.*

▷ *c.n* **2** trader, often in wholesale(1) goods of a particular kind: *a timber merchant.*

,merchant ma'rine/'navy *c/def.n* (often capitals **M** and **M/N**) ships and seamen concerned with a country's trade.

'merchant ,ship *c.n* ship that carries trading goods.

merciful(ly/ness), merciless(ly/ness) ⇒ mercy.

Mercury /'mɜːkjʊrɪ/ *unique n* (*astronomy*) planet nearest the sun.

mercury /'mɜːkjʊrɪ/ *u.n* heavy silver liquid metal used in thermometers etc, *chem.symb* Hg.

mercurial /mɜːˈkjʊərɪəl/ *adj* **1** of, like, containing, mercury. **2** (*fig; formal*) (of a person) active; lively; who changes (feelings, preferences etc) often: *He has such a mercurial mind.*

mercy /'mɜːsɪ/ *n* (*pl -ies*) **1** *u.n* (often *ask for —; show —* (*to s.o*)) (ask for, show (s.o)) forgiveness, kindness for s.t wrong one/s.o has done, esp when it is in s.o's power to punish one/s.o: *The thief asked the shopkeeper for mercy and promised never to steal from him again. The judge told the criminal he would show no mercy to people who harm young children.* **2** *c.n* thing to be grateful for or relieved about: *It was a mercy that she wasn't killed in the accident.* **ask for mercy** ⇒ mercy(1). **be at s.o's mercy** be in s.o's power so that he/she can do what he/she wants to one: *Unions are not always at the mercy of employers as they can always refuse to work.* **be thankful for small mercies** be relieved that at least there are a few things that are good (even though most things are bad). **have mercy (on s.o)** show forgiveness, kindness, (to s.o in one's power): *Have mercy on me — please don't tell my parents about it.* **leave s.o to s.o's (tender) mercies, to the mercy of s.o/s.t** cause s.o to be in the (cruel) power of s.o/s.t: *If you don't stop complaining about my driving I'll leave you to the mercy of the night.* **show mercy (to s.o)** ⇨ mercy(1).

'**merciful** *adj* having or showing mercy(1): *a merciful judgement.* Opposite merciless.

,**merciful 'death** *c.n* death that ends terrible suffering, e.g after a painful illness.

'**mercifully** *adv* **1** in a merciful way. **2** luckily; thankfully: *Mercifully, the rain didn't last long.*

'**mercifulness** *u.n.*

'**merciless** *adj* having or showing no mercy(1) or pity: *The speaker was merciless in his criticism of the newspapers.*

'**mercilessly** *adv.* '**mercilessness** *u.n.*

'**mercy ,killing** *c/u.n* (act of) killing s.o who is suffering from an illness for which there is no cure in order to end pain and suffering. ⇨ euthanasia.

mere /mɪə/ *attrib.adj* (*superl* merest) no more than: *He's a mere boy — you expect too much from him. The mere mention of his name makes me sad.* **the merest (s.t)** the least or smallest possible (s.t): *The merest whisper makes him angry.*

'**merely** *adv* only; simply: *I merely asked if you knew where the biscuits were; I didn't say you ate them all.*

merge /mɜːdʒ/ *v* **1** *tr/intr.v* (often — (one company) with (another company)) (of businesses, companies etc) come together, join, (one with another) to form one company: *When Trend merges with Savemore they'll form the biggest supermarket in the city.* **2** *intr.v* (often — into s.t) gradually come together, change and become one: *In the distance the clouds and mountains seemed to merge until it was difficult to tell one from the other.* **3** *intr.v* (often — into s.t) gradually change or disappear (into s.t else): *One day merged into the next and he never knew whether it was Sunday or Monday.*

'**merger** *c.n* an act of joining of two or more companies: *a business merger.*

meridian /mə'rɪdɪən/ *c.n* imaginary line drawn anywhere around the earth's surface that passes through the poles²(1), used to show positions on maps; any line of longitude: *Which meridian passes through New York?*

meridiem /mə'rɪdɪəm/ *c.n* (*Latin*) (*abbr m* used in *am, pm*). ⇨ am, pm.

meringue /mə'ræŋ/ *c/u.n* (small cake made of the) white(8) of egg that is beaten with sugar until stiff and then baked slowly.

merino /mə'riːnəʊ/ *c/u.n* (*pl* -s) (also *attrib*) (type of sheep which provides) very soft wool.

merit /'merɪt/ *n* **1** *u.n* quality deserving approval, praise: *You have produced work of merit. It is merit that has won you the prize, not your family name. What merit is there in telling me about this when I can do nothing about it?* **2** *c.n* (good) quality: *Your plan has its merits but it's too expensive.* **on s.o's/s.t's merits** according to s.o's (good) value or the facts of the matter: *The case will be judged on its merits not on opinions.*

▷ *tr.v* **3** deserve (praise, criticism etc): *This news merits a celebration.*

meritocracy /,merɪ'tɒkrəsɪ/ *c/def.n* (*pl* -ies) (system of government by) people judged to have the greatest ability to rule.

meritorious /,merɪ'tɔːrɪəs/ *adj* (*formal*) worthy of praise.

,**meri'toriously** *adv.* ,**meri'toriousness** *u.n.*

mermaid /'mɜː,meɪd/ *c.n* imaginary woman with a fish's tail instead of legs, who lives in the sea.

merman /'mɜː,mæn/ *c.n* (*pl* -,men) imaginary man with a fish's tail instead of legs, who lives in the sea.

merry /'merɪ/ *adj* (*-ier, -iest*) **1** cheerful; happy; lively: *a merry party; a time to be merry, not sad.* **2** (*informal*) a little drunk: *We all got a little merry last night.* **make merry** have fun, esp at a party or celebration. ⇨ merrymaking.

'**merrily** *adv.*

'**merriment**, '**merriness** *u.n* fun; enjoyment: *There's a lot of merriment next door.*

,**Merry 'Christmas** *interj/c.n* (greeting to s.o wishing her/him a) happy time at Christmas: *We wish you a Merry Christmas.*

'**merry-go-,round** *c.n* = roundabout(3).

'**merry,maker** *c.n* person who is enjoying herself/himself.

'**merry,making** *u.n* enjoyment or fun, esp at a party or celebration.

mesh /meʃ/ *n* **1** *c/u.n* (also *attrib*) (piece of) material, net, made of a fine network of threads with small holes in between: *Put a wire mesh under the wood to hold the hot coals. We used some strong mesh to make a home for our rabbit.* **2** *c.n* (often *sing*) one of the small (regular) holes in a net: *I need a net with very small meshes (or a very small mesh).* **3** *c.n* (often *pl*) (thread of a) network: *caught in the meshes of a* spider's web(1). **4** *c.n* (*fig*) complicated network (of different ideas, opinions, systems etc): *She hated being caught up in the mesh of social activities expected of a film-star.*

▷ *v* **5** *tr.v* catch (a fish, butterfly etc) in a net. **6** *intr.v* (usu — with s.t) (of a (wheel) cog) connect (with s.t else) or hold together: *The bicycle chain meshes with the* cogs *of the* gear(1) *system to turn the wheel.* **7** *intr.v* (of ideas etc) fit or go together well: *They can't work together — their ideas never mesh.* Compare enmesh.

mesmerize, -ise /'mezmə,raɪz/ *tr.v* make (s.o, an animal) unable to move or make a sound; hypnotize(1) (s.o, an animal): *The rabbit was mesmerized by the side-to-side movements of the snake's head. The children were mesmerized by the* magician's *skill.*

mess¹ /mes/ *n* **1** *c/u.n* (usu *sing*) (often *in a* —) (person who lives in a) state of confusion caused by things not being finished, organized or in order: *He left his office in a mess when he resigned. Your life's a mess. You must start to organize your life — you're a real mess.* **2** *sing.n* state of confusion where everything is untidy, out of its usual place and often dirty: *Your room's a mess — please tidy it up. There was such a mess after the party that we spent hours cleaning up.* **3** *c/def.n* dirt: *Your dog's been sick all over the house — please clean up the mess* (or *its little messes*). **4** *c.n* (usu *sing*) (often *in a* —) trouble; difficult, confused or complicated situation: *You shouldn't have lied — it's put us all in a real mess. What a mess I've caused!* **get (s.o) into a mess (a)** (cause (s.o) to) be in trouble: *If we break a window we'll get into a real mess.* **(b)** (*informal*) (cause (s.o) to) become worried.

confused, (about s.t): *Don't get yourself into a mess about it — it's not so important.* **in a mess** (**a**) in trouble. ⇨ mess¹(4). (**b**) dirty, untidy: *The kitchen's in a mess! What have you been doing?* ⇨ mess¹(2). (**c**) in confusion; not finished, not organized. ⇨ mess¹(1). **make a mess (of s.t)** (**a**) cause a mess¹(4) (in s.t): *Don't make a mess (of the house) while I'm out, please. The storm made a mess of the garden.* (**b**) do (s.t) badly: *I made such a mess of my second examination paper — I'm sure I'll fail.* (**c**) ruin, spoil, (s.t): *You've made a mess of your life by chasing wild and impossible dreams.*

▷ *tr.v* **5** make (s.t) dirty or untidy: *Please don't do that; you're messing my hair.* **6** allow waste matter from the body to dirty (one's clothes): *The baby's rather smelly — he must have messed his* nappy. **mess about/around** (**a**) behave badly, foolishly: *As soon as I leave the classroom you start messing around and making a noise.* (**b**) do nothing in particular; be lazy: *You've been messing around all afternoon — don't you think you should do some homework? The children are messing about in the garden.* (**c**) work with no particular aim: *I've been messing about in the kitchen.* **mess s.o about/around** (**a**) cause confusion for s.o: *I wish you'd make up your mind and stop messing me about.* (**b**) treat s.o badly, roughly: *The boys messed him about a bit and took his gold watch.* **mess about/around with s.o/s.t** (**a**) spend one's free time with s.o, doing s.t: *I usually mess around with Pete after school.* (**b**) treat s.o/s.t badly: *You shouldn't mess around with someone so young.* (**c**) handle, treat, s.o/s.t badly or roughly: *Stop messing around with my record player.* **mess s.t up** (**a**) spoil s.t: *You'll really mess up our plans if you decide not to come.* (**b**) make s.t untidy: *Please don't mess up the house — I've spent all day cleaning and tidying up.* ⇨ mess-up. **mess with s.o/s.t** cause trouble to, interfere with, s.o/s.t: *You can't mess with people like him — he'll really hurt you. Don't mess with things you know nothing about.*

'messily *adv* in an untidy way: *He did it so messily that he'll have to do it again.*

'messiness *u.n* state of being messy or untidy.

'mess-,up *c.n* mistake that causes (a state of) confusion: *There's been a mess-up with the tickets — we've both been given the same seat.*

'messy *adj* (*-ier, -iest*) (that makes s.o, or causes s.t to be) dirty, untidy: *Don't clean your bike inside — it's too messy. You always give me the messiest jobs.*

mess² /mes/ *c.n* **1** place where a group of people, esp in the army, navy etc, eat together.

▷ *intr.v* **2 mess with s.o** eat with a group of people. **3 mess in together** (*informal*) share whatever there is: *The campers messed in together and shared their food.*

message /'mesɪdʒ/ *c.n* **1** spoken or written information, request passed on, sent to s.o: *Could you take this message to Mr Jones in room 4? May I leave a message for her please? Jane's not here at the moment but I'll take a message if you like.* **2** (usu *sing*) moral(2) or social teaching (in a story, piece of writing). **get the message** (*informal*) understand what is meant: *Fine, I get the message; you don't love me any more.*

messenger /'mesɪndʒə/ *c.n* person who carries messages from one person or place to another: *The messenger wants to know if there's any reply to take back.*

Messiah /mɪ'saɪə/ *def/unique n* leader promised by God to come and save the Jews and the world, believed by Christians to be Jesus.

Messrs /'mesəz/ *pl.n* (*written pl* of **Mr**, used esp to address a company): *Messrs Jones and Jones, Printers.*

messy ⇨ mess¹.

Met /met/ *attrib.adj* (*informal*) meteorological: *the* Met Office.

met /met/ *p.t,p.p* of meet¹.

metabolism /mɪ'tæbəˌlɪzəm/ *u.n* (*technical*) process by which the body produces energy(2) for its activities.

metabolic /ˌmetə'bɒlɪk/ *adj* (usu *attrib*) of metabolism: *He eats so much but he doesn't get fat because he has a high metabolic rate.*

metabolize, -ise /mɪ'tæbəˌlaɪz/ *tr.v* change (food) in the body chemically into a form of energy(2) that can be used by the body.

metal /'metl/ *adj* **1** of or referring to any of a group of substances that are shiny, malleable(1) and conduct(6) heat and electricity, e.g copper, gold, iron: *a metal door. I prefer wooden windows to metal ones.*

▷ *c/u.n* **2** substance of this kind; metal(1) object: *Tin is a metal. Put a piece of metal over the hole.*

'metal fa,tigue *u.n.* ⇨ fatigue(2).

metallic /mɪ'tælɪk/ *adj* of, like, metal: *metallic paint; a metallic sound.*

metallurgical /ˌmetə'lɜːˌdʒɪkl/ *adj* (*technical*) of metals and their uses.

metallurgist /me'tælɜːdʒɪst/ *c.n* (*technical*) person who studies and knows about metals and their uses.

metallurgy /me'tælədʒɪ/ *u.n* (*technical*) study of metals and their uses.

'metal,work *u.n* **1** objects shaped from metal. **2** (study of) making things from metal.

metamorphose /ˌmetə'mɔːfəʊz/ *intr.v* (often — *into* s.t) (*technical*) change into a different form: *The tadpole metamorphosed into a frog.*

metamorphosis /ˌmetə'mɔːfəsɪs/ *c.n* (*pl* metamorphoses /ˌmetə'mɔːfəˌsiːz/) **1** (*technical*) complete change in shape of certain animals, esp insects, as they grow into an adult, e.g from an egg to a caterpillar and then to a butterfly: *The development of a frog from the egg into a tadpole and finally to the adult frog is called metamorphosis.* **2** change in shape, character etc, esp of a person growing up from a plain young person into a handsome adult: *I haven't seen you for two years and you've been through a complete metamorphosis in that time.*

metaphor /'metəfə/ *c/u.n* (example of the) description of s.o/s.t using the name of s.t (or words normally used to describe s.t) in order to make a comparison, without using 'like', e.g: *'Don't trust her, she's a snake.' 'She flew out of the room in anger.'* Compare simile. **mixed metaphor** description that uses two or more metaphors, sometimes in an unsuitable or unsatisfactory way, e.g: *'Honesty, clothed in sorrow, strayed(6) from my mind.'*

metaphorical /ˌmetə'fɒrɪkl/ *adj* of, like, using.

a metaphor: *I used the word in its metaphorical meaning.*

,meta'phorically *adv.*

metaphysics /,metə'fızıks/ *u.n* **1** science of being and knowing. **2** deep and detailed discussion or thought about abstract(1) ideas.

metaphysical /,metə'fızıkl/ *adj* **1** of or referring to metaphysics(1,2). **2** (of poetry) philosophical(1) poetry of 17th century poets, e.g John Donne, who described thoughts of death, love, the nature of being etc using detailed metaphorical language.

mete /mi:t/ *tr.v* **mete s.t out (to s.o)** (*formal*) give a (share of) punishment, reward, (to s.o): *The judge meted out long sentences to the men who were found guilty of the crime.*

meteor /'mi:tıə/ *c.n* (also **'falling/'shooting ,star**) small object that travels through space very fast and burns brightly when it enters the earth's atmosphere(1).

meteoric /,mi:tı'ɒrık/ *adj* **1** of a meteor. **2** of or referring to the earth's atmosphere(1). **3** (*fig*) (esp of success etc) happening very quickly or suddenly but often only lasting for a short time: *The success of his first book resulted in a meteoric rise to fame. Her success was meteoric.*

,mete'orically *adv.*

meteorite /'mi:tıə,raıt/ *c.n* small (piece of a) meteor that has landed on earth.

meteoroid /'mi:tıə,rɔıd/ *c.n* small body of matter(1) that travels around the sun and burns brightly (like a meteor) if it enters the earth's atmosphere(1).

meteorology /,mi:tıə'rɒlədʒı/ *u.n* study of climate and weather.

meteorological /,mi:tıərə'lɒdʒıkl/ *adj* (*informal met*) of meteorology: *a meteorological report on tomorrow's weather.*

meteorologist /,mi:tıə'rɒlə,dʒıst/ *c.n* person who studies and understands meteorology.

Met Office /'met ,ɒfıs/ *def.n* (UK) group of officials who study and give reports on the weather.

meter¹ /'mi:tə/ *c.n* **1** instrument for measuring the amount (of gas, electricity, water, time) used: *I've come to read your electricity meter. This parking meter allows two hours for shopping.*

▷ *tr.v* **2** measure (gas, electricity, water, time, force, rain etc) using a meter¹(1): *This instrument meters the amount of gas you use.* **3** (*fig*) measure (s.t); keep an account of (the amount of time etc used, of progress made etc): *I shall be metering your performance to see if you improve.*

meter² ⇨ metre¹, metre².

methane /'mi:θeın/ *u.n* kind of gas that has no colour and that burns easily, *chem.form* CH_4.

method /'meθəd/ **1** *c.n* way of doing s.t: *It's not the results I'm complaining about but your methods for getting those results.* **2** *c.n* set of steps or actions for doing s.t: *If you follow the method described in the guidebook you will have no problems.* **3** *u.n* use of organization and careful planning: *There's no sign of method in your work.* **method in s.o's madness** (real or good) reason behind what appears to be foolish.

methodical /mı'θɒdıkl/ *adj* **1** (of work) done in an organized, planned way: *If your work is not methodical you will leave out important details. We must organize a methodical search for your watch.* **2** (of a person) acting, behaving, in an

organized or planned way so as to produce careful, thorough work: *a methodical doctor. He's very methodical and does the job well but his work is not very exciting.*

me'thodically *adv.*

methodology /,meθə'dɒlədʒı/ *c/u.n* system of methods for doing s.t: *a methodology for teaching mathematics.*

methodological /,meθədə'lɒdʒıkl/ *adj* of, using, methodology.

Methodism /'meθə,dızəm/ *unique n* belief in, following of the beliefs of, a Protestant(1) group developed in the early 18th century by John Wesley and others, with importance given to personal moral(1) responsibility and God's willing protection and love.

Methodist /'meθə,dıst/ *adj* **1** of or referring to Methodism: *the Methodist church.*

▷ *c.n* **2** person who believes in and practises Methodism.

meths /meθs/ *u.n* (*informal*) methylated spirits.

methylated spirits /,meθı,leıtıd 'spırıts/ *u.n* (*informal meths*) (esp UK) form of alcohol(1) used for burning, e.g in lamps.

meticulous /mı'tıkjuləs/ *adj* very careful, esp about detail: *a meticulous worker. She's meticulous about her work.*

me'ticulously *adv.* **me'ticulousness** *u.n.*

métier /'metı,eı/ *c.n* (*French*) profession or type of work.

Met Office ⇨ meteorology.

metre¹ /'mi:tə/ *c.n* (US **'meter**) (*written abbr m*) unit for measuring length in the metric system: *This room is 5 m wide. She ran 100 metres in 11 seconds. May I have 4 metres of this material please?* ⇨ centimetre, kilometre, millimetre.

metric /'metrık/ *adj* of the metre or metric system: *metric size.* **go metric** change to the metric system of money and measurement (from the old system that used £ s d, feet and inches etc): *Britain began to go metric in 1971.*

metrical /'metrıkl/ *adj* of, in, poetic metre²(1).

metricate /'metrı,keıt/ *tr/intr.v* (*formal*) change (a system of money, measuring etc) to the metric system. ⇨ go metric. Compare decimalize.

metrication /,metrı'keıʃən/ *u.n.*

,metric 'mile *def.n* (*athletics*) 1500 metres (race).

'metric ,system *def.n* measuring system based on units of 10 in which the metre is the basic unit of length, the gram(me) is the basic unit of mass, the litre is the basic unit of capacity, and the unit of money is divided into 100 parts.

,metric 'ton *c.n* 1000 kilos; tonne.

metre² /'mi:tə/ *u.n* (US **'meter**) (in poetry) rhythm(1) formed by a pattern of stressed(4) and unstressed sounds.

metro /'metrəʊ/ *def/u.n* (often with capital **M**) underground railway system, esp in Paris: *I'll come by metro. Let's take the Metro.*

metronome /'metrə,nəʊm/ *c.n* (*music*) instrument that can be set to make a required number of beats per minute in order to mark musical time.

metropolis /mı'trɒpəlıs/ *c.n* (*pl -es*) large busy city, esp the main or capital city of a country: *I've always preferred to live in a small town but I enjoy going to a big metropolis sometimes.*

metropolitan /,metrə'pɒlıtən/ *adj* **1** of, in, a

capital city: *I live outside the metropolitan area.
He wants to join the Metropolitan Police.*
▷ *c.n* **2** person who lives in the capital city.

mettle /'metl/ *u.n* (*formal*) spirit(2); courage: *She
showed her mettle by finishing the race although
she was clearly in terrible pain*. **be on one's mettle**
be in a position that makes one do one's best in
order to be successful: *You'll need to be on your
mettle among all those* world-class athletes. **put
s.o on her/his mettle** cause s.o to be on her/his
mettle.

mew /mju:/ ⇒ miaow.

mews /mju:z/ *c.n* (*pl* **mews**) (with capital **M** in
names) (name for a) street or square formerly
used as stables: *I live at 14 Cromwell Mews.*

mezzanine /'mezə,ni:n/ *c.n* (also *attrib*) floor
between the ground and first floors often acting
as an intermediate stage between them.

mg *symb* milligram.

Mgr *written abbr* Manager.

MHz *symb* megahertz.

MI5, MI6 /,em ,aɪ 'faɪv, 'sɪks/ *abbr* Military
Intelligence, section 5, 6 (UK's government
departments for obtaining information about
enemies).

miaow, miaou /mi:'aʊ/ *c.n* (also **mew**) **1** crying
sound of a cat.
▷ *intr.v* **2** (of a cat) cry: *The cat is miaowing for
food.*

mice /maɪs/ *pl* of mouse.

mickey /'mɪkɪ/ *def.n* **take the mickey (out of
s.o)** (*informal*) tease(2) (s.o).

micro /'maɪkrəʊ/ *c.n* (*informal*) microcomputer.

micro- *adj* showing that the object, system etc
described in the second part of the word is very
small: *micro-toys.*

microbe /'maɪkrəʊb/ *c.n* (*technical*) very small
organism, esp one that causes disease and that can
only be seen under a microscope.

microbiology /,maɪkrəʊbaɪ'ɒlədʒɪ/ *u.n* scientific study of very small organisms, e.g bacteria.
microbiological /,maɪkrəʊ,baɪə'lɒdʒɪkl/ *adj.*
microbiologist /,maɪkrəʊbaɪ'ɒlədʒɪst/ *c.n* person skilled in, or student of, microbiology.

microchip /'maɪkrəʊtʃɪp/ *c.n* (also **chip**) very
small thin piece of material (e.g silicon) used
to make an integrated circuit that operates
an electronic machine such as a computer.

microcomputer /'maɪkrəʊkəm'pju:tə/ *c.n*
small computer, e.g one that one can use in
the home. ⇒ personal computer.

microcosm /'maɪkrə,kɒzəm/ *c.n* thing representing life, the universe etc but on a very much
smaller scale.

microelectronics /,maɪkrəʊ,ɪlek'trɒnɪks/ *u.n*
(making use of) very small electronic instruments.

microfiche /'maɪkrəʊ,fi:ʃ/ *c.n* (*informal* **fiche**)
piece of microfilm.

microfilm /'maɪkrəʊ,fɪlm/ *c/u.n* **1** film for
photographing s.t in a very small size: *microfilms
of books and journals.*
▷ *tr.v* **2** photograph (s.t) using microfilm to produce a
very small picture: *microfilm newspaper articles.*

micrometer /maɪ'krɒmɪtə/ *c.n* (*technical*)
instrument for measuring (the size, length etc
of) very small objects.

micron /'maɪkrɒn/ *c.n* (*technical*) unit of length
equal to one millionth of a metre, *symb* μ.

micro-organism /,maɪkrəʊ 'ɔ:gə,nɪzəm/ *c.n*
very small living creature that can only be seen
under a microscope.

microphone /'maɪkrə,fəʊn/ *c.n* (*informal* mike)
instrument used to make sounds louder or carry
further. ⇒ loudspeaker.

microphysics /,maɪkrəʊ'fɪzɪks/ *u.n* scientific
study of very small matter and energy, e.g
atoms(1), electrons etc.

microprocessor /,maɪkrəʊ'prəʊsesə/ *c.n*
(*technical*) very small integrated circuit in a
small computer.

microscope /'maɪkrə,skəʊp/ *c.n* instrument
that has lenses(1) to make it possible to examine
very small objects. **put s.o/s.t under the microscope** (*fig*) examine s.o/s.t very carefully: *Before
the secret service employs anyone, they put them
under the microscope.*

microscopic /,maɪkrə'skɒpɪk/ *adj* **1** so small
that it can only be seen under a microscope: *a
microscopic* organism. **2** (*informal*) very small:
You only gave me a microscopic piece of cake.
micro'scopically *adv.*

microwave /'maɪkrə,weɪv/ *c.n* **1** (also *attrib*)
very short electric wave(2) used in sending messages, cooking food etc: *Many people have begun
to buy microwave ovens because they cook very
fast.* **2** oven using microwaves(1).

midair /,mɪd'eə/ *u.n* (also *attrib*) (usu *in —*)
somewhere above the ground in the air: *They
both jumped for the ball and crashed in midair.
There was a midair accident.*

midcourse /,mɪd'kɔ:s/ *u.n* (also *attrib*) (usu *in
—*) somewhere along the course, route(1), of an
aircraft etc: *lose control in midcourse.*

midday /,mɪd'deɪ/ *unique n* (also *attrib*) in the
middle of the day; at 12 o'clock in the day: *It's
too hot to do anything at midday. I prefer not to
eat a large midday meal.* ⇒ noon, noonday.

middle /'mɪdl/ *attrib.adj* **1** at the same distance
from the ends or edges; at, in, the central point:
*'T' is the middle letter in 'meter'. Can you find
the middle point of this* triangle(1)? **2** at, near, a
point that is the centre of an ordered group (in
time, quality, rank, size etc): *a middle standard/
height/amount; the middle period of the war.*
▷ *def.sing.n* **3** point at the same distance from the
ends or edges: *standing in the middle of the room.*
4 (*informal*) waist(1): *a pain in my middle.* **in
the middle of (doing) s.t (a)** at, near, a middle(2)
point in s.t: *in the middle of the night/road/race.*
(b) during the course of s.t: *in the middle of the
conversation.* **(c)** busy with s.t: *I'm in the middle
of my dinner so can you wait?*
middle 'age *u.n* period of life between being
young and being old.
middle-'aged *adj* (of a person, behaviour,
ideas) (like a person) of middle age: *feel
middle-aged; middle-aged habits such as worry
about health.*
middle-,age 'spread *u.n* tendency to put on
weight during middle age.
Middle 'Ages *def.pl.n* period of history, about
AD 1000–1500 in Europe.
'middle-,brow *adj* (often *derog*) having ordinary interests, values and average ability to
judge books, plays, music etc. Compare high-
brow, low-brow.
middle 'C *unique n* (*music*) a note in the

middle of the standard range of notes used to play music.

,middle 'class *def/def.pl.n* **1** class of people including business and professional people and their families. **2** (*derog*) this class of people considered to be too interested in money, possessions and public respect.

,middle-'class *adj* (often *derog*) of, for, like, suitable for, (the values of) the middle class: *middle-class clothes/ambitions/ideas.*

,middle 'course *def.n* way of acting, behaving, that is between two or more extremes: *He took the middle course and wrote a letter rather than go there or telephone.*

,middle 'distance *def.n* (often *in the* —) part between the front and the back (of a scene in a photograph, painting etc).

,middle-'distance *attrib.adj* (*sport*) over a distance between long and short: *middle-distance running*; *a middle-distance runner.*

,Middle 'East *def.n.* countries east of the Mediterranean from Turkey to Iran.

'middle ,finger *c.n* finger that is second from the thumb.

'middle,man *c.n* (*pl* -,men) **1** person who buys things from manufacturers and sells them to shops, sends them to areas for selling etc. **2** person who helps two sides in a quarrel etc to find agreement.

,middle 'name *c.n* name between a first name and a family name.

,middle-of-the-'road *adj* (of a person, political beliefs etc) between extremes: *a middle-of-the-road politician.*

'middle ,school *c/u.n* (UK) school for children between 8 and 12.

,middle-'sized *adj* of a middle(2) size: *a middle-sized house.*

'middle,weight *c.n* (also *attrib*) boxer weighing about 75kg: *a middleweight fight.*

middling /'mɪdlɪŋ/ *adj* **1** of a middle(2) standard: *Her new record player is middling.* **fair to middling** ⇒ fair(*adj*).

▷ *adv* **2** (*informal*) quite: *The new sports bicycle is middling fast.*

midfield /,mɪd'fiːld/ *u.n* (also *attrib*) (in sport) middle area of the field: *a midfield player.* ⇒ forward(11), defender.

midge /mɪdʒ/ *c.n* small flying insect that can bite.

midget /'mɪdʒɪt/ *adj* **1** (*attrib*) very small: *a midget radio/camera.*

▷ *c.n* **2** (*derog*) small person.

midi /'mɪdɪ/ *attrib.adj* between the knee and the ankle in length: *wearing a midi dress/skirt.* Compare maxi, mini.

midland /'mɪdlənd/ *def.n* (also *attrib*) central part (of a country etc): *the midland states of India.*

'Midlands *def/def.pl.n* area in the middle of England, esp that around Birmingham.

midnight /'mɪd,naɪt/ *unique n* (also *attrib*) 12 o'clock in the night: *I arrived at midnight. Be home before midnight. After midnight the television closes down. By midnight most people are in bed asleep. We took the midnight train.* ⇒ midday. **burn the midnight oil** ⇒ oil(*n*).

,midnight 'sun *def.n* sun seen at midnight during summer at the poles²(1).

midpoint /'mɪd,pɔɪnt/ *def.n* **1** place, time, in the middle of an event, process, action etc: *He fell at the midpoint of the race.* **2** position half way along a line or other measurement: *Draw the circle at the midpoint of the line.*

midriff /'mɪdrɪf/ *c/def.n* part of the front of the body between the chest and the waist.

midst /mɪdst/ *def.n* **1 in the midst of s.t** in the middle of an activity: *In the midst of the crisis the leader was shot.* **2 in our**, **your** etc **midst** among us/you/them (all): *Suddenly a stranger appeared in our midst.*

▷ *prep* **3** (*literary*) amidst.

midstream /,mɪd'striːm/ *unique n* **in midstream** while speaking: *She paused in midstream to drink some water.*

midsummer /'mɪd,sʌmə/ *unique n* (also *attrib*) middle of the summer: *English gardens look lovely in midsummer. Let's give a midsummer party.*

,Mid,summer 'Day *unique n* (also ,Mid-,summer's 'Day) 24th June.

midway /'mɪd,weɪ/ *adj/adv* (often — *between s.t* (*and s.t*)) in the middle; halfway (between two points): *The train stopped midway between the bridge and the station.*

midweek /,mɪd'wiːk/ *adv* **1** in the middle of the week: *Let's have lunch midweek.*

▷ *unique n* (also *attrib*) **2** middle of the week: *It was nearly midweek before I heard from him. We took a midweek flight because it was cheaper.*

midwife /'mɪd,waɪf/ *c.n* (*pl* midwives) professional person who helps a woman to give birth to a baby.

midwifery /'mɪd,wɪfərɪ/ *u.n* job, practice, of a midwife.

midwinter /,mɪd'wɪntə/ *unique n* (also *attrib*) middle of the winter: *Many trees are bare in midwinter. We took a midwinter holiday in southern Spain.*

midyear /,mɪd'jɪə/ *unique n* (also *attrib*) middle of the year, esp a financial or academic(1) year: *We hope to sell most of the stock by midyear. Do you have midyear examinations?*

mien /miːn/ *c.n* (*literary*) person's appearance, way of behaving, type of voice etc: *a serious mien.*

might¹ /maɪt/ *aux.v* (no *pres.p*, *p.p* or *p.t* forms; negative forms **might not** or **mightn't** /'maɪtnt/; **might have** can be **might've** /'maɪtəv/; 'might' is followed by the infinitive form of a verb without *to*) Compare may. **1** (used after a *p.t* as the past tense of 'may' to show a possibility in the past): *I warned you that it might rain.* Compare may(1). **2** (used to express less probable present or future possibility than may(1)): *If you're not careful, you might fall.* **3** (used to give advice hesitantly): *You might like to try the police station.* **4** (*formal*) (used to ask permission more hesitantly than may(3)): *Might I speak to you for a moment?* **might have** + **p.p** (**a**) = may have + *p.p* (but with lesser probability): *John might have been too ill to go out.* (**b**) (used to express past unfulfilled possibility): *With a little more luck he might have won.* (**c**) (used to express s.t one should have done as a duty etc): *He might at least have paid her train* fare (but he did not). **s.o/s.t might well have** + **p.p** s.o was likely to have done s.t (but he/she did not); s.t was likely to have happened (but did not): *Boris might well have won but he was too tired at the end. It might well have rained if you'd gone earlier.* **s.o might (just) as well do s.t** ⇒ may.

might² /maɪt/ *u.n* (often (with) *all one's —*) physical(1) strength or mental(1) power: *They tried with all their might but the stone would not move. The committee used all its might to persuade the government, but failed.* **Might is right** (*proverb*) A more senior(1) or powerful position allows one the right to do s.t, esp s.t thought by some to be unfair: *When the old man complained about his house being pulled down to build a new road he soon discovered that might is right.* **by/with** (**all one's**) **might and main** using all one's strength or power: *He pulled with all his might and main but the boat would not move.*

'mightily *adv* to a large amount or extent: *She's mightily tired.*

'mighty *adj* (*-ier, -iest*) **1** having great physical(1) strength or mental(1) power: *A mightier man than you couldn't have stopped John from falling.* **high and mighty** ⇒ high.
▷ *adv* **2** (*informal*) very: *I'm mighty grateful.*

mightn't /'maɪtnt/ = might not. ⇒ might¹.

migraine /'miːɡreɪn/ *c/u.n* serious headache, usu one making it difficult to see.

migrate /maɪˈɡreɪt/ *intr.v* **1** (of a person) change the place where one lives, often for a limited length of time: *Some groups of Africans migrate across the desert in search of food and water.* **2** (often *— (from s.w) to s.w*) (of birds, fish) move from one part of the world to another at the same time each year: *Millions of birds migrate from the cold winter in the north to warm regions in the south during October.*

migrant /'maɪɡrənt/ *c.n* (also *attrib*) **1** person who moves from place to place, either to find work or with all her/his group to find food and water: *migrant workers.* **2** bird or fish that migrates(2).

migration /maɪˈɡreɪʃən/ *c/u.n.*

migratory /maɪˈɡreɪtərɪ/ *adj* (of people, animals) who/that migrate(1,2): *a migratory population*; *migratory routes*(1) *across central America.*

mike /maɪk/ *c.n* (*informal*) microphone.

milage ⇒ mileage.

mild /maɪld/ *adj* **1** (of food, drink, any substance with smell or taste) not strong in smell or taste: *a mild mustard*(2); *a mild beer*; *mild cheese*; *a mild cigarette*; *a mild perfume*(2); *a mild smell of burning.* **2** (of a person, personality(1)) gentle; easy to please and reach agreement with: *a mild mother/husband/boss*; *have a mild temperament.* **3** (of climate, weather) not very hot or very cold: *a mild winter.* Opposite hard(4). **4** (of a crime, punishment, illness, feeling etc) not serious or severe: *a mild form of measles; a mild sentence*(2); *a mild feeling of fear; mild drugs*(2). **meek and mild** ⇒ meek(*adj*).

'mildly *adv* to a small extent or degree: *It tastes mildly of soap. He seemed to be only mildly concerned about her health.* **to put it mildly** (describing s.t) without showing the strength of one's anger, disapproval etc: *When I discovered that my car had been repaired badly I was angry to put it mildly.*

'mildness *u.n.*

mildew /'mɪldjuː/ *u.n* **1** kind of disease that affects plants. **2** = mould²(1).

mile /maɪl/ *n* **1** *c.n* measurement of length, distance (1609 metres) over land, up into the air etc; 1760 yards²(1): *Many people can run a mile in under 4 minutes.* **2** *c.n* (usu *pl*, *for —s*) (*informal*) very long distance: *We walked (for) miles before we found a café.* **3** *def.n* race over a measured mile(1): *He ran the mile in 3.47 minutes.* **a miss is as good as a mile** ⇒ miss²(*n*). **be miles out** (**in s.t**) (*fig*) be wrong to a great extent (in a calculation, a measurement etc). **miss** (**s.t**) **by a mile** not succeed (in hitting s.t, reaching one's objective(2)) by a very great amount or extent. **nautical mile** ⇒ nautical. **run a mile** (**from s.o/ s.t**) (*fig*) go far away (from s.o/s.t): *She'd run a mile if she saw you looking like that.* **stand/stick out a mile** be very easy to see or understand: *It stands out a mile that Fred will fail because he never does any work.* **statute mile** ⇒ statute.

mileage /'maɪlɪdʒ/ *c/u.n* (also **'milage**) (example of) distance travelled measured in miles: *I bought the car because it had done a low mileage* (i.e had not been driven very far). **get** (**a lot of, no, some**) **mileage out of s.t** (*fig*; *informal*) be able to make (a lot of, no, some) use of information, conditions, an opportunity etc: *The lawyer hoped to get some mileage out of the fact that the police had no strong evidence*(1).

mileometer /maɪˈlɒmɪtə/ *c.n* (also **mi'lometer**) instrument that records mileage in a vehicle.

'miler *c.n* person who runs in the mile(3).

'mile,stone *c.n* (often *— in s.t*) important event, occasion, (in life or history): *The introduction of small computers has become a milestone in business practice.*

milieu /'miːljɜː/ *c.n* (*pl -s, milieux* /'miːljɜːz/) (*French*) social setting (of a person or group): *Her favourite milieu is dinner parties with the best wines.*

militant /'mɪlɪtənt/ *adj* **1** (of a person, political group or a philosophy(2)) very willing and ready to use force to win s.t, esp power: *She writes for a militant newspaper.*
▷ *c.n* **2** militant(1) person: *Several militants joined the trade union in an effort to take control of the members and destroy the factory.*

militancy /'mɪlɪtənsɪ/ *u.n.* **'militantly** *adv.*

military /'mɪlɪtrɪ/ *attrib.adj* **1** of or referring to the armed forces or war: *a military operation/ force/ response*(2). **2** like (a member of) the armed forces or their activities: *We organized the preparations for the expedition² with military precision.*
▷ *def.pl.n* **3** armed forces: *The military have been asked to help during the emergency.*

,military a'cademy *c.n* (*pl -ies*) place where young officers are trained.

,military 'honours *pl.n* (often *with full —*) ceremony by the military, e.g when burying a member of the armed forces: *The soldiers were buried with full military honours.*

,military po'lice *def.pl.n* (*abbr MP*) part of an army acting as police to keep law and order in the armed forces.

,military 'service *u.n* (often *on —*) (length of time of) being a soldier.

militarism /'mɪlɪtə,rɪzəm/ *u.n* **1** (support for)

political control by the military(3). **2** strong desire to succeed as a member of the military(3).

militarist /'mɪlɪtərɪst/ *c.n* person who believes in militarism.

militaristic /ˌmɪlɪtə'rɪstɪk/ *adj* of, like, a militarist(2).

militia /mɪ'lɪʃə/ *def/def.pl.n* group of men, not regular soldiers, trained to act as a military(1) force in an emergency.

militate /'mɪlɪˌteɪt/ *intr.v* **militate against s.o/s.t** (formal) be a force or power against, have an effect that is against, s.o/s.t: *The bad weather militated against him as he climbed the mountain* (or *against an attempt on the world speed record*).

milk /mɪlk/ *u.n* **1** white liquid formed by a woman and other female mammals, used to feed their young. **2** this liquid from cows (or sometimes goats, sheep etc) used by people as food: *a bottle of milk; cheese and butter are made from milk*. **3** white liquid in a coconut(1) or inside some plants and trees. **cry over spilt milk** (*fig*) be sad about a bad result, loss etc that cannot be changed: *You did not get the job but it's no good crying over spilt milk*. **the milk of human kindness** (*fig*) (of an action, person) showing a large amount of sympathy and understanding: *Her mother is the milk of human kindness*.

▷ *v* **4** *tr/intr.v* take milk(1) from (a female mammal): *Cows must be milked twice a day*. **5** *intr.v* (of a cow etc) produce milk: *Is the brown cow still milking?* **6** *tr.v* (often — *s.o* (out) of *s.t*) (*fig*; informal) take money, information etc from (s.o/ s.t) gradually: *The old woman was milked of all her savings by her lazy son. The journalists milked the story of the robbery out of the unwilling man*. **milk s.o/s.t dry** (*fig*) milk(6) a person, situation, until there is nothing of value left.

milk 'chocolate *c/u.n* (piece of) chocolate made with milk. ⇨ plain chocolate.

'milkiness *u.n* (of a liquid) state of being or looking milky.

'milking ˌmachine *c.n* device for getting milk(2) from a cow etc.

'milk ˌjug *c.n* container for milk(2) with a handle and a lip(2), used in a home.

'milkˌmaid *c.n* woman who milks(4) cows, goats etc.

'milkman *c.n* (*pl -men*) **1** man who milks(4) cows, goats etc. **2** man who delivers milk(2) to homes.

ˌmilk of mag'nesia ⇨ magnesia.

ˌmilk 'pudding *c/u.n* (kind of) food made by boiling or baking a cereal(2) with sugar in milk(2).

'milk ˌshake *c.n* drink of milk(2) mixed with a fruit or chocolate etc flavour: *a strawberry milk shake*.

'milk ˌtooth *c.n* (*pl milk teeth*) one of the first set of teeth, with short roots.

'milky *adj* (*-ier, -iest*) **1** containing a lot of milk(2): *milky coffee*. **2** (of a liquid) white or unclear(1): *Some trees produce a milky liquid when the bark is cut*.

ˌMilky 'Way *def/unique n* long narrow area made up of light from millions of stars seen across the sky at night.

mill /mɪl/ *c.n* **1** (building for a) large machine for producing flour from cereal(2). ⇨ windmill. **2** (building for) machinery used to make s.t, esp

by turning or crushing: *a cotton mill; a paper mill; a mill for crushing fruit*. **3** small machine that turns to crush coffee beans, polish metal etc. **4** large machine used to print cloth. **be put, go, through the mill** (*fig*) experiences.t as a usual routine(2), esp one considered to be unpleasantly necessary: *be put through the educational mill*. **run-of-the-mill** ⇨ run.

▷ *tr.v* **5** produce (flour, paper, coffee powder etc) using a mill(1–3). **6** produce small grooves(1) across the edge of (a coin). **mill about/around (s.o/s.t)** (of a group of people, animals etc) move between one another (or s.o/s.t) in a disorganized way: *We saw some boys milling about on the corner of the street*.

'miller *c.n* person who works a mill(1).

'mill,pond *c.n* small area of water made to provide water to turn a millwheel. **as calm as, like, a millpond** (of the sea etc) calm; without waves.

'mill,stone *c.n* **1** one of the two heavy stones turned on each other to make flour from cereal(2). **2** (usu *a* — *round s.o's neck*) (*fig*) responsibility, duty, promise, person etc that/ who is difficult or hard to bear: *Her children were a millstone (round her neck) for years*.

'mill,wheel *c.n* large wheel, esp a wooden one that turns in water, used to work a mill(1). ⇨ waterwheel.

millennium /mɪ'lenɪəm/ *n* (*pl -s, millennia* /mɪ'lenɪə/) **1** *c.n* period of 1000 years. **2** *def.n* (imaginary) period in the future when people will be always happy: *It's no good waiting for the millennium; you must solve your own difficulties*.

millet /'mɪlɪt/ *u.n* small round seed of some cereals(2), used as food: *Indian millet. Pearl millet is used to feed animals*.

millibar /'mɪlɪˌbɑː/ *c.n* (*technical*) unit of measurement of air pressure.

milligram /'mɪlɪˌɡræm/ *c.n* (also **'milli,gramme**) thousandth part of a gram, *symb* mg.

millilitre /'mɪlɪˌliːtə/ *c.n* (US **milli,liter**) thousandth part of a litre, *symb* ml.

'milli,metre /'mɪlɪˌmiːtə/ *c.n* (US **millimeter**) thousandth part of a metre, *symb* mm.

milliner /'mɪlɪnə/ *c.n* **1** person who makes and sells women's hats etc. **2** (also **'milliner's**) shop that sells hats etc.

millinery /'mɪlɪnrɪ/ *u.n* goods (hats, lace(2) etc) sold by a milliner.

million /'mɪljən/ *det/pron* (*cardinal number*) (used with 'a' (*a million*) unless there is another det; e.g *one million, your million*, *pl million* after another number, e.g *two million*, but otherwise *millions*, e.g *millions of people*) **1** 1 000 000; a thousand times a thousand: *Five million families own a washing-machine. People promised in their millions* (i.e several million people promised) *to send money to the Children in Need* appeal(1). **'millions** *pl.n* (often — *of s.o/s.t*) **1** several million (people, things etc) (usu more than two or three million): *The family business is now worth millions*. **2** (*informal*) extremely large amount/ number (of people, things etc): *Millions of people saw the event on television*.

millionth /'mɪljənθ/ *det/pron* (*ordinal number*) **1** (person or thing) following 999 999 in order; 1 000 000th.

▷ *c.n* **2** fraction(2) produced by dividing s.t into 1 000 000 equal parts; $\frac{1}{1\,000\,000}$.

millipede /'mɪlɪˌpiːd/ *c.n* kind of long insect with many pairs of short legs. ⇒ centipede.

millpond, millstone, millwheel ⇒ mill.

milometer ⇒ mileometer.

mime /maɪm/ *n* **1** *c/u.n* (example of) expressing an idea, a feeling, an activity or kind of personality(1) using movements of the face and body only and not words, detailed scenery etc. **2** *u.n* entertainment, e.g in a theatre, using mime(1). **3** *c.n* person who uses mime(1).

▷ *tr/intr.v* **4** use mime(1) to describe, imitate, (s.o) or to express (s.t): *He was miming a weak man trying to break down a locked door.*

¹**mimer** *c.n* mime(3), esp when entertaining.

mimic /'mɪmɪk/ **1** person who imitates s.o/ s.t, esp as entertainment. **2** animal, e.g a parrot(1) or chimpanzee, that can imitate s.o/s.t.

▷ *v* (-ck-) **3** *tr/intr.v* (of a person) pretend to be (s.o, a kind of personality) by using similar movements, speech etc: *He was mimicking his teacher's walk when she came into the classroom. Paul can mimic (people) very well.* **4** *tr.v* (of animals) pretend to be (another animal) as a form of protection: *Some harmless insects mimic poisonous ones.* **5** *tr.v* (of animals) copy (the voice or movements of humans): Parrots(1) *can mimic a person's voice so well that it is often impossible to tell the difference.*

mimicry /'mɪmɪkrɪ/ *u.n* **1** act of mimicking(3–5). **2** mimicking(4), esp to avoid danger.

min *written abbr* **1** minimum. **2** minute(s). **3** (**M**) Minister(1); Ministry(1).

minaret /ˌmɪnəˈret/ *c.n* tall narrow tower of a mosque.

mince /mɪns/ *u.n* **1** (also ¹**minced ˌmeat**) meat made into very small pieces using a mincer.

▷ *v* **2** *tr.v* make (meat) into very small pieces using a mincer. **3** *intr.v* (usu — *about, around, in, out* etc) (usu *derog*) use a way of walking that tries to make one appear elegant(1) and cultured in order to impress(2) or attract others: *The young woman was mincing down the steps in her high-heeled shoes hoping that the man would notice her.* **not mince one's words**; **not to mince matters** speak openly and clearly and not try to hide one's true opinion or be polite: '*Not to mince matters,*' he said, '*you're a fool!*' *He didn't mince his words but told her that she was boring.*

¹**minced ˌmeat** *u.n* ⇒ mince(1).

¹**mince ˌmeat** *u.n* **1** (also *attrib*) mixture of dried fruit: *mincemeat pies.* **2** = minced meat. **make mincemeat (out) of s.o/s.t** (*fig*) completely defeat s.o, an argument, s.o's plans etc: *The cruel examiner made mincemeat of the nervous students.*

ˌ**mince ¹pie** *c.n* pie filled with mincemeat(1).

¹**mincer** *c.n* machine that minces(2) meat by cutting it.

¹**mincing ma,chine** *c.n* mincer(1).

mind¹ /maɪnd/ *n* **1** *c/u.n* activity in s.o's brain so that he/she can think, imagine and have feelings: *Her mind is not on her job and so she makes lots of mistakes. Don't fill his mind with useless ideas.* **2** *u.n* memory: *Her name is in my mind but I can't say it.* **3** *u.n* state or manner of thought: *I need peace of mind in order to work well.* **4** *c.n* purpose; intention: *I have a mind to report you*

to the police but *I won't if you return all my things.* **5** *c.n* attention: *Television can take your mind off your problems.* **6** *c.n* opinion: *They seem to be of the same mind about the value of your car.* **7** *c.n* person with very good intelligence and imagination: *Some of the greatest minds of this century are trying to find a cure for* cancer(1).

absence of mind ⇒ absence. ⇒ absent-minded. **be all in the mind** be s.t one imagines and not real: *Her backache is all in the mind.* **be in two minds (about s.t, whether to do s.t)** find difficulty in deciding what to do or what opinion to have (about s.t etc): *She's in two minds about going to China for her holiday.* **be of a, one, the same, mind (about s.o/s.t)** have the same opinion (about s.o/s.t); agree: *We're of one mind about who should become chairman.* **be out of one's (tiny) mind** be very foolish; mad: *You must be out of your mind to pay so much for such an old bicycle.* **bear/keep s.o/s.t in mind**; **bear** etc **in mind that . . .** continue to be conscious of s.o/s.t (or that . . .); remember s.o/s.t (or that . . .): *You must bear in mind that he has been very ill and will look older when you see him.* **blow s.o's mind** (*fig; informal*) cause s.o to be extremely surprised or excited: *One quick look at all the expensive equipment(2) in the music centre they gave me for my birthday and it really blew my mind!* ⇒ mind-blowing. **bring/call s.o/s.t to mind** cause one to remember s.o/s.t: *Your story brings to mind a similar(1) experience I had years ago.* **change one's mind (about s.o/s.t)** change one's opinion or decision (about s.o/s.t): *Are you sure you won't change your mind and come with us?* **close one's mind to s.t** refuse to consider s.t: *He has closed his mind to any idea of seeing her again.* **come to mind**; **come into s.o's mind** be remembered: *Her name came to mind a minute ago but now it's gone again.* **cross s.o's mind** come into s.o's thoughts: *The idea that John might have taken your pen never even crossed my mind!* **dismiss s.o/s.t from one's mind** put thoughts about s.o/s.t out of one's head: *You must dismiss from your mind any idea of getting your job back.* **drive s.o out of her/ his mind** (often passive) cause s.o to become very worried or mad: *She was driven out of her mind with worry.* **ease/relieve s.o's mind** make s.o feel less anxious: *The doctor's news that she will recover has eased our minds greatly.* **enter s.o's head/mind (to do s.t)** ⇒ head(*n*). **flit through one's mind** ⇒ flit(*v*). **give/put/set/ turn one's mind to s.t** give all one's attention to an activity: *If you put your mind to it, you could finish the work by Friday.* **give s.o a piece of one's mind** be very angry and blame s.o; tell s.o one's poor opinion of her/him. **go out of one's mind (with s.t)** become (almost) mad (with worry etc): *She's going out of her mind with anxiety about her missing child.* **go (clean) out of s.o's mind** (of a name, arrangement, time etc) be (completely) forgotten. **have a closed mind (about s.t)** = close one's mind to s.t. **have a good mind to do s.t** feel strongly that one should do s.t: *I've a good mind to tell your mother how badly you've been behaving at school.* **have half a mind to do s.t** be interested in doing s.t but unable to decide: *I've half a mind to join the youth club but I'm not sure.* **have (got) s.o/**

s.t in mind be thinking about s.o/s.t to choose (as a solution to a problem). **have it in mind to do s.t** have decided to do s.t (but have not yet done it): *I have it in mind to order a newspaper each day but I haven't done it yet.* **have a mind of one's own** be able to decide for oneself, not be dependent on others: *You must let your son decide what university to apply for — he has a mind of his own.* **have one's mind on s.o/s.t** have one's attention on s.o/s.t (so that other matters are ignored or forgotten): *He didn't think about feeding the dog because he had his mind on more important things.* **have an open mind (about s.o/s.t)** be still undecided(1) (about s.o/s.t): *Peter has an open mind about his future.* ⇒ open-minded. **(in a) good, bad** etc **frame of mind** ⇒ frame(*n*). **in one's/the mind's eye** ⇒ eye(*n*). **in one's right mind** ⇒ right(*adj*). **keep s.o/s.t in mind** ⇒ bear/keep s.o/s.t in mind. **keep one's mind on s.t** keep one's attention on an activity: *The teacher told the children to keep their minds on their work.* **know one's own mind** be able to decide (because one knows what one wants, has a strong opinion etc): *First you want a camera and then you want a bicycle — you don't know your own mind!* **lose one's mind** become mad, esp because of anger or worry: *He completely lost his mind and hit the policeman.* **make up one's mind (about s.o/s.t, to do s.t)** make a decision, arrive at an opinion (about s.o/s.t, about what to do): *I can't make up my mind about which television programme to watch. I've made up my mind to go and apologize. My mind's made up — I'm not going to marry you.* **s.o's mind's a blank; s.o's mind went blank** s.o's memory has gone/failed: *I can't remember his name — my mind's a blank. As soon as I entered the examination room my mind went blank and I could remember nothing.* **mind over matter** (being in favour of) feelings and mental(1) powers rather than the body and the material(1) world: *Love is often a question of mind over matter.* **(not) enter s.o's head/mind (to do s.t)** ⇒ head(*n*). **nothing is, can be, farther/further from s.o's mind** an idea, opinion, intention etc already mentioned is definitely not in one's thoughts: *'Will you ask Mary to the party on Saturday?' 'Nothing could be farther from my mind!'* **of sound/unsound mind** (*law*) sane/insane. **on one's mind** in one's thoughts, usu in a worrying way: *I've had her on my mind all day — do you think I ought to telephone her?* **a one-track/single-track mind** ⇒ track(*n*). **open one's mind to s.t** be willing to consider s.t: *I wish she would open her mind to other possibilities.* ⇒ open-minded. **peace of mind** ⇒ peace. **presence of mind** ⇒ presence. **prey on s.o's mind** cause one to be worried all the time. **put one's mind to s.t** ⇒ give/put/set/turn one's mind to s.t. **put s.o in mind of s.o/s.t** cause s.o to remember s.o/s.t: *Your experience puts me very much in mind of my own time in the army.* **read s.o's mind** know what s.o is thinking, planning etc: *I sat opposite him trying to read his mind in order to win the argument.* ⇒ mind-reader. **run through s.o's mind** be s.t that s.o is thinking about. **set/turn one's mind back (to s.t)** think about s.t in the past: *I want you to set your mind back to your childhood and tell me about your parents.* **set one's mind on s.t** decide completely to have

s.t or to do s.t: *I've set my mind on buying that watch.* **set s.o's mind at ease/rest** take away s.o's feelings of anxiety: *The doctor was able to set our minds at rest about the operation on David's leg.* **set one's mind to s.t** ⇒ give/put/set/turn one's mind to s.t. **slip s.o's memory/mind** ⇒ memory. **speak one's mind** say exactly what one is thinking: *Can I speak my mind and tell you my true opinion of your writing?* **state of mind** ⇒ state(*n*). **stick in s.o's mind** be often remembered; be remembered clearly: *Her speech about words being bridges that take one from one place to another has stuck in my mind for years.* **take s.o's mind off s.o/s.t** help to take s.o's attention away from s.o/s.t: *She thought a holiday might help to take her mind off her sister's illness.* **The mind boggles** (*informal*) One cannot imagine such a strange, extraordinary etc idea, event etc: *The mind boggles when one thinks of the possibility of taking a holiday on the moon.* ⇒ mind-boggling. **to one's mind** in one's opinion: *To my mind air travel should be cheaper.* **turn one's mind to s.t** ⇒ give/put/set/turn one's mind to s.t. **turn one's mind back (to s.t)** ⇒ set/turn one's mind back (to s.t). **turn s.t over in one's mind** think about s.t carefully: *He turned the idea of becoming a policeman over in his mind but could not decide.* **Two minds with but a single thought** (used when two people say or do the same thing at the same time). **the way, how, one's/s.o's mind works** how one/s.o decides, thinks, arrives at an opinion: *I'd love to know how his mind works when he plans a robbery.* **weigh, be a weight, on s.o's mind** make s.o feel worried about s.t all the time.

'mind-,blowing *adj* (*informal*) causing great surprise or excitement: *a mind-blowing model of a spacecraft.* ⇒ blow s.o's mind (⇒ mind¹).

'mind-,boggling *adj* (*informal*) difficult to imagine because so strange, extraordinary etc: *a mind-boggling journey to another planet.* ⇒ The mind boggles (⇒ mind¹).

-minded *adj* (state of) having or showing the kind, condition, of mind(1) mentioned in the first part of the word: *a tough-minded head teacher.* ⇒ broad-minded, high-minded, narrow-minded, open-minded, small-minded.

'mindful *pred.adj* (usu — of s.o/s.t) (*formal*) giving care or thought (to s.o/s.t): *He's mindful of his duty to his parents.* Opposite unmindful.

'mindless *adj* **1** (*derog*) careless: *a mindless error.* **2** not needing or using intelligence or thought: *have a mindless job in a factory; watching acts of mindless violence on television.* **3** (*pred*) (usu — of s.o/s.t) giving no care or thought (to s.o/s.t): *mindless of the danger.*

'mindlessly *adv.* **'mindlessness** *u.n.*

'mind-,reader *c.n* = thought-reader.

'mind-,reading *u.n* act/ability of a mind-reader.

mind² /maind/ *v* **1** *tr.v* take care or charge of (s.o/s.t): *Who is minding the baby while you are shopping? We're minding their house for them during the holidays.* ⇒ minder. **2** *intr/tr.v* (not in continuous tenses; usu in questions or negative statements) be opposed (to s.t); not like (s.t): *Would he mind waiting for me if I am a little late? She doesn't seem to mind if I come or not. I don't mind children being lively but I do mind rudeness. 'Do you mind if I smoke?' 'Yes, I do* *mind.'* We wouldn't mind (We'd like) *a holiday but there's no time.* **3** *intr/tr.v* (usu imperative) be careful (about/of s.t): *Mind that coffee — you'll spill it. Mind you don't fall down the stairs. Mind your head, the bridge is very low. Mind that you remember to lock the door.*

Do you mind! (used to show one's opposition to s.o's behaviour, speech, concerning oneself): *Do you mind! Some people are trying to listen to the music* (i.e so could you please stop talking).

Do you mind (. . .-ing/if . . .)? Do you have any objection to (s.o doing s.t)?

Don't mind me (usu ironic) pay no attention to me or what I prefer: *Your music is very loud but don't mind me, I only live here!*

I don't mind if I do (used as a polite way of accepting s.t): *'Would you like a chocolate?' 'I don't mind if I do.'*

If you don't mind (usu used to show annoyance) if it is no trouble to you: *If you don't mind I'd like my pen back.*

I wouldn't mind, but . . . (usu used to show surprised anger): *She asked me for £2 and I wouldn't mind but she borrowed £5 last week and hasn't paid me back.*

mind one's own business ⇨ business.

mind one's language ⇨ language.

mind one's p's and q's be careful about what one says or does.

mind one's/the step ⇨ step(*n*).

mind out (often as an order) be careful; take care: *Mind out — that handle is loose. Mind out because she'll try to cheat you.*

Mind you . . . (used when giving more information) (a) but: *I like the house; mind you I don't like the furniture.* (b) note or remember: *Paul broke the chair but he did apologize, mind you.*

never mind it does not matter; don't worry about it: *'I've broken a cup.' 'Never mind, we have lots of them.'* **never you mind** I refuse to tell you: *'What's on TV?' 'Never you mind — get on with your work.'*

ˈ**minder** *c.n* person who minds²(1) s.o/s.t: *a baby minder; a machine-minder.*

mine¹ /main/ *c.n* **1** underground system of tunnels where valuable minerals are taken out: *a coal/gold/tin mine.* **2** kind of explosive (to be) buried in the ground, used to make large holes in the ground, to make rocks loose, to destroy an enemy etc. **3** kind of bomb made by putting an explosive into a metal container; it is used in the sea to destroy enemy ships. **a mine of information (about s.o/s.t)** (*fig*) a person, book etc who/that provides a lot of information (about s.o/s.t): *Our dad is a mine of information about the development of space travel.*

▷ *v* **4** *intr/tr.v* (often *— for* s.t) dig up (s.t), look for (s.t) by digging in a mine(1): *Copper has been mined in Zambia for many years. We shall need to mine for coal more seriously when our oil supplies run out.* **5** *tr.v* put, bury, use, a mine(2,3) in (a place): *The rivers and the forests have been mined to prevent harm from any army coming too near.*

ˈ**mine deˌtector** *c.n* instrument for finding the position of mines(2,3).

ˈ**mine-disˌposal** *u.n* (also *attrib*) act of making mines(2,3) useless by removing or separating parts: *a mine-disposal expert.*

ˈ**mineˌfield** *c.n* **1** place where several mines(1) have been dug. ⇨ field(2). **2** place where many mines(2,3) have been placed. **3** (*fig*) thing that is very difficult to get through or understand: *This catalogue(1) is a minefield of badly arranged information.*

ˈ**mineˌlayer** *c.n* ship, aircraft, that carries and lays mines(3).

ˈ**miner** *c.n* person who works in a mine(1).

ˈ**mineˌsweeper** *c.n* ship that finds and destroys mines(3).

ˈ**mining** *u.n* (also *attrib*) act, process, of mining (⇨ mine¹)(4): *the mining industry.*

mine² /main/ *possessive pron* the one(s) belonging to, for, me: *Your coat is there and mine is over here. His children are at school but mine are much older. Are they yours or mine?* **of mine** of, belonging to, me: *She's a friend of mine. That's a silly habit of mine.* ⇨ I², me, my, myself.

mineral /ˈmɪnərəl/ *c.n* (also *attrib*) **1** substance, e.g a metal, jewel, kind of rock, forming part of the ground and obtained by mining: *The mineral wealth of parts of Africa is huge. Iron is the world's most common mineral.* **2** chemical substance that is not an animal or plant: *We need to eat or drink very small quantities of certain minerals to keep us healthy.* **3** drink made of water flavoured with fruit juice etc and with gas in it.

ˈ**mineral ˌkingdom** *def.n* all substances that are not animals or plants, e.g rocks, soil, stones etc. ⇨ animal kingdom, vegetable kingdom.

mineralogical /ˌmɪnərəˈlɒdʒɪkl/ *adj* of mineralogy: *mineralogical science.*

mineralogist /ˌmɪnəˈrælədʒɪst/ *c.n* expert in mineralogy.

mineralogy /ˌmɪnəˈrælədʒɪ/ *u.n* study of minerals(1,2).

ˈ**mineral ˌoil** *u.n* oil that is mined¹(4): *Petroleum is a mineral oil.*

ˈ**mineral ˌsalt** *c.n* kind of chemical substance (compound(1)) forming a particular group of minerals, often used in medicines.

ˈ**mineral ˌwater** *u.n* **1** water with gas in it prepared as a drink and sometimes flavoured with fruit juice etc. ⇨ mineral(3). **2** supply of natural water containing mineral salt, used for bathing or drunk for pleasure or as medical treatment.

minestrone /ˌmɪnɪˈstrəʊnɪ/ *u.n* (also *attrib*) (*Italian*) soup made of a mixture of vegetables and pasta: *Let's have some minestrone soup.*

mingle /ˈmɪŋgl/ *intr/tr.v* (cause s.o/s.t to) mix (with other people, things): *We mingled with the other people on the beach. The different kinds of birds (were) mingled together in the same cage.*

mingy /ˈmɪndʒɪ/ *adj* (-ier, -iest) (*derog; informal*) not at all generous; miserly: *He's so mingy with his sweets.*

ˈ**mingily** *adv*. ˈ**minginess** *u.n*.

mini /ˈmɪnɪ/ *attrib.adj* **1** very small: *a mini camera/computer.* **2** very short: *a mini skirt/dress.* Compare maxi, midi.

▷ *c.n* **3** very short skirt or dress: *Do girls wear minis in winter?* **4** kind of small car: *He drives a mini.*

ˈ**mini ˌbus** *c.n* small bus.

ˈ**mini ˌcab** *c.n* small car used as a taxi.

miniature /ˈmɪnɪtʃə/ *attrib.adj* **1** very much smaller in size than is usual or normal: *a miniature railway; a miniature painting of a rose; a miniature breed(1) of dog.*

▷ *c.n* **2** copy or model that is very much smaller than

the original: *This* statue *is a miniature of the one in Paris.* **3** very small painting of a person, thing: *Miniatures were popular as presents a hundred years ago.* **4** very small breed(1) of dog: *My terrier is a miniature.*

minim /'mɪnɪm/ *c.n* (*music*) note with twice the value of a crotchet, *symb* ♩.

minimum /'mɪnɪməm/ *attrib.adj* (*written abbr min*) **1** smallest (amount, size of s.t): *What's your minimum cost for doing the work? The minimum quantity I can sell you is ten. The minimum age for leaving school is 16.* Opposite maximum(1).

▷ *c.n* (*pl* -s, or, much less usu, *minima* /'mɪnɪmə/) **2** least possible or known amount, size, extent etc: *We have managed to reduce our prices to a minimum. You ought to eat a minimum of 1000 calories a day.* Opposite maximum(2).

minimal /'mɪnɪməl/ *adj* of the smallest amount, size, extent etc possible: *We have only a minimal quantity of food left. The amount of work Alex does is minimal.* ⇨ maximal.

minimize, -ise /'mɪnɪmaɪz/ *tr.v* **1** make (possible failure, a risk etc) least likely to happen: *Good brakes will minimize the possibility of an accident while driving.* **2** treat (s.t) as having very little size, importance or value: *It is no good minimizing the work needed to pass examinations.* Opposite maximize.

,minimum 'wage *c.n* lowest wage allowed by law or union agreement.

minion /'mɪnɪən/ *c.n* (*derog*) **1** person who obeys a boss, officer etc in an exaggerated way in order to gain favour: *Some managers seem to enjoy reducing their staff to minions.* **2** person who has less or little power, rank etc: *minions in the government offices who seem unable to take a decision.*

minister /'mɪnɪstə/ *c.n* **1** (often with capital **M**; *written abbr Min*) person who leads a government department: *the Minister for Trade and Industry.* ⇨ prime minister. **2** (in some Protestant(1) churches) clergyman. Compare priest, vicar.

▷ *intr.v* **3** (often — *to s.o/s.t*) (*formal*) take care (of s.o, s.o's needs): *ministering to (the needs of) the poor. A priest ministers to the religious needs of the* community(1).

ministerial /ˌmɪnɪ'stɪərɪəl/ *adj* of or referring to a minister(1,2) or her/his duties: *ministerial papers.*

,mini'sterially *adv*: *ministerially efficient.*

,minister of 'state *c.n* (UK) government minister(1), esp one not in the cabinet(2).

ministration /ˌmɪnɪ'streɪʃən/ *c/u.n* (*formal*) (example of) ministering(3), esp on religious matters: *the devoted ministrations of the nurses in the refugee camp.*

ministry /'mɪnɪstrɪ/ *n* (*pl* -ies) **1** *c.n* (with capital **M** in titles) government department: *the Ministry of Transport.* **2** *c.n* office, duties, of a government minister(1). **3** *def.n* profession of a priest, vicar or minister(2): *He entered the ministry (became a priest etc) at 18.*

mink /mɪŋk/ *c/u.n* (*pl* -(s)) (coat, jacket etc made from the) valuable brown fur of a kind of small animal that lives near water.

minor /'maɪnə/ *adj* (usu *attrib*) **1** less important than others: *I have made only minor changes to the plan you suggest. The minor roads on the map are brown or yellow. He took only a minor part in*

the robbery. *Luckily her injuries seem to be minor.* Compare major(1).

▷ *c.n* **2** (*law*) person who is not an adult (under 18 in age). Compare major(3).

minority /maɪ'nɒrɪtɪ/ *attrib.adj* **1** (agreed by) less than half the members of a group: *The minority parties had wanted more time to consider the matter.* Compare majority(1).

▷ *n* (*pl* -ies) **2** *c.n* smaller number, amount or part: *The racial minorities* (i.e groups of people who are not of the same race as the majority(2)) *would like their languages to be taught in schools. Only a minority of his wages was spent on feeding his family.* Opposite majority(2,3). **be in the minority** be in the group with the smallest number (of people in favour etc): *Why do you continue to argue when you know you are in the minority?*

mi,nority 'government *c/u.n* (example of) government by a group who do not have enough support or members to win on matters discussed.

mint¹ /mɪnt/ *u.n* (also *attrib*) kind of herb with strong smelling and tasting leaves, used in cooking, for flavouring chocolate etc: *I like mint sauce with roast* lamb(2).

mint² /mɪnt/ *attrib.adj* **1** as good as new. **in mint condition (a)** (esp of books, stamps etc) as good as new; not used. **(b)** (also of second-hand goods) still in excellent condition: *I've hardly used the sewing machine — it's in mint condition.*

▷ *n* **2** *c/def.n* (often with capital **M**) place where money is made (by the government). **3** *sing.n* (*informal*) large amount of money: *He earned a mint selling insurance.*

▷ *tr.v* **4** make (coins): *When did Britain start minting pound coins?*

minuet /ˌmɪnjʊ'et/ *c.n* (piece of music for a) slow, graceful dance popular in the 17th century in Europe.

minus /'maɪnəs/ *attrib.adj* (*mathematics*) **1** (of the sign '—' that shows a number) less than 0: *Minus six plus minus two is equal to minus eight* (−6 + −2 = −8). *The temperature last night dropped to minus six degrees* (−6°).

▷ *c.n* **2** mathematics sign '—' to show the operation of subtracting or that a number is less than 0.

▷ *prep* **3** (*mathematics*) used to show the operation of subtracting: *Fifteen minus four is equal to eleven* (15 − 4 = 11). **4** (*informal*) without: *We were minus several glasses after that party.*

minuscule /'mɪnɪˌskjuːl/ *adj* very small: *He used a minuscule tool to open the watch.*

minute¹ /maɪ'njuːt/ *adj* **1** very small (in size, degree): *The baby mice were minute when they were born. The glass vase fell on the stone floor and broke into the minutest pieces.* **2** accurate and including even the smallest details: *Please report this event in the minutest detail.*

mi'nutely *adv* carefully and accurately: *They examined the area minutely.*

mi'nuteness *u.n.*

minutiae /mɪ'njuːʃɪˌaɪ/ *pl.n* very small details: *You're wasting a lot of time on the minutiae and there is no time for the more important things.*

minute² /'mɪnɪt/ *c.n* (also *attrib*) (*written abbr min*; *symb* ') **1** sixty seconds; one sixtieth part of an hour: *It's four minutes to six. It starts in two minutes. Can you wait (for) a few minutes? I'll be*

five minutes late. **2** (*informal*) a very short time: *He won't be a minute — why don't you sit and wait for him. I'll just be a minute.* Compare moment. **3** (*mathematics*) sixty seconds, one sixtieth part of a degree (in measuring an angle): *The angle measures sixty-four degrees forty minutes (64° 40').* **4** (usu *pl*) notes that record what was said and decided at a meeting etc: *The secretary read the minutes of the last meeting.* (**at**) **any minute** very soon: *We're expecting him to arrive (at) any minute.* **at that minute** at that particular point in time: *At that minute the door opened and there they were.* **the minute that . . .** as soon as . . . : *We hadn't met but I knew who he was the minute he walked in.* **to the minute** exactly: *She phones every day at 7 o'clock to the minute.* **up to the minute** (**up-to-the-minute** when *attrib*) including, providing, the very latest information: *He is always up to the minute about what films are showing. Stay with Radio 4 for an up-to-the-minute account of the peace talks in Geneva.*
▷ *tr.v* **5** make notes or minutes²(4) to record (what was said and decided at a meeting etc): *I would like my personal opinion to be minuted as I disagree with the decision being taken.*
'minute ,hand *c/def.n* longer of the two main moving pointers on a clock or watch which shows the minutes when reading the time. ⇨ hour/second hand, hand(4).

minx /mɪŋks/ *c.n* (*informal*) young girl who is naughty, mischievous(1).

miracle /'mɪrəkl/ *c.n* **1** surprising event that produces a happy and unexpected result: *It's a miracle you weren't all killed in that accident.* **2** event or result that cannot be explained because it does not follow the known laws of nature: *The* Bible *describes many miracles, as when* Christ *gave a blind man his sight.* **3** (esp *a — of s.t*) surprising and wonderful example (of science, medicine, technology etc): *It's a miracle of nature that life can grow from plants that look dead all winter.* **work miracles** have a result or effect that people think is not possible: *The new* drug(1) *worked miracles.*
miraculous /mɪ'rækjʊləs/ *adj* producing an unexpected and happy result: *She made a miraculous recovery. It is miraculous that they escaped.*
mi'raculously *adv*: *Miraculously, no one was hurt.*

mirage /'mɪrɑːʒ/ *c.n* effect of hot air rising off a surface, esp a hot road, desert, which makes one see s.t that is not there or makes one imagine that s.t is nearer than it really is: *The driver thought he saw a large lake in the distance but he soon realized that it was just a mirage.*

mire /'maɪə/ *u.n* **1** thick soft mud. **2** (often *be in the —*) (*fig*) a difficult situation, esp one that causes shame, dishonour. **drag s.o, s.o's name, through the mire** (*fig*) cause s.o shame, dishonour, by making certain information public: *He threatened to drag her name through the mire if she left him.*

mirror /'mɪrə/ *n* **1** piece of glass, metal etc that has a shiny surface that reflects an image(2): *Have a look in the mirror and see if you like the coat on you. Always look in your rear-view mirror before you* overtake(1) *another car.* **2** *c.n* (often *a — of s.t*) (*fig*) thing that reflects a situation or presents

a true picture (of a situation): *The feelings of the people in this village will be a mirror of opinion in all similar villages.*
▷ *tr.v* **3** (often *passive*) produce an image(2) of (s.t) like a mirror does: *The clouds were mirrored in the calm lake.*
,mirror 'image *c.n* (*formal*) reflection, copy of s.t, showing it the other way round as if in a mirror.

mirth /mɜːθ/ *u.n* (*formal*) amusement; laughter.

misadventure /ˌmɪsəd'ventʃə/ *c/u.n* (*law*) (accident, event caused by) bad luck. **death by misadventure** death caused by an accident (and not the result of a crime).

misanthrope /'mɪzənˌθrəʊp/ *c.n* (*formal*) person who does not like or trust people and avoids being with other people.
misanthropic /ˌmɪzən'θrɒpɪk/ *adj* (*formal*) (of a person, action etc) not liking or trusting people.
,misan'thropically *adv*. **misanthropy** /mɪ'zænθrəpɪ/ *u.n*.

misapply /ˌmɪsə'plaɪ/ *tr.v* (*-ies, -ied*) (*formal*) use (one's skill, s.o's money etc) for a wrong purpose: *The company's money has been misapplied for his personal needs.*
misapplication /ˌmɪsæplɪ'keɪʃən/ *c/u.n* (*formal*) (example of the) wrong use (of s.t): *He was asked to resign from the club because of his misapplication of the funds.*

misapprehend /ˌmɪsæprɪ'hend/ *tr.v* (*formal*) wrongly understand (s.o's intentions, a situation etc): *You have completely misapprehended my intentions.*
misapprehension /ˌmɪsæprɪ'henʃən/ *c/u.n* (*formal*) misunderstanding: *Her misapprehension was not her fault because William never made his true intentions clear.* (**be**) **under a misapprehension** (**about s.o/s.t**) (be) in a state of not understanding (s.o, a situation) correctly: *If you think he intends to pay you for your work you are under a misapprehension.*

misappropriate /ˌmɪsə'prəʊprɪˌeɪt/ *tr.v* (*formal*) take, use, (s.o's money) in a dishonest way, esp for oneself: *He was asked to resign when it was discovered that a large sum of money had been misappropriated.*
misappropriation /ˌmɪsəˌprəʊprɪ'eɪʃən/ *c/u.n*.

misbehave /ˌmɪsbɪ'heɪv/ *tr/intr.v* (often — *oneself*) behave badly: *If you continue to misbehave (yourself) in this way I shall have to punish you.*
misbehaviour /ˌmɪsbɪ'heɪvɪə/ *u.n*.

miscalculate /mɪs'kælkjʊˌleɪt/ *tr.v* calculate or judge (cost, money, time etc) incorrectly: *He miscalculated the cost.*
miscalculation /ˌmɪskælkjʊ'leɪʃən/ *c/u.n*.

miscarry /mɪs'kærɪ/ *intr.v* (*-ies, -ied*) **1** (of a pregnant(1) woman) have a miscarriage(1): *She miscarried after nine weeks of* pregnancy *because of a car accident.* **2** (*formal*) (of a plan etc) be unsuccessful, fail to produce the required result: *They lost in their attempt to win a large order when their plans miscarried.*
miscarriage /mɪs'kærɪdʒ/ *c/u.n* **1** (of a pregnant woman) (example of the) loss of a developing baby before it is ready and able to survive: *She has not yet recovered(1) from the miscarriage she had last month.* **2** (*formal*) (example of the) failure (of a plan etc): *His lack*

of real preparation led to the miscarriage of his plans. **3** (example of the) failure (of goods, letters, parcels etc) to reach s.w at a particular time: *I'm afraid there was a miscarriage of your order as it was sent to the wrong address.* **miscarriage of justice** *(law)* mistake or wrong judgement made by a court of law, esp in punishing a person who is not guilty: *He was sent to prison because of a miscarriage of justice when his lawyer gave him the wrong advice.*

miscast /ˌmɪsˈkɑːst/ *tr.v (p.p,p.t miscast)* (usu passive) choose (an actor) for a part in a play or film for which he/she is not suitable or good enough: *She was miscast because she was too old for the part.*

miscellaneous /ˌmɪsəˈleɪnɪəs/ *adj* consisting of, containing, several different kinds: *a miscellaneous group of students studying a variety of subjects.*

miscellany /mɪˈselənɪ/ *c.n (pl -ies) (formal)* collection, mixture, of things: *The market has miscellanies of old clothes and tools for sale.*

mischance /mɪsˈtʃɑːns/ *c/u.n (formal)* (example of) bad luck: *It was only (a) mischance that they didn't meet because they both saw the same film at the same time.* **by mischance** (happening) as a result of a mischance.

mischief /ˈmɪstʃɪf/ *u.n* **1** (esp of a child) activity or behaviour that causes some annoyance and damage but not a lot: *Most children enjoy a little mischief. Do you think you two boys can stay out of mischief for an hour while I do some shopping?* **2** expression that shows a naughty(1) intention: *Her smile was full of mischief.* **3** trouble; damage: *Some insects cause mischief to farmers.* **do oneself/s.o a mischief** *(informal)* hurt oneself/s.o: *I almost did myself a mischief when I jumped over that fence.* **get into**, **up to**, **mischief** do s.t that will cause some trouble: *You're always getting into mischief — I daren't leave you alone for a minute.* **make mischief (between s.o and s.o)** say or write s.t that will cause trouble, a quarrel, (between two or more people): *Don't listen to what he says; he's just trying to make mischief between us.* **mean mischief** be determined to cause trouble.

'mischief-,maker *c.n* person who causes trouble between other people.

'mischief-,making *u.n* act of causing trouble between other people, esp by saying s.t.

mischievous /ˈmɪstʃɪvəs/ *adj* **1** (esp of a child) enjoying tricks and behaviour that cause a little trouble and annoyance: *What a mischievous little boy you are!* **2** (of an expression, eyes etc) showing an enjoyment of fun, a small joke, trick etc: *She's got such mischievous eyes.* **3** *(formal)* causing trouble: *You really must stop your mischievous stories about them before you really cause a quarrel.*

'mischievously *adv.* **'mischievousness** *u.n.*

misconceive /ˌmɪskənˈsiːv/ *tr.v* (usu passive) *(formal)* produce (ideas, plans) that are wrong, not suitable: *His plans were totally misconceived because he refused to ask advice.*

misconception /ˌmɪskənˈsepʃən/ *c.n* wrong idea; misunderstanding: *There has been a misconception about our rates which include only bed and breakfast and no other meals.* **be under a misconception (about s.t)** have a wrong or

mistaken idea (about s.t): *We have all been under a misconception about why the meeting was called.*

misconduct /mɪsˈkɒndʌkt/ *u.n (formal)* **1** bad behaviour: *He was asked to leave the school because of his misconduct.* **2** bad management, esp of business affairs.

misconstrue /ˌmɪskənˈstruː/ *tr.v (formal)* give a wrong meaning to (s.t said, done): *He's misconstrued my meaning/words.*

misconstruction /ˌmɪskənˈstrʌkʃən/ *c/u.n.*

miscount /ˈmɪsˌkaʊnt/ *c.n* **1** result of counting s.t, esp votes, incorrectly: *The results were not accepted because of a miscount.*

▷ *tr/intr.v* /ˌmɪsˈkaʊnt/ **2** count (votes etc) wrongly: *We miscounted the number of people and did not provide enough chairs.*

miscreant /ˈmɪskrɪənt/ *c.n (formal)* person who does wrong.

misdeed /ˌmɪsˈdiːd/ *c.n (formal)* bad or wrong act: *You will have to be punished for all your misdeeds.*

misdemeanour /ˌmɪsdɪˈmiːnə/ *c.n* **1** *(formal)* small act of bad behaviour: *I won't punish you for your misdemeanours this time but make sure your behaviour improves.* **2** *(law)* (esp until 1967) crime that is not very serious.

misdirect /ˌmɪsdɪˈrekt/ *tr.v* send (s.o/s.t) in the wrong direction or to the wrong place: *The letter was misdirected because it had an incomplete address on it.* ⇒ miscarriage(3).

misdirection /ˌmɪsdɪˈrekʃən/ *c/u.n.*

misdoing /mɪsˈduːɪŋ/ *c.n* (usu pl) *(formal)* bad deed: *You'll be punished for your misdoings.*

miser /ˈmaɪzə/ *c.n (derog)* person who does not like to spend money but prefers to keep it and live as if he/she has no money.

'miserly *adj.* **'miserliness** *u.n.*

miserable /ˈmɪzrəbl/ *adj* **1** very unhappy and sad: *I feel miserable. It was miserable going home to an empty house.* **2** (of life, conditions etc) very poor: *They live in miserable conditions in a hut outside the town.* **3** *(informal)* (of a person) who does not enjoy herself/himself or find any reason to smile: *He's such a miserable old man — I've never seen him smile.* **4** (of weather) wet and dark: *What a miserable day!* **5** poor in quality or quantity: *They gave us a miserable meal.*

'miserably *adv* **1** very sadly: *You've been wandering about miserably all day — please smile!* **2** in poor and unhappy conditions: *They live miserably on a few pounds a month.* **3** (in quality, quantity) very badly: *They treat/pay their staff miserably.*

misery /ˈmɪzərɪ/ *n (pl -ies)* **1** *u.n* great unhappiness, sadness: *The earthquake left the town in misery. She could not hide her misery when she received the news of the* hijacking. **2** *c.n* (often *pl*) suffering; misfortune: *The miseries among poor people.* **3** *c.n (informal)* person who is unhappy, sad and difficult: *You're such a misery — you haven't stopped complaining all day.* **make s.o's life a misery** make s.o unable to enjoy her/his (ordinary) life: *The children are making my life a misery with all their demands and complaints.*

misfire /ˌmɪsˈfaɪə/ *c.n* **1** failure of (a gun, engine or plan) to work properly.

▷ *intr.v* **2** (of a gun) fail to shoot a bullet. **3** (of an engine) fail to start or work properly: *I can't get*

the car to start because the engine keeps misfiring.
4 (of a plan) fail to succeed or to produce the right result: *Their plan to ruin the party misfired when the party was moved to another address.* **5** (*informal*) (of a joke, trick) fail to produce the effect required: *His trick misfired (on him) when someone was badly hurt because of the confusion he had caused.*

misfit /ˈmɪsˌfɪt/ *c.n* **1** person who is different from the rest of the people who live and work around her/him and who cannot change to be like them: *a social misfit.* **2** thing, e.g clothing, that does not fit properly.

misfortune /mɪsˈfɔːtʃən/ *c/u.n* (*formal*) (example of) bad luck: *We had the misfortune to meet our old head teacher yesterday. Our journey consisted of one misfortune after another.* Opposite fortune(2).

misgiving /mɪsˈɡɪvɪŋ/ *c/u.n* (*formal*) (often *have a* — or *—s about s.o/s.t*) **1** lack of certainty (about s.o/s.t), doubt (about s.o/s.t in the present or future): *I do have some misgiving(s) about our holiday plans. There's a lot of misgiving surrounding the plans for the new shopping centre.* **2** regret (about s.t in the past): *Do you have any misgivings about the way you have lived your life?*

misgovern /mɪsˈɡʌvən/ *tr.v* govern (a country) badly.
misˈgovernment *u.n.*

misguide /ˌmɪsˈɡaɪd/ *tr.v* (*formal*) (often passive, *be —d into doing/thinking s.t*) (of a person, an action etc) allow (s.o) to do, think, s.t that is wrong or foolish; lead (s.o) in the wrong direction: *You have been misguided into thinking he wants to marry you.*
misˈguided *adj* **1** (of a person) acting from wrong or foolish expectations: *He's a misguided young man who has not learnt that there is no easy way to become rich.* **2** (of behaviour) influenced by wrong or foolish reasons: *Your treatment of the child is misguided because if you never correct him he'll never learn the difference between right and wrong.*

mishandle /mɪsˈhændl/ *tr.v* handle (s.t), treat (s.o/s.t), without care, skill, understanding: *I don't want the children playing with the new video(3) because if they mishandle it they may damage it.*

mishap /ˈmɪshæp/ *c/u.n* (example of an) unlucky, usu not serious, accident: *He had a slight mishap in the kitchen when he let the bread burn. Fortunately the holiday went without mishap.*

mishear /ˌmɪsˈhɪə/ *tr/intr.v* (*p.p,p.t* misheard /ˌmɪsˈhɜːd/) hear (s.o/s.t) incorrectly: *You must have misheard — no one said anything like that.*

mishit /ˈmɪsˌhɪt/ *c.n* **1** incorrect or faulty hit (in cricket¹, tennis etc).
▷ *tr/intr.v* /ˌmɪsˈhɪt/ **2** hit (a ball) in an incorrect way.

mishmash /ˈmɪʃˌmæʃ/ *sing.n* (*informal*) mixture that has no order or purpose: *Your report is a mishmash of ideas.*

misinform /ˌmɪsɪnˈfɔːm/ *tr.v* (often passive) (*formal*) give (s.o) wrong information: *I'm afraid you've been misinformed — the play only starts next week.*
misinformation /ˌmɪsɪnfəˈmeɪʃən/ *u.n.*

misinterpret /ˌmɪsɪnˈtɜːprɪt/ *tr.v* understand (s.o/s.t) wrongly: *He misinterpreted her nod for agreement when in fact she hadn't heard what he'd said.*
misinterpretation /ˌmɪsɪnˌtɜːprɪˈteɪʃən/ *c/u.n* (example of) understanding s.t in the wrong way: *It is often misinterpretation of a question that causes students to fail an examination.*

misjudge /ˌmɪsˈdʒʌdʒ/ *tr/intr.v* make an incorrect judgement (about a person, time, distance, speed etc): *He misjudged (the corner) and drove off the road. I think you have misjudged Alice — she's a very serious student.*
misˈjudgement *c/u.n* (also **misˈjudgment**) (example of the) act of making an incorrect judgement (about s.o/s.t).

mislay /mɪsˈleɪ/ *tr.v* (*p.p,p.t* mislaid /mɪsˈleɪd/) lose (s.t), usu only for a short time until one remembers where it was left: *I seem to have mislaid the car keys.*

mislead /mɪsˈliːd/ *tr/intr.v* (*p.p,p.t* misled /mɪsˈled/) (often — s.o into (doing s.t)) (cause (s.o) to) think, act, wrongly: *You misled me into believing you. Don't be misled by his size; he's still a child.*
misˈleading *adj* (of s.t said, done etc) that misleads (s.o): *That sign is very misleading — it looks like a cross, not an arrow.*

mismanage /ˌmɪsˈmænɪdʒ/ *tr.v* (*formal*) manage (a business, event, s.o's affairs) badly: *My lawyer mismanaged my brother's affairs.*
misˈmanagement *u.n.*

mismatch /ˈmɪsˌmætʃ/ *c.n* **1** result of putting two players, articles of clothing etc together who/that are not suitable together: *I didn't enjoy the game — it was a mismatch between a good player and a lazy one.*
▷ *tr.v* /ˌmɪsˈmætʃ/ **2** put (two people, articles of clothing etc) together who/that do not match or are not suitable together.

misnomer /ˌmɪsˈnəʊmə/ *c.n* (*formal*) unsuitable use of a word to name s.o/s.t: *It would be a misnomer to call our little piece of grass a garden.*

misogynist /mɪˈsɒdʒɪˌnɪst/ *c.n* (*formal*) person who hates women.
misogyny /mɪˈsɒdʒɪnɪ/ *u.n* condition of hating women.

misplace /ˌmɪsˈpleɪs/ *tr.v* (*formal*) **1** put (s.t) in a place one cannot remember: *I seem to have misplaced your book for the moment.* **2** (usu passive) put (s.t) in the wrong place, in an unsuitable or unwise place: *That chair is rather misplaced in this room. My trust in you was clearly misplaced.*
misˈplacement *u.n.*

misprint /ˈmɪsˌprɪnt/ *c.n* **1** mistake in s.t printed.
▷ *tr.v* /ˌmɪsˈprɪnt/ **2** print (a date, word, number etc) with a mistake in it.

mispronounce /ˌmɪsprəˈnaʊns/ *tr.v* say (a word) incorrectly: *I always try very hard not to mispronounce people's names.*
mispronunciation /ˌmɪsprəˌnʌnsɪˈeɪʃən/ *c/u.n.*

misquote /ˌmɪsˈkwəʊt/ *tr.v* make mistakes while repeating (what s.o else has said, written): *She criticized the newspaper for misquoting her.*
misquotation /ˌmɪskwəʊˈteɪʃən/ *c/u.n.*

misread /ˌmɪsˈriːd/ *tr.v* (*p.p,p.t* misread /ˌmɪsˈred/) **1** read (s.t) wrongly: *I misread* *the time and arrived an hour early for the meeting.* **2** misunderstand (s.t): *You misread my meaning/intentions.*

misrepresent /ˌmɪsreprɪ'zent/ *tr.v* (often passive) (*formal*) give a false description, explanation, about (s.o/s.t): *She was misrepresented as an unkind mother.*

misrepresentation /ˌmɪsreprɪzen'teɪʃən/ *c/u.n.*

misrule /ˌmɪs'ru:l/ *u.n* (*formal*) **1** bad or weak government: *It will take some time for the country to* recover(1) *from the misrule of the last government.* **2** confusion; lack of order: *There was general misrule in the classroom.*

▷ *tr.v* **3** (*formal*) govern, rule, (a country) badly.

miss¹ /mɪs/ *c.n* (usu with capital **M**) (title placed before the name of a girl or woman who is not married): *Would you ask Miss Jones to come in?* Compare Mrs, Ms, Mr.

miss² /mɪs/ *c.n* **1** failure to catch, hit etc s.t: *After the first few misses, she found the* target(1). ***A miss is as good as a mile*** (*proverb*) Failure by even a little is the same as failing by a lot. ***a near miss*** **(a)** result that fails to be successful by a very small amount. **(b)** example of two vehicles that avoid hitting each other by a very small distance. ***give s.t a miss*** (*informal*) decide not to do s.t, go s.w: *I think I'll give the film a miss tonight — I'm too tired.*

▷ *v* **2** *tr/intr.v* fail to catch, hit, (s.t that one is aiming for): *She missed the ball and it went through the window. He tried to hit the nail but missed and hit his finger.* **3** *tr.v* be unable to do (s.t), go (s.w); lose an opportunity of doing (s.t), going (s.w): *I'll have to miss the party — I've got too much work to do. If we don't go tonight we'll miss the opportunity of hearing) the Rolling Stones. You missed a good programme on television last night.* ⇨ miss out (on s.t). **4** *tr.v* arrive too late for (s.t): *She missed her train and had to take a later one.* **5** *tr.v* feel sad because of the absence of (s.o/s.t/s.w): *Do you miss your family? Most of all I miss the mountains near my home.* **6** *tr.v* notice the absence, lack of, (s.o/s.t): *No one will miss me if I don't go to the party tonight. I must have left my* suitcase *in the taxi — I didn't miss it till now.* **7** *tr.v* fail to hear, meet, see, understand, (s.o/s.t): *I missed that — what did she say? The post office is a hundred metres up the road — you can't miss it!* ⇨ miss the point (of s.t). **8** *tr.v* avoid, escape (s.o/s.t): *If you leave now you'll miss the traffic. We narrowly missed being killed.* ⇨ a near miss. **9** *tr.v* (of an engine) fail to work or run smoothly: *There's something wrong with my car — the engine keeps missing.* ⇨ misfire(1,3). ***miss the boat/bus*** (*fig*) lose an opportunity (to do, get, s.t): *Adult education services are very important for those people who missed the boat when they were younger.* **miss** (**s.t**) **by a mile** ⇨ mile. **miss the mark** ⇨ mark(*n*). **miss out** (**on s.t**) lose an opportunity (of doing s.t, going s.w, enjoying oneself): *If you don't come now you're going to miss out (on all the fun).* **miss s.o/s.t out** fail to include s.o/s.t: *Why did you miss me out when you were offering the drinks? You've missed out two very important points.* **miss the point** (**of s.t**) ⇨ point(*n*).

'missing *adj* (often — *from* s.t/s.w) not able to be found (s.w); not in the correct place: *There*

is a page missing (from my book). She checked to see if anything was missing from her bag. **go missing** be, get, lost: *Four members of the group went missing during the storm.*

missing 'link *c.n* fact, information, which must still be found in order to complete an investigation.

missal /'mɪsl/ *c.n* book containing the religious service for mass²(1) in the Roman Catholic church.

misshapen /ˌmɪs'ʃeɪpən/ *adj* (esp of (part of) the body) (*formal*) badly or wrongly formed: *He has a misshapen foot.*

missile /'mɪsaɪl/ *c.n* **1** (also *attrib*) weapon that moves by its own power and therefore can travel a long distance to its target(1) which it destroys by exploding when it hits it: *There are enough* atomic *missiles to destroy the whole world several times.* **2** any weapon thrown or shot: *The pupils threw paper missiles at one another while the teacher was out of the classroom.* **guided missile** ⇨ guide.

missing ⇨ miss².

mission /'mɪʃən/ *c.n* **1** group of people working in or sent to another country etc for a particular, usu trade or political, purpose: *the British mission in Bonn; a trade mission.* **2** purpose for which a person or group of people is sent s.w: *Their mission was to find a way to the top of the mountain.* **3** group of missionaries sent to teach people, esp about a religion. **4** place where missionaries live and work. **s.o's mission in life** purpose that a person believes is the reason for which he/she was born: *Her mission in life is to teach people in poor countries.*

missionary /'mɪʃənrɪ/ *c.n* (*pl* -ies) (also *attrib*) person sent to another country to teach, esp about her/his religion: *She wanted to be a missionary in a poor country. Her missionary work has taken her all over Africa.*

missive /'mɪsɪv/ *c.n* (*informal* or *joking*) very long letter.

misspell /ˌmɪs'spel/ *tr.v* (*p.p,p.t* misspelled, misspelt /-'spelt/) spell (a word) incorrectly: *He always misspells 'separate' by writing 'seperate'.* **mis'spelling** *c/u.n.*

misspend /ˌmɪs'spend/ *tr.v* (*p.p,p.t* misspent /ˌmɪs'spent/) use (money, time etc) wrongly or unwisely.

misspent /ˌmɪs'spent/ *adj* used or spent wrongly or unwisely: *When you get older you'll regret your misspent youth.*

mist /mɪst/ *n* **1** *c/u.n* (area when there is) air that has become darker and thicker near the ground because it is heavy with water vapour: *The view was hidden by the mist.* Compare fog(1). **2** *c.n* film of water, esp one caused by tears, that makes it difficult to see: *She smiled at her son through a mist of tears.* **3** *c.n* (often *pl*) (*fig*) thing (esp a long time) that makes understanding or knowledge unclear: *The real facts are lost in the mists of time.*

▷ *tr/intr.v* **4** (often — (s.t) over/up) (cause (s.t) to) become covered (over) with mist(1): *The steam from the kettle has misted (up) the windows. Towards midday the hills misted over and we had to wait for them to clear.* Compare fog(3).

'mistily *adv* (as if) covered with a mist(2): *She looked mistily at him.*

'mistiness *u.n* fact or state of being misty.

'misty *adj* (-*ier*, -*iest*) **1** full of mist(1); covered with mist(1): *a misty evening. It was misty when we woke up but it had turned into a sunny day by 11 o'clock.* **2** (as if) in a mist(2): *Her eyes grew misty when she remembered the past.*

mistake /mɪ'steɪk/ *c.n* **1** wrong act, idea, thought etc: *Don't make any mistakes when you add these numbers. I didn't do it on purpose — it was a mistake.* **by mistake** as a result of an accident, of being careless: *She went to the wrong place by mistake.* Opposite deliberately, intentionally. **be/make no mistake (about it)** (used to give force to a statement) be/make certain, without any doubt (about s.t): *If you don't work harder you'll fail your examinations — make no mistake (about it)! It was he who stole my bag — there's no mistake (about it)!*
▷ *tr.v* (*p.t* mistook /mɪ'stʊk/, *p.p* mistaken /mɪ'steɪkən/) **2** be wrong about (s.o/s.t): *I must have mistaken the date — our tickets are for tomorrow. He mistook what she said.* ⇒ unmistakable. **3** (usu — *s.o/s.t* for *s.o/s.t*) think wrongly that (s.o/s.t) is s.o/s.t else: *I mistook her for her younger sister.* **there's no mistaking s.o/s.t** it is not possible to make a mistake about s.o/s.t or think anything else is true: *There's no mistaking her work.*
mi'staken *adj* **1** (of a person) wrong: *You're mistaken if you think I'm going there alone. She's mistaken in thinking he's a liar.* **2** (of an action, thought) wrong; badly judged: *She acted in the mistaken belief that everyone would support her. Your opinion of your son is mistaken — he's much cleverer than you think.* **3** (of a statement etc) understood in the wrong way: *If you don't speak clearly, your intentions will be mistaken.* **be mistaken (about s.o/s.t)** be wrong (about s.o/s.t): *You are mistaken about that hotel — the food is very good. If I'm not mistaken there's an excellent Chinese restaurant in this road.*
mi'stakenly *adv* wrongly: *She mistakenly thought I was you.*
mister /'mɪstə/ *c.n* **1** (*abbr* Mr) (title, usu in the abbr form, placed in front of the name of a man): *Has Mr Jones arrived yet?* Compare miss¹, Mrs, Ms. **2** (*informal*) (used, esp by children, to address a man whose name is not known): *Excuse me, mister — can you tell me where Oxford Street is?*
mistily, mistiness ⇒ mist.
mistime /ˌmɪs'taɪm/ *tr.v* (*formal*) **1** time (s.t) badly: *She mistimed her speech and spoke for an hour too long.* **2** do, say, (s.t) at a wrong or unsuitable time: *She mistimed her arrival and had to interrupt their meeting.*
ˌmis'timed *adj* done, said, at a wrong or unsuitable time: *a mistimed arrival/remark.*
mistletoe /'mɪsl̩ˌtəʊ/ *u.n* plant with white berries which grows on trees and is used in Christmas decorations.
mistook /mɪ'stʊk/ *p.t* of mistake.
mistress /'mɪstrɪs/ *c.n* **1** (*formal*) woman teacher: *the games mistress.* ⇒ headmistress, master(2). **2** woman who is having a love affair with a man to whom she is not married. **3** (*formal*) (usu — *of s.t*) woman who controls s.t: *She's mistress of her own life/affairs.* **4** (*old use; formal*) woman who is the head of the household: *The cook told her friend*

that her mistress was very good to her and her family.
mistrust /ˌmɪs'trʌst/ *u.n* **1** (*formal*) lack of trust: *They decided not to go further because of their mistrust of the old bridge.*
▷ *tr.v* **2** have no trust in (s.o/s.t): *She mistrusts her own ability to judge people.*
ˌmis'trustful *adj* (usu — *of s.o/s.t*) having no trust (in s.o/s.t): *He's mistrustful of her new ideas.*
ˌmis'trustfully *adv.* **ˌmis'trustfulness** *u.n.*
misty ⇒ mist.
misunderstand /ˌmɪsʌndə'stænd/ *tr/intr.v* (*p.p,p.t* misunderstood /-'stʊd/) understand (s.o/s.t) incorrectly; get the wrong meaning from (s.t said, written etc): *She misunderstood the instructions and took the wrong road. I'm sorry, I must have misunderstood (you).*
ˌmisunder'standing *n* **1** *c/u.n* mistake in the meaning of s.t said, done etc: *There seems to have been a misunderstanding — I never made any such promise.* **2** (*informal*) disagreement that is not serious: *It was a little misunderstanding but we've sorted it out now.*
misuse /ˌmɪs'juːs/ *c/u.n* **1** (example of the) bad or wrong use (of s.t): *The television has been damaged by misuse.*
▷ *tr.v* /ˌmɪs'juːz/ **2** use (s.t) for a wrong purpose: *Since you have misused your freedom I shall have to be stricter with you.* **3** treat (s.o/s.t) roughly or badly: *I doubt if you would misuse it if you had to pay for it.*
mite /maɪt/ *c.n* **1** small insect. **2** (*informal*) very small child, esp one for whom one feels sympathy: *the poor little mite.*
miter ⇒ mitre¹, mitre².
mitigate /'mɪtɪˌgeɪt/ *v* **1** *tr.v* (*law*) make (a crime) less severe: *The judge did not send her to prison for murdering her husband because her husband's terrible treatment of her and their children mitigated her crime.* **2** *tr.v* (*formal*) reduce (the anger, pain, damage etc caused by s.o/s.t): *Nothing I say will mitigate her anger.* ⇒ unmitigated. **3** *intr.v* (usu — *against s.o/s.t*) make it less likely (that s.o will manage to do s.t successfully or that s.t will happen): *The weather mitigated against our breaking the record.*
'miti.gating *attrib.adj* (*formal*) (of a remedy) that makes pain, sadness etc less painful.
ˌmiti.gating 'circumstances *pl.n* conditions, reasons, that make a crime less serious, esp when deciding the punishment. ⇒ extenuating circumstances.
mitigation /ˌmɪtɪ'geɪʃən/ *u.n* (usu *in* — *of s.t*) facts that reduce the seriousness (of a crime etc and therefore the punishment).
mitre¹ /'maɪtə/ *c.n* (US **'miter**) kind of tall hat worn by a bishop(1).
mitre² /'maɪtə/ *c.n.* (US **'miter**) (*technical*) **1** (also **'mitre ˌjoint**) joint made by cutting one end of two pieces (of wood) at 45° and joining those ends to form a right angle (90°).
▷ *tr.v* **2** join ((two) pieces of wood etc) with a mitre(1): *You'll only get a good corner if you mitre the wood for your picture frame.*
mitt /mɪt/ *c.n* **1** (*informal*) mitten. **2** special kind of covering which protects the hands: *oven mitts.* **3** (usu *pl*) (*slang*) hand: *Get your mitts off my new car!*

mitten /'mɪtn/ *c.n* (*informal* **mit**) kind of glove that has one place for the thumb and another place for all four fingers.

mix /mɪks/ *c/u.n* **1** collection of all the parts of a particular kind of mixture: *I didn't use a recipe for the bread — I used a bread mix.* **2** collection of different kinds of people, things: *There was such a mix (of people) at the party that no one knew anyone else. Make sure there's a good mix of things for the children to do.*
▷ *v* **3** *tr.v* put (different things) together: *They mixed all their sweets together and had a feast. I don't believe in mixing business with pleasure.* **4** *tr/ intr.v* combine (different things) so that a new substance is formed: *First mix the butter and sugar and then add the eggs. Mix red and yellow to make orange. Oil and water don't mix.* **5** *tr.v* make (s.t) by mixing(1) the different parts together: *mix cement for the bricks. Mix me a drink, please.* **6** *intr.v* (of people) be, do s.t, come, together easily: *Very few people knew anyone at the party but everyone mixed very well.* **mix s.t in(to s.t) (a)** put the parts in(to a bowl, bucket etc) and mix(4). **(b)** put s.t with s.t else and combine together: *Mix in the flour and the milk. Mix the beaten eggs into the rest of the mixture.* **mix s.t up (a)** put different things together and combine them well: *If you don't have enough I'll have to mix up some more. Mix up all the playing cards and then I'll do the trick again.* **(b)** confuse two or more dates, activities etc: *He mixed up the dates and went on the wrong night.* ⇨ mixed up, mix-up. **mix s.o/s.t up (with s.o/s.t)** confuse, mistake, s.o/s.t (for s.o/s.t else): *I'm always mixing you up with your sister (or mixing the two of you up). You're mixing up last year with the year before.*

mixed *adj* **1** done, used, by people of both sexes: *I wish I'd gone to a mixed school.* **2** consisting of different kinds: *We were able to choose from a tray of mixed cakes.* **have mixed feelings (about s.o/ s.t)** ⇨feelings. **mixed up** confused: *I don't know what to believe any more — I'm so mixed up.* **mixed up in s.t** connected with s.t bad: *He's mixed up in something that is going to get him into trouble.* **mixed up with s.o/s.t** connected with s.o/s.t bad: *He got (himself) mixed up with a group of boys who have nothing better to do than cause trouble.*

,**mixed 'bag** *c.n* (*fig*; *informal*) collection of many different kinds, qualities etc of things: *The exhibition(1) was a bit of a mixed bag — some paintings were good and others were bad.*

,**mixed 'doubles** *pl.n* (in tennis etc) (game for) four players in which each team consists of one man and one woman.

,**mixed 'grill** *c.n* meal which consists of different kinds of meat cooked on a grill.

,**mixed 'marriage** ⇨ marriage.

,**mixed 'metaphor** ⇨ metaphor.

,**mixed 'salad** *c.n* salad(1) made with various kinds of vegetables.

'**mixer** *c.n* **1** (often as the second part of a word) person, instrument, machine who/that mixes: *a food-mixer; a cement mixer.* **2** person who mixes(6) (easily) with other people: *I like having her at my parties because she's such a good mixer.*

mixture /'mɪkstʃə/ *n* **1** *c/u.n* combination of particular parts, substances etc for a particular purpose: *Take some cough mixture before you go*

to bed. **2** *u.n* act of mixing different things: *The mixture of copper(1) and zinc produces brass.* **3** *c/ u.n* result of putting different people or things together: *Our group was such a mixture of people. We did a mixture of things such as walking and swimming and also sailing.*

'**mix-,up** *c.n* (*informal*) state of confusion caused by mixing s.t up(b): *There was a bit of a mix-up because no one really knew what we had to do.*

ml *symb* millilitre(s).

mm *symb* millimetre(s).

mnemonic /nɪ'mɒnɪk/ *c.n* (also *attrib*) easy way to remember s.t by using rhyme, music, a set of rules etc.

mne'monically *adv.*

moan /məʊn/ *c.n* **1** low sound of pain or suffering: *moans from a child in hospital.* **2** (*fig*) low sound as if of pain: *the moan of the wind in the trees.* **3** (*informal*) (sound of) complaint: *She answers every request with a moan.*
▷ *intr.v* **4** (often — *with* s.t) make a low sound of pain, suffering, unhappiness etc (because of s.t): *The sick child moaned with pain.* **5** (*informal*) (often — *about* s.t) complain (about s.t): *She's always moaning about how poor she is.*
'**moaner** *c.n* person who moans(5).

moat /məʊt/ *c.n* deep wide ditch round a castle etc that is filled with water for defence purposes.

mob /mɒb/ *c.n* (also *attrib*) **1** crowd of noisy, often violent, people: *A mob of young boys ran onto the football field.*
▷ *tr.v* (**-bb-**) **2** (of a crowd of people) surround (s.o/ s.t) in order to admire or attack her/him/it: *The film-star was mobbed by a large group of fans. Hundreds of people mobbed the police station to try and get the prisoner set free.*

mobile /'məʊbaɪl/ *adj* Opposite immobile for (1,2). **1** able to move or be moved easily: *At 90 years old my grandmother was still completely mobile.* **2** (*informal*) having a vehicle to go about in: *I'm not mobile at the moment because my car is in the garage.* **3** (of s.o's face, expression) changing often or easily: *Her face is so mobile — one minute she seems to be laughing, the next crying!*
▷ *c.n* **4** structure(2) that consists of several hanging parts that move slightly in the air and sometimes make sounds: *I hung a colourful mobile in the baby's room.*

mobility /məʊ'bɪlɪtɪ/ *u.n* fact or state of being mobile(1–3). Compare immobility.

mobilization, -isation /ˌməʊbɪlaɪ'zeɪʃən/ *u.n* act or state of mobilizing s.o/s.t or of being mobilized.

'**mobi,lize, -ise** *tr/intr.v* prepare (an army etc) for war, action: *He was asked to mobilize his men. The army is mobilizing.* Compare immobilize.

moccasin /'mɒkəsɪn/ *c.n* kind of shoe made of soft leather like those worn by American Indians.

mock /mɒk/ *attrib.adj* **1** not real; being a copy of the real or final thing: *a coat of mock leather. This is only a mock examination.*
▷ *tr/intr.v* **2** make (s.o/s.t) the object of a joke or of joking (often by copying her/him/it in an exaggerated way): *They mocked the little boy because*

he was fat. The naughty boy was mocking the old man's walk.

'mockery *n* (*pl* -*ies*) **1** *u.n* act of criticizing and laughing at s.o or mocking (⇒ mock(2)) s.o: *I hate the mockery in her eyes when she looks at me.* **2** *c.n* person or thing who/that is or should be mocked(1): *The meeting was a mockery.* **3** *c.n* (usu *a* — of *s.t*) very bad example (of s.t): *Their marriage is a mockery.* **make a mockery of s.o/ s.t** cause s.o/s.t to look or seem foolish: *Their excellent ability made a mockery of our attempt.* **'mocking** *adj* that mocks(2): *a mocking smile.* **'mockingly** *adv.*

'mock-,up *c.n* full-size copy, model, of the final thing that is made for tests: *We built a mock-up of the new car to test its wind resistance.*

modal ⇒ mode.

mod cons /ˌmɒd 'kɒnz/ *pl.n* (*formal* modern conveniences) objects that make a home more comfortable and life easier, e.g a microwave oven, a freezer, central heating etc: *Our new home has all mod cons.*

mode /məʊd/ *c.n* **1** (*formal*) manner, style, way, (of doing or saying s.t): *an unusual mode of talking.* **2** kind, style, type, (of s.t): *What mode of* transport(5) *do you prefer?* **3** fashion; style(2): *What's the latest mode — long or short skirts?* **4** (*grammar*) = mood² (of a verb).

modal /'məʊdl/ *adj* (*grammar*) concerned with, showing, the mood² of a verb, as in 'I *would* come, if I *could*'.

,modal au'xiliary (ˌverb) *c.n* (*grammar*) one of the verbs that express ability, condition, duty, possibility or permission as an auxiliary(3) as in: You *must* go. *Can* you see? *Could* I speak to you? I *may* see you later. He said he *might* come. I *will* be there. I *wouldn't* do that if I were you. He *should* be there. I *ought* to go but I don't really want to. You *need* not stay.

'modish *adj* (*formal*) fashionable: *a modish young man.*
'modishly *adv.* **'modishness** *u.n.*

model /'mɒdl/ *attrib.adj* **1** of a very small copy of s.t: *a model railway.* **2** having all the necessary good qualities; deserving to be copied: *He's a model pupil.*
▷ *c.n* **3** small copy of s.t: *I was given an aeroplane model to build while I was ill.* ⇒ model(1). **4** (*informal*) person or thing who/that is (almost) a copy of (s.o/s.t else): *She's the model of her grandmother.* **5** person or thing who/that is perfect and deserves to be copied or used as an example for s.t: *He's a model of healthy living. Virginia Woolf is my model for writing.* ⇒ model(2). **6** (example of a) particular kind of manufactured article: *Our washing machine is the latest* electronic(2) *model.* **7** person trained to show new clothes to buyers by wearing them. **8** person who is painted, photographed etc for money.
▷ *tr/intr.v* (-*ll*-; US -*l*-) **9** work as a model(7,8), (showing (s.t)): *I am modelling new summer clothes this week. She models for a famous photographer.* **10** form clay etc into a particular shape or copy of (s.o/s.t): *He models famous dancers in clay. She likes to model in her spare time.* **model oneself/s.t (up)on s.o/ s.t** make oneself/s.t a copy of s.o/s.t else: *He's modelling his acting on Clint Eastwood.*

moderate /'mɒdərɪt/ *adj* **1** within reasonable limits; not extreme: *You can get a good meal there for a moderate price. His ideas have become moderate since he bought a house.* **2** (often *derog*) average; some; fairly good: *moderate improvement/intelligence. Their standard is moderate.* Compare immoderate.
▷ *c.n* /'mɒdərɪt/ **3** person whose ideas, opinions etc are not extreme.
▷ *tr/intr.v* /'mɒdəˌreɪt/ **4** (make (s.o/s.t)) become less extreme: *You must moderate your expectations/demands. His temper gradually moderated during the evening.*
'moderately /'mɒdərətlɪ/ *adv* to an average degree; fairly (well, badly etc): *She did moderately well in the examination.*
moderation /ˌmɒdə'reɪʃən/ *n* **1** *u.n* (often — in *s.t*) quality of being moderate(1) (about s.t): *Moderation in drinking is essential.* **2** *c/u.n* act of moderating(4) s.t: *You will have to make some moderations to your plans if you don't want to spend more money.* **in moderation** in a moderate(1) way: *If you eat in moderation you will not get fat.*
modern /'mɒdn/ *adj* of the present or recent time; up-to-date: *modern languages/ideas/buildings. She wears very modern clothes.*
,modern 'history *u.n* history(1) from AD 1500.
modernity /mɒ'dɜːnɪtɪ/ *u.n.*
modernization, -isation /ˌmɒdənaɪ'zeɪʃən/ *c/ u.n* fact or state of modernizing s.t.
'moder,nize, -ise *tr.v* make (a house, factory etc) suitable for modern needs; bring (s.t) up to date: *modernize an old house by building a new bathroom and a kitchen.*
modest /'mɒdɪst/ *adj* Opposite immodest. **1** (of a person) not having or showing too high an opinion of one's own abilities etc: *She's such a modest person. He's very modest about his success.* **2** not too/very large: *His father gives him a modest allowance to live on. His needs are modest so he manages.* **3** (often — in *s.t*) taking care not to be extreme, shocking, esp in the way one dresses, behaves, talks: *He has a very modest taste in clothes. He is modest in his speech.*
'modestly *adv.*
'modesty *u.n* fact or state of being modest(1–3): *It's surprising to find modesty in such a famous person.* **in all modesty** being modest: *She told everyone in all modesty that she didn't deserve such praise.*
modicum /'mɒdɪkəm/ *sing.n* (usu — of *s.t*) small or least amount (of s.t): *If he showed a modicum of regret for what he's done, I wouldn't mind.*
modify /'mɒdɪˌfaɪ/ *tr.v* (-*ies*, -*ied*) **1** (*formal*) make (s.t) (slightly) different; change (s.t) (slightly), esp in order to improve it: *We will modify the plans according to your suggestions. You'll have to modify the way you dress when you start a job.* **2** (*grammar*) (of an adv, adj) change the meaning of a (noun, verb) by giving extra information about it: *In 'She shouted angrily at the naughty child', 'angrily' modifies 'shouted' and 'naughty' modifies 'child'.* ⇒ qualify(2).
modification /ˌmɒdɪfɪ'keɪʃən/ *n* **1** *u.n* act of modifying(1) s.t or of being modified: *The modification of these plans will take longer than drawing new ones.* **2** *c.n* change; result of modifying(1) s.t:

We can use the same engine if we make some *modifications to it.*
modifier /'mɒdɪ,faɪə/ *c.n* (*grammar*) word that modifies(2) another word.
modish(ly/ness) ⇒ mode.
modulate /'mɒdjʊ,leɪt/ *tr.v* (*formal*) make a change in the frequency(2), pitch¹(4), tone(5) of (a sound): *Can you modulate your voice more because you're speaking too loudly?*
modulation /,mɒdju'leɪʃən/ *c/u.n.*
module /'mɒdju:l/ *c.n* **1** part of a manufactured article that is made separately (and in large quantities) to fit a standard size etc: *We won an order to supply certain modules for the new shopping centre.* **2** (*technical*) independent and separate part of a spacecraft usu with a particular function(1). **command module** ⇒ command.
modular /'mɒdjʊlə/ *adj* that is manufactured in/as modules(1): *modular furniture*; *a modular kitchen.*
mohair /'məʊ,heə/ *u.n* (also *attrib*) (wool, thread made from the) silky hair of an Angora goat: *I bought some mohair to knit a jersey*(1). *She was wearing a mohair sweater.*
Mohammed /məʊ'hæmɪd/ *unique n* (also **Mu'hammad**) prophet(2) and founder of Islam.
Mo'hammedan, Mo'hammeda,nism = Muslim, Islam.
moist /mɔɪst/ *adj* damp; a little wet: *The soil should be moist — not wet. Her eyes were moist with tears. Wipe the table with a moist cloth.*
moisten /'mɔɪsn/ *tr.v* make (s.t) damp or very slightly wet: *Moisten the cloth and try to remove the stain.*
'moistness *u.n.*
moisture /'mɔɪstʃə/ *u.n* small drops of water or liquid in/on s.t: *There's a lot of moisture in the air.*
moisturize, -ise /'mɔɪstʃə,raɪz/ *tr.v* put moisture into/onto (one's skin): *This cream will moisturize your skin.*
'moistu,rizer, -iser *c.n* substance used to add moisture to the skin.
'moistu,rizing, -ising ,cream *c.n* creamy substance, usu with a sweet smell, which is used as a moisturizer.
molar /'məʊlə/ *c.n* (also *attrib*) any one of the back teeth which are used for grinding(2) food.
molasses /mə'læsɪz/ *u.n* thick dark liquid from sugar plants produced while sugar is being made.
mole¹ /məʊl/ *c.n* small dark spot on the human skin.
mole² /məʊl/ *c.n* **1** small animal covered with fur which lives under the ground. **2** (*informal*) person in an organization etc who gives secrets about it to s.o outside it: *My mole in the government tells me that tax changes are being planned.*
'mole,hill *c.n* small pile of earth caused by a mole while tunnelling underground. **make a mountain out of a molehill** ⇒ mountain.
molecule /'mɒlɪ,kju:l/ *c.n* smallest unit, usu of a group of atoms(1), into which a substance can be divided without changing its chemical structure(1): *One molecule of water equals two atoms of hydrogen and one atom of oxygen.*
molecular /mə'lekjʊlə/ *adj.*
molest /mə'lest/ *tr.v* (*formal*) interfere with (s.o), esp sexually: *The police are looking for a*

young man who has been molesting children in the park.
molestation /,məʊle'steɪʃən/ *c/u.n.*
mollify /'mɒlɪ,faɪ/ *tr.v* (-ies, -ied) (*formal*) make (s.o) calmer or less angry: *She mollified the child with a piece of chocolate.*
mollification /,mɒlɪfɪ'keɪʃən/ *u.n.*
mollusc /'mɒləsk/ *c.n* (*technical*) one of a group of animals that have soft bodies that are usu protected by a hard shell, e.g a snail.
mollycoddle /'mɒlɪ,kɒdl/ *tr.v* protect (a child, an animal) excessively: *Her children are so molly-coddled — what will they do when they have to face the world on their own?*
molten /'məʊltən/ *attrib.adj* (of s.t solid, esp metal, rock) melted by great heat; in a liquid form: *molten lava/rock.*
mom /mɒm/ *c.n* (US) mum¹.
moment /'məʊmənt/ *c.n* very short, small, amount of time: *Will you wait (for) a moment? I'll be ready in a moment. She'll only be a few moments. Can I see you for a moment? Just a moment. It will only take a few moments.* Compare minute²(2). **at any moment** at any time from now on; very soon: *We're expecting her to arrive at any moment.* **at the last moment** at the (very) last possible time (before s.t starts or before it is too late): *She said no all the time until at the last moment she suddenly agreed to take us.* **at the moment** now; at this particular time: *I can't come at the moment as I'm busy.* **at this moment (in time)** right now: *At this moment in time she's probably lying on the beach.* **in a moment** a little later; very soon: *I'll be back in a moment.* **not for a moment** not at all: *I didn't for a moment think she'd really do it!* **of (great) moment** (*formal*) (very) important: *I have a problem of great moment to discuss with you.* **on the spur of the moment** ⇒ spur(*n*). **the moment of truth** the very important point in time when one realizes the truth and has to accept reality at last. **the moment (that) . . .** immediately (that) . . .; at exactly the time when (s.t happens): *Phone me the moment that you hear any news.*
momentarily /'məʊməntərɪlɪ/ *adv* for a short amount of time: *She paused momentarily and then continued.*
momentary /'məʊməntrɪ/ *adj* lasting for a short time only: *There was a momentary hesitation in her voice.*
momentous /məʊ'mentəs/ *adj* (usu *attrib*) very important: *a momentous occasion.*
'moments *pl.n* (usu important, enjoyable) short lengths of time: *Remember the moments we shared during that summer.* **have (had) one's moments** know (or have known) times that are good, successful, happy: *We're not very happy but we've had our moments.*
momentum /mə'mentəm/ *u.n* **1** amount, force, of motion in a moving body: *The momentum of the cart was so great that it continued to roll along the street after we stopped pushing it.* **2** (*fig*) force, strength, esp when caused and increased by the movement of events. **gain/gather momentum** go faster; become stronger. **lose momentum** go slower, become less serious, important etc.
Mon written abbr Monday.
monarch /'mɒnək/ *c.n* (*formal* or *literary*) ruler of a country, esp by birth, e.g a king, queen.

monarchic /mə'nɑːkɪk/ *adj* of, like, a monarch: *monarchic laws.*

monarchism /'mɒnəˌkɪzəm/ *u.n* (belief in a) system of government by a monarch.

monarchist /'mɒnəkɪst/ *c.n* person who supports and believes in monarchism.

monarchy /'mɒnəkɪ/ *c/u.n* (*pl -ies*) (country that is under the) rule of a monarch: *There are not many monarchies left in the world.*

monastery /'mɒnəstrɪ/ *c.n* (*pl -ies*) building in which a group of monks live.

monastic /mə'næstɪk/ *adj* (*usu attrib*) of, like, monks or monasteries: *a monastic way of life.*

monaural /mɒn'ɔːrəl/ *adj* (*abbr mono*) of or referring to sound recordings, record players etc that have sound coming from only one direction: *a monaural record player.* Compare stereo.

Monday /'mʌndɪ/ *c/unique n* (*written abbr Mon*) (also *attrib*) first working day of the week in Christian(1) (and some other) countries; day after Sunday and before Tuesday. **last Monday** the last Monday before today. **next Monday** the first Monday after today. **on a Monday** on a day of one week that is/was a Monday. **on Monday** on the nearest Monday before/after today or on the Monday of the week being referred to: *I saw him on Monday.* **on Mondays** every Monday: *I'm always late for work on Mondays.* **Monday after next** the second Monday after today. **Monday before last** the Monday before last Monday. **Monday morning, afternoon** etc the morning, afternoon etc of last, next, Monday.

monetarism /'mʌnɪtəˌrɪzəm/ *u.n* economic(1) system of reducing a country's money supply in order to control the economy(2).

monetarist /'mʌnɪtrɪst/ *adj* **1** of or referring to monetarism: *monetarist policy.*
▷ *c.n* **2** person who supports monetarism.

monetary /'mʌnɪtrɪ/ *adj* (*usu attrib*) of money and/or finance: *monetary policy.*

money /'mʌnɪ/ *u.n* coins and/or notes that are used in buying and selling: *Do you have enough money to buy me a drink? You shouldn't carry so much money around. I don't earn much money. I'd love to win lots of money and spend it all.* **bet s.o (any money) that . . .** ⇒ bet(v). **be coining money** ⇒ coin(v). **get one's money's worth** get the full value of the money one has paid. **a (good) run for one's money** ⇒ run(n). **in the money** being wealthy; having a lot of money. **make money (at/by, out of, s.t)** get, earn, (a lot of) money (by doing s.t, selling s.t etc). **money for old rope** ⇒ rope(n). **pin money** ⇒ pin(n). **pocket money** ⇒ pocket. **put money into s.t** lend money to a business etc, esp with the aim of making a profit in the future. **raise money (on s.t)** get money (by selling s.t); borrow money (by using s.t of the same value as a promise of repayment): *raise money on one's house.* **rolling in money** very wealthy. **throw one's money about/around** spend money foolishly.

'money-,box *c.n* box with a small long hole for putting coins in which is kept for saving money.

'money,lender *c.n* person who earns money by lending money at interest.

moneyless /'mʌnɪləs/ *adj* having no money.

'money,maker *c.n* person or thing who/that earns (plenty of) money: *Our new restaurant is a real moneymaker.*

'money,making *adj.*

'money ,order *c/u.n* way of paying money to a named person through the post office: *I bought a £10 money order to send my sister.*

'moneys *pl.n* (also **'monies**) (*old use*) amounts of money.

'money-,spinner *c.n* (*informal*) thing that earns a lot of money: *His latest idea has been a real money-spinner.*

mongol /'mɒŋɡɒl/ *c.n* (*old use*) person with Down's syndrome.

mongolism /'mɒŋɡəˌlɪzəm/ *u.n* (*old use*) Down's syndrome.

mongoose /'mɒŋɡuːs/ *c.n* (*pl -s*) kind of small animal that eats rats and snakes.

mongrel /'mʌŋɡrəl/ *c.n* (also *attrib*) animal, esp a dog, of mixed breed(1).

monies ⇒ moneys.

monitor /'mɒnɪtə/ *c.n* **1** pupil who checks that other pupils behave. ⇒ prefect. **2** instrument for checking the quality of sounds, pictures etc, e.g a screen in a television studio. **3** device with a screen(3) for looking at text put into a computer.
▷ *tr.v* **4** check how well (a person, machine, engine etc) works or progresses.

monk /mʌŋk/ *c.n* member of a religious group of men who live according to strict rules, usu in a monastery. Compare nun.

monkey /'mʌŋkɪ/ *c.n* **1** kind of animal with a long tail and fur which belongs to the group of animals that is most like humans. **2** (*informal*) child who is fond of playing tricks: *He's a naughty little monkey.* **make a monkey (out) of s.o** (*informal*) make s.o seem foolish.
▷ *intr.v* **3** monkey about/around (with s.o/s.t) (*informal*) play in a foolish way (with s.o/s.t): *Those boys are always monkeying about. Stop monkeying around with my clothes.*

'monkey ,business *u.n* (*informal*) act, behaviour etc that is not legal: *There's some monkey business here!*

'monkey ,wrench *c.n* kind of tool with an adjustable opening, used for loosening and tightening things.

mono /'mɒnəʊ/ *adj* (*informal*) monaural.

monochrome /'mɒnəˌkrəʊm/ *adj* having, using, showing, various shades of one colour only: *A monochrome television is a black and white one.*

monocle /'mɒnəkl/ *c.n* lens(1) for one eye only.

monogamy /mə'nɒɡəmɪ/ *u.n* (*formal*) (system of) having only one wife or husband.

mo'nogamist *c.n* person who practises monogamy.

mo'nogamous *adj* (of a marriage etc) between two people only (at one time).

monogram /'mɒnəˌɡræm/ *c.n* two or more letters, esp from s.o's name, formed into a pattern on an article of clothing or on paper etc.

'mono,grammed *adj.*

monograph /'mɒnəˌɡrɑːf/ *c.n* written detailed account or study of a particular subject.

monolingual /ˌmɒnə'lɪŋɡwəl/ *adj* speaking, using, referring to, one language only: *This is a monolingual dictionary.* Compare bilingual, multilingual.

monolith /'mɒnəˌlɪθ/ *c.n* very large upright block of stone, sometimes used as a monument.

‚mono'lithic *adj* **1** consisting of one or more monoliths. **2** very large.

monologue /ˈmɒnəˌlɒg/ *c.n* long speech by one person, esp in a play etc.

monopoly /məˈnɒpəlɪ/ *c.n* (*pl -ies*) (also *fig*) **1** right of, or control by, one group, person, company etc to do, make or supply s.t: *They have a monopoly here and so they can charge whatever prices they want. I can visit her too — you don't have a monopoly over her.* **2** thing that is controlled by only one person, group, company: *They have a petrol monopoly.*

mo'nopo‚list *c.n* person who has a monopoly.

mo‚nopo'listic *adj.* **mo‚nopo'listically** *adv.*

monopolization, -isation /məˌnɒpəlaɪˈzeɪʃən/ *u.n* act or fact of monopolizing s.t.

mo'nopo‚lize, -ise *tr.v* (also *fig*) get or keep control of (the supply of s.t) completely: *I couldn't say a word — he totally monopolized the conversation.*

monorail /ˈmɒnəˌreɪl/ *c.n* (also *attrib*) railway (system) with one main rail on which a train rides, or sometimes from which the train hangs down. **by monorail** on a monorail: *go/travel by monorail.*

monosyllable /ˈmɒnəˌsɪləbl/ *c.n* word containing only one syllable, e.g *come*.

monosyllabic /ˌmɒnəsɪˈlæbɪk/ *adj* **1** having only one syllable. **2** speaking using only words of one syllable.

monotony /məˈnɒtənɪ/ *u.n* state of being dull and without variety: *The monotony of his voice annoys me.*

monotonous /məˈnɒtənəs/ *adj* (usu *derog*) having no variety; continuing in the same way; dull: *Their music has a monotonous beat.*

mo'notonously *adv.*

monoxide /mɒˈnɒksaɪd/ *c/u.n* (*technical*) chemical substance (oxide) with one oxygen atom(1) in each molecule: *carbon monoxide.*

monsoon /mɒnˈsuːn/ *c.n* (also *attrib*) **1** wind that blows in the Indian Ocean from the south-west between April and October (= *wet monsoon*) and from the north-east during the rest of the year (= *dry monsoon*). **2** rains that are brought by the monsoon between April and October, e.g in India.

monster /ˈmɒnstə/ *c.n* **1** (in children's stories) imaginary, usu large and frightening, creature. **2** bad or evil person: *Don't be such a monster to your brother.* **3** (also *attrib*) animal or plant that is unusual in size, shape or appearance: *monster apples.*

monstrosity /mɒnˈstrɒsɪtɪ/ *c.n* (*pl -ies*) thing that is large and very ugly: *Are they really going to pull down this lovely old building to build that monstrosity?*

monstrous /ˈmɒnstrəs/ *adj* **1** huge and horrible, ugly or disgusting: *He's got a monstrous pimple on his nose. What a monstrous building!* **2** (*formal*) shocking; unfair: *It's monstrous of you to talk to your mother like that.*

'monstrously *adv.*

montage /ˈmɒntɑːʒ/ *c.n* (*French*) picture, piece of music etc made by combining several different pictures or parts.

month /mʌnθ/ *c.n* one of the twelve divisions of the year each of which is between 28 and 31 days long: *The month of January has 31 days. This work*

will take six months. She's only two months old. I see her twice a month. **a month last/next/this Friday** etc exactly one month after last/next/this Friday etc. **a month on Friday** etc exactly one month after next Friday. **a month today, tomorrow** etc exactly one month after today, tomorrow etc. **month in, month out** for a long time without any rest etc. Compare week. **never/not in a month of Sundays** almost never.

'monthly *adj* **1** (happening, printed etc) once a month: *monthly meetings; a monthly magazine.* ▷ *adv* **2** once a month: *We'll meet monthly. It's printed monthly.* ▷ *c.n* **3** magazine, newspaper etc that is produced once a month.

monument /ˈmɒnjʊmənt/ *c.n* (often — *to s.o/s.t*) thing (built) in memory of a person, event etc: *I don't want to visit any more monuments. That's a monument to their bravery.*

monumental /ˌmɒnjʊˈmentl/ *adj* of great size: *monumental success/stupidity.*

‚monu'mentally *adv* extremely: *monumentally stupid.*

moo /muː/ *c.n* (*pl -s*) **1** sound made by a cow. ▷ *intr.v* **2** make a moo(1).

'moo-‚cow *c.n* (child's word for a) cow.

mooch /muːtʃ/ *intr.v* (esp — *about/around*) (*informal*) spend time wandering around without reason and without doing anything or going anywhere in particular: *You've spent the whole morning mooching about; — why don't you work?*

mood¹ /muːd/ *c.n* **1** state of s.o's mind, feelings etc: *What's her mood like this morning? She's in a good/bad/terrible mood.* **2** state of bad temper: *Why are you in such a mood today? He's in one of his moods.* **in no mood for s.t; not in the mood (for s.t)** not in the right state of mind to do, for, s.t: *I'm tired and in no mood for your nonsense. I'm not in the mood (for watching television).* **in the mood for s.t, to do s.t** wanting s.t, to do s.t: *I'm in the mood for a night out.*

'moodily *adv* in a moody way.

'moodiness *u.n* fact or state of being moody.

'moody *adj* (*-ier, -iest*) having moods¹(2) that often change; often bad-tempered: *a moody child.*

mood² /muːd/ *c.n* (*grammar*) one of the sets of forms of a verb that show if the action is a fact, command, possibility etc: *the imperative(3) mood.*

moon¹ /muːn/ *n* **1** *def/unique n* body that moves round the earth once a month and reflects light from the sun at night: *The moon is bright tonight.* **2** any of the similar bodies that move round other planets: *It has recently been discovered that Uranus has 15 moons.* **crescent moon** shape of the moon when it looks curved and less than half a circle. **full moon** (time of the month when) the moon is seen as a big round ball. **half moon** shape of the moon when the side facing earth is seen as half a circle. **new moon** (time when only a thin curve of) the moon is seen before it grows and becomes a half moon. **once in a blue moon** ⇒ once. **over the moon (about s.t)** (*fig*) extremely pleased (about s.t): *She's over the moon about her success.* **promise (s.o) the moon** (*fig*) promise to give (s.o) s.t that is impossible to give.

'moon,beam *c.n* beam of light reflecting from the moon.

'moonless *adj* (usu *attrib*) (of a night) very dark and without moonlight.

'moon,light *u.n* **1** (often *attrib*) light from the moon: *Let's go for a walk in the moonlight.* **do a moonlight flit** ⇒ flit(1).

▷ *intr.v* **2** have a second job that is done outside the working hours of the first job.

'moon,lit *adj* having light from the moon on it: *a moonlit path.*

'moon,shine *u.n* nonsense.

'moon,struck *adj* slightly wild and mad.

moon² /muːn/ *tr/intr.v* **1 moon about/around (s.w)** wander around (a place) sadly and without any purpose, esp when in love: *Stop mooning about (the house) — go and phone him if you want to talk to him.* **2 moon over s.o** spend time thinking about s.o one loves.

moor¹ /muə/ *c/u.n* large open stretch of land that is not farmed or fenced and is often covered with heather.

'moorland *u.n* large area of moor¹.

moor² /muə/ *tr/intr.v* tie (a boat etc) with rope etc to the side of a river, canal etc.

'moorings *pl.n* place where a boat etc is tied safely.

moose /muːs/ *c.n* (*pl* -(s)) largest kind of deer with big antlers, found in North America, North Asia and Northern Europe (in Northern Europe it is called an elk).

moot /muːt/ *tr.v* (usu *passive*) raise, state, (a question etc) for discussion so that a decision can be made.

,moot 'point *c.n* (usu *sing*) matter that is uncertain or not decided.

mop /mɒp/ *c.n* **1** bundle of thick string or a sponge(3) pad attached to a (long) handle for washing floors, dishes etc. **2** act of cleaning (the floor) with a mop(1): *Please give the floor a mop.* **3** head of thick untidy hair: *a mop of black hair.*

▷ *tr.v* (-pp-) **4** rub, wash, wipe, (the floor etc) with a mop(1). **5** wipe (a sweaty face etc): *mop one's brow.* **mop (s.t) up (a)** use a mop(1), cloth etc to clean (s.t away): *Go and fetch a cloth to mop up the milk.* **(b)** capture(4), destroy etc, the last remaining groups (e.g of an enemy): *Soldiers are mopping up after the victory.*

mope /məup/ *intr.v* (often — about/around) be sad or in low spirits and not wanting to do anything in particular: *Stop moping around — do something.*

moped /'məuped/ *c.n* motorbike with a very small, usu 50cc, engine.

moral /'mɒrəl/ *adj* (usu *attrib*) **1** of or referring to behaviour that is good or right: *a moral judgement/question*; *She's a very moral person. They live a moral life.* Opposite immoral. **2** that describes/teaches correct behaviour, the difference between right and wrong: *a moral lesson/ story.* **give (s.o) moral support** provide help (to s.o) by one's presence rather than by physical(1) or financial help: *Please come and watch me — you'll give me moral support.*

▷ *c.n* **3** lesson that one learns from a story, experience etc: *The moral of the story is 'Don't take a lift from someone you don't know'.* ⇒ morals.

'moralist *c.n* person who makes moral(2) judgements about other people's behaviour, ideas etc.

,mora'listic *adj* (*derog*) of, referring to, teaching, narrow-minded ideas about correct or good behaviour.

,mora'listically *adv.*

morality /mə'ræliti/ *n* (*pl* -ies) **1** *u.n* correct behaviour: *I don't know about the morality of his business dealings but he is successful.* Opposite immorality. **2** *c.n* particular system of moral beliefs: *the moralities of right and wrong.*

moralize, -ise /'mɒrəlaiz/ *intr.v* (usu — about/ on s.t) (*derog*) speak, write, in a moralistic way about matters of right and wrong etc: *Stop moralizing about other people's behaviour.*

'morally *adv* **1** in, referring to, the correct way of behaving: *You behaved very morally.* Opposite immorally. **2** concerning what is considered right or wrong: *She is morally correct in this matter.*

'morals *pl.n* one's own rules of good or correct behaviour: *He has no morals so I would never trust him.*

morale /mə'rɑːl/ *u.n* level of courage, spiritual(1) strength and enjoyment: *The work was hard but everyone's morale was high.*

morass /mə'ræs/ *c.n* (usu *sing*) situation that is difficult and full of problems: *Progress was difficult because of the morass of papers we had to complete.*

moratorium /,mɒrə'tɔːriəm/ *c.n* (*pl* -s or, less usu, moratoria /,mɒrə'tɔːriə/) **1** (often — on s.t) agreement that allows a debt to be paid later than originally stated. **2** amount of time allowed for delay in paying a debt.

morbid /'mɔːbid/ *adj* (of a person, ideas, thoughts) very concerned with death and unhappiness: *She's so morbid these days — all her conversation is about dying.*

'morbidly *adv.* **'morbidness** *u.n.*

more /mɔː/ *adv* **1** (used to form the comparative of many adjs and advs, esp those with three or more syllables): *They finished it more quickly than we did. She is more interesting than he is. That way is more possible than this.* ⇒ less(1). **2** to a greater amount or degree: *I can work more than I used to be able to. You should paint more.* ⇒ less(2). **and what is more . . .** (used as an expression when one wishes to add) another point, reason: *I'm not giving you any money this week and what's more, if you don't tidy your room I won't give you any money next week either.* **any more** ⇒ anymore. **more and more** (also *det*) increasingly; (in a way that is becoming) greater all the time: *It is becoming more and more easy to travel all over the world.* **more often than not** on most occasions. **more or less (a)** approximately: *It's an hour's drive from here more or less. It'll cost you £200 more or less.* **(b)** almost: *We're more or less finished.* **more than glad, happy** etc **(to do s.t)** (used to express a feeling that is stronger than the adj, adv that is being used): *I shall be more than happy to look after you for the evening.* **more . . . than . . .** it is more (true to say) that he/she/it is . . . than (to say that) (he/she/it is) . . .: *He's more lazy than unintelligent.* **no more . . . than . . .** in no better way than . . .: *I can no more help you with your mathematics than climb Mt Everest.* **once more** ⇒ once. **the more . . . the**

more . . . to the degree that (s.t happens) so (will s.t else happen) to the same degree: *The more you practise the more you'll improve.*

▷ *det* (comparative of *much*, *many*) **3** additional amount, number, quantity: *We'll need more milk. May I have some more sweets? How many more miles must we walk? Do you need (any) more help?* **4** (often — *s.o/s.t than* . . .) a greater amount, number, quantity: *There were more visitors to the island last year. You've got more cake than I have.* ⇨ most (*det*). **the more . . . the more/less . . .** the amount of s.t that one does, gives, sees etc has a greater/ lesser effect on what s.o else does, on what other things one does etc: *The more help you give her the more/less help she'll need.*

▷ *pron* **5** (often — *of s.t, than* . . .) greater, additional amount, number, quantity: *I've given you so much already — you can't want more. I've seen more of you this holiday than I usually do. There aren't any more. How many more do you need? More are going on strike than are returning to work.* ⇨ most (pron). **any more** (in questions and negative statements) anything left, extra etc: *Is there any more? Have you any more to say?* ⇨ anymore. **more (in/to s.t) than meets the eye** ⇨ eye(*n*). **see more of s.o** meet s.o again, often: *I enjoyed our evening — I'd like to see more of you.* **the more . . . the more/less . . .** the amount that one does, sees etc s.t affects the amount that one does s.t else: *The more I understand of this business, the less I like it.*

moreover /mɔː'rəʊvə/ *adv* in addition; also: *It's very expensive and moreover it's not really what we want.*

mores /'mɔːreɪz/ *pl.n* (*formal*) customs, standards, that are accepted by a particular group at a particular time.

morgue /mɔːg/ *c.n* building where dead bodies are kept until it is discovered who they were.

moribund /'mɒrɪ,bʌnd/ *adj* (*formal*) in the process of dying or coming to an end: *a moribund custom.*

morning /'mɔːnɪŋ/ *c/unique n* (also *attrib*) first part of the day until noon: *I'll see you tomorrow/Monday morning. Let's go for a morning swim.*

morning star *def.n* the planet Venus when it appears in the sky just before sunrise. ⇨ evening star.

moron /'mɔːrɒn/ *c.n* **1** person with very low intelligence. **2** (*derog*) stupid person: *Don't be such a moron!*

moronic /mə'rɒnɪk/ *adj*. **mo'ronically** *adv*.

morose /mə'rəʊs/ *adj* (*formal*) (of a person, a mood[1](1)) silently bad-tempered or angry: *He's in such a morose mood that no one dares go near him.*

mo'rosely *adv*. **mo'roseness** *u.n*.

morpheme /'mɔːfiːm/ *c.n* (*grammar*) smallest meaningful part of a word: *'Cups' contains the two morphemes, 'cup' and 's', and 'cupfuls' has three, 'cup', 'ful' and 's'.*

morphia /'mɔːfɪə/ *u.n* (also **morphine** /'mɔːfiːn/) kind of drug(2) used to stop pain.

morphology /mɔː'fɒlədʒɪ/ *u.n* **1** (*grammar*) study of the morphemes of a language and the ways they are joined together to form words.

2 (*technical*) study of the structure of plants and animals.

morphological /,mɔːfə'lɒdʒɪkl/ *adj*. **morpho-logically** *adv*.

morrow /'mɒrəʊ/ *def.sing.n* (*formal*, *literary*) next day or morning.

Morse /mɔːs/ *u.n* (also **Morse 'code**) system of communication(1), esp in signalling, telegraphs etc, that consists of dots and dashes, or long and short sounds or flashes of light, for the letters of the alphabet.

morsel /'mɔːsl/ *c.n* very small piece (of food): *There isn't a morsel of food in the house.*

mortal /'mɔːtl/ *adj* **1** who/that cannot live for ever: *We are all mortal beings.* Opposite immortal(*adj*). **2** (usu *attrib*) causing death: *a mortal disease.* **3** (*informal*) very great: *mortal fear; a mortal enemy* (i.e s.o one hates very much).

▷ *c.n* **4** person: *We are all mortals.* Compare immortal(3).

mortality /mɔː'tælɪtɪ/ *n* **1** *u.n* state of being mortal(1). Opposite immortality. **2** *def.n* (also *attrib*, usu *the — rate*) number of deaths caused by accidents, violence, an earthquake etc; deathrate: *The mortality rate in air travel was very high in 1985.*

mortally /'mɔːtəlɪ/ *adv* **1** in a way that causes death: *She was mortally injured(1) in a car accident.* **2** greatly; extremely: *I was mortally hurt by what you said.*

mortal 'sin *c.n* (esp in the Roman Catholic(1) church) extremely serious crime against one of God's laws.

mortar[1] /'mɔːtə/ *u.n* mixture of sand, water and cement(1), used to fix bricks together.

'mortar board *c.n* **1** (also **hawk**) small square board with a handle underneath for carrying mortar[1]. **2** flat black cap worn by university academics(1).

mortar[2] /'mɔːtə/ *c.n* bowl made of stone etc for crushing substances with a pestle.

mortar[3] /'mɔːtə/ *c.n* (shell from a) kind of gun with a short wide barrel.

mortgage /'mɔːgɪdʒ/ *c.n* **1** (agreement for an) amount of money that is borrowed by a person or a company to buy a house, a building or some land.

▷ *tr.v* **2** provide, offer, (one's house, a building) as a guarantee(4) when one needs to raise money: *We can always mortgage our house to raise money for our business.*

mortice ⇨ mortise.

mortify /'mɔːtɪ,faɪ/ *tr.v* (*-ies*, *-ied*) (often passive) (*formal*) make (s.o) feel very ashamed or upset: *She was mortified when she learned that her son was in trouble with the police.*

mortification /,mɔːtɪfɪ'keɪʃən/ *u.n*.

mortise /'mɔːtɪs/ *c.n* (also **'mortice**) (*technical*) hole in a piece of wood etc where another piece (the tenon) will fit.

mortuary /'mɔːtjʊərɪ/ *c.n* (*pl -ies*) building or room, e.g in a hospital, where dead bodies are kept before they are buried.

mosaic /mə'zeɪɪk/ *c.n* (also *attrib*) pattern made by laying together small pieces of different coloured stones, glass etc: *a mosaic floor.*

Moslem /'mɒzləm/ ⇨ Muslim.

mosque /mɒsk/ *c.n* Muslim(1) place of worship.

mosquito /məs'kiːtəʊ/ *c.n* (*pl -es*) (also *attrib*) kind of small flying insect that bites.

moss /mɒs/ c/u.n (kind of) small plant with no flowers that grows on rocks, trees etc in cool damp places: *The forest floor was covered with many different kinds of mosses.* **a rolling stone gathers no moss** ⇨ roll(v).
'mossy adj (-ier, -iest) (usu attrib) covered with, like, moss: *a mossy rock.*
most /məʊst/ adv **1** (used to form the superlative of many adjs and advs, esp those with three or more syllables): *She is the most beautiful/interesting/amusing person I know. That is most likely.* **2** to the greatest degree: *What hurts most? What made me most angry was that he seemed not to care. I like all kinds of cake but most of all I love chocolate cake.* ⇨ more (adv). **3** (formal) extremely; very: *You have been most kind. I am most grateful for all your help. It has been a most enjoyable evening.*
▷ det **4** (often the —) greatest possible amount, number, quantity (of s.t): *Who ate the most cake/sweets? Which year did we get the most rain?* ⇨ many, more, much (det). **5** (usu without the) greater part (of s.t): *I enjoy most music. Most people disagree with you. I like most kinds of food.* **for the most part** ⇨ part(n).
▷ pron **6** (often the —) greatest amount, number, quantity: *The most I can do is offer my help.* ⇨ many, more, much (pron). *We bought a lot but they bought the most.* **7** (often — of (the) people, time etc) the greatest part: *Most of us passed the examination. It was warm and sunny most of the time. We spend most of the year in Paris. Everyone wanted to go but most didn't manage it.* **at (the very) most** the largest possible amount, number etc; not more than: *There were two thousand people at the most. I can stay for three days at the very most.* **make the most of s.t** use an opportunity in the best possible way: *You'll only go to the Himalayas once in your life so make the most of it.*
'mostly adv **1** nearly always: *We mostly go to France for our holidays.* **2** nearly all; mainly: *I got mostly A's in the last examinations.*
motel /məʊ'tel/ c.n hotel mainly used by people travelling by car, bus etc.
moth /mɒθ/ c.n kind of flying insect seen mainly at night when it is attracted by light; some kinds eat cloth etc. Compare butterfly.
'moth,ball c.n chemical ball used to protect clothing etc from moths.
'moth-,eaten adj **1** (of clothes etc) eaten, ruined, by moths. **2** (fig) old; worn-out: *That's a rather moth-eaten sweater.*
'moth-,proof adj **1** (of material, clothes etc) treated so as not to be attacked, ruined, by moths.
▷ tr.v **2** treat (material etc) in this way so that moths will not attack it.
mother /'mʌðə/ c.n **1** female parent: *My mother and father were married 20 years ago.* **2** woman who looks after children in a boarding house, school etc: *She has a job as a house-mother during the week only.* **3** (usu with capital **M**; also **Mother Su'perior**) (title of a) leader of a female religious group: *Mother Augusta.* **expectant mother** ⇨ expect.
▷ tr.v **4** (often derog) care for (s.o) in the way a mother does; protect (s.o) (often too much): *Stop mothering me!* Compare father(7).

'mother ,country c/def.n country where one was born.
'mother,hood u.n state of being a mother: *I don't think I'm suited to motherhood.*
'mother-in-,law c.n (pl mothers-in-law) mother of one's wife, husband.
'motherliness u.n quality of being, acting, like a mother.
'motherly adj having, showing, the qualities of a mother(1): *I need some motherly love and attention.*
,Mother 'Nature unique n the natural forces that control the world: *If Mother Nature will give us a warm dry day tomorrow we'll have a picnic.*
,Mother Su'perior c.n ⇨ mother(3).
,mother-to-'be c.n (pl mothers-to-be) pregnant(1) woman.
'mother ,tongue c.n first language one learns to speak as a child.
motif /məʊ'tiːf/ c.n (main) pattern or important part that is repeated often in a design(2), in music, in a play etc.
motion /'məʊʃən/ n **1** u.n act, way, of moving: *The snake moves with a sideways motion.* **2** c.n single movement: *She made a motion with her head which warned me to be quiet.* **3** c.n proposal to be discussed at a meeting: *At the end of the meeting the chairperson counted the number of votes for and against the motion.* **go through the motions (of s.t)** do all the things that are needed although they are not important, do not mean very much to one etc: *I'll have to go through the motions of mourning at his funeral but I didn't really like him.* **in motion** (of a vehicle etc) moving: *The car was in motion as I got to it.* **(in) slow motion** (esp of a film) with the speed slowed down (so that one can examine movements etc more closely): *Let's see that goal again but this time in slow motion.* **put/set s.t in(to) motion** cause s.t to start moving, working, happening: *This switch sets the whole system in motion. Their plans were put into motion when they got the money.*
▷ tr/intr.v **4** make a sign, movement, (at/to s.o/s.t), esp when directing s.o to do s.t: *She motioned (to) her daughter to leave the room. He motioned me (to come) closer.*
'motionless adj not moving: *She remained motionless in the dark hoping she wouldn't be noticed.*
'motion ,picture c.n film for the cinema.
motive /'məʊtɪv/ c.n (often — for (doing) s.t) reason (for doing s.t or choosing to act, behave, in a particular way): *I don't understand your motive for being so unkind. No one has discovered the motive for the murder.* **ulterior motive** ⇨ ulterior.
motivate /'məʊtɪ,veɪt/ tr.v (usu passive) be the reason for (s.o's actions, behaviour etc): *Her actions are motivated by greed.*
motivation /,məʊtɪ'veɪʃən/ c/u.n (example of a) purpose; state of being motivated: *If you have no motivation you'll never win.*
motley /'mɒtlɪ/ attrib.adj consisting of a variety of different colours, kinds etc: *a motley group of people.*
motor /'məʊtə/ c.n (also attrib) **1** machine that uses power from electricity, petrol etc to produce motion: *an electric motor. Does this motor work*

by electricity or on petrol? Motor vehicles *are not allowed in this street.*

▷ *intr.v* **2** (*old use*) travel by car: *We motored to the coast for the day.*

'**motor,bike** also '**motor,cycle** *c.n* strong and heavy vehicle with two wheels and a petrol engine.

'**motor,boat** *c.n* boat with a motor that (usu) uses petrol.

'**motor,cade** *c.n* procession of motorcars.

'**motor,car** *c.n* (also **car**) motor vehicle with usu four wheels and space inside for two to six people.

'**motor,cycle** *c.n* = motorbike.

'**motor,cyclist** *c.n* person who rides a motorcycle, motorbike.

'**motor,horn** *c.n* = horn(3).

'**motoring** *u.n* (also *attrib*) driving (in a car): *I'm going to have a few driving lessons at the school of motoring. We had a motoring holiday in Europe.*

'**motorist** *c.n* person who drives a car.

motorized, **-ised** /'məʊtə,raɪzd/ *adj* (usu *attrib*) fitted with a motor: *a motorized toy.*

'**motor ,nerve** *c.n* (*technical*) part of the body that carries a message to a muscle(1) and starts it moving.

'**motor,scooter** *c.n* (also '**scooter**) small motorbike, usu with a small engine.

'**motor ,vehicle** *c.n* = vehicle(1).

'**motor,way** *c.n* (*written abbr* M) wide road with separate lanes(3) for vehicles travelling in opposite directions used by fast traffic which goes round towns etc and not through them: *Since the motorway has been opened it takes less than an hour to reach the airport.*

mottled /'mɒtld/ *adj* having spots and marks of many shapes and colours: *a mottled pattern.*

motto /'mɒtəʊ/ *c.n* (*pl* -(e)s) short sentence expressing a general rule of behaviour etc: *She lives by the motto 'Never leave for tomorrow what you can do today!'*

mould¹ /məʊld/ *u.n* **1** hollow shape into which a substance is poured in liquid or soft form so that it will harden in the desired shape: *The molten metal is poured into the mould.* **2** thing shaped in this way.

▷ *tr.v* **3** make, form, (s.t) in a mould¹(1): *Steel is moulded into huge long poles¹(1).* **4** make (s.t) into a shape: *mould the clay into the shape of a dish.* **5** make (s.t) by shaping it out of, in, s.t: *mould a vase out of a piece of clay.* **6** (*fig*) shape, influence, (behaviour, ideas, character): *Her opinions have been moulded since her early childhood.*

'**moulding** *u.n* moulded¹(4) decorations for walls, ceilings, picture frames etc.

mould² /məʊld/ *u.n* **1** white or green growth on food, leather, walls etc caused by damp air. **2** soil made from old leaves, bark etc.

'**moulder** *intr.v* (often — *away*) slowly become rotten and useless: *Those letters have been mouldering away in my cupboard for many years.*

'**mouldiness** *u.n* fact or state of being mouldy.

'**mouldy** *adj* (-ier, -iest) **1** (of food etc) covered with mould(1): *There's only a mouldy piece of cheese left.* **2** (esp *attrib*) (*derog*) old and worn out: *I hate this mouldy old coat — I want a new*

one. **go mouldy** become full of mould²(1): *The cake's gone mouldy.*

moult /məʊlt/ *intr.v* (of a bird, cat, dog etc) lose old hair, feathers, skin etc: *The cat is moulting — look how much fur she's left on the chair.*

mound /maʊnd/ *c.n* small hill or pile of earth: *Throw that old chair on that mound of rubbish.*

Mount /maʊnt/ *c.n* (*written abbr* Mt) (esp before the name) mountain: *Mount Kilimanjaro.*

mount /maʊnt/ *c.n* **1** (*formal*) animal, esp a horse, that one rides. **2** piece of card on which to place a (smaller) picture, photograph etc, e.g when framing.

▷ *v* **3** *tr/intr.v* get on (a horse etc): *He mounted (his horse) and rode off in a cloud of dust.* **4** *tr.v* climb up (higher) on (s.t): *She mounted the ladder.* **5** *intr.v* become greater; increase: *Pressure on the government to resign is mounting.* **6** *tr.v* put (a picture, photograph) in a frame, book, box etc for display(1): *He mounted his butterfly collection on a large board.* **7** *tr.v* organize (an exhibition(1), an attack etc): *We are mounting an exhibition of our year's work.* **8** *tr.v* (of a male animal) get on to (a female's back) in a mating(7) position.

mountain /'maʊntɪn/ *c.n* **1** (also *attrib*) mass of high land, often with bare rocks near the top: *If you want to climb a mountain there are lots in Austria.* ⇒ Mount. Compare hill. **2** (often — *of* s.t) (*fig*) big pile (of s.t): *I have a mountain of papers to read and mark.* **make a mountain out of a molehill** (*fig*) treat a small matter, problem etc as s.t very important, serious etc.

mountaineer /,maʊntɪ'nɪə/ *c.n* person who is skilled at climbing mountains.

,**mountai'neering** *u.n* activity, sport, of climbing mountains.

'**mountainous** *adj* **1** having many mountains: *Lesotho is a very mountainous country.* **2** (*fig*) very big: *a mountainous meal.*

'**mountain ,range** *c.n* group of mountains.

mourn /mɔːn/ *tr/intr.v* (often — (*for*) s.o/s.t) be very sad or show one's sorrow (because of s.o's death, the end of s.t etc): *She is still mourning her father's death. He's mourning for his wife. He mourned the passing of old customs.*

'**mourner** *c.n* person who mourns (for) s.o.

'**mournful** *adj* (*formal*) sad: *Why are you looking so mournful?*

'**mournfully** *adv.* '**mournfulness** *u.n.*

'**mourning** *u.n* (also *attrib*) sadness shown for s.o's death: *The Americans declared a week's mourning after the earthquake.* **be in mourning (for s.o)** spend a length of time in which one shows one's sadness for the death of s.o by wearing black clothes, staying at home etc.

mouse /maʊs/ *c.n* (*pl* mice /maɪs/) **1** kind of small animal with fur, a pointed nose and a long tail: *The cat brought a mouse into the house.* **2** quiet shy person: *She's such a little mouse — she never says anything.* **play cat and mouse (with s.o)** ⇒ cat. **poor as a church mouse** very poor.

'**mousiness** *u.n* fact or state of being mousy.

'**mousy** *adj* (-ier, -iest) (usu *derog*) **1** (of hair) light brown. **2** (of a person) dull.

mousse /muːs/ *c/u.n* mixture of eggs, cream, fruit etc to give a soft, fluffy kind of pudding: *chocolate mousse.*

moustache /mə'stɑːʃ/ *c.n* hair growing above the top lip.

mouth /maʊθ/ *c.n* (*pl* -s /maʊðz/) **1** opening on the face through which people, animals make sounds, talk, eat: *Don't talk with food in your mouth. What has he got in his mouth?* **2** opening; entrance of a bottle, cave, river etc. **by word of mouth** by speaking (and not in a written form): *Send me a message by word of mouth.* **keep one's mouth shut** (*slang*) not talk about s.t or tell anyone else about s.t. (**not/never**) **look a gift-horse in the mouth** ⇨ gift-horse. **make one's mouth water** make one hungry for s.t: *That cake is making my mouth water.* **put words into s.o's mouth** (**a**) tell s.o what to say, how to answer: *Don't put words into his mouth — I want to hear what he has to say.* (**b**) suggest falsely that s.o has said s.t: *You're putting words into my mouth — that's not at all what I said.* **shoot one's mouth off** (*slang*) talk loudly about s.t that one doesn't know anything about or that one shouldn't be talking about. **take the words out of s.o's mouth** be, say, exactly what s.o else was going to say or would have said: *You took the words right out of my mouth!*

▷ *tr/intr.v* /maʊð/ **3** make movements of the lips to form the words one wants to say but without making any sound: *He mouthed to me to meet him outside.*

mouthful /ˈmaʊθfʊl/ *c.n* **1** as much food as can be put in one's mouth: *He ate that whole sandwich in one mouthful.* **2** (*fig*) (of a word, name etc) hard to pronounce: *The title of his new book is quite a mouthful!* **3** (often **get**, **give** s.o, **a —**) (*informal*) angry criticism: *She gave me such a mouthful for being late.*

ˈmouth ˌorgan *c.n* small musical instrument played by blowing and sucking air into it.

ˈmouth ˌpiece *c.n* **1** part of a telephone into which one speaks. **2** part of a musical instrument etc which is placed at or between the lips. **3** (*fig*) person, newspaper etc who/that expresses the opinions, feelings, ideas of others: *I'm not buying that newspaper — it's just the government's mouthpiece.*

ˈmouth ˌwash *c/u.n* liquid containing an antiseptic for cleaning out the mouth.

ˈmouth- ˌwatering *adj* **1** (of food) that makes one want to eat it. **2** (*fig*) (of an advertisement, experience etc) that makes one want to do s.t: *a mouth-watering film on a visit to China.*

move /muːv/ *c.n* **1** act of moving(5); movement(1): *One move and you're dead!* **2** act of changing the position in a board game: *It's your move. I can beat you at chess in less than five moves.* **3** act or step in a plan or action: *Our next move is very important — it could win or lose us the order.* **4** act of taking one's furniture, possessions, to another home: *Who is going to do your move?* **be on the move** be moving around from one place to another. **get a move on** (usu as an order) hurry up. **make a move**; **make the first move** begin or prepare to leave, act: *If we don't make a move now we'll never get there before dark. They're waiting for us to make the first move.*

▷ *v* **5** *tr/intr.v* (cause (s.o/s.t) to) change position, go to a different place: *What was that moving? Could you move your car, please? Everything was still — not a leaf moved.* **6** *intr.v* (often — *house*; — *to* s.w) take one's furniture, possessions etc to another home: *Where are you moving to?*

When are you moving? ⇨ move in, move out. **7** *tr.v* (often passive) make (s.o) feel pity or have strong feelings about s.o/s.t: *Millions of people were moved by the television pictures of people dying in Ethiopia.* ⇨ unmoved, move s.o to tears (⇨ tear[1]). **8** *tr/intr.v* (often — *that . . .*) suggest (a form of action, question, subject etc) at a meeting to be discussed and a decision made, usu by a vote: *He moved that a committee be set up to study the problems.* **9** *intr.v* make progress: *If the work continues to move this fast we'll finish earlier than expected.*

get things moving cause s.t to begin well and effectively: *Put some music on — that'll get things moving.*

keep things moving cause s.t that is happening to continue.

move (**s.t**) **about/around** (**a**) (cause (s.t) to) change position: *Stop moving the furniture around. There's something moving about in the grass.* (**b**) change one's/s.o's job, home etc often: *She never lives in one place for long as she likes to move around.*

move (**s.o/s.t**) **along/on** (cause (s.o/s.t) to) move(5): *The police moved us on as they said we were blocking the way. We slowly moved along with the rest of the crowd.*

move (**s.o/s.t**) **away** (**a**) (cause (s.o/s.t) to) move(5) from one place to another: *Could you move those books away as I want to work there?* (**b**) (cause (s.o/s.t) to) leave s.w to go to another house: *They don't live here; they moved away about a year ago.*

move (**s.o/s.t**) **back** (cause (s.o/s.t) to) move(5) from a position in front to one further back: *Would you please move back to let these other people come in.*

move (**s.o/s.t**) **down** (**s.t**) (**a**) (cause (s.o/s.t) to) change from a higher position to a lower one: *Move those books down as I need the space.* (**b**) (cause (s.o/s.t) to) change position and go forwards (in a bus, queue(1) etc): *Move right down (the bus), please.*

move heaven and earth (**to do s.t** (**for s.o**)) ⇨ heaven.

move in ⇨ move (s.o/s.t) in(to s.w). **move in on s.o/s.t** (**a**) start to take advantage of s.o/s.t, esp s.o/s.t who/that is beginning to be successful: *As soon as there are signs of large profits to be made, the big companies will move in on the smaller ones and take them over.* (**b**) get into a position to attack s.o/s.t. **move** (**s.o/s.t**) **in** (**to s.w**) (cause (s.o/s.t) to) enter a new home, place, position: *When are they moving the new machinery in (to the factory)? Who's moving in next door?* **move in the best**, **highest** etc **circles** ⇨ circle(*n*).

move off (of a person, vehicle etc) start to move(5) from a place: *The trucks moved off slowly.*

move (**s.o/s.t**) **on** ⇨ move (s.o/s.t) along/on.

move (**s.o/s.t**) **out** (**of s.w**) (cause (s.o/s.t) to) leave a place, home, position: *We plan to move out (of the house) on the 22nd of August.*

move over change one's position so as to allow more room for s.o/s.t else: *Could you move over a bit so that I can sit next to you?*

move to s.w ⇨ move(6).

move s.o to do s.t cause s.o to act or do s.t: *The film moved millions of people to send money* to help those suffering from the drought. ⇨ move(7).

move s.o to tears ⇨ tear¹.

move towards s.o/s.t move(5) and get nearer to s.o/s.t: *We could see a storm moving towards us in the distance.*

move (s.o/s.t) up (to s.t/s.w) (a) (cause (s.o/s.t) to) move(5) to a higher position from a lower one: *Move those books up so that I can fit these ones in.* (b) (cause (s.o/s.t) to) change position, come closer together etc (in a bus, queue(1) etc): *Move up (the bus) please.* (c) (cause (soldiers, vehicles etc) to) get closer (to the enemy, a battle etc): *The enemy has started moving its tanks up to the front line.* (d) (cause (prices, shares(3) etc) to) increase in value etc: *The company's shares(3) have been moving up steadily.*

'moveable *adj* (also **'movable**) Opposite immoveable. 1 that can be moved; not fixed: *This doll has movable arms and legs.* 2 (*law*) (of possessions) that can be moved, sold etc, esp when compared to things that cannot be moved, e.g a house: *a person's movable estate(3).*

'moveables *pl.n* (also **'movables**) personal property and furniture that is not fixed: *Do you want to sell any movables with your house?* Compare immoveables.

'movement *n* 1 *c/u.n* (act of) moving, being moved, changing position: *I saw a movement in the bush.* 2 *c/u.n* activity; ability to move: *After the accident I had no movement in my left arm for six months.* 3 *c.n* (with capital **M** in names) organization of people with the same aims: *the Peace Movement.* 4 *c.n* general direction of ideas, ways of thinking etc; trend(1): *The movement is towards healthy living and eating.* 5 *c.n* (*music*) one of the parts of a long piece of music: *I loved the second movement.* 6 *c.n* (*formal*) (example of, waste matter from) emptying the bowels.

'mover *c.n* person who moves(8) a question, a motion(3), at a meeting.

'movie /'muːvɪ/ *c.n* (*informal*) film.

'movie ,star *c.n* film-star.

'movies *def.pl.n* cinema: *Let's go to the movies tonight.*

'moving *adj* 1 having a strong effect on one's feelings: *What a moving story! The ceremony was very moving.* 2 (*attrib*) that is not fixed: *Oil the moving parts regularly.* **moving staircase =** escalator.

mow /məʊ/ *tr.v* (*p.p* mowed, mown /məʊn/) cut (grass) with a machine: *Have you mowed the grass yet?* **mow s.o down** kill or destroy many people at one time.

'mower *c.n* machine for cutting grass. ⇨ lawnmower.

MP /,em 'piː/ *abbr* 1 Member of Parliament. 2 Military Policeman.

mpg /,em ,piː 'dʒiː/ *abbr* miles per gallon.

mph /,em ,piː 'eɪtʃ/ *abbr* miles per hour.

Mr /'mɪstə/ *abbr* mister(1).

Mrs /'mɪsɪz/ (title used in front of the name of a married woman): *I'm meeting Mrs Williams for tea.*

ms /,em 'es/ (*pl* mss /,em 'es ,ɪz/) *abbr* manuscript.

Ms /'mɪz/ (title used in front of the name of a woman who is married or not married): *Make

an appointment to see Ms Best.* Compare miss¹, Mr, Mrs.

MS /,em 'es/ *abbr* multiple sclerosis.

MSc /,em ,es 'siː/ *abbr* Master(3) of Science.

Mt *written abbr* Mount: *Mt Kenya.*

much /mʌtʃ/ *adv* 1 (used with a comparative or a superlative) by a large amount, degree: *He's much stronger than she is. She's much more intelligent than he is. You'll have to try much harder. That's much the best film I've seen this year.* 2 often: *We don't go out much. I don't see him very much now.* 3 (to) a great or certain degree: *Thanks very much. I don't much like that place. It doesn't matter much. It's much too late to phone him. He talks too much. I so much want to meet him. 'How much does she mean to you?' 'Not very much.'* 4 in most ways: *She's much the same as yesterday* (i.e her condition is no better/worse). *He's much the same as ever* (i.e He has not changed a lot). **much less . . .** (used to show that what is stated in the first part of the sentence has even greater force in the second part): *I've never met her much less spoken to her.* **much to s.o's regret, surprise, horror** etc (used to show s.t that happens in spite of s.o's strong opinion, feelings): *Bob passed his examination much to everyone's surprise.*

▷ *det* (*comp/superl* more/most) (used mainly in negative statements and questions; in affirmative statements 'much' is formal; instead we usu use 'a lot of' or 'plenty of', except in sentences where 'much' is used with 'too', 'so', 'as' and 'how'). 5 (used with uncountable nouns) a large amount or quantity of: *How much time do we have left? Is there much milk left? Eat as much food as you like. She drank so much wine that she felt sick. You put too much salt in the food.* Compare many(1).

▷ *pron* 6 a large amount: *She doesn't say much. 'Did he leave much?' 'No, not much.' Take as much as you want. Is it too much to ask you to play your music more softly? 'Did you do much at school today?' 'No, nothing much really.'* Compare many(2). **as much** that is what is true: *I realized as much as yesterday.* (**as**) **much as . . .** although . . . : *Much as I'd like to see the film I must work tonight.* **as much again** double that amount: *We paid £50 000 for the cottage and as much again on the repairs.* **be a bit much** (a) be too expensive. (b) (*informal*) be asking, expecting, an excessive amount: *I don't mind you using my phone but isn't it a bit much to phone Australia?* **be not so much (that) . . . as/but (that . . .)** be not (one reason) but more (another reason) why one dislikes s.o/s.t or cannot do s.t: *It's not so much the dress I don't like as the colour.* **be not up to much** be not very good: *That meal wasn't up to much.* **be too much (for s.o)** (a) be too difficult, tiring etc (for s.o): *That walk was too much for her — she's only a little dog.* (b) (*informal*) (of bad behaviour) be more than one can take, handle: *Your rudeness is just too much!* **in as much as**; **inasmuch as** ⇨ in². **make much of s.o/s.t** (a) treat s.o/s.t as important: *He makes much of the fact that you were once friends.* (b) understand s.o/s.t: *I couldn't make much of him or his speech.* **not be/have much of a s.t** not be/have a very good example of s.t: *I'm not much of a dancer. She doesn't have much of an ability for this kind of* *thing.* **not think much of s.o/s.t** have a low opinion of s.o/s.t: *I didn't think much of her speech.* **so much for s.o/s.t** now that s.o's/that's decided, finished: *So much for that idea — does anyone else have a suggestion?* **so much so that . . .** to the extent that . . . : *We arrived early — so much so that we still had time for lunch.* Compare many(*pron*).

'muchness *c.n* **much of a muchness** (of several things) like each other, usu without being particularly good: *They were all much of a muchness so I didn't buy any of them.*

muck /mʌk/ *n* **1** *u.n* manure(1). **2** dirt; rubbish: *What's all this muck in the road?* **make a muck of s.t** (a) make s.t dirty: *How did you make such a muck of yourself?* (b) spoil s.t; do s.t unsuccessfully: *I made a muck of my chemistry paper.*

▷ *tr.v* **3** (usu — *s.t up*) make (s.t) dirty or messy: *You've mucked* (*up*) *my clean floor with your muddy boots.* **muck about/around** (**with s.o/s.t**) (*informal*) (a) do s.t (with s.o/s.t) without much purpose: *We spent our time mucking about with a football in the back yard.* (b) do s.t foolish (with s.o/s.t): *Stop mucking about with that hammer or you'll hurt someone.* **muck s.o about** (*slang*) annoy or harm s.o, esp by delaying s.t, not coming to a decision etc: *Stop mucking me about and tell me when you are going to pay me the money you owe.* **muck in** (**with s.o**) (*informal*) share work, costs etc (with s.o): *We all mucked in together and bought her a present.* **muck s.t up** (a) ⇨ muck(3). (b) (*informal*) spoil s.t: *I'm sorry if I mucked up your evening.*

'mucky *adj* (*-ier, -iest*) very dirty or sticky: *mucky work. My hands are very mucky.*

mucus /'mju:kəs/ *u.n* (*technical*) sticky substance, esp one produced in the nose or by an insect etc: *You can see a snail's been eating this cabbage because it's left mucus on the leaf.*

mucous /'mju:kəs/ *adj* of, like, covered with, mucus.

,mucous 'membrane *u.n* (*technical*) thin skin covered with mucus that protects certain parts of the body, e.g inside the nose, covering the eye etc.

mud /mʌd/ *u.n* very soft wet earth: *Take your shoes off — I don't want any mud in the house.* **s.o's name is mud** (*fig*) s.o is very unpopular: *My name is mud in their house since I broke the vase.* **sling mud at s.o/s.t** use damaging insults to spoil s.o's reputation. ⇨ mud-slinging.

'mud,bath *c.n* dirty and muddy place: *Our garden is a mudbath since those heavy rains.*

'muddiness *u.n* **1** fact or state of being muddy, slippery and dirty: *We had to drive slowly because of the muddiness of the road.* **2** (*fig*) confusion.

'muddy *adj* (*-ier, -iest*) **1** covered with mud: *muddy boots. The roads are muddy.* **2** like mud, esp in colour: *muddy brown shoes.* **3** (*fig*) not clear; confused: *muddy thoughts.*

▷ *tr.v* (*-ies, -ied*) **4** make (s.t) dirty with mud: *I've muddied my new shoes! Don't muddy the carpet.*

'mud,guard *c.n* guard over the wheel of a bicycle, car etc to prevent mud, rainwater etc from splashing.

'mud,pack *c.n* mixture (like mud) placed on the face to clean the skin as it dries.

'mud-,slinging *u.n* (*fig*) act of using damaging insults to spoil s.o's reputation. ⇨ sling mud at s.o/s.t.

muddle /'mʌdl/ *c.n* **1** (often *be in, get into, a —*) confused state: *How did these papers get into such a muddle? He left things in a muddle and it's taken a week to sort it all out. I got into a muddle and forgot what I was supposed to do.*

▷ *tr.v* **2** confuse (s.o): *Don't talk so fast — you're muddling me.* **3** (often — *s.t up*) make a muddle(1) of (s.t); get, put, (s.t) into disorder: *You've muddled* (*up*) *all my papers. He muddled* (*up*) *all the arrangements and now I don't know what's happening.* **4** (often — *s.o/s.t up*) confuse, mix up, (two different people, things etc): *Everyone muddles us up and doesn't know if I'm me or my sister. I muddled* (*up*) *the dates and went to see the doctor two days early.* **muddle along/ on** make some progress in spite of inefficiency and lack of understanding. **muddle through** (**s.t**) manage to finish (s.t) although without much efficiency or organization: *He's so disorganized but he always manages to muddle through* (*the work*) *somehow.* **muddle s.o/s.t up** ⇨ muddle(3,4).

,muddle-'headed *adj* (*derog*) confused; not able to think clearly.

,muddle-'headedly *adv.* **,muddle-'headedness** *u.n.*

muesli /'mju:zlɪ/ *u.n* mixture of nuts, dried fruit, grains etc, usu eaten with milk.

muff¹ /mʌf/ *c.n* warm covering for hands, ears etc worn in winter.

muff² /mʌf/ *tr.v* (*informal*) spoil (an opportunity): *You had a chance to get into the team and you muffed it.*

muffle /'mʌfl/ *tr.v* **1** (often — *oneself/s.o up* (*in s.t*)) cover (oneself/s.o) for warmth (in clothes etc): *Everyone muffled up before going out into the wintry night.* **2** reduce the noise or sound of/ from (s.t): *Their voices were muffled so I couldn't hear what they were saying.*

'muffler *c.n* **1** (woollen) cloth worn around the neck for warmth. **2** (*technical*) thing used to reduce noise, e.g an engine silencer.

mug¹ /mʌg/ *c.n* **1** kind of large cup used without a saucer: *a coffee mug.* **2** (often — *of s.t*) as much as a mug'(1) holds: *May I have a mug of coffee?* **'mugful** *c.n* = mug¹(2).

mug² /mʌg/ *c.n* (*slang*) fool: *I was such a mug to trust him.* ⇨ muggins.

mug³ /mʌg/ *c.n* (*slang*) face: *What an ugly mug!*

mug⁴ /mʌg/ *tr.v* (*-gg-*) attack (s.o) with the intention of stealing: *I was mugged on my way home last night.*

'mugger *c.n* person who mugs⁴ s.o.

'mugging *c.n* attack: *Old people are afraid to go out at night because of the increase in muggings.*

muggins /'mʌgɪnz/ *c.n* (*pl -es*) (*informal*) fool: *Don't be a muggins!* ⇨ mug².

muggy /'mʌgɪ/ *adj* (*-ier, -iest*) (of weather) damp, warm and with very little fresh air: *It's usually too muggy there at this time of the year.*

'mugginess *u.n* hot and sticky air or weather: *I can't breathe in such mugginess.*

Muhammad /mʊ'hæməd/ = Mohammed.

mule /mju:l/ *c.n* animal that is the offspring of a horse and donkey. **be as stubborn as a mule** be unwilling to cooperate or agree with s.o's advice, ideas etc.

'mulish adj (derog) refusing to agree, take advice etc.

'mulishly adv. **'mulishness** u.n.

mull¹ /mʌl/ tr.v make (wine etc) into a warm drink with spices.

'mulled adj (of wine) made hot and spicy: mulled wine.

mull² /mʌl/ tr.v **mull over s.t**; **mull s.t over** think about s.t very carefully: Don't make a decision now; mull over it for a few days (or take a few days to mull it over).

mullet /'mʌlɪt/ c.n (pl mullet) kind of seafish that can be used as food: grey/red mullet.

multifarious /ˌmʌltɪ'feərɪəs/ adj (formal) of many different kinds: She has multifarious skills.

multilateral /ˌmʌltɪ'lætərəl/ adj referring to two or more different groups or countries: a multilateral trade agreement between France, Spain and England; multilateral disarmament. Compare bilateral, unilateral.

multilingual /ˌmʌltɪ'lɪŋgwəl/ adj 1 expressed in many different languages. 2 able to speak many different languages. Compare bilingual, monolingual.

multimillionaire /ˌmʌltɪˌmɪlɪə'neə/ c.n person who owns several million pounds, dollars etc.

multinational /ˌmʌltɪ'næʃənl/ c.n (also attrib) company, business, that has offices etc in many different countries: He works for a multinational oil company and travels all over the world.

multiple /'mʌltɪpl/ adj (usu attrib) 1 having, referring to, many parts: a multiple-choice examination paper; receive multiple injuries in an accident; a multiple crash in foggy weather when six cars hit each other.

▷ c.n 2 (mathematics) number that contains another number an exact number of times: 20 is a multiple of 4. **lowest common multiple** (abbr lcm) smallest number that is a multiple(2) of all the numbers in a group. ⇒ highest common factor (⇒ factor).

multiple sclerosis /ˌmʌltɪpl ˌsklɪə'rəʊsɪs/ u.n (abbr MS) disease of the nervous system that affects movement and control of the body.

multiply /'mʌltɪˌplaɪ/ v (-ies, -ied) 1 tr.v (mathematics) (often — s.t by s.t; also shown by the sign 'X') add a number to itself a stated number of times and find the answer: Multiply 2 by 4. 2 multiplied by 4 is 8. 2 × 4 = 8. 2 tr/intr.v (cause (s.t) to) increase in number, amount: The world population is multiplying fast.

multiplication /ˌmʌltɪplɪ'keɪʃən/ c/u.n.

multiplicity /ˌmʌltɪ'plɪsɪtɪ/ n (often — of s.t) 1 sing.n (formal) state of being many (things): the multiplicity of nations. 2 c.n great number, variety, (of s.t): We listed a multiplicity of ways of raising money.

multiracial /ˌmʌltɪ'reɪʃəl/ adj consisting of or referring to many races of people: a multiracial society.

multistorey /ˌmʌltɪ'stɔːrɪ/ adj (esp of a high building) consisting of many levels: a multistorey car park.

multitude /'mʌltɪˌtjuːd/ n 1 c.n great number (of people, things): multitudes of people; a multitude of excuses/reasons/answers. 2 def.pl.n people in general: The multitude love his jokes. **cover a multitude of sins** (fig) be a useful or easy excuse: I'll say I wasn't feeling well — that'll cover a multitude of sins.

multitudinous /ˌmʌltɪ'tjuːdɪnəs/ adj (formal) large in number: a gadget with multitudinous uses.

mum¹ /mʌm/ c/unique n (also **'mummy**) (child's name for her/his) mother: Do you know where my mum is?

mum² /mʌm/ pred.adj 1 silent: keep mum about this.

▷ unique n 2 **Mum's the word!** Don't say anything about this.

mumble /'mʌmbl/ tr/intr.v say (s.t) softly or not very clearly and without opening one's mouth (much): He mumbled something about his daughter. What's Charlotte mumbling?

mummy¹ /'mʌmɪ/ c.n (pl -ies) ⇒ mum¹.

mummy² /'mʌmɪ/ c.n (pl -ies) dead body that has been treated with substances that prevent rotting etc.

mumps /mʌmps/ u/pl.n disease that affects the glands, esp in the neck area.

munch /mʌntʃ/ tr/intr.v chew (s.t), usu noisily: I can hear you munching your apple. **munch away (at s.t)** eat (s.t) in a noisy, active way: She munched away at her nuts throughout the film.

mundane /mʌn'deɪn/ adj (derog) ordinary; that happens every day: Life is so mundane — I want to do something exciting.

municipal /mju:'nɪsɪpl/ adj referring to (the parts of) a town or city controlled by itself: the municipal swimming pool/library/buildings.

municipality /ˌmju:nɪsɪ'pælɪtɪ/ c.n (pl -ies) 1 town, city, area with its own local government. 2 building where all matters of local government are dealt with. 3 governing body of a municipality(1).

munificent /mju:'nɪfɪsənt/ adj (formal) very generous; generously large: a munificent gift/person.

mu'nificence u.n.

munitions /mju:'nɪʃənz/ pl.n (also attrib) weapons etc, esp for war: This factory made munitions during the war. It was a munitions factory.

mural /'mjʊərəl/ c.n (also attrib) painting done directly on a wall.

murder /'mɜ:də/ n 1 c/u.n (example of an) unlawful deliberate(1) killing of s.o: The police are treating her death as murder. The young boy was found guilty of murder (or guilty of the murder of a policeman). 2 u.n (fig) thing that is extremely difficult to do or handle: This heat is murder. The examination was murder! **get away with murder** (fig) (be able to) escape punishment easily. **scream blue murder** (fig) shout very loudly and angrily.

▷ tr.v 3 kill (s.o) unlawfully and deliberately: They murdered a helpless old lady to steal her £2. 4 spoil, ruin, (s.t): You've murdered that song for me.

'murderer c.n person who murders(3) s.o.

murderess /'mɜ:dərɪs/ c.n woman who murders(3) s.o.

'murderous /'mɜ:dərəs/ adj (of s.o/s.t who/ that looks) able to kill: a murderous look in his eyes.

'murderously adv. **'murderousness** u.n.

murk /mɜːk/ *u.n* gloomy(1) darkness.
   '**murky** *adj* (*-ier*, *-iest*) **1** dark and gloomy(1): *a murky back street.* **2** (*fig*) suggesting evil or harm: *a man with a murky past.*
murmur /'mɜːmə/ *c.n* **1** quiet and continuous sound, esp from s.w distant: *the murmur of the traffic from the top floor of a building*; *the murmur of the trees in the wind.* **2** sound (often of complaint): *a murmur of happiness/ dissatisfaction*; *She gave him the money without a murmur. There are murmurs from the office that she's going to resign.*
   ▷ *v* **3** *tr/intr.v* speak, say (s.t), quietly and usu not clearly: *She murmured something about her brother.* **4** *intr.v* (often *— about s.o/s.t*) complain (about etc s.o/s.t): *I've heard people murmuring about the way you are handling the matter.*
   '**murmuring** *c/u.n* (also *attrib*) sound, usu of complaining, dissatisfaction: *The town is full of murmurings about the new law.*
muscle /'mʌsl/ *n* **1** *c/u.n* bundle of fibres(2) in the body by which one controls one's movements: *I've got strong leg muscles.* **2** *u.n* (*fig*) power; influence: *He has a lot of muscle in this town.*
   ▷ *intr.v* **3** **muscle in** (**on s.t**) gain (part of s.t) by force: *This time we will not allow you to muscle in on our success.*
   '**muscled** *adj* (often as the second part of a word) having muscles(1) of the kind described in the first part of the word: *a tight-muscled body.*
muscular /'mʌskjʊlə/ *adj* **1** of or referring to the muscles(1): *It's a muscular pain.* **2** having strong muscles(1): *a muscular body.*
   muscular dystrophy /ˌmʌskjʊlə 'dɪstrəfɪ/ *u.n* disease that weakens the muscles(1).
muse[1] /mjuːz/ *n* **1** *c.n* (in Greek mythology) one of the nine goddesses of poetry, music etc. **2** *def.n* spirit(1) that inspires(2) a poet, writer etc.
muse[2] /mjuːz/ *intr.v* (usu *— over/(up)on s.t*) think quietly (about s.t) while partly in a dream: *She sat under a tree musing on the quiet farming scene below. He lay in bed musing over the evening's events.*
museum /mjuː'zɪəm/ *c.n* place where collections of things of historic, artistic, scientific etc interest can be studied: *Ben loves the Science Museum because there he can learn about processes(1) through activities.*
   mu'**seum** ,**piece** *c.n* **1** thing that is (old, rare/ valuable and therefore) suitable for a museum. **2** (*joking*) old-fashioned person or thing.
mush /mʌʃ/ *u.n* soft mixture, esp of food that has been cooked too much: *I'm not paying for that mush.*
   '**mushy** *adj* (*-ier*, *-iest*) **1** soft, esp from being cooked too much: *mushy peas*(1). **2** (*fig*) (of words, writing) too sentimental: *a mushy film.*
mushroom /'mʌʃrʊm/ *n* **1** *c/u.n* (also *attrib*) kind of fungus, usu shaped like an umbrella, many kinds of which can be eaten: *I love chicken and mushroom soup.* **2** *c.n* (usu *attrib*) sudden large development, growth: *the mushroom development of large towns in the north.* **3** *c.n* shape of the cloud that follows the explosion of a nuclear bomb.
   ▷ *intr.v* **4** grow or spread very quickly: *Since the government began offering easy loans(2), small businesses have mushroomed.*
music /'mjuːzɪk/ *u.n* **1** (also *attrib*) (composition

of sounds produced by the) arranging of different combinations of sounds in a rhythm(2): *I'm studying music at university. She's a music teacher.* **2** written form of a composition of music(1) which can be read and played by other musicians: *I bought some new piano music.* **be music to one's ears** (*fig*) (of s.t said etc) be welcome and exactly what one wants to hear: *His long apology was music to my ears.* **face the music** (*fig*) accept responsibility and punishment for s.t bad that one has done. **put/set s.t to music** write the music for a poem etc so that it becomes a song.
musical /'mjuːzɪkl/ *adj* **1** (*attrib*) of, producing, music(1): *a musical instrument*; *a musical box.* **2** like music: *whistle a musical tune.* **3** having a feel, understanding, skill, for music(1): *My younger daughter is very musical.*
   ▷ *c.n* **4** (also *attrib*) film or play in which large parts are performed to music(1): *'West Side Story' is a very popular musical.*
   ,**musical 'instrument** ⇒ instrument(2).
   '**musically** *adv.*
   '**music ,centre** *c.n* set of equipment(2), including a record player, a tape deck, loudspeakers etc for playing records'(1), tapes(3) etc.
musician /mjuː'zɪʃən/ *c.n* person skilled in playing (and sometimes composing) music(1).
   '**music ,stand** *c.n* stand with a frame for holding music(2).
musk /mʌsk/ *u.n* substance with a strong smell taken from the male of a kind of deer and used in perfume(2).
   '**muskiness** *u.n* fact or state of being musky.
   '**musky** *adj* (*-ier*, *-iest*) having a strong smell of or like musk.
Muslim /'mʊslɪm/ (also **Moslem**) *adj* **1** of or referring to the Islamic religion etc: *Muslim architecture.*
   ▷ *c.n* **2** person who is a follower of the Islamic religion.
muslin /'mʌzlɪn/ *u.n* (also *attrib*) thin cotton cloth: *I made cheese by straining sour milk through a piece of muslin.*
mussel /'mʌsl/ *c.n* kind of shellfish that can be eaten..
must (strong form /mʌst/, weak form /məst/) *aux.v* (no *pres.p*, *p.p* or *p.t* forms; negative forms *must not* or *mustn't* /'mʌsnt/; *must have* can be *must've* /'mʌstəv/; 'must' is followed by the infinitive form of a verb without *to*) **1** (to express an obligation(2) or duty to do s.t): *He must telephone her. We must do some shopping this afternoon.* **2** (used to express necessity or a rule) have to; be necessary to: *You must be 16 to become a member. All applications must reach the office by Friday. 'You lost my bag so you must buy me a new one.' 'Must I?'* **3** (used to express strong probability, certainty) be likely, be certainly: *He must be very tired after such a long journey. You must be relieved that they are all safe.* **4** (used to introduce an opinion or preference in a polite way): *I must say it's not the way I would have handled it.* **5** (used to express that s.t is not convenient): *Must you ask me now? Can't you see I'm busy? Must I go now? Isn't it a bit early?* **must have done s.t** it is (almost) certain that s.o has done s.t: *He must have forgotten.* Compare should, ought to.

▷ *c.n* /mʌst/ **6** (usu *sing*) (*informal*) thing that is essential and has to be seen, done etc: *The latest film at the cinema is an absolute must.*

mustard /'mʌstəd/ *n* **1** *u.n* plant with leaves that have a strong hot(2) taste and yellow flowers. **2** *c/ u.n* yellow powder made by crushing the seeds of mustard(1) plants and used to flavour food. **3** *c/ u.n* powder made of mustard(2) and mixed with water or vinegar to make a paste that is used in small quantities with food. **as keen as mustard** very eager. **mustard and cress** *u.n* small young plants from seeds of mustard(1) and cress(1), eaten in salads etc.

muster /'mʌstə/ *c.n* **1** (*formal*) gathering of people. **pass muster** be accepted as satisfactory.

▷ *v* (often — (*s.o/s.t*) *up*) **2** *tr/intr.v* (cause(s.o/s.t)to) gather, come together: *Muster up all the children and meet me in 10 minutes.* **3** *tr.v* gather, build up, (one's strength etc): *I'm trying to muster (up) the courage to ask if I can use the car tonight.*

mustn't /'mʌsnt/ = must not. ⇨ must.

must've /'mʌstəv/ = must have. ⇨ must.

musty /'mʌsti/ *adj* (-ier, -iest) (esp of a smell) stale and damp: *It's rather musty in here — leave the door open.*
'**mustiness** *u.n.*

mutable /'mju:təbl/ *adj* (*formal*) able or likely to change. Opposite immutable.
mutability /ˌmju:tə'bɪlɪti/ *u.n.*

mutant /'mju:tənt/ ⇨ mutation(2).

mutation /mju:'teɪʃən/ **1** *c/u.n* (example of the) act, process, of changing the natural form of s.t: *New plants sometimes develop by mutation.* **2** *c.n* (also '**mutant**) plant or animal that is different from its parent and can pass the difference on to its young.

mute /mju:t/ *adj* **1** (of a person) unable to speak. **2** silent: *He looked at me in mute amusement.* **3** (of a letter in a word) that is not sounded: *The 'k' in 'knife' is mute.*

▷ *c.n* **4** person who is unable to speak.

▷ *tr.v* **5** reduce the strength of (sounds, colours etc). '**muted** *adj* (of a sound, colour) not so loud or bright: *the muted sounds of distant traffic*; *a picture painted in muted shades of blue.*

mutilate /'mju:tɪˌleɪt/ *tr.v* destroy or remove an important part of (s.t): *photographs of the mutilated bodies killed in the war.*
mutilation /ˌmju:tɪ'leɪʃən/ *c/u.n.*

mutiny /'mju:tɪni/ *c/u.n* (-ies) **1** (example of the) refusal to obey an officer, a leader, esp in the armed forces.

▷ *intr.v* (-ies, -ied) **2** refuse to obey an officer or a leader, esp in the armed forces: *The sailors mutinied because they wanted to go home.*
mutineer /ˌmju:tɪ'nɪə/ *c.n* soldier, sailor etc who mutinies(2).
mutinous /'mju:tɪnəs/ *adj* taking part in a mutiny(1) or likely to mutiny(2): *The angry sailors were becoming mutinous.*

mutter /'mʌtə/ *c.n* **1** quiet words, usu of anger, spoken so that they are not clearly heard.

▷ *tr/intr.v* **2** complain quietly so that the exact words are not heard: *He walked away muttering (something) to himself.*
'**mutterer** *c.n* person who mutters(2).

mutton /'mʌtn/ *u.n* (also *attrib*) meat from an adult sheep: *mutton* chops(2). Compare lamb(2).

mutual /'mju:tʃʊəl/ *adj* **1** (of feelings) shared; of the same kind, extent etc that the other person has: *They had mutual respect for one another. 'I hate you!' 'Well, the feeling is mutual!'* **2** (common) to two or more people, places: *We have a mutual friend — Peter.* **3** (given) to one another: *mutual support.*
mutuality /ˌmju:tʃʊ'ælɪti/ *u.n* (*formal*) condition of being mutual.
'**mutually** *adv.*

Muzak /'mju:zæk/ *u.n* (*t.n*) (usu *derog*) music played as background in restaurants etc.

muzzle /'mʌzl/ *c.n* **1** nose and mouth of an animal, e.g a dog. **2** straps shaped to fit over a dog's mouth, muzzle(1) to prevent it biting. **3** open end of a gun.

▷ *tr.v* **4** put a muzzle(2) on (a dog). **5** (*fig*) prevent (s.o, a newspaper etc) from expressing an opinion: *The government is trying to muzzle the newspapers.*

muzzy /'mʌzi/ *adj* (-ier, -iest) (of thoughts) confused; not clear: *This wine is making my head muzzy.*
'**muzzily** *adv.* '**muzziness** *u.n.*

MW written abbr **1** medium wave (⇨ medium).

▷ *symb* **2** megawatt.

my /maɪ/ *possessive pron* **1** belonging to, for, me: *You stood on my toe. That's my bus. Where's my mum?* ⇨ mine². **2** (used as part of an address, exclamation): *How are you, my dear? Come, my love.*

▷ *interj* **3** (often *My, my!*) (used to express (pleased) surprise): *My — what a big boy you are now!*

my'self *pron* **1** *reflex.pron* (used when the object of the verb or preposition is the same (person, animal, thing) as the subject): *I hurt myself when I fell over. I looked at myself in the mirror.* ⇨ I, me. **2** (used to emphasize(1) I): *I myself saw him steal it.* **3** without help: *I did it myself — no one helped me.* (**all**) **by myself** (**a**) without help: *I can't carry it by myself.* (**b**) alone: *I've been waiting (all) by myself at the station.*

mynah /'maɪnə/ *c.n* (also '**mynah ,bird**; also '**myna**) kind of large bird from Asia, which is mostly dark in colour and can be taught to talk.

myopia /maɪ'əʊpɪə/ *u.n* (*technical*) ability to see only near things clearly.
myopic /maɪ'ɒpɪk/ *adj* (*technical*) able to see only near things clearly.
my'opically *adv.*

myriad /'mɪrɪəd/ *c.n* (also *attrib*) (usu — of s.o/ s.t) (*formal*) great number of people/animals/ things: *myriads of people*; *a myriad of stars*; *myriad kinds of plants.*

myrrh /mɜ:/ *u.n* substance from certain kinds of bushes or trees used to make products that smell sweet, e.g incense¹.

myself ⇨ my.

mystery /'mɪstəri/ *n* (*pl* -ies) **1** *c.n* thing that cannot be explained or understood: *It's still a mystery to me why she went away. Ask Joe to help you — he's good at solving mysteries.* **2** *u.n* condition of being difficult or impossible to explain or understand: *She's full of mystery about where the money comes from.*
mysterious /mɪ'stɪərɪəs/ *adj* full of mystery(2); difficult to understand or explain: *You're being very mysterious — what's this all about?*
my'steriously *adv.* **my'steriousness** *u.n.*

mystic /'mɪstɪk/ *adj* (also '**mystical**) **1** of or

referring to the means of trying to reach an understanding of the universe, nature etc by religious, magical(1) and not scientific means: *a mystic ceremony.*

▷ *c.n* **2** mystic(1) person; person who practises or studies mysticism.

'mystical ⇨ mystic(1).

mysticism /'mɪstɪˌsɪzəm/ *u.n* practice of trying to reach a real understanding and knowledge of nature, the universe and truth etc, esp through spiritual(1) means, meditation etc.

mystify /'mɪstɪˌfaɪ/ *tr.v* (*-ies*, *-ied*) confuse, surprise, (s.o) because of the lack of any explanation: *I am totally mystified by her disappearance. This matter mystifies me.*

mystification /ˌmɪstɪfɪ'keɪʃən/ *u.n.*

mystique /mɪ'stiːk/ *c.n* (usu *sing*) quality of mystery that surrounds a special skill, important person etc: *The medical profession has a mystique that makes patients have total confidence in their doctors.*

myth /mɪθ/ *n* **1** *c.n* ancient story that deals with the origins of life, the history and old heroes(1) of a race and often describes events that have a moral lesson: *When we were children our grandmother told us the myths that she had heard from her grandmother.* **2** *c/u.n* (example of a) story like a myth(1) and accepted without question as true by some and known not to be true by others: *The idea that women are better cooks than men is pure myth.* **3** *c/u.n* person or thing who/that does not exist: *Her story that she got an important job in London is a myth.*

mythical /'mɪθɪkl/ *adj* **1** (of a person, event) from a myth(1): *Apollo is a mythical hero.* **2** imaginary: *David has a mythical rich aunt.*

'mythically *adv.*

mythology /mɪ'θɒlədʒɪ/ *n* (*pl -ies*) **1** *c/u.n* (collection of) myths(1): *I love reading African mythology.* **2** *u.n* study of myths(1).

mythological /ˌmɪθə'lɒdʒɪkl/ *adj* of or referring to mythology(1).

mythologist /mɪ'θɒlədʒɪst/ *c.n* person skilled in, or student of, mythology(2).

Nn

N, n /en/ *c/unique n* **1** 14th letter of the English alphabet.

▷ *written abbr* **2** noun.

▷ *symb* (**N**) **3** north. **4** Nitrogen.

nab /næb/ *tr.v* (*-bb-*) (*informal*) catch (s.o) (for doing s.t): *The boys were nabbed by the police for stealing a car.*

nadir /'neɪdɪə/ *c.n* (*fig*) **1** lowest point (of hope, worry etc). **2** time of greatest weakness, unhappiness etc. Opposite zenith.

nag /næg/ *c.n* **1** small, weak, old horse. **2** (*derog*;

informal) person who asks for s.t continually: *You're such a nag!*

▷ *tr/intr.v* (*-gg-*) **3** (often — *at* s.o) criticize (s.o), complain, continually: *She's always nagging (at) her children to tidy their room.* **4** ask (s.o) for a particular thing continually: *The children have been nagging me to take them to the cinema. What are you nagging for now?* **5** worry (s.o) continually: *This toothache has been nagging me all day.*

'nagger *c.n* person who nags(3,4).

'nagging *adj* (usu *attrib*) that worries, hurts: *a nagging headache. I have a nagging feeling that something's wrong.*

nail /neɪl/ *c.n* **1** hard substance that grows at the tips of the fingers (fingernail) and toes (toenail): *Stop biting your nails. Why do you paint your toenails?* **2** small piece of metal which is pointed at one end and flat on the other end, used to join pieces of wood etc together etc: *I'll hammer the nail into the wall where you want to hang the picture.* **as hard as nails** (*fig*) (of a person) without pity/feelings for other people: *Don't expect help from her — she's as hard as nails.* **be a nail in s.o's coffin** (*fig*) be s.t that will cause s.o's ruin. (**fight**) **tooth and nail** (**for s.o/s.t**) ⇨ tooth. **hit the nail on the head** (*fig*) be completely right about s.t: *You've hit the nail on the head — that's exactly why she's been behaving so strangely.* **on the nail** (*fig*) (*informal*) (**a**) immediately: *I prefer to pay cash on the nail if I have the money.* (**b**) at exactly the right time: *The birthday card arrived on the nail.*

▷ *tr.v* **3** fasten (s.t) with nails: *He nailed the picture to the wall. Nail the boards together. We nailed down the corners of the tablecloth so that it wouldn't blow away.* **4** (*informal*) find/catch (s.o): *She's been avoiding me for weeks but I finally nailed her at her office.* **nail s.o down** (**to s.t**) (*fig*) force s.o to make a decision (about s.t): *She's finally agreed to do the job but I can't nail her down to a date.* **nail s.t up** (**a**) nail(3) s.t in a high position. (**b**) close s.t with nails so that it cannot be opened: *They nailed up the doors and windows of their house when they left.*

'nail-ˌbrush *c.n* small hard brush for cleaning the nails(1).

'nail-ˌfile *c.n* flat metal or hard paper with a rough surface for shaping the nails(1).

'nail-ˌpolish *u.n* (also **'nail-ˌvarnish**) brightly coloured substance for painting the nails(1).

'nail-ˌscissors *pl.n* small sharp scissors for cutting/shaping the nails(1).

'nail-ˌvarnish *u.n* = nail-polish.

naive /naɪ'iːv/ *adj* (also **naïve**) **1** simple and young in one's way of behaving and in one's ideas, beliefs etc: *a naive suggestion.* **2** (slightly *derog*) ignorant; simple and pure because lacking experience or knowledge of reality: *It's rather naive to believe that people are always willing to help others. How can you be so naive as to believe his promises?*

na'ively, na'ïvely *adv.*

na'ivety, na'ïvety *u.n.*

naked /'neɪkɪd/ *adj* **1** wearing no clothes: *You're allowed to be naked on that beach.* **2** (*attrib*) (also *fig*) without the usual covering, protection: *Naked flames can be dangerous. That naked light is blinding. She didn't believe that he was not at work but the naked truth forced her to realize*

the fact. (**see s.t with**) **the naked eye** ⇒ eye(*n*).
strip naked remove all one's clothes: *She stripped naked and jumped into the river.*
'**nakedly** *adv.*
'**nakedness** *u.n.*

name /neɪm/ *n* **1** *c.n* word(s) by which a person, animal, place, thing, is known: *What's her name? My name is Sue. Do you know the name of this plant? What's the name of the street? What's your cat's name? I know her by name but I've never spoken to her.* **2** *sing.n* reputation, fame: *Book your holiday through 'Funaways' — they have a name for being cheap and good.* **3** *c.n* famous, well known, person: *There'll be some great names at the opening night.* **brand name** ⇒ brand. **call s.o names** insult s.o by telling her/him that she/he is a coward, liar, fool etc: *'They're calling me names,' the little boy told his mother. 'They called me "fatty" and "spotty".'* **give s.o/s.t a bad/good name** cause s.o/s.t to have a bad/good reputation. **go by the name (of) s.t** have s.t as one's usual name(1) although this is not the official or formal one: *Barbara goes by the name (of) Babs.* **one's/s.o's/s.t's good name** one's/s.o's/s.t's good reputation: *Your behaviour could spoil your family's good name.* **in name only** having the title but not the meaning, rights, power etc of that title: *He's my father in name only — he's never cared about me.* **in the name of s.o/s.t** (a) by the power of s.o/s.t: *Stop in the name of the law!* (b) for the sake of: *Please help us — in the name of freedom!* **know s.o by name** know s.o's name but (usu) nothing else about them: *Do you know all the members by name?* **make a name for o.s/s.o** (cause s.o to) become well known: *She gets a lot of work now that she's made a name for herself.* **not have a penny to one's name** be completely without money. **s.o's name is mud** ⇒ mud. **the name of the game** the most important thing: *In this business honesty is the name of the game.* **under the name of s.o** using another name instead of one's own: *Emily Brontë wrote under the name of Ellis Bell.*
▷ *tr.v* **4** give (s.o/s.t) a name: *They named their baby Ben. Let's name the dog 'Spot'.* **5** say/list the names of (s.o/s.t): *She could name every child in her class after only two days. Can you name the five senses?* **6** state (the price, date etc) that is wanted: *I'll give you any amount for that painting — just name your price. I'd love to come for a weekend — name the date. Have they named the day (for their wedding) yet?* **7** appoint (s.o) to a position: *Have they named the new President yet? Who's been named (as) the new chairperson?* **name s.o after s.o** give a child etc the name of s.o who is important to one: *She named her first child after her father. The mountain was named after the first person to reach its top.*
'**name,drop** *intr.v* (-pp-) mention the names of important people in a conversation as if they were friends (esp to make oneself seem important).
'**name,dropper** *c.n* person who namedrops.
'**name,dropping** *u.n.*
'**nameless** *adj* **1** (esp *attrib*) not having a name; not known by name: *a nameless disease, river.* **2** (esp *pred*) not referred to by name: *The person who gave me my information shall remain nameless.*

'**namely** *adv* (used to identify the subject(s) that have been referred to) the one(s) I mean: *I like the science subjects at school namely mathematics, physics, chemistry and biology.*
'**name,plate** *c.n* piece of metal, plastic(3), wood, with the name of the person who works in the room or lives in the house where it is fastened.
'**name,sake** *c.n* person or thing with the same name.

nanny /'nænɪ/ *c.n* (*pl -ies*) woman who looks after children, esp in a family where both parents are employed or too busy to look after them: *She got a job as a nanny with a family that was going to spend two years in Brazil.*
nanny goat /'nænɪ ˌgəʊt/ *c.n* female goat. ⇒ billy goat.

nap /næp/ *c.n* **1** short sleep during the day: *I'll have a quick nap before we go out.*
▷ *intr.v* (-pp-) **2** have a short sleep: *Don't disturb him — he's napping.* **catch s.o napping** (a) see s.o resting, playing etc while he/she should be doing s.t else: *They came home early and caught him napping instead of studying.* (b) find s.o unprepared: *We were all caught napping when we were asked for the end-of-year reports earlier than usual.*
napalm /'neɪpɑːm/ *u.n* petrol in the form of jelly(4) which is used to make fire bombs.
nape /neɪp/ *c.n* back of the neck.
napkin /'næpkɪn/ *c.n* (also '**table ,napkin**) piece of cloth or paper used at meals to protect clothing, wipe the hands, lips etc.
'**napkin-,ring** *c.n* silver, wooden etc ring to hold a napkin.
nappy /'næpɪ/ *c.n* (*pl -ies*) piece of cloth or soft paper for wrapping round a baby's bottom to collect urine etc.
narcissus /nɑːˈsɪsəs/ *c.n* (*pl -es, narcissi* /nɑːˈsɪsaɪ/) plant that grows from a bulb(1) and produces a sweet-smelling yellow or white flower in spring: *The garden is full of narcissi in April.*
narcotic /nɑːˈkɒtɪk/ *c.n* (also *attrib*) drug(1) that can stop pain, cause a person to feel sleepy etc but is dangerous when taken often or in large quantities: *Opium is a narcotic. It is a very serious crime to bring narcotics into the country illegally. She is studying the narcotic effects of a new pain-killing drug(1).*
narrate /nəˈreɪt/ *tr.v* (*formal*) tell (a story); describe (an experience).
narration /nəˈreɪʃən/ *n* **1** *u.n* telling of a (long) story: *The narration will take a few hours.* **2** *c.n* (long) story/account(2): *That was quite a narration you gave.*
narrator /nəˈreɪtə/ *c.n* person who tells a story: *Who's the narrator in the book?*
narrow /'nærəʊ/ *adj* **1** measuring a small amount/distance from one side to the other: *a narrow mountain path. This cloth is too narrow for the table. I need a narrower piece to fit in here. That space looks much too narrow for our car.* Opposite broad(1), wide(1). **2** (*attrib*) successful by a very small amount: *a narrow win; a narrow escape; a narrow miss.* Compare a close/narrow shave (⇒ shave(*n*)). **3** limited; not wide or great: *a narrow circle of friends. He's always lived such a narrow life. Her experience in such matters has been very narrow.* **4** = narrow-minded. **a narrow**

shave = a close shave (⇨ close¹ (*adj*)). (**on**) **the straight and narrow** ⇨ straight.

▷ *tr/intr.v* **5** (cause (s.t) to) become narrow(1-3): *Having such a protected life narrows one's experience. The river narrows as it goes through the valley. Our chances of winning were seriously narrowed when one of the members of the team was hurt.*

'**narrowly** *adv* by only a small amount/distance: *That car only narrowly missed my foot.*

,**narrow¹-minded** *adj* not willing to agree with, listen to, other people's ideas, opinions. Opposites broad-minded, open-minded.

,**narrow-¹mindedly** *adv.* ,**narrow-¹mindedness** *u.n.*

'**narrowness** *u.n* state of being narrow.

'**narrows** *pl.n* (with capital **N** in names) narrow place in a river or sea.

nasal /'neɪzl/ *adj* **1** of the nose: *Nasal hairs prevent dirt from entering the body through the nose.* **2** (also *technical*) of/having sounds produced through the nose, e.g 'm', 'n', 'ng': *My voice is rather nasal because of my cold.*

▷ *c.n* **3** nasal(2) sound.

nasalize, -ise /'neɪzə,laɪz/ *tr.v* cause (a sound) to pass through the nose: *When you speak French you must try to nasalize some of your sounds.*

nasty /'nɑːstɪ/ *adj* (*-ier, -iest*) **1** unpleasant (esp to the senses): *What's that nasty smell? That medicine left a nasty taste in my mouth.* **2** unpleasant, cruel, unfriendly (esp of behaviour): *Don't be so nasty to your sister. That was a nasty thing to say. He turned nasty when he realized that no one was going to give him what he wanted. I wouldn't tell her about it — she has a nasty temper.* **3** (usu *attrib*) immoral, wicked: *What a nasty mind you have!* **4** difficult: *They asked some nasty questions.* **5** (*attrib*) dangerous, unpleasant: *She had rather a nasty experience in town today. How did you get into such a nasty situation? I've got a nasty cold.* **6** (of the weather) cold, wet, windy etc: *There's only one thing to do in such nasty weather — stay in bed.* **a nasty piece of work** ⇨ piece(*n*).

'**nastily** *adv.* '**nastiness** *u.n.*

natal /'neɪtl/ *adj* of birth. ⇨ antenatal, postnatal, prenatal.

nation /'neɪʃən/ *c.n* large group of people with the same history and often speaking the same language and living in the same country under one government: *Are the British a nation of animal lovers?*

national /'næʃənl/ *adj* (usu *attrib*) **1** of/for a whole nation: *the national bank*; *a national champion*(3); *national pride.*

▷ *c.n* **2** member of a particular nation: *Most foreign nationals decided to leave the country before war began.*

,**national ¹anthem** *c.n* official song of a nation which is usually played/sung on important occasions.

,**national ¹debt** *c/def.n* total amount of money owed by the government of a country.

,**National ¹Giro** *def.n* ⇨ giro.

,**national ¹government** *c.n* government formed by all or most of the country's political parties.

,**National ¹Health ¹Service** *def.n* (*abbr* NHS) medical service for people in Britain that is paid for by the government from taxes.

,**national ¹holiday** *c.n* day on which all shops, factories, schools etc in the country are closed.

,**National In¹surance** *u.n* (*written abbr* NI) (UK) government system of collecting money from workers and employers in order to provide for times of illness, unemployment and retirement.

nationalism /'næʃənə,lɪzəm/ *u.n* **1** pride in one's country. **2** political desire/effort to govern one's own country: *Welsh nationalism.*

nationalist /'næʃənəlɪst/ *c.n* person who believes in nationalism.

nationalistic /,næʃənə'lɪstɪk/ *adj* showing (too) great love of one's country.

nationality /,næʃə'nælɪtɪ/ *n* (*pl -ies*) **1** *u.n* belonging to a particular nation: *What nationality are you? I have German nationality.* **2** *c.n* person or group belonging to a particular nation: *The meeting was attended by people of all nationalities.*

nationalization, -isation /,næʃənəlaɪ'zeɪʃən/ *u.n.*

'**nationa,lize, -ise** *tr.v* **1** make (an industry etc) the property of the nation (instead of a private person, group): *Will they nationalize the postal service?* **2** make (s.o) a national(2) of a country: *The government refuses to nationalize any more new immigrants.*

'**nationally** *adv.*

,**national ¹park** *c.n* area of land that is preserved in its natural state for the enjoyment of the people.

,**national ¹service** *u.n* fact of young people serving in the armed forces for a length of time.

,**National ¹Trust** *def/def.pl.n* (also *attrib*) private organization in Britain for preserving buildings and areas of beauty or historic importance.

,**nation¹wide** *adj/adv* (happening) everywhere in the country: *a nationwide search for the murderers*; *a nationwide demand for the government to resign. We looked nationwide for a suitable actor.*

native /'neɪtɪv/ *adj* **1** (*attrib*) of the place where one was born: *I haven't returned to my native land for over 20 years. What's his native language?* **2** (of qualities) belonging to a person naturally and not taught: *native ability/intelligence/talent*(1). **native to s.w** (of plants, animals) growing/living in a place naturally and not having been brought from somewhere else: *Horses are not native to this area — they were brought here from the Middle East.*

▷ *c.n* **3** person born in a particular place: *a native of Oxford/Scotland/England.* **4** (also *attrib*; now *derog*) one of the original people in a particular country: *the native inhabitants of Britain.*

,**native ¹speaker** *c.n* (often — *of s.t*) person whose first language is (a particular language): *Are you a native speaker of French?*

Nativity /nə'tɪvɪtɪ/ *def.n* birth of Jesus.

na¹tivity ,play *c.n* play about the Nativity.

natter /'nætə/ *sing.n* **1** (*informal*) talking that continues for some time and is usually not very important: *She enjoys a good natter every now and again. Let's meet for a natter.*

▷ *intr.v* **2** (*informal*) (often — *away/on* (*about s.o/ s.t*)) talk continuously usu about matters that are not very important: *What are you two nattering (on) about? We were nattering away and we didn't realize how late it was getting.*

natty /'nætɪ/ adj(-ier, -iest) (informal) smart¹(1) and tidy: a natty dresser (⇒ dress(5)). You look natty today!
'**nattily** adv.
'**nattiness** u.n.
natural /'nætʃrəl/ adj Opposite unnatural. **1** (attrib) of, produced by, nature and not people: At the park you can see animals living in their natural environment. Some of our natural resources(1) are oil, coal, natural gas, tin. **2** (usu attrib) (of an ability, quality etc) born in a person and not taught: He's a natural actor. She has a natural beauty. She has a natural ability in working with wood. Kindness is natural to him. **3** normal, to be expected: It's natural to be happy on your wedding day. That was a perfectly natural thing to do. It's only natural that you should be angry. **4** simple, honest and direct (way of doing s.t): Don't try to be someone you're not — just be natural. She has such a natural style. Try to look natural otherwise they'll know something is wrong.
▷ c.n **5** (often a — for s.t) person who is born with an ability to do s.t: Look at her run — she's a natural. He's a natural for the job.
,**natural** '**child,birth** c/u.n (example of) giving birth to a child in a natural way with no drugs(1).
,**natural** '**death** c/u.n (example of) dying from old age, illness etc and not as a result of an accident etc.
,**natural** '**gas** u.n gas that is found underground in a form that can be used for burning.
,**natural** '**history** u.n study of plants and animals.
'**natura,lism** u.n **1** drawing, painting, describing things etc in a way that is true to nature. **2** system of thought by which everything is explained by natural causes and effects.
'**naturalist** c.n **1** person who studies animals and plants. **2** person who believes in naturalism(2).
naturalistic /,nætʃrə'lɪstɪk/ adj of naturalism(1): a naturalistic writer.
,**natura'listically** adv.
naturalization, -isation /,nætʃrələr'zeɪʃən/ u.n. act of naturalizing s.o/s.t.
'**natura,lize, -ise** tr.v **1** make (s.o) a citizen of a country where he/she was not born: She was naturalized after 10 years and given a British passport. **2** accept (a word from another language) as part of the language: Many French words and phrases(1) have been naturalized in (to) English. **3** bring (an animal/plant from another part of the world) to live/grow in a country: Does the bee come from these parts or has it been naturalized?
,**natural** '**law** c/u.n = law of nature (⇒ law).
,**natural** '**life** c.n expected length of one's life on earth.
naturally /'nætʃrəlɪ/ adv **1** in a natural way and not done, made, taught, by people: She's naturally good with her hands. Kindness comes naturally to her. He's naturally gentle. Animals live there naturally as they have done for hundreds of years. Is your hair naturally that colour? Try to act naturally and stop being so nervous. **2** of course: Naturally I'd like to come with you — but how can I? 'Did you win?' 'Naturally.'
'**naturalness** u.n.

,**natural** re'**sources** pl.n wealth of a country in the form of things that are naturally there, e.g the forests, minerals etc.
,**natural** '**science** c/u.n (often pl) area of study of the natural world, e.g biology, chemistry, physics, geology etc. Compare social science.
,**natural** se'**lection** u.n process by which plants and animals that are strong and best suited to their surroundings continue to live while those that are weaker and less suited die.
'**natural** ,**world** def.n world as it is before people do things to change it.
nature /'neɪtʃə/ n **1** unique n the physical world, e.g the animals, plants, rivers, seas, mountains, weather, stars etc and all that controls it: Nature is at its most exciting in the spring. The forces of nature could be seen on that stormy night. **2** unique n simple life without the influences of the civilized world: They decided to give up their city comforts and return to nature by farming a small piece of land in the country. **3** sing/u.n natural quality, characteristic(1): She has a good nature (or She is good-natured). He is quiet by nature. It is the nature of things that some days everything is perfect and other days everything goes wrong. **4** sing.n (usu the — of s.t) exactly what a thing is, does or consists of: Today we are going to study the nature of air. Can you explain the nature of her illness? What is the nature of the job? **5** sing.n kind, sort: What nature of excuse is that? Was the crime of a sexual nature? I'd like to study the behaviour of plants and things of that nature. **call of nature** (polite way of expressing a need to go to the lavatory). **freak of nature** ⇒ freak(n). **(go) against nature** (be/become) unnatural. **human nature** ⇒ human. **(not) in s.o/s.t's nature (to do s.t)** (not) natural for s.o/s.t (to do s.t): It's not in my nature to be lazy, unkind. Is it in his nature to tell such lies? **in the nature of s.t** (formal) having the qualities of s.t: The love letter was written in the nature of a poem. **let nature take its course** allow things to happen naturally and without any help from anyone: If you let nature take its course you'll find that everything works out for the best. **Mother Nature** ⇒ mother.
-**natured** adj having the quality shown by the first part of the word: good/ill-natured; pleasant-natured.
'**nature** ,**study** c/u.n (pl -ies) (esp at school) study of animals, plants etc.
naturism /'neɪtʃə,rɪzəm/ u.n practice of not wearing clothes in order to be healthy. ⇒ nudism.
naturist /'neɪtʃərɪst/ c.n person who likes wearing no clothes. ⇒ nudist.
naught /nɔːt/ u.n (old use) nothing. **care naught for s.o/s.t** not care about s.o/s.t at all. **come to naught** fail: All their effort came to naught. ⇒ nought(2).
naughty /'nɔːtɪ/ adj (-ier, -iest) **1** (usu of children) badly-behaved; causing trouble: a naughty child. It was very naughty (of you) to swear at them. **2** (of a story, joke etc, esp about sexual matters) intended to shock: She loves telling naughty jokes.
'**naughtily** adv. '**naughtiness** u.n.
nausea /'nɔːzɪə/ u.n feeling of sickness: She was filled with nausea at the sight of such terrible

poverty. The mixture of rich food and stormy weather gave her a feeling of nausea.

nauseate /'nɔːzɪˌeɪt/ *tr.v* cause (s.o) to feel sick.

'nause,ating *adj*: *a nauseating smell. Your behaviour is nauseating.*

nauseous /'nɔːzɪəs/ *adj (formal)* **1** causing a feeling of nausea: *The medicine has a nauseous taste but it's good for you.* **2** affected by nausea: *I don't usually feel nauseous on car journeys.*

'nauseousness *u.n.*

nautical /'nɔːtɪkl/ *adj* of sailors, ships: *nautical magazines.*

,nautical 'mile *c.n* unit of length (1852 metres) used to measure the distance of a journey across the sea.

naval /'neɪvl/ ⇨ navy.

nave /neɪv/ *c.n* middle of a church where people sit.

navel /'neɪvl/ *c.n* small place on one's stomach where one was joined to one's mother before birth.

navigate /'nævɪˌgeɪt/ *v* **1** *tr.v* (also *fig*) direct, guide, and sometimes also move, (an aircraft, ship etc) in a particular direction: *He navigated the ship safely through the storm.* **2** *intr.v* find/follow a route(1): *You take the map and navigate and I'll drive. He can navigate by the stars.* **3** *tr.v* find a way across, through, over (s.t) safely: *Be careful how you navigate that muddy road. Has that river been navigated?*

navigability /ˌnævɪgəˈbɪlɪtɪ/ *u.n.*

navigable /'nævɪgəbl/ *adj* **1** (esp of rivers, seas etc) able to be crossed or followed safely (by ships etc). **2** (esp of ships etc) able to be sailed, driven safely: *How long will it take to get that boat navigable again?*

navigation /ˌnævɪˈgeɪʃən/ *u.n* **1** skill of navigating(2): *Without your navigation we would never have found the place.* **2** (often — of s.t) act of directing/moving oneself/s.o/s.t safely s.w: *Navigation of that river is not going to be easy.*

'navi,gator *c.n* person who navigates(1,2): *Navigators on aeroplanes are often not necessary nowadays because of modern machinery.*

navy /'neɪvɪ/ *n* **1** *c/def/pl.n* (pl -ies) country's warships and sailors who work in them: *He's joined the navy.* **2** *u.n* (also **,navy 'blue**) (also *attrib*) very dark blue colour: *She's always dressed in navy (blue). I want a pair of navy trousers.*

naval /'neɪvl/ *attrib.adj* of a navy, its ships: *a naval uniform; a naval officer.*

nay /neɪ/ *interj (old use)* no. **say yea or nay (to s.t)** say yes or no (to s.t): *All those who say nay put up their hands.*

NE *written abbr* northeast(ern).

near /nɪə/ *adj* **1** not far (in time or space): *It's quite near now. She hid behind the nearest tree. Is there a toilet anywhere near? The holidays are very near now. I don't expect any change in the near future.* **2** *(attrib)* (of relatives, friends) close: *He's not a near relation but we call him uncle. We're only inviting near friends and relatives.* **3** (of vehicles) side closer to the pavement; left side in UK: *It's the front window on the near side that is broken.* ⇨ nearside. **a near miss** ⇨ miss²(n). **a near thing** ⇨ thing. **in the near future** ⇨ future(n). **near and dear (to s.o)** loved very much (by s.o): *She's near and dear to us.* ⇨ nearest and dearest. **near to s.t**

close to s.t; almost s.t: *We were near to bursting (with joy, excitement). Leave him alone — can't you see he's near to tears.*

▷ *adv* **4** (also **,near'by**) to/at a short distance: *Do you live near/nearby? She won't come near. Don't go near!* **as near as** as closely as (possible): *We stood as near as we could. As near as I could see, no one was seriously hurt.* **come near to s.t** be close to doing s.t: *She was so angry she came near to screaming.* **near and far and near/wide** everywhere: *They came from near and far to see the show. I've looked near and far for someone suitable.* **near at/to hand** ⇨ hand(n). **not anywhere, nowhere, near as clever, rich etc as s.o/s.t** (not) at all as clever, rich etc as s.o/s.t: *He's nowhere near as successful as I am. Is her sister anywhere near as intelligent as she is?*

▷ *prep* **5** at a short distance from (s.o/s.t): *Don't go too near the water. Sit near me.*

▷ *tr/intr.v* **6** *(formal)* come near to (s.t): *As we neared the station we saw the train arrive. Winter is nearing and soon there'll be no leaves on the trees.*

near- *adj* almost having the state shown by the second part of the word: *near-perfect; near-white.*

nearby /'nɪəˌbaɪ/ *adj* **1** near(1): *We stopped at a nearby house to ask the way.*

▷ *adv* /ˌnɪəˈbaɪ/ **2** ⇨ near(4).

,nearest and 'dearest *adj/pl.n* (of) one's closest friends and relations: *We're only inviting our nearest and dearest to the party.*

nearly /'nɪəlɪ/ *adv* not far from; almost: *We're nearly there. It's nearly time to go. Are you nearly ready? Hurry up — it's nearly 5 o'clock!* **not nearly** far from; not near at all: *I'm not nearly finished! She isn't even nearly ready. We won't have nearly enough food for all these people.*

,near 'miss *c.n* ⇨ miss²(n).

'nearness *u.n* state of being very close (to s.o/s.t): *The nearness of those noises is making me nervous.*

'near,side *adj/def.n* (of the) side (of a vehicle) nearer the pavement: *the nearside front door. Get out of the car on the nearside.*

,near-'sighted *adj* = short-sighted(1). ⇨ long-sighted(1).

,near-'sightedness *u.n.*

,near 'thing *c.n* act of just avoiding s.t, e.g an accident or being caught doing s.t wrong.

neat /niːt/ *adj* **1** tidy; having everything in its right place: *I hope your room is neat this morning.* **2** (of appearance) simple, pleasing: *You're looking clean and neat — where are you going?* **3** done with skill; clever: *a neat trick/answer/description.* **4** (of physical appearance, the body) well proportioned and small: *He has such a neat little body.* **5** (of alcoholic(1) drinks) without anything, e.g water, added: *Do you want your whisky neat or with water?*

'neatly *adv.* **'neatness** *u.n.*

nebula /'nebjʊlə/ *c.n* (pl -s, nebulae /'nebjʊˌliː/) area of light in the sky caused by a group of distant stars.

nebulous /'nebjʊləs/ *adj* **1** unclear; cloudy. **2** *(fig)* having no clear/definite form: *a nebulous plan/idea. That's a rather nebulous solution.*

necessary /'nesɪsrɪ/ *adj* that must be (done);

essential: *Is it necessary to bring our own food? Take everything necessary to make you feel comfortable. The necessary things in life are free. Is it necessary for you to be so nasty to your brother?* Opposite **unnecessary**.

necessarily /'nesɪsərɪlɪ/ *adv* (esp *not* —) in a way that has to, must, be; that cannot be avoided: *'Will we all have to go?' 'Not necessarily!' It doesn't necessarily mean that we can't see each other again.* Opposite **unnecessarily**.

necessitate /nɪ'sesɪˌteɪt/ *tr.v* (*formal*) make (s.t) necessary, essential: *Starting a new business will necessitate borrowing money.*

necessity /nɪ'sesɪtɪ/ *n* (*pl -ies*) **1** *c.n* thing that is essential: *The necessities of life include food, shelter and clothing. A water-bottle is an absolute necessity on this trip.* **2** *u.n* great need: *Necessity has made a thief of a good person.* (**the**) **bare necessities** those things that one definitely cannot manage without: *Please bring only the bare necessities as there is very little room in the car.* **by necessity** because of a great need: *She was forced by necessity to leave school and get a job.* **of necessity** without doubt: *That must of necessity be right.* **make a virtue of necessity** ⇒ virtue.

neck /nek/ *c.n* **1** part of the body between the head and shoulders: *Tie this round your neck to keep warm.* **2** this part of an animal used as meat: *keep the neck (of the chicken) for soup.* **3** thing that is shaped like a neck(1): *the neck of a bottle*, guitar. **4** part of a shirt etc worn at the neck. ⇒ collar(1). **break one's neck** (*fig*) work very hard (in order to manage to do s.t): *I'll have to break my neck to finish this job on time.* **breathe down s.o's neck** (*fig*) (**a**) stand very close to s.o esp while he/she is doing s.t. (**b**) watch closely (and offer advice, give orders) while s.o is doing s.t: *I can't work properly with her breathing down my neck the whole time.* **get it in the neck** (*fig*; *slang*) get into serious trouble; be punished: *You'll get it in the neck for breaking that window.* **a millstone round s.o's neck** ⇒ millstone(2). **neck and neck** (**with s.o/ s.t**) (esp in a competition) side by side; having an equal chance of winning, succeeding: *They were running neck and neck right until the end when Jones fell.* **a pain in the neck** ⇒ pain(*n*). **risk one's neck** (*fig*) do s.t that might badly affect one's life or position: *I'm not going to risk my neck for such an unimportant matter.* **save one's (own) neck** (*fig*; *informal*) save oneself from punishment: *All he cared about was saving his own neck — he didn't care about the rest of us.* **stick one's neck out (for s.o)** (*fig*; *informal*) do/ say s.t (to help s.o) which may be dangerous or cause one trouble: *Are you prepared to stick your neck out in order to support the workers?* **up to one's neck (in s.t)** (*fig*; *informal*) (**a**) very busy (with s.t): *I'm up to my neck in paperwork.* (**b**) in great trouble because of s.t: *She's up to her neck in that nasty business.* (**c**) having a great amount, number (of s.t): *He's up to his neck in debts.*

▷ *intr.v* **5** (*slang*) kiss etc one another: *They're necking in the back of the car.*

-necked *adj* (of an article of clothing, a bottle etc) having the kind of neck(3,4) shown by the first part of the word: *V-necked*, *round-necked*; *an open-necked shirt*; *a wide-necked jar*.

necklace /'neklɪs/ *c.n* string of beads, jewellery etc worn round the neck: *She wore a gold necklace.*

'neck,line *c.n* edge of the neck of an article of clothing: *That dress has a low neckline.*

'neck,tie *c.n* ⇒ tie(1).

nectar /'nektə/ *u.n* sweet liquid found in flowers and collected by bees to make honey.

nectarine /'nektərɪn/ *c.n* kind of fresh fruit like a mixture between a peach(2) and a plum(2) with a large stone (seed) in the middle.

née /neɪ/ *adj* (*French*) (used after a woman's married(1) name(1) to show her family name before her marriage): *Emily Green, née Jones.*

need /niːd/ *n* **1** *c.n* (often *pl*) thing that is thought to be essential for one to have: *My main need at this moment is peace and quiet. Their first needs were food and water. What are your greatest needs?* **2** *u.n* (usu *in* — (*of s.t*)) state of lacking the essential thing(s) in life: *They are in need of food and blankets. It is an organization which helps people in need — the old, unemployed etc. You are in need of nothing.* **3** *sing/u.n* important reason for (doing) s.t; necessity: *There was no need to be so rude. Is there any need to rush? There's a need for caution in this matter.* **as/if/ when the need arises** when it becomes necessary: *We'll deal with the problem if the need arises.* **a crying need** very important and essential thing that is needed(5). **hour of need** ⇒ hour.

▷ *v* **4** *aux.v* (no *pres.p*, *p.p* or *p.t* forms; negative forms *need not* or *needn't* /'niːdnt/; *need have* can be *need've* /'niːdəv/; *need not have* can be *needn't have*; 'need' is followed by the infinitive form of a verb without *to*) (used only in questions and in the negative) be essential/necessary, have, to: *It need not be understood in that way. You needn't come if you don't want to. Need you shout all the time? Need I say how angry I was? I don't think I need go. I don't think I need have gone. We needn't have hurried — we're the first here!* Compare *has/have* (got) to do s.t (⇒ have(*aux.v*)). Compare 'You needn't shout' meaning 'It is not necessary to shout' and 'You mustn't shout' meaning 'You are not allowed to shout'. **5** *tr.v* (often *need to . . .*; *need . . .-ing*) have an important reason for (s.o/s.t); require(1) (s.t) (to happen): *If you need help call me. Do you need anything from the shop? The car needs more oil. My hair needs to be cut. My hair really needed cutting. What you need is a holiday. Will you be needing anything for tonight?* **need to (do s.t)** (esp with *if*) have an important reason to do s.t; be required(1) (to do s.t) (in order for s.t to happen): *You'll need to apologize if you want their continued support. They'll need to try much harder if they're going to win.*

'needful *adj* (*formal*) necessary: *I'll do whatever is needful.*

'needfully *adv.*

'needless *adj* unnecessary: *needless arguing, fighting, work, pain.* **needless to say, . . .** it's not necessary to say, . . .: *Needless to say, I still haven't received my money.*

'needlessly *adv.*

'needy *adj/def.pl.n* (*-ier, -iest*) (often *the poor and* —) (of) poor people: *We should all try to help the needy.*

needle /'niːdl/ *c.n* **1** small piece of thin steel with a point at one end and a hole at the other end for thread, used in sewing: *Give me a needle and cotton and I'll sew your button on.* **2** long thin piece of steel, plastic(3) etc with one pointed end that is used for knitting: *I'll need size 8 needles to knit you a pair of socks.* **3** (in a compass(1)) thin steel pointer that always shows magnetic north. **4** small sharp steel object of varying size and used for different purposes, e.g a needle on a record player for playing records¹(1), a needle for injecting medicine etc into a person or an animal. **5** thin pointed leaf of a pine(1)/fir tree: *The forest floor was covered with pine(1) needles.* **6** thing that has a narrow sharp appearance, e.g the pointed top of a mountain or monument. (**find**, **look for**) **a needle in a haystack** (*fig*) (find, look for) an impossible or very difficult thing: *Looking for that receipt in all these papers will be like trying to find a needle in a haystack.* **give s.o the needle** (*fig*; *slang*) annoy (s.o) or make s.o angry: *Why do you behave like that? You know it gives her the needle.*

▷ *tr.v* **7** (*fig*; *informal*) annoy (s.o) or make (s.o) angry: *Stop needling me! You're doing that just to needle me.*

'**needle,craft** *u.n* skill, activity etc of sewing.

'**needle,woman** *c.n* (*pl* -,*women*) woman who is good at sewing or makes money by sewing.

'**needle,work** *u.n* **1** = needlecraft. **2** cloth etc being sewn: *leave your needlework on the table.*

'**needling** *attrib.adj* (*informal*) annoying, worrying: *a needling fear/thought/pain.*

needn't /'ni:dnt/ = need not. ⇒ need.

need've /'ni:dəv/ = need have. ⇒ need.

needy ⇒ need.

ne'er /neə/ *adv* (*literary*) never.

nefarious /nɪ'feərɪəs/ *adj* (*formal*) wicked; evil: *a nefarious crime.*

negate /nɪ'geɪt/ *tr.v* cause (s.t) to be worthless, useless or no longer effective(1): *What you said negates everything I've tried to teach you.*

negation /nɪ'geɪʃən/ *sing/u.n* (*formal*) **1** act of causing s.t to be no longer effective or not to have any force: *Their present view is a negation of their earlier interest in this matter.* **2** act of refusing: *Raise your hand to show negation of the plan.*

negative /'negətɪv/ *adj* **1** (*formal*) (esp of an answer) that means 'no', 'not': *We got a negative answer to our request. All the replies to our requests were negative. The negative form of 'can' is 'can't'.* Opposite affirmative(1). **2** only concerned with failing and the bad things about s.t: *Don't be so negative about everything. If you're so negative you'll never get the job.* Opposite positive(6). **3** (*attrib*) (*mathematics*) (of a number, quantity) less than zero(1): *−6 is a negative number.* **4** (in electricity) (of charge(4)) that is carried by electrons: *Rubbing a plastic(3) bag or a balloon with a cloth produces a negative charge. The negative terminal(4) of a battery is the place where there are more electrons.* Opposite positive(11) charge(4) and positive(11) terminal(4). **5** (in photography) showing the dark areas as light and the light areas as dark (on a piece of film).

▷ *n* **6** *def.n* word or form that says 'no': *The negative of 'You can go' is 'You cannot go'. You can expect the answer to be in the negative.* Opposite affirmative(2). **7** (*mathematics*) negative(3) number, quantity: *−8 and −2x are negatives.*

8 *c.n* (*photography*) piece of film that has been developed(6) showing the dark areas as light and the light areas as dark.

'**negatively** *adv* in a negative(1,2,4) way: *She answered everything negatively. If you treat everything so negatively you'll never get anywhere. A material that is negatively charged means that it has more electrons than neutrons or protons.*

,**negative** '**pole** *def.n* (*technical*) (of a magnet(1)) end that naturally turns away from the earth: *Two negative poles move away from one another. A negative and a positive pole will move towards one another.*

neglect /nɪ'glekt/ *u.n* **1** lack of attention, caring etc: *I'm suffering from neglect. The house was in a terrible state of neglect when we bought it.*

▷ *tr.v* **2** not give enough attention to (s.o/s.t): *Don't neglect your health! He works so hard that he neglects his family.* **3** (usu — to do s.t) (*formal*) fail (to do s.t): *He neglected to tell his parents where he was going and made them very angry. He was thrown out of his flat because he neglected to pay the rent.*

ne'glectful *adj* (esp — of oneself/s.o/s.t) (*formal*) careless; in the habit of not giving enough attention (to oneself/s.o/s.t): *I have been very neglectful of everyone over the last month and I promise to change.*

ne'glectfully *adv*. **ne'glectfulness** *u.n*.

negligee /'neglɪˌʒeɪ/ *c.n* (also '**négli,gé**) thin nightdress for women.

negligent /'neglɪdʒənt/ *adj* careless; not giving enough attention: *We cannot afford to employ someone who is so negligent in his work.*

'**negligence** *u.n* **1** fact of being careless; carelessness: *The accident was caused by the driver's negligence. He was dismissed for negligence.* **2** (*law*) not taking enough care (esp of children, conditions of safety, health etc): *After the accident the company was sued for criminal negligence.* **contributory negligence** ⇒ contribute.

'**negligently** *adv*.

negligible /'neglɪdʒəbl/ *adj* hardly noticeable; too small, unimportant to be considered: *a negligible improvement in standards; a negligible rise in profits.*

negotiate /nɪ'gəʊʃɪˌeɪt/ *v* **1** *tr/intr.v* discuss (s.t) in order to reach an agreement about s.t: *I've got the job but we're still negotiating my salary and hours of work. Is it worth trying to negotiate with them over the conditions of work? We might have found a buyer for our house — we're still negotiating.* **2** *tr.v* get past or through (s.t difficult): *Be careful when you negotiate some of those mountain roads — they're very dangerous.*

negotiable /nɪ'gəʊʃɪəbl/ *adj* **1** that can still be discussed, changed: *Is your price negotiable?* **2** (usu *pred*) (of cheques, forms of payment) that can be changed into cash: *This cheque is not negotiable — you'll have to put it into your bank account.* **3** (of roads etc) that can be passed, travelled on safely: *Will the roads still be negotiable after these heavy rains?*

negotiation /nɪˌgəʊʃɪ'eɪʃən/ *c/u.n* discussion in order to reach agreement: *Have the negotiations begun yet? Have the negotiations been successful? Is your offer open to negotiation? We'll settle the problem by negotiation.* **under negotiation**

being negotiated(1): *Our proposal is still under negotiation.*

ne'goti,ator *c.n* person who negotiates(1).

neigh /neɪ/ *c.n* **1** cry made by a horse.
▷ *intr.v* **2** make the cry of a horse.

neighbour /'neɪbə/ (US **neighbor**) *c.n* **1** person who lives near someone; country next to another country: *We used to be neighbours. Do you have nice neighbours? France and Germany are neighbours.* **nextdoor neighbours** people whose houses are next to one another.
▷ *tr/intr.v* **2** (usu — *on s.t*) (*formal*) be next to (another country, place etc): *Which countries neighbour (on) Switzerland? Our house neighbours on a large open field.*

'neighbour,hood (US **neighborhood**) *c.n* particular area in a town: *She lives in a poor neighbourhood.* **in the neighbourhood (of s.t)** **(a)** area near or surrounding (another area): *He lives somewhere in the neighbourhood (of the swimming pool).* **(b)** about (a stated amount of something): *It'll cost in the neighbourhood of £1000.*

'neighbouring (US **neighboring**) *attrib.adj* next to one another: *We live in neighbouring towns. Austria and Italy are neighbouring countries.*

'neighbourly (US **neighborly**) *adj* kind, helpful: *That was very neighbourly of her.*

'neighbourliness (US **neighborliness**) *u.n.*

neither /'naɪðə, 'niːðə/ *adv* (used in short answers) **1** and (I, you, he, she, they, we etc) also do not (want s.t), cannot (do, see etc s.o/s.t): *'I don't want to go.' 'Neither do I.' She didn't know about it.' 'Neither did Harry.'* **2** (*formal*) and (he, she etc) also cannot, does not etc (do s.t else): *I can't see anything and neither can I hear anything. She doesn't visit her brother, neither does she visit her parents.* ⇒ either(*adv*).
▷ *conj* **3 neither . . . nor . . .** not the first (person, thing, group etc) and not the second (person, thing, group etc): *Neither this house nor the one you showed us yesterday interests us. I can neither read nor write Chinese but I can understand it. Neither of my brothers nor my father came to my wedding.* ⇒ either(4).
▷ *det* (used with a sing noun/pron) (of two people, things etc) **4** not the one and not the other: *Neither school agreed to accept her. Did neither team score a goal?* ⇒ either(4), no(2).
▷ *pron* **5** (often — *of s.o/s.t*) not the one and not the other (of two people, animals, things): *Neither of my parents can come to the meeting tonight. Neither will be acceptable. I could see neither of them. Neither of these two pieces of work is good enough.* ⇒ either(6), none(2).

neoclassical /ˌniːəʊ'klæsɪkl/ *adj* **1** (of buildings, paintings etc) done in the style of ancient Greece or Rome. **2** (*music*) done in the style of early music: *Stravinsky was a neoclassical composer.*

neocolonial /ˌniːəʊkə'ləʊnɪəl/ *adj* of the economic control/power of a strong and developed country over a less developed one.

,neoco'lonia,lism *u.n.*

neon /'niːɒn/ *u.n* (also *attrib*) colourless(1) gas used in some kinds of electric lighting, *chem.symb* Ne: *This glass tube is filled with neon and lights up when an electric current is sent through it.*

,neon 'light *c.n* (also **,neon 'lamp**) glass tube filled with neon which lights up when electricity is sent through it: *I don't like working under neon lights all day. From the top of the hill we could see the city's neon lights.*

,neon 'sign *c.n* glass tubes filled with neon in the shape of the name of a place or product.

nephew /'nefjuː/ *c.n* son of one's brother or sister. Compare niece.

nepotism /'nepə,tɪzəm/ *u.n* (*formal*) giving of favours (esp a job) to a member of one's family.

nerve /nɜːv/ *n* **1** *c.n* bundle of fibres(2) that sends messages between the brain and various parts of the body causing the body to move and feel etc: *The dentist hit a nerve in my tooth which made me jump.* ⇒ nerves(2). **2** *def/u.n* courage: *I don't have the nerve for rock-climbing any more. You need a lot of nerve to hang-glide* (⇒ hang-gliding(*n*)). ⇒ unnerve. **3** *u.n* confidence to do s.t rude or not generally acceptable; cheek(2): *You've got a nerve to come here after all you've done!* **have the nerve (to do s.t)** **(a)** have the courage (to do s.t): *I didn't have the nerve to jump.* **(b)** = have the cheek to do s.t (⇒ cheek(2)). **hit/touch a nerve** (*fig*) do/say s.t that is a difficult/painful subject: *I must have hit a nerve when I mentioned her husband because she went very quiet.* **lose one's nerve** no longer have the courage to do s.t: *I've lost my nerve since my friend had a climbing accident.*

'nerve ,cell *c.n* (also **'neuron** or **'neurone**) part of the nervous system that takes messages to different parts of the body.

'nerve ,centre *c.n* **1** group of a particular kind of nerve cells. **2** (*fig*) place in an organization from which it is controlled.

'nerve-,racking *adj* causing great fear and anxiety: *a nerve-racking drive through the storm.*

nerves *pl.n* **1** *pl* of nerve(1). **2** condition of being, easily becoming, anxious, afraid, annoyed, excited: *I need something to calm my nerves.* **a bundle of nerves** (*informal*) very nervous: *She's a bundle of nerves before every race.* **get on s.o's nerves** (*informal*) annoy s.o; cause s.o to be irritated(1): *That habit of yours really gets on my nerves.* **live on one's nerves** be in a continuous nervous(2) state because of working too hard, doing too many things etc. **war of nerves** competition that depends on courage, determination, confidence etc.

nervous /'nɜːvəs/ *adj* **1** of the nerves(1): *a nervous shake; a nervous disease; the nervous system.* **2** anxious, afraid; a nervous person. *She gets very nervous before examinations. Stop doing that — you're making me nervous. What are you so nervous about?*

,nervous 'break,down *c.n* mental illness caused by worry, extreme tiredness etc.

,nervous 'energy *u.n* energy(1) produced by great activity and excitement.

'nervously *adv* in a nervous(2) way: *She tapped the table nervously.*

'nervousness *u.n.*

'nervous ,system *c.n* brain, nerves and spinal cord in an animal or person.

'nervy *adj* (-ier, -iest) (*informal*) easily excited.

nest /nest/ *c.n* **1** place chosen or made by birds and some animals and insects for their eggs or young to develop and grow in safely. **2** (usu *a*

—*of s.t*)comfortable place: *We made a nest of cushions to sleep on.* **3** (usu *a* — *of s.t*) (*fig*) safe place (esp where criminals can hide or do illegal things): *a nest of crime.* **feather one's nest** ⇨ feather(v).

▷ *intr.v* **4** build and live in a nest and have young there: *Our pigeons(1) are nesting.*

'nest ,egg *c.n* (*fig*) money that is saved for a future use: *Every month we put £5 in the bank so that we'll have a nest egg when we retire.*

'nestling *c.n* young bird (still in the nest).

nestle /'nesl/ *intr.v* **1** (often — *down s.w*) make oneself comfortable (s.w): *She nestled down on the bed of leaves and fell asleep. I love nestling on the cushions in front of the fire with a book.* **2** (often — *up to s.o/s.t*) go very close (to s.o/s.t): *The little girl nestled up to her mother. The young dog nestled against its mother for the night. They nestled together for warmth.*

net¹ /net/ *c/u.n* **1** material made of lengths of string, wire, rope, plastic(3) etc knotted together so that there are small holes in it and used for particular purposes (e.g a *fishing net* is used to catch fish; a *tennis net* is stretched between two poles on a tennis court for the players to hit the tennis ball over; a net is hung around goal posts in netball, football, hockey etc to catch the ball when a goal is scored).

▷ *tr.v* (*-tt-*) **2** catch, put, (s.t) in a net or nets: *We net tons of fish every day. The player netted the ball with a hard straight kick.* **3** cover (s.t) with a net: *Have you netted the strawberries(2)?*

'net,ball *c.n* ball game for seven girls or women in each team in which the aim is to throw the ball into a net that hangs from a ring at the top of a pole. Compare basketball.

'netting *u.n* material made like a net¹(1): *use wire netting to make a cage for some birds.*

'net,work *c.n* **1** system that consists of many lines that cross one another: *a network of roads; a railway network.* **2** large system that is made of many connecting parts: *a radio network; a communications(2) network.*

net² /net/ *adj* (also **nett**) **1** (of an amount of money) left after all other amounts have been taken away: *It cost £250 net.* Opposite gross²(1). ⇨ net price, net profit.

▷ *tr.v* (*-tt-*) **2** gain (an amount of money) as profit: *We netted £50.*

,net 'price *c.n* final price after all discounts(1) have been allowed: *What is the net price?*

,net 'profit *c/u.n* amount of money left after all expenses have been taken away: *We made £500 net profit* (or *a net profit of £500*).

,net re'sult *c.n* (often — *of s.t*) final result (of s.t) after everything has been considered: *The net result of all our effort is that no decisions will be made without a vote.*

nettle /'netl/ *c.n* **1** (also *attrib*) wild plant that stings anyone who touches it: *I walked into nettles and got a very painful nettle rash¹.*

▷ *tr.v* **2** (usu passive) make s.o angry, annoyed: *He was really nettled by what you said.*

network ⇨ net¹.

neural /'njʊərəl/ *adj* (*technical*) of the nerves(1).

neuralgia /ˌnjʊə'rældʒə/ *u.n* (*technical*) sharp pain of the nerves, esp those in the head.

neuralgic /njʊə'rældʒɪk/ *adj*.

neurology /njʊə'rɒlədʒɪ/ *u.n* medical study of the nerves(1).

neurological /ˌnjʊərə'lɒdʒɪkl/ *adj* (of a disease) of or referring to the nerves(1).

neu'rologist *c.n* person who is studying, or is skilled in, neurology.

neuron /'njʊərɒn/ *c.n* (also **neurone** /'njʊərəʊn/) ⇨ nerve cell.

neurosis /njʊə'rəʊsɪs/ *c.n* (*pl* **neuroses** /njʊə'rəʊsiːz/) (*medical; informal*) illness of the mind causing the person to suffer great anxiety and (often unreasonable(1)) fear which affects behaviour etc (esp towards other people): *have a neurosis about untidy rooms.*

'neuro,surgeon *c.n* doctor who is qualified to perform medical operations on the nervous system.

neurotic /njʊə'rɒtɪk/ *adj* **1** (usu *informal*) (of a person) suffering from neurosis; excessively nervous, anxious etc: *Just because I'm neurotic it doesn't mean they aren't trying to ruin me. She's neurotic about her children — she doesn't let them do anything alone.*

▷ *c.n* **2** person who is excessively concerned with everything.

neuter /'njuːtə/ *adj* (*grammar*) of a form that is neither feminine(4) nor masculine(5). **2** (of plants and animals) having neither female nor male sexual parts.

▷ *c.n* **3** (usu *the* —) (*grammar*) neuter(1) form (of a noun, adj etc): *Write the neuter of the following adjectives.*

▷ *tr.v* **4** make (a male animal) no longer able to produce young: *We've had our cat neutered.* Compare spay.

neutral /'njuːtrəl/ *adj* **1** neither helping nor supporting any particular side in an argument, fight, war etc: *If there is another war we intend to remain neutral. We need a neutral person to help us settle this matter.* **2** (esp of colour, pattern etc) not so bright/strong as to be too noticeable: *We need a neutral colour for the carpet in this room because there are too many colours already.* **3** (of electricity) that carries no charge: *The black or blue wire is the neutral wire.* **4** (*chemistry*) neither more acid(2) nor more alkaline: *Water is a neutral substance. We can make acids(4) neutral by adding a little alkaline solution.* **5** (of gears in a vehicle) of the position in which no power can pass from the engine to the wheels.

▷ *n* **6** *c.n* (*formal*) neutral(1) person, country. **7** *u.n* (esp *in* —) neutral(5) position of the gears(1) of a vehicle: *Remember to check that the car is in neutral before you turn the engine on.*

neutrality /njuː'trælɪtɪ/ *u.n* state of being neutral(1).

neutralization, -isation /ˌnjuːtrəlaɪ'zeɪʃən/ *u.n* process of making a substance neutral(4).

'neutra,lize, -ise *tr.v* make (s.t) neutral(4)/ harmless by causing or having the opposite effect: *We neutralized the acid(2) sting of a bee.*

neutron /'njuːtron/ *c.n* (*physics*) one of the particles(1) with no electric charge which forms part of the nucleus(2) of an atom. ⇨ proton.

never /'nevə/ *adv* **1** not at any time or on any occasion; not ever: *I've never been to America. He's never done that before. I've never seen anything so beautiful.* **2** (used to add force to the idea of 'not'): *Never in all my life have I heard such nonsense. I never knew my father.* **never mind** ⇨ mind². **never you mind** ⇨ mind². **That**

will never do! That is not good enough! **Well I never!** (used to express great surprise).

‚never-'ending adj of s.t that is very long and seems to have no end: *a never-ending story.*

‚never'more adv never again.

‚never-'never def.n (esp *on the —*) (*informal*) borrowing money; hire purchase: *If we need a new fridge we'll have to buy it on the never-never.*

nevertheless /‚nevəðə'les/ adv even so; however, still: *I don't want to come — nevertheless I shall because I feel I have to. It's kind of you to offer; nevertheless we don't really need any more help. He's not clever but he's quite successful nevertheless.*

new /njuː/ adj **1** not existing (or owned) before; only now happening or being built; made, produced, bought etc for the first time: *There's a new book by John le Carré in the shops. Have you seen the new Bond film? I've never seen those shoes before — are they new? When the new road is finished it'll take half the time to reach London.* **2** just discovered: *I try to learn ten new words every day. Have you heard anything new about that robbery? That's new to me; I've never heard that before. So, what else is new?* **3** (*attrib*) changed; having a new(1) start: *It's not too late to begin a new life. I feel like a new person since I've been swimming every day.* **4** just arrived; about to start s.t the first time and still not familiar with things: *I'm new to this kind of work. Are you the new secretary? We've got a new boy in our class.* Compare old. **as good as new** as good as when first made/bought: *We'll soon have your bicycle as good as new. A little paint will make your car look as good as new.*

▷ adv **5** happening not long before: *new-laid* (*eggs*); *a new-born baby.*

▷ def.pl.n **6** new people/things: *We mixed the old with the new and no one noticed.*

'new,comer c.n person who has just arrived s.w.

‚new-'fangled /-'fæŋgld/ adj (*informal*; slightly *derog*) (of ideas/things) new and not yet liked or accepted by everyone: *She's full of new-fangled ideas. I can't use all these new-fangled machines.*

'newly adv of s.t done recently: *newly married.*

'newly,wed c.n person who has just got married.

'new 'moon ⇒ moon¹.

'newness u.n.

‚New 'Testament def/unique n (abbr NT) second part of the Bible(1) which contains the life and teachings of Jesus. ⇒ Old Testament.

‚New 'World def.n America.

‚new 'year c/def.n (also *attrib*) (often with capital **N** and **Y**) year that has just begun or has not yet begun: *a New Year party. Happy New Year!*

‚New ‚Year's 'Day unique n 1 January.

‚New ‚Year's 'Eve unique n 31 December.

New Year resolution ⇒ resolution.

news /njuːz/ u.n (also *attrib*) new information about s.t that is happening or has just happened: *Did you hear the 7 o'clock news? Have you heard the news — Joan's getting married! I'll just listen to the news* headlines(2). *The news is all bad.* **break the (bad etc) news (to s.o)** be the first to tell (s.o) (bad etc) news: *I suppose I'll have to be the one to break the news to him about his bad examination results.* (*it's, that's*) **news**

to s.o (that is) information that was not known before by s.o (suggesting that it may not be true): *'I hear you're getting married tomorrow!' 'That's news to me!'*

'news ‚agency c.n (*pl -ies*) organization that collects information and supplies it to newspapers, radio and television.

'news,agent c.n **1** owner of a shop that sells newspapers, magazines, stationery etc. **2** (also 'news,agent's) shop selling newspapers etc.

'news ‚bulletin c.n (special) news on radio or television.

'news,cast c.n news broadcast(1).

'news,caster c.n = newsreader.

'news,flash c.n piece of important news that interrupts(1) a radio or television programme.

news item ⇒ item(2).

'news,letter c.n information sent to members of a group once a week, month etc.

'news,paper c.n printed paper containing news etc that is sold to the public usu every day: *Do you get a daily newspaper delivered to you?*

'news,reader c.n person who presents a news broadcast(1).

'news,stand c.n small place where newspapers (and sometimes magazines) are sold: *I always buy my newspaper from the newsstand on the corner.* Compare kiosk(2).

'news,worthy adj interesting or important enough to be read and therefore reported in the newspapers etc.

'newsy adj (*-ier, -iest*) (*informal*) full of news of friends' activities etc: *I wrote her a very newsy letter which I'm sure she'll enjoy.*

newt /njuːt/ c.n kind of small animal like a lizard that lives on the land and in the water.

next /nekst/ adv **1** immediately after in order, space, time: *What happened next? First we'll have some soup and next (we'll have) the fish. I have to finish some work first but I'll help you next.* **next but one** one after the next one: *be next but one in the* queue. **next to s.o/s.t** near/close to s.o/s.t: *Come and sit next to me, the fire. Try to get a seat next to the window. May I have a room next to hers? Can you reach those blue plates next to the white ones?* **next to impossible** almost impossible: *It's next to impossible to see anything in this weather/rain.* **next to nothing** ⇒ nothing(*pron*).

▷ det/pron **2** immediately after in order, space, time: *Ours is the next train. Can I see the next person, please? Who's next? Are you going on holiday next year? What film is on next week? Let's meet next Monday. They arrived on Tuesday and left the next day. The next time I see you doing that I'll report you to the boss.* ⇒ first(5), last(3).

▷ def.n **3** person, thing, moment etc that comes immediately after: *The first two questions were easy but the next were very difficult. One moment we were all talking happily and the next there was terrible shouting and arguing.* ⇒ first(7), last(7).

‚next 'door adj/adv (**'next,door** when *attrib*) in/to the next house: *We're going to be nextdoor neighbours. Go next door and borrow some sugar. Who lives next door?*

‚next of 'kin c.n (*pl next of kin*) (*law*) one's nearest relation(1), e.g parent(1), child(2).

nib /nɪb/ c.n metal point at the end of a pen which

controls the flow of ink: *I need a* medium(1) *nib for my handwriting.*

nibble /'nɪbl/ *c.n* **1** (often *a — of s.t*) small bite (of s.t): *Can I have a nibble of your sandwich?*
▷ *tr/intr.v* **2** (often *— at s.t*) take small bites: *I can feel something nibbling* (*at*) *my toes. You should stop nibbling between meals.*

nice /naɪs/ *adj* **1** pleasant: *a nice person/day/ meal. Did you have nice weather? Taste this — is it nice? That wasn't a very nice thing to do/say. It was nice to meet you. Were they nice to you?* **2** (*attrib*) good, exact: *a nice sense of timing.* **3** (*joking*) bad: *What a nice friend you are! That's nice — my own father won't help me!* **nice and clean**, **warm**, **tidy** *etc* comfortably, pleasantly clean etc.

'nice-,looking *adj* pretty; handsome: *He's a nice-looking young man.*

'nicely *adv* **1** in a nice(1) way: *She dresses nicely.* **2** very well: *They're progressing nicely.* **doing nicely** (esp of a patient) making good progress.
'niceness *u.n.*

nicety /'naɪsɪti/ *n* (*pl -ies*) **1** *u.n* (usu *— of s.t*) (*formal*) exactness (of s.t): *Nicety of judgement is necessary in this situation.* **2** *c.n* careful and correct way of doing things in a particular situation: *She hasn't yet learnt the niceties of entertaining important people.*

niche /niːʃ/ *c.n* **1** small hollow in a wall etc for an ornament etc: *The niche by the fireplace will be perfect for this statue.* **2** (esp *find a — for oneself/ s.o*) (*fig*) right/suitable place (for oneself/s.o): *She just hasn't found her niche in life yet. He found a niche for himself in his father's business.*

nick /nɪk/ *c.n* **1** small hole caused by a cut etc: *Do you have another piece of cloth — this one has a nick on the edge?* **2** (*slang*) prison: *They put him in the nick for the night because he was so drunk.* **in good**, **bad**, **excellent**, **poor** *etc* **nick** (*informal*) (used to describe the condition of s.o/s.t): *I bought a second-hand car in very good nick.* **in the nick of time** only just in time: *She woke up in the nick of time — a few minutes later and they may not have escaped the fire.*
▷ *tr.v* **3** make a small cut in (s.o/s.t): *The ball nicked him just above the eye.* **4** (*informal*) steal (s.t): *Who nicked my ruler? Someone's nicked my bicycle.* **5** (*slang*) arrest (s.o): *The police nicked him for stealing a car.*

nickel /'nɪkl/ *n* **1** *u.n* hard metal used esp for mixing with other metals, *chem. symb* Ni. **2** *c.n* US and Canadian coin worth five cents.

nickname /'nɪk,neɪm/ *c.n* **1** informal name for s.o: *His name is Mr Jones but his nickname is 'Fats'.*
▷ *tr.v* **2** give (s.o/s.t) a nickname(1): *She was nick-named 'the Iron Lady'.*

nicotine /'nɪkə,tiːn/ *u.n* substance in tobacco which is dangerous for the body.

niece /niːs/ *c.n* daughter of one's brother or sister. Compare nephew.

nifty /'nɪfti/ *adj* (*-ier*, *-iest*) (*informal*) clever; efficient; fast: *a nifty car.*

niggardly /'nɪgədlɪ/ *adj* **1** (of a person) not willing to give (esp money): *He's such a nig-gardly person — he always complains if you ask him to do anything.* Compare miserly, stingy(1). **2** having little value or importance: *After all his promises he gave me such a niggardly increase in salary that I decided to resign.*

niggle /'nɪgl/ *v* **1** *intr.v* (often *— about/over s.t*) argue, worry, complain, (esp about the less important things): *You're spending so much time niggling over what food to take and we haven't even decided where we're going.* **2** *tr/intr.v* annoy (s.o): *You're only doing that to niggle me.*

'niggling *attrib.adj* **1** a little worrying: *I have a niggling feeling that we've made the wrong decision.* **2** small and less important: *We'll save an hour at the end to discuss all the niggling details of the trip so that we don't forget anything.*

night /naɪt/ *n* **1** *u.n* dark time of a whole day: *Night comes early during the winter months.* **2** *c.n* length of time between sunset and sunrise: *It was a lovely still night and the sky was full of stars. How many nights did you sleep there? We meet every Monday night. I saw her* (*on*) *the night after you left. I woke up four times during the night because of the storm. The first night we were too tired to do anything but the next night we danced till four in the morning.* ⇨ overnight. **all night** (**long**) during the whole night. **at night** (**a**) at the end of the day when it is dark: *I like to read in bed at night.* (**b**) during the night: *We leave this light on at night for the baby.* **by night** during the night: *It was so hot that we travelled by night and slept during the day. New York is a different city by night.* **night and day** ⇨ day and night. **have a bad/good night** sleep badly/well (used esp when s.o is ill): *Did he have a good night?* **make a night of it** go out and enjoy oneself during the whole night. **night after night** every night for a long time: *She used to sit there night after night waiting for him to come home.* **night off** free night when one does not have to work etc: *I get one night off a week.* (**on**) **the night of s.t** (on) the particular night stated: *Where were you on the night of March 14?*

'night,cap *c.n* **1** cap worn at night: *No one wears a nightcap any more, do they?* **2** drink before bed.

'night,clothes *pl.n* any clothing worn for bed.

'night,club *c.n* club open at night for dancing, drinking etc.

'night,dress *c.n* (also **'nightie**) loose-fitting kind of dress worn in bed by a woman.

'night,fall *u.n* beginning part of a night: *Don't expect us before nightfall.*

'night,gown *c.n* (*formal*) = nightdress.

nightie /'naɪtɪ/ *c.n* = nightdress.

'night,life *u.n* entertainment available at night: *The nightlife in New York is very exciting.*

'night,long *adj/adv* (lasting) the whole night: *a nightlong journey. We worked nightlong to finish.*

'nightly *attrib.adj* **1** that happens every night: *a nightly tv programme(5).*
▷ *adv* **2** every night: *showing nightly at 10 o'clock for two weeks.*

nightmare /'naɪt,meə/ *c.n* **1** frightening dream. **2** frightening/bad experience: *That trip over the mountains was a nightmare.*

'night,marish *adj* of s.t that is a nightmare(2): *a nightmarish journey.*

'night ,porter *c.n* person who works at night at a hotel.

nights *adv* at night: *Do you ever work nights?*

'night ,school *c/u.n* place where classes are

held in the evening: *She goes to night school to improve her English.* ⇒ evening class.

'night ‚shift *n* **1** *c/u.n* (often *on* —) work done by a group of people during the night: *I'm on night shift that week.* **2** *def/def.pl.n* people who do the night shift: *The night shift was/were just leaving as we arrived.*

'night‚shirt *c.n* long loose shirt for wearing in bed.

'night‚time *u.n* (also *attrib*) night: *a nighttime activity. Most crimes are done at nighttime.* ⇒ daytime.

'night‚watchman *c.n* (*pl* -men) person whose job is to look after a building at night.

nightingale /'naɪtɪŋ‚geɪl/ *c.n* kind of small bird that sings beautifully, esp at night.

nil /nɪl/ *u.n* (used esp to give a score) nothing: *We won the football match two-nil* (2–0) (*or by two goals to nil*). ⇒ nought(1).

nimble /'nɪmbl/ *adj* **1** able to move quickly and easily: *The piano player has very nimble fingers. The dancer is nimble on her feet.* **2** (of the mind) able to think/understand quickly.

'nimbleness *u.n.* **'nimbly** *adv.*

nimbus /'nɪmbəs/ *c.n* (*pl* -es, nimbi /'nɪmbaɪ/) **1** rain cloud. **2** shining ring as often painted above a saint's(1) head. Compare halo.

nincompoop /'nɪŋkəm‚puːp/ *c.n* (*informal*) foolish person.

nine /naɪn/ *det/pron/c.n* (*cardinal number*) number 9 (between 8 and 10): *There will be nine of us for dinner. See you at 9 (o'clock) tonight. I'll be nine (years old) next birthday. We'll need 9 metres of material.* **nine times out of ten** on most occasions: *I'm right nine times out of ten.* **nine days' wonder** thing that starts very well or causes great excitement in the beginning but ends quickly, is soon forgotten.

'nine‚pin *c.n* wooden bottle used in the game of ninepins.

'nine‚pins *pl/u.n* game with a heavy ball and nine wooden bottles in which one rolls the ball along the floor and tries to knock all the bottles down.

nineteen /‚naɪn'tiːn/ *det/pron/c.n* (*cardinal number*) number 19 (between 18 and 20): *Have you turned 19 (years old) yet? Only nineteen people came to the meeting.* (**talk**) **nineteen to the dozen** (talk) very fast or for a very long time.

nineteenth /‚naɪn'tiːnθ/ *det/pron* (*ordinal number*) **1** (person or thing) following 18 in order; 19th.
▷ *c.n* **2** one of nineteen equal parts; ¹⁄₁₉.

ninety /'naɪntɪ/ *det/pron/c.n* (*pl* -ies) (*cardinal number*) number 90 (between 89 and 91): *The temperature reached ninety (degrees) today. I got 90% (per cent) for the test. She is ninety-three (93) years old. I'm not paying £90 for that old thing.* **in one's nineties** between 90 and 99 years old: *They're all in their nineties.* **the nineties** (or **the 90(')s**) (**a**) (of speed, temperature, marks etc) between 90 and 99: *It was in the nineties today. Most of her examination marks are in the nineties.* (**b**) (years) between '90 and '99 in a century: *Gold had been discovered by the nineties.* **ninety-nine times out of a hundred** nearly always.

ninetieth /'naɪntɪəθ/ *det/pron* **1** (*ordinal*

number) (person or thing) following 89 in order; 90th.
▷ *c.n* **2** one of ninety equal parts; ¹⁄₉₀.

ninth /naɪnθ/ *det/pron* **1** (*ordinal number*) (person or thing) following 8 in order; 9th.
▷ *c.n* **2** one of nine equal parts; ¹⁄₉.

ninny /'nɪnɪ/ *c.n* (*pl* -ies) (*informal*) foolish person who is easily afraid.

nip /nɪp/ *c.n* **1** small bite or pinch: *I felt a nip on my toe — it was a fish!* **2** (*fig*) feeling of cold: *There's a nip in the air tonight.* **3** small quantity/measure of alcohol: *a nip of vodka.*
▷ *v* (-pp-) **4** *tr/intr.v* pinch/bite (s.o/s.t): *Something nipped my leg in the water. That dog nips — be careful.* **5** *tr.v* (often — s.t off) cut s.t (off), esp with a small instrument: *For the first year you should nip off the young fruit.* **6** *intr.v* (usu — *into* s.t; — down, out, off etc) (*informal*) go quickly: *I'll nip into town and buy some flowers. Nip down to the shop and buy me a newspaper. He nipped out for a few minutes — he'll be back soon. Do you mind if I nip in front of you — I only have one thing to buy.* **nip s.t in the bud** stop s.t right at the beginning before it gets too big or difficult to deal with: *We should have nipped that idea in the bud — it's too late to stop them going now.*

nippers /'nɪpəz/ *pl.n* kind of tool for holding s.t in a tight position.

nippy /'nɪpɪ/ *adj* (-ier, -iest) (*informal*) **1** quick. **2** (esp of the weather) icy cold: *The air is rather nippy tonight.*

nipple /'nɪpl/ *c.n* **1** darker pointed tip on a woman's breast(1) from where a baby gets milk. **2** one of two darker pointed tips on a man's chest. **3** small pointed part of a machine etc, esp for oiling an engine: *the greasing nipples.*

nirvana /nɪə'vɑːnə/ *u.n* (in Buddhism) state of perfect calm and happiness reached after a person has freed herself/himself from desire.

nit /nɪt/ *c.n* **1** egg of a tiny insect, esp the kind in a person's hair. **2** (also **'nit‚wit**) (*informal*) foolish person: *Don't be a silly nit!*

'nit‚pick *intr.v* look for unimportant mistakes/faults in s.t: *You're just nitpicking — it was very good.*

'nit‚picking *u.n* act of looking for unimportant mistakes, faults etc in s.t: *That kind of nitpicking is very destructive; criticize the work but also explain how it could be improved.*

'nit‚wit *c.n* = nit(2).

nitrate /'naɪtreɪt/ *c/u.n* substance in the soil that contains nitrogen in a form that can be used by plants as food: *Ammonium nitrate is especially important for growing green vegetables.*

nitric /'naɪtrɪk/ *adj* containing nitrogen: *nitric acid.*

nitrogen /'naɪtrədʒən/ *u.n* gas that has no colour or smell and forms four-fifths of the air. *chem. symb* N.

nitroglycerin /‚naɪtrəʊ'glɪsərɪn/ *u.n* (also **‚nitro'glyce‚rine** /-‚riːn/) kind of powerful explosive(2).

nitty-gritty /‚nɪtɪ 'grɪtɪ/ *def.n* (often *get down to the* —) (*informal*) difficult parts or details of a problem: *It's easy to talk about what we want but it will be hard work when we get down to the nitty-gritty of how it can happen.*

nitwit ⇒ nit(2).

no /nəʊ/ *adv* **1** (used with comparatives) not (in

any way): *She's no prettier than you are. I'm no more happy with him than without him. Go no further — the bridge ahead has been destroyed. Drive no faster than 60 mph.*

▷ *det* **2** not any: *I have no more money left. We have no eggs. There will be no football match tonight. No two pictures are exactly the same. She would accept no other way. There's no easy way of winning. I phoned her but there was no reply.* **3** (in commands) not permitted: *No dogs! No smoking! No entry!* **4** (*formal*) not a/an: *Leaving such a good friend is no easy thing. He's no friend of mine.* **by no means** ⇒ means. **in no time (at all)** ⇒ time(*n*). **no claim(s) bonus** ⇒ bonus. **no doubt** ⇒ doubt. **no end of s.t** ⇒ end(*n*). **It's no good/use (. . . ing)** It's useless to (worry etc): *It's no good waiting — they're not coming.* ⇒ be no good (⇒ good(*n*)). **no way** (*informal*) certainly not: *'Are you going to the meeting?' 'No way!' There's no way that I'd do anything like that!* (or *No way would I do anything like that!*) **there's no (. . . ing)** it's impossible to (know, say, tell etc): *There's no knowing where they'll go next.* **there's no point in (. . . ing)** it's useless to (do s.t): *There's no point in worrying about it — it's too late now. There's no point in saying you're sorry now!*

▷ *interj* **5** (used to say that s.t is not true, right, wanted etc): *'Would you like some more?' 'No, thank you.' 'Is this right?' 'No, it's not.' 'Can you see anything?' 'No, I can't.' 'Can I come?' 'No.'* Opposite yes(1).

▷ *c.n* (*pl* noes) **6** vote against s.t: *There were more noes than yeses.* ⇒ aye(2). **7** refusal: *When I asked for more I got a very loud no!*

nobody /'nǝʊbǝdɪ/ *c.n* (*pl* -ies) **1** person who is not important and will never be successful: *He's just a nobody — why worry about what he says?*

▷ *pron* **2** (also **'no one**) no person: *Nobody you know will be there. Did nobody help him? What he does with his life is nobody's business but his own.* **like nobody's business** (*informal*) very well, fast etc; in a way that not many people can: *He can run like nobody's business.* Compare anybody(1), somebody(2).

no 'go *u.n* (*informal*) not successful, possible: *I tried to get permission but it's no go — we'll have to try again next year.*

no-'go area *c.n* (*informal*) **1** area where people (esp police) do not enter because it is not safe for them. **2** subject which one does not discuss because of differences of opinion etc.

'no-,man's-,land *c/unique n* (esp in war) area that is not controlled by any army, government etc.

'no one *pron* = nobody(2).

No *written abbr* (also **No.**) (*pl* Nos) number(1): *No 31.* **No 10** Number 10 Downing Street (home of the British Prime Minister).

nobble /'nɒbl/ *tr.v* (*informal*) gain (s.o's) attention in order to discuss/win s.t or persuade s.o about s.t: *I'll try to nobble him at dinner tonight and I'll mention your name.*

noble /'nǝʊbl/ *adj* (*formal*) **1** worthy of honour: *a noble deed/sacrifice.* **2** of high birth, rank, title.

▷ *c.n* **3** (esp in history) person born into a noble(2) family, e.g a duke, earl.

nobility /nǝʊ'bɪlɪtɪ/ *u.n* **1** (*formal*) quality/state of being noble(1) or acting nobly: *The nobility of*

his action was honoured. **2** (esp in history) class of people with a title and often with land and power.

'nobleman *c.n* (*pl* -men) (esp in history) man who is a noble(3).

,noble-'minded *adj* of a person who is noble(1) in thought.

'noble,woman *c.n* (*pl* -,women) (esp in history) woman who is a noble(3).

'nobly *adv* in a noble(1) way.

nobody ⇒ no.

nocturnal /nɒk'tɜ:nl/ *adj* active at night: *Nocturnal animals look for their food at night.*

nod /nɒd/ *c.n* **1** up and down movement of the head, usu as a greeting or to show agreement etc: *He looked across the room at his mother who gave him a nod of encouragement.*

▷ *v* (-dd-) **2** *tr/intr.v* move (the head) up and down quickly as a greeting or to show agreement, approval, encouragement etc: *She nodded (her head) at her teacher when she saw her in the restaurant. She nodded (her head) without saying anything. The manager nodded to his secretary to come in.* **3** *tr.v* show (s.t) by nodding(2): *She nodded her agreement/approval.* **4** *intr.v* allow one's head to fall loosely when falling asleep: *Most of the passengers were nodding in their seats.* **nod off** fall asleep: *What happened — I must have nodded off for a few minutes?*

node /nǝʊd/ *c.n* place on the stem of a plant where a new shoot or leaf grows.

nodule /'nɒdju:l/ *c.n* small lump: *She felt the nodules under her skin as she rubbed her aching neck.*

Noel /nǝʊ'el/ *c/unique n* ⇒ Christmas.

noise /nɔɪz/ *n* **1** *c.n* sound: *What was that noise? We could hear the noises of the busy city far below us.* **2** *c/u.n* sounds that are loud and usu unpleasant: *Stop making such a noise. I can't sleep when there's noise around me.* **a big noise** (*informal*) an important person: *He's become a big noise in television.* **make a noise (about s.t)** show one's dissatisfaction (about s.t); complain (about s.t): *He made such a noise about the quality of their work that they had to do the whole job again.*

'noiseless *adj* who/that does not make any sounds.

'noisily *adv* with, while making, a lot of noise(2): *Try not to play so noisily.*

'noisiness *u.n* fact or state of being noisy: *I must get away from the noisiness of this house.*

'noisy *adj* (-ier, -iest) **1** making a lot of noise(2): *The engine is very noisy. It is a noisy machine.* **2** full of loud noises(2): *The room was so noisy we couldn't hear ourselves speak.*

nomad /'nǝʊmæd/ *c.n* person (usu one of a group) who has no fixed home and moves from place to place with everything that he/she owns: *The San of the Kalahari Desert are nomads.*

nomadic /nǝʊ'mædɪk/ *adj* like/of nomads: *The San are a nomadic people.*

no-man's-land ⇒ no.

nom de plume /,nɒm dǝ 'plu:m/ *c.n* (*pl noms de plume* /,nɒm dǝ 'plu:m/) (*French*) name used by a writer instead of her/his own name: *'Ellis Bell' was the nom de plume of the writer Emily Brontë.*

nominal /'nɒmɪnl/ *adj* **1** in name, title, only: *We need a nominal leader but we can all share* *the responsibilities of the job.* **2** small: *We only have to pay a nominal* fee(3) *to join the club.* **3** (*grammar*) of nouns.

'nominally *adv* in a nominal(1) way: *He's only nominally the manager and can't take any important decisions.*

nominate /'nɒmɪˌneɪt/ *tr.v* **1** (usu — s.o as/for s.t) suggest s.o as a suitable person (for a particular job): *I would like to nominate* Ms *Jones for the job* (or *as* chairperson). *Five people were nominated for the position but most people voted for Jones.* **2** (usu — s.o to s.t) appoint s.o to a particular job/ position: *Who was nominated to the committee?*

nomination /ˌnɒmɪ'neɪʃən/ *c/u.n* (example of the) act of nominating: *They asked for five nominations for the position. Next week's meeting will be mainly for the nomination of a new secretary.*

nominee /ˌnɒmɪ'niː/ *c.n* person who is nominated(1) for a particular job, position.

nominative /'nɒmɪnətɪv/ *adj/c.n* (*grammar*) (of the) form of a word when it is the subject of a sentence: *The nominative form of the pronoun in the first person singular is 'I'.* ⇨ accusative.

non- /nɒn-/ who/that is not the kind of person or thing mentioned in the second part of the word: non-fiction; non-resident.

ˌnon-agˈgression *u.n* (also *attrib*) state of not wanting to start a fight, war etc: *a non-aggression treaty.*

ˌnon-ˌalcoˈholic *adj* (of a drink) that does not contain alcohol.

ˌnon-aˈligned *adj* (*formal*) not linked to any particular side in world politics: *Which countries are still non-aligned?*

ˌnon-aˈlignment *u.n.*

ˌnon-ˈcombatant *c.n* person (in a war etc) who is not a member of the armed forces.

ˌnon-comˈmissioned *adj* not given a commission(3).

ˌnon-comˈmittal *adj* not expressing a firm opinion: *He was very non-committal about it — I don't know what he really thinks.*

ˌnon-comˈmunicable *adj* not communicable.

non compos mentis /ˌnɒn ˌkɒmpɒs 'mentɪs/ *adj* (*Latin*) (esp *law*) not in control of one's mind and therefore not responsible. ⇨ compos mentis.

ˌnonconˈformist *adj/c.n* (of a) person who does not live, act, think etc in the same way as other people usually do: *He likes to think of himself as a nonconformist but he behaves and dresses like all boys of his age.*

ˌnonconˈformity *u.n.*

nondescript /'nɒndɪˌskrɪpt/ *adj* having no noticeable, distinguishing, interesting characteristics: *I don't know what to say about their new house — it's rather nondescript.*

ˌnon-esˈsential *adj* = inessential.

ˌnon-eˈvent *c.n* occasion that is not as successful as expected: *The celebration was a non-event — most people came for a few minutes and left.*

ˌnon-ˈfiction *u.n* books etc concerning information and descriptions that are true. ⇨ fiction(1).

'non-ˌfinite *adj* ⇨ finite(2).

ˌnon-ˈflammable *adj* (also ˌnon-inˈflammable) that does not burst into flames or burn easily: *Seats in planes should be covered with non-flammable material.*

ˌnon-ˈflowering *adj* that does not produce

flowers: *non-flowering plants.* Opposite flowering.

ˌnon-inˈflammable ⇨ non-flammable.

ˌnon-interˈvention *u.n* (also ˌnon-ˌinterˈference) (*formal*) not taking sides or interfering in world politics, esp in quarrels between governments: *a policy¹ of non-intervention.*

ˌnon-ˈiron *adj* (of clothing) made of material that does not need to be ironed after washing: *He wears only non-iron shirts.*

ˌnon-obˈservance *u.n* (often — of s.t) (*formal*) failure to obey (a law, rule etc): *He was thrown out of school for non-observance of the rules.*

ˌnon-ˈpayment *u.n* (often — of s.t) failure to pay (rent, tax etc): *He was forced to leave his flat because of non-payment of rent.*

ˌnon-ˈpoisonous *adj* not poisonous(1).

ˌnon-ˈprofit-ˌmaking *adj* **1** organized to provide a service and not to make a profit: *It's a non-profit-making organization that offers a place to sleep for homeless people.* **2** not making the profit that one wants: *Your idea is a good one but it's non-profit-making.*

ˌnon-reˈnewable *adj* that cannot be renewed.

ˌnon-ˈresident *adj/c.n* (of a) person who does not live in a hotel etc: *It's a non-resident job but you can take your meals here. Non-residents are not allowed in the swimming area.*

ˌnon-reˈstrictive *attrib.adj* (*grammar*) (of a clause(1) or phrase(1)) that does not limit the (pro)noun it refers to, to a (more) particular one, e.g 'who is sitting over there' in 'My father, who is sitting over there, is sixty'. ⇨ restrictive clause.

ˌnon-ˈrust *adj* that does not rust(3).

ˌnon-ˈsmoker *c.n* Opposite smoker. **1** person who does not smoke. **2** part of a train etc in which one is not allowed to smoke.

ˌnon-ˈsmoking *attrib.adj* for non-smokers(1): *a non-smoking area of a cinema.* Opposite smoking(1).

ˌnon-ˈstandard *adj* not accepted as good, right, standard(2).

ˌnon-ˈstarter *c.n* (*informal*) person, idea, plan etc who/that has no chance of succeeding: *The plan was a non-starter from the beginning — we didn't think about it carefully enough.*

ˌnon-ˈstick *adj* (of pots, pans etc) having a surface that prevents food from sticking to it.

ˌnon-ˈstop *adj/adv* without stopping: *Is it a non-stop flight? She talked non-stop for four hours.*

ˌnon-ˈtoxic *adj* (*technical*) = non-poisonous.

ˌnon-ˈtransˈferable *adj* not transferable.

ˌnon-ˈunion *adj* not belonging to a trade union: *They only employ non-union labour.*

ˌnon-ˈviolence *u.n* refusal to use violent methods to gain s.t.

ˌnon-ˈviolent *adj* without using violence: *There are non-violent ways of winning equal rights.*

nonchalant /'nɒnʃələnt/ *adj* having or showing no interest, concern: *He was so nonchalant when I told him about it that I don't know what he really feels.*

ˈnonchalance *u.n.* **ˈnonchalantly** *adv.*

none /nʌn/ *adv* **1** in no way. (**none the poorer, healthier** etc **for s.t**) in no way (poorer, healthier etc) because of s.t: *His behaviour is none the better for that warning you gave him. My children didn't go to a private school and they're none the*

worse for it. **none too** . . . not very (good, fast, successful etc): *The beds in this hotel are none too comfortable.* **none the wiser** not knowing anything (more) about it: *If we leave before they arrive, they'll be none the wiser.*
▷ *pron* **2** not any/one: *'Is there any cake?' 'No there's none left.' None of us want(s) to go but we have to. None of that! I'll have none of your rudeness, young man.* **none but** only: *She will accept none but the best.* **none other than s.o/s.t** the very person, thing: *We were talking about my family when there was a knock at the door and it was none other than my parents.*

nonentity /nɒnˈentɪtɪ/ *c.n* (*pl* -ies) (*derog*) person who is not important or special in any way: *How can you appoint a nonentity to such an important position?*

nonetheless /ˌnʌnðəˈles/ *adv* = nevertheless.

nonplus /nɒnˈplʌs/ *tr.v* (-ss-) (usu passive) (cause s.o to) be confused, surprised, puzzled: *Her refusal completely nonplussed him. She was nonplussed by his rudeness.*

nonsense /ˈnɒnsəns/ *interj* **1** (way of saying that one disagrees strongly).
▷ *sing/u.n* **2** thing that is foolish and without meaning: *That's nonsense — how can you say such a thing! Don't talk such nonsense. What nonsense! That's just (a) silly nonsense.* **stand no** etc **nonsense** refuse to allow bad behaviour: *I will not stand any more of your nonsense — next time you do that you'll go straight home.*

nonsensical /nɒnˈsensɪkl/ *adj* foolish; that does not make sense: *It's nonsensical to expect them to pay. What a nonsensical thing to say!*

noodle /ˈnuːdl/ *c.n* (also *attrib*) flour, water and eggs made into long thin strips and boiled in water as food: *chicken-noodle soup. Should we have noodles or rice with the meat?*

nook /nʊk/ *c.n* small area that is hidden from view: *They bought a very old house that has lots of nooks for the children to play games in.* **nook and cranny** (*informal*) small place: *I've looked in all the nooks and crannies and I still can't find my glasses.*

noon /nuːn/ *unique n* 12 o'clock in the day: *We are expected there at noon.* Compare midnight.
'noon,day *attrib.adj* of the middle of the day; midday: *the noonday sun.*

no one ⇨ no.

noose /nuːs/ *c.n* loop(1) in a rope which is tied so that it becomes tighter when pulled: *Shall I show you how to tie a noose?*

nope /nəʊp/ *interj* (*slang*) no(5).

nor /nɔː/ *conj* (used after a negative statement) and not: *She didn't see it and nor did I. They aren't going — nor are we.* ⇨ neither . . . nor . . .

norm /nɔːm/ *c.n* standard of behaviour or level of s.t expected by most people: *live by the social norms of the people around one. Her reading and writing ability is below the norm of other children her age.*

normal /ˈnɔːml/ *adj* average, usual: *In normal conditions I can make one toy a day. Everything looked normal but I knew someone had been there. A person's normal temperature is about 37°.*

normality /nɔːˈmælɪtɪ/ *u.n* state of being normal: *It will take a long time before our lives are back to normality after such a terrible experience.*

normalization, -isation /ˌnɔːməlaɪˈzeɪʃən/ *u.n* fact or act of returning to normal.

'norma,lize, -ise *tr/intr.v* (cause (s.t) to) return to normal: *It took years for life to normalize after the earthquake.*

'normally *adv* **1** in a usual way: *Try to act normally otherwise they'll know something is wrong.* **2** usually; most times: *What time do you normally get back?*

north /nɔːθ/ *adj* (often with capital **N**) **1** in or coming from the direction that is on one's left when one is facing the rising sun; at a point on a compass(1) that is usu at the top in a drawing, *symb* **N**: *a north wind.* Opposite south(1).
▷ *adv* **2** towards a north(1) direction: *Drive north for about 10 km. We live north of London.* Opposite south(2). **up north** (*informal*) in/towards a north(1) direction. Opposite down south (⇨ south(*adv*)).
▷ *n* **3** *def/unique n* direction that is north(1). **4** *def.n* part of a country or of the world that is further north(1) than the rest of it: *People talk of a division between the North and the South.* **go north** go/ travel towards the north(3). **in the north** (**a**) in the direction that is north(1): *We could see clouds gathering in the north.* (**b**) in that part of the country or the world that is further north(1) than the rest: *He lives in the north.* **in the north of s.t** inside the northern part of s.t. (**to the**) **north of s.t** further north(1) than s.t.

'north,bound *adj* going towards the north(3).

,north'east *adj* **1** (often with capital **N**) coming from/in a direction or point on a compass(1) halfway between north(3) and east(3).
▷ *adv* **2** towards a northeast(1) direction.
▷ *def/unique n* **3** northeast(1) direction.

,north'easter *c.n* strong wind/storm from the northeast(3).

,north'easterly *adj* **1** from, in, towards, the northeast(3).
▷ *c.n* **2** wind from the northeast(3).

,north'eastern *adj* of, belonging to, the northeast(3), usu of a place.

northeastward /ˌnɔːˈθiːstwəd/ *adj* towards the northeast(3).

northeastwards /ˌnɔːˈθiːstwədz/ *adv* (US **,north'eastward**) towards the northeast(3); northeast(2).

northerly /ˈnɔːðəlɪ/ *adj* from, in, towards, the north(3): *a northerly wind. We travelled in a northerly direction.*

northern /ˈnɔːðən/ *adj* (often with capital **N**) of, belonging to, the north(3) of a place: *Northern Europe.*

Northerner /ˈnɔːðənə/ *c.n* person who lives in or comes from the northern part of a place.

,Northern 'Hemi,sphere *def.n* ⇨ hemisphere.

'northern,most *adj* that is furthest to the north(*n*).

'north,facing *adj* that looks towards, faces, the north(3): *a northfacing window.*

,North 'Pole *def.n* ⇨ pole²(1).

northward /ˈnɔːθwəd/ *adj* towards the north(3).

northwards /ˈnɔːθwədz/ *adv* (US **'northward**) towards the north(3).

,north'west *adj* (often with capital **N**) **1** coming from a direction or point on a compass(1) halfway between north(3) and west(3).
▷ *adv* **2** towards a northwest(1) direction.

⊳ *def/unique n* **3** northwest(1) direction.

,north'wester *c.n* strong wind/storm from the northwest(3).

,north'westerly *adj* **1** from, in, towards, the northwest(3).

⊳ *c.n* **2** wind from the northwest(3).

,north'western *adj* of, belonging to, the northwest(3).

northwestward /,nɔː'θ'westwəd/ *adj* towards the northwest(3).

northwestwards /,nɔː:θ'westwədz/ *adv* (US **,north'westward**) towards the northwest(3); northwest(2).

Nos *written abbr* numbers. ⇒ No.

nose /nəuz/ *c.n* **1** part of the face used for breathing and smelling. **2** sense of smell: *My dog has an excellent nose.* **3** (usu (*have*) *a — for s.t*) (*fig*) ability to find/discover something without too much difficulty: *He has a nose for trouble. She has a nose for a good story.* **4** thing that is the shape or is in the position of, a nose: *the nose of a plane.* **blow one's nose** hold a handkerchief/tissue(3) over one's nose and blow into it to remove dirt or extra mucus. **cut off one's nose to spite one's face** (*fig*) spoil s.t for oneself because of anger and an attempt to harm s.o else. **follow one's nose** (a) go in the direction that feels right. (b) go straight. **keep one's nose clean** (*fig*; *informal*) keep out of trouble. **keep one's (big) nose out of s.t** (*fig*; *informal*) not interfere in s.t; not take an interest in s.t (esp s.t that does not concern one): *Keep your nose out of my private life — it's none of your business!* **keep s.o's nose to the grindstone** ⇒ grindstone(*n*). **lead s.o by the nose** (*fig*; *informal*) make s.o do whatever one wants her/him to do: *If you always lead your children by the nose they'll never be able to do anything by themselves.* **look down one's nose at s.o/s.t** show that one feels superior(3), does not like s.o/s.t. **pay through the nose (for s.t)** (*fig*; *informal*) pay too much money (for s.t): *I paid through the nose for that coat but it was worth it!* **pick one's nose** clean one's nostril by using one's fingers. **poke/stick one's nose in(to s.t)** (*fig*; *informal*) interfere with s.t that does not concern one: *She's always poking her nose into everything. I wish you'd stop sticking your nose into my affairs — they do not concern you.* **put s.o's nose out of joint** (*fig*; *informal*) hurt/offend s.o. **rub s.o's nose in it** (*fig*; *informal*) remind s.o continuously about her/his mistake or failure: *I know I made a mistake — you don't have to rub my nose in it.* **turn up one's nose (at s.o/s.t)** (*fig*; *informal*) treat s.o/s.t as if he/she/it is not good enough: *They don't talk to us — we're the poor relations so they turn up their noses at us. He turned up his nose at the cheap wine we provided with lunch.* **under s.o's (very) nose** (*fig*; *informal*) (a) directly in front of s.o; obvious: *I found my glasses — they were right under my nose all the time.* (b) while one is present: *They must have stolen the money from under my nose.* **wipe one's nose (on/with s.t)** clean one's nose (on one's sleeve, with a handkerchief etc) (and stop crying).

⊳ *v* **5** *tr/intr.v* (often — *one's way*) move forward carefully: *They nosed their way slowly through the tall grass. The boat nosed (its way) between the rocks.* **6** *tr.v* (usu — *s.t out*) discover (s.t) (as

if) by smelling: *The dog nosed out the rabbit. The child nosed out the biscuits his mother had hidden. The police nosed out the thieves.* **7** *tr/intr.v* (usu — *about/around* (for s.t)) search (for s.t) (esp s.t that does not concern one): *She's been nosing around your desk. What are you doing nosing about here?* **8** *intr.v* (usu — *into* s.t) interfere (in s.o else's affairs); try to be included in things that do not concern one: *He's always nosing into our affairs.*

'nose,dive *c.n* **1** very fast fall with the front first: *The plane went into a nosedive and crashed.*

⊳ *intr.v* **2** fall very fast with the front (of the plane) first. **3** (also **dive**) (of prices etc) fall heavily.

'nosy *adj* (*-ier, -iest*) (also **'nosey**) (*derog*; *informal*) taking too much interest in other people's affairs: *Don't be so nosy! She's such a nosy person and always wants to know everything.*

,nosy-'parker *c.n* (*derog*; *slang*) person who takes too much interest in other people's affairs.

nosh /nɒʃ/ *u.n* (*informal*) **1** food: *What's the nosh like there?* **2** act of eating: *Do you want a quick nosh before we go?*

⊳ *tr/intr.v* **3** (*informal*) eat (esp small amounts of food): *What are you noshing?*

nostalgia /nɒ'stældʒə/ *sing/u.n* (often — *for* s.t) (*formal*) sadness because of a memory or longing for s.t in the past: *Seeing her mother gave her a nostalgia for her youth. The film filled her with nostalgia for her home and children.*

no'stalgic /nɒ'stældʒik/ *adj* of/causing nostalgia: *The film made me feel so nostalgic.*

no'stalgically *adv.*

nostril /'nɒstril/ *c.n* one of the two openings in the nose.

nosy ⇒ nose.

not /nɒt/ *adj* (often shortened to *-n't*, esp after forms of the verbs 'have' and 'be' (except 'am'), e.g: *wouldn't, needn't, didn't, hasn't, aren't*) **1** (used to make a negative): *He's not coming* (or *He isn't coming*). *I didn't see anything* (or *did not see anything*). 'Is the shop open?' 'No, *it's not.*' **2** (used to put verbs that have no subject into the negative): *He told me not to come. I asked you not to make a noise.* **3** (used as the object of verbs such as 'suppose', 'hope', 'believe', 'think', 'expect', 'must', 'appear' and 'be afraid' to form the negative): *'Did she win?' 'It appears not.' 'Are we going to be too late?' 'I hope not.' 'Aren't they coming then?' 'I suppose not.' 'Are you coming to the party tonight?' 'I'm afraid not.'* Compare so[3]. **not a/one (single)** *s.o/s.t* not even one person, animal or thing: *There's not a (single) piece of bread to eat in this house! Is there not one drop left? There was not a person/soul in the street. He didn't leave me one single chocolate from that whole box.* **not at all** (a) not in any way: *'Are you hungry?' 'Not at all.' I was not at all frightened.* (b) (as a polite reply) it is a pleasure: *'Thank you for your advice.' 'Not at all.'* **not half!** ⇒ half(*adv*). **not half bad (at s.t)** ⇒ bad(*adj*). **not half as bad, ill** etc **as (expected** etc) ⇒ half(*adv*). **not only . . . but (also)** . . . (used when mentioning an additional thing): *She not only plays the piano but she sings too. He not only came first but he also broke the record.* **not that** although one doesn't (care, mind etc), wouldn't (do it): *'Where were you last night — not that I care, of course?'*

I told him that if he didn't pay me more I'd leave — not that I would!

notable ⇨ note.

notary /ˈnəʊtərɪ/ *c.n* (*pl* -ies) (also **,notary ˈpublic**) official who does particular kinds of legal(2) work, e.g making sure that a (legal(2)) document(1) has the correct signature on it.

notation /nəʊˈteɪʃən/ *n* **1** *u.n* use of signs, symbols etc to represent numbers, musical notes etc: mathematical *notation*. **2** *c.n* signs and symbols etc that represent numbers, musical notes etc when written down.

notch /nɒtʃ/ *c.n* **1** small V-shaped cut.
▷ *tr.v* **2** cut a notch(1) in/on (s.t): *He notched the tree at the level of his head every year so he could see how much he was growing.* **notch s.t up** gain/ win s.t: *How many goals have you notched up this season?*

note /nəʊt/ *n* **1** *c.n* (usu *pl*) thing written down to remind one of s.t, esp s.t heard or seen: *Can I borrow your* lecture(1) *notes? She wrote notes for her speech on small cards.* **2** *c.n* short explanation about s.t written in a book etc: *My copy of 'Hamlet' is full of notes written by my brother when he was studying it.* ⇨ footnote. **3** *c.n* short letter: *Write me a note when you've fixed the date. Give me a note about this new idea of yours.* **4** *c.n* amount of money in paper form: *a five pound note. English bank notes come in amounts of five, ten, twenty and fifty pounds.* **5** *c.n* musical sound: *She can't sing a note. I'll never reach that high note.* **6** *c.n* written or printed musical note(5). **7** *sing.n* (usu *a* — of s.t) sign (of fear, pleasure etc): *There was a note of fear in her voice. The meeting ended on a high* (pleasant, optimistic etc) *note.* **compare notes (with s.o)** share ideas, opinions etc about s.t (with s.o): *After the performance they had a cup of coffee and compared notes.* **make a note of s.t** record s.t: *I'll make a note of the books you want to borrow. She made a note of the date in her diary.* **of note** having fame, importance: *an actor of some note.* **take note (of s.t)** listen carefully (to what s.o says) and remember: *Take note of all he says and do exactly what he tells you.*
▷ *tr.v* **8** (often — *s.t down*) write (notes(1)): *The police officer noted* (*down*) *my name and address.* **9** (*formal*) notice (s.t): *She noted a strange smell in the room.*

notable /ˈnəʊtəbl/ *adj* **1** (*formal*) who/that deserves attention: *He has written a notable book on the disease. A number of notable speakers have been invited to talk tonight.*
▷ *c.n* **2** (*formal*) important/notable(1) person: *Which notables have accepted your invitation?*

ˈnotably *adv* **1** particularly: *A number of students did very well in the examinations, notably Liz James.* **2** noticeably: *His performance on stage was notably better on the second night.*

ˈnote,book *c.n* book of paper for writing notes(1) in.

ˈnoted *adj* (often — *as/for s.t*) well known: *She's a noted writer. He is noted as an excellent cook. She is noted for her work on bees.*

ˈnote,paper *u.n* paper for writing notes(3).

ˈnote,worthy *adj* (usu *pred*) unusual, important, worth mentioning: *Did anything noteworthy happen in the office while I was away?*

nothing /ˈnʌθɪŋ/ *adv* **1** (often — *like s.o/s.t*) not in any way (like s.o/s.t): *It was nothing like he said*

it would be. She's nothing like her sister. **nothing like/near as . . . as s.o/s.t** not at all as (ill, bad etc) as s.o/s.t: *nothing like as ugly as his father*; *nothing near as painful as you'd think it'd be.*
▷ *c.n* **2** person, animal, thing without value, worth; the number nought, 0: *He's a nothing — he won't be able to help you in any way.* **sweet nothings** words of love that are not very serious: *He whispers sweet nothings in all the girls' ears.*
▷ *pron* **3** not a thing; not anything: *There's nothing left to eat. Nothing I can say satisfies you. I know nothing about it. Is there nothing we can do to help? Nothing is as bad as you think it is. Have you got nothing to do? She said nothing that we haven't already heard.* Compare anything, something. **be nothing (compared to s.o/s.t)** be unable to match (what s.o else is/does): *'I swim one mile a day.' 'That's nothing — I do three times that!' Our worries are nothing compared to theirs.* **care nothing for s.o/s.t** not care at all about s.o/ s.t: *I care nothing for his money.* **come to nothing** be unsuccessful: *Their plan to open a restaurant came to nothing.* **for nothing (a)** without having to pay (money); free: *He gave me the batteries for nothing.* **(b)** without reason, need, a good result: *Did we do all that work for nothing? It's not for nothing that he's been bringing her gifts and flowers all this time.* **have nothing on (a)** have no clothes on. **(b)** have made no plans, promises etc: *I'll work this evening since I've nothing on.* **have nothing on s.o** have no proof that s.o has done s.t illegal, wrong: *You can't arrest me — you have nothing on me.* **have nothing to do with s.o/s.t (a)** refuse to deal with s.o/s.t: *He's had nothing to do with that company since he left it.* **(b)** not be connected with s.t; not be part of s.t: *'What about Peter?' 'He had nothing to do with it.'* This has nothing to do with the robbery. **(c)** not concern/ interest s.o: *I don't have to ask him whether I can come — it has nothing to do with him.* **look like nothing on earth** look very bad, ill etc: *I don't know where he found those clothes — he looks like nothing on earth.* **make nothing of s.t (a)** be unable to understand s.t: *I can make nothing of this strange message he left me.* **(b)** treat s.t as being unimportant: *He made nothing of having to pay thousands of pounds' worth of damages.* ⇨ think nothing of s.t. **mean nothing to s.o (a)** ⇨ nothing to s.o(a). **(b)** have no meaning for s.o; not able to be understood by s.o: *This message means nothing to me — what is it trying to say?* **next to nothing** almost nothing: *They paid me next to nothing when I worked there.* **nothing at all** absolutely nothing: *There's nothing at all you can do to help her now.* **nothing but** nothing except for: *We've had nothing but a sandwich all day. You're nothing but a cheat and a liar.* **nothing doing (a)** absolutely not: *'Can I use your car tonight?' 'Nothing doing — not after the way you treated it last time!'* **(b)** no chance of s.t happening: *I tried to see him again today but there was nothing doing.* **(c)** nothing happening (at s.w): *There's nothing doing at the club tonight so let's go to the cinema.* **nothing for it but (to do s.t)** nothing else to do except (to do s.t): *When it began to get dark there was nothing for it but to find a place to sleep.* **nothing in s.t/it** no truth in a story etc: *There's nothing in what he says.* **nothing like (a)** no other thing the same

as: *There's nothing like this feeling in the whole world. Nothing like it is produced in this country.* (**b**) nothing better than: *There's nothing like a fire and a good book on cold wet weekends. There's nothing like a good friend when one is in trouble.* **nothing like as bad**, **good** etc (**as s.o/s.t**) not nearly as bad, good etc (as s.o/s.t). **nothing much** not a lot: *'What's on television tonight?' 'Nothing much.' 'What's news?' 'Nothing much.'* **nothing of the kind** (used to give force) absolutely not that: *I said nothing of the kind. You'll do nothing of the kind — you're staying home tonight.* **nothing to s.o** (**a**) not important to s.o: *We used to be close but she means/is nothing to me now.* (**b**) ⇒ mean nothing to s.o(b). **nothing to s.t** no difficulty (about s.t): *He'll have no trouble learning how to use the machine — there's nothing to it.* **nothing whatsoever** = nothing at all. **think nothing of** (**doing**) **s.t** consider s.t to be simple, ordinary: *She thinks nothing of baking eight loaves of bread a day.* **Think nothing of it!** (used as a polite way of saying) Don't let it worry you! **to say nothing of s.o/s.t** (that is) without mentioning (other people, things); as well as: *He has six children by his first two marriages to say nothing of the boy he has since adopted.*

'nothingness *u.n* state of not being, happening etc; state of feeling empty and without purpose: *She was left with a feeling of nothingness after her children left home.*

notice /'nəʊtɪs/ *n* **1** *c.n* printed/written information of an event that has happened or is going to happen: *Did you see the notice about the change in the arrangements? There will be a notice on the board informing you of the date and time of the next meeting.* **2** *u.n* (often give — to s.o) advice of an intention to dismiss s.o or to leave a job: *We have all been given two weeks' notice which is not enough time to look for another job. I do not intend to give/hand in my notice until I've found another job.* **3** *u.n* (esp **bring s.t**, **come**, **to s.o's** —) attention: *He promised to bring the matter to the manager's notice. It has come to my notice that you have not paid taxes for five years.* (**do s.t**) **at short**, **an hour's**, **a moment's** etc **notice** with only a little time, an hour etc, to prepare: *Can you start work at short notice? We had to leave at a moment's notice so I left everything behind.* **notice to quit** ⇒ quit(*v*). **sit up and take notice** become interested, pay attention etc suddenly. **take notice of s.o/s.t** (usu negative) treat/regard (s.o/s.t) in a serious way: *Don't take any notice of her — she doesn't mean what she said. I tried to warn her but she took no notice. He never takes any notice of me — I'm too young.* **until further notice** until more information is provided: *The restaurant will be closed for repairs from 1 May until further notice.* **without notice** without any warning: *The management reserves the right to change the prices without notice.*
▷ *tr/intr.v* **4** see/observe (s.t): *Did you notice how fat she's getting? He noticed that she was wearing a new ring. He left without noticing the letter she'd left for him. Did you notice anyone playing near the river? Did you notice whether there was a light on when you left? I didn't notice who was there.*

'noticeable *adj* able to be noticed(4) easily: *Is this mark noticeable? Is there any noticeable difference between the two rooms?*

'notice ,board *c.n* large board on which to pin, stick etc notices(1).

notify /'nəʊtɪ,faɪ/ *tr.v* (*-ies*, *-ied*) (usu — s.o about s.o/s.t; — s.o of s.t) (*formal*) inform/tell (s.o) (about s.t): *Have you been notified about the change in the programme? I shall have to notify the police about this. It is important to keep us notified of all his movements.*

notification /,nəʊtɪfɪ'keɪʃən/ *c/u.n* (*formal*) (example of) act or fact of informing; thing that informs one of s.t: *Have you received any notification of the changes to be made?*

notion /'nəʊʃən/ *c.n* idea, thought: *I had a notion that you'd be here. What a strange notion!* **have no notion**; **not have the faintest/slightest/vaguest notion** not know/understand s.t at all: *I have not the slightest notion what you're talking about. I don't have the vaguest notion where he is.*

notional /'nəʊʃənl/ *adj* based on an idea but not yet proved: *a notional profit.*

notorious /nəʊ'tɔːrɪəs/ *adj* well known (esp for s.t bad or not quite accepted): *a notorious bank robber; notorious as a dancer in certain clubs. He's notorious for his attacks on the government.*

notoriety /,nəʊtə'raɪɪtɪ/ *u.n* fact or state of being notorious: *His speeches won him notoriety throughout the country.*

no'toriously *adv* in a way that is well known: *He is a notoriously bad liar.*

notwithstanding /,nɒtwɪð'stændɪŋ/ *adv* **1** (*formal*) in spite of this; nevertheless: *Notwithstanding, all the work was finished on time. We all said they'd never manage it alone but they did it notwithstanding.*
▷ *prep* **2** (*formal*) in spite of: *Notwithstanding his lack of practice, he performed well. The weather notwithstanding, we had an excellent walk.*

nougat /'nuːgɑː/ *u.n* kind of white chewy(2) sweet with nuts etc in it.

nought /nɔːt/ *n* **1** *c.n* (*mathematics*) number 0: *A thousand has three noughts. You write one point nought as 1.0 and point nought three as 0.03. Three centimetres written in metres is 0.003 (nought point nought nought three).* Compare nil, zero(1). **2** *u.n* (esp **come to** —) (*old use*) nothing. ⇒ naught.

noun /naʊn/ *c.n* (*grammar*) word used to name s.o/s.t (and shown in this dictionary as *n*): *Peter is a proper noun. In the sentence 'The child didn't eat his food' 'child' and 'food' are both nouns. 'Beauty', 'freedom' and 'happiness' are also nouns.* Compare pronoun. **count(able) noun** ⇒ count[1]. **definite (plural) noun** ⇒ definite. **uncountable noun** ⇒ uncountable. **unique noun** ⇒ unique.

nourish /'nʌrɪʃ/ *tr.v* **1** (esp of food) cause (s.o, an animal) to grow and keep healthy: *Children often don't like food that will nourish them.* **2** feed (esp the soil, skin etc): *Manure nourishes the soil.* ⇒ undernourished. **3** (*fig*) cause (fear, doubt, anger, feeling etc) to grow: *Not talking about problems usually nourishes them.*

'nourishing *adj* (esp of food) providing what is healthy: *Eat nourishing food not cakes and sweets.*

'nourishment *u.n* (*formal*) food that encourages healthy growth: *Powdered milk does not usually provide babies with enough nourishment.*

nouveau riche /,nuːvəʊ 'riːʃ/ *c.n* (*French*) (pl

nouveaux riches /ˌnuːvəʊ ˈriːʃ/) (usu *derog*) person who has recently become rich and enjoys a high standard of living, esp in a vulgar way.

novel¹ /ˈnɒvl/ *c.n* long story about imaginary people: *I have read all of Dickens' novels.*

novelist *c.n* writer of novels¹: *I'm reading the life-story of the novelist Henry James.*

novel² /ˈnɒvl/ *adj* new; not previously known, experienced or thought of: *It's a novel idea if not very practical.*

novelty /ˈnɒvltɪ/ *n* (*pl -ies*) **1** *c.n* thing that is new or not yet familiar: *She'll enjoy the first few weeks while everything is still a novelty.* **2** *u.n* newness: *Once the novelty has gone he'll lose interest.* **3** *c.n* (usu *pl*) cheaply made toy, ornament etc: *The novelties in that shop would make good cheap presents to take home.*

November /nəʊˈvembə/ *c/unique n* (also *attrib*) (*written abbr* Nov) 11th month of the year: *There are thirty days in November. She was born on November 5* (say 'November the fifth' or 'the fifth of November'). *This is typical November weather.*

novice /ˈnɒvɪs/ *n* **1** *c.n* person who is beginning s.t, still learning: *He can't play very well — he's still a novice.* **2** *c.n* person training to be a monk, nun.

noviciate /nəˈvɪʃɪət/ *c/u.n* (also **no'vitiate**) (period of) being a novice(2): *She's doing her noviciate.*

now /naʊ/ *adv* **1** at this very moment; immediately: *I told you to do it now.* **2** (at) this moment, the present time: *Where are you working now? What are you doing now? We've been living here for ten years now.* **3** (used in stories or descriptions in the past tense) at that time; then: *They were now very tired and hungry.* **4** because of that: *Now I'll never be able to go there again. Now we're really in trouble.* **5** (used in exclamations or to introduce a statement, warning etc): *Now stop all this fighting — it's enough. Do be careful now — it's very dangerous on those cliffs. Now look what's happened!* (**every**) **now and again/then** sometimes; from time to time: *I go and visit her every now and again. We watch television now and then but not often.* **just now** ⇒ just². **Now now! Now then!** (used before a warning or statement of disapproval): *Now now! That wasn't a very nice thing to do, was it? Now then, what's happening here?* **now . . . , now/then . . .** at one moment (s.t happens) and at another moment (s.t different happens): *Now you see it — now you don't. Now it's hot then it's cold — no one knows what to wear.* **now that** because (s.t has happened): *Will you start thinking about having a family now that you're married?* **There now** (**a**) (used as an expression when comforting s.o): *There now, it's not so serious — don't worry!* (**b**) = there²: *There now, I told you he wouldn't fall and he didn't.*

▷ *unique n* **6** the present time: *Now is a good time for buying flowers.* **as of now** from this moment: *As of now everyone over the age of twelve will have to pay the whole amount for a ticket.* ⇒ from now/then on. **by now** by this time: *They'll have arrived by now.* (**enough**) (**s.t**) **for now** (enough) (s.t) for this time, until another time: *That's enough (work) for now — you can do some more tomorrow.* **from now on** ⇒ from. **up to, till, until, now** before, until, this time: *Everything*

has been working very well up till now. I've never been afraid until now.

nowadays /ˈnaʊədeɪz/ *adj* during the present time (and opposed to other times): *Travel is much easier nowadays.*

nowhere /ˈnəʊˌweə/ *adv* in/to no place: '*Where are you going?*' '*Nowhere really.*' *There's nowhere to go. They are nowhere to be found.* **from**, **out of**, **nowhere** from an unexpected place: *We looked for him everywhere and suddenly he appeared from nowhere. The winner seemed to come out of nowhere.* **get s.o nowhere** not help s.o get the result wanted: *Shouting will get you nowhere. Your threats will get you nowhere.* **go nowhere** buy very little: *Nowadays £10 goes nowhere.* **go**, **lead/take s.o**, **nowhere** not help to find a solution: *All this talk is leading us nowhere. The discussion is going nowhere — let's stop.* **miles from nowhere** very far away from a town etc: *The farm is miles from nowhere so we must take everything we need with us.* **nowhere near** (**s.o/ s.t**) (**a**) not nearly (s.t): *I'm nowhere near finished/ ready. That's nowhere near enough time/money.* (**b**) not at all close to (s.o/s.t): *We were nowhere near where we thought we were.*

noxious /ˈnɒkʃəs/ *adj* (*formal*) harmful, poisonous: *Is that a noxious gas?*

nozzle /ˈnɒzl/ *c.n* narrow piece that is fitted to the end of a pipe for directing the air, gas or liquid.

-n't /-nt/ = not. ⇒ not.

nuance /ˈnjuːɑːns/ *c.n* very small difference in meaning, colour etc: *The artist has produced lovely nuances of blue in the painting. It was difficult to understand the nuances in his argument.*

nub /nʌb/ *c.n* (usu *sing*) (most) important point: *That's the nub of his whole argument.*

nubile /ˈnjuːbaɪl/ *adj* (of young girls) attractive and the right age for marriage.

nucleus /ˈnjuːklɪəs/ *c.n* (*pl* nuclei /ˈnjuːklɪˌaɪ/) **1** (*biology*) central part of an animal or plant cell(4) that controls growth and development. **2** (*physics*) central part of an atom(1) that consists of protons and neutrons. **3** central part of s.t around which other things develop, collect, happen: *When she is having problems she always likes to return to her grandparents' home which is the nucleus of her family life.*

nuclear /ˈnjuːklɪə/ *adj* (usu *attrib*) **1** of a nucleus: *the nuclear family.* **2** of/using energy(2) or power that is produced by splitting the nucleus(2) of an atom(1): *nuclear power.* **3** of or referring to military(1) power that includes nuclear(2) weapons: *a nuclear war.*

nuclear 'bomb *c.n* very powerful and destructive bomb that uses nuclear(2) power.

nuclear dis'armament *u.n* agreement not to use, develop or collect nuclear(2) weapons.

nuclear 'energy *u.n* modern form of power produced by splitting the nucleus(2).

nuclear 'fall-out *u.n* = fall-out(3).

nuclear 'family *c.n* social group consisting of a married man and woman and their children.

nuclear 'fission *u.n* splitting of the nucleus(2) of an atom.

nuclear 'physics *pl.n* study of the nucleus(2), its behaviour and what it consists of etc.

nuclear 'physi,cist/'scientist *c.n* person who studies or is skilled in nuclear physics.

,nuclear 'power *u.n* **1** nuclear energy. **2** country that has nuclear(3) weapons.

,nuclear-'powered *adj* working by nuclear energy.

,nuclear 'power ,plant/,station *c.n* place where nuclear energy is produced.

,nuclear re'actor *c.n* machine that produces nuclear energy.

,nuclear 'scientist ⇒ nuclear physicist.

,nuclear 'war *c/u.n* (example of a) war using nuclear(2) weapons: *A nuclear war would destroy the world. Is it possible to avoid nuclear war?*

nude /njuːd/ *adj/c.n* (of a person) who is not wearing any clothes: *a nude* statue. *Was that a nude man I saw run past?* **in the nude** not wearing any clothes: *I love swimming in the nude.*

'nudism *u.n* practice of not wearing any clothes because it is believed to be healthy.

'nudist *c.n* (also *attrib*) person who practises nudism.

'nudity *u.n* fact or state of not wearing any clothes.

nudge /nʌdʒ/ *c.n* **1** slight push, usu with the elbow or side of the arm/shoulder: *Give him a nudge — he's fallen asleep.*

▷ *tr.v* **2** give (s.o) a nudge(1): *He nudged his sister to try to warn her not to say any more.* **nudge one's way through (s.t)** push oneself through (a crowd etc).

nugget /'nʌgɪt/ *c.n* piece of metal (esp gold) found in the ground: *a gold nugget.*

nuisance /'njuːsəns/ *c.n* person or thing causing trouble/discomfort: *Sorry to be a nuisance but can you give me a lift to town? Don't be such a nuisance! It's a nuisance to have to work tonight but I did promise to finish it. What a nuisance!* **make a nuisance of oneself** be annoying.

null /nʌl/ *adj* having no value; useless. **null and void** having no legal(2) force.

nullify /'nʌlɪ,faɪ/ *tr.v* (-*ies*, -*ied*) cause (s.t) to have no effect esp in law: *This will nullifies all previous wills. Your behaviour last night nullified all your efforts to please me.*

numb /nʌm/ *adj* having lost the ability to feel or move: *My toes have gone numb (with cold). The news left her numb with shock.*

▷ *tr.v* **2** cause (s.o/s.t) to feel numb(1): *The dentist gave him an injection to numb his mouth. The medicine numbed the pain.*

'numbness *u.n.*

number /'nʌmbə/ *c.n* **1** (*abbr* No, *pl* Nos) word/figure that shows how many: *My lucky number is four. What number is your house, 34 or 35? What's your room number? You're in room No 6. We have to do Nos 1–20 in Exercise A.* ⇒ cardinal, ordinal. **2** (usu *a — of s.o/s.t*) several; (large) quantity (of people or things): *I'll leave you a number of books to choose from. I have a number of things to do before I can leave the office. A number of people have refused to come.* **3** dance, song, piece of music: *Play that number again. That's a rather sad number — sing something cheerful.* **4** one of the magazines, journals(1) etc produced monthly or weekly etc: *I didn't receive last month's number of 'New Internationalist'.* ⇒ issue(2). **by force/weight of numbers** because of having more people, soldiers etc. **few in number** not many: *We were few in number but we managed to do a*

lot of work. **in number** forming a group of the stated number of people/things: *We were six in number.* **without number** (almost) too many to be counted: *We waited days without number for some news.*

▷ *tr.v* **5** give a number to (s.o/s.t): *Have you numbered the pages? We were all numbered as we went in.* ⇒ unnumbered(2). **6** add up to, be a total of, (a certain/stated number) altogether: *We numbered fifty in all. The complaints we received can be numbered in the thousands.* ⇒ unnumbered(1). **7** (usu — *s.o/s.t among s.t*) include (s.o/s.t as s.t): *She numbers you among the most exciting people she's ever met.* **back number** ⇒ back. **be numbered** be going to end soon: *Her days as head of this organization are numbered.* **opposite number** ⇒ opposite.

,number 'one *def/sing.n* most important person, e.g in an organization: *There's no point in talking to anyone except the number one in this office.*

'number ,plate *c.n* piece of metal with letters and numbers showing the registration(1) number of a vehicle.

'numbers *pl.n* arithmetic: *I've never been very good at numbers.*

numbskull ⇒ numskull.

numeral /'njuːmərəl/ *adj/c.n* (of a) figure, sign that represents a number: *Numbers written like 1,2,3 etc are called 'Arabic numerals'.*

numerate /'njuːmərɪt/ *adj* (*formal*) having some knowledge of mathematics and science. Compare literate.

numerator /'njuːmə,reɪtə/ *c.n* (*mathematics*) number that is above the line in a fraction: *In ⁶⁄₇ 6 is the numerator.* Compare denominator.

numerical /njuː'merɪkl/ *adj* of/using numbers: *a numerical system of grades(3) for an examination.* (**in**) **numerical order** (according to) the correct order of the numbers: *Put these pages in numerical order.* Compare alphabetical.

nu'merically *adv* **1** in size of numbers: *Their group is numerically greater but we have more experience in our group.* **2** using numbers: *You say we've made more money this year — can you show me how well the sales have done numerically?*

numerous /'njuːmərəs/ *adj* (*formal*) many: *We've had numerous complaints about the quality of the food. I've told you numerous times (or on numerous occasions) that I don't eat meat.*

numskull /'nʌm,skʌl/ *c.n* (also **'numb,skull**) (*informal*) fool; silly, stupid person: *Don't be such a numskull.*

nun /nʌn/ *c.n* woman who has taken religious vows(1) and chosen to work for the church. Compare monk.

nunnery /'nʌnəri/ *c.n* (*pl* -*ies*) place where nuns live. ⇒ convent. Compare monastery.

nuptial /'nʌpʃəl/ *attrib.adj* (*formal*) of marriage: *nuptial happiness.*

'nuptials *pl.n* (*formal*) wedding.

nurse /nɜːs/ *c.n* **1** person who cares for people who are sick etc, esp in a hospital: *She's training to become a nurse. He's a male nurse in a large hospital.* **2** (also **'nurse,maid**) woman who looks after young children. **State enrolled nurse** ⇒ state. **State registered nurse** ⇒ state.

▷ *v* **3** *tr/intr.v* care for (s.o who is sick etc), esp

in a hospital. **4** *tr/intr.v* feed (a baby) milk from one's breast(1): *Mother asks if you will wait a few minutes while she finishes nursing (the baby).* **5** *tr.v* hold (s.o/s.t) very gently, carefully: *The little boy nursed the baby bird in his hands.* **6** *tr.v* take great care of (s.t): *She nurses that kitten as if it were a baby.* **nurse a fear**, **grudge**, **hope** etc keep in one's mind a fear etc: *She is still nursing a grudge(1) against him for leaving her and her child so many years ago. He nursed a hope that his wife would live.* **nurse s.o back to health** look after s.o until he/she is healthy again.

'nurse,maid ⇒ nurse(2).

nursery /'nɜːsrɪ/ *c.n* (*pl -ies*) **1** room for a young child: *They are decorating a nursery for the new baby.* **2** place where young plants, trees etc are grown.

'nurseryman *c.n* (*pl -men*) person who works in a nursery(2).

'nursery ,rhyme *c.n* short traditional poem or song for young children.

'nursery ,school *c.n* first school for children from the ages of 3 to 5.

'nursing *u.n* **1** profession of a nurse: *She always wanted to study nursing.* **2** act of looking after s.o/s.t: *This patient needs a lot of careful nursing.*

'nursing-,home *c.n* place that is smaller than a hospital where old or sick people can live.

nurture /'nɜːtʃə/ *u.n* **1** (*formal*) help in developing and growing.

▷ *tr.v* **2** (*formal*) help(s.o/s.t) develop, grow etc: *He nurtures his mind by reading good books. He's been nurturing his love for her since he first saw her.*

nut /nʌt/ *c.n* **1** fruit inside a hard dry shell: *She put a bowl of nuts on the table. I don't like salted nuts. We have a* **hazel-nut** *tree and a* **walnut(1)** *tree in our garden. It's impossible to grow* **peanuts** *in this country.* **2** small round piece of metal with a threaded (⇒ thread(3)) hole in the middle where a bolt²(2) is screwed to hold s.t together. **3** (*slang*) head: *That apple hit me on the nut.* ⇒ off one's nut. **4** (*derog; slang*) slightly foolish, mad person: *She's a nut — she wears the strangest clothes.* ⇒ nutcase, nuts(1), nutty(2). **a hard/tough nut to crack** (*fig; informal*) a difficult person, problem etc to understand. **do one's nut** (*slang*) be very worried. **off one's nut** (*slang*) not in one's right mind; mad; silly; crazy: *He's off his nut!* **the nuts and bolts (of s.t)** the simple facts (about s.t): *Before you buy your own business go and work somewhere where you can learn the nuts and bolts about running a business.* **wing nut** ⇒ wing.

'nut,case *c.n* (*derog; slang*) person who is slightly foolish, mad or does mad things: *She's a complete nutcase.*

'nut,cracker *c.n* (also *a pair of* —s) tool for breaking the hard shell of a nut: *Pass the nutcrackers please.*

'nut,house *c.n* (*derog, slang*) mental hospital.

nuts *pred.adj* **1** (*slang*) crazy; behaving in a foolish, slightly mad way: *You must be nuts — I'd never do that!* **be nuts about s.o/s.t** (*slang*) be in love with s.o; love (doing) s.t: *He's nuts about her. She's nuts about horses.* **go nuts** (*slang*) become crazy, mad: *I'll go nuts if I don't get some peace and quiet.*

▷ *interj* **2** = nonsense(1).

'nut,shell *c.n* hard covering of a nut. (**put s.t**)

in a nutshell (*fig; informal*) (express s.t) very simply, directly and in a few words only: (*To put my feelings about him*) *in a nutshell — he's a fool.*

'nutty *adj* (*-ier, -iest*) **1** containing, tasting of, nuts: *Have you any nutty chocolates?* **2** (*derog; slang*) crazy, slightly mad: *She's nutty!* **as nutty as a fruitcake** ⇒ fruitcake. **be nutty about s.o/s.t** (*informal*) be very fond of s.o/s.t: *He's nutty about his baby.*

nutmeg /'nʌtmeg/ *c/u.n* hard seed that has a strong smell and is ground(1) into powder and used to flavour food.

nutrient /'njuːtrɪənt/ *c.n* (*formal*) substance (in food) that helps growth and development: *It is important to add nutrients to the soil after harvesting.*

nutriment /'njuːtrɪmənt/ *c/u.n* substance that encourages healthy growth and development: *A drop of this gives the soil all the nutriment it needs to produce healthy plants.*

nutrition /njuːˈtrɪʃən/ *u.n* (*formal*) **1** study of the value of different kinds of foods for the body. **2** act of providing or receiving healthy food: *She takes a lot of care about her children's nutrition.*

nu'tritional *adj* (usu *attrib*) (*formal*) of nutrition(2): *Is there any nutritional value in white bread?*

nutritious /njuːˈtrɪʃəs/ *adj* (*formal*) (of food) providing the body with substances that encourage growth and development: *nutritious food. Her meals are always very nutritious.*

nuzzle /'nʌzl/ *tr/intr.v* push the nose against (s.o/s.t): *The dog nuzzled (against) her neck/ arm.*

NW *written abbr* northwest(ern).

nylon /'naɪlɒn/ *adj/u.n* (made of a) kind of artificial material used to make rope, clothes etc: *I can't wear nylon clothes. The strongest rope contains nylon.*

nylons *pl.n* stockings made of nylon.

nymph /nɪmf/ *c.n* **1** (in Greek/Roman(1) mythology(1)) small lively person, usu a young woman, living in woods etc. **2** (*biology*) young form of an insect.

nympho /'nɪmfəʊ/ *adj/c.n* (*pl -s*) (*informal*) nymphomaniac.

nymphomaniac /ˌnɪmfəˈmeɪnɪˌæk/ *adj/c.n* (*informal nympho*) (of a) woman with too much sexual desire.

Oo

O, o /əʊ/ *n* **1** *c/unique n* 15th letter of the English alphabet. **2** *c.n* nil, nought, zero: *Five minus(3) five equals nought (5 − 5 = 0). My telephone number is 0* (/əʊ/) *five three four (0534).*

▷ *written abbr* (**O**) **3** Ocean. **4** Order.

▷ *interj* **5** = oh.

▷ *symb* **6** (O) oxygen.

o' /ə/ (*informal*) shortened form of 'of': *the streets o' London; a bottle o' milk.*

oaf /əʊf/ *c.n* (*derog*) foolish and clumsy(1) person (usu male).
'oafish *adj.* **'oafishness** *u.n.*

oak /əʊk/ *n* **1** *c.n* kind of large tree with hard wood. **2** *u.n.* (also *attrib*) this wood used to make furniture and buildings: *an oak chest; shelves of oak.*

oar /ɔ:/ *c.n* long piece of wood with a flat end, used, often in pairs, to move a boat in water. **put/ shove/stick one's oar in** (*derog; informal*) take part in s.o else's personal affairs without being asked.
'oarsman *c.n* (*pl -men*) man who uses an oar or oars to move a boat.
'oars,woman *c.n* (*pl -,women*) woman who uses an oar or oars to move a boat.

oasis /əʊ'eɪsɪs/ *c.n* (*pl oases* /əʊ'eɪsi:z/) small place in a desert where there are plants, water etc.

oatmeal ⇒ oats.

oath /əʊθ/ *c.n* (*pl -s* /əʊðz/) **1** serious promise to be honest, loyal etc or to do something: *I give you my oath that I shall look after your children.* **2** wrong use of the name of God or other holy person to express one's anger, hatred etc: *The crowd shouted oaths at the rich politicians.* Compare curse(1). **on/under oath** (*law*) having made an oath(1), esp in a court of law. **swear/take an oath** make a formal oath(1) in public.

oats /əʊts/ *pl.n* kind of grain plant or its seeds, used as food. **sow one's wild oats** (*fig*) enjoy a period of pleasure and excitement while young before beginning a serious and respectable life.
'oat,meal *u.n* crushed(3) oats used to make biscuits etc.

obdurate /'ɒbdjʊrɪt/ *adj* (*formal*) determined to do or have what one wants. Compare obstinate(1), stubborn(1).
'obduracy *u.n.*
'obdurately *adv.*

OBE /,əʊ ,bi: 'i:/ *abbr* (Officer of the) Order(10) of the British Empire (a British honorary(2) title).

obedience, obedient ⇒ obey.

obelisk /'ɒbɪlɪsk/ *c.n* tall pointed pillar(1).

obese /əʊ'bi:s/ *adj* (*formal*) (of a person) too/ very fat.
obesity /əʊ'bi:sɪtɪ/ *u.n.*

obey /ə'beɪ/ *tr/intr.v* do what (s.o) tells one to do; carry out (an order): *obey one's parents; obey orders; obey the law/rules.* Opposite disobey.
obedience /ə'bi:dɪəns/ *u.n* **1** (often — *to s.o/s.t*) act of obeying s.o/s.t. **2** willingness to obey: *prove one's obedience by coming back early.* Opposite disobedience.
obedient /ə'bi:dɪənt/ *adj* showing obedience(2): *obedient children.* Opposite disobedient.
o'bediently *adv.*

obituary /ə'bɪtjʊərɪ/ *c.n* (*pl -ies*) statement, e.g in a newspaper, on television, about a famous person's death with a report on her/his life and/ or work.

object¹ /'ɒbdʒɪkt/ *c.n* **1** thing that can be seen or touched: *His pockets were full of many different objects.* **2** purpose, aim: *What was his main object*

in going to Japan? Her object in life is to become famous. **3** (usu — *of s.t*) person/thing who/that an act, thought etc is meant for: *She is the object of his love. The country is the object of the world's attention.* **4** (*grammar*) word or words in a sentence to which the action of the verb is directed, e.g 'ice-cream' in 'I love ice-cream' and 'a story' in 'She told us a story'. ⇒ direct object, indirect object. **be no object** not be a problem: *His age is no object.*
'object ,lesson *c.n* (often — *in s.t*) ideal practical example (of s.t): *His speech was an object lesson in the art of public speaking.*

object² /əb'dʒekt/ *intr.v* (often — *to s.o/s.t*) say that one dislikes or disapproves (of s.o/s.t): *He objected to being treated like a child. We object to her as our manager.*
objection /əb'dʒekʃən/ *c.n* (often — *to s.t*) **1** statement of dislike or disapproval (of s.t): *He stated his objection to the plan.* **2** cause for dislike or disapproval: *His objection to the plan is that it will cost too much money.* **have a rooted objection to s.t** ⇒ root(*n*). **make/raise an objection** (**to s.t**) state one's disapproval (of s.t): *There will be a chance to raise objections at the end of the discussion.*
ob'jectionable *adj* unpleasant and not acceptable: *objectionable language/behaviour.*
ob'jector *c.n* person who objects. ⇒ conscientious objector.

objective /əb'dʒektɪv/ *adj* **1** not caused/affected by personal feelings or opinion: *an objective view of conditions in the factory.* Opposite subjective(2).
▷ *c.n* **2** = object¹(2): *His main objective was to sell cameras. Her objective in life is to win an Olympic medal.*
ob'jectively *adv* without personal feelings or opinion: *Considered objectively, the idea is a good one but I would not benefit(5) personally.*
ob'jectivity /,ɒbdʒek'tɪvɪtɪ/ *u.n* fact or state of being objective(1): *Objectivity is an essential in scientific experiments.*

oblige /ə'blaɪdʒ/ *tr.v* **1** (usu passive, *be —d to do s.t*) make (s.o) doing something: *He was obliged to sell his car when he lost his job.* **2** (often — *s.o by doing s.t*) (*formal*) do s.t for (s.o) as a favour: *Would you oblige me by opening that door? I hope she will oblige me with an interview(2).*

obligate /'ɒblɪgeɪt/ *tr.v* (usu passive) (*formal*) force (s.o) (to do s.t), esp by law or morals: *We felt obligated by our friendship to help each other.*

obligation /,ɒblɪ'geɪʃən/ *n* **1** *u.n* fact or state of being obliged(2). **2** *c.n* (esp *feel an/no* — (*to do s.t*)) duty, promise, (to do s.t) which cannot be ignored, esp because of the law or morals: *I feel no obligation to pay the bill.* **be under an/ no obligation** (**to do s.t**) have, not have, a duty (to do s.t): *You are under an obligation to tell us if you are not able to come to work.*

obligatory /ə'blɪgətərɪ/ *pred.adj* which must be done, esp because of the law or morals: *Having a visa is obligatory for travelling to China.*

obliged /ə'blaɪdʒd/ *pred.adj* **1** (usu — *to s.o* (*for s.t*)) feeling grateful (to s.o for doing s.t): *I'm much obliged to her (for helping my daughter).* **2** (usu — *to do s.t*) having to (do s.t): *Members are obliged to sign the visitors' book.*

o'bliging *adj* having the desire/will to help: *She'll let you stay for one night — she's very obliging.*

o'blingingly *adv.*

oblique /ə'bliːk/ *adj* **1** (*attrib*) not aimed directly or straight: *make an oblique reference to poor sports training in schools by describing the low standard of young competitors.* **2** (of a line) drawn as a slope and not upright or horizontal.

▷ *c.n* **3** oblique(2) line as used in this dictionary to separate alternatives(2), e.g in s.o/s.t.

o'blique ,angle *c.n* (*mathematics*) angle that is smaller or larger than 90°.

o'bliquely *adv.* **o'bliqueness** *u.n.*

obliterate /ə'blitəˌreit/ *tr.v* **1** (often passive) destroy (s.t) completely: *That hotel was obliterated by the bomb.* **2** hide (s.t) completely, e.g under a cover of s.t: *The snow obliterated every sign of the path.*

obliteration /əˌblitə'reiʃən/ *u.n.*

oblivion /ə'bliviən/ *u.n* **1** (usu *fall/sink into —*) state of being ignored or forgotten: *She fell into oblivion when she gave up international tennis competitions.* **2** state of not knowing s.t: *They left me in oblivion about our money problems.*

oblivious /ə'bliviəs/ *pred.adj* (usu — *of/to s.o/s.t*) not knowing (s.o/s.t); not aware(1) (of s.o/s.t): *I was oblivious of his problems at college. I sat in the sun oblivious to the noise of the children.*

ob'liviously *adv.* **ob'liviousness** *u.n.*

oblong /'bblɒŋ/ *c.n* (also *attrib*) shape with four straight sides and corners of 90° with one pair of sides longer than the other: *an oblong table.*

obnoxious /əb'nɒkʃəs/ *adj* (*derog; formal*) very unpleasant: *an obnoxious smell/child*; *obnoxious behaviour.*

ob'noxiously *adv.* **ob'noxiousness** *u.n.*

oboe /'əubəu/ *c.n* kind of wooden musical instrument like a pipe that has stops over holes to make notes and is played by blowing through a double reed(3): *He plays the oboe.*

oboist /'əubəuist/ *c.n* person who plays the oboe.

obscene /əb'siːn/ *adj* causing disgust esp because of sexual references: *obscene jokes/language/behaviour.*

ob'scenely *adv.*

obscenity /əb'seniti/ *c/u.n* (*pl -ies*) (example of) obscene language or behaviour: *shout obscenities at the speaker*; *disapprove of obscenity on television.*

obscure /əb'skjuə/ *adj* **1** difficult to see, find, understand etc: *living in an obscure part of the country*; *an account of how the accident happened that was very obscure*; *obscure meanings in a dictionary.* **2** not known by many people: *an obscure writer/painter.*

▷ *tr.v* **3** (often passive) make (s.t) obscure(1): *a house obscured by tall trees.*

ob'scurely *adv.*

ob'scurity *n* (*pl -ies*) (*formal*) **1** *u.n* state of being obscure: *remain in obscurity in order to avoid people.* **2** *c.n* thing that is difficult to understand: *He found too many obscurities in the report to consider it valuable.*

obsequies /'bbsikwiz/ *pl.n* (*formal*) usual ceremonies at a funeral.

obsequious /əb'siːkwiəs/ *adj* (*derog; formal*) too willing to agree with s.o, do things for s.o, esp to get s.o's favour: *Some secretaries are too obsequious to their bosses.*

ob'sequiously *adv.* **ob'sequiousness** *u.n.*

observe /əb'zɜːv/ *v* **1** *tr.v* notice or watch (s.o/s.t): *observe that the key is missing*; *observe a fly on the window*; *observe her preparing the vegetables.* **2** *tr/intr.v* be at (a meeting) and listen but not speak, vote etc: *I have been invited to observe (at) the next Council meeting.* **3** *tr.v* (*formal*) obey, pay attention to, (the law, rules, local customs etc): *You must observe the speed limit, the rules of the game. Do you observe Sunday as a religious day in your country?* **4** *tr.v* (often — *that . . .*) (*formal*) comment(2) (that): *She observed (that) the journey was long and tiring.*

observance /əb'zɜːvəns/ *c/u.n* (often — *of s.t*) (*formal*) (example of) paying attention to the law, rules, local customs etc (of s.t): *observance of the rules of the game, the wishes of the owner, the speed limit, a religious* festival(1). ⇒ non-observance.

ob'servant *adj* **1** ready and quick to notice: *an observant birdwatcher.* **2** (often — *of s.t*) (*formal*) ready and careful to observe(3) (s.t): *observant of conditions for membership.*

observation /ˌɒbzə'veiʃən/ *n* **1** *u.n* fact of observing(1): *use one's powers of observation when on a walking holiday.* **2** *c.n* comment(1): *a thoughtless observation to a friend about his mother looking ill.* **3** *c.n* act of recording the position of the sun etc to find one's position on the ground or at sea. **under observation** being carefully watched: *He is under observation in the general hospital.*

observatory /əb'zɜːvətri/ *c.n* (*pl -ies*) building used for observing(1) the moon, stars, sun etc.

ob'server *c.n* **1** person who observes(1): *an observer of changing weather conditions.* **2** person who observes(2): *I'm only an observer at the meeting so I can't vote.*

obsess /əb'ses/ *tr.v* (usu passive) take up (s.o's) attention completely: *He was obsessed by the fear of being very ill.*

obsession /əb'seʃən/ *n* (usu — *about/with s.o/s.t*) **1** *c/u.n* state of being obsessed (about/with s.o/s.t): *obsession with possible failure.* **2** *c.n* act, feeling, idea etc that obsesses one/s.o: *have an obsession about failing. Loving her is a splendid obsession.*

obsessive /əb'sesiv/ *adj* (usu *derog*) concerning/having an obsession: *An example of obsessive behaviour is often checking that the door is locked. She's obsessive about having clean hands.*

ob'sessively *adv.* **ob'sessiveness** *u.n.*

obsolescent /ˌɒbsə'lesnt/ *adj* (*formal*) going out of date or out of use: *obsolescent machines.*

obso'lescence *u.n.*

obsolete /'bbsəˌliːt/ *adj* out of date or no longer used: *Word-processors have made many typewriters obsolete.*

obstacle /'bbstəkl/ *c.n* **1** thing that is a barrier(2). **2** (often — *to s.t*) thing that stops progress or success (in s.t): *Your age is an obstacle to getting the job. Don't put obstacles in the way of her career(1).*

'obstacle ,race *c.n* **1** race in which people must get over or under obstacles such as fences.

2 (*fig*) following of an ambition etc with many difficulties to deal with: *A* career(1) *in business is an obstacle race.*

obstetrics /ɒbˈstetrɪks/ *u.n* (*medical*) science and practice of helping women have babies.

obˈstetric (also **obˈstetrical**) *adj* (usu *attrib*) of or referring to obstetrics: *obstetric instruments.*

obstinate /ˈɒbstɪnɪt/ *adj* **1** (usu *derog*) not willing to accept s.o's opinion, do what s.o wants etc: *an obstinate son who refuses to go to bed.* **2** (of an illness etc) not easy to control or defeat: *an obstinate pain/fear/cough.*

obstinacy /ˈɒbstɪnəsɪ/ *u.n* fact or state of being obstinate.

ˈobstinately *adv.*

obstreperous /əbˈstrepərəs/ *adj* (*derog*; *formal*) badly behaved and noisy, esp when being obstinate(1): *obstreperous children.*

obˈstreperously *adv.* **obˈstreperousness** *u.n.*

obstruct /əbˈstrʌkt/ *tr.v* **1** cause (s.t) to be blocked: *The tall building obstructed our view of the sea. Your car is obstructing my way out.* **2** make the progress or development of (s.t) difficult: *His dislike of me is obstructing my* career(1). **3** make it (almost) impossible for (s.o) to act or take a decision: *The students obstructed the speaker. They are trying to obstruct the meeting by shouting.*

obstruction /əbˈstrʌkʃən/ *n* **1** *c.n* thing that obstructs: *an obstruction in front of the door*; *obstructions to taking a decision.* **2** *u.n* (often — of s.o/s.t) act or fact of obstructing: *use obstruction to prevent a discussion. Obstruction of justice is foolish.*

obˈstructive *adj* **1** likely to obstruct(2,3): *obstructive behaviour.* **2** intended to obstruct(2,3): *an obstructive* policy(1).

obtain /əbˈteɪn/ *v* (*formal*) **1** *tr.v* get possession or ownership of (s.t): *obtain permission from the manager to leave work early*; *obtain a copy of an important newspaper article. Where can I obtain a map of Europe? I've seen the stamp you wanted and I'll try to obtain it for you.* **2** *intr.v* (of a custom, law etc) be accepted, used: *Which rules of membership obtain for foreign students?*

obˈtainable *adj* (*formal*) that can be obtained(1): *Is the book obtainable from your local library?* Opposite unobtainable.

obtrusive /əbˈtruːsɪv/ *adj* (often *derog*; *informal*) (too) obvious; that makes one (too) noticeable: *obtrusive remarks about her hair*; *wearing an obtrusive hat.* Opposite unobtrusive.

obˈtrusively *adv.* **obˈtrusiveness** *u.n.*

obtuse /əbˈtjuːs/ *adj* (*formal*) **1** unkind and not polite: *make obtuse comments.* **2** not able to understand s.t easily: *an obtuse student.* **3** (*mathematics*) (of an angle) that is larger than 90°. Compare acute(6).

obˈtusely *adv.* **obˈtuseness** *u.n.*

obverse /ˈɒbvɜːs/ *def.n* side (of a coin, medal etc) with the main design, e.g the head of the ruler. Compare reverse(5).

obviate /ˈɒbvɪˌeɪt/ *tr.v* (*formal*) make (s.t) unnecessary: *The agreement obviated the need for more discussions.*

obviation /ˌɒbvɪˈeɪʃən/ *u.n* (*formal*).

obvious /ˈɒbvɪəs/ *adj* easy to see or understand: *an obvious mistake*; *an obvious attempt to deceive*

me. It is obvious that they need our help. She loves you — that's obvious!

ˈobviously *adv* (esp) it is obvious that: *Obviously he likes her very much.*

occasion /əˈkeɪʒən/ *n* **1** *c.n* (often on this/that —) particular time for s.t: *She has visited us on many occasions. On this occasion he brought his wife. During those rare occasions when the weather is good, we eat outside.* **2** *c.n* special event, e.g a celebration: *Let's make our wedding an occasion to remember.* **3** *c.n* opportunity: *There will be plenty of occasions to buy postcards. If the occasion presents itself, I shall speak to him.* **4** *u.n* (*formal*) reason: *I hope you'll have no occasion to criticize our hotel.* **on occasion** (*formal*) sometimes: *I ride my bicycle on occasion.* **on the occasion of s.t** (*formal*) at the time of celebrating (a special event): *We bought her the picture on the occasion of her 70th birthday.* **rise to the occasion** show ability, courage etc to deal with a situation. **(have a) sense of occasion** ⇒ sense(*n*). **take the/that/this occasion to do s.t** use the etc opportunity to do s.t.

▷ *tr.v* **5** (*formal*) be the cause of (s.t): *Kindly explain what occasioned her rude behaviour.*

ocˈcasional *attrib.adj* done, happening, sometimes: *I smoke the occasional cigarette.*

ocˈcasionally *adv* sometimes: *I eat brown rice but only occasionally.*

occult /ɒˈkʌlt/ *def.n* (also *attrib*) magic(3) or mystery produced by unnatural forces: *Some societies cure illnesses using the power of the occult* (or *of occult medicine*).

occupy /ˈɒkjuˌpaɪ/ *tr.v* (-ies, -ied) **1** (*formal*) live in, possess, (a house, farm etc): *We occupy the top flat.* **2** be in, use, (a space, seat etc): *Is this chair occupied?* **3** use, take up, (an amount of time, space): *The examinations occupy most of my evenings. The piano seemed to occupy the whole room.* **4** (often passive) use the attention or energy of (s.o): *He's occupied with his model trains.* **5** (*formal*) have (a job or position): *She occupies an extremely important position on the committee.* **6** take possession of (a place), e.g to show one's opposition(2) to s.t or during a war etc: *The workers have occupied the factory.* **occupy oneself** keep oneself busy: *Occupy yourselves for a few minutes while I finish my work.*

occupancy /ˈɒkjupənsɪ/ *n* **1** *c.n* length of time occupying(1) s.t: *The papers give me an occupancy of five years.* **2** *u.n* act or state of occupying(1) s.t: illegal *occupancy.*

occupant /ˈɒkjupənt/ *c.n* person occupying(1,2) a place or position: *Who is the occupant of that house? Every occupant of a seat on the Council has resigned.*

occupation /ˌɒkjuˈpeɪʃən/ *n* **1** *c.n* job, work, hobby that s.o does: *Write down her occupation. I have many occupations to use up my free time.* **2** *u.n* act or state of occupying(1): *No one can refuse to accept our* legal(1) *occupation of this land.* **3** *c.n* length of time occupying(1,6) a house, country etc: *How did you live during the occupation of the town by the rebels*(1)*?*

ˌoccuˈpational *attrib.adj* of, referring to, caused by, one's occupation(1): *occupational risks/diseases.*

ˌoccuˌpational ˈtheraˌpist *c.n* expert in occupational therapy.

,occu,pational 'therapy *u.n* treatment of mental(3) or physical(1) illness by giving s.o work, e.g knitting or sewing.

'occu,pied *pred.adj* being used; not free: *All our flats/chairs/tables are occupied.*

occupier /'ɒkjʊ,paɪə/ *c.n* person having, living in, a place: *I own the house but I am not the occupier.*

occur /ə'kɜ:/ *intr.v* (-rr-) 1 (*formal*) happen: *When did the robbery occur? Several murders occur during the last act of the play. Quarrels occur in every family.* 2 (*formal*) be found: Germs(1) *occur in most drinking water.* 3 (*usu — to s.o*) come into (s.o's) thoughts: *Did it ever occur to you that she needs you? The idea of selling the farm has never occurred to me before.*

occurrence /ə'kʌrəns/ *n* (*formal*) 1 *c.n* thing that happens; event: *Such expensive weddings are a rare occurrence.* 2 *u.n* act of happening: *Cruelty to children is of increasingly rare occurrence. The regular occurrence of headaches is a sign of the disease.*

ocean /'əʊʃən/ *n* 1 *c/def.n* (also *attrib*) area of salt water round the masses of land on the earth: *sail across the ocean*; ocean waves. Compare sea(1). 2 *c.n* (with capital **O** in names) one part of the ocean(1): *There are seven oceans and the Pacific Ocean is the biggest.* Compare sea(3).

'ocean,going *adj* able/built to travel long distances on the ocean: *an oceangoing yacht*(1).

oceanic /,əʊʃɪ'ænɪk/ *adj* of, referring to, living in, the ocean: *oceanic winds/fish.*

'oceans *pl.n* (usu — of s.t) (*fig*) a large amount (of s.t): *You have oceans of space/time.*

ochre /'əʊkə/ *u.n* (also *attrib*) yellow-brown earth or its colour: *ochre lines on the walls.*

o'clock /ə'klɒk/ *adv* (also *attrib.adj*) (used after a number to refer to an hour when stating the time): *It's nearly 5 o'clock. I must leave by 6 o'clock. Is it 5 o'clock already? I'll arrive some time between 9 and 10 o'clock. We didn't finish until 12 o'clock midnight. They went on the 3 o'clock bus.*

Oct *written abbr* October.

octagon /'ɒktəgən/ *c.n* (*mathematics*) flat shape with eight sides.

octagonal /ɒk'tægənl/ *adj.*

octahedron /,ɒktə'hi:drən/ *c.n* (*mathematics*) solid figure with eight faces.

octave /'ɒktɪv/ *c.n* 1 (*music*) series of notes between one note and the one that is seven notes above it. 2 (*poetry*) poem/verse with eight lines.

octet /ɒk'tet/ *c.n* 1 (*music*) eight musicians playing together. 2 = octave(2).

October /ɒk'təʊbə/ *c/unique n* (also *attrib*) (*written abbr* Oct) 10th month of the year: *It's usually cold in October. I'll meet you on October 1st* (say 'October the first' or 'the first of October'). *This is typical October weather.*

octogenarian /,ɒktəʊdʒɪ'neərɪən/ *c.n* (also *attrib*) person aged 80–89.

octopus /'ɒktəpəs/ *c.n* kind of sea animal with eight long arms (tentacles).

oculist /'ɒkjʊlɪst/ ⇨ ophthalmologist.

'ocular *attrib.adj* (*technical*) of or referring to the eyes, the ability to see: *ocular problems.*

odd /ɒd/ *adj* 1 (of a number) that cannot be divided by 2 without producing a fraction(2): *31 and 103 are odd numbers.* Opposite even(1).

2 (*attrib*) one of a pair with the other one not there: *an odd sock.* 3 a little more than the stated amount: *It cost me £10 odd.* 4 unusual, strange, not expected: *She gave me an odd look. That was an odd thing to say. It's odd but I feel that I've been here before. My teacher has the oddest way of talking.* 5 (*attrib*) not fixed, occupied or regular: *I'd like to speak to you when you've an odd moment. I do see her on odd occasions. He helps me with odd jobs in the house.* 6 (*attrib*) additional or extra: *have odd pieces of cloth left over.* ⇨ oddments. **odd jobs** ⇨ job. **the odd man/ one/person out** person or thing left when others form groups, teams or sets: *I'm always the odd person out at parties.*

'odd,ball *c.n* (*informal*) strange person.

oddity /'ɒdɪtɪ/ *n* (*pl -ies*) 1 *c.n* odd(4) person or thing: *My aunt is a bit of an oddity in the village.* 2 *u.n* (*formal*) fact or state of being odd(4): *oddity of behaviour/dress/speech.*

'oddly *adv* strangely: *behave oddly.* **oddly enough** ⇨ enough.

'oddments *pl.n* pieces (of s.t) left over: *They sell all kinds of oddments of cloth in the market.*

'oddness *u.n* state of being odd(4).

odds *pl.n* 1 chances: *The odds are that she'll be here later on. All the odds are against us winning the football match.* 2 differences in amount or strength: *We played against impossible odds.* 3 (statement when betting of) the number of times more than the money paid for a bet(1) that s.o will get if he/she wins: *Odds of 2 to 1 means the person will get twice the money paid for the bet.* **be at odds (with s.o) (about/over s.t)** be having a quarrel (with s.o) (about s.t): *They are at odds over who can keep the piano.* **be odds on (that s.t)** be very likely (that s.t will happen): *It's odds on that the weather will be hot.* **make no odds (to s.o)** not be important (to s.o): *You can sleep here or upstairs — it makes no odds to me.* **odds and ends** different things, pieces etc together, esp as oddments. **odds and sods** (*slang*) different kinds of people. **over the odds** more than is necessary or expected: *Do Americans tip²(2) waiters over the odds?*

ode /əʊd/ *c.n* kind of poem, usu about a strong feeling or noble idea: *John Keats wrote 'Ode to Autumn'.*

odious /'əʊdɪəs/ *adj* (*derog; formal*) disgusting: *an odious smell/taste/colour/person.*

'odiously *adv.* 'odiousness *u.n.*

odour /'əʊdə/ *c.n* (*formal*) smell: *flowers with a pleasant odour.* **be, hold s.o/s.t, in bad/good odour** (*fig*) be thought of as bad/good; have a bad/good opinion about s.o's/s.t's qualities: *After the fight, his neighbours held him in bad odour.*

odorous /'əʊdərəs/ *adj* (*formal*) having a smell (good or bad).

'odourless *adj* having no smell.

o'er /'əʊə/ *adv/prep* (*literary*) = over¹.

oesophagus /i:'sɒfəgəs/ *def.n* (US e'sophagus) (*technical*) long passage from the back of the mouth to the stomach, used to take food in.

oestrogen /'i:strədʒən/ *u.n* (US 'estrogen) (*technical*) chemical substance (called a hormone) produced in a woman's body to help her to be able to have children.

of (strong form /ɒv/, weak form /əv/) *prep*

1 belonging to, connected with, forming part of, (s.o/s.t): *the people of Africa; the back of the house; the capital of Spain; the bottom of the sea; a friend of mine* (or *one of my friends*). **2** produced by: *the music of Elton John; the poetry of Shelley; the paintings of Goya.* **3** looking like; showing: *a drawing of a bridge; a photograph of a tree.* **4** referring to; about: *a report of a meeting; told of a possibility; a story of a farm.* **5** containing: *a bottle of milk; a box of matches; a packet of tea; a tube of toothpaste; a crowd of people; a group of students; a pile of books.* **6** (joining a stated amount etc and the contents, material etc): *a litre of milk; a metre of cloth; a teaspoonful of sugar; full of fun; all of them; none of the time.* **7** (often *made — s.t*) using as material: *a dress made of cotton; a house of stone; a heart of gold.* ⇒ from (6), out (26). **8** having; with regard to: *a lady of high rank; charm of manner.* **9** (introducing age): *a child of six.* **10** (showing cause): *died of her injuries; accused of murder; smelling of cheese.* **11** (showing removal or loss): *cured of a disease; get rid of a poor worker; short of supplies.* **12** (showing separation in time or space): *a city north of Paris; within a space of five minutes.* **13** (showing relationship between an action and the performer): *a good maker of bread; a poor player of Mozart's music.* **14** (referring to the object'(4) and showing association or connection): *the love of a mother for her children.* **15** having (a particular quality or character): *a person of good judgement; a subject of great importance.* **16** that is called: *the city of Oxford; the post of headteacher.*

off /ɒf/ *adj* **1** not of the usual or expected standard: *It has been an off year for English cricket.* **2** (*pred*) in the condition stated by the adj: *If you'd make less noise we'd all be better off. He'll be worse off without her.* **3** (*pred*) not available: *The carrot soup is off today.* ⇒ off (6–11).
▷ *adv* **4** away: *The thief ran off with the money. She's gone off and got married. We ought to be off soon or we'll be late.* **5** so as to be no longer worn: *Do take your coat/hat/boots off.* Opposite on (2). **6** (also *pred.adj*) (of a machine, apparatus) (so as to be) no longer in use: *turn the television/light/switch/tap off. Are the brakes off?* Opposite on (4). **7** (also *pred.adj*) (of a form of power) (so as to be) no longer being used: *Who turned the gas/electricity off? Is the gas off?* Opposite on (5). **8** (also *pred.adj*) (of food) not good or fresh: *I think this meat/milk has gone off* (or *is off*). **9** (also *pred.adj*) cancelled (1): *The meeting has been called off* (or *is off*). ⇒ on (1). **10** (also *pred.adj*) free from work: *He gave us the afternoon off. I'm off on Saturdays.* **11** (also *pred.adj*) out of a bus, train etc: *You must get off at Oxford Street. Are all the children off?* ⇒ off (15). Compare out (8). **12** completely: *finish a meal off; kill a man off.* **13** not as good as usual or expected: *Her singing has been rather off lately.* **badly/well off** (a) poor/rich: *I was badly off as a student but now I'm quite well off.* (b) (usu — *for s.t*) having a small/large amount (of s.t): *She's badly off for shoes at the moment.* **off and on** (also **on and off**) occasionally but not regularly: *I've had a headache off and on all day.*
▷ *prep* **14** away from: *Who took the money off the table? He drove off the road into a tree. He was knocked off the ladder. She took £1 off the price because of the dirty mark. Please keep off the grass.* **15** out of (a bus, train etc): *We got off the bus at Victoria Station.* Compare out of (23). ⇒ on (11). **16** near or going away from: *The hotel is off the main road. There is a small road off the High Street. The house is on an island off the west coast of Scotland.* **17** not able or willing to enjoy, do etc: *She's off smoking/beer/her food.* **off the cuff, duty, one's head, the map** etc ⇒ cuff, duty, head, map etc.

ˌoff-'beat *adj* ('off-ˌbeat when *pred*) (*informal*) (pleasantly) unusual: *off-beat hair/clothes/music.*

'off ˌchance *sing.n* (*informal*) slight possibility: *There's only an off chance that he'll get well. We waited on the off chance that the weather would improve.*

ˌoff-'colour *pred.adj* unwell: *be/feel off-colour.*

ˌoff'hand *adj* **1** without thinking first (and often rude): *remarks that were a little offhand.*
▷ *adv* **2** without thinking first: *Offhand, I'd say he's about 15 years old.*

ˌoff 'key *adv* **1** (*music*) not in tune. **2** (*fig*) not in agreement with expected behaviour.

'off-ˌlicence *c.n* shop selling beer, wines, spirits (9) etc.

ˌoff-'load *tr/intr.v* get rid of (s.o/s.t unpleasant): *Don't try to off-load your old car, younger brother, on me!*

ˌoff-'peak *attrib.adj* available for use when general use or need is small (and so cheaper): *off-peak electricity.*

'off-ˌputting *adj* (*informal*) upsetting one's ability to think clearly or to keep one's attention fixed: *I find the noise of people eating chocolates in the theatre very off-putting.*

'off-ˌset *tr.v p.t, p.p* 'offˌset (-*tt-*) (often — *s.t against s.t*) form a balance with (s.t else): *You need to offset her lack of experience against her willingness. He worked as a waiter to offset his expenses as a student.* **web offset** ⇒ web.

'offˌshoot *c.n* **1** branch growing out of a main stem of a plant. **2** (*fig*) thing that develops from the main part: *Producing cameras is an offshoot from his interest in* designing (5) *microscopes.*

ˌoff'shore *adj* **1** (also *adv*) a small distance away from the coast: *an offshore island; moored² offshore.* **2** in a direction away from the coast: *an offshore breeze.* ⇒ onshore.

ˌoff'side *attrib.adj* **1** on the side near the middle of a road: *an offside wheel.* Opposite nearside.
▷ *adv* (also *adj*) **2** (in football etc) (of a player) in a wrong position between the ball and opposite goal: *play/be offside.*

'offˌspring *unique n* (*pl* 'offˌspring) (*formal; technical*) child; young of an animal.

ˌoff-the-'record *adj/adv* not official; not to be made public: *My comments are strictly off-the-record.*

ˌoff-'white *u.n* (also *adj*) colour that is almost white.

offal /'ɒfl/ *u.n* inside parts of an animal eaten as food, e.g liver (2), heart.

off-beat, off chance, off-colour ⇒ off.

offend /ə'fend/ *v* **1** *tr.v* make (s.o) feel angry or upset: *Your criticism offended me very much. I'll be very offended if you don't buy me a birthday* *card*. **2** *tr.v* annoy (s.o) because unpleasant: *Ash-trays on restaurant tables offend me*. **3** *intr.v* (usu — *against s.o/s.t*) (*formal*) act against expected or usual behaviour, the law, tradition(1,2) etc: *Her language offends against religion*. ⇒ offence(2).

offence /əˈfens/ *n* (US **of'fense**) **1** *c.n* illegal act: *I was taken to the police station and charged with a driving offence*. **2** *c.n* (often — *against s.o/s.t*) act that offends(3) (s.o/s.t): *an offence against tradition, the rules, human rights*. **3** *c/u.n* (usu — *to s.o/s.t*) (cause of) hurting s.o, s.o's feelings etc: *Some modern buildings are an offence to the landscape. I hope my remarks will not give/cause offence to your parents*. **take offence** (**at s.t**) be made angry or upset (because of s.t): *You take offence too easily. He took great offence at your refusal to help*.

o'ffender *c.n* person who offends(1).

offensive /əˈfensɪv/ *adj* **1** used for attack in war or battles: *offensive weapons*. Compare defensive(1). **2** causing s.o to feel angry or upset because very unpleasant: *offensive language/ behaviour*. Opposite inoffensive. **3** disgusting: *an offensive smell*. Opposite inoffensive.
▷ *c.n* **4** (usu — *against s.o/s.t*) attack (on s.o/s.t): *begin an offensive against the enemy*. **be on the offensive** (usu *fig*) be attacking s.o, s.o's opinions etc: *He's been on the offensive since the manager criticized his report*.

of'fensively *adv*. **of'fensiveness** *u.n*.

offer /ˈɒfə/ *c.n* **1** act/example of offering (⇒ offer 3): *We received many offers of help/money/food*. **2** (usu — *of s.t* (*to s.o*) (*for s.t*)) offering (⇒ offer 4) of (an amount of money) (for s.t): *We have already had an offer of £500 (for the car)*. **make an offer** (**of s.t**) (**for s.t**) offer(4) (an amount of money) (for s.t): *They made me an offer I couldn't refuse*. **on offer** for sale at a lower price. **open to offers** willing to sell and consider prices offered(4). **under offer** (of a house etc) to be sold for the price and conditions offered(4) but not yet having a signed agreement.
▷ *v* **3** *tr/intr.v* (often — *to do s.t*) say or show that one is ready and willing (to help, do s.t etc): *I offered to carry her bag. We offered but he didn't need any more help*. **4** *tr.v* (often — (*to do*) *s.t for s.t*) say or show (what one is willing to do, pay, give etc) (for s.t): *She offered me £20 for my old bicycle. He offered to exchange his dictionary for my pen*. **5** *tr/intr.v* ask (guests etc) if they want (food, drinks etc): *Offer your friends some biscuits* (or *Offer the biscuits to your friends*). **6** *tr.v* say what one is willing to give (usu in response to a situation): *Can I offer you some advice? He offered me his arm as I crossed the street. The terrorists offered no resistance when the soldiers came in*. **7** *tr.v* (usu — *up s.t to God*) (*formal*) give (s.t); present (s.t): *She offered up prayers to God*. **offer s.t around/round** take food, sweets etc to friends, guests and ask if they want s.t.

'offering *n* **1** *c.n* money given to a religious group, e.g during a church service. **2** *u.n* act of offering (⇒ offer 4): *The offering of money to the police is a serious crime*.

offhand ⇒ off.

office /ˈɒfɪs/ *n* **1** *c.n* (also *attrib*) (often —*s*) room(s) used by a business company; room(s) in a school, factory, shop etc used for general administration(2), e.g typing, telephoning, keeping records etc: *Our offices are in the centre of town. The office is at the back of the factory. We met during an office party*. **2** *c.n* room used by one person in a business company etc: *the manager's office. Come to my office after lunch, please*. **3** *c.n* (usu with capital **O**) place that has a government department in it: *the Foreign Office; the Home Office; the Cabinet Office*. **4** *c.n* position of public duty or authority(1): *What office does she have/hold on the committee?* **5** *u.n* (esp in —, hold —) the ruling position, authority(1), esp in government: *Which political party was in office in 1980? The Liberals have not held office for many years*. ⇒ box office, post office, ticket office etc.

'office-,block *c.n* large building with several offices(1) in it.

'office ,hours *pl.n* period in the day when an office(1) is open for business.

'officer *c.n* **1** person with authority to order others in the army, navy, airforce etc: *I would like to be an officer in the navy*. **2** person with authority(1) and special duties, esp in the police force: *She's a police officer, a customs officer*.

'offices *pl.n* (*formal*) services (⇒ **of service** (**to s.o/s.t**)): *She learned about the job through the offices of a friend*.

official /əˈfɪʃəl/ *adj* Opposite unofficial. **1** (*attrib*) of or referring to a position of authority(1) or formal duty: *official uniform; an official form of address; official duties/statements*. **2** done/ produced by a person with authority(1): *This information is official*.
▷ *c.n* **3** person with a position of authority(1), esp in government.

of'ficialdom *u.n* (often *derog*) officials(3) as a group.

of'ficially *adv* **1** with reference to what is official(2) (but possibly not true): *Officially she's unable to go because she has a headache but actually she doesn't want to go*. Opposite unofficially. **2** according to established rules or ceremony: *The building will be opened officially by the Queen*. **3** as an official: *He will be present officially and so he will be near the front*.

officiate /əˈfɪʃɪˌeɪt/ *intr.v* (often — *at s.t*) carry out the duties of an official, esp at a religious ceremony: *Which priest will be officiating at your wedding?*

officious /əˈfɪʃəs/ *adj* (*derog; formal*) too willing to use one's authority(1): *an officious manager/ teacher/soldier*.

of'ficiously *adv*.

offing /ˈɒfɪŋ/ *def.n* **in the offing** likely (but not certain): *A pay rise is in the offing*.

off key, off-licence, off-load, off-peak, off-putting, offset, offshoot, offshore, offside, offspring, off-the-record, off-white ⇒ off.

oft /ɒft/ *adv* (*literary*) often: *'For oft, when on my couch(1) I lie...'*

often /ˈɒfn/ *adv* many times; a lot of the time: *I often eat in this café. She often has headaches. You must visit your dentist more often. How often do you wash your hair? We quite often (on many occasions) have eggs for breakfast*. Opposite seldom. **as often as not** on many occasions: *She forgets her glasses as often as not*. **every so often** ⇒ every. **more often than**

not on most occasions: *We meet at the bus stop more often than not.*

ogle /'əʊgl/ *tr/intr.v* (*derog*) look at (s.o), esp with sexual desire: *He was ogling the young women in the train.*

ogre /'əʊgə/ *c.n* **1** (in stories) very large ugly and cruel man. **2** (*fig*) cruel man: *Her uncle is an ogre towards his children.*

ogress /'əʊgrɪs/ *c.n* woman ogre.

oh /əʊ/ *interj* (used to express surprise, fear, agreement etc according to what is happening): *Oh! There's a snake! Oh dear! Oh, there you are. Oh, now I understand. Oh, I'm so sorry. Oh, oh, — here comes that bore again!*

ohm /əʊm/ *c.n* (*technical*) unit of measurement of resistance(4) in an electric circuit(4), *symb* Ω.

OHMS *written abbr* (used on government envelopes and paper) on Her/His Majesty's Service.

oho /əʊˈhəʊ/ *interj* (*old use*) used to express satisfaction, scorn, surprise etc: *Oho! Now you can't possibly win!*

oil /ɔɪl/ *u.n* **1** one of many kinds of thick liquid that will not mix with water, used as fuel, food, to make paint, to make machine parts move or turn smoothly, to make one's skin feel soft etc: *vegetable/mineral oil*; *cooking oil*; *olive(1) oil*; *engine oil. The car engine needs some oil. Do you use oil on your hair?* **burn the midnight oil** (*fig*) work, read etc very late at night. **strike oil** find mineral oil in the ground after searching with a deep pipe.

▷ *tr.v* **2** put oil on (machine parts, cooking dishes etc): *My bicycle needs oiling. Oil the pan before you put the potatoes in.*

'oil ˌdrum *c.n* large round container for mineral oil.

'oil ˌfield *c.n* area where mineral oil is taken out of the ground.

'oil-ˌfired *attrib.adj* using mineral oil as fuel: *oil-fired central heating.*

'oil ˌpaint *c/u.n* (kind of) paint made from oil.

'oil ˌpainting *n* **1** *u.n* art of painting using oil paint. **2** *c.n* picture made using oil paints.

'oilˌrig ⇨ rig(1).

oils *pl.n* oil paints: *Do you paint in oils or watercolours(1)?*

'oilˌskin *u.n* (also *attrib*) kind of cloth treated with oil to make it waterproof(1); jacket etc made of this.

'oil ˌslick *c.n* area of oil on the sea, e.g produced by a damaged ship.

'oil ˌtanker *c.n* ship designed to carry mineral oil from one part of the world to another.

'oil ˌwell *c.n* deep hole in the ground to take out mineral oil.

oily /'ɔɪlɪ/ *adj* (*-ier, -iest*) containing, covered with, feeling/looking like, oil: *oily skin/hair/fingers.*

ointment /'ɔɪntmənt/ *c/u.n* (kind of) thick, oily substance, used on the skin to help an injury to mend or as protection: *She put some ointment on the cut.*

OK /ˌəʊˈkeɪ/ *pred.adj* (also **oˈkay**) (*informal*) **1** all right; satisfactory: *Are you feeling OK? Will it be OK for me to leave early? Is this OK for the job?*

▷ *interj* **2** (used to express approval, agreement etc): *OK, you can come in now. OK, I'll try. 'Can I borrow your car?' 'OK.'*

▷ *tr.v* **3** (usu **oˈkay**) approve of an idea, suggestion, request etc: *She has okayed your expenses.*

old /əʊld/ *adj* **1** having existed or lived for a long time: *an old man/building/city/story/song/joke. I'm getting too old for camping. It's a very old university. The older I get, the more I need to sleep.* Opposite young(1). **2** (*pred*) having the age mentioned: *This tree is a hundred years old. I'm twenty-one years old. How old are you? The winner was an eighteen-year-old student* (or *an eighteen-year-old*). ⇨ elder¹. **3** having the qualities of an old(1) person: *That poor child looks old even though he is only a boy.* Opposite young(2). **4** (*pred; formal*) (of a period of time) at a late stage: *The night is old and I must sleep.* Opposite young(4). **5** (also with capital **O**) (of two or more kinds) having existed or been used earlier: *the old* method(1,2)/edition(1)/version; *Old English*; *the Old Testament. I've never been back to my old school.* **6** (*attrib*) known for a long time: *an old friend*/acquaintance(2). **7** (*attrib*) experienced: *an old soldier/member.* ⇨ old hand. **8** no longer modern, used or fashionable: *old clothes*; *an old style of hat*; *an old way of expressing it.* Compare young(3). **9** (*informal*) (used to express kindness, approval or friendship towards s.o): *Hello, old fellow/thing. Good old Mary – I knew she'd help us.* **any old s.t** (*informal*) it does not matter which: *Any old shoes/paper/thing will do.* **as old as the hills** very old(1): *That joke's as old as the hills.* **in days of old** a long time ago. ⇨ olden. **old hat** ⇨ hat.

▷ *def.pl.n* **10** old people: *The old deserve our care.* **of old** from/during an earlier time: *stories of old*; *in days of old.*

ˌold 'age *u.n* later period of a person's life; being old(1): *Old age doesn't stop him from swimming every day. Who'll look after you in your old age?*

ˈold ˌcountry *def.n* country in which one (or one's father etc) was born.

ˌold 'crock *c.n* person/car who/that is old and ill/broken.

olden /'əʊldən/ *attrib.adj* (**in**) **the olden days/times** a long time ago.

ˌold-ˈfashioned *adj* (*derog*) = old(8): *old-fashioned clothes/ideas/expressions.*

ˌold 'hand *c.n* (*informal*) (often *an — at s.t*) person with much experience (of s.t): *I'm an old hand at mending bicycles.* ⇨ old(7).

ˈoldish *adj* becoming/rather old(1,6): *an oldish man*; *an oldish-looking dress.*

ˌold 'maid *c.n* (*derog*) woman who will probably not marry.

ˌold 'man *c.n* (*slang*) husband or father.

ˌOld 'Nick *unique n* the devil.

ˌOld 'Testament *def/unique n* (*abbr* OT) first part of the Bible(1) telling a history of the Hebrew people. ⇨ New Testament.

ˌold 'timer *c.n* (*informal*) person who has lived or worked somewhere for a long time.

ˌold 'wives' ˌtale *c.n* (*informal*) story (often about illness or a difficulty), not based on science: *Believing that touching frogs can cause warts is an old wives' tale.*

ˌOld 'World *def.n* Europe, Asia and Africa. Compare New World.

ˈold-ˌworld *attrib.adj* of or referring to earlier times: *old-world beliefs.*

oligarchy /'ɒlɪˌgɑːkɪ/ *c/u.n* (*pl -ies*) (country

with) government by a small group of people.

,oli'garchic adj.

olive /'ɒlɪv/ n 1 c.n (also attrib) (kind of tree with a) small black or yellowish-green fruit having a bitter taste, used as food and to make oil: salad(1) with olives; olive oil. 2 u.n (also attrib) yellow-green colour: olive green.

'olive ,branch c.n (fig) offer of peace: It is better to hold out an olive branch to one's enemies.

Olympics /ə'lɪmpɪks/ def.n (also **the O,lympic 'Games**) (in modern times) international competition for athletics, sports and games, held every four years.

O'lympic attrib.adj at, during, of, referring to, the Olympics: win an Olympic medal.

OM /,əʊ 'em/ abbr (UK honorary title) Order(10) of Merit.

ombudsman /'ɒmbʊdsmən/ c.n (pl -men) government official who considers complaints by ordinary people about the way government departments have treated them.

omelette /'ɒmlɪt/ c.n kind of food made by frying a mixture of beaten eggs: a cheese omelette.

omen /'əʊmen/ c.n sign of s.t (good or bad) that will happen: A blue sky is a good omen for warm weather.

ominous /'ɒmɪnəs/ adj suggesting that s.t bad will happen: Those grey clouds look ominous (or are an ominous sign of bad weather).

'ominously adv. **'ominousness** u.n.

omit /əʊ'mɪt/ tr.v (-tt-) (formal) 1 (often — s.o/ s.t from s.t) not include (s.o/s.t) (in s.t): I omitted the more serious criticisms from my speech. He's been omitted from the team. 2 (usu — to do s.t) fail (to do s.t): I omitted to give her your message.

omission /əʊ'mɪʃən/ n (formal) 1 c.n thing that is/was not included: a serious omission. There are several omissions in your report. 2 u.n act of not including s.t: The omission of his name from the list caused great confusion.

omnibus /'ɒmnɪbəs/ adj 1 (attrib) (of a book) containing several stories, novels', plays etc: an omnibus edition of Shakespeare's plays.

▷ c.n 2 (old use) bus(1).

omnipotent /ɒm'nɪpətənt/ adj (formal) having total/unlimited power or control: an omnipotent ruler.

om'nipotence u.n. **om'nipotently** adv.

omnivorous /ɒm'nɪvərəs/ adj (technical) eating both plants and animals as food.

omnivore /'ɒmnɪvɔː/ c.n (technical) animal or person that/who eats both plants and animals as food. ⇒ carnivore, herbivore.

on /ɒn/ pred.adj 1 going to happen as agreed or planned; in progress: What's on at the cinema? Is the meeting still on for Friday? ⇒ off(9).

▷ adv 2 being worn; so as to be worn: Have you got a vest' on? Put your coat on. Compare off(5). 3 (of movement) forward; (of a state) that is continuing: The police moved us on. Carry on with your work. From this moment on I'll be more careful. 4 (also pred.adj) (of a machine, apparatus etc) so as to be/begin working: He turned on the radio/tap. Is the television/record player/ tap/switch/light on? Opposite off(6). Compare out(7). 5 (also pred.adj) (of a form of power) (so as to start to be) in use: She turned on

the gas/water. I think the gas/electricity is on. Opposite off(7). **and so on** ⇒ so'(adv). **later on** ⇒ late(adv). **on and off** = off and on ⇒ off(13). **on and on** (used for emphasis) continuing without stopping: They ran on/drove on and on through the night. She went on and on (= complained a lot) about the weather. For other expressions using a verb, adj, noun etc with 'on', e.g add s.t on, earlier on, head on, ⇒ the verb, adj or noun etc entries.

▷ prep 6 touching, fixed to, the surface or side that is on top or facing forward: She was sitting on the grass. There's a fly on the ceiling. The picture was glued on the door. 7 being carried by (s.o): Have you any money on you? 8 supported by (s.t): The bird was standing on one leg. The house is built on brick columns. 9 at the date, occasion etc mentioned; when a particular moment, occasion etc happens: I was born on April 1st. Let's meet on Friday. On that occasion I was ill. On the same day my son lost his pen. On your arrival please come to the main hall. 10 (referring to the apparatus, instrument, method(1,2) etc used): She played a tune on the piano. I saw it on television. I heard it on the radio. She arrived on her bicycle, on foot (walking), on horseback (riding a horse). Be quiet, I'm (talking to someone) on the telephone. 11 in/into a bus, coach(1), train etc: We met on the train. Sheila got on the bus. ⇒ off(15). 12 (showing position with reference to s.t): the first road on the left; on the second floor. 13 near; at the side of: We live on the coast. The garage is on the corner, on the main road. 14 towards, esp in order to attack: We marched on the enemy's camp. 15 about: a book on Shakespeare; a television programme on public health. 16 taking part as a member of: I'm on the committee, council, board of directors. 17 active, busy doing, having: She's on holiday, away on a business trip. 18 taking or using: She lives on salads. He's on a diet(1). How can they manage on a small pension? 19 in the act/state of: on fire/sale/strike. 20 (— + -ing) when (+ clause(1)): On entering the hall, please take off your hats. 21 fastened by: on a rope/chain. For other uses of a verb, noun, adv etc with 'on', e.g decide on s.t, on s.o's advice, on one's own, be down on s.o/s.t, ⇒ the verb, noun, adv etc entries. **on Her/His Majesty's Service** (abbr OHMS) (used on government stationery).

'on,coming attrib.adj coming towards or forwards: oncoming traffic.

'on,going attrib.adj happening now, without stopping: an ongoing discussion.

,on'shore adj in a direction towards the coast: an onshore wind. ⇒ offshore(2).

onto (strong form /'ɒntu/, weak form /'ɒntə/) prep (also **on to**) 1 to a position that is touching, fixed to, a surface or side that is on the top or facing forward: glue a picture onto a door; fix a carpet onto the floor. 2 to a position supported by: Turn onto your back. 3 (informal) having information about s.t wrong or bad, or s.o doing wrong: The tax officials are onto them. 4 into a bus, coach(1), train etc: climb/get onto a train. Opposite off(15). 5 towards: The house looks onto a lake. For verb + 'onto' + s.o/s.t, e.g get onto s.o/s.t, ⇒ the verb entries.

onward /'ɒnwəd/ adj of the next stage: Do

you have a ticket for your onward journey? ⇒ return(1).

onwards /'ɒnwədz/ (US **onward**) adv to a further, later or advanced position in space or time: *We moved onwards towards the the river.* Opposite back(4).

once /wʌns/ adv **1** on one occasion: *He'd met her only once but he remembered her. I'll say it once and once only.* **2** on one occasion, for a period, in the past: *I once tried to ride a camel. There were elephants living in Europe once.* **all at once** suddenly: *All at once a face appeared at the window.* **at once** immediately: *Come here at once.* **for once** on this one occasion: *Why don't you pay for once?* **once again** one more time: *If you're late once again, you'll lose your job.* **once and for all** on this occasion only and never again; for the last time: *I'm telling you once and for all that I will not pay for it.* **once in a blue moon** very rarely: *I see her once in a blue moon.* **once in a while** sometimes: *They eat in this restaurant once in a while.* **once more** again. **once or twice** a few times: *We've met at the bus stop once or twice.* **once upon a time** (used to begin a story) during a period in the past: *Once upon a time there lived a girl called Snow White.*
▷ conj **3** as soon as; when: *Once I'd turned the corner I felt safe. Once you've learned the method it will be easy.*

oncoming ⇒ on.

one /wʌn/ det/c.n (cardinal number) **1** number 1: *one man/day/thought/opportunity. It costs £1. Let's meet at one (o'clock), at a quarter to one. The baby will be one (year old) tomorrow. One moment she's happy and then she's sad. Oxford United won the game one-nil* (or *1–0*). **one day** ⇒ day.
▷ pron **2** person, animal, thing etc: *He was the first one to find it. This one is bigger than that one. Which ones shall I buy? She's one of my friends. I haven't got one.* **3** (formal) you(2): *One must never shout in a church.* ⇒ oneself. **all in one** together as one unit: *It was a dress and coat all in one.* **for one** being one example: *I for one will not be there.* **for one thing** ⇒ thing. **one after another** one(2) after the other: *One after another they refused to sign.* **one by one** one person, thing etc happening, moving etc after the one before: *We were allowed in one by one.* **one and all** everyone: *Thank you, one and all, for the present.* **one and only s.t** one single example of (s.o/s.t): *This is my one and only coat.* **one and the same** (s.o/s.t) (used for emphasis) the same person, thing: *Your boyfriend and my brother are one and the same* (person). **one another** (used of two people, things etc when the action refers to both): *They smiled at one another, waited for one another, gave presents to one another.* ⇒ each other. **one or two** a few: *There are one or two minutes left for questions.* **one up on s.o** having an advantage over s.o: *Having very rich parents makes her one up on her friends.*

one- having only one of the person/thing shown by the second part of the word: *a ‚one-‚parent ’family; a ‚one-‚room ’flat; a ‚one-‚man ’show; a ‚one-‚piece ’swimming ‚costume.*

‚one-‚night ’stand c.n ⇒ stand(n).

‚one-’off c.n (also attrib) thing that is the only one made or available: *a one-off opportunity.*

oneself /wʌn'self/ pron (formal) **1** reflexive pron of one(3) (used when the person being referred to is connected with the action of the verb): *Washing oneself every day is important.* **2** (used to emphasize one): *It is better if one checks the money oneself.* ⇒ one(3). **(by) oneself** (often all by —) (a) alone: *One must not go by oneself.* (b) without help: *One could do it (by) oneself but it would be difficult.* (not) **be/feel oneself** (not) be/feel as healthy, active etc as usual. **keep s.t to oneself** not tell any other person about s.t.

‚one-’sided adj **1** giving information about or representing only one opinion, method, possibility etc: *a one-sided argument.* **2** with one player, team etc having more ability, experience etc than the other or others: *a one-sided competition.*

’one-‚time attrib.adj former: *a one-time dancer.*

‚one-to-’one adj (of two people, groups etc) with one member on each side: *one-to-one teaching* (one teacher with one student).

’one-‚way adj **1** in which vehicles can move in only one direction: *a one-way street; one-way traffic.* **2** with which a person can travel to a place but not back: *a one-way ticket.* ⇒ return(1).

onerous /'ɒnərəs, 'əʊnərəs/ adj (formal) difficult to put up with or do: *an onerous responsibility/task.*

ongoing ⇒ on.

onion /'ʌnjən/ c/u.n (also attrib) kind of vegetable that is a round white bulb of several layers(1); it has a strong taste and smell and is eaten as food: *hamburgers with onions; onion soup.*

onlooker /'ɒn‚lʊkə/ c.n person who watches but does not take an active part.

only /'əʊnlɪ/ attrib.adj **1** that is the one or ones made, existing etc without there being others: *He was the only person who came to see me. They were the only passengers on the bus.* **2** (informal) so good that there is no other possible choice: *Running is the only way to get fit.* **one and only s.t** ⇒ one(pron). **only child** person with no brothers or sisters: *I am an only child.*
▷ adv **3** and no/nothing more: *It only costs* (or *costs only*) *£5. I only drove as far as Dover and then the car broke down. They've only 50p left. I've room for one more person only.* **4** and no other person: *Only Peter came to visit me.* **5** no earlier than: *We met only a week ago but we are already good friends.* **6** with one possible result: *That ice-cream will only make you sick.* **7** referring to one of several possibilities: *I only said you're sometimes late — I didn't say you could not be trusted.* **if only** ⇒ if. **not only ... but** (also) ⇒ not. **only just** ⇒ just²(3). **only too** (used for emphasis) very: *We're only too pleased that you've arrived safely.*
▷ conj **8** but (it is/was necessary, impossible etc because): *I'm sorry to telephone you so late only I've lost my key. I'd pay for you only I don't have enough money.*

onrush /'ɒn‚rʌʃ/ c/u.n (often — of s.t) strong forward movement or flow (of s.t): *an onrush of football supporters, passengers, water.*

onset /'ɒn‚set/ def.n (often — of s.t) (formal) beginning (of s.t): *the onset of her illness.* Compare outset.

onshore /'ɒn‚ʃɔː/ attrib.adj **1** towards the land: *an onshore wind.*
▷ adv /ɒn'ʃɔː/ **2** towards the land: *a wind blowing onshore.*

onslaught /'ɒn‚slɔːt/ *c.n* (often — on s.o/s.t) determined or strong attack (on s.o/s.t).

onto ⇒ on.

onus /'əʊnəs/ *def.n* (often the — on s.o to do s.t) task that is s.o's responsibility: *The onus is on him to apologize to her. The onus of apologizing is with him.*

onward, onwards ⇒ on.

oodles /'uːdlz/ *pl.n* (usu — of s.t) (*informal*) large amounts (of s.t): *oodles of money/ ice-cream.*

oops /uːps/ *interj* (*informal*) (used to suggest surprise, e.g because of a mistake, dropping s.t etc): *Oops! I almost dropped it!*

ooze /uːz/ *u.n* **1** slow flow: *an ooze of blood.*
▷ *v* **2** *intr.v* (of liquid) flow slowly out of, through, s.t: *Blood was oozing from, out of, the wound. The paint oozed through the cloth.* **3** *tr.v* produce a slow flow of (s.t liquid): *The wound was oozing blood.* **ooze away** gradually go away: *His strength was oozing away.*

opal /'əʊpl/ *c.n* kind of valuable stone used to make jewellery.

opaque /əʊ'peɪk/ *adj* (*technical*) not allowing light through; not able to be seen through: *opaque glass.*

opacity /əʊ'pæsɪti/ *u.n* (*technical*) state of being opaque.
o'paquely *adv.* **o'paqueness** *u.n.*

OPEC /'əʊpek/ *abbr* Organization of Petroleum Exporting Countries.

open /'əʊpən/ *adj* **1** allowing people, things etc to go in, out, through etc: *an open door, gate. Who left the window open?* Opposite closed[2](2), shut(1). **2** ready and willing to be active: *Are you open on Saturday afternoon? The road/airport will not be open until the police have gone.* Opposite closed[2](3), shut(3). **3** without anything to stop a person seeing or moving inside: *an open flower/hand; open countryside/spaces.* **4** without a cover or roof: *an open boat/car; open eyes.* **5** not kept secret or hidden: *an open dislike of him; open opposition(2) to the government. Their relationship is an open one.* Opposite secret(1), hidden. **6** willing to be honest, tell the truth: *an open discussion. Please be open with me and tell me your opinion.* **7** allowing everyone to take part: *an open meeting. Is the competition open to all students?* Opposite closed(*adj*). **8** being, or to be, considered: *They left the decision open until they had more information.* **9** available: *Your job is being left open. Is your offer of money still open? Leave some time open for a discussion.* **10** (usu — to s.t) not kept safe, protected, (from s.t): *open to criticism/attack.* **with one's eyes open** ⇒ eye(*n*). **with open arms** ⇒ arm[1].
▷ *def.n* **11** area or space outside buildings: *We slept in the open under the stars.*
▷ *tr/intr.v* **12** cause (s.t) to (be/become) open: *Please open the window, your books. I opened the lid. The door opened and a man came in.* Opposite close[2](2), shut(1). **13** be/make a way along, through or towards (s.t): *They've opened a path through the forest. The front door opens onto the street.* **14** (cause (s.t) to) be ready and willing to be active: *We're not allowed to open (our shop) on Sundays.* Opposite close[2](3). **15** (often — (s.t) with s.t) begin (a meeting, discussion, activity etc) (by doing s.t): *He opened the discussion with a*

statement of the facts. *The show opened with a collection of old songs. I've opened a savings account at the bank.* Opposite close[2](4). **open one's heart/mind (to s.o)** give personal information, thoughts etc (to s.o). **open up (a)** (of a business, shop etc) open(14). **(b)** (of a person) tell the truth; give the necessary information. **(c)** (usu *imperative*) open the door of a room, house etc.

‚open 'air *def.n* (‚open-'air when *attrib*) (often in the —) open(11): *We like to eat in the open air. There's an open-air concert in the park.*

'opener *c.n* **1** kind of device for opening a container: *a tin-opener; a bottle-opener.* **2** person who begins a game, e.g of bridge, cricket.

‚open 'fire *intr.v* begin to shoot(3).

‚open-'handed *adj* generous.

‚open-'hearted *adj* kind and friendly.

‚open 'house *u.n* (esp keep —) willingness to have visitors in one's home.

'opening *n* **1** *c.n* free area; hole: *an opening in a wall, forest.* **2** *def.n* (also *attrib*) beginning: *the opening of a debate; her opening remarks. The opening night of the play was a disaster(2).* **3** *u.n* act or process(2) of becoming, making s.t, open: *the opening of a door, one's eyes.* **4** *c.n* opportunity of a job: *openings in the coal industry. We have an opening for an accountant.*

'opening ‚time *u.n* time when pubs open in Britain.

'openly *adv* without keeping anything secret or hidden: *speak openly; be openly angry.*

‚open 'market *u.n* (*technical*) economic(1) situation in which prices depend on the relationship between the amount of goods available and the amount of goods wanted.

‚open 'mind *c.n* (esp have/keep an — (about s.t)) willingness to consider all the facts (about s.t): *She kept an open mind about how the fire started.*

‚open-'minded *adj* willing to consider new ideas, opinions etc. Opposite narrow-minded.

‚open-'mindedly *adv.*

‚open-'mouthed *adj* **1** with one's mouth open. **2** (*fig*) very surprised.

'openness *u.n* fact or state of being open(6).

‚open-'plan *adj* having only a few walls inside: *an open-plan office.*

‚open 'prison *c.n* prison without walls to stop prisoners from escaping.

‚open 'sea *def.n* area of sea away from land.

‚open 'secret *c.n* thing that is supposed to be a secret but is known by everyone.

‚Open Uni'versity *def.n* (*abbr* OU) university for older students using radio and television programmes and correspondence(1) with tutors(2).

‚open 'verdict *c.n* a verdict(1) saying the jury(1) have been unable to decide one way or the other.

opera /'ɒprə/ *n* **1** *c.n* play with music in which all or most of the words are sung. **2** *u.n* plays of this kind. **3** *pl* of opus. ⇒ soap opera.

operatic /‚ɒpə'rætɪk/ *attrib.adj* of or referring to an opera(1): *an operatic company/singer.*

operate /'ɒpə‚reɪt/ *v* **1** *tr.v* make (a machine) work: *I was operating the lathe when the accident happened. Can you operate this computer?* **2** *intr.v* (of a machine, engine) be active, work: *The engine seems to be operating normally.*

3 *intr/tr.v* (*usu — on s.o, an animal* (*for s.t*)) (of a surgeon) cut open (s.o, an animal) (in order to cure her/him/it of a disease): *She will operate* (*on her*) *tomorrow. How often have you been operated on?* **4** *tr.v* (*formal*) own and run (a business): *He operates a factory in Leeds.*

operable /'ɒpərəbl/ *adj* **1** (*medical*) able to be cured by an operation(1). Opposite inoperable. **2** (of a plan, machine etc) that can be made to work properly: *Is his idea really operable?*

'ope,rating ,table *c.n* table used for operating(3).

'operating ,theatre *c.n* (*informal* **'theatre**) room in a hospital for operating(3).

operation /,ɒpə'reɪʃən/ *n* **1** *c.n* (often — *on s.o/s.t* (*for s.t*)) act of operating(3) (on a part of the body) (in order to cure s.o of a disease): *have, perform an operation on the* liver(1) *for* cancer(1). **2** *c.n* organized process(2) or set of actions: *We planned to move everything in one complete operation. The whole operation took less than an hour.* **3** *u.n* process(2) of how a machine works: *understanding the operation of a computer.* **4** *c.n* organized movements, activities of soldiers: *military operations.* **bring s.t into operation** (**a**) begin to use a plan, process(2) etc. (**b**) make a machine start working. (**c**) order soldiers, military(1) equipment(2) etc to begin to move etc as part of a plan etc. **in operation** (**a**) (of a machine) working. (**b**) (of a plan, activity, organized process(2)) being carried out; active.

operational /,ɒpə'reɪʃənl/ *adj* **1** referring to the way any operation(2) etc works: *operational methods.* **2** (of a machine, factory etc) working (well): *Is the new factory fully operational?*

operative /'ɒprətɪv/ *adj* **1** (*pred*) in operation: *The factory, plan, school will not be fully operative until we have mended the broken water pipe.* **2** (*pred*) (of a law etc) being used: *Is the rule about wearing school uniform still operative?* Opposite inoperative. **3** of or referring to an operation(1): *operative instruments/methods.* Compare operable. **the operative word** word that is the most important and useful: '*Energetic*' *is the operative word when describing his business success.*

'ope,rator *c.n* **1** person who controls a machine. **2** official who works for a telephone company and connects people who want to talk to each other by telephone: *If you cannot get through to him on the telephone, ask the operator to help you.* **3** (*usu derog*) ambitious person with good judgement of other people's weaknesses: *a clever/smooth operator.*

ophthalmic /ɒf'θælmɪk/ *adj* (*technical*) of the eye: *an ophthalmic specialist.* ⇒ ocular.

ophthalmologist /,ɒfθæl'mɒlədʒɪst/ *c.n* (also **oculist**) expert(1) in the treatment of eye diseases.

ophthalmology /,ɒfθæl'mɒlədʒɪ/ *u.n* study/ treatment of diseases of the eye.

opiate /'əʊpɪət/ *c.n* (*technical*) **1** drug containing opium. **2** kind of drug that makes a person sleep.

opinion /ə'pɪnjən/ *n* **1** *c/u.n* personal belief: *It is my opinion that dogs are nicer than cats. Don't become too concerned with public opinion.* **2** *c.n* (often — *of s.o/s.t*) personal idea of the value, beauty, usefulness etc (of s.o/s.t): *What's your opinion of her, the new building? Our opinions*

differ. **3** *c.n* professional judgement: *a* legal/ medical opinion; scientific opinion. **be of the opinion that . . .** think/believe that . . .: *I'm of the opinion that you don't like my father.* **consensus of opinion** ⇒ consensus. **difference of opinion** ⇒ difference. **a matter of opinion** ⇒ matter(*n*). **a second opinion** (**about s.t**) another opinion(3) after a doctor, lawyer etc has given hers/his (about s.t). **s.o's informed opinion** ⇒ informed(*adj*).

opinionated /ə'pɪnjə,neɪtɪd/ *adj* (*usu derog*) expressing one's opinions often and being unwilling to accept any argument against them.

o'pinion ,poll *c.n* ⇒ poll(2).

opium /'əʊpɪəm/ *u.n* kind of drug(1,2) made from poppies, used in medicine and as a narcotic.

opponent /ə'pəʊnənt/ *c.n* **1** person who plays against s.o in a game, sport. **2** person who attacks, fights against, s.o in a battle. **3** person who acts against a person, government, business, opinion, idea etc, e.g in an argument, election, business deal, law court etc. ⇒ oppose(2).

opportunity /,ɒpə'tjuːnɪtɪ/ *c/u.n* favourable time, occasion, chance etc for doing s.t: *I'll ring you later if I get an opportunity. You've missed the opportunity of a place at university. There isn't much opportunity for work at the moment. Opportunities in Canada seem to be better.* **the opportunity of a lifetime** an extremely favourable chance for getting or doing s.t important. **take the, this** etc **opportunity (of doing, to do, s.t)** make use of a favourable occasion (to do s.t): *Take this opportunity of a hot meal because we will be travelling for a long time.*

opportune /'ɒpə,tjuːn/ *adj* (*formal*) suitable; coming at a favourable time: *find an opportune time to mention your request. Meeting her then was most opportune since I was able to give her the message.* Opposite inopportune.

'oppor,tunely *adv.*

opportunist /,ɒpə'tjuːnɪst/ *c.n* (*usu derog*) person who uses any (fair or unfair) opportunity to make a personal gain.

oppose /ə'pəʊz/ *tr.v* **1** fight against (s.o) in a battle. **2** act against (a person, team, government, plan, opinion etc), e.g in an argument, election, sport, competition, law court: *Why did you oppose my suggestion?*

op'posed *pred.adj* (*usu — to s.o/s.t*) against (a person, activity, plan etc): *I'm opposed to the idea, their marriage.* **as opposed to s.o/s.t/s.w** and/but not s.o/s.t/s.w: *We're going to the seaside this year as opposed to the mountains.*

op'posing *attrib.adj* who/that opposes(2): *the opposing player/team.*

opposition /,ɒpə'zɪʃən/ *n* (often — *to s.o/s.t*) **1** *u.n* fact or act of opposing(1) s.o/s.t: *The army met with very little opposition as it entered the town.* **2** *u.n* (expression of) being opposed(2): *Her opposition (to the idea) was obvious. Opposition to the government is increasing.* **3** *def.n* person, organization etc opposing(2) oneself/s.o: *We must watch the opposition's prices.* **4** *def.n* (with capital **O**) (also *attrib*) group of MPs opposing the Government in Parliament: *Who is the leader of the Opposition? She's a member of the Opposition (party).* **in opposition** (*politics*) opposing the Government in Parliament: *The Labour Party is in opposition.*

opposite /ˈɒpəzɪt/ *adj* **1** facing: *We sat on opposite sides of the table.* **2** as completely different as possible: *We have opposite opinions. There are cafés at opposite ends of the* motorway. *They went their opposite ways after their quarrel. I live in the opposite direction* (*to you*). *The club is not open to members of the opposite sex.*
▷ *adv* **3** on the opposite side: *Who's that man opposite?*
▷ *c.n* **4** (usu — *of s.t*) person or thing who/that is as completely different (from s.t) as possible: *'Hot' is the opposite of 'cold'. My opinion is the exact opposite.*
▷ *prep* **5** (often — *to*) (on the other side of and) facing: *The cars were parked opposite each other. The new* stadium *will be built opposite* (*to*) *the car park.*
ˌopposite ˈnumber *c.n* person who does the same job etc as someone else; counterpart: *My opposite number in that company earns a lot more than I do.*

opposition ⇨ oppose.

oppress /əˈpres/ *tr.v* **1** govern, rule, manage, (people) using cruel or violent methods: *The government was accused of oppressing the workers.* **2** (*formal*) cause anxiety, sadness, suffering to (s.o): *The long wait for news oppressed him.*
oppression /əˈpreʃən/ *n* **1** *u.n* fact or state of oppressing or being oppressed: *oppression of opinion, the workers.* **2** *c/u.n* period(1) of oppressing or being oppressed: *The political oppression in that country has lasted ten years.*
oppressive /əˈpresɪv/ *adj* **1** using oppression(1): *oppressive government/laws/measures. His management was oppressive.* **2** (often of weather) causing sadness/suffering because hot etc.
opˈpressively *adv.* opˈpressiveness *u.n.*
oppressor /əˈpresə/ *c.n* person who oppresses(1).

opt /ɒpt/ *tr/intr.v* (usu — *for s.o/s.t, to do s.t*) decide (in favour of s.o/s.t etc) by choosing: *She opted for a quieter life in the country. He opted to study engineering at university.* **opt out** (**of s.t**) decide/choose not to take part, be involved(2), (in s.t): *It's too late to opt out of the meeting.*

optician /ɒpˈtɪʃən/ *c.n* expert(2) who makes or sells glasses (and sometimes binoculars etc).
optic /ˈɒptɪk/ *attrib.adj* (*technical*) of or referring to the eye: *the optic nerve.*
optical /ˈɒptɪkl/ *adj* of or referring to the power to see or what is seen: *optical instruments.*
ˌoptical ilˈlusion *c.n* example of seeing s.t that does not exist because of a wrong impression of one's eyes.
ˈoptics *u.n* study of the laws of light and the power of vision(1).

optimism /ˈɒptɪˌmɪzəm/ *u.n* feeling or idea that nothing bad will happen, that one will be successful etc: *be filled with optimism.* Opposite pessimism.
ˈoptimist *c.n* person who is optimistic. Opposite pessimist.
optimistic /ˌɒptɪˈmɪstɪk/ *adj* believing/feeling that nothing bad will happen, that one will be successful etc. Opposite pessimistic.
ˌoptiˈmistically *adv.*

optimum /ˈɒptɪməm/ *adj* (*formal*) most favourable; best: *the optimum size/time/conditions.*

option /ˈɒpʃən/ *n* **1** *c.n* (*formal*) choice: *You have two options; either stay home and work or come to the film with us. My option is to go to Tibet.* **2** *u.n* right/power to choose: *He had little option but to agree.* (**take** (**out**)) **an option on s.t** (get) an opportunity to buy s.t within a stated period of time. **leave one's options open** not make a decision; not choose.
ˈoptional *adj* allowing one to choose to agree, act, buy, wear etc or not: *Hats are now optional in most churches. You can have a telephone fitted in the car as an optional extra.*

opulent /ˈɒpjʊlənt/ *adj* (*formal*) very wealthy, usu in a showy way: *an opulent country house.*
ˈopulence *u.n* (usu — *of s.t*) state of being opulent.
ˈopulently *adv.*

opus /ˈəʊpəs/ *c.n* (*pl* -es or, less usu, *opera* /ˈɒpərə/) (used with capital **O** in names, *written abbr* Op) musical work: *Beethoven's Symphony No. 9, Op 125.* ⇨ magnum opus.

or (strong form /ɔː/, weak form /ə/) *conj* **1** (joining alternatives(2)): *Is it Monday or Tuesday, ready or not? I'll accept tomatoes, lettuce or carrots.* **2** (often — *else*) if not; otherwise: *Decide now or* (*else*) *I'll give it to Peter.* **3** (often — *rather*) (joining different ways of saying the same thing): *Come upstairs to my flat or* (*rather*) *apartment as you Americans say.* **either . . . or . . .** ⇨ either. **or else** (**a**) ⇨ or(2). (**b**) (*informal*) if not you'll be in trouble: *Come back before midnight or else!* **or so** approximately; about that (number etc): *I've seen that film ten or so times* (or *ten times or so*). *We were able to sell a hundred or so* (*of them*). **or something, somewhere** ⇨ something, somewhere.

oracle /ˈɒrəkl/ *c.n* **1** (in ancient Greece, Rome etc) (place where one can obtain) information about the future from the gods. **2** (*informal*) wise person.

oral /ˈɔːrəl/ *adj* **1** of, or referring to, using, the mouth: *oral medicine.* **2** spoken and not written: *an oral examination.* Compare aural.
▷ *c.n* **3** (*informal*) oral(2) examination.
ˈorally *adv* using the mouth: *This medicine should not be taken orally.*

orange /ˈɒrɪndʒ/ *adj* **1** having the colour of the sun that is between red and yellow: *an orange skirt. The walls are orange!* **2** (*attrib*) tasting of, made from, oranges: *orange juice.*
▷ *c/u.n* **3** (also *attrib*) kind of round fruit with (usu) an orange(1) skin (when ripe) and juicy flesh: *an orange tree/drink. It tastes of oranges* (or *has an orange taste*). **4** orange(1) colour.
ˌorangeˈade *u.n* fizzy orange juice.

orang-utan /ɔːˌræŋ uːˈtæn/ (also **oˌrang-uˈtang** /uːˈtæŋ/) *c.n* kind of large ape with orange fur.

orate /ɔːˈreɪt/ *intr.v* (*formal*) make a formal speech.
oration /ɔːˈreɪʃən/ *c.n* (*formal*) formal speech.
orator /ˈɒrətə/ *c.n* person who makes speeches: *A good orator knows how to please a crowd.*
oratory /ˈɒrətrɪ/ *u.n* art of speaking well in public.

orb /ɔːb/ *c.n* **1** thing with the shape of a ball, e.g the moon. **2** ball covered with jewels and having a cross on top, used as a symbol of a king's or queen's authority(1).

orbit /ˈɔːbɪt/ *c.n* **1** path of an object, e.g a moon, round a planet, the sun etc. **2** (*informal*) area of

influence or control: *When children are out of the family orbit they sometimes behave badly.*
▷ *tr.v* **3** travel round (a planet, the sun etc): *How long does it take for the Earth to orbit the Sun?*
orbital /'ɔːbɪtl/ *adj.*

orchard /'ɔːtʃəd/ *c.n* area containing fruit trees: *an apple orchard.*

orchestra /'ɔːkɪstrə/ *c.n* (also *attrib*) large group of people playing violins, cellos, flutes etc together: *an orchestra company.*
orchestral /ɔː'kestrəl/ *attrib.adj* by/for/of an orchestra: *orchestral instruments/music.*
'orchestra ‚pit ⇨ pit'(4).
orchestrate /'ɔːkɪ‚streɪt/ *tr.v* **1** arrange (music) for an orchestra to play. **2** (*fig*) arrange (things) to get a particular result: *She orchestrated the quarrel. The meeting was well orchestrated.*
orchestration /‚ɔːkɪ'streɪʃən/ *c/u.n.*
orchestrator /'ɔːkɪ‚streɪtə/ *c.n* person who orchestrates.

orchid /'ɔːkɪd/ *c.n* kind of plant with unusual, colourful(1) and often waxy(1) flowers.

ordain /ɔː'deɪn/ *tr.v* **1** make (s.o) a priest etc. ⇨ ordination. **2** (often — *that* . . .) (*formal*) (esp of fate, God) give a formal command (that . . .): *Fate had ordained that he would be ill on the day of the race.*

ordeal /ɔː'diːl/ *c.n* severe test of one's (esp mental(1)) strength or character: *Watching him suffer was a difficult ordeal. Don't make such an ordeal out of a small problem.*

order /'ɔːdə/ *n* **1** *c.n* statement (spoken or written) (esp from an official) telling a person he/she must do s.t: *I have my orders and I must obey them. He received an order from the law court to pay the money to his wife. I told you to leave her alone and that's an order!* **2** *c.n* piece of paper giving an order(1) to pay money: *a postal order.* **3** *c.n* (also *attrib*) (often — *for* s.t) statement asking a person or business to supply s.t: *We haven't had many orders for our cars this month.* Export(2) *orders have increased. Use the correct order form.* **4** *u.n* organized, peaceful way of living, working, behaving etc: *Without order life would be very difficult.* ⇨ keep order. **5** *u.n* (usu in —) organized, correct condition or state: *Are your papers, Is the house, in good order? Everything seems to be in order. The car is in poor working order.* **6** *c/u.n* (often in (a particular kind of) —; in — of s.t) arrangement: *in alphabetical order; in order of size/age/importance.* **7** *c.n* sort(1); standard: *This is education of the highest order.* **8** *c.n* (*technical*) class; division: *Apes(1) and humans belong to the same order.* **9** *c.n* (often with capital **O**) religious group (esp of nuns or monks). **10** *c.n* (with capital **O**) honorary(2) title or rank: *The Order of* Merit(1). **11** *c.n* (with capital **O**) group of people having the same Order(10). **by order (of s.o)** (*formal*) as an order(1) (from an official). **call s.o/s.t to order** state that s.o, a meeting etc must stop behaving against the rules. **keep order** make certain that a group etc remains organized, behaves well etc. **in order** ⇨ order(5). **in order of s.t** ⇨ order(6). **in the order of s.t** about(7), s.t, approximately: *Your new bike will cost in the order of £100.* **in order that . . ., to do s.t** so that (s.t) is possible; for the purpose of doing s.t: *I'm writing in order to explain what happened.* **in**

running order ⇨ run(*v*). **law and order** ⇨ law. **made to order** produced in the shape, colour etc asked for: *Her dresses are made to order.* **of the order of s.t** = in the order of s.t. **on order** for which an order(3) has been made (but not yet supplied): *The red plates are on order and will be in the shop next week.* **Order! Order!** (used to demand attention, silence etc). **out of order** **(a)** not working well: *My bicycle is out of order at the moment.* **(b)** not in the correct place in an arrangement: *This book is out of order.* **(c)** not done according to the rules: *She spoke out of order.* **point of order** ⇨ point(*n*). **take holy orders** become a priest. **tall order** (*informal*) request, duty, task etc that is difficult. **under orders (to do s.t)** having been ordered(12) (to do s.t). **under starter's orders** ready for the signal to begin to take part in a race.
▷ *v* **12** *tr.v* give an order(1) to (s.o): *We were ordered to leave.* **13** *tr.v* give an order(3) for (s.t): *I didn't order these pink shoes!* **14** *tr/intr.v* ask for (a meal, drink in a restaurant etc): *Are you ready to order? We ordered coffee a long time ago.* **15** *tr.v* arrange (things, ideas, people etc) in an organized way: *I'll explain how to order these papers. I need time to order my thoughts before I speak.* **order s.o about** give many orders(1) to s.o: *She orders me about as if I was a servant.*
'orderliness *u.n* state of being orderly(1).
'orderly *adj* **1** in good order(5): *an orderly desk/kitchen/report.* **2** organized and well-behaved: *an orderly group of children.*
▷ *c.n* (*pl* -ies) **3** person who does small regular duties in a hospital, e.g taking patients to the operating theatre. **4** (*military*) soldier who does small duties for an officer.

ordinal /'ɔːdɪnl/ *c.n* (also ‚ordinal 'number) number that shows position in a list, line etc, e.g 'first', 'second', 'third' (1st, 2nd, 3rd). Compare cardinal.

ordinance /'ɔːdɪnəns/ *c.n* (*formal*) official law(1), order(1), decree(1) etc.

ordinary /'ɔːdɪnrɪ/ *adj* **1** usual; common; normal: *wearing her ordinary clothes; an ordinary way of cooking chicken.* ⇨ special(2). **2** (*derog*) not exciting enough: *The colours in the pattern are very ordinary.* ⇨ extraordinary.
▷ *def.n* **3** **out of the ordinary** unusual: *Did you notice anything out of the ordinary when you visited him?*
ordinarily /'ɔːdɪnrɪlɪ/ *adv* usually; on most occasions: *Ordinarily I would take the bus but today I think I'll walk.*
ordination /‚ɔːdɪ'neɪʃən/ *c/u.n* (example of an) act of making a person a priest.

Ordnance Survey /‚ɔːdnəns 'sɜːveɪ/ *def.n* (*abbr* OS) (organization producing) government maps of Great Britain and Northern Ireland.

ore /ɔː/ *c/u.n* (particular kind of) rock, stone etc containing metal: *iron/tin ore.*

oregano /‚ɒrɪ'gɑːnəʊ/ *u.n* (*Italian*) kind of herb used in cooking.

organ[1] /'ɔːgən/ *c.n* **1** part of (the inside of) the body, with a particular purpose: *The* liver(1) *and heart are* internal(1) *organs. The ear is the organ of hearing.* **2** part of any living thing with a particular purpose: *the reproductive organs of plants.* **3** (*fig*) organization, system to get work done: *The* Civil Service *is the organ of government* administration(2). **4** organization used as a way of giving out information: *Some newspapers are organs of government policy.* **vital organ** ⇨ vital.

organic /ɔːˈgænɪk/ *adj* **1** of an organ[1](1,2): *an organic disease.* **2** grown without using manmade(1) chemicals, i.e using only fertilizers produced by animals or plants: *organic vegetables.* **3** (*technical*) that has life; of or referring to any chemical compound(1) containing carbon(1). Opposite inorganic.

orˈganically *adv* **1** referring to an organ[1](1): *Is there something wrong organically?* **2** using organic(2) methods: *grown organically.*

orˌganic ˈchemistry *u.n* branch of chemistry concerned with the study of organic(3) substances. Compare inorganic chemistry.

organism /ˈɔːgənɪzəm/ *c.n* very small and simple living animal or plant: *The sea is full of organisms used as food by fish.*

organ² /ˈɔːgən/ *c.n* (also *attrib*) musical instrument with a keyboard(1) which makes sounds by sending air through pipes: *a church organ*; *organ music.* ⇨ electric(2) organ, mouth organ.

organist /ˈɔːgənɪst/ *c.n* person who plays an organ².

organize, -ise /ˈɔːgənaɪz/ *v* **1** *tr.v* put/form (s.t, e.g units or parts) in a particular arrangement: *The classes have been organized according to ability.* **2** *tr.v* prepare/arrange (a group or activity): *organize a meeting/party/trip for fifty people.* **3** *tr.v* arrange (workers) in a trade union. **4** *intr.v* become members of a trade union: *We must organize if we are to improve our working conditions.*

organization, -isation /ˌɔːgənaɪˈzeɪʃən/ *n* **1** *u.n* act/state/process of being or becoming organized: *I don't understand the organization of this office.* **2** *c.n* (with capital **O** in names) group of businessmen, government officials, political workers etc working for a particular purpose: *an organization for training sales staff in the computer industry*; *the Organization of African Unity.*

ˈorgaˌnized, -ised *adj* **1** having or using a particular arrangement: *an organized room/ desk/ discussion/demonstration(3)/student.* ⇨ disorganized. **2** having become a member of a trade union.

ˈorgaˌnizer, -iser *c.n* person who organizes(2).

orgasm /ˈɔːgæzəm/ *c/u.n* strongest point of sexual feeling.

orgasmic /ɔːˈgæzmɪk/ *adj.*

orgy /ˈɔːdʒɪ/ *c.n* (*pl -ies*) **1** wild gathering of people where there is too much alcoholic(1) drink, sexual freedom etc. **2** (*informal*) period of (too) many pleasant experiences: *an orgy of theatre visits.*

oriental /ˌɔːrɪˈentl/ *adj* (sometimes with capital **O**) of, from or referring to, the eastern part of the world: *oriental food/fashions.*

Orient /ˈɔːrɪənt/ *def.n* (*old use*) eastern part of the world.

orientate /ˈɔːrɪənˌteɪt/ *reflex.v* **1** organize one's thoughts; decide about one's position according to one's surroundings: *It was difficult to orientate myself in the mist.* **2** make oneself familiar with new surroundings: *It takes time to orientate oneself after changing one's job.* ⇨ disorientate.

orientation /ˌɔːrɪənˈteɪʃən/ *u.n.*

orifice /ˈɒrɪfɪs/ *c.n* (*technical*) opening in the body, e.g the mouth, ear, nostril.

origami /ˌɒrɪˈgɑːmɪ/ *u.n* Japanese art of making models of things by folding paper.

origin /ˈɒrɪdʒɪn/ *c/u.n* **1** (often *pl*) point at which s.t began; first stage: *AIDS has its origin(s) in Africa.* **2** *c.n* (usu — *of s.t*) cause of s.t beginning: *Can you explain the origin of the war?* **of English/French** etc **origin**; **English/French** etc **by/in origin** coming from an English/French etc family: *She is of Russian origin* (or *is Russian by origin*). ⇨ origins.

original /əˈrɪdʒɪnl/ *adj* **1** of, from or referring to, the beginning: *This is the original map before the forest was cut down. Who were the original people who lived in these mountains?* **2** new and not copied: *an original painting/design/ idea.* **3** (*informal*) particularly interesting because new: *That's an original suggestion!* **4** able to produce original(2) things: *an original mind/writer/ thinker.* **5** (*attrib*) being the one from which copies have been produced: *Please send the original letter/certificate(1) and not a photocopy(1).* ▷ *n* **6** *def.n* earliest form or example: *I have the original and you have a copy.* **7** *c.n* (*informal*) person able to produce original(2) things.

originality /əˌrɪdʒɪˈnælɪtɪ/ *u.n* fact or quality of being original(3,4): *a writer who produces novels' of great originality.*

originally /əˈrɪdʒɪnəlɪ/ *adv* **1** at/in the beginning: *Originally I wanted to be a doctor, but I discovered that I hate blood. The bicycle was mine originally and I gave it to Sally.* **2** using original(2) ideas, methods etc: *He designs(5) originally.*

originate /əˈrɪdʒɪˌneɪt/ *tr/intr.v* (often — *in s.t*; — *with s.o*) (cause (s.t) to) come into existence: *Life originated in the sea. Who originated this particular style(2) of dressing? Geometry originated with the ancient Greeks.* **originate from s.w** (*formal*) come originally(1) from a place: *These plants originate from Nepal.*

origination /əˌrɪdʒɪˈneɪʃən/ *u.n.*

oˈrigiˌnator *c.n* (usu — *of s.t*) person who originates s.t.

ˈorigins *pl.n* (person's) family background: *She was ashamed of her origins.*

ornament /ˈɔːnəmənt/ *n* **1** *c.n* thing used to make s.o/s.t more attractive: *She has many china ornaments in the room.* **2** *u.n* ornaments(1) as a group; state of being an ornament: *I prefer very little ornament on my clothes.* ▷ *tr.v* /ˌɔːnəˈment/ (*formal*) **3** make (s.o/s.t) more attractive using ornaments(1): *ornament a garden with pots of flowers.* **4** act as an ornament(1): *flowers ornamenting the living-room.*

ornamental /ˌɔːnəˈmentl/ *adj* used as an ornament(1): *ornamental flowers.*

ornate /ɔːˈneɪt/ *adj* having (too) many decorations: *an ornate pattern/design(2).*

orˈnately *adv.* **orˈnateness** *u.n.*

ornithology /ˌɔːnɪˈθɒlədʒɪ/ *u.n* study of birds.

ornithological /ˌɔːnɪθəˈlɒdʒɪkl/ *adj.*

ornithologist /ˌɔːnɪˈθɒlədʒɪst/ *c.n* expert(1) in ornithology.

orphan /ˈɔːfən/ *c.n* (also *attrib*) child whose parents are dead: *an orphan girl.*

orphanage /ˈɔːfənɪdʒ/ *c.n* place where orphans live.

orthodox /ˈɔːθəˌdɒks/ *adj* **1** having or using

beliefs, standards, methods etc that are generally accepted: *have orthodox views*; *use orthodox methods*; *be a member of an orthodox political party*. Opposite unorthodox. **2** (with capital **O**) being a member of the Christian church of Greece and eastern Europe.
'ortho,doxy *u.n* (*formal*) state of having orthodox(1) beliefs, using orthodox(1) methods: *We're worried about the orthodoxy of his teaching style.*

orthography /ɔːˈθɒgrəfɪ/ *u.n* (*technical*) system of spelling.
orthographic /ˌɔːθəˈgræfɪk/ *adj*.

orthopaedics /ˌɔːθəˈpiːdɪks/ *sing.n* (US **,ortho'pedics**) (also *attrib*) medical science concerning diseases and repair of the bones.
,ortho'paedic *attrib.adj* (US **,ortho'pedic**) of, from or referring to orthopaedics: *an orthopaedic surgeon.*

OS *written abbr* Ordnance Survey.

oscillate /ˈɒsɪˌleɪt/ *intr.v* (usu — *between s.t and s.t*) (*formal*) **1** move backwards and forwards, up and down etc (between two amounts, sides, points etc): *The needle on the* dial(1) *was oscillating between 30 and 40.* **2** move (between two decisions, opinions etc): *She was oscillating between buying a record and going to the cinema.*
oscillation /ˌɒsɪˈleɪʃən/ *u.n*.

osmosis /ɒzˈməʊsɪs/ *u.n* **1** (*technical*) mixing of two liquid substances having different strengths until both have the same strength. **2** (usu *by* —) (*informal*) slow, unconscious taking in of knowledge, ideas etc: *We learn the grammar of the language we speak by osmosis.*

osprey /ˈɒsprɪ/ *c.n* (also **'fish ,eagle/,hawk**) kind of bird of prey that eats fish.

ossify /ˈɒsɪfaɪ/ *intr.v* (*-ies, -ied*) **1** (*technical*) become bone. **2** (*formal*) (of a person's ideas, habits, beliefs etc) become impossible to change or adapt(1).
ossification /ˌɒsɪfɪˈkeɪʃən/ *u.n*.

ostensible /ɒˈstensɪbl/ *attrib.adj* apparent or stated (but not necessarily true): *The weather was the ostensible reason for his untidy garden but the true reason was his lack of interest.*
o'stensibly *adv*.

ostentation /ˌɒstenˈteɪʃən/ *u.n* (*derog*; *formal*) exaggerated way of doing s.t, showing wealth etc.
,osten'tatious *adj* (*derog*; *formal*) showing/using ostentation: *an ostentatious way of speaking*; *ostentatious clothes/people.*
,osten'tatiously *adv*: *ostentatiously dressed.*

osteoarthritis /ˌɒstɪəʊɑːˈθraɪtɪs/ *u.n* serious and painful swelling and inflammation of the bone joints.

osteopath /ˈɒstɪəˌpæθ/ *c.n* person who studies, is skilled in, osteopathy.
osteopathy /ˌɒstɪˈɒpəθɪ/ *u.n* treatment of injuries by moving bones and muscles into their correct positions.

ostracize, -ise /ˈɒstrəˌsaɪz/ *tr.v* refuse to have contact with (a particular person): *The other students ostracized her because of her behaviour.*
ostracism /ˈɒstrəˌsɪzəm/ *u.n*.

ostrich /ˈɒstrɪtʃ/ *c.n* (also *attrib*) kind of very large bird that cannot fly and has large tail feathers used to make hats, dusters etc.

other /ˈʌðə/ *det* **1** (*the, her, your* etc — . . .) (referring to the second of two people, things, groups etc): *I found one shoe but I can't see the other one. He's parked on the other side of the road. My other brother is a policeman.* **2** different: *'Can you help me?' 'Some other time — I'm busy at the moment.' 'No other person would be so willing.* **3** more; additional: *I have other colours in stock.* **every other . . .** ⇨ every. **one's/s.o's other half** ⇨ half(n). **on the other hand** ⇨ hand. **other than** (a) except for: *No one other than her relatives went to her wedding.* (b) different from: *I need a tool other than the one you gave me yesterday.* ⇨ no/none other than. **the other day, evening** etc on a recent day, evening etc: *I met John the other night at the football game.*
▷ *pron* **4** (usu *the* —) second of two people, things, groups etc: *I've got one sock but I can't find the other.* ⇨ another(1). **each other** ⇨ each. **no/none other than** the same person, thing as: *The strange visitor was no/none other than my old aunt.* **(s.o/s.t/s.w/somehow) or other** (used to show lack of certainty about what, who, which etc): *Someone or other telephoned you this morning. He's somewhere or other. I'll get there somehow or other.*

'others *pron* **1** different ones: *I like these, but have you any others I can look at?* **2** more; additional/extra ones: *I have six helpers but I need some others.* **3** people, things etc remaining: *The others will be ready next week.*

otherwise /ˈʌðəˌwaɪz/ *adv* **1** in a different way: *She believes he took it but I believe otherwise.* **2** except for that: *The garden is too small but otherwise I like the house.*
▷ *conj* **3** if not: *Come early otherwise you may not get a seat. Stop it, otherwise I'll tell your dad.*

otter /ˈɒtə/ *c.n* small animal with dark fur that lives near rivers, swims well and eats fish.

OU /ˌəʊ ˈjuː/ *def.n abbr* Open University.

ouch /aʊtʃ/ *interj* (used to express sudden pain).

ought /ɔːt/ *aux.v* (no *pres.p, p.p* or *p.t* forms; negative forms *ought not* or *oughtn't* /ˈɔːtnt/; 'ought to have' can be *ought've* /ˈɔːtəv/; 'ought not to have' can be *oughtn't to have*; 'ought' is always followed by the infinitive form of a verb with *to*) **1** be s.o's duty or responsibility; be advisable that . . .: *'You ought to go.' 'Ought I?' He ought to have paid for the damage. You oughtn't to have been so rude. She ought not to stay out so late. We ought to apologize, oughtn't we?* **2** be likely, reasonable etc that . . .: *He ought to be here soon. That ought to be enough money for the holiday. These trousers ought to last for a few months. You ought to win if you try hard. You oughtn't to be here yet!* **3** be desirable that . . .; be a good thing if . . .: *Teachers ought to earn more money. They oughtn't to be outside in this weather. You oughtn't to have left so late. We ought to be told about the dangers. You ought to have warned me.* Compare should(5,6).

oughtn't /ˈɔːtnt/ = ought not. ⇨ ought.
ought've /ˈɔːtəv/ = ought to have. ⇨ ought.

ounce /aʊns/ *n* **1** *c.n* (*written abbr* oz) unit of weight equal to about 28.4 grams: *There are 16 ounces to the pound. The bird weighs 5 oz.* **2** *sing.n* (*fig*) (used with a negative) even a small amount: *She doesn't have an ounce of intelligence. There's not an ounce of spare flesh on her.*

our /auə/ *possessive adj* belonging to, for, us: *This is our home. Where's our bus?* ⇒ us(*pron*), we(*pron*).

ours /auəz/ *possessive pron* the one(s) belonging to, for, us: *This hotel room is ours. Ours is here and yours is over there.*

ourselves /auə'selvz/ *pron* 1 *reflex.pron* (used when the object of the verb or preposition is the same (people, animals, things as the subject)): *We washed ourselves and our clothes in the river.* 2 (used to emphasize 'us', 'we'): *We painted the room ourselves. They're trying to save £100 but we ourselves hope to save £150.* (**by**) **ourselves** (often *all by* —) (**a**) alone: *We travelled all by ourselves.* (**b**) without help: *We did it* (*by*) *ourselves.*

oust /aust/ *tr.v* (often — *s.o from s.t*) (*formal*) cause/force (s.o) to leave a job, position: *The members ousted him from the committee. She was ousted from the team by the younger players.*

out /aut/ *adj* 1 (*attrib*) (showing the direction of movement out of s.t/s.w: *leave through the out door.* Opposite in²(1). 2 (*pred*) not possible or acceptable: *No, that plan is out because we could hurt someone.* 3 (*pred*) not in power any longer: *The Liberals are out.* ⇒ in²(3), out(14). 4 (*pred*) known: *The news/secret is out.* 5 (*pred*) (of time) finished: *We must complete this job before the week is out.* 6 (*pred*) not correct: *The bill/ account is out by £5.*

▷ *adv* 7 (also *pred.adj*) away from one's home, work etc: *They've gone out for a meal. I was sent out to buy some milk. They slept out under the stars. I'm sorry but Mary's out tonight.* ⇒ in²(4). 8 (also *pred.adj*) so as to be no longer burning or working: *The lights/fire went out. The lights are out.* 9 leaving from, looking at etc a place from the inside: *They walked/ran out. She opened the window and looked out.* ⇒ in²(5). 10 from the inside (of s.t): *Take your pens out and write this down.* ⇒ in²(6). 11 so as not to include (s.o/s.t): *If it's dangerous, count me out!* ⇒ in²(8). 12 (also *pred.adj*) so as to be no longer working: *The men are, have.come, out* (*on strike*). 13 so as to be no longer present, seen: *We were told to rub/ scratch/paint the words out.* 14 (also *pred.adj*) (of styles of clothes etc) so as to be no longer in fashion: *When did wide trousers go out? Thin ties are out.* ⇒ in²(10). 15 (also *pred.adj*) available for sale: *When does her new record come out? His new book is out.* Compare in²(11). 16 (also *pred.adj*) existing; visible(1): *All the flowers have come out. The stars are out.* 17 so as to be completed, have a successful result: *They must fight/work it out.* 18 so as to be beyond the limit or surface: *His ears stick/stand out.* 19 (of members of a team in some sports, esp cricket¹ and baseball) so as to be defeated while in the batting (⇒ bat²(2)) position: *I was caught/run out. He's out! They were all out for only 50 runs*(8). Compare in²(13) 20 (also *pred.adj*) (esp of a ball in some sports, e.g tennis, football) outside the boundary lines: *The ball bounced out. That ball was out.* ⇒ in²(14). 21 (also *pred.adj*) (of the tide) at, or going to, its lowest point: *The tide has gone, is, out.* ⇒ in²(16). For a verb, or a verb followed by a noun (phrase)/pron, followed by 'out', e.g *come out, knock s.o out, spread* (*s.t*) *out,* ⇒ the verb. **inside out** ⇒ inside. **out and about** in the

open air and busy, active. **out for s.t**; **out to do s.t** determined to do, get, have etc s.t: *He's out for the job of captain. She's out to win a medal.*

▷ *interj* 22 (used to order s.o to leave): *Out! Out you go!* **out with it** (used to order s.o to tell s.t): *Out with it; what did she say to you?*

▷ *prep* **out of** 23 from inside: *She walked out of the room. I got out of bed and looked out of the window. She took the money out of her pocket.* ⇒ into(1). 24 away from; not in, not inside: *John is out of town for the day. We live ten miles out of London.* ⇒ in²(17,18). 25 not busy with; not engaged in: *He's out of work. I'm out of a job at the moment.* ⇒ in²(25). 26 (made) using (s.t) as material: *built out of wood; made out of paper; sewn out of pieces of silk.* ⇒ from(6), in²(26), of(7). 27 using: *drink out of a cup/bowl.* 28 not in the state or condition mentioned: *She's out of danger now. We've fallen out of love.* ⇒ in²(28). 29 (showing that s.o/s.t is not in an order or arrangement: *These books are out of* (alphabetical/numerical) *order.* ⇒ in²(29). 30 having none left: *out of breath/matches/petrol.* ⇒ in²(30). 31 from (a larger amount): *Nine out of ten people prefer butter.* ⇒ in²(23). 32 because of: *She did it out of sympathy. He stole out of hunger.* 33 (used to show the result or effect(1) of s.t causing loss, a decision not to act etc): *He went out of his mind with worry. I'll talk her out of doing it.* ⇒ into(6). For a verb followed by 'out of' and then a noun (phrase(1))/pron, e.g *grow out of one's clothes,* ⇒ the verb. **out of doors** ⇒ door. **out of it** (**a**) not wanted: *I felt out of it at their party.* (**b**) not, no longer, involved(2): *The business is doing well and I'm sorry to be out of it.* **out of order** ⇒ order(*n*). **out of the ordinary** ⇒ ordinary(3). **out of the red** ⇒ red(*n*). **out of sorts** ⇒ sort(*n*). **out of s.o's/the way** ⇒ way. **the ins and outs** (**of s.t**) ⇒ ins (*def.pl.n*). For verb + 'out of' + noun (phrase)/ pron, e.g *grow out of one's clothes,* ⇒ the verb.

,out-and-'out *attrib.adj* complete, thorough: *an out-and-out liar.*

'outer *attrib.adj* 1 situated/falling outside: *the outer walls; outer garments.* 2 near the edge: *the outer limits.* 3 at a great distance: *outer space.* Opposite inner.

'outer,most *adj* furthest from the inside, centre; at the greatest distance. Opposite innermost.

,outer 'space *unique n* space(3) that is far away or outside the earth's atmosphere(1).

,out-of-'date *attrib.adj* (,**out of 'date** when *pred*) ⇒ date¹.

,out-of-the-'way *attrib.adj* 1 far from towns, cities etc: *visit out-of-the-way places.* 2 unusual: *out-of-the-way ideas.*

'out-,tray *c.n* tray in which papers, letters etc are put when they have been dealt with. ⇒ in-tray.

outward /'autwəd/ *attrib.adj* 1 of/on the outside or surface: *the outward signs of illness; ignore outward appearances.* ⇒ inward(1). 2 away from s.w: *an outward journey.*

'outwardly *adv* according to what is seen on the outside: *Outwardly he looks brave but he is actually very frightened.* ⇒ inwardly.

outwards /'autwədz/ *adv* towards the outside, edge: *stretch one's legs outwards. Her knees bend outwards.* ⇒ inwards.

outbid /,aut'bid/ *tr.v* (-dd-, *p.t,p.p* outbid) offer a larger amount of money than s.o else for s.t.

outbreak /'aʊtˌbreɪk/ c.n (usu — of s.t) sudden strong start (of an illness, a war, anger etc). ⇒ break out (⇒ break(v)).

outbuilding /'aʊtˌbɪldɪŋ/ c.n small building near a larger/main building.

outburst /'aʊtˌbɜːst/ c.n (usu — of s.t) sudden strong expression (of feeling or emotion): an outburst of anger; outbursts of laughter. ⇒ burst out (⇒ burst(v)).

outcast /'aʊtˌkɑːst/ c.n (also attrib) person who is not allowed to be a friend, member of a group etc. ⇒ cast s.o out (⇒ cast(v)).

outcome /'aʊtˌkʌm/ c.n (usu — of s.t) result (of an activity, event): What was the outcome of your argument, the meeting?

outcry /'aʊtˌkraɪ/ c.n (pl -ies) general show of strong feeling (against s.t): an outcry against the rising price of food. ⇒ cry out (⇒ cry(v)).

outdated /ˌaʊt'deɪtɪd/ adj out of fashion; no longer useful: outdated methods/ideas. ⇒ out-of-date.

outdistance /ˌaʊt'dɪstəns/ tr.v (formal) go far ahead of (s.o) in a race etc.

outdo /ˌaʊt'duː/ tr.v (3rd pers sing pres.t outdoes /ˌaʊt'dʌz/, p.t outdid /ˌaʊt'dɪd/, p.p outdone /ˌaʊt'dʌn/) (often passive) (formal) be more successful than (s.o/s.t); do more than (s.o/s.t): I will not be outdone by a younger colleague.

outdoor /'aʊtˌdɔː/ attrib.adj happening, used etc outside any buildings: outdoor sports and games. Opposite indoor.

outdoors /ˌaʊt'dɔːz/ adv outside any buildings: eat/play/sleep outdoors. It's warmer outdoors than indoors. Opposite indoors.

outer, outermost ⇒ out.

outface /ˌaʊt'feɪs/ tr.v (formal) oppose (s.o) with courage.

outfit /'aʊtˌfɪt/ c.n 1 set of clothes: a sports/ wedding outfit. 2 (informal) set of people in an organization, esp business or military(1): We have a hardworking outfit in the factory.
▷ tr.v (-tt-) 3 provide an outfit(1) for (s.o). ⇒ fit s.o out (⇒ fit').

'outˌfitter c.n person/shop selling clothes: a men's outfitter.

outflank /ˌaʊt'flæŋk/ tr.v 1 go round (soldiers) that are flanking(2) one's army. 2 (fig) to outdo (s.o) by using their chosen method more successfully than they have.

outfox /ˌaʊt'fɒks/ tr.v be more cunning(1) than (another person).

outgoing /ˌaʊt'gəʊɪŋ/ adj 1 (attrib) leaving (a place, job etc): the outgoing government/chairperson/tenant(1). 2 pleasant and friendly: have an outgoing personality(1). She's very outgoing.

outgrow /ˌaʊt'grəʊ/ tr.v (p.t outgrew /ˌaʊt'gruː/, p.p outgrown /ˌaʊt'grəʊn/) 1 grow too big for (one's clothes, shoes etc). 2 become too mature(1) for (an activity, habit, attitude etc): I've outgrown childish games. ⇒ grow out of s.t(a). 3 grow bigger or faster than (another person).

outhouse /'aʊtˌhaʊs/ c.n (pl -s /-ˌhaʊzɪz/) = outbuilding.

outing /'aʊtɪŋ/ c.n short journey to s.w and back for pleasure: go on a day's outing to the seaside.

outlandish /aʊt'lændɪʃ/ adj (often derog) deliberately made to look/be very unusual, strange: outlandish clothes. Her language is outlandish! **ˌout'landishly** adv. **ˌout'landishness** u.n.

outlast /ˌaʊt'lɑːst/ tr.v last/live longer than (another person, thing).

outlaw /'aʊtˌlɔː/ c.n 1 person who has done s.t that is against the law.
▷ tr.v 2 make (s.o) an outlaw. 3 make (s.t) officially not allowed: Smoking has been outlawed on most trains.

outlay /'aʊtˌleɪ/ c/u.n 1 (usu — of s.t) spending of money: an outlay of at least £200.
▷ /ˌaʊt'leɪ/ tr.v (p.t,p.p outlaid /ˌaʊt'leɪd/) 2 spend (s.t): How much do you have to outlay on a new carpet?

outlet /'aʊtlɪt/ c.n (usu — for s.t) 1 opening for liquid etc to go out. 2 means/method for expressing feelings, emotions etc. 3 shop etc that sells certain goods: It's a good outlet for modern dresses. They are sold through many outlets.

outline /'aʊtˌlaɪn/ c.n (usu — of s.t) (also attrib) 1 line drawn to show the shape of the edges/limit of s.t esp without other details: an outline map. She drew an outline of the new house. 2 short account, description with the important matters only and no details: This is an outline of the story, her theory(1). **in outline** without details: I'll describe the plot of the play in outline.
▷ tr.v 3 give a short account or description of (s.t): He outlined his plan/idea.

outlive /ˌaʊt'lɪv/ tr.v 1 live longer than (another person). 2 live long enough for (s.t bad that is known about oneself) to be forgotten: He'll never be able to outlive their criticism.

outlook /'aʊtˌlʊk/ c.n 1 view looking out of s.t, esp a window: The house has a pleasant outlook. 2 person's general attitude(2) towards life: She has an optimistic outlook/on life. 3 (often — for s.t) thing that seems likely to happen (to s.t): a miserable weather outlook. What's the outlook for our sales to America next year?

outlying /'aʊtˌlaɪŋ/ attrib.adj in a position far from the centre: outlying villages.

outmanoeuvre /ˌaʊtmə'nuːvə/ tr.v (US **ˌoutma'neuver**) get an advantage over (s.o) by using better methods etc than that person.

outnumber /ˌaʊt'nʌmbə/ tr.v be more in number than (s.o/s.t): The girls outnumbered the boys. We were outnumbered.

out-of-date, out of date ⇒ date'.

out of doors ⇒ door.

out-of-the-way ⇒ way.

outpatient /'aʊtˌpeɪʃənt/ c.n person treated in a hospital but not sleeping there: go to the outpatients' department of the hospital.

outplay /ˌaʊt'pleɪ/ tr.v (often passive) play a game, sport etc better than (another person, team).

outpoint /ˌaʊt'pɔɪnt/ tr.v get a bigger score than (another person, team).

outpost /'aʊtˌpəʊst/ c.n (usu — of s.t) 1 place for soldiers that is far from the main centre of military(1) activity. 2 place where people have settled far from the main country or city: visit the outposts of the company's offices overseas.

outpourings /'aʊtˌpɔːrɪŋz/ pl.n long exaggerated expressions of sadness, worry etc.

output /'aʊtˌpʊt/ n 1 u.n act or fact of producing finished goods: slow/fast output. 2 c.n (usu — of s.t) amount (of goods) produced: a high/low output of cars. 3 c.n (usu — of s.t) amount (of work, power etc) produced by a person, machine, kind of fuel(1) etc: *Her output was low last week. This coal has a high output of heat.* **4** *c.n* piece of information produced when a computer is working. **5** *c.n* (also *attrib*) part of a machine etc used to produce an article, the power etc.

outrage /ˈaʊtˌreɪdʒ/ *n* **1** *c.n* (often — *against s.t*) activity, decision etc that makes people angry, hurt etc because it is cruel, immoral, indecent(1) etc: *Hitting babies is an outrage. Putting people in prison because of their beliefs is an outrage against human rights.* **2** *c/u.n* extremely cruel act or action: *The people demonstrated about the outrages committed by their government.* **3** *u.n* state of being very angry or offended(1): *a feeling of outrage; filled with outrage.*
▷ *tr.v* **4** (usu passive) cause outrage(3) in (a person): *be outraged by the decision.*

outrageous /aʊtˈreɪdʒəs/ *adj* **1** very cruel, immoral, indecent(1) etc: *an outrageous act of violence; outrageous behaviour/language.* **2** (*informal*) terrible; shocking: *outrageous prices.*
ouˈtrageously *adv.* **ouˈtrageousness** *u.n.*

outrider /ˈaʊtˌraɪdə/ *c.n* official (esp a policeman) on a motorbike at the side of, in front of, another vehicle as a guard.

outright /ˈaʊtˌraɪt/ *attrib.adj* **1** complete and without others: *the outright winner; outright ownership.* **2** complete, thorough: *an outright liar/refusal.*
▷ *adv* /aʊtˈraɪt/ **3** completely and without others: *win the race, own the house, outright.* **4** completely and thoroughly: *refuse outright to help.* **5** clearly and without hiding anything: *tell her one's opinion outright.* **6** immediately: *be killed outright.*

outrun /aʊtˈrʌn/ *tr.v* (*-nn-, p.t* outran /aʊtˈræn/, *p.p* outrun) (*formal*) run faster than (another person or animal) in a race.

outsell /aʊtˈsel/ *tr.v* (*p.t,p.p* outsold /aʊtˈsəʊld/) sell, be sold, in larger numbers than (another person, company, product).

outset /ˈaʊtˌset/ *def.n* **at/from the outset** (**of** *s.t*) at/from the beginning (of an activity): *I knew from the outset that we would win.*

outshine /aʊtˈʃaɪn/ *tr.v* (*p.t,p.p* outshone /aʊtˈʃɒn/) (*formal*) **1** shine more than (another thing). **2** (*fig*) be more successful, attractive etc than (another person).

outside /ˈaʊtˌsaɪd/ *adj* **1** in, leading to, the outer area that is away from a building, edge or limit: *an outside swimming pool; an outside door; an outside broadcast in front of the palace.* ⇒ inside(1). **2** (*attrib*) unlikely; very small: *an outside chance, possibility.* **3** (*attrib*) largest possible or likely: *an outside estimate(1).* **4** not part of one's usual work or activity: *an outside interest, hobby.* **5** not from the group etc one is part of: *We used outside help.*
▷ *adv* /aʊtˈsaɪd/ **6** out of a building etc: *go outside. I'll be outside if you need me.* **7** on the outer surface: *Our house is painted white outside.* **8** in the outer area away from a building, edge etc: *I'll be waiting outside.* Compare inside(3). **9** (*slang*) no longer in prison. Compare inside(4).
▷ *def.n* /ˈaʊtˌsaɪd/ **10** (often *the* — *of s.t*) outer part, surface area, (of s.t): *The outside (of the house) was painted blue.* Compare inside(5).
at the outside (*informal*) at the most: *It*

will cost £10, I'll be five minutes, at the outside.
▷ *prep* /aʊtˈsaɪd/ **11** in/into the area that is not in: *live outside the city; work outside the office.* Compare inside(6). **12** past, away from, the limits of: *outside my control/experience.* Opposite within. **13** not during: *do it outside working hours.* Opposite during(2). **14** (often — *of*) apart from: *Outside (of) the family no one knows about it.*

outˈsider *c.n* **1** person not able or not allowed to take part in the activities of a group: *Those people are not friendly towards outsiders.* Compare insider. **2** person or animal that is considered unlikely to win a race or competition.

outsize /ˈaʊtˌsaɪz/ *adj* **1** (*abbr* OS) for, of, people who are very big: *outsize clothes.* **2** unusually big: *outsize vegetables.*

outskirts /ˈaʊtˌskɜːts/ *def.pl.n* (usu *on the* — *of s.t*) areas, e.g of a city, near the outside edge: *I live on the outskirts of town.*

outsmart /aʊtˈsmɑːt/ *tr.v* be (more) successful by being more clever than (another person): *be outsmarted by the police.*

outspoken /aʊtˈspəʊkən/ *adj* expressing one's thoughts, opinion etc freely and without hiding anything: *an outspoken critic.*

outspread (/aʊtˈspred/, when *attrib* /ˈaʊtˌspred/) *adj* (of arms etc) straight and wide open: *She was waiting for me with outspread arms, arms outspread.*

outstanding /aʊtˈstændɪŋ/ *adj* **1** of extremely good quality: *an outstanding singer. He gave an outstanding performance.* **2** not yet dealt with, done etc: *have work outstanding; outstanding debts.*
outˈstandingly *adv* extremely: *outstandingly good/bad.*

outstay /aʊtˈsteɪ/ *tr.v* stay longer than (a time, another person). **outstay one's welcome** stay longer than the person who invited one wants.

outstretched (/aʊtˈstretʃt/, when *attrib* /ˈaʊtˌstretʃt/) *adj* (of arms, legs etc) straight out and not bent: *sit with one's legs outstretched.* ⇒ stretch out (⇒ stretch(*v*)).

outstrip /aʊtˈstrɪp/ *tr.v* (*-pp-*) be more successful than (another person).

outvote /aʊtˈvəʊt/ *tr.v* be successful by getting more votes than (another person).

outward, outwards ⇒ out.

outwear /aʊtˈweə/ *tr.v* (*p.t* outwore /aʊtˈwɔː/, *p.p* outworn /aʊtˈwɔːn/) **1** grow/develop until one is too big, experienced etc for (s.t): *You've outworn your clothes, such toys.* ⇒ wear s.t out. **2** become no longer what is needed for (s.t) because of developments: *You've outworn your usefulness.*
outˈworn *adj* **1** (of clothes, toys, machines etc) that have become old from too much use, wear etc: *an outworn coat, car.* **2** no longer used because not modern: *outworn methods.*

outweigh /aʊtˈweɪ/ *tr.v* be more important, larger etc than (s.o/s.t): *The difficulties outweigh the benefits(1). The costs outweigh the advantages.*

outwit /aʊtˈwɪt/ *tr.v* (*-tt-*) be more successful than (another person) by being more clever; trick (s.o).

ova ⇒ ovum.

oval /ˈəʊvl/ *adj* **1** shaped like an egg: *an oval face.*

▷ *c.n* **2** shape like an egg.

ovary /ˈəʊvərɪ/ *c.n* (*pl* -*ies*) one of two inside parts of a female where eggs are formed for reproduction(1).

ovation /əʊˈveɪʃən/ *c.n* (*formal*) expression of approval etc esp by clapping. **standing ovation** one made by people standing up in a theatre etc.

oven /ˈʌvn/ *c.n* space with a door in a cooker, used for baking, roasting etc: *I have an electric oven. Your dinner is in the oven keeping warm.*

over¹ /ˈəʊvə/ *pred.adj* **1** finished: *The game/play/storm is over. Their marriage is nearly over.* **over and done with** (**a**) finished: *Let's get this horrible task over and done with.* (**b**) now forgotten completely; no longer important: *You were very rude but that's over and done with now.*

▷ *adv* **2** in/to a position above (s.o/s.t): *A bird flew over.* **3** to another, the other side: *The river is wide and I can't jump over. I turned over onto my back.* **4** description of s.o/s.t after falling: *I fell over.* **5** so as to cross an edge: *The milk boiled over. She stood on the edge and looked over.* **6** at/to another place: *Come over when you have time. They came over from Africa many years ago. I went over to their table. Over in Europe people eat more salad.* **7** from beginning to end; in detail: *Please read/think/talk it over.* **8** more (in age, number, amount etc): *The boots could cost as much as £50 and over. The film is only for people of 18 and over.* ⇨ below(7), under(2). **9** remaining: *We've sold 48 balls and we have 2 left over.* **10** so as to cover s.t: *The wound will soon heal over.* **11** (often *all* —) finished: *Do get it over quickly.* (**all**) **over again** once more: *You'll have to count the balls all over again.* **over and over** (**again**) often: *I've told you over and over again not to do that.* For verb + 'over', e.g *change over, cross over, have s.o over* ⇨ the verb.

▷ *prep* **12** in or to a position above the top of: *A plane flew over the town.* Opposite under(4). **13** on the other side of: *They live over the road.* **14** covering the top of: *Put that cloth over the table. I hung my coat over a chair.* Opposite beneath(3), under(4). **15** so as to cross an edge: *Don't fall over the edge/ cliff!* **16** from one side to another of: *She swam over the river. I looked over the wall.* **17** (often *all* —) across, covering, the surface of: *There was mud (all) over the floor. We travelled over most of southern Europe.* **18** through every part of: *I'll take you over the factory tomorrow.* **19** more than: *He's over two metres tall. I paid over £10 for it. She's over sixteen years of age. We didn't meet for over ten years.* Opposite under(6). **20** concerning; because of: *They argued over a silly mistake. He's crying over nothing.* **21** using: *I spoke to her over the telephone.* **22** during: *Let's discuss it over dinner. Would you like to stay over the weekend?* **23** having become happy, well etc again: *You'll get over losing Peter. Are you completely over your illness?* **all over** ⇨ over(17) and all. **over and above** as well as: *She gets her room and meals over and above £20 a week.* **over/here there** at/in this/that place: *There's a strange animal over there in the bushes, You've been to Japan — what's it like over there?* For noun + 'over' + s.o/s.t or verb + 'over' + noun (phrase), e.g *an advantage over s.o , over age , over s.o's head , over the worst,* ⇨ the noun. For verb

+ 'over' s.o/s.t, e.g *get over s.t , watch over s.t ,* ⇨ the verb.

over² /ˈəʊvə/ *c.n* (in cricket¹) series of six balls bowled²(3) from the same end of the wicket(2).

overact /ˌəʊvərˈækt/ *tr/intr.v* behave, show one's feelings etc in an exaggerated way.

overall /ˌəʊvərˈɔːl/ *attrib.adj* **1** including everything: *overall expenses; the overall length.*

▷ *adv* /ˌəʊvərˈɔːl/ **2** including everything: *How much did it cost overall? What is the size overall?*

▷ *c.n* /ˈəʊvəˌrɔːl/ **3** piece of clothing worn over other clothes as protection: *Wear your overall in the kitchen.*

ˈoverˌalls *pl.n* (often *pair of* —) piece of clothing (trousers with a front flap or attached shirt) worn by workers, often over other clothes, as protection: *He needs a clean pair of overalls.*

overarm /ˈəʊvərˌɑːm/ *adj/adv* (done) with the arm above one's shoulder.

overawe /ˌəʊvərˈɔː/ *tr.v* make (s.o) feel full of awe(1), quiet, afraid, surprised etc: *The size of the room overawed her.*

overbalance /ˌəʊvəˈbæləns/ *intr.v* lose control of one's balance and fall over.

overbearing /ˌəʊvəˈbeərɪŋ/ *adj* (*derog*) too certain of one's opinion and demanding agreement from others.

overblouse /ˈəʊvəˌblaʊz/ *c.n* kind of blouse that is worn over the top of a skirt or trousers.

overboard /ˈəʊvəˌbɔːd/ *adv* over the side of a boat etc into the water: *He's fallen overboard.* **go overboard** (*fig*) be very/too enthusiastic: *I know you like that singer but there's no need to go overboard in your praise.*

overburden /ˌəʊvəˈbɜːdn/ *tr.v* (usu — *s.o with s.t*) give (s.o) too much work to do.

overcame ⇨ overcome(2).

overcast /ˌəʊvəˈkɑːst/ *adj* **1** full of dark clouds: *an overcast sky.* **2** (*fig*) very quiet and sad.

overcharge /ˌəʊvəˈtʃɑːdʒ/ *tr/intr.v* (often — (s.o) *for s.t*) ask (s.o) for too much money as payment (for s.t). Opposite undercharge.

overcoat /ˈəʊvəˌkəʊt/ *c.n* heavy coat worn in cold weather.

overcome /ˌəʊvəˈkʌm/ *pred.adj* **1** (— *by/with s.t*) very affected (by s.t); made to feel helpless (because of s.t): *I was overcome with tiredness/ joy/fear. He was overcome by the heat/smoke.*

▷ *tr.v* **2** (*p.t* overcame /ˌəʊvəˈkeɪm/, *p.p* overcome) (*formal*) win a victory over (s.o/s.t): *I wasn't able to overcome my fear.*

overcrowded /ˌəʊvəˈkraʊdɪd/ *adj* containing too many people: *The poor people live in overcrowded conditions on the edge of the city.*

ˌoverˈcrowding *u.n* state of being overcrowded: *They closed the gates of the stadium to avoid overcrowding.*

overdo /ˌəʊvəˈduː/ *tr.v* (*3rd pers sing pres.t* overdoes /ˌəʊvəˈdʌz/, *p.t* overdid /ˌəʊvəˈdɪd/, *p.p* overdone /ˌəʊvəˈdʌn/) **1** (usu *p.p*) cook (meat etc) for too long: *The steak*(2) *was overdone.* **2** do (s.t) with too much energy, for too long etc: *She overdid her part in the play. If you overdo your concern, no one will believe you.* **overdo it/things** work much too long or hard: *If you overdo it you'll be ill.*

ˌoverˈdone *adj* (of meat) cooked for too long: *an overdone steak*(1). Opposite underdone, rare(2).

overdose /ˈəʊvəˌdəʊs/ *c.n* (often — *of s.t*) too

much of a drug: *She died of an overdose (of heroin).*

overdraft /ˈəʊvəˌdrɑːft/ *c.n* amount of money (allowed to be) owed to a bank: *We were given an overdraft of £1000.*

overdrawn /ˌəʊvəˈdrɔːn/ *pred.adj* (usu — *by an amount of money*) having taken more money from the bank than one has in an account: *You are overdrawn by £800 (or You are £800 overdrawn).*

overdress /ˌəʊvəˈdres/ *intr.v* (usu *p.p*) (*derog*) put on clothes that are too formal, expensive etc for an occasion: *You look overdressed in that suit. Don't overdress, wear something simple.*

overdrive /ˈəʊvəˌdraɪv/ *u.n* highest gear(1) in some vehicles, used when driving very fast.

overdue /ˌəʊvəˈdjuː/ *adj* (usu *pred*) **1** late: *The buses are always overdue. The train is an hour overdue.* **2** past the agreed time (for action): *The baby is already 10 days overdue. The cheque is overdue — I expected it last week. A charge will be made on all overdue equipment.*

overeat /ˌəʊvərˈiːt/ *intr.v* (*p.t* overate /ˌəʊvərˈet/, *p.p* overeaten /ˌəʊvərˈiːtn/) eat too much.

overestimate /ˌəʊvərˈestɪmət/ *c.n* **1** estimate(1) that is higher or larger than the correct one. Opposite underestimate(1).

▷ *tr.v* /ˌəʊvərˈestɪˌmeɪt/ **2** make an overestimate(1) of (s.t).

overflow /ˈəʊvəˌfləʊ/ *n* **1** *def.n* amount (of liquid, people etc) that cannot be contained in s.t: *This room can be used for the overflow.* **2** *c.n* pipe for overflowing(3) liquid.

▷ *v* /ˌəʊvəˈfləʊ/ (*p.t,p.p* overflowed) **3** *tr/intr.v* become too much for (a container etc) and so flow over the edge: *The River Nile overflowed its banks.* **4** *tr/intr.v* (*fig*) become too many for (a particular area, space): *The crowds overflowed onto the pavement.* **5** *intr.v* (usu — *with s.t*) (*fig*) have (almost) too much (of an emotion, feeling): *overflowing with pride and joy.*

overgenerous /ˌəʊvəˈdʒenərəs/ *adj* too generous.

overgrown /ˌəʊvəˈɡrəʊn/ *adj* **1** (usu *pred*) having too many (big) plants: *My garden is very overgrown with weeds.* **2** (usu *attrib*) having grown too big: *an overgrown tree.*

overhaul /ˈəʊvəˌhɔːl/ *c.n* **1** act of overhauling(2) s.t: *My bicycle needs a complete overhaul.*

▷ *tr.v* /ˌəʊvəˈhɔːl/ **2** examine (a machine, engine etc) and mend anything that is wrong. **3** (*formal*) catch up with (and pass) (s.o/s.t): *The police overhauled the thieves on the motorway.*

overhead /ˈəʊvəˌhed/ *attrib.adj* **1** above one's head: *overhead telephone wires.* **2** over one's head: *play an overhead stroke in tennis.*

▷ *adv* /ˌəʊvəˈhed/ **3** above one's head: *looking at the sky overhead.*

overheads /ˈəʊvəˌhedz/ *pl.n* expenses such as rent, heating costs etc of a business, family etc.

overhear /ˌəʊvəˈhɪə/ *tr/intr.v* (*p.t, p.p* overheard /ˌəʊvəˈhɜːd/) hear (s.o, a conversation etc) when one is not supposed to: *I overheard Paul talking about me in the next room. I'm sorry but I couldn't help overhearing (you).*

overheat /ˌəʊvəˈhiːt/ *tr/intr.v* (cause (s.t) to) become too hot: *Our car has been overheating.*

over'heated *adj* **1** that has become too hot: *an*

overheated car engine. **2** (*fig*) having too much strong feeling: *an overheated discussion.*

overjoyed /ˌəʊvəˈdʒɔɪd/ *pred.adj* extremely pleased or glad: *I was overjoyed at your news (or to hear your news) that you won.*

overkill /ˈəʊvəˌkɪl/ *u.n* **1** state of owning more nuclear(2) weapons than is necessary. **2** ability or action that is stronger than necessary.

overladen /ˌəʊvəˈleɪdn/ *adj* having too much weight, electricity etc: *an overladen circuit(4).* ⇨ overload.

overland /ˈəʊvəˌlænd/ *attrib.adj* **1** across land: *use an overland route.*

▷ *adv* **2** across land: *travel overland to Moscow.*

overlap /ˈəʊvəˌlæp/ *c/u.n* **1** (amount of) overlapping(2,3): *allow a 10 cm overlap all round the cloth. There is always some overlap in a set of talks.*

▷ *tr/intr.v* /ˌəʊvəˈlæp/ (-pp-) **2** cover/go over the edge or limit of, (s.t): *The pieces of leather should overlap (each other).* **3** (*fig*) be partly the same; partly cover the same area/time: *Her job overlaps with mine. Their experiments overlap (each other) in several important areas.*

overleaf /ˌəʊvəˈliːf/ *adv* on the other side of a page: *The photograph is overleaf.*

overload /ˈəʊvəˌləʊd/ *c/u.n* **1** (amount of) too much of s.t.

▷ *tr.v* /ˌəʊvəˈləʊd/ **2** (often — *s.t with s.t*) put too much weight or too many things on or in s.t: *Don't overload your suitcase (with books). The lift(1) broke because it was overloaded.* **3** put too much electricity into (a circuit(4)): *If you use a fire, television, record-player and lamp on the same socket, you'll overload it.* ⇨ overladen.

overlook /ˌəʊvəˈlʊk/ *tr.v* **1** have a view of (s.o/s.t): *Their kitchen overlooks our garden.* **2** not take (s.t) into account: *I'll overlook his rudeness because his mother is so ill. You seem to have overlooked the fact that I'm older than you.*

overmanned /ˌəʊvəˈmænd/ *adj* having too many workers in a factory, industry etc. Opposite undermanned, understaffed, shorthanded.

over'manning *u.n* state of being overmanned.

overnight /ˈəʊvəˌnaɪt/ *attrib.adj* **1** for/during the night: *take the overnight train; pack an overnight bag.* **2** immediate: *an overnight success.*

▷ *adv* /ˌəʊvəˈnaɪt/ **3** for the night: *You can stay here overnight.* **4** immediately: *She became a success overnight.*

overpaid /ˌəʊvəˈpeɪd/ *adj* (of a worker) paid too much money. Opposite underpaid.

overpass /ˈəʊvəˌpɑːs/ *c.n* part of a main road that crosses above another. Opposite underpass. Compare flyover.

overplay /ˌəʊvəˈpleɪ/ *tr.v* Opposite underplay. **1** make s.t seem more important, special etc than it really is. **2** = overact. **overplay one's hand** (*fig*) make one's position etc seem stronger, more important etc than it really is.

overpopulated /ˌəʊvəˈpɒpjʊˌleɪtɪd/ *adj* containing too many people or animals. Opposite underpopulated.

overpopulation /ˌəʊvəˌpɒpjʊˈleɪʃən/ *u.n.*

overpower /ˌəʊvəˈpaʊə/ *tr.v* use greater strength, numbers etc to win a victory over (s.o, an animal): *The escaped prisoners were overpowered by the police.*

over'powering *adj* (esp of a smell) very strong.

overrate /ˌəʊvəˈreɪt/ *tr.v* say/consider that (s.o/ s.t) is better than he/she/it really is: *He overrated her ability.* Opposite underrate.

over'rated *adj* considered better than he/she/ it really is: *an overrated book. Margaret's ability/ intelligence is overrated.*

overreach /ˌəʊvəˈriːtʃ/ *reflex.v* fail in one's desires because one has tried to do or get too much: *He overreached himself when he borrowed £1000 and he couldn't pay it back.*

overriding /ˌəʊvəˈraɪdɪŋ/ *adj* being first, ahead, in importance or strength: *Their safety is of over- riding importance. My overriding* impression(1) *was of a badly organized meeting.*

overripe /ˌəʊvəˈraɪp/ *adj* too ripe.

overrule /ˌəʊvəˈruːl/ *tr.v* (*formal*) not allow a decision, opinion to be expressed or accepted by using one's higher position of authority: *The judges overruled the decision of the officials and allowed the* athlete *to take part.* Opposite sustain(5).

overrun /ˌəʊvəˈrʌn/ *v* (*-nn-*, *p.t* overran /ˌəʊvəˈræn/, *p.p* overrun) **1** *tr/intr.v* continue for (a period that is) longer than the (time agreed or allowed): *Please try not to overrun the time allowed you. The speaker overran by several minutes.* **2** *tr.v* (usu passive, — *by/with* s.t) spread over and fill (s.t) (with s.t): *The grass was overrun by/with weeds.* **3** *tr.v* (usu passive, — *by/with s.o/s.t*) attack (s.o/s.t) (with s.o/s.t) and win a complete victory: *Very soon the area was overrun by/with enemy soldiers.*

overseas /ˈəʊvəˈsiːz/ *attrib.adj* **1** of/for/from/ to countries across the sea: *overseas* aid(1); *over- seas trade/markets.*
▷ *adv* /ˌəʊvəˈsiːz/ **2** in, from or to countries across the sea: *go/travel overseas.*

oversee /ˌəʊvəˈsiː/ *tr.v* (*p.t oversaw* /ˌəʊvəˈsɔː/, *p.p overseen* /ˌəʊvəˈsiːn/) be in charge of and watch (workers, a task being carried out etc).

overseer /ˈəʊvəˌsɪə/ *c.n* person in charge of workers.

oversew /ˌəʊvəˈsəʊ/ *tr.v* (*p.t oversewed* /ˌəʊvəˈsəʊd/, *p.p oversewn* /ˌəʊvəˈsəʊn/) sew (two pieces of cloth) together with long stitches(2) over the top of both edges.
over'sewn *attrib.adj*: *an oversewn edge.*

oversexed /ˌəʊvəˈsekst/ *adj* too interested in sexual activity. Opposite undersexed.

overshadow /ˌəʊvəˈʃædəʊ/ *tr.v* **1** (often pas- sive) make (s.o/s.t) appear less important, clever, attractive etc when compared: *My successes at school were always overshadowed by my sister's.* **2** (*formal*) make (a situation, scene etc) appear very sad: *Their son's death overshadowed their happy marriage.*

overshoe /ˈəʊvəˌʃuː/ *c.n* rubber or plastic shoe worn over ordinary shoes as protection against rain etc.

overshoot /ˌəʊvəˈʃuːt/ *tr.v* (*p.t,p.p overshot* /ˌəʊvəˈʃɒt/) go past (the point or mark aimed at): *The plane overshot the* runway *and hit a tree.*

oversight /ˈəʊvəˌsaɪt/ *c/u.n* (example of a) mistake or failure to notice s.t: *Because of an oversight they did not find the cor- rect way. It was oversight that caused the accident.*

oversimplify /ˌəʊvəˈsɪmplɪˌfaɪ/ *tr/intr.v* (*-ies*, *-ied*) make (s.t) appear too easy or straight- forward: *an oversimplified account of the difficulties.*

oversimplification /ˌəʊvəˌsɪmplɪfɪˈkeɪʃən/ *u.n.*

oversized /ˈəʊvəˌsaɪzd/ *attrib.adj* bigger than usual or normal. Opposite undersized. ⇒ -sized.

oversleep /ˌəʊvəˈsliːp/ *intr.v* (*p.t,p.p overslept* /ˌəʊvəˈslept/) sleep longer than the agreed or intended time.

overspend /ˌəʊvəˈspend/ *intr.v* (*p.t,p.p overspent* /ˌəʊvəˈspent/) (usu — *by*) spend more money than agreed or intended (by spending s.t): *overspend by £10.*

overstaffed /ˌəʊvəˈstɑːft/ *adj* having more workers, managers etc in an office etc than necessary. Opposite understaffed, undermanned. Compare overmanned. ⇒ -staffed.

overstate /ˌəʊvəˈsteɪt/ *tr.v* (*formal*) express (one's opinion, argument etc) too strongly. Opposite understate.
over'statement *c/u.n* (example of a) fact of overstating. Opposite understatement.

overstay /ˌəʊvəˈsteɪ/ *tr.v* (esp — *one's welcome*) stay longer than (the time that the person who invited one wants). ⇒ outstay.

overstep /ˌəʊvəˈstep/ *tr.v* (*-pp-*) (esp — *the mark*) go further than (one's authority, the correct limit etc): *She overstepped the mark when she ordered the children to run the next 10 km.*

oversubscribed /ˌəʊvəsəbˈskraɪbd/ *adj* (usu pred) having more requests from buyers than supplies available: *Tickets for the finals of the game are oversubscribed.*

overt /ˈəʊvɜːt/ *adj* done/shown clearly and pub- licly: *an overt dislike of the manager.* Opposite covert(2).
'overtly *adv.*

overtake /ˌəʊvəˈteɪk/ *v* (*p.t overtook* /ˌəʊvəˈtʊk/, *p.p overtaken* /ˌəʊvəˈteɪkən/) **1** *tr/intr.v* pass (another moving car etc): *Don't overtake on corners.* **2** *tr/intr.v* do better than (a business) competitor): *Our sales have overtaken our most important competition in Japan.* **3** *tr.v* (usu pas- sive, — *by/with* s.t) happen to (s.o) suddenly or without warning: *She was overtaken by/with fear.*

overtax /ˌəʊvəˈtæks/ *tr.v* **1** make (s.o, a business etc) pay too much tax. **2** put too much strain(3) on (s.o/s.t): *The problems were overtaxing his strength/savings.*

overthrow /ˈəʊvəˌθrəʊ/ *c.n* **1** (usu — *of s.t*) defeat/ruin (of a government, ruler etc).
▷ *tr.v* **2** /ˌəʊvəˈθrəʊ/ (*p.t overthrew* /ˌəʊvəˈθruː/, *p.p overthrown* /ˌəʊvəˈθrəʊn/) defeat/destroy the power of (a government, ruler etc).

overtime /ˈəʊvəˌtaɪm/ *u.n* (also *attrib*) **1** work done after one's usual working hours: *I did 10 hours' overtime last week.* **2** money paid for working after one's usual hours: *earn £50 overtime. What's the overtime rate of pay?*

overtones /ˈəʊvəˌtəʊnz/ *pl.n* (usu — *of s.t*) (suggestions of) additional and deliberate(1) meanings: *a speech with suspicious overtones. I recognized overtones of jealousy in their conversation.*

overture /ˈəʊvəˌtjʊə/ *c.n* **1** piece of music played at the beginning of an opera. **2** (often *pl*) offer, act etc intended to begin negotiations.

make overtures show willingness to come to
an agreement.
overturn /ˌəʊvəˈtɜːn/ *tr/intr.v* (cause (s.t) to)
turn over: *The car overturned in a ditch*(1). *The
lorry was overturned by the wind.* ⇨ turn over.
overview /ˈəʊvəˌvjuː/ *c.n* general account without details.
overweight /ˌəʊvəˈweɪt/ *adj* **1** more heavy than
is usual, allowed or healthy: *overweight footballers. Your luggage is overweight.* Opposite
underweight.
▷ *u.n* /ˈəʊvəˌweɪt/ **2** amount by which s.o/s.t is too
heavy: *The horse is carrying 2 kg overweight.*
overwhelm /ˌəʊvəˈwelm/ *tr.v* (usu passive)
1 greatly affect the emotions of (s.o): *feel
overwhelmed by your kindness*; *be overwhelmed
with fear.* **2** win a complete victory over (s.o): *The
enemy overwhelmed our soldiers.* **3** be too much/
difficult for (s.o): *I'm overwhelmed with work.*
ˌoverˈwhelming *adj* **1** causing s.o to be greatly
affected: *Their encouragement was overwhelming. They gave me overwhelming support.* **2** great
in force or amount: *an overwhelming amount
of letters to answer*; *win by an overwhelming
majority*(3).
overwork /ˌəʊvəˈwɜːk/ *u.n* **1** act of over-
working(2): *tired because of overwork.*
▷ *tr/intr.v* **2** (cause (s.o) to) work too hard or too
long: *She overworks her staff. If you overwork
you'll be ill.*
overwrought /ˌəʊvəˈrɔːt/ *adj* (*formal*) very
nervous (esp because very tired): *Andy was so
overwrought that he began to cry with impatience.*
Compare wrought-up.
overzealous /ˌəʊvəˈzeləs/ *adj* (*formal*) too
eager.
ˌoverˈzealously *adv.*
oviduct /ˈəʊvɪˌdʌkt/ *c.n* (*technical*) passage
from an ovary to the womb.
ovum /ˈəʊvəm/ *c.n* (*pl* ova /ˈəʊvə/) (*technical*)
female's egg before it is fertilized(2).
ow /aʊ/ *interj* (used to express sudden pain).
owe /əʊ/ *tr.v* **1** be in a position where one must
give (an amount of money etc) back to s.o who
has lent it to one: *I owe you £5. What do I
owe you for the petrol you paid for?* **2** be in
a position where one must pay (s.o) (for s.t):
What do I owe you for the meal? **3** (often —
s.t to s.o/s.t) have (s.t) because of (s.o/s.t); feel
the need to thank (s.o) (because of s.t): *I owe
all my success to you, to my education.*
ˈowing *pred.adj* to be paid: *There is £10 owing
(to you).*
ˈowing to *prep* because of: *The walk has been
postponed owing to the bad weather.*
owl /aʊl/ *c.n* kind of bird with eyes at the front
(and not at the sides) that flies at night and eats
small animals.
own /əʊn/ *det* **1** (*my, her, your, their* etc — *s.t*)
(used for emphasis) belonging to the person
mentioned: *This is my own car. Even his own
mother refused to help. It's your own fault that
you failed.*
▷ *pron* **2** (*my, his, our* etc —) (used for emphasis)
that belongs to the person mentioned: *Is it your
own or did you borrow it?* (**all**) **on one's own** =
(all) by oneself (⇨ oneself). **come into one's own**
become as good, interesting etc as one can be:
*She comes into her own when the conversation

is about horses.* **get one's own back** (**on s.o**)
(**for s.t**) (*informal*) have one's revenge(1) (on
s.o) (for s.t): *I'll get my own back on you for
telling my mother about it.* **have a mind of one's
own** ⇨ mind¹. **hold one's own** not be defeated in
an argument or difficult situation: *She was able
to hold her own during the discussion even
though most people didn't agree with her.*
▷ *tr.v* **3** have (s.t) as one's possession: *Do you own this
house or do you rent it? You don't own this park
— it belongs to everyone.* **own that . . .** (*formal*)
admit s.t as being true: *I will own that you have
cause to be angry but I was also hurt.* **own up** (**to
s.t**) admit that one has done s.t wrong: *He owned
up (to having broken the window). Who took my
pen? Come on — own up!*
ˈowner *c.n* (usu — *of s.t*) person who owns(3) s.t:
*Who is the owner of this bicycle? Please return this
book to its owner.*
ˈownerˌship *u.n* (usu — *of s.t*) fact, legal right,
of owning(3) s.t.
ox /ɒks/ *c.n* (*pl* oxen /ˈɒksn/) (also *attrib*) **1** castrated bull¹(1), used to pull a plough(1) or cart
in some countries: *an ox cart.* **2** kind of animal
belonging to the cattle(1) family.
oxtail /ˈɒksˌteɪl/ *c/u.n* (also *attrib*) tail of a
bull¹(1) or cow used as food: *oxtail soup.*
oxide /ˈɒksaɪd/ *c/u.n* (*technical*) chemical com-
pound(1) having an atom(1) of oxygen.
oxygen /ˈɒksɪdʒən/ *u.n* chemical element that
forms part of the air and is essential for life,
chem.symb O.
ˈoxygen ˌmask *c.n* (*medical*) device put over
s.o's mouth to allow her/him to breathe
oxygen.
ˈoxygen ˌtent *c.n* (*medical*) device put over
s.o's bed to help her/him to breathe more
easily.
oyster /ˈɔɪstə/ *n* (also *attrib*) **1** *c.n* kind of sea
creature with two rough shells, in which pearls
are sometimes formed. **2** *u.n* this creature as food:
order oysters; *oyster soup.*
oz *written abbr* ounce(s)(1).

Pp

P, p /piː/ *c/unique n* **1** 16th letter of the English
alphabet.
▷ *written abbr* **2** (*pl* pp) page¹(2). **3** (*grammar*)
past. **4** (*grammar*) participle. **5** per. **6** (**P**) *President.*
7 (**P**) Priest.
▷ *symb* **8** (UK) pence; penny. **9** (*science*) pressure.
10 (**P**) parking(2). **11** (**P**) Phosphorus. **mind one's
p's and q's** ⇨ mind².
pa /pɑː/ *c.n* (*informal*) father (used by a daughter
or son): *Pa, can I borrow your car tonight?*
PA /ˌpiː ˈeɪ/ *abbr* personal assistant.
pace /peɪs/ *n* **1** *c.n* (length of a) step: *Take two

paces forward/back. **2** sing.n rate of moving: *go at a fast/slow/even pace*. (**at**) **a snail's pace** ⇨ snail.
keep pace (**with s.o/s.t**) (**a**) go at the same speed (as s.o/s.t): *keep pace with the other runners*. (**b**) keep informed about modern ideas, developments etc: *keep pace with the latest fashions/news/scientific* equipment(2). **put s.o through her/his paces** test s.o's ability, intelligence etc. **set a/the pace** (**for s.o/s.t**) move/do things at a speed that others must try to match. **show one's paces** show what one is able to do.
▷ v **3** tr.v control the speed of (s.o/s.t): *pace oneself in a race*; *pace the changes to allow people to get used to them*. **4** tr/intr.v (often — *about, up and down*) walk forward and back: *She paced the floor trying to decide what to do. He paced up and down waiting for news*. **pace s.t out** measure the length of s.t by using long paces(1): *I'll pace out the room to give us an idea of the size for a new carpet*.
'pace,maker c.n **1** person or animal used to establish(1) the speed during a race. **2** person or business considered to be the best in a particular kind of activity. **3** (*medical*) device used to help a person's heart to work correctly.
'pace,setter c.n = pacemaker(2).
pacify /'pæsɪ,faɪ/ tr.v (-*ies*, -*ied*) make (s.o, an animal) calm and not afraid: *It was impossible to pacify the passengers during the storm*.
pacific /pə'sɪfɪk/ adj (*formal*) **1** helping to make s.o calm: *a pacific tone of voice*. **2** believing in, involving(1), pacificism: *a pacific foreign policy*.
pa'cifically adv.
pacification /,pæsɪfɪ'keɪʃən/ u.n process of pacifying.
pacifism /'pæsɪ,fɪzəm/ u.n belief that all acts of violence, including all wars and sports involving fighting, are wrong.
pacifist /'pæsɪfɪst/ adj **1** of, referring to, supporting, pacifism.
▷ c.n **2** believer in pacifism.
pack /pæk/ c.n **1** (also *attrib*) (things in a) container that is carried on the back of a person or animal: *a pack horse*; *a day pack*. ⇨ backpack, haversack, rucksack. **2** set of similar things or bad people: *a pack of cards/lies*; *a pack of thieves/liars/criminals*. **3** group of animals, esp concerned with hunting(1): *a pack of hounds/wolves*; *a hunting pack*. **4** (usu **'packet**) small container made of paper or cardboard: *a pack of needles/cigarettes*. **5** mass of a thick semi-liquid substance that goes hard when dry: *a facepack*; *a mudpack*.
▷ v **6** tr/intr.v arrange (things, esp personal belongings) in a container such as a suitcase: *Have you packed (your things) for the holiday? Don't forget to pack the camera*. Opposite unpack(1). **7** tr/intr.v put things into (a container): *Pack your bags and go*. Opposite unpack(2). **8** tr.v force s.t into (a space): *pack a hole with cement*. **9** tr/intr.v (usu — s.o/s.t in; — (s.o/s.t) into s.t) fill a room etc (with s.o/s.t): *The supporters packed (into) the hall. They packed the books into boxes. We were so packed in it was difficult to breathe*. ⇨ packed out. **10** tr.v (usu — s.t with s.o/s.t) fill (a room etc) with people, things etc: *Pack these boxes with books. Students packed the hall*. **11** tr.v put a pack(1) on an animal: *pack camels for a journey across the desert*. **12** tr.v (*informal*) fill (s.t) with

supporters in order to win a vote: *They accused the extreme left of packing the meeting*.
pack s.t away put clothes, tools, games etc in a container, drawer, cupboard etc until they are needed again: *The camping* equipment(2) *was packed away after the holiday*.
pack one's bags (*informal*) (esp as an order) pack(6,7) and leave a house etc. ⇨ send s.o packing.
pack s.o in (*slang*) stop seeing a person socially as a girlfriend or boyfriend. **pack s.t in** (*informal*) give up a habit, job, hobby etc: *I hate getting up early so I'm packing in my job*. **pack it in** (*informal*) (usu as an order) stop doing that: *I've warned you about making a noise, now pack it in!*
pack s.o off (**to s.w**) (*informal*) make arrangements and send a person away (to another place): *I was packed off to* boarding school *when I was 11 years old*.
pack up (*informal*) (usu *may/might as well* —) stop an activity and not try again: *I'll never be a successful student so I may as well pack up*. **pack** (**s.t**) **up** put (things) in a container: *Everyone pack up now — it's time to go home. She packed up (her clothes) and left the hotel without paying her bill*. **pack it up** (**a**) = pack it in. (**b**) = pack s.t in. **pack up** (**on s.o**) (*informal*) (of an engine, machine) stop working correctly: *My car packed up on me on the motorway*.
package /'pækɪdʒ/ c.n **1** thing or things put into a box, wrapping paper etc. **2** (also *attrib*) several parts put together and offered for sale as a single unit: *Their holiday package* (or *package holiday*) *includes travel, hotels and meals. The price is for the whole package including the* computer, *two* programs(1) *and spare* disks(2).
▷ tr.v **3** put (s.t) in, make (s.t) into, a package(1). **4** (often — s.t *together*) put (parts) together to make a single unit, package(2).
'packaging u.n **1** the act of packing(6,7), packaging (⇨ package(3)), things for posting, storing etc. **2** material used to make packages(1): *Use a lot of packaging round these plates*.
,packed 'out pred.adj (of a room etc) completely full of people: *The theatre/meeting was packed out*. ⇨ jam-packed.
'packer c.n person/machine/business company who/that packages(3).
packet /'pækɪt/ n **1** c.n (usu — of s.t) small container, made of paper or cardboard (containing several things); pack(4): *a packet of cigarettes/biscuits*. Compare carton. **2** sing.n (*informal*) large amount of money: *His new car cost a packet!*
'pack ,ice u.n mass of pieces of ice in the sea, a lake etc.
pact /pækt/ c.n (often *make a* — (*with s.o*) (*to do s.t*)) formal agreement: *Let's make a pact and stop competing with each other. The two countries made a pact never to fight each other again*.
pad /pæd/ c.n **1** set of pieces of paper fixed along one edge and used to write letters, notes etc: *a pad of paper*; *a notepad*; *a writing pad*. **2** soft material or object used esp to stop damage, make s.t comfortable etc: *These shoes have pads for the ankles. The nurse used a* cotton-wool *pad to clean the baby's eyes*. **3** soft part under the foot of

a cat, dog, lion etc. **4** (*informal*) home: *You can stay at my pad.* ⇨ launching pad.

▷ *v* (*-dd-*) **5** *tr.v* fill (s.t) with pads(2); put pads(2) in/on s.t: *The jacket has padded sleeves.* **6** *intr.v* (esp of a cat, dog etc) walk very quietly: *The lion padded through the trees.* **pad s.t out** (**with s.t**) (**a**) put soft material inside s.t: *The jacket(1) was padded out with feathers.* (**b**) (often passive) make a report, story, explanation etc longer by adding unnecessary details.

'padding *u.n* **1** soft material used to pad(5) s.t. **2** unnecessary details in a report etc. ⇨ pad s.t out(b).

paddle /'pædl/ *c.n* **1** small, usu short length of wood etc with a flat end used to move a canoe etc. Compare oar. **2** act of paddling (⇨ paddle(4,5)).

▷ *v* **3** *tr/intr.v* move (a canoe(1) etc) using a paddle(1): *The boys paddled* (*their small boat*) *along the river and out to sea.* **4** *intr.v* (often — about (*in s.t*)) walk, jump, run etc in shallow water: *The baby was paddling about in the water/ river.* **5** swim with quick circular arm and leg movements like a dog. ⇨ dog paddle.

'paddling ,pool *c.n* small shallow pool for young children.

paddock /'pædək/ *c.n* **1** small field for a horse. **2** enclosed field at a race-course where the horses can be looked at before or after races.

paddy /'pædɪ/ *c.n* (*pl -ies*) (also **'paddy ,field**) field for growing rice: *rice paddies.*

padlock /'pæd,lɒk/ *c.n* **1** lock with a movable piece shaped like a 'U' that can be fastened to a lid, door etc.

▷ *tr.v* **2** lock (a lid, door etc) with a padlock(1): *Can I padlock my bicycle to yours?*

paediatrics /,pi:dɪ'ætrɪks/ *sing.n* (US **,pedi-'atrics**) study of children's development and illnesses.

,paedi'atric *attrib.adj* (US **,pedi'atric**).

,paediatrician /,pi:dɪə'trɪʃən/ *c.n* (US **,pedia-'trician**) expert in paediatrics.

pagan /'peɪgən/ *c.n* (also *attrib*) (*derog*; do not use!) person who does not believe in a world religion such as Christianity, Islam, Judaism etc.

page¹ /peɪdʒ/ *c.n* **1** one piece of paper in a book, newspaper etc. **2** (*written abbr* p) usu numbered side of a page¹(1): *Turn to page 16, p 16.*

page² /peɪdʒ/ *c.n* **1** boy who takes messages, does small jobs, in a hotel etc. **2** (also **'page,boy**) boy who is an attendant to the bride at a wedding. Compare bridesmaid.

▷ *tr.v* **3** use a loudspeaker etc to call out (s.o's name) in order to tell her/him a message: *Paging Mrs Smith; please come to the telephone.*

'page,boy *c.n* ⇨ page²(2).

pageant /'pædʒənt/ *c.n* colourful procession(1), esp one showing historical scenes.

'pageantry *u.n* colourful rich show: *a traditional annual event full of pageantry.*

pagoda /pə'gəʊdə/ *c.n* temple, esp in eastern Asia, like a tower with several overhanging storeys.

paid /peɪd/ *p.t,p.p* of pay. **put paid to s.t** ⇨ put.

pail /peɪl/ *c.n* metal, plastic(1), bucket.

pain /peɪn/ *n* **1** *c/u.n* sharp feeling of hurt in one's body or mind: *I've got a pain in my tooth/stomach. He couldn't bear the pain of being separated from his family. 'Can you feel any pain in your leg?' 'I can feel some pain but not much.'* **aches and pains** ⇨ ache(1). **a pain in the neck** (*slang*) an annoying person.

▷ *tr.v* **2** cause mental(1) suffering, anxiety etc to (s.o): *It pained her to watch her son suffering.*

pained *attrib.adj* having/showing pain(1): *a pained expression/look.*

'painful *adj* **1** causing mental pain(1): *a painful duty.* **2** having/producing pain(1): *a painful cut/ finger/injury.* **3** (*informal*) very bad: *Her singing was painful.*

'painfully *adv.*

'pain,killer *c.n* thing, esp a drug(1), that takes away pain(1).

'pain,killing *adj* that takes away pain(1).

'painless *adj* **1** not causing mental(1) pain(1), anxiety etc: *The examination was painless.* **2** not having/producing pain(1): *a painless injection.*

'painlessly *adv.*

pains *pl.n* (esp be at, take, — to do s.t) trouble, personal effort: *He was at pains (or took great pains) to provide every detail. You've been so helpful; what can I give you for your pains?*

'pains,taking *adj* giving much effort and care to be thorough: *You've been so painstaking in your work. Writing a dictionary is a painstaking task.*

paint /peɪnt/ *n* **1** *c/u.n* (also *attrib*) (example of a) substance used to put colour on s.t: *a new paint brush. I use that as a paint cloth. I need a paint suitable for outdoor wood. Is there enough paint for all the windows? I need outdoor paint for the fence.* ⇨ dye(1). **2** *c/u.n* (usu *pl*) paint(1) used by an artist. ⇨ oils(1), watercolours(1).

▷ *tr/intr.v* **3** put paint(1) on (a surface): *We're painting the living-room. Your door needs painting.* ⇨ dye(2). **4** produce (a picture etc) using paints(2): *She paints flowers and small animals.* **paint the town red** ⇨ town.

'paint,brush *c.n* brush used to paint(3).

'painter *c.n* **1** person who paints(3) surfaces. **2** person who paints(4) pictures.

'painting *n* **1** *c.n* picture produced using paints(2). **2** *u.n* act/art of using paint(1,2): *Painting is her only interest.*

'paint,work *u.n* area/parts with paint(1) on the surfaces, e.g doors and windows or the body of a car: *Don't drive near the bushes or you'll scratch the paintwork of the car.*

pair /peə/ *c.n* (*pl -(s)*) (often — of s.o/s.t) **1** two similar or related(2) things that form a complete set: *a pair of boots/gloves. I bought two pairs* (or, *informal, two pair*) *of socks. These boots are a matching pair.* **2** one thing that is made up of two similar parts: *a pair of trousers/scissors.* **3** two people, animals, things etc used or thought of as a set: *Ben and Emma make a nice pair. I don't trust that pair (of children). The cart was pulled by a pair of horses.* **in pairs** two at a time: *leave the room in pairs.*

▷ *tr.v* **4** arrange (s.o/s.t) in pairs: *Please pair your socks before you put them in the drawer.* **pair s.o** (**off**) (**with s.o**) put one person with another to make a pair: *I was paired off with their best player. They soon paired off at the party.*

paisley /'peɪzlɪ/ *u.n* (also *attrib*) pattern of long curved shapes with flowers: *a paisley skirt.*

pajamas ⇨ pyjamas.

pal /pæl/ *c.n* **1** (*informal*) friend: *You're a real pal to lend me the money.*

▷ *intr.v* (*-ll-*) **2 pal up** (**with s.o**) (*informal*) become friends or partners (with s.o): *She palled up with Tom for the party.*

'pally *adj* (*-ier, -iest*) (*informal*) friendly.

palace /'pælɪs/ *c.n* **1** (with capital **P** in names) home of a king, queen or chief: *Buckingham Palace*; *the chief's palace in Kumasi.* **2** large and richly furnished house.

palatial /pə'leɪʃəl/ *adj* large and richly furnished (like a palace(1)): *a palatial room in a* luxury *hotel.*

palaeolithic /ˌpælɪə'lɪθɪk/ *adj* of or referring to the life and social development of human beings about 2.5 million years ago: *palaeolithic stone tools.*

palaeontology /ˌpælɪən'tɒlədʒɪ/ *u.n* study of fossils(1).

ˌpalaeontoloˌgist *c.n* person who studies, is skilled in, palaeontology.

palatable /'pælɪtəbl/ *adj* **1** (*formal*) pleasant to taste. **2** (*fig*) that can be accepted: *a palatable idea.* Opposite unpalatable.

palate /'pælɪt/ *n* **1** *def.n* roof of the mouth with bone at the front (**'hard ˌpalate**) and fleshy only at the back (**'soft ˌpalate**). **2** *sing.n* (often — for s.t) (*formal*) ability to recognize and enjoy particular food or drink: *I have no palate for* olives(1).

palatial ⇒ palace.

palaver /pə'lɑːvə/ *u.n* (*informal*) trouble; bother(1): *Why must I go to the palaver of providing four photographs and two application forms?*

pale /peɪl/ *adj* **1** (usu *attrib*) (of a colour) less strong than usual: *pale blue/yellow.* **2** with less colour than usual: *Her face went pale.* **3** (*fig*) not as convincing or strong as usual: *a pale excuse*; *a pale copy of her former self.*

▷ *intr.v* **4** become pale: *These books have paled in* the sun. Her face paled. **pale before s.t** become less important or significant(1) when compared with s.t: *His examination successes paled before those of his friends.*

ˌpale 'ale *u.n* kind of light beer.

'paleness *u.n*.

'palish *adj* a little pale.

palette /'pælɪt/ *c.n* **1** piece of wood with a place for the thumb, used by an artist to mix paints on. **2** range of paints used: *She uses a wide/small palette in her work.*

'palette-ˌknife *c.n* knife with a flat wide and rounded end, used (**a**) by artists to mix paints; (**b**) for mixing, spreading etc in cookery.

paling /'peɪlɪŋ/ *c.n* **1** (often *pl*) fence made of wooden poles. **2** (also *attrib*) one of the upright wooden poles of such a fence: *a paling fence.*

pall¹ /pɔːl/ *c.n* **1** dark cloth put over a coffin. **2** (*fig*) dark covering: *a pall of black smoke.* **3** (*fig*) sad atmosphere: *The disaster produced a pall over the whole* community.

'pall,bearer *c.n* person who carries, walks near, a coffin at a funeral.

pall² /pɔːl/ *intr.v* (often — on s.o) become dull or boring (to s.o): *Her lessons are beginning to pall* (*on me*).

pallet /'pælɪt/ *c.n* wooden base used when carrying goods.

pallid /'pælɪd/ *adj* (*formal*) pale and looking ill: *pallid skin.*

'pallidness *u.n*.

pallor /'pælə/ *u.n* condition of being pallid.

pally ⇒ pal.

palm¹ /pɑːm/ *c/def.n* **1** inside surface of the hand or a glove: *She was holding the* puppy(1) *in the palms of her hands.*

▷ *tr.v* **2 palm s.o/s.t off** (**on s.o**); **palm s.o off with s.t** persuade/force a person to accept s.o/s.t by using deceit: *It was immoral to try to palm that old man off with a useless bicycle. Don't try to palm your aunt off on me this afternoon.*

palm² /pɑːm/ *c.n* **1** (also *attrib*) kind of tree that comes from hot countries, with wide long leaves growing at the top of a straight trunk(2): *a palm tree*; *a* coconut/date(2) *palm.* **2** (leaf made into a) symbol of victory.

'palm ˌoil *u.n* oil from a kind of palm²(1), used in cooking and to make soap.

palpable /'pælpəbl/ *attrib.adj* (*formal*) **1** obvious: *a palpable mistake/lie.* **2** able to be touched or felt: *a palpable hit.*

'palpably *adv*.

palpitate /'pælpɪˌteɪt/ *intr.v* (*formal*) produce small regular beats: *a palpitating heart.*

palpitations /ˌpælpɪ'teɪʃənz/ *pl.n* many small beats of the heart because of fear, anxiety, hard work, love etc.

palsy ⇒ cerebral palsy.

paltry /'pɔːltrɪ/ *adj* (*-ier, -iest*) worthless because too small: *a paltry sum of money*; *a paltry meal of bread and water.*

pampas /'pæmpəs/ *def./def.pl n* flat areas of South America which are covered with grass.

pamper /'pæmpə/ *tr.v* give (s.o, esp a child) too many gifts and allow her/him to do what she/he wants. ⇒ pander, spoil¹(2).

pamphlet /'pæmflɪt/ *c.n* (often — about/on s.t) set of pages fastened together containing information, a description etc, about a particular subject: *Write a pamphlet on the dangers of smoking.*

pan¹ /pæn/ *c.n* **1** metal pot with a handle used for cooking: *Put the* peas *in a pan of boiling water.* ⇒ frying pan, saucepan. **2** shallow metal dish as used on scales. **3** = lavatory pan. **4** natural shallow hole in the surface of the ground, esp one used to collect salt. **a flash in the pan** ⇒ flash(*n*).

pan² /pæn/ *tr.v* (*-nn-*) (*informal*) criticize (s.o/ s.t) severely: *The newspaper panned the England football team.* **pan out** (*informal*) turn out; make progress: *The new painting is panning out well.*

panacea /ˌpænə'sɪə/ *c.n* (usu *sing, a* — for s.t) **1** thing that can cure any illness or disease: *Is chicken soup a panacea for everything?* **2** (*fig*) activity, event etc that cures problems or difficulties: *A good book is an excellent panacea for long cold winter evenings.*

panache /pə'næʃ/ *u.n* bold and attractive style(3): *She plays cards with panache.*

panatella /ˌpænə'telə/ *c.n* kind of long thin cigar.

pancake /'pænˌkeɪk/ *c.n* (also *attrib*) flat round piece of fried batter¹ eaten with sugar, lemon, ice-cream etc: *a pancake mixture.* **as flat as a pancake** ⇒ flat(*adj*).

ˌpanˌcake 'roll *c.n* ⇒ spring roll (⇒ spring¹).

pancreas /'pæŋkrɪəs/ *def.n* (*technical*) organ near the stomach which produces chemical substances to help digest(3) food.

pancreatic /ˌpæŋkrɪˈætɪk/ *adj* of the pancreas: *pancreatic juices.*

panda /ˈpændə/ *c.n* (also ˌgiant ˈpanda) black and white animal like a bear living in forests in China: *There are very few pandas left in the world.*

pandemic /pænˈdemɪk/ *adj* affecting people in a very large area: *a pandemic disease.* Compare endemic, epidemic.

pandemonium /ˌpændɪˈməʊnɪəm/ *u.n* wild noisy and confused state: *The referee's(2) decision produced pandemonium in the crowd.*

pander /ˈpændə/ *intr.v* **pander to s.o/s.t** give s.o everything he/she wants, let him/her make all the decisions etc: *It is harmful to pander to a child's every wish.* ⇨ pamper, spoil¹(2).

pane /peɪn/ *c.n* (also ˌpane of ˈglass) = window pane.

panel /ˈpænl/ *c.n* **1** flat piece of a wall, door etc. **2** part of a structure, e.g of the body of a car, of a skirt etc. **3** (also *attrib*) group of people who answer questions, usu on television or radio: *a panel game.* **4** list of patients registered(6) with a general practitioner.

▷ *tr.v* (-ll-) **5** put (wooden etc) panels(1) on/in (s.t): *panel a ceiling.*

panelling /ˈpænəlɪŋ/ *u.n* **1** material, e.g wood, used to make panels(1). **2** act of putting panels(1) on/in.

pang /pæŋ/ *c.n* (often — *of s.t*) sudden uncomfortable feeling (because of s.t): *a pang of pain/ hunger; guilt pangs.*

panic /ˈpænɪk/ *c/u.n* **1** sudden uncontrolled fear, esp among many people: *The news of the war filled us with panic. The whole town was in a state of panic. A wild panic gripped(7) the audience.*

▷ *intr.v* (-ck-) **2** become affected by panic(1): *They panicked when they saw the fire and ran towards the doors. If you see a snake, stand still and don't panic.*

ˈ**panicky** *adj* affected by panic(1): *The sound of the guns made him panicky.*

ˈ**panic-ˌstricken** *adj* filled with panic(1): *a panic-stricken crowd.*

pannier /ˈpænɪə/ *c.n* one of two bags or baskets on the sides of a motorbike, donkey etc.

panorama /ˌpænəˈrɑːmə/ *c.n* (often — *of s.t*) **1** wide view (of an area): *a panorama of Cape Town from the top of Table Mountain.* **2** (fig) wide general survey(1) (of a subject): *provide a panorama of the condition of our schools.*

panoramic /ˌpænəˈræmɪk/ *adj.*

pant /pænt/ *c.n* **1** (example of an) act of panting(2): *breathing with short pants.*

▷ *v* **2** *intr.v* breathe using short quick breaths: *The dog was panting after a long run along the beach.* **3** *tr.v* (often — *s.t out*) say (s.t) while panting(2): *He panted his apology and ran on.*

pantheism /ˈpænθiːˌɪzəm/ *u.n* belief that God is the actual universe and is inside everything.

ˈ**panthe,ist** *adj* **1** of, referring to, believing in, pantheism.

▷ *c.n* **2** believer in pantheism.

pantheistic /ˌpænθiːˈɪstɪk/ *adj.*

panther /ˈpænθə/ *c.n* = leopard, esp one that is black.

panties /ˈpæntɪz/ *pl.n* pants(1) for girls and women.

pantihose /ˈpæntɪˌhəʊz/ *u.n* = pantyhose.

pantomime /ˈpæntəˌmaɪm/ *c.n* **1** (also *attrib*) popular play telling a traditional story and produced around Christmas time with singing, dancing, jokes etc: *the pantomime horse.* **2** (*informal*) ridiculous event or situation: *The meeting was a pantomime with no one able to control the speakers.*

pantry /ˈpæntrɪ/ *c.n* (*pl* -ies) small room or cupboard in/near a kitchen for storing food.

pants /pænts/ *pl.n* **1** = underpants. ⇨ panties. **2** (esp US) trousers. **a kick in the pants** ⇨ kick(*n*).

ˈ**panty,hose** *u.n* (also ˈpanti,hose) = tights(1).

pap /pæp/ *u.n* **1** semi-liquid food, e.g for babies or ill people. **2** useless or valueless ideas: *newspaper articles that are full of pap.*

papa /pəˈpɑː/ *c.n* (*informal*) father.

papacy, papal ⇨ pope.

papaya /pəˈpaɪə/ *c/u.n* = pawpaw.

paper /ˈpeɪpə/ *n* **1** *u.n* (also *attrib*) substance (often made from wood pulp(2)) in the form of flat pieces, used for writing and drawing on, covering or wrapping s.t etc: *a piece of writing paper; a paper bag; paper money.* ⇨ wallpaper(1). **2** *c.n* piece of paper(1): *The wind blew the papers everywhere.* **3** *c.n* written lecture: *give a paper on Plato.* **4** *c.n* written examination on a subject: *When do you write your biology paper?* **5** *c.n* (*informal*) = newspaper: *Do you get a Sunday paper?* **on paper** according to theory(1) but not tested: *The plan looks good on paper but is it really possible?* **put/set pen to paper** ⇨ pen¹(*n*).

▷ *tr.v* **6** (also ˈwall,paper) cover (s.t) with wallpaper(1): *Do you know how to paper corners? We're having the dining-room repapered (papered with new wallpaper(2)).* **paper over s.t** (fig) hide s.t unpleasant or embarrassing, esp using an unsatisfactory cover: *She tried to paper over her mistake with excuses but no one believed her.*

ˈ**paper,back** *c.n* (also *attrib*) book with a thin cardboard or plastic(1) cover. ⇨ hardback.

ˈ**paper-,clip** *c.n* piece of bent wire for holding papers together.

ˈ**paper ,round** *c.n* job of delivering newspapers to people's homes.

ˈ**papers** *pl.n* printed pieces of paper used as identity: *Are your papers in order?*

ˈ**paper,work** *u.n* work that includes writing letters, putting papers into files³(1) etc.

papist ⇨ pope.

papoose /pəˈpuːs/ *c.n* kind of bag in a stiff frame used to carry a baby on one's back.

paprika /ˈpæprɪkə/ *u.n* (powder made from a) kind of sweet red pepper which is often not hot, used in cooking.

par /pɑː/ *u.n* **1** (esp (*not*) up to —; *below* —) usual or normal standard: *Your work is below par, not up to par.* **2** (in golf) score for a hole that a good player is expected to get. ⇨ birdie(2), bogey(2), eagle(2). **on a par (with s.o/s.t)** equal in standard (to s.o/s.t): *His singing is on a par with many famous popstars.* ⇨ parity. **be below/under par** be feeling unwell.

parable /ˈpærəbl/ *c.n* short story, esp from the Bible(1), used to demonstrate(2) a particular point about moral(1) behaviour.

parabola /pəˈræbələ/ *c.n* flat curved shape made by cutting a cone(1).

parabolic /ˌpærəˈbɒlɪk/ *adj* shaped like a parabola: *a parabolic roof.*

paracetamol /ˌpærəˈsiːtəˌmɒl/ *c/u.n* (tablet containing a) drug(1) that takes away pain.

parachute /ˈpærəˌʃuːt/ *c.n* 1 (also *attrib*) device like a large umbrella, used to slow down a person or thing falling to the ground from an aircraft: *a parachute jump; parachute silk.*

▷ *intr.v* 2 jump/fall from an aircraft using a parachute(1).

ˈparaˌchutist *c.n* person using a parachute. ⇨ paratrooper.

parade /pəˈreɪd/ *c.n* 1 procession(1) of people, animals, vehicles etc in colourful(1) clothes etc as a celebration: *a royal parade through the streets of London.* 2 line or succession(2) of moving people to display(3) s.t: *a fashion parade.* 3 (*military*) (also *attrib*) organized line or succession(2) of soldiers, army vehicles etc: *a parade ground.* **be on parade** (**a**) be on show: *There were many new designs(2) on parade in the* exhibition(1). (**b**) be showing one's (good) qualities: *Remember you'll be on parade this afternoon at the tea party.* (**c**) (of soldiers) be taking part in a parade(3).

▷ *v* 4 *tr/intr.v* (esp — (s.o/s.t) along, round, through etc *s.w*) (cause (s.o/s.t) to) take part in a parade(1): *They paraded (the winner's cup) through the streets.* 5 *tr.v* show (s.t) in public in a deliberately obvious way: *He was parading his wealth by wearing several gold rings.* 6 *intr.v* (esp — *up and down*) walk about in a public place in order to be seen: *They were parading up and down in front of the government buildings.* 7 *tr/intr.v* (*military*) (cause (soldiers etc) to) take part in a parade(3).

paradise /ˈpærəˌdaɪs/ *n* 1 *unique n* heaven. 2 *sing/u.n* (example/place of) complete beauty or happiness: *The scenery in parts of Africa is paradise. Living with my aunt was paradise compared to being at home.* **a fool's paradise** ⇨ fool.

paradox /ˈpærəˌdɒks/ *c.n* statement that expresses two ideas etc that are true but which seem to be opposites: *We work to make money but it's a paradox that people who work hard and long often do not make the most money.*

paradoxical /ˌpærəˈdɒksɪkl/ *adj*.

ˌparaˈdoxically *adv*.

paraffin /ˈpærəfɪn/ *u.n* (also **ˈkeroˌsene**) (also *attrib*) kind of oil made from petrol, used as fuel: *a paraffin heater/lamp.*

paragon /ˈpærəgən/ *c.n* excellent example: *a paragon of virtue/patience.*

paragraph /ˈpærəˌɡrɑːf/ *c.n* 1 part of a piece of writing made up of a group of sentences and shown by starting a new line.

▷ *tr.v* 2 divide (writing) into paragraphs(1).

parakeet /ˈpærəˌkiːt/ *c.n* kind of parrot with a long tail.

parallel /ˈpærəˌlel/ *adj* (often — *to/with* s.t) 1 (of lines, long structures(2) or pieces) always the same distance from each other at every point: *parallel lines. The opposite sides are parallel. The fence is parallel to/with the wall.* 2 similar; same: *parallel responsibilities/situations/difficulties.* ⇨ unparalleled.

▷ *adv* 3 (often — *to/with* s.t) in parallel(1) lines or directions: *They planted trees parallel to/with the road.*

▷ *c.n* 4 line that is parallel(1) to another. 5 (esp — *between* s.t and s.t) comparison (between s.t and s.t): *She described a parallel (or drew parallels) between the human lung and a balloon.* 6 (usu in — or *attrib*) (*technical*) way of joining electrical parts so that the same electrical supply passes through each part. Compare series(3). **on a parallel** (**with** s.o/s.t) of the same standard (as s.o/s.t): *The two actors are on a parallel (with each other).*

▷ *tr.v* (*-l-* or *-ll-*) be, describe as, represent as, similar: *Her career paralleled his in many ways.*

paralleled (*adj*) **be paralleled** be equalled (by anyone/anything else): *Her success couldn't be paralleled.*

ˌparallel ˈbars *pl.n* pair of wooden poles across uprights, used by gymnasts.

parallelogram /ˌpærəˈleləˌɡræm/ *c.n* shape with four straight sides and opposite sides parallel(1). ⇨ square(9), rhombus.

paralyse /ˈpærəˌlaɪz/ *tr.v* 1 affect (s.o, an animal) with paralysis(1). 2 make (a part of the body) unable to feel pain or touch by using an anaesthetic. 3 (*fig*) cause loss of activity or progress in (s.t): *High costs have paralysed the building industry.*

paralysis /pəˈrælɪsɪs/ *c/u.n* (often — *of* s.t) 1 (disease causing) loss of ability or strength to move some or all parts of the body. ⇨ paraplegia, quadriplegia. 2 (*fig*) loss of ability to act or make progress: *the paralysis of the shipping industry because of lack of orders.*

paralytic /ˌpærəˈlɪtɪk/ *adj* 1 of or referring to paralysis(1). 2 (*informal*) (usu *pred*) very drunk.

paramedical /ˌpærəˈmedɪkl/ *adj/c.n* (of or referring to a) person or activity that supports the work of doctors and surgeons.

parameter /pəˈræmɪtə/ *c.n* fact that limits s.t: *Every business works within the parameters of money available, market size and opportunities.*

paramilitary /ˌpærəˈmɪlɪtərɪ/ *adj* (usu *attrib*) organized like an army, e.g with uniforms, rules etc but not part of an official army: *a paramilitary political organization.*

paramount /ˈpærəˌmaʊnt/ *adj* most important or significant(1): *The children's safety is paramount (or is of paramount importance).*

paranoia /ˌpærəˈnɔɪə/ *u.n* 1 mental(3) illness in which a person has ideas of being extremely important and of being threatened by others. 2 (*informal*) strong fear of being hurt by other people.

paranoid /ˈpærəˌnɔɪd/ *adj/c.n* (of or referring to a) person who suffers from paranoia, esp one who thinks other people want to hurt her/him: *My mother is paranoid about going out in the evening.*

paranormal /ˌpærəˈnɔːml/ *adj* not able to be explained using normal human experience: *Some people claim to have seen paranormal objects in the sky.*

parapet /ˈpærəpɪt/ *c.n* low wall, e.g along a roof or balcony.

paraphernalia /ˌpærəfəˈneɪlɪə/ *u.n* small objects, esp tools or equipment needed to work: *The workmen left their paraphernalia all over the house.*

paraphrase /ˈpærəˌfreɪz/ *c.n* 1 (often — *of* s.t) piece of writing expressing the content of a speech, piece of writing, using new words and

sentences: *make a paraphrase of the committee's report.*
▷ *tr.v* **2** make/provide a paraphrase(1) of (s.t).
paraplegia /ˌpærəˈpliːdʒə/ *u.n* paralysis(1) of both legs. ⇨ quadriplegia.
para'plegic *adj/c.n* (of or referring to a) person suffering from paraplegia. ⇨ quadriplegic.
parasite /ˈpærəˌsaɪt/ *c.n* **1** animal/plant living in or on another animal/plant: *Fleas and tapeworms are parasites.* **2** (*derog*; *fig*) person taking food, shelter and money from another person and giving or doing nothing.
parasitic /ˌpærəˈsɪtɪk/ *adj.*
parasol /ˈpærəˌsɒl/ *c.n* umbrella used to keep off the sun.
paratrooper /ˈpærəˌtruːpə/ *c.n* soldier trained to use a parachute(1).
para,troops *pl.n* paratroopers as a group.
parboil /ˈpɑːˌbɔɪl/ *tr.v* boil (food) until partly cooked (before cooking it later or in a different way): *Parboil the potatoes.*
parcel /ˈpɑːsl/ *c.n* **1** (also *attrib*) (often — *of s.t*) thing wrapped, esp to be posted: *a parcel of clothes*; *a food parcel*; *send the books by parcel post.* **2** particular area (of land): *a parcel of grassland.* **part and parcel of s.t** ⇨ part(*n*).
▷ *tr.v* (*-ll-*) **3** (often — *s.t up*) make a parcel(1) of (s.t): *parcelling up the birthday presents.* **4** (often — *s.t out*) divide (and give out) (s.t) in parts (among several people, organizations etc): *The money was parcelled out among/between several families/charities(3).*
parch /pɑːtʃ/ *tr.v* cause (s.o/s.t) to become hot and very dry: *The tropical sun parched the fields.*
parched *adj* **1** hot and very dry: *parched earth.* **2** (*fig*; *informal*) very thirsty: *I am parched after that long walk.*
parchment /ˈpɑːtʃmənt/ *c/u.n* (piece of) animal skin made into a thin material for writing on.
pardon /ˈpɑːdn/ *interj* **1** (also **pardon me, I beg your pardon**) would you kindly repeat what you said.
▷ *n* **2** *u.n* (often — *for s.t*) (*formal*) forgiveness: *seek a person's pardon for one's bad behaviour.* **3** *c.n* (document(1) stating an) agreement to let s.o free from punishment, prison etc: *He was given a pardon because he gave information to the police.* **I beg your pardon** (a) ⇨ pardon(1): *I beg your pardon but could you repeat that address?* (b) (used to express regret after doing s.t wrong): *I beg your pardon — did I step on your toe?* (c) (polite expression used before saying s.t that is possibly unfriendly(1) or critical): *I beg your pardon but you've no right to speak to her in that manner.*
▷ *tr.v* **4** (esp — *me (but)* . . .) excuse (me for disturbing you) (but): *Pardon me but aren't you Peter's sister?* ⇨ pardon(1). **5** (*formal*) forgive (s.t): *How can I pardon such rude language?* **6** give (s.o) a pardon(3).
'pardonable *adj.*
pare /peə/ *tr.v* **1** cut off or peel (the outside of fruit or vegetables) using a knife. **2** cut (fingernails or toenails) shorter. **pare s.t down** gradually make s.t smaller in amount, size etc: *paring down costs by reducing one's travel expenses.*
'parer *c.n* (also **'paring-,knife**) small, sharp knife used for peeling fruit or vegetables.
parent /ˈpeərənt/ *c.n* (also *attrib*) **1** father or

mother: *The school has organized parent inter-views(2) to discuss the children's progress.* **2** living thing (animal or plant) that has produced a similar living thing: *This old rose is the parent (plant).* **3** organization that has smaller offices in other areas: *This office is controlled by the parent (company) in New York.*
parentage /ˈpeərəntɪdʒ/ *u.n* immediate family or origin: *Are you of British parentage?*
parental /pəˈrentl/ *attrib.adj* of or referring to parents: *parental responsibility.*
'parent,hood *u.n* condition of being a parent: *Are you ready for parenthood at such a young age?*
parenthesis /pəˈrenθəsɪs/ *c.n* (*pl* parentheses /pəˈrenθəˌsiːz/) **1** (often *pl*) (esp *in* —) one or both round brackets ( ) used in writing. **2** words inside parentheses(1) put in the middle of a sentence etc to explain, give details etc.
parenthetical /ˌpærənˈθetɪkl/ *adj.* **,paren-'thetically** *adv.*
par excellence /ˌpɑːr ˈeksələns/ *adv* (*French*) so excellent that there is no person or thing as good or better: *Florence is a beautiful city par excellence!*
pariah /pəˈraɪə/ *c.n* person sent away from, or ignored by, a community(1): *After I came out of prison I felt like a social pariah.*
paring-knife /ˈpeərɪŋ ˌnaɪf/ *c.n* = parer.
parish /ˈpærɪʃ/ *c/def.pl.n* (also *attrib*) (people living in a) place with a Christian(1) church and priest: *the parish church. Do you live in this parish? The whole parish refused to help.* ⇨ parochial(2), parson.
,parish 'council *c.n* division of a county(1) or district council in England.
parishioner /pəˈrɪʃənə/ *c.n* member of a parish.
parity /ˈpærɪti/ *u.n* (*formal*) equality of amount, value, rank etc: *ask for parity between teachers' salaries and those of the police.* ⇨ on a par (with s.o/s.t) (⇨ par).
park /pɑːk/ *c.n* **1** area of land with grass, trees etc in a town or city: *a public park. Let's play football in the park.* **2** large area of land round a house in the countryside. **3** area of land containing things, animals etc for public entertainment: *an amusement park*; *a wild life park.* ⇨ national park, carpark.
▷ *v* **4** *tr/intr.v* put (and leave) (a vehicle) in a particular place: *Where can I park? You can't park on a corner. I'll park my car next to yours.* **5** *tr.v* (often — *s.o/s.t on s.o*) (*informal*) put (s.o/s.t) in a place and leave her/him/it: *She parks the baby on us almost every Saturday.* **park oneself (down)** (*informal*) sit down: *Park yourself (down) in that chair for a few minutes.*
'parking *u.n* (also *attrib*) **1** act of parking (⇨ park(4)) a vehicle: *a parking space/ticket.* **2** area or space where one is allowed to park(4), usu shown by *symb* P. **No parking!** Parking(1) is not allowed.
'parking ,meter *c.n* device at, near, a parking(2) area which one puts money into and which shows how long one can legally park there.
'park,land *u.n* large grassy area with trees and bushes.
parka /ˈpɑːkə/ *c.n* quilted short coat to protect one against wind, rain and cold.

parky /'pɑːkɪ/ *adj* (*-ier, -iest*) (*slang*) cold: *feeling parky.*

parlance /'pɑːləns/ *u.n* (*formal*) way of speaking: *using scientific parlance.*

parliament /'pɑːləmənt/ *c.n* (with capital **P** when referring to a particular one, e.g in Britain) (meeting of the) people who make the laws and control the general political affairs of a country: *The British Parliament has two* assemblies(3), *the* House of Commons *and the* House of Lords. *Who was the leader of the French parliament in 1980?*

parliamentarian /ˌpɑːləmen'teərɪən/ *adj* **1** of or referring to a parliament: *parliamentarian duties.*

▷ *c.n* **2** expert in how a parliament is run. **3** (often with capital **P**) member of a parliament.

parliamentary /ˌpɑːlə'mentərɪ/ *adj* by, of, referring to, a parliament: *parliamentary government.*

parlour /'pɑːlə/ *c.n* (also *attrib*) (*old use*) small room in a house for entertaining: *a parlour maid.* ⇨ beauty parlour.

parochial /pə'rəʊkɪəl/ *adj* **1** (*derog*) showing limited interest and lacking imagination: *She has a parochial mind.* **2** of or referring to a parish: *parochial affairs.*

pa'rochia,lism *u.n* **pa'rochially** *adv.*

parody /'pærədɪ/ *c.n* (*pl* *-ies*) (often — *of s.t*) **1** amusing copy (of the style of a person's writing, music, acting etc). **2** copy or example (of s.t) that is so bad that it seems deliberate(1): *The trial was a parody of justice.*

▷ *tr.v* **3** produce a parody(1) of (s.t).

parole /pə'rəʊl/ *n* **1** *u.n* (*law*) freeing of a person from prison on condition that he/she will not commit another crime: *He was given his parole.* **2** *sing.n* (*law*) document(1)/permission allowing parole(1): *I hope to get my parole next month.* (**out**) **on parole** in a state of having parole(1) for an amount of time: *She's coming out of prison and will be on parole for two years.*

▷ *tr.v* **3** allow (s.o) out of prison and on parole: *I'm hoping to be paroled next month.*

paroxysm /'pærəkˌsɪzəm/ *c.n* (usu *pl*) (often — *of s.t*) uncontrollable attack (of anger, laughter, guilt, pain etc): *The audience was sent into paroxysms of laughter.*

parrot /'pærət/ *c.n* kind of brightly coloured bird with a sharp hooked beak.

'parrot,fashion *adv* (esp *do/learn s.t* —) without thinking: *learn a science* formula *parrot-fashion.*

parsimonious /ˌpɑːsɪ'məʊnɪəs/ *adj* (*derog*; *formal*) miserly: *a parsimonious relative.*

,parsi'moniously *adv.* **parsimony, ,parsi'moniousness** *u.n.*

parsley /'pɑːslɪ/ *u.n* (also *attrib*) kind of herb used in cooking, esp in sauces: *parsley butter.*

parsnip /'pɑːsnɪp/ *c.n* (also *attrib*) kind of vegetable with a long white root, cooked and eaten: *parsnip soup*; *roast parsnips.*

parson /'pɑːsn/ *c.n* Church of England priest, usu one who has a parish.

parsonage /'pɑːsnɪdʒ/ *c.n* home of a parson.

part /pɑːt/ *attrib.adj* **1** not the whole: *I took his bicycle in part payment for the* motorbike.

▷ *adv* **2** partly: *The animal was part brown and part white.*

▷ *n* (often — *of s.t*) **3** *c/unique n* piece of a whole;

some: *Part of the land has been planted with trees.* (*A*) *part of me is still in Venice — it was so beautiful! Can you name the parts of a flowering plant? Part(s) of the time we were able to swim in the sea. I'll walk with you part of the way. That's only part of the story.* **4** *c.n* equal amount: *Mix two parts flour to one part butter. A centimetre is a hundredth part of a metre. I've divided the money into three parts.* **5** *c.n* person's share of duty or responsibility: *We expect everybody to do her or his part to make the* festival(2) *a success.* **6** *c.n* (words etc for an) actor's role in a film, play, television programme etc: *the leading part*; *a small part in a television commercial. Please learn your parts by Saturday.* **7** *c.n* (notes for a) musician's/singer's contribution(1) to a group work: *The trumpet's part is extremely difficult.* **8** *c.n* piece of a machine, engine etc that can be taken off and changed: *Do you have any spare parts for an old sports car?* **for the most part** (*formal*) generally; mostly: *It's warm in August for the most part.* **for my, your** etc **part** in my etc opinion. **in part** partly: *I was wrong in part but I think you were also wrong.* **s.o of many parts** person with many abilities: *She's a woman of many parts in this town.* **on the part of s.o**; **on s.o's part** (*formal*) representing s.o; on behalf of s.o: *I'm replying on the part of my client(1).* **part and parcel (of s.t)** necessary or central contribution(1) (to s.t): *Getting up early is part and parcel of being a farmer.* **play a/one's part (in s.t)** share (in s.t); be involved(2) (in s.t): *Did you play a part in the* riot(1)? *I don't like war but I suppose one must play one's part.* **take part (in s.t)** be a member (of a group activity): *I refused to take part (in their quarrel). I enjoyed taking part in sports activities at school.* ⇨ partake in s.t. **take s.o's part** support s.o in an argument or quarrel.

▷ *v* **9** *tr/intr.v* (often — (*s.o/s.t*) *from s.o/s.t*) separate (s.o/s.t) (from another or each other): *We parted (from our families) at the railway station. The clouds parted and the sun came through. Our* routes(1) *part soon. We tried to part the two men but they continued to fight.* **10** *tr/intr.v* (cause (s.o and s.o) to) go away from one another and not return: *We lived together for a year and then parted. It was the problem of money that parted us.* ⇨ depart. **part company (with s.o/s.t)** ⇨ company. **part with s.o/s.t** give s.o/s.t up, esp when not wanting to: *I could never part with my old bicycle.*

'parting *n* **1** *c/u.n* (also *attrib*) (often — *from s.o/s.t*) act of leaving: *Parting (from you) is so painful. Our parting was sad. This is my parting gift to you.* **2** *c.n* line made when hair is made to go in opposite directions. **the parting of the ways** time/occasion when people must do different things in their lives, take different decisions about their lives.

'partly *adv* to a certain amount or extent: *I was partly angry and partly disappointed. It was mainly my fault but he was also partly to blame.*

,part of 'speech *c.n* (*pl* parts of speech) (*grammar*) set into which words are grouped according to how they are used in sentences: *Nouns, verbs, adjectives and adverbs are parts of speech.*

parts *pl.n* (esp *these/those* —) area: *Do you come from these parts (or live in these parts)?*

part-'time *attrib.adj* for some of a working day: *a part-time job*. ⇨ part-time (⇨ time(*n*)). Compare full-time.

partake /pɑːˈteɪk/ *intr.v* (*p.t* partook /pɑːˈtʊk/, *p.p* partaken /pɑːˈteɪkən/) (usu — *of s.t*) (*formal*) take a portion of (food): *Have you time to partake of a meal with us?* **partake in s.t** take part in s.t: *partake in the meeting/discussion/events*.

partial /ˈpɑːʃəl/ *adj* **1** (usu *attrib*) affecting/ forming a part only; not complete: *a partial success/recovery*. **2** (often — *towards s.o/s.t*) favouring one person, side etc more than another: *a partial referee; be partial towards the visiting players/team*. Opposite impartial. Compare partisan(1). **partial to s.o/s.t** having a liking for s.o/s.t: *I'm very partial to ice-cream*. **partiality** /ˌpɑːʃiˈælɪtɪ/ *n* **1** *u.n* (often — *towards s.o/s.t*) act/state of being partial(2). Opposite impartiality. **2** *c.n* (often *have a* — *for s.o/s.t*) liking (for s.o/s.t). **partially** /ˈpɑːʃəlɪ/ *adv*.

participate /pɑːˈtɪsɪpeɪt/ *intr.v* (often — (*with s.o*) *in s.t*) (*formal*) take part (with s.o) (in a group activity): *I refused to participate (in their quarrel). I wanted to participate with the others but my parents wouldn't let me*. **participant** /pɑːˈtɪsɪpənt/ *c.n* (often — (*with s.o*) *in s.t*) person who participates (with s.o) (in s.t): *a list of instructions for the participants*. **participation** /pɑːˌtɪsɪˈpeɪʃən/ *u.n* (often — (*with s.o*) *in s.t*).

participle /ˈpɑːtɪsɪpl/ *c.n* (*written abbr* p) (*grammar*) form of a verb used as an adjective, e.g a '*broken* finger'; 'a *parting* gift', and to make certain tenses[2], e.g 'We're *coming*', 'They have *gone*'. ⇨ past participle, present participle. **participial** /ˌpɑːtɪˈsɪpɪəl/ *attrib.adj* (*grammar*): *a participial adjective/clause(1)*. **participially** /ˌpɑːtɪˈsɪpɪəlɪ/ *adv*.

particle /ˈpɑːtɪkl/ *c.n* **1** (often — *of s.t*) very small piece (of s.t): *particles of dust*. **2** (*grammar*) small word used as a preposition or part of a phrasal verb, e.g 'get *up*'. ⇨ adverbial particle.

particular /pəˈtɪkjʊlə/ *attrib.adj* **1** belonging/ referring to, of, a single person, group, thing etc and not others: *a particular student/reason/ day/time/team*. **2** exceptional; more than usual: *It's of particular importance/interest/concern to me*. **3** (often — *about s.t*) difficult to please or satisfy because of high personal standards: *He's a particular eater/dresser* (⇨ dress(5)). *She's very particular about her choice of hotels*.
▷ *c.n* **4** (often *in every, this* etc —) (*formal*) separate item(1) of detail: *In this particular I'm sure he's wrong*. **in particular** especially: *I don't love anyone in particular. In particular, I enjoy a walking holiday. I want you to check the temperature in particular*. **par'ticularly** *adv* especially: *I'm particularly grateful to my parents*. **par'ticulars** *pl.n* (often — *of s.t*) details of infor- mation (esp personal details, e.g name, address etc): *Please leave me all your particulars and I'll see if I can help you*.

parting ⇨ part.

partisan /ˌpɑːtɪˈzæn/ *adj* **1** (usu *pred*) (*formal*) extremely loyal or committed to one person, group, idea etc: *have partisan opinions. A chair- person must not be partisan*. Compare partial(2).

▷ *c.n* **2** extremely loyal supporter. **3** person fighting an enemy that has occupied(6) her/his country.

partition /pɑːˈtɪʃən/ *n* **1** *c.n* thing, e.g a wall, fence etc, that separates an area into parts: *Partitions have been put up in the office*. **2** *c/u.n* (often — *of s.t*) act/state of separating (a country) into parts: *the partition of Ireland*.
▷ *tr.v* **3** (often — *s.t off*) separate (an area) into parts: *The office has been partitioned off*.

partly ⇨ part.

partner /ˈpɑːtnə/ *c.n* **1** one of a pair of players in an activity, game or sport: *a dancing/tennis partner*. **2** member of a (usu) business partnership. **3** one of a pair consisting of a husband or wife: *married partners*. **sleeping partner** ⇨ sleep.
▷ *tr.v* **4** (cause (s.o) to) be a partner(1): *I partnered (or was partnered with) Sally in the card game*. **'partnership** *c/u.n* condition of being/be- coming partners, joint owners in a business etc: *They've formed a business partnership. Navratilova and Shriver were a good doubles partnership*. **go into partnership (with s.o)** become a partner(2) (of s.o): *The two brothers have gone into partnership with their cousins*.

partook /pɑːˈtʊk/ *p.p* of partake.

partridge /ˈpɑːtrɪdʒ/ *c/u.n* (also *attrib*) (flesh of a) kind of game(7) bird, eaten as food: *partridge pie*.

party /ˈpɑːtɪ/ *c.n* (*pl* -ies) **1** (also *attrib*) social meeting for pleasure with music, dancing etc or for a meal: *a dinner/tea party; a birthday party; party music. We're having a* farewell(2) *party for* (i.e to say goodbye to) *my sister on Saturday*. **2** (often — *of s.o*) group (of people) sharing an activity: *the wedding party; a search party; a party of tourists*. **3** (often with capital **P**) (also *attrib*) group of people sharing a political opinion and working together in politics: *the Labour Party; party politics; a party political broadcast*. **4** (often — *to s.t*) (*formal*) person taking part in a group activity (often an illegal one): *be a party to the discussions; be a party to the crime/murder*. **5** (*law*) person involved in a case[1](5): *the guilty party*. **hen/stag party** ⇨ hen, stag.
'party line *c.n* **1** (esp *follow the* —) collection of policies[1] of a political party. **2** telephone line shared by people at two different addresses. **party 'politics** *u/pl.n* political policies and activities of one party(3). **party 'spirit** *u.n* happy and friendly atmos- phere at a party(1). **party 'wall** *c.n* wall shared by two buildings.

pass /pɑːs/ *c.n* **1** act of passing (⇨ pass(8)). **2** (with capital **P** in names) way through an area esp by travelling between hills or mountains: *a pass through the mountains; a mountain pass. The Brenner Pass connects Austria with Italy*. **3** document(1) giving official permission to do s.t, go s.w: *a travel pass. Please show your pass to the guards at the gate*. **4** (also *attrib*) passing (⇨ pass(14)) of an examination but not at a high standard: *gain a pass in mathematics; a pass mark*. **5** act of sending the ball to another player in football etc. **6** (esp *make a* — (*at s.o*)) (*informal*) try, by using words or movement, to attract s.o to the idea of sexual activity with one. **come to, reach, a fine/pretty/sad/sorry pass** reach a bad state(1): *Things in the school have* come to a sad/sorry pass when no one offers to teach football after school.

▷ *v* **7** *tr/intr.v* go forward and move beyond (s.o/ s.t): *We passed the garage an hour ago. A plane passed over our heads. What time does the bus pass?* ⇒ pass by(a). **8** *tr/intr.v* (often — *s.t to s.o*) (cause (s.t) to) go/move from one person/place to another: *Pass me that pen, please. He passed the ball to the captain. The responsibility passed to the deputy*(2). *She passed the rope round the pole, the letter under the door. Would you like to pass these biscuits round (to everyone)?* **9** *intr.v* go by; happen: *The time passed quickly. We let the matter pass. I don't know what passed between them.* **10** *tr.v* go beyond (a standard, level etc): *His success passed all our expectations.* ⇒ surpass. **11** *tr/intr.v* get, make a path, across, through etc (s.t): *Their route passes through several places of beauty.* **12** *intr.v* (often — *from s.o/s.t to s.o/s.t*) spread; transfer(5): *The disease passes from the mother to the baby. The money will pass from my daughter to her children.* ⇒ pass down. **13** *intr.v* come to an end: *This bad weather, Her anger, will soon pass.* **14** *tr/intr.v* get, decide that s.o/s.t has, the necessary standard or grade in an examination, test etc: *I've passed (my examinations)! Who passed these cups as perfect? The examiner passed all of us.* **15** *tr.v* officially agree to, accept, (a rule, law, policy(1) etc): *They've passed a law about smoking in theatres. Has your application for a visa been passed?*

pass as/for s.o be accepted or mistaken for s.o: *He'll never pass as a waiter with those hands! You could pass for a younger man in those clothes.* ⇒ pass oneself/s.o off (as s.o).

pass away (*informal*) die: *My father passed away last week.*

pass by (s.o/s.t) (**a**) go past (s.o/s.t). (**b**) not pay attention to (s.o/s.t who/that is a problem).

pass (s.t) down (from s.o) (to s.o) (of the ownership of money, property) transfer(5) s.t, be transferred(5), (from s.o) (to s.o else).

pass off (**a**) gradually come to an end: *The ache will soon pass off.* (**b**) (of an event) happen: *The meeting passed off peacefully.* **pass oneself/s.o off (as s.o)** cause oneself/s.o to be accepted as s.o else: *He tried to pass her off as his wife.* ⇒ pass as/for s.o. **pass s.t off (as s.t)** cause s.t to be accepted as s.t else: *Don't try to pass off those cheap jewels as genuine*(1).

pass on (**a**) (*informal*) die. (**b**) move beyond or further. **pass s.t on** give s.t (esp s.t given to oneself) to s.o else: *When you've read the letter, pass it on.*

pass out (**a**) (*informal*) become unconscious. (**b**) leave after successfully completing a course, e.g at a military college. **pass s.t out** give things to several people: *Please pass out these books.*

pass s.o over/up not give s.o a job (that she/he has a right to), but instead give it to s.o less senior(1). *I've been passed over for a younger woman.*

pass sentence (on s.o) ⇒ sentence(*n*).

pass the time (by doing s.t); pass the time of day (with s.o) ⇒ time(*n*).

pass (s.t) to s.o (**a**) ⇒ pass(8). (**b**) = pass (s.t) down to s.o.

pass s.t up (*informal*) refuse an offer, opportunity etc: *Don't pass up the chance of earning more money.*

pass water ⇒ water(*n*).

'passable *adj* **1** (*pred*, usu with a negative) (of a barrier etc) that can be passed: *The path through the mountain isn't passable.* Opposite impassable. **2** (*formal*) of an acceptable but not high standard: *This meal is passable.*

,passer-'by *c.n* (*pl* passers-by) person walking past s.o, a place: *We stood on the bridge watching the passers-by.*

'passing *attrib.adj* **1** going past: *We stopped a passing car.* **2** lasting a short time (and so not serious or detailed): *a passing interest/ comment*(1). *a* **passing fancy** ⇒ fancy (6). **in passing** in the course of a conversation, discussion etc: *He told me in passing that he was very rich.*

'pass,port *c.n* (also *attrib*) document(1) giving one's nationality(1) and other personal details, used to travel to another country: *passport number.*

'pass,word *c.n* secret word etc that (proves one's identity(1) and) allows one to enter or be accepted.

passage /'pæsɪdʒ/ *c.n* **1** (also **'passage,way**) long narrow space in a building leading to a room or rooms: *The stairs are at the end of the passage.* Compare corridor. **2** long path or way through s.w: *find a passage through the rocks, the crowds.* **3** (often — (*by s.t*) (*from s.w to s.w*)) journey (in s.t) by sea: *a passage by boat from Cairo to Aswan.* **4** piece of writing/music taken from a longer one. **passage of time** (*formal*) act or fact of time passing. **work one's passage (to s.w)** get a job on the ship one is travelling in in order to pay the fare.

'passage,way *c.n* = passage(1).

passenger /'pæsɪndʒə/ *c.n* (also *attrib*) person who travels in a car, bus, train, boat etc who is not the driver: *a passenger vehicle.*

passer-by ⇒ pass.

passion /'pæʃən/ *c/u.n* (usu — *for s.o/s.t*) strong feeling or emotion(1) (esp of love or anger) (for s.o/s.t): *She felt a great passion for him, has a passion for music..I was in such a passion that I hit him.*

passionate /'pæʃənɪt/ *adj* **1** having very strong feelings: *a passionate lover of music.* **2** having strong sexual desires: *a passionate man*; *feeling passionate (about him).* ⇒ dispassionate, impassioned.

'passionately *adv.*

passive /'pæsɪv/ *adj* **1** showing no emotion, feeling or interest: *The bird was passive in my hand. She remained passive during the storm.* ⇒ impassive. **2** not violent: *use passive means to express political* opposition(2). **3** (*grammar*) (of a verb) the subject(4) of which is acted on by the verb. ⇒ active(3).

▷ *c/def.n* **4** (*grammar*) (verb in the) passive voice.

,passive re'sistance *u.n* use of methods that do not include violence to express (esp political) opposition.

,passive 'voice *def.n* (*grammar*) form of a verb in a sentence used when the subject(4) is acted on by the verb, e.g 'The photograph *was taken* by my brother', 'Which window *was broken?*' ⇒ active voice.

'passi,vism *u.n* belief/practice of not being violent when opposing s.o/s.t.

passport ⇒ pass.

past /pɑːst/ *adj* **1** ended, finished, at a time before now: *past actions*; *past experiences*. **2** of a period of time immediately before now: *during the past week/month/year*. **3** (*attrib*) of a person who has had (but no longer has) a position of power: *a past chairman/president*. **4** (*grammar*) (of verb tenses²) showing actions or states completed before now.
▷ *adv* **5** later than; after: *'Is it ten o'clock yet?' 'Yes, it's five past!'* **6** by(2); so as to pass: *Two men walked/drove past.* ⇨ flypast.
▷ *n* **7** *sing.n* person's life, actions etc before now: *She has a strange past. My past was a happy one.* **8** *def.n* time before now: *We never think about the past. During/In the past most people lived on farms.* **9** *def.n* (*grammar*) = past tense.
▷ *prep* **10** after, beyond, in time: *It's well past 10 o'clock. It was past midnight before she returned. It's 5 (minutes) past 7.* **11** up to and beyond: *She was walking past the bus stop.* **12** after/beyond in position: *My house is past the park.* **13** beyond the reach of; no longer capable(2) of: *That old horse is past hope.* **be/feel past it** (*informal*) be/feel unable to be as active as when young. **would not put it past s.o (to do s.t)** ⇨ put.

past 'participle *c.n* (*written abbr* p.p used in this dictionary) (*grammar*) form of verb used to make one of the perfect tenses, e.g 'He has *gone*', 'We had *seen* it'.

past 'perfect ('tense) *def.n* (*grammar*) verb form used to show action, an event etc that had already finished (before the action of the main verb which is in the past (8), e.g 'We *had seen* it a month before they saw it', 'They*'d arrived* an hour earlier than we did'.

past 'tense *def.n* (*written abbr* p.t used in this dictionary) (*grammar*) verb form used to show an action, event or state completed in the past, e.g 'He *went*', 'We *saw* it', 'They *arrived*'.

pasta /ˈpæstə/ *u.n* shaped pieces of a dried mixture of flour, eggs and water such as macaroni, spaghetti, eaten as food.

paste /peɪst/ *n* **1** *u.n* soft mixture of flour or glue and water, used to join pieces of paper, cardboard etc. **2** *u.n* (also *attrib*) soft mixture of cooked and creamed meat, fish etc esp for cooking, spreading on bread, biscuits etc: *fish paste sandwiches*; *tomato paste*. **3** *u/sing.n* soft mixture: *use paste to spread on the surface*; *mix the flour and water to a smooth paste*. ⇨ toothpaste. **4** *u.n* substance used to make artificial jewels.
▷ *tr.v* **5** join (s.t) to s.t using paste(1): *She was pasting down a picture, pasting up a notice, pasting the cardboard pieces together.*

pastel /ˈpæstl/ *adj* **1** (of a colour) pale: *pastel green*.
▷ *c/u.n* **2** (kind of crayon(1) made from a) mixture of glue and coloured chalk used to draw pictures. **3** *c.n* (also *attrib*) picture made using pastels(2).

pasteurize, -ise /ˈpæstjəˌraɪz/ *tr.v* (*technical*) kill bacteria in (milk etc) by heating it.
 pasteurization, -isation /ˌpæstjərəˈzeɪʃən/ *u.n*.

pastille /ˈpæstl/ *c.n* small tablet or sweet, esp one containing medicine to help a sore throat: *fruit pastilles*; *throat pastilles*.

pastime /ˈpɑːstaɪm/ *c.n* activity done to spend free time pleasantly: *My favourite pastime is watching football matches.*

pastor /ˈpɑːstə/ *c.n* priest etc with responsibility for all the people attending a particular church.

pastoral /ˈpɑːstrəl/ *attrib.adj* **1** of (the work of) a pastor. **2** (*formal*) of (life in) the countryside: *pastoral beauty, scenery*. **3** of or referring to the care of people in a community(1) such as a school: *a teacher with responsibility for pastoral care.*

pastry /ˈpeɪstrɪ/ *c/u.n* (*pl* -ies) (item of food made using a) soft mixture of flour, water etc baked to make a pie, tart¹(1) etc.

pasture /ˈpɑːstʃə/ *c/u.n* (also **'pasture ˌland**) piece of grassland, esp used for cows and sheep.

pasty¹ /ˈpeɪstɪ/ *adj* (of the skin on the face) pale and looking unwell: *have a pasty complexion*(1).

pasty² /ˈpæstɪ/ *c.n* (*pl* -ies) piece of folded pastry with meat and/or vegetables inside.

pat /pæt/ *adv* **1** (usu off —) (of knowledge) (until) known thoroughly: *learn the words off pat.*
▷ *c.n* **2** (often — *on s.t*) gentle touch with the fingers on a person, animal or thing: *a pat on the shoulder*. **3** small shaped piece (of butter). **pat on the back (for (doing) s.t)** (*informal*) show of approval, thanks etc (for (doing) s.t): *We were given, gave ourselves, a pat on the back for completing so much work.*
▷ *tr.v* (-tt-) **4** give (s.o/s.t) a pat(2): *pat a horse*; *pat a ball.* **pat s.o on the back** (*informal*) give s.o one's approval, congratulations etc.

patch /pætʃ/ *c.n* **1** (often — *of s.t*) small piece of cloth (to be) sewn over a hole. **2** (often — *of s.t*) small area: *patches of blue between the clouds.* **3** small area of land: *a vegetable patch*; *get off my patch.* **be not a patch on s.o/s.t** (*informal*) be not nearly as good as s.o/s.t: *Her cooking isn't a patch on yours.* **a bad patch** a difficult period: *Business is in (or has hit/struck) a bad patch.*
▷ *tr.v* **4** sew a patch(1) on (s.t): *patch (a hole in) one's jeans.* **5** (often — *s.t up* (*with s.t*)) mend (s.t) quickly and roughly (using s.t): *patch (up) a hole in the wall with cardboard.* **patch s.t up** (*fig*) agree to end a disagreement etc: *patch up a quarrel, their differences.*

'patchˌwork *u.n* (also *attrib*) cloth made by sewing patches(1) together: *a patchwork blanket.*

'patchy *adj* (-ier, -iest) not the same quality throughout: *patchy work.*

pate /peɪt/ *c.n* (old use) head: *a bald pate.*

pâté /ˈpæteɪ/ *u.n* (also *attrib*) paste(2) of cooked liver(2), minced(1) fish etc (to be) spread on toast¹(1) or biscuits: *chicken liver(2) pâté.*

patella /pəˈtelə/ *c/def.n* (*technical*) = kneecap.

patent /ˈpeɪtnt/ *adj* **1** obvious: *a patent liar, lie. It was patent to us all that he was lying.*
▷ *c.n* **2** (esp *take out a* — (*on s.t*)) official government permission to be the only maker of a particular thing.
▷ *tr.v* **3** get a patent(2) for (s.t): *I've patented my invention.*

ˌpatent 'leather *u.n* (also *attrib*) leather made to have a hard shining surface: *black patent leather shoes.*

'patently *adv* obviously: *He's patently telling the truth.*

paternal /pəˈtɜːnl/ *adj* **1** of, referring to, characteristic of, a father: *paternal responsibilities.* **2** (*attrib*) from one's father's relatives: *my*

paternal grandmother (i.e my father's mother).
⇨ maternal.

pa,ternal 'love *u.n* love like a father has for his child (and not romantic or sexual).

paternity /pə'tɜːnɪtɪ/ *u.n* state of being a father.

path /pɑːθ/ *c.n* (*pl -s* /pɑːðz/) **1** small narrow way through, across etc a place: *a footpath*; *a path over the mountains, through the fields.* **2** (often — *of s.t*) course of the movement of s.o/s.t: *the path of a storm. He blocked her path. We followed the path of the* satellite(2) *using a* telescope(1). **cross s.o's path** meet s.o during one's usual activities. **lead s.o up the garden path** ⇨ garden(*n*). **stand in s.o's path** make oneself a barrier(2) to s.o's personal progress or success.

'path,way *c.n* = path(1).

pathetic /pə'θetɪk/ *adj* **1** expressing, causing, pity: *the poor dirty houses looked pathetic* (or *were a pathetic sight*). *He was a pathetic-looking child.* **2** (*informal*) useless because not at all good or strong enough: *a pathetic fire*; *a pathetic excuse/attempt/answer.* **3** (*informal*) very bad: *Her singing was pathetic.*

pa'thetically *adv.*

pathos /'peɪθɒs/ *u.n* (*formal*) power or quality of causing feelings of pity.

pathology /pə'θɒlədʒɪ/ *u.n* (*medical*) science of the causes and types of diseases.

pathological /ˌpæθə'lɒdʒɪkl/ *adj* **1** of or referring to pathology. **2** (*informal*) (of bad feelings or behaviour) very strong and uncontrollable: *a pathological liar.*

,patho'logically *adv.*

pathologist /pə'θɒlədʒɪst/ *c.n* person who studies, is skilled in, pathology.

patient /'peɪʃənt/ *adj* **1** bearing delay, trouble, difficulty, an annoying person etc without becoming angry or complaining: *Be patient! A teacher must be patient with his pupils.* Opposite impatient(1).

▷ *c.n* **2** person being given medical care by a doctor, nurse, dentist etc. ⇨ inpatient, outpatient.

'patience *u.n* **1** ability or quality of being patient(1). Opposite impatience. **2** kind of card game played by one person alone.

'patiently *adv.*

patio /'pætɪˌəʊ/ *c.n* small area outside a house for sitting or eating outdoors: *a breakfast patio.*

patisserie /pə'tiːsərɪ/ *c.n* shop (making and) selling cakes and pastries.

patna rice /ˈpætnə ˌraɪs/ *u.n* (often with capital **P**) kind of rice with long grains.

patriarch /'peɪtrɪˌɑːk/ *c.n* **1** (with capital **P**) senior bishop(1) in the Christian(1) (Orthodox(2)) Church of eastern Europe: *a Greek Patriarch.* **2** male head of a community(1). ⇨ matriarch.

patriarchal /ˌpeɪtrɪ'ɑːkl/ *adj* of, ruled by, patriarchs(2). ⇨ matriarchal.

patricide /'pætrɪˌsaɪd/ *u.n* (esp *law*) act of killing one's father.

patrimony /'pætrɪmənɪ/ *u.n* things given to s.o by or through her/his dead father.

patrimonial /ˌpætrɪ'məʊnɪəl/ *adj.*

patriot /'pætrɪət/ *c.n* person proud of and supporting her/his country.

patriotic /ˌpætrɪ'ɒtɪk/ *adj* having or showing pride and love for one's country: *a patriotic speech.* Opposite unpatriotic.

,patri'otically *adv.*

'patrio,tism *u.n* great pride and love for one's country, esp with a strong commitment to defending it.

patrol /pə'trəʊl/ *n* **1** *u.n* (also *attrib*) (esp *on* —) act of going round an area guarding and watching it: *The police were on patrol at the football* stadium. *There were several patrol cars in the area.* **2** *c.n* group of officials, ships etc on patrol(1): *an army/naval patrol.*

▷ *tr/intr.v* (*-ll-*) **3** take part in a patrol(1) of (s.t): *patrolling the streets.*

patron /'peɪtrən/ *c.n* (often — *of s.o/s.t*) **1** person, business, company etc giving money and encouragement to artists etc: *a patron of the arts.* **2** person who visits a particular shop etc regularly.

patronage /'pætrənɪdʒ/ *u.n* (often — *of s.t*) support (of s.t) by a patron(1,2).

patronize, -ise /'pætrəˌnaɪz/ *tr.v* **1** (*formal*) be a patron(2) of (a particular shop, restaurant etc): *I always patronize that café because their coffee is excellent.* **2** (*derog*) behave towards (s.o) as if friendly but really thinking of oneself as more important, intelligent etc: *Don't patronize me by saying things that are obviously not true.*

'patro,nizing, -ising *adj* (*derog*) behaving as, caused by, a person who patronizes(2) s.o: *a patronizing way of talking.*

,patron 'saint *c.n* saint(1) connected with a particular country or group of people: St Christopher is the patron saint(1) *of travellers.*

patter /'pætə/ *n* **1** *c.n* (often — *of s.t*) sound of short quick drops or taps: *the patter of rain, children's feet.* **2** *u.n* (*informal*) quick talk of s.o trying to sell one s.t: *sales patter.*

▷ *intr.v* **3** make a patter(1): *rain pattering on the roof; children pattering down the stairs.* ⇨ pitter-patter.

pattern /'pætn/ *c.n* **1** design on cloth, paper etc that is repeated: *a floral pattern.* **2** (often — *for s.t*) thing used as a guide for making s.t: *a dress, knitting pattern.* **3** (often — *of s.t*) way in which s.t happens, is done: behavioural *patterns*; *patterns of life on a farm. His movements yesterday did not follow their usual pattern.* **4** (usu — *of s.t*) excellent example (of s.t): *a pattern of generosity.*

▷ *tr.v* **5** (— *oneself/s.t on s.o/s.t*) use s.o/s.t as a model for oneself/s.t: *She patterns herself, her writing, on her mother.*

'patterned *adj* having a pattern(1): *patterned cloth.*

paucity /'pɔːsɪtɪ/ *sing/u.n* (usu — *of s.t*) (*formal*) small amount or number (of s.t): *a paucity of food, understanding.*

paunch /pɔːntʃ/ *c.n* stomach, esp a fat one: *a beer paunch.*

pauper /'pɔːpə/ *c.n* very poor person.

pause /pɔːz/ *c.n* **1** (often — *in s.t, for s.t*) short stop (during an activity) (in order to do/have s.t): *a pause in the conversation/music; a pause for breath.*

▷ *intr.v* **2** (often — *for s.t*) stop an activity for a short time (in order to do/have s.t): *pausing for breath/ food. Let's pause for a short while.*

pave /peɪv/ *tr.v* (usu — *s.t* (*with s.t*)) cover (a road etc) (with flat pieces of stone, etc): *We paved the path with bricks.* **pave the way for s.t** ⇨ way(*n*).

'pavement *c.n* paved or concrete(1) area at the side of a road for people to walk on: *Please keep to the pavement. The child stepped off the pavement and was almost hit by a cyclist.*

'paving *u.n* stone etc shaped in flat pieces to pave s.t with. **crazy paving** ⇨ craze.

'paving-,stone *c.n* piece of paving.

pavilion /pə'vɪlɪən/ *c.n* **1** very large tent for an exhibition(1) etc. **2** small building near a sports ground for the use of players: *a cricket' pavilion.*

paw /pɔː/ *c.n* **1** foot of any animal with claws(1): *a cat's/dog's paws.*

▷ *v* **2** *tr/intr.v* feel, touch etc (s.o/s.t) with a paw: *The cat was pawing the mouse.* **3** *tr/intr.v* (often — *at s.t*) (of a horse etc) touch (the ground etc) several times using a front leg: *The horse was pawing (at) the ground, gate.* **4** *tr.v* (often — *s.o about*) (*informal*) (of a person) touch (s.o) rudely or to suggest sexual interest: *Some men try to paw girls at parties.*

pawn /pɔːn/ *c.n* **1** chess piece of lowest value. **2** (esp — *in s.t*) (*fig*) person, thing, animal used by s.o else for her/his own advantage: *He was only a pawn in their plans.* **in pawn** having been pawned(3).

▷ *tr.v* **3** give (s.t) to s.o, a shop etc as a security(3) for borrowing money: *We'll have to pawn the jewels in order to pay the electricity bill.*

'pawn,broker *c.n* person whose business is lending money in return for things that are pawned(3).

'pawn,shop *c.n* (also **'pawn,broker's**) shop where one can pawn(3) things.

pawpaw /'pɔːpɔː/ *c/u.n* (also *attrib*) (also **pa'paya**) (kind of tree with a) large fruit with pale orange flesh and many black seeds: *a pawpaw tree; pawpaw ice-cream.*

pay /peɪ/ *u.n* **1** (also *attrib*) money given in return for regular work: *What's your monthly pay? My pay is £100 a week. We've been given a pay increase of £10 a month.* ⇨ salary, wages. **be in the pay of s.o/s.t** be secretly paid by the police, enemy etc in return for one's services.

▷ *v* (*p.t,p.p* paid /peɪd/) **2** *tr/intr.v* (usu — *s.o* *for s.t*) give (s.o) (money) in return for work, goods etc: *I'm paid on Fridays. How much will you pay for this old cooker? This job pays well. I'm paid £100 a week.* ⇨ overpay. **3** *tr/intr.v* give (s.o) (money that one owes): *I always pay my debts. When can you pay me?* ⇨ pay back, pay up, repay. **4** *tr/intr.v* be a benefit(1), be useful, (to (s.o)): *It would pay you to work harder. Honesty always pays.* **5** *tr.v* (often — *s.t to s.o*) give (s.t, e.g attention, respect) to s.o: *Please pay attention (to me)! We paid our respects to the organizers. You never pay me any compliments(1).*

make s.o pay (for s.t) make sure that s.o is punished (for doing s.t wrong).

pay s.o back (for s.t) (a) punish s.o (for doing one harm): *I'll pay you back for telling lies about me.* (b) do or give a similar(1) thing in return for a favour: *Thanks for your help — I'll pay you back!* **pay s.t back** give back money that one owes.

pay a call (on s.o) ⇨ call(*n*).

pay s.t down pay(2) an amount of money as a deposit(4): *I can pay £10 down and the other £90 next month.*

pay (s.o) for s.t (a) ⇨ pay(2). (b) (*fig*) be punished for a bad act: *He'll make you pay!* **pay s.o (s.t) (for s.t)** (a) pay(2) s.o (an amount of money) (for s.t): *I'll pay you £25 for that bicycle.* (b) (*fig*) punish s.o for an insult, injury etc: *I'll pay you for that insult!*

pay off be successful; have a good result: *Ben's hard work paid off and he passed all his examinations.* **pay s.o off** (a) (*informal*) give s.o money so that he/she will not say anything to the police etc. (b) pay a worker an amount of money and dismiss her/him from a job. **pay s.t off** (a) pay a small amount of money each week, month etc until a larger amount has been paid: *We bought the car with a loan that we're paying off (over two years).* (b) pay the full amount of money that one owes: *pay off one's debts, taxes.*

pay (s.t) out give (money) to pay(3) what one owes. **pay s.t out** gradually allow (more rope etc) to become available.

pay s.t over (to s.o) pay money (to s.o).

pay through the nose (for s.t) ⇨ nose(*n*).

pay up (often as an order) pay(3) all the money one owes immediately.

pay a visit (on s.o) = pay a call (on s.o).

pay one's way ⇨ way(*n*).

put paid to s.t ⇨ put.

'payable *pred.adj* (often — *to s.o/s.t*) that must be paid (⇨ pay(3)) (to s.o, a business company, bank etc): *Make the cheque payable to me.*

'pay,day *c.n* day when one is paid (⇨ pay(2)).

payee /peɪ'iː/ *c/def.n* person to whom money, a cheque, postal order etc is to be paid.

,paying 'guest *c.n* (*abbr PG*) person who lives in (a room in) s.o's house, sometimes as part of the family, and who pays money for it.

'payment *n* **1** *c.n* (usu — (*to s.o*) *for s.t*) amount of money (to be) paid (to s.o) (for s.t): *There are six monthly payments.* **2** *c.n* punishment (for doing s.t wrong). **3** *u.n* act of paying (⇨ pay(3)): *Payment is due by next Monday. On payment of £10 the goods will be given to you. This £10 is in payment for the food.* ⇨ non-payment, repayment.

'pay-,off *def.sing.n* (*informal*) result or climax(1) of an event, story etc esp one not considered likely: *The pay-off was that the police caught the thieves but never found the money.*

'pay-,packet *c.n* small bag or envelope for one's pay(1): *Joe always gives his pay-packet to his wife.*

'pay-,phone *c.n* public telephone that accepts coins as payment.

'pay,roll *c/def.n* list of all the workers and their pay(1): *How many women are on our payroll?*

'pay,slip *c.n* piece of paper showing one's pay(1), deductions² etc.

PC /,piː 'siː/ *c.n abbr* **1** personal computer. **2** Police Constable.

PE /,piː 'iː/ *abbr* physical(1) education (as a school subject).

pea /piː/ *c.n* (also *attrib*) **1** small round green seed that forms in a pod(1) of a climbing plant and is eaten as a vegetable: *garden peas; pea soup; pea green.* **2** any similar seed: chickpeas.

peace /piːs/ *n* **1** *u/sing.n* (also *attrib*) (written agreement for a) (period of) freedom from war: *We want peace not war. The two countries signed a peace treaty. We hope this will be a lasting peace.* **2** *u.n* freedom from violence, disorder(1,2) or breaking laws: *peace and* prosperity. ⇨ Justice of the Peace. **3** *u.n* state of being quiet and calm: *I need peace in order to study*. **be at peace** (**with s.o/s.t**) (**a**) not be fighting or taking part in a war: *We've been at peace for 40 years*. (**b**) be quiet and calm: *At last he was at peace with his family*. (**c**) (of a person) be dead. **breach of the peace** ⇨ breach(*n*). **disturb the peace** ⇨ disturb. **in peace** in a state of peace(2): *live in peace*. **keep the peace** (**a**) not cause public disorder(1,2) or break the law. (**b**) stop s.o from causing public disorder(1,2) or breaking the law. **make one's peace** (**with s.o**) (**a**) end a quarrel (with s.o). (**b**) agree to end a fight or war. **peace of mind** state or condition of not being worried: *I need peace of mind in order to work*. **rest in peace** ⇨ rest[2].

'peacefully *adv*: *sleeping peacefully*.
'peace,maker *c.n* person who encourages others to end a quarrel, war etc.
'peace-,offering *c.n* thing given to s.o as a sign that one wants to end a quarrel etc.
'peace,time *u.n* period(1) of peace(1).

peach /piːtʃ/ *adj* **1** yellow-pink in colour: *peach skin*; *paint the walls pale peach*.
▷ *n* **2** *c.n* (also *attrib*) (kind of tree with a) usu round fruit with pink flesh and yellow-red skin that has small soft hairs: *a peach tree*; *peach jam*. **3** *u.n* yellow-pink colour: *Choose peach for the walls*. **4** *sing.n* (*informal*) person, animal, thing who/ that gives particular pleasure: *You're a peach!*

peacock /'piːˌkɒk/ *c.n* (also *attrib*) (female **peahen** /'piːˌhen/) kind of large male bird with long blue-green tail feathers: *peacock blue*. **as proud as a peacock** very proud.

peak /piːk/ *c.n* (often — *of s.t*) **1** top (of a mountain or hill): *We climbed to the peak of Everest*. **2** pointed top or edge: *a roof peak*. **3** highest point (of s.o's ability or progress in an activity): *She's at the peak of her* career(1), *fitness*. **4** (also *attrib*) period(1) of being most busy: *Work/Traffic was at a peak. Don't travel during peak traffic, peak hours*. ⇨ off-peak. **5** front part (of a cap over the top of the face).
▷ *intr.v* **6** reach the highest point of ability, activity, size etc: *Prices/Temperatures peaked last month. I hope the English team hasn't peaked too early because the competition is still a month away*.
peaked *attrib.adj* having a peak(5): *a peaked cap*.

peal /piːl/ *c.n* **1** act or period(1) of ringing (church) bells.
▷ *v* **2** *intr.v* (often — *out*) (of a bell) ring: *The church bells pealed out, are pealing (out)*. **3** *tr.v* (of a person) ring (bells). **4** *intr.v* (of thunder) make a repeated sound.
peals *pl.n* (often — *of s.t*) set of repeated sounds: *peals of laughter/thunder*.

peanut /'piːˌnʌt/ *c.n* (also *attrib*) kind of nut growing in a thin shell under the ground: *peanut oil*.
,peanut 'butter *u.n* (also *attrib*) soft mixture made of crushed peanuts: *peanut butter sandwiches*.

pear /peə/ *c.n* (also *attrib*) (kind of tree with a) fruit like an apple but with a long top: *a pear tree*. **avocado pear** ⇨ avocado.
'pear-,shaped *adj* having a bottom part that is wider than the top.

pearl /pɜːl/ *adj* **1** shiny white in colour: *pearl paper*.
▷ *c.n* **2** (also *attrib*) small round usu white object (as) found in an oyster(1), valued as a gem(1): *a pearl necklace*; *pearl white*. **3** (usu *pl*) (*fig*) small detail, object etc that is highly valued: *pearls of good advice/wisdom*.

peasant /'peznt/ *c.n* (also *attrib*) **1** person living a simple life on farms, esp in poor countries: *peasant farmers*. **2** (*derog*) person who behaves in an unpleasant way: *peasant behaviour*.
'peasantry *def.n* peasants(1) as a social group.

peat /piːt/ *c/u.n* (also *attrib*) (piece of a) dark brown substance made from rotting plants, used as fertilizer or dried and used as fuel: *peat blocks*.
'peaty *adj* (-*ier*, -*iest*): *peaty soil*.

pebble /'pebl/ *c.n* (also *attrib*) small smooth stone as found in rivers or on a beach: *a pebble beach*.

peck /pek/ *c.n* **1** light tap or bite using a beak: *a quick peck at the bread*. **2** (*esp* — *on s.t*) (*fig*) light touch or kiss with the mouth: *I gave her a peck on the cheek*.
▷ *v* **3** *tr/intr.v* (often — (*away*) *at s.t*) (of a bird) tap or bite (s.t) using a beak: *pecking food*; *pecking* (*away*) *at a piece of bread*. ⇨ woodpecker. **4** *tr.v* (*fig*) (of a person) give (s.o) a light kiss: *She pecked me on the cheek*. **5** *tr/intr.v* (usu — *at s.t*) (*informal*) eat a small amount of (food): *He was pecking at his potatoes*.
'pecking ,order *c.n* **1** natural acceptance(1) by birds etc of an order of importance, power based on strength etc. **2** (*fig*) any similar social order based on importance, strength etc: *Where do you come in the pecking order among your friends?*
'peckish *pred.adj* a little hungry: *feel peckish*.

pectin /'pektɪn/ *u.n* chemical substance found in some fruit that makes jam become solid.

pectoral /'pektərəl/ *adj* (*technical*) of or referring to the breast or chest: *pectoral muscles*(1).

peculiar /pɪ'kjuːlɪə/ *adj* **1** unusual; strange: *a peculiar way of walking*; *a peculiar taste, suggestion*. **2** (often — *to s.o/s.t*) belonging to one person, thing, area, group etc: *It's their peculiar concern. This animal is peculiar to Australia*. **3** (*formal*) special: *A peculiar group of children need extra help when learning to read and write*.
peculiarity /pɪˌkjuːlɪ'ærɪtɪ/ *c/u.n* (*pl* -*ies*) (often — *of s.t*) (example of) being unusual or strange: *Notice the peculiarity of this* design.
pe'culiarly *adv* **1** unusually; strangely: *acting peculiarly*. **2** more than usually: *peculiarly difficult/interesting*.

pecuniary /pɪ'kjuːnɪərɪ/ *adj* (*formal*) of or referring to money: *pecuniary problems*.

pedagogic /ˌpedə'gɒdʒɪk/ *adj* (also **peda-'gogical**) (*formal*) of or referring to the science of learning and teaching.

pedal /'pedl/ *c.n* **1** part of a machine worked by pushing with the foot: *a bicycle pedal*; *the* accelerator(1)/*brake pedal of a car*.
▷ *tr/intr.v* (-*ll*-, US -*l*-) **2** move (a bicycle etc) by pushing the pedals(1): *She was pedalling along the street. I couldn't pedal* (*my bicycle*) *up the hill*.

pedant /'pednt/ *c.n* (*derog*) person who gives too much importance to her/his personal knowledge, esp to unnecessary detail or facts.

pedantic /pɪ'dæntɪk/ adj of, referring to, like, a pedant: a pedantic person/speech.
pe'dantically adv.
peddle /'pedl/ tr/intr.v go from one house etc to another trying to sell (things): She was peddling her garden plants at different markets in the area.
pedlar /'pedlə/ c.n person who tries to sell a variety of small things, esp by going from one house to another.
pedestal /'pedɪstl/ c.n bottom part of a column or statue.
pedestrian /pɪ'destrɪən/ adj 1 (usu attrib) of or for people walking and not travelling in vehicles: a pedestrian crossing. 2 (derog) too ordinary and dull: a pedestrian way of speaking; be pedestrian in one's thinking.
▷ c.n 3 person walking and not travelling in a vehicle: This road is for pedestrians only.
pedigree /'pedɪˌgriː/ n 1 c.n (also attrib) line or list of high quality ancestors etc of an animal or sometimes a person: This dog comes from a long pedigree (of champions(3)). These are pedigree cats. 2 u.n (formal) state of having (high quality) ancestors: horses of great pedigree. It's of unknown pedigree.
pedlar ⇒ peddle.
pee /piː/ c.n 1 (slang) act of peeing (⇒ pee(2)): go for a pee; have a pee. ⇒ piddle(1).
▷ intr.v (slang) 2 pass water from the body; urinate. ⇒ piddle(2).
peek /piːk/ c.n 1 (informal) quick look: have/take a peek at a cake cooking in the oven.
▷ intr.v 2 have a quick look: peek through the window, into a room, round the door, over a wall.
peel /piːl/ u.n 1 (thick) skin of some fruit and vegetables: apple/banana/orange peel; potato peel.
▷ v 2 tr.v take peel(1) off (fruit or vegetables): peeling an orange/potato. 3 tr/intr.v (often — s.t off) (cause (s.t) to) come off in thin pieces or layers(1): The hot sun made her skin peel (off). He peeled off his shirt. The paint on the door is peeling off. **keep one's eyes peeled** (informal) keep a careful watch for s.o/s.t.
'peeler c.n small device for peeling(2).
'peelings pl.n pieces of peel(1): potato peelings.
peep¹ /piːp/ c.n 1 (often have/take a — at s.o/s.t) quick (usu secret) look (at s.o/s.t): I took a peep at the birthday presents hidden in the cupboard.
▷ intr.v 2 (often — at s.o/s.t) have a peep(1) (at s.o/s.t): peeping through the trees at the girls swimming in the river.
peep² /piːp/ c.n (usu sing) 1 (often — of s.t) short high sound (made by s.t): the peep of a whistle. Be quiet, children — I don't want to hear another peep out of you!
▷ tr/intr.v 2 (cause (s.t) to) make a peep²(1): She peeped (the car horn(3)) as she drove into the garden.
peer¹ /pɪə/ c.n 1 (also ˌpeer of the 'realm) person who has a title such as Baron(1), Viscount, Earl, Marquess, Duke etc; person who is a member of the House of Lords. 2 (also attrib) person of about the same age: Children need to be liked by their peers. He is no different from other boys in his peer group. **life peer** ⇒ life.
peerage /'pɪərɪdʒ/ n 1 c.n peer(1)'s title or rank. 2 u/def.n peers(1) as a group: the British peerage. **life peerage** ⇒ life.

peer² /pɪə/ intr.v look (as if) with difficulty: peering into dirty water; peering at a notice in the distance.
peeved /piːvd/ pred.adj (informal) a little angry: She felt peeved because no one told her the news.
peg /peg/ c.n 1 piece of wood, metal, plastic(3) etc used to fasten s.t to s.t, to show the position of s.t, to hang things on etc: The cloth was held down with pegs. Tent pegs are used to hold a tent in position. Clothes pegs are used to fasten clothes etc to a line. Put your hat on that peg. **off the peg** (informal) (of clothes) bought in a shop when already made and not specially made for a particular person). **take s.o down a peg or two** (informal) make s.o lose her/his idea of being more able, more important etc.
▷ tr.v (-gg-) 2 (often — s.t out) fasten or mark (s.t) using pegs(1): peg washing (out) on the line; peg (out) the place where the path will be made; peg down the tent. 3 (informal) decide and keep (prices, costs, wages etc) at a particular level: The price of petrol has been pegged by the government. ⇒ level pegging. **peg out** (slang) (a) die: The old man should peg out soon. (b) sleep or be able to do nothing because of being very tired.
pejorative /pɪ'dʒɒrətɪv/ adj/c.n (of a) word etc expressing disapproval, dislike, lack of respect etc: 'Old maid' is a pejorative description of an unmarried woman.
pe'joratively adv.
pelican /'pelɪkən/ c.n kind of big bird with a large orange beak that has a soft bag underneath it for keeping fish in.
ˌpelican 'crossing c.n (UK) place where people can cross a road by pressing a button to change the traffic lights.
pellet /'pelɪt/ c.n 1 small round object. 2 small metal ball (to be) fired from a gun: gun pellets.
pelmet /'pelmɪt/ c.n long piece of wood etc in front of the top of curtains.
pelt¹ /pelt/ c.n skin taken from an animal that has fur or wool.
pelt² /pelt/ unique n 1 at full pelt as fast as possible: We drove down the motorway at full pelt.
▷ v 2 tr.v (usu — s.o with s.t) throw s.t at (s.o/s.t): They pelted the speaker with tomatoes. 3 intr.v (often — down (with s.t)) fall in large amounts for a long time: It was pelting (down) with rain.
pelvis /'pelvɪs/ c.n (technical) group of bones between the waist and the top of the legs.
'pelvic attrib.adj of the pelvis: pelvic muscles(1).
pen¹ /pen/ c.n 1 instrument used to write in ink: My pen needs filling. **put/set pen to paper** (informal) begin to write: Think carefully before you put pen to paper. **ball point pen** ⇒ ball¹. **felt-tip pen** ⇒ felt². **fountain pen** ⇒ fountain.
▷ tr.v (-nn-) 2 (formal) write (s.t): He penned a reply to her.
'penˌfriend c.n person (living in another country) to whom one writes letters as a friend and often never meets.
'penˌknife c.n (pl -ˌknives) small knife with one or more blades that fold into the handle.
'penˌname c.n name used by a writer that is not her/his real name: 'John le Carré' is the pen-name of John David Cornwell.
'penˌpal c.n (informal) = penfriend.

'pen-,pusher *c.n* (usu *derog*; *informal*) person who has to write most of the time when at work.

pen² /pen/ *c.n* **1** fenced area for farm animals: *a sheep pen*. **2** = play-pen.
▷ *tr.v* (*-nn-*) **3** keep, put, (farm animals) in a pen(1).

penal /'pi:nl/ *adj* (usu *attrib*) (*law*) of or referring to places, rules, types etc of punishment: *penal institutions*(1)/*laws*/*practices*.
'penal ,code *def.n* (*law*) laws of a country about crime and punishment.
penalize, -ise /'pi:nə,laɪz/ *tr.v* punish (s.o) because he/she has not obeyed the rules or the law: *I was penalized for arriving ten minutes late for the examination. The football player was penalized for dangerous play*.
penalty /'penltɪ/ *c.n* (also *attrib*) **1** punishment for doing wrong: *The penalty for armed robbery can be* imprisonment *for life. Are you in favour of the death penalty?* **2** advantage, e.g a free kick, given to the other player or team because a rule has not been obeyed: *The other team was given a penalty because their player had been knocked down*. **pay the penalty (for s.t)** be punished (for doing wrong): *If you are caught stealing you will have to pay the penalty*. **on penalty of s.t** (*formal*) with s.t as the punishment: *People must not enter on penalty of six months' imprisonment*.
'penalty ,area *c.n* marked area in front of a goal where a free kick at the goal can be awarded as a penalty(2).
'penalty ,kick/*,shot* *c.n* free kick at goal as a penalty(2), with only the goalkeeper to beat.
penance /'penəns/ *c/u.n* (*formal*) punishment given to s.o because he/she has done wrong, behaved badly etc: *I'm washing my dad's car as a penance for being rude to him*.
pence ⇒ penny.
pencil /'pensl/ *c.n* **1** (also *attrib*) long instrument containing a stick of lead¹(3), coloured wax etc, used for writing and drawing: *a pencil drawing*. **in pencil** using a pencil: *write in pencil*.
▷ *tr.v* (*-ll-*, US *-l-*) **2** (often *— s.t in*) write, draw etc (s.t) using a pencil: *Pencil in your answers*.
pendant /'pendənt/ *c.n* (also *attrib*) object etc (designed(6) to be) hung on a chain: *a gold pendant*; *a pendant watch*.
pending /'pendɪŋ/ *pred.adj* **1** not yet decided: *The result of the competition is still pending*. **2** coming (soon): *The scientists warned that the* earthquake *had been pending for a long time*.
▷ *prep* (*formal*) **3** until: *She waited in a hotel near the station pending his return. There will be no statement pending a decision by the committee*.
pendulous /'pendjʊləs/ *adj* (*formal*) hanging down: *pendulous fruit on the trees*.
pendulum /'pendjʊləm/ *c.n* (also *attrib*) heavy object or piece hanging down and moving from side to side to make a machine work: *a pendulum clock*.
penetrate /'penɪ,treɪt/ *v* **1** *tr/intr.v* force, make, a way into or through (s.o/s.t): *The sun couldn't penetrate the dark clouds. A piece of glass has penetrated the left eye. Luckily the knife didn't actually penetrate*. **2** *intr.v* be understood: *She suddenly smiled as the importance of the news penetrated*.
'pene,trating *adj*: *a penetrating look*/*voice*; *a penetrating mind*. ⇒ impenetrable.

penetration /,penɪ'treɪʃən/ *u.n*.
penguin /'peŋgwɪn/ *c.n* kind of black and white seabird that cannot fly and is found mostly in very cold areas.
penicillin /,penɪ'sɪlɪn/ *u.n* (also *attrib*) kind of powerful medicine that kills many kinds of bacteria: *a penicillin injection*.
peninsula /pə'nɪnsjʊlə/ *c.n* long piece of land almost surrounded by (usu sea) water: *Italy is a peninsula*.
pe'ninsular *adj* of or like a peninsula.
penis /'pi:nɪs/ *c/def.n* male organ used for passing water and sexual intercourse.
penitent /'penɪtənt/ *adj* (*formal*) very sorry about having behaved badly or done wrong: *feel penitent*; *a penitent criminal*. Opposite impenitent.
'penitence *u.n*.
'penitently *adv*.
pennant /'penənt/ *c.n* flag shaped like a long triangle(1), as used on boats.
penny /'penɪ/ (in combinations, e.g 'tenpenny', *-pənɪ*/) *c.n* (*pl -ies* for coins, *pence* /pens/ for cost, amount etc) (*abbr* (*informal*) *p* /pi:/) (coin with the) value of 100th of £1: *100 pennies weigh a lot. It cost me 80p* (or *80 pence*). *They are 10p each. I need a 50 pence* (or *a 50p coin*) *for the parking meter. I'd like a tenpenny ice-cream. This is a fivepenny piece* (or *a 5p piece*). ⇒ halfpenny.
a bad penny ⇒ bad(*adj*). **a pretty penny** (*informal*) a lot of money: *It cost a pretty penny*. **spend a penny** (*informal*) go to the lavatory: *I must spend a penny before I go*. **ten a penny** ⇒ ten. **two a penny** ⇒ two.
'penniless *adj* with (almost) no money: *I'm penniless until Friday*.
'penny-,pincher *c.n* (*derog*) person who is too careful about saving money; miser.
'penny-,pinching *adj* (*derog*) too careful about saving money; miserly.
'penny-,wise *adj* (usu *— and pound-foolish*) careful about saving small amounts of money (but not careful about bigger expenses).
pension /'penʃən/ *c.n* **1** (also *attrib*) amount of money given to s.o each week, month etc because he/she has retired, was wounded during a war etc: *My mother gets a widow's pension. I belong to a private pension* scheme(2).
▷ *tr.v* **2** (usu *— s.o off*) (usu passive) let, make, (s.o) retire(1) and give her/him a pension: *I was pensioned off at 50 years of age*.
'pensionable *adj* old enough to be pensioned(2): *pensionable age*.
'pensioner *c.n* person receiving a pension(1). esp s.o who has retired from work.
pensive /'pensɪv/ *adj* (*formal*) thinking seriously and for a long time: *He had a pensive look*.
'pensively *adv*. **'pensiveness** *u.n*.
pentagon /'pentəgən/ *c.n* flat figure with five sides.
pentathlon /pen'tæθlən/ *def/c.n* athletic(1) competition which consists of five different events, running, swimming, riding, shooting and fencing. Compare decathlon.
penthouse /'pent,haʊs/ *c.n* (*pl -s* /-,haʊzɪz/) (also *attrib*) expensive flat built on the top of a (tall) building: *a penthouse flat*.
pent-up /,pent 'ʌp/ *adj* very strong, excited etc

but not expressed: *pent-up anger*; *feeling pent-up before the race*.

penultimate /pe'nʌltɪmɪt/ *adj* next to the last: *the penultimate day of our holiday.* ⇒ ultimate(1).

penury /'penjʊrɪ/ *u.n* (*formal*) great poverty: *The failure of the business reduced them to a life of penury.*

people /'piːpl/ *n* **1** *pl.n* men, women and children in general: *People think you don't care. The city was filled with people from all over the world.* **2** *def.pl.n* ordinary men and women (not peers(1)) belonging to a country or society: *The people will never accept such high prices. We demand government by the people. It is the people's wish.* **3** *pl.n* two or more persons: *How many people went to the party? There were six people on the bus.* ⇒ person(1). **4** *pl.n* particular group of persons: *deaf/poor/rich people.* **5** *pl.n* relatives: *My people come from northern England.* **6** *c.n* nation; race²(3): *the peoples of Asia.*

▷ *tr.v* **7** (often — *s.w with s.o*) (*formal*) provide (a place) with people: *Northern America was peopled with Europeans during the last century.*

pep /pep/ *u.n* (*informal*) **1** mental(1) or physical(1) energy(1).

▷ *tr.v* (*-pp-*) (*informal*) **2** *pep s.o up* give mental(1) or physical(1) energy or courage to s.o: *This medicine, That good news, should pep her up.*

'pep ,talk *c.n* (*informal*) talk by s.o in order to encourage a person or group to act with energy(1) and determination.

pepper /'pepə/ *n* **1** *u.n* (also *attrib*) powder from the fruit of a kind of climbing plant which tastes hot and is used to flavour food: *white/black pepper*; *pepper steak(2)*; *a pepper pot.* **2** *u.n* (also ,**red 'pepper**, ,**cayenne** ('**pepper**)) red powder from the seeds of certain plants which tastes very hot and is used to flavour food. **3** *c.n* (also ,**sweet 'pepper**, '**capsicum**) kind of large hollow, usu green or red, fruit growing on a small bush and eaten as a vegetable: *onions and green peppers.*

▷ *tr.v* **4** flavour (food) with pepper. **pepper s.o with s.t** fire, throw etc many small objects at s.o: *He was peppered with small metal balls.* **pepper s.t with s.t** (*fig*) add many small amounts of a certain style, character etc to a speech or piece of writing: *an essay peppered with spelling mistakes*; *a speech peppered with praise for his efforts.*

'pepper,corn *c.n* small round berry used to make pepper(1) from.

'pepper,mill *c.n* device held in the hand and turned to crush peppercorns.

'pepper,mint *n* **1** *c/u.n* (kind of plant with a) hot, minty' flavour, used in ice-cream, sweets etc. **2** *c.n* sweet that tastes of peppermint.

'peppery *adj* (*-ier*, *-iest*) **1** tasting strongly of pepper(1): *peppery soup.* **2** (*fig*) quickly made angry or annoyed: *a peppery character, old man.*

per (strong form /pɜː/, weak form /pə/) *det/prep* for each or every: *20p per mile*; *£30 per person*; *three weeks' holiday per year.* **as per** as stated or shown by: *as per your instructions.*

per annum /pər 'ænəm/ *adv* for each year: *costing £1000 per annum.*

per capita /pə 'kæpɪtə/ *adj/adv* for each person: *needing £100 per capita*; *a per capita income of £100 a week.*

per cent /pə 'sent/ *adv* for each hundred, *symb* %: *You need at least 51 per cent* (or *51%*) *of the votes to win. We are 100 per cent* (i.e completely) *against the plan, behind you.*

c.n (also **per'cent**) amount, number etc that is a part of each hundred: *What per cent are you offering as a reduction on the price for regular customers?* ⇒ percentage.

percentage /pə'sentɪdʒ/ *c.n* **1** amount, number etc that is a part of a hundred: *What percentage did you get in the mathematics examination?* **2** (often — *of s.t*) amount of s.t as a part of a hundred: *What percentage of cats in England are orange? A small percentage* (i.e much less than 50%) *could not swim.* ⇒ percent.

perambulator /pə'ræmbjʊ,leɪtə/ *c.n* (*formal*) = pram.

perceive /pə'siːv/ *tr.v* (*formal*) (usu — *that s.t*) become aware of, realize, s.t: *She perceived that there would be many difficulties.* ⇒ perception.

per'ceivable *adj*.

per'ceptible *adj* (*formal*) that can be seen or noticed: *a perceptible difference between the two colours.* Opposite imperceptible.

per'ceptibly *adv*.

perception /pə'sepʃən/ *c/u.n* (*formal*) (often — *of s.t*) (example of an) act, ability or effect, of seeing, noticing, understanding etc (s.t): *What is your perception of the economic(2) needs of Africa? She is an architect(1) with great visual(2) perception.*

per'ceptive *adj* showing ability to see, notice or understand: *a perceptive mind*; *realizing her true intention was very perceptive of him.*

per'ceptively *adv*. **perceptiveness** *u.n*.

percent(age) ⇒ per.

perch /pɜːtʃ/ *c.n* **1** branch, pole etc used by a bird to rest on. **2** (*fig*) high position: *The boy found a perch on the wall where he could watch the football game.*

▷ *v* (usu — (*s.t*) *on s.t*) **3** *intr.v* (of a bird) rest on a perch(1): *The little bird perched on the telephone wire.* **4** *tr.v/intr.v* (cause (s.t) to) rest on s.t: *He perched the hat on the side of his head. He perched himself on the roof.*

'perched *adj* in a position on a perch: *Many birds were perched* (*on a branch*) *in the apple tree. The builder was perched on the roof.*

percolate /'pɜː kə,leɪt/ *intr.v* (usu — *through* (*s.t*)) **1** (of liquid) pass through (a material): *The water has percolated through the tablecloth.* **2** (*fig*) (of information etc) pass between individuals and groups: *The news of the fire took a long time to percolate through* (*to the villagers*). **percolate coffee** make coffee by pouring boiling water through powdered coffee.

'perco,lator *c.n* (also '**coffee ,perco,lator**) kind of pot used to percolate coffee.

percussion /pə'kʌʃən/ *u/def.n* (also *attrib*) (musical instruments producing) (sounds made by) hitting s.t with s.t or striking two parts together: *Drums are percussion instruments. The percussion is responsible for rhythm(1) in an orchestra.*

per'cussionist *c.n* person playing a percussion instrument.

peremptory /pə'remptərɪ/ *adj* (*derog*; *formal*) having a manner showing belief in one's superior(1) importance, e.g that one must be

obeyed: *The chairman's peremptory style of talking made him very* unpopular.
pe'remptorily *adv.*

perennial /pə'renɪəl/ *adj* **1** (of a plant) lasting more than two years: *A garden is easy to keep if it is planted with perennial flowers.* Compare annual (3). **2** (*fig*) lasting a very long time: *It seems to be a perennial problem.*
▷ *c.n* **3** plant that is perennial(1).
pe'rennially *adv.*

perfect /'pɜːfɪkt/ *adj* **1** not having any mistakes, faults etc: *a perfect* essay(1)/*answer*/*student*; *perfect weather for a walk.* **2** accurate: *a perfect circle*/*square*; *a perfect* reproduction(2) *of an old map.* Opposite imperfect(1). **3** (*informal*) complete: *a perfect stranger.* **4** (*grammar*) of or referring to the perfect tense. **perfect for s.o**/**s.t** completely suitable, right etc for s.o/s.t: *This weather is perfect for swimming.* **a perfect match** ⇒ match¹ (*n*). **future perfect tense** ⇒ future. **past perfect tense** ⇒ past. **present perfect (tense)** ⇒ perfect tense.
▷ *def.n* **5** (*grammar*) perfect tense: *In 'She has gone' the verb is in the perfect.* **practice makes perfect** ⇒ practice.
▷ *tr.v* /pə'fekt/ **6** (*formal*) make (s.t) free from all faults etc: *perfecting one's English.*

perfect 'tense *def.n* (also **present 'perfect**) (*grammar*) verb form used to show action that finished before the present time, e.g 'We *have* seen it', 'They *have* arrived'.

perfection /pə'fekʃən/ *u.n* **1** quality or state of being perfect(1): *Is it possible to find complete perfection in one's wife or husband?* ⇒ imperfection. **2** (often — *of s.t*) (*formal*) act of making s.t perfect(1): *They are working on the perfection of their sales plans.* **to perfection** (esp of food) so that it is perfect(1): *The vegetables have been cooked to perfection.*

per'fectionist *c.n* person who works to, asks for, the highest possible standards.

'perfectly *adv* **1** extremely well; without mistakes: *He speaks English perfectly.* Opposite imperfectly. **2** completely: *perfectly obvious*/*happy*/*miserable.*

perfidious /pə'fɪdɪəs/ *adj* (*derog*; *formal*) not at all honest or faithful: *a perfidious husband.*

perforate /'pɜːfəˌreɪt/ *tr.v* (usu passive) (*formal*) make a hole or many holes in (s.t): *The ticket has been perforated so that it can easily be torn in half.*

perforation /ˌpɜːfə'reɪʃən/ *n* **1** *c.n* small hole or line of holes, e.g separating stamps. **2** *u.n* act or fact of perforating or being perforated.

perform /pə'fɔːm/ *v* **1** *tr.v* (*formal*) do (s.t, e.g one's work, duty or s.t one has promised): *perform one's duties.* **2** *tr*/*intr.v* be an actor in (a play or film): *perform on television*; *perform 'Macbeth' in the theatre.* **3** *tr*/*intr.v* (often — (*s.t*) *on s.t*) play (a piece of music) (on a musical instrument): *perform on the piano*/ guitar. **4** *intr.v* (*informal*) behave in a bad-tempered way: *He often performs if he can't get what he wants.*

performance /pə'fɔːməns/ *n* (often — *of s.t*) **1** *u.n* (*formal*) act of performing(1) (s.t): *The accident happened during the performance of his duties.* **2** *c.n* acting of a play, film etc; act of playing music: *We have tickets for tomorrow's performance. It happened during a performance*

of 'Carmen'. **3** *c*/*u.n* way s.o/s.t does s.t: *What do you think of her performance as 'Mother Courage'? The engine's performance is not very good.* **4** *c.n* example of behaving in a bad-tempered way: *His performance when she refused was very surprising.* **gala performance** ⇒ gala.

per'former *c.n* person who performs, esp in a play, film etc.

per'forming ˌarts *def.pl.n* artistic activities such as acting, dancing, playing music etc. Compare visual arts.

perfume /'pɜːfjuːm/ *c*/*u.n* **1** (often — *of s.t*) (*formal*) pleasant smell (of s.t): *the perfume of fresh coffee.* **2** (example of a) liquid made by mixing pleasant-smelling oils and other substances in alcohol, used on the body: *French perfumes.* ⇒ scent(2).
▷ *tr.v* **3** give a perfume(2) to (s.t): *perfuming the skin with soap.*

perfunctory /pə'fʌŋktərɪ/ *adj* (*derog*; *formal*) done without any serious interest or care: *a perfunctory attempt to repair the damaged roof.*
per'functorily *adv.*

perhaps /pə'hæps/ *adv* possibly: *Perhaps I can help you. She is, perhaps, much happier than you realize. 'Will you be there?' 'Perhaps.'*

peril /'perɪl/ *c*/*u.n* (often *in* — (*of s.t*)) (example of) extreme danger (of s.t): *The climbers were in great peril* (or *in peril of losing their lives*). *We met many different perils during our journey through the forests.* ⇒ imperil.

'perilous *adj* (*formal*) extremely dangerous: *a perilous voyage.*

'perilously *adv.* **'perilousness** *u.n.*

perimeter /pə'rɪmɪtə/ *c.n* (often — *of s.t*) (length of the) outside edge (of a shape or area): *They are building a wall round the perimeter of the airport.*

period /'pɪərɪəd/ *c.n* **1** (often — *of s.t*) amount of time (of s.t): *for long*/*short periods*; *periods of warm weather*; *cold periods*; *during a period of several months*; *lived for a period in Italy*; *suffered periods of bad health.* **2** (also *attrib*) (often — *of s.t*) particular stage in the progress of life on earth, of a person's work, of a society's development etc: *the period of Queen Victoria* (or *the Victorian period*); *the prehistoric period*; *Picasso's blue period*; *wearing* costumes *belonging to that period* (or *wearing period* costume); *period furniture.* **3** amount of time of a lesson at school: *Come and see me during my free period this afternoon. How many periods do you teach each week?* **4** monthly flow of blood etc from the uterus. **5** (US) full stop.

periodic /ˌpɪərɪ'ɒdɪk/ *adj* happening at regular intervals(1) or occasionally: *I would like to have periodic accounts of your progress. She suffers from periodic backache.*

periodical /ˌpɪərɪ'ɒdɪkl/ *c.n* magazine produced regularly each month, 3 months etc.

ˌperi'odically *adv*: *I phone him periodically.*

ˌperi'odic ˌtable *c.n* (*technical*) arrangement of all the chemical elements(1) in order of their atomic number (i.e the number of protons in each).

peripatetic /ˌperɪpə'tetɪk/ *adj* (*formal*) travelling from one place to another: *Our peripatetic teachers visit many different schools.*

periphery /pə'rɪfərɪ/ *c.n* (*pl* -*ies*) (usu *the* — (of *s.t*)) (*formal*) outer edge of an area, subject of study etc: *We've planted trees along the periphery of the farm. Your book deals only with the peripheries of the problem.*

peripheral /pəˈrɪfərəl/ *adj* (*formal*) **1** of, referring to, forming, the periphery: *a peripheral fence.* **2** of or referring to areas of interest, study etc that are much less important: *Your book is of peripheral interest to me.*

periscope /ˈperɪˌskəʊp/ *c.n* device that allows things above one's head to be seen, esp the surface of the sea from a submarine(2).

perish /ˈperɪʃ/ *intr.v* **1** die, esp in a violent way or in an accident: *Many families perished in the storm/war.* **2** (of a substance such as rubber) break, rot etc and lose its ability to stretch, become hard etc often because of age: *These tyres have perished.* **3** (esp — *with s.t*) become badly affected (by *s.t* unpleasant): *He was perishing* (*with cold*).

'perishable *adj* likely to rot quickly: *perishable food; perishable elastic.*

'perished *adj* (usu *pred*) (*informal*) extremely cold: *I'm perished.*

'perishing *adj/adv* (*informal*) extremely cold: *It's perishing outside.*

perjure /ˈpɜːdʒə/ *reflex.v* (*law*) not tell the truth in a court of law after swearing to do so.

'perjurer *c.n* person who perjures herself/himself.

perjury /ˈpɜːdʒərɪ/ *c/u.n* (*pl -ies*) (example of the) act of perjuring: *commit perjury.*

perk¹ /pɜːk/ *tr/intr.v* **perk** (**oneself/s.o**) **up** (cause *s.o* to) become (more) active, energetic etc: *I need a coffee to perk me up.* **perk s.t up** lift up the head/ears to show (more) interest, energy etc: *The dog perked up its ears at the noise.*

'perkily *adv* in a perky way. **'perkiness** *u.n* fact or state of being perky.

'perky *adj* (*-ier, -iest*) (*informal*) full of, showing, energy, interest etc: *She's looking perky today.*

perk² /pɜːk/ *c.n* (*formal perquisite*) extra money, a car, meals etc given to a person as an addition to her/his salary: *The job has attractive perks such as a car and free petrol.*

perm /pɜːm/ *c.n* **1** permanent (wave); treatment of the hair to make it curly: *Oh, you've had a perm — it looks very nice.*

▷ *tr.v* **2** give (*s.o's* hair) a perm(1): *have one's hair permed.*

permanent /ˈpɜːmənənt/ *adj* **1** expected to exist for a long time: *Please write your permanent address here. This new arrangement is now permanent. I was a temporary*(1) *member of staff but now I've got a permanent post.*

▷ *c.n* **2** = permanent wave.

'permanently *adv.*

'permanence *u.n.*

ˌpermanent 'wave *c.n* (*formal*) = perm(1).

permeate /ˈpɜːmɪˌeɪt/ *tr/intr.v* (*formal*) **1** enter, spread, into (*s.t*): *Luckily the oil didn't permeate the carpet.* **2** (*fig*) enter (people's minds, thoughts): *The news quickly permeated* (*through*) *the whole college.*

permeable /ˈpɜːmɪəbl/ *adj* able to be permeated(1). Opposite impermeable.

permit /ˈpɜːmɪt/ *c.n* **1** (often — *to do s.t*) official written statement allowing a person to do *s.t*, go *s.w* etc: *a visitor's permit; a student's permit to travel cheaply.*

▷ *tr.v* /pəˈmɪt/ (*-tt-*) **2** (usu — *s.o to do s.t*) (*formal*) allow (*s.o* to do *s.t*); let (*s.o* do *s.t*): *Smoking is not permitted. Would you permit me to offer some advice?*

permissible /pəˈmɪsɪbl/ *adj* (*formal*) (able to be) allowed: *Using a dictionary in the examination is not permissible.* Opposite impermissible.

permission /pəˈmɪʃən/ *u.n* (often — *to do s.t*) written or spoken statement allowing a person to do *s.t*, go *s.w* etc: *You have my permission to leave early. Have you asked anyone's permission to do that?*

permissive /pəˈmɪsɪv/ *adj* allowing (too) much sexual, moral etc freedom: *Is the lack of discipline in our schools a result of parents being too permissive?*

per'missively *adv.* **per'missiveness** *u.n.*

permutation /ˌpɜːmjʊˈteɪʃən/ *c.n* (*technical*) (change in the) arrangement, esp of individual numbers or members of a set: *Do you know the permutation of this bicycle lock?*

pernicious /pəˈnɪʃəs/ *adj* (*formal*) causing much harm: *a pernicious lie.*

per'niciously *adv.* **per'niciousness** *u.n.*

peroxide /pəˈrɒksaɪd/ *u.n* (also **'hydrogen per'oxide**) chemical substance used as a bleach(1), *chem.form* H_2O_2.

perpendicular /ˌpɜːpənˈdɪkjʊlə/ *adj* **1** (often — *to s.t*) in a position that is pointing, standing etc straight up: *a perpendicular line. The wall must be perpendicular to the floor.* Compare vertical(1).

▷ *c.n* **2** perpendicular line, e.g one from the bottom to the top of a triangle(1).

ˌperpen'dicularly *adv.*

perpetual /pəˈpetjʊəl/ *adj* (*formal*) lasting always; happening often and for a very long time: *The laughter in their house seems to be perpetual. I have had a perpetual desire to drive a racing car.*

per'petually *adv* lasting for a very long time: *perpetually tired.*

perpetuate /pəˈpetjʊˌeɪt/ *tr.v* (*formal*) cause (*s.t*) to continue or be remembered for a long time.

perpetuation /pəˌpetjʊˈeɪʃən/ *u.n* (*formal*) act or state of perpetuating (⇒ perpetuate) (*s.t*).

perpetuity /ˌpɜːpɪˈtjuːɪtɪ/ *u.n* **in perpetuity** (*law*) for always: *The money is yours in perpetuity.*

perplex /pəˈpleks/ *tr.v* (*formal*) make (*s.o*) confused or puzzled: *Her smile as she walked away perplexed me.*

per'plexed *adj* confused; puzzled: *He had a perplexed expression.*

per'plexing *adj* causing confusion: *a perplexing smile.*

per'plexity *n* (*pl -ies*) **1** *u.n* state or fact of being perplexed. **2** *c.n* thing that perplexes *s.o.*

perquisite /ˈpɜːkwɪzɪt/ *c.n* (*formal*) = perk².

persecute /ˈpɜːsɪˌkjuːt/ *tr.v* (often — *s.o for s.t*) treat (*s.o*) badly (because one disapproves of her/his beliefs or opinions): *It is wrong to persecute people for their religion or politics.*

persecution /ˌpɜːsɪˈkjuːʃən/ *c/u.n* (example of the) act of persecuting (⇒ persecute).

'perse,cutor *c.n* person who persecutes *s.o.*

persevere /ˌpɜːsɪˈvɪə/ *intr.v* (usu — *at/in/with s.o/s.t*) continue to make an effort to do *s.t* difficult: *persevering at/in/with his attempt to learn Japanese.*

,perse'verance *u.n.*

persist /pə'sɪst/ *intr.v* **1** continue to try (to do s.t difficult): *He couldn't find a job for a long time but he persisted and now he's a* shop assistant. **2** (often — *in/with* s.t) refuse to stop doing/believing s.t: *If you persist in believing that you can win, you probably will.* **3** (usu of s.t unpleasant) continue to exist: *The rain persisted so the tennis match was cancelled* (1).

persistence /pə'sɪstəns/ *u.n.*

per'sistent *adj*: *a persistent refusal*; *a persistent lawyer.*

per'sistently *adv.*

person /'pɜːsn/ *n* **1** *c.n* (*pl* persons, people) man, woman or child: *Only one person got the answer right. Which person asked for a pencil? The bus will take one more person. How many persons can this lift carry?* ⇒ people. **2** *c/u.n* (*pl* persons) (*grammar*) one of three forms of pronouns and verbs according to who they refer to. **in person** being actually present: *You must come in person to sign the* certificate(1). **on s.o's person** (*formal*) carried in s.o's pocket, on s.o's body etc: *He didn't have the money on his person but the police still believe he took it.* **first/second/third person** ⇒ first, second, third.

'personable *adj* attractive and pleasant: *a personable hotel* receptionist.

'personal /'pɜːsənl/ *adj* **1** of the speaker or person referred to; private: *This is my personal opinion. My diary is personal. He's leaving the job for personal reasons and not because of the company he works for.* **2** (*attrib*) referring to a person's body: *taking care about one's personal health/appearance.* **3** (*attrib*) for, belonging to, a particular person: *This key is for your personal use.* **4** (*attrib*) being actually present: *You will have to make a personal appearance to prove you are well.* **5** (*derog*) referring to a particular person in an insulting way: *making personal remarks about his big feet. It is rude to be so personal.* ⇒ impersonal(1).

,personal as'sistant *c.n* (*abbr* PA) person who helps a senior official, e.g by organizing her/his diary.

'personal ,column *c.n* part of a newspaper or magazine where there are requests or advertisements by individuals(3) or small groups, e.g for homes, friends, holidays.

,personal com'puter *c.n* (*abbr* PC) small computer used at home.

personality /,pɜːsə'næliti/ *n* (*pl* -ies) **1** *c.n* person's individual(2) way of behaving, thinking, responding (⇒ respond(1,3)) emotionally etc: *a strong personality.* **2** *u.n* ability to be confident, energetic and to persuade: *A good salesperson must have lots of personality.* **3** *c.n* well-known person in a particular field: *a sports/television personality*; *personalities in the theatre*, *the* pop world. ⇒ celebrity(2).

personalize, -ise /'pɜːsənə,laɪz/ *tr.v* (*formal*) mark (s.t) to show that it belongs to a particular person: *personalized* stationery(2)/*shirts.*

'personally *adv* **1** oneself; in person: *I'd like to thank her personally. He's promised to deal with it personally. It won't affect me personally.*

2 expressing one's own opinion: *Personally, I'd prefer to watch television tonight.*

,personal 'pronoun *c.n* (*grammar*) pronoun used to show person(2), e.g 'I, we; you; he, she, it, they' and used in the sentence like the noun (phrase) it refers to.

personification /pə,sɒnɪfɪ'keɪʃən/ *c/u.n* (often — of s.t) (example of the) act of representing an object, idea, quality etc as a person: *the personification of the sea or beauty as 'she'.* **the personification of s.t** excellent example of a quality: *We're the personification of happiness.*

personify /pə'sɒnɪ,faɪ/ *tr.v* (-*ies*, -*ied*) **1** talk about (an object, idea, quality etc) as a person: *A car is often personified as 'she'.* **2** be an excellent example of (a quality): *My neighbours are happiness personified.* Compare impersonate.

personnel /,pɜːsə'nel/ *pl.n* (also *attrib*) members of a business company's staff, of the army, navy or airforce etc: *We need more personnel in the factory. Go and see the personnel manager if you are unhappy about your job.*

,person'nel ,officer *c.n* (*abbr* PO) person in a large company, factory etc who attends to the staff and their problems etc.

perspective /pə'spektɪv/ *u.n* **1** way of looking at facts, conditions etc and forming a judgement: *Try to understand the problem from my perspective. Why not consider the offer in the perspective of new opportunities?* **2** *c.n* (*formal*) particular opinion: *What's your perspective on the government's plans?* **3** (also *attrib*) (*technical*) way of representing solid objects in a flat drawing to give the size, shape, distances etc: *This is a perspective drawing of the new building.* **in**, **out of**, **perspective** with(out) the correct perspective(1,3): *The scene has been drawn in, out of, perspective. She gets her difficulties out of perspective by* ignoring many other possibilities.

perspire /pə'spaɪə/ *intr.v* (*formal*) sweat: *After the race he was perspiring heavily.*

perspiration /,pɜːspɪ'reɪʃən/ *u.n* (*formal*) sweat.

persuade /pə'sweɪd/ *tr.v* **1** cause (s.o) (not) to do s.t, agree etc by giving facts, opinion, advice, threats etc: *I persuaded her to come, to reduce the price. Her huge partner persuaded me not to argue!* **2** (often — s.o of s.t, that . . .) (*formal*) cause s.o to believe (s.t): *We couldn't persuade her that eating meat is healthy.* ⇒ dissuade.

persuasion /pə'sweɪʒən/ *n* **1** *u.n* (often — to do s.t) act, power, of persuading (s.o to do s.t): *I didn't need much persuasion to come.* **2** *c.n* (*formal*) (group having a) particular belief: *people with different political persuasions. Which persuasion do you belong to?*

persuasive /pə'sweɪsɪv/ *adj* able to persuade s.o: *a persuasive personality*(1)/*politician.*

per'suasively *adv.* **per'suasiveness** *u.n.*

pert /pɜːt/ *adj* **1** a little rude, often in an amusing way: *a pert child/reply/letter.* **2** (*old use*) lively and attractive: *a pert little dress.*

'pertly *adv.* **'pertness** *u.n.*

pertain /pə'teɪn/ *intr.v* (often — to s.t) (*formal*) be relevant or appropriate (to s.t): *These facts do not really pertain to the argument.*

pertinent /'pɜːtɪnənt/ *adj* (often — to s.t) (*formal*) relevant (to s.t): *Are these facts pertinent to the discussion?* Compare impertinent.

'pertinently *adv*.

pertinacity /ˌpɜːtɪˈnæsɪtɪ/ *u.n* (*formal*) determination(1).

pertinacious /ˌpɜːtɪˈneɪʃəs/ *adj*.

pertinent ⇨ pertain.

perturb /pəˈtɜːb/ *tr.v* (*formal*) cause (a person) to become anxious: *I was perturbed by the bad weather report.* Compare imperturbable.

peruse /pəˈruːz/ *tr.v* (*formal*) read (s.t) carefully: *perusing the newspapers in search of a job.*

perusal /pəˈruːzl/ *u.n*.

pervade /pəˈveɪd/ *tr.v* (*formal*) (of a smell, emotion(1) etc) enter or spread into an area, among a group etc: *A bad smell pervaded the house. Sadness seemed to pervade the whole town.*

pervasion /pəˈveɪʒən/ *u.n*.

pervasive /pəˈveɪsɪv/ *adj* (*formal*) able to enter or spread easily: *a pervasive smell/influence.*

perʹvasively *adv*.

perverse /pəˈvɜːs/ *adj* 1 (esp *be — of s.o* (*to do s.t*)) (of a person) continuing to believe or do s.t one knows is wrong or will annoy others: *It was perverse of her to refuse to agree.* 2 (of behaviour) consciously wrong or annoying others.

perʹversely *adv*. **perʹverseness** *u.n*.

perʹversity *c/u.n* (example of the) act or state of being perverse.

pervert /ˈpɜːvɜːt/ *c.n* 1 (*derog*) person who practises abnormal sexual activities or has too much interest in sexual activities.

▷ *tr.v*/pəˈvɜːt/ 2 cause (s.o) to behave as a pervert(1): *Some people believe that certain films or scenes on television can pervert children, children's minds.* 3 (*formal*) use (s.t) wrongly: *perverting the course of justice.*

perverted /pəˈvɜːtɪd/ *adj* (*derog*) 1 (of a person) behaving as a pervert(1). 2 (of behaviour etc) immoral, esp referring to sexual matters: *a perverted sense of humour.*

perʹverter *c.n* person who perverts(2) (s.o).

perversion /pəˈvɜːʃən/ *c/u.n* 1 (*formal*) (example of) sexually abnormal behaviour. 2 (often *— of s.t*) (example of the) act of perverting(3): *a perversion of justice.*

pessimism /ˈpesɪmɪzəm/ *u.n* belief that bad things will happen, that one will not be successful etc. Opposite optimism.

'pessimist *c.n* person who behaves or thinks according to pessimism: *A person who is certain that he or she will fail is a pessimist.* Opposite optimist. ⇨ realist.

pessimistic /ˌpesɪˈmɪstɪk/ *adj*.

ˌpessiʹmistically *adv*.

pest /pest/ *c.n* 1 insect, creature, animal etc that causes damage to food plants, farm animals, soil etc: *garden/farm pests; pest control.* 2 person, animal etc that annoys, esp by being s.w where he/she/it is not wanted and causing trouble: *Her young son is such a pest when he comes into our house. Your dog's a pest!*

pesticide /ˈpestɪˌsaɪd/ *c/u.n* (kind of) chemical used to kill insects and creatures that are pests(1).

pester /ˈpestə/ *tr.v* (often *— s.o for/with s.t*) annoy (s.o) often, esp by wanting s.o's attention, advice etc: *She's always pestering me with silly questions. Stop pestering me for money.*

pestilence /ˈpestɪləns/ *c/u.n* (*formal; old use*) (example of a) serious disease affecting a community(1).

pestle /ˈpesl/ *c.n* stick used as a tool to crush s.t to powder in a kind of bowl called a mortar[2].

pet /pet/ *attrib.adj* 1 favourite; strongest: *a pet theory/hate.* 2 kept as a pet(4): *a pet dog/rabbit.* 3 for/of pets(4): *pet food/biscuits; a pet shop.*

▷ *c.n* 4 animal kept at home for pleasure: *Cats and dogs are the most common pets.* 5 person who is treated as a favourite: *the teacher's pet.*

▷ *v* (*-tt-*) 6 *tr.v* pat or stroke (an animal) to show affection: *She was petting the dog.* 7 *intr.v* (*informal*) (of two people) kiss and touch to show love or affection.

ˌpet aʹversion *c.n* ⇨ aversion.

ˌpet ʹname *c.n* name used to show love or affection: *My real name is Margaret but 'Silver' is my pet name.*

petal /ˈpetl/ *c.n* one of many white or coloured pieces that make a flower.

petard /pɪˈtɑːd/ *c.n* ⇨ hoist(*v*).

peter /ˈpiːtə/ *intr.v* **peter away/out** gradually become smaller, weaker etc and stop: *The sound of the car slowly petered out. Our food supply is petering away.*

petition /pɪˈtɪʃən/ *c.n* 1 written request, opinion etc signed by a large number of people and (to be) sent to a government, authority(2) etc: *We signed the petition asking for more books for schools.* 2 (*law*) written request to a law court asking for s.t: *a divorce(1) petition.*

▷ *tr.v* 3 (*formal*) (usu *— s.o/s.t for s.t*) prepare and hand over a petition(1,2) (to s.o for s.t): *We are petitioning the government for more money. They have petitioned for a divorce.*

peʹtitioner *c.n* person who petitions.

petrify /ˈpetrɪˌfaɪ/ *tr.v* (*-ies, -ied*) 1 cause (s.o) to become extremely afraid or nervous: *When they asked me to speak at the meeting I was petrified. I'm petrified of failing the examination.* 2 (*technical*) cause (a substance) to become stone.

petrol /ˈpetrəl/ *u.n* (also *attrib*) liquid made from petroleum, used as a fuel(1) for vehicles: *I've run out of petrol. Is this a petrol engine?*

petroleum /pəˈtrəʊlɪəm/ *u.n* kind of oil found in the ground, used to make petrol, paraffin etc.

'petrol ˌpump *c.n* machine which is used to send petrol through a pipe into vehicles.

'petrol ˌstation *c.n* (also **'filling ˌstation**) place with petrol pumps to sell petrol for vehicles.

petticoat /ˈpetɪˌkəʊt/ *c.n* piece of underwear (usu a thin skirt and often with a top attached(1)) worn under a dress etc by a woman.

petty /ˈpetɪ/ *adj* (*-ier, -iest*) 1 small and not important: *petty details/mistakes; costs that are petty compared to others.* 2 having little authority(1): *petty officials.* 3 (*derog*) unpleasant and critical about small details: *make petty remarks about her hair.* 4 (*derog*) unkind and ungenerous: *He was petty about lending his bicycle.*

'pettily *adv*. **'pettiness** *u.n*.

ˌpetty ʹcash *u.n* money for/from small expenses.

petulant /ˈpetjʊlənt/ *adj* (*derog; formal*) behaving in an unpleasant and impatient way because of small or unimportant reasons.

'petulance *u.n*. **'petulantly** *adv*.

pew /pjuː/ *c.n* long seat in a church.

pewter /ˈpjuːtə/ *u.n* (also *attrib*) (things made of

a) grey metal made from lead and tin: *a pewter mug.*

PG /ˌpiː ˈdʒiː/ *c.n abbr* paying guest.

phallic /ˈfælɪk/ *adj* shaped like a penis to represent sexual power or fertility(1): *a phallic* symbol.
phallus /ˈfæləs/ *u.n* image of a penis.

phantom /ˈfæntəm/ *c.n* (also *attrib*) ghost(1): *a phantom shape.*

pharmacy /ˈfɑːməsɪ/ *n* (*pl -ies*) **1** *c.n* (part of a) shop supplying medicines, ointments etc. ⇨ chemist(3). **2** *u.n* act or profession of preparing medicines.
pharmaceutical /ˌfɑːməˈsjuːtɪkl/ *adj* (*technical*) of or referring to the preparation of medicines: *a pharmaceutical company.*
ˈpharmacist *c.n* professional person who prepares medicines; chemist.
pharmacologist /ˌfɑːməˈkɒlədʒɪst/ *c.n* person who studies, is skilled in, pharmacology.
pharmacology /ˌfɑːməˈkɒlədʒɪ/ *u.n* science of drugs(1) and medicines.

pharynx /ˈfærɪŋks/ *c.n* (*technical*) area at the back of the mouth.
pharyngitis /ˌfærɪnˈdʒaɪtɪs/ *u.n* inflammation of the pharynx.

phase /feɪz/ *c.n* (often — *of s.t*) **1** stage during the development of s.t: *the first/last phase of a disease.* **2** stage during the regular changes in shape or appearance of s.t: *the phases of the moon.* **in**, **out of**, **phase** (**with s.t**) (not) at the same stage, (not) doing the same thing, (as s.t else): *The two machines are out of phase* (*with each other*).
▷ *tr.v* **3 phase s.t in**/**out** gradually introduce/stop s.t: *phasing in the new laws over two years.*
phased *adj* done gradually: *a phased distribution of food.*

Ph.D /ˌpiː eɪtʃ ˌdiː/ *abbr* (also in some universities **D.Phil**) Doctor of Philosophy.

pheasant /ˈfeznt/ *c/u.n* (*pl pheasant(s)*) (also *attrib*) (flesh of a) kind of long-tailed bird, eaten as food: *pheasant pie.*

phenomenon /fɪˈnɒmɪnən/ *c.n* (*pl phenomena* /fɪˈnɒmɪnə/) **1** (*formal*) thing known to exist because it can be seen, heard, touched, smelled or tasted. **2** unusual, special, extraordinary etc thing, event, idea, result etc: *Electricity has produced some unusual phenomena.*
phenomenal /fɪˈnɒmɪnl/ *adj* very unusual, special, extraordinary etc: *She won the race with the phenomenal time of nine seconds. The amount he earns is quite phenomenal.*
pheˈnomenally *adv.*

phew /fjuː/ *interj* (used to express surprise, relief, tiredness etc): *Phew! I'm glad that's done! Phew! It's so hot today!*

philanthropy /fɪˈlænθrəpɪ/ *u.n* (*formal*) (general love for other people, esp shown by) being kind, generous, helpful etc towards others.
philanthropic /ˌfɪlənˈθrɒpɪk/ *adj* kind, generous, helpful etc: *a philanthropic person/action.*
philanthropist /fɪˈlænθrəpɪst/ *c.n* person who is philanthropic.

philately /fɪˈlætəlɪ/ *u.n* (*formal*) collecting of, study of (the history of), postage stamps.

philology /fɪˈlɒlədʒɪ/ *u.n* study of historical written materials and literature.
philological /ˌfɪləˈlɒdʒɪkl/ *adj* of or referring to philology: *philological studies.*

philoˈlogically *adv.*
phiˈlologist *c.n* person who studies, is skilled in, philology.

philosophy /fɪˈlɒsəfɪ/ *n* (*pl -ies*) **1** *u.n* study of the meaning of existence, knowledge of the natural world, what is good behaviour etc: *moral/political philosophy.* **2** *c.n* particular system of ideas, theories(2) etc used to explain existence, morality etc: *Do you understand Russell's philosophy concerning mathematics and language?* **3** *c.n* (*informal*) way of thinking, living, behaving etc: *I live by the philosophy that we must always try to reach agreement.*
phiˈlosopher *c.n* **1** person who studies, is skilled in, philosophy(1,2). **2** (*informal*) person who is reasonable, wise, patient etc.
philosophical /ˌfɪləˈsɒfɪkl/ *adj* **1** of or referring to philosophy: *a philosophical argument/theory(2).* **2** (also **ˌphiloˈsophic**) (of a person, her/his way of thinking) reasonable, patient and calm: *a philosophic(al)* loser. *She's being philosophic(al) about losing.*
ˌphiloˈsophically *adv.*
philosophize, -ise /fɪˈlɒsəˌfaɪz/ *intr.v* (*formal*) think about, discuss seriously, the nature of existence, meaning of an event, what is good behaviour etc.

phlegm /flem/ *u.n* thick liquid brought up into the mouth by coughing.
phlegmatic /flegˈmætɪk/ *adj* (*formal*) calm and reasonable: *be phlegmatic during a* crisis(1).
phlegˈmatically *adv.*

phobia /ˈfəʊbɪə/ *c.n* (often — *about s.t*) extreme fear or dislike (of s.t): *a phobia about* spiders. ⇨ agoraphobia, claustrophobia, hydrophobia.
phobic /ˈfəʊbɪk/ *adj.*

phone /fəʊn/ *c.n* **1** (also *attrib*) telephone: *Can I use your phone? What's your phone number?* **by phone** using the telephone: *We can make the final arrangements by phone.* **on the phone** talking to s.o by using the telephone: *I was on the phone when it happened.*
▷ *tr/intr.v* **2** (*informal*) (often —(s.o)up) telephone (s.o): *Phone me* (*up*) *tomorrow. I never phone* (*anyone*) *after 11 o'clock. I'll phone for a doctor. Phone* (*them*) *up and ask if they're open.*
ˈphone-ˌbox *c.n* tall structure(2) with a public telephone inside.
ˈphone-ˌin *c.n* radio or television programme during which people can telephone with questions or information.
ˈphone-ˌtapping *u.n* act of tapping(3) s.o's telephone.

phoneme /ˈfəʊniːm/ *c.n* (*technical*) one of a set of sounds in a language that makes one word different from another: *The words 'feel' and 'fill' differ by one phoneme.*
phonemic /fəˈniːmɪk/ *adj.*

phonetic /fəˈnetɪk/ *adj* of or referring to the sounds of a language: *A phonetic* alphabet *uses a different symbol to represent each sound.*
phoˈnetically *adv.*
phonetician /ˌfəʊnəˈtɪʃən/ *c.n* person who studies, is skilled in, phonetics.
phonetics /fəˈnetɪks/ *sing.n* **1** study of the sounds of a language. **2** system of letters and symbols showing the sounds of a language.

phoney /ˈfəʊnɪ/ *adj* (*-ier, -iest*) (also **ˈphony**)

(*slang*) **1** not genuine(1): *a phoney passport.*
2 (*derog*) (of a person) not sincere.
▷ *c.n* (*pl -ies*) **3** insincere person: *She's not in love —*
she's a phoney.

phosphorus /'fɒsfərəs/ *u.n* element that shines
in the dark and burns easily, *chem.symb* P.

photo /'fəʊtəʊ/ *c.n* (*informal*) photograph. ⇨
photograph(1).

photocopy /'fəʊtəˌkɒpɪ/ *c.n* (*pl -ies*)
1 photographic copy of s.t written, drawn
etc.
▷ *tr/intr.v* **2** make a photocopy(1) (of (s.t)).
'photo,copier *c.n* machine that photocopies(2).

photoelectric /ˌfəʊtəʊɪ'lektrɪk/ *adj* (*technical*)
of or referring to (the effects of) electricity produced by light: *a photoelectric cell.*

photofinish /ˌfəʊtəʊ'fɪnɪʃ/ *c.n* end of a race in
which people, horses etc are so close that a
photograph is needed to decide the winner(1).

photogenic /ˌfəʊtə'dʒenɪk/ *adj* looking attractive in photographs.
,photo'genically *adv.*

photograph /'fəʊtəˌɡrɑːf/ *c.n* **1** (also **'photo**
/'fəʊtəʊ/) (often — *of* s.t) picture (of s.o/s.t)
made using a camera and film: *a photograph of*
a fly. Compare slide(6).
▷ *tr.v* **2** take a photograph of (s.o/s.t): *I'm*
photographing the wedding.

photographer /fə'tɒɡrəfə/ *c.n* (professional)
person who takes photographs.

photographic /ˌfəʊtə'ɡræfɪk/ *adj* **1** of or referring to photography: *photographic equipment.* ⇨
photogenic. **2** (of a memory) able to remember
details after looking at s.t: *She has a photographic*
memory for scenery.

photography /fə'tɒɡrəfɪ/ *u.n* (study of the) act
or process of taking photographs.

Photostat /'fəʊtəˌstæt/ *c.n* (*t.n*) = photo-
copy(1).

phrase /freɪz/ *c.n* **1** group of words (without a
verb) forming part of a sentence, e.g *'in other*
words', 'the cost of living', 'slow but sure', 'not
in the least'. **2** (*music*) group of notes forming
part of a longer piece of music. **3** (*music*) sign
used in music to show that two notes should be
played or sung without a pause between them. ⇨
tie(3). **to coin a phrase** ⇨ coin(v). **turn of phrase**
⇨ turn(n).
▷ *tr.v* **4** (*formal*) express (s.t) in words: *Be careful*
how you phrase your argument.

phrasal /'freɪzl/ *adj* of or referring to a
phrase(1): *a phrasal part of a sentence.*
,phrasal 'verb *c.n* (*technical*) verb with one or
more adverbs and/or prepositions, e.g *'come in',*
'go out of', 'set to', 'take off'.

phraseology /ˌfreɪzɪ'ɒlədʒɪ/ *u.n* (*formal*) way
of using words to say s.t: *He explained the mistake*
using unfortunate phraseology which sounded as
if he was accusing his parents.

phut /fʌt/ *adv* **go phut** (*informal*) (of a machine
etc) break down: *My bicycle went phut!*

physical /'fɪzɪkl/ *adj* **1** of or referring to the body
(and not the mind): *physical education/exercise.*
2 of or referring to anything that can be seen,
heard, smelled or touched: *the physical world.*
3 of or referring to the structure of the earth or
the world: *physical geography; a physical map of*
Europe. **4** of or referring to bodies, substances,
energy(2) etc and how they act scientifically: *It is*

a physical impossibility to balance upside-down
on one's nose. **5** (*informal*) using one's body
and strength, e.g when fighting: *be/feel physical*
when angry.
▷ *c.n* **6** (*informal*) examination of one's body by a
doctor: *If you don't pass your physical you can't*
join the army.
'physically *adv.*

physician /fɪ'zɪʃən/ *c.n* (*formal*) medical practitioner who is not a surgeon.

physics /'fɪzɪks/ *sing.n* (also *attrib*) study of
substances and energy(2), e.g heat, electricity,
magnetism(1), mechanics(2) and the atom(1), and
how they act scientifically: *a physics teacher/*
lecture; nuclear physics.
physicist /'fɪzɪsɪst/ *c.n* person who studies, is
skilled in, physics.

physio /'fɪzɪəʊ/ *c.n* (*informal*) physiotherapist.

physiognomy /ˌfɪzɪ'ɒnəmɪ/ *c.n* (*usu sing*)
(often — *of* s.o/s.t) **1** (*technical*) outward
appearance of a geographical region. **2** (*formal*) judgement of a person's character using
a person's facial expressions and appearance.

physiology /ˌfɪzɪ'ɒlədʒɪ/ *u.n* (*technical*) study
of the way living things, esp animals' bodies,
work.
physiological /ˌfɪzɪə'lɒdʒɪkl/ *adj* (*technical*)
of or referring to physiology: *the physiological*
symptoms *of an illness.*
,physio'logically *adv.*
,physi'ologist *c.n* person who studies, is skilled
in, physiology.

physiotherapy /ˌfɪzɪə'θerəpɪ/ *u.n* (study of the)
treatment of an illness using exercise, massage(1)
etc: *Your bruised ankle will need physiotherapy.*
You'll need to have physiotherapy on that knee.
,physio'therapist *c.n* (*informal* **'physio**) professional person who gives people physiotherapy.

physique /fɪ'ziːk/ *c/u.n* form of a person's body:
have a strong/weak physique.

piano /pɪ'ænəʊ/ *c.n* (also *attrib*) musical instrument with a long row of black and white keys that
are pressed to make small hammers hit strings: *I*
can play the piano well. We listened to some music
played on the piano. It was a piano concert. ⇨
grand piano, upright piano.
pianist /'pɪənɪst/ *c.n* person who plays the piano.
pianoforte /pɪˌænəʊ'fɔːtɪ/ *c.n* (*formal*) piano.

piccolo /'pɪkələʊ/ *c.n* musical instrument like a
small flute.

pick¹ /pɪk/ *c.n* **1** act of picking(2,4,5): *a pick*
through the pile of shoes; a pick at one's teeth.
the pick of s.t the best of them all: *This fruit*
is the pick of the bunch. I got the pick of the
holiday offers. He was the pick of his class. **take**
your pick (expression used to tell s.o that he/
she is free to choose): *'Which cake can I have?'*
'Take your pick.'
▷ *tr.v* **2** remove and take (s.t) with the fingers: *pick*
apples off a tree; pick flowers; pick a piece of dirt
from a collar; pick a leaf out of her hair. **3** make
(s.t) by picking(1): *He picked a hole in his jumper.*
⇨ unpick. **4** choose (s.o/s.t) (carefully) from a
group: *Pick the clothes you want. I hope I have*
been picked to play in the team tomorrow. **5** (also
— *at* s.t) **(a)** (of a bird) remove small pieces of (s.t,
usu food) using the beak. **(b)** (*fig*) (of a person)
take and eat small amounts of (food): *He wasn't*
very hungry and only picked at his dinner. **6** (usu

— *s.t with s.o*) be the cause of (s.t concerning disagreement) between two people: *pick a fight/ argument/quarrel with him.*

pick at s.o make critical remarks about s.o: *She's always picking at me.* **pick at s.t** ⇨ pick¹(5).

pick s.o's brains ⇨ brain(*n*).

pick and choose choose very carefully, often too carefully: *You must accept that job — you can't afford to pick and choose.* ⇨ picky.

pick holes in s.o/s.t ⇨ hole(*n*).

pick a lock ⇨ lock(*n*).

pick one's nose ⇨ nose(*n*).

pick s.o off (*informal*) kill s.o who is in a group by shooting her/him: *He was picking off the soldiers one by one.*

pick on s.o (a) choose s.o, often to do s.t unpleasant or difficult: *He always picks on me to do the nasty jobs.* **(b)** = pick at s.o: *Stop picking on me!*

pick s.o/s.t out (a) recognize s.o/s.t in a group: *I can pick her out in any crowd because of her red hair.* **(b)** choose s.o/s.t from a group for a special reason: *pick out the best players/fish.* **pick s.t out** paint, draw etc s.t in a different colour etc to make it more obvious: *We picked out the flowers in the pattern using bright red paint.*

pick s.o's pocket ⇨ pocket(*n*), pickpocket.

pick a quarrel (with s.o) ⇨ quarrel(*n*).

pick up (a) (of a person's health) improve: *She was ill for a time but is picking up now.* ⇨ pick-me-up. **(b)** (of a business, market etc) improve: *The tourist industry is picking up in this warm weather.* **pick up (speed)** (of a vehicle etc) go faster; increase (speed): *My old car only picks up (speed) going down a hill.* **pick s.o up (a)** talk to s.o (e.g at a party) and invite her/him to become a girlfriend or boyfriend. ⇨ pick-up(4). **(b)** stop and give s.o a lift in a bus, taxi, one's car etc: *pick up passengers.* **(c)** (of the police etc) stop and arrest s.o: *The thief was picked up by the police the next day.* **pick s.o/s.t up (a)** take or lift s.o/s.t up in one's hand(s): *pick up a baby. Pick up your clothes.* **(b)** (of a radio, television etc) manage to receive sound, pictures etc: *My radio can't pick up the World Service.* **(c)** hear and collect facts, information etc: *I pick up all sorts of* gossip(1) *in the pub.*

'picker *c.n* person or thing that picks(2) s.t: *a fruit picker.*

'pickings *pl.n* money, profits, rewards etc, esp those obtained easily or dishonestly: *The discovery of North and South America provided rich pickings for Europeans.*

'pick-me-,up *c.n* (*informal*) thing that helps a person to feel better, have more energy(1): *The holiday, hot meal, medicine, was a perfect pick-me-up.*

'pick,pocket *c.n* **1** person who pickpockets(2). ⊳ *tr/intr.v* **2** steal from s.o's clothes, bag etc.

'pick-,up *c.n* **1** part like an arm on a record player that has the needle(4) in it. **2** small van. **3** (*informal*) (order to) stop in order to collect s.o/s.t: *I have four pick-ups to make before lunch.* **4** (*slang*) person who is picked up(a,b).

'picky *adj* (-ier, -iest) (*informal*) difficult to please; choosy: *be picky about what one eats.*

pick² /pɪk/ *c.n* **1** (also **'pick,axe**) tool with a long usu wooden handle and a pointed steel head, used to break the ground, roads etc. **2** any small or large tool used to break

or remove a hard substance: *an icepick; a toothpick.*

'pick,axe *c.n* ⇨ pick²(1).

picket /'pɪkɪt/ *c.n* **1** (also *attrib*) (member of a) group of workers on strike outside a factory etc trying to persuade others not to go to work: *picket duty.* **2** (member of a) small group of soldiers on guard against attack: *put a picket at the entrance.* **3** small upright post in the ground used to support a fence.

⊳ *tr/intr.v* **4** act as a member of a picket(1,2): *They were picketing the factory all night. Soldiers picketed the whole boundary.*

'picketer *c.n* person who is part of a picket(1).

'picket ,line *c.n* group of picketers.

pickle /'pɪkl/ *n* **1** *c/u.n* vegetable(s) or fruit in vinegar and sugar: *fruit pickle; cheese with pickles.* ⇨ chutney. **2** *sing.n* (esp in *a* —) (*informal*) **(a)** difficult situation: *We were high up the mountain when the rain began which left us in a real pickle.* **(b)** untidy state: *My son's room is always (in) a pickle.*

⊳ *tr.v* **3** preserve (vegetable(s) or fruit) in vinegar and sugar etc: *pickle small onions.*

'pickled *adj* (*informal*) drunk.

pickpocket, pick-up ⇨ pick¹.

picnic /'pɪknɪk/ *c.n* **1** (also *attrib*) meal eaten outdoors as part of a trip to the country etc: *have a picnic by the river; a picnic basket; a picnic lunch/ meal.* **2** (often be no —) easy occasion, event or job: *It's no picnic doing both jobs when you're away. Do you think* housework *is a picnic?*

⊳ *intr.v* **3** (-ck-) have a picnic: *picknicking by the sea.*

pictorial /pɪk'tɔːrɪəl/ *adj* (usu *attrib*) **1** of or involving(1) pictures; expressed using pictures: *a pictorial record.* **2** (of the mind) using pictures: *a pictorial memory; a pictorial* image(4) *of what happened.* **3** (of language) very descriptive and lively(2): *written in a pictorial style.*

⊳ *c.n* **4** magazine with many illustrations and some text.

pic'torially *adv.*

picture /'pɪktʃə/ *c.n* (often — of s.t) **1** (also *attrib*) drawing, painting etc: *draw a picture of her house; a picture postcard.* **2** (usu take a — (of s.o/s.t)) photograph: *We took some pictures of the mountains.* **3** (*informal*) cinema film: *'Out of Africa' was a good picture.* ⇨ pictures. **4** mental(1) impression: *have a clear picture in one's mind of what happened.* **5** general situation: *the political/ economic picture in the developing world.* **6** (usu the — of s.o/s.t) person, thing, scene etc who/ that is a typical or good example of s.o/s.t: *She's the picture of her grandmother. As he left the examination room he was the picture of misery. You look the picture of health after your holiday.*

as pretty as a picture very pretty. **be, put s.o, in the picture (about s.o/s.t)** (*informal*) have, give s.o, all the necessary information: *be, put her, in the picture about his illness.* **get the picture** (*informal*) (usu as a question) understand s.o's description of an event or situation.

⊳ *tr.v* **7** imagine (s.o/s.t): *I'd like you to picture a small boy lost on a beach.* **8** (usu *passive*) make a drawing, painting etc of s.o/s.t: *She was pictured sitting under a tree.*

'picture-,book *c.n* child's book with many pictures.

'**pictures** *def.pl.n* (*informal*) cinema: *Let's go to the pictures tonight.*

picturesque /ˌpɪkʃəˈrɛsk/ *adj* (*formal*) attractive to look at: *a picturesque cottage.*
ˌpictu'**resquely** *adv.*

piddle /'pɪdl/ *u.n* **1** (*slang*) urine: *cat's piddle.* **go for**, **have**, **a piddle** urinate. ⇨ pee(1).
▷ *intr.v* **2** (*slang*) urinate. ⇨ pee(2). **piddle about** (*informal*) pass one's time doing silly, unnecessary things: *Stop piddling about.*

piddling /'pɪdlɪŋ/ *adj* (usu *attrib*) (*informal*) (small and) unimportant: *a piddling amount*; *piddling little waves/jobs/details.*

pidgin /'pɪdʒɪn/ *u.n* (also *attrib*) language that is a mixture of a local language and English, French etc as spoken by traders etc in developing countries: *pidgin English.*

pie /paɪ/ *c/u.n* (example, shaped portion(2) of) food made by baking fruit, meat or vegetables inside pastry: *apple/steak(3)/cheese pie*; *a pork pie.* **as easy as pie** (*informal*) very easy. **have a finger in every pie** ⇨ finger(*n*). **pie in the sky** (*informal*) hope or idea of future success, happiness etc that is unlikely.
'**pie ˌchart** *c.n* circular diagram showing relative(1) quantities.

piece /piːs/ *c.n* **1** (often — *of s.t*) particular amount, part etc of a thing or substance: *a piece of cheese/meat/paper/cloth/wood. I can't find all the pieces of the puzzle.* **2** (usu — *of s.t*) example or item(1) (of s.t): *a piece of furniture/advice/news/information/luck.* **3** coin: *a 50p piece.* **4** small shaped object used in board games: *a chess piece.* **5** item(1) of art, literature, music etc: *a lovely piece of china/writing*; *a jazz(1) piece.* **cut to pieces** ⇨ cut(*v*). **give s.o a piece of one's mind** ⇨ mind¹. **go to pieces** (of a person) lose self-control, esp because of anxiety. **in one piece** not damaged or hurt: *I was glad to see her get out of the car in one piece.* **in pieces** (**a**) broken: *The pot was in pieces on the floor.* (**b**) in separate parts: *The car was in pieces on the ground.* **a nasty piece of work** (*derog*; *informal*) a cruel or very unpleasant person. **piece by piece** one part, item(1), detail etc at a time: *We had to check the rubbish piece by piece before we found the ring.* **be a piece of cake** (*fig*; *informal*) a thing that is easy to do or get: *That job was a piece of cake.* **pull s.o/s.t to pieces** (*fig*; *informal*) criticize s.o/s.t severely: *The report pulled the actor* (or *his acting*) *to pieces.* **say one's piece** express one's opinion. **to pieces** (**a**) into the separate parts: *I took the puzzle to pieces but I couldn't put it together again.* (**b**) into broken parts: *The cup came/fell to pieces in my hand.*
▷ *tr.v* **6 piece s.t together** put the parts, details etc of s.t together to make a whole: *piecing together a broken teapot*; *piecing together an accurate report of what happened.*
'**pieceˌmeal** *adj/adv* (doing) one part, item(1) etc at a time: *piecemeal methods*; *working piecemeal.*

pièce de résistance /piːˌes də ˌrezɪˈstɑːns/ *c.n* (*pl* pièces de résistance, same pronunciation) (*French*) best of all the examples of an artist's, cook's, writer's etc work: *Chocolate cake is her pièce de résistance.*

pied-à-terre /ˌpɪˌed ɑː 'teə/ *c.n* (*pl* pieds-à-terre

same pronunciation) (*French*) small flat or other home, esp one used only occasionally.

pier /pɪə/ *c.n* long structure(2) built out from the coast, used for fastening boats to, for people to walk about on etc: *Brighton pier.*

pierce /pɪəs/ *tr.v* **1** make a hole in (s.o/s.t) with a sharp or pointed instrument: *The nail pierced the wall. The stick pierced his skin. You must pierce the tin in two places so that the liquid will pour out.* **2** (*fig*) go through or into (s.t): *The sunlight pierced through the clouds. Her loud cry pierced the silence. The cold wind was piercing my chest.*
'**piercing** *adj* (of sound, cold, light etc) very powerful: *a piercing noise/wind/cry.*
'**piercingly** *adv.*

piety ⇨ pious.

piffle /'pɪfl/ *u.n* (*informal*) nonsense. *You're talking complete piffle.*

pig /pɪg/ *c.n* **1** (also *attrib*) kind of farm animal with a flat round nose, eaten as bacon, ham(1,2), pork: *a pig farm*; *pig meat.* ⇨ hog(1), sow(1). **2** (*derog*; *fig*) unpleasant or dirty person. **3** (*fig*) difficult task or problem: *This sum is a pig.* **guinea pig** ⇨ guinea. **make a pig of oneself** (*informal*) eat far too much food. **pigs might fly** (expression used to show one has no belief in what s.o says). **a pig in a poke** (*fig*) a thing that is bought without looking at it or knowing its value.
'**piggish** *adj* (*derog*; *informal*) greedy.
'**piggy** *c.n* (*pl* -ies) (child's word for a) pig.
'**piggy-ˌback** *adv* **1** (*informal*) carried on s.o's back.
▷ *c.n* **2** act of being carried piggy-back(1): *Give me a piggy-back.*
'**piggy-ˌbank** *c.n* small box (often shaped like a pig) for a child to save money in.
ˌpig-'**headed** *adj* (*derog*) too determined and stubborn(1).
piglet /'pɪglɪt/ *c.n* young pig.
ˌpig's 'ear *sing.n* (esp make a — of s.t) (*informal*) mess; bad job.
'**pigˌsty** *c.n* (*pl* -ies) **1** building for keeping pigs in. **2** (*derog*) dirty, untidy place: *Your bedroom is a pigsty.*
'**pigˌtail** *c.n* long hair twisted into a plait(1): *wear pigtails.*

pigeon /'pɪdʒən/ *c.n* **1** (also *attrib*) one of many kinds of birds with heavy bodies and small heads, some very common in cities: woodpigeons; *pigeon pie.* **2** victim: *be a pigeon in an argument.* **it is her/his pigeon** (*informal*) it is her/his responsibility.
ˌpigeon-'**hearted** *adj* (*derog*) lacking courage.
'**pigeon-ˌhole** *c.n* **1** small open box for letters etc. **2** (*informal*) particular category.
▷ *tr.v* **3** put (s.o/s.t) in a particular category: *I hate to be pigeon-holed.* **4** put (s.t) to one side and not deal with it.
'**pigeon-ˌtoed** *adj* having feet that turn inwards at the front.

pigment /'pɪgmənt/ *c/u.n* **1** (example of a) substance that produces a colour, e.g for paint. **2** (example of a) substance that produces colour in a plant or animal: *Which pigment makes plants green, blood red?*
pigmentation /ˌpɪgmənˈteɪʃən/ *u.n* (often — *of s.t*) natural colouring (of s.t): *the pigmentation of plants, the skin.*

pigmy ⇨ pygmy.

pike /paɪk/ *c.n* **1** kind of long spear(1). **2** (*pl pike(s)*) kind of long fish found in rivers.

pilaff /'pɪlæf/ *u.n* = pilau.

pilau /pɪ'laʊ/ *u.n* (also **'pilaff**) dish of flavoured rice with meat, fish and/or vegetables added.

pilchard /'pɪltʃəd/ *c.n* (*pl pilchard(s)*) (also *attrib*) kind of small grey sea fish like a herring(1), eaten as food: *a tin of pilchards; pilchard paste.*

pile¹ /paɪl/ *c.n* (often — *of s.t*) **1** quantity (of things) in a heap: *a pile of clothes/bricks; a wood pile.* **2** (*informal*) large amount (of s.t): *I have piles of work to finish.* **make a pile** (*informal*) earn/get a large amount of money.

▷ *v* **3** *tr/intr.v* (often — (*s.t*) *up*) form, cause (s.t) to be, (as if) a pile: *I piled* (*up*) *the books in the corner. My work is piling up.* ⇨ pile-up. **4** *intr.v* (usu — *in, into s.t, off* (*s.t*)*, out* (*of s.t*)) (*informal*) move as a group quickly or in an unorganized way: *We piled off the bus, into the cinema, out of the room. Come on everyone, pile in.* **pile it on** (*informal*) exaggerate pain, difficulties, sadness etc.

'pile-,up *c.n* (*informal*) accident involving many vehicles.

pile² /paɪl/ *c.n* post of wood or length of metal in the ground, used as a support for a building etc.

'pile-,driver *c.n* (*technical*) machine for hammering a pile² into the ground.

pile³ /paɪl/ *c/u.n* soft surface formed by the short threads that stand up in some carpets and cloths, e.g velvet.

piles /paɪlz/ *pl.n* (*informal*) haemorrhoids.

pilfer /'pɪlfə/ *tr/intr.v* (*informal*) steal (small things, often of little value): *pilfering paper and pens from work.*

'pilferer *c.n* person who pilfers.

pilgrim /'pɪlgrɪm/ *c.n* person who goes to a holy place for religious reasons: *pilgrims to Mecca.*

pilgrimage /'pɪlgrɪmɪdʒ/ *c.n* journey by a pilgrim.

pill /pɪl/ *n* **1** *c.n* small tablet of medicine, usu to be swallowed whole: *Don't forget to take* (swallow) *your pills before you go to bed.* **2** *def.n* contraceptive(1) pill. **a bitter pill to swallow** (*fig*) something that one has to accept even though it is bitter(2). **be on the pill** be taking the pill(2) regularly.

pillage /'pɪlɪdʒ/ *u.n* **1** act of pillaging (⇨ pillage(2)).

▷ *tr/intr.v* **2** steal (things) from a community(1), esp during a war: *The soldiers pillaged the town.*

pillar /'pɪlə/ *c.n* **1** long upright support of stone, brick etc, e.g one of many in a row supporting a roof. **2** (usu — *of s.t*) thing like a pillar(1) in shape (consisting of s.t): *a pillar of smoke.* **3** (usu — *of s.t*) (*fig*) strong supporter (of s.t): *a pillar of freedom/ Christianity.* **from pillar to post** (*fig*) from one place to another: *We were driven* (made to go) *from pillar to post looking for somewhere to live.* **a pillar of strength** a person who supports s.o strongly during difficulties: *My husband was a pillar of strength while I was ill.*

'pillar-,box *c.n* red metal container like a short pillar(1), put by the side of the road for posting letters etc in.

pillion /'pɪlɪən/ *adv* **1** on a pillion(2): *riding pillion.*

▷ *c.n* **2** (also *attrib*) seat behind the rider of a motorbike, horse etc: *a pillion seat.*

pillow /'pɪləʊ/ *c.n* **1** cushion for resting the head on in bed.

▷ *tr.v* **2** (*formal*) rest (one's head) (as if) on a pillow(1): *pillowing her head in his arms.* Compare cushion(1).

'pillow-,case,,slip *c.n* loose cover for a pillow(1).

pilot /'paɪlət/ *attrib.adj* **1** done as a trial: *a pilot scheme to solve parking problems.* ⇨ pilot study.

▷ *c.n* **2** (also *attrib*) person trained to control an aircraft: *The crash was not due to* (*a*) *pilot error(1). The sleeve is only person trained to direct ships into and out of a harbour etc.*

▷ *tr.v* **4** act as a pilot(2) of (an aircraft or ship). **5** start or guide (a new idea, scheme(2) etc): *piloting a new method of learning French.* ⇨ pilot(1).

'pilot ,light *c.n* small flame in a gas cooker, heater etc that lights a burner when the gas is turned on.

'pilot ,study *c.n* (*pl -ies*) limited study used as a trial for one covering more people, details etc.

pimp /pɪmp/ *c.n* **1** man who earns money by finding customers for a prostitute.

▷ *intr.v* **2** act as a pimp(1).

pimple /'pɪmpl/ *c.n* small sore swelling on the skin.

'pimply *adj* (*-ier, -iest*) having pimples on it: *a pimply skin.*

pin /pɪn/ *c.n* **1** short thin pointed piece of metal, used to hold pieces of paper, cloth etc together: *a box of pins for dressmaking. The sleeve is only held on by/with pins at the moment.* **2** pin(1) with a decorated head, used as an ornament or badge. **3** long thin piece of wood or metal for holding things together or s.t in position: *a wooden pin in a fence for strength; a metal pin in a broken bone.* ⇨ drawing-pin, hairpin(1), rolling-pin, safety-pin.

▷ *tr.v* (*-nn-*) **4** fasten (s.t) (together, down etc) with a pin or pins: *I pinned the* sleeve(1) *to the cloth. Pin the flower in your hair. James pinned the papers together, pinned out the map.* Opposite unpin. **5** hold (s.o) using one's weight: *The police pinned the thief against the wall. They pinned the man to the floor.* **pin s.o down** (**to s.t**) (*fig; informal*) manage to make s.o decide or agree (to a particular time, action etc): *I wasn't able to pin her down to a date for finishing the work.*

pin s.t on s.o cause s.o to seem responsible for a bad act: *They're trying to pin the blame on me.*

pin one's hopes on s.o/s.t ⇨ hope(*n*).

'pin-,cushion *c.n* small pad for holding pins(1).

'pin,head *c.n* **1** flat end of a pin(1). **2** (*derog; slang*) stupid person.

'pin,headed *adj* (*derog; slang*) stupid.

'pin,hole *c.n* very small hole (as if) made by a pin(1).

'pin ,money *u.n* small amount of money earned regularly by doing small jobs.

'pin,point *tr.v* identify (a place, time) exactly: *Can you pinpoint the time of the accident, the place on this map?*

,pins and 'needles *pl.n* tingling(2) feelings in one's arms or legs: *I got pins and needles in my legs from sitting on my feet for so long.*

'pin,stripe *c.n* (also *attrib*) thin line in cloth: *pinstripe cloth/trousers.*

'pin-,up *c.n* (*informal*) picture of s.o with few or no clothes on.

pinafore /'pınəˌfɔ:/ *c.n* (*informal pinny*) apron with a top attached (⇒ attach(1)), used to protect the front of one's clothes.

'pinafore ,dress *c.n* dress without sleeves(1) and worn over a blouse etc.

pincer /'pınsə/ *c.n* (*usu pl*) (large) claw(1) of a crab(1), lobster, insect etc.

'pincers *pl.n* **1** ⇒ pincer. **2** (often *a pair of* —) tool with two flat edges, used to hold s.t firmly.

pinch /pıntʃ/ *c.n* **1** act of pinching(3). **2** (often — *of s.t*) small amount (of s.t, esp a powder): *a pinch of salt*. **at a pinch** if really necessary: *I could be there by five o'clock at a pinch*. **feel the pinch** (*informal*) be needing money: *We felt the pinch when we had to pay for a new television*. **with a pinch of salt** (*fig*) (while) not fully believing s.t: *We always take what he says with a pinch of salt*.

▷ *v* **3** *tr.v* press (s.o's) skin firmly between the fingers and thumb: *Stop pinching me*. **4** *tr/intr.v* (of shoes) hurt (s.o) by pressing the toes or foot tightly: *These new shoes pinch (me)*. **5** *tr.v* (usu — *s.t back, off, out*) remove the top of (a plant) to make new shoots grow: *pinching back the tomato(1) plants*. **6** *tr.v* (*informal*) steal (usu s.t small): *Who's pinched my pen?* ⇒ penny-pinching.

pinched *adj* (of the face) looking thin, pale and tired.

pine¹ /paın/ *n* (also *attrib*) **1** *c.n* kind of tree with leaves like needles and hard fruit with overlapping (⇒ overlap(2)) scales (called cones(2)): *pine trees*; *pine needles*; *pine cones*(2). **2** *u.n* soft light wood of this tree used for building, furniture etc: *a pine table*; *pinewood*.

pine² /paın/ *intr.v* **1** (often — *for s.o/s.t*; — *to do s.t*) want s.o/s.t, to do s.t, so much that one feels sad: *pining for one's parents, for home*; *pining to join friends on holiday*. **2** (usu — *away*) become weak and ill because of great sadness, pain etc: *When John left Mary she seemed to pine away*.

pineapple /'paın,æpl/ *c/u.n* (also *attrib*) (kind of plant from a hot country with prickly leaves and a) large juicy fruit: *grow pineapples*; *eat some pineapple*; *a tin of pineapple pieces/juice*.

ping /pıŋ/ *c.n* **1** short high sound (as) made by a stone hitting metal.

▷ *intr.v* **2** make a ping(1).

ping-pong /'pıŋ ,pɒŋ/ *u.n* table tennis.

pinhead(ed), **pinhole** ⇒ pin.

pinion¹ /'pınıən/ *c.n* **1** part of a bird's wing furthest from its body. **2** feather on a bird's wing that is used for flying.

▷ *tr.v* **3** remove the outer part of (a bird)'s wing so that it cannot fly. **4** hold, tie up, (s.o) so that he/ she cannot move: *The man pinioned the boy's arms so that he couldn't get away*.

pinion² /'pınıən/ *c.n* (*technical*) cogwheel that is fitted to a rack(2).

pink¹ /pıŋk/ *adj* **1** having the colour that is between white and red: *pink flowers. Her cheeks were pink with cold*.

▷ *c/u.n* **2** pink(1) colour: *dressed in pink. Which pink do you like?* **in the pink (of health)** very healthy: *She's feeling/looking in the pink (of health)*. **in pink** having pink clothes on.

'pinkish *adj* a little pink in colour.

'pinkness *u.n*.

pink² /pıŋk/ *tr.v* cut (cloth) with pinking scissors to stop fraying¹(1).

'pinking ,scissors/,shears *pl.n* kind of scissors that produce a wavy or jagged edge for pinking².

pinnacle /'pınəkl/ *c.n* (often — *of s.t*) **1** highest point (of a mountain, tower etc). **2** highest point (of success, fame etc): *This is the pinnacle of my fame as a singer*.

pinny /'pını/ *c.n* (*pl -ies*) (*informal*) pinafore.

pinpoint, **pinstripe** ⇒ pin.

pint /paınt/ *c.n* **1** (*written abbr pt*) (often — *of s.t*) (also *attrib*) unit of liquid measurement (= 0.57 litres): *4 pints equal 1 gallon*; *a pint of milk/ beer*; *a pint glass*. **2** (*informal*) pint of beer: *Let me buy you a pint*.

pin-up ⇒ pin.

pioneer /ˌpaıə'nıə/ *c.n* **1** (also *attrib*) person who explores, settles in, a new area, country etc: *early pioneers in North America*; *have a pioneer spirit*. **2** (often — *of s.t*) person who explores new methods, ideas etc: *Fleming was a pioneer of penicillin*.

▷ *tr.v* **3** be first to do, use, (s.t): *pioneer a new cure for cancer(1)*.

,pio'neering *adj* ready and willing to explore new methods, ideas etc.

pious /'paıəs/ *adj* having or showing serious belief in and love of God. Opposite impious.

piety /'paıətı/ *u.n*. **'piously** *adv*.

pip¹ /pıp/ *c.n* small seed of a fruit such as an orange or apple.

pip² /pıp/ *c.n* **1** very short high sound as used on the radio to mark the exact time or made by electronic(2) equipment(2): *I hate the pips of digital watches¹ in the cinema*. **2** spot or mark on a playing card or dice(1) to show the value.

▷ *intr.v* (*-pp-*) **3** make a pip²(1).

pip³ /pıp/ *def.n* (*esp give s.o the* —) (*slang*) angry feeling: *His continual criticism gives me the pip*.

pip⁴ /pıp/ *tr.v* (*-pp-*) (often passive, *be* —*d at the post*) defeat (s.o who has almost won): *I thought I'd got the job but I was pipped at the post by a younger man*.

pipe /paıp/ *n* **1** *c/u.n* (also *attrib*) (length of a) hollow tube for liquid, gas etc: *a gas/water pipe*; *a long piece of pipe*. ⇒ drainpipe. **2** *c.n* small object for smoking tobacco that consists of a hollow stem with a bowl at one end. **3** *c.n* (also *attrib*) musical instrument in which sounds are made by blowing air through a hollow tube: *pipe music*; *organ pipes*. ⇒ bagpipes. **4** *c.n* part of the body like a tube: *the windpipe*.

▷ *v* **5** *tr.v* send (gas, liquid etc) through pipes(1): *piping water to the cities*, *oil to the factory*. **6** *tr/intr.v* make (music), give (a signal etc), on a pipe(3): *piping a signal to the sailors*. **7** *tr.v* put (lengths of) piping(5,6) on the edge of (a cake, cushion etc). **8** *intr.v* (of a bird) make high sounds. **9** *tr/intr.v* (of a person) speak, say (s.t), using high sounds. **pipe down** (*informal*) make less noise; speak quietly: *I wish the children would pipe down*. **pipe up** (*informal*) begin to speak suddenly (and in a high voice): *Then a voice piped up at the back of the crowd*.

'pipe ,dream *c.n* impossible idea or wish.

'pipe ,line *c.n* system of pipes(1) for sending gas, oil etc to other places. **in the pipeline** (*fig*) on the way; in the process (⇒ process(n)) of being done/produced: *A new plan is in the pipeline.*

'piper *c.n* person who plays a pipe(3), the bag-pipes etc.

'pipes *def.pl.n* musical instrument made using a set of pipes(3); bagpipes: *play (on) the pipes.*

'piping *u.n* **1** length or lengths of pipes(1). **2** act of sending gas or liquid to a place through pipes(1): *piping of gas to the city.* **3** act of making music, giving a signal etc, on a pipe(3). **4** act of putting lengths of icing(1) on a cake, cord(1) round a cushion, jacket(1) etc. ⇒ pipe(7). **5** thin length or lengths of icing(1) piped(7) on a cake: *blue piping round a cake.* **6** thin length or lengths of cord(1), often covered with material and sewn onto the edge of a cushion, shirt etc. ⇒ pipe(7).

,piping 'hot *adj* (*informal*) extremely hot: *piping hot coffee.*

pipette /pɪ'pet/ *c.n* very narrow glass tube used by scientists to measure the volume of a liquid.

pipsqueak /'pɪp,skwiːk/ *c.n* (*derog*; *informal*) unimportant and disliked person.

piquant /'piːkənt, 'piːkaːnt/ *adj* (*formal*) having a pleasantly sharp taste: *a piquant sauce.*

'piquancy *u.n.* **'piquantly** *adv.*

pique /piːk/ *c/u.n* **1** (example of a) feeling of mild anger and annoyance esp because one's pride has been affected: *In a fit of pique she threw the cup on the floor.*

▷ *tr.v* **2** (usu passive) make (s.o) feel pique(1): *be piqued by his refusal to come.*

pirate /'paɪərɪt/ *c.n* **1** (also *attrib*) person who stops ships at sea and steals goods etc from them: *a pirate leader/ship.* **2** (also *attrib*) person who acts, uses s.t etc without legal(1) right: *video(1) pirates; a pirate radio station. A pirate writer uses parts of another writer's work.*

▷ *tr.v* **3** copy/use (s.t) without legal(1) right: *pirating a pop³(1) record, a book.*

'piracy *u.n* (often — *of s.t*) act of a pirate: *piracy at sea; piracy of another writer's work.*

piratical /paɪ'rætɪkl/ *adj.*

pirouette /,pɪruːˈet/ *c.n* **1** fast turn of the body by a dancer etc, usu on the tips of her/his toes.

▷ *intr.v* **2** make a pirouette(1): *a skater pirouetting on the ice.*

Pisces /'paɪsiːz/ *n* **1** *unique n* one of the 12 signs of the zodiac. **2** *c.n* person born under this sign.

piss /pɪs/ *u.n* **1** (*slang*; do not use!) urine. **take the piss out of s.o** laugh at s.o cruelly; mock(2) s.o.

▷ *intr.v* **2** (*slang*; do not use!) urinate. **piss (down) (with rain)** rain very much. **piss off** (esp as an order) go away. **be pissed off (with s.o/s.t)** be very annoyed or angry (with s.o/s.t).

pissed *adj* (*slang*; do not use!) drunk(1).

pistachio /pɪ'staːʃɪəʊ/ *c.n* (also *attrib*) (kind of tree with a) small green nut that has a pleasant taste: *buy some pistachios; pistachio ice-cream; pistachio green.*

pistil /'pɪstɪl/ *c.n* (*technical*) part of a flower that produces the seeds.

pistol /'pɪstl/ *c.n* small gun.

piston /'pɪstn/ *c.n* (*technical*) part of an engine like a rod or pipe that moves up and down or backwards and forwards to make a vehicle move.

pit¹ /pɪt/ *c.n* **1** wide hole in the ground, esp one out of which a substance such as coal is taken:

a coal/sand pit; dig a pit to catch wild animals. **2** hollow place like a pit(1) on a surface: *an armpit; the pit of the stomach; huge pits on the moon; small pits on the skin left after certain illnesses.* **3** (usu *pl*) area at the side of a racing track where cars are checked: *He came into the pits for a wheel change.* **4** (also **'orchestra ,pit**) area in front of a stage in a theatre for the orchestra. **5** (people in the) ground floor of a theatre or cinema.

▷ *tr.v* (*-tt-*) **6** (often — *s.o/s.t against s.o/s.t*) make (s.o/s.t) compete with another: *The old car was pitted against a newer model in the race. We were pitted against a much stronger team.* **7** (often — *s.t with s.t*) mark (s.t) with holes: *a skin/landscape(1) pitted with ugly holes.*

'pit,fall *c.n* unexpected difficulty or danger: *She ignored the pitfalls of marrying a stranger.*

'pit,head *c.n* entrance to a coalmine.

pits *def.n* (*informal*) worst possible example, situation etc: *This music/book is the pits!*

pit² /pɪt/ *c.n* **1** (*formal*) stone or hard seed of a fruit such as a cherry(1).

▷ *tr.v* (*-tt-*) **2** remove pits(1) from (fruit).

pitch¹ /pɪtʃ/ *n* **1** *c.n* marked area of ground for certain games: *a cricket'/hockey/football pitch.* **2** *c.n* (usu — *of s.t*) (degree of a) slope: *the pitch of a field.* **3** *c.n* (*informal*) public place used regularly by a seller, singer etc: *They have a regular pitch in the market.* **4** *u.n* (degree of) high or low quality of the voice, music etc: *high/low pitch.* **5** *c.n* act or way of pitching(9) a ball. **6** *sing.n* (*informal*) way of talking in order to persuade s.o: *He gave me his usual sales pitch.* **7** *c.n* act or way of a ship pitching(12).

▷ *v* **8** *tr/intr.v* (cause (s.o) to) move/fall forward suddenly: *I was pitched (forward) out of my seat.* **9** *tr/intr.v* throw/send (a ball etc) through the air. **10** *tr.v* set up (a tent or tents): *Let's pitch camp (or the tent) over there.* **11** *intr.v* (of ground) slope down. **12** *intr.v* (of a ship) move in such a way that the front goes up and down in the water: *pitching dangerously in rough seas.* Compare roll(5). **13** *tr.v* produce (sound (voice or music)) at a certain level: *The music/singing is pitched too high/low for me.* **pitch in** (*informal*) (**a**) begin to help, do s.t etc, esp with energy: *We all pitched in and finished the work in an hour.* (**b**) give money towards s.t: *All of us pitched in to buy you this present.* **pitch into s.o** attack s.o. **pitch into s.t** = pitch in(a). **pitch s.o out** (*informal*) force a person to leave a building etc. **pitch up (at s.t)** (*informal*) suddenly appear, arrive (at a place): *Guess who pitched up at our house last night!*

'pitch,fork *c.n* large fork with a long handle for lifting straw etc.

pitch² /pɪtʃ/ *u.n* thick black semi-liquid substance used in floors and on roofs to make them waterproof.

,pitch-'black *adj* (of the night, a colour etc) completely dark: *a pitch-black night/room.*

pitcher /'pɪtʃə/ *c.n* large jug.

piteous ⇒ pity.

pitfall ⇒ pit¹.

pith /pɪθ/ *n* **1** *u.n* white layer(1) inside the skin of oranges, lemons etc. **2** *u.n* soft white substance inside the stem of some plants. **3** *def.n* (often — *of s.t*) essential, most important, part or point: *the pith of his argument.*

'pithily *adv.* In a pithy way.

'pithy *adj* (*-ier*, *-iest*) short, detailed and relevant: *a pithy speech.*

pitiful, **pitiless** ⇨ pity.

pitta /'pɪtə/ *c/u.n* kind of flat oval(1) bread (to be) filled with food.

pittance /'pɪtəns/ *c.n* (usu *sing*) very small amount of money: *earn a pittance as a writer.*

pitter-patter /'pɪtə ˌpætə/ *u.n* **1** sound of a series of light taps: *the pitter-patter of small feet in a primary school.* ⇨ patter(1).
▷ *intr.v* **2** make a pitter-patter(1): *The rain pitter-pattered on the window.* ⇨ patter(3).

pity /'pɪtɪ/ *n* **1** *u.n* feeling of sadness or sympathy for the difficulties, sufferings etc of s.o: *Haven't you any pity for that poor child? She showed him no pity when she left him.* **2** *sing.n* (thing that is a) cause of feeling sad or sorry about s.o/s.t: *It's a pity that you weren't able to be there. Not getting the job was a great pity.* **do s.t out of pity (for s.o)** do s.t because one feels sorry (for s.o): *I gave her the money out of pity (for her children).* **for pity's sake** ⇨ sake(4). **have/take pity on s.o** help s.o because one feels sorry for her/him: *I took pity on him and offered him a lift in my car.* **more's the pity** unfortunately: *I didn't succeed, more's the pity.* **What a pity!** How sad, unfortunate etc.
▷ *tr.v* **3** feel pity for (s.o, an animal etc): *She pities you having to work so hard.*

'piteous *adj* deserving pity(1) or causing feelings of pity(1).

'pitiable *adj* deserving one's low opinion: *a pitiable attempt to win the game.*

'pitiful *adj* **1** causing a feeling of sadness or sympathy: *The poor old woman was a pitiful sight.* **2** = pitiable: *a pitiful effort.* **3** very small, bad etc: *a pitiful wage.*

'pitifully *adv.* **'pitifulness** *u.n.*

'pitiless *adj* (*formal*) having or showing no sympathy or mercy: *a pitiless employer.*

'pitilessly *adv.* **'pitilessness** *u.n.*

'pityingly *adv* showing one feels pity(1): *I watched pityingly as the old woman searched the* dustbin.

pivot /'pɪvət/ *c.n* (often — *of* s.t) **1** central point on which s.t turns: *the pivot of a spinning coin.* **2** (*fig*) most important person or part on which s.t depends: *This information is the pivot of her argument. He is the pivot of the sales department.*
▷ *tr/intr.v* **3** (often — (oneself/s.o/s.t) on s.t) (cause (s.o/s.t) to) turn round and round on a central point: *pivoting (herself) on her heels; pivoted a coin on its edge.*

pix /pɪks/ *pl.n* (often — *of* s.o/s.t) (*informal*) pictures; photographs (of s.o/s.t).

pixie /'pɪksɪ/ *c.n* (also **'pixy**) (*pl -ies*) (in stories) kind of naughty fairy(2).

pizza /'piːtsə/ *c/u.n* (also *attrib*) layer(1) of dough(1) covered with cheese, vegetables, meat etc and cooked: *eat a/some pizza; a pizza lunch.*

pl *written abbr* **1** (with capital **P** in names) place(3): *St Martin's Pl.* **2** plural.

placard /'plækɑːd/ *c.n* large written or printed notice: *The students carried placards asking for more money.*

placate /plə'keɪt/ *tr.v* (*formal*) make s.o calm and not angry: *The angry woman could not be placated by the promise of another house.* ⇨ implacable.

place /pleɪs/ *c.n* **1** particular point, position or space: *There's a place for everything in her kitchen. Find an empty place for it.* **2** area such as a city, town, park: *I can't find the place on the map. What's the name of this place? We visited some interesting places during our holiday.* ⇨ place-name. **3** (with capital **P** in names; written *abbr Pl*) open area with houses around the edge in a town: *I live at Queen's Place.* **4** point or position in an order, series(1) etc: *I'm in (the) third place on the list.* **5** job, duty, position etc: *What's your place in the office, football team? Kate's got a place (i.e as a student) at York University. It's your place to look after the children.* **6** seat: *Is there a place for one more at the dinner-table? There are a few more places in the bus.* **7** particular point in a book etc: *I can't find my place now that you've closed the book.* **8** (*informal*) home: *Come over to my place tonight.* **9** (*mathematics*) position of a particular digit(1) in a decimal(2) number: *When you multiply by ten move the decimal point one place to the right, e.g $10.55 \times 10 = 105.5$.* **all over the place** in a disorganized state: *His clothes were lying all over the place.* **change places (with s.o)** (of two people, groups) take each other's place: *I'm before you but I can wait so why don't we change places?* **fall into place** become clear(3): *Once she'd understood the reason, all the other facts fell into place.* **find one's place (a)** ⇨ place(7). **(b)** (*fig*) identify and feel comfortable (in a social group). **give place to s.o/s.t (a)** make space for s.o/s.t. **(b)** be replaced by s.o/s.t: *Small shops have given place to the supermarkets.* Compare take the place of s.o/s.t. **go places (a)** travel widely. **(b)** (*informal*) be successful in one's career(1). **in place** in the correct or suitable position. **have one's heart, one's heart is, in the right place** ⇨ heart(*n*). **in the first, second etc place** firstly etc: *In the first place I don't like them and in the second place they live far away.* **in s.o's place** if one was s.o: *I don't know what I'd do in your place (i.e if I were you).* **in place of s.o/s.t** instead of s.o/s.t: *I went in place of my husband.* **keep/put s.o in her/his place** keep/make s.o less arrogant, proud etc. **know one's place** know (or believe) that one is less important, senior(1) etc. **out of place** not in the correct or suitable position: *These books are out of place. I feel out of place in expensive restaurants.* **pride of place** ⇨ pride. **put s.o in her/his place** ⇨ keep/put s.o in her/his place. **put oneself in s.o else's place** imagine that one is another person: *Put yourself in her place and imagine how you'd feel.* **take place** happen: *Describe to me exactly what took place.* **take one's place** take one's seat at a table, in a theatre etc. **take the place of s.o/s.t (a)** = change places (with s.o/s.t). **(b)** replace s.o/s.t: *Supermarkets have taken the place of small shops.*
▷ *tr.v* **10** put, arrange, (s.o/s.t) in a particular position: *She placed the cups back in the cupboard. Please place the books in alphabetical order. I'm placing you in charge of the department.* **11** consider (s.o/s.t) as being s.t: *I place honesty above profit.* **12** find, decide, a job, position etc for (s.o): *Can we place all the young people in jobs? I placed her in the food department. Many parents place their own children above others.*

13 (usu passive) put (s.o) in first, second etc position in a race: *The favourite wasn't placed.* ⇒ unplaced. **14** make (an order, bet etc): *We've placed an order for a hundred packets. He placed a bet(1) on the last race.* **15** put (an advertisement) (in a newspaper).

'**placement** *c.n* (*formal*) job: *There are a few placements for trained mechanics.*

'**place-,name** *c.n* name of a geographical area, town etc. ⇒ place(2).

'**place-,setting** *c.n* plate with a knife, fork etc where a person will sit at a table. ⇒ place(6).

placenta /pləˈsentə/ *def.n* (*technical*) layer(1) inside a womb which gives a baby food before it is born. ⇒ afterbirth.

placid /ˈplæsɪd/ *adj* calm and not quickly upset: *She is placid* (or *has a placid nature*).

'**placidly** *adv.* '**placidness** *u.n.*

plagiarize, -ise /ˈpleɪdʒəˌraɪz/ *tr/intr.v* take and use (another writer)'s work without permission.

plagiarism /ˈpleɪdʒəˌrɪzəm/ *u.n.*

'**plagiarist** *c.n* person who plagiarizes.

plague /pleɪg/ *c.n* **1** very serious disease that quickly spreads through a community(1), killing many people. **2** (usu — *of s.t*) (*fig*) very large number (of *s.t* unpleasant): *a plague of flies.* **avoid s.o/s.t like the plague** try as hard as one can to avoid s.o/s.t.

▷ *tr.v* **3** (often — *s.o with s.t*) (usu passive) annoy (s.o) with s.t unpleasant: *I've been plagued with a bad headache, lots of little problems.*

plaice /pleɪs/ *n* (*pl* plaice(s)) **1** *c.n* kind of flat fish with spots. **2** *c.n* (also *attrib*) flesh of this fish eaten as food: *plaice fillets.*

plain /pleɪn/ *adj* **1** simple, ordinary; not decorated: *a plain dress; plain cooking; plain furniture.* **2** clear and easy to understand: *plain English/speech/writing; the plain truth.* **3** honest: *a plain speaker. I'll be plain about my feelings.* ⇒ plain-spoken. **4** (of a person, building etc) not attractive(2); not special in any way: *a plain child/design(1,2).* **5** (of a stitch(3) or style(4) of knitting) using the basic(1) and simplest method: *a plain stitch(3); plain knitting.*

▷ *adv* **6** (*informal*) very: *I'm plain bored.*

▷ *c.n* **7** large area of land which is (almost) flat. **8** *u.n* plain(5) knitting style(4): *knit in plain.*

,**plain 'chocolate** *u.n* dark chocolate made with little or no milk. Compare milk chocolate.

'**plain-,clothes** *attrib.adj* not in uniform(2): *a plain-clothes policeman.*

,**plain 'sailing** *u.n* (*informal*) easy regular progress: *After the first examination the rest were plain sailing.*

,**plain-'spoken** *adj* honest and open when speaking: *a plain-spoken critic.*

plaintiff /ˈpleɪntɪf/ *c.n* (*law*) person who brings a case against another person in court. ⇒ defendant.

plaintive /ˈpleɪntɪv/ *adj* (*formal*) sounding sad: *a plaintive cry.*

'**plaintively** *adv.* '**plaintiveness** *u.n.*

plait /plæt/ *c.n* **1** length of hair, straw etc in a pattern made by twisting three sections together: *wearing her hair in plaits.*

▷ *tr.v* **2** make (hair, straw etc) into plaits: *plaiting hair.*

'**plaited** *adj.*

plan /plæn/ *c.n* **1** (often — *of s.t*) drawing (of a building, garden etc) showing edges, sizes, positions etc: *a plan of the rooms, the new shopping centre.* **2** (often — *of s.t*) simple map (of s.t): *a street plan of a city.* **3** detailed idea, arrangement etc of how to do s.t, what to do etc: *We're making plans to win the race. Keep to the agreed plan.* **4** intention: *What are the government plans for this area? We've big plans for you. Their plan is to visit India first.*

▷ *v* (*-nn-*) **5** *tr.v* make a plan(1) of (s.t): *The new houses have been planned in detail.* **6** *tr/intr.v* discuss and agree an idea, arrangement, method etc (for (s.t)): *We must plan ahead by saving for the future. They're busy planning their next business trip.* ⇒ unplanned. **plan on doing s.t; plan to do s.t** intend to do s.t: *We're planning on leaving* (or *to leave*) *early.*

'**planner** *c.n* person who plans(5) s.t: *a town planner.*

'**planning** *u.n* (also *attrib*) act of making plans(1): *town planning; planning permission.*

plane¹ /pleɪn/ *adj* **1** flat; level: *a plane surface; a plane figure/shape.*

▷ *c.n* **2** (also *attrib*) (*informal*) aeroplane: *a plane journey.* **3** flat/level surface: *It's safer to drive on the plane.* **4** level of a standard: *His work isn't on the same plane as hers.* **by plane** in a plane(2): *go/travel by plane.*

▷ *intr.v* **5** glide(2) through the air.

plane² /pleɪn/ *c.n* **1** tool with a wide blade, used to level a surface by gradually cutting off the bumps(3).

▷ *tr/intr.v* **2** use a plane²(1) to level the surface of (s.t): *planing wood (down/off).*

plane³ /pleɪn/ *c.n* (also *attrib*) kind of tree with wide pointed leaves.

planet /ˈplænɪt/ *c.n* one of several large bodies travelling round the sun: *Mercury, Venus, Earth, Mars, Jupiter, Saturn, Uranus and Pluto are all planets.*

'**planetary** /ˈplænɪtərɪ/ *adj.*

plank /plæŋk/ *c.n* **1** (often — *of s.t*) long flat length (of wood), used in building etc.

▷ *tr.v* **2** (usu — *s.t with s.t*) build/cover (s.t) with planks(1) of wood.

'**planking** *u.n* floor made of planks(1).

plankton /ˈplæŋktən/ *u.n* kind of very small animals and plants on or near the surface of water, esp the sea, used as food by fish etc.

plant /plɑːnt/ *n* **1** *c.n* (also *attrib*) living thing, usu with leaves, which is not an animal: *flowering plants; plant life.* **2** *c.n* factory for making large complicated things: *a car plant.* **3** *u.n* machinery for industry: *agricultural plant.* **4** *u.n* something illegal placed in a person's possession without her or his knowledge, esp to get her/him into trouble.

▷ *v* **5** *tr/intr.v* (often — *s.t out*; — *s.t with s.t*) put (seeds, small plants(1), bushes etc) in the ground (in (a place)) so that they will grow: *planting (out) beans/flowers/trees; be busy planting; plant an area with grass.* **6** *tr.v* put (s.t) down firmly: *plant one's feet on the floor; plant oneself in a chair.* **7** *tr.v* establish(2) (s.t) (in the mind): *She planted (in his mind) the idea of a weekend in the country.* ⇒ implant(2). **8** *tr.v* (usu — *s.t on s.o*) (*informal*) put (s.t stolen or illegal) in a person's pocket etc, esp to cause her/him trouble: *The* *young man said that the stolen money had been planted on him.*

'plant ,kingdom *def.n* plants as a category of living things. ⇨ animal kingdom, mineral kingdom, vegetable kingdom.

plantation /plæn'teɪʃən/ *c.n* (often — *of s.t*) area planted with a particular tree or crop: *a tea plantation*; *a plantation of pine¹(1) trees.*

plaque /plɑːk/ *n* **1** *c.n* piece of decorated clay, china etc (to be) fixed to a wall. **2** *u.n* (*technical*) hard substance on the teeth in which bacteria etc can live.

plasma /'plæzmə/ *u.n* (*technical*) liquid part of the blood.

plaster /'plɑːstə/ *n* (also *attrib*) **1** *u.n* substance made by mixing sand, lime¹(1) and water, used to cover walls, ceilings etc: *a plaster ceiling.* **2** *u.n* similar substance that dries quickly and is often used to support broken bones: *Her leg is in plaster. She has a plaster cast(5).* **3** *c.n* (also **'sticking ,plaster**) strip of cloth or plastic(3) with a medicated pad, used to cover a small cut, scratch etc: *Put a plaster on that bad cut.*
▷ *tr.v* (often — *s.t with s.t*) **4** put plaster(1) on (a surface): *plaster a wall.* **5** put plaster(2) round (a part of the body): *plaster an ankle.* **6** put a thick semi-liquid on (s.t): *shoes plastered with mud*; *plaster one's face with cream.*

'plastered *pred.adj* (*informal*) drunk(1).

'plasterer *c.n* person who plasters(4).

plastic /'plæstɪk/ *adj* **1** made of plastic(3): *a plastic cup. Are these shoes plastic?* **2** (*attrib*) (*formal*) changing shape, bending etc easily: *a plastic substance such as rubber.*
▷ *u.n* **3** any kind of manmade(1) substance that is shaped while soft and then goes hard, used to make objects that need to be light, waterproof, non-rust etc: *Plates, bowls, shoes, cloth and pipes are often made of plastic.*

plasticity /plæ'stɪsɪtɪ/ *u.n* (*formal*) (of a substance) quality of easily changing shape, bending etc.

,plastic 'money *u.n* (*informal*) credit cards.

,plastic 'surgeon *c.n* surgeon who repairs, replaces etc bones and skin.

,plastic 'surgery *u.n* work of a plastic surgeon.

plat du jour /,plɑː du 'ʒuə/ *c.n* (*pl plats du jour*, same pronunciation) (*French*) special or suggested dish of the day in a restaurant: *Today's plat du jour is chicken in wine.*

plate /pleɪt/ *n* **1** *c.n* flat dish of china etc for holding food: *a dinner plate.* **2** *c.n* (also **'plateful**) as much of s.t as a plate(1) holds: *a plate of meat.* **3** *c.n* (also *attrib*) flat piece of metal, glass etc: *plate glass*; *metal plates used for printing. The doctor's name was on a brass plate*; *a name plate.* ⇨ hot plate, number plate. **4** shaped piece of plastic(3) with artificial teeth attached: *my bottom/ top plate of teeth.* **5** *u.n* (also *attrib*) things made of or covered with brass(1), gold, silver etc: *gold/ silver plate*; *plate brass*; *plate spoons.* **on a plate** (*fig*; *informal*) very easily; without any problems: *She was given the job on a plate.* **on one's plate** (*fig*; *informal*) waiting for one to do: *I've got a lot (of work) on my plate at the moment.*
▷ *tr.v* **6** cover (an object) with a metal such as brass(1), gold, silver.

'plated *adj* covered with silver etc (⇨ plate(5)): *silver-plated spoons.*

'plateful *c.n* plate(2).

plateau /'plætəʊ/ *c.n* (*pl -s, plateaux* /'plætəʊz/) **1** area of high land with an (almost) flat top. **2** (*fig*) period(1) of an unchanging or standard amount: *My salary has reached a plateau.*
▷ *intr.v* **3** (*informal*) reach a plateau(2): *Costs have plateaued this year.*

platform /'plætfɔːm/ *c.n* **1** part of a floor, stage etc that is higher than the rest: *The speaker stood on the platform.* **2** (also *attrib*) part of a railway station where people can stand or walk by the side of the railway line: *He was waiting for me on the platform. Your train leaves from platform 10 at 6 o'clock.* **3** aims, promises etc of a political party: *Will the parties keep to their platforms if they are elected? They won on a platform of reducing unemployment.*

platinum /'plætɪnəm/ *u.n* (also *attrib*) very valuable silvery metal, *chem. symb* Pt: *a platinum ring*; *an electric contact made of platinum.*

,platinum-'blond *adj/u.n* (esp of hair) (having a) silver-yellow colour.

platitude /'plætɪˌtjuːd/ *c.n* remark (usu about s.t unimportant) that is obviously true and has been made so often that it has lost its force: *It is an old platitude that people who criticize others are usually weak themselves.*

platitudinous /ˌplætɪ'tjuːdɪnəs/ *adj.*

platonic /plə'tɒnɪk/ *adj* (of a relationship) not including sexual love: *a platonic friendship.*

pla'tonically *adv.*

platoon /plə'tuːn/ *c.n* (*military*) division of a company of soldiers.

platter /'plætə/ *c.n* large shallow dish, used for serving food.

plaudits /'plɔːdɪts/ *pl.n* (*formal*) expressions of approval or praise, esp clapping.

plausible /'plɔːzəbl/ *adj* Opposite implausible. **1** seeming to be possible, true etc: *a plausible excuse.* **2** believable: *a plausible speaker.*

plausibility /ˌplɔːzə'bɪlɪtɪ/ *u.n.*

'plausibly *adv.*

play /pleɪ/ *n* **1** *c.n* (also *attrib*) story written in conversations to be acted on the stage, on television etc: *Shakespeare's plays*; *a play reading.* **2** *c.n* performance of a play(1): *She was taken ill during the play last night.* **3** *u.n* (often *at* —) activity done for pleasure, esp by children: *The children are at play in the park. All work and no play can make you ill.* **4** *u.n* activity of playing a game: *We must try harder during tomorrow's play. Rain stopped play.* **5** *c.n* turn/chance for a person to play a game: *It's your play now.* **6** *c.n* (often — *to do s.t*) act/activity whose purpose is to make s.t untrue seem to be true: *Saying she had a headache was a play to be allowed to go home early.* **7** *u.n* (amount of) freedom in the movement of a rope etc: *give the rope lots of play.* **8** *u.n* activity of light etc moving about: *the play of the sun on water.* **be child's play** ⇨ child(*n*). **give play to s.t** express a particular feeling openly: *give play to one's anger.* **in**, **out of**, **play** inside, outside, the field (during a game of football, hockey etc): *The ball was in, out of, play.* **make a play for s.o/s.t** try to get a person or thing for oneself: *He made a play for her at the party by offering to buy her a drink.* **a play on words** = pun(1). ⇨ wordplay.
▷ *v* **9** *intr.v* (often — *about*) do things for pleasure: *The children have gone out to play. They were*

playing (*about*) *in the park. Come and play with us.* **10** *tr/intr.v* take part in (a game, sport etc): *play football/cards with friends; playing him at* chess; *play well/badly; play* (rugby) *for England. It's your turn to play.* **11** *tr/intr.v* take a particular position, job, in a team game: *play the main* attacker; *play in the* midfield. **12** *tr/intr.v* act (a particular part) in a play(1): *play* (*the lead*) *in the school production of 'Hamlet'.* **13** *tr/intr.v* perform (a play(1)): *Where is 'Death of a Salesman'* playing? *The National Theatre is playing it.* **14** *tr/ intr.v* (often — *the s.t*) perform on (a musical instrument): *play the* guitar. **15** *tr/intr.v* perform (music): *play Elton John's music on the piano; play with one hand.* **16** *tr.v* make (a radio(2), record player etc) work: *play* (*Beatles music on*) *the* record player *too loudly; play one's radio in the* bathroom; *play* (*a tape on*) *her* cassette-player. **17** *intr.v* pretend: *I wasn't serious when I said that — I was only playing.* **18** *tr/intr.v* (cause (light, water etc) to) move across/over a surface: *play water onto the lawns and flowers; with light playing on the river.*
play s.o along; play along (with s.o) agree with, help, s.o, usu to get an advantage for oneself: *I only played along with her to get the information I wanted.*
play at s.t (a) pretend to be/do s.t: *play at being in love, at studying.* **(b)** (usu used to show anger because one disapproves of what s.o is doing) do s.t without being serious: *He's only playing at becoming a lawyer — he never does any work. What are you playing at?*
play s.t back (a) play music, a tape(2) etc in order to listen to it again or after it has been recorded. ⇒ playback. **(b)** send a ball etc to the player one got it from.
play s.t by ear ⇒ ear.
play s.t down make a mistake, problem, illness etc seem less serious or important: *The manager played down the firm's* financial *difficulties.*
play fair (with s.o) ⇒ fair¹(7).
play the fool ⇒ fool(n).
play a game ⇒ play(10). **play s.o's game; play the game** ⇒ game(n).
play to the gallery ⇒ gallery.
play hard to get ⇒ hard(adj).
play into s.o's hands ⇒ hand(n).
play the market ⇒ market(n).
play off play the last deciding game in a competition. ⇒ play-off. **play s.o/s.t off against s.o/s.t else** make a person, organization etc act against another in a way that gives oneself an advantage: *He played the unions off against each other in order to force an agreement.*
play on continue playing a game: *It was raining but we played on.* **play on s.t** use s.o's weakness, fear etc to get s.t: *He plays on her kindness to get his clothes washed.*
play (it) rough ⇒ rough(adv).
play (it) safe ⇒ safe(adj).
play a sport ⇒ play(10).
play for time ⇒ time(n).
play truant ⇒ truant.
play with fire ⇒ fire(n).
'playable *adj* good enough, ready, to be used for a game: *wait for the tennis courts to be playable.* Opposite unplayable.

'play₁acting *u.n* (*informal*) act or fact of pretending.
'play₁back *c.n* act of playing a tape(2) etc again or after it has just been recorded.
'play₁boy *c.n* (*informal*) young rich man who enjoys a life of (wild) pleasure.
'player *c.n* person taking part in a game, sport etc: *a football player.*
'playful *adj* (of a person, animal) lively and enjoying being happy: *a playful* kitten/child.
'playfully *adv.* **'playfulness** *u.n.*
'play₁goer *c.n* person who goes to a theatre to watch a play(2).
'play₁ground *c.n* area outside a school etc for children to play.
'play₁group *c.n* daily class for very young children: *My three-year-old daughter goes to a playgroup.*
'play₁house *c.n* theatre: *the Oxford Playhouse.*
'playing ₁card *c.n* ⇒ card(5).
'play₁mate *c.n* (*informal*) friend of a young person.
'play-₁off *c.n* game that will decide a competition.
'play-₁pen *c.n* set of four fences linked in a square where a child can play safely.
'play₁room *c.n* room for children to play in.
'play₁school *c.n* school for children below five years old.
'play₁thing *c.n* **1** toy. **2** (*informal*) person treated as not important: *I'm only your plaything, you never did love me.*
'play₁time *u.n* period of time for play between lessons at school.
playwright /'pleɪ₁raɪt/ *c.n* person who writes plays(1).
plc /₁piː el 'siː/ *abbr* public limited company. ⇒ ltd.
plea /pliː/ *c.n* **1** (often — *for s.t*) (*formal*) serious request (for s.t): *a plea for more money; pleas from the organizers for a peaceful* demonstration(3). **2** (usu — *of s.t*) (*law*) person's reply to an accusation in court: *enter a plea of guilty, not guilty.* **3** (usu — *of s.t*) (*formal*) excuse (based on s.t): *a plea of bad health.*
plead /pliːd/ *v* (*p.t,p.p* -ed, pled /pled/) **1** *intr.v* (usu — (*with s.o*) *for s.t, to do s.t*) make a serious request (to s.o) (to do s.t): *plead with the government for more help.* **2** *tr.v* (*law*) make a plea(2) of (s.t): *plead* insanity. *What do you plead? Do you plead guilty or not guilty?* **3** *tr/intr.v* (usu — (*s.t*) (*for s.o*)) (*law*) (of a lawyer) present (s.o's case) in court: *Mr Martin will plead* (*my case*) *for me.* **4** *tr.v* (*formal*) give (s.t) as an excuse: *plead* ignorance, *poverty.*
'pleading *adj* showing one is seriously wanting s.t: *a pleading expression.*
pleasant /'pleznt/ *adj* causing a feeling of pleasure: *a pleasant smell/sound/taste; pleasant* weather; *a pleasant journey/holiday/evening/ smile/conversation.* Opposite unpleasant.
'pleasantly *adv.* **'pleasantness** *u.n.*
please /pliːz/ *interj* **1** (used with a polite request, question etc): *Please come in. Can you help me, please? Please go away. 'Can I join you?' 'Please do.' 'Would you like some coffee?' 'Yes, please.'*
▷ *v* **2** *tr.v* give pleasure, happiness, satisfaction etc to (s.o): *It's impossible to please everyone. She's very difficult to please. He's so pleased that you could come. I'm very pleased to meet you at last.* ⇒

displease. **3** _intr.v_ (esp _as s.o_ —_s_) want: _He thinks he can do exactly as he pleases. Do as you please — I don't care._ **pleased** (**with s.o/s.t**) (**about s.t**) feeling happy, satisfied etc (with s.o/s.t) (about s.t): _Your teacher is very pleased with you_ (or _your work_). _He's not very pleased about the damage to his car._ **please yourself** (used to show mild anger when one disagrees or disapproves): _If you must buy it, please yourself, but I don't like it._

'**pleasing** _adj_ that pleases(2) one: _a pleasing smile._

pleasure /'pleʒə/ _n_ **1** _c/u.n_ (also _attrib_) act, event, occasion etc that pleases(2): _the pleasure of a pretty garden. Seeing him so happy is a great pleasure to us_ (or _gives us so much pleasure or was such a pleasure_). _May we have the pleasure of your company at dinner? 'Have you met Jane?' 'I don't think I've had the pleasure.'_ **2** _u.n_ (also _attrib_) amusement/enjoyment (and not a necessity or work): _Is it a trip for pleasure or work? It's a pleasure trip._

'**pleasurable** _adj_ (_formal_) enjoyable; satisfying: _a pleasurable hobby._

'**pleasure ,boat**/,**craft** _c.n_ boat designed(6) and used for enjoyment.

pleat /pliːt/ _c.n_ **1** vertical fold made in cloth: _a skirt with pleats._
▷ _tr.v_ **2** make a pleat(1) or pleats in cloth.

'**pleated** _adj_: _a pleated skirt._

pleb /pleb/ _adj/c.n_ (_informal_) plebeian(2,4).

plebeian /plə'biːən/ _adj_ **1** of or referring to ordinary people. **2** (_informal_ **pleb**) (_derog_) (of a person, behaviour etc) having, showing, low class or vulgar(1) qualities: _a plebeian style of writing_; _a plebeian writer._
▷ _c.n_ **3** ordinary person, not an aristocrat. **4** (_informal_ **pleb**) (_derog_) person who is plebeian(2).

'**plebby** _adj_ (-ier, -iest) (_informal_) ordinary and dull: _a plebby life in London._

plebiscite /'plebɪ,saɪt/ _c.n_ (_formal_) vote by everyone on a particular matter; referendum.

pled /pled/ _p.t_ of plead.

pledge /pledʒ/ _n_ **1** _c/u.n_ (_formal_) serious promise: _I've given you my pledge. We exchanged news under pledge of complete secrecy._ **2** _c.n_ thing given to s.o to be kept until s.t else is done, returned etc: _We gave them the car as a pledge that we would repay the money._
▷ _tr.v_ **3** (_formal_) promise (s.t): _I've pledged my support._ **4** give (s.t) as a pledge(2).

plenary /'pliːnərɪ/ _adj_ (_formal_) **1** involving all the members: _a plenary meeting._ **2** unlimited: _have plenary powers._

plenty /'plentɪ/ _pron_ (esp — of s.o/s.t) **1** large amount/number (of s.o/s.t): _We've plenty of time/money/food. There are plenty of plates/ reasons/methods._ **2** enough: _£5 will be plenty for the ticket._

'**plentiful** _adj_ (_formal_) to be found in large amounts: _Oranges are plentiful in May._ Opposite scarce.

plethora /'pleθərə/ _sing.n_ (usu _a_ — of s.t) (_formal_) large amount (of s.t); too many (of s.t): _a plethora of goals; a plethora of silly excuses._

pleurisy /'plʊərɪsɪ/ _u.n_ serious illness with a sore and inflamed lining around the lungs.

pliable /'plaɪəbl/ _adj_ **1** (of a substance) easily bent, shaped etc. **2** (of a person, mind) easily persuaded or influenced.

pliability /,plaɪə'bɪlɪtɪ/ _u.n._

pliant /'plaɪənt/ _adj_ = pliable. ⇨ compliant.

pliers /'plaɪəz/ _pl.n_ (often _a pair of_ —) kind of hand tool with two long pieces that can be closed to bend, hold etc s.t firmly.

plight /plaɪt/ _c.n_ seriously bad situation, state etc: _the plight of poor and hungry children._

plimsoll /'plɪmsəl/ _c.n_ (_old use_) kind of light canvas(1) tennis shoe: _a pair of plimsolls._

plinth /plɪnθ/ _c.n_ (usu square) bottom part of a column, base of a statue etc.

plod /plɒd/ _c.n_ **1** act or sound of plodding (⇨ plod(2)).
▷ _v_ (-dd-) **2** _tr/intr.v_ walk slowly (as if) with much effort(1): _plodding along the road in the hot sun._ **3** _intr.v_ work slowly and with much effort(1): _plodding through a dull book._

'**plodder** _c.n_ (_derog_) person who plods(3).

plonk[1] /plɒŋk/ _c.n_ **1** (often — of s.t) act or deep sound of dropping s.t flat and heavy: _the plonk of a heavy bag on the floor._
▷ _tr.v_ **2** (esp — s.t down (on s.t)) put or drop (s.t heavy or oneself) on a surface with a dull soft sound: _He plonked his bag_ (_down_) _on the table. She plonked herself down on the floor._

plonk[2] /plɒŋk/ _u.n_ (_informal_) cheap wine.

plop /plɒp/ _c.n_ **1** (usu — of s.t) act or short sound (like that) of s.t falling (into water etc): _the plop of the rain; the plop of a stone falling in the river._
▷ _intr.v_ (-pp-) **2** fall with, make, the sound of a plop(1): _The fish was plopping about in the water. The rain plopped down._

plot /plɒt/ _c.n_ **1** secret plan to do s.t (esp s.t bad): _a plot to steal the winner(1)'s cup._ **2** story in a play, novel[1], film etc: _I can't understand the plot. What's the main plot of the film?_ **3** small area (of land) for a particular use: _a building plot; a vegetable plot; a plot of land._
▷ _v_ (-tt-) **4** _tr/intr.v_ take part in a plot(1) to do (s.t): _plotting to kill the leader._ **5** _tr.v_ make (a plan, map etc): _plot a map of the area; plot a route through the mountains; plot a graph of the different replies._

'**plotter** _c.n_ person who plots (esp 4).

plough /plaʊ/ _c.n_ (US **plow**) **1** kind of large tool usu pulled by a tractor, horses etc, used on a farm to turn and break up the soil. ⇨ snowplough.
▷ _v_ (US **plow**) **2** _tr/intr.v_ use a plough (on (s.t)): _ploughing the fields._ **3** _tr.v_ (_informal_) decide that (s.o) has failed an examination or test. **plough s.t back** put money earned back into a business, project(1) etc. **plough into s.t** hit s.t with great force: _The lorry ploughed into the back of our car._ **plough through s.t** make one's way through s.t with difficulty: _plough through the mud; ploughing through a dull book._

'**ploughman** _c.n_ (US '**plowman**) (_pl_ -men) person who ploughs(2).

,**ploughman's** ('**lunch**) _c.n_ meal of cheese, bread etc: _order a ploughman's in a pub._

'**plough,share** _c.n_ (US '**plow,share**) long, wide blade of a plough(1).

ploy /plɔɪ/ _c.n_ skilful planned method(1,2) in a conversation, activity etc in order to achieve(1) s.t: _She said she needed more information as a ploy to gain more time before being forced to act._

pluck[1] /plʌk/ _u.n_ courage: _The young competitor showed lots of pluck._

pluck² /plʌk/ *c.n* **1** short pull: *a pluck of her sleeve.*

▷ *v* **2** *tr.v* remove (feathers, hairs, fruit etc) from (s.t) by pulling: *plucking apples from a tree*; *plucking a chicken.* **3** *tr/intr.v* (often — *at* s.t) pull (s.t): *I plucked (at) her sleeve.* **4** *tr/intr.v* (often — *at* s.t) play (a stringed musical instrument) by pulling the strings: *plucking (at) a guitar.* **pluck up (the) courage (to do s.t)** become brave (enough to do s.t): *I'd swim across if I could pluck up enough courage.*

'plucky *adj* (-ier, -iest) brave; determined: *The plucky young girl learned to walk again after her accident.*

plug /plʌg/ *c.n* **1** piece of rubber etc used to block the hole in a sink. **2** piece of wood, metal etc used to block a hole: *a plug in a barrel.* **3** device with two or three pins on one side, used to make an electrical connection. ⇔ socket. **4 =** sparking plug. **5** (often — *for* s.t) (*informal*) favourable statement about the good qualities of s.o/s.t, esp on television, the radio etc: *a plug for a new record on the radio.*

▷ *tr.v* (-gg-) **6** (often — *s.t up* (*with* s.t)) block or fill (a hole etc) (as if) with a plug(1,2) (using s.t): *We plugged (up) the leak with a piece of cloth. She plugged her ears with* cotton-wool. **7** (often — *s.t into* s.t) put (s.t) into anything that has a hole: *She plugged* cotton-wool *into her ears.* **8** (*informal*) make a plug(5) about (s.t): *plug a new record.* **plug away (at s.t)** (*informal*) work hard (at s.t): *He was plugging away at learning English grammar.* **plug s.t in** use a plug(3) to make an electrical connection for (a piece of apparatus): *plug in a kettle.*

plum¹ /plʌm/ *adj* **1** (dark) purple-red in colour: *a plum hat*; *plum shoes*; *paint the gate plum.*

▷ *n* **2** *c.n* (also *attrib*) (kind of tree with a) dark red, purple or yellow round fruit with soft flesh and a stone inside: *a plum tree*; *plum jam.* **3** *u.n* (dark) purple-red colour: *Choose plum for the curtains.*

plum² /plʌm/ *attrib.adj* **1** (*informal*) (of a job etc) very good: *a plum post in the government.* **plum³** /plʌm/ *adv* ⇒ plumb(1).

plumage /'pluːmɪdʒ/ *u.n* feathers on a bird's body.

plumb /plʌm/ *adv* **1** (also **plum**) extremely: *plumb crazy.* **2** exactly: *plumb in the middle.*

▷ *c.n* **3** weight at the bottom of a rope etc, used to show a vertical line, the depth of water etc.

▷ *tr.v* **4** join (a tap etc) to a pipe for water. **5** understand or solve (a problem): *plumb the cause of the accident.* **6** experience (the extreme of s.t unpleasant): *plumb the depths of despair.*

'plumber *c.n* person who fits and repairs pipes, taps etc, esp for water in a house.

'plumbing *u.n* fitting and repair of pipes, taps etc.

'plumb,line *c.n* line to which a plumb(3) is fixed.

plume /pluːm/ *c.n* large showy feather: *a peacock's plumes.*

plummet /'plʌmɪt/ *intr.v* drop/fall quickly and directly: *The bag plummeted to the bottom of the mountain. Prices have plummeted.*

plummy /'plʌmɪ/ *adj* (-ier, -iest) (*derog*; *informal*) (of a voice) using a style to appear upper-class, rich etc: *a plummy voice/accent(1).*

plump¹ /plʌmp/ *adj* **1** fat and round: *a plump chicken*; *a plump-looking woman.*

▷ *tr.v* **2** (usu — s.t out/up) make (a cushion, pillow etc) fat and round: *I'll plump up your pillow for you.*

plump² /plʌmp/ *sing.n* **1** sudden heavy fall: *He sat down with a plump.*

▷ *tr/intr.v* **2** (usu — (oneself/s.t) down) (cause (oneself/s.t) to) fall suddenly and heavily: *She plumped herself down in a chair. The old woman plumped down on the wall.* **plump for s.o/s.t** (*informal*) decide to choose s.o/s.t, esp after considering other possibilities: *We've plumped for a holiday in Greece.*

plunder /'plʌndə/ *u.n* **1** (*formal*) goods stolen, esp during a war: *The paintings were part of the enemy's plunder.*

▷ *tr/intr.v* **2** (*formal*) steal things from (a place), esp during a war: *The soldiers plundered the village for food, the valuables in the town.*

plunge /plʌndʒ/ *c.n* **1** act of plunging (⇒ plunge(2)): *a plunge from the boat into the water.* **take the plunge** (*informal*) **(a)** (decide to) do s.t after hesitating. **(b)** get married.

▷ *v* **2** *intr.v* throw oneself head first (into water): *The bird flew down and plunged into the river.* **3** *tr.v* (usu — s.t into s.t) **(a)** put/push (s.t) quickly into s.t: *He plunged the hot metal into the water.* **(b)** (often passive) (*fig*) create a (usu unpleasant) situation in (s.t) suddenly and violently: *The country was plunged into war. The room was plunged into darkness.* **plunge in** (*informal*) join in a conversation, begin an activity etc with energy(1) and determination: *He plunged in and gave his opinion.*

'plunger *c.n* device with a rubber cap on a handle, used to clear a blocked pipe.

pluperfect (tense) /pluːˈpɜːfɪkt/ *def.n* (*grammar*; *old use*) **=** past perfect (tense).

plural /'plʊərəl/ *adj* **1** (*written abbr* pl) (*grammar*) showing that more than one person, thing etc is included: *The plural form of 'child' is 'children'.* Opposite singular(1).

▷ *c/def.n* **2** (*written abbr* pl) (often *in* the —; the — of s.t) (*grammar*) state or word that is plural(1): *'Children' is in the plural. What is the plural of 'mouse'?* Opposite singular(3).

plus /plʌs/ *adj* **1** (*attrib*) (*mathematics*) (of the sign '+' that shows a number) more than 0: *The temperature was +10°C last night.* **2** (*pred*) with a value above the stated standard: *I got B+ for the examination.* **3** (*pred*) and more: *There were sixteen plus in the boat. You must be aged 18+ to be able to join.* Opposite minus.

▷ *c.n* **4** (also **'plus ,sign**) sign (+) showing addition: *4 + 5 = 9.* **5** advantage; good thing: *This job has a lot of pluses.* Compare minus.

▷ *prep* **6** with the addition of: *He earns £13000 a year plus a car.*

'plus ,sign *c.n* ⇒ plus(n).

plush /plʌʃ/ *adj* **1** (also **'plushy** (-ier, -iest)) richly furnished or decorated: *a plush room.*

▷ *u.n* **2** kind of cloth like velvet.

plutocracy /pluːˈtɒkrəsɪ/ *c/u.n* (*pl* -ies) (country with a) government by the rich people in the community(2).

plutocrat /'pluːtəˌkræt/ *c.n* **1** person who supports and believes in plutocracy. **2** (*derog*) rich person.

plutocratic /ˌpluːtəˈkrætɪk/ *adj* of or referring to plutocracy: *a plutocratic government.*

Pluto /ˈpluːtəʊ/ *unique n* (*astronomy*) farthest known planet from the sun.

plutonium /pluːˈtəʊnɪəm/ *u.n* chemical substance found in very small amounts in uranium and used in nuclear power/weapons(1), *chem. symb* Pu.

ply[1] /plaɪ/ *u.n* often as the second part of a word showing the number of threads(1), layers(1) etc): *4-ply wool; 3-ply wood.*

'ply,wood *u.n* kind of flat wooden material made by joining thin layers(1) of wood.

ply[2] /plaɪ/ *v* (*-ies, -ied*) **1** *tr.v* (usu — *s.o with s.t*) give (s.o) the same thing often: *She plied me with whisky(1). Stop plying her with questions.* **2** *tr.v* (*old use*) work at (s.t): *plying one's trade in the market.* **3** *intr.v* (*formal*) (of a ship etc) travel regularly: *The boats ply between England and France.*

pneumatic /njuːˈmætɪk/ *attrib.adj* (*technical*) **1** filled with air: *pneumatic tyres.* **2** operated by using a rush of air: *a pneumatic drill.*

pneumonia /njuːˈməʊnɪə/ *u.n* serious illness of the lungs.

po /pəʊ/ *c.n* (*informal*) pot for urine.

PO /ˌpiː ˈəʊ/ *abbr* **1** post office: *PO Box 32.* **2** personnel officer. **3** postal order.

poach[1] /pəʊtʃ/ *tr.v* boil (eggs) without a shell; cook (fish etc) by boiling gently: *poached eggs; fish poached in milk.*

poach[2] /pəʊtʃ/ *tr/intr.v* **1** steal (animals, birds, fish etc) from s.o's land. **2** take (another person's or business's ideas, staff etc): *He poached the idea for his painting from his brightest student.*

'poacher *c.n* person who poaches[2].

pocket /ˈpɒkɪt/ *c.n* **1** (also *attrib*) thing like a bag sewn on/in clothes, used for carrying small things: *a pocket dictionary/handkerchief. Take your hands out of your pockets.* **2** (also **'pocketful**) as much as a pocket(1) holds. **3** (often — *of s.t*) small area/place filled with s.o/s.t: *pockets of air; an air-pocket; pockets of gold in the ground; pockets of opposition(3) to the new government policy.* **in, out of, pocket** having gained/lost money after a business deal. **line one's (own) pockets** make money for oneself, esp dishonestly. **pick s.o's pocket** steal from s.o's clothes etc while he/she is wearing them. ⇒ pickpocket.

▷ *tr.v* **4** put (s.t) in one's pocket: *She pocketed the change from the shopping.* **5** steal (s.t) and put it in one's pocket: *I saw you pocketing the money.*

'pocket ,calcu,lator *c.n* = calculator(1).

'pocketful *c.n* = pocket(2).

'pocket ,knife *c.n* = penknife.

'pocket ,money *u.n* amount of money given by a parent etc to a child, grandchild etc each month, week etc.

pod /pɒd/ *c.n* **1** long green case grown on a plant and containing beans, peas or seeds: *a bean pod.*

▷ *tr.v* (*-dd-*) **2** remove (beans etc) from pods(1): *podding peas.*

podgy /ˈpɒdʒɪ/ *adj* (*-ier, -iest*) (*informal*, sometimes *derog*) (of a person) short and fat.

'podginess *u.n.*

poem /ˈpəʊɪm/ *c.n* piece of writing organized in lines with a rhythm(1) (and sometimes rhyme(3))

to suit the ideas or feelings being expressed: *a love poem.*

poet /ˈpəʊɪt/ *c.n* person who writes poems.

poetess /ˈpəʊɪtɪs/ *c.n* (*rare*) woman poet.

poetic /pəʊˈetɪk/ *adj* of, referring to, like, poems or poets: *a poetic style of writing.*

po,etic 'justice *u.n* suitable but not planned punishment for s.t, e.g unkind behaviour.

po,etic 'licence *u.n* freedom (as if) of a poet to use unusual language, logic(1) etc.

poetry /ˈpəʊɪtrɪ/ *u.n* (art of writing) poems in general.

po-faced /ˈpəʊ ˌfeɪst/ *adj* (*informal*) having a fixed expression of disapproval.

pogrom /ˈpɒgrəm/ *c.n* organized killing of a particular racial(1) or religious group of people.

poignant /ˈpɔɪnɪənt/ *adj* **1** (*informal*) causing feelings of pain, sadness etc: *poignant descriptions of life in poor areas of the country.* **2** relevant and important: *a poignant argument.*

point /pɔɪnt/ *c.n* (*written abbr* pt) **1** (often *the — of s.t*) smaller sharp end of a needle, pin, nail etc: *the point of a pencil, knife; a knife-point.* **2** small round mark (as if) made by a point(1): *a decimal point.* **3** particular place on a map, in a view etc: *I can't find the point where the river begins. Find a point on that hill near the trees.* **4** (with capital **P** in names) long narrow piece of land going out to sea: *fishing off the point; Cape Point.* **5** one of the marked positions of a compass(1). ⇒ cardinal point. **6** unit in a system of scoring or on a scale: *We won by 16 points to 8* (or *16 pts to 8*). *Extra points are scored for difficult questions. What is the freezing-point of petrol?* **7** particular moment: *I'm not able to help at this point. From that point the journey became even more difficult.* **8** particular characteristic(2): *All students, political opinions, buildings, have their good and bad points. That's my strong/weak point.* **9** (often *the — of s.t*) particular reason, subject, detail etc in speech or writing: *What's the main point of the story? Another point of her argument is the need to save lives. What's the point of worrying? The point is that no one believes you. We are agreed on that point.* **10** one of two parts of an electric circuit(4) that may be joined. ⇒ power-point. **be beside the point** not be relevant. **be on the point of doing s.t** be close to the moment when one will do s.t: *I was on the point of leaving when you telephoned.* **a case in point** ⇒ case. **come to a point** (of a stick etc) have a pointed end. **come to the point** (esp as an order) stop avoiding the main reason for speaking. **in point of fact** (used when giving an explanation or making s.t clear) actually: *You say I did it but in point of fact I was with Anne at the time of the murder.* **I take your point (but . . .)** I understand your opinion (but . . .). **make a point of (doing) s.t** make certain that one does s.t: *I made a point of turning out the lights before I left.* **make a/one's point** explain an idea, one's opinion etc about s.t clearly. **miss the point (of s.t)** fail to understand the point(9) (of s.t said or written). **not to put too fine a point on it** speaking without hiding one's true opinion. **on the point of s.t** about to reach/do s.t: *She's on the point of death.* **the point at issue** ⇒ issue(*n*). **the point in question** ⇒ question(*n*). **a point of honour** thing that one must do because it is one's moral(1) responsibility, duty etc. **point of order** thing that concerns (a detail of) a rule: *He was refused membership on a point of order.* **point of view** opinion. ⇨ viewpoint. **stretch a point** make an exception. **the finer points of s.t** the very small details about s.t. **to the point** relevant. **up to a point** to a certain extent but not completely: *I believe you* (or *You're right*) *up to a point.*

▷ *v* **11** *tr.v* aim (s.t) at a particular person, thing, place etc: *He pointed a gun at the thief.* **12** *tr/intr.v* aim (one's finger) at a person, thing etc to identify her/him/it or when making a point etc: *She pointed to/towards the window. Stop pointing* (*your finger*) *at me.* **point s.o/s.t out** point(12) to identify a person, thing etc in a group.

‚point-'blank *adj* **1** (of a gun) aimed/fired from a position very close to the person, thing etc (to be) hit.
▷ *adv* **2** (*informal*) plainly: *I told her point-blank that I was angry.*

'pointed *adj* **1** having a point(1): *pointed shoes.* **2** clearly aimed at a particular person: *a pointed remark about his smelly feet.*
'pointedly *adv* in a pointed(2) way.
'pointer *c.n* **1** person or thing who/that points(11). **2** long pointed(1) part that moves to show a particular measurement in an instrument. **3** (often — *to s.t*) fact or piece of information etc that helps one to understand or decide s.t: *The increased sales are a useful pointer* (*to a better future for the business company*).
'pointless *adj* (esp) not worth doing, saying etc: *It's pointless to argue.*
'pointlessly *adv.* 'pointlessness *u.n.*
points *pl.n* two short rails(3) that move to allow a train to change from one railway line to another.

poise /pɔɪz/ *u.n* **1** confidence and quiet pride: *She shows remarkable poise when she meets important people.* **2** state of being able to balance well: *Dancers have to have a lot of poise.*
▷ *tr.v* (*formal*) **3** balance (s.t): *The plate was poised on the edge of the table. He poised the spoon on the end of his finger.*
poised *adj* (usu *pred*) in a state and position ready for an activity: *He was poised to start running. Is the party poised to win a sudden election?*

poison /'pɔɪzn/ *u.n* **1** substance that causes death or serious illness if eaten, drunk, injected etc. **2** thing that destroys or harms s.o's reputation etc: *poison in his criticism of the play.* **One man's meat is another man's poison** ⇨ meat.
▷ *tr.v* **3** use poison(1) to kill/harm (a person or an animal).
'poisoned *adj* **1** containing poison: *poisoned meat.* **2** affected by poison: *a poisoned dog.* **3** very harmful: *poisoned words of criticism.*
'poisoner *c.n* person who tries to poison(3) s.o.
'poisoning *u.n* **1** poison(1). **2** act of affecting s.o with, by adding, poison.
'poisonous *adj* **1** able to kill or cause serious illness: *Are these berries poisonous?* Opposite non-poisonous. **2** (*fig*) causing great harm: *a poisonous review of a new play.*
‚poison 'pen ‚letter *c.n* letter, usually anonymous(2), that contains serious criticism of a person and is intended to hurt or frighten her/him.

poke[1] /pəʊk/ *c.n* **1** act of poking (⇨ poke(2)): *a poke in the eye with a stick.*
▷ *v* **2** *tr/intr.v* (often — *at s.o/s.t*) push one's finger, a stick etc into (s.o/s.t): *He poked me in the back with his umbrella. He poked at the ground.* **3** *tr/intr.v* (cause (s.o/s.t) to) be seen (over an edge etc): *She poked her head out of the window, round the door. Be careful, there's a stick poking out of the water.* **poke about/around** (**for s.t**) look (for s.t) by poking (⇨ poke(2)): *He was poking about in the dark for his keys.* **poke fun at s.o/s.t** ⇨ fun. **poke one's nose into s.t** ⇨ nose(*n*).
poker[1] /'pəʊkə/ *c.n* long piece of metal used to poke(2) a fire.
poke[2] /pəʊk/ *c.n* **a pig in a poke** ⇨ pig.
poker[2] /'pəʊkə/ *u.n* (also *attrib*) kind of card game, often used for gambling(1): *a poker player.*
poky /'pəʊkɪ/ *adj* (*-ier, -iest*) (*informal*) (of a room, space) too small.

polar, polarity ⇨ pole[2].
Polaroid /'pəʊlərɔɪd/ *unique n* (also *attrib*) (*t.n*) **1** kind of material(4) used in sunglasses etc to prevent glare(2): *Polaroid glasses.* **2** kind of camera or photographic film used to produce photographs after a few seconds: *a Polaroid camera.*
'Pola‚roids *pl.n* (*t.n*) (*informal*) Polaroid(1) sunglasses.
pole[1] /pəʊl/ *c.n* long round piece of wood, metal etc, esp used as a support: *a tent pole; bean poles.* **up the pole** (*slang*) mad.
'pole ‚vault *c/def.n* **1** athletic(1) activity or competition using a long pole to get over a high bar.
▷ *intr.v* **2** take part in a pole vault(1).
'pole ‚vaulter *c.n* person who pole vaults(2).
pole[2] /pəʊl/ *n* **1** *def.n* (also with capital **P**) one of two points at the top and bottom of the earth: *the North/South Pole.* **2** *def.n* one of two opposite ends of a bar magnet(1). **3** *c/n* one of two different terminals(4) on a battery: *the positive(11)/negative(4) pole.* **be poles apart** have very different opinions, ways of living etc.
polar /'pəʊlə/ *attrib.adj* of or referring to (the regions near) one or both poles[2](1): *polar ice.*
‚polar 'bear *c.n* kind of white furry bear living near the North Pole[2](1).
polarity /pəʊ'lærɪtɪ/ *u.n* **1** (*technical*) condition of having two opposite poles[2](2). **2** (often — *of s.t*) tendency (of s.t) to progress, separate and go in two opposite directions: *the polarity of the two main parties in British politics.*
polarization, -isation /‚pəʊləraɪ'zeɪʃən/ *u.n.*
'pola‚rize, -ise *tr/intr.v* (cause (s.t) to) divide into two opposite groups: *Opinion about nuclear(2) weapons(1) has polarized.*
police /pə'liːs/ *def.pl.n* (also *attrib*) group of trained men and women whose job is to keep law and order in society and to try to stop crime: *If you don't go away, I'll call the police. The police are guarding the entrance. That's a police car/dog. He's not in police uniform(2).*
▷ *tr.v* **2** (watch in order to) keep law and order in (a place): *policing the gardens of the house.*
po‚lice 'constable *c.n* = constable.
po‚lice ‚force *n* **1** *c.n* group of police responsible for an area: *the police force in London.* **2** *def.n* all groups of police.

po'liceman c.n (pl -men) male member of the police.

po'lice ,officer c.n policeman or policewoman.

po'lice ,state c.n country with a very strict government that prevents political opposition(1,2) by using the police.

po'lice ,station c.n office of a particular police force in an area: *Come with me to the police station. He's at the police station.*

po'lice,woman c.n (pl -,women) female member of the police.

policy[1] /'pɒləsɪ/ c/u.n (pl -ies) (also attrib) planned way of acting, behaving etc based on beliefs, purposes etc: *What is the policy of the government towards aid(1) for developing countries? In this instance, patience is the better policy. The minister made a policy statement.*

policy[2] /'pɒlɪsɪ/ c.n (pl -ies) (also attrib) official written statement agreeing to conditions for insurance: *a policy document; an insurance policy.*

'policy-,holder c.n person who owns a policy[2] for herself/himself or her/his things.

polio /'pəʊlɪəʊ/ u.n (formal **poliomyelitis** /,pəʊlɪəʊ,maɪə'laɪtɪs/) serious disease causing weakness and wasting of muscles(1) and paralysis(1).

polish /'pɒlɪʃ/ n 1 u.n kind of paste or semi-liquid substance used to make surfaces smooth and shiny: *furniture polish; car polish.* 2 sing.n act or result of polishing (⇒ polish(4)): *give the table top a good polish.* 3 u.n well-trained and fine manners, way of writing etc: *write/speak with polish.*

▷ v 4 tr/intr.v cause the surface of (s.t) to be smooth and shiny by rubbing, usu with polish(1): *polishing shoes, the furniture.* 5 tr.v (often — s.t up) improve (s.t): *polish (up) one's English/manners.* **polish s.t off** (informal) quickly eat all of s.t: *polish off a whole chicken.*

'polished adj 1 done to a high standard: *a polished performance.* 2 showing very good ability, training etc: *a polished speech/accent.*

'polisher c.n 1 person who puts a smooth shiny surface on furniture. 2 device used to polish(4) s.t: *a floor polisher.*

polite /pə'laɪt/ adj showing respect for others, good manners when speaking or writing etc: *a polite letter/request. A child should be polite to/with teachers.* Opposite impolite.

po'litely adv. **po'liteness** u.n.

politics /'pɒlɪtɪks/ n 1 sing.n (practice or study of the) science of organizing and running a country through a government and administration: *Politics is an interesting subject to study.* 2 pl.n ideas, opinions, activities etc related to government: *party politics. What are your politics?*

'politic adj (formal) showing good practical judgement: *a politic decision, reply, business manager.*

political /pə'lɪtɪkl/ adj of or referring to (the science of) government: *political studies; a political party/speech/discussion; political problems. The causes of the country's poverty are political and not economic(1).*

po,litical a'sylum u.n ⇒ asylum(3).

po,litical 'prisoner c.n prisoner held because of her/his political opinions and not because of a crime.

po,litical 'science u.n politics(1) as an academic(2) subject.

po'litically adv.

politician /,pɒlɪ'tɪʃən/ c.n 1 person who is a member of a body that governs a country, e.g a member of parliament: *I do not trust politicians in any political party.* 2 (informal) person with ability to express opinions and get agreement: *She's an intelligent politician in management meetings.*

politicize, -ise /pə'lɪtɪ,saɪz/ tr.v cause ((a group of) people) to become aware of, interested in, their political rights.

politicking /'pɒlɪ,tɪkɪŋ/ u.n (often derog; informal) activity used to gain support for one's opinions.

polka /'pɒlkə/ c/def.n (music for a) kind of lively skipping dance.

poll /pəʊl/ c.n 1 (voting, counting votes, number of votes etc in an) election: *a poll to choose the new leader, government, manager. It was a heavy/light poll.* 2 (also (,public) o'pinion ,poll) (results from the) activity of asking a selection(3) of people for their opinions about a particular matter in order to determine what people in general think about it: *The poll in yesterday's newspaper shows that support for the government is growing. Polls are often wrong.* **go to the polls** (a) vote in an election. (b) put one's political party, opinions, policy etc forward to be chosen or decided by an election.

▷ tr.v 3 gain (a particular number of votes): *He polled over half the votes.* 4 ask questions of (a person or group) as part of a poll(2).

'polling ,booth c.n small enclosed place where one can vote secretly.

'polling ,station c.n place in a town etc where one can vote in an election.

'pollster c.n person who organizes polls(2).

pollen /'pɒlən/ u.n powder produced by a flower containing male reproductive cells(4) to fertilize(2) (female parts of) (other) flowers.

'pollen ,count c.n measurement of the amount of pollen in the air.

pollinate /'pɒlɪ,neɪt/ tr.v fertilize(2) (a plant) with pollen.

pollination /,pɒlɪ'neɪʃən/ u.n.

pollute /pə'luːt/ tr.v 1 fill (the air, sea etc) with dirty (and harmful) substances: *Traffic pollutes our cities. Chemicals from industry are polluting the rivers and killing the fish.* 2 (of bad, wrong or harmful ideas) affect (a person, her/his mind) badly: *Many people think that violent films pollute children's minds.*

pol'lutant c.n substance that pollutes(1).

pollution /pə'luːʃən/ u.n.

polo /'pəʊləʊ/ u.n kind of outdoor sport played on horses, using sticks with a long handle to hit a wooden ball. ⇒ water polo.

'polo-,neck u.n (also attrib) rolled or turned neck of a sweater fitting closely round the neck: *a polo-neck sweater.*

poly /'pɒlɪ/ c.n (pl -ies) (informal) polytechnic.

polyester /,pɒlɪ'estə/ u.n (also attrib) (technical) one of many kinds of manmade(1) substances used to make cloth(1), plastics(3) and glue: *a polyester shirt.*

polygamy /pə'lɪgəmɪ/ u.n practice or state of having more than one wife.

po'lygamist *c.n* person who practises polygamy.

po'lygamous *adj.* **po'lygamously** *adv.*

polyglot /'pɒlɪˌglɒt/ *adj* **1** (*formal*) written in, using, many languages: *a polyglot arrangement for publishing a new book.*

▷ *c.n* **2** (*formal*) person able to speak and use many languages.

polygon /'pɒlɪˌgɒn/ *c.n* (*technical*) flat shape with many sides: *A regular polygon has sides of equal length.*

polyhedron /ˌpɒlɪ'hiːdrən/ *c.n* (*technical*) solid figure with many faces or sides: *A regular polyhedron has faces which are the same shape and size.*

polymorphous /ˌpɒlɪ'mɔːfəs/ *adj* (also **polymorphic**) (*technical*) passing through many very different stages while developing: *polymorphous animals such as* frogs.

polystyrene /ˌpɒlɪ'staɪriːn/ *u.n* (also *attrib*) (*technical*) kind of manmade(1) substance in the form of a white material with many small holes in it, used to protect things, to stop heat from escaping from hot water tanks etc.

polysyllabic /ˌpɒlɪsɪ'læbɪk/ *adj* (*technical*) (of a word) containing more than two syllables.

polytechnic /ˌpɒlɪ'teknɪk/ *c.n* (*informal poly, tech*) (also *attrib*) college with advanced educational courses, esp in scientific, technical(1), industrial and vocational training: *polytechnic students. I'm studying engineering at the local poly/tech/polytechnic.* Compare university(1).

polythene /'pɒlɪˌθiːn/ *u.n* (also *attrib*) (*technical*) kind of tough manmade(1) material, used for packaging, pipes, toys etc: *a polythene bag.*

polyunsaturated /ˌpɒlɪʌn'sætʃəˌreɪtɪd/ *adj* (*technical*) of a group of fats that are considered to be less harmful in food than ordinary fats.

polyurethane /ˌpɒlɪ'jʊərəˌθeɪn/ *u.n* (also *attrib*) (*technical*) kind of tough manmade(1) substance used in hard foams(1) to make packaging, or in paint etc to make it hard-wearing.

pomegranate /'pɒmɪˌgrænɪt/ *c.n* (also *attrib*) (kind of small tree with a) round fruit containing many juicy red seeds and having a tough skin.

pomp /pɒmp/ *u.n* rich and colourful(1) ceremony for a special occasion.

pomposity /pɒm'pɒsɪtɪ/ *u.n* (*formal*) show or quality of being pompous.

'pompous *adj* (*derog*) (of a person, behaviour, way of speaking or writing etc) having or showing too much self-importance and pride: *a pompous politician.*

'pompously *adv.* **'pompousness** *u.n.*

pompom /'pɒmpɒm/ *c.n* (also **pompon** /'pɒmpɒn/) ball made of short pieces of wool as on the top of a knitted hat.

poncho /'pɒntʃəʊ/ *c.n* piece of cloth, blanket, with a hole in the middle through which one puts one's head, worn as a cloak(1).

pond /pɒnd/ *c.n* (also *attrib*) small lake, usually manmade(2): *a fish/duck pond; pond water.*

ponder /'pɒndə/ *tr/intr.v* (often — *about/on/over s.t*) give serious and determined thought to (s.t) before deciding one's opinion, what to do etc: *I'm pondering over what she said. He pondered his reply carefully. Don't ponder too long or the chance will be lost.* ⇨ imponderable.

'ponderous *adj* (of movement, one's way of speaking or writing) slow, dull and heavy.

'ponderously *adv.* **'ponderousness** *u.n.*

pong /pɒŋ/ *c.n* **1** (*slang*) unpleasant smell.

▷ *intr.v* **2** (*slang*) make a pong(1).

pontiff /'pɒntɪf/ *def.n* Pope.

pontificate /pɒn'tɪfɪˌkeɪt/ *intr.v* (often — *about/on/over s.o/s.t*) speak/write in a pompous way: *pontificating on the need to eat less meat.*

pontoon¹ /pɒn'tuːn/ *c.n* (also *attrib*) (*technical*) flat-bottomed boat or similar structure(2), as used to support a road over a river etc: *a pontoon bridge.*

pontoon² /pɒn'tuːn/ *u.n* kind of card game, often used for gambling(1).

pony /'pəʊnɪ/ *c.n* (*pl -ies*) (also *attrib*) kind of small horse: *go for a pony ride; ride a pony.*

'pony-ˌtail *c.n* way of arranging the hair into the shape of a tail at the back of the head.

poodle /'puːdl/ *c.n* kind of dog with curly hair.

pooh /puː/ *interj* (used to express mild annoyance, often because of an unpleasant smell).

ˌpooh-'pooh *tr.v* (*informal*) say/write that (a suggestion etc) has no value: *He pooh-poohed our idea of opening a restaurant.*

pool¹ /puːl/ *c.n* **1** small area of water as made by rain. **2** (often — *of s.t*) small quantity (of a liquid) on a surface: *pools of blood.* **3** = swimming pool: *No dangerous games are allowed in the pool.* **4** deep part of a river etc: *diving into pools near the rocks.* ⇨ rock pool.

pool² /puːl/ *n* **1** *c.n* quantity of people, things etc as a supply: *a pool of money/ideas.* **typing pool** ⇨ type.

▷ *tr.v* **2** put (money, ideas etc) together for general use: *Let's pool our money and buy a computer.*

pools *def.n* = football pools: *I do the pools each week.*

pool³ /puːl/ *u.n* (also *attrib*) indoor game with a large table and balls that must be hit with long sticks (cues(3)) into holes along the edges of the table: *a pool table.* ⇨ billiards, snooker.

poor /pʊə/ *adj* **1** having not enough money or other basic(1) needs: *a poor student. Do so many countries need to be so poor? Are they deliberately kept poor?* Opposite rich(1). **2** not enough in amount: *a poor wage; a poor harvest(2).* **3** (of quality) not good: *a poor attempt, performance, piece of writing; in poor health; poor examination results. Your work is poor.* Opposite good(1). **4** (*attrib*) deserving sympathy: *Poor Mary has lost her job again. Oh, you poor thing!* **poor in s.t** badly supplied with s.t: *Some rivers are now poor in fish.* **a poor loser** ⇨ loser(*n*).

▷ *def.pl.n* **5** poor people: *We must help the poor. The poor are the first to suffer in bad* economic(1) *conditions.*

'poorly *adj* **1** ill: *He's (feeling) poorly.* **poorly off** poor(1): *You'll be even more poorly off if you buy a car.* Opposite well off(1). ⇨ impoverished(1).

▷ *adv* **2** badly: *a poorly furnished home.*

'poorness *u.n* (often *the* — *of s.t*) bad quality or condition (of s.t): *the poorness of the soil, her work.*

poverty /'pɒvətɪ/ *n* **1** *u.n* state of being poor(1): *living in poverty.* ⇨ impoverish(1). **2** *u.n* (often *the* — *of s.t*) bad quality or condition (of s.t): *The small vegetables are due to the poverty of the soil.* **3** *sing.n* (usu *a* — *of s.t*) (*formal*) too small an amount (of s.t): *There is a poverty of ideas in your report.*

'poverty-,stricken *adj* extremely poor: *poverty-stricken countries. She was poverty-stricken after her husband's death.*

pop[1] /pɒp/ *c.n* (*informal*) (used by a daughter or son) father: *Hi, pop.*

pop[2] /pɒp/ *adv* **1 go pop** make the sound of a pop(2): *The balloon went pop!*

▷ *n* **2** *c.n* short loud sound as made by a bag bursting suddenly: *There was a loud pop when the balloon burst.* **3** *u.n* kind of fizzy non-alcoholic drink.

▷ *v* (-pp-) **4** *tr/intr.v* (cause (s.t) to burst and) make a pop[2](2): *The bag popped. The boys popped all the balloons.* **5** *tr.v* put (s.t) quickly into s.t: *She popped the papers behind the chair, the keys into her bag, the pill in her mouth.* **6** *intr.v* (usu — *in*(to s.w), *out* (of s.w), *across* (s.t), *across* to s.w etc) (*informal*) go or come (in etc) quickly or for a short time: *I'll pop across to the shop. He can pop in this afternoon. She's popped out for a minute. They've popped down to the shops.* **7** *intr.v* (of the eyes) become wide with surprise, excitement etc. **pop the question** ⇨ question(*n*). **pop up** (*informal*) (**a**) suddenly appear: *He pops up in the most unlikely places. Something urgent has popped up.* (**b**) speak suddenly in a conversation: *She often pops up with difficult questions.*

'pop-,up *attrib.adj* made to cause s.t to pop up(a): *a pop-up toaster; a pop-up book.*

pop[3] /pɒp/ *u.n* (also *attrib*) **1** modern style of music and singing enjoyed by many young people: *pop group, records. Do you like pop? He's a famous pop singer/musician/star.* **2** modern style of painting, writing etc: *He paints in a pop style(1). He's a pop artist. All this pop in political speeches is done to get votes.*

pope /pəʊp/ *c/def.n* (also with capital **P**) leader of the Roman Catholic(1) church living in Rome: *Who elects the Pope? Did any of the early popes marry?*

papacy /'peɪpəsɪ/ *u.n* position or authority of popes: *The papacy decides all the main religious matters in the* Roman Catholic(1) *church.*

papal /'peɪpl/ *attrib.adj* of or referring to the Pope or papacy: *papal power.*

'papist *c.n* (*derog*) Roman Catholic(2).

poplar /'pɒplə/ *n* (also *attrib*) **1** kind of tall tree with wide leaves and a soft wood: *a poplar tree.* **2** *u.n* soft wood from this tree: *Does poplar burn well?*

poppet /'pɒpɪt/ *c.n* (*informal*) pleasant kind child.

poppy /'pɒpɪ/ *adj* **1** bright red in colour.

▷ *n* (*pl* -ies) **2** *c.n* (also *attrib*) kind of wild plant having (usu) red, white or orange flowers with large floppy leaves: *a poppy field.* **3** *u.n* bright red colour.

'poppy,seed *u.n* (also *attrib*) round grey-blue seed of a particular kind of poppy, used in cooking: *a poppyseed loaf.*

poppycock /'pɒpɪˌkɒk/ *u.n* (*old use*; *slang*) nonsense: *She talks poppycock.*

populace /'pɒpjʊləs/ *u.n* (*formal*) all the people of a place.

popular /'pɒpjʊlə/ *adj* Opposite unpopular. **1** liked, enjoyed, favoured etc by many people: *popular music,* styles(2) *of clothes; a popular teacher, member of the committee,*

neighbour. He's very popular with the older students. Motorbikes *are not so popular as they were.* ⇨ pop[3](1). **2** (*attrib*) felt/held by most people: *popular* enthusiasm, opinion. **3** (*attrib*) intended to be enjoyed by everyone and not only people with a special ability or interest: *popular television programmes; a popular account of how electricity works.*

,popular 'front *c/def.n* (also with capitals **P** and **F**) group of socialist parties who have united to gain political power.

popularity /ˌpɒpjʊ'lærɪtɪ/ *u.n* condition or degree of being popular(1): *Her popularity went down/up after the strike. Politicians must never lose their popularity (with the voters).*

popularize, -ise /'pɒpjʊləˌraɪz/ *tr.v* make (s.o/s.t) popular(1): *The prince popularized colourful(1) shirts for men.*

'popularly *adv.*

populate /'pɒpjʊˌleɪt/ *tr.v* (usu passive) **1** live in (a place): *This part was once populated by small farming* communities(1). **2** fill (an area) (with s.t): *The hills are now heavily populated with trees.* Opposite depopulate. ⇨ overpopulated, underpopulated.

population /ˌpɒpjʊ'leɪʃən/ *c/u.n* (number of) people living in a country, area etc: *What's the total population of France/London/Africa? It has a population of more than 100 000. The Black population fought hard for equal opportunities.*

populous /'pɒpjʊləs/ *adj* (*formal*) having a large population: *populous cities.*

porcelain /'pɔːslɪn/ *c/u.n* (thing(s) made using a) kind of delicate china(1): *made of porcelain; a porcelain bowl. She owns some fine porcelain.*

porch /pɔːtʃ/ *c.n* small room or covered area in front of a door as an entrance: *Leave your wet shoes in the porch.*

porcupine /'pɔːkjuˌpaɪn/ *c.n* (also *attrib*) kind of animal like a large hedgehog with long sharp quills(3) on its body: *a porcupine quill.*

pore[1] /pɔː/ *c.n* (*technical*) very small hole in the skin for sweat to come out.

porous /'pɔːrəs/ *adj* (*technical*) able to absorb(1) liquid, esp because of having very small holes: *porous rocks. Metals are not porous.*

pore[2] /pɔː/ *intr.v* **pore over s.t** make a detailed study of s.t: *She was poring over the map, her notes.*

pork /pɔːk/ *u.n* (also *attrib*) flesh of a pig used as food: *a pork pie; roast pork.* ⇨ bacon, ham(1,2).

porn /pɔːn/ *u.n* (also *attrib*) (*informal*) pornography: *a porn shop; porn magazines.*

pornography /pɔː'nɒgrəfɪ/ *u.n* (*informal* **porn**) writing, photography, jokes, films etc that encourage sexual excitement: *Does pornography encourage* rape(1)*?*

por'nographer *c.n* person who writes, draws etc or sells pornography.

pornographic /ˌpɔːnə'græfɪk/ *adj*: *pornographic literature.*

porous ⇨ pore[1].

porpoise /'pɔːpəs/ *c.n* kind of animal that lives in the sea and is related(1) to the dolphin.

porridge /'pɒrɪdʒ/ *u.n* soft mixture of oatmeal and water or milk, boiled and eaten for breakfast.

port[1] /pɔːt/ *c.n* (also *attrib*) (town by the sea with a) place where ships can stop: *We sailed into port*

*early in the morning. The port of London is not
used much today. You need permission from the
port* authorities(2). ⇨ harbour(1).

port² /pɔːt/ *u.n* (also *attrib*) (*technical*) left side
of a ship: *We were on the port* (*side*) (*of the boat*).
⇨ starboard.

port³ /pɔːt/ *adj* **1** dark red in colour: *His tie was
a deep port colour.*
▷ *n* **2** *c/u.n* kind of strong dark red wine: *A glass of
port and lemon, please.* **3** *u.n* dark red colour.

portable /'pɔːtəbl/ *adj* able to be moved or
carried easily: *a portable computer.*

portals /'pɔːtlz/ *pl.n* (*formal*) large decorated
entrance: *We rode through the portals of the
city.*

portcullis /pɔːt'kʌlɪs/ *c.n* network of iron or
thick wood that can be raised or lowered at the
entrance to a castle.

portend /pɔː'tend/ *tr.v* (*formal* or *literary*) warn
about, foretell, (s.t in the future): *Such intelligence
portends a great future as a lawyer.*

portent /'pɔːtent/ *c.n* (*formal*) (usu very
strange) thing that warns or tells of the future:
*A few hundred years ago people thought that bad
weather was a portent of* (*a*) disaster(1).

portentous /pɔː'tentəs/ *adj* (*formal*) acting as
a portent: *a portentous sign.*
por'tentously *adv.*

porter¹ /'pɔːtə/ *c.n* person in charge of the
entrance to a hotel, set of offices, building with
flats etc: *a hotel porter; ask the porter for the
keys.*

porter² /'pɔːtə/ *c.n* person who carries bags etc
in a station, airport etc: *I must find a porter to
help me with my luggage.*

portfolio /pɔːt'fəʊlɪəʊ/ *c.n* **1** (large flat case for
carrying a) collection of drawings, plans etc: *a
leather portfolio. She has built up a varied portfolio of her work as a photographer.* **2** duties and
authority(1) of a senior(1) government official: *the
portfolio for foreign affairs.* **3** (*informal*) duties of
a senior(1) manager in a business or organization:
Such responsibilities are outside my portfolio.
4 all the investments(2) held by one person or
group.

porthole /'pɔːt,həʊl/ *c.n* small, usu round, window in the side of a ship.

portion /'pɔːʃən/ *c.n* **1** (often — *of* s.t) part (of a
whole): *a portion of the blame; during several portions of the day; divide the cake into 12 portions.*
2 (often — *of* s.t) amount of s.t, esp given to s.o as
a share: *a portion of ice-cream; gave his portion of
the profits to the poor.* **3** (*formal*) person's fate:
What will be her portion in Australia?
▷ *tr.v* **4** (esp — s.t *out*) divide (s.t) among several
people: *portion* (*out*) *the work between the two
departments.* **5** give a part of (money, responsibilities, duties etc) to s.o: *be portioned the largest
share.* ⇨ apportion, disproportionate.

portly /'pɔːtlɪ/ *adj* (-*ier*, -*iest*) (often *joking* or
derog) (of a person) fat.
'portliness *u.n.*

portmanteau /pɔːt'mæntəʊ/ *c.n* (*pl* -*s*,
portmanteaux /-təʊz/) (*old use*) kind of large
suitcase that opens in two parts.

portrait /'pɔːtrɪt/ *c.n* (often — *of* s.o) **1** (also
attrib) drawing, painting etc of s.o: *a photographic portrait of the Queen; a portrait gallery*(1).
2 description in writing or speech (of a person

etc): *write a life portrait of Mozart; a portrait of
a marriage.*

portraitist /'pɔːtrɪtɪst/ *c.n* person who makes
portraits(1).

portraiture /'pɔːtrɪtʃə/ *u.n* art or practice of
making portraits(1).

portray /pɔː'treɪ/ *tr.v* **1** make a portrait(1) of
(s.o): *portray the scientist working at her desk.*
2 describe (s.o/s.t) in writing, speech etc: *The film
portrays the developing world as the most exciting
place to work.* **3** (*formal*) play the part of (s.o):
I've never portrayed Hamlet on the stage.
por'trayal *c/u.n* (often — *of* s.o/s.t) (example of
an) act of portraying(2) s.o/s.t: *the portrayal of life
on a Greek farm; a convincing portrayal of a blind
man.*

pose /pəʊz/ *c.n* **1** particular way of standing,
sitting etc, esp for a photograph or drawing.
2 way of behaving to get a particular effect that
will be to one's advantage: *His interest in books
was only a pose to get her attention.*
▷ *v* **3** *intr.v* (often — *for* s.o/s.t) put oneself in a
pose(1) for a photograph or drawing: *posing for
the photographers, for a painting; pose in the nude
for an artist.* **4** *intr.v* (usu — *as* s.o) pretend to like
s.t or to be s.o: *posing as an Englishwoman. He's
only posing when he says he enjoys opera*(1). **5** *tr.v*
(*formal*) ask (a question etc): *pose a difficulty/
question to an official; pose students a problem
about electrical force.*
'poser *c.n* **1** person who poses(3). **2** difficult
question. ⇨ pose(5).

poseur /pəʊ'zɜː/ *c.n* (*French*; *derog*) person
who poses(4).

posh /pɒʃ/ *adj* (*informal*) **1** expensive; fashionable: *posh clothes; a posh car.* **2** (also *adv*) (often
derog) in a manner to show one is upper class,
rich, important etc: *a posh English accent; talking
posh.*

posit /'pɒzɪt/ *tr.v* (*formal*) state (s.t) as the
basic(1) information or reason in an argument:
*She posited that money would be more useful to
him because with it he could choose his present.*

position /pə'zɪʃən/ *n* **1** *c.n* particular way of
standing, sitting etc: *The nurse helped the man
to find a comfortable position. The baby was in a
sitting position.* **2** *c.n* place where s.o/s.t is: *The
house is in* (or *has*) *a good position near the sea.*
3 *c.n* (often — *in* s.t) person's rank or place
(in an order): *What position do you hold in the
army/office/factory? She's in second position in
the race.* **4** *c.n* person's job or responsibility: *I've
applied for the position of manager. What position
does Gary have/play in the team?* **5** *c.n* (usu *sing,
in a good, bad* etc —) state, situation: *That puts
me in a very difficult position.* **6** *c.n* opinion or
policy(1): *My position regarding political rights
is well known. What is the government position
on private education?* **7** *u.n* rank, importance,
wealth, status(1): *a family with position; a man of
position.* **be in a position to do s.t** be able to do
s.t because of conditions that have an influence:
I'm not in a position to lend you money. **in, out
of, position** in, out of, the place where s.o/s.t is
supposed to be: *A bone in your neck is out of
position* (not in the right place). *Put the furniture
back in position.*
▷ *tr.v* **8** put (s.o/s.t) in a particular place: *I positioned
the fruit tree in the centre of the garden.*

po'sitional *adj.*

positive /ˈpɒzɪtɪv/ *adj* Opposite negative for 3,4,6,8–11. **1** (*pred*) certain about one's opinion; sure: *I'm positive that I can win. Jack is positive that he saw you. He's feeling very positive.* **2** (*attrib*) certain; exact and confident; definite: *They need positive proof that you own the house. She had positive reasons for saying no.* **3** expressing certainty or complete agreement: *He gave me a positive answer.* **4** having practical, useful, helpful etc qualities: *a positive advantage; positive criticism.* **5** (*attrib*) (*informal*) (of s.o/ s.t bad, poor etc) extreme; complete: *a positive idiot/lie.* **6** showing confidence about the future: *a positive view of one's future; positive thinking.* **7** (*grammar*) (of an adj/adv) showing a form that is not the comparative(4) or superlative(2): *The positive form of 'better' and 'best' is 'good'.* **8** (*technical*) meaning 'yes': *Her answer was positive.* **9** (*medical*) showing that a disease is present: *The test was positive and you'll need to have an operation.* **10** (*mathematics*) (of a number or quantity) larger than 0. **11** (*technical*) of or for the kind of electricity having fewer electrons: *a positive charge; the positive end of a battery* (marked +). **12** (*technical*) (of photographic film) showing light and dark as in nature and not the other way round. Compare negative(8).
▷ *adv* **13** (*informal*) in a positive(6) way: *think positive about the examinations.*
▷ *c.n* Opposite negative. **14** (*mathematics*) positive(10) number or quantity. **15** (*grammar*) positive(7) form of an adj/adv. **16** (*technical*) positive(12) photograph or film.
'positively *adv* **1** in a positive(6) way: *talk positively about the future; argue positively for another computer.* Opposite negatively. **2** (*informal*) extremely; completely: *Your reaction was positively criminal.*
'positive ˌsign *c.n* (*technical*) plus sign.

poss /pɒs/ *adj* (*informal*) possible(1): *If poss, I'll come in dad's car.*

possess /pəˈzes/ *tr.v* **1** (*formal*) have (s.t); own (s.t): *Do you possess a licence(1) for this car? The thief took all we possessed.* **2** take control of the mind of (s.o): *Extreme anger possessed her and she hit the taxi driver. Whatever possessed you to do that!*
pos'sessed *pred.adj* with one's mind controlled by an evil spirit: *He fought like a man possessed.* ⇒ self-possessed.
possession /pəˈzeʃən/ *n* **1** *c.n* thing that a person, group, organization etc has or owns: *I have few valuable possessions.* **2** *u.n* condition of having/owning s.t: *Can you explain how this car came into your possession? Are you in possession of a university degree? Which player had possession of the ball at the time?* **gain/take possession (of s.t)** get, begin to have, (legal(1)) ownership, use etc of s.t: *When did you take possession of your house/car?* **regain possession (of s.t)** gain possession (of s.t) again.
pos'sessive *adj* **1** (*derog*) showing too much interest and enjoyment in owning things: *a possessive personality.* **2** (*derog*) behaving as if one has complete control and rights over s.o: *possessive parents; a possessive husband.* **3** (*grammar*) of the form of an adj, pronoun

etc showing possession(1), e.g a *child's*, the *children's*, *Mary's* game; *her*, *its*, *their* playground; it's *hers*.
▷ *c.n* **4** (*grammar*) possessive(3) form of a noun/pronoun: *The possessive of 'him' is 'his'.*
pos'sessively *adv.* **pos'sessiveness** *u.n.*
pos'sessor *c.n* (often the — of s.t) person who has or owns s.t.

possible /ˈpɒsɪbl/ *adj* **1** able or likely to exist, happen, be done etc: *Are* ghosts(1) *possible? Is it possible for England to win? I don't think it's possible to arrive before 9 o'clock. There will be a possible delay.* ⇒ impossible(1). **2** (*attrib*) likely to be satisfactory: *That's one possible way of doing it. Her idea is a possible* winner(2).
possibility /ˌpɒsɪˈbɪlɪti/ *n* (*pl -ies*) **1** *u.n* condition or degree of being possible(1): *There is always the possibility of losing* (or *that we shall lose*). **2** *c.n* thing that is possible: *There is a strong possibility of rain. There are several possibilities to choose from. We think there are good possibilities for you in the Rome office.* ⇒ impossibility.
'possibly *adv* **1** in a way that is possible(1): *This is possibly the last time we'll ever meet.* **2** (used for emphasis, usu with 'not'): *I couldn't possibly tell you her secret.* **3** perhaps: *'Will you be there?' 'Possibly.'* **4** (*informal*) (used to make a polite request): *Could you possibly tell me where the station is?*

post¹ /pəʊst/ *u.n* **1** letters, parcels etc (to be) delivered by a special (government) organization: *Please take this letter to the post. Is there any post today? The present was sent by parcel post.* **by return (of post)** ⇒ return(n). Compare mail¹(1).
▷ *tr.v* **2** send (letters, parcels etc) by post¹(1): *Did you post my letter? I've posted you a long letter. They've posted the letter to my old address.* Compare mail¹(2). **3** write down or enter (an item(1)) in a business account: *These costs must be posted to the general account.*
postage /ˈpəʊstɪdʒ/ *u.n* charge (to be) made for sending post¹(1).
'postage ˌstamp *c.n* ⇒ stamp(1).
'postal *adj* of or referring to post¹(1): *postal charges/services.*
'postal ˌorder *c.n* (*written abbr PO*) printed order for payment of an amount of money to a particular person at another post office.
'post ˌbox *c.n* **1** = pillar-box. **2** place in a building where post¹(1) is put for collection.
'post ˌcard *c.n* piece of card, usu with a picture on one side, used to send informal messages or greetings.
'post ˌcode *c.n* group of letters and numbers used to identify an address for post¹(1).
ˌpost'haste *adv* as quickly as possible: *She travelled posthaste to the hospital.*
'postman *c.n* (*pl -men*) person who delivers post¹(1) to homes, offices etc.
'post ˌmark *c.n* mark put on the stamp on a letter etc showing the date and where it is posted¹(2).
'post ˌmaster/-ˌmistress *c.n* man/woman in charge of a post office.
'post ˌoffice *c.n* **1** (*written abbr PO*) official place selling stamps, paying out pensions(1), collecting or paying national savings etc. **2** (government) organization for postal services in a country.

'post ,office ,box *c.n* (*abbr PO Box*) numbered box in a post office for a person's or business company's post[1](1): *Write to PO Box 100, Kenfield.*

'post,woman *c.n* (*pl* -,women) woman who delivers post[1](1) to homes, offices etc.

post² /pəʊst/ *c.n* **1** long upright piece of wood, metal etc, used as a support, marker(2) etc: *a goal post*; *a gatepost*; *the winning post.* **from pillar to post** ⇒ pillar.

▷ *tr.v* **2** (often — *s.t up*) put (a notice etc) in a public place: *The new rules have been posted on walls throughout the town. We've posted up the information about the election.* **keep s.o posted** give s.o information regularly: *Keep me posted about his illness.*

post³ /pəʊst/ *c.n* **1** job, esp one to which a person is appointed: *I've been given a post in South America.* **2** position or place where a soldier is sent to be on duty: *Is he at his post?* **3** established(4) place for a unit of the army, navy or airforce: *naval posts along the south coast.* ⇒ trading post. **4** (*military*) one of two calls made by blowing a bugle at the end of the day: *the first/ last post.*

▷ *tr.v* **5** (usu passive) appoint (s.o) to a job, esp in another place: *I've been posted to our offices in Kenya.* **6** send (a soldier etc) to a post³(3).

'posting *c.n* appointment for a job, esp in another place.

postdate /pəʊst'deɪt/ *tr.v* **1** put a future date on (a cheque etc) so that it cannot be used until then. ⇒ antedate(1), predate. **2** happen/exist later than s.o/s.t ⇒ antedate(2).

poster /'pəʊstə/ *c.n* notice or picture put up in a public place as an advertisement.

posterior /pɒ'stɪərɪə/ *adj* **1** (*technical*) situated at the back: *the posterior muscles*(1) *of the hand.* **2** (*formal*) coming after another or others in an order: *a posterior position in the list.* ⇒ anterior(1).

▷ *c.n* **3** person's bottom(3).

posterity /pɒ'sterɪtɪ/ *u.n* (usu for —) people who will live in the future: *These paintings will be left here for posterity. Posterity will judge its value.*

postgraduate /pəʊst'grædjuɪt/ *c.n* (also *attrib*) student with a first degree from a university who is studying for a higher qualification: *a postgraduate in science*; *postgraduate courses.* Compare graduate(1–3), undergraduate.

posthaste ⇒ post[1].

posthumous /'pɒstjʊməs/ *adj* (*formal*) existing, happening etc after s.o's death: *a posthumous award for bravery.*

'posthumously *adv.*

posting ⇒ post³.

postman, postmark, postmaster ⇒ post[1].

post meridiem /,pəʊst mə'rɪdɪəm/ *adj* (*abbr* pm, p.m.) (*formal*) in the afternoon. Compare ante meridiem.

postmistress ⇒ post[1].

postmortem /pəʊst'mɔːtəm/ *c.n* (also *attrib*) **1** examination of a dead body to decide the cause of death: *a postmortem examination.* **2** (*fig*) examination of the causes of failure or defeat: *They held a postmortem to decide why sales had been so poor.*

postnatal /pəʊst'neɪtl/ *adj* happening after childbirth. ⇒ antenatal, prenatal.

post office (box) ⇒ post[1].

postpone /pəʊs'pəʊn/ *tr.v* delay (doing/deciding (s.t)) until a later time: *The meeting has been postponed until next week. I'll postpone my decision for another day.*

post'ponement *c/u.n.*

postscript /'pəʊs,skrɪpt/ *c.n* (*abbr* ps, PS) message added to a letter after the signature.

postulate /'pɒstjʊ,leɪt/ *tr.v* (*formal*) claim (s.t) as a true fact or basis for an argument: *He postulated that if she won the next tennis match she would go on to win the competition.*

posture /'pɒstʃə/ *c/u.n* **1** (particular) way of standing, sitting etc: *painted in a* relaxed(1) *posture. Be careful about your posture while picking up heavy objects.*

▷ *intr.v* **2** (*derog*; *formal*) hold oneself in an affected way so that one appears important: *She postures every time she meets a person with influence.*

postwoman ⇒ post[1].

posy /'pəʊzɪ/ *c.n* (*pl* -ies) (often — *of s.t*) small bunch (of flowers): *a posy of roses.*

pot¹ /pɒt/ *n* **1** *c.n* deep container for holding things, for cooking in etc: *a flower pot*; *a cooking pot*; *a teapot*; *pots and pans.* **2** *c.n* (also **'potful**) as much as a pot[1](1) holds: *She drank a whole pot of coffee.* ⇒ potful. **3** *u.n* (*informal*) marijuana. **4** *c.n* = potbelly. **go to pot** (*informal*) (**a**) lose self-control because of worry or anger. (**b**) be gradually ruined: *Her examinations went to pot in the second week.* **pots of money** (*slang*) lots of money.

▷ *tr.v* (-tt-) **5** put (s.t, esp a plant) in a pot[1](1). **6** (*informal*) put (a baby) on a potty[1].

'pot'bellied *adj* having a fat round belly(1).

'pot,belly *c.n* (*pl* -ies) fat round belly(1).

'pot,boiler *c.n* (*derog*; *informal*) piece of writing produced quickly to make money.

'potful *adj* ⇒ pot[1](2).

'pot,head *c.n* (*informal*) person who often uses pot[1](3).

'pot,hole *c.n* **1** (*technical*) deep hole made by an underground river. **2** hole in a road surface.

'pot,holer *c.n* person who explores potholes(1).

,pot 'luck *u.n* **take pot luck** accept what is available without being given a choice: *You're too late to choose the meal you want so you'll have to take pot luck.*

'pot ,plant *c.n* indoor plant kept in a pot[1](1).

,pot-'shot *c.n* (often *take a — at s.o/s.t*) quick shot or one taken without aiming carefully.

'potted *attrib.adj* **1** (put) in a pot[1](1): *potted plants.* **2** (of food) (put) in a pot[1](1) or jar until used: *potted* crab(2) *meat.* **3** (of information) made short and simple: *a potted history of Europe.*

'potter¹ *c.n* person who makes clay pots(1).

'pottery *n* (*pl* -ies) **1** *c.n* place where a potter works. **2** *u.n* (clay used to make) pots[1](1) made by a potter[1]. **3** *u.n* art of making pots[1](1): *studying pottery.*

'potty¹ *c.n* (*pl* -ies) (*informal*) chamberpot. ⇒ potty².

pot² /pɒt/ *tr.v* **1** shoot (an animal, esp a bird). **2** hit/knock (a ball) into a pocket in the game of snooker etc.

potassium /pə'tæsɪəm/ *u.n* shining silvery(1) chemical element(1), used in fertilizers and in the production of nuclear power(1). *chem. symb* K.

potato /pə'teɪtəʊ/ c/u.n (pl -es) (also attrib) (kind of plant grown for its) swollen underground stems that are cooked and eaten as a vegetable: a field planted with potatoes; boiled potatoes; potato soup; potato crisps(4).

potbellied, potbelly, potboiler ⇒ pot¹.

potent /'pəʊtnt/ adj 1 having a large amount of power or strength: a potent drug(1); a potent drink. 2 (of an argument) able to persuade s.o easily: a potent argument in favour of learning Spanish. Compare impotent.

'potency u.n (often the — of s.t) power or strength (of s.t).

potential /pə'tenʃəl/ attrib.adj 1 able to exist or happen but not yet existing or happening: a potential first class football team; potential power/wealth/success/failure.

▷ sing/u.n 2 possibility of existing (esp at a high standard) but not yet shown: He has potential as a lawyer. There is good potential in her work, in the European markets, in their suggestions.

po'tentially adv.

potful, pothead, pothole(r) ⇒ pot¹.

potion /'pəʊʃən/ c.n small drink of medicine, poison, magic liquid etc: a love potion.

pot luck, pot plant ⇒ pot¹.

potpourri /ˌpəʊpʊ'riː/ c.n (pl -s) mixture of petals, spices(1) etc kept in a bag or pot with holes and used to provide a pleasant smell.

pot-shot, potted ⇒ pot¹.

potter¹ ⇒ pot¹.

potter² /'pɒtə/ intr.v potter about move around tidying things etc without a definite plan. ⇒ pot¹.

pottery, potty¹ ⇒ pot¹.

potty² /'pɒti/ adj (-ier, -iest) (informal) mad; crazy: She's potty. **potty about s.o/s.t** (informal) very much in love with s.o/s.t: I'm potty about him, his paintings.

pouch /paʊtʃ/ c.n 1 small bag (to be) carried in a pocket: a tobacco pouch. 2 flap(2) in the front of certain animals, used to carry young: a kangaroo's pouch. 3 place like a bag on/in part of a person's or animal's body: pouches under the eyes; a squirrel's pouches for carrying nuts in the sides of its cheeks.

pouf /puːf/ c.n (also **pouffe**) large solid cushion, used as a seat.

poultice /'pəʊltɪs/ c.n special mixture placed on the skin to treat injury, pain etc.

poultry /'pəʊltrɪ/ u.n (also attrib) chickens, ducks, turkeys(1), geese etc as a group, used as food: poultry farms.

pounce /paʊns/ c.n 1 sudden attack: The cat hid behind the bushes ready for a pounce on(to) a young bird.

▷ intr.v 2 (often — at/on/upon s.o/s.t) make a sudden attack in order to get a hold on s.o/s.t: The cat pounced at/on the bird. **pounce on s.o/ s.t** attack s.o/s.t suddenly in an argument: She pounced on him (or his mistake) and was able to force him to end his opposition(2). **pounce on s.t** quickly take an opportunity to do s.t: He pounced on the idea of buying the house.

pound¹ /paʊnd/ c.n 1 (also attrib) unit of British money equal to 100 pence. symb £: a pound note; costing £100. 2 (written abbr lb) unit of weight equal to 16 ounces (or 0.37 kg): Two pounds of potatoes, please. I'd like half a pound

of butter. It weighs 12 lb. How many pounds do you weigh?

pound 'sterling c.n (pl pounds sterling) British £1; British money.

pound² /paʊnd/ v 1 tr/intr.v (often — at/on s.t) hit (s.o/s.t) heavily: pound meat flat; pound at/ on the door; pound one's feet on the floor. 2 tr/ intr.v run or walk heavily (along (s.t)): pound the streets; pound up and down. 3 intr.v (of the heart) beat heavily: Her heart was pounding. 4 tr.v (usu — s.t into/to s.t) break (s.t) into small pieces or powder: pound a block of salt into/to a powder.

pound³ /paʊnd/ c.n enclosed place for keeping animals that have no home or vehicles that have been taken by the police: a dog pound; a police pound for illegally parked cars. ⇒ impound.

pour /pɔː/ v 1 tr/intr.v (cause (a liquid) to) flow out: Shall I pour the tea? The water poured over the edge. 2 intr.v (often — down) rain heavily: It's pouring (down)! It was pouring with rain. 3 intr.v — down ⇒ rain(v). **It never rains but it pours** ⇒ rain(v). **pour out (of s.w)** (of people) leave (a place) in large numbers: The children poured out of school.

pout /paʊt/ c.n 1 act or state of pouting (⇒ pout(2)): a sullen pout.

▷ tr/intr.v 2 push (the lips) out to show disappointment/anger: He pouted to show his anger. Don't pout your lips like that.

poverty(-stricken) ⇒ poor.

powder /'paʊdə/ n 1 c/u.n substance in the form of a collection of extremely small pieces like flour: soap powder; talcum powder; a strong washing powder.

▷ tr.v 2 make (a substance) into a powder(1): powdered milk. 3 put powder on (s.o/s.t): powder one's face; powder a cake.

powder 'blue adj/u.n very pale blue (colour).

'powder ˌroom c.n lavatory for women in a restaurant etc.

'powdery adj (dry and loose) like powder(1): powdery snow.

power /'paʊə/ n 1 u.n (often — (of s.o/s.t) to do s.t) ability or strength (to do s.t): the power of sight, to see; the power to influence the government; the power of God. Is it within your power to help us? 2 u.n (source or means of) strength: the power of electricity, a magnet(1); water power. He has great physical(1)/mental(1)/intellectual(1) power. ⇒ horsepower, nuclear power. 3 u.n authority(1)/control; influence: the power of the police, the law; government/union power. When did the Liberals(5) gain power? 4 c.n organization with power(3): The church, civil service, is a great power in the land. 5 c.n authority(1) given to a person or group: What powers does he have in this factory? Can you list the powers of the prime minister? We have special powers to arrest anyone causing trouble. 6 c.n country with a strong influence or authority(1) in the world: the European powers. 7 c.n (technical) result of multiplying a number by itself a stated number of times: 10 to the power of 3 (10³) is 1000. **gain power** get control of a government etc, e.g in an election. **in power** having authority, control: What political party is in power in France?

'power,boat c.n boat with an engine, esp used in races.

'power ,cut *c.n* (sudden) break in the supply of electricity.

'powered *adj* using a (stated) form of energy(2): *powered by electricity*; *an electrically-powered machine.* ⇨ high-powered(1).

'powerful *adj* **1** having much power(2): *a powerful motor*; *a powerful politician.* **2** extremely effective(1): *a powerful poison*; *a powerful telescope*(1).

'powerfully *adv.*

'power,house *c.n* **1** = power station. **2** (*fig*) powerful(2) person or thing: *He's a powerhouse in the business.*

'powerless *adj* (esp — *to do s.t*) having no power(3,5) or authority(1) (to do s.t); not able to act: *powerless sections of the community*; *be powerless to help.*

'powerlessly *adv.* **'powerlessness** *u.n.*

,power of at'torney *u.n* ⇨ attorney.

'power-,point *c.n* place (called a socket) in a wall etc where electricity can be taken using a plug(3).

,power 'politics *u/pl.n* threat of using force in international politics.

'power ,station *c.n* place where electricity is made.

pp *written abbr* **1** on behalf of: *pp G Jones, the Manager.* **2** pages¹. **3** (*p.p* in this dictionary) past participle.

pps, PPS *written abbr* (used to identify a message written after a postscript). ⇨ PS.

pr, PR *abbr* **1** (*written abbr*) pair(1,2). **2** (*written abbr*) price. **3** (*written abbr*) (**Pr**) Priest. **4** (*written abbr*) (**Pr**) Prince. **5** (**PR**) proportional representation. **6** (**PR**) Public Relations. ⇨ PRO.

practicable /'præktɪkəbl/ *adj* (*formal*) able to be carried out: *a practicable plan. Your suggestion is extremely practicable.* Opposite impracticable.

practicability /,præktɪkə'bɪlɪtɪ/ *u.n.*

'practicably *adv.*

practical /'præktɪkl/ *adj* **1** of or referring to the act of actually doing s.t and not only thinking about the possibility of it: *There are practical reasons for delaying the building of the new bridge. We see no practical difficulties except finding money for the materials.* Compare theoretical, pragmatic. **2** (of a suggestion, plan etc) useful; able to be carried out: *a practical idea, way of avoiding a* crisis(1). *Your plan can't be practical if it needs so many people.* Opposite impractical. **3** (of a person) able to do things well, esp using the hands or having an organized mind: *She's very practical in the house.* Opposite unpractical.

practicality /,præktɪ'kælɪtɪ/ *c/u.n* (*pl -ies*) (usu *the — of s.o/s.t*) (*formal*) (example of the) condition of being practical(2): *Consider the practicality of moving 800 tonnes of soil!*

,practical 'joke *c.n* joke in which s.t is done to s.o to make her/him seem stupid.

'practically *adv* **1** when (considering) doing s.t (and not planning it): *Practically, the idea is impossible.* **2** almost: *I've practically no money. It's practically empty.*

practice /'præktɪs/ (US **practise**) *n* **1** *c/u.n* usual or normal activity, method or way of behaving: *My practice is to get up early. Will England follow other countries' practice of allowing shops to open on Sundays?* **2** *c/u.n* business

of a doctor, lawyer, accountant etc: *She has a practice in London. He's set up practice as a solicitor.* ⇨ general practice, group practice. **3** *u.n* regular activity done to improve one's skill: *piano practice*; *an evening practice for the tennis team. You'll need some extra practice with English conversation.* **in practice** (**a**) able to do something well because of practice(3): *I can't play in the competition because I'm not in practice at the moment.* (**b**) when doing/using s.t instead of thinking about it: *Your idea seems good but will it work in practice? In practice there will be many problems.* ⇨ in theory. **out of practice** not able to do s.t well because lacking practice(3): *I used to play tennis well but now I'm out of practice.* **Practice makes perfect** (*saying*) Practice(3) will make one able to do s.t well. **put s.t into practice** actually do/use s.t instead of only thinking about it: *We won't know if the plan will work until we put it into practice.*

practise /'præktɪs/ *v* **1** *tr/intr.v* do (s.t) to improve one's skill: *practise (the piano) every evening*; *practise balancing on a rope.* **2** *tr/intr.v* work in the profession of (medicine, law etc): *He's practising (medicine) in India.* **3** *tr.v* (*formal*) do (s.t) regularly or as one usually does: *practise one's religion even when on holiday.* **practise what one preaches** do what one advises others to do.

'practised *attrib.adj* having a high standard because of practice(3): *a practised speaker.*

'practising *adj* **1** doing one's work as a doctor/lawyer: *a practising lawyer. Are you practising at the moment?* **2** (*attrib*) actively involved(2): *I'm not a practising* Christian *because I never go to church but I do believe in* Jesus.

practitioner /præk'tɪʃənə/ *c.n* (*formal*) active professional person: *a medical practitioner*; *a practitioner of international law.* ⇨ general practitioner.

pragmatic /præg'mætɪk/ *adj* concerned with practical(1) matters and not theory(2): *a pragmatic suggestion for raising the money*; *a pragmatic politician.*

prag'matically *adv.*

pragmatist /'prægmə,tɪst/ *c.n* person who is pragmatic when deciding what to do.

prairie /'preərɪ/ *c.n* area of flat land with grass and few trees.

praise /preɪz/ *u.n* (often — *of s.o/s.t*) **1** expression of approval, one's high opinion of the quality, (of s.o/s.t): *show one's praise of her work. Her kindness received a lot of praise from the teachers.* **2** (*formal*) show of one's high respect (for God): *praise of God.* **sing s.o's praises** (*fig*) express one's high opinion of s.o, s.o's ability.

▷ *tr.v* **3** express praise(1) of (s.o/s.t): *praising her work.* **4** express praise(2) of (God): *praise God by singing* hymns. **praise s.o/s.t to the skies** ⇨ sky(*n*).

'praise,worthy *adj* (*formal*) deserving praise(1): *a praiseworthy performance/attempt.*

pram /præm/ *c.n* (also *attrib*) (*formal* perambu-*lator*) kind of small carriage on wheels for a baby: *a pram cover. The pram rolled into a tree.*

prance /prɑːns/ *c.n* **1** act of prancing (⇨ prance(*v*)).

▷ *intr.v* **2** (of an animal) jump from the back legs:

The horse was prancing about in the fields. **3** (of a person) leap or skip in big dancing movements: *The girl pranced across the stage.*

prank /præŋk/ *c.n* (often *play a — on s.o*) practical joke.

prattle /'prætl/ *u.n* **1** (*derog; old use*) example of prattling (⇨ prattle(2)).
▷ *intr.v* **2** (*derog; old use*) talk a lot about unimportant things, esp in a self-important way: *He prattled (on) about his holidays.*

prawn /prɔːn/ *c.n* (also *attrib*) kind of shellfish with a long tail and ten legs, eaten as food: *fried prawns; a prawn salad*(1). ⇨ shrimp.

pray /preɪ/ *tr/intr.v* speak to God to give praise, ask for s.t etc: *We prayed for good weather. They prayed to God for the child to recover from the illness. Let's pray that our team wins.*

prayer¹ /preə/ *n* **1** *c.n* (often *pl*) set of words used when praying, esp to God: *Do you say your prayers every night?* **2** *c.n* (often *pl*) set of learned words used regularly, e.g in a church or by a family, when praying, esp to God: *the Lord's prayer; school prayers at the beginning of the day.* **3** *u.n* act of (regularly) praying, esp to God: *Nuns spend much of their time in prayer. He knew his illness had been cured through prayer.*

prayer² /'preɪə/ *c.n* person who prays.

'prayer ‚book *c.n* book of prayers¹(2) used in church.

'prayer ‚rug *c.n* mat used by a Muslim(2) when praying (⇨ pray).

'prayer ‚wheel *c.n* round container with many written prayers²(2) inside that turns on a pole¹, used by Buddhists.

praying mantis /ˌpreɪɪŋ 'mæntɪs/ *c.n* (also **'mantis**) carnivorous insect with a long body and large eyes.

preach /priːtʃ/ *tr/intr.v* **1** give a religious talk, esp in church or during a religious occasion (saying (s.t)): *He preached (to us) (about) the love of God.* **2** give advice about how to behave well (saying (s.t)): *She preached (about) the rewards of helping others.*

'preacher *c.n* person who preaches(1) in a Protestant(1) church.

preamble /priː'æmbl/ *c.n* first part of a speech, written agreement etc that introduces it, explains the purpose etc of it: *In his preamble he described the main reasons for organizing the meeting.*

prearrange /ˌpriːə'reɪndʒ/ *tr.v* arrange or agree (s.t) in advance: *The result of the election could have been prearranged.*
‚prear'ranged *adj*: *at a prearranged time.*
‚prear'rangement *u.n*.

precarious /prɪ'keərɪəs/ *adj* (*formal*) **1** dangerous: *The car stopped in a precarious position on the edge of the slope. It was a precarious journey through the snow.* **2** likely to fail: *I live the precarious life of a writer.*
pre'cariously *adv*.

precaution /prɪ'kɔːʃən/ *c/u.n* (esp *as a —* (against s.t); *take —s*; *take the — of doing s.t*) (example of an) action taken to avoid an unwanted or harmful event: *wear a hat as a precaution against the hot sun; take the precaution of wearing a hat; take precautions against the hot sun by wearing a hat.*

pre'cautionary *adj* done as a precaution against s.t.

precede /priː'siːd/ *tr/intr.v* (*formal*) be, go, happen, before (s.o/s.t) in position, order etc: *How many people precede me on the list? He took my luggage and preceded me up the stairs.*

precedence /'presɪdəns/ *u.n* (often *take — over s.o/s.t*) (right of) being first in importance, position (compared with s.o/s.t): *Your health must take precedence over all other considerations. In order of precedence he comes before you.*

precedent /'presɪdənt/ *c.n* (often *establish/set a —*) (*formal*) earlier example of an event, decision etc used as a rule for a similar one happening later: *They established(1) a precedent by sending the man to prison for kicking his dog.* ⇨ unprecedented.

preceding /prɪ'siːdɪŋ/ *adj* coming before in position, order etc: *during the preceding two weeks.* ⇨ following.

precinct /'priːsɪŋkt/ *c.n* (often *pl*) area (as if) inside walls or similar boundaries: *a shopping precinct; inside the church precincts; growing vegetables around the precincts of the town.*

precious /'preʃəs/ *adj* **1** having much value: *precious jewels.* **2** (esp *— to s.o*) much loved (by s.o): *You are very precious to me.* **3** (*informal*) (of a person) acting/speaking with too much self-importance.

‚precious 'metal/'stone *c/u.n* (example of a kind of) metal/stone that has a high value e.g gold, silver, diamond, emerald(1), ruby(1). ⇨ semi-precious.

'preciously *adv*. **'preciousness** *u.n*.

precipice /'presɪpɪs/ *c.n* **1** dangerously steep side of a mountain etc: *be blown over the precipice.* Compare cliff. **2** (*fig*) dangerous situation: *be on a financial precipice.*

precipitous /prɪ'sɪpɪtəs/ *adj* (*formal*) dangerously steep: *a precipitous route down the mountain.*
pre'cipitously *adv*. **pre'cipitousness** *u.n*.

precipitate /prɪ'sɪpɪtɪt/ *c/u.n* **1** (*technical*) substance precipitated(3).
▷ *v* /prɪ'sɪpɪˌteɪt/ *tr.v* (*formal*) cause (s.t) to happen suddenly (sooner than wanted or expected): *The fire precipitated the business's financial ruin.* **3** *tr/intr.v* (*technical*) (cause (a substance) to) separate from a solution in the form of very small pieces. **4** *tr/intr.v* (*technical*) (cause (damp air) to) become rain, snow etc and fall.

precipitation /prɪˌsɪpɪ'teɪʃən/ *c/u.n*.

precis, précis /'preɪsiː/ *c.n* **1** (*pl* precis, précis /'preɪsiːz/) summary(3) of the content of a speech or piece of writing.
▷ *tr.v* (*p.t,p.p -ed* /'preɪsiːd/) **2** make a precis(1) of (s.t): *We precised the report for the meeting.*

precise /prɪ'saɪs/ *adj* Opposite imprecise. **1** exact; particular: *a precise measurement/number/date.* **2** accurate: *precise scientific instruments; her precise address.* **3** (of a person) determined to keep to the agreed rules or standards: *be precise in one's business methods.*

pre'cisely *adv* **1** exactly: *Be here at 9 o'clock precisely.* **2** clearly and accurately: *explain precisely what one wants.* **3** (used to express one's total agreement) yes, that is exactly right: 'You'd obviously need extra time to finish the work if we change the design(1,3).' 'Precisely.'

precision /prɪ'sɪʒən/ *u.n* (also *attrib*) fact or

quality of being accurate: *precision instruments*; *use precision when measuring.*

preclude /prɪˈkluːd/ *tr.v (formal)* prevent (s.t) (by making s.t impossible): *The evidence before us precludes any doubt that he was in the house that night.*
pre'clusion /prɪˈkluːʒən/ *u.n.*

precocious /prɪˈkəʊʃəs/ *adj (often derog; formal)* (esp of a child) (trying to seem) advanced in mental(1) development/ability: *Mozart was a precocious child.*
pre'cociously *adv.* **pre'cociousness** *u.n.*

preconceived /ˌpriːkənˈsiːvd/ *attrib.adj* formed before any personal knowledge or direct experience: *a preconceived idea/opinion of life as a student.*
preconception /ˌpriːkənˈsepʃən/ *c.n* preconceived idea, opinion etc: *going to university without any preconceptions of/about life as a student.*

precondition /ˌpriːkənˈdɪʃən/ *c.n (formal)* condition that is necessary before a particular result can be had: *One precondition for getting into university is to have a good report from your teachers.*

precursor /prɪˈkɜːsə/ *c.n* person or thing coming in advance as a sign of what will come later: *She was a precursor of many women prime ministers. This invention was a precursor of television.*
pre'cursory *adj.*

pred *written abbr* predicative.

predate /priːˈdeɪt/ *tr.v* (of an event, happening etc) occur earlier than (s.t): *His successful attempt at getting a driving licence predates mine by about two years.* ⇒ postdate.

predator /ˈpredətə/ *c.n* animal that kills another animal for food, e.g a lion, eagle(1), spider or human.

predecessor /ˈpriːdɪˌsesə/ *c.n* **1** person who has a particular job before another person: *My predecessor worked from nine to six but I prefer to work from eight to five.* **2** ancestor: *His predecessors were born in eastern Europe.*

predestine /priːˈdestɪn/ *tr.v* (usu passive) *(formal)* (with God or fate(1) as the agent) decide (s.t) in advance: *He seemed predestined to become a lawyer.*
predestination /priːˌdestɪˈneɪʃən/ *u.n* (esp) religious belief that God has decided the future.

predetermine /ˌpriːdɪˈtɜːmɪn/ *tr.v* (usu passive) decide (s.t) in advance: *Her future was predetermined by her parents' wealth.*

predeterminer /ˌpriːdɪˈtɜːmɪnə/ *c.n (grammar)* determiner used in front of another, e.g 'all the money', 'both the wheels'.

predicament /prɪˈdɪkəmənt/ *c.n* (often *be in a — (about s.o/s.t)*) difficult, embarrassing or puzzling situation (about s.o/s.t): *We're in a predicament about which way to choose.*

predicate /ˈpredɪkət/ *c.n (grammar)* part of a statement saying s.t about the subject[1](4), e.g *The house is beautiful, is a mess, cost £50 000.*

predicative /prɪˈdɪkətɪv/ *adj (written abbr pred) (grammar)* referring to, situated(1) with, the predicate (and not placed before the noun): *'Awake' is a predicative adjective.* Compare attributive.

predict /prɪˈdɪkt/ *tr.v* say (what will happen) in

advance: *I've predicted sunshine (or that the weather will be good) tomorrow. It's impossible to predict who will win the competition.*
pre'dictable *adj* that can be predicted: *predictable behaviour; a result that was predictable.* Opposite unpredictable.
pre'dictably / *adv.*
prediction /prɪˈdɪkʃən/ *c/u.n* (example of the) act of predicting: *make predictions about the weather.*

predilection /ˌpriːdɪˈlekʃən/ *c.n* (often *— for s.o/ s.t) (formal)* obvious preference (for s.t): *She has a predilection for fast cars.*

predispose /ˌpriːdɪˈspəʊz/ *tr.v* (usu *— s.o to s.t) (formal)* cause (s.o) to act, feel, in a particular way in advance: *John's childhood living on an island predisposed him to a love of the sea.*
predisposition /ˌpriːdɪspəˈzɪʃən/ *c/u.n* (often *— to s.t) (formal)* condition of being likely to do, feel, suffer etc s.t: *She has a predisposition to backaches.*

predominate /prɪˈdɒmɪˌneɪt/ *intr.v* (often *— over s.o/s.t) (formal)* **1** be greater in number, strength etc (than s.o/s.t): *In this area cattle predominate (over sheep).* **2** have control/power (over s.o/s.t): *The Liberals seem to predominate (over other political parties) in the southwest.*
predominance /prɪˈdɒmɪnəns/ *c/u.n* fact or state of being predominant.
pre'dominant *adj* having greater numbers, strength, power, influence etc: *The predominant cause of the illness was dirty water.*
pre'dominantly *adv.*

pre-eminent /priːˈemɪnənt/ *adj (formal)* far greater than others in influence, importance, merit etc: *Her skill was pre-eminent in her school.*
pre-'eminence *u.n.*
pre-'eminently *adv.*

pre-empt /priːˈempt/ *tr.v (formal)* do, get or take (s.t) before another person has an opportunity: *My bid(1) for the house was pre-empted by their ability to settle a price quickly.*
pre-'emptive *adj* that pre-empts: *a pre-emptive offer.*

preen /priːn/ *v* **1** *tr.v* (of a bird) keep (its feathers) healthy by cleaning and arranging them: *The pigeons sat preening themselves, each other, their feathers.* **2** *intr/reflex.v (derog; fig)* arrange one's clothes in a self-important way: *He was preening himself in front of the mirror.*

prefab /ˈpriːˌfæb/ *c.n (informal)* prefabricated house.
prefabricated /priːˈfæbrɪˌkeɪtɪd/ *adj* (of parts of a structure) produced in advance so that s.t can be put together more quickly and easily: *prefabricated houses.*

preface /ˈprefɪs/ *c.n* **1** writer's personal introduction at the beginning of a book.
▷ *tr.v* **2** *(formal)* begin (a speech, book etc) with remarks as an introduction: *He prefaced his speech by explaining that the law prevented him from speaking freely.*
prefatory /ˈprefətərɪ/ *attrib.adj* that prefaces(2) s.t: *prefatory remarks.*

prefect /ˈpriːfekt/ *c.n* senior(1) pupil given special responsibilities in a school. ⇒ monitor(1).

prefer /prɪˈfɜː/ *tr.v (-rr-)* **1** choose (s.o/s.t) because one likes her/him/it better: *I prefer* *butter to* margarine. *Which dress do you prefer? I'd prefer to wait, thanks.* **2** (of the police) make (a charge(3)) against s.o in a law court.

preferable /'prefərəbl/ *adj* (often — *to* s.o/s.t) liked more (than another or others): *This method is preferable (to that one).*

'preferably *adv.*

preference /'prefərəns/ *c/u.n* (example of) preferring (⇒ prefer(1)): *Do you have any preference for a particular kind of music? My preference would be a holiday in the mountains. A* referee(2) *must not show any preference for either team during the match.* **in preference to s.o/s.t** instead of s.o/s.t because he/she/it is better liked: *I'd always go walking in preference to lying on a beach.*

preferential /,prefə'renʃəl/ *attrib.adj* giving or showing preference: *He gives his own children preferential treatment.*

prefix /'pri:fɪks/ *c.n* set of letters or word put in front of another word to change its meaning, e.g 'dis-', 'pre-', 'over-', 'un-', 'under-'.

pregnant /'pregnənt/ *adj* carrying one or more unborn children or young animals in the body: *My sister's pregnant. Do you think the cat is pregnant?* **pregnant with s.t** (*fig; formal*) having signs of (s.t); filled with (s.t): *Her smile was pregnant with meaning.*

'pregnancy *n* **1** *c.n* (*pl -ies*) example of being pregnant: *I had an easy pregnancy.* **2** *u.n* condition of being pregnant: *Smoking during pregnancy is dangerous.*

,pregnant 'pause *c.n* pause in a speech etc having obvious importance that is not actually expressed in words.

prehistoric /,pri:hɪ'stɒrɪk/ *adj* of the period(2) before history was written down: *prehistoric animals/societies.*

prejudge /pri:'dʒʌdʒ/ *tr.v* make a judgement of (s.o/s.t) before all the facts are known: *Don't prejudge other people, the situation.*

pre'judgement *c/u.n* (also **pre'judgment**).

prejudice /'predʒudɪs/ *c/u.n* **1** (often — *against* s.o/s.t) poor opinion (of s.o/s.t) formed unfairly, e.g because one refuses to consider all the facts: *He has a prejudice against young men with* earrings. Racial(2) *prejudice is a social disease.* **2** opinion, good or bad, formed without considering all the facts: *She seems to have a prejudice in favour of children who enjoy sports. The appointment must be made without prejudice towards any* candidate(1).

▷ *tr.v* **3** cause (s.o) to have or show prejudice (*n*): *I like her photographs but then I'm prejudiced because she's a close friend.* **4** cause (s.o) a disadvantage: *Her hair could prejudice her chances of getting the job.*

'prejudiced *adj* (*derog*) using or showing prejudice(*n*): *a prejudiced opinion of foreigners; a prejudiced manager.* Opposite unprejudiced.

preliminary /prɪ'lɪmɪnərɪ/ *adj* **1** (usu *attrib*) done, happening before, esp as a preparation or introduction: *a preliminary search/ report/* interview(1); *preliminary remarks before giving a speech.*

▷ *c.n* (*pl -ies*) **2** (usu *pl*) preliminary(1) action or event: *Let's get the preliminaries finished so that the main meeting can begin.*

prelude /'prelju:d/ *c.n* **1** (usu — *to* s.t) action or event that is an introduction (to the main one):

These lessons are a prelude to the actual language course. **2** (*technical*) piece of music forming the first part of a longer piece.

premarital /pri:'mærɪtl/ *attrib.adj* (usu of sexual relations) happening before marriage: *premarital sex.*

premature /'premə,tjʊə/ *adj* **1** coming, happening before, the usual or expected time: *I was a premature baby and was born two months early* (or *I was two months premature*). **2** done quickly without enough time or thought: *Wasn't it premature to sell your house before buying another one? Your decision was premature.*

'prema,turely *adv.*

premed /pri:'med/ *c.n* (*informal*) premedication.

premedication /,pri:medɪ'keɪʃən/ *u.n* (*informal premed*) drugs(1) used to make a patient calm before surgery(1).

premeditated /pri:'medɪ,teɪtɪd/ *adj* decided and planned in advance: *The murder was premeditated.*

premier /'premɪə/ *attrib.adj* **1** first in importance, order, rank etc: *a premier politician/ writer.*

▷ *c/def.n* **2** prime minister: *Britain's premier; the premier's car.*

premiere, première /'premɪ,eə/ *c.n* (also *attrib*) (often — *of* s.t) first performance (of a film, play, musical composition etc): *a Royal premiere of Stoppard's new play.*

premise /'premɪs/ *c.n* (also **'premiss**) statement used as the basis for one's opinion, feeling of certainty etc in an argument etc: *If you accept the premise that most children like sugar then you'll understand why sweets are so popular.*

premises /'premɪsɪz/ *pl.n* area of land and its buildings: *business/private premises. Were there any staff on the premises at the time? I want you off the premises immediately.*

premium /'pri:mɪəm/ *c.n* **1** amount of money (to be) paid for insurance(1). **2** great value: *I put a high premium on assistants who are prepared to work hard.* **at a premium** costing a high price or difficult to get because there is only a small supply: *Hotel rooms were at a premium during the Olympic games.*

premonition /,premə'nɪʃən/ *c.n* strong feeling that s.t (bad) is going to happen: *have a premonition that he will fail, of a serious fall in sales.*

prenatal /pri:'neɪtl/ *adj* happening during pregnancy: *prenatal problems.* ⇒ antenatal, postnatal.

prenominal /pri:'nɒmɪnl/ *adj* (*grammar*) (of an adj) placed before a noun; attributive.

preoccupy /pri:'ɒkjʊ,paɪ/ *tr.v* (*-ies, -ied*) (often passive, — *s.o* (*with* s.o/s.t)) fill (s.o)'s mind with thoughts (about s.o/s.t): *I was preoccupied with financial worries. A wish to visit Tibet preoccupied them.*

preoccupation /pri:,ɒkjʊ'peɪʃən/ *c/u.n* (often — *with* s.o/s.t) state of being preoccupied (about s.o/s.t): *preoccupation with planning the journey.*

pre'occu,pied *adj* (usu *pred*) with all one's attention on one's own thoughts: *She didn't hear me because she was preoccupied.*

prep *written abbr* **1** preposition.

▷ *n* /prep/ (*informal*) **2** *u.n* homework. ⇒ preparation(3). **3** *c.n* = preparatory school.

prepare /prɪ'peə/ *tr/intr.v* (often — (s.o/s.t) *for*

s.o/s.t, *to do s.t*) get/make (s.o/s.t) ready (for a person, purpose, use, occasion etc): *prepare for an examination*; *prepare a meal for one's friends*; *prepare oneself for bad news*; *prepare the ground for plants*; *prepare to meet guests*. **be prepared for s.t** be mentally ready for s.t and expect it to happen: *I knew the game would be difficult but I wasn't prepared for such excellent playing*. **be prepared to do s.t** be able and willing to do s.t: *I'm prepared to lend the money. Are you prepared to work hard?*

preparation /ˌprepəˈreɪʃən/ *n* **1** *u.n* activity of preparing: *Preparation for examinations includes getting enough sleep*. **2** *c.n* mixture made for a particular purpose or use: *a chemical/medical preparation*. **3** (usu **prep**) (in a (private) school) homework.

preparations *pl.n* things done while preparing: *make preparations for one's wedding*.

preparatory /prɪˈpærətəri/ *adj* (*formal*) done or used when preparing or as an introduction: *preparatory exercises/discussions*. **preparatory to s.t** (*formal*) in advance and as preparation for s.t: *read one's notes preparatory to making a speech*.

preˈparatory ˌschool *c.n* (also **ˈprep ˌschool**) private school for children up to about 14 years of age.

preparedness /prɪˈpeərɪdnɪs/ *u.n*.

prepay /priːˈpeɪ/ *tr.v* (*p.t,p.p* **prepaid** /priːˈpeɪd/) pay (money for) (s.t) in advance: *The postage was prepaid*.

preˈpayment *c/u.n*.

preponderant /prɪˈpɒndərənt/ *adj* (usu *pred*) (*formal*) larger in number, weight, strength etc: *Many families live in houses but flats are preponderant in the cities*.

preˈponderance *sing/u.n* (often — *of s.o/s.t*): *a preponderance of flats in the cities*.

preˈponderantly *adv*.

preposition /ˌprepəˈzɪʃən/ *c.n* (*written abbr* **prep** as used in this dictionary) (*grammar*) word used in front of a noun or pronoun to show its relation to one or more other words, e.g 'come *into* a room', '*over* his shoulder', '*up* a mountain'.

ˌprepoˈsitional *adj* (*grammar*) containing, acting as, referring to, a preposition: *a prepositional phrase*(1) *such as 'in place of'; a prepositional verb such as 'look at'*.

prepossessing /ˌpriːpəˈzesɪŋ/ *adj* (often with a negative) (*formal*) giving a favourable impression(1): *This hotel doesn't look very prepossessing*. Opposite unprepossessing.

preposterous /prɪˈpɒstərəs/ *adj* very silly, esp because clearly impossible: *a preposterous excuse/idea/plan*.

preˈposterously *adv*. **preˈposterousness** *u.n*.

prerecord /ˌpriːrɪˈkɔːd/ *tr.v* make a recording of (a television programme, interview(2) etc) for later use: *This programme has been prerecorded*. ⇒ live¹(2).

prerequisite /priːˈrekwɪzɪt/ *c.n* (also *pred*) (*formal*) necessary (thing): *A driving licence is (a) prerequisite for the job*.

prerogative /prɪˈrɒgətɪv/ *c.n* (often — *to do s.t*) (*formal*) personal right or privilege(3) (to do s.t) because of one's power, rank etc: *They have the prerogative to send away lazy students. Who has the prerogative to pardon*(6) *a criminal? It's my prerogative to change my decision if I want to.*

Pres *written abbr* President.

Presbyterian /ˌprezbɪˈtɪəriən/ **1** *adj/c.n* ((of a) member of the) Protestant(1) churches run by senior(2) people who belong to it (called **ˈpresbyters**) and now forming part of the United Reform Church. **2** *adj* of these churches.

preschool /priːˈskuːl/ *attrib.adj* **1** of or referring to children too young to go to school: *preschool education*.
▷ *c.n* **2** (also *attrib*) educational establishment(2) for children under five years old: *preschool classes*.

prescribe /prɪˈskraɪb/ *tr.v* **1** order the use of (s.t): *prescribe which books to use*; *prescribe drugs*(1) *for an illness*. ⇒ proscribe. **2** give a ruling on (which action to take): *These are the fines prescribed by the law*. Compare proscribe.

prescription /prɪˈskrɪpʃən/ *n* **1** *u.n* act or fact of prescribing (⇒ prescribe). **2** *c.n* (also *attrib*) doctor's/optician's written order for medicines, drugs(1) etc: *prescription glasses*. **on prescription** as/if ordered by a doctor: *This drug*(1) *is only available on prescription*.

prescriptive /prɪˈskrɪptɪv/ *adj* (*formal*) established/given because of a right, rule, order etc: *One's prescriptive rights include the right to a fair trial*.

present¹ /ˈpreznt/ *adj* **1** (*pred*) (being) in a particular place: *I was present when they got married. How many students are present this morning?* **2** (*attrib*) existing at the time when s.t is said or written; now: *The present government supports that idea. At the present time I'm living in Oxford.* **3** (*attrib*) now being discussed or mentioned: *the present topic of conversation*. **4** (*grammar*) of or referring to the present tense.
▷ *def.n* **5** time now: *She worries more about the present than the future*. **6** (*grammar*) present tense: *In 'He shouts when he's angry', 'shouts' is in the present*.

presence /ˈprezns/ *u.n* **1** fact or state of being present¹(1): *Is my presence necessary at tomorrow's meeting? After two weeks as manager he soon made his presence felt*. **2** (*formal*) impressive way of standing, talking etc: *Olivier has such great presence when he's on stage*. **presence of mind** ability to be calm and act sensibly during a crisis(1): *During the fire he showed great presence of mind by closing the doors*. ⇒ absence of mind.

ˌpresent-ˈday *attrib.adj* modern, current: *present-day life in the city*.

ˌpresent ˈparticiple *c.n* (*written abbr* **pres.p** used in this dictionary) (*grammar*) form of a verb used to make the present tense, e.g 'He is *going*', 'We are *reading*'.

ˌpresent ˈperfect (ˌtense) *def.n* = perfect tense.

ˌpresent ˈtense *def.n* (*grammar*) verb form used to show an action happening or a state existing, now, e.g 'She's *laughing*', 'They're *arriving*', 'He *worries*'.

present² /ˈpreznt/ *c.n* thing given freely to show affection, thanks etc: *a birthday present*; *make a present of one's favourite record*.

present³ /prɪˈzent/ *tr.v* **1** (often — *s.t to s.o*) (*formal*) give (s.t) (to s.o): *I was presented with a certificate*(1). *You must present your letter of* *introduction to the manager.* **2** (often — *s.o* (*to s.o*)) (*formal*) introduce: *May I present my eldest son (to you)?* **3** give a performance of (a play): *present 'King Lear' at Stratford.* **4** suggest in one's mind: *That presents a difficulty/problem.* **5** (*commerce*) give/produce (a bill, estimate(1) etc).

pre'sentable *adj* fit to be introduced to s.o: *look presentable.* Opposite unpresentable.

presentation /ˌprezən'teɪʃən/ *n* **1** *u.n* (also *attrib*) act of giving s.t formally: *the presentation of a medal*(1); *a presentation ceremony.* **2** *c.n* performance of a play etc: *an interesting presentation of 'Figaro'.* **3** *u.n* way in which written work is produced: *neat/untidy presentation.*

presently /'prezəntlɪ/ *adv* (*formal*) **1** soon: *I'll be there presently.* **2** (esp US) now; at present.

preserve /prɪ'zɜ:v/ *n* **1** *sing.n* particular (area of) activity: *Teaching mathematics is not my preserve.* **2** *c/u.n* (*formal*) jam: *strawberry preserve.* ▷ *tr.v* **3** (*formal*) keep (s.o/s.t) safe from harm: *using seat belts to preserve people from serious injury.* **4** keep (s.t) from being destroyed: *preserving old buildings.* **5** (*formal*) keep (food) from going bad by boiling, freezing etc: *preserve plums.*
preservation /ˌprezə'veɪʃən/ *u.n.*
preservative /prɪ'zɜ:vətɪv/ *c/u.n* (example of a) substance used to keep food from going bad: *Are there too many preservatives in our food?*

preside /prɪ'zaɪd/ *intr.v* (often — at/over s.t) have the main position of authority in a group activity: *preside at a meeting, over a committee.*

president /'prezɪdənt/ *c.n* (with capital **P** in names) (*written abbr* Pres) **1** head of state in a republic: *President Lincoln of the USA.* **2** head of some business companies, organizations, colleges etc: *the president of the students' union.*
presidency *c/def.n* (*pl -ies*) **1** period(2) of being a president: *during the presidencies of Reagan and Bush.* **2** office or rank of a president: *It was a difficult battle to win the presidency.*
presidential /ˌprezɪ'denʃəl/ *attrib.adj* of, for, referring to, a president: *a presidential speech.*

press /pres/ *n* **1** *c.n* act of applying pressure or weight, e.g by pushing against s.o/s.t: *with a press of her hand*; *felt a press on his arm.* **2** *c.n* act of pressing (⇒ press(8)): *Your trousers need a press.* **3** *c.n* close/tight group of people: *a press outside the doors waiting for the new shop to open.* ⇒ press(7). **4** *def.n* (also *attrib*) people concerned with getting and giving out news, e.g in newspapers, magazines, on television and radio: *Are you willing to talk to the press? Is there freedom of the press in your country? He's at a press conference. Do you have a press card?* **5** *u.n* newspapers, news reports etc: *I read it in today's press.* **6** *c.n* machine that makes or changes something using pressure: *a flower-press*; *a printing-press*; *a wine-press.* **hot off the press** (of news, information) very new and not known yet by anyone else.
▷ *v* **7** *tr/intr.v* apply pressure or weight (to (s.o/s.t)) by pushing: *I pressed the button and the machine started. She pressed my hand to her face. His nose was pressed against the window. We pressed together on the station* platform(2). **8** *tr.v* apply heat and pressure to (cloth or clothes) to make it/them flat: *Would you press the* sleeves(1) *for me?* ⇒ iron(5). **9** *tr.v* press(7)

(s.t) between two or more surfaces, esp to get liquid etc out: *You must press the two* lemons *and save the juice.* **10** *tr.v* (esp — (s.o) for, to do, s.t) make a serious and very urgent request to (s.o) (for s.t etc): *They're pressing (me) for a decision* (or *me to decide quickly*). **be hard pressed (for, to do, s.t)** be in great difficulties (about getting, doing etc s.t): *We're hard pressed (for money* or *to find the money) at the moment.* **be pressed for s.t** have (almost) not enough of s.t: *I'm pressed for money/space/time.* **press for s.t** demand s.t strongly: *The unions have pressed for better working conditions.* **press s.t home (to s.o)** ⇒ home(*adv*). **press s.t on s.o** (try to) make s.o accept s.t offered: *She tried to press the money on me but I refused to take it.* **press on (with s.t)** continue (doing s.t) with great effort: *We pressed on (with our journey) even though it was raining hard.*
'pressing *adj* needing quick or immediate attention: *a pressing problem.*
'press re,lease *c.n* official statement from a government department, important person etc to the press(4).
'press ,stud *c.n* small device used to fasten cloth etc with one part having a small knob and the other part having a hole; the parts fasten when pressed(7) together.
'press-,up *c.n* physical(1) exercise by lying face down on the floor and lifting one's body by pressing against the floor with one's hands.

pressure /'preʃə/ *n* **1** *u.n* (amount of) force against, on, through etc s.t: *It would need a lot of pressure to hold it down. I could feel the pressure of the crowd behind me.* **2** *u.n* (used in combinations) kind of pressure(1) produced by s.t: *air pressure*; *blood pressure.* **3** *c/u.n* quality that is difficult to put up with, produces tiredness, strain(3) etc: *pressure of work. I have so many pressures at the moment.* **4** *u.n* (esp under — (to do s.t); put — on s.o (to do s.t)) strong influence, esp to persuade s.o (to do s.t): *I'm under pressure to change the team. They're putting pressure on us to agree a price for the house.*
'pressure ,cooker *c.n* kind of saucepan with an airtight lid so that food can cook quickly at a very high temperature using steam.
'pressure ,group *c.n* group of people trying to use their influence to persuade a government, politician, organization etc to agree to do s.t.
'pressure ,point *c.n* **1** part of the body where bleeding can be stopped if pressed firmly. **2** part of a process(2) where there are the most problems.
pressurize, -ise /'preʃəraɪz/ *tr.v* **1** put pressure(4) on (s.o) to do s.t: *I refuse to decide who to vote for while I feel so pressurized.* **2** (usu passive) increase air pressure inside (an aircraft) so that it is the same as normal air pressure on the ground.

prestige /pre'sti:ʒ/ *u.n* good reputation, esp because of personal position, success etc: *His prestige is due to his family, business successes.*
prestigious /pre'stɪdʒəs/ *adj.*

presume /prɪ'zju:m/ *v* **1** *tr/intr.v* accept (s.t), think of (s.t), as true without proof: *I presume that you have decided not to go. You are Mark's wife, I presume. We must presume that they are not to blame until we have* evidence(1) *that they* *are.* **2** *intr.v* (usu — *to do s.t*) (*formal*) have the courage (to do s.t) without first getting permission: *How dare you presume to tell me what to do!*

pre'sumably *adv* one supposes (that . . .): *Presumably you've decided not to go.*

presumption /prɪ'zʌmpʃən/ *n* (*formal*) **1** *sing.n* (esp *on the — that . . .*) thing considered to be true but without proof: *I'm sending another cheque on the presumption that the other was lost.* **2** *u.n* way of behaving in order to seem very important, clever etc: *He had the presumption to suggest that he could do my job better than me.*

presumptive /prɪ'zʌmptɪv/ *pred.adj* (*formal*) considered as true but not yet proved: *an heir presumptive.*

presumptuous /prɪ'zʌmtjʊəs/ *adj* (*derog*) having or showing presumption(2): *a presumptuous act/person.*

presuppose /ˌpriːsə'pəʊz/ *tr.v* (*formal*) suggest that (s.t) is true, esp because it is a necessary condition etc: *Having a university degree presupposes that you are intelligent.*

presupposition /ˌpriːsʌpə'zɪʃən/ *c/u.n.*

pretend /prɪ'tend/ *tr/intr.v* **1** try to make s.o believe (s.t) is true when it is not: *She pretended that she was rich* (or *to be rich*). *I wasn't really asleep — I was only pretending.* **2** make s.o/s.t seem to be (another person, thing etc), esp as a game: *Let's pretend to be famous explorers. They're pretending that they are travelling under the sea.*

pretence /prɪ'tens/ *c/u.n* (example of the) act of pretending (⇨ pretend): *It was only a pretence of loyalty.* **(by/under) false pretences** ⇨ false(*adv*).

pre'tension *n* **1** *c.n* (often *pl*, —s to s.t) (*formal*) (false) claim: *I make no pretensions to being able to sew.* **2** *u.n* state of being pretentious: *She spoke without pretension about her books.*

pretentious /prɪ'tenʃəs/ *adj* (*derog; formal*) having or showing self-importance: *a pretentious speaker.* Opposite unpretentious.

pre'tentiously *adv.* **pre'tentiousness** *u.n.*

pretext /'priːtekst/ *c.n* untrue reason used to hide the real one: *It was a pretext for not joining the others.* **on the pretext of doing s.t** pretending that one is doing s.t: *She stayed behind on the pretext of helping to wash up.*

pretty /'prɪtɪ/ *adj* **1** (*-ier, -iest*) (**a**) (of a woman or girl) attractive, pleasant to look at: *a pretty little girl.* (**b**) (esp of female clothes, young or small animals, designs(2) etc) pleasant to look at: *a pretty dress/hat; pretty little lambs*(1); *a pretty pattern; a pretty garden/house.* Opposite ugly(1). Compare beautiful(1). **2** (used ironically) good: *After the accident she looked a pretty mess*[1](1)/ *sight!* **as pretty as a picture** ⇨ picture(*n*).

▷ *adv* **3** (*informal*) quite(2); rather(1): *a pretty large house.* **pretty much/well** almost: *pretty much/ well the same thing.* **pretty nearly** almost: *The work is pretty nearly finished.* **a pretty penny** ⇨ penny. **sitting pretty** (*informal*) (of a person) in a good personal position: *With an interesting job and a nice home she is sitting pretty.*

'prettily *adv.* **'prettiness** *u.n.*

prevail /prɪ'veɪl/ *intr.v* (often — *against/over s.o/ s.t*) be successful (against s.o/s.t); prove to be better (than s.o/s.t): *Justice must prevail* (*against*

any attempt to prevent it). *Our* policies(1) *will prevail over all the others.* **prevail on/upon s.o (to do s.t)** (*formal*) persuade s.o (to do s.t): *prevail on/upon them to tell the truth.*

pre'vailing *adj* **1** happening most often; general: *the prevailing violence in some countries.* **2** (*attrib*) most frequent: *prevailing winds.* **3** existing now: *It is difficult to make money under the prevailing* economic(1) *conditions.*

prevalence /'prevələns/ *u.n* (usu *the — of s.t*) (*formal*) condition of being prevalent: *the prevalence of anger among unemployed people.*

prevalent /'prevələnt/ *adj* (*formal*) common among many people or in a large area: *Poverty is prevalent in too many countries.*

prevaricate /prɪ'værɪˌkeɪt/ *intr.v* (*formal*) act or speak in a way that avoids being completely honest or truthful: *We needed the full facts about the situation but the government prevaricated.*

prevarication /prɪˌværɪ'keɪʃən/ *u.n.*

prevent /prɪ'vent/ *tr.v* (do s.t to) stop (s.t) happening: *They had injections to prevent the spread of the disease.* **prevent s.o (from doing s.t)** stop s.o (from doing s.t): *I was prevented from speaking by the noisy crowd.*

pre'ventable *adj* that can be prevented: *Is* nuclear war *preventable?*

prevention /prɪ'venʃən/ *u.n* act of preventing s.t: *Prevention of disease avoids problems of curing it.*

pre'ventive *adj* used, intended, to prevent s.t: *take preventive measures against disease.*

pre,ventive de'tention *u.n* act or policy of keeping people in prison because they are considered dangerous.

pre,ventive 'medicine *u.n* science, practice, of keeping people healthy and preventing disease: *Clean air in factories is a kind of preventive medicine.*

preview /'priːvjuː/ *c.n* (often — *of s.t*) **1** act of showing a film, play, show etc before it is officially available to the general public: *a preview of a new play.* **2** study or report used as a preparation for a more detailed one.

▷ *tr.v* **3** view (a film, play, show etc) in advance.

previous /'priːvɪəs/ *attrib.adj* coming, happening, before another in position or time: *the previous meeting/day/event/* chairperson. **previous to s.o/s.t** (*formal*) before s.o/s.t: *Previous to that occasion we'd never travelled abroad.*

'previously *adv.*

prey /preɪ/ *n* (*pl* prey) **1** *c/u.n* animal, bird etc taken and killed by another for food. ⇨ bird of prey. **2** *sing.n* (often — *to s.o/s.t*) (*fig*) victim of a pain, illness, enemy etc: *He's a prey to severe pain, her anger, disease.*

▷ *intr.v* **prey on/upon s.o/s.t 3** take and kill an animal for food: Eagles(1) *prey on small animals.* **4** (often — *on s.o's mind*) (*fig*) have a strong effect(1) that causes great sadness, anxiety etc: *Their huge debts prey on his mind.*

price /praɪs/ *c.n* (often — *of s.t*) **1** amount of money asked or paid (for s.t): *What's the price of this coat? That's a fair price to pay. Prices are increasing.* **2** thing one must do or give in order to get or keep s.t: *Is killing too high a price to pay for one's freedom? Illness was the price of her success at work.* **at a price** if one is willing to pay a high price: *You can get a house in London at a* *price! at any price* it doesn't matter how high the price may be: *I wouldn't sell the painting at any price.* **beyond/without price** too valuable to be given a price; priceless. **set a price on s.t** give s.t a price(1) (that one is not willing to reduce).

▷ *tr.v* **3** (often — *s.t at s.t*) give (s.t) a price (of a particular amount): *How much have you priced these tomatoes at?* **4** find out the price of (s.t): *I've visited other shops to price their vegetables and yours are much too high.* **price oneself/s.t out of the market** ask a price (for one's work etc) that is so high that people refuse to pay.

'priceless *adj* too valuable to be given a price: *priceless jewels. One's health is priceless.*

'price ,war *c.n* situation in which prices are reduced to beat competition from other shops.

'pricey *adj* (also **'pricy**) (*-ier, -iest*) (*informal*) expensive: *Bananas are pricey at the moment.*

prick /prɪk/ *c.n* **1** small hole made with a pointed object: *a pin prick.* **2** act of pricking (⇨ prick(5)): *pricks from a rose branch.* **3** short sudden pain caused by pricking (⇨ prick(5)): *feel a prick on one's finger.* **4** (*slang; do not use!*) penis.

▷ *tr.v* **5** make a prick(1) in (s.o/s.t): *The rose pricked my fingers.* **prick a hole (in s.t)** make a hole (in s.t) by pricking (⇨ prick(5)): *You need to prick a hole in the bag to let the air out.* **prick up one's ears** ⇨ ear.

prickle /'prɪkl/ *c.n* **1** small pointed piece on a plant or animal: *a bush/leaf with sharp prickles; a hedgehog's prickles.* ⇨ quill(3), spine(3), thorn(1). **2** feeling of short quick pricks(3): *the prickle of sunburn(1).*

▷ *tr/intr.v* **3** (cause (s.o) to) feel prickles(2): *These rose stems prickle (me).*

'prickly *adj* (*-ier, -iest*) **1** having prickles(1): *prickly leaves.* **2** causing prickles(2): *a prickly feeling.* **3** (*derog*) (of a person) easily made angry: *a prickly customer.* **4** difficult: *a prickly problem/situation.*

,prickly 'heat *u.n* prickly(2) feeling and red marks on the skin, caused by hot weather.

,prickly 'pear *c.n* (kind of cactus with a) round fruit with many very small prickles(1) on the outside.

pricy ⇨ price.

pride /praɪd/ *n* **1** *u.n* feeling of personal satisfaction, pleasure, honour etc because of one's ability, success, family etc: *I was filled with pride after my success. Our daughter's examination results gave us great pride.* ⇨ proud(1). **2** *u.n* feeling of high self-respect: *You can apologize without any loss of pride.* **the pride of s.t** the best example in a group, set: *He's the pride of the school.* **a pride of lions, peacocks** a group of lions, peacocks. **pride of place** the best, most important position: *Pride of place in the* exhibition(1) *was given to the Greek statues.* **swallow one's pride** not allow one's pride(2) to prevent one doing s.t: *Lisa swallowed her pride and apologized.* **take pride in s.t** (a) feel proud because of s.t: *You can take pride in your success so far.* (b) treat s.t in a way that deserves pride: *You must take more pride in your appearance.*

▷ *reflex.v* **3 pride oneself on s.t** feel proud because of s.t: *He prides himself on being good at English, on his scientific ability.*

pried, pries ⇨ pry¹, pry².

priest /priːst/ *c.n* **1** person in a Christian(1)

church, esp the Roman Catholic(1) one, who is trained to administer(1) a church service, preach, bless etc. ⇨ clergyman. **2** man who has a similar position in another religion. ⇨ priestess.

'priestess *c.n* woman who is a priest(2).

'priest,hood *def.pl n* priests as a group, profession: *join the priesthood.* ⇨ clergy.

prig /prɪg/ *c.n* (*derog*) person who is too eager for moral purity, perfection etc. Compare prude.

'priggish *adj.*

prim /prɪm/ *adj* (*-mm-*) (esp — *and proper*) (*usu derog*) very formal, well-mannered and (too) critical of other people's standards of behaviour: *looking prim and proper in a plain dress.*

'primly *adv.* **'primness** *u.n.*

prima ballerina /ˌpriːmə ˌbæləˈriːnə/ *c.n* leading woman ballet(3) dancer.

primacy /'praɪməsɪ/ *c.n* (*pl -ies*) **1** (*formal*) fact or state of being the first in position, importance etc. **2** position of an archbishop or other priest of very high rank. ⇨ primate².

prima donna /ˌpriːmə ˈdɒnə/ *c.n* **1** leading woman opera(1) singer. **2** (*derog*) woman with too much self-importance who is often bad-tempered.

primaeval ⇨ primeval.

primary ⇨ prime.

primate¹ /'praɪmeɪt/ *c.n* (*technical*) animal belonging to the group that have high intelligence, good eyesight and fingers and thumbs able to move and hold things easily: *People, apes(1) and monkeys are primates.*

primate² /'praɪmət/ *c.n* archbishop or other priest of very high rank.

prime /praɪm/ *attrib.adj* **1** highest in quality: *prime beef; in prime condition.* **2** highest in authority: *the prime minister.* **3** first in importance: *of prime concern/importance.*

▷ *u.n* **4** (often *in one's* —; *in the* — *of s.t*) (*formal*) (at the) time when s.o/s.t is at her/his/its best: *in the prime of life, one's youth. Jeff is in his prime.*

▷ *tr.v* **5** get (s.t) ready for use: *prime wood before painting it.* **6** give (s.o) facts, information etc as a preparation for s.t: *Your duty is to prime the manager about the company's activities so that she can prepare her speech.*

primarily /'praɪmərəlɪ/ *adv* mainly; chiefly: *My duties are primarily to keep the patients comfortable and happy.*

primary /'praɪmərɪ/ *adj* first in importance, order etc: *her primary duties; of primary concern/importance.*

,primary 'colour *c.n* one of three colours (red, blue and yellow) used to produce all the other colours. ⇨ cyan, magenta, yellow.

,primary 'industry *c.n* (*pl -ies*) industry that gets raw materials, food etc from natural sources, e.g farming, fishing, mining.

'primary ,school *c/u.n* school for children up to 9 or 11 years old. Compare preschool(2), secondary school, high school.

,primary 'stress *c.n* (*technical*) (mark¹ used to show the) strongest stress when saying a word, phrase(1) etc, e.g in 'population' the primary stress is on the third syllable, i.e /ˌpɒpjʊˈleɪʃən/. ⇨ secondary stress.

,prime 'minister *c.n* leading minister(1) in a government.

,prime 'number c.n (*mathematics*) number that can only be divided equally by itself or 1, i.e 3, 5, 7, 11, 13, 17 etc.

'primer c/u.n substance used on a surface before the undercoat of paint.

,prime 'time u.n time when the highest number of people watch television (and therefore when advertising rates are highest).

primeval /praɪˈmiːvl/ adj (also priˈmaeval) of (the time of the) earliest period of the world's development: *primeval forests.* ⇨ primordial.

primitive /ˈprɪmɪtɪv/ adj 1 of or referring to the earliest period of history: *primitive man*, *tools*. 2 very simple: *primitive weapons such as sticks and stones*; *primitive societies.* 3 rough and difficult to bear: *primitive conditions.*

▷ c.n 4 (*rare*) primitive(1) person.

primordial /praɪˈmɔːdɪəl/ adj (*technical*) belonging to the earliest times: *small primordial legs on some kinds of snakes.* ⇨ primeval.

primrose /ˈprɪmrəʊz/ adj 1 light yellow in colour: *primrose curtains.*

▷ n 2 c.n kind of short plant with light yellow flowers. 3 u.n light yellow colour.

prince /prɪns/ c.n (with capital P in names) 1 son of a king or queen: *Prince Charles.* 2 title of the ruler of some small states: *Prince Rainier of Monaco.* 3 noble of high rank in countries such as Germany and Italy.

'princely adj (-*ier*, -*iest*) 1 showing great generosity or kindness: *a princely gift/welcome.* 2 of a prince: *princely responsibilities.*

prin'cess c.n (with capital P in names) 1 daughter of a king or queen: *Princess Anne.* 2 wife of a prince(1,2).

principality /ˌprɪnsɪˈpælɪtɪ/ c.n (*pl -ies*) state ruled by a prince(2): *the principality of Monaco.*

principal /ˈprɪnsɪpl/ attrib.adj 1 first in importance, rank etc; main: *my principal source of income; the principal speaker.*

▷ n 2 c.n head of a college etc. 3 c.n leading dancer, singer etc in a performance on stage. 4 u.n (*technical*) amount of money owed on which interest is (to be) charged.

'principally adv.

principality ⇨ prince.

principle /ˈprɪnsɪpl/ n 1 c/u.n general rule or standard of (usu good) behaviour: *live up to one's principles. It's against her principles to lie.* 2 c.n general law, rule, theory(2): *I've never understood the principles of electricity.* ⇨ first principles. in principle (a) according to general theory(2): *We expect it to work in principle but we've yet to try.* (b) in general: *I agree with you in principle but I'd like to discuss a few details.* on principle because of one's principles(1): *I disagree with all violence on principle.* man/woman of principle person who has strong principles(1).

'principled adj (often used in combinations) having certain personal principles(1): *a high-principled politician.* Opposite unprincipled.

print /prɪnt/ n 1 u.n printed (⇨ print(5)) words: *This is easy print to read. Is the print too small?* 2 c.n photograph: *It was impossible to see some of the views in my holiday prints.* 3 c.n design, picture printed (⇨ print(5)) by using a wooden or metal block. 4 c.n mark etc made by pressure on a surface: *There's the print of her toes. There were many fingerprints, footprints in the sand.* ⇨ imprint(1). in, out of, print (of a book etc) available, not available, for buying.

▷ v 5 tr/intr.v produce (words, a design(2), picture etc) on paper, cloth etc by ink pressed on a surface: *print newspapers/books*; *print patterns on cloth.* 6 tr.v produce (a photograph) on paper: *Who printed your holiday photographs?* 7 tr/intr.v write (s.t) without joining the letters to each other as in normal handwriting: *Please print your name and address.* ⇨ block letters. 8 tr.v (usu — s.t out) (of a part of a computer) produce (words, tables(4), graphs etc) on paper. ⇨ printout.

'printable pred.adj (usu) suitable for being printed in a newspaper, book etc because not offensive(2): *What she said isn't printable.* Opposite unprintable.

,printed 'circuit c.n (*technical*) kind of electric(1) circuit(4) made by printing (⇨ print(5)) a system of electrical connections in metal on a flat board, used in radios, washing machines etc.

'printed ,matter u.n magazines, newspapers, leaflets etc (that can be sent at a cheap rate when posted).

'printer c.n 1 factory etc used to print(5) books, magazines etc. 2 person who prints(5) books, magazines etc. 3 device for printing (⇨ print(8)) information from a computer.

'print,out u.n printed (⇨ print(8)) information from a computer.

prior[1] /ˈpraɪə/ attrib.adj 1 earlier; already agreed: *I can't come because I have a prior arrangement to visit my parents.* 2 more important: *Would you agree that the examinations have a prior claim on your time?* prior to s.t (*formal*) before s.t in time: *Prior to that, to going to university, I worked in Brazil for a year.*

priority /praɪˈɒrɪtɪ/ n (*pl -ies*) 1 u.n (esp give — to s.o/s.t; have/take — over s.o/s.t) (*formal*) right of s.o/s.t to be first because already agreed or more important: *You must give priority to your family.* 2 c.n activity etc that must be first: *He must get his priorities right if he wants to be a lawyer. Being healthy is a top priority.*

prior[2] /ˈpraɪə/ c.n head of a priory.

'prioress c.n woman who is head of a priory.

'priory c.n (*pl -ies*) Christian(1) community(1) and the buildings it lives in, often as part of an abbey.

prise /praɪz/ tr.v 1 use force to get (s.t) off, open etc: *I prised off the lid with a spoon.* 2 (*fig*) force (information) out of s.o: *We prised the information out of her by threatening to tell her parents.*

prism /ˈprɪzəm/ c.n (*technical*) solid figure, usu transparent, with sides that are rectangles or triangles(1): *A glass prism will produce the colours of the rainbow when light is shone through it.*

prismatic /prɪzˈmætɪk/ adj.

prison /ˈprɪzn/ n 1 c/unique n (also *attrib*) place where criminals are kept as punishment: *He was sent to prison for five years. How long was she in prison? The prison officers want more pay.* ⇨ gaol(1), jail, open prison. 2 c.n (*fig*) place that seems like a prison(1): *After her accident, the house was a prison for several months.* ⇨ imprison.

'prisoner c.n 1 criminal who is in prison. 2 person kept in a place by force: *I was a prisoner in my* house for several months while my legs got better. ⇒ political prisoner. **keep s.o prisoner** force s.o to be a prisoner.

‚**prisoner of 'conscience** c.n prisoner held because of her/his religious etc beliefs and not because of a crime.

‚**prisoner of 'war** c.n prisoner who is an enemy soldier, officer etc captured during a war.

prissy /'prɪsɪ/ adj (-ier, -iest) (derog; informal) too concerned or worried about morals, good manners etc. Compare priggish, prude.
'**prissily** adv. '**prissiness** u.n.

pristine /'prɪstiːn/ attrib.adj in the earliest, most genuine(1) and pure state: The old house was in pristine condition.

private /'praɪvɪt/ adj 1 of, for, referring to, one particular person or group: This is a private conversation/letter. You interfered in my private affairs. I have a private office where I can work quietly. 2 secret: I have private information that he will leave tomorrow. Keep the news private until tomorrow. 3 without any official position: I'm here in my private capacity(3), not as a doctor. **in private** with no other person involved(2): May I see you, speak to you, in private?
▷ c.n 4 (written abbr Pte) soldier of the lowest rank in the army: Private/Pte Jones.

privacy /'praɪvəsɪ, 'prɪvəsɪ/ u.n (esp in the — of s.t) condition of being alone (s.w): I enjoy the privacy of my own garden. Would you like some privacy?

‚**private 'bill** c.n bill'(3) presented by an individual member of parliament, not by the government or a political party.

‚**private 'company** c.n business company that does not offer shares(3) to the public.

‚**private de'tective** c.n detective who is not a member of the police force but works for herself/himself.

‚**private 'enter,prise** c.n ⇒ enterprise.

‚**private 'eye** c.n (informal) private detective.

‚**private 'income/'means** c/u.n money obtained by any method(1) except employment, e.g from rich parents, investments(2) etc.

'**privately** adv 1 (usu) in one's own mind and often with no one else knowing: I spoke in favour of the idea but privately I was very worried about it. 2 without a dealer(2): I sold my car privately through the newspaper.

‚**private 'parts** pl.n (informal) external sexual organs.

‚**private 'practice** c.n medical practice that is not part of the state-controlled health service.

‚**private 'school** c/u.n school that is not part of the state education system and where fees(2) are charged.

‚**private 'secretary** c.n (often — to s.o) secretary(1) who works for one person only.

privatization, -isation /ˌpraɪvɪtaɪ'zeɪʃən/ u.n (often the — of s.t) act or process of privatizing (s.t).

'**priva,tize, -ise** tr.v give or sell control/ ownership of a state-controlled business or organization to individuals(3): Will the government privatize the railways?

privation /praɪ'veɪʃən/ c/u.n (formal) (example of the) condition of lacking necessities such as food, clothes and a home: Some families suffer many privations. ⇒ deprivation(1).

privilege /'prɪvɪlɪdʒ/ n 1 c.n special benefit(1)/ favour allowed under certain conditions: The older members have many extra privileges at the club. 2 c.n basic(1) right given to people according to the constitution(1) of a country: Education is a privilege that must be available to all our children. 3 c.n right given to a person because of her/his profession or position: It is my privilege as a lawyer to see the prisoner. 4 u.n benefit(1)/advantage given to a rich, powerful etc group in society: He should not get a place at university through privilege. **be a privilege to do s.t** (formal) be a great honour to do s.t: It was a privilege to know her.
'**privileged** adj enjoying the advantages of privilege(1,4). ⇒ underprivileged.

privy¹ /'prɪvɪ/ pred.adj **privy to s.t** knowing secret information about s.t: I was privy to the arrangements/decision.

‚**privy 'council** c.n group (now without real authority(1)) of senior(1) members of parliament etc appointed to advise the king or queen.

privy² /'prɪvɪ/ c.n (pl -ies) (old use or joking) lavatory.

prize /praɪz/ c.n 1 (also attrib) reward, honour etc for success in a competition, effort, good work etc: He won first prize. I got a prize for English at school. The prize money was given to the first four to finish.
▷ tr.v 2 consider (s.o/s.t) to have a high value: I prize my health above being wealthy.

pro¹ /prəʊ/ adv/prep (often as the first part of a word) in favour of: Are you pro the idea or anti? She's pro-Irish. ⇒ anti.

pros /prəʊz/ pl.n **pros and cons (of s.t)** arguments for (pros) and against (cons) s.t: They discussed the pros and cons of going by train.

pro² /prəʊ/ adj/c.n (informal) professional(1) (player): She turned pro six years ago (or has been a pro for six years).

PRO /ˌpiː ɑː 'əʊ/ abbr Public Relations Officer.

probable /'prɒbəbl/ adj that is likely to be, happen etc: The probable cause is her bad health. A win for Spain will be the probable result. Hot weather in England is possible but not probable. Opposite improbable.

probability /ˌprɒbə'bɪlɪtɪ/ c/u.n fact, condition or degree of being probable: What is the probability of finishing the work by Friday? There's a probability of rain tonight. Opposite improbability. **in all probability** it is extremely likely: In all probability he'll decide not to come.

'**probably** adv 1 it is probable that; in a way that is probable: They will probably arrive on Friday evening. 2 very likely: 'Will you need more bread?' 'Probably.'

probate /'prəʊbeɪt/ c/u.n (law) act of proving that a will²(1) is valid(1).

probation /prə'beɪʃən/ u.n (often on —) 1 period(1) during which s.o's abilities etc are watched: Teachers are usually put on probation for the first year. I did four years' probation before I became a car mechanic. 2 period(1) during which s.o who has committed a crime is watched by a probation officer instead of going to prison: one year probation. **on probation** being watched by a probation officer: The young man was put on probation because the theft was his first offence. Compare parole(1).

pro'bationary *adj.*

pro'bationer *c.n* person on probation.

pro'bation ,officer *c.n* officer of the law court who watches and helps a person on probation(1).

probe /prəʊb/ *c.n* **1** formal inquiry or search: *a police probe into the spread of* drugs(2). **2** (*technical*) kind of instrument used by a doctor, surgeon or dentist to examine an internal organ¹(1), infected area of the body, a tooth etc. ⇒ space probe.

▷ *v* **3** *tr/intr.v* (often — *into s.t*) inquire into (a problem): *probing (into) the causes of mass unemployment.* **4** *tr/intr.v* use a probe(2) to examine (a part of the body). **5** *tr/intr.v* use a long object to examine (s.t): *probing a hole with one's finger.* **6** *tr.v* use equipment(2) on a spacecraft to collect information about (s.t in the universe): *probing space to* identify *chemical structures of planets.*

problem /'prɒbləm/ *c.n* **1** (also *attrib*) person, animal, thing etc who/that is difficult to deal with: *We've had no problems with the new car. It is a problem car. You'll meet many problems during the journey. Her son is a real problem* (or *problem child*). **2** question, esp in an examination, that is to be solved: *I answered only four of the problems. The problem is what to do about the bad weather?* **the heart of the problem** ⇒ heart(*n*).

problematic /,prɒblə'mætɪk/ *adj* (also **,proble'matical**) (esp) causing doubt; not sure: *Whether we will ever own a house is problematic.*

proboscis /prə'bɒsɪs/ *c.n* (*pl* -es) (*technical*) **1** long mouth of certain insects, e.g a fly. **2** long nose of certain animals, e.g an elephant.

procedure /prə'si:dʒə/ *c/u.n* (often — *for doing s.t*) established(1) way (of doing s.t): *follow the normal/standard/usual procedure. What are the procedures for becoming a member?*

procedural /prə'si:dʒərəl/ *adj.*

proceed /prə'si:d/ *intr.v* (*formal*) **1** (often — *to s.t/s.w*) go forward (to s.t/s.w); carry on: *The group proceeded down the hill to the main gate. Let's proceed to the next item on the* agenda. **2** (often — *with s.t*; — *to do s.t*) begin or continue (to do) an activity: *We proceeded with the meeting, to talk about the difficulties.* **3** begin and then continue a course of action: *If you want to become a qualified* accountant *I'll explain how you should proceed.* **4** (usu — *against s.o*) (*law*) take legal(2) action (against s.o): *The police decided not to proceed against her.* **proceed from s.t** have its origins in s.t: *The illness proceeded from the lack of clean water.*

pro'ceeding *u.n* way of doing s.t, behaving: *Becoming qualified is your best way of proceeding.*

proceedings *pl.n* **1** (esp legal — (against s.o)) legal(2) action (against s.o): *They've begun* (or *taken out*) *legal(2) proceedings against their* neighbours. **2** records²(1) of the discussions, activities etc of a meeting, club, group etc.

proceeds /'prəʊsi:dz/ *pl.n* profit made by a business deal, the sale of s.t, a public entertainment etc: *She has given the proceeds of her prize to* charity(2).

process /'prəʊses/ *c.n* **1** organized way of producing things: *They have a new process for making bricks.* **2** series(1) of actions done to get a particular result: *follow the process of* reproduction(1) *in plants. Applying to enter a university is a complicated process.* **in the process** (of doing **s.t**) during or in the activity (of doing s.t): *I burnt my hand in the process of cooking the vegetables. I'm in the process of getting ready.*

▷ *tr.v* **3** deal with, produce, (s.t) using a process(2): *process film to make* negatives(8); *process information using a* computer; *processed cheese.*

'processor *c.n* device used to process(3).

procession /prə'seʃən/ *n* **1** *c.n* (also *attrib*) group of people, vehicles etc moving in an organized way, esp as part of a ceremony: *procession music. The royal procession moved slowly towards the church.* **2** *u.n* (*formal*) act of proceeding (⇒ proceed(1)): *They moved in procession down the street.*

pro'cessional *adj.*

proclaim /prə'kleɪm/ *tr.v* (*formal*) state or show (s.t) publicly and clearly: *War/Peace was proclaimed. The man proclaimed his* innocence(1) *in the law court.*

proclamation /,prɒklə'meɪʃən/ *n* **1** *u.n* act of proclaiming. **2** *c.n* official statement: *a government proclamation; a proclamation of war.*

proclivity /prə'klɪvɪtɪ/ *c.n* (*pl* -ies) (usu — *to/towards s.t*) (*formal*) tendency: *a proclivity towards laziness; a proclivity to be better at science subjects.*

procrastinate /prə'kræstɪ,neɪt/ *intr.v* (*formal*) delay doing s.t until a later time, esp delay many times in an attempt to avoid doing it.

procrastination /prə,kræstɪ'neɪʃən/ *c/u.n.*

pro'crasti,nator *c.n* person who procrastinates.

procreate /'prəʊkrɪ,eɪt/ *tr/intr.v* (*formal*) produce (children or young).

procreation /,prəʊkrɪ'eɪʃən/ *u.n.*

procure /prə'kjʊə/ *v* **1** *tr.v* (*formal*) obtain, get, (s.t): *procure a* divorce(1). **2** *tr/intr.v* (*law*) get/provide prostitutes.

prod /prɒd/ *c.n* **1** act of prodding (⇒ prod(2)): *a prod in the back with a stick.*

▷ *v* (-dd-) **2** *tr/intr.v* push or touch (s.o/s.t) with s.t long: *He prodded my arm. I prodded (the dead fish) with a stick but it didn't move.* **3** *tr.v* (usu — s.o *to do s.t, into doing s.t*) encourage (s.o) (to do s.t): *My conscience was prodding me to help them. What will prod them to act* (or *into action*)?

prodigal /'prɒdɪgl/ *adj* **1** using money, supplies etc too quickly and carelessly: *You'll be sorry later if you continue to be prodigal with the* water.

▷ *c.n* **2** person who is prodigal.

prodigy /'prɒdɪdʒɪ/ *c.n* (*pl* -ies) **1** child with great and special ability or talents(1). **2** (*formal*) thing that is particularly unusual and wonderful: *prodigies such as deep sea fish.*

prodigious /prə'dɪdʒəs/ *adj* (*formal*) **1** particularly unusual and wonderful. **2** very large: *the prodigious costs of space travel.*

pro'digiously *adv.*

produce /'prɒdjuːs/ *u.n* **1** thing that is produced(2), esp food from farms, gardens etc: *farm produce.*

▷ *v* /prə'djuːs/ **2** *tr/intr.v* give birth or existence to (s.o/s.t): *Our cat produced three* kittens. *Can the garden produce enough potatoes to feed us all? The tree produced many apples.* **3** *tr.v* use effort to bring (s.t) into existence: *He always produces* *a hot meal when we arrive.* **4** *tr.v* have (s.t) as a result: *The speech produced a large pile of letters of complaint.* **5** *tr.v* present (s.t) so that it can be considered: *produce evidence*(1)/*proof.* **6** *tr.v* (*formal*) take (s.t) out and show it: *He produced the missing money from under the bed.* **7** *tr/intr.v* arrange the performance of (a play, film etc): *I've produced many of Shakespeare's plays for television. He prefers producing to acting.*

pro'ducer *c.n* (often — *of* s.t) **1** person or thing who/that produces(2) s.t: *Is Brazil the biggest producer of coffee in the world?* ⇨ consumer. **2** person who produces(7) s.t: *a film producer.*

product /ˌprɒdʌkt/ *c.n* **1** thing that is made by s.o or a machine: *factory products.* **2** thing made by natural processes(2): *agricultural products.* **3** (often — *of* s.t) result (of an activity, process(1)): *The design was the product of many years of experience and experiment.* **4** (often — *of* s.o/s.t) result of reproduction(1): *I'm the product of two very determined people. It's the product of a white cat and a* ginger(2) *one.* **5** (*mathematics*) result of multiplying two or more numbers, quantities together: *The product of 2, 4 and 6 is 48.*

production /prə'dʌkʃən/ *n* **1** *u.n* act or process of producing(v) s.t: *Agricultural production is expensive.* **2** *u.n* (also *attrib*) amount produced: *Industrial production is decreasing. The production rate is very good.* **3** *c.n* (also *attrib*) organization and performance of a film, television programme etc: *production assistants/costs; radio productions; a splendid production of 'Othello'.* **in production** in the process of being produced(2), built: *A new car is in production.* **on production of s.t** if/when one shows, produces(5,6), s.t: *You can go on production of a driving* licence(1).

pro'duction ,line *c.n* system in a factory where parts are sent to several places for assembly(2), painting etc so that the finished product is ready at the end of the line.

productive /prə'dʌktɪv/ *adj* Opposite unproductive. **1** producing many or much of s.t: *productive mines/land/factories.* **2** producing good results: *a productive meeting/discussion.*

productivity /ˌprɒdʌk'tɪvɪtɪ/ *u.n* (power/rate of) being productive: *There was a fall/rise in productivity last year.*

prof¹ *written abbr* **1** professional(1). **2** (with capital **P** in names) Professor: *Prof B. Bright.*

prof² /prɒf/ *c.n* (*informal*) **3** professor: *Who's the prof in your* faculty(3)?

profane /prə'feɪn/ *adj* (*derog; formal*) having/showing no respect for God or religion: *profane language.*

pro'fanely *adv.*

profanity /prə'fænɪtɪ/ *c/u.n* (*pl -ies*) (*formal*) (example of) using profane language or being profane.

profess /prə'fes/ *tr.v* (*formal*) state (s.t) publicly and clearly: *She professed that she'd never seen him before, professed her* innocence(1). **profess to be s.o/s.t** state one's claim to be s.o/s.t: *She professes to be a qualified teacher.*

profession /prə'feʃən/ *n* **1** *c.n* (*formal*) public statement: *make a profession of one's* innocence(1). **2** *c.n* job that needs formal qualifications after training, e.g law, medicine,

teaching, acting. **3** *def/def.pl.n* people in a profession(2): *The medical profession say(s) the disease is very dangerous.*

pro'fessional *adj* Opposite unprofessional. **1** (*written abbr* prof) earning money by playing a game, acting etc: *a professional actor, football player.* Opposite amateur(1). **2** of a high standard: *a professional piece of work; a professional performance.* **3** of a profession(3); using the accepted rules, morals, behaviour etc of a profession(3): *professional ability; professional behaviour.* ▷ *c.n* **4** (*informal* pro) professional(1) person. Opposite amateur(3).

pro'fessionally *adv.*

professor /prə'fesə/ *c.n* (also **prof**) (also with capital **P**; *informal* and *abbr* in names Prof) head of a university department; teacher of the highest rank: *the Professor of* Biology; *Professor R U Thick.*

professorial /ˌprɒfɪ'sɔːrɪəl/ *adj.*

pro'fessor,ship *c/u.n* position or rank of (a) professor.

proficient /prə'fɪʃənt/ *adj* (esp — *in* s.t) having or showing ability (in s.t), usu after training: *a proficient piano player.*

pro'ficiency *u.n.*

pro'ficiently *adv.*

profile /'prəʊfaɪl/ *c.n* **1** view of the head from the side: *draw a profile of her face.* **2** (often — *of* s.o/s.t) description of (s.o, a business company, plan etc) with the main details only. **in profile** as a profile(1): *His nose looks bigger in profile.* ▷ *tr.v* **3** produce a profile(2) of (s.o/s.t): *The newspaper profiled her as an* irresponsible *parent.*

profit /'prɒfɪt/ *n* **1** *c/u.n* (amount of) money gained after paying expenses in a business activity, selling s.t etc: *I made a profit of £10 on the sale of my bicycle.* Gross²(1) *profit is the money gained before expenses such as wages, rent, reducing value of* equipment(2) *etc are taken into account.* Net²(1) *profit is the money gained after including all these expenses.* Opposite loss(2). ⇨ non-profit-making. **2** *u.n* (*formal*) advantage; benefit(1): *No one denies the profits of a good education.* ▷ *intr.v* **3** (often — *by/from* s.t) gain an advantage (by/from s.t): *profit by going to university; profit from experience.*

'profitable *adj* Opposite unprofitable. **1** producing profit(1): *a profitable business.* **2** (esp — *to* s.o) producing benefits(1) (for s.o); useful (to s.o): *a skill that will be profitable to you later on.*

,profita'bility *u.n.* **'profitably** *adv.*

profiteer /ˌprɒfɪ'tɪə/ *c.n* **1** (*derog*) person making large (and usu unfair) profits(1), e.g during a war or by selling goods at a high price because there is only a small supply of them. ▷ *intr.v* **2** (usu — *from* s.t) act as a profiteer(1): *profiteering from the war, his illness.*

'profit ,margin *c.n* difference between the amount earned/gained and the costs of production.

profligate /'prɒflɪgət/ *adj* (*derog; formal*) **1** immoral and not caring about it: *a profligate father.* **2** spending far too much money, wasting far too much time, using far too many supplies etc: *a profligate business manager.* ▷ *c.n* **3** (*derog; formal*) profligate(1) person.

profound /prə'faʊnd/ *adj* **1** very strong or deep:

a profound sleep; profound sadness; a profound silence. **2** showing much intelligence, knowledge, seriousness etc: *a profound statement; a profound mind/thinker.* **3** complete; total: *make profound changes to the basic(1) design.*

pro'foundly *adv (formal)* extremely: *I profoundly regret my bad behaviour. I'm profoundly sorry.*

profundity /prə'fʌndɪtɪ/ *u.n (formal)* (often *the — of s.t*) great depth (of s.t): *the profundity of his knowledge.*

profuse /prə'fjuːs/ *adj (formal)* (too) many or much: *profuse apologies/compliments.*

pro'fusely *adv.* **pro'fuseness** *u.n.*

profusion /prə'fjuːʒən/ *c/u.n (formal)* (often *— of s.o/s.t*) great number; too many or much: *a profusion of flags in the sports stadium.* **in profusion** in large numbers/amounts: *They grew vegetables in profusion.*

progeny /'prɒdʒɪnɪ/ *c/u.n (formal)* children of a person; young of an animal: *die without progeny.*

prognosis /prɒg'nəʊsɪs/ *c.n (pl prognoses /-siːz/) (medical)* statement of an opinion of the outcome of an illness: *make a prognosis.*

prognostic /prɒg'nɒstɪk/ *adj.*

prognosticate /prɒg'nɒstɪˌkeɪt/ *tr/intr.v (formal)* foretell (s.t in the future) using present information, signs etc.

programme /'prəʊgræm/ *c.n* (also, esp US, **'program**) **1** details of events, performers, times etc in a public entertainment: *a cinema/ theatre programme; a programme of the artists and their pictures in the* exhibition(1). **2** details of performances (to be) on television or the radio. **3** organized group of activities: *I have a busy programme tomorrow. What's on the programme for this morning?* **4** (details of the parts of a) plan: *the government programme for introducing new school examinations.* **5** broadcast(2) shown on television or radio.

▷ *tr.v* **6** organize, arrange, (s.t) as a programme (esp 3): *I've programmed my visits for the week.*

'program *c.n* **1** coded(4) information (to be) put into a computer. **2** (US) = programme.

▷ *tr.v* **3** supply (a computer) with a program(1).

'programmable *adj* able to be (coded(4) and) put into a computer.

,programmed 'learning *u.n* system of learning in which the subject or task is divided into small parts.

'programmer *c.n* person who prepares one or more programs(1).

progress /'prəʊgres/ *u.n* **1** (often *make —*) improvement: *She's making good progress after the* operation(1). *There has been no progress in the* economy(3) *during the past two months.* **2** (also *attrib*) advance towards completing s.t: *The news came during the progress of the race. Here is a progress report on the building of the new school.* **3** (usu *the — of s.o/s.t*) movement forwards (of s.t): *the progress of time,* economic(1) *development.* **in progress** happening at this moment: *The meeting is still in progress.* **report progress** ⇒ report[1].

▷ *intr.v* /prə'gres/ *(formal)* **4** improve: *She's progressing well after the accident.* **5** advance towards completion: *How is the work progressing?* **6** *(formal)* move forwards, esp in a formal, organized

group: *The bride and her father progressed towards the* altar(2).

progression /prə'greʃən/ *u.n (formal)* **1** improvement: *I've noticed an obvious progression in his behaviour.* ⇒ regression. **2** (often *— of s.o/s.t*) movement forwards (of s.t): *Are they making any progression towards* democratic(1) *government?*

progressive /prə'gresɪv/ *adj* **1** *(formal)* moving forwards in a regular way: *a progressive advance towards full health.* **2** using or favouring new ideas or methods: *a progressive education; a progressive thinker.* **3** (also with capital **P**) (in politics) favouring (much) change in government policies(1) to benefit(4) the majority(2). **4** *(grammar)* = continuous.

▷ *def.n* **5** *(grammar)* = continuous tense[2].

pro'gressively *adv.*

pro'gressive ,tense *def.n* = continuous tense[2].

prohibit /prə'hɪbɪt/ *tr.v* **1** not allow (s.o/s.t) by rule or law: *Visitors are prohibited before 2 o'clock. They should prohibit smoking in restaurants.* **2** (esp *— s.o from doing s.t*) stop (s.o from doing s.t): *He was prohibited from seeing her by her father.*

prohibition /ˌprəʊɪ'bɪʃən/ *n* **1** *c.n* rule or law that does not allow s.t: *a prohibition against smoking in trains.* **2** *u.n* act of prohibiting(1) s.o/ s.t: *The prohibition of visitors was a cruel act.*

prohibitive /prə'hɪbɪtɪv/ *adj* **1** having the result of prohibiting(1) s.t: *prohibitive rules.* **2** (of prices or costs) so high that buying, making etc is difficult, not encouraged: *prohibitive prices, rents, costs of production.*

project /'prɒdʒekt/ *c.n* **1** organized plan: *accept a project to* design(5) *a new car.* **2** particular piece of study: *a project on the life of a fish.*

▷ *v* /prə'dʒekt/ **3** *tr.v* (usu passive) put (s.t) forward as a plan: *A tunnel has been projected between England and France.* **4** *tr.v* (often *— s.t onto s.t*) cause an image(2) of (s.t) to be produced (on a surface): *project light, a photograph, onto a wall.* **5** *tr.v* throw (s.t) forward: *use a rubber band to project a stone into the air.* **6** *tr/intr.v* (cause (s.t) to) stand out from the edge or surface: *a pipe that projects over the top of the wall.*

projection /prə'dʒekʃən/ *n* **1** *u.n* act of projecting(*v*) s.t. **2** *c.n* (part of an) object that projects(6). **3** *u.n (technical)* act or process of causing a film to be seen on a screen(3).

pro'jectionist *c.n* (professional) person who projects(4) a film onto a screen(3).

pro'jector *c.n* machine that causes s.t to be projected(4): *a film/* slide(6) *projector.*

prole /prəʊl/ *c.n (derog)* proletarian(3).

proletarian /ˌprəʊlɪ'teərɪən/ *adj* **1** of or referring to one or more proletariats. **2** *(derog)* of ordinary working people considered as less important, not as good etc.

▷ *c.n* **3** (also **prole**) (usu *derog*) person who is proletarian(2).

prole'tariat *def/c.n* **1** ordinary working people as a group: *government by the proletariat.* **2** *(derog)* ordinary working people considered as less important, able etc. ⇒ bourgeoisie.

proliferate /prə'lɪfəˌreɪt/ *intr.v (formal)* **1** increase quickly: *Germs(1) proliferate in dirty homes.* **2** exist in large numbers: *Insects proliferate in warm wet climates.*

proliferation /prə,lɪfə'reɪʃən/ c/u.n (often — of s.t) act or fact of proliferating: *the proliferation of* germs(1) *in dirty places*; *a proliferation of committees.*

prolific /prə'lɪfɪk/ adj producing very many or very much: *a prolific worker, fruit tree.*

prologue /'prəʊlɒg/ c.n **1** introduction to a play or poem. **2** first part that prepares for s.t: *Their discussions are a prologue to the main meeting.*

prolong /prə'lɒŋ/ tr.v (formal) make (s.t) longer in time: *Can't you prolong your visit for one more week?*

prolongation /,prəʊlɒŋ'geɪʃən/ u.n.

pro'longed adj existing for a long time: *a prolonged silence.*

prom /prɒm/ c.n (informal) **1** promenade(1). **2** promenade concert: *We listen to the proms every summer.*

promenade /,prɒmə'nɑːd/ c.n **1** (informal **prom**) (place for a) pleasant walk, esp by the sea in a holiday town.

▷ intr.v **2** walk about slowly for pleasure, e.g at the seaside or round the deck of a ship.

,prome'nade 'concert c.n (informal **prom**) concert of classical(2) music at which people stand as well as sit.

prominent /'prɒmɪnənt/ adj **1** standing out from the edge or surface (and therefore easy to see): *prominent teeth. A yellow border will make the words more prominent.* ⇨ promontory. **2** well known: *a prominent artist.*

'prominence n **1** u.n fact or state of being prominent. **2** c.n thing that is prominent(1).

'prominently adv.

promiscuous /prə'mɪskjʊəs/ adj tolerant of or having casual intercourse with many people: *They live in a promiscuous society.*

promiscuity /,prɒmɪ'skjuːɪtɪ/ u.n promiscuous behaviour: *Sexual promiscuity can cause the spread of* infectious *diseases.*

pro'miscuously adv.

promise /'prɒmɪs/ n **1** c.n statement by s.o that he/she will (not) do, give, say etc s.t: *I gave you my promise and I will keep it. You've broken your promise that you would work hard.* **2** u.n sign of good quality or success that will happen in the future: *His work shows great promise.* **3** c.n (often — of s.t) (formal) sign of s.t that will happen: *I can feel a promise of better weather.* **make a promise** promise(1): *She made a promise that she would not do it again.*

▷ v **4** tr/intr.v (often — (s.o) to do s.t; — that . . .) give a promise(1) to (s.o): *I promise not to tell. He promised her a new bicycle. 'Will you promise that you'll try hard?' 'I promise.'* **5** tr.v (formal) be a sign of (s.t) that will happen: *This sun promises a good harvest.* **I promise you** (used to show one's certainty about s.t): *He'll never forgive you, I promise you.* **promise (s.o) the moon** ⇨ moon¹.

'promising adj showing promise(2): *Her work, The weather, looks promising.*

'promisingly adv.

promontory /'prɒməntərɪ/ c.n (pl -ies) long high part of land that stands out from the coast.

promote /prə'məʊt/ tr.v **1** give (s.o, a team etc) a higher position, rank etc: *I was promoted from* lieutenant(1) *to* captain. *She promoted him to*

sales manager. Will Bristol City be promoted to the first division? **2** encourage the improvement, progress etc of (s.t): *promoting health and happiness in society.* **3** (commerce) encourage the increased sale of (s.t) by advertising, demonstrating(1) etc: *give away free samples to promote the new product.*

pro'moter c.n **1** person who promotes(2,3). **2** person or business company that organizes and finds the money for a sporting event: *Should cigarette companies be promoters of sports?*

promotion /prə'məʊʃən/ n **1** c/u.n (example of) being promoted(1): *I've been promised (a) promotion next month.* **2** u.n (also attrib) (often the — of s.t) act of promoting(2,3) s.t: *the promotion of healthy eating habits*; *a promotion campaign(2).* **3** c.n example of promoting(3) s.t: *a sales promotion.*

prompt /prɒmpt/ adj **1** done, happening etc as quickly as possible: *a prompt reply*; *be prompt in replying.*

▷ adv **2** exactly: *Be there at 2 o'clock prompt!*

▷ v **3** tr.v (often — s.o to do s.t) encourage/urge (s.o to do s.t): *I was prompted by your own efforts to try again. What prompted you to steal my pen?* **4** tr.v cause (s.o) to remember s.t: *I forgot her birthday but your letter prompted me.* **5** tr/intr.v tell (an actor, speaker etc) what to say or do if he/she forgets.

'prompter c.n person who prompts(5).

'promptly adv quickly; at once.

'promptness u.n.

pron written abbr **1** pronoun. **2** pronounced; pronunciation.

prone /prəʊn/ adj **1** (of a person) lying flat with the face downwards: *in a prone position.* **2** (pred) (usu — to s.t) likely (to do, suffer etc s.t unpleasant): *He's prone to illness. Helen is so accident-prone.*

prong /prɒŋ/ c.n long pointed part of a fork.

pronged adj.

pronoun /'prəʊnaʊn/ c.n (abbr **pron** as used in this dictionary) (grammar) word used to replace a noun or noun phrase, e.g 'he', 'it', 'them', 'ours', 'yourself'. ⇨ personal pronoun, possessive pronoun.

pronominal /prəʊ'nɒmɪnl/ adj (grammar) of or referring to a pronoun.

pro'nominally /-nəlɪ/ adv.

pronounce /prə'naʊns/ tr.v speak (words etc) (esp when referring to the method of speaking): *How do you pronounce 'clothes'?* **pronounce s.o s.t** say officially that s.o is s.t: *The doctors pronounced him dead. She was pronounced guilty by the judge.*

pro'nounceable adj (usu with a negative) that can be spoken: *His name isn't easily pronounceable.* Opposite unpronounceable.

pro'nounced adj strong and therefore obvious: *Her American accent is very pronounced.*

pro'nouncement c.n official statement, esp one expressing a decision taken at a meeting.

pronunciation /prə,nʌnsɪ'eɪʃən/ c/u.n (example of the) act or way of pronouncing s.t.

pronto /'prɒntəʊ/ adv (informal) immediately; at once: *I order you to come pronto!*

proof /pruːf/ pred.adj **1** (also — against s.t; usu as the second part of a word) able to keep out or stop s.t: *Is the material rainproof/bulletproof?*

The glass is proof against bullets. ⇨ heatproof, waterproof.

▷ *n* **2** *c/u.n* (example of a) thing used to show the truth of s.t: *Have you any proof that the pen is yours? He produced his* diary *as proof of his innocence*(1). **3** *u.n* system of steps in mathematics, philosophy or science used to show that s.t is definitely true or false. **4** *c.n* (*technical*) copy of a newly printed set of words used to check for mistakes. **5** *u.n* (also *attrib*) strength of an alcoholic drink.

prove /pruːv/ *v* **1** *tr.v* use proof(2) to show the truth of (s.t): *Can you prove that the pen is yours? You say it's yours but can you prove it?* **2** *tr.v* use proof(2) to show that (s.t) is definitely(1) true or false: *Scientists must prove that the medicine will work.* Opposite disprove. **3** *intr.v* be discovered or seen to be: *That book proved (to be) very useful.* **4** *intr.v* (of dough(1)) increase in size before being baked.

provable /ˈpruːvəbl/ *adj* able to be proved(1,2).
proven /ˈpruːvn/ *adj* **1** (*law*) proved (⇨ prove(1)). **2** tested and shown to be successful: *a proven method for curing backache.*

prop¹ /prɒp/ *c.n* **1** thing used to give support: *a stick used as a prop for a* washing line. **2** (*informal*) person who helps another person who is weaker: *She used me as a prop after her husband was killed.*

▷ *tr.v* (-pp-) (usu — *s.o/s.t up*) **3** support (s.o/s.t) using a firm object: *I propped up the* washing line *with a stick. The nurse propped her up in bed with several pillows.* **4** lean (s.t) on s.t else for support: *Prop your bicycle (up) against the wall.*

prop² *written abbr* **1** proprietor.
▷ *c.n* /prɒp/ **2** (*informal*) propeller. **3** property(4).

propaganda /ˌprɒpəˈgændə/ *u.n* (also *attrib*) (organized methods used for the) activity of spreading information etc in order to influence opinion: *political propaganda; a propaganda film.*

propagate /ˈprɒpəˌgeɪt/ *v* **1** *tr.v* (*formal*) cause (information etc) to spread: *propagate news about the victory.* **2** *tr/intr.v* (cause (a plant etc) to) produce seeds, reproduce, and grow: *We propagate our own vegetables in our greenhouse. How do worms propagate?*

propagation /ˌprɒpəˈgeɪʃən/ *u.n.*
propagator /ˈprɒpəˌgeɪtə/ *c.n* (heated) box used to propagate(2) seeds.

propane /ˈprəʊpeɪn/ *u.n* (also **propane gas**) colourless gas made from petrol which burns easily, used as a fuel(1).

propel /prəˈpel/ *tr.v* (-ll-) cause (s.t) to move (forward), esp using a machine: *The model plane is propelled by a small engine.*

propeller *c.n* (*informal* **prop**) part of a machine (usu with long blades that turn round a central part) used to propel a boat, plane etc: *Don't go near the propellers of that plane.*

propulsion /prəˈpʌlʃən/ *u.n* (way of) causing s.t to move: jet propulsion.

propensity /prəˈpensɪtɪ/ *c.n* (*pl* -ies) (usu — *to do s.t*) (*formal*) tendency (to do s.t): *have a propensity to tell lies.*

proper /ˈprɒpə/ *adj* **1** (*attrib*) correct or suitable for a purpose or reason: *Put the book in its proper place. That's not the proper way to spell*

it. **2** (placed after the noun) only the object, quality etc named and not anything else that is connected with it: *This affects the house proper and not the land around it.* **3** (esp *prim and* —) ⇨ prim: *a proper old lady.* ⇨ improper(1). **4** (*attrib*) (*informal*) complete: *a proper liar/ fool.* **5** (*attrib*) (*informal*) thorough: *a proper search.*

▷ *adv* **6 good and proper** (*informal*) thoroughly: *I'll punish you good and proper.*

proper fraction *c.n* (*technical*) fraction(2) that has a smaller number above the line than below it, e.g ⅜. ⇨ improper fraction.

properly *adv* correctly: *Do it properly.*

proper noun/name *c.n* (*grammar*) name of a particular person, place, object etc, e.g David, Canada, Venus. ⇨ common noun.

property /ˈprɒpətɪ/ *n* (*pl* -ies) **1** *u.n* thing that s.o owns: *Is this your property? That's my personal property.* **2** *c/u.n* (also *attrib*) buildings, land etc that s.o owns: *Get off my property! I own several properties in town. She's a property owner.* **3** *c.n* (often — *of s.t*) particular quality or feature(2) (of a substance or material): *One property of stainless steel is that it will not rust.* **4** *c.n* (also **prop**) object, e.g a chair, vase, used on a stage during the performance of a play, making of a film etc.

prophecy /ˈprɒfɪsɪ/ *n* (*pl* -ies) **1** *c.n* statement or action that tells what will happen in the future: *His prophecies about their marriage came true. The clouds are a prophecy of rain.* **2** *u.n* ability or power to tell what will happen in the future: *She has the power of prophecy.*

prophesy /ˈprɒfɪˌsaɪ/ *tr.v* (-ies, ied) tell (what will happen): *She prophesied that the girl would become famous.*

prophet /ˈprɒfɪt/ *c.n* **1** person who tells what will happen: *a prophet of world peace.* **2** (also with capital **P**) person who (claims that he) knows God's will.

prophetess *c.n* woman prophet.

prophetic /prəˈfetɪk/ *adj* **1** of or referring to a prophecy: *a prophetic statement.* **2** containing a prophecy: *a prophetic sign of good weather.*

prophetically *adv.*

propitious /prəˈpɪʃəs/ *adj* (*formal*) favourable: *a propitious occasion.*

propitiously *adv.* **propitiousness** *u.n.*

proponent /prəˈpəʊnənt/ *c.n* (*formal*) (often — *of s.t*) person who speaks in favour (of s.t): *a proponent of more sports in schools.*

proportion /prəˈpɔːʃən/ *n* **1** *c.n* (often — *of s.t*) part or share (of a whole): *A large proportion of the fruit is bad. He has done his fair proportion of the driving.* **2** *c/u.n* (often *the* — *of s.t to s.t*) relationship between s.t and another thing when comparing number, amount, size etc: *What is the proportion of boys to girls in the mathematics class?* ⇨ well-proportioned. **in**, **out of**, **proportion (to s.t)** having, not having, a correct relationship when compared (with s.t): *The punishment is out of all proportion (to the seriousness of the crime). We pay in proportion to the amount of work done.*

sense of proportion good understanding of how important or not s.t is.

proportional *adj* of or referring to proportion(2); having a correct relationship when compared: *proportional distribution of the money.*

pro'portionally *adv.*

pro,portional ,represen'tation *u.n* (*abbr* PR) system of electing members to a committee, parliament etc according to the number of votes for the particular group, political party etc.

proportionate /prə'pɔːʃənɪt/ *adj* (often — *to* s.t) (*formal*) having a correct relationship when compared (to s.t): *earn money proportionate to one's qualifications.* Opposite disproportionate.

pro'portionately *adv.*

pro'portions *pl.n* size: *a building, city, business company, of huge proportions.*

propose /prə'pəuz/ *v* **1** *intr.v* (often — *to* s.o) offer to marry (s.o): *He proposed to me last night and I accepted.* **2** *tr.v* put forward (an idea, plan etc) for consideration: *I propose going by train* (or *that we go by train*). *If you don't like his suggestion, what do you propose we should do?* **3** *tr.v* suggest (s.o) for a position or job: *Mr Brown has proposed Jane for the post of chairperson* (or *as* chairperson). **propose to do s.t** (*formal*) intend to do s.t: *He proposes to go later tonight.*

pro'posal *c.n* **1** offer to marry s.o: *a proposal of marriage.* **2** idea, plan etc that is suggested: *a new proposal to build a sports centre.*

pro'posed *adj* already suggested: *a proposed design.*

pro'poser *c.n* person who proposes(2,3) s.t/ s.o.

proposition /ˌprɒpə'zɪʃən/ *c.n* **1** proposal(2): *That's an interesting proposition.* **2** (*informal*) immoral request for sexual intercourse.

▷ *tr.v* **3** make (s.o) a proposition(2).

propound /prə'paund/ *tr.v* (*formal*) put forward (an idea etc) for consideration: *propound a theory(1).*

proprietor /prə'praɪətə/ *c.n* (*abbr* prop) owner of a shop, restaurant etc.

pro'prietary *attrib.adj* owned, used, made etc by a proprietor: *a proprietary brand(1) of biscuit.*

pro'prietress *c.n* woman proprietor.

propulsion ⇨ propel.

pro rata /ˌprəu 'rɑːtə/ *adj/adv* (*Latin*) according to the (fair) share belonging to each when compared: *a pro rata share; be paid pro rata.*

pros ⇨ pro¹.

prosaic /prəu'zeɪɪk/ *adj* (*derog; formal*) lacking interest or imagination; dull(3): *a prosaic talk.*

pro'saically *adv.*

proscribe /prəu'skraɪb/ *tr.v* (*formal*) say officially that (s.t) is not allowed, esp because dangerous: *proscribe the use of* asbestos *in buildings.*

proscription /prəu'skrɪpʃən/ *c/u.n.*

proscriptive /prəu'skrɪptɪv/ *adj.*

prose /prəuz/ *u.n* (also *attrib*) spoken or written language that is not poetry: *write prose; write in prose* style(1).

prosecute /'prɒsɪˌkjuːt/ *tr/intr.v* begin a legal action against (s.o): *He refused to build the wall again so I've decided to prosecute (him).* ⇨ defend(3).

prosecution /ˌprɒsɪ'kjuːʃən/ *n* **1** *c/u.n* act of prosecuting (s.o): *face prosecution for not paying a debt.* **2** *def/def.pl.n* (also *attrib*) person or group prosecuting: *a witness for the prosecution; a prosecution witness.* ⇨ defence(5).

'prose,cutor *c.n* person who begins or manages a prosecution(1).

prospect /'prɒspekt/ *n* **1** *c.n* (often *pl*) chance or idea of future success (based on the standard of present activities): *If she works that hard, her prospects are very good.* **2** *c.n* long or wide view: *a house with a prospect of the sea.* **3** *c.n* possibility/ thought (of what may or will happen): *I don't like the prospect of being without a job.* **4** *c.n* possible buyer, helper, member of a team, winner etc: *She's a bright/good/poor prospect.* **5** *u.n* (often — *of doing* s.t) hope: *He has no prospect of becoming a manager.*

▷ *intr.v* /prə'spekt/ **6** (usu — *for* s.t) search (for valuable metals, oil etc): *prospecting for gold in West Africa.*

prospective /prə'spektɪv/ *attrib.adj* likely; possible: *a prospective customer/* candidate(1).

prospector /prə'spektə/ *c.n* person who prospects(6) for s.t.

prospectus /prə'spektəs/ *c.n* short book containing information about a school, new product, course of study etc: *a university prospectus.*

prosper /'prɒspə/ *intr.v* (continue to) succeed, esp financially.

prosperity /prɒ'sperɪtɪ/ *u.n* state of prospering: *enjoy prosperity as a professional football player.*

'prosperous *adj* successful, esp financially: *a prosperous businessman/writer.*

'prosperously *adv.*

prostitute /'prɒstɪˌtjuːt/ *c.n* person who has sexual intercourse to earn money.

prostitution /ˌprɒstɪ'tjuːʃən/ *u.n.*

prostrate /'prɒstreɪt/ *adj* (*formal*) **1** prone(1), esp as a sign of obedience: *lying prostrate before the cruel king.* **2** very tired, weak. **3** (often — *with* s.t) in a state of great shock (because of s.t).

▷ *reflex.v* /prɒ'streɪt/ **4** put (oneself) in a prostrate(1) position: *prostrate oneself as a sign of submission(1).*

prostration /prɒ'streɪʃən/ *u.n.*

protagonist /prəu'tægənɪst/ *c.n* **1** main character in a play, story etc. ⇨ antagonist(2). **2** (often — *of* s.t) supporter of a (usu political) idea or opinion: *a protagonist of women's rights.*

protect /prə'tekt/ *tr.v* (often — *s.o/s.t against/ from* s.o/s.t) keep (s.o/s.t) safe, defend (s.o/s.t) (from attack, danger, harm etc): *protect the children against disease; protect society from dangerous criminals; wear gloves to protect one's hands.*

protection /prə'tekʃən/ *n* (often — *against/from* s.o/s.t) **1** *u.n* act or state of protecting (s.o/s.t): *ask for protection against an angry neighbour; go under the tree for protection from the rain.* **2** *c.n* thing that protects s.o/s.t: *White paint offers a good protection against the heat.*

pro'tective *adj* giving protection: *protective clothing.*

pro'tector *c.n* person or thing who/that protects s.o/s.t.

protégé /'prəutɪˌʒeɪ/ *c.n* (*French; formal*) person given usu financial help or encouragement by a rich or influential person.

'proté,gée *c.n* (*French*) woman protégé.

protein /'prəutiːn/ *c/u.n* (example of a) kind of essential chemical substance in food that encourages good health, energy(1) and growth.

pro tem /ˌprəu 'tem/ *adv* (*Latin*) for the moment; for the time being: *Her boss is on holiday so she's the manager pro tem.*

protest /'prəʊtest/ *c.n* (also *attrib*) **1** (usu — *against s.o/s.t*) public statement or show of strong disapproval or opposition(2): *a protest against war*; *a protest march.* **in protest (against s.t)** as a protest(1) (against s.t): *write to the manager in protest against low wages.*
▷ *v* /prə'test/ **2** *intr.v* (often — *against s.o/s.t*) make one or more protests(1) (against s.o/s.t): *I've decided to protest (against being refused membership).* **3** *tr.v* (*formal*) make a strong statement, show clearly one's opinion or belief, about s.t: *She protested her innocence(1) (or that she did not do it).*
protestation /ˌprɒtɪ'steɪʃən/ *c.n* (*formal*) thing that one protests(3): *a protestation of her innocence(1).*
pro'tester *c.n* person who protests(2).
Protestant /'prɒtɪstənt/ *adj* **1** of or referring to one of the Christian(1) churches that left the Roman Catholic(1) church in the 16th century.
▷ *c.n* **2** member of a Protestant(1) church.
protocol /'prəʊtəˌkɒl/ *u.n* way of behaving or acting in official, very formal, situations: *Do you know the protocol when writing to the Bishop(1)?*
proton /'prəʊtɒn/ *c.n* (*technical*) particle(1) with a positive electric charge(4) which forms part of the nucleus(2) of an atom. ⇨ neutron.
prototype /'prəʊtəˌtaɪp/ *c.n* (often — *of s.t*) original/first example of s.t from which others are copied: *This is the prototype of the modern car.*
protracted /prə'træktɪd/ *adj* continuing for a long time or for too long: *protracted discussions.*
protractor /prə'træktə/ *c n* (*technical*) flat instrument usu shaped like half a circle, used for measuring or drawing angles.
protrude /prə'truːd/ *intr.v* (*formal*) stand out from the edge or a surface: *An arm was protruding through the hole in the curtain, over the edge.*
pro'truding *adj*: *protruding teeth.*
protuberance /prə'tjuːbərəns/ *c.n* (*formal*) thing that protrudes; bulge(1).
proud /praʊd/ *adj* **1** (often — *of s.o/s.t*) very pleased or satisfied (because of one's ability, success, possessions, family etc): *My daughter won and I'm so proud of her. He's so proud of his new bicycle. This is a proud day for our family. I'm proud to say that our team has been chosen.* **2** (*derog*) having an opinion of oneself that is too high: *He's too proud to admit he was wrong.* ⇨ pride.
'proudly *adv.* **'proudness** *u.n.*
prove, proven ⇨ proof.
proverb /'prɒvɜːb/ *c.n* short well-known statement that gives advice, e.g about life, how to act etc, e.g 'Smile and the world smiles with you'.
proverbial /prə'vɜːbɪəl/ *adj* of/like a proverb: *a proverbial saying.*
pro'verbially *adv.*
provide /prə'vaɪd/ *tr.v* (often — *for s.o/s.t*) supply (s.o/s.t) (with what is necessary): *provide food and clothes*; *provide for one's children.*
provident /'prɒvɪdənt/ *adj* (*formal*) (careful about) providing (⇨ provide) what will be needed in the future. Opposite improvident.
pro'vider *c.n* person who provides.
provision /prə'vɪʒən/ *n* (often — *of s.t*) **1** *u.n*

act or fact of providing (⇨ provide) s.t: *Who is responsible for the provision of food and water?* **2** *c.n* particular quantity provided (⇨ provide): *a large provision of food.* **make provision for s.o/ s.t** provide enough money etc for s.o/s.t to use in the future: *Have you made provision in your will²(1) for your children?*
pro'visions *pl.n* (*formal*) supplies of food: *Take enough provisions for the journey.*
provided /prə'vaɪdɪd/ *conj* (also **pro'viding**) (often — *that...*) on condition: *I'll come provided (that) you drive slowly.*
providence /'prɒvɪdəns/ *c/u.n* (example proving) God's care and interest: *The ending of the storm was divine(1) providence.* **tempt providence** ⇨ tempt.
providential /ˌprɒvɪ'denʃəl/ *adj* (*formal*) (because of providence and therefore) fortunate: *a providential meeting.*
provident ⇨ provide.
providing /prə'vaɪdɪŋ/ *conj* = provided.
province /'prɒvɪns/ *n* **1** *c.n* large area with a separate local government in a country. **2** *c.n* (usu *s.o's* —) area of s.o's knowledge, responsibility etc: *Your question is out of my province as a mathematics teacher. Cooking is well within his province.*
'provinces *def.pl.n* all the areas that are not inside the capital city of a country: *the people in the provinces.*
provincial /prə'vɪnʃəl/ *adj* **1** of or referring to a province(1): *provincial government.* **2** (often *derog*) of, from, referring to, the provinces(2): *a provincial way of behaving*; *a provincial accent(1).*
▷ *c.n* **3** (often *derog*) person from the provinces.
pro'vincially *adv.*
provision ⇨ provide.
provisional /prə'vɪʒənl/ *adj* (*formal*) **1** for the present time only: *a provisional government.* **2** that depends on certain conditions being met: *be given a provisional place at a university.* **provisional on s.t** that depends on certain conditions being met: *Getting a new bicycle is provisional on continued good behaviour.*
pro'visionally *adv.*
proviso /prə'vaɪzəʊ/ *c.n* (*pl* -(e)s) (often *on/ with the — that...*) (written) condition that has to be met (which is that...): *You can come on the proviso that you pay your fare.*
provoke /prə'vəʊk/ *tr.v* **1** make (s.o) angry esp by doing/saying many small annoying things: *Don't provoke me!* ⇨ unprovoked. **2** cause (a particular feeling or response such as anger, smiles, laughter): *She was trying to provoke a smile.* **provoke s.o into doing s.t** cause s.o to become angry and do s.t: *She was provoked into telling the teacher that he was a nuisance.*
provocation /ˌprɒvə'keɪʃən/ *c/u.n* (example of an) act of provoking or being provoked: *Provocation made me break her pen. After many provocations I decided to leave the house.*
provocative /prə'vɒkətɪv/ *adj* **1** causing, likely to cause, an angry response(2): *provocative behaviour.* **2** intended to encourage a sexual interest: *a provocative smile.*
pro'vocatively *adv.*
pro'voking *adj* causing anger; annoying: *be provoking*; *provoking children.*

pro'vokingly *adv.*

prow /praʊ/ *c.n* front part of a boat or ship. ⇒ bow¹(1).

prowess /'praʊɪs/ *u.n* (*formal*) unusually good ability or skill: *show prowess as a painter* (or *at painting*).

prowl /praʊl/ *c.n* **1** act of prowling (⇒ prowl(2)). **on the prowl** moving about secretly looking for something to steal etc: *The cat's on the prowl.*
▷ *tr/intr.v* **2** move quietly about (a place) etc in order to steal: *prowling the streets for food*; *prowling about downstairs.*
'prowler *c.n* person who prowls.

proximity /prɒk'sɪmɪtɪ/ *u.n* (usu *in* (*close*) — *to s.o/s.t/s.w*) (*formal*) (in a state of) nearness (to s.o etc) in space or time: *The garage is in proximity to the post office. They were born in close proximity to each other.*

proxy /'prɒksɪ/ *c/u.n* (*pl -ies*) (often *by* —) (written paper giving) authority(3) to act for another person: *vote by proxy.*

prude /pruːd/ *c.n* (usu *derog*) person who is (too) concerned with moral behaviour. Compare prig, prissy.
'prudery *u.n* prudish behaviour.
'prudish *adj.* **'prudishly** *adv.* **'prudishness** *u.n.*

prudent /'pruːdənt/ *adj* careful and wise when managing one's affairs: *a prudent wife.* Opposite imprudent.
'prudence /-əns/ *u.n.* **'prudently** *adv.*

prune¹ /pruːn/ *c.n* dried plum¹(2).

prune² /pruːn/ *tr.v* **1** cut (parts of a tree, bush etc) off: *pruning roses.* **2** (*fig*) remove (parts of a piece of writing): *prune a letter to make it fit one piece of paper.*

pry¹ /praɪ/ *intr.v* (*-ies, -ied*) (usu — *into s.t*) ask too many questions in order to find out about s.t esp s.o's private affairs: *She's always prying into my family business.*

pry² /praɪ/ *tr.v* (*-ies, -ied*) (esp — *s.t open*) use force to open (a container, door etc).

psalm /sɑːm/ *c.n* kind of religious song, esp one from the Bible(1).

pseudonym /'sjuːdəˌnɪm/ *c.n* name used by a writer that is not her/his real name: *write under a pseudonym.*
pseudonymous /sjuː'dɒnɪməs/ *adj* (of a piece of writing) written under a pseudonym.

PS /ˌpiː 'es/ *abbr* postscript.

psyche /'saɪkɪ/ *c.n* (*technical*) human mind or soul: *a disease that affected his psyche.*

psychedelic /ˌsaɪkɪ'delɪk/ *adj* **1** (of a drug(2)) affecting one's senses and feelings so that one feels extreme excitement, fear etc. **2** (*informal*) having a strong effect on one's senses and feelings: *psychedelic music/colours/patterns.*

psychiatry /saɪ'kaɪətrɪ/ *u.n* (also *attrib*) (study of the) medical treatment of mental illness: *practise psychiatry; a psychiatry student.*
psychiatric /ˌsaɪkɪ'ætrɪk/ *adj* (usu *attrib*) of, referring to, needing, psychiatry: *a psychiatric hospital/patient.*
psychiatrist /saɪ'kaɪətrɪst/ *c.n* professional medical person who treats mental illness.

psychic /'saɪkɪk/ *adj* **1** of, referring to, using, influences that have no physical or natural cause, e.g helping a sick person to become well by using her/his own will to be well or by shared meditation. **2** (*informal*) (of a person) able to say what will happen in the future: *You said there would be an accident — you must be psychic!*

psychical /'saɪkɪkl/ *adj* of or referring to psychic(1) influences: *psychical healing.*

psychoanalyse /ˌsaɪkəʊ'ænəˌlaɪz/ *tr.v* (also **'ana,lyse**) (US also **-lyze**) use psychoanalysis to treat (s.o who is mentally(3) ill).

psychoanalysis /ˌsaɪkəʊə'nælɪsɪs/ *u.n* (also **a'nalysis**) treatment of mental illness and emotional(1) suffering by discovering and discussing events and people that have influenced s.o's past.

psycho'ana,lyst *c.n* (also **'analyst**) professional person who uses psychoanalysis to treat s.o.

psycho,ana'lytical *adj* (also **psycho,ana'lytic**).

psychology /saɪ'kɒlədʒɪ/ *u.n* (also *attrib*) study of all kinds of human (or animal) behaviour: *the psychology department.*
psychological /ˌsaɪkə'lɒdʒɪkl/ *adj* **1** of psychology. **2** of/in the mind or thought: *The pain in her back is purely psychological. Making a person think that he will definitely lose if he fights you is a form of psychological attack.*
psychologist /saɪ'kɒlədʒɪst/ *c.n* professional person who studies human behaviour.

psychopath /'saɪkəˌpæθ/ *c.n* person who is seriously mentally(3) ill and who is dangerous because he/she can become extremely violent.
psychopathic /ˌsaɪkə'pæθɪk/ *adj.*

psychosis /saɪ'kəʊsɪs/ *c.n* (*pl psychoses* /saɪ'kəʊsiːz/) (*technical*) kind of serious mental illness.
psychotic /saɪ'kɒtɪk/ *adj* **1** of a psychosis.
▷ *c.n* **2** person suffering from a serious mental illness.

psychosomatic /ˌsaɪkəsə'mætɪk/ *adj* **1** of/ describing a physical pain or condition caused by mental(1) stress(1). **2** (*informal*) existing only in the mind: *His aching knee is psychosomatic.*

psychotherapy /ˌsaɪkə'θerəpɪ/ *u.n* (also **'therapy**) use of the way a person thinks and feels to treat mental illness, emotional(1) problems.
psycho'therapist *c.n* (also **'therapist**) professional person who uses psychotherapy to treat s.o.

psychotic ⇒ psychosis.

pt *written abbr* **1** pint(1). **2** point. **3** (**Pt**) Point. **4** (**Pt**) Port¹. **5** (*p.t* in this dictionary) past tense. **6** (**PT**) Physical Training.

PTA /ˌpiː ˌtiː 'eɪ/ *abbr* Parent Teacher Association (in a school).

Pte *written abbr* (*military*) Private(4).

PTO /ˌpiː ˌtiː 'əʊ/ *abbr* (usu at the bottom of a page) please turn over.

pub /pʌb/ *c.n* (*informal*) (**,public 'house**) building where alcoholic(1) drinks are bought and drunk: *They've gone to the pub for a drink.*
'pub ,crawl *c.n* (*informal*) visit to several pubs during one evening.

publican /'pʌblɪkən/ *c.n* person who owns or manages a pub.

puberty /'pjuːbətɪ/ *u.n* period(2) (of change in the human body) between being a child and becoming sexually mature(1).

pubic hair /ˌpju:bɪk 'heə/ *u.n* hair growing round the sexual organs.

public /'pʌblɪk/ *adj* **1** of, referring to, for, all the people in a community(2) or country: *public health*; *public opinion*; *a public lavatory/library*. **2** done for, known to etc all the people: *a public performance*, disgrace(1); *make the information public*. **3** (*attrib*) (of a person) known to everyone: *a public sports* personality(3). **be in the public eye** ⇨ eye(*n*). **go public** (*commerce*) allow members of the public to buy shares(3) in a company: *The family business is going public next year*.

▷ *def/def.pl.n* **4** people in a community(2) or in general: *The library is open to the public. Will the public enjoy the film?* ⇨ general public.

ˌpublic conˈvenience *c.n* (esp in notices) public(1) lavatory.

ˌpublic ˈholiday *c.n* official holiday when businesses, shops etc are closed.

ˌpublic ˈhouse *c.n* = pub.

ˌpublic ˌlimited ˈcompany *c.n* (*pl -ies*) (*abbr plc*) business whose shareholders are responsible for any debts only to the total amount of money they provided for the business. ⇨ limited liability (company).

publicity /pʌb'lɪsɪtɪ/ *u.n* **1** (also *attrib*) way/process(2)/method(1) of getting public attention, e.g by advertising: *use publicity to sell a product*; *a publicity* campaign(2). **2** condition of being known to the public: *get publicity by appearing on television*. ⇨ publication.

publicize, -ise /'pʌblɪˌsaɪz/ *tr.v* use publicity(1) to make (s.o/s.t) known.

ˈpublicly *adv*.

ˌpublic oˈpinion ˌpoll *c.n* ⇨ poll(2).

ˌpublic reˈlations *pl.n* (*abbr PR*) (also *attrib*) getting and keeping good will and trust between a business company, person, institution(1) etc and the public: *Are your public relations good? The party is a public relations exercise. She's our public relations officer*.

ˌpublic ˈsector ⇨ sector(*n*).

ˌpublic ˈschool *c/u.n* (UK) private secondary school, esp a well known one that was established(1) a long time ago. ⇨ prep school.

publican ⇨ pub.

publication /ˌpʌblɪˈkeɪʃən/ *n* **1** *u.n* act or process of publishing (⇨ publish): *the publication of a magazine/newspaper/book*; *the official publication of the government's plans for education*. **2** *c.n* thing that has been published(1).

publish /'pʌblɪʃ/ *tr.v* **1** produce and publicize (a book, magazine, newspaper etc). **2** make (s.t) known officially to the public: *The Liberal Party will publish its plans for unemployment at the meeting tonight*.

ˈpublisher *c.n* **1** person who publishes(1) s.t. **2** (also **ˈpublishers**) business company of a publisher(1).

ˈpublishing *u.n* (also *attrib*) act or business of publishing (⇨ publish): *educational publishing*; *a publishing house*.

puce /pju:s/ *adj/u.n* (usu *derog*) (of a) colour between red and dark purple (considered to show lack of artistic judgement).

puck /pʌk/ *c.n* flat rubber disc(1) used instead of a ball when playing ice hockey.

pucker /'pʌkə/ *tr/intr.v* (often — (s.t) *up*) (cause (s.t) to) get wrinkles(1) or folds in it: *pucker (up) one's eyebrows*.

pudding /'pʊdɪŋ/ *c/u.n* **1** kind of soft usu sweet food, esp one eaten at the end of a meal: *rice pudding*; *plum*[1](2) *pudding. Shall we have pudding now or later? Baked apple is a tasty pudding*. **2** kind of soft cooked food, usu with pastry: *cheese pudding*; *a meat pudding with gravy*(2).

puddle /'pʌdl/ *c.n* small pool of rain water.

pudenda /pju:'dendə/ *pl.n* (*technical*) external genital organs[1](2), esp of a woman.

puerile /'pjʊəˌraɪl/ *adj* (*derog*) childish and silly: *puerile behaviour*.

puerility /pjʊə'rɪlɪtɪ/ *u.n*.

puff /pʌf/ *c.n* **1** (often — *of s.t*) short, quick sending out of s.t, e.g air: *a puff of smoke/wind*. **2** short quick breath: *I could hear his puffs as he walked up the stairs. I had a quick puff of his cigarette*. **3** (also *attrib*) kind of light pastry containing many spaces filled with air: *a jam puff*; *puff pastry*. **4** (*informal*) short statement of praise: *Will you give my new book a puff at the meeting?*

▷ *v* **5** *intr.v* make short quick breaths, esp because one is tired: *puffing up the stairs*. ⇨ blow[2](8). **6** *tr.v* produce (s.t) in short quick breaths: *puffing smoke into my eyes*. **7** *tr/intr.v* (often — *at s.t*) breathe in air through (a cigarette, cigar or pipe): *puff (at) a cigarette*. **puff s.t out/up** cause s.t to become larger (as if) by filling it with air: *puff up a pillow*; *be puffed out with pride*.

ˈpuffy *adj* (*-ier, -iest*) swollen: *puffy eyes/cheeks*.

puffin /'pʌfɪn/ *c.n* kind of black and white sea bird with a short colourful(1) beak.

pug /pʌg/ *c.n* kind of small dog with a short flat nose.

pugnacious /pʌg'neɪʃəs/ *adj* (*formal*) ready and willing to fight or quarrel.

pugˈnaciously *adv*. **pugnacity** /pʌg'næsɪtɪ/ *u.n*.

puke /pju:k/ *u.n/tr/intr.v* (*informal*) = vomit.

pull /pʊl/ *n* **1** *c.n* act of pulling(5): *The chain needed a strong pull. I gave a pull at her skirt*. **2** *c/u.n* influence/force of pulling(5): *the pull of a magnet*(1), *the* underwater current(3); **3** *u.n* (*informal*) power to attract people: *the pull of the mountains that makes him travel to Nepal. The speaker has a lot of pull and there is always a large crowd round her*. ⇨ pull(8). **4** *u.n* (*informal*) ability to influence important or powerful people: *My father has a lot of pull in our town*.

▷ *v* **5** *tr/intr.v* use force to (try to) move (s.o/s.t) towards oneself or in the same direction as oneself with oneself in front: *The horse was pulling the cart. I pulled the table away from the wall. I pulled on the string and it broke. He pulled off his socks. She pulled the boy out of the river. Stop pulling my hair! Pull up a chair and sit down*. ⇨ push(5). **6** *tr/intr.v* (usu — (s.t) *away* (*from s.t*); — *out* (*of s.t*); — *over* (*to s.t*) etc) drive (a vehicle) in the direction stated: *I pulled away from the side of the road, out of the car park, over to the side of the road*. **7** *tr.v* damage (a muscle(1) or other internal(1) part of the body) by stretching it: *I've pulled a muscle/tendon in my leg*. **8** *tr.v* (*informal*) attract (s.o): *The speaker can pull a large crowd*. ⇨ pull(3). **9** *tr/intr.v* move (a boat etc) using oars: *We pulled away from the edge*.

pull s.t apart = pull s.t to pieces.

pull back move to a position further back: *The soldiers were forced to pull back.*

pull s.t down destroy a building etc: *pull down an old house.*

pull a face; ***pull faces*** ⇒ face(*n*).

pull a fast one (on s.o) (*informal*) give s.o false information in order to deceive: *'She said she'd be at the station at 3 but left on the 2 o'clock train.'* — *'She certainly pulled a fast one on you!'*

pull in (to s.t) (of a train, bus etc) arrive at a station etc. ⇒ pull(6).

pull s.o's leg ⇒ leg.

pull s.t off be successful in persuading s.o to do s.t, getting one's plan accepted etc: *I never thought you'd pull off that business deal!*

pull s.t on put clothing on quickly: *She pulled on her coat and scarf.*

pull out (of s.t) **1** (of a train, bus etc) leave a station etc. ⇒ pull(6). **2** stop taking part in s.t: *I have to pull out of the team until after the examinations.* ***pull s.t out (of s.t)*** take s.t out (of a pocket etc): *He pulled out his handkerchief/ gun.* ***pull one's finger out*** ⇒ finger(*n*).

pull s.o/s.t to pieces ⇒ piece(*n*).

pull (s.o) round (*informal*) (help s.o to) wake up, become healthier etc, e.g after an operation(1): *She took an hour to pull round after her operation(1).*

pull strings ⇒ string(*n*).

pull through recover from a serious illness: *I never thought he would pull through.*

pull together cooperate with one another to be successful: *If we all pull together we can make this business a successful one.* ***pull oneself together*** begin to have control of one's feelings and behave or act responsibly: *Stop crying and pull yourself together!*

pull (s.o/s.t) up cause (s.o, a vehicle etc) to stop: *He pulled up at the corner.* ***pull s.o up*** tell s.o about her/his personal faults.

pull one's weight ⇒ weight(*n*).

pullet /ˈpʊlɪt/ *c.n* young hen.

pulley /ˈpʊlɪ/ *c.n* wheel over/round which a rope or chain turns in order to lift heavy objects.

pullover /ˈpʊləʊvə/ *c.n* kind of knitted sweater.

pulmonary /ˈpʌlmənərɪ/ *adj* (*technical*) of or referring to the lungs: *a pulmonary illness.*

pulp /pʌlp/ *u.n* **1** soft substance (like) inside some fruit, e.g a peach(2), melon. **2** soft wet substance made by beating wood, used to make paper: *wood pulp.* ***beat s.o to a pulp*** (*fig*) beat s.o very hard. ***to a pulp*** so that s.t becomes like pulp(1): *boil the potatoes to a pulp.*

▷ *tr.v* **3** make (wood etc) into pulp.

pulpit /ˈpʊlpɪt/ *c.n* small raised part in a church from which the priest gives his sermon(1).

pulse¹ /pʌls/ *c.n* **1** regular beat of the heart as felt in a blood vessel. **2** (*technical*) sudden change in size, strength etc that is greater than the usual amount in a system or series(1).

▷ *intr.v* **3** = pulsate.

pulsate /pʌlˈseɪt/ *intr.v* (*formal*) beat regularly or move along because of regular beats: *I could feel the blood pulsating through my head.*

pulsation /pʌlˈseɪʃən/ *c/u.n.*

pulse² /pʌls/ *c/u.n* (*technical*) (example of) seeds used for food, e.g peas and beans.

pulverize, -ise /ˈpʌlvəˌraɪz/ *tr.v* **1** make (a substance) into a powder or soft mass by beating it. **2** (*fig*) completely defeat (s.o) in a fight, match etc.

puma /ˈpjuːmə/ *c.n* wild grey-brown animal like a large cat, found in North America.

pumice /ˈpʌmɪs/ *c/u.n* (also **ˈpumice ˌstone**) (piece of) a kind of light grey stone (lava), used to clean and polish things, e.g to make one's heels soft and smooth.

pummel /ˈpʌml/ *tr.v* (-ll-) (*formal*) hit (s.o/s.t) many times with one's closed hands: *pummelling on the door.*

pump /pʌmp/ *c.n* **1** device that forces air, water etc into or out of s.t: *a bicycle pump.*

▷ *tr.v* **2** use a pump(1) on (s.t): *pump water onto the fields.* **3** (*informal*) (try to) get information from (s.o) by asking many questions: *They were pumping him for new information about the plan.* **4** (*informal*) put in large amounts of (money): *They are pumping thousands of pounds into the business company.* ***pump s.t up*** use a pump(1) to put air into s.t: *He pumped up the tyres.*

pumpkin /ˈpʌmpkɪn/ *c/u.n* (also *attrib*) (example of a) kind of very large orange or yellow vegetable: *pumpkin pie.*

pun /pʌn/ *c.n* **1** use of a word or phrase(1) with two or more meanings(2), usu to be funny.

▷ *intr.v* (-nn-) **2** tell a pun(1).

punch¹ /pʌntʃ/ *n* **1** *c.n* strong hit with one's closed hand: *a punch on the chin.* **2** *u.n* (*fig*) strong effect: *His speech has no punch.*

▷ *tr/intr.v* **3** hit (s.o/s.t) with a punch¹(1): *He punched me in the stomach.*

ˈpunch-ˌup *c.n* (*informal*) fight in which people punch¹(3) each other.

punch² /pʌntʃ/ *c.n* **1** tool that makes holes in paper, leather etc.

▷ *tr.v* **2** make (holes) in (s.t) using a punch²(1): *punch holes in paper.*

punch³ /pʌntʃ/ *u.n* kind of (usu hot) drink made by mixing fruit juice, alcoholic(1) drink and spices(1).

punctilious /pʌŋkˈtɪlɪəs/ *adj* (*formal*) paying much attention to details, esp to behaving in a socially acceptable way.

puncˈtiliously *adv.* **puncˈtiliousness** *u.n.*

punctual /ˈpʌŋktjʊəl/ *adj* (of a person) arriving or doing something at the agreed time: *She's not very punctual and is sure to be late again.* Opposite unpunctual.

punctuality /ˌpʌŋktjʊˈælɪtɪ/ *u.n.* **ˈpunctually** /-əlɪ/ *adv.*

punctuate /ˈpʌŋktjʊˌeɪt/ *v* **1** *tr/intr.v* put punctuation marks in (a piece of writing). **2** *tr.v* (usu passive) (*formal*) interrupt (a speech, meeting etc): *The meeting was punctuated by several rude shouts.*

punctuation /ˌpʌŋktjʊˈeɪʃən/ *u.n* use of punctuation marks.

ˌpunctuˈation ˌmark *c.n* sign used in writing to show the end of a sentence, type of statement, when to pause etc, e.g a comma, colon(1), full stop, question mark.

puncture /ˈpʌŋktʃə/ *c.n* **1** (act of making a) small hole in s.t that is filled with air: *a puncture in a tyre.*

▷ *tr/intr.v* **2** (cause (s.t) to) have a puncture(1): *These new tyres seem to puncture easily.*

pundit /'pʌndɪt/ c.n expert(2), esp one able to say what will happen: *political pundits*.

pungent /'pʌndʒənt/ adj **1** (of smell or taste) very strong: *a pungent (smell of) fish*. **2** (*fig*; *formal*) (of an argument, statement, joke etc) very strong and effective(1,2): *pungent criticism*.
'**pungency** u.n. '**pungently** adv.

punish /'pʌnɪʃ/ tr.v (usu passive) make s.o suffer because he/she has done wrong: *If you steal you will be punished. She was punished for being late. He punished the boy for telling lies.*
'**punishable** adj that should be, deserves to be, punished: *stealing is a punishable offence.*
'**punishing** adj causing s.o to suffer: *It was a punishing walk to the top of the mountain.*
'**punishment** n **1** u.n. act or fact of punishing s.o or being punished: *punishment by a fine.* **2** c.n thing suffered because of doing wrong: *be given extra duties as a punishment.*

punitive /'pjuːnɪtɪv/ adj (*formal*) related to, involving(1), punishment: *punitive measures against lazy students; punitive taxes.*

punk /pʌŋk/ adj/c.n (also *attrib*) (of a) type of person of the 1970s and 1980s who deliberately shocked ordinary people by using rude or obscene words, having strange and coloured hair, wearing strange clothes: *punk music.*

punnet /'pʌnɪt/ c.n small container for fruit when it is sold: *a punnet of* strawberries(1).

punt¹ /pʌnt/ c.n kind of long flat boat moved by pushing a long pole on the bottom of a river etc.
'**punter¹** c.n person who pushes a punt¹ along with a pole.

punt² /pʌnt/ intr.v gamble on horse races.
'**punter²** c.n person who punts².

puny /'pjuːnɪ/ adj (*-ier*, *-iest*) (*derog*) **1** small and weak: *puny arms; a puny man.* **2** too small: *a puny wage, amount of sugar.*

pup /pʌp/ c.n (*informal*) puppy.

pupa /'pjuːpə/ c.n (pl *-s*, pupae /'pjuːpiː/) (*technical*) = chrysalis.

pupil¹ /'pjuːpɪl/ c.n **1** schoolboy or schoolgirl. **2** person being given personal teaching: *a pupil of a music master.*

pupil² /'pjuːpɪl/ c.n (*technical*) round black opening in the middle of the iris¹ of the eye.

puppet /'pʌpɪt/ c.n **1** (also *attrib*) kind of doll that can be moved by pulling strings (string puppet) or by putting one's hand inside its body which is shaped like a glove (glove puppet): *a puppet show.* **2** (*fig*) (also *attrib*) person or group controlled by another: *We are puppets in their hands. The country has a puppet king who is controlled by the army.*

puppy /'pʌpɪ/ c.n (pl *-ies*) (*informal* pup) **1** (also *attrib*) very young dog: *puppy food.* **2** (*derog*; *informal*) young and arrogant man.
'**puppy ,fat** u.n extra weight on a young person that (usu) disappears later.
'**puppy ,love** u.n inexperienced feeling of love for s.o by a young person.

purchase /'pɜːtʃɪs/ n (also *attrib*) (*formal*) **1** c.n thing bought: *Are these your purchases?* **2** u.n act of buying s.t: *the purchase of a new house; purchase tax.* ⇨ hire purchase.
▷ tr.v **3** (*formal*) buy (s.t): *purchase a car.*
'**purchaser** c.n person who purchases(3) s.t.

pure /pjʊə/ adj **1** not mixed with another substance: *pure air/water/wool.* Opposite impure(1). **2** without any faults: *a pure English accent.* **3** without any immorality: *pure thoughts/love.* Opposite impure(2). **4** (*formal*) moral and innocent(2): *a pure young girl.* ⇨ impure(2). **5** (*attrib*) complete: *pure arrogance; a pure coincidence.* **6** (of an academic(2) subject) studying the theory(2) of it and not the way it can be used: *pure science/mathematics.* **pure and simple** (*informal*) (used after a noun) completely: *It was her mistake pure and simple.*
'**purely** adv (esp) only; entirely: *I came purely to tell you I'm sorry. It was purely by chance that you found me here.*

purification /ˌpjʊərɪfɪ'keɪʃən/ u.n act of purifying.

purify /'pjʊərɪˌfaɪ/ tr.v (*-ies*, *-ied*) make (a substance) pure(1) or clean: *purify the air/water.*

purist /'pjʊərɪst/ adj/c.n (of a) person who pays attention to details of correct forms of speaking, writing etc: *a purist way of speaking English.*

purity /'pjʊərɪtɪ/ u.n quality or fact of being pure.

purée /'pjʊəreɪ/ u.n **1** kind of food made by beating vegetables, fruit etc to a soft mass: *tomato purée.* ⇨ pulp(1).
▷ tr.v **2** make (food) into a purée(1): *puréed fish.*

purgative /'pɜːgətɪv/ u.n (also *attrib*) (*technical*) medicine that clears waste from the bowels(1).

purgatory /'pɜːgətrɪ/ u.n **1** (esp Roman Catholic(1)) place where souls go for a limited period of suffering before being pure(3) and able to go to heaven. **2** (often *in* —) (*fig*) situation of suffering: *I was in (or It was) purgatory waiting for news.*

purge /pɜːdʒ/ tr.v (*formal*) make (s.o/s.t) free of immorality, faults etc: *purging one's mind of bad thoughts; purging one's soul.*

purification, purify, purist ⇨ pure.

puritan /'pjʊərɪtn/ c.n (also *attrib*) (*derog*) person who is too severe and does not allow any pleasures such as dancing, jewellery, telling jokes etc: *puritan* attitudes(2).
puritanical /ˌpjʊərɪ'tænɪkl/ adj.

purity ⇨ pure.

purl /pɜːl/ u.n **1** way of knitting a stitch(3) that produces a plain(5) stitch(4) back to front.
▷ tr/intr.v **2** knit (s.t) in purl(1): *then purl two rows.*

purloin /pɜː'lɔɪn/ tr.v (*formal*) steal (s.t).

purple /'pɜːpl/ adj/u.n (of a) colour between dark red and blue: *purple fruit; go purple with anger; a coat of purple.* Compare mauve(1).

purport /pə'pɔːt/ intr.v **purport to be/do s.t** (*formal*) seem or claim to be/do s.t (esp when it is not true): *He purports to be sixteen years old.*

purpose /'pɜːpəs/ n **1** c/u.n reason/use for (doing) s.t: *What's the purpose of having a bicycle if you don't use it? Do you have a purpose for this old tool? The main purpose of this lesson is to learn how electricity works.* **2** u.n (*formal*) firm/definite intention to do etc s.t: *study/work with purpose; a woman of purpose.* **on purpose** intentionally; deliberately; not by mistake: *You broke it on purpose!* **to all intents and (purposes)** ⇨ intent.
,**purpose-'built** adj designed(5) for an individual(3)'s needs: *a purpose-built flat.*

'purposeful *adj* showing/with purpose(2): *I gave her a purposeful look.*
'purposefully *adv.*
'purposeless *adj* without any fixed intentions, reasons etc: *a purposeless way of living.*
'purposelessly *adv.* **'purposelessness** *u.n.*
'purposely *adv* intentionally; deliberately: *I rang you purposely to see if you were back home.*
purr /pɜː/ *c/u.n* **1** low vibrating sound of a cat when it is happy. **2** (*fig*) similar low sound of an engine.
▷ *intr.v* **3** make a purr.
purse¹ /pɜːs/ *c.n* **1** small bag for money. **2** amount of money, esp offered as a prize.
purse² /pɜːs/ *tr.v* (usu — *one's lips*) pull (one's lips) tightly together.
purser /'pɜːsə/ *c.n* officer on a ship who is responsible for supplies, the comfort of passengers etc.
pursue /pə'sjuː/ *tr.v* (*formal*) **1** follow (s.o, an animal, vehicle etc) esp to catch her/him/it: *The police car pursued the criminals to the edge of the city.* **2** carry out, follow, (one's studies, interests, way of living etc): *I hope to pursue my studies at the University of London. He's still pursuing a lazy life.*
pursuance /pə'sjuːəns/ *def.n* **in the pursuance of s.t** (*formal*) during the course of doing an action, carrying out a plan, one's duties etc.
pur'suer *c.n* person who pursues(1) s.o, an animal etc.
pursuit /pə'sjuːt/ *n* **1** *u.n* act of pursuing (⇒ pursue(1))(s.o/s.t): *His pursuit of the thief led him into an unknown area of town.* **in (hot) pursuit (of s.o/s.t)** chasing s.o/s.t (strongly): *They drove down the street with the dog in pursuit.* **2** *c.n* personal interest or activity: leisure *pursuits.* **in the pursuit of s.t** (while) trying to get s.t: *in the pursuit of justice.*
pus /pʌs/ *u.n* thick yellow liquid produced in a poisoned wound.
pustule /'pʌstjuːl/ *c.n* (*technical*) small poisoned place on the skin with pus in it.
push /pʊʃ/ *n* **1** *c.n* act of pushing (s.o/s.t): *I gave the door a push.* **2** *c.n* (also *attrib*) (part of a) device for working a machine: *the push button.* **3** *u.n* (*informal*) strong desire and energy to do s.t, esp to succeed: *She has plenty of push.* **4** *c.n* (*informal*) special effort: *One more push and we'll get to the top!* **at a push** (*fig*; *informal*) only just: *We can afford the rent at a push.* **be given, get, the push** (*informal*) be dismissed from one's job.
▷ *v* **5** *tr/intr.v* use pressure to (try to) move (s.o/s.t) away from oneself or in the same direction as oneself with oneself behind: *The man was pushing the baby's pram along the road. I pushed the table against the wall. That boy pushed me over. I hate people pushing past me in the city. Stop pushing!* ⇒ pull(5). **6** *tr/intr.v* put pressure on (a knob(2), button etc) in order to make a machine start to work, ring a bell etc: *I pushed the button and the lights came on.* **7** *tr.v* encourage/urge (s.o) to do s.t, work hard etc: *My parents are always pushing me to try to get into Oxford University. If my teacher hadn't pushed me I would never have passed the examination.* **8** *tr.v* use one's influence to (try to) get (s.o/s.t) accepted: *She's always pushing her own family for*

important positions on the committee. ⇒ push for s.t. **9** *tr.v* (*informal*) sell (illegal drugs(2)): *push heroin on the streets.*
push s.o about/around (*fig*; *informal*) make s.o do things; order s.o to do things in an angry and unfriendly(1) way.
push s.t down force costs, prices etc to fall.
push for s.t use one's energy(1) and influence to get agreement, acceptance(1) etc for s.t: *He's pushing for changes in the system.*
push oneself forward (*fig*) make others notice one, one's qualities etc in order to get a job, favour etc.
push one's luck ⇒ luck.
push off (usu as an order) (*informal*) go away!
push on (with s.t) continue energetically (with an activity, plan etc) regardless of opposition(1): *Let's push on because time is limited. They pushed on with the* scheme(1) *although some people tried to stop them.*
push s.t up force costs, prices etc to increase.
push up the daisies ⇒ daisy.
'push,bike *c.n* (*informal*) bicycle.
'push ,button *c.n* (**'push-,button** when *attrib*) button(2) that is operated by pushing(6) it: *push-button controls.*
'push,chair *c.n* chair with wheels for a young child. Compare pram.
'pusher *c.n* (*informal*) **1** person who pushes(9) drugs(2). **2** person who pushes(8).
'pushing *adv* **be pushing forty** etc (*informal*) be almost forty etc years old: *My dad's pushing sixty.*
'push,over *c.n* (*informal*) **1** person or group etc who/that is easily defeated: *Their team will be no pushover.* **2** thing that is easy to do: *Getting into the college was a pushover.*
'pushy *adj* (*-ier, -iest*) (*derog*; *informal*) using one's influence or energy(1) to get what one wants in a rude and unpleasant way.
puss /pʊs/ *c.n* (also **'pussy** (*pl -ies*), **'pussy-,cat**) (*informal*) cat.
pustule ⇒ pus.
put /pʊt/ *tr.v* (*-tt-, p.t,p.p put*) **1** move (s.o/s.t) to a certain place, position or state; place (s.o/s.t) s.w: *I put the book on the table. Please put it in the cupboard. Put the cups over there. Shall I put milk in your coffee? Put that knife back where you found it. I was putting the clothes into a box. Please put all these books in* alphabetical *order. She put the picture straight, the cloth right.* **2** order or organize (s.o) to do s.t, work etc: *I've been put to work on the new* design(1–3). **3** write or mark (s.t): *put a cross against your choice.* **4** offer/suggest (s.t): *put an idea/plan to the meeting.* **5** state (s.t): *I want to say I'm sorry but I don't know how to put it. To put it plainly, I don't like you.*
put s.t about cause information, news etc to become known: *Who's putting about the idea that I'm getting married?*
put s.t across (to s.o) be successful at getting s.o to understand s.t: *I want to explain but I don't seem able to put it across.*
put s.t aside (a) stop using/doing s.t for a short time: *He put his book aside and listened to the conversation.* (**b**) save an amount of money for later: *You should try to put aside a few pounds each month.*

put s.o at (her/his) ease ⇒ ease(*n*).

put s.t at s.t guess/estimate(2) s.t to be s.t: *I'd put her age at twenty, the distance at a hundred metres.*

put s.o away place s.o in prison or a mental hospital. **put s.t away (a)** = put s.t aside(b). **(b)** (*informal*) eat s.t: *He put away a huge meal.*

put s.t back (a) put(1) s.t in the place one took it from. **(b)** move a date, time etc of a meeting, ceremony etc to a later time. **(c)** move the hands(4) on a clock, watch etc to an earlier time. **(d)** cause production, progress etc to be delayed.

put the blame on s.o ⇒ blame(*n*).

put s.t by = put s.t aside(b).

put s.o to death = death.

put s.o down criticize s.o. **put (an animal) down** give (a usu very old, sick etc animal) something that makes it die painlessly. **put s.t down to s.o/ s.t** decide/state that s.t was caused by s.o/s.t: *I put his bad behaviour down to his parents.*

put an end to s.t ⇒ end(*n*).

put one's feet up; **put one's foot down** ⇒ foot(*n*).

put s.o forward suggest s.o as suitable for a position(4). **put s.t forward (a)** suggest an idea, plan etc at a meeting. ⇒ put(4). **(b)** move the hands(4) on a clock, watch etc to a later time.

put s.t in (s.t) (a) include s.t (in s.t): *We can't put all the expressions in without making the dictionary very big.* **(b)** have s.t built or fitted in a building: *They're putting new cupboards in the office.* **(c)** do a particular amount of time on an activity, work etc: *I put in eight hours work yesterday.* **put in for s.t (a)** enter for a competition etc. **(b)** ask permission to have a holiday etc: *I've put in for leave*[1](2). **put s.o in the picture (about s.o/s.t)** ⇒ picture(*n*). **put s.o in her/his place** ⇒ place(*n*). **put s.o in touch (with s.o)** ⇒ touch(*n*).

put s.t into s.t translate s.t into another language. **put s.t into s.o's head** ⇒ head(*n*).

put s.o off cancel a meeting, arrangement etc with s.o: *Do you mind if I put you off for tonight, I'm so tired?* **put s.t off** delay the agreed time for s.t: *Can I put off our meeting until Thursday?* **put s.o off (s.o/s.t)** cause s.o to lose interest in, liking for, s.o/s.t: *Her bad breath put me off (her).*

put s.t on (a) get dressed in clothes: *What shirt shall I put on?* Opposite take s.t off. **(b)** = turn s.t on: *Who put the light/television/radio on?* Opposite turn s.t off(d). ⇒ put s.t out(a). **(c)** become heavier or fatter (by a certain amount): *I've put on two kilos. You've put on weight.* Opposite lose weight (⇒ weight(*n*)). **(d)** produce s.t for the public: *put on a play/exhibition(1).* **put it on** pretend to be ill, upset etc: *You're not really so ill — you're just putting it on.* **put on a bold, good etc face** ⇒ face(*n*). **put pressure on s.o (to do s.t)** ⇒ pressure(4). **put s.t on one side** ⇒ side(*n*). **put years on s.o** ⇒ year.

put s.o out (a) cause trouble to, annoy, s.o, esp because an agreed plan, arrangement etc is changed: *I hope my late arrival has not put you out too much.* **(b)** make s.o unconscious(1): *Those tablets will put her out for hours.* **put s.t out (a)** make a fire, light etc stop burning: *The wind put the candle out. Please put out the lights.* ⇒ put

s.t on(b). **(b)** state/publish(1) s.t for the public to know: *The radio puts out news reports every hour. We've put out a report on our* financial position. **(c)** (of a plant) produce leaves etc: *The tree has put out some new branches.* ⇒ output.

put paid to s.t destroy s.o's hopes, plans etc: *The rain put paid to our idea of a walk.*

would not put it past s.o (to do s.t) consider s.o as likely to do s.t unpleasant, deceitful etc: *I wouldn't put it past her (to tell lies about us).*

put s.o right (about s.t) ⇒ right[1]. **put s.t right** do s.t to correct a mistake, example of bad behaviour etc.

put s.o through (to s.o) connect s.o to another person by telephone. **put s.o through s.t** force s.o to suffer s.t.

put s.o to shame; **put s.o/s.t to shame** ⇒ shame(*n*). **put s.t to s.o** suggest s.t to s.o; ask s.o a question formally: *I put it to you that you were the person who stole the key.* **put a match to s.t** ⇒ match[2]. **put pen to paper** = pen[1](1). **put a stop to s.t** = put an end to s.t. **put s.t to music** ⇒ music. **put s.t to the test** ⇒ test(*n*).

put s.t together use the parts (of s.t) to build s.t: *I can't put this puzzle together.* **put our etc heads together** ⇒ head(*n*). **put two and two together** ⇒ two.

put s.t towards s.t give money as a contribution(2) to the cost of s.t.

put s.o up give s.o a place to sleep in one's home: *We can put you up for the night.* **put s.o up to s.t** encourage s.o to do s.t wrong: *You took the bicycle but who put you up to it?* **put s.t up (a)** raise a flag, one's hand etc. **(b)** put a notice etc on a wall where it can be seen. **(c)** build s.t; set s.t up: *put up a new factory; put up a tent.* **(d)** cause prices etc to increase: *The government has put up our taxes again.* **put up with s.o/s.t** (*informal*) tolerate an unpleasant person, noise, uncomfortable hotel etc usu for a short time.

putative /ˈpjuːtətɪv/ *attrib.adj* (*formal*) generally accepted as being: *He's the putative father.*

putrefy /ˈpjuːtrɪˌfaɪ/ *intr.v* (*-ies*, *-ied*) (of dead plants/animals, food) rot and produce a strong bad smell.

putrid /ˈpjuːtrɪd/ *adj* rotten and smelling bad: *putrid meat.*

putt /pʌt/ *c.n* **1** example of putting(2) a golfball(1).

▷ *tr/intr.v* **2** hit a golfball(1) gently to get it into a hole.

putty /ˈpʌtɪ/ *u.n* (also *attrib*) kind of soft sticky mixture of oil and powder, used to fit glass into windows: *a putty knife.*

puzzle /ˈpʌzl/ *c.n* **1** kind of toy, activity or game that presents a problem and needs intelligent thought or skill to find a solution: *a jigsaw puzzle; a crossword puzzle.* **2** problem that is not easy to solve: *How she managed to feed them all with only one loaf is a puzzle to me.*

▷ *v* **3** *tr.v* make (s.o) find it difficult to understand s.t, answer a question, solve a problem etc: *What puzzles me is where he got the money from. She was puzzled by his refusal to help.* **puzzle s.t out** solve a problem after much thought: *puzzle out the cause of the fire.* **puzzle over s.t** think about s.t and try to find the answer: *I've been puzzling over how the dog got into the house.*

'puzzlement *u.n* state of being puzzled(3).

'puzzling *adj* difficult to understand or solve: *a puzzling remark/question.*

PVC /ˌpiː ˌviː ˈsiː/ *u.n* kind of plastic(1) material, used to make boots, clothes, pipes etc.

pygmy /ˈpɪɡmɪ/ *c.n* (also **'pigmy**) (*pl -ies*) (*derog*) very small person.

pyjamas /pɪˈdʒɑːməz/ *pl.n* set of trousers and shirt for sleeping in.

py'jama *attrib.adj* forming part of a pair of pyjamas: *pyjama bottoms/tops/trousers.*

pylon /ˈpaɪlən/ *c.n* tall steel tower, used to hold cables(2) etc.

pyramid /ˈpɪrəmɪd/ *c.n* **1** (also *attrib*) solid figure with a flat (usu square) base and sides that meet together at a point at the top: *a pyramid shape.* **2** large stone structure of this shape in Egypt.

'Pyramids *def.pl.n* pyramids(2) found in Egypt.

pyre /paɪə/ *c.n* pile of wood etc, used to burn a dead person: *a funeral pyre.*

pyromaniac /ˌpaɪrəʊˈmeɪnɪˌæk/ *adj/c.n* (of a) person with an uncontrollable desire to cause large fires. Compare arsonist.

python /ˈpaɪθən/ *c.n* kind of large snake that kills by twisting itself round an animal and crushing it.

Qq

Q, q /kjuː/ **1** *c/unique n* 17th letter of the English alphabet.

▷ *written abbr* **2** (*pl qq*) question. **3** (**Q**) Queen.

▷ *symb* (**Q**) **4** (*physics*) heat. **5** (*chess*) Queen(6). *mind one's p's and q's* ⇒ mind².

QC /ˌkjuː ˈsiː/ *c.n abbr* (often after a person's name) Queen's Counsel : *Sir Frederick Smith, QC.* ⇒ KC.

QED /ˌkjuː iː ˈdiː/ *abbr* (*Latin*) ('quod erat demonstrandum') 'which was to be proved', used esp at the end of geometric(1) problems that have been solved.

QM *written abbr* Quartermaster.

qq *pl* of q(2).

qr *written abbr* quarter¹.

qt *written abbr* quart.

qty *written abbr* quantity.

qu *written abbr* **1** (**Qu**) Queen. **2** question.

quack¹ /kwæk/ *c.n* **1** sound made by ducks.

▷ *intr.v* **2** make one or more sounds of a quack(1).

quack² /kwæk/ *adj* **1** who/that pretends to be a qualified medical practitioner etc when he/she is not.

▷ *c.n* **2** quack²(1) person: *Don't go to 'Dr' Jones; he's a quack.*

quad¹ /kwɒd/ *c.n* (*informal*) quadrangle(2).

quad² /kwɒd/ *c.n* (*informal*) quadruplet.

quadrangle /ˈkwɒdræŋɡl/ *c.n* **1** (*geometry*) figure that has four sides. ⇒ quadrilateral. **2** (also

quad) square area out of doors, with buildings on all or most sides of it, e.g in a university.

quadrangular /kwɒdˈræŋɡjʊlə/ *adj* shaped like a quadrangle(1).

quadrant /ˈkwɒdrənt/ *c.n* **1** quarter of a circle; right angle; 90°. **2** (*technical*) instrument used for measuring angles. Compare sextant.

quadratic equation /kwɒˌdrætɪk ɪˈkweɪʒən/ *c.n* (*mathematics*) equation(1) that contains x^2, e.g $3x^2 - 9x + 6 = 0$.

quadrilateral /ˌkwɒdrɪˈlætərəl/ *adj* **1** having four sides.

▷ *c.n* **2** quadrilateral(1) figure.

quadriplegia /ˌkwɒdrɪˈpliːdʒɪə/ *u.n* paralysis(1) of all four limbs. ⇒ paraplegia.

quadri'plegic *adj/c.n* (of or referring to a) person suffering from quadriplegia. ⇒ paraplegic.

quadruped /ˈkwɒdrʊˌped/ *c.n* animal that has four legs.

quadruple /ˈkwɒdrʊpl/ *det* **1** (often — *the amount/number* (*of s.t*)) four times the amount/number (of s.t)

▷ *adj* **2** four times as many/much as before, usual etc: *a quadruple supply of food.*

▷ *def.n* **3** (often *the — of s.t*) four times as many/much (as s.t).

▷ *tr/intr.v* **4** (cause (s.o/s.t) to) increase to four times the amount/number.

quadruplet /ˌkwɒˈdruːplɪt/ *c.n* (usu *pl*) (*informal quad*) one of four children born to one mother at one time.

quadruplicate /kwɒˈdruːplɪkət/ *unique n* **in quadruplicate** consisting of four copies: *I'd like this letter in quadruplicate, please.*

qua'druply *adv.*

quagmire /ˈkwæɡˌmaɪə/ *c.n* bog(1).

quail¹ /kweɪl/ *n* (*pl quail(s)*) **1** *c.n* kind of small bird that is shot and eaten. **2** *u.n* meat from a quail(1).

quail² /kweɪl/ *intr.v* (often — *at/with s.t*) be afraid (and tremble) because of s.t: *quail with fear at the thought of having to cross a stormy river.* ⇒ quake(2).

quaint /kweɪnt/ *adj* pleasantly or attractively strange (and old-fashioned).

'quaintly *adv.* **'quaintness** *u.n.*

quake /kweɪk/ *c.n* **1** (*informal*) earthquake.

▷ *intr.v* **2** (often — *at/with s.t*) tremble or shake (because of s.t, e.g fear). ⇒ quail².

Quaker /ˈkweɪkə/ *c.n* (also *attrib*) person who belongs to a branch of Christianity which is against fighting of any kind.

'Quake,rism *u.n* this branch of Christianity.

qualify /ˈkwɒlɪˌfaɪ/ *v* (*-ies, -ied*) **1** *tr/intr.v* (often — *as/for s.t*; — (*s.o*) *to do s.t*) (cause (s.o) to) reach the level needed for s.t, or to do s.t; get a qualification(2): *qualify as* (or *to become*) *a lawyer; qualify for a competition. This examination qualifies you to become a teacher.* **2** *tr.v* limit (s.t that one has said or written before) so that it does not cover so wide an area or so that it is more exact: *Joe's boss gave him permission to leave early but qualified it by adding, 'But not before 3 p.m'.* **3** *tr.v* (*grammar*) add s.t to the meaning of (s.t), often in a way that limits it: *In 'I like polite boys', 'polite' qualifies 'boys'; and in 'Mary can ride well', 'well' qualifies 'ride'.* ⇒ modify(2). **qualify s.o/s.t as s.t** (*formal*) describe s.o/s.t as s.t: *I qualify the party as a great success.*

qualification /ˌkwɒlɪfɪˈkeɪʃən/ n 1 u.n act or fact of qualifying (⇒ qualify(1)). 2 c.n (often pl) thing that qualifies(1) s.o for, to do, s.t: a legal(2) qualification. What qualifications do you need to become a teacher in your country? 3 c.n (often pl) (often with the — that . . . ; with —s; without —) thing that qualifies(2) s.t: He was given permission to leave with the qualification that he had to report to the police station once a week.

'quali,fied adj Opposite unqualified. 1 (often (highly) — for, to do, s.t) who has the qualifications(2) for s.t: a qualified doctor. 2 that has one or more qualifications(3): a qualified agreement to their terms.

'quali,fier c.n (grammar) word that qualifies(3).

'quali,fying ,round c.n round(19) before a competition which one has to win before one can play in the competition itself.

quality /ˈkwɒlɪtɪ/ n (pl -ies) 1 c.n (often the — of s.t) thing that distinguishes s.o/s.t from other people/animals/things: The quality of her voice that I like best is its richness. 2 c/u.n (often of good etc —) level or degree of goodness, excellence etc: cloth of good/high/low/poor quality. It is the quality of one's food that is important not its quantity.

qualitative /ˈkwɒlɪtətɪv/ adj referring to quality.

'qualitatively adv.

qualm /kwɑːm/ c.n (often pl) (often (have) —s (about (doing) s.t); without a —) unpleasant feeling, of sickness, worry, doubt etc (about whether one is right to do s.t): The young mother had qualms about leaving her child alone with another woman all day.

quandary /ˈkwɒndərɪ/ sing.n (usu in a — (about (doing) s.t, about whether. . .)) state of uncomfortable doubt (about (doing) s.t): We were in a quandary about whether to go or stay.

quantity /ˈkwɒntɪtɪ/ n (pl -ies) (written abbr qty) 1 c.n (often a — of s.t) amount/number (of s.t): What quantity of paint will you need for this job? 2 u.n thing about s.t which can be measured in size, number, weight etc: When buying cloth for our factory we are less interested in quantity than in quality. **an unknown quantity** (a) a person or thing about which one knows nothing yet. (b) (mathematics) a number that one does not yet know the size of and that one represents by x until one works it out. **quantities of s.t** large quantities(1) of s.t.

'quantity sur,veyor c.n person whose job is to work out the quantities of materials needed for doing a job and how much they will cost.

quarantine /ˈkwɒrənˌtiːn/ sing.n 1 (often (keep s.o/s.t) in —; put s.o/s.t in(to) —) state of being kept away from other people/animals to prevent one/it spreading a disease to them; time during which one/it is kept away in this way.

▷ tr.v 2 put (s.o, an animal) in quarantine(1).

quarrel /ˈkwɒrəl/ c.n 1 (often have a — (with s.o)) argument; fight, usu without using force. 2 (often have no — with s.o/s.t) disagreement (with s.o or about s.t): We have no quarrel with your plans. **pick a quarrel** (with s.o) start an argument (with s.o).

▷ intr.v (-ll-, US -l-) 3 (often — with s.o (about/over s.o/s.t)) have a quarrel(1) (with s.o) (about s.o/

s.t). **quarrel with s.t** disagree about s.t; not be satisfied with s.t: I don't mind your stopping for tea but I am quarrelling with the length of time you spend doing it.

'quarrelsome adj (of a person, animal) who/ that often picks quarrels(1).

'quarrelsomeness u.n.

quarry¹ /ˈkwɒrɪ/ c.n (pl -ies) 1 place where stone etc is dug out for use in building etc.

▷ tr/intr.v (-ies, -ied) 2 dig (stone etc) out of a quarry(1).

quarry² /ˈkwɒrɪ/ sing.n thing that is hunted by people, dogs, birds of prey(1) etc.

quart /kwɔːt/ c.n (written abbr qt) measure of capacity(1) equal to about 1.14 litres; there are two pints(1) in a quart and four quarts in a gallon.

quarter¹ /ˈkwɔːtə/ attrib.adj 1 that is (equal to) one of four equal parts that make the whole: a quarter bottle of milk (i.e a bottle that is a quarter(2) of the size of an ordinary one); a quarter chicken for each person; a quarter mile race; a quarter century (= 25 years etc). **quarter the amount, size, number** etc (of s.t) (equal to only) one of four (almost) equal parts: I want only quarter the amount of food you gave Peter. We had enough books for quarter the number of people. We finished the work in quarter the time they did. **one, two** etc **and a quarter** one, two etc wholes and one quarter(2) of a whole: two and a quarter hours; an hour and a quarter delay (75 minutes); four and a quarter miles.

▷ c.n (written abbr qr) 2 one or other of the four equal parts that make a whole or into which s.t can be divided equally: a mile and a quarter (1¼m); a quarter of mushrooms (¼ of a pound/
kilogram). We've finished a quarter (of the work). 3 (often a — past/to s.t) 15 minutes (past/to an hour). 4 fourth part of a year: The rent for this quarter is now due. 5 (informal) four ounces(1): I bought a quarter of chocolates to eat in the cinema. 6 old measure of weight that is a quarter(1) of a hundredweight(1); 28 pounds¹(2). 7 (in the US etc) coin worth a quarter of a dollar. 8 quarter of an animal, with one of the legs. ⇒ forequarters, hindquarters (⇒ hind¹). 9 (of the moon) time when the moon looks like half a plate, because one can see one quarter of it (another quarter is towards us but dark and the other half is on the other side of the moon): The moon is in its first/last quarter tonight. 10 direction: Policemen suddenly arrived from every quarter to search the village. 11 part of the world, a country, town etc: We have students from every quarter of the earth in our classes. This is the Arab quarter of the town.

▷ tr.v 12 divide (s.t) into four parts.

'quarter ,day c.n day on which one of the quarters(3) into which a year is officially divided begins; it is the day on which certain payments have to be made.

'quarter,deck c/def.n part of the upper deck of some ships that is further back than the last mast and is where officers live, work etc.

,quarter'final c.n (also attrib) one of four matches in a competition, the winner of which goes on to the semifinals.

'quartering u.n division into quarters(1,11).

'quarterly adj/adv 1 done etc every three months: quarterly rent payments.

▷ *c.n* (*pl -ies*) **2** magazine etc that comes out every three months.
'quarters[1] *pl* of quarter[1](*n*). **at close quarters** near each other.
quartet, quartette /kwɔː'tet/ *c.n* **1** group of four singers or musicians who play together. **2** music written for a quartet(1).
quarter[2] /'kwɔːtə/ *tr.v* provide (s.o, usu soldiers) with quarters[2].
'quartering[2] *u.n* giving or finding of quarters[2] for people, usu soldiers.
'quarter,master *c.n* (*written abbr* QM) **1** (in the army) officer who looks after a regiment's(1) supplies of food, clothing, quarters[2] etc. **2** sailor who steers a ship.
'quarters[2] *pl.n* places given to people, usu soldiers, to live in. **married quarters** places where soldiers etc live with their families.
quarter[3] /'kwɔːtə/ *u.n* (often *ask for*, *give s.o*, (*no*) —) mercy; allowing a beaten enemy to live.
quartz /kwɔːts/ *u.n* kind of rock in the form of crystals(2) that often have attractive colours and patterns.
,quartz 'clock/'watch *c.n* clock/watch that is extremely accurate because of the use of quartz in it.
quasar /'kweɪzɑː/ *c.n* (*technical*) object in space that is like a star; it gives off light and radio waves.
quash /kwɒʃ/ *tr.v* (*law*; *formal*) stop (s.t) being valid(1) any longer, usu by giving a judgement in a court of law or by an official statement. ⇒ annul.
quaver[1] /'kweɪvə/ *c.n* **1** shaking or trembling of one's voice, sometimes because one is frightened or very old.
▷ *v* **2** *intr.v* make the sound of a quaver(1). **3** *tr.v* say (s.t) while quavering(2): *'I don't know what to say to that,'* the old man quavered uncertainly.
'quavery *adj* that quavers(2).
quaver[2] /'kweɪvə/ *c.n* musical note the sign for which is ♪ ; it is half a crotchet. ⇒ semiquaver.
quay /kiː/ *c.n* place beside, sticking out into, the sea, a river etc, usu built of stone or metal, where ships can come and tie up.
queasy /'kwiːzɪ/ *adj* (*-ier, -iest*) **1** feeling sick in one's stomach. **2** (often — *about/at* (*doing*) s.t) feeling very uncomfortable in one's mind (about (doing) s.t unpleasant, wrong, dangerous etc).
'queasily *adv*. **'queasiness** *u.n*.
queen /kwiːn/ *c.n* **1** (often with capital **Q**; *the* — *of s.t*) female ruler (of a country). **2** (often with capital **Q**; *the* — *of s.o*) wife of a king. **3** (often *the* — *ant/bee/wasp* etc) most important insect in a group which lays the eggs. **4** (usu *the* — *of s.t*) most important female person, city, ship etc (in s.t): *Venice is often called the Queen of the Adriatic*. **5** (often with capital **Q**; *the* — *of diamonds* etc) playing card below a king(2) but above a jack(2) in value with a picture of a queen(1) on it, *symb* Q. **6** piece in the game of chess that one can move as many places as one wants straight forwards/back, from side to side or diagonally, *symb* Q. **7** (*slang*; *derog*) male homosexual(2).
▷ *tr.v* **8** **queen it over s.o** (*informal*; *derog*) (of a female) treat s.o as one's inferior(2).
,queen 'consort ⇒ consort(1).
'queenly *adj* like (what one expects for/from) a queen(1,2).

,queen 'mother *c.n* mother of a ruler who is a king/queen.
,Queen's 'Counsel *c.n* (*abbr* QC) (UK) (title of a) barrister who is appointed to act for the Crown(2) when a queen(1) is on the throne(2). Compare King's Counsel.
,queen's 'evidence ⇒ evidence(*n*).
queer /kwɪə/ *adj* **1** unpleasantly strange. **2** ill: *feel queer*. **3** (*informal*; *derog*) (of a male) homosexual(2). **queer in the head** (*informal*) mad.
▷ *c.n* **4** (*informal*; *derog*) homosexual(1) man.
▷ *tr.v* **5** **queer one's/s.o's pitch** (*informal*) cause one's/s.o's ideas, plans etc to fail.
'queerly *adv*. **'queerness** *u.n*.
'queer ,street *unique n* **in queer street** (*slang*) in difficulties, often because of lack of money.
quell /kwel/ *tr.v* force (s.t) to stop; suppress(1) s.t: *quell a rebellion*.
quench /kwentʃ/ *tr.v* **1** put (a fire etc) out. **2** (often — s.t *in/with* s.t) stop (one's thirst) (by drinking s.t).
'quenchless *adj* unquenchable.
querulous /'kwerjuləs/ *adj* (*formal*) complaining, usu in an irritating way.
'querulously *adv*. **'querulousness** *u.n*.
query /'kwɪərɪ/ *c.n* (*pl -ies*) **1** question; doubt.
▷ *tr.v* (*-ies, -ied*) **2** (often — *whether*...) question (s.t, whether . . .); raise doubts about (s.t, whether . . .): *Joan queried whether it was wise to leave so late*. **3** ask (s.t): *'Are you ready?'* she queried.
quest /kwest/ *c.n* (*formal*) **1** (often — *for s.o/s.t*) search (for s.o/s.t); attempt to find s.o/s.t. **in quest of s.o/s.t** trying to find s.o/s.t: *David has gone off in quest of a taxi*.
▷ *intr.v* **2** **quest for s.o/s.t** (*literary*) search, look for s.o/s.t.
question /'kwestʃən/ *n* (*written abbr* q, qu; *pl* qq) **1** *c.n* word or words asking for an answer, (from s.o): *'Oh?' 'What?' 'Is it?' 'Are you ready?' 'Where's your sister?'* are all questions. **2** *c.n* (often *a* — *of s.t*) difficulty/problem (that consists of s.t). **3** *u.n* (often *a* — *about, as to, s.t/whether* . . .) doubt (about s.t, whether . . .): *There's some question as to whether we can get there in time*. **call s.t in(to) question** express doubts about s.t. **come into question** begin to be talked, thought etc about. **leading question** ⇒ leading. **out of the question** impossible; not to be accepted at all. **(only) a question of time, a few years** etc that will certainly happen, the only problem being when. **pop the question** ask s.o to marry one. **(the point) in question** (matter) being talked, thought etc about. **there's no question of (doing) s.t**; **there's no question that** . . . s.t has certainly not been, is certainly not going to be, done: *There's no question of stopping now we have got as far as this*.
▷ *tr.v* **4** (often — s.o *about* s.o/s.t) ask (s.o) a question(1) (about s.o/s.t). **5** (often — *whether*. . .) doubt (s.t, /whether . . .): *I question whether we really need to spend so much on a radio*.
'questionable *adj* that can be doubted; doubtful(2). Opposite unquestionable.
'questionably *adv*.
'questioner *c.n* person who asks a question(1).
'questioning *adj* that seems to ask a question(1): *a questioning look*. ⇒ unquestioning.
'questioningly *adv*.
'question ,mark *c.n* mark **?** showing that a

question is being asked. *a question mark over s.t* (*fig*) a doubt about s.t: *There is now a question mark over the football match because of the weather.*

'**question** ,**master** *c.n* person who asks the questions(1) in a competition etc, e.g on television.

'**questionnaire** /ˌkwestʃə'neə/ *c.n* list of questions(1) to be answered in writing, e.g to find out what kind of people live in a place.

'**question** ,**tag** *c.n* words added at the end of a statement to turn it into a question(1), e.g 'isn't it?' in 'It's warm today, isn't it?'

'**question** ,**time** *unique n* time during which people can ask questions(1): *In Parliament any member can ask a minister a question at question time.*

queue /kjuː/ *c.n* **1** (often *form, join, get into, a* —; *a* — *of people, vehicles* etc) line (of people etc) waiting, usu in an orderly way, for, to do, s.t. **2** (*fig*) (often (*join*) *a* — (*of people* etc)) list of people waiting for s.t, e.g council houses. *jump the queue* (*informal*) join a queue(1) but not in one's right place at the end of it.
▷ *intr.v* **3** form, stand in, a queue(1): *We queued for hours to get tickets.*

quibble /'kwɪbl/ *c.n* **1** argument that is unnecessary, not important, annoying and is usu used because one does not want to admit that one was wrong about s.t.
▷ *intr.v* **2** (often — *with s.o* (*about/over s.t*)) argue in this way (with s.o) (about s.t).
'**quibbler** *c.n* (*derog*) person who quibbles(2).
'**quibbling** *adj* that is a quibble(1).

quick /kwɪk/ *adj* **1** (often — *about/at* (*doing*) *s.t*; — *to do s.t*; — *with s.t*) who/that does s.t or that happens etc with speed; fast(1); rapid; speedy. Opposite slow(1). *be quick off the mark* ⇒ mark(*n*).
▷ *adv* **2** in a quick(1) way; quickly; fast(6): *Come quick, there's been an accident! How can one get rich quick?* (*as*) *quick as a flash* ⇒ flash(*n*). *Quick march!* ⇒ march(*v*).
▷ *n* **3** *u/def.n* part of one's body that can feel pain, usu of the part on which nail grows. **4** *def.pl.n* (*old use*) people who are alive: *the quick and the dead. be quick on the draw* ⇒ draw(4). *cut s.o to the quick* (*fig*) hurt s.o's feelings very much.
'**quicken** *tr/intr.v* (cause (s.t) to) go faster.
,**quick-'freeze** *tr.v* (*p.t* quick-froze, *p.p* quick-frozen) freeze (food) quickly so as to keep the natural taste etc: *quick-frozen meat.*
'**quickie** *c.n* (*informal*) thing, e.g a question or a film, that takes only a very short time.
'**quickly** *adv*. '**quickness** *u.n*.
'**quick**,**sand** *c/u.n* area of sand that is loose so that anyone who steps on it sinks down into it.
,**quick-'tempered** *adj* having a quick temper that easily turns to anger.
'**quick** ,**time** *u.n* (often (*march*) *in* —) (usu of soldiers) way of marching that is very fast without actually running. ⇒ double, quick march (⇒ march).
,**quick-'witted** *adj* clever; able to understand and think quickly.

quid /kwɪd/ *c.n* (*pl* quid) (*informal*) pound¹(1); £: *Paul owes me five quid.*

quiet /'kwaɪət/ *adj* **1** not making any/much noise: *a quiet car.* **2** not having any/much noise in it: *a*

quiet room. **3** calm; not busy or rough: *a quiet lake; the quiet time between rush hours.* **4** not behaving in a way that makes people notice one: *a quiet look around the room.* **5** (of a colour) not bright.
▷ *u.n* **6** (often (*in*) *peace and* —; *in the peace and* — *of s.t*) state or fact of being quiet(1–3). *on the quiet* (*informal*) secretly.
'**quieten** *tr/intr.v* (often — (*s.o/s.t*) *down*) (cause (s.o/s.t) to) become quiet(er).
'**quietly** *adv*. '**quietness** *u.n*.

quill /kwɪl/ *c.n* **1** bird's feather, usu a big strong one. **2** (also ,**quill** '**pen**) (*old use*) pen made from a quill(1). **3** sharp thing like a needle that grows out of the body of a hedgehog etc.

quilt /kwɪlt/ *c.n* thing that one puts on a bed, usu over the blankets, for warmth; it is made of two pieces of cloth sewn together with padding between.
'**quilted** *adj* made as, like, a quilt: *The Chinese often wear quilted coats in winter.*

quin /kwɪn/ *c.n* (*informal*) quintuplet.

quince /kwɪns/ *c.n* (also *attrib*) kind of sour yellow fruit that looks rather like an apple; it is cooked with sugar or made into jelly(2): *quince jelly(2).*

quinine /kwɪ'niːn/ *u.n* substance made from the bark of a tree and used against malaria etc.

quintet /kwɪn'tet/ *c.n* (also **quin'tette**) **1** group of five singers or musicians who play together. **2** music written for a quintet(1).

quintuplet /'kwɪntjʊplɪt/ *c.n* (*informal* quin) (usu *pl*) one of five children born to one mother at one time.

quip /kwɪp/ *c.n* **1** remark that is intended to sound clever but is usu unkind.
▷ *v* (*-pp-*) **2** *intr.v* make one or more quips(1). **3** *tr.v* say (s.t) as a quip(1): '*John always was quick with his hands,*' *Peter quipped.*

quirk /kwɜːk/ *c.n* **1** strange happening that one did not expect. **2** strange way of behaving. *a quirk of fate* a quirk(1) that one thinks is a result of fate(1).

quit /kwɪt/ *pred.adj* **1** *quit of s.t* having got rid of s.t; no longer troubled by s.t.
▷ *v* (*-tt-*, *p.t,p.p* quit) **2** *tr/intr.v* (often — *doing s.t*) leave (s.t); stop doing (s.t). *notice to quit* order to leave one's home, job etc.

quits *pred.adj* (after an argument, contest etc) even (⇒ be/get even (with s.o)). *call it quits* agree that one is even with s.o in an argument, contest etc.
'**quitter** *c.n* (*derog*; *informal*) person who gives up doing s.t too easily.

quite /kwaɪt/ *det/adv* **1** completely; absolutely; perfectly: *a quite white bird*; *quite the oldest man in our club*; *quite beyond my knowledge.* **2** rather; more than the average: *quite pleasant*; *quite a small house.* **3** rather; to some but not a great, extent: *almost but not quite all the way*; *almost but not quite enough people, money. not quite the man he etc was* less good, strong etc man than he etc was before. *quite a/some girl* etc (*informal*) unusually interesting etc girl etc: *That was quite a journey, wasn't it? quite a few/lot (of s.t)* not really a small number/amount (of s.t). *quite a/some time* rather a long time. *quite all right* not at all bad, ill etc. *quite (so)* I agree: '*We'd better stop now.*' '*Quite (so).*' *quite something* (*informal*) unusually good, interesting etc: *It's quite something to be invited to dinner by a film-star!* **quite the nicest** etc **s.o/s.t** (*I have ever seen* etc) without any doubt the nicest etc.

quits ⇨ quit.

quiver¹ /'kwɪvə/ *c.n* **1** movement of trembling: *A quiver of excitement ran through the crowd as the film-star got out of her car.*

▷ *tr/intr.v* **2** (often — *at/with s.o*) (cause (one's lips etc) to) tremble (because of excitement, fear etc).

quiver² /'kwɪvə/ *c.n* long case for holding arrows.

quiz /kwɪz/ *c.n* **1** game or competition in which one or more people have to answer questions.

▷ *tr.v* (-zz-) **2** (often — *s.o about s.t*) ask (s.o) (a lot of) questions (about s.t): *Why are you quizzing me about my relations with her?*

'quiz ,master *c.n* = question master.

'quizzical *adj* (esp of a look) as if asking a question: *She gave me a quizzical look.*

quoit /kɔɪt/ *c.n* ring, often made of rope, used in the game of quoits.

quoits *u.n* (usu *play* (*a game of*) —) game in which one tries to throw a quoit over a vertical peg(1), often played on the decks of ships.

quorum /'kwɔːrəm/ *c.n* minimum(1) number of people needed to hold a meeting, e.g of a committee.

quota /'kwəʊtə/ *c.n* (*pl* -s) (often *the* — *of s.t*) number or amount (of s.t) that has been fixed or agreed, usu as a limit: *The government has fixed yearly quotas for the* import(1) *of cars.*

quote /kwəʊt/ *adv* **1** (word used to warn a listener that one is about to begin a quotation(2); at the end of the quotation one then says unquote): *The man said (quote) 'Give me all your money or I'll shoot' (unquote).*

▷ *c.n* **2** thing quoted(1); quotation(2). **in quotes** in quotation marks.

▷ *v* **3** *tr/intr.v* (often — (*s.t*) *from s.t*; — *what . . .*) repeat (s.t s.o has said or written, usu s.t that one thinks important, beautiful etc): *To finish her lecture, Joan quoted two lines from Shakespeare. The journalist asked the politician if he could quote what she had said.* **4** *tr.v* give the name of (s.o/s.t) to support what one says: *Peter didn't believe George was correct about his illness, so George quoted his doctor.* **5** *tr.v* (often — *s.o s.t*) tell s.o (a price) for s.t he/she wants to buy/sell: *In the next shop a man quoted Mary £5 for the same stockings.*

quotation /kwəʊ'teɪʃən/ *n* **1** *u.n* act or fact of quoting (⇨ quote(*v*)) (s.t). **2** *c.n* (often — *from s.t*) thing quoted (s.t): *a quotation from Shakespeare's 'Hamlet'.* **give s.o a quotation (for s.t)** tell s.o what the price (of s.t) will be.

quo'tation ,mark *c.n* punctuation mark ' or " at the beginning and ' or " at the end of s.t quoted(1). **in quotation marks** with ' or " before and ' or " after it: *In 'Come here,' he said, 'Come here' is in quotation marks.*

quotient /'kwəʊʃənt/ *c.n* (*mathematics*) number that one gets by dividing one number by another: *The quotient of 16 ÷ 8 is 2.*

qv /ˌkjuː 'viː/ *abbr* (*Latin*) (*'quod vide'*) 'which see'; used to tell a reader to look somewhere else in the book etc to find the information referred to.

Rr

R, r /ɑː/ *c/unique n* **1** 18th letter of the English alphabet. **roll one's r's** ⇨ roll(*v*).

▷ *written abbr* (**R**) **2** Railway(s). **3** (*Latin*) Regina or Rex. **4** Republican. **5** River. **6** Royal.

rabbi /'ræbaɪ/ *c.n* (with capital **R** in names) Jewish religious teacher and leader.

rabbit /'ræbɪt/ *n* **1** *c.n* kind of small animal with fur and long ears that lives in holes in the ground and eats grass and vegetables. ⇨ hare(1). **2** *u.n* (also *attrib*) meat or fur of this animal. **Welsh rabbit** ⇨ Welsh.

'rabbit ,hutch *c.n* **1** cage in which rabbits are kept. **2** (*derog*; *informal*) very small home/house.

'rabbit ,warren *c.n* **1** area of land with many rabbit holes in which wild rabbits live. **2** (*fig*; *informal*) place, e.g in a town or building, in which it is difficult to find one's way because of many small streets, passages etc.

rabble /'ræbl/ *n* **1** *sing/def.pl.n* disorderly(2) crowd; mob(1). **2** *def.pl.n* (*derog*) common people; lower classes.

rabies /'reɪbiːz/ *u.n* kind of very dangerous disease that all animals with a backbone(1) can get; it makes the person or animal mad and then kills her/him/it.

rabid /'ræbɪd/ *adj* **1** who/that has rabies. **2** (*derog*) (of a person, her/his beliefs etc) extreme: *a rabid hatred of foreigners.*

RAC /ˌɑːr ˌeɪ 'siː/ *def.n abbr* Royal Automobile Club.

race¹ /reɪs/ *c.n* **1** (often — *between s.o/s.t and s.o/s.t*; — *against s.o*) competition (between s.o/s.t and s.o/s.t etc) to see who can run, row, drive a car etc fastest over a certain distance: *a 100 metres race.* **a race against time** an attempt to complete s.t before s.t else happens: *It was a race against time to get the roof repaired before the rains came.*

▷ *v* **2** *tr/intr.v* (often — *against s.o/s.t*) have, or take part in, a race¹(1) (against s.o/s.t): *I'll race you to the gate!* **3** *tr/intr.v* (often — *by*) (cause (s.o/s.t) to) go (by) very fast: *As she ran to him, her heart was racing. Summer is racing by and soon it will be autumn again. The only way to save the child is to race him to a doctor.*

'race-,course *c.n* ground for horse races.

'race,horse *c.n* horse used for racing.

'race ,meeting *c.n* (date for) people meeting at a certain place for horse racing.

'races *def.pl.n* (*informal*) = race meeting: *a day at the races.*

'race,track *c.n* course, usu with two parallel sides and a curve at each end, for racing round.

'racing *u.n* (also *attrib*) sport of taking part in, watching etc races (⇨ race¹(1)): *a racing car.*

race² /reɪs/ *n* **1** *c.n* group of creatures (of the kind shown by an adjective etc): *the human race.* **2** *c.n* group of people or animals who/that are (treated as) having the same origins or descent: *the white races*; *the* Caucasian(1) *race.* **3** *c.n* group (of people) belonging to a particular country or region: *the German race.* **4** *unique n* fact that people are divided into different races: *Race is becoming a serious problem in the modern world.* **of a . . . race** descended from a certain kind of background: *These people are of noble race.*

,race re'lations *pl.n* treatment of each other by people of different races²(2).

racial /'reɪʃəl/ *adj* (usu *attrib*) **1** referring to race²(2). **2** that attacks one's/s.o's race²(2): *a racial remark.*

'racia,lism *u.n* (also **'racism**) (*derog*) feeling that one's own race²(2) is better than others; behaviour based on this feeling.

'racialist *c.n* (also *attrib*) (also **'racist**) (*derog*) person/thing showing racialism: *a racialist remark.* **'racially** *adv.*

'racism, 'racist ⇒ racialism, racialist.

rack /ræk/ *c.n* **1** framework of bars, rods etc, sometimes with hooks or pegs(1) on it, for putting or hanging things on tidily: *a plate rack; a luggage rack over the seats in a train.* ⇒ roof rack. **2** (*technical*) strip of metal with teeth that fit into the teeth on a wheel called a pinion² so that one can move the other. **3** (in history) frame used for stretching people's bodies to try to get them to confess their crimes.

▷ *tr.v* **4** (often passive, —*ed by/with s.t*) cause (s.o) great pain. **rack one's brains (to do s.t)** ⇒ brain(*n*).

,rack and 'ruin *u.n* **be in, go to, rack and ruin** (usu of a building) be in, get into, a very ruined state because of not being looked after.

racket¹ /'rækɪt/ *c.n* (also **'racquet**) instrument consisting of a frame with strings stretched tightly across it to form a network, used for hitting the ball in tennis etc.

racket² /'rækɪt/ *n* **1** *sing.n* (often **make a —**) loud unpleasant noise: *What a racket! I'm trying to sleep!* **2** *u.n* busy activity that tires some people and makes them nervous: *the racket of modern life in a big city.* **3** *c.n* (*derog; informal*) dishonest activity or behaviour: *The man had a wonderful racket selling bottles of English rainwater to tourists.* **4** *c.n* (*informal; joking*) kind of work; business: *I'm in the newspaper racket.*

,racke'teer *c.n* (*derog*) person who is in a racket²(3).

,racke'teering *u.n* activity of a racketeer.

racquet /'rækɪt/ *c.n* = racket¹.

radar /'reɪdɑː/ *u.n* (also *attrib*) way of finding the position and distance of things by sending out radio waves that hit them and then come back: *a radar screen.*

radial /'reɪdɪəl/ *c.n* (also **,radial 'tyre**) kind of tyre on a car etc that has lines, bars etc in it which help to prevent skidding(1).

radiant /'reɪdɪənt/ *adj* **1** sending out light and/ or heat. **2** (*attrib*) (*technical*) (of heat) sent out from a hot body. **3** (usu — **with s.t**) (of a person, her/his face etc) showing great happiness, love etc (because of s.t): *radiant with delight at the good news.*

'radiance *u.n.* **'radiantly** *adv.*

radiate /'reɪdɪ,eɪt/ *tr.v* send (s.t, e.g light, heat, happiness) out. **radiate from s.t** spread out from s.t. ⇒ irradiate.

radiation /,reɪdɪ'eɪʃən/ *n* **1** *u.n* act or fact of radiating s.t. **2** *c.n* thing that is radiated. **3** *u.n* radioactivity: *atomic radiation.*

,radi'ation ,sickness *u.n* illness caused by radiation(3).

radiator /'reɪdɪ,eɪtə/ *c.n* **1** part of a car that has water in it to keep the engine cool. **2** device, usu fixed to a wall, that can be heated so that it sends out heat into a room.

radical /'rædɪkl/ *adj* **1** (of a change) complete; covering everything: *Computers have produced a radical change in our ways of doing business.* **2** (*politics*) belonging to, supporting, ideas for great, sometimes extreme, change.

▷ *c.n* **3** person who is radical(2).

'radica,lism *u.n* **1** fact or quality of being radical(2). **2** idea of radicals(3).

'radically *adv.*

radii /'reɪdɪ,aɪ/ *c.n pl* of radius.

radio /'reɪdɪəʊ/ *n* (*pl -s*) (also *attrib*) **1** *u.n* (often **by —**) (system of) sending and/or receiving sounds through the air in the form of electrical waves. **2** *c.n* device for both sending and/ or receiving. ⇒ wireless(3). **3** *u.n* radio broadcasting as an industry: *radio programmes. Wendy works in radio.* **on the radio (a)** as (part of) a radio broadcast: *We get some good music on the radio.* **(b)** speaking, playing music etc during a radio broadcast: *We heard Mary on the radio yesterday evening.*

▷ *tr/intr.v* (*radioes, radioed*) **4** send (a message) (to s.o) by radio (asking for s.t etc): *He radioed for help when his boat started sinking. We radioed that we were safe.*

'radio ,frequency *c.n* (*pl -ies*) frequency(3) used in radio(1).

'radio,gram *c.n* (becoming *old use*) radio(2) and record player in one.

'radio ,ham = ham(4).

'radio ,set *c.n* = radio(2).

,radio 'tele,scope *c.n* device used to look at the stars, outer(3) space(3) etc using radio(1) waves(2).

radioactive /,reɪdɪəʊ'æktɪv/ *adj* having radioactivity: *radioactive dust.*

,radio'actively *adv.*

,radioac'tivity *u.n* act or fact of atoms breaking up spontaneously which produces energy(2) that can be dangerous to living things.

radiographer /,reɪdɪ'ɒɡrəfə/ *c.n* person who produces X-ray(1) photographs.

,radi'ography *u.n* work of producing X-ray(1) photographs.

radio-isotope /,reɪdɪəʊ 'aɪsə,təʊp/ *c.n* (*technical*) one of the radioactive forms that an element(1) can appear in.

radiology /,reɪdɪ'ɒlədʒɪ/ *u.n* practice of using radioactivity to find and treat illnesses in a person.

,radi'ologist *c.n* person whose job concerns radiology.

radiotherapy /,reɪdɪəʊ'θerəpɪ/ *u.n* treatment of diseases by using radioactive substances and/or X-rays(1).

,radio'thera,pist *c.n* person whose job concerns radiotherapy.

radish /'rædɪʃ/ *c.n* kind of small vegetable with a red or white root that is eaten raw.

radium /'reɪdɪəm/ *u.n* (also *attrib*) radioactive metal element(1) used in treating some diseases, *chem.symb* Ra: *radium treatment.*

radius /'reɪdɪəs/ *c.n* (*pl radii* /'reɪdɪ,aɪ/) **1** half the distance across a circle along a line that passes through its centre. **2** (*informal*) distance all round, or in every direction, measured from a point: *There are only two other farms within a radius of 50 kilometres (of us)*.

RAF /ˌɑːr ˌeɪ 'ef/ *def.n abbr* Royal Air Force.

raffia /'ræfɪə/ *u.n* (also *attrib*) soft fibre(1) from a kind of palm²(1) tree, used for tying plants, making baskets etc.

raffle /'ræfl/ *c.n* (also *attrib*) **1** sale of s.t by selling a lot of tickets to different people; the person with the winning ticket can then have the thing: *raffle tickets*. Compare lottery(1).
▷ *tr.v* **2** (often — *s.t off*) sell (s.t) by means of a raffle(1).

raft /rɑːft/ *c.n* kind of flat thing, made of pieces of wood or logs or of plastic(3), that floats on water and is used to carry people etc, e.g to save them from drowning. *life raft* ⇒ life.

rafter /'rɑːftə/ *c.n* sloping beam that is one of those holding a roof up.

rag¹ /ræg/ *n* **1** *c/u.n* (small irregular piece of) old cloth. **2** *c.n* (*derog*; *informal*) newspaper, usu one that one does not like. **feel like a wet rag** (*informal*) feel very tired. **in rags** (a) torn: *Their clothes were in rags at the end of the fight.* (b) wearing ragged(1) clothes: *The poor people were in rags.* (**like**) **a red rag to a bull** (*informal*) making s.o very angry: *Telling those men that they don't deserve a rise in wages is like a red rag to a bull.*

ragged /'rægɪd/ *adj* **1** (of clothes, curtains etc) torn. **2** (of a person) dressed in ragged(1) clothes. **3** having rough ends, edges etc: *a ragged cloud.* **4** in which people etc go at a different speed, do different things etc instead of all doing the same: *a ragged rowing crew¹(1).*
'raggedly *adv.* **'raggedness** *u.n.*

rag² /ræg/ *n* **1** *c.n* rough noisy piece of fun. **2** students' procession in strange clothes etc to collect money for charity(2).
▷ *v* (*-gg-*) **3** *intr.v* take part in a rag²(1). **4** *tr.v* (usu — s.o about, for doing, s.t) make fun of, tease(2), (s.o) (because of s.t).
'rag ,day/,week *c/unique n* day/week during which students have a rag²(2).

rage /reɪdʒ/ *n* **1** *c/u.n* (often *in a* — (*about s.t*); scream etc *with* —) (state of) violent anger (about s.t etc). **2** *u.n* violence (of a storm, flood etc). **3** *c.n* strong interest or fashion (for s.t): *There was a rage for shoes with pointed toes some years ago.* (**all**) **the rage** (*informal*) very fashionable. **fly into a rage** ⇒ fly².
▷ *intr.v* **4** (often — *against/at s.o/s.t*) be violently angry (with s.o/s.t). **5** be violent: *The storm raged all night.* **rage oneself/itself out** rage(4,5) until one/it is finished: *The storm finally raged itself out as the sun came up.*
'raging *attrib.adj* (of pain) very severe: *raging toothache.*

ragged(ly/ness) ⇒ rag¹.

raglan coat/jacket /ˌræglən 'kəʊt/'dʒækɪt/ *c.n* coat/jacket(1) that has raglan sleeves.
,raglan 'sleeve *c.n* sleeve(1) that is not sewn on to the coat etc in the usual place round the shoulder, but near the neck instead.

ragtime /'rægˌtaɪm/ *u.n* (also *attrib*) kind of syncopated music particularly popular in the 1920s.

raid /reɪd/ *c.n* **1** (often — *on s.t*) sudden quick attack or visit after which one goes away again: *a raid on an enemy position*; *a police raid*; *a midnight raid on the kitchen to find something to eat.* ⇒ air raid.
▷ *tr/intr.v* **2** make a raid(1) (on (s.o/s.t)).
'raider *c.n* person, plane etc who/that raids(2).

rail /reɪl/ *attrib.adj* **1** by rail: *a rail journey.*
▷ *c.n* **2** horizontal or sloping bar, or set of bars that are part of a fence, used for hanging things on or for holding onto. **3** metal rail(1) along which trains run. ⇒ monorail. **by rail** in a train: *go/travel by rail.*
▷ *tr.v* **4** (often — *s.t in/off*) use rails(1) to close s.t in or to separate it from s.t else.
'rail,car *c.n* kind of vehicle that can travel alone on rails(2), driven by its own power. **by railcar** in a railcar: *go/travel by railcar.*
'rail,head *c.n* place where a railway line ends.
'railing *c.n* (often *pl*) fence made of rails(2).
'rail,road *c.n* (US) railway.
rails *pl.n* = rail(3). (**go**) **off the rails** (a) (of a train) (having) come off the rails. (b) (*fig*) (of a person) (having) become (rather) mad, or (be) quite wrong. **jump the rails** (of a train) go off the rails(a).
'rail,way *n* (also *attrib*) **1** *c.n* system of rails(3) that trains travel on: *the railway network*; *a railway system.* **2** *def.n* company that runs trains. **a job etc on/with the railway** a job etc working for a railway(2) company.
'railway ,engine *c.n* part of a train with a steam, electric or diesel engine that pulls the coaches or trucks.

rain /reɪn/ *n* **1** *u.n* water falling from clouds in the form of drops. Compare dew, hail¹(1), mist(1), sleet(1), snow(1). **2** *u.n* fall of such water: *We had rain last night.* **3** *c.n* rain(2) of the kind shown by an adjective etc: *There was a very welcome rain today after several dry months.* **4** (often *a* — *of s.t*) a large number/amount of s.t all coming at about the same time: *a rain of stones thrown by angry boys*; *a rain of rude remarks.* (**as**) **right as rain** (*informal*) completely well; not at all ill. (**come**) **rain or shine** (*informal*) whatever the weather may be; whatever may happen: *I'll be there come rain or shine.* **in the rain** in a place where the rain is falling on one: *Don't stand there in the rain; come in.* **it looks like rain** (*informal*) it looks as if it is going to rain.
▷ *v* **5** *intr.v* (*it rains; it is/was —ing* etc) (of rain(1)) fall from the clouds: *It rains quite a lot here.* **6** *tr/intr.v* (often — (s.t) (**down**) ((up)on s.o/ s.t)) (cause (s.t) to) come down ((on) s.o/s.t) like rain: *The enemies' arrows rained down on the soldiers.* **rain cats and dogs** ⇒ cat¹. **It never rains but it pours** (*proverb*) When one, usu bad, thing happens, other ones like it also happen. **rain itself out** rain so much that the rain stops (because there is no more left). **rain s.t off** (usu passive) (of rain) cause s.t, e.g a tennis match, to stop: *The football match was rained off.*
'rain,bow *c.n* arch of seven colours that is sometimes seen in the sky, usu after rain. **all the colours of the rainbow** (*informal*) many different colours.
'rain ,check *c.n* **take a rain check on s.t** (*fig*; *informal*) not accept s.t that has been offered now but agree to take it another time: *I can't come to*

the cinema with you tonight, but can I take a rain check on it?

'rain,coat *c.n* coat for wearing over one's clothes to keep one dry when one is in the rain(2).

'rain,drop *c.n* drop of rain(1).

'rain,fall *c/u.n* amount of rain(1), that falls in a place in a certain time.

'rain ,forest *c/u.n* thick forest in hot wet countries, e.g Brazil.

'rain ,gauge *c.n* kind of instrument that measures rainfall.

'rain,proof *adj* that does not let rain through. Compare showerproof.

rains *def.pl.n* season of heavy rain in some hot countries. ⇨ monsoon(2).

'rain,storm *c.n* sudden heavy fall of rain.

'rain,water *u.n* water that fell as rain(1).

'rainy *adj* (-ier, -iest) that has a lot of rain(2): *a rainy country; a rainy week.* **put s.t by**, **save up**, **for a rainy day** (*fig*) save s.t, usu money, for a time when one may/will need it.

raise /reɪz/ *c.n* **1** increase in one's salary, wages etc; rise(4): *I've asked for a raise. Did you get a raise last month?* ⇨ raise(4).

▷ *tr.v* **2** cause (s.o/s.t) to go up or to move upwards. **3** cause (s.o/s.t) to become vertical, sometimes after having fallen down: *Whenever the baby fell, its little sister raised it to its feet again.* **4** cause (s.t) to go up in price, cost, amount, number etc: *When rents were raised we had to move to a cheaper flat.* ⇨ raise(1). **5** bring up (a family), grow (crops etc) or breed(2) animals: *She raised five children with very little help from her husband. The farmers raise corn here.* Compare rear²(1). **6** collect (s.t) together: *We need to raise money for a new sports club.* **7** (*formal*) build (s.t tall): *We want to raise a monument to our last prime minister.* **8** (usu — *a cheer/shout*) make (a noise of some kind). **9** (usu — *a laugh* etc) cause s.o to make (a noise of some kind). **10** cause people to feel (s.t, esp doubts or fears). **11** put (a subject) forward for discussion: *Helen raised several interesting points during the meeting.* **12** cause (s.t) to stop or finish: *The government has raised the ban(1) on* imports(1). **13** (in a card game) make a higher bid(2) than (the last player): *I'll raise you one pound.* **raise Cain/hell/the roof** (*informal*) become very angry; cause a lot of trouble. **raise a family** ⇨ family. **raise one's hat** (**to s.o**) ⇨ hat. **raise s.o's hopes** ⇨ hope(*n*).

raisin /'reɪzn/ *c.n* kind of dried grape used for eating, e.g in cakes. Compare currant(1), sultana².

rake /reɪk/ *c.n* **1** kind of tool used for collecting leaves etc together or smoothing earth; it has a long usu wooden handle with a metal bar at one end with metal teeth on it. **2** kind of tool like a very big rake(1), pulled by a horse or a tractor. **3** kind of tool like a small rake(1), used to collect people's stakes(1) in gambling.

▷ *v* **4** *tr/intr.v* (often — *s.t over*) use a rake(1,2) (on(s.t, e.g leaves, earth)). **5** *tr.v* (often — *s.t in*, *together*, *up* etc) collect (s.t, e.g leaves or money), using a rake. **6** *intr.v* (often — *about/around* (among, in etc *s.t*)) dig (about) (in s.t), usu in search of s.t. **7** *tr.v* cover the whole of s.t by shooting (with a gun etc): *Our guns raked the enemy ship.* **rake s.t in** (**a**) ⇨ rake(5). (**b**) (*informal*) earn, win etc a

lot of money etc. **rake it in** (*informal*) earn, win etc a lot of money etc. **rake s.t up** (**a**) ⇨ rake(5). (**b**) break up the surface of earth with a rake(1,2). (**c**) (*informal*) collect s.t together with difficulty: *Can you rake up a few pounds to lend me until Friday?* (**d**) (*informal*) start talking about s.t that happened in the past and that other people want to forget: *Why must you go on raking up that mistake Jill once made?*

'rake-,off *c.n* (usu *get*, *give s.o*, *a* —) usu dishonest share of money received by s.o: *When Sam brings a new customer to that shop he gets a 5% rake-off.*

rally /'rælɪ/ *c.n* (*pl* -ies) **1** act or fact of people coming together for some purpose, usu to show unity or support for s.o/s.t. **2** big public meeting that is a rally(1). **3** (usu long) car race that is on public roads. **4** long exchange of shots in a tennis game before one of the players/teams wins the point.

▷ *v* (-ies, -ied) **5** *tr.v* bring (a group, esp soldiers) together, e.g in order to fight again. **6** *intr.v* (often — *round/to s.o/s.t*) come together to show unity or support (of s.o/s.t): *In former times soldiers often rallied to their flag when a battle was going badly for them.* **7** *tr/intr.v* (cause (s.o) to) improve in health, e.g after an operation. **8** *tr/intr.v* (cause (s.t) to) increase in value after falling in value: *The pound rallied towards the end of the day.*

RAM /ræm/ *abbr* random-access memory.

ram¹ /ræm/ *c.n* adult male sheep that has not been castrated. Compare ewe, lamb(1), wether.

ram² /ræm/ *c.n* **1** = battering ram (⇨ batter²). **2** machine that drops a weight on s.t, or pushes s.t into s.t, again and again. **3** part of a ram²(2) that is dropped or pushed in these ways.

▷ *tr.v* (-mm-) **4** run into (s.t) hard: *The police stopped the thieves by ramming their car.* **5** (often — *s.t down*; — *s.t in(to s.o/s.t)*) push (s.t, e.g earth round a newly planted bush) (down etc) hard: *He rammed a letter into her hand and ran away.* **ram s.t down s.o's throat** ⇨ throat.

ramble /'ræmbl/ *c.n* **1** (often **go for/on a** —) walk, usu a long slow one for pleasure, usu in the country.

▷ *intr.v* **2** go for a ramble(1). **3** (of a plant, often a climbing one) grow in an irregular way in different directions. **4** (usu — *on* (*about s.o/s.t*)) talk/write (about s.o/s.t) in a confused way (for a long time).

'rambler *c.n* **1** person who rambles(2,4). **2** = rambler rose.

,rambler 'rose *c.n* kind of rose that rambles(3).

'rambling *adj* **1** who/that rambles(4): *a rambling letter written by an old man.* **2** (of streets etc) twisting about irregularly.

▷ *u.n* **3** talking or writing in a rambling(1) way: *I had to listen to the old man's rambling for ages.*

'ramblings *pl.n* = rambling(3).

ramp¹ /ræmp/ *c.n* slope built for going up from one level to another instead of having to use steps: *There's a ramp for wheelchairs beside the steps.*

ramp² /ræmp/ *c.n* (*informal*) = racket²(3).

rampage /ræm'peɪdʒ/ *def.n* **1** (**be/go**) **on the rampage** (be/start) rushing around in an excited and violent way.

▷ *intr.v* **2** (often — *about/around*) be on the rampage(1).

rampant /'ræmpənt/ *adj* **1** (of s.t bad) so widespread that it is very difficult or impossible to control or stop: *Crime is rampant in our city.* **2** (of a plant) growing out of control: *Weeds are rampant in our garden.* **'rampantly** *adv.*

rampart /'ræmpɑ:t/ *c.n* (often *pl*) **1** big earth wall built to protect s.o/s.t (from s.o/s.t). **2** (*fig*) thing that protects one strongly (from s.o/s.t).

ramshackle /'ræmʃækl/ *adj* (of a building etc) so badly built, or so badly looked after, that it is almost falling down.

ran /ræn/ *p.t* of run(*v*).

ranch /rɑ:ntʃ/ *c.n* (mostly in North America) **1** very big farm for cattle(1), sheep and/or horses. **2** farm that produces the thing shown by the word(s) before: *a chicken ranch.* **'rancher** *c.n* person who owns or works on a ranch(1).

rancid /'rænsɪd/ *adj* (often go —) (of oil or fat, or s.t with oil or fat in it) smelling and tasting unpleasant because it is too old and has gone bad. **ran'cidity, 'rancidness** *u.n.*

rancour /'ræŋkə/ *u.n* (US **'rancor**) (often — against s.o/s.t) feeling of bitter hatred (for s.o/s.t). **'rancorous** *adj.* **'rancorously** *adv.*

random /'rændəm/ *adj* **1** made or done by chance; not aimed: *a random collection of fruits*; *a random thought.*

▷ *unique.n* **2** **at random** in a random way: *The soldiers were firing at random.*

,random-'access ,memory *u.n* (*abbr* RAM) memory (device) in a computer that stores information that can be found at any point and that can be added to, changed etc. Compare read-only memory. **'randomly** *adv.* **'randomness** *u.n.*

,random 'sample *c.n* sample(1) (taken from a much larger number of people, animals or things) without choosing any particular ones.

randy /'rændɪ/ *adj* (-ier, -iest) (*informal*) feeling that one wants sex(2): *a randy old man.* **'randily** *adv.* **'randiness** *u.n.*

rang /ræŋ/ *p.t* of ring²(*v*).

range /reɪndʒ/ *n* **1** *c.n* line or row (of hills etc): *a mountain range.* **2** *c.n* big area of land with grass, usu in North America, where cattle(1) can feed or people can hunt. **3** *c/u.n* area within which one can find a particular kind of animal, plant etc. **4** *c.n* piece of land where there are targets(1) for soldiers etc to shoot at. **5** *sing.n* (often *the — of s.t*) distance that a gun etc can shoot, a plane can fly without having to land for fuel(1) etc. **6** *c/u.n* (often *a — of 2000 metres* etc) distance (of s.t etc) between a gun etc and the thing it is trying to shoot at. **7** *sing.n* limits within which s.t varies: *That girl's voice covers an extraordinary range of* pitch¹(4). **at close range** very near to the person or thing who/that is the target: *He was shot at close range.* **beyond, out of, within, range (of s.o/s.t)** too far away, close enough, to be hit, seen etc (by a gun, s.o's eyes etc). **(come) within range (of s.o/s.t)** (come) near enough to be shot at, seen etc (by s.o/s.t). ⇒ range(6).

▷ *v* **8** *intr.v* (of hills, mountains etc): form a range(1): *The hills range across the country to the sea.* **9** *intr.v* vary: *The creatures in our zoo range from insects to elephants.* **10** *tr/intr.v* (often

— over/through s.t) move about freely, wander (over etc s.t): *The lions range the plains, living on the animals they catch.* **range over s.t** (a) ⇒ range(10). (b) (of a discussion etc) cover various subjects.

'range ,finder *c.n* instrument used to find the range(6) of a target(1).

'ranger *c.n* **1** forest guard. **2** (US) policeman in country areas. **3** (with capital **R**) senior Guide(5).

rank¹ /ræŋk/ *adj* **1** unpleasantly strong in smell or taste: *the rank smell of cigarettes.* **2** (of a plant) growing too strongly and without control. **3** (*attrib*) absolute; complete: *Her horse is a rank outsider* (very unlikely to win) *in the race.* **'rankly** *adv.* **'rankness** *u.n.*

rank² /ræŋk/ *n* **1** *c/u.n* position in a scale going from higher to lower: *The highest rank in the army is Field Marshal. Mary is a tennis player of top rank.* **2** *c/u.n* (often of (high etc) —) social position; importance in the world: *People of all ranks swim here.* **3** *c.n* line (of people) side by side: *Come on, boys, form three ranks facing this way!* **4** *c.n* = taxi rank.

▷ *v* **5** *tr/intr.v* have, put (s.o/s.t) in, a rank²(1) (that is above etc that of s.o/s.t, or that is high etc within s.t): *Joe ranks* (or *I rank Joe*) *quite low among the people I like to meet.* **6** *tr.v* arrange (s.o/s.t) in an orderly way. **rank s.o/s.t as s.o/s.t** consider s.o/s.t to be s.t: *I rank Helen as a friend.*

,rank and 'file *def/def.pl.n* (also *attrib*) **1** soldiers of the lowest rank(1). **2** people in a company etc who are not in important positions.

'ranking *c.n* order in which s.t is ranked²(5).

ranks *pl.n* (*pl* of rank²). **break ranks** get out of being in a line. ⇒ ranks(3). **join the ranks (of s.t)** become a member (of s.t): *Many people are joining the ranks of the unemployed.* **keep rank(s)** remain in a line. ⇒ rank(3). **other ranks** soldiers who are not officers.

rankle /'ræŋkl/ *intr.v* (often — with s.o) be s.t that s.o resents, or remembers with anger or bitterness.

ransack /'rænsæk/ *tr.v* (often — s.t for s.t) search (s.t) thoroughly and roughly (to find s.t, or to steal things).

ransom /'rænsəm/ *c/u.n* **1** (money paid for the) freeing of s.o who has been kidnapped or taken prisoner, or for s.t that has been stolen. **hold s.o/s.t to ransom** demand a ransom before freeing s.o/s.t. **a king's ransom** (*literary*) a very great amount of money.

▷ *tr.v* **2** free (s.o/s.t) by paying a ransom(1) for her/him/it.

rap /ræp/ *c.n* **1** (usu — at/on s.t) (sound of a) quick light knock, e.g at a door.

▷ *v* (-pp-) **2** *tr/intr.v* (usu — at/on s.t) knock or hit (s.o/s.t): *Who's that rapping at the window?* **rap s.o on s.t** hit s.o's hands etc: *My grandfather rapped me on the* knuckles(1).

rapacious /rə'peɪʃəs/ *adj* (*formal*) who/that seizes things in a greedy way. **ra'paciously** *adv.* **ra'paciousness, rapacity** /rə'pæsɪtɪ/ *u.n.*

rape /reɪp/ *c/u.n* **1** act or crime of having sex with s.o against her/his will. **2** (usu the — of s.t) process or act of ruining or damaging (s.t): *The rape of our great forests in order to make paper* *out of them is one of the saddest things we are doing.*

▷ *tr.v* **3** have sex with (s.o) against her/his will. **4** ruin or damage (s.t).
'rapist *c.n* person who rapes (3) s.o.

rapid /'ræpɪd/ *adj* **1** fast; very quick. **2** (of a slope) going down steeply.

▷ *c.n* (usu *pl*) **3** place, usu rocky and shallow, in a river where the water flows very fast. **shoot the rapids** (of a boat) go quickly through rapids (3).
rapidity /rə'pɪdɪtɪ/ *u.n.* **rapidly** /'ræpɪdlɪ/ *adv.*

rapier /'reɪpɪə/ *c.n* kind of light thin sword for thrusting (1) and not cutting.

rapist ⇒ rape.

rapture /'ræptʃə/ *u.n* great joy: *I was filled with rapture when I saw her.* ⇒ enrapture.
'raptures *pl.n* (usu *be in, go into,* —) state of rapture.
'rapturous *adj.* **'rapturously** *adv.*

rare /reə/ *adj* **1** not happening at all often; found in only very small quantities: *a rare animal; a rare sight.* **2** (of meat) not cooked very much. Compare well-done. **3** (of air, esp at a great height) having less oxygen in it than normal. **have a rare old time** ⇒ time (*n*).
'rarely *adv* not at all often: *He rarely comes here.*
'rareness *u.n.*
'rarity /'reərɪtɪ/ *n* (*pl -ies*) **1** *u.n* =rareness. **2** *c.n* thing that is rare (1).

rarebit /'reəbɪt/ ⇒ Welsh rarebit.

rascal /'rɑːskl/ *c.n* **1** person who is dishonest. **2** (*joking*) naughty person, usu a child.
'rascally *adj* of, referring to, like, a rascal (1).

rash¹ /ræʃ/ *c.n* red area on one's skin caused by a disease, e.g measles, an illness, heat etc: *a heat rash.* **come out in a rash** start having a rash¹. **a rash of s.t** (*fig*) a large number of s.t unpleasant which appear suddenly: *a rash of complaints about the food.*

rash² /ræʃ/ *adj* dangerously hasty. **in a rash moment** at a time when one was being rash². **'rashly** *adv.*
'rashness *u.n.*

rasher /'ræʃə/ *c.n* thin slice (of bacon or ham (1)).

rasp /rɑːsp/ *c.n* **1** kind of tool that has a metal blade with sharp points over its surface, used for rubbing metal, wood etc to make it smooth. **2** feeling or sound (like that) of a rasp (1).

▷ *v* **3** *tr.v* rub (s.t) (as if) with a rasp (1). **4** *tr/intr.v* disturb or irritate (1) (s.o, s.o's feelings etc): *Some people have rasping voices that annoy everyone.* **5** *tr.v* (often — *s.t out*) say (s.t) in a voice that rasps (4).
'raspingly *adv* in a way that rasps (4).

raspberry /'rɑːzbərɪ/ *c.n* (*pl -ies*) (also *attrib*) **1** kind of plant that usu grows as a bush and has raspberries (2) on it. **2** kind of soft sweet red (or sometimes yellow) fruit with a lot of seeds in it: *raspberry jam.* **3** (*slang*) (often *blow* —s) rude sound made by putting one's tongue between one's rounded lips and blowing wetly.

rat /ræt/ *c.n* **1** kind of small animal like a mouse but bigger and with a long tail, often found in buildings, old ships etc. **2** (*informal*) bad person, esp one who does not behave loyally. (**look**) **like a drowned rat** (look) very wet. **smell a rat** (*fig*; *informal*) suspect s.t.

▷ *intr.v* (*-tt-*) **3 rat on s.o** (*slang*) give information about s.o, what he/she has done etc, esp so that he/she gets caught, punished etc.
'rat ‚race *def.n* (*derog*; *informal*) daily competition among people in a society for better jobs, more money etc.

rats *interj* (*slang*) **1** nonsense (1). **2** bother (5).
'rattily *adv* in a ratty (1) way.
'rattiness *u.n* fact or state of being ratty (1).
'ratty *adj* (*-ier, -iest*) **1** (*informal*) angry; annoyed. **2** having rats (1) in it.

ratable ⇒ rate.

rat-a-(-tat)-tat /‚ræt ə(‚tæt) 'tæt/ *sing.n* (also **‚rat-'tat**) sound made by s.o knocking, usu on a door using the knocker.

ratchet /'rætʃɪt/ *c.n* (usu metal) wheel or bar with sloping teeth on it into which a kind of catch fits so that the wheel or bar can move in one direction but not in the other.
'ratchet ‚wheel *c.n* wheel that is a ratchet.

rate /reɪt/ *n* **1** (often *at a* — of *50 kilometres an hour* etc) speed (of s.t) measured by comparing distance travelled and time taken. **2** (often *at a* — *of . . .*) cost, price etc (of s.t) measured by comparing sums of money etc with numbers of units: *They're sold at the rate of £10 for twenty.* ⇒ birthrate, deathrate. **3** amount one has to pay, or is paid, (for s.t), based on a list of charges or pay levels: *Postal rates have gone up. The rate for a letter under 60 grams is now 20p. Rates of pay in this industry are good.* **4** (usu *pl*) tax paid to the local government by people who own/live in a building: *Rates are high in this town. We must pay our water rates.* **at any rate** whatever may happen; in any case. **at that/this rate** if things continue as they were/are doing.

▷ *tr.v* **5** (often — *s.o/s.t highly, low* etc (*as s.o/s.t*)) consider (s.o/s.t) to be worth a certain amount (as s.o/s.t, e.g a teacher). ⇒ overrate, underrate. **6** set a rate (4) for (a building).
‚rateable 'value *c.n* (also **‚ratable 'value**) value set on a building on which the rates (4) are based.
‚rate of ex'change *c/def.n* = exchange rate.
'rate‚payer *c.n* person who pays rates (4).
'rating *n* **1** *c/u.n* (also *attrib*) amount fixed as a rate (4): *The job of the rating officer is to decide on rates.* **2** *c.n* rank given to s.t in a scale. Compare rate (5). **3** *c.n* position given to a record¹ (1), television programme etc according to how popular it is. **4** *c.n* (in the British navy) sailor who is not an officer. **credit rating** ⇒ credit (*n*).

rather /'rɑːðə/ *adv* **1** a little; not very; somewhat: *a rather old coat* (or *rather an old coat*); *rather small feet*; *rather (too) slowly*; *rather a lot of mistakes. A zebra is rather like a horse. I rather enjoy cold weather in spite of the discomfort.* **or rather . . .** or it would be truer, more correct, to say . . . : *John's a teacher — or rather, a man who is hoping to become one.* **rather than** + *verb* instead of doing s.t else, because one thinks it better: *I'll help you rather than sit and watch you struggle. Rather than wait for the bus she took a taxi.* **s.o/s.t rather than s.o/s.t else** s.o/s.t instead of s.o/s.t else, because the first is preferable to the other: *We'll get Joan to help us rather than Peter.* **rather than what, where** etc . . . instead of what, where etc . . ., because that is less suitable etc: *I'll look for it in this part of the garden rather than where* *you were looking for it.* **tired** *etc* **rather than ill** *etc* not so much ill etc as tired etc instead. **would rather do s.t** (**than do s.t else**) would prefer to do s.t: *I'd rather stay at home than go out.* **would rather not** prefer not to do what has just been said: *'Would you like to stay to dinner?' 'No, I'd rather not, thank you.'*

▷ *interj* /rɑːˈðɜː/ **2** (becoming *old use*) Yes, (very much): *'Would you like some lemonade?' 'Rather!'*

ratify /ˈrætɪˌfaɪ/ *tr.v* (*-ies, -ied*) (*formal*) confirm(1) (an agreement etc) formally or make it official and legal(1), esp by signing it.
ratification /ˌrætɪfɪˈkeɪʃən/ *u.n.*

rating ⇨ rate.

ratio /ˈreɪʃɪˌəʊ/ *c.n* (*pl -s*) (often (*in the*) — *of s.t to s.t*) relation between two numbers based on how many times one can be divided by the other; proportion(2) (of s.t to s.t): *150 and 100 are in the ratio of 3 to 2* (*150 : 100 = 3 : 2*).

ration /ˈræʃən/ *c.n* **1** amount of s.t, e.g food or clothing, that one person is allowed to have each week, year etc, when supplies are limited.

▷ *tr.v* **2** allow people only a ration(1) of (s.t): *Is bread rationed?* **3** allow (s.o) only a ration(1) of s.t. **ration s.t out** (**to s.o**) share s.t out (to s.o).
rations *pl.n* food given to members of the armed forces. **iron rations** ⇨ iron. **on short rations** receiving less food than usual: *We're on short rations this weekend because we forgot to go shopping.*

rational /ˈræʃənl/ *adj* based on, using, reason rather than feelings. Opposite irrational.
rationalism *u.n* idea that reason should be the basis for our beliefs and behaviour instead of feeling, religious dogmas etc.
rationalist *c.n* (also *attrib*) person who believes in rationalism.
rationality /ˌræʃəˈnælɪtɪ/ *u.n* fact of being rational.
rationalization, -isation /ˌræʃənəlaɪˈzeɪʃən/ *c/u.n* fact or example of rationalizing.
rationalize, -ise *v* **1** *tr/intr.v* find rational reasons or explanations for (s.t that seemed strange). **2** *tr.v* make (s.t) more efficient, usu by cutting out waste, using faster ways of doing things etc.
rationally *adv.*

rat-tat ⇨ rat-a(-tat)-tat.

rattily, rattiness ⇨ ratt.

rattle /ˈrætl/ *c.n* **1** several short sharp hard sounds e.g made by small stones thrown at a window, by an old car as it goes over rough ground etc. **2** kind of baby's toy that gives a rattle(1) when one shakes it. **3** kind of instrument that one swings round and round to make the sound of a rattle(1), e.g at a football match when one wants to encourage one's team.

▷ *v* **4** *tr/intr.v* (cause (s.t) to) make the sound of a rattle(1): *Stop rattling that box of chalks!* **5** *intr.v* (often — *along, by, past* etc) move (along etc) while rattling(4). **6** *tr.v* make (s.o) nervous, anxious or frightened. **rattle away/on** (**about s.o/s.t**) talk quickly and for a long time (about s.o/s.t). **rattle s.t off** say s.t that one has learnt by heart quickly and without difficulty. Compare reel s.t off (⇨ reel¹). **rattle through s.t** do s.t quickly: *rattle through one's work.*
rattled *adj* nervous, anxious or frightened: *He often gets rattled when he's on his own.*

rattlesnake *c.n* (also, *informal*, **rattler**) kind of poisonous snake found in America that rattles(4) its tail as a warning.

ratty ⇨ rat.

raucous /ˈrɔːkəs/ *adj* (of a person, voice, s.o's behaviour) rough and noisy.
raucously *adv.* **raucousness** *u.n.*

ravage /ˈrævɪdʒ/ *tr.v* (*formal*) **1** destroy, ruin or wreck (s.t): *Storms ravaged the farmer's corn.* **2** rob (a place) violently. Compare loot(2), pillage(2).
ravages *pl.n* (often *the* — *of s.o/s.t*) serious damage done (by s.o/s.t): *the ravages of time.*

rave /reɪv/ *attrib.adj* (*informal*) full of praise and admiration: *This film has been getting rave notices from the* critics(1).

▷ *c.n* **2** (*informal*) wild party. **in a rave** (**about s.o/s.t**) (*slang*) feeling, showing etc great admiration (for s.o/s.t).

▷ *intr.v* **3** (often — *about s.o/s.t*) talk or write with great admiration about s.o/s.t. **4** (often — *against/at s.o/s.t*) talk or write very angrily (while attacking s.o/s.t). **5** behave, talk etc as if one is delirious(1) etc.
raver *c.n* (*informal*) person who people rave(3) about, or who leads a very exciting modern social life.
rave-up = rave(2).
raving *attrib.adj/adv* (*informal*) complete(ly); absolute(ly): *raving mad.*
ravings *pl.n* wild behaviour (like that) of a mad person.

ravel /ˈrævl/ *tr/intr.v* (*-ll-*, US *-l-*) **1** (cause (s.t) to) become tangled(2) and knotted. **2** (often — (s.t) *out*) (cause (cloth etc) to) become loose so that the threads are not tied. ⇨ unravel(1).

raven /ˈreɪvn/ *c.n* kind of big shiny black bird like a crow(1).
raven-haired *adj* having shiny black hair.

ravenous /ˈrævənəs/ *adj* very hungry.
ravenously *adv.* **ravenousness** *u.n.*

raver, rave-up ⇨ rave.

ravine /rəˈviːn/ *c.n* kind of deep narrow valley.

raving(s) ⇨ rave.

ravioli /ˌrævɪˈəʊlɪ/ *u.n* (*Italian*) kind of pasta that consists of small squares, usu filled with meat.

ravish /ˈrævɪʃ/ *tr.v* **1** (*literary*) = rape(3). **2** seize or rob (s.t) violently; ravage(2) (s.t). **3** (usu passive) please (s.o) very much; delight (s.o).
ravishing *adj* very beautiful/pleasing.
ravishingly *adv.* **ravishment** *u.n.*

raw /rɔː/ *adj* **1** not cooked: *raw vegetables/fruit.* **2** not yet manufactured or changed by man: *raw cotton.* **3** not yet trained; without experience yet: *a raw* recruit(1). **4** (of weather) unpleasantly cold (and damp). **5** (of a place on s.o's or an animal's body) having had the skin torn or rubbed until the flesh underneath can be seen. **a raw deal** ⇨ deal(n).

▷ *def.n* **6** **in the raw** (**a**) without any clothes on; naked(1). (**b**) without any of the comforts of civilization.
rawly *adv.*
raw material *c/u.n* (often *pl*) raw(2) things from which things are manufactured or made.
rawness *u.n.*

ray¹ /reɪ/ *c.n* **1** line or narrow beam (of light), often one of a number going out from one central point, e.g a lamp: *a ray of light in the darkness;*

the rays of the sun. **2** (*science*) straight line of energy(2): X-rays(1). **3** (*fig*) very small amount (of s.t good in a situation that is otherwise bad): *a ray of hope. The baby is a ray of sunshine in their poor life.*

ray² /reɪ/ *c.n* kind of big flat fish with a long tail, found in the sea.

rayon /'reɪɒn/ *u.n* (also *attrib*) kind of artificial silk: *a rayon blouse*.

raze /reɪz/ *tr.v* (usu — s.t to the ground) (*formal*) knock (s.t) completely flat: *The bomb razed the building to the ground.*

razor /'reɪzə/ *c.n* instrument used for shaving one's face etc: *an electric razor; a safety razor.*
'razor ,blade *c.n* ⇒ blade(1).

RC /,ɑːˈsiː/ *abbr* Roman Catholic.

Rd *written abbr* Road.

RE /,ɑːˈriː/ *abbr* Royal Engineers.

re /riː/ *prep* (*formal*, usu in business letters) regarding; with reference to.

're = 'are', as in 'we're', 'you're'.

reach /riːtʃ/ *n* **1** *u.n* (often *beyond, out of, within, s.o's* —) area that (one) can cover when one puts out one's hand as far as one can: *I always keep a rubber within easy reach when I am writing.* **2** *sing.n* distance one's hand can stretch to: *That nasty boy gets all the best food on the table because he has the longest reach.* **3** *c.n* straight part of a river between two bends. **beyond, out of, within s.o's reach, the reach of s.o/s.t; within (easy) reach (of s.o/s.t) (a)** ⇒ reach(1). **(b)** (*fig*) (im)possible for s.o to have: *I am afraid that a university education is beyond the reach of most children in that country.*

▷ *v* **4** *tr/intr.v* be able, or long etc enough, to touch, or take hold of, (s.o/s.t) (because he/she/it is within reach(1)): *I tried to put my foot on the ladder but I couldn't reach (it). Her dress doesn't quite reach her ankles.* ⇒ overreach. **5** *intr.v* (usu — (across, out etc) for s.t) put one's hand across etc (as far as one can) (to get s.t): *reach across for the salt; reach out your hand for the salt.* **6** *tr.v* arrive at, get to, (s.o/s.t): *When does the train reach Newcastle? When you reach page 30, please tell me. I have reached retirement age. Your letter hasn't reached Jane yet.* **7** *tr.v* be able to make contact(2) with s.o/s.t: *You can always reach me by telephone.* **as far as the eye can reach** ⇒ eye(*n*).

react /rɪˈækt/ *intr.v* **1** (often — *to s.o/s.t* (by doing *s.t*)) do s.t because of s.t done by s.o/s.t else: *Margaret reacts to criticism by becoming angry. Some plants react to being touched by closing their leaves up.* **2** (often — (up)on/with *s.t*) (*chemistry*) cause a change (in s.t etc) or be changed (by s.t). **react against s.o/s.t** react(1) in a way that goes in the opposite direction.

reaction /rɪˈækʃən/ *n* **1** *c.n* (often — *to s.t*) example of reacting(1,2). **2** *u.n* (*technical*) force that balances opposite force: *When you are sitting on a chair, your weight is pushing downwards and the chair is pushing upwards; without the chair's reaction you would fall.* **3** *sing.n* return to an earlier condition. **4** *sing.n* change to a feeling of tiredness, weakness, fear etc, usu after a time of great effort: *After working hard, reaction set in and we sat down to rest.* **5** *u.n* (often *the forces of* —) political ideas and/or feelings that are against change, esp towards liberal(1) or Socialist policies. ⇒ reactionary.

re'actionary *c.n* (also *attrib*) person who believes in, or supports, reaction(5).

re'actor *c.n* **1** = nuclear reactor. **2** thing in which a chemical reaction(1) takes place.

read /riːd/ *c.n* (usu *sing* only) **1** act of reading(2) s.t: *Just give this report a quick read, please.*
▷ *v* (*p.t,p.p* read /red/) **2** *tr/intr.v* (see, look at and) understand (s.t that is written or printed): *Can your little boy read yet? Did you read the news about Peter in the paper yesterday? I read what he had been doing.* ⇒ well-read. **3** *tr.v* (look at and) understand (a language, a map, musical signs, an electricity meter¹(1), a code(3) etc): *I read Russian but I don't speak it. Mary hasn't learnt to read music yet.* **4** *tr.v* (often — s.o *s.t*; — *s.t* (aloud/out) *to s.o*) read (s.t) (aloud etc) in such a way that another person, or other people, can hear it: *The children like to have stories read to them.* **5** *tr/intr.v* (often — *for s.t*) (at university level) study (s.t) (for an examination or a degree). **6** *intr.v* be written (as s.t): *The two copies of the telegram read differently! One reads 'Come tomorrow' and the other 'Don't come tomorrow.'* **7** *tr.v* (of a device that measures s.t) show (s.t): *The thermometer reads 42°.*

read as if . . . give the idea that . . .; make one think that . . .: *Joan's letters always read as if she wasn't really happy in Australia.*

read between the lines ⇒ line¹(*n*).

read s.t for s.t put s.t in the place of s.t when one is reading it: *You must read 'feet' for 'feel'.*

read s.t into s.t think that s.t really means s.t: *You mustn't read your own ideas into what is a perfectly simple letter.*

read s.o's mind ⇒ mind¹.

read s.t over/through read the whole of s.t.

read s.t up; read up on s.t (*informal*) study s.t, esp a subject, carefully.

take s.t as read (/red/) accept s.t without examining it (any more).

,reada'bility *u.n* fact or state of being readable.

'readable *adj* Opposite unreadable. **1** that it is possible to read; legible. **2** that one can enjoy reading because it is interesting and/or not too difficult.

'reader *n* **1** *c.n* person who reads s.t or reads in a certain way: *readers' letters in a newspaper; a slow reader.* **2** *c.n* book used for teaching children to read. **3** *c/unique n* person whose job is to read books to see whether they should be published, or to correct them before they are printed. **4** *c/unique n* teacher at a university who is below a professor in rank but above a senior(1) lecturer.

'reader,ship *c.n* **1** number of people who read s.t, e.g a newspaper. **2** (often *a* — *in s.t*) job as reader(4) (in a subject).

'reading *attrib.adj* **1** that is used when one is reading (⇒ read(1)): *a reading light; a reading room in a library.*
▷ *n* **2** *u.n* act of reading (⇒ read(1)): *The three Rs are reading, writing and arithmetic.* **3** *u.n* knowledge that comes from books, not life. **4** *u.n* things that one reads: *Is this book suitable reading for your girls?* **5** *c.n* meeting of people at which s.t, e.g poetry, is read aloud. **6** case of reading through (s.t): *In the British House of Commons a bill¹(3) has to have three readings before it is voted on.* **7** *c.n* (often — *of s.t*) way in which one person understands and/or

explains (s.t): *Three different lawyers gave three different readings of the law.* **8** *c.n* temperature etc shown by an instrument: *What is the reading on our gas* meter¹(1)?

'**reading** ,**matter** *u.n* books, magazines, newspapers etc: *holiday reading.*

'**read-,only ,memory** *u.n* (*abbr ROM*) memory (device) in a computer that has information stored in it that cannot be changed or added to. Compare random-access memory.

'**read,out** *c.n* **1** written material, pictures etc produced by a computer. **2** action of producing a readout(1).

ready /'redɪ/ *adj* (*-ier*, *-iest*) **1** (*pred*) in a state in which one/it can start whenever needed or wanted: *The doctor had his bag ready in case he was needed. We're ready to help if you need us. The children are ready for the journey.* **2** (*pred*) (often — *to do s.t*) (of a person) willing (to do s.t). Opposite unready. **3** (often — *with s.t*) pleased and eager (to give s.t): *Some people are always ready with criticisms of others.* **4** (of a person's brain or the way he/she uses it) quick: *Liz has a ready* wit(2) *and a ready tongue* (i.e she thinks quickly and talks clearly). **rough and ready** ⇒ rough(4).

▷ *adv* **5** (often as the first part of a word/phrase) already: *You can buy this meat ready cooked. This is a ready-made suit.*

▷ *interj* **6** (word used to warn children that a race is going to start): *Ready, steady, go!* ⇒ mark(*n*).

'**readily** *adv*. '**readiness** *u.n* **hold oneself in readiness** be ready(1), prepared.

,**ready 'cash**/'**money** *u.n* money in the form of bank notes and/or coins, not cheques etc.

'**ready-,made** *adj* **1** very suitable: *a ready-made excuse.* **2** produced or manufactured for a customer to buy and use: *ready-made clothes.* **3** used often (and so having lost its meaning or value): *a ready-made apology.*

,**ready-to-'wear** *adj* (of clothes) that is already made before one buys it. Compare made-to-measure (⇒ measure(*n*)).

reafforest /,ri:ə'fɒrɪst/ = reforest.

real /rɪəl/ *adj* **1** who/that does truly exist. Opposite unreal. **2** who/that is what he/she/ it is supposed to be and not false; true: *He's a real gentleman. This can't be a real diamond!*

▷ *unique n* **3 for real** (*informal*) real; serious(ly); intended seriously: *After all the training, at last the football match was for real.*

'**real e,state** *u.n* (esp US) property such as buildings or land.

'**rea,lism** *u.n* **1** practice of looking at people and things as they really are, not as one would like them to be or imagines them. **2** (in art, literature etc) fact or style of presenting things as they really are. Compare romanticism. **3** belief that things really exist and are not just in our minds. Opposite idealism(3).

'**realist** *c.n* person who follows realism(1,2) in her/his behaviour, art etc.

,**rea'listic** *adj*. Opposite unrealistic. **1** showing realism(1). **2** (of art etc) representing what is seen etc as it really is.

,**rea'listically** *adv*.

reality /rɪ'ælɪtɪ/ *n* (*pl -ies*) **1** *u.n* quality or state of being real(1) or of really existing. **2** *u.n* the real world as it is: *Drugs*(2) *enable one to*

escape from reality into a world of dreams. **3** *c.n* fact; thing that is real: *Kate's dreams of getting that job have become a reality at last.* **in reality** actually; in contrast(1) to what was thought etc: *He said he was a professor but in reality he's only a lecturer.*

realizable, -isable /'rɪə,laɪzəbl/ *adj* that can be realized(2).

realization, -isation /,rɪəlaɪ'zeɪʃən/ *n* **1** *sing.n* (often *a/the* — of s.t, that . . .) fact of realizing(1) s.t. **2** *u.n* (usu *the* — of s.t) fact of (s.t) becoming a reality(3): *the realization of all my dreams.* **3** *u.n* (usu *the* — of s.t) (*formal*) selling (of shares(3) etc).

realize, -ise /'rɪəlaɪz/ *tr.v* **1** understand (s.t); be/become completely conscious of (s.t): *I hadn't realized what a clever girl you were! I realized that I'd misunderstood him.* **2** put (s.t) into effect; carry (s.t) out; turn (s.t) into a reality(3): *John has at last realized his ambition to become a writer.* **3** sell (s.t) and get the money for it. **4** get (money) from the sale of s.t: *'How much did your jewellery realize?' 'I realized £500 on it.'*

'**really** *adv* **1** actually; in fact: *She really did say that.* **2** very (much): *She's a really kind person. I really hate this weather!* **3** (used to show that one is interested in what someone has said, angry at s.t that has been done, said etc): *'I saw Helen at the market.' 'Really?'* (or *'Oh, really?'*). *'Really! I wish you'd be more careful!'* **s.o/s.t ought really to, should really, do s.t** it would be better if s.o/s.t did s.t: *You ought really to speak to your teacher about it, not to me.* **really and truly** actually and honestly: *He really and truly said that.*

realm /relm/ *n* **1** *c.n* (*literary*; *law*) kingdom. **2** *def.n* (often *the* — (s) of s.t) area (in which s.o/ s.t operates, exists etc): *the realms of music.*

reap /ri:p/ *tr/intr.v* **1** cut and collect up (a grain crop). **2** (*fig*) collect, gather up or receive (s.t, usu a reward or punishment for what has been done): *reap one's reward.* **reap the harvest of s.t** ⇒ harvest(*n*).

'**reaper** *c.n* person or machine who/that reaps(1).

rear¹ /rɪə/ *attrib.adj* **1** who/that is at the back: *the rear line of soldiers; the rear window of a car.* ⇒ forward(7).

▷ *def.n* **2** (often *at the* — (of s.t); *in the* —) back: *We have a small garden at the rear of our house. Tall children should stand in the rear.* **3** (*informal*) bottom(3). **bring up the rear** (**of s.t**) be the last in a moving group (of people, vehicles etc).

,**rear 'admiral** *c.n* lowest rank of admiral.

'**rear,guard** *c/def.n* part of an army etc that guards the rear¹(2). Opposite vanguard(1).

,**rear,guard 'action** *c.n* (often — *against s.o/s.t*) **1** (of a rearguard) fight to try to keep back an enemy that is following one. **2** (*fig*) attempt to prevent change, e.g in politics.

'**rear,most** *adj* °who/that is furthest to the rear¹(2).

,**rear-,view 'mirror** *c.n* mirror in a car etc that one looks into to see what is happening behind or at the side of the car etc.

rear² /rɪə/ *v* **1** *tr.v* raise(4), bring up, (a family, animals etc). **2** *tr.v* raise(2), lift up, (s.t, e.g one's head to see s.t). **3** *intr.v* (usu — *up*) (of a horse etc) stand on its two back legs with the front ones in the air.

reason /ˈriːzn/ *n* **1** *c.n* thing that explains s.t; thing that shows (why s.t happens, why s.o wants s.t etc): *I have good reasons for what I do. The reason that/why I am late is that my car broke down. John has a reason to hate Peter because he is responsible for him losing his job. What is your reason for wanting this key?* **2** *u.n* ability to think things out and to reason(4) that makes human beings different from animals: *Use reason!* **3** *u.n* (common) sense; sensible thinking. ⇨ reasoning(1). **beyond/past (all) reason** not (at all) reasonable(1). **by reason of s.t** (*formal*) because of s.t. (**do**, **say** etc **s.t**) **for that/this**, **a** (**good** etc), **reason** (do etc s.t) because one has a particular, a (good, etc), reason for it. **for no reason (at all)** without any reason(1): *She shouted at me for no obvious reason.* **hear**, **listen to**, **see**, **reason** allow oneself to be persuaded to be sensible. **lose one's reason** become mad. **past (all) reason** ⇨ beyond (all) reason. **rhyme or reason** ⇨ rhyme(*n*). **see reason** ⇨ hear etc reason. **stand to reason**; **it stands to reason that** ... all reasonable people will believe s.t. **the voice of reason** ⇨ voice. **with reason** rightly; correctly: *The naughty boy was punished and with reason.* **within reason** (to an extent) that is reasonable.
▷ *v* **4** *intr.v* (often — **with s.o** (**about s.t**)) use reason(2,3) and reasons(1) (to try to persuade s.o about s.t). **reason that** ... say or think that ..., basing what one says or thinks on reason(3): *I reasoned that, if I rang at 9 they would be back home but not yet asleep.* **reason s.t out** find an/ the answer to s.t by using one's reason(3).

ˈreasonable *adj* Opposite unreasonable. **1** who/ that shows reason(3). **2** (of a price, an offer etc) not too high; fair.

ˈreasonableness *u.n*.

ˈreasonably *adv* **1** in a reasonable(1) way. Opposite unreasonably. **2** enough to be accepted: *We live in a reasonably quiet part of the town.*

ˈreasoned *adj* (of an argument etc) based on good reasons(1) (that are given).

ˈreasoning *u.n* **1** use of one's reason(3): *one's powers of reasoning.* **2** reasons(1): *What is the reasoning behind your decision?*

reassure /ˌriːəˈʃʊə/ *tr.v* (often — **s.o about s.t**) stop (s.o) feeling anxious or worried (about s.t). **ˌreasˈsurance** *c/u.n.* **ˌreasˈsuringly** *adv*.

rebate /ˈriːbeɪt/ *c.n* (often — **on s.t**) deduction² from money that one has to pay. Compare discount(1).

rebel /rebl/ *c.n* (also *attrib*) **1** (often — **against** s.o/s.t) person who refuses to obey (s.o/s.t) (and who fights her/him/it).
▷ *intr.v* /rɪˈbel/ (*-ll-*) **2** (often — **against** s.o/s.t) be a rebel(1) (against s.o/s.t).

rebellion /rɪˈbeljən/ *c/u.n*.

reˈbellious *adj* who rebels or would like to rebel; that shows s.o rebels or would like to rebel.

reˈbelliously *adv.* **reˈbelliousness** *u.n*.

rebound /rɪˈbaʊnd/ *intr.v* (often — **from** s.o/s.t) bound²(2) back (after hitting s.o/s.t). **rebound (up)on s.o/s.t** (*formal*) have a bad effect on the person or thing that started s.t: *His refusal to help rebounded on him because no one gave him money when he needed it.*

rebuff /rɪˈbʌf/ *c.n* **1** rude or unkind way of not

accepting s.o's attempt to be polite, helpful etc. **meet with**, **suffer**, **a rebuff** be rebuffed(2).
▷ *tr.v* **2** give (s.o) a rebuff(1).

rebuke /rɪˈbjuːk/ (*formal*) *c.n* **1** scolding, usu a short official one: *receive a rebuke from a teacher.*
▷ *tr.v* **2** (usu — **s.o for s.t**) give (s.o) a rebuke(1) (because of s.t).

recall /rɪˈkɔːl/ *n* **1** *sing/u.n* act of calling back s.o, e.g an ambassador, or s.t, e.g a product (from s.w). **2** *u.n* fact of bringing s.t back to one's memory. **beyond/past recall** (so that it is) impossible to recall(4) any more.
▷ *tr.v* **3** (often — **s.o/s.t from** s.w)) call (s.o/s.t back (from s.w)): *He has been recalled for consultations. The new car is being recalled because there is a fault in it.* **4** remember (s.o/s.t).

recd *written abbr* received.

recede /rɪˈsiːd/ *intr.v* **1** (often — **from** s.o/s.t) go back or (further) away (from s.o/s.t): *When the tide recedes you find all sorts of interesting things on the beach. John's hair is beginning to recede.* **2** slope backwards: *a receding chin/forehead.*

recession /rɪˈseʃən/ *n* **1** *u.n* act or fact of receding(1). **2** *c/u.n* time during which trade is becoming less; slump(1). **in recession** (a) receding(1). (b) suffering from recession(2).

reˈcessive *adj* **1** receding. **2** (*science*) (of a gene) not likely to produce the same features in an offspring unless it is paired with another recessive gene. ⇨ dominant(4).

receive /rɪˈsiːv/ *v* **1** *tr.v* (often — **s.t from** s.o/s.t) get (s.t that is given or that has been sent etc to one) (from s.o etc); accept delivery of (s.t). **2** *tr.v* have (s.t unpleasant) done to one; suffer (s.t): *receive a blow in the stomach; receive punishment.* **3** *tr.v* be the place into which (s.t) is put, flows etc: *This river receives all the dirt that people throw away.* **4** *tr.v* (of a radio or television set) (be able to) pick up ((the waves(2) sent out by) a station): *We receive the World Service quite easily. Hullo, hullo, are you receiving me?* **5** *tr/intr.v* (usu — **s.o into s.t**) (*formal*) allow (s.o) to join a certain church(2). **6** *tr.v* take part in a religious ceremony and get (absolution(1) etc).

receipt /rɪˈsiːt/ *n* **1** *u.n* (often **the** — **of** s.t) fact or act of receiving (s.t). **2** *c.n* (often — **for** s.t) written statement that one has received s.t **3** (*old use*) = recipe. **be in receipt of s.t** (*formal*) be receiving s.t, e.g a pension(1). **make out a receipt** (**for s.t**) write a receipt(2) (for s.t). **on receipt** (**of s.t**) (*formal*) as soon as one receives s.t.
▷ *tr.v* **4** write or print a receipt(2) on/for (s.t).

reˈceipts *pl.n* money received, e.g by a shop. Compare expenditure(2).

reˌceived proˌnunciˈation *u.n* (*abbr RP*) way of pronouncing English that is the one accepted as correct by educated people.

reˈceiver *c.n* **1** thing that receives s.t, e.g the sound on a telephone or radio, or the picture and sound in a television set. **2** criminal who accepts/buys and sells stolen property. **the** (**official**) **receiver** (also with capital **O** and **R**) (*law*) person whose job is to look after the affairs of bankrupts(1). **in the hands of the receiver** being looked after by the Official Receiver.

reˈceiving ˌset *c.n* (*technical*) radio receiver(1).

reception /rɪˈsepʃən/ *n* **1** *c.n* (often — **of** s.o/

s.t) act or fact of receiving(1,4) (s.o/s.t). **2** *c.n* big formal party (for s.o), e.g after a wedding, or to meet s.o important. **3** *c/unique n* place in a hotel, big office etc where people are received(5) when they come in.

re'ception ,desk *c.n* desk at reception(3).

re'ceptionist *c.n* person whose job is to receive(5) people when they arrive at an hotel, a doctor's office etc.

receptive /rɪ'septɪv/ *adj* (often — *to s.t*) willing and able to receive (new ideas). Opposite unreceptive.

re'ceptiveness, receptivity /,resep'tɪvɪtɪ/ *u.n*.

recipient /rɪ'sɪpɪənt/ *c.n* (often — *of s.t*) (*formal*) person who receives (s.t, e.g a pension(1)).

recent /'riːsnt/ *adj* (usu *attrib*) that happened or began, or who came etc, only a short time ago: *a recent visitor to our house; the recent good weather; Joan's recent baby.*

'recently *adv.* **'recentness** *u.n*.

receptacle /rɪ'septəkl/ *c.n* (*formal*) (often — *for s.t*) container (for putting/keeping s.t in).

reception(ist), receptive(ness), receptivity ⇒ receive.

recess /rɪ'ses/ *n* **1** *c.n* place in a wall that is set back from the main surface so that one can have shelves etc in it which do not stick out beyond that surface. Compare alcove, niche(1). **2** *c/u.n* holiday or vacation(1). **3** *c/u.n* time of rest, e.g between lectures during a university day. **4** *c.n* (usu *pl*) (usu *in the —es of s.t*) (*literary*) deepest and most secret part (of a person's mind etc). **in recess** having a recess(2,3): *The committee is in recess.*

recession, recessive ⇒ recede.

recharge /riː'tʃɑːdʒ/ *tr.v* charge(11) (s.t, esp a battery²) again so that it becomes full of electricity.

recipe /'resɪpɪ/ *c.n* statement of what is needed (for making s.t and of how to make it out of these things): *Have you got a recipe for a Christmas cake? The government's new plans are a recipe for disaster(1).*

recipient ⇒ receive.

reciprocal /rɪ'sɪprəkl/ *adj* **1** given, done etc in return for s.t received: *He sent me a present and I sent him a reciprocal one.* **2** reciprocal(1) in both directions: *Francis and I have a reciprocal arrangement to help each other.* ⇒ mutual(3).

re'ciprocally *adv*.

reciprocate /rɪ'sɪprəkeɪt/ *tr/intr.v* (*formal*) give s.t in return for (s.t received): *She sent me a present and I reciprocated by sending her a book.*

reciprocation /rɪ,sɪprə'keɪʃən/ *u.n*.

reciprocity /,resɪ'prɒsɪtɪ/ *u.n* (*formal*) principle(1) or practice of reciprocating, e.g of two countries treating each other in the same ways.

recite /rɪ'saɪt/ *v* **1** *tr/intr.v* repeat (a poem etc) aloud from memory. **2** *tr.v* (*formal*) mention (several things) one after the other.

re'cital *c.n* **1** example of reciting (s.t). **2** performance (of music).

recitation /,resɪ'teɪʃən/ *n* **1** *u.n* act or art of reciting(1). **2** *c.n* thing recited(1).

reckless /'reklɪs/ *adj* (often— *of s.t*) foolishly brave (in spite of s.t); not caring (about s.t): *She jumped into the water to save the child, reckless of the danger.*

'recklessly *adv*. **'recklessness** *u.n*.

reckon /'rekən/ *tr.v* **1** (often — *that . . .*) think, consider, believe (that . . .): *I reckon (that) we'll arrive home at about six.* **2** (*informal*) (often — *so/not*) guess, suppose, imagine, (that s.t is, is not, so): *'Could it perhaps snow?' 'I reckon so/not.'* **3** calculate, count, (an amount): *Interest on this money is reckoned at 1% below bank rate.*

reckon s.o/s.t as, to be, s.t reckon(1,2) that s.o/s.t is s.t: *Helen is reckoned to be the best piano player in our town.*

reckon s.o/s.t among s.t reckon(1) that s.o/s.t is one of s.t: *I reckon Fred among my best friends.*

reckon s.t in (s.t) include s.t (in s.t).

reckon (up)on s.o/s.t base one's plans etc on s.o/s.t; count (up)on s.o/s.t. **reckon (up)on s.o/s.t doing s.t** expect s.o/s.t to do s.t and base one's plans etc on that.

reckon (s.t) up add up (a bill etc) to see what the total is.

reckon with s.o/s.t (a) deal with s.o/s.t; do what is necessary with s.o/s.t. (b) not forget or overlook s.o/s.t because he/she/it is important: *Irena is a woman to be reckoned with.*

reckon without s.o/s.t make the mistake of not considering s.o/s.t when making one's plans etc.

'reckoning *n* **1** *u.n* act or fact of reckoning (⇒ reckon). **2** *c.n* (*old use*) bill¹(1). **by s.o's reckoning** according to what s.o has worked out.

reclaim /rɪ'kleɪm/ *v* **1** *tr/intr.v* (often — *s.t from s.o*) ask (s.o) for (s.t) to be given back to one; get (s.t) back (from s.o): *You can reclaim your bags from us as you leave the* museum. **2** *tr.v* change part of the sea etc into (dry land). **3** *tr.v* (often — *s.t from s.t*) produce (s.t useful) (from s.t useless): *You can reclaim rubber from old tyres.*

reclamation /,reklə'meɪʃən/ *u.n*.

recline /rɪ'klaɪn/ *v* **1** *intr.v* (often — *against/on s.t*) lie (down) (on s.t); lean (back) (against/on s.t). **2** *tr.v* (often — *s.t against/on s.t*) lean (one's head, shoulder etc) (against/on s.o/s.t).

re,clining 'seat *c.n* seat with a back the angle of which can be changed so that one can recline(1) if one wants.

recognize, -ise /'rekəg,naɪz/ *tr.v* **1** know who/ what (s.o/s.t) is because one has seen, heard etc her/him/it before. **2** (often — *s.o/s.t as s.o/s.t*) agree, admit or say that (s.o/s.t) is s.o/s.t: *The people of this part of the country recognize the prince as their chief.* **3** (often — *that, what, why etc . . .; — s.o/s.t to be s.t*) be willing to admit, agree or say (that etc . . .): *I now recognize that I was wrong. Charlie recognized Lucy to be a better singer than him.* **4** (often — *s.t by doing s.t*) show one's appreciation(1) of s.t (by doing s.t): *Our company recognized Ted's loyalty by presenting him with a gold watch.*

recognition /,rekəg'nɪʃən/ *n sing/u.n* (often *in — of s.o/s.t*) act or fact of recognizing (s.o/s.t) or of being recognized. **change beyond, out of, all recognition** change so much that one/it can no longer be recognized (⇒ recognize(1)).

'recog,nizable, -isable *adj*.

'recog,nizably, -isably *adv*.

'recog,nized, -ised *adj* generally accepted: *a recognized expert(2) on 18th century paintings.*

recoil /'riːkɔɪl/ *sing/u.n* **1** sudden movement backwards, often of a gun when it is fired.

▷ *intr.v* /rɪˈkɔɪl/ **2** (of a gun) jump back when it is fired. **3** (often — *from s.t*) move back suddenly (away from s.t), usu because one is afraid or disgusted.

recollect /ˌrekəˈlekt/ *tr.v* (often — *that, what, where* etc . . .; — *doing s.t*) (*formal*) remember (that . . . etc). **as far as s.o recollects, can recollect** to the best of s.o's recollection: *As far as I can recollect, Julie has been with us for ten years.*

recollection /ˌrekəˈlekʃən/ *n* **1** *u.n* fact or act of remembering; ability to remember. **2** *c.n* (often — *of s.o/s.t*) person or thing who/that one remembers. **to the best of s.o's recollection** if s.o remembers correctly.

recommend /ˌrekəˈmend/ *tr.v* **1** (often — *s.o/ s.t to s.o* (*as/for s.t*)) give (s.o) the name of s.o/ s.t) with the suggestion that he/she/it is good, suitable etc (as s.t): *John was recommended to me as a good electrician.* **2** (often — *that . . .; — doing s.t*) advise s.o (to do s.t): *I recommend that you* (*should*) *be more careful in future.* **have s.t, nothing, little** etc **to recommend one/it** have s.t, nothing etc that makes people like one/it: *I am afraid that this shop has nothing to recommend it.*

recommendation /ˌrekəmenˈdeɪʃən/ *n* **1** *u.n* act or fact of recommending s.o/s.t. **2** *c.n* statement recommending(1) s.o/s.t. **3** *c.n* thing that makes people recommend(1) s.o/s.t. **on s.o's recommendation** because s.o has recommended s.o/s.t: *I took Henry on in our office on Jane's recommendation.*

recompense /ˈrekəmˌpens/ *sing/u.n* **1** (often — *for s.t*) (*formal*) money etc that one is given to reward one (for doing s.t) or to make amends (for s.t one has suffered). **in recompense** (**for s.t**) as a recompense(1) (for s.t).

▷ *tr.v* **2** (often — *s.o for s.t*) give (s.o) a recompense(1) (for s.t).

reconcile /ˈrekənˌsaɪl/ *tr.v* **1** make (people) friendly with each other again. **2** (often — *s.t with s.t*) (find out how to) make (s.t) agree (with s.t): *How does Fred reconcile his love of animals with the fact that he eats meat?* **reconcile oneself/ s.o to s.t** cause s.o to accept s.t unpleasant: *You will just have to reconcile yourself to the fact that a better job means being away from home more.* **ˈreconˌcilable** *adj* who/that can be reconciled. Opposite irreconcilable.

ˈreconˌcilement, reconciliation /ˌrekən-ˌsɪlɪˈeɪʃn/ *sing/u.n* (often (a) — *between s.o/s.t and s.o/s.t*).

reconnoitre /ˌrekəˈnɔɪtə/ *tr/intr.v* (US **recon-ˈnoiter**) (usu of a unit of the armed forces) go towards the enemy to find out where (his positions) are, how many men he has etc.

reconnaissance /rɪˈkɒnɪsəns/ *c.n* example of reconnoitring.

reconsider /ˌriːkənˈsɪdə/ *tr/intr.v* think about (s.t) again, sometimes with the result that one changes one's mind about it.

reconsideration /ˌriːkənˌsɪdəˈreɪʃən/ *u.n*.

reconstruct /ˌriːkənˈstrʌkt/ *tr.v* **1** build (s.t) again. **2** (often — *s.t from s.t*) build up a complete picture or description of (s.t, often a crime) (by putting together all the pieces of information one has about it).

reconstruction /ˌriːkənˈstrʌkʃən/ *n* **1** *u.n* act

or fact of reconstructing s.t. **2** *c.n* (often — *of s.t*) result of reconstructing s.t.

record¹ /ˈrekɔːd/ *c.n* **1** (also **ˈgramoˌphone ˌrecord** (becoming *old use*) or **disc**) flat circular piece of plastic(3) with a spiral(2) groove(2) cut into it to store sound that is reproduced on a record player.

▷ *tr/intr.v* /rɪˈkɔːd/ **2** put (s.t, e.g music or a play) on one or more records¹(1) or tapes. **ˈrecord ˌdeck** *c.n* ⇒ deck(4). **reˈcorder¹** *c.n* = tape recorder. **ˈrecord ˌlibrary** *c.n* collection of records¹(1), often that people can borrow. **ˈrecord ˌplayer** *c.n* machine with a turntable, an arm¹(2) and a needle that plays records¹(1). **recording** /rɪˈkɔːdɪŋ/ *c.n* song, piece of music etc that is recorded¹(2). **reˈcording ˌstudio** *c.n* place where recordings are made.

record² /ˈrekɔːd/ *c.n* **1** written report or notes (of s.t), usu to prevent one forgetting. **2** (often **have a good** etc — (*as/for s.t*)) facts known about one/it (as etc s.t): *This kind of plane has a good safety record.* **3** *c.n* thing that gives us information about the past: *Archaeologists provide us with records of ancient civilizations.* **be/go on record as saying s.t** be/become known as having said s.t. **for the record** in order that it should be on record. **a matter of record** thing that is known to be true (because it has been recorded²(4)). **off the record** on condition that it is not reported: *The politician said that off the record so you mustn't mention it in your newspaper.* **on record** (**a**) well known (because it has been recorded). (**b**) that has (ever) been recorded: *Last summer was the sunniest on record here.* **place/put** (**s.t**) **on record** make s.t a matter of record. **put/set s.o straight**; **put/set the record straight** explain s.t to s.o so that he/she can know the correct facts.

▷ *tr.v* **4** make a record²(1) of (s.t); put (s.t) on record. **5** (of an instrument that measures s.t) show (s.t): *An electricity* meter¹(1) *records the amount of electricity used.*

reˌcorded deˈlivery *u.n* way of sending a letter etc through the post which makes it necessary for the person receiving it to sign for it so that one knows that it has reached her/him. Compare register(7), registered letter/mail/post.

reˈcorder² *c.n* title of a judge in some courts.

record³ /ˈrekɔːd/ *attrib.adj* **1** (also **ˈrecord-ˌbreaking**) that breaks the last record³(2).

▷ *c.n* **2** (often in a sport) best yet done (in s.t), e.g the fastest in a kind of race or the highest in a kind of jump. **break/establish/set a record** (**for s.t**) do better than the last record³(2) (in s.t). **equal the record** do as well as the last record³(2).

recorder¹ ⇒ record¹.

recorder² ⇒ record².

recorder³ /rɪˈkɔːdə/ *c.n* a musical instrument like a flute but played by blowing into a hole at the top.

recover /rɪˈkʌvə/ *v* **1** *intr.v* (often — *from s.t*) get well, strong etc again (after s.t): *recover from an illness; recover from a long run.* **2** *tr.v* get (s.t) back after losing etc it: *recover a lost bag; recover one's health.* **recover oneself** return to one's normal state after having left it: *He began to cry but then recovered himself and wiped his eyes.* **recover consciousness** become conscious again. Opposite lose consciousness (⇒ consciousness(*n*)).

re'coverable *adj* that one can recover(2): *Tax on these goods is recoverable when one leaves the country again.* Opposite irrecoverable.

re'covery *c/u.n* (usu no *pl*) (often — *from s.t*; *the* — *of s.t*) fact or act of recovering (s.t), or of being recovered(2). *make a quick etc recovery (from s.t)* recover(1) quickly etc (after having s.t).

re-cover /ˌriː ˈkʌvə/ *tr.v* put a new cover(1) on (s.t, e.g a chair).

recreation /ˌrekrɪˈeɪʃən/ *c/u.n* thing one does in one's free time for pleasure and to relax(1).

recre'ational *adj* of, referring to, providing, recreation.

recre'ation ,ground *c.n* public place for recreation.

recruit /rɪˈkruːt/ *c.n* 1 (often — *to s.t*) new member (of s.t, e.g a team or the armed forces).
▷ *v* 2 *tr/intr.v* (often — *s.o into s.t*) persuade, bring etc (people) to join s.t as recruits(1). 3 *tr.v* produce (a team etc) by finding recruits(1) to it.

re'cruitment *u.n*.

rectangle /ˈrekˌtæŋgl/ *c.n* (*geometry*) shape that has four straight sides, usu ones that are not all the same length, and four right angles. Compare square(9).

rectangular /rekˈtæŋgjʊlə/ *adj* having the shape of a rectangle.

rectify /ˈrektɪˌfaɪ/ *tr.v* (*-ies*, *-ied*) put (s.t, usu a mistake) right.

rector /ˈrektə/ *c.n* 1 (in the Church of England) priest who is in charge of a parish and who is paid directly by it. Compare vicar. 2 (title of the) head (of certain colleges and schools).

'rectory *c.n* (*pl -ies*) house in which a rector(1) lives.

rectum /ˈrektəm/ *c.n* lowest part of the large intestine ending in the anus.

recuperate /rɪˈkuːpəˌreɪt/ *v* 1 *intr.v* (often — *from s.t*) get well again (after having been ill, worried etc). 2 *tr.v* (*formal*) get (one's health etc) back.

recuperation /rɪˌkuːpəˈreɪʃən/ *u.n*.

recur /rɪˈkɜː/ *intr.v* (*-rr-*) 1 happen again; happen two or more times. 2 (of a number or numbers after a decimal point): continue to be repeated to infinity(2): *10 divided by 3 is 3.3 recurring.*

recurrence /rɪˈkʌrəns/ *c/u.n* (usu *a* — *of s.t*) example of happening again, or happening two or more times (of s.t).

recurrent /rɪˈkʌrənt/ *adj* that recurs(1).

re'currently *adv*.

red /red/ *adj* (*-dd-*) 1 having the colour of fresh blood etc. 2 (of some people's hair) between red and brown in colour. 3 (of wine) dark red in colour. Compare rosé (⇒ rose¹), white(5). 4 (often *derog*) Communist(1). 5 (usu with capital **R**) concerning the USSR, China or other Communist(1) countries. *go/turn red (with s.t)* (of the skin of one's face) become red(1) (because of s.t, e.g shame); blush.
▷ *n* 6 *c/u.n* red(1) colour. 7 *c.n* (often *derog*) Communist(2). *in red* having red(1) clothes on: *dressed in red*. *in the red* owing money, usu to a bank. Opposite in the black (⇒ black(*n*)). *get into, out of, the red* begin to be, stop being, in the red. *paint the town red* ⇒ town.

see red (*fig*; *informal*) suddenly become very angry.

,red 'admiral *c.n* kind of butterfly that has red bands on mostly black wings.

,red 'blood ,cell *c.n* (also **,red cor'puscle**) one of the two kinds of blood cell (the other is the white blood cell): *Red blood cells carry oxygen around the body.*

,red 'carpet *def.n* (**,red-'carpet** when *attrib*) (*fig*) way of welcoming a very important visitor: *She received red-carpet treatment when she visited the town. roll out the red carpet (for s.o)* welcome s.o as (if he/she is) very important.

,red cor'puscle *c.n* = red blood cell.

,Red 'Cross *def.n* (also *attrib*) organization that gives medical help, food, blankets etc to people all over the world who need them.

,red'currant *c.n* (also *attrib*) 1 kind of small red berry that hangs in bunches on a bush: *redcurrant jam.* 2 kind of bush on which redcurrants(1) grow.

,red 'deer *c.n* (*pl red deer*) kind of big deer whose colour is between red and brown.

'redden *tr/intr.v* (cause (s.t) to) become red(der)(1).

'reddish *adj* rather red(1,2).

,red 'ensign *c/def.n* British flag most of which is red(1) and which is used by ships that do not belong to the Royal Navy.

,red 'flag *n* 1 *c.n* red(1) flag, usu a sign of danger. 2 *def.n* red(1) flag as a sign of Communism or other left-wing parties. 3 *def.n* song used by Communists(2) and other left-wing parties.

,red-'handed *adj* (often *catch s.o* —) while actually doing s.t wrong.

'red,head *c.n* person who has red(2) hair.

,red 'herring *c.n* ⇒ herring.

,red-'hot *adj* 1 so hot that it is red: *a red-hot piece of iron.* 2 (*fig*) very enthusiastic. 3 (*fig*) very new or recent: *red-hot news.*

,red 'lead *u.n* lead¹(2) oxide which is a poisonous red powder used in paint and to protect seeds from insects, *chem.form* Pb_3O_4.

,red-'letter ,day *c.n* important, happy day that people remember.

,red 'light *c.n* red light used to show danger, on the back of a car at night etc. *see the red light* (*fig*) realize that one is doing s.t dangerous and therefore stop.

,red-'light ,district *c/def.n* part of a town etc where prostitutes are.

'redly *adv*.

,red 'meat *u.n* meat from animals which is bright red in colour, e.g beef¹(1), lamb(2). Compare white meat(2).

'redness *c.n*.

,red 'pepper *n* ⇒ pepper(*n*).

,red 'rag *c.n* (*like*) *a red rag to a bull* ⇒ rag¹.

,red 'tape *u.n* (*fig*) condition of following all the details in doing a job too closely so that there are unnecessary delays.

redeem /rɪˈdiːm/ *tr.v* 1 (often — *s.o from s.t*) get freedom for (s.o) (from s.t, e.g sin(1)). 2 (often — *s.t from s.o*) get (s.t) back (from s.o) by paying s.t: *I pawned(3) my medals on Monday and redeemed them on Friday. redeem a promise* (*formal*) do what one promised.

Re'deemer *def.n* (often *our* —) Jesus Christ.

re,deeming 'feature *c.n* one thing that is

good about s.o/s.t who/that is otherwise bad.

redemption /rɪ'demʃən/ *u.n* fact or act of redeeming (s.t) or being redeemed. **beyond/ past redemption** too bad to be able to be redeemed(1).

rediffusion /,ri:dɪ'fju:ʒən/ *u.n* (*technical*) passing on of radio and/or television broadcasts to a number of other places.

reduce /rɪ'dju:s/ *v* **1** *tr.v* (often — *s.t* (*from s.t*) *to s.t*) make (s.t) less (expensive etc) by bringing it down (from s.t) (to s.t): *This suit is reduced from £110 to only £55.* **2** *tr/intr.v* try to lose (weight): *I'm trying to reduce (my weight) by two kilos. Joan has lost two kilos on her reducing* diet(1). **reduce s.t to s.t (a)** ⇒ reduce(1). **(b)** change s.t into s.t smaller: *The fire soon reduced the secret papers to ashes.* **(c)** divide s.t into the parts that make it up: *You can reduce all the argument to two simple facts: one side wants the new road and the other doesn't.* **reduce s.o/s.t to (doing) s.t** change s.o/s.t into, make s.o do, s.t less free, important, happy etc: *reduce s.o to begging in the streets; reduce s.o to silence* (make her/him stop talking); *reduce s.o to tears* (make her/him cry).

re,duced 'circumstances *pl.n* (usu *in* —) a state of poverty compared with what one had before.

reduction /rɪ'dʌkʃən/ *n* **1** *c/u.n* (often — (*from s.t*) *to s.t*) fact or act of reducing (s.t), or of s.t being reduced, (from s.t) (to s.t): *He has offered us a price reduction of 10%.* Opposite increase(1). **2** *c.n* smaller copy (of a photograph etc). Opposite enlargement(2).

redundant /rɪ'dʌndənt/ *adj* (usu *pred*) not needed (any more): *Our factory is making 100 workers redundant next month. In 'a young baby', 'young' is redundant because all babies are young.*

re'dundancy *c/u.n* (*pl* -*ies*) (example of the) fact of being redundant.

re'dundancy ,pay *u.n* money given to a worker as compensation for being made redundant.

reed /ri:d/ *n* **1** *c.n* tall strong straight hollow stem of some kinds of plants, often ones that grow near water. **2** *u.n* number of reeds(1) growing together. **3** *c.n* device that one puts in some musical instruments and that produces musical notes by vibrating when air is blown over it.

'reed ,instrument *c.n* musical instrument with a reed(3) in it.

'reediness *u.n* fact or state of being reedy(2).

'reedy *adj* (-*ier*, -*iest*) **1** having reeds(1) in it. **2** (of a sound) high and thin.

reef /ri:f/ *c.n* **1** dangerous shallow place in the sea where rocks, sand etc are just below, or just above, the surface. **2** layer(1) of a particular rock, ore etc when one is mining: *a gold reef.*

reefer /'ri:fə/ *c.n* (*informal*) cigarette with marijuana in it.

reek /ri:k/ *c.n* **1** strong unpleasant smell; stink(1).

▷ *intr.v* **2** give out smoke, usu with an unpleasant smell. **reek of s.t (a)** have an unpleasant smell of s.t: *His clothes always reek of tobacco.* **(b)** = reek with s.t have an unpleasant air of s.t about it: *His behaviour reeks with dishonesty.*

reel¹ /ri:l/ *c.n* (often — *of s.t*) **1** round thing that

s.t, e.g cotton or a film, can be wound round to keep it tidy: *a reel of film; a cotton reel.* **2** amount (of s.t) that a reel(1) can hold: *I used two reels of silk to make that dress.*

▷ *tr/intr.v* **3** (usu — (*s.t*) *in, out, up* etc) make (s.t) come in, go out etc by turning the reel(1) it is on: *The fishermen were reeling in a large fish.* **reel s.t off** (*fig*) say s.t quickly and easily; rattle s.t off.

reel² /ri:l/ *intr.v* **1** stand, walk etc unsteadily, e.g because one is drunk or fainting. **2** (often *make s.o's head* —) (of a person's brain or s.o/s.t one is looking at) seem to go round and round: *The speed with which she talks makes my head reel. Suddenly the whole scene reeled before my eyes and I fell down.* **reel back (from s.o/s.t)** bend or step back unsteadily (because of s.t, e.g a blow or an unpleasant sight or smell).

reel³ /ri:l/ *c.n* kind of lively(1) Scottish or Irish dance.

ref¹ /ref/ *c.n* (*informal*) referee(2).

ref² *written abbr* reference; (*informal*) in/with reference to.

refectory /rɪ'fektərɪ/ *c.n* (*pl* -*ies*) dining hall (in a college, monastery etc).

refer /rɪ'fɜ:/ *tr/intr.v* (-*rr*-) **refer to s.o/s.t (a)** mention, speak about, s.o/s.t: *Who were you referring to when you said you had a good friend here? It is rude to refer to your wife as the old lady.* **(b)** try to get information from s.o/s.t: *If you want the answer to that question, refer to Mary* (or *refer to your French dictionary*). **(c)** concern, deal with, s.o/s.t: *The rule about not walking on the grass also refers to teachers.* **refer s.o/s.t (back) to s.o/s.t** ask s.o to refer to s.o/s.t(b): *It's no good complaining to him because he will only refer you back to the manager.*

referee /,refə'ri:/ *c.n* **1** person who one can refer(b) to for s.t, e.g information about a person who is applying for a job. ⇒ reference(4). **2** (*informal ref*) person who blows the whistle during a game of football etc and who decides whether the players are behaving properly etc. Compare umpire(1). **3** person to whom both sides in an argument refer(b) and who decides which of them is right.

▷ *tr/intr.v* **4** act as a referee(2) ⇒ umpire(2).

reference /'refərəns/ *n* **1** *c/u.n* (often — *to s.o/ s.t*) mention, or (example of) speaking (about s.o/s.t). **2** *c/u.n* (often — *to s.o/s.t*) act or fact of referring to(b) s.o/s.t: *Reference to a medical book will soon solve that problem.* **3** *c.n* piece of information, usu in writing, about a person who is applying for a job. **4** *c.n* person who gives a reference(3). for (easy) reference** ready to be referred(b) to (easily). **frame of reference** ⇒ frame(*n*). **in/with reference to s.o/s.t** referring(a) to s.o/s.t; about/regarding s.o/s.t. **without reference to s.o/s.t** having nothing to do with s.o/s.t.

'reference ,book/,library/,work *c.n* book etc where one can find useful information, e.g a dictionary.

referendum /,refə'rendəm/ *c.n* (*pl* -*s* or, less usu, *referenda* /,refə'rendə/) (often *hold a* — on s.t, *to decide s.t*) vote (about s.t) by all the voters individually and not through their elected representatives (to decide s.t). **by referendum** in this way: *decide by referendum.*

refine /rɪ'faɪn/ *tr.v* make (s.t) pure(r). **refine**

(**up**)**on** *s.t* (*formal*) improve s.t, make s.t better.

re'fined *adj* **1** made pure(r). **2** (of a person, her/his behaviour etc) well mannered; showing good education, training etc. Compare genteel.

re'finement *n* **1** *u.n* (often *the — of s.t*) act of refining s.t. **2** *u.n* fact or quality of being refined(2). **3** *c.n* (usu — (*up*)*on s.t*) thing that refines (up)on s.t.

re'finery *c.n* (*pl -ies*) place where refining is done: *a sugar refinery.*

reflate /ri:'fleɪt/ *tr/intr.v* increase the supply of money in (the economy(3) of a country etc). Compare deflate(4), inflate(2).

reflation /ri:'fleɪʃən/ *u.n.*

reflect /rɪ'flekt/ *v* **1** *tr.v* throw/bounce(3) (s.t, e.g a picture, light, sound or heat) back. Compare echo(2), mirror(3). **2** *tr.v* show (s.t); give a correct idea of (s.t): *His actions do not always reflect his words. Does this letter reflect what Graham really thinks?* **3** *intr.v* think carefully. **reflect that . . .** think or say that . . . after careful thought. **reflect** (**up**)**on** *s.o/s.t* (**a**) think carefully about s.o/s.t. (**b**) cause people to think badly of s.o/s.t: *What you have said about Joe reflects on his honesty.* **reflect s.t on s.o/s.t** cause people to give s.t good or bad, usu credit(6) or discredit(1), to s.o/s.t as their opinion about her/him/it.

reflection /rɪ'flekʃən/ *n* **1** *u.n* act or fact of reflecting(1) or being reflected(1). **2** *c.n* thing that one sees because it is reflected(1), e.g in a mirror or clear water. **3** *c/u.n* (often — *on s.o/s.t*) careful thought (about s.o/s.t). **be/cast a reflection**, **cast reflections**, (**up**)**on s.o/s.t** reflect (up)on s.o/s.t(b). **on reflection** after thinking carefully (about it): *I didn't want to go but on reflection I decided that I ought to.*

re'flective *adj* (*formal*) thoughtful.

re'flector *c.n* thing that reflects(1).

reflex¹ /'ri:fleks/ *attrib.adj* **1** (of a movement, e.g that of closing one's eyes without wanting to when s.t comes close to them) not controlled or even conscious; instinctive: *a reflex action.*
▷ *c.n* **2** reflex(1) action: *The doctor tested Molly's reflex(es) by tapping her knees.* ⇒ reflexes. **a conditioned reflex** a reflex(2) that is the result of training, not instinct: *You can train a dog to go to the kitchen whenever it hears a bell by always ringing one before giving it food, and so develop a conditioned reflex in it.*

,reflex 'camera *c.n* camera that has a mirror that throws a picture of what the camera is pointing at onto a small glass screen in the camera so that one can see exactly what one is going to photograph.

'reflexes *pl.n* actions that are done in reply to outside stimuli (⇒ stimulus(n)): *When two cars are about to crash the driver with the fastest reflexes is likely to get out of the way.*

reflex² *written abbr* reflexive(1).

reflexive /rɪ'fleksɪv/ *adj* (*written abbr* reflex as used in this dictionary) **1** (*grammar*) that shows that the subject of the verb has the action done to it: *In 'I always help myself to food', 'myself' is a reflexive pronoun.*
▷ *c.n* **2** (*grammar*) word that is reflexive(1).

reforest /ri:'fɒrɪst/ *tr.v* (also **,reaf'forest**) to plant a forest in (an area) which had a forest before.

reform /rɪ'fɔːm/ *c/u.n* **1** (also *attrib*) change, usu a political or social one, which is intended to improve things: *reform movements.*
▷ *v* **2** *tr/intr.v* (cause (s.o/s.t) to) improve. **3** *tr.v* make reforms(1) in (s.t, e.g a country or a system of doing things).

reformation /,refə'meɪʃən/ *n* **1** *c/u.n* act or fact of reforming(1) (s.o/s.t) or state of being reformed. **2** *def.n* (with capital **R**) 16th century reform(1) movement leading to the setting up of the Reformed and Protestant(1) churches.

reformatory /rɪ'fɔːmətrɪ/ *c.n* (*pl -ies*) (*old use* or *US*) = approved school.

Re,formed 'Church *c/def.n* church that was originally set up to try to reform the Roman Catholic Church but then became independent(1) of it.

re'former *c.n* person who reforms(1), or tries to reform, s.t.

refrain¹ /rɪ'freɪn/ *c.n* words in a song etc that are repeated at the end of each verse.

refrain² /rɪ'freɪn/ *intr.v* (usu — *from* (*doing*) *s.t*) (*formal*) not do (s.t, usu s.t one would like to do); prevent oneself (doing s.t): *Please refrain from talking while the lecture is going on.*

refresh /rɪ'freʃ/ *tr.v* stop (s.o) feeling tired any more; make (s.o) feel fresh again. **refresh one's/s.o's memory (of s.o/s.t)** ⇒ memory.

re'fresher ,course *c.n* course that aims to remind professional people of ways of doing things that they may have forgotten, to teach them new ones that have appeared since they were first trained etc.

re'freshing *adj* **1** that refreshes. **2** interesting and pleasing, usu because it is s.t new to one: *the refreshing simplicity of a country girl.*

re'freshment *u.n* **1** fact of refreshing (⇒ refresh) or being refreshed. **2** (esp *take* —) food and/or drink.

re'freshment ,room *c.n* café or restaurant, usu at a bus or railway station etc.

re'freshments *pl.n* food and drink, but usu not a full meal.

refrigerate /rɪ'frɪdʒə,reɪt/ *tr.v* make (s.t) (very) cold; freeze (s.t).

re'frigerant *c/u.n* substance that refrigerates.

refrigeration /rɪ,frɪdʒə'reɪʃən/ *u.n* act or fact of making/keeping things cold so that they do not go bad. **under refrigeration** being refrigerated.

re'frige,rator *c.n* (*informal* fridge) place in which refrigerated food etc is kept.

refuel /ri:'fjuːəl/ *tr/intr.v* to put fuel into (a vehicle); (of a vehicle) have fuel put in.

refuge /'refjuːdʒ/ *c/u.n* (often *find/seek — from s.o/s.t*) (a place that gives one) safety or protection (from s.o/s.t dangerous). **take refuge (from s.o/s.t) (in s.t)** find a safe place (against s.o/s.t) (s.w).

refugee /,refjʊ'dʒiː/ *c.n* (often — *from s.o/s.t*) person who finds or seeks(1) refuge (from s.o/s.t, esp in a time of war, fighting etc).

refund /'ri:fʌnd/ *c/u.n* **1** paying back (of s.t, esp money) (to s.o).
▷ *tr.v* /ri:'fʌnd/ **2** pay (s.t) back (to s.o).

refuse¹ /'refjuːs/ *u.n* things that have been thrown away because they are no longer useful; rubbish.

'refuse ,bin *c.n* container in which refuse¹ is thrown.

'refuse col,lector *c.n* (also **'dustman**) person who is paid, usu by the local government, to take refuse¹ away from people's houses etc.

'refuse ,dump *c.n* place to which large pieces of refuse¹ are taken.

refuse² /rɪ'fjuːz/ *tr/intr.v* not accept (s.o/s.t); say that one does not agree (to do, have etc s.t, to give s.o s.t): *He refused my offer to help. I refuse to answer that question. Joe asked Mary to marry him but she refused (him).*

re'fusal *c.n* act or fact of refusing² (s.t, e.g help). **(give s.o, have) (the) first refusal (on s.t)** (give s.o, have the) right to make an offer to buy s.t before other people are allowed to make offers.

refute /rɪ'fjuːt/ *tr.v* prove (s.t) is not correct: *refute a statement,* theory(1) etc.

refutable /'refjʊtəbl/ *adj* able to be refuted. Opposite irrefutable.

refutation /,refjʊ'teɪʃən/ *c/u.n.*

regain /rɪ'geɪn/ *tr.v* **1** get back (s.t one had lost): *regain one's health; regain one's position in society.* **2** reach (a place) again, sometimes with difficulty, after having gone away from it: *I had to swim very hard to regain the boat after falling into the water.* **regain one's balance/footing** ⇒ balance(*n*), footing. **regain consciousness** ⇒ consciousness. **regain possession (of s.t)** ⇒ possession.

regal /'riːgl/ *adj* of, like, suitable for, a king or queen; very splendid.

'regally *adv.*

regard /rɪ'gɑːd/ *u.n* **1** respect (for s.o/s.t). **2** (often have — for/to s.o/s.t) consideration, thought, care (for s.o/s.t): *That boy has no regard for his little sister's safety and encourages her to climb trees with him.* **hold s.o/s.t in high/ low regard** consider s.o/s.t to be a good/bad person, example etc. **in that/this regard** (*formal*) on the subject of that/this. **in/with regard to s.o/s.t** on the subject of s.o/s.t.

▷ *tr.v* **3** (*formal*) (often — s.o/s.t with s.t) look at, think of, (s.o/s.t) (in a certain way): *The child regarded the dog suspiciously* (or *with suspicion*). **4** (*formal*) listen carefully to (s.o/ s.t). **as regards s.o/s.t** on the subject of (⇒ subject¹) s.o/s.t. **regard s.o/s.t as s.t** think that s.o/s.t is s.t: *I have always regarded Miriam as a friend.*

re'garding *prep* about (s.o/s.t); on the subject of (s.o/s.t): *What do you know regarding yesterday's robbery?*

re'gardless *adv* (*informal*) without any regard(1) for anything: *He doesn't want me to go but I shall go regardless.* **regardless of s.o/s.t** without having any regard(1) for s.o/s.t.

re'gards *pl.n* (often give/send s.o one's —) good wishes or greetings. **with kind regards** (way of ending a letter instead of 'with good wishes' etc, before adding 'Yours sincerely, faithfully' etc).

regatta /rɪ'gætə/ *c.n* sports meeting for rowing or sailing races.

regent /'riːdʒənt/ *adj* **1** (with capital **R**; placed after the noun) who is a regent: *the Prince Regent.*

▷ *c.n* **2** person who is the ruler of a place instead of the real ruler when he/she is ill, mad etc.

'regency *n* (*pl* -ies) **1** *c/u.n* (often the — of s.o) time when s.o is a regent(1). **2** *def.n* (also *attrib*) (with capital **R**) time from 1811–1820 in Britain

when the Prince Regent was the ruler: *Regency furniture.*

regime /reɪ'ʒiːm/ *c.n* (*French*) **1** rule; government: *live under a cruel regime.* **2** course of exercise, diet(1) etc that is for the good of one's health: *follow a strict regime* prescribed(1) *by one's doctor.*

regiment /'redʒɪmənt/ *c.n* **1** (often with capital **R**) army unit of about 500 men commanded by a Lieutenant-Colonel: *the 6th Royal Tank Regiment.* **2** army unit consisting of several battalions or regiments(1).

regimental /,redʒɪ'mentl/ *adj* of or referring to a regiment: *regimental music.*

,Regi,mental ,Sergeant 'Major *c.n* (*abbr* **RSM**) warrant officer of the highest rank in a regiment(1).

Regina /rɪ'dʒaɪnə/ *unique n* (*abbr* **R**) **1** (title put after the name of the Queen when she is the ruler): *Elizabeth Regina; ER.* Compare Rex(1). **2** (used in lawsuits when the Queen is the ruler) the State(3); the Crown(2): *Regina v Smith* (i.e the plaintiff is the State, and the defendant is s.o called Smith). Compare Rex(2).

region /'riːdʒən/ *c.n* big part of a country or of the world: *the frozen regions of the North.* **in the region of s.t** about s.t: *There are in the region of 1000 families in that town.*

'regional *adj* of or referring to one or more regions: *regional differences between the west and the east.*

'regionally *adv.*

register /'redʒɪstə/ *n* **1** *c.n* list or book in which information that one wants to keep is entered: *a church's marriage register; a class attendance register.* Compare roll(4). **2** *c/u.n* (*music*) spread of pitch¹(4) covered by a voice or by a musical instrument: *the upper register.* **3** *c.n* instrument or machine for registering(8) amount, speed etc: *a cash register.* **4** *c/u.n* (*technical*) kind of language used in a particular situation: *In this dictionary we have a formal, an informal and a slang register.*

▷ *v* **5** *tr.v* enter (s.o/s.t) in a register(1). **6** *intr.v* put one's own name in a register(1), or have this done for one: *The first thing I did when I got to the hotel was to register at the desk. Are you registered with a local doctor?* **7** *tr.v* send (a letter etc) by registered post. **8** *tr.v* (of a measuring device) show (s.t): *The thermometer registers 41° so you have a fever.*

,registered 'letter/'mail etc *c.n* letter, mail etc sent by registered post.

,registered 'nurse *c.n* (*US*) person who is officially registered and allowed to work as a trained nurse. Compare state registered nurse.

,registered 'post *u.n* (often *by* —) way of sending a letter etc for which one pays extra, but in which the post office has to pay one if the letter etc is lost. Compare recorded delivery.

'register office *c.n* = registry office.

registrar /'redʒɪ,strɑː/ *c.n* person whose job is to keep a register(1) or registers, e.g in a register office or university.

registration /,redʒɪ'streɪʃən/ *n* **1** *u.n* act or fact of registering(5–7) or being registered. **2** *c.n* thing that has been registered(5,6).

,regi'stration ,book *c.n* (also **'log ,book**) book in which things are registered(5,6): *Every car has* *to have a registration book giving information about it.*

regi'stration number *c.n* official numbers and/or letters that a car has at the front and back.

'registry *c.n* (*pl -ies*) place where registers(1) are kept.

'registry office *c.n* office where one can be married according to the law, and where one registers(5) births, marriages and deaths.

regress /rɪˈgres/ *intr.v* return to an earlier condition, especially to childish behaviour when an adult.

regression /rɪˈgreʃən/ *u.n*.

regret /rɪˈgret/ *u.n* 1 (often — *at s.t*) feeling of sorrow (because s.t has happened that one would have liked (not) to have happened). (**greatly/much**) **to s.o's regret** that is s.t that s.o regrets(2) (very much): *Much to my regret, I can't come this evening.* **with** (**much** etc) **regret** I am (very) sorry to say.

▷ *tr.v* (*-tt-*) 2 (often — *that . . .*; — *doing s.t*) feel regret(1) at (s.t), because of (having done) s.t, or that . . .): *I regret (that) I can't help. Bill now regrets not having visited the old lady while she was still alive.* 3 feel sorrow at having lost s.t: *The fire destroyed everything but the only things I really regret are my books.* **regret to inform/tell s.o that . . .** (*formal*) be sorry because one has to tell s.o that . . .

re'gretful *adj* feeling, showing or causing regret(1).

re'gretfully *adv* 1 in a regretful way. 2 I am sorry to say that . . .: *Regretfully, my wife can't come tomorrow.*

re'gretfulness *u.n*.

re'grets *pl.n* polite words of regret(1). **have no regrets** not feel sorry about s.t that has happened.

re'grettable *adj* that is, or should be, regretted(2).

re'grettably *adv* 1 in a regrettable way. 2 I am sorry to say that . . .: *Regrettably, my wife can't come tomorrow.*

regular /ˈregjʊlə/ *adj* Opposite irregular for 1–3, 8. 1 happening or being at intervals(3) of time or place that follow a pattern, usu a good one, and/or one in which the intervals are (almost) the same each time: *the regular beat of a person's heart.* 2 (usu *attrib*) that does not change: *a regular habit; walking at a regular speed.* 3 that is pleasant and/or normal in shape: *regular teeth.* 4 (usu *attrib*) real; proper: *There are people in that country who give medical treatment although they are not regular doctors.* 5 (*attrib*) professional; full-time: *a regular soldier.* Compare reserve(4), territorial(2). 6 (*attrib*) (*informal*) absolute; complete: *That little boy is a regular nuisance!* 7 (*attrib*) normal; usual: *You can buy this toothpaste in the regular or the extra large family size.* 8 (*grammar*) behaving in the same way as a lot of other ones: *'Can' is a regular noun because its plural is 'cans', but 'man' is irregular(4) because its plural is 'men'.*

▷ *c.n* 9 regular(5) soldier. 10 (*informal*) regular(1) customer, visitor etc: *the regulars of the local pub.*

regularity /ˌregjʊˈlærɪtɪ/ *u.n* fact of (s.t) being regular(1,3).

regularization,-isation /ˌregjʊləraɪˈzeɪʃən/ *u.n*.

'regula,rize, -ise *tr.v* make (s.t, e.g the fact that a man and a woman have been living together without being married) lawful and official after it has not been so.

'regularly *adv* in a regular(1–3, 8) way. Opposite irregularly. (**as**) **regularly as clockwork** ⇒ clockwork.

regulate /ˈregjʊˌleɪt/ *tr.v* make (s.t) regular(1,2); control (s.t, e.g an engine or a clock) so that it behaves regularly.

regulation /ˌregjʊˈleɪʃən/ *n* 1 *c.n* official rule: *If you don't follow regulations you will have to leave.* 2 *u.n* (often *the* — *of s.t*) act or fact of regulating s.t. **rules and regulations** ⇒ rule(*n*).

'regu,lator *c.n* thing that regulates s.t, e.g a device on a motor that prevents it going at more than a certain speed.

rehearse /rɪˈhɜːs/ *v* 1 *tr/intr.v* practise (s.t, e.g a play or a speech) with the purpose of making it as good as possible before one does it in public. 2 *tr.v* make (s.o) rehearse(1) in detail.

re'hearsal *c/u.n* act or fact of rehearsing s.t. **dress rehearsal** ⇒ dress. **in rehearsal** being rehearsed(1).

reheel /riːˈhiːl/ *tr.v* to put a new heel(3) on a shoe etc.

rehouse /riːˈhaʊz/ *tr.v* put (s.o) in a new, another, house or flat, usu because of damage to their own one or because its condition is bad.

reign /reɪn/ *c.n* 1 time during which s.o reigns(2). **in the reign of s.o** during s.o's reign(1).

▷ *intr.v* 2 (often — *over s.o/s.t*) be the ruling king/queen/emperor/empress (of s.o/s.t). 3 exist: *The children had all gone and silence reigned in the school until the next day.*

reign of 'terror *c.n* time during which there is a lot of cruelty, killing etc in a place, esp by the government.

reimburse /ˌriːɪmˈbɜːs/ *tr.v* (*formal*) 1 pay (s.t) back (to s.o): *You will have to pay for your ticket but the cost will be reimbursed to you.* 2 pay (s.t) back to (s.o): *I'll reimburse you later.*

reim'bursement *c/u.n*.

rein /reɪn/ *c.n* (sometimes *pl* with *sing* meaning) long strip, usu made of leather, used to control a horse, or sometimes a small child. **assume/take the reins** (**of s.t**) (*fig*) take control (of s.o/s.t). **draw rein** go more slowly. **drop the reins** (**of s.t**) stop controlling s.t. **give** (**free**) **rein to s.t** (*fig*) allow s.t to behave/happen freely. **hold the reins** (**of s.t**) (*fig*) have control (of s.t). **keep a tight rein on s.o/s.t** (*fig*) prevent s.o/s.t doing what he/she/it wants.

reincarnation /ˌriːɪnkɑːˈneɪʃən/ *n* 1 *c/u.n* the fact of s.o being born again after death (in the form of s.t, e.g an animal). 2 *c.n* form in which one is born again in this way. 3 *c.n* case of reincarnation(1): *He believes that in his last reincarnation he was a woman.*

reindeer /ˈreɪndɪə/ *c.n* (*pl reindeer*) kind of deer that lives in the far north of Europe.

reinforce /ˌriːɪnˈfɔːs/ *tr.v* 1 (often — *s.t with s.t*) make (s.t) strong(er) (by using s.t): *This wall may break so we had better reinforce it with iron strips.* 2 make (an army, the police etc) stronger (by adding more men, ships etc); make (a place) stronger by bringing in more soldiers, guns etc. 3 make (an argument, an order etc) stronger (by adding s.t, e.g a threat).

,rein,forced 'concrete *u.n* concrete(4) with iron bars in it.

,rein'forcement *u.n* act of reinforcing(1,3).

,rein'forcements *pl.n* men/women, ships etc brought in to reinforce(2) s.t.

reinstate /,ri:in'steit/ *tr.v* (often — s.o as/in s.t) put (s.o) back in a position he/she had before (as s.t etc).

,rein'statement *c/u.n*.

reject /'ri:dʒekt/ *c.n* **1** person or thing who/that is rejected(3).

▷ *tr.v* /rı'dʒekt/ **2** (often — s.o/s.t for s.t) refuse to accept (s.o/s.t) (for s.t, e.g a job). **3** (often — s.t from s.t) throw (s.t) away (out of s.t) because it is not good enough etc.

rejection /rı'dʒekʃən/ *u.n*.

rejoice /rı'dʒɔıs/ *intr.v* (often — at/over s.t; — to do s.t) (*formal*; *literary*) feel/show great happiness (because of s.t). **rejoice in s.t** have s.t that seems silly: *Joan's new boyfriend rejoices in the name of Ivor Goodname.*

re'joicing *c/u.n*: *There was great rejoicing at the news of the victory.*

relaid /ri:'leid/ *p.t,p.p* of relay².

relapse /rı'læps/ *c.n* **1** act or fact of returning to an earlier and worse state, e.g of health.

▷ *intr.v* **2** (often — into s.t) have a relapse(1) (into s.t).

relate /rı'leit/ *tr.v* (*formal*) **1** (often — s.t to s.o) tell (s.t, e.g a story) (to s.o). **2** (often — s.t to/with s.t) see, show, the relation(2) between (s.t and s.t): *I can't relate what you say happened to/with what I saw.* **relate to s.o/s.t** (a) have a (good) relationship with s.o/s.t: *Success in this job depends entirely on how you relate to people.* (b) refer to s.o/s.t. **strange to relate** ⇒ strange.

re'lated *adj* **1** (often — to s.o (by s.t)) being a relation(1) (of s.o) by blood(2) or marriage, or by having been adopted(1). **2** (often — to s.t) connected (with s.t): *Blood pressure and health are related problems.*

re'latedness *u.n*.

relation /rı'leıʃən/ *n* **1** *c.n* (often — of s.o('s)) person who is a member of (one's) family, either by blood(2) or by marriage etc. **2** *c/u.n* (often — between s.t and s.t) way or ways in which (s.t and s.t) are connected. **3** *c/u.n* (often — of s.t) act of telling (s.t, e.g a story). **bear little, no, some** etc **relation (to s.t)** have only a small, no, some etc connection (with the way in which s.t varies): *The amount of money you spend in this shop bears little relation to how the staff treat you.* **blood relation** ⇒ blood(*n*). **in/with relation to s.o/s.t** with reference/regard to s.o/s.t; about s.o/s.t.

re'lations *pl.n* (often — between s.o/s.t and s.o/ s.t; — with s.o/s.t) **1** ways in which people, countries etc behave towards, talk or think about etc each other. **2** connections; things that people do with each other: *business relations between the two companies.* **establish/have friendly relations (with s.o)** (begin to) be friendly (with s.o). **have (sexual) relations (with s.o)** (*formal*) have sex (with s.o). **public relations** ⇒ public.

re'lation,ship *c/u.n* (often — between s.o/s.t and s.o/s.t; — of s.o/s.t to s.o/s.t) fact of (s.o/s.t and s.o/s.t) being related.

relative /'relətıv/ *adj* **1** (often — to s.o/s.t) when

compared (with s.o/s.t): *What are the relative advantages of living here and in town?* Opposite absolute(2). **relative to s.o/s.t** (*formal*) connected with s.o/s.t; about s.o/s.t: *I want everything you know relative to the accident.*

▷ *c.n* **2** relation(1).

,relative 'adverb *c.n* (*grammar*) adverb that joins a subordinate clause to another clause: *In 'the house where I was born', 'where' is a relative adverb.*

,relative 'clause *c.n* (*grammar*) kind of subordinate clause that limits a noun or pronoun in another clause: *In 'the man (who/that) I saw yesterday', '(who/that) I saw yesterday' is a relative clause.*

'relatively *adv* compared with another or others: *It's relatively cold this month.* **relatively speaking** when one looks at it relatively.

,relative 'pronoun *c.n* (*grammar*) pronoun used to join a relative clause to another clause: *In 'the man who/that I saw yesterday', 'who/that' is a relative pronoun.*

,rela'tivity *u.n* (often the — of s.t) fact of (s.t) being relative(1). **Einstein's theory of relativity** belief that we can only measure relative(1) motion, that the speed of light is always the same and that the mass of a body varies with its speed.

relax /rı'læks/ *v* **1** *tr/intr.v* (cause (s.o/s.t) to) become less tight, tense¹(2), stiff, worried, excited etc. **2** *tr.v* (often — one's efforts (to do s.t)) make (s.t) less strong; weaken (s.t).

relaxation /,ri:læk'seıʃən/ *n* **1** *u.n* act of s.t relaxing; fact of being relaxed. **2** *c/u.n* thing that one does in order to relax(1), for pleasure etc.

relay¹ /'ri:leı/ *n* **1** *c.n* group of people, horses etc who/that work for a certain time and are then replaced by a fresh, less tired group, and so on. **2** *c.n* (*informal*) = relay race. **3** *c/u.n* broadcast (of a radio or television programme) passed on from one station, receiver etc to another: *the relay of a tennis match from America.* **by relay** using a relay¹(3). **by/in relay(s)** one relay¹(1) after the other.

▷ *tr.v* /rı'leı/ **4** pass on (a broadcast) using a relay¹(3): *This programme is being relayed from America.* **5** (often — s.t to s.o) (*formal*) pass on (news etc) (to s.o): *Could you relay the information to him?*

'relay ,race *c.n* running race in which teams take part with each member of a team running part of the distance.

relay² /rı'leı/ *tr.v* (*p.t,p.p* relaid /ri:'leıd/) lay (s.t, e.g a carpet) again after having taken it up.

release /rı'li:s/ *n* **1** *c/u.n* (often — (of s.o/s.t) from s.o/s.t) setting free (of s.o/s.t) (from s.o/s.t); allowing (of s.o/s.t) to leave (e.g a prison). **2** *c.n* paper giving information **3** *c.n* new record¹(1), tape(3), film etc that has just come out. **4** *c.n* = press release. **5** *c.n* (also *attrib*) device that releases(6) s.t when one presses, switches¹(4) etc it: *You can't take your safety belt off without pressing this release (button).* **on general release** (of a film) allowed to be shown at all cinemas (in a place): *The film was shown to the President and his family before it was put on general release.*

▷ *tr.v* **6** (often — s.o/s.t from s.t) free (s.o/s.t) (from s.t); set (s.o/s.t) free (from s.t); allow (s.o/s.t) to leave (s.t). **7** allow (a new film) to be shown in cinemas. **8** publish(1), usu in newspapers, on television etc, (a story, picture etc, often one that was kept secret before). **9** press/move (s.t) so that it no longer holds/stops s.t: *Before you start you have to release the* handbrake. **10** (*law*) stop claiming (s.t, e.g a building or a right).

relegate /'relə,geɪt/ *tr.v* (usu — *s.o/s.t to s.t*) make (a team) go down (to a lower division) because it was one of the least successful teams in its division. Opposite promote(1). *relegate s.o/s.t to s.t* (*in s.t*) put s.o/s.t down to a lower position (in s.t).

relegation /,relə'geɪʃən/ *u.n*.

relent /rɪ'lent/ *intr.v* (change one's mind and) become less severe/cruel; show pity/mercy.
re'lentless *adj* not relenting ⇒ unrelenting.
re'lentlessly *adv*. **re'lentlessness** *u.n*.

relevant /'reləvənt/ *adj* (often — *to s.o/s.t*; — *to what, where* etc . . .) having a connection (with s.t, with what . . .): *What you are saying is not relevant* (*to the matter we are discussing*). Opposite irrelevant.
'relevance, 'relevancy *u.n*.

reliability, reliable, reliably, reliance, reliant ⇒ rely.

relic /'relɪk/ *c.n* (often — *of s.o/s.t*) **1** thing that is still left after s.o/s.t no longer exists, and that reminds one of her/him/it: *Relics of the lives of earlier* generations *of my family are in the* attic. **2** (*religion*) part of the body, clothes, possessions etc of a dead saint(1) etc which people feel reverence(1) for.
'relics *pl.n* what is left (of a person's body, a building etc) after he/she/it has died, been ruined etc.

relief[1] /rɪ'li:f/ *u.n* way of shaping s.t, e.g a coin, so that parts of it stick out further from the surface than others. (*stand out*) *in* (*bold/sharp*) *relief* (*against s.t*) (be able to be seen) contrasted(5) (strongly) (with s.t behind): *The dark cliffs stand out in sharp relief against the pale sky. in high/ low relief* cut so that it stands out a long/short way from the rest of the surface of s.t, e.g a coin. Compare relief[2] (⇒ relieve).
re'lief ,map *c.n* map showing differences in height by different colours, lines etc.

relieve /rɪ'li:v/ *tr.v* **1** make (a pain, worry, boredom etc) go away or become less strong. ⇒ unrelieved. **2** make (s.t, e.g a meeting) more enjoyable: *We sometimes relieve our political meetings with a few songs.* **3** take the place of (s.o) so that he/she can go and rest etc: *The guards are relieved every two hours.* **4** stop (a place) being surrounded and cut off by the enemy: *Our army has relieved the town at last. relieve oneself* (*formal*) urinate and/or defecate. *relieve s.o's mind* ⇒ mind[1]. *relieve s.o of s.t* take s.t from s.o to help her/him: *Can I relieve you of that heavy bag? You are relieved of all your duties so that you can visit your wife in hospital.*

relief[2] /rɪ'li:f/ *n* **1** *c/u.n* fact of relieving(1) s.o/ s.t, or of being relieved(1): *It was a relief to learn that he was safe.* **2** *u.n* (also *attrib*) help for s.o in trouble: *It's a relief*(1) *for hungry children.* **3** *u.n* fact of being allowed not to pay s.t because of certain circumstances: *If you are looking after your old mother at home, you can get tax relief for this.* **4** *c/pl.n* (also *attrib*) person, group of people, vehicle etc who/that relieve(s)(3) s.o or

another vehicle etc: *a relief bus* (*to help when the regular bus is full*). **5** (often *the* — *of s.t*) act of relieving(4) (a place). (*give/heave*) *a sigh of relief* ⇒ sigh(*n*). *light relief* thing that relieves(2) s.t serious by providing s.t light and amusing. (*much*) *to s.o's relief* which relieved(1) s.o (very much): *At last the bus arrived, much to our relief, and we could get home. to s.o's great relief =* much to s.o's relief. Compare relief[1].

re'lieved *adj* (often — (*to hear* etc) *that* . . .) feeling relief[2](1) (because one has heard etc that . . .).

religion /rɪ'lɪdʒən/ *n* **1** *u.n* belief in one or more gods or powers that are outside our physical(2) world. **2** *c.n* system of faith, worship etc based on religion(1): *the* Christian(1)/Hindu(1)/Buddhist *religion.* **3** *u.n* state of being a monk or nun: *enter into religion.* **4** *sing.n* thing that one is very serious about: *Football is a religion with some people. make a religion of s.t* treat s.t as a religion(4).

re'ligious *adj* **1** of or referring to religion: *religious liberty; a religious procession.* **2** (of a person, the way he/she behaves etc) doing etc what a religion demands. Opposite irreligious. **3** great; showing great care: *She looks after her pupils with religious care/* devotion(1).
re,ligious 'feast *c.n* = feast(2).
re'ligiously *adv* **1** in a religious(3) way. **2** acting as if it was a religion(4): *He follows the local team religiously.*
re'ligiousness *u.n*.

relinquish /rɪ'lɪŋkwɪʃ/ *tr.v* (*formal*) give (s.t) up; stop trying to keep (s.t). *relinquish one's hold on s.t* (**a**) open one's hand so that s.t that one was holding can come out of it. (**b**) give up s.t that one has had or owned.

relish /'relɪʃ/ *sing/u.n* **1** (often *with* (a) —) (great) enjoyment. **2** *c/u.n* thing put in or on food to give it a (strong/interesting) taste. Compare pickle(1). *have a relish for s.t* = relish(3) s.t.
▷ *tr.v* **3** (often — *doing s.t*) enjoy ((doing) s.t).

reluctant /rɪ'lʌktənt/ *adj* (often — *to do s.t*) not (very) willing (to do s.t).
re'luctance *sing/u.n with reluctance =* reluctantly(1).
re'luctantly *adv* **1** in a reluctant way. **2** I am sorry, but . . .: *Reluctantly, I have had to leave Joe behind.*

rely /rɪ'laɪ/ *intr.v* (-*ies*, -*ied*) *rely* (*up*)*on s.o/s.t* (*doing s.t, for s.t, to do s.t*) trust, or confidently depend on, s.o/s.t etc (for s.t etc): *I rely on you to help us* (or *on your help*(ing) *us*). Compare count (up)on s.o/s.t.
reliability /rɪ,laɪə'bɪlɪtɪ/ *u.n* fact or state of being reliable.
reliable /rɪ'laɪəbl/ *adj* who/that can be relied on. Opposite unreliable.
re'liably *adv* in a way that can be relied on: *I am reliably informed that you missed school yesterday.*
reliance /rɪ'laɪəns/ *u.n* (often — (*up*)*on s.o/s.t*) fact of relying on s.o/s.t. *place reliance* (*up*)*on s.o/s.t* rely on s.o/s.t.
re'liant *adj* (often — *on s.o/s.t*) in a state of relying on s.o/s.t. Compare self-reliant.

remain /rɪ'meɪn/ *intr.v* **1** stay; not go away; be left behind after another or others have gone. **2** continue to be (s.t, e.g a certain rank, a certain condition, e.g cold etc). *it only remains for s.o/ s.t to do s.t*, *for s.t to be done* the only thing that still needs doing is for s.o/s.t to do s.t etc: *Well, dinner is finished and it only remains for me to thank you all for coming.* *it remains to be seen what*, *where etc . . .*; *that remains to be seen* we do not yet know (what etc . . .).

re'mainder *def/def.pl.n* rest (of s.t/s.o); what is left (of s.t/s.o): *You are free for the remainder of the day. The remainder of us did another hour's study.*

re'mains *pl.n* (often *the — of s.o/s.t*) **1** thing(s), or part(s) (of s.o/s.t), that remain(s). **2** (*formal*) corpse.

remand /rɪ'mɑːnd/ *c/u.n* **1** (*law*) act or fact of remanding(2). *on remand* in prison after having been remanded(2).

▷ *tr.v* **2** (*law*) (of a judge etc in a law court) send (s.o) back to prison to wait for later trial so that more information can be collected about her/his case. *remand s.o in custody* = remand s.o.

re'mand ,home *c.n* place to which young people are remanded(2) until a court decides what to do with them.

remark /rɪ'mɑːk/ *n* **1** *c.n* thing said or written (about s.o/s.t): *I listened to her remarks about/ on the painting with interest. Don't make rude remarks! make/pass a remark (about s.o/s.t)* say or write s.t (about s.o/s.t). *worthy of remark* (*formal*) worth noticing.

▷ *tr/intr.v* **2** (often *— (up)on s.t; — that . . .*) say or write (s.t, that . . .) as a remark(1) (about s.t).

re'markable *adj* (often *— for s.t*), worth noticing, striking, (because of s.t): *These forests are remarkable for beautifully coloured birds.* Opposite unremarkable.

re'markably *adv* (before an adj or adv) noticeably; unusually: *They are remarkably similar.*

remedy /'remɪdɪ/ *c/u.n* (*pl -ies*) **1** (often *— for s.t*) cure (for s.t); thing that makes s.t bad better: *No real remedy for colds has yet been found. beyond/past remedy* so bad that it can no longer be cured.

▷ *tr.v* (*-ies, -ied*) **2** be/provide a remedy(1) for (s.t).

remedial /rɪ'miːdɪəl/ *adj* that remedies(2), is intended to remedy(2), s.t: *remedial exercises/lessons.*

remember /rɪ'membə/ *v* **1** *tr/intr.v* bring (s.t that happened or s.o/s.t one knew etc in the past) back to one's mind; have (s.t that happened or s.o/s.t one knew etc in the past) in one's mind: *Do you remember Joe? I remember seeing him last summer. I remember him saying he would be here in December. I can't remember where I put my pen. 'What did you do with my shirt?' 'I can't remember.'* **2** *tr/intr.v* (often *— to do s.t*) be careful not to forget (s.o/s.t): *'Did you remember to lock the door?' 'Yes, I remembered.' Remember me when you next invite people to dinner.* **3** *tr.v* not forget to give (s.o) a present/tip/legacy(1) etc, or to pray for her/him. *remember s.o/s.t as s.t* remember s.o/s.t when he/she/it was (like) s.t: *I remember Pat as a young girl and now she's 40! remember s.o to s.o* give s.o's greetings to s.o: *Please remember me to your mother.* ⇨ memory.

re'membrance *n* (*formal*) **1** *c/u.n* fact or state of remembering(1) (s.o/s.t). **2** *c.n* thing remembered. **3** *c.n* thing by which one remembers s.o/

s.t; memento. *in remembrance of s.o/s.t* in order to remember s.o/s.t.

remind /rɪ'maɪnd/ *tr.v* cause (s.o) to, make (s.o), remember(1,2) (s.o, s.t, that . . .): *That woman reminds me of my aunt Mabel. Mrs Jones reminded her son that she wanted him to help her in the garden on Saturday. Remind me to buy some fruit when we go to town. 'It's raining.' 'That reminds me — Sheila has got my umbrella.'*

re'minder *c.n* (often *as a — (of s.t)*) thing that reminds s.o (of s.t, e.g of the fact that one owes money).

remit /rɪ'mɪt/ *v* (*-tt-*) **1** *tr/intr.v* (*formal*) send (s.t, esp money) (to s.o). **2** *tr.v* (*law*) no longer make s.o have (a long or severe punishment): *remit s.o's sentence of five years in prison.*

remission /rɪ'mɪʃən/ *n* **1** *u.n* (often *— of s.t*) act or fact of remitting(2) (s.t) or (of s.t) being remitted(2). ⇨ unremitting. **2** *c/u.n* shortening of the time to which s.o has been sentenced to prison, usu for good behaviour. **3** *c.n* (*medical*) time during which an illness is less severe before becoming worse again. *the remission of sins* God's forgiveness of people's sins(1).

re'mittance *n* (*formal*) **1** *u.n* remitting(1) of money. **2** *c.n* money remitted(1).

remnant /'remnənt/ *c.n* **1** (often *— of s.t*) thing that remains after the rest (of s.t) has gone: *the remnants of a defeated army.* **2** (also *attrib*) piece of cloth left after most of the bale[1](1) has gone and therefore being sold cheaply: *a remnant sale.*

remonstrate /'remən,streɪt/ *intr.v* (*formal*) (often *— (with s.o) about s.t; — against s.t*) (*formal*) complain (to s.o) (about s.t).

remorse /rɪ'mɔːs/ *u.n* (often *feel, be filled with, — (for s.t)*) sorrow because of having done s.t bad, cruel etc. *without remorse* cruel(ly).

re'morseful *adj* feeling, showing, remorse.

re'morsefully *adv.* **re'morsefulness** *u.n.*

re'morseless *adj* without remorse.

re'morselessly *adv.* **re'morselessness** *u.n.*

remote /rɪ'məʊt/ *adj* (often *— from s.o/s.t*) **1** far away (from s.o/s.t) in space or time; distant(1). **2** (of a farm, village etc) far away from towns etc. **3** not at all close(ly connected) (to s.o/s.t): *a remote relative of mine; have a remote connection with what I was thinking about.* **4** (of a person or her/his behaviour) not friendly; distant(3). **5** slight; very small: *There is a remote chance/ possibility that the letter has already arrived. There isn't the remotest chance of that, I am afraid. not have the remotest idea (what, where etc . . .)* (*informal*) not know at all what etc (to) . . .: *I haven't the remotest idea where Dorothy lives.*

re,mote con'trol *u.n* (often *by —*) control of s.t, e.g the programme, colour, brightness etc of a television picture, from a distance by using radio waves.

re'motely *adv.*

re'moteness *u.n.*

remove /rɪ'muːv/ *v* **1** *tr.v* (often *— s.o/s.t from s.o/s.t*) take (s.o/s.t) off (s.o/s.t), away (from s.o/ s.t) or out (of s.o/s.t): *The dentist had to remove two teeth. Remove your hat when you go inside.* **2** *tr.v* (often *— s.o from s.t*) dismiss (s.o) (from a job): *The teacher was removed for smoking in class.* **3** *intr.v* (often *— (from s.w) to s.w*) (*formal*) = move(5): *During the war, the factory was removed to a safer part of the country.* **far removed from s.t** not at all like s.t: *His story is far removed from the truth.* **once**, **twice** etc **removed** (of cousins) of a generation(2) that is one, two etc away from one, or from each other: *My uncle's grandchild is my first cousin once removed.*

re'moval *c/u.n* (example of the) act or fact of removing (s.o/s.t).

re'moval ,van *c.n* kind of large van used for moving furniture etc from one house, office etc, to another.

renaissance /rɪ'neɪsəns/ *n* **1** *c.n* (*formal*) new interest in s.t after it has been neglected for some time. **2** *def.n* (with capital **R**) time in Europe from the 14th to the 17th centuries when the ideas etc of ancient Greece were studied again and influenced thought, art etc.

render /'rendə/ *tr.v* (*formal*) **1** cause (s.o/s.t) to be (s.t): *The accident has rendered him helpless* (or *unable to use his arms*). **2** (often — *s.o s.t*; — *s.t to s.o*) give (s.o, usu s.t useful, or s.t to s.o): *You would be rendering me a great service if you could phone for a taxi.* **3** perform (s.t, e.g a song). **render an account (to s.o)** ⇨ account(*n*). **render s.t down** melt fat so as to make it pure. **render thanks (to s.o) (for s.t)** thank s.o, usu God (for s.t).

'rendering /'rendərɪŋ/ *c.n* (often — *of s.t*) **1** performance (of a song etc). **2** translation (of s.t).

rendezvous /'rɒndɪ,vuː/ *c.n* (*pl* **rendezvous** /'rɒndɪ,vuːz/) (*French*) **1** (often — *with s.o*) agreement (with s.o) to meet s.w at a certain time. **2** meeting as a result of a rendezvous(1): *I was ten minutes late for my rendezvous with Jane.* **3** (often — *for s.o*) place where a lot of people (of a certain kind) meet: *a rendezvous for journalists.*

▷ *intr.v* **4** meet as a result of a rendezvous(1).

renew /rɪ'njuː/ *tr.v* **1** put a new one in place of (one that is old, worn out etc): *I'll have to renew the* washer(2) *on this tap.* **2** get (a new one) in place of one that is out of date: *It's time to renew our insurance.* **3** do (s.t) again: *renew attempts to save the trapped men.* **4** bring (s.t) back to its original good state: *The stay in hospital gave me renewed health.*

re'newable *adj* that can or must be renewed(1,2). Opposite non-renewable.

re'newal *n* **1** *c/u.n* (often — *of s.t*) act or fact of renewing(1–3) s.t, or of being renewed. **2** *c.n* thing that is used to take the place of s.t else in a renewal(1).

renounce /rɪ'naʊns/ *tr.v* give up (s.t, often a claim or religion); say that one no longer claims or wants (to keep/follow) (s.t).

renunciation /rɪ,nʌnsɪ'eɪʃən/ *c/u.n.*

renown /rɪ'naʊn/ *u.n* (often — *as s.o/s.t*) (*formal*) fame (as s.o/s.t).

re'nowned *adj* (often — *as/for s.t*) famous (as/ for s.t).

rent¹ /rent/ *c.n* big tear²(1).

rent² /rent/ *c/u.n* **1** money paid every week etc to s.o, usu the owner, for being allowed to use s.t, e.g a house, field. **at a rent of s.t** paying s.t as rent: *I have this place at a rent of £45 a week.* **for rent** offered to be rented(3): *Is this house for rent?* **free of rent** = rent-free.

▷ *v* **2** *tr/intr.v* (often — (*s.t*) *from s.o*) pay rent²(1)

(to s.o) (for (s.t)): *'Have you got your own house?' 'No, we rent.'* **3** *tr.v* (often — *s.t* (*out*) *to s.o*) make s.o pay rent²(1) for (s.t). **rent for s.t** bring in s.t as rent²(1): *This house rents for £200 a month.*

'rental *c.n* (often *at a* — *of s.t*) rent²(1) (of a certain amount).

'rent col,lector *c.n* person whose job is to collect rents²(1).

,rent-'free *adj/adv* without having to pay rent²(1) (for a house etc): *His room is rent-free. He lives rent-free.*

renunciation ⇨ renounce.

reorganize, -ise /rɪ'ɔː gənaɪz/ *tr/intr.v* organize (s.t) again and in a different way.

rep /rep/ *c.n* (*informal*) representative(4).

repair /rɪ'peə/ *c/u.n* **1** (often — *to s.t*) act or result of putting (s.t) back into good condition or mending (it). **carry out repairs (on s.t)** repair(2) (s.t). **in a bad**, **good** etc **state of repair**; **in bad**, **good** etc **repair** in a good, bad etc condition; needing, not needing, repair(1). **under repair** being repaired(2).

▷ *tr.v* **2** make repairs(1) on (s.t). **3** put right (s.t that has been done wrongly, unfairly etc); right (s.t); make amends for (s.t).

re'pairer *c.n* person who repairs(2) things.

re'pairable *adj* that can be repaired(2). ⇨ irreparable.

reparations /,repə'reɪʃənz/ *pl.n* money, goods etc a country that has lost a war has to give to the country or countries that have won it.

repartee /,repɑː'tiː/ *n* **1** *u.n* quick amusing answers given during a conversation. **2** *u.n* ability to give such answers. **3** *c.n* one of these answers.

repay /rɪ'peɪ/ *tr.v* (*p.t,p.p* **repaid** /rɪ'peɪd/) pay (s.t) back. **repay s.o (for s.t) (by doing s.t, with s.t)** reward/punish s.o (for s.t) (by doing s.t, by giving her/him s.t (not always s.t good)). **repay s.t by doing s.t**, **with s.t** do/give s.t in return for s.t: *John repaid Helen's generosity by painting her house.*

re'payable *adj* that can/must be repaid.

re'payment *c/u.n.*

repeal /rɪ'piːl/ *u.n* **1** (often *the* — *of s.t*) (*law*) action of repealing(2) (s.t).

▷ *tr.v* **2** (*law*) cause (a law) to stop being in operation.

repeat /rɪ'piːt/ *c.n* (also *attrib*) **1** thing, e.g a radio or television programme or a statement, that is repeated(2): *There are so many repeats* (*of old films*) *on television. That is a repeat of what I have just said. She is giving a repeat performance next week.*

▷ *v* **2** *tr.v* say (s.t) again; do (s.t) again. **3** *tr.v* say (to s.o) (s.t one has heard or read): *Now you mustn't repeat what I'm going to tell you to a living soul!* **4** *intr.v* (of a decimal(2)) recur(2). **not bear repeating** (of s.t said) be too bad to be repeated(2,3). **not to be repeated** (**a**) that one must not repeat(2). (**b**) (of an offer) that will not be repeated(2) (so one should do s.t about it now). **repeat a course**, **year** etc (in a school etc) do the same course again (for a year etc), usu because one failed the first time. **repeat oneself** (often *derog*) say again s.t that one has already said. **repeat an order** (in a shop etc) ask for, supply, the same thing(s) again.

re'peated *adj* happening, done, again and again.

re'peatedly *adv.*

repetition /ˌrepɪ'tɪʃən/ *n* 1 *c/u.n* (often — *of s.t*) act of repeating(2,3) (s.t). 2 *u.n* repetition(1) of s.t, e.g a list of words, in order to learn it by heart.

ˌrepe'titious, repetitive /rɪ'petɪtɪv/ *adj* full of repetitions(1) (and therefore boring).

repe'titiously, re'petitively *adv.*

ˌrepe'titiousness, re'petitiveness *u.n.*

repel /rɪ'pel/ *v* (-ll-) 1 *tr.v* drive, force, (s.o/s.t) back: *The soldiers repelled all the enemy's attacks.* 2 *tr/intr.v* cause (s.o) to feel disgust: *The smell of his breath repelled her.*

re'pellent *adj* 1 (often — *to s.o*) (*derog*) who/ that repels(2) (s.o).

▷ *c/u.n* 2 substance that repels(1) s.t: *an insect repellent.*

repulse /rɪ'pʌls/ *c.n* 1 act of repelling(1) s.o/s.t. 2 act of rejecting(2) s.o/s.t, e.g s.o's attempt to be polite.

▷ *tr.v* 3 repel(1) (s.o/s.t). 4 reject(2) s.o/s.t. ⇒ repulse(2).

repulsion /rɪ'pʌlʃən/ *sing/u.n* (often *feel* (a) — *for s.o/s.t*) feeling of being repelled(2) (by s.o/ s.t).

repulsive /rɪ'pʌlsɪv/ *adj* (*derog*) repellent(1).

re'pulsively *adv.* **re'pulsiveness** *u.n.*

repent /rɪ'pent/ *tr/intr.v* (often — *of s.t*) (*formal*) be sorry (for s.t wrong that one has done).

re'pentance *u.n.*

re'pentant *adj* 1 feeling or showing that one repents.

▷ *def.pl.n* 2 people who repent.

repercussion /ˌriːpə'kʌʃən/ *c.n* (often *pl*) (often *have* —s (*on s.o/s.t*); *the* —s *of s.t*) effect (of s.t that has been done/said etc) that was not expected (and that covers a wide field).

repertoire /'repətwɑː/ *c.n* (*French*) collection of pieces of music, plays, stories etc that a person or group has/have learnt so that he/she/they can produce them easily.

repetition, repetitious(ly/ness), repetitive(ly/ness) ⇒ repeat.

replace /rɪ'pleɪs/ *tr.v* 1 put (s.t) back in the place it was in before. 2 (often — *s.t by/with s.t*) provide s.t to take the place of (s.t else, usu s.t broken, lost etc). 3 (often — *s.o as s.t*) take the place of (s.o, e.g s.o who is ill or has left).

re'placeable *adj* that can be replaced(2). Opposite irreplaceable.

re'placement *n* 1 *u.n* (often (*the*) — (*of s.o/s.t*) (*by/with s.o/s.t*)) (the) act/fact of replacing(2, 3) (s.o/s.t) (with s.o/s.t). 2 *c.n* (often — *for s.o/s.t*) person or thing who/that replaces(2, 3) (s.o/s.t).

replay /'riː,pleɪ/ *c/u.n* (often — *of s.t*) 1 football etc match that is played again. 2 act of playing back (s.t recorded, e.g on a tape recorder).

▷ *v* /riː'pleɪ/ 3 *tr/intr.v* play (a match) again. 4 *tr.v* play (a piece of music) again.

replenish /rɪ'plenɪʃ/ *tr/intr.v* (often — (s.o/s.t) *with s.t*) fill (s.o/s.t, e.g a store cupboard) up again (with s.t) after all/some of the things that were there before have been finished.

re'plenishment *u.n*

replica /'replɪkə/ *c.n* person or thing who/that is exactly like s.t; copy (of s.o/s.t): *Jimmy is an exact replica of his father.* Compare reproduction(2).

reply /rɪ'plaɪ/ *c.n* (*pl* -ies) 1 (often — *to s.t*) answer (to s.t). *in reply* (*to s.o/s.t*) as an answer (to s.o/s.t). *make no reply* not answer.

▷ *tr/intr.v* (-ies, -ied) 2 (often — *to s.o/s.t.*; — *that* . . .) answer (s.o/s.t) (by saying that . . .): *'No, I'm sorry but I can't come,' she replied.* **reply for s.o** answer on behalf of s.o; answer as a representative of s.o.

re,ply-'paid *adj* (usu of a telegram) with the answer already paid for by the person who has sent it.

report¹ /rɪ'pɔːt/ *c.n* 1 spoken or written statement about s.t that happened, s.o's activities etc. 2 (also **'school re,port**) written statement sent to a pupil's parents etc giving details of her/his progress, behaviour etc during the term that has just finished.

▷ *v* 3 *tr.v* make a report¹(1) about (s.o/s.t) (to s.o): *I'll report you/it to the manager. Have you reported on the meeting yet? She reported what happened.* 4 *tr.v* (of a journalist) write about (s.t that has happened) in a newspaper etc. 5 *tr.v* (often — *s.o* (*to s.o*) *for* (*doing*) *s.t*) make a report¹(1) (to s.o) about s.o, saying that he/she has done s.t bad: *I shall report you to the head teacher for causing trouble unless you stop at once!* 6 *intr.v* (often — *to s.o* (*for s.t*)) go s.w (and say (to s.o) that one is there or that one is ready to do s.t): *All units will report for duty at 0900 hours tomorrow morning.* **report back** (*to s.o*) report¹(3) to the person who sent one to find s.t out. **report progress** state what progress has been made so far.

reportedly /rɪ'pɔːtɪdlɪ/ *adv* according to what is reported¹(3,4) (which may be untrue).

re,ported 'speech *u.n* = indirect speech.

re'porter *c.n* person who reports(4) s.t.

report² /rɪ'pɔːt/ *c.n* sharp noise made by an explosion, shot etc.

represent /ˌreprɪ'zent/ *tr.v* 1 (of a picture, statue etc) show (s.o/s.t); be a picture, statue etc of (s.o/ s.t). 2 be a sign or symbol of (s.o/s.t); stand for (s.o/s.t): *In mathematics, the sign ∞ represents* infinity(2). 3 act the part of (s.o in a play, film etc). 4 act for (another person, or other people who has/have agreed to one acting for her/him/ them in this way): *I am not here as a private person but to represent all the village.* 5 be the person elected to represent(4) people. 6 be one specimen(1) of s.t: *Our collection is quite small but we have something to represent each main branch.*

representation /ˌreprɪzen'teɪʃən/ *n* (often — *of s.o/s.t*) 1 *u.n* act or fact of representing(1) (s.o/s.t). 2 *c.n* thing that represents(1) s.o/s.t. **proportional representation** ⇒ proportional.

ˌrepresen'tational *adj* (in art) showing things as they actually are. Compare abstract¹(2).

ˌrepre'sentative *adj* 1 (often — *of s.o/s.t*) that represents(6), is typical of, (s.o/s.t): *This painting is quite representative of late 19th century art.* Opposite unrepresentative. 2 in which people are elected to represent(4) others.

▷ *c.n* 3 (often — *of s.o/s.t*) person or thing who/ that represents(1,4–6) s.o/s.t. 4 (*informal rep*) travelling salesman.

repress /rɪ'pres/ *tr.v* 1 stop (s.o) behaving freely. 2 prevent (s.t) from appearing, coming out etc: *We had to repress our laughter so as not to hurt the man's feelings.* 3 crush (s.t, e.g a rising by the people of a place) by using the police, soldiers, etc.

re'pressed *adj* **1** (of a feeling etc) not allowed to show itself; kept down because one thinks it is bad. **2** (of a person) whose feelings are repressed(1).

repression /rɪ'preʃən/ *n* **1** *u.n* (often *the — of s.o/s.t*) act or fact of repressing (s.o/s.t); state of (s.o/s.t) being repressed (⇨ repress). **2** *c/u.n* state or fact of being repressed(1,2).

repressive /rɪ'presɪv/ *adj* (*derog*) who/that represses(1) s.o.

re'pressively *adv.* **re'pressiveness** *u.n.*

reprieve /rɪ'priːv/ *c/u.n* **1** delay of execution(1,4) (usu done by a judge, a government etc). **2** (*fig*) delay in the happening of s.t bad: *After her heart attack she was expected to die soon, but in fact she had five years' reprieve.*

▷ *tr.v* **3** give (s.o) a reprieve.

reprimand /'reprɪˌmɑːnd/ *c/u.n* **1** severe official scolding (because of s.t).

▷ *tr.v* /ˌreprɪ'mɑːnd/ **2** (often *— s.o for s.t*) give (s.o) a reprimand(1) (because of s.t).

reprint /'riːˌprɪnt/ *c.n* **1** (often *— of s.t*) second, third etc printing (of s.t), usu because the first one has been sold out.

▷ *v* /riː'prɪnt/ **2** *tr/intr.v* make a reprint(1) (of (s.t)). **3** *intr.v* be reprinted(2): *We can send you a copy of the book soon — it's reprinting at the moment.*

reprisal /rɪ'praɪzl/ *c/u.n* (often *pl* or *as a — (for s.t)*) (an act of) retaliating (for s.t); (an act of) doing s.t bad to s.o in return (for s.t bad he/ she has done to one). *in reprisal (for s.t)* as a reprisal (for s.t).

reproach /rɪ'prəʊtʃ/ *n* **1** *u.n* fact of reproaching(3). **2** *c.n* thing said or written that reproaches(3) s.o. *above/beyond reproach* so good that there is absolutely nothing about her/him/it that deserves reproach(1). *a reproach to s.o/s.t* (*formal*) a person or thing who/that should cause one to reproach(3) s.o: *The dirty condition of the office is a reproach to all who work in it.*

▷ *tr.v* **3** (often *— oneself/s.o for (doing) s.t, with s.t*) blame (oneself/s.o) in a sad, not angry, way (because of s.t): *Don't worry, you have nothing to reproach yourself with.*

re'proachful *adj* feeling, showing, reproach(1). **re'proachfully** *adv.* **re'proachfulness** *u.n.*

reproduce /ˌriːprə'djuːs/ *v* **1** *tr/intr.v* give birth to young. **2** *tr.v* produce a copy of (s.t), e.g by photography. **3** *tr.v* produce (s.t that has been recorded, e.g music or a film). **4** *intr.v* (be able to) be reproduced(2,3): *This kind of picture reproduces well.*

reproduction /ˌriːprə'dʌkʃən/ *n* (often *— of s.t*) **1** *u.n* act or way of reproducing(1–3) (s.o/ s.t). **2** *c.n* copy (of s.t), often not a very good one and done in a way that is different from the original: *a reproduction of a famous painting on a Christmas card.* Compare replica.

ˌrepro'ductive *adv* of or referring to reproduction(1,2). ⇨ organ¹(2).

reproof /rɪ'pruːf/ *c.n* (*formal*) scolding; blame.

reprove /rɪ'pruːv/ *tr.v* (*formal*) (usu *— s.o for (doing) s.t*) scold s.o (for (doing) s.t).

re'proving *adj* (*formal*) that shows reproof: *He gave me a reproving look.*

re'provingly *adv.*

reptile /'reptaɪl/ *c.n* one of many kinds of creature that crawls on the ground and is cold-blooded(1): *Snakes, crocodiles(1) and tortoises are reptiles.*

republic /rɪ'pʌblɪk/ *c.n* (with capital **R** in names) nation whose head is a president, not a king, queen, emperor or empress.

re'publican *adj* **1** of or referring to a republic or republics. **2** in favour of republics (instead of monarchies etc). **3** (with capital **R**) of, about, as a member of, the Republican Party. Compare Democratic(2).

▷ *c.n* **4** person who has republican(2) beliefs. **5** (with capital **R**) person who supports the Republican Party. Compare Democrat.

re'publicaˌnism *u.n.* republican(2) beliefs.

Re'publican ˌParty *def.n* one of the two main US political parties. Compare Democratic Party.

repudiate /rɪ'pjuːdɪˌeɪt/ *tr.v* **1** refuse to accept, obey, (s.o/s.t) (any more). **2** state that (s.t) is not true. **3** (*formal*) refuse to pay (s.t, e.g a bill that one has received).

repudiation /rɪˌpjuːdɪ'eɪʃən/ *u.n.*

repulse, repulsion, repulsive(ly/ness) ⇨ repel.

reputation /ˌrepjʊ'teɪʃən/ *sing/u.n* what people think, say, write etc about s.o/s.t: *Mary has a high reputation in our village for good works. He has the reputation of always being late* (or *for arriving late*). *live up to one's reputation* behave as people expect one to because of one's (good or bad) reputation.

reputable /'repjʊtəbl/ *adj* who/that has a good reputation.

'reputably *adv.*

reputed /rɪ'pjuːtɪd/ *adj* (usu *— to be/do s.t; — as s.t*) considered by a lot of people (to be s.t): *Joe was the reputed inventor* (or *reputed to be the inventor*) *of a new way of making money quickly.*

re'putedly *adv.*

request /rɪ'kwest/ *c.n* **1** act of asking (politely) for s.o/s.t. **2** thing asked for (politely). *at s.o's request; by request (of s.o)* because s.o has asked for it. *grant s.o's request (for s.t)* do what s.o has asked; give s.o what he/she has asked for. *make a request (for s.o/s.t)* ask for s.o/s.t. *on request* when s.o asks for it: *Anyone can have the book on request.*

▷ *tr.v* **3** ask for (s.t) politely (from s.o); ask s.o (to do s.t): *All I request (of you) is that you should not interfere. I am requested to ask you for your keys. I have requested an answer from her.*

re'quest ˌstop *c.n* place where a bus will stop only if s.o who is, or wants to be, a passenger on it wants it to: *Our next stop is a request stop.*

require /rɪ'kwaɪə/ *tr.v* (*formal*) **1** need (s.o/s.t); need to be done: *This job requires strength. This tyre requires mending.* **2** (often *— s.t of s.o; — (of s.o) that...*) demand (s.t) (from s.o, that...); make it a rule that s.o should do s.t: *The bank requires of its employees that they should be* smartly¹(1) *dressed.*

re'quirement *c.n* (*formal*) thing that is required. *meet s.o's requirements* do/provide what s.o requires. *meet the requirements for s.t* have the qualities etc required for s.t.

requisite /'rekwɪzɪt/ *attrib.adj* **1** (*formal*) required: *I have the requisite information.*

▷ *c.n* **2** (*formal*) thing required.

rescue /'reskju:/ *c.n* (also *attrib*) **1** act of rescuing(2) s.o/s.t. **come/go to s.o's rescue** come/go to try to rescue(2) s.o.

▷ *tr.v* **2** (often — *s.o/s.t from s.o/s.t*) save (s.o/s.t) (from a danger, a dangerous person etc).

'rescuer *c.n* person who rescues(2) s.o/s.t.

research /rɪ'sɜːtʃ/ *n* (often — *in(to)/on s.t*) **1** *u.n* (also *attrib*) careful attempt(s), usu by a highly qualified person or team, to make a scientific discovery (about s.t): *carry out research into the causes of* cancer(1). **2** *c.n* (often *pl* with *sing* meaning) piece of research(1).

▷ *tr/intr.v* **3** (often — *into/on s.t*) do research(1) (on/for (s.t)).

re'searcher *c.n* (also **re'search ,worker**) person who does research(1).

resemble /rɪ'zembl/ *tr.v* (often — *s.o/s.t in s.t*) be, look, taste etc like (s.o/s.t) (in a certain way).

re'semblance *c/u.n* (often — *between s.o/s.t and s.o/s.t; — to s.o/s.t*) fact of (s.o/s.t) resembling (s.o/s.t).

resent /rɪ'zent/ *tr.v* show, feel, annoyance about, indignation against, (s.o/s.t).

re'sentful *adj* (often — *ofs.o/s.t*) showing/having a feeling of resenting (s.o/s.t).

re'sentfully *adv*.

re'sentfulness, re'sentment *u.n*. **bear** (**s.o**) **resentment** resent s.o.

reserve /rɪ'zɜːv/ *n* **1** *c.n* (sometimes *pl* with *sing* meaning; also *attrib*) (a quantity of a thing kept, or not used now, in case it is needed later, e.g when there is a shortage; store; stock. **2** *c.n* (usu *pl* with *sing* meaning) amount of s.t, e.g strength or will-power, that one has in one but does not usu have to use. **3** *c.n* (in games) person who is not in the team but is ready to enter it if a member of the team is ill, hurt etc. **4** *c/def.n* (sometimes *pl* with *sing* meaning) (member of the) armed forces not being used at the moment but kept in case of need, e.g in an emergency. ⇨ reservist. **5** *c.n* land kept aside or separate for a special purpose: *a game reserve* (i.e one for wild animals). **6** *c.n* (often *put a* — (*of s.t*) *on s.t*) price below which one is not willing to sell s.t, usu at auction(1). **7** *u.n* quality or fact of being reserved(2). **in reserve** kept back for later use if/when needed. (**accept s.t** etc) **without reserve** (**a**) (accept s.t) completely. (**b**) (accept s.t) without making any conditions.

▷ *tr/intr.v* **8** book(6) (a seat in a theatre etc): *Do you think we need to reserve* (*seats*)? **reserve s.t for s.o/s.t** allow only s.o/s.t to have or use s.t: *These parking places are reserved for* handicapped(1) *drivers*.

reservation /ˌrezə'veɪʃən/ *n* **1** *c/u.n* fact of reserving(8) s.t. **2** *c.n* (often *pl*) (often *have a — about s.t; with/without —s*) doubt (about s.t) that makes one not sure that one is willing to do s.t: *I have reservations about going on holiday with all those noisy children.* **3** *c/u.n* (often *with the — that . . .; without —(s)*) limitation(1) put on s.t: *I accept your offer with the reservation that you'll pay half the costs.*

re'served *adj* **1** that has been booked(6) in advance: *reserved seats on a train.* Opposite unreserved(1). **2** (of a person, behaviour etc) not liking (or showing that one does not like)

to make friends easily, to show one's feelings, to talk much etc. Compare distant(3), shy(1).

re'servist *u.n* person who is in the reserve(4).

reservoir /'rezəˌvwɑː/ *c.n* **1** place in which liquid, usu a large amount of water for use in homes and industry, is kept. **2** (often — *of s.t*) (*fig*) big supply/collection (of s.t, e.g information), as in a library.

resettle /riː'setl/ *tr/intr.v* (cause or help (s.o) to) begin to live in a different (part of a) country: *After the* earthquake *the people were resettled a hundred kilometres from the mountain.*

residence /'rezɪdəns/ *n* (*formal*) **1** *c.n* place where s.o lives; house. Compare abode¹. **2** *u.n* fact or state of living (s.w). **3** *u.n* (*law*) place where one is considered by law to live. Compare domicile(1). **in residence** (**a**) (sometimes of students and/or staff of a college, university, hospital etc) living where they work (**b**) (*formal*) at home *The Queen is in residence today.* **take up residence** (**s.w**) begin to live (s.w).

'residency *c/def.n* (*pl* -*ies*) (often with capital **R**) official house of an ambassador, High Commissioner or other head of a British mission(1).

'resident *adj* **1** (often — *in s.t*) living (s.w).

▷ *c.n* **2** (often — *of s.t*) person who lives in a certain place: *a resident of Cambridge.* ⇨ non-resident.

residential /ˌrezɪ'denʃəl/ *adj* (of part of a town etc) where people live, not where they work.

residue /'rezɪˌdju:/ *c.n* (often *the* — *of s.t*) **1** what is left, e.g after a chemical process(2). **2** (*law*) what is left in a dead person's estate(3) after all debts and bequests have been paid.

residual /rɪ'zɪdjuəl/ *adj* left, remaining, as a residue.

resign /rɪ'zaɪn/ *tr/intr.v* (often — *from s.t*) leave, give up, (a job etc): *John is thinking of resigning from the government. She's resigned her post as manager.* **resign oneself/s.o/s.t to s.o/s.t** (*formal*) give oneself/s.o/s.t (to s.t, or into the hands of s.o). **resign oneself to** (**doing**) **s.t** become resigned to (doing) s.t: *At first Donald was unhappy about staying in England but then he resigned himself to doing so.*

resignation /ˌrezɪg'neɪʃən/ *n* **1** *c/u.n* (often — *from s.t*) act or fact of resigning (from a committee etc): *I had to accept his resignation from the political party.* **2** *c.n* (often *hand/send in one's —*) written statement saying that one is resigning (from a job etc). **3** *u.n* (often *with —*) state or feeling of being resigned.

re'signed *adj* (often — *to s.t*) accepting (s.t unpleasant) patiently: *Mary is resigned to the fact that her son will never be a great musician.*

resin /'rezɪn/ *c/u.n* **1** substance like glue that comes out of some trees when one cuts them, used for making varnish(1), oil for thinning paint etc. **2** kind of artificial plastic(1) substance.

'resinous *adj* containing resin.

resist /rɪ'zɪst/ *v* **1** *tr/intr.v* try to stop (s.o/s.t); not allow (s.o/s.t) to do what he/she/it wants; not yield to (s.o/s.t). **2** *tr.v* be strong enough not to be damaged by (s.t, e.g damp). **3** *tr.v* keep oneself from ((having, taking, doing) s.t): *Children can't resist ice-cream.*

re'sistance *n* **1** *sing/u.n* (often — *to s.o/s.t*) fact or act of resisting (s.o/s.t); ability to resist (s.o/s.t): *resistance to disease; sales resistance* (i.e ability to

resist(1) attempts to sell one s.t. *The army put up a strong resistance.* **2** *u/def.n* (often with capital **R**) = underground(6). **3** *sing/u.n* resistance(1) of air/water etc to s.t moving through/towards it: *Modern cars are shaped in such a way as to cut down wind resistance as much as possible.* **4** *u.n* (*technical*) power, measured in ohms, of a wire etc to cut down the amount of electricity that can go through it. **passive resistance** ⇒ passive. (*take*) **the line of least resistance** (choose) the easiest, least dangerous etc way of doing s.t.
re'sistant *adj* (often — *to* s.o/s.t) who/that resists (s.o/s.t).

resolute /'rezə,lu:t/ *adj* (*formal*) determined. Opposite irresolute.
'reso,lutely *adv.* **'reso,luteness** *u.n.*
resolution /,rezə'lu:ʃən/ *n* **1** *u.n* quality or fact of being resolute. **2** *c.n* thing that one resolves(3) to do: *I've made a resolution to keep my room tidy.* **3** *c.n* (often — *against/for* s.t) formal resolution(2), arrived at by a vote, (against, in favour of, s.t). **4** *u.n* (often *the* — *of* s.t) resolving (⇒ resolve(4)) (of s.t). **make good resolutions** resolve(3) to work hard, be polite etc. **New Year resolution** good resolution(2) made on January 1st for the whole of that year.
resolve /rɪ'zɒlv/ *n* **1** *c.n* (often (*make*) a — *to do* s.t) = resolution(2). **2** *u.n* = resolution(1).
▷ *v* **3** *tr/intr.v* decide, sometimes formally as a result of a vote, (against, or in favour of, s.t, *to do* s.t): *I have resolved against staying here and for going to London. Derek has resolved to get another job.* **4** *tr.v* find a way of dealing successfully with (a difficulty).
resonance, resonant(ly), resonate ⇒ resound.
resort /rɪ'zɔ:t/ *n* **1** *c.n* place that people go to for their holidays, their health etc: *a popular holiday resort*; *a health resort in the mountains.* **2** *c.n* place that one often visits: *Pubs are some people's favourite evening resorts.* **3** *u.n* (often *have* — *to* s.t) (*formal*) thing that one resorts to(1). (**as**) **a last resort**; **in the last resort** if/ when everything else one has tried has failed. **have resort to s.t** = resort(4). (**without**) **resort to s.t** (without) resorting to(1) s.t: *I always do puzzles without resort to a dictionary.*
▷ *intr.v* **4 resort to** (**doing**) **s.t** start (doing) s.t, often s.t bad: *When people can't earn money honestly, they sometimes resort to stealing.*
resound /rɪ'zaʊnd/ *intr.v* **1** (of a sound) be heard loudly, clearly and usu in an echoing(2) way. **2** (*fig*) (of fame etc) be heard and talked about widely. **resound with s.t** be filled with echoing(2) sounds, with s.o's praise etc.
resonance /'rezənəns/ *c/u.n* quality or fact of being resonant.
resonant /'rezənənt/ *adj* (of a sound) continuing to sound, usu on a deep strong note; echoing(2): *the resonant note of a big bell.*
'resonantly *adv.*
resonate /'rezə,neɪt/ *intr.v* (of a sound) be resonant(1).
re'sounding *attrib.adj* **1** that resounds. **2** (*attrib*) (*fig*) very great: *The play was a resounding success.*
re'soundingly *adv.*
resource /rɪ'zɔ:s/ *c.n* **1** (often *pl*) means of supplying needs, wants etc: *huge resources of*

oil. A country's natural resources can be coal, oil, water power. **2** *c.n* means of giving one happiness, amusement etc. **3** *u.n* skill in finding or inventing ways of solving difficulties. **have resource to s.o/ s.t** (*formal*) go to s.o, or usu s.t, as a way of doing s.t. **leave s.o to her/his own resources** leave s.o to fill her/his time in any way she/he can. **without resource to s.t** (*formal*) without having resource to s.o/s.t.
re'sourceful *adj* showing resource(3).
re'sourcefully *adv.* **re'sourcefulness** *u.n.*
respect¹ /rɪ'spekt/ *n* **1** *sing/u.n* (often — *for* s.o/ s.t) feeling that s.o deserves to be treated, listened to etc politely: *He showed her no respect.* ⇒ self-respect. **2** *u.n* (often — *for/to* s.t) willingness to do what one should do (about s.t): *Some people have no respect for the law.* **hold s.o/s.t in great, the greatest, respect** respect¹(3) s.o/s.t very much (indeed).
▷ *tr.v* **3** (often — *s.o/s.t for* s.t) feel respect¹(1,2) for, show respect¹(1,2) to, (s.o/s.t) (because of s.t). **respect oneself** have self-respect.
res,pecta'bility *u.n.* fact or quality of being respectable(1).
re'spectable *adj* **1** who/that can be respected¹(3). **2** (of an amount or number of s.t) reasonable; quite good: *Sue has a very respectable salary.*
re'spectableness *u.n.* **re'spectably** *adv.*
re'spectful *adj* feeling, showing, respect¹(1).
re'spectfully *adv.* **re'spectfulness** *u.n.*
re'spects *pl.n* polite formal greetings: *Please give my respects to your parents.* **pay s.o one's respects** (*formal*) visit s.o formally and politely.
respect² /rɪ'spekt/ *c.n* **in one/this etc respect**; **in many etc respects** with regard to one, this etc thing or many etc things; in one etc way or in many etc ways: *In some respects this is a nice place to live, but in one respect it is not — it is very crowded.* **in respect of s.t** (a) as far as s.t is concerned; with regard to s.t: *This hotel is fine in respect of scenery but terrible in respect of the food.* (b) (*technical*) in payment for s.t. **with respect to s.o/s.t** about or concerning s.o/s.t. **without respect to s.t** without considering s.t; without taking s.t into account.
re'specting *prep* (*formal*) about or concerning: *I am writing respecting your query.*
respective /rɪ'spektɪv/ *attrib.adj* each one's own separately: *After the meeting, we each returned to our respective classrooms.* ⇒ irrespective.
re'spectively *adv* in the order given: *Mary, Helen and Polly scored five, three and two goals, respectively.*
respiration /,respɪ'reɪʃən/ *u.n* (*formal*) breathing. **artificial respiration** ⇒ artificial(2).
respiratory /'respərətrɪ/ *adj* (*formal*) of or referring to breathing: *respiratory diseases.*
respond /rɪ'spɒnd/ *v* **1** *intr.v* (often — *to* s.t (*by doing* s.t)) answer (s.t) (by doing s.t). **2** *tr.v* say (s.t) in answer: *'No, I can't come now,' she responded.* **3** *intr.v* (often — *to* s.t (*by doing* s.t, *with* s.t)) do s.t as an answer (to s.t): *I responded to Peter's offer to help by saying that I would tell him if I needed him. The child responded to the woman's kind words with a smile.* **respond to s.t** (a) ⇒ respond(1,3). (b) get better as a result of s.t, e.g medicine or treatment.

re'spondent *c.n* (*law*) person who is accused of s.t, esp in a divorce case. ⇨ co(-)respondent.

response /rɪ'spɒns/ *n* **1** *c.n* (often — *to s.o/s.t*) answer (to so/s.t). **2** *c/u.n* (often — *to s.t*) thing done as an answer (to s.t). **in response** (**to s.t**) as a response(1,2) (to s.t).

re'sponsive *adj* Opposite unresponsive. **1** (often — *to s.t*) who/that responds(3) easily and willingly (to s.t). **2** that shows that s.o is responsive(1): *a responsive look in s.o's eyes.*

re'sponsively *adv.* **re'sponsiveness** *u.n.*

responsible /rɪ'spɒnsəbl/ *adj* **1** (often — (*to s.o*) *for* (*doing*) *s.t*) being in a position where one can be blamed (by s.o) (for (doing) s.t) if it goes wrong: *John is responsible to the manager for seeing that all doors are locked at night.* **2** who/that one can trust; who one can safely give responsibility(4) to. Opposite irresponsible. **3** that needs s.o responsible(2) to do it: *a responsible job.* **hold oneself/s.o responsible** (**for s.t**) consider oneself/s.o to be responsible(1) for s.t.

re,sponsi'bility *n* (*pl -ies*) **1** *u.n* (often — (*to s.o*) *for* (*doing*) *s.t*) fact or state of being responsible(1) (to s.o) (for (doing) s.t). **2** *c/u.n* thing for which one is responsible(1). **3** *u.n* quality of being responsible(2). Opposite irresponsibility. **4** *u.n* (often *the* — *of s.t*) condition or fact of being responsible(3) (for s.t): *a position of great responsibility.* **on one's own responsibility** without anyone else being responsible(1) in any way: *I gave the children an afternoon's holiday on my own responsibility.* **a sense of responsibility** a feeling that makes one behave in a responsible(2) way. **take** (**full**) **responsibility** (**for s.t**) say that one is the (only) person responsible(1) (for s.t).

re'sponsibly *adv.*

responsive(ly/ness) ⇨ respond.

rest¹ /rest/ *def/def.pl.n* people or thing(s) who/ that remain(s) or is/are left: *The rest of us went by train.* **all the rest** (**of s.t** *etc*) all the remaining amount/number (of s.t etc). **for the rest** as far as the rest is/are concerned.

rest² /rest/ *n* **1** *c/u.n* (often — *from s.t*) time during which one is free (from s.t, e.g work). ⇨ unrest. **2** *c/u.n* sleep: *After a good night's rest you'll feel much better.* **3** *c.n* (often as the second part of a word) support (for s.t); thing on which s.t rests(8): *a foot-rest.* **4** *c.n* (*music*) fixed length of time during which one does not sing/play. **5** *c.n* (*music*) sign, e.g ♩ ‿ , for a rest²(4). **at rest** (**a**) not moving at all. (**b**) (of a person) dead. **come to rest** stop after having been moving before. **lay s.o to rest** (of a dead person) bury s.o. **set s.o's mind at rest** ⇨ mind¹. **lay s.t to rest** remove a fear, suspicion etc.

▷ *v* **6** *intr.v* have a rest²(1): *After our long walk we rested for an hour.* **7** *tr.v* allow (s.o/s.t) to have a rest²(1): *We'd better rest the horses for a bit.* **8** *tr/ intr.v* (often — (*s.t*) *against/on s.o/s.t*) (cause (s.t) to) be supported by s.o/s.t. ⇨ rest²(3). **9** *intr.v* be left without further talk etc about it: *It's not worth going on and on about Jill's mistake — let the matter rest!* **rest assured that . . .** ⇨ assured(*adj*). **may God rest s.o's soul** (prayer for a dead person, asking God to let her/his soul feel at peace). **rest in peace** (*abbr* RIP) (wish that a dead person shall be allowed by God to rest²(6) quietly). **not rest till/until . . .** go on working

etc until . . .. **rest** (**up**)**on s.o/s.t** (**a**) ⇨ rest²(8). (**b**) (of s.o's eyes or their looks) look at s.o/s.t. (**c**) depend on s.o/s.t: *Our choice of where to go must rest on what the weather is like tomorrow.* **rest with s.o** be the responsibility(2) of s.o.

'rest ,cure *c.n* rest²(1) for the purpose of getting well, strong etc again after an illness, too much work etc.

'restful *adj* who/that helps or allows one to rest²(6); during which one can rest²(6).

'restfully *adv.* **'restfulness** *u.n.*

'rest ,home *c.n* place where people who are old and/or ill can live and be looked after.

'rest ,house *c.n* house where travellers can stay, usu in a place with no hotels etc.

'resting-,place *c.n* place where s.o/s.t is buried.

'restless *adj* (in which one is) moving about (a lot); (in which one is) not keeping still: *a restless night*; *feel restless.*

'restlessly *adv.* **'restlessness** *u.n.*

'rest ,room *c.n* (US) lavatory in a hotel, club etc for use by customers.

restaurant /'restərɒnt/ *c.n* place where one can go to have a meal sitting down. Compare café, cafeteria.

'restaurant ,car *c.n* = dining car.

restaurateur /,restərə'tɜː/ *c.n* (*French*) person who owns and (usu) runs a restaurant.

restore /rɪ'stɔː/ *v* **1** *tr.v* (often — *s.o/s.t to s.o*) give (s.o/s.t) back (to s.o). **2** *tr.v* (often — *s.o/s.t to a state, position* etc) bring or put (s.o/s.t) back into the state, position etc in which he/she/it was before: *restore s.o to full health*; *restore s.o to her/his former job*; *restore an old painting.* **3** *tr.v* bring back (s.t that had stopped (being done)): *Some people want to restore capital punishment for* terrorists.

restoration /,restə'reɪʃən/ *n* **1** *u.n* (often *the* — *of s.t* (*to s.o*)) (*formal*) act of restoring(1) (s.t) (to s.o). **2** *c/u.n* (often — *of s.o/s.t* (*to s.t*)) act or fact of restoring(2) (s.o/s.t) (to a former state or condition). **3** *c/u.n* (— *of s.t*) act or fact of restoring(3) s.t. **4** *def.n* (with capital **R**) (also *attrib*) return of King Charles II as King of England in 1660; the period(2) following this.

restrain /rɪ'streɪn/ *tr.v* (often — *s.o/s.t from* (*doing*) *s.t*) hold or keep (s.o/s.t) back (from (doing) s.t); prevent (s.o/s.t) from doing s.t.

re'strained *adj* **1** (of a person or how he/she behaves, talks etc) showing restraint(3). Opposite unrestrained. **2** (of decoration etc) avoiding all excess or exaggeration.

re'straint *n* **1** *u.n* fact of being restrained (⇨ restrain). **2** *c.n* thing that restrains (s.o/s.t). **3** *u.n* quality of showing great control over one's feelings etc. **keep/put s.o under restraint** keep/put s.o, esp s.o who is mad, in a place where he/she is restrained (⇨ restrain). **show great restraint** (**in doing s.t**) behave, speak etc in a very restrained(1) way (by doing s.t). **wage restraint** ⇨ wage. **without restraint** free(ly); without being restrained (⇨ restrain).

restrict /rɪ'strɪkt/ *tr.v* (usu — *oneself/s.o/s.t to* (*doing*) *s.t*) limit (oneself/s.o/s.t) (to (doing) s.t): *I haven't much time so I shall restrict myself to the important details.*

re'striction /rɪ'strɪkʃən/ *n* **1** *u.n* act or fact of restricting (s.o/s.t) or of being restricted.

2 *c.n* (often — *against s.t*) thing that restricts (s.t). **without restriction** without anything that restricts (one/it).

restrictive /rɪ'strɪktɪv/ *adj* that restricts s.o/s.t.

re'strictive ,clause *c.n* (*grammar*) clause that limits the meaning of its antecedent(2); relative clause: *In 'The man who is standing there is my father', 'who is standing there' is a restrictive clause. In 'My father, who is standing there, is 60', 'who is standing there' is a* non-restrictive clause.

re'strictively *adv.* **re'strictiveness** *u.n.*

re,strictive 'practices *pl.n* things done by or to trade unions etc to limit the freedom of other workers or management, e.g allowing only one trade union for all the workers.

result /rɪ'zʌlt/ *n* **1** *c/u.n* thing that happens because of s.t else, which is the cause: *The result of Jim's fall was a broken ankle.* **2** *c.n* (often *pl*) (information about) how s.o has done in s.t, e.g an examination or a football match: *The football results will be on television at 5 o'clock. What was the result of Mary's test?* **3** *c.n* answer arrived at through calculation: *'If I divide 112 by 14, what is the result?'* **as a result** for that reason. **as a result of s.t** because of s.t. **with the result that . . .** and the result(1) is, was etc that *. . .*. **without** (**much**) **result** (rather) unsuccessful(ly).

▷ *intr.v* **4** (often — *from s.t*) be a result(1) of s.t. **result in s.t** have s.t as its result(1).

resume /rɪ'zjuːm/ *v* **1** *tr/intr.v* start ((doing) s.t) again: *The governments have resumed talking/ talks* (or *Talks between the governments have resumed*). **2** *tr.v* take, get into, (s.t) again: *Please resume your seats* (i.e sit down again). *After resting, the dancers resumed their positions and began again.*

resumption /rɪ'zʌmpʃən/ *u.n.*

resumé /'rezjuːˌmeɪ/ *c.n* (*French*) (often — *of s.t*) summary(3) (of s.t).

resurrection /ˌrezə'rekʃən/ *u.n* (often *the* — *of s.o/s.t*) **1** bringing back to life or into use (of s.o/ s.t). **2** *def.n* (with capital **R**) rising again of Jesus after his death and burial.

resuscitate /rɪ'sʌsɪˌteɪt/ *tr.v* bring (a person or animal who/that is almost dead) back to life, e.g by using artificial respiration.

re,susci'tation *u.n.*

retail /'riːteɪl/ *attrib.adj/adv* **1** (sold) in small quantities to customers in a shop and not in large quantities to a shop etc: *a retail business; the retail price of s.t; buy/sell s.t retail.* Compare wholesale(1).

▷ *u.n* **2** selling of things to customers and not to shops. Compare wholesale(2).

▷ *tr.v* **3** sell (s.t) retail(1).

'retailer *c.n* person who sells things retail(1).

retain /rɪ'teɪn/ *tr.v* (*formal*) **1** keep (s.o/s.t); not lose, not give away etc (s.t): *When one pays a builder one often retains 10% for a time in case of bad work. He slipped but managed to retain his balance. A good memory retains all important information.* **2** prevent (s.t) falling, running etc out: *a retaining wall at the side of a canal.* **3** (*law*) make a payment so as to get (a lawyer, her/his services) at a future date: *We have retained the services of Mr Brown for our case next month.*

retention /rɪ'tenʃən/ *u.n* act or state of retaining (s.o/s.t).

retentive /rɪ'tentɪv/ *adj* that retains(1) things well: *a person with a retentive memory.*

re'tentively *adv.* **re'tentiveness** *u.n.*

retaliate /rɪ'tælɪˌeɪt/ *intr.v* (often — (*against s.o/ s.t*) *by doing s.t*) do s.t bad (to s.o/s.t) to pay her/him/it back for s.t bad she/he/it did to one before.

retaliation /rɪˌtælɪ'eɪʃən/ *u.n* act or fact of retaliating. **in retaliation** (**for s.t**) as a way of retaliating (because of s.t).

retard /rɪ'tɑːd/ *tr.v* (*formal*) cause (s.t) to become slower or to happen later.

retardation /ˌriːtɑː'deɪʃən/ *u.n.*

re'tarded *adj* **1** that has been retarded (⇒ retard). **2** (of a child, its development etc) making slower than average educational or emotional(1) progress.

retch /retʃ/ *intr.v* make the movements of being sick, vomiting(3), but without being able to bring anything up.

retd *written abbr* retired(1).

retention, retentive(ly/ness) ⇒ retain.

reticent /'retɪsənt/ *adj* (often — *about s.o/s.t*) (showing that one is) not willing to talk (much) (about s.o/s.t); silent (about s.o/s.t).

'reticence *u.n.* **'reticently** *adv.*

retina /'retɪnə/ *c.n* (*pl* -s, *retinae* /'retɪˌniː/) (*medical*) area of nerve endings at the back of one's eye that are sensitive to light.

retinue /'retɪˌnjuː/ *c/def.pl.n* group of people who go about with an important person to advise, protect, serve etc her/him.

retire /rɪ'taɪə/ *v* **1** *tr/intr.v* (often — (*s.o*) *from s.t*) (cause (s.o) to) stop doing a job, e.g because he/ she is old or too ill to continue: *People in our office retire at 60.* **2** *tr/intr.v* (often — (*s.o*) *from s.t* (*with s.t*)) (cause (s.o) to) stop playing in a match, competition etc, e.g because he/she is ill etc: *Our best player was forced to retire with a bad knee.* **3** *intr.v* (often — (*from s.t*) *to s.t*) leave (a place) (for another place): *After lunch the President retired to his office.* **4** *intr.v* (of armed forces) move to a position or positions further back, without being forced to do so. Compare retreat(3).

re'tired *adj* **1** (*written abbr* **retd**) who has retired (⇒ retire(1)). **2** (of a place) a long way from towns, busy roads etc.

re'tirement *c/u.n* **1** act or fact of retiring (⇒ retire(1)). **2** time after one has retired (⇒ retire(1)). **go into retirement** retire(1). **in retirement** in a state of having retired (⇒ retire(1)). **on** (**s.o's**) **retirement** when, as soon as, one/s.o retires(1).

re'tirement ,age *def/unique n* age at which one usu retires(1).

re'tiring *adj* liking, showing that s.o likes, to be alone rather than to mix with other people.

retort /rɪ'tɔːt/ *c.n* **1** (*formal*) quick, sometimes clever and/or angry reply.

▷ *tr.v* **2** (often — *that . . .*) (*formal*) answer in this way, saying (s.t, or that . . .): *'It was you who made me spill the water,' she retorted.*

retreat /rɪ'triːt/ *n* **1** *c/u.n* (often — (*from s.t*) *to s.t*) act or fact of retreating(3,4) (from s.t) (to s.t). **2** *c.n* place to which one retreats(4). **beat a** (**hasty**) **retreat** retreat(4) (quickly), usu to avoid s.o/s.t unpleasant. **in full retreat** retreating(3) without any attempt to stop. **make good one's retreat** retreat(4) successfully. **retreat into s.t** go into a

certain state in order to escape s.t unpleasant: *When the questions became too painful, she retreated into silence.*
▷ *intr.v* (often — (*from s.t*) *to s.t*) **3** (usu of armed forces) go back, usu because one is forced to do so. Compare retire(3). **4** go away, escape (from s.t unpleasant) (to s.t pleasanter): *When life in the city becomes too tiring we retreat to the country for a few days' rest.*

retribution /ˌretrɪˈbjuːʃən/ *sing/u.n* (often — *for s.t*) (*formal*) punishment (for s.t) that is deserved.

retrieve /rɪˈtriːv/ *v* **1** *tr.v* (often — *s.o/s.t from s.o/s.t*) (go and) get (s.o/s.t) back (from s.o/s.t): *I managed to retrieve my money from the hole it had fallen into. It is easy to retrieve information stored in this* computer. **2** *tr.v* save, rescue, (s.o) from danger, evil etc. **3** *tr.v* put (s.t, e.g a mistake) right. **4** *tr/intr.v* (of a dog) go and find (birds that have been shot) and bring them to s.o, usu its owner. ⇒ retriever.
re'trieval *u.n* act or fact of retrieving (1–3) (s.t). **beyond/past retrieval** too bad to be, so bad that it cannot be, retrieved (1–3).
re'triever *c.n* dog trained to retrieve(4) birds.

retrospect /ˈretrəˌspekt/ *u.n* **in retrospect** when one looks back at it, in one's memory, from a later time: *In retrospect, I am not as happy with my results as I was at the time.*
ˌretro'spective *adj* **1** that looks back in this way. **2** affecting the past as well as the present and future: *a retrospective law.*
ˌretro'spectively *adv.*

return /rɪˈtɜːn/ *attrib.adj* **1** (of a ticket, journey etc) there and back. Compare single(3). **2** (of a match etc) played after an earlier one, and usu on the other team's ground. Compare away(3), home(3).
▷ *n* **3** *c.n* (often — (*from s.o/s.t*) *to s.o/s.t*) act or fact of going back (from a place etc) to another place etc. **4** *u.n* (often *the* — *of s.t* (*to s.o*)) act or fact of giving (s.t) back (to s.o): *Kim asked for the return of the umbrella she had lent Paul.* **5** *c.n* (usu *the* — *of s.t*) coming back or starting again (of s.t): *the return of winter; the return of coughs and colds as the weather gets bad.* **6** *c.n* (often *pl*) money earned from an investment(2). **7** *c.n* official report showing money earned, number of things in store etc: *Every year I fill in my tax return.* **8** *c.n* (*informal*) return(1) ticket: *Two returns to Manchester, please.* Compare single(9). **bring in a good etc return**; **bring in good etc returns** earn a good amount of interest. Compare return(6). **by return** (**of post**) (of a letter etc sent) immediately; as soon as one receives it so that it leaves by the next post: *Please let me have the money you owe me by return.* **in return** (**for s.t**) to pay s.o back (for s.t). **on s.o's return**; **on the return of s.o/s.t** when s.o/s.t comes back.
▷ *v* **9** *intr.v* (often — (*from s.o/s.t*) *to s.o/s.t*) come/go back (from a place etc) (to another place etc). **10** *tr.v* (often — *s.o s.t*; — *s.o/s.t to s.o*) give (s.o/s.t) back (to s.o). **11** *intr.v* come, happen, again: *The holidays return surprisingly quickly.* **12** *tr.v* answer, say, (s.t): '*And the same to you!*' *he returned.* **13** *tr.v* produce (interest, a profit etc). ⇒ return(7). **14** *tr.v* make a return(7) of (s.t). **15** *tr.v* (often — *s.o* to parliament etc (*as s.t*)) (of electors) elect (s.o) (to parliament etc) (as one's

representative). **return a favour** ⇒ favour(*n*).
return s.o (**not**) **guilty**; **return a verdict** (**of** (**not**) **guilty**) (of a jury in a court of law) declare a defendant (not) guilty. **return to s.t** go back to talking, writing, about s.t. **return s.t to s.o** ⇒ return(10). **return s.t to s.t** put s.t back in/on s.t: *After using the knife he returned it to its drawer.*
re'turns *pl.n* (**wish s.o**) **many happy returns** (**of the day**) (give) good wishes to s.o on her/his birthday; (wish that s.o may have) many more birthdays in the future.

Rev *written abbr* Reverend(3).

rev /rev/ *c.n* (*informal*) revolution²(2) (⇒ revolve).

revalue /riːˈvæljuː/ *tr/intr.v* increase the value of (money, a country's currency(1) etc). Compare devalue(1).
re,valu'ation *u.n.*

reveal /rɪˈviːl/ *tr.v* (often — *s.t to s.o*) allow (s.t) to be seen, known etc (by s.o) after it has been hidden, kept secret etc. **reveal s.o/s.t as**, **to be**, **s.t** show that s.o/s.t is s.t after this was not known before.
re'vealing *adj* **1** that allows things that are not usu seen to be seen: *a revealing blouse.* **2** that reveals s.t that was not known before: *a revealing speech by a politician.*
revelation /ˌrevəˈleɪʃən/ *n* **1** *u.n* (often *the* — *of s.t, that . . .*) fact or act of revealing (⇒ reveal) (s.t). **2** *c.n* (often — *about s.o/s.t*) thing that is revealed (about s.o/s.t).

revel /ˈrevl/ (-*ll*-, US -*l*-) *intr.v* (*old use*) enjoy oneself dancing, eating, drinking etc. **revel in** (**doing**) **s.t** enjoy (doing) s.t very much.
'reveller *c.n* (US **'reveler**) person who revels.
'revelries *pl.n.* **'revelry** *u.n.*
'revels *pl.n* examples of revelling (⇒ revel).

revenge /rɪˈvendʒ/ *sing/u.n* **1** (often — (*on s.o*) *for s.t*) bad thing one does (to s.o) to pay her/him back (for s.t bad she/he did to one before). **give s.o her/his revenge** allow s.o whom one has beaten in a match etc to try to beat one in another. **have one's revenge** (**on s.o**) (**for s.t**) do s.t that gives one revenge(1) (in return for s.t). **in revenge** (**for s.t**) as a revenge(1) (for s.t). **out of revenge** (**for s.t**) because one wants to have one's revenge(1) (for s.t). **take revenge** (**on s.o**) (**for s.t**) have one's revenge (on s.o) (for s.t).
▷ *tr.v* **2** do s.t to get one's revenge(1) for (s.t). **3** do s.t to get one's revenge(1) for s.t done to (s.o): *He joined the army to revenge his brother who had been killed by the enemy the year before.* **revenge oneself on s.o/s.t** (**for s.t**) do s.t that gives one one's revenge(1) (for s.t s.o did before).

revenue /ˈrevɪˌnjuː/ *u.n* money that one receives; income. Compare expenditure(2).

reverence /ˈrevərəns/ *n* **1** *sing/u.n* (often — *for s.o/s.t*) fact or feeling of (great) respect (for s.o/s.t). **hold s.o/s.t in** (**great**) **reverence** feel great reverence(1) for s.o/s.t. **his/your reverence**; **your/their reverences** (*old use*) (way of addressing or speaking about a priest).
▷ *tr.v* **2** (*formal*) respect (s.o/s.t) very much.
'reverend *adj* **1** (*formal*) deserving reverence(1). **2** (*formal*) who is a priest: *There is a reverend gentleman at the door.* **3** (with capital **R**); (*written abbr* Rev) (title used in addressing or talking about a priest or the head of a monastery or convent): *The Reverend*

Peter Jones is here. Good morning, Reverend Father/Mother.
▷ *n* (with capital **R**) **4** *def.n* priest: *Where's the Reverend gone?* **5** *unique n* (way of addressing a priest): *Good morning, Reverend.*
'reverent *adj* feeling, showing, reverence(1).
'reverently *adv.*
reverse /rɪ'vɜːs/ *adj* **1** opposite (of s.t); (towards/at the) back: *the reverse side of a piece of cloth*; *reverse gear*(1) *on a car.* Opposite forward(2). **in reverse order** starting from the end instead of the beginning: *I shall read the names and marks of those who took the test in reverse order.*
▷ *n* **2** *unique n* (often *be in, get into, put s.t into* —) reverse(1) gear(1) on a car. **3** *def.n* (often *the* — *of s.t*) opposite side or back (of s.t): *the reverse of a piece of cloth.* **4** *def.n* (often *the* — *of s.t*) opposite (of s.t or of what . . .); the other way round: *You can say all dogs are animals but not the reverse. What he said happened was the exact reverse of what really happened.* **5** *def.n* side of a coin that does not show the head of the Queen etc. Opposite obverse. **6** *c.n* (often — *for s.o/s.t*) defeat or piece of bad fortune (for s.o/s.t): *She suffered many reverses.*
▷ *v* **7** *tr/intr.v* (cause (a car etc) to) go backwards: *I always reverse (the car) into the garage.* **8** *tr.v* turn (s.t) over so that the other side is on top or in front: *When I have to ride in the rain on my motorbike I reverse my coat.* **9** *tr.v* change the order of (s.t) to the opposite: *If you reverse the letters in 'lived' you get 'devil'.* **10** *tr.v* change (a judgment in a law court etc) into the opposite. ***reverse (the) charges*** ⇨ charge(n).
re'versal *c/u.n* (often — *of s.t*) act or fact of reversing(8–10) (s.t).
re,verse 'charge ,call *c.n* telephone call in which one reverses (the) charges (⇨ charge(n)).
re'versible *adj* that can be reversed(7–10). Opposite irreversible.
revert /rɪ'vɜːt/ *intr.v* **1** (usu — *to* (*doing*) *s.t*) return to a former state or practice. **2** (usu — *to s.o*) (*law*) return to the ownership (of s.o). **3** (usu — *to s.t*) go back to speaking (about s.t). ***revert to type*** ⇨ type(n).
reversion /rɪ'vɜːʃən/ *u.n* (usu — *to s.t*) act or fact of reverting(1) (to s.t). ***reversion to type*** ⇨ type(n).
review /rɪ'vju:/ *n* **1** *c.n* (usu careful and thorough) examination (of s.t that happened or was done in the past). **2** *c.n* parade(3) and formal inspection of armed forces etc for show rather than for serious purposes. **3** *c.n* magazine etc that has articles about current events, new plays, books etc. **4** *c.n* article in a magazine etc giving opinions about a new play, book etc. **5** *u.n* (also *attrib*) fact of reviewing(8) or being reviewed: Reviewers *get free review copies of new books for review.* **be/come under review** be, or start to be, reviewed(6,8).
▷ *tr.v* **6** carry out a review(1) of (s.t). **7** carry out a review(2) of (soldiers etc). **8** *tr/intr.v* write a review(4) of /reviews (of (a book or books etc)).
re'viewer *c.n* person who writes one or more reviews(4).
revise /rɪ'vaɪz/ *v* **1** *tr.v* read (s.t) and make any changes to (it) that one thinks necessary. **2** *tr.v* change (one's opinion, ways of doing things etc)

because one has new and better information than before. **3** *tr/intr.v* (often — *for s.t*) prepare (for an examination etc) by going through (what one has learnt before).
revision /rɪ'vɪʒən/ *n* **1** *c/u.n* act or work of revising(1,2) (s.t). **2** *c.n* (usu — *of s.t*) revised(2) version (of a speech, piece of writing, etc). **3** *u.n* (often *for s.t*) work of revising(3) (for an examination etc).
revitalize, -ise /ri:'vaɪtə,laɪz/ *tr.v* give (s.o/s.t) energy(1), health etc after being in a bad state.
revive /rɪ'vaɪv/ *v* **1** *tr/intr.v* (of a person or animal) (cause (s.o/s.t) to) become conscious again. **2** *tr/intr.v* (of a plant etc) (cause (s.t) to) become healthy, strong etc again: *You can revive those flowers by watering them.* **3** *tr/intr.v* (cause (s.t) to) start being done, fashionable etc again: *We are trying to revive the old dances of this area.*
re'vival *c/u.n* (often — *of s.t*) act or fact of reviving(3) (s.t).
revoke /rɪ'vəʊk/ *tr.v* (*formal*) stop (s.t, often a law) being in operation any more; cancel(1) (s.t).
revocation /,revə'keɪʃən/ *c/u.n.*
revolt /rɪ'vəʊlt/ *n* **1** *c/u.n* (often — *against s.o/s.t*) (sometimes violent) refusal to continue obeying (s.o, e.g the ruler or the government). **in revolt** **(a)** revolting (⇨ revolt(2)). **(b)** feeling revolted.
▷ *v* **2** *intr.v* (often — *against s.o/s.t*) start a revolt(1) (to try to destroy the power of s.o/s.t over one). **3** *tr.v* make (s.o) feel revolted. ***revolt against/at/from s.t*** feel revolted by s.t.
re'volted *adj* feeling sick, disgusted, shocked (and angry).
re'volting *adj* who/that makes one feel revolted.
revolution[1] /,revə'lu:ʃən/ *n* **1** *c/u.n* (time of a) big revolt(1), sometimes including the overthrow(1) of the ruler, government etc one is revolting(2) against. **2** *c.n* (often — *in s.t*) very big, or sometimes complete, change (in s.t): *The invention of the petrol engine brought about a revolution in* transport(4). Compare revolution[2] (⇨ revolve).
,revo'lutionary *adj* **1** of or referring to (a) revolution[1](1). **2** causing a revolution[1](2).
▷ *c.n* (*pl -ies*) **3** person who supports (and takes part in) (a) revolution[1](1).
revolutionize, -ise /,revə'lu:ʃə,naɪz/ *tr.v* change (s.t) greatly or completely. ⇨ revolution[1](2).
revulsion /rɪ'vʌlʃən/ *c/u.n* (often — *against s.o/s.t*) feeling of being revolted (by s.o/s.t).
revolve /rɪ'vɒlv/ *v* **1** *tr/intr.v* (cause (s.o/s.t) to) turn round and round (a point in the centre): *The earth revolves (on its* axis(1)). **2** *intr.v* (of thoughts in one's mind) be thought of one after the other. **3** *tr.v* (formal) think about (s.t) for some time. ***revolve about/round s.t*** move in a circle round s.t: *The earth revolves round the sun.* ***revolve around s.t*** have s.t as its main interest or subject: *When I'm hungry my thoughts tend to revolve around food.*
revolution[2] /,revə'lu:ʃən/ *n* **1** *c/u.n* (example of) revolving (⇨ revolve(1)) (around s.t) (once). **2** *c.n* (*informal rev*) (of a wheel in a machine etc) single revolution[2](1). **(at a speed of) 100** etc **revolutions a/per minute, second** etc (*abbr rpm, rps* etc) (at a speed of) 100 etc complete

revolutions[2](1) during each minute, second etc. Compare revolution[1] (⇒ revolt).

re'volving *adj* that revolves(1): *revolving doors.*

revolver /rɪ'vɒlvə/ *c.n* kind of small gun held in one's hand which can fire several (often six) shots because it has a part that revolves(1) bringing a new bullet into position for firing each time.

revue /rɪ'vju:/ *n* **1** *c.n* amusing play that does not have much of a story, or that consists of a number of separate scenes, and that deals with current events, fashions etc. **2** *u.n* shows of this kind in general.

revulsion ⇒ revolt.

reward /rɪ'wɔ:d/ *n* **1** *c/u.n* (often — *for* s.t) (good or sometimes bad) thing given to, or received by, s.o (in return for s.t done): *Her reward for 25 years of public service was to be made a* baroness(2). *All the reward I got for having tried to help was a broken arm.* **2** *c.n* (often *a* — of £10 etc *(for (doing)* s.t)*)* money etc offered for bringing back s.t that has been lost/stolen, for information etc.

▷ *tr.v* **3** (often — *s.o with* s.t *(for (doing)* s.t)*)* give (s.o) a reward(1,2) (for s.t he/she has done). **4** (often — *s.t with* s.t) give or do s.t as a reward(1) for (s.t): *All his work was rewarded with nothing but criticism.*

re'warding *adj* that gives or brings a good reward(1), usu in the form of satisfaction and happiness. Opposite unrewarding.

re'wards *pl.n* (often *the* — *of* s.t) rewarding things.

Rex /reks/ *unique n* (*abbr* R) **1** (title put after the name of the King when he is the ruler: *George Rex*; *GR*. Compare Regina(1). **2** (used in lawsuits when the King is the ruler) the State(3); the Crown(2): *Rex v Smith* (i.e the plaintiff is the State, and the defendant is s.o called Smith). Compare Regina(2).

rhetoric /'retərɪk/ *u.n* **1** art of speaking, or sometimes writing, in ways that persuade and impress(2) people. **2** (*derog*) things said or written that seem wonderful but are really dishonest or without (much) meaning.

rhetorical /rɪ'tɒrɪkl/ *adj* **1** of or referring to rhetoric(1). **2** showing or using rhetoric(2).

rhe'torically *adv.*

rhe,torical 'question *c.n* question that is asked not to get information but to produce a rhetorical(1) effect.

rheumatism /'ru:mətɪzəm/ *u.n* kind of disease that causes pains and inflammation in one's joints.

rheumatic /ru:'mætɪk/ *adj* **1** of, referring to, having, rheumatism.

▷ *c.n* **2** person who suffers from rheumatism.

rheu,matic 'fever *u.n* serious form of rheumatism that can affect the heart too.

rheumatoid arthritis /,ru:mətɔɪd ɑ:'θraɪtɪs/ *u.n* chronic(1) disease causing inflammation of the joints.

rhino /'raɪnəʊ/ *c.n* (*pl* -(s)) (*informal*) rhinoceros.

rhinoceros /raɪ'nɒsərəs/ *c.n* (*pl* -(es)) kind of big very heavy animal with a thick skin and one or two horns on its nose, found in Africa or Asia.

rhododendron /,rəʊdə'dendrən/ *c.n* (also *attrib*) kind of large evergreen(1) bush that produces big bunches of red, pink etc flowers.

rhombus /'rɒmbəs/ *c.n* (*pl* -es or, less usu,

rhombi /'rɒmbaɪ/) (*mathematics*) parallelogram with four equal sides.

rhubarb /'ru:bɑ:b/ *u.n* (also *attrib*) kind of vegetable with big leaves that have thick, usu red, stems; these stems are cooked with sugar and eaten.

rhyme /raɪm/ *n* **1** *c.n* short not serious poem in which the lines rhyme(4). **2** *c.n* (often — *for* s.t) word that rhymes (with another): *'Earn' and 'burn' are rhymes. Is there a rhyme for 'curiosity'?* **3** *u.n* practice of using rhymes(4) in poetry: *Rhyme did not enter English literature until about 700 years ago.* **in rhyme** written with rhyming(4)lines. **rhyme or reason** sense(3): *There often seems to be no rhyme or reason in what small children do.*

▷ *v* **4** *intr.v* (often — *with* s.t) (of words or lines in a poem etc) end with stressed(4) syllables (followed by one or more unstressed ones) that sound the same except at the beginning, e.g 'house', 'mouse'; 'money'; 'funny'; 'fearfully', 'tearfully'. **5** *tr.v* (often — *s.t and/with* s.t) put (a word) with another one so that they rhyme(4): *You can rhyme 'too' with 'through'.*

rhythm /'rɪðəm/ *n* (often *the* — *of* s.t) **1** *u.n* way in which s.t happens again and again at regular intervals(3) of time, e.g in music, speaking, moving one's body: *The steady rhythm of the rain falling on the roof soon sent the child to sleep. The life of the farmer is governed by the rhythm of the seasons.* **2** *c.n* example of rhythm(1): *I like the rhythm of this poem.*

rhythmic /'rɪðmɪk/ *adj* (also **'rhythmical**) that has (a) rhythm.

'rhythmically *adv.*

rib /rɪb/ *n* **1** *c.n* curved bone joined to the backbone of a person or an animal and coming round to the front of her/his/its chest. **2** *c.n* rib(1) (of beef[1] etc) with meat on it which is used as food. **3** *c.n* thing like a rib(1) but made of wood etc and used to strengthen s.t, e.g an umbrella or a boat. **4** *c.n* thing like a rib(1) that is higher than the surface of the thing of which it is a part: *Most leaves have ribs that end in their stems.* **5** *c/u.n* part of s.t knitted with some columns of stitches that are higher than the surface, e.g round the bottom of a jumper: *knitted in rib stitch.* **dig/ poke s.o in the ribs** push s.o's side with one's finger, elbow etc to attract her/his attention.

▷ *tr/intr.v* **6** knit in rib(5).

ribbed *adj* (often of s.t knitted) having ribs(5).

ribbon /'rɪbn/ *n* **1** *c/u.n* (piece of) fine material woven into a long narrow band and used for decoration, for tying up parcels prettily etc. **2** *c.n* ribbon(1) to which a medal(1) etc is fixed. **3** *c.n* thing like a ribbon(1) but used for a different purpose: *a typewriter ribbon* (a ribbon(1) with ink in it that produces marks on paper when a typewriter key hits it). **4** *c.n* (often — *of* s.t) strip (of s.t, e.g cloud) that looks like a ribbon(1). **cut to ribbons** ⇒ cut(*v*). **in ribbons** torn into narrow strips: *After fighting their way through the forest, their clothes were in ribbons.*

,ribbon de'velopment *u.n* (building of) houses etc along the sides of a road that leads out of a town or village.

rice /raɪs/ *u.n* kind of cereal(2) forming the main food in many areas in Asia; the grains are usu polished until they are white, and then boiled. *Brown rice is rice that has not been polished.*

'rice ,paper *u.n* 1 thin sheets of rice that look like paper but can be eaten. 2 real paper that looks like rice paper(1) and is used mostly for making pictures on.

,rice 'pudding *c/u.n* kind of pudding(1) made by cooking rice, milk, sugar, eggs etc together.

rich /rɪtʃ/ *adj* 1 (of a person) having a lot of money, possessions etc. 2 (of a thing) expensive. 3 (of food) having a lot of fat, cream etc in it. 4 (of land) containing things that enable one to grow very good crops. 5 (of a sound, colour, smell etc) full(7); strong in a beautiful way. **strike it rich** suddenly win, gain, inherit(1) etc a lot of money.

▷ *def.pl.n* 6 rich(1) people.

'riches *pl.n* (often the — of s.t) wealth, rich possessions or rich things (to be found s.w): *the mineral riches of Northern Canada.*

'richly *adv* 1 in a rich(2,5) way. 2 very much: *a richly decorated church*; *richly deserved punishment.*

'richness *u.n.*

rick[1] /rɪk/ *c.n* big pile of straw or hay, esp one shaped like a small house. ⇨ haystack.

rick[2] /rɪk/ *tr.v* twist (one of one's joints, e.g one's ankle or neck) accidentally and often painfully.

rickety /'rɪkɪtɪ/ *adj* (-ier, -iest) (of furniture etc) having loose joints so that it is not steady or strong.

rickshaw /'rɪkʃɔ:/ *c.n* kind of small cart for one or two passengers; it is usu either pulled by a person or driven by s.o cycling.

rid /rɪd/ *v* (-dd-, *p.t.p.p* rid) **rid oneself/s.o/s.t of s.o/s.t** free oneself/s.o/s.t from s.o/s.t, sometimes by destroying her/him/it or by driving her/him/it away: *How can we rid our house of mosquitoes?* **be rid of s.o/s.t** be in a state of having rid oneself of s.o/s.t: *She was very glad to be rid of all duties for a week.* **get rid of s.o/s.t** rid oneself of s.o/s.t.

riddance /'rɪdəns/ *sing/u.n* (informal) getting rid of s.o/s.t. **Good riddance!** I am glad to be rid of her/him/it!

ridden /'rɪdn/ *p.p* of ride.

riddle /'rɪdl/ *c.n* 1 puzzling question or problem, often of an amusing kind: *'Ask me a riddle.' 'All right, why do some birds fly across the world each year?' 'I don't know.' 'Because it's too far to walk.'* 2 (often the — of s.t) mystery (about s.t); thing that is very difficult or impossible to understand (about s.t).

ride /raɪd/ *c.n* 1 (often go for, have etc, a — in/on s.t) example of riding in etc (s.t). ⇨ ride in (s.t). 2 path, often through a wood, which has a soft surface on which one can ride horses comfortably. **take s.o for a ride (a)** ⇨ ride(2). **(b)** (fig) cheat s.o.

▷ *v* (*p.t* rode /rəʊd/, *p.p* ridden /'rɪdn/) 3 *tr/intr.v* move along while sitting on (a horse, bicycle etc). **ride in s.t** travel inside s.t, e.g a car, ship or plane. **ride on s.o/s.t (a)** ⇨ ride(1). **(b)** sit on s.o/s.t, e.g s.o's shoulders, as if on a horse. **ride smoothly** (of a car etc) travel smoothly etc even over rough roads. **ride up** (of a piece of clothing) move up into an uncomfortable position, usu as a result of the person's movements: *These trousers ride up between my legs.*

'rider *c.n* person who rides horses, motorbikes etc.

'riderless *adj* not having a rider(1): *Riderless horses are a danger in a race.*

'riding *u.n* = horse riding.

'riding ,breeches *pl.n* breeches specially designed for riding horses in.

'riding 'crop *c.n* ⇨ crop(4).

ridge /rɪdʒ/ *c.n* line where two (sloping) surfaces meet at the top: *a ridge of mountains*; *the ridge of a roof/tent*; *the ridge of one's mouth*; *a ridge of high/low pressure* (i.e where there is a change in the weather).

ridicule /'rɪdɪ,kju:l/ *u.n* 1 making fun of, laughing at, s.o/s.t in a nasty way. **hold s.o/s.t up to ridicule** try to make people ridicule(2) s.o/s.t. **lay oneself open to ridicule** behave, talk etc in a way that makes it likely that people will ridicule(2) one.

▷ *tr.v* 2 treat (s.o/s.t) with ridicule(1).

ridiculous /rɪ'dɪkjʊləs/ *adj* (derog) deserving ridicule(1); stupid; foolish; silly.

ri'diculously *adv*. ri'diculousness *u.n.*

riff-raff /'rɪf ,ræf/ *def.pl.n* (derog) rabble(2).

rifle /'raɪfl/ *c.n* kind of long gun that one puts to one's shoulder and that fires bullets. Compare airgun, shotgun.

rig /rɪg/ *c.n* 1 (often with a noun coming before, to show the purpose of the thing) thing built for doing s.t: *an oil rig*; *a drilling rig.*

▷ *tr.v* (-gg-) 2 *tr.v* arrange (s.t, e.g an election) in such a way that one will win by cheating. **rig s.o (out) (in/with s.t)** dress s.o in, supply s.o with, (certain) clothes. **rig s.o out as s.t** make s.o look like s.t by putting suitable clothes on her/him. **rig s.t up** (informal) build s.t roughly and usu quickly, so that it will last until one can build s.t better: *It's starting to rain — let's rig up a place to spend the night.*

'rigging *u/def.n* ropes, sails etc of a ship.

'rig-out *c.n* (informal) clothes s.o is wearing.

right[1] /raɪt/ *adj* Opposite wrong. 1 (usu pred) correct; true: *'Are you Tom's sister?' 'Yes, that's (quite) right.'* *Would I be right in thinking that Jackie lives here? You were right to bring your own food. This is the right side of the cloth.* 2 (often — to do s.t) morally good or proper (to do s.t); as he/she/it ought to be: *right behaviour. Would it be right to take this without asking?* 3 (most) successful or suitable: *the right way to prepare for this examination.* **(as) right as rain** ⇨ rain(*n*). **get on the right side of s.o** ⇨ side(*n*). **get s.t right** get the correct answer to s.t; do s.t successfully. **keep on the right side of the law** ⇨ law. **on the right side of 40** etc ⇨ side(*n*). **put/set s.o/s.t right** correct s.o/s.t; give s.o the correct information etc; arrange s.t in the correct position etc. **right in one's/the head/mind**; **in one's right mind** (informal) sensible; not mad; sane(1). **Rightoh!**; **Rightyouare!** (informal) Yes, all right! **right side out** ⇨ side(*n*).

▷ *adv* 4 in a/the right[1](1) way; correctly: *Did you guess it right?* Opposite wrong(4). 5 straight: *Now go right up to bed without any more arguing!* 6 (informal) exactly: *The train should be arriving right now.* *'Where are you, Mary?' 'Right here, Mum!'* 7 the whole way; completely: *If you make a mistake, you have to go right back and start again.* 8 in a morally right[1](2) way: *If you treat people right, they will treat you right too.* **9** in the right[1](3) way: *If you do it right, that bottle opens easily.* **10** (with capital **R**, used in some titles(2)) very: *the Right Honourable member for Oxford East; the Right Reverend the Bishop of Portsmouth.* **11** (*informal*) all right; yes; I agree: *'Catch hold of this rope, will you?' 'Right.'* **all right** ⇒ all(*adv*). **right away/off** immediately; at once; without waiting. **right enough** (**a**) good enough. (**b**) = sure enough. **serve s.o right** ⇒ serve(*n*). **too right** ⇒ too.

▷ *n* **12** *u.n* what is right[1](2): *A baby doesn't know the difference between right and wrong.* Opposite wrong(5). **13** *c/u.n* (often **have a/the — to** (**do**) *s.t*) fair claim (to (do) s.t); claim based on law or on accepted moral ideas (to (do) s.t): *What right have you to refuse to help your mother?* ⇒ rights. **as of right** because it is a right[1](13) under the law. **in one's own right** not through anyone else but directly: *Joan is a* viscountess(2) *in her own right.* **in the right** right[1](1) in what one has said etc. Opposite in the wrong.

▷ *tr.v* **14** put (s.t) right: *right a wrong.* **15** put (s.t) upright after it has fallen down.

'right ˌangle *c.n* (*mathematics*) angle of 90°. **at right angles** (**to s.t**) at an angle of 90° (to s.t).

ˌright-ˌangled 'triangle *c.n* (*mathematics*) triangle(1) one of the angles of which is a right angle.

'rightful *adj* lawful. **'rightfully** *adv.* **'rightfulness** *u.n.*

'rightly *adv* **1** in a right[1](1–3) way. **2** (*informal*) in a way that one would be sure about: *I don't rightly know what time I got here.*

'rightness *u.n.*

ˌright of 'way *n* (*pl* rights of way) **1** *c.n* right to walk, drive etc on a path that crosses s.o else's land. **2** *c.n* path on which one has a right of way(1). **3** *u/def.n* (of vehicles on a certain road etc) right[1](3) to go before others on other roads etc.

rights *pl.n* rights[1](13) in society generally. ⇒ civil rights, human rights. **by rights** lawfully. **put/set s.o/s.t to rights** = put/set s.o/s.t right. **stand on one's rights** insist(5) on having one's rights; refuse to give up one's rights. **the rights and wrongs of s.t** the truth about s.t. **within one's rights** not doing, demanding etc more than what are one's rights: *I'm within my rights to complain.*

right² /raɪt/ *adj* Opposite left. **1** (*attrib*) that is on or towards the side of a person's body opposite to the left one in which the heart is; of the side of s.o/s.t that is towards the east when one faces north: *I write with my right hand. If you do a right turn here you will get to the station.* **2** (*attrib*) worn on a right²(1) hand or foot: *a right shoe.* **3** (usu *attrib*) often with capital **R**) (in politics) (in favour) of the Conservatives(3) in the UK, the Republicans(5) in the US etc, and therefore against Socialism, Communism(2) etc.

▷ *adv* Opposite left. **4** in or towards a right²(1,3) direction: *Turn right here.* **right and left**; **right, left and centre** in every direction; everywhere: *Our company's losing orders and money right and left.*

▷ *n* Opposite left. **5** *def.n* right²(1) side or direction: *Keep to the right as you go down these steps. The*

first turning on the right will take you straight to the station. **6** *c/def.n* (blow with one's) right²(1) hand: *A right to the jaw knocked him out.* **7** *def/def.pl.n* (usu with capital **R**) (in politics) people, parties etc who are right²(3).

ˌright 'hand *c.n* **1** ⇒ right²(1). **2** person who is one's best and most important helper.

ˌright-'hand *attrib.adj* on, to, the right(5): *the right-hand drawer. If you do a right-hand turn here you will get to the station.*

ˌright-ˌhand 'man *c.n* = right hand(2).

ˌright-'handed *adj* using one's right²(1) hand (more than one's left): *Most people are right-handed.*

ˌright 'wing *n* (**'right-ˌwing** when *attrib*) **1** *c.n* (in football etc) (player who is in the) position on the extreme right²(5) of the front line of players. **2** *def/def.pl.n* (often with capital **R** and **W**) (extreme) right²(7).

ˌright-'winger *c.n* person holding right²(3) views.

rigid /'rɪdʒɪd/ *adj* **1** very stiff; that does not bend (easily). **2** (of a person, character etc) who/that does not let herself/himself/itself be changed (at all easily).

ri'gidity *u.n.*

'rigidly *adv.* **rigidly against**, **opposed to**, **s.o/s.t** very strongly against s.o/s.t.

rigour /'rɪgə/ *n* (US **'rigor**) **1** *u.n* severe/harsh(1) treatment (caused or given by s.t). **2** *c.n* (usu *pl*) severe/harsh(2) conditions (of s.t): *the rigours of a northern winter.* **3** *u.n* (*formal*) strict following of rules (in s.t).

'rigorous *adj* showing rigour(1,2). **'rigorously** *adv.* **'rigorousness** *u.n.*

rig-out ⇒ rig.

rim /rɪm/ *c.n* outer edge of s.t, usu s.t round: *It is often not easy to get a tyre on to the rim of a wheel.*

'rimless *adj* that does not have a rim: *rimless spectacles.*

rind /raɪnd/ *c/u.n* thick, usu hard, outside of some fruits, cheeses etc.

ring¹ /rɪŋ/ *n* **1** *c.n* (an arrangement or thing in the shape of a) circle: *a key ring* (for holding one's keys together); *a ring around an address* (i.e a circle drawn around it). **2** *c.n* ring¹(1) worn on a finger as a decoration or to show s.t, e.g that one is engaged(1) (*an* engagement(2) *ring*), or married (*a wedding ring*), or what family one belongs to (*a signet ring*): *a diamond ring*; *a gold ring.* **3** *c.n* piece of round metal, or a coil, (as on a cooker). **4** *c/def.n* enclosure or space, whether circular or not, where people and/or animals perform, or animals or things are shown: *a boxing ring*; *a circus ring*; *a show ring.* **5** *c/def.n* group of people who work together to control s.t, often dishonestly: *One usually finds the ring at all big* auctions(1). **in a ring** in the shape of a ring¹(1): *sitting in a ring round a fire.*

▷ *tr.v* **6** make/put a ring¹(1) in/round (s.t): *During the match, thousands of people ringed the field. Ring anything you want in this list* (i.e. draw a circle around it) *and I'll try to get it for you.* **ring s.o/s.t in** (**with s.t**) surround s.o/s.t (with s.t).

'ring ˌbinder *c.n* looseleaf notebook that has (usu) metal rings(1) to hold its pages together.

'ring ˌfinger *c/def.n* finger on which one puts

one's wedding ring, in the UK the third finger of the left hand.

'ring,leader *c.n* person who leads (a group of bad people).

ringlet /'rɪŋlɪt/ *c.n* long curl of hair that hangs down.

'ring ,road *c.n* road round a town that allows traffic to avoid having to go through it.

'ring,side *adj/adv/def.n* (of a seat etc) (close to the) side of a boxing etc ring'(4).

'ring ,spanner *c.n* spanner that has a hollow end that fits over a nut(2) or bolt²(2).

ring² /rɪŋ/ *c.n* **1** sound (like that) of a bell: *the ring of coins on a glass table top*; *the ring of children's happy voices*. **give s.o a ring** (*informal*) telephone s.o (**have**) **a/the ring of truth** *etc* sound true etc.

▷ *v* (*p.t* rang /ræŋ/, *p.p* rung /rʌŋ/) **2** *tr/intr.v* (cause (a bell) to) make a musical sound: *I can hear the telephone ringing*. **3** *tr/intr.v* (often — (s.o) *up*) telephone (s.o): *I'll ring (Robert)* (*up*) *and ask him to come*. **4** *tr.v* (of a clock) make a ringing sound to give (the time): *The church clock rang a quarter to five*. Compare strike(9). **5** *intr.v* (often — *in s.o's ears*) give an echoing(1) sound like that of a bell (in one's ears): *If you take too much of that medicine, it will make your ears ring. The team left the field with the cheers of the crowd ringing in their ears*.

ring at s.t ring²(2) s.t, usu several times.

ring (s.o) back telephone s.o again later: *I'm sorry, I can't talk to you just now; I'll ring (you) back in ten minutes*.

ring the changes (on s.t) ⇒ change(*n*).

ring down the curtain (on) ⇒ curtain(*n*).

ring false/true sound as if it is (not) true.

ring for s.o/s.t ring²(2) so that s.o/s.t will come, be brought etc.

ring hollow ⇒ hollow(*adj*).

ring off (when telephoning) finish one's call by putting the receiver down.

ring out (of a person's voice etc) be heard loudly and clearly.

ring (s.o/s.t) up telephone (s.o/s.t).

rink /rɪŋk/ *c.n* **1** (also **'ice ,rink**) ice surface made for skating on. **2** smooth hard surface made for roller-skating on.

rinse /rɪns/ *c/u.n* **1** (often *give s.t a* —) example of rinsing(3). **2** liquid used for colouring a person's hair.

▷ *tr.v* **3** (often — *s.t out* (*in/with s.t*)) wash (clothes, one's mouth etc) (with clean water) to get rid of dirt, soap, toothpaste etc. **rinse s.t down** (with s.t) make it easier to swallow s.t by drinking (s.t) with it. **rinse s.t out (of s.t)** remove s.t, e.g soap, (from s.t) by rinsing(3).

riot /'raɪət/ *n* **1** *c.n* noisy dangerous and often violent public disturbance by a crowd. **2** *sing.n* (*informal*) very funny and popular happening or person: *Susan's party was a riot; we all had great fun*. **a riot of colour** a mass of different colours, usu not arranged in any special way. **put down a riot** stop a crowd from rioting(3). **run riot** (a) riot(3). (b) (of plants, esp weeds) grow without any control.

▷ *intr.v* **3** take part in a riot(1).

'rioter *c.n* person who is rioting(3).

'riotous *adj* **1** wild and disorderly(2). ⇒ riot(1). **2** enjoyably noisy and exciting. ⇒ riot(2).

'riotously *adv*. **'riotousness** *u.n*.

RIP /ˌɑːr ˌaɪ 'piː/ *abbr* rest in peace (⇒ rest²).

rip /rɪp/ *c.n* **1** (often — *in s.t*) tear²(1) or cut, usu a long one, (in s.t). **2** area of rough, sometimes dangerous, water caused by the meeting of two currents. ⇒ riptide.

▷ *v* (-pp-) **3** *tr.v* (often — *s.t in half/two*; — *s.t in(to) pieces*) tear²(2) (s.t) quickly, violently and intentionally (in half etc). **4** *tr.v* (usu — *s.t on s.t*) tear²(2,3) (s.t) accidentally (on s.t): *I ripped my coat on some wire*. **5** *intr.v* become torn in this way. **rip s.t from s.o/s.t**; **rip s.t off (s.o/s.t)** remove s.t (from s.o/s.t) quickly and violently. **rip s.o/s.t off** (*fig; informal*) cheat or rob s.o/s.t. **rip s.t open** open s.t by ripping(3) it. **rip s.t up** tear²(2) s.t into pieces by ripping(3) it.

'rip,tide *c.n* tide that produces a rip(2).

ripe /raɪp/ *adj* **1** (of fruit, corn etc) ready for picking or cutting and eating. Opposite unripe. ⇒ overripe. **2** (of cheese, wine etc) ready to be eaten or drunk. ⇒ overripe. **3** (of a person's knowledge etc) mature(1); fully developed; experienced. (**reach**) **a ripe old age** (of a person) (become) old. **ripe for s.t** ready or suitable for s.t. **ripe in s.t** (*formal*) having plenty of s.t, e.g experience. **the time is ripe (for s.t)** ⇒ time(*n*).

'ripely *adv*.

'ripen *tr/intr.v* (cause (s.t) to) become ripe.

'ripeness *u.n*.

ripple /'rɪpl/ *c.n* **1** gentle movements up and down like/of small waves (on water, a field of grass etc). **2** mark made on sand by a ripple(1) of water. **3** sound of or like (that made by) a ripple(1): *the gentle ripple of a stream. A ripple of laughter ran through the audience*.

▷ *v* **4** *tr/intr.v* (cause (s.t, e.g water or a field of grass) to) have ripples(1,2). **5** *intr.v* make the sound of a ripple(3).

rise /raɪz/ *n* **1** *c/u.n* (often — *in s.t*) upward movement (of s.t) in space, amount, rank, importance etc: *a rise in prices; the rise and fall of political parties*. Opposite fall(2). **2** *c.n* increase in height: *You go up a small rise and our house is at the top*. **3** *c.n* higher piece of land; hill: *Our house is on top of the rise*. **4** *c.n* (usu *get, give s.o, a* —) (*informal*) increase in pay. ⇒ raise(1). **get/take a rise out of s.o** (**by doing s.t**) (*fig; informal*) intentionally make s.o angry, make her/him do s.t silly etc, (by doing s.t). ⇒ rise(16). **give rise to s.t** (*formal*) cause s.t (to happen).

▷ *intr.v* (*p.t* rose /rəʊz/, *p.p* risen /'rɪzn/) **5** go up, get higher, in position, amount, rank, importance etc. Opposite fall(2). **6** (of the sun, the moon or a star) come up above the horizon. Opposite set²(14). ⇒ sunrise. **7** go up to a higher level: *The river/tide is rising. Their voices rose* (i.e became louder, or reached a higher pitch'(4)) *as they became angrier*. **8** get up from one's bed. Opposite go to bed (⇒ bed(*n*)). **9** (often — *up*) stand up. ⇒ arise(2). **10** (*formal*) (of people at a meeting, in a court of law etc) end one's work, usu for a rest. **11** slope upwards: *The road rises sharply here so you'd better push your bicycle*. **12** (of a river) start (s.w): *The Amazon rises in the Andes*. **13** (of bread, a cake etc before or while it is baked) swell because of the yeast in it. **14** (of a person's feelings) become happier. **15** (of wind, a storm) become stronger. **16** (often — *to s.t*) become angry, or behave in a silly etc

way, (because of s.t). ⇨ get/take a rise out of s.o.
rise above/over s.o/s.t (a) ⇨ rise(5–7). (b) be
able to be seen because he/she/it is higher than
s.o/s.t. **rise above (doing) s.t** overcome s.t, e.g
a weakness or fault; be good, strong etc enough
not to (want to) do s.t that is bad: *Lisa used
to get angry when people made remarks about
her hair but now she rises above such things.*
rise again; **rise from the dead** become alive
again after having been dead. **rise against s.o/
s.t** revolt(2) against s.o/s.t. **rise from, out of, s.t** be
the result of s.t; stem from s.t. **rise to the occasion**
⇨ occasion(*n*).

'**riser** *c.n* person when he/she gets out of bed: *a
late riser.*

'**rising** *adj* **1** that is rising (⇨ rise(5–7,14,15)):
rising damp (*in the walls of a house*).
▷ *c.n* **2** (usu small) revolt(1). ⇨ uprising.
▷ *prep* **3 rising 20** etc nearly 20 etc years old.

risk /rɪsk/ *n* **1** *sing/u.n* (often — of s.t, that . . .)
danger (that s.t may happen): *There's no risk of
losing your umbrella here. There's a great risk
that this rain may cause floods.* **2** *c.n* example of
risk(1). **3** *c.n* particular danger against which one
insures: *fire risk*; *all risks.* **4** *c.n* person or thing
who/that is considered from the point of view
of how dangerous he/she/it is for an insurance
company to insure: *I am afraid Joe is a poor risk
because he has a weak heart.* **at risk (from s.o/
s.t)** (*formal*) in danger (from s.o/s.t). **at s.o's own
risk** without being the responsibility of anyone
else: *Passengers leaving their luggage here do so
at their own risk.* **at risk to s.t** with danger to
s.t: *He saved the dog from drowning at risk to
his own life.* **at the risk of (doing) s.t** with the
danger of (doing) s.t: *At the risk of seeming rude,
could I ask how much you paid for that watch?*
face/run/take a risk, risks, or **the risk of s.t** do
s.t that could be dangerous (in a certain way).
▷ *tr.v* **5** put (s.t) in danger: *risk one's life to save him.*
6 run the risk of (s.t): *risk failure*; *risk her scorn.*

'**riskily** *adv* in a risky way.

'**riskiness** *u.n* fact or state of being risky.

'**risky** *adj* (*-ier, -iest*) dangerous.

risotto /rɪˈzɒtəʊ/ *c/u.n* (*pl -s*) (*Italian*) rice
cooked with other things: *a chicken risotto.*

rissole /ˈrɪsəʊl/ *c.n* fried ball etc of mashed(3)
potato, breadcrumbs etc mixed with small pieces
of meat, fish etc.

rite /raɪt/ *c.n* (often *pl* with *sing* meaning) fixed
and formal way (of doing s.t, usu of a religious
kind): *the rites of the Church of England.*

ritual /ˈrɪtʃʊəl/ *adj* **1** done as a rite.
▷ *c/u.n* **2** (often go through the — of (doing) s.t)
rite(s) or ritual(1) ceremony or ceremonies (of
doing s.t): *They go through the ritual of locking
all doors and windows before going to bed.*

rival /ˈraɪvl/ *adj* **1** who/that competes: *The manager of that company was rude to me so now I
buy my things from a rival company.*
▷ *c.n* **2** (often a — for s.o/s.t, in s.t) person, company
etc who/that competes (for s.o/s.t, in s.t).
▷ *tr.v* **3** (*-ll-*, US *-l-*) **3** be as good as (s.o/s.t). Compare
unrivalled.

'**rivalry** *c/u.n* (*pl -ies*) (often — in s.t; — with s.o/
s.t (for s.t)) competition (with s.o/s.t (to try to get
s.t)); fact of competing (with s.o/s.t) (to get s.t).

river /ˈrɪvə/ *c.n* wide stream of water flowing
naturally, often into the sea or a lake. Compare

canal(1). **down/up river** towards, away from, the
mouth of the river. **rivers of blood** a lot of blood:
Rivers of blood flowed during the revolution. **sell
s.o down the river** (*fig*) harm s.o by not being
loyal to her/him; betray(2) s.o.

'**river ,basin** *c.n* area of land containing the
main stream and all the tributaries(2) of a river.

'**river,bed** *c.n* bottom of a river as far up on each
side as the surface of the water can reach.

'**river,side** *def.n* (also *attrib*) land along the bank
of a river: *a riverside hotel.*

rivet /ˈrɪvɪt/ *c.n* **1** kind of nail for joining pieces
of metal together; one end is put through a hole
in them and then flattened so that it will not come
out again.
▷ *tr.v* (*-t-*) **2** fasten or join (s.t) with one or more
rivets(1). **3** (often — one's attention etc) cause
one to fix (one's attention on her/him/it): *The
man's strange movements riveted the children's
attention.* **rivet one's attention, eyes** etc (**up)on
s.o/s.t** fix one's attention on s.o/s.t.

RN /ˌɑːr ˈen/ *abbr* Royal Navy.

road /rəʊd/ *c.n* (also *attrib*) (*written abbr* in
names *Rd*) strip of land along which vehicles etc
can go from one place to another: *Edgware Road.
Follow this road until you get to the town.* Compare path(1), street, track(2). **by road** going in a
car etc along a road, not in a train, plane or ship:
go/travel by road. **hit the road** (*fig*; *informal*)
begin one's journey (back, home etc). **hog the
road** ⇨ hog(*v*). **hold the road** (of a car etc) be
stable(1) on the road when travelling. **the rule(s)
of the road** ⇨ rule(*n*). **take to the road** become
a tramp(1).

'**road,block** *c.n* thing put across (part(s) of) a
road, usu by the police or army, to stop vehicles
and people on foot, usu so that they can be
searched and/or questioned.

'**road ,hog** *c.n* (*informal*) driver who drives
badly, uses too much space on the road and
makes it difficult for other cars etc to pass.

'**road ,map** *c.n* map for drivers of vehicles etc
showing the roads in a place.

'**road,mender** *c.n* person who repairs damaged
roads.

'**road ,metal** *u.n* stones used for making or
repairing roads.

'**road ,safety** *u.n* rules and advice for avoiding
accidents on the road.

'**road ,sense** *u.n* skill in avoiding accidents on
the road.

'**road,side** *def.n* (also *attrib*) (often at/by the —)
land at the edge of a road.

'**road ,sign** *c.n* sign beside, above or on a road
giving drivers information, warnings etc.

'**road,way** *def.n* main part of a road where
vehicles travel.

'**road,works** *pl.n* repairs to a road.

'**road,worthiness** *u.n* fact or state of being
roadworthy.

'**road,worthy** *adj* (of a vehicle) in safe condition
for being driven on a road.

roam /rəʊm/ *tr/intr.v* (often — around; — over/
through s.t) wander about (in (s.t)): *The animals
roam the plains in search of food.*

roar /rɔː/ *c.n* **1** (often the — of s.t) loud deep
sound (made by s.o/s.t) that continues for some
time: *the roar of a lion*; *the roar of an excited
crowd*; *the roar of an engine.* **a roar, roars, of**

s.t a roar(1) caused by, showing, s.t: *a roar of laughter*; *roars of pain*; *roars of approval*.

▷ *v* **2** *intr.v* (often — *at s.o/s.t*; — *with s.t*) make the sound of a roar(1) (when shouting at s.o, about s.o/s.t or showing s.t): *roar with laughter*; *roar with pain*. **3** *tr.v* (often — *s.t out*) shout s.t in a roaring (⇒ roar(2)) voice: *'Come here!' he roared* (*out*). **4** *tr.v* show (s.t) by roaring (⇒ roar(2)): *The crowd roared their approval of what the prime minister was saying*. **5** *intr.v* (*informal*) laugh or cry(2) loudly and a lot. **be a roaring success** ⇒ success(2). **do a roaring trade** ⇒ trade(*n*). **roar s.o down** make so much noise that s.o cannot be heard speaking. **roar oneself hoarse** roar until one becomes hoarse.

roast /rəʊst/ *adj* **1** that has been roasted(3): *English roast beef*[1](1).

▷ *c.n* **2** big piece of roasted(3) meat.

▷ *tr/intr.v* **3** (cause (s.t) to) cook in an oven, or in front of, or over, an open fire. **roast** (**oneself**) (**in the sun**) (*fig*) sunbathe(2).

'roasting *adj* **1** very hot.

▷ *adv* **2 roasting hot** very hot.

rob /rɒb/ *tr/intr.v* (-*bb-*) steal from (s.o/s.t): *rob a bank*; *go around robbing and killing*. **rob s.o/ s.t of s.o/s.t** steal s.o/s.t from s.o/s.t; take s.o/ s.t away from s.o/s.t: *You have robbed me of my house; are you now going to rob me of my children too?*

'robber *c.n* (often *a band/gang of* —*s*) person (in a band/gang(1)) who robs: *bank robbers*.

'robbery *c/u.n* (*pl -ies*) (example of) robbing. (**charge s.o with**) **robbery** (**with violence**) (accuse s.o of) stealing (and using violence to do s.t). **daylight robbery** (*fig; informal*) charging too much for what one is selling.

robe /rəʊb/ *c.n* long loose outer piece of clothing, often one worn informally at home, or one worn formally by a judge, mayor etc: *a bathrobe*.

robin /'rɒbɪn/ *c.n* (also, usu said by or to children, **,robin 'red,breast**) kind of small brown bird with a red breast(2).

robot /'rəʊbɒt/ *c.n* (also *attrib*) **1** machine that can do things like a human being does them, e.g that can make parts of cars in a factory. **2** machine that is made to look like a human being and that can walk, talk etc. **3** person who obeys orders etc without questioning them.

robust /rəʊ'bʌst/ *adj* strong and/or healthy. **ro'bustly** *adv*. **ro'bustness** *u.n*.

rock[1] /rɒk/ *n* **1** *c/u.n* (big piece of the) natural stone that forms part of our earth: *the Rock of Gibraltar*. **2** *c.n* (*US*) stone: *Stop throwing rocks!* **3** *u.n* (often *a stick of* —) hard sweet in the shape of a stick, sold mostly in seaside towns with the name of the town in it. **as firm/solid/steady as a rock** (**a**) absolutely firm etc; that will not move. (**b**) who/that one can trust completely.

,rock 'bottom *unique n* lowest point/level: *This share touched rock bottom a month ago but has been going up ever since*.

,rock-'bottom *attrib.adj* that is offered, sold, at the lowest price: *a rock-bottom price*.

'rock,bound *adj* (of a shore or coast) having rocks[1](1) along its edge.

,rock 'bun *c.n* (also **'rock ,cake**) kind of small cake with a rough hard surface.

'rock-,climbing *u.n* (also *attrib*) sport or practice of climbing rocks[1](1).

'rock ,crystal *c/u.n* kind of quartz.

'rockery *c.n* (*pl -ies*) place in a garden for growing rock plants among rocks[1](1).

'rock ,garden *c.n* = rockery.

'rockiness *u.n* fact or state of being rocky.

'rock ,plant *c.n* kind of plant that likes growing among rocks[1](1).

'rock ,pool *c.n* deep pool[1](4) in an area with rocks.

rocks *pl.n* = rock[1](1,2). **on the rocks** (*fig*) (**a**) having troubles about money etc: *I am afraid Adam's marriage is on the rocks*. (**b**) (of a strong drink) with ice but not water in it: *John likes his whisky*(1) *on the rocks*.

'rock ,salt *u.n* salt from mines, not from the sea. Compare sea salt.

'rocky[1] *adj*(-*ier*, -*iest*) **1** full of rocks[1](1). **2** very hard. Compare rocky[2] (⇒ rock[2]).

rock[2] /rɒk/ *v* **1** *tr/intr.v* (often — (*s.o/s.t*) *to and fro*) (cause (s.o/s.t) to) move from side to side and/or backwards and forwards. **2** *tr.v* shock (s.o) greatly. **rock the boat** ⇒ boat. **rock s.o to sleep** rock[2](1) s.o (usu a baby) until he/she goes to sleep.

'rocker *c.n* one of the pair of curved pieces of wood under a cradle(1), rocking chair or rocking horse that make it possible to rock[2](1) it. (**be/go** etc) **off one's rocker** (*slang*) (be/become) mad.

'rocking ,chair *c.n* chair that has rockers so that one can rock[2](1) (in) it.

'rocking ,horse *c.n* big toy horse that has rockers so that children can sit on it and rock[2](1).

'rocky[2] *adj* (-*ier*, -*iest*) (*informal*) **1** (of furniture etc) not very firm. **2** (of a business etc) not very safe, likely to fail: *His company is very rocky*. Compare rocky[1] (⇒ rock[1]).

rock[3] /rɒk/ *u.n* (also *attrib*) **1** kind of popular modern dance music that has a very strong loud beat; it is played mostly on electric(2) guitars.

▷ *intr.v* **2** dance to this music.

,rock and/'n' roll *u.n/intr.v* = rock[3].

rocket /'rɒkɪt/ *c.n* **1** (often *fire, let off, a* —) device consisting of a cardboard, metal etc tube filled with explosive(2) that can be lit so that it shoots high up into the air as a signal or for amusement. **2** kind of bomb etc that has its own oxygen in it and is driven through the air by burning gases. **3** device like a rocket(2) that is used to drive a plane, or for space travel. **get, give s.o, a rocket** (*fig; informal*) get, give s.o, a severe scolding.

▷ *intr.v* **4** suddenly and quickly become greater in amount, level etc: *The cost of oil rocketed in the 1970s*.

rockiness ⇒ rock[1].

rocking chair/horse ⇒ rock[2].

rock 'n' roll ⇒ rock[3].

rocks ⇒ rock[1].

rocky ⇒ rock[1], rock[2].

rod /rɒd/ *c.n* long thin straight round piece of wood, metal etc, e.g one used for fishing. ⇒ fishing-rod. **rod and line** fishing-rod and line[1](1).

rode /rəʊd/ *p.t* of ride.

rodent /'rəʊdənt/ *c.n* kind of animal (e.g a mouse, rabbit, rat) with strong sharp front teeth.

roe[1] /rəʊ/ *u.n* **1** eggs of a fish, sometimes cooked for food (soft roe). **2** sperm(2) of a male fish, sometimes cooked for food (hard roe).

roe[2] /rəʊ/ *c.n* (also **'roe ,deer** (*pl* roe deer)) kind of small deer found in forests in Europe and Asia.

'roe,buck *c.n* (*pl* **roebuck**) male roe[2].

rogue /rəʊg/ *c.n* **1** (*derog*) very bad and dishonest person. **2** (*joking*) naughty child.

'roguish *adj*.

'roguishly *adv*. **'roguishness** *u.n*.

role, rôle /rəʊl/ *c.n* part acted by an actor/actress in a play, film etc. **have/play a role** (**in s.t**) take part (in s.t); be one of the people or things who/that do s.t (in s.t): *Lessons in cooking should play a role in every person's education*. **fulfil one's role** (**as s.t**) do what it is one's job to do (because one is s.t, e.g a parent). **title role** ⇒ title.

'role,play *u.n* playing roles in a class to practise language, or in a psychiatrist's place to overcome character problems etc.

roll /rəʊl/ *c.n* **1** example of rolling(5): *A lot of animals enjoy having a roll on the grass*. **2** (often — of s.t) thing that has been produced by rolling(7) (s.t): *a roll of film*; *a toilet roll*. **3** small loaf of bread for one person. **4** (sometimes with capital **R**) official list, register(1) etc. **call the roll** read a roll(4) out aloud to see who is present, e.g in a class. ⇒ roll call. **sausage roll** ⇒ sausage.

▷ *v* **5** *tr/intr.v* (cause (s.o/s.t) to) turn or swing from side to side, over (and over) sideways etc, often while moving about: *a ship rolling in rough seas*; *an elephant rolling over on its back in the dust*; *a stone rolling down a slope*; *children rolling a snowball along*. **6** *intr.v* move smoothly (as if) on wheels: *clouds rolling by* (or *rolling across the sky*). **7** *tr/intr.v* (often — (s.t) up) curl (s.t) round and round into a round shape such as a tube, circle etc: *You can roll your umbrella up again now; it's stopped raining*. Hedgehogs *roll* (*themselves*) *up into a ball when they are frightened*. Opposite unroll(1). **8** *tr.v* produce (s.t, usu a cigarette) by rolling(7) s.t. **9** *tr.v* (often — s.t out) make (s.t, e.g a new road surface, pastry) flat with a roller(1), or thin with a rolling-pin. **10** *intr.v* make a sound like/of a drum being hit again and again very quickly or thunder echoing(2).

keep the ball rolling ⇒ ball[1].

roll about (**laughing**) laugh so much that one throws one's body about.

roll (**s.o/s.t**) **back** force (s.o/s.t, e.g enemy soldiers) to go back, usu over a wide front.

roll by (**a**) = roll(6). (**b**) (of time) pass.

roll one's eyes (**at s.o**) ⇒ eye(*n*).

roll in (*informal*) arrive in large numbers or quantities. **roll s.o/s.t in s.t** put s.o/s.t in s.t by rolling(7) it round her/him/it. **roll s.t in s.t** cover s.t with s.t by rolling (⇒ roll(5)) it in it: *After you make the fish balls, roll them in flour*. **rolling in money.** ⇒ money.

roll on (**a**) (of a big river etc) go on flowing in an impressive way. (**b**) (of time) continue to pass; roll by(b). **roll on s.t** (*informal*, as an order) (of a future time) come quickly: *I'm tired of work; roll on the holidays!*

roll s.t out (**a**) = unroll s.t. (**b**) ⇒ roll(9). (**c**) (*informal*) produce s.t in large quantities. (**d**) say, sing, s.t in a voice that reminds one rather of a drum. ⇒ roll(10).

roll one's r's pronounce the sound /r/ so that it sounds rather like a drum rolling(10).

roll up (**for s.t**) (**a**) (often as an order) come in to see a show, performance in a circus etc: *Roll up, roll up, and see the greatest show on earth!* (**b**) arrive, often late or otherwise in a rude way, (to attend etc s.t). **roll s.t up** (**a**) ⇒ roll(7). (**b**) shorten s.t, e.g one's sleeves or trousers, by rolling(7).

set the ball rolling ⇒ ball[1].

'roll ,call *c/unique n* calling of the roll(4).

,rolled 'gold *u.n* (also *attrib*) (thing that has a) thin coat(4) of gold (on it).

'roller *c.n* **1** kind of instrument or tool that has the shape of a tube and is used for flattening, pressing, shaping, printing etc s.t: *a garden roller*; *hair rollers*. ⇒ steamroller(1). **2** rod round which s.t is rolled: *The screen on which I show films has a wooden roller*.

'roller ,coaster *c.n* kind of small train on a track that goes up and down very steep slopes and round very sharp corners at a fair[2](2), amusement park etc.

'roller-,skate ⇒ skate[1](2,4). device with four wheels for fixing on one's shoe so that one can slide on it; one of a pair of shoes with four such wheels on it.

'roller-,skate *intr.v* (also **skate**) go around on roller skates.

'roller-,skater *c.n* (also **'skater**) person who roller-skates.

'roller-,skating *u.n* (also **'skating**) activity of going around on roller-skates.

'roller ,towel *c.n* long towel with the ends joined together, that is on a roller(2).

'rolling *adj* **1** (*attrib*) (of land) having gentle slopes. **2** (also **rolling in it/money**) (*informal*) (of a person) very rich.

'rolling-,pin *c.n* piece of wood etc shaped like a tube and used for rolling(9) pastry etc.

'rolling ,stock *u.n* (in a railway system) engines, carriages, trucks and all other vehicles with wheels.

,rolling 'stone *c.n* (*fig*) person who never stays in one place for long. **A rolling stone gathers no moss** (*proverb*) A person who is always moving from place to place and job to job does not become rich, successful etc.

,roll of 'honour *c.n* list of people who deserve to be honoured, usu because they died for their country in a war.

,roll-,on ,roll-'off *adj* (of a ferry(1)) that vehicles can drive directly onto and off.

rolls *def.pl.n* (often with capital **R**) official list of qualified lawyers. **strike s.o off the rolls** not allow s.o to act as a lawyer any more.

,roll,top 'desk *c.n* desk with a lid that rolls back out of sight when it is opened.

ROM /rɒm/ *abbr* read-only memory (⇒ read).

roman /'rəʊmən/ *u.n* (also *attrib*) ordinary letters used in printing: This is printed in roman (letters). Compare italic, bold(4).

Roman /'rəʊmən/ *adj* **1** of or referring to the ancient empire of Rome. **2** of or referring to the city of Rome.

▷ *c.n* **3** citizen of the ancient empire of Rome. **4** citizen of the city of Rome.

,Roman 'Catholic *adj* **1** of or referring to the Roman Catholic Church.

▷ *c.n* **2** = Catholic(2).

,Roman ,Catholic 'Church *def.n* (also **,Catholic 'Church**) branch of the Christian(1) religion that has the Pope as its head. Compare Church of England, Protestant(1) Church.

,Roman Ca'tholi,cism *u.n* ⇒ Catholicism.

,Roman 'numeral *c.n* symbol used by the ancient Romans for a number; e.g X = 10, and C = 100. Compare Arabic numeral.

romance /rəʊ'mæns/ *n* **1** *c.n* story about strong feelings, often of love, strange places, exciting events (sometimes long ago) etc that helps people to escape, in their minds, from their own dull, unsatisfactory and/or unhappy lives. **2** *u.n* quality that such stories have. **3** *u.n* tendency in one's mind to want and enjoy romance(2). **4** *c.n* love affair, often a short one.

▷ *intr.v* **5** (often — about *s.t*) tell romances(1) (about s.t); say things that are exciting but probably not true ⇒ romanticize. **6** (often — with *s.o*) have a romance(4) (with s.o).

ro'mantic *adj* **1** of, referring to, full of, romance(2). **2** who/that romances(5); exciting and enjoyable in a romantic(1) but not practical way. **3** concerning, showing romanticism.

▷ *c.n* **4** person who thinks (and tries to live) in a romantic(1) way. **5** (sometimes with capital **R**) person, often a writer, artist etc, who belongs to, or favours, the Romantic Movement.

ro'manti,cism *u.n* (sometimes with capital **R**) love of romantic(1) things; tendency to prefer feelings to thought and reason, nature to the works of man, and wild to orderly things. Compare classicism, realism.

ro'manticist *c.n* person who likes romanticism.

romanticize, **-ise** /rəʊ'mæntɪ,saɪz/ *tr/intr.v* (*derog*) make (s.t) seem more romantic(1) than it really is.

Ro'mantic ,Movement *def.n* fashion that began towards the end of the 18th century and continued into the first part of the 19th century for romance(2) in art, literature, clothes etc.

romp /rɒmp/ *c.n* **1** example of romping(2) (with s.o/s.t).

▷ *intr.v* **2** play about happily, usu with a lot of jumping around. **romp home** (*informal*) (of a horse etc in a race) win easily. **romp through s.t** (*informal*) finish s.t, e.g a piece of work, quickly and easily.

'romper *c.n* (also **'rompers** *pl.n*; often *a pair of* —s) piece of clothing for a small child consisting of an upper and a lower part all in one.

roof /ru:f/ *c.n* **1** upper covering of a building, car etc which is usu supported by the walls. Compare ceiling(1). (**have**) **a/no roof over one's head** (have) somewhere/nowhere to live. **hit the roof** become very angry. **raise the roof** ⇒ raise(2). **the roof of one's/the mouth** one's/the hard palate(1).

▷ *tr.v* **2** (often — s.t (*in/over*) with s.t) cover s.t as/ with a roof (made of s.t).

'roof ,garden *c.n* garden on the flat roof of a house, restaurant or hotel.

'roofing *u.n* material for roofs.

'roof ,rack *c.n* rack(1) fixed on top of a car for carrying things on.

rook[1] /rʊk/ *c.n* kind of big black bird found in Europe.

'rookery *c.n* (*pl -ies*) place where there are a lot of rooks's nests.

rook[2] /rʊk/ *c.n* (in chess) = castle(2).

rook[3] /rʊk/ *tr.v* cheat (s.o) so that one gets s.t from her/him, esp by overcharging.

room /ru:m/ *n* **1** *c.n* any part of a building (e.g an office, sitting-room) that is separated from the rest of it by walls: *a bedroom*; *a dining room*. **2** *unique/pl.n* person/people using a room in an hotel, office etc: *Room 21 want(s) tea now.* **3** *u.n* (often — for s.o/s.t, to do s.t) empty space (that s.o/s.t can use, fit into etc, do s.t in): *Is there room for another person on the back seat of your car? There's hardly room to move in our flat when the children are home.* **4** *u.n* (often — for s.t, to do s.t*) opportunity, chance, possibility (sometimes that needs to be taken) (for s.t etc): *There is a lot of room for improvement in John's work. Mary has finished her studies and now she needs room to practise what she has learnt.* **a double/single/ twin-bedded room** a room in a hotel etc that is for two people in the same bed, or for one person, or for two people in separate beds. **make room (for s.o/s.t)** move (s.t) so that there is room(3) (for s.o/s.t). **room for doubt** possibility that s.t may not be true. **take up room** fill a space or spaces, usu one(s) really needed for s.o/s.t else.

▷ *intr.v* **5** (usu — with s.o) (*informal*) have a room or rooms (that one shares with s.o, or in s.o's house).

'roomful *c.n* (usu *a — of people* etc) (almost) as many (people etc) as can fit into a room.

'roominess *u.n* fact or state of being roomy.

'room,mate *c.n* person with whom one shares a room, e.g at university.

rooms *pl.n* rooms that one has rented in a building that has other rooms too; lodgings.

'room ,service *u.n* (in a hotel etc) service of food etc that one can have in one's room instead of having to go down to the restaurant, bar etc.

'roomy *adj* (*-ier, -iest*) having plenty of room(3).

roost /ru:st/ *c.n* **1** place, e.g branch of a tree or wooden pole, on which birds rest (and sleep), usu at night. **at roost** roosting(2).

▷ *intr.v* **2** sit on a roost(1) and sleep.

root /ru:t/ *c.n* **1** (often *pl*) part of a plant that is under the ground. **2** part of a hair, tongue, tooth etc that is buried in the flesh or attached to the rest of one's body. **3** (*grammar*) base of a word to which prefixes and/or suffixes can be added: *The root of 'unkindness' is 'kind'.* **cube root** ⇒ cube. (**get at/to**) **the root of s.t** (*fig*) (find/reach) the real cause, reason for etc, s.t. **have deep, strong** etc **roots** (*fig*) have a strong base; be strongly believed in etc: *This religion has deep roots here.* **root and branch** (when getting rid of s.t bad) completely. **square root** ⇒ square. **strike/take root** (**a**) (of a seed, plant etc) begin to put down roots. (**b**) (of an idea etc) begin to be established (⇒ establish(1,3)).

▷ *v* **4** *tr/intr.v* (cause (s.t, e.g a plant) to) put down roots. **root s.o/s.t out** (**a**) destroy, get rid of, s.o/ s.t completely. (**b**) (usu — s.o out s.t; — s.t out for s.o) (*informal*) find s.t (for s.o): *Your clothes are wet; I'll root you out something dry to put on.* **root oneself/s.o up** make oneself/s.o leave a place where one/he/she has lived for some time. ⇒ pull up one's roots (⇒ roots); uproot(2). **root s.t up** pull s.t out of the ground. ⇒ uproot(1).

'root ,crop *c.n* crop, e.g turnips, the roots of which are the parts mostly eaten.

'rooted *adj* (usu **,deep-'rooted**) (*fig*) (of a

belief etc) strong. **rooted in s.t** having s.t as its base, reason etc. **rooted to the spot** ⇨ spot(n).

,**rooted ob'jection** c.n. **have a rooted objection to s.t** dislike s.t very much indeed.

'**rootless** adj having no roots(1,2).

'**rootlessness** u.n.

roots pl.n 1 ⇨ root(1-3). 2 feeling that one belongs to a particular place because one was born there or one's parents were etc. **pull up one's roots** stop living in the place where one's roots(2) are and move somewhere else. ⇨ root oneself/s.o up; uproot(2). **put down (new) roots** begin to fit into a new place by finding friends there etc.

rope /rəʊp/ n 1 c/u.n (piece of) strong thick cord(1) (made by twisting dried pieces of a plant, nylon, leather or wires, together), used for tying things, holding things up etc: *Tie that horse to this tree with a rope. Pull the sails up with these ropes.* ⇨ cable(1), string(1). 2 c.n (usu — of s.t) string of s.t, e.g pearls, as a necklace. **give s.o plenty of rope** (fig) allow s.o a lot of freedom. **a length of rope** a piece of rope. **money for old rope** (fig; informal) a bargain; getting a lot for very little money etc: *This job is money for old rope; I get £200 a week for sitting around waiting for someone to phone!*

▷ tr.v 3 tie (s.o/s.t) with rope(1): *The climbers roped themselves together* (or *to each other*). 4 (usu — s.t up) put rope(1) round (s.t) so that it will not open etc. 5 catch (s.t, e.g an animal or a branch of a tree) by throwing a rope(1). **rope s.o in (to do s.t)** (fig; informal) get s.o to help, often unwillingly, (to do s.t). **rope s.t off (from s.t)** separate (part of) s.t from the rest with one or more ropes(1).

'**ropey** ⇨ ropy.

'**ropiness** u.n fact or state of being ropy.

'**ropy** adj (-ier, -iest) (also '**ropey**) (informal) 1 in a bad, sometimes dangerous condition: *a ropy old car with no brakes.* 2 cheap and badly made: *a ropy pair of trousers.*

rosary /'rəʊzəri/ c.n (pl -ies) 1 string of beads for keeping count of the number of prayers said, mostly by Roman Catholics(2). 2 (often say the — (for s.o/s.t)) saying of a set of such prayers (to help s.o/s.t).

rose¹ /rəʊz/ c.n 1 kind of bush that usu has thorns on its stems and that produces beautiful flowers, often with a beautiful scent. 2 flower on a rose(1). 3 flower that looks rather like a rose: *Christmas rose*; *rock rose*; *rose of May.* 4 metal, plastic etc device with a lot of small holes in it that is put on the end of a watering can or hose'(1) so that one can water plants gently. **a bed of roses** (fig) a pleasant, easy situation: *Working in London is no bed of roses, however good the pay.* **s.t is not all roses** s.t has unpleasant things about it as well as pleasant ones. **There's no rose without a thorn** (proverb) It is not possible to have only pleasant things without any unpleasant ones too.

rose- adj pink: *rose-red.*

rosé /'rəʊzeɪ/ u.n (French) kind of pink wine.

'**rose,bud** c.n bud(1) of a rose'(2).

rosette /rəʊ'zet/ c.n prize/ornament, rose/ shaped, of ribbons, carved(1) in stone etc.

'**rose,wood** u.n (also attrib) kind of hard dark red wood from a tree that is found

in the tropics, used to make very good furniture.

'**rosiness** u.n state or fact of being rosy.

'**rosy** adj (-ier, -iest) 1 pink, often as a sign of health: *rosy cheeks.* 2 hopeful; giving one hope: *a rosy future.*

rose² /rəʊz/ p.t of rise.

rosemary /'rəʊzməri/ u.n (also attrib) kind of herb with long pointed leaves that smell sweet, used in cooking.

roster /'rɒstə/ c.n list showing people's names, the jobs they have to do and the times at which they have to take turns to do them.

rostrum /'rɒstrəm/ c.n (pl -s, rostra /'rɒstrə/) platform(1) on which a person stands in order to give a lecture, conduct(5) an orchestra etc.

rosy ⇨ rose'.

rot /rɒt/ u.n 1 (action of) rotting(4,5). 2 (after an adj or attrib n) (disease like, or causing) rot(1) of the kind shown by the adj etc: *dry/damp rot in the beams of an old house*; *foot rot in an animal.* 3 (slang) nonsense: *talk (a lot of) rot.* **the rot sets in** (fig) bad things begin to happen one after the other: *Jim was healthy until he passed 70 but then the rot set in.* **stop the rot** (fig) prevent things continuing to be bad: *This new government will soon stop the rot.*

▷ v (-tt-) 4 tr/intr.v (often — (s.t) away) (cause (s.t) to) decay(3), go bad, as a natural result of becoming old, wet, damaged by insects etc (until there is nothing left). 5 intr.v (fig) (of a person) live a life that is bad for one's health, mind etc: *men rotting in prison.* **rot off** rot(4) until it falls off.

'**rotten** adj 1 that has rotted(4) or gone bad. 2 (often — to s.o) (informal) (of a person, her/his behaviour) bad; unkind; cruel (to s.o). 3 (often — for s.o) (slang) bad; unpleasant (for s.o): *We had a rotten time at the party last night*; *there was nothing to eat or drink, and no music.* **feel rotten** (informal) feel ill, unhappy etc. **rotten to the core** ⇨ core(n).

'**rottenly** adv. '**rottenness** u.n.

'**rotter** c.n (old use or joking) rotten(3) person.

rota /'rəʊtə/ c.n = roster.

rotary /'rəʊtəri/ adj (usu attrib) 1 going round and round like a wheel: *rotary motion.* 2 having a rotary(1) part: *a rotary engine.*

rotate /rəʊ'teɪt/ tr/intr.v 1 (cause (s.t) to) go round and round like a wheel. 2 (cause (s.t) to) be done in turns, one after the other: *We rotate our crops every year so that the soil remains good.* 3 (cause (s.o/s.t) to) take turns: *The guards rotate on a four-hour basis.*

rotation /rəʊ'teɪʃən/ n 1 u.n act or fact of rotating (s.o/s.t). 2 c.n one turn of s.t that is rotating(1). **in rotation (a)** taking turns. **(b)** following one after the other in a fixed order.

ro,tation of 'crops u.n = crop rotation.

rotatory /rəʊ'teɪtəri/ adj that rotates(1).

rotisserie /rəʊ'tɪsəri/ c.n (French) 1 device for cooking food on a rotating(1) rod. 2 restaurant that cooks food in this way.

rotor /'rəʊtə/ c.n 1 part of some machines which rotates(1). 2 (also '**rotor-,blade**) thing like a big horizontal propeller on top of a helicopter with which it flies.

rote /rəʊt/ u.n (also attrib) way of learning that uses memory rather than reason. **learn s.t by rote**

learn s.t by memorizing it instead of thinking about it.
'**rote** ,**learning** *u.n* learning by rote.
rotten(ly/ness), **rotter** ⇨ rot.
rotund /rəʊˈtʌnd/ *adj* (*formal*) (of a person) round in shape because one is fat.
roˈtunda *c.n* (*formal*) round building, usu with a dome(1) on top.
rouge /ruːʒ/ *u.n* (*French*) **1** red substance for colouring one's cheeks etc, used mostly by women and actors.
▷ *tr.v* **2** put rouge(1) on (s.o/s.t).
rough /rʌf/ *adj* **1** having a surface that is not even, regular or smooth: *You can make this rough piece of wood smooth with a plane²*(1). *Put some oil on your rough skin. The sea is very rough today.* **2** (of weather) stormy and very windy. **3** during which there is a lot of unpleasant movement, up and down, from side to side etc: *a rough crossing from England to France; a rough flight from London to New York; a rough ride on a* camel. ⇨ bumpy. **4** (also **rough and ready**) (of living conditions, food etc) without any of the comforts of modern life. **5** (*derog*) (of people, their behaviour etc) not showing the signs of civilization, polite society etc. **6** (not *derog*) (of people, their behaviour) pleasantly simple and without any affectation: *the rough kindness of the workers.* **7** using (too much) force; not at all gentle: *Boys often play rough games.* **8** (of a plan, drawing, idea etc) not yet in its finished form; only at an early stage, before details have been put in. **9** (of a sound, e.g a person's voice) harsh(3); not gentle. **10** (often — *on s.o*) (*informal*) showing bad luck (for s.o); unfortunate (for s.o): *'I've broken a tooth!' 'That's rough — especially on a Saturday evening when you won't be able to find a dentist.'* (**at**) **a rough estimate** ⇨ estimate(*n*). **rough and ready** ⇨ rough(4).
▷ *adv* **11** in rough(4) conditions: *sleep rough* (sleep out of doors because one is poor and has no home). **12** in a rough(7) way: *play rough.* **cut up rough** (*fig; informal*) become angry (and fight). **play it rough** behave, or do s.t, in a rough(7) way.
▷ *n* **13** *c.n* man who behaves in a rough(7) way. **14** *c.n* drawing etc that is still rough(8). **15** *u/ def.n* parts of a golf course where the grass has not been cut short. Compare green(7). **in rough** in a rough(8) or unfinished state. **take the rough with the smooth** patiently accept bad things as well as good ones.
▷ *tr.v* **16 rough** *s.t* **in/out** draw the rough(8) shape/ outlines of s.t before filling in the details. **rough it** live rough(11). **rough** *s.o/s.t* **up** (*informal*) attack and hurt s.o/s.t, usu as a threat. **rough** *s.t* **up** make s.t rough(1) or untidy: *The boy roughed up his bed to make his mother think he had slept in it.*
'**roughage** *u.n* coarse(2) material that one does not digest(3) but which is useful because it helps one's bowels(1) to work properly.
'**roughen** *tr/intr.v* (cause (s.t) to) become rough(1).
,**rough** '**luck** *u.n* bad luck, usu that makes the speaker sad. ⇨ rough(10).
'**roughly** *adv* **1** in a rough(1-9) way. **2** about: *There are roughly 350 pupils in our school.* **roughly speaking** = roughly(2).

'**roughness** *n* **1** *u.n* fact or quality of being rough(1-9). **2** *c.n* rough(1) place on s.t.
,**rough** '**paper** *u.n* paper on which to write, draw etc rough(8) things.
'**rough** ,**stuff** *u.n* (*informal*) violence; fighting.
,**rough** **trans**'**lation** *c.n* translation of s.t that gives the general meaning but is not detailed, careful or exact.
roulette /ruːˈlet/ *u.n* (often *play* —) gambling game in which a small ball is put on a wheel that is spinning round; the wheel has numbers on it, and the number in which the wheel stops is the winning one.
rouˈlette ,**wheel** *c.n* wheel used in roulette.
round /raʊnd/ *adj* **1** having the shape of a circle or a ball. **2** curved; fat: *round cheeks.* **3** (of a number) exactly and particularly not less than: *a round dozen.* **in round figures** (of a number) not exactly, but to the nearest 10, 100 etc: *It will cost you £97.75 — in round figures £100.*
▷ *adv* (US usu a'**round**) **4** (often — *and* —) with a circular motion, e.g coming back again to the point of starting, like a wheel or moving through part of a circle as when one looks behind one. **5** (often *all* —) in the shape of a circle, without turning: *She has a house with fields* (*all*) *round.* **6** (after a phrase(1) showing size) in circumference; measured in a complete circle: *The moon is about 11 000 kilometres round.* **7** to, at, or affecting, various people, places etc: *The postman goes round every morning delivering letters.* **8** (of a journey etc) not straight; going out of one's way: *I'll be home late this evening because I'm going round to the shops first.* **9** to s.o's home: *I went round to see Emma yesterday.* **all the year round** ⇨ year. **be/ come round** (**again**) ⇨ be, come. **gather** (**s.o**) **round** ⇨ gather(*v*). **hand** *s.t* **round** (**to s.o**) ⇨ hand(*v*). **have a look round** ⇨ look(*n*). **have** *s.o* **round** (**for** *s.t*) ⇨ have(*v*). **show** *s.o* (**a**)**round** ⇨ show(*v*). (*s.w*) **round about 60** etc about 60 etc. **the right/wrong way round**; **the other/opposite way round** ⇨ way(*n*).
▷ *prep* (US usu a'**round**) **10** (often *all/right* —; — *and* — *s.o/s.t*) with a more or less circular motion, with s.o/s.t as her/his/its centre: *I walked right round the park.* Compare round(4). **11** in the shape of a circle (without turning), with (s.o/ s.t) as her/his/its centre: *a large house with fields all round it.* Compare round(5). **12** to, at, affecting, (various people, places etc): *The postman goes round all the houses.* Compare round(7). **13** to, at, the other/far side of (s.t): *Go round the next bend carefully. Our house is round the next corner.* **14** (often *somewhere* — *s.t*; — *about s.t*) (of a number or quantity) about (s.t): *We have somewhere round 200 sheep. Mike is round about 30 years old.* **have a look round** *s.t* ⇨ look(*n*). (**a**)**round the clock** ⇨ clock(*n*). **show** *s.o* (**a**)**round** *s.t* ⇨ show(*v*).
▷ *c.n* **15** (often — *of s.t*) thing that is round(1) (and made of s.t): *a round of beef¹*(1); *a round of toast¹*(1) (i.e a slice of bread cut off a loaf and toasted). **16** example of going round (s.o/s.t). Compare round(7,12), rounds, roundsman. **17** (in golf) act of going round(12) the whole course, hole by hole, once. **18** (*boxing*) one of the parts of a match, usu lasting three minutes. **19** (in sports competitions) one set of matches, the winners of

which then play each other in the next round: *the first round of the Football Association Cup*; *the* semifinal *round*. **20** series(1) or set of s.t, one after the other: *Christmas is one long round of parties here. Each year there is a new round of wage claims from the workers in various industries.* **21** (often — *of s.t*) example of giving s.t (of a certain kind) to everyone in a group: *Who's paying for this round of drinks?* **22** kind of song sung by three or four people, each starting the first line as the person before starts the second. **one's/the daily round** the same jobs that one has to do every day. **it is s.o's round** it is s.o's turn to pay for the drinks. ⇨ round(21). **paper round** ⇨ paper(*n*). **a round of applause** ⇨ applause(*n*). **stand s.o a round** pay for a round(21) of drinks for s.o.

▷ *v* **23** *tr/intr.v* (cause (s.t) to) become round(1) (because of s.t): *Round your lips when you pronounce /u:/. Her eyes rounded with surprise when she saw William dancing.*

round a corner ⇨ corner(*n*).

round s.t down/up (to s.t) bring a number etc down/up (to the nearest 10, 100 etc): *We are asking £32.50 for this but I am prepared to round it down to £30 for you.*

round s.t off bring s.t down/up to the nearest 10, 100 etc. **round s.t off (by doing s.t, with s.t)** finish s.t pleasantly, neatly etc (by doing s.t, with s.t): *We rounded our meal off with coffee and chocolates.*

round (s.t) out (cause (s.t) to) become rounder/ fatter: *A few weeks of good food soon rounded out the child's cheeks.*

round s.o/s.t up bring together, catch, s.o/s.t, e.g criminals or animals that have strayed(5). **round s.t up (to s.t)** ⇨ round s.t down/up (to s.t).

round (up)on s.o/s.t suddenly (turn and) attack s.o/s.t, either with blows etc or with words.

'rounda,bout *attrib.adj* **1** not direct; not the shortest/straightest: *He went home by a round-about way to avoid the police. I heard of Penny's marriage in a roundabout way.*

▷ *c.n* **2** circle in the middle of a place where roads meet or cross, around which cars etc have to go. **3** (also **,carou'sel**(1), **'merry-go-,round**) device having a circle with toy horses etc on it which goes round and round; children can ride on the horses for pleasure.

,round 'bracket *c.n* (usu *pl*) ⇨ bracket(2).

'rounded *adj* that has become, has been made, round(1): *rounded stones on a beach.*

'rounders *u.n* kind of game like baseball, usu played by children.

,round-'eyed *adj* with eyes wide open in surprise etc. ⇨ round(23).

'roundish *adj* almost round(1).

'roundly *adv* (often *be — defeated*) completely (beaten, e.g in a match).

'roundness *u.n.*

rounds *pl.n* **1 do/go/make one's rounds** go to all the people/places etc one usu goes to as part of one's work/duties. ⇨ round(7,12,16). **2 go the rounds** (of a story etc) be passed on from person to person.

,round 'shoulders *pl.n* shoulders (and back) that are bent forward.

,round-'shouldered *adj*.

roundsman /'raʊndzmən/ *c.n* (*pl -men*) person

who is employed to go round delivering things to people at their houses: *a milk roundsman.* ⇨ round(7,12,16), rounds.

,round-the-'clock *adj*. ⇨ round the clock (⇨ clock(*n*)).

'round ,trip *c.n* journey to a place and then back again, either along the same route(1) or along a different one.

'round,up *c.n* (usu — *of s.o/s.t*) **1** example of rounding people or animals up. **2** (in television, radio etc) collection of the latest news etc.

rouse /raʊz/ *v* **1** *tr.v* (often — *s.o/an animal, from, out of, s.t*) awaken (s.o/an animal) (after he/she/ it has been asleep etc). **2** (often — *s.o from, out of, s.t*) excite, interest, (s.o) (so that he/she stops doing s.t): *rouse s.o out of her/his apathy.* **rouse s.o to s.t** (*formal*) rouse(2) s.o so that he/she begins to do s.t: *He roused her to anger.*

'rousing *adj* (usu *attrib*) **1** exciting. **2** (of shouting) loud and happy: *a rousing cheer/welcome for the team after they have won their match.*

rout /raʊt/ *c.n* **1** complete defeat, chasing away etc of another team, army etc. **put s.o to rout** rout(2) s.o.

▷ *tr.v* **2** defeat (s.o) completely; chase (her/him) away. **rout s.o out (of s.t)** find s.o and make her/him come out (of the place where he/she is).

route /ru:t/ *c.n* **1** way of going from one place to another: *The quickest route from here to the town is not the shortest.*

▷ *tr.v* **2** (often — *s.o/s.t by/through/via s.w*) send (s.o/s.t) along a route(1) (that passes through s.w).

'route ,march *c.n* long march by members of the armed forces, usu as part of their training.

routine /ru:'ti:n/ *adj* **1** done regularly as part of normal practice (and sometimes therefore boring): *The police asked the man some routine questions and then let him go. I am looking for a less routine job.*

▷ *n* **2** *u.n* routine(1) way in which things are done, in which one lives etc. **3** *c.n* set of actions etc that are done in the same way each time: *a dance routine* (i.e a particular set of dance steps).

rove /rəʊv/ *tr/intr.v* (*literary*) wander over (s.t): *Pirates*(1) *used to rove the seas looking for ships to rob.*

'rover *c.n* (usu *literary*) person who roves.

,roving 'eye *sing.n* (often *have a —*) interest in sex which does not concentrate(3) on any one person for long.

row[1] /rəʊ/ *c.n* **1** (often *go for, have, a —*) example of rowing.

▷ *v* **2** *intr.v* make a boat move through the water by using oars. **3** *tr.v* make (a boat) move in this way. **4** *tr.v* take (s.o) s.w in a boat by rowing(2) it: *Get in and I'll row you across to the other side of the river.* **row (a race) against s.o** have a race against s.o in rowing boats.

'rower *c.n* person who rows[1].

'rowing *u.n* (also *attrib*) (often *go —*) sport done by rowing (⇨ row[1](2)): *Our rowing club does its rowing mostly at weekends.*

'rowing ,boat *c.n* boat that one rows[1](3).

row[2] /rəʊ/ *c.n* line (of people etc) side by side: *a row of children*; *a row of cabbages.* **in a row** arranged to form a row[2]: *Now stand in a row, girls, so that the princess can see you all.*

row[3] /raʊ/ *c.n* **1** (often *make a —*) unpleasant

noise. **2** (often *have a* — (*with s.o*)) quarrel, usu
a noisy one, (with s.o). **get in a row** be scolded:
*You'll get in a row if your mother sees you doing
that!* **kick up**, **make**, **a row** (**about s.t**) = kick up,
make, a fuss (about s.o/s.t) (⇒ fuss(*n*)).
▷ *intr.v* **3** (usu — *with s.o* (*about s.t*)) have a row[3](2)
(with s.o) (about s.t).

rowdy /'raʊdɪ/ *adj* (*-ier*, *-iest*) **1** (*informal*)
unpleasantly noisy and sometimes rather violent.
▷ *c.n* (*pl -ies*) **2** (*slang*) rowdy person.
'**rowdily** *adv*. '**rowdiness** *u.n.*

rower, **rowing**, **rowing boat** ⇒ row[1].

royal /'rɔɪəl/ *adj* **1** (sometimes with capital **R**) of
or referring to a king or queen. **2** (often *right* —)
(*formal* or *old use*) (very) splendid: *a right royal
welcome*.
▷ *c.n* **3** (*informal*) member of a royal family.
,**Royal 'Air ,Force** *def.n* (*abbr RAF*) branch of
the British armed forces that has planes.
,**Royal 'Automobile ,Club** *def.n* (*abbr RAC*)
one of the two main British drivers' clubs that
help them on and off the road. ⇒ Automobile
Association.
,**Royal ,Engi'neers** *def.pl.n* (*abbr RE*) branch
of the armed forces that deals with building,
repairing things etc.
,**Royal 'Highness** *c.n* (often *Her/His/Your* —;
Their/Your —*es*) title of a prince(ss).
'**royalist** *c.n* (also *attrib*) person who supports a
king or queen, or believes that a country should
have one. Compare republican(2,4).
'**royally** *adv* in a royal(2) way.
,**Royal Ma'rines** *pl.n* soldiers trained to fight on
or from ships.
,**Royal 'Navy** *def.n* (*abbr RN*) branch of the
British armed forces that has ships.
,**royal pre'rogative** *def.n* special right that the
king or queen of a country has.
,**Royal So'ciety** *def.n* British society started in
1662 for the improvement of science. *Fellow of
the Royal Society* (*abbr FRS*) member of this
society, chosen from among the best scientists.

RP /,ɑː 'piː/ *unique n abbr* received pronunciation.

rpm /,ɑː ,piː 'em/ *pl.n abbr* revolutions per minute
(⇒ revolution[2](2) at revolve).

rps /,ɑː ,piː 'es/ *pl.n abbr* revolutions per second (⇒
revolution[2](2) at revolve).

RSM /,ɑːr ,es 'em/ *c.n abbr* Regimental Sergeant
Major.

RSVP /,ɑːr ,es ,viː 'piː/ *abbr répondez s'il vous
plaît* (*French*) (put on invitations), 'please answer'.

rub /rʌb/ *c.n* **1** (often *give s.o/s.t a* —) example
of rubbing(2).
▷ *v* (*-bb-*) **2** *tr.v* slide s.t, often one's hand or s.t held
in it, along, over, up and down etc the surface
of (s.o/s.t), using pressure: *Is your back hurting
again? I'll rub it with oil.* **3** *intr.v* (often —*against/
on s.o/s.t*) slide (against/on s.o/s.t) with pressure,
sometimes causing pain or damage: *New shoes
sometimes damage the skin by rubbing.*
rub s.t away/out/off (**s.o/s.t**) remove s.t (from
s.o/s.t) by rubbing.
rub s.o/s.t clean/dry (**with s.t**) rub s.o/s.t until
he/she/it is clean/dry (using s.t).
rub s.o, **an animal**, **down** dry s.o, an animal, by
rubbing her/him/it. **rub s.t down** (**with s.t**) make
s.t smooth(er) made by rubbing it (with s.t).
rub one's hands ⇒ hand(*n*).
rub s.t/it in; **rub it in that . . .** (*fig*) try to stop

s.o forgetting s.t by saying it again and again: *The
manager kept on rubbing it in that the customer
is always right. 'You shouldn't have said that!' 'I
know, but don't keep rubbing it in.'* **rub s.t in** (**to
s.o/s.t**) make s.t, e.g oil, go into the surface of
one's skin etc by rubbing(2).
rub s.t on s.o/s.t put s.t, e.g oil, on s.o's skin etc
and rub(2) it in.
rub out go away as a result of being rubbed(2):
Pencil marks rub out easily. Compare rub s.t
away/out.
rub shoulders with s.o ⇒ shoulder(*n*).
rub s.t (**and s.t**) **together** rub(2) s.t against s.t.
rub s.t up (**a**) make s.t shine etc by rubbing(2) it.
(**b**) (*fig*) study s.t again so as not to forget it;
revise(3) s.t. **rub up on s.t** = rub s.t up(b). **rub
s.o up the wrong way** ⇒ way(*n*).

'**rubber**[1] *c.n* **1** thing used for rubbing(2) s.t away
or off, e.g for cleaning a blackboard. **2** person,
machine etc who/that rubs(2).

rubber[2] /'rʌbə/ *n* **1** *u.n* (usu *attrib*) material
that comes out of a rubber tree as a thick
white liquid and is then made solid and used
for making tyres, boots etc: *a rubber ball.* **2** *u.n*
(also *attrib*) material like rubber[2](1) but made
from chemicals. **3** *c.n* piece of rubber[2](1,2) used
for rubbing out pencil marks etc; eraser. **4** *c.n* =
condom.
,**rubber 'band** *c.n* round strip of rubber used
for holding things together etc.
,**rubber 'dinghy** *c.n* small boat made of rubber
that one blows air into.
'**rubber ,plant** *c.n* plant of the rubber tree family
that has big shiny leaves.
,**rubber 'sheath** *c.n* = condom.
,**rubber 'stamp** *c.n* **1** device with a handle and a
rubber base on which there is s.t in raised letters,
numbers, pictures etc used to print the letters,
numbers etc on paper etc. **2** (*derog*) person,
office etc who/that rubber-stamps everything.
,**rubber-'stamp** *tr.v* (usu *derog*) approve (s.t, e.g
a decision made by s.o one is afraid of) without
thinking whether it is right or wrong.
'**rubber ,tree** *c.n* tree that grows in hot damp
countries from which we get rubber by cutting
its sides and letting the liquid rubber flow out.
'**rubbery** *adj* (*derog*) (of food) tough like
rubber[2](1).

'**rub-,down** *c.n* (often *give s.o/s.t a* —) example
of rubbing s.o/s.t down.

rubbish /'rʌbɪʃ/ *interj* **1** nonsense(1).
▷ *u.n* **2** things that one is throwing away. **3** (often *a
load of* (*old*) —; *talk* —) (*derog*) nonsense(2).
▷ *tr.v* **4** (*informal*) try to make (s.o/s.t) appear
to be no good, worthless etc: *He's doing his
best to rubbish the government's report on
unemployment.*
'**rubbish ,bin** *c.n* = dustbin.
'**rubbish col,lector** *c.n* = dustman.
'**rubbish ,heap** *c.n* pile of rubbish(2), often the
place in a garden where one puts dead leaves
etc.
'**rubbishy** *adj* (*derog*; *informal*) that is
rubbish(3); that is not worth anything.

rubble /'rʌbl/ *u.n* pieces of broken stone, bricks
etc left after building or destroying a house etc.

rub-down ⇒ rub(*v*).

rubella /ruːˈbelə/ *u.n* (*medical*) German
measles.

ruby /ˈruːbɪ/ n (pl -ies) (also attrib) **1** c.n kind of red precious stone: a ruby ring. **2** u.n red colour of this stone.

rucksack /ˈrʌkˌsæk/ c.n bag carried on a person's back, usu by straps(1) that go over her/his shoulders, used by people having a walking holiday, to carry their clothes etc. ⇨ backpack, haversack, knapsack.

rudder /ˈrʌdə/ c.n device at the back of a ship, plane etc for steering it by turning it to one side or the other.

ruddy¹ /ˈrʌdɪ/ adj (-ier, iest) **1** (of a person's face etc) red (and therefore looking healthy). **2** (attrib) (literary) (rather) red: the ruddy glow(1) of a fire.
ˈruddiness u.n.

ruddy² /ˈrʌdɪ/ attrib.adj **1** (used to show anger, with no real meaning): I wanted a rest but the ruddy telephone's ringing!
▷ adv **2** very: I'm ruddy glad it isn't raining.

rude /ruːd/ adj **1** (derog) (of a person, the way he/she behaves etc) not at all polite; who/that hurts a person's feelings. **2** (of a story, joke etc) shocking because of references to sex etc. **3** simple; not decorated or elaborate(1).
ˌrude aˈwakening c.n (usu have a —) sudden unpleasant realization of s.t one did not know before.
ˈrudely adv **1** in a rude way. **2** suddenly and unpleasantly: I was sleeping happily when I was rudely awakened by the telephone.
ˈrudeness u.n **1** fact or state of being rude. **2** (usu the — of s.t) fact of (s.t) being sudden and unpleasant.
ˌrude ˈshock c.n sudden and unpleasant shock.

rudiments /ˈruːdɪmənts/ def.pl.n (often the — of s.t) things that form the basis (of s.t); things (about s.t) that one learns first, before going on to the details.
rudimentary /ˌruːdɪˈmentərɪ/ adj **1** consisting only of the rudiments of s.t. **2** (of an organ in a person's or an animal's body) not fully developed: We each have a rudimentary tail.

rueful /ˈruːfʊl/ adj (formal) feeling or showing regret.
ˈruefully adv. **ˈruefulness** u.n.

ruffian /ˈrʌfɪən/ c.n bad, rough, sometimes cruel, person.

ruffle¹ /ˈrʌfl/ c.n frill of lace(2) etc sewn round the neck or wrist of a shirt etc as a decoration.

ruffle² /ˈrʌfl/ tr.v **1** cause (s.t, e.g the surface of water, a person's hair, a bird's feathers) to stop being smooth and become untidy, rough etc. **2** tr/intr.v (cause (s.o, s.o's feelings) to) become disturbed, worried, angry etc. **smooth s.o's ruffled feathers** ⇨ feather(n).
ruffled adj (of a person) disturbed, worried etc. Opposite unruffled(2).

rug /rʌg/ c.n **1** kind of small carpet. ⇨ hearthrug. **2** thing like a blanket but often thicker used for putting round oneself when one is sitting, e.g in a car.

rugby /ˈrʌgbɪ/ u.n (also **ˌrugby ˈfootball**, **ˈrugger**) u.n game played by teams of 15 with a ball shaped like an egg which can be held when one runs as well as kicked.

rugged /ˈrʌgɪd/ adj **1** having a rough irregular surface: a rugged mountain; a man with a rugged face. **2** (of a person, usu a man, or his character)

strong and rough but good and to be trusted. He was rugged and true.
ˈruggedly adv. **ˈruggedness** u.n.

rugger /ˈrʌgə/ u.n (informal) rugby.

ruin /ˈruːɪn/ n **1** u.n (often the — of s.o/s.t) example of ruining(3,4) (s.o/s.t). **2** c.n (often pl with sing meaning) thing, e.g a building, or sometimes person, that/who has been ruined(3,4). **be in**, **go to**, **rack and ruin** ⇨ rack and ruin (⇨ rack). **face ruin** be likely to be ruined(4). **fall into ruin** become ruined(3). **in ruins** that has been ruined(3,4).
▷ tr.v **3** destroy, completely spoil, (s.t, e.g a building, a person's hopes of doing s.t, a child's character). **4** make (s.o/s.t) lose all her/his money.
ˈruinous adj **1** causing ruin(3,4). **2** (of a building etc) partly or completely in ruins.
ˈruinously adv in a way that is likely to ruin(4) s.o: ruinously expensive.

rule /ruːl/ n **1** c.n written or spoken words that tell one what one must (not) or ought (not) to do: One of the rules in our school is that there must be no running in the passages. Compare law(1), regulation(1). **2** c.n normal fact or state of s.t etc …): There's no rule about which people will prove to be brave in battle; the most surprising people are and are not. **3** u.n (often the — of/over s.t) control or government (of s.t); time during which this lasts: The rule of the Romans(3) in Britain lasted hundreds of years. **4** c.n ruler(2): a foot rule (i.e one that measures in feet (⇨ foot(4)) and inches(1)). ⇨ slide rule. **according to rule** in the way the rule(1) states it should be done. **against the rules (of s.t)** not according to rule. **as a (general) rule** usually. **bend/stretch the rules** do s.t that is not quite according to rule. **(do s.t) by rule** = (do s.t) according to rule. **go by the rules** ⇨ go by the book/ rules (⇨ book(n)). **(the) golden rule** ⇨ golden. **make it a rule to do s.t** have the habit of doing s.t. **the rule of law** situation in which everybody has to do what the law says, instead of what he/ she wants. **the rule(s) of the road** law telling one which side of the road one should drive on etc. **rules and regulations** (a) rules(1). (b) (derog) usu large number of small unimportant rules that only make life difficult. **under British** etc **rule** ruled(5) by Britain etc. **work to rule** strike(5) by following every rule carefully so that work is very slow. ⇨ work-to-rule (⇨ work).
▷ v **5** tr/intr.v (often — over s.o/s.t) have the rule(3) (over s.o/s.t). **6** tr/intr.v (often — against/on s.t; — that …) (usu of a judge in a court of law or an official) decide officially (against/about s.t, that …). **7** tr.v draw (a straight line) using a ruler(2). **8** tr.v draw straight lines on (a piece of paper etc) using a ruler(2). **be ruled by s.t** have s.t that guides or influences one: You should be ruled by your head, not your heart, when it comes to business. **rule s.t off** draw a line under s.t, usu a list of numbers, to show that it is finished. **rule s.t out** say that s.t is not possible, allowed etc: We can rule out the possibility of murder in this case because the door was locked from the inside. **rule (s.o/s.t) with an iron hand, a rod of iron** ⇨ iron(n).
ˈrule book c/def.n book/set of rules(1) for doing s.t, e.g one given to workers by their trade union. **go by the rulebook** do only what is in the rulebook.

'ruler *c.n* **1** (often *the — of s.o/s.t*) person who rules(5) (s.o/s.t). **2** long flat device with which one can rule(7) straight lines; it is marked with centimetres etc so that one can use it for measuring lengths.

'ruling *attrib.adj* **1** (of a person, a class of people etc) who has/have the power in a country etc: *the ruling class(es) of a country.* **2** (of a feeling etc) most important; strongest: *Many children here have one ruling passion and that is riding horses.*
▷ *c.n* **3** (often *a — on s.t, that...*) official decision. ⇒ rule(6).

rum /rʌm/ *u.n* (also *attrib*) strong alcoholic(1) drink made from sugar cane(1) juice.

rumba /'rʌmbə/ *c/def.n* **1** kind of dance that started in Cuba. **2** music for such a dance.
▷ *intr.v* **3** dance a/the rumba(1).

rumble /'rʌmbl/ *c.n* **1** (often *— of s.t*) deep rolling sound (like that) of thunder or a cart going over a rough stone street (made by s.t).
▷ *intr.v* **2** make the sound of a rumble(1): *My stomach's rumbling because I haven't eaten all day.*

ruminate /'ruːmɪˌneɪt/ *intr.v* **1** (*formal*) (often *— about/over s.t*) think (about s.t), usu for a long time. **2** (of some kinds of animals, e.g cows and deer) bring food up again out of the stomach and chew it again. ⇒ chew the cud (⇒ cud(*n*)).

rumour /'ruːmə/ *c/u.n* (US **'rumor**) (example of) general talk (about s.o/s.t) which may or may not be true: *I heard a rumour about your party. Have you heard the rumour that we're going to have a holiday tomorrow? Rumour has it that...* There is a rumour that....

'rumoured *adj* (US **'rumored**) that is only a rumour: *Have you heard of Joan's rumoured marriage? It is rumoured that...* There is a rumour that....

'rumour-,monger *c.n* (US **'rumor-,monger**) (*derog*) person who (starts and) spreads rumours.

rump /rʌmp/ *n* **1** *c.n* buttocks of an animal, bird or sometimes (*joking*) person. **2** *u.n* (also **,rump 'steak**) meat off the rump(1) of a cow, ox etc. **3** small, poor or useless part of s.t that is left after the rest has gone.

rumple /'rʌmpl/ *tr.v* make (s.t, e.g bedclothes or a person's hair) untidy.

run /rʌn/ *c.n* **1** act or example of running(13,14). **2** time during which s.o/s.t (e.g a train or ship) runs(15). **3** distance s.o/s.t (e.g a train or ship) runs(15). **4** (often *go for a —*) short journey in a vehicle, boat etc, usu for pleasure. **5** (often *— from s.w to s.w, across/through s.t*) journey (from s.w to s.w etc). **6** (in a sport such as skiing(2)) slope down which one goes: *a ski-run.* **7** place in which animals, chickens etc are kept and in which they can run about. **8** (in cricket¹ etc) point scored by running from one place to another. **9** (often *— in s.t*) ladder(3) (in a stocking etc). **10** (of a play, film etc) period(1) (of a year etc) during which there are regular performances. **11** (often *— of s.t*) (of production in a factory, printing press etc) one thing produced regularly after another. **12** (often *a — of s.t*) (of things of the same kind happening) one happening (of s.t) after another: *a run of good luck at cards.* **at a run** while running(13): *The man crossed the road at a run.* **break into a run** start to

run(13,14). **the common/ordinary run of s.t** the ordinary kind of s.t. **give s.o the run of s.t** allow s.o to use s.t (e.g a house) freely. **a (good) run for one's money** (*fig*) **(a)** (*informal*) a fair or generous return for what one pays or for one's time and trouble. **(b)** a good chance to win. **have the run of s.t** be allowed to use s.t (e.g a house) freely. **in the long/short run** looking at the distant/near future: *In the short run Fred will earn less in his new job but in the long run he will be much better off.* **make a run (for it)** run away. **on the run (a)** (often *— from s.o/s.t*) running away to escape (from s.o/s.t). **(b)** working hard; busy. **a run on s.t** a sudden demand for s.t with the result that there is not enough of it. **a run on a/the bank** a time when a lot of people try to get money out of a/the bank at the same time so that there is a danger of it failing.
▷ *v* (*-nn-*, *p.t* ran /ræn/, *p.p* run /rʌn/) **13** *intr.v* (of a person, some birds etc) go along by moving one's feet one after another in such a way that both are never on the ground at the same time. Compare hop¹(3), walk(7). **14** (of an animal with four legs, an insect) move along at a speed faster than walking. **15** *tr/intr.v* (cause (s.t, often a vehicle or ship) to) move, usu quickly: *Could you please run the car to the petrol pump and get some petrol. When the storm began the boats all ran into port.* **16** *intr.v* (often *— across/over (to s.o/s.t)*) go (to s.o/s.t) quickly and informally, usu on a short visit: *I'll just run over to Pam's and tell her the news.* **17** *tr.v* (usu *— s.o s.w*) take (s.o) s.w in one's car etc: *Can I run you home (or to the station)?* **18** *tr/intr.v* (cause (a train, bus, ferry(1) etc) to) operate, go or follow its usual course: *This company runs a bus service down to the port.* **19** *intr.v* (usu *— along/over/through s.t*; *— from s.t to s.t*) go, extend, cover, a certain distance, (along etc s.t): *Our part of the coast runs from here to Dover.* **20** *tr/intr.v* (cause (s.o, an animal) to) take part in a race, an election etc (against s.o/s.t): *We aren't running any horses today. Our party is running candidates(1) in every constituency except three. John is running for mayor next year. Who will run against him?* Compare stand(19). **21** *tr.v* organize (an election, a campaign(2) etc). **22** *tr.v* control, direct, be the boss of, (s.t, e.g a company, government, country, shop). **23** *tr/intr.v* (cause (an engine etc) to) work, operate or be in motion: *Run the engine till it is warm before you put any load on it.* **24** *intr.v* (*fig*) work; operate; function(3): *How are things running in your university these days?* **25** *tr/intr.v* (cause (s.t, e.g water or sand) to) flow: *If you run the water for a few seconds, it will get hot.* **26** *intr.v* (of a person's nose, a tap, a river etc) flow; have liquid coming out of it. **27** *intr.v* (of a coloured thing) spread its colour when it is wet: *Don't wash that blue handkerchief with the white ones because it runs.* **28** *intr.v* (of a colour) spread in this way. **29** *intr.v* (of s.t that melts when it is heated) become liquid and spread: *Butter runs when it is put on something hot.* **30** *intr.v* (of a material) have a ladder(3) in it. **31** *intr.v* continue to be in operation, to be performed etc: *Our agreement hasn't ended yet; it has another year to run. The film we saw in London last May is still running in the same cinema.* **32** *tr/intr.v* (usu *— like this*) (of the words of a poem etc) consist

exactly of (s.t); be made up exactly of (s.t): *Her telegram runs (like this)*: *'Come soonest; child ill'.*

cut and run ⇒ cut(*v*).

make s.o's blood run cold ⇒ blood.

run across s.o find or meet s.o (usu s.o one is pleased to see) by chance. ⇒ come across s.o/s.t; run into s.o, run up against s.o. **run across s.t (a)** run to the other side of s.t, e.g a road. **(b)** find s.t, by chance. **run across (to s.o/s.t)** ⇒ run(16).

run after s.o/s.t run to try and catch (up with) s.o/s.t.

run (s.t) aground (on s.t) ⇒ aground.

run along (usu imperative, to a child etc) go away. **run along s.t** ⇒ run(19).

run amok ⇒ amok(*adv*).

run around together; **run around with s.o** (*fig*) often go to places together, with s.o.

run at s.o/s.t run towards s.o/s.t to try hit her/ him/it with one's head or body.

run away (from s.o/s.t) (sometimes *fig*) try to escape (from s.o/s.t). **run away/off with s.o** run away taking s.o with one; elope with s.o. **run away with s.o** (of feelings etc) control s.o completely and dangerously: *It's not very wise to let your emotions*(1) *run away with you.* **run away with the idea etc that . . .** believe that . . . when this idea is, or may be, wrong: *You shouldn't run away with the idea that the job is easy.* **run away with s.t (a)** steal and take s.t with one. **(b)** use s.t up; cost s.t that one does not want to spend: *His new boat is running away with most of his salary every month.* **(c)** win a match easily: *The other side was so poor that our team ran away with the game.* **run back (s.w or to s.o/s.t)** run, return, (to the place, person etc) one has just left: *He ran back to his mother and gave her a kiss.* **run s.t back** make a film etc go backwards, esp so that one can look at a part of it again. **run back over s.t** discuss, read, etc s.t again.

run (oneself/s.o) a bath ⇒ bath(*n*).

run behind (schedule/time) be late (in one's/its schedule(1)/time), esp in a planned programme: *The production schedule is running about two weeks behind.*

run the chance/danger/risk of s.t be, or put oneself, in danger etc of s.t.

run by electricity etc have electricity etc as the thing that makes it work. **time runs by** ⇒ time(*n*).

run down (a) (of a clock, battery, machine etc) lose power or become weaker and weaker, sometimes until it stops completely. **(b)** (of a factory etc) do less and less work, sometimes until it stops completely. ⇒ run-down(2). **run down to s.w** (of a garden etc) go, stretch, slope down, as far as s.w: *The park runs down to a small stream.* **run s.o/s.t down (a)** hit s.o, an animal, with the car etc one is driving. **(b)** chase and catch s.o, an animal. **(c)** find s.o/s.t after searching for her/him/it. **(d)** say nasty things about s.o/s.t to try to make people think he/she/it is no good. **(e)** allow s.t, e.g a factory, to do less and less work, often until it stops completely. ⇒ run down(b), run-down(2).

run (s.t) dry ⇒ dry.

run for dear/one's life; **run for it** run (very hard) in order to escape. **run for s.t** ⇒ run(20).

run high ⇒ high(*adv*).

run s.o home ⇒ run(17).

run s.o in (*informal*) arrest s.o. **run (s.t) in** (let a new (engine of a) car etc) run rather slowly and carefully until it is ready to be driven at full speed.

run in the family ⇒ family.

run into s.o (*informal*) meet s.o by chance. ⇒ run across s.o, run up against s.o. **run into s.o/s.t** hit s.o/s.t with a vehicle, boat etc. **run into s.t** reach the amount of s.t: *The amount he spends on clothes every month runs into hundreds of pounds.*

run low ⇒ low[1].

run a mile (from s.o/s.t) ⇒ mile(*n*).

run off run from s.o, a place etc: *She ran off, leaving him standing there.* **run off s.t** be powered by s.t, e.g a battery: *The lights run off a small generator.* **run s.t off (a)** cause or allow a liquid to flow out. **(b)** print s.t: *I'll run off a few extra copies of the report for you.* **(c)** have (the heats(4) of) a race: *The heats are run off during the week and the finals are on Saturday.* **run off with s.o/ s.t** ⇒ run away with s.o, run away with s.t(a). **run s.o off her/his feet** ⇒ foot(*n*).

run on (a) continue. **(b)** (*informal*) talk for a long time, usu boringly: *He does run on a bit when he starts talking about his favourite subject.* **run on s.o/s.t** ⇒ run (up)on s.o/s.t. **run s.t on** continue writing or printing s.t without a break, new line etc: *Run this paragraph*(1) *on.* **run (s.t) on s.t** use s.t, e.g oil, as the fuel(1) (for s.t): *This car runs on diesel.*

run out (of an agreement etc) finish; be no longer in force; be no longer valid(2): *The lease*(1) *on my flat runs out in a year's time.* **run out (of s.t)** not be/have any more (of s.t) left, because it has all been used up. **run s.o out** (in cricket[1]) cause a player to be out(19) by hitting the wicket(1) with the ball when he/she is not in the crease(3). ⇒ runout. **run (s.t) out** (cause (s.t that is rolled up etc) to) stretch out: *Run a rope out to the boat and tie it to the shore.* **run out on s.o** (*informal*) leave s.o whom one has a duty etc not to leave: *He just ran out on his wife and children without a word.* ⇒ walk out on s.o.

run over (into s.t) spill (and flow into s.t) because it is too full. **run over s.o/s.t**; **run s.o/s.t over** (of a car etc or its driver) knock s.o/s.t down and then go over her/him/it. **run over s.t** = run through s.t(a).

run riot ⇒ riot(*n*).

run a risk, risks ⇒ risk(*n*).

run short (of s.t) ⇒ short(*adv*).

run a temperature ⇒ temperature(*n*).

run through s.t (a) look at, examine, s.t, usu again or quickly: *Let's just run through the main points again.* ⇒ run-through(1). **(b)** read a play, scene etc or act it, esp during a rehearsal: *Can you run through your lines again, please?* ⇒ run-through(2). **(c)** spend s.t, usu much faster than one should: *He has had several fortunes and run through them all.* **(d)** be in every part of s.t; permeate(2) s.t: *A belief in the goodness of human beings runs through all Mary's writings.* **run through s.o's mind** ⇒ mind[1]. **run s.o through (with s.t)** pierce(1) s.o's body (with a sword etc) so that it comes out the other side.

run to s.o/s.t have/be enough to pay for s.o/s.t: *I can't run to a secretary.* **run to s.t** have a tendency towards s.t: *Some families run to fat.*

run (s.o/s.t) to s.w ⇨ run(15–17). **run to seed** ⇨ seed(*n*).

run up (*sport*) run towards the place where one jumps or (in cricket[1]) where one bowls[2](3): *He's now running up to take his third and final jump.* ⇨ run-up(2). **run up s.t** (start to) have bills, debts etc because one is getting things one cannot pay for: *He ran up a large overdraft because of his wife's medical expenses.* **run up against s.o** (*informal*) meet s.o by chance. ⇨ run across s.o; run into s.o. **run up against s.o/s.t (a)** hit s.o/s.t with one's body, car etc. **(b)** (*informal*) meet s.o/s.t that causes one trouble: *We're running up against a few problems and can't get very far.*

run (up)on s.o/s.t (of a person's mind) be thinking a lot about s.o/s.t: *My thoughts were running on all our problems and I couldn't get to sleep.*

'run,bout *c.n* small car that one uses for short journeys, e.g in a town to go to the shops.

'run-a,round *c/def.n* **get, give s.o, a/the run-around** (*informal*) get etc bad treatment: *She's giving him a real run-around and won't say whether she'll marry him or not.*

'runa,way *attrib.adj* **1** who has run away, usu from home: *a runaway child.* **2** that is done by running away: *a runaway marriage to escape a jealous father.* **3** that one cannot control: *a runaway horse; runaway* inflation(2).
▷ *c.n* **4** runaway(1) person.

,run 'down *adj* (**'run-,down** when *attrib*) tired and/or weak, esp because one has been working too hard, has been ill etc: *He looked very run down after working 18 hours a day. He was in a very run-down state.*

'run-,down *adj* **1** = run down. **2** (of a factory etc) working less, badly etc: *The industry is in a run-down condition because of lack of orders.* ⇨ run down(b).
▷ *c.n* **3** reduction in the number of things produced, people employed etc: *There has been a steady run-down in the armed forces.* **4** (often *a — on s.t*) giving of the main facts, information etc, usu in a brief way (on s.t): *Can you give me a run-down on the present situation?*

'runner *c.n* **1** person who runs, e.g in a race. **2** vertical metal blade on which a skate[1](1) slides over the ice. **3** one of the two horizontal strips of metal etc on which a sleigh etc slides over the snow. **4** thing along which s.t, e.g a curtain, slides. **5** strip of cloth for putting along the middle of a table, usu for decoration, or along a floor to keep it clean where people walk on it.

'runner ,bean *c.n* (also **,scarlet 'runner, ,string 'bean**) **1** kind of bean plant that climbs, and usu has red flowers. **2** bean from such a plant.

,runner-'up *c.n* (*pl* runners-up, runner-ups) person/team that does not win a race etc but comes second.

'running *adj* **1** (of a liquid) that flows/runs(26), sometimes out of taps: *a room with running hot and cold water.* **2** out of which liquid flows: *a running nose/sore/tap.* **3** needed or used for running (⇨ run(23,24)) s.t: *the running costs/expenses.*
▷ *adv* **4** (*twice, three etc times, two years etc —*) (twice etc) one after the other without a break: *Our college has won the* football cup three times (or three years) running.
▷ *u.n* **5** act or sport of running (⇨ run(13)). **in, out of, the running (for s.t)** (*informal*) having a/no chance of getting, winning etc (s.t): *Kate is in the running for* promotion(1) *to manager.*

,running 'commentary *c.n* ⇨ commentary(*n*).

'running ,mate *c.n* **1** person who runs(20) for s.t in which he/she will be the partner of s.o else if both are successful. **2** less important of two running mates(1): *President Reagan's running mate was George Bush* (the man who became Vice-President (⇨ vice(-)[3])).

'running ,order *u.n* (often *in* (*good*) —) condition that allows good running (⇨ run(23)).

'runny *adj* (*-ier, -iest*) **1** more liquid than is usual or normal: *runny jam.* **2** (of one's nose or eyes) = running(2).

'run-,off *c.n* final race, competition etc to find a winner after all/both the competitors are equal at that stage.

,run-of-the-'mill *adj* (usu *derog*) very ordinary; not interesting, good etc.

'run,out *c.n* (in cricket[1]) act of running s.o out or of being run out (⇨ run s.o out).

'run-,through *c.n* (usu *— of s.t*) **1** examination (of s.t), usu again or quickly. ⇨ run through s.t(a). **2** reading of a play etc, esp during a rehearsal. ⇨ run through s.t(b).

'run-,up *c.n* (often *a/the — to s.t*) **1** (time of) preparation for s.t, e.g an election, when the people taking part in it are trying to win votes. **2** (in jumping sports etc) run(1) that is done to give one impetus(1) before one jumps etc. ⇨ run up(a).

'run,way *c.n* wide hard surface at an airport on which planes take off and land.

rung[1] /rʌŋ/ *c.n* **1** step of a ladder. ⇨ tread(2). **2** thing like a rung(1) that is between the legs of a chair, usu to strengthen them. **the highest/lowest, the top/bottom, rung of the ladder** (*fig*) the highest/lowest etc rank in s.t: *In our office, you start at the bottom rung of the ladder and hope to reach the top one day.*

rung[2] /rʌŋ/ *p.p* of ring[2].

runt /rʌnt/ *c.n* animal that is smaller than normal: *the runt of the* litter[1](2) (i.e the smallest of the babies produced by a cat etc).

run-through, run-up, runway ⇨ run.

rupture /'rʌptʃə/ *c/u.n* **1** sudden breaking, bursting or tearing (of s.t, e.g an organ in one's body, or (*fig*) relations between two countries). ⇨ hernia.
▷ *tr/intr.v* **2** (cause (s.t) to) break, burst or tear suddenly: *The pipe has ruptured.* **rupture oneself** suffer a rupture(1).

rural /'rʊərəl/ *adj* (usu showing that one likes it) in, like or concerning the country, not the town: *rural life.* Opposite urban. Compare rustic(1).

ruse /ru:z/ *c.n* trick(4–6).

rush[1] /rʌʃ/ *n* **1** *c/u.n* (often *in a —*) hurry; (in) haste: *We're all in a rush because we're late for our train.* **2** *u.n* (too) busy activity: *I get up at 7 and go straight to work to beat the rush.* ⇨ rush hour. **3** *c.n* sudden quick movement (to get/reach s.t): *The soldiers advanced in short rushes.* **a rush for s.t, to do s.t** sudden unusually big demand for s.t, e.g tickets for a match, or to do s.t, e.g to buy gold. ⇨ gold(-)rush. **there is no rush for s.t, to do**

s.t it is not urgent to do, have etc s.t. **What's (all) the rush?** Why are you hurrying? (because it is not necessary to do so).

▷ *v* **4** *tr/intr.v* (often — (s.o/s.t) *in*(to s.t), *out* (of s.t)) (cause (s.o/s.t) to) hurry or move (in etc) fast: *She's badly hurt — we must rush her to hospital.* **5** *tr.v* do (s.t) quickly, sometimes so quickly that one does not or cannot do it properly: *When you are rowing a race you must never rush your strokes.* **6** *tr.v* (often — s.o *into* (doing) s.t) (try to) force (s.o) to rush¹(4) (and do s.t): *It's a difficult decision so don't rush him (into anything).* **7** *tr.v* attack (s.o, an animal) suddenly and all/both together: *Let's rush the sheep from all sides; then we should catch it all right.* **rush into print** print s.t in a newspaper etc without waiting and thinking whether it is wise to do so (yet). **rush into s.t** do s.t in too great a hurry, without thinking carefully first: *It is foolish to rush into marriage before you are sure.* ⇨ rush(6). **rush s.o off her/his feet** ⇨ foot(*n*). **rush s.t out** produce s.t, e.g a story in a newspaper, in a great hurry. **rush s.t through** do s.t in a hurry until it is finished.

'rush ˌhour *c/def.n* time when the traffic is very heavy in a place, when the trains, buses etc are crowded, e.g when everybody is travelling to or from work.

ˌrush ˌhour 'traffic *u.n* traffic at the rush hour.

ˌrush 'job *c.n* job that has to be done urgently.

rush² /rʌʃ/ *c.n* kind of plant that grows in or near water and has long bare stems, sometimes dried and woven into mats etc.

rusk /rʌsk/ *c.n* piece of bread that has been cut off a loaf and baked slowly until it is hard.

rust /rʌst/ *u.n* (also *attrib*) **1** red-brown substance that forms on iron etc when it is not kept dry, oiled or polished. **2** colour of rust(1).

▷ *tr/intr.v* **3** (cause (s.t) to) become covered with rust(1). **rust (s.t) away** (cause (s.t) to) be destroyed by rust(1). **rust (s.t) up** (cause (s.t) to) become so covered with rust(1) that it does not move any more.

'rustiness *u.n* state or fact of being rusty.

'rustless *adj* without rust(1) on it.

'rustˌproof *adj* **1** unable to get rust(1) on it. Compare non-rust, stainless(1).

▷ *tr.v* **2** make (s.t) rustproof(1).

'rusty *adj* (-*ier*, -*iest*) **1** having rust(1) on it. **2** (of a person, s.o's knowledge or memory of s.t) having forgotten (some of s.t): *I used to speak Russian well but now I am* (or *my Russian is*) *rusty.*

rustic /'rʌstɪk/ *adj* **1** of, referring to, suitable for, the country, not the town: *rustic furniture*, *rustic simplicity.* ⇨ rural, urban. **2** roughly made of wood without removing the bark¹: *a rustic seat in a garden.*

rustle /'rʌsl/ *sing.n* **1** (often *the — of* s.t) small sound(s) (like that/those) made when dry leaves, sheets of paper etc are moved by the wind and rub against each other or s.t else.

▷ *tr/intr.v* **2** cause (s.t) to make this sound.

rustless, rustproof, rusty ⇨ rust.

rut /rʌt/ *c.n* deep line left, usu in soft ground, by the wheel of a cart etc. **be in**, **get into**, **a rut** (*fig*) be in, get into, a situation in which one is doing the same boring things every day. **get out of a/ the rut** (*fig*) get out of a situation of this kind.

'rutted *adj* (of a path etc) having ruts in it.

ruthless /'ruːθlɪs/ *adj* **1** (*derog*) very cruel;

feeling and/or showing no pity. **2** firm in doing s.t necessary but unpleasant.

'ruthlessly *adv.* **'ruthlessness** *u.n.*

rye /raɪ/ *u.n* **1** kind of plant grown for making bread etc. **2** (also *attrib*) grain of this plant: *rye bread*; *rye* whisky(1).

Ss

S, s /es/ *c/unique n* **1** 19th letter of the English alphabet.

▷ *written abbr* **2** second (of time). **3** singular. **4** (**S**) Saturday. **5** (**S**) Sunday.

▷ *symb* (**S**) **6** small size. **7** south. **8** sulphur.

Sabbath /'sæbəθ/ *c/def.n* **1** Saturday, considered by Jews and some Christians(3) as the day on which one does not work. **2** Sunday, considered by most Christians(3) as the day on which one does not work.

sabbatical /sə'bætɪkl/ *attrib.adj* **1** of or referring to the Sabbath. **2** during which one has a sabbatical(3): *sabbatical leave.*

▷ *c.n* **3** free period of time given to university teachers during which they do not have to do any work so that they can study, write, travel etc. **4** similar freedom given by organizations to their employees. Compare secondment (⇨ second⁴). **on sabbatical** having a sabbatical (3, 4): *Mary is on sabbatical at present.*

sable /'seɪbl/ *n* **1** *c.n* small animal that has beautiful dark fur. **2** *u.n* (also *attrib*) fur of this animal: *a sable coat.*

sabotage /'sæbətɑːʒ/ *u.n* **1** damage done (to buildings, vehicles, people's plans etc), usu secretly, for political or moral purposes: *Acts of sabotage will not make this government give them what they want.*

▷ *tr.v* **2** use sabotage(1) against (s.t): *The soldiers' job was to sabotage the enemy's railway lines. A few of the workers are trying to sabotage the new agreement on pay by going slow.*

saboteur /ˌsæbə'tɜː/ *c.n* person who does sabotage.

sabre /'seɪbə/ *c.n* (US **saber**) kind of curved sword used mostly by the cavalry in former times and now used for one kind of fencing² . Compare foil².

sac /sæk/ *c.n* part of an animal or plant like a bag, usu with liquid in it.

saccharin /'sækərɪn/ *u.n* chemical substance that has a very sweet taste, used instead of sugar by people who do not want to get/stay fat or who are not allowed to eat sugar.

sachet /'sæʃeɪ/ *c.n* **1** small flat container, usu made of plastic (which contains enough liquid etc for use once): *a sachet of* shampoo(1). **2** small flat packet (of powder or dried leaves etc) for putting in a cupboard etc to make clothes smell nice.

sack¹ /sæk/ *c.n* **1** bag made of rough cloth or strong plastic, used for storing or carrying things: *a coal sack*. **2** (often — *of s.t*) as much as a sack¹(1) holds: *a sack of coal*. **hit the sack** = hit the hay (⇒ hay).

'sack,cloth *u.n* cloth from which sacks are made.

'sackful *c.n* = sack¹(2).

'sacking *u.n* = sackcloth.

sack² /sæk/ *def.n* **1** dismissal; loss of one's job. **get the sack** be dismissed. **give s.o the sack** dismiss s.o from her/his job.

▷ *tr.v* **2** dismiss (s.o) from her/his job.

sack³ /sæk/ *sing.n* **1** (*literary*) action of burning, robbing, damaging etc a place (and attacking and killing the people living in it), usu in a war: *the sack of Rome*.

▷ *tr.v* **2** (*literary*) destroy (a place) in this way.

sacrament /'sækrəmənt/ *c.n* one of the important ceremonies of Christianity, e.g baptism or marriage. **the (Blessed/Holy) Sacrament** (Holy) Communion (⇒ communion(3)).

sacramental /,sækrə'mentl/ *adj* of or referring to a sacrament.

sacred /'seikrid/ *adj* **1** of or referring to religion; religious: *sacred music.* ⇒ secular. **2** considered to be holy (in some way): *a sacred mountain; a wood sacred to the goddess of wisdom.* **3** having the greatest importance without actually being holy; solemn: *a sacred promise. Is nothing sacred (to you) any more?*

,sacred 'cow *c.n* (*fig*) thing(s) that one is not allowed to criticize: *Although it is too expensive, keeping the old theatre open is a sacred cow for the town council.*

'sacredness *u.n.*

sacrosanct /'sækrə,sæŋkt/ *adj* (*formal*) so important or holy that one is not allowed to change or harm it etc: *My Friday evenings are sacrosanct and I refuse to work then.*

sacrifice /'sækrɪ,faɪs/ *c/u.n* **1** act of giving up, state of not having, s.t one likes because of s.t one considers to be more important or because one is forced to do so: *It was a great sacrifice not to have a holiday abroad but we needed the money to paint the house.* **2** things offered to God or to a god(dess) as part of one's religion, e.g a sheep killed at an altar(1). **make sacrifices (to do s.t)** sacrifice(3) things (in order to do s.t).

▷ *tr/intr.v* **3** (usu — *s.t for s.o/s.t, to do s.t*) give (s.t) up as a sacrifice(1) (for the sake of s.o/s.t, in order to do s.t). **4** (usu — (*s.t*) *to s.o/s.t*) offer (s.t) as a sacrifice(2) (to a god etc). **5** (*informal*) sell (s.t) at much less than its value, usu because one needs money very much. **sacrifice on s.t** save money, time etc by not using it for s.t: *Is it worth sacrificing on one's family in order to be rich?* **sacrifice one's life (for s.o/s.t, to do s.t)** allow oneself to be killed (to save etc s.o/ s.t).

sacrificial /,sækrɪ'fɪʃəl/ *adj* (usu *attrib*) used as or in sacrifice(2).

,sacri'ficially *adv.*

sacrilege /'sækrɪlɪdʒ/ *c/u.n* (example of the) act of being disrespectful to a holy person, place etc.

sacrilegious /,sækrɪ'lɪdʒəs/ *adj* guilty of sacrilege.

sacrosanct ⇒ sacred.

sad /sæd/ *adj* (*-dd-*) **1** not happy; feeling sorrowful. Opposite happy(1). **2** causing or likely to cause (s.o) to feel sad(1): *the sad death of a friend.* **3** (often — *state of affairs*) bad or not pleasant; not what one considers to be right: *It is a sad state of affairs when so many young people have no jobs.* **sad to say** unfortunately; I am sorry that I have to say it: *Sad to say, my uncle is ill again.* **sadder but wiser** who has learnt a useful but unpleasant lesson as a result of s.t: *John finished the match a sadder but wiser man, having realized that he needed a lot more practice before he could win anything.*

sadden /'sædn/ *tr.v* make (s.o) sad(1): *It saddens me to hear you say that.*

'sadly *adv* unfortunately: *Mary tried her best but sadly that was not good enough.* **sadly mistaken** very wrong: *If you expect to get to the station in ten minutes, you are sadly mistaken.*

'sadness *u.n.*

saddle /'sædl/ *n* **1** *c.n* kind of seat, usu made of leather, that is put on the back of a horse etc so that a person can sit on it. **2** *c.n* seat (of a bicycle etc). **3** *c.n* part of an animal's back that is behind its stomach. **4** *c/u.n* meat from this part: *a saddle of* lamb(2). **5** *c.n* line of high land joining two hills etc that are higher than it. **in the saddle (a)** riding an animal, bicycle etc. **(b)** (*fig; informal*) in control or in charge; in the position of being boss etc.

▷ *tr.v* **6** put a saddle(1) on (a horse etc). **7** (often — *s.o with s.t; — s.t* (*up*)*on s.o*) give (s.o) a job etc to do that he/she does not want or like: *When I started teaching I was saddled with the worst class in the school.*

sadism /'seidɪzəm/ *u.n* (love of) cruelty to people, sometimes giving one sexual pleasure. Compare masochism.

'sadist *c.n* person who enjoys sadism. Compare masochist.

sadistic /sə'dɪstɪk/ *adj* (*derog*) cruel; enjoying or showing sadism.

sa'distically *adv.*

sadly, sadness ⇒ sad.

s.a.e. *written abbr* stamped addressed envelope.

safari /sə'fɑːrɪ/ *c.n* (*pl* -s) trip in East Africa whose purpose is usu to find and watch wild animals such as elephants and lions. **be/go on safari** take part in a safari.

sa'fari ,park *c.n* park in which one can drive around in a car looking at wild animals that are not in cages.

safe /seif/ *adj* **1** (often — *from s.o/s.t*) not being in any danger (because of s.o/s.t): *You will be safe from attack here.* **2** (often — (*for s.o/s.t*) *to do s.t*) not causing, not able to cause, any danger (to s.o/s.t): *Is this bridge safe for us to walk on?* Opposite unsafe. **3** (also **safe and sound**) without having been hurt or damaged: *The children have arrived home quite safe (and sound).* **4** that one is sure to win: *a safe seat in* parliament (i.e a seat that the same party is sure to win again in the elections). **a safe bet** a bet(*n*) that one is sure to win. **(as) safe as houses** (*informal*) very safe. **It's safe to say (that)** ... One can say (that) ... without any fear that one will be wrong. **play (it) safe** (*informal*) not do anything that might be dangerous or risky: *We played safe and waited for the weather to improve.* **a safe place for s.t,**

to do s.t a place in which one can keep or do s.t safely. (*to be*) *on the safe side* (to be) in a position where one does not do anything that might be dangerous or risky: *It takes ten minutes to get to the station but to be on the safe side we'll allow twenty.*

▷ *c.n* **5** strong container for money and valuable things. ⇨ **strongbox. 6** container for food with net on all sides to keep flies etc out while letting air in.

,safe-'conduct */u.n* permission to go into or through a place where most people are not normally allowed: *The women were given a safe conduct to leave the battle area.*

'safe-de,posit *u.n* (also *attrib*) storing of money and valuables for customers in a bank etc: *safe-deposit box.*

'safe,guard *c.n* **1** (usu — *against s.o/s.t*) thing that protects one or is intended to protect one (against s.o/s.t).

▷ *tr.v* **2** (usu — *oneself/s.o/s.t against s.o/s.t*) protect (oneself/s.o/s.t) (against s.o/s.t).

,safe'keeping *u.n* (usu *for/in* —) the act or result of putting or keeping things in a safe place so that they are not stolen, lost etc.

'safely *adv.*

'safety *u.n* (also *attrib*) fact or state of (s.o/s.t) being safe: *safety* conscious(2). *road safety* ⇨ road. *There is safety in numbers* (*proverb*) One is safer when one is with other people than when one is alone.

'safety ,belt *c.n* **1** (also **'seat ,belt**) belt fixed across the shoulder and/or across one's stomach, worn in a car, plane etc to protect one in an accident. **2** belt worn by a person who is doing s.t dangerous, e.g working on a roof.

'safety ,catch *c.n* device on a gun that prevents it being fired accidentally.

'safety ,curtain *c.n* curtain that can be let down in front of the stage in a theatre to stop a fire spreading.

'safety ,lamp *c.n* lamp used by miners in which the flame is covered so that it cannot make dangerous gases explode.

'safety ,match *c.n* kind of match that can only be lit by striking it against a special surface, usu on the matchbox.

'safety-,pin *c.n* kind of curved pin that cannot prick(5) one easily because its point is covered when the pin is closed.

'safety ,valve *c.n* **1** (*technical*) device on an engine that opens to let steam, gas etc out when the pressure becomes so great that an explosion is likely. **2** (*fig*) activity that allows people to get rid of violent feelings in a safe way: *Writing letters to the newspaper is a safety valve for many people because it allows them to give their opinion about matters that are important to them.*

saffron /'sæfrən/ *u.n* **1** (also *attrib*) yellow-orange colour. **2** powder of this colour made from the pollen of the crocus and used to give colour and/or taste to food.

sag /sæg/ *c/u.n* (often — *in s.t*) **1** downward bend (in s.t), usu because of being too heavy or weak: *a sag in a bed.* **2** (*fig*) downward movement (in amounts): *a sag in prices, in quantities of sales.*

▷ *intr.v* (*-gg-*) **3** hang down lower than it should, usu because of weight or weakness: *That bridge looks like it's going to break; it's sagging badly in the*

middle. **4** (*fig*) become less strong, interesting, happy etc: *The soldiers' courage sagged as their food ran out. The play was very amusing at the beginning but it sagged in the middle. sag at the knees* feel weak in one's knees because very tired.

saga /'sɑːgə/ *c.n* **1** long story (of a person, family or place during a period etc), sometimes a long story about brave men in ancient Scandinavian times. **2** (long account of an) exciting event.

sagacious /sə'geɪʃəs/ *adj* (*formal* or *literary*) wise.

sagacity /sə'gæsɪtɪ/ *u.n.* **sa'gaciously** *adv.* **sa'gaciousness** *u.n.*

sage[1] /seɪdʒ/ *attrib.adj* **1** (*literary*) wise: *sage opinions.*

▷ *c.n* **2** (*literary*) person who is wise.

'sagely *adv.*

sage[2] /seɪdʒ/ *u.n* (also *attrib*) **1** kind of herb with grey-green leaves used in cooking. **2** (also **,sage 'green**) grey-green colour.

Sagittarius /,sædʒɪ'teərɪəs/ *n* **1** *unique n* one of the 12 signs of the zodiac. **2** *c.n* person born under this sign.

sago /'seɪgəʊ/ *u.n* (also *attrib*) small round pieces of a starch(1) substance, used in food etc: *sago pudding.*

said /sed/ *attrib.adj* **1** (*formal*) who/that has already been mentioned: *the said Peter Jones; the said children.*

▷ *v* **2** *p.t,p.p* of say.

sail /seɪl/ *c.n* **1** large piece of strong cloth which is put up on a boat or ship so that the wind can push the boat or ship along. **2** trip in a sailing-boat: *On Sunday we had an hour's sail in our new boat.* **3** thing shaped like a sail(1) on a windmill(1) etc. *go for a sail* have a trip in a sailing-boat or ship. *hoist sail* ⇨ hoist(*v*). *set sail* (*for s.w*) start a voyage (to s.w).

▷ *v* **4** *tr/intr.v* (cause (a ship, boat etc) to) move on water with or without using a sail, sometimes using an engine: *Our ship sailed along the African coast. We sailed our boat to Greece. I sail every weekend.* **5** *intr.v* start a voyage or trip in a ship: *Our ship sails at 5; don't be late! sail by, through etc* (*s.t*) (*fig*) walk past etc (s.t) proudly, majestically or without any trouble: *The queen sailed through the hall and sat down on her* throne(1). *sail through s.t* (*fig*) do s.t very easily: *He sailed through the examination.*

'sail,cloth *u.n* kind of strong cloth from which sails are made.

'sailing *n* **1** *u.n* (also *attrib*) sport of racing or doing trips in a sailing-boat: *go sailing; a sailing hat.* **2** *unique n* act of starting a voyage by ship: *Our time of sailing is 5.30.*

'sailing-,boat *c.n* boat with sails(1).

sailor /'seɪlə/ *c.n* **1** person who works on a ship, usu not as an officer. **2** person who is serving in a country's navy, usu not as an officer. *a bad/good sailor* a person who gets sick, does not get sick, on a ship or boat when the sea is rough.

saint /seɪnt/ *c.n* **1** (*written abbr* St) person who lived a very holy life and has been given the official title of Saint after her/his death. **2** person who is always very patient and kind: *Mrs Hall is a real saint – look at the way she helps the poor and the sick.*

'saint,hood *u.n* fact or state of being a saint(1).

'saintliness *u.n* fact or state of being saintly.

'saintly *adj* (-ier, -iest) like (that of) a saint.

'saint's ,day *c.n* day on which a particular saint(1) is celebrated each year (and on which people with that name celebrate too).

Saint (strong form /seɪnt/, weak form before a person's name /sənt/) *c.n* (*written abbr* St) (title put before the name of a person who has been officially declared to be a saint(1)): *Saint John*; *Saint Theresa*; *St Margaret*.

sake /seɪk/ *u.n* **1 for the sake of s.o**; **for s.o's sake** in order to do s.t good to/for s.o: *If you won't stop smoking for your own sake, do it for the sake of your family!* **2 for the sake of s.t**; **for s.t's sake** (a) in order to do s.t good to/for s.t. (b) for the purpose of s.t: *Sometimes the children just shout for shouting's sake.* **3 for argument's sake** so that one can discuss it: *No one likes to think of dying but let's imagine for argument's sake that you died, how would your family live?* **4 for Christ's, God's, goodness', pity's** *etc* **sake** (way of making a request stronger or for showing that one is annoyed): *For goodness' sake stop talking such nonsense!* (Notice that there is no *-s* after *goodness'*; some people write it without the '.)

salable ⇒ sale.

salad /'sæləd/ *n* **1** *c/u.n* cold food, usu made of one or more raw or cooked vegetables and sometimes with meat, fish, egg etc added: *chicken salad*. **2** *u.n* green vegetable that is usu eaten raw in a salad(1). *fruit salad* ⇒ fruit. *green salad* ⇒ green. *mixed salad* ⇒ mix.

'salad ,cream *u.n* thick yellow salad dressing. Compare mayonnaise.

'salad ,dressing *u.n* liquid, or thick yellow substance like cream, used for putting on a salad(1) to make it taste good.

salami /sə'lɑːmɪ/ *u.n* (also *attrib*) kind of big hard sausage that has a strong salty taste: *salami sandwiches*.

salary /'sælərɪ/ *c/u.n* (*pl* -ies) fixed amount of money paid to a person each month for work in a profession, as a manager etc. Compare wage¹.

'salaried *adj* paid by means of a salary, not a wage: *a salaried position*.

sale /seɪl/ *c.n* **1** fact or action of selling (s.t) for money: *The sale of the house will be on Monday.* **2** selling of things at a lower price than usual: *I bought this coat in a sale.* **3** (often *pl*) total amount of (s.t) that is sold: *Sales in our shop have gone up this month.* **for sale** being offered to people who want to buy it: *Is that car for sale?* **jumble sale** ⇒ jumble. **make a sale** be successful in selling s.t. **on sale** available to people who want to buy it: *The new car is now on sale in England.*

saleable *adj* (US **'salable**) that can (easily) be sold. Opposite unsaleable.

'sale ,price *c.n* price at which one can buy s.t in a sale(2).

'sale,room *c.n* room in which an auction(1) is held.

sales *attrib.adj* **1** of or referring to selling: *the sales department of a big office.*

⊳ *n* **2** *pl.n* ⇒ sale. **3** *def.pl.n* special time in the year when shops sell goods at prices that are (much) lower than usual ⇒ sale(2).

'sales,clerk *c.n* (*old use*) = shop assistant.

'sales,lady *c.n* (*pl* -ies) female shop assistant.

'salesman *c.n* (*pl*-men) male shop assistant; male sales representative: *A travelling salesman visits many homes or companies selling things.*

'salesman,ship *u.n* skill in selling s.t or in persuading s.o to do s.t.

'sales,person *c.n* male or female sales representative.

'sales ,repre,sentative *c.n* (*informal* **'sales ,rep**) person whose job is to sell things, sometimes by going to people's houses, offices etc.

'sales ,slip *c.n* piece of paper one gets when one has bought s.t in a shop.

'sales ,talk *c/u.n* things said by a sales representative when he/she is trying to sell one s.t.

'sales ,tax *c/u.n* tax that one has to pay in some places when one buys s.t (called Value Added Tax in the UK).

'sales,woman *c.n* (*pl* -,women) female sales representative.

salient /'seɪlɪənt/ *attrib.adj* most important or noticeable; more important or noticeable than the rest: *the salient features(2) of a painting/ speech/plan.*

saline /'seɪlaɪn/ *adj* (*technical*) of or referring to salt; having salt in it: *a saline solution(1) of water and salt.*

saliva /sə'laɪvə/ *u.n* liquid produced in the mouth of a person or animal, esp when eating.

sa'livary ,glands *pl.n* glands that produce saliva.

sallow /'sæləʊ/ *adj* looking pale, yellow and not healthy: *sallow skin.*

'sallowness *u.n*.

salmon /'sæmən/ *n* (*pl* salmon) (also *attrib*) **1** *c.n* kind of big fish with orange-pink flesh that lives in the sea but goes up rivers to lay its eggs: *salmon fishing*. **2** *u.n* flesh of this fish as food: *salmon salad.* **3** *u.n* orange-pink colour of a salmon's flesh.

salmonella /,sælmə'nelə/ *u.n* (also *attrib*) group of bacteria that cause typhoid, food poisoning etc: *salmonella poisoning.*

salon /'sælɒn/ *c.n* **1** shop that sells expensive clothes: *a dress salon.* **2** (*formal*) big living-room, usu with expensive furniture. *beauty salon* ⇒ beauty.

saloon /sə'luːn/ *c.n* **1** room in a hotel, ship etc where people can buy alcoholic drinks, sit and talk etc. ⇒ saloon bar. **2** (US) bar or pub. **3** car that has seats for four or more passengers and without an inside space for baggage etc. Compare convertible(3), estate car, hatchback, sedan, station wagon.

sa'loon ,bar *c.n* bar in a pub which is more comfortable and more expensive than the public bar.

sa'loon ,car *c.n* = saloon(3).

salt /sɔːlt/ *attrib.adj* **1** tasting of salt(2); having salt(2) in it: *salt water*; *salt fish.*

⊳ *n* **2** *u.n* chemical found in the earth and sea called sodium chloride, *chem.form* NaCl: *Salt gives the sea its taste.* **3** (*chemistry*) chemical substance consisting of an acid plus a base(5) or metal, e.g sulphuric acid. *cooking/rock/sea/ table salt* ⇒ cooking, rock¹, sea, table. *rub salt into s.o's wound* make s.o's suffering even worse. *the salt of the earth* (*fig*) person or group of the best kind; excellent person: *The nurses in the hospital were the salt of the earth.* *take s.t with a grain/*

pinch of salt (*fig*) not believe s.t (completely): *Mary told wonderful stories about what she did at school but one had to take them with a pinch of salt.*

▷ *tr.v* **4** put salt(2) in or on (s.t). **5** put (food) in salt to preserve it. **6** (often — *s.t with s.t*) (*fig*) make (s.t) more exciting or interesting (by putting s.t in it): *He salted his account of the voyage with many* vivid(2) *details.* **salt s.t away** (*informal*) save s.t, usu money, for use in the future instead of spending or using it now. **worth one's salt** valuable; worth paying for.

'salt,cellar *c.n* container for salt(2) used during meals.

'saltiness *u.n* state or fact of (s.t) being salty. ⇒ saltness.

'saltness *u.n* fact or degree of s.t being salty. ⇒ saltiness.

salts *pl.n* kinds of salt(3) used for medical purposes: smelling salts. *bath salts* ⇒ bath.

'salt,shaker *c.n* container out of which one can shake salt(2) onto food etc.

,salt'water *attrib.adj* **1** of or referring to salty water, esp the sea. **2** that lives in salt water: *saltwater fish.*

'salty *adj* (*-ier*, *-iest*) having salt(2) in it or tasting of salt(2).

salute /sə'luːt/ *c.n* **1** way of greeting s.o or of showing respect to s.o/s.t in the armed forces etc: *Some salutes are made with the hand, some by firing guns and some by pulling a flag down and then pulling it up again.* ⇒ salvo(1). **2** *c/u.n* (*literary*) greeting of any kind. **in salute** (*formal*) as a greeting or sign of respect: *When Alex passed us he turned his head and smiled in salute.* **take the salute** (*military*) (of an officer of high rank or a very important person) stand and watch while soldiers etc go past and give a salute.

▷ *tr/intr.v* **3** do a salute to greet or honour (s.o/s.t).
salutation /,sælju'teɪʃən/ *c/u.n* (*formal*) **1** = salute(2). **2** words at the beginning of a letter such as 'Dear Mr Brown', 'My dearest Mary' or 'Dear Sir'.

salvage /'sælvɪdʒ/ *u.n* **1** things that have been saved from a wreck, fire etc: *All salvage belongs to the insurance company.* **2** (also *attrib*) act or fact of saving things from a wreck, fire etc: *Salvage operations were carried out by two small ships.*

▷ *tr.v* **3** save (things) from a wreck etc.

salvation /sæl'veɪʃən/ *n* **1** *u.n* act or state of saving or being saved, sometimes by Jesus etc. **2** *c.n* fact, reason, that saves one: *Helen was late for the examination but her salvation was the fact that her examiner was even later!*

Sal,vation 'Army *def.n* religious organization with ranks like the army that tries to help the poor in many countries and to make people (better) Christians(3) etc.

sal'vationist *c.n* (usu with capital **S**) member of the Salvation Army.

salve /sælv/ *c.n* thick oily substance that one puts on cuts, sore places etc to make them better; ointment: *lip salve.*

salver /'sælvə/ *c.n* (*formal*) metal tray, usu made of silver, on which food, drinks etc are served to people.

salvo /'sælvəʊ/ *c.n* (*pl* -(e)s) **1** (*military*) set of shots from more than one gun fired at (almost) the same time, often as a salute(1). **2** (usu — *of s.t*)

(*formal*) a lot (of s.t) all at the same time: *As the princess came out, a salvo of cheers greeted her.*

samba /'sæmbə/ *c/def.n* **1** kind of South American dance in which one takes fast bouncing (⇒ bounce(4)) steps. **2** music for this kind of dance.

same /seɪm/ *adj* (usu *the* —) **1** (often *the* — *s.o/ s.t* (*as s.o/s.t*)) not or never different: *She and I have the same grandparents. And I have the same grandparents as Mary has. Do you live in the same house as before* (or (*that*) *you had before*)*? Everybody in the country gets the same television programmes.* **2** not exactly the same; similar(1): *All the young women in our town wear the same clothes.* **about the same (s.o/s.t)** (**as/ that . . .**) almost the same (s.o/s.t) (as/that . . .). **amount/come to (much) the same thing** have (almost) the same(1) meaning, result etc. **at the same time** (**a**) (happening) at a simultaneous time. (**b**) but; however(5): *I would like to go but at the same time I don't want to leave my parents without help.* **much the same (s.o/s.t)** (**as/that . . .**) nearly the same s.o/s.t (as/that . . .). **not the same** (**thing**) (**without s.o/s.t**) not as pleasant, enjoyable etc (if s.o/s.t is missing): *Weekends are not the same* (**thing**) *without the children at home.* **one and the same (s.o/s.t)** ⇒ one(*pron*). **the same old story** ⇒ story. **the very same (s.o/s.t)** exactly the same(1) (s.o/s.t).

▷ *pron* **3 the same** (*adj*) person, animal or thing: *We don't have separate food for students and teachers; they all get the same.* **about the same** (**as/that . . .**) ⇒ same(*adj*). **all the same**; **all the same to/with s.o** ⇒ all(*adv*). **just the same** = at the same time(b). **much the same** (**as/that . . .**) ⇒ same(*adj*). **not the same** (**without s.o/s.t**) ⇒ same(*adj*). **one and the same** ⇒ one(*pron*). **same here**(*informal*) I agree, would like etc the same(3): '*I like Jane.*' '*Same here.*' '*I'd like a cake, please.*' '*Same here.*' (**the**) **same again, please** I would like to have another drink, cake etc of the same(2) kind, please. (**the**) **same to you** I wish you the same(2) thing (good or bad) that you have just wished me. **the very same** ⇒ same(*adj*).

▷ *adv* **4 the same** (**as s.o/s.t** (**does** etc)) in the same(1) way (as s.o/s.t (does etc)): *This flower looks the same as that one. I like animals, the same as you do.*

'sameness *u.n* (often *the* — *of s.t*) fact of (s.t) being the same(3,4), often with the result of being boring: *The sameness of the scenery soon made me stop looking out of the train window.*

sample /'sɑːmpl/ *c.n* (also *attrib*) **1** (often — *of s.t.*) example (of s.t) that is (supposed to be) typical of the rest or of the whole: *a blood sample from a sick person; a sample tube of toothpaste.* **free sample** thing one gives to s.o to try to persuade her/him to buy the product.

▷ *tr.v* **2** test, try, a sample(1) of (s.t) to find out what it is like.

'sampling *u.n* act of trying to find out s.t about a whole group by asking a representative group questions about it, e.g how people intend to vote in the next elections. Compare poll(2).

sanatorium /,sænə'tɔːrɪəm/ *c.n* (*pl* -s or, less usu, *sanatoria* /-rɪə/) kind of hospital for people who need to spend a long time there, often to get better quietly after an illness etc.

sanctify /'sæŋktɪ,faɪ/ *tr.v* (*-ies*, *-ied*) **1** make (s.t) holy. **2** (*fig*; *formal*) make (s.t) accepted: *Some bad habits become sanctified by custom and are therefore not questioned by most people.*

sanctification /ˌsæŋktɪfɪˈkeɪʃən/ *u.n.*

sanctimonious /ˌsæŋktɪˈməʊnɪəs/ *adj* (*derog*) trying too hard to seem religious or holy.

ˌsanctiˈmoniously *adv.* **ˌsanctiˈmoniousness** *u.n.*

sanction /ˈsæŋkʃən/ *n* **1** *u.n* (*formal*) act of being allowed to do s.t: *You can only be absent from school with the sanction of the head teacher.* **2** (usu *pl*) (often —*s against s.o/s.t*) action taken against s.o or a country etc because he/she/it has done s.t. illegal or wrong: *Trade sanctions have now been approved against that country.*
▷ *tr.v* **3** (*formal*) allow (s.t) officially.

sanctity /ˈsæŋktɪtɪ/ *u.n* (often *the* — *of s.o/ s.t*) fact of s.o/s.t being holy: *the sanctity of a church.*

sanctuary /ˈsæŋktjʊərɪ/ *n* **1** *c.n* (*pl -ies*) place where one is safe from danger: *a bird sanctuary* (where birds are officially protected from hunters etc). **2** *u.n* state of being safe from danger: *The women found sanctuary in the church.* **3** *c.n* holiest part of a church in front of the altar(2).

sand /sænd/ *u.n* **1** fine material made of very small pieces of rock, shells etc that is often found on beaches and in deserts. **build (s.t) on sand** (*fig*) do s.t in such a foolish or inefficient way that it cannot succeed. **bury one's head in the sand** ⇒ head(*n*). ⇒ quicksand.
▷ *tr.v* **2** (often — *s.t down*) make (s.t) smooth(er) by rubbing it with sandpaper(1) etc. **3** put sand(1) on (a road etc) to make it less slippery, e.g when there is ice on it.

ˈsandˌbag *c.n* bag full of sand(1) or earth and used to protect people, buildings etc from floods, enemy shots, etc.

ˈsandˌbank *c.n* bank of sand(1) under the water (at high tide and sometimes above it at low tide).

ˈsandˌbar *c.n* sandbank at the mouth of a harbour, river etc.

ˈsandˌcastle *c.n* shape made of sand(1) using a small bucket, usu by children on a beach.

ˈsandˌdune *c.n* ⇒ dune.

ˈsander *c.n* machine for sanding (⇒ sand(2)) things.

ˈsandˌfly *c.n* (*pl -ies*) kind of small fly that bites.

ˈsandˌglass *c.n* glass device with a narrow waist through which sand(1) runs and which is used to measure time.

ˈsandiness *u.n* fact or state of being sandy.

ˈsanding maˌchine *c.n* = sander.

ˈsandˌmartin *c.n* small bird (martin) with white feathers underneath which lives near sand, rivers etc.

ˈsandˌpaper *u.n* **1** strong paper with sand(1) or some other abrasive(3) stuck on one side, used to sand(2) wood etc.
▷ *tr.v* **2** (often — *s.t down*) = sand(2).

sands *pl.n* area of sand(1), usu on a beach or in a desert. **The sands (of time) are running out** (*fig*) There is not much more time left (for s.t).

ˈsandˌstone *u.n* rock formed of sand(1) pushed together by the pressure of other rocks etc.

ˈsandˌstorm *c.n* strong wind with sand(1) blown through the air.

ˈsandy *adj* (*-ier*, *-iest*) **1** having sand(1) in or on it. **2** looking like sand(1), esp in colour; between yellow and pale brown: *sandy hair*.

sandal /ˈsændl/ *c.n* kind of shoe with a sole³(2) and strips of leather etc on top to hold it on the foot.

sandwich /ˈsænwɪdʒ/ *c.n* **1** two pieces of bread with food between them: *a cheese sandwich*; *a chicken sandwich*; *a toasted sandwich.* **2** (also **ˈsandwich ˌcake**) cake made by putting jam, cream etc between a top piece and a bottom piece.
▷ *tr.v* **3** (often — *s.o/s.t* (*in*) *between* (*s.o/s.t and s.o/ s.t*)) put s.o/s.t tightly (between two other people/things): *The train was crowded and I found myself sandwiched between two old women. Our car was sandwiched in (between two other cars) and we couldn't move.* **4** (often — *s.t in* (*between s.t and-s.t*)) fit s.t in among the things one has to do (between other things): *She is busy all day but usually manages to sandwich in a few minutes with her family (between meetings).*

ˈsandwich ˌboard *c.n* two boards that are joined at the top so that a person can carry them about, one in front and the other behind, to advertise s.t.

ˈsandwich ˌcake *c.n* = sandwich(2).

ˈsandwich ˌcourse *c.n* course during which one studies for some months, then does practical work for some months, then studies again (etc) so that one can have practice in what one is learning.

sandy ⇒ sand.

sane /seɪn/ *adj* Opposite insane. **1** not mad; able to use one's brain like normal people. **2** not silly or foolish; sensible.

ˈsanely *adv.* **sanity** /ˈsænɪtɪ/ *u.n.*

sang /sæŋ/ *p.t* of sing¹.

sanitary /ˈsænɪtrɪ/ *adj* **1** clean; not dirty and so not dangerous to one's health: *Sanitary conditions in a hospital are of the greatest importance.* Opposite insanitary. **2** (*attrib*) of or referring to things that are made or provided for health purposes.

ˈsanitary ˌtowel *c.n* (*abbr* ST) pad worn by women when they are menstruating to absorb(1) the blood.

sanitation /ˌsænɪˈteɪʃən/ *u.n* arrangements for avoiding danger to health by keeping the water supply clean, getting rid of waste products carefully etc.

sanity ⇒ sane.

sank /sæŋk/ *p.t* of sink².

Santa Claus /ˈsæntə ˌklɔːz/ *n* **1** *unique n* = Father Christmas. **2** *c.n* (*informal*) person who is very generous to s.o.

sap¹ /sæp/ *u.n* liquid inside a plant that carries its food etc.

sap² /sæp/ *c.n* (*informal*) fool.

sap³ /sæp/ *tr.v* (*-pp-*) make (a person's health, confidence, strength etc) weaker, usu gradually.

sapling /ˈsæplɪŋ/ *c.n* young tree.

sapper /ˈsæpə/ *c.n* (*informal*; *military*) member of the regiment(2) of Royal Engineers in the British army.

sapphire /ˈsæfaɪə/ *c/u.n* (also *attrib*) kind of precious stone that is bright blue and transparent: *a sapphire ring.*

,sapphire 'blue *u.n* (also *attrib*) bright blue colour like sapphire.

sarcasm /'sɑːkæzəm/ *u.n* nasty, usu ironic, remark(s) that is/are intended to hurt a person's feelings.

sarcastic /sɑːˈkæstɪk/ *adj* showing or using sarcasm.

sar'castically *adv*.

sardine /sɑːˈdiːn/ *c.n* (also *attrib*) kind of small young fish, usu sold already cooked and in oil in flat tins: *sardine sandwiches*. **like sardines** (*informal*) crowded tightly together: *During the rush hour passengers are packed into the trains like sardines*.

sardonic /sɑːˈdɒnɪk/ *adj* (*derog*; *formal*) scornful; showing that one considers oneself very superior(3): *sardonic humour*.

sar'donically *adv*.

sash¹ /sæʃ/ *c.n* **1** piece of cloth that is worn round one's waist like a belt. **2** strip of cloth that is worn over one's shoulders and across one's chest and back, e.g as worn by a beauty queen.

sash² /sæʃ/ *c.n* frame of a window or of a door etc that has glass in it.

,sash-'window *c.n* window that has two sashes² that slide up and down parallel(1) to each other so that the window can be open at the top and/or bottom.

sat /sæt/ *p.t* of sit.

Satan /'seɪtn/ *unique n* (name for the) Devil.

satchel /'sætʃəl/ *c.n* kind of strong bag in which children carry their things to school.

satellite /'sætəlaɪt/ *c.n* (also *attrib*) **1** (*technical*) moon or other body in space that circles around (a bigger one). **2** artificial satellite(1) sent up from the earth by human beings: *A communications satellite sends radio and television signals from one place on earth to another*. **3** country etc that is controlled by a stronger one: *the USSR and its satellites* (or *its satellite states*). **by satellite** using a satellite(2).

,satellite 'town *c.n* town near a city or bigger town where people live who work in the city or bigger town.

satiate /'seɪʃɪˌeɪt/ *tr.v* (often — *s.o* with *s.t*) (*formal*) give (s.o) so much (of s.t) that he/she feels he/she has had enough or even too much.

satin /'sætɪn/ *u.n* (also *attrib*) kind of cloth that is very thin and shiny on one side only.

satire /'sætaɪə/ *n* **1** *u.n* way of criticizing s.o/s.t, usu in a clever and amusing way. **2** *c.n* (often — *on s.o/s.t*) poem or play (criticizing s.o/s.t).

satirical /səˈtɪrɪkl/ *adj* showing, using etc satire(1).

sa'tirically *adv*.

satirize, -ise /'sætɪˌraɪz/ *tr.v* criticize (s.o/s.t) by using satire(1).

satisfy /'sætɪsˌfaɪ/ *v* (-ies, -ied) **1** *tr/intr.v* give (s.o) all that he/she wants or needs. **2** *tr.v* be, do, enough for (s.t): *It is useless to apply for a job unless you satisfy the requirements for it*. **3** *tr.v* succeed in making (s.o) believe (s.t, that . . .): *She is still not satisfied that we tried to help*. **satisfy the examiner** do well enough in an examination to pass. **satisfy one's/s.o's curiosity (by doing s.t)** find out, say, write etc what one/s.o was curious to know (by doing s.t).

satisfaction /ˌsætɪsˈfækʃən/ *u.n* (often the — of (*doing*) *s.o/s.t*) fact of satisfying (s.o/s.t); state of being satisfied: *At least she had the satisfaction of seeing her daughter before she died*. **get (great) satisfaction from, out of, s.t** be (very) pleased about/by s.t. **take (great) satisfaction in doing s.t** enjoy doing s.t (very much). **to s.o's (complete) satisfaction** (*formal*) in such a way as to satisfy s.o (completely): *Was the dinner (cooked) to your satisfaction?*

satisfactorily /ˌsætɪsˈfæktərɪlɪ/ *adv* in a satisfactory way.

satisfactory /ˌsætɪsˈfæktərɪ/ *adj* good enough to satisfy (s.o/s.t) without necessarily being very good. Opposite unsatisfactory.

'satis,fying *adj* (often of food) that satisfies(1).

satsuma /sætˈsuːmə/ *c.n* kind of small fruit like a tangerine(1) that has no pips¹.

saturate /'sætʃəˌreɪt/ *tr.v* (often — *s.t* with *s.t*) **1** put as much liquid onto or into (s.t) as it can take. Compare soak(4). **2** (of a market for s.t one is selling etc) provide (s.t) with so many goods etc that demand is satisfied.

saturation /ˌsætʃəˈreɪʃən/ *u.n* act of saturating (s.t) or result of being saturated.

,satu'ration ,point *c/def/unique n* (often reach (a/the) —) level of complete saturation.

Saturday /'sætədɪ/ *c/unique n* (also *attrib*) (*written abbr* Sat) sixth working day of the week in Christian(1) (and some other) countries; day after Friday and before Sunday; first day of the weekend. **last Saturday** the last Saturday before today. **next Saturday** the first Saturday after today. **on a Saturday** on a day of one week that is, was, will be, a Saturday. **on Saturday** on the nearest Saturday before/after today or on the Saturday of the week being referred to: *I'll come on Saturday*. **on Saturdays** every Saturday: *I go swimming on Saturdays*. **Saturday after next** the second Saturday after today. **Saturday before last** the Saturday before last Saturday. **Saturday morning, afternoon** etc the morning, afternoon etc of last, next, every Saturday.

Saturn /'sætɜːn/ *unique n* sixth planet away from the sun.

sauce /sɔːs/ *c/u.n* **1** (usu thick) liquid put on food to make it taste good: *apple sauce*; *tomato sauce*; *cheese sauce*. Compare gravy. **2** (often have the — to do s.t) (*informal*) cheek(2): *He had the sauce to tell me I was wrong*. **What's sauce for the goose is sauce for the gander** (*proverb*) If one person is allowed to do s.t, s.o else should be allowed to do the same too.

'sauce-,boat *c.n* deep oval(1) container with a stand, used to serve sauce(1) during meals.

saucepan /'sɔːspən/ *c.n* deep metal container with a handle and often a lid, used for cooking things on a cooker or fire.

saucer /'sɔːsə/ *c.n* kind of small plate which one puts under a cup.

saucy /'sɔːsɪ/ *adj* (-ier, -iest) rude in a usu amusing and not serious way; cheeky.

'saucily *adv*. **'sauciness** *u.n*.

sauna /'sɔːnə/ *c.n* (also **'sauna ,bath**) room with hot air in which one sits so that one's pores¹ will open to clean one's skin. Compare Turkish bath.

saunter /'sɔːntə/ *intr.v* (often — *along/by*) walk without hurrying at all, usu just for pleasure.

sausage /'sɒsɪdʒ/ *n* **1** *c.n* piece of skin filled with meat etc and closed at both ends, eaten as food. **2** *u.n* (also **'sausage ,meat**) meat used to make sausages(1).

,sausage 'roll *c.n* small roll made of pastry with sausage meat inside it.

sauté /'səʊteɪ/ *c/u.n* **1** (*French*) (also *attrib*) food that has been cooked quickly in a little butter, oil etc: *sauté potatoes.*
▷ *tr.v* (*pres.p sautéing, p.t,p.p sauté(e)d*) **2** (*French*) cook (s.t) in a little butter etc: *sautéing potatoes.*

savage /'sævɪdʒ/ *adj* **1** (*old use*) that comes from a wild place that has not yet been civilized: *savage people.* **2** (*derog*) (of a person, animal) cruel and fierce: *a savage dog.*
▷ *c.n* **3** (*old use*) person who is savage(1). **4** (*derog*) person who is savage(2).
▷ *tr.v* **5** attack (s.o/s.t) violently, usu by biting: *The child was savaged by the dog.*

'savagely *adv.* **'savageness** *u.n.* **'savagery** *c/u.n.*

savanna /sə'vænə/ *c/u.n* (also **sa'vannah**) area of flat land in hot damp places, covered with grass and having very few trees.

save /seɪv/ *prep* **1** (*old use*) (usu — *that* . . .) except (that . . .): *She is a good worker save that she is quite often ill.*
▷ *c.n* **2** (in football etc) successful attempt, usu by the goalkeeper, to prevent the other side scoring a goal.
▷ *v* **3** *tr.v* (often — *s.o/s.t from s.o/s.t*) keep (s.o/s.t) from danger, harm etc (caused by s.o/s.t): *I ran to save the child from being hit by a car.* **4** *tr.v* (often — *s.t for s.t*) not use (s.t) now so as to have it for later use: *save money; save time; save your strength for tomorrow's hard work.* **5** *intr.v* (often — *up* (*for, to do, s.t*)) keep the money one gets instead of spending it so that one can use it (for s.t) later: *I'm saving up for a new car, to buy a car.* **6** *tr.v* (often — *s.o/s.t; — (s.o) doing s.t; — s.o from having to do s.t*) make it unnecessary (for s.o) to do s.t: *Working at home saves me a lot of travelling every day. Using the telephone saves (us from) having to go to town so often.* **7** *tr/intr.v* (usu — *s.o from s.t*) (in religions) save(3) s.o (from the devil, hell(1) etc). **save face** ⇨ face(*n*). **save one's/s.o's skin** ⇨ skin(*n*).

'saver *c.n* person who saves(4,5), usu money.
-,saver *c.n* person or thing who/that saves the thing that is the first part of the word: *a life-saver. The telephone is a great time-saver.*

'saving *attrib.adj* **1** that lets one accept s.t that would otherwise be unpleasant: *The one saving thing about the rain was that it kept the tourists away and gave us a quiet Sunday.* **s.o's (one) saving grace** ⇨ grace(*n*).
▷ *c.n* **2** (often — (*of s.t*) (*on s.t*)) amount (of s.t) that is saved (out of s.t): *a saving of £20 on the price of a new table; a saving of time.*
▷ *prep* **3** (*old use*) = save(1).

'savings *pl.n* things, usu money, that have been saved(4), usu by putting them in a bank.
'savings ac,count *c.n* account in a bank that earns interest (at a higher rate than a deposit account).
'savings ,bank *c.n* bank in which one can put one's savings but which does not have the other services of ordinary banks.

saviour /'seɪvɪə/ *n* **1** *c.n* person who saves (s.o/ s.t). **2** *def.n* (usu *our Saviour*) Jesus.

savour /'seɪvə/ *c/u.n* (US **'savor**) (*formal*)

1 (often — *of s.t*) taste or smell (of s.t): *Don't wait too long before cooking those vegetables or they will lose their savour.* **2** (*fig*) interest or bit of excitement: *Danger adds savour to many sports.* Compare spice(2).
▷ *tr.v* **3** taste, eat, drink, (s.t) carefully and/or slowly to get its taste: *You need to savour this wine to get its full flavour.* **4** (*fig*) enjoy (s.t): *Can't you just savour the excitement of being on holiday?*

'savoury *adj* (US **'savory**) **1** (*formal*) having a pleasant taste. **2** not having a sweet taste: *savoury biscuits.* ⇨ savoury(4). **3** (*fig*) good in a moral way: *That man does not have a very savoury reputation in business circles.* Opposite unsavoury.
▷ *c.n* **4** kind of food, e.g cheese, that is not sweet and that is sometimes served at the end of a meal.

saw[1] /sɔː/ *p.t* of see[1].

saw[2] /sɔː/ *c.n* **1** tool for cutting wood, metal etc that has teeth. **chain saw** ⇨ chain.
▷ *v* (*p.t sawed, p.p sawn*/sɔːn/ or *sawed*) **2** *tr/intr.v* cut (s.t) with a saw[2](1). **3** *intr.v* be able to be sawn[2](2): *This wood saws easily.*
saw (**away**) **at s.t** (**a**) try to cut s.t with a saw[2](1). (**b**) move one's hand etc across s.t as if sawing[2](2): *He was sawing away at his violin without producing any tune I recognized.*
saw away go on sawing[2](2) for some time.
saw s.t off (**s.t**) remove s.t (from s.t) with a saw[2](1).
saw through s.t cut through s.t with a saw[2](1).
saw s.t through saw[2](2) s.t until one gets right through it.
saw s.t (**up**) (**into s.t**) cut s.t into more than two pieces with a saw[2](1).
'saw,dust *u.n* very small pieces of wood that fall when one is sawing[2](2) s.t.
'saw,mill *c.n* place where large amounts of wood are sawn[2](2) into pieces for use in building etc.
,sawn-,off 'shot,gun *c.n* shotgun whose barrel has been shortened, esp so that it is easier to hide.

sax /sæks/ *c.n* (*informal*) saxophone.

saxophone /'sæksəfəʊn/ *c.n* (*informal* **sax**) kind of musical instrument, shaped like the letter S and usu made of brass, played by blowing into it: *The saxophone is used a lot in* jazz(1) *bands.*
saxophonist /sæk'sɒfənɪst/ *c.n* person who plays the saxophone.

say /seɪ/ *interj* **1** (mostly US) (used to get attention): *Say, haven't I seen you before?*
▷ *sing.n* **2** (often — (*in s.t*); *have/say one's* —) opinion (about s.t): *I demand a say in how the new office will be run. I shall have my say and then leave it to them to decide.*
▷ *tr.v* (*3rd pers sing, pres.t says* /sez/, *p.t,p.p said* /sed/) **3** put (s.t) into words; express (s.t) in words: *'Come in,' said the girl. I said that it was raining. The man didn't say whether he was going to come back. Did your mother say where she was going?* **4** speak (a word or words): *How do you say 'clothes'?* **5** show (s.t) without using words: *What time does your watch say?*
be easier said than done be easier to suggest than to carry out.
have s.t to say (**for oneself**) have an opinion.
I'd rather not say I prefer not to give

the information you ask for: *'What did your brother do last night?' 'I'd rather not say.'*

I say! (expression showing surprise or trying to get s.o's attention): *I say, look at those strange birds!*

I should say not! (showing anger etc) certainly not!

I wouldn't say no (to s.t) (*informal*) I'd be quite pleased to accept (s.t): *'Are you thirsty?' 'Well, I wouldn't say no to a nice cup of tea.'*

it goes without saying (that . . .) of course . . .; it is not necessary to say (that) . . . .

it says here etc (that) . . . it is written here etc (that) . . .: *It says on this notice that one can't swim here.*

it's not for me to say (whether, what etc . . .) I am not the person who should say (whether etc . . .).

(let us) say . . . I want to make the suggestion that . . .: *We can meet at the gate to the park —* (*let us*) *say at 5 o'clock.*

no sooner said than done (used to state one's willingness to carry out a request immediately).

not have a good word (to say) for s.o/s.t ⇒ word(*n*).

not to say s.o/s.t and also, or even, s.o/s.t: *He was not helpful — not to say rude.*

say no more! (*informal*) you do not need to say anything more as I have understood (and will do what you want).

say one's prayers (to s.o) pray (to God): *the little boy says his prayers for his family every night.*

say the word ⇒ word(*n*).

say s.t to oneself think s.t without saying it aloud.

say what you like/want/will, . . . whatever you may say, ... **so you/he/she say(s)** yes, you/he/she say(s) that, but . . . .

that is to say which means: *She is your mother — that is to say, someone you should respect.*

there is very little to be said for s.o/s.t s.o/s.t is bad in nearly every way.

they say (that) . . . it is said (that) . . .; people in general say (that) . . . .

to say nothing of s.o/s.t and also of course s.o/s.t: *The house is full every Saturday with friends and strangers, to say nothing of the numerous members of our own family.*

what do you say . . .? (*informal*) I suggest that we should . . .?: *It's raining, so what do you say we stay at home this afternoon?*

what do you say to (doing) s.t? (*informal*) I suggest (doing) s.t.

what have you got to say for yourself? (a way of asking s.o to apologize for doing s.t wrong, to defend herself/himself against an accusation).

Who can say? I don't know and probably other people don't either: *'Is it going to rain next Sunday?' 'Who can say?'*

you can say that again! (*fig*; *informal*) I agree completely.

you don't say (so)! (*informal*) (showing surprise) oh, (really)?

you said it (*informal*) you're right; I agree.

'saying *c.n* thing that is said and that a lot of people know: *There is a saying that only the good die young.*

'say-,so *c.n* **on s.o's say-so** (**a**) just because s.o has said it. (**b**) with s.o's permission.

scab /skæb/ *n* **1** *c/u.n* dry rough crust(4) that forms over a wound while it is healing. **2** *c.n* (*derog*; *slang*) worker who continues to go to work during a strike(1).

scabbard /'skæbəd/ *c.n* cover for a sword or similar weapon, usu made to hang from one's belt.

scaffold /'skæfəld/ *n* **1** *c.n* framework made of poles with boards on them, used for people to stand on while they are working on the outside of a building. **2** *c.n* board hanging on ropes, used for people to stand on while they are cleaning windows, painting a building etc. **3** *c.n* (usu *the* —) raised platform(1) on which criminals used to be executed(1).

'scaffolding *u.n* scaffolds(1).

scald /skɔːld/ *c.n* **1** damage to the skin caused by a hot liquid or steam. Compare burn(1).

▷ *tr.v* **2** damage the skin of (an animal, s.o, part of one's body) with a hot liquid or steam: *I scalded myself yesterday.*

'scalding *adj* **1** boiling. **2** very hot: *Last summer was scalding.* **3** (*fig*) fiercely critical: *scalding remarks about a person's behaviour.*

▷ *adv* **4 scalding hot** very hot: *scalding hot water.*

scale¹ /skeɪl/ *n* **1** *c.n* fixed list (of numbers etc) with which one can compare things to see where they fit in: *Our company has a scale of salaries that begins at £6000 a year and goes up to £20 000.* **2** *c.n* scale(1) shown by numbers, small lines etc on a ruler etc. **3** *c.n* ruler etc with such marks on it. **4** *c.n* (often — *of s.t to s.t*) amount of one measurement that represents(2) a certain amount of another measurement (and that goes from s.t to s.t): *The scale of this map is 1 centimetre to 2 kilometres* (= 1 : 200 000). **5** *c/u.n* (often *the* — *of s.t*) size (of s.t) usu compared with that of other things of the same kind: *The scale of our company's operations seems big but it is nothing compared to that of many others.* **6** *c.n* (often *the* — *of A* etc) (*music*) fixed set of musical notes (called A etc which is) arranged in an order so that each note is a certain distance in pitch'(4) above/below the next one: *The scale of C major is the set of notes C D E F G A B.* (**draw s.t etc**) **to scale** (draw s.t etc) in such a way that it is accurately based on a scale(4). **on a large, small etc scale** in a way that is big, small etc. ⇒ scale(5). **out of scale** not to scale. **sliding scale** ⇒ slide. **to a scale of s.t** based on a scale(4) of s.t. **to scale** ⇒ (draw s.t etc) to scale.

▷ *tr.v* **7** climb to the top of (a mountain, wall etc). **8** make, draw, (a picture, model etc) using a scale(4). **scale s.t up/down** draw, make, s.t bigger/smaller by using a scale(4).

-,scale *adj* that is on the scale(4) shown in the first part of the word: *large-scale; a small-scale operation.*

,scale 'drawing/'model *c.n* (often — *of s.t*) drawing/model (of s.t) that is to scale.

scales *pl.n* (often *a pair of* —) kind of device for weighing things: *Some scales have two trays, one for the weights and the other for the thing to be weighed; others have an arrow that goes round or up and down to show the weight; others have one or more pieces of metal that slide along a bar with* *a scale on it to show the weight.* **tip the scales at s.t** weigh a certain amount. **tip/turn the scales** (*against s.o/s.t*) (*fig*) be just enough to make s.o/s.t succeed against s.o/s.t else.

scale² /skeɪl/ *n* **1** *c.n* thin small hard piece on the body of a fish, snake etc that protects the skin underneath: *A fish's scales overlap(2) each other.* **2** *c/u.n* thing like a scale²(1) that forms on metal, stone etc (and that consists of s.t): *scales of rust on an old stove.*
▷ *tr.v* **3** take off the scales from (a fish) before cooking.
'scaliness *u.n* fact or state of being scaly.
'scaly *adj* (*-ier, -iest*) having scales²(1).

scallop¹ /'skɒləp/ *c.n* (also *attrib*) (also **'scollop**) kind of shellfish that has two wide shells shaped like hand fans(1) and is good to eat: *scallop shells.*

scallop² /'skɒləp/ *c.n* (also **scollop**) **1** small curve that is part of a row of such curves decorating a dress etc, usu along an edge.
▷ *tr.v* **2** make scallops²(1) in (a dress etc).
'scalloped *adj* (also **'scolloped**) shaped like a scallop²(1).

scalp /skælp/ *c.n* **1** skin (and hair) on the top and back of a person's head. **2** (*fig; informal*) sign that one has defeated s.o: *The sportsman had the scalps of many great opponents(1) under his belt.*
▷ *tr.v* **3** (in history) cut off the scalp(1) of (s.o) as a proof of victory.

scalpel /'skælpəl/ *c.n* (*medical*) kind of small knife that doctors use for operations.

scaly ⇨ scale².

scamp /skæmp/ *c.n* naughty young person whom one is fond of.

scamper /'skæmpə/ *c.n* **1** quick short run, often for pleasure.
▷ *intr.v* **2** (often — *along, by* etc; — *after s.o/s.t*) have a scamper(1) (chasing s.o/s.t etc): *The dog scampered after the ball.*

scampi /'skæmpɪ/ *n* (*Italian*) **1** *pl.n* kind of shellfish that are like big prawns. **2** *u.n* kind of food made from scampi(1).

scan /skæn/ *c.n* **1** careful examination of s.t by looking at it closely, sometimes with a machine.
▷ *v* (*-nn-*) **2** *tr.v* (often — *s.t for s.t*) examine (s.t) carefully by looking at it, sometimes with an instrument (to try to find s.t). **3** *tr.v* read through (s.t) very quickly, without examining every word. **4** (often — *s.o for s.t*) (*medical*) examine (s.o) with X-rays(1) etc (to see whether he/she has cancer(1) etc). **5** *intr.v* (of (one or more lines of) a poem) have a regular pattern of stressed(4) and unstressed syllables, e.g 'To bé, or nót to bé'.
'scanner *c.n* (*informal*) machine used in a hospital etc to scan(4) people.
scansion /'skænʃən/ *u.n* way in which s.t scans(5). Compare stress(2).

scandal /'skændl/ *n* **1** *c/u.n* action or state that shocks people. **2** *c.n* shocked feelings that result from (a) scandal(1): *Their affair caused a scandal in the village.* **3** *u.n* nasty, often lying talk (about s.o/s.t); gossip(1): *Those old people spend hours talking scandal about their neighbours.* **breath of scandal** rumour or slight talk that suggests s.t scandalous: *The slightest breath of scandal will make him lose the election.*
scandalize, -ise /'skændəˌlaɪz/ *tr.v* shock (s.o or her/his feelings).

scandalmonger /'skændlˌmʌŋgə/ *c.n* (*derog*) person who spreads scandal(3).
'scandalous *adj* (*derog*) causing scandal(1).
'scandalously *adv*.

scant /skænt/ *adj* (usu *attrib*) hardly, only just, enough: *pay scant attention to what one is told.*
'scantily *adv* in a scanty way.
'scantiness *u.n* fact of being scanty.
'scanty *adj* (*-ier, -iest*) hardly, only just, (big etc) enough; skimpy: *a scanty dress. The food was rather scanty.*

-scape /skeɪp/ *c.n* painting of the thing that is the first part of the word: *a landscape; a seascape.*

scapegoat /'skeɪpˌgəʊt/ *c.n* person or thing that is unfairly blamed for s.t when it is really the fault of s.o/s.t else.

scapula /'skæpjʊlə/ *c.n* (also **'shoulder ˌblade**) big flat triangular bone below the outer end of a shoulder.

scar /skɑː/ *c.n* **1** mark left on the skin after a wound has healed. **2** mark on s.t which is the result of damage: *scars on a field made by motorbikes.* **3** (*fig*) result of damage that cannot actually be seen: *She still had the scars of her terrible experience long after it had passed.*
▷ *tr.v* (*-rr-*) **4** make/leave a scar on (s.o/s.t). **scar s.o for life** leave a scar(1,3) on s.o that will remain for all her/his life.
'scar ˌtissue *u.n* (*medical*) material of which a scar(1) is made.

scarce /skeəs/ *adj* not at all common or easy to find: *Elephants are becoming scarce in most parts of Africa.* Opposite plentiful.
'scarcely *adv* almost not: *I could scarcely see the boat against the dark sky. Scarcely anyone came to the dance. Scarcely had we entered when the gates were closed.* Compare barely(2), hardly(1).
scarcity /'skeəsɪtɪ/ *c/u.n* (*pl -ies*) (often — *of s.t*) lack (of s.t); state or condition of being/having not as many/much (of s.t) as one would like.

scare /skeə/ *c.n* **1** sudden feeling of being afraid; fright: *That loud noise gave me a bad scare. She got a scare when the lights went out.* **2** thing that frightens people unnecessarily because they think s.t is going to happen but it does not: *There was a scare last week that the banks had run out of money but luckily it was not true.*
▷ *v* **3** *tr.v* make (s.o, an animal) feel afraid: *You can't scare me with those silly stories.* **4** *tr.v* (often — *s.o/s.t away/off*) frighten (s.o, an animal) (so that he/she/it goes away or does not come near). **scare easily** become easily afraid: *I don't scare easily.* **scare s.o into, out of, doing s.t** force s.o (not) to do s.t by making them feel afraid. **scare s.o stiff** scare(3) s.o very much.
'scareˌcrow *c.n* **1** figure (of a person) put in a field to frighten birds away so that they do not eat the things that are growing there. **2** (*fig; derog; informal*) person who is wearing very old or very ugly clothes or who does not look at all tidy.
scared *adj* (often — *of s.o/s.t;* — *that . . .*) afraid (of s.o/s.t, that . . .). **scared out of one's wits**; **scared silly/stiff**; **scared to death** (*fig*) very frightened.
scaremonger /'skeəˌmʌŋgə/ *c.n* (*derog*) person who tries to scare(3) people. ⇨ alarmist.
'scary *adj* (*-ier, -iest*) (*informal*) **1** who/that frightens one; frightening: *a scary film.* **2** easily frightened.

scarf /skɑːf/ *c.n* (*pl -s, scarves* /skɑːvz/) **1** long narrow piece of cloth worn round the neck by men or women, usu to keep warm or to show that one belongs to a certain club, college etc. **2** square piece of cloth worn by women round the neck, over the shoulders or on the head. ⇨ headscarf.

scarlet /'skɑːlɪt/ *u.n* (also *attrib*) bright red colour. Compare crimson.

,**scarlet 'fever** *u.n* kind of illness that spreads easily, causing red spots and sore throat, found mostly among children.

,**scarlet 'runner** *c.n* = runner bean.

scarves /skɑːvz/ *pl.n* ⇨ scarf.

scary ⇨ scare.

scathing /'skeɪðɪŋ/ *adj* (usu *attrib*) (of s.t said or written as an opinion about s.o/s.t) extremely cruel and critical.

'**scathingly** *adv.*

scatter /'skætə/ *tr/intr.v* (cause (several people, animals, things) to) go off, each in a different direction; throw things so that they go in different directions: *Scatter the grass seeds evenly over the earth. The crowd scattered* (*in all directions*) *when the police charged.*

'**scatter,brain** *c.n* (*derog; informal*) person who cannot, or does not want to, remember things so that he/she is often confused and careless, although not in a way that causes trouble.

'**scatter,brained** *adj* (*derog*) like (that of) a scatterbrain.

'**scattered** *adj* spread about; not close together: *scattered showers* (i.e rain showers in various places).

'**scattering** *c.n* small amounts or groups in various places: *When we got to the square, there was only a scattering of tourists there.*

scavenge /'skævɪndʒ/ *tr/intr.v* look for (things one can use, eat etc) among rubbish, things that have been thrown away etc: *He was scavenging in the boxes for something to eat.*

'**scavenger** *c.n* person/animal who/that scavenges, sometimes as her/his/its main way of getting food.

scenario /sɪ'nɑːrɪəʊ/ *c.n* (*pl -s*) description of what one plans should happen in a play, film etc, or in real life.

scene /siːn/ *n* **1** *c.n* part of (an act in) a play, film etc that does not have a change of place in it: *Act 1, Scene 1 of our radio play is in Jane's living room.* **2** *c.n* setting(2) or place in which a scene(1) takes place: *The scene is now the kitchen of the same house.* **3** *c.n* things that can be seen from a particular place at a particular time; view: *The scene as we came out of the building was wonderful.* **4** *c.n* (often *the — of s.t*) place where s.t happens: *By the time we reached the scene of the accident everything had been cleared up.* **5** *c.n* happening or event that people can see: *There were great scenes of rejoicing when the young men arrived back home.* **behind the scenes** (*of s.t*) (*fig*) in a place where one is not seen or noticed: *In many offices the people visitors meet are much less important than the ones who work quietly behind the scenes.* **come on the scene** appear for the first time; come into one's life. **make a scene** cause a disturbance by angry etc behaviour: *You mustn't make a scene in the restaurant just because you can't get the table you want!* **on the scene** (*of s.t*) where s.t is happening or has happened etc: *We were very happy until you arrived on the scene.* ⇨ scene(4). **set the scene** (*for s.o/s.t*) describe the background (of s.t, for s.o) so that the person one is talking or writing to can understand one's story better. **steal the scene** (*from s.o*) take attention (from another person). **the business** etc **scene** (*informal*) the world of business etc: *Joe is very interested in the fashion scene although he does not make clothes himself.* **the scene of the crime** the place where a crime was committed.

scenery /'siːnərɪ/ *u.n* **1** things one can see when one is in the country and not in a town: *desert scenery.* **2** things made for use on a stage as the background etc.

'**scenic** *adj* of or referring to scenery, either in the country or on a stage.

'**scenically** *adv.*

scent /sent/ *n* **1** *c.n* (often *— of s.t*) smell (of s.t), usu a pleasant one. **2** *c/u.n* liquid etc that one puts on one in order to smell pleasant. ⇨ perfume(2). **3** smell left by an animal etc which can be followed by dogs etc. **4** *sing.n* ability of people/animals to smell scents(3): *Dogs and cats have a much better scent than people have.* **5** *sing.n* (often *a — of s.t*) (*fig*) feeling that s.t is present: *There is a scent of* scandal(1) *about the way the company lost so much money for so many people.* (**follow**) **a false scent** (follow) a scent(3,5) that misleads one. **on the scent** (*of s.t*) following s.t by its scent(3,5). **throw s.o off** (**the scent**) ⇨ throw(*v*).

▷ *tr.v* **6** smell (s.t); notice that s.o/s.t is there by smelling (her/him/it): *The cat has scented a mouse.* **7** (*fig*) have a feeling/idea that (s.t) is there: *I scent danger; be careful.* **8** put scent(2) on (s.o/s.t).

'**scented** *adj* (often *— with s.t*) having a scent(1,2) (of s.t) in/on it: *scented soap.* Opposite unscented.

'**scentless** *adj* who/that does not have any scent(1,3).

sceptic /'skeptɪk/ *c.n* (US '**skeptic**) person who often or usu doubts things, e.g those that religious people believe.

'**sceptical** *adj* (US '**skeptical**) (often *— about/ of s.t*) not believing (s.t); very doubtful (about s.t).

'**sceptically** *adv* (US '**skeptically**). **scepticism** /'skeptɪ,sɪzəm/ *u.n* (US '**skepti,cism**).

schedule /'ʃedjuːl/ *c.n* **1** (often *— of s.t*) list (of things that need to be done), sometimes with the times arranged for them: *Here is my schedule* (*of* engagements(3)) *for this week.* **2** list (of prices, times of buses, things one can buy etc). **ahead of schedule** earlier than the scheduled(3) time. **behind schedule** later than the scheduled(3) time. **on schedule** at the scheduled(3) time.

▷ *tr.v* **3** put s.t on or into a schedule(*n*) (for a certain time): *The train is scheduled to arrive at 6 pm.*

,**scheduled 'flight** *c.n* flight by a plane that follows a regular timetable. Compare charter(2).

scheme /skiːm/ *c.n* **1** plan or arrangement, often a clever one, and sometimes one that is not honest: *a scheme to earn money by growing vegetables.* **2** way in which s.t is arranged or organized; plan: *There must be some scheme* *behind this way of working but I haven't discovered it yet.* **colour scheme** ⇨ colour(*n*). **the scheme of things** the natural situation in which things are in real life and which one cannot change.

▷ *intr.v* **3** plot(4); use schemes(1) (against, in favour of, s.o/s.t or to do s.t).

schizophrenia /ˌskɪtsəˈfriːnɪə/ *u.n* kind of disease of the mind, marked by a breakdown(3) in the relation(2) between thoughts, feelings and actions. **schizophrenic** /ˌskɪtsəˈfrenɪk/ *adj* 1 of, referring to, showing signs of, schizophrenia.

▷ *c.n* **2** schizophrenic(1) person.

school /skuːl/ *n* **1** *c.n* (also *attrib*) place where children go to be taught by teachers: *I teach in the local school.* **2** *unique n* work done in such a place or time spent in it: *Do you like school? School starts at 8.30 in the morning. What are you going to do when you finish school next year?* **3** *c/def.n* all the students (and sometimes also the teachers) of a particular school: *The whole school came to see the match.* **4** *c/unique n* (with capital **S** in names) place where a particular subject or subjects is/are taught, sometimes to adults as well as, or instead of, children and sometimes as part of a university etc: *Joe goes to dancing school twice a week. The London School of Economics is part of London University.* **5** *c.n* (often with capital **S**) group of people who are united by common beliefs, ways of doing things etc: *the* Expressionist(1) *School of painting.* **6** *c.n* (*fig*) (often — *of s.t*) thing that teaches one (s.t): *Life is a hard school. I learnt how to look after myself in the school of life itself, not from any teacher.* **7** *c.n* (often — *of fish,* herring(1) etc) group (of fish) that all move about together. **after/before school** after lessons finish or before they begin. **at school** in a school(1) as a pupil or teacher. **comprehensive / grammar / law / medical / middle / night / primary / private / public / secondary / Sunday school** ⇨ comprehensive etc. **go to school** go (regularly) to a school(1), esp as part of one's education: *My daughter will be going to school next year.* **leave school** finish one's education at a school(1): *He's going to leave school when he's sixteen and get a job.* **the, my** etc **old school** the school(1) to which one went as a student and which one therefore usu feels loyalty to. **the old school tie** (a) a special tie worn by boys who were at a particular school(1). (b) (*fig*) (a sign of the) loyalty of men to their old school and to each other.

▷ *tr.v* **8** teach or train (a person or animal) to do (s.t that needs control): *Before you can win any prizes with that horse it will have to be schooled. In the army you must school yourself to stand motionless for minutes at a time.*

scholar /ˈskɒlə/ *c.n* **1** person who studies and knows a lot about s.t, e.g ancient Roman history. **2** person who has a scholarship(2) at a school, university etc. **3** (*old use*) schoolboy, schoolgirl. **4** (*informal*) (usu *not much of a* —) well-educated person; person who is, has been, good at studying.

'scholarly *adj* of or referring to a scholar(1), her/ his work.

'scholar,ship *n* **1** *u.n* (*formal*) (piece of) study by scholars(1). **2** *c.n* money, prize, given to a

clever student to help her/him pay for her/his studies. Compare bursary, exhibition(3).

scholastic /skəˈlæstɪk/ *adj* of or referring to schools(1) and/or teaching.

scho'lastically *adv.*

,school 'age *unique n* (often *of* —) age at which one should or must go to school(1).

'school,boy *c.n* boy who goes to school(1).

'school,days *pl.n* time of one's life during which one is at school(1).

'school,fellow *c.n* (also **'school ,mate**) boy or girl who goes to the same school(1) as s.o.

'school,girl *c.n* girl who goes to school(1).

'schooling *u.n* (often — *in s.t*) **1** education in a school(1) (to learn s.t). **2** training (in s.t). ⇨ school(8).

'school,master *c.n* man who teaches in a private school(1).

'school,mistress *c.n* (*old use*) woman who teaches in a school(1).

,school of 'thought *c.n* (*pl* schools of thought) people who share the same opinion. ⇨ school(5).

,school re'port *c.n* ⇨ report¹(2).

'school,teacher *c.n* person who teaches in a school(1).

sciatica /saɪˈætɪkə/ *u.n* pain in the nerve that goes down the back of the leg as far as the knee.

science /ˈsaɪəns/ *n* (also *attrib*) **1** *u.n* knowledge (of s.t) that follows a system or systems and is (claimed to be) based on facts that can be observed and tested: *medical science.* **2** *u.n* study (of such knowledge): *science students; the science of how diseases spread.* **3** *c/u.n* branch of such study or knowledge: *natural/pure/social science. Chemistry is a science course at a university and literature is an arts course.* **have s.t down to a science** be very clever and successful at doing s.t because one knows exactly how to do it.

sci-fi /ˌsaɪ ˈfaɪ/ *u.n* (*informal*) science fiction.

,science 'fiction *u.n* (*informal sci-fi*) literary works about the future and new scientific discoveries and inventions that may affect people's lives then.

'sciences *def.pl.n* branches of science(3).

scientific /ˌsaɪənˈtɪfɪk/ *adj* **1** of or referring to science. **2** following scientific(1) rules and therefore properly organized in every detail: *a scientific approach to management studies.*

,scien'tifically *adv.*

'scientist *c.n* person whose work is on a science(3).

scissors /ˈsɪzəz/ *pl.n* (often *a pair of* —) two pieces of metal (or plastic) fastened together in the middle so that they can open and shut, with sharp blades at one end and holes for one's fingers at the other, used to cut cloth, paper etc. Compare shears(1).

sclerosis ⇨ multiple sclerosis.

scoff /skɒf/ *intr.v* (often — *at s.o/s.t*) laugh in a rude or critical way (at s.o/s.t); speak scornfully (about s.o/s.t).

scold /skəʊld/ *tr/intr.v* speak critically and usu angrily (to s.o) because of s.t he/she has (not) done, said etc.

'scolding *c.n* (often *get a* —) angry criticism etc: *You'll get a scolding if you're late again.*

scollop /ˈskɒləp/ = scallop¹, scallop².

scone /skɒn/ *c.n* small round cake that one usu cuts in half horizontally so that one can spread each half with butter, jam and sometimes also cream before eating it.

scoop /sku:p/ *c.n* **1** thing shaped like a deep spoon, used for picking up and holding liquids, soft substances, grains of things like corn etc: *an ice-cream scoop.* **2** thing like a scoop(1) used for measuring the amount of s.t or for holding it while it is being weighed. **3** (*informal*) (by a newspaper, radio programme, journalist etc) success in printing or reporting an exciting piece of news before anyone else does. **4** success in getting s.t else, e.g a business chance, before one's competitors.
▷ *tr.v* **5** (often — *s.t out* (*of s.t*); — *s.t up*) take s.t out (of s.t), lift s.t up, with a scoop(1,2) or with one's hand(s). **6** (of a newspaper, business company etc) beat (a competitor) by getting a scoop(3,4) first: *We scooped the market* (i.e our competitors) *by producing boxes cheaper than anyone else.*

scooter /'sku:tə/ *c.n* **1** vehicle shaped like an 'L', used by a child, who stands on the base of the L with one foot and pushes against the ground with the other foot to make it move. **2** = motorscooter.

scope /skəʊp/ *u.n* **1** area within which s.t operates, applies etc: *This job is within/outside the scope of his duties.* **2** (often — *for s.t*) opportunity or chance offered (for s.t): *There is little scope for doing anything new in our company as the manager is very old-fashioned.*

scorch /skɔ:tʃ/ *c.n* **1** (also **'scorch ,mark**) mark made on s.t by burning.
▷ *v* **2** *tr/intr.v* (cause (s.t) to) burn enough to leave marks on it but not enough to destroy it. **3** *tr.v* (of hot dry weather) cause (plants etc) to become dry and withered(1). **4** *intr.v* (*informal*) drive very fast: *Peter has a fast car and loves scorching along for hours on end.*
'scorcher *sing.n* (*informal*) very hot day: *It looks as though it's going to be a scorcher.*
'scorching *adj* **1** very hot; burning. **2** (*informal*) (of s.t said, written etc) very strong or fierce: *a scorching attack on the government.* ⇒ scathing.
▷ *adv* **3** **scorching hot** very hot.

score¹ /skɔ:/ *n* **1** *c.n* total of points, goals etc gained (so far) by one side in a match etc. **2** *def.n* total score¹(1) of all the competitors in a match etc: *'What's the score now?'* **3** *c.n* (often — *against/off s.o*) success (against s.o) which is the result of s.t clever one has said, written etc. ⇒ score¹(10). **4** *c.n* written copy of music that a person or an orchestra etc has to play, sing etc or that has been produced for a film etc. **full score** score¹(4) that has the parts for all the singers and players, each on a different line. **have a score to settle** (**with s.o**) (*informal*) have s.t that one wants to fight or argue about (with s.o). **keep the score** mark the score¹(1) on a card, in a book etc as each goal, point etc is made. **know the score** (*informal*) understand s.t, often in spite of s.o else's efforts to prevent one doing so. **make a score** (**of s.t**) score¹(5) (a certain number of points etc). **on that/this score** for that/this reason. **the score stands at s.t** the present score¹(2) is a certain number of points etc. **vocal score** score¹(4) for one or more singers.

▷ *v* **5** *tr/intr.v* be successful in winning (one or more points etc) in a match etc. **6** *tr/intr.v* give (s.o) (a certain score¹(1)) (for (doing) s.t): *The judges scored her 19 marks out of 20* (*for her performance*). **7** *intr.v* be the person who writes down the score¹(1) (of a team) as points etc are scored¹(5). ⇒ scorekeeper, scorer(1). **8** *tr/intr.v* gain (a certain number of marks etc) in an examination, competition etc: *You've scored 60 points.* **9** *intr.v* be successful: *The photographer scored again last week when she sold another large photograph.* **10** *intr.v* (often — *against/off/over s.o*) be successful (against s.o) by saying or writing s.t clever etc. ⇒ score¹(3). **score a hit** be successful and become popular as a result.
'score,board *c.n* board showing what the score¹(2) is.
'score,book *c.n* book in which one keeps the score¹(2).
'score,card *c.n* card on which one keeps the score¹(2), esp in golf¹(1).
,score 'draw *c.n* final result of a (football) match in which both sides have scored¹(5) the same number of goals, points.
'score,keeper *c.n* person whose job is to keep the score¹(2), usu in cricket¹.
,scoreless 'draw *c.n* final result of a (football) match in which neither side has scored¹(5).
'scorer *c.n* **1** = scorekeeper. **2** person who scores¹(5) a goal etc.

score² /skɔ:/ *pron* (*old use*), (pl score except in *scores* (*and scores*) *of s.t*) (*cardinal number*) twenty: *four score* (= 80). **scores** (**and scores**) **of s.t** a lot of people, animals, things.

scorn /skɔ:n/ *u.n* **1** (often — *for s.o/s.t*) fact of not respecting (s.o/s.t) at all or of despising(1) (her/him/it); contempt(1). **hold s.o/s.t up to scorn** = hold s.o/s.t up to ridicule (⇒ ridicule(*n*)). **laugh s.o/s.t to scorn** (try to) make other people scorn(2) s.o/s.t. **pour scorn on s.o/s.t** scorn(2) s.o/s.t.
▷ *tr.v* **2** feel scorn(1) for (s.o/s.t). **3** (*formal*) refuse to accept (help etc) because one thinks one is too clever etc to need it.
'scornful *adj* (often — *of s.o/s.t*) feeling and/or showing scorn(1) (for s.o/s.t).
'scornfully *adv.*

Scorpio /'skɔ:pɪ,əʊ/ *n* **1** *unique n* one of the 12 signs of the zodiac. **2** *c.n* person born under this sign.

scorpion /'skɔ:pɪən/ *c.n* kind of insect found in hot countries that has a long tail with a poisonous sting at the end.

Scot /skɒt/ *c.n* person who comes from Scotland.

Scotch /skɒtʃ/ *adj* **1** belonging to, coming from, Scotland.
▷ *n* **2** *u.n* (also *attrib*) whisky(1) made in Scotland. **3** *c.n* one glass of this.
,Scotch 'whisky *c/u.n* (pl -ies) = Scotch(*n*).
,Scotland 'Yard *unique n* **1** headquarters(1) of the London police. **2** (*informal*) detective branch of this.
Scots /skɒts/ *adj* (also **Scottish** /'skɒtɪʃ/) from, of or referring to, Scotland.
scot-free /,skɒt 'fri:/ *adj* (often *escape/get off* —) without having to pay what one should; without being punished for what one has done; without being hurt etc.

scoundrel /'skaʊndrəl/ c.n (derog) very bad man.

scour /skaʊə/ tr.v **1** (often — s.t out) rub (s.t) hard with s.t rough to clean or polish it (thoroughly): We had to scour out the old pots. **2** (often — s.t off (s.t); — s.t out (of s.t)) get (rust, dirt etc) off or out (of s.t) by scouring(1) it. **3** (usu — s.t out) (technical) (of moving water) make (a way through s.t) by the force of its action: Over millions of years the river had scoured out a deep gorge(1) across the plain. **4** (often — s.t for s.o/s.t) search (a place) very carefully (to try to find s.o/s.t).

'scourer c.n (also **'scouring pad**) device used for scouring(1), often made of wire or plastic net, used to clean pots and pans.

scourge /skɜːdʒ/ c.n (usu — of s.t) thing that punishes or harms people greatly (and that consists of s.t): the scourge of hunger in much of Africa.

scout /skaʊt/ c.n **1** (usu with capital **S**) member of an organization that is intended to improve a boy's/girl's character, ability etc. ⇨ Girl Guide (guide(5)). **2** person, usu in the army, whose job is to go out in front of the others to find out the positions etc of the enemy. **3** person who tries to find good professional people to join a sports team, group of actors etc. **talent scout** ⇨ talent.
▷ v **4** intr.v (usu — about/around (for s.o/s.t)) look here and there (to try to find s.o/s.t). **5** tr.v (often — s.t out (for s.o/s.t)) search (a place) (to see if one can find s.o/s.t).

'scout,master c.n (also with capital **S**) man who is the leader of a group of Scouts(1).

scowl /skaʊl/ c.n **1** angry look on a person's face.
▷ intr.v **2** (often — at s.o/s.t) look angrily (at s.o/s.t). Compare frown.

scrabble /'skræbl/ intr.v (often — about/around (for s.t)) move one's hands and fingers about in a fast erratic way, often while trying to find s.t: The prisoners were scrabbling about in the straw for small pieces of food that had fallen off the table.

'scraggy /'skrægɪ/ adj (-ier, -iest) thin and with one's/its bones very noticeable.

scram /skræm/ intr.v (-mm-) (slang; usu as an order) go/run away: I'm too busy to talk to you just now, so scram!

scramble /'skræmbl/ c.n **1** (often — for s.t) hurried and badly organized attempt (to get s.t). **2** difficult walk up or down a steep rough slope. **3** race on motorbikes over rough ground.
▷ v **4** intr.v struggle in a badly organized way: The hungry men scrambled with each other to get the food. **5** intr.v (usu — up, down etc (s.t)) climb (up, down etc (s.t)) with difficulty and often in a way that is not well organized. **6** tr.v mix (s.t) up: In this puzzle, you have ten scrambled words that you have to make into a sentence. ⇨ jumble(v). **7** tr.v mix up (the letters or sounds in a radio or telephone message) so that no one else can understand if they try to listen. ⇨ unscramble. **8** tr.v mix (one or more eggs) to make scrambled egg.

,scrambled 'egg(s) u.n kind of food made by mixing or beating an egg (or eggs), often with a little milk, and then cooking it.

scrap¹ /skræp/ n **1** c.n (often — of s.t) small, not important, piece (of s.t): a scrap of paper. **2** u.n (also attrib) thing or things that has/have been thrown away but may still be useful for making other things out of: scrap paper/metal. Joe buys up scrap and sells it to factories. **sell s.t for scrap** sell s.t that can be used only as scrap¹(2).
▷ tr.v (-pp-) **3** throw (s.t) away because it is no longer needed and sometimes turn it into scrap¹(2). **4** abandon or reject(3) (a plan, idea, method etc) because it is useless.

'scrap,book c.n book used for sticking in things that interest one, e.g articles and pictures cut out of newspapers.

'scrap ,heap n **1** c.n pile of scrap¹(2). **2** def.n (fig) place where things, ideas, people etc that are or have become useless are thrown: I used to think that people who had reached the age of 50 were ready for the scrap heap.

'scrap ,paper u.n **1** paper that has already been used but perhaps on one side only so can be used again to save paper and money. **2** paper that has been used or is not needed and is sold to factories for making new paper.

'scrappily adv in a scrappy(2) way.

'scrappiness u.n fact or state of being scrappy(2).

'scrappy adj (-ier, -iest) (informal) **1** consisting of scraps(2). **2** not as well arranged or complete as it should be: a scrappy report; a scrappy meal.

scraps pl.n **1** bits of food, esp that have remained after a meal and are thrown away, given to an animal etc. **2** pl of scrap¹(1).

scrap² /skræp/ c.n **1** (informal) fight, usu a short and not very serious one.
▷ intr.v (-pp-) **2** (often — with s.o) (informal) have a scrap²(1) (with s.o).

scrape /skreɪp/ c.n **1** act or sound of rubbing or scratching against s.t, often leaving a mark, wound etc. **2** mark, wound etc left by a scrape(1). **3** (often get into a — (with s.o)) (fig; informal) dangerous or unpleasant situation (with s.o), often as a result of behaving badly: That boy is always getting into scrapes with his teachers because he is careless.
▷ v **4** tr.v (often — s.t from/off s.t) remove (mud etc) (from s.t) by scratching it with a tool such as a knife: I scraped the dirt off my shoes before going inside. **5** tr.v remove s.t from (s.t) in this way: I scraped my shoes before going inside. **6** tr/intr.v (often — (s.t) against/on s.t) (cause (s.t) to) rub against s.t in a way that scratches, often leaving a mark, wound etc: I scraped my knee on a stone. **7** tr.v (often — s.t in s.t) make (a hole etc) (in s.t) by scraping (⇨ scrape(4)). **bow and scrape (to s.o)** ⇨ bow(v). **scrape along/by (on s.t)** (informal) earn only enough to live on (using a certain amount of money): Those old people have to scrape along on £30 a week. **scrape s.t clean** scrape(4) s.t until it is clean. **scrape s.t out** clean the inside of s.t by scraping (⇨ scrape(4)) it. **scrape through (s.t)** (a) manage to get through s.t narrow with difficulty. (b) manage to pass an examination etc but only just. **scrape s.t together/up** (fig) manage to collect s.t with difficulty: He managed to scrape together enough money to buy the house.

'scraper c.n device used for scraping (⇨ scrape(4)) things: a paint scraper.

'scrapings pl.n (often — of s.t) pieces (of s.t)

that have been scraped(4) off s.t: *scrapings of paint.*

scrappily, scrappiness, scrappy, scraps ⇨ scrap[1].

scratch /skrætʃ/ *attrib.adj* **1** (of a sportsperson etc) so good that her/his handicap(3) is zero(1).

▷ *c.n* **2** long mark or wound made with s.t sharp or rough. **3** act of rubbing with one's nails etc, sometimes causing a scratch(2) but usu to stop an itch(1) etc. **4** sound made by a scratch(3). (**be/come**) **up to scratch** (*fig*; *informal*) (be etc) at a level that can be accepted: *Peter's work hasn't really been up to scratch this term.* **from scratch** (*informal*) beginning right at the beginning, with nothing: *John built this car from scratch. Mary started from scratch and is now a very rich woman.* **without a scratch** (*informal*) without having suffered any damage in body or mind: *Peter survived the car accident without a scratch.*

▷ *v* **5** *tr/intr.v* make one or more marks or wounds (in or on (s.t)) with s.t sharp or rough: *Be careful; that cat scratches! The dust in that dirty cloth has scratched the paint on my car! I've scratched my hand on an old nail!* **6** *tr.v* (often — *s.t in/on s.t*) write (one or more letters), make (one or more marks), (in/on s.t) by scratching(5): *Someone has scratched 'M.L loves P.N' on this gate.* **7** *tr/intr.v* rub (the skin, part of the body, oneself), usu with one's nails, to stop an itch(1): *You often see dogs scratching themselves. When I* itch(3)*, I scratch. Stop scratching!* **8** *intr. v* (often — *about* (for s.t) ; — *at s.t*) use one's nails or claws(1) to dig on the surface of s.t to try to find, open etc s.t, and usu making a scratch(4): *When our cat wants to come in, it scratches at our door. You often see chickens scratching about on the ground for grains of corn.* **9** *tr/intr.v* withdraw(1) (oneself, s.o, an animal) from a race etc before it starts: *Helen's too ill to play tennis today so we'll have to scratch her, I'm afraid.* **scratch s.t from/off s.t**; **scratch s.t off/out** remove words etc written on a surface, (from s.t) by scratching(5).

'scratchy *adj* (*-ier, -iest*) that scratches(5,7) or is scratched, often producing a sound at the same time: *a scratchy pen* (i.e one that scratches(5,7) the paper while it writes); *a scratchy record.*

scrawl /skrɔːl/ *c.n* **1** bad (piece of) handwriting: *I find it difficult to read Wendy's scrawl.*

▷ *tr.v* **2** write (s.t) quickly and in a way that is difficult to read.

scream /skriːm/ *c.n* **1** (often — *for s.o/s.t*) very loud cry on a high note (to try to get s.t): *I gave a scream for help when I saw him.* **2** (*slang*) very funny person or thing: *Jane's a real scream! It was a scream when Joe's car slid backwards into the water.*

▷ *v* **3** *intr.v* (often — *out*) give a scream(1). **4** *tr.v* (often — *s.t out*) say (s.t) while screaming(3). **scream about s.t** cause a disturbance by complaining loudly about s.t one does not like: *What are they screaming about now?* **scream blue murder** ⇨ murder(*n*). **scream with s.t** scream because of s.t: *scream with pain.*

'screamingly *adv* (usu — *funny*) (*informal*) very (funny).

screech /skriːtʃ/ *c.n* **1** loud unpleasant sound on a high note: *the screech of brakes as a car stops suddenly; the screech of a frightened child; the screech of an* owl.

▷ *v* **2** *intr.v* (often — *out*) make a loud unpleasant sound, on a high note: *The car screeched to a stop.* **3** *tr.v* (often — *s.t out*) say (s.t) while screeching(2).

screen /skriːn/ *n* **1** *c.n* thing that is made, put up, to protect s.o/s.t from being seen or from wind, fire, insects etc: *a screen of trees; a screen round a patient's bed in a hospital; screens on windows to keep flies out.* ⇨ smokescreen, windscreen. **2** *c.n* kind of net etc that allows s.t to go through while preventing other things from doing so. ⇨ sieve(1). **3** *c.n* flat surface on which films etc are shown: *a television screen; a cinema screen.* **4** *def/unique n* (industry of) making and acting in films: *This play was originally written for the screen, not the stage. He was a star of stage and screen as well as of radio.* ⇨ screenplay. **screen for s.t** (*fig*) thing that one uses for hiding an activity: *His clothes shop is a screen for his* illegal *activities.*

▷ *tr.v* **5** (often — *s.o/s.t (off) from s.t*) provide (s.o/s.t) with a screen(1), be a screen(1) for (s.o/s.t) (to protect her/him/it against s.t). **6** provide (a window) etc with a screen(1) to keep flies etc out. **7** show (a film etc): *This is the first time the film has been screened on television.* **8** (often — *s.o/s.t from s.t*) (*fig*) protect (s.o/s.t) (from s.t): *The film-star tried to screen her family from the curiosity of the journalists.* **9** examine (s.o/s.t) carefully to find out whether he/she/it is suitable etc for s.t: *We have to screen all those who apply for jobs in* Military *Intelligence.* **10** (*medical*) (often — *s.o for s.t*) examine s.o, usu with X-rays(1) (to find out whether he/she has a disease, e.g cancer(1)).

'screening *c/u.n* **1** showing of a film. ⇨ screen(7). **2** testing of a person. ⇨ screen(9,10).

'screen,play *c.n* story written for television or a film, not a stage play.

'screen ,test *c.n* test to see whether s.o is suitable as a film or television actor/actress.

screw /skruː/ *n* **1** *c.n* thing like a nail(2) with a thread(3) running round it and a slot(1) in its head so that one can turn it with a screwdriver to make it go into, or (by turning it the other way) come out of, a piece of wood etc. **2** *c.n* device made of wood or metal that looks like a screw(1), used in a machine etc to pull, push or press s.t. **3** *c.n* (often *give s.t a —*) (one) turn (of a screw(1) or a lid etc with the inside like a screw(1)).

▷ *v* Opposite unscrew. **4** *tr.v* fix (s.t) (to s.t) with one or more screws(1): *I screwed the legs onto the table. We screwed the two pieces of wood together.* **5** *tr.v* (often — *s.t up*) turn a screw(1) etc to tighten s.t. **6** *intr.v* (often — *together/up*) be able to be tightened by screwing(4): *Do these two pipes screw together?* **screw s.t down** (**a**) cause (a lid etc with the inside like a screw) to be fastened on the jar etc. (**b**) cause (s.t) to be held in place by screws(1). **screw s.t on(to s.t)** close (a lid etc) (on(to a jar etc)) by turning it: *screw the lid on tightly so it won't leak.* ⇨ unscrew. **screw one's eyes up** press or twist the skin round one's eyes together because of bright light or to show doubt, etc. **screw up one's courage (to do s.t)** try to be brave enough (to do s.t). **screw s.t up** (**a**) ⇨ screw(5). (**b**) ⇨ screw(6). (**c**) force s.t, e.g paper, into a bundle(1) with one's hands. (**d**) (*fig*; *slang*) make a mess(4) of s.t: *That has really screwed up the deal!*

'screw,driver *c.n* kind of tool with one flat end

that fits into the slot on the head of a screw so that one can turn it.

'screw ,top *c.n* (also *attrib*) **1** metal etc top for a jar etc which has a thread(3) so that it can be screwed onto the jar. **2** upper part of a jar etc which has a thread(3) so that a metal etc top can be screwed onto it.

screwy /'skruːɪ/ *adj* (*-ier*, *-iest*) (*derog*; *informal*) mad; stupid; absurd: *a screwy person*; *screwy ideas.*

scribble /'skrɪbl/ *n* **1** *c/u.n* (word(s) written in) handwriting that is bad and/or careless. **2** *c.n* thing that looks like writing but has no meaning.
▷ *tr/intr.v* **3** write (s.t) in a scribble(*n*).

script /skrɪpt/ *n* **1** *u.n* kind of handwriting in which the letters are joined to each other. **2** *c/ u.n* system of letters used for writing and printing a language: *Can you read Russian script?* **3** *c.n* written text(2) of what a person is going to say in a talk or lecture or what actors and actresses have to say in a television programme, film etc. **in script** using script(1), not another form of handwriting or typing etc.
▷ *tr.v* **4** write the script(3) of (a television programme, film etc).
'script,writer *c.n* person who writes the script(3) of a television programme, film etc.

scriptures /'skrɪptʃəz/ *pl.n* **1** holy books of a religion: *Hindu scriptures.* **2** *def.n* (with capital **S**) the Bible(1).
'scriptural *adj* of, referring to, found in, scriptures or the Scriptures.

scroll /skrəʊl/ *c.n* **1** roll (of parchment etc), used mostly in ancient times for writing on: *A scroll was often rolled on a handle at one end or on handles at both ends and one turned the handle(s) to find the place that one wanted to read.*
▷ *tr/intr.v* **2** (often — (s.t) *down/up*) (in a computer) cause (a program to) move down/up the screen so that one can see earlier/later parts of it.

scrotum /'skrəʊtəm/ *c.n* (*pl scrotums* or, less usu, *scrota* /'skrəʊtə/) bag of skin etc which holds the testicles of a male person or animal.

scrounge /skraʊndʒ/ *tr/intr.v* (*derog*) (try to) get (s.t) without paying for it. **scrounge around** (*for s.t*) look in various places to scrounge s.t.
'scrounger *c.n* (*derog*) person who scrounges.

scrub /skrʌb/ *c.n* **1** hard rub, (usu with a brush) to make her/him/it clean: *Give that dirty floor a good scrub with this brush.*
▷ *tr/intr.v* (*-bb-*) **2** rub (s.t) hard to clean it. **scrub s.t clean** scrub(2) s.t until it is clean. **scrub s.t off** (*s.t*) remove s.t (from s.t) by scrubbing(2): *scrub mud off shoes.* **scrub s.t out** remove (words etc, e.g on walls) by scrubbing(2).
'scrubbing ,brush *c.n* hard brush used for scrubbing(2) floors etc.

scruff /skrʌf/ *def.n* (**by**) **the scruff of the neck** (using) the back of a person's/animal's neck (usu to stop her/him/it from escaping): *Jack grabbed the boy by the scruff of the neck.*

scruffy /'skrʌfɪ/ *adj* (*-ier*, *-iest*) (*derog*) not at all tidy and sometimes also dirty: *scruffy children/ clothes.*
'scruffily *adv.* **'scruffiness** *u.n.*

scrum /skrʌm/ *c.n* **1** (in rugby) tight grouping of forwards(*n*) of both teams who push against

each other and use their feet to try to get the ball back to their own side when it is thrown in between them. **2** (*informal*) crowd of people who are pushing each other about.

scrumptious /'skrʌmpʃəs/ *adj* (*informal*) that tastes very good or looks very attractive.
'scrumptiousness *u.n.*

scruple /'skruːpl/ *c.n* **1** (usu *pl* (*have —s*), but also *u.n* (*without —*)) feeling that it is, may be, morally wrong to do s.t: *Mary began to have scruples about the work she was doing when she saw that it was harming others and finally she left the job. John behaves quite without scruple(s) in his attempts to get rich.*
▷ *intr.v* **2** (often — *about s.t*; — *to do s.t*) have scruples(1) (about (doing) s.t): *Some shops wouldn't scruple to charge poor people high prices for food during a famine.*

scrupulous /'skruːpjʊləs/ *adj* trying to be completely honest or correct: *a scrupulous official.* Opposite unscrupulous.
'scrupulously *adv.* **'scrupulousness** *u.n.*

scrutiny /'skruːtɪnɪ/ *c/u.n* (*pl -ies*) examination (of s.o/s.t) by looking at her/him/it carefully.

scrutinize, -ise /'skruːtɪˌnaɪz/ *tr.v* look at (s.o/ s.t) carefully in order to find anything wrong, errors etc.

scuba /'skuːbə/ *c.n* device that one wears on one's back while swimming under water which provides air to enable one to breath.
'scuba ,diver *c.n* person who uses a scuba.
'scuba ,diving *u.n* using a scuba as a sport etc.

scuffle /'skʌfl/ *c.n* **1** (often *have a —* (*with s.o*)) fight (with s.o), usu a short not very hard or well organized one: *He was involved in a scuffle with the police.*
▷ *intr.v* **2** (often — *with s.o*) have a scuffle(1) with s.o).

scull /skʌl/ *c.n* **1** one of a pair of small oars with which a person moves a boat along the water. **2** example of sculling(3). Compare row¹(1).
▷ *tr/intr.v* **3** use sculls(1) to move (a boat) along the water.
'sculler *c.n* person who sculls(3).

scullery /'skʌlərɪ/ *c.n* (*pl -ies*) room (in a usu big old house) in which dishes are washed up etc.

sculpt /skʌlpt/ *v* **1** *tr/intr.v* (often — *s.t into s.o/ s.t*) remove parts of (s.t) in order to produce a new shape (which is that of s.o/s.t): *The artist sculpted the stone into a battle scene. Years of wind and rain had sculpted the rocks into strange shapes.* **2** *tr.v* (often — *s.o/s.t out of, in, s.t*) make the shape of (s.o/s.t) by sculpting(1) (using a particular material): *She sculpted a bird out of ice.*

sculptor /'skʌlptə/ *c.n* person who sculpts.
sculptress /'skʌlptrəs/ *c.n* woman who sculpts.
sculptural /'skʌlptʃərəl/ *adj* of or referring to sculpture(1).

sculpture /'skʌlptʃə/ *n* **1** *u.n* art of sculpting. **2** *c/u.n* work produced by a sculptor/sculptress.
▷ *v* **3** *tr/intr.v* = sculpt(1) (s.t). **4** *tr.v* = sculpt(2) (s.o/s.t).

scum /skʌm/ *n* **1** *c/u.n* thin covering of dirty material that often forms on a liquid when it has remained without moving for some time or after it has been boiled: *After boiling the jam, remove the scum and allow it to cool.* **2** *u.n* (*derog*; *fig*) very bad people who are harmful to society. **the scum of the earth** = scum(2).

'scummy adj (*-ier, -iest*) covered with scum(1).

scurf /skɜːf/ u.n small bits of loose dry skin, esp in the hair. ⇨ dandruff.

'scurfy adj (*-ier, -iest*) having scurf.

scurrilous /'skʌrɪləs/ adj (*derog; formal*) very rude in a vulgar(1) way: *a scurrilous attack on the government.*

scurrility /skə'rɪlɪtɪ/ u.n. **'scurrilously** adv. **'scurrilousness** u.n.

scuttle¹ /'skʌtl/ c.n (also **'coal-,scuttle**) container in which coal is kept beside a fire.

scuttle² /'skʌtl/ intr.v (usu — *away/off*) (usu of a small animal or person) move (away) quickly, usu to escape.

scuttle³ /'skʌtl/ tr.v make a hole in (a boat, ship) to make it sink.

scythe /saɪð/ c.n 1 kind of tool with a long curved metal blade and a long wooden handle, used to cut grass, corn etc. Compare sickle.
▷ tr.v 2 (often — *s.t down/off*) cut (grass etc) with a scythe(1).

SDP /,es ,diː 'piː/ def/unique n abbr Social Democratic Party.

SE written abbr southeast(ern).

sea /siː/ n 1 u/def.n area of salty water that covers most of our earth: *The temperature of the sea changes more slowly than that of the land. Most of our earth is covered by (the) sea.* Compare ocean(1). 2 def.n any part of the sea(1), when one is contrasting(3) it with the land: *I went down to the shore and ran into the sea.* 3 c.n (usu in names with capital **S**, after 'the') area of the sea(1) that is considered to form one unit of it, sometimes almost completely surrounded by land: *the Caspian Sea; the Dead Sea; the Black Sea; the North Sea.* Compare bay², gulf(1), lake, ocean(2). 4 c.n (often *pl*) movement of waves on a/the sea(1-3): *There was a big sea running that day.* 5 c.n (often — *of people/animals/things*) (*fig*) large mass (of people etc): *The fields were a sea of beautiful wild flowers in spring.* **all at sea** (*fig*) (of a person, her/his mind etc) confused: *I'm sorry but I'm all at sea; will you please repeat what you said?* **at sea** (a) (esp of a sailor) on a ship or boat that is away from the land: *My son is at sea at the moment.* (b) (*fig*) = all at sea. **by sea** in a ship, boat etc: *Let's go/travel by sea.* **go to sea** become a sailor or officer on a ship. **lost at sea** drowned in the sea. **. . .-on-Sea** (in the name of a place that is beside the sea): *Southend-on-Sea.* **on the sea** (a) in a ship etc floating or moving on the sea. (b) beside the sea: *Brighton is on the sea.* **put (out) to sea** leave land in a ship or boat.

'sea ,a'nemone c.n sea animal that looks like a flower, with many narrow feelers round an opening.

'sea,bed c/def.n bed(3) of the sea.

'sea,bird c.n bird that spends some or most of its time on or over the sea to catch its food.

'sea ,breeze c.n breeze blowing from the sea on to the land.

'sea ,captain c.n captain of a merchant ship.

'sea,coast c.n land lying alongside the sea.

'sea,food u.n (also *attrib*) food that comes from the sea; fish and shellfish: *a seafood cocktail(2).*

'sea,front c/u/def.n part of a town that is alongside the sea, often with a road or path so that people can walk or drive along and look at the sea: *We walked along the seafront.*

'sea,gull c.n = gull¹.

'sea,horse c.n kind of very small fish whose head looks like a horse's.

'sea ,level unique n (*above/at/below* — etc) average level of the sea from which the heights of places on land are measured: *The Dead Sea is below sea level. The highest mountain in Britain is 1343 metres above sea level.*

'sea ,lion c.n kind of seal¹(1) found in the Pacific Ocean.

'seaman c.n (*pl -men*) 1 sailor who is not an officer. 2 person who is experienced in handling ships at sea.

'seaman,like adj behaving or done in the way a seaman(2) would do it.

'seaman,ship u.n skill of a seaman(2).

'sea ,mile c.n = nautical mile.

'sea,plane c.n plane that can land on the sea and take off from it.

'sea,port c.n (big town or city with a) port¹ on the sea or on a big river etc which ships can reach from the sea.

'sea ,power n 1 u.n naval strength. 2 c.n country that has a large navy.

seas pl.n = sea(4): *heavy seas.* (**on**) **the high seas** ⇒ high seas (⇨ high).

'sea ,salt u.n salt produced by evaporating(2) sea-water. Compare rock salt (⇨ rock¹), table salt.

'sea ,shanty c.n (*pl -ies*) = shanty².

'sea,shell c.n shell of a creature that lives on or beside the sea.

'sea,shore u/def.n part of the land that is alongside the sea.

'sea,sick adj feeling sick because of the movement of waves on the sea.

'sea,sickness u.n.

'sea,side def.n (also *attrib*) (often *at/by the —*) area close to the edge of the sea, esp when it is considered as a place for a holiday: *a seaside town; a seaside holiday; go to the seaside for the day.*

'sea ,urchin c.n sea animal with a hard round body and spines(3), found in shallow(1) water.

seaward /'siːwəd/ adj (facing) towards the sea. ⇨ landward.

'seawards adv (US **'seaward**) towards the sea. ⇨ landwards.

'sea-,water u.n (also *attrib*) salty water that is in, comes from, the sea(1): *sea-water fish.*

'sea,weed u.n plant or plants that grow(s) in the sea, not on land.

'sea,worthiness u.n fact or state of being seaworthy.

'sea,worthy adj well enough built, in good enough condition, to go to sea safely.

seal¹ /siːl/ n 1 c.n kind of mammal that lives in and near the sea and has flippers(1) and a tail like a fish has. 2 u.n (also *attrib*) skin or fur of this animal used for making clothes: *a seal coat.*

'seal,skin u.n (also *attrib*) = seal¹(2).

seal² /siːl/ c.n 1 symbol of a country, group of people, important person etc that can be stamped, often in sealing wax, after a signature on an official letter etc. 2 mark pressed into paper, sealing wax etc by a seal²(1). 3 round piece of paper, sometimes with a seal²(1) stamped on it, which one sticks beside one's signature etc on an official document(1). **4** metal instrument with a seal²(1) on it, used for stamping the seal²(1) on paper, sealing wax etc. **5** piece of paper, sealing wax, wire etc used to close s.t in such a way that it cannot be opened without breaking the seal²(2,3). **6** device, material etc put between parts of a machine etc to stop water, gas, air etc leaking between them. **7** fact of water, gas etc not being allowed to leak because of such a seal²(6).

▷ *tr.v* **8** make or put a seal²(2,3) on (s.t). **9** (often — *s.t down/up/shut* (*with* s.t)) close s.t (with a seal²(5) or) by sticking it: *You can seal this envelope by wetting the glue.* **seal s.o/s.t off** (*from s.o/s.t*) surround s.o/s.t, close an area, so that there is no contact(2) (with s.o/s.t).

'**sealing ,wax** *u.n* hard often red material that melts when one heats it and hardens again when it cools, used to seal(*v*) s.t.

seam /si:m/ *c.n* **1** place where two pieces of cloth etc are joined together, usu by sewing along or near their edges. **2** layer(1) of coal etc between two layers of rock etc. **bursting at the seams** (a) very/too full. (b) wanting very much (to do, say s.t): *When I came home, Sue was bursting at the seams to tell me her good news.* **come apart at the seams** break open along the seams(1).

seaman(like/ship), seaplane, seaport ⇒ sea.

search /sɜ:tʃ/ *c.n* **1** (often — *for* s.o/s.t) act of trying to find (s.o/s.t) by looking in places, examining s.t etc: *a search for the missing jewels.* **in search of s.o/s.t** trying to find s.o/s.t: *We went in search of the lost boys.*

▷ *v* **2** *intr.v* (often — *after/for* s.o/s.t) try to find (s.o/s.t) by looking in places, examining s.t: *I searched for the keys but I couldn't find them. We searched everywhere.* **3** *tr.v* (often — s.o/s.t for s.o/s.t) examine (s.o/s.t) (in order to try to find s.o/s.t). **search into s.t** examine (a situation, problem etc) carefully. **search through s.t** (for **s.t**) examine all the parts of s.t (to try to find s.t).

'**searching** *adj* (of a look, question etc) that is intended to find the truth of s.t: *Her searching questions forced him to admit what he had done.*

'**search,light** *c.n* very powerful light used at night to find enemy aircraft, stop prisoners escaping from s.w etc.

'**search ,party** *c.n* (*pl* -*ies*) group of people who are trying to find s.o who is lost etc.

'**search ,warrant** *c.n* written permission to search(3) a place, usu given by a judge to the police so that they can try to find things that have been stolen.

seas, seashell, seashore, seasick-(ness), seaside ⇒ sea.

season¹ /'si:zn/ *c.n* one of the parts into which people divide a year esp according to the weather or into lengths of time suitable, good etc for s.t: *the growing season; the football season.* In England we have the four seasons of spring, summer, autumn and winter. In India they have a monsoon(2) *season each year. For shops, the time before Christmas is a busy season.* **high season** ⇒ high. **in season** (a) (of fruit, vegetables etc) able to be found fresh and therefore not needing to be

imported(2). Opposite out of season. (b) (of female animals) = in/on heat. ⇒ heat(*n*). (c) during the high season. **low season** ⇒ low¹. **out of season** = not in season(a).

'**seasonable** *adj* Opposite unseasonable. **1** normal for that season¹: *seasonable weather.* **2** suitable for that season¹: *seasonable amusements.*

'**seasonably** *adv.*

seasonal /'si:zənl/ *adj* that happens or is found only at certain seasons¹: *seasonal jobs in seaside hotels.*

'**seasonally** *adv.*

,**season of ,good 'cheer** *def.n* Christmas season¹.

,**Season's 'Greetings** *pl/def.pl.n* greetings that are suitable for this particular season¹, usu Christmas and the New Year.

'**season ,ticket** *c.n* ticket that one can use as often as one likes for a certain length of time, e.g for a week or a month, to travel on trains, go to sports etc.

season² /'si:zn/ *v* **1** *tr.v* (often — s.t with s.t) put salt, pepper(1) etc on food to make it taste good. **2** *tr/intr.v* (cause (wood) to) become suitable for use in building etc by drying (it) slowly.

'**seasoned** *adj* (*fig*) who has had so much experience of s.t that he/she is quite used to it: *a seasoned traveller.*

'**seasoning** *c/u.n* thing(s) used to season²(1) food.

seat /si:t/ *c.n* **1** thing on which one sits, e.g a chair or bench. **2** part of one's body on which one sits; bottom(3). **3** part of a piece of clothing that covers one's seat(2): *the seat of my trousers.* **4** position, job etc on a committee etc: *have a seat on the club committee; win a seat in Parliament.* **back-seat driver** ⇒ back. (**be in**) **the hot seat** ⇒ hot(*adj*). **have/take a seat** sit down. **in the driving seat** ⇒ driving. **lose/win a seat** succeed in being, fail to be, elected to a seat(4). **seat of government** etc (*formal*) place from which a government etc operates: *London is the seat of government in Britain.* **seat of learning** (*formal*) university or other place which is important for its teaching work. **take a back seat** ⇒ back(*adj*). **take a seat** ⇒ have/take a seat. **win a seat** ⇒ lose/win a seat.

▷ *tr.v* **5** cause (s.o) to sit down: *I seated the child in the chair.* ⇒ unseat. **6** be able to give seats to (a certain number of people): *This cinema seats 500 people.* ⇒ seating. (**please**) **be seated** (*formal*) (please) sit down. **seat oneself** (*formal*) sit down: *After we had all seated ourselves the lecture began.*

'**seat ,belt** *c.n* ⇒ safety belt.

-'**seater** *c.n* vehicle, plane etc that has the number of seats shown in the first part of the word: *a four-seater.*

'**seating** *u.n* supply or arrangement of seats: *This cinema has seating for 500 people. We are going to change the seating in the room so that everyone can see the new stage.* ⇒ seat(6).

'**seating ,plan** *c.n* plan showing where people are to sit, e.g at a big dinner.

sea-water, seaweed, seaworthiness, seaworthy ⇒ sea.

sec /sek/ *abbr* **1** secretary.

▷ *c.n* **2** (*informal*) second²(3): *I'll only be a sec. Wait a sec, I'm coming with you.*

seclude /sɪ'klu:d/ tr.v (often — s.o from s.t) (formal) keep (s.o) away (from taking part in s.t etc): Some countries still seclude women from public view.

se'cluded adj quiet and hidden away from people: a nice secluded spot in the garden.

seclusion /sɪ'klu:ʒən/ u.n **1** state of being secluded: She chose seclusion in a small country cottage. **2** (often — of s.o (from s.t)) act or fact of secluding (s.o) (from s.t): We demand the seclusion from the stadium of people who are violent. **in seclusion** in a state of being secluded: He kept her in seclusion in his small house.

second¹ /'sekənd/ det/pron (ordinal number) **1** number two in an order; 2nd: Mary was first and John was second in the examination. Peter passed at his second attempt. **second to none** the best: She (or Her work) is second to none.
▷ c.n **2** grade(1) between the top and the bottom one in a British university examination (sometimes this class is divided into two sections, an upper second and a lower second): John got a second in his examination (or a second class degree).

secondarily /'sekəndərɪlɪ/ adv in secondary(1) place.

secondary /'sekəndrɪ/ adj **1** (often of — importance) less important than the best or top. **2** (of schools, educational systems etc) for children of between about 11 and 18 years old. ⇨ higher education, middle school, primary school, secondary school, tertiary(1). **3** that comes, has spread, from the original one: a secondary symptom of the disease.

'secondary ,school c/u.n school that students go to after primary school and before getting a job or going to university etc, usu between the ages of about 11 and 16 or 18.

,secondary 'stress c/u.n stress(2) on part of a word or group of words that is less strong than primary stress: In ,secondary 'stress', the primary stress is on 'stress' and is marked by the sign¹, and the secondary stress is on 'sec' and is marked by ₁.

,second 'best adj not the best but the next thing after that. **come off second best** (informal) lose in a fight, argument etc. **settle for second best** decide to accept s.t even though it is not as good as the best one had hoped for.

,second 'childhood u.n (derog) act or fact of behaving like a child again when one is older.

,second 'class adj (,second-'class when attrib) **1** (informal) not (quite) of the best quality etc: second-class fruit. **2** (also adv) (of travel) (by a) cheaper class than first class. **3** (also adv) (of the British postal services) (by a) slower and therefore cheaper class than first class.
▷ c.n (also attrib) **4** = second¹(2).

,second 'cousin c.n child of either of one's parents' cousin.

,second-de'gree attrib.adj of a middle level of seriousness: second-degree burns; second-degree murder. ⇨ first-degree, third-degree burn.

,second 'floor def.n (also attrib) (US ,third 'floor) two floors higher than ground level. ⇨ ground floor.

,second-'hand adj/adv **1** not new; already used by s.o else: a second-hand car; I bought it second-hand. **2** from s.o who did not see it herself/himself: I got the report of the accident second-hand from a woman whose son had been in it. Compare second hand (⇨ second²).

,second-in-co'mmand c.n person in an army unit, business etc who is next in rank after the commander, boss etc.

,second lieu'tenant c.n (military) lowest rank of commissioned officer in the British army.

'secondly adv number two in a list: I'm staying at home tonight, firstly because I'm tired and secondly because I want to wash my hair.

,second 'nature u.n (often — to s.o) (informal) part of the firm, usual habits (of s.o): It's second nature to her to offer help when it is needed.

,second 'person def.n (grammar) (form used with the) person to whom one is writing or speaking, i.e 'you', not 'I', 'we', 'he', 'she' or 'they': The second person singular and plural of 'be' is 'are'. Compare first person, third person.

,second-'rate adj (derog; informal) not as good as the best.

'seconds pl.n **1** (in the serving of food) second helping of the same food. **2** goods that are imperfect(1) and are sold at a cheap price.

,second 'sight u.n ability to see things in the future or things that are far away, not with one's eyes but with other powers: She seems to have second sight.

,second-'string adj (mostly in sports and games) in the second rank: a second-string player.

,second 'thoughts pl.n doubts about whether one is correct in saying, doing or thinking s.t: He's having second thoughts about going. **on second thoughts** having thought about it again: I said I would go out this evening but on second thoughts I had better stay in.

second² /'sekənd/ c.n **1** (of time) sixtieth of a minute: There are sixty seconds (60″) in a minute. **2** (of measures of angles) sixtieth of a minute: There are 3 600 seconds (3 600″) in a degree. **3** (informal sec) very short time but usu longer than a second³(1): Wait a second, I'm not ready yet. I'll be ready in a second.

'second ,hand c/def.n thin long pointer on some watches/clocks that shows the seconds²(1). Compare second-hand (⇨ second¹). ⇨ hour/minute hand, hand(4).

second³ /'sekənd/ c.n **1** person who seconds³(2,3) s.o in a duel(1), for an election etc or who seconds a motion.
▷ tr.v **2** support (and act as the agent of) (s.o) in an argument, duel(1) etc. **3** be the second person to propose s.o for election or s.t for voting on: The suggestion was proposed by Helen and seconded by Dave. **second a motion** second³(3) a proposal so that it can be voted on.

'seconder c.n second³(1).

second⁴ /sɪ'kɒnd/ tr.v (often — s.o from s.t (to s.t)) move (s.o) from her/his usual job (to another one), usu for a short time.

se'condment c/u.n.

secret /'si:krɪt/ adj **1** not known by anyone else, or only by a few chosen people: a secret plan to attack; a secret passage from the house to a hollow tree in the garden; my secret love for Joan. **2** = secretive. **keep s.t secret (from s.o)** try to prevent anyone (or a particular person) finding out about s.t.
▷ c.n **3** thing that is kept private, secret(1). **4** (often

the — of s.t) thing that no one has yet discovered (about s.t): *the secrets of how the brain works.* **5** (often *the — of s.t*) thing that one must know in order to be able to do or understand etc (s.t); key(5) (to s.t): *The secret of opening this door is to press the wall just here.* **dark secret** ⇨ dark. **in secret** secretly. **keep a secret** not tell anyone s.t that one has been told as a secret(3). **let s.o into a secret** tell s.o s.t that is/was a secret(3). **an open secret** a thing that is said to be a secret(3) but that everyone knows. **remain a secret** not be discovered by anyone.

secrecy /'si:krɪsɪ/ *u.n* fact of being, keeping s.t, secret(1). **in (complete) secrecy** (absolutely) secretly. **veil of secrecy** ⇨ veil.

‚secret 'agent *c.n* person who tries to find out the secrets(3) of an enemy etc by secret(1) means; spy(1).

secrete /sɪ'kri:t/ *tr.v* **1** hide (s.o/s.t) away. **2** (*technical*) (of a (gland in a person/animal or of a plant) produce (a (liquid) substance, e.g saliva or resin(1)). Compare excrete.

secretion /sɪ'kri:ʃən/ *c/u.n* (*technical*) substance secreted(2).

'secretive /'si:krɪtɪv/ *adj* liking to keep, in the habit of keeping, things secret(1).

'secretively *adv.* **'secretiveness** *u.n.*

'secretly *adv* in a secret(1) way: *Secretly, I admired her.*

‚secret 'service *c/def.n* department in a government that does secret(1) work, trains and sends out secret agents, esp to try to find dangerous people or find out important, useful information etc.

secretary /'sekrətrɪ/ *c.n* (*pl -ies*) **1** (*abbr sec*) person working in an office, answering the telephone, typing letters, filing³(4) papers, making appointments(1) etc: *My secretary is responsible for the success of this office.* **2** (*abbr sec*) person of quite high rank in a company, club etc whose job is to look after the ordinary business, write official letters etc. **3** (with capital **S**) rank of minister in the British government: *the Secretary of State for Foreign Affairs, for Trade; the Foreign/Home Secretary.* **4** high rank in the British Civil Service: *The highest rank is Permanent Secretary, the next is* Deputy(1) *Secretary, then Undersecretary and then* Assistant(1) *Secretary.* **5** (with capital **S**) rank in British embassies(1), High Commissions and consulates(2): *The highest rank is a First Secretary, the next a Second Secretary and the lowest a Third Secretary.* **honorary secretary** ⇨ honorary(1). **private secretary** ⇨ private.

secretarial /ˌsekrə'teərɪəl/ *adj* of or referring to a secretary(1,2) or her/his work.

secretariat /ˌsekrə'teərɪət/ *c.n* office of a secretary(2) or secretary-general.

‚secretary-'general *c.n* secretary(2) of a very big and important organization, often an international one, e.g the United Nations.

secrete, secretive(ly/ness) ⇨ secret.

sect /sekt/ *c.n* group of people which is usu part of a bigger group but has certain beliefs etc that are different from other parts of the bigger group.

sectarian /sek'teərɪən/ *adj* (often *derog*) **1** of or referring to a sect (usu with the result that one disagrees with other people): *sectarian violence.* ▷ *c.n* **2** person who is sectarian(1).

sec'tarian‚ism *u.n.*

section /'sekʃən/ *c.n* **1** separate part of (s.t bigger): *This section of the audience is from Ireland. You can divide oranges easily into sections but you can't do the same with apples.* **2** (*technical*) diagram of s.t that looks as if one has cut through it and then drawn a picture of one of the resulting flat areas: *a section through a lung.* **in section** showing what one can see in a section(2). ▷ *tr.v* **3** cut or divide (s.t) into sections(1).

'sectional *adj* **1** consisting of sections(1) that one can put together and then take apart again: *a sectional bookcase.* **2** of or referring to only one section(1) or only certain sections, of the population: *sectional interests.* **3** happening between different sections(1) of the population: *sectional fights.* ⇨ faction(1).

sector /'sektə/ *c.n* area or group that is a separate part (of a bigger one): *There are more new houses in the northern sector of the city. Most businesses belong to the private sector (i.e not owned by the government) but some are still in the public sector (i.e owned by the government).*

secular /'sekjʊlə/ *adj* (usu *attrib*) **1** not part of, under, a religious body: *secular education.* **2** opposed to control or interference by religion: *a secular society.*

secure /sɪ'kjʊə/ *adj* Opposite insecure **1** (often — *against/from s.o/s.t*) safe (from s.o/s.t); not in danger (of attack by s.o/s.t or of being lost or broken into etc): *a secure military position; a secure job.* **2** (*formal*) (often — *in s.t*) confident (because of s.t); not affected by any doubts or worries: *She was secure in her knowledge that her mother was always there to help her.* ▷ *tr.v* (*formal*) **3** (often — *s.t against/from s.o/s.t*) make (s.t) secure(1) (against/from s.t); lock(5) (s.t): *Before we go out, we always secure all doors and windows.* **4** manage to get or obtain(1) (s.t): *We have secured the services of the best lawyer in town for our case.*

se'curely *adv.*

security /sɪ'kjʊərɪtɪ/ *n* (*pl -ies*) **1** *u.n* state of feeling or being secure(1,2) (in s.t): *security of mind.* **2** *c/u.n* (also *attrib*) (often — *against s.t*) thing that makes one secure(1,2) (against s.o/s.t bad): *Our new central heating is a security against a hard winter. We have put in a new security system to protect us from thieves.* **3** *u.n* thing, e.g a house, offered or given to a lender by a borrower which the lender keeps if the borrower does not pay back the loan. **4** *c.n* (*commerce*) paper showing that a person is the owner of a stock(10,11), bond(5) etc, usu one sold by a government as a way of borrowing money. (**for**) **security reasons** (because of the) need to have security(2) from spies(1), terrorists etc. **maximum/minimum security** (also *attrib*) the greatest/least amount of security(2): *a maximum security prison.*

Se'curity ‚Council *def.n* group in the United Nations with representatives of 15 countries that has the job of trying to prevent wars.

se'curity ‚forces *pl.n* police and military(1) forces whose job is to look after security(2) from terrorists etc.

se'curity ‚risk *c.n* person or thing who/that is dangerous to security(2).

sedan /sɪ'dæn/ *c.n* (mainly *US*) kind of saloon(3) (car) for four or more people.

sedate /sɪ'deɪt/ *adj* **1** calm; not or never excited: *My grandmother is that tall sedate figure sitting in the garden chair.*
▷ *tr.v* **2** give (s.o) medicine to make her/him sleepy or to prevent her/him being worried, excited etc.
se'dately *adv.* **se'dateness** *u.n.*
sedation /sɪ'deɪʃən/ *u.n* act or fact of sedating(2) s.o. **under sedation** in a state of having been sedated(2).
sedative /'sedətɪv/ *adj* **1** causing sedation.
▷ *c/u.n* **2** medicine etc that sedates(2) s.o.
sedentary /'sedəntrɪ/ *adj (formal)* **1** not moving about much; staying in the same place most of the time: *sedentary groups in the desert.* Compare nomadic. **2** not needing much movement; making one sit most of the time: *Writing books is usually a sedentary job.*
sediment /'sedɪmənt/ *n* **1** *c/u.n* solid matter in a liquid that settles on the bottom: *coffee grounds² are a sediment.* **2** *u.n* matter like sediment(1) that has been carried along by moving water or ice and left s.w.
sedimentary /ˌsedɪ'mentərɪ/ *adj* of, referring to or consisting of, sediment: *sedimentary rock.* Compare igneous.
sedimentation /ˌsedɪmen'teɪʃən/ *u.n* process(2) of becoming sediment(1).
sedition /sɪ'dɪʃən/ *u.n* words or actions that try to persuade people to rebel(2) against the government etc, especially violently.
se'ditious *adj* who/that persuades, tries to persuade, people to rebel(2) against the government etc.
se'ditiously *adv.* **se'ditiousness** *u.n.*
seduce /sɪ'djuːs/ *tr.v* **1** persuade (s.o) to have sex(3), usu when he/she is too young, afraid etc. **2** (often — *s.o* (*away*) *from s.o/s.t*; — *s.o into* (*doing*) *s.t*) persuade (s.o) (to leave s.o/s.t, do s.t) by making her/him think that this is a pleasant thing to do when it is really wrong.
se'ducer *c.n* person who seduces(*v*) s.o.
seduction /sɪ'dʌkʃən/ *n* **1** *u.n* act or fact of seducing(*v*) s.o. **2** *c.n* thing that seduces(2) s.o.
se'ductive *adj* that seduces(2) one; very attractive.
se'ductively *adv.* **se'ductiveness** *u.n.*
sedulous /'sedjʊləs/ *adj (formal)* trying very hard; diligent: *sedulous attempts to gain the love of a woman.*
'sedulously *adv.* **'sedulousness** *u.n.*
see¹ /siː/ *v* (*p.t* saw /sɔː/, *p.p* seen /siːn/) *v* **1** *intr.v* be able to receive information and impressions through one's eyes; have the sense of sight: *There's a beautiful bird in the tree — come and see. Turn the light on; I can't see in the dark.* **2** *tr.v* use one's sense of sight to get information about (s.o/s.t (doing s.t etc)) or to understand, (s.t, that etc...): *Can you see John? I saw him come in. Did you see him playing football? Did you see where your mother put my cup? I could see that it was raining outside. Did you actually see Mary take the bicycle?* **3** *tr/intr.v* understand (s.t, that etc...); have read (s.t, that etc...): *I see in the paper that England won the match last night. 'Do you see how you have to fix the wires now?' 'Yes, I see.'* **4** *tr/intr.v* try to find out (s.t); try to decide (about s.t): *Please see who that is at the door. Can you see if Helen's arrived? See what you can do to help.* **5** *intr.v* think about (s.t) and decide: *I*

haven't decided whether to go yet; I'll have to see. ⇒ wait and see (⇒ wait(*v*)). **6** *tr.v* (usu — *that*...) be certain (that ...); arrange things in such a way (that ...): *See that you are not late this time.* **7** *tr.v* (often — *oneself/s.o/s.t doing s.t*) imagine (s.t, that one is doing s.t etc); think (s.t) possible: *I can't see ourselves getting up at five to go and play tennis! I can see a big future for you if you continue to practise hard.* **8** *tr.v* be the time of (an event); be the time when (s.t happens): *The end of the discussion saw the division of the department into two offices.* **9** *tr.v* experience (s.t); enjoy (s.t pleasant); suffer (s.t unpleasant): *That old man has seen both success and failure in his long life.* **10** *tr.v* pay a visit to (s.o); accept a visit from (s.o): *I'm seeing the doctor at 2.30. You can go in now, Mr Jones; the doctor's ready to see you.* **11** *tr.v* take or guide (s.o) (s.w): *I saw the old man across the road, up the stairs. Let me see you home.* ⇒ see s.o in/out. **12** *tr.v* look at (a page etc in a book, a notice on a wall etc): *See chapter 16, page 20, the notice near the door.*
be seeing things ⇒ things.
s.o/s.t has seen better days/times (*informal*) s.o/s.t is old, worn etc. ⇒ see¹(9).
I'll be seeing you, **him** etc (*later* etc) (an informal way of saying I'm going to see you etc (later etc), used esp when one is leaving, saying goodbye).
I'll/We'll see I/We won't decide yet; I/We will wait to see¹(5) what happens first.
let me see (way of showing that one has not decided what to say yet): *You're leaving at 6 o'clock and Jane comes at 7.30 so – let me see – yes, I'll have an hour and a half to have a rest.*
See? (*informal*) Do you understand?
see about s.o/s.t. (*informal*) find out what is happening about s.o/s.t; make arrangements about s.o/s.t. **We'll see about that!** (threatening suggestion that the person who has just said s.t will not be allowed to do what he/she wants): *'I'm not going to do this work.' 'We'll see about that!'*
see the back/last of s.o/s.t (*informal*) stop having to see s.o/s.t unpleasant because he/she/it finishes or goes away etc: *Do you think we've seen the last of this bad weather?*
see eye to eye (**with s.o**) (**about s.t**) ⇒ eye(*n*).
See here! ⇒ here(*adv*).
see s.o in take s.o into a room (to meet s.o): *The doctor is ready now, so I'll see you in.* **see s.t in s.o** (*informal*) believe that s.o has s.t in her/his character, appearance etc: *I don't know what you see in him; I think he's terrible!*
see the last of s.o/s.t ⇒ see the back/last of s.o/s.t.
see a lot, very little etc **of s.o/s.t** see, meet etc s.o/s.t often, rarely etc.
see s.o/s.t off (**a**) watch while s.o/s.t leaves (and usu say goodbye): *When James left, we went to the station to see him off.* (**b**) (*informal*) force a person/animal to go away: *When strangers come to our house, our dog sees them off.*
see s.o out take or guide s.o out (of a room, house etc): *Can you wait a moment while I see my sister out?*
see over/round s.t see the whole of a house etc. e.g to decide whether to buy it.
see red ⇒ red.

see round s.t ⇨ see over/round s.t.

see something of s.o ⇨ something(*pron*).

see through s.o/s.t understand the truth about s.o/s.t so that one is not cheated by her/him/it. **see s.t through** continue with s.t until it is finished; not give up.

see to s.o/s.t do what is necessary about s.o/s.t: *I've got to go upstairs; will you see to the soup on the stove, please?* **see one's way to doing s.t** ⇨ way(*n*).

see s.t s.o's way ⇨ way.

s.o will never see 30 etc again (*informal*) s.o is certainly over 30 etc years old.

see s.t with one's own eyes actually see s.t oneself, not just hear about it from s.o else.

See you later/soon etc (*informal*) friendly way of saying goodbye and that one will meet again.

wait and see ⇨ wait(*v*).

you see (*informal*) (way of trying to persuade a person to accept what one is saying): *'Why haven't you finished your work?' 'Well, you see, Joan wanted to talk to me and I didn't want to be rude to her.'*

'seeing *conj* (also **seeing as, that, as how** (*informal*)) in view of the fact that; since(6): *Seeing* (or *Seeing as, that, as how*) *you asked, yes, I am pleased.*

'see-,through *attrib.adj* (usu of clothes) that one can see through; transparent.

see² /si:/ *c.n* area that a bishop(1) is responsible for; office of a bishop(1).

seed /si:d/ *attrib.adj* **1** that is kept to provide seed(4) for sowing: *seed corn; seed potatoes.* **2** very small because not completely grown: *seed pearls.*

▷ *n* **3** *c.n* small hard thing produced by a plant from which another plant of the same kind can grow: *flower seeds.* **4** *u.n* quantity of seeds(3) taken together: *I've sown grass seed here so I'm trying to keep the birds off.* **5** *c.n* (usu *pl*, *—s of s.t*) (*fig*) thing(s) out of which s.t is likely to grow, happen: *Letting children do what they like all the time is sowing(2) the seeds of future trouble.* **6** *c.n* (in tennis etc) person who has been seeded(11). **go/run to seed (a)** (of a plant) reach the stage of having seeds(3) (and therefore usu be too old to eat etc). **(b)** (*fig*) (of people) become old, tired etc. **in seed** (of a plant) having seeds(3) in/on it.

▷ *v* **7** *intr.v* (of a plant) form seeds(3). **8** *tr.v* (often *— s.t with s.t*) spread seeds(3) (of s.t) on, plant seeds(3) (of s.t) in, (a field etc). **9** *tr.v* take the seeds(3) out of (fruit). **10** *tr.v* (often *— s.t with s.t*) (*fig*) put s.t into (s.t) hoping that it will produce the results one wants: *If you seed this company with clever people, in a few years the business will show big improvements.* **11** *tr.v* (in tennis etc) choose (a player) as one of those who have the best chance of winning and put her/him on a list in order of likelihood of her/his doing so. **seed itself** (of a plant) produce seeds(3) and drop them in the ground so that they can grow: *Most wild flowers seed themselves.*

'seed,bed/,box/,tray *c.n* bed(2) or container in which seeds(3) are planted and from which the plants will be moved when they are bigger.

'seedily *adv* in a seedy(3) way.

'seediness *u.n* fact or state of being seedy(3).

'seedless *adj* having no seeds(3) in it: *seedless grapes.*

'seedling *c.n* very young plant that has grown from a seed(3). Compare cutting(4).

'seedy *adj* (*-ier, -iest*) **1** having (a lot of) seeds(3) in it. **2** (*informal*) not feeling very well. **3** (*derog; informal*) (of a place) not clean and tidy; (of clothes etc) old and worn; (of people) dressed in old dirty clothes.

seeing ⇨ see¹.

seek /si:k/ *v* (*p.t,p.p* sought /sɔ:t/) **1** *tr/intr.v* (*literary; formal*) try to find (s.o/s.t) by looking or searching; try to get (s.t) by asking: *They are seeking him everywhere. The scientists are seeking an answer to the problem.* **2** *tr.v* be attracted to (s.t) by a natural force (usu gravity², magnetism(1)): *Water seeks its own level so it is always flat on top when it is at rest. A magnet seeks the north.* **not far to seek** not difficult to understand or find. **seek after s.o/s.t** (*formal*) try to find s.o/s.t: *seeking after a cure for cancer*(1). **seek one's fortune** ⇨ fortune. **seek s.o/s.t out** try to find s.o/s.t who/that has disappeared or cannot easily be found. **seek to do s.t** (*formal*) try to do s.t.

'seeker *c.n* (often *— after s.t*) (*formal*) person who seeks(1) s.t: *a seeker after truth.*

'sought ,after *adj* (**'sought-,after** when *attrib*) (often *much —*) wanted (by a lot of people).

seem /si:m/ *intr.v* (often *— to be s.t; — like s.t*) give the appearance of (being) s.t; appear (to be s.t); look, sound etc (as if one is s.t). **it seems as if/though . . . ; it seems that . . .** what one can see, hear etc suggests that . . . : *It seems as if Bob won't be coming to the party.* **it seems not** (way of answering in the negative(6) while suggesting that one is not sure): *'Does John like this place?' 'It seems not; he's leaving tomorrow.'* **it seems so; so it seems** (way of agreeing, answering in the affirmative(2) while at the same time showing some doubt): *'A storm is coming.' 'Yes, it seems so; I can see the clouds.' 'Helen likes this place.' 'So it seems; she comes here whenever she can.'*

'seeming *attrib.adj* who/that seems to be (s.t) though there is some doubt about it: *with seeming pleasure.*

'seemingly *adv.*

seemly /'si:mlɪ/ *adj* (*-ier, -iest*) (*formal*) suitable for the place, time etc; decent(2): *seemly dress for a funeral.* Opposite unseemly.

'seemliness *u.n.*

seen /si:n/ *p.p* of see¹.

seep /si:p/ *intr.v* (usu *— in*(to s.t); *— out* (of s.t); *— through* (s.t)) (of a liquid) move very slowly and gradually (in(to s.t) etc).

seesaw /'si:,sɔ:/ *n* **1** *c.n* long flat piece of wood etc that is balanced in the middle and on which children play by sitting at each end and going up and down in turn. **2** *u.n* game of going up and down in this way on a seesaw(1). **3** *c.n* (*fig*) fact of winning and losing in turn in a match, fight etc.

▷ *intr.v* **4** play on a seesaw(1). **5** (*fig*) (of prices, success and failure in a match, battle etc) go up and down, be winning and losing etc, one after the other.

seethe /si:ð/ *intr.v* **1** (often *— with s.t*) (of a person, feeling etc) be very angry or excited (because of s.t): *My father seethed with anger* when he saw his damaged car. **2** (*literary*) (of the sea, waves) move about violently: *waves seething against the cliffs.*

'**seething** *adj* (often — *with s.o/s.t*) having many people, insects etc: *a seething crowd of ants; shops that are seething with people.*

see-through ⇨ see¹.

segment /'segmənt/ *c.n* **1** (often — *of s.t*) part (of s.t) that can be divided off easily; section(1) (of s.t): *segments of an orange. You can divide an orange into segments but not an apple.* **2** (*technical*) part of a line that is between two points on it.
▷ *v* /seg'ment/ (*formal*) **3** *tr.v* (often — *s.t into s.t*) divide (s.t) into segments. **4** *intr.v* (usu — *into s.t*) be able to divide into segments.
segmentation /,segmən'teıʃən/ *c/u.n*.

segregate /'segrı,geıt/ *tr/intr.v* (often — (s.o/ s.t) *into s.t, from s.o/s.t*) (cause (s.o/s.t) to) be divided and kept apart (from s.o/s.t) (in a separate group or separate groups): *The slower learners have been segregated from the others so that they can have special education.*

'**segre,gated** *adj* **1** who/that is kept separated. **2** that provides different things for different segregated(1) groups: *segregated classes in schools.* **3** that provides s.t for one segregated(2) group: *a segregated class for slow learners.*

,**segre'gation** *sing/u.n* fact or act of segregating: racial(1) *segregation.*

seismic /'saızmık/ *adj* (*technical*) of or referring to earthquakes and other movements of the earth.

seismograph /'saızmə,grɑːf/ *c.n* (*technical*) kind of instrument for measuring and recording earthquakes and other such movements.

seismologist /saız'mɒlədʒıst/ *c.n* person who works on seismology.

seis'mology *u.n* (*technical*) science of earthquakes and other such movements of the earth.

seize /siːz/ *v* **1** *tr.v* catch (s.o/s.t) usu quickly and strongly: *He seized the boy as he tried to run away.* **2** *tr.v* take (s.o/s.t) usu by force and often as part of an operation against criminals: *The enemy have seized one of our ships. The police seized five million pounds' worth of drugs(2).*
seize hold of s.o/s.t = seize(1). **seize up** (of (part of) a machine, one's body) stop working and become fixed in one position because of lack of oil, being tired etc. **seize (up)on s.t** accept s.t with great eagerness: *Mary seizes upon every opportunity to practise her French.*

seizure /'siːʒə/ *n* (*formal*) **1** *u.n* (often — *of s.o/s.t*) act of seizing (s.o/s.t) or the fact of being seized. **2** *c.n* sudden attack of a disease or illness: *have a heart seizure.*

seldom /'seldəm/ *adv* rarely: *We seldom go to parties. Seldom have I seen a better table.* Opposite often. ⇨ scarcely. **seldom if ever** very rarely: *We seldom if ever go by train.*

select /sı'lekt/ *attrib.adj* **1** that has been chosen out of a bigger number, usu because it is better than the rest: *select fruit.* **2** that is for people who are rich (and upper class): *a select school.* ⇨ exclusive(1).
▷ *tr.v* **3** (often — *s.o/s.t from s.o/s.t*) choose (s.o/s.t) (from a number), usu because he/she/it is the one that one needs, likes best etc.
se,lect com'mittee *c.n* committee of Members

of Parliament chosen to discuss and make a report on a certain subject.

selection /sı'lekʃən/ *n* **1** *u.n* (often — *of s.o/ s.t* (*for s.t*)) act of selecting(3) (s.o/s.t (for s.t)). **2** *c.n* person(s)/animal(s)/thing(s) who/ that has/have been selected(3): *Which horse is your selection for the first race?* **3** *c.n* (often — *of s.t*) number (of different things) so that one has a good choice among them. **natural selection** ⇨ natural.

se'lective *adj* **1** affecting only certain people or things, not all of them: *a selective pay increase for the lower paid workers only.* Opposite general(2). **2** (usu *pred*) (of a person) who chooses carefully instead of just taking anyone or anything: *be selective about what one eats.*

se'lectively *adv*. **se'lectiveness** *u.n*. ,**selec'tivity** *u.n*.

se'lector *c.n* person who selects(3) s.o/s.t, esp people to play in a team.

self /self/ *n* (*pl* selves /selvz/) **1** *c/u/def.n* a person's own particular nature that makes her/ him different from other people and that she/he can examine by looking into her/his own mind: *Everyone has a self that he or she can learn to know; such knowledge of self can help one to avoid mistakes but the self can probably never be fully understood.* **2** *c.n* one part or form of one's self(1): *Do you know your true self? My better self tells me to do one thing but my weaker self often wins. Don't worry, you won't feel like this for long; you'll soon be your old self again* (i.e you will again feel as you did before). **3** *u.n* one's own selfish interests or pleasure: *That man thinks of nothing but self.*

-self /self/ *pron* (*pl* -selves /selvz/) ⇨ herself, himself, itself, myself, oneself, yourself; ourselves, themselves, yourselves.

self- **1** (the object of the second part of the word): *self-defeating* (= that defeats oneself/ itself); self-defence. **2** by, through the agency of, oneself: self-imposed exile(2). **3** to oneself: *a self-addressed envelope.* **4** in oneself: self-absorbed. **5** of oneself: self-assertion. **6** about oneself: self-assured. **7** on oneself: self-reliance.

,**self-ab'sorbed** *adj* too concerned about oneself. ⇨ self(4).

,**self-ab'sorption** *u.n*.

,**self-a'buse** /self-ə'bjuːs/ *u.n* = masturbation.

,**self-'acting** *adj* who/that does not need to be controlled but acts alone or automatically: *a self-acting switch.*

,**self-ad,dressed 'enve,lope** *c.n* (*abbr* s.a.e) one that has been addressed to oneself.

,**self-ap'pointed** *adj* who has not been properly chosen by others but has given herself/himself the job without being asked or wanted.

,**self-as'sertion** *u.n* the act or fact of being self-assertive.

,**self-as'sertive** *adj* showing one's confidence by stating one's opinions, desires, needs etc. ⇨ assert oneself, assertive.

,**self-as'sertiveness** *u.n*.

,**self-as'surance** *u.n* confidence in oneself.

,**self-as'sured** *adj* = confident about oneself.

,**self-as'suredness** *u.n*.

,**self-'centred** *adj* (*derog*) selfish; thinking only of oneself.

,**self-'centredness** *u.n*.

,self-co'mmand *u.n* = self-control.

,self-con'fessed *attrib.adj* who has herself/himself confessed to s.t: *a self-confessed thief.*

,self-'confidence *u.n.*

,self-'confident *adj* having confidence in one's own ability, opinions, power, etc.

,self-'conscious *adj* shy; nervous about what other people are thinking of one.

,self-'consciously *adv.* **,self'consciousness** *u.n.*

,self-con'tained *adj* **1** (of a flat(13) etc) having all its parts, e.g bathroom, toilet etc, inside so that one does not have to share with others. **2** (of a person, her/his character) independent; not needing other people; not showing much feeling.

,self-,contra'dictory *adj* having in it things that are the opposites of each other so that they cannot both be true.

,self-con'trol *u.n* ability, power to control one's actions, anger, feelings etc. ⇨ control(2).

,self-con'trolled *adj* having self-control.

,self-de'fence *u.n* act or fact of defending oneself, one's ideas, opinions, etc. ⇨ defend(1).

,self-de'nial *u.n* (*formal*) fact or habit of not letting oneself have things that one wants to have.

,self-de'nying *adj* (*formal*) showing self-denial.

,self-de,termi'nation *u.n* (of (part of) a country) act or right of choosing one's own form of government.

,self-'discipline *u.n* control of one's actions, thoughts etc by oneself, not because one is doing what s.o else tells one. Compare self-indulgence.

,self-'disciplined *adj* having self-discipline. Compare self-indulgent.

,self-'drive *attrib.adj* (of a hire car etc) that one drives oneself instead of having s.o else to drive it.

,self-'edu,cated *adj* educated or taught by oneself and not at school etc. Compare self-taught.

,self-ef'facing *adj* (*formal*) modest; trying not to be noticed by other people.

,self-em'ployed *adj* **1** working in one's own business, not for s.o else.
▷ *def.pl.n* **2** people who have their own business and work for themselves, not for s.o else.

,self-e'steem *u.n* belief that one is a good, useful etc person.

,self-'evident *adj* so easy to see or understand that it is not necessary to mention it; obvious.

,self-e,xami'nation *u.n* questioning oneself, often to decide whether one is behaving well or badly etc.

,self-ex'planatory *adj* that does not need any further explanations as they are already in what has been said.

,self-'governing *adj* (of (part of) a country etc) that governs itself instead of being governed by anyone else. Compare autonomous.

,self-'government *u.n* act or fact of governing oneself. ⇨ self-governing, self-rule, autonomy.

,self-'help *u.n* doing things for oneself instead of having them done for one by other people.

,self-im'portance *u.n* feeling that one is more important than one really is. ⇨ pomposity.

,self-im'portant *adj* (*derog*) showing self-importance. ⇨ pompous.

,self-im'portantly *adv.*

,self-im'posed *adj* forced on one by oneself: *a self-imposed punishment.* ⇨ impose(2).

,self-in'dulgence *u.n* allowing oneself to have and do what one wants, even if it is a bad thing. Compare self-discipline. ⇨ indulge(1).

,self-in'dulgent *adj* (*derog*) showing self-indulgence. Compare self-disciplined.

,self-in'dulgently *adv.*

,self-'interest *u.n* selfishness; being selfish.

,self-'interested *adj* (*derog*) selfish.

'selfish *adj* (*derog*) interested only in what is useful or interesting for oneself and not in what is useful or interesting for others. Opposite unselfish.

'selfishly *adv.* **'selfishness** *u.n.*

'selfless *adj* interested only in what is useful or good for other people and not at all in what is useful or good for oneself.

'selflessly *adv.* **'selflessness** *u.n.*

,self-'made *adj* (usu *attrib*) who has become rich by her/his own efforts alone.

,self-'moti,vated *adj* having in oneself purpose, motivation, etc to do s.t and not needing others to force, encourage one.

,self-,moti'vation *u.n.*

,self-o'pinio,nated *adj* (usu *derog*) having and/or expressing very strong opinions, often ones that other people do not agree with (because they are wrong).

,self-'pity *u.n* feeling and/or complaining that one is unhappy, unlucky etc, often so much that it annoys other people.

,self-pos'sessed *adj* very calm and in control of oneself. Compare composed.

,self-pos'session *u.n* fact or state of being self-possessed. Compare composure.

,self-,preser'vation *u.n* natural wish to keep oneself from being hurt or killed.

,self-,raising 'flour *u.n* flour that has baking powder in it.

,self-re'liance *u.n* fact of trusting one's own ability etc. ⇨ rely.

,self-re'liant *adj* showing, feeling self-reliance.

,self-re'spect *u.n* reasonable pride in what one is and does. ⇨ respect¹(1).

,self-re'specting *adj* feeling self-respect.

,self-'righteous *adj* (*derog*) too interested in showing that one is good or right so that it annoys other people.

,self-'righteously *adv.* **,self-'righteousness** *u.n.*

,self-'rule *u.n* = self-government.

,self-'sacri,fice *u.n* fact of sacrificing one's own interests and/or pleasures for the good of other people or for s.t that one thinks is more important.

,self-'sacri,ficing *adj* showing self-sacrifice.

'self,same *attrib.adj* (*informal*) exactly the same.

,self-,satis'faction *u.n* (*derog*) state of feeling satisfied about s.t one has done etc.

,self-'satis,fied *adj* (*derog*) showing or feeling self-satisfaction.

,self-'service *u.n* (also *attrib*) arrangement by which people collect their own goods in a shop, food in a restaurant etc, instead of being served by staff: *a self-service restaurant.*

,self-'starter *c.n* (*technical*) (switch for an)

electrical device for starting an engine in a vehicle.

ˌself-ˈstyled *attrib.adj* (often *derog*) using a description chosen by oneself, often without it being a true, correct one: *a self-styled poet/expert*(2) *on roses.*

ˌself-sufˈficiency *u.n* state or fact of being self-sufficient.

ˌself-sufˈficient *adj* **1** (often — *in s.t*) having or producing everything one needs (of s.t) so that one does not need to buy etc anything from outside: *Nepal is trying to become self-sufficient in food.* **2** (of a person) thinking (often wrongly) that he/she does not need help from anyone else.

ˌself-supˈporting *adj* not needing money from anyone else because one has/earns enough oneself.

ˌself-ˈtaught *adj* who has learnt s.t herself/himself and not by having had a teacher. Compare self-educated.

ˌself-ˈwill *u.n* (*derog*) fact of wanting very much to do only what one wants to do oneself.

ˌself-ˈwilled *adj* (*derog*) showing self-will: *a self-willed child.*

ˌself-ˈwinding *adj* (of a watch) that winds itself as a result of the movements of the person wearing it.

sell /sel/ *sing.n* **1** thing that is not as good as s.o/s.t suggests: *'I ordered some plants by post, but when they arrived they were all dead.' – 'What a sell!'* **hard sell** way of selling things by using a lot of clever pressure on buyers. **soft sell** way of selling things by seeming not to be putting pressure on the buyers so that they are not frightened away.

▷ *v* (*p.t,p.p* sold /səʊld/) **2** *tr.v* (often — *s.o s.t*, —*s.t to s.o*) (try to) give (s.t) in return, exchange s.t, for a money payment (to s.o) etc: *Do you sell beer here? Have you sold your furniture yet? I sold my boat to Helen. Mary is selling us one of her pictures.* **3** *tr.v* help to persuade people to buy (s.t): *They say that a clever title or an attractive picture on the cover sells more books than the stories inside it.* **4** *intr.v* (often — *at/for s.t*) (can) be bought: *This cheese sells for £1.54 a kilo in the market. These blouses are not selling* (are not being bought). **5** *tr.v* (*fig*) (often — *s.t to s.o; — s.o s.t*) persuade s.o to do, accept etc (s.t): *I had a lot of trouble selling my partners the idea of starting a new factory.*

be sold on s.t (*informal*) be convinced about the value, importance etc of s.t: *My mother is quite sold on her new stove; she thinks it's the best she's ever seen.*

s.o has been sold (*informal*) s.o has been cheated.

sell badly, well etc be bought by few, a lot of etc people: *Our fruit is selling well in the market this year.*

sell s.o down the river ⇨ river.

sell s.t for s.t sell(2) s.t for a certain amount of money. ⇨ sell(4).

sell like hot cakes ⇨ cake(*n*).

sell s.t off get rid of s.t by selling it, often cheaply.

sell oneself (a) persuade people to like one, do what one wants etc. (b) do things that one thinks wrong, dishonest etc in return for money, love etc.

sell (s.o/s.t) out (*fig*) not be faithful (to s.o/s.t);

betray(1) s.o/s.t ⇨ sell-out(2). **sell (s.t) out** (**to s.o**) (a) sell the whole of s.t (to s.o): *When I tried to get a ticket for the match I found that they were all sold out.* ⇨ sell-out(1). (b) sell what one owns of s.t (to s.o): *When I retired from the business I sold out to my partners.*

sell (s.o/s.t) short ⇨ short(*adv*).

sell one's soul (to the devil) (for s.t) ⇨ soul.

sell s.o up make s.o sell everything he/she has in order to pay what he/she owes one. **sell (s.t) up** sell the whole of s.t.

ˈseller *c.n* person who sells(2) s.t.

ˌsellers' ˈmarket *c.n* situation in which it is easy to sell things because there are more people wanting to buy than to sell. Opposite buyers' market.

ˈselling ˌpoint *c.n* good thing about s.t that helps a seller to sell it: *This car's main selling point is that it only needs to be serviced once a year.*

ˈsell-ˌout *c.n* (*informal*) **1** match, performance etc for which all the tickets have been sold. ⇨ sell (s.t) out. **2** act of selling (s.o/s.t) out; betrayal.

sellotape /ˈseləˌteɪp/ *u.n* (*t.n*) **1** (roll of) thin sticky transparent ´tape, used for sticking paper etc together.

▷ *tr.v* **2** stick (s.t) with sellotape(1).

selves, -selves ⇨ self.

semantic /sɪˈmæntɪk/ *adj* (*technical*) of or referring to the meaning of writing, words etc: *a semantic study of a poem.*

seˈmantically *adv.*

seˈmantics *u.n* science of the meanings of words.

semaphore /ˈseməˌfɔː/ *u.n* (also *attrib*) system of sending messages by holding two flags in one's hands and putting them in various positions to show different letters and numbers.

semblance /ˈsembləns/ *c.n* (often a/some — of s.t) (*formal*) appearance (of s.t); thing that makes one think that s.t is s.t: *I hope there will be a semblance of discipline in the team by the time we play in the competition.*

semen /ˈsiːmen/ *u.n* thick white liquid produced from the penis during sex and carrying sperm(1).

semester /sɪˈmestə/ *c.n* one of the two halves of the year into which some universities, esp US ones, divide their activities. Compare term(2).

semi /semɪ/ *c.n* (UK *informal*) **1** semi-detached (house). **2** semifinal: *reach the semis in the tournament.*

semi /ˌsemɪ-/ **1** exactly half of the thing that is shown in the second half of the word: *a semicircle.* **2** happening twice as frequently as shown by the second part of the word: *a semi-annual event; semi-annually.* **3** having some of the quality etc of what is shown in the rest of the word: *semi-skilled; a semi-official report; semi-smile.*

ˈsemiˌbreve *c.n* (*music*) note in music that is twice the length of a minim, *symb* ○.

ˈsemiˌcircle *c.n* half a circle. **in a semicircle** in such a way as to form a semicircle.

ˌsemiˈcircular *adj* having/in the shape of a semicircle.

ˌsemiˈcolon *c.n* punctuation mark ; used in writing English etc to show a pause(1) that is longer than one shown by a comma but shorter than one shown by a full stop.

,semicon'ductor *c.n* (*technical*) substance through which electricity can pass more easily when it is hot than when it is cold.

,semi-de'tached *adj* **1** (of a house) joined to another house on one side only.
▷ *c.n* **2** (*informal* semi) semi-detached(1) house.

,semi'final *c.n* (also *attrib*) (*informal* semi) match to decide the players, team etc who/which go(es) into the final(3).

,semi'finalist *c.n* player, team etc who/that is in a semifinal.

,semi-'liquid *adj* very thick and not able to run(25), be poured etc easily.

,semi-'precious *adj* (of a jewel, stone etc) quite high in value but not as high as a gem(1).

'semi,quaver *c.n* (*music*) note in music that is an eighth as long as a minim, *symb* ♪.

,semi-'solid *adj* almost firm¹(1) or rigid(1).

'semi,tone *c.n* (*music*) half interval of tone(4) in a musical scale; smallest difference between notes in ordinary European music.

seminar /'semɪˌnɑː/ *c.n* **1** small group of students who meet to study a particular subject with a teacher. **2** class/talk attended by a seminar(1).

seminary /'semɪnərɪ/ *c.n* (*pl -ies*) college where priests, usu Roman Catholic(1) ones, are trained.

semi-precious, semiquaver, semitone ⇒ semi-.

semolina /ˌseməˈliːnə/ *u.n* (also *attrib*) wheat that has been crushed into very small pieces, used in making both sweet and not sweet kinds of food: *semolina* pudding(1).

senate /'senɪt/ *c/def.n* (often with capital **S**) **1** body of people who are the higher of two parts of a parliament etc in some countries: *Britain has a House of Lords and a House of Commons and the United States has a Senate and a House of Representatives*. **2** group of people in some British universities who govern the university.

'senator *c.n* (with capital **S** in names) member of a senate(1).

senatorial /ˌsenəˈtɔːrɪəl/ *adj* of or referring to a senate or a senator: *senatorial duties*.

send /send/ *v* (*p.t,p.p* sent/sent/) **1** *tr.v* (often — s.o s.t, —s.t to s.o) cause (s.o/s.t) to go, be taken, (away etc (to s.o or to get s.t)): *Joan sends you her love. She couldn't take the letter herself so she sent her son with it. She sent her secretary to meet me. I arrived without my books and so I was sent home to get them.* **2** *tr.v* (usu — s.o/s.t -ing (s.w)) cause (s.o/s.t) to move (s.w): *The crash sent the child (flying) through the car window.* **3** *tr.v* (*fig*) cause (s.t) to move in the way shown, esp strongly: *The bad weather sent the price of vegetables up.* **4** *tr.v* transmit(1) (a message): *send a telegram.* **5** *tr.v* cause (s.o) to be in a certain state: *That loud music will send me mad!* **6** *tr.v* (*slang*) cause (s.o) to feel very excited and happy: *Soul music really sends some people!*

send away (for s.t) write etc to s.o, a business company etc (asking for information, application forms, a catalogue(1) etc).

send s.o down (a) send(1) s.o downstairs. (b) (of a university) not allow a student to continue studying at a university because he/she has done s.t wrong. (c) (*informal*) send s.o to prison.

send for s.o/s.t send(1) a message that s.o/ s.t must come, be brought, to one. **send**

s.o for s.o/s.t send(1) s.o to bring s.o/s.t to one.

send s.t forth (*literary*) produce s.t: *The chimney sent forth black smoke.* **send s.o/s.t forth (to do s.t)** (*literary*) = send(1) s.o (to do s.t).

send (s.t) in (for s.t) apply (to get s.t) by sending a letter etc.

send s.o into s.t cause s.o to have or experience s.t: *The funny man sent the children into* fits²(1) *of laughter.* ⇒ send(5).

send s.o off (in football etc) make one of the players leave the field because he/she has done s.t bad.

send (s.o) out (for s.t) = send(1) (s.o) for s.t.

send s.t out (a) = distribute(2) s.t from a centre: *We are sending out invitations to the party.* **(b)** produce (smoke etc); cause s.t to come out: *The hoover is sending out a lot of dust.*

send s.o packing send s.o away because one does not want to be with her/him any more.

send s.o/s.t up (*informal*) make fun of s.o/s.t, usu by copying her/him/it. ⇒ send-up. **send s.t up** cause s.t, e.g smoke from a fire, prices in a market, to go up.

send word (about/of s.o/s.t) (to s.o); **send word (to s.o) to do s.t** ⇒ word(*n*).

'sender *c.n* person/device, e.g a radio transmitter, who/that sends a letter, message etc.

'send-,off *c.n* (*informal*) (example of) saying goodbye to s.o/s.t who/that is leaving, giving good wishes to s.o/s.t who/that is beginning s.t new: *A large group of people joined in giving her, the business, a send-off.*

'send-,up *c.n* making fun of s.o/s.t. ⇒ send s.o/ s.t up.

senile /'siːnaɪl/ *adj* so old that her/his mind (and/or sometimes body) is not working properly any more.

senility /sɪˈnɪlɪtɪ/ *u.n*.

senior /'siːnɪə/ *adj* Opposite junior. (with capital **S** in names or titles) **1** (often — to s.o) higher in rank (than s.o): *He is Senior Manager.* **2** (often — to s.o) older (than s.o). **3** (often — to s.o) who has been in s.t, e.g a company, longer (than s.o): *Peter is senior to me.* **4** (*written abbr* Snr, Sr) (placed after the name) title of the father etc of s.o with the same name: *Peter Robinson Senior.* Compare elder¹(3).
▷ *c.n* **5** (often s.o's — (by . . . years)) person who is (ten etc years) senior(1–3) (to s.o): *He's my senior by four years.*

,senior 'citizen *c.n* person who is old enough to retire(1); pensioner: *In Britain, a man over 65 or a woman over 60 years old is a senior citizen.*

seniority /ˌsiːnɪˈɒrɪtɪ/ *u.n* (often — over s.o) fact or state of being senior(1–3) (to s.o), usu with the advantages this gives one.

sense /sens/ *n* **1** *c.n* one of the five ways in which we learn about the things that are around us in the world: *Our five senses are sight, hearing, taste, smell and touch.* **2** *u.n* meaning (of a word, phrase etc): *'Go' means 'move away from me' but it has many other senses too. In what sense are you using this word?* **3** *u.n* ability to understand (and follow) (s.t): *a sense of honour; business sense. I've got a terrible sense of direction. Haven't you got enough sense to see that Michael's trying to cheat you?* **4** *sing.n* (often *a* — of s.t, that . . .) feeling (of s.t, that . . .), usu one that is not at all

clear: *As I entered the room, I had a sudden sense
of danger.* **a** (**good, poor** etc) **sense of direction**
⇒ direction. **commonsense** ⇒ common. (**have
a**) **sense of occasion** (have an) awareness of
the importance of an occasion and show it by
dressing, behaving etc correctly. **in a sense** in
one way; in one of its meanings: *In a sense, it is
wrong to hate rain in summer because without it
the plants would die.* **in its broadest** etc **sense**
looking at it from every etc angle. **in the true(st)
sense** (**of the word**) ⇒ true. **knock** (**some**)
sense into s.o to s.o to understand the need
to believe, decide etc in a sensible(1) way. **make**
(**good** etc) **sense** be (very) reasonable. **make
sense** (**out**) **of s.t** manage to understand the
sense(2) of s.t. **sixth sense** ⇒ sixth. **talk sense**
(*informal*) say things that are reasonable. **there's
no sense in s.t** (*informal*) it is not reasonable to
say, do etc s.t: *There's no sense in lying because
everyone knows the truth.* **What's the sense of**
(**doing**) **s.t?** What good reason can there be in
(doing) s.t?

▷ *tr.v* **5** have a sense(4) of (s.t, that etc ...): *Although
no one said so, I sensed that people at the party
were very glad to see us.* **6** (of a machine etc) notice
(and record) (s.t): *When this device senses smoke
in the room, it makes a terrible noise.*

sensation /sen'seɪʃən/ *n* **1** *c/u.n* feeling (of s.t,
that . . .): *After being out in the cold for so long,
she had no sensation in her feet. When I am just
going to sleep I often have a sensation of falling.*
2 *c.n* person or thing who/that causes great
excitement and interest: *She was a sensation
when she first sang in London.* **3** *c.n* (often
cause a- —) strong feelings of excitement and
interest.

sen'sational *adj* **1** causing, intended to be/cause,
a sensation(2,3). **2** (*informal*) wonderful: *John's
getting married at last? That's sensational!*

sen'sationa,lism *u.n* (*derog*) wish to produce a
sensation(3), e.g in a newspaper by writing about
s.t in a very exaggerated way.

sen'sationalist *c.n* (*derog*) person who produces sensationalism.

sen'sationally *adv.*

,**sense of pro'portion** ⇒ proportion(*n*).

'**sense ,organ** *c.n* part of one's body through
which one of our senses(1) tells us what is
happening in the world around us: *The nose is
a sense organ.*

'**senseless** *adj* **1** (*derog*) stupid, silly.
2 unconscious(1).

'**senselessly** *adv.* '**senselessness** *u.n.*

'**senses** *pl.n* **bring s.o to her/his senses** make
s.o think properly after he/she has taken leave
of her/his senses. **come to one's senses** (**again**)
(**a**) become conscious (again). (**b**) become reasonable (again) after having taken leave of one's
senses. **take leave of one's senses** (usu as a
question) go mad: *You can't go alone; have you
taken leave of your senses?*

sensibility /,sensɪ'bɪlɪtɪ/ *n* (*pl -ies*) **1** *c/u.n*
(often *pl*) specially sensitive(1) ability to feel
and understand the right way to do s.t. **2** *u.n*
(often *— to s.t*) fact of being sensitive(1, 2) (to
s.t): *People's sensibility to pain varies greatly. Her
sensibility to the sufferings of the poor led her to
train as a nurse.*

sensible /'sensɪbl/ *adj* **1** reasonable; behaving

etc in a useful or helpful way. **2** styled to be
comfortable, practical: *sensible shoes.* **3** (*formal*)
(often *— to s.t*) = sensitive(1) (to s.t). **sensible of
s.t** (*formal*) knowing about s.t; knowing that s.t
exists: *We are very sensible of the need for caution
over this matter.* Opposite insensible(2).

'**sensibly** *adv.*

sensitive /'sensɪtɪv/ *adj* **1** (often *— to s.t*) showing (sometimes too much) feeling (caused by s.t):
*sensitive plants. Her eyes are very sensitive to
bright lights. Oh, stop being so sensitive; nobody's
trying to be rude to you!* Opposite insensitive. **2** (of
a measuring device etc) able to show very small
differences: *a sensitive instrument.* **3** (of an actor
etc) able to show very small differences in feeling,
meaning etc. **4** (of reports, a person's work etc)
secret; that should not be seen by the wrong
people.

'**sensitively** *adv.* '**sensitiveness** *u.n.*

,**sensi'tivity** *u.n.*

,**sensory** *adj* of, referring to, using, the senses
(⇒ sense(1)).

,**sensory per'ception** *u.n* ability to collect
information, result of doing this, by sensory
means.

sensual /'sensjʊəl/ *adj* **1** of or referring to the
pleasures one feels through one's senses (⇒
sense(1)), esp sexual pleasures. **2** seen, felt etc
through these senses: *sensual pain* (compared
with pain caused by one's thoughts).

'**sensualist** *c.n* (*derog*) person who is very or
too interested in sensual(1) pleasures.

sensuality /,sensjʊ'ælɪtɪ/ *u.n* fact or state of
being sensual(1).

'**sensually** *adv.*

'**sensuous** *adj* (*formal*) of or referring to one's
feelings, esp those of pleasure from one's senses
(⇒ sense(1)): *the sensuous enjoyment of the
sun.*

'**sensuously** *adv.* '**sensuousness** *u.n.*

sent /sent/ *p.t,p.p* of send.

sentence /'sentəns/ *c.n* **1** group of words that
begins with a capital letter and ends with **.** or **!**
or **?**, e.g *It is raining. Run! Will you help me if
I need you?* **2** punishment for a crime ordered
by a judge in a court of law; the judge's order for
such a punishment. **await sentence** wait until the
judge decides and states one's sentence(2). **death
sentence** ⇒ death. **give/pass/pronounce sentence** (**on s.o**) say what s.o's sentence(2) is to be.
life sentence ⇒ life(4). **heavy, light** etc **sentence**
(**for s.t**) severe, merciful etc sentence(2) (for a
crime). **under sentence of death** having been
given the death sentence but not yet having been
killed.

▷ *tr.v* **3** (usu *— s.o to s.t*) give (s.o) a sentence(2)
(of s.t): *She was sentenced to death, five years'*
imprisonment.

sentiment /'sentɪmənt/ *n* **1** *c/u.n* (often *pl*)
opinion, thing that one thinks/says/writes,
which is usu based on one's feelings rather
than on reason: *The general sentiment after
the strike was that the government could have
prevented it.* **2** *u.n* kind emotion(1) (of gentle
love, pity, nostalgia etc). **3** *c.n* words showing
a wish/feeling for s.o etc, often on a Christmas
or birthday card etc.

sentimental /,sentɪ'mentl/ *adj* (often *derog*)
feeling or showing (too much) sentiment(2):

Peter's a sentimental old fool; he only talks about his happy times as a child.

ˌsentiˈmentaˌlism *u.n* fact of being sentimental.

ˌsentiˈmentalist *c.n* (often *derog*) person who is sentimental.

sentimentality /ˌsentɪmenˈtælɪtɪ/ *u.n* = sentimentalism.

ˌsentiˈmentaˌlize, -ise *v* (*derog*) **1** *intr.v* (often — *about/over s.o/s.t*) behave, talk etc in a sentimental way (about s.o/s.t). **2** *tr.v* think etc of (s.o/ s.t bad or serious) in a sentimental way: *I dislike films that sentimentalize crime.*

ˌsentiˈmentally *adv.*

sentinel /ˈsentɪnl/ *c.n* (*old use*) sentry; guard.

sentry /ˈsentrɪ/ *c.n* (*pl -ies*) soldier guarding a place.

ˈsentry ˌbox *c.n* small place in which a sentry stands while he is on duty.

sepal /ˈsepl/ *c.n* (*technical*) one of the green parts under a flower that look like small leaves.

separate /ˈseprɪt/ *adj* **1** different; not the same: *I cut the cake into five separate pieces. This coat is sold in four separate sizes.* **2** (often — *from s.o/s.t*) not together (with s.o/s.t); divided (from s.o/s.t): *We keep the cleaning things separate from the food in our shop.* **go one's separate ways** each go a different way: *After school we went our separate ways – some of us into jobs and some into college or university.*

▷ *v*/ˈsepəˌreɪt/ **3** *tr/intr.v* (often — (s.o/s.t) (*out*) *from s.o/s.t*) (cause (s.o/s.t) to) divide (from s.o/s.t), no longer be joined (to s.o/s.t): *If you try to mix oil and water, they will soon separate. We separated the bad apples from the rest.* **4** *tr/intr.v* split (s.t) (into its different parts): *The weight on the rope was too great, and it separated, letting the load fall to the street below. You can separate the grains of cooked rice by pouring boiling water over it.* **5** *tr.v* (usu — *s.o/s.t from s.o/s.t*) be s.t that divides (two or more people/things): *A wide road separates us from the rest of the village.* **6** *tr/intr.v* (*law*) (cause (a husband and wife) to) (agree formally to) stop living together, without actually divorcing(3).

separability /ˌseprəˈbɪlɪtɪ/ *u.n* (*formal*) ability to separate, be separated(3,4).

separable /ˈseprəbl/ *adj* who/that can be separated(3,4) or treated separately. Compare **inseparable**.

ˈseparably *adv.* **ˈseparately** *adv.* **ˈseparateness** *u.n.*

separation /ˌsepəˈreɪʃən/ *n* **1** *c/u.n* (often — (*of s.t*) (*into s.t*)) dividing (of s.t) (into different parts). **2** *c.n* thing or distance that separates (s.o/s.t and s.o/s.t): *This wall acts as a separation between the two gardens.* **3** *c/u.n* (usu — *from s.o/s.t*) act of splitting away (from s.o/s.t) or fact of being split in this way: *The child suffers from anxiety because of his separation from his parents when he was small.* **4** *c/u.n* (*law*) formal agreement by a husband and wife not to live together any more, without actually divorcing(3).

ˈsepaˌratism *u.n* **1** wish to become separate(2) from the rest of one's country, church etc; belief that one should do this. **2** wish to keep different groups separate(2) from each other; belief that they should be separate(2).

ˈseparatist *c.n* person who believes in separatism.

ˈsepaˌrator *c.n* device that separates(3–5) (s.t).

sepia /ˈsiːpɪə/ *u.n* (also *attrib*) brown colour used esp for painting and drawing: *painting in sepia*; *a sepia drawing.*

September /sepˈtembə/ *c/unique n* (also *attrib*) (*written abbr* Sept) 9th month of the year: *There are thirty days in September. School begins on September 5* (say 'September the fifth' or 'the fifth of September'). *It was a warm September evening.*

septic /ˈseptɪk/ *adj* (*medical*) that has been poisoned by bacteria. Compare **antiseptic**.

ˌseptic ˈtank *c.n* container in which sewage is made pure by using bacteria.

sepulchre /ˈsepəlkə/ *c.n* (*old use*) place in which s.o is buried; tomb.

sequel /ˈsiːkwəl/ *c.n* **1** (usu — *to s.t*) thing that follows and is the result (of s.t): *The sequel (to their argument) was a fight in which both were hurt.* **2** second part/episode (of a film, television etc series(1)): *We saw the first part of the film on television last night and we shall see the sequel next Sunday.*

sequence /ˈsiːkwəns/ *n* **1** *c.n* (often — *of s.t*) collection (of s.t), one of which follows the other: *You can see from this sequence of photographs exactly how the accident happened.* Compare **series(1)**. **2** *u.n* (usu *the — of s.t*) order in which things happen (in s.t): *Everything happened so fast after the train crash that each of us has a different account of the sequence of events.* **3** *c.n* scene(1) in a film etc. **in/out of sequence** each following, not following, the other in a certain order: *Please arrange the cards in sequence with aces(1) first.*

sequential /sɪˈkwenʃəl/ *adj* (*formal*) of or referring to a sequence.

seˈquentially *adv.*

sequin /ˈsiːkwɪn/ *c.n* small circle of bright metal etc with a hole in the middle, used for sewing on to clothes for decoration.

ˈsequined *adj* having sequins on it.

serenade /ˌserəˈneɪd/ *c.n* **1** song that is (intended to be) sung, music that is (intended to be) played, outside at night, usu by a man for the woman he loves. **2** piece of music written to be played by a small group of musicians.

▷ *tr.v* **3** sing or play a serenade(1) for (s.o, usu the woman one loves).

serene /sɪˈriːn/ *adj* absolutely calm and peaceful, sometimes in spite of danger etc: *a serene disregard for all the noise and struggle around one*; *a serene evening beside a warm fire.*

seˈrenely *adv.* **serenity** /sɪˈrenɪtɪ/ *u.n.*

serf /sɜːf/ *c.n* (in history) person who was forced to work on her/his master's/mistress's land and was not allowed to go away without his/her permission. Compare **slave(1)**.

ˈserfdom *u.n* fact or state of being a serf.

serge /sɜːdʒ/ *u.n* (also *attrib*) strong woollen cloth, usu for making clothes that will have a lot of rough wear: *serge trousers.*

sergeant /ˈsɑːdʒənt/ *c.n* (*written abbr* Sgt) (*military*) **1** kind of non-commissioned officer in the army, air force or Royal Marines: *A sergeant has three chevrons on the upper part of each sleeve to show her/his rank.* **2** police officer whose rank is one above a constable, which is the lowest.

ˌsergeant ˈmajor *c.n* (*written abbr* Sgt Maj) (*military*) warrant officer in the British army or Royal Marines.

series /'sɪərɪz/ *c.n* (*pl* series) **1** group of things, usu of the same kind, that follow each other in a certain order: *a television series* (i.e a number of films etc of the same kind that follow each other on television once a week etc). Compare sequence(1). **2** group of different books, coins, stamps, football matches etc that form one unit, often because they are like each other in one or more ways: *a series of butterfly stamps* (i.e in which each has a picture of a kind of butterfly on it). **3** (usu in — or *attrib*) (*technical*) way of joining electrical parts in one line so that the same current goes through all of them one after the other: *a series circuit*(4). Compare parallel(6).

serial /'sɪərɪəl/ *adj* **1** of, referring to, in, a series.
▷ *c.n* **2** story in two or more parts, e.g in different editions(2) of a magazine or different television programmes.

serialization, **-isation** /,sɪərɪəlaɪ'zeɪʃən/ *u.n* serializing of s.t.

serialize, -ise /'sɪərɪə,laɪz/ *tr.v* produce (a story etc) in parts, as a serial(2).

'serially *adv*.

'serial ,number *c.n* number given to one of a group of people, animals or things to distinguish it from others.

,serial 'order *u.n* (often *in* —) correct order in the series(1).

serious /'sɪərɪəs/ *adj* **1** (of a person, the way he/ she says, does etc s.t) solemn (and after thinking carefully); not joking, cheerful or trying to be funny: *a serious look on s.o's face*. **2** severe; dangerous; bad; not at all easy to bear or to deal with: *a serious illness*.

'seriously *adv* **1** in a serious way. **2** (used at the beginning of a sentence to introduce s.t serious(1) that one wants to say, often after a joke etc): *But seriously, you shouldn't let the children play with that ball so near the house*. **take s.o/s.t seriously** treat s.o/s.t as deserving careful thought, either because he/she/it is important or because he/ she/it is difficult or dangerous.

'seriousness *u.n*.

sermon /'sɜːmən/ *c.n* **1** (usu by a priest) formal talk as part of a church service. **2** (*informal*; often *derog*) long talk, advice etc that is often too moral: *My teacher gave me a sermon about being late for school*.

sermonize, -ise /'sɜːmə,naɪz/ *intr.v* (often — *on s.t*) (usu *derog*) give a sermon(2) (about s.t).

serpent /'sɜːpənt/ *c.n* **1** (*literary*) snake. **2** (*derog* or *religion*) very bad person who persuades other people to be bad too.

serrated /se'reɪtɪd/ *adj* (of a knife, mountain tops etc) having an edge with things like pointed teeth: *the serrated edge of a saw*.

serum /'sɪərəm/ *n* (*pl* —s or, less usu, sera /'sɪərə/) **1** *u.n* clear yellow liquid that is part of one's blood. **2** *c/u.n* serum(1) taken from an animal that has had a certain disease and put into a person/animal who/that is ill with this disease to cure her/him/it.

serve /sɜːv/ *c.n* **1** (in tennis etc) kind of hard hit of the ball etc by the server at the start of a point. ⇒ serve(10), service(11).
▷ *v* **2** *tr.v* (*formal*) work, esp well and faithfully, for (s.o/s.t): *serve the cause of liberty*. **3** *intr.v* (often — *as/in/on s.t*; — *under s.o*) work or do a job

(as an assistant(2) etc): *serve on a committee*. **4** *tr.v* provide a service(9) for (s.o/s.t): *This post office serves three villages*. **5** *tr.v* spend (a certain length of time) (as/in/on s.t, under s.o or in prison): *serve three years in the army*; *serve a life* sentence(2), *six years in prison*. ⇒ serve time (for s.t). **6** *tr/intr.v* (often — (s.o) as/for s.t, to do s.t) be suitable (for s.o) (as/for s.t, to do s.t): *Will this pen serve you? We didn't have a garden table so an old box had to serve as one. This old axe will serve to cut up this wood*. **7** *tr/ intr.v* (often — *up* (food) for s.o; — (s.o) food etc) give (food) to the people who are having a meal (at a table); offer/give food to (s.o): *Call everyone to the table; I'm serving up now. Will you please serve the soup at that table? Do you serve your guests or let them help themselves?* **8** *tr.v* (of food and drink) be enough for (a certain number of people): *This tin of fruit serves four people*. **9** *tr/intr.v* (in a restaurant, shop etc) find out what a customer wants and try to get it for (her/him): *Have you been served?* (or *Are you being served?*) **10** *tr/intr.v* (in tennis etc) start play for a point by hitting (the ball) to the other player or member of the other team who has to hit it back. ⇒ serve(1). **11** *intr.v* help the priest during (Holy) Communion. **serve s.o's purpose** be suitable for what one wants. ⇒ serve(6). **serve s.o right** (*informal*) be what s.o deserves for s.t bad he/she has done. **serve a summons/writ** etc (**on s.o**) (*law*) deliver a summons(1)/writ etc (to s.o) in a way that is accepted by law. **serve at table** (*formal*) (of a waiter etc) serve(7) food to people sitting round a table. **serve time** (**for s.t**) be in prison (because of a certain crime). ⇒ serve(5).

servant /'sɜːvənt/ *c.n* **1** (becoming *old use*) person who is paid to work for a rich or important person, e.g to clean the house. ⇒ staff(1). **2** (usu — *of s.o*) (*literary*) person who does what (s.o else) needs or wants: *The president promised to be the servant of the people*.

'server *c.n* person who serves(7,9,10,11) s.o/s.t. ⇒ assistant(2), waiter.

service /'sɜːvɪs/ *attrib.adj* **1** for use by staff, not visitors or customers: *a service entrance/lift*.
▷ *n* **2** *c/u.n* (often (*in*) the — of s.o/s.t) (*formal*) work (for s.o/s.t): *Eric is in the service of the government. Mary has been made a* baroness(2) *for her services to the country*. **3** *u.n* (often *of* — (to s.o/s.t)) use (to s.o/s.t): *This dictionary has been of great service to me*. **4** *c.n* (usu *pl*) one of the armed forces. **5** *c/def.n* one of the government departments: *the consular/ diplomatic(1) service*. **6** *u.n* way of serving(7,9) in a shop, restaurant etc: *Service is good/slow in this place*. **7** *c.n* set of plates etc needed for serving(7) a meal at the table: *We have a dinner service with flowers on it*. **8** *c/u.n* formal meeting at which there are prayers, singing etc: *morning service*; *the marriage service*. **9** *c.n* (also *attrib*) (company, group of people etc, for the) doing of s.t that people need, often without making any goods: *a bus service*; *the postal services*. ⇒ service industry. **10** *c/u.n* (also *attrib*) (often — *on s.t*) (of cars, machines etc) checking (of s.t) including changing the oil etc and repairing if necessary: *May I speak to your service department please; my car needs a service*. **11** *c.n* = serve(1): *Whose service is it?* (= Whose turn is it to serve(10)?)

active service ⇨ active. **armed services** ⇨ arm². **at s.o's service** (*formal*) ready to help s.o. **be in the services** be a member of the armed forces. **civil service** ⇨ civil. **do s.o a service** do s.t to help s.o, usu out of kindness. **of service (to s.o/s.t)** helping (s.o/s.t); useful (to s.o/s.t). **room service** ⇨ room. **social service(s)** ⇨ social.

▷ *tr.v* **12** give a service(10) to (a car etc).

'service ,charge *c.n* money charged by a restaurant, bank etc for providing (a) service(2,9).

'service ,flat *c.n* flat in which cleaning etc is provided.

'service ,industry *c.n* (*pl -ies*) industry that does not produce goods but provides services(9).

'service ,station *c.n* place where one can buy petrol etc for one's car etc and often where car repairs and services(10) are done.

,servicea'bility *u.n* (*formal*) usefulness; extent to which one can use s.t.

'serviceable *adj* useful, helpful; that can be used for a long time without giving trouble.

'serviceman *c.n* (*pl -men*) man who is in one of the armed forces.

'service,woman *c.n* (*pl -,women*) woman who is in one of the armed forces.

servile /'sɜ:vaɪl/ *adj* (*derog*; *formal*) **1** (too) humble and obedient. **2** (usu in art or literature) copying other people's way of doing things without showing any originality.

'servilely *adv*. **servility** /sɜ:'vɪlɪtɪ/ *u.n*.

'serving *attrib.adj* **1** who is an active member of a service(2,4,5): *a serving member of a committee*; *a serving soldier*.

▷ *n* **2** *c.n* (often — *of s.t*) amount of (a certain) food that is intended for one person: *a large/ second serving of meat*.

'servi,tude *u.n* (*formal*) state of being (like) a slave(1).

serviette /,sɜ:vɪ'et/ *c.n* = napkin often made of paper.

sesame /'sesəmɪ/ *u.n* (also *attrib*) kind of plant whose seeds and oil are used in cooking etc: *sesame oil*.

session /'seʃən/ *c.n* meeting, often formal and regularly held, of a court of law, group of people etc: *Our club has a bridge² session every week*. **in session** actually meeting now: *When the court is in session there is a red light above the door*.

'sessions *pl.n* one of certain regular meetings of British courts of law.

set¹ /set/ *n* **1** *c.n* (often — *of s.t*) collection/group (of things) that form a whole: *a set of knives and forks*; *a complete set of Shakespeare's plays*; *a set of rules*. **2** *c.n* group of people who are like each other in certain ways, e.g in what they do and like: *the racing set*; *the literary set*. **3** electrical or mechanical device used for listening to, looking at, playing with etc: *a radio set*; *a television set*; *a train set* (i.e toy trains, rails etc). **4** *c.n* scene built for actors to act in either a play or a film: *a stage/film set*. **5** *c.n* one of the parts of a tennis match: *You can win a set with a score of 6 games but if the score reaches 6 games each, the set is usually won by a tiebreak*. **jet set** ⇨ jet¹. **on the set** actually acting in a play or film. ⇨ set¹(4).

set² /set/ *adj* **1** (usu *attrib*) fixed: *set ideas and opinions*; (*at*) *set hours* (regularly and at times fixed before); *a set smile on one's face* (i.e a smile

that is not natural but that one keeps on one's face). **2** (*pred*; usu (*all*) — *for, to do, s.t*) ready (for, to do, s.t): *We were all set to leave when the telephone rang*. **set in one's ways** always thinking and behaving in the same ways and not wanting or able to change. **set (up)on s.t** absolutely determined to do s.t.

▷ *c.n* **3** (often *shampoo and —*) (an act of a) setting (⇨ set²(15)) of a person's hair. **4** (usu *the — of s.t*) position in which one holds (part of one's body): *I could see by the set of his jaw that he was not going to let himself be persuaded*.

▷ *v* (*-tt-*, *p.t,p.p* set) **5** *tr.v* put (s.o/s.t) (s.w): *She set her heavy load down and sat on it to rest*. **6** *tr.v* cause (s.o/s.t) to become (free etc): *He set the house on fire! Mary is setting all the birds free*. **7** *tr.v* arrange, fix, choose, (s.t): *Have they set their wedding date? We have to set a limit on the time we will allow for the building of the house*. **8** *tr.v* give (s.o) s.t to do: *The manager set us a difficult task when he asked us to find a cheaper way to do this work. We set the students difficult questions in the examination*. **9** *tr.v* adjust(1) s.t so that it is correct or ready to do exactly what one wants it to do: *Please set your watches; it is exactly 9.33 now. Have you set the alarm clock?* **10** *tr.v* put (a broken bone etc) into the correct position for it to set²(11). **11** *intr.v* (of a broken bone etc) grow together again. **12** *tr.v* put (part of one's body) into a particular position: *When he did not want to do something, he always set his jaw and said nothing*. **13** *tr/intr.v* (cause (a liquid) to) become solid or (cause (s.t soft) to) become hard: *Has the jelly(1) set yet?* **14** *intr.v* (of the sun, moon etc) go down. Opposite rise(6). ⇨ sunset. **15** *tr.v* arrange, put curlers into, (wet hair) in the way one wants it to look when it dries. **16** *intr.v* (of hair) become dry in the shape in which one has set²(15) it. **17** *tr.v* (usu — *s.t in s.t*) fix (a jewel etc) (in silver etc). ⇨ setting(5). **18** *intr.v* (of plants) produce seeds and fruit properly. **19** *tr.v* (often — *s.t in s.t*) give a setting(2) to (a play, film etc): *This story is set in London*. **20** *tr/intr.v* use a keyboard(1) to type(7) letters, numbers etc for (a book, newspaper etc).

set about (doing) s.t start (doing) s.t. **set about s.o/s.t** (*informal*) attack s.o/s.t.

set s.o against s.o cause s.o to dislike s.o. **set s.t against s.t** (*commerce*) balance s.t, e.g costs, against s.t, e.g income.

set s.t alight cause s.t to begin burning.

set s.o apart (from s.o) cause s.o to be different (from s.o): *Her great beauty has always set her apart from the other students*.

set s.t aside (**a**) (often — *s.t aside for s.o/s.t*) not use s.t now, but keep it for the future (for s.o/s.t). (**b**) not take s.t into account: *Setting aside what your parents want, what do you yourself want?* (**c**) (*law*) overrule (a decision etc).

set s.o back cause s.o to lose an advantage, get a disadvantage: *Mary's illness has set her back a lot*. ⇨ setback. **set s.o back £20** etc (*informal*) cost s.o £20 etc. **set s.t back** (**a**) put s.t in a position that is further back than it was or than other things: *Our house is set back thirty metres from the road and has a garden in front*. (**b**) cause s.t to be late: *The cold weather has set fruit back several weeks*. Opposite bring s.t on.

set s.t before s.t prefer s.t to s.t: *You should always set duty before pleasure.*

set s.o/s.t beside s.o/s.t compare s.o/s.t to s.o/s.t.

set s.t by = set s.t aside(a).

set one's cap at s.o ⇒ cap(*n*).

set a day/time etc **for s.t** decide on what day etc to do s.t. ⇒ set²(7).

set s.o/s.t doing s.t cause s.o/s.t to start doing s.t: *set s.o thinking*; *set s.t going.*

set s.o down (of a bus etc) allow passengers to get out. **set s.t down** (a) put down s.t one is carrying. (b) write s.t: *set down your ideas (on paper).*

set eyes on s.o/s.t see s.o/s.t (suddenly): *I've loved her from the first time I set eyes on her. I've never set eyes on anything so beautiful before.*

set fire to s.t; **set s.t on fire** ⇒ fire(*n*).

set foot in/on s.t ⇒ foot(*n*).

set forth (*formal*) start a journey.

set s.o/s.t free ⇒ free(*adj*).

set one's heart on s.t ⇒ heart(*n*).

set in (of bad weather, winter, illness etc) begin: *Buy plenty of supplies because once winter sets in, we won't be able to go out much.* **the rot sets in** ⇒ rot(*n*).

set a match to s.t ⇒ match².

set s.o's mind at ease/rest; **set one's mind on s.t** ⇒ mind¹.

set off start on a journey etc. **set s.o/s.t off** (**doing s.t**) cause s.o/s.t to start (doing s.t): *The clown set the children off laughing. The report in the newspaper set off a big hunt for the criminals.* **set s.t off** (a) cause s.t, e.g a bomb, to explode. (b) make s.t look more attractive because of being beside s.t else: *That green dress sets Emma's red hair off perfectly.* (c) (in writing, printing) separate s.t from s.t: *These darker letters set this word off from the rest of the sentence.* **set s.t off against s.t** (*commerce*) place, balance, (an amount, e.g of expenditure(2)) against (another amount, e.g profit): *These losses will have to be set off against our profit on other sales.*

set (**s.o/s.t**) **on s.o/s.t** (cause a person, animal to) attack s.o/s.t: *The old man set his dog on us.*

set out (**on s.t**) begin a journey etc. **set out to do s.t** begin or plan to do s.t. **set s.t out** (a) arrange several things tidily in various places. (b) (*formal*) arrange various points in an argument etc in a particular order and write or speak them.

set pen to paper ⇒ pen¹(*n*).

set a price on s.t ⇒ price(*n*).

set a record (**for s.t**) ⇒ record³(*n*).

set s.o/s.t right ⇒ right¹(*adj*).

set sail (**for s.w**) ⇒ sail(*n*).

set the stage (**for s.o/s.t**) ⇒ stage¹(*n*).

set store by s.o/s.t ⇒ store(*n*).

set s.o straight; **set the record straight** ⇒ straight(*adj*).

set s.o's teeth on edge ⇒ tooth.

set to (a) begin doing s.t in an eager or a determined way. (b) start fighting with words and/or actions. ⇒ set-to. **set s.t to music** ⇒ music. **set s.o/s.t to rights** ⇒ rights (⇒ right¹). **set to work** (**on s.t**) ⇒ work(*n*).

set s.o up (**as s.t, for/with s.t**) give s.o what is needed (to become s.t or in the way of s.t): *Mary has set herself up as a hairdresser. After our successful trip yesterday we're well set up with*

fish for the next few weeks. **set s.t up** (a) build s.t, put s.t up in its place: *They're setting up camp.* (b) make (a device etc) ready for use: *set up a camera.* (c) form or start a company, club etc. (d) cause s.t to start or happen: *Dropping the stone into the water sets up disturbances that cause fish to move about.* (e) begin a loud noise etc: *When Alex fell into the water, his sister set up a cry that quickly brought people to her help.*

'set₁back *c.n* (often — *to s.o/s.t*; *suffer a* —) thing that puts s.o/s.t in a worse state than before: *Helen was getting better after her illness but now she has suffered a setback.* ⇒ set s.o back.

₁set 'book *c.n* book that one has to study for an examination. Compare unseen(3).

₁set 'meal *c.n* meal in a hotel, restaurant etc, planned and cooked without any choice by the customer.

'set ₁square *c.n* triangle(1) of wood, plastic(3) etc used to help draw angles, straight lines etc.

'setting *c.n* (often — *of s.t*) **1** surroundings or background (of s.t): *The house is ugly but its setting is beautiful. What a perfect setting for a party.* **2** place and time in which (a story etc) is set²(19). **3** going down (of the sun etc). ⇒ set²(14), sunset. **4** way/position in which (a machine etc) is set²(9). **5** way in which (a jewel) is set²(17), or the metal etc in which it is set²(17).

set-to /₁set 'tu:/ *c.n* (*informal*) short fight with actions or angry words.

'set-₁up *c.n* (*informal*) way in which things are organized/arranged: *Their set-up suits them well. He's got a good set-up* (His business is well organized).

settee /se'ti:/ *c.n* = sofa.

setter /'setə/ *c.n* kind of dog with long hair, sometimes used in hunting.

settle /'setl/ *v* **1** *tr/intr.v* (cause/help (s.o) to) begin to live in a place, usu one to which he/she has moved from s.w else: *We settled in Oxford many years ago.* **2** *tr.v* provide (a place) with people to live there: *This part of the country was settled by sheep farmers over a hundred years ago.* **3** *tr/intr.v* (cause (s.o/s.t) to) get into a comfortable and/or steady position: *Settle into your chairs and I'll read you a story. She settled her chair/herself (down) on the rocky beach.* **4** *intr.v* (of a bird, dust etc) fly or float down and then stop (on s.t): *The bird settled on a branch. The sand settled on the bottom of the river.* **5** *tr/intr.v* (usu — *down* when intr) (cause (s.o/s.t) to) become calm or quiet: *Settle down, children; I'm starting the lesson. You're feeling sick, are you? Well, this medicine will settle your stomach.* ⇒ unsettle. **6** *tr/intr.v* (cause (s.t) to) become more tightly packed together: *The flour will settle in the jar and you can put more in.* **7** *intr.v* (of a building, the ground etc) slowly become lower, usu because the earth is settling(6): *We can't build the roof until the walls have settled.* **8** *tr.v* decide (s.t, that etc . . .); agree (with s.o) (about s.t, that etc . . .) (sometimes after an argument or law case): *Have you settled which college to go to? We haven't settled where to meet yet.* **9** *tr/intr.v* (often — *up* (*with s.o*)) pay (s.o) (what one owes): *Let's settle our bill and go. You pay the taxi and then we'll settle up in the hotel* (i.e we will divide up the cost among ourselves). **10** (often —(*s.t*) *in, out of, court*) ⇒ court(*n*).

settle an account, accounts, (with s.o) ⇨ account(*n*).

settle one's affairs ⇨ affair.

settle down (a) ⇨ settle(3,5). **(b)** begin to live a regular life (s.w): *I'm tired of travelling; I'd like to settle down — probably in a small town.* **(c)** become accustomed to new conditions: *I found my new job difficult at first but now I have settled down and I'm enjoying it.* **settle down to (doing) s.t** start doing s.t seriously: *It's time you settled down to some work studying for your examinations.*

settle for s.t agree (with s.o) to accept s.t, usu s.t that is not as good as one had expected or hoped: *We'd hoped to get £100 000 for our house but we settled for £90 000 because we were in a hurry to sell.*

settle (s.o) in(to s.t) (help/cause (s.o) to) become pleasantly accustomed to s.t new.

settle (up)on s.o/s.t choose s.o/s.t, usu after considering several people or things.

settle up (with s.o) ⇨ settle(9).

that settles it (*informal*) that gives the final answer: *'It's started to rain so that settles it; we can't have a picnic.'*

'settled *adj* **1** (of people) living in one place; not moving about. Opposite nomadic. **2** that has been decided on: *It is all settled that we should leave together.* **3** that is not likely to change soon or easily: *settled weather.* Opposite unsettled.

'settlement *n* **1** *u.n* settling(1) of people in a place. **2** *c.n* place where people have settled(1), usu not long before. **3** *u.n* (often — *of s.t*) settling(4) (of s.t, e.g leaves to the bottom of a pot of tea). **4** *u.n* (often — *of s.t*) settling(7) (of s.t). **5** *c.n* (often — *of s.t*) settling(8,9) (of s.t). **6** *c.n* (often (*make*) *a* — (*on s.o*)) gift (to s.o) by means of a legal(1) document. **in settlement of s.t** in order to settle(9) s.t.

'settler *c.n* **1** person who settles(1) s.w. **2** person who settles(8,9) s.t.

set-to, set-up ⇨ set².

seven /'sevn/ *det/pron/c.n* (*cardinal number*) number 7 (between six and eight): *Seven of us came to the meeting. He arrived at 7 (o'clock). She'll be 7 (years old) tomorrow. It was 7 metres long.* **at sixes and sevens (with s.o) (about s.t)** ⇨ six.

seventeen /ˌsevn'tiːn/ *det/pron* (*cardinal number*) number 17 (between sixteen and eighteen).

seventeenth /ˌsevn'tiːnθ/ *det/pron* (*ordinal number*) **1** 17th; (person or thing) following 16 in order.
▷ *c.n* **2** one of seventeen equal parts; 1/17.

seventh /'sevnθ/ *det/pron* (*ordinal number*) **1** 7th; (person or thing) following 6 in order.
▷ *c.n* **2** one of seven equal parts; 1/7.

ˌseventh 'heaven *def/unique n* (usu *in* —) state of the greatest possible happiness: *I'm in seventh heaven!*

seventieth /'sevntɪəθ/ *det/pron* (*ordinal number*) **1** 70th; (person or thing) following 69 in order.
▷ *c.n* **2** one of seventy equal parts; 1/70.

seventy /'sevntɪ/ *det/pron* (*pl -ies*) (*cardinal number*) number 70 (between sixty-nine and seventy-one): *The temperature reached seventy (degrees) yesterday. 70% (per cent) of them*

were bad. He's seventy (years old). It cost £70.*
in one's seventies between 70 and 79 years old. **(in/into) the seventies** (*or* **the 70('·)s**) **(a)** (speed, temperature, marks etc) between 70 and 79: *The temperature was well into the seventies.* **(b)** (years) between '70 and '79 in a century.

ˌseventy-'eight *c.n* former kind of record¹(1) that one plays at a speed of 78 revolutions²(1) a minute.

sever /'sevə/ *tr/intr.v* break or cut (s.t) (off) (from s.t): *He severed the rope with one blow of his sword. In the accident one finger was severed from his hand.* **sever (diplomatic) relations (with s.t)** stop having (diplomatic(1)) relations(1) (with another country or government).

'severance *n* (*formal*) **1** *c/u.n* act or state of severing (s.t). **2** *u.n* cancelling(1) (of a contract(1), usu one concerning a person's job).

'severance ˌpay *u.n* money paid to an employee when her/his contract(1) of employment is severed.

several¹ /'sevrəl/ *det/pron* a number (of us, them etc); more than two but fewer than many (of us, them etc). Compare some.

several² /'sevrəl/ *attrib.adj* (*formal*) separate; a different one for each person or thing; various; respective: *The girls walked to the square together and then went their several ways home.*

'severally *adv* (*formal*).

severe /sɪ'vɪə/ *adj* **1** strict; not gentle or weak; hard(6): *a severe teacher. Her haircut makes her look too severe.* **2** very strong or bad and therefore usu causing a lot of damage, pain etc: *a severe storm; a severe punishment; a severe headache.* **3** very strong: *His behaviour during the match came in for severe criticism by the club committee.* **4** very difficult to do: *Climbing that mountain is a severe test of one's fitness.* **5** very simple and without decoration; austere(2): *severe clothes/countryside. Some religions prefer very severe buildings.*

se'verely *adv*.

severity /sɪ'verɪtɪ/ *n* (*pl -ies*) (often — *of s.t*) **1** *u.n* fact or quality of (s.t) being severe: *the severity of the climate, sentence.* **2** *c.n* (usu *pl*) severe(2,3) conditions or actions (of s.t): *the severities of the northern winter.*

sew /səʊ/ *v* (*p.t* sewed, *p.p* sewn /səʊn/) **1** *tr/intr.v* join (two or more pieces of s.t together), join (s.t) to s.t, using a needle and thread. ⇨ oversew. **2** *tr.v* make (s.t, e.g a picture) by using a needle and thread. **sew s.t on(to s.t)** fix s.t to s.t by sewing (⇨ sew(1)). **sew s.t up (a)** close s.t by sewing it: *He sewed up the hole in his shirt.* **(b)** (*fig; informal*) successfully finish what one is trying to do about s.t: *The business was sewn up after a day of secret meetings.*

'sewing *u.n* work (to be) done with a needle and thread.

'sewing maˌchine *c.n* machine used to sew(1) s.t, worked by turning a handle, moving one's feet or by electricity.

sewage /'suːɪdʒ/ *u.n* solid and liquid waste substances from houses etc that runs through pipes into sewers.

'sewage disˌposal *u.n* way of removing sewage.

sewer /'suːə/ *c.n* very big pipe or small tunnel under the ground along which sewage is carried.

sewerage /'su:ərɪdʒ/ *u.n* (also *attrib*) removal and treatment or disposal of sewage: *We have a very modern sewerage system in our town.*

sex /seks/ *n* **1** *u.n* (also *attrib*) fact or state of being male or female: *sex organs. Do you know the sex of that little bird?* **2** *c.n* either all males or all females: *It is often difficult for the sexes to understand each other.* **3** *u.n* (usu *have* — (with *s.o*)) (*informal*) sexual intercourse (with s.o). **4** *u.n* (also *attrib*) talking, writing, showing pictures etc, about sex(3) and activities connected with it: *All that some people seem to want on television is sex and violence. He reads sex magazines.* (**a member of**) **the opposite sex** (person who is of) the sex(1) that one is not oneself, e.g when a woman talks about the opposite sex she means men.

'sex ap,peal *u.n* (*informal*) power or fact of being attractive to a person.

'sex ,drive *u.n* strength of one's desire or need for sexual intercourse: *have a high/low sex drive.*

-sexed *adj* having the amount of sex drive shown in the first part of the word: *highly-sexed*; *undersexed.*

'sexily *adv* in a sexy way: *sexily dressed.*

'sexiness *u.n* fact or amount of being sexy.

'sexism *u.n* belief or idea that women are not as good, useful, efficient etc as men (or sometimes that men are not as good etc as women).

'sexist *adj* **1** (*derog*) who/that shows sexism: *sexist literature.*

▷ *c.n* **2** (*derog*) person who shows sexism.

'sexless *adj* **1** neither male nor female; neuter(2). **2** (*derog*) not sexy.

sexual /'seksjʊəl/ *adj* of or referring to sex(1,3,4).

,sexual 'inter,course *u.n* (also **'inter,course, sex**) (often *have* — (with *s.o*)) activity that takes place between two people or animals in which the male's penis goes into the female's vagina.

,sexu'ality *u.n* fact of, or reference to, one's sexual state.

'sexually *adv.*

'sexy *adj* (*-ier, -iest*) exciting or attractive in a sexual way: *a sexy man; a sexy photograph.*

sextant /'sekstənt/ *c.n* (*technical*) instrument used to find the position (usu of a ship or plane) by measuring angles of stars in the sky etc. Compare quadrant(2).

sextet /seks'tet/ *c.n* (*music*) **1** group of six singers or musicians. **2** piece of music written for such a group.

sextuplet /sek'stju:plɪt/ *c.n* one of six people (or sometimes animals) born at the same time of the same mother.

SF /,es 'ef/ *abbr* science fiction. ⇨ sci-fi.

Sgt *written abbr* sergeant.

Sgt Maj *written abbr* sergeant major.

sh /ʃ/ *interj* (also **shh, ssh**) (sound made to ask/ tell s.o to stop talking, making a noise or to do it more quietly). Compare shush.

shabby /'ʃæbɪ/ *adj* (*-ier, -iest*) (*derog*) **1** (of clothes etc) looking old and untidy etc. **2** (of a person) wearing shabby(1) clothes. **3** (*fig*) unfair; dishonourable: *a shabby trick.*

'shabbily *adv.* **'shabbiness** *u.n.*

shack /ʃæk/ *c.n* small hut, usu badly built.

shackle /'ʃækl/ *tr.v* (usu — *s.o/s.t* to *s.o/s.t*; — *s.o/s.t together*) prevent s.o/s.t from acting freely by using shackles (joining her/him/it to s.o/s.t or people/animals/things together).

'shackles *pl.n* **1** pair of metal rings for putting round a person's/animal's leg etc so as to fix her/ him/it to s.t, often by a metal chain. **2** (*fig; literary*) things that prevent one from having one's freedom: *In some countries the government's shackles on newspapers mean that it is difficult to find out the truth.*

shade /ʃeɪd/ *n* **1** *u.n* (usu *in the* — (of *s.t*)) darker area caused by s.t being between the sun, a light etc and oneself: *We sat in the shade of a big umbrella while the sun beat down around us.* **2** *c.n* thing that gives shade(1). ⇨ eyeshade, lampshade. **3** *c/u.n* darker part of a picture: *That artist is a real master of the use of light and shade.* **4** *c.n* (often — *of s.t*) different kind (of a colour), usu because it is lighter or darker: *Look at all the different shades of green in that garden!* **5** *c.n* (often *a* — *of s.t*) (*fig*) small difference in (the) meaning (of s.t). **a shade of s.t** a little of s.t: *Did you notice a shade of doubt in what she said?* **a shade too big** etc a little too big etc: *That piece of glass is a shade too small.* **put s.o/s.t in the shade** (*fig; informal*) be so good, clever etc that one makes s.o/s.t else look very poor etc by comparison: *I thought Peter swam well but his younger sister put him in the shade.*

▷ *v* **6** *tr.v* (often — *s.o/s.t from s.t*) give (s.o/s.t) shade(1) (from the sun etc). **7** *tr.v* (often — *s.t in*) put (s.t) into a picture using shade(3). **shade (off)** (**into s.t**) (sometimes *fig*) gradually change from s.t (into s.t): *This paper starts pink at the top and shades off into white at the bottom. In this poem dream and reality shade into each other in a wonderful way.*

'shading *u.n* act or fact of drawing or painting shade(3).

'shady *adj* (*-ier, -iest*) **1** in the shade(1): *a shady spot.* **2** giving shade(1): *a shady tree.* **3** (*fig; informal*) who/that may easily be dishonest.

shadow /'ʃædəʊ/ *attrib.adj* **1** (of a person who would be a government minister etc if her/his party was in power; of the job of such a person) who has been chosen for the job or has the job itself: *the Shadow Foreign Secretary; the Shadow Cabinet(2); a shadow post in the party.*

▷ *c.n* **2** (often (*in*) *the* — *of s.t*) area of darkness produced by s.t which prevents the sun or other light falling on s.t else: *The shadow of a cloud came over us and it was cold for a few minutes. In the evenings when the sun is low, shadows grow longer.* **3** dark area that looks rather like a shadow(2): *shadows under a tired person's eyes.* **4** person/animal who/that follows s.o closely: *The secret policemen had to be the prime minister's shadows day and night.* **5** (often *the* — *of s.t*) danger or threat (of s.t): *We are living in the shadow of another world war.* **afraid of one's own shadow** (*fig; informal*) easily frightened. **beyond a/any shadow of** (**a**) **doubt** absolutely certain. ⇨ not a, no, shadow of s.t. **cast a/one's shadow** (**on s.o/s.t**) (**a**) cause a shadow(2) to be seen (on s.o/s.t). (**b**) (*fig*) threaten (s.o/s.t): *The knowledge that our mother was ill cast a shadow on our party.* **cast a shadow over s.o/s.t** = cast a shadow on s.o/s.t. **in shadow** covered by a shadow(2): *Our faces were in shadow in the photograph.* **live in the shadow of s.o** (*fig*) be very strongly influenced

by s.o; (appear to be) less important etc than one really is because of comparison with s.o else near one who is very important etc. **not a**, **no**, **shadow of (a)** **s.t** not the smallest amount of s.t, esp doubt: *There is no shadow of* (*a*) *doubt in my mind that he did it.* **a shadow of one's former self** (*fig*) much less strong, fat etc than one was before, usu because of illness, worry etc. **wear oneself/s.o (down) to a shadow** make oneself/s.o work so hard etc that one/he/she becomes a shadow of one's/her/his former self.
▷ *tr.v* **6** make (s.t) darker because one throws a shadow(2) on it. **7** follow and watch (s.o/s.t) while trying not to let her/him/it know that one is doing this. Compare shadow(4).
shadows *def.pl.n* (often *in the* —) = shadow(2).
shadowy *adj* **1** in shadow. **2** (*fig*) who/that is not at all clear; about whom/which little is known.
shady ⇒ shade.
shaft /ʃɑːft/ *c.n* **1** long usu vertical or sloping hole, e.g one in which a lift goes up and down or which miners use to go down a mine. **2** long thin piece of wood etc used as the main part of a weapon that one throws or shoots, e.g an arrow, the handle of a tool, e.g an axe, or for hitting a ball, e.g a golf club(1). **3** one of two long pieces of wood fixed to the front of a cart etc so that a horse etc can be put between them to pull it. **4** axle of a machine around which s.t turns: *a ship's propeller shaft.* **5** beam of light: *shafts of sunlight coming through the trees.*
shaggy /ˈʃæɡɪ/ *adj* (-ier, -iest) rough, hairy and untidy: *shaggy hair; a shaggy coat.*
shaggily *adv.* **shagginess** *u.n.*
shake /ʃeɪk/ *c.n* **1** (often — *of s.t*) act of moving (s.t) from side to side and/or up and down: *In Greece a shake of the head means 'Yes', not 'No'.* **2** ⇒ milk shake. **give s.o/s.t a shake** shake(3) s.o/s.t. **in two shakes** (*informal*) very quickly or soon: *I'll be with you in two shakes.*
▷ *v* (*p.t* shook /ʃʊk/, *p.p* shaken) **3** *tr/intr.v* (cause (s.o/s.t) to) move from side to side and/or up and down: *One sometimes sees 'Shake well before taking' on bottles of medicine. She was shaking with cold, fear. He shook the cloth and the* crumbs(1) *fell out.* **4** *tr.v* shake(3) a container so that (s.t) comes out: *She shook powder onto the floor, pepper on the food.* **5** *tr.v* (often — *s.o up*) (*fig*) disturb (s.o)'s mind; make (s.o) feel worried: *Everyone was shaken by the bad news.* ⇒ unshakeable. **6** *tr.v* make (s.o/s.t) weaker: *Nothing could shake her belief that her husband was not guilty.*
shake (on s.t) one's fist(s) (at s.o) ⇒ fist.
shake hands (with s.o); **shake s.o's hand**; **shake s.o by the hand** ⇒ hand(*n*).
shake one's head; **shake one's head (at s.o/ s.t)** ⇒ head(*n*).
shake s.o/s.t off escape from s.o/s.t; get rid of s.o/s.t: *The car chased us for several kilometres but then we managed to shake it off. I started to get a cold but managed to shake it off.* **shake s.t off** shake(3) s.t in order to get rid of s.t: *shake off the dust.*
shake (on s.t) (*informal*) shake hands to show one's agreement about s.t.
shake oneself (a) move one's body about, e.g to get water off it. **(b)** (*fig*) try to force

oneself to become more awake, sensible etc.
shake s.t out (a) shake(3) s.t so that s.t comes out: *Go outside and shake out the cloth.* **(b)** cause s.t to open or become flatter by shaking it: *Shake the blankets out before you put them on the bed.*
shake (oneself) out of it/s.t (*informal*) make oneself more conscious, awake etc.
shake s.o/s.t up (a) ⇒ shake(5). **(b)** mix s.t by shaking it. **(c)** (*fig*) make changes in s.t to try to improve it: *Our factory needs shaking up.* ⇒ shake-up.
shaker *c.n* container in which one shakes(3) s.t: *a cocktail*(1) *shaker.*
shakes *def.pl.n* **get/have the shakes** be shaking(3) because one is afraid, ill etc. **give s.o the shakes** cause s.o to get the shakes. **(be) no great shakes (as/at s.t)** (*informal*) not (be) very good, skilful etc (as/at s.t): *John is no great shakes as a typist* (or *at typing).*
shake- *c.n* example of shaking s.t up(c): *The factory has been given, needs, a good shake-up.*
shakily *adv* in a shaky way.
shakiness *u.n* fact or state of being shaky.
shaky *adj* (-ier, -iest) **1** shaking(3), sometimes because of illness, fear etc. **2** (*fig*) not firm or strong: *a shaky knowledge of French.*
shale /ʃeɪl/ *u.n* rock made of layers(1) of clay that have become hard.
shall (strong form /ʃæl/, weak form /ʃəl/) *aux.v* (*pres.t* (all persons) shall; no *pres.p*; *p.t* should (strong form /ʃʊd/, weak form /ʃəd/); no *p.p*; negative forms shall not or shan't /ʃɑːnt/, should not or shouldn't /ˈʃʊdnt/; 'I shall' can be *I'll* /aɪl/, 'you shall' can be *you'll* /juːl/, 'he/she shall' can be *he'll/she'll* /hiːl, ʃiːl/, 'it shall' can be *it'll* /ˈɪtl/, 'we shall' can be *we'll* /wiːl/, 'they shall' can be *they'll* /ðeɪl/); 'shall' is followed by the infinitive form of a verb without *to*) Compare will. **1** (used in questions with 'I', 'we' and in *formal* or *old use* with 'he', 'she', 'it', 'they' or a noun, to ask the opinion of s.o): *Shall I stay or go home? Shall John come and help you? We'll make the tea for you, shall we?* **2** (*formal* or *old use*) (used with 'I' and 'we' to show future action or state without any other meaning, now usu replaced by will¹(1), esp in the US): *I shall see you again soon.* **3** (*formal*) (used with 'you', 'he', 'she', 'it', 'they' etc to show a promise or a command, order, sometimes a threatening one, using the strong form of 'shall'): *You shall have the book back tomorrow. 'I won't sit down!' 'You shall sit down, or else!'*
shalt /ʃælt/ *aux.v* (*old use*) (form of shall used with 'thou'): *Thou shalt not steal.*
shallot /ʃəˈlɒt/ *c.n* kind of small onion.
shallow /ˈʃæləʊ/ *adj* **1** not far from the top to the bottom; not deep: *a river that is so shallow that one can stand in it easily; a shallow pan.* **2** (of breathing) not taking much breath into one's lungs. **3** (*derog; fig*) not showing a lot of careful thought: *That man is handsome but shallow so one soon gets bored with him.*
shallows *pl.n* shallow(1) area in the sea etc.
shalt ⇒ shall.
sham /ʃæm/ *adj* **1** (*derog*) false; not real; pretending to be s.t different from what he/she/it really is: *sham flowers made of paper; a sham attempt to make peace.*

▷ *n* (*derog*) **2** *c.n* thing that is sham(1): *He wasn't crying; it was just a sham.* **3** *u.n* fact or state of being sham(1).

▷ *tr/intr.v* (*-mm-*) **4** pretend (s.t): *You don't need to feel sorry for him; he's not really hurt; he's only shamming. The children were shamming sleep; they were really wide awake.*

shamble /'ʃæmbl/ *intr.v* walk unsteadily, usu dragging one's feet along the ground: *The tired old man shambled down the road slowly.*

shambles /'ʃæmblz/ *sing.n* place that is very untidy or badly damaged; mess(2): *After the car accident the whole street was a shambles. Small children can turn a room into a shambles in a few minutes.* **make a shambles of s.t** wreck s.t: *The loss of all his money has made a shambles of all his wonderful plans.*

shame /ʃeɪm/ *u.n* **1** feeling of having lost the right to be proud of oneself because of s.t dishonest, dishonourable etc that one has done or that s.o for whom one feels responsible has done: *The child hung his head in shame.* **2** *u.n* ability to feel shame(1): *Some people have no shame.* **3** *sing.n* (*formal*) thing that causes shame(1) (to s.o): *His behaviour at the party was a shame to us all.* **4** *sing.n* a pity(2): *It's a shame (that) you couldn't come. What a shame! To miss the chance of a holiday was a great shame.* **a crying shame** a great pity. **bring shame on s.o** produce results that (should) make s.o feel shame(1): *His behaviour brought shame on his family.* **put s.o to shame** cause s.o to feel shame(1). **put s.o/s.t to shame** make s.o/s.t seem very poor, stupid etc by comparison: *Her house was so clean that it put all the others in the street to shame.* **Shame (on s.o)!** S.o ought to be ashamed!

▷ *tr.v* **5** cause (s.o/s.t) shame(1): *You have shamed your family's name.* **6** (usu — s.o into/out of (doing) s.t) (try to) make s.o feel shame(1) (so that he/she does (not do) s.t): *We tried to shame him into helping but he still refused.*

,shame'faced *adj* showing shame(1) or timidity. **shamefacedly** /ʃeɪm'feɪsɪdlɪ/ *adv.*

'shameful *adj* that makes, ought to make, s.o feel shame(1).

'shamefully *adv*. **'shamefulness** *u.n*.

'shameless *adj* (*derog*) **1** (of a person) not feeling shame(1). **2** (of an action etc) done without showing any shame(1).

'shamelessly *adv*. **'shamelessness** *u.n*.

shammy /'ʃæmɪ/ ⇒ chamois leather(2).

shampoo /ʃæm'puː/ *n* (*pl -s*) **1** *c/u.n* special liquid etc made for washing people's/animals' hair or for cleaning carpets etc. **2** *c.n* (often *give s.o/s.t a —; have a —*) use of shampoo(1) for one of these purposes: *I have, give my dog, a good shampoo twice a week.* **shampoo and set** ⇒ set²(3).

▷ *tr.v* **3** give (s.o/s.t) a shampoo(2). ⇒ set²(15).

shamrock /'ʃæmrɒk/ *c/u.n* kind of plant that has three or rarely four, leaves arranged in a pattern at the end of each stem: *The shamrock is the national emblem of Ireland.*

shandy /'ʃændɪ/ *c/u.n* (*pl -ies*) (one glass of a) drink made by mixing beer and a soft drink, usually lemonade.

shan't /ʃɑːnt/ = shall not. ⇒ shall.

shanty¹ /'ʃæntɪ/ *c.n* (*pl -ies*) = shack.

'shanty ,town *c.n* group of shanties in which very poor people live.

shanty² /'ʃæntɪ/ *c.n* (*pl -ies*) (also **'sea ,shanty**) kind of song that used to be sung by sailors on sailing ships and that fitted in with the movements they made while working.

shape /ʃeɪp/ *n* (often — of s.o/s.t) **1** *c/u.n* form (of s.o/s.t) when one looks at her/him/it; bodily appearance (of s.o/s.t): *'What's the shape of your new garden?' 'It's not quite square.' I prefer the shape of this vase. My hair's got no shape.* **2** *u.n* (*fig*) way in which s.t is arranged, organized: *Nobody knows the exact shape of things to come.* **get s.t into shape** organize s.t into the right shape(2). **(in/of) all shapes and sizes** (having) every kind of shape(1) and size: *The children in our school are all shapes and sizes.* **in any shape or form** whatever kind it may be: *He refuses to accept orders from me in any shape or form.* **in good etc shape** (*informal*) in good etc state or condition: *Joan's in good shape again after her operation.* **in shape** in a good state or condition: *We keep in shape by walking a lot every day.* Opposite out of shape. **in the shape of s.t** (a) ⇒ shape(1). (b) (*fig*) (appearing) as s.t; by way of s.t: *What do you have in the shape of fruit in your shop today?* **knock s.t into shape** change s.t in order to get it into the right shape(2). **out of shape** not in shape. **put s.t into shape** = get s.t into shape. **take shape** begin to have a shape: *As the fog became less thick, objects on the shore began to take shape. Our plans are at last beginning to take shape.*

▷ *v* **3** *tr.v* (often — s.t from, out of, s.t; — s.t into s.t) give (s.t) (more) form; make (s.t) into a certain shape(1) (using a certain material or producing s.t as a result): *shape the clay into a vase. Can you shape the back of my hair a little more?* **4** *tr.v* (*fig*) cause (s.t) to take a certain form, be organized in a certain way: *The development of computers has shaped the future of industry for many years.* ⇒ shape(2). **5** *intr.v* (usu — up (into s.t)) take (a certain) shape(2) (and in this way become s.t); begin to be what one wants her/him/it to be (which is s.t): *The new students are shaping up well.*

-shaped *adj* who/that has the shape of the person/thing who/that is shown by the first part of the word: *a diamond-shaped garden.*

'shapeless *adj* (usu *derog*) not having a (clear or pleasant) shape(1).

'shapelessly *adv*. **'shapelessness** *u.n*.

'shapeliness *u.n* fact or quality of being shapely.

'shapely *adj* (*-ier, -iest*) having a pleasant shape(1): *shapely legs.*

share /ʃeə/ *c.n* **1** part (of s.t) into which it is divided (and which is one particular person's): *Here's your share of the money. Everyone will get a share of the profits.* **2** (usu — in s.t) share(1) of the ownership (of s.t). **3** (usu *pl*) (often —s in s.t) (*commerce*) one of the parts into which the ownership of a company is divided and for which one is given a share certificate: *I've got/own shares in British Oil.* ⇒ stock(10). **a fair share (of s.t)** as much (of s.t) as one ought to have: *Don't cheat your little brother! Give him a fair share of the sweets!* **have a/no share in s.t** (a) (not) own a share(1) in s.t. (b) (not) have part of the responsibility for s.t: *I had no share in stealing the money.*

▷ *v* **4** *tr/intr.v* do/have(s.t)together(with others),not alone: *All the owners of flats here share one big garden. Don't be selfish; share your toys with your little sister.* **5** *tr.v* (often — *s.t out*) divide s.t so that two or more people get shares(1) of it. **6** *tr.v* (usu — *s.t with s.o*) tell s.o (s.t) so that he/she can know it too: *She has decided to share the news of her good luck with her friends.* **7** *tr.v* have the same (opinions etc) as s.o: *I am sorry but I can't share your belief that everything will be all right if we do nothing.* **share and share alike** (*informal*) have/having equal shares in everything: *Let's share and share alike. We decided to divide all our food among us, share and share alike.*

'share cer,tificate *c.n* paper proving that one is the owner of a certain number of shares(3).

'share,holder *c.n* (often — *in s.t*) person who owns shares(3) (in a business etc).

'share-,out *c.n* (often — *of s.t*) dividing (of s.t) into shares(1).

'share ,prices *pl.n* prices at which shares(3) are bought and sold.

'sharer *c.n* (often — *in s.t*) person who shares(4,5) (s.t).

shares *pl.n* **fair shares** (**of s.t**) a division of s.t that is fair to all those who are given a part. **go shares** (**in s.t**) (**with s.o**) share(4) (s.t) (with s.o): *Do you want to go shares with us in buying a box of wine?*

shark /ʃɑːk/ *c.n* **1** kind of large grey fish with sharp teeth, some kinds of which are very dangerous to people swimming in the sea. **2** (*derog; informal*) person who gets money from other people by cheating them or by taking advantage of their need or weakness in a cruel way: *a loan shark.*

sharp /ʃɑːp/ *adj* **1** ending in a narrow point, like the end of a pin. **2** having a narrow edge that cuts well, like the blade of a knife: *Be careful, the knife is very sharp.* Opposite blunt(1). **3** not as curved as is usual: *sharp* features(1). **4** that hurts suddenly and strongly: *a sharp pain*; *a sharp wind.* **5** (of a kick etc) quick and strong: *a sharp blow in the stomach.* **6** (of things said or written) angry; strong; severe: *a sharp scolding for being late.* **7** (of a change in direction) sudden: *a sharp turn in the road*; *a sharp rise in the cost of petrol*; *a sharp fall in farm prices.* **8** (of s.o's brain, sight etc) quick and clear: *John has a sharp brain. You've got sharp eyes, Diana, so could you look for my needle, please?* **9** clever, often in a dishonest way. ⇒ sharp practice. **10** clear in shape; having clear outlines; in focus(2): *a sharp photograph.* **11** (*informal*) (of clothes etc) smart(1) in appearance: *He's a sharp* dresser(1). **12** (*music*) (of a note) half a tone(1) higher than the natural(3) note: *F sharp* (*F♯*). (Notice that 'sharp' comes after the name of the note.) ⇒ flat(6). **13** (*music*) higher than the correct note(5): *That girl's not singing the notes right; she's quite often sharp.* ⇒ flat(7).

▷ *adv* **14** exactly (the time stated): *The race will start at 2.30 sharp* (or *sharp at 2.30*) *so don't be late.* **15** in a sharp(7) way: *When you get to the end of the street, turn sharp right.* **16** in a sharp(13) way: *You're singing sharp.* **look sharp** (*informal*) (**a**) hurry up. (**b**) be careful.

▷ *c.n* **17** (*music*) note that is half a tone(1) higher than the natural(3) note, *symb* ♯. ⇒ sharp(12). ⇒ flat(15).

,sharp 'contrast *c.n* (usu — *to s.o/s.t*) person or thing who/that is strikingly different (from s.o/s.t else). **in sharp contrast** (**to s.o/s.t**) in a way that is very different (from s.o/s.t else). ⇒ sharp(10).

'sharpen *tr/intr.v* (cause (a pencil, knife etc) to) become sharp(er)(1,2,4,6,8). **sharpen one's hunger** cause one to be more or very hungry.

'sharpener *c.n* instrument for sharpening things: *a pencil/knife sharpener.*

,sharp-'eyed *adj* able to see things very clearly. ⇒ sharp(8).

'sharply *adv.* **'sharpness** *u.n.*

,sharp 'practice *u.n* dishonest behaviour. ⇒ sharp(9).

'sharp,shooter *c.n* person who is very good at shooting, esp at shooting very straight.

sharp-tongued /,ʃɑːp 'tʌŋd/ *adj* (*derog*) who says nasty things; who scolds in a sharp(6) way.

shat /ʃæt/ *p.t, p.p* of shit.

shatter /'ʃætə/ *v* **1** *tr/intr.v* (cause (s.t) to) smash(1), break into small pieces suddenly. **2** *tr/intr.v* (cause (s.t) to) become very bad; ruin/wreck (s.t): *The loss of the business shattered all his hopes of becoming rich.* **3** *tr.v* shock (s.o) severely: *He was shattered by his wife's death.*

shave /ʃeiv/ *c.n* **1** act of removing hair from one's/s.o's face: *I have a shave every morning. It's time for your shave.* **a close shave** ⇒ close¹ (*adj*). Compare narrow(2).

▷ *v* **2** *tr.v* (often — *s.t off* (*s.t*)) remove(hair)etc(from a person's face etc) by scraping it off, usu with a razor: *He shaved his beard off. If you shave pieces of ice off that block, you can put them in our drinks.* **3** *intr.v* shave(2) one's own face etc: *I shave every morning. Some women shave under their arms.* **4** *tr.v* shave(2) (s.o or s.t): *The nurse shaved me before my visitors arrived.* **5** *tr.v* remove thin pieces from (s.t): *If you shave the edge of this window it will close more easily.* **6** *tr.v* (*informal*) almost or just touch (s.t) while passing it: *I turned the* steering-wheel *sharply and just shaved the side of the other car.*

-,shaven *adj* having had a shave(1) of the kind shown in the first part of the word: *a cleanshaven man* (i.e a man who has no moustache or beard).

'shaver *c.n* instrument used to shave(2–4) oneself/s.o: *an electric shaver.*

,shaving *n* **1** *u.n* act of shaving(2–4). **2** *c.n* (usu *pl*) thin piece that has been shaved(2,6) off s.t: *wood shavings.*

'shaving ,brush *c.n* brush used for putting lather(1) or shaving cream on the face etc.

'shaving ,cream *u.n* paste put on the face etc to make shaving(1) easier.

shawl /ʃɔːl/ *c.n* piece of usu knitted cloth put round a woman's shoulders and/or over her head or used to wrap a small child.

she /ʃiː/ *c.n* **1** female: *'Here's my cat.' 'Is it a he or a she?'*

▷ *pron* (strong form /ʃiː/, weak form /ʃi/) **2** (as the subject¹(4) of a verb or (*formal*) a subjective(3) complement(3)), female person or animal (or thing thought of as female) who/that has recently been mentioned or is clear from the context(1):

Do you see that girl? She's in my class. 'Whose cow is that?' 'She belongs to my brother.' 'That's a beautiful boat.' 'Yes, she's lovely, isn't she?' Look, it is she — the woman I was telling you about. Compare her. ⇒ he, it, her, hers.

'she- *adj* female of the animal shown in the second part of the word: *a she-elephant.*

sheaf /ʃiːf/ *c.n* (*pl* sheaves /ʃiːvz/) (often — *of* s.t) **1** big bunch (of corn) etc still on the stalks[1](1) and tied up after being reaped(1). **2** bundle (of other stiff things, e.g pieces of paper).

shear /ʃɪə/ *v* (*p.t* sheared, *p.p* sheared or shorn /ʃɔːn/) **1** *tr.v* cut the wool off (sheep). **2** *tr.v* (usu *literary*) cut hair off (s.o/s.t). **3** *tr.v* cut (hair) off s.o/s.t. **4** *tr/intr.v* (usu — (s.t) *off*) (*technical*) (cause (s.t) to) break (off) as a result of twisting, pressure from one side: *We tried to lift the car but it was too heavy and the bolts[2](2) on the engine sheared off.* **be shorn of s.t** (*literary*) have s.t taken away from one: *It is sad to see such a good politician shorn of all influence in old age.*

shears *pl.n* (often *pair of* —) **1** big scissors. **2** tool that works like shears(1) and is used for cutting plants, metal etc: *garden shears.*

sheath /ʃiːθ/ *c.n* (*pl*/ʃiːðz/) **1** cover for a sword, knife etc to protect its sharp edge(s) and prevent it/them from hurting any one. **2** condom.

sheathe /ʃiːð/ *tr.v* **1** put (a sword etc) in a/ its sheath(1). **2** (usu — s.t *in/with* s.t) cover (s.t) (with s.t) to protect it: *a young tree sheathed in a* plastic(1) *pipe.*

'sheath-ˌknife *c.n* (*pl* -knives) knife that is carried in a sheath(1) and cannot be folded like a penknife.

sheaves /ʃiːvz/ *pl* of sheaf.

shed[1] /ʃed/ *c.n* building, usu built of wood and often with open sides, used for storing things in, keeping animals in etc: *a cow shed; a bicycle shed. We have a garden shed for our tools.* ⇒ hut.

shed[2] /ʃed/ *v* (-dd-, *p.t.p.p* shed) **1** *tr/intr.v* (allow (leaves, hair etc) to) fall naturally: *Many trees shed their leaves in autumn. Snakes shed their skins when they grow too big for them.* **2** *tr.v* allow (s.t) to fall out by mistake: *The truck went round the corner so fast that it shed all the hay it was carrying.* **3** *tr.v* not allow (a liquid) to stay on or in it: *Some birds have oily feathers that shed water as soon as it falls on them.* **shed blood** wound (and kill) a person/animal. ⇒ bloodshed. **shed (new) light on s.o/s.t** ⇒ light[1](n). **shed tears** cry; weep(1).

she'd (strong form /ʃiːd/, weak form /ʃid/) = she had/would. ⇒ have, would.

sheen /ʃiːn/ *c/u.n* bright, shining appearance; shininess: *the sheen of a silk dress, of sunlight on a lake.*

sheep /ʃiːp/ *c.n* (*pl* sheep) animal kept by farmers for its wool and meat: *a large* flock[1](1) *of sheep.* ⇒ ewe, lamb(1), mutton, ram[1]. **a black sheep** (*fig; informal*) a person who people consider to be bad, dishonest etc: *Fred is the black sheep of our family; he has been in prison three times so far.* **make sheep's eyes at s.o** (*fig; informal*) look at s.o in a loving but shy way, usu with the result that people think one silly. **s.o might as well be hanged for a sheep as a lamb** (*fig; informal*) if s.o is going to be punished etc even for s.t that is not very serious, he/she might as well do s.t really bad etc. **separate the sheep from**

the goats (*fig*) find/show the better, stronger etc people in a group.

'sheep,dog *c.n* kind of dog that can be trained to look after sheep.

'sheep,fold *c.n* enclosure in which sheep can be kept.

'sheepish *adj* looking or feeling ashamed. **'sheepishly** *adv.* **'sheepishness** *u.n.*

'sheep,skin *c/u.n* (also *attrib*) skin of a sheep, usu with the wool still on it, used for clothing etc: *a warm sheepskin coat.*

sheer[1] /ʃɪə/ *adj* **1** (almost) vertical: *a sheer rock which is almost impossible to climb up.* **2** (*fig*) pure; not mixed with anything else: *She is not so clever but she does well by sheer hard work.* **3** (of cloth) so thin and fine that one can (almost) see through it.
▷ *adv* **4** (almost) vertically: *Here the land falls sheer down to the sea.*

sheer[2] /ʃɪə/ *intr.v* (also *fig*) turn sharply (away) (from s.o/s.t), usu so as not to hit her/him/it: *sheer away from certain subjects; sheer to the left to avoid a dog in the road.*

sheet /ʃiːt/ *c.n* **1** piece of cloth for putting on a bed: *a bottom/top sheet. I use a fitted sheet on the bottom and a duvet on top.* **2** piece of paper: *500 sheets of writing paper.* **3** flat, thin piece (of metal, ice etc). **4** wide area of water, fire etc moving upwards or downwards: *rain coming down in sheets; a sheet of flame coming from a burning petrol tank.* **(as) white as a sheet** very pale because of fear, illness etc. **change the sheets** take the used or dirty sheets off a bed and put clean ones in their place. **(start with) a clean sheet/slate** ⇒ slate[1](n).

,sheet 'lightning *u.n* lightning(2) that covers a wide area of the sky. Compare forked lightning.

,sheet 'metal *u.n* metal that is in sheets(3).

'sheet ,music *u.n* music that is written or printed on sheets of paper that are not bound together.

sheik /ʃeɪk/ *c.n* (also **sheikh**) **1** chief or prince in Arab countries. **2** important person in the Muslim(1) religion.

'sheikdom *c.n* (also **'sheikhdom**) place ruled by a sheik.

shelf /ʃelf/ *c.n* (*pl* shelves /ʃelvz/) **1** long flat narrow board on a wall or in a cupboard, on which one keeps books, ornaments, things that one is selling etc: *We need more bookshelves.* **2** (usu — *of* s.t) all the things on a shelf(1): *I have three shelves of pretty plates in my living room.* **3** thing that looks like a shelf(1) but is made of rock etc: *We climbed to the top of the mountain and sat on a shelf to look at the view.*

shelve /ʃelv/ *v* **1** *intr.v* (usu — *down/up*) (*formal*) slope (down/up) gradually. **2** *tr.v* stop planning to do or use (s.t), sometimes with the intention of doing or using it at a later date: *The accident to the truck meant shelving deliveries until we knew how long repairs would take.*

'shelving *u.n* shelves(1): *We need a lot more shelving in this room.*

shell /ʃel/ *n* **1** *c/u.n* hard outside covering of an egg, nut, snail, tortoise etc. **2** *c.n* outside of a building, often before the inside has been built or after the inside has been destroyed. **3** *c.n* hard case of a pie or tart[1](1) in which the filling is put.

4 *c.n* thing fired from a big gun. *bring s.o out of her/his shell* (*fig*; *informal*) make s.o less shy and afraid of talking etc to other people. *come out of one's shell* stop being shy and begin to talk and mix with other people.

▷ *v* **5** *tr.v* take the shell(1) off (a nut, pea(1) etc). **6** *tr/intr.v* drop bombs (on (s.o/s.t)); fire shells(4) (at (s.o/s.t)).

-shell *c.n* kind of shell(1) shown by the first part of the word: *a seashell*.

'shell,fish *c.n* (*pl shellfish*) **1** invertebrate(1) creature that lives in water, e.g a crab(1) or a mussel. **2** *u.n* (also *attrib*) flesh of such creatures used as food: *shellfish soup*.

she'll (strong form /ʃiːl/, weak form /ʃɪl/) = she shall/will. ⇨ will.

shelter /'ʃeltə/ *n* **1** *u.n* fact or state of being protected (from bad weather, danger etc): *shelter from a storm*; *under the shelter of a large tree*. **2** *c.n* place where one can get such protection: *a bus shelter*. **3** *u.n* (*formal*) place in which to live: *In cold countries shelter is as important to life as food and water*. *take shelter (from s.t)* get into a position where one is protected (from s.t): *Let's take shelter (from the rain) in that cave*.

▷ *v* (often — (s.o/s.t) from s.o/s.t) **4** *tr.v* protect (s.o/s.t) (from s.o/s.t). **5** *intr.v* protect oneself (from s.o/s.t) by getting into shelter(1): *We sheltered in an old hut*.

'sheltered *adj* (usu *attrib*) who/that is protected from the weather, danger, worry etc: *He has lived a sheltered life and knows very little about the outside world*.

shelve(s), shelving ⇨ shelf.

shepherd /'ʃepəd/ *c.n* **1** (male) person who looks after sheep.

▷ *tr.v* **2** help, guide, lead (s.o, one or more animals) (in(to) s.t) etc).

'shepher,dess *c.n* (usu *literary*) female person who looks after sheep.

,shepherd's 'pie *u.n* mince(1) covered with mash(1) and baked.

sherbet /'ʃɜːbət/ *n* (also *attrib*) *c/u.n* kind of sweet powder that fizzes(4) when it is put in water or one's mouth and is used for making sweets and cold drinks for children: *sherbet lemons*.

sheriff /'ʃerɪf/ *c.n* (often with capital **S**; often *the* — *of s.t*) **1** (Great Britain and Northern Ireland) high official in a county(1) (where he/she is often called the **,High 'Sheriff**) or city who has duties connected with the law and ceremonial duties. **2** (US) official who is in charge of law and order in a county(2).

sherry /'ʃerɪ/ *n* (*pl -ies*) **1** *u.n* dry or sweet, pale or dark, fortified wine, originally produced in Spain and mostly drunk before meals in Britain. **2** *c.n* glass of sherry(1).

she's (strong form /ʃiːz/, weak form /ʃɪz/) **1** = she is. ⇨ be. **2** = she has. ⇨ have.

shield /ʃiːld/ *c.n* **1** thing made of metal, plastic(1) etc carried for protection against stones etc, e.g by policemen. ⇨ windshield. **2** picture of a shield(1) with a pattern on it, used as a coat of arms etc. **3** thing like a shield(1) fixed to a machine etc (and used as protection against danger, e.g from moving parts of the machine). **4** (often a — *against s.o/s.t*) (*fig*) thing, e.g one's faith, that protects one (against s.o/s.t dangerous).

▷ *tr.v* **5** (usu — s.o/s.t *against/from* s.o/s.t) protect (s.o/s.t) (from s.t) with a shield(1,3,4).

shift /ʃɪft/ *c.n* **1** (often — *in s.t*) move or change in (the) position or direction (of s.t): *A shift in the wind caused the smoke to move towards us*. **2** group of people who work together at certain hours, e.g during the day, while other groups work at other hours: *Which nurses are on the night shift this week?* **3** length of time that a shift(2) works: *In our factory we work in shifts of 8 hours – a morning shift, an afternoon shift and a night shift*. **4** (*old use*) petticoat or loose dress worn by a woman. ⇨ makeshift.

▷ *v* **5** *tr/intr.v* (cause (s.o/s.t) to) change position or direction: *We shifted the piano into the other room. The smoke has shifted to the other side of the fire*. **6** *tr/intr.v* (often — (down/up) *into* second etc *gear*) (cause (a gear of an engine) to) change position: *I shifted (down) into second gear to slow down before turning*. *shift for oneself* do everything for oneself instead of having things done for one by others. *shift one's ground* ⇨ ground²(*n*). *shift s.t onto s.o* say that s.o else is responsible for s.t that one is being blamed for oneself. *shift over* (*informal*) move over to make some space: *Shift over so that I can sit down*. *shift to s.t* stop doing, using etc one thing and start doing, using etc another.

'shift ,key *c.n* key(4) on a typewriter, word-processor etc that is pressed when one wants to type capital letters etc.

shiftless /'ʃɪftlɪs/ *adj* (*derog*) not behaving in a responsible way; not really trying to do anything useful.

'shiftlessly *adv*. **'shiftlessness** *u.n*.

shifty /'ʃɪftɪ/ *adj* (*-ier, -iest*) (*derog*) not to be trusted; (in the habit of being) dishonest: *a man with shifty eyes*.

'shiftily *adv*. **'shiftiness** *u.n*.

shilling /'ʃɪlɪŋ/ *c.n* (*abbr* s) **1** twelve (old) pence (=5 (new) pence) or one twentieth of a pound (£) in Britain until 1971. **2** 100 cents in some African countries.

shilly-shally /'ʃɪlɪ ˌʃælɪ/ *intr.v* (*-ies, -ied*) (*derog*; *informal*; becoming *old use*) waste time doing nothing (useful).

shimmer /'ʃɪmə/ *c.n* **1** (often — *of s.t*) weak gently flickering(3) light (of s.t): *the shimmer of moonlight on the sea*.

▷ *intr.v* **2** shine with a shimmer(1).

shin /ʃɪn/ *n* **1** *c.n* hard front part of a person's leg between the knee and the ankle. **2** *c/u.n* (usu — *of beef*(1)) lower part of the leg of a cow, bull¹(1), ox etc used as food.

▷ *tr/intr.v* (*-nn-*) **3** (usu — *down/up* (s.t)) (*informal*) climb (down/up (s.t)), usu quickly and easily, by using one's hands and legs like a monkey.

'shin,bone *c.n* bone in the shin.

shine /ʃaɪn/ *n* **1** *c/u.n* quality or fact of giving out or reflecting light: *There was a shine on their faces*. **2** *c.n* (often *give s.t a* —) polish to make s.t shine(3). (*come*) *rain or shine* ⇨ rain(*n*). *take a shine to s.o* (*informal*) begin to like s.o, often for no reason.

▷ *v* (*p.t,p.p* shone /ʃɒn/, except in 6, shined) **3** *intr.v* (often — (*down*) *on* s.o/s.t) give out or reflect light (that can be seen from s.w): *The sun and moon shine down on us. There's a light shining under the door. The light's shining in my eyes*.

4 *tr.v* (often — *a light* etc *on s.o/s.t*) cause (a light etc) to shine(3) (on s.o/s.t): *Shine your torch over here.* **5** *intr.v* (often — *at s.t*) be seen to be very good at s.t: *Mary shines at mathematics.* **6** *tr.v* polish (a shoe, furniture etc) to make it shine(3): *Have you shined your shoes?*

'shininess *u.n* fact or state of being shiny.

'shining *adj* having a shine(1): *a shining pair of shoes; shining faces.* **a shining example of s.t** a particularly good example of s.t.

'shiny *adj* (-ier, -iest) bright; reflecting light: *shiny metal.*

shingle /'ʃɪŋgl/ *u.n* small pieces of stone which cover some beaches.

'shingly *adj* (-ier, -iest) having shingle(1) on it.

shingles /'ʃɪŋglz/ *pl.n* painful skin disease round the waist etc.

ship /ʃɪp/ *c.n* **1** big vessel that travels on the sea. Compare boat(1). **2** (*informal*) airship; spaceship. **by ship** in a ship: *We went to America by ship not by plane.* **on board ship** on or in a ship.

▷ *tr.v* (-pp-) **3** send (s.t) by ship. **4** send (s.t big) by train, post etc. **ship s.o off** send s.o (to s.w): *After a month's training in London, Paul was shipped off to our Edinburgh office.* **ship water** have water coming over the side and into the boat or ship.

-ship *c.n* vessel of the kind shown by the first part of the word: warship; airship.

'ship,builder *c.n* person who builds ships(1).

'ship,building *u.n* building of ships(1).

'ship,mate *c.n* sailor who is working with one on the same ship(1).

'shipment *n* **1** *c/u.n* act or fact of shipping (⇨ ship(v)) s.t. **2** *c.n* all the goods sent together by a ship, train etc.

'shipper *c.n* person or business who/that sends shipments(2).

'shipping *u.n* **1** ships(1) in general or all the ships in a particular place or area: *Shipping is warned to expect severe storms this evening.* **2** (also *attrib*) fact or act of making shipments(2): *arrange for the shipping of all our household goods; a shipping company.*

'shipping ,agent *c.n* person or business who/that represents a shipping(2) company in a particular place, usu a port.

,ship's 'chandler *c.n* person who sells equipment for ships, e.g ropes etc.

'ship,shape *adj* tidy and clean.

'ship,wreck *n* **1** *u.n* (of a ship) fact of being wrecked. **2** *c.n* (of a ship) example of being wrecked. **3** *u.n* (usu *the* — *of s.t*) (*fig*) ruin (of one's hopes etc).

▷ *tr.v* **4** cause (a ship etc) to be wrecked. **5** (*fig*) ruin (s.o's plans etc).

'ship,wright *c.n* person whose job is building and/or repairing ships(1).

'ship,yard *c.n* place for building and/or repairing ships(1) in.

shire /ʃaɪə/ *c.n* (*old use* except in names /-ʃə/) = county(1): *Yorkshire; Wiltshire.*

shirk /ʃɜːk/ *tr/intr.v* try to avoid (work, duties etc).

'shirker *c.n* (*derog*) person who shirks duties etc.

shirt /ʃɜːt/ *c.n* piece of clothing with short or long sleeves (and a collar), worn by a man or boy (or sometimes a woman or girl) from the neck down

to below the waist. ⇨ blouse, nightshirt, sweatshirt, T-shirt. **keep your shirt on** (*fig*; *slang*) don't get angry. **lose one's shirt** (**on s.t**) (*fig*; *informal*) lose (all) one's money by betting(4) (on a horse etc). **put one's shirt on s.t** (*fig*; *informal*) bet(4) (all) one's money on a horse etc. **a stuffed shirt** ⇨ stuff.

'shirt,front *c.n* front part of a shirt.

'shirt,sleeve *c.n* sleeve of a shirt. **in** (**one's**) **shirtsleeves** (*informal*) not wearing a jacket(1) or coat.

'shirt,tail *c.n* part of a shirt that hangs below one's waist, especially at the back.

shish kebab /'ʃɪʃ kə,bæb/ *c/u.n* = kebab.

shit /ʃɪt/ *n* (*slang*; do not use!) **1** *u.n* excrement, faeces. **2** *c.n* (often *have a* —) act of defecation. **3** *u.n* nonsense(2); lies(1): *You talk shit!* **4** *c.n* unpleasant or worthless person. **not care/give a shit** (**for s.o/s.t**) not care at all (about s.o/s.t). **not worth a shit** not worth anything.

▷ *intr.v* (-tt-, *p.t,p.p* shit(ted), shat /ʃæt/) **5** (*slang*; do not use!) defecate.

'shitty *adj* (-ier, -iest) (*derog*; do not use!) very nasty; very unpleasant: *a shitty job.*

shiver /'ʃɪvə/ *c.n* **1** (feeling of) shaking, usu because of cold or illness but sometimes caused by fear: *When I heard the noise, a shiver ran down my* spine(1).

▷ *intr.v* **2** (of a person, animal) shake, usu because of cold or illness but sometimes because of fear. Compare tremble(2). **shiver in one's boots/ shoes** (*fig*; *informal*) be very afraid.

'shivers *def.pl.n* (*informal*) act of shivering(2), esp because of fear or cold. **get the shivers** begin to shiver(2). **give s.o the shivers** (*fig*) frighten s.o. **have the shivers** be shivering(2). **send shivers** (**up and down**) **one's spine** (often *fig*) make one feel very excited, frightened etc.

'shivery *adj* shaking; cold.

shoal[1] /ʃəʊl/ *c.n* (usu — *of fish*) large number, group (of fish).

shoal[2] /ʃəʊl/ *c.n* **1** (dangerous) sandbank under the water.

▷ *intr.v* **2** (of the sea) become shallow.

shock[1] /ʃɒk/ *n* **1** *c/u.n* strong sudden unpleasant feeling caused to one's body or mind by an electric current, explosion, bad news etc: *The electric shock killed him at once. The shock of the explosion blew down trees hundreds of metres away. She got a shock when she saw the price of the shoes. The shock of hearing about her husband's accident was too much for my aunt.* **2** *c.n* (usu a — *to s.o*) thing that causes (s.o) shock[1](1): *Her death was a shock to all of us.* **3** *u.n* (*medical*; *fig*) state of a person's body or mind when one's heart beats slowly, one's temperature is low etc as a result of a big burn, wound or of great strain[1](3): *He almost died from shock when he saw her.*

▷ *v* **4** *tr/intr.v* (cause (s.o) to) feel shock[1](1). **5** *tr.v* cause (s.o) to feel angry surprise: *Some people are shocked by the sex and violence on television.*

'shock ab,sorber *c.n* (*technical*) device in a car, plane etc that makes it move up and down less violently when the car goes over rough ground or the plane lands etc.

'shocker *c.n* (*derog*; *informal*) person or thing who/that shocks[1](5) s.o: *Joey is a real shocker; listen to the way he screams when he doesn't get what he wants.*

'shocking *adj* (*derog*) who/that shocks¹(5) s.o: *shocking behaviour*.

'shock,proof *adj* (of a watch etc) protected against shock¹(1).

'shock ,tactics *pl.n* way of trying to get what one wants by using sudden, sometimes violent, surprise means.

'shock ,therapy/,treatment *u.n* (*medical*) way of treating disturbances of the mind by using electric shocks¹(1) etc.

shock² /ʃɒk/ *c.n* (usu — *of hair*) big untidy mass (of hair).

shod /ʃɒd/ *adj* **1** (*literary*) having shoes.
▷ *v* **2** *p.t.p.p* of shoe(4).

-shod *adj* having shoes of the kind shown by the first part of the word: *well-shod*.

shoddy /'ʃɒdɪ/ *adj* (*-ier, -iest*) (*derog*) **1** badly made or done, using cheap/poor materials: *a shoddy job*. **2** not fair or generous: *It was a shoddy trick to get those people to give you money for the repairs and then use it to go on holiday!*
'shoddily *adv*. **'shoddiness** *u.n*.

shoe /ʃuː/ *c.n* **1** (often *pair of* —s) thing worn on one's foot, usu over a sock etc: *Shoes usually have leather or rubber soles³(2) and heels. Put your shoes on. Take those dirty shoes off.* Compare boot(1), sandal, slipper. ⇒ overshoe. **2** = horseshoe(1). **3** (also **'brake ,shoe**) device that presses on the wheel of a bicycle etc to slow it down when the brake is put on. **fill s.o's shoes** (*fig; informal*) take the place/job of s.o else. **in s.o's shoes** (*fig; informal*) in the same position as s.o is in: *If I were in your shoes I would refuse to pay for such poor work.*
▷ *tr.v* (*pres.p shoeing, p.t.p.p shod* /ʃɒd/, *shoed*) **4** put horseshoes on (a horse etc).

'shoe,horn *c.n* device that one puts between one's heel and the back of a shoe to help one get a shoe(1) on.

'shoe,lace *c.n* piece of string or strip of leather etc used for keeping the top front of a shoe(1) closed: *Please tie your shoelace; it's come undone*.

'shoe,string *c.n* **on a shoestring** (*informal*) having or with very little money: *When he left school, he had to live on a shoestring but now he is a rich man.*

'shoe ,tree ⇒ tree(2).

shone /ʃɒn/ *p.t.p.p* of shine.

shoo /ʃuː/ *interj* **1** (*informal*) go away.
▷ *tr.v* (*pres.p shooing, p.t.p.p shooed*) **2** (*informal*) make (a person, animal) go away (from s.o/s.t) (by saying 'Shoo(1)!' to her/him/it): *I shooed away the cat, shooed the cat off, shooed it out of the kitchen.*

shook /ʃʊk/ *p.t* of shake.

shoot /ʃuːt/ *c.n* **1** new piece that is beginning to grow out (of a plant). **2** occasion during which people fire guns etc for practice, as a sport etc. **put out shoots** (of a plant) start to grow new shoots(1).
▷ *v* (*p.t.p.p shot* /ʃɒt/) **3** *tr.v* hit (s.o/s.t) with a bullet, arrow etc that one fires. **4** *tr/intr.v* (often — *s.t off*) cause (a gun etc) to fire, (an arrow) to fly from a bow: *Stop shooting; there are people crossing in front of us.* ⇒ shot¹(1). **5** *intr.v* move very fast: *I saw the boys shoot past my window. They shot out of the room, through the gates. As I bent my arm, a nasty pain shot through my elbow.* **6** *intr.v* (of

a plant) put out shoots(1). **7** *tr/intr.v* kick (a ball) and try to score (a goal). ⇒ shot¹(3). **8** *tr/intr.v* make (a photograph etc) of (s.t): *I shot my uncle as he dived into the river. She will shoot many photographs/films/pictures during her holiday.* ⇒ shot¹(8,9). **9** *intr.v* (used only as an order) (*informal*) say what you want to say: '*Can I say something now, please?' 'OK, shoot!*'

shoot a goal score a goal.

shoot (s.t) at s.o/s.t try to hit s.o/s.t with a bullet, arrow etc or by firing a gun etc.

shoot s.o/s.t dead kill a person, animal by shooting(3) her/him/it.

shoot s.o/s.t down cause s.o/s.t, e.g a plane, to fall by shooting(3) her/him/it.

shoot to kill shoot(4) with the intention of killing.

shoot (s.o) a line ⇒ line(*n*).

shoot one's mouth off ⇒ mouth(*n*).

shoot it out have a fight with s.o with guns etc until one (side) or the other loses. ⇒ shoot-out.

shoot questions (at s.o) ask (s.o) questions very quickly one after the other.

shoot the rapids ⇒ rapid(*n*).

shoot one's way out (of s.t), into s.t etc get out (of s.t) etc by shooting(4).

-,shooter *c.n* person or thing who/that shoots(4) what is shown, in the way shown, in the first part of the word: *a sharpshooter; a six-shooter.*

'shooting ,brake *c.n* (*old use*) = estate car.

'shooting ,star *c.n* = meteor.

'shooting ,stick *c.n* stick with a folding seat on top on which one can sit.

'shoot-,out *c.n* (*informal*) fight between two or more people using guns etc. ⇒ shoot one's way out (of s.t).

shop /ʃɒp/ *c.n* **1** place in which things are normally sold or certain services provided: *a gift shop* (in which one can buy presents for people); *a beauty shop*. **2** = workshop(2): *a repair shop*.

all over the shop (*informal*) (**a**) scattered about untidily: *When we got home, our possessions were lying all over the shop.* (**b**) everywhere; to a lot of different places: *I have looked all over the shop but I can't find a pair of red shoes.* **close up shop** shut one's shop, stop one's work, usu in the evening or because of a holiday etc. **closed shop** ⇒ closed. **set up shop** start business (as s.t): *John has decided to set up shop as a house painter.* **shut up shop** = close up shop. **talk shop** (*informal*) talk about business matters, usu when one should be talking about more personal or general matters: *Do you mind if Mary and I talk shop for a minute before we join you?*
▷ *v* (*-pp-*) **3** *intr.v* (often — *for s.t; go —ping (for s.t)*) go to one or more shops(1) to try to buy s.t: *I go shopping twice a week.* ⇒ window shop. **4** *tr.v* (*slang*) report (a criminal) to the police so that they can arrest her/him. **shop around (for s.t)** go to various shops(1) (to look for s.t), usu in order to find the one where s.t is cheapest or best.

-shop *c.n* shop(1) in which the thing shown in the first part of the word is sold, provided etc: *a sweet-shop.*

'shop as,sistant *c.n* person who serves people in a shop(1).

,shop 'floor *def.n* (often *on the* —) (*informal*) part of a factory etc where things are made: *The* *workers on the shop floor are determined to make this business successful.*

'shop,keeper *c.n* person who owns or manages a shop(1).

'shop,lift *tr/intr.v* steal (s.t) from a shop(1).

'shop,lifter *c.n* person who shoplifts.

'shopper *c.n* person who is shopping (⇒ shop(3)).

'shopping *u.n* **1** act of buying things one needs etc: *Can you do my shopping for me?* ⇒ shop(3). **2** things that one buys in a shop(1): *I saw an old woman carrying her shopping home.*

'shopping ,bag *c.n* bag in which one carries one's shopping(2).

'shopping ,centre *c.n* place where there are several shops(1) near each other so that one can buy everything one wants without having to go long distances between shops.

'shop,soiled *adj* that has been kept in a shop(1) for so long that it is no longer in very good condition and is often sold cheaply.

,shop 'steward *c.n* trade union member who is elected by her/his fellow workers to represent them in all business with management.

shore¹ /ʃɔː/ *c.n* land along the edge of the sea, a lake, big river etc. Compare bank(1), beach(1), coast(1), seaside. **off shore** away from the shore¹: *The boat is a kilometre off shore.* **on shore** on the land, not the sea etc. ⇒ ashore, inshore, offshore, onshore.

'shore ,leave *u.n* free time that s.o working on a ship is allowed to spend on shore.

shore² /ʃɔː/ *c.n* **1** piece of wood etc used to hold s.t up, prevent it falling over etc. Compare prop(1).

▷ *tr.v* (often — *s.t up* (*with s.t*)) **2** use one or more shores²(1) to hold (s.t) up. Compare prop¹(3). **3** (*fig*) try to protect or save (a business etc) (using s.t): *The government has refused to shore up the car company with any more loans(2).*

shorn /ʃɔːn/ *p.p* of shear.

short /ʃɔːt/ *adj* **1** that measures little from one end to the other in space or time: *short hair*; *a short visit*; *short for her age*. *The string is too short. Cut the wood a little shorter.* Opposite (for height) tall(1); (for length in space or time) long¹(1). **2** not having enough or not having the correct or normal number or amount (of s.t): *We can't start yet because our team is short of two men. I can't let you have any milk this morning because I'm two litres short myself.* **3** (often — *with s.o*) rude and unwilling to say more than a very little to s.o: *I tried to get the boss to tell me what was wrong but he was very short with me.* **4** (of a drink) of a kind that is usu drunk out of a small glass because it is strong and not mixed with water etc. Compare long(5). **5** (of the odd(s) for a bet(1)) likely to win so favourable to the person accepting a bet(1). ⇒ long(6). **6** (*technical*) (of a syllable in a word or poem etc) unstressed. Opposite long(7). **7** (of pastry) that breaks easily into small pieces. **8** (of a ball that is kicked or bowled²(3)) that hits the ground quite a long way from the target. **be short on s.t** not have as much of s.t as one should have: *Those children are rather short on good manners.* **for short** as a quick, easier way of saying or writing it: *His name is Christopher and we call him Chris for short.* **have a short memory** ⇒ memory. **in short** saying or writing it in one word, very few words:

'The weather was wet, cold and cloudy and – in short, terrible!' **in short supply** ⇒ supply²(n). **little/nothing short of s.t** almost/completely s.t: *The way she sings without ever having had any training is little short of* miraculous. **make short work of s.o/s.t** ⇒ work(n). **short and/but sweet** (*informal*) finished in a pleasantly short time. **short of s.t (a)** ⇒ short(2). **(b)** not having reached a place (that one was moving towards or hoping to reach): *We stopped the car a few hundred metres short of the village. We managed to stop the car just short of a ditch.*

▷ *adv* **9** in a sudden way: *He* stopped me short *in the middle of a sentence before I told his secret. Peter stopped short when he saw her.* **be caught/taken short** (*informal*) have a sudden urgent need to go to the lavatory. **cut s.o/s.t short** stop s.o doing or saying s.t; stop doing s.t, usu suddenly: *When he continued talking she tried to cut him short. I had to cut short my holiday as my mother was ill.* **fall short (of s.t)** not reach (s.t) that one was expecting or hoping to reach. **go , run etc short (of s.t)** not have enough of s.t. **sell (s.o/s.t) short** give (s.o) less (of s.t) than the correct amount that has been paid for: *It wasn't till I got home and weighed the apples that I found I had been sold short.* **stop (s.o/s.t) short** (cause s.o/s.t to) stop suddenly. **stop short of (doing) s.t** not go quite as far as (to do) s.t, usu s.t dangerous or wrong: *He is sometimes very nasty to the children but he stops short of hitting them.* **be taken short** ⇒ be caught/taken short.

▷ *c.n* **10** short(4) drink. **11 =** short circuit. **12** short(1) film shown before the main film in a cinema. **the long and the short of it** ⇒ long(n).

▷ *tr/intr.v* **13** (cause (s.t) to) have a short circuit.

'shortage *c/u.n* (often — *of s.t*) state of there not being enough (of s.t): *a shortage of staff*; *no shortage of food.*

'short,bread *u.n* kind of thick biscuit made of flour, sugar and butter.

'short,cake *u.n* large kind of shortbread.

,short 'change *u.n* not enough change(5) given to s.o when he/she has paid for s.t.

,short-'change *tr.v* give (s.o) short change.

,short 'circuit *c.n* fault in an electric connection that causes a fuse(1) to cut the electricity off.

,short-'circuit *v* **1** *tr/intr.v* (cause (s.t) to) have a short circuit. **2** *tr.v* (*fig*) avoid (the officials etc one is supposed to go to): *Jane managed to short-circuit the management and arrange a meeting of the workers during the lunch break.*

'short,comings *pl.n* things that are wrong about s.o/s.t: *I still love her in spite of her shortcomings.*

,short 'cut *c.n* (often *take a* —) way of getting from one place or situation to another in a shorter and/or quicker way than the usual one: *I took a short cut across the field.*

'shorten *tr/intr.v* (cause (s.t) to) become shorter(1). Opposite lengthen.

'shortening *n* **1** *c.n* act of making (s.t) shorter(1). **2** *u.n* fat mixed with flour etc while making pastry.

'short,fall *c.n* amount or number by which s.t is short(2) of what is expected, hoped for etc: *Her parents offered to make up her shortfall of £10 so she could pay for a ticket to Greece.*

'short,hand *u.n* (often *in* —) system of writing quickly by using signs or abbreviations instead of words. Compare longhand. **s.t is shorthand for s.t** s.t is a short way of saying s.t: *For some people, 'the greens' is shorthand for people or groups who care about the* environment.

,short'handed *adj* not having as many people to do the work as are really or normally needed. Opposite overmanned.

,short,hand 'typist *c.n* typist who can also do shorthand.

'shortie *c.n* ⇒ shorty.

'short ,list *c.n* (often *on the* — (*for s.t*)) final list of people chosen out of longer lists for consideration (for a job).

'short,list *tr.v* put (s.o) on the short list for s.t.

short-lived /ˌʃɔːt-'lɪvd/ *adj* that does not last long: *The good weather was short-lived.*

'shortly *adv* **1** soon: *We'll meet again shortly.* **2** using only a few words. **3** in a short(3) way. **4** (often — *after/before s.o/s.t*) a short distance or time (after/before s.o/s.t): *Peter arrived shortly after Sally.*

,short 'measure ⇒ measure(*n*).

'shortness *u.n.*

,short-'range *attrib.adj* of or referring to a short(1) length of time or distance only: *a short-range weather forecast*; *short-range* missiles(1).

,short 'rations ⇒ rations.

shorts *pl.n* short(1) trousers that finish at or above the knee.

,short 'shrift *u.n* (usu *get/give s.o* —) fact of not getting/giving enough care, attention etc: *When we are at our busiest, the cooking of meals gets short shrift.*

,short'sighted *adj* **1** (also **,near-'sighted**) not able to see clearly as far as people with normal eyesight can. ⇒ longsighted(1). **2** (*fig*) not thinking carefully about the future results of what is being done now: *It was shortsighted of Joe to leave school at 16 and without a job.* Opposite farsighted.

,short'sightedly *adv.*, **,short'sightedness** *u.n.*

,short 'story *c.n* (*pl -ies*) piece of fiction(1) writing that is much shorter than a novel¹.

,short-'tempered *adj* (*derog*) (of a person, animal) who/that easily becomes angry.

,short-'term *adj* of or referring to a short(1) length of time only, usu in the near future: *a short-term solution to the problem.*

,short 'time *u.n* **on short time** working fewer hours a day or week than usual: *When our factory has few orders, the workers have to be put on short time.*

,short 'wave *u.n* (**,short-'wave** when *attrib*) system for sending and receiving radio messages using waves that are less than 60 metres long. ⇒ long wave, medium wave, ultrahigh frequency, very high frequency.

,short-'winded *adj* who loses her/his breath easily when making an effort such as walking fast.

'shorty *c.n* (also **'shortie**) (*pl -ies*) (*informal*; *derog*) person who is short.

shot¹ /ʃɒt/ *n* **1** *c.n* thing fired from a gun, bow etc (at s.o/s.t): *His first shot missed but the second one hit me in the leg.* **2** *c.n* (often *have a* — (*at s.o/s.t*)) attempt to hit s.o/s.t with a shot¹(1). **3** *c.n* (often — *at s.t*) attempt to score a goal or point by kicking, hitting or throwing a ball (at a goal, net etc): *Her first shot at the goal missed but the second scored.* **4** *c.n* (often *have a* — (*at*

s.t)) (*informal*) attempt (to do s.t): *I've never used this kind of machine but I'll have a shot at it.* **5** *c.n* firing of a rocket(3), spacecraft etc. **6** *c.n* heavy metal ball used in shotput. **7** *u.n* small metal balls fired together from a shotgun or old-fashioned big gun. **8** *c.n* (often — *of s.o/ s.t*) photograph (of s.o/s.t). **9** *c.n* part of a cinema film taken by one camera at one time: *Did you see the shot of Helena swimming around the lake?* ⇒ take(1). **10** *c.n* (often — *of s.t*) (*informal*) injection (of s.t): *The doctor gave me a shot in the arm.* **11** *c.n* (often — *of s.t*) (*informal*) small drink (of s.t), esp that is swallowed all in one. **12** *c.n* gamble(2): *That horse is a 100 to 1 shot in the race* (i.e if you put £1 on it and it wins, you will win £100). ⇒ a long shot. **action shot** shot¹(9) in which there is (a lot of) movement. **a long shot** guess, suggestion etc with only a little chance of success: *It's a long shot but you may find it in the garage.* **a shot in the arm** (*fig*; *informal*) a thing that gives one new strength, courage, hope etc: *The arrival of a few experienced builders was a shot in the arm for our company.* **a shot in the dark** a guess made with little or no information. **big shot** ⇒ big. **crack shot** ⇒ crack(1). **like a shot** (*informal*) very quickly, willingly or without waiting a moment. **not by a long shot** not at all: *You haven't won by a long shot.* **penalty shot** ⇒ penalty(2). **put the shot** try to throw a shot(6) further than others. ⇒ shotput.

'shot,gun *c.n* gun that one holds to one's shoulder for firing and which fires shot(7) from one barrel, or more usu two, one after the other. ⇒ sawn-off shotgun (⇒ saw²).

'shot,put *def.n* kind of sport in which one has to throw the shot(6) as far as one can.

shot² /ʃɒt/ *p.t,p.p* of shoot.

shot³ /ʃɒt/ *adj* mixed in colour because of being woven in two different colours, one going along the cloth and the other across it, so that the colour of the cloth changes as one looks at it from different angles: *Ann's new dress is made of shot silk – red shot with yellow.* **be/get shot of s.o/s.t** (*informal*) be/get rid of s.o/s.t.

should (strong form /ʃʊd/, weak form /ʃəd/) *aux.v* (no *pres.p*; negative forms **should not** or **shouldn't** /'ʃʊdnt/; should have can be **should've** /'ʃʊdəv/; 'should' is followed by the infinitive of a verb without *to*) **1** *p.t* of 'shall' in reported speech: *He asked whether he should stay or go home* (direct speech: '*Shall I stay or go home?*'). **2** (*formal*) (used instead of would(2) after 'I' and 'we' in the main clauses of conditional sentences): *If he came tomorrow, I should ask him for the book he borrowed. I should have been as frightened as you if the man had attacked me too.* **3** (used in conditional clauses to show that s.t is not probable): *Should it rain tomorrow the picnic will not be held.* **4** (used after certain verbs and adjectives in clauses beginning, that could begin, with 'that'): *I proposed (that) we should all go together. I am eager that nothing should go wrong this time.* **5** ought(1) to, be s.o's duty to, be necessary for s.o to, (do s.t): *You should always be kind to the sick. You shouldn't worry so much about your examinations; you're sure to pass.* **6** ought(2) to, am/are/is likely to, will probably, (do s.t): *This should be the house we were told about; it has a red door.* **7** should(5) not; does/not need to: *So her boyfriend has left her, has he? She should worry! He was useless!* **I should think (that) . . .; I should think so; I should have thought (that) . . .; I should have thought so** I think it is probable *(that . . .): I should think you would pass the examination easily. 'Is Mary likely to be there?' – 'I should have thought so.'* **I should think not/so** Certainly (not)! Of course (not)!: *'Shall I help Mother with the washing up?' 'I should think so!'* **who**, **what**, **where** *etc* **should . . . but . . .** (showing a person's surprise at s.t): *Then who should come round the corner but a man I hadn't seen for ten years! Then what should happen but (that) he slipped and fell into my arms!*

shoulder /'ʃəʊldə/ *c.n* **1** part of the body between the neck and the outside of the top of the arm. **2** part of a coat etc that covers a shoulder(1): *The shoulder's torn.* **3** (often — *of s.t*) upper part of the front leg (of a lamb(2) etc) used as meat. **4** thing that is shaped like a shoulder(1): *the shoulder of a mountain.* **5** side of a road, motorway etc beyond the edge of the part normally used for driving on. ⇨ hard shoulder. Compare verge(1). **get, give s.o, the cold shoulder** ⇨ cold(*adj*). **head and shoulders above s.o** ⇨ head(*n*). **put one's shoulder to the wheel** (*fig*) start working (hard). **shoulder to shoulder (a)** (*fig*) in a united way: *If we stand shoulder to shoulder over this business we are sure to win.* **(straight) from the shoulder** without trying to hide anything or to make anything seem less bad etc than it really is: *I like Harry because he speaks straight from the shoulder and one knows what he is thinking.*
▷ *tr.v* **6** put (s.o/s.t) on one's shoulder(s)(1) in order to carry her/him/it. **7** (*fig*) accept or take on (a job, duty etc): *Do you think Helen is old enough to shoulder so much responsibility?* **8** use one's shoulders to push so that one can get through (a crowd), past (s.o) etc: *She shouldered the crowd aside as she pushed her way to the front.* **shoulder arms** (in the British armed forces) hold one's gun vertically against one's right side with one's hand about half way down the gun.

'shoulder ˌblade *c.n* = scapula.

'shoulders *pl.n* top part of one's back, including both shoulders(1) and the part between them: *He was carrying his son on his shoulders so that he could see over the heads of the crowd.* **have broad shoulders** (*fig*) be able to take a lot of responsibility etc. **rub shoulders with s.o** (*fig*) meet s.o socially and informally.

'shoulder ˌstrap *c.n* strip of cloth etc for putting over a shoulder(1) to hold up a dress etc.

shouldn't /'ʃʊdnt/ = should not. ⇨ should.

shouldst /ʃʊdst/ (*old use*) = should.

shout /ʃaʊt/ *c.n* **1** loud sound when one is calling s.o or saying s.t to s.o who is a long way away or when one is angry, excited etc: *We heard shouts coming from the back of the house and found people fighting there.*
▷ *v* **2** *tr/intr.v* give a shout(1); (also **shout s.t out**) say (s.t) in a very loud voice: *She shouted out my name.* **shout s.o down** stop s.o speaking (any more) by shouting so that he/she cannot be heard. **shout for s.o/s.t** shout for s.o to come, to get s.t: *Shout for Ben; he's wanted on the telephone. We're locked in; shout for help.*

shout oneself hoarse ⇨ hoarse. **shout (s.t) out** = shout(2).

'shouting *attrib.adj* **1 within shouting distance (of s.o/s.t)** so near (s.o/s.t) that one can be heard by her/him or from there, if one shouts.
▷ *u.n* **2 all over bar the shouting** (of a result of a game, election etc) decided and clear although there is still a little time left: *When Joe scored a goal a minute before the end of the match it was all over bar the shouting.*

shove /ʃʌv/ *c.n* **1** (often *give s.o/s.t a* —) (*informal*) push: *He gave the queue(1) a little shove to make more space.*
▷ *v* **2** *tr/intr.v* (*informal*) push (s.o/s.t), often in an unpleasant way: *Don't shove! There's plenty of time to get on to the train. Everybody was pushing and shoving so we got the children out of the crowd for safety.* **shove s.o around (a)** = shove(2). **(b)** (*fig*) make s.o do things that he/she does not want to do. **shove off (a)** (often — *off from s.t*) push against s.t so that one's boat moves away (from it): *We got down into the boat and shoved off from the shore.* **(b)** (usu as an order) (*informal*) go away; leave: *Tell those children to shove off; they're being a nuisance.* **shove over** (usu as an order) (*informal*) move to one side, usu to allow s.o else to sit down too.

shovel /'ʃʌvl/ *c.n* **1** kind of spade used for moving things from one place to another rather than for digging. **2** thing shaped like a shovel(1) on a bulldozer etc. **3** (also **'shovelful**) as much as a shovel(1,2) holds.
▷ *tr/intr.v* (*-ll-*, US *-l-*) **4** use a shovel(1,2) (to move (s.t) (away etc)).

'shovelful *c.n* = shovel(3).

show /ʃəʊ/ *n* **1** *c.n* (often — *of s.t*) act of making (s.t) be seen, looked at; display(2) (of s.t): *His show of anger was enough to stop the children's noise.* **2** *sing.n* (usu — *of s.t*) pretence (of s.t): *Her show of politeness did not last long and it was soon clear that she wanted us to leave.* **3** *u.n* fact or act of trying to seem very important or beautiful etc: *Don't think he's really successful; all this is just empty show.* **4** *c.n* public exhibition(1) of s.t so that people can come and see it: *There is a big boat show in London every winter.* **5** *c.n* play, performance etc in a theatre etc: *What time does the show begin this evening?* **6** *sing.n* (often *the whole* —) (*informal*) business/work: *I'm running the show now so just do as I tell you.* **floor show** ⇨ floor(*n*). **give the game/show away** ⇨ game(*n*). **Good show!** (*informal*) (way of congratulating s.o or of showing that one is pleased about s.t). **make a show of s.t** pretend to be or do s.t: *He always makes a show of helping with the cooking but really he does nothing.* **on show** being shown(12); in a place where people can see it: *We very seldom have our best silver on show because we are afraid of thieves.* **put on a (good etc) show (for s.o)** try to look good, successful for s.o. **put up a good etc show** try hard and do well in s.t: *He isn't a very good player but he always puts up a good show when his parents come to watch a match.* **a show of hands** an act of putting up of hands to vote: *After the discussion the chairman asked for a show of hands and the motion was defeated.* **steal the show (from s.o)** ⇨ steal.
▷ *v* (*p.t* showed, *p.p* shown /ʃəʊn/) **7** *tr.v* try to get

a person, animal to look at (s.o/s.t); allow a person, animal to do this: *Show me your hands. 'I've found a pretty butterfly.' 'Oh, do show me* (or *show it to me*)!' **8** *intr.v* be able to be seen: *Your* petticoat *is showing. 'Can you still see where I spilt tea on my trousers?' 'No, it doesn't show any more.' The moon is beginning to show through the clouds.* **9** *tr.v* (of an instrument that measures s.t) display (the time, temperature etc); cause (the information being recorded) to show(8): *That clock shows 5.15 but my watch says 5.05.* **10** *tr.v* allow (s.t) to be seen, noticed (sometimes s.t that one would like to hide): *Her answers to the questions showed that she had learnt the subject well. His nervousness was shown by the way he kept on dropping things. White is not a good colour for children because it shows the dirt so easily.* **11** *tr/ intr.v* (often — s.o what, where, how etc to do s.t) teach (s.o) (s.t, what etc . . .) by doing it oneself or by drawing a map etc: *This map shows the way to* (or *how to get to*) *the station from here. Could you please show me what to do next?* **12** *tr.v* (of a cinema, theatre, public exhibition(1) etc) offer (s.t) for people to come and see: *What's, What film is, showing tonight?* **13** *tr.v* (*literary*) behave with s.t (towards s.o): *When he has any power he shows no mercy to those under him.* **14** *intr.v* (*slang*) appear; come to the place one is supposed to come to: *Whenever a big plane leaves there are always several passengers who have booked on it but not shown.* ⇨ show up(a).

be showing (at a cinema) ⇨ show(12).

have nothing etc **to show for s.t** have done s.t but without any result that can be seen: *We worked hard for a week but had little to show for our efforts at the end of it all.*

it (all) goes to show (that) s.t . . . (*informal*) that is proof of the fact (that . . .): *Mary has done very well in her examinations, which all goes to show that hard work pays after all.*

show s.o (a)round/over (s.t) go with s.o to show her/him all the parts of s.t: *This castle is open to the public and there are guides to show people around.*

show one's face (s.w) ⇨ face(*n*).

show one's hand ⇨ hand(*n*).

show s.o in, **out**, **up** etc help s.o to find the way in etc by showing it to her/him.

show (s.o/s.t) off (to s.o) behave proudly by showing what one or s.o/s.t else, can do etc: *Don't pay any attention to the children; they're just showing off. Peter's mother likes showing him off to other parents.* ⇨ show-off.

show s.o over/round (s.t) ⇨ show s.o (a)round/ over (s.t).

show signs of s.t allow it to be seen that one/ it has s.t: *Peter is showing signs of old age at last. This table is showing signs of wear.*

show through (s.t) be able to be seen through (s.t): *That dress is so thin that one's underclothing shows through.*

show s.o to s.t go with s.o to show her/him where s.t is: *I'll show you to your room, seat, Mr Lee's office, the lavatory.*

show up appear; come when one is (not) expected. **show (s.t) up** (allow s.t to) be seen clearly: *This carpet shows up the dirt so badly. Dirt shows up terribly on this white dress.* ⇨ show(8).

show s.o/s.t up let people see the bad things

about s.o/s.t: *Peter claimed to be a film-star but when his brothers arrived they soon showed him up to be a liar.*

show biz /'ʃəu ˌbiz/ *u.n abbr* (*informal*) show business.

'show ˌbusiness *u.n* business of entertaining people with films, plays etc.

'show ˌcase *c.n* case²(1) in which things are on show.

'show,down *c.n* (usu have a — (with s.o)) (*informal*) ending of a disagreement etc (with s.o) by arguing it out (with her/him) to the end.

'show,girl *c.n* girl or woman who is in the chorus(1) in a musical show.

'showily *adv* in a showy way.

'showiness *u.n* fact or state of being showy.

'showing *n* **1** *c.n* (often — of s.t) act or fact of showing (⇨ show(7)) s.t. **2** *sing.n* standard reached in performing s.t: *After our team's poor showing in the match, they began to train more seriously.* **on any showing** in whatever way one may judge her/him/it: *It has been a very good summer for tourists on any showing.* **on s.o's showing** judging her/him/it according to what s.o says: *The winter was a very good one for farmers even on their own showing — and they usually try to pretend that they are poor!*

'show ˌjumper *c.n* rider or horse who/that takes part in jumping competitions at shows(4).

'show ˌjumping *u.n* jumping competitions at horse shows(4).

'showman *c.n* (*pl* -men) **1** person whose job is to produce shows(4). **2** person who behaves in a showy way to try to impress(2) people: *A lot of people come to Joe's restaurant not because the food is good but because Joe is a good showman.*

'showman,ship *u.n* quality or skill of a showman(2).

'show-,off *c.n* (*derog*) person who shows off.

'show,piece *c.n* building, piece of furniture etc that is so good that people should be encouraged to see it.

'show,place *c.n* place that is a showpiece.

'show,room *c.n* room in a big shop, office etc in which one can look at things that may be sold there or bought somewhere else.

'showy *adj* (-ier, -iest) (*derog*) full of show(3).

shower /'ʃauə/ *c.n* **1** (often *a* — of s.t) fall (of rain or snow) that does not last long. **2** (often *a* — of s.t) fall (of usu small things or drops of liquid): *The politician ran under a shower of rotten eggs and tomatoes.* **3** (often *a* — of s.t) large number or amount (of s.t) all coming at the same time: *The actor left the stage amid a shower of praise.* **4** device that produces many fast streams of water, used for washing oneself under. **5** (usu have/take a —) wash under a shower(4). **6** (*derog*; *informal*) group of unpleasant people: *Look at those people! What a shower!*

▷ *v* **7** *intr.v* (also — *down*) come down in showers(1–3): *It's showering (down).* **8** *tr.v* (often — s.t on s.o; — s.o/s.t with s.t) pour (s.t) on s.o/s.t, pour s.t on (s.o/s.t), in showers(2,3); give (s.o/ s.t s.t) in large quantities: *She always showers her grandchildren with presents when she visits.* **9** *intr.v* have a shower(5): *She's showering.*

'showery *adj* bringing/having showers(1) of rain: *showery weather.*

showgirl, showily, showiness, showing, showman(ship), show-off, showpiece, showplace, showroom, showy ⇒ show.

shrank /ʃræŋk/ *p.t* of shrink.

shrapnel /'ʃræpnəl/ *u.n* pieces of metal that come from a shell(4) or bomb when it explodes.

shred /ʃred/ *c.n* (often — *of s.t*) **1** small strip (of s.t) after it has been torn or roughly cut off a bigger piece: *shreds of cloth from an old shirt that has been torn up.* **2** (usu negative) (*fig*) very small piece: *There isn't a shred of truth in the story.*
▷ *tr.v* (-dd-) **3** tear, cut etc (s.t) into shreds(1).
'shredder *c.n* **1** tool for shredding(3) vegetables etc. **2** machine for shredding(3) papers, usu secret ones that are no longer needed but that one does not want other people to be able to read.

shrew /ʃru:/ *c.n* **1** very small kind of animal that looks like a mouse with a very long nose. **2** (*derog*) unpleasant woman who scolds a lot.
'shrewish *adj* (*derog*) like a shrew(2).
'shrewishly *adv.* **'shrewishness** *u.n.*

shrewd /ʃru:d/ *adj* **1** clever at deciding what will be to one's best advantage. **2** cleverly worked out: *a shrewd guess.*
'shrewdly *adv.* **'shrewdness** *u.n.*

shriek /ʃri:k/ *c.n* **1** scream: *shrieks of laughter.*
▷ *v* **2** *intr.v* (often — *with s.t*) give one or more screams (because of s.t): *They shrieked with laughter whenever the old man spoke.* **3** *tr.v* say (s.t) in a shrieking(2) voice: *'Stop!' she shrieked.*

shrift /ʃrɪft/ *u.n* **short shrift** ⇒ short.

shrill /ʃrɪl/ *adj* **1** (of a sound, voice etc) unpleasantly high and piercing. **2** (of a way of complaining, attacking s.o/s.t in words etc) going on and on in an unpleasant way.
'shrillness *u.n.* **'shrilly** *adv.*

shrimp /ʃrɪmp/ *c.n* (also *attrib*) kind of small creature like a prawn but smaller that lives in the sea and is eaten for food: *a shrimp cocktail(2).*

shrine /ʃraɪn/ *c.n* **1** box in which a part or parts of the dead body of a holy person is/are kept. **2** place that is sacred to the memory of s.o/s.t and where people go to show respect to her/ him/it or to pray etc.

shrink /ʃrɪŋk/ *v* (*p.t* shrank /ʃræŋk/, *p.p* shrunk /ʃrʌŋk/) *tr/intr.v* (cause (s.t) to) become smaller by heating it, putting it in water etc: *Don't wash that dress or it will shrink; send it to the dry-cleaner's.* **shrink away/back** (**from s.o/s.t**), **shrink from s.t** (often *fig*) move away (from s.o/ s.t), usu because of fear, disgust etc; be afraid (to do s.t); not do s.t because of fear.
shrinkage /'ʃrɪŋkɪdʒ/ *u.n* act, fact or amount of shrinking(1): *allow for some shrinkage of this material.*
shrunken /'ʃrʌŋkən/ *adj* that has (been) shrunk (⇒ shrink(1)): *shrunken cloth; a shrunken old man.*

shrivel /'ʃrɪvl/ *tr/intr.v* (-ll-, US -l-) (often — (*s.o/ s.t*) *up*) (cause (s.o/s.t) to) become smaller, usu by drying and becoming wrinkled(2).

shroud /ʃraʊd/ *c.n* **1** cloth that is put over a dead body. **2** (usu *a* — *of s.t*) (*fig*) thing that hides s.t (in s.t): *There's a shroud of secrecy around the factory's new product.* **3** one of a pair of ropes that help to support a ship's mast.
▷ *tr.v* **4** (usu — *s.o/s.t in s.t*) cover (s.o/s.t) with a shroud(1,2) (of s.t) in order to hide her/him/

it: *The tops of the mountains are nearly always shrouded in cloud. His disappearance is shrouded in mystery.* ⇒ enshroud.

shrub /ʃrʌb/ *c.n* small bush that has more than one stem.
shrubbery /'ʃrʌbərɪ/ *c/u.n* (*pl -ies*) shrubs growing in the same area, e.g in a garden.

shrug /ʃrʌg/ *c.n* **1** (usu *a* — *of one's shoulders*) example of shrugging(2).
▷ *tr/intr.v* (-gg-) **2** raise (one's shoulders), usu to show that one doesn't know s.t or doesn't care about it: *When I asked him what to do about the car he just shrugged (his shoulders) and said nothing.* **shrug s.t off** not worry or care about s.t: *You must learn to shrug off remarks like his and not let them affect you.*

shrunk /ʃrʌŋk/ *p.p* of shrink.

shrunken /'ʃrʌŋkən/ ⇒ shrink.

shudder /'ʃʌdə/ *c.n* **1** (often — *of s.t*) act of shaking one's body (caused by fear, disgust etc).
▷ *intr.v* **2** (often — *with s.t*) shake (because of fear, disgust etc): *shudder (with* horror) *at the thought of what might have happened.* Compare shiver, tremble(2).

shuffle /'ʃʌfl/ *n* **1** *c.n* (often *give s.t a* —) act of mixing playing cards in one's hands so that no one knows what order they are in. **2** *sing.n* way of walking by moving one's feet slowly and dragging them along on the ground.
▷ *v* **3** *tr/intr.v* give (playing cards) a shuffle(1): *Have you shuffled (the cards)?* **4** *tr.v* (usu — *s.t about*) move (s.t) from one place to another, usu in a random(1) way: *Some people think that civil servants spend all their time shuffling papers about to look busy.* **5** *tr/intr.v* move (one's feet) in a shuffle(2): *Don't shuffle (your feet)! Lift them up as you walk!*
'shuffler *c.n* person who shuffles(3,5).

shun /ʃʌn/ *tr.v* (-nn-) avoid (s.o/s.t).

shunt /ʃʌnt/ *v* **1** *tr/intr.v* (cause (a train or part of one) to) move from one line to another by using points(10). **2** *tr.v* (often — *s.o/s.t from s.o/s.t to s.o/s.t*) (*fig*) move (s.o/s.t) (to another position, job etc, usu one that is not better or more helpful than the one before): *I'm tired of being shunted from one department to another.*
'shunter *c.n* person or railway engine who/that shunts(1) trains.

shush /ʃʊʃ/ *interj* **1** be quiet; shut up.
▷ *v* **2** *tr.v* (often — *s.o up*) tell (s.o) to be quiet; say 'Sh' or 'Shush(1)' to (s.o). **3** *intr.v* (usu as an order) be quiet; stop talking etc.

shut /ʃʌt/ *v* (-tt-, *p.t,p.p* shut) **1** *tr/intr.v* move (s.t) into a position where there is no longer an opening left; close (s.t): *Will you please shut the door to keep the kitchen smells out. Her eyes were tired so she shut them for a minute.* Opposite open(12). **2** *tr.v* stop (oneself/s.o/s.t) getting out (of s.t), being troubled etc, by shutting(1) s.t: *When I want to write I shut myself away in a small room at the top of the house. Shall I let the dog out? He's been shut in for several hours. My house is shut off from the noise of the traffic by a high wall. Let's go out tonight; I've been shut up in the house all day.* **3** *tr/intr.v* (often — (s.t) *down/up*) (cause (a shop, factory etc) to) stop work for the night, weekend etc or permanently: *Our shop shuts at 5.30. The factory had to shut down because it wasn't getting any new orders.* **shut one's eyes**

to s.t ⇒ eye(*n*). **shut s.o/s.t out** (*of s.t*) not allow s.o/s.t to enter s.t. **shut (s.o) up** (a) (*slang*) (cause s.o to) stop talking. (b) ⇒ shut(2). **shut up** (**shop**) stop work (and prepare one's place of work for the night, weekend etc when one will not be there).

'shut,down *c.n* stopping of work because of holidays, a strike(1) etc.

'shut-,eye *u.n* (*informal*) sleep: *I need a bit of shut-eye before we go out tonight.*

shutter /'ʃʌtl/ *c.n* **1** thing like a door made of wood or metal that is hinged to each/one side of a window and can be shut to protect it from wind, sun etc or to keep out thieves. **2** device on a camera that opens to allow light in to photograph s.t on the film. **put up the shutters** (*informal*) close the shop etc for the night etc.
▷ *tr.v* **3** (often *fig*) shut (s.t) (as if) with shutters(1).

shuttle /'ʃʌtl/ *c.n* **1** instrument used for taking the threads of the weft through the warp(1) when weaving. **2** device on a sewing machine that holds the lower thread. **3** (also **'shuttle ,service**) regular bus, train, plane etc service from one place to another and then back again: *The next shuttle to Belfast leaves in ten minutes.* **4** = space shuttle. **5** = shuttlecock.
▷ *tr/intr.v* **6** (often — (s.o/s.t) *between s.t and s.t*) (cause (s.o/s.t) to) move from one place to another and then back again. **7** (cause (s.o) to) move from one place to another by a shuttle(3).

'shuttle,cock *c.n* small object like half a ball with feathers on top of it that one hits about in the game of badminton.

shy /ʃaɪ/ *adj* **1** (of a person, animal) who/that feels uncomfortable in her/his/its mind when with people she/he/it does not know well: *It is a good thing for small children to be shy with strangers.* **2** showing that a person/animal is shy(1): *a shy look.* **fight shy of s.o/s.t** try to avoid s.o/s.t.
▷ *intr.v* (-*ies*, -*ied*) **3** (often — *at s.o/s.t*) (usu of a horse) move suddenly, usu because of fear (of s.t): *My horse shied at the snake and I nearly fell off.* **4** (often — *away from, at, s.t*) (*fig*) avoid (doing) s.t because one does not like it: *Very few people come into Pam's new shop because they shy at the high prices.*

-,shy *adj* avoiding or trying to avoid the thing shown in the first part of the word: *workshy.*

'shyly *adv.* **'shyness** *u.n.*

Siamese cat /ˌsaɪəmiːz 'kæt/ *c.n* kind of cat that has short pale hair, blue eyes and a loud cry.

Siamese twin /ˌsaɪəmiːz 'twɪn/ *c.n* twin(2) joined to her/his sister/brother at birth.

sibilant /'sɪbɪlənt/ *adj* **1** (*technical*) hissing(1) or made in a hissing(1) way: *In English, /s/, /z/, /ʃ/ and /ʒ/ are sibilant sounds.*
▷ *c.n* **2** (*technical*) sibilant(1) sound.

sick /sɪk/ *adj* **1** ill; not well in one's health; having a disease: *feel/be sick; a sick child/animal/plant.* Compare healthy(1). **2** (usu *pred*) (caused by) being or wanting to be sick(b): *I feel sick. I'm going to be sick.* **3** (often *be* — *at* (doing) *s.t*) very sad, sorry or upset(1) (because of (doing) s.t): *She was quite sick at the sight of so much damage to her beautiful house.* **4** (of things said, written, drawn etc) unpleasantly nasty, cruel etc; morbid: *a sick joke; a person who has a sick mind.* **be sick** (a) ⇒ sick(1). (b) bring up what is in one's

stomach; vomit(3). **be worried sick** ⇒ worry(*v*). **feel sick** (a) ⇒ sick(1,3). (b) feel that one wants to or is going to be sick(b). **sick for s.o/s.t** wanting s.o/s.t so much that it makes one feel ill. **go sick** leave one's work because one says one) is ill. **look sick** (a) ⇒ sick(1–3). (b) (*informal*) seem inferior(1) by comparison: *Helen is so good at mathematics that she makes the rest of the class look quite sick.* **make s.o sick** (a) ⇒ sick(1–3). (b) (*informal*) make s.o angry, jealous etc: *Look at the way that small boy plays the piano! It makes me sick!* **sick and tired of s.o,** (**doing**) **s.t** bored or angry because one has had too much of s.o or of (doing) s.t: *I'm sick and tired of you, your complaints.* **report sick** go to the doctor etc to say that one is ill. **be/feel sick to one's stomach** (*informal*) (a) be/feel very sick(3). (b) feel that one is going to be sick(b). **sick at heart** ⇒ heart(*n*). **sick to death of s.o/s.t** ⇒ death.
▷ *def.pl.n* **5** people who are ill: *The old and the sick were taken off the boat first.*
▷ *tr.v* **6 sick s.t up** bring s.t up out of one's stomach when one is being sick (⇒ be sick(b)).

-sick *adj* feeling sick because of the movement caused by the vehicle one is travelling in or the kind of travel which is shown in the first part of the word: *airsick; carsick; seasick.*

'sick,bay *c.n* place in a school, ship, factory etc in which sick(1) people can lie in bed and be looked after.

'sick,bed *c.n* (often *on one's* —) bed in which a person is lying ill.

'sicken *v* **1** *tr.v* (often — *s.o of s.t*) cause (s.o) to feel sick(3) (about s.t). **2** *intr.v* (usu — *for s.t*) begin to feel ill (with a certain disease): *I think Joan is sickening for measles.* **sicken of s.t** begin to be bored, tired etc of s.t.

'sickening *adj* that sickens(1) s.o.

'sick ,leave *u.n* (usu *on* —) leave¹(2) given or allowed a person while he/she is ill: *She's on (or gone on) sick leave.*

'sick ,list *c.n* (often *on the* —) list of people who are ill: *Who's on the sick list today?*

'sickly *adj* (-*ier*, -*iest*) **1** often ill; likely to be ill: *a sickly child.* **2** (*derog*) making one feel sick(1–3): *a sickly smell.* **3** (*derog*) looking unpleasantly pale, weak etc: *The room was painted a sickly green.* **4** (*derog*) false: *a sickly smile.*

'sickly-,looking *adj* who/that looks sickly.

'sickness *u.n* **1** state or fact of being ill. Opposite health(1). **2** disease; illness. **3** feeling of wanting to be sick(b).

-sickness *u.n* state or fact of being -sick: *airsickness.*

'sickness ,benefit *u.n* money paid to s.o under an insurance plan, usu one run by the government, while he/she is too ill to work.

'sick ,pay *u.n* money paid to s.o while he/she is away from work because of illness.

sickle /'sɪkl/ *c.n* kind of short tool with a curved blade, used for cutting grass, corn etc. Compare scythe(1).

side /saɪd/ *attrib.adj* **1** that is at, from etc, one of the (vertical) surfaces of s.t but not the top or bottom or the front or back: *the side entrance to the house; a side view of her face.* ⇒ side(5,6). **2** less important: *a side issue.*
▷ *c.n* **3** one of the lines that are at the edges of a surface: *A square has four sides.* **4** one of the

surfaces of s.t: *A cube(1) has six sides.* **5** one of the (vertical) surfaces of s.t but not the top or bottom: *The four sides of the box are all painted red but the top and bottom are green.* **6** (as 5 but not at the front, back or ends): *The front and back of the house are white but the two sides are grey. The sides of the box are blue but the ends are black.* **7** one of the two surfaces of s.t, e.g a piece of paper, that has a front and a back: *In an examination one usually has to write on one side of the paper only.* **8** part of the body that is on the left or right half, esp the part that is between the armpit (⇒ arm¹) and the hip¹ of a person or the front leg and the back leg of an animal: *I have a pain in my left side. He lay on his side reading a book. I want to buy a whole side of* lamb(2), *please.* **9** (often (*on*) *the left/ right — of* s.t) part (of s.t) that is either at the left or at the right when one looks at it: *We keep our accounts in this book; on the left is the* credit(2) *side and on the right the* debit(1) *side. Don't walk in the middle of the road; keep to the side!* **10** place near the side(8,9) of s.o/s.t: *The dog always stayed at its master's side. The policeman didn't leave my side during the whole time I was there.* **11** one of the ways of looking at or thinking about s.t: *We examined the question from all sides before deciding what to do.* **12** team: *our football side.* **change sides** go from one side(11) to another, esp in an argument, a war etc. **err on the side of s.t** ⇒ err. **from side to side** ⇒ from. **get on the right/wrong side of s.o** become s.o's friend/ enemy. **hold/split one's sides** (**laughing**) (*fig*) laugh very much. **on the high**, **low** etc **side** rather high, low etc: *My mother isn't fat; in fact she's rather on the thin side.* (**on/through**) **one's father's/mother's side** (inheriting s.t) from one's father/mother and his/her ancestors. **on s.o's side** supporting s.o's position in a fight, argument etc: *Whose side are you on?* **look on the bright side** consider the fortunate or good results of a disadvantage (e.g it could have been worse). **on the right/wrong side of 40** etc less/ more than 40 etc years old. **on the side** besides or as well as the main thing, sometimes in a dishonest way: *Fred is a postman but he is also a house painter on the side.* **put s.t on/to one side** not use, think of etc s.t now but keep it for possible later use, consideration etc. **right/ wrong side out** with the correct/wrong side outside: *You're trying to put that shirt on wrong side out.* **side by side** (**with s.o/s.t**) beside (s.o/ s.t or each other): *Our two boats were side by side in the water.* **split one's sides** (**laughing**) ⇒ hold/ split one's sides (laughing). **take sides** support the side(11) one agrees with. **take sides against/with s.o** support the opposite/same side(11) (to/as s.o). **this side of s.t** (**a**) (on) the side(10) of s.t that is nearest one: *We live this side of the town.* (**b**) before a time or an event: *I'm afraid my report won't be ready this side of Christmas.* **this side up** (sign on a box etc that is being sent by train etc, to show which side(4) should be kept at the top). (**to be**) **on the safe side** ⇒ safe(*adj*).

▷ *intr.v* **13 side with s.o** (**against s.o**) support s.o's side(11) (against s.o else's).

'**side,board** *c.n* low kind of cupboard in a dining room for keeping plates, glasses etc in and for putting things on the top of.

'**side,boards**, '**side,burns** *pl.n* (*informal*) = sidewhiskers.

'**side,car** *c.n* small vehicle for a passenger that is fixed to the side of a motorbike and has one wheel only.

-sided *adj* having the number or kind of sides shown in the first part of the word: *three-sided*; *flat-sided*; *an open-sided lorry.*

'**side ,dish** *c.n* food that is not the main part of a course but is an addition to it: *Usually when one serves meat or fish one also has potatoes and other vegetables as side dishes.*

'**side ef,fect** *c.n* result (of doing or using s.t) that is not the one intended but that happens in addition to that: *The medicine was taken off the market because of its dangerous side effects.*

'**side ,issue** *c.n* subject that is not the main one and is therefore not so important.

'**side,kick** *c.n* (*derog*; *informal*) person who is less important than the one he/she is with.

'**side,light** *n* **1** *c.n* one of the small lights on a car etc that are less strong than the headlights: *If you park here at night, you must leave your sidelights on.* **2** *u.n* light coming from the side(6), not from in front: *The artist opened a curtain to give him some sidelight.*

'**side,line** *c.n* **1** line at the side(9) of a football etc field within which one can play the ball. **2** thing one does in addition to one's main job or activity: *Sue is an actress and she plays the piano as a sideline.* **on the sideline(s)** outside the limits of the football etc field, the area of activity etc: *The team manager sat on the sidelines watching the game. He waited on the sidelines hoping that she would get tired of the new job and return to him.*

'**side,long** *adj/adv* from one side(10): *He gave the girl a sidelong look as he passed.*

'**side ,plate** *c.n* usu small plate for bread etc that is often put at the side(10) of one's main plate at the table.

'**side,show** *c.n* small show at a fair²(2) etc in a separate place from the other or main shows.

'**side,splitting** *attrib.adj* that makes one laugh very much: *a sidesplitting performance.*

'**side,step** *tr/intr.v* (*-pp-*) **1** step to one side(9), e.g to avoid (danger). **2** (*fig*) avoid (s.t unpleasant etc).

'**side ,street** *c.n* (less important) street that goes off from the side(9) of a main street. Compare back street.

'**side,stroke** *u/def.n* **1** (often *do* (*the*) —) way of swimming during which one is lying on one's side(8).

▷ *adv* **2** in this way: *swim sidestroke.*

'**side,track** *c.n* **1** less important and irrelevant line of thought which takes one away from the main one.

▷ *tr.v* **2** take (s.o/s.t) away from the main line of thought into a different and irrelevant one.

'**side,walk** *c.n* (US) = pavement.

'**side,ways** *adj* **1** towards one side(10): *Before taking the box he gave some sideways* glances(1) *to see if anyone was looking.*

▷ *adv* **2** towards one side: *look sideways.*

'**side,whiskers** *pl.n* hair that grows on the sides of a man's face in front of his ears but does not go across his chin.

'**siding** *c.n* short railway track for a train to leave

the main track for a short time, often to leave carriages and trucks on until they are needed etc.

sidle /'saɪdl/ *intr.v* (usu — *up to s.o*) move close (to s.o) in a nervous or secretive way.

siege /siːdʒ/ *c.n* attempt by an army, navy etc to force a town, country etc to surrender(2) by surrounding it, preventing it from getting food etc and often attacking it. **lay siege to s.t** besiege(1) s.t. **raise a siege** (force an army etc to) stop besieging(1) s.t.

siesta /sɪ'estə/ *c.n* (often *have a* —) (*Spanish*) sleep during the day, usu after lunch in hot weather.

sieve /sɪv/ *c.n* **1** device made of wire or plastic with holes in it that lets through liquids but not solids, small bits of solid material but not bigger ones. **(have) a head/memory like a sieve** (*informal*) (have) a mind that does not remember things (easily). ▷ *tr.v* **2** (often — *s.t out*) put (s.t) through a sieve(1) (to remove (s.t)): *Once I've sieved out the lumps this soup will be very good.* ⇒ sift(1).

sift /sɪft/ *v* **1** *tr/intr.v* (usu — *s.t out* (*from s.t*)) sieve(2) (s.t) (to remove (s.t)) (from s.t). **2** *tr/intr.v* (usu — *through s.t*) go through (s.t) carefully, usu in order to try to find s.t in it: *Will you please sift through these letters and try to find one from Jones & Company.* **3** *intr.v* (of a substance made up of small pieces, e.g sand) get through one or more holes or narrow openings: *The sand sifted (through) into the water.*

'sifter *c.n* container with holes in the top, used for shaking sugar, salt, flour etc onto food etc.

sigh /saɪ/ *c.n* **1** act of breathing in deeply and letting one's breath come out of one's mouth in a way that can easily be heard, because one is tired, sad, pleased etc about s.t. **2** (of wind etc) noise like a sigh(1). **(give/heave) a sigh (of relief)** (give) a sigh(1) (showing relief²(1) about s.t): *We all heaved a sigh of relief when it was over.* ▷ *intr.v* **3** make a sigh(1). **4** (of wind etc) make a noise like a sigh(1). **sigh for s.o/s.t** (*literary*) feel sad in a sentimental way because one cannot have s.o/s.t one wants or used to have.

sight /saɪt/ *n* **1** *u.n* ability to see, which is one of the five senses. ⇒ eyesight, vision(1). **2** *u.n* area that can be seen (by s.o): *At last the boat came into sight (or came within sight of us) and we saw that it was flying a French flag. Don't let that girl out of your sight while I call the police.* **3** *c.n* act, fact, or example of seeing s.o/s.t: *I'm trying to get a sight of a rare bird that nests here.* **4** *sing.n* (*derog; informal*) person or thing who/ that looks silly, ugly etc: *Isn't Joe a sight in those red and blue trousers!* ⇒ sight¹(det). **5** *c.n* part (on the front/rear¹(2)) of a telescope, gun etc which one uses to help one in aiming it: *Get the front sight in line with the middle of the back sight before you fire.* **a damn/darn sight bigger, less ugly etc (than . . .)** (*informal*) much bigger, less ugly etc (than . . .). **at/on sight** as soon as he/ she/it is seen: *When dealing with such dangerous animals you may have to shoot on sight.* **at first sight** ⇒ first(det). **catch sight of s.o/s.t** (manage to) see s.o/s.t, usu only for a short time: *I caught sight of her getting onto the train.* ⇒ lose sight of s.o/s.t. **come within sight (of s.t)** get near

enough to see s.t and be seen. **have s.o/s.t in one's sights** (sometimes *fig*) be aiming at s.o/s.t; able to see s.o/s.t: *I had the bird in my sights but it seems to have flown away. Don't stop walking until you have the camp in your sights.* ⇒ sight(5), set one's sight on s.t. **know s.o by sight** recognize s.o when one sees her/ him without knowing her/his name or without having spoken to her/him. **look a sight** look ugly, absurd, silly etc. ⇒ sight(4). **lose sight of s.o/s.t** be no longer able to see s.o/s.t: *I lost sight of him when he disappeared into the crowd.* ⇒ catch sight of s.o/s.t. **on sight** ⇒ at/on sight. **set one's sights high** have big ambitions. **set one's sights on s.t** aim to do, get etc s.t: *I've set my sights on the manager's job when he retires.* **a sight for sore eyes** (*informal*) a person or thing that gives one pleasure to see. **sight unseen** (of s.t one buys, pays for etc) without seeing whether it is in good condition: *I signed for the goods sight unseen because I could not open them just then.* **test s.o's sight** (usu of an optician) give s.o tests to see whether he/she needs glasses, and if so, what kind. **within sight (of s.o/s.t)** near enough to be seen (by s.o, from s.t). ▷ *v* **6** *tr.v* manage to see (s.o/s.t), usu after some difficulty in finding her/him/it: *The escaped prisoner has been sighted several times during the past week but each time he has got away.*

'sighted *adj* able to see; not blind. Opposite sightless.

-,sighted *adj* having the kind of sight(1) or ability to understand things shown in the first part of the word: *longsighted; clear-sighted.*

'sighting (often — *of s.o/s.t*) example of sighting (⇒ sight(6)) (s.o/s.t): *There have been several sightings of a rare bird here recently.*

'sightless *adj* (*literary*) unable to see; blind: *sightless fish living in caves.* Opposite sighted.

'sightlessness *u.n*.

'sightliness *u.n* fact of being sightly.

'sightly *adj* (*-ier, -iest*) pleasing to look at. Opposite unsightly.

sight-read /'saɪt ˌriːd/ *tr/intr.v* (*p.t,p.p* sight-read /'saɪt ˌred/) play or sing (music) by reading it, not by hearing or practising it first.

sights /saɪts/ *def.pl.n* interesting places or things that tourists etc go to see: *We went to London to see the sights.* ⇒ sightsee, sightseer.

'sight,see *intr.v* see the sights.

'sight,seer *c.n* person who sightsees.

'sight,seeing *u.n* (often *go* —) seeing the sights.

sign /saɪn/ *c.n* **1** (often — *of s.t*; — *that . . .*) thing that shows (s.t, that . . .): *The falling of the leaves is a sign of autumn. Those clouds are signs that we are going to have a fine day.* **2** information in the form of words and/or pictures/symbols for any people who see it, e.g telling drivers to turn left or warning people that s.t is dangerous. **3** signal, movement of one's hand etc: *Don't do anything until you see my sign. When he puts his flag up that is the sign to get ready. Our sign that we are ready is a nod of the head.* **a sign of the times** a thing that is just what one would expect at this time: *It is a sign of the times that people buy animals and then find that they do not have enough money to feed them.* **(all) the signs are that . . .** everything seems to show that . . . . **road sign** ⇒ road. **show**

signs of s.t ⇒ show(*v*). **sign of life** (**a**) thing that shows s.o is alive: *After the earthquake rescuers were looking for any sign of life.* (**b**) (*informal*) thing that shows that s.o is there or not asleep: *I looked through the windows but there was no sign of life downstairs in the house.*

▷ *v* **4** *tr/intr.v* write one's name on (a cheque etc), in (a guest book etc) in a way that allows people to recognize that one has written it oneself: *sign here. I forgot to sign the cheque. Sign (your name) next to each cross, please.* **5** *intr.v* (often — *to s.o* (*to do s.t*)) give a sign(3) (to s.o to tell her/him to do s.t): *I signed to the children to be quiet while I was phoning.* **6** *tr.v* (usu — *s.o on/up*) give (s.o) a job and let her/him sign(4) to show that she/he accepts it: *The agent signed* (*up*) *three new singers last week.* **7** *intr.v* (usu — *on/up*; — *with s.o*) show that one accepts a job (with s.o) by signing(4) s.t: *I've signed on to work three days a week.* **8** *intr.v* use sign language. **sign s.t away** sign(4) a paper etc to show that one is giving s.t away: *If you sign that paper you will be signing away all your rights.* **sign for s.t** sign(4) to show that one has received s.t. **sign in/out** sign(4) to show that one has arrived, is leaving: *When you get to the office you have to sign in in this book and when you leave you have to sign out again.* **sign off** (**s.t**) (of a radio/television station, a performer etc) end (one's broadcasting, performance etc). **sign s.t over** (**to s.o**) sign(4) to show that one is giving s.t away to s.o.

signatory /'sɪgnɪtrɪ/ *c.n* (*pl -ies*) (often — *to s.t*) person who signs(4) or has signed(4) s.t.

signature /'sɪgnɪtʃə/ *c.n* name signed(4) in the usual way by a person. **witness s.o's signature** sign(4) to show that one has seen s.o else signing(4) s.t: *When you sign your will you must get two people to witness your signature or else the will is not valid(1).*

'signature ,tune *c.n* tune that is always played at the beginning and end of a particular radio/television programme or person's performance etc.

'sign ,language *u.n* system for exchanging information by signs(3) instead of by speaking or writing words, e.g one used by deaf people.

,sign of the 'zodiac *c.n* ⇒ zodiac.

'sign,post *c.n* sign(2) showing the direction(s) to a place or places and sometimes also the distance(s) to it/them.

'sign,posted *adj* marked by one or more signposts.

signal¹ /'sɪgnəl/ *c.n* **1** (also *attrib*) thing that gives information by its shape, colour, movement etc, and not in words: *That signal means 'Stop'. Railways would not be able to operate without signals.* **2** movement etc that shows s.t or that tells s.o to do s.t: *What's the signal for wanting to turn right?* **3** = traffic light. **4** picture(s), sound(s) etc sent by radio, television etc waves: *I'm getting a good signal now that I've tuned the radio in.* **a signal** (**for s.o**) **to do s.t** thing that causes s.t to happen: *The appearance of a politician on television is always a signal for us to change to another programme.*

▷ *v* (*-ll-*, US *-l-*) **5** *tr/intr.v* give/send (s.o) a signal¹(2) (to show that one wants s.t or that s.o should do s.t): *We signalled* (*to*) *the child to cross the road.* **6** *tr.v* be a sign of (s.t); mark (s.t):

Most people believe that his speech signals the beginning of a new political movement.

'signal ,box *c.n* small building in which the people who control the signals¹(1) on a railway work.

'signa,lize, -ise *tr.v* (*formal*) show the importance of (s.t); mark (s.t): *Their marriage was signalized by a big party in the village hall.*

'signaller *c.n* (US **'signaler**) person who signals¹(5), usu as a member of the armed forces.

'signalman *c.n* (*pl -men*) **1** man who controls railway signals¹(1), usu in a signal box. **2** signaller.

signal² /'sɪgnəl/ *attrib.adj* (*literary*) especially good, noticeable etc: *It's a signal achievement(2) for such a young girl to win the race.*

'signally *adv.*

signatory, signature ⇒ sign.

'signet /'sɪgnɪt/ *c.n* = seal²(1,2).

'signet ,ring *c.n* ring with a signet on it made to be worn on a finger so that one can use it for sealing²(8) s.t.

signify /'sɪgnɪˌfaɪ/ *tr.v* (*-ies, -ied*) (*formal*) be a sign of (s.t): *Those clouds signify rain.*

significance /sɪg'nɪfɪkəns/ *c/u.n* **1** importance: *That letter is of no significance to us.* **2** meaning: *Do you know what the significance of his remarks is?*

significant /sɪg'nɪfɪkənt/ *adj* **1** important; so big that one has to take notice of it: *There has been a significant increase in crime in our city this year.* Opposite insignificant. **2** having a particular meaning: *She gave me a significant look but said nothing.*

sig'nificantly *adv.*

signpost(ed) ⇒ sign.

silage *u.n* ⇒ silo.

silent /'saɪlənt/ *adj* **1** without any noise; absolutely quiet: *a silent corner of the room*; *a silent child.* **2** (usu — *on s.t*) not containing any information (about s.t): *This is supposed to be a history of modern Britain but it is completely silent on the trade unions.* **3** (of a letter in a word) not pronounced: *The 't' in 'listen' is silent.*

'silence *n* **1** *u.n* quietness; lack or absence of any sound: *I love the silence of the country after months in a town.* **2** *u.n* not saying or writing anything: *I am afraid his silence about his examination results means that he has failed.* **3** *c.n* length of time during which there is silence(1,2): *There's a strange silence before a storm. After her first letter there was a long silence and then a postcard.* **break a/the silence** start speaking, writing or making a noise after a quiet time. **in silence** silently; without speaking or making a noise. **reduce s.o/s.t to silence** make s.o/s.t stop speaking, writing or making a noise.

▷ *tr.v* **4** cause (s.o) to stop speaking or writing; cause (s.o/s.t) to stop making a noise: *She silenced the children by putting a finger to her lips. Her speech soon silenced her critics.*

'silencer *c.n* device fitted to a gun, car exhaust(1) etc to reduce the noise it makes.

,silent 'film *c.n* film made without any recorded speech etc.

'silently *adv.*

silhouette /ˌsɪluːˈet/ *c.n* **1** shape or picture of s.o/s.t in which the whole area within the outline is one solid colour, usu black. **2** shape; outline:

the silhouette of the mountains against the blue of the sky. **in silhouette** seen in the form of a shape of one colour against a background of a different colour: *As the moon came up we suddenly saw a big ship in silhouette*.

▷ *tr.v* **3** (usu passive) cause (s.o/s.t) to be seen in silhouette: *The ship was silhouetted against the moonlight*.

silica /'sɪlɪkə/ *u.n* sand or some other hard substance, *chem.form* SiO_2.

silicon /'sɪlɪkən/ *u.n* one of the elements(1) of which silica is formed, *chem.symb* Si.

͵silicon 'chip *c.n* very small piece of silicon used to make a microchip.

silk /sɪlk/ *u.n* **1** (also *attrib*) thread produced by a silkworm. **2** thread for sewing and weaving made from silk(1). **3** kind of cloth woven from silk(2). **'silken** *adj* **1** made of silk(2). **2** feeling or looking like silk(3); silky.

'silkiness *u.n* fact or state of being silky.

͵silk 'screen *u.n* way of printing in which ink or paint is pressed through a stencil(1) made of silk(3) or cloth like it.

'silk͵worm *c.n* kind of caterpillar(1) that makes a cocoon(1) out of silk(1) from its body.

'silky *adj* (-ier, -iest) feeling or looking like silk(3).

sill /sɪl/ *c.n* (also **'window͵sill**) flat horizontal piece of stone, wood etc at the bottom of a window etc.

sillabub /'sɪlə͵bʌb/ *c/u.n* = syllabub.

silly /'sɪlɪ/ *adj* (-ier, -iest) (*derog*) **1** (of a person or animal) foolish; stupid; not thinking, behaving etc in a sensible, reasonable way. **2** (of an action etc) that makes one think that the person or animal who/that does or makes it is silly(1): *a silly remark*. **bore s.o silly** (*informal*) bore s.o so much that he/she cannot think properly any more.

▷ *c.n* (*pl* -ies) **3** (*informal*) silly(1) person.

silo /'saɪləʊ/ *c.n* (*pl* -s) **1** very big container, usu like a tower, in which silage is stored. **2** (also **'missile ͵silo**) large vertical hollow tube, usu underground, in which missiles(1) are stored and kept ready for firing.

silage /'saɪlɪdʒ/ *u.n* grass etc that is put in a silo(1) so that cows etc can be fed on it in winter.

silt /sɪlt/ *u.n* **1** mud etc carried by moving water and dropped on the bottom.

▷ *tr/intr.v* **2** (usu — *up* (s.t)) (cause (part of a river etc) to) fill with silt(1).

silver /'sɪlvə/ *adj* **1** made of silver(3). **2** grey-white colour that looks like silver(3): *an old woman with silver hair*. **born with a silver spoon in one's mouth** (*fig*) born to a rich family.

▷ *n* **3** *u.n* kind of precious metal that is a shining grey-white in colour, used for making forks, spoons, ornaments, jewellery, coins etc, *chem.symb* Ag. **4** *u.n* (often *in* —) coins: '*How would you like the £30, madam?*' '*Two ten-pound notes, one five-pound note and the rest in silver, please.*' **5** *u.n* spoons, forks etc made of silver(3) or silver-plated. **6** *c.n* = silver medal. **in silver (a)** ⇒ silver(4). **(b)** made of silver(3): *make a piece of jewellery in silver*.

▷ *v* **7** *tr.v* cover (s.t) with silver(3) or s.t that looks like it.

͵silver 'birch *c.n* kind of birch(1) tree that has white bark'.

͵silver 'foil *u.n* strong thick silver paper, used esp in cooking.

͵silver ͵jubi'lee/'wedding *c.n* 25th year after an important event, e.g a wedding, usu celebrated in some way. Compare golden jubilee/wedding, diamond jubilee/wedding.

'silver ͵medal *c.n* medal given for coming second in a race or contest.

͵silver 'paper *u.n* (*informal*) thin light sheet(s) of shiny metal, used mostly for wrapping chocolates etc.

'silver ͵plate *u.n* metal covered with silver(3).

͵silver-'plated *adj* covered with silver(3).

'silver͵smith *c.n* person who makes ornaments etc out of silver(3).

'silver͵ware *u.n* = cutlery.

͵silver 'wedding ⇒ silver jubilee.

'silvery *adj* **1** looking like silver(3). **2** (of a sound) pleasantly clear and high: *the silvery sound of a small bell*.

similar /'sɪmɪlə/ *adj* **1** (often — *to* s.o/s.t) like (s.o/s.t); (almost) the same (as s.o/s.t, e.g who/that has just been mentioned): *The two houses are rather similar but the prices aren't. We hold similar views on this subject*. Opposite dissimilar. **2** (*geometry*) having exactly the same shape but not of the same size: *similar* triangles(1).

similarity /͵sɪmɪ'lærɪtɪ/ *n* (*pl* -ies) (often — *between* s.o/s.t and s.o/s.t; — *to* s.o/s.t) **1** *u.n* fact of being similar(1) (to s.o/s.t etc). **2** *c.n* thing in which s.o/s.t is similar(1): *What are the similarities between Amy's results and Mary's?*

'similarly *adv*: *Those* twins(2) *are always similarly dressed. Frank stays at home in the evening and, similarly, he does not let his children go out then*.

simile /'sɪmɪlɪ/ *c.n* group of words comparing a person or thing to s.o/s.t else, using the word 'as' or 'like', e.g 'as black as thunder'. Compare metaphor.

similitude /sɪ'mɪlɪ͵tjuːd/ *n* (*literary*) **1** *u.n* form, appearance (that looks like s.o/s.t): *Some quite harmless insects appear in the similitude of dangerous ones so that nothing will try to eat them*. **2** *c.n* simile; comparison.

simmer /'sɪmə/ *sing.n* **1** (usu *bring* s.t *to a* —) state of boiling gently.

▷ *v* **2** *tr/intr.v* (cause (s.t) to) boil gently: *Simmer the mixture till it sets but don't allow it to boil strongly*. **3** *intr.v* (usu — *with* s.t) feel (anger etc) so strongly that one finds it difficult to control it. **simmer down** become less angry etc.

simper /'sɪmpə/ *c.n* **1** silly smile when one is pretending s.t.

▷ *intr.v* **2** smile in this way.

simple /'sɪmpl/ *adj* **1** ordinary; plain; not complicated or difficult; easy to understand: *The children can already do simple arithmetic. We cook our own simple food*. **2** consisting only of one part: *a simple leaf*. Opposite complex(1). **3** (*attrib*) not mixed with anything else; pure: *All I want is the simple truth about the matter*. **4** honest and not affected by thoughts of what is to one's advantage; not artificial in any way: *a woman with a simple heart*. **5** so simple(4) that one is foolish or easily cheated: *I'm not so simple as to believe that story!* **6** (usu *pred*; *derog*) not intelligent: *I'm afraid she's a bit simple.* **7** (*attrib*; *literary*) being one of the ordinary people, not a rich or important person: *a simple country girl.* **pure and simple** ⇒ pure.

,simple 'fracture *c.n* fracture(1) in which a broken bone does not push through the skin. ⇒ compound fracture.

,simple-'hearted *adj* (*literary*) simple(4).

,simple 'interest *u.n* interest(4) calculated only on the amount borrowed or lent. Compare compound interest (⇒ compound).

,simple-'life *def.n* ⇒ life.

,simple-'minded *adj* simple(4–6).

simpleton /'sɪmpltən/ *c.n* (*derog*) simple(5,6) person.

simplicity /sɪm'plɪsɪtɪ/ *u.n* fact or state of being simple(1,4,5). **be simplicity itself** (*informal*) be very easy to do, understand etc: *Making this cake is simplicity itself.*

simplification /,sɪmplɪfɪ'keɪʃən/ *c/u.n* (*formal*) act or fact of simplifying (s.t). ⇒ oversimplification.

simplify /'sɪmplɪ,faɪ/ *tr.v* (-*ies*, -*ied*) make (s.t) simple(r)(1). ⇒ oversimplify.

'simply *adv* **1** in a simple(1,4,5) way. **2** only; just: *I wasn't rude to him; I simply told him I was busy and to come back later.* **3** (*informal*) really; absolutely: *'You've passed your examination? That's simply wonderful!'*

simulate /'sɪmju,leɪt/ *tr.v* (*formal*) imitate (s.o/ s.t); pretend to be, have etc (s.t): *Some creatures simulate death to avoid being eaten by their enemies.*

'simu,lated *adj* that is an imitation: *simulated pearls.* Opposite real(2), genuine(1).

simulation /,sɪmju'leɪʃən/ *c/u.n* (*formal*) **1** (often — *of s.t*) imitation (of s.t); pretence (of s.t). **2** way of trying to find out the future results of different events, actions etc by getting a computer etc to work them out.

'simu,lator *c.n* device that simulates the movements of a plane, car etc so that pilots, drivers etc can learn to fly, drive etc in safety.

simultaneous /,sɪməl'teɪnɪəs/ *adj* happening or being done at exactly the same time: *Six simultaneous refusals could not have happened by chance.*

simultaneity /,sɪməltə'niːɪtɪ/ *u.n.* ,simul'taneously *adv.* ,simul'taneousness *u.n.*

sin /sɪn/ *n* **1** *c/u.n* action, thought etc that is against moral or religious laws or rules: *Is it always a sin to tell a lie? We have to fight sin wherever we find it.* **2** *c.n* thing that one ought not to do, although it is not really a sin(1): *Some women think that it is a sin to eat lots of cakes.* **commit a sin** do s.t that is sinful. **cover a multitude of sins** ⇒ multitude. **for one's sins** (*informal*; *joking*) as a punishment for s.t one has done, said etc. **live in sin** (*informal*) (of a man and a woman who are not married to each other) live together as if married to each other. **mortal sin** ⇒ mortal. **sin against s.o/s.t** sin(1) that harms s.o or that breaks a moral or religious law etc. **wages of sin** ⇒ wage¹.

▷ *intr.v* (-*nn*-) **3** (often — *against s.o/s.t*) commit a sin(1) (against s.o/s.t).

'sinful *adj* (*derog*) **1** that is a sin. **2** who commits a sin.

'sinfully *adv.* 'sinfulness *u.n.*

'sinless *adj* without sin.

'sinlessness *u.n.*

'sinner *c.n* person who sins(3), has sinned.

since /sɪns/ *adv* **1** (often *ever* —) from then till now: *I bought my first car in 1971 and have had one ever since.* **2** at some time between then and now: *I bought a new car two years ago but I've since sold it.* **long since** ⇒ long¹ (*adv*).

▷ *conj* **3** (often *ever* —) from the time that … until now (without stopping): *I have been working (ever) since I finished my breakfast.* **4** (often *ever* —) from the time that … until a certain time (without stopping): *At 10 I stopped for some tea having been working (ever) since I got up at 7.* **5** because; as(5): *Since it is raining I shall stay at home this morning. Helen took a lot of clothes with her since she didn't know what the weather was going to be like.* **6** because (you took the trouble to): *Since you asked, yes I am pleased.* seeing.

▷ *prep* **7** from (an earlier time, the time of doing s.t) up to now or a time later than the first time: *I have been here since 1 o'clock. I had been in France since the year before. Since getting up this morning I haven't stopped working. It isn't long since we had a railway station in our village.* **ever since s.t** the whole of the time since(7) s.t: *We've been friends ever since that day.* Compare for(1).

sincere /sɪn'sɪə/ *adj* honest; not pretending at all. Opposite insincere.

sin'cerely *adv* in an honest way. **Yours sincerely** (way of ending a letter to s.o one knows by name but not very well; one signs one's name after this). Compare Yours faithfully, Yours truly.

sincerity /sɪn'serɪtɪ/ *u.n* honesty: *She spoke with sincerity.* ⇒ insincerity. **in all sincerity** being completely sincere.

sine /saɪn/ *c.n* (*mathematics*) quantity arrived at by dividing the length of the side of a right-angled triangle (⇒ right¹) that is opposite an angle by the length of the side that is opposite the right angle: *If the sides of a triangle are 3, 4 and 5 centimetres long, the sine of the angle opposite the 3 centimetre side will be 3 divided by 5 = 0.6.* Compare cosine, tangent(2).

sinecure /'saɪnɪ,kjuə/ *c.n* (*formal*) job or position that is usu well paid or important but that needs little or no work.

sinew /'sɪnju:/ *c/u.n* thing like a piece of strong string that joins a muscle(1) and a bone in one's body.

'sinewy *adj* **1** (of meat) tough. **2** having strong muscles(1).

sinful(ly/ness) ⇒ sin.

sing¹ /sɪŋ/ *v* (*p.t* sang /sæŋ/, *p.p* sung /sʌŋ/) **1** *intr.v* (often — *about/of s.o/s.t*) (of a bird, person etc) make pleasant musical sounds with one's voice (about s.o/s.t): *sing softly about a secret place.* ⇒ unsung. **2** *tr.v* (usu — *s.t to s.o* (*about s.o/s.t*)) cause (a song etc (about s.o/s.t)) to be heard (by s.o) in this way: *You sing the first line and I'll sing the second.* **3** make a sound like s.o singing (⇒ sing¹(1)) on one note: *When the kettle(1) begins to sing, take it off the stove. A bullet sang past my head and hit the wall behind me.* **4** *tr.v* cause s.o to hear a sound like s.o singing (⇒ sing¹(1)) on one note: *After the long climb, my ears were singing.* **cannot sing a note** not be able to sing¹(1) at all. **sing (s.t) out** shout (s.t) loudly. **sing s.o's praises** ⇨ praise(*n*). **sing s.o**, *usu **a baby**, **to sleep** sing¹(1) to s.o till he/she goes to sleep. **sing up** sing¹(1) (more) loudly: *'Come on, sing up! They can't hear us at the back of the hall.'*

'singable *adj* that it is possible to sing¹(2).

'singer *c.n* person who sings¹(1).

'singing *u.n* fact or act of singing (⇨ sing¹(1–3)) s.t.

'sing,song *attrib.adj* **1** (of a voice) that goes up and down in tone(1) in a boring way. ▷ *c.n* **2** singsong(1) sound. **3** occasion for getting together of people for singing songs, usu informally.

sing² *written abbr* singular(1,3).

singe /sɪndʒ/ *c.n* **1** act of burning the ends of s.t, e.g hair, or the outside of s.t slightly; mark left by doing this. ▷ *tr.v* (*pres.p* singeing) **2** burn off the ends of (hair etc): *She singed her eyebrow as she lit her cigarette.* **3** burn the outside of (s.t) slightly: *Don't get too near the fire or it might singe your clothes.*

singer, singing ⇨ sing¹.

single /'sɪŋgl/ *adj* **1** not married. **2** (*attrib*) for one person only: *a single bed*; *a single room.* Compare double(4). **3** (*attrib*) (of a bus, train etc ticket) for going one way but not returning. Compare return(1). **4** (*attrib*) (of a flower) having only one set of petals: *a single rose.* Compare double(1). **5** (*attrib*) consisting only of one part: *He was hanging from the cliff by just a single thickness of rope.* **6** (*attrib*) separate; one compared with all others: *The hospital's biggest single source(1) of money is from the government.* **7** (*attrib*) only: *The old man's single pleasure was walking.* **not a single s.o/s.t** not even one person/animal/thing: *Not a single student came to the lecture. Have you got a single piece of furniture that is not broken?* **every single s.o/s.t** ⇨ every. ▷ *c.n* **8** single(2) room. Compare double(10). **9** single(3) ticket: *A single to Manchester, please.* Compare return(8). **10** (in cricket') one run(8). **11** small record¹(1) with one song on each side. Compare LP. ▷ *tr.v* **12 single s.o/s.t out (from s.o/s.t) (for s.t)** choose s.o/s.t out of a group (of people, animals or things) (for some special purpose).

,single-'breasted *adj* (of a coat or jacket(1)) having one row of buttons to close it in the front. Compare double-breasted.

,single 'cream *u.n* cream(3) as a liquid that cannot be whipped(9).

,single-'decker *c.n* (also *attrib*) bus that only has one floor: *a single-decker bus.* Compare double-decker.

,single 'file *c.n* one line of people etc in which one follows behind the other. **in single file** in such a line: *The students went forward in single file to receive their prizes.*

,single-'handed *adj/adv* by oneself and without the help of anyone else: *He managed to carry the cupboard upstairs single-handed.*

,single-'minded *adj* keeping one's mind on one thing only without becoming distracted from it.

,single-'mindedly *adv.* **,single-'mindedness** *u.n.*

'singleness *u.n* state of being single(1).

singleness of mind/purpose fact of being single-minded.

'singles *n* **1** *c.n* (*pl singles*) game or competition of tennis etc in which there is one person on each side. Compare doubles. **2** *pl.n* (also *attrib*) (esp US) single(1) people as a group: *a place where singles can meet*; *a singles bar.*

,single 'spacing *u.n* ⇨ spacing (⇨ space).

singlet /'sɪŋglɪt/ *c.n* piece of clothing without sleeves or collar, worn mostly by men under a shirt or instead of a shirt for sports.

'singly *adv* each by herself/himself/itself; separately; one by one: *The students had to come in singly to have their oral(2) test.*

singsong ⇨ sing¹.

singular /'sɪŋgjulə/ *adj* **1** (*written abbr* sing) (*grammar*) of, referring to, representing, only one: *'Child' is singular and 'children' is plural.* Opposite plural(1). **2** (*formal*) extraordinary; unusual: *The diamond was of singular quality.* ▷ *c/def.n* **3** (*written abbr* sing) (often *in the —*; *the — of s.t*) (*grammar*) state or word that is singular(1): *The singular of 'men' is 'man'. We seldom talk of 'beans' in the singular.* Opposite plural(2).

singularity /,sɪŋgju'lærɪtɪ/ *c/u.n* (*pl -ies*) (*formal*) singular(2) quality or fact.

'singularly *adv* (*formal*) extraordinarily; unusually: *a singularly fortunate meeting.*

sinister /'sɪnɪstə/ *adj* that seems dangerous, threatening: *sinister clouds on the horizon.*

sink¹ /sɪŋk/ *c.n* = kitchen sink. **everything but the kitchen sink** ⇨ kitchen.

sink² /sɪŋk/ *v* (*p.t* sank /sæŋk/, *p.p* sunk /sʌŋk/) **1** *tr/intr.v* (cause (s.t) to) go down below a surface of water etc, to the bottom of s.t or so that one can no longer see it: *I sank his paper boat with a big stone. As the sun sank below the horizon the clouds turned red.* **2** *intr.v* (often *— down*) become less high: *The level of the water in our river is sinking.* **3** *intr.v* become smaller, less strong, less loud etc (and reach a certain level): *The money in our bank account has sunk by £500 in two months. Slowly the engine warmed up and the noise from it sank to a hum(1).* **4** *intr.v* fall asleep; sit/lie down because one is very weak, tired etc: *The child sank into its mother's arms and she had to carry it home.* **5** *intr.v* (often *be sinking fast/slowly*) be dying (fast etc). **6** *tr.v* make a hole for/as (s.t): *We shall have to sink these posts one metre into the ground. To get water here you have to sink a deep well.* **7** *tr.v* (*fig; informal*) cause (s.t) to fail: *This rain will sink all our hopes of a good harvest this year.* **8** *tr.v* (*fig*) stop thinking about (s.t); get rid of (s.t): *The two women decided to sink their jealousies and become friends again.*

sink in(to s.t) (a) (of a liquid entering s.t solid) slowly go in(to s.t): *Pour the melted sugar over the cake and let it sink in.* (b) (of an idea entering s.o's mind) be slowly understood: *Her father's leaving has not sunk in (to her head) yet.* **sink into s.t** slowly reach a state of s.t: *She put her head down and soon sank into a deep sleep.* **sink s.t in(to) s.t** (a) push s.t in(to s.t): *She sank her arm into the mud and tried to find the missing bag.* (b) (*fig*) put money etc in (a company etc); invest(1) s.t in s.t. **sink or swim** (*fig*) be successful or fail without help from anyone: *After giving children the best education you can, you must let them sink or swim; you can't live their lives for them.* **sink to s.t**

(a) ⇨ sink²(3,4). **(b)** (*fig*) go down so far morally as to do s.t: *He is a bad man but he hasn't yet sunk to stealing from children.*

'**sinking ˌfund** *c.n* (*commerce*) money kept as a reserve for paying debts in the future.

'**sunken** *attrib.adj* **1** that has (been) sunk (⇨ sink²(1)): *sunken treasure.* **2** lower in level than what is around it: *sunken eyes in a person's face; a sunken garden where the wind cannot harm the plants.*

sinless(ness), sinner ⇨ sin.

sinuous /'sɪnjʊəs/ *adj* (*formal*) twisting or curving about; winding: *the sinuous movements of a snake.*

sinuosity /ˌsɪnjʊ'ɒsɪtɪ/ *n* (*pl* -ies) (*formal*) **1** *u.n* fact of being sinuous. **2** *c/u.n* sinuous movement(s).

'**sinuously** *adv.*

sinus /'saɪnəs/ *c.n* (usu *pl* except when *attrib*) hollow place, esp one in the bones of one's face: *blocked sinuses; a sinus headache.*

sip /sɪp/ *c.n* (often *have/take a — (of s.t)*) little amount that one drinks at a time, usu from a glass or cup.

▷ *tr/intr.v* (-pp-) **2** drink a little (of s.t) at a time: *Don't drink that all at once; sip it!*

siphon /'saɪfn/ *c.n* (also '**syphon**) **1** (curved) pipe through which liquid can rise and then fall to a lower level by atmospheric pressure. **2** (also '**soda ˌsiphon**) strong bottle from which soda water is forced out by the pressure of gas.

▷ *tr.v* (often — *s.t off (s.t)*; — *s.t out (of s.t)*) **3** take (a liquid) out (of s.t) using a siphon(1): *Some people steal petrol by siphoning it out of the tanks of cars.* **4** (*fig*) take or lead (s.o/s.t) away: *When this road gets crowded, the police siphon off some of the traffic into other roads. Some dishonest managers siphon off the profits of their company so that the owners do not get them.*

sir /sɜː/ *c.n* (usu *sing*) Compare madam. **1** (also with capital **S**) (polite way of speaking to a man, esp when he is a customer in a shop, to show respect or because he is higher in rank, older etc than oneself): *Pupils address their teachers as sir, soldiers do the same to their officers and people who work in shops do so to customers.* **2** (with capital **S**) written form of address in a formal letter to a man whose name is not known: *Dear Sir.* **3** (with capital **S**) title put before a man's first name to show that he is a knight(3) or baronet: *Sir Winston Churchill* (or *informal: Sir Winston*).

sire /saɪə/ *c.n* **1** father of an animal, usu a horse. ⇨ dam².

▷ *tr.v* **2** be the father of (an animal, usu a horse).

siren /'saɪərən/ *c.n* **1** device that makes a loud warning noise, e.g on an ambulance, fire engine, police car or ship, or to warn that enemy planes are coming. **2** (usu *pl*) (in ancient Greek stories) creature like a woman who sang so beautifully that passing ships were attracted onto rocks and wrecked. **3** dangerously beautiful woman.

sirloin /'sɜːˌlɔɪn/ *c/u.n* (also ˌ**sirˌloin 'steak**) (piece of) beef¹(1) cut from the best part of the loin(2).

sis /sɪs/ *unique n* (*informal*) (way of speaking to one's sister): *Hullo, Sis, where have you been?*

sisal /'saɪsl/ *u.n* (also *attrib*) **1** kind of plant from whose leaves rope, mats etc are made. **2** fibres(1)

from the leaves of this plant used for making ropes etc.

sissy /'sɪsɪ/ *adj* (-ier, -iest) **1** (*derog*; *informal*) like a sissy(2); effeminate.

▷ *c.n* (also '**cissy**) (*pl* -ies) **2** (*derog*; *informal*) cowardly boy.

sister /'sɪstə/ *attrib.adj* **1** belonging to the same group, association etc: *sister ships; our sister office in Edinburgh.*

▷ *n* **2** *c.n* female child of the same parents (as oneself): *My sister's name is Laura. Those three girls are sisters.* ⇨ half-sister, stepsister. **3** *c/unique n* (with capital **S** in names) woman in a hospital who is in charge of a ward and is above a nurse but below a matron(2) in rank: *Sister Jones is in charge here tonight.* **4** *c/unique n* (with capital **S** in names) woman who belongs to a religious order; nun: *Sister Theresa.* ⇨ brother(3). **5** *c.n* woman who is in the same group, e.g a trade union or women's rights movement: *We must unite to get what is owed to us, sisters!* ⇨ brother(4).

'**sister-ˌhood** *n* **1** *u.n* feeling that one sister(*n*) has, or should have, towards another. **2** *c.n* group of people who are sisters(4,5).

'**sister-in-ˌlaw** *c.n* (*pl* '**sisters-in-ˌlaw**) sister(2) of one's husband, wife; wife of one's brother or brother-in-law. ⇨ brother-in-law.

'**sisterliness** *u.n* feeling of being sisterly.

'**sisterly** *adj* of, or like a sister(2); like what a loving sister(2) would be/do.

sit /sɪt/ *v* (-tt-, *p.t.p.p* sat /sæt/) **1** *intr.v* (often *be sitting down*) (of a person, animal) have one's bottom on s.t with one's weight on it and with the upper part of one's body more vertical than horizontal (if it is more horizontal, one is lying and not sitting). **2** *tr/intr.v* (often — (*s.o*) *down*) (cause (s.o) to) get into the position of sitting (⇨ sit(1)): *Please sit down. You can sit your children on that bench.* **3** *intr.v* (of an official group of people) have one or more meetings: *Is Parliament sitting today?* **4** *intr.v* be in a position without moving: *Our house sits on the edge of the sea.* **5** *tr.v* take (a written examination): *When are you sitting your finals?* ⇨ sit for s.t(a). **6** *intr.v* (of a bird) sit on eggs to hatch²(1) them out: *Don't disturb that nest; the birds are sitting.*

sit about/around sit s.w, usu doing nothing (and often while others are busy).

sit back (a) move from an upright position in a chair to a more comfortable one further back. **(b)** (*fig*) take no part in s.t that others are doing: *It's all right for you to sit back but there's work to be done.*

sit badly *etc* (of a piece of clothing) fit badly etc.

sit by = sit back(b).

sit down sit(1,2). **sit down under s.t** (*fig*) do s.t without complaining about it.

sit for s.o have one's picture painted by s.o; have oneself photographed by s.o. **sit for one's portrait** have one's portrait(1) painted. **sit for s.t (a)** prepare for, take, an examination. ⇨ sit(5). **(b)** be a member of Parliament etc for a place.

sit in take part in a sit-in. **sit in (as s.t) (for s.o)** take s.o else's place (as s.t) while he/she is absent.

sit in on s.t attend s.t, e.g a meeting, without being a member and without speaking etc.

sit on s.o (*fig*; *informal*) rudely stop s.o doing s.t: *Whenever the little boy tried to join in the game he* *was sat on by the bigger boys.* **sit on s.t (a)** not do anything about s.t that one is supposed to do s.t about: *I don't know who is sitting on my letters but I never get any answers to them.* **(b)** (also — *upon s.t*) have a meeting to deal with s.t. **(c)** be a member of a committee etc.

sit s.t out (a) stay until the end of s.t, usu without enjoying it. **(b)** not take part in a dance: *After dancing continuously for an hour Mary and John agreed to sit the next one out.*

sit pretty ⇨ pretty(*adv*).

sit s.t through; **sit through s.t** = sit s.t out(a).

sit tight ⇨ tight(*adv*).

sit (s.o) up (cause s.o to) change from a lying to a sitting (⇨ sit(1)) position. **sit up and take notice** ⇨ notice(*n*). **sit up (at/to a table)** sit down for a meal at a table. **sit up (for s.o)** not go to bed (yet) (because one is waiting for s.o). **sit up (straight)** sit in a vertical position, esp to be/look more attentive: *Come on, boys, sit up straight!*

sit upon s.t = sit on s.t(b).

sit with s.o help to look after s.o who is ill (in bed) etc.

'sit-,down *attrib.adj* **1** (of a meal) at which people sit and are served the food. Compare buffet¹, self-service.

▷ *c.n* **2** (also **,sit-down 'strike**) strike(1) in which the workers refuse to leave their place of work although they stop doing any work.

'sit-,in *c.n* (also *attrib*) way of protesting(2) against an organization by entering its offices etc, interfering with its work and refusing to leave.

'sitter *c.n* **1** person who sits for a painting or photograph (⇨ sit for s.o). **2** = baby-sitter.

'sitting *attrib.adj* **1** who now has the position of (a Member of Parliament etc).

▷ *c.n* **2** time during which one sits s.w without getting up: *I finished the book in two or three sittings.* **3** = session. **4** act of providing a meal for one group of people at the same time: *We have so many passengers that we have to feed them in two sittings.*

,sitting 'duck *c.n* person, animal or thing who/ that is easy to hit, catch, cheat etc.

'sitting-,room = living-room.

,sitting-'tenant *c.n* person who rents s.t and cannot be got rid of by law.

site /saɪt/ *c.n* **1** place where s.t is, was or is intended to be: *This is the site of a famous battle. Which site has been chosen for the new factory?* ⇨ building(1). **on site** at the place where s.t, usu building, is taking place.

▷ *tr.v* **2** put or build (a house etc) s.w: *The factory is ideally sited for supplying the shops.*

situated /'sɪtjʊˌeɪtɪd/ *pred.adj* **1** found/located(2) (in a certain place): *The factory is situated near the motorway.* **2** (often — *for s.t*) (*informal*) in a certain condition (with regard to s.t): *How are you situated for money at the moment?*

situation /ˌsɪtjʊ'eɪʃn/ *c.n* position in which s.o/s.t is situated: *My situation is that I've got no job but I have a place to stay and a little money.*

,situ'ation ,comedy *c/u.n* kind of funny serial(2) on the stage, television etc.

,situ,ations 'vacant *pl.n* column(s) in a newspaper etc for people to advertise jobs.

,situ,ations 'wanted *pl.n* column(s) in a newspaper etc in which people who are looking for work advertise.

six /sɪks/ *n* **1** *det/pron/c.n* (*cardinal number*) number 6 (between five and seven): *Six of us went in the same car. She's 6 (years old). It's 6 (o'clock). It will cost £6.* **2** *c.n* (in cricket¹) hit by a batsman which makes the ball cross the boundary(2a) without touching the ground and for which he/she gets six runs(8). **at sixes and sevens (with s.o) (about s.t)** (*informal*) not able to agree (with s.o) (about s.t); not able to decide; confused.

,six-'footer *c.n* (*informal*) person who is at least six feet but not as much as seven feet tall.

sixpence /'sɪkspəns/ *n* **1** *c.n* old silver coin worth six pennies (now 2½ new pence). **2** *unique n* sum of six old pennies.

,six-'shooter *c.n* revolver that one can load with six bullets at a time.

sixteen /sɪks'tiːn/ *det/pron/c.n* (*cardinal number*) number 16 (between fifteen and seventeen).

sixteenth /sɪks'tiːnθ/ *det/pron* (*ordinal number*) **1** 16th; (person or thing) following 15 in order.

▷ *c.n* **2** one of sixteen equal parts; $\frac{1}{16}$.

sixth /sɪksθ/ *det/pron* **1** (*ordinal number*) 6th; (person or thing) following 5 in order.

▷ *c.n* **2** one of six equal parts; $\frac{1}{6}$.

,sixth 'form *def.n* (also *attrib*) highest class in a British secondary school.

,sixth 'former *c.n* student who is in the sixth form.

,sixth 'sense *sing.n* (*informal*) = intuition.

sixtieth /'sɪkstɪəθ/ *det/pron* (*ordinal number*) **1** (person or thing) following 59 in order; 60th.

▷ *c.n* **2** one of sixty equal parts; $\frac{1}{60}$.

sixty /'sɪkstɪ/ *det/pron/c.n* (*pl -ies*) (*cardinal number*) number 60 (between fifty-nine and sixty-one): *The temperature is only sixty (degrees). He's sixty (years old).* **in one's sixties** between 60 and 69 years old. **(in/ into) the sixties** (or **the 60(')s**) **(a)** (speed, temperature, marks etc) between 60 and 69: *The temperature is in the sixties.* **(b)** (years) between '60 and '69 in a century.

size¹ /saɪz/ *n* **1** *c/u.n* (often — *of s.t*) length and/ or breadth(1) and/or thickness (of s.t): *I couldn't take a photograph of all the children at the same time because of the size of the group. These socks will fit feet of every size.* **2** *c/unique n* one of the fixed standards of measurement for clothes etc: *I take size 9 shoes. Have you got these trousers in children's sizes? What size tube of toothpaste do you usually buy?* **be of some** /sʌm/ **size** be quite big. **cut s.o down to size** show that s.o is not as clever, important etc as he/she seemed to be. **That's about the size of it** (*fig*; *informal*) That's a correct description of what happened etc.

▷ *tr.v* **3** **size s.o/s.t up** (*informal*) decide what one thinks of s.o/s.t.

'sizeable *attrib.adj* (also **'sizable**) rather big; considerable: *They have a sizeable number of buildings on their farm.*

-sized *adj* of the size¹(*n*) shown by the first part of the word: *a small-sized pair of socks*; *a fair-sized* (reasonably big) *crowd.* ⇨ oversized, undersized.

size² /saɪz/ *u.n* **1** (also **'sizing**) kind of glue

mixed with water, used for making paper stiff, putting on wood before varnish(1) to stop the varnish going into the wood etc.
▷ *tr.v* **2** put size²(1) on (s.t).

sizzle /'sɪzl/ *intr.v* **1** make a hissing(1) sound like that of s.t frying in hot fat. **2** (*fig*) be very hot: *It was a sizzling hot day last Sunday.*

skate¹ /skeɪt/ *c.n* (often *pair of* —s) **1** (also '**ice-,skate**) device with metal blades for fixing to one's shoe, shoe/boot with metal blade fixed underneath, for sliding over the ice. **2** (also '**roller-,skate**) device with four wheels for fixing on one's shoe, shoe/boot with four wheels fixed underneath, for sliding across a hard surface. ⇨ skating. **get/put one's skates on** (*fig*; *informal*) hurry.
▷ *intr.v* **3** (also '**ice-,skate**) move on skates¹(1). **4** (also '**roller-,skate**) move on skates¹(2). **skate on thin ice** ⇨ ice(*n*). **skate over/round s.t** (*fig*) (try to) avoid talking etc about s.t (seriously); gloss over s.t (⇨ gloss(*v*)).

'**skate,board** *c.n* short piece of wood etc with small wheels under it, used for standing on and moving as a sport.

'**skater** *c.n* = ice-skater, roller-skater.

'**skating** *u.n* = ice-skating, roller-skating. **go skating** = skate¹(*v*).

skate² /skeɪt/ *n* (*pl skate*, -(*s*)) **1** *c.n* kind of flat fish found in the sea and cheap to buy as food. **2** *u.n* (also *attrib*) flesh of this fish as food.

skein /skeɪn/ *c.n* (often — *of s.t*) loose coil(1) (of wool etc).

skeleton /'skelɪtn/ *attrib.adj* **1** just enough to keep things going: *We don't close our factory completely at weekends but there is only a skeleton staff on duty.*
▷ *c.n* **2** all the joined bones of a human or animal body. **3** (*fig*; *informal*) very thin person: *After his years in prison he was just a skeleton.* **4** (usu — *of s.t*) framework (of a building, story etc) without any added pieces, details etc. **skeleton in the cupboard** (*fig*) shameful secret: *Every family has a skeleton in the cupboard and ours is Uncle Bill who was in prison for many years.*

'**skeleton ,key** *c.n* key that can open several doors.

skeptic(al/ally), skepticism ⇨ sceptic.

sketch /sketʃ/ *c.n* **1** (often — *of s.o/s.t*) outline, or rough drawing, picture (of s.o/s.t) without details: *a quick sketch of the house.* **2** (often — *of s.t*) written or spoken outline (of s.t) without details. **3** short play, story, amusing act etc: *She's written a funny sketch about English food.*
▷ *v* **4** *intr.v* (of an artist) make one or more sketches(1). **5** *tr.v* make a sketch(1) of (s.o/s.t). **6** *tr.v* make a sketch(2) of (s.t). **sketch s.t in** add s.t to a sketch(1,2). **sketch s.t out** make a sketch(2) of s.t.

'**sketch,book** *c.n* book of paper for making sketches(1) on.

'**sketchily** *adv* in a sketchy way.

'**sketchiness** *u.n* fact or state of being sketchy.

'**sketch,pad** *c.n* = sketchbook.

'**sketchy** *adj* (-ier, -iest) not complete; lacking (necessary) detail; rough: *His knowledge of French is sketchy.*

skew /skju:/ *adj* **1** (usu *pred*) not straight or level. ⇨ askew.
▷ *def.n* **2** **on the skew** = skew(1).

skewer /skjuə/ *c.n* **1** metal or wooden rod for pushing through pieces of meat etc to hold them over a fire for cooking: *a meat skewer.* **on a skewer** having a skewer(1) through it.
▷ *tr.v* **2** put a skewer(1) through (meat etc).

ski /ski:/ *c.n* (*pl* -s) **1** (often *pair of* —s) long narrow piece of wood etc turned up at the front and fixed to one's boot for going over snow.
▷ *intr.v* (*pres.p skiing* /'ski:ɪŋ/, *p.t,p.p skied* /ski:d/) **2** move on skis(1) as a sport or to get from one place to another.

skier /'ski:ə/ *c.n* person who skis(2).

skiing /'ski:ɪŋ/ *u.n* (doing the) sport of going on skis(1): *We go skiing every winter.*

'**ski ,jump** *n* **1** *u.n* sport of skiing (⇨ ski(2)) down a steep slope and then jumping off a cliff or a kind of ramp¹ at the end to see who can jump farthest. **2** place on which this sport is done.

'**ski ,lift** *c.n* cable(1) with seats hanging from it on which skiers can go up and down mountains.

'**ski-,run** *c.n* course where one skis(2).

'**ski ,stick** *c.n* one of two special sticks which a skier uses to help her/him balance, move forward and stop.

skid /skɪd/ *c.n* **1** (of a car, driver) act of sliding sideways, esp when one cannot prevent it. **get/go into a skid** begin to skid(2). **put the skids under s.o/s.t** (*slang*) (**a**) stop s.o doing s.t he/she wants to do; prevent s.t happening. (**b**) make s.o/s.t hurry.
▷ *tr/intr.v* (-dd-) **2** (cause (a car etc) to) go into a skid(1).

skiff /skɪf/ *c.n* small light boat.

skiing ⇨ ski.

skill /skɪl/ *c/u.n* ability to do s.t (well), usu as a result of training and/or practice.

'**skilful** *adj* (US '**skillful**) having or showing skill.

'**skilfully** *adv* (US '**skillfully**).

skilled *adj* Opposite unskilled. **1** (often — *in s.t*) having skill (in s.t): *a skilled driver*; *skilled in the art of reading one's fortune.* **2** needing skill: *Making glasses for people's eyes is a skilled job.*

skillet /'skɪlɪt/ *c.n* kind of small shallow(1) frying pan.

skim /skɪm/ *v* (-mm-) **1** *tr.v* remove s.t, e.g dirt, foam(1) etc, that is floating on (a liquid). **2** *tr.v* (often — *s.t off*) remove (s.t that is floating) (from a liquid): *skim the leaves off the pond before swimming.* **3** *tr/intr.v* (usu — *over s.t*) move over (s.t) in such a way as almost or just to touch its surface: *birds skimming over the waves.* **4** *tr/intr.v* (often — *over/through s.t*) (*fig*) read (s.t) very quickly to get the main meaning.

,**skim(med) 'milk** *u.n* milk that has had the cream taken out of it.

skimp /skɪmp/ *tr/intr.v* (usu — *on s.t*) not provide or use enough (of s.t); not use as much (of s.t) as is really necessary: *One should never skimp on nourishing food for children.*

'**skimpily** *adv* in a skimpy way.

'**skimpiness** *u.n* fact or state of being skimpy.

'**skimpy** *adj* (-ier, -iest) (giving) too little; scanty: *a skimpy helping of food. Don't be skimpy; there's plenty of food.*

skin /skɪn/ *n* **1** *c/u.n* (also *attrib*) elastic material that covers the flesh of a human or animal body and that often has hair growing out of it. **2** *c/u.n* skin(1) of an animal used as leather, fur etc: *sheep-skin*. **3** *c/u.n* covering of a fruit or vegetable: *a banana skin*; *the skin of a* tomato(1). Compare peel(1). **4** *c.n* thing like a skin(1) which is the outside of a sausage. **5** *c.n* more solid surface found on a liquid after it has been cooked or after the air has got to it: *the skin on milk in a pan*; *the skin on oil paint left in an open tin*. **by the skin of one's teeth** (*fig*; *informal*) with great difficulty; only just: *She passed the examination by the skin of her teeth*. **get under s.o's skin** (*fig*; *informal*) annoy s.o; make s.o angry. **save one's/s.o's skin** save oneself/s.o from a dangerous situation, esp at the last moment, at the expense of others etc: *In order to save his own skin he told the police all he knew*. **skin and bone(s)** (*informal*) very thin: *After her long illness Ruth was skin and bone*. **under the skin** (*fig*) when one looks more deeply than the outside appearance: *All human beings are the same under the skin*.

▷ *tr.v* (*-nn-*) **6** *tr.v* take the skin(1–3) off (s.t), either intentionally or accidentally: *Skin the rabbit before you cook it. The little girl fell and skinned her knees*. ⇨ peel(2).

,skin-'deep *pred.adj* (often *fig*) not serious; only on the surface: *Her wound was skin-deep. His love for her is only skin-deep.*

'skin di,sease *c/u.n* disease that affects the skin.

'skin-,dive *intr.v* go diving without wearing a diving suit.

'skin-,diver *c.n* person who skin-dives.

'skin-,diving *u.n* sport or job of a skin-diver.

'skin,flint *c.n* = miser.

'skin ,graft *c.n* operation for taking a piece of good skin(1) from part of a person's body and putting it on another part to take the place of damaged skin.

'skin,head *c.n* (UK) (*informal*) young person in about 1969 to 1975 who had very short hair and behaved violently.

-skinned *adj* having skin of the kind shown in the first part of the word: *light-skinned*. ⇨ thick-skinned, thin-skinned.

'skinniness *u.n* fact or state of being skinny.

,skin-'tight *adj* fitting very tightly: *skin-tight trousers.*

'skinny *adj* (*-ier, -iest*) (*derog*) very or too thin.

skint /skɪnt/ *adj* (*slang*) having no money at all; broke(1).

skip¹ /skɪp/ *c.n* **1** act of jumping lightly up and down, first on one foot and then the other, while moving forwards, backwards or sideways: *He gave a little skip when he heard the good news.*

▷ *v* (*-pp-*) **2** *intr.v* move with skips¹(1): *I often see small children skipping along beside their mothers.* **3** *intr.v* move a rope over one's head and jump over it as it comes to one's feet again and again as a kind of amusement or exercise: *Joe skips every morning to help him to keep fit. Betty's two friends held the ends of the rope so that she could skip.* **4** *intr.v* change (from s.t to s.t) without following any fixed order: *A bad teacher skips from one subject to another without giving full explanations.* **5** *tr/intr.v* (often — *over s.t*) leave (s.t) out; not deal with (s.t) completely: *During his account of what he had done the week before he skipped (over) his accident with his bicycle.* **6** *tr.v* not do, have etc (s.t one normally does, has etc): *Let's skip lunch today and have an early dinner instead.* **7** *intr.v* (usu — *off/out*) (*informal*) escape; go away quickly and secretly: *He skipped off before anyone saw him.* **skip town** leave a place quickly and secretly, esp to escape punishment etc.

'skipping *u.n* (also *attrib*) act of skipping (⇨ skip²).

'skipping-,rope *c.n* rope used for skipping.

skip² /skɪp/ *c.n* big metal container used by builders etc to take away rubbish etc.

skipper /'skɪpə/ *c.n* **1** captain of a ship, team etc.

▷ *tr.v* **2** be the skipper(1) of (a team etc).

skirmish /'skɜːmɪʃ/ *c.n* **1** usu short fight between small units, often as a preparation for a bigger battle between bigger units. **2** (*fig*) small argument or quarrel between two or more people, sometimes before a more serious one.

▷ *intr.v* **3** (often — *with s.o*) have a skirmish(*n*) (against s.o).

skirt¹ /skɜːt/ *c.n* **1** piece of clothing worn by women and girls over their underclothes from their waist down. **2** part of a dress or coat that hangs below the waist. **3** device on a machine, vehicle etc that is used to prevent it dirtying or doing damage to people or things. **4** length of rubber, plastic(3) etc like a skirt(1) that hangs down from the sides of a hovercraft and keeps the air inside when it is moving.

skirt² /skɜːt/ *tr.v* **1** be or go round (s.t) without going into it: *Here the river skirts the mountains.* **2** (*fig*) avoid (s.t): *Mr and Mrs Gray have tried to talk to their daughter but she always skirts the question of what she wants to do after leaving school.* **skirt (a)round s.t** = skirt² s.t.

'skirting ,board *c/u.n* board fixed to the bottom of the walls of a room.

skit /skɪt/ *c.n* (often — *on s.t*) short funny story or play (about s.t), usu by copying it.

skittish /'skɪtɪʃ/ *adj* **1** (of a person or animal) jumping about; not serious; always changing one's mind; lively(1) (⇨ live¹). **2** (of an animal, usu a horse) having a nervous nature.

'skittishly *adv*. **'skittishness** *u.n*.

skittle /'skɪtl/ *c.n* thing that is like a wooden bottle, used in a game of skittles.

skittles *u.n* (often *play* —) game in which there are nine skittles (⇨ skittle) and one has to try to knock down as many of them as one can with a ball. Compare bowls (⇨ bowl²), ninepins.

skive /skaɪv/ *intr.v* (often — *off*) (*informal*) avoid doing s.t that one ought to do, often by keeping away from people who can make one do it: *skive off school.*

'skiver *c.n* (*derog*) person who skives.

skulduggery ⇨ skullduggery.

skulk /skʌlk/ *intr.v* hide, usu while moving about, because one has done, wants to do, s.t bad: *There is someone skulking (about) in the bushes.*

'skulker *c.n* person who skulks.

skull /skʌl/ *c.n* bone around one's brain. **get s.t into one's/s.o's (thick) skull** (*fig*; *derog*) manage to (make s.o) understand s.t.

,skull and 'cross,bones *c/def.n* **1** picture of a skull with two bones crossed behind it, used as a warning of danger, e.g on a bottle of poison. **2** the same kind of picture used on pirates'(1) flags in the past.

skullduggery /skʌl'dʌgərɪ/ *u.n* (US **skul-'duggery**) (*informal*) secret, dishonest or unfair action(s).

skunk /skʌŋk/ *c.n* **1** small black and white animal found in North America which protects itself against attack by giving out a very nasty smelling liquid. **2** (*fig*) unpleasant and/or unfair person.

sky /skaɪ/ *n* (*pl* **-ies**) **1** *def.n* air above our earth: *The sky is bright blue today. There are clouds in the sky.* **2** *c.n* (sometimes *pl* with a *sing* meaning) appearance of the sky(1): *We started our voyage under a blue sky* (or *blue skies*). **pie in the sky** ⇒ pie. **praise s.o/s.t to the skies** praise s.o/s.t very much. **the sky's the limit** (*informal*) there is no limit to how much one can spend. ⇒ sky-high.
▷ *tr.v* (**-ies, -ied**) **3** hit (a ball) high into the air, usu by mistake.
,sky 'blue *u.n* colour of a clear sky.
,sky-'blue *adj* having the colour of sky blue.
'sky-,diver *c.n* person who engages in the sport of parachuting(2) and performs tricks in the air before opening her/his parachute(1).
'sky-,diving *u.n* sport of sky-divers.
,sky-'high *adj/adv* (*fig; informal*) very high: *The cost of meat has gone sky-high.* ⇒ skyrocket.
'sky,lark *c.n* **1** kind of small bird that flies up high while singing.
▷ *intr.v* **2** = lark that (⇒ lark²(2)).
'sky,light *c.n* kind of flat window in a roof.
'sky,line *c/def.n* outline of things seen at the edge of the sky.
'sky,rocket *intr.v* (*informal*) (of prices etc) go up quickly and steeply: *The price of petrol skyrocketed in 1981.*
'sky-,scraper *c.n* very tall building.

slab /slæb/ *n* **1** *c.n* (usu — of s.t) thick flat piece (of s.t): *a slab of chocolate; a* marble(1) *slab to prepare food on.* **2** *def.n* (*informal*) kind of table on which dead bodies are put in a hospital etc.

slack /slæk/ *adj* **1** (of a rope etc) not tight(ened). **2** (*derog*) (of a person, behaviour etc) a little lazy; not very careful or diligent. **3** (of business etc) not busy: *Business is slack in the umbrella trade because the weather is so good.* **4** (of controls over s.t etc) not strong or effective(1).
▷ *u.n* **5** part of a rope etc that is not tight. **6** time when business etc is slack(3). **take in/up the slack** tighten s.t so that the slack(5) becomes tight.
▷ *v* **7** *intr.v* be slack(*adj*).
'slacken *tr/intr.v* (often — (s.t) off/up) (cause (s.o/s.t) to) become slack(er)(*adj*): *The sailors slackened off the ropes and let them go. Business slackens at this time of year.*
'slacker *c.n* (*derog; informal*) person who is slack(2).
'slackly *adv.* **'slackness** *u.n.*
slacks *pl.n* (often *pair of* —) informal, loose trousers.
'slack ,season *c/def.n* season when things are not busy. ⇒ slack(3).

slag /slæg/ *u.n* waste material that is not wanted after ore has been melted to make metal.
'slag,heap *c.n* pile of slag that has been thrown away after making metal.

slain /sleɪn/ *p.p* of slay.

slake /sleɪk/ *tr.v* (usu — one's thirst) (*literary*) drink enough to satisfy (one's thirst).

slalom /'slɑːləm/ *c/def.n* race on skis(1) down a hill in which one has to follow a winding course marked by pairs of flags.

slam /slæm/ *c.n* **1** act of shutting a door etc with a lot of noise and force; noise made by doing this: *He closed the cupboard door with a slam. I was woken up by the slam of a car door.* **a/the grand slam** (**a**) (in sport, esp tennis) winning of all the most important tournaments. (**b**) (in bridge²) winning of all 13 tricks(7).
▷ *tr/intr.v* (**-mm-**) **2** (often — (s.t) shut) (cause (a door etc) to) shut with a lot of noise and force: *The angry man went out slamming the door behind him. The door slammed shut and the boys found themselves trapped.* **slam the door** (**in s.o's face**) (**a**) leave in an angry way, often in the middle of an argument etc and often closing a door etc with a bang. (**b**) (*fig*) rudely refuse to do s.t for s.o. **slam s.t down** put s.t down with a lot of noise and force: *The woman slammed the books down on my table and walked out of the room.* **slam the telephone down** (**on s.o**) put down the telephone suddenly and rudely in the middle of an argument etc (with s.o). **slam on the brake(s)** ⇒ brake(*n*).

slander /'slɑːndə/ *n* **1** *c.n* lie spoken about s.o which causes her/him harm. **2** *u.n* speaking such a lie, esp when the person who made it is sued for making it. Compare libel(1).
▷ *tr.v* **3** tell a lie about (s.o) which is a slander(1). Compare libel(2).
'slanderer *c.n* person who slanders(3) s.o.
'slanderous *adj* that is or contains a slander(1).
'slanderously *adv.*

slang /slæŋ/ *u.n* (also *attrib*) **1** very informal (and often *derog*) language not considered to be polite, suitable etc: *A slang word for 'girl' is 'bird'.* **2** special language used by a particular kind of person: schoolboy *slang.*
▷ *tr.v* **3** attack (s.o) rudely with words.
'slanginess *u.n* fact of being slangy.
'slanging ,match *c.n* rude argument between two or more people in which each slangs(3) the other(s).
'slangy *adj* (**-ier, -iest**) **1** that is (like) slang(*n*). **2** that is rude (and slangy(1)).

slant /slɑːnt/ *c.n* **1** position or direction that is at an angle neither horizontal nor vertical; slope(1). **2** way of looking at, writing etc about, s.o/s.t that is different from other ones (sometimes in an unfair way): *I don't like that newspaper because it always gives its own political slant to news.* **at/on a slant** not horizontal(ly) or vertical(ly): *She always wears her hat at a slant.*
▷ *v* **3** *tr/intr.v* (cause (s.t) to) be at a slant. ⇒ tilt(2). **4** *tr.v* give a slant(2) to (s.t): *This newspaper slants the news.*
'slantingly *adv* at a slant.
'slant,wise *adj/adv* at a slant.

slap /slæp/ *adv* **1** (*informal*) right; exactly: *The apple from the tree landed slap on top of my head. I went round the corner and ran slap into the middle of a crowd of children.*
▷ *c.n* **2** quick hit with the palm¹(1) of one's hand. **a slap in the face** (**for s.o**) (*fig; informal*) action, words etc that is/are, seems/seem to be, intended to reject(3) s.o/s.t rudely. **a slap on the back** (*fig*) congratulations for s.o.
▷ *tr.v* (**-pp-**) **3** give (s.o/s.t) one or more slaps(2): *She's crying because I slapped her for being rude.*

Sheila slapped me on the back and wished me good luck. **4** (often — *s.t down* (*on s.t*)) put (s.t) down or on s.t with a lot of force and noise or carelessly: *He slapped the book down on my table. Don't slap the paint on like that; do it carefully.* **slap s.o down** (*fig; informal*) = give s.o a slap in the face.

slap-'bang *adv* (*informal*) = slap(1).

'**slap,dash** *adj* (*derog; informal*) careless: *a slap-dash worker; slapdash work.*

'**slap,happy** *adj* (-*ier*, -*iest*) (*informal*) **1** happy in a careless way, without any control of oneself. **2** = slapdash.

'**slap,stick** *u.n* (also *attrib*) comedy(2) in which the action and words are of a very simple and rough kind, e.g people throwing cream in each other's faces: (*a*) *slapstick comedy.*

'**slap-,up** *attrib.adj* (*informal*) very good; very high-class: *a slap-up dinner in the best restaurant in town.*

slash /slæʃ/ *c.n* **1** act of cutting s.o/s.t with a sword, knife etc, usu with a quick or strong stroke: *He gave the weeds several slashes with his stick.* **2** cut made in this way: *There was a slash on his arm that was bleeding quite heavily.*

▷ *v* **3** *tr.v* give (s.o/s.t) one or more slashes(1). **4** *tr/ intr.v* (usu — (*s.t*) *about/around* etc) (cause (a sword etc) to) move about as if trying to slash(3) s.o/s.t. **5** *tr/intr.v* (often — *against/at s.t*) (of rain etc) beat hard (against s.t). **6** *tr.v* reduce (prices, costs etc) very much.

slat /slæt/ *c.n* long thin narrow flat piece of wood, plastic etc, usu found in furniture or venetian blinds: *a bed with slats instead of springs.*

'**slatted** *adj* that has slats: *a chair with a slatted back.*

slate¹ /sleɪt/ *n* **1** *u.n* (also *attrib*) rock made of grey clay that has become hard by heat and pressure while under the earth; it is mined and split into sheets: *a slate roof.* **2** *c.n* piece of this material or of wood etc used for putting on roofs in overlapping(2) rows to keep out rain etc. **3** *c.n* piece of slate¹(1), wood etc used for writing on. (**start with**) **a clean sheet/slate** (*fig*) a completely new situation in which there is nothing that is the result of past actions etc: *We are going to forget about what you did last week and start again with a clean slate.* **wipe the slate clean** (*fig*) remove all record or memory of a bad past: *Let's wipe the slate clean and start again.*

▷ *tr.v* **4** cover (a roof etc) with slates(2).

slate² /sleɪt/ *tr.v* (usu — *s.o for* (*doing*) *s.t*) attack (s.o) strongly in words (for (doing) s.t).

slatted ⇒ slat.

slaughter /'slɔːtə/ *n* **1** *u.n* killing (of an animal) to use it for meat. **2** *c/u.n* killing (of s.o, an animal, esp a lot of them) in a cruel and/or unnecessary way. **3** *c.n* (*fig; informal*) heavy defeat (of s.o) in a match etc: *The tennis match was a slaughter as the champion(3) was just too good.*

▷ *tr.v* **4** kill (an animal) to use it for meat; butcher(4) (an animal). **5** (*derog*) kill (s.o, an animal, esp a lot of people, animals) in a cruel and/or unneces-sary way; massacre(3) (s.o, an animal): *Hundreds of people are slaughtered on the roads every year by drivers who have drunk too much.* **6** (*fig; informal*) beat (s.o) very easily in a match etc.

'**slaughter,house** *c.n* (*pl* -s /-,hauzɪz/) place where animals are slaughtered(4); abattoir.

slave /sleɪv/ *c.n* **1** person who is the property of another person. **2** (usu — *of s.o/s.t;* — *to s.t*) per-son who does everything that he/she is told to do by s.o or that s.t, e.g fashion or habit, makes her/ him want to do: *She refused to be her husband's slave. John is a slave to duty.* **3** (*informal*) person who has a hard and/or boring job that he/she has to do in order to earn a living: *a wage slave.*

▷ *intr.v* **4** (usu — (*away*) *at/over s.t*) work very/too hard (doing s.t).

'**slave-,driver** *c.n* (*derog*) person who makes one or more other people work too hard.

,**slave 'labour** *u.n* very hard work for very little or no money.

'**slavery** *u.n* **1** state of being a slave(1). **2** system of having slaves(1).

'**slavish** *adj* **1** like the work, life etc of slaves(1). **2** (usu *attrib*) (*derog*) that copies/follows s.o/s.t exactly without showing any originality: *a slavish copy/imitation of s.t.*

'**slavishly** *adv.*

slaver /'slævə/ *u.n* **1** saliva that is coming out of s.o's, an animal's, mouth.

▷ *intr.v* **2** produce slaver(1).

slay /sleɪ/ *tr.v* (*p.t* slew /sluː/, *p.p* slain /sleɪn/) (*literary*) kill (s.o).

'**slayer** *c.n* person who slays s.o.

SLD /,es ,el 'diː/ *def/unique n abbr* Social Liberal Democratic Party.

sleazy /'sliːzɪ/ *adj* (-*ier*, -*iest*) (*derog*) cheap, dirty and unpleasant: *The man was living in a sleazy little hotel because he had lost most of his money.*

'**sleaziness** *u.n.*

sled /sled/ = sledge.

sledge /sledʒ/ *c.n* (also **sled**) **1** vehicle for going over snow and ice with runners(3) underneath instead of wheels. Compare sleigh.

▷ *intr.v* (also **sled**, -*dd*-) **2** use a sledge(1) for sport or for going from one place to another.

'**sledging** *u.n* (usu *go* —) use of a sledge(1) for sport or for going from one place to another.

sledgehammer /'sledʒ,hæmə/ *c.n* large heavy hammer, used esp for breaking stones, hammering in posts etc.

sleek /sliːk/ *adj* **1** (usu of hair or fur) smooth and shining because it is healthy. **2** (of a person, her/his appearance etc) (too) well groomed (⇒ groom(*v*)).

'**sleekly** *adv.* '**sleekness** *u.n.*

sleep /sliːp/ *n* **1** *u.n* state of not being awake; state of unconsciousness which is a natural way of resting. **2** *sing.n* period of time during which one is in a state of sleep(1): *I hope you have, can get, a good night's sleep. He was in a deep sleep when I found him.* **get** (**off**) **to sleep** manage to go to sleep(a), usu after some difficulty. **go to sleep** (**a**) begin to sleep(1); lose consciousness, usu to enter a state of sleep(1) but sometimes as a result of an anaesthetic. (**b**) (of a part of one's body) become unable to feel anything; get pins and needles (⇒ pin); become numb(1). **lose sleep over s.t** (usu negative) (*informal*) be very worried about/by s.t: *I'm sorry about Joe's accident but I'm not going to lose any sleep over it.* **put s.o, an animal, to sleep** (**a**) give s.o, an animal, an anaesthetic to make her/him/it unconscious. **(b)** give an animal an injection that kills it in a gentle way. **read oneself/s.o to sleep** read (to s.o) until one, he, she goes to sleep. ⇒ asleep.

▷ *v* (*p.t,p.p* slept /slept/) **3** *intr.v* be in a state of sleep(1): *Peter's sleeping.* ⇒ oversleep. **4** *tr.v* provide a place where (s.o) can sleep(3): *Our boat sleeps four people.*

sleep around (*informal*) have sex(3) with a lot of different people; be promiscuous.

sleep in **(a)** sleep(3) in the house etc in which one also works: *Our school has a cook but she doesn't sleep in; she sleeps out.* **(b)** = lie in (⇒ lie²).

sleep it/s.t off **(a)** sleep(3) in order to stop feeling s.t: *I had a headache this evening but I slept it off.* **(b)** sleep(3) long enough to stop being drunk.

sleep like a log/top ⇒ log(*n*), top¹.

sleep on s.t (*informal*) postpone deciding about s.t until the next day so that one can have time to think about it.

sleep out **(a)** sleep(3) in a different place from where one works, usu when it is possible to sleep in(a). **(b)** sleep(3) outdoors or in a different place from one's own home.

sleep through s.t not be woken up by s.t: *Did you manage to sleep through all the noise last night?*

sleep tight ⇒ tight(*adv*).

sleep together (*informal*) (of two people) have sex(3).

sleep well (words often said to s.o before he/ she goes to bed/sleep): *Good night, Helen. Sleep well.*

sleep with s.o (*informal*) have sex(3) with s.o.

'sleeper¹ *c.n* **1** person who sleeps(3). **a deep/ heavy/light/sound sleeper** ⇒ deep(6), heavy(8), light²(8), sound¹(2). **2** train that has sleeping-cars. ⇒ sleeper².

'sleepily *adv* in a sleepy(1) way.

'sleepiness *u.n* fact or state of being sleepy.

'sleeping ,bag *c.n* padded (⇒ pad(5)) bag for sleeping(3) in when one is camping etc.

'sleeping-,car *c.n* carriage on a train with beds for sleeping(3) in.

,sleeping 'partner *c.n* partner in a business company etc who does not work for it.

'sleeping ,pill *c.n* pill(1) that one takes to help one to sleep(3).

'sleeping ,sickness *u.n* kind of disease caused by the bite of the tsetse fly in Africa which makes animals and people very tired etc and can also kill them.

'sleeping ,tablet = sleeping pill.

'sleepless *adj* **1** (usu — *night*) during which one is unable to sleep(3). **2** (of a person, animal) who/ that cannot or does not sleep(3).

'sleeplessly *adv.* **'sleeplessness** *u.n.*

'sleep,walk *intr.v* get up and walk about while one is asleep.

'sleep,walker *c.n* person who sleepwalks.

'sleep,walking *u.n* fact or act of getting up and walking about while one is asleep.

'sleepy *adj* (*-ier, -iest*) **1** wanting to go to sleep(a). **2** (of a place) very quiet; not busy: *a sleepy little village.*

'sleepy,head *c.n* (*informal*) person, usu a child, who is sleepy(1).

sleeper¹ ⇒ sleep.

sleeper² /'sli:pə/ *c.n* piece of wood, metal etc joining the two rails of a railway track(3).

sleet /sli:t/ *u.n* **1** mixture of rain and ice falling from the sky.

▷ *intr.v* **2** (of sleet) fall from the clouds: *It's been sleeting all day.*

'sleety *adj* (*-ier, -iest*) in the form of sleet.

sleeve /sli:v/ *c.n* **1** part of a coat etc that covers (part of) one's arm: *'Do you want a shirt with long or short sleeves?'* **2** cover like an envelope that fits over a record¹(1) and usu has information about the record¹(1) printed on it. **3** cover that fits closely over s.t, e.g a book or a moving part of a machine. **have/keep s.t up one's sleeve** (*fig; informal*) have s.t secretly for use when it is needed. **laugh up one's sleeve** (*fig; informal*) laugh secretly. **roll up one's sleeves** **(a)** make one's sleeves(1) shorter by rolling the cloth so as to have one's arms free. **(b)** (*fig; informal*) get ready for some serious or hard work. **wear one's heart on one's sleeve** ⇒ heart(*n*).

-sleeved *adj* having sleeves(1) of the kind shown in the first part of the word: *a short-sleeved shirt.*

'sleeveless *adj* (of a piece of clothing) having no sleeves(1).

sleigh /slei/ *c.n* vehicle like a sledge(1) but usu bigger that can carry people; it is pulled by a horse.

sleight of hand /,slait əv 'hænd/ *n* **1** *u.n* skill in doing tricks with cards etc using one's hands so quickly and cleverly that people do not see how one does them. **2** *c/u.n* (*fig*) act of deceit: *He got a loan from the bank by sleight of hand.*

slender /'slendə/ *adj* **1** not fat; thin in a pleasant way; slim(1): *a slender girl; a slender branch on a tree.* Compare skinny. **2** not thick; slim(2): *a slender book of poems.* **3** slight; very small; hardly big enough; slim(3): *There is still a slender chance that we can catch our train.*

,slender 'means *pl.n* (often *of* —) having very little or hardly enough money.

'slenderly *adv.* **'slenderness** *u.n.*

slept /slept/ *p.t,p.p* of sleep.

sleuth /slu:θ/ *c.n* (*joking*) = detective.

slew¹ /slu:/ *tr/intr.v* (cause (s.o/s.t) to) turn or swing violently: *When the giant wave struck the ship it slewed (around) and hit a rock.*

slew² /slu:/ *p.t* of slay.

slice /slais/ *c.n* **1** (often — *of s.t*) thin flat piece that has been cut from s.t: *a slice of bread.* **2** instrument with a flat wide blade, used in cooking to lift up food, e.g slices(1) of meat. **3** way of hitting a ball so that it does not go straight but twists at an angle: *a backhand slice.* Compare hook(3).

▷ *v* **4** *tr.v* (often — *s.t up*) cut (a loaf of bread) etc into slices(1). **5** *tr/intr.v* cut (one's hand etc), usu accidentally, with a knife etc. **6** *tr.v* hit (a ball) so that it twists instead of going straight. ⇒ slice(3).

slice s.t (up) into s.t cut s.t, e.g a loaf, up in such a way that one produces s.t, e.g thick slices(1).

slice s.t off (s.t) cut a slice(1) of s.t off (s.t). **slice s.t thin** slice(4) s.t in such a way as to produce thin slices(1).

,sliced 'bread *u.n* bread that one buys already cut into slices(1).

slick¹ /slik/ *adj* **1** smooth and slippery: *Be careful how you drive this morning; there is slick ice on the roads.* **2** looking smart¹(1), well dressed etc (but often unpleasant underneath it all). **3** clever and successful (but sometimes not honest).

▷ *tr.v* **4** *slick one's hair* etc **down** make one's hair etc look straight, tidy and shiny by putting water, grease etc on it.

'**slickly** *adv.* '**slickness** *u.n.*

slick² /slɪk/ *c.n* ▬ oil slick.

slide /slaɪd/ *c.n* **1** movement along a smooth surface while remaining touching it all the time: *We had a slide on the ice.* **2** place down which people, esp children, or things can slide(8): *The children are playing on the swings and slides.* **3** (often as part of a word) sudden and often dangerous fall of s.t: *a landslide.* **4** (*fig*) steady fall: *The slide in the value of the pound is continuing.* **5** ▬ hair-slide. **6** single frame(5) of a film that has been put in a frame(1) so that it can be seen on a screen or in a viewer(2): *a colour slide.* **7** thin piece of glass on which one puts s.t one wants to examine with a microscope.

▷ *v* (*p.t,p.p* slid /slɪd/) **8** *tr/intr.v* (cause (s.o/s.t) to) move along in a slide(1): *The children slid down the hill on a tray. Slide the* bolt²(1) *across the door to lock it, please.* **9** *intr.v* walk, run etc quietly in order not to be noticed: *During the meeting the secretary slid out of the room several times to collect papers. As we came nearer the rabbits slid away into the trees.* **let s.t slide** (*fig; informal*) not interfere in s.t, often when such interference would have been a good thing.

'**slide pro,jector** *c.n* projector for showing slides(6), usu one after another.

'**slide ,rule** *c.n* instrument like a ruler but with a piece that slides(8) along it, used for doing certain calculations in mathematics.

'**slide ,show** *c.n* kind of film show in which only slides(6) and not moving films are shown.

,**sliding 'door** *c.n* door that opens and shuts by sliding(8) across the doorway.

,**sliding 'scale** *c.n* (often *on a —*) scale¹(1) that varies when there are other changes: *We are paid on a sliding scale* linked(5) *to the cost of living.*

slight¹ /slaɪt/ *adj* **1** small; not strong: *a slight taste of fish in the soup.* **2** very little; low in probability: *There's only a slight chance of him living beyond tomorrow.* **3** thin; who/that does not look strong: *a girl with a slight figure.* **not in the slightest** not at all; absolutely not: *I don't care in the slightest.*

'**slightly** *adv.* '**slightness** *u.n.*

slight² /slaɪt/ *c.n* (*formal*) **1** (often *— on/to s.o/ s.t*) insult (aimed at s.o/s.t); thing that is done to try to make s.o feel less important.

▷ *tr.v* (*formal*) **2** insult (s.o); try to make (s.o) feel less important: *She felt slighted.*

'**slightingly** *adv* in a way that slights²(2) s.o.

slim /slɪm/ *adj* (*-mm-*) **1** (of a person) not fat; pleasantly thin. **2** (of an object) not thick: *a slim book of poems.* **3** slight; not at all good: *John hasn't worked enough but there is still a slim chance that he will pass his examination.*

▷ *tr/intr.v* (*-mm-*) **4** (often *— (s.o/s.t) down*) (try to) (cause (oneself/s.o/s.t) to) become slim(mer)(1) or lose weight: *I don't want to eat much — I'm slimming.*

'**slimly** *adv.*

'**slimmer** *c.n* person who slims(4).

'**slimming** *u.n* (also *attrib*) action of making oneself/s.o/s.t slim(mer)(1).

'**slimness** *u.n* fact of being slim(*adj*).

slime /slaɪm/ *u.n* **1** very wet mud. **2** sticky liquid that is on the bodies of some fish or that is produced by snails etc.

'**sliminess** *u.n* state or fact of being slimy.

'**slimy** *adj* (*-ier, -iest*) **1** consisting of, like, covered with, slime. **2** (*derog; fig*) very unpleasant.

sling /slɪŋ/ *c.n* **1** piece of cloth etc put under one's arm and round one's neck to support a damaged arm or hand. **2** support(s) made of rope etc put underneath s.t heavy when lifting it, often with a crane(2). **3** weapon usu made of rope and leather and used to throw a stone hard and far.

▷ *tr.v* (*p.t,p.p* slung /slʌŋ/) **4** throw (s.t) (at/to s.o/ s.t), sometimes carelessly or with some difficulty. **5** (often *— s.t up*) lift, hold, move, s.t in a sling(2). *sling mud at s.o/s.t*; *mud-slinging* ⇒ mud.

'**sling,shot** *c.n* ▬ catapult(1).

slink /slɪŋk/ *intr.v* (*p.t,p.p* slunk /slʌŋk/) move quietly and secretly, usu because one does not want to be seen.

slip¹ /slɪp/ *n* **1** *c.n* accidental movement as a result of being on a surface that is too smooth to let one stand etc on it safely. **2** *c.n* (often *a — of the pen/tongue*) mistake (in writing/speech) that is not very important or is done accidentally. **3** *c.n* piece of women's underclothing that is like a thin dress with no sleeves and a low neck. **4** *c.n* (also '**slip,way**) slope running down from the land into the water so that ships and boats can be pulled up it or so that boats can stop there for people to get in and out. **5** *c.n* (in cricket¹) person who stands near the batsman (⇒ bat²) but to her/his right (if she/he is right-handed) and a little behind. **6** *u.n* position of a slip¹(5) on the field. *give s.o the slip* (*informal*) escape from s.o secretly.

▷ *v* (*-pp-*) **7** *intr.v* move accidentally as a result of being on a surface that is too smooth to let one stand etc on it safely: *The boy slipped on the mud and fell. My foot slipped and I hit a wall.* **8** *intr.v* become worse, lower etc: *The pound is slipping on the money markets. Standards in our schools are slipping.* **9** *intr.v* start to make mistakes or be careless: *You're slipping; you forgot to buy the vegetables I asked for.* **10** *tr.v* get free from (s.t that is fastening one): *The man was so thin that he was able to slip his* handcuffs(1) *and escape.* **let s.t slip** (**a**) allow a secret to come out through being careless etc. (**b**) miss a chance.

slip away, *in*, *out* etc go away etc quietly and secretly.

slip by/past (of time) pass, usu in a way that seems very fast.

slip a disc get a slipped disc. ⇒ disc.

slip one's memory/mind be forgotten: '*Why didn't you bring the fruit?*' '*It slipped my mind.*'

slip s.t off/on (*over* (s.t)) (*informal*) take a piece of clothing or a cover off or put it on (over s.t else), usu quickly and without much care.

slip s.o s.t; *slip s.t to s.o* give s.o s.t (often a bribe) secretly.

slip up make a mistake that is not very important. ⇒ slip-up.

'**slip,knot** *c.n* knot that is tied in such a way that one can tighten it by pulling one end of the string.

'**slip-,on** *attrib.adj* that one can slip on (⇒ slip s.t off, on etc): *a slip-on dress.*

'**slip,over** ▬ pullover.

,slipped 'disc ⇒ disc.

'slipper *c.n* kind of light shoe, sometimes with no back, for wearing in the house.

'slipperiness *u.n* fact or state of being slippery.

'slippery *adj* (*-ier, -iest*) **1** smooth, wet etc so that one can easily slip¹(7) on it or so that one cannot hold it easily. **2** (*derog; informal*) who/that one cannot trust because he/she/it is dishonest etc. **as slippery as an eel** ⇒ eel.

'slip ,road *c.n* road that leads on to, off, a motorway or other main road.

'slip,shod *adj* (*derog*) careless: *slipshod work.*

'slip,stream *c.n* (*technical*) **1** stream of air left by a plane's propeller or jet engine (⇒ jet¹). **2** area behind a vehicle that is moving very fast in which air resistance is less than usual: *If a cyclist gets into a car's slipstream he/she can move faster than usual.*

'slip-,up *c.n* mistake that is not very important. ⇒ slip up.

'slip,way *c.n* = slip¹(4).

slip² /slɪp/ *c.n* small piece of paper, e.g for writing on: *sales slips. Put a slip of paper into your book so you remember your place.* **slip of a boy/girl** small thin boy/girl.

slit /slɪt/ *c.n* **1** narrow cut or opening: *a skirt with a slit at the back.*

▷ *tr.v* (*-tt-, p.t,p.p slit, slitted*) **2** make a slit(1) in (s.t). **slit s.t open** make s.t open by slitting(2) it: *He slit the letter open with a knife.*

slither /'slɪðə/ *intr.v* slip and slide, usu following a twisting or unsteady course: *We saw snakes slithering through the grass.*

'slithery *adj* that looks or feels slippery(1).

sliver /'slɪvə/ *c.n* (often — *of s.t*) small thin (broken, cut etc) piece (of s.t): *a sliver of broken glass; slivers of meat.*

slob /slɒb/ *c.n* (*derog; informal*) unpleasant and lazy person.

slobber /'slɒbə/ *tr/intr.v* (allow (saliva) to) run down out of one's mouth. **slobber over s.o/s.t** (*fig*) praise or show love etc for s.o/s.t in an unpleasantly excessive way.

sloe /sləʊ/ *c.n* small dark purple fruit of the blackthorn.

,sloe 'gin *u.n* strong alcoholic(1) drink made from sloes and gin¹.

slog /slɒɡ/ *n* **1** *c/u.n* (example of s.t that is) long, hard and often unpleasant work etc: *Digging the garden was a slog. Today's walking was all slog.* **2** *c.n* time or course of slog(1). **3** *c.n* hard careless hit given to a ball etc.

▷ *v* (*-gg-*) **4** *intr.v* (often — *away at s.t*) work hard, continuously and often unpleasantly at s.t. **5** *tr/intr.v* hit (a ball, person etc), usu hard and carelessly.

'slogger *c.n* person who slogs(*v*).

slogan /'sləʊɡən/ *c.n* word(s) saying s.t that one wants people to believe esp because one is trying to get them to vote for one or to buy one's product: *'First Choice' is that fruit shop's slogan.*

sloop /sluːp/ *c.n* **1** very small kind of warship. **2** small kind of sailing ship with one mast.

slop /slɒp/ *u.n* (usu *pl* with *sing* meaning) **1** food that is mainly liquid and has very little taste or has been made for sick people. **2** food left after preparing, cooking and serving it to people and often given to animals.

▷ *v* (*-pp-*) **3** *tr/intr.v* (often — *(s.t) about/over*)(cause (a liquid) to) move about from side to side in a container (so that some of it spills). ⇒ slosh(1). **4** *intr.v* (often — *about/around* — *through s.t*) go about etc in mud, water etc. ⇒ slosh(2).

slope /sləʊp/ *c.n* **1** (surface that is at an) angle between horizontal and vertical: *A slope of one in ten is a slope of nine degrees.*

▷ *intr.v* **2** be or move at an angle between horizontal and vertical: *The park slopes down to a river.* **slope off** (*informal*) go away secretly, usu to avoid s.t.

sloppy /'slɒpɪ/ *adj* (*-ier, -iest*) (*derog*) **1** rather wet or damp. **2** (of s.o's appearance, clothes etc) not tidy; unpleasantly informal, dirty etc. **3** (of s.o's work etc) careless. **4** showing love in an unpleasantly soft way: *a sloppy film.*

'sloppily *adv.* **'sloppiness** *u.n.*

slosh /slɒʃ/ *v* **1** *tr/intr.v* (often — *about/around*) = slop(3). **2** *intr.v* move through water, mud etc, usu making a splashing noise. ⇒ slop(4). **3** *tr.v* (*slang*) hit (s.o).

sloshed *adj* (*informal*) drunk(1).

slot /slɒt/ *c.n* **1** long narrow rectangular opening in a machine, tool etc into which one puts s.t else: *If you put a 50p coin in the slot, a ticket will come out. The screw has a slot on its head for a screwdriver.* **2** (*informal*) place that is intended for s.o/s.t: *I found a slot for me in the factory. This television programme has frequent slots for advertisements.*

▷ *v* (*-tt-*) **3** *tr/intr.v* (usu — *(s.o/s.t) into s.t;* — *(s.t) together*) (cause (s.t) to) go into a slot(*n*) in s.t: *This bit that sticks out slots into the one with the hole in it. I think we can find a job to slot you into.*

'slotted *adj* that has slots(1) in it.

slouch /slaʊtʃ/ *c.n* **1** position of standing, walking etc with one's shoulders hanging forward because, as if, one was tired: *We knew he had failed by the slouch in his shoulders.* **2** (*derog; informal*) careless, useless person.

▷ *intr.v* **3** stand, walk etc with a slouch(1): *Stop slouching and stand up straight!*

'slouchingly *adv.*

slough¹ /slaʊ/ *c.n* (*formal* or *literary*) place where there is deep mud; swamp(1).

slough² /slʌf/ *tr.v* (usu — *s.t off*) (of a snake etc) throw off (its old dead skin).

slovenly /'slʌvənlɪ/ *adj* (*derog*) who does not look tidy, clean etc.

'slovenliness *u.n* state or fact of being slovenly.

slow /sləʊ/ *adj* **1** not moving or happening quickly; taking a long time to go from one place to another or to do s.t; moving or happening with less speed than usual: *He's usually very slow in the morning and takes a long time to wake up properly. I got on the slow train by mistake.* Opposite fast¹(1), quick(1). **2** (of business etc) not busy: *Business is slow in summer because so many people are on holiday.* Opposite brisk. **3** (of a person, her/his brain etc) not able to think quickly; not able to understand things easily. **4** (*pred*) (of a clock or watch) showing an earlier time than the correct one: *Your clock is five minutes slow.* Opposite fast¹(2). **(be) slow in doing s.t** do s.t slowly; delay doing s.t. **be slow off the mark** ⇒ mark(*n*). **(be) slow to do s.t** not do s.t except after some delay. **slow but sure** slow(1) but safe: *My old car is slow but sure.*

▷ *adv* **5** slowly. **go slow** ⇨ go, go-slow.

▷ *tr/intr.v* **6** (often — (s.o/s.t) down/up) (cause (s.o/ s.t) to) go more slowly.

'**slow,coach** *c.n* (*derog*; *informal*) person who does things very or too slowly.

'**slow-,down** *c.n* (often *a* — *in/of s.t*) slowing(6) down (of work).

'**slowly** *adv.*

,**slow 'motion** *u.n* (often *in* —) movement that happens more slowly than in real life, usu in a film, often so that one can see details that one cannot usually see: *Let's watch that goal in slow motion to see who actually scored it.*

'**slowness** *u.n.*

,**slow 'poison** *c/u.n* kind of poison that acts slowly.

'**slow,worm** *c.n* kind of small lizard that has no legs and looks like a snake.

sludge /slʌdʒ/ *u.n* **1** thick mud. **2** dirty oil in an engine after it has been used too long. **3** sewage after it has been treated to clean it.

slug[1] /slʌg/ *c.n* kind of creature like a snail without a shell, often found in gardens eating vegetables and other plants.

slug[2] /slʌg/ *c.n* **1** (*slang*) bullet. **2** piece of metal made for some purpose.

slug[3] /slʌg/ *tr.v* (-gg-) (*informal*) hit (s.o/s.t) hard, usu with one's fist. **slug it out** (*informal*) fight hard until one person or side wins or both are unable to go on.

sluggish /'slʌgɪʃ/ *adj* moving slowly; feeling tired.

'**sluggishly** *adv.* '**sluggishness** *u.n.*

sluice /sluːs/ *c.n* **1** place through which water can be allowed to flow in a controlled way by using a sluice gate or valve(1) to reduce or stop it.

▷ *v* **2** *tr.v* (often — *s.t* down (*with s.t*); — *s.t* out (*with s.t*)) wash (s.t) (or sometimes s.o) by pouring a lot of water over or along (her/him/it): *sluice down the dirty walls and floors.* **3** *intr.v* (often — *down* (*from s.t*)) flow strongly (down) (from s.t).

'**sluice ,gate** *c.n* kind of gate that can be raised, lowered etc, to control the flow of water in a sluice(1).

'**sluice,way** *c.n* kind of small canal along which water can be made to flow fast, e.g to wash earth from gold when mining.

slum /slʌm/ *c.n* (also *attrib*) (*derog*) **1** (sometimes *pl* with *sing* meaning) area, usu of a city, in which the houses are very poor, dirty and in a bad condition: *a slum part of the town.* **2** (*informal*) dirty untidy place: *Your room is an absolute slum inside; tidy it now.*

▷ *intr.v* (-mm-) **3 slum it** live in a poorer, cheaper way than one is used to: *When we stay in a hotel in London we often have to slum it.*

'**slummy** *adj* (-ier, -iest) (*informal*) of/like a slum(*n*).

slumber /'slʌmbə/ *c/u.n* **1** (sometimes *pl* with a *sing* meaning) (*literary*) sleep: *I was awakened from my slumbers by a knock at the door.*

▷ *intr.v* **2** (*literary*) sleep.

slump /slʌmp/ *c/u.n* **1** time during which business is very bad; depression(2). Opposite boom[3](1).

▷ *intr.v* **2** (often — *down*) fall (down) heavily; collapse(4): *When she got home she was very tired and just slumped in a chair to rest.* **3** (of business etc) become (very) bad, sometimes suddenly. Opposite boom[3](2).

slung /slʌŋ/ *p.t,p.p* of sling.

slunk /slʌŋk/ *p.t,p.p* of slink.

slur[1] /slɜː/ *c.n* nasty and untrue suggestion about s.o/s.t. (**cast/put**) **a slur on s.o/s.t** (make) such a suggestion about s.o/s.t.

slur[2] /slɜː/ *sing.n* **1** way of speaking in which one pronounces sounds unclearly and/or in such a way that one sound runs into another: *There was a slur in his voice as a result of the damage to his throat.*

▷ *tr/intr.v* **2** pronounce (a sound etc) with a slur[2](1): *People who are drunk often slur their words.*

slurp /slɜːp/ *c.n* **1** unpleasant noise made when eating food with a liquid in it or when drinking s.t: *He finished the bowl of soup with a final slurp.*

▷ *tr/intr.v* **2** eat (food with liquid in it) or drink (liquid) in a noisy unpleasant way.

slush /slʌʃ/ *u.n* **1** mixture of snow and water, usu when the snow is melting. **2** (*derog*) love stories that are too sentimental.

'**slush ,fund** *c.n* money collected and kept for dishonest purposes, usu to help s.o to be elected or to help one's business by bribing people.

'**slushiness** *u.n* state or fact of being slushy.

'**slush ,money** *u.n* money in a slush fund.

'**slushy** *adj* (-ier, iest) consisting of slush; having slush in/on it.

slut /slʌt/ *c.n* (*derog*) immoral or dirty woman.

'**sluttish** *adj* of or like a slut.

sly /slaɪ/ *adj* **1** (trying to be) clever in a secret and not honest way; cunning(1). **2** unkind but in a joking way: *Those children make sly jokes about their teacher's clothes.*

▷ *def.n* **3 on the sly** secretly; not telling anyone: *He gave the children some sweets on the sly although he knew their mother disapproved.*

'**slyly** *adv.* '**slyness** *u.n.*

smack[1] /smæk/ *adv* **1** (of a way of hitting etc s.o/s.t) suddenly and hard: *As he ran around the corner he ran smack into a woman.* **2** (almost) exactly: *The church is smack in the middle of the village.*

▷ *c.n* **3** hit with one's open hand: *If you do that again, I'll give you a smack.* **4** noise (like that) made by a smack(3): *She threw the papers on the table with a loud smack.* (**give s.o**) **a smack on the cheek/ lips** (*informal*) (give s.o) a quick noisy kiss.

▷ *tr.v* **5** give a smack(3) to (s.o/s.t). **6** put/throw (s.t) ((down) on s.t) with a smack(4): *She smacked the papers down on his desk and left.* **smack one's lips** make a noise like a smack(4) by opening and closing one's lips, usu because one enjoys eating or drinking s.t.

'**smacker** *c.n* (*slang*) **1** loud kiss. **2** pound (£); dollar ($).

smack[2] /smæk/ *c.n* **1** (usu have a — of s.t) (often *fig*) special taste (of/like s.t); suggestion(3) of s.t: *This drink has a smack of apples.*

▷ *intr.v* **2 smack of s.t** (usu *fig*) = have a smack[2](1) of s.t: *The whole business smacks of bribery.*

smack[3] /smæk/ *c.n* (also '**fishing ,smack**) small fishing-boat with sails.

small /smɔːl/ *adj* **1** not big or large; having little size, number etc: *He is rather small for his age. We bought a small house in the village. Only a small number of people came to the meeting.* **2** very little; not much; low in probability; slight¹(2): *We have small chance of catching the train now.* **3** (of letters in writing and printing) not capital: *This is a capital 'C' and this is a small 'c'.* **4** who/that does not do much business: *She has a small printing company.* **feel small** feel ashamed or humble. **in a small way** on a small(4) scale: *Chris is a farmer in a small way; he has only one field and a few cows.* **small wonder (that . . .)** it is not surprising that . . . .

▷ *adv* **5** in such a way that the result is small(1): *He writes so small that I can hardly read his letters.*

▷ *def.n* **6 in the small of one's/s.o's back** in the narrowest part of one's/s.o's back.

'**small ,arms** *pl.n* (also *attrib*) weapons that a person can easily carry: *small arms fire.*

'**small 'beer** *u.n* (*derog*) person or people, ideas, problems etc who/that are not important. **be small beer** be unimportant.

'**small 'change** *u.n* money in coins of little value.

'**small ,fry** *unique/pl.n* (*informal*) **1** baby fish. **2** (*derog*) unimportant person or people.

'**small,holder** *c.n* person who owns or rents a small amount of land for farming etc.

'**small,holding** *c.n* small amount of land, usu used for farming.

'**small 'hours** *def.pl.n* early hours of the morning.

'**small in'testine** *def/c.n* part of the alimentary canal between the stomach and the colon. ⇨ large intestine.

'**small-'minded** *adj* (*derog*) interested only in a few things, usu only in ones that are of advantage to oneself. Opposites broadminded, open-minded.

'**small-'mindedly** *adv.* '**small-'mindedness** *u.n.*

'**smallness** *u.n.*

'**small,pox** *u.n* dangerous disease that spread easily from person to person and left big marks, mostly on people's faces: *Smallpox has now been eradicated.*

smalls *pl.n* (*informal*) underclothing etc, usu ready for washing.

'**small-,talk** *u.n* talk about unimportant things.

'**small-,time** *adj* doing things on a small scale: *a small-time thief.*

smarmy /'smɑːmɪ/ *adj* (*-ier, -iest*) (*derog; slang*) so polite that he/she/it sounds unpleasant and dishonest.

smart¹ /smɑːt/ *adj* **1** who/that looks well dressed, fashionable etc. **2** clever; intelligent; having a quick brain. **3** (of a rise, fall etc) sudden and quite big: *There has been a smart rise in the value of the pound today.* **play it smart** (*informal*) do s.t in a smart¹(2) way.

'**smarten** *tr/intr.v* (usu — (s.o/s.t) **up**) make (s.o/s.t) smart(er)¹(1).

'**smartly** *adv.* '**smartness** *u.n.*

smart² /smɑːt/ *adj* **1** (of a hit etc) quick and hard: *a smart slap*(2).

▷ *c.n* **2** sharp stinging pain, usu not lasting long.

▷ *intr.v* **3** feel, give s.o, a smart²(2): *The smoke is making my eyes smart.* **smart over/under s.t** feel hurt in one's feelings because of s.t.

smash /smæʃ/ *c.n* **1** act of breaking into pieces violently as a result of being dropped, thrown etc: *the smash of plates; a car smash.* **2** sound made by a smash(1): *We heard the smash when she dropped the tray.* **3** (in tennis etc) hard hit of the ball from above.

▷ *v* **4** *tr/intr.v* (often — (s.t) **up**) break (s.t) into pieces violently. **5** *tr/intr.v* (usu — (s.t) *into/through* etc *s.t*) (cause (s.t) to) go into etc s.t violently: *The train smashed into the back of the empty carriages. He smashed his fist through the thin wall.* **6** *tr.v* destroy or ruin (s.t): *The police have smashed the drug*(2) *ring.* **7** *tr/intr.v* (in tennis etc) hit (the ball) hard from above. **smash one's way in(to s.t)** get in(to s.t) etc by smashing(4) s.t.

'**smash-and-'grab** *adj* (usu — *raid*) breaking the window of a shop etc, stealing things from inside and then running away.

smashed *adj* (*slang*) drunk(1) (⇨ drink).

'**smash 'hit** *c.n* ⇨ hit(*n*).

'**smashing** *adj* (*informal*) excellent; wonderful: *We had a smashing time at the dance last night.*

'**smash-,up** *c.n* (*informal*) crash of one or more vehicles.

smattering /'smætərɪŋ/ *c.n* (usu *a* — of *s.t*) very small amount (of knowledge etc): *He has a smattering of German which is useful when he travels.*

smear /smɪə/ *c.n* **1** dirty or untidy(1) mark made when s.t greasy, sticky etc touches s.t. Compare smudge(1). **2** (*medical*) very thin piece of s.t put on a slide(7) so that it can be examined under a microscope, usu to see if it shows signs of disease. **3** (often *attrib*) (*fig*) nasty, usu untrue, thing(s) said or written about s.o to try to make other people dislike her/him: *a smear campaign*(2).

▷ *v* **4** *tr/intr.v* (usu — *s.t on/over s.o/s.t; — s.o/s.t with s.t*) (cause (s.t) to) make a smear(1) (on s.o/s.t etc): *smear glue on the back of the picture and stick it down.* **5** *tr/intr.v* (cause (s.t) to) spread in such a way that it makes a smear(1): *If you try painting on that wet paper it will only smear.* ⇨ smudge(3). **6** *tr.v* make a smear(3) against (s.o): *smearing their name.*

'**smear ,test** *c.n* = cervical smear (⇨ cervix).

smell /smel/ *n* **1** *u.n* one of our five senses that we use our noses for: *Most animals have a much better sense of smell than we have.* **2** *c/u.n* quality in s.o/s.t that we experience by means of our sense of smell(1): *That rose has a beautiful smell.* **3** *c.n* (usu *have a —* (*at/of s.t*)) example of using one's sense of smell(1) for some purpose: *Have a smell at this fish and tell me if you think it's bad.*

▷ *v* (*p.t,p.p* smelled, smelt /smelt/) **4** *tr/intr.v* use one's sense of smell(1) (to experience s.o/s.t); have a smell(3) (at s.o/s.t); know by means of one's sense of smell(1) (that etc . . .): *This apple is ripe; smell (it). I can smell that there is something wrong with the drains*(1). *Smell that fresh air!* **5** *intr.v* give off an unpleasant smell(2): *The fish is bad; it smells.* **6** *intr.v* give off a certain kind of smell(2): *This rose smells beautiful. That food smells good/burnt.* **smell like/of s.o/s.t** have a smell(2) that is like or that reminds one of s.o/ s.t. **smell s.t out** (**a**) find something by using one's sense of smell(1): *Dogs are trained to smell out drugs*(2). (**b**) discover s.t by using one's instinct, knowledge etc.

'**smelliness** *u.n* fact or state of being smelly.

-smelling *adj* who/that has the kind of smell shown by the first part of the word: *a strong-smelling chemical.*

'smelling ,salts *pl.n* chemical (usu ammonia) with a very strong smell that was used to help people become conscious again after fainting.

'smelly *adj* (*-ier, -iest*) (*derog*) having an unpleasant smell(2): *smelly feet.*

smelt¹ /smelt/ *tr.v* melt ore by heating it to get the metal out.

smelt² /smelt/ *p.t,p.p* of smell.

smile /smaɪl/ *c.n* **1** raising of the sides of the mouth to show that one is happy, glad or amused etc: *She met me with a bright smile. He gave me a friendly smile as I came in.* **be all smiles** be very happy. **smile of s.t** smile showing s.t: *smiles of triumph*(3).

▷ *v* **2** *intr.v* give a smile(1): *I smiled when he looked at me.* **3** *tr.v* show (s.t) by smiling instead of speaking: *When I opened the door for her she smiled her thanks but said nothing.* **smile at s.o/ s.t** (a) look at s.o/s.t while smiling(2). (b) smile(2) because of s.o/s.t: *He smiled at the little girl's enjoyment of her ice-cream.* **smile on s.o/s.t** (*fig*) (often of the weather or fate) be helpful or favourable to s.o/s.t: *The weather smiled on us during our holiday.*

'smilingly *adv* in a smiling way.

smirch /smɜːtʃ/ *c.n* **1** (often — *on s.t*) dishonour (to one's character(5) etc).

▷ *tr.v* **2** dishonour (s.t, esp s.o's character(5)). ⇨ besmirch.

smirk /smɜːk/ *c.n* **1** silly smile, often because of shyness or pride.

▷ *intr.v* **2** (usu — *at s.o/s.t*) give a smirk(1) (while looking at s.o/s.t or because of s.o/s.t).

smite /smaɪt/ *tr.v* (*p.t smote* /sməʊt/, *p.p smitten* /'smɪtn/) (*old use*) **1** hit (s.o/s.t) hard. **2** (often *fig*) attack, destroy or ruin (s.o/s.t).

smitten /'smɪtn/ *adj* (usu — *by/with s.t*) **1** attacked (by a disease etc). **2** feeling (love etc) very strongly.

-smitten *adj* smitten (⇨ smite(2)) by the thing that is the first part of the word: *conscience-smitten.*

smith /smɪθ/ *c.n* = blacksmith.

-smith *c.n* **1** person who makes things out of the metal shown in the first part of the word: *a silversmith.* **2** person who makes the thing shown in the first part of the word: *a gunsmith.*

smithy /'smɪðɪ/ *c.n* (*pl -ies*) place in which a blacksmith works.

smithereens /ˌsmɪðə'riːnz/ *pl.n* **in(to), to, smithereens** in(to) very small pieces because of smashing, with the result that the person or thing is ruined or destroyed: *The vase lay in smithereens on the floor. He was blown to smithereens by the bomb.*

smitten /'smɪtn/ ⇨ smite.

smock /smɒk/ *c.n* **1** loose piece of clothing worn over other clothes to keep them clean while working. **2** loose piece of clothing like a shirt worn by a woman, e.g when she is pregnant.

'smocking *u.n* decoration on a dress etc produced by making small folds in the cloth and then joining them together in pretty patterns with a needle and cotton.

smog /smɒg/ *u.n* harmful mixture of fog and smoke from chimneys, car exhausts(1) etc.

smoke /sməʊk/ *n* **1** *u.n* product of burning that one can see in the air and that is a mixture of gas and very small pieces of solid materials: *smoke from a fire/cigarette*; *smoke from a car exhaust*(1). **2** *c.n* (usu *have a —*) act of smoking a cigarette etc: *John often has a smoke after a meal.* **3** *c.n* (*informal*) cigarette: *Have you got a smoke?* **go up in smoke** ⇨ go up(f). **There's no smoke without (a) fire**; **Where there's smoke there's fire** (*proverb*) When people say s.t nasty about s.o/s.t, it may not all be true but there is sure to be some truth in it.

▷ *v* **4** *intr.v* give off (sometimes too much) smoke(1): *Jim, the fire's smoking; will you do something about it, please? When I see a smoking chimney on a cold day I am happy because it means a warm fire.* **5** *tr/intr.v* take smoke(1) into one's mouth (and lungs) from (a cigarette etc): *'Does Norah smoke?' 'Yes, she smokes 20 cigarettes a day.'* **6** *tr.v* put (meat etc) in smoke(1) to give it a good taste and esp so it can be stored. **7** *tr.v* put glass in smoke(1) to make it darker so that it makes lights less bright when one looks through it. **smoke s.o/s.t out** (a) force s.o, an animal, out of a place by putting smoke(1) in the place. (b) (*fig*) find s.o who was hiding and tell people where he/she is.

,smoked 'glass *u.n* glass that has been smoked(7).

'smoker *c.n* **1** person who smokes(5). **2** part of a train etc in which one is allowed to smoke(5). Opposite non-smoker.

'smoke,screen *c.n* **1** cloud of smoke(1) created to hide s.t from an enemy. **2** (*fig*) thing that one does, says etc to hide what is really happening.

'smoke,stack *c.n* very tall chimney on a factory etc.

'smokiness *u.n* fact or state of being smoky.

'smoking *attrib.adj* **1** where one is allowed to smoke(5): *a smoking carriage on a train.* Opposite non-smoking.

▷ *u.n* **2** activity or habit of smoking (⇨ smoke(5)).

'smoky *adj* (*-ier, -iest*) **1** having in it, producing, (too much) smoke(1): *a smoky room.* **2** looking, smelling, tasting like/of, smoke(1).

smolder ⇨ smoulder.

smooch /smuːtʃ/ *c.n* **1** example of smooching.

▷ *intr.v* **2** (*informal*) kiss and cuddle(2).

smooth /smuːð/ *adj* **1** having a flat surface without lumps etc: *smooth skin*; *a smooth sea.* **2** (of s.t mixed with a liquid) without lumps in it: *a smooth paste.* **3** moving in a regular way and without sudden changes in speed etc: *a comfortable car with smooth* acceleration(2); *a smooth journey.* **4** (of the taste of s.t) not sharp or bitter etc: *a smooth old wine.* **5** very polite, pleasant etc: *a smooth way of talking.* **6** (*derog*) too smooth(5) and therefore dangerous or unpleasant: *He has a smooth way with women.*

▷ *def.n* **7** **take the rough with the smooth** ⇨ rough(*n*).

▷ *tr.v* **8** (usu — *s.t down/out*) make (a surface etc) smooth(1,2). **smooth s.t away** (a) make (a problem etc) appear less difficult or important. (b) make (a pain etc) less strong by rubbing an injury gently. **smooth s.t over** (*fig*) make s.t, e.g anger, worry etc, appear less strong. **smooth the way for**

s.o/s.t (*fig*) make things easy or easier for s.o.

'smoothie *c.n* (also **smoothy**) (*pl* -ies) (*derog*; *informal*) person who is smooth(6).

'smoothly *adv.* **'smoothness** *u.n.*

smote /sməʊt/ *p.t* of smite.

smother /'smʌðə/ *v* **1** *tr.v* (usu — *s.o/s.t in/with s.t*) put a thick or complete covering (of s.t) over or round (s.o/s.t): *All the food was smothered in sauces or cream.* **2** *tr.v* cause (s.o) to die by preventing her/him from breathing. **3** *intr.v* die in this way. **4** *tr.v* prevent (s.t) starting or getting stronger: *The police tried to smother the hooligans' activities by arresting their leaders before the football match.*

smoulder /'sməʊldə/ *intr.v* (US **'smolder**) **1** burn without a flame: *If you blow on these smouldering pieces of wood they will burst into flames again.* **2** (often — *with s.t*) (*fig*) show a deep feeling, usu of rage, jealousy etc, often without expressing it fully: *He (or His eyes) smouldered with anger.*

smudge /smʌdʒ/ *c.n* **1** mark made or left by s.t dirty or by s.t wet being spread: *There was a smudge on the letter because of the rain.* ▷ *v* **2** *tr.v* make a smudge(1) on (s.t). **3** *tr.v* make (s.t) dirty or spoil (s.t) by spreading it while it is (still) wet: *Don't smudge the new sign I have painted on the gate; it's still wet.* **4** *tr.v* (*fig*) spoil (one's/s.o's reputation etc) by doing, saying etc s.t bad.

'smudgy *adj* (-ier, -iest) that has smudges(1) on it; that has been smudged(3).

smug /smʌg/ *adj* (-gg-) (of a person, expression etc) showing too great satisfaction with oneself, one's ability etc; self-satisfied: *a smug look on his face.*

'smugly *adv.* **'smugness** *u.n.*

smuggle /'smʌgl/ *tr/intr.v* take (a person, animal or thing) into, out of, a place or country against the law or without paying duty(4) on it.

'smuggler *c.n* person who smuggles.

'smuggling *u.n* practice or crime of smuggling (⇒ smuggle).

smut /smʌt/ *n* **1** *c/u.n* (small piece of) black, very dark, dirt, usu from s.t that has burnt. **2** *u.n* (*fig*) obscene talk, writing etc.

'smuttily *adv* in a smutty way.

'smuttiness *u.n* fact of being smutty.

'smutty *adj* (-ier, -iest) (*derog*) that contains or consists of smut(2): *smutty conversations.*

snack /snæk/ *c.n* small amount of food, usu eaten between meals rather than as a meal.

'snack ,bar *c.n* place where one can buy and eat snacks.

snag /snæg/ *c.n* **1** difficulty, esp that one was not expecting: *The snag is that we don't have enough money at the moment.* **2** rough or sharp piece of s.t that can cause damage, e.g a broken part of a piece of metal. **3** thread in knitted clothes etc that has been pulled out of its proper place. *hit a snag* find, encounter(4), a snag(1). ▷ *tr.v* (-gg-) **4** (of a snag(2)) catch (on) (s.t): *A sharp rock snagged my shorts and tore them.*

snail /sneɪl/ *c.n* small soft creature with a shell which does a lot of damage to plants in gardens etc. *(at) a snail's pace* (moving at) a very slow speed.

snake /sneɪk/ *c.n* **1** long thin creature, (usu) with eyes and teeth, with no legs which moves along the ground by twisting itself: *Some snakes have a poisonous bite.* *snake in the grass* (*derog*; *fig*) person who pretends to be one's friend but is really one's enemy. ▷ *v* **2** *intr.v* move like a snake(1). *snake (one's way) through s.t* go through s.t moving like a snake(1).

'snake,bite *c/u.n* bite by a snake(1), usu a poisonous one.

'snake ,charmer *c.n* person who charms(6) snakes.

,snakes and 'ladders *u.n* (often *play* —) game played on a board by moving pieces along a course the number of spaces shown by throwing dice(1); if a piece lands on the bottom of a ladder it moves up to the top of it and if it lands on the head of a snake(1) it moves down to the end of its tail.

'snaky *adj* (-ier, -iest) twisting like a snake(1).

snap /snæp/ *attrib.adj* **1** sudden; done without warning: *a snap election to try to catch the other parties* unprepared. ▷ *interj* **2** word used in the game of snap(8). **3** word used when one notices two things of the same kind, e.g when two people are wearing the same dress etc. ▷ *n* **4** *c.n* act or sound of biting quickly and suddenly: *The dog's teeth fastened on the bone with a snap.* **5** *c.n* (sound of a) sudden break, e.g of a piece of wood: *The branch broke with a snap.* **6** *c.n* (also **'snap,shot**) photograph, usu one taken quickly: *holiday snaps.* **7** *c.n* kind of hard thin sweet biscuit: brandy(1)/ginger(1) *snaps.* **8** *u.n* card game in which one has to say 'snap(2)' when two cards of the same kind are turned up by the players. *cold snap* ⇒ cold. ▷ *v* (-pp-) **9** *tr/intr.v* (try to) bite (s.o/s.t) quickly and suddenly: *The dog snapped the bone and ran away. That dog snaps but it never really bites.* **10** *tr/intr.v* (cause (a piece of wood etc) to) break suddenly, usu with a noise: *As I stepped on the branch it snapped.* **11** *intr.v* (*fig*) (of one's feelings, nerves(2) etc) suddenly stop being under one's control: *Something snapped in my brain and I began to hit out at the man violently.* **12** *tr/intr.v* (cause (s.t) to) make a sound (like that) of snapping(10). **13** *tr.v* say (s.t) in a sharp quick angry way: *'Shut up!' she snapped. Why is she snapping at everyone?* **14** *tr.v* (*informal*) photograph (s.t), usu quickly. *snap at s.o/s.t* (a) make the movements of snapping(9) but without actually biting s.o/s.t. (b) (also — *back at s.o*) attack s.o with words (in answer to s.t he/she has said). ⇒ snap(13). *snap at/up s.t* buy or accept s.t eagerly: *John snapped at the chance of a holiday in the sun. I'd snap up the offer of such a job. snap one's fingers; snap one's fingers at s.o/s.t* ⇒ finger(n). *snap s.o's head off* ⇒ head(n). *snap out of it* (*informal*) quickly stop feeling sad, tired, bored etc. *snap to it* (*informal*) hurry up. *snap s.t up* ⇒ snap at/up s.t.

'snap,dragon *c.n* = antirrhinum.

,snap 'fastener *c.n* device used mostly to close dresses etc having two small metal parts, one of which fits into the other.

'snappily *adv* in a snappy way.

'snappiness *u.n* fact of being snappy.

'snappish *adj* speaking in a snapping way (⇒ snap(13)); bad-tempered.

'snappishly *adv.* **'snappishness** *u.n.*

'snappy *adj* (*-ier*, *-iest*) **1** who/that snaps(9,13): *a snappy dog*; *a snappy person*. **2** smart'(1); dressed fashionably. **3** quick and eager. **look snappy**; **make it snappy** (*informal*) hurry up.

'snap.shot *c.n* = snap(6).

snare /sneə/ *c.n* **1** trap for catching animals, esp one that uses string, wire etc to go round the animal's foot, neck etc. **2** (often *a — and a delusion*) (*fig*) dangerous thing that may look nice but will trap one.
▷ *tr.v* **3** catch (an animal) in a snare(1). **4** (*fig*) trap (s.o) by means of a snare(2).

'snare ,drum *c.n* small drum with springs stretched across the bottom to make a rattling (⇒ rattle(4)) sound.

snarl¹ /snɑːl/ *c.n* **1** (of an animal) growl(1) with lips pulled back to show the teeth: *I heard the snarl of a dog*. **2** (of a person) unkind expression on one's face, way of speaking angrily: *He spoke with a cruel snarl. He always seems to have a snarl on his face*. Compare sneer(*n*).
▷ *v* (often *— at s.o/s.t*) **3** *intr.v* (of an animal) make a snarl¹(1) (at s.o/s.t). **4** *tr/intr.v* (of a person) speak with a snarl¹(2); have a twisted expression, a snarl on one's face: *Stop snarling*.

snarl² /snɑːl/ *c.n* **1** mixed up state that is difficult to straighten out. **in a snarl** in a tangle(1): *My hair is in a snarl*.
▷ *tr.v* **2** (usu *— s.t up*) cause (s.t) to get into a snarl²(1): *The road repairs snarled up the traffic*.

'snarl-,up *c.n* snarl²(1) (usu of traffic on the roads).

snatch /snætʃ/ *c.n* **1** (often *— at s.o/s.t*) sudden attempt to catch (s.o/s.t), sometimes a successful one. **2** short piece of a conversation etc that one hears while not hearing the rest. **in snatches** in short lengths of time separated by other things: *The nurses listened to the radio in snatches between visits to the patients*.
▷ *v* **3** *tr.v* take hold of (s.o/s.t) quickly and suddenly; grab(2) (s.o/s.t): *The thief snatched the girl's handbag and ran away*. **4** *tr/intr.v* take (s.t) quickly and in a hurry when one gets a chance, sometimes when one should not do so: *snatch a bite to eat, a few minutes' sleep. Now children, don't snatch!* **snatch at s.o/s.t** try to snatch(3) s.o/s.t.

snazzy /'snæzɪ/ *adj* (*-ier*, *-iest*) (*informal*) fashionably dressed, sometimes too much so.

'snazzily *adv.*

sneak /sniːk/ *attrib.adj* (*informal*) **1** kept secret until it is done so that it is not expected: *a sneak attack*.
▷ *c.n* **2** (*derog*; *slang*) (used mostly by children) person who tells s.t (bad) about s.o so that s.o gets into trouble. **3** (*derog*; *informal*) person who does bad things secretly.
▷ *v* **4** *intr.v* move quietly and secretly, so as not to be seen or heard: *Several boys sneaked out of the room during the speech*. **5** *tr.v* take (s.t) while sneaking(4): *Let's sneak some food into the classroom*. **6** *intr.v* (usu *— on s.o*) (*slang*) act as a sneak(2) (so that s.o gets into trouble). **sneak up (on s.o/s.t)** get near (s.o/s.t) in a sneaking (⇒ sneak(4)) way.

'sneaker *c.n* kind of shoe with a cloth top and rubber sole³(2) for sports or informal wear; trainer(2).

'sneakily *adv* in a sneaky way.

'sneakiness *u.n* fact of being sneaky.

'sneaking *attrib.adj* (of a feeling, idea) kept secret because one is ashamed of it or not sure that one is right about it: *a sneaking sympathy for the thief*; *a sneaking doubt. I've a sneaking feeling that he never intended to do anything.*

'sneaky *adj* (*-ier*, *-iest*) (*derog*; *informal*) secret in a nasty or dishonest way.

sneer /snɪə/ *c.n* **1** way of showing scorn by raising one side of one's nose and mouth: *Take that sneer off your face*. Compare snarl¹(2). **2** thing said or way of saying it that shows scorn. Compare snarl¹(2).
▷ *intr.v* **3** (often *— at s.o/s.t*) show scorn (of s.o/s.t) with a sneer(*n*).

'sneeringly *adv* with a sneer(*n*).

sneeze /sniːz/ *c.n* **1** (sound made by a) sudden rush of air out of one's nose (and mouth) which is difficult to prevent and is usu caused by s.t unpleasant, e.g dust, affecting one's nose.
▷ *intr.v* **2** give a sneeze(1). **not to be sneezed at** (*fig*; *informal*) worth having or thinking about: *Even though the job is not wonderful it is not to be sneezed at*. ⇒ not to be sniffed at (⇒ sniff(*v*)).

snick /snɪk/ *c.n* **1** small cut.
▷ *tr.v* **2** make a snick(1) on/in (s.t).

snide /snaɪd/ *adj* (usu *attrib*) (*derog*) that is meant to hurt s.o's feelings while pretending to be a joke: *He made a snide remark about how some people got the better jobs by always agreeing with the boss.*

'snidely *adv.* **'snideness** *u.n.*

sniff /snɪf/ *c.n* **1** sharp breathing in through one's nose, e.g because one's nose is running(26) or to identify s.t by smelling it: *Have a sniff and tell me what you think it is.*
▷ *v* **2** *tr/intr.v* (often *— at s.o/s.t*) give one or more sniffs(1) (while smelling s.o/s.t). **3** *tr.v* say (s.t) while sniffing(2), e.g because one is, has been, crying. **sniff at s.t (a)** ⇒ sniff(2). **(b)** (*fig*) refuse s.t because one is too proud to accept it. **not to be sniffed at** worth having. ⇒ not to be sneezed at (⇒ sneeze(*v*)).

sniffle /'snɪfl/ *c.n* **1** repeated acts of sniffing(2), usu because one's nose is running(26) as a result of having a cold, crying etc.
▷ *intr.v* **2** make a sniffle(1).

snigger /'snɪgə/ *c.n* **1** quiet, scornful and often secret way of laughing.
▷ *intr.v* **2** (often *— at s.o/s.t*) laugh (at s.o/s.t) in this way.

snip /snɪp/ *c.n* **1** small cut (in s.t) with a pair of scissors or other tool that has two blades: *Make a snip in the material where it must be cut.* **2** (often *— of s.t*) small piece cut off (s.t). **3** (*informal*) bargain(2): *Two pounds for that shirt is a real snip!*
▷ *tr.v* (*-pp-*) **4** (often *— s.t off* (s.t)) cut (a piece) (off (s.t)) with scissors or some other tool with two blades, by making small quick cuts.

snipe¹ /snaɪp/ *c.n* (*pl* snipe(s)) kind of bird with a long thin beak which lives in wet places.

snipe² /snaɪp/ *intr.v* (often *— at s.o/s.t*) **1** shoot (at s.o/s.t) while hiding so as not to be seen. **2** (*fig*) attack (s.o/s.t) with words, usu repeatedly but not very strongly.

'sniper *c.n* person who snipes²(1).

snippet /'snɪpɪt/ *c.n* (often *— of s.t*) small piece

(of information etc), part (of a conversation etc).

snivel /'snɪvl/ *intr.v* (-ll-, US -l-) **1** = sniffle(2). **2** (*derog*) cry in a miserable way.

'**sniveller** *c.n* (US '**sniveler**) (*derog*) person who snivels(2).

snob /snɒb/ *c.n* (also *attrib*) (*derog*) person who thinks herself/himself very important or clever etc, or too important to have anything to do with ordinary people: *a snob who looks down on working people*; *an art snob who only likes very expensive paintings*.

'**snobbery** *u.n* behaviour, talk etc of a snob.

'**snobbish** *adj* (*derog*) who/that is (like that of) a snob: *snobbish values*.

'**snobbishly** *adv*. '**snobbishness** *u.n*.

'**snobby** *adj* (-ier, -iest) = snobbish.

snog /snɒg/ *c.n* **1** (usu *have a* —) (*informal*) kiss (and a cuddle(1)).

▷ *intr.v* (-gg-) **2** (*informal*) have a snog(1): *snogging in the park*.

snook /snuːk/ *sing.n* **cock a snook** (**at s.o/s.t**) (**a**) put one's thumb on one's nose and spread out one's four fingers to show disrespect (for s.o/s.t). (**b**) (*fig*) speak, write etc disrespectfully (about s.o/s.t).

snooker /'snuːkə/ *u.n* **1** game like billiards but with one white ball, 15 red balls and 6 balls of other colours.

▷ *tr.v* **2** leave the balls in a difficult position for (the other player) after one's turn in a game of snooker(1). **3** (*fig*) put (s.o/s.t) in a difficult or dangerous position.

snoop /snuːp/ *c.n* (*informal*) **1** person who tries to find out things in a way that interferes with another person's right to be private.

▷ *intr.v* (*informal*) **2** be, act like, a snoop(1).

'**snooper** *c.n* (*informal*) = snoop(1).

snooty /'snuːtɪ/ *adj* (-ier, -iest) (*derog*; *informal*) too proud and therefore rude; snobbish.

'**snootily** *adv*. '**snootiness** *u.n*.

snooze /snuːz/ *c.n* **1** (usu *have a* —) (*informal*) short sleep or nap(1).

▷ *intr.v* **2** (*informal*) have a snooze(1).

snore /snɔː/ *c.n* **1** deep noise made in one's throat while one is asleep, esp when one is lying on one's back with one's mouth open.

▷ *intr.v* **2** make this noise.

'**snorer** *c.n* person who snores(2).

snorkel /'snɔːkl/ *c.n* **1** short tube used by a person (also a submarine etc) while under water to get air from above the surface.

▷ *intr.v* (-ll-, US -l-) **2** swim using a snorkel(1): *We go snorkelling in the sea every morning*.

snort /snɔːt/ *c.n* **1** loud sound made by blowing through the nose as by a pig or horse, and often by s.o to show anger, scorn etc.

▷ *v* **2** *intr.v* give a snort(1): *Joan snorted when Fred said he had forgotten to buy the bread*. **3** *tr.v* say (s.t) while snorting(2): *'I don't believe it!' she snorted*.

snot /snɒt/ *u.n* (do not use!) mucus that comes out of one's nose.

'**snotty** *adj* (-ier, -iest) (*slang*; do not use!) **1** (often *have a* — *nose*) (of a nose) that has snot in/on it. **2** (*derog*; *informal*) snobbish.

'**snotty-,nosed** *adj* (= snotty(*adj*).

snout /snaʊt/ *c.n* long nose of a pig etc.

snow /snəʊ/ *n* **1** *u.n* rain that has become frozen

into soft flakes and not into ice or hail'(1): *Thick snow covered the fields*. **2** *c.n* one fall of snow(1). **3** *u.n* (*slang*) powdered cocaine.

▷ *intr.v* **4** (of snow(1)) fall from the clouds: *It snowed last night*. **snow s.o/s.t in/up** surround s.o/s.t with thick snow(1) so that he/she/it cannot get out (of it). **snow s.o under** (**with s.t**) (*fig*; *informal*) give s.o too much (of s.t): *I was snowed under with work when two people in the office were away sick*. **snow s.o/s.t up** ⇨ snow s.o/s.t in/up.

'**snow,ball** *c.n* **1** ball made by pressing or rolling snow(1) until it is round.

▷ *intr.v* **2** (*fig*) get bigger and bigger, faster and faster, often so that it cannot be controlled: *The whole movement snowballed until there were thousands of members*.

'**snow-,blind** *adj* blind, but not permanently, as a result of having looked at bright snow(1) for too long.

'**snow-,blindness** *u.n*.

'**snow,bound** *adj* trapped, unable to move, because of snow(1).

'**snow-,capped** *adj* (of a mountain etc) having snow(1) on its top.

'**snow-,clad** *adj* (*literary*) covered with snow(1).

'**snow,drift** *c.n* ⇨ drift(1).

'**snow,drop** *c.n* kind of small white flower that comes up towards the end of winter, sometimes through the snow(1).

'**snow,fall** *n* **1** *c.n* fall of snow(1). ⇨ snow(2). **2** *c/u.n* amount of snow(1) that falls.

'**snow,field** *c.n* big area of land covered with snow(1).

'**snow,flake** *c.n* small piece, flake(1) of snow(1).

'**snowiness** *u.n* fact or state of being snowy.

'**snow,line** *c.n* level on a mountain etc above which there is always snow.

snowman /'snəʊˌmæn/ *c.n* (*pl* -men) shape of a human being made out of snow(1), usu by or for children. **abominable snowman** ⇨ abominate.

'**snow,plough** *c.n* (US '**snow,plow**) vehicle or device for clearing snow(1) from roads, railway lines etc.

'**snow,shoe** *c.n* thing that looks like a tennis racket and is fixed under one's shoe so that one can walk on deep snow(1) more easily.

'**snow,storm** *c.n* very heavy fall of snow(1), usu with strong wind at the same time. Compare rainstorm.

,**snow 'white** *adj* very white/clean.

'**snowy** *adj* (-ier, -iest) **1** covered with snow(1). **2** during which snow(1) falls: *a snowy afternoon*. **3** very white/clean like fresh snow(1).

Snr *written abbr* senior: *John Smith Snr*. Compare Jnr/Jr.

snub¹ /snʌb/ *attrib.adj* (of a nose) short and flat or turned up at the end.

,**snub-'nosed** *adj* having a snub¹(1) nose.

snub² /snʌb/ *c.n* **1** rude way of (not) treating, speaking/writing to, s.o to try to make her/him feel unimportant or not wanted.

▷ *tr.v* (-bb-) **2** treat, speak/write to, (s.o) in a way that is a snub²(1).

snuff¹ /snʌf/ *u.n* powdered tobacco for breathing up one's nose.

snuff² /snʌf/ *tr.v* (mostly *old use*) cut the burnt end of the wick(1) off (a candle). **snuff it** (*slang*) die. **snuff s.t out** put a candle etc out by pinching it with one's fingers etc.

'snuffer *c.n* tool for snuffing[2] candles.

snuffle /'snʌfl/ *c.n* **1** (quiet noise of) breathing through one's nose with a low liquid sound.
▷ *intr.v* **2** breathe in this way, often when one has a cold.

snug /snʌg/ *adj* (-gg-) **1** warm, comfortable and pleasant; cosy. **2** (of clothes etc) fitting closely: *a snug coat.*
'snugly *adv*. **'snugness** *u.n.*

snuggle /'snʌgl/ *intr.v* (usu — *up* (*to s.o/s.t*)) be/get close (to s.o/s.t) in order to be snug(1); nestle(2): *We all snuggled up together to keep warm.*

so¹ /səʊ/ *adv* **1** (often *just* —) in this way; (exactly) thus: *You open the bag so.* **2** (*formal*) in that way; doing that: *You will work for us for one month and while you are so employed you will not take on any other jobs.* **3** to such an extent (that . . . etc): *She was so happy (that) she actually cried. It was so cold that day as to freeze the sea. Sam fainted he was so hot. Stop being so stupid! That animal has so small a mouth that it can hardly eat anything. I love your house because it is so comfortable* (or *so much more comfortable than ours*). **4** (*informal*) very: *It was so kind of you to help us.* **5** (often *just* — *many, much, big* etc) up to a certain (number etc) and no further: *I can stand just so much pain and then I start to sweat.* **6** (followed by aux.verbs such as 'be', 'can', 'have', 'do', 'must'; used to avoid repeating a main verb) also: *Helen may see him and so may Fred* (i.e and Fred may also see him). *I saw him and so did Kate* (i.e and Kate also saw him). *I thought he would fall and so he did* (and he did fall). *John is a student and so am I* (I am also a student). *Peter has a pen and so have I.* **and so forth/on**; **and so on and so forth** (a) and other people/animals/things of the same kind; etc: *In the zoo we saw lions, tigers and so on.* (b) and on from there: *We put money on every fifth square, 5, 10, 15 and so on.* **as . . . so . . .** when, to the extent that, (s.t happens) (s.t else happens): *As you go higher up so the trees get smaller.* **even so** ⇒ even(*adv*). **ever so . . .** ⇒ ever. **in so far as . . .** ⇒ far(*adv*). **it so happens that . . .**; **as it so happens, . . .** ⇒ happen. **just as . . . , so . . .** ⇒ just². **quite so** ⇒ quite. **just so** carefully and tidily arranged: *That woman always wants her house to be just so in case a visitor comes.* **more so** more in that way: *'Is Mary nice?' 'Yes, more so than her husband.'* **or so** ⇒ or. **not so big** etc **as . . .** not big etc to the extent that . . . : *That idea wasn't so stupid as it sounded.* Compare *as . . . as . . .* (*adv*). **quite so** ⇒ just/quite so. **like so** ⇒ like¹(*prep*). **so . . . as . . .**; **so . . . that . . . . . .** in such a way that . . . : *The house is so built that you can enter it directly from the sea* (or *as to have an entrance from the sea*). **so as to do s.t** (a) in order to do s.t; for the purpose of doing s.t. (b) with the result of doing s.t. **so far; so far as; so far as s.o/s.t is concerned; so far (and no farther/further); so far so good** ⇒ far(*adv*). **so it is** (usu to show surprise) that is true: *'It's raining.' 'So it is!'* **so long; so long as . . .** ⇒ long(*adv*). **so many/much** (a) ⇒ so(5). (b) a certain number/amount: *You get so many free cigarettes for every box of two hundred you buy.* **so much as . . .**; **so much the better** etc; **so much for s.o/s.t**; **so much nonsense** etc

⇒ much. **so to speak** ⇒ speak. **too much so** ⇒ too.

so² /səʊ/ *conj* **1** (often — *that* . . .) with the result (that . . .); and the result is (that . . .): *The car failed to start so that we missed the plane.* ⇒ so¹(3). **2** (often — *that* . . .) with the purpose (that . . .); the purpose being (that . . .): *Could you all please keep quiet so that we can hear what he's saying.* **3** (without much more meaning than well¹(4)): *So, what do you want to eat? So, the guests have arrived at last. So, it's raining; what do you want me to do about it?* **so what?** ⇒ what(*pron*).

so³ /səʊ/ *pron* (used to avoid repeating a clause): *'You must go home now.' 'If you say so'* (i.e I will go home if you say that I must). **expect so** think that s.t will happen, is true etc: *'Will you be at the meeting tonight?' 'Yes, I expect so'.* **if so** if you are right: *You may be right after all; if so I apologize.*

'so-and-,so *n* (*pl* **so-and-sos**) **1** *unique n* person/animal/thing whose name is not mentioned, has been forgotten etc. **2** *c.n* (*derog*) unpleasant person: *Peter's children are real little so-and-sos.*

,so-'called *adj* (usu *attrib*) who/that has that name, usu without deserving it: *We stayed at that so-called hotel one night and that was enough!*

-soever (*old use*) at all; of any kind. ⇒ howsoever, whatsoever, whensoever, wheresoever, who(m)soever.

soak /səʊk/ *c.n* **1** act of putting s.t in liquid to get it thoroughly wet, e.g in order to clean it: *Give that dirty shirt a good soak in hot water.*
▷ *v* **2** *tr.v* (often — *s.t in s.t*) (put and then) keep (s.t) in a liquid long enough for it to get thoroughly wet. **3** *intr.v* (often — *in s.t*) remain (in a liquid) in such a way. **4** *tr/intr.v* (often — *into/through s.t*) (of a liquid) enter (s.t) completely: *This dirty water has soaked* (*into*) *all our carpets.* Compare saturate(1). **5** *tr.v* (*fig*; *informal*) make (s.o) pay too much for s.t. **soak s.t out** (**of s.t**) remove s.t (from s.t) by soaking (⇒ soak(2)) it in a liquid. **soak s.t up** (a) fill s.t with a liquid by absorbing(1) it: *You can use that cloth to soak up the spilt milk.* (b) (*fig*) take in (a lot of) information, knowledge etc: *Children can soak up a lot of facts at an early age.*

soaked *adj* (often — *through*) very wet.

'soaking *adj* **1** very wet.
▷ *adv* **2 soaking wet** ⇒ wet(*adj*).
▷ *c.n* **3** (often *get/give s.o a* —) fact or act of being made wet: *When the boat turned over we all got a soaking.*

soap /səʊp/ *n* **1** *u.n* solid substance made by mixing fat and alkali and used for washing one's body, clothes etc when one wets it: *a bar of soap.* **2** *c/u.n* = soap opera.
▷ *tr.v* **3** put wet soap(1) on (s.o/s.t); clean (s.o/s.t) with soap(1).

'soap-,box *c.n* box on which s.o stands so that he/she can be seen better while giving a speech, usu outdoors. **get on one's soap-box** (*fig*) begin to talk to s.o (as if) giving a speech.

'soap,bubble *c.n* bubble(1) formed by soap(1) in water.

'soap,flakes *pl.n* soap(1) in the form of flakes(1), usu for washing clothes etc.

'soapiness *u.n* fact or state of being soapy.

'soap ,opera *c/u.n* (also **soap**) (*informal*)

regular serial(2) on radio or television that deals with the lives of a group of people.

'soap ,powder *u.n* detergent in the form of a powder, used to wash clothes.

'soap,suds *pl.n* soapy(1) water with bubbles(1), esp when washing clothes etc.

'soapy *adj* (*-ier, -iest*) **1** having soap(1) in/on it. **2** like soap(1). **3** (*derog; informal*) too pleasant so that one dislikes her/him/it or suspects that she/he/it is not honest.

soar /sɔː/ *intr.v* **1** fly, usu high and slowly. **2** (of mountains, tall buildings etc) be very high; tower(3). **3** (of prices, temperature etc) go up, usu fast and high. **4** (of feelings etc) go up very high: *Tempers soared during the discussions.*

sob /sɒb/ *c.n* **1** short sudden breath while crying: *I heard a sob in the corner of the classroom.*
▷ *v* **2** *intr.v* make short sudden sounds by breathing while crying hard: *The child was sobbing because of his broken toy.* **3** *tr.v* (often — *s.t out*) say (s.t) while sobbing(2): *'I can't do it!' sobbed the child.* **sob oneself to sleep** sob(2) until one goes to sleep. **sob with s.t** sob(2) because of pain, grief etc.

'sobbingly *adv* while sobbing(2).

'sob ,story *c.n* (*pl -ies*) (*informal*) story that is told to try to make people feel sorry for oneself or s.o, esp to get money etc from them.

sober /'səʊbə/ *adj* **1** not drunk(1). **2** serious; dressed, behaving etc, in a proper respectable way. **3** (of clothes etc) not brightly coloured. (**as**) **sober as a judge**; **stone cold sober** not at all drunk(1).
▷ *tr/intr.v* **4** (usu — (*s.o*) *up*) (cause (s.o) to) become sober(1) again.

sobriety /sə'braɪətɪ/ *u.n* (*formal*) fact or state of being sober(*adj*).

so-called ⇒ **so**.

soccer /'sɒkə/ *u.n* = (Association) football.

sociable /'səʊʃəbl/ *adj* (also **'social**) **1** liking to be with other people; friendly. **2** at/in which people are sociable(1): *a sociable evening of games and dancing.* ⇒ **unsociable**.

sociability /,səʊʃə'bɪlɪtɪ/ *u.n.* **'sociably** *adv*.

social /'səʊʃəl/ *adj* **1** of or referring to the ways in which people or animals live and/or work together or the things that happen to them in their lives: *Liz has an interesting social life in Oxford.* **2** (*technical*) (of animals, esp insects) that normally live together in groups: *Ants and bees are social insects.* **3** = **sociable**.
▷ *c.n* **4** meeting or party to which friends or members of a club, church etc can go.

,social 'class *c/u.n* class(2) in society: *People of different social class(es) belong to our sports club.*

,social 'climber *c.n* (*derog*) person who tries to rise into a higher social class.

,social de'mocracy *u.n* political system that is like socialism.

,social 'demo,crat *c.n* person who supports social democracy or the Social Democratic Party.

,Social ,Demo'cratic ,Party *def/unique n* (*abbr SDP*) (UK) political party supporting moderate(1) change.

,Social ,Liberal ,Demo'cratic ,Party *unique n* (*abbr SLD*) (UK) political party formed out of Liberal(4) supporters and others, supporting moderate(1) change. ⇒ **democrat(3)**.

'socia,lism *u.n* (often with capital **S**) political system that is in favour of public ownership of the means of production, and of everybody having equal opportunities. Compare communism(1).

'socialist *c.n* (also *attrib*) person, party or policy who/that supports socialism.

socialite /'səʊʃə,laɪt/ *c.n* person who goes to a lot of fashionable parties.

,socialization, -isation /,səʊʃəlaɪ'zeɪʃən/ *u.n* fact of becoming or making s.o/s.t socialized.

'socia,lize, -ise /'səʊʃəlaɪz/ **1** *intr.v* (often — *with s.o*) meet people socially. **2** *tr.v* cause (s.t) to come into public ownership or to be paid for by the state: *Medical care was socialized in Britain quite a long time ago.*

,social 'science *n* **1** *u.n* study of the ways in which societies of people are organized, behave, change etc which includes economics, politics, anthropology etc. **2** *c.n* (often *pl*) one of the kinds of social science(1). Compare natural science.

'socially *adv*.

,social se'curity *u.n* (system of using) public money paid to unemployed people, people who are too ill to work, pensioners etc.

,social 'service *c.n* (usu *pl*) service paid from public money, e.g a bus service, medical care, the police.

,social 'studies *pl.n* = social science(1).

'social ,work *u.n* work done to help people who are poor, ill, weak etc.

'social ,worker *c.n* person who does social work, either as a paid job or voluntarily.

society /sə'saɪətɪ/ *n* (*pl -ies*) **1** *u.n* (of people or sometimes animals) fact or state of being grouped together in a social(1,2) way: *Most human beings live and work in society.* **2** *u.n* people in society(1). **3** *c.n* group of such people usu sharing a common interest. **4** *u.n* kind of group of such people: *Words that are not suitable for use in polite society are marked 'do not use!' in this dictionary.* **5** *u.n* (often *in the — of s.o; in s.o's —*) (*formal*) companionship. **6** *u.n* (also *attrib*) fashionable, upper-class people: *a big society wedding.*

sociological /,səʊsɪə'lɒdʒɪkl/ *adj* of or referring to sociology.

,socio'logically *adv*.

sociologist /,səʊsɪ'ɒlədʒɪst/ *c.n* person who studies, or is skilled in, sociology.

sociology /,səʊsɪ'ɒlədʒɪ/ *u.n* study of societies(3) and the ways in which the people in them behave as groups.

sock¹ /sɒk/ *c.n* (often *pair of —s*) short covering of cotton, wool etc for the foot and usu (part of) the leg below the knee. ⇒ **stocking**. **pull one's socks up** (*fig; informal*) start to behave better, more properly etc. **put a sock in it** (*fig; slang*) = shut up (⇒ shut (s.o) up(a)).

sock² /sɒk/ *adv* **1** (of a strong hit) (almost) exactly: *The ball hit him sock in the eye.*
▷ *c.n* **2** strong hit: *He gave me a sock on the jaw.*

socket /'sɒkɪt/ *c.n* device or place in s.t that is hollow or has a hole or holes in it into which a plug(3) or a light bulb etc fits: *Our eyes and teeth are in sockets. That pole fits into a socket in the floor.*

sod¹ /sɒd/ *c/u.n* (piece of) earth cut out of the ground often with grass still growing in it.

sod² /sɒd/ *c.n* (*slang*; do not use!) **1** (*derog*) unpleasant person: *Go away, you silly sod!*

2 person whom one likes, usu in a rather condescending way: *Mr Evans is a nice old sod really.* **3** thing that is troublesome or a nuisance: *That old car's a real sod to start in the cold weather.*

▷ *v* **4** (*slang*; do not use!) **sod it** (expression used to show anger, annoyance etc with s.t): *Oh, sod it! I've left my glasses at home.* **sod off** go away: *Sod off, you silly old fool!*

soda /'səʊdə/ *u.n* **1** = soda water. **2** = ice-cream soda. **3** = bicarbonate of soda.

'**soda ,siphon** *c.n* ⇨ siphon(2).

'**soda ,water** *u.n* water that is fizzy because it contains carbon dioxide.

sodden /'sɒdn/ = soaked.

sodium /'səʊdɪəm/ *u.n* metal that looks like silver and is only found combined with other substances in natural conditions, *chem.symb* Na.

,**sodium 'chloride** *u.n* (*technical*) = salt(2), *chem.form* NaCl.

sodomy /'sɒdəmɪ/ *u.n* sexual intercourse through the anus.

'**sodo,mist** /'sɒdə,mɪst/ *c.n* (also '**sodo,mite** /'sɒdə,maɪt/) man who takes part in sodomy.

-**soever** ⇨ so.

sofa /'səʊfə/ *c.n* soft seat with a back and arms for two or sometimes more people.

'**sofa ,bed** *c.n* sofa(1) that can be opened flat to make a bed.

soft /sɒft/ *adj* **1** that changes shape, yields or does not resist, when one presses it: *a soft bed/cushion. The ground is soft today because of the rain.* Opposite hard(1). **2** less hard than the average: *a soft metal.* **3** that feels smooth and pleasant when one touches it: *the soft skin of a baby.* **4** that is pleasant because it does not look, sound, smell, taste or feel too strong: *the soft light of evening; the soft sound of distant voices; the soft smell of pine'*(1) *trees; a soft breeze.* **5** gentle; not angry, attacking or violent: *When someone is angry with you, a soft reply is often the best way of dealing with her or him.* **6** (*informal*) easy; not needing (much) effort: *Joe has a soft job; he only has to drive the manager five kilometres to work and back.* **7** (often go —) (of a person's muscles(1) etc) weak; not in good bodily condition: *Peter was a good sportsman when he was young but now he has gone soft.* **8** (*informal*) (of a person's character) weak; easily influenced: *Soft teachers don't stay long at that school.* **9** (of water) not having certain chemicals in it and therefore producing bubbles easily when soap is added. Opposite hard(7). **10** (of the sound of the letters 'c' and 'g') pronounced /s/ and /dʒ/ (not /k/ and /g/). Opposite hard(8). **11** not of one of the very harmful kinds: *soft drugs*(2); *soft drink.* Opposite hard(9). **go soft** become soft(1,8): *The ice-cream has gone soft because it's been out of the freezer too long.* **soft in the head** (*informal*) stupid; mad. **soft on s.o/s.t** (**a**) not strongly against s.o/s.t; not resisting or fighting s.o/s.t strongly (enough): *The police here seem to be soft on drinking and driving.* Opposite hard on s.o/s.t. (**b**) fond of s.o/s.t. ⇨ soft spot.

'**soft,ball** *u.n* game like baseball played with a larger ball.

,**soft-'boiled** *adj* (of an egg) boiled only for a short time so that the yellow part has not become hard. Opposite hard-boiled(1).

,**soft 'drink** *c.n* one not having any alcohol in it, e.g orange juice. ⇨ hard drink, long drink.

soften /'sɒfn/ *tr/intr.v* (often — (s.o/s.t) *up*) (cause (s.o/s.t) to) become soft(er) (1,3,4,5,7–9).

'**softener** *c.n* thing that makes s.o/s.t soft(er)(1,3,5,6,8,9): *a water softener.* ⇨ soft(9).

,**soft 'furnishings** *pl.n* curtains, carpets, cloth coverings of chairs and other soft parts of the furnishings of a room.

,**soft-'hearted** *adj* kind; easily feeling sympathy or pity for s.o/s.t. ⇨ hard-hearted.

,**soft-'heartedness** *u.n*.

'**softie** *c.n* (also '**softy**) (*pl* -*ies*) (*informal*) soft-hearted, soft(8), person.

,**soft 'landing** *c.n* gentle landing of a space vehicle etc without damaging itself.

'**softly** *adv.* '**softness** *u.n*.

,**soft-'pedal** *tr/intr.v* (-*ll*-, US -*l*-) (try to) make (s.t) seem less important than it really is; play s.t down.

,**soft por'nography** *u.n* (*informal* ,**soft 'porn**) thing that suggests sexual activity without being explicit(2) ⇨ hard pornography.

,**soft 'sell** *c.n* **1** ('**soft-,sell** when *attrib*) way of selling without using pressure.

▷ *tr.v* **2** sell (s.t) (to s.o) without using any pressure ⇨ hard sell.

,**soft-'soap** *tr.v* (*informal*) (try to) persuade (s.o) to do s.t by flattery(1), politeness etc.

,**soft-'spoken** *adj* who speaks gently and kindly.

'**soft ,spot** *c.n* (usu have a — for s.o/s.t) (*informal*) fondness (for s.o/s.t), often a fondness that is not to be expected. ⇨ soft on s.o.

'**soft ,top** *c.n* car with a roof made of a waterproof(1) cloth that can be folded back in warm dry weather. ⇨ hardtop.

'**soft,ware** *u.n* (*technical*) programs written for computers. Compare hardware(2).

'**soft,wood** *u.n* wood that one can cut easily, e.g pine(2). Compare hardwood.

'**softy** *c.n* ⇨ softie.

soggy /'sɒgɪ/ *adj* (-*gg*-) (of s.t solid) having so much liquid in it that it is unpleasant: *a soggy piece of ground near a river; soggy bread.*

'**soggily** *adv.* '**sogginess** *u.n*.

soil[1] /sɔɪl/ *n* **1** *u.n* top layer(1) of earth which is what plants grow in: *poor soil* (i.e soil in which it is difficult for plants to grow); *rich soil* (in which plants grow well). **2** *def.n* (*literary*) farms and farming: *men of the soil* (farmers). **3** *c/u.n* (*literary*) place where one lives or comes from: *my native soil.*

soil[2] /sɔɪl/ *u.n* **1** dirt. **2** sewage.

▷ *v* **3** *tr.v* make (s.o/s.t) dirty. **4** *intr.v* become dirty: *This material soils easily.*

,**soiled 'goods** *pl.n* things that are being sold more cheaply because they have been in the shop some time and are not as clean as new goods.

sojourn /'sɒdʒɜːn/ *c.n* **1** (*literary*) stay in a place that is not one's home, usu for quite a long time.

▷ *intr.v* **2** (*literary*) live in such a place.

solace /'sɒlɪs/ *c/u.n* **1** (*formal*) thing that makes one feel less sad; comfort for the mind.

▷ *tr.v* **2** (*formal*) give (s.o) solace(1).

solar /'səʊlə/ *adj* (usu *attrib*) of or referring to the sun.

,**solar 'cell** *c.n* device for producing electricity from sunlight.

solarium /sə'leərɪəm/ *c.n* (*pl* —*s*, or less usu. solaria /sə'leərɪə/) place where one can sit in the sun, usu protected from wind etc by glass.

,**solar 'panel** *c.n* flat structure for collecting heat from the sun to heat water etc, often containing solar cells to produce electricity.

solar plexus /,səulə 'pleksəs/ *def.n* **1** group of nerves between one's stomach and backbone. **2** (*informal*) place between one's middle ribs(1): *If the solar plexus is hit hard, one loses one's breath.*

'**solar ,power** *u.n* power produced by sunlight, e.g to drive a machine: *a solar power system.*

'**solar ,system** *def.n* **1** our sun and its planets. **2** any other star and its planets.

,**solar 'year** *c.n* time taken by our earth to go round the sun once; 365 days 5 hours and 49 minutes.

sold /səuld/ *p.t,p.p* of sell.

solder /'səuldə/ *u.n* **1** metal that can easily be melted and used to join other pieces of metal together.

▷ *tr.v* **2** (often — *s.t together/up*) join (s.t) (together etc) with solder(1).

'**soldering ,iron** *c.n* tool used for soldering(2) things by heating the solder(1).

soldier /'səuldʒə/ *c.n* **1** person who is in an army and usu not an officer. **2** (*fig*) person who is working hard for s.t, e.g a religious purpose.

▷ *intr.v* **3** work as a soldier. **soldier on** (*fig*; *informal*) continue doing s.t in spite of difficulties, boredom etc.

'**soldier,like** *adj* (also '**soldierly**) as a soldier is/does or should be/do.

sole¹ /səul/ *attrib.adj* **1** only; not having any other: *Mary was her mother's sole support in her old age.* **2** not shared by anyone else: *Pat has sole command of our group.*

solely /'səullɪ/ *adv.*

sole² /səul/ *n* **1** *c.n* kind of flat fish found mostly in warm seas. **2** *u.n* flesh of this fish as food.

sole³ /səul/ *c.n* **1** front under part of one's foot. **2** part of a shoe etc that covers one's sole³(1). ⇨ heel(2).

▷ *tr.v* **3** put a sole³(2) on (a shoe etc): *I'm going to have these old boots soled and heeled.*

-**soled** *adj* having a sole or soles of the kind shown in the first part of the word: *rubber-soled.*

solely ⇨ sole¹.

solemn /'sɒləm/ *adj* (usu *attrib*) serious, often in a religious way: *I give you my solemn promise not to be late.*

solemnity /sə'lemnɪtɪ/ *n* (*pl -ies*) (*formal*) **1** *u.n* fact or state of being solemn. **2** *c.n* (usu *pl*) action, activity etc suitable for a solemn important event.

solemnization, -isation /,sɒləmnaɪ'zeɪʃən/ *u.n* (usu *the — of s.t*) (*formal*) formal carrying out (of a religious ceremony, usu a marriage).

'**solem,nize, -ise** *tr.v* (*formal*) carry out a ceremony of solemnization: *solemnize a marriage.*

sol-fa /,sɒl 'fɑː/ *def.n* (*music*) system in which each of the seven different notes in the octave(1) is given a different name (do, re, mi, fa, sol, la, ti (do)).

solicit /sə'lɪsɪt/ *v* **1** *tr/intr.v* (often — *for s.t*; — *s.t*

from s.o) (*formal*) ask (s.o) for (money, advice, help etc). **2** *intr.v* (of a beggar) ask for money. **3** *intr.v* (of a prostitute) try to get s.o to have sex(3) with one for money.

solicitation /sə,lɪsɪ'teɪʃən/ *c/u.n.*

solicitor /sə'lɪsɪtə/ *c.n* (UK and some other countries but not US) lawyer who is not allowed to work in high courts. Compare barrister, attorney.

So,licitor 'General *c.n* (*pl solicitors general*) second highest rank of law officer in a country. Compare Attorney-General.

solicitous /sə'lɪsɪtəs/ *adj* (usu — *about/for/of s.o/s.t*) (*formal*) full of helpful thought (for s.o/s.t); very willing and eager to help (s.o/ s.t), sometimes because one is worried (about her/him/it).

so'licitously *adv.* **so'licitousness, solici-tude** /sə'lɪsɪ,tjuːd/ *u.n.*

solid /'sɒlɪd/ *adj* **1** not liquid and not in the form of a gas; that does not need to be kept in a container to stop it running away or disappearing into the air: *When ice gets warm it changes from a solid into a liquid state.* **2** not hollow; not empty inside: *The first cars had solid tyres.* **3** (*attrib*) without holes, breaks, empty spaces or mixtures of anything else in it: *solid rock. This ring is solid gold.* **4** (*attrib*) (*geometry*) (of a figure) having depth as well as length and height: *A cube is a solid figure.* **5** (usu *attrib*) that is or seems to be very well made, built, written etc: *a solid piece of work. The building is solid, it just needs painting.* **6** that/whom one can trust absolutely: *Our town is full of solid but rather boring citizens.* **7** united: *There was solid support in favour of the plan.* **8** (*attrib* or after the noun) without a break or pause: *We had to wait two solid days* (or *two days solid*) *for a plane.* **9** without a hyphen in it: *One can write ice-cream with a hyphen, in two words or solid* (i.e 'icecream'). **freeze s.t solid** (cause (s.t) to) become solid(1) by freezing (it).

▷ *c.n* **10** thing or part of s.t that is solid(1,4): *milk solids. A cube is a solid.* **11** (usu *pl*) food that contains solids(10): *Peter isn't well enough to take solids yet.*

solidarity /,sɒlɪ'dærɪtɪ/ *u.n* (often — *with s.o*) support (for s.o); agreement to support each other: *show solidarity by attending the meeting.*

solidification /sə,lɪdɪfɪ'keɪʃən/ *u.n* process or fact of solidifying.

solidify /sə'lɪdɪ,faɪ/ *tr/intr.v* (-*ies*, -*ied*) **1** (cause (s.t) to) become solid(1). **2** (*fig*) (cause (s.t) to) become clear and strong: *People were in doubt at first but then opinion solidified in favour of the proposal.*

solidity /sə'lɪdɪtɪ/ *u.n* fact or state of being solid(1,5).

'**solidly** *adv.*

soliloquy /sə'lɪləkwɪ/ *c/u.n* (*pl -ies*) (piece of) speech in which one is talking to oneself, usu about one's thoughts and feelings.

soliloquize, -ise /sə'lɪlə,kwaɪz/ *tr/intr.v* (often — *about s.t*) say (s.t) (about s.t) in the form of a soliloquy.

solitaire /,sɒlɪ'teə/ *n* **1** *c.n* (also *attrib*) (of a diamond etc ring) having only one stone. **2** *u.n* = patience(2).

solitary /'sɒlɪtərɪ/ *adj* **1** alone; without any other one. **2** liking to be alone. **3** that is in a lonely

place. **4** (*attrib*) single; just one: *I haven't seen one solitary person I'd like to speak to.*
▷ *n* (*pl -ies*) **5** *c.n* person who lives quite alone; hermit. **6** *u.n* (often *in —*) solitary confinement. **'solitarily** *adv.*
,solitary con'finement *u.n* (often *in —*) state of being in prison alone without being allowed to see, talk to etc any other prisoner.
solitude /'sɒlɪˌtjuːd/ *u.n* fact or state of being solitary(1).
solo /'səʊləʊ/ *adj/adv* **1** alone; without any other person: *fly solo.* **2** (*music*) used, heard, played etc by one person only, without any accompaniment.
▷ *c.n* (*pl -s*) **3** job, activity etc done solo(1). **4** (*music*) piece sung or played solo(2).
▷ *intr.v* **5** (*informal*) do s.t solo(1,2).
'soloist *c.n* (*music*) person who plays solo(1,2).
solstice /'sɒlstɪs/ *c/def.n* (**a**) **the summer solstice**: the longest day in the year, around June 22nd. (**b**) **the winter solstice**: the shortest day in the year, around December 22nd. Compare equinox.
soluble /'sɒljʊbl/ *adj* Opposite insoluble. **1** that can be dissolved(1): *soluble medicine.* **2** that can be solved. ⇨ solvable. **soluble in s.t** that dissolves(1) in a liquid.
solubility /ˌsɒljʊ'bɪlɪtɪ/ *u.n* fact of being soluble(1).
solution /sə'luːʃən/ *c/u.n* **1** liquid in which a solid or gas has been dissolved(1). **2** (often — *to s.t*) answer to, thing that solves, a mystery, problem, puzzle etc. **admit solution** (*formal*) be possible to be solved; be solvable. **in solution** in a state of having been dissolved(1) in a liquid.
solve /sɒlv/ *tr.v* find an/the answer to (a mystery, problem, puzzle etc); find out the thing one wants to know about (s.t).
'solvable *adj* that can be solved. ⇨ soluble(2). Opposite insoluble.
'solver *c.n* person who solves s.t.
solvent[1] /'sɒlvənt/ *adj* having more money than one owes; having enough money to pay one's debts. Opposite insolvent.
solvent[2] /'sɒlvənt/ *c/u.n* (*technical*) liquid that can dissolve(1) solids, e.g one that can dissolve(1) grease so that it can be removed from one's clothes etc.
sombre /'sɒmbə/ *adj* (US **'somber**) **1** dark. **2** serious and sad; gloomy(1).
'sombrely *adv* (US **'somberly**). **'sombreness** *u.n* (US **'somberness**).
sombrero /sɒm'breərəʊ/ *c.n* (*pl -s*) Mexican hat with a high crown(6) and very wide brim(2) that is turned up at the edges.
some /sʌm/ *adv* **1** about: *We have some dozen* (about a dozen) *eggs left.* **some few** (**people** etc) quite a lot (of people etc): *We had to wait some few hours for a train.* **some little time** etc quite a lot of time etc.
▷ *det* (strong form /sʌm/, weak form /səm/) **2** (usu /səm/) a certain number/amount of; a little/few of; not many/much of: *I want some bread and some eggs.* Compare any(2). **3** (/sʌm/) a certain number/amount but not all of: *Some people like this town but I don't. I enjoy some meat but not this kind.* Compare any(3). **4** (/sʌm/) who/ which is not (yet) known or not mentioned: *We'll probably meet again some day.* Compare any(4). **5** (/sʌm/) quite a large number/amount of: *We*

have lived here for some years now. **6** (/sʌm/) (*informal*) a really good: *That was some jump! It must have been at least six metres.* **some day** ⇨ day. **go some way towards s.t** ⇨ way. **some . . . or (an)other** = some(4): *We saw some child or other in your garden last night.*
▷ *pron* /sʌm/ **7** (usu — *of it, us, you, them* etc) a certain number/amount (but not all); a few/ little; not many/much: *Some of our friends can't come. Have we got any butter? I need some.* Compare any(5).
somebody /'sʌmbədɪ/ *c.n* (*pl -ies*) **1** important person. Compare nobody(1).
▷ *pron* (also **'some,one**) **2** (often — *or other*) a person (but one does not know which one): *Hide; somebody's coming! Somebody or other telephoned you.* Compare anybody, nobody(2). **or somebody** or a person like that: *If you don't know the way, ask a policeman or somebody.*
'some,day *adv* (often — *or other*) at some time in the future.
'some,how *adv* (often — *or other*) **1** in a way that is not mentioned or not known: *Don't worry, we'll get to our hotel somehow.* **2** for a reason that is not mentioned or is not known: *Somehow I can't find Joan's telephone number.*
'some,one *pron* = somebody(2). Compare anyone, no one.
'some,thing *adv* **1** rather; somewhat: *I think she's something under 40 years old.* **something like** (**a**) rather like. (**b**) about: *The town is something like 2000 years old.*
▷ *pron* **2** (often — *or other*) a thing (but one does not know which one). **3** (used when one cannot remember something(2)): *Her telephone number's 3-8-5-something, I think.* **4** an important/ encouraging thing or a thing that should make a person grateful: *John only got a third class degree but he did pass which is something.* (**get**) **something for nothing** (get) something that one has not had to give/pay anything for. **make something of oneself, one's life** be successful in one's life. **something of a s.t** rather a s.t: *Mary's considered something of a beauty in our village.* **or something** or a thing like that: *Would you like a coffee or something?* **quite something** ⇨ quite. **see something of s.o** see s.o occasionally: *Now that Julie's living in London I hope we'll be seeing something of her.* **something like . . .** about . . .: *It'll cost something like £10.* **Something tells me** (**that**) . . . (*informal*) I think (that) . . .; I have a feeling (that) . . . . **something to do with s.o/s.t** something that concerns, is connected with, s.o/ s.t. **there is something in/to s.t** there is a certain amount of truth in s.t: *I believe there's something in what you say.*
'some,time *adj* = former(1).
'some,times *adv* at some times; from time to time; occasionally; not always.
'some,what *adv* (*formal*) rather; a little: *This hat is somewhat small for me. These shoes hurt my feet somewhat.* **somewhat of a s.t** (*informal*) rather a s.t: *Mollie is somewhat of an expert(2) on tax affairs.*
'some,where *adv* (often — *or other*) at/in/to a place, without saying exactly where: *This cat must have a home somewhere but I haven't found out where.* **get somewhere** (*fig; informal*) be successful. ⇨ anywhere(1). **or somewhere** or at/in/

to another place, without saying exactly where: *Peter has a house in Oxford or somewhere.*

somersault /'sʌmə,sɔːlt/ *c.n* **1** (often *do a —*) act of turning right over either forwards or backwards in the air or while remaining on a surface, e.g so that one's feet go right over one's head: *a back(ward) somersault.*
▷ *intr.v* **2** do a somersault(1) either intentionally or accidentally: *The car left the road and somersaulted down the hill.*

somnolent /'sɒmnələnt/ *adj* (*formal*) almost asleep; feeling very sleepy; drowsy(1).
'somnolence *u.n.* **'somnolently** *adv.*

son /sʌn/ *c.n* **1** one's/s.o's male child: *His son is a lawyer.* ⇨ daughter(1). **2** (usu *pl*) male descendant. **3** (way in which an older person sometimes speaks to a much younger man or a boy): *Where do you live, son?* **the Son of God** = Jesus.
'son-in-,law *c.n* (*pl* sons-in-law) husband of one's/s.o's daughter. ⇨ daughter-in-law.
'sonny *unique n* son(3), usu used only when speaking to a child.
,son of a 'bitch *c.n* (*pl* sons of bitches) (*slang*; do not use!) very unpleasant person.

sonar /'səʊnɑː/ *u.n* (*technical*) system that shows one where things are under the water by bouncing(3) sound waves off them. Compare radar.

sonata /sə'nɑːtə/ *c.n* (*music*) piece of music usu divided into three or four movements(5) of different speeds to be played by a piano (and one other instrument).

song /sɒŋ/ *n* **1** *c.n* piece of music (usu) with words that people sing: *He sang a song about the sea.* **2** *u.n* poem that can be sung. **3** *u.n* singing in general: *I don't like men who are only interested in wine, women and song.* **4** *c/u.n* attractive sound of a bird etc. (**get s.t, go**) **for a song** (manage to buy s.t, be sold) very cheaply. **a song and dance routine/show** a carefully prepared and practised arrangement of songs and dance steps or a show with them. **make a song and dance about s.t/it** (*fig, informal*) make a fuss(1); be angry, excited etc: *You've only cut your finger a little; you don't need to make such a song and dance about it!*
'song,bird *c.n* kind of bird that sings.
'song,book *c.n* book that contains a number of songs(1), usu with the music as well as the words.

sonic /'sɒnɪk/ *adj* (*technical*) **1** of or referring to sound waves. **2** of or referring to the speed of sound through the air. ⇨ subsonic, supersonic.
,sonic 'bang/'boom *c.n* short loud sound made when a plane breaks the sound barrier (⇨ sound²).

son-in-law ⇨ son.

sonnet /'sɒnɪt/ *c.n* poem that is 14 lines long and has one of several rhyming(4) patterns.

sonny ⇨ son.

sonorous /'sɒnərəs/ *adj* (*formal*) (of a voice, bell etc) having a pleasantly deep loud sound.
sonority /sə'nɒrɪtɪ/ *u.n.* **'sonorously** *adv.*

soon /suːn/ *adv* after a short time; before much time has passed: *It's six o'clock so it will soon be dark.* **at the soonest** not earlier than that: *I'm very busy so I can't see you till Friday at the soonest.* (**just**) **as soon as . . .** no later than . . .: *Come just as soon as you are ready.* (**just**)

as soon as possible (just) as soon as it can be done. (**just**) **as soon do s.t** (**as** (**do**) **s.t**) be equally willing to do s.t (instead of (doing) s.t): *I would just as soon eat at home this evening* (*as go to a restaurant*). (**just**) **as soon not** (**do s.t**) be equally willing not to do s.t: *'Would you like to go to the cinema?' 'I would just as soon not as I want to wash my hair.'* **no sooner . . . than . . .** as soon as (s.t happens) (s.t else happens): *No sooner had the doors opened than the crowd rushed in.* **no sooner said than done** as soon as it is said it is done. **soon after s.o/s.t; soon after . . .** a short time after . . .; not much time after . . .: *John arrived soon after Barbara. Soon after I received the letter the parcel arrived.* **sooner or later** at some time in the future, perhaps soon, perhaps not. **speak too soon** speak as if s.t is certain before it really is: *Don't speak too soon — they haven't decided to leave yet.* **would sooner do s.t** (**than** (**do**) **s.t**) would prefer to do s.t (rather than (do) s.t).

soot /sʊt/ *u.n* **1** (also *attrib*) black powder produced by flames esp from coal: *a soot brush. One often finds soot inside chimneys.*
▷ *tr/intr.v* **2** (often *— (s.t) up*) (cause(s.t) to) become covered etc with soot(1).
'sooty *adj* (*-ier, -iest*) **1** covered or full of soot(1). **2** black like soot(1).

soothe /suːð/ *tr.v* **1** cause (s.o) to become calmer, less worried, angry etc. **2** (cause (s.t) to) become less painful: *A warm drink often soothes a sore throat.*
'soothingly *adv* in a way that soothes.

sop /sɒp/ *c.n* **1** thing that one gives/offers (to s.o) to make her/him friendly, willing to help etc. **2** piece of solid food, e.g bread, soaked (⇨ soak(2)) in a liquid, e.g milk.
▷ *tr.v* (*-pp-*) **3** (often *— s.t in s.t*) put (s.t solid) (in s.t liquid). **sop s.t up** collect all of a liquid into s.t solid: *Use a cloth to sop up the spilt milk* (*from the floor*).
'sopping *adj* **1** very (wet).
▷ *adv* **2 sopping wet** = sopping(1).
'soppy *adj* (*-ier, -iest*) (*derog*; *informal*) silly because too sentimental.

sophisticated /sə'fɪstɪ,keɪtɪd/ *adj* Opposite unsophisticated. **1** knowing how to behave, what to say etc in society or showing such knowledge: *a sophisticated person; sophisticated clothes.* **2** complicated: *a sophisticated telephone system; sophisticated arguments.*
sophistication /sə,fɪstɪ'keɪʃən/ *u.n.*

soporific /,sɒpə'rɪfɪk/ *adj* **1** (*formal*) causing one to (want to) sleep: *This music is soporific.*
▷ *c.n* **2** thing that is soporific(1), e.g a drug.
,sopo'rifically *adv.*

sopping, soppy ⇨ sop.

soprano /sə'prɑː,nəʊ/ *adj/adv* **1** having a woman's highest singing voice: *She sings soprano.*
▷ *c.n* (*pl -s*) (also *attrib*) **2** woman's highest singing voice. **3** woman with such a voice. Compare contralto, tenor¹.

sorbet /'sɔːbeɪ/ *c/u.n* (*French*) (US **'sherbet**) food like ice-cream made of fruit juices with little or no cream in it: *lemon sorbet.*

sorcerer /'sɔːsərə/ *c.n* person who is supposed to be able to do bad magic(3).
'sorceress *c.n* woman who is supposed to be able to do this.
'sorcery *u.n* magic(3) done by a sorcerer etc.

sordid /ˈsɔːdɪd/ adj (derog) **1** particularly unpleasant and shameful: a sordid murder. **2** very poor and dirty: a sordid little hotel. **ˈsordidly** adv. **ˈsordidness** u.n.

sore /sɔː/ adj **1** painful; hurting: a sore head after too much wine; sore arm muscles(1) after rowing. My toe is sore where my shoe has been rubbing. **2** (often — (with s.o)) (informal, US) angry (with s.o). **a sight for sore eyes** ⇒ sight(n).
▷ c.n **3** sore(1) place on one's body where the skin is broken.
ˈsorely adv (formal) very (much): sorely tempted to miss the lecture. He's sorely in need of advice.
ˈsoreness u.n.

sorority /səˈrɒrɪtɪ/ c.n (pl -ies) (US) society for women who are students of a university. Compare fraternity(3).

sorrow /ˈsɒrəʊ/ n (formal) **1** c/u.n sad, unhappy feeling (caused by s.t): She was filled with sorrow for the sick child, over the loss of her son. Forget your sorrows and enjoy yourself. **2** c.n (often — to s.o) cause of sorrow(1) (to s.o): Losing the job was a great sorrow to me.
▷ intr.v **3** (literary) feel sorrow(1): It's no use sorrowing over a past mistake.
ˈsorrowful adj feeling, showing or causing sorrow(1); very sad.
ˈsorrowfully adv. **ˈsorrowfulness** u.n.
ˈsorrowing attrib.adj feeling/showing sorrow(1): a sorrowing mother.

sorry /ˈsɒrɪ/ adj (-ier, -iest) (pred except in 4) **1** sad; rather sorrowful: 'It rained during the whole of our holiday.' 'I'm sorry about that.' I'm sorry (to hear) (that) Jane's ill. **2** feeling regret (that one has done s.t bad): I'm sorry about the bad egg I gave you. John says he's sorry (that) he broke your toy engine. **3** (usu I'm — but . . .) (used as a polite way of refusing, disagreeing etc): 'Could I borrow your bicycle, please?' 'I'm sorry but it's broken.' **4** (attrib) (literary) that makes one feel pity: She looked a sorry sight. **be/feel sorry for s.o/s.t** feel pity for s.o/s.t. **be sorry to say (that)** . . . say (that) . . . while apologizing or expressing one's sorrow about it: I'm sorry to say that he's broken his leg.
▷ interj **5** = I'm sorry(2,3): Sorry I'm late! 'Can I have a ticket?' 'Sorry, they've all been sold.' **6** (informal) What? I beg your pardon?: 'What time is it, please?' 'Sorry?' 'I asked you the time.'

sort /sɔːt/ c.n **1** (often — of s.o/s.t) kind², type (of s.t); collection (of people, animals, things all of whom/which have certain qualities that are the same): 'What sort of ice-cream do you want?' 'Lemon, please.' All sorts of people can be found in our town. People of all sorts come and live here. **a good/nice sort** a nice etc person. **a sort of s.t** not a very definite or strong kind of s.t: I've had a sort of idea of starting a shop. **It takes all sorts (to make a world)** (proverb) People vary very much so one should not expect them to be alike. **of a sort; of sorts** of some kind (but not very good or easy to recognize as such): Fred is a clerk of sorts. **out of sorts** feeling ill, angry etc. **these/those sort of people** etc (slang) people of this/that sort(1).
▷ v **2** tr.v (often — s.t out) arrange (s.t) into different groups or into the correct order: Will you please sort all these letters out and arrange them in order of date. **3** intr.v (use — over/through s.t) sort(2) s.t.

sort s.o out (slang) attack and beat s.o. **sort s.t out (a)** sort(2) s.t. **(b)** take s.t out of s.t while one is sorting(2): Will you please sort out all the blue clothes from the washing. **(c)** settle s.t; deal with s.t in order to solve the problems it presents: The trade union and the management are trying to sort out the trouble in the factory.
ˈsorter c.n person whose job is to sort(2) things.
ˈsort-ˌout c.n (often have a —) example of sorting(2) things.

sortie /ˈsɔːtɪ/ c.n **1** (often — into s.t) short visit (to a place, usu where one feels strange or not welcome): After a quick sortie into the city centre, we returned to the safety of our hotel. **2** (often — into s.t) (fig) short attempt (to do s.t difficult, dangerous etc): Jones has made a few sorties into business but he is happier as a writer. **3** (military) attack made by soldiers from a defended position.

SOS /ˌes ˌəʊ ˈes/ c.n **1** (often (send out) an — (for s.t)) international call (for help etc), e.g when a ship is in danger. Compare mayday. **2** broadcast message for s.o to do s.t urgently, e.g for the parents of a lost child to go to it.

sot /sɒt/ c.n person who drinks too much alcohol.

soufflé /ˈsuːfleɪ/ c/u.n (French) very light fluffy(2) food made from baked flour, milk and eggs.

sought /sɔːt/ p.t,p.p of seek.
sought-after ⇒ seek.

soul /səʊl/ n **1** c.n part of a person that is not her/his body and that is said by some people to continue living after the body dies. **2** u.n (informal) ability to experience and express feelings in a satisfying way: That music has such/no soul. **3** c.n person, usu a nice one: Joyce's mother is a sweet old soul. **4** c.n (often a (living —) (often used in the pl after a number, meaning people) (one) single person: I didn't speak to a (living) soul (anyone at all) while I was on holiday. **5** u.n = soul music. **keep body and soul together** ⇒ body. **heart and soul** ⇒ heart(n). **the life and soul of the party** ⇒ life. **sell one's soul (to the devil) (for s.t)** want s.t so much that one is willing to do anything, however bad, to get it. **the soul of s.t** a perfect example of s.t: Joe is the soul of politeness to all his customers — but not to his family!
ˈsoul-deˌstroying attrib.adj (derog) very uninteresting, boring etc: soul-destroying work.
ˈsoulful adj showing or expressing sadness or feeling: a soulful look.
ˈsoulfully adv. **ˈsoulfulness** u.n.
ˈsoulless adj having no soul(2); cold(2).
ˈsoullessly adv. **ˈsoullessness** u.n.
ˈsoul ˌmusic u.n popular music expressing strong feelings.
ˈsoul-ˌsearching u.n thinking very deeply about one's conscience, moral behaviour etc.

sound¹ /saʊnd/ adj Opposite unsound. **1** (usu attrib) not damaged or spoilt in any way; in a good state: a sound engine; in sound health. **2** (usu attrib) complete; deep: a sound sleep/ sleeper. ⇒ sound¹(7). **3** solid; thorough: a sound knowledge of medicine. **4** correct; well reasoned: sound advice. **5** (of a person) who can be trusted. **6** (of a hit etc) hard: a sound smack¹(3) on the bottom. **of sound mind** ⇨ mind¹. **safe and sound** ⇨ safe(3).

▷ *adv* **7 sound asleep** deeply or completely asleep. **'soundly** *adv* **1** in a sound(2,3,6) way. **2** thoroughly: *Our team was soundly beaten in the match.*

'soundness *u.n.*

sound² /saʊnd/ *attrib.adj* **1** that is for listening to: *a sound film; sound radio.*

▷ *n* (also *attrib*) **2** *c/u.n* thing that one can hear; thing that one experiences by one's ears: *sounds of an argument; the loud sound of a bell ringing in the darkness. Sound travels through the air at a speed of about 344 metres per second. Where are those sounds coming from?* **3** *sing/u.n* (of s.t one hears or reads) quality: *sound problems. Today's news has a more cheerful sound about it. My new* hi-fi(2) *has excellent sound.* **consonant/ vowel sound** the sound and not the letter(s) to represent a consonant(1)/vowel(1). **by the sound of it** from what one hears about it.

▷ *v* **4** *intr.v* (often — *like s.t.; — as if . . .*) seem (like s.t etc) when one hears (about) it: *That game sounds easy but it's very difficult to play. That sounds (like) a clever idea. It sounds as if it's raining outside.* **5** *tr/intr.v* (cause (s.t) to) make a sound²(2): *When the bell sounds we have to get up. Drivers are not allowed to sound their horns in a town.* **6** *tr.v* give the signal for/of (s.t) by making one or more sounds²(2): *The enemy is attacking! Sound the* alarm(2)! **7** *tr.v* pronounce (s.t): *The 'k' in 'know' is not sounded.* **sound off** (**about s.o/ s.t**) (*informal*) say what one thinks (about s.o/ s.t) strongly and without hiding anything.

'sound ,barrier *def.n* sudden increase in air resistance as s.t gets close to the speed of sound, producing a loud noise. **break the sound barrier** go faster than the speed of sound.

'sound ef,fects *pl.n* sounds used in a play, film, radio show etc to make the story more real.

'sound'proof *adj* **1** that prevents sound getting in or out: *soundproof material on the walls.*

▷ *tr.v* **2** make (s.t) soundproof(1).

'sound'track *c.n* **1** strip at the edge of a film on which the sounds are recorded. **2** recording of the music, speech and sound effects of a film.

'sound 'wave *c.n* (usu *pl*) wave of air that carries sound.

sound³ /saʊnd/ *n* **1** *c.n* long wide piece of sea with land on most sides. **2** channel(3) between two larger areas of water. Compare strait.

sound⁴ /saʊnd/ *tr.v* (try to) find how deep (water etc) is. **sound s.o out** (**about/on s.o/s.t**) ask questions in order to find out what s.o thinks, plans to do etc, (about s.o/s.t).

'sounding ,line *c.n* rope etc with a weight at the end, used for sounding⁴.

'soundings *pl.n* (often *take* —) **1** measurements by sounding⁴. **2** (*fig*) attempts to find out what people are thinking, planning etc. ⇨ sound s.o out (about/on s.o/s.t).

soup /suːp/ *u.n* **1** (also *attrib*) kind of food that is mostly liquid; it is usu cooked and often has pieces of meat, vegetable etc in it: *fish soup; a soup spoon.* **clear soup** soup that is a transparent liquid. **in the soup** (*fig; informal*) in trouble.

▷ *tr.v* **2 soup s.t up** (*informal*) (**a**) make an engine, car etc more powerful by using a special device. (**b**) make s.t bigger, more exciting etc: *You'll have*

to soup that story up a lot before anyone will make a film of it.

sour /saʊə/ *adj* **1** that tastes acid, e.g like a lemon that has no sugar with it; that is not sweet or bitter or salty. **2** (of milk, cream) that has fermented(2); no longer fresh: *use sour cream in the sauce. The milk tastes, has gone, sour.* **3** showing that one is not in a good temper: *a sour look on one's face.* **go/turn sour** (**a**) become sour(2). (**b**) (*informal*) change from being pleasant to being unpleasant, disappointing etc: *The meeting began well enough but it turned sour when the workers asked for more money.*

▷ *tr/intr.v* **4** (cause (s.t) to) go sour.

,sour 'grapes *u.n* (*fig; informal*) thing that one pretends one did not really want so as not to seem unsuccessful: *If Jack says he wouldn't have accepted that job even if it was offered to him, that is just sour grapes; he wants it very much.*

'sourly *adv.* **'sourness** *u.n.*

source /sɔːs/ *c.n* (often — *of s.t*) **1** place/thing/ person from which s.t starts or comes: *Nobody knows the source of his wealth. Government sources say that there will be changes in the law.* **2** place where a river begins: *the source of the River Thames.*

south /saʊθ/ *adj* (often with capital **S**) **1** in or coming from the direction that is on one's right when one is facing the rising sun; at a point on a compass(1) that is usu at the bottom in a drawing, *symb* **S**: *a south wind.* Opposite north(1).

▷ *adv* **2** towards a south(1) direction: *We travelled south.* Opposite north(2). **down south** (*informal*) in/towards a south(1) direction. Opposite up north (⇨ north(*adv*)).

▷ *n* **3** *def/unique n* direction that is south(1). **4** *def.n* part of a country or of the world that is further south(1) than the rest of it: *The South has lower unemployment than the North.* **go south** go/ travel towards the south(3) (esp because it is warmer). **in the south** (**a**) in the direction that is south(1): *We could see the rain in the south.* (**b**) in that part of a country or the world that is further south(1) than the rest: *He lives in the south.* **in the south of s.t** inside the southern part of s.t. (**to the**) **south of s.t** further south(1) than s.t.

'south,bound *adj* going towards the south(3).

,south'east *adj* (often with capital **S**) **1** coming from/in a direction or point on a compass(1) halfway between south(3) and east(3).

▷ *adv* **2** towards a southeast(1) direction.

▷ *def/unique n* **3** southeast(1) direction.

,south'easter *c.n* strong wind/storm from the southeast(3).

,south'easterly *adj* **1** from, in, towards, the southeast(3).

▷ *c.n* **2** wind from the southeast(3).

,south'eastern *adj* of, belonging to, the southeast(3), usu of a place.

southeastward /,saʊθˈiːstwəd/ *adj* towards the southeast(3).

southeastwards /,saʊθˈiːstwədz/ *adv* (US **,south'eastward**) towards the southeast(3); southeast(2).

southerly /'sʌðəlɪ/ *adj* from, in, towards, the south(3): *a southerly wind. Our room has a southerly view.*

southern /'sʌðən/ *adj* (often with capital **S**) of,

belonging to, the south(3) of a place: *Southern Europe.*

Southerner /'sʌðənə/ *c.n* person who lives in or comes from the southern part of a place.

,**Southern 'Hemi,sphere** *def.n* ⇒ hemisphere.

'**southern,most** *adj* that is furthest to the south(*n*).

'**south,facing** *adj* that looks towards, faces, the south(3): *a southfacing house.*

,**South 'Pole** *def.n* ⇒ pole²(1).

southward /'saʊθwəd/ *adj* towards the south(3).

southwards /'saʊθwədz/ *adv* (US **southward**) towards the south(3).

,**south'west** *adj* (often with capital **S**) **1** coming from a direction or point on a compass(1) halfway between south(3) and west(3).

▷ *adv* **2** towards a southwest(1) direction.

▷ *def/unique n* **3** southwest(1) direction.

,**south'wester** *c.n* strong wind/storm from the southwest(3).

,**south'westerly** *adj* **1** from, in, towards, the southwest(3).

▷ *c.n* **2** wind from the southwest(3).

,**south'western** *adj* of, belonging to, the southwest(3), usu of a place.

southwestward /,saʊθ'westwəd/ *adj* towards the southwest(3).

southwestwards /,saʊθ'westwədz/ *adv* (US ,**south'westward**) towards the southwest(3); southwest(2).

sou'wester /saʊ'westə/ *c.n* oilskin hat worn, usu in storms, to keep the rain and wind off one's head.

souvenir /'su:və,nɪə/ *c.n* thing that one keeps to remind one of s.o/s.t, e.g a place one has been to.

sovereign /'sɒvrɪn/ *adj* **1** that rules a country: *sovereign power.* **2** (*attrib*) that is not ruled by anyone else: *a sovereign state.*

▷ *c.n* **3** king, queen, emperor or empress. **4** (in history) British £1 gold coin.

'**sovereignty** *u.n* **1** (fact of having) sovereign(1) power. **2** fact of being sovereign(2).

soviet /'səʊvɪət/ *attrib.adj* **1** (usu with capital **S**) of or referring to the USSR: *the Soviet Union.*

▷ *c.n* **2** group of people elected to act as a kind of council or parliament in a communist(1) country.

sow¹ /saʊ/ *c.n* adult female pig. Compare boar, hog(1).

sow² /səʊ/ *tr/intr.v* (*p.p* sowed, sown) **1** put (seeds) in/on the ground so that they can become plants. **2** (*fig; literary*) cause (s.t) to start: *Those who sow trouble often reap(2) it too.*

'**sower** *c.n* person who sows² s.t.

sox /sɒks/ *pl.n* (*informal*) socks¹.

soya /'sɔɪə/ *u.n* (also *attrib*) (also **soy** /sɔɪ/) sauce, flour etc made from soya beans.

'**soya ,bean** *c.n* (also '**soy ,bean**) **1** kind of plant from Asia that produces beans rich in protein. **2** bean produced by this plant.

'**soy ,sauce** *u.n* dark brown liquid made from soya beans, used in cooking.

sozzled /'sɒzəld/ *adj* (*slang*) drunk(1) (⇒ drink).

spa /spɑ:/ *c.n* place where natural mineral water comes out of, is found under, the ground and where usu fashionable people go to drink it, wash in it etc for the good of their health.

space /speɪs/ *n* **1** *c/u.n* empty place between things, solids, edges etc: *the space between the*

words in a line. **2** *c/u.n* (often — *for s.o/s.t*) big enough empty space (to fit s.o/s.t): *There is space for three cars in this garage.* **3** *u.n* area round all our earth which contains air lower down and nothing higher up. **4** *c.n* (usu — *between s.t and s.t*) length of time (between s.t and s.t): *We fill the spaces between lessons with amusing games.* **5** *c.n* width of one letter or space(1) on a typewriter etc: *'Would have done' takes up 15 spaces.* **air space** ⇒ air. **during/in the space of a week, kilometre** etc within a week/kilometre etc. **open spaces** ⇒ open(3). **outer space** ⇒ out. **parking space** ⇒ parking(1).

▷ *tr.v* **6** (often — *s.o/s.t out*) arrange (people etc) in such a way that there are spaces(1) between them.

'**space,craft** *c.n* (*pl* spacecraft(s)) vehicle used for taking people and/or things into space, e.g to the moon.

'**space ,probe** *c.n* spacecraft sent to collect information about planets etc.

'**space,ship** *c.n* = spacecraft, esp in stories.

'**space ,shuttle** *c.n* kind of spacecraft that can be used again and again, e.g to launch(6)/repair satellites(1).

'**space ,suit** *c.n* suit worn in space(3) which covers the whole person and in which air is provided.

'**spacing** *u.n* amount of space(1) allowed, wanted etc between people or things. **single/double/triple spacing** (in typing etc) one/two/three spaces between one line and the next.

spacious /'speɪʃəs/ *adj* having a lot of space(2); roomy: *a spacious sitting room.*

'**spaciously** *adv.* '**spaciousness** *u.n.*

spade¹ /speɪd/ *c.n* **1** tool with a flat wide blade fixed to a wooden handle for making holes in and moving earth. Compare shovel(1), trowel(1). **2** (often — *of s.t*) = spadeful (of s.t). **call a spade a spade** (*fig; informal*) speak absolutely truthfully without hiding anything or trying to be polite.

'**spadeful** *c.n* amount that one can carry on a spade(1).

'**spade,work** *u.n* (usu do the —) hard work done to prepare for s.t.

spade² /speɪd/ *c.n* one of a set of playing cards with one or more black shapes on it that look like this ♠: *a seven of spades.* Compare club³, diamond(3), heart(6).

spaghetti /spə'getɪ/ *u.n* (*Italian*) kind of pasta that is shaped like long solid strings. Compare macaroni, vermicelli.

span¹ /spæn/ *c.n* **1** (often — *of s.t*) length (of time or distance): *Her life covered a span of 80 interesting years.* ⇒ wingspan. **2** span¹(1) of time during which s.t lasts or remains efficient: *Children usually have a short attention span.* **3** (length of) part of a building, bridge etc that hangs in the air between supports: *That bridge has two spans of 120 metres each.*

▷ *tr.v* (**-nn-**) **4** form a span¹(3) over (a river etc). **5** cover a span¹(1) of (s.t): *Her life spanned 80 troubled years.*

span² /spæn/ *p.t* of spin.

span³ ⇒ spick and span.

spangle /'spæŋgl/ *c.n* **1** small piece of shiny metal, plastic(3) etc used to decorate clothes etc. Compare sequin.

▷ *tr.v* **2** put spangles on (s.t). **3** make (s.t) glitter(3) as if it had spangles(1) on it: *a star-spangled sky*; *the star-spangled banner* (the US national flag).

spaniel /'spænɪəl/ *c.n* kind of small dog with soft hair and long ears.

spank /spæŋk/ *c.n* **1** (one) act of spanking(2).
▷ *tr.v* **2** hit (s.o/s.t) usu with one's hand on the bottom: *Should parents spank their children when they are naughty?*
'**spanking** *c.n* (usu *get, give s.o, a* —) punishment with a spank(1).

spanner /'spænə/ *c.n* tool used for tightening and loosening nuts(2) and bolts²(2) by turning them. *adjustable spanner* ⇨ adjust. *ring spanner* ⇨ ring¹. *a spanner in the works* (*fig*; *informal*) a thing that causes a lot of trouble or that ruins what s.o is trying to do.

spar¹ /spɑː/ *c.n* thick round length of wood etc, used to support a sail etc. Compare mast.

spar² /spɑː/ *intr.v* (-rr-) (often — *with s.o*) **1** box² (with s.o) without hitting hard for practice or to find out how good the other person is. **2** argue (with s.o), usu not very seriously.
'**sparring** ,**partner** *c.n* person with whom one spars².

spare /speə/ *adj* **1** not needed immediately but ready to be used when needed: *a spare tube of toothpaste; a spare room for guests. 'Have you got any spare eggs I could buy?'* **2** not being used for anything; free: *spare time.* **3** (of a person's body) thin; having no unnecessary fat on it; lean(1). *go spare* (*slang*) become very worried/cross: *I went spare when they said my son was not at school.*
▷ *c.n* **4** thing that is spare(1): *Never travel with only one razor; always carry a spare.* **5** = spare tyre/ wheel. **6** (often *pl*) = spare part.
▷ *tr.v* **7** (often — *s.o s.t*) allow s.o to have s.t because it is spare(1,2): *Can you spare (me) a cup of sugar till Monday? Could you spare five minutes to talk about arrangements for tomorrow?* **8** avoid attacking, hurting, punishing (s.o/s.t): *The merciful king spared his enemies' lives.* **9** (often — *oneself/s.o s.t*) save (oneself/s.o) from having to do (s.t unpleasant etc): *Peter decided to spare himself a lot of work by employing a gardener. You can spare David your advice; he won't take it. spare no expense* ⇨ expense. *spare no trouble* do all that is possible. *to spare* left over or extra: *We arrived at the station with ten minutes to spare before our train left.*
,**spare** '**part** *c.n* piece for putting into a machine, car etc to replace one that is broken, worn out etc.
,**spare** '**ribs** *pl.n* ribs(2), usu of a pig, with meat still on them which are cooked and eaten.
,**spare** '**tyre**/'**wheel** *c.n* tyre/wheel, usu kept in a car etc, that can replace a damaged one when necessary. ⇨ spare(1,5).
'**sparing** *adj* using very little (of s.t); not at all generous/liberal(1) (with s.t): *A sparing use of salt and sugar is good for one's health. He was very sparing with his praise.* Compare unsparing.
'**sparingly** *adv.*

spark /spɑːk/ *c.n* **1** very small piece of burning material etc that suddenly jumps out from a fire or that is produced when hard objects, e.g stones, hit each other. **2** flash of light produced when electricity jumps across a gap. **3** (*fig*) thing that starts trouble, e.g a war. **4** (usu — *of s.t*) very small amount (of s.t): *That child occasionally shows a*

spark of interest in what the teacher says. **bright spark** (*informal*) person who is clever, cheerful or who has a quick mind.
▷ *intr.v* **5** produce one or more sparks(1,2). *spark into s.t* cause s.t bad or worse to begin: *The row soon sparked into a fight. spark s.t off* be the spark(3) that causes s.t: *The fight was sparked off by something rude David said about Ted's wife.*
'**spark** ,**plug** *c.n* (also '**sparking** ,**plug**) (*technical*) device that is screwed into the engine of a vehicle which produces sparks(2) to make the mixture of petrol and air explode to start the engine working.

sparkle /'spɑːkl/ *c/u.n* (often — *of s.t*) **1** quick repeated flashes (of a diamond, the sea in the sun etc). **2** (*fig*) quick repeated clever or amusing things said: *the sparkle of witty conversation.*
▷ *intr.v* **3** flash with sparkles(1). **4** be clever or amusing: *The conversation sparkled that evening.*
'**sparkler** *c.n* small metal rod with a chemical(2) on it that gives off sparks(1) when it is lit; children hold it in their hands as a kind of firework.
'**sparkling** *adj* (esp — *wine*) that gives off small bubbles(2) of gas. Compare fizzy. Opposite still(4).

sparrow /'spærəʊ/ *c.n* kind of small mostly brown bird commonly found in many parts of the world.

sparse /spɑːs/ *adj* not at all numerous; not growing etc at all close together: *the sparse vegetation(2) of desert areas.*
'**sparsely** *adv.* '**sparseness** *u.n.*

spartan /'spɑːtn/ *adj* (also with capital **S**) not having any consideration for, not providing any, comfort or luxury(1); very simple: *the spartan conditions of life as a poor student.*

spasm /'spæzəm/ *n* **1** *c/u.n* sudden tightening of a muscle(1) without it being controlled or intentional. **2** (often — *of s.t*) sudden violent attack (of pain, coughing, laughing, sadness etc); fit²(3).
spasmodic /spæz'mɒdɪk/ *adj* **1** happening like a spasm. **2** happening at irregular times or in an irregular way.
spas'modically *adv* in a spasmodic(2) way.

spastic /'spæstɪk/ *adj* **1** having, referring to, spastic paralysis.
▷ *c.n* **2** person who has spastic paralysis.
,**spastic pa'ralysis** *u.n* disease that causes spasm(1) in some muscles(1).

spat /spæt/ *p.t* of spit¹.

spate /speɪt/ *c.n* (often *a* — *of s.t*) flood (of s.t); big amount/number (of s.t) coming all together: *a spate of work.*

spatial /'speɪʃəl/ *adj* (*formal*) of or referring to space.
'**spatially** *adv.*

spatter /'spætə/ *c.n* **1** drop of s.t that has fallen on s.t. **2** (often — *of s.t*) small amount/number (of a liquid or pieces of solid matter): *spatters of mud. We were hoping for plenty of rain but there was only a spatter (of it).*
▷ *v* **3** *tr.v* drop a spatter(*n*) of s.t) (on s.t): *You've spattered mud on my shoes.* **4** *tr.v* drop a spatter(*n*) of s.t on (s.t): *You've spattered my shoes with mud.* **5** *intr.v* (often — *on s.t*) fall (on s.t) in the form of a spatter(*n*).

spatula /'spætjʊlə/ *c.n* (*technical*) **1** kind of tool with a wide flat blade used for spreading, mixing and/or picking up soft substances. **2** device used for pressing down the back of a person's tongue so that one can look down her/his throat.

spawn /spɔːn/ *u.n* **1** eggs of a fish, frog etc laid in water in a mass that looks like jelly(1). ⇒ frogspawn.
▷ *v* **2** *tr/intr.v* produce(spawn(1)). **3** *tr.v* (*fig*)produce (s.t), usu in large numbers or quantities: *Many big cities now spawn large numbers of young criminals.*

spay /speɪ/ *tr.v* prevent (a female animal) producing young by removing her ovaries: *We're having our cat spayed.* Compare neuter(4).

speak /spiːk/ *v* (*p.t* spoke /spəʊk/, *p.p* spoken /ˈspəʊkən/) **1** *intr.v* (often — *to/with s.o*) (about *s.o/s.t*) say s.t, talk, use one's voice, to express what one thinks aloud (to s.o) (about s.o/s.t): *Will you speak to them about their children's behaviour or shall I?* ⇒ unspeakable. **2** *intr.v* (often — *of s.t*) express s.t but not with one's voice: *Nicki's latest letter speaks of very hot weather in Spain. Everything we saw that summer spoke of preparations for war.* **3** *intr.v* (often — *about/on s.o/s.t*) make a formal speech, e.g at a meeting, (about s.o/s.t). **4** *tr.v* be able to say things in (a language): *Do you speak German?* **5** *tr.v* say (s.t); express (s.t) while speaking (⇒ speak(1)): *He was so surprised that he couldn't speak a (single) word. It's difficult to know when she is speaking the truth and when she is lying.* **6** *intr.v* (often — *to s.o*) be willing to speak(1) (to s.o): *For years John and Peter weren't speaking to each other because of a family quarrel but now they are speaking again.* **7** *intr.v* (*literary*) (of a musical instrument, gun, bell etc) make a (loud) sound: *Now the politicians fell silent and the guns began to speak.* **8** *tr.v* recite(1) (s.t); say (s.t that one has planned to say): *speak one's lines in a play.*
so to speak rather; more or less; as one way of saying it.
speak for s.o be the representative of s.o, usu for giving their opinions to s.o. **speak for s.t** **(a)** (often *speak well for s.t*) be a (good etc) sign of what happens, will happen. Compare speak volumes for s.t. **(b)** reserve(8) s.t in advance: *You can't have this table, I'm afraid; it's already spoken for.* **speak for itself** not need to be explained, because it is already clear; be self-evident: *You don't have to ask a lot of questions about these pictures as they speak for themselves.*
speak one's mind ⇒ mind¹.
speak out (about s.t) say what one thinks (of s.t) freely and without hiding anything.
speak to s.o (a) ⇒ speak(1). **(b)** scold s.o. ⇒ speaking-to. **(c)** (*informal*) give s.o a feeling of pleasure, understanding etc: *Modern music doesn't speak to Sue at all.* **speak to s.t** (*formal*) talk about a certain subject without wandering off it.
speak too soon ⇒ soon.
speak up (a) speak(1) more loudly. **(b)** = speak out.
speak volumes (for s.t) ⇒ volumes.
to speak of (usu in negative sentences) of much value/use; worth speaking of: *We have no friends to speak of in this town* (not many, no real, friends).
ˈspeaker *c.n* **1** person who is speaking (⇒ speak(1)) or who makes a speech. **2** person who

speaks(1) in the way, the language etc shown: *a fast speaker; a speaker of English/French.* **3** = loudspeaker. **4** *def.n* (with capital **S**) official in a parliament etc who controls its meetings. *Mr Speaker* (title of the Speaker(4)).
ˈspeaking *adj/adv* **1** *generally, personally, properly* etc *speaking* if one is to say s.t in a general, personal etc way. *(not) on speaking terms (with s.o)* ⇒ terms (⇒ term²).
▷ *u.n* **2** act of speaking (⇒ speak(1,3)): *the art of public speaking.*
-speaking *adj* who speaks(4) the language shown in the first part of the word: *an Arabic-speaking official.*
ˈspeaking-ˌto *c.n* scolding. ⇒ speak to s.o(b).
-spoken *adj* who speaks(1) in the way shown by the first part of the word: *soft-spoken.*
ˈspokesman *c.n* (*pl* -men) male spokesperson.
ˈspokesˌperson *c.n* person who speaks(1) as a representative of other people (as well as herself/himself).
ˈspokesˌwoman *c.n* (*pl* -ˌwomen) female spokesperson.

spear /spɪə/ *c.n* **1** weapon with a long handle and a sharp metal head, used in the past for fighting and hunting. **2** long thin leaf of grass etc that looks like a spear(1).
▷ *tr.v* **3** catch or make a hole in (s.t) with a spear(1), fork etc.
ˈspearˌhead *c.n* **1** head of a spear(1). **2** (usu — *of s.t*) (often *fig*) leading part (of s.t) that goes first: *the spearhead of an attack.*
▷ *tr.v* **3** act as a spearhead(2) for (s.t): *The church is spearheading the* opposition *to child poverty.*
ˈspearˌmint *u.n* (also *attrib*) kind of mint¹ used in chewing-gum, sweets etc: *spearmint toothpaste.*

spec /spek/ *u.n* **on spec** knowing that it is risky but hoping to be lucky: *We chose a place for our holiday on spec and we were very pleased with it.*

special /ˈspeʃəl/ *adj* **1** that is different from and often additional to, the usual ones; that is not an ordinary one: *a special train to take people to a football match; a special edition of a newspaper after a big event.* **2** extra good, important etc: *Mary is my special friend. January 11th is a special day for us because that is when we were married.* ⇒ especial.
▷ *c.n* **3** special(1) thing: *The bus company is putting on some specials for the match.*
ˌspecial deˈlivery *u.n* delivery of mail to s.o at an earlier time than the regular one: *One has to pay more to send a letter by special delivery.*
ˈspecialist *c.n* person who specializes in a particular activity, field of medicine, study etc: *a skin specialist* (dermatologist); *a specialist in 17th century art.*
speciality /ˌspeʃɪˈælɪtɪ/ *c.n* (*pl* -ies) (US **specialty** /ˈspeʃəltɪ/) **1** field in which one is a specialist. **2** thing that s.o/s.t does particularly well: *John's speciality is double backward somersaults(1). I'll cook you my speciality tonight.*
specialization, -isation /ˌspeʃəlaɪˈzeɪʃən/ *u.n* fact or act of specializing.
ˈspeciaˌlize, -ise (often — *in s.t*) concentrate(3) one's studies, interests etc (on a particular field etc): *Carol specializes in American history.*
ˈspeciaˌlized, -ised *adj* particularly suited to a

thing as a result of training, natural development etc: *specialized instruments for heart* surgery(1).

'specially *adv* **1** (often — *for s.o/s.t*) for a particular person or purpose: *This ship was specially built for use in shallow waters.* **2** in a different way from the usual one: *Mary is not allowed salt so I specially cooked this cabbage without any.* **3** especially; more than usually.

,special 'offer *c.n* thing offered for sale in a shop at a low price to sell it more quickly or to attract customers to the shop. **on special offer** being offered in this way.

'specialty ⇒ speciality.

species /'spi:ʃi:z/ *c.n* (*pl* **species**) (often — *of s.t*) kind (of animal or plant) that consists of individuals(3) that are alike in certain ways and that produce young of the same kind when they breed(3) with each other. Compare genus.

specific /spɪ'sɪfɪk/ *adj* **1** clear and exact in meaning: *I gave him specific* instructions(3) *as to what to say but he forgot them.* **2** (often — *to s.t*) referring to, suitable for, only one thing or a limited number of things: *This disease is specific to pigs.*

spe'cifically *adv* **1** in a specific way. **2** to say it more exactly: *We live near Bournemouth - specifically at a place called Canford.*

specification /,spesɪfɪ'keɪʃən/ *n* (often — *of s.t*) **1** *u.n* fact of specifying s.t. **2** *c.n* (usu *pl*) one of the details laid down in the plans, rules etc (for s.t): *What are the specifications of the new house you want to build?*

spe,cific 'gravity *u.n* (*technical*) density(2) of s.t compared with that of water; weight of a particular liquid or solid divided by the weight of pure water of the same volume(3): *The specific gravity of gold is 19.3.*

specificity /,spesɪ'fɪsɪtɪ/ *u.n.*

spe'cifics *pl.n* details (of s.t) of which one knows the general nature.

specify /'spesɪ,faɪ/ *tr.v* (*-ies*, *-ied*) say (s.t) exactly or in detail: *Have you specified the taps you want on the new bath? Could you please specify exactly where you want the roses planted?*

specimen /'spesɪmən/ *c.n* (often — *of s.t*) **1** one example (of s.t) that has all the usual characteristics(2) of that kind of thing: *an excellent specimen* of tulip. **2** small piece/amount of s.t for testing to see if it has any disease etc: *a blood specimen.*

specious /'spi:ʃəs/ *adj* (*formal*) appearing to be good, right etc when it is not: *a specious argument against eating meat.*

'speciously *adv.* **'speciousness** *u.n.*

speck /spek/ *c.n* (often — *of s.t*) **1** very small piece (of dirt, dust etc). **2** (*fig*) very small amount (of s.t): *There wasn't a speck of honesty among the lot of them.*

speckle /'spekl/ *c.n* (usu *pl*) small mark or irregular shape.

'speckled *adj* having speckles: *speckled feathers.*

specs /speks/ *pl.n* (*informal*) spectacles (⇒ spectacle²).

spectacle¹ /'spektəkl/ *c.n* thing that there is to be seen, often a particularly beautiful, interesting one; spectacular(1) sight. **make a spectacle of oneself** behave in a silly way that makes people notice, laugh at, one.

spectacular /spek'tækjʊlə/ *adj* **1** unusually wonderful, exciting etc: *a spectacular jump.*
▷ *c.n* **2** spectacular(1) show.

spec'tacularly *adv.*

spectacle² /'spektəkl/ *attrib.adj* used for spectacles: *a spectacle case.*

'spectacles *pl.n* (*informal specs*) glasses for wearing in front of the eyes to see better.

spectator /spek'teɪtə/ *c.n* person who watches a sport etc without being a player etc in it.

spectre /'spektə/ *c.n* (US **'specter**) **1** ghost(1). **2** (often the — *of s.t*) thing that frightens or worries one when one thinks (about it): *the spectre of unemployment.*

spectrum /'spektrəm/ *c.n* (*pl* **spectra** /'spektrə/) **1** bands of coloured light like those in a rainbow arranged in the order of their wavelengths: *A spectrum can be produced by breaking up a white light with a prism.* **2** all the wavelengths of other kinds, e.g sound or radio waves, within certain limits. **3** collection of different ideas etc arranged in an order: *There is a wide spectrum of opinions in our village about the new road.*

speculate /'spekjʊ,leɪt/ *v* **1** *tr/intr.v* (often — *about s.t*) think (about s.t) in a guessing kind of way without having any proof. **2** *intr.v* (often — *in s.t*) buy and/or sell things to try to make a profit when one may in fact make a loss instead: *Eric is speculating in gold shares.*

speculation /,spekjʊ'leɪʃən/ *c/u.n* example/ fact of speculating.

speculative /'spekjʊlətɪv/ *adj* **1** based only on thought and not on scientific facts. **2** in which one is speculating(2): *speculative buying of* shares(3).

'speculatively *adv.*

'specu,lator *c.n* person who speculates(2).

sped /sped/ *p.t,p.p* of speed.

speech /spi:tʃ/ *n* **1** *u.n* fact, act or power of speaking; system of language when spoken not written: *Monkeys use language but not speech as we know it.* **2** *u.n* way of speaking of a particular person or group of people; accent(1): *Can you tell from that girl's speech which part of Italy she comes from?* **3** *c.n* (often *give/make a —*) formal talk to an audience. ⇒ maiden speech. **4** *c.n* words spoken in a speech(3). **5** *c.n* set of words spoken by one actor/actress in a play, film etc: *Antony's famous speech to the crowds in Rome.*

'speechless *adj* (often — *with s.t*) (temporarily) not able to speak (because of surprise, anger etc): *Her rudeness left us all speechless.*

'speechlessly *adv.* **'speechlessness** *u.n.*

'speech ,therapist *c.n* person who gives speech therapy.

'speech ,therapy *u.n* treatment to help people who have trouble in speaking, esp in making certain speech sounds.

speed /spi:d/ *n* **1** *c.n* amount of quickness/ slowness; distance divided by the time taken; rate at which s.o/s.t moves: *The speed of sound through the air is about 344 metres a second. He drove at a speed of more than 140 kilometres an hour.* **2** *u.n* fact or state of moving quickly; ability to do this: *Speed is much less important than safety when driving.* **3** *u.n* (*slang*) amphetamine. **at speed** moving very quickly. **gain/gather speed** (of a vehicle etc) move more quickly: *As the* avalanche(1) *gained speed it brought more and* *more rocks down with it.* **get up speed** (of a train etc) start to move more quickly. **lose speed** (of a vehicle etc) (start to) move more slowly.

▷ *v* (*p.t,p.p* sped /sped/, speeded) **4** *intr.v* (usu — by) move, pass (by), quickly: *During holidays the hours usually speed by.* **5** *tr.v* (often — s.o/s.t up) cause (s.o/s.t) to move, happen etc (more) quickly: *A good lawyer will speed the sale of the house. Lots of good food will speed up your recovery.* **6** *intr.v* go faster than the law allows; break the speed limit: *Don't speed; there's lots of time.* **speed** (s.t) **up** (a) ⇒ speed(5). (b) (cause (a car etc) to) go faster.

'speed- *adj* (of the activity shown in the second part of the word) **1** that can be done very quickly: *speed-reading.* **2** in which one tries to win by going faster than others: *speed-skating.*

-speed *adj* that has the number of different gears(1) shown in the first part of the word: *a ten-speed bicycle.*

'speed,boat *c.n* small boat with an engine that allows it to be driven very fast.

'speedily *adv* in a speedy way.

'speediness *u.n* fact of being speedy.

'speeding *u.n* driving faster than the law allows: *be fined²(2) for speeding.*

'speed ,limit *c.n* fastest speed(1) allowed by the law: *There is a speed limit of 50 kilometres an hour in our village.* **break/exceed the speed limit** go faster than this speed. **keep to the speed limit** not go faster than this speed.

speedo /'spiːdəʊ/ *c.n* (*informal*) = speedometer.

speedometer /spɪ'dɒmɪtə/ *c.n* instrument for showing what speed a vehicle is going at.

'speed ,trap *c.n* place where police hide to catch drivers who break the speed limit.

'speed,way *n* **1** *c.n* race track for motorbikes etc. **2** *u.n* sport of motorbike racing on speedways(1).

'speedy *adj* (-*ier*, -*iest*) fast; quick; not taking, seeming to take, a long time.

spell¹ /spel/ *v* (*p.t,p.p* spelled, spelt /spelt/) **1** *tr.v* write (a word etc) using letters: *'How do you spell* /'kɑːsl/?' *'C-A-S-T-L-E.'* **2** *tr.v* (of the letters in a word) go together to make (a word): *C-A-S-T-L-E spells 'castle'.* **3** *intr.v* be able to spell¹(1) (correctly): *Jim is five and he is learning to spell.* **4** *tr.v* (*informal*) mean (s.t) or have (s.t) as its result: *The rain spelt the end of our wonderful days on the beach.* **spell s.t out** (a) write or say a word etc with each letter clear and separate. (b) (*fig*) explain s.t very simply and clearly with every detail.

'speller *c.n* person who spells¹(3): *Peggy is a very good speller* (she spells¹(3) very well).

'spelling *n* **1** *u.n* action of spelling (⇒ spell¹(1)). **2** *u.n* ability to spell¹(3). **3** *c.n* way in which s.t is spelt¹(2): *The British spelling is 'centre' and the American spelling is 'center'.*

spell² /spel/ *c.n* **1** piece of magic(1). **2** words used for a spell²(1). **3** strong attraction: *Ted felt the spell of Jill's smile the first time they met.* **be/ come/fall under a/s.o's/s.t's spell** (begin to) be affected by magic(3); be strongly attracted to s.o/ s.t. **cast a spell (on/over s.o/s.t)** cause s.o/s.t to be affected by magic(3).

'spell,bind *tr.v* (*p.t,p.p* spellbound /'spel,baʊnd/) interest (s.o) so much that he/she cannot think of anything/anyone else.

'spell,binder *c.n* person who spellbinds s.o.

'spell,binding *adj* holding one's attention or interest completely.

'spell,bound *adj* having one's attention or interest held completely.

spell³ /spel/ *c.n* (often — of s.t) **1** length of time (during which s.t goes on): *After a spell of bad weather we had beautiful sunshine for a week.* **2** usu short attack (of coughing, illness etc).

spend /spend/ *v* (*p.t,p.p* spent /spent/) **1** *tr/ intr.v* (often — s.t for/on s.t) give (money etc) to buy or pay (for s.t): *How much money do you spend on food every week?* ⇒ overspend. **2** *tr.v* (often — s.t in (doing) s.t) pass/use (time) (on/ in doing s.t): *We spent two weeks (driving) in France last summer.* **3** *tr.v* (*formal*) use (s.t) up till nothing is left: *After three days the winds had spent their strength and the sea was calm again.* **spend a penny** ⇒ penny(*n*).

'spender *c.n* person who spends(1): *a big spender* (i.e a person who spends a lot of money).

'spending ,money *u.n* = pocket money.

'spend,thrift *c.n* person who spends too much money, usu wasting some of it.

spent *adj* **1** (usu *pred*) so tired that one cannot do any more; exhausted. ⇒ spend(3). **2** (usu *attrib*) used; having lost its original force: *a spent bullet*; *a spent force.*

sperm /spɜːm/ *n* (*pl* -(s)) **1** *c.n* cell produced by a male person or animal which may enter an egg in a female so that a baby is produced. **2** *u.n* (also *attrib*) = semen.

spermatozoon /ˌspɜːmətə'zəʊɒn/ *c.n* (*pl* spermatozoa /ˌspɜːmətə'zəʊə/) (*technical*) sperm(1).

'sperm ,whale *c.n* kind of blue whale.

spew /spjuː/ *tr/intr.v* (usu — (s.t) out) (cause (a liquid etc) to) pour out. **spew (s.t) up** (*slang*) vomit(3) (s.t).

sphere /sfɪə/ *c.n* **1** object that has the shape of a perfect ball in which every point on the surface is the same distance from the centre. **2** area in which s.t exists, happens etc: *Poland is within Russia's sphere of influence.*

-sphere *n* **1** of a sphere(1): *a hemisphere* (half of a sphere). **2** sphere(1) of the kind shown by the first part of the word: *atmosphere.*

spherical /'sferɪkl/ *adj* having the shape of a sphere(1).

spheroid /'sfɪərɔɪd/ *c.n* (*technical*) shape that is almost a sphere(1) but is usu more like an egg with two equal ends.

sphinx /sfɪŋks/ *c.n* **1** (mostly ancient Egyptian) statue or other image of a lion with a human head. **2** person who speaks and/or behaves in (secret) ways that are very difficult to understand; person who stays silent.

spice /spaɪs/ *n* **1** *c/u.n* kind of powder etc made from a vegetable and used to give a taste/flavouring to other food: *Pepper(1) is a spice.* **2** *sing.n* (often *add* — *to* s.t) (*fig*) thing that makes s.t more exciting or interesting: *Danger adds spice to some sports.*

▷ *tr.v* **3** add spice to s.t.

'spicily *adv* in a spicy(2) way.

'spiciness *u.n* fact or state of being spicy.

'spicy *adj* (-*ier*, -*iest*) **1** having, tasting as if it has, spice(1) in it. **2** exciting, often because it is rather rude or immoral.

spick and span /ˌspɪk ən 'spæn/ *adj* (**spick-and-span** when *attrib*) (*informal*) clean and tidy.

spider /'spaɪdə/ *c.n* kind of small creature with eight legs: *Spiders spin webs*(1) *to catch insects in.*

'**spidery** *adj* long and thin: *spidery writing.*

spies /spaɪz/ 1 *pl.n* ⇒ spy(*n*). 2 *3rd pers pres.t* of spy(*v*).

spike /spaɪk/ *c.n* 1 long piece of metal with a point at one end: *Spikes are used on the bottoms of shoes for running races.*
▷ *tr.v* 2 put spikes(1) on/in (s.t). 3 add a strong alcoholic(1) drink to (one that has little or no alcohol). **spike s.o's guns** (*fig*) make it impossible for s.o to do, be successful in, s.t.

'**spiky** *adj* (-*ier*, -*iest*) 1 having spikes(1). 2 (*informal*) easily offended.

spill¹ /spɪl/ *c.n* 1 act of pouring s.t out, usu accidentally: *There's a spill of oil from the tanker.* 2 (amount of) thing spilt(4). 3 = spillway. 4 fall (from a horse etc). ⇒ spill(7).
▷ *v* (*p.t,p.p* spilled, spilt/spɪlt/) 5 *tr/intr.v* (cause(s.t) to) pour out, usu accidentally, over the edge: *Don't spill the milk; we haven't got any more. The pan fell over and all the vegetables spilled onto the floor.* 6 *intr.v* (often — (over) *into* s.t) spread from within s.t (into s.t): *There were so many people at the meeting that they spilled over into the passages outside the hall.* 7 *tr/intr.v* (*informal*) tell (s.t that is supposed to be a secret). 8 *tr.v* (of a horse etc) throw (s.o); cause (s.o) to fall off. **cry over spilt milk** ⇒ milk(*n*). **spill the beans** ⇒ bean. **spill blood** (*literary*) kill people: *A lot of blood has been spilt over religion.*

'**spill,way** canal or place on a dam, river etc where water flows when the level gets too high, esp to prevent flooding.

spill² /spɪl/ *c.n* thin piece of wood or twisted paper, used for lighting a fire etc.

spin /spɪn/ *n* 1 *u.n* (usu — *of* s.t) fast turning movement (of s.t) on its own axis(2): *the spin of a coin/wheel.* 2 *c.n* act of making s.t spin(8): *I'll give this coin a spin to see which side it falls on.* 3 *c.n* (often **go for a —**) short trip, in a car etc: *I'm going to take my motorbike for a quick spin.* 4 (of a plane) act of spinning (⇒ spin(8)) steeply downwards: *The plane went into a spin. The spin was impossible to control.* **in a** (**flat**) **spin** (*fig*; *informal*) in a state of panic(1), serious worry etc: *Joe is in a flat spin because he is making a speech this evening.* **send s.t into a spin** (*fig*) cause s.t to fall steeply: *The news about the troubles have sent shares*(3) *into a spin.*
▷ *v* (-*nn*-, *p.t* spun /spʌn/, span /spæn/, *p.p* spun) 5 *tr/intr.v* make (thread) (out of wool, cotton etc) by twisting it. 6 *tr.v* (usu — s.t *into* thread etc) make thread out of (wool, cotton etc) in this way. 7 *tr.v* (of a spider, silkworm etc) produce (thread, a web(1), cocoon(1) etc). 8 *tr/intr.v* (cause (s.o/ s.t) to) go round very fast in a spin(1). 9 *intr.v* (of a vehicle or the people in it) drive fast: *We were spinning along at 100 kilometres an hour.* 10 *tr.v* invent (and say/write) (a story etc). ⇒ spin (s.o) a yarn. **spin s.t out** (*fig*) make s.t longer than it needs to be: *Val wanted to stay till three o'clock so she spun lunch out till then.* **spin round** turn round quickly and suddenly to face the opposite way. **spin (s.o) a yarn** ⇒ yarn². ⇒ spin(10).

'**spin ,bowler** *c.n* (in cricket¹) bowler(1) who makes the ball spin(8). ⇒ spinner(2).

,**spin-'dry** *tr.v* (-*ies*, -*ied*) get the water out of (clothes etc that have been washed) by spinning(8) them in a spin-dryer.

,**spin-'dryer** *c.n* machine that spin-dries.

'**spinner** *c.n* 1 person who spins(5). 2 (in cricket¹) ball that spins(8); spin bowler.

-**spinner** *c.n* ⇒ money-spinner.

'**spinning-,top** *c.n* child's toy that can be made to spin(8).

'**spinning ,wheel** *c.n* machine used for spinning (⇒ spin(5)) by hand using one's foot to make a spindle(1) go round.

'**spin-,off** *c.n* (*informal*) = by-product.

spina bifida /ˌspaɪnə 'bɪfɪdə/ *u.n* (also *attrib*) (*medical*) condition in which one is born with one's backbone(1) divided vertically.

spinach /'spɪnɪdʒ/ *u.n* (also *attrib*) kind of vegetable with broad green leaves, used as food: *spinach soup.*

spindle /'spɪndl/ *c.n* 1 rod with a point at one end, used for twisting the wool etc into a thread while one is spinning (⇒ spin(5)). 2 thin rod/axis(2) around which s.t in a machine turns.

'**spindly** *adj* (-*ier*, -*iest*) long, thin and (seeming to be) weak: *spindly legs.*

spin-dry(er) ⇒ spin.

spine /spaɪn/ *c.n* 1 line of bones down the back of a person and some animals; backbone(1). ⇒ vertebrate(2). 2 back of a book where the pages are fixed together and covered by s.t on which the title is usu printed. 3 sharp piece sticking out of some animals and plants; prickle(1): *A hedgehog has spines.*

'**spinal** *adj* of or referring to the spine(1).

'**spinal ,column** *c.n* = spine(1).

'**spinal ,cord** *c.n* thick cord(3) inside the spine(1) that carries messages from and to the brain through the central nervous system.

'**spineless** *adj* 1 having no spine(1). ⇒ invertebrate. 2 (*fig*) weak; cowardly.

'**spinelessly** *adv.* '**spinelessness** *u.n.*

'**spiny** *adj* (-*ier*, -*iest*) 1 having spines(3). 2 like a spine(3).

spinner ⇒ spin.

spinney /'spɪnɪ/ *c.n* small group of trees and bushes.

spin-off ⇒ spin.

spinster /'spɪnstə/ *c.n* 1 woman who has never been married. Compare bachelor(1). 2 (often *derog*) woman considered unlikely to marry.

'**spinster,hood** *u.n* fact or state of being a spinster.

spiny ⇒ spine.

spiral /'spaɪərəl/ *adj* 1 having a shape that is produced by going round and round a central axis(1) remaining at the same distance from it but going up/down: *a spiral staircase.* 2 having a shape that is produced by going round and round a central point while getting either further and further away or nearer and nearer: *Some watches have spiral springs in them.*
▷ *c.n* 3 (often **in a —**) spiral(*adj*) shape: *The steps go up to the top of the tower in a gentle spiral.* 4 (often **— of** s.t) continuous change (in s.t) which takes it lower and lower, or more often, higher and higher: *The spiral of increasing wages is threatening our country's future.*

▷ *intr.v* (*-ll-*, US *-l-*) **5** (often — *down*) form, move in, a spiral(3): *The fire escape spirals down to the street.* **6** go down or (usu) up, in a spiral(4): *Prices are spiralling.*

spire /spaɪə/ *c.n* tall (part on a) roof with a point at the top, usu on the tower of a church; top of a steeple.

spirit /'spɪrɪt/ *n* **1** = soul(1). ⇨ Holy Spirit. **2** *u.n* strong and active character; energy(1): *Maureen has spirit.* ⇨ spirited, spirits(1). **3** *u.n* loyalty to the thing shown by the word before: *team spirit.* **4** *u.n* (often — *of s.t*) feeling (of s.t) that strongly influences and guides one: *There is a new spirit of confidence in our country since this government came in.* **5** *c.n* (often *in the* (*right* etc) — . . .) way of looking at s.t; attitude(2): *I did say I didn't like the paintings but if he takes my remarks in the spirit in which they were intended he will learn a lot from my criticism.* **6** *def.n* (often *the* — *of s.t*) real intended meaning (of s.t) rather than its actual words: *I try to obey the spirit of the law.* Compare to the letter (⇨ letter). **7** *u.n* life or mind considered by some people to exist independently from individual(1) people: *Some religions believe that spirit is everywhere in the world.* **8** *c.n* person who has the character shown by an adjective that is with it: *a generous spirit.* **9** *c/u.n* strong alcoholic(1) liquid produced by distilling(2) a weaker one: *Gin¹ is a spirit.* **10** *u.n* kind of liquid such as alcohol used as a fuel(1) or to clean things etc. ⇨ methylated spirits, white spirit. **11** *c.n* = ghost(1). **be s.w, with s.o** etc **in spirit** not actually be s.w, with s.o etc but have one's thoughts there: *We were too far away to visit Wendy in hospital but we were there, with her, in spirit.*

▷ *tr.v* **12 spirit s.o/s.t away, off, out** (**of s.t**) take/carry s.o/s.t away in a secret or mysterious way: *The leader of the troubles was spirited out of the prison that night.*

'spirited *adj* **1** full of spirit(2); showing a lot of spirit(2): *a spirited defence of one's side.* **2** (often -*spirited*) having the kind of spirit shown by the first part of the word or by the word before: *high-spirited*; *public spirited* (unselfish).

'spiritless *adj* **1** (*derog*) showing little or no spirit(2); weak; lazy. **2** sad; in low spirits(1).

'spiritlessly *adv.* **'spiritlessness** *u.n.*

'spirit ,level *c.n* instrument with a bubble(1) that moves along a tube and stays in the middle when the spirit level is completely horizontal, used for finding out whether s.t is completely horizontal.

'spirits *pl.n* **1** degree of happiness, sadness etc: *in high/low spirits* (cheerful/sad). **2** = spirit(9): *I drink wine but not spirits.* **3** (often — *of s.t*) spirit(10) (consisting/made of s.t): *You can clean that with spirits of salt.* **kindred spirits** ⇨ kindred. **lift one's/s.o's spirits** make oneself/s.o feel happier, more confident etc: *Let's go for a walk; fresh air will lift our spirits.*

spiritual /'spɪrɪtjʊəl/ *adj* **1** of or referring to the spirit(1) not the body. **2** religious: *The Pope is a spiritual leader.* **3** that is close to s.o's spirit(4); that one feels one's spirit(1) belongs to: *Mecca is the spiritual home of Moslems.* **4** (*pred*) (*formal*) of the church: *the lords spiritual.* Opposite temporal(2).

▷ *c.n* **5** kind of religious song: *The original spirituals were sung by black people in the US.*

'spiritua,lism *u.n* belief that one can communicate(2) with dead people through a medium(7).

'spiritualist *c.n* person who believes in spiritualism.

spiritualistic /,spɪrɪtjʊə'lɪstɪk/ *adj* of or referring to spiritualism.

'spiritually *adv.*

spirt /spɜːt/ = spurt.

spit¹ /spɪt/ *u.n* **1** = saliva.

▷ *v* (*-tt-*, *p.t,p.p* spat /spæt/) **2** *tr/intr.v* make (s.t) come out of one's mouth, often by pulling the tip of one's tongue back suddenly and blowing at the same time: *The notice read 'NO SPITTING'. She spat into the dish. If that fish tastes bad, spit it out.* **3** say s.t with a lot of force, sometimes after having had difficulty in speaking: *She spat angry words at him.* **spit it out** (*fig*; *informal*) say what you want to say without hesitating (any more). **spit s.t up** bring s.t up from one's stomach, lungs etc and spit¹(2) it out. **spit** (**s.t**) **up** (*informal*) vomit(3) (s.t). **the spitting image of s.o** ⇨ image.

'spittle *u.n* = saliva.

spittoon /spɪ'tuːn/ *c.n* container provided for spitting(1) s.t out, e.g in a hospital.

spit² /spɪt/ *c.n* **1** thin metal/wooden rod that one puts through pieces of meat etc so that one can roast them over a fire or under a grill, often while turning them at the same time. **2** small narrow piece of land running out into the sea, a lake etc. **3** depth of earth that is the same as the length of the blade of a spade.

▷ *tr.v* (*-tt-*) **4** put (pieces of meat etc) on a spit²(1).

spite /spaɪt/ *u.n* **1** (often *for, out of,* —) feeling of wanting to be nasty to s.o, usu without any good reason. **in spite of s.o/s.t** although s.o does not like it, s.t is against it, s.o/s.t is not suitable for it etc; despite s.o/s.t: *She failed in spite of her efforts, her parents' support. Mary is a very good driver in spite of being so old.*

▷ *tr.v* **2** do s.t to (s.o) out of spite(1): *She did it to spite her parents.*

'spiteful *adj.*

'spitefully *adv.* **'spitefulness** *u.n.*

spittle, spittoon ⇨ spit¹.

splash /splæʃ/ *adv* **1** with a splash(2): *She slipped and fell splash into the river.*

▷ *c.n* **2** noise and/or disturbance when s.o/s.t hits a liquid: *She dived into the pool with hardly a splash and swam to the other side.* **3** (often — *of s.t*) mark (of s.t) caused by s.t splashing (⇨ splash(6)) on s.t: *After the car had passed I was covered with splashes of mud, mud splashes.* **4** (often — *of s.t*) very small amount (of a liquid): *I always have a splash of soda(1) in my whisky.* ⇨ dash(2). **make a splash** (*informal*) make a very strong impression: *Their victory made a big splash in all the newspapers.* ⇨ splash(7).

▷ *v* **5** *tr/intr.v* (often — (*s.t*) *about*) (cause (a liquid) to) make a spash(2): *The children were splashing about in the water.* **6** *tr.v* throw s.t on (s.o/s.t): *The passing cars splashed us with mud* (or *splashed mud on us*). **7** *tr.v* (*informal*) (of a newspaper etc) make (s.t) seem very important: *Her success was splashed all over the newspapers.* **splash s.t about; splash** (**s.t**) (**out**) (**on s.t**) spend (usu money) in large amounts, often in an unnecessary/wasteful way or to celebrate s.t. **splash**

down (of a spacecraft) come down in the sea instead of on land.

splat /splæt/ *adv* **1** with a splat(2): *He threw the egg and hit the speaker splat on his leg.*

▷ *c.n* **2** noise of s.t flat and wet hitting a surface.

splatter /'splætə/ *tr/intr.v* = spatter(*v*).

splay /spleɪ/ *tr/intr.v* (often — (s.t) out) (cause (s.t) to) spread out or be wider at one end: *Peter has strange feet that splay out very noticeably.*

spleen /spliːn/ *n* **1** *c.n* organ that lies behind the stomach on one's left side, used to store blood and make new blood cells. **2** *u.n* (fig) anger.

splendid /'splendɪd/ *adj* **1** glorious; wonderful; very striking: *splendid news.* **2** (*informal*) very good; excellent: *'I've finished.' 'Splendid! So we can go now.'*

'**splendidly** *adv*.

splendour /'splendə/ *u.n* (US **'splendor**) (often the — of s.t) (*formal*) fact or state of (s.t) being splendid(1): *enjoy the splendour of the occasion.*

'**splendours** *pl.n* = splendour.

splice /splaɪs/ *c.n* **1** fact or act of joining one end of string, film etc to one end of another. **2** place where film, rope etc is joined.

▷ *tr.v* **3** join (rope, film etc) (to s.t or together) using one or more splices(1). **get spliced** (*informal*) get married.

'**splicer** *c.n* device for splicing (⇒ splice(3)) film, tapes(2) etc.

splint /splɪnt/ *c.n* flat piece of wood etc to which a broken leg etc is tied while it is mending.

splinter /'splɪntə/ *attrib.adj* **1** that has left a bigger group of which it was a part: *a splinter group.*

▷ *c.n* **2** (often — of s.t) small sharp piece (of glass, wood etc) that has been broken off s.t bigger: *When I broke the stick I got a splinter in my hand.*

▷ *v* **3** *tr/intr.v* (cause (s.t) to) break into splinters(2). **4** *intr.v* (usu — off) (of a group) leave a bigger group.

split /splɪt/ *c.n* **1** cut or break along/down the length of s.t, not across it: *The lightning(2) hit the tree leaving a split down it from top to bottom.* **2** division or difference of ideas etc (between s.o/ s.t and s.o/s.t): *There is a split in our party between those who want more action and those who don't.* **3** sweet(8) made by splitting (⇒ split(4)) fruit and putting ice-cream inside: *a banana split.*

▷ *v* (-tt-, *p.t,p.p* split) **4** *tr/intr.v* (often — (s.o/s.t) up (into parts)) (cause (people/things) to) divide (into parts): *split* (*up*) *a class of children into three groups.* **5** *intr.v* break/separate so that there is a split(1,2): *The wood splits easily.* **6** *tr.v* (often — s.t among/between s.o/s.t) share or divide (s.t) (between two people etc or among more than two): *Split the last piece of cake between you.* **7** *intr.v* (usu — on s.o) (*slang*) tell s.t that was a secret (about s.o): *Joe split on Fred for cheating.* **8** *intr.v* (*slang*) go away quickly and often secretly: *Quick, let's split — the police are coming!* **split** (*up*) (**with s.o**) stop seeing, living with etc s.o: *Mike and Pat have split up and are getting divorced* (⇒ divorce(3)). **split an infinitive** put a word or words between 'to' and its infinitive (e.g 'to clumsily fall' instead of 'to fall clumsily'), which used to be considered bad grammar. **split hairs** ⇒ hair. **split one's sides**

(*laughing*) ⇒ side(*n*). **split the difference** ⇒ difference.

,**split in'finitive** *c.n* example when one splits an infinitive (⇒ split(*v*)).

,**split-'level** *adj* (usu *attrib*) **1** (of a floor) divided into two different levels. **2** (of a building) having split-level(1) floors.

,**split 'pea** *c.n* pea(1) that has been dried and split(4) into its two parts.

,**split ,perso'nality** *c.n* (*informal*) = schizophrenic(2).

splits *def.pl.n* (usu do the —) movement in which a person's legs are spread out horizontally to the sides.

,**split 'second** *c.n* (**'split-,second** when *attrib*) (*informal*) very short time that is less than a second; instant(3): *split-second timing.*

'**splitting** *attrib.adj* (usu of a headache) very strong or painful.

splurge /splɜːdʒ/ *c.n* **1** one example or act of splurging(2).

▷ *tr/intr.v* **2** (usu — out on s.t; — s.t on s.t) spend more (money) than is reasonable (buying s.t).

splutter /'splʌtə/ *c.n* (also '**sputter**) **1** noise as when drops of water fall on fire or when a person makes a coughing sound when there is a lot of saliva in her/his mouth.

▷ *v* (also '**sputter**) **2** *intr.v* make the noise of a splutter(1). **3** *tr.v* say (s.t) with a splutter(1), usu because one is angry, surprised etc.

spoil¹ /spɔɪl/ *v* (*p.t,p.p* spoiled, spoilt /spɔɪlt/) **1** *tr/intr.v* (cause (s.t) to) become bad or no longer able to be used/eaten etc: *Our holiday was spoilt by rain. Don't leave that food out of the* fridge *or it will spoil.* **2** *tr.v* treat (a child etc) too kindly, allow (it) to do what it wants etc, so that it becomes selfish and has no discipline. **3** *tr.v* treat (s.o) very/too well: *It is nice to go to an expensive hotel that spoils one occasionally.* **spoil for a fight** etc want a fight etc very much. **spoil s.o for s.t** be so good, pleasant etc that it makes one dissatisfied with others: *The sports we see on television spoil us for small local matches.*

'**spoil,sport** *c.n* (*derog*) person who spoils(1) other people's pleasure.

spoils /spɔɪlz/ *pl.n* things that have been taken, stolen or won during a war etc: *the spoils of war.*

spoke¹ /spəʊk/ *c.n* one of the rods between the rim/circle of a wheel and its hub(1)/centre. **put a spoke in s.o's wheel** (fig) prevent s.o doing what he/she wants to do.

spoke² /spəʊk/ *p.t* of speak.

spoken /'spəʊkən/ *p.p* of speak.

-spoken, **spokesman**, **spokesperson**, **spokeswoman** ⇒ speak.

sponge /spʌndʒ/ *n* **1** *c.n* kind of simple creature that lives in the sea fixed to a rock etc and has a body with a lot of holes in it. **2** *c/u.n* (part of) one of these creatures used for washing because it can absorb a lot of water. **3** *c/u.n* thing like a sponge(2) but made of rubber etc. **4** *c/u.n* = sponge cake. **throw in/up the sponge** (*informal*) give up; surrender(2).

▷ *v* **5** *tr.v* (usu — s.o/s.t down/off; — s.t out) clean, wipe, rub etc s.o/s.t with a sponge(2,3), cloth etc. **6** *tr.v* (often — s.t up) absorb(1) (liquid) using a cloth etc (so as to remove it from s.t): *As the blood came out I sponged it up.* **7** (often — off/on s.o/s.t) (*informal*) get money etc from s.o, usu so as not to have to work oneself.

'sponge ,bag *c.n* waterproof bag for putting one's soap, toothbrush etc in.

'sponge ,cake *c/u.n* cake that is light because it has little or no fat in it.

'sponger *c.n* (*derog*) person who sponges(7).

'sponginess *u.n* fact or state of being spongy.

'spongy *adj* (*-ier, -iest*) soft, full of holes and wet or absorbent, like a sponge: *spongy ground at the edge of a river.*

sponsor /'spɒnsə/ *c.n* (often — *of s.o/s.t*) **1** person who takes the responsibility for supporting and helping (s.o/s.t): *The Minister for Education is the sponsor of this new bill.* **2** company that gives the money (for a match, play etc) so that it can get publicity(1) and often also advertising from it.

▷ *tr.v* **3** act as sponsor for (s.o/s.t).

'sponsor,ship *u.n* (often — *of s.o/s.t*) act or fact of sponsoring (⇒ sponsor(3)) s.o/s.t.

spontaneous /spɒn'teɪnɪəs/ *adj* done quickly and suddenly without any planning or outside influence: *spontaneous applause.*

spontaneity /ˌspɒntə'niːɪtɪ/ *u.n.*

spon,taneous com'bustion *u.n* (*science*) fact of a substance beginning to burn because of oxygen from the air and without any other source of heat etc.

spon'taneously *adv.* **spon'taneousness** *u.n.*

spoof /spuːf/ *c.n* **1** (also *attrib*) amusing copy (of a well-known person, style of writing etc).

▷ *tr/intr.v* **2** joke with (s.o) by saying, writing etc things that are not true.

spook /spuːk/ *c.n* (*informal*) ghost(1).

'spooky (*-ier, -iest*) *adj* (*informal*) who/that frightens one like a ghost(1).

spool /spuːl/ *c.n* **1** round thing, usu with a hole through the middle, used for holding rolled up thread, wire, film, tape etc. **2** (often — *of s.t*) amount (of s.t) that a spool(1) holds.

spoon /spuːn/ *c.n* **1** tool with a round bowl on a handle, used for picking up, carrying, serving etc liquid and sometimes solid food. ⇒ dessertspoon(1), tablespoon(1), teaspoon(1). **2** (also **'spoonful**) amount a spoon(1) can hold. **wooden spoon** ⇒ wood.

▷ *v* **3** *tr.v* pick (s.t) up or move (s.t) with a spoon. **spoon s.t out** serve s.t with a spoon.

'spoon,feed *tr.v* (*p.t,p.p* spoonfed /'spuːnˌfed/) **1** feed (s.o, usu a baby) with a spoon. **2** (*fig*) give (s.o) information needed, esp in small very easy amounts.

'spoonful *c.n* = spoon(2).

spoonerism /'spuːnəˌrɪzəm/ *c.n* way in which the first sounds of two words are changed over, usu accidentally, e.g 'It's pouring with rain' becomes 'It's roaring with pain'.

spoonfeed, spoonful ⇒ spoon.

spoor /spuə/ *c.n* (*technical*) signs left behind by a wild animal or person and which can be seen and followed by s.o trying to catch her/him/it.

sporadic /spə'rædɪk/ *adj* happening at irregular times: *sporadic rainfall.*

spo'radically *adv.*

spore /spɔː/ *c.n* (*science*) cell(4) or group of cells(4) produced by a low form of plant or creature from which a new one can grow: Fungi *produce spores.*

sporran /'spɒrən/ *c.n* kind of bag or purse¹(1) with fur on it worn by a Scot in front of her/his kilt.

sport /spɔːt/ *n* **1** *c/u.n* (also *attrib*) kind of activity, usu a game with its own rules, for which one needs to use strength and/or skill: *Football and tennis are sports.* ⇒ sports(3). **2** *u.n* thing one does that is pleasant: *The children found it great sport to slide down the muddy bank.* **3** *c.n* (*old use; slang*) person: *Hello, old sport.* **make sport of s.o/s.t** make fun of s.o/s.t; laugh at s.o/s.t. **the sport of kings** horse racing. **the world of sport** the people who take part in, organize etc sport(1).

▷ *v* **4** *intr.v* (*literary*) play about; enjoy oneself, usu running about; frolic(2). **5** *tr.v* wear (s.t), usu so that people can see and admire it: *Joe is sporting his college tie.*

'sportily *adv* in a sporty way: *sportily dressed.*

'sportiness *u.n* fact of being sporty.

'sporting *adj* **1** fair(1); giving one a fair chance of winning, sometimes when one does not have to do so: *a sporting chance of winning the race. Tessa was sporting enough not to race until Mary was well again.* **2** (*attrib*) of or referring to sport(1): *sporting events.*

'sportingly *adv.*

'sportive *adj* (usu *literary*) of, referring to, enjoying, sport(2); playful.

'sportively *adv.* **'sportiveness** *u.n.*

sports *attrib.adj* **1** of, referring to, used for, sports(*n*): *the sports pages in a newspaper.* **2** (of clothes, esp coats and jackets(1)) informal.

▷ *pl.n* **3** different kinds of sport(1). **4** athletic(1) sports(1) meeting. **field sports** ⇒ field. **indoor/outdoor sports** sports played inside/outside a building.

'sports ,car *c.n* car built for going fast and for pleasure rather than for practical purposes.

'sportsman *c.n* (*pl -men*) **1** man who takes part in, enjoys seeing, sports(3). **2** man who is fair, sporting(1).

'sportsman,like *adj* = sporting(1).

'sportsman,ship *u.n* sporting(1) behaviour.

'sports,person *c.n* = sportsman or sportswoman.

'sports,woman *c.n* (*pl -ˌwomen*) **1** woman who takes part in or enjoys watching sports(3). **2** woman who is fair and sporting(1).

'sports,wear *u.n* clothes for playing sports(3).

'sporty *adj* (*-ier, -iest*) (*informal*) **1** attractively bright and informal: *a sporty red and yellow shirt.* **2** very good at sports(3).

spot /spɒt/ *attrib.adj* **1** being or done suddenly and without warning: *a spot check.* **2** that has to be paid for immediately: *a spot fine. What are the spot prices for gold today?*

▷ *adv* **3** (*informal*) **spot on** (ˌspot-'on when *attrib*) exactly right. **spot on time** at exactly the right time.

▷ *c.n* **4** small unpleasant usu round mark on s.t: *grease spots on a dress; spots on a young girl's face.* Compare pimple. **5** thing like a spot(4) but intentional: *a blue tie with white spots.* **6** place: *There is a spot near York where we often go for a picnic. Here's a good spot for watching the football match.* **7** job: *Alice has found a really good spot as a sports journalist.* **8** = spotlight(1). **blind spot** ⇒ blind¹. **have a soft spot for s.o/s.t** ⇒ soft spot (⇒ soft). **a holiday spot** a place where one goes for a holiday. **in a spot** (*informal*) in trouble; in a difficult/dangerous position. **knock spots off s.o/s.t** (*fig*; *informal*) be much better than s.o/s.t; beat s.o/s.t easily. **a spot of s.t** (*informal*) a small amount of s.t: *Would you like a spot of lunch now? We had a spot of bother/trouble with our car yesterday.* **on the spot (a)** right in that place. **(b)** immediately; without warning. **put s.o on the spot** (*fig*; *informal*) force s.o to decide what to do/say. **rooted to the spot** unable to move because of fear etc. **trouble spot** ⇒ trouble. **X marks the spot** the place (where it happened etc) is marked by the sign X.

▷ *tr.v* (-tt-) **9** notice (s.o/s.t); manage to see (and recognize) (s.o/s.t): *Tell me when you spot your luggage and I'll help you get it.* **10** make spots(4,5) on (s.t): *Her dress was spotted with ink.* **11** place (s.t) in a position or positions: *Ashtrays are spotted everywhere around the room.* **be spotting (with rain)** be raining very lightly.

,spot 'cash *u.n* money paid immediately.

,spot 'check *tr.v* carry out a spot(1) check of (s.t).

'spotless *adj* perfectly clean.

'spotlessly *adv.* **'spotlessness** *u.n.*

'spot,light *n* **1** *c.n* lamp that can throw a narrow beam of light on s.t, often used in a theatre. **2** *c.n* beam thrown by a spotlight(1). **3** *def.n* (*fig*) (often *in the* —) situation where everyone is looking at, reading about etc, s.o: *The royal family are always in the spotlight.*

▷ *tr.v* **4** put (s.o/s.t) in the spotlight(3).

,spot-'on *attrib.adj* ⇒ spot on (⇒ spot(3)).

'spotted *adj* that has spots(4,5) on it.

'spotter *attrib.adj* **1** that is used for spotting(9): *a spotter plane* (one that tries to find s.o/s.t).

▷ *c.n* **2** person who tries to spot(9) s.t: *a train spotter* (a person who tries to see as many different kinds and numbers of trains as possible).

'spottiness *u.n* fact or state of being spotty.

'spotty *adj* (-ier, -iest) having spots(4,5) on her/him/it.

spouse /spaʊz/ *c.n* (*law*) husband or wife.

spout /spaʊt/ *c.n* **1** cylindrical or U/V-shaped device out of which a liquid pours or is poured: *the spout of a teapot.* **2** stream of water etc moving strongly, usu upwards: *an oil spout.* ⇒ waterspout.

▷ *v* **3** *tr/intr.v* (often — (s.t) out) (cause (a liquid) to) flow out strongly. **4** *tr.v* (*fig*) speak about (s.t) loudly and usu for a long time: *He's always spouting politics.*

sprain /spreɪn/ *c.n* **1** damage to an ankle, wrist etc by twisting it, e.g when one falls.

▷ *tr.v* **2** damage (an ankle etc) in this way.

sprang /spræŋ/ *p.t* of spring(*v*).

sprat /spræt/ *c.n* kind of small fish that is caught and eaten.

sprawl /sprɔːl/ *c/u.n* **1** example of spreading out: *urban sprawl* (an ugly and irregular mass of buildings in a town).

▷ *v* **2** *tr/intr.v* (often — (s.t) out) stretch or spread (one's body, arms etc) (out) in an irregular, usu unattractive shape.

spray[1] /spreɪ/ *n* **1** *u.n* very small drops of water moving through the air: *When a wave hits the rocks the spray rises to a great height. The spray from the shower in our bathroom is too fine.* **2** *u.n* (also *attrib*) liquid made to be used as

a spray(1): *hair spray* (for holding one's hair in place); *insect spray* (for killing insects); *a spray can.* **3** *c.n* device/container for spray(2).

▷ *v* **4** *tr.v* make (a liquid) come out of s.t in a spray(1): *We must spray insecticide on the roses.* **5** *tr.v* (often — s.o/s.t with s.t) put spray(2) on (s.o/s.t): *We must spray the roses. Spray me with water.* **6** *intr.v* (often — out) come out in the form of spray(1).

'sprayer *c.n* person or device who/that sprays(4,5).

'spray ,gun *c.n* kind of pump for spraying (⇒ spray(4,5)) with.

spray[2] /spreɪ/ *c.n* (often — of s.t) **1** small branch (of s.t) with flowers (and leaves) still on it. **2** flowers, jewels etc in the shape of a spray(1): *a spray of diamonds.*

spread /spred/ *n* **1** *sing.n* (often *the* — of s.t) fact of (s.t) spreading(7): *the spread of a disease.* **2** *c.n* (often — of s.t) area or time that is covered: *a spread of ten kilometres, five years. The college offers a wide spread of subjects.* ⇒ middle-age spread. **3** *c.n* big meal or large amount of food spread out on a table. **4** *c.n* cloth used for covering s.t. ⇒ bedspread. **5** *c/u.n* soft food used for spreading(11) on bread etc: *sandwich spread.* **6** *c.n* article, advertisement etc in a newspaper/magazine that covers two or more pages: *a centre-page spread.*

▷ *v* (*pt,p.p* spread) **7** *tr/intr.v* (cause (s.o/s.t) to) cover a bigger area/space, longer time or to affect more people, places etc: *The water spread over the kitchen floor. She spread her arms out wide. The disease is spreading fast. Their lunch hour now spreads from 12 to nearly tea time. The fog spread for miles across the hills.* **8** *tr.v* divide, share, scatter, s.t (so that several people, places etc get some of it or so that there is some of it at different times): *If you spread the cost among you it will not be so difficult to pay. We spread the work over two months.* **9** *tr/intr.v* (often — s.t around (s.t)) (cause (information, news etc) to) become known by more people. **10** *tr.v* (often — s.t on s.t) put (butter etc) (on bread etc) in such a way that the first thing covers the surface of the second. **11** *tr.v* (often — s.t with s.t) cover (bread etc) (with butter etc), in this way.

,spread-'eagle *tr/intr.v* (cause (s.o) to) spread(7) her/his arms and legs out into the position of a cross.

spree /spriː/ *c.n* (often *go on/have a* —) happy carefree time when one spends a lot and enjoys oneself without (much) control.

sprig /sprɪg/ *c.n* small end of a plant with the leaves on it: *Put a sprig of mint' in your drink.*

sprightly /'spraɪtlɪ/ (-ier, -iest) *adj* bright, cheerful and happy; lively'(1).

'sprightliness *u.n.*

spring[1] /sprɪŋ/ *c/u/def.n* (also *attrib*) (often with capital **S**) season of the year between winter and summer when trees begin to have leaves again: *spring flowers. The garden looks lovely in the spring. We met in the spring of 1984.*

spring-clean /'sprɪŋ ,kliːn/ *c.n* **1** (often *give s.t a* —) example or act of spring-cleaning (⇒ spring-clean(2)).

▷ *tr/intr.v* /,sprɪŋ 'kliːn/ **2** clean (a room, house etc) thoroughly, usu after the winter has ended.

,spring 'onion *c.n* kind of long thin onion that is eaten (usu raw in salad).

,spring 'roll *c.n* (also **,pan,cake 'roll**) Chinese food with vegetables (and sometimes also meat) inside pastry.

'spring,time *u/def.n* (often *in* (*the*) —) spring[1]; time when the climate is getting warmer and the trees are beginning to have leaves again.

spring² /sprɪŋ/ *c.n* **1** place where water comes out of the ground naturally.

▷ *intr.v* (*p.t* sprang /spræŋ/, *p.p* sprung /sprʌŋ/) **2** (often — *from s.t*) (of a liquid) come out (of s.t): *Here water springs from the rocks and flows down to the valley. Tears sprang to her eyes when she saw the dead bird.* **spring from s.t** (*fig*) be the result of s.t; have s.t as one's/its origin: *Much crime springs from poverty.*

spring³ /sprɪŋ/ *n* **1** *c.n* strip of metal etc that goes back into its original shape when it has been tightened, moved etc and then let free: *Many modern watches do not have springs. There is a spring on this door that closes it when you let go.* **2** *u.n* quality that makes a spring(1) able to do this; elasticity; springiness. **3** *c.n* (often — *at s.o/ s.t*) jump (to try to catch s.o/s.t): *The cat made a spring at the fly.* **have a spring in one's step** walk with long, bouncing (⇨ bounce(3)) steps.

▷ *v* (*p.t* sprang /spræŋ/, *p.p* sprung /sprʌŋ/) **4** *intr.v* jump. **5** *intr.v* move quickly: *She cried out and her brother sprang to her help.* **6** *tr.v* (*slang*) help (s.o) to escape from prison secretly.

spring a leak ⇨ leak(*n*).

spring into life suddenly begin to be active: *The party did not spring into life until the band arrived.*

spring s.t on s.o surprise s.o by telling, showing etc her/him s.t that she/he did not expect.

spring open open suddenly and strongly.

spring to one's feet stand up suddenly and strongly.

spring up begin (to be there): *The wind sprang up and the boat began to move at last. Villages are springing up all over the country.*

'spring,board *c.n* **1** springy board that one jumps on in order to go up in the air, e.g when diving into water. **2** (often — *to s.t*) (*fig*) thing that helps one a lot in one's preparations or effort (to do s.t): *Jane's springboard to success was finding an excellent music teacher.*

'springiness *u.n* state or fact of being springy.

'springy *adj* (*-ier, -iest*) having spring³(2) in it; elastic; going back to its original shape when free to do so.

spring-clean ⇨ spring¹.

springtime ⇨ spring¹.

sprinkle /'sprɪŋkl/ *c.n* **1** (often — *of s.t*) small amount (of a liquid, powder etc) that is scattered: *a sprinkle of sugar on a cake.*

▷ *tr.v* **2** scatter (a sprinkle(1) of s.t): *Peter sprinkled sugar on his grapefruit.* **3** (often — *s.t with s.t*) put a sprinkle(1) of s.t on (s.t): *Tina sprinkled the carpet with soapy water.*

'sprinkler *c.n* **1** device for spraying (⇨ spray¹(4)) water, e.g on a garden. **2** device in a building that can put out fires by spraying (⇨ spray¹(4)) water.

'sprinkling *c.n* (usu — *of s.t*) few (of s.t) scattered about in various places: *We had a sprinkling of children at the meeting last night.*

sprint /sprɪnt/ *c.n* **1** very fast short run. **2** short running race, e.g 100 metres.

▷ *intr.v* **3** take part in a sprint(*n*).

'sprinter *c.n* person who sprints(*v*).

sprite /spraɪt/ *c.n* (in stories) fairy(2), usu a live-ly(1)/graceful one.

sprocket /'sprɒkɪt/ *c.n* (*technical*) **1** (also **'sprocket ,wheel**) wheel that has teeth around its edge so that it can turn s.t with holes in it, e.g a bicycle chain or a film in a camera. **2** one of the teeth of a sprocket(1).

sprout /spraʊt/ *c.n* **1** thing that is just growing or has just grown, out of a plant or root; shoot(1): *bean sprouts.* **2** = Brussels sprout.

▷ *tr/intr.v* **3** (cause (s.t) to) begin to grow: *In spring the leaves begin to sprout. I hardly recognized Fred — he's sprouted a red beard.*

spruce¹ /spru:s/ *adj* **1** clean and tidy; smart¹(1): *a spruce appearance; looking spruce.*

▷ *tr/reflex.v* **2** (often — *oneself/s.o/s.t up*) make (oneself/s.o/s.t) spruce(1).

'sprucely *adv.* **'spruceness** *u.n.*

spruce² /spru:s/ *n* **1** *c.n* kind of coniferous tree. **2** *u.n* (also *attrib*) light coloured wood from this tree.

sprung /sprʌŋ/ *adj* **1** having springs³(1): *a well sprung bicycle.*

▷ *v* **2** *p.p* of spring², spring³.

spry /spraɪ/ *adj* active; able to move quickly and easily; lively(1): *a spry old man of 80.*

'spryly *adv.* **'spryness** *u.n.*

spud /spʌd/ *c.n* (*slang*) potato.

spun /spʌn/ *p.p* of spin.

spunk /spʌŋk/ *u.n* (*informal*) courage.

spur /spɜ:/ *c.n* **1** device put on the heel of a rider's boot which he/she can use to kick the horse to make it go faster or to make it turn. **2** thing like a spur(1) that grows on the back of the legs of some birds. **3** (*fig*) (often — *to s.t*) thing that encourages or urges s.o (to do s.t); incentive (to s.t): *Success is an excellent spur to further effort.* **4** piece of a mountain that sticks out from the main part. **on the spur of the moment** suddenly, without any preparation or plan before.

▷ *v* (*-rr-*) (often — *s.o/s.t on*) **5** *tr.v* use spurs(1) on (a horse) to make it go faster. **6** *tr.v* (*fig*) urge (s.o) to go faster, work harder etc.

,spur-of-the-'moment *attrib.adj* done on the spur of the moment: *a spur-of-the-moment idea.*

spurious /'spjʊərɪəs/ *adj* (*formal*) false; not what he/she/it is said to be: *a spurious excuse.*

'spuriously *adv.* **'spuriousness** *u.n.*

spurt /spɜ:t/ *c.n* (also **spirt**) **1** (often *put on a* —) sudden short increase in speed, force etc: *The runner made a spurt for the line* (or *put on a spurt towards the end of the race*). **2** (often — *of s.t*) sudden rush (usu of a liquid). **do s.t in spurts** do s.t and then stop then do it again etc: *study in spurts.*

▷ *v* **3** *intr.v* make a spurt(1). **4** *tr/intr.v* (often — *out* (*from*) *s.t*) (cause (s.t) to) come out (of s.t) in spurts(2).

sputter /'spʌtə/ ⇨ splutter.

spy /spaɪ/ *c.n* (*pl -ies*) (also *attrib*) **1** person who watches/listens secretly, usu to try to get information for her/his country: *a spy plane.*

▷ *v* **2** *intr.v* (*-ies, -ied*) (often — *into s.t;* — *up(on) s.o/s.t*) act as, behave like, a spy(1) (against s.o/s.t). **3** *tr.v* (*old use*) (manage to) see (s.o/s.t): *I spied a small bird in the tree.*

'spy,glass *c.n* (*old use*) small telescope(1).

'spying *u.n* activity of a spy(1).

sq *written abbr* square: *10 sq cm* (or *10 cm²*).

Sqn Ldr *written abbr* Squadron Leader.

squabble /'skwɒbl/ *c.n* **1** (often — *about/over s.o/s.t*) (*informal*) argument or quarrel, usu one that is noisy, goes on for quite a long time (and is about s.t that is not important): *The children squabbled over the apple.*

▷ *intr.v* **2** (often — *about/over s.o/s.t*) take part in a squabble(1) (about s.o/s.t).

squad /skwɒd/ *c.n* **1** (*military*) small group of soldiers etc, collected together for some special purpose. Compare platoon, section(1), troop(2). **2** any small group of people doing s.t together.

'squad ,car *c.n* (US) police car; patrol car (⇒ patrol(1)).

squadron /'skwɒdrən/ *c.n* (with capital **S** in names) (*military*) **1** army unit of cavalry, tanks or engineers of about the same size as a company(3) in the infantry. **2** naval unit consisting of a number of warships. **3** air force unit.

,squadron 'leader *c.n* (*written abbr* Sqn Ldr) commander of a squadron(3) with the same rank as a major(2) in the army.

squalid /'skwɒlɪd/ *adj* (*derog*) **1** very dirty and untidy; filthy(1): *a squalid hut in a* slum(1). **2** morally very low; sordid(2): *a squalid affair with a married man.*

'squalidly *adv.* **squalor** /'skwɒlə/ *u.n.*

squall¹ /skwɔːl/ *c.n* sudden strong wind that lasts only a short time.

'squally *adj.*

squall² /skwɔːl/ *c.n* **1** loud unpleasant cry, e.g of an unhappy baby.

▷ *intr.v* **2** make the sound of a squall²(1).

squalor ⇒ squalid.

squander /'skwɒndə/ *tr.v* spend (money etc) in a wasteful way.

'squanderer *c.n* (*derog*) person who squanders.

square /skweə/ *adj* **1** that has four equal sides and four right angles: *a square table.* **2** that forms (almost) a right angle: *a field with square corners.* **3** (often — *with s.o*) fair or honest (towards s.o): *I could see he wasn't being square with me because he could not look me in the face.* ⇒ square deal **4** (*informal*) old-fashioned. **5** (often *all* —) paid so that nothing more is owing: *Here's £5; that makes us* (*all*) *square.* **6** (often *all* —) having the same number of goals, points etc, usu in a match: *Then Helen scored another goal and the teams were square again.* **two metres** etc **square** two metres long and two metres wide. **a square metre** etc an area that is (the same as) one metre etc long and one metre etc wide: *Our room is five metres long and three metres wide so it has an area of 15 square metres* (15 sq m or 15 m²).

▷ *adv* **7** straight; exactly: *The ball hit him square on the chin.* **8** fairly or honestly. ⇒ square(3). **fair and square** ⇒ fair¹(adv).

▷ *c.n* (*written abbr* sq) **9** square(1) shape, figure, thing. **10** (with capital **S** in names) open space in a town etc: *a market square; St Mark's Square.* **11** (with capital **S** in names) houses round a square(10): *Mary lives in Bryanston Square.* **12** place on a board in a game in which one

can put one of one's pieces: *A chess board has 64 squares.* **13** (usu triangular(1) or L-shaped) tool for measuring right angles and drawing straight lines. ⇒ set square, T-square. **14** (often *the* — of *s.t*) number that is equal to another number multiplied by itself: *The square of 12 is 144.* **15** square(4) person.

▷ *v* **16** *tr.v* (often — *s.t up*) make (s.t) square(2). **17** *tr.v* (often — *s.t off*) divide (s.t) into squares(9), often with a pen etc. Compare squared(2) paper. **18** *tr.v* multiply (a number) by itself: *12 squared is 144.* **19** *tr/intr.v* (often — (*s.t*) *with s.t*) (cause (s.t) to) fit or suit (s.t) exactly; reconcile(2) (s.t) or be reconciled(2) (with s.t): *How do you square what you have just said with what the police say happened? The two accounts don't square.* **20** *tr.v* make (scores in a match etc) square(6). **square an account** pay an account so that nothing more is owed. Compare square(5). **square one's shoulders** push one's shoulders back defiantly. **square up (with s.o)** pay what one owes (to s.o). **square up to s.o/s.t** face s.o/s.t with strength and courage. **square s.t with s.o** make sure that s.o agrees to an arrangement etc: *Have you squared your plan with the manager?*

'square-,bashing *u.n* (*informal*, usu *derog*) drill¹(2) by soldiers, usu in a barracks.

,square 'bracket *c.n* ⇒ bracket(2).

squared *adj* **1** (*pred*) multiplied by itself. ⇒ square(18). **2** (*attrib*) having squares(1) on it: *squared paper.* Compare square(17).

,square 'deal *c.n* fair/honest treatment: *I buy from that shop because I always get a square deal.* Compare square(3).

'squarely *adv.* **'squareness** *u.n.*

,square 'one *unique n* (usu *back to* —) the place where one started: *The manager has not accepted our plan so we are back to square one again.*

,square 'root *def.n* (*mathematics*) number that, when multiplied by itself, produces a certain number: *The square root of 16 is 4.*

squash¹ /skwɒʃ/ *c.n* **1** act or sound of s.t soft being crushed by being pressed between two things, falling on the floor etc: *We heard a squash as the bag of grapes dropped.* **2** uncomfortably tight overcrowding together: *There was a terrible squash at Joan's party with over a hundred people in a small hall.* **3** *c/u.n* (example, portion of a) sweet drink made from crushed fruit or fruit juice without alcohol in it: *orange squash.*

▷ *v* **4** *tr/intr.v* (cause (s.o/s.t) to) be crushed or pressed unpleasantly: *Don't drop those grapes or they'll squash.* **5** *tr/intr.v* (cause (s.o/s.t) to) push (into, through etc, s.t) tightly: *All the students squashed into the hall to hear the results.* **6** *tr.v* (*fig*) make (s.o) stop doing s.t, esp using critical or sarcastic remarks to make (s.o) feel inferior(1): *Every time the boy tried to speak his sister squashed him.* **7** *tr.v* (*fig*) prevent (s.t) (continuing): *That teacher squashes all attempts at originality.*

'squashiness *u.n* fact or state of being squashy.

'squashy *adj* (*-ier, -iest*) **1** soft and easy to squash¹(4). **2** (of ground) soft and wet.

squash² /skwɒʃ/ *u.n* (also *attrib* **'squash ,rackets**) indoor game played in a walled area with rackets and a small rubber ball: *I'm a good squash player.*

'squash ,rackets *u.n* (*formal*) = squash².

squat¹ /skwɒt/ *adj* (*derog*) unattractively low or short compared with her/his/its height/length: *a squat house*; *a squat little man*.

squat² /skwɒt/ *c.n* **1** position of a person in which he/she is almost sitting on the ground but is taking his/her weight on the front of his/ her feet. **2** building where people squat²(4): *live in a squat.*
▷ *intr.v* (*-tt-*) **3** be in, get into, the position of a squat²(1). **4** (*informal*) live in a place (usu an empty one) without paying and usu without the owner's permission.
'squatter *c.n* person who squats²(*v*).
,squatter's 'rights *pl.n* rights of a person living on land, in a building etc, that are a result of having been there for some time.

squawk /skwɔːk/ *c.n* **1** loud angry or frightened cry, e.g of a disturbed hen. **2** (*informal*) loud complaint.
▷ *intr.v* **3** give a squawk(1). **4** (*informal*) complain loudly.

squeak /skwiːk/ *c.n* **1** high-pitched usu short and not very loud sound, e.g that of a mouse or a door that needs oiling. **a narrow squeak** (*fig*; *informal*) a narrow escape from s.t; a near thing.
▷ *intr.v* **2** make the sound of a squeak(1): *New shoes sometimes squeak.* **3** (*slang*) give away a secret; squeal(4). **squeak by/through** (**s.t**) (*fig*; *informal*) manage to pass/get through s.t but only just: *Danny squeaked through the fence.*
'squeaky *adj* (*-ier*, *-iest*) that squeaks(2).

squeal /skwiːl/ *c.n* **1** high-pitched usu long cry or noise, e.g of tyres on a wet road, excited children.
▷ *v* **2** *intr.v* give a squeal(1). **3** *tr.v* say (s.t) while squealing(2). **4** *intr.v* (*slang*) (often — *on s.o*) inform (against s.o), often a criminal.
'squealer *c.n* (*slang*) person who squeals(2,3).

squeamish /'skwiːmɪʃ/ *adj* easily made to feel sick; easily shocked.
'squeamishly *adv* etc. **'squeamishness** *u.n*.

squeegee /'skwiːˌdʒiː/ *c.n* (also *attrib*) kind of mop(1) with a sponge(3) on the end of a long handle: *a squeegee mop.*

squeeze /skwiːz/ *n* **1** *c.n* act of pressing s.o/s.t, either from the sides or against s.t: *One squeeze of the bottle is enough. He gave his wife's hand a squeeze.* **2** *c.n* (often — *of s.t*) small amount (of a liquid) that is got by giving s.t a squeeze(1): *a squeeze of lemon.* **3** *sing.n* (*informal*) squash¹(2). **4** *c.n* difficult situation, esp in business, when there is not enough of what is needed. **credit squeeze** ⇒ credit. **a tight squeeze** (*informal*) a situation in which it is difficult but just possible to be successful.
▷ *v* **5** *tr.v* give (s.o/s.t) a squeeze(1). **6** *tr.v* manage to get s.t within a narrow space or short length of time: *We were standing squeezed between two fat men. I think I can squeeze a meeting with the staff into my diary.* **7** *tr.v* make things difficult for (s.o) because of a squeeze(4). **squeeze s.t out** (**of s.o**) manage to get (money, information) from (s.o) with great difficulty. **squeeze up** (often as an order) move together to allow room for other people, e.g on a bus or seat.
'squeezer *c.n* device for squeezing(5) juice etc out of s.t: *a lemon squeezer.*

squelch /skweltʃ/ *c.n* **1** sound made when s.t soft

and wet is pressed and then let go: *I could hear the squelch of people walking through the thick mud outside.*
▷ *v* **2** *intr.v* (move in such a way as to) produce a squelch(1): *squelch through mud.*

squib /skwɪb/ *c.n* small firework that explodes. **a damp squib** (*fig*; *informal*) thing that is not as exciting, successful etc as intended: *The advertising campaign(2) was a damp squib.*

squid /skwɪd/ *n* **1** *c.n* kind of sea creature that has a long narrow body with ten arms round its mouth. **2** *u.n* flesh of these creatures used as food.

squidgy /'skwɪdʒɪ/ *adj* (*-ier*, *-iest*) (*informal*) soft and wet, usu in an unpleasant way.

squiggle /'skwɪgl/ *c.n* (*informal*) short twisting line, usu one that has been drawn or printed.
'squiggly *adj* (*-ier*, *-iest*) in the shape of one or more squiggles.

squint /skwɪnt/ *c.n* **1** condition of the eyes in which each looks in a different direction. **2** (often — *at s.o/s.t*) look (at s.o/s.t) with one's eyes only slightly open.
▷ *intr.v* **3** have a squint(1). **4** (often — *at s.o/s.t*) look with a squint(2) (at s.o/s.t).

squire /skwaɪə/ *c.n* (*old use*) most important owner of land in an area of the country.

squirm /skwɜːm/ *c.n* **1** twisting of one's body because one has an itch, is ashamed etc.
▷ *intr.v* **2** move with a squirm(1). **squirm out of s.t** (*fig*) escape s.t, e.g punishment, by being clever etc.

squirrel /'skwɪrəl/ *c.n* kind of small grey or red animal with a bushy tail that lives mostly in trees.

squirt /skwɜːt/ *c.n* **1** thin stream of liquid that is pressed out of s.t strongly; jet¹(1): *I put a squirt of lemon juice in my drink.* **2** (*derog*; *informal*) young weak person: *You little squirt!*
▷ *v* **3** *tr.v* make a squirt(1) of (s.t) come out: *He squirted paint in my eye.* **4** *tr.v* (often — *s.o/s.t with s.t*) cover, wet etc (s.o/s.t) by squirting(3) s.t at her/him/it. **5** *intr.v* produce a squirt(1): *Be careful of that tap; it squirts.*

Sr *written abbr* **1** Senior(4). **2** Sister(3,4).

SRN /ˌes ˌɑːr 'en/ *abbr* State Registered Nurse.

SS /ˌes 'es/ *unique n abbr* (used before the name of a ship) steamship.

ssh /ʃ/ = sh.

St *written abbr* **1** Saint (used before her/his name): *St Peter.* **2** Street (after the name of the street): *Regent St.*

stab /stæb/ *n* **1** *c.n* attack (on s.o/s.t) with a sharp weapon/tool. **2** *c.n* wound made by a stab(1). **3** *sing.n* (often — *of s.t*) sudden sharp painful feeling (caused by s.t): *a stab of pain*; *a stab of guilt*(3). **have/make a stab at s.t** (a) ⇒ stab(2). (b) (*informal*) try to do s.t, usu when the chances of success are not good. **a stab in the back** (*fig*) an act of betrayal.
▷ *tr.v* (*-bb-*) **4** make a stab(1) at (s.o/s.t) producing a wound or cut. **stab at s.o/s.t** try to stab(4) s.o/ s.t: *He stabbed at her but missed.*
'stabbing *attrib.adj* (usu of a pain) sharp and sudden.

stable¹ /'steɪbl/ *adj* Opposite unstable. **1** firm; steady; not easily changed, shaken etc: *stable government.* **2** (of a person, her/his character etc) who/that one can trust to do the right thing.

3 (of a chemical etc) that does not (easily) change its form.

stability /stə'bɪlɪtɪ/ *u.n* fact or state of being stable[1]. Opposite instability.

stabilization, -isation /ˌsteɪbɪlaɪ'zeɪʃən/ *u.n* fact or act of stabilizing (s.t).

stabilize,-ise/'steɪbɪˌlaɪz/ *tr/intr.v* (cause(s.t)to) become stable[1] (1,2).

'stabiˌlizer, -iser *c.n* thing that stabilizes s.t: *Some ships have stabilizers on their sides to reduce*(1) *their roll in rough seas.*

'stably *adv.*

stable² /'steɪbl/ *c.n* (often *pl* with *sing* meaning) **1** building, yard etc where horses (or sometimes other animals) are kept and looked after. **2** several horses owned or trained by one person or group of people and used for racing.

▷ *tr.v* **3** put/keep (horses etc) in a stable(1).

'stabling *u.n* (often — *for 10 horses* etc) (enough) space in a stable²(1) (for 10 horses etc).

staccato /stə'kɑːtəʊ/ *adj/adv* (*music*) (of a way of playing music) with each note played shortly and very separately from the note before and the one after. Opposite legato.

stack /stæk/ *c.n* **1** (often — *of s.t*) pile (of s.t), usu carefully arranged: *a stack of wood.* **2** = haystack. **3** = smokestack. (**whole**) **stack** (**of s.t**) (large) number/amount (of s.t).

▷ *v* **4** *tr.v* (often — *s.t up*) make (s.t) into a stack(1). **5** *tr.v* (often — *s.t with s.t*) put stacks(1) of s.t in/on (s.t). **6** *tr/intr.v* (often — (s.t) *up*) (cause planes to) wait with others before being allowed to land; (cause (traffic) to) wait in a long line: *The road repairs meant that cars were stacked* (*up*) *for many kilometres.* **7** *tr.v* (usu — *s.t against s.o*) make the chances against s.o winning (s.t) unfairly or dishonestly high.

stadium /'steɪdɪəm/ *c.n* (*pl* -s or, less usu, stadia /'steɪdɪə/) big, usu oval(1), open building with rows of seats round the sides and a place in the middle for games etc: *a football stadium.*

staff¹ /stɑːf/ *n* **1** *c/pl.n* all (the) people who work s.w: *Our staff is/are fully trained. We have 20 on our staff* (or *a staff of 20*). **2** *u/pl.n* (also *attrib*) members of a staff(1): *the staff entrance. We are looking for staff for our office. Only staff are allowed here.* **3** *c/def.pl.n* (also *attrib*) (*military*) group of officers who work for another officer instead of commanding their own units: *a staff officer.* **4** *unique n* (informal way of addressing a staff nurse/sergeant). **general staff** ⇒ general.

▷ *tr.v* **5** be/provide the staff¹(1) for (s.t): *How can we staff our new library? Our company is staffed only with women.*

-staffed *adj* having the amount of staff(1) shown in the first part of the word: *understaffed*; *well-staffed.*

ˌstaff 'nurse *c.n* senior(1) rank of nurse in a hospital etc.

'staff ˌoffice *c.n* office in a big company etc that looks after staff(2) affairs.

ˌstaff 'sergeant *c.n* (*military*) **1** highest rank of sergeant(1) in the British army. **2** sergeant(1) of middle rank in the US armed forces.

staff² /stɑːf/ *c.n* (*pl* -s, staves /steɪvz/) **1** stick usu carried by an official to show his rank or position. **2** = flagstaff (⇒ flag¹). **3** (*music*) = stave¹(2).

stag /stæg/ *attrib.adj* **1** for men only: *a stag party.* Compare hen(2).

▷ *c.n* **2** adult male deer.

stage¹ /steɪdʒ/ *n* **1** *c.n* raised part of a theatre etc on which plays are performed. **2** *def.n* work, life etc of actors, actresses, theatre managers etc. **3** *c.n* (*fig*; *formal*) place where s.t important, interesting etc happens: *Will Europe be the stage for the next world war?* **go on the stage** become an actor/actress. **off stage** not actually on the stage while a play is being performed. **on stage** actually on the stage then. **set the stage** (**for s.o/ s.t**) get things ready (for s.t); make it possible for s.t to happen. ⇒ downstage, upstage.

▷ *tr.v* **4** arrange for (a play) to be performed: *The students are staging 'Macbeth' in the gardens.* **5** (*fig*) organize (s.t) to happen, esp in order to impress(2) people: *The event is being staged to show how successful the business is.*

'stage diˌrection *c.n* direction(3) written in a play etc telling actors etc where to move to, what to do etc.

ˌstage 'door *c/def.n* door at the back/side of a theatre that the actors, actresses and staff use.

'stage ˌfright *u.n* nervousness that some people feel when they have to act, give a speech etc in public.

ˌstage-'manage *tr.v* (*informal*) organize (s.t, usu s.t aimed at influencing or impressing(2) people), often in a way that people do not know about: *The whole trouble was stage-managed by people trying to defeat the government.*

ˌstage 'manager *c.n* person who is in charge of the stage in a theatre.

'stage ˌset *c.n* ⇒ set¹(4).

'stage,struck *adj* loving everything about the theatre(2), and esp wanting to be an actor/ actress.

'staging *c/u.n* **1** (often — *of s.t*) example or way of staging (⇒ stage¹(4)) a play: *the staging of 'Othello'.* **2** *u.n* floor and supports used during building only; scaffolding.

stage² /steɪdʒ/ *c.n* **1** state of s.t at a certain time during its development; particular time when s.t is at a certain step (in development): *an early stage in the development of a frog. At this stage of the meeting I do not know what will be decided.* **2** (often *early, late* etc — *of s.t*) one of the (early etc) divisions (of s.t) according to time: *The first stages of our journey were the most difficult.* **by** (**easy**) **stages** gradually without trying to do too much at any particular time.

'stage,coach *c.n* (*old use*) carriage pulled by horses, used to carry people from one town etc to another.

stagger /'stægə/ *c.n* **1** unsteady movement made by a person/animal when he/she/it is finding it difficult not to fall.

▷ *v* **2** *intr.v* move with a stagger(1): *When the bullet hit the man he staggered on for a few steps and then fell.* **3** *tr.v* (usu *passive*) shock (a person, her/his mind etc) so much that he/she/it does not know what to think: *I was staggered when I heard he had won the competition.* **4** *tr.v* arrange (times of work etc) in such a way that they do not all happen at the same time: *If we stagger office hours there won't be so much traffic at five o'clock.* **stagger to one's feet** stand up with a stagger(1).

'staggered *adj* **1** shocked; very surprised. ⇒ stagger(3). **2** not in a straight line one behind the other. **3** ⇨ stagger(4): *staggered working hours.*

'staggering *adj* very surprising. ⇨ stagger(3).

staging ⇨ stage¹.

stagnant /'stægnənt/ *adj* **1** (of water etc) not flowing or moving (and therefore having a bad smell). **2** (of business, life etc) in which nothing is happening.

'stagnantly *adv.*

stagnate /stæg'neɪt/ *intr.v* be/become stagnant.

stagnation /stæg'neɪʃən/ *u.n.*

staid /steɪd/ *adj* (*derog*) (of a person, her/his behaviour etc) quiet, serious (and usu boring).

'staidly *adv.* **'staidness** *u.n.*

stain /steɪn/ *n* **1** *c.n* mark (left by ink, blood etc) that is difficult to remove. **2** *c/u.n* liquid made for changing the colour of wood etc. **3** *c.n* (often — on s.o/s.t) (*formal*) thing that brings shame (on s.o/s.t): *Bob's bad behaviour in school was a stain on his* character(5).

▷ *v* **4** *tr.v* make/put a stain(*n*) on (s.o/s.t): *Let's stain the fence brown. His bad behaviour stained his family's honour.* **5** *intr.v* be able to be stained(4): *Be careful, this material stains easily.*

,stained 'glass *u.n.* glass that has colour put in it while it is melted, and is then used, esp in church windows, to make pictures.

'stainless *adj* **1** (*attrib*) that does not stain(5) or rust easily: *stainless steel knives.* **2** (*literary*) not having any stain(3): *a stainless reputation.*

stair /steə/ *c.n* (one step in a) staircase.

'stair ,carpet *c/u.n* carpet fixed to a staircase.

'stair ,case *c.n* (also **'stair ,way**) set of steps one above the other (and their framework and banisters), usu in a building to get from one floor to another. ***moving staircase*** ⇨ move.

stairs *pl.n* staircase; steps(5). ***flight of stairs*** ⇨ fly². ⇨ downstairs, upstairs.

'stair ,way *c.n* ⇨ staircase.

'stair ,well *c.n* space in a building inside which there is a staircase.

stake¹ /steɪk/ *c.n* **1** piece of wood, metal etc with a sharp end that is fixed in the ground as a support, e.g in a fence etc. ***pull up stakes*** (*fig; informal*) stop doing s.t or living s.w, usu in order to start doing s.t else or living s.w else.

▷ *tr.v* **2** tie (s.t, e.g a young tree) to one or more stakes¹(1) so that it does not fall or break. ***stake a place off/out*** put stakes¹(1) round a place to show where its boundaries are. ***stake (out) a/one's claim (to s.t)*** (*fig*) claim s.t. ***stake (a place) out*** (*slang*) watch (a place) secretly or arrange for it to be watched, to try to catch criminals etc. ⇨ stakeout.

'stake ,out *c.n* act of staking (a place) out.

stake² /steɪk/ *c.n* **1** (often *have* (*got*) *a* — *in* s.t) share (in s.t) that can bring one profit or loss: *I bought a large stake in the business. All people have a stake in the success of their country.* **2** stake²(1) that is the result of betting(3) money on a horse in a race, in card games etc. ***at stake*** being risked. ***put s.o/s.t at stake*** risk s.o/s.t: *He knew that taking on the job meant putting his life at stake.*

▷ *tr.v* **3** (often — *s.t on s.o/s.t*) risk/bet(3) (money) (on s.t, e.g a horse in a race).

'stake ,holder *c.n* person who holds everybody's stakes(1) so that he/she can give them to the winner when he/she has won.

stakes *n* **1** *pl.n* amounts of money staked²(3) in a game etc. **2** *sing.n* horse race in which the owner of each horse puts in the same amount of money which is then given to the winner(s) after the race. **3** *pl.n* prize in a race etc.

stalactite /'stælək ,taɪt/ *c.n* long piece of rock that hangs down from the roof of some caves where water drips(4).

stalagmite /'stæləg ,maɪt/ *c.n* thing like a stalactite but rising from the floor of a cave.

stale /steɪl/ *adj* **1** (of food, smells etc) old and therefore not fresh or pleasant any more. **2** (of news etc) old, already known etc and therefore not interesting any more. **3** (of a person) tired, bored or having no interest in things because one is not doing anything new.

'stale ,mate *c/unique n* **1** (in chess) situation in which neither player wins. **2** (*fig*) situation in which neither side in a quarrel etc can win; deadlock.

▷ *tr.v* **3** cause (s.t) to reach stalemate(*n*).

'staleness *u.n.*

stalk¹ /stɔːk/ *c.n* **1** part of a plant (but not a tree) that comes up out of the ground. Compare trunk(2). **2** stem on a plant/tree which is not the main one and is smaller than a branch in trees.

stalk² /stɔːk/ *v* **1** *tr.v* follow (s.o, an animal) secretly to try to catch, photograph etc her/him/it. **2** *intr.v* walk proudly with long steps. **3** *tr/intr.v* (of ghosts(1) etc) move (through a place) in a frightening way.

'stalker *c.n* person who stalks²(1) animals.

stall¹ /stɔːl/ *c.n* **1** enclosed part of a stable²(1) etc for keeping one animal in. Compare pen²(1). **2** small open shop or table for selling things in a market etc. ⇨ stand(3). **3** seat in the front part of the ground floor in a theatre. **4** one of the seats on the side of a big church in which the choir(1), important priests sit.

'stall ,holder *c.n* person who has/rents a stall¹(3).

stalls *pl/def.pl.n* seats in the front part of a theatre.

stall² /stɔːl/ *c.n* **1** (of a plane) loss of climbing power and tendency to fall backwards as a result of having the nose turned up while the speed is too slow. **2** (of a car etc) act of stopping because there is not enough power from the engine.

▷ *v* **3** *tr/intr.v* (cause (a plane) to) go into a stall²(1). **4** *tr/intr.v* (cause (a car etc) to) stop because of a stall²(2). **5** *intr.v* cause delay intentionally: *Stop stalling and tell me the truth!* **6** *tr.v* delay (s.t) intentionally. **7** *tr.v* cause (s.o) to be delayed: *Could you stall them for a few days while I try to get the money I owe them?*

stallion /'stæliən/ *c.n* adult male horse that has not been gelded (⇨ geld). Compare gelding.

stalwart /'stɔːlwət/ *adj* **1** strong; who/that one can trust not to give in.

▷ *c.n* **2** stalwart(1) person.

'stalwartly *adv.* **'stalwartness** *u.n.*

stamen /'steɪmen/ *c.n* (*science*) part of a flower that holds the bags in which pollen is produced.

stamina /'stæmɪnə/ *u.n* power to go on doing s.t without getting tired, bored etc: *You have no stamina.*

stammer /ˈstæmə/ *c.n* **1** difficulty in speaking causing repeating of sounds and/or stopping in the middle of words etc, often because of being nervous etc. ⇨ stutter.

▷ *v* **2** *intr.v* speak with a stammer(1). **3** *tr.v* (often — *s.t out*) say (s.t) with a stammer(1): *'C-c-come . . . in!' he stammered.* ⇨ stutter.

'stammerer *c.n* person who stammers(2).

'stammeringly *adv.*

stamp /stæmp/ *c.n* **1** (also **'postage ˌstamp**) piece of paper with glue on the back which one buys from a post office and sticks on letters etc before posting them. **2** piece of paper like a stamp(1) but used for other official purposes, e.g to show that one has paid s.t. Compare stamp duty. **3** (also **'trading ˌstamp**) piece of paper like a stamp(1) but given to customers in some shops, petrol stations etc when they buy goods there, used to buy other goods. **4** device for making a mark on paper etc, either in ink or by pressing a shape on the paper etc: *It is much quicker to put the date on all these letters with a stamp than to write it by hand.* Compare rubber stamp. **5** mark made by a stamp(4). **6** (often (*bear*) *the* — *of s.o/s.t*) (*fig*) thing that is typical (of s.o/s.t) so that one can recognize her/him/it by it: *This crime bears the stamp of Fred Sykes.* Compare hallmark(1), mark(5). **7** (often *leave its/one's* — *on s.t*) effect (on s.t) that is strong and lasts a long time. **8** strong, heavy step on the ground with one's foot. (*have*) **the stamp of truth** (give) the appearance of being true. **of that/this stamp** of that/this kind.

▷ *v* **9** *tr.v* put a stamp(1–3,5) on (s.t). **10** *tr.v* (often — *s.t out*) produce (s.t, e.g a coin) by using a machine that presses out the shape. **11** *intr.v* (often — *about*) step heavily on the ground with one's feet. **stamp one's feet** = stamp(11). **stamp s.o/s.t as s.t** class(7) s.o/s.t as s.t; say that s.o/s.t is a s.t: *That child's bad behaviour stamps him as a* hooligan. **stamp s.t off s.t** remove s.t (e.g mud) from s.t (e.g one's shoes) by stamping(11). **stamp s.t out** (**a**) ⇨ stamp(10). (**b**) destroy or put an end to s.t completely: *How are we going to stamp out violence at football matches?*

'stamp ˌduty *u.n* kind of tax that one buys stamps(2) to pay.

stamped *adj* already having the necessary stamp(s)(1) on it: *We can send you the information if you send us a stamped addressed envelope.*

stampede /stæmˈpiːd/ *c.n* **1** sudden wild rush of animals, usu because they are frightened. **2** sudden rush by people to do s.t, e.g buy goods before prices go up.

▷ *tr/intr.v* **3** (often — *s.o/s.t into s.t*) (cause (s.o/s.t) to) begin a stampede(*n*) (to do s.t).

stance /stæns/ *c.n* **1** way in which s.o, an animal, stands. **2** way in which one thinks about s.o/s.t; attitude(2), standpoint.

stanch /stɑːntʃ/ = staunch².

'stanchly *adv.* **'stanchness** *u.n.*

stand /stænd/ *c.n* **1** raised place on which s.o stands/sits for s.t. ⇨ bandstand. **2** outdoor place with rows of seats and/or areas where one can stand to watch football matches etc. ⇨ grandstand. **3** place, often in a market, at the side of a street, where things are being sold etc; stall*(2). **4** thing where one stands(12) s.t: *an umbrella stand.* **5** place where taxis wait for

hire; rank²(4): *a taxi stand.* **6** (often *make a* —) determined effort, e.g to defend a position in a battle or to avoid losing a match. **7** opinion that one sticks to: *What is your stand on unemployment?* **one-night stand** (**a**) performance on one night only. (**b**) person one has sex(3) with on one night only. **take a/one's stand** decide on one's stand(7). **take the stand** (*law*) (in a court) go into the witness box to answer questions.

▷ *v* (*p.t,p.p* stood /stʊd/) **8** *intr.v* (of a person) be in an (almost) vertical position supported by one's feet: *There are seats for 100 people and the rest of the audience must stand.* **9** *intr.v* (of an animal) be supported only by its feet: *I can see three ducks; one is standing keeping guard and the others are lying down.* **10** *intr.v* (of a thing, e.g a table, building) be in a position where the bottom part is on a base: *The school stands at the corner of two small streets.* **11** *tr/intr.v* (often — *s.o/s.t up*) (cause (s.o/s.t) to) change from a lying, sitting etc position to a standing (⇨ stand(1,2)) position: *The children stood (up) as the teacher came in.* **12** *tr.v* put s.o/s.t in a standing (⇨ stand(8–10)) position: *Stand your umbrella in that corner.* **13** *intr.v* (followed by a prep, adj or phrase) change to, stay in, the position shown by the prep etc: *Stand away from the edge, please. Stand back (or to one side) and let the ambulance pass.* **14** *intr.v* remain without moving: *After you have put the powder in the milk let it stand in a warm place until it sets. That car has been left standing there since the beginning of the month.* Compare idle(1). **15** *tr.v* (often — *to do s.t*; — *doing s.t*) bear(5), put up with, tolerate, (s.o/s.t, doing s.t); suffer (s.o/s.t, doing s.t) successfully: *I can't stand Norman because he is so rude. Mary can stand a lot of pain which was useful when she broke her arm. She can't stand (going to) meetings.* **16** *tr.v* do (s.t), allow (s.t) to be done to one, usu as part of one's job. **17** *intr.v* appear; be seen: *Learn the speech just as it stands; don't change a single word of it.* **18** *intr.v* remain as before: *The rule that all students must be in by 10 pm still stands.* **19** *intr.v* (often — *for s.t*) be/become a candidate(1) for s.t: *stand for* presidency(2) *of the club.*

as s.t stands in the present situation regarding s.t: *As things stand, none of us can have a holiday because there is still too much work to do.*

How do things stand with s.o/s.t? What is the situation regarding s.o/s.t?

How does s.o stand in s.t? What is s.o's position about s.t, e.g which side does he/she support?

know how/where one stands (with s.o) know what one's situation is (regarding s.o).

leave s.o/s.t standing (**a**) start running, driving etc so fast that one leaves s.o/s.t far behind. (**b**) (*fig*) make such fast progress that one leaves s.o far behind.

stand against s.o/s.t be against s.o/s.t; oppose s.o/s.t: *stand against his brother in the elections; stand against the new law.* ⇨ stand for s.t.

stand a (*good* etc) **chance** (**of** (*doing*) *s.t*) ⇨ chance(*n*).

stand at ease ⇨ ease(*n*).

stand at/to attention ⇨ attention. **stand at £100** etc be £100 etc at present: *My bank account stands at £150.32.*

stand by (**a**) (often — *for, to do, s.t*) get ready (for, to do, s.t). (**b**) (often — *idly by* (*while . . .*))

remain without doing anything when one should be helping etc. (c) be near/there. ⇨ bystander. (d) **stand by s.o/s.t** (still) support s.o or keep a promise etc.

stand down stop standing (19). **stand (s.o) down** (*law*) (allow (a witness) to) leave the witness stand.

stand easy ⇨ easy.

stand (close) examination be good enough not to fail when examined (carefully).

stand fast/firm not allow oneself to be moved or one's opinion etc to be changed: *We must stand firm about our demand for better working conditions.*

stand for s.t (a) ⇨ stand (19). (b) support s.t: *stand for peace.* ⇨ stand against s.o/s.t. (c) represent (2) s.t: *'SS' in 'SS Canton' stands for 'steamship'.* (d) (*usu cannot/can't* —) allow s.t to happen; tolerate s.t; put up with s.t.

stand one's ground = stand firm.

stand guard/watch (over s.o/s.t) act as a guard to see that nothing bad happens (to s.o/s.t).

stand high (in s.o's opinion) be thought highly of (by s.o).

stand idle remain doing nothing; remain without being used. Compare stand (14). ⇨ idle (1).

stand in (for s.o) do s.o else's work, usu while he/she is away, ill etc. ⇨ stand-in.

stand s.o s.t pay for s.o to have s.t, e.g a drink at a bar; treat s.o to s.t (⇨ treat (*v*)).

stand s.o off stop employing s.o, usu only while there is little work for her/him to do; lay s.o off (⇨ lay²).

stand on one's hands/head stand upside-down supporting oneself on one's hands, or one's head and hands.

stand on one's own (two) feet ⇨ foot (*n*).

stand s.t on its head (a) turn s.t upside-down. (b) (*fig*) cause s.t to change very much, sometimes even to be completely changed to the opposite: *The discovery that the world is round not flat stood geography on its head.*

stand out (a) be easy to see because it is very different from what is around it etc: *If you wear white clothes you will stand out in the dark.* (b) (often — *among/from s.t*) be very noticeably (one of) the best (of s.t). **stand out against s.o/s.t** resist (s.o/s.t). **stand out for s.o/s.t** support s.o/ s.t and not allow oneself to be changed in this.

stand out a mile ⇨ mile.

stand to (*military*) (in the armed forces) get ready to fight.

stand to gain, win etc **(s.t)** be in a position where one has a chance of gaining etc (s.t).

stand to reason ⇨ reason (*n*).

stand trial (for s.t) (*law*) ⇨ trial (⇨ try).

stand up (a) ⇨ stand (11). (b) be able to be accepted: *What you say about Julia would never stand up in a court of law.* **stand s.o up** (*informal*) not meet s.o at a place where one had arranged to meet her/him. **stand up for s.o/s.t** support/ defend s.o/s.t against attacks. **stand up to s.o** resist s.o; not allow oneself to be frightened by s.o. **stand up to/under s.t** be strong enough to resist, not be damaged or worn down by, s.t.

-stand *c.n* stand (1–5) for the thing shown in the first part of the word: *a bandstand; a hatstand.*

'stand,by *u.n* (also *attrib*) person or thing who/ that is not at work at present but is ready for work

as soon as needed. **on standby** (a) ready for work in this way. (b) ready to take a seat on a plane if one becomes available.

'stand-,in *c.n* person who does another person's work while he/she is ill etc or when s.t difficult or dangerous needs to be done, e.g by an actor/ actress.

'standing *attrib.adj* **1** that is always there: *a standing army* (i.e a regular one, not a reserve or part-time one); *a standing invitation to (do) s.t* (i.e an invitation to (do) s.t at any time one wants).
▷ *u.n* **2** rank or position in an organization. **of (high etc) standing** who has a high etc rank or position in s.t. **of (long etc) standing** who has been in that position for a long etc time or that has existed etc for a long time.

,standing 'order *c.n* **1** order to a bank to pay a certain amount of money every week, month, year etc. **2** (usu *pl*) rule that is always in operation and does not have to be repeated every time.

,standing o'vation *c.n* applause after a good speech etc, during which (almost) all the audience stand up.

'standing ,room *u.n* **1** (often — *only*) state of having no seats left so that anyone who still wants to come has to stand. **2** place where there are no seats so that people have to stand.

,stand'offish *adj* (*derog*; *informal*) not friendly; aloof.

,stand'offishly *adv*.

'stand,point *c.n* point of view; way of looking at things: *What is your standpoint on* hanging (⇨ hang (5))? *We can consider the problem from several standpoints.*

'stand,still *sing.n* complete stop; state of not moving at all: *The traffic was at* (or *came to*) *a complete standstill.*

'stand-,up *attrib.adj* **1** (of a collar) that is not made for folding down (over a tie) but for wearing with the edge up. **2** where people stand up instead of sitting down etc: *a stand-up dinner.* **3** (of a funny act or performer) using jokes and talk while standing: *a stand-up comedian* (1).

standard /'stændəd/ *adj* **1** (*written abbr* std) of the usual, ordinary kind: *the standard size/quality.* **2** accepted as good, right etc: *standard pronunciation.* ⇨ non-standard, substandard.
▷ *c.n* **3** level or amount of s.t compared with other possible levels or amounts of it: *The standard of the work in that university is below average for the country.* **4** (*written abbr* std) fixed level/amount of s.t or set of such levels/amounts, against which things can be measured or compared: *Which standard do you use for weighing fruit – pounds or kilograms?* **5** thing on which s.t stands (10): *a lamp standard.* **6** bush that is grown with a main trunk like a tree. **7** special kind of flag, e.g the British royal standard. **gold standard** ⇨ gold. **living standard** ⇨ standard of living. **set a high** etc **standard (for s.o/s.t)** (a) expect people to be of, work to etc, a high etc standard. (b) be s.o/s.t whose standard is high etc so that others can try to reach the same standard.

standardization, -isation /,stændədaɪ'zeɪʃən/ *u.n* fact of being/becoming standardized.

'standar,dize, -ise *tr/intr.v* (cause (s.t) to) become standard (2) or to be measured against a standard (4).

,standard 'lamp *c.n* lamp at the top of a kind of tall pole[1] that stands on the floor.

,standard of 'living *c.n* (also **'living ,standard**) standard(3) of wealth, comfort etc: *Western countries mostly have a high standard of living.*

standby, stand-in, standing, standoffish, standpoint, standstill, stand-up ⇨ stand.

stank /stæŋk/ *p.t* of stink(*v*).

stanza /'stænzə/ *c.n* group of usu four or more lines in a poem, usu ones that rhyme(4).

staple[1] /'steɪpl/ *attrib.adj* **1** that is the main one produced, used etc: *The staple product of Fiji is sugar. One of the staple foods of Africa is* maize.
▷ *c.n* **2** staple(1) food, product etc.

staple[2] /'steɪpl/ *c.n* **1** short thin piece of wire that is pushed through sheets of paper etc (usu with a stapler) to fasten them together. **2** small piece of strong wire, shaped like the letter U with pointed ends so that it can be hammered into wood, usu to hold wire in a fence etc.
▷ *tr.v* **3** (often — *s.t to s.t*; — *s.t together*) fasten (s.t) (to s.t etc) with one or more staples[2](*n*).

'stapler *c.n* device used to staple[2](3) s.t.

star /stɑː/ *c.n* **1** very big bright body that we see in the sky: *Our sun is a star.* **2** (*informal*) any distant body that we can see shining in the sky at night. **3** figure/shape usu with five points that looks like a star(1,2): *My child was given a gold star at school today. The Turkish flag has a star and a crescent(1) moon on it.* **4** asterisk. **5** (often *pl*) star(1,2) thought of as influencing a person's fate: *Dorothy was born under a lucky star. What do the stars* foretell *for you this month?* **6** (also *attrib*) person who is very good at, famous for, s.t: *a film-star; a football star.* ⇨ all-star. **shooting star** ⇨ shoot. **s.o's star is rising/falling** s.o is becoming more/less successful.
▷ *v* (**-rr-**) **7** *intr.v* (often — *ins.t*) be a star(6) (in a film, play etc). **8** *tr.v* (of a film, play etc) have (s.o) in it as a star(6): *'Goldfinger' starred Sean Connery as 007.* **9** *tr.v* mark (s.t) with a star(4).

stardom /'stɑːdəm/ *u.n* state or fact of being a star(6).

'star,fish *c.n* (*pl* **-(es)**) kind of creature that lives in the sea and has the shape of a star(1–3) with five arms.

starlet /'stɑːlɪt/ *c.n* young actress who is hoping to become a star(6).

'star,light *u.n* light from the stars(2).

'star,lit *adj* (*literary*) having light only from the stars(2): *a starlit night.*

'starry (**-ier, -iest**) *attrib.adj* full of stars(2): *a starry sky.*

,starry-'eyed *adj* (*derog*) having hopes that are (stupidly) unreasonable.

stars *pl.n* ⇨ star(5). **have stars in one's eyes** be starry-eyed. **reach for the stars** (*fig*; *literary*) try to get s.t that is impossible. **see stars** see flashes of light, usu because one has had a blow on the head. **thank one's lucky stars (that . . .)** be thankful (usu because one has escaped s.t unpleasant).

,Stars and 'Stripes *def/def.pl.n* US flag.

,Star-,Spangled 'Banner *def.n* **1** Stars and Stripes. **2** US national anthem.

'star-,studded *adj* (*usu attrib*)(*informal*) having a lot of stars(3,6) on/in it.

starboard /'stɑːbəd/ *def.n* (also *attrib*) right side of a ship/plane when one is looking forwards. Opposite port[2].

starch /stɑːtʃ/ *n* **1** white substance found mostly in corn, potatoes, beans etc. **2** *u.n* powder etc made from starch(1) and used to stiffen clothes after. they have been washed. **3** *c/u.n* food that has a lot of starch(1) in it.
▷ *tr.v* **4** put starch(2) in (clothes).

'starchy *adj* (**-ier, -iest**) **1** having a lot of starch(1) in it. **2** that is like starch(1). **3** (*fig*; *informal*) stiff and formal in one's manner.

stardom ⇨ star.

stare /steə/ *c.n* **1** long look at s.o/s.t, usu with one's eyes wide open and without looking away.
▷ *intr.v* **2** (often — *at s.o/s.t*) look (at s.o/s.t) with a stare(1). **stare back** stare(2) at s.o who is staring (⇨ stare(2)) at one. **stare into space** look in an absent-minded way. **stare s.o in the face** face(*n*). **stare s.o out** succeed in staring(2) at s.o longer than he/she is able to stare back.

'staring *attrib.adj* **1** (of eyes) that are very/unpleasantly wide open. **2** that is unpleasantly noticeable, usu because it is very bright and unsuitable: *a staring red and yellow suit.* **stark staring mad** ⇨ mad.

starfish ⇨ star.

stark /stɑːk/ *adj* **1** (unpleasantly) bare, simple, without any softness or decoration: *stark life in prison; stark countryside.* **2** (of s.t unpleasant) complete; utter[1]. *stark terror(1).*
▷ *adv* **3** **stark naked** completely naked(1). **stark staring mad** ⇨ mad.

'starkers *adj* (*slang*) stark naked.

'starkly *adv*. **'starkness** *u.n*.

starlet, starlight ⇨ star.

starling /'stɑːlɪŋ/ *c.n* very common kind of bird with shiny purple and green feathers.

starlit, starry(-eyed), stars, starstudded ⇨ star.

start /stɑːt/ *n* **1** *c.n* (often (*at*) *the* — of *s.t*; (*right*) *from the* (*very*) — (of *s.t*)) beginning (of s.t); place where s.t begins; fact or act of beginning: *At the start of the race I was at the back. I knew I would win right from the start.* **2** *sing.n* sudden movement of part of one's body that happens without one wanting it usu because of surprise, fear etc: *wake with a start.* **3** *sing/u.n* (often *a* — (of *five metres, hours* etc) *on/over s.o/s.t*) difference between the place, time etc where s.o starts (e.g a race) and the place, time etc where s.o else starts further behind (which consists of five metres, hours etc): *We'll give her 20 metres start in the race as she is so young.* **for a start** this is the first thing I want to say: *I don't want to go out; for a start it's going to rain.* **get off to a bad/good start** have a bad/good beginning: *The meeting got off to a good start.* ⇨ flying(*adj*). **by/in fits and starts** ⇨ fit[2].
▷ *v* **4** *tr/intr.v* (often — *off/out* (*for s.w*) (*from s.w*)) begin (s.t, e.g a journey etc) (to go towards s.w) (from s.w). **5** *tr/intr.v* (often — (*s.t*) *up*) (cause (s.t) to) begin/happen: *The argument started (up) when Lynne said something rude about Peter's wife. Who started it?* **6** *tr/intr.v* (cause (s.o/s.t) to) begin (an activity, doing s.t): *At what time are we, is the meeting, starting? It started snowing (or to snow) early in the morning. Start the watch (going) when the flag is dropped. We started our lunch with some soup.* **7** *intr.v* (usu —

at/from s.t) begin a distance (at a certain place): *The road to the coast starts at Greenfield.* **8** *intr.v* (usu — *at/from s.t)* begin (at a certain point in a scale): *Prices for holidays start from £150.* **9** *tr.v* begin using (s.t): *Once we start this cheese we'll have to finish it quickly.* **10** *intr.v* (usu — *at s.t)* give a start(2) (because of s.t): *She started at the sight of her mother looking so ill.* **start for s.t** suddenly begin to move quickly towards s.t. **start s.t** *(informal)* cause trouble. **to start with (a)** at first: *They were shy to start with but soon became friendly.* **(b)** = for a start.

'**starter** *c.n* **1** person whose job is to tell or signal the competitors in a race when to start. **2** competitor who is at the start of a race: *Some horses are entered for a race but are not actually starters.* Opposite non-starter. **3** person who starts(6) to do s.t: *Julia was a slow starter at arithmetic but now she's the best in her class.* Compare beginner. **4** device for starting an engine etc. Compare self-starter. **5** *(informal)* (often *pl* with a *sing* meaning) first course in a meal, e.g soup. **for starters** *(informal)* first of all; to start (a meal etc) with.

'**starting ,block** *c.n* pair of blocks fixed to the ground so that people starting to run a short race can push against them to get more speed.

'**starting ,gate** *c.n* set of gates that all open at exactly the same time so that all the horses etc in a race can start together.

'**starting ,price** *c.n* odds(3) against/on a horse etc at the moment racing begins.

startle /'stɑ:tl/ *tr.v* surprise (s.o) suddenly, sometimes so that he/she gives a start(2).

'**startlingly** *adv* in a way that startles.

starve /stɑ:v/ *tr/intr.v* **1** (often — *(s.o/s.t) to death)* (cause (s.o, an animal) to) die through lack of food. **2** (cause (s.o, an animal) to) be very hungry: *What's for breakfast? I'm starving!* **starve for s.t** want s.t very much when one finds it difficult or impossible to get it: *One sees many children who are starving for a little love.* **starve s.o/s.t of s.t** not give s.o/s.t s.t he/she/it needs: *Many children are starved of companionship too.*

starvation /stɑ:'veɪʃən/ *u.n.*

stash /stæʃ/ *tr.v* (often — *s.t away)* *(informal)* store s.t, usu in a secret place.

state /steɪt/ *n* **1** *c.n* (often — *of s.o/s.t)* condition in which (s.o/s.t) is; way of existence (of s.o/s.t): *What state is the football field in today? Joan is in a state of despair.* **2** *(informal)* (often *be in, get into, a —)* bad state(1) sometimes as a result of being nervous or worried: *Henry's in such a state over work.* **3** *c/u/def.n* (often with capital **S**) organized group of people with a government; nation. **4** *def.n* (also *attrib*) government of a state(3): *state ownership of the means of production.* ⇒ police state, welfare state. **5** *c.n* (often *the — of Virginia* etc) part of a state(3) that has its own government for its own affairs (and is called s.t): *The US is divided into 50 states.* **6** *u.n* (also *attrib*) dignity/pomp; dignified ceremonious way: *the state opening of* Parliament. **affairs of state** ⇒ affair. **lie in state** (of an important person who has just died) be put in a place where people can come and pay their respects. **state of affairs** present situation. **state of mind** way in which one is thinking; condition of one's mind. **Secretary of State** ⇒ secretary(3).

▷ *tr.v* **7** say (s.t), give (information etc), usu in a formal way. ⇒ overstate, understate. **8** fix (s.t); specify (s.t): *Only officers of the stated ranks can enter.*

'**state,craft** *u.n* ability to govern a state(3); statesmanship.

,**state en,rolled 'nurse** *c.n* (*abbr* SEN) nurse of a lower rank than a State Registered Nurse.

,**state 'enter,prise** *c.n* ⇒ enterprise.

statehood /'steɪthʊd/ *u.n.* fact or state of being a state(3,5).

'**stateless** *adj* (of a person) not being a member, able to use the passport, of any state(3).

'**statelessness** *u.n.*

'**stateliness** *u.n* fact of being stately.

'**stately** *adj* dignified; ceremonious; formal.

,**stately 'home** *c.n* big house in the country, often open to the public to see the interesting and beautiful things it contains.

'**statement** *n* **1** *u.n* act or way of stating (⇒ state(7)) s.t. **2** *c.n* thing that one states(7). **3** *c.n* (often *bank —*) list of money received, spent, still owing etc and the balance.

,**state-'owned** *adj* owned by the state(4).

,**state ,registered 'nurse** *c.n* (*abbr* SRN) nurse who is fully trained and recognized by the state(4). ⇒ state enrolled nurse.

'**state,room** *c.n* passenger's cabin on a ship.

States *def.pl.n* (*informal*) US.

,**state 'secret** *c.n* secret known only by people the state(4) allows to do so.

,**state's 'evidence** *unique n* **turn state's evidence** agree/decide to be a witness in a court of law against one's fellow criminals, usu in return for not being punished oneself.

'**statesman** *c.n* (*pl* -men) important person in government, politics, esp a wise one.

'**statesman,like** *adj* as a wise statesman would be, do: *a statesmanlike decision.*

'**statesman,ship** *u.n* qualities of a statesman.

,**state 'visit** *c.n* official visit by a king, president etc to another country.

static /'stætɪk/ *adj* **1** not moving or changing; stationary(1). **2** (*derog*) boring because of lacking action. Compare dynamic(2). **3** (*technical*) of or referring to things that are not moving. Compare dynamic(1). **4** (of electricity) not moving in a current like ordinary electricity: *Often when one combs one's hair on a dry day one can hear the static electricity produced.*

▷ *u.n* **5** (*technical*) noise that interferes with radio signals caused by electricity in the air.

'**statics** *u.n* (*technical*) part of the science of mechanics that deals with things that are not moving. Compare dynamics.

station /'steɪʃən/ *c.n* **1** (also *attrib*) building at a place where trains/buses stop to take on and/or let off passengers and/or goods: *a railway/bus station*; *a station café.* ⇒ stop(3). **2** building/place that is for the service/work shown by the word that comes before: *a fire/petrol/police station*; *an animal care station.* **3** place that broadcasts radio and/or television programmes: *Which station produces the best news in English?* **4** (in Australia) big farm for cattle(1) and/or sheep. **5** small place where traders etc live and/or work in a wild place, e.g the far north of Canada. **6** place where one or more of the armed forces has men, ships etc. **7** (*literary*) position in society:

In the old days everyone knew her or his station in life. **above one's station** above one's position in society. **(at) action stations** (*military*) (in) the positions ready for action, a battle.

▷ *tr.v* **8** put (s.o/s.t) in a certain position.

'station,master *c.n* person who is in charge of a railway station.

'station ,wagon *c.n* kind of car that has a door at the back through which goods, animals etc can be loaded into it; estate car. ⇨ convertible(3), hatchback, sedan.

stationary /'steɪʃənərɪ/ *adj* **1** not moving: *a stationary train.* **2** not intended, made, to be moved.

stationer /'steɪʃənə/ *c.n* **1** person who sells stationery(1). **2** (also **'stationer's**) shop that sells stationery(1).

'stationery *u.n* **1** things used for writing, e.g paper and pens. **2** paper for writing letters on (and envelopes to send them in).

statistic /stə'tɪstɪk/ *c.n* item(1) in statistics(1).

sta'tistical *adj* of or referring to statistics(2).

sta'tistically *adv.*

statistician /,stætɪ'stɪʃən/ *c.n* person who works with statistics.

sta'tistics *n* **1** *pl.n* information in the form of numbers which has been collected in a systematic organized way, e.g to show how the number of university students in different countries compare with each other. **2** *u.n* science of collecting, organizing and using statistics(1). **vital statistics** ⇨ vital.

statue /'stætʃu/ *c.n* (often — of s.o/s.t) figure (usu of a person or animal), made of stone, metal etc. ⇨ statuette, figurine.

statuary /'stætjʊərɪ/ *adj* **1** (*formal*) of or referring to statues.

▷ *u.n* **2** (*formal*) art of making statues. **3** statues in general.

statuesque /,stætjʊ'esk/ *adj* like, having the dignity, beauty etc of, a statue.

statuette /,stætjʊ'et/ *c.n* small statue for putting on a shelf etc in a house.

stature /'stætʃə/ *c/u.n* **1** importance, rank etc that is the result of one's own work: *a person of stature.* **2** (*formal*) height, usu of a person. **grow to full stature** reach full adult height.

status /'steɪtəs/ *n* **1** *c/u.n* position, rank etc compared with other people. **2** *u.n* high social status(1); prestige. **3** *c.n* (often *the* — of s.t) situation (regarding s.t): *What is the present status of your law case?*

status quo /,steɪtəs 'kwəʊ/ *def.n* (*Latin*) present status(3), arrangement of things.

statute /'stætʃu:t/ *c.n* written law. **by statute** as a result of a statute.

'statute ,book *def.n* (*informal*) book(s) or papers containing the statute law.

'statute ,law *u.n* all the laws that have been passed by Parliament. Compare case law.

'statute ,mile *c.n* legal(1) name for a mile.

statutory /'stætjʊtərɪ/ *adj* that is fixed or governed by statute.

staunch[1] /stɔ:ntʃ/ *attrib.adj* loyal; whom one can trust absolutely: *a staunch friend.*

'staunchly *adv.* **'staunchness** *u.n.*

staunch[2] /stɔ:ntʃ/ *tr.v* stop (usu blood) coming out of a wound etc.

stave[1] /steɪv/ *c.n* **1** curved piece of wood that

is fitted to others of the same kind to form the outside of a barrel. **2** (*music*) one or more groups of five lines on which notes are written down.

staves *pl.n* **1** *pl* of stave(n). **2** *pl* of staff[2](1).

stave[2] /steɪv/ *tr/intr.v* **1** (*p.t,p.p* staved, stove /stəʊv/) **stave (s.t) in** (cause (s.t) to) break inwards: *Our boat was thrown onto the rocks and its side stove in.* **2** (*p.t,p.p* staved) **stave s.o/s.t off** manage to keep (s.o/s.t) away; manage to delay s.t or to prevent it happening; fend(2) s.o/s.t off.

stay /steɪ/ *n* **1** *c.n* (short) time during which s.o/s.t remains s.w: *a two week(s') stay in a hotel.* **2** *c/u.n* delay/postponement ordered by a judge: *stay of execution(4).* **3** *c.n* rope supporting a mast. **4** *c.n* (*literary*) person or thing that supports s.o, esp in difficult times: *She was my stay in times of need.*

▷ *v* **5** *intr.v* continue to be s.w; not leave or go away. **6** *intr.v* continue in the position, direction, state etc shown by the following word(s): *stay home*; *stay on the same course*; *stay warm.* **7** *intr.v* (often — at a place; — with s.o) have a stay(1) (at a place, with s.o) as a guest or visitor. ⇨ overstay. **8** *tr.v* (usu — three days etc) stay(7) for (three days etc). **9** *tr.v* manage to keep going for (a certain distance). **10** *tr.v* (*formal*) order a stay(2) of (s.t): *stay a decision for one hour.* **11** *tr.v* (*literary*) delay, satisfy the need for, (s.t) for a time: *We stayed our thirst with a little water from the engine of the car.* **12** *intr.v* (*old use*) (usu as an order) stop; wait a little. **s.t has come**, **is here**, **to stay** (*informal*) s.t is not just a short passing fashion. **stay the course** manage to keep going right to the end. ⇨ stay(9). **stay one's hand** ⇨ hand(n). **stay on (as s.t)** not go when one had planned, was expected, to go but remain (in the job etc of s.t). **stay out (on strike)** remain on strike(1). **stay put** remain where one is; not move. ⇨ stay[1](5).

'stay-at-,home *c.n* (also *attrib*) (*informal*) person who prefers staying at home to going out, travelling etc.

'stayer *c.n* (*informal*) person, horse etc who/ that has stamina , will stay(9).

'staying ,power *u.n* ability to stay(9); stamina.

stays *pl.n* old-fashioned piece of underclothing for making one's waist look narrower; it has bones to stiffen it. Compare corset.

std *written abbr* standard(1,4).

STD /,es ,ti: 'di:/ *abbr* Subscriber Trunk Dialling; *an STD call.*

stead /sted/ *n* **in s.o's/its/their stead** instead of s.o/s.t; as a replacement for s.o/s.t. ⇨ instead. **stand s.o in good stead** (*literary*) be useful to s.o.

steadfast /'stedfəst/ *adj* (*formal*) **1** that cannot be moved or changed (at all easily): *a steadfast expression on his face.* **2** who/that is absolutely loyal and to be trusted: *a steadfast friend.*

'steadfastly *adv.* **'steadfastness** *u.n.*

steady /'stedɪ/ *adj* (*-ier, -iest*) **1** not shaking or moving about at all; firm: *You need a steady hand to pour that coffee out without spilling any.* *Soldiers need steady nerves(2).* Opposite unsteady. **2** (usu *attrib*) not changing (much); remaining (about) the same all the time: *a steady speed of 60 kilometres an hour.* **3** regular: *a steady job.* **4** whom one can trust not to do anything wild or foolish: *a steady husband.* **hold steady** don't move about. ⇨ steady(1).

▷ *adv* **5** **go steady** (**with s.o**) be s.o's regular boyfriend/girlfriend.

▷ *interj* **6** (often — *on!*) (*informal*) be careful.

▷ *tr/intr.v* (*-ies, -ied*) **7** (cause/help (s.o/s.t) to) be/ become steady(1).

'steadily *adv.* **'steadiness** *u.n.*

steak /steɪk/ *n* **1** *c.n* (thick) slice of (usu good quality) meat, fish. **2** *u.n* meat for cutting into steaks(1); one or more steaks: *I love steak and chips.* ⇒ sirloin. **3** *u.n* beef(1) of lower quality that is cut into small pieces and cooked with other things: stewing *steak.*

steal /stiːl/ *v* (*p.t* stole /stəʊl/, *p.p* stolen /'stəʊlən/) **1** *tr/intr.v* take (s.o/s.t that belongs to s.o else) from a person, place etc without permission. **2** *tr.v* take (a look at s.o/s.t, kiss etc) quickly and when one should not do so. **3** *intr.v* move quietly and/or secretly: *We stole quietly out of the meeting.* **steal a march on s.o** ⇒ march(*n*). **steal the scene/show** (**from s.o**); **steal s.o's thunder** ⇒ thunder(*n*).

stealth /stelθ/ *u.n* (*formal*) fact or act of doing s.t secretly and quietly. **by stealth** in a stealthy way.

'stealthily *adv* in a stealthy way.

'stealthy *adj* (*-ier, -iest*) secret and quiet.

steam /stiːm/ *u.n* (also *attrib*) **1** kind of gas/vapour produced when water boils: *a steam engine.* **2** mist(1) that water vapour changes into when it becomes cool, e.g by touching a cold window; condensation. **3** use of steam(1) engines in a railway system: *Some railways still use steam instead of electricity.* **blow/let/work off steam** (**a**) (of a steam engine) allow steam(1) to escape so as not to get too much pressure. (**b**) (*fig*; *informal*) allow one's feelings of anger to come out instead of keeping them in. **full steam ahead** forwards at full speed. **get up steam** (**a**) (of a steam engine) get ready to work by heating water to produce steam(1). (**b**) (*fig*) begin to move faster and faster and/or more and more strongly. **under one's, its, etc own steam** (*fig*) without any help from anyone else.

▷ *v* **4** *intr.v* produce steam(1), usu because s.t is hot. **5** *intr.v* move by steam(3): *We steamed out of port at 5.15.* **6** *tr.v* cook (s.t), using steam(1): *steam potatoes.* **steam s.t off s.t** remove s.t, e.g a stamp, that was stuck on s.t, e.g an envelope, by melting the glue with steam(1). **steam s.t open** open s.t, e.g an envelope, using steam. **steam** (**s.t**) **up** (cause (a window etc) to) become covered with steam(2).

steam- *n* using steam(3) to work the thing named in the second part of the word: *steamboat*; *steamship.*

'steam ,boat *c.n* boat with an engine that works by steam(3).

steamed *adj* cooked with steam(1). ⇒ steam(6). (**all**) **steamed up** (**about s.t**) (*informal*) very angry, worried etc (because of s.t).

'steam ,engine *c.n* engine that works by steam(1).

'steamer *c.n* **1** = steamship. ⇒ steam-. **2** container to steam(6) food in.

'steaming *adv* **steaming hot** very hot.

'steam ,iron *c.n* iron(2) that one fills with water to produce steam when it is hot, used to iron(5) creases(1).

'steam,roller *c.n* **1** heavy vehicle with very wide metal wheels, used for flattening newly made roads etc. **2** (*fig*; *informal*) thing that crushes any attempts to stop it.

▷ *tr.v* **3** (*informal*) stop (s.t) from being successful.

'steam,ship *c.n* ship with an engine that works by steam(3).

steed /stiːd/ *c.n* (*literary*) horse, esp when it is used for riding.

steel /stiːl/ *u.n* **1** very strong metal made by adding other things to iron when it is melted.

▷ *reflex.v* **2** make (oneself) strong and hard: *He had to steel himself to kill the wounded animal.*

,steel 'band *c.n* band²(2) with drums made from metal oil barrels prepared in such a way that one can play different musical notes on them.

,steel 'wool *u.n* fine steel threads used to make things smooth, remove old paint etc.

'steel,worker *c.n* person who works in a place that makes steel(1).

'steel,works *c.n* (*pl* steelworks) factory that makes steel.

'steely *adj* (*-ier, -iest*) **1** as hard as steel. **2** of a silver blue colour like steel.

steep¹ /stiːp/ *adj* **1** that goes up/down at a sharp angle: *The hill was so steep that we were very tired by the time we got to the top.* **2** that increases/ decreases quickly: *There has been a steep rise in the cost of petrol this year.* **be a bit, rather, etc steep** (*informal*) be too much, not reasonable: *It's a bit steep expecting us to make our own beds in a hotel!*

'steepen *intr.v* become steep(er)(1): *The hill steepens towards the top.*

'steeply *adv.* **'steepness** *u.n.*

steep² /stiːp/ *tr/intr.v* (often — *s.t in s.t*) (cause (s.t) to) remain in a liquid, usu until it is clean or the colour/taste has gone into the liquid etc. **be steeped in s.t** (*fig*) know a lot about s.t; have a lot of experience of s.t: *This town is steeped in history.*

steeple /'stiːpl/ *c.n* tall (part of a) building, usu consisting of a tower with a spire on top.

'steeple,jack *c.n* person whose job is building, mending etc tall buildings.

steeplechase /'stiːpl,tʃeɪs/ *c/def.n* **1** long race across country for horses with things to jump over on the way. **2** 3000 metre running race for people during which they have to do 35 jumps.

steeply, steepness ⇒ steep¹.

steer¹ /stɪə/ *tr/intr.v* control the direction in which (a boat, car, argument etc) goes: *We often have arguments but I always manage to steer them away from religion.* **steer** (**a course**) (**for s.t**) follow a course (that aims in the direction of s.t): *steer for the shore.*

steer clear (**of s.o/s.t**) (*informal*) avoid s.o/ s.t.

'steering com,mittee *c.n* committee whose job is to decide in what order to arrange the business for a conference etc.

'steering ,gear *u.n* all parts of a ship that are used for steering it.

'steering-,wheel *c.n* wheel in a car, ship etc that is turned in order to steer.

'steersman *c.n* (*pl* -men) person who steers a ship or boat; helmsman.

steer² /stɪə/ *c.n* castrated bull(1), esp a young one grown for its meat. Compare bullock, ox.

stellar /'stelə/ *adj* (*usu attrib*) (*technical*) of or referring to the stars: *stellar groups.*

stem¹ /stem/ *c.n* **1** part of a plant that comes up from the ground and has leaves, flowers and smaller stems¹(2) growing on it. **2** piece of a plant that sticks out of the bottom of a leaf, flower or out of a branch or other stem(1). **3** narrow vertical part of the bottom of a wine glass etc. **4** narrow part of a pipe used for smoking. **5** wooden or metal continuation of the keel of a ship at its bow¹(1). *from stem to stern* from the front end to the back end.

▷ *intr.v* (*-mm-*) **6** *stem from s.t* have s.t as one's origin.

-stemmed *adj* having a stem of the kind shown by the first part of the word: *thick-stemmed.*

stem² /stem/ (*-mm-*) *tr.v* **1** stop (s.t, usu a liquid) from flowing out. **2** (often — *the tide of s.t*) stop (the progress of) s.t, (e.g a movement towards freer government).

Sten gun /'sten ˌgʌn/ *c.n* (*military*) kind of small machine-gun held by one person.

stencil /'stensl/ *c.n* **1** thin piece of plastic(3), metal etc with a design(1) cut in it, used to reproduce the design(1) by spreading ink or paint etc over it. **2** sheet of wax paper, used to make a stencil(1) of s.t typed which can be printed.

▷ *tr/intr.v* (*-ll- US -l-*) **3** make (a design(1) etc) using a stencil(1).

step /step/ *c.n* **1** act of putting one foot forward, backwards, to one side, up etc so as to move in one of those directions. **2** sound made by a step(1): *I can hear steps outside the door.* **3** distance covered by a step(1): *Our house is only a few steps from the bus station.* **4** distance: *It is only a short step to the shops.* **5** thing on which one puts one's foot when going up/down from one horizontal level to another: *If you go down these steps you will come to the village square.* Compare rung, stair. ⇒ stepladder. *flight of steps* ⇒ flight² (⇒ fly²). **6** particular way of moving one's foot or feet as part of a dance: *I learnt a new step at the dance last night.* **7** difference between one point on a scale and the next point: *This weighing machine goes up in steps of 50 grams.* **8** act, usu one of several aimed at reaching a certain result: *Jane's first step towards becoming a singer was to find a good teacher.* *break step* stop being in step. *in step* (*with s.o/s.t*) (a) taking steps at the same time (as s.o), e.g with everybody's left leg moving at the same time and then everybody's right leg and so on. (b) (*fig*) in a way that fits in well with other people/things: *Your ideas are in step with mine.* Opposite out of step (with s.o/s.t). *keep step* remain in step. *mind one's step* (*fig*) be careful about what one does and so avoid trouble. *mind the step* be careful not to fall on a step(5). *out of step* (*with s.o/s.t*) not in step (with s.o/s.t). *step by step* (*fig*) gradually; not all at the same time. *take steps* (*to do s.t*) (*fig*) begin certain activities (in order to be successful at doing s.t). *watch one's step* (a) be careful where one puts one's feet, so as not to fall etc. (b) (*fig*) = mind one's step.

▷ *intr.v* (*-pp-*) **9** take a step. **10** (usu — *in*(*side*), *up*, *over here* etc) walk: *The shopkeeper asked us to step inside and look at his goods.* *step aside/ down* (*in favour of s.o*) give up one's position, job etc (so that s.o else can have it). *step in* (a) ⇒

step(10). (b) enter an argument etc. *step on it* (*informal*) (esp when driving) go faster. *step out of line* (*fig*) not do what one is expected to do, usu with the result that one annoys or worries others. *step s.t up* produce more of s.t: *step up production in a factory.*

'step,brother/'sister etc *c.n* person who is connected as a brother, sister etc by the fact of another marriage (i.e a stepson may be the son of one's wife by a former husband): *stepdaughter/ son*; *stepfather/mother.*

'step,ladder *c.n* ladder with legs hinged at the top which can be folded out to support it, so that the shape is like the letter A.

'stepping-,stone *c.n* **1** large stone (put) in a stream so that one can cross without getting one's feet wet. **2** (esp — *to s.t*) (*fig*) thing that one can use to help one make progress: *Training offers stepping-stones to better jobs.*

steps *pl.n* **1** two or more steps, sometimes forming a flight(4) of steps(5). Compare staircase. **2** = stepladder.

steppe /step/ *c.n* (often *pl* with a *sing* meaning) big flat plain with no trees on it, found mostly in the USSR.

stereo /'sterɪˌəʊ/ *adj* (*usu attrib*) producing, made with, sound from two different directions so that it seems more natural: *a stereo set*; *a stereo recording.*

stereophonic /ˌsterɪəʊ'fɒnɪk/ *adj* (*formal*) = stereo.

'stereo,scope *c.n* instrument that allows one to see two pictures of the same thing at the same time each with one of one's eyes so that the thing seems to be solid or three-dimensional.

stereoscopic /ˌsterɪəʊ'skɒpɪk/ *adj* seeing/seen three-dimensionally.

stereotype /'sterɪəʊˌtaɪp/ *c.n* **1** (often — *of s.o/ s.t*) fixed idea (of s.o/s.t) that one has and that influences all one's opinions about her/him/it, often wrongly: *Sarah does not fit the stereotype of the tired old grandmother; she's always busy.*

▷ *tr.v* **2** think of (s.o/s.t) as a stereotype(1): *It is unwise to stereotype people because they are all very different.*

sterile /'steraɪl/ *adj* **1** (of people, animals) who/ that cannot produce young. **2** (of land) that does not produce any crops. **3** that has no bacteria or other things that could be harmful in it: *Put a sterile dressing(2) on his wound.* **4** (*formal*) (of s.t one thinks, says etc) not containing anything new, interesting etc.

sterility /ste'rɪlɪtɪ/ *u.n* fact or state of being sterile.

sterilization, -isation /ˌsterɪlaɪ'zeɪʃən/ *u.n* fact of sterilizing or being sterilized.

'steri,lize, -ise *tr.v* make (s.o/s.t) sterile(1,3).

sterling /'stɜːlɪŋ/ *attrib.adj* **1** who/that one can trust completely; reliable; loyal: *sterling qualities.* **2** (*technical*) (of gold and silver) of the standard value or purity: *a sterling silver spoon.* *pound sterling* ⇒ pound¹.

▷ *u.n* **3** (*technical*) kind of money used in Britain, consisting of pounds (£) and pence (p).

stern¹ /stɜːn/ *adj* **1** severe; strict; keeping discipline strongly: *a stern teacher.* **2** severe; difficult to bear: *a stern test of a person's character.* **3** (of the way a person looks, speaks etc) showing that one is not pleased: *a stern word to a careless boy.*

'sternly adv. **sternness** /ˈstɜːnnɪs/ u.n.

stern² /stɜːn/ c.n back end of a ship or boat. Compare bow¹(1).

sternum /ˈstɜːnəm/ (pl -s or, less usu, sterna /ˈstɜːnə/) c.n (medical) breastbone.

steroid /ˈstɪərɔɪd/ c.n (also attrib) kind of chemical found in the human body and also used to strengthen muscles(1) etc: Steroids can be very dangerous if wrongly used and are not allowed by sports authorities(2).

stethoscope /ˈsteθəˌskəʊp/ c.n (medical) instrument used by a doctor for listening to a person's heart, lungs etc.

stetson /ˈstetsən/ c.n (also **'stetson ,hat**) kind of hat with a wide brim(2).

stevedore /ˈstiːvəˌdɔː/ c.n person whose job is to load and unload ships. Compare docker.

stew /stjuː/ n 1 c/u.n (also attrib) mixture of vegetables and often meat etc cooked together in a liquid: lamb/vegetable stew. **in a stew** (fig; informal) worried; anxious; not knowing what to do.
▷ tr/intr.v 2 cook (s.t) slowly on a low heat in liquid, usu with the lid on the container. **stew in one's own juice** (fig; informal) suffer as a result of one's own (unwise or stupid) actions.

stewed adj (usu attrib) **1** ⇨ stew(2): stewed meat. **2** (of tea) allowed to stand or continue boiling slowly, for a long time before it is poured out so that it becomes very strong and bitter. **3** (informal) drunk(1).

steward /ˈstjuːəd/ c.n **1** male member of the crew of a ship or plane who serves and looks after the passengers. **2** man who does similar work in a club: a wine steward. **3** man who looks after the supply of food in a club, college etc. **4** man who helps to organize and control a meeting, e.g a sports meeting or conference. **5** man whose job is to look after a house, farm etc for s.o else.

stewardess /ˈstjuːədɪs/ c.n woman who does the same work as a steward(1).

'steward,ship u.n job or duties of a steward(5).

stick¹ /stɪk/ c.n **1** (piece of a) stem of a tree that has been cut so that it can be used for burning, building, supporting one while one is walking or standing etc. **2** (usu — of s.t) piece (of s.t) that looks like a stick¹(1): carrot cut into sticks; a stick of celery. **get (hold of) the wrong end of the stick** (fig) have the wrong idea about what s.o has said, a situation etc. **give s.o stick** (fig; informal) scold or criticize s.o. **walking stick** ⇨ walk.

sticks pl.n **1** def.pl.n (often out in the —) (informal) place right out in the country away from towns etc. **2** pl.n (usu — of furniture) furniture that is worth very little.

stick² /stɪk/ v (p.t,p.p stuck /stʌk/) : tr.v (often — s.t in(to s.t)) push (s.t) (in(to s.t)) so that it makes a hole. **2** tr.v (usu — s.t on(to s.t); — s.t over s.t; — s.t together) cause s.t to become fixed (to s.t) by using glue etc: Stick the stamps (on) here, please. ⇨ unstuck. **3** intr.v (often — to s.t) remain fixed (to s.t) by glue etc. ⇨ non-stick. **4** intr.v (often — in s.t) become fixed (in s.t) so that one cannot move it: My shoe is stuck in the door. The door has stuck. ⇨ unstuck. **5** tr.v (usu — s.t in, on, under etc s.t) (informal) put s.t (in, on etc s.t) usu in a quick informal way: 'Where shall I put my umbrella?' 'Just stick it behind that

door.' **6** tr.v (usu s.o can't — s.o/s.t; s.o can't — doing s.t) (informal) bear (s.o/s.t, doing s.t); be able to put up with (s.o/s.t, doing s.t): He had to leave Greece because he couldn't stick the heat.

stick around (slang) stay/wait s.w.

stick at nothing be ready and willing to do anything, however bad and wrong.

stick at s.t continue doing s.t even though it is difficult, boring etc.

stick by s.o/s.t continue to support s.o/s.t.

stick in s.o's mind ⇨ mind(n). **stick in s.o's throat** ⇨ throat.

stick out for s.t refuse to stop demanding s.t; insist on getting s.t. **stick out a mile** ⇨ mile. **stick s.t out** manage to continue s.t right to the end: You'll have to stick the course out because you need the qualification(2). **stick (s.t) out (from/of s.t)** (cause (s.t) to) go out further than the rest of the thing it is part of: The doctor told the little girl to stick her tongue out. Joe's ears stick out a lot.

stick to s.o/s.t not leave s.o/s.t. **stick to s.t** not stop doing s.t, usu s.t difficult or boring.

stick together remain together or united.

stick up a bank etc (informal) (try to) rob a bank etc using a gun. ⇨ stick-up.

stick with s.o/s.t remain loyal to s.o/s.t.

'sticker c.n (informal) label(1) etc that one sticks²(2) on s.t to give certain information: I always have stickers with my name and address on all my luggage.

'stickily adv in a sticky way.

'stickiness u.n fact or state of being sticky.

'sticking ,plaster ⇨ plaster(3).

'stick-in-the-,mud c.n (derog; informal) person who is not able, willing, to accept new ideas or to change her/his opinions.

'stick-,on attrib.adj that is made for sticking (⇨ stick²(2)) onto s.t: a stick-on label(1).

'stick-,up c.n (informal) example of sticking up a bank etc.

'sticky adj (-ier, -iest) **1** (often — with s.t) that sticks²(3) (because of s.t): a sticky sweet; fingers sticky with jam. **2** (informal) awkward; difficult: She was in a sticky position. **3** (often — about s.t) (informal) not helpful or willing (to do s.t). **come to a sticky end** (fig; informal) die unpleasantly; finish by being ruined etc. **on a sticky wicket** ⇨ wicket.

stickler /ˈstɪklə/ c.n (usu — for s.t) person who strongly demands (s.t) from herself/himself and others: Sharon is very successful because she is a stickler for accurate work.

stiff /stɪf/ adj **1** difficult to bend: stiff cardboard. **2** (of muscles(1) etc) painfully tight. Opposite loose. **3** firm; able to stand up by itself: You have to beat the cream till it is stiff. **4** difficult: a stiff test of one's driving skill; stiff competition. **5** not friendly; formal: He gave me a stiff bow and then turned away. **6** (informal) too much; excessive: stiff prices. **7** (of an alcoholic(1) drink) containing a lot of alcohol and not much water etc. **bore s.o stiff** ⇨ bore¹(v). **scare s.o stiff** ⇨ scare(v).
▷ c.n **8** (slang) dead person.

'stiffen tr/intr.v (often — (s.o/s.t) up) (cause (s.o/s.t) to) become stiff(er)(1–5).

'stiffener c.n thing that stiffens s.o/s.t.

'stiffly adv in a stiff(5) way.

'stiffness u.n.

stifle /ˈstaɪfl/ v **1** tr/intr.v (cause (s.o) to) stop breathing normally, usu because of bad air, smoke etc. **2** *tr.v* stop (s.t) being said, written, done etc: *The new government tried to stifle free thought.*

'stifling *adj* (often — *hot*) very hot and close(6).

stigma /'stɪgmə/ *c.n* **1** stain(3) on the reputation of s.o/s.t; shameful thing said, thought etc about s.o/s.t. **2** (*science*) top end of the stem that comes out of the place where seeds are formed in a flower and on which the pollen falls.

stigmatize, -ise /'stɪgmətaɪz/ *tr.v* (often — *s.o/s.t as s.t*) put one or more stigmas(1) on s.o/s.t (by calling her/him/it s.t).

stile /staɪl/ *c.n* place with (usu) two steps where one can climb over a fence or wall in the country.

stiletto /stɪ'letəʊ/ *c.n* (*pl -s*) **1** small dagger. **2** (*informal*) = stiletto heel.

sti,letto 'heel *c.n* tall very thin heel on a woman's shoe: *We do not allow stiletto heels in here because they damage the floor.*

still¹ /stɪl/ *adv* **1** continuing up to the present moment or the moment shown by the tense² of the verb: *The weather is still warm although it is October. Don't worry; there will still be plenty of food left when we reach the hall.* Compare already, yet. **2** in spite of that; however; nevertheless: *That was a slow journey; still, it was quite comfortable so we mustn't complain.* **3** (usu — *bigger* etc; — *more/less beautiful* etc) even, yet(3) (bigger etc): *More people arrived and still more.* **worse still** ⇒ worse.

still² /stɪl/ *adj* **1** not moving; not making any noise: *Keep still or I can't do your buttons up.* **2** without any wind: *a still evening.* **3** calm; peaceful; quiet: *a still mind.* **4** (of a drink) without gas bubbles(2) in it; not fizzy. Opposite sparkling. **hold still** stay still(1).

▷ *c.n* **5** single scene from a film in the form of a photograph or slide. (*in*) *the still of s.t* (during) the quietness of s.t, e.g the evening.

▷ *tr.v* **6** cause (s.t) to become still²(1-3).

'still,born *adj* born dead: *a stillborn child.*

,still 'life *c/u.n* (*pl still lifes*) painting of things, usu flowers and fruit, not people or animals.

'stillness *u.n*.

still³ /stɪl/ *c.n* device for distilling(2) liquid (to make alcoholic(1) drinks).

'still,room *c.n* room in which there is a still³.

stilt /stɪlt/ *c.n* (usu *pl*) one of a pair of usu wooden poles that have supports for one's feet so that one can walk with one's feet raised some distance from the ground.

stilted /'stɪltɪd/ *adj* (*derog*) (of one's way of speaking, writing) very formal and unnatural; pompous.

Stilton /'stɪltən/ *u.n* (also *attrib*) kind of soft usu English cheese with green bits in it: *Stilton cheese.*

stimulate /'stɪmjʊ,leɪt/ *tr.v* cause (s.o/s.t) to become more active, energetic etc or to do s.t: *Rubbing the body stimulates the circulation(1) of the blood. A cut in taxes stimulates demand for goods.*

'stimulant *c.n* medicine, advice etc that stimulates (s.o/s.t). Compare depressant.

,stimu'lation /,stɪmjʊ'leɪʃən/ *u.n*.

stimulus /'stɪmjʊləs/ *c.n* (*pl -es, stimuli* /'stɪmjʊ,laɪ/) thing that stimulates (s.o/s.t).

sting /stɪŋ/ *c.n* **1** sharp part of a bee etc used for attack and/or defence by injecting a painful liquid or poison into the skin. **2** substance in the hairs of nettles(1) etc that causes pain when one touches them. **3** result of a sting(1,2) that can be felt. **4** feeling like a sting(3) but not caused by a sting(1,2): *the sting of salt spray*(1) *against one's face.* *a sting in s.t's tail* an unpleasant part of s.t that was expected to be pleasant: *You can have the money you asked for but there's a sting in the tail — you'll have to work extra hours for it.*

▷ *v* (*p.t,p.p stung* /stʌŋ/) **5** *tr.v* hurt (s.o, an animal) with a sting(1,2). **6** *intr.v* be able to sting(5). **7** *intr.v* hurt as (if) a result of being stung (⇒ sting(5)): *My eyes are stinging.* **sting s.o** (*for s.t*) (*slang*) charge s.o too much money (for s.t).

'stinging ,nettle *c.n* common kind of nettle(1) that stings(6).

'sting,ray *c.n* kind of big flat fish that has a strong sting(1) in its tail.

stingy /'stɪndʒɪ/ *adj* (*-ier, -iest*) (*derog*) **1** not generous; mean¹(1); miserly. **2** not big or generous enough: *a stingy offer.*

'stingily *adv*. **'stinginess** *u.n*.

stink /stɪŋk/ *n* **1** *c.n* (often — *of s.t*) strong bad smell (caused by s.t). **2** *sing.n* (*informal*) trouble: *She caused a stink at work.*

▷ *intr.v* (*p.t stank* /stæŋk/, *p.p stunk* /stʌŋk/) **3** (often — *of s.t*) have a stink(1) ((like that) of s.t). **4** (*fig; slang*) be very bad: *That idea stinks.* **stink s.t out** make a place smell very bad.

'stinker *c.n* (*derog; slang*) very unpleasant person or thing.

'stinking *attrib.adj* **1** who/that smells very bad. **2** (*slang*) that stinks(4).

▷ *adv* **3** (*informal*) very: *stinking hot; stinking rich.*

stint /stɪnt/ *c.n* **1** (often *do a/one's —*) fixed/ limited share of s.t, usu work. **without stint** without limit: *His high opinion of her work was without stint.* ⇒ unstinting.

▷ *tr.v* **2** (often — *oneself/s.o of s.t*) be stingy(1) with (s.o/s.t): *We don't need to stint ourselves of butter; there's plenty.* **stint on s.t** be stingy(1) about s.t: *Don't stint on the jam; I like it thick.*

stipend /'staɪpend/ *c.n* salary etc paid to a priest, magistrate etc.

stipendiary /staɪ'pendɪərɪ/ *adj* who is paid a stipend: *a stipendiary magistrate.*

stipple /'stɪpl/ *tr/intr.v* make (a picture) using dots and not lines.

stipulate /'stɪpjʊ,leɪt/ *tr.v* (*formal*) demand (s.t) as a condition for doing etc s.t: *We stipulated that the painter should give everything three coats.*

stipulation /,stɪpjʊ'leɪʃən/ *c/u.n* thing that is stipulated. **make a stipulation** (*that . . .*) stipulate (that . . .).

stir¹ /stɜː/ *c.n* **1** (often *give s.t a —*) example of stirring (⇒ stir¹(2)). **cause a stir** cause trouble, excitement, interest etc.

▷ *v* (*-rr-*) **2** *tr.v* move (a liquid, powder etc) round, with a spoon etc to mix it: *If you stir your tea the sugar will melt more quickly.* **3** *tr/intr.v* (cause (s.o, an animal) to) move, wake, change position: *She waited until the children were stirring before making the tea.* **4** *tr.v* make (s.t) move about: *The wind began to stir the leaves.* **5** *tr.v* excite (s.o/s.t); make (s.o/s.t) feel s.t: *Her paintings are stirring a lot of interest.* **stir s.o's, the blood** excite s.o. **stir s.t into s.t** add s.t to s.t and stir¹(2) while putting it in: *Stir the flour into the milk.* **stir s.t up** (usu — *up trouble*) cause (trouble etc).

'stirring *attrib.adj* that stirs[1](5)/excites: *stirring music; a stirring speech.*

stir[2] /stɜː/ *u.n* (*slang*) (often *in* —) prison.

stirrup /'stɪrəp/ *c.n* **1** piece of metal shaped like an upside-down U with a bar across the bottom for a rider to put her/his foot into so that she/ he can ride steadily on a horse. **2** (*technical*) one of the bones inside one's ear that helps one to hear.

stitch /stɪtʃ/ *c.n* **1** (in sewing) act of putting a needle and thread into cloth etc in one place and pulling it out in another place so that a length of thread is left in; act of putting a special kind of thread into a person's skin to mend a cut. **2** length of thread left in s.t after a stitch(1): *That cut will need a few stitches.* **3** (in knitting) act of putting the wool etc round the needle once; length of wool etc round the needle. **4** *c/ u.n* particular way of sewing or knitting: *chain stitch*; ribbed *stitch.* **5** *c.n* sharp pain in one's side, usu after running. **be in stitches** (*fig; informal*) laugh very much. **drop a stitch** (in knitting) let one of the stitches(3) come off the needle. **have s.o in stitches** (*fig; informal*) make s.o laugh very much. **not have a stitch on** (*informal*) be completely naked(1). **not have a stitch** (**to wear**) (*informal*) not have any clothes that one likes or can wear. **A stitch in time saves nine** (*proverb*) It is better to do s.t quickly before it gets worse and then needs more work. **put a stitch in s.t** stitch(6) s.t with one stitch(2).
▷ *tr/intr.v* **6** sew (s.t); put stitches(2) in (s.t). **stitch s.t up** (*fig; informal*) successfully finish organizing a plan, business deal etc.

stoat /stəʊt/ *c.n* kind of small thin brown animal that catches and eats rabbits etc. ⇨ ermine(1), weasel.

stock /stɒk/ *attrib.adj* **1** (most) often used or to be found: *Our manager's stock reply to all difficult questions is 'I'm sorry but I can't help you.' If you aren't a stock size you will find it very difficult to buy a ready-made(2) shirt here.*
▷ *n* **2** *c.n* (often — *of s.t*) supply (of s.t); quantity/ number (of s.t) ready to be used: *We always keep a good stock of candles in case the electricity fails.* **3** *c/u.n* quantity/number of goods ready to be sold. **4** *u.n* animals kept on a farm etc, esp ones that are used for breeding(1). ⇨ livestock. **5** *u.n* family line of a person/animal of the kind shown by an adj etc: *He comes of good stock.* **6** *u.n* liquid made by boiling bones, food that has been left over etc until the juices have gone into the water, used for making soups etc. **7** *c.n* main part of a plant, tree etc onto which one can graft(3) other pieces or which one can use as a cutting(4). **8** *c.n* kind of flower grown in gardens for its sweet smell and pretty flowers. **9** *c.n* piece of wood that is the handle, support etc of s.t, e.g a gun. **10** *c/u.n* capital(8) of a company which is divided into shares(3). **11** *c/u.n* money lent to a government (for a certain length of time) at a fixed rate of interest. **in stock** ready to be sold. Opposite out of stock. **laughing stock** ⇨ laugh. **lock, stock and barrel** ⇨ lock(*n*). **out of stock** (**of s.t**) all sold; sold out: *I'm sorry but we're out of stock of size 10 at the moment.* Opposite in stock. **rolling stock** ⇨ roll. **take stock** count the

stock(3) to check what has been sold and what needs to be ordered etc. ⇨ stocktaking. **take stock** (**of the situation**) examine s.t in order to be able to decide what to do about it.
▷ *tr.v* **12** get/keep a stock(2,3) of (s.t). **stock s.t up** (**with s.t**) put a stock(2,3) of s.t in s.t. **stock up** (**with s.t**) collect a good stock(2,3) of s.t.

'stock,breeder *c.n* person who breeds(2) stock(4).

'stock,broker *c.n* person who buys and sells stocks(10) and shares(3) as a job.

'stock,broking *u.n* work done by a stock-broker.

'stock ,cube *c.n* cube(2) that produces stock(6) when it is mixed in water.

stocked *adj badly*, *well* etc **stocked** (**with s.t**) having a bad/good etc stock(2,3) of s.t.

'stock ex,change *n* **1** *c/def.n* (often with capital **S** and **E**) place where stocks(10) and shares(3) are traded. **2** *def.n* this kind of trade.

'stock,holder *c.n* person who has stock(10); shareholder.

,stock-in-'trade *u.n* **1** stock(3) used for one's business. **2** (*fig*) things that one often does: *Joe never does any work; his stock-in-trade is getting rich women to support him.*

'stockist *c.n* person who stocks(12) s.t.

'stockman *c.n* (*pl -men*) man whose job is to look after animals on a farm.

'stock ,market *c/def.n* = stock exchange.

'stock,pile *c.n* **1** (often — *of s.t*) big stock(2,3) (of s.t) so that one will have enough when it is difficult to get later.
▷ *tr.v* **2** make a stockpile(1) of (s.t).

'stock,pot *c.n* container in which stock(6) is made or kept.

'stock,room *c.n* room in which stock(3) is stored.

'stock,taking *u.n* act of checking and/or listing stock(3).

'stock,yard *c.n* place where stock(4) is kept, usu only for a short time, e.g before being sold.

stockade /stɒˈkeɪd/ *c.n* wooden wall round a place so that it is difficult or impossible to attack it from the outside.

stockbreeder, stockbroker, stock cube, stock exchange, stockholder ⇨ stock.

stockily, stockiness ⇨ stocky.

stocking /'stɒkɪŋ/ *c.n* (often *pair of* —*s*) tight covering for a woman's foot and leg made of silk, wool, cotton etc and coming up higher than the knee. Compare sock[1], tights. **in one's stockinged feet** wearing stockings but no shoes: *Lisa is one and a half metres tall in her stockinged feet.*

stock-in-trade, stockist, stockman, stock market, stockpile, stockpot, stockroom ⇨ stock.

stocks /stɒks/ *pl.n* (*old use*) wooden frame with holes to hold one's feet so that one could not escape, used as a punishment.

stock-still /ˌstɒk ˈstɪl/ *adv* absolutely without moving: *standing stock-still.*

stocktaking ⇨ stock.

stocky /'stɒkɪ/ *adj* (*-ier*, *-iest*) (of a person's body) short, broad and strong. **'stockily** *adv*. **'stockiness** *u.n*.

stockyard ⇨ stock.

stodge /stɒdʒ/ *u.n* (*derog; informal*) **1** heavy, thick food that does not have much taste.

2 heavy, difficult subject that one is reading, learning etc.

'**stodginess** u.n fact of being stodgy.

'**stodgy** adj (-ier, -iest) (derog) **1** (of food) heavy, thick and without much taste. **2** (of books etc) difficult and boring. **3** (of a person) boring.

stoic /'stəʊɪk/ adj **1** (formal) patient and not showing signs of suffering, pain etc.
▷ c.n **2** (formal) person who is stoic.
'**stoical** adj = stoic(1).
'**stoically** adv. **stoicism** /'stəʊɪˌsɪzəm/ u.n.

stoke /stəʊk/ tr/intr.v (often — (s.t) up (with s.t)) put (more) coal etc in (a furnace etc) so that it can be used to give heat etc.
'**stoker** c.n person or machine who/that stokes s.t.

stole[1] /stəʊl/ c.n **1** piece of cloth, fur etc worn by women round their shoulders, usu for formal parties etc. **2** thing like a stole[1](1) worn by priests in some Christian(1) churches.

stole[2] /stəʊl/ p.t of steal.

stolen /'stəʊlən/ p.p of steal.

stolid /'stɒlɪd/ adj (often derog) always calm even when other people would be excited; not showing one's feelings (often because of a dull personality).
stolidity /stɒ'lɪdɪtɪ/ u.n. '**stolidly** adv. '**stolidness** u.n.

stomach /'stʌmək/ c.n **1** part of the inside of one's body in which the food one eats is digested(3). **2** (informal) part of the front of one's body below one's lungs: Look at that man's fat stomach! (**do s.t**) **on an empty stomach** (work, play, run etc) without having eaten anything. **have no stomach for s.t** (fig) not want/like s.t, e.g fighting.
▷ tr.v **3** be able to eat (s.t) without trouble: I can't stomach a lot of fat. **4** accept (s.t) willingly: I can't stomach rudeness. ⇒ have no stomach for s.t.
'**stomach,ache** c/u.n pain in (and around) one's stomach.
'**stomachful** c.n (often — of s.t) as much (of s.t) as one can stomach(4).
'**stomach,pump** c.n device used by doctors to pump the food out of a person's stomach through a tube when he/she has swallowed s.t dangerous.

stomp /stɒmp/ intr.v (often — about) (informal) walk putting one's feet down heavily. ⇒ stamp(11).

stone /stəʊn/ n **1** u.n (also attrib) hard natural material found in/on the earth and formed by the pressing together of sand etc; material of which rocks are made. **2** c.n piece of stone(1) either found naturally or shaped by s.o. ⇒ gravestone, milestone, millstone, stepping-stone. **3** c.n = precious stone. **4** c.n thing that is like a stone(2) but is not made of stone(1): Some fruits such as cherries have a stone in them. Compare pip[1]. Sometimes people get stones in their bladder(1) or kidneys(1). **leave no stone unturned** (fig) do absolutely everything one can (in order to do s.t). **rolling stone** ⇒ roll.
▷ tr.v **5** throw stones at (s.o, an animal): The cruel children stoned the cat to death. **6** take the stones(4) out of (fruit).
'**Stone ,Age** def.n (also attrib) time many centuries ago when the only tools and weapons people had were made of stone. ⇒ Iron Age.

'**stoneless** adj (of fruit) not having any stones(4) in it.

'**stone,mason** c.n person who cuts stone(1) into shapes. Compare sculptor.

'**stone's ,throw** sing.n (usu a — from s.w) very short distance (from s.w).

'**stone,wall** tr/intr.v (formal) try to prevent or delay (s.t) by wasting time; prevent (s.o) from making progress, e.g by not giving necessary information.

'**stone,ware** u.n pottery(2) made from a kind of very hard clay or from clay with flint(1) in it.

'**stone,work** u.n parts of a building made of, and/or decorated with, stone(1).

'**stonily** adv in a stony(2) way.

'**stoniness** u.n fact or state of being stony(1,2).

'**stony** adj (-ier, -iest) **1** having stones(2) in/on it: a stony path. **2** showing no pity or other warm feelings; hard-hearted. **stony broke** ⇒ broke(adj).

stood /stʊd/ p.t of stand.

stooge /stuːdʒ/ c.n **1** actor/actress who pretends to be stupid so that another actor/actress can make fun of her/him on the stage. **2** (derog) person who does everything that s.o else tells her/him to do so that he/she seems stupid.

stool[1] /stuːl/ c.n small seat that has no back or arms. ⇒ footstool. Compare bench(1). **fall between two stools** (fig) fail to get either of two things that one could have got: Joe fell between two stools by refusing our help and then being unable to do the job himself.

stool[2] /stuːl/ c.n (formal; technical) faeces.

stool pigeon /'stuːl ˌpɪdʒɪn/ c.n person, usu a criminal, acting as a decoy(1) to help the police etc catch (other) criminals.

stoop /stuːp/ c.n **1** position of one's body in which one's head and shoulders are (always) bent forward and down: Many old people have, suffer from, a stoop.
▷ v **2** tr/intr.v (cause (one's head and/or shoulders) to) bend forward and down. **3** have a stoop(1). (**not**) **stoop to** (**doing**) **s.t** (not) be so shameless or lacking in self-respect as to do s.t.

stop /stɒp/ c.n **1** change from a moving state to a state where one is not moving. ⇒ non-stop. **2** length of time during which one is not moving, travelling etc: We had an hour's stop at Bombay. **3** place where buses etc regularly pick passengers up and put them down. Compare station(1). **4** = full stop. **5** device in a musical instrument that one moves in order to change the pitch(4). **6** row of pipes in an organ that allows one to make a certain set of notes. **come to a stop** = stop(9). **pull out all the stops** (**to do s.t**) (fig) do absolutely everything one can (so as to try to do s.t).
▷ v (-pp-) **7** tr/intr.v (cause (s.o/s.t) to) change from a moving state to a state where he/she/it is not moving. **8** tr/intr.v (often — (s.o/s.t (from)) doing s.t)) (make (s.o/s.t)) not do s.t (any more): Has it stopped snowing yet? Our teacher has stopped us using dictionaries in class. **9** tr/intr.v (cause (s.t) to) end, not continue (any more), sometimes only for a short time: The snow has stopped at last. This shop has stopped its deliveries to the house. The gas company has stopped our gas supply till we pay our bill. **10** tr.v (often — s.t up) block (s.t); fill s.t so that nothing can get through. Opposite

unstop. **11** *intr.v* (often — *to* s.t) stay, remain (for s.t); not go away (before s.t): *Is Mary stopping to lunch?* **12** *tr.v* put a finger on (a string or hole of a musical instrument) so as to produce a particular note.

stop a cheque ⇒ cheque.

stop at nothing (to do s.t) be ready and willing to do anything, however bad or evil (in order to get s.t etc).

stop by/round visit s.o.

stop dead ⇒ dead(*adv*).

stop off/over stop during a trip etc, usu to visit s.o/s.t.

stop the rot ⇒ rot(*n*).

stop round ⇒ stop by.

stop short ⇒ short(*adv*).

'stop,cock *c.n* kind of tap/valve(1) that turns the water in a pipe on and off.

'stop,gap *c.n* (also *attrib*) person or thing who/ that takes the place of s.o/s.t else for a short time when he/she/it is ill, absent etc.

'stop,over *c.n* short stop(2) during a journey.

'stoppable *adj* that can be stopped. Opposite unstoppable.

'stoppage *n* (often — *of* s.t) **1** *c.n* state of (s.t) being stopped(7,10). **2** act of stopping(9) (s.t): *stoppage of wages until damage has been paid for.* **3** *c.n* strike(*n*): *a stoppage at work.*

'stopper *c.n* thing put in the neck of a bottle etc to stop liquid etc coming out. Compare cork(2).

put the stopper(s) on s.t (*informal*) stop s.t happening, becoming publicly known etc.

,stop 'press *def.n* (also *attrib*) fresh news added to a newspaper after the rest has already been printed.

'stop,watch *c.n* special watch that enables one to measure the exact time taken by s.o/s.t, e.g the winner of a race.

store /stɔː/ *c.n* **1** (often — *of* s.t) amount or number (of s.t) that has/have been collected for future use: *In summer we make a store of bottled fruit for the winter.* **2** room etc in which stores(1) are kept. **3** big shop: *a clothing store.* ⇒ chain store, department store, drugstore. **4** (US) shop, even a small one. **5** (often — *of* s.t) collection, number or amount (of s.t): *Mandy has a store of funny stories that she tells at parties.* **(keep s.t) in store (for s.t)** (keep s.t) ready to be used (for s.t). **set (great etc) store by s.o/s.t** consider s.o/s.t to be (very etc) important, useful etc.

▷ *tr.v* **6** (often — s.t *up*) put/keep (s.t) in a store(1,2). **7** (often — s.t *with* s.t) put stores(1) (of s.t) in (s.t), e.g a room; stock(12) (s.t) (with supplies of s.t).

storage /'stɔːrɪdʒ/ *u.n* **1** fact of storing(6) s.t. **2** money paid to s.o for storing(6) s.t. **in storage** being stored(6): *Our furniture is in storage until we find a house.*

'store,house *c.n* (*pl -s* /-,haʊzɪz/) **1** (part of a) building where things are stored(6). **2** (*fig*) (often *a* — *of information* etc) person or place who/that contains a lot of information etc.

'store,keeper *c.n* **1** person who looks after a store(1,2). **2** shopkeeper.

'store,room *c.n* room in which one stores(6) things.

stores *n* **1** *pl.n* things that are stored(6), often by the armed forces; supplies. **2** *def/unique n* (*military*) place where supplies are kept: *the quartermaster's stores.*

storey /'stɔːrɪ/ *c.n* one level of a building; floor(3): *the top storey of our house.*

-storeyed *adj* having the number of storeys shown in the first part of the word: *a three-storeyed building.*

stork /stɔːk/ *c.n* kind of bird, usu white, with very long legs, a long neck and/or a long beak.

storm /stɔːm/ *n* **1** *c/u.n* bad weather in which there is a lot of wind, rain, thunder etc. **2** *c.n* (*technical*) weather condition between whole gale and hurricane. **3** *sing.n* (often *a* — *of* s.t) sudden violent showing (of feeling): *a storm of anger; a storm of* abuse(1) *from angry customers.* **a storm in a teacup** (*fig*) an argument, fight etc about s.t that is not at all important. **take s.t by storm** (a) conquer s.t, e.g an enemy position, by a sudden violent attack. (b) be very successful in winning the admiration of s.t: *Her new play is taking its audiences by storm.*

▷ *v* **4** *tr.v* attack (s.t) violently. Compare take s.t by storm(a). **5** *intr.v* (of wind) blow violently. **6** *intr.v* (often — *at* s.o/s.t) behave (towards s.o/s.t) or speak (to s.o or about s.t) very angrily.

-storm *c.n* storm of the kind shown by the first part of the word: *a sandstorm; a snowstorm; a thunderstorm.*

'storm,bound *adj* prevented by a storm(1) from travelling.

'storm ,centre *c.n* **1** place that is the centre of a storm(1). **2** (*fig*) place or person who is at the centre of troubles.

'storm ,cloud *c.n* **1** dark cloud that makes one think that a storm(1) is coming. **2** (usu *pl*) (*fig*) thing that makes one think that s.t dangerous is coming.

'stormily *adv* in a stormy way.

'stormy *adj* (*-ier, -iest*) **1** having a storm(1) or storms: *stormy weather; a stormy night.* **2** angry, upset etc in a noisy way: *a stormy argument.*

story /'stɔːrɪ/ *c.n* (*pl -ies*) **1** (often — *of* s.o/s.t) things that a person says or writes (about real or imaginary people and/or happenings): *tell a story about three bears; a love story* (i.e one about people who love each other). **2** lie[1](1). **a likely story** excuse, information etc that is not easy to believe. **a sob story** ⇒ sob. **a tall story** a daring lie[1](1). **tell stories** (a) ⇒ story(1). (b) tell lies[1](1). **the same old story** the same excuse that s.o has used before.

'story,book *c.n* (also *attrib*) book of children's stories, usu with happy endings and often about magic(3) and fairies: *Their marriage was a story-book ending to all their troubles.*

'story ,line *c.n* = plot(2).

'story,teller *c.n* **1** person who tells stories, usu to children. **2** liar.

stout[1] /staʊt/ *adj* **1** (of a person, (part of) her/his body) fat. **2** (of a person, her/his character etc) brave; not giving in easily. **3** (of a thing) strong; that does not break easily: *a stout pair of shoes for walking.*

,stout-'hearted *adj* (*literary*) = stout[1](2).

'stoutly *adv*. **'stoutness** *u.n*.

stout[2] /staʊt/ *u.n* kind of strong dark beer.

stove[1] /stəʊv/ *c.n* **1** device for cooking things on, using wood, coal, gas or electricity. Compare cooker(1). **2** similar thing for heating a room, water etc: *Light the stove and we'll soon be warm.* ⇒ heater.

'stove,pipe *c.n* pipe that carries the smoke away from the inside of a stove.

stove² /stəʊv/ *p.t,p.p* of stave.

stow /stəʊ/ *tr.v* (often — *s.t away*) put (s.t) (away) in a place where it will not be in the way. **stow away** hide on a ship or plane so as to make a journey secretly, usu so as not to have to pay.

'stowage *u.n* **1** fact of stowing s.t. **2** space in which things can be stowed, usu on a ship. **3** cost of stowing things, usu on a ship.

'stowa,way *c.n* person who stows away.

straddle /'strædl/ *tr/intr.v* sit on (s.t) with one leg on one side and the other leg on the other side, of (s.t).

strafe /streɪf/ *tr.v* (of a plane) shoot at (s.t, usu s.t that is on the ground) from a low altitude.

straggle /'strægl/ *intr.v* **1** spread out in an untidy, usu long and narrow, shape/way: *the straggling houses of a small village.* **2** fail to remain with the rest of one's group, usu by not moving fast enough: *Come on children, don't straggle or you may get lost!*

'straggler *c.n* person or animal who/that straggles(2): *The teacher followed behind encouraging the stragglers to hurry up.*

'straggly *adj* (-ier, -iest) that straggles(1): *with long straggly hair.*

straight /streɪt/ *adj* **1** that follows the course/line that is the shortest distance from one end to the other: *a straight road; a dancer with a nice straight back.* **2** (with the sides) vertical or with the bottom horizontal: *Wait a moment, your tie isn't straight.* **3** tidy; arranged as it should be: *Will you please put things straight in your bedroom before you go out.* **4** honest; not trying to hide anything: *He is very straight. I want straight answers to my questions.* **5** correct; without any mistakes in it: *Are your accounts straight yet?* **6** (in the performing arts, e.g plays or films) serious; of the traditionally accepted kind. **7** (of an alcoholic(1) drink) without any water etc added; neat(5): *He was drinking straight gins.* **be straight with s.o** tell s.o the truth. **keep a straight face** ⇒ face(*n*). **put/set s.o straight; put/set the record straight** record²(*n*).

▷ *adv* **8** in a straight(1) way: *Sit up straight!* **9** without waiting, taking the shortest way and without doing anything else meanwhile: *I'm going straight to London after breakfast.* **come/go straight to the point** say what one wants to say without any delays or irrelevant talk. **get s.t, it etc straight** (*informal*) understand s.t/it clearly: *You'd better get this straight – I don't like you.* **give it to s.o straight** tell s.o s.t (usu s.t unpleasant or critical) in a completely frank way. **go straight** (*informal*) stop being a criminal and start being honest. **straight away** ⇒ straightaway. **straight off** immediately. **straight out** without delay and without trying to hide anything: *say 'no' straight out.* ⇒ straight-out. **tell s.o (s.t) straight** (*informal*) = give it to s.o straight.

▷ *c.n* **10** straight(1) part of s.t, e.g a race track: *The horses are coming into the last straight now!*

,straight and 'narrow *def.n* **on the straight and narrow** behaving in an honest way, usu after having been dishonest. Compare go straight.

,straighta'way *adv* (also **,straight a'way**) immediately; without waiting at all: *Please come straightaway.*

,straighten *tr/intr.v* (often — (*s.o/s.t*) *up*) (cause (s.o/s.t) to) become straight(er)(1–3). **straighten s.o out** (*informal*) give s.o the necessary information about s.t important. **straighten s.t out** make s.t straight(1–3,5).

,straight 'fight *c.n* honest fight, without any cheating, when trying to get elected to s.t.

,straight'forward *adj* **1** honest; not hiding anything: *a straightforward answer.* **2** simple; not difficult to do, understand etc: *a straightforward job.*

,straight'laced *adj* (*derog*) having too narrow ideas about what is morally right and wrong.

'straightness *u.n.*

,straight-'out *attrib.adj* (*informal*) that is made or given straight out: *I want straight-out answers to my questions.*

strain¹ /streɪn/ *n* **1** *c/u.n* (often — *on s.t*) force that pulls/stretches (s.t). **2** *c.n* state of being subjected to a strain(1). **3** *c/u.n* (often (*put*) *a* — *on s.o*; — *s.o's body, mind* etc) difficult and therefore painful or worrying demand on (a person, her/his body, mind etc): *Jim's illness put a great strain on his family.* **4** *c/u.n* damage to part of one's body or mind caused by a strain(3). Compare sprain. (**be**) **under strain** (be) suffering from strain(3).

▷ *tr.v* **5** pull/stretch (s.t) hard. ⇒ strain at s.t. **6** hurt (s.t, e.g a muscle(1)) as a result of a strain(2): *I've strained my elbow.* **7** separate (s.t) into its solid and its liquid parts, usu by using a strainer: *strain vegetables.* **strain against/at s.t** press hard on s.t. **strain one's ears** (**at s.t, to hear s.o/s.t**) try very hard to hear s.o/s.t. **strain one's eyes** (**to see s.o/s.t**) try very hard to see s.o/s.t. ⇒ eyestrain. **strain at s.t** pull s.t very hard, usu to get away: *The dog was straining at its lead.* **strain to do s.t** try very hard to do s.t, e.g to hear, see, understand, s.t.

strained *adj* **1** that has been strained(5,6). **2** tense'(2), usu because of being tired, worried etc. **3** (of a person's behaviour etc) not natural; very formal. **4** (of an explanation, excuse etc) not very probable; difficult to believe.

'strainer *c.n* kitchen device with holes in it, used for separating solid parts of s.t from the liquid parts. ⇒ colander, sieve.

strain² /streɪn/ *c.n* (often —*s of s.t*) **1** (often *pl* with a *sing* meaning) (*music*) sound, tune, note (of s.t): *We dined to the strains of Indian music.* **2** quality (of s.t) or tendency (towards s.t), sometimes one that is inherited(2): *strains of daring in his family.* **3** particular breed(1) (of animal or plant): *There are new strains of corn that produce bigger crops than before.* **in a (pleasant etc) strain** showing certain (e.g pleasant) characteristics(2): *'Do you receive many short stories in this strain?' 'Yes and also poems in a similar strain.'*

strait /streɪt/ *c.n* (with capital **S** in names) (usu *pl*) narrow stretch of water, usu joining two big areas of land: *France and England are separated by the Straits of Dover.*

'strait,jacket *c.n* **1** piece of clothing like a jacket(1) with long sleeves, used to prevent mad people from hurting themselves. **2** (*fig*) thing that prevents one doing what one wants to, should, do.

straits *pl.n* **1** = strait. **2** (usu *in bad, serious* etc —) (in) difficulties, often because of lack of money.

strand¹ /strænd/ *c.n* one of the number of threads or wires of s.t: *the strands of a rope.*

strand² /strænd/ *def.n* **1** (*poetry*) beach; shore.
▷ *tr.v* **2** cause (a ship) to run ashore.

'stranded *adj* **1** lying on a beach after having been stranded (⇒ strand²(2)). **2** (*fig*) in a position where one is helpless: *The sudden bus strike left us stranded in London that evening.*

strange /streɪndʒ/ *adj* **1** that it is difficult to believe or understand; that surprises one: *Fred told me a strange story about that house.* **2** that one has not seen, heard, been in etc before: *I don't sleep well in a strange bed.* **strange to relate** it is strange(1) to tell but . . . **strange to s.t** (*formal*) not used to s.t; not having any experience of s.t: *I am strange to this work so I'll be very slow at first.*

'strangely *adv* **1** in a strange(1) way. **2** (*often* — *enough*) it is strange(1) but . . .: *His wife soon left him but strangely enough he did not mind at all.*

'strangeness *u.n.*

'stranger *c.n* **1** person who one does not know, has not met before etc: *Children should be taught never to speak to strangers.* 'Have you met Linda before?' 'No, we're strangers.' **2** (*usu* — *to s.t*) person who has not been (to s.t), done (s.t), before: *'Could you tell me the way to the station?' 'I'm sorry but I'm a stranger here myself.' Peter is no stranger to acting; he was in several school plays.*

strangle /'stræŋgl/ *tr.v* **1** kill (s.o, an animal) by pressing her/his/its throat. **2** prevent (s.t) from growing, developing: *The weeds are strangling these young plants.*

'strangle,hold *c.n* (*often* get/have a — *on s.o/s.t*) **1** firm hold round s.o's neck. **2** (*fig*) strong control (of s.t) which often prevents it making progress etc.

strangulation /ˌstræŋgjʊ'leɪʃən/ *u.n* act of strangling (s.o/s.t) or fact of being strangled.

strap /stræp/ *c.n* **1** strip, narrow piece, of leather etc used to fasten or put round s.t, e.g a trunk(1).
▷ *tr.v* (-pp-) (*often* — *s.t up*) **2** fasten (s.t, e.g a trunk(1)) with one or more straps(1). **3** put bandages round (part of one's body that is hurt). **strap s.o/s.t in** put one or more straps(1) round s.o/s.t to stop her/him/it falling out or hitting against s.t esp while travelling.

'strapless *adj* (of a woman's dress etc) not having any straps(1) over the shoulders to support it.

'strapping *attrib.adj* big and strong: *a big strapping boy.*

strata /'strɑːtə/ *pl* of stratum.

stratagem /'strætədʒəm/ *c.n* clever plan or trick aimed at getting s.t one wants.

strategy /'strætədʒɪ/ *c/u.n* (*pl* -ies) **1** *c/u.n* (example of the) art of war or way of controlling and moving armed forces so as to get an advantage over the enemy. Compare tactics. **2** *c/u.n* way of arranging things in order to be successful against one's competitors, e.g in football, business, marriage: *Our strategy will increase sales and keep down costs.*

strategic /strə'tiːdʒɪk/ *adj* (also **stra'tegical**) that is part of (a) strategy.

stra'tegically *adv.*

strategist /'strætɪdʒɪst/ *c.n* person who has the skill of strategy.

stratosphere /'strætəˌsfɪə/ *unique/def.n* (*technical*) layer of air round our earth that begins where our atmosphere(1) ends, about 10 kilometres above the earth.

stratum /'strɑːtəm/ *c.n* (*pl* strata /'strɑːtə/) **1** (*technical*) layer(1) of rock or earth in the ground: *When digging out ancient cities, one has to be careful to keep the different strata from different periods(2) separate.* **2** (*formal*) class of people in society: *People from every stratum come to our meetings.*

stratification /ˌstrætɪfɪ'keɪʃən/ *u.n* **1** act of stratifying or state of being stratified (⇒ stratify). **2** way in which s.t is stratified (⇒ stratify).

stratified /'strætɪˌfaɪd/ *adj* arranged in strata. ⇒ stratum.

stratify /'strætɪˌfaɪ/ *tr/intr.v* (-ies, -ied) (cause (s.t) to) be arranged in strata. ⇒ stratum.

straw /strɔː/ *n* **1** *u.n* dry cut stems of corn etc, used for animals to sleep on and for making mats, hats etc. Compare hay. **2** *c.n* stem of straw(1). **3** *c.n* thin tube made of plastic, paper etc used for drinking through, usu out of a bottle or can. **a straw in the wind** (*fig*) a thing that gives one some idea of what is going to happen, what s.o is planning etc. **clutch at straws** (*fig*) try even the most unlikely and hopeless ways of saving oneself. **not care/give a straw (for s.o/s.t, what etc . . .)** not care at all (about s.o/s.t, what etc . . .): *I don't care a straw where Ted goes.* **not give a straw for s.o/s.t** not give anything of value for s.o/s.t: *I wouldn't give a straw for his chances of winning.* **not worth a straw** not worth the smallest amount: *His opinions aren't worth a straw.* **the last straw (that breaks the camel's back)** (*fig*) the one thing after many others that finally causes s.t unpleasant to happen.

'straw-,coloured *adj* (US **'straw-,colored**) pale yellow in colour.

ˌstraw 'poll/'vote *c.n* = unofficial opinion poll.

strawberry /'strɔːbərɪ/ *n* (*pl* -ies) **1** *c.n* (also *attrib*) soft red fruit with small yellow pips¹ on it: *strawberry jam.* **2** *c.n* (also *attrib*) plant on which strawberries(1) grow. **3** *u.n* (also *attrib*) colour of this fruit: *strawberry pink.*

stray /streɪ/ *attrib.adj* **1** (of an animal) that has been lost, abandoned(1) by, its owner(s) or the rest of its group: *stray cats and dogs.* **2** met with here and there by chance; scattered: *stray houses in the valley.*
▷ *c.n* **3** stray(1) animal. **4** person or thing who/that is not among other people/things where one would not expect to find her/him/it. **waif and stray** ⇒ waif.
▷ *intr.v* **5** (*often* — (*away*) *from s.o/s.t*) wander (away) (from s.o/s.t), often with the result that one is lost: *We strayed from the path and soon we were lost.* **6** (of a person's thoughts, words) leave the present subject and wander off into other ones.

streak /striːk/ *c.n* (*often* — *of s.t*) **1** thin line or band (of s.t, e.g colour or cloud): *streaks of white in the sky.* **2** quality/strain²(2) (of s.t) that is part of a person's character: *Sometimes even the people who seem the kindest can have a hidden streak of cruelty in them.* **losing/winning streak** length of time during which one loses/wins again and again.
▷ *v* **3** *tr.v* (*often* — *s.t with s.t*) put streaks(1) on (s.o/

s.t) (using s.t). **4** *intr.v* move very fast. **5** *intr.v* (*informal*) run fast in a public place with no clothes on the main parts of one's body.

'**streaker** *c.n* person who streaks(5).

'**streaky** *adj* (*-ier, -iest*) having streaks(1) in/on it.

,**streaky** '**bacon** *u.n* bacon that has streaks(1) of fat in the meat.

stream /striːm/ *c.n* **1** natural flow of water that is smaller than a river. Compare brook¹. **2** (often — *of s.t*) amount/number (of people, animals, things) moving along: *a stream of traffic across a bridge.* **3** (in a school) one of the levels into which children of the same age are divided according to how clever they are: *the top stream in history.* **a stream of abuse** ⇒ abuse(*n*). (**go**) **against/with the stream** (**a**) (go) in the opposite/same direction as the water is flowing. (**b**) (*fig*) (behave/think) in the opposite way to, the same way as, most other people. (**be**) **on stream** (*technical*) (of oil from a well etc) (be) in production. **come on stream** begin to be in production.

▷ *v* **4** *intr.v* (of water etc (in s.t)) flow strongly: *Smoke makes my eyes stream.* **5** *intr.v* (often — *in*(to), *out* (*of*) etc *s.t*) move all together (into etc s.t): *Look at all those people streaming in*(*to the cinema*). **6** *tr.v* (of students in a school) put (s.o) into streams(3).

'**streamer** *c.n* long narrow piece of paper, cloth etc used for decorating buildings, boats etc, usu on special occasions.

'**stream,line** *tr.v* **1** make (a car, ship etc) able to move fast by reducing its resistance to air/water. **2** make (a business, factory etc) more efficient by using fewer staff, less machinery etc to do the same amount of, more, work.

street /striːt/ *c.n* (also *attrib*) (with capital **S** in names) (*written abbr* St) road in a town or village that has houses, shops etc along one or both sides: *Regent Street. My house is in a small street.* **be on the streets** (**a**) have no home. (**b**) be a prostitute. **the man in the street** ⇒ man(*n*). **not in the same street** (**as s.o/s.t**) (*fig*) not at all as good (as s.o/s.t); not in the same class (as s.o/s.t). **streets ahead** (**of s.o/s.t**) (*fig*) very much better (than s.o/s.t). (**right**) **up s.o's street** (exactly) what s.o wants or is interested in. **walk the streets** = be on the streets(b).

'**street,car** *c.n* (US) = tram.

'**street,walker** *c.n* = prostitute.

strength(en) ⇒ strong.

strenuous /'strenjuəs/ *adj* that needs/shows a lot of effort, energy(1) etc.

'**strenuously** *adv.* '**strenuousness** *u.n.*

streptomycin /,streptə'maɪsɪn/ *u.n* (*medical*) kind of strong drug(1) used to kill harmful bacteria.

stress /stres/ *c/u.n* **1** force that puts pressure on s.o/s.t: *the stresses put on a floor by the people walking on it; the stresses put on a person by the pressures of modern life.* **2** (*technical*) amount of strength or emphasis(2) put on a syllable of a word to show how important it is or how strongly it should be pronounced: *In this dictionary stress is shown by* ' (*primary stress*) *and* , (*secondary stress*). (**lay/put**) **stress on s.t** (put) special emphasis(1) on s.t; stress(3) s.t. **under stress** suffering/feeling stress(1).

▷ *tr.v* **3** show that (s.t) is particularly important;

emphasize(1) (s.t). **4** pronounce (a syllable) more strongly. ⇒ stress(2). Compare unstressed.

'**stress ,mark** *c.n* mark (' or , in this dictionary) that shows stress(2).

stretch /stretʃ/ *n* **1** *c.n* act of stretching(8–10). **2** *u.n* (also *attrib*) ability to be stretched(8): *These stretch socks will fit anyone.* **3** *u.n* amount that s.t can be stretched(8). **4** *c.n* (usu — *of s.t*) piece of land, sea, river etc) over a certain distance that is usu rather narrow: *We often fish along this stretch of the river.* **5** *c.n* (often *the final/finishing/home* — (*of s.t*)) straight part of a race-course etc. **6** *c.n* (often *a* — *of five years* etc) length of time (consisting of five years etc). **7** *c.n* (*slang*) stretch(6) in prison. **at a stretch** without stopping: *I work four hours at a stretch and then have a rest.* **at full stretch** as hard, fast etc as one can. **by any stretch of the imagination** however hard one tries to imagine it: *He isn't an actor by any stretch of the imagination.* **have a** (**good**) **stretch** (**a**) ⇒ stretch(3). (**b**) stretch(10) (pleasantly).

▷ *v* **8** *tr/intr.v* (cause (s.t) to) become longer and/or wider: *I want wool that won't stretch when it is washed.* Opposite shrink(1). **9** *tr/intr.v* (cause (s.t) to) tighten and/or straighten by pulling from one or more ends/sides or pushing (away) from the centre: *Stretch this rope across to that tree. When I get up in the morning I always stretch my arms.* **10** *intr.v* stretch(2) one's arm(s) etc to exercise one's muscles(1) or to reach s.t: *It's rude to stretch across the table; ask for what you want instead.* **11** *intr.v* be able to be stretched(8): *elastic stretches.* **stretch between s.t and s.t** extend(2)/reach from s.t to s.t. **stretch it a bit**; **stretch a point**; **stretch the rules** not do exactly what is the right thing; do s.t that is outside the rules etc: *You're late with your application but I'm prepared to stretch a point and accept it this time.* **stretch one's legs** (*fig*) go for a walk to have some exercise. **stretch** (**s.t**) **out** = stretch(8,9) (s.t). **stretch over s.t** reach/extend(2) far enough to cover s.t. **stretch s.o's patience** make it difficult for s.o to be patient.

stretcher /'stretʃə/ *c.n* flat thing like a bed with no legs on which people who are too ill etc to walk are carried.

'**stretcher,bearer** *c.n* person who carries a stretcher.

'**stretcher ,party** *c.n* (*pl* -ies) group of people whose job is to find people who need to be carried on stretchers and then carry them.

strew /struː/ *tr.v* (*p.t* strewed, *p.p* strewn /struːn/) **1** (often — *s.t on/over s.t*) scatter (s.t) (on/over s.t): *They strew the seeds on the ground.* **2** (usu — *s.t with s.t*) scatter s.t on/over (s.t): *They strew the ground with seeds.*

striated /straɪ'eɪtɪd/ *adj* (*technical*) having stripes on it: *a striated pattern.*

stricken /'strɪkən/ *adj* (often — *by/with s.t*) feeling/showing worry, sadness, illness etc: *stricken with pain.* ⇒ strike(*v*).

-stricken *adj* stricken by the thing that is the first part of the word: *conscience-stricken*; grief-stricken.

strict /strɪkt/ *adj* **1** severe; not allowing any indiscretion. **2** exact; not containing any changes or mistakes: *When we are dancing we are careful to keep strict time.* **3** absolute: *We were given the information in the strictest secrecy.*

'strictly adv. **'strictness** u.n.

stricture /'strɪktʃə/ c.n **1** (usu pl) (often —s on s.o/s.t) criticism (of s.o/s.t). **2** (medical) narrowing of part of a tube in one's body, usu through disease.

stride /straɪd/ c.n **1** long step during walking. **get into one's stride** (a) begin walking with one's usual strides, often after having walked less well to begin with. (b) (fig) begin doing s.t properly, usu after having started less well: After stammering a bit the speaker got into his stride and gave us a really good talk. **make great strides** (fig) make good progress. **take s.t in one's stride** (fig) not allow s.t to interfere with what one is doing.
▷ intr.v (p.t strode /strəʊd/, p.p stridden /strɪdn/) **2** take one or more long steps: They strode across the hills.

strident /'straɪdənt/ adj (derog; formal) making a loud harsh(3) unpleasant sound, often on a high note: Margaret's strident voice.
'stridency u.n fact or quality of being strident.
'stridently adv.

strife /straɪf/ u.n arguments, quarrels or fights between people.

strike /straɪk/ c.n **1** time when people refuse to work because they want better working conditions, higher wages etc. ⇒ general strike. **2** hit: He gave her a strike across the face. **3** attack, usu by planes on an enemy position. **4** finding of oil, gas etc under the ground after drilling. **go on strike** begin a strike(1). **on strike** not working because of a strike(1).
▷ v (p.t,p.p struck /strʌk/) **5** intr.v go on strike. **6** tr.v (often — s.o/s.t with s.t) hit (s.o/s.t) (with s.t): He struck the nail with a hammer. **7** intr.v (often — out (at s.o/s.t)) try to hit, bite etc (s.o/s.t): The snake struck at my hand but missed. **8** tr/intr.v (usu — s.o/s.t down) (of illness, poverty etc) attack (s.o/s.t) (and make her/him/it fall). **9** tr/intr.v (cause (s.t) to) produce (a sound): The clock struck half past two. The child struck the piano keys and made a loud unpleasant sound. **10** tr.v (usu — s.o as s.t) seem (like s.t) to s.o: Does the house strike you as rather cold? **11** tr.v find (s.t), usu suddenly and when one was not expecting it: After four months they finally struck gas. We walked across the desert for hours before we struck the coast. **12** tr.v (often — a cutting) put (a piece of a plant) into earth so that it can grow into a full plant. **13** tr.v (technical) make (a coin etc). **14** tr.v (technical) pull down (a flag, sail etc). **15** tr.v get into (a position): When he wants to impress people, he strikes a pose(1) with his chin in the air and his chest out.
be struck by s.t be impressed(2) by s.t; find s.t interesting, wonderful etc.
be struck dumb ⇒ dumb.
strike a balance (**between s.o/s.t and s.o/s.t**) ⇒ balance(n).
strike a bargain ⇒ bargain(n).
strike a blow against/for s.o/s.t ⇒ blow(n).
strike camp ⇒ camp(n).
strike fear into s.o ⇒ fear(n).
strike a happy medium ⇒ medium(n).
strike a light ⇒ light(n).
strike a match ⇒ match(n).
strike off (**in a certain direction**) start going (towards the coast etc). **strike s.o/s.t off** (**s.t**) remove s.o/s.t from a list etc: Doctors and lawyers are sometimes struck off (i.e they are not allowed to continue as doctors etc) for very bad behaviour in their official positions.
strike out (**for/towards s.t**) = strike off (in a certain direction). **strike out** (**on one's own**) begin to do s.t (new) alone. **strike s.t out** ⇒ cross s.t out.
strike it rich ⇒ rich(1).
strike terror into s.o ⇒ terror.
it strikes s.o that . . . s.o suddenly realizes/thinks that . . . .
strike s.t through = strike s.t out.
strike while the iron is hot ⇒ iron(n).
strike (s.t) up begin to play and/or sing (a piece of music). **strike up an acquaintance/friendship** (**with s.o**) begin an acquaintance/friendship.
strike (up)on s.t find s.t, e.g a new idea, by chance; discover s.t.
'strike,bound adj unable to work, move etc because of a strike(1).
'strike,breaker c.n person who works while other workers are on strike.
'strike,breaking u.n working while other workers are on strike.
'strike ,fund c.n trade union money that has been saved up, given by others, so that strikers(1) can get strike pay.
'strike ,pay u.n money paid to strikers(1) out of a strike fund.
'striker c.n **1** person who is on strike. **2** (in football) forward(11).
'striking adj that people notice particularly because he/she/it is unusually beautiful, interesting etc.
'strikingly adv.

string /strɪŋ/ n **1** c/u.n (example, piece, of a) thing like rope but thinner, used for tying up parcels etc. **2** c.n thing like a string(1) on a musical instrument which one pulls or hits to make a note: a guitar string. **3** c.n (often — of s.t) number (of beads etc) on one string(1). **4** c.n (often — of s.t) number (of people, animals, things) one following the other: a string of arguments, each worse than the one before. **have s.o on a string** (fig) be able to do whatever one wants with s.o: Mary has her new boyfriend on a string. **have more than one string to one's bow; have a second string to one's bow** (fig) have another way of doing s.t, another job etc in addition to one's first one. **play second string (to s.o)** (fig) be treated as less important (than s.o).
▷ tr.v (p.t,p.p strung /strʌŋ/) **5** put (beads etc) on a string(1). **6** put strings (⇒ string(2)) on (a violin etc). **string along** (**with s.o**) (fig; informal) go to places and/or do things with s.o but only for as long as it suits one. **string s.o along** (informal) deceive s.o by making her/him think that she/he will have what she/he wants. **string (s.o/s.t) out** (cause (s.o/s.t) to) spread out in a line or on a rope etc. **string s.t together** manage to produce s.t by putting pieces together but often not in a very successful way. **string s.o up** (slang) hang (s.o).
,string 'band c.n band²(2) that plays music on stringed instruments.
,string 'bean c.n = runner bean.
,stringed 'instrument c.n musical instrument, such as a violin, that has strings (⇒ string(2)).
'stringiness u.n fact of being stringy.

,string 'orchestra c.n orchestra that plays music on stringed instruments.

'string-,puppet c.n ⇨ puppet(1).

strings pl.n players of stringed instruments in an orchestra that has other kinds of instruments too. **have two strings to one's bow** (fig) = have a second string to one's bow. **no strings attached** (fig) with nothing to limit it. **pull strings** (fig) use one's influence in order to get s.t one wants: *When Dick wanted a job in a bank his uncle pulled a few strings for him.*

'stringy adj (-ier, -iest) (derog) having thin fibres(2), muscles(1) etc in it: *a stringy mango; stringy meat; stringy legs.*

strung adj highly strung very sensitive, nervous, easily offended. (all) strung up very nervous, worried or excited.

stringent /'strɪndʒənt/ adj (formal) 1 strict; severe: *There are stringent rules governing the work here.* 2 (of the money that can be borrowed, spent etc) in short supply; difficult to find.

'stringency u.n.

strip /strɪp/ c.n 1 (often — of s.t) long narrow piece (of s.t, e.g paper or land). 2 particular colour(s) of clothes worn by a football team etc; uniform(2). **comic strip** ⇨ comic. **do a strip** take off (almost) all one's clothes, usu as an entertainment for others. **tear s.o off a strip** be angry and very critical when talking to s.o.

▷ v (-pp-) 3 tr.v (often — s.t from/off (s.o/s.t)) take (s.t) off (s.o/s.t): *His mother stripped his dirty clothes off (him) and put them straight in the wash.* 4 tr.v (often — s.o/s.t of s.t) take s.t off, away from (s.o/s.t): *He was stripped of his power.* 5 intr.v (often — off) take off all one's clothes. **strip s.t down** take s.t to pieces; remove all the parts that can be removed from s.t, usu a motor; dismantle s.t.

'strip ,artist c.n = stripper.

,strip car'toon c.n row of cartoons(1) that tell a joke, funny story etc.

'strip ,lighting u.n light(4) made using a long bulb (neon light).

'stripper c.n person who does a striptease.

'strip ,show c.n = striptease.

'strip,tease c.n act of taking off all one's clothes to entertain other people in a nightclub etc.

stripe /straɪp/ c.n 1 long narrow band, usu of the same width over all its length and of a different colour, texture etc from what is beside it: *Tigers have stripes but lions do not.* 2 sign of rank, length of service etc on some uniforms(2): *A sergeant in the British army has three stripes.*

striped adj having stripes(1) on it: *a striped shirt.*

stripling /'strɪplɪŋ/ c.n (literary) young man who is not yet fully grown.

strive /straɪv/ intr.v (p.t strove /strəʊv/, p.p striven /strɪvn/) (usu — after, against, for, to do, s.t) try very hard (to do/get, overcome, prevent s.t).

strode /strəʊd/ p.t of stride.

stroke /strəʊk/ c.n 1 hit/blow, usu with a weapon: *with one stroke of a whip/sword.* 2 hit with a racket(1), golf club etc in a game: *a good stroke.* 3 (in rowing) act of putting an oar in the water and pulling it to move the boat. 4 person in a rowing crew(1) who is nearest the stern² and from whom the rest of the crew take their time. 5 strong movement, e.g of a bird's wings.

6 mark drawn or painted without taking one's pencil, brush etc off the paper etc. 7 = oblique(2). 8 illness that affects one's brain suddenly and can lead to one being unable to move part(s) of one's body. **at a/one stroke** all with one single action: *The closure of the factory changed the lives of many families at one stroke.* **give s.t a stroke** = stroke(9) s.t. **on the stroke of midnight** etc exactly when it is midnight etc; exactly when the clock strikes 12 etc. **a stroke of luck** a piece of good luck.

▷ tr.v 9 rub one's hand over (s.t, e.g a person's hair, an animal) gently. 10 act as stroke(4) of a crew(1)/ boat etc.

stroll /strəʊl/ c.n 1 (often go for, take, a —) slow walk for pleasure.

▷ intr.v 2 walk about slowly for pleasure.

'stroller c.n 1 person who strolls(2). 2 folding pushchair for a small child.

'strolling attrib.adj who goes from place to place playing music or doing acts, usu outdoors: *strolling players.*

strong /strɒŋ/ adj 1 firm; tough; having power to resist damage, pressure etc; not easily damaged, broken, worn etc: *a strong chair; a strong healthy baby; strong cloth.* Opposite weak(1). 2 powerful; having a lot of force or strength: *a strong smell; a strong pull; a strong wind.* 3 (of an alcoholic(1) drink) having a lot of alcohol in it. Opposite weak(4). 4 (of tea, coffee etc) having a lot of tea etc in it and not very much water. Opposite weak(4). 5 (grammar) (of a verb) that does not make its p.t,p.p by adding '(e)d': *'Buy' is a strong verb because its past tense is 'bought'.* Opposite weak(6). 6 (of a country's money) having a high value compared with the money of other countries: *The dollar is stronger today.* Opposite weak(7). **be a bit strong** (informal) be not fair¹(1): *It's a bit strong expecting us to make our own beds in a hotel.* (still) going strong (still) alive, working properly, usu in spite of being old. **60 etc strong** consisting of 60 etc people: *The factory was 2 000 strong five years ago.*

strength /streŋθ/ n (often — of s.t) 1 u.n fact of (s.t) being strong(1-4,6) (in s.t): *strength of mind.* 2 u.n degree to which s.o/s.t is strong(1-4,6): *a man of great strength.* 3 u.n thing that gives s.t strength(1): *The strength of her arguments lies in her long experience.* **a strength of 60** etc people who number 60 etc: *Our club has a strength of 326.* **a tower of strength** (to s.o/s.t) = tower(n). **above/below strength** having more/ fewer people, animals or things in it than the correct/usual number: *Our sales department is five people below strength.* **brute strength** ⇨ brute. **in strength** in large numbers: *The soldiers attacked the enemy position in strength.* **on the strength of s.t** because of s.t: *We accepted him on the strength of your recommendation.* **up to strength** having the number of people, animals or things needed.

'strengthen tr/intr.v (cause (s.o/s.t) to) become strong(er)(1-4,6).

'strong,arm attrib.adj using (too much) force: *strongarm ways of controlling crowds.*

'strong,box c.n strong box or safe(5) for keeping money and valuables in.

'strong ,form c/def.n (technical) form of a word that is used when it has some stress(2) on it: *The strong form of 'of'* (/ɒv/) *is used in 'What are you thinking of?' and the* weak form (/əv/) *is used in 'I'm thinking of tomorrow'.* Compare weak form.

'strong,hold *c.n* **1** fort. **2** (often — of *s.o/s.t*) place where *s.o/s.t* is particularly strong: *South America is a stronghold of* Catholicism.

,strong 'language *u.n* cursing; swearing: *use strong language.*

'strongly *adv.*

,strong-'minded *adj* keeping strongly to what one believes, wants etc.

,strong 'point *c.n* thing *s.o* is particularly good at: *Politeness is not Richard's strong point.*

'strong ,room *c.n* room with very strong doors and walls in which to keep money, valuables etc, usu in a bank.

,strong 'verb *c.n* (*grammar*) ⇒ strong(5).

strove /strəʊv/ *p.t* of strive.

struck /strʌk/ *p.t,p.p* of strike.

structure /'strʌktʃə/ *n* **1** *u.n* (often *the* — of *s.t*) way in which (*s.t*) is composed of various parts. **2** *c.n* thing, often a building, that is composed of various parts.

▷ *tr.v* **3** form (the parts of *s.t*) into a well arranged structure(2).

structural /'strʌktʃərəl/ *adj* of or referring to structure(1,2): *a structural weakness in a bridge.*

'structurally *adv.*

struggle /'strʌgl/ *c/u.n* **1** difficult effort/fight: *It was a struggle to catch the end of the rope. There was a struggle between the two men. For many people life is one long struggle.*

▷ *intr.v* **2** make great efforts (to do *s.t* etc): *Many animals are struggling to* survive(1) *in the last areas of forest. The dress was tight but she managed to struggle into it.*

'struggling *attrib.adj* who is making great efforts to do *s.t*: *a struggling poet.*

strum /strʌm/ *v* (-*mm*-) **1** *tr/intr.v* play (music) on a stringed instrument with one or more of one's fingers, usu in an informal and often unskilful way. **2** *tr.v* play music in this way on (a stringed instrument): *strum a* guitar.

strung /strʌŋ/ *p.t,p.p* of string.

strut[1] /strʌt/ *c.n* piece of metal etc that supports the weight of *s.t*: *The roof was held up by struts while the walls were being repaired.*

strut[2] /strʌt/ *c.n* **1** way of walking in which one tries to look important by pushing one's chest out, holding one's head high and swinging one's arms.

▷ *intr.v* (-*tt*-) **2** walk with a strut[2](1).

strychnine /'strɪkniːn/ *u.n* kind of strong poison used in very small quantities as a medicine.

stub /stʌb/ *c.n* **1** (often — of *s.t*) small piece (of *s.t*, esp a pencil, cigarette) that remains after the rest has been used. **2** piece at the side of a cheque in a cheque book or ticket in a book of tickets, that is left after one has torn the cheque/ticket out of the book.

▷ *tr.v* (-*bb*-) **3** hit (one's toe) against *s.t* accidentally and usu painfully. **stub a cigarette** *etc* **out** put a cigarette etc out by pressing it against *s.t*, e.g an ashtray.

'stubby *adj* (-*ier*, -*iest*) short and thick: *stubby fingers.*

stubble /'stʌbl/ *u.n* **1** short stiff pieces of straw or stems left in a field after the harvest. **2** short stiff hairs on a man's

chin etc when he has not shaved for some time.

'stubbly *adj* (-*ier*, -*iest*) like, covered with, stubble.

stubborn /'stʌbən/ *adj* **1** (often *derog*) having/ showing a strong will; (showing that one is) determined to do or believe what one wants and not what other people want. **2** stiff; difficult to move, remove etc: *a stubborn door handle that refuses to turn; a stubborn ink stain.*

'stubbornly *adv.* **'stubbornness** *u.n.*

stubby ⇒ stub.

stucco /'stʌkəʊ/ *u.n* (also *attrib*) plaster(1) that is used to cover walls, make decorations etc.

stuck /stʌk/ *pred.adj* **1** not able to be moved: *The car's stuck in the mud.* ⇒ unstuck. **2** not able to do *s.t* (any more) because of difficulties: *Could you please help me? I'm stuck because I've forgotten my key.* **get stuck in(to** *s.t*) (*informal*) start (*s.t*), usu in an energetic way: *Here's your dinner — get stuck in, boys!* **be stuck on** *s.o* (*informal*) like *s.o* very much. **be stuck on(to)** *s.o/s.t* be fixed to *s.o/s.t* by *s.t* sticky. **be stuck with** *s.o/s.t* (*informal*) be forced to deal with *s.o/s.t* although one does not want to: *I'm afraid we're stuck with boring visitors the whole of this weekend.*

▷ *v* **3** *p.t,p.p* of stick.

,stuck-'up *adj* (*derog*; *informal*) proud; thinking that one is better than other people.

stud[1] /stʌd/ *c.n* **1** = collar-stud. **2** = press stud. **3** (thing like a) nail, usu with a rounded top, that is knocked into *s.t* as an ornament, to mark the lanes(3) along a road etc. Compare cat's-eye.

▷ *tr.v* (-*dd*-) **4** (often — *s.t* with *s.t*) put things here and there on (*s.t*) like studs(3): *The sky was studded with stars.* ⇒ star-studded.

stud[2] /stʌd/ *c.n* **1** (also **'stud ,farm**) place where horses are bred (⇒ breed(*v*)). **2** horses at a stud(1).

student /'stjuːdənt/ *c.n* (also *attrib*) person who studies at a college, university etc and in the older groups in a school. Compare pupil[1](1). **a student of** *s.t* a person who studies, is interested in, *s.t*, e.g history, human nature.

,student 'nurse, 'teacher etc *c.n* person who is learning to be a nurse, teacher etc.

,students' 'union *c.n* **1** kind of association to which the students of a university, college etc belong and which organizes debates(1), social activities etc. **2** place where students meet etc.

studied /'stʌdɪd/ *adj* ⇒ study.

studio /'stjuːdɪəʊ/ *c.n* (*pl* -s) **1** room in which an artist, photographer etc does her/his work. **2** room from which radio or television broadcasts are made. **3** (often *pl*) place where films are made for the cinema; room where films are shown.

'studio a,partment *c.n* flat with one room to live and sleep in and usu a small kitchen and bathroom or shower room.

'studio ,audience *c/def.pl.n* audience during the recording of a radio or television programme.

'studio ,couch *c.n* kind of couch(1) that can be changed into a bed for sleeping on; bedsettee, sofa bed.

study /'stʌdɪ/ *n* (*pl* -ies) **1** *c/u.n* (often — of *s.o/s.t*) act or fact of studying(7) (*s.o/s.t*). **2** *c/ u.n* (often *pl*) thing that one studies(7): *I'm busy* *with my studies.* **3** *c.n* (often — *of s.o/s.t*) example of studying(8) s.o/s.t: *a careful study of a map.* **4** *c.n* (often — *of s.o/s.t*) picture (of s.o/s.t) often drawn or painted as a preparation for including it as part of a bigger picture. **5** *c.n* piece of music written for giving practice in s.t. **6** *c.n* room in which one studies(1), writes etc. **make a study of s.o/s.t** study(8) s.o/s.t.

▷ *v* (*-ies, -ied*) **7** *tr/intr.v* try to learn (s.t): *What did you study at university? I studied English.* **8** *tr.v* look at, listen to etc, (s.o/s.t) carefully in order to try to find out (more) about her/him/it, or help etc her/him/it: *study a map.*

studious /'stju:dɪəs/ *adj* (*formal*) **1** liking to study(7); studying(7) a lot. **2** (*formal*) the result of a very careful study(3): *a studious attempt to get the background of a picture right.*

'studiously *adv.* **'studiousness** *u.n.*

stuff /stʌf/ *u.n* **1** (*informal*) material(1) things: *'What's this stuff doing on my table?' 'Those are the things I bought this morning.'* **2** (*informal*) thing that s.t is made of: *The soup was made from some stuff I had never heard of before.* **do/ know one's stuff** (*informal*) do/know what one is supposed to do, usu s.t that needs skill.

▷ *v* **3** *tr.v* (often — *s.t with s.t*) fill (s.t) (using s.t): *stuff a cushion with cotton; stuff a chicken with* herbs *and then cook it.* **4** *tr.v* fill the skin of (an animal) to make it look as if it is alive. **5** *tr/intr.v* (often — *oneself/s.o with s.t*) (cause (s.o) to) eat a lot (of s.t): *Stop stuffing (yourself); you've had enough to eat.* **get stuffed** (*slang*) (used to show anger, strong disagreement etc): *I told her to get stuffed — I refuse to do her work as well as my own.* **stuff s.t in(to s.t)** put s.t in(to s.t), usu carelessly and pushing rather hard. **stuff s.t up with s.t** put s.t into s.t so that nothing else can pass: *This pipe is stuffed up with wet paper. My nose is (all) stuffed up so I have to breathe through my mouth.*

,stuffed 'shirt *c.n* (*derog*) person who considers herself/himself to be very important.

'stuffily *adv* in a stuffy way.

'stuffiness *u.n* fact or state of being stuffy.

'stuffing *u.n* material used to stuff(3,4) s.t. **knock the stuffing out of s.o** (of an illness, fight etc) make s.o feel very weak: *His row with his parents knocked the stuffing out of Peter for a week.*

'stuffy *adj* (*-ier, -iest*) **1** (of air in a room etc) not fresh. **2** (of a room etc) not having fresh air in it. **3** (*derog*) (of a person) very formal, old-fashioned and boring.

stultify /'stʌltɪˌfaɪ/ *tr.v* (*-ies, -ied*) (*formal*) **1** make (s.t) seem absurd or wasted. **2** make (s.o, her/his mind etc) dull and slow: *boring work stultifies the mind.*

stultification /ˌstʌltɪfɪ'keɪʃən/ *u.n.*

stumble /'stʌmbl/ *c.n* **1** act of almost falling, caused by catching one's foot on s.t; trip(5).

▷ *intr.v* **2** (often — *on s.t*) almost fall after catching one's foot (on s.t). **3** (often — *at/over s.t*) have difficulty in speaking (when one tries to say s.t), with the result that one stops, repeats oneself, makes mistakes etc: *David isn't very good at reading aloud; he stumbles at every long word.* **stumble across/(up)on s.o/s.t** meet s.o/s.t by chance. **stumble into s.t** start doing s.t, usu s.t bad: *A lot of people stumble into debt without intending to.*

'stumbling ,block *c.n* thing that makes it difficult for s.o to do s.t.

stump /stʌmp/ *c.n* **1** short piece of a tree trunk that is left after the rest has been cut down. **2** part of an arm or leg that is left after the rest has been cut off etc. **3** thing like a stump¹ that is left after s.t has been worn down or used a lot: *a pencil stump.* **4** (in cricket¹) one of three vertical pieces of wood that the bowler(1) tries to hit.

▷ *v* **5** *intr.v* (often — *about*; — *across s.t*) walk (about etc) with heavy steps. **6** *tr.v* (in cricket¹) put a batsman out(19) by hitting the stumps(4) with the ball when he/she is not inside the crease(3). **7** *tr.v* (*informal*) ask, say, do, s.t that (s.o) has no answer for: *His first question stumped me completely. It stumps me how anyone can trust that man.*

'stumpy *adj* (*-ier, -iest*) short and thick; stubby. Compare stocky.

stun /stʌn/ *tr.v* (*-nn-*) **1** make (a person, animal) unconscious with a hit on the head. **2** make (s.o) unable to think, hear, feel etc anything for a usu short time: *The explosion stunned John for a few moments.* **3** shock (s.o) very much. **4** fill (s.o) with admiration.

'stunner *c.n* (*informal*) very attractive person (usu a woman), animal or thing.

'stunning *adj* (*informal*) very attractive, beautiful etc: *a stunning dress. You look stunning in that white* jacket(1).

stung /stʌŋ/ *p.t,p.p* of sting.

stunk /stʌŋk/ *p.t,p.p* of stink.

stunt¹ /stʌnt/ *c.n* **1** difficult and/or dangerous action done by a person, plane etc, usu to entertain people: *In films stunts like jumping out of a plane into a car are usually not done by the film stars but by* stunt men *or* stunt women. Compare feat. **2** thing that is done to attract attention, often as an advertisement. **pull a stunt** do a trick, often a foolish one.

▷ *intr.v* **3** do stunts¹(1).

'stunt ,man *c.n* (*pl* stunt men) man who does stunts¹(1).

'stunt ,woman *c.n* (*pl* stunt women) woman who does stunts¹(1).

stunt² /stʌnt/ *tr.v* prevent (s.o/s.t) growing to her/his/its full height: *These trees have been stunted by the icy winds.* **stunt the growth of s.o/s.t** stunt² s.o/s.t.

stupefy /'stju:pɪˌfaɪ/ *tr.v* (*-ies, -ied*) (*formal*) **1** stop (s.o) being able to think. **2** surprise s.o very much.

stupefaction /ˌstju:pɪ'fækʃən/ *u.n.*

stupendous /stju:'pendəs/ *adj* (*formal*) very, often surprisingly, big: *a stupendous achievement.*

stu'pendously *adv.* **stu'pendousness** *u.n.*

stupid /'stju:pɪd/ *adj* (*derog*) **1** foolish; silly; not showing wisdom or common sense. **2** (usu — *with s.t*) (*old use*) behaving in a stupid(1) way (because of drink(3)).

stu'pidity *n* (*pl -ies*) **1** *u.n* fact or state of being stupid(1). **2** *c/u.n* (often *pl*) stupid action, thing said etc.

'stupidly *adv.*

stupor /'stju:pə/ *c/u.n* (usu *in a* —) state in which one is still conscious but unable to think properly, e.g because of drugs(2).

sturdy /'stɜ:dɪ/ *adj* (*-ier, -iest*) **1** (of a person's body, a tree, building etc) strong; firmly built.

2 (of the way in which s.o behaves, talks etc) firm; not giving in to anyone.
'**sturdily** adv. '**sturdiness** u.n.
sturgeon /'stɜːdʒən/ n **1** c.n kind of big fish that is caught and eaten and from which one gets caviar. **2** u.n flesh of this fish as food.
stutter /'stʌtə/ c.n **1** = stammer(1).
▷ intr.v **2** = stammer(2).
'**stutterer** c.n person who stutters(2).
'**stutteringly** adv in a stuttering (⇨ stutter(2)) way.
sty¹ /staɪ/ c.n (pl -ies) = pigsty.
sty² /staɪ/ c.n (pl -ies) = stye.
stye /staɪ/ c.n (pl styes) inflamed(1) swelling on the edge of one's eyelid.
style /staɪl/ n **1** c/u.n not the actual contents of what one writes, says or does but the way in which one writes etc it: a modern style of speaking. **2** c.n (often (in) the — of s.o/s.t) fashion (of s.o/s.t): Popular styles in the 1960s were very short skirts for women and long hair for men. **3** u.n style(1) that shows good sense, ability etc: I like Jennifer because she has style. **4** c.n (often — of s.t) kind, sort (of s.t): We have all styles of handbags in our shop. **5** c.n (formal) form of a title: A baron(1) has the style 'the Right Honourable the Lord . . .'. **6** c.n (technical) very thin stem in a flower which joins the ovary to the stigma(2).
▷ tr.v **7** arrange (s.t) in a certain style(2): How do you like your hair styled? **8** (formal) address (s.o) by a certain style(5): John is now styled the Right Honourable.
-style adj of the style(1,2) shown by the first part of the word: an old-style watch.
'**styleless** adj lacking style(1–3).
'**stylish** adj fashionable.
'**stylishly** adv. '**stylishness** u.n.
'**stylist** c.n **1** person who does things in a good style(1). **2** person who does work that needs style(1): a hair stylist who styles(7) women's hair.
sty'listic adj of or referring to style(1).
sty'listically adv.
sty'listics u.n study of style(1), esp that of literary work.
stylize, -ise /'staɪlaɪz/ tr.v write, paint etc (s.o/s.t) in a way that follows a particular style(1,2) instead of being true to nature.
stylus /'staɪləs/ c.n (pl styluses) **1** pointed device in the arm of a record player that goes along the grooves in a record¹(1) and picks up the sounds to pass them to the speaker(s); needle on a record player for playing records¹(1). **2** pointed device for cutting glass, making designs in metal etc.
suave /swɑːv/ adj (often derog) pleasantly polite (often with the purpose of cheating people).
'**suavely** adv. '**suavity** u.n.
sub /sʌb/ c.n abbr (informal) **1** subscription(3). **2** subsidy. **3** submarine(2). **4** substitute(2). **5** subeditor.
▷ v (-bb-) (informal) **6** intr.v (often — for s.o) be a substitute(2) (for s.o). **7** tr/intr.v give a (sub(2)) to (s.o/s.t); get a sub(2) from s.o/s.t. **8** tr.v subedit (s.t).
subaltern /'sʌbəltən/ c.n (military) (UK) commissioned officer in the army below the rank of captain.
subarctic /sʌb'ɑːktɪk/ adj (technical) not quite arctic: subarctic temperatures.

subatomic /ˌsʌbə'tɒmɪk/ adj (technical) smaller than an atom(1): subatomic particles(1).
subcommittee /'sʌbkəˌmɪtɪ/ c/def.pl.n committee that is organized or appointed by a more important or larger one.
subconscious /sʌb'kɒnʃəs/ adj **1** (of a person's thoughts, feelings etc) not consciously known, felt, understood etc.
▷ def.n **2** part of one's mind (and the thoughts, feelings etc in it) which one is not conscious of. ⇨ unconscious.
sub'consciously adv.
subcontinent /sʌb'kɒntɪnənt/ c.n large part of a continent(1), e.g India, Pakistan, Bangladesh, Sri Lanka etc taken together.
subcontract /sʌb'kɒntrækt/ c.n **1** contract(1) that is given by the main contractor to another one.
▷ tr/intr.v /ˌsʌbkən'trækt/ **2** give the contract(1) for (s.t) to another contractor.
ˌ**subcon'tractor** c.n person who is given a subcontract(1).
subcutaneous /ˌsʌbkju:'teɪnɪəs/ adj (medical) under the skin: a subcutaneous injection.
ˌ**subcu'taneously** adv.
subdivide /ˌsʌbdɪ'vaɪd/ tr/intr.v cause (s.t that has already been divided) to) be divided into still smaller parts.
subdivision /'sʌbdɪˌvɪʒən/ n **1** u.n fact or act of subdividing. **2** c.n one of the parts into which s.t has been subdivided.
subdue /səb'dju:/ tr.v (formal) bring (s.o/s.t) under control (so that he/she/it is no longer free, violent etc).
sub'dued adj quiet(er); gentle(r); less/not bright, loud, happy etc: subdued lights; subdued discussion; feel subdued because one is not well.
subedit /sʌb'edɪt/ tr.v do the work of a subeditor.
sub'editor c.n assistant(2) to an editor; person who reads what others have written, e.g for a newspaper or magazine, and makes changes to it.
subheading /'sʌbˌhedɪŋ/ c.n heading inside an article in a newspaper etc.
subhuman /sʌb'hju:mən/ adj (derog) so bad that one would not expect it from a human being; inhuman: subhuman cruelty.
subject¹ /'sʌbdʒɪkt/ c.n **1** thing that is being thought, spoken, written, about: The subject of our lesson today is the life of Shakespeare. **2** one of the things that one studies in school etc, e.g history, mathematics. **3** (formal) person who has, is likely to have, s.t that is described by the adjective before: an easily upset subject; an asthmatic subject. **4** (grammar) part of a sentence/clause(1) that represents the person, animal or thing about which some new information is given. **change the subject** stop talking about one subject(1) and start another one. **a subject for s.t** s.o/s.t that causes s.t or about whom/which s.o thinks, writes etc s.t: John's new hairstyle is a subject for much joking in the factory. Her life is a good subject for a film. **the subject of s.t** (formal) **(a)** ⇨ subject¹(1,2). **(b)** the person, animal or thing with which s.t deals: The new laws are the subject of much discussion here. **(c)** the particular person, animal etc to which s.t is done: The subject of the

children's interest was a big snake. **off the subject** not relevant to the subject(1) being discussed. **on the subject of s.o/s.t** about, referring to, s.o/s.t.

'subject ,matter *u.n* person, animal or thing that is the subject'(1) of a talk, piece of writing etc.

subject² /'sʌbdʒɪkt/ *adj* **1** not independent; ruled by s.o else: *the subject peoples of an ancient empire.* **subject to s.t (a)** governed by s.t; dependent on s.t: *The date of holidays is subject to the work in the factory.* **(b)** likely/liable(1) to get/have s.t: *Dick is subject to coughs and colds.*

▷ *c.n* /'sʌbdʒɪkt/ **2** (often — *of s.t*) person who is a citizen (of a country): *a British subject.*

▷ *tr.v* /səb'dʒekt/ **3 subject s.o to s.o/s.t** cause s.o to be ruled by s.o/s.t.

subjection /səb'dʒekʃən/ *u.n* (often — *of s.o/s.t*) *to s.o/s.t*) (*formal*) fact or state of (s.o/s.t) being subjected²(3) (to s.o/s.t). **in complete subjection (to s.o/s.t)** in a state of being completely subjected²(3) (to s.o/s.t).

subjective /səb'dʒektɪv/ *adj* **1** (of thought) that is the result of the activity of thinking only, instead of being based on the real world around one; imaginary. **2** that depends on one's own personal opinions instead of being based on facts. **3** (*grammar*) of or referring to a subject'(4). Opposite objective(1).

subjectivity /,sʌbdʒek'tɪvɪtɪ/ *u.n.*

sub'jectively *adv.*

sub judice /,sʌb 'dʒuːdɪsɪ/ *adj* (*Latin*) (of a case in a law court) still being dealt with and therefore not allowed to be discussed in the press etc.

subjugate /'sʌbdʒʊ,geɪt/ *tr.v* (*formal*) conquer (s.o, a country etc); bring (s.o, a country etc) under one's power.

subjugation /,sʌbdʒʊ'geɪʃən/ *u.n.*

subjunctive /səb'dʒʌŋktɪv/ *def.n* (*grammar*) verb that is in the subjunctive mood.

sub,junctive 'mood *def.n* (*grammar*) form of a verb that is used mostly to show that s.t is not definitely known to be a fact but is just a possibility, hope, s.t imagined etc: *In 'I wouldn't do that if I were you', 'were' is in the subjunctive mood.*

sublease /'sʌb,liːs/ *c.n* **1** lease(1) of (part of) s.t to another person, group of people, by s.o who already leases it from s.o else: *a sublease of a room to a friend.*

▷ *tr/intr.v* /sʌb'liːs/ **2** lease (s.t) to s.o in this way: *sublease a flat(13) to a friend.*

sublet /sʌb'let/ *tr/intr.v* (*-tt-*, *p.t,p.p sublet*) let(4) to s.o else ((part of) s.t) that one rents oneself.

sublieutenant /,sʌblef'tenənt/ *c.n* (*military*) (UK) commissioned officer of the lowest rank in the navy.

sublimate /'sʌblɪ,meɪt/ *tr.v* get rid of (feelings, usu sexual ones, that one does not want to have) by developing other interests etc to take their place.

sublimation /,sʌblɪ'meɪʃən/ *u.n.*

sublime /sə'blaɪm/ *adj* (*formal*) **1** of the highest, grandest kind: *the sublime joys of heaven.* **2** (*informal*; often *derog*) very surprising: *a sublime lack of concern for others.*

sub'limely *adv.* **sub'limeness, sublimity** /sə'blɪmɪtɪ/ *u.n.*

subliminal /sʌb'lɪmɪnl/ *adj* (*formal*) that affects only the subconscious(1) mind: *subliminal advertising.*

submachine gun /,sʌbmə'ʃiːn ,gʌn/ *c.n* (*military*) kind of small machine gun that one person can carry.

submarine /'sʌbmə,riːn/ *attrib.adj* **1** lower than the surface of the sea; submarine *life* (things that live in the sea).

▷ *c.n* (*informal sub*) **2** ship, usu a warship, that can travel under water as well as on the surface.

submariner /sʌb'mærɪnə/ *c.n* member of the crew'(1) of a submarine(2).

submerge /səb'mɜːdʒ/ *v* **1** *tr/intr.v* (cause (s.o/s.t) to) go below the surface of water. **2** *tr.v* (*fig*) cause (s.t) to be covered by s.t else: *The main points of her report were submerged in unnecessary details.*

sub'merged *adj* hidden under the water: *submerged rocks.*

sub'mergence *u.n.*

submit /səb'mɪt/ *v* (*-tt-*) (usu — (*oneself/s.o/s.t*) *to s.o/s.t*) (*formal*) **1** *tr/intr.v* (allow (oneself/s.o/s.t) to) give in, surrender(3) control, (to s.o/s.t): *After a lot of argument he agreed to submit (himself) to the decision of the committee.* **2** *tr.v* offer (s.t, e.g a plan) (to s.o) (for a certain reason, action): *You must submit your plans to the management for their approval.* **3** *tr.v* (*law*) (usu — *that ...*) respectfully suggest (that ...): *I would like to submit that the witness is mistaken.*

submission /səb'mɪʃən/ *n* (often — *to s.o/s.t*) **1** *c/u.n* act of submitting(1) or state of being submitted(2) (to s.o/s.t). **2** *c.n* thing that is submitted(2,3) (to s.o/s.t).

submissive /səb'mɪsɪv/ *adj* ready or willing to submit(1); docile.

sub'missively *adv.* **sub'missiveness** *u.n.*

subnormal /sʌb'nɔː,məl/ *adj* below what is normal or average: *subnormal temperatures.* Compare abnormal.

subnormality /,sʌbnɔː'mælɪtɪ/ *u.n.* **sub'normally** *adv.*

subordinate /sə'bɔːdɪnɪt/ *adj* **1** (usu — *to s.o/s.t*) (*formal*) lower in rank, importance etc (than s.o/s.t).

▷ *c.n* /sə'bɔːdɪnɪt/ **2** (often — *of s.o*) person who is subordinate(1) (to s.o).

▷ *tr.v* /sə'bɔːdɪ,neɪt/ **3** (usu — *s.o/s.t to s.o/s.t*) (*formal*) make s.o/s.t subordinate(1) (to s.o/s.t).

su'bordinate ,clause *c.n* (*grammar*) clause(1) that qualifies part of a main clause(1) or another subordinate clause or is the subject'(4)/object'(4) of its verb: *In 'I told you I had seen the boy you were looking for', both 'I had seen the boy you were looking for' and 'you were looking for' are subordinate clauses.* Compare coordinate clause.

sub'ordi,nating con,junction *c.n* (*grammar*) conjunction used to introduce a subordinate clause, e.g 'if', 'although'. Compare coordinating conjunction.

subordination /sə,bɔː,dɪ'neɪʃən/ *u.n* **subordinative** /sə'bɔː,dɪnətɪv/ *adj.*

subplot /'sʌb,plɒt/ *c.n* plot(2) in a play, film etc that is less important than the main one.

subpoena /səb'piːnə/ *c.n* **1** (*law*) written order telling one to appear at a court of law.

▷ *tr.v* (*pres.p subpoenaing*, *p.t,p.p subpoenaed*) **2** (*law*) give/send (s.o) a subpoena(1).

subscribe /səb'skraɪb/ *v* (*formal*) **1** *tr/intr.v*

(often — (s.t) to s.t) pay (money) usu regularly (to s.t, often a charity(3)). **2** *intr.v* (often — to s.t) **(a)** pay regularly for a newspaper, magazine, telephone service etc. **(b)** (*formal*) agree with, support, be in favour of, s.t: *I don't subscribe to such rudeness.* ⇨ oversubscribed.

sub'scriber *c.n* (often — to s.t) **1** person who subscribes (to a magazine etc). **2** person who has a telephone.

ˌSubscriber ˌTrunk 'Dialling *u.n* (*abbr STD*) way of telephoning s.o who lives a long way away by calling the number oneself and not using an operator(2).

subscription /səb'skrɪpʃən/ *attrib.adj* **1** for which one has to pay a subscription(3): *a subscription dinner.*
▷ *n* (often — to s.t) **2** *u.n* act or fact of subscribing (to s.t). **3** *c.n* amount of money given when one subscribes (to s.t).

subsequent /'sʌbsɪkwənt/ *adj* (often — to s.t) that comes later (than s.t) and sometimes as a result (of it): *the subsequent result; information subsequent to the meeting.*
'subsequently *adv.*

subservient /səb'sɜːvɪənt/ *adj* (often — to s.o/ s.t) (*derog*) too obedient (to s.o/s.t).
sub'servience *u.n.*

subside /səb'saɪd/ *intr.v* **1** (*technical*) (of water) go down in level: *The floods are subsiding at last.* **2** (*formal*) (of the strength of wind, feelings etc) become less strong. **3** (of a building, road etc) sink down lower into the ground, usu because the foundations(4) are not firm. **4** (usu — into/ onto s.t) (*informal*) sit, lie or kneel down on s.t etc, usu rather suddenly, because one is tired, bored etc.
sub'sidence *c/u.n* act, fact or result of subsiding(3).

subsidiary /səb'sɪdɪərɪ/ *adj* **1** (often — to s.t) part of, controlled by, but less important than, the main one: *a subsidiary company; an office subsidiary to the main one.*
▷ *c.n* (*pl* -ies) **2** (often — of s.t) subsidiary(1) thing (that is part of, controlled by, s.t else).

subsidy /'sʌbsɪdɪ/ *c/u.n* (*pl* -ies) (often — on s.t) part of the cost (of s.t) that is paid by the government etc so that the people who have to buy or pay for it can get it cheaper.
subsidization, -isation /ˌsʌbsɪdaɪ'zeɪʃən/ *u.n* act or fact of subsidizing (s.t).
'subsiˌdize, -ise *tr.v* pay a subsidy on (s.t): *Some countries subsidize food.*

subsist /səb'sɪst/ *intr.v* (often — on s.t) (*formal*) manage to keep alive (by having s.t, e.g certain food or a certain amount of money).
sub'sistence *u.n* ability to subsist.
sub'sistence ˌcrop *c.n* crop that s.o grows for her/his own use, not for sale. Compare cash crop.
sub'sistence ˌlevel *unique n* level at which it is just possible for s.o to subsist.

subsoil /'sʌbˌsɔɪl/ *u.n* level of coarse soil that is between the topsoil and the rock below.

subsonic /sʌb'sɒnɪk/ *adj* (going at) less than the speed of sound: *a subsonic (journey in a) plane.* Opposite supersonic.

substance /'sʌbstəns/ *n* **1** *c.n* thing of which s.t is made or composed; (kind of) material: *I found a strange substance at the bottom of my cup after I had drunk my tea.* **2** *def.n* (often the — of s.t) important part (of s.t) without the details: *The substance of what she said was that we would have to change our methods of doing things.* **3** *u.n* solid substance(1) of s.t: *The meal looks big but it has little substance.* **4** *u.n* firm facts about s.t: *There is no substance to his accusations.*

substantial /səb'stænʃəl/ *adj* **1** quite big, important etc: *A substantial part of Vicky's wealth is in stocks(10) and shares(3).* **2** big; generous: *a substantial dinner; a substantial gift.* Opposite insubstantial. **3** (*formal*) strongly built; solid: *a substantial chair.* **4** rich and important: *a substantial member of the community.* **5** that refers to the main points of s.t: *Although they had some disappointments they had substantial success in their efforts.*
sub'stantially *adv.*

substantiate /səb'stænʃɪˌeɪt/ *tr.v* (*formal*) prove that (s.t, e.g a claim, accusation) is true.
substantiation /səbˌstænʃɪ'eɪʃən/ *u.n.*

substandard /sʌb'stændəd/ *adj* below the average or expected standard.

substantive /'sʌbstəntɪv/ *c.n* (*grammar*) noun.
substantival /ˌsʌbstən'taɪvl/ *adj* (*grammar*) of, referring to, or acting as, a noun.
'substantive ˌverb *def.n* (*grammar*) verb 'to be'.

substation /'sʌbˌsteɪʃən/ *c.n* place where electricity arrives from a power station and is sent out to the people who use it.

substitute /'sʌbstɪˌtjuːt/ *c.n* (often — for s.o/s.t) **1** person, animal or thing who/that takes the place (of the real/usual/former one), sometimes only for a short time: *Margarine is often used as a substitute for butter.* **2** (*informal sub*) (in football etc) member of a team who takes the place of another player during a game: *When Joe was hurt in the football match our team was allowed to bring Fred on as a substitute.*
▷ *v* (*abbr sub*) **3** *tr.v* (often — s.o/s.t for s.o/s.t) make (s.o/s.t) a substitute(1) (for s.o/s.t else). **4** *intr.v* act as a substitute(1) for s.o/s.t else.
substitution /ˌsʌbstɪ'tjuːʃən/ *c/u.n.*

substratum /sʌb'strɑːtəm/ *c.n* (*pl* substrata /sʌb'strɑːtə/) (often — of s.t) (*technical*) thing, e.g rock, that is in/under (s.t else) but that one cannot see (easily).

substructure /'sʌbˌstrʌktʃə/ *c.n* = foundation(4).

subsume /səb'sjuːm/ *tr.v* (often — s.t under s.t) (*formal*) include (s.t) (under a rule or in a class(1)).

subtenant /sʌb'tenənt/ *c.n* person to whom a tenant has sublet s.t.

subtend /səb'tend/ *tr.v* (*geometry*) (of a line in a triangle etc) have (a certain angle) opposite one: *Each side of an equilateral triangle subtends an angle of 60°.*

subterfuge /'sʌbtəˌfjuːdʒ/ *c/u.n* (*formal*) trick(s); way(s) of getting s.t by secret, usu dishonest, means.

subterranean /ˌsʌbtə'reɪnɪən/ *attrib.adj* (*formal*) underground: *a subterranean river.*

subtitle /'sʌbˌtaɪtl/ *c.n* title that is under, less important than, the main title (of a book etc).
'subˌtitles *pl.n* written version for deaf people or

translation (into another language) at the bottom of a film of what is being said in it.

subtle /'sʌtl/ *adj* **1** slight, usu in a clever and pleasant way: *a subtle taste of onion in the soup.* **2** cleverly done, arranged etc: *a subtle plan.* **3** able to work things out well, even when they are complicated or hidden: *a subtle brain.* **'subtlety** *n* (*pl -ies*) **1** *u.n* quality of being subtle. **2** *c.n* thing that is subtle(2). **'subtly** *adv.*

subtract /səb'trækt/ *tr.v* (often — *s.t from s.t*) take (a number or part of s.t) away (from a number or the whole of s.t): *If you subtract 10 from 25 you get 15. Here's £17 for you; I've already subtracted the money you owe me.* Compare **deduct**. **subtraction** /səb'trækʃən/ *n* **1** *c/u.n* act of subtracting. **2** *c.n* thing subtracted.

subtropical /sʌb'trɒpɪkl/ *adj* **1** not quite in the tropics: *subtropical areas.* **2** suitable for, like in, a subtropical(1) place.

suburb /'sʌbɜːb/ *c.n* (often *the* —*s*) place on the edge of a town or city where people have their homes. **suburban** /sə'bɜːbən/ *adj* **1** of or referring to a suburb. **2** (*derog*) boring, lacking excitement etc: *suburban life.* **suburbia** /sə'bɜːbɪə/ *unique n* (often *derog*) places, life, habits etc of a suburb. **'suburbs** *def.pl.n* (often *the* — *of s.t*) area(s) at the edge(s) (of a town) in which people have their homes.

subvert /sʌb'vɜːt/ *tr.v* (*formal*) try to destroy the power, influence etc, of (s.o/s.t). **subversion** /səb'vɜːʃən/ *u.n.* **subversive** /səb'vɜːsɪv/ *adj* who/that subverts. **sub'versively** *adv.* **sub'versiveness** *u.n.*

subway /'sʌbˌweɪ/ *n* **1** *c.n* path that goes under a road, railway line etc so that people can get across safely. **2** *def.n* (US) underground railway in a town; tube(5). **by subway** using the subway(2): *go/travel by subway.*

subzero /sʌb'zɪərəʊ/ *attrib.adj* that is under 0° (in temperature).

succeed /sək'siːd/ *v* **1** *intr.v* (often — *in* (*doing*) *s.t*) manage (to do s.t); be successful (in (doing) s.t). Opposite **fail**. **2** *intr.v* get what one wants to get; become rich, famous etc: *She has all the qualities one needs to succeed in life.* **3** *tr.v* come after (s.t); follow (s.t): *The wet summer was succeeded by a beautiful autumn.* **4** *tr/intr.v* (often — *to s.t*) be the next person to get s.t (after s.o else); be the person who next inherits s.t (after (s.o else)): *Queen Elizabeth II succeeded (George VI) to the* throne(2) *in 1952.* **success** /sək'ses/ *n* **1** *c/u.n* act or fact of succeeding(3). **2** *person or thing who/that succeeds(1,2).* **meet with success** succeed(1,2). **be a roaring success** be a very great success(2). **successful** /sək'sesful/ *adj* who/that succeeds(1,2) or has succeeded(1,2). Opposite **unsuccessful**. **suc'cessfully** *adv.* **succession** /sək'seʃən/ *n* **1** *u.n* fact or act of succeeding(3). **2** *c.n* (often — *of s.t*) several (people, animals, things) following one after the other: *a succession of sunny days.* **3** *u.n* (often — *to s.t*) succeeding(4) (to s.t): *the Queen's succession to the throne.* **in** (**quick**) **succession** one following the other (quickly).

suc'cessive *attrib.adj* one following the other: *We had rainy weekends for three successive weeks.* Compare **consecutive**. **suc'cessively** *adv.* **suc'cessor** *c.n* **1** person or thing who/that succeeds(3) s.o/s.t else. **2** person who succeeds(4) s.o else.

succinct /sək'sɪŋkt/ *adj* (*formal*) (of s.t said or written) short and clear: *a succinct reply.* **suc'cinctly** *adv.* **suc'cinctness** *u.n.*

succour /'sʌkə/ *u.n* **1** (*formal*) help given when s.o/s.t is in trouble.
▷ *tr.v* **2** (*formal*) give (s.o/s.t) succour(1).

succulent /'sʌkjʊlənt/ *adj* **1** (*formal*) (of food) juicy and tasting good. **2** (*technical*) (of a plant or part of it) thick and soft inside.
▷ *c.n* **3** (*technical*) succulent(2) plant, e.g a cactus. **'succulence** *u.n.*

succumb /sə'kʌm/ *intr.v* (often — *to s.o/s.t*) (*formal*) **1** give in or surrender (to s.o/s.t): *John has succumbed to Helen's request. The small boy succumbed to temptation and stole some sweets.* **2** die (as a result of s.t): *She finally succumbed to her illness.*

such /sʌtʃ/ *det* **1** of that/this or the same kind: *I don't trust anyone who is very clever; such people can be dangerous. This net keeps out flies, mosquitoes and all such insects. I have never met such a strange person before.* **2** so great, enjoyable etc: *We had such fun at the party last night!* **any/no/some such** (*formal*) any etc of this/that kind: *'Have you seen a boy with red hair here?' 'We have no such boys in our school.'* **such and such a person**, **animal or thing** (*informal*) a certain person etc: *We were always invited on such and such a day and then on the same morning we had a telephone call to say it had been postponed.* **such (a) . . . as . . .** (a) . . . like . . .: *such a man as Peter; such fruit as apples; such weather as we have never had before.* **such things** etc **as . . .** (*formal*) any/whatever things etc (that) . . .: *Such money as still remains after her death will go to her children.* **such a big**, **nice etc s.o/s.t** (a) person or thing as big, nice etc as this/that. (b) very big, nice etc person/thing: *She has such a beautiful garden. We had such a good time at the party!* **such good** etc **s.o/s.t** (a) s.o/s.t as good etc as this/that. (b) very good etc s.o/s.t: *The Joneses are such nice people!* **such a lot** (**of s.t**) so many/much (of s.t): *There were such a lot of people there that there wasn't enough food.*
▷ *pron* **3** (often — *that . . .*) so great etc (that . . .): *Her help was such (or Such was her help) that we could never have succeeded without it. They had to take on fifty extra workers, such was the business they had over Christmas.* **and such** and others of the same kind. **as such** (a) as being what has just been said: *Mary is an honest person and everyone knows her as such.* (b) in its true meaning: *This is not a restaurant as such but one can always get something to eat here.* **such as it is**; **such as they are** even though it/they may not be very good, useful etc: *If you're cold you can borrow my old coat such as it is.* **such as to do s.t** so great etc that it does s.t: *His help was such as to make our job twice as easy as before.* **such is life** (usu said when s.t sad or unlucky has happened) life is like that. **such is s.t that . . .** s.t

is so great etc that . . .: *Such was the violence of the storm that boats were sinking all around us.*
'such,like *adj* **1** of this/that kind; such(1).
▷ *pron* **2 and suchlike** and suchlike(1) things.
suck /sʌk/ *c.n* **1** (often — *at/on s.t*) example of sucking(2,3): *a suck at/on a* lolly(1).
▷ *v* **2** *tr/intr.v* pull (liquid) into one's mouth (out of s.t) by using the muscles(1) of one's mouth etc, usu with one's lips pressed into a small circle: *suck juice (in/up) through a straw; suck juice out of an orange.* **3** *tr/intr.v* (often — (away) *at/ on s.t*) hold (s.t) in one's mouth while pulling at it with the muscles(1) of one's tongue etc so as to melt and swallow s.t: *Don't suck your thumb! Tom likes sucking sweets.* **4** *tr.v* (of a machine, wave etc) pull (s.o/s.t): *You can suck the dust out of the carpet with this machine.* **suck s.t dry** empty s.t by sucking(2,3) all the liquid out of it. **suck s.o/s.t under** (of a wave in the sea etc) pull s.o/s.t down below the surface. **suck s.t up** pull s.t into oneself/s.t by sucking: *suck up dust with a* hoover. **suck up (to s.o)** (*derog; informal*) try to make s.o like one by being nice to her/him in a way that other people find unpleasant.
'sucker *c.n* **1** person or animal that sucks(2). **2** device that allows one to fix s.t to a surface by suction. **3** organ that some animals have that makes them able to stick to even a vertical surface without slipping or falling. **4** shoot(1) that comes out of the root or the lower part of the stem of a plant. **5** (*derog; informal*) person whom one can cheat easily.
suckle /'sʌkl/ *tr/intr.v* give milk to (a baby or young animal) from one's breast, udder etc.
suction /'sʌkʃən/ *u.n* act or ability of sucking(1) a liquid, gas or air, sometimes with the result that a vacuum is left.
'suction ,pump *c.n* pump that works by suction.
sudden /'sʌdn/ *adj* happening very quickly when it is not expected: *a sudden storm.* **all of a sudden** suddenly.
'suddenly *adv.* **'suddenness** *u.n.*
suds /sʌdz/ *pl.n* = soapsuds.
sue /suː/ *tr/intr.v* (often — (s.o) *for s.t*) (*law*) make a claim (against s.o) (for a certain amount of money).
suede, suède /sweɪd/ *u.n* (often *attrib*) soft leather that has not been made smooth and shiny: *a suede coat.*
suet /'suːɪt/ *u.n* (also *attrib*) hard fat from the kidneys(2) etc of an animal used for cooking: *suet pudding.*
'suety *adj* like suet.
suffer /'sʌfə/ *v* **1** *intr.v* feel pain, sadness etc (as a result of s.t); be damaged (because of s.t): *Irena suffered badly from colds this winter. When parents fight children suffer for it. The plants have suffered badly as a result of this bad weather.* **2** *tr.v* (*formal*) have (s.t) unpleasant happen to one: *Our team suffered its second defeat last Saturday. Sarah suffered the loss of her husband bravely.* **suffer fools gladly** be patient with foolish people: *Our boss doesn't suffer fools gladly.*
'sufferable *adj* that can be suffered(1). Opposite insufferable.
'sufferance *u.n* **on sufferance** accepted but not willingly.

'sufferer *c.n* (often — *from s.t*) person who suffers(1) (from an illness etc).
'suffering *n* **1** *u.n* fact or state of suffering (⇨ suffer(1)). **2** *c.n* (usu *pl*) one case of suffering (⇨ suffer(1)).
suffice /sə'faɪs/ *tr/intr.v* (often — *for s.o/s.t*) (*formal*) be enough (for (s.o/s.t)). **Suffice it to say that . . .** I will only say that . . . .
sufficiency /sə'fɪʃənsɪ/ *n* **1** *u.n* fact of sufficing. **2** *sing.n* (often *a* — *of s.t*) (*formal*) sufficient amount/number (of s.t).
sufficient *adj* (often — *for s.o/s.t*) enough (for s.o/s.t). Opposite insufficient.
sufficiently *adv.*
suffix /'sʌfɪks/ *c.n* (*grammar*) letter or syllable(s) added to the end of a word to change it into a different part of speech, different meaning of the same part of speech: *If we add the suffix '-less' to 'sugar', we get 'sugarless'. If we add the suffix '-n' to 'grow', we get 'grown'.* Compare prefix.
suffocate /'sʌfəˌkeɪt/ *tr/intr.v* (cause (s.o, an animal) to) die or suffer as a result of not having enough air to breathe.
suffocation /ˌsʌfə'keɪʃən/ *u.n.*
suffrage /'sʌfrɪdʒ/ *u.n* (*formal*) right to vote in national elections: *universal suffrage* (where everyone above a certain age has the right).
suffragette /ˌsʌfrə'dʒet/ *c.n* woman in Britain at the beginning of the 20th century who campaigned for the right of women to vote in national elections.
suffuse /sə'fjuːz/ *tr.v* (often — *s.o/s.t with s.t*) (*formal*) (of a colour, liquid, light) come up/out and spread over (s.o/s.t): *The room was suffused with the early morning sun.*
suffusion /sə'fjuːʒən/ *u.n.*
sugar /'ʃʊgə/ *n* **1** *u.n* sweet substance made usu from sugar beet or sugar cane and used in foods: *brown/white sugar.* **2** *c.n* (*technical*) kind of sweet substance found in a plant.
▷ *tr.v* **3** put sugar in/on (s.t). **4** (*fig*) make (s.t) less unpleasant by using polite words etc. **sugar the pill** (*fig*) make s.t unpleasant seem more acceptable or pleasant.
'sugar ,beet *u.n* kind of plant from the roots of which beet sugar, a kind of sugar(1), is made.
'sugar ,cane *u.n* kind of tall grass that grows in tropical countries and from whose stems we can get cane sugar.
,sugar-'coated *attrib.adj* that has a hard coat of sugar over it, often to hide the unpleasant taste inside it: *sugar-coated pills.*
'sugar ,daddy *c.n* (*pl* -ies) (*informal*) older man who gives a young girlfriend money, presents etc.
'sugarless *adj* not having any sugar(1) in it.
'sugary *adj* **1** having (too much) sugar(1) in/on it. **2** (*derog; fig*) (of a person's words, behaviour etc) unpleasantly kind, sweet etc.
suggest /sə'dʒest/ *tr.v* **1** (often — *that*; — *doing s.t*) put (s.t) forward (to s.o) as an idea to be thought about: *I suggested to Paul that we should wait. He suggested going immediately.* **2** cause one to think of (s.o, (doing) s.t); be a sign of (s.t): *Those clouds suggest rain. The storm suggested going back early.* **suggest itself (to oneself/s.o)** come into one's/s.o's mind: *Then another plan suggested itself to her.*
sug'gestible *adj* easily influenced.

suggestion /səˈdʒestʃən/ n 1 u.n act or fact of suggesting (s.t). 2 c.n thing suggested. 3 c.n (usu — of s.t) very small sign/amount (of s.t): *There was a suggestion of impatience in his voice. There was just a suggestion of onion in the soup.* ⇨ suggest(2). 4 u.n (*technical*) putting an idea etc into s.o's mind, not directly but by association with other ideas. **make a suggestion** suggest(1) s.t.

sug'gestive adj (often — of s.t) that suggests(1) (s.t) sometimes s.t sexual or bad.

sug'gestively adv. **sug'gestiveness** u.n.

suicide /ˈsuːɪˌsaɪd/ n 1 u.n act of killing oneself. 2 c.n example of s.o doing this. 3 c.n person who does this. 4 u.n (*fig*) very dangerous action that will almost certainly lead to complete ruin etc: *To give up now would be suicide.* **commit suicide** kill oneself.

suicidal /ˌsuːɪˈsaɪdl/ adj 1 wanting/likely to kill oneself. 2 likely/certain to be suicide(4).

ˌsuiˈcidally adv.

suit /suːt/ c.n 1 jacket(1) and trousers/skirt (and sometimes also waistcoat) that match each other: *He wears a suit to work.* ⇨ bathing suit. 2 one of the four sets (clubs³, diamonds(3), hearts(6) and spades²) into which a pack of cards is divided. 3 = lawsuit. **follow suit** (a) (in card games) play the same suit(2) as was played before. (b) (*fig*) do the same as s.o has done (just) before: *The president stood up and we all followed suit.* **suit of armour** ⇨ armour(1). **wet suit** ⇨ wet.

▷ v 4 tr/intr.v be what (s.o) wants/needs; fit in well with the needs of (s.o/s.t): *Working mornings only suits me* (or *suits my needs*) *very well.* 5 tr.v look right for (s.o/s.t): *That hat doesn't suit you at all; it's for a much taller woman.* 6 tr.v be good, healthy etc for (s.o/s.t): *Late nights don't suit me because I get too tired.* ⇨ suitable. **suit s.o down to the ground** ⇨ ground³(n). **suit oneself** (*informal*) do what one wants to do oneself instead of what other people want: *'I'm not going to the cinema with you.' 'Suit yourself.'* **be suited for/to s.t** have qualities that make one good or right for s.t. **suit s.t to s.t** make s.t fit in well with s.t.

ˌsuitaˈbility u.n (often — for s.t) fact or degree of being suitable (for s.t).

'suitable adj (often — for s.o/s.t) who/that suits(4–6) (s.o/s.t). Opposite unsuitable.

'suitableness u.n. **'suitably** adv.

'suit,case c.n piece of luggage, usu in the shape of a rectangle, used for holding one's clothes etc when one is travelling.

'suiting c/u.n material out of which a suit(1) can be made.

suitor /ˈsuːtə/ c.n 1 (*formal*) man who tries to persuade a woman to marry him. 2 (*law*) person who brings a lawsuit.

suite /swiːt/ c.n 1 (often — of s.t) set (of s.t, e.g furniture, rooms in a hotel): *A bathroom suite includes a bath and a basin.* 2 (*music*) piece of music consisting of several parts that do not have much connection with each other. **three-piece suite** set of furniture consisting of a sofa and two armchairs.

sulk /sʌlk/ intr.v show that one is dissatisfied, unhappy etc by not talking, keeping the corners of one's mouth turned down etc.

'sulkily adv in a sulky(1) way.

'sulkiness u.n fact or state of being sulky.

sulks def.pl.n (often have the —) act or state of sulking.

'sulky adj (-ier, -iest) 1 showing that one is sulking. 2 who often sulks.

sullen /ˈsʌlən/ adj 1 silently sulky. 2 (*literary*) dark and depressing: *the sullen skies of a northern winter.*

'sullenly adv. **'sullenness** u.n.

sully /ˈsʌlɪ/ tr.v (-ies, -ied) (*literary*) make (s.o/ s.t) dirty; make (s.o/s.t) less worthy of respect etc: *sully someone's reputation.*

sulphate /ˈsʌlfeɪt/ c/u.n (often — of s.t) (*chemistry*) salt(2) of sulphuric acid.

sulphide /ˈsʌlfaɪd/ c/u.n (often — of s.t) (*chemistry*) compound(1) of sulphur and s.t else, usu a metal.

sulphur /ˈsʌlfə/ u.n chemical element, usu in the form of a yellow powder, used in medicines etc, *chem.symb* S.

sulphuric acid /sʌlˌfjʊərɪk ˈæsɪd/ u.n kind of strong acid used in car batteries, for making explosives etc, *chem.form* H_2SO_4.

'sulphurous adj of, like or containing sulphur.

sultan /ˈsʌltən/ c.n Muslim ruler.

sultana¹ /sʌlˈtɑːnə/ c.n mother/wife/daughter of a sultan.

sultanate /ˈsʌltəˌneɪt/ c/def.n (often — of s.o/ s.t) 1 country ruled by a sultan (the name of which is s.t). 2 position or rule (of the sultan whose name is s.t).

sultana² /sʌlˈtɑːnə/ small dried grape. ⇨ raisin.

sultry /ˈsʌltrɪ/ adj (-ier, -iest) 1 (of weather) hot and with no wind or fresh air. 2 (usu of a woman, her smile etc) who/that attracts one sexually.

'sultrily adv. **'sultriness** u.n.

sum /sʌm/ c.n 1 simple example of adding, subtracting, multiplying, dividing, of the kind taught to young children. 2 (also pl with a sing meaning) (often — of s.t) amount (of s.t): *A small sum of money is missing from my desk.* **a lump sum** large sum(2) of money paid or given in one amount. **in sum** putting it shortly. **the sum of s.t** the total/whole of s.t: *The sum of 50 and 100 is 150. The sum of my knowledge of how a car engine works is that it needs petrol and water.*

▷ v (-mm-) **sum (s.t) up** 3 give the main points (of a lecture, discussion etc). 4 (*law*) (of a judge) give a summary(3) (of a court case). 5 (often — s.o/ s.t up as s.t) give a quick opinion (about s.o/s.t) (as s.t).

ˌsumming-'up c.n (pl summings-up) one example of summing up (⇨ sum(v)).

ˌsum 'total def.n (often the — of s.t) whole/all (of s.t): *The sum total of our expenses is £40.*

summary /ˈsʌmərɪ/ adj (usu attrib) 1 short, sometimes in the form of a summary(3). 2 (usu of a punishment, e.g execution(1) or dismissal) done immediately and without going through the usual formal steps.

▷ c.n (pl -ies) 3 (often — of s.t) short report (of s.t) giving only the main points.

'summarily adv.

summarize, -ise /ˈsʌməˌraɪz/ tr/intr.v make a summary(3) (of (s.t)); sum(3) s.t up. **to summarize** as a summary(3).

summer /ˈsʌmə/ c/u/def.n 1 (also attrib) (often with capital **S**) season of the year between spring and autumn when one has the warmest weather:

summer clothes. When it is summer in Europe it is winter in Australia. We spend a lot of time outside in (the) summer.

▷ *intr.v* **2** (usu — (in) s.*w*) spend the summer: *They summer away, in the South of France.*

'**summer,house** *c.n* (*pl /-,*haʊzɪz/) small building where one can sit in the shade in a garden.

'**summer ,school** *c.n* course of lessons etc held during the summer holidays.

'**summer,time** *def.n* (often *in* (the) —) summer months.

'**summer ,time** *unique.n* time, during the spring and summer months, when some countries put their clocks forward.

'**summery** *adj* **1** of or like summer(1): *summery weather.* **2** suitable for summer(1): *a summery dress.*

summing-up ⇨ sum.

summit /'sʌmɪt/ *attrib.adj* **1** at the highest level: *a summit meeting* (i.e for world leaders).

▷ *c.n* **2** (often *the — of s.t*) top or highest point (of s,t, esp a mountain). **3** (usu *the — of s.t*) (*formal*) highest level or degree (of s.t): *His behaviour was the summit of rudeness.* **4** meeting between the top leaders of two or more countries.

summon /'sʌmən/ *tr.v* (*formal*) order (s.o) to come, do s.t etc; order (s.o) to appear in a court of law.

'**summons** *c.n* (*pl -es*) **1** order, usu in writing, to appear in a court of law.

▷ *tr.v* **2** give (s.o) a summons(1).

sump /sʌmp/ *c.n* **1** place at the bottom of the engine of a car where the oil collects when it is not circulating(1). **2** place at the bottom of a hole, e.g a mine, where water collects.

sumptuous /'sʌmptjʊəs/ *adj* (*formal*) expensive and generous: *a sumptuous dinner.*

'**sumptuously** *adv.* '**sumptuousness** *u.n.*

sun /sʌn/ *n* **1** *def.n* heavenly body that the earth goes round once every year and from which we get light and heat. **2** *c.n* fixed star that planets go round. **3** *u/def.n* light and warmth from the sun(1): *It's nice to feel the sun on one's body again after a long cold winter.* **4** *u/def.n* place on which the sun(1) is shining: *Let's sit in the sun and talk.* **a place in the sun** (*fig*) a very favourable/fortunate situation. **under the sun** in the world: *Nowhere under the sun can one find nicer people than here.*

▷ *reflex.v* **5** sit, lie etc s.w where the sun(1) is shining on (one). ⇨ sunbathe.

'**sun,baked** *adj* **1** made hard by the sun(3). **2** (*informal*) = sundrenched.

'**sun,bathe** *c.n* **1** act of lying etc in the sun(3) to let it make one's body brown.

▷ *intr.v* **2** lie etc in the sun in this way.

'**sun,bather** *c.n* person who sunbathes(2).

'**sun,beam** *c.n* beam of light from the sun.

'**sun,blind** *c.n* device that keeps the sun(3) from coming in through a window or door and can usu be rolled up or down.

'**sun,burn** *u.n* **1** redness and pain when one has been burnt by the sun. **2** area of skin affected by this.

'**sun,burned** *adj* (also '**sun,burnt**) **1** affected by sunburn(1). **2** (also '**sun,tanned**) browned by the sun.

'**sun,deck** *c.n* one of the top decks, the top deck, of a ship where one can get a lot of sun(3).

'**sun,dial** *c.n* device for showing the time using the sun's shadow: *As the position of the sun in the sky changes, a rod standing on the sundial throws its shadow on different numbers on a circular plate.*

'**sun,down** *u.n* (US) = sunset.

'**sun,downer** *c.n* alcoholic(1) drink that one has in the early evening.

'**sun,drenched** *adj* that receives a great amount of sun(3): *a sundrenched beach.*

,**sun'dried** *adj* that has been dried in the sun(4).

'**sun,flower** *c.n* (also *attrib*) kind of tall plant with a very big yellow flower that turns to follow the sun: *Sunflower oil that we use for cooking is made from sunflower seeds.*

'**sun,glasses** *pl.n* dark glasses used to protect one's eyes from the sun(3).

'**sun ,god** *c/def.n* god of the sun in some ancient religions.

'**sun,lamp** *c.n* (also '**sun,ray ,lamp**) kind of lamp using ultra-violet light for browning one's skin.

'**sunless** *adj* that does not get or have any sun(3): *a sunless corner of the garden.*

'**sun,light** *u.n* light from the sun. **in the sunlight** in a place that the sun is shining on.

'**sun,lit** *adj* on which the sun is shining.

'**sun ,lounge** *c.n* room in which one gets a lot of sun because it has glass sides (and a glass roof).

'**sunnily** *adv* in a sunny(1,3) way.

'**sunniness** *u.n* fact or state of being sunny.

'**sunny** *adj* (*-ier, -iest*) **1** full of sun(3); in/on which the sun(1) is shining: *a sunny spot*; *a sunny afternoon.* **2** in which there are no clouds to hide the sun(1): *a voyage under sunny skies.* **3** (*fig*) cheerful: *a sunny character.*

'**sun,ray** *attrib.adj* that uses ultra-violet light: *a sunray lamp* (a sunlamp); *sunray treatment.*

'**sun,rise** *c/unique n* time when the sun comes up above the horizon. Opposite sunset. **at sunrise** at this time.

'**sun,roof** *c.n* sliding piece in the roof of a car that allows the sun(3) to come in when it is opened.

'**sun,set** *c/unique n* time when the sun goes down behind the horizon. Opposite sunrise. **at sunset** at this time.

'**sun,shade** *c.n* **1** thing like an umbrella used to protect one from the sun. **2** sunblind or blind[2] on the front of a shop, restaurant etc.

'**sun,shine** *u.n* **1** sunlight. **2** sun(4). **a ray of sunshine** (*fig*) (a) happiness during an unhappy time or in an unhappy place etc. (b) a person who brings a ray of sunshine(a).

,**sun,shine 'roof** *c.n* = sunroof.

'**sun,spot** *c.n* **1** dark spot on the surface of the sun. **2** (*informal*) place where the sun often shines and summers are long and hot.

'**sun,stroke** *u.n* illness caused by too much sun(3), esp on one's head: *You'll get sunstroke if you sit on the beach without a hat.* Compare heatstroke.

'**sun,tan** *c.n* (also *attrib*) brown colour of the skin which is the result of being in the sun: *I got a lovely suntan on holiday last year. Did you use suntan* lotion?

'**sun,tanned** *adj* having a suntan.

'**sun,trap** *c.n* place which gets a lot of sun.

'**sun-,up** *unique n* (*informal*) = sunrise. **at sun-up** at the time the sun rises.

'sun ,visor *c.n* ⇨ visor(1).

sundae /'sʌndeɪ/ *c.n* mixture of ice-cream, fruit, fruit juice, nuts etc.

Sunday /'sʌndɪ/ *c/unique n* (also *attrib*) (*written abbr* Sun) day after Saturday and before Monday on which most people in European and American countries do not work; second day of the weekend. *last Sunday* the last Sunday before today. *next Sunday* the first Sunday after today. *not/never in a month of Sundays* not for a very long time; it is very unlikely. *on a Sunday* on a day of one week that is/was, will be, a Sunday. *on Sunday* on the nearest Sunday after/before today or on the Sunday of the week being referred to: *I wrote to you on Sunday*. *on Sundays* every Sunday: *I get up late on Sundays*. *Sunday after next* the second Sunday after today. *Sunday before last* the Sunday before last Sunday. *Sunday afternoon*, *evening etc* the afternoon, evening etc of the last, next, every Sunday.

'Sunday ,school *c/unique n* **1** lessons about religion given to children on Sundays. **2** place where such lessons are given.

sundeck, sundial, sundown, sundrenched, sundried ⇨ sun.

sundry /'sʌndrɪ/ *attrib.adj* various: *There are sundry articles for sale cheaply in that box.* *all and sundry* everyone; all kinds of people: *All and sundry came to the meeting.*

'sundries *pl.n* various small things that are not important enough to be listed separately, e.g in an account.

sunflower ⇨ sun.

sung /sʌŋ/ *p.p* of sing¹.

sunglasses, sun god ⇨ sun.

sunk /sʌŋk/ *p.p* of sink².

sunken ⇨ sink².

sunlamp, sunless, sunlight, sunlit, sun lounge, sunny, sunray, sunrise, sunroof, sunset, sunshade, sunshine, sunspot, sunstroke, suntan(ned), suntrap, sun-up ⇨ sun.

super¹ /'suːpə/ *adj* (*informal*) excellent; very good: *That was a super party.*

super² /'suːpə/ *c.n* (*informal*) superintendent, usu in the police.

superabundant /ˌsuːpərə'bʌndənt/ *adj* (usu *attrib*) (*formal*) existing in very large numbers/ quantities, usu more than what is needed.

,supera'bundance *c/u.n*. **,supera'bundantly** *adv*.

superannuate /ˌsuːpər'ænjuˌeɪt/ *tr.v* cause (s.o) to stop doing a job when he/she has reached an age where he/she is thought too old for it.

,super'annu,ated *adj* (of a person) who has been superannuated (⇨ superannuate).

superannuation /ˌsuːpərˌænjuˈeɪʃən/ *u.n*.

superb /suː'pɜːb/ *adj* extremely good; wonderful: *a superb meal.*

su'perbly *adv*.

supercilious /ˌsuːpə'sɪlɪəs/ *adj* (*derog; formal*) treating other people as less important, clever etc than oneself.

,super'ciliously *adv*. **,super'ciliousness** *u.n*.

superduper /ˌsuːpə'duːpə/ *adj* (*slang*) excellent; very good; super¹.

superego /ˌsuːpər'iːgəʊ/ *c/def.n* (*technical*)

partly conscious idea that a person has of herself/himself as she/he would like to be rather than as she/he really is that makes her/him do what she/he thinks right and not do what she/he thinks wrong. Compare ego.

superficial /ˌsuːpə'fɪʃəl/ *adj* **1** only of/on the surface and not deep: *a superficial cut.* **2** not (the result of) thinking deeply and carefully: *superficial remarks.*

superficiality /ˌsuːpəˌfɪʃɪ'ælɪtɪ/ *u.n*. **,super-'ficially** *adv*.

superfine /'suːpəˌfaɪn/ *adj* very fine: *cloth of superfine quality.*

superfluity /ˌsuːpə'fluːɪtɪ/ *c/u.n* (*pl* -ies) (*formal*) (often — of s.t) too much, more than is needed, (of s.t); excess (of s.t).

superfluous /suː'pɜːfluəs/ *adj* excessive; too much; more than is needed.

su'perfluously *adv*. **su'perfluousness** *u.n*.

superhuman /ˌsuːpə'hjuːmən/ *adj* (almost) beyond what a human being can do: *superhuman strength/courage.*

superimpose /ˌsuːpərɪm'pəʊz/ *tr.v* (often — s.t on s.t) put (s.t) over (s.t else), often so that one can see both at the same time.

superintend /ˌsuːpərɪn'tend/ *tr.v* manage, arrange and inspect (s.t, e.g the work of others).

,superin'tendent *c.n* (*written abbr* Supt) **1** person who superintends the work of others. **2** rank in the British police.

superior /suː'pɪərɪə/ *adj* **1** (often — to s.o/s.t) higher in position, rank, quality, value etc (than s.o/s.t). Opposite inferior. **2** higher than the average in quality, ability etc: *a superior quality of cloth.* **3** (*derog*) showing that one thinks oneself better, cleverer etc than other people: *a superior smile.* *superior to s.t* (a) ⇨ superior(1). (b) (*formal*) too good, strong etc to need to do s.t bad: *Dorothy is superior to revenge.*

▷ *c.n* **4** (usu s.o's — (in s.t)) person who is higher in rank or greater in ability etc (than s.o) (in s.t). Opposite inferior. **5** (in printing) number, letter written or printed above the line. *Father/Mother Superior* head of a monastery etc.

superiority /suːˌpɪərɪ'ɒrɪtɪ/ *u.n* fact or quality of being superior(*adj*): *my superiority to him as a writer.* Opposite inferiority. *superiority in numbers* fact or state of having more people etc than s.o/s.t else.

,superi'ority ,complex *c.n* (*informal*) feeling or belief that one is superior(1) to other people which makes one behave rudely to them. Opposite inferiority complex.

superl *written abbr* superlative(2).

superlative /suː'pɜːlətɪv/ *adj* **1** extremely good; as good as it is possible to have/be.

▷ *n* (*written abbr* superl) **2** *def.n* (*grammar*) highest degree of comparison of an adj or adv: *The comparative*(4) *of 'big' is 'bigger' and the superlative is 'biggest'.* **3** *c.n* example of the superlative(2).

su,perlative de'gree *def.n* = superlative(2).

su'perlatively *adv* (*formal*) extremely: *superlatively good.*

supermarket /'suːpəˌmɑːkɪt/ *c.n* big shop selling food etc where one chooses goods oneself and takes them to a place on the way out to pay for them.

supernatural /ˌsuːpə'nætʃrəl/ *adj* **1** having, the

result of, magical(1) powers that are not the natural ones in our world and that do not follow our laws of cause and effect(1).

▷ *def.n* **2** things that are supernatural(1).

super'naturally *adv.*

supersede /ˌsuːpəˈsiːd/ *tr.v* take the place of (s.t that has become out of date).

supersonic /ˌsuːpəˈsɒnɪk/ *adj* faster than the speed of sound. Opposite subsonic.

superstar /ˈsuːpəˌstɑː/ *c.n* very famous and successful star(6).

superstition /ˌsuːpəˈstɪʃən/ *c/u.n* belief that is not based on reason and on facts but on the supernatural(2), magic(3) etc.

super'stitious *adj* believing in, based on, superstition.

super'stitiously *adv.*

superstructure /ˈsuːpəˌstrʌktʃə/ *c.n* **1** structure(1), often the upper parts of a ship, that is on top of s.t else. **2** part of a building that is above ground level. **3** (often — *of s.t*) organization or system (of beliefs etc) that has been built up or grown from a certain base.

supertax /ˈsuːpəˌtæks/ *u.n* (also **'sur,tax**) special extra tax that people with very high incomes pay.

supervise /ˈsuːpəˌvaɪz/ *tr/intr.v* direct or watch with the power to give orders (the work done by others).

supervision /ˌsuːpəˈvɪʒən/ *u.n.*

supervisor /ˈsuːpəˌvaɪzə/ *c.n* person who supervises.

super'visory *adj* (usu *attrib*) of or referring to supervision.

supper /ˈsʌpə/ *c/u.n* last meal of the day, often an informal one instead of a more formal dinner, sometimes late at night.

'supperless *adj* without having had supper: *The children were sent to bed supperless.*

supplant /səˈplɑːnt/ *tr.v* take the place of (s.o), often by dishonest or forceful means.

supple /ˈsʌpl/ *adj* bending easily; flexible(1): *Athletes have supple limbs(1).*

'suppleness *u.n.* **supply¹** /ˈsʌplɪ/ *adv.*

supplement /ˈsʌplɪmənt/ *c.n* **1** thing added to s.t, e.g a person's diet(1) or the main part of a newspaper.

▷ *tr.v* /ˌsʌplɪˈment/ **2** (often — *s.t by/with s.t*) add s.t to (s.t).

supple'mentary *adj* **1** (often — *to s.t*) that is a supplement(1) (to s.t). **2** (*geometry*) (of angles) that total 180°: *An angle of 60° and an angle of 120° are supplementary angles.* **supplementary to s.t** (of an angle) totalling 180° with another angle.

supple,mentary 'benefit *u.n* extra money given by the British government to s.o who already receives sickness benefit(2) etc but still does not have enough money to live on.

suppleness ⇒ supple.

suppliant /ˈsʌplɪənt/ *c.n* (also *attrib*) (*literary*) person who asks for s.t humbly.

'supplicant *c.n* = suppliant.

supplicate /ˈsʌplɪˌkeɪt/ *tr/intr.v* (often — (s.o) for s.t) (*formal*) ask (s.o) humbly for s.t; ask s.o humbly for (s.t).

supplication /ˌsʌplɪˈkeɪʃən/ *u.n.*

supply¹ ⇒ supple.

supply² /səˈplaɪ/ *n* (*pl -ies*) **1** *c.n* (often — *of s.t*) amount or store (of s.t) that is ready to be used. **2** *u.n* (often *the* — *of s.t*) (act of providing a supply(1) (of s.t). **3** *c.n* (often — *of s.t*) amount (of s.t): *You need a large supply of patience for this work.* **in short supply** not there in as large numbers/amounts as one wants.

▷ *tr.v* (*-ies, -ied*) (often — *s.o/s.t with s.t*; — *s.t to s.o/ s.t*) **4** provide (a supply(1) (of s.t)) to (s.o/s.t): *I was supplied with paper and a pen. We supply fruit to the market.* **5** provide a supply(1) (of s.t) to (s.o/s.t): *We provide the hospital with doctors.* **6** satisfy or fill (a need).

sup'plier *c.n* (often — *of s.o/s.t*) person or shop etc who/that supplies (⇒ supply(4,5)) (s.o/s.t).

sup'plies *pl.n* things needed for living, for s.t to be able to work etc: *Without supplies we cannot continue our journey through the mountains.*

sup,ply and de'mand *u.n* amount of s.t that can be supplied, compared with the amount that is wanted: *The prices of goods are largely governed by the law of supply and demand.*

sup'ply ,teacher *c.n* teacher who takes the place of regular teachers while they are ill etc.

support /səˈpɔːt/ *n* **1** *c.n* (often — *for/of s.o/s.t*) person or thing who/that holds (s.o/s.t) up so that he/she/it does not fall. **2** *u.n* (often — *for/ of s.o/s.t*) act or fact of holding (s.o/s.t) up to prevent her/him/it falling. **3** *c.n* (often — *of s.o*) person who provides the money etc (for s.o, e.g her/his family) to live on: *He is the sole¹ support of his old mother.* **4** *u.n* help, encouragement etc, sometimes from the number of people who come to meetings, matches etc: *Our team gets a lot of support on Saturdays. Can we rely on your support at the meeting?* **in support of s.o/s.t** in order to support(7,8) s.o/s.t. **means of support** ⇒ means.

▷ *tr.v* **5** be a support(1) for (s.o/s.t): *These walls support the roof.* **6** be a support(3) for (s.o). **7** give support(4) to (s.o/s.t). **8** tend to show that (s.t) is correct: *The results of tests support Dorothy's idea that the cat was poisoned.* **s.o can(not) support s.t** (*formal*) s.o can(not) bear(5) s.t: *How does your wife support the heat here? I cannot support the noise.*

sup'porter *c.n* (often — *of s.o/s.t*) person who supports(6,7) s.t.

sup,porting 'part/'role *c.n* small part in a play, film etc which is less important than those of the stars.

sup,porting 'programme *c.n* less important film, show etc before the main one in a cinema, theatre etc: *Our cinema usually has a supporting programme of cartoons(2) before the main film.*

sup'porting 'role *c.n* ⇒ supporting part.

sup'portive *adj* who/that supports(7) (s.o/s.t).

suppose /səˈpəʊz/ *conj* **1** (what would happen) if; let us imagine that: *'Suppose the bus is late; what happens then?' 'We miss our plane.'*

▷ *tr.v* **2** (often — *that...*) believe, think, assume(1). (s.t) without having facts: *I suppose you're right. I suppose we should be going home.* **3** (*formal*) have (s.t) as a condition; presuppose (s.t): *Smoke supposes fire burning somewhere.* **suppose s.o/ s.t to be s.t** think, believe, etc that s.o/s.t is s.t without having facts: *Everyone supposes Mary to have a lot of money.* **suppose so/not** think that it is probably (not) true that . . .: *'Is John right about the time of the lecture?' 'Yes, I suppose so.'* **be supposed to be/do s.t** (a) be thought/ believed to be/do s.t: *Fred is supposed to be a very* good teacher. **(b)** be expected to be/do s.t; have the duty of being/doing s.t: *Why are you here, Alan? You're supposed to be at school!* **not be supposed to be/do s.t** not be allowed to be/do s.t: *You're not supposed to bring dogs in here.*

sup'posed *adj* who/that people believed, imagined etc to be so: *Anna's supposed boyfriend turned out to be her brother.*

supposedly /sə'pəʊzɪdlɪ/ *adv* according to what people believe to be true: *Supposedly yesterday was the hottest day of the year but it didn't seem all that hot to me.*

sup'posing *conj* = suppose(1).

supposition /ˌsʌpə'zɪʃən/ *n* **1** *u.n* act or fact of believing (s.t) to be true, guessing, without any proof. **2** thing supposed (⇒ suppose(2)).

suppository /sə'pɒzɪtərɪ/ *c.n* (*pl -ies*) small mass of medicine, usu mixed with wax etc that melts easily, that is put into the anus or vagina instead of being swallowed.

suppress /sə'pres/ *tr.v* **1** put an end to (s.t), prevent (s.t) starting, by force: *Any attempt to cause trouble at the match was quickly suppressed by the police. The boys were afraid of their teacher so they suppressed their laughter when he could not open the door.* **2** prevent (s.o) doing s.t: *The students could not be suppressed for long.* **3** prevent (s.t, e.g a piece of news) being made public.

suppression /sə'preʃən/ *u.n.*

suppressor /sə'presə/ *c.n* **1** (often — *of s.o/s.t*) person or thing who/that suppresses (s.o/s.t). **2** (*technical*) device that prevents a machine interfering with the sound on a radio or with the sound and/or picture on television.

suppurate /'sʌpjʊˌreɪt/ *intr.v* (*formal*) (of a wound or sore) form pus.

suppuration /ˌsʌpjʊ'reɪʃən/ *u.n.*

supreme /su'priːm/ *adj* **1** highest in rank, degree, importance etc: *the supreme head of state*; *a supreme example of* self-sacrifice. **2** greatest possible: *the supreme test of honesty.*

supremacy /su'preməsɪ/ *u.n* **1** (often — *of s.o/ s.t*) fact or state of (s.o/s.t) being supreme(1). **2** (often — *over s.o/s.t*) supreme(1) position (over s.o/s.t): *gain/win supremacy over the others as an actor.*

Su,preme 'Being *def.n* (*literary*) God.

Su,preme 'Court *def.n* highest court in the US or one of its states.

su,preme 'sacri,fice *def.n* (often *make the —*) dying for one's country, beliefs etc.

Supt *written abbr* superintendent.

surcharge /'sɜːˌtʃɑːdʒ/ *c.n* **1** extra amount that one is asked to pay in addition to the ordinary charge for s.t: *If you do not put enough stamps on a letter, the person who receives it has to pay a surcharge.*

▷ *tr.v* **2** make (s.o) pay a surcharge(1) (of a certain amount).

sure /ʃʊə/ *adj* **1** that cannot be doubted; that is absolutely true; certain(4): *One thing is sure and that is that nobody was killed in the accident.* **2** (often — *that, whether, when, where* etc . . .) knowing/feeling that s.t is sure(1): *I think it's 12 o'clock but I'm not quite sure (that it is). I'm not sure how one gets to the station from here.* **be sure to do s.t** be certain, not forget, to do s.t: *she's sure to be at the meeting today.*

Be sure to lock the door when you leave. **make sure (of s.t)** check (s.t) so that one does not make a mistake: *'Does John know we're here?' 'I think so but I'll make sure.'* **make sure (of s.t, that . . .)** arrange (that . . .) so that there will be no mistake: *Make sure you're not late for the bus.* **slow but sure** ⇒ slow(*adj*). **sure of oneself** trusting one's abilities, knowledge etc; self-confident. **to be sure** certainly; of course; one must admit that: *To be sure it's a long walk to the shops but you're young and strong.*

▷ *adv* **3** (mostly US) certainly; really; yes: *'May I borrow your pen?' 'Sure (you may borrow it).'* *Mary sure is pretty.* **as sure as . . .** and that is as sure(1) as the fact that . . .: *Freda is getting married next week as sure as my name's Ted.* **as sure as fate** ⇒ fate(*n*). **for sure** absolutely a fact. **sure enough** as had been expected: *The train is due at 11.35 and sure enough at 11.33 it came into sight.*

,sure'fire *attrib.adj* (*informal*) absolutely certain; that cannot fail: *a surefire reason for failure.*

,sure'footed *adj* that never slips or falls because he/she/it always puts his/her/its feet down in the right places.

,sure'footedness *u.n.*

surely *adv* **1** (used to show that one would think it surprising if what one is saying is wrong): *Surely you don't think I'm going to pay for your ticket! You surely know how to spell lawyer, don't you?* **2** safely; without accident: *slowly but surely.* ⇒ slow but sure (⇒ slow(*adj*)). **3** certainly; without any doubt.

'sureness *u.n.*

,sure 'thing *interj* **1** = sure(3).

▷ *sing.n* **2** certainty: *Put all your money on my horse; it's a sure thing for the second race.*

'surety /'ʃʊərətɪ/ *c/u.n* (*pl -ies*) (*law*) **1** (often — *for s.o*) person who agrees to be responsible, usu to a court of law, (for s.o else's behaviour, the payment of money). **2** money given, promised, to a court of law so as to try to make sure that s.o appears in court when told to do so. ⇒ bail'(1).

surf /sɜːf/ *u.n* **1** foam(1) and disturbance of the sea, a lake etc when waves come towards the shore, rocks etc and break on them.

▷ *intr.v* **2** ride on the surf(1) as a sport.

'surf,board *c.n* wooden, plastic(1) etc board for surfing (⇒ surf(2)) on.

'surf,boat *c.n* light boat for going over/through surf(1) in.

'surfer *c.n* person who surfs(2).

'surfing *u.n* (often *go —*) sport of surfing (⇒ surf(2)).

'surf ,ride *c.n* **1** example of surf riding.

▷ *intr.v* **2** = surf(2).

'surf ,riding *u.n* = surfing.

surface /'sɜːfɪs/ *attrib.adj* **1** (of post) by land and/or sea, not by air: *by surface mail.* **2** that does not go deep: *a surface wound.* Compare superficial(1). **3** (of a ship) that is not a submarine: *a surface* vessel .

▷ *c.n* (often *the — of s.t*) **4** outside (of s.t): *The surface of the wall must be smooth.* **5** top (of s.t, e.g the sea). **on the surface (a)** ⇒ surface(4,5). **(b)** when one does not know her/him/it very well and when one therefore does not know what she/ he/it is really like: *On the surface Kate was very* *quiet but underneath she was angry.* Opposite under the surface(b). **under the surface** (a) on the inside; under water etc. (b) when one knows a person well and understands, knows what he/ she is really like, thinking, etc: *What's she like under the surface?* .

▷ *intr.v* **6** come to the surface of s.t liquid: *The submarine surfaced only at night.* **7** (*fig; informal*) appear; come into a position where it can be seen, noticed etc: *At first everyone seemed happy but slowly problems began to surface.* **8** (*fig; informal*) appear for the first time in the morning having woken up or got out of bed.

,surface-to-'air *adj* (*military*) (of a missile(1) etc) fired from the ground at s.t in the air.

'surface ,worker *c.n* mine worker who works above ground.

surfboard, surfboat ⇨ surf.

surfeit /'sɜːfɪt/ *c.n* (usu *sing*) (often *a — of s.t*) too many/much (of s.t, e.g food).

surfer, surfing, surf riding ⇨ surf.

surge /sɜːdʒ/ *c.n* (often *— of s.t*) **1** wave (of s.t); thing that moves forward or gets stronger like a wave (and is composed of s.t): *a surge of people into the theatre; a sudden surge in the electrical current; a surge of feeling in a person's heart.*

▷ *intr.v* **2** (usu *— forward, out, up* etc) move (forward etc) in a surge(1): *Anger surged up in him.*

surgeon /'sɜːdʒən/ *c.n* doctor who operates on s.o, an animal etc e.g cutting her/him/it open to remove a diseased part of the body. ⇨ dental surgeon, tree surgeon.

surgery /'sɜːdʒərɪ/ *n* (*pl -ies*) **1** *u.n* work of a surgeon(1). **2** *c.n* place where one or more doctors/dentists receive and deal with patients who come to them. **3** *u.n* time during which patients can visit a surgery(2): *I'm sorry but you've missed surgery; it's from 2.30 to 5.30 today.*

surgical /'sɜːdʒɪkl/ *adj* **1** of, for, referring to, surgery(3): *surgical instruments.* **2** (of a piece of clothing) made to help or cure a medical condition: *surgical boots.*

,surgical 'spirit *u.n* (*technical*) alcohol(1) used for cleaning wounds etc.

surly /'sɜːlɪ/ *adj* (*-ier, -iest*) (*derog*) rude, usu by not being willing to talk, help etc; not friendly.
'surliness *u.n.*

surmise /sɜːˈmaɪz/ *c.n* **1** (*formal*) reasonable guess.

▷ *tr/intr.v* **2** (often *— that . . .*) (*formal*) make a surmise(1) (that . . .).

surmount /sɜːˈmaʊnt/ *tr.v* (*formal*) **1** overcome (difficulties etc); manage to get over (s.t difficult). **2** manage to jump over (s.t). **3** (usu passive) be above or on top of (s.t): *The hill was surmounted by trees.*

sur'mountable *adj* (*formal*) that can be surmounted(1). Opposite insurmountable.

surname /'sɜː,neɪm/ *c.n* (also **'family ,name**) name that one shares with one's parents, grandparents, brothers and (until they marry) sisters. Compare Christian name, forename.

surpass /sɜːˈpɑːs/ *tr.v* (often *— s.o/s.t at/ in s.t*) (*formal*) do better than (s.o/s.t) (in s.t).

sur'passing *adj* (*literary*) better than anyone/ anything else: *surpassing beauty.* ⇨ unsurpassed.

surplice /'sɜːplɪs/ *c.n* loose white piece of clothing with big sleeves, worn over other clothes by priests and members of the choir at religious services.

surplus /'sɜːpləs/ *adj* **1** (often *— to s.t*) more than is needed or used (for/in s.t): *Mrs Brown says these are surplus to her requirements.*

▷ *c.n* **2** (often *— of s.t*) number or amount (of s.t) that is surplus(1).

surprise /səˈpraɪz/ *attrib.adj* **1** that gives s.o a surprise(2): *a surprise attack.*

▷ *n* **2** *sing/u.n* feeling caused by s.t happening when one is not expecting it. **3** *c.n* thing that causes a surprise(2): *It was a surprise to find Ian already up and dressed so early.* **give s.o a surprise** do s.t that makes s.o feel surprise(1). **take s.o/s.t by surprise** find s.o/an animal not expecting one/it: *Our attack took the enemy completely by surprise.*

▷ *tr.v* (rare in continuous tenses) **4** give (s.o) a surprise; cause surprise(2) to (s.o): *His success surprised us all.* **5** take (s.o, an animal) by surprise. **6** shock (s.o) because he/she did not expect anything so bad: *His rudeness to his mother surprises me.*

sur'prising *adj* that surprises(4–6): *What I find surprising is that he didn't apologize.*

surreal /səˈrɪəl/ *adj* (*formal*) strange (and disturbing to the mind); like a dream; not like real life.

sur'rea,lism *u.n* modern kind of art and literature that tries to express what goes on in a person's unconscious mind in a set of pictures like dreams.

sur'realist *adj* **1** of or referring to surrealism.

▷ *c.n* **2** artist or writer using surrealism.

sur,rea'listic *adj* **1** surreal. **2** of or referring to surrealism.

sur,rea'listically *adv.*

surrender /səˈrendə/ *c/u.n* **1** (example of) stopping fighting, arguing etc and allowing one's enemy or opponent(1,2) to win (s.t).

▷ *v* **2** *tr/intr.v* stop fighting, arguing etc and allow one's enemy or opponent(1,2) to win (s.o/s.t). **3** *tr.v* give up (one's claim to s.t sometimes in return for s.t else, e.g money); no longer keep (s.t): *You have to surrender your ticket as you go out of the railway station. You can surrender your insurance policy² at any time.* **surrender to s.t** stop trying to control a feeling, resist pressure etc and allow it to defeat one: *After being brave for several hours he surrendered to the pain and had an injection.*

surreptitious /ˌsʌrəpˈtɪʃəs/ *adj* (*formal*) secret.
,surrep'titiously *adv.* **,surrep'titiousness** *u.n.*

surrogate /'sʌrəgɪt/ *attrib.adj* **1** taking the place of, used instead of, the real or ordinary one: *a surrogate mother; a surrogate priest; a surrogate material.*

▷ *c.n* **2** person or thing that is surrogate(1).

surround /səˈraʊnd/ *c.n* **1** thing that is round (the edge of) s.t: *I don't like the surround of the painting.*

▷ *tr.v* **2** (often *— s.o/s.t with s.t*) be or move into positions all round (s.o/s.t): *surround ourselves with friends. Come out with your hands up! You're surrounded (by police officers).* **3** (often passive) be easy to find in many places near one: *We are surrounded by good restaurants in this part of the country.*

sur'rounding *adj* (usu *attrib*) that is all round one: *the surrounding country.*

sur'roundings *pl.n* (often *the — of s.t*) **1** area round (s.t). **2** conditions in which s.o/s.t exists: *I'm not happy in these surroundings.*

surtax /'sɜː‚tæks/ *u.n* = supertax.

surveillance /sə'veɪləns/ *u.n* close watch on s.o/s.t to protect her/him/it or to prevent her/him/it escaping etc. *under surveillance* being closely watched in this way: *We have them under surveillance.*

survey /'sɜːveɪ/ *n* **1** (often *— of s.t*) inspection (of s.o/s.t); look, report, either a general or a detailed one; viewing (of s.t): *The purpose of a survey is to make a map of an area or to find out the condition of something such as a house before a person buys it.* **2** *c.n* map (of s.t). *Ordnance Survey* ⇒ ordnance. *under survey* being surveyed(3), usu to find out its condition before s.o buys it.

▷ *tr.v* /sə'veɪ/ **3** make a survey(1,2) of (s.o/s.t).

surveyor /sə'veɪə/ *c.n* person whose job is to survey(3) (s.t). *quantity surveyor* ⇒ quantity.

survive /sə'vaɪv/ *v* **1** *intr.v* continue to exist; not be killed or die; not stop being done etc: *Only two of his children survive now. Few of their old customs still survive.* **2** *tr.v* not be killed (by (s.t)): *25 passengers survived the crash.* **3** *tr.v* be still alive after the death of (s.o): *Mrs Green died last night and is survived by two of her children.*

sur'vival *n* **1** *u.n* (often *— of s.t*) fact of s.o/s.t surviving(1,2) (s.t): *Their survival of the crash was a miracle(1).* **2** *c.n* (usu *a — from s.t*) thing that has survived(1) (from s.t): *This ceremony is a survival from very ancient times.*

sur'vival ‚kit *c.n* small collection of things that will make it possible for s.o to survive(1) anywhere, e.g in the desert after a crash.

sur‚vival of the 'fittest *def/unique n* = natural selection.

sur'vivor *c.n* person who has survived(1,2) (s.t).

susceptible /sə'septɪbl/ *adj* (*formal*) **1** (often *— to s.t*) easily influenced or attacked (by s.t): *Peter is very susceptible to colds.* **2** whose feelings, esp ones of love, are easily affected. *susceptible of s.t* (*formal*) that can have done to it the thing shown by a noun: *susceptible of proof* (that can be proved).

sus‚cepti'bility *u.n* (often *— to s.t*) fact of being susceptible (to s.t).

suspect /'sʌspekt/ *adj* **1** that one should suspect(3); that one cannot trust or be sure about: *a radio that is suspect because it is so cheap.*

▷ *c.n* /'sʌspekt/ **2** person who is suspected (⇒ suspect(4)), esp of having done s.t criminal.

▷ *tr.v* /sə'spekt/ **3** (often *— that...*) think (that there is s.t) without being sure or without having proof: *Be careful — I suspect (that there is) a trap.* **4** (often *— s.o of s.t*; *— s.o to be s.t*) think that (s.o/s.t) is (doing), has done, s.t: *I suspect David of lying to us. Wendy suspects that man to be a murderer.* **5** be suspicious(1) about (s.t): *He says he is doing it only for his children but I suspect his reasons.* **6** (*informal*) suppose (that...): *I suspect the children will want to go home soon.*

suspected /sə'spektɪd/ *attrib.adj* that people suspect(3,4) to be s.t: *He has a suspected broken ankle.*

suspicion /sə'spɪʃən/ *n* **1** *u.n* fact of suspecting

s.t. **2** *c.n* (often *have a — (that) ...*) feeling of suspecting (that ...). *a suspicion of s.t* (*fig*) a very small amount of s.t: *There is just a suspicion of onion in the soup. above suspicion* too respected to be suspected(4). *under suspicion* being suspected(4). *(treat s.o/s.t) with suspicion* (treat s.o/s.t) in a suspicious(1) way.

suspicious /sə'spɪʃəs/ *adj* **1** (often *— about/of s.o/s.t*) who/that suspects(4) (s.o/s.t). **2** who/that makes one suspicious(1) about her/him/it: *We saw a suspicious character looking into cars parked in the streets and told the police. We noticed his suspicious behaviour.*

su'spiciously *adv.*

suspend /sə'spend/ *tr.v* (*formal*) **1** (often *— s.o/s.t from s.t*) hang (s.o/s.t) down (from s.t): *The light was suspended from the branch of a tree.* **2** (usu passive) cause (s.t) to remain in the air or a liquid without moving: *Low clouds hung suspended over the area.* **3** postpone (s.t); delay (s.t) for a certain time; stop (s.t) being in force for a certain time: *suspend payment until the work is completed.* **4** stop (a person, team etc) taking part in s.t, e.g a match, usu as a punishment: *British teams have been suspended from international football because of bad crowd behaviour.*

su'spenders *pl.n* **1** pair of garters for men's socks. **2** (US) braces.

su'spender ‚belt *c.n* device worn round the hips by a woman to keep her stockings up.

suspension /sə'spenʃən/ *n* **1** *u.n* (often *the — of s.o/s.t*) act of suspending(1,3,4) s.o/s.t or being suspended(1-4). **2** *c.n* (*technical*) liquid in which very small solid pieces are suspended(2). **3** *c.n* part of a car etc that helps to make it more comfortable by absorbing(4) (some of) the shocks when one goes over rough places. *in suspension* in a state of being suspended(1-3). *under suspension* in a state of being suspended(4).

su'spension ‚bridge *c.n* bridge that hangs by cables(1) from towers.

suspense /sə'spens/ *u.n* state of waiting anxiously for s.t to happen: *The suspense was almost impossible to bear. We were kept in suspense all day waiting to hear whether Ann had been hurt in the accident.*

suspicion, suspicious(ly) ⇒ suspect.

sustain /sə'steɪn/ *tr.v* **1** (*formal*) bear the weight of (s.t); hold (s.t) up (so that it does not fall). **2** support and/or encourage (s.o); help (s.o) to bear(5) s.t. **3** (of food) help (s.o) to remain strong: *A meal like that can sustain you all day.* **4** bear(5) (s.t); not be beaten by (s.t). **5** (*law*) (of a court, judge) decide in favour of (s.t). Opposite overrule. **6** suffer (s.t); experience (s.t unpleasant): *The car sustained a lot of damage in the crash.* **7** keep (s.t) going; not stop (s.t): *The team started off very fast but they could not sustain it for long and soon fell back. You must sustain that note for at least ten seconds.*

sustenance /'sʌstɪnəns/ *u.n* food that sustains(3).

svelte /svelt/ *adj* (*formal*) (usu of a woman) slim(1).

SW *written abbr* **1** short wave. **2** southwest(ern).

swab /swɒb/ *c.n* (*medical*) **1** pad used to collect liquid, e.g from a wound. **2** liquid taken with a swab(1).

▷ *tr.v* (*-bb-*) **3** (often — *s.t up*) collect (liquid) with a swab(1).

swaddle /'swɒdl/ *tr.v* (often — *s.o/s.t in s.t*) wrap (s.o/s.t) up by winding s.t round her/him/ it several times: *Babies always used to be swaddled in cloth.*

swag /swæg/ *u.n* (*old use*; *slang*) things stolen by a thief.

swagger /'swægə/ *sing.n* **1** way of walking, usu moving one's shoulders a lot, which shows pride.

▷ *intr.v* **2** walk with a swagger(1).

  '**swaggeringly** *adv* with a swagger(1).

swallow[1] /'swɒləʊ/ *c.n* kind of small bird with long pointed wings and a long tail like a V. Compare martin, swift[2].

  '**swallow ,dive** *c.n* kind of dive into water in which one starts with one's arms at one's sides and lifts them so they are at right angles to one's body as one dives.

  '**swallow,tailed** *adj* (of some birds etc or long coats) having a tail like a V.

swallow[2] /'swɒləʊ/ *c.n* **1** act of swallowing[2](2).

▷ *v* **2** *tr.v* (also — *s.t down*) cause (food, liquid etc) to go down from one's mouth into one's throat. **3** make the movements of swallowing[2](2) but without any food or liquid, e.g because one is nervous or afraid. **4** *tr.v* (*fig*) accept (s.t unpleasant) patiently: *She had to swallow a lot of criticism from the other students.* **5** believe (s.t that is not very likely): *Did your mother swallow your story about being late because you missed your bus?* **swallow one's pride** ⇨ pride. **swallow s.t up** cause s.t to disappear; use up all of s.t: *That cave has swallowed up many people. Our holiday swallowed up all our savings.*

swam /swæm/ *p.t* of swim.

swamp /swɒmp/ *c/u.n* **1** soft wet (piece of) land; bog(1).

▷ *tr.v* **2** fill (a boat etc) with water so that it (almost) sinks. **3** fill a boat etc that (s.o) is in so that it (almost) sinks: *A big wave swamped us.* **4** (often passive) (often — *s.o with s.t*) (*fig*) put so much work etc on (s.o) that he/she cannot do it all.

  swampy *adj* (*-ier*, *-iest*) soft and wet because of being a swamp(1).

swan /swɒn/ *c.n* **1** kind of big, usu white, bird with a long graceful neck usu found on or near rivers, lakes etc.

▷ *intr.v* (*-nn-*) **2** (*informal*) **swan about/around** go about freely. **swan off** (**to s.t**) go off (to a place), usu without telling anyone.

  '**swan,song** *c.n* last work produced by an artist, composer(1) etc.

swank /swæŋk/ *n* (*informal*) **1** *u.n* (also *attrib*) act or fact of showing off; behaving or talking in a proud and boastful way. **2** *c.n* person who behaves or talks like this.

▷ *intr.v* **3** (*informal*) behave like a swank(2).

  '**swankily** *adv* in a swanky way.

  '**swankiness** *u.n* state of being swanky.

  '**swanky** *adj* (*-ier*, *-iest*) **1** behaving or talking like a swank(2). **2** (of clothes, a restaurant, party etc) very fashionable.

swansong ⇨ swan.

swap /swɒp/ *c.n* (also **swop**) **1** (often *do* (s.o) *a* — (*of s.t*) (*for s.t*)) (*informal*) exchange (of s.t) (with s.o) (for s.t): *I'll do you a swap of my toy boat for your kite.* **2** thing that one exchanges in a swap(1): *My swap was a toy boat.*

▷ *tr/intr.v* (also **swop**) (*-pp-*) **3** (often — *s.o* (*s.o/s.t*) *for s.o/s.t*) (*informal*) exchange (s.o/s.t) (with s.o) (for s.o/s.t): *I'd swap Mike my car for his one any day!* **swap places** (**with s.o**); **swap round** change places etc: *My seat was too big for me and Peter's was too small for him so we swapped round,* (or *so I swapped places with him*).

swarm /swɔːm/ *c/def.pl.n* **1** (often — *of s.t*) large number (of insects, animals, people) all in one mass: *a swarm of bees.*

▷ *intr.v* **2** (of a swarm(1) of bees) leave the hive(1) to find another place to live. **3** move in a swarm(1). **swarm with s.t** be full of s.t: *The market was swarming with people.*

swarthy /'swɔːði/ *adj* (*-ier*, *-iest*) (of a person, her/his skin) dark in complexion(1).

  '**swarthiness** *u.n*.

swat /swɒt/ *c.n* **1** hit or blow with s.t flat. **2** = swatter.

▷ *tr.v* (*-tt-*) **3** (often — *s.o/s.t with s.t*) give (s.o/s.t) a swat(1) (using s.t).

  '**swatter** *c.n* instrument used to swat(2) insects: *a fly swatter.*

swatch /swɒtʃ/ *c.n* (often — *of s.t*) (*commerce*) sample piece (of cloth).

swathe /sweɪð/ *tr.v* (often — *s.o/s.t in s.t*) (*formal*; *literary*) wrap (s.o/s.t) up (in s.t, e.g a bandage). Compare swaddle.

swatter ⇨ swat.

sway /sweɪ/ *u.n* **1** side to side movement, usu of the upper part of s.t: *the sway of trees in the wind.* **2** (*formal*) influence. **3** (*old use*) rule; government. **under the sway of s.o/s.t** (*old use*) (**a**) being influenced by s.o/s.t. (**b**) being ruled or governed by s.o/s.t.

▷ *v* **4** *tr/intr.v* (cause (s.o/s.t) to) swing from side to side. **5** *tr.v* influence (s.o/s.t): *Television advertisements try to sway us to buy things.* **sway to s.t** swing from side to side in time with music etc.

swear /sweə/ *v* (*p.t* swore /swɔː/, *p.p* sworn /swɔːn/) *intr.v* use bad language; curse: *I don't allow swearing in my classroom.* **swear at s.o/ s.t** use bad language in speaking to s.o or about s.o/s.t. **swear by s.t** (*informal*) have complete confidence in s.t so that one encourages others to use/do it: *I swear by my new typewriter.* **swear (by/on s.t)** (**that . . .**, **to do s.t**) promise formally and faithfully (while taking an oath(1) on s.t) (that . . ., to do s.t): *She swore on the Bible, on her honour, that she would tell the truth* (or *to tell the truth*). **swear s.o in** (**a**) (*law*) cause a witness in a court etc to take an oath(1) that he/she will tell the truth. (**b**) cause s.o who is about to start a new job (e.g a new President of the US) to swear that he/she will do it honestly. **swear an oath** make a formal promise, usu in a court of law. **swear s.o to silence** make s.o promise to keep s.t secret. **swear (that) . . .** (*informal*) say strongly (that) . . .; promise (that) . . .: *I'll swear Peter was still there when I left.* **swear to s.t** (*informal*) say s.t strongly because of being certain about it: *I'd swear to it that I left my coat here but now it's gone.*

  '**swearer** *c.n* person who swears.

  '**swear ,word** *c.n* word that is part of bad language, e.g shit.

,sworn 'enemy *c.n* (often *pl*) person who is completely s.o's enemy.

sweat /swet/ *n* **1** *u.n* liquid that comes out through one's skin when one is hot; perspiration. **2** *u.n* liquid that comes out of s.t else, e.g cheese, usu when it is hot. **3** *c.n* case of sweat(1) coming out, usu because one has a fever. **4** *c.n* (*informal*) hard, usu unpleasant, work: *We had to clean the whole floor — what a sweat!* **in a cold sweat (about s.t)** sweating(5) because one is worried or frightened (about s.t): *I was in a cold sweat over my exams.*
▷ *intr.v* **5** *intr.v* (often — *with* s.t) have sweat(1,2) coming out of one (because of s.t, e.g heat or fear). **sweat blood (to do s.t)** (*fig*; *informal*) work extremely hard (in order to do s.t). **sweat it out** (*informal*) go through s.t unpleasant waiting only for it to end and not able to do anything about it: *The soldiers had to sweat it out under heavy bombing for several hours.* **sweat s.t out** get rid of (a fever etc) by sweating(5).

'sweat,band *c.n* **1** strip of cloth worn round one's head or wrist to stop sweat(1) from running down onto one's face/hand. **2** leather strip inside a hat to stop sweat(1) damaging the cloth.

'sweater *c.n* woollen piece of clothing worn on the top half of the body. ⇒ jumper.

'sweat ,gland *c.n* (*technical*) organ under one's skin out of which the sweat(1) comes.

'sweatiness *u.n* fact or state of being sweaty.

'sweat,shirt *c.n* informal piece of clothing with long sleeves, usu of cotton or nylon, worn on the upper half of the body. Compare T-shirt (⇒ T, t).

'sweaty *adj* (*-ier, -iest*) **1** who/that is sweating(5). **2** having sweat(1,2) on it. **3** smelling of sweat(1,2). **4** that makes one sweat(5), usu because of heat.

swede /swiːd/ *c/u.n* kind of big round yellow root vegetable like a turnip.

sweep /swiːp/ *c.n* **1** example of sweeping (⇒ sweep(7)): *This room needs a good sweep.* **2** (often — *of* s.t) sweeping (⇒ sweep(9)) movement (of s.t): *With one sweep of her brush the painter produced a wonderful sunset.* **3** (often — *of* s.t) big and usu impressive curve (of s.t): *the sweep of the bay.* **4** movement by soldiers, police etc over a wide area to try to find the enemy, a criminal etc. **5** = sweepstake. **6** (*informal*) = chimneysweep. **(make) a clean sweep (of s.o/ s.t)** **(a)** (have) a complete win or success (in which one gets everyone/everything). **(b)** (make) a complete removal (of everyone/everything).
▷ *v* (*p.t,p.p* swept /swept/) **7** *tr.v* clean (s.t, e.g a floor or a room) by brushing it with a broom(1) etc (until it no longer has any dirt etc in/on it): *She swept the kitchen clean.* **8** *tr.v* (often — *s.t up*) get rid of (s.t, e.g dirt) by sweeping(1): *I swept the dust into a bag. Every autumn we have to sweep up leaves day after day.* **9** *tr/intr.v* (often — (s.t) *across* etc (s.t)) (cause (s.t) to) swing or move quickly (across etc) (s.t): *The plane swept across the sky and was gone in a moment. She swept her hand across her face to get rid of the flies. His eyes swept the faces in the crowd trying to find his lost friend.* **10** *tr.v* cover, affect, be successful in, the whole of s.t: *The fire swept the village.* The Liberals(5) *swept the country in the elections.* **11** *tr.v* hang so far down as to touch (s.t): *Her dress swept the floor.* **12** *intr.v* (often — *in*(to s.t), *out* (of s.t)) move (in etc) in a strong

proud way: *The woman swept into the room and sat down.* **sweep the board** ⇒ board[1]. **sweep s.o off her/his feet** (*fig*) ⇒ foot(*n*). **sweep over s.o** (of a feeling) suddenly affect s.o strongly. **sweep round** have the shape of a curve: *The coast sweeps round to a cape here.* **sweep up** clean a place by sweeping (⇒ sweep(7)).

'sweeper *c.n* **1** person or thing who/that sweeps(7,8): *a road sweeper.* ⇒ carpet sweeper. **2** (in football etc) player whose job is to stop the other team coming close to her/his goal.

'sweeping *attrib.adj* covering a lot of things or everything, usu in too general a way to be quite correct: *You should avoid making sweeping statements about things you don't know enough about.*

'sweep,stake *c.n* form of gambling in which everybody puts in money and the winner(s) take(s) it all.

'sweep,stakes *pl.n* = sweepstake.

,swept-'back *attrib.adj* **1** (of hair) that is combed/brushed back off one's face. **2** (of the wings of a plane) not sticking out at right angles to the body but at an angle towards the back.

sweet /swiːt/ *adj* **1** having a taste like sugar. Compare sour. **2** having sugar in it: *Do you like your coffee sweet?* **3** pleasant in its taste, smell or sound; pleasant to look at. **4** (of water) not salty like the sea; fresh(3). **5** (of wine) tasting (a little) sweet. Opposite dry. **6** gentle and charming in character, behaviour etc: *a sweet child; a sweet nature.* **short and/but sweet** ⇒ short(*adj*). **sweet nothings** ⇒ nothing(*n*). **sweet on s.o** (*informal*) in love with s.o: *I think you're sweet on that girl you were talking to.*
▷ *n* **7** small sweet(1) thing that one eats for pleasure and not as food: *Most children love sweets but they are bad for their teeth.* **8** *c/u.n* sweet food usu eaten (almost) at the end of a meal; dessert, pudding. **my sweet** my darling/sweetheart.

,sweet-and-'sour *attrib.adj* (usu in Chinese cooking) using sweet(1) and sour tastes at the same time.

'sweet,bread *c.n* pancreas of an animal eaten as a food.

'sweet,corn *u.n* kind of maize that is cooked and eaten. ⇒ corn-on-the-cob.

'sweeten *tr/intr.v* **1** (cause (s.t) to) become sweet(er)(1,3,5,6). **2** (often — *s.o with* s.t) (*informal*) bribe (s.o) (with s.t).

'sweetener *c/u.n* **1** thing, usu a chemical substance used instead of sugar, which sweetens(1) s.t. **2** (*informal*) bribe.

'sweetening *u.n* substance used to make food sweet(er)(1).

'sweet,heart *c.n* person whom one loves.

'sweetie *c.n* (*informal*) **1** sweet(7). **2** sweetheart. **3** lovable person (usu a child).

'sweetish *adj* (rather/too) sweet(1).

'sweetness *u.n*.

,sweet 'pea *c.n* kind of climbing plant whose flowers have a very sweet smell and can be of many different colours.

,sweet 'pepper *c.n* = pepper(3).

,sweet po'tato *c.n* (*pl -es*) kind of plant growing in hot countries with a yellow root that is eaten as a vegetable.

,sweet 'tooth *sing.n* (usu *have a —*) liking/taste for sweet things.

swell /swel/ n (often the — of s.t) **1** sing/u.n up and down movement (of the ocean or sea) without the breaking(18) of waves. **2** sing.n outward curving shape (e.g of the muscles(1) in a person's arm). **3** sing.n increase in loudness (esp of the music played on an organ).
▷ v (p.p swelled, swollen /'swəulən/) **4** (often — up) become bigger because of liquid, inflammation etc inside: His arm swelled up after the bee stung him. **5** tr/intr.v (often — (s.t) out) fill (s.t) so that it becomes round in shape: The wind swelled our sails and the boat began to move. The balloon swelled out as I blew into it. **6** tr/intr.v (cause (s.t) to) become bigger in number or amount: The money from the sale swelled our bank account. **7** tr/intr.v (usu — with s.t) (fig) fill (s.t) (with a feeling): Their hearts swelled with pride (or Pride swelled their hearts) as their daughter went up to receive her prize.

'swelling n **1** u.n act or fact of swelling (⇒ swell(4)). **2** c.n place on one's body that has swollen (⇒ swell(4)).

swollen /'swəulən/ adj **1** that has swollen (⇒ swell(4–6)): the swollen waters of a river after heavy rainfalls. **2** (of ideas etc) too great or proud: a swollen opinion of oneself. **get/have a swollen head** ⇒ head(n).

,swollen'headed adj (derog) too proud. **'swollenly** adv. **'swollenness** u.n.

swelter /'sweltə/ intr.v feel unpleasantly hot, sweat a lot etc, because of the weather, heating in a room etc.

'sweltering adj unpleasantly hot: a sweltering summer evening. **'swelteringly** adv.

swept /swept/ p.t of sweep.

swept-back ⇒ sweep.

swerve /swɜːv/ c.n **1** sudden turn to one side, e.g by a car to avoid hitting s.o/s.t.
▷ v **2** intr.v (often — to the left/right) make a swerve(1) (towards the left/right). **3** tr/intr.v (formal) (cause (s.o) to) change what he/she plans to do or what he/she believes in etc: Nothing will swerve us from the path of duty.

swift¹ /swift/ adj **1** quick; fast: send a swift reply. **2** that does not last long: a swift lunch between pieces of work.
'swiftly adv. **'swiftness** u.n.

swift² /swift/ c.n kind of small bird that is like a swallow¹ but with a shorter tail like a V and with long curved wings that cross each other when the bird is not flying.

swig /swig/ c.n **1** (often have/take a — of s.t) (slang) drink, usu one big swallow, (of s.t).
▷ tr.v (-gg-) **2** (often — s.t down) (slang) drink quickly by swallowing swigs(1) one after the other.

swill /swil/ u.n **1** food given to pigs, usu very liquid and consisting mostly of what people have left.
▷ v **2** tr.v (usu — s.t down/out) wash (s.t) by pouring a lot of water on it. **3** tr.v (slang) = swig(2).

swim /swim/ c.n **1** example of swimming (⇒ swim(2)): Let's go for a swim. My hair's wet because I've just had a swim. **in the swim** (informal) up to date; knowing the latest things.
▷ v (-mm-, p.t swam /swæm/, p.p swum /swʌm/) **2** intr.v (of a person, animal, fish etc) move in water by using one's arms, legs, tail etc: I swim 500 metres every day. A water snake swims by moving

its body from side to side. **3** tr.v go from one side of (s.t) to the other by swimming (⇒ swim(2)): swim a river. **4** intr.v (usu — in/with s.t) (of food etc) have (liquid) all round/over it: I hate food that is swimming in fat. **5** intr.v (of a person's brain) seem to be going round and round; be dizzy; feel faint: His head was swimming after all the drink.`
sink or swim ⇒ sink². **swim against/with the tide** ⇒ tide(n).

'swimming u.n act or sport of swimming (⇒ swim(2)): Do you do (or have) swimming at your school?

'swimming ,bath c.n (also **'swimming ,baths** pl.n) public swimming pool, usu indoors.

'swimming ,costume c.n clothing used by a woman or girl for swimming.

'swimming ,pool c.n pool, e.g in a garden or sports centre, for swimming.

'swimming ,trunks pl.n (often pair of —) short piece of clothing worn by a man or boy on the lower part of his body for swimming.

swindle /'swindl/ c.n **1** example of cheating. **2** (informal) thing that one has paid for that is not worth the money: That visit to the castle was a swindle; all we saw for our £2 was one room.
▷ tr.v **3** (often — s.o out of s.t) cheat (s.o) (in a way that gets s.t from her/him).
'swindler c.n (derog) person who swindles(3).

swine /swain/ c.n (pl swine) **1** (becoming old use) pig. **2** (derog; slang) person who one dislikes very much: Get out, you swine!

swing /swiŋ/ n **1** c/u.n (often the — of s.t) movement (of one end of s.t) from side to side, backwards and forwards, round and round etc once or more than once, while the other end stays in the same place: the swing of a pendulum. **2** c.n distance covered by a swing(1): a swing of ten metres. **3** c.n device on which children can sit and swing(7,8) backwards and forwards for amusement. **4** c.n ride on a swing(3). **5** c.n (often — in s.t) big change (in s.t), e.g in the value of the pound, in what people think about s.t etc. **6** u.n (also attrib) kind of jazz(1) with a strong regular rhythm that was particularly popular in the 1930s and 1940s: swing dancing. **get (back) into the swing of things** find the best, correct ways of doing s.t (again): It won't take you long to get into the swing of things in the office. **(go) with a swing** (happen) successfully: Our party went with a swing. **in full swing** working very busily or at its full rate: The party started slowly but by ten o'clock it was in full swing.
▷ v (p.t,p.p swung /swʌŋ/) **7** tr/intr.v (cause (s.o/s.t) to) move with a swing(1): walk along swinging our arms and laughing. **8** intr.v ride on a swing(3). **9** intr.v (often — for s.t) (slang) (of a person) be hanged as a punishment (for s.t). **10** intr.v (often — along, down etc s.t) walk quickly and strongly: The sailors came swinging down the street towards their ship. **11** tr/intr.v (cause (s.o/s.t) to) change a lot, once or more than once (from one limit) (to another limit): The price of gold swung sharply as the news came in each day. Our hearts swung between hope and fear. **swing (s.o/s.t) (a)round** turn (s.o/s.t) round suddenly. **not enough, no, room to swing a cat** (informal) very little space. **swing (oneself) down** etc **(from s.t)** get down etc (from s.t) by holding on with one's hand(s) and swinging one's body. **swing into action** ⇒ action.

swing open/shut (of a door, window etc) swing into a position where it is open/shut.

'swinger *c.n* (*informal*) person who leads a happy, free, modern life.

'swinging *adj* (*informal*) suitable for swingers: *swinging clothes/music.*

'swingingly *adv.*

'swing-,wing *adj* (*technical*) (of a plane) having wings whose angle can be changed to suit slower and faster speeds.

swipe /swaɪp/ *c.n* **1** hard, often swinging, hit or blow: *The cruel man gave the boy a swipe.* **2** (often *take a — at s.o/s.t*) attack (on s.o/s.t) with words, not blows: *I took a swipe at the answer but I was wrong.*

▷ *tr.v* **3** give (s.o/s.t) a swipe(1). **4** (*informal*) take (and steal) (s.t): *Who's swiped my pen?* **swipe at s.o/s.t** try to give s.o/s.t a swipe(1).

swirl /swɜːl/ *c.n* **1** movement round and round, e.g of water going down a hole. **2** (often — *of s.t*) thing (consisting of water, smoke etc) which is swirling(3): *swirls of dust.*

▷ *v* **3** *intr.v* move round and round: *The fast stream swirled round our feet as we crossed.* **4** *tr.v* (usu — *s.o/s.t about, along, (a)round, away* etc) carry or push (s.o/s.t) (along etc) in a swirling(3) way.

swish[1] /swɪʃ/ *adj* (usu *attrib*) (*informal*) very fashionable or expensive: *a swish party.*

swish[2] /swɪʃ/ *c.n* **1** (often — *of s.t*) sound like a long 'sh' (made by s.t moving through the air quickly or by brushing against s.t): *the swish of a golf club; the swish of a horse's tail; the swish of a silk dress.*

▷ *tr/intr.v* **2** (usu — (*s.t*) *about, around* etc) (cause (s.t) to) make a swish (as it moves about etc).

Swiss roll /,swɪs 'rəʊl/ *c.n* kind of thin sponge cake that is spread with jam and/or cream and then rolled up.

switch[1] /swɪtʃ/ *c.n* **1** device for turning electric current etc on and off, usu by moving s.t down or up with one's hand: *an electric light switch.* **2** device for controlling which line a train follows at points. **3** (often *a — in/of s.t*) big change (in s.t), usu one that is not expected: *There has been a switch in classes between the teachers. We have had a switch of plan.*

▷ *v* **4** *tr/intr.v* (usu — (*s.o/s.t*) (*over*) (*from s.o/s.t*) *to s.o/s.t*) (cause (s.o/s.t) to) change (from s.o/s.t) (to s.o/s.t): *The lights switched from green to red. This device switches trains from one line to another. Let's switch (over) to the other television station.* **5** *tr/intr.v* (usu — *s.t for s.t; — s.t over* (*from s.t*) (*to s.t*)) exchange (s.t) (for s.t): *You don't like your chair and I don't like mine so let's switch.* **switch off** (*fig; informal*) stop listening or thinking, usu when one is bored or tired. **switch (s.t) off/on** stop/start (s.t, e.g the light) by moving a switch(1).

'switch,board *c.n* **1** central place connecting a number of telephone lines in a building, hotel etc. **2** staff of a switchboard(1).

,switched-'on *adj* **1** (*informal*) modern; in fashion; up to date. **2** (*informal*) alert(1); following everything that is going on. **3** (*slang*) under the influence of a drug(2).

'switch,over *c.n* (usu *a — (from s.t) (to s.t)*) (*informal*) big or complete change (from s.t) (to s.t).

switch[2] /swɪtʃ/ *c.n* **1** small thin stick that bends easily.

▷ *tr.v* **2** hit (a person, horse etc) with a switch[2](1).

swivel /'swɪvl/ *c.n* **1** joint that makes it possible for one or both of the things joined to turn independently of the other.

▷ *tr/intr.v* (-ll-, US -l-) **2** (often — (*s.o/s.t*) *round, to the left/right*) (cause (s.t) to) turn to face in a different direction without moving from the place one/it is on. Compare pivot(3).

swollen, swollen-headed ⇒ swell.

swoon /swuːn/ *c.n* **1** (*old use*) faint(7).

▷ *intr.v* **2** (*old use*) (almost) faint(8).

swoop /swuːp/ *c.n* (often — *on s.o/s.t*) **1** (of a bird, plane etc) steep descent through the air, usu to attack (s.o/s.t). **2** sudden quick attack, usu by police (to catch criminals). **at/in/with one fell swoop** using one action or method: *have a party to see all one's friends in one fell swoop.*

▷ *intr.v* **3** (often — (*down*) *on s.o/s.t*) make a swoop(1,2) (on s.o/s.t).

swop /swɒp/ ⇒ swap.

sword /sɔːd/ *c.n* weapon with a long blade and a handle, used in former times for fighting and now sometimes worn or carried by officers on formal occasions. **cross swords (with s.o)** have a serious quarrel (with s.o). **draw one's sword** pull one's sword out of its scabbard. **put s.o to the sword** (*literary*) kill s.o.

'sword ,dance *c.n* dance in which one jumps about over swords lying on the ground or waves swords about and hits them against each other.

'sword,fish *c.n* (*pl* 'sword,fish(es)) **1** kind of big fish that has a very long sharp upper jaw like a sword. **2** *u.n* flesh of this fish as food.

swore /swɔː/ *p.t* of swear.

sworn /swɔːn/ *p.p* of swear.

sworn enemy ⇒ swear.

swot /swɒt/ *c.n* **1** (often *derog; informal*) person who studies very (or too) hard.

▷ *tr/intr.v* (-tt-) **2** (*informal*) study (s.t) to prepare for an examination etc. **swot s.t up** study a particular subject, set of information etc for an examination or to get a job.

'swotter *c.n* (usu *derog*) person who swots(2).

swum /swʌm/ *p.p* of swim.

swung /swʌŋ/ *p.t,p.p* of swing.

sycamore /'sɪkəmɔː/ *n* (also *attrib*) **1** *c.n* kind of tree that includes the maple and has lobed leaves, yellow flowers and winged seeds. **2** *u.n* wood from this kind of tree.

sycophant /'sɪkəfænt/ *c.n* (*derog*) person who flatters rich and/or important people to try to get things he/she wants.

,syco'phantic *adj* (acting) like a sycophant.

syllable /'sɪləbl/ *c.n* (*technical*) word or part of a word that contains one vowel sound, diphthong or consonant behaving like a vowel (and one or more consonants before and/or after it): *There are two syllables in 'swimming' and three in 'syllabic'.* **not a syllable** (*informal*) no part at all of s.t said: *I don't want a syllable of what I've just told you to be passed on to anyone else.*

syllabic /sɪ'læbɪk/ *adj* forming a syllable: *The 'l' is syllabic in* /'bɒtlɪŋ/*, and the 'n' is syllabic in* /'bʌtnd/.

-syllabic *adj* having the number of syllables shown in the first part of the word: *trisyllabic* (having three syllables).

syllabification /ˌsɪləˌbɪfɪˈkeɪʃən/ *u.n* division (of a word) into syllables.
syllabify /sɪˈlæbɪˌfaɪ/ *tr.v* (*-ies*, *-ied*) divide (a word) into its syllables.
-syllabled *adj* having the number of syllables shown in the first part of the word: *four-syllabled*.
syllabub /ˈsɪləˌbʌb/ *c/u.n* (also **ˈsillˌabub**) cold dessert made by mixing cream, sugar, wine and lemon.
syllabus /ˈsɪləbəs/ *c.n* (*pl -es*, or, less usu, syllabi /ˈsɪləˌbaɪ/) list of things to be studied or learned.
syllogism /ˈsɪləˌdʒɪzəm/ *c.n* (*formal*) way of reasoning in which a conclusion(2) is drawn from two premises.
syllogistic /ˌsɪləˈdʒɪstɪk/ *adj* of or referring to syllogisms.
syiph /sɪlf/ *c.n* **1** (in stories) kind of fairy. **2** slim(1) and graceful woman.
ˈsylphˌlike *adj* slim(1) and graceful.
symbol /ˈsɪmbl/ *c.n* (often — *of/for s.t*) thing that is used to represent (s.t): *The letter 'P' is the symbol for a car park. A lion is the symbol of courage.*
symbolic /sɪmˈbɒlɪk/ *adj* (also **symˈbolical**) (often — *of s.t*) that is a symbol (of s.t).
symˈbolically *adv*.
symbolism /ˈsɪmbəˌlɪzəm/ *u.n* **1** use of symbols. **2** system of art and literature in which symbols are used which was particularly fashionable in late 19th century France.
ˈsymbolist *c.n* artist, writer etc who uses symbolism(2).
symbolization, -isation /ˌsɪmbəlaɪˈzeɪʃən/ *u.n* fact or act of symbolizing (s.t).
ˈsymboˌlize, -ise *tr.v* **1** be a symbol of (s.t). **2** represent (s.t) in one or more symbols.
symmetry /ˈsɪmɪtrɪ/ *u.n* (beauty that is the result of a) right balance or harmony(1) between the parts of s.t, often its two halves when it is divided down the middle.
symmetrical /sɪˈmetrɪkl/ *adj* (also **symˈmetric**) having symmetry. Opposite asymmetrical.
symˈmetrically *adv*.
sympathy /ˈsɪmpəθɪ/ *n* (*pl -ies*) *u.n* (often — *for s.o/s.t*) feeling of sharing s.o else's worries, pains, beliefs etc: *She felt sympathy for him, his parents, when he failed the test. I have a lot of sympathy for poor families.* ⇒ empathy(1). **be in sympathy (with s.o/s.t)** share s.o's feelings, beliefs etc (about s.t). **come out in sympathy (with s.o)** (esp) go on strike to support (s.o else who is on strike).
sympathetic /ˌsɪmpəˈθetɪk/ *adj* (often — *to s.o/s.t*) feeling sympathy (for s.o/s.t); being in sympathy (with s.o/s.t).
ˌsympaˈthetically *adv*.
ˈsympathies *pl.n* **1** feelings of sympathy. **2** statement of these feelings given or sent to s.o, esp s.o whose husband, wife, parent, child etc has died. **s.o's sympathies are/lie with s.o** s.o supports s.o/s.t.
sympathize, -ise /ˈsɪmpəˌθaɪz/ *intr.v* (often — *with s.o/s.t*) feel sympathy for, support, (s.o/s.t).
ˈsympaˌthizer, -iser *c.n* person who sympathizes (with s.o/s.t).
ˈsympaˌthizingly, -isingly *adv* in a way that sympathizes (with s.o/s.t).

symphony /ˈsɪmfənɪ/ *c.n* (*pl -ies*) (*music*) long musical composition, usu consisting of four movements, for playing by an orchestra.
symphonic /sɪmˈfɒnɪk/ *adj* of/like a symphony: *symphonic music.*
symposium /sɪmˈpəʊzɪəm/ *c.n* (*pl -s* or, less usu, *symposia* /sɪmˈpəʊzɪə/) (often — *on s.t*) conference of specialists (referring to one or more particular subjects).
symptom /ˈsɪmptəm/ *c.n* (often — *of s.t*) sign that one can see, feel etc (and that shows that s.t one cannot see, feel etc is happening, likely to happen): *Fever can be a symptom of various diseases.*
symptomatic /ˌsɪmptəˈmætɪk/ *adj* (usu — *of s.t*) that is a symptom (of s.t).
ˌsymptoˈmatically *adv*.
synagogue /ˈsɪnəˌɡɒɡ/ *c.n* place where Jews worship God.
synchromesh /ˈsɪŋkrəʊˌmeʃ/ *u.n* (*technical*) system used in the engine of a car etc that makes the speed of two gears(1) the same just before one changes gear(1).
synchronization, -isation /ˌsɪŋkrənaɪˈzeɪʃən/ *u.n* (often *the* — *of s.t* (*with s.t*)) fact or act of (s.t) synchronizing (with s.t) or of synchronizing (s.t) (with s.t).
ˈsynchroˌnize, -ise *v* (often — (*s.t*) *with s.t*) **1** *tr/intr.v* (cause (s.t) to) happen or be done at the same time (as s.t): *If we synchronize our efforts they will be much more successful.* **2** *tr.v* cause (the sounds on a film) to fit in (with the things one can see), e.g make the sounds fit the movements of a person's lips as he/she speaks. **3** *tr.v* cause the sounds on (a film) to do this. **synchronize clocks/watches** set two or more clocks/watches so that they show exactly the same time.
syncopate /ˈsɪŋkəˌpeɪt/ *tr.v* (*music*) change the places where the beats are in music so that ones with a strong beat now have a weak one and vice versa, as in jazz.
ˈsyncoˌpated *adj*.
syncopation /ˌsɪŋkəˈpeɪʃən/ *u.n*.
syndicate /ˈsɪndɪkɪt/ *c/def.pl.n* **1** group of people or companies working together. **2** company that sells reports or articles to several newspapers at the same time.
▷ *v* /ˈsɪndɪˌkeɪt/ **3** *tr/intr.v* form (s.t) into a syndicate(1). **4** (of a syndicate(2)) supply (articles etc) to various newspapers.
syndication /ˌsɪndɪˈkeɪʃən/ *u.n*.
syndrome /ˈsɪndrəʊm/ *c.n* group of symptoms, often medical ones, that together show s.t. ⇒ AIDS, Downe's syndrome.
synod /ˈsɪnəd/ *c.n* big important official meeting to discuss church business.
synonym /ˈsɪnənɪm/ *c.n* (*technical*) word that means (almost) the same as another one in the same language. Opposite antonym.
synonymous /sɪˈnɒnɪməs/ *adj* (often — *with s.t*) having (almost) the same meaning (as s.t): *Our hotel's name is synonymous with good service.*
syˈnonymously *adv*.
synopsis /sɪˈnɒpsɪs/ *c.n* (*pl synopses* /sɪˈnɒpˌsiːz/) (often — *of s.t*) summary(3) (of s.t).
syˈnoptic *adj* that is, refers to, a synopsis.
syˈnoptically *adv*.

syntax /'sɪntæks/ *u.n* (*grammar*) (rules for the) arrangement of words to form sentences and phrases(1). Compare morphology(1).
syn'tactic *adj* of or referring to syntax.
syn'tactically *adv.*
synthesis /'sɪnθəsɪs/ *n* (*pl syntheses* /'sɪnθə-ˌsiːz/) **1** *u.n* act or fact of putting different things together to form a whole. Compare analysis. **2** (often — *of s.t* (*and s.t*)) result of (the) synthesis(1) (of s.t (and s.t else)).
synthesize, -ise /'sɪnθəˌsaɪz/ *tr.v* produce (s.t) by putting different things together to form it: *Artificial rubber was synthesized many years ago.* Compare analyse.
'synthe,sizer, -iser *c.n* (person using a) machine that synthesizes, esp one that produces music artificially by combining various sound frequencies(2).
synthetic /sɪn'θetɪk/ *adj* **1** of or referring to synthesis(1). **2** produced by synthesizing; artificial: *synthetic cloth/rubber.*
▷ *c.n* **3** synthetic(2) material.
syn'thetically *adv.*
syphilis /'sɪfɪlɪs/ *u.n* dangerous venereal disease that is usually passed from one person to another by sexual intercourse but that can also be inherited(2).
ˌsyphi'litic *adj* **1** having, referring to, syphilis.
▷ *c.n* **2** person who has syphilis.
syphon ⇨ siphon.
syringe /sɪ'rɪndʒ/ *c.n* **1** (*medical; science*) device for sucking up liquids and then pushing them out again strongly. ⇨ hypodermic(2).
▷ *tr.v* **2** (often — *s.t out*) use a syringe on (s.t) (to clean it out): *syringing (out) one's ears.*
syrup /'sɪrəp/ *u.n* **1** sweet liquid, sometimes sugar cane juice that has been treated in different ways, e.g to produce treacle. **2** sugar melted in water and boiled until it is thick.
'syrupy *adj* **1** like, consisting of, containing, syrup. **2** (*derog*) unpleasantly sentimental.
system /'sɪstəm/ *n* **1** *c/u.n* (often — *of s.t*) arrangement (of a number of things) into an organized whole. **2** *u.n* good organization: *One has to have some system in an office or one will never be able to find anything one wants.* **3** *c.n* way of doing things: *I prefer my own system of work.* **4** *c.n* body of a person as a whole: *Very cold water is a shock to one's system.*
systematic /ˌsɪstə'mætɪk/ *adj* using a system(1–3).
ˌsyste'matically *adv.*
systematization, -isation /ˌsɪstəmətaɪ'zeɪʃən/ *u.n* (*formal*) act or fact of systematizing or of being systematized.
'systema,tize, -ise *tr/intr.v* (*formal*) arrange (s.t) into, according to, a system(1).
systemic /sɪ'stemɪk/ *adj* affecting the whole system(4) not just part(s) of it: *a systemic disease.*

Tt

T, t /tiː/ *c/unique n* 20th letter of the English alphabet.
'T-,junction *c.n* place where one street or road enters another but does not cross it, so that the two streets or roads form the shape of a T.
'T-,shirt *c.n* (also **'tee-,shirt**) tight shirt with no buttons or collar and usu with short sleeves and round neck.
'T-,square *c.n* big ruler that has the shape of a T.
ta /tɑː/ *interj* (*informal*) (often used by or to small children) thank you. **ta ever so** (*slang*) thank you very much.
TA /ˌtiː 'eɪ/ *def.n abbr* Territorial Army.
tab /tæb/ *c.n* **1** small piece of paper, cloth etc fixed to s.t used to provide identity(1), to hang s.t (e.g a coat) up etc: *name tab.* Compare tag(1). **2** (*informal*) tabulator. **keep a tab, tabs, on s.o/s.t** (*informal*) pay close attention to or watch s.o/s.t to see what he/she/it is doing.
TAB /ˌtiː ,eɪ 'biː/ *u.n abbr* (typhoid A and B) injection to prevent one getting either the A type or the B type of typhoid.
tabasco /tə'bæskəʊ/ *u.n* (*t.n*) (also **ta,basco 'sauce**) kind of sauce made from red peppers(2) and with a very hot(2) taste.
tabby /'tæbɪ/ *c.n* (*pl -ies*) (also **,tabby 'cat**) cat with fur that has darker lines or marks on a grey or brown background.
table /'teɪbl/ *n* **1** *c.n* piece of furniture with a flat top and usu four legs: *a dining table. Your pen is on that table.* **2** *sing.n* food that one gets at meals or in a place etc: *Mrs Robinson always has an excellent table.* **3** *c/def.pl.n* all the people sitting at a table: *Our table all want white wine.* **4** *c.n* list of information (e.g dates) arranged in lines and columns. **5** arrangement, usu in a column, of results of multiplying sets of numbers, e.g $2 \times 2 = 4$, $2 \times 3 = 6$ etc: *Do you know your tables* (or *your multiplication tables*, or *your three times table*)? **drink s.o under the table** ⇨ drink(*v*). **know one's tables** be able to multiply numbers from memory. **lay the table** put plates, cups, knives etc on a table for people to eat a meal with. **on the table** being discussed or considered. Compare table(6). **turn the tables** (**on s.o**) get into a winning position (against s.o) after having been in a losing position before. **under the table** (*fig*) (**a**) very drunk; so drunk that one falls down. (**b**) secretly and dishonestly, to get s.o to do s.t wrong: *If you pass that official some money under the table, he won't ask any more questions.*
▷ *tr.v* **6** suggest or propose (s.t) for discussion at a meeting etc.
'table,cloth *c.n* cloth for putting on the top of a table.
table d'hôte /ˌtɑːbl 'dəʊt/ *adj* (*French*) (of a meal at a restaurant) consisting of several dishes, one after the other (e.g soup, meat, sweet and cheese) offered at a fixed price. Opposite à la carte(1).
'table ,lamp *c.n* lamp for standing on a table.

'**table,land** *c/u.n* flat high piece of land.

'**table ,linen** *u.n* cloth, napkins etc for use on a table at meals.

'**table ,manners** *pl.n* polite ways of eating, drinking and behaving during meals.

'**table,mat** *c.n* small mat used to stop the heat from hot dishes, plates etc from damaging tables.

'**table ,napkin** *c.n* = napkin.

,**table of 'contents** *c.n* list of the subjects etc dealt with in a book etc. Compare table(4), index(1).

'**table ,salt** *u.n* salt as a fine powder for putting in a container for the dining table. ⇒ cooking salt.

'**table,spoon** *c.n abbr* tbsp **1** big spoon used for taking food out of a dish and putting it on a plate. **2** (often — *of* s.t) as much as a tablespoon(1) holds: *You have to put two tablespoons of flour in the mixture.*

'**table,spoonful** *c.n* = tablespoon(2).

'**table ,tennis** *u.n* (also '**ping-,pong**) game played on a table with a net across the middle by one or two players at each end who hit a small ball with special bats²(1).

'**table ,top** *c.n* top of a table.

'**table,ware** *u.n* plates, spoons, forks, glasses etc used on a table during a meal.

'**table ,wine** *u.n* wine for drinking during meals.

tablet /'tæblɪt/ *c.n* **1** small hard piece of medicine: *an* aspirin *tablet.* **2** small lump (of s.t hard) that has a flat top and bottom: *a tablet of soap.* **3** metal or stone plaque(1) with writing cut into it, fixed to a wall to show that s.t important happened at that place or in memory of s.o/s.t.

tabloid /'tæblɔɪd/ *c.n* (also *attrib*) popular(1) newspaper with small pages, many photographs and less serious news: *tabloid* journalism.

taboo /tə'buː/ *adj* **1** disapproved of; so bad that it must not be spoken, written etc: *Do we hear too many taboo words on television? Politics is taboo in this pub!* **2** (in some societies) so holy or bad that one must not speak, touch etc it: *This stone is taboo for all but chiefs.*

▷ *n* **3** *c.n* thing that is taboo. **4** *c/u.n* (often — *against* s.t) rule making (s.t) taboo(1,2). **under a taboo** not allowed because of a taboo(4) against it.

tabular /'tæbjʊlə/ *adj* arranged in the form of a table(4).

tabulate /'tæbjʊ,leɪt/ *tr.v* arrange (information, facts etc) in the form of a table(4).

tabulation /,tæbjʊ'leɪʃən/ *u.n.*

tabulator /'tæbjʊ,leɪtə/ *c.n* (*informal* **tab**) device on a typewriter or computer that helps one to tabulate by moving the thing that controls the columns to the column one wants.

tacit /'tæsɪt/ *adj* (usu *attrib*) accepted without actually being expressed in words: *John and I have a tacit agreement never to compete with each other in the same race.*

'**tacitly** *adv.*

taciturn /'tæsɪ,tɜːn/ *adj* (*formal*) talking very little, often with the result that people think one is not friendly.

,**taci'turnity** *u.n.* '**taci,turnly** *adv.*

tack¹ /tæk/ *c.n* **1** kind of small nail with a flat top. **2** long stitch(1) used to hold pieces of cloth together until one sews them properly. **get down to brass tacks** (*fig*; *informal*) begin to discuss s.t seriously and realistically.

▷ *v* **3** *tr.v* (often — *s.t down*) fix (s.t) (down) with tacks(1). **4** *tr.v* (often — *s.t to s.t*; — *s.t together*) sew s.t (to s.t/together) with tacks(2). **tack s.t on (to s.t)** (*fig*) add s.t (to s.t): *He tried to tack an extra cup of coffee on to our bill but Eric noticed it.*

tack² /tæk/ *c.n* **1** change of direction of a sailing ship or boat, made by moving the sail(s). **2** way of doing things: *We can't get home by bus, so let's try another tack — let's pretend you're ill and telephone your parents!* **a change of tack** (*fig*) a change in the way one is trying to do s.t. **on the right/wrong tack** (*fig*) doing things the right/wrong way.

▷ *intr.v* **3** change the direction of a sailing ship or boat by one or more tacks²(1).

tackiness ⇒ tacky.

tackle¹ /'tækl/ *n* **1** *u.n* things one uses when doing a particular sport, e.g one's rods, hooks etc when one fishes: *sports tackle.* **2** *c/u.n* arrangement of ropes used for lifting heavy things, e.g sails on a ship. ⇒ pulley.

tackle² /'tækl/ *c.n* **1** attempt in some games (e.g football, hockey) to take the ball away from s.o who has it. **2** attempt in rugby to make s.o who has the ball fall down by catching him round his legs or the lower part of his body.

▷ *v* **3** *tr/intr.v* to take the ball from (s.o who has it). ⇒ tackle²(1). **4** *tr/intr.v* try to make (the person who has the ball) fall down in rugby. ⇒ tackle²(2). **5** *tr.v* try to stop (s.o) but not in a game: *The policeman tackled the armed thief and managed to take his gun from him.* **6** *tr.v* (often — *s.o about s.t*) speak to (s.o) (about s.t) when this means one has to face her/his unwillingness to be spoken to: *I've decided to tackle my boss about a pay rise.* **7** *tr.v* try to deal with (s.t difficult): *We'll have to tackle indiscipline in class soon.*

tacky /'tækɪ/ *adj* (*-ier, -iest*) **1** (*informal*) rather sticky, usu because not yet quite dry. **2** (*derog*) bad of its kind: *tacky jewellery.*

'**tackiness** *u.n.*

tact /tækt/ *u.n* quality of avoiding offending people by saying, writing etc things that hurt them. **lack tact** not have this quality.

'**tactful** *adj* having or showing tact.

'**tactfully** *adv.* '**tactfulness** *u.n.*

'**tactless** *adj* not having or showing tact.

'**tactlessly** *adv.* '**tactlessness** *u.n.*

tactic /'tæktɪk/ *c.n* way of getting what one wants to get: *If you want his agreement, your best tactic is to be particularly nice to him.*

'**tactical** *adj* of or referring to tactics.

'**tactically** *adv.*

tactician /tæk'tɪʃən/ *c.n* person who uses tactics (successfully).

'**tactics** *u/pl.n* **1** art of using one's military, naval and/or air forces for a particular battle. Compare strategy(1). **2** art of using whatever one has or can get to be successful: *One of the first things a teacher must learn is the tactics of dealing with difficult parents.*

tactile /'tæktaɪl/ *adj* (*formal*) of or referring to the sense of touch: *tactile skills.*

tadpole /'tæd,pəʊl/ *c.n* small creature that lives

in water and becomes a frog or toad when it grows.

taffeta /'tæfɪtə/ *u.n* (also *attrib*) kind of thin cloth that is smooth, stiff and shiny: *a taffeta skirt.*

tag /tæg/ *c.n* **1** small strip of paper, cloth etc fixed to s.t as a label(1): *a name tag; a price tag.* Compare tab(1). **2** small metal etc tube round the end of a shoelace etc to make it easier to push through a hole. **play tag** play a child's game in which one person has to try to touch one of the others. **question tag** ⇨ question.
▷ *tr.v* **3** fix a tag(1) to (s.t). **tag along (behind s.o/ s.t)** (*informal*) follow (s.o/s.t) often when one is not wanted or needed. **tag on; tag onto s.o/ s.t** (*informal*) join (and follow) s.o/s.t, usu when one is not wanted. **tag s.t (on) to s.t; tag s.t on(to) s.t** add s.t (to s.t).

tail /teɪl/ *c.n* **1** part of an animal, bird or fish that is joined to the end of its spine(1) at the opposite end to its head. **2** part of s.t else that is in the same kind of position as a tail(1): *the tail of a kite; the tails of a coat; a plane's tail; the tail of a column of soldiers.* **3** (*informal*) person who tails(4) s.o. **have one's tail between one's legs** (*fig*) be afraid or ashamed, like a dog when its tail is in this position. **heads or tails** ⇨ head(*n*). **(not be able to) make head or/nor tail of s.t** ⇨ head(*n*). **put a tail on s.o** arrange for s.o to be followed. Compare tail(4). **turn tail** ⇨ turn(*v*).
▷ *tr.v* **4** follow (s.o), usu to find out where he/she goes and what he/she does: *The police tailed the man from the airport to a big block of flats but then lost him there.* **tail away/off** gradually become less strong, quick etc. **tail back** (of a long line of people, cars etc) go back a long way. **top and tail s.t** ⇨ top(*v*).

'tail,back *c.n* long line of waiting people, cars etc, e.g because of a delay.

'tail,coat *c.n* (also **tails**) old-fashioned or formal coat that has tails(2).

-,tailed having a tail like the first part of the word: *a bushy-tailed cat.*

'tail 'end *c/def.n* (usu *the — of s.t*) (*informal*) last part (of s.t long): *the tail end of a* queue(1).

'tail,light *c.n* red light at the back of a car etc that can be seen at night. Compare brake-light.

'tails *pl.n* **1** = tailcoat. **2** ⇨ heads or tails(head(*n*)).

'tail,spin *c.n* dangerous fall by a plane in which the tail spins in a wider circle than the nose.

'tail,wind *c.n* wind coming from behind: *Our plane arrived twenty minutes early because it had a tailwind all the way.* Opposite headwind.

tailor /'teɪlə/ *c.n* **1** person who makes coats, trousers etc (but not usu shirts), usu for men only. **2** (also **'tailor's**) place/shop where a tailor(1) works.
▷ *tr.v* **3** make (a coat, trousers etc but not usu a shirt) by measuring, cutting and sewing cloth. **tailor s.t to s.t** (*fig*) make s.t fit what is needed: *We can tailor holidays to anyone's special wishes.*

,tailor-'made *adj* (usu *pred*) **1** tailored(3) to fit a particular person. Compare made to measure (⇨ measure(*n*)), ready-made(2). **2** (usu *— for s.o/s.t*) (*fig*) very suitable (for a person, purpose): *She's tailor-made for this kind of work.*

tails, tailspin, tailwind ⇨ tail.

taint /teɪnt/ *n* **1** *c/u.n* slight amount (of s.t unpleasant or bad) which one can usu notice because of its smell or taste: *The meat has a taint. There is a taint of madness in his family.*
▷ *tr.v* **2** cause (food etc) to become tainted(1). **3** (*fig*) cause (s.o/s.t) to become evil or immoral.

'tainted *adj* (often *— with s.t*) having a taint(1) (of s.t): *tainted meat. The village felt tainted with their evil behaviour.*

take /teɪk/ *c.n* **1** photograph taken as part of a film(2). **2** amount of money paid to a shop etc; takings.
▷ *v* (*p.t* took /tʊk/, *p.p* taken /'teɪkən/) **3** *tr.v* get hold of (s.o/s.t) with one or both hands: *Take this book, please. I took her arm and led her to a chair.* **4** *tr.v* move or guide (s.o/s.t) from one place to another: *Take the plates to the kitchen, please. Will you take me to your father? Someone's taken my umbrella!* **5** *tr.v* get (s.o/s.t) by force; capture(3,4) (s.o/s.t): *Our army has taken 1000 prisoners.* **6** *tr.v* get (s.t); be given (s.t): *If the President dies, the Vice-President (⇨ vice³) takes his position.* **7** *tr.v* have enough space for (s.o/s.t); hold(10) (s.o/s.t): *This container takes 25 litres.* **8** *tr.v* (be able to) use (s.t): *This machine takes 10p coins.* **9** *tr.v* write down (s.t): *We took notes during the speech.* **10** *tr.v* accept and make use of (s.t): *If you'll take my advice, you'll apologize. He took the opportunity to ask for extra money.* **11** *intr.v* (of a dye(1), vaccination etc) act successfully: *The dye(1) took perfectly so now my old white blouse is bright blue. If your arm becomes hot and red, it means that the vaccination has taken.* **12** *tr.v* get or determine (a measurement or similar information): *He took a reading from the electricity meter¹(1)/the dial(1). The doctor took my pulse¹(1).* **13** *tr.v* make (a photograph): *We took several shots(9) of the mountains.* **14** *tr.v* begin to travel in (s.t): *I'll take the bus to the station.* **15** *tr.v* study, enter for an examination in, (s.t): *I'm taking English at college.* **16** *tr.v* buy (a newspaper, magazine etc), usu regularly every day etc. **17** *tr.v* rent (a room, flat etc): *They've taken a house by the sea for a holiday.* **18** *tr.v* need (a certain amount of time, effort etc) if one wants (s.o/s.t) to do s.t: *The journey will take five hours. It takes a lot of money to build a garage. That statement took courage.* **19** *tr.v* accept (people) to live in one's house, or (students) to teach etc: *Mrs Jones takes lodgers. Do you take private students?* **20** *tr.v* eat or drink (s.t): *Do you take sugar in your coffee? Why don't you take two aspirins and go to bed?* **21** *tr.v* teach: *Could you take my class for me tomorrow as I'm going to the doctor?* **22** *tr.v* treat (s.o/s.t) (as being serious etc): *When he dresses like that I can't take him seriously.* **23** *tr.v* feel or experience (s.t): *She takes great* pride(1) *in her son's success.* **24** *tr.v* get and accept (s.t) in a particular way: *He took the news of his son's death badly.* **25** *tr.v* (usu *can't — s.t*; *not be able to — s.t*) (*informal*) be strong enough in body or mind to be able to tolerate s.t: *I can't take much more of this criticism.* For 'take' + noun, e.g take a bath, take one's time, ⇨ the noun.

be taken by/with s.o/s.t be attracted by s.o/s.t: *I was so taken by her when we first met. We're greatly taken with the new houses for sale.*

be taken ill suddenly become ill.

give or take s.t ⇨ give.

take s.o aback ⇨ aback.

take after s.o be like s.o, usu one of one's

parents or grandparents: *Anne takes after her grandfather; they both have red hair and green eyes.*
It takes all kinds (to make a world) (*proverb*) One mustn't expect everybody to be the same; one must tolerate differences between them.
take s.o/s.t apart ⇨ apart.
take s.t as meaning, **to mean**, **s.t** treat s.t as if it means s.t; believe that s.t means s.t.
take s.t as read ⇨ read.
take s.o/s.t at face value ⇨ face(*n*).
take away from s.t make s.t less beautiful etc; detract from s.t: *Those old shoes take away from your appearance.* **take s.t away (from s.o/s.t)** remove(1) s.t from s.o/s.t; not let s.o/s.t have s.t any more. **take s.t away (from s.t)** subtract s.t (from s.t): *If you take 38 away from 62, you are left with 24.*
take s.t back (a) (of a shop etc) be willing to receive goods back and to return the money paid for them if the buyer is not satisfied. **(b)** say that one wants s.t that one said or wrote before to be forgotten because one is sorry one said or wrote it: *If you take back what you said about my wife, we can be friends again.*
take s.o by the arm etc put one's hand or hands on s.o's arm etc and hold it. **take s.o by surprise** ⇨ surprise(*n*).
take s.o down a peg (or two) ⇨ peg(*n*). **take s.t down** write s.t down, usu while listening to s.o saying it.
take s.o/s.t for s.o/s.t think (wrongly) that s.o/s.t is s.o/s.t: *Oh, I'm sorry — I took you for a friend of mine! What do you take me for — a fool?* **take s.t for s.t** drink or eat a medicine etc to try to cure oneself of s.t. **take s.o/s.t for granted** ⇨ granted. **take s.o for a ride** ⇨ ride(*n*).
take form = take shape (⇨ shape(*n*)).
take it from s.o (that . . .) believe s.o when he/she says that . . .: *You can take it from me that she's very sorry.* **take it from s.t** copy s.t down from s.t: *I took the recipe from a Chinese cookery book.*
take s.o in cheat s.o. **take s.t in (a)** make a dress etc narrower by sewing. **(b)** accept things, e.g dirty clothes, for working on, e.g washing, at one's home. **(c)** understand s.t: *I was so worried I didn't take in what he said.* **take s.o/s.t in hand** ⇨ hand(*n*). **take s.t in one's stride** ⇨ stride(*n*).
take s.o into care ⇨ care(*n*). **take it into one's head to do s.t** ⇨ head(*n*).
take hold of s.o/s.t ⇨ hold(*n*).
take issue with s.o/s.t ⇨ issue(*n*).
take off (a) (of a plane) leave the ground. **(b)** start to leave. **(c)** start being successful: *Our business began very slowly but then it took off about a year ago.* **take s.o off** mimic(3) s.o; copy s.o, usu for fun. **take s.t off (a)** remove s.t (e.g one's coat from one's body). **(b)** stop s.t (e.g a bus) giving its regular service: *Because there are so few passengers on a Saturday, the 7.35 train is being taken off.* **take one's hands off (s.o/s.t)** ⇨ hand(*n*).
take on (*informal*) become worried: *Don't take on so - no one's going to hurt you.* **take s.o on (a)** give s.o a job. **(b)** begin to fight s.o, either with words or with blows. **take s.t on (a)** begin to do s.t; begin to deal with s.t: *I'm sorry but I*

can't take on any new work at present. **(b)** begin to show or to have s.t: *The leaves take on a rather yellow colour at this time of year.*
take s.o out go to a restaurant etc, taking s.o with one: *Those two take their grandchild out every Saturday.* **take s.t out (a)** remove s.t: *I had a tooth taken out last week.* **(b)** arrange to have s.t: *take out insurance on one's house.* **take s.t out of s.t (a)** remove s.t from inside s.t. **(b)** copy s.t from s.t. **take it out of s.o** tire s.o. **take s.o out of herself/himself** make s.o forget her/his daily problems by giving her/him s.t nicer to think about. **take s.t out on s.o/s.t** relieve one's feelings of anger etc about s.t by attacking s.o/s.t with words or blows: *When he is bored, he takes it out on the furniture by kicking it.*
take s.t over (from s.o) begin to do s.t instead of s.o else when he was doing it before.
take first etc **place (in s.t)** come first etc (in a race etc).
take shape ⇨ shape(*n*).
take to s.o/s.t begin to like s.o/s.t. **take to s.t** begin doing or using s.t: *When he was unhappy, he often took to drink.* **take to one's heels** ⇨ heel(*n*). **take to the road** ⇨ road. **take s.o to task** ⇨ task.
take s.t to mean s.t = take s.t as meaning s.t.
take s.t up begin to do s.t (e.g a sport): *You're getting fat; why don't you take up tennis?* **take s.t up (with s.o)** begin to talk about a problem etc (with s.o). **take up residence** ⇨ residence. **take up space/time** need space/time: *I'm sorry but we can't print your whole letter because it takes up too much space. Every complaint we receive takes up time.* **take up with s.o** begin to be friendly with s.o; begin to do things with s.o. **taken up with s.t** busy with s.t.
take s.o/s.t with one go s.w with s.o/s.t.
'take,away *c.n* (also *attrib*) **1** restaurant etc in which customers can take food away (e.g to their homes) and eat it there. **2** food taken away in this way: *takeaway meals.*
'take-,home ,pay *u.n* pay after tax etc has been taken off.
'take-,off *n* **1** *c/u.n* (by a plane etc) act of leaving the ground. ⇨ take off(a). **2** *c.n* mimicry(1); copying. ⇨ take s.o off.
'take,over *c.n* (also *attrib*) act of taking control of s.t (usu a business company), usu by buying it. ⇨ take s.o/s.t over.
'taker *c.n* person who takes or accepts s.t: *We are trying to sell this house but there have been no takers yet.*
'takings *pl.n* money etc paid to a shop etc: *Our takings today were over £1000.*
talc /tælk/ *u.n* **1** soft smooth kind of mineral(1) that is used for making talcum powder etc. **2** = talcum powder.
talcum powder /'tælkəm ,paʊdə/ *u.n* kind of very soft fine powder for putting on one's skin, made by crushing talc(1) and (usu) adding s.t to it to make it smell nice.
tale /teɪl/ *c.n* story (usu about things that have never actually happened): *the tale of the three bears.* **fairy tale** ⇨ fairy. **old wives' tale** (*informal*) old story about how to cure s.o, prevent failure etc that includes superstition. **tale of woe** account(2) of all one's troubles, difficulties etc.
tell (s.o) tales (a) tell lies[1](1) (to s.o). **(b)** pass

on (to s.o) information that one should keep secret.

talent /'tælənt/ n **1** c/u.n (often — for s.t) special (usu natural) ability (to do s.t better than most people): *She has a great talent for making speeches.* **2** u.n people who have talent(1): *We have plenty of commercial talent in our town.*
'talent ,scout c.n person who goes around trying to find talented people of a particular kind, e.g footballers or singers.
'talented adj having talent(1).

talisman /'tælɪzmən/ c.n (pl -s) thing that often has special words or signs on it and is supposed to give one magical(1) protection from dangers etc.

talk /tɔːk/ n **1** c.n (often — about/on s.o/s.t) informal speech (about s.o/s.t). **2** u.n way of talking (⇨ talk(5)): *baby talk.* **3** u.n sounds made by an animal which sound like human talk(2). **4** u.n (usu all/just —) talking about things but not doing them: *His wonderful plans for becoming rich were all talk; he remained poor all his life.*
▷ v **5** intr.v (often — (to/with s.o) about s.o/s.t) use speech to tell s.o (about s.o/s.t) (and to hear what he/she has to say). **6** tr.v express (s.t) in a spoken form: *You're talking nonsense now!* **7** tr.v speak about (a particular subject): *You won't be interested in the conversation in that room; they're talking business.* **8** tr.v (be able to) speak (a particular (kind of) language): *Everyone at the party talked English.* **9** intr.v gossip(4); say usu nasty things about people and/or things: *You must be careful not to do anything that makes people talk.* **10** intr.v give information, usu after being beaten or threatened, which one wanted to keep secret: *Has the prisoner talked yet?* **11** intr.v communicate, not by speaking or writing but by using other kinds of signal: *Deaf and dumb people talk by using signs.* **12** intr.v speak human words without knowing what they mean: *One can teach several kinds of birds to talk.*
talk big ⇨ big(adv).
talk down to s.o speak to s.o as if he/she was more stupid than he/she really is: *A lot of audiences hate being talked down to by the lecturer.* **talk s.o down** (informal) talk so loudly or continuously that one stops s.o else being able to say something too.
talk s.o into (doing) s.t persuade s.o to do s.t that he/she did not really want to do by talking to him/her.
talk nineteen to the dozen ⇨ nineteen. **talk s.t out (a)** discuss s.t until one reaches a decision. **(b)** discuss a bill in parliament for so long that it does not get voted on etc. ⇨ guillotine(3,6).
talk s.o out of (doing) s.t persuade s.o not to do s.t that she/he wanted to do by talking to her/him. **talk one's way out (of s.t)** ⇨ way.
talk s.t over discuss s.t. **talk over s.o's head** ⇨ head.
talk round s.t talk in such a way that one is always avoiding the subject one is supposed to be talking about. **talk s.o round (to s.t)** persuade s.o to change his/her mind (and accept s.t that she/he did not want before).
talk rot ⇨ rot(n).
talk sense ⇨ sense(n).
talk shop ⇨ shop.

talk through one's hat ⇨ hat.
talk turkey ⇨ turkey(n).
talkative /'tɔːkətɪv/ adj who talks a lot or too much.
'talker c.n (usu a good etc —) person who talks (well etc).
'talking ,point c.n subject that is particularly interesting to talk about.
'talking-,to sing.n (often get, give s.o, a (good) —) (severe) scolding.
talks pl.n (often have — (with s.o)) discussions (with s.o). **peace talks** discussions between two sides to try to end a war, fight etc.

tall /tɔːl/ adj **1** higher than the average: *a tall person*; *a tall building.* Opposites short(1) (for people), low¹(1) (for things). **2** in height: *He is 1.82 m tall. That mountain is over 8000 metres tall.* Compare high(2).
'tall,boy c.n kind of tall chest of drawers.
'tallish adj rather tall.
'tallness u.n.
,tall 'order sing.n (informal) thing that one is asked to do that is very difficult or perhaps even impossible: *To be ready for that examination in three months' time is a tall order.*
,tall 'story c.n (pl -ies) (informal) story that is difficult to believe because it seems exaggerated or not true.

tally /'tælɪ/ tr/intr.v (-ies, -ied) (often — with s.t) (cause (s.t) to) agree (with s.t), usu in number: *Do the figures the waiter gave you for your bill tally with the ones on the menu?*

talon /'tælən/ c.n sharp curved nail on the foot of a bird of prey; claw(1).

tamable ⇨ tame.

tambourine /,tæmbə'riːn/ c.n kind of musical instrument with skin stretched tightly over a frame that has small circles of metal loosely fastened to it, played by hitting it against s.t so that the skin makes a noise like a drum and the pieces of metal make a jingling(1) sound.

tame /teɪm/ adj **1** (of an animal) accustomed to living with human beings and therefore not wild or dangerous. **2** (informal) not at all exciting; boring: *a tame end to a day that had seemed full of promise.* **3** not at all brave or adventurous.
▷ tr.v **4** make (a wild and/or dangerous animal) tame(1). **5** control (s.t that was free and perhaps even dangerous): *If we can tame the waters of this river, we can use them to produce electricity.*
'tameable adj (also **'tamable**) that can be tamed.
'tamely adv. **'tameness** u.n.
'tamer c.n person who tames a wild animal: *a lion tamer.*

tamper /'tæmpə/ intr.v (usu — with s.t) interfere (with s.t); do s.t (often s.t dangerous) (to s.t) without having permission to do it.

tampon /'tæmpɒn/ c.n long pad of cotton wool a woman puts inside her vagina when she is menstruating to collect the blood.

tan¹ /tæn/ n **1** u.n brown colour of the skin resulting from the action of the sun or a sunlamp etc. **2** u.n (also attrib) light brown colour.
▷ tr/intr.v (-nn-) **3** (cause (s.o or s.o's skin) to) become brown: *The sun will quickly tan you here. I tan easily.*

tan² /tæn/ (-nn-) tr.v **1** make (the skin of an animal) into leather by using tannin. **2** (informal) beat (s.o) hard. **tan s.o's hide** (*informal*) beat s.o very hard.

'tanner¹ *c.n* person whose job is to make leather.

'tannery *c.n* (*pl* **-ies**) place where leather is made.

,tannic 'acid *u.n* (also **'tannin**) acid used for making the skin of an animal into leather.

'tanning *n* 1 *u.n* making of animal skins into leather. 2 *c.n* (*slang*) beating. ⇨ tan²(2).

tan³ /tæn/ *c.n* (*informal*) tangent(2).

tandem /'tændəm/ *c.n* bicycle that has two seats and two pairs of pedals(1) so that two people can ride on it at the same time. **(work) in tandem (with s.o)** (work) together closely (with s.o).

tang /tæŋ/ *c.n* (often — *of s.t*) strong smell or taste.

'tangy /'tæŋɪ/ *adj* (*-ier* /'tæŋɪə/, *-iest* /'tæŋɪəst/) having a tang.

tangent /'tændʒənt/ *c.n* 1 straight line that touches but does not cross a curved line, e.g the edge of a circle. 2 (*informal tan*) (often *the* — *of an angle*) (*mathematics*) (of an angle in a right-angled triangle which is not the right-angle) length of the side opposite (the angle) divided by the length of the shorter of the other two sides. Compare cosine, sine. **fly/go off at a tangent** (*informal*) change suddenly from one belief, subject etc to another different one.

tangerine /,tændʒə'riːn/ *n* 1 *c.n* fruit that is like an orange but is usu smaller and sweeter. 2 *u.n* (also *attrib*) dark orange colour.

tangible /'tændʒɪbl/ *adj* (usu *attrib*) 1 that one can feel by touching it. 2 real; certain(1); not just imagined: *tangible* evidence(1) *that the world goes round the sun.* Opposite intangible.

,tangible 'assets *pl.n* actual tangible(1) things that a company owns as against its goodwill(2).

,tangi'bility *u.n.*

tangle /'tæŋgl/ *c.n* 1 mixed up state of s.t, e.g wool, hair. **in a tangle** in a tangled(2) state. **(get into) a tangle with s.o** (*informal*) (begin) a quarrel or fight with s.o.

▷ *tr/intr.v* 2 (cause (s.t) to) be in a tangle(1). Opposite untangle. **tangle (s.t) (up) (with s.t)** (cause (s.t) to) become entangled(1) (with s.t). **tangle with s.o** (*informal*) get into a quarrel or fight with s.o.

tango /'tæŋgəʊ/ *n* (*pl* **-s**) 1 *c/def.n* kind of South American dance: *dance the tango.* 2 *c.n* music for this kind of dance.

▷ *intr.v* (*tangoes, tangoed*) 3 dance the tango(1).

tangy ⇨ tang.

tank /tæŋk/ *c.n* 1 kind of container in which one puts water, petrol etc: *a car's petrol tank*; *a fish tank* (in which live fish are kept in water). 2 kind of army vehicle with thick armour and tracks instead of wheels.

tankard /'tæŋkəd/ *c.n* 1 kind of container with a handle, and usu a lid, out of which one drinks beer. 2 (often — *of s.t*) as much as a tankard(1) holds: *That man has already drunk three tankards.*

tanked up /,tæŋkt 'ʌp/ *adj* (*slang*) drunk(1).

tanker /'tæŋkə/ *c.n* ship, vehicle, plane that has the job of carrying oil, gas, water etc.

tanner¹ ⇨ tan².

tanner² /'tænə/ *c.n* (*old use*; *slang*) sixpenny(1) coin.

tannery, tannic acid, tannin, tanning ⇨ tan².

tannic /'tænɪk/ *u.n* ⇨ tannic acid(tan²).

tantalize, -ise /'tæntə,laɪz/ *tr.v* offer (a person or an animal) s.t that he/she/it wants very much but not let him/her/it have it, with the result that he/she/it is unhappy or angry: *She tantalized me with the promise of a holiday if I work harder.*

tantamount /'tæntə,maʊnt/ *adj* (usu — *to s.t*) just about the same as (s.t): *Paying the money is tantamount to agreeing that you owe it.*

tantrum /'tæntrəm/ *c.n* sudden fit²(3) of violent anger or bad temper: *Young children often have tantrums* (or *go into tantrums*).

tap¹ /tæp/ *c.n* (US usu **'faucet**) 1 device (e.g in a bath, basin or sink) for controlling the amount of water, gas etc passing through a pipe etc: *We have a hot tap and a cold tap on our bath.*

▷ *tr.v* (**-pp-**) 2 get water, gas, beer etc from (s.t): *To get rubber, one has to tap rubber trees. A nation can only keep up with international progress by tapping its people's best brains.* 3 listen to (other people's conversations) secretly by putting s.t on their telephone wires. ⇨ phone-tapping. 4 put s.t on (telephone wires) so that one can listen to such conversations.

tap² /tæp/ *c.n* 1 gentle hit: *I gave him a tap on the shoulder.*

▷ *tr/intr.v* (**-pp-**) 2 hit (s.o/s.t) gently. **tap at/on s.t** hit s.t gently: *He tapped at the window.*

'tap ,dancer *c.n* person who dances with small pieces of metal on her/his shoes so that she/he can make loud rhythmical sounds with them.

'tap ,dancing *u.n* dancing in this way.

tape /teɪp/ *n* 1 *c/u.n* long narrow strip of cloth etc: *The woman sewed a piece of tape round the neck of the shirt to strengthen it.* 2 *c/u.n* (also **mag,netic 'tape**) long narrow strip of plastic(3) used for recording music etc on. 3 *c.n* particular strip of tape(2) on which (s.t) is recorded: *I'm going to play you a tape of our last show.* 4 *c.n* = tape measure. **have s.t on tape** have a tape(3) on which s.t is recorded. **put s.t on tape** tape(6) s.t. **red tape** ⇨ red.

▷ *tr.v* 5 (often — *s.t up*) tie (s.t) with tape(1). 6 record (s.t) on tape(2). **have s.o/s.t taped** (*fig*; *informal*) know exactly how to deal with s.o/s.t successfully.

'tape ,deck *c.n* device for recording things on tape(2) and for playing them back, but not the loudspeakers etc for listening to the recordings.

'tape ,measure *c.n* tape(1) with centimetres etc marked on it so that one can use it for measuring things.

'tape-re,cord *tr/intr.v* record (s.t) on tape(2).

'tape re,corder *c.n* (also **re'corder**) device for recording things on tape(2) and playing them back, with one or more built-in or separate speakers.

'tape-re,cording *c.n* = tape(3).

tapeworm /'teɪp,wɜːm/ *c.n* kind of long flat worm that lives in human and animal bowels(1).

taper /'teɪpə/ *c.n* 1 thing that becomes narrower as it comes closer to one end.

▷ *tr/intr.v* 2 (often — *off*) (cause (s.t) to) become narrower as it comes closer to one end: *I prefer my trousers to taper.*

tape-record, tape recorder, tape-recording ⇨ tape.

tapestry /'tæpɪstrɪ/ c/u.n (pl -ies) picture made by sewing wool etc on cloth and usu hung on a wall.

tapeworm ⇒ tape.

tapioca /ˌtæpɪ'əʊkə/ u.n (also attrib) white grains from cassava(1) roots, usu cooked with milk and sugar in Western countries: tapioca pudding.

tar /tɑː/ n 1 u.n kind of black substance used in making roads.
▷ tr.v (-rr-) 2 cover or paint (s.t) with tar(1). **tarred with the same brush** having the same (bad) habits: If you don't like Jenny you can't like any of her family — they're all tarred with the same brush.
'tarry¹ adj (-ier, -iest) covered with, smelling like, tar(1).

tarantula /tə'ræntjʊlə/ c.n kind of big poisonous spider.

target /'tɑːgɪt/ c.n 1 thing that one fires at with a gun, bow etc, either for practice or to kill etc. 2 (often — of s.t) person or thing who/that is attacked (with criticism, jokes etc): The boy was so stupid that he soon became the target of all the other boys' fun. 3 thing (that consists of s.t, e.g a certain amount of money and) that one is trying to get, reach: We are collecting money for a new youth club and our target is £100 000 in six months.

tariff /'tærɪf/ c.n 1 price list, e.g in a hotel: Our tariff shows the prices of our various rooms, the cost of meals and the service charges. 2 tax on imports(1) into a country, and sometimes on exports(2) too.

tarmacadam /ˌtɑːmə'kædəm/ u.n (formal) tarmac(1).

tarmac /'tɑːmæk/ n 1 u.n (formal ˌtarma-'cadam) (also attrib) mixture of tar(1) and stones used for putting on the top of a road. 2 c/ def.n piece of ground covered with tarmac(1), esp when it is part of an airport, parking lot or playground.
▷ tr.v (-ck-) 3 cover (s.t, usu a road or runway) with tarmac(1).

tarnish /'tɑːnɪʃ/ c/u.n 1 result of tarnishing(2,3) s.t.
▷ tr/intr.v 2 (cause (s.t that was bright, e.g brass) to) become dull(1). 3 (fig) (cause (s.t that was good) to) seem less good: Politicians should be careful not to tarnish their reputations by doubtful business deals.

tarpaulin /tɑː'pɔːlɪn/ c/u.n kind of thick heavy waterproof cloth, used for covering things, e.g piles of wood.

tarragon /'tærəgən/ u.n kind of herb used in cooking.

tarry¹ ⇒ tar.

tarry² /'tærɪ/ intr.v (-ies, -ied) (old use; literary) wait; spend time s.w: Tarry a while, pretty lady.

tart¹ /tɑːt/ c/u.n 1 kind of food consisting of meat, cheese, cooked fruit or jam etc with pastry under it and round its sides. Compare pie. 2 (derog; slang) prostitute.

tart² /tɑːt/ adj 1 having a sharp rather sour or bitter taste. 2 (fig) (of a person or the things he/ she says) nasty; trying to hurt s.o.
'tartly adv in a tart²(2) way.
'tartness u.n.

tartan /'tɑːtn/ n 1 u.n (also attrib) cloth made of wool and with a special pattern of bands of different colours and widths: Each Scottish clan(1) has a different pattern on its tartan. 2 c.n pattern of tartan(1) belonging to a particular Scottish clan(1).

tartar¹ /'tɑːtə/ u.n 1 hard white or brown substance formed on the teeth by the action of saliva. 2 (also ˌcream of 'tartar) kind of white powder used for making baking powder and some medicines.

tartar² /'tɑːtə/ c.n (derog) person who is very strict, severe or fierce.

tartar sauce /ˌtɑːtə 'sɔːs/ u.n sauce made by mixing mayonnaise with very small pieces of kinds of pickled (⇒ pickle(3)) vegetables, eaten with fish.

tartness ⇒ tart².

task /tɑːsk/ c.n piece of work, usu one that is hard or not pleasant but must be done. **take s.o to task** scold s.o.
'task ˌforce c.n group of people from the armed services or the police who have a particular task.
'task,master/-,mistress c.n (often a hard —) person (e.g a boss or a teacher) who gives (hard) tasks to people, e.g employees or students.

tassel /'tæsl/ c.n pieces of cord, wool, thread etc fixed together at one end but loose at the other, used as a decoration on curtains etc.

taste /teɪst/ n 1 u.n one of our five senses that we use our tongues for, e.g to know whether s.t is sweet or sour. 2 c/u.n quality in food etc that we experience by means of our sense of taste(1): This soup has a sour taste/a taste of lemons. Some food has little or no taste. 3 c.n (often have a — of s.t) small amount (of s.t) that is just enough for one to find out its taste(2) or to find out what it is like: You can have a taste of this cheese before you buy it. After having had a taste of life in a big city, Mary returned to her quiet life in the country. 4 u.n (often — in s.t) personal way of judging whether things (of a particular kind) are beautiful, ugly etc: That woman has good taste in jewellery but her sister seems to have no taste. **get/have a taste for s.t** (begin to) like s.t. **in bad, good etc taste** showing good etc taste(4): I think the furniture in her house is in very good taste. **a matter of taste** ⇒ matter(n).
▷ v 5 tr/intr.v use one's sense of taste(1) (to experience s.t); know by means of one's sense of taste(1) (that etc . . .): This pie is burnt; taste (it). 6 intr.v have a certain kind of taste(2): This fish tastes rotten. This soup tastes of onions. 7 tr.v have (s.t to eat): I've never tasted goat's cheese. 8 tr.v (fig) have a taste(3) of (s.t, e.g life in a foreign country).
'taste ˌbuds pl.n collections of cells(4) on one's tongue which allow one to taste(5) s.t.
'tasteful adj showing good taste(4); in good taste.
'tastefully adv. **'tastefulness** u.n.
'tasteless adj not having any taste(2,4).
'tastelessly adv. **'tastelessness** u.n.
'tastily adv in a tasty way.
'tastiness u.n fact of being tasty.
'tasty adj (-ier, -iest) having a pleasant taste(2).

tat /tæt/ ⇒ tit for tat.

tata /tæ'tɑː/ interj (informal, usu used by and to small children) goodbye.

tattered /'tætəd/ *adj* torn in many places: *He was wearing a tattered old shirt.*

'tatters *pl.n* things (e.g clothes) that are torn in many places. **in tatters (a)** torn in many places: *The wind was so violent that it left our sails in tatters.* **(b)** (*fig*) seriously damaged; ruined: *His failures have left his confidence in tatters.*

tattily, tattiness ⇒ tatty.

tattle /'tætl/ *intr.v* talk a lot about things that are not important or about other people's private affairs; gossip(4). ⇒ tittle-tattle.

tattoo¹ /tə'tu:/ *c.n* (*pl* -s) **1** thing drawn or written on s.o's skin in such a way that it stays there permanently.
▷ *tr.v* **2** mark (s.o on her/his skin) with a tattoo(1): *The old woman tattooed a lion on the sailor's chest. His arm was tattooed with a snake.*
tattooist /tə'tu:ɪst/ *c.n* person who tattoos(2) people.

tattoo² /tə'tu:/ *c.n* big military show for the public, with one or more bands²(2), usu at night.

tatty /'tætɪ/ *adj* (-ier, -iest) (*derog*) untidy and worn.
'tattily *adv.* **'tattiness** *u.n.*

taught /tɔ:t/ *p.t,p.p* of teach.

taunt /tɔ:nt/ *c.n* **1** thing said to s.o in order to make her/him feel angry or hurt: *Because Edward had a big nose, he suffered many taunts from the other boys in the school.*
▷ *tr.v* **2** (often — s.o with s.t) say nasty things to (s.o) (about s.t) in order to make her/him feel angry or hurt.
'tauntingly *adv* in a way that taunts(2).

Taurus /'tɔ:rəs/ *n* **1** *unique n* one of the 12 signs of the zodiac. **2** *c.n* person born under this sign.

taut /tɔ:t/ *adj* **1** tight(5); stretched. **2** tense¹(1); not at all relaxed(1).
'tautly *adv.* **'tautness** *u.n.*

tautology /tɔ:'tɒlədʒɪ/ *c/u.n* (example of) saying s.t twice, each time using different words, when this does not help people to understand better, e.g 'He decided to leave his own country and to go abroad'.
tautological /ˌtɔ:təˈlɒdʒɪkl/ *adj* showing or referring to tautology.

tavern /'tævən/ *c.n* (*old use*) inn; small hotel and/or pub.

tawdry /'tɔ:drɪ/ *adj* (-ier, -iest) (*derog*) not showing any taste(4): *tawdry jewellery.*
'tawdrily *adv.* **'tawdriness** *u.n.*

tawny /'tɔ:nɪ/ *adj* (-ier, -iest) (esp of an animal, its fur etc) between brown and yellow in colour.
,tawny 'owl *c.n* kind of brown European owl.

tax /tæks/ *n* **1** *c/u.n* money that has to be paid to a government every year or when one buys or sells s.t, etc: *I earned £400 before tax.* ⇒ capital gains tax, income tax, purchase(2) *tax,* value added tax. **tax on s.t** tax that one has to pay on the cost of goods bought, profit etc.
▷ *tr.v* **2** make (s.o/s.t) pay tax(1). **3** put a strain¹(3) on (s.o/s.t); tire (s.o/s.t); put too much pressure on (s.o/s.t): *tax s.o's patience or strength.* ⇒ overtax. **tax s.o with s.t** accuse s.o of s.t.
taxation /tæk'seɪʃən/ *u.n* **1** act of taxing (⇒ tax(2)). **2** money that a government gets from taxes(1).
'tax col,lector *c.n* person whose job is to collect taxes(1).

,tax-'free *adj* that does not have to have any taxes(1) paid on it.

'tax ,haven *c.n* (*informal*) (part of a) country where there are no, or very small, taxes(1).

'taxing *adj* tiring: *a taxing climb up the hill.*

'tax,payer *c.n* person who pays taxes(1).

taxi¹ /'tæksɪ/ *c.n* (*pl* -s) car with a driver that one can hire to take one from one place to another. Compare hire car. **by taxi** in a taxi: *go/travel by taxi.*
'taxi,cab *c.n* (*formal*) = taxi¹.
'taxi,meter *c.n* machine in a taxi that shows how much one has to pay.
'taxi ,rank/,stand *c.n* (also **'cab ,rank/,stand**) special place where taxis, but not other vehicles, are allowed to wait.

taxi² /'tæksɪ/ *tr/intr.v* (*pres.p* taxiing, *p.t,p.p* taxied) (cause (a plane) to) move along the ground, not in the air: *Our plane taxied out to the runway and then waited there for a few minutes before taking off.*

TB /ˌtiː 'biː/ *abbr* tuberculosis.

tbsp *written abbr* (*pl* tbsps) tablespoon(ful).

tea /ti:/ *n* **1** *u.n* drink made from the leaves, and sometimes the roots, of certain plants, mostly special bushes grown in India, China etc for the purpose of making this drink: *a cup/pot of (China/Indian) tea.* **2** *u.n* dried leaves from which tea(1) is made. **3** *u.n* bush(es) with white flowers from which most kinds of tea(2) are made. **4** *c.n* cup of tea(1). **5** *c/u.n* meal eaten usu in the middle of the afternoon in Britain and some other countries: *We are having chocolate cake for tea today. At what time do you have tea?* **(not) s.o's cup of tea** (*informal*) (not) what s.o likes: *I know that a lot of people like this music but it isn't my cup of tea at all.*

'tea,bag *c.n* small bag made of a special kind of paper which has enough tealeaves in it for one cup of tea.

'tea ,break *c.n* period of stopping work so that one can have some tea and a rest.

'tea ,caddy *c.n* (*pl* -ies) container in which one keeps tea(2).

'tea,cake *c.n* kind of small cake.

'tea ,chest *c.n* large square wooden box in which tea(2) is carried from the place where it is made to the place where it is sold to people: *Tea chests are often used by people to pack their belongings when they move to a new house.*

'tea ,cloth *c.n* (also **'tea ,towel**) cloth used to dry plates, spoons etc after washing them.

'tea ,cosy *c.n* (*pl* -ies) padded cover put over a teapot to keep it hot.

'tea,cup *c.n* cup out of which tea is drunk. **a storm in a teacup** (*fig; informal*) a lot of trouble and worry about s.t that is not important: *Their quarrel(1) was just a storm in a teacup.*

'tea,cupful *c.n* as much as a teacup can hold.

'tea,house *c.n* (*pl* -s /-ˌhaʊzɪz/) restaurant, usu in Asia, where one can drink tea(1) and usu also have a small meal.

'tea,leaf *c.n* (*pl* -leaves) small piece of the dried leaves used to make tea(1).

'tea ,party *c.n* (*pl* -ies) party at which one gets tea(1) (and usu also food).

'tea,pot *c.n* pot in which one makes tea(1).

'tea,room *c.n* restaurant where one can get tea(1) and small meals. Compare café.

'**tea** ,**service**/,**set** *c.n* cups, saucers, plates, tea-pot etc which are all of the same pattern.

'**tea**,**spoon** *c.n abbr tsp* **1** small spoon as used for putting sugar in tea(1) and then stirring it. **2** (often — *of s.t*) as much as a teaspoon(1) holds: *a teaspoon of sugar.*

'**tea**,**spoonful** *c.n* = teaspoon(2).

'**tea** ,**strainer** *c.n* device, usu made of metal, which has a lot of small holes in it, so that one can pour tea(1) into a cup without any of the tealeaves passing through.

'**tea**,**time** *unique n* (often *at* —) time at which one is having, or usu has, tea(5).

'**tea** ,**towel** *c.n* tea cloth.

'**tea** ,**tray** *c.n* tray on which the things for tea(5) are carried.

'**tea** ,**trolley** *c.n* = trolley(2).

teach /tiːtʃ/ *tr/intr.v* (*p.t,p.p* taught /tɔːt/) give s.o one or more lessons; help s.o to learn (s.t): *'What does your brother do?' 'He teaches.' Vera teaches mathematics. John teaches adults English. He taught his children to ride bicycles. The church teaches (us) that kindness is better than riches. Our teacher taught us how people make carpets.* **cannot teach an old dog new tricks** ⇒ dog(*n*). **teach one's grandmother to suck eggs** ⇒ egg(*n*). **teach s.o a lesson**; **teach s.o (not) to do s.t** punish s.o as an example (not) to do s.t another time.

'**teachable** *adj* who/that can be taught (s.t). Opposite unteachable.

'**teacher** *c.n* person who teaches: *He's an English teacher* (or *a teacher of English*).

'**teaching** ,**hospital** *c.n* hospital that not only treats patients but also teaches medical students who work and study there.

'**teachings** *pl.n* (often *the* — *of s.o/s.t*) things that (s.o/s.t) teaches: *The teachings of all religions agree on many points.*

teacup(ful), teahouse ⇒ tea.

teak /tiːk/ *n* **1** *c.n* (also '**teak** ,**tree**) kind of big tree found in South (East) Asia whose wood is very hard and very good for making furniture etc. **2** *u.n* (also *attrib*) wood of this tree.

tealeaf, tealeaves ⇒ tea.

team /tiːm/ *c.n* **1** group of people who do s.t (e.g work or play a game) together in an organized way: *There are eleven people in a football team.* **2** group of animals working together: *a team of horses pulling a heavy load.*

▷ *intr.v* **3** **team up** (**with s.o/s.t**) join (s.o/s.t) in order to do s.t all together: *We're not good enough but if we team up with other players we could win.*

'**team** ,**game** *c.n* kind of game, e.g football, that is played by teams, not by one person against another.

'**team** ,**spirit** *u.n* feeling that one is playing, working etc for one's team and not for oneself.

'**teamster** *c.n* person who drives a lorry or a team of animals.

'**team**,**work** *u.n* working together in a team and not just for oneself.

teapot ⇒ tea.

tear[1] /tɪə/ *c.n* drop of water that comes out of s.o's eye when he/she is sad, cold etc. **bore s.o to tears** (*informal*) bore[1](2) s.o very much. **burst into tears** begin to cry(7). **in tears** crying(3); weeping (⇒ weep(2)). **move s.o to tears** make s.o

cry(7). **tears of s.t** tears[1] caused by s.t: *tears of anger/shame.*

'**tear**,**drop** *c.n* = tear[1].

'**tearful** *adj* crying(3); weeping (⇒ weep(2)); (as if) wanting to cry(7): *feeling tearful.*

'**tearfully** *adv*. '**tearfulness** *u.n*.

'**tear**,**gas** *u.n* kind of gas that makes tears flow from one's eyes so much that one cannot see, sometimes used by police etc against crowds.

'**tear**,**jerker** *c.n* (*informal*) story, film etc that is so sad that it makes people (want to) cry(7).

'**tearless** *adj* not having tears[1].

tear[2] /teə/ *c.n* **1** irregular cut in s.t which is made by pulling, not by cutting etc. **wear and tear** ⇒ wear.

▷ *v* (*p.t* tore /tɔː/, *p.p* torn /tɔːn/) **2** *tr.v* (cut (s.t) by pulling, not by cutting etc. **3** *intr.v* be able to be torn; become torn: *Be careful of this paper; it tears easily. When I tried to fly my kite in a strong wind, it tore.* **4** *intr.v* (often — *across*, *down*, *past* etc (s.o/s.t)) move very, or too, fast (across etc s.t): *Cars tear through our village streets at a dangerous speed.*

be torn between s.o/s.t and s.o/s.t find it very difficult to choose between s.o/s.t and s.o/s.t because one likes them both equally.

tear s.o/s.t apart (*fig*) criticize or scold s.o/s.t severely.

tear at s.o/s.t (**with s.t**) (try to) pull s.o/s.t violently (with one's nails etc).

tear s.o away (**from s.t**) make s.o leave (s.t) in spite of the person not wanting to do so.

tear s.t down pull s.t away from a wall etc, often roughly or angrily, so that it falls down.

tear into s.o/s.t attack s.o/s.t violently, with blows or words.

tear s.o off a strip ⇒ strip(*n*).

tear s.t off (**s.t**) pull s.t (e.g a piece of paper) off the top (e.g of the rest of the pad).

tear s.t out (**of s.t**) pull s.t (e.g a page) out (of s.t, e.g a book). **tear one's hair** (**out**) ⇒ hair. **tear s.o's heart out** ⇒ heart.

tear s.t up tear s.t into pieces.

'**teara**,**way** *c.n* (*derog*) (young) person who behaves badly, usu by being wild and noisy.

tearoom ⇒ tea.

tease /tiːz/ *c.n* **1** person who teases(2).

▷ *v* **2** *tr/intr.v* say or do things to s.o to make her/him feel worried, sometimes as a joke but sometimes to hurt her/him: *The children knew that Peter was fond of Mary but too shy to speak to her, so they used to tease him about it.* **3** *tr.v* (usu — *s.t out*) divide (s.t, e.g a mass of wool) into its separate strands[1], usu by combing it.

'**teaser** *c.n* **1** tease(1). **2** (*old use*) difficult problem.

teaspoon(ful) ⇒ tea.

teat /tiːt/ *c.n* **1** part of a woman's breast(1) or of a cow's etc udder from which the baby or young animal sucks milk. **2** rubber device like a teat(1) which is put round the mouth of a bottle so that a baby can suck milk etc from it.

teatime ⇒ tea.

tech /tek/ *c.n* (*informal*) polytechnic or technical college.

technical /'teknɪkl/ *adj* **1** (usu *attrib*) of or referring to one or more practical (rather than pure(6) or academic(2)) sciences (i.e sciences that help one to use one's hands as well as one's brain). **2** (usu *pred*) needing much knowledge of one particular subject; specialized: *I am sorry but this magazine about cars is too technical for the general reader.* **3** (usu *attrib*) only on a technicality(2): *Our side suffered a technical defeat in the vote but when the rest of the committee arrived we won easily.*

'technical ,college *c.n* (*informal tech*) college at which technical(1) subjects are taught; polytechnic.

technicality /ˌteknɪˈkælɪtɪ/ *c.n* (*pl* -*ies*) **1** technical(2) detail, way of saying things etc: *I know a certain amount about a car engine but not all its technicalities.* **2** idea, point etc that tries to be so perfect that it does not seem reasonable: *They lost their case on a technicality because they had not filled a form in properly.*

,technical 'knock,out *c.n* (in boxing) instance when a boxer is not actually knocked out(a), but is stopped from fighting any more by the referee(2) because he is too badly hurt, weak etc to continue.

'technically *adv.*

technician /tekˈnɪʃən/ *c.n* person who has one or more technical(1) skills.

technique /tekˈniːk/ *c.n* special way in which one does s.t: *Watch that player's technique as she hits the ball. Every artist has a different technique which an art* expert(2) *can usually recognize at once.*

technocracy /tekˈnɒkrəsɪ/ *n* (*pl* -*ies*) **1** *u.n* control of a country or a kind of business etc by a group of technicians or technologists. **2** *c.n* country controlled by such people.

technocrat /ˈteknəˌkræt/ *c.n* member of, supporter of, a technocracy(1).

technological /ˌteknəˈlɒdʒɪkl/ *adj* of or referring to technology.

,techno'logically *adv.*

technologist /tekˈnɒlədʒɪst/ *c.n* person who knows a lot about technology.

tech'nology *u.n* practical (as against pure(6)) science; science dealing with the development and use of practical ways of doing things in factories etc. ⇒ high technology, information technology.

teddy /ˈtedɪ/ *c.n* (also **,teddy 'bear**) toy bear, usu stuffed with some soft material.

tedious /ˈtiːdɪəs/ *adj* boring.

'tediously *adv.* **'tediousness** *u.n.*

tedium /ˈtiːdɪəm/ *u.n.*

tee /tiː/ *c.n* **1** place or thing from which the ball is hit at the start of each hole(4) of golf(1).
▷ *tr.v* **2 tee off** hit the ball from a tee(1) in golf(1).

tee shirt /ˈtiː ˌʃɜːt/ *c.n* = T-shirt (⇒ T,t).

teem /tiːm/ *intr.v* **1** exist in very large numbers: *Rabbits teem in some parts of Australia.* **2** (usu *it is/was* —*ing* (*down*)) (of rain) fall very heavily.
teem with s.o/s.t be full of s.o/s.t; have large numbers of s.o/s.t in or on it: *At weekends this beach teems with people.*

teenage /ˈtiːnˌeɪdʒ/ *adj* (also **'teen,aged**) (usu *attrib*) older than 12 but younger than 20.

'teen,ager *c.n* person who is teenage.

teens *pl.n* (usu *in one's* —) age that is more than 12 but less than 20.

teeny /ˈtiːnɪ/ *adj* (also **,teeny 'weeny**) (-*ier*, -*iest*) (*informal*) very small.

teeter /ˈtiːtə/ *intr.v* (often — *on the edge/brink*

(*of s.t*)) (sometimes *fig*) be unsteady (and almost falling into or over (s.t)): *After teetering on the edge of the bridge for a few seconds she fell into the water. Our team teetered on the brink of defeat for most of the match but in the last minute we scored a goal so the match was a draw.*

teeth, teethe, teething troubles ⇒ tooth.

teetotal /tiːˈtəʊtl/ *adj* (of a person) never drinking or providing alcoholic(1) drinks.

tee'totaller *c.n* person who is teetotal.

Teflon /ˈteflɒn/ *u.n* (*t.n*) material put on the insides of pans to stop food sticking to them.

telecommunications /ˌtelɪkəˌmjuːnɪˈkeɪʃənz/ *unique/pl.n* ways of sending and/or receiving messages by telephone, telegraph etc using wires, or radio or television signals.

telegram /ˈtelɪˌɡræm/ *c.n* message sent by telegraph. **by telegram** in the form of a telegram: *We will send her the news by telegram.*

telegraph /ˈtelɪˌɡrɑːf/ *n* **1** *u.n* way of sending written messages from one place to another along wires by using electricity. **2** *c.n* machine for doing this.
▷ *tr/intr.v* **3** send (a piece of news, or order etc) by telegraph(1).

telegrapher /tɪˈleɡrəfə/ *c.n* (also **te'legraphist**) person whose job is to send messages by telegraph.

telegraphic /ˌtelɪˈɡræfɪk/ *adj* of or referring to telegraphs; for telegrams: *a company's telegraphic address.*

,tele'graphically *adv.*

telegraphist /tɪˈleɡrəfɪst/ *c.n* ⇒ telegrapher.

'tele,graph ,pole/,post *c.n* pole supporting telegraph wires.

telepathy /tɪˈlepəθɪ/ *u.n* act or fact of sending and receiving messages from one person to another without using speech, writing or any other physical means: *Some people believe that they can send thoughts to other people across great distances by telepathy.*

telepathic /ˌtelɪˈpæθɪk/ *adj* of, referring to, by, telepathy.

,tele'pathically *adv.*

telepathist /tɪˈlepəθɪst/ *c.n* person who (says he/she) is able to send messages by telepathy.

telephone /ˈtelɪˌfəʊn/ *n* (also **phone**) **1** *u.n* (also *attrib*) way of sending and receiving spoken messages and other sounds from one place to another by electrical signals, either along wires or by radio: *telephone wires.* **2** *c.n* (also *attrib*) device that one talks into etc and listens to etc when using the telephone(1): *telephone numbers.* **by telephone** using the telephone. **on the telephone** (**a**) engaged in telephoning: *The manager can't talk to you just now because he's on the telephone.* (**b**) connected to the telephone system: *We are not on the telephone yet.*
▷ *v* (also **phone**) **3** *tr/intr.v* use the telephone(1) (to speak to s.o or to a place): *I'll telephone/phone you next week. Please telephone our London office for that information.* **4** *tr.v* send (a message) by telephone: *I'll telephone the details later.*

'telephone ,book *c.n* book in which people's names and telephone numbers (and addresses) are listed.

'telephone ,booth *c.n* small booth on a wall with a telephone inside, e.g at a station, for use by the public.

'telephone ,box ⇒ call box, phone-box(*n*).

'telephone di,rectory *c.n* = telephone book.

'telephone ex,change *c.n* place where the telephone lines in an area come in so that they can be connected with each other, either by a telephone operator or automatically.

'telephone ,ope,rator *c.n* person whose job is to answer telephone calls and connect people who are telephoning with the person etc they want to speak to.

telephonist /tɪˈlefənɪst/ *c.n* = telephone operator.

telephoto /ˈtelɪˌfəʊtəʊ/ *c.n* 1 photograph of s.o/ s.t that has been taken through a telephoto lens. 2 picture sent from one place to another by telegraph or radio.

,tele,photo 'lens *c.n* lens(1) on a camera that makes things bigger.

telephotography /ˌtelɪfəˈtɒɡrəfɪ/ *u.n* 1 photographing with a telephoto lens. 2 sending telephotos(2).

teleprinter /ˈtelɪˌprɪntə/ *c.n* machine like a typewriter that sends and receives written messages from one place to another by telegraph or radio. ⇒ telex.

telescope /ˈtelɪˌskəʊp/ *c.n* 1 device for looking through which makes things look bigger and nearer than they really are.

▷ *tr/intr.v* 2 (cause (s.t) to) become shorter, either by crushing, usu as a result of a crash, or because one part fits into another: *When the two trains hit each other head on, several of the carriages were telescoped. One can telescope this umbrella so that it is 15 centimetres long.*

telescopic /ˌtelɪˈskɒpɪk/ *adj* 1 referring to, acting as, a telescope(1): *a telescopic lens(1) on a camera.* 2 that is made in such a way that it can telescope(2).

televise /ˈtelɪˌvaɪz/ *tr.v* broadcast (an event etc) on television.

television /ˌtelɪˈvɪʒən/ *n* (*informal* telly) (*abbr* TV) 1 *u.n* (also *attrib*) broadcasting of pictures as well as sound: *television news.* Compare radio. 2 *u.n* programmes broadcast by television(3). 3 *u.n* (also *attrib*) industry that produces television programmes: *television companies. John hopes to go into television when he leaves college.* 4 *c.n* (also **,tele'vision ,set**) device with a screen in front, used for receiving and viewing television programmes. **on television** being televised.

,tele'vision ,set *c.n* = television(4).

telex /ˈteleks/ *n* 1 *u.n* system of sending messages by teleprinter. 2 *c.n* machine for sending messages by telex(1). 3 *c.n* message sent by telex(1).

▷ *v* 4 *tr.v* send (s.o) s.t by telex(1). 5 *tr/intr.v* send (s.t) by telex(1).

tell /tel/ *v* (*p.t,p.p* told /təʊld/) 1 *tr.v* give s.o (certain information): *He told the children a story. You can tell that to your friends. She told me that she did not know. Tell us where you are going. Can you tell me how to get to the station?* 2 *tr.v* (with special stress(2) on 'tell') advise or warn (s.o) (about s.t etc): *I told him that was dangerous but he didn't believe me and now he's in hospital. Your mother told you not to go near the water and look at your shoes now! 3 *tr.v* know, understand, (which etc): *I can never tell which of those two boys will do best in school. How do you tell which switch to put on?* 4 *tr.v* show, inform,

(s.o): *If this light comes on, that tells you (that) you need petrol.* 5 *intr.v* (often — *on* s.o) pass on information that is supposed to be kept secret (and in this way not be faithful to s.o): *If you give me the name of the man you are going to marry, I promise I won't tell (on you).* 6 *intr.v* (often — *on* s.o/s.t) have a bad effect (on s.o/s.t): *That man's age is beginning to tell (on him) — he's finding it more and more difficult to climb stairs.*

all told ⇒ all.

I told you so! I warned you that that would happen!

tell against s.o be s.t that is to s.o's disadvantage: *In some countries, the fact that one is a woman still tells against one when trying to get certain jobs.*

Tell me another! (*informal*) I don't believe what you have just said.

tell s.o/s.t from s.o/s.t be able to recognize the difference between two or more people/things: *Helen and Mary are so alike that I can never tell one from the other.*

tell s.o off scold s.o.

tell on s.o ⇒ tell(5). **tell on s.o/s.t** ⇒ tell(6).

tell the time ⇒ time(*n*).

tell s.o to do s.t order s.o to do s.t; give s.o the order to do s.t: *The teacher told the children to be quiet.*

tell the truth ⇒ truth.

there is no telling, you can never tell, (*where* etc ...) it is impossible to know (where etc ...).

'teller *c.n* 1 cashier in a bank. 2 person who counts votes when people are voting about s.t.

'tell,tale *attrib.adj* 1 that shows s.t that would otherwise remain secret or hidden: *We could see from the telltale marks on the river bank that there were water rats there.*

▷ *c.n* 2 (*derog; informal*) person who gives away information that should be secret.

telly /ˈtelɪ/ *u/c.n* (*pl* -ies) (*informal*) television.

temerity /tɪˈmerɪtɪ/ *u.n* (*formal*) (often have the — *to* do s.t) cheek(2) or rude boldness (to do s.t): *She arrived late and had the temerity to ask for the afternoon off!*

temp /temp/ *c.n* (*informal*) temporary(2) secretary etc.

temper /ˈtempə/ *n* 1 *c.n* (tendency to have an) angry state of mind: *Polly has quite a temper.* 2 *u.n* hardness or strength of a metal etc resulting from tempering (⇒ temper(3)). **fly into a temper** ⇒ fly². **get in(to) a temper** become angry. **have a gentle** etc **temper** be gentle etc in one's character. **have a quick temper** have a temper(1) that easily turns to anger. ⇒ quick-tempered. **(in a) bad, good** etc **temper** (in a state of) anger, happiness etc. **in a temper** angry. **keep one's temper** not show that one is angry; prevent oneself getting angry. **lose one's temper** become angry.

▷ *tr.v* 3 harden or strengthen (a metal etc) by heating and then cooling or by other treatments. 4 make (s.t) less severe: *The heat of the summer here is tempered by pleasant winds.* **temper s.t with s.t** (*formal*) prevent s.t being too nasty by mixing it with s.t: *Our system of law tempers justice with mercy.*

-tempered *adj* having a temper of the kind shown by the first part of the word: *good-tempered; evil-tempered.*

temperament /'temprəmənt/ c/u.n nature of a person or animal which makes her/him/it tend to think and behave in certain ways: *Mary has a very calm temperament which makes her a good nurse.* **by temperament** as far as her/his/ its temperament is concerned: *Mike is impatient by temperament.*

temperamental /ˌtemprə'mentl/ adj **1** sometimes calm, sometimes excited etc: *You never know how Sally is going to behave when you take her somewhere because she is so temperamental.* **2** referring to a person's temperament: *She has a temperamental hatred of cold weather.*
ˌtempera'mentally adv.

temperance /'tempərəns/ u.n (*formal*) fact or state of being temperate(1,2).

temperate /'temprət/ adj **1** (*formal*) calm; having control of oneself. **2** drinking little or no alcohol. **3** neither very hot nor very cold: *a temperate climate.*

temperature /'temprɪtʃə/ u.n amount of heat or cold: *The temperature today is 18°. The water has a temperature of 25°.* **a change in temperature** a change to a colder or hotter temperature. **have/ run a temperature** (of people who are ill) have a higher temperature than normal. **take s.o's temperature** (try to) find out a person's temperature by using a thermometer.

-tempered ⇨ temper.

tempest /'tempɪst/ c.n (*literary*) violent storm.
tempestuous /tem'pestjʊəs/ adj (*formal*) **1** stormy; violent: *tempestuous seas.* **2** (*fig*) angry; having violent fighting with words: *a tempestuous argument.*
tem'pestuously adv. **tem'pestuousness** u.n.

template /'templɪt/ c.n specially cut shape that can be used as a guide for cutting others: *If you want to make the shelves exactly the same, first make a template out of cardboard.*

temple¹ /'templ/ c.n place in which people of certain religions, e.g Hindus(1), Buddhists and some kinds of Christians(3), worship.

temple² /'templ/ c.n part of a person's face next to the outside edge of her/his eyebrows.

tempo /'tempəʊ/ c.n **1** (*music*) (pl -s or, less usu, tempi /'tempiː/) speed. **2** (pl -s) rate(1) at which s.t happens: *The slow tempo of life in our village is a great relief from that of town life.*

temporal /'tempərəl/ adj (*formal*) **1** (*attrib*) of or referring to time: *A temporal conjunction shows time* (e.g 'when' but not 'where' or 'how'). **2** of or referring to things that are not religious: *temporal power* (i.e power over matters that do not concern religion). Opposite spiritual(4).

temporary /'tempərərɪ/ adj **1** who/that does s.t only for a short time: *a temporary secretary*; *a temporary delay/repair.* Opposite permanent.
▷ c.n **2** (*informal temp*) temporary(1) secretary etc.
'temporarily adv. **'temporariness** u.n.

tempt /tempt/ tr.v (often — s.o with s.t, to do s.t) **1** try to get (a person or an animal) to do s.t (by offering her/him/it s.t attractive): *Can I tempt you with another ice-cream* (or *to have another potato*)? **2** make (a person or an animal) want to do s.t: *The size of the prize tempted many people to enter the competition.* **tempt Providence** do s.t that could be very dangerous: *It is tempting Providence to try to cross the river when it is running so strongly.*

temptation /temp'teɪʃən/ n **1** c.n thing that tempts(2) s.o. **2** u.n state of being tempted(2); fact of tempting (⇨ tempt(2)): *In our church we pray to God not to lead us into temptation.*
'tempter c.n person who tempts(1).
'tempting adj that tempts(2): *a tempting offer in a shop.*

ten /ten/ det/pron/c.n (cardinal number) number 10 (between 9 and 11): *Ten of us went by bus. She's ten (years old). It's 10 (o'clock).* **ten a penny** (*fig*) found in large numbers: *Clever students are ten a penny at our university.* **ten to one (that . . .)** very probable (that . . .): *I bet(3) you ten to one that it will rain tomorrow.*

tenth det/pron **1** (ordinal number) (person or thing) following nine in order; 10th.
▷ c.n **2** one of ten equal parts; 1/10.

tenable /'tenəbl/ adj **1** that it is possible to hold or defend successfully: *a tenable position in a battle/argument.* Opposite untenable. **2** that can be held by s.o as a job: *This position is tenable for life* (i.e for as long as one lives).

tenacious /tɪ'neɪʃəs/ adj (*formal*) **1** refusing to change or give up (s.t); remaining firmly fixed (in s.t): *These shellfish are very tenacious — I can't get a single one off the rocks.* **2** determined to succeed: *He's a tenacious student, businessman, tennis player.*
te'naciously adv. **te'naciousness, tenacity** /tɪ'næsɪtɪ/ u.n.

tenant /'tenənt/ c.n **1** person who rents a room, house, land etc.
▷ tr.v **2** be a tenant(1) of (s.t).
'tenancy n (pl -ies) (often — of s.t) **1** u.n fact of being a tenant(1) (of s.t): *He has the tenancy of this farm.* **2** c.n time during which a tenancy(1) is in operation: *Your tenancy will come to an end soon.*
ˌtenant 'farmer c.n farmer who rents farmland from s.o.

tend¹ /tend/ tr/intr.v (usu — to do s.t; — towards (doing) s.t) show the beginnings of a movement in the direction of (doing or being) s.t: *Her pupils tended to be noisy unless they were kept busy. These apples tend towards the smaller size. Prices in the shops are tending upwards again.*
tendency /'tendənsɪ/ c.n (pl -ies) (often — to do s.t; — towards (doing) s.t) beginnings of a movement towards (doing or being) s.t: *The children have a tendency to be noisy. These dogs show a tendency towards (becoming) fat.*

tend² /tend/ tr.v look after or take care of (s.o/ s.t, e.g a sick person, a child, animal, garden or machine that needs to be watched).
'tender¹ c.n person who tends² s.o/s.t.

tendentious /ten'denʃəs/ adj (*derog; formal*) trying to make people believe or accept s.t, usu in a way that one considers bad or dishonest.
ten'dentiously adv. **ten'dentiousness** u.n.

tendency ⇨ tend¹.

tender¹ /'tendə/ ⇨ tend².

tender² /'tendə/ adj **1** (of meat etc) not tough; pleasantly soft when one bites or chews it. **2** (of plants etc) not strong; easily damaged or broken. **3** (of people and their feelings) kind; gentle. **4** (of a part of one's body) painful because of damage, illness etc: *I hit my finger with a hammer a week ago and it is still quite tender.* **5** that can cause s.o unhappiness or embarrassment(1): *Sex is a very tender subject with many people.* **leave s.o to s.o's (tender) mercy** ⇨ mercy.

,tender'hearted *adj* having tender[2](3) feelings; kind.

tenderize, -ise /'tendə,raɪz/ *tr.v* make (meat etc) tender[2](1) by beating it, or by putting it in certain liquids etc: *tenderize* steak(2). Compare marinate.

'tender,loin *c/u.n* (also *attrib*) specially tender[2](1) pieces of beef[1](1) or pork from the sides of the animal: *tenderloin* steak(2).

'tenderly *adv.* **'tenderness** *u.n.*

tender[3] /'tendə/ *c.n* **1** one of the parts of a train that comes just behind the engine and carries the coal etc for it. **2** boat that takes passengers, luggage etc from the shore to a ship and back.

tender[4] /'tendə/ *c.n* **1** (in business) offer that shows how much one is willing to pay or be paid for s.t. **legal tender** ⇨ legal.

▷ *tr.v* **2** offer (s.t to s.o) as one's payment for s.t. **tender for s.t** make a tender[4](1) to try to get s.t. **tender one's resignation (to s.o)** (make an) offer to resign (to s.o).

tenderhearted, tenderize, tenderloin, tenderness ⇨ tender[2].

tendon /'tendən/ *c.n* strong band by which a muscle(1) is fixed to a bone.

tendril /'tendrɪl/ *c.n* stem of a climbing plant that twists round things so that it can climb.

tenement /'tenɪmənt/ *c.n* (also **'tenement ,house,** *pl* **-s** /,hauzɪz/) block of (usu cheap) flats.

tenet /'tenɪt/ *c.n* (*formal*) idea that a person or a group of people believes in strongly.

tenner /'tenə/ *c.n* (*informal*) ten pound note.

tennis /'tenɪs/ *u.n* (also *attrib*) game in which two people, or two teams of two people each, play against each other by hitting a ball over a net with special rackets[1]: *tennis players/balls*; *a tennis court*; *a game of tennis. Can you play tennis?* ⇨ table tennis.

,tennis 'elbow *c/u.n* pain in the elbow(1) caused by using it too much, e.g in playing tennis.

tenon /'tenən/ *c.n* end of a piece of wood that has been shaped to fit exactly into a space cut in another piece of wood; when the two pieces are put together, they make a tight joint.

tenor[1] /'tenə/ *c.n* (also *attrib*) **1** man's singing voice higher than bass[1]. **2** man with such a singing voice. Compare bass[1], soprano.

▷ *adj/adv* **3** having the musical range of a tenor[1](1): *a tenor* saxophone. *He sings tenor.*

tenor[2] /'tenə/ *n* (*formal*) (usu **the — of s.t**) **1** *def.n* general meaning (of s.t) but not every detail: *There were so many long words but I think I got the tenor of his argument.* **2** *c/def.n* general way in which s.t is going: *He shows no interest in the tenor of her career*(1).

tenpin /'ten,pɪn/ *c.n* one of the ten wooden objects one tries to knock down in tenpin bowling.

,ten,pin 'bowling *u.n* game in which one rolls a big wooden ball along a special track in order to knock down tenpins at the end of it.

tense[1] /tens/ *adj* **1** (of muscles(1) etc) very tight and sometimes therefore painful. **2** (showing that one is) feeling anxious and worried: *the tense*

moments before the start of a race. Opposite relaxed(1).

▷ *tr/intr.v* **3** (often — (s.t) up) (cause (a muscle etc) to) become tense[1](1,2). Opposite relax(1).

'tensely *adv.* **'tenseness** *u.n.*

tensile /'tensaɪl/ *adj* (usu *attrib*) (*formal*) **1** of or referring to tension(2,3): *the tensile strength of a wire.* **2** that can be stretched to a certain extent without breaking: *Rubber and elastic are tensile.*

tension /'tenʃən/ *n* **1** *u.n* tenseness. **2** *c/u.n* amount of tightness of s.t; the amount of pull that s.t is subjected to: *This wire can stand a tension of 10 kilos per square millimetre.* **3** *u.n* electric power or current. **4** *c/u.n* tense[1](2) situation that could lead to violence: *international tension*; *tensions between a mother and son*; *the tension of city life.* **high-tension** ⇨ high. **nervous tension** worry; anxiety. **under tension** feeling tense[1](2): *We were under tension for most of the match before our side finally scored the winning goal.*

tense[2] /tens/ *c.n* (*grammar*) form taken by a verb to show the time of an action or state and/or whether it is, was or will be finished or still continuing: *'Give(s)', 'was giving' and 'will have given' are three of the tenses of the verb 'give'.*

tent /tent/ *c.n* kind of small shelter made of cloth and supported by poles[1] and ropes, used when camping etc. ⇨ oxygen tent.

'tent ,peg *c.n* small piece of wood, metal etc that is put into the ground to hold the end of a rope supporting a tent.

tentacle /'tentəkl/ *c.n* very long part of an animal that can bend and twist, used as an arm, leg, feeler(1) etc: *An octopus has eight tentacles.*

tentative /'tentətɪv/ *adj* **1** not yet certain or agreed; only suggested: *We made tentative plans to meet at 11 the next day and* confirmed (⇨ confirm(2)) *them later.* **2** not finding it easy to make up one's mind; hesitating.

'tentatively *adv.* **'tentativeness** *u.n.*

tenterhooks /'tentə,hʊks/ *pl.n* **on tenterhooks** waiting in a state of worry or anxiety for s.t to happen: *We were all on tenterhooks until the telegram arrived saying our mother was all right.*

tenth ⇨ ten.

tenuous /'tenjʊəs/ *adj* (*formal*) **1** very thin; fine(4): *a tenuous thread.* **2** weak: *a tenuous excuse*; *a tenuous* link(2) *between the families.*

tenuity /te'njuːɪtɪ/ *u.n* (*formal*) weakness: *No one believes him because of the tenuity of all his arguments.*

'tenuously *adv.* **'tenuousness** *u.n.*

tenure /'tenjʊə/ *u.n* (*formal*) **1** (s.o's right of) using or owning (land). **2** (s.o's time of) holding (of a position, e.g that of being a mayor): *She had many successes during her tenure of office.*

tepid /'tepɪd/ *adj* **1** not completely cold and also not very warm: *tepid water.* **2** (*fig*) not showing interest or enthusiasm: *a tepid welcome.*

tepidity /te'pɪdɪtɪ/ *u.n.* **'tepidly** *adv.* **'tepidness** *u.n.*

tercentenary /,tɜː'sentɪnərɪ/ *c.n* (*pl* -ies) (often **the — of s.t**) 300th anniversary (of s.t).

term[1] /tɜːm/ *n* **1** *c.n* particular length of time; period: *Each Lord Mayor of London is elected for a one-year term only.* **2** *c.n* division of the working year of a school, university etc: *There are three school terms in Britain, the autumn, the Easter and the summer terms.* **3** *unique* *def.n* time during which a school is open and teaching: *The boys at our school are not allowed to go abroad during (the) term.* **in the long/short term** if one looks at it from the point of view of a long/short time: *If you buy the most expensive paint, it could save you a lot of money in the long term.* **near one's/its term** near the end of the time arranged or expected: *I lent the money for three years and the loan is now near its term. Mrs Jones is expecting a baby and she is near her term now* (she is expected to have the baby soon).

term² /tɜːm/ *c.n* **1** word or group of words that is used in a particular job or activity and which has a special meaning in this: *The term 'out' is used in football when the ball crosses one of the lines along the sides of the* pitch¹(1). **2** one of the parts of a mathematical statement: *In* $2x + y = 20$*, the three terms are* $2x$*,* y *and* 20.
▷ *tr.v* **3** call (s.o/s.t) a certain name; give (s.o/s.t) the name of (s.t): *We term these kinds of animals 'crustaceans'.*

terms *pl.n* conditions on which s.t is agreed or sold etc: *On what terms are you willing to let us have this field? The shop was offering generous payment terms to people buying its goods.* **a contradiction in terms** ⇨ contradiction. **be on intimate terms (with s.o)** ⇨ intimate¹. **come to terms (with s.o)** agree s.t (with s.o). **come to terms with s.t** learn to live with s.t (e.g a long illness, an unpleasant fact) after difficulties in doing so. **in financial** etc **terms**; **in terms of finance** etc when one looks at s.t from the point of view of finance(1) etc: *These people do not have much in money terms but they are perfectly happy.* **make terms (with s.o)** reach an agreement (with s.o). **on equal/unequal terms (with s.o/s.t)** without any, with many, differences (between s.o/s.t and s.o/s.t). **on friendly terms** in a friendly way; as friends. **on generous** etc **terms** in a generous etc way; with generous etc conditions: *We have been offered the use of the house on very* advantageous *terms.* **(not) on speaking terms (with s.o)** (not) willing to speak to each other: *Chris and her old boyfriend are no longer on speaking terms.* **think in terms of s.t** think in a way that is limited to s.t: *I want a quiet holiday and am thinking in terms of a small hotel by the sea.*

terms of reference *pl.n* limits of what an official committee etc is allowed to deal with: *Our terms of reference in this inquiry do not go beyond our own town.*

terminable ⇨ terminate.

terminal /ˈtɜːmɪnl/ *adj* **1** of or referring to the end of s.t, sometimes the end of a person's life: *Some hospitals are very suitable for people with terminal illnesses* (illnesses from which they cannot get better).
▷ *c.n* **2** place where trains, buses etc start or finish their journeys: *a bus terminal.* Compare terminus. **3** building at an airport where one goes before one gets onto, or after one gets off, a plane. **4** place where one can add things (e.g wires) to an electrical circuit(4). **5** device that can be used to send messages to, and receive messages from, a computer.

terminate /ˈtɜːmɪˌneɪt/ *tr/intr.v* (*formal*) (cause (s.t) to) stop or finish: *After long arguments, the president decided to terminate the meeting and make her own decision.*

terminable /ˈtɜːmɪnəbl/ *adj* that can be terminated: *This agreement is terminable by either side giving three months' notice.* Compare interminable.

termination /ˌtɜːmɪˈneɪʃən/ *n* **1** *c/u.n* act of terminating s.t. **2** *c.n* (*grammar*) part at the end of a word etc: *You can change 'terminate' into 'termination' by adding the termination '-ion'.* Compare suffix. **3** *c/u.n* abortion(1).

terminology /ˌtɜːmɪˈnɒlədʒɪ/ *c/u.n* (*pl -ies*) way of describing things in language, usu in a particular job: *If you know Greek, you can understand a lot of medical terminology without ever having studied medicine.*
terminological /ˌtɜːmɪnəˈlɒdʒɪkl/ *adj.* **,termin-o'logically** *adv.*

terminus /ˈtɜːmɪnəs/ *c.n* (*pl -es, termini* /ˈtɜːmɪˌnaɪ/) place where buses or trains finish their journey. Compare terminal(2).

termite /ˈtɜːmaɪt/ *c.n* kind of insect that looks like an ant, lives in hot countries and builds tall hills to live in.

terrace /ˈterɪs/ *c.n* **1** flat piece of ground made by cutting into a slope, e.g to grow rice on the side of a hill. **2** place by the side of a house or on a roof or balcony(1) where one can sit in the open air. **3** one of the areas with wide steps at the side of a pitch¹(1) where one can stand and watch a football match. **4** (with capital **T** in names) line of houses in a street which are joined to each other: *My address is No 10, Seaview Terrace.*
▷ *tr.v* **5** make (s.t, e.g the side of a hill) into terraces(1), e.g by digging earth away.
'terraced *adj* formed into terraces(1): *a terraced house.*

terracotta /ˌterəˈkɒtə/ *u.n* (also *attrib*) **1** (things, e.g pots made of) baked clay. **2** colour between red and brown.

terrain /təˈreɪn/ *c/u.n* area of land of a particular kind: *difficult terrain for camping;* stony(1) *terrain.*

terrestrial /təˈrestrɪəl/ *adj* (*formal*) **1** of or referring to the earth we live on and not the stars, outer space etc: *terrestrial beings.* **2** of or referring to the land and not the sea and other waters: *terrestrial animals.*

terrible /ˈterəbl/ *adj* (*derog*) very unpleasant or bad: *a terrible climate; a terrible smell.*
'terribly *adv* **1** very unpleasantly or badly: *It smells terribly.* **2** (*informal*) very; extremely: *Oh, I'm terribly sorry; I didn't know you were in there.*

terrier /ˈterɪə/ *c.n* kind of small dog that has a lot of energy(1) and is very good at catching rats etc.

terrific /təˈrɪfɪk/ *adj* (*informal*) **1** very pleasant or good: *We had a terrific time at Jane's party.* **2** very great: *A terrific wave turned our boat over.*
te'rrifically *adv* (*informal*) very; extremely: *John's terrifically clever.*

terrify /ˈterɪˌfaɪ/ *tr.v* (*-ies, -ied*) frighten (s.o/s.t) very much.
'terri,fied *adj* (often *— of s.o/s.t*) very frightened (of s.o/s.t).
'terri,fying *adj* who/that terrifies s.o.

territory /ˈterɪtərɪ/ *c/u.n* (*pl -ies*) area of land that a country, an animal etc treats as its own, and that it defends against others: *This part of the South* Pole²(1) *is American territory. Each* *large male deer knows its own territory. In our office, all matters dealing with food supplies are the territory of my department.*

territorial /ˌterɪˈtɔːrɪəl/ *adj* **1** of or referring to territory(1).

▷ *c.n* **2** (often with capital **T**) soldier who is in the Territorial Army.

ˌTerriˌtorial 'Army *def/def.pl.n* (*abbr* **TA**) part of the British Army that consists of people who are not regular(5) soldiers but train part-time so as to be ready to fight in a war.

ˌterriˌtorial 'waters *pl.n* area of sea round a country in which that country has special rights, e.g for fishing.

terror /ˈterə/ *n* **1** *u.n* (often *in* —) (state of) great fear: *When we saw the animal so near us, we ran away in terror.* **2** *c.n* person, animal or thing that causes terror(1). **3** *c.n* (*informal*) (*derog*) nasty unpleasant child: *Jimmy can be a real little terror sometimes.* **strike terror into s.o** fill s.o with terror(1).

'terroˌrism *u.n* act or policy of using violence, or threats of violence, to try to change a political system etc.

'terrorist *c.n* person who uses terrorism.

terrorize, -ise /ˈterəˌraɪz/ *tr.v* frighten (s.o) very much, usu by using violence or threats.

'terror-ˌstricken, 'terror-ˌstruck *adj* very frightened; filled with terror(1).

terse /tɜːs/ *adj* (often *derog*) (of a person who is speaking or writing, or what or how he/she speaks or writes) using as few words as possible: *a terse reply.*

'tersely *adv.* **'terseness** *u.n.*

tertiary /ˈtɜːʃərɪ/ *adj* **1** (*formal*) third: *The tertiary level of education includes universities.* **2** (*medical*) of the third and worst level: *tertiary burns are worse than* secondary(1) *ones.*

terylene /ˈterɪˌliːn/ *u.n* (also *attrib*) (*t.n*) kind of cloth made from artificial materials: *a terylene shirt.*

tessellated /ˈtesəˌleɪtɪd/ *adj* made up of regular shapes of stone, paper etc of different colours: *a tessellated floor.* Compare mosaic.

test /test/ *c.n* **1** short examination using questions, pictures etc by which one tries to find out how much s.o knows about s.t: *an English test*; *a driving test*; *an eye test* (to see whether a person needs glasses). **2** (often — *of s.t*) trial (of s.t) to see how good, suitable etc it is: *No medicines are sold until they have had a careful test to see that they are not dangerous.* **3** (often — *of s.t*) thing with which one compares other things to see whether they are good enough etc: *My test of a good car is that it should be able to go up this hill even when it is icy.* **4** = test match. **give s.o/s.t a test (for s.t)** test(5) s.o/s.t (to find out whether he/she/it has an illness etc). **have a test (for s.t)** be tested(6) (to see whether one has an illness etc). **put s.o/ s.t to the test** test(5) s.o/s.t to find out about her/his/its qualities. **means test** ⇒ means.

▷ *tr.v* **5** examine (s.o) to find out how much he/she knows about s.t. **6** examine (s.o/s.t) to find out certain things about her/him/it (e.g whether he/ she is in good health or what it is made up of). **7** show any weaknesses in (s.o/s.t) by making things difficult for her/him/it: *Jumping from a plane really tests one's courage.* **have s.t tested** get s.o to test s.t: *If your eyes are getting very red,*

you should have them tested. **test (s.o/s.t) for s.t** give (s.o/s.t) a test to see whether he/she/it has a disease etc.

'test ˌban *c.n* ban(1) on testing(6) nuclear bombs.

'test ˌcase *c.n* example that is used as a sample to cover others as well: *John's trial is a test case; if he is found guilty, other people will also be prosecuted.*

ˌtest 'drive *c.n* drive in a car to find out how good it is and usu whether one wants to buy it.

'test-ˌdrive *tr.v* drive (a car etc) to test(6) it.

'tester *c.n* **1** person who tests(5,6) people or things. **2** product, e.g hand cream, available in a shop for testing(6) before buying.

'testing ˌtime *c.n* time when one is really tested(7).

'test ˌmatch *c.n* important match between two countries, usu in cricket[1] or rugby.

'test ˌpilot *c.n* person who pilots planes when they are being tested(6), usu when they have not yet begun to be used by ordinary pilots.

'test ˌtube *c.n* glass tube closed at the bottom and used for chemicals in laboratories etc.

'test-ˌtube ˌbaby *c.n* baby that has not been conceived(3) in the usual way, but with donated sperm(1), and an ovum that may have been outside a woman's body for some time.

testament /ˈtestəmənt/ *c.n* (*formal* or *old use*) will[2](1). **last will and testament** = will[2](1). **the New/Old Testament** ⇒ new, old.

testate /ˈtesteɪt/ *adj* (*law*) of person having made a will[2](1) before he/she died. Opposite intestate.

tester ⇒ test.

testicle /ˈtestɪkl/ *c.n* (also **'testis**) one of the two male organs that produce sperm(2) and that hang in a kind of bag of skin under the penis.

testify /ˈtestɪˌfaɪ/ *tr/intr.v* (*-ies, -ied*) give evidence(1) (usu in a court of law) (in favour of or against s.o): *She refused to testify against her husband. He testified that he knew nothing about the robbery.* **testify to s.t** support s.t by giving evidence(1) about it: *The woman was able to testify to the truth of everything I had said.*

testily ⇒ testy.

testimonial /ˌtestɪˈməʊnɪəl/ *c.n* **1** report on a person's abilities which that person can use when he/she wants to get another job. **2** (often — *to s.o/s.t*) formal statement or action to show one's admiration, respect etc (concerning s.o/s.t).

ˌtesti'monial ˌgame/ˌmatch *c.n* game/match held for a player who is going to retire(1) and who gets (some of) the money people pay to watch.

testimony /ˈtestɪmənɪ/ *c/u.n* (*pl -ies*) formal statement, often in a court of law, of what one has seen, heard etc; evidence(1).

testiness ⇒ testy.

testis /ˈtestɪs/ *c.n* (*pl testes* /ˈtestiːz/) (*medical*) = testicle.

test-tube (baby) ⇒ test.

testy /ˈtestɪ/ *adj* (*-ier, -iest*) (also **'tetchy**) (*derog*) easily becoming angry; showing that one easily becomes angry; showing impatience.

'testily *adv.* **'testiness** *u.n.*

tetanus /ˈtetənəs/ *u.n* (also **'lock,jaw**) disease that can kill, caused by bacteria in the earth, esp where there is animal dung.

tetchy /ˈtetʃɪ/ *adj* (*-ier, -iest*) = testy.

'tetchily *adv.* **'tetchiness** *u.n.*

tête-à-tête /ˌteɪt ɑː 'teɪt/ *adj/adv* **1** (*French*) (of two people) private(ly); with no one else there: *We are going to discuss the matter tête-à-tête.*

▷ *c.n* (also *attrib*) **2** (*French*) private meeting between two people only.

tether /'teðə/ *c.n* **1** rope etc used to keep an animal from going beyond a certain area. **at, come to, the end of one's tether** (*fig*) (become) so tired, angry etc that one cannot bear s.t annoying any more.

▷ *tr.v* **2** (often — *s.t to s.t*) tie (an animal) (to s.t) using rope etc.

text /tekst/ *n* **1** *c/u.n* main written part of a book, magazine etc (i.e not the pictures, the words under the pictures etc). **2** *c/u.n* actual words used or intended to be used by s.o, not the reports of what he/she said nor anything he/she said in addition or instead: *I don't believe newspaper reports of most speeches so I have to wait till I see the original text. During his speech yesterday, the president* departed(3) *from his text in several places to refer to the day's fresh events.* **3** *c.n* one of two or more versions of a written work: *There is a more accurate text of that old book than the one you have.* **4** *c.n* short piece out of the Bible(1) that a priest etc chooses as a subject for a sermon(1) etc. **5** *c.n* (part of a) textbook(2), usu one that students have to study for a particular examination: *This is one of our* prescribed(1) *texts for our examination in July.*

'text,book *attrib.adj* **1** so perfect that it can be used as an example to show to other people: *a textbook landing of a plane.*

▷ *c.n* **2** book that gives information about a subject that people study, esp in school.

textual /'tekstjʊəl/ *adj* (usu *attrib*) of or referring to texts(3): *textual criticism; textual differences between two copies of a poem.*

textile /'tekstaɪl/ *c.n* (also *attrib*) cloth etc made by weaving threads together: *the textile industry.*

textual ⇒ text.

texture /'tekstʃə/ *c/u.n* (often *the* — *of s.t*) **1** way in which (s.t) is woven (e.g whether it is tightly or loosely woven and whether it feels rough or smooth). **2** way (s.t) feels to one's touch (i.e whether it feels rough, smooth etc): *I don't like the texture of this cheese on my tongue.*

-,textured *adj* having the texture shown by the first part of the word: *a fine-textured coat.*

than (strong form /ðæn/, weak form /ðən/) *conj/ prep* (used to join two (groups of) words when one is comparing them to show that they are not equal in some way; if one is comparing equals, one uses 'as compared with': *John is taller than me* (or, more formally, *John is taller than I*). *I came earlier than you* (*did*). *Sitting in the garden is nicer than staying indoors on such a hot day. What is pleasanter than to spend Sunday at home with one's family?* **more** ... ⇒ more(*adv*). **than** ... ⇒ more(*adv*). **no/none other than s.o** ⇒ other(*pron*).

thank /θæŋk/ *tr.v* (often — *s.o for* (*doing*) *s.t*) say or write that one is grateful to (s.o) (because of s.t); say or write that one feels that s.o has been very kind to one (in doing s.t): *Please thank Mary for the book.* **have oneself to thank** (**for s.t**) be oneself entirely responsible (for s.t): *Dick has himself to thank for failing his examination*

because he didn't work hard enough. **have s.o/ s.t to thank** (**for s.t**) be the responsibility of s.o/ s.t (that s.t happened): *We have Mr Jones to thank for this wonderful party. The children had the bad weather to thank for their colds.* **thank God/ goodness/heaven(s)** (**that** . . .) I am grateful (that . . .): *'Mary hasn't been hurt badly.' 'Thank God!' Thank heaven you've come.* **thank you** (**for** (**doing**) **s.t**) I thank you (for (doing) s.t): *Thank you for coming* (or *for the present*). **No, thank you** (polite way of refusing an offer): *'Would you like some tea?' 'No, thank you.'* Opposite 'Yes(1), please.' ⇒ thanks.

'thankful *adj* feeling grateful: *I am thankful that we don't have to go out on a night like this. Joe was thankful to have finished the work before it got dark.* **be thankful for small mercies** ⇒ mercy.

'thankfully *adv.* **'thankfulness** *u.n.*

'thankless *attrib.adj* that one does not get any reward for and therefore usu unpleasant: *Trying to teach those children good manners is a thankless task.*

'thanklessness *u.n.*

thanks *pl.n* (often — *for* (*doing*) *s.t*) word or words (that show that one is grateful): *Thanks for lending me your pen* (or *for the pen*). *'You can borrow my pen.' 'Thanks.'* **give thanks** (**to s.o**) (**for s.t**) (*formal*) thank s.o (for s.t). **thanks to s.o/s.t** because of s.o/s.t; as a result of s.o/s.t: *Thanks to Jenny's cleverness, we have all managed to get home safely. Thanks to the teacher's mistake, his pupils were late for the match.*

,thanks'giving *c/u.n* saying that one is grateful, usu to God.

,Thanks'giving *unique n* (also **,Thanks'giving ,Day**) the fourth Thursday in November, on which the US thanks God for the autumn harvest.

thankyou /'θæŋkju/ *c.n* (also *attrib*) (often — (*for s.t*)) act, statement, gift etc that show(s) one is grateful (for s.t): *I'll write a thankyou letter. This is a small thankyou from all of us for your kind help.*

that¹ /ðæt/ *det* (*pl* those /ðəʊz/) **1** which is over there: *Please bring me that book. Is that one still for sale?* **2** which was mentioned some time ago: *Do you remember that old man who came to the house last Monday?* Compare this(1,2). **at that/ this point** ⇒ point(7).

▷ *adv* **3** (often *all — clever, easily* etc) so (clever, easily etc); to such an extent; as (clever, easily etc) as what has just been said or suggested: *A lot of children have trouble with mathematics but it isn't (all) that difficult if it is well taught.* Compare this(3). (**all**) **that many/much** as many/much as has just been mentioned or suggested.

▷ *pron* **4** the one over there: *Do you see that? It's my new desk. Who's that?* Compare this(4). **5** the thing that has just been mentioned: *'The sun is out again.' 'That's good; we can have a swim.' I'm going to the shops this morning but before that I'm going to wash my hair.* Compare this(5). **6** the one; the kind: *Let's take one name out of the hat at a time and that which is left at the end will be the winner. My first Christmas card this year was that from my Australian uncle.* (Notice that we cannot use 'that' for a person in these cases.) **all that/those** ⇒ all. **and** (**all**) **that** and so on; et cetera: *She was tired of the silly talk* *and arguments and all that.* **at that** (**a**) when that happened; then: *Suddenly a bell rang and at that all the children began to put away their books.* (**b**) in addition: *John talks too much, and stupidly at that.* **don't be like that** ⇨ like¹. **for all that** in spite of everything: *We paid for extra lessons but for all that we still failed the examination.* **that is** (*abbr i.e*); **that is** (**to say**) to say it in another (more correct) way: *It's raining; that is to say, a few drops are falling from time to time.* **that's that** the thing is finished now: *Well, that's that; now we can go home.* **that is how**, **where**, **why** *etc* . . . that is the way, place etc in which . . ., or the reason why . . . etc. **this and that**; **this, that and the other** ⇨ this(*pron*). **with that** ⇨ with. **Who's that?** (used, e.g when hearing s.o make a noise) Who are you? Who is that person?

that² (strong form /ðæt/, weak form /ðət/) *conj* **1** (used to introduce clauses(1) used in the same places as nouns or pronouns): *I know that he is here* (compare, 'I know it.'). *That he will help is certain* (compare, 'It is certain.'). *He made* (*it*) *known that he wanted the job* (compare, 'He made it known.'). (Notice that 'that' can be left out except when it comes first in the sentence.) **2** (used to introduce clauses(1) after a noun that has a verbal(1) meaning, to introduce a clause that would be the object of the verb): *my belief that I am right.* **3** (used after 'it' and a form of the verb 'be'): *It is true that he is here.* (Notice 'that' can be left out in such cases.) **4** (used after certain adjs) because: *He's annoyed that you are late.* (Notice 'that' can be left out in such cases.) **5** (used after an adj to introduce its object): *I'm afraid that I may fall. She is anxious that you should not be late.* (Notice 'that' can be left out in such cases.) **6** (used to introduce a clause(1) that is in apposition to a noun): *The fact that he is not willing to help means that we shall have to get rid of him.* **7** (used as part of certain compound(2) conjs). **for fear that** . . . ⇨ fear(*n*). **in order that** . . . ⇨ order(*n*). **on condition that** . . . ⇨ condition(*n*). **so that** . . . ⇨ so¹.

that³ (strong form /ðæt/, weak form /ðət/) *relative pron* (used instead of relative 'who(m)', 'which', except after a preposition or in sentences where 'who(m)', 'which' does not introduce a clause(1) that qualifies(3) s.t in the clause before, but another clause that is coordinate'(3) with it): *There's the man that I saw yesterday.* (Notice, when 'that' is the object¹(4), it can be left out; we must use 'that', and not 'who', in cases where it is the complement(3) of a form of the verb 'be', e.g 'She's no longer the noisy child *that* she was a year ago'; we can leave 'that' out in such cases.)

that⁴ (strong form /ðæt/, weak form /ðət/) *relative adv* when; in/on which: *It happened on the day that it snowed so heavily.* (Notice 'that' can be left out in such cases.)

thatch /θætʃ/ *n* **1** *c/u.n* roof made of straw etc that has usu been tied tightly so that rain cannot get through. **2** *c.n* (often *derog*; *informal*) thick or untidy hair on s.o's head.

▷ *tr.v* **3** cover (s.t) on top with thatch(1). **a thatched roof** *etc* a roof etc made of, covered with, thatch(1).

thaw /θɔː/ *c.n* **1** (period of time when there is) melting of snow and/or ice. **a thaw in s.t** (*fig*) an improvement of relations between countries

etc; an improvement of feelings in a quarrel etc.

▷ *tr/intr.v* **2** (often — (s.t) out) (cause (snow or ice, or frozen food etc) to) melt. **3** (*fig*) (cause (bad relations) to) improve, become more friendly.

the¹ (strong form /ðiː/, weak form before consonant(2) sounds /ðə/, weak form before vowel(1) sounds /ðɪ/) *det* (or *definite article*) **1** (one(s) that is/are unique, i.e the only one(s) in this/that situation): *the sun, the moon and the stars*; *the north*; *the top/bottom*; *in the middle/centre. Did you bathe in the sea when you went to Africa or in a river? There is a* swimming pool *and a river near our house but I prefer the* swimming pool. *There are flies on the walls* (i.e the walls of this room). *John is the tallest person in the family.* (Notice that sometimes a noun or pronoun that has 'the' before it is followed (or sometimes preceded) by a phrase(1) that shows the situation in which it is the only one; e.g 'the Queen of England'; 'Queen Elizabeth the Second'; 'the girl with the green eyes'.) **2** (used in the names of): (rivers) *the Nile*; (seas) *the Atlantic*; (pl of mountains, countries and islands) *the Alps*; *the Philippines*; *the United States*; (peoples) *the English*; *the Chinese*; (places whose names contain adjs other than geographical ones such as North, South, Central) *the German Democratic Republic*; (places whose names contain a prepositional phrase(1)) *the Republic of Ireland*; (places qualified(3) by a phrase(1) or a clause(1)) *the England I knew when I was a boy.* **3** (not referring to one particular person or thing but to the person or thing as a general class): *People in this country usually go to the office at 9. Do you often go to the cinema? I'm going to the doctor('s) now. I play the piano. I heard it on the radio.* (Notice, with some very familiar words, we do not use 'the', e.g 'We go to church on Sundays.' 'Jimmy's at school.' 'Do you play football?' Notice also the difference between, e.g 'go to church' (for the purpose of taking part in a church service) and 'go to the church' (just to visit it, to take some flowers there etc). Notice that we say 'by car, bus, plane, road, sea, air etc', without 'the' (e.g I go to work by train/road) but we can say 'I go to work in the train or bus'.) **4** (used instead of 'my', 'your' etc for parts of the body): *I have a pain in the stomach* (but we can also say 'I have a pain in my stomach.') **5** (used in certain phrases(1) of time): *in the morning/afternoon/evening*; *during the morning/afternoon/evening/day/night* (but we say 'at night/sunrise/sunset', 'by day/night', 'on Monday etc', 'in January etc', 'in 1988 etc'). (Notice that we can say 'in the autumn/spring/ summer/winter' or just 'in autumn/spring etc', and that if we have a phrase(1) or clause(1) that qualifies(3) a noun, we need 'the' before it, e.g on 'the Monday after I got there'.) **6** (used in the strong form /ðiː/) to mean 'the best', 'the most important' etc: *Monte Carlo is the place in Europe for rich people. This painting is by a man called Michelangelo but not the Michelangelo or it would be worth millions of dollars.* **7** (used with a negative(6)) enough; the necessary: *He didn't have the sense to say 'No' when his friend suggested they should steal a car.* **8** ('the' + *sing* meaning *pl*): *Summer is the best time here*

Summers in general are the best times here). *The cat is a very independent animal* (Cats are . . .). **9** ('the' + adj = adj + people/animals/ things): *the poor* (poor people in general). *We can't do the impossible.* **10** (used in prepositional phrases(1) of rate or quantity): *We now sell cloth by the metre. How many kilometres does your car do to the litre?* (**in**) *the 60s etc* between the beginning of 1960 and the end of 1969 (or 1860 and 1869 etc). (Notice, we do not use 'the' in 'make s.o s.t', e.g 'They made her queen'; 'They appointed him manager'; also, when we are talking to s.o, we do not use 'the' before her/his title; e.g we say 'Good morning, captain/dad'.)

the² (strong form /ðiː/, weak form before consonant(2) sounds /ðə/, weak form before vowel(1) sounds /ðɪ/) *adv* **1** (used in the pattern 'the' + comparative(3) + 'the' + comparative(3) to show that the second adj/adv varies according to the first): *the faster the better* (i.e things get better as the speed increases). **2** (used before a superlative(2)): *This is the biggest coat we sell. Simone speaks English the best. We had the greatest difficulty finding your house.* (Notice that we cannot leave 'the' out before adjs but we can before advs, e.g we cannot say 'This is biggest coat', but we can say 'Simone speaks English best'.)

theatre /ˈθɪətə/ *n* (US **'theater**) **1** *c.n* place where plays(1) are performed. **2** *u/def.n* writing, acting, directing etc plays(1) in general: *The theatre was very important in ancient Greece.* **3** *c.n* hall in a university etc where people sit in rows that are one above and behind the other to listen to a lecture or to watch s.t being done. **4** *c.n* = operating theatre. **5** *c.n* one of the areas in which a war is fought: *The Pacific Ocean would be an important theatre in a world war.*

theatre,goer *c.n* (US **'theater,goer**) person who goes (usu regularly) to a theatre to see plays.

theatrical /θɪˈætrɪkl/ *adj* **1** of or referring to a/the theatre(1,2): *a theatrical performance.* **2** (*derog*) (of a person, her/his way of behaving etc) exaggerating; more dramatic(3) than is normal: *theatrical behaviour.*

the'atrical ,company *c.n* (also **'theatre ,company**) group of actors who perform together in plays(1).

the'atrically *adv.*

the'atricals *pl.n* (usu *amateur* —) performing of plays(1) (by amateurs(3)).

thee /ðiː/ ⇒ thou.

theft ⇒ thief.

their /ðeə/ *possessive adj* belonging to, for, them: *That's their train. Their coats are in the cupboard.*

theirs /ðeəz/ *possessive pron* the one(s) belonging to, for, them: *That car is theirs. Theirs is the house with the blue door.*

them (strong form /ðem/, weak form /ðəm/) *pron* (form of 'they' used when it is the object'(4) of a verb or preposition, or (*informal*) when it is a subjective complement(3): *They own them. I travelled with them. It was them who broke the window.*

them'selves *pron* **1** *reflex.pron* (used when the object'(4) of the verb or preposition is the same (people, animals, things) as the subject'(4)): *They saw themselves in the mirror. The boys were too interested in themselves to care about the others.*

2 (used to emphasize 'they'): *They themselves know the way home.* **3** without help: *Did they build it themselves or did someone help them?* (**all**) **by themselves** (**a**) without help: *Did they build it (all) by themselves?* (**b**) alone: *They were (all) by themselves in a small house by the sea.*

theme /θiːm/ *c.n* **1** subject dealt with (in s.t, e.g a lecture): *What is the theme of the play (or for your next talk)?* **2** short simple group of notes which is the basis for a longer piece of music: *a theme by Mozart.*

'theme ,music/,song/,tune *c.n* piece of music that is heard again and again during a film, play etc. Compare signature tune (⇒ sign).

themselves ⇒ them.

then /ðen/ *attrib.adj* **1** that was/existed at that time: *The then president refused to agree to this.*
▷ *adv* **2** at that time: *I was born in 1973; my parents lived in London then.* **3** (often *after/before/by* —) that time: *Come at 6; I won't be ready before then. We couldn't leave until 8 and by then it was dark.* **4** after that: *The door opened slowly and then closed again.* **5** if that is so: *'I'm cold!' 'Then go and put some more clothes on.'* **6** the result is, was etc that: *Go and put some more clothes on; then you won't feel so cold. If two men can dig a field in six hours, then four men can dig the same field in three hours.* **but then** (**again**) but also; at the same time: *Sometimes Nicholas can be a nasty little boy. Mary hasn't written, but then I never really expected her to.* **from then on** ⇒ from. **just then** ⇒ just². **now and then** ⇒ now(*adv*). **there and then** ⇒ there(*adv*).

thence /ðens/ *adv* (*old use; formal*) **1** from there: *I went home to get my wife and thence to the restaurant.* **2** for that reason: *Mary's parents have brown eyes, thence we know that she got her blue eyes from her grandparents.*

,thence'forth *adv* (also **,thence'forward**) (*old use; formal*) from that time on.

theology /θɪˈɒlədʒɪ/ *n* (*pl -ies*) **1** *u.n* study of religion. **2** *c/u.n* one particular religious system.

theologian /θɪəˈləʊdʒɪən/ *c.n* person who studies, or is skilled in, theology.

theological /θɪəˈlɒdʒɪkl/ *adj* of or referring to theology: *a theological college.*

,theo'logically *adv.*

theorem /ˈθɪərəm/ *c.n* (*technical*) statement in mathematics that can be proved.

theory /ˈθɪərɪ/ *n* (*pl -ies*) **1** *c/u.n* idea that has not yet been proved to be true: *My mother had a theory that eating cabbage makes your hair curly. What you say is just theory — can you prove it?* **2** *u.n* side of s.t that concerns general ideas about it and not details or practical examples: *After studying the human body at school, I had to put theory into practice when I went to medical college.* **in theory** when one is only thinking about it and not actually trying it: *Passing the examination may be easy in theory but it is not so easy in practice.* See in practice(b).

theoretical /θɪəˈretɪkl/ *adj* dealing with, based on, theory(2), not practical experience; using theory only: *theoretical knowledge.*

,theo'retically *adv: Theoretically it is possible to find snakes here, but I have not seen one in twenty years.*

'theorist *c.n* person who makes or uses theories(1), not practical things.

theorize, -ise /ˈθɪəˌraɪz/ *intr.v* (often — *about/ on s.o/s.t*) make or have theories(1) (about s.o/ s.t).

therapeutic /ˌθerəˈpjuːtɪk/ *adj* **1** of or referring to therapeutics. **2** that can, is intended to, help to cure troubles of the body or mind.

ˌtheraˈpeutically *adv*.

ˌtheraˈpeutics *u.n* science or practice of curing diseases of the body or mind.

therapist /ˈθerəpɪst/ *c.n* **1** person who practises therapy: occupational/*speech therapist*. **2** = psychotherapist.

therapy /ˈθerəpɪ/ *c/u.n* (*pl -ies*) (one example of) treatment of people for troubles of the body or mind without using medicines or operations. ⇒ psychotherapy. **occupational therapy** ⇒ occupational. **speech therapy** ⇒ speech.

there¹ /ðeə/ *adv* **1** at, in or to that place: '*Where's my umbrella?' 'There.' I went to the park yesterday; there I met an old friend*. **2** (used with the verbs 'is/was/go(es)' when pointing to s.o/s.t in the distance; the main stress is on 'there') **(a)** (if the subject is a pronoun, the order is 'there' + subject¹(4) + verb): *There it is! There he goes!* **(b)** (if it is a noun (phrase(1)), the order is 'there' + verb + subject¹(4)): *There's the bus! There goes Mary!* Compare there³, here(2). **3** (used after a noun or 'one') (*informal*) that is in that place: *That boy/one there is my brother*. ⇒ here(3). **4** at that point in time: *And there I must stop because I have some other work to do*. ⇒ here(4). **all there** ⇒ all(*adv*). **get there (in the end** *etc*) succeed in doing what one wants to do (finally etc): *Don't give up hope of passing your examination; you'll get there in the end!* **out there** at, in or to that place, which is outside, or on the sea (and not on the land), or in space (and not on our earth). **over there** in, to that distant place: *Your books are over there. When I get over there, I'll telephone you.* **there and back** from the starting point to the end of the journey and then back again: *A single ticket costs £1 and a ticket there and back costs £1.75.* **there and then; then and there** at once; without waiting. **There you are (a)** (said when giving or offering s.o s.t): '*Can I have a cup of tea, please?' 'There you are.'* **(b)** (with the main stress(2) on 'there' meaning 'so that is where you are', 'I have only just noticed you' etc.): *Ah, there you are!* **(c)** I told you so: *There you are — I said it would rain!* **there you go** (**again**) you are again doing s.t (usu s.t bad or annoying) that you have done before: *There you go again, making the same mistake in your English!* Compare here.

thereabouts /ˈðeərəˌbaʊts/ *adv* (usu *or —*) (*informal*) close to it/them: *I think he lives in Bristol or thereabouts. He is fifty years old or thereabouts.* Compare hereabouts.

thereafter /ˌðeərˈɑːftə/ *adv* (*formal*) after that/ those/it/them (in time or order): *He apologized and thereafter behaved well.* Compare hereafter.

ˌthereˈby *adv* (*formal*) by doing etc that/it; in that way: *He paid the money thereby being certain of a ticket for the show.* Compare hereby.

therein /ˌðeərˈɪn/ *adv* (*formal*) in that/those/ it/them: *He owns the house and the furniture therein.* Compare herein.

thereon /ˌðeərˈɒn/ *adv* (*formal*) on that/those/ it/them: *I have read the official letter and checked the signature thereon.* Compare hereon.

thereto /ˌðeəˈtuː/ *adv* (*formal*) to that/those/ it/them: *He signed the official letter and I was a witness thereto.* Compare hereto(1).

thereupon /ˌðeərəˈpɒn/ *adv* (*formal*) **1** about that/those/it/them: *Are we all agreed thereupon?* **2** immediately after that/it: *Her husband came home at six and thereupon they left the house to go to the party.* ⇒ hereupon.

there² /ðeə/ *interj* (used to draw attention to what one is going to say next which is often an expression of one's feelings, e.g the feeling of wanting to comfort s.o): *There, that'll stop your hand bleeding.* **there, there** (used to comfort s.o who is crying, unhappy etc): *There, there, don't cry little girl.*

there³ /ðeə/ *pron* **1** (used in sentences in which the verb is a form of 'be' and the subject¹(4) is indefinite(2) (i.e it does not have 'the/this/that' etc)): *There is a man in our garden. There are some cars in that street.* (Notice, if the subject¹(4) is definite, we do not use 'there', e.g 'That man is in our garden.' 'The cars are in the street.') **2** (*literary*) (used with other verbs and an indefinite(2) subject¹(4)): *There grew up new trees to take the place of the ones that had died.*

therefore /ˈðeəˌfɔː/ *adv* for that reason; as a result of which; so²(1): *He arrived late, therefore he missed the bus.*

therein, thereon, thereto, thereupon ⇒ there¹.

therm /θɜːm/ *c.n* (*technical*) unit for measuring the amount of gas used in a building.

ˈthermal *attrib.adj* **1** of or referring to heat: *the thermal efficiency of an engine.*

▷ *c.n* **2** warm air going upwards which gliders use for climbing in the air.

ˌthermal ˈunderˌwear *u.n* underclothing made of a special kind of cloth that keeps the body warm.

thermodynamics /ˌθɜːməʊdaɪˈnæmɪks/ *u.n* (used with a sing.verb) (*technical*) mathematical study of the ways in which heat is related to other forms of energy, e.g work(4).

thermometer /θəˈmɒmɪtə/ *c.n* device for measuring temperature. **clinical thermometer** one used for measuring people's temperature.

thermonuclear /ˌθɜːməʊˈnjuːklɪə/ *adj* (*technical*) of or referring to the great heat produced when atoms(1) fuse¹(4).

thermos /ˈθɜːmɒs/ (*t.n*) = flask(1).

thermostat /ˈθɜːməˌstæt/ *c.n* device for keeping the temperature of a building etc between certain limits.

ˌthermoˈstatic *adj*. **ˌthermoˈstatically** *adv*.

thesaurus /θɪˈsɔːrəs/ *c.n* (*pl -es*) book etc in which words with a similar meaning are arranged together. Compare dictionary(1).

these ⇒ this.

thesis /ˈθiːsɪs/ *c.n* (*pl theses* /ˈθiːsiːz/) **1** idea or opinion supported by good reasons for having it: *The woman's thesis was that taxes only make the differences between rich and poor greater.* **2** piece of writing presenting the results of advanced study which a student prepares in order to get a master's(3) degree (MA etc) or a doctorate (Ph.D etc) at a university.

they /ðeɪ/ *pron* (object¹(4) form *them*, possessive adj *their*, possessive pron *theirs*, emphatic and reflexive pron *themselves*) **1** persons about

whom one is speaking or writing: *They can use
my car. Dave's family are very nice and they often
visit us. John and Mary are here; they want to see
you. The girls are here but they've forgotten their
books. I haven't seen Peter and Bob for a long time
— how are they?* ⇨ them, themselves. (Notice
that 'they' is used when it is the subject[1](4),
e.g 'They are here', and 'them' is used when
it is the object[1](4) of a verb or preposition, e.g
'I saw them.' 'I got it from them', and in informal
English when it is the subjective complement(3),
e.g 'Look, it's them at last!'.) **2** people in general:
*They say that it's going to be a very hot summer
this year.* Compare one(3).

they'd /ðeɪd/ **1** they had. ⇨ have[1]. **2** = they
would. ⇨ will[1], would.

they'll /ðeɪl/ = they shall/will. ⇨ will[1], shall.

they're /ˈðeɪə/ = they are. ⇨ be.

they've /ðeɪv/ = they have. ⇨ have.

thick /θɪk/ *adj* **1** big in size from the front to
the back or the top to the bottom: *It's a thick
wall/slice. This piece of wood is two metres long,
30 centimetres wide and five centimetres thick.*
Opposite thin(1). **2** (of a thing that is round,
e.g a rope or wire) big in diameter. Opposite
thin(2). **3** (of a liquid) that does not flow as
easily as water: *thick oil.* Opposite thin(4). **4** in
which the parts are very close to each other:
a thick fog; a thick forest. Compare dense(1).
Opposite thin(5). **5** (usu — *with s.t*) (of air) made
dirty (by s.t, e.g smoke). **6** (of a person's voice)
rough; not clear, usu because one has a cold
etc. **7** (of an accent(1) in speaking a language)
strong(2); very noticeable. **8** (*derog; informal*) (of
a person) stupid. **9** (*informal*) not able to think
well: *My head is quite thick this morning after all
the drink I had last night.* **(as) thick as thieves**
(*informal*) (of two or more people) very friendly
with each other. **s.t is a bit thick** (*informal*) s.t
is really too much to accept: *'We have to go to
school on Saturday because an important visitor
is coming.' 'That's a bit thick, isn't it?'* **thick with
s.o** (*informal*) very friendly with s.o.

▷ *adv* **10** thickly; in a thick(4) way: *These bushes
grow thickest in damp places.* **lay it on thick**
(*informal*) exaggerate (s.t); do too much of s.t,
e.g praise s.o so highly that it is stupid.

▷ *def.sing.n* **11** the thickest part (of s.t): *The pain was
strongest in the thick of his leg.* **(in) the thick of
s.t** (in) the busiest or most active part of s.t: *We
were caught in the thick of the traffic.* **through
thick and thin** whatever the conditions may be
(good and bad): *She helped her husband through
thick and thin.*

thicken *tr/intr.v* (cause (s.t) to) become
thick(er)(1–4).

thickener *c/u.n* (also **thickening**) thing,
e.g flour, that makes s.t thick(3,4). Compare
thinner(2).

thick-headed *adj* (*derog; informal*) stupid(1).

thickly *adv.*

thickness *u.n* **1** fact of being thick(*adj*). **2** *c.n*
layer(1) of s.t: *If you put several thicknesses of
cloth under the hot dishes, the table will not
be damaged by the hot dishes.* **in thickness**
when one measures how thick it is: *This ice is
5 centimetres in thickness.*

thick'set *adj* (of a person or her/his body) short
and broad.

thick-'skinned *adj* **1** having a thick skin: *a
thick-skinned orange.* **2** (*fig*, usu *derog*) not
easy to make feel ashamed: *It's no use telling
Steve that he's rude; he's so thick-skinned that
he doesn't care.*

thicket /ˈθɪkɪt/ *c.n* mass of bushes and small trees
growing close together.

thief /θiːf/ *c.n* (*pl* thieves /θiːvz/) person who
steals or has stolen. Compare burglar, robber.
(as) thick as thieves ⇨ thick(*adj*).

theft /θeft/ *n* **1** *u.n* act or fact of stealing. **2** *c.n*
example of this.

thieve /θiːv/ *intr.v* steal things.

thieving *attrib.adj* **1** (of a person or animal)
who/which steals or has stolen.
▷ *u.n* **2** act of stealing things.

thigh /θaɪ/ *c.n* upper part of a human leg or of an
animal's back leg, from the knee to the trunk.

thimble /ˈθɪmbl/ *c.n* object, usu made of metal
or plastic(3), which is put over the end of one's
finger so that one can push a needle while sewing
without hurting one's finger.

thin /θɪn/ *adj* (-nn-) **1** (of things) small in size
from the front to the back or from the top to
the bottom: *a thin slice of bread; a thin book.*
Opposite thick(1). **2** (of a thing that is round,
e.g a thread or wire) small in diameter. Opposite
thick(2). **3** (of a person, animal, or (part of) her/
his/its body) not having much fat(1) on her/him/
it: *Look at that poor boy's thin legs.* Opposite
fat(1). **4** (of a liquid) that flows easily, rather like
water: *thin glue.* Opposite thick(3). **5** in which
the parts are not very close to each other: *a thin
mist.* Opposite thick(4). **6** not strong in flavour,
contents: *a thin soup.* **thin on the ground** not
found in large numbers. **thin on top** (*informal*)
not having much hair on one's head; rather
bald(1).

▷ *adv* **7** so that it is thin after one has finished with
it: *I like my meat cut very thin.* **wear thin** ⇨
wear(*v*).

▷ *tr/intr.v* (-nn-) **8** (often — (s.o/s.t) *down*) (cause
(s.o/s.t to) become thinner(1–4)): *Mary will have
to thin down before she can get a job as a dancer
again. Thin the soup down with wine.* **9** (often —
(s.o/s.t) *out*) cause (s.t or a group of people) to
become thinner(5): *The trees thin out as one gets
closer to the river.*

▷ *u.n* **10 through thick and thin** ⇨ thick(*n*).

thinner *adj* **1** comp of thin.
▷ *u.n* **2** liquid, e.g white spirit, used to make a
liquid substance, e.g paint, less thick. Compare
thickener.

thin-'skinned *adj* **1** having a thin skin. **2** (*fig*)
very sensitive to criticism.

thine ⇨ thou.

thing /θɪŋ/ *n* **1** *c.n* material object that is not a
person; abstract[1](1) idea or event: *'What's that
thing?' 'It's my new watch.' One thing I don't
understand is why you didn't come earlier. His
return was the best thing that could have happened to us.* **2** (used after some adjs, for persons,
usu to show fondness or sympathy): *Our daughter is a pretty little thing. Mary's broken a leg, poor
thing.* **a near thing** almost an accident, or s.t else
that is dangerous: *It was a near thing when our
tyre burst on a sharp corner.* **do one's (own)
thing** (*informal*) do exactly what one wants to
do, without troubling about others. **first thing**

⇒ first. **for one thing** one reason is that . . . : *She can't help us; for one thing she has a child to look after, and for another, she lives far away.* **be a good thing** ⇒ good(*adj*). **be onto a good thing** ⇒ good. **it is a good** etc **thing to do** s.t doing s.t is good etc: *It's a sensible thing to clean your teeth after meals.* **have a good thing about s.o/s.t** (*informal*) like or dislike s.o/s.t very much, often for no clear reason. **just the thing** exactly what is needed etc. Compare the thing below. **not have a thing to wear** have no clothes that one wants to wear. **not know the first thing about s.t** not know anything at all about s.t. **(not) (quite) the thing** (not) (exactly) who/what is fashionable or accepted. **taking one thing with another** in general; when one considers everything. **the thing** (with the strong form of 'the') exactly what is needed or suitable. Compare just the thing. **the done thing** what is considered the correct way to behave in polite society. **the last thing** thing that is completely unlikely, not wanted: *The last thing I want to do is to hurt you.* **the latest thing (in s.t)** the newest fashion (with regard to s.t): *It's the latest thing in shoes.* **not a living thing** no person or animal: *In some parts of the desert you won't see a living thing for miles.* **the thing is . . .** what I mean is . . . : *I don't really like the fish here; the thing is, they're never fresh.*

thingamabob /'θɪŋəmɪˌbɒb/ *c/u.n* (also **thingamajig**, **thingumajig** /'θɪŋəmɪˌdʒɪg/, **thingummy** /'θɪŋəmɪ/) (informal way of referring to s.o/s.t whose real name one has forgotten) *I met thingamabob yesterday. Please pass me that thingamajig — that screwdriver.*

things *pl.n* **1** more than one thing. **2** the situation or condition of the country, of a person etc: *Things are getting better now that we have a new government. 'How are things with you?' 'Not too bad, thank you.'* **all things being equal** ⇒ equal(*adj*). **(and) to make things better, worse** etc (and) what makes the situation better, worse etc: *I've got a bad cold, and to make things worse my husband's getting one too.* **be seeing things** imagine one sees people, objects, events etc that are not there: *Pat wasn't at the meeting — you must have been seeing things.* **my, your** etc **things** my, your etc clothes. **the breakfast** etc **things** the plates, spoons etc used for breakfast etc: *Who's going to help wash up the dinner things?* **(well,) of all things** (exclamation showing that what one has just seen, heard etc surprises one very much): *Well, of all things! Simon is getting married!*

think /θɪŋk/ *sing.n* **1** (usu have a — (about s.t)) (*informal*) example of thinking(2) (about s.t): *I can't answer that question at once; I'll have a think about it.* **have another think coming** have the wrong idea: *If you expect me to let you stay out till two in the morning, you've got another think coming.*

▷ *v* (*p.t,p.p* thought /θɔːt/) **2** *tr/intr.v* produce ideas and pictures in one's brain; use one's mind to work (s.t) out, e.g how, where etc (to) . . . : *Think before you speak! He's thinking about his family. She always tried to think beautiful thoughts. That man thinks only money. Now try to think where you left your coat. Now think how to get back to the station.* **3** *tr.v* (often — that . . .) believe (s.t);

have (s.t) as one's opinion: *I thought (that) you were ready. He thought himself cleverer than he really was.* **4** *tr.v* (usu — that . . .) expect (that) . . . : *I didn't think (that) you'd be able to come so I didn't save any food for you.* **5** *intr.v* (usu — about/of doing s.t) have a plan, although one is not sure one will want to carry it out: *I was thinking of asking Barbara to join us tomorrow; what do you think?*

can't/couldn't think how, what etc **(to)** . . . can't/couldn't etc understand or imagine how/ what etc (to) . . . : *I still can't think why the manager wants to see us.*

can/could/will/would not think of doing s.t (often with the main stress(2) on 'think') be so strongly against doing s.t as never to do it: *Elizabeth wouldn't think of cheating in an examination.*

I thought as much what I have just heard, seen is just what I expected: *The rain's coming through the roof! I thought as much when I saw those holes.*

little does/did s.o think (that) . . . s.o does/did not at all expect (that) . . . : *Dick was very critical of teachers a few years ago; little did he think that he would soon be one himself!*

think about/of s.o/s.t (a) ⇒ think(5). **(b)** consider s.o; have s.o/s.t as one's main concern: *When he refused that very good job abroad, he was thinking of his mother who needs him here.*

think aloud say aloud what one is thinking, usu without having worked it out finally: *Don't pay any attention to what I say; I'm only thinking aloud.*

think big ⇒ big.

think in English etc use English etc as the language in which one thinks.

think not ('not' takes the place of a negative(1) clause(1)): *'Is it going to rain?' 'I think not'* (i.e I think it is not going to rain). Compare think so.

think of s.o/s.t (a) ⇒ think(2,5). **(b)** ⇒ can/could/ will/would not think of doing s.t. **(c)** ⇒ think about/ of s.o/s.t.

think better of it/doing s.t ⇒ better². **think highly/well/little/poorly of s.o/s.t** have a high/ low opinion of s.o/s.t. **not think much of s.o/ s.t** have a low opinion of s.o/s.t. **think nothing of it/s.t** ⇒ nothing(*pron*).

think s.t out/through consider s.t in detail until one has worked it out completely.

think s.t over think about s.t for some time (usu in order to decide what to do about it).

think so ('so' takes the place of a positive(8) clause(1)): *'Is it going to rain?' 'I think so'* (i.e I think that it is going to rain). Compare think not.

think twice (before doing s.t) ⇒ twice.

think s.t up (*informal*) invent s.t: *Can you think up a way of letting our cat come in without other animals getting in too?*

What/who do you think . . .? What is your opinion or guess about . . .?: *Who do you think broke our window?*

Who do you think you are? (way of protesting(3) angrily about a person's words or actions when one thinks he/she is being rude).

'thinkable *adj* that can be thought (⇒ think(2,3)). Opposite unthinkable.

'thinker *c.n* person who thinks(2).

'thinking *attrib.adj* **1** who thinks(2) seriously and a lot: *a thinking person.*

▷ *u.n* **2** act of thinking (⇒ think(2)): *'Let's book our holiday early this year.' 'That's good thinking!'* **3** opinion; view: *Our company's thinking about the new tax is that it will not affect us much.* **wishful thinking** ⇒ wish.

'think ‚tank *c.n* group of clever people who meet together to consider the best ways of doing things.

thinner ⇒ thin.

third(-degree/rate) ⇒ three.

thirst /θɜːst/ *sing/u.n* **1** feeling of wanting, needing, to drink. **be dying of thirst** be very thirsty. **(have a) thirst for s.t** (*fig*) (have a) strong desire for s.t (e.g knowledge).

▷ *intr.v* **2 thirst after s.t** (*literary*) want s.t (e.g knowledge) very much.

'thirstily *adv* in a thirsty way.

'thirstiness *u.n* fact of being thirsty.

'thirsty *adj* (*-ier, -iest*) feeling thirst(1). **thirsty for s.t** having a thirst for s.t.

thirteen /θɜː'tiːn/ *det/pron/c.n* (*cardinal number*) number 13 (between 12 and 14): *Some people think 13 is an unlucky number. Thirteen people went to the meeting. I'm 13 (years old).*

thir'teenth *det/pron* **1** (*ordinal number*) (person or thing) following 12 in order; 13th.

▷ *c.n* **2** one of thirteen equal parts; ¹⁄₁₃.

thirty /'θɜːtɪ/ *det/pron/c.n* (*pl -ies*) (*cardinal number*) number 30 (between 29 and 31): *There were thirty-four (34) children on the bus.* **in one's thirties** between 30 and 39 years old. **the thirties** (or **the 30(')s**) **(a)** (speed, temperature, marks etc) between 30 and 39: *The temperature was well into the thirties.* **(b)** (years) between '30 and '39 in a century.

thirtieth /'θɜːtɪəθ/ *det/pron* **1** (*ordinal number*) (person or thing) following 29 in order; 30th.

▷ *c.n* **2** one of thirty equal parts; ¹⁄₃₀.

this /ðɪs/ *det* (*pl these* /ðiːz/) **1** which is here: *Take this letter to the post, please. This pencil is sharper than that one.* Compare that¹(1). **2** (referring to s.o/s.t who/that has just been mentioned, is going to be mentioned next, or who/that the listener knows about): *When you hear this story you'll laugh, I'm sure. Where's this new cinema I've heard about?* Compare that¹(2). **this morning/afternoon/evening** the morning etc of today. **this one** the one that is here, near or that has just been, or is about to be, referred to. **at this point** ⇒ point(7).

▷ *adv* **3** so; so . . . as this: *I didn't know it could be this hot here in summer. I want this much cheese, please.* Compare that¹(3).

▷ *pron* **4** the one that is here or that is rather near: *Who's this? This is my seat and that's yours.* (Notice that we do not use the pronoun 'this/these' to refer to a person or people except with a form of the verb 'be', e.g 'This is Margaret speaking' (i.e on the telephone).) Compare that¹(4). **5** the one that has just been or is soon to be mentioned: *I made a mistake in my first addition and this made all the other sums wrong. Listen to this; Dick thinks it's going to be cold tonight.* Compare that¹(5). **like this** ⇒ like¹. **this and that**; **this, that and the other** various kinds of things.

thistle /'θɪsl/ *c.n* kind of wild plant with lots of sharp points on its leaves and usu purple flowers.

thither /'ðɪðə/ *adv* (*old use*) to that place; in that direction. **hither and thither** ⇒ hither.

thong /θɒŋ/ *c.n* strip of leather used for tying things etc.

thorax /'θɔːræks/ *c.n* (*pl -es or, less usu, thoraces* /'θɔːrəsiːz/) (*technical*) **1** (in people and animals but not insects) chest; part of the body in which the lungs are. **2** (in insects) middle part of the body to which the legs and wings are fixed.

thorn /θɔːn/ *c.n* **1** thing growing out of a plant which has a sharp point at the end: *Most rose bushes have a lot of thorns.* **2** *c.n* bush, tree etc that has thorns(1). **a thorn in s.o's flesh/side** (*fig*) a person or thing that often troubles or annoys s.o.

'thorniness *u.n* fact of being thorny.

'thorny *adj* (*-ier, -iest*) **1** having thorns(1) on it: *a thorny bush.* **2** (*fig*) causing difficulty or problems: *a thorny problem.*

thorough /'θʌrə/ *adj* **1** complete; very careful: *a thorough search of the building.* **2** absolute; complete: *He has made a thorough fool of himself.*

'thoroughly *adv.* **'thoroughness** *u.n.*

those ⇒ that.

thou /ðaʊ/ *pron* (*old use*) (subject¹(4) form of the pronoun meaning 'you' (sing); the object¹(4) form is *thee* /ðiː/, the possessive adj *thy* /ðaɪ/, the possessive pron *thine* /ðaɪn/, the reflexive(2) and emphatic(1) form *thyself* /ðaɪ'self/).

though /ðəʊ/ *adv* **1** however; nevertheless; in spite of that: *It's raining; I didn't get wet, though, because I had my big umbrella.* (Notice that one cannot put the adv 'though' at the beginning of a sentence.)

▷ *conj* **2** (also **al'though**) in spite of the fact that: *Though it was very late, the child would not go to sleep. We had cold weather during our holiday, though it was already June.* **3** but at the same time; but nevertheless: *She is small though strong.* **as though** as if: *He closed his eyes, as though to shut out his unpleasant memories.* **big etc though s.t is, was etc . . .** even though s.t is etc big etc . . .: *Cold though it is, I'm going out for my walk.* **even though** ⇒ even(adv).

thought /θɔːt/ *n* **1** *u.n* ability to think(2). **2** *c.n* thing that is thought. ⇒ think(3). **3** *u.n* (usu *have some etc — for s.o/s.t, give some etc — to s.o/s.t*) consideration(2); attention; care: *He really has no thought for anyone but himself. Will you please give some thought to what you would like for dinner tonight?* **4** *u.n* way of thinking: *modern thought on the treatment of criminals.* **5** *u.n* (often *— of (doing) s.t*) intention, expectation, (of doing s.t): *When she decided to go to London she had no thought of meeting us there again.* **(deep) in thought** (very) busy thinking (⇒ think(2)). **food for thought** ⇒ food. **give up (all) thought of (doing) s.t** stop wanting or hoping for s.t or to do s.t. **train of thought** ⇒ train¹.

▷ *v* **6** *p.t,p.p* of think(*v*).

'thoughtful *adj* **1** (of a person) who thinks(2) a lot or is thinking now. **2** (of a person or s.t he/she does, gives etc) (showing that one is) thinking (⇒ think(2)) about s.o kindly (and in a practical way): *A thoughtful present to a new mother would be something she could use for her baby.* Compare thoughtless. **thoughtful of**

s.o (a) thinking (⇨ think(2)), caring about, s.o. (b) (usu *be — to do s.t*) showing thought(3) or care by s.o: *It was very thoughtful of her to ask whether she could help in any way.*

'**thoughtfully** *adv.* '**thoughtfulness** *u.n.*

'**thoughtless** *adj* not thinking (⇨ think(2)); not caring. Compare thoughtful(2), unthinkable. *thoughtless of s.o* (a) not thinking (⇨ think(2)); not caring about s.o. (b) (usu *be — to do s.t*) showing lack of thought(3) or care by s.o: *It was very thoughtless of you to say such things to a sick old man.*

'**thoughtlessly** *adv.* '**thoughtlessness** *u.n.*

,**thought-'out** *adj* (usu *well, poorly* etc —) produced after a lot of thinking(2) (which may be good, bad etc).

'**thought-,reader** *c.n* (also '**mind-,reader**) person who (says he/she) can know what other people are thinking (⇨ think(2)) without their saying or writing etc anything.

thoughts *pl.n* (often — *on s.o/s.t*) ideas (about s.o/s.t); things s.o thinks(2) (about s.o/s.t). **second thoughts** ⇨ second thoughts (⇨ second¹).

thousand /'θaʊzənd/ *det/pron/c.n* (*cardinal number*) (used with 'a' (*a thousand*) unless there is another det, e.g *one thousand*, *your thousand*; *pl thousand* after another number, e.g *two thousand*, otherwise *thousands*, e.g *thousands of people*) 1000; ten times a hundred. *a thousand and one* (*informal*) very many: *Before a long journey, one always has a thousand and one things to do.* **one in a thousand** very, unusually, good: *My secretary is one in a thousand; I don't know what I would do without her.*

'**thousands** *pl.n* (often — *of s.o/s.t*) 1 several thousand (people, things etc) (usu more than 2000 or 3000 but less than a million): *It'll cost thousands (of pounds) to build a swimming pool.* 2 (*informal*) a lot, large amount/number (of people, things etc) but less than a million: *There were thousands of people at the match.* Compare hundreds(2), millions.

thousandth /'θaʊzəndθ/ *det/pron* (*ordinal number*) 1 (person or thing) following 999 in order; 1000th.
▷ *c.n* 2 one of a thousand equal parts; $\frac{1}{1000}$.

thrash /θræʃ/ *tr.v* 1 beat, hit, (s.o, an animal) a number of times to punish her/him/it. 2 beat, defeat, win against, (s.o, a team etc) easily. *thrash about* move violently from side to side and/or up and down: *When the animal felt the rope round its neck, it thrashed about to try to get away.* *thrash s.t out* (*fig*) (a) discuss s.t very fully to try to find an answer. (b) produce s.t, e.g a plan, in this way.

thrashing *c.n* 1 beating(1). ⇨ thrash(1). 2 (usu *get, give s.o, a* —) heavy defeat. ⇨ thrash(2).

thread /θred/ *n* 1 *c/u.n* very thin length of wool, cotton etc, used for sewing and weaving cloth etc: *cotton thread.* 2 *c.n* very thin line of s.t, e.g light. 3 *c.n* raised spiral(2) round the outside of a screw etc or the inside of a nut(2). *follow/lose the thread (of s.t)* be able, not be able, to understand (the various parts of) a story: *I listen to a lot of French programmes on the radio but sometimes I lose the thread when they speak very fast.* *hang by a (single) thread* ⇨ hang(v).
▷ *tr.v* 4 put (a thread(1), film etc) through the hole,

e.g in a needle or a camera, intended for it. 5 put a thread etc through the hole of (a needle etc). *thread one's way through* (*s.t, a crowd of people etc*) go through (s.t) or between the people in a crowd etc by carefully finding spaces. *thread s.t on* (*a string etc*) put beads etc on a piece of string etc by passing it through them. *thread s.t together* join beads etc together by passing a thread through one after the other.

'**thread,bare** *adj* (of cloth etc) very thin because of having been rubbed or used a lot.

'**thread,like** *adj* looking like one or more threads(1).

threat /θret/ *c.n* 1 (often — *of s.t*) statement that one is going to do (s.t unpleasant), usu if the person one is talking or writing to does s.t one does not want her/him to do, or does not do s.t one wants her/him to do: *We have received threats of violence if we do not do what the men want.* 2 (often — *to s.o/s.t*) person or thing that is dangerous (to s.o/s.t): *The floods were a threat to our village.* 3 (usu — *of s.t*) sign that a danger may be coming: *The distant sounds of thunder were our first threat of bad weather.* **under threat of s.t** (a) being threatened with s.t: *Our factory is still under threat of closure.* (b) because of the threat(1) of s.t: *At last the criminals came out of the house under threat of being shot by the police.* *veiled threat* ⇨ veil.

'**threaten** *v* 1 *tr.v* (often — *s.o with s.t*) make threats(1) (of s.t) against (s.o): *The whole school was threatened with punishment unless the boy who had broken the door confessed.* 2 *tr.v* be a sign or warning of (s.t): *Those black clouds threaten rain.* 3 *tr.v* be a threat(2) against (s.o/s.t): *The destruction of the rain forests threatens the whole of our civilization.* 4 *intr.v* be a threat(2): *When danger threatens, we go down into our underground rooms.* *threaten to do s.t* say that one is going to do s.t unpleasant, usu unless s.t else is done.

'**threateningly** *adv* in a way that threatens(1).

three /θriː/ *det/pron/c.n* (*cardinal number*) number 3 (between 2 and 4): *Three tickets to London, please. Three of us are going by train. He's 3 (years old).* *in threes* in ranks/groups of three people etc each: *The police walked around the area in threes.* *the three R's* (/ɑːz/) reading, writing and arithmetic when they are being referred to as the basis of education.

third /θɜːd/ *det/pron* 1 (*ordinal number*) (person or thing) following 2 in order; 3rd: *Helen is my first child, Harry is my second and Peter's my third.*
▷ *c.n* 2 one of three equal parts; $\frac{1}{3}$. 3 lowest level of degree in most British universities with which one passes: *Gordon got a third in his BA examination.*

,**third de'gree** *def.n* very cruel treatment, usu of a prisoner, in order to get information out of her/him; torture(2).

,**third-de,gree 'burn** *c.n* very bad burn on a person's body.

,**third 'party** *c.n* (*law*) 1 person who is neither the plaintiff nor the defendant in a law case. 2 person who is not one of the main ones covered by an insurance policy(2) but who will be covered in case of an accident (e.g not the driver or a passenger but a person who is hit by the car).

,**third** ,**party in'surance** *u.n* insurance to cover people of this kind.

,**third 'person** *def.n* (*grammar*) not the person speaking/writing or the person spoken/written to, but another person: *'I' refers to the first person, 'you' to the second person, and 'he', 'she' and 'it' to the third person.*

,**third-'rate** *adj* (*derog*) of low quality.

,**Third 'World** *adj/def.n* (countries) that are less economically(2) advanced than Europe, North America, Russia etc.

,**three-'cornered** *adj* taking place between three people or teams etc: *a three-cornered election for a seat in* parliament.

,**three-di'mensional** *adj* (*abbr* three-D, 3-D) having, or seeming to have, not only length and width but also depth. **in three-D**, **in 3-D** (shown/made) in three dimensions(1): *It is possible to see certain films or photographs in three-D if one wears special glasses of different colours.*

'**three,fold** *adj/adv* (*formal*) three times: *a threefold increase in temperature.*

threepence /'θrepəns/ *u.n* three pence; 3p.

,**three-,piece 'suite** *c.n* ⇨ suite.

'**three-,ply** *adj/c.n* **1** (wool etc) having three threads or lengths: *three-ply wool.* **2** (s.t) having three layers: *three-ply wood.*

,**three-'quarter** *attrib.adj* (of a coat etc) neither long nor short; going down three quarters of the way: *a three-quarter (length) skirt.* ⇨ quarter¹(1).

'**threesome** /-səm/ *c.n* group of three: *My daughter always goes about in a threesome.*

thresh /θreʃ/ *tr/intr.v* beat (corn etc) to get the grains out of the husks(1).

'**thresher** *c.n* person or machine who/that threshes.

'**threshing ma,chine** *c.n* machine that threshes.

threshold /'θreʃ,həʊld/ *c.n* **1** piece of wood or stone in the ground across the bottom of the entrance to a building, room etc. **2** (often (on) the — of s.t) (*fig*) place where s.t starts: *These little children, who are on the threshold of life, need good food.* **3** (usu the — of s.t) (*technical*) lowest level at which (s.t) appears: *Some people have a low pain threshold, others a high one.*

threw /θru:/ *p.t* of throw.

thrift /θrɪft/ *u.n* careful use of money etc so as not to waste any.

'**thriftily** *adv* in a thrifty way.

'**thriftiness** *u.n* = thrift.

'**thrifty** *adj* (-ier, -iest) using money etc carefully so as to avoid wasting any.

thrill /θrɪl/ *c.n* **1** strong feeling of pleasure, excitement, fear etc that goes through one's body suddenly. **2** thing causing such a feeling. **get a thrill (from s.t)** feel thrilled(3) (by s.t). **give s.o a thrill** thrill(3) s.o.

▷ *v* **3** *tr.v* give (s.o) a thrill(1). **4** *intr.v* (usu — at/to s.t) (*formal*) feel a thrill(1) (as a result of s.t): *This is a story that thrills. The dancers thrilled to the beat of the drums.*

'**thriller** *c.n* story, film etc that thrills(4).

'**thrilling** *adj* that thrills(4).

'**thrillingly** *adv*. '**thrillingness** *u.n*.

thrive /θraɪv/ *intr.v* (*p.t* throve /θrəʊv/, thrived, *p.p* thriven /'θrɪvn/, thrived) (often — on s.t) be very successful (because of s.t); make very good progress (using s.t): *The trees we planted last year*

are thriving on all the rain they have been getting. *Business in our city is thriving.*

'**thriving** *adj* that is making good progress, is successful etc: *He owns a thriving business company.*

throat /θrəʊt/ *c.n* **1** passage inside the neck of a person or animal: *I've got a sore throat.* **2** front of a person's or animal's neck: *She had a large* woollen scarf(1) *round her throat.* **clear one's throat** cough to free one's throat of mucus etc before speaking, because it feels uncomfortable etc. **force**, **thrust** etc **s.t down s.o's throat** (*fig*) (try to) make s.o accept s.t (e.g an opinion) by force or rudeness. **have a frog in one's throat** ⇨ frog. **jump down s.t's throat** (*fig*) suddenly criticize s.o or speak angrily to s.o for no known reason. **stick in s.o's throat** (*fig*) be very difficult for s.o to accept.

-**throated** *adj* having a throat(2) of the kind shown in the first part of the word: *a white-throated bird.*

'**throatily** *adv* in a throaty way.

'**throatiness** *u.n* fact of being throaty.

throaty *adj* (-ier, -iest) (*informal*) sounding as if one has a sore throat; sounding rougher and speaking on a lower tone than normal: *a throaty voice*; *a throaty speaker.*

throb /θrɒb/ *c.n* **1** (one) beat(2) of a person's heart, a machine etc: *There was one last throb and then the machine stopped.* **2** (often the — of s.t) continuous, usu regular, not very loud beating(3) (of s.t, e.g a drum, an engine). ⇨ heartthrob.

▷ *intr.v* (-bb-) **3** beat(9) once or regularly. ⇨ throb(1,2). **throb with s.t** (**a**) throb(3) repeatedly and strongly because of emotion etc. (**b**) be excited or exciting because of s.t: *a city throbbing with life.*

'**throbbing** *adj* **1** that throbs(3): *a throbbing headache.*

▷ *c.n* **2** throb(2).

throes /θrəʊz/ *pl.n* **in the throes of s.t** very busy doing s.t difficult and/or painful.

thrombosis /θrɒm'bəʊsɪs/ *c/u.n* (*pl* thromboses /θrɒm'bəʊ,si:z/) (*medical*) (formation/existence of a) clot(1) (i.e a solid lump of blood) in an artery(1), a vein(1) or the heart.

throne /θrəʊn/ *n* **1** *c.n* chair on which a king or queen sits on special formal occasions. **2** *def.n* rank or position of being a king or queen. **come to the throne** become king or queen.

throng /θrɒŋ/ *c/def.pl.n* **1** (often — of people etc) big crowd (of people etc).

▷ *v* **2** *intr.v* come, arrive etc in crowds: *The people thronged into the small theatre to see the film-star.* **3** *tr.v* fill (s.t) with a crowd: *The people thronged the streets to see the successful football team.*

throttle /'θrɒtl/ *c.n* **1** device that controls the amount of petrol etc coming into an engine, used to make it go faster/slower.

▷ *v* **2** *tr.v* strangle(1) (s.o or an animal); prevent (s.o or an animal) breathing by holding her/his/its throat tightly.

through /θru:/ *adj* (US *thru*) **1** (*attrib*) going from one place to another without a break or without having to get out and change: *a through road*; *a through train* (*to s.w*). **2** (*pred*) (often — with s.o/s.t) finished: *Wait a few minutes; I'm not through (with my work) yet.* **3** (*pred*) (often — with s.o/s.t) (*informal*) not wanting to have anything more to do with s.o/s.t because one is angry etc: *'Isn't Tom your boyfriend any more?'* *'No, we're through'* (or *'I'm through with him'*). **4** (*pred*) (*informal*) finished; dismissed from a job.

▷ *adv* (US **thru**) **5** entering from one side of s.t, crossing it and going out from the other side: *Please go right through into the hall.* Compare through(12), across(1). **6** going from one side of s.t (e.g a doorway, hole) to the other side of it. Compare through(13). **7** passing between the various units of s.t: *He came to the trees and ran through to the other side.* Compare through(14). **8** (with abstract[1](1) things) successfully to the end of s.t: *Not many people* survive(2) *this disease but my brother came through all right. What happened in your examination? Did you get through?* Compare through(15). **9** (often *all* —) from beginning to end of s.t: *Have you read that book through yet?* Compare through(16). **10** (of a journey) without having to change trains etc anywhere: *You can go right through from London to Venice now. Can I book my luggage through to Chicago?* **11** (often *you're* —) (in telephoning) connected with the person one wants to speak to. **halfway** *etc* **through** in a state of having got through(5—7) half etc of s.t: *'Have you finished your examinations?' 'No, I'm only a quarter of the way through.'* Compare through(17). **all** (**the**) **winter** *etc* **through** during the whole of the winter etc. Compare through(16). **wet through** wet right down to one's skin. For verb + 'through', e.g *break through*, ⇨ the verb.

▷ *prep* (US **thru**) **12** entering from one side of (s.t), crossing (it) and going out from the other side: *Go through the hall and into the dining-room.* Compare through(5), across(1). **13** going from one side of (s.t, e.g a doorway, hole) to the other side of (it): *Will this thick rope go through that small hole?* Compare through(6). **14** passing between the various units of (s.t): *We walked through the trees to the side of the river.* Compare through(7). **15** (with abstract[1](1) things) successfully to the end of (s.t): *Mary has got through all her examinations.* Compare through(8). **16** (often *all* — *s.t*) from beginning to end of (s.t): *There was rain all through that night.* Compare through(9). **17** entering (s.t, e.g a factory or college) having certain things done to one while one is there and then leaving: *I went through university with my cousin Amy. The cars have to pass through the paint workshop before they finish.* **18** within (a place) without first entering from outside or leaving afterwards: *We flew to Rome, got a car and drove through Italy for a week.* Compare across(1). **19** everywhere in (s.t); all over (s.t): *My family are scattered through the world.* **20** in spite of (noise): *I could hear the sound of children crying through the sound of the storm.* **halfway** *etc* **through s.t** in a state of having got through(5—7) half etc of s.t: *I'm only halfway through my dinner.* For 'through' + verb and/or noun, e.g *pay through the nose*, ⇨ the verb or noun. **through and through** (**a**) through(1) again and again: *The arrows* pierced(1) *him through and through.* (**b**) thoroughly; in all parts: *The tea soon warmed her through and through. I love you through and through. He's an Englishman through and through* (a perfect example of an Englishman).

through'out *adv* **1** during the whole of that time: *We had one week's holiday and it rained throughout.* **2** in/on every part of it: *The hotel is furnished in the best taste throughout.*
▷ *prep* **3** (often *right* —) during the whole time of (s.t): *We were there* (*right*) *throughout the summer.* **4** in/on every part of (s.t): *There were desks and chairs throughout the hall.*

'through put *c.n* amount of materials dealt with by a factory etc in a certain time.

throw /θrəʊ/ *c.n* **1** (often *a* — *of a certain distance*) example of throwing(2): *The competition was won by my friend Jane with a good throw of over 50 metres.*
▷ *v* (*p.t* **threw** /θru:/, *p.p* **thrown** /θrəʊn/) **2** *tr/intr.v* (often — *s.t to s.o*; — *s.o s.t*) make (s.t) go (a certain distance) through the air by pushing it hard and suddenly with one's hand(s): *She threw the ball to her little son. Can you throw this stone twenty metres? Throw me that towel, please.* Compare throw s.t at s.o/s.t. **3** *tr.v* move (a switch, handle etc) so as to turn electricity, a machine etc on or off. **4** *tr/intr.v* make (one or more dice(1)) roll so that one can see what numbers come up: *It's your turn to throw.* **5** *tr.v* score (a certain number) by throwing one or more dice(1): *You can't start the game until you throw a six.* **6** *tr.v* cause (s.o) to fall down: *She was thrown by her horse.* **7** *tr.v* (*fig; informal*) puzzle (s.o); present (s.o) with a problem that he/she finds it difficult or impossible to solve. **8** *tr.v* give s.o (s.t) quickly: *He threw me an angry look.* **9** *tr.v* (*informal*) give, arrange, (a party, dinner etc): *I'm going to throw a big lunch for the visiting manager.* **10** *tr.v* make (a pot etc) out of soft clay by throwing it on a potter's[1] wheel and then shaping it.

throw oneself at s.o (*fig; informal*) try to make s.o love one by very obvious means. **throw oneself at s.o/s.t** try to hit s.o/s.t with one's body. **throw s.t at s.o/s.t** throw s.t in order to try to hit s.o/s.t. Compare throw s.t to s.o (⇨ throw(1)).

throw s.t away (**a**) get rid of s.t, usu by throwing it s.w. (**b**) fail to make use of an opportunity.

throw s.t back at s.o accuse s.o of s.t that he/she has accused one of himself/herself.

throw a fit ⇨ fit[2].

throw s.t in (**a**) (in football) throw the ball on to the field again after it has gone out(20). ⇨ throw-in. (**b**) (*fig; informal*) add s.t extra without making s.o pay for it: *The club charges £30 a week, with all sports* equipment *thrown in.* **throw in one's hand, throw one's hand in** ⇨ hand(*n*).

throw oneself into s.t (*fig*) (begin to) do s.t with great energy(1). **throw s.o/s.t into confusion** ⇨ confusion.

throw s.o off (**the scent**) (*fig*) cause s.o to stop being able to continue doing s.t, to try to find s.t out. **throw s.t off** take one or more pieces of clothing off quickly.

throw s.t on put one or more pieces of clothing on quickly.

throw s.o out cause s.o to make a mistake, e.g in counting. **throw s.o/s.t out** (**of s.t**) remove s.o/s.t (from s.t), either by actually throwing(1) her/him/it or by ordering her/him to go.

throw s.o over (*fig*) stop having anything to do with s.o.

throw s.o and s.o together (*fig*) cause s.o and s.o

to meet. **throw s.t together** make s.t quickly (and often rather badly) by putting parts together: *When her family suddenly arrived, I had to throw a meal together in a few minutes.*

throw up (*slang*) be sick(b); vomit(3). **throw s.t up** (**a**) (*fig*) produce s.t by chance or when it is not expected. (**b**) (*fig; informal*) stop doing s.t; resign from s.t, e.g a job. (**c**) bring s.t up out of one's stomach when one vomits(3).

'throwa,way *attrib.adj* **1** that can be thrown away after use: *throwaway paper plates for a picnic.* **2** (of a usu clever or important remark) said in such a way that one seems not to care what people think of it (although one really does).
▷ *c.n* **3** (*informal*) thing that is made to be thrown away after use. Compare throwaway(1).

'throw,back *c.n* (often — *to s.t*) (*informal*) case in which a person or an animal shows characteristics(2) of people/animals from whom/which he/she/it is descended: *This dog is a throwback to an earlier version of the* breed(1).

'thrower *c.n* person who throws, e.g in a game or sport.

'throw-,in *c.n* example or act of throwing the ball in again after it has gone out(20) in football.

thru /θru:/ *adj/adv/prep* (US) through.

thrum /θrʌm/ *c.n* **1** (often — *of s.t*) (usu of a machine that is vibrating) dull continuous sound (of s.t).
▷ *v* (*-mm-*) **2** *intr.v* make the sound of a thrum(1). **3** *tr/intr.v* (often — (*s.t*) *on s.t*) make (sounds) by playing on the strings of (a guitar etc), often without playing an actual piece of music.

thrush /θrʌʃ/ *c.n* kind of brown bird with spots on its breast(2) which sings prettily.

thrust /θrʌst/ *n* **1** *c.n* (one) example of thrusting(3). **2** *u.n* pushing force that is spread over an area, e.g the force with which an aircraft's engines push it forward. **cut and thrust (of s.t)** ⇒ cut(*n*).
▷ *tr/intr.v* (*p.t,p.p* thrust) **3** push (s.o/s.t) forward strongly and suddenly (through a crowd, person's body etc). **thrust oneself forward** (sometimes *fig*) push forward in order to be noticed. **thrust s.t (up)on s.o** (try to) force s.o to accept/take s.t.

thud /θʌd/ *c.n* **1** dull sound (like one) made by s.t heavy hitting s.t, e.g the ground.
▷ *intr.v* (*-dd-*) **2** make the sound of a thud(1).

thug /θʌg/ *c.n* (*derog*) criminal who uses violence.

'thuggery *u.n* (*derog*) bad behaviour of thugs.

thumb /θʌm/ *c.n* **1** part of a human hand that is at the side of the four fingers and that can be bent so as to hold things between itself and one or more of the fingers. **2** part of a glove that goes over a thumb(1). **be all (fingers and) thumbs** ⇒ finger(*n*). **stick out like a sore thumb** (*fig; informal*) be very obvious. **give (s.o) the thumbs up** (*informal*) give s.o a sign made by putting one or both of one's thumbs upwards to show (hope of) success. **under s.o's thumb** (*fig; informal*) doing what s.o says; not free: *That man is under his wife's thumb.* **twiddle one's thumbs** (*fig; informal*) have no work to do; be idle.
▷ *tr.v* **3** do s.t to (s.t) with one's thumb, e.g turn the pages of a book. **thumb a lift** = hitchhike. **thumb through s.t** look at the pages of a book, magazine etc quickly.

'thumb,nail *c.n* nail(1) on a thumb(1).

thump /θʌmp/ *c.n* **1** (often — *on s.t*) (sound made by a) heavy blow (on s.t), e.g hitting s.o on the back with one's hand.
▷ *v* **2** *tr/intr.v* (often — *against s.o/s.t*) hit (s.o/s.t) heavily. **3** *intr.v* make a noise (which is like one) caused by a thump(1).

'thumping *attrib.adj* **1** (*informal*) like a thump(1). **2** (*fig*) big; very bad: *a thumping headache.*
▷ *adv* **3** (*informal*) very: *a thumping great horse; a thumping big lie.*
▷ *c.n* **4** (*informal*) beating as a punishment or in a fight.

thunder /'θʌndə/ *u.n* **1** loud noise in the sky which follows lightning(2). **2** (often *the* — *of s.t*) loud noise (made by s.t) that sounds like thunder(1): *the thunder of horses'* hooves. (**as**) **black as thunder** (*fig; informal*) looking very angry. **steal s.o's thunder** (*fig*) spoil what s.o was trying to do to win admiration etc by doing it first oneself.
▷ *v* **3** *intr.v* make a noise like thunder(1). **4** *tr.v* (often — *s.t out*) shout (s.t) very loudly.

'thunder,bolt *c.n* **1** flash of lightning followed (sometimes very quickly) by thunder(1). **2** (*fig*) sudden (news of a) very bad happening: *His death came as a thunderbolt to us all.*

'thunder,clap *c.n* (one) loud sudden noise caused by thunder(1).

'thunder,cloud *c.n* dark cloud that produces thunder(1).

'thundering *attrib.adj* **1** (*informal*) great: *I've got a thundering headache.*
▷ *adv* **2** (*informal*) very: *He made a thundering big mistake in not being kind to his rich aunt.*

'thunderous *adj* **1** producing thunder(1). **2** (*fig*) very loud: *thunderous applause.*

'thunder,storm *c.n* storm during which there is thunder(1).

'thunder,struck *adj* (usu *pred*) extremely (and usu very unpleasantly) surprised.

'thundery *adj* threatening thunder(1): *thundery weather.*

Thursday /'θɜːzdɪ/ *c/unique n* fourth working day of the week in Christian(1) (and some other) countries; day after Wednesday and before Friday. **last Thursday** the last Thursday before today. **next Thursday** the first Thursday after today. **on a Thursday** on a day of one week that is/was a Thursday. **on Thursday** on the nearest Thursday before/after today; on the Thursday of the week being referred to: *I saw Mary on Thursday.* **On Thursdays** every Thursday: *We play* bridge² *on Thursdays.* **Thursday after next** the second Thursday after today. **Thursday before last** the Thursday before last Thursday. **Thursday morning, afternoon** etc the morning, afternoon etc of last, next, Thursday.

thus /ðʌs/ *adv* (*formal*) **1** in this/that way: *You open the bottle thus.* **2** therefore; as a result: *It rains a lot here; thus we always have plenty of fresh vegetables.* **thus far** ⇒ far(*adv*).

thwack /θwæk/ *c.n/tr.v* = whack.

thwart /θwɔːt/ *tr.v* **1** prevent (s.o or an animal) from doing s.t he/she/it is trying to do. **2** prevent (s.t) from being successful: *We were able to thwart the rival business company.*

thy /ðaɪ/ ⇒ thou.

thyme /taɪm/ *u.n* kind of small herb (with small leaves), used in cooking.

thyroid /ˈθaɪrɔɪd/ *c.n* (also ˌthyroid ˈgland) gland in the lower front part of one's neck which controls one's growth and activity.

thyself /ðaɪˈself/ ⇒ thou.

tiara /tɪˈɑːrə/ *c.n* small crown that a woman can wear on her head at formal parties.

tibia /ˈtɪbɪə/ *c.n* (*pl* -s, or, less usu, *tibiae* /ˈtɪbɪˌiː/) straight front bone in a person's leg below the knee.

tic /tɪk/ *c.n* sudden sharp movement of a muscle(1) which is not controlled by the person who has it and which does not hurt.

tick¹ /tɪk/ *c.n* **1** short sharp sound (as) made by a watch or clock. **2** mark(3) that one makes opposite or after s.t (e.g one of the things on a list) to show that it is present, correct etc. *in a couple of ticks*; *in a tick* (*informal*) very soon; in a moment.
▷ *v* **3** *intr.v* (of a watch, clock etc) make one or more ticks¹(1). **4** *tr.v* (often — *s.t off*) make a tick¹(2) opposite (s.t) to show that it is correct or that it has been done. **tick away** go on ticking for some time. **tick s.o off (for s.t)** (*informal*) scold s.o (because of bad behaviour). **tick over** (**a**) (of an engine) run very slowly without moving the thing it drives. (**b**) (of things that are done) happen, work etc, sometimes slowly: *'How's business this month?' 'Oh, it's ticking over.'*
ˈ**ticking¹** *u.n* sound of a series(1) of ticks¹(1): *the ticking of a clock.*
ˌticking ˈoff *c.n* (usu *get/give s.o a* —) scolding.

tick² /tɪk/ *c.n* kind of small insect that goes under the skin of animals, and sometimes people, and sucks blood.

tick³ /tɪk/ *u.n* **on tick** (*informal*) being allowed to take s.t with the agreement that one will pay for it later; on credit(1): *I don't believe in getting things on tick; I think one should not buy anything until one has the money to pay for it.*

ticket /ˈtɪkɪt/ *c.n* **1** card or piece of paper with things printed on it which one gets to show that one has paid (to travel on a train or bus, to go into a theatre etc): *a bus ticket.* **2** card or piece of paper fixed to s.t to show its price, size etc. Compare label(1), tag(1). **3** (*informal*) (often *parking* —) paper put on one's car etc to tell one that one has broken the law and that one has to pay a fine²(1). **by ticket** only if one has a ticket: *Admission to the party is by ticket.* **just the ticket** (*fig*; *informal*) exactly what is needed.
▷ *tr.v* **4** put a ticket(2,3) on (s.t).
ˈ**ticket col⟨ector** *c.n* person whose job is to examine and/or collect tickets on a train, bus, at a station etc.
ˈ**ticket ˌoffice** *c.n* place that sells tickets in a theatre, station etc.

ticking¹ /ˈtɪkɪŋ/ ⇒ tick¹.

ticking² /ˈtɪkɪŋ/ *u.n* kind of thick strong cloth from which the covers of pillows and mattresses are made.

ticking off ⇒ tick¹.

tickle /ˈtɪkl/ *c.n* **1** act or example of tickling (⇒ tickle(2,3)).
▷ *v* **2** *tr.v* touch (s.o or an animal) with one's hand(s) or with s.t else in such a way as to make her/him/it laugh. **3** *intr.v* make s.o's nerves behave in this way: *I can't wear wool next to my skin because it tickles.*
ˌtickled ˈpink *pred.adj* (*fig*, *slang*) very pleased or amused.
ˈ**ticklish** *adj* sensitive, made to laugh, when being tickled (⇒ tickle(2,3)).
ˈ**ticklishness** *u.n*.

tidal ⇒ tide.

tiddler /ˈtɪdlə/ *c.n* very small fish or child.

tiddly /ˈtɪdlɪ/ *adj* (-ier, -iest) (*informal*) **1** a little drunk(1). **2** very small: *This is a tiddly piece of cake!*

tiddlywinks /ˈtɪdlɪˌwɪŋks/ *u.n* game in which one tries to make round pieces of plastic(3) jump into a cup by pressing their sides with other round pieces of plastic.

tide /taɪd/ *c.n* **1** rise and fall of the level of the sea about every six hours as a result of the attraction of the moon: *The tide is coming in/going out* (is rising/falling). **2** movement of water in a certain direction (e.g up or down a river) as a result of a tide(1). **3** (often *a* — *of s.t*) (*fig*) feeling (of s.t) that a lot of people have: *The government came into power on a great tide of support from the farmers.* (**at**) **high/low tide** (at) the time when the tide(1) has brought the water right up/down. **go/swim against/with the tide** (*fig*) (not) do what other people do. **the turn of the tide** ⇒ turn(*n*).
▷ *tr.v* **4 tide s.o over** (**s.t**) help s.o to get through (a difficult time): *Peter didn't have enough money to pay the rent last month but Mary tided him over (this difficult time) by lending him the money.*
ˈ**tidal** *adj* (usu *attrib*) caused, affected, by the tides(1): *a tidal river.*
ˌtidal ˈwave *c.n* very big and dangerous wave caused by an earthquake etc under the water.
ˈ**tideˌmark** *c.n* **1** line of the tide(1) when it is highest. **2** (*informal*) dirty line round the inside of an empty bath showing how high the water was before it was let out.

tidiness ⇒ tidy.

tidings /ˈtaɪdɪŋz/ *pl.n* (*old use*) (often — *of s.o*/s.t) news about s.o/s.t).

tidy /ˈtaɪdɪ/ *adj* (-ier, -iest) Opposite untidy for (1,2). **1** well arranged; with nothing out of its right place: *tidy hair.* **2** (of a person, an animal, her/his/its behaviour etc) liking or wanting everything to be tidy(1). **3** (*attrib*) (*informal*) quite big in quantity: *When she died she left a tidy fortune to her son.* **neat and tidy** ⇒ neat(1).
▷ *tr/intr.v* (-ies, -ied) **4** (often — (*s.o/s.t*) *up*) make (s.o/s.t) tidy(1). Opposite untidy(2). **tidy s.t away** put s.t away in order to make a place tidy(1).
ˈ**tidily** *adv*. ˈ**tidiness** *u.n*.

tie /taɪ/ *c.n* **1** (also ˈneckˌtie) long piece of clothing worn round the neck under the collar of a shirt. ⇒ bow tie (⇒ tie³). **2** thing used for tying (⇒ tie(7)) s.o/s.t or for joining and holding things together. **3** (*music*) sign used in music to show that where two notes of equal pitch¹(1) have a curve over them, the first note only is sounded, and is held on for its own length plus that of the next (*tied*) note. ⇒ phrase(3). **4** (usu *pl*, often —*s of s.t*) thing that joins people in friendship etc: *family ties*; *the ties of friendship.* **5** thing that prevents one doing what one wants to do: *Having old parents to look after is a tie.* **6** situation in which both sides in a competition, an election etc have the same number of points, votes etc.

▷ v **7** *tr/intr.v* (*pres.p.* tying /'taɪɪŋ/, *p.t.p.p* tied) fix or join (s.o/s.t) (to s.t) (with a rope, string etc): *I tied the box on the car with string. Tie those ropes together.* Opposite untie. **8** *intr.v* (often — *up*) be tied(7): *This robe you have to wear in the hospital ties (up) at the back.* **9** *tr.v* make a knot in (a tie(1) etc) so that it is properly arranged. **10** *intr.v* (often — (*with s.o*) *for s.t*) have a tie(6) (when competing with s.o) (to try to win s.t). **tie a bow/knot (in s.t)** tie s.t in such a way that it has a bow/knot in it. **tie in (with s.t)** (*fig*) fit in well (with s.t). **tie s.o down (to s.t)** (*fig*) force s.o to agree (about s.t). **tie s.t up** (**a**) tie(7) s.t properly. (**b**) (*fig*) finish s.t successfully. (**c**) (*fig*) put limits on the use of s.t (e.g money left in a will). **tie s.t up (in s.t)** (*fig*) put money etc in a business etc so that it is difficult or impossible to get it out again. **tie up** ⇒ tie(8). **tie s.t up (with s.t)** (**a**) make a parcel etc secure(1) (by winding string etc round it). (**b**) tie(7) an animal etc to s.t (using rope etc). **tied up (with s.o/s.t)** (*informal*) very busy (doing s.t (with s.o)).

'tie,break *c.n* (also 'tie,breaker) final part of a competition/match to decide who wins when two or more people or teams have tied(10) up to that point.

'tie-,on *attrib.adj* that one ties on s.t instead of sticking it on: *a tie-on* label(1).

'tie,pin *c.n* decorative pin that is put in a tie(1) to keep the front and back parts of it together.

tier /tɪə/ *c.n* one of two or more rows² of which each is higher and further back than the one in front: *Students often sit in tiers of benches inside* lecture(1) *halls.*

tiff /tɪf/ *c.n* (often *have a* — (*with s.o*)) quarrel, usu not a serious one, (with s.o).

tiger /'taɪgə/ *c.n* **1** kind of big wild Asian animal of the cat family that has black and yellow stripes. **2** (*fig*) person who is very brave or fierce.

'tiger ,lily *c.n* orange flower of the lily family which has black spots on it.

'tigerish *adj* like a tiger; fierce.

tigress /'taɪgrɪs/ *c.n* female tiger.

tight /taɪt/ *adj* Opposite loose for (1–4). **1** closed in so much that it is difficult or impossible to move: *a tight cork in a bottle.* **2** pressing (too) closely: *a tight collar.* **3** stretched enough to keep it quite straight: *Before you walk along the rope you must make sure that it is tight.* **4** fitting so closely that nothing can get past: *Unless the ship has tight joints it will leak.* Compare airtight, watertight(1). **5** making one feel that one is held in a tight(1) way: *I had a tight feeling in my chest.* **6** having so many things to do that it is difficult to find the time for them: *a tight* schedule(1). **7** (*pred*) (*technical*) (of money and other things one wants) difficult to get: *Money is very tight just now* (i.e lots of people want to borrow it but few want to lend it). **8** (*attrib*) in which neither side, team etc is winning at all easily: *a tight match.* **9** (*slang*) drunk(1).

▷ *adv* **hold (s.o/s.t) tight** hold (s.o/s.t) firmly or strongly so that it is difficult for her/him/it to escape. **pack s.t tight** pack s.t (e.g a bag) so that there is no room left in it. **pull s.t tight** pull s.t until it is quite tight(3). **sit tight** (*informal*) do not move; do not go away; do not change. **sleep tight** (*informal*) sleep well.

,tight 'corner *c.n* (usu *in a* —) (*fig*) difficult or dangerous situation.

'tighten *tr/intr.v* (often — (*s.t*) *up*) (cause (s.t) to) become tight(er)(1–4). **tighten one's belt** ⇒ belt(*n*). **tighten up on s.t** start doing s.t, making other people do s.t, more carefully or correctly: *Our students are not working as hard as they were; we'd better tighten up on their discipline.*

,tight-'fisted *adj* (*derog*; *informal*) not at all generous; mean'(1).

'tight-'fistedness *u.n.*

,tight-'lipped *adj* (usu *pred*) (*fig*) not willing to talk (much).

'tightly *adv.* 'tightness *u.n.*

'tight,rope *c.n* rope or wire stretched tightly above the ground so that people can walk along it as an entertainment. **walk a tightrope (between s.t and s.t)** (*fig*) be very careful to avoid a danger.

'tight,rope ,walker *c.n* person who performs on a tightrope.

tights *pl.n* **1** (often *pair of* —) piece of clothing worn by women and girls which covers the legs and the lower half of the body tightly. **2** piece of clothing which covers the whole body from the neck to the feet, as worn by some dancers etc.

,tight 'spot *c.n* (usu *in a* —) = tight corner.

tigress ⇒ tiger.

tile /taɪl/ *c.n* **1** flat thing made out of clay, slate'(2) etc for putting on the roofs of houses to keep the rain etc out. **2** square or oblong thing made of baked clay, plastic(3) etc for putting on floors and walls for decoration and so that they can be cleaned easily etc. (**out**) **on the tiles** (*informal*) having a good time away from one's home at night.

▷ *tr.v* **3** (fix tiles) on (a roof, wall etc).

tiled *adj* having tiles(1) on it: *a tiled path.*

'tiler *c.n* person whose job is putting tiles on roofs etc.

'tiling *u.n* cover made of tiles.

till¹ /tɪl/ *conj/prep* (*informal*) = until.

till² /tɪl/ *c.n* drawer in a shop, bank etc in which money is kept.

till³ /tɪl/ *tr.v* dig, plough etc (land) in order to grow things on it; cultivate(1) (land).

tiller /'tɪlə/ *c.n* long handle used to steer a small boat.

tilt /tɪlt/ *c/u.n* **1** action or result of tilting(2) s.t. **at a tilt** at an angle to the horizontal position: *Many hats are worn at a tilt.* (**at**) **full tilt** (*informal*) moving as fast as possible: *The riders rode across the fields at full tilt.*

▷ *tr/intr.v* **2** (cause (s.o/s.t) to) change from a (more) vertical to a less vertical position: *Every time the ship tilted, the bottle rolled across the table.*

timber /'tɪmbə/ *n* **1** *u.n* wood that has been cut for use in building s.t. **2** *u.n* trees that are still growing, esp when one is thinking of them as future timber(1). **3** *c.n* piece of timber(1) that is part of a building, ship etc.

timbre /'tæmbə/ *c/u.n* (often *the* — *of s.t*) (*technical*) special quality (of an individual sound) that distinguishes it from other sounds having the same note, loudness etc: *I could recognize her voice anywhere by its timbre alone.*

time /taɪm/ *n* **1** *u.n* flow of the seconds, minutes, days, years etc: *We live our lives in space and time so we can show where and when something* *happens by describing the place and giving the year, month, hour etc.* **2** *unique n* abstract[1](1) idea of time(1): *Time is a great healer*(2) *after you have been made sad.* **3** *c.n* length of time(1): *I was there a short time.* **4** *u/def.n* enough time(3) for s.t: *'Can you help me?' 'No, I'm sorry, I haven't (the) time.'* **5** *c/u.n* occasion: *That time I was lucky — the car knocked me down but did not hurt me.* **6** *c/u.n* point in time(1): *At what time shall I come? It's time for dinner.* **7** *c.n* (often *pl*) particular length of time(1) in history; period(2); age(3): *in King Henry VIII's time; in modern times.* **8** *c.n* (sometimes *pl*) experience(1) one has at a particular time(6): *I hope you have a good time at the dance. We experienced difficult times in the 1970s.* **9** *def.n* hour, minute and, sometimes, second: *What's the time? The time is 6 o'clock.* **10** *c/u.n* time(3) taken by s.o/s.t (to do s.t): *My time for the race was 5 minutes 3.4 seconds. The first race was won in (a) record time.* **11** *unique n* (often with capital **T**) particular system of measuring time(1): *British Summer Time.* **after s.o's time** too late for s.o to have been there, seen it etc. **ahead of one's time** so modern in one's ideas etc that some people do not understand or like one. Opposite behind the times. **ahead of time** earlier than the normal or agreed time: *We needn't hurry because we are an hour ahead of time.* Opposite behind time. **(all) in good time** without hurrying; when the right time comes: *'Where's our dinner?' — 'Don't worry, it will come all in good time.'* **all the time** without stopping; continually. **at the same time** happening together in time; simultaneously. **at the time** at that time(6): *She was born in May 1978; at the time her parents lived in London.* **at the time of s.t** when s.t happened or was happening. **beat time** make movements, usu with one or both hands, at the same time as the strong beats of music. **before one's time** = ahead of one's time. **before s.o's time** too early before for s.o to be there or to be alive etc: *I never saw a tram in London; they were before my time.* **behind the times** old fashioned. **behind time** late; later than the normal or agreed time. **bide one's time** wait till the right or suitable moment comes. **closing time** time when shops, pubs etc shut. **die before one's time** die at an earlier age than might be expected. **do time** be a prisoner. **double time** twice the ordinary rate of pay for the work: *We sometimes have to work on Sundays but then we get double time.* Compare overtime(2), time and a half. **everytime**; **every time (that)** ⇒ every time. **for the first, second, last** etc **time** the first etc time that one does s.t: *I'm visiting London for the first time. I'm telling you for the hundredth time not to shout like that!* **for the time being** ⇒ being(*adj*). **from/since time immemorial** ⇒ immemorial. **from time to time** occasionally; every now and then. **full time (a)** ('**full-,time** when *attrib*) all the hours of the working week: *work full time.* Compare part time. **(b)** ⇒ full time (⇒ full). **gain time** (of a clock, watch) go too fast so that the time shown is ahead of the true time. Opposite lose time. **half time** time halfway through a match (e.g of football) during which the teams have a rest and change sides. **have a good time** enjoy oneself. **have a rare old time** enjoy a party, holiday etc very much. **have an easy time (of it)** not have

too much or too difficult work to do. **have no time for s.t/to do s.t** not have enough free time in which to do s.t. **have the time of one's life** enjoy oneself very much. **have (the) time for s.t/to do s.t** have enough free time to do s.t. **in good time (for s.t)** early enough not to miss s.t. **in the fullness of time** ⇒ fullness. **in the nick of time** ⇒ nick(*n*). **in no time (at all)** very quickly or soon. **in one's own (good) time** when one wants to do it oneself without letting oneself be hurried. **in one's own time** during the time when one is free, not during working hours: *If you want to get your hair cut you'll have to have it done in your own time.* **in time** if one waits long enough: *I know you are very sad about losing your girlfriend but you'll forget her in time.* **in time (for s.t)** not too late (for s.t). **in time (to/with s.o/s.t)** doing s.t at the same rate as s.o/s.t: *Swing your arms in time to/with the music.* **it is time (to do s.t)** the right/suitable time (for doing s.t) has arrived. **just in time** ⇒ just[2]. **keep good time** be punctual. **kill time** (*informal*) help time to seem to pass more quickly by doing s.t: *He used to kill time by counting the cars that passed his house.* **lose time** (of a clock, watch) go too slowly so that the time shown is behind the true time. Opposite gain time. **make good time** go reasonably fast so that one is not late. **make up (for) lost time** do s.t now to take the place of opportunities that no longer exist. **many a time** often. **many's the time that/when...** there have been a large number of occasions that/when...: *Many's the time when I've wanted to give him my true opinion.* **mark time (a)** (in marching in the army etc) raise one foot at a time as if walking but without moving forward. **(b)** (*fig*) not make any progress but also not go backwards at all: *During August business always marks time because so many people are on holiday.* **now's the time (for s.t)** the best or most suitable time (for s.t) is now. **on time** at the correct time; not late but also not early. Compare in time (for s.t). **a race against time** ⇒ race[1](*n*). **once upon a time** (way in which many children's stories start) at a point in time in the past. **(only) a matter/question of time** sure to happen, the only question being when. **only time will tell (whether, what** etc) one cannot know in advance (whether, what etc) and one will have to wait to find out. **opening time** time when shops, pubs etc open. **part time** ('**part-,time** when *attrib*) not all the hours of the working week: *John works part time in a shop* (or *John has a part-time job*). **pass the time (by doing s.t)** use up free time (by doing s.t). **pass the time of day (with s.o)** ⇒ day. **passage of time** ⇒ passage(*n*). **play for time** cause a delay hoping that it will allow one to avoid s.t unpleasant. **serve time** = do time. **take one's time (over s.t)** not hurry (about s.t). **take (s.o/s.t) a long** etc **time (to do s.t)** need a lot etc of time ((for s.o) to do s.t). **take time** need (quite a lot of) time to do: *It takes time for wounds to heal completely.* **tell the time** (of a clock etc) give or show the time(9). **the time is ripe (for s.t)** this is the best time (for s.t). **time and (time) again** very often. **time and a half** payment for work at the full rate for the job plus half the rate (e.g because it is overtime). **time runs by** time passes quickly.

▷ *tr.v* **12** find the speed of (s.o/s.t) or the time he/

she/it takes to do s.t: *We timed the car over 20 kilometres.* **13** choose just the right moment for (s.t): *If you time the ball just right, you can hit it wherever you want it to go.* **time s.t to do s.t** arrange things in such a way that s.t will do s.t at a certain time: *The men timed her arrival just as people were starting to leave the building.*

-time *u.n* period(1) during which the thing in the first part of the word exists or happens: *summertime.*

'**time ,bomb** *c.n* bomb that can be timed to explode at a certain time.

'**time-con,suming** *adj* taking up, using up, a lot of time.

-timed *adj* that is timed (⇨ time(13)) in the way described by the first part of the word: *badly-timed.*

'**time ex,posure** *c/u.n* (in taking photographs) exposure made with a longer than normal delay between the time the lens(1) opens and the time it shuts.

'**time ,fuse** *c.n* fuse² fixed to an explosive so that one can set the time that it will go off.

'**time-,honoured** *attrib.adj* respected because of its age.

,**time ,imme'morial** *unique n* from/since **time immemorial** back in time for as long as people can remember.

'**time,keeper** *c.n* person or thing that keeps a record of the time.

'**time ,lag** *c.n* delay (of a certain length of time) between s.t and s.t.

'**timeless** *adj* never ending; never changing.

'**timelessly** *adv.* '**timelessness** *u.n.*

'**time ,limit** *c.n* (often *set a — (on s.t)*) time before which (s.t) has to be done.

'**timeliness** *u.n* fact of being timely.

'**timely** *adj* (-ier, -iest) happening at just the right moment for s.t: *If it had not been for your timely help, I would have lost everything.* Compare untimely.

'**timer** *c.n* device that times(12) s.o/s.t: *An egg-timer will show you when your boiled egg is cooked.*

times *prep* **1** multiplied by: *Five times five is 25* (5 × 5 = 25).
▷ *pl.n* **2** (*pl* of time(3,5–8,10). **at all times** always. **at the best of times** even when things are going very well: *Peter is rude at the best of times, but when he is angry he is really terrible.* **at times** sometimes; occasionally. **behind the times** old-fashioned; not modern. **for old times' sake** because of past friendship etc. **hard times** a difficult period(1) or difficult periods that s.o has to suffer. Compare time(8). (**in**) **ancient times** very long ago. Compare time(7). **march/move with the times** keep up with modern advances; not get behind the times. **other times** on other occasions: *Sometimes I stay at home; other times I go to my sister's house.* **time(s) without number** so many times that it is impossible to count them.

'**time,saving** *attrib.adj* that saves time.

'**time ,signal** *c.n* signal which tells one the exact time: *There is a time signal before the news on the radio.*

'**time ,switch** *c.n* switch that turns things on and off at times that one has set before.

'**time,table** *c.n* list of times at which trains

etc leave and arrive or at which other things happen: *Here is the timetable for examinations next week.*

'**time,worn** *attrib.adj* damaged by having existed for a long time or been used for too long or too often: *timeworn jokes/ phrases* (1).

'**time ,zone** *c.n* area of land and/or sea within which the clocks show a certain time: *When you fly from England to Greece in winter, you have to put your watch back two hours because Greece is in a different time zone.*

'**timing** *u.n* way in which s.t is timed (13).

timid /'tɪmɪd/ *adj* easily becoming afraid.

timidity /tɪ'mɪdɪtɪ/ *u.n.* '**timidly** *adv.* '**timidness** *u.n.*

timing ⇨ time.

timorous /'tɪmərəs/ *adj* (*formal*) easily becoming afraid; timid.

'**timorously** *adv.* '**timorousness** *u.n.*

timpani /'tɪmpənɪ/ *def/def.pl.n* set of kettledrums as played in an orchestra.

timpanist /'tɪmpənɪst/ *c.n* person who plays the timpani.

tin /tɪn/ *n* **1** *u.n* (also *attrib*) kind of soft pale metal that shines like silver and is used mostly to put over other metals, *chem.symb* Sn: *a tin box.* **2** *c.n* (US **can**) metal container, esp a small one covered with tin(2): *a tin of tomatoes.*
▷ *tr.v* (-nn-) **3** (US **can**) put (food, e.g fruit) in one or more tins(2).

'**tin,foil** *u.n* very thin sheet of metal that shines like silver, used for putting round things, e.g food.

tinned *attrib.adj* (US **canned**) that has been put in tins(2): *tinned fruit.* ⇨ tin(3).

'**tinniness** *u.n* fact of being tinny.

'**tinny** *adj* (-ier, -iest) (*derog*) poor in quality; cheap and nasty.

'**tin-,opener** *c.n* (US '**can-,opener**) tool for opening tins(2).

'**tin,plate** *u.n* very thin sheets of metal covered with tin(1) and used, for example, in making tins(2).

'**tin,tack** *c.n* short nail made of iron with tin(1) over it.

tincture /'tɪŋktʃə/ *c/u.n* medicine made from a medical substance and alcohol.

tinfoil ⇨ tin.

ting /tɪŋ/ *c.n* **1** sound made when s.t, e.g a bell, tings(2).
▷ *tr/intr.v* **2** (cause (a bell etc) to) make a musical sound on a high note.

tingaling /,tɪŋə'lɪŋ/ *c.n* repeated tings(2), e.g those made by a bicycle bell.

tinge /tɪndʒ/ *c.n* **1** (often — *of s.t*) very small amount (e.g of redness in a person's cheeks).
▷ *tr.v* **2** (usu passive) give (s.t) a tinge(1). **tinged with s.t** (*fig*) mixed with a little of s.t: *Her joy at her daughter's marriage was tinged with sadness at losing her.*

tingle /'tɪŋgl/ *c.n* **1** (often — *of s.t*) feeling (caused by s.t) which makes one tingle(2).
▷ *intr.v* **2** (often — *with s.t*) have a slight feeling like that of having pins stuck into one (because of s.t): *After playing in the snow, the children's fingers began to tingle with cold.*

tininess ⇨ tiny.

tinker /'tɪŋkə/ *c.n* **1** person who goes from house to house offering to repair pots, pans and other metal things. **2** (*derog*; *informal*) naughty child: *Come here, you little tinker!*

▷ *intr.v* **3** (usu — *about* (with s.t)) work at s.t, e.g trying to repair it, but not efficiently or very seriously: *'What's Pat doing?' 'Nothing much; she's just tinkering about in the garage.'*

tinkle /'tɪŋkl/ *c.n* **1** sound of s.t tinkling(1): *the tinkle of glasses in the bar of the hotel.*

▷ *tr/intr.v* **2** (cause (s.t) to) make one or more sounds like glasses hitting each other gently.

tinniness ⇒ tin.

tin-opener, tinplate ⇒ tin.

tinsel /'tɪnsl/ *u.n* **1** decorations made of shiny material that glitters(3). **2** (*derog*; *fig*) thing that looks valuable but is really not.

'tinselly *adj* (often *derog*) made of, like, tinsel.

tint /tɪnt/ *c.n* **1** slight amount (of a colour). **2** dye(1) for colouring a person's hair slightly.

▷ *tr.v* **3** give (one's hair etc) a slight amount of a colour: *She tints her hair. It's tinted red.*

tintack ⇒ tin.

tiny /'taɪnɪ/ *adj* (*-ier, -iest*) very small: *tiny insects.*

'tininess *u.n.*

tip[1] /tɪp/ *c.n* **1** (often *the* — *of* s.t) piece right at the end (of s.t): *the tips of my fingers*; *the tip of an umbrella.* **have s.t on the tip of one's tongue** almost remember s.t that one is trying to remember. **the tip of the iceberg** (*fig*) only that small part of the whole which one can notice: *Someone in the shop had stolen £5 but that was only the tip of the iceberg because big thefts of money had been going on for years.* **2** place where people tip(4) rubbish: *a rubbish tip.*

▷ *tr.v* (*-pp-*) **3** hit (s.t) slightly: *I tipped the ball into the net.* **4** move a container (slightly) and empty (the contents) (into or out of s.t): *She tipped the dirty water out of the bucket* (or *into the* sink). *Don't tip rubbish over this bridge.* **tip (s.o/s.t) over** (knock (s.o/s.t) slightly and cause (her/him/it) to) fall down: *I'm sorry but I've tipped the bottle over. I knocked the table and the bottle tipped over.*

tipped *adj* having a tip[1](1): *tipped cigarettes.*

'tip,toe *intr.v* (*pres.p -toeing*) walk on tiptoe.

'tip,toe(s) *u/pl.n* **on tiptoe(s)** **(a)** with only the tips[1](1) of one's toes touching the ground: *walk on tiptoe.* **(b)** (*fig*) excited or keen (because of a feeling one has): *on tiptoes with excitement.*

,tip-'top *adj* (usu *attrib*) of the best kind: *fruit of tip-top quality.*

tip[2] /tɪp/ *c.n* **1** (usu *give* s.o, *get, a* — (*for* s.t)) present, usu of money, given to a porter, waiter etc for service he/she has given one, or service one hopes he/she will give.

▷ *tr/intr.v* **2** (*-pp-*) give a tip[2](1) to (s.o) (for a service): *Have you tipped the porter? That woman tips well.*

'tipper *c.n* person who tips[2](2) s.o: *That woman is a good tipper* (she gives generous tips[2](1)).

tip[3] /tɪp/ *c.n* **1** piece of useful advice or information (about s.t, e.g a horse race).

▷ *tr.v* (*-pp-*) **2** say that (s.o/s.t) is going to win etc: *Which horse do you tip (to win) in the next race?* **tip s.o off** (*that . . .*) warn s.o, often secretly, that . . .: *The police were tipped off that there was going to be an attack on the National Bank that morning.* ⇒ tip-off.

'tip-,off *c.n* warning (about s.t that is going to happen). ⇒ tip s.o off (that . . .).

tipster /'tɪpstə/ *c.n* person who gives tips[3](1), usu about which horses are going to win races.

tipple /'tɪpl/ *c.n* **1** (*informal*) alcoholic(1) drink: *My favourite tipple is* whisky(1).

▷ *intr.v* **2** drink alcohol regularly and/or too much. ⇒ tipsy.

'tippler *c.n* (*informal*) person who tipples(2).

tipsily, tipsiness ⇒ tipsy.

tipster ⇒ tip[3].

tipsy /'tɪpsɪ/ *adj* (*-ier, -iest*) rather drunk(1).

'tipsily *adv.* **'tipsiness** *u.n.*

tiptoe, tip-top ⇒ tip[1].

tirade /taɪ'reɪd/ *c.n* (*formal*) long angry scolding.

tire[1] /taɪə/ *tr/intr.v* (*formal*) (cause (s.o or an animal) to) become tired(1). **tire of (doing) s.t** become bored with (doing) s.t; become tired of (doing) s.t. **tire s.o/s.t out** make s.o or an animal extremely tired.

tired *adj* **1** feeling that one has lost one's strength of body or mind, usu as a result of having worked too much: *If you're tired, why don't you go to bed and have a rest?* **2** (*attrib*) that has been used so often that it has become boring: *We hear the same tired old jokes every day.* **tired of s.o/s.t** no longer interested in s.o/s.t; bored with s.o/s.t.

'tiredly *adv.* **'tiredness** *u.n.*

'tireless *adj* never getting tired(1).

'tirelessly *adv.* **'tirelessness** *u.n.*

'tiresome /-səm/ *adj* (*derog*) causing tiredness, boredom or annoyance: *a tiresome journey*; *a tiresome lecture*; *a tiresome child.*

'tiresomely *adv.* **'tiresomeness** *u.n.*

'tiring *adj* who/that makes one tired(1). Compare untiring.

tire[2] ⇒ tyre.

tissue /'tɪʃuː/ *n* **1** *c/u.n* material out of which a particular part of a living thing is made: *nervous tissue* (out of which nerves(1) are made). **2** *u.n* (also **'tissue ,paper**) very thin paper, often used for wrapping things up. **3** *c.n* piece of tissue(2) that one can blow one's nose on or use for cleaning one's face etc. **a tissue of lies** (*fig*) a story built up by putting lies together.

tit[1] /tɪt/ *c.n* kind of small bird: *a blue tit*; *a coal tit.*

tit[2] /tɪt/ *c.n* (also **'titty**) (*slang*) breast(1); nipple(1).

tit[3] /tɪt/ *c/u.n* **tit for tat** (*informal*) giving s.t unpleasant in return for s.t unpleasant that one has received: *'Why did you take Pauline's umbrella?' 'It was tit for tat; she took mine yesterday.'*

titanic /taɪ'tænɪk/ *adj* (*literary*) very powerful in body, importance etc.

titanium /taɪ'teɪnɪəm/ *u.n* pale light strong metal used in industry, *chem.symb* Ti.

titbit /'tɪt,bɪt/ *c.n* **1** specially tasty little piece of food. **2** interesting piece (of information etc).

titillate /'tɪtɪ,leɪt/ *tr.v* give (s.o, s.o's curiosity etc) a pleasantly exciting feeling.

titillation /,tɪtɪ'leɪʃən/ *u.n.*

titivate /'tɪtɪ,veɪt/ *tr/intr.v* (*informal*) make (oneself, another person, one's clothes etc) tidy or attractive.

title /'taɪtl/ *c.n* **1** name by which a book, film etc is known: *I gave my poem the title 'Wings* *over the Sea'.* **2** word(s) put before a person's name to show her/his rank, social position etc, e.g Mr, Ms, Mrs, Lady, Sir, Captain, Professor. **3** *c.n* position (of champion(3)), usu in a sport: *Who holds the world title for the high jump at present?* **4** *c/u.n* (*law*) right to own or have s.t: *Who has the title to this property?*

ˈ**titled** *adj* having the title(2) of Lady, Sir etc, not just of Mr, Mrs, Ms etc.

ˈ**title ˌdeed** *c.n* (often *pl*) official paper to prove one's title(4) to s.t.

ˈ**title ˌfight** *c.n* boxing match to decide who will have a title(3).

ˈ**title ˌholder** *c.n* person who has a title(4) to s.t; owner.

ˈ**title ˌpage** *c.n* page at the beginning of a book on which the title(1) is shown.

ˈ**title ˌrole** *c.n* person in a play, film etc from whom it gets its title: *Sir Laurence Olivier played the title role in the film 'King Henry V'.*

titles *pl.n* = credit titles (⇒ credits).

titular /ˈtɪtjʊlə/ *attrib.adj* (*formal*) as far as the title(3,4) is concerned without having any of the powers or duties that one would expect to go with it: *The* chancellor(2) *is the titular head of the university but the real head when it comes to work is the* vice-chancellor (⇒ vice³).

titter /ˈtɪtə/ *c.n* **1** quiet laugh because one is too ashamed or too polite to do it loudly.
▷ *intr.v* **2** laugh in this way.

tittle-tattle /ˈtɪtl ˌtætl/ *u.n* **1** (*informal*) gossip(1).
▷ *intr.v* **2** (*informal*) gossip(4).

titty /ˈtɪtɪ/ *c.n* (*pl -ies*) ⇒ tit².

titular ⇒ title.

tizzy /ˈtɪzɪ/ *c.n* (*pl -ies*) (often *get into, be in a,* —) (*slang*) state of nervousness that makes it difficult or impossible for one to do things properly.

T-junction ⇒ T,t.

TM /ˌtiː ˈem/ *abbr* transcendental meditation.

TNT /ˌtiː ˌen ˈtiː/ *abbr* trinitrotoluene (an explosive(2)).

to¹ /tuː/ *adv* before (a time): *'Is it ten o'clock yet?' 'No, it's five to.'* *He promised to come at twenty to, but it's already five o'clock and he isn't here.* Compare to²(12). Opposite past(10). For verb + 'to', e.g *bring s.o to, come to,* ⇒ the verb. **to and fro** first in one direction and then in another.
ˌ**toings and ˈfroings** *n.pl* movement (of people, animals etc) in one direction and then back again often.

to² (strong form /tuː/, weak form before a vowel(1) sound or in final position /tʊ/, weak form before a consonant(3) sound /tə/) *prep* **1** in the direction of and actually reaching: *We went to the station.* **2** ('to' + noun without 'a/an/the') in the direction of and actually reaching (a place, building etc for the purpose shown by the noun): *Did you go to school yesterday? They went to sea* (They became sailors). *He was sent to prison* (i.e as a prisoner). *They went to war* (began to fight). Compare at(10). **3** (noun + 'to' + noun) with one (thing, part etc) touching the other: *If you put all those pencils end to end they will go right across the hall. Some people like dancing cheek to cheek.* **4** towards but without actually reaching; in the direction of: *She pointed to her house. We have to go to the north now. Turn to the left here.* (*fig*) *She has a tendency to* headaches. **5** towards but

without movement; in the direction of: *Is this the road to Cambridge? We had our backs to the wall.* **6** as far as or so as to reach (s.t): *The bill came to £11.12. All our plans have come to nothing. She can count from 1 to 100. It is 15 kilometres from here to the coast.* **7** so as to become (a state or condition): *Ice turns to water when it is warmed. Stop pulling those bushes to pieces! Our village only comes to life at weekends. The thief was at last brought to justice.* **8** (verb + 'to' + noun (phrase(1))/pronoun in which verb + 'to' is a compound(2) verb, with noun (phrase(1))/pronoun as its object): *Listen to me!* (Sometimes the pattern is verb + 'to' + noun (phrase(1))/pronoun + 'for' + noun (phrase(1))/pronoun (which shows the reason for the action of the verb)): *They always look to us for help.* **9** (introducing the person/animal/thing addressed): *Did you speak to her? Greetings to you all!* **10** (introducing the person/animal/thing receiving s.t that is given, offered or used): *Give this to your teacher. This shop delivers to its customers. Thanks to you, we are all right now. John is no trouble to us. Your umbrella has been very useful to me. He lacks the respect due to teachers. The sun does a lot of good to your body.* **11** (introducing s.o/s.t to which s.t belongs or with which it is connected, or to which it is stuck, tied etc): *Who does this house belong to? Where's the key to this door? Tie the dog to this post.* **12** before (a certain time): *It is ten minutes to five. How long is it to dinner?* Compare to¹. **13** until: *We work from 9 to 5. From beginning to end, I have enjoyed these holidays. To this day I haven't discovered where Alice lives* (I still do not know). *She was faithful to the last* (She never stopped being faithful). **14** (introducing s.o/s.t with which s.o/s.t is compared) as against; as compared with: *£50 a week is equal to £200 a month. His skill on the piano is nothing to his sister's. This restaurant is second to none. It is 10 to 1 that Emily will win.* **15** (number + 'to' + distance, weight etc) in every: *There are about 24 people to the square kilometre here. There are about 2.2 pounds to the kilo.* **16** (introducing s.t that is answered): *And what was her answer to that? I have no objection to your going too.* **17** (joining a word showing addition and the thing(s) to which the adding is done): *That will only add to our work.* **18** (noun + 'to' + noun) between ... and ...: *He is 50 to 60 years old.* **19** (introducing the person/animal/thing to which the word(s) just before 'to' is/are limited): *I am not used to such work. Unknown to my mother, my brother left the house at midnight. What is your decision with reference to this letter? This holiday means a great deal to us. He is a stranger to London. Our street is at right angles to the main road.* **20** in honour of; to show respect for: *Let us drink to the happy* couple(3)*! They built a temple to their gods.* **21** (introducing s.t one has a right or claim to have): *He gave up his claim to the money in return for a field.* **22** for the purpose of: *Several people came to the man's help when he fell through the ice.* **23** causing or resulting in (s.t): *He rocked the baby to sleep. To my great surprise, Peter arrived early.* **24** (introducing a high level of s.t): *We enjoyed our holiday to the full* (completely). *After the rain we were wet to the skin* (right down to our skins). **25** (combining extent and result): *After the meal we were all full to bursting. He loves her to distraction*(1). **26** according to; to the extent of: *To the best of my knowledge, he isn't married.* **27** suitable to; in accordance with: *I found the film very true to life.* For noun/verb/adj/adv + 'to' + noun (phrase(1))/pronoun, e.g *in relation to s.o, answer to s.o/s.t, jump to one's feet,* ⇨ the noun/ verb/adj/adv; for 'to' + noun, e.g *to date,* ⇨ the noun.

to³ (strong form /tuː/, weak form before a vowel(1) sound or in final position /tʊ/, weak form before a consonant(3) sound /tə/) **1** (used before an infinitive (phrase(1)): *my wish to help you; something nice to eat; pleased to meet you; cool enough to drink; too heavy to lift; a pleasant place to have a picnic. It is easy (for us) to talk but more difficult to act. To make mistakes is natural. Do you know what to do next?* (Sometimes 'to' forms part of a tense² of a verb, e.g 'I am to leave tomorrow.' 'He is going to help us.' 'You ought to be more careful.' 'I used to live in Turkey.') **2** (taking the place of 'to' + infinitive(1) phrase(1) to avoid repetition): *I asked him to go but he refused to* (i.e. he refused to go). **(so as) to**, **(in order) to**, **do s.t** for the purpose of doing s.t: *He has come to see you. To be honest, I forgot to post your letter. I came early (so as) to clean my office. I have to stop here (in order) to get some petrol.*

to-do /tə'duː/ *c.n* (*informal*) state of confusion; upset; fuss(1): *There was such a to-do in the house while the workmen were there.*

toad /təʊd/ *c.n* kind of creature that is like a frog but spends most of its time on land: *A toad only goes into water to* breed(3).

‚toad-in-the-'hole *c/u.n* sausage(s) that has/ have been covered with a mixture of flour, eggs and milk and then baked.

'toad‚stool *c.n* kind of plant that is like a mushroom(1) but some kinds are poisonous. ⇨ fungus.

toast¹ /təʊst/ *u.n* **1** slice(s) of bread that has/ have been toasted¹(2).

▷ *tr.v* **2** make (bread etc) brown and hard by putting it near s.t very hot, e.g in front of a fire or into a toaster.

'toaster *c.n* device for toasting¹(2) bread using electricity.

toast² /təʊst/ *n* **1** *c.n* fact or action of toasting²(3) (s.o/s.t). **2** *def.n* person or thing that is toasted²(3). **drink a toast to s.o/s.t** drink s.t in honour of s.o/s.t, to wish her/him/it success etc. **propose a toast to s.o/s.t** ask people to drink a toast to s.o/s.t. **the toast of s.o/s.t** the person, animal etc that is being praised in a certain place: *After the race, our horse was the toast of the town.*

▷ *tr.v* **3** (ask people to) drink s.t in honour of (s.o/ s.t), to wish (s.o/s.t) success etc: *At the party after a wedding it is usual to toast the* bride *and* bridegroom. **toast s.o/s.t in s.t** drink s.t, e.g wine, in order to toast²(3) s.o.

'toast‚master *c.n* person at a big dinner etc party who introduces the speakers and says the toasts²(1) in a loud voice.

tobacco /tə'bækəʊ/ *n* (also *attrib*) **1** *u.n* plant with big leaves used for making cigarettes etc. **2** *c/u.n* (one kind of) product made from the leaves of this plant and used in cigarettes etc.

tobacconist /tə'bækənɪst/ *c.n* **1** person who sells cigarettes etc. **2** (also **to'bacconist's**) shop that sells cigarettes etc.

toboggan /tə'bɒgən/ *c.n* **1** small vehicle without wheels made for sliding down slopes that are covered with snow, usu for pleasure.

▷ *intr.v* **2** use a toboggan(1).

to'bogganing *u.n* sport of riding down snow-covered slopes in a toboggan(1). **go tobogganing** do this sport.

tod /tɒd/ **on one's tod** (*slang*) alone; with no one else there.

today /tə'deɪ/ *adv* **1** on the day on which one is speaking or writing this: *Let's go for a walk today.* **2** now; in the times in which we are living: *There is much less poverty in England today than when I was a child.* Compare nowadays.

▷ *unique n* **3** the day on which one is speaking or writing this: *Today is the first day of spring.* **4** (often *of* —) the times in which we are living now: *The clothes of today are not made to last.*

toddle /'tɒdl/ *intr.v* walk unsteadily like a very small child does.

'toddler *c.n* very small child who cannot walk steadily yet.

toddy /'tɒdɪ/ *c/u.n* (*pl -ies*) (example of a) drink made by mixing whisky(1) or brandy(1), sugar and hot water.

to-do ⇨ to³.

toe /təʊ/ *c.n* **1** one of the five parts like fingers on a person's foot. **2** part of a sock, shoe etc that goes over a person's toes(1). **on one's toes** (*fig*) ready and waiting to begin s.t. **tread on s.o's toes** (*fig*) do s.t that hurts s.o's feelings.

▷ *tr.v* (toes, toed) **3 toe the line** ⇨ line(*n*).

'toe‚cap *c.n* separate part of a shoe that is fixed over the front above the toes.

'toe‚hold *c.n* enough room to support oneself (e.g on a piece of rock when climbing a mountain) by having the toes of one foot on s.t: *She had only a toehold on the rock.* Compare foothold.

'toe‚nail *c.n* nail(1) on a toe.

toffee /'tɒfɪ/ *c/u.n* (one piece of a) sweet made from sugar, butter and water by boiling these until the mixture is hard, sticky and brown.

'toffee ‚apple *c.n* apple that has been covered with toffee before it goes hard.

'toffee-‚nosed *adj* (*derog; slang*) behaving as if one is very important; snobbish.

tog /tɒg/ *tr.v* (-gg-) **tog oneself/s.o out/up** (*informal*) dress (oneself/s.o) (to look like s.t or by putting on certain clothes).

togs *pl.n* (*informal*; becoming *old use*) clothes: *swimming togs.*

together /tə'geðə/ *adv* **1** with or to each other; in such a way as not to be apart or separated: *Mary and her parents are together at last. The animals collect together for warmth. Will you please join these wires together? Can you multiply 25 and 25 together?* **2** at the same time: *The rain and the earthquake* arrived *together.* **3** not taken separately but all in one: *India is much bigger than all the West European countries* (put) *together.* For verb + noun ((phrase(1))/pronoun + 'together', 'stick them together', ⇨ the verb. **all together** ⇨ all(*pron*). **close/near together** near each other. **fasten s.t together** ⇨ fasten. **together with s.o/ s.t** with s.o/s.t: *We went home together with our friends.*

to'getherness *u.n* (fact of) friendly feeling of wanting to be with another person or other people.

toggle /'tɒgl/ *c.n* small piece of plastic(3), wood etc sewn to a coat and used instead of a button.

toil /tɔɪl/ *u.n* (*formal*; *literary*) **1** (usu hard and/or unpleasant) work.
▷ *intr.v* **2** work (usu hard and/or unpleasantly).

toilet /'tɔɪlɪt/ *n* **1** *c.n* lavatory; (room in which there is a) device where one empties one's bowels(1) and/or bladder(1). **2** *u.n* (*formal*) act of washing, dressing, doing one's hair etc. **go to the toilet** empty one's bowels(1) and/or bladder(1).

'toilet ˌpaper *u.n* paper used for wiping oneself after going to the toilet.

'toilet ˌroll *c.n* roll of toilet paper.

'toilet ˌtrain *tr.v* train (a child) to use a toilet(1) when he/she wants to empty his/her bowels(1) and/or bladder(1).

'toiletries *pl.n* things one uses to wash oneself, one's hair etc.

'toiletry *attrib.adj* that sells toiletries.

toings and froings ⇒ to¹.

token /'təʊkən/ *attrib.adj* **1** not serious; done only to show that s.t exists without doing it fully or properly: *There was only token resistance to the enemy's advance.*
▷ *c.n* **2** (often (as) a — of s.t) sign (showing that s.t does in fact exist): *Please accept this small gift as a token of my thanks.* **3** (often (as) a — of s.t) thing that helps one remember (s.t): *I kept the vase as a token of a wonderful holiday.* **4** card or piece of metal, plastic(3) etc that one can exchange for s.t else of a certain value: *a book token*; *a gift token.* **by the same token** in the same way. **in token of s.t** as a token(2,3) of s.t.

'token ˌpayment *c.n* **1** sum of money paid which is not the whole amount owed but is intended as a sign that the rest will be paid. **2** small payment made to show good will rather than as a full payment for what one is getting.

'token ˌstrike *c.n* strike(1) that is intended as a warning rather than to cause serious trouble.

told /təʊld/ *p.t* of tell.

tolerate /'tɒləˌreɪt/ *tr.v* be willing or able to suffer (s.o/s.t unpleasant) without getting angry or objecting etc.

tolerable /'tɒlərəbl/ *adj* (*formal*) Opposite intolerable. **1** that can be tolerated: *a tolerable noise level.* **2** reasonable; not too great: *live in tolerable comfort.*

'tolerably *adv.*

tolerance /'tɒlərəns/ *c/u.n* ability or willingness to tolerate (s.o/s.t). Opposite intolerance.

'tolerant *adj* willing or able to tolerate s.o/s.t. Opposite intolerant.

'tolerantly *adv.*

toleration /ˌtɒləˈreɪʃən/ *u.n* act or fact of allowing other opinions: *religious toleration.*

toll¹ /təʊl/ *c.n* **1** tax that one pays when one uses s.t, e.g a road or a bridge. **2** unpleasant things that one suffers as a result of s.t: *The death toll on our roads caused by people who drink and drive is becoming huge.*

'tollˌgate *c.n* gate across a road at which tolls¹(1) are collected.

toll² /təʊl/ *c.n* **1** sound of tolling²(2).
▷ *v* **2** *tr/intr.v* (cause (a bell) to) make a series of slow ringing sounds. **3** *tr.v* tell people (the time etc) by tolling²(2): *As the church bell tolled six, the shops began to close.*

tomato /təˈmɑːtəʊ/ *n* (*pl* -es) **1** *c.n* kind of vegetable that is red when it is ripe and can be cooked or eaten raw. **2** *u.n* (also *attrib*) amount of this vegetable when it has been cut up and/or cooked: *tomato sauce.* **3** *c.n* (also *attrib*) plant on which this vegetable grows.

tomb /tuːm/ *c.n* grave; thing built on top of a grave, usu of stone, on which the name etc of the dead person is cut.

'tombˌstone *c.n* stone which is put at the head of a grave.

tombola /tɒmˈbəʊlə/ *u.n* kind of game in which everyone gets a ticket and then tickets with certain numbers win prizes.

tomboy /'tɒmˌbɔɪ/ *c.n* girl who behaves as a boy is thought to behave, i.e roughly and noisily.

'tomˌboyish *adj* like a tomboy.

tombstone ⇒ tomb.

tomcat /'tɒmˌkæt/ *c.n* male cat.

tome /təʊm/ *c.n* (*formal*) big book.

tomfoolery /ˌtɒmˈfuːləri/ *c/u.n* (*pl* -ies) (example of) foolish behaviour.

tomorrow /təˈmɒrəʊ/ *adv* **1** on or during the next day after today: *I promise to do it tomorrow.* **tomorrow afternoon/evening/morning** the afternoon, evening or morning of tomorrow.
▷ *n* **2** *unique n* the day after today: *Tomorrow will be Tuesday.* **3** *c/unique n* the future: *all our tomorrows. Tomorrow is another day.*

ton /tʌn/ *c.n* **1** measure of weight that is divided into 2240 pounds in Britain (called *a long ton*) and divided into 2000 pounds in the US (called *a short ton*). ⇒ tonne. **2** (*technical*) unit for measuring the size of ships that equals 100 cubic(2) feet. **3** (*technical*) unit for measuring how much a ship can carry that equals 40 cubic(2) feet. **by the ton** measured by one ton(1) at a time. **come down (on s.o) like a ton of bricks** (*informal*) scold or attack s.o suddenly and violently. **weigh a ton** (*fig*) weigh a lot.

tonnage /'tʌnɪdʒ/ *c/u.n* (*technical*) **1** amount of tons(2) (of a ship). **2** amount of tons(3) (of a ship. **3** total amount of tons(2,3) (of a number of ships, e.g of a country's whole merchant navy or of the ships passing through a canal in one year). **4** amount one has to pay for having each ton(1) of s.t carried, e.g in a train.

tonne /tʌn/ *c.n* measure of weight that is divided into 1000 kilograms. ⇒ ton(1).

'tonˌup *attrib.adj* who is in the habit of driving or riding at 100 miles an hour and more.

tone /təʊn/ *n* **1** *c.n* sound of s.t when one is interested in its quality, pitch¹(4) etc. **2** *c.n* abilities of a musical instrument, person's voice etc to produce tones(1): *That violin has a beautiful tone.* **3** *c.n* way in which one says s.t, esp to show one's feelings: *She spoke in a quiet, sincere tone. I could tell by the tone of his voice that he was very tired.* **4** *c.n* (*music*) one of five of the seven units into which an octave(1) is divided (the other two are called semi tones). **5** *c.n* way in which the voice rises or falls in pitch¹(4), or remains on the same pitch¹(4), in speaking but not singing. **6** *c.n* shade(4) (of a colour); (one) variety of a colour that is different from other varieties because it is darker or lighter, or has a little of another colour in it: *We painted the room in tones of yellow.* ⇨ highlight(3). **7** *u.n* (often *bring down*, *raise*, *the —* *(of s.t)*) general spirit, way of behaving etc of a group of people. **8** *u.n* healthy condition of one's body or of part of it: *His* muscle(1) *tone is poor because he does not take enough exercise.*

▷ *tr/intr.v* **9 tone s.t down** make s.t less violent or rude etc: *Before you send that letter you had better tone the language down a little.* **tone (s.t) in (with s.t)** (cause (s.t) to) match (s.t), usu in colour: *I want some curtains that will tone in with these walls.*

'**tonal** *adj* of or referring to tone(1–6,8).

-toned *adj* having the kind of tone(1,2) or the number of tones(1,2,6) shown in the first part of the word: *a gentle-toned voice*; *a two-toned horn on a car.*

,**tone-'deaf** *adj* unable to distinguish between different levels of pitch'(4).

'**toneless** *adj* without (enough) emotion, brightness etc; dull: *a toneless voice.*

'**tonelessly** *adv.* '**tonelessness** *u.n.*

tongs /tɒŋz/ *pl.n* (often *a pair of —*) instrument with two arms joined at one end, used for picking things up without dirtying them or one's hands: *sugar tongs.* **hammer and tongs** ⇨ hammer(*n*).

tongue /tʌŋ/ *n* **1** *c.n* long organ in one's mouth which one can move about and with which one licks, tastes and talks. **2** *c/u.n* (also *attrib*) tongue(1) from an animal used as food: *tongue sandwiches.* **3** *c.n* thing that looks like a tongue(1), e.g the piece of leather in a shoe that is between the shoelaces and the top of one's foot. **4** *c.n* spoken language. **get one's tongue (a)round s.t** (*fig*; *informal*) manage to pronounce s.t difficult. **hold one's tongue** (*fig*; *informal*) keep quiet; stop talking. **keep a civil tongue (in one's head)** not speak rudely. **mind one's tongue** be careful about what one says. **mother tongue** ⇨ mother. **on the tip of one's tongue** ⇨ tip'(*n*). **set tongues wagging** behave in a way that makes people talk about one (usu saying unpleasant things). **tongue in cheek**; **with one's tongue in one's cheek** (*fig*) not speaking seriously; jokingly.

-tongued *adj* **1** having a tongue(1) like the first part of the word: *white-tongued.* **2** speaking in the way of the first part of the word: *a sharp-tongued person.*

'**tongue-,tied** *adj* unable to speak because one is shy, nervous etc.

'**tongue ,twister** *c.n* word or group of words that it is difficult to pronounce without a mistake when one speaks quickly, e.g 'She sells seashells on the seashore'.

tonic¹ /'tɒnɪk/ *adj* **1** (*formal*) that acts as a tonic'(2,3): *the tonic effects of a warm day in the garden.*

▷ *n* **2** *c/u.n* kind of medicine that is intended to make people stronger. **3** *c.n* thing that helps to make people healthier, stronger or more cheerful: *Our holiday was a real tonic for us.* **4** *u.n* = tonic water.

'**tonic ,water** *u.n* kind of fizzy bitter-sweet liquid that is often added to gin' etc to give it a different taste and to make it less strong.

tonic² /'tɒnɪk/ *adj* **1** (*music*) of or referring to the tonic²(2).

▷ *def.n* **2** (*music*) first note of an octave(1).

tonight /tə'naɪt/ *adv* **1** on or during the night following the day on which one is speaking or writing this: *I'm going to the* disco *tonight.* **2** on the night on which one is speaking or writing this: *It's cold tonight, isn't it?*

▷ *unique n* **3** night following the day on which one is speaking or writing this: *Tonight will be cold, they say.* **4** night on which one is speaking or writing this: *I've been looking forward to tonight's party for weeks, and now it's nearly over.*

tonnage, tonne ⇨ ton.

tonsil /'tɒnsɪl/ *c.n* one of two small glands at the back of the mouth that protect the throat from infection.

tonsilitis /,tɒnsɪ'laɪtɪs/ *u.n* inflammation of the tonsils.

ton-up ⇨ ton.

too /tuː/ *adv* **1** also; in addition; as well: *Is your brother at home too? I too have feelings, you know! In these countries, too, there are very high mountains.* (Notice that 'too' can only come at the end of the clause(1) or after the first phrase(1) (or word if there is not a phrase at the beginning).) **2** (often *— big*, *quickly* etc *for s.o/s.t (to do s.t)*) more than is good or suitable: *People who drive too quickly on this road often have accidents. John thinks he is far too old/much too fat. It's too big an apple for him to eat. He ran too fast for the policeman to catch him.* **not too bad/badly** etc really quite good, well etc: 'How are you feeling today?' 'Not too bad, thank you.' **only too glad/happy** etc really very glad etc: *I shall be only too willing to help.* **rather too small**, **quickly** etc a little too small etc. **too much of a fool** etc **to understand** etc so foolish etc that he/she/it cannot understand etc. **too much so** too much of that. **too right** (*slang*) you are right.

took /tʊk/ *p.t* of take.

tool /tuːl/ *c.n* **1** instrument or device that is used to do a job such as cutting, digging, hitting nails, pulling out nails etc. **2** (*fig*) person who is forced to do what s.o else wants her/him to do: *Eric is not a bad man but he has become the tool of evil people.* **down tools** stop work, usu because one is going on strike(1). **machine-tool** ⇨ machine.

▷ *tr.v* **3** use a tool to do s.t to (s.t), esp to draw pictures on leather. **tool (s.o/s.t) up** get (s.o/ s.t) ready for production by giving her/him/ it the tools that are needed: *Our factory is just tooling up and will start production in June.*

toot /tuːt/ *c.n* **1** one sound of tooting(2).

▷ *tr/intr.v* **2** (cause (s.t, e.g a car horn) to) make one or more short sounds showing that one wants s.o else to get out of the way etc: *As soon as the lights change the drivers begin to toot their horns.*

tooth /tuːθ/ *c.n* (*pl* teeth /tiːθ/) **1** one of the set of hard white things like bones that grow in one's jaws and are used for biting and chewing things. **2** thing like a tooth(1) on a saw, comb or some parts of a machine, where they are made to fit into other teeth so that one part of the machine can drive another. **(fight) tooth and nail (for s.o/s.t)** (*fig*) (fight) very violently (for s.o/s.t). **long in the tooth** (*fig*, *informal*) (of a person) old (and therefore experienced).

teeth *pl.n* **1** ⇨ tooth. **2** (*fig*; *informal*) strength and power: *These laws have no teeth because there is nothing the police can do about people who break them.* **armed to the teeth** (*fig*) having many weapons. ***bare one's teeth*** (of a dog etc) show one's teeth by pulling back one's lips, usu as a threat. **buck teeth** ⇒ buck[1]. ***canine tooth*** ⇒ canine. ***cast/throw s.t in s.o's teeth*** (*fig*) blame s.o rudely for s.t. ***cut one's teeth*** grow one's teeth when a baby. ***cut one's teeth on s.t*** (*fig*) gain experience by doing s.t for the first time: *Lesley cut her political teeth by giving a speech at the meeting.* ***escape by the skin of one's teeth*** (*fig*) only just escape. ***false teeth*** teeth that are not real but are made by a dentist to replace one's own. ***get one's teeth into s.t*** (*fig*) start doing s.t really strongly and with determination. ***grit one's teeth*** ⇒ grit. ***in the teeth of s.t*** against s.t strong and/or dangerous. ***a kick in the teeth*** ⇒ kick(*n*). ***lie through one's teeth*** tell obvious lies without caring. ***set s.o's teeth on edge*** **(a)** (of lemon juice etc) make one's teeth feel unpleasantly sensitive. **(b)** (*fig*) make one feel irritable or uncomfortable. ***show one's teeth*** (*fig*) behave, talk etc in a threatening way.

teethe /tiːð/ *intr.v* (of babies) grow teeth.

'teething ,troubles *pl.n* (*fig*) troubles one has with s.t new until it is operating properly.

'tooth,ache *c/u.n* pain in one or more of one's teeth: *I've got (a) toothache.*

'tooth,brush *c.n* brush made for cleaning one's teeth.

-toothed *adj* having teeth like the first part of the word or having as many teeth as the number in the first part of the word: *long-toothed.*

'toothless *adj* **1** having no teeth(1) (left). **2** (*fig*) having no teeth(2).

'tooth,paste *u.n* paste used for cleaning one's teeth: *a tube of toothpaste.*

'tooth,pick *c.n* thin stick of wood, plastic(3) etc used for cleaning between one's teeth.

'tooth ,powder *u.n* powder used for cleaning one's teeth.

tootle /'tuːtl/ *c.n* **1** noise made by tootling(2): *give a tootle on a car horn.*
▷ *tr/intr.v* **2** toot(1) (a car horn etc) for some time but not very loudly. **tootle along/off** etc (*informal*) move along etc in a car etc without hurrying.

top[1] /tɒp/ *attrib.adj* **1** of, referring to, at, the highest point or place; highest in rank, position, standard etc: *I'm in the top class in our school. He is the top lawyer in our town. My room is on the top floor. Who got the top marks in the examination? Is that* record[1](1) *in the top twenty?*
▷ *n* (often — of s.t) **2** *c/def.n* highest point or place (on/in s.t): *the top of a bottle/building; the tops of the mountains; a hill/mountain top.* **3** *c/def.n* upper surface (of s.t): *a desk/table top; the top of a box.* **4** *c/def.n* highest rank, position etc: *You are clever so if you work hard you should get to the top (of your* profession(2)) *by the time you are 30.* **5** *c/def.n* cover, often one that is screwed on to the top[1](2) of a bottle etc. **6** *c.n* piece of clothing worn on the upper part of one's body: *Here's my* pyjama *bottom but where's the top?* **blow one's top** (*informal*) become very angry. **from top to bottom** the whole way, starting at the highest level and going down to the lowest. **get on top of s.o** (*informal*) be too difficult for s.o so that he/she becomes tired, nervous etc. **get on top of s.t** (*informal*) manage to master s.t, e.g a job one was finding difficult. **on top** in the highest

position in s.t. **on top form** ⇒ form(*n*). **on top of s.t** (*fig*) in addition to s.t; as well as s.t: *He has a headache and on top of that he feels he's going to be sick.* **on top of the world** feeling very cheerful. (**shout** etc) **at the top of one's voice** (shout etc) as loudly as one can. **thin on top** ⇒ thin(*adj*). **work one's way to the top** get to the top(4) stage by stage.
▷ *tr.v* (-pp-) **7** reach the top(2) of (a slope). **8** give, make, a top(2) for (s.t): *The house was topped by a tall chimney.* **9** cut the top off (a vegetable etc) to prepare it for eating etc. **10** be more or better than (s.t): *Our speed topped 100 miles an hour in some places.* **11** tell a better (joke, story etc) than s.o else: *I've read every Dickens novel so top that!* **top and tail s.t** cut the top and bottom off vegetables, e.g carrots. **top the bill** be the most important performer in a show. (**and**) **to top it all** ... and this is even more important...: *It rained all through our picnic and to top it all Jim fell into the river.* **top s.o up** (**with s.t**) fill s.o's glass (with s.t, e.g beer). **top s.t out** have a special ceremony at the end of s.t, e.g the building of a new school. ⇒ topping-out. **top s.t up** (**with s.t**) fill s.t to the top(2) (with s.t).

,top 'brass *def/def.pl.n* (*slang*) most important people in a group, e.g the generals in an army.

'top,coat *c.n* **1** = overcoat. **2** *c/u.n* final or last coat of paint put on s.t (e.g wood) that one is painting. ⇒ primer, undercoat.

,top 'dog *def/unique n* (*informal*) most important or successful person: *After a year of competition, Judy came out top dog.*

'top ,dressing *c.n* = dressing(2).

,top-'flight *attrib.adj* belonging to the highest level, rank etc of s.t: *a top-flight lawyer.*

,top 'gear *def/unique n* highest gear(1) of an engine.

,top 'hat *c.n* tall hat, sometimes made of black silk and sometimes of grey felt[2], used on formal occasions.

,top-'heavy *adj* with a top(2) that is too heavy so that the thing is likely to fall over: *a top-heavy boat.*

'topless *adj* **1** (of a woman) not wearing any clothes on the upper half of one's body. **2** (*attrib*) (of a piece of clothing) not covering any part of the upper half of one's body. **3** (*attrib*) (of a place) in which women can go about without any clothing on the upper part of their body: *a topless beach.*

'top,most *adj* highest in position, rank etc.

,top-'notch *adj* (*informal*) = top-flight.

'topper *c.n* (*informal*) = top hat.

'topping *c/u.n* covering (of s.t) put on food for decoration or to give a taste.

,topping-'out *u.n* (also *attrib*) ceremony when a building is finished: *a topping-out ceremony.*

tops *def.n* (*slang*) best: *For me, Clint Eastwood has always been the tops among film-stars.*

,top-'secret *adj* completely secret.

'top,side *u.n* meat from the upper part of the leg of an animal, considered to be very good.

'top,soil *u.n* top layer(1) of earth in a garden etc.

top[2] /tɒp/ *c.n* kind of toy that remains upright by spinning fast. **sleep like a top** sleep very well.

topaz /'təʊpæz/ *u/c.n* (also *attrib*) (piece of)

yellow transparent semi-precious stone, used in rings etc.

topcoat, top dog, top-flight, top gear, top hat, top-heavy ⇨ top[1].

topic /'topɪk/ c.n subject (in a conversation, report etc): *the main topic of conversation.*

'**topical** adj concerning s.t that is of interest to people now: *This magazine only prints articles of topical interest.*

topicality /ˌtopɪ'kælɪtɪ/ c/u.n fact of being, thing that is, topical.

'**topically** adv.

topless, topmost, top-notch ⇨ top[1].

topography /tə'pogrəfɪ/ u.n (*technical*) 1 character of a place giving all the details of the shape, height etc of the land. 2 science that describes and/or makes maps etc of the topography(1) of places.

to'**pographer** c.n person who does topography.

topographical /ˌtopə'græfɪkl/ adj of or referring to topography.

ˌtopo'**graphically** adv.

topper, topping ⇨ top[1].

topple /'topl/ tr/intr.v 1 (often — (s.o/s.t) over) (cause (s.o/s.t) to) become so unsteady that he/she/it falls (over): *The pile of bricks toppled over.* 2 (*fig*) (force a government) to) give up power, control: *The army tried to topple the government of the country.*

tops, top-secret, topside, topsoil ⇨ top[1].

topsy-turvy /ˌtopsɪ 'tɜːvɪ/ adj/adv all mixed up and confused.

tor /tɔː/ c.n small hill.

torch /tɔːtʃ/ c.n 1 electric light that one can carry about and switch on and off. 2 one or more pieces of wood etc which burn to give light.

'**torch,light** u.n (also *attrib*) (often by —) light given by torches(2): *a torchlight procession.*

tore /tɔː/ p.t of tear[1].

toreador /'torɪəˌdɔː/ c.n man who takes part in a bullfight, usu on a horse.

torment /'tɔːment/ c/u.n 1 thing that torments(3) s.o. 2 state of being tormented(3).

▷ tr.v /tɔː'ment/ 3 cause (s.o or an animal) pain, great sorrow or annoyance: *The picnic was spoilt by the flies that tormented us. Those boys torment their teacher mercilessly.*

tor'mentor c.n person who torments(3) s.o.

torn /tɔːn/ p.p of tear[1].

tornado /tɔː'neɪdəʊ/ c.n (pl -(e)s) very strong wind that spins round and round. Compare hurricane, typhoon.

torpedo /tɔː'piːdəʊ/ c.n (pl -es) 1 long device that is fired (usu from a submarine(2)) at ships so as to try to hit them under the water and sink them.

▷ tr.v (-es, -ed) 2 (try to) sink (a ship) with a torpedo(1). 3 (*fig*) (try to) destroy (s.t, e.g a plan).

torpid /'tɔːpɪd/ adj (*formal*) 1 weak and slow, sometimes because of laziness. 2 (of animals in a state of hibernation) unconscious.

tor'pidity u.n. '**torpidly** adv. '**torpidness** u.n.

torpor /'tɔːpə/ u.n.

torrent /'torənt/ c.n (often — of s.t) strong big flow (usu of water but sometimes also of strong language): *a torrent of rain; a torrent of abuse[1](1).*

in torrents very heavily: *The rain came down in torrents.*

torrential /tə'renʃəl/ adj flowing in torrents: *torrential rain.*

tor'rentially adv.

torrid /'torɪd/ adj (*formal*) very, usu unpleasantly, hot.

torso /'tɔːsəʊ/ c.n (pl -s) (sculpture(2) of the) body of a person except for her/his head, arms and legs.

tort /tɔːt/ c.n (*law*) wrong done to s.o which is a civil(3) matter, not a criminal one.

tortoise /'tɔːtəs/ c.n kind of animal that lives on the land and has a hard shell into which it can pull its head, legs and tail when it is afraid. Compare turtle.

'**tortoise,shell** n (also *attrib*) 1 u.n (part(s) of the) shell of a turtle or sometimes tortoise which is/are polished and used as a decoration or to make things: *a tortoiseshell comb.* 2 c.n (also *attrib*) cat that has fur of various colours: *a tortoiseshell cat.* 3 c.n kind of butterfly with brown and yellow markings.

tortuous /'tɔːtjʊəs/ adj (*formal*) 1 twisting a lot; winding (⇨ wind[2]): *a tortuous mountain road.* 2 dishonest; not saying or writing things at all simply: *a tortuous argument.*

'**tortuously** adv. '**tortuousness** u.n.

torture /'tɔːtʃə/ n 1 c.n great pain, either of the body or of the mind. 2 c/u.n act of causing such pain, often to punish s.o or to try to get information out of her/him. 3 c.n particular way of giving torture(2): *The worst torture is not to know what is going to be done to one.*

▷ tr.v 4 cause torture(1) to (s.o or an animal).

'**tortured** adj = tortuous(1).

'**torturer** c.n person who tortures(4) s.o.

Tory /'tɔːrɪ/ adj 1 belonging to, referring to, the Conservative Party in British politics.

▷ c.n (pl -ies) 2 person who belongs to this party.

'**Tory,ism** u.n ideas etc of this party.

toss /tos/ n 1 c.n (often — of s.t) example of tossing(1) (s.t): *a toss of a coin.* ⇨ toss(4). 2 sing/def.n (often the — of s.t) movement in a tossing(2) way (of s.t): *The toss of the waves soon made him sick.* **argue the toss** (*fig; informal*) object to s.t when it has already been decided (and can therefore not be changed). **lose/win the toss** lose/win as a result of throwing a coin. **take a toss** fall, usu off a horse.

▷ v 3 tr.v (often — s.t to s.o; — s.o s.t) throw (s.t) (to s.o), often in a careless way. 4 tr/intr.v (often — (s.o/s.t) about/around) (cause (s.o/s.t) to) move up and down: *We were tossing about in the waves. The waves tossed the little boat about.* 5 tr.v mix (salad(2) etc) (with a sauce etc) by lifting it and moving it about. 6 intr.v (often — (s.o) for s.t) (try to) decide who is to win (s.t) by tossing a coin (in competition with s.o). **toss and turn** move about in bed and not be able to keep still because one is worried or in pain. **toss s.t off** (*informal*) (a) drink s.t quickly. (b) produce s.t (e.g a report) quickly and without much work.

'**toss-,up** c.n (often a — between s.o/s.t and s.o/s.t) (*informal*) situation in which it is not more likely that either one side will win rather than the other, or that one thing will happen etc rather than the other: *'Are we going to get there in time or not?' 'I don't know; it's a toss-up.'*

tot[1] /tot/ c.n 1 (often tiny —) very small child.

2 (often — *of s.t*) small quantity (of a liquid, usu a strong alcoholic(1) one).

tot² /tɒt/ *tr/intr.v* (-*tt*-) **tot s.t up** add s.t up. **tot up to s.t** (of an amount) add up to s.t: *Her earnings this month tot up to £1000.*

total /'təʊtl/ *attrib.adj* **1** if one takes all of it/ them together; complete: *His total earnings last year were £15 000.*

▷ *c/def.n* **2** total(1) number or quantity (that is s.t): *Two weeks at £300 per week and three weeks at £200 per week make a total of £1200.* **in total** in all; taking everything together: *There were five tonnes of the stuff in total.*

▷ *tr.v* (-*ll*-, US -*l*-) **3** make or come to a total(2) of (s.t): *Our bill totalled £53.64.* **total s.t up** add all the parts of s.t together to reach a total(2).

totality /təʊ'tælɪtɪ/ *n* (*formal*) **1** *u.n* state or fact of being one complete whole. **2** *sing/def.n* (often the — *of s.t*) total(1) number or amount (of s.t).

'totally *adv.*

totalitarian /təʊˌtælɪ'teərɪən/ *adj* of or referring to a system of government in which one person or group of people have full power over everything. ⇒ dictator.

to,tali'taria,nism *u.n* this system of government.

totter /'tɒtə/ *intr.v* **1** lean to one side and then to the other so that one seems likely to fall: *When the earthquake started, several old trees tottered and then fell.* **2** move along unsteadily: *The old man got up and tottered off to bed.*

'tottery *attrib.adj* who/that totters(1): *a tottery old woman.*

toucan /'tuːkən/ *c.n* kind of bird that lives in hot countries and has a very big beak and usu bright feathers.

touch /tʌtʃ/ *n* **1** *def/u.n* one of our senses (taste, smell etc) that gives us information through the skin of our fingers etc: *This cloth feels rough to the touch.* **2** *c.n* act or way of touching(9,10) s.o/ s.t. **3** *c.n* gentle blow or movement: *This car just needs a touch of the brake to make it slow down.* ⇒ touch(11). **4** *c.n* feel of s.t when one touches it: *I love the silky touch of a baby's skin.* **5** *c.n* small part of s.t one is doing or making that gives it a special character, taste etc: *Thanking the teacher for something she did not do was a clever touch, wasn't it? This dish needs a touch more salt.* **6** *sing.n* special ability or skill in s.t: *When she hits a tennis ball, she has a surprisingly clever touch.* **7** *c.n* (often — *of s.t*) slight attack (of an illness, e.g a cold or flu). **8** *u.n* (often be in/go into —) (in games such as football) area outside the one within which the ball is in play. **be, get, keep, put s.o, in touch (with s.o/ s.t)** in contact(2) (with s.o/s.t) by writing letters, telephoning, visiting etc: *Do keep in touch — ring me sometimes.* **lose one's touch** stop being skilful or good at s.t: *She used to be a very good tennis player but she seems to be losing her touch now.* **lose touch (with s.o/s.t)** stop being in touch (with s.o/s.t). **out of touch (with s.o/s.t)** not, or no longer, in touch (with s.o/s.t). **put the finishing touches to s.t** add the last part, do one last act, to complete s.t well.

▷ *v* **9** *tr/intr.v* be in bodily contact(1) (with s.o/s.t); not be divided (from s.o/s.t) by any space: *The two balls were touching (each other).* **10** *tr/intr.v* come into bodily contact(1) (with s.t) intentionally: *You must not touch (those cakes)!* **11** *tr.v* hit or push (s.o/s.t) gently: *You just have to touch the brake and the car stops.* ⇒ touch(3). **12** *tr.v* (with 'not' and other negatives(6)) have any contact(1) with (s.o/s.t); put one's hand on (s.o/s.t); do anything one should not do to (s.o/ s.t): *'You've broken my glasses!' 'I didn't touch them!' 'What have you done to John?' 'I never touched him!' He promised he would never touch another drop of whisky(1). I think the cat isn't well; it hasn't touched its food for two days.* **13** *tr.v* (fig, usu with negatives(6) or in questions) (almost) equal (s.o/s.t) in s.t: *Mike can't touch Mary as an artist.* **14** *tr.v* (*formal*) concern (s.o/s.t); have to do with (s.o/s.t): *What I have to say now touches your sister more than it does you.* **15** *tr.v* (fig) make (s.o or s.t, e.g a person's heart) feel sad, sympathetic etc: *The sight of sick children touches me deeply.*

touch bottom ⇒ bottom(*n*).

touch down (esp of a plane) touch the ground for the first time when landing.

touch s.o for s.t (*informal*) borrow money from s.o: *Could I touch you for £5 till I get my pay tomorrow?*

touch s.t off do s.t that suddenly causes s.t to happen or to explode: *Her remarks touched off a violent argument.*

touch s.t up make some small additions or improvements to s.t, e.g a painting.

touch (up)on s.t (in a speech, letter etc) mention s.t; refer to s.t; deal with s.t.

,touch-and-'go *adj* (usu *pred*) dangerous; that might just as easily lead to failure as to success: *It was touch-and-go whether we'd catch our train.*

touched *pred.adj* **1** (often — *by s.t*) moved in one's feelings: *I was very touched by her kind words.* **2** (*informal*) a little mad.

'touchily *adv* in a touchy way.

'touchiness *u.n* fact of being touchy.

'touching *adj* that makes one touched(1). ⇒ touch(15).

'touch,line *c.n* one of the lines at the sides of a football etc field: *If the ball crosses the touchline, it goes into touch(8).*

'touch,stone *c.n* thing that is treated as the standard against which other things are judged; criterion.

'touch-,type *intr.v* (be able to) type on a typewriter or word-processor without having to look at the keys because one knows where each letter etc is by heart.

'touchy *adj* (-*ier*, -*iest*) **1** (*derog*) easily hurt in one's feelings; easily annoyed: *Don't be touchy — I was only joking!* **2** that can easily lead to trouble and that therefore needs to be treated carefully: *The situation in their family is very touchy at the moment.*

tough /tʌf/ *adj* **1** (of things one eats) hard to chew: *tough meat.* **2** difficult to cut or break: *a tough pair of shoes.* **3** difficult or hard to do: *a tough climb to the top of the mountain.* **4** strong; able to resist pain etc: *tough soldiers.* **5** not able to feel sympathy or not showing sympathy: *a tough teacher/manager.* **6** violent; badly behaved: *a tough gang(3) of children.* **7** (*informal*) (sometimes — *luck*) unfortunate; unlucky: *'My mother's ill again.' 'That's tough (luck)!'* (**as**) **tough as**

old boots very tough(1,2,4,5). **get tough with s.o** begin to treat s.o in a tough(5) way.

'**toughen** *tr/intr.v* (often — *s.o/s.t up*) (cause (s.o/s.t) to) become tough(er)(1–5).

'**toughly** *adv.* '**toughness** *u.n.*

toupee /'tu:peɪ/ *c.n* kind of wig made to cover only the top part of a man's head when it is bald(1).

tour /tʊə/ *c.n* **1** trip or journey during which one visits (several places): *a tour round/of the museum.* **2** length of time during which one has to do s.t (often as part of one's job), in a particular place or area: *a tour of duty in the Far East*; *a tour of six months in Scotland*; *the England team's tour in Australia.* **a guided tour (of s.w)** a tour(1) (of s.w) during which one has a guide to show one things and explain them. **on tour** doing a tour(2), sometimes as part of one's job.

▷ *tr/intr.v* **3** go on a tour(1): *We toured the museum.* **tour round s.w** tour(3) s.w.

'**tourism** *u.n.* activities of tourists and of the people who do things for them: *Tourism is one of the main industries of many countries.*

'**tourist** *c.n* **1** person who travels for pleasure. **2** member of a sports team which goes to another country to play official matches.

'**tourist class** *adj/adv* ('**tourist-class** when *attrib*) by the cheap class on a plane etc: *a tourist-class hotel. We always go to Italy tourist class.* Compare club class, economy class, first class(2).

tournament /'tʊənəmənt/ *c.n* knock-out(2) competition to find the best player, team etc: *an international tennis tournament.*

tourniquet /'tʊənɪkeɪ/ *c.n* device twisted round an arm or leg to stop a wound from bleeding.

tousled /'taʊzəld/ *adj* (usu of hair) not combed or brushed tidily.

tout /taʊt/ *c.n* **1** person who buys tickets for very popular entertainments and later sells them at a higher price to people who cannot get them in any other way: *a ticket tout.* **2** person who sells advice about horse races.

▷ *v* **3** *tr/intr.v* sell (tickets, advice etc) in these ways. **4** *intr.v* (often — *for s.t*) try to persuade people to buy s.t or to use one's services etc: *Guides were touting for business outside the castle.*

tow /təʊ/ *c.n* **1** act of pulling of a boat, car etc: *The man gave me a tow to the garage.* **(be) in tow (a)** (be) being towed(2): *The motorboat had a sailing-boat in tow.* **(b)** (*fig*) (be) behind one or in one's care: *The teacher had twenty children in tow.* **take s.o in tow** (*fig*) begin to look after or help s.o. **take s.t in tow** begin to tow(2) a boat, a car etc.

▷ *tr.v* **2** pull (a car, boat etc) behind one.

'**tow,line** *c.n* = towrope for towing a boat/ship.

'**tow,path** *c.n* path along which horses used to walk while they towed(2) a barge¹ on a canal etc.

'**tow,rope** *c.n* rope used for towing(2) a car, barge¹ etc.

towards /tə'wɔ:dz/ *prep* (also **to'ward**) **1** (sometimes *fig*) in the direction of: *He came towards us but then stopped. The village lies towards the west. Her face was towards me so I saw her clearly. He has a tendency towards laziness.* **2** (introducing the object of behaviour, feeling etc): *She behaves very well towards her*

teachers. *He never showed his feelings of love towards her.* **3** near, nearly as late as, (a time): *It gets cool here towards evening.* **4** in such a way as to help with (s.t): *Your mother is giving us £10 towards the cost of the party.*

towel /'taʊəl/ *c.n* **1** thing made of (usu thick) cloth used for drying oneself, a person or an animal after a wash, bath etc. **throw in the towel** (*fig*) stop trying to do something, e.g win a race, complete a job.

▷ *tr.v* (-ll-, US -l-) **2** (often — *s.o/s.t down*) dry or rub (s.o, an animal) with a towel.

'**towelling** *u.n* (US '**toweling**) *u.n* thick cloth from which towels are made.

tower /'taʊə/ *c.n* **1** tall (part of a) building, often part of a castle or church. **2** tall construction(2) made out of lengths of metal and usu used for sending radio, television etc signals. **a tower of strength (to s.o/s.t)** (*fig*) a person or thing that is very helpful (to s.o/s.t): *My boss was a tower of strength to me during my wife's illness.*

▷ *intr.v* (often — *above/over s.o/s.t*) **3** be very tall (compared with s.o/s.t): *The mountains towered above us.* **4** (*fig*) be much more clever, important etc (compared with s.o/s.t): *She towers over her fellow scientists.*

'**tower-,block** *c.n* tall block of offices, flats etc: *live in a tower-block.*

'**towering** *attrib.adj* **1** that towers(3). **2** (*fig*) very strong: *be in a towering temper with s.o.*

towline ⇒ tow.

town /taʊn/ *n* **1** *c.n* group of buildings (houses, offices, shops etc) which is bigger than a village. Compare city. **2** *def/unique n* part of a town(1) where (most of) the shops and offices are: *I'm going into (the) town today to shop.* **3** *unique n* town(1) that one considers the most important place in one's part of the country (in England this is often London): *I'm going up to town tomorrow to see my lawyer.* **4** *def.n* (living in) towns and cities rather than in the country and villages: *I prefer the town to the country.* **5** *def/def.pl.n* all the people who live in a particular town(1): *The town is/are in favour of the new rules about parking cars.* **go to town (a)** go to the town(2,3). **(b)** (*fig*; *informal*) behave without (much) control, e.g by spending a lot of money. **hit town** (*fig*; *informal*) arrive in town. **(out) on the town** (*fig*; *informal*) having a very enjoyable time, usu at night. **paint the town red** (*fig*; *informal*) go out on the town.

,**town 'clerk** *c.n* official who is a kind of secretary to the government of a town and who advises them on questions of law.

,**town 'council** *c/def/def.pl.n* elected representatives of the people of a town who are its government.

,**town 'crier** *c.n* (in history) person whose job was to go about the town shouting the latest news.

,**town 'hall** *c.n* building in which a town council meets and where the government of the town has its offices.

'**town ,house** *c.n* house in a town, sometimes the property of s.o who also has another house in the country.

'**towns,folk** *pl.n* people who live in a particular town or in towns in general: *townsfolk and country folk(1).*

'townsman *c.n* (*pl -men*) man who lives in a town.

'towns,people *pl.n* people who live in a town.

'towns,woman *c.n* (*pl -,women*) woman who lives in a town.

towpath, towrope ⇒ tow¹.

toxaemia /tɒkˈsiːmɪə/ *u.n* (US **toˈxemia**) (*technical*) state in which the blood has something poisonous in it.

toxic /ˈtɒksɪk/ *adj* (*technical*) **1** poisonous. Opposite non-toxic. **2** of or referring to poisons. **3** caused by one or more poisons.

toxicity /tɒkˈsɪsɪtɪ/ *u.n.*

toxicologist /ˌtɒksɪˈkɒlədʒɪst/ *c.n* (*technical*) person studying, or skilled in, with toxicology.

toxicology /ˌtɒksɪˈkɒlədʒɪ/ *u.n* science dealing with poisons.

toxin /ˈtɒksɪn/ *c.n* (*technical*) poison, esp one produced by bacteria and causing a particular disease.

toy /tɔɪ/ *c.n* (also *attrib*) **1** thing that children play with: *a toy train*. **2** kind of small dog: *a toy spaniel*.

▷ *v* **3 toy with s.t** (a) think about doing s.t but not very seriously: *I'm toying with the idea of going to work in Africa*. (b) play with s.t without thinking what one is doing: *Instead of eating, the child was toying with its food*.

'toy,shop *c.n* shop that sells toys(1).

Tpr *written abbr* Trooper.

tr *written abbr* (used in this dictionary) transitive(1).

trace /treɪs/ *n* **1** *c.n* (often — *of s.t*) very small amount (of s.t) (which is just enough to notice). **2** *c/u.n* thing left behind by s.o/s.t because of which one can tell that he/she/it was there: *The police could find no trace of the thieves*. **lose (all) trace (of s.o/s.t)** no longer know where s.o/s.t is, what is happening to her/him/it etc. **without trace** without leaving any trace(2) behind: *Mary has disappeared without trace*.

▷ *tr.v* **3** follow the traces(2) of (s.o/s.t): *The hunters traced the wounded animal to the place where it had died*. **4** follow (the history etc of s.o/s.t) through the past years etc. **5** find (s.t) by searching for the things that have happened to it: *The secretary tried to trace the letter but it had disappeared*. **6** copy (s.t) by putting transparent paper over it and then drawing what one can see through it. **trace s.t (back) (to s.t)** follow the history etc of a family etc back (to a certain date, place, event etc).

'traceable *adj* that can be traced(3–6).

'trace ,element *c.n* chemical substance that occurs in very small quantities in animals and plants and without which they cannot live as they should.

tracery /ˈtreɪsərɪ/ *c.n* (*pl -ies*) (example of a) way of decorating things, often windows in churches, by using lines that form patterns.

'tracing *c.n* drawing that has been made by tracing (⇒ trace(6)).

'tracing ,paper *u.n* transparent paper used for making tracings.

trachea /trəˈkiːə/ *c.n* (*medical*) = windpipe (⇒ wind¹).

tracing ⇒ trace.

track /træk/ *n* **1** *c.n* mark(s) made by s.o/s.t as he/she/it moves which can be seen (and followed) by others. (Notice that when there is more than one mark made by the same person etc, we usu talk of 'tracks'.) **2** *c.n* path that people have not made smooth. **3** *c/u.n* rails for a train etc: *a railway track*. **4** *c.n* course made for racing on: *a race track*. **5** *c.n* (also *fig*) line followed by s.o/s.t as he/she/it moves: *follow the track of a satellite(2). If you follow the same track for too long in your work, your products will soon be old-fashioned*. **6** *c.n* belt that goes round the wheels of a tank, some kinds of tractor etc so that they can go over rough or muddy ground easily. **7** *c.n* one of the parts of a recording on a disc(2) or tape(2). **8** *c.n* one of the bands on a tape(2) on which things can be recorded. **be stopped in one's tracks** (*fig*; *informal*) be suddenly stopped when one is not expecting to be. **cover (up) one's tracks** (*fig*) hide the traces(2) one has left in the hope that no one will know what one has done, where one is etc. **have a one-track/single-track mind** not be able or willing to think outside very narrow limits. **keep/lose track (of s.o/s.t)** manage/fail to continue following the track(s)(1) (of s.o/s.t). **make tracks** (*fig*; *informal*) (start to) leave or go away: *Well, it's nearly midnight, so I'd better be making tracks*. **off the beaten track** away from the places that most people go to or live in. **on s.o's track; on the track of s.o/s.t** following s.o/s.t's track(1,5), sometimes in order to try to catch her/him/it. **on the right/wrong track** (not) on successful lines(10). **stop in one's tracks** stop suddenly.

▷ *tr.v* **9** follow the track(s)(5) of (s.o/s.t). **track s.o/s.t down** find s.o/s.t by following her/his/its tracks(1,5).

'tracker *c.n* person who tracks(9) people, animals etc.

'track e,vent *c.n* event(2) in a sports meeting when one uses a track(4), e.g running but not jumping, throwing etc.

'tracking ,station *c.n* place from which the movements of space(3) satellites(2) etc are tracked(9).

'track,suit *c.n* warm clothing (loose trousers and a sweatshirt) covering the whole body and worn by athletes, people playing games etc.

'track,suited *adj* wearing a tracksuit.

tract /trækt/ *c.n* **1** area of land: *mountain tracts*. **2** part of the body of a person or animal that is made up of different kinds of organs but is used for one thing: *the digestive tract*. **3** (small) book, article in a newspaper etc, usu about religion or morals.

traction /ˈtrækʃən/ *u.n* **1** act of pulling s.t heavy over the ground etc. **2** kind of power used for doing this: *steam traction*. **3** friction(2) that stops s.t (e.g a wheel) from moving easily over s.t underneath it (e.g a rail). **4** (*medical*) (often *be in —*) pull on an arm, a leg etc to ease pressure on a nerve(1) or to help a broken bone to set etc.

tractor /ˈtræktə/ *c.n* kind of vehicle used on farms etc for pulling ploughs etc; it has big wheels with very thick tyres. **caterpillar tractor** ⇒ caterpillar.

trad /træd/ *adj* **1** (*informal*) traditional.

▷ *u.n* **2** (also *attrib*) traditional jazz.

trade /treɪd/ *n* **1** *u.n* activity of buying, selling and/or exchanging things: *trade between countries; international trade*. **2** *def.n* particular kind

of trade(1): *the tourist trade.* **3** *def/def.pl.n* people who have a particular trade(2): *You can only buy from this wholesaler if you are in the trade* (i.e if your job is selling that kind of product). **4** *c.n* particular kind of job, usu one needing a course of training. **by trade** as far as one's trade is concerned; *Mary is an electrical engineer by trade.* **do a good/roaring trade (in s.t)** sell, buy or exchange a lot etc (of s.t).
▷ *v* **5** *intr.v* (often — *in s.t*) carry on trade(1) (buying, selling or exchanging s.t): *We trade in postage stamps only.* **6** *tr.v* (often — *s.t for s.t*) do a trade(1) in s.t (exchanging it for s.t): *Would you be interested in trading your apples for our tomatoes?* **7** *intr.v* shop regularly (at a particular person's shop). **trade s.t in (for s.t)** give s.o s.t as part of the price one pays (for s.t one is buying): *I'm going to trade my old car in for a new one.* ⇒ trade-in. **trade (up) on s.t** (*fig*; *formal*) take unfair advantage of s.o's kindness, weakness etc to get s.t from her/him.
'trade ,gap *c.n* difference between what one gets by selling and what one has to pay for what one buys: *Japan has a big trade gap in its favour.*
'trade-,in *c.n* act of trading s.t in (for s.t).
'trade,mark *c.n* **1** mark, sign, name etc a company has registered(5) with the government which it puts on the things it makes and which cannot be used by any other company. **2** (*fig*) way of doing things that a person or animal uses so regularly that one can recognize her/him/it by it.
'trade ,name *c.n* name under which s.t is sold and by which buyers can recognize it.
'trade ,price *c/unique n* price at which s.t is sold wholesale(1) to people in the trade(3): *We can let you have the goods at trade price.*
'tradesman *c.n* (*pl -men*) **1** man who trades(5); shopkeeper. **2** man who has a trade(4).
'trades,people *pl.n* people who trade(5); shopkeepers.
,trades 'union *c.n* = trade union.
,Trades ,Union 'Congress *def.n* (*abbr TUC*) association of trade unions in Britain.
,trade 'union *c.n* (also — **'union**) union of workers which represents them in dealings with employers and the government.
,trade 'unio,nism *u.n* idea or practice of workers forming trade unions.
,trade 'unionist *c.n* person who belongs to a trade union.
'trading *u.n* (also *attrib*) act or business of trading (⇒ trade(5)).
'trading e,state *c.n* area of land with buildings on it, usu owned by the government and let to companies for factories, wholesale(1) trade etc.
'trading ,post *c.n* shop in an area where there are very few people living that sells supplies to hunters, farmers etc.
'trading ,stamp *c.n* = stamp(3).
tradition /trə'dɪʃən/ *n* **1** *u.n* group of ideas, habits etc that one generation(2) of people passes on to the next, and so on. **2** *u.n* fact or process(2) of passing on such ideas etc. **3** *c.n* one such idea etc: *It is a tradition in our family to all have Christmas together.*
traditional /trə'dɪʃənəl/ *adj* of or referring to (a) tradition.
tra'ditionalist *c.n* person who is in favour of following tradition(s).

tra'ditional ,jazz *u.n* (*informal trad*) kind of jazz(1) with a strong fast rhythm.
tra'ditionally *adv.*
traffic /'træfɪk/ *u.n* **1** moving about of people and/or vehicles in the streets etc, of ships etc on the sea, rivers etc, of planes from one airport to another etc. **2** people and vehicles etc who/ that form part of the traffic(1). **3** (often — *in s.t*) trade(1) (in s.t): *the traffic in the furs of rare animals.* **4** business of carrying people and goods which trains, planes, ships etc do: *goods traffic*; *passenger traffic.*
▷ *intr.v* (**-ck-**) **5** (often — *with s.o*) in s.t) trade(5) (with s.o) (in s.t, usu s.t bad): *trafficking in drugs(2).* ⇒ trafficker.
'traffic ,block *c.n* = traffic jam.
'traffic ,indi,cator *c.n* = indicator(1) (⇒ indicate).
'traffic ,island *c.n* raised place in the middle of a road where people can stand while waiting to cross the road.
'traffic ,jam *c.n* long line of vehicles waiting to move.
'traffic ,light/,signal *c.n* (often *pl*) red, amber(3) and/or green light(s) that tell(s) traffic to stop or go.
'traffic ,warden *c.n* official whose job is to see that vehicles are not parked in the wrong places or for longer than they are allowed, and who reports¹(3) ones that break these laws.
trafficator /'træfɪ,keɪtə/ *c.n* = traffic indicator.
'trafficker *c.n* (*derog*) (often — *in s.t*) person who traffics(5) (in s.t bad): *drug(2) traffickers.*
tragedy /'trædʒɪdɪ/ *n* (*pl -ies*) **1** *c.n* sad serious play, film etc. **2** *u.n* plays etc of this kind in general: *One does not see as much tragedy as comedy in the British theatre today.* **3** *u.n* kind of drama(1) that concerns such plays etc. **4** *c/ u.n* very sad happening: *Her death at the age of 21 was a real tragedy for the family.*
tragedian /trə'dʒiːdɪən/ *c.n* man who acts in or writes tragedies(1).
tragedienne /trə,dʒiːdɪ'en/ *c.n* woman who acts in or writes tragedies(1).
tragic /'trædʒɪk/ *adj* **1** of or referring to tragedy(3): *a tragic actor.* **2** very sad: *a tragic accident.*
'tragically *adv.*
,tragi'comedy *n* (*pl -ies*) **1** *c.n* play etc that is partly a tragedy(1) and partly a comedy(1). **2** *u.n* kind of drama(1) that concerns such plays.
trail /treɪl/ *c.n* **1** (often *on the* — *of s.o/s.t*) track(1) or line of smells left (by s.o/s.t). **2** track(2) that people or animals follow. **3** (often — *of s.t*) line (of people, animals, rubbish, smoke etc). **blaze a/the trail (for s.o/s.t)** (*fig*) do s.t that no one has done before (for s.o/s.t). **hard/hot on s.o's trail**; **hard/hot on the trail of s.o/s.t** trailing(4) s.o/s.t closely so that one is likely to catch her/ him/it very soon.
▷ *v* **4** *tr.v* follow (s.o/s.t) by finding her/his/its trail(1). **5** *tr/intr.v* (often — (s.o/s.t) *along* (*behind s.o/s.t*)) (cause (s.o/s.t) to) move (s.o/s.t), sometimes slowly and in a tired way and sometimes on the ground (behind one): *Be careful, your coat's trailing in the mud. The children trailed along behind their teacher.* **6** *intr.v* (of a plant etc) grow (and spread) along the ground.
'trailer *c.n* **1** vehicle that is pulled behind

another one. **2** short piece of a film shown in a cinema, on television etc to advertise it. **3** plant that trails(6).

train[1] /trein/ *n* **1** *c.n* railway engine and the carriage(s) and/or truck(s) it is pulling. **2** *c.n* (often — *of people*, *animals*, *cars* etc) (*formal*) procession or long line (of people etc). **3** *c.n* lower part of a long dress which lies on the ground. **4** *c/pl.n* people who an important person takes with her/him when she/he goes s.w to give advice, act as assistants(2) etc. **by train** in a train: *go/travel by train.* **train of s.t** events, ideas etc that follow each other: *a train of events.* **train of thought** the ideas that follow each other in s.o's mind.

train[2] /trein/ *v* **1** *tr.v* teach (s.o) (how etc) to do s.t that needs skill and experience rather than, or as well as, theoretical knowledge: *train him to be a doctor/teacher/footballer.* **2** *intr.v* (often — *as*, *for*, *to be*, *s.o/s.t*) receive training in such things: *train as, to be, a doctor; train for a teaching job.* **3** *intr.v* (often — *for s.t*) do what is necessary in order to become good (at s.t) (including doing exercises, eating the right foods, not smoking etc). **4** *tr.v* make (a plant) grow in the direction(s) one wants.
'trainable *adj* that can be trained[2](1): *Lions and tigers are surprisingly trainable.*
trained *adj* having had some training: *a trained nurse.* Opposite untrained.
trainee /treɪˈniː/ *c.n* (also *attrib*) person who is being trained[2](1): *a trainee manager.*
'trainer *c.n* **1** person who trains[2](1) people or animals. **2** = sneaker.
'training *u.n* act or fact of training (⇒ train[2]). **go into training** start to train[2](3). (**be**) **in training** (be) training (⇒ train[2](3)). (**be**) **out of training** (be) no longer fit because one has not been training (⇒ train[2](3)).

traipse /treips/ *intr.v* (usu — *along*) (*informal*) walk in a tired, often bored, way.

trait /trei/ *c.n* quality or characteristic(2) of s.o/ s.t that makes her/him/it different from others or particularly noticeable.

traitor /'treɪtə/ *c.n* (often — *to s.o/s.t*) (*derog*) person who is not faithful (to s.o/s.t); person who betrays(1,2) s.o/s.t. **turn traitor** become a traitor.
traitorous /'treɪtərəs/ *adj* (*formal*) behaving like a traitor; treacherous.
'traitorously *adv.*

trajectory /'trædʒɪktərɪ/ *c.n* (*pl -ies*) (often *the* — *of s.t*) (*technical*) arched line made by a bullet, a ball etc as it flies through the air.

tram /træm/ *c.n* passenger vehicle that runs along rails, usu in a town.
'tram,car *c.n* (one car of a) tram.
'tram,line *c.n* rail on which trams run.

tramp /træmp/ *c.n* **1** person who has no home or job and who wanders about (begging). ⇒ hobo. **2** ship that takes on goods anywhere it can and then takes them wherever they have to go; ship that does not have a regular schedule(2). **3** walk, usu a long hard one. **4** sound made by s.o walking heavily.
▷ *v* **5** *intr.v* walk heavily. **6** *tr.v* walk through/along (s.t, e.g the streets of a town), usu with some difficulty or tiringly.
'tramp ,steamer *c.n* = tramp(2).

trample /'træmpl/ *tr/intr.v* (often — *on s.o/s.t*; — *s.o/s.t down*) step on s.o/s.t heavily so that one crushes her/him/it. **trample s.o, an animal, to death** kill s.o, an animal by doing this.

trampoline /'træmpəˌliːn/ *c.n* device consisting of a cloth base with springs at the sides to stretch it tight, used by people to jump up and down on and do tricks in the air.

trance /trɑːns/ *c.n* state in which one is not conscious of what is going on around one, although one is not really asleep: *She was in a trance during the boring speech.*

tranquil /'træŋkwɪl/ *adj* quiet; peaceful; without any worries.
tranquillity /træŋˈkwɪlɪtɪ/ *u.n* (US **tran'quility**).
'tranquilly *adv.*
tranquillize, -ise /'træŋkwɪˌlaɪz/ *tr.v* (US **'tranqui,lize**) make (s.o, an animal) tranquil, usu with a tranquillizer.
'tranqui,lizer, -iser *c/u.n* (US **'tranqui,lizer**) drug(1.) that tranquillizes s.o, an animal.

transact /træn'zækt/ *tr.v* carry out, do, (a piece of business etc) successfully.
transaction /træn'zækʃən/ *n* **1** *c.n* thing that is transacted: *business transactions.* **2** *u.n* act of transacting a piece of business etc.
trans'actions *pl.n* (often — *of s.t*) written or printed reports of meetings (of a group).

transatlantic /ˌtrænzətˈlæntɪk/ *attrib.adj* **1** that crosses the Atlantic Ocean. **2** of, referring to or in a place or places that is/are on the other side of that ocean. **3** between people, countries etc on both sides of that ocean: *a transatlantic treaty.*

transcend /træn'send/ *tr.v* (*formal*) go further or higher than (s.t): *The wealth of some old kings transcended anything one could imagine.*
tran'scendence, tran'scendency *u.n* (*formal*) state or fact of transcending s.t.
transcendental /ˌtrænsen'dentl/ *adj* transcending what human beings can know, understand etc through their normal senses, knowledge etc.
,transcen,dental ,medi'tation *u.n* (*abbr TM*) meditation that is supposed to put one in direct touch with powers we cannot know through our normal senses.
,transcen'denta,lism *u.n* belief that one can learn about transcendental things by using the powers of one's mind.
,transcen'dentalist *c.n* person who believes in transcendentalism.
,transcen'dentally *adv.*
transcendently /træn'sendntlɪ/ *adv.*

transcontinental /ˌtrænz,kɒntɪ'nentl/ *attrib. adj* that goes across a continent(1): *a transcontinental bus service.*

transcribe /træn'skraɪb/ *tr.v* (often — *s.t from s.t*) *into s.t*) copy (s.t written or printed) (changing it into another form, sometimes into another language or into phonetics(2)).
transcript /'trænskrɪpt/ *c.n* (often — *of s.t*) **1** piece of writing or a printed piece that has been transcribed (from s.t). **2** written or printed copy (of s.t, e.g a speech s.o has made).
transcription /træn'skrɪpʃən/ *n* **1** *u.n* act of transcribing s.t. **2** *c.n* thing that has been transcribed.

transept /'trænsept/ *c.n* (in a church whose ground plan is in the shape of a cross) part that crosses the main length (the nave) of the church.

transfer /'trænsˌfɜː/ *n* **1** *c/u.n* (example of the) act of transferring(4–6) (s.o/s.t) (from s.o/s.t) (to s.o/s.t). **2** *c.n* person or thing who/that has (been) transferred(4–6). **3** *c.n* ticket that can be used on more than one train or bus, one after the other.
▷ *v* /træns'fɜː/ (*-rr-*) **4** *tr/intr.v* (cause (s.o/s.t) to) move (from one job, place, vehicle etc) (to another): *My employers want to transfer me to York. You have to transfer from the train to a bus here.* **5** *tr.v* take (s.t) away (from s.o) and give it (to s.o else). **6** *tr.v* take (a picture, s.t written etc) off one surface and put it on to another.
transferability /trænsˌfɜːrə'bɪlɪtɪ/ *u.n.*
trans'ferable *adj* that can be transferred(4,5) (from s.o/s.t) (to s.o/s.t). Opposite non-transferable.
transference /'trænsfərəns/ *u.n.* act of transferring(4–6) or fact of being transferred(4–6) (from s.o/s.t) (to s.o/s.t).
transfix /træns'fɪks/ *tr.v* **1** push a knife, sword etc through (s.o/s.t). **2** surprise or shock (s.o) so much that he/she cannot move.
transform /træns'fɔːm/ *tr.v* **transform s.o/s.t** (**from s.t**) (**into s.t**) change (s.o/s.t) (so that he/she/it stops being s.t) (and becomes s.t else): *The hall was transformed into a* magic(1) *cave for the party. A* caterpillar(1) *is transformed into a butterfly.*
trans'formable *adj* that can be transformed (from s.t) (into s.t).
transformation /ˌtrænsfə'meɪʃən/ *c/u.n* (example of the) act or fact of transforming (s.o/s.t) (from s.o/s.t) (into s.o/s.t).
trans'former *c.n* (*technical*) device for changing the voltage of electricity, e.g from the 220 volts provided by an electricity company to the 6 volts needed by a radio.
transfuse /træns'fjuːz/ *tr.v* take (blood) out of s.o and put it in s.o else.
transfusion /træns'fjuːʒən/ *c/u.n* (also **'blood trans'fusion**) (one example of) transfusing blood.
transgress /træns'gres/ *v* (*formal*) **1** *tr.v* go outside or beyond (s.t that is right or lawful): *transgress the laws of nature.* **2** *intr.v* sin(3); do s.t that is wrong or against the law.
transgression /træns'greʃən/ *c/u.n.*
transgressor /træns'gresə/ *c.n* (*formal*) person who transgresses.
tranship /træn'ʃɪp/ *tr.v* (*-pp-*) (also **trans'ship**) take s.o/s.t out of one ship or vehicle and put her/him/it into another.
tran'shipment, trans'shipment *u.n.*
transient /'trænzɪənt/ *adj* (*formal*) **1** lasting only a short time: *a transient pain.* **2** (of people or animals) staying in a place only a short time.
▷ *c.n* **3** person or animal who/that is transient(2).
'transience, 'transiency *u.n.*
transistor /træn'sɪstə/ *c.n* **1** (*technical*) small solid device that controls the flow of electricity in a radio etc. ⇔ microchip. **2** (also **tran,sistor 'radio**) radio that uses transistors(1).
transit /'trænsɪt/ *u.n* passing from one place to another. **in transit** (**from s.w**) (**to s.w**) (while) passing (from one place) (to another); not finishing one's journey at an airport etc but spending some time there while the plane refuels etc.

'transit ,camp *c.n* camp in which people stay for a short time when they are on their way from s.w to s.w.
transition /træn'sɪʃən/ *c/u.n* (example of the) changing or passing (of s.t) (from s.t) (to s.t): *The transition from school to university can sometimes be a difficult one.*
tran'sitional *adj* (usu *attrib*) that is in a changing state.
tran'sitionally *adv.*
transitorily /'trænsɪtərɪlɪ/ *adv* (*formal*) in a transitory way.
'transitoriness *u.n.* fact of being transitory.
transitory /'trænsɪtərɪ/ *adj* = transient(1,2).
transitive /'trænsɪtɪv/ *adj* **1** (*written abbr* tr) (*grammar*) (of a verb) taking a direct object: '*Enjoy' is a transitive verb.* Compare intransitive(1).
▷ *c.n* **2** (*written abbr* tr.v) transitive(1) verb.
translate /træns'leɪt/ *v* **1** *tr/intr.v* change (a spoken or written word or words) from one language into another: *The book was translated from English into French.* **2** *intr.v* be (able to be) translated(1): *English translates more easily into German than into Japanese.* **3** *tr.v* explain (s.t difficult or technical(2)) in simpler language: *Let me translate what the doctor has just said into ordinary English for you.* **4** *tr.v* (*formal*) move or transfer(4) s.o from one job, place etc to another.
trans'latable *adj* that can be translated(1,3).
translation /træns'leɪʃən/ *c/u.n* (example of) translating(1,3,4) (from one language, place) (into/to another). **in translation** not in the original language in which it was spoken or written but in a language into which it has been translated(1): *He has only read Shakespeare in translation, not in English.* **a rough translation** ⇒ rough(*n*).
translator /træns'leɪtə/ *c.n* person who translates(1) (s.t) (from one language) (into another language).
translucent /træns'luːsənt/ *adj* (*technical*) allowing light to pass through without actually being transparent.
trans'lucence, trans'lucency *u.n.*
transmit /trænz'mɪt/ *v* (*-tt-*) **1** *tr/intr.v* broadcast or send out (a radio programme etc) along wires or through the air. **2** *tr.v* (*formal*; *technical*) pass (information, energy(2), a disease etc) on from one person, place, part of a machine etc, to another. **3** *tr.v* (*technical*) allow (heat, electric current, sound etc) to pass through: *Rubber does not transmit electricity.*
transmission /trænz'mɪʃən/ *n* **1** *u.n* (*formal*; *technical*) act or fact of transmitting or of being transmitted. **2** *c.n* programme etc transmitted(1): *a television programme transmission.* **3** *c/def.n* (*technical*) part(s) of a car etc that transmit(s)(2) power from the engine to the wheels.
trans'mitter *c.n* (*technical*) device, person etc that transmits.
transoceanic /ˌtrænzˌəʊʃɪ'ænɪk/ *attrib.adj* that crosses an ocean: *a transoceanic airline.*
transparent /træns'pærənt/ *adj* **1** that one can see through: *Most glass is transparent.* **2** (*fig*) easy to understand. **3** (*fig*) obvious; impossible not to understand or notice: *a transparent lie.*
trans'parency *n* (*pl -ies*) **1** *u.n* fact or state

of being transparent. **2** *c.n* small piece of film(3) put in a frame for showing in a projector or viewer(2).

transpire /træn'spaɪə/ *v* **1** *intr.v* (*formal*) happen: *What transpired at your meeting with the boss?* **2** *tr/intr.v* (*technical*) (of a person, animal or plant) give off or produce (s.t, usu sweat or another liquid that is not needed) from one's pores¹ etc. *it transpires/transpired that . . .* (*formal*) it has become, became, known gradually that . . .: *He told us he could not come because he was ill but it transpires that he just wanted a holiday.*

transpiration /ˌtrænspɪ'reɪʃən/ *u.n* (*technical*) act or fact of transpiring(2).

transplant /'træns,plɑːnt/ *c.n* **1** thing that has been transplanted(3). **2** operation in which s.t is transplanted(3): *a heart transplant.*

▷ *tr.v* /træns'plɑːnt/ **3** remove s.o/s.t (from s.w) and take, move etc her/him/it (to s.w else).

transplantation /ˌtrænsplɑːn'teɪʃən/ *u.n.*

transport /'trænspɔːt/ *n* (also *attrib*) **1** *u.n* act of transporting(4) or of being transported (from s.w) (to s.w) (by ship, sea etc). **2** *u.n* means (vehicles, ships, planes etc) used to do this. **3** *c.n* ship or plane used to carry military personnel or supplies.

▷ *tr.v* /træns'pɔːt/ **4** carry or move (s.o/s.t) (from one place to another). **5** (*literary*) make (s.o) feel very happy, excited etc.

trans'portable *adj* that can be transported(4).

transportation /ˌtrænspɔː'teɪʃən/ *u.n* = transport(1).

'transport ˌcafé *c.n* small restaurant beside a road where lorry drivers etc can get cheap meals.

trans'porter *c.n* kind of long lorry that can carry several cars, or a long tank etc.

transpose /træns'pəʊz/ *tr.v* (*formal*) **1** do s.t to (two or more things) which changes their order or position relative(1) to each other: *If you transpose the letters in 'on', you get 'no'.* **2** (*music*) change the key(6) of (a piece of music) (into another key).

transposition /ˌtrænspə'zɪʃən/ *c/u.n.*

transship /træns'ʃɪp/ *tr.v* = tranship.

transverse /trænz'vɜːs/ *attrib.adj* (*technical*) that is (put) across: *a transverse beam in a ceiling.* Compare traverse¹(1).

trans'versely *adv.*

transvestism /trænz'vestɪzəm/ *u.n* practice of wearing, the wish to wear, clothes that the opposite sex usu wears.

transvestite /trænz'vestaɪt/ *c.n* (also *attrib*) person who wears, wants to wear, such clothes.

trap /træp/ *c.n* **1** device used for catching, and sometimes killing, animals: *a mouse trap; a fish trap.* **2** thing used to catch people who are not expecting it: *a speed trap to catch drivers who are driving faster than the speed allowed.* **3** thing like a box which opens at the start of a dog race to allow a dog to begin running at exactly the same time as the other dogs in the race. *keep your trap shut* (*slang*) don't speak. *set a trap (for, to catch, s.o/s.t)* prepare a trap(1,2) (to catch a person, animal). *shut your trap* (*slang*) stop talking.

▷ *v* (*-pp-*) **4** *tr/intr.v* catch (an animal) in a trap(1). **5** *tr.v* catch (a person) in a trap(2). **6** *tr.v* prevent

(s.t) from moving freely: *He tried to move his foot but it was trapped in the door.*

'trap,door *c.n* small door that covers a hole in the floor (esp of a stage in a theatre) or ceiling of a room etc.

'trapper *c.n* person who traps(1) animals.

trapeze /trə'piːz/ *c.n* short bar that hangs down from a rope at each end and is used to do acrobatics(2).

tra'peze ˌartist *c.n* person who performs on a trapeze.

trapezium /trə'piːzɪəm/ *c.n* (*pl -s* or, less usu, *trapezia* /trə'piːzɪə/) (US **'trape,zoid**) (*geometry*) figure that has two sides that are parallel(1) and two that are not.

trapezoid /'træpɪ,zɔɪd/ *c.n* (US **tra,pezium**) (*geometry*) figure that has four sides of which none is parallel(1) to another.

trapper ⇒ trap.

trappings /'træpɪŋz/ *pl.n* clothes, decorations etc usu worn to show one's position or job: *When Joe Davis was wearing all the trappings of a judge, I could hardly recognize him.*

trash /træʃ/ *n* **1** *u.n* rubbish; thing(s) that is/are so poor in quality that it is, or they are, not worth anything. **2** *u.n* (US) rubbish; garbage(1); things that one throws away. **3** *pl.n* (US) (*derog*) people who are of low quality or class.

'trash,can *c.n* (US) dustbin.

'trashiness *u.n* fact of being trashy.

'trashy *adj* (*-ier, -iest*) (*derog*) so poor in quality that he/she/it is not worth anything.

trauma /'trɔːmə/ *c.n* (*pl -s* or, less usu, *traumata* /'trɔːmətə/) (*medical*) **1** wound. **2** damage to one's mind caused by severe shock or by a wound to one's body.

traumatic /trɔː'mætɪk/ *adj* **1** (*medical*) of or referring to traumas. **2** causing severe shock or one's mind.

trau'matically *adv.*

travel /'trævl/ *u.n* **1** fact or act of travelling(2).

▷ *v* (*-ll-*, US *-l-*) **2** *intr.v* go from one place to another in a vehicle, ship or plane; make a journey or voyage. **3** *intr.v* (often — *at a certain speed*, — *a certain distance*) go, move, (at a certain speed, a certain distance): *We travelled 100 kilometres, at 50 kilometres an hour.* **4** *tr.v* travel(2) in (a place): *The man travelled America in his search for a place to live. travel light* carry very little luggage with one while travelling(2).

'travel ˌagency *c.n* shop or office that arranges travel, hotels etc for people.

'travel ˌagent *c.n* **1** person who owns or works in a travel agency. **2** (also **'travel ˌagent's**) shop or office of a travel agent(1).

'travel ˌbureau *c.n* = travel agency.

'travelled *attrib.adj* (US **'traveled**) **1** (often *well, widely* etc —) who has travelled (⇒ travel(1)) a lot etc. **2** along which a lot etc of people, vehicles etc travel(1): *the much travelled road to Delhi.*

'traveller *c.n* (US **'traveler**) person who makes journeys, voyages etc. *fellow traveller* ⇒ fellow.

'traveller's ˌcheque *c.n* (US **'traveler's ˌcheck**) cheque that one can buy from a bank and then use while travelling to buy foreign money, to pay hotel, restaurant and shop bills etc.

'travelling *attrib.adj* (US **'traveling**) that one

uses while one is travelling(2): *a travelling iron*(2).

'travelling com,panion *c.n* person who travels with one.

,travelling 'salesman *c.n* (*pl -men*) salesman who travels from one place to another selling things.

travelogue /'trævə,lɒg/ *c.n* (US **'trave,log**) film, lecture etc about travel, sometimes to persuade people to visit certain places.

'travels *pl.n* journey(s): *We met last year during my travels in Tibet.*

'travel,sick *adj* feeling sick because of the movement of the ship, plane or vehicle one is travelling in.

traverse /'trævɜːs/ *attrib.adj* **1** (*technical*) that crosses from one side of s.t to the other: *a traverse beam in the floor.* Compare transverse.

▷ *c.n* **2** (*technical*) thing that does this.

▷ *tr/intr.v* /trə'vɜːs/ **3** (*technical*) cross from one side of (s.t) to the other.

travesty /'trævɪstɪ/ *c.n* (*pl -ies*) (often — *of s.t*) completely false representation(2) (of s.t); thing that gives a completely false picture or account (of s.t): *a travesty of justice.*

trawl /trɔːl/ *c.n* **1** big net that a fishing-boat pulls along the bottom of the sea etc to catch fish.

▷ *intr.v* **2** (often — *for s.t*) use a trawl(1) (to try to catch s.t).

'trawler *c.n* fishing-boat that uses a trawl(1).

tray /treɪ/ *c.n* **1** flat piece of wood, plastic(3) etc on which one carries food, cups of coffee, plates etc. **2** (usu — *of s.t*) things carried on a tray: *a tray of medical supplies for an operation.* **3** thing like a tray(1) but with raised sides that is used for putting letters, files³(1) etc in. **in-tray** ⇨ in². **out-tray** ⇨ out.

'trayful *c.n* (usu — *of s.t*) = tray(2).

treachery /'tretʃərɪ/ *c/u.n* (*pl -ies*) (example of) being unfaithful or (of) being a traitor.

'treacherous *adj* behaving with treachery.

'treacherously *adv*.

treacle /'triːkl/ *u.n* kind of sweet sticky black liquid that is a by-product of sugar refining. ⇨ molasses.

'treacly *adj* (*-ier, -iest*) **1** thick and sticky like treacle: *treacly coffee.* **2** (*derog*; *fig*) (of a way of speaking) unpleasantly thick and trying too hard to be pleasant.

tread /tred/ *n* **1** *c.n* way of walking or sound made by s.t, e.g s.o's boots, when walking. **2** *c.n* one of the horizontal parts of a staircase or ladder on which one steps. **3** *c/u.n* parts on the surface of a tyre that stick out so that they help to stop a car etc from slipping.

▷ *v* (*p.t trod* /trɒd/, *p.p trodden* /'trɒdn/) **4** *intr.v* (usu — *on s.t*) step (on s.t) with one's foot or feet. **5** *tr.v* (often — *s.t down*) push (s.t) down with one's foot or feet. **6** *tr.v* (*formal*) walk along (a path etc). **tread on air** (*fig*) be so happy that one feels one is floating in the air. **tread s.t in(to s.t)** force s.t in(to s.t) by treading(4) on it: *Stop treading mud into our best carpet!* **tread on s.o's heels** ⇨ heel(*n*). **tread on s.o's toes** ⇨ toe(*n*). **tread water** ⇨ water(*n*).

treadle /'tredl/ *c.n* **1** device allowing one to turn a wheel by pushing s.t up and down with one's foot or feet: *the treadle of a sewing-machine.*

▷ *intr.v* **2** use a treadle(1).

treason /'triːzn/ *u.n* (crime of) being unfaithful to one's country, usu by working for its enemies. Compare treachery.

'treasonable *adj* of, referring to or showing treason.

'treasonably *adv*.

'treasonous *adj* = treasonable.

treasure /'treʒə/ *n* **1** *u.n* things that are very valuable: *The thieves buried their stolen treasure hoping to come back for it later.* **2** *c.n* thing that is very valuable or that one treasures(4). **3** *c.n* person who is very useful to one or whom one loves very much: *My secretary is a real treasure. Come and see what I've bought for you, my treasure.*

▷ *tr.v* **4** treat (s.t) as a treasure(2). **treasure s.t up** keep s.t carefully so that one can use or enjoy it later: *She treasured up all the useful facts that the old man spoke about.*

'treasure ,house *c.n* (often — *of s.t*) place that is full of treasures(2) (of a certain kind): *a treasure house of knowledge.*

'treasurer *c.n* (often — *of s.t*) person whose job is to look after the money (and accounts) (of a group of people).

'treasure ,trove *u.n* treasure(1), money etc found buried in the ground and not belonging to anyone.

'treasury *c.n* (*pl -ies*) **1** office whose job is to look after the money (and accounts) of a government. **2** (usu — *of s.t*) place that contains treasures(2) (in the form of s.t): *a treasury of famous paintings.* **3** *def/def.pl.n* (with capital **T**) British government treasury(1): *the Treasury is/are trying to limit losses.*

treat /triːt/ *c.n* **1** thing that one enjoys very much and that one gets as a special favour and not very often: *When I was a child, going to the cinema was such a treat.*

▷ *v* **2** *tr.v* (often — *s.o/s.t well* etc; — *s.o/s.t as/like s.t*) behave towards or use (s.o/s.t) in a certain way: *Don't let your boss treat you as a servant.* ⇨ ill-treat. **3** *tr.v* (*medical*) try to make (a person who is ill or an illness) better by using medicines etc. **4** *tr.v* (often — *s.t with s.t*) do s.t to (s.t) in order to change it in some way (using s.t): *If you treat the cloth with this chemical, it will be waterproof.* **5** *intr.v* (often — *with s.o*) (*formal*) have discussions (with a government) to try to reach an agreement about s.t. **treat s.o to s.t** give s.o s.t as a treat(1); buy s.o s.t, usu s.t to drink or eat: *After dinner, Harry treated all his guests to a glass of his special wine.*

'treatable *adj* that can be treated(3,4).

'treatment *n* **1** *c/u.n* fact or way of treating(3,4) s.o/s.t. **2** *c.n* thing used in treating(3) s.o.

treatise /'triːtɪz/ *c.n* (often — *on s.o/s.t*) piece of writing (dealing with s.o/s.t).

treaty /'triːtɪ/ *c.n* (*pl -ies*) agreement between governments about s.t: *a peace treaty.* **by private treaty** by means of a private agreement, not through an agent: *I sold my house by private treaty.*

treble¹ /'trebl/ *attrib.adj* **1** that is three times as much/many as usual or normal: *He was so hungry that he ate a treble portion*(2) *of chips.*

▷ *adv* **2** three times: *He earns treble my salary.* Compare double.

▷ *tr/intr.v* **3** (cause (s.t) to) be multiplied by three (in number, weight etc): *Those rabbits seem to treble in number every month.* Compare double.

treble² /'trebl/ *c.n* (also *attrib*) **1** a very high singing voice. **2** person, esp a boy before puberty, with such a singing voice. Compare soprano, tenor¹.

▷ *adj/adv* **3** having the musical range of a treble(1): *a treble recorder³. He sings treble.*

,**treble 'clef** *c.n* (*in music*) sign (𝄞)that shows that the notes in a piece of music are from middle C upwards. Compare bass clef.

tree /tri:/ *c.n* **1** kind of large plant with a thick stem from which one can get wood: *Most trees have a trunk(2) and branches.* **2** (also '**shoe ,tree**) thing made of wood put in shoes to keep them stretched. **3** *c.n* = family tree.

'**treeless** *adj* having no trees(1) in or on it.

'**tree ,surgeon** *c.n* person trained to cut down trees or cut branches etc from a tree.

'**tree,top** *c.n* (often *pl*) top of a tree(1).

'**tree ,trunk** *c.n* trunk(2) of a tree(1).

trek /trek/ *c.n* **1** journey on land, often on foot, and usu long and hard.

▷ *intr.v* (-*kk*-) **2** do a trek(1).

trellis /'trelɪs/ *c/u.n* framework made of strips of wood, used to help plants to climb.

tremble /'trembl/ *c.n* **1** example of trembling(1) (caused by fear etc): *A tremble of excitement went through the crowd as the film-star's car came into sight.* **be all of a tremble** (*informal*) be trembling(1) because one is excited or nervous.

▷ *intr.v* **2** (often — *with s.t*) shake (because one is afraid, nervous, excited): *We trembled with excitement.* Compare shiver(2). **3** be shaken by s.t, e.g an earthquake.

'**tremblingly** *adv* in a trembling(1) way.

tremor /'tremə/ *c.n* shaking movement caused by an earthquake, fear, fever etc. **earth tremor** ⇒ earth.

tremulous /'tremjʊləs/ *adj* (*formal*) trembling(2); shaking, usu because one is nervous.

'**tremulously** *adv.* '**tremulousness** *u.n.*

tremendous /trɪ'mendəs/ *adj* **1** (*attrib*) very big: *a tremendous storm*; *a tremendous number of people.* **2** (*informal*) very enjoyable; good in quality: *a tremendous performance.*

tre'mendously *adv.*

trench /trentʃ/ *c.n* **1** long narrow hole made in the ground, usu with straight sides: *Sometimes a trench is for soldiers to get into so as to protect themselves from enemy attack.*

▷ *tr.v* **2** dig trenches in or round (a place).

trend /trend/ *c.n* **1** general direction of ways of thinking or behaving: *the latest political trend.*

▷ *intr.v* **2** have a tendency (towards s.t).

'**trendily** *adv* in a trendy way.

'**trendiness** *u.n* fact or state of being trendy.

'**trend,setter** *c.n* person or thing that sets a fashion.

'**trendy** *adj* (-*ier*, -*iest*) (*informal*) following the latest fashions.

trepidation /,trepɪ'deɪʃən/ *u.n* (*formal*) fear; anxiety; nervousness.

trespass /'trespəs/ *c.n* **1** example of trespassing(2).

▷ *intr.v* **2** (often — *on s.t*) go onto land or into a building etc without having the right to do so: *Anyone who trespasses (on our land) will be*

prosecuted. **trespass (up)on s.t** (*formal*) take advantage of s.t, e.g a person's kindness, to take more than is right or fair: *Could I trespass a little longer upon your time and ask you a few questions?*

'**trespasser** *c.n* person who trespasses(2): *One sometimes sees a sign outside a field or a building which says 'Trespassers will be prosecuted'.*

tresses /'tresɪz/ *pl.n* (*literary*) curls in long hair, usu on a woman's head.

trestle /'tresl/ *c.n* **1** length of wood supported at each end by two fixed legs that spread outwards and downwards, used as a support for wood etc that one is working on. **2** bridge made of lengths of metal or wood fixed together to form a framework.

,**trestle 'bridge** *c.n* = trestle(2).

,**trestle 'table** *c.n* flat surface that has trestles(1) as its legs.

trews /tru:z/ *pl.n* tight trousers made in a special Scottish pattern (tartan(1)).

trial ⇒ try.

triangle /'traɪæŋgl/ *c.n* **1** shape or thing (consisting of s.t) which has three (almost) straight sides and therefore three corners. **2** metal musical instrument shaped like a triangle(1) that makes a sound like a bell when one hits it with another piece of metal. **the eternal triangle** one man and two women, or one woman and two men, when this leads to competition between two for the love of the other one.

triangular /traɪ'æŋgjʊlə/ *adj* **1** having three sides; like a triangle(1). **2** between three people or groups of people: *a triangular sports competition.*

triathlon /traɪ'æθlɒn/ *def.c.n* athletic(1) competition which consists of three different events, running, swimming and cycling.

tribe /traɪb/ *c.n* group of people who are related(1) to each other and share a language, traditions etc.

tribal /'traɪbl/ *adj* of or referring to one or more tribes: *tribal costume/customs* (⇒ custom²).

'**triba,lism** *u.n* arrangement of one or more groups of people into tribes.

tribulation /,trɪbjʊ'leɪʃən/ *n* (*formal*) **1** *c/u.n* (feeling of) unhappiness. **2** *c.n* thing that causes this.

tribunal /traɪ'bju:nl/ *c/def.pl.n* court whose job is to decide about a particular thing or things: *a rent tribunal* (i.e one that decides how much rents should be).

tribute /'trɪbju:t/ *c.n* (often *pay s.o/s.t a —; pay a — to s.o/s.t*) thing that shows that one admires or respects s.o/s.t: *As a tribute to the retiring head teacher, a tree was planted in front of the school. He paid me a great tribute by visiting me at home.* **floral tribute** present of flowers given as a tribute.

tributary /'trɪbjʊtrɪ/ *adj* **1** (of a river etc) that runs into a bigger river etc.

▷ *c.n* (*pl* -*ies*) **2** tributary(1) river.

trice /traɪs/ *sing.n* **in a trice** very quickly.

triceps /'traɪseps/ *c.n* (*pl* -(es)) muscle(1) at the back of the arm: *When the triceps is tightened, the arm straightens.*

trick /trɪk/ *attrib.adj* **1** used in a trick(5): *a trick box with a false bottom.* **2** that is done as a trick(5): *trick cycling.* **3** who does tricks(6): *a trick cyclist.*

▷ *c.n* **4** thing done to cheat s.o. ⇨ play a trick (on s.o). **5** thing done to make s.o look foolish, to amuse one or more other people. ⇨ play a trick (on s.o). **6** skilful action that needs to be learnt and practised, used to surprise people or to make them laugh: conjuring tricks. **7** (in some card games) round(16) of cards (one from each player) won by the player with the best card. **a card trick** a trick(6) played with cards. **a dirty**, **nasty** etc **trick** an unfair or unkind trick(4). **do the trick** (*informal*) be just what is needed for s.t: *I need something to open this tin with; ah, this screwdriver should do the trick!* **never/not miss a trick** (*fig*) never fail to notice things that are important. **play a trick (on s.o)** (a) cheat (s.o) with a trick(4). (b) make s.o look foolish by a trick(5).
▷ *tr.v* **8** cheat (s.o) with a trick(4). **9** make (s.o) look foolish with a trick(5). **trick s.o into (doing) s.t** make or persuade s.o to do s.t by a trick(4).
'trickery *u.n* fact or act of using tricks(4).
'trickily *adv* in a tricky(1) way.
'trickiness *u.n* fact of being tricky.
,trick 'question *c.n* question that is difficult to answer because it is different from what it seems to be.
'trickster *c.n* person who plays tricks(4,5).
'tricky *adj* (*-ier*, *-iest*) **1** (of a person, her/his behaviour etc) playing tricks(4). **2** difficult to answer, deal with etc: *a tricky question.*
trickle /'trɪkl/ *c.n* **1** (often — *of s.t*) slight flow (of water, people etc): *There was only a trickle of water in the stream. We had only a trickle of visitors during the first week.*
▷ *tr/intr.v* **2** (cause (s.t) to) flow in very small quantities or amounts: *The blood trickled down her arm.*
trickster, tricky ⇨ trick.
tricolour /'trɪkələ/ *n* **1** *c.n* flag that has three bands, each being the same in width but different in colour. **2** *def.n* (with capital **T**) the French flag, which is red, white and blue.
tricycle /'traɪsɪkl/ *c.n* machine like a bicycle but with three wheels, two of them at the back.
trident /'traɪdənt/ *c.n* (in history) kind of big spear with three points on the end.
tried *p.t,p.p* of try.
trier ⇨ try.
trifle /'traɪfl/ *n* **1** *sing.n* (also *attrib*) a little bit: *I'm a trifle cold. 'Are you worried?' 'Yes, a trifle.'* **2** *c.n* (often *derog*) thing that is small in value or importance. **3** *c/u.n* sweet or pudding made of sponge cake, cooked fruit etc, custard and cream.
▷ *intr.v* **4** **trifle with s.o/s.t** treat s.o/s.t in a rudely careless way: *Don't trifle with me; I want to know the true story.* **5** **trifle with s.t** play with s.t instead of doing s.t with it seriously: *I could see that she was only trifling with her food.*
'trifler *c.n* person who trifles with s.o/s.t.
'trifling *attrib.adj* very small and unimportant: *You can have this machine for the trifling sum of £10.*
trigger /'trɪgə/ *c.n* **1** small piece of metal in a gun etc which one pulls when one wants to fire a shot or shots.
▷ *tr.v* **2** (often — *s.t off*) cause (s.t) to start: *The sight of the old place triggered off a chain of happy memories of my childhood.*

'trigger-,happy *adj* **1** eager to fire one's gun: *The soldiers there are trigger-happy.* **2** (*fig*) dangerously irresponsible in what one says, does etc.
trigonometry /,trɪgə'nɒmɪtrɪ/ *u.n* (*mathematics*) branch of mathematics that deals with triangles(1).
trilateral /traɪ'lætərəl/ *adj* between three (groups of) people: *a trilateral peace treaty.*
tri'laterally *adv.*
trilby /'trɪlbɪ/ *c.n* (*pl -ies*) (also **,trilby 'hat**) kind of soft hat, usu made of felt², with a brim(2) and a dent(1) along the top.
trilingual /traɪ'lɪŋgwəl/ *adj* **1** knowing three languages. **2** written or spoken in three languages.
tri'lingually *adv.*
trill /trɪl/ *c.n* **1** (in music, or in the song of a bird) act of singing or playing two notes very quickly one after the other again and again. **2** (*technical*) (in phonetics) consonant(3) sound used in some languages and made by causing two parts of the mouth or throat to beat against each other rapidly several times: *In Spanish /r/ is a trill.*
▷ *tr/intr.v* **3** sing etc (s.t) with a trill.
trillion /'trɪlɪən/ *det/pron* (*cardinal number*) (*pl* trillion after another number, e.g *three trillion dollars*); otherwise *trillions*, e.g *There were trillions of ants at our picnic*) **1** (UK) million times a million times a million. **2** (US) million millions.
trilogy /'trɪlədʒɪ/ *c.n* (*pl -ies*) three books, films etc, each telling a complete story but all three of them connected with each other, e.g because they deal with the same family.
trim /trɪm/ *adj* (*-mm-*) **1** neat; tidy.
▷ *c.n* **2** example of trimming (⇨ trim(3)) hair. **in (good) trim (for s.t)** in good condition (for (doing) s.t): *You had better lose some weight so as to be in trim for the summer season.*
▷ *v* (*-mm-*) **3** *tr.v* cut (hair, bushes etc) neatly and tidily, usu taking off only small amounts. **4** *tr.v* make (s.t) less: *We have more workers than we need so we shall have to trim our staff.* **5** *tr.v* (often — *s.t with s.t*) decorate (clothing etc) (using s.t); add s.t to (clothing etc) to make it look more attractive: *Her blouse was trimmed with gold lace(2).* **6** *tr.v* change the position or angle of (a sail on a boat or ship).
'trimly *adv.*
'trimming *c.n* **1** thing cut off when one trims(3,4) s.t. **2** thing added to s.t when one trims(5) it.
'trimmings *pl.n* things usu served or given with s.t else that is the main thing: *We had roast chicken for lunch, with all the trimmings — potatoes, bread sauce and gravy(2).*
trimaran /'traɪmə,ræn/ *c.n* kind of sailing-boat with three joined hulls parallel(1) to each other. Compare catamaran.
trimester /trɪ'mestə/ *c.n* (US) term at a university etc that lasts for three months.
trimly, trimming(s) ⇨ trim.
trinitrotoluene /traɪ,naɪtrəʊ'tɒlju,i:n/ *u.n* (usu as *abbr* TNT) kind of explosive.
trinity /'trɪnɪtɪ/ *n* **1** *c.n* (*formal*) group of three people etc. **2** *unique n* (with capital **T**) Sunday after Whitsun(1). **3** *def.unique n* (with capital **T**) (in Christianity) God the Father, God the Son (Jesus) and God the Holy Spirit considered together as one God.
,Trinity 'Sunday *unique n* = Trinity(2).

trinket /'trɪŋkɪt/ c.n small ring, vase etc that is not worth very much.

trio /'triː:əu/ n **1** c/def.pl.n group of three people, animals or things. **2** c/def.pl.n group of three people who sing or play music together. **3** c.n piece of music for three singers or players.

trip /trɪp/ c.n **1** journey or voyage, usu a fairly short one (to a place, and sometimes back again): *They're on a school trip to France.* **2** example of tripping(5). **3** device for switching s.t on or making it start. ⇒ tripwire. **4** (*slang*) time during which one is under the influence of certain kinds of drugs(2). *day trip* ⇒ day. *round trip* ⇒ round. *a slip/trip of the tongue* a mistake in saying s.t which is accidental and not the result of not knowing s.t.
▷ tr/intr.v (-pp-) **5** (often — (s.o) up; — over s.o/s.t) (cause (s.o) to) (almost) fall because of hitting s.t with a foot: *I tripped over the mat and fell down. The football player tripped up a member of the other team.* **6** tr.v cause a trip(3) to act: *If you touch that window you will trip the* alarm(2) *bell.* **7** tr/intr.v (usu — s.o up) (*fig*) **(a)** (cause (s.o) to) make a mistake because of a trick question etc. **(b)** show that (s.o) is lying etc: *She said she knew John well but I tripped her up by saying how much I liked his red hair; she agreed but his hair is actually black! trip out* (*slang*) have a trip(4).
'tripper c.n person who goes for a trip(1), usu one that finishes up where it started. *day tripper* ⇒ day.

tripartite /traɪ'pɑː:taɪt/ attrib.adj between three people or groups: *a tripartite treaty.*

tripe /traɪp/ u.n **1** lining of the stomach of a cow etc which can be eaten: *Tripe and onions is an old English dish.* **2** (*informal*) nonsense: *Don't talk such tripe!*

triple /'trɪpl/ attrib.adj **1** that is three times the amount or number that is usual or normal: *a triple helping of potatoes.* Compare double.
▷ adv **2** three times as much or many: *He asked for triple the amount of money the last man had wanted.*
▷ tr/intr.v **3** (cause (s.o/s.t) to) become three times more in size, amount etc: *The extra work should triple our profits.*
'triple 'jump sing/def.n sport in which one has to jump and land on one foot, then jump again and land on the other foot, and finally jump again and land on both feet.

triplet /'trɪplɪt/ c.n **1** one of three children to whom a mother gives birth at the same time. **2** (*literature*) group of three lines in a poem etc. **3** (*music*) group of three notes that have to take as long to play as two notes usu do.

triplex /'trɪpleks/ u.n (t.n) (often with capital **T**) kind of glass used for car windows etc that is not as dangerous as ordinary glass when it breaks because it has three layers(1), the two outside ones of glass, and the middle one of plastic(3).

triplicate /'trɪplɪkɪt/ c.n copy, usu the last one, of s.t of which three have been made. *in triplicate* typed, written etc with the original and two exact copies.

tripod /'traɪpɒd/ c.n device with three legs on which one can put a camera etc.

tripper ⇒ trip.

trisect /traɪ'sekt/ tr.v (*technical*) divide (s.t) into three, usu equal, parts. Compare bisect.

trite /traɪt/ adj (*derog*) boring because too ordinary: *a trite remark.*
'tritely adv. **'triteness** u.n.

triumph /'traɪʌmf/ n **1** c.n great or absolute success or victory. **2** u.n (often — (of s.o/s.t) over s.o/s.t) fact of (s.o/s.t) being very or absolutely successful or victorious (in fighting or competing with s.o/s.t). **3** u.n feeling of great pleasure caused by triumph(2).
▷ intr.v **4** (often — over s.o/s.t) win completely (against s.o/s.t). **5** feel great pleasure because of triumphing(4).
triumphal /traɪ'ʌmfəl/ attrib.adj of, referring to, showing, (a) triumph(1,2): *a triumphal arch; triumphal music.*
tri'umphant adj triumphing (⇒ triumph(v)).
tri'umphantly adv.

trivia /'trɪvɪə/ pl.n things that are not at all important or valuable; trifles(2).
'trivial adj (*derog*) not at all important, valuable or interesting.
triviality /ˌtrɪvɪ'ælɪtɪ/ n (pl -ies) **1** u.n fact or state of being trivial. **2** c.n thing that is trivial.
'trivia,lize, -ise tr.v make (s.t) (seem) trivial.

trod /trɒd/ p.t of tread.

trodden /'trɒdn/ p.p of tread.

troll /trəul/ c.n kind of magical(1) creature like a human being that one finds in ancient Scandinavian stories and poems.

trolley /'trɒlɪ/ n **1** c.n kind of small cart that is pushed or pulled by a person: *a luggage trolley at an airport; a trolley for carrying the things one buys in a* supermarket. **2** (also **'tea ,trolley**) small table with wheels, used for taking drinks and/or food from one place to another.
'trolley,bus c.n electric bus that gets power from an overhead wire. *by trolleybus* in a trolleybus: *go/travel by trolleybus.*

trollop /'trɒləp/ c.n (*derog*) woman or girl who is very untidy and dirty, or who is immoral.

trombone /trɒm'bəun/ c.n (also *attrib*) kind of musical instrument made of brass which one blows and changes the notes by pushing a tube backwards or forwards inside it: *a trombone player.*
trom'bonist c.n person who plays a trombone.

troop /truː:p/ n (often — of s.o/s.t) **1** group (of people or animals) moving etc together: *a troop of monkeys.* **2** (in the army) small unit (of soldiers, tanks etc). Compare regiment(1), squadron(1). **3** small unit (of scouts).
▷ intr.v **4** (often — along, in etc) go (along etc) together. *troop the colour* (in the British army) perform a ceremony in which the flag of a regiment(1) is shown to its members.
'troop ,carrier c.n (written abbr Tpr) ship, plane or vehicle that carries troops(2).
'trooper c.n ordinary soldier in the cavalry, tanks etc. *swear like a trooper* use a lot of swearwords.
troops pl.n soldiers of all ranks.
'troop,ship c.n ship that carries troops.

trope /trəup/ c.n figurative way of using a word; figure of speech, e.g 'sunny' in 'a sunny smile' but not in 'a sunny day'.

trophy /'trəufɪ/ c.n (pl -ies) prize that a person gets for doing s.t difficult, dangerous etc, e.g a silver cup for winning a race.

tropic /'trɒpɪk/ c.n (usu with capital **T**) *the*

Tropic of Cancer/Capricorn the imaginary line round the earth that marks the northern/southern limit of the tropics about 23° north/south of the equator.

'**tropical** adj from, found in, the tropics; very hot (and at the same time damp): tropical heat; tropical rain forests.

'**tropically** adv.

'**tropics** def.pl.n (often with capital **T**) area of the world that lies between the Tropics of Cancer and Capricorn.

trot /trɒt/ c.n **1** one of the ways in which a horse moves, faster than a walk but not as fast as a canter(1). **2** ride on a horse while it is doing a trot(1). **3** way of moving by a person or an animal that is not a horse, which is faster than walking but not as fast as running. **4** trip during which one moves at a trot. **at a trot** at the speed of a trot(1). **break into a trot** begin to move at this speed. **get/have the trots** (slang) get/have diarrhoea. **on the trot** (informal) **(a)** busy: We've been on the trot ever since the children started their holidays. **(b)** without a change: We've been to Italy for our holidays for five summers on the trot.

▷ v (-tt-) **5** tr/intr.v (cause (a horse) to) go at a trot(1). **6** intr.v (often — along, by etc) (of a person, animal) move at a trot(3). **trot s.t out** (informal) say or write s.t in a boring way: He trots out the same things every time we visit him.

'**trotter** c.n **1** horse that has been trained to trot(5). **2** pig's foot that is cooked for eating.

Trot /trɒt/ c.n (informal) Trotskyist.

Trotskyist /'trɒtskɪˌɪst/ c.n (also **Trotskyite** /'trɒtskɪˌaɪt/) (also attrib) (informal **Trot**) (often derog) supporting the ideas of Leon Trotsky, esp the idea that workers must seize power so that socialism can be established.

trotter ⇨ trot.

trouble /'trʌbl/ n **1** u.n state of being worried, anxious, annoyed or in difficulty or danger. **2** c.n thing that causes one to be in such a state. **3** c/u.n work that is unpleasant or that one does not want: 'I'm sorry to give you all this trouble.' 'Oh, it's no trouble at all!' The children were a great trouble to keep amused during the holidays. **4** c/u.n thing that is wrong (with s.o/s.t): engine trouble in a car; heart trouble. The trouble with you is that you are too lazy. **5** u.n dissatisfaction, strikes, unrest etc among the people of a country etc: We have had a lot of trouble among the miners this year. **ask for trouble** (fig) do s.t dangerous that is likely to lead to trouble. **get a girl into trouble** (informal) make a girl pregnant. **get (s.o) into trouble (with s.o/s.t)** (cause (s.o) to) get into a position where there is trouble(1) (with the police, the law etc). **have trouble doing s.t** find it difficult to do s.t. **have trouble with s.o/s.t** be caused worry, annoyance etc by s.o/s.t: We're having trouble with the neighbours. John's having trouble with his English grammar. **in trouble** having trouble. **in trouble with s.o/s.t** in a difficult or dangerous situation because of s.o/s.t. **look for trouble** = ask for trouble. **make trouble (for s.o)** be the cause of trouble (for s.o). **put s.o to a lot of trouble**; **put s.o to the trouble of doing s.t** cause s.o to have a lot of trouble(3), to do a certain thing that causes her/him trouble(3). **take the trouble to do s.t** be kind, efficient etc enough to do s.t:

The secretary took the trouble to show me the way to his office. Dave never takes the trouble to check what he has written. **take trouble** try to do s.t properly by effort and hard work: You'll never be successful unless you take trouble. **that's the least of s.o's troubles** s.o has other troubles that are greater than that one. **the trouble with s.o/s.t** the thing that is wrong with s.o/s.t: The trouble with Bob is that he has never learnt the meaning of hard work.

▷ v **6** tr/intr.v cause trouble(3–5) to (s.o/s.t). **Can/Could/May/Might I trouble you for s.t, to do s.t?** (polite ways of asking s.o for s.t or to do s.t): May I trouble you for the time? (i.e Please tell me what time it is.) Could I trouble you to pass the wine? **I'm sorry to trouble you, but . . .** (a polite way of asking s.o for s.t or to do s.t). **(please) don't trouble (to do s.t)** (please) don't give yourself the trouble (of doing s.t).

'**trouble,maker** c.n (derog) person who causes trouble(n).

'**trouble,shooter** c.n person who deals with problems when they happen, e.g in an office or a factory.

'**troublesome** adj (derog) who/that causes trouble or difficulties.

'**trouble ,spot** c.n place where there is trouble(5).

trough /trɒf/ c.n **1** long narrow container in which food or water for animals or earth for plants is put. **2** (technical) long narrow area that is lower than two long high areas, e.g between waves on the sea. **3** (technical) (in weather reporting) long area of lower pressure between two areas of higher pressure.

trounce /traʊns/ tr.v beat (a player, team etc) easily in a match etc.

troupe /truːp/ c.n group (of people) who do s.t (e.g act or sing) together.

'**trouper** c.n person who belongs to a troupe.

trousers /'traʊzəz/ pl.n (often a pair of —) piece of clothing with two legs to cover a person below the waist. ⇨ pants(2), slacks, underpants. **wear the trousers** (fig) be the boss in a house: In some homes the wife wears the trousers.

'**trouser** attrib.adj **1** that is part of a pair of trousers: my left trouser leg; a trouser button. **2** that makes, is for, trousers: a trouser factory.

'**trouser ,press** c.n device for making trousers neat by pressing them.

trousseau /'truːsəʊ/ c.n (pl -s, trousseaux /'truːsəʊz/) clothes, brushes, combs, linens etc that a woman brings with her when she marries; clothes that a woman is going to get married in.

trout /traʊt/ n (pl trouts) (also attrib) **1** c.n kind of fish that is found in rivers and is considered to be very good to eat: trout fishing. **2** u.n flesh of such fish used as food: smoked trout. **3** c.n (pl trouts) (usu old —) (derog; fig) person (usu old woman) who one does not like.

trove /trəʊv/ c.n ⇨ treasure trove.

trowel /'traʊəl/ c.n **1** kind of very small spade with curved sides, used for making small holes in the ground, digging up small plants etc. **2** small flat tool used for putting plaster(1) etc on walls and then spreading it.

troy /'trɔɪ/ u.n (also attrib) system used for weighing jewels and precious metals: troy weight.

In the troy system a pound[1](2) *is divided into* 12 ounces(1). Compare avoirdupois.

truant /'tru:ənt/ *c.n* (also *attrib*) boy or girl who stays away from school without permission. **play truant** stay away from school without permission.

'truancy *u.n* act or fact of being a truant.

truce /tru:s/ *c/u.n* agreement between countries, people etc who have been fighting to stop doing so for some time. Compare armistice.

truck[1] /trʌk/ *c.n* **1** (usu **'lorry** in GB) large heavy vehicle for carrying goods along roads. **2** vehicle used in the same way as a truck(1) but as part of a railway train: *a goods truck.* **3** small vehicle with two wheels used to push or pull goods along on in a factory etc. Compare trolley(1).

truck[2] /trʌk/ *u.n* **have no truck with s.o/s.t** refuse to do business etc with s.o/s.t.

truculent /'trʌkjʊlənt/ *adj* (*derog*; *formal*) ready to argue, fight or cause trouble.

'truculence, 'truculency *u.n.* **'truculently** *adv.*

trudge /trʌdʒ/ *c.n* **1** tiring and/or boring walk.

▷ *intr.v* **2** walk in a slow and unpleasant or boring way (for a distance): *To get home from the station we had to trudge (for) one and a half kilometres over rough paths.*

true /tru:/ *adj* (*comp* -r /'tru:ə/, *superl* -st /'tru:ɪst/) Opposite untrue for (1,3,6). **1** correct; not lying ⇒ lie[1](2); accurate: *What I am about to tell you is a true story.* **2** real; not imitation; not cheating in any way: *The path of true love never did run smooth.* **3** (often — to s.o/s.t) who/ that one can trust; faithful (to s.o/s.t): *Mary has always been a true friend to all of us. He remained true to his promises.* **4** (often — to life) exact; not different in any way from the (living) original: *a true copy of s.t; a painting that is true to life.* **5** never wrong or mistaken: *The truest sign of love is being willing to* ignore *all faults.* **6** exact in measurement, position etc: *The lid of your desk isn't true; it needs to be taken off and straightened.* **come true** happen in the way in which one had hoped, wished etc that it would: *When he married, all his wishes came true.* **in the true(st) sense (of the word)** absolutely truly. **out of true** not true(6); crooked(1). **true to type** ⇒ type. **true to life** ⇒ true(4).

▷ *adv* **7** in a true(1,4,6) way. **ring true** ⇒ ring[2](*v*).

,true'born *attrib.adj* real; actually born as (s.t): *a trueborn English farmer.*

,true'hearted *adj* faithful.

,true-'life *attrib.adj* that really happened; who was really that in her/his own life: *a true-life story*; *a true-life princess.*

'true,love *c.n* person one really loves.

truism /'tru:ɪzəm/ *c.n* thing that is so clearly true that it is unnecessary to say or write it.

'truly *adv* **well and truly** ⇒ well[1](*adv*). **Yours truly** (way of ending a letter that is more formal than Yours sincerely but less so than Yours faithfully).

truth /tru:θ/ *n* (*pl* /tru:θs/, /tru:ðz/) **1** *u.n* fact, quality or state of (s.t) being true: *The truth of the matter is that she doesn't like you.* **2** *c/u.n* thing that is true: *Truth is often stranger than* fiction(1). ⇒ untruth. **3** *u.n* honesty: *You could see the truth of her love from her face.* **have a ring of truth about/in it** ⇒ ring[2](*n*). **in truth** truly; really. **the**

moment of truth ⇒ moment. **tell the truth** say what is true; not tell lies. **to tell the truth** (if I am) to be honest: *I ate the food but, to tell the truth, I did not enjoy it.*

'truthful *adj* Opposite untruthful. **1** (of s.t s.o says, writes etc) true. **2** (of a person) known to usually be honest.

'truthfully *adv.* **'truthfulness** *u.n.*

truffle /'trʌfl/ *c.n* **1** very expensive and tasty fungus that grows under the ground, esp in France. **2** kind of soft chocolate, usu with rum in it.

truism, truly ⇒ true.

trump /trʌmp/ *c.n* **1** (in card games) card belonging to the suit(2) that has been chosen to be the most powerful one in a particular game: *Play your lowest trump.*

▷ *tr.v* **2** beat (s.o else's card) by playing a trump(1). **trump s.t up** invent s.t false or untrue (e.g a lying accusation against s.o).

,trump 'card *c.n* (*fig*) thing that gives one a big advantage over other people.

trumps *pl.n* (with a sing or pl verb) suit(2) in bridge[2] etc that has been chosen to be the most powerful one in a particular game: *Which suit is trumps? What are trumps?*

trumpet /'trʌmpɪt/ *c.n* **1** kind of short brass musical instrument played by blowing into it, with three keys on top that one presses to change the note. **2** thing that looks like the end of a trumpet(1): *The trumpet at the centre of a* daffodil(1). **3** noise made by an elephant. **blow one's own trumpet** (*fig*) praise oneself.

▷ *v* **4** *intr.v* (of an elephant) give a cry. **5** *tr.v* shout (s.t, esp to praise oneself).

'trumpeter *c.n* person who plays a trumpet(1).

truncate /trʌŋ'keɪt/ *tr.v* (*formal*) cut (s.t) short; shorten (s.t) by cutting part of it off/out: *a truncated version of a film.*

truncheon /'trʌntʃən/ *c.n* kind of thick stick carried by police officers.

trundle /'trʌndl/ *tr/intr.v* (cause (s.t, usu s.t that is not easy to move) to) roll along on wheels: *The old man was trundling all he owned in the world on a little truck he had made himself.*

trunk /trʌŋk/ *c.n* **1** big piece of luggage. **2** long wooden stem of a tree often with branches growing out of it. **3** elephant's long nose. **4** (US) = boot(2).

'trunk ,call *c.n* telephone call to a place outside one's own area.

'trunk ,line *c.n* (**a**) telephone line along which trunk calls go. (**b**) main railway line.

'trunk ,road *c.n* main road in the country joining towns or cities.

trunks *pl.n* (often *a pair of —*) short piece of clothing worn below the waist by men and boys for swimming.

truss /trʌs/ *c.n* **1** (*formal*) hay or straw tied up into a package. **2** (*medical*) belt worn by people who have a hernia. **3** (*technical*) wooden, metal etc framework holding up a bridge, roof etc.

▷ *tr.v* **4** (often — s.o/s.t up) tie (s.o/s.t) tightly with a rope etc. **5** (often — s.t up) tie a (bird's) wings and legs to its sides before cooking it. **6** support (s.t) with a truss(3).

trust /trʌst/ *n* **1** *u.n* (often — in s.o/s.t) confidence, faith or absolute belief (that s.o/s.t is honest, safe etc). **2** *c.n* arrangement by which money, property etc is owned and managed by a group of people for the advantage of one or more other people. **3** *c.n* money, property etc owned and managed in this way. **4** *c.n* group of companies etc that have agreed not to compete with each other etc, in order to keep prices high etc. **hold s.t in trust (for s.o/s.t)** be a trustee(1) of s.t (for s.o/s.t). **place one's trust in s.o/s.t** trust(5) s.o/s.t. **position of trust** job etc in which one is trusted(5). **(take s.t) on trust** (believe s.t) without trying to find out whether it is true or not: *I take everything the children say to me on trust.*

▷ *v* **5** *tr.v* have trust(1) in (s.o/s.t). **6** *tr.v* (often — *s.o/ s.t to do s.t*) be sure (that s.o/s.t will do s.t): *You can trust me to be there whenever you need me.* **7** *tr/intr.v* (*formal*) hope((that)…): *I trust you had a good time. You enjoyed yourself, I trust.* **trust in s.o/s.t** have confidence in s.o/s.t. **trust s.o with s.o/s.t** allow s.o to have s.o/s.t feeling sure that he/she will look after her/him/it well.

'trust ,fund *c.n* money controlled by one person or group of people for the benefit(1) of another person or other people.

trustee /trʌs'tiː/ *c.n* (often — *of s.t*) **1** person, business company etc who/that has the job of looking after a trust(3). **2** person who has the job of looking after, or helping to look after, the money, property etc of a club, university etc.

trus'teeship *c/u.n* job or fact of being a trustee.

'trustful *adj* (*formal*) feeling that one can trust(5) s.o/s.t.

'trustfully *adv.* **'trustfulness** *u.n.*

'trusting *adj* = trustful: *She's very trusting.*

'trustingly *adv.*

'trust,worthiness *u.n* fact of being trustworthy.

'trust,worthy *adj* who/that can be trusted(5).

'trusty *adj* (-ier, -iest) **1** = trustworthy.

▷ *c.n* **2** (*informal*) prisoner who has behaved so well that he/she is given special privileges(1) while still in prison.

truth(ful), truthfully, truthfulness ⇒ true.

tr.v *written abbr* (used in this dictionary) transitive verb (⇒ transitive(2)).

try /traɪ/ *c.n* (*pl -ies*) **1** act of doing, or beginning to do, s.t to see whether one can do it or what it is like to do it; attempt. **2** (in rugby) score of four points when one touches the ball on the ground behind the opposite side's goal line(5), after which one can try to kick a goal. **(have) a try (at (doing) s.t** (make) an attempt (to do s.t), esp to see whether one can do it or what it is like; try(3) to do s.t.

▷ *v* (-ies, -ied) **3** *tr/intr.v* attempt (to do s.t): *Try to be early tomorrow.* **4** *tr.v* make use of (s.o/s.t) to see if he/she/it is suitable or successful for one's purposes: *If you want a good hairdresser, try Mr Jones. Try this soup and see if you like it.* ⇒ well-tried. **5** *tr.v* make an attempt to open (s.t): *The thief tried the doors of the car but they were all locked.* **6** *tr.v* (*law*) try(3) to find out whether (s.o) is guilty of s.t or not by hearing evidence(2) in front of a judge etc: *He was tried in London and found guilty.* **7** *tr.v* make (s.o/s.t) suffer: *This very bright light tries my eyes. Small children often try their parents' patience.*

try and do s.t (*informal*) = try(3) to do s.t.

try doing s.t do s.t to see if it is pleasant, successful etc: *We tried making a garden*

behind our house but the earth was not good enough.

try for s.t try to get, win etc s.t: *Mary has passed her BA and now she is going to try for the MA.* **try s.o for s.t** (*law*) try(6) s.o to find out whether he/ she is guilty of s.t: *He was tried for murder.*

try s.t on (a) put a piece of clothing on to see whether it fits, whether one likes it etc. **(b)** (*informal*) pretend s.t in order to see how far s.o will accept s.t: *Don't pay any attention to that naughty boy; his tooth isn't really hurting — he's just trying it on.* ⇒ try-on.

try one's hand (at s.t) ⇒ hand(*n*).

try s.o/s.t out test s.o/s.t (thoroughly) by making her/him/it do what she/he/it is supposed to do.

trial /'traɪəl/ *n* **1** *c.n* example of trying (⇒ try(6)) (s.o). **2** *c.n* attempt; try(1). **3** *c/u.n* (example of) trying (⇒ try(4,5)): *Don't buy that machine without giving it a trial first.* **4** *c.n* (*derog*) person or thing who/that tries(7) (s.o/s.t). **on trial** being tried (⇒ try(4,6)). **put s.o on trial** decide to try(6) s.o. **stand trial (for s.t)** be tried (⇒ try(6)). **trial and error** testing s.t just by trying (⇒ try(4)) various things one after the other to see whether they are right or not, instead of doing the testing in a scientific way: *You'll find the best restaurant only by trial and error.*

,trial 'marriage *c/u.n* (example of) living together before marrying each other to see whether one likes it or not.

'trial ,period *c.n* length of time during which one is trying (⇒ try(4)) s.o/s.t.

,trial 'run *c.n* test of s.t, usu a vehicle, by actually going for a trip in it.

trials *pl.n* test of animals as a kind of sport: *horse trials.*

tried *adj* tested and found good, suitable etc. ⇒ well-tried.

trier /'traɪə/ *c.n* person who always tries (⇒ try(3)) hard to do things properly.

trying /'traɪɪŋ/ *adj* (*derog*) annoying; tiring to one's mind or body.

'try-,on *c.n* example of trying s.t on(b).

'try-,out *c.n* test; trial(3).

tsar /zɑː/ *c.n* (also **tzar, czar**) (in history) emperor of Russia.

tsarina /zɑː'riːnə/ *c.n* (also **tza'rina, cza'rina**) (in history) empress of Russia.

tsetse fly /'tsetsɪ ,flaɪ/ *c.n* (*pl -ies*) kind of fly found in Africa that bites people and animals and gives them sleeping sickness etc.

T-shirt *c.n* ⇒ T,t.

tsp *written abbr* (*pl tsps*) teaspoon(ful).

T-square *c.n* ⇒ T,t.

TT /,tiː 'tiː/ *abbr* teetotal.

tub /tʌb/ *c.n* **1** big round container, e.g for keeping a plant in. **2** (*informal*) = bathtub. **3** (also **'tubful**) (often — *of s.t*) as much as a tub(1) holds.

'tubful *c.n* = tub(3).

tuba /'tjuːbə/ *c.n* kind of big brass musical instrument, played by blowing into it and producing low notes.

tubby /'tʌbɪ/ *adj* (-ier, -iest) (*informal*) (of a person) shorter and fatter than the average.

tube /tjuːb/ *n* **1** *c.n* long round hollow pipe made of glass, metal, rubber etc, used to carry liquids, air etc. **2** *c.n* long container closed at one end and

with a kind of lid (a cap that one usu opens by unscrewing it) at the other end, used for holding toothpaste, paint etc. **3** *c.n* thing like a tube(1) in the body of a person or animal: bronchial tubes. **4** *c.n* = cathode ray tube. **5** *def.n* (often with capital **T**) underground railway in London. **by tube** (**train**) in the tube(5): *go/travel by tube.*
'tube ,train *c.n* train on the tube(5).
'tubeless *adj* (of a tyre) that does not have an inner tube(1).
'tubing *u.n* (system of) one or more tubes(1).
tubular /'tju:bjʊlə/ *adj* shaped like, made out of, a tube(1) or tubes.

tuber /'tju:bə/ *c.n* kind of root that is fat and round from which new plants can grow: *Some kinds of tubers, such as potatoes, can be eaten.*
tuberculosis /tju:,bɜ:kjʊ'ləʊsɪs/ *u.n* (*abbr* TB) dangerous kind of disease that attacks the lungs etc of people and animals.
    tubercular /tju:'bɜ:kjʊlə/ (also **tuberculous** /tju:'bɜ:kjʊləs/) *adj* having, referring to, tuberculosis.
tubful ⇒ tub.
tubing, tubular ⇒ tube.
TUC /,ti: ,ju: 'si:/ *def.n/abbr* Trades Union Congress.
tuck¹ /tʌk/ *c.n* **1** fold made in a piece of cloth and then sewn so that it does not unfold: *sew a tuck in a skirt.*
▷ *tr.v* **2** make one or more tucks¹(1) in (s.t). **tuck s.o in/up** push the ends of sheets and blankets under the mattress when s.o is in bed. **tuck s.t away**; **tuck s.t under** *etc* **s.t** put s.t away, under s.t etc in a way that makes it safer, more comfortable etc: *When he finished reading his newspaper, he tucked it away in his bag. Tuck your shirt into the top of your trousers. Our house is very quiet because it is tucked away behind a thick wood.*
tuck² /tʌk/ *u.n* **1** (*informal*) sweets, chocolates etc eaten by children, e.g during breaks at school.
▷ *v* **2 tuck in**(**to s.t**) (*informal*) eat (s.t) hungrily. **tuck s.t away** (*informal*) eat (usu a lot of) s.t.
'tuck ,shop *c.n* shop, usu at a school, where tuck²(1) is sold.
Tues *written abbr* Tuesday.
Tuesday /'tju:zdɪ/ *unique n* (also *attrib*) second day of the week in Christian(1) (and some other) countries; day after Monday and before Wednesday. **last Tuesday** the last Tuesday before today. **next Tuesday** the first Tuesday after today. **on a Tuesday** on a day of one week that is/was a Tuesday. **on Tuesday** on the nearest Tuesday before/after today or on the Tuesday of the week being referred to: *We arrived on Tuesday.* **On Tuesdays** every Tuesday: *What do you do on Tuesdays?* **Tuesday after next** the second Tuesday after today. **Tuesday before last** the Tuesday before last Tuesday. **Tuesday morning**, **afternoon** *etc* the morning, afternoon etc of last, next, Tuesday.
tuft /tʌft/ *c.n* bunch (of hair, grass etc) which is fixed at one end and loose at the other.
tug /tʌg/ *c.n* **1** sudden sharp pull: *He gave my sleeve a tug.* **2** kind of small ship with strong engines, used for pulling and pushing big ships, e.g when they are coming into, or leaving, port.
▷ *v* (**-gg-**) **3** *tr/intr.v* pull (s.o/s.t) suddenly and

sharply. **4** *tr.v* (often — **at** *s.t*) pull (s.o/s.t heavy) with difficulty.
'tug,boat *c.n* = tug(2).
,tug-of-'war *c/u/def.n* kind of sport in which two teams pull a thick rope, each from one end, to see which is the stronger.
tuition /tju:'ɪʃən/ *u.n* **1** (also *attrib*) (often — *in s.t*) teaching (of a certain subject). **2** money people have to pay for tuition(1).
tulip /'tju:lɪp/ *c.n* kind of plant that grows from a bulb(1) and has a colourful(1) flower that looks like a small cup.
tum /tʌm/ *c.n abbr* tummy.
tumble /'tʌmbl/ *c.n* **1** sudden fall. (**all**) **in a tumble** all mixed up; not in an orderly state. **take a tumble** = tumble(2).
▷ *intr.v* **2** fall suddenly without intending to. **3** roll in a way that is not orderly: *The children loved tumbling about in the hay.* **4** (often — **down**) fall into pieces: *As they had no money, they had to allow their old house to tumble down.* **5** *intr.v* do tricks with one's body by rolling, twisting in the air etc. **6** *intr.v* (of prices) fall suddenly and far: *Shares*(3) *on the* stock exchange(1) *tumbled yesterday.* **tumble clothes dry** (of a washing machine) dry clothes after washing them by making them turn over and over in hot air. **tumble** (**to s.t**) (*informal*) understand (s.t) suddenly after not having understood (it) for some time: *It took her some time to tumble to what her children were doing in the garden.*
'tumble,down *attrib.adj* having tumbled(4) almost right down: *a tumbledown old castle.*
'tumble ,drier *c.n* machine which tumbles clothes dry.
tumbler /'tʌmblə/ *c.n* kind of heavy glass for drinking out of that has no handle and no stem.
tumescent /tju:'mesənt/ *adj* (*medical*) more swollen than normal.
    tu'mescence *u.n.*
tumid /'tju:mɪd/ *adj* (*medical*) = tumescent.
    tu'midity *u.n.*
tummy /'tʌmɪ/ *c.n* (*pl* -ies) (also **tum**) (*informal*) (often used by, or when speaking to, children) stomach.
tumour /'tju:mə/ *c.n* (US **'tumor**) (*medical*) swelling caused by cells(4) in the body that have multiplied too fast.
tumult /'tju:mʌlt/ *c/u.n* (*formal*) state of disorder(1) and noise, e.g of an angry crowd.
    tumultuous /tju:'mʌltjʊəs/ *adj* (usu *attrib*) (*formal*) noisy and disorderly(2), sometimes in a friendly way: *The film-star received a tumultuous welcome from the crowd.*
    tu'multuously *adv.*
tuna /'tju:nə/ *n* (*pl* -(s)) **1** *c.n* (also **'tunny**) kind of big fish caught in the sea for eating. **2** *u.n* (also *attrib*) flesh of this fish as food: *tuna* salad(1).
    'tuna ,fish *u.n* = tuna(2).
tundra /'tʌndrə/ *u/def.n* flat land south of the North Pole²(1) that has no trees on it and is covered with thick ice in winter.
tune /tju:n/ *c.n* **1** short piece of music consisting of a number of notes (heard in a song etc): *Do you know the tune of 'Land of Hope and Glory'?* **call the tune** (*fig*) be the person who can give all the orders because he/she is the head, boss etc. **change one's tune** (*fig*) change what one says, thinks etc about s.t, or the way in which

one speaks etc: *When the man realized that I knew much more about the subject than he did, he quickly changed his tune.* **in tune (with s.o/s.t)** (a) in musical harmony(1) with s.o/s.t, e.g because both people's instruments have been tuned(2) in the same way. (b) (*fig*) thinking, behaving etc in the same way as s.o/s.t. **out of tune (with s.o/ s.t)** not in tune (with s.o/s.t)(a,b). **sing a different tune** (*fig*) = change one's tune. **to the tune of s.t** (a) using the tune of s.t: *The crowd welcomed the singer to the tune of his most successful song* (i.e they welcomed him by singing the tune of that song). (b) (*informal*) to a certain amount of money: *The damage to the roof needed repairs to the tune of £500.*

▷ *tr.v* **2** (sometimes — *s.t up*) change the pitch[1](4) of (a musical instrument) so that all the strings etc produce the right notes. **3** do things to (an engine) so that it works as efficiently as it can. **tune (a radio etc) in (to s.t)** change the controls (of a radio etc) so that one can hear a particular radio station or programme. **tune up** tune(2) one's instrument(s) ready for playing.

tuned adj **tuned in (to s.t)** (a) (of a radio) adjusted(1) in such a way that one can hear a particular station or programme. (b) (*fig*) (of a person) able to understand exactly what s.o is thinking, feeling etc: *A good teacher is one who is tuned in to her or his students' hopes and wishes.*

'tuneful *adj* pleasant to listen to.

'tunefully *adv.* **'tunefulness** *u.n.*

'tuneless *adj* not pleasant to listen to.

'tunelessly *adv.* **'tunelessness** *u.n.*

'tuner *c.n* **1** person who tunes(2) musical instruments: *a piano tuner.* **2** part of a radio or television which receives the signals and changes them into sounds and/or pictures.

'tune-,up *c.n* tuning(3) of an engine.

'tuning ,fork *c.n* metal device like a fork with two long points which produces a certain musical note when one hits it against s.t, used to tune(2) musical instruments.

tungsten /'tʌŋstən/ *u.n* (*technical*) kind of hard metal used in making steel etc, *chem. symb* W.

tunic /'tjuːnɪk/ *c.n* **1** short coat worn by soldiers etc. **2** loose dress with sleeves, e.g worn by women for some sports etc.

tuning fork ⇨ tune.

tunnel /'tʌnl/ *c.n* **1** hole made under the ground through which people, cars, trains etc can go.

▷ *v* (*-ll-*, US *-l-*) **2** *intr.v* (often — *through/under s.t*) make a tunnel(1) (through/under s.t). **3** *tr.v* make (s.t) by tunnelling(2): *We tunnelled a hole through the fallen earth wide enough to get the children out.*

'tunneller *c.n* (US **'tunneler**) person who tunnels(2).

tunny /'tʌnɪ/ *c/u.n* (*pl tunny, -ies*) = tuna.

'tunny ,fish *c/u.n* (*pl tunny fish*) = tunny.

turban /'tɜːbən/ *c.n* **1** piece of clothing worn on the head by Arabs, Indians etc and consisting of a long piece of cloth that is wound round the head like a bandage. **2** small hat sometimes worn by women which looks like a turban(1).

turbine /'tɜːbaɪn/ *c.n* machine driven by steam or a (usu very hot) liquid or gas, which turns a kind of wheel to produce power.

turbojet /ˌtɜːbəʊ'dʒet/ *c.n* (also *attrib*) **1** engine

that drives s.t, usu a plane, forward by means of a jet[1](1) of hot air and gases going through it. **2** plane driven by one or more such engines.

turboprop /ˌtɜːbəʊ'prɒp/ *c.n* (also *attrib*) **1** engine using a turbine to make a propeller go round. **2** plane with one or more such engines and propellers.

turbot /'tɜːbət/ *n* (*pl turbot*) **1** *c.n* kind of big flat fish with flesh that is very good to eat. **2** *u.n* (also *attrib*) flesh of this fish as food.

turbulent /'tɜːbjʊlənt/ *adj* very strong and irregular; behaving in a wild way: *the turbulent waters of a big river; turbulent winds causing trouble to planes; the turbulent history of South America.*

'turbulence, 'turbulency *u.n.*

turd /tɜːd/ *c.n* (*slang*; do not use!) piece of excrement.

tureen /tə'riːn/ *c.n* kind of big container for serving soup from during a meal, with a lid to keep it hot: *a soup tureen.*

turf /tɜːf/ *n* (*pl -s, turves* /tɜːvz/) **1** *u.n* top part of the soil with grass growing in it. **2** *c.n* piece of turf(1) used to make a new lawn[1]. **3** *c.n* piece of peat like a turf(2) but dug out for burning on a fire. **4** *def.n* turf(1) on which horse races are run. **5** *def.n* horse racing in general.

▷ *tr.v* **6** cover (a piece of land) with turves(3). **turf s.o/s.t out (of s.t)** (*informal*) (a) throw s.o/s.t out (of s.t). (b) (*fig*) get rid of s.o/s.t (from s.t): *The man made so much trouble in the pub that the owner turfed him out.*

'turf a,ccountant *c.n* person whose job is to take people's bets on horse races; bookmaker.

turgid /'tɜːdʒɪd/ *adj* (*derog*) (of a way of speaking or writing etc) pompous.

tur'gidity *u.n.* **'turgidly** *adv.*

turkey /'tɜːkɪ/ *n* **1** *c.n* kind of bird like a very big chicken, eaten esp at Christmas time in Britain. **2** *u.n* (also *attrib*) flesh of such a bird as food: *turkey sandwiches.* **cold turkey** (*fig; slang*) (a) way of stopping people needing drugs(2) such as cocaine by not letting them have any. (b) feeling of great discomfort caused by this treatment. **talk turkey** (*fig; informal*) talk really seriously, esp in doing business with s.o.

Turkish bath /ˌtɜːkɪʃ 'bɑːθ/ *c.n* kind of bath in which one cleans one's pores[1] by being in a very hot damp room, then washes the dirt off in a bath. Compare sauna.

Turkish coffee /ˌtɜːkɪʃ 'kɒfɪ/ *u.n* kind of coffee that is ground very fine and then boiled in the water so that it is thick.

Turkish delight /ˌtɜːkɪʃ dɪ'laɪt/ *u.n* kind of sweet that is like lumps of jelly(1) that are covered in powdered sugar.

turmeric /'tɜːmərɪk/ *u.n* powdered root of a kind of plant from Asia that gives a special taste to curries (⇨ curry(2)) etc and makes them yellow.

turmoil /'tɜːmɔɪl/ *sing/u.n* (often *in (a)* —) state of being all mixed up, confused, worried etc: *The streets were in turmoil after the attack on the government. Her mind was in a turmoil of excitement.*

turn /tɜːn/ *n* **1** *c.n* movement forming (part of) a circle or in such a way that one finishes up facing in a different direction. **2** *c.n* change in direction without movement: *a turn in a road.*

3 *c.n* time or chance to do s.t that other people are doing too, not at the same time as them but in a certain order one after the other: *John hit the ball first, then it was Peter's turn and then came my turn. She had learnt to fly planes so she sometimes took a turn at flying her private one.* **4** *c.n* (*informal*) sudden attack of illness, giddiness etc. *at every turn* (*fig*) whatever one tries to do and wherever one tries to do it: *We tried all sorts of ways of finding where she lived but failed at every turn.* *by turns* one after another. ⇨ turn(3). *do s.o a good/bad turn* do s.t nice/unpleasant for s.o. *give s.o quite a turn* frighten s.o; surprise s.o in a way that makes her/him nervous. *have one of one's turns* suddenly feel ill, giddy(1) etc, as one had done before. ⇨ turn(4). *in turn* one after the other. ⇨ turn(3). *miss one's turn* fail to have one's turn(3). *out of turn* not in one's correct turn(3): *John answered one of the teacher's questions out of turn.* *take a turn for the better/worse* suddenly become better/worse. *take turns* (*at s.t*) do s.t in turn. (*at*) *the turn of the century* (at) the time when one century ends and another begins: *Paris was a wonderful city at the turn of the century.* *the turn of the tide* the time when the tide has just finished going out and is about to start coming in again, or the opposite. *to a turn* (of s.t that is cooked) just the right amount; not cooked too much, nor too little: *The meat was done to a turn.* *turn and turn about* taking turns(3), first one then the other, then the first one again etc. *the turn of events* the way in which events happen. *turn of phrase* a particular way of saying/phrasing(3) s.t. *wait one's turn* (*to do s.t*) wait until it is one's turn(3) (to do s.t).

▷ *v* **5** *tr/intr.v* (cause (s.o/s.t) to) make a turn(1): *The cow turned and looked at us.* **6** *intr.v* do a turn(2) (to the left etc): *The road turns to the right here.* **7** *intr.v* (be forced to) change from lying on one side to lying on the other: *The child woke up, turned and saw the parcel. The car turned in circles as it rolled down the hill.* **8** *tr/intr.v* (cause (s.t) to) change position so that the front becomes the back, the top moves to the bottom etc: *If you turn the page you will see a picture of the plane on the other side.* **9** *tr.v* (often — *s.t back, down, in* etc) fold (s.t) (in a certain direction): *I hate people who turn the pages of a book down to show where they have got to.* **10** *tr.v* plough (a field, the earth etc). **11** *tr.v* make (s.t, usu wood or metal) into a particular shape, using a lathe. **12** *tr.v* make (s.t, e.g wooden columns) a particular shape, using a lathe. **13** *tr/intr.v* (cause (s.o/s.t) to) change (from s.t) to s.t; (cause (s.o/s.t) to) become (s.t) (after having been s.t): *The motion of the waves turned him almost green. The children turn quite brown after a few days in the sun. You can easily turn this garage into a kitchen. She has turned from a/not very pretty child into a beautiful woman.* **14** *tr.v* get (money etc) by trading: *Our shop turned £5000 last summer.* **15** *tr.v* be/become just past; just later than: *Oh, no, Peter isn't a young man — he's turned 40. 'What's the time?' 'It's just turned half past 12.'* *about turn* ⇨ about(*adv*). *toss and turn.* ⇨ toss(*v*). *turn (s.o) against s.o/s.t* (make s.o) stop liking s.o/s.t.

turn one's attention, thoughts etc to s.o/s.t stop paying attention to, or thinking of etc, s.o/s.t and start paying attention etc to s.o/s.t else. *turn away (from s.o/s.t)* stop facing in the direction of s.o/s.t and face in another direction. *turn s.o away* refuse to let s.o come in: *When the theatre was full, they began to turn people away.* *turn back* stop going in the direction of s.t (and start going in the opposite direction). *turn s.o/s.t back* refuse to allow s.o/s.t to go on in the same direction. *turn the clock(s) back* ⇨ clock(*n*). *turn for the better/worse* start becoming better/worse. *turn a blind eye (to s.t)* ⇨ eye(*n*). *turn a/the corner* ⇨ corner(*n*). *turn a deaf ear (to s.t)* ⇨ ear. *turn s.o/s.t down* refuse to accept s.o/s.t: *They have turned down my application for a job.* *turn a radio etc down* make a radio etc play less loudly. *turn (from s.o/s.t) (to s.o/s.t)* stop looking at, talking to or dealing with s.o/s.t and start doing this to s.o/s.t else. ⇨ turn(13). *turn a gun, hose etc on s.o/s.t* point a gun etc at s.o/s.t and (threaten to) fire it, turn the water on etc. *not turn a hair* ⇨ hair(*n*). *turn one's hand to s.t* ⇨ hand(*n*). *turn s.o's head* ⇨ head(*n*). *turn in* (*fig*; *informal*) go to bed. *turn s.o in* (*fig*) hand s.o over to the police. *turn s.t in* hand s.t in to the people who should have it: *When you have finished your practice, you have to turn your racket(1) in.* *turn into s.t* change (from s.t) into s.t: *Caterpillars(1) turn into butterflies or moths.* *turn into a street etc* turn and go into a street. *turn s.o/s.t into s.t* change s.t into s.t. ⇨ turn(13). *turn s.o, an animal, loose* free s.o or an animal. *turn nasty* become unpleasant, rude, dangerous etc. *turn off (from s.t)* stop going along a street etc and turn to go into another one. *turn s.o off* (*fig*; *informal*) not seem pleasant to s.o: *Violence in films turns me off.* *turn s.t off* stop s.t (e.g a tap or the water) from running. *turn the gas, light etc off/out* stop the gas etc burning. *turn on s.o/s.t* ⇨ turn (up)on s.o/s.t. *turn s.o on* (*fig*; *informal*) seem pleasant to s.o: *Do pretty faces turn you on? turn s.t on* make s.t (e.g a tap or water) start running. *turn out* happen; have a result; finish up in a certain way: *Our plans turned out well. How did your job turn out in the end? The day started rainy but it turned out warm and sunny.* *turn s.o/s.t out* (**a**) produce s.o/s.t: *This university turns out good scientists.* (**b**) provide s.o with the clothes etc he/she needs: *She was always beautifully turned out when I met her.* *turn s.o out* (*of s.t*) force s.o to leave (s.t): *The teacher turned the naughty boy out (of his class).* *turn a cupboard, drawer etc out* take all the things out of a cupboard etc so as to arrange them more tidily again. *turn the gas, light etc* ⇨ turn the gas, light etc off/out. *turn over* = turn(7): *She turned over and went to sleep. The car turned over in the road as it went round the corner.* ⇨ overturn. *turn (s.t) over* (of an engine) (cause an engine to) run very slowly. *turn s.t over* earn a certain amount of money by one's trade: *Our factory turns over a million or* *more pounds a year.* **turn over (from s.t) to s.t** stop doing or using s.t and start doing or using s.t else: *Our factory is turning over from coal to oil.*

turn s.o/s.t over (to s.o) give s.o/s.t to the police or to the person who is supposed to receive her/him/it. **turn s.t over (in one's mind)** think (carefully) about s.t.

turn s.o's stomach ⇒ stomach.

turn the tables (on s.o) ⇒ table(*n*).

turn tail (*informal*) turn and begin to run away or escape from danger.

turn to s.t start directing one's attention to s.t. **turn to crime** *etc* change from being honest etc to being a criminal etc. **turn to s.o (for s.t)** apply to s.o (for s.t). **turn to page 20** *etc* (**for s.t**) look at page 20 etc (to find s.t).

turn turtle ⇒ turtle.

turn up appear when one/it is not expected. **s.t will turn up** s.t will happen if one waits: *I don't know what we can do tomorrow but something will probably turn up.* **turn s.t up** (**a**) cause s.t to appear when it is not expected. (**b**) look for s.t in a book etc and find it: *I don't know exactly where he lives but I can turn his address up in my address book if you like.* **turn a dress** *etc* **up** make a dress shorter by turning the bottom up and sewing it. Opposite let s.t down(b). **turn it up** (*slang*) (usu as an order) stop doing what one is doing. **turn up one's nose (at s.t)** ⇒ nose(*n*).

turn (up)on s.o/s.t (**a**) suddenly attack s.o/s.t, either with blows or with words etc. (**b**) (*fig*) depend on s.t: *Whether his story can be proved or not turns on whether anyone saw him in the park that morning or not.*

turn (s.o/s.t) upside down (cause (s.o/s.t) to) turn in such a way that what was the top becomes the bottom. **turn s.t upside down** make s.t very untidy.

'turna,bout *c.n* (sometimes *fig*) change from going in one direction to going in another, usu the opposite one.

'turn,coat *c.n* (*derog*) person who does not remain loyal to her/his beliefs etc.

-turned *adj* shaped, spoken, written etc in the way shown in the first part of the word: *His speeches were always made in well-turned sentences.*

'turner *c.n* person who turns(11) wood etc.

'turning *c.n* place where one can turn(5) off one road into another.

'turning ,circle *c.n* smallest width of a circle that a car etc can turn in.

'turning ,point *c.n* point in time at which things change in an important way: *The invention of the steam engine was a turning point in British industry.*

'turn-,off *c.n* place where one turns(5) off a road, usu into a less important one.

'turn,out *c.n* **1** total number of people who come to a meeting etc. **2** way in which s.o is dressed, in which a horse and carriage are decorated, etc. **3** (often — *of s.t*) example of turning (a drawer etc) out.

'turn,over *c.n* **1** (often — *of s.t*) money earned or goods sold etc, usu in a certain time (totalling an amount): *Our shop had a turnover of £3500 last week but after paying wages only £1000 was left.* **2** number of times s.t goes from one owner, tenant(1) etc to another in a certain time: *The flats*

in this building have a rapid turnover because they are rented mostly by foreigners. **3** change of people doing a particular job: *There is a rapid turnover among clerks in our office because they are all looking for better jobs.* **4** kind of small pie in which the filling is covered by folding over part of the pastry: *an apple turnover.*

'turn-,round *c.n* time taken to deal with s.t after it has arrived and to get it ready for leaving again: *The plane only had an hour's turn-round between arriving at the airport and leaving again.*

'turn,stile *c.n* kind of small gate that turns on an axle in the middle so that only one person can pass at a time, usu after having paid to go into a stadium etc.

'turn,table *c.n* flat circle on a record player on which records[1](1) are put in order to play them.

'turn-,up *c.n* piece at the bottom of some trousers that is turned up. **a turn-up for the book(s)** (*informal*) surprising, usu pleasant, thing that happens: *I thought I would have to travel alone, so it was a turn-up for the book when I found my old friend Margaret on the train.*

turnip /'tɜ:nɪp/ *n* **1** *c.n* kind of root eaten by people and cows etc. **2** *c.n* plant that has such a root. **3** *u.n* (also *attrib*) this root as food.

turnout, turnover, turnstile, turntable, turn-up ⇒ turn.

turpentine /'tɜ:pən,taɪn/ *u.n* (*informal* **turps**) kind of oil made from pine[1] etc trees, used to clean oil paint off brushes, clothes etc, or to make oil paint thinner etc.

turps /tɜ:ps/ *u.n* (*informal*) turpentine.

turquoise /'tɜ:kwɔɪz/ *n* **1** (also *attrib*) *u.n* light blue-green colour. **2** *c/u.n* semi-precious stone of this colour.

turret /'tʌrɪt/ *c.n* **1** small tower on a castle etc for fighting from or for decoration. **2** (*military*) (on a tank, warship, plane) place in which guns are protected by steel armour and that can be turned so that they can be fired in any direction.

turtle /'tɜ:tl/ *c.n* kind of animal like a tortoise but usu flatter and living in water. **turn turtle** (usu of boats and ships) turn upside down.

'turtle,dove *c.n* kind of dove(1).

'turtle,neck *c.n* (also *attrib*) sweater etc having a neck that is not open in front but that goes right round.

tusk /tʌsk/ *c.n* long sharp tooth of an elephant, warthog etc.

tussle /'tʌsl/ *c.n* **1** (*informal*) struggle: *have a tussle with a large dog.*
▷ *intr.v* **2** struggle: *We tussled over whether to buy the house or not.*

tussock /'tʌsək/ *c.n* tuft of grass growing close together.

tut /tʌt/ *interj* (sound made by clicking(2) the tip of the tongue against the back of the front top teeth, used to show disapproval): *Tut, tut, child, you can't run about with no clothes on!*

tutelage /'tju:tɪlɪdʒ/ *n* (*formal*) **1** *u.n* job of looking after a person's business, education, property etc when he/she is too young or ill to do it himself/herself. Compare guardianship. **2** *sing/u.n* state or time of being under s.o's tutelage(1).

tutor /'tju:tə/ *c.n* **1** teacher who teaches one pupil or a very few pupils privately. **2** teacher in a British university who gives a small number of students help in their studies.

either one at a time or in very small groups.

▷ *v* **3** *tr/intr.v* (often — (*s.o*) *in* s.t) be (like) a tutor(1,2) to s.o (in a particular subject).

tutorial /tju:'tɔ:rɪəl/ *adj* **1** of or referring to a tutor(1,2) or her/his work.

▷ *c.n* **2** lesson given by a tutor(2).

tutti frutti /ˌtu:tɪ 'fru:tɪ/ *u.n* (*Italian*) kind of ice-cream that has small pieces of fruit and sometimes nuts in it.

tut-tut /ˌtʌt 'tʌt/ *interj* **1** = tut.

▷ *intr.v* (-*tt*-) **2** say tut-tut(1).

tutu /'tu:ˌtu:/ *c.n* short very full kind of ballet(3) skirt.

tux /tʌks/ *c.n* (*informal*) tuxedo.

tuxedo /tʌk'si:dəʊ/ *c.n* (*pl* -s) (*informal tux*) (mostly US) = dinner jacket.

TV /ˌti: 'vi:/ *abbr* television.

twaddle /'twɒdl/ *u.n* (*derog*; *informal*) nonsense: *Don't talk twaddle!*

twang /twæŋ/ *c.n* **1** sound made by a very tight wire, string etc when it is pulled and let go. **2** sound made while speaking when one lets air come out of one's nose at the same time.

▷ *tr/intr.v* **3** (cause (s.t) to) make a twang(1).

'twas (strong form /twɒz/, weak form /twəz/) (*poetry*) = it was.

tweak /twi:k/ *c.n* **1** sudden pull and twist at the same time.

▷ *tr.v* **2** suddenly pull and twist (a person's nose or ear).

twee /twi:/ *adj* (*derog*; *informal*) too precious(3); too dainty(1) to be pleasant.

tweed /twi:d/ *u.n* (also *attrib*) kind of rough woollen cloth that is made with threads of various colours: *tweed trousers.*

tweeds *pl.n* clothes made of tweed.

'tween /twi:n/ *prep* (*poetry*) between.

tweet /twi:t/ *c.n* **1** sound made by a small bird, or a sound like this. Compare chirp(1), twitter(1).

▷ *intr.v* **2** make a tweet(1).

'tweeter *c.n* (part of a) loudspeaker that gives the high notes. Compare woofer.

tweezers /'twi:zəz/ *pl.n* (often *a pair of* —) instrument like a pair of scissors but with flat ends with which one can pull out hairs, pick up very small pieces etc.

twelve /twelv/ *det/pron/c.n* (*cardinal number*) number 12 (between 11 and 13): *I bought twelve apples. I bought twelve of them.* ⇒ dozen.

twelfth /twelfθ/ *det/pron* **1** (*ordinal number*) (person or thing) following 11 in order; 12th.

▷ *c.n* **2** one of twelve equal parts; 1/12: *A month is a twelfth of a year.*

twenty /'twentɪ/ *det/pron/c.n* (*pl* -*ies*) (*cardinal number*) number 20 (between 19 and 21): *It costs twenty pounds. Twenty-two of them were broken.* **in one's twenties** between 20 and 29 years of age. (**in/into**) **the twenties** (or **the 20(')s**) (**a**) (speed, temperature, marks etc) between 20 and 29: *the marks are only in the twenties.* (**b**) (years) between '20 and '29 in a century.

twentieth /'twentɪəθ/ *det/pron* **1** (*ordinal number*) (person or thing) following 19; 20th.

▷ *c.n* **2** one of twenty equal parts; 1/20.

'twere (strong form /twɜ:/, weak form /twə/) (*poetry*) = it were.

twerp /twɜ:p/ *c.n* (*derog*; *slang*) stupid or unpleasant person.

twice /twaɪs/ *adv* two times: *He's twice as big as you. She visits me twice a week. He earns twice my salary.* **once or twice** ⇒ once. **think twice** (**before doing s.t**) hesitate and think carefully (before doing s.t). **twice the person** (**he/she used to be** etc) (*fig*) much stronger, healthier etc (than before etc).

twiddle /'twɪdl/ *tr.v* move (s.t) in different directions without any purpose or without thinking: *twiddle one's fingers*; *twiddle the* knobs(2) *of a radio.* **twiddle at s.t** = twiddle s.t.

twig¹ /twɪg/ *c.n* long thin bit of a tree that grows out of a branch and that can have leaves etc on it.

twig² /twɪg/ *tr/intr.v* (-*gg*-) (*slang*) understand (s.t).

twilight /'twaɪˌlaɪt/ *u.n* **1** time between darkness and light in the morning, or between light and darkness in the evening: *There's no sound after twilight.* **2** light that one sees in the sky at these times. **3** (also *attrib*) (often *the* — *of s.o/s.t*) (*fig*) period in the life, history etc (of s.o/s.t) when he/she/it is losing his/her/its power, glory etc: *in the twilight of my life*; *the twilight of the British Empire.*

twill /twɪl/ *u.n* kind of strong cloth for making army uniforms(2) etc that has slightly raised lines very close together across it: cavalry *twill* breeches.

'twill /twɪl/ (*poetry*) = it will.

twin /twɪn/ *attrib.adj* **1** of one of two people, places etc that are very like each other, or that are twinned(3).

▷ *c.n* **2** (also *attrib*) one of two children born at the same time to the same mother: *John and David are twins. Paul is my twin brother.*

▷ *tr/intr.v* (-*nn*-) **3** (often — (s.t) *with* s.t) form a kind of special friendship with (another town etc, usu one in another country): *St Helier in Jersey is twinned with Avranches in France.*

ˌtwin 'bed *c.n* one of two single beds in the same room: *We would like a room with twin beds, please.* Compare double bed.

ˌtwin-'bedded *attrib.adj* having twin beds in it: *a twin-bedded room in a hotel.*

ˌtwin-'engined *adj* (usu *attrib*) (of a plane etc) having two engines.

'twin ˌset *c.n* woman's jumper and cardigan of the same colour and style which she wears together.

twine /twaɪn/ *u.n* **1** kind of strong string made of two or more strands' twined(2) together.

▷ *tr/intr.v* **2** (cause (s.t) to) twist round s.t: *Climbing plants like to twine round trees. The plants were twined together.* ⇒ entwine, intertwine.

twinge /twɪndʒ/ *c.n* (often — *of* s.t) sudden painful feeling in the body or mind (caused by s.t): *twinges of* neuralgia; *twinges of conscience after doing something wrong.*

twinkle /'twɪŋkl/ *n* **1** *sing.n* bright shine that comes and goes (and is produced by s.t): *the twinkle of the reflections of light on water.* **2** *c.n* light that becomes brighter, less bright, then bright again like the light of the stars in the sky. **3** *c.n* bright shining of a person's eyes (when he/she is happy, amused etc): *The cheerful conversation soon brought a twinkle to the old man's tired eyes.*

▷ *intr.v* **4** shine with a twinkle(*n*).

'twinkling *sing.n* **in a twinkling**; **in the twinkling of an eye** very quickly. ·

twirl /twɜːl/ *c.n* **1** fast twist round and round; spin(1,2).

▷ *tr/intr.v* **2** (cause (s.o/s.t) to) go round and round fast; (cause (s.o/s.t) to) spin: *twirl a stick in the air.* **3** *tr.v* curl (s.o's hair).

'twirly *adj* (*-ier, -iest*) **1** that twirls(2). **2** that curls.

twist /twɪst/ *n* **1** *c.n* turn(1), usu a sudden and/or sharp one. **2** *c.n* (often *a — of s.t*) thing made by twisting(7) s.t or by twisting two or more things together: *He lit the fire with a twist of paper.* **3** *c.n* bend in a road etc, usu a sharp bend: *After many twists and turns we arrived at the village.* **4** *c.n* (*fig*) direction, sometimes one that is not expected, in which a person's mind, character, life etc goes: *It was a twist of fate that brought him riches at the age of 55.* **5** *def.n* kind of dance that was popular in the 1960s when one had to move one's hips¹ from side to side and wave one's arms: *dance/do the twist.* **round the twist** (*derog; slang*) mad; round the bend (⇒ bend(*n*)).

▷ *v* **6** *tr/intr.v* (cause (s.o/s.t) to) turn and go or face in a different direction, once or more than once. **7** *tr/intr.v* (cause (s.t) to) go round (and round) (s.t): *She twisted the rope round a post on the shore to stop the boat. You can twist this wire into any shape you want.* **8** *tr.v* (often *— (s.t) together*) (cause (s.t and s.t) to) go round each other once or more than once: *If you twist these pieces of string together they will be stronger. The snakes were twisting together on the ground.* **9** *tr.v* make (s.t) by twisting(7) s.t and s.t: *You can twist a thread out of these pieces of cotton.* **10** *tr.v* hurt (one's ankle etc) by bending it accidentally: *He fell and twisted an ankle badly.* **11** *intr.v* dance the twist(5). **twist s.o's arm** ⇒ arm¹. **twist s.t off s.t** remove s.t from s.t by twisting(6) and pulling it. **twist s.o round one's little finger** ⇒ finger(*n*).

'twisty *adj* (*-ier, -iest*) that twists(6) (a lot): *a twisty path through the woods.*

twit /twɪt/ *c.n* (*derog; slang*) stupid person.

twitch /twɪtʃ/ *c.n* **1** sudden movement (or several movements) of a muscle(1) without the person intending it. **2** sudden short quick pull at s.t, e.g a rope.

▷ *v* **3** *intr.v* (often *— with s.t*) move with a twitch(1) (because of s.t). **4** *tr.v* cause (one's nose etc) to move as if it is twitching(3): *Animals often twitch their ears when flies try to settle on them.* **5** *tr.v* pull (s.t) suddenly with a twitch(2). **twitch at s.t** = twitch(5) s.t.

twitter /'twɪtə/ *sing/u.n* **1** sounds made by small birds. Compare chirp(1), tweet(1). **2** sound of excited talk.

▷ *intr.v* **3** (of small birds) make a twitter(1). **4** talk fast and usu in an excited way because one is worried or excited.

twixt, 'twixt /twɪkst/ *prep* (*poetry*) = between.

two /tuː/ *det/pron/c.n* (*cardinal number*) number 2 (between 1 and 3): *I ran two miles. Two of us went. He's two (years old).* **in two** so that s.t divides into two parts: *He broke the biscuit in two.* **one or two** ⇒ one(*pron*). **put two and two together** (*fig*) (try to) work s.t out by looking at the facts: *I didn't know where the children had gone but I saw they had taken their toy boats so I put two and two together and found them by the*

pond. **two a penny** (**a**) of small value: *Bicycles like his are two a penny.* (**b**) easily available: *People with her ability are two a penny.* **two can play at that game** (*fig*) if one person can do that, so can another person: *Jim sometimes goes out without doing the housework but two can play at that game, and I have now started to do the same.*

,two-'edged *attrib.adj* **1** (of a sword etc) having two sharp edges instead of only one. **2** (*fig*) having two possible meanings or effects, one of which is good and the other bad: *Saying to someone that he has a voice like a trumpet can be a two-edged* compliment(1).

,two-'faced *adj* (*derog*) not honest; saying one thing to one person and the opposite to another.

,two-'handed *adj* (usu *attrib*) that needs two hands or two people to use it: *a two-handed sword; a two-handed saw.*

twopence /'tʌpəns/ *c/u.n* (coin worth) two pennies. **not care twopence (about s.o/s.t)**; **not give twopence (for s.o/s.t)** (*informal*) not care anything at all (about s.o/s.t).

twopenny /'tʌpənɪ/ *adj* costing twopence.

twopenny piece /ˌtʌpənɪ 'piːs/ *c.n* coin worth twopence.

,two-'piece *attrib.adj* **1** consisting of two parts that go together: *a two-piece suit* (coat and trousers); *a two-piece* suite(1) *of furniture.*

▷ *c.n* **2** suit consisting of two parts (e.g a coat and skirt/trousers).

'two-ply *adj* **1** (usu *attrib*) made of two thicknesses or of two threads together: *two-ply board; two-ply wool.*

▷ *u.n* **2** board, wood etc that is two-ply(1).

'twosome *c.n* two people or things together.

'two-,time *tr/intr.v* (*informal*) cheat (one's boyfriend, girlfriend) by having another one secretly.

,two-'timer *c.n* (*derog*) person who two-times.

,two-'tone *adj* (usu *attrib*) **1** (usu *attrib*) painted in two colours or two different shades of the same colour. **2** (of a car horn etc) producing two musical tones.

,two-'way *attrib.adj* **1** going in two opposite directions: *two-way traffic.* Compare one-way. **2** (of a radio etc) allowing one both to speak to others and to listen to them.

tycoon /taɪ'kuːn/ *c.n* very important (and rich) businessman or factory owner etc.

tying /'taɪɪŋ/ *pres.p* of tie.

type /taɪp/ *n* **1** *c.n* (often *— of s.t*) special kind² or sort(1) (of s.t): *We sell pens but not ones of this type.* (Notice that we can use a count noun without 'a/an' after 'type of', e.g 'What type of man do you prefer?' 'This type of car is very fast.') **2** *c/u.n* (also *attrib*) kind of: *French type bread; a German type sausage.* **3** *c.n* (*informal*) sort of person: *Pleasant types live in our street.* **4** *c.n* metal etc block with a raised letter, number or symbol on it, used on a typewriter. **5** *u.n* metal letters, numbers etc made into a block or blocks, and used in printing books etc. **6** *c.n* one style or block of this kind: *italic type.* **reversion to type** fact of reverting to type. **revert to type** go back to what s.o/s.t was by nature: *He tries to be nice but soon gets angry and reverts to type.* **true to type** behaving, looking etc like a normal one of that type(1).

▷ *tr/intr.v* **7** write (s.t) using a typewriter.

'type,cast *tr.v* class (s.o) (as s.t), esp for acting in plays, films etc: *Valerie is always typecast as the simple little country girl.*

'type,face *c.n* kind and size of type(4) used in printing, on a typewriter etc.

'type,script *c/u.n* thing that has been written on a typewriter. *in typescript* written on a typewriter. Compare manuscript.

'type,set *tr/intr.v* set(20) type(5).

'type,setter *c.n* person who sets(20) type(5).

'type,writer *c.n* machine that prints letters, numbers etc on paper when one hits keys(4). Compare word-processor.

'type,written *adj* that has been written on a typewriter.

typical /'tɪpɪkl/ *adj* (often — *of s.o/s.t*) normal or usual (for that type(1,3) of person, animal, thing): *Our typical Sunday is spent driving around the villages.*

'typically *adv* and what I am about to say is typical: *Typically, although the man was hungry, he gave his food to the poor children.*

typify /'tɪpɪˌfaɪ/ *tr.v* (*-ies*, *-ied*) (*formal*) be a typical example of (s.o/s.t): *Mary typifies the best in our young women.*

'typing ,pool *c.n* group of typists who type things for anybody in the office etc where they work.

'typist *c.n* person whose main job is to type(7) letters etc. *shorthand typist* ⇒ short.

typographer /taɪˈpɒgrəfə/ *c.n* person skilled in designing typefaces or in designing books and choosing the typefaces for them.

typographical /ˌtaɪpəˈgræfɪkl/ *adj* (also **typo-graphic**) of or referring to typography.

,typo'graphically *adv.*

typography /taɪˈpɒgrəfɪ/ *u.n* (*technical*) **1** preparing things before one prints them. **2** kind, size, arrangement etc of type(5) used in printing.

typhoid /'taɪfɔɪd/ *u.n* (also **,typhoid 'fever**) kind of disease that one can catch by eating or drinking contaminated(1) things and that attacks one's bowels(1), causing fever and sometimes death.

typhoon /taɪˈfuːn/ *c.n* kind of very strong storm with violent winds moving round and round and over a wide area in the Pacific Ocean or the China Seas. Compare cyclone(1), hurricane, tornado.

typhus /'taɪfəs/ *u.n* kind of disease that can be caught by being bitten by lice (⇒ louse(1)) or fleas and that gives one a high fever.

typical(ly), typify, typing, typist, typog-rapher, typographic(al), typography ⇒ type.

tyrant /'taɪərənt/ *c.n* (*derog*) **1** cruel and unfair person (esp a ruler) who can do whatever he/she wants with other people without being limited by any laws etc. **2** person who behaves as if he/she was a tyrant(1), e.g a husband towards his wife or a parent towards children.

tyrannical /tɪˈrænɪkl/ *adj* of, like, a tyrant.

ty'rannically *adv.*

tyrannous /'tɪrənəs/ *adj* = tyrannical.

tyrannize, -ise /'tɪrəˌnaɪz/ *tr/intr.v* behave like a tyrant (towards s.o/s.t).

tyranny /'tɪrənɪ/ *n* (*pl -ies*) **1** *u.n* behaviour of, or treatment by, a tyrant. **2** *c.n* example of such

behaviour or treatment. **3** *c.n* country etc ruled by a tyrant(1). **4** *u.n* (*fig*) power that cannot be resisted: *the tyranny of having to earn a living so that one is not free to do what one wants to do.*

tyre /taɪə/ *c.n* (US **tire**) thing made of rubber that is put round the wheel of a car, bicycle etc to make driving or riding more comfortable.

tzar /zɑː/ *c.n* ⇒ tsar.

tzarina /zɑːˈriːnə/ *c.n* ⇒ tsarina.

Uu

U, u /juː/ *c/unique n* 21st letter of the English alphabet.

,U-'turn *c.n* **1** turn by a driver, cyclist etc to face the opposite direction. **2** (*fig*) complete change of opinion, a decision etc.

U /juː/ *adj* (*informal*) upper class. Opposite non-U.

ubiquitous /juːˈbɪkwɪtəs/ *adj* (*formal*) existing or done (almost) everywhere: *ubiquitous chips on English menus.*

u'biquitousness *u.n.*

udder /'ʌdə/ *c.n* part of a cow, female goat etc in which her milk is kept.

UDI /ˌjuː diː 'aɪ/ *abbr* Unilateral Declaration of Independence. *declare UDI* declare that one's country is going to make itself politically independent in spite of opposition from other governments.

UFO /ˌjuː ,ef 'əʊ/ *abbr* unidentified flying object.

ugh /ʊh/ *interj* (sound made when one thinks s.o/ s.t is unpleasant).

ugly /'ʌglɪ/ *adj* (*-ier*, *-iest*) **1** not pleasant to look at; not at all beautiful or pretty: *ugly buildings; an ugly face/expression.* **2** not pleasant to listen to: *ugly sounds from a broken piano.* **3** unpleasant and dangerous or threatening: *an ugly scene outside the offices with crowds shouting and throwing things; an ugly cloud (threatening rain).*

,ugly 'duckling *c.n* person who seems less beautiful, clever etc than others when young but who later becomes more beautiful, clever etc than them.

'ugliness *u.n.*

UHF /ˌjuː ,eɪtʃ 'ef/ *abbr* ultrahigh frequency.

UK /ˌjuː 'keɪ/ *def.n abbr* United Kingdom.

ukulele /ˌjuːkəˈleɪlɪ/ *c.n* kind of small musical instrument with 4 strings.

ulcer /'ʌlsə/ *c.n* open sore on a person's or animal's skin or inside her/his/its body.

ulterior /ʌlˈtɪərɪə/ *adj* **1** (*technical*) coming later in time. **2** further away.

ul,terior 'motive *c.n* (often — *for s.t*) real (secret) reason (for doing or saying s.t) hidden behind the (false) reason one gives people.

ultimate /'ʌltɪmɪt/ *adj* **1** final; last (of a group of events etc): *The ultimate decision belongs to* *the judge.* **2** furthest away: *The ultimate place to find these flowers is a long way up the mountain.* **3** basic and most important: *A minister has ultimate responsibility for mistakes and dishonesty in a government department.*

'ultimately *adv* in the end; as the last thing: *We seemed to be losing the game but ultimately we won by 3 points.*

ultimatum /ˌʌltɪˈmeɪtəm/ *c.n* (*pl* -s or, less usu, *ultimata* /ˌʌltɪˈmeɪtə/) threat to do s.t (often to attack) if s.o else refuses to do s.t else (e.g to surrender(1)).

ultrahigh frequency /ˌʌltrəˌhaɪ ˈfriːkwənsɪ/ *u.n* (usu as *abbr* UHF) (*formal*) frequency(2) of radio waves between 300 million and 3000 million hertz; this makes the quality of the sound extremely good. Compare very high frequency.

ultramarine /ˌʌltrəməˈriːn/ *u.n* (also *attrib*) very bright blue colour.

ultramodern /ˌʌltrəˈmɒdən/ *adj* extremely modern.

ultrasonic /ˌʌltrəˈsɒnɪk/ *adj* (of a sound wave) so high in frequency(2) that human beings cannot hear it.

ultraviolet /ˌʌltrəˈvaɪələt/ *adj* (of light waves) frequency(2) which is higher than the highest that human beings can see.

ˌultraˌviolet 'lamp *c.n* lamp using ultraviolet rays.

ˌultraˌviolet 'rays *pl.n* light waves of ultraviolet frequency(2) used for medical or scientific purposes. Compare infrared.

umbilical cord /ʌmˌbɪlɪkl ˈkɔːd/ *c.n* tube carrying blood etc from a mother to her child before it is born.

umbrage /ˈʌmbrɪdʒ/ *u.n* **take umbrage (at s.t)** take offence (because of s.t): *She took umbrage at not receiving an invitation.*

umbrella /ʌmˈbrelə/ *c.n* **1** round piece of cloth etc on a frame with a handle in the centre; it can be opened and closed; used to protect from rain. **2** (*fig*) thing that protects: *We travelled secretly under the umbrella of darkness.* **3** (*fig*) political or administrative responsibility: *These expenses come under the umbrella of the sales department.*

umpire /ˈʌmpaɪə/ *c.n* **1** judge in certain kinds of games and sport, e.g tennis and cricket[1]. Compare referee(2).
▷ *tr/intr.v* **2** act as umpire(1) in (a game).

umpteen /ʌmpˈtiːn/ *det/pron* (*informal*) very many (of s.t): *I've asked you umpteen times to close the door.*

'umpteenth /ʌmpˈtiːnθ/ *det/pron* (usu *for the — time*) so often that it becomes annoying etc.

UN /ˌjuː ˈen/ *def.n abbr* United Nations.

unabashed /ˌʌnəˈbæʃt/ *adj* (usu *pred*; *formal*) not afraid or ashamed in spite of danger or embarrassing events: *Sue seemed unabashed after the criticism of her work in the newspaper.* Compare abashed.

unabated /ˌʌnəˈbeɪtɪd/ *adj* not stopping or growing less strong; continuing as strongly as before: *The rain continued unabated for several days.*

unable /ʌnˈeɪbl/ *adj* **unable to do s.t** not able to do s.t: *I'm unable to help you.* ⇒ inability.

unabridged /ˌʌnəˈbrɪdʒd/ *adj* not abridged; in

its full original form: *an unabridged report of a meeting.*

unacceptable /ˌʌnəkˈseptəbl/ *adj* not acceptable(1).

unaccompanied /ˌʌnəˈkʌmpənɪd/ *adj* **1** not being carried or taken by s.o: *unaccompanied luggage/children.* **2** not with music as support: *an unaccompanied song/singer.*

unaccountable /ˌʌnəˈkaʊntəbl/ *adj* (*formal*) impossible to explain the reasons for: *an unaccountable delay in sending a reply.*
ˌunacˈcountably *adv.*

unaccustomed /ˌʌnəˈkʌstəmd/ *adj* **1** (usu — *to s.t*) not used[3]/accustomed (to s.t): *I am unaccustomed to speaking in public.* **2** not usual: *Athens had unaccustomed rain during our holiday there.*

unaffected /ˌʌnəˈfektɪd/ *adj* **1** (often — *by s.t*) not involved, influenced, damaged etc (by s.t): *She was unaffected by the decision to reorganize the department.* **2** simple and natural and not trying to make an impression(1) on s.o: *Her pleasure at the news of her rival's success was quite unaffected.*

un-American /ˌʌn əˈmerɪkən/ *adj* (usu — *activities*) against or not favourable to the US.

unanimous /juːˈnænɪməs/ *adj* (with) everybody in agreement: *unanimous approval.*

unanimity /ˌjuːnəˈnɪmɪtɪ/ *u.n* fact of being unanimous.

unˌanimous 'verdict *c.n* verdict(1) agreed by everyone on a jury(1).

uˈnanimously *adv.*

unannounced /ˌʌnəˈnaʊnst/ *adj* without warning; without having been announced before (it happened): *When the manager returned to the factory unannounced, there was a rush to get back to work.*

unanswerable /ʌnˈɑːnsərəbl/ *adj* impossible to answer.

unappealing /ˌʌnəˈpiːlɪŋ/ *adj* not attractive.

unappetizing /ʌnˈæpɪˌtaɪzɪŋ/ *adj* not appetizing.

unapproachable /ˌʌnəˈprəʊtʃəbl/ *adj* not easy to talk to; seeming not to want people to talk to her/him: *A manager must not be unapproachable.*

unarmed /ʌnˈɑːmd/ *adj* without or not using any weapons or arms: *unarmed combat(1).*

unasked /ʌnˈɑːskt/ *adj* (often — *for*) that has not been asked for; not necessary: *That rude remark was unasked for.*

unassuming /ˌʌnəˈsjuːmɪŋ/ *adj* modest; behaving quietly; not seeming to want to be thought important.

unattached /ˌʌnəˈtætʃt/ *adj* without a husband, wife, regular boyfriend or regular girlfriend.

unattainable /ˌʌnəˈteɪnəbl/ *adj* that cannot be attained.

unattended /ˌʌnəˈtendəd/ *adj* (often *leave s.o/s.t —*) without anyone looking after, watching or guarding her/him/it.

unavailable /ˌʌnəˈveɪləbl/ *adj* not available.

unavailing /ˌʌnəˈveɪlɪŋ/ *adj* (*formal*) not successful: *unavailing efforts to save her life.*

unavoidable /ˌʌnəˈvɔɪdəbl/ *adj* not avoidable.

unawares /ˌʌnəˈweəz/ *adv* **take s.o unawares** come when not expected: *He came to the party and took us unawares* (surprised us).

unbalance /ʌnˈbæləns/ *tr.v* cause (s.o) to lose

her/his balance(1,2) of body or mind: *The shock unbalanced his mind.*

un'balanced *adj* having lost, or showing that one has lost, normal balance of mind: *an unbalanced person; unbalanced behaviour.*

unbar /ʌn'bɑː/ *tr.v* (*-rr-*) **1** remove the bar(s)(1) from (s.t): *They unbarred the door.* **2** (*fig*) remove the thing(s) restricting (s.t) or holding (s.t) back: *The law unbarred the opportunities for women in industry.*

unbearable /ʌn'beərəbl/ *adj* impossible to put up with; impossible to bear[1](5): *unbearable cold/ pain/behaviour.*

un'bearably *adv.*

unbecoming /ˌʌnbɪ'kʌmɪŋ/ *adj* not suiting s.o well; not becoming.

unbelievable /ˌʌnbɪ'liːvəbl/ *adj* too great, bad etc to believe: *Mike's unkindness/generosity is unbelievable.*

ˌunbe'lievably *adv: unbelievably wealthy.*

ˌunbe'liever *c.n* person who does not have faith (in a religion).

unbend /ʌn'bend/ *intr.v* (*p.t,p.p* **unbent** /ʌn'bent/) (*fig*) become less formal in speech or behaviour.

un'bending *adj* (usu *derog*) never willing to change one's ideas, beliefs etc.

unbind /ʌn'baɪnd/ *tr.v* (*p.t,p.p* **unbound** /ʌn'baʊnd/) untie (s.o/s.t); loosen or remove (s.t that binds s.o/s.t): *She unbound the bandage.*

un'bound[1] *adj* (usu of a book) not bound[1].

unborn /ʌn'bɔːn/ *adj* **1** alive but not yet born: *an unborn child.* **2** (*fig*) not yet existing: *unborn generations(4).*

unbound[2] /ʌn'baʊnd/ *p.t,p.p* of unbind.

unbounded /ʌn'baʊndɪd/ *adj* (*formal*) very great; without any limits or bounds: *an unbounded faith in his son's ability.*

unbreakable /ʌn'breɪkəbl/ *adj* that cannot be broken.

unbridled /ʌn'braɪdld/ *adj* (*fig*) not controlled or limited: *unbridled curiosity.*

unbuckle /ʌn'bʌkl/ *tr.v* loosen or open the buckle(1) (of a belt, shoe etc).

unburden /ʌn'bɜːdn/ *tr.v* (often — *oneself* (*of s.t*) (*to s.o*)) (*formal*) tell (s.o) about s.t unpleasant that has been secretly worrying one and by doing so feel some relief: *He unburdened himself to his doctor. Talking may help you to unburden yourself of the guilt you are feeling.*

unbutton /ʌn'bʌtn/ *tr.v* take the buttons of (s.t) out of their buttonholes: *He unbuttoned his coat.*

un'buttoned *adj.*

uncalled-for /ʌn'kɔːld ˌfɔː/ *adj* (of unpleasant behaviour, words etc) not deserved; unfair: *uncalled-for rudeness.*

uncanny /ʌn'kænɪ/ *adj* (*-ier, -iest*) very strange(1); very unusual; difficult to explain: *That man has an uncanny resemblance to his cat.*

un'cannily *adv.* **un'canniness** *u.n.*

uncared-for /ʌn'keəd ˌfɔː/ *adj* (seeming to be) not (properly) looked after: *an uncared-for appearance.*

unceremonious /ˌʌnserɪ'məʊnɪəs/ *adj* (*formal*) **1** (so great as to be) rude: *unceremonious haste.* **2** without (too) much ceremony(1): *an unceremonious wedding.*

ˌunceremoniously *adv.* **ˌuncere'monious-ness** *u.n.*

uncertain /ʌn'sɜːtn/ *adj* (often — *about/of s.o/ s.t*) not sure (about/of s.o/s.t): *He was uncertain of the way to the station. I'm uncertain where to go next.*

un'certainly *adv.* **un'certainness** *u.n.*

un'certainty *n* (*pl -ies*) **1** *u.n* (often — *about/ of s.t*) fact of being uncertain (about s.t): *She felt uncertainty about her ability to do the work.* **2** *c.n* thing that is uncertain: *the uncertainties of politics.*

uncertifiable /ˌʌnsɜːtɪ'faɪəbl/ *adj* not certifiable.

unchanged /ʌn'tʃeɪndʒd/ *adj* not changed(11).

uncharitable /ʌn'tʃærɪtəbl/ *adj* (*formal*) not kind or generous(1,2); cruel and nasty: *uncharitable criticism.*

un'charitably *adv.*

uncharted /ʌn'tʃɑːtɪd/ *adj* not having been mapped; about which few or no details are known: *uncharted seas; uncharted areas of the brain.*

unchecked /ʌn'tʃekt/ *adj* **1** not having been checked (⇒ check(7)): *unchecked reports of an explosion.* **2** (usu *go* —) without being controlled or stopped: *This disease will go unchecked unless we tell everyone how serious it is and give useful advice.* ⇒ check(8).

unchivalrous /ʌn'ʃɪvlrəs/ *adj* not chivalrous.

unchristian /ʌn'krɪstʃən/ *adj* unkind; not what one expects from a Christian(3): *unchristian thoughts.*

uncivil /ʌn'sɪvl/ *adj* not civil.

uncivilized /ʌn'sɪvɪˌlaɪzd/ *adj* not civilized.

uncle /'ʌŋkl/ *c.n* **1** brother of one's mother or father; husband of one's aunt: *her uncle Bob.* **2** man whose brother/sister has a daughter/ son: *Fred has just become an uncle.* **3** man friend who is old enough to be a young child's uncle(1).

unclean /ʌn'kliːn/ *adj* **1** (considered) immoral: *unclean thoughts.* **2** considered unsuitable to eat etc for religious or moral reasons.

un'cleanness *u.n.*

unclear /ʌn'klɪə/ *adj* **1** not easy to see through; cloudy: *unclear water.* **2** not easy to understand: *an unclear explanation.* **3** (*pred*) not certain: *I am unclear about what you want me to do.*

unclouded /ʌn'klaʊdɪd/ *adj* (often — *by s.t*) **1** not having anything in it that makes seeing difficult: *unclouded sight.* **2** (*fig*) pure; not mixed with anything that makes it less perfect: *unclouded happiness.*

uncoloured /ʌn'kʌləd/ *adj* (*US* **un'colored**) **1** not having any colour in it: *uncoloured glass.* **2** not having any additions to it to make it more interesting etc: *an uncoloured report of a discussion.*

uncomfortable /ʌn'kʌmftəbl/ *adj* not at ease in one's body or mind; not comfortable: *an uncomfortable feeling/chair.*

un'comfortably *adv* **1** in an uncomfortable way: *sitting uncomfortably.* **2** so much as to be unpleasant: *The suggestions about who is to blame came uncomfortably close to us.*

uncommercial /ˌʌnkə'mɜːʃəl/ *adj* not commercial(2).

uncommitted /ˌʌnkə'mɪtɪd/ *adj* (often — *to s.t*) not having agreed to support one side or another in an argument, disagreement etc: *an uncommitted voter.*

uncommon /ʌnˈkɒmən/ *adj* rare; not usual: *uncommon flowers*; *uncommon behaviour.*
un'commonly *adv* (*formal*) unusually; very: *Our neighbours are uncommonly helpful to us.*

uncommunicative /ˌʌnkəˈmjuːnɪkətɪv/ *adj* not communicative.

uncomplicated /ʌnˈkɒmplɪˌkeɪtɪd/ *adj* not complicated.

uncompromising /ʌnˈkɒmprəˌmaɪzɪŋ/ *adj* not changing one's beliefs, ideas etc at all; refusing to compromise(2): *uncompromising politicians.*
un'compro,misingly *adv.*

unconcern /ˌʌnkənˈsɜːn/ *u.n* (often — *for s.o/ s.t*) (*formal*) lack of worry, interest, (about s.o/ s.t): *unconcern for the future.*
,uncon'cerned *adj* **1** (often — *about s.t*) not feeling worried, disturbed or concerned (about s.t): *I'm unconcerned about his late arrival.* **2** (often — *with s.t*) not involved(1) with s.t: *I'm unconcerned with that part of the work.*

unconditional /ˌʌnkənˈdɪʃənl/ *adj* (often — *surrender*) complete (surrender(1) etc) without any conditions being allowed or agreed. ⇨ conditional.
,uncon'ditionally *adv.*

unconfirmed /ˌʌnkənˈfɜːmd/ *adj* not confirmed(2).

unconnected /ˌʌnkəˈnektɪd/ *adj* not connected; not connected (with s.o/s.t).

unconscionable /ʌnˈkɒnʃənəbl/ *adj* (*formal*) more, greater, than is reasonable: *She spends an unconscionable time in front of the mirror.*
un'conscionably *adv.*

unconscious /ʌnˈkɒnʃəs/ *adj* **1** having lost consciousness; not conscious(1,2). **2** (often — *of s.t*) not conscious(2) (of s.t); not knowing (s.t): *unconscious of the danger.*
▷ *def.n* **3** part of the mind containing feelings etc that one is not conscious of. Compare subconscious.
un'consciously *adv.* **un'consciousness** *u.n.*

unconsidered /ˌʌnkənˈsɪdəd/ *adj* (*formal*) **1** done without careful thought: *unconsidered actions.* **2** not thought to be at all important: *unconsidered papers left in an untidy pile.*

unconstitutional /ʌnˌkɒnstɪˈtjuːʃənl/ *adj* not constitutional(1).
un,consti'tutionally *adv.*

unconstructive /ˌʌnkənˈstrʌktɪv/ *adj* not constructive.

uncontrollable /ˌʌnkənˈtrəʊləbl/ *adj* not controllable.

uncontrolled /ˌʌnkənˈtrəʊld/ *adj* not controlled.

unconventional /ˌʌnkənˈvenʃənl/ *adj* not conventional.

unconvincing /ˌʌnkənˈvɪnsɪŋ/ *adj* not convincing.

uncooperative /ˌʌnkəʊˈɒprətɪv/ *adj* not cooperative.

uncork /ʌnˈkɔːk/ *tr.v* remove the cork of (a bottle of wine etc).

uncountable /ʌnˈkaʊntəbl/ *adj* (*grammar*) (of a noun) that cannot have a plural and has 'some', 'a lot of' etc in front of it, not numbers etc (marked *u.n* in this dictionary). Compare count noun.

uncouple /ʌnˈkʌpl/ *tr.v* (often — *s.t from s.t*) stop (s.t) remaining joined together or to s.t

else: *They are uncoupling the train from its engine.*

uncouth /ʌnˈkuːθ/ *adj* (*derog*; *formal*) rude; showing bad manners: *It was uncouth of Ben to walk out without saying goodbye.*
un'couthly *adv.* **un'couthness** *u.n.*

uncover /ʌnˈkʌvə/ *tr.v* **1** take the cover off (s.t): *Leave the meat uncovered.* **2** find out (s.t that was hidden or secret before): *uncover a plot(1) to kill the president.*

uncritical /ʌnˈkrɪtɪkl/ *adj* (often — *about/of s.o/ s.t*) accepting (s.o/s.t) without thinking about whether he/she/it has any faults; not critical(2) (about s.o/s.t).
un'critically *adv.*

uncross /ʌnˈkrɒs/ *tr.v* (usu — *one's legs, arms*) move (one's legs, arms) apart from a crossed position.

uncrushable /ʌnˈkrʌʃəbl/ *adj* **1** (of cloth etc) that does not have creases(1) after having been crushed. **2** (*fig*) (of people, beliefs, feelings etc) that cannot be defeated.

unctuous /ˈʌŋktjuəs/ *adj* (*derog*; *formal*) (of a person, behaviour) insincere, oily, showing too much willingness to please, help etc.
'unctuously *adv.* **'unctuousness** *u.n.*

uncultivated /ʌnˈkʌltɪˌveɪtɪd/ *adj* not cultivated.

uncultured /ʌnˈkʌltʃəd/ *adj* not cultured.

uncured /ʌnˈkjʊəd/ *adj* not cured.

uncurl /ʌnˈkɜːl/ *intr.v* bend straight after being curled(4).

uncut /ʌnˈkʌt/ *adj* **1** (of precious stones etc) not cut and polished for use in jewellery. **2** (of films etc) complete; without having had any parts taken away. **3** (of a book) having some edges of pages still joined to each other.

undaunted /ʌnˈdɔːntɪd/ *adj* not frightened by the dangers and difficulties that might frighten other people: *Bill was undaunted by the storm as he sailed round the coast.*

undecided /ˌʌndɪˈsaɪdɪd/ *adj* **1** (often — *about s.t*) not yet having come to a decision (about s.t): *I'm still undecided about what colour to paint the house.* **2** without a result one way or the other: *The game continued until darkness when both players stopped, leaving the result still undecided.*
,unde'cidedly *adv.*

undemanding /ˌʌndɪˈmɑːndɪŋ/ *adj* not demanding.

undemocratic /ʌnˌdeməˈkrætɪk/ *adj* not democratic.

undemonstrative /ˌʌndɪˈmɒnstrətɪv/ *adj* not demonstrative.

undeniable /ˌʌndɪˈnaɪəbl/ *adj* not possible to deny(1).
,unde'niably *adv.*

under /ˈʌndə/ *adv* **1** in or to a lower position: *The sail broke in the storm and the ship went under* (sank). **2** less (in age, number, amount etc): *Children of 16 and under are not allowed in. If there are 20 or under who sign for the journey, the fare(1) will have to be increased.* ⇨ below(7), over(8). **3** (often *keep s.o —*) in a state of being strictly controlled by using force: *The population refused to be kept under by their cruel ruler.* **down under** ⇨ down¹ (*adv*). For 'under' + noun (phrase(1)) e.g *under age*, ⇨ the noun.
▷ *prep* **4** in or to a position below (and touching

or not touching): *The cat is under the table. He hid under the blankets.* Compare beneath(2). Opposite over(12,14). **5** in or into a position below the surface of: *under the ground/water.* Compare beneath(4). Opposite above(10). **6** less or fewer than: *We were there for under an hour. Children under 2 years old travel free. There are under 50 members now.* Opposite over(19). **7** lower in rank than: *A lieutenant*(1) *is under a captain.* Opposite above(12). **8** with (s.o) as one's leader, chief etc: *My department in the office is under Mr Jones. The shop is under new management.* **9** in a position at the bottom of and next to: *We sat under a tree and talked.* **10** because of the weight or pressure of: *The horse sank to the ground under the man's weight.* **11** (introducing the conditions in which s.t is done): *We bathed under a hot sun. We work under great difficulties.* **12** subject to or being affected by: *He's under orders to come. The whole affair is under discussion at the moment. He's under threat of being reported to the police.* ⇒ under fire (⇒ fire(*n*)). **13** according to: *Under the rules you must wear white clothes. Under this agreement I shall be paid monthly.* **14** (by) using: *He signed under a false name. The man got into the office under false pretences.* **15** (introducing the headings etc of a list, dictionary etc): *You will find 'hopeful' under 'hope' in this dictionary.* **under grass, corn** etc having grass etc growing on it: *That field is under grass at present.* **under the weather** ⇒ weather.

,under'act *tr/intr.v* (of actors, producers etc in plays, films etc) act (one's part) in a quieter, less dramatic(3), way than usual or expected. Opposite overact.

,under'arm *adj/adv* (usu in games) (throw etc) with the hand lower than the shoulder. Opposite overarm.

'under,belly *c.n* (*pl -ies*) softest part of an animal's belly(3).

,under'bid *tr.v* (*-dd-*, *p.t,p.p* underbid) put in a lower bid(1) than (s.o else); offer to sell s.t more cheaply than (s.o else). Compare undercut².

'under,carriage *c.n* part of a plane that is below the body and on which it lands; usu it has wheels, but sometimes it has floats for landing on water or skis(1) for landing on snow and ice.

,under'charge *tr/intr.v* (often — (s.o) for s.t) ask (s.o) for too little money (for s.t). Opposite overcharge.

'under,clothes *pl.n* = underclothing.

'under,clothing *u.n* clothes, e.g vests¹ and underpants, worn under one's shirt, blouse, trousers, skirt etc.

'under,coat *c.n* coat of paint put on after the primer but before the topcoat(s)(2).

,under'cover *adj* secret: *an undercover agent/ meeting/organization.*

'under,current *c.n* **1** current that flows below the surface of the water and is therefore often not noticed. **2** (*fig*) (often — of s.t) people's feelings, opinions etc (of a certain kind) that are not openly expressed and are therefore often difficult to notice.

'under,cut¹ *c/u.n* piece of meat cut from the lower part of a sirloin.

,under'cut² *tr.v* (*-tt-*, *p.t,p.p* undercut) sell s.t more cheaply than (s.o else). Compare underbid.

,underde'veloped *adj* not as advanced in economy(3) or politics as others: *an under-developed country.* Compare developing.

'under,dog *c.n* person, place etc treated less well, generously etc than others because he/she/ it is weaker, less important etc.

,under'done *adj* (of meat) not cooked thoroughly. Opposite overdone. Compare rare(2).

underestimate /,ʌndər'estimət/ *c.n* **1** estimate(1) that is lower or smaller than the correct one. Opposite overestimate(1).
▷ *tr.v* /,ʌndər'esti,meit/ **2** make an underestimate(1) of (s.t). Opposite overestimate(2).

'under,felt *u.n* kind of underlay².

'under,floor *attrib.adj* that is under the floor: *underfloor heating.*

,under'foot *adv* under one's foot or feet: *The grass was soft and warm underfoot.*

'under,garment *c.n* (*formal*) piece of underclothing.

,under'grad *c.n* (*informal*) undergraduate.

undergraduate /,ʌndə'grædjuət/ *c.n* university student who has not yet passed her/his bachelor's examination (BA, BSc etc). Compare graduate(*n*), postgraduate.

underground /'ʌndə,graund/ *adj* **1** below the surface of the ground: *an underground stream.* **2** (*fig*) secret because it would be dangerous to appear publicly: *an underground political party.*
▷ *adv* /,ʌndə'graund/ **3** below the surface of the ground: *Some small animals spend a lot of their time underground.* **4** (*fig*) secretly. Compare underground(2,4). **go underground** begin to act secretly. Compare underground(2, 4).
▷ *def.n* /'ʌndə,graund/ **5** system of underground(1) trains in a city etc. **6** (*fig*) secret group of people, usu fighting against the government. Compare resistance(2). **by underground**; **on the underground** in an underground(1) train: *go/ travel by underground* (or *on the underground*). ⇒ tube(5).

'under,growth *u.n* thick mass of bushes under and around trees.

'under,hand, 'under,handed *adj* (*derog*) unfair or dishonest in a secret way: *underhand plans to win the* contract(1).

,under'handedly *adv*.

,under'lain *p.p* of underlie.

,under'lay¹ *p.t* of underlie.

'under,lay² *u.n* (pieces of a) soft material put between a carpet and the floor to make the carpet feel softer under one's feet, to protect it from damage by the floor and to keep the room warmer.

,under'lie *tr.v* (*pres.p* underlying /,ʌndə'laiiŋ/, *p.t* underlay /,ʌndə'lei/, *p.p* underlain /,ʌndə'lein/) be the (unseen(1)) reason for (s.t): *What really underlay his delay in answering our letter was his inability to make a decision.*

,under'lying *adj* that underlies s.t: *the underlying reason.*

,under'line *tr.v* **1** draw a line under (s.t), usu to show that it is important. **2** (*fig*) make (s.t) seem important by emphasizing it; stress(3) (s.t): *I must underline the need for speed if we are to finish the job this year.*

'under,ling *c.n* (*derog*) person who is lower in rank than s.o else.

underlying ⇒ underlie.

,under'manned *adj* not having enough workers

etc to do the job properly. Opposite **overmanned**. Compare **understaffed**, **shorthanded**.

'under,mentioned *adj* ⇨ **-mentioned**.

,under'mine *tr.v* **1** remove the supporting earth of (s.t) so that it falls or is in danger of falling. **2** (*fig*) make (s.t) weaker; damage or destroy (s.t): *Smoking undermines people's health.*

,under'neath *adj* **1** lower: *the underneath part of a car.*

▷ *adv/prep* **2** in or into a position below or beneath (and touching or not touching): *We live on the top floor and we never hear the people who live underneath* (*us*). *I found my pen underneath the chair. Put a mat underneath* (*that hot dish*). **3** on the lower side of (s.t): *These leaves are smooth on top and hairy underneath.* Notice that 'underneath' can be used for 'under' (esp 4,5,9,10,15), e.g *swimming underneath the water*; *standing underneath the street light*; *bending underneath a heavy load*; *'gaiety' is underneath 'gay' in this dictionary.* **from underneath** (**s.o/ s.t**) coming from below (s.o/s.t): *The new plant is growing from underneath the old stem.*

▷ *def.sing.n* **4** (often *the — of s.t*) lower part or surface (of s.t): *the underneath of the carpet.*

,under'nourish *tr.v* not give enough nourishing food to (a person or an animal).

,under'nourished *adj* not getting, not having had, enough nourishing food.

,under'nourishment *u.n.*

,under'paid *adj* (of a worker etc) paid too little money. Opposite **overpaid**.

'under,pants *pl.n* (also **pants**) (often *a pair of —*) underclothing for the lower part of a man's body, from the waist down to the top of the legs or a little below. ⇨ **panties**.

'under,pass *c.n* road, street, path etc by which one can cross another road or street by going under it. Opposite **overpass**.

,under'pin *tr.v* (**-nn-**) **1** support (a wall etc) by building s.t under it. **2** (*fig*) support (an idea, a statement etc), e.g with facts etc.

,under'play *tr.v* Opposite **overplay**. **1** act (one's part in a play, film etc) in a quieter way than usual or expected. **2** aim to get (an effect) by pretending to be less concerned etc: *He underplayed his interest in buying the house in order to keep the price low.* **underplay one's hand** (*fig*) hide (some of) the advantages one has so that people will not notice them and protect themselves against them.

,under'popu,lated *adj* not having enough people, animals. Opposite **overpopulated**.

,under'privileged *adj* not having (had) the same educational, financial etc opportunities as other people in society.

,under'rate *tr.v* judge (s.o/s.t) as less good, useful etc than he/she/it really is. Opposite **overrate**.

,under'score *tr.v* (*formal*) = **underline**.

,under'secretary *c/def/unique n* (*pl* **-ies**) person with a high rank in a government department.

,under'sell *tr.v* (*p.t,p.p* **undersold** /-'sǝʊld/) **1** sell s.t for a lower price than (another business, company). **2** (*fig*) give a wrong low impression of the value of (a person, a person's ability etc).

,under'sexed *adj* having less strong sexual desires or urges (1) than the average. Opposite **oversexed**.

'under,side *def.n* (usu *the — of s.t*) lower surface (of s.t).

'under,signed *def.n* (also *attrib*, *the —* (*person(s)*)) person(s) whose signature(s) is/are below.

,under'sized *adj* (also **,under'size**) smaller than the average. Opposite **oversized**. ⇨ **-sized**.

,under'staffed *adj* not having enough office workers, managers etc to do the job properly. Opposite **overstaffed**, **overmanned**. Compare **undermanned**. ⇨ **-staffed**.

,under'state *tr.v* talk or write about (s.t) as if it is less important, dangerous etc than it really is. Opposite **overstate**. Compare **undersell**(2).

,under'statement *c/u.n* fact of understating; statement that makes s.t seem less important, dangerous etc than it really is: *In Britain, understatement is often used; we say 'Not bad' when we really mean 'Very good'.* Opposite **overstatement**.

'under,study *c.n* (*pl* **-ies**) **1** actor or actress who is ready to replace another if he/she becomes ill etc.

▷ *tr.v* (**-ies**, **-ied**) **2** act as an understudy (1) for (an actor or actress).

,under-the-'counter *adj* (*informal*) bought or sold etc secretly and often when the law does not allow this. Compare **black market**.

'under,tone *c.n* (often *in an —*; *in —s*) quiet voice, usu so that other people cannot hear: *speaking in undertones.*

'under,tow *c/def.n* force that pulls the water under a wave back towards the sea when the wave is moving towards the land.

,under'value *tr.v* judge or treat (s.o/s.t) as less good, useful etc than he/she/it really is.

,under'water *adj/adv* (that is or is used) below the surface of the water: *an underwater camera*; *swim underwater.*

'under,wear *u.n* (*informal* **undies**) underclothing.

,under'weight *adj* less than the average or expected weight: *This bag of onions is supposed to weigh five kilos but is 400 grams underweight.* Opposite **overweight**(1).

'under,world *n* **1** *def.n* (*old use*; *literary*) place under the earth where the spirits of dead people were supposed to go. **2** *def.pl.n* criminals who know each other and work in groups.

,under'write *tr.v* (*p.t* **underwrote** /,ʌndǝ'rǝʊt/, *p.p* **underwritten** /,ʌndǝ'rɪtn/) **1** promise to buy (any of a group of newly offered shares that other people do not buy). **2** promise to pay for (s.t that is risky, usu an agreement to insure a ship) if necessary (e.g if the ship sinks).

'under,writer *c.n* person who underwrites (1,2) as a job.

undergo /,ʌndǝ'gǝʊ/ *tr.v* (*p.t* **underwent** /,ʌndǝ'went/, *p.p* **undergone** /,ʌndǝ'gɒn/) suffer (s.t); have (s.t) done to one: *Joe has to undergo an operation at the hospital tomorrow.*

undergrad(uate), **underground**, **undergrowth**, **underhand(edly)**, **underlay**, **underlie**, **underline**, **underling**, **underlying**, **undermanned**, **undermentioned**, **undermine**, **underneath**, **undernourish(ed/ment)**, **underpaid**,

underpants, underpass, underpin, underplay, underpopulated, under- privileged, underrate, underscore, undersecretary, undersell, under- sexed, underside, undersigned, un- dersize(d), understaffed ⇒ under.

understand /ˌʌndəˈstænd/ v (p.t,p.p understood /ˌʌndəˈstʊd/) **1** tr/intr.v know or succeed in discovering what (s.t) means: Can you under- stand everything she says? **2** tr.v (often — (s.t) by s.t, — by s.t that . . .) believe (s.t) because of what one has heard, seen etc: I understand that you are not satisfied with the food in the hotel. **3** tr.v know or succeed in discovering (what s.o feels, thinks etc) and feel sympathy towards her/ him/it: I understand your position in this matter completely. **4** tr.v know or realize (how (to do s.t) etc) using information: I don't understand how to do it, where he's gone. We didn't understand why he left until we heard that he felt ill. **give s.o to understand that** . . . give s.o the (perhaps wrong) idea that . . .: Valerie gave us to understand that she could not go out today but she is sitting over there. **make oneself understood** speak or write etc (e.g in a foreign language) sufficiently well to be understood. **so I understand** that is what I understand(2). **s.t is understood** s.t is known although it is not actually mentioned by the speaker or writer: When a person answers a question with the words 'Don't know', the word 'I' is understood before 'don't'. **understand each other, one another** (a) each understands(1) what the other means. (b) each knows what makes the other happy, sad etc. Compare understand(3).

ˌunderˈstandable adj that can be under- stood(1,3).

ˌunderˈstandably adv.

ˌunderˈstanding adj **1** showing sympathy; able to judge well what s.o feels: My teacher was very understanding when I explained why I was late.

▷ n **2** u.n act or fact of understanding. ⇒ understand(1,2). **3** c.n ability to know or judge: Her behaviour is beyond my understanding, I am afraid. According to my understanding, each of us must pay £10 for a ticket. **4** sing/u.n (often an — between s.o and s.o) agreement based on each person treating s.t as true but without spoken or written proof: We have an understanding that neither of us will enter the competition. **come to, reach, an understanding (with s.o)** (**about s.t, to do s.t** etc) make (usu an informal) agreement (with s.o) (about s.t, or to do s.t etc). **on the understanding that . . .** on condition that . . .: We agreed to help on the understanding that no one else was told.

understate(ment) ⇒ under.

understood /ˌʌndəˈstʊd/ p.t,p.p of understand.

understudy ⇒ under.

undertake /ˌʌndəˈteɪk/ tr.v (p.t undertook /-ˈtʊk/, p.p undertaken /-ˈteɪkən/) (usu — to do s.t) (agree to) accept (a responsibility etc) or start (to do s.t): I've undertaken to make a cake for the meeting. Who'll undertake all this work?

ˌunderˈtaking c.n **1** piece of work that one has agreed or promised to do. **2** activity needing a lot of hard work: It was quite an undertaking to teach so many children in one classroom. **3** (often give (s.o), make, an — (to do s.t)) promise (to do s.t): She made an undertaking to stop being late

for work. **4** business organization: a profitable undertaking.

undertaker /ˈʌndəˌteɪkə/ c.n person whose job is to arrange funerals.

under-the-counter, undertone, under- tow, undervalue, underwater, under- wear, underweight ⇒ under.

underwent /ˌʌndəˈwent/ p.t of undergo.

underworld, underwrite(r) ⇒ under.

undesirable /ˌʌndɪˈzaɪərəbl/ adj **1** not desir- able.

▷ c.n **2** person who is not desirable(1).

ˌundeˈsirably adv.

undetached /ˌʌndɪˈtætʃt/ adj having or showing a personal opinion, prejudice etc: He's my son so I am not undetached in my opinion.

undeveloped /ˌʌndɪˈveləpt/ adj still in its natu- ral state; not (yet) having been developed(1).

undid /ʌnˈdɪd/ p.t of undo.

undies /ˈʌndɪz/ pl.n (informal) women's underclothing.

undignified /ʌnˈdɪgnɪˌfaɪd/ adj not dignified.

undiminished /ˌʌndɪˈmɪnɪʃt/ adj not diminished in any way.

undiplomatic /ʌnˌdɪpləˈmætɪk/ adj not diplo- matic.

undistinguished /ˌʌndɪsˈtɪŋgwɪʃt/ adj not very good in any way; poor in quality; not distin- guished: an undistinguished performance in a film.

undivided /ˌʌndɪˈvaɪdɪd/ adj complete; not shared with anything else: I want your undivided attention. We were undivided in our opinion. ⇒ be divided (⇒ divide(v)).

undo /ʌnˈduː/ tr.v (3rd pers sing pres.t undoes /ʌnˈdʌz/, p.t undid /ʌnˈdɪd/, p.p undone /ʌnˈdʌn/) **1** untie (s.o/s.t); remove (the thing fastening s.o/s.t). **2** change the action of (s.t) back to what it was before: Unless he undoes all the damage he caused, we will make him pay.

undoing /ʌnˈduːɪŋ/ u.n (formal) cause of ruin, failure etc: Laziness was his undoing.

undone /ʌnˈdʌn/ adj **1** (usu be/come —) not tied or fastened: Be careful because your shoes are coming undone and you may fall! **2** (pred) in a state of not (yet) having been done: He went home leaving a lot of work undone.

▷ tr.v **3** p.p of undo.

undoubted /ʌnˈdaʊtɪd/ attrib.adj (formal) absolutely certain or sure: I don't like her in spite of her undoubted charm.

unˈdoubtedly adv.

undreamed-of /ʌnˈdriːmd ˌɒv/ adv (also **undreamt-of** /ʌnˈdremt ˌɒv/) that one would never have dared hope or expect to have, do etc: undreamed-of riches.

undress /ʌnˈdres/ u.n **1** (formal) (usu in a state of —) not wearing any clothes or wearing only one's underclothes etc.

▷ v **2** intr.v take (some of) one's clothes off. **3** tr.v take (some of) the clothes off (s.o).

unˈdressed adj **1** without clothes on. **2** (of foods) not (yet) dressed(5–8) or prepared: an undressed salad. **3** (of a wound) still without medicines, bandages etc on it. **get undressed** take (some of) one's clothes off (e.g before going to bed).

▷ v **4** p.t,p.p of undress(v).

undrinkable /ʌnˈdrɪŋkəbl/ adj not drinkable.

undue /ʌnˈdjuː/ *attrib.adj* (*formal*) more than is suitable: *undue haste*.

unˈduly *adv* (*formal*) too: *unduly hopeful*.

undulate /ˈʌndjuˌleɪt/ *v* (*formal*) **1** *tr/intr.v* (cause (s.t) to) move up and down like waves. **2** *intr.v* be shaped like waves: *undulating scenery*.

undulation /ˌʌndjuˈleɪʃən/ *n* **1** *u.n* fact of undulating(*v*). **2** *c.n* curve of an undulating(*v*) movement or surface.

unduly ⇒ undue.

undying /ʌnˈdaɪɪŋ/ *attrib.adj* (*formal*) continuing for ever or for all one's life: *his undying love for her.*

unearth /ʌnˈɜːθ/ *tr.v* **1** dig (s.t) up from under the ground. **2** (*fig*) discover (s.t); find (s.t) that was hidden.

unearthly /ʌnˈɜːθlɪ/ *adj* (*-ier, -iest*) **1** terrible; not seeming to be from our world: *an unearthly scream*(1). **2** (*informal*) not at all what one would like: *In a hospital one is always woken up at an unearthly hour in the morning.* Compare ungodly, unholy.

unˈearthliness *u.n*.

unease /ʌnˈiːz/ *u.n* (*formal*) feeling of being uneasy.

unˈeasily *adv*. **unˈeasiness** *u.n*.

unˈeasy *adj* (*-ier, -iest*) **1** not calm or comfortable: *an uneasy sleep.* **2** (often — *about s.t*) worried or anxious (because of s.t).

uneatable /ʌnˈiːtəbl/ *adj* not fit to be eaten because cooked badly etc. Compare inedible.

uneconomic /ˌʌnˌiːkəˈnɒmɪk/ *adj* (also **unˌecoˈnomical**) not economic(2) or economical; wasting too much time, money etc to be worth doing, using etc.

uneducated /ʌnˈedjuˌkeɪtɪd/ *adj* not (well) educated; not having gained enough knowledge, good manners etc from one's school, parents etc.

unemployed /ˌʌnɪmˈplɔɪd/ *adj* **1** (of a person) without work or a job. **2** (of a thing) not being used.

▷ *def.pl.n* **3** people who are without work or a job.

ˌunemˈployment *u.n* fact or state of being unemployed. Opposite employment.

unenlightened /ˌʌnɪnˈlaɪtənd/ *adj* (*formal*) without (right) knowledge, either of one or more particular things or in general.

unending /ʌnˈendɪŋ/ *adj* that does not stop or reach an end(2).

unentertaining /ˌʌnˌentəˈteɪnɪŋ/ *adj* not entertaining.

unenviable /ʌnˈenvɪəbl/ *adj* that people do not envy one for; bad: *This airport has an unenviable reputation for crashes.*

unequal /ʌnˈiːkwəl/ *adj* (often — *in s.t*) not equal or not the same (in length, size etc): *These curtains are of unequal length* (or *are unequal in length*). ⇒ inequality. **unequal to s.t** not having enough strength, skill etc for s.t: *Jim is still ill so he is unequal to climbing stairs at present.*

unˈequalled *adj* (US **unˈequaled**) (*formal*) having no equal(s)(2); impossible to find s.o/s.t as good etc as he/she/it is.

unˈequally *adv*.

unequivocal /ˌʌnɪˈkwɪvəkl/ *adj* (*formal*) impossible to misunderstand or make a mistake about.

ˌuneˈquivocally *adv*.

unerring /ʌnˈɜːrɪŋ/ *adj* (*formal*) not making any mistakes: *unerring aim*; *unerring judgement.*

unˈerringly *adv*.

UNESCO /juːˈneskəu/ *abbr* United Nations Educational, Scientific and Cultural Organization.

uneven /ʌnˈiːvn/ *adj* **1** not flat, smooth; not regular: *an uneven surface*; *uneven teeth.* Opposite even(2). **2** not equal or equally balanced: *Her examination results are uneven.* Opposite even(4). **3** (of numbers) odd(1); that cannot be divided by two without leaving s.t over; not even(1). **4** not steady: *an uneven rhythm.* Opposite even(5).

unˈevenly *adv*. **unˈevenness** *u.n*.

uneventful /ˌʌnɪˈventfʊl/ *adj* in which nothing unusual, interesting, exciting etc happens; calm; quiet: *an uneventful week.*

ˌuneˈventfully *adv*.

unexpected /ˌʌnɪkˈspektɪd/ *adj* surprising because not thought likely or possible: *an unexpected letter from the bank. The bad report was unexpected.* Compare unforeseen.

unexpurgated /ʌnˈekspɜːˌgeɪtɪd/ *adj* not expurgated.

unfailing /ʌnˈfeɪlɪŋ/ *adj* (*formal*) never growing less or worse: *an unfailing supply of water*; *unfailing kindness.*

unˈfailingly *adv*.

unfair /ʌnˈfeə/ *adj* not fair¹(1).

unfaithful /ʌnˈfeɪθfʊl/ *adj* (often — *to s.o/s.t*) not faithful (to s.o), usu one's husband or wife by having a love affair with another man or woman.

unˈfaithfully *adv*. **unˈfaithfulness** *u.n*.

unfaltering /ʌnˈfɔːltərɪŋ/ *adj* who/that never hesitates, weakens, doubts or falters: *unfaltering devotion to one's duty.* Compare unflagging, unflinching, unwavering.

unˈfalteringly *adv*.

unfashionable /ʌnˈfæʃənbl/ *adj* not fashionable.

unfasten /ʌnˈfɑːsn/ *tr/intr.v* (cause (s.t) to) be loose or open after being fastened.

unfathomable /ʌnˈfæðəməbl/ *adj* (*formal*) **1** so deep that it is impossible to measure or explore its depths. **2** (*fig*) impossible to understand completely: *the unfathomable variety of insects in the world.*

unˈfathomably *adv*.

unˈfathomed *adj* **1** the depths of which have never been measured or explored. **2** (*fig*) that has never been (completely) understood.

unfavourable /ʌnˈfeɪvərəbl/ *adj* (US **unˈfavorable**) (often — *for/to s.o/s.t*) not likely to help (s.o/s.t); not favourable (to s.o/s.t): *unfavourable weather.*

unˈfavourably *adv* (US **unˈfavorably**).

unfeeling /ʌnˈfiːlɪŋ/ *adj* (*formal*) not sympathetic or kind; cruel; indifferent(1).

unˈfeelingly *adv*.

unfinished /ʌnˈfɪnɪʃt/ *adj* not finished(1): *an unfinished piece.*

unfit /ʌnˈfɪt/ *adj* (*-tt-*) (usu — *for s.t*; — *to do s.t*) not good or well (enough for s.t, to do s.t): *This meat is unfit for human consumption*(1). *John can't play in the match today because the doctor has declared him unfit.*

unflagging /ʌnˈflægɪŋ/ *adj* never getting tired

or weaker; never hesitating: *unflagging support.*
Compare unfaltering, unflinching, unwavering.
un'flaggingly *adv.*

unflappable /ʌn'flæpəbl/ *adj* (*informal*) very calm; impossible to disturb, worry or frighten in any way. ⇒ flap(5,8).

unflinching /ʌn'flɪntʃɪŋ/ *attrib.adj* (*formal*) who/that never weakens: *unflinching determination.* Compare unfaltering, unflagging, unwavering.
un'flinchingly *adv.*

unfold /ʌn'fəʊld/ *tr/intr.v* **1** (cause (s.t) to) open, or become flat after having been closed or folded: *The bud(1) unfolded into a beautiful rose.* **2** (*fig*) (cause (s.t) to) develop so that more and more of it can be seen, heard etc: *As the story unfolded I realized that it described my own childhood.*

unforeseeable /ˌʌnfɔː'siːəbl/ *adj* that cannot be known, sensed in advance. Opposite foreseeable.

unforeseen /ˌʌnfɔː'siːn/ *adj* not expected; not thought about before (so that plans could be made to deal with it): *Our visit has had to be postponed owing to unforeseen* circumstances(1). Compare unexpected.

unforgettable /ˌʌnfə'getəbl/ *adj* impossible to forget.
ˌunfor'gettably *adv.*

unforgivable /ˌʌnfə'gɪvəbl/ *adj* not forgivable.
unforgiving /ˌʌnfə'gɪvɪŋ/ *adj* not willing to forgive.

unforthcoming /ˌʌnfɔː'θkʌmɪŋ/ *adj* not forthcoming(3).

unfortunate /ʌn'fɔːtʃənɪt/ *adj* **1** not fortunate or lucky: *an unfortunate accident.* **2** who/that has suffered misfortune so that he/she/it deserves pity: *the unfortunate children in poor countries.* **3** badly chosen for the situation; not suitable: *Peter was doing well until he made an unfortunate remark about his manager's wife being fat.*
▷ *c.n* **4** (*formal*) person who is unfortunate(2).
un'fortunately *adv* **1** in an unfortunate(1,3) way. **2** it is unfortunate(1), but . . . : *Unfortunately George can't come to lunch because he has to go to London.*

unfounded /ʌn'faʊndɪd/ *adj* (*formal*) not based on facts and therefore probably not true: *unfounded accusations.*

unfrequented /ˌʌnfrɪ'kwentɪd/ *adj* to which few people go; lonely.

unfriendly /ʌn'frendlɪ/ *adj* (*derog*) **1** not kind or willing; not friendly(1): *an unfriendly remark.* **2** hostile(1): *an unfriendly country.*

unfrock /ʌn'frɒk/ *tr.v* dismiss (a priest) for behaving badly, saying or writing the wrong things etc.

unfulfilled /ˌʌnfʊl'fɪld/ *adj* **1** not achieved: *unfulfilled hopes.* **2** not satisfying the conditions(3) (of a rule).

unfurl /ʌn'fɜːl/ *tr.v* open up (s.t, e.g a flag or a sail, that is furled or rolled up); unroll(1) (s.t).

unfurnished /ʌn'fɜːnɪʃt/ *adj* containing no furniture.

ungainly /ʌn'geɪnlɪ/ *adj* (*derog*) awkward; not graceful in appearance and/or movements.
un'gainliness *u.n.* Notice that 'gainly' and 'gainliness' do not exist.

ungenerous /ʌn'dʒenərəs/ *adj* not willing to give money etc or to be kinder than absolutely necessary; not generous.

un'generously *adv.*

ungodly /ʌn'gɒdlɪ/ *adj* (*-ier, -iest*) **1** not behaving etc in a way that is expected of people with religious beliefs. **2** unpleasantly unsuitable: *In hospitals they wake one up at an ungodly hour in the morning.* Compare unearthly, unholy.
un'godliness *u.n.*

ungovernable /ʌn'gʌvənəbl/ *adj* (*formal*) impossible to control: *ungovernable anger.*

ungracious /ʌn'greɪʃəs/ *adj* (*formal*) rude; unkind.
un'graciously *adv.*

ungrammatical /ˌʌngrə'mætɪkl/ *adj* not following the rules of grammar correctly; not grammatical.

ungrateful /ʌn'greɪtfʊl/ *adj* (*derog*) not behaving, speaking etc in a way that shows one is thankful for kind treatment etc; not grateful: *ungrateful children.* ⇒ gratitude.
un'gratefully *adv.* **un'gratefulness** *u.n.* ⇒ ingratitude.

unguarded /ʌn'gɑːdɪd/ *adj* **1** not guarded by anyone or anything: *an unguarded entrance¹(1) to the museum.* **2** (usu *in an — moment*) not being careful about avoiding telling secrets etc (when one has always been careful about this in the past).

unhappy /ʌn'hæpɪ/ *adj* (*-ier, -iest*) **1** not joyful or happy(1). **2** unfortunate(3); badly chosen; not happy(4): *a purple coat was an unhappy choice for a girl with such red hair.*
un'happily *adv* **1** in an unhappy way. **2** it was unfortunate(1) but: *Unhappily, his mother was still awake when Joe got home so she knew how late he was.*
un'happiness *u.n.*

unhealthy /ʌn'helθɪ/ *adj* (*-ier, -iest*) **1** (of a person) not in good health; not healthy(1). **2** not showing that one is in good health; not healthy(3): *an unhealthy look/paleness.* **3** likely to cause bad health; not healthy(2): *an unhealthy climate/diet(1).* **4** likely to cause bad thoughts, feelings etc; not healthy(4): *an unhealthy interest in violence.*
un'healthily *adv.* **un'healthiness** *u.n.*

unheard /ʌn'hɜːd/ *adj* (often *go —*) not heard; not listened to: *Her request for more money went unheard* (was ignored).

unheard-of /ʌn'hɜːd ˌɒv/ *adj* never heard or seen etc before; very surprising: *Snow is quite unheard-of here.*

unhinge /ʌn'hɪndʒ/ *tr.v* **1** take (a door etc) off its hinges(1). **2** (*fig*) cause (s.o) to go mad.

unholy /ʌn'həʊlɪ/ *attrib.adj* (*-ier, -iest*) **1** bad from a religious point of view. **2** (*informal*) terrible; very bad: *an unholy* row³(2). Compare unearthly, ungodly.

unhook /ʌn'hʊk/ *tr.v* **1** unfasten (s.t) by taking one or more hooks out: *The mother unhooked the little girl's dress.* **2** take (s.t) off a hook: *unhook a towel from the wall.*

unhoped-for /ʌn'həʊpt ˌfɔː/ *adj* so good that one had not dared hope that it would happen: *an unhoped-for win.*

unhygienic /ˌʌnhaɪ'dʒiːnɪk/ *adj* not clean and therefore likely to cause disease.

UNICEF /'juːnɪˌsef/ *abbr* United Nations International Children's Emergency Fund.

unicorn /ˈjuːnɪˌkɔːn/ c.n imaginary horse with one horn in the middle of its forehead.

unidentified /ˌʌnaɪˈdentɪˌfaɪd/ adj the nature of which has not yet been discovered; that has not (yet) been identified: *an unidentified cause of the illness.*

ˌuniˌdentiˌfied ˌflying ˈobject c.n (usu as abbr UFO) thing flying in the sky the nature of which has not yet been discovered.

unification ⇒ unify.

uniform /ˈjuːnɪˌfɔːm/ adj 1 (often — with s.t) (formal) the same in colour, size, value etc (as s.t): *If you build a house in this row it must be uniform with all the other houses.*

▷ c/u.n 2 clothes of a certain colour, shape etc worn by all the members of a group, e.g an army, the police, a school or club. **in uniform (a)** wearing a uniform(2). **(b)** in one of the armed services. **out of uniform** not wearing one's uniform: *The bars were full of sailors out of uniform.*

ˈuniˌformed adj wearing uniform(1).

ˌuniˈformity u.n state of being the same in colour, size etc.

ˈuniˌformly adv in the same way; having the same colour, value etc.

unify /ˈjuːnɪˌfaɪ/ tr.v (-ies, -ied) make (two or more things) into one; make (two or more things) both or all the same.

unification /ˌjuːnɪfɪˈkeɪʃən/ u.n.

unilateral /ˌjuːnɪˈlætərəl/ adj affecting, agreed to by, only one side, country etc: *unilateral disarmament.* Compare bilateral, multilateral.

ˌuniˈlaterally adv.

unimaginable /ˌʌnɪˈmædɪnəbl/ adj not able to be imagined(1).

unimaginative /ˌʌnɪˈmædʒɪnətɪv/ adj not imaginative.

unimportant /ˌʌnɪmˈpɔːtənt/ adj not important.

ˌunimˈportance u.n.

unimposing /ˌʌnɪmˈpəʊzɪŋ/ adj not imposing.

uninformed /ˌʌnɪnˈfɔːmd/ adj 1 (often — about s.t) not having information (about s.t). 2 without much knowledge; ignorant(1); without enough knowledge to make reasonable judgements: *uninformed criticism.*

uninhabitable /ˌʌnɪnˈhæbɪtəbl/ adj impossible to live in; not at all suitable for living in.

uninhabited /ˌʌnɪnˈhæbɪtəd/ adj with no one living in it; not inhabited.

uninhibited /ˌʌnɪnˈhɪbɪtɪd/ adj behaving, speaking, writing etc freely and without worry or embarrassment; not inhibited.

ˌuninˈhibitedly adv.

uninspired /ˌʌnɪnˈspaɪəd/ adj not inspired.

uninspiring /ˌʌnɪnˈspaɪərɪŋ/ adj not inspiring.

unintelligent /ˌʌnɪnˈtelɪdʒənt/ adj not intelligent.

unintelligible /ˌʌnɪnˈtelɪdʒɪbl/ adj not intelligible.

unintentional /ˌʌnɪnˈtenʃənl/ adj not intentional.

uninterested /ʌnˈɪntrɪstɪd/ adj (often — in s.o/s.t) not interested (in s.o/s.t). Compare disinterested.

uninteresting /ʌnˈɪntrɪstɪŋ/ adj not interesting.

uninterrupted /ˌʌnɪntəˈrʌptɪd/ adj not broken or interrupted by anyone or anything: *an uninterrupted sleep; an uninterrupted view across the plains.*

ˌuninterˈruptedly adv.

uninvited /ˌʌnɪnˈvaɪtɪd/ adj not invited s.w.

uninviting /ˌʌnɪnˈvaɪtɪŋ/ adj not attractive.

union /ˈjuːnjən/ n 1 u.n act of joining together. 2 u.n fact or state of being joined together. 3 c.n (often with capital U) group of people, countries, parts of a country, which are joined together. 4 c/u.n state of being joined together in marriage. 5 c.n (often with capital U) club; society: *a students' union at a university.* 6 c.n (often with capital U) = trade union. **the state of the Union** the conditions in which the USA is at a certain time as described by the President in a speech once a year. **trade union** ⇒ trade.

ˈunioˌnism u.n (often with capital U) 1 belief that certain countries, or parts of a country (e.g Great Britain and Northern Ireland or the Northern and the Southern States of the US), should be or remain united. 2 belief that there should be trade unions: *trade unionism.*

ˈunioˌnist adj 1 that is the result of unionism: *unionist policies¹.*

▷ c.n 2 person who supports unionism. **trade unionist** ⇒ trade.

ˌUnion ˈJack c/def.n flag of the UK.

unique /juːˈniːk/ adj who/that is the only one of that kind.

uˈniquely adv. **uˈniqueness** u.n.

uˈnique ˌnoun c.n (grammar) noun that represents s.t that is only one of its kind and is not used with 'a', 'some' or 'any' (marked *unique n* in this dictionary), e.g London, Easter, November.

unisex /ˈjuːnɪˌseks/ attrib.adj used without any differences both by men and by women: *unisex clothes; a unisex hairdresser's.*

unison /ˈjuːnɪsən/ u.n (usu in — (with s.o)) 1 condition of singing the same notes (as s.o). 2 state of agreeing completely or saying exactly the same thing (as each other): *All the children answered in unison.*

unit /ˈjuːnɪt/ attrib.adj 1 for each one separately: *the unit cost of making each book.* 2 that is divided into separate units(5): *unit furniture in a kitchen.*

▷ c.n 3 thing that is complete in itself: *The land is being sold in units of 50 hectares.* 4 group that is a complete part of a bigger whole: *an army unit; the accounts unit in an office.* 5 piece of furniture that can be used with other pieces to form a set: *a kitchen unit* (e.g a set of cupboards). 6 (often — of s.t) thing used as a fixed standard (of s.t) against which other things are measured: *The unit of temperature that we use is the degree.* 7 any of the numbers from one to nine.

ˌunit ˈtrust c.n company through which one can spread one's investments(1) over a number of different kinds of shares(3) instead of having to buy each kind separately oneself; the unit trust buys and sells the shares(3) of different companies and tries in this way to make a profit for the people who buy its own shares(3).

unite /juːˈnaɪt/ tr/intr.v (often — s.o/s.t with s.o/ s.t) join (s.o/s.t) together: *be united in marriage.*

uˈnited adj 1 joined together, esp politically: *the United States (of America).* 2 all agreeing with each other; all working together: *a united effort to do s.t.*

Uˌnited ˈKingdom def.n (abbr UK) England, Scotland, Wales and Northern Ireland. Compare Great Britain.

Uˌnited ˈNations def.n (with sing/pl v) (abbr

UN) international(1) organization of countries to encourage economic(1) and political cooperation(1) and world peace.

U,nited ,Reform 'Church *def.n* Church(2) that is made up of several Protestant Churches(2) (who united in 1972).

unity /'juːnɪtɪ/ *c/u.n* (*formal*) (often — *between s.o/s.t* and *s.o/s.t*; — *of s.o/s.t*) state or fact (of s.o/s.t) being united.

universe /'juːnɪˌvɜːs/ *n* **1** *def.n* (our) world, sun, moon, stars etc and all the space around them. **2** *c.n* any universe(1), whether it is ours or another one.

universal /ˌjuːnɪ'vɜːsl/ *adj* **1** affecting or given by everybody (in the group) or by a very large number of people: *universal approval.* **2** found in, affecting, all our world: *a universal problem.*

,uni,versal 'joint *c.n* (*technical*) (in a machine) joint that can bend in any direction.

universality /ˌjuːnɪvɜː'sælɪtɪ/ *u.n* fact of being universal.

,uni'versally *adv.*

university /ˌjuːnɪ'vɜːsɪtɪ/ *n* (*pl -ies*) **1** *c.n* (often with capital **U**) (also *attrib*) place where students are taught and which gives them degrees (BA(1), MA etc) if they are successful: *Oxford University; the University of Bristol; a university student.* Compare polytechnic. **2** *def/def.pl.n* all the teachers and students of a university(1). **be at university** be at a university(1) for the purpose of studying. **go to university** go to a university(1) for the purpose of studying.

unjustifiable /ʌn'dʒʌstɪˌfaɪəbl/ *adj* not justifiable.

un'justi,fiably *adv.*

unkempt /ʌn'kempt/ *adj* (*derog*) **1** (of a person) having untidy hair and/or clothes. **2** (of hair) not brushed or combed tidily.

unkind /ʌn'kaɪnd/ *adj* (*derog*) not kind¹: *an unkind thought/action/parent.*

un'kindly *adv* **not mean s.t unkindly** not intend that s.t should be unkind.

un'kindness *u.n.*

unknot /ʌn'nɒt/ *tr.v* (*-tt-*) **1** untie the ends of string, rope etc. **2** cause (hair etc) to lose its knots(1).

unknowingly /ʌn'nəʊɪŋlɪ/ *adv* without knowing (about) s.t: *She accepted the stolen goods unknowingly.*

un'known *adj* **1** not known: *The cause of the fire is unknown.* **an unknown quantity** ⇒ quantity. ▷ *c.n* **2** person or thing who/that is not known: *In x + 2 = 10, x is the unknown.*

unlawful /ʌn'lɔːfʊl/ *adj* against the law; not allowed by the law; not lawful.

un'lawfully *adv.* **un'lawfulness** *u.n.*

unlearn /ʌn'lɜːn/ *tr.v* remove from one's mind (s.t that has been previously learnt), usu because it is wrong.

unleash /ʌn'liːʃ/ *tr.v* **1** free (a dog etc) by removing its leash. **2** (often — *s.t against/(up)on s.o/s.t*) (*fig*) remove the controls on (s.t) (so that it can attack s.o/s.t): *The newspapers unleashed their anger against the decision to introduce censorship.*

unleavened /ʌn'levənd/ *adj* (of bread) containing no yeast so that the dough(1) does not rise, and the bread is flat and hard; not leavened.

unless /ʌn'les/ *conj* if ... not; except if: *Unless*

you apologize, I will refuse to come. Don't open the door unless the bell rings four times.

unlikeable /ʌn'laɪkəbl/ *adj* (also **un'likable**) not likeable.

unlike /ʌn'laɪk/ *adj* **1** different; not like each other. **be unlike s.o to do s.t** be surprising when s.o does s.t because he/she does not usu do it. ▷ *prep* **2** different from; not like.

unlikely /ʌn'laɪklɪ/ *adj* (*-ier, -iest*) not probable; not likely. **s.o is unlikely to do s.t** it is not likely that s.o will do s.t.

un'likeli,hood *u.n.*

unlimited /ʌn'lɪmɪtɪd/ not limited: *an unlimited amount of time.*

unlined /ʌn'laɪnd/ *adj* not lined¹/lined².

unload /ʌn'ləʊd/ *v* **1** *tr.v* (often — *s.t (from s.t) onto s.t*) remove the load from (s.t) (and put it on s.t). **2** *intr.v* have its load removed: *The bus unloaded and then went back for the rest of the students.* **3** *tr.v* take the bullet(s), shell(s) etc out of (a gun etc). **4** *tr.v* take the film out of (a camera). **5** *tr.v* (often — *s.t on(to) s.o/ s.t*) (**a**) get rid of (s.t) (by giving it to s.o): *Don't let that old man unload all his broken furniture on you.* (**b**) (*fig*) free oneself of (feelings etc) (by attacking s.o/s.t, or by telling s.o s.t): *He unloaded all his frustrations on the door by kicking it.*

unlock /ʌn'lɒk/ *tr/intr.v* turn a key so that (a door etc) is no longer locked. Opposite lock(v).

unlooked-for /ʌn'lʊkt ˌfɔː/ *adj* (usu *literary*) not at all expected.

unloose /ʌn'luːs/ *tr.v* (usu *literary*) untie (s.o/ s.t); loose(12) (s.o/s.t).

un'loosen *tr.v* loosen (s.t); make (s.t) looser.

unlovable /ʌn'lʌvəbl/ *adj* not lovable.

unlucky /ʌn'lʌkɪ/ *adj* not lucky.

un'luckily *adv.*

unmade /ʌn'meɪd/ *adj* (of a bed) not (yet) made. ⇒ make a bed (⇒ bed(*n*)).

unmanly /ʌn'mænlɪ/ *adj* (*-ier, -iest*) (*derog*) (of a man, boy) not courageous, determined etc; not manly.

unmanned /ʌn'mænd/ *adj* (esp of a machine, spacecraft) not having humans using or in it to control it.

unmarketable /ʌn'mɑːkɪtəbl/ *adj* not marketable.

unmarried /ʌn'mærɪd/ *adj* single(1); not married(1): *an unmarried mother.*

unmask /ʌn'mɑːsk/ *tr.v* **1** remove the mask(1–3) from (s.o). **2** (*fig*) let the truth about (s.o/s.t) come out after it has remained hidden for some time.

unmatched /ʌn'mætʃt/ *adj* (*formal*) having no equal or match(2): *unmatched beauty.*

unmentionable /ʌn'menʃənəbl/ *adj* so bad that one ought not to talk or write about her/him/it.

unmindful /ʌn'maɪndfʊl/ *adj* (usu — *of s.o/s.t*) having forgotten (about s.o/s.t); not thinking (about s.o/s.t).

unmistakable /ˌʌnmɪ'steɪkəbl/ *adj* so clear or obvious that one cannot mistake her/him/it (for anyone/anything else).

,unmi'stakably *adv.*

unmitigated /ʌn'mɪtɪˌgeɪtɪd/ *adj* (*formal*) not limited or weakened by anything else; complete: *These flies are an unmitigated nuisance.*

unmoved /ʌn'muːvd/ *pred.adj* not showing any feelings; not worried or afraid; quite calm.

unnatural /ʌnˈnætʃərəl/ adj 1 not natural: *an unnatural interest in violent crimes.* 2 behaving in a way in which normal people or animals do not behave: *an unnatural mother* (i.e one who does not love her child).
unˈnaturally adv. **unˈnaturalness** u.n.

unnecessary /ʌnˈnesəsrɪ/ adj not needed or wanted; harmfully or unpleasantly more than is necessary: *Your rude reply was unnecessary.*
unˈnecessarily adv.

unnerve /ʌnˈnɜːv/ tr.v make (s.o) nervous or frightened when he/she was not before; make (s.o) lose her/his nerve(2).

unnumbered /ʌnˈnʌmbəd/ adj 1 so many that it is impossible to count them. 2 that has not been given a number: *an unnumbered ticket.*

UNO /ˈjuːnəʊ/ abbr (rare; usu UN) United Nations.

unobtainable /ˌʌnəbˈteɪnəbl/ adj not obtainable.

unobtrusive /ˌʌnəbˈtruːsɪv/ adj (careful to be) seen, heard etc as little as possible; discreet; not obtrusive. **make oneself unobtrusive** try to be seen, heard etc as little as possible.
ˌunobˈtrusively adv. **ˌunobˈtrusiveness** u.n.

unofficial /ˌʌnəˈfɪʃəl/ adj not (yet made) official.
ˌunoˈfficially adv.

unorthodox /ʌnˈɔːθəˌdɒks/ adj not done, said etc in the way that most people think normal or correct; not orthodox(1).

unpack /ʌnˈpæk/ v 1 tr.v take (s.t) out of the thing in which it is packed. 2 intr.v take one's clothes etc out of one's luggage.

unpalatable /ʌnˈpælətəbl/ adj not palatable.

unparalleled /ʌnˈpærəleld/ adj (formal) having no equal because so extreme: *unparalleled hate.*

unpatriotic /ʌnˌpætrɪˈɒtɪk/ adj not patriotic.

unpick /ʌnˈpɪk/ tr.v 1 remove (stitches(2)) in cloth etc. 2 remove the stitches(2) from (cloth etc).

unpin /ʌnˈpɪn/ tr.v (-nn-) take the pins out of (material etc).

unplaced /ʌnˈpleɪst/ adj (in racing) not first, second or third.

unplanned /ʌnˈplænd/ adj not planned.

unplayable /ʌnˈpleɪəbl/ adj not playable.

unpleasant /ʌnˈpleznt/ adj 1 (of things) making one feel unhappy, ill, angry etc; not pleasant: *an unpleasant journey.* 2 (of people, things they say or write etc) not kind; intended to hurt; not pleasant:
unˈpleasantly adv.
unˈpleasantness n 1 u.n state of being unpleasant. 2 c.n unpleasant event.

unpopular /ʌnˈpɒpjʊlə/ adj not popular.

unpractical /ʌnˈpræktɪkl/ adj (of a person) not good at doing things with the hands; not practical(3). Compare impractical.

unprecedented /ʌnˈpresɪˌdentɪd/ adj never having been done, seen etc before; without precedent: *an unprecedented fall of snow in July.*
unˈpreceˌdentedly adv.

unpredictable /ˌʌnprɪˈdɪktəbl/ adj not able to be predicted.

unprejudiced /ʌnˈpredʒʊdɪst/ adj not showing any unfairness caused by favouring one side more than the other; not showing any prejudice(n).

unprepared /ˌʌnprɪˈpeəd/ adj not ready (because one has failed to organize oneself in advance); not prepared.

unprepossessing /ˌʌnˌpriːpəˈzesɪŋ/ adj not giving a favourable impression(1).

unpretentious /ˌʌnprɪˈtenʃəs/ adj modest; not seeming, or trying to seem, rich, important etc; not pretentious (⇒ pretend).
ˌunpreˈtentiously adv. **ˌunpreˈtentiousness** u.n.

unprincipled /ʌnˈprɪnsɪpəld/ adj (derog; formal) not following any rules of good behaviour, honesty etc; having or showing no principles(1).

unprintable /ʌnˈprɪntəbl/ adj so rude, immoral etc that it cannot be printed(5).

unproductive /ˌʌnprəˈdʌktɪv/ adj not productive.

unprofessional /ˌʌnprəˈfeʃənəl/ adj said, done etc in a bad way that is not suitable for the job one is doing: *unprofessional behaviour by a doctor or lawyer.*
ˌunproˈfessionally adv.

unprofitable /ʌnˈprɒfɪtəbl/ adj not profitable.

unprompted /ʌnˈprɒmptɪd/ adj said, done etc of one's own free will, without any suggestion, advice etc from anyone else; voluntary(1).

unpronounceable /ˌʌnprəˈnaʊnsəbl/ adj not pronounceable.

unprovoked /ˌʌnprəˈvəʊkt/ adj (of an attack, rudeness etc) done, said etc without being deserved: *unprovoked anger.*

unqualified /ʌnˈkwɒlɪˌfaɪd/ adj 1 (often — to do s.t) not having any/the necessary training, qualifications(2) etc (for (doing) s.t): *an unqualified nurse.* 2 not limited in any way; complete: *an unqualified success.*

unquenchable /ʌnˈkwentʃəbl/ adj that cannot be quenched.

unquestionable /ʌnˈkwestʃənəbl/ adj impossible to doubt or question.
unˈquestionably adv.
unˈquestioning adj having or showing no doubts; absolutely certain: *unquestioning faith.*

unquote /ʌnˈkwəʊt/ adv end of a quotation(2): *The defendant said* (quote(3)) *'Give me your money or I'll kill you'* (unquote).

unravel /ʌnˈrævl/ tr/intr.v (-ll-, US -l-) 1 (cause (threads that are part of cloth etc) to) divide up so that the threads become separated. 2 (fig) (cause (a complicated story etc) to) develop and become clearer.

unreadable /ʌnˈriːdəbl/ adj too difficult or boring to read.

unready /ʌnˈredɪ/ adj not ready(2).

unreal /ʌnˈrɪəl/ adj different from what is the real one: *Some film-stars live in an unreal world of admiration and wealth.*

unrealistic /ˌʌnrɪəˈlɪstɪk/ adj not realistic.

unreasonable /ʌnˈriːzənəbl/ adj 1 not sensible; not showing common sense. 2 (of prices, costs etc) too high.
unˈreasonableness u.n. **unˈreasonably** adv.

unrelenting /ˌʌnrɪˈlentɪŋ/ adj never allowing oneself/itself to become less or weaker: *unrelenting hatred.*
ˌunreˈlentingly adv.

unreliable /ˌʌnrɪˈlaɪəbl/ adj not reliable.

unrelieved /ˌʌnrɪˈliːvd/ adj never being made

less or weaker by anything: *unrelieved boredom.*

unremarkable /ˌʌnrɪˈmɑːkəbl/ *adj* not special or noticeable in any way.

unremitting /ˌʌnrɪˈmɪtɪŋ/ *adj* going on continuously without stopping or weakening: *unremitting efforts.*
  ˌunreˈmittingly *adv.*

unrepentant /ˌʌnrɪˈpentənt/ *adj* not willing to repent.

unrepresentative /ˌʌnreprɪˈzentətɪv/ *adj* (often — *of s.o/s.t*) not a typical example (of s.o/s.t); not representative(1).

unrequited /ˌʌnrɪˈkwaɪtɪd/ *adj* (of love) felt by s.o but not felt by the other person.

unreserved /ˌʌnrɪˈzɜːvd/ *adj* 1 (of a seat etc) not reserved(1). 2 (*formal*) showing willingness to be honest about one's feelings: *She has an unreserved personality.*
  unreservedly /ˌʌnrɪˈzɜːvɪdlɪ/ *adv* without any wish to hide what one truly feels or thinks.

unresponsive /ˌʌnrɪˈspɒnsɪv/ *adj* not responsive(1,2).

unrest /ʌnˈrest/ *u.n* disturbance; absence of calm; state or feeling of being dissatisfied and sometimes also angry: *political unrest.*

unrestrained /ˌʌnrɪˈstreɪnd/ *adj* not held back or controlled in any way: *unrestrained laughter.*

unrewarding /ˌʌnrɪˈwɔːdɪŋ/ *adj* not rewarding.

unripe /ʌnˈraɪp/ *adj* not ripe(1). Compare overripe.

unrivalled /ʌnˈraɪvəld/ *adj* (US **unˈrivaled**) (*formal*) having no equal (because so good of its kind): *unrivalled success/skill.*

unroll /ʌnˈrəʊl/ *tr/intr.v* 1 (cause (s.t that is rolled up) to) open by flattening out. 2 (cause (s.o/s.t) to) become uncovered by unrolling(1) the thing covering her/him/it.

unruffled /ʌnˈrʌfəld/ *adj* 1 (of water) smooth; calm; without even the smallest waves on it. 2 (*fig*) (of a person) calm; not at all disturbed.

unruly /ʌnˈruːlɪ/ *adj* (*-ier, -iest*) (*derog*) 1 without discipline: *unruly people.* 2 difficult to do what one wants with it: *unruly hair.*
  unˈruliness *u.n.*

unsaddle /ʌnˈsædl/ *tr/intr.v* take the saddle off (a horse etc).

unsafe /ʌnˈseɪf/ *adj* not safe; dangerous.

unsaid /ʌnˈsed/ *adj* (of thoughts, ideas etc) remaining silently in one's mind without being spoken. **leave s.t unsaid** think (s.t) but not say it.

unsaleable /ʌnˈseɪləbl/ *adj* that cannot be sold easily.

unsatisfactory /ˌʌnsætɪsˈfæktərɪ/ *adj* not good enough: *an unsatisfactory explanation.*

unsatisfying /ʌnˈsætɪsˌfaɪɪŋ/ *adj* not satisfying.

unsavoury /ʌnˈseɪvərɪ/ *adj* (US **unˈsavory**) (*derog*; *formal*) dirty or unpleasant, usu morally.

unscathed /ʌnˈskeɪðd/ *adj* not hurt in any way. (Notice that there is no word 'scathed'.)

unscented /ʌnˈsentɪd/ *adj* that has no scent(1,2).

unscramble /ʌnˈskræmbl/ *tr.v* arrange (s.t that is all mixed up) in the right order (again).

unscrew /ʌnˈskruː/ *tr.v* 1 turn (a lid, cap(4) etc) so that it comes off. 2 unscrew(1) screws to allow (s.t) to be taken off, out etc: *You can unscrew*

that shelf and take it down if you want more room.

unscrupulous /ʌnˈskruːpjʊləs/ *adj* (showing that one is) willing to do anything, however dishonest or evil, to get what one wants; not having or showing any scruples(1).
  unˈscrupulously *adv.* **unˈscrupulousness** *u.n.*

unseasonable /ʌnˈsiːzənəbl/ *adj* not normal or suitable for that season[1].

unseat /ʌnˈsiːt/ *tr.v* 1 (of a horse etc) throw (one's rider) off one's back. 2 (cause (a rider on a horse, bicycle etc) to) fall off: *The sudden noise unseated the girl.* 3 (*fig*) cause (s.o) to lose her/his position or job, e.g as a Member of Parliament.

unseemly /ʌnˈsiːmlɪ/ *adj* not suitable, usu morally; not decent(2) or seemly: *unseemly behaviour.*
  unˈseemliness *u.n.*

unseen /ʌnˈsiːn/ *adj* 1 not seen; without being seen: *He managed to get into the building unseen.*
  ▷ *n* 2 *def.n* world that we cannot see in which spirits(7) are supposed to live. 3 *c.n* piece written in a foreign language which a student has to translate into her/his own language without having been allowed to see it before. Compare set book (set²).

unselfish /ˌʌnˈselfɪʃ/ *adj* concerned about other people and not thinking of oneself; not selfish.

unsettle /ʌnˈsetl/ *tr.v* cause (s.o/s.t) to become disturbed: *Not having any news is very unsettling.*
  unˈsettled *adj* 1 (of weather) changing from time to time, e.g sometimes sunny and sometimes rainy. 2 changing (in position, kind etc): *lead an unsettled life.* 3 anxious and insecure(1): *feel unsettled; an unsettled mind.*

unshakeable /ʌnˈʃeɪkəbl/ *adj* (also **unˈshakable**) (*fig*) (of people and their ideas, beliefs etc) not able to be affected by any doubts; absolutely fixed.

unsightly /ʌnˈsaɪtlɪ/ *adj* (*-ier, -iest*) ugly in appearance: *an unsightly advertisement on a beautiful building.*
  unˈsightliness *u.n.*

unskilled /ʌnˈskɪld/ *adj* 1 not having learnt a skill; not trained to do s.t needing skill: *an unskilled workman.* 2 not needing a particular skill: *an unskilled job.*

unsociable /ʌnˈsəʊʃəbl/ *adj* (also **unˈsocial** /ʌnˈsəʊʃl/) 1 not enjoying being or doing things with other people. Compare antisocial. 2 (of a place etc) not friendly: *an unsociable street.* 3 (usu — *hours*) that interferes with one's social life.

unsophisticated /ˌʌnsəˈfɪstɪˌkeɪtɪd/ *adj* 1 (of a person) not having had (much) experience of life in society and therefore able to behave only in simple natural ways; not sophisticated(1). 2 (of things) not complicated: *an unsophisticated textbook.* 3 not fashionable: *unsophisticated clothes.* 4 (of ideas etc) simple and showing that a person is unsophisticated(1).

unsound /ʌnˈsaʊnd/ *adj* (*formal*) 1 (of ideas etc) not true; not to be trusted: *an unsound argument.* 2 (of (part of) a person's body) not in good health; not well: *an unsound heart.* 3 (of a building etc) not as strong as it should be because of damage, bad work etc. **of unsound mind** ⇨ mind¹.

unsparing /ʌnˈspeərɪŋ/ adj (often — of s.t) (formal) not limiting (s.t); not holding (any of) s.t back: She is always unsparing in her efforts to help. Compare sparing.
unˈsparingly adv.

unspeakable /ʌnˈspiːkəbl/ adj very bad; so bad that one does not want to speak of it (although one does in fact do so): unspeakable cruelty.
unˈspeakably adv.

unstable /ʌnˈsteɪbl/ adj not stable.

unstated /ʌnˈsteɪtɪd/ adj not mentioned; not spoken or written down.

unsteady /ʌnˈstedɪ/ adj not steady(1).

unstinting /ʌnˈstɪntɪŋ/ adj generous and without limit: unstinting praise. ⇨ without stint (⇨ stint(1)).

unstop /ʌnˈstɒp/ tr.v take out s.t that is keeping s.t in (s.t) or preventing s.t getting out (of (s.t)): unstop a bottle; unstop a blocked pipe.

unstoppable /ʌnˈstɒpəbl/ adj who/that cannot be stopped.

unstressed /ʌnˈstrest/ adj (of a syllable etc) that is not stressed(4).

unstuck /ʌnˈstʌk/ adj 1 free from being glued, fixed, blocked etc. **come unstuck** (a) stop being stuck on, often accidentally: The label came unstuck. (b) (fig; informal) go wrong; not be successful: Our plans for a short holiday by the sea came unstuck when the railway workers went on strike.
▷ v 2 p.t,p.p of unstick.

unsuccessful /ˌʌnsəkˈsesfəl/ adj not successful.
ˌunsucˈcessfully adv.

unsuitable /ʌnˈsjuːtəbl/ adj not suitable.

unsung /ʌnˈsʌŋ/ adj given no public or official praise: Her help with the plans went unsung. She was an unsung heroine.

unsure /ʌnˈʃʊə/ adj 1 not having confidence in one's opinion, ability etc. 2 not sure about having enough knowledge.

unsurpassed /ˌʌnsəˈpɑːst/ adj too good of its kind for s.o/s.t to be better.

unswerving /ʌnˈswɜːvɪŋ/ adj that never changes; always remaining the same: unswerving loyalty; unswerving commitment to one's studies.

untangle /ʌnˈtæŋgl/ tr.v straighten (s.t); separate (s.t) into its different parts after it was tangled(2) or mixed up.

untapped /ʌnˈtæpt/ adj that has not (yet) had any part of it taken out: the untapped mineral wealth under the sea.

unteachable /ʌnˈtiːtʃəbl/ adj not able to be taught.

untenable /ʌnˈtenəbl/ adj (formal) that it is impossible to defend: I am sorry but that argument is quite untenable.

unthinkable /ʌnˈθɪŋkəbl/ adj that is so terrible that one would not even think that it was true or that it could be done etc: To leave my baby alone all night would be unthinkable!

unˈthinking adj that is done, said etc without first thinking what the result might be: an unthinking remark. Compare thoughtless.
unˈthinkingly adv.

unthought-of /ʌnˈθɔːt ˌɒv/ adj beyond the limits of one's powers of imagination: After

her success in films she lived in unthought-of luxury.

untidy /ʌnˈtaɪdɪ/ adj (-ier, -iest) 1 not neat and organized.
▷ tr.v 2 to make (s.t) untidy(1).

untie /ʌnˈtaɪ/ tr.v (pres.p untying, p.t,p.p untied) 1 free (a rope etc) from s.t to which it was fixed by loosening and removing it. 2 free (s.o/s.t) by loosening (and removing) the rope etc holding her/him/it.

until /ʌnˈtɪl/ conj 1 up to the time that; during the whole of the time before; till¹: She promised to wait until I arrived. He cried until he fell asleep.
until s.o is blue in the face ⇨ face(n).
▷ prep 2 up to the time of; during the whole of the time before; till¹: We watched TV until midnight. 3 as far as (a place): They stayed on the train until Paris.

untimely /ʌnˈtaɪmlɪ/ adj (-ier, -iest) (formal) not usual for that time; coming earlier than it should: We had some untimely snow in September. Her death was untimely. **come to an untimely end** finish or die earlier than normally expected.
unˈtimeliness u.n.

untiring /ʌnˈtaɪərɪŋ/ adj (usu attrib) not (showing that one is) getting tired: an untiring helper; untiring efforts.
unˈtiringly adv.

unto /ˈʌntʊ/ prep (old use; in the Bible) to².

untold /ʌnˈtəʊld/ adj 1 that has not been told: Her experiences as an explorer are still untold. 2 (attrib) so many/much that one cannot count them/it: untold centuries; untold wealth.

untrained /ʌnˈtreɪnd/ adj not trained.

untrue /ʌnˈtruː/ adj not true.
unˈtruth c.n (often tell an —) lie¹(1).
unˈtruthful adj 1 (of s.t said, written etc) not true. 2 (of a person) (often) not telling the truth.
unˈtruthfully adv. **unˈtruthfulness** u.n.

unusable /ʌnˈjuːzəbl/ adj that cannot be used; not usable: The tool is rusty so it's unusable. Compare useless(1).

unused¹ /ʌnˈjuːzd/ adj that has not been used: an unused ticket; a ticket that is unused.

unused² /ʌnˈjuːst/ pred.adj **unused to s.o/s.t** not accustomed or used³ to s.o/s.t: John is unused to having to work hard.

unusual /ʌnˈjuːʒʊəl/ adj not common; different from others; rarely seen, heard etc; not usual: a blouse of an unusual colour.
unˈusually adv 1 in an unusual manner: dress unusually. 2 more than is usual: We are having an unusually warm winter. Compare usually.

unutterable /ʌnˈʌtərəbl/ adj (formal) (of s.t bad) very great: unutterable poverty. ⇨ utter², utmost.
unˈutterably adv extremely.

unveil /ʌnˈveɪl/ v 1 tr.v remove from (s.o/s.t) the veil or other covering that hides her/him/ it: The president unveiled the memorial to those who died in the accident. 2 intr.v remove the veil covering one's face etc: Many Arab women never unveil before a man who is not a close relative.

unvoiced /ʌnˈvɔɪst/ adj 1 not spoken aloud although thought in the mind. 2 (technical) pronounced without vibration(2) of the vocal cords; not voiced.

unwanted /ʌn'wɒntɪd/ *adj* not wanted.

unwarranted /ʌn'wɒrəntɪd/ *adj* done, said etc without a good reason for it or without being deserved: *unwarranted rudeness to a parent*.

unwavering /ʌn'weɪvərɪŋ/ *adj*. not wavering.

unwell /ʌn'wel/ *adj* (usu *pred*) ill or sick(1), usu not for a long time: *I feel unwell*.

unwieldy /ʌn'wiːldɪ/ *adj* (-*ier*, -*iest*) **1** difficult to use, move etc because of its shape, weight etc: *an unwieldy chair*. **2** (*fig*) difficult to control or use because it is too big, complicated etc: *an unwieldy organization*.
un'wieldiness *u.n.*

unwilling /ʌn'wɪlɪŋ/ *adj* not willing: *an unwilling helper*.
un'willingly *adv.*

unwind /ʌn'waɪnd/ *v* (*p.t,p.p* **unwound** /ʌn'waund/) **1** *tr/intr.v* (often — *s.t from s.t*) (cause (*s.t*) to) become less wound up by turning it: *She unwound her arms from the child and let it go. Don't let go of that spring or it will unwind.* **2** *intr.v* (*fig*) develop (often while at the same time becoming easier to understand): *As the old woman's story unwound, we began to realize how much she had suffered.* **3** *intr.v* (*fig*) (of a person) become calmer or less tense¹(2); relax(1).

unwise /ʌn'waɪz/ *adj* (often — *of s.o* (*to do s.t*)) foolish; not wise(1): *an unwise decision. It was unwise of you to say that.*
un'wisely *adv.*

unwitting /ʌn'wɪtɪŋ/ *attrib.adj* (*formal*) not done consciously: *unwitting lies*/slander(1).
un'wittingly *adv.*

unworkable /ʌn'wɜːkəbl/ *adj* that cannot be done, managed etc successfully.

unworldly /ʌn'wɜːldlɪ/ *adj* **1** not caring about material benefits. **2** simple and lacking experience or knowledge about life.

unworthy /ʌn'wɜːðɪ/ *adj* (-*ier*, -*iest*) shameful; without value: *unworthy behaviour/remarks.* **unworthy of s.o** not of the high standard expected of s.o (because so bad, unpleasant etc): *Such rude remarks were unworthy of you.* **unworthy of s.t** not deserving s.t: *Such bad behaviour is unworthy of* comment. **unworthy to do s.t** not good enough to do s.t: *She's unworthy to continue to be his friend.* ⇒ worthy.
un'worthiness *u.n.*

unwound /ʌn'waund/ *p.t,p.p* of unwind.

unwrap /ʌn'ræp/ *tr.v* (-*pp*-) remove the paper cover from (s.t): *unwrap a present.*

unwritten /ʌn'rɪtn/ *adj* (esp — *law*) that people know and obey although it has never been officially made.

unzip /ʌn'zɪp/ *tr.v* (-*pp*-) open the zip(1) of (clothing, a bag etc).

up /ʌp/ *adv* **1** from a lower to a higher position: *He climbed up and looked over the wall. She lifted up the lid. This lift is going up (to the top floor).* Compare up(21). Opposite down(1). **2** from a (more) horizontal position to a (more) vertical one: *She stood up and walked towards me. Sit up! Can you put up the tent/sail?* Compare down(3). **3** out of bed: *Are the children up yet?* **4** in or towards a position or direction that is higher: *He looked up and saw me. The bedroom is three floors up. The moon isn't up yet. The sun comes up in the east.* Opposite down¹(4). **5** so as to be out

of the ground, water etc: *Let's dig up all those old bushes. The storm threw up some dead fish. She was almost dead when she finally came up, having been under the water for several minutes.* **6** to or towards the place or direction referred to: *He walked up to the post office. She came up (to me) and shook my hand.* Compare along(1), down¹(6). **7** from a place considered less important to one considered more important: *We went up to town/London yesterday.* Compare down¹(7). **8** in or towards the north: *They live up north, up in Scotland.* Compare down¹(8). **9** in or towards a place or position further away from the mouth of a river: *Is it possible to row from London up to Oxford? We are in the City of London and Chelsea is a few kilometres up.* Compare up(23). Opposite down¹(9). **10** from a lower rank, grade etc to a higher one: *He's moving up to the first class next week.* Opposite down¹(10). **11** higher in amount, degree etc: *The temperature/cost/price/ fare has gone up. The river is up by 10 metres.* Opposite down¹(11). **12** in or into a more active, lively state: *Wake up! Cheer up! Hurry up! The wind is up.* **13** (so as to be) finished: *Drink up your coffee. Eat up—we are late. The fire burnt up all our furniture. It's your turn to wash up. Carry on and I'll tell you when your time is up.* **14** so as to be fastened, closed, covered etc: *Button up your coat. Do up your* shoelace. *Have you tied up the parcel?* Compare down¹(13). **15** so as to be together: *Fold up the sheets. We rolled up the carpet. Dead leaves were piled up in the corner.* **16** so as to be separated into parts or pieces etc: *The group broke up and everyone went home. Tear that letter up.* **17** together so as to reach a total: *I can't add up these large numbers. Please count up how many days you have been away this month. I'm saving up (my money) to buy a bicycle.* **18** to s.o's attention (often for discussion, agreement etc): *Bring it up for discussion next week. The problem could easily come up again.* **19** better than a competitor: *We finished the match two goals up.* Opposite down¹(15). For verb (+ s.o/s.t) + 'up', e.g *bring s.t up, catch up*, ⇒ the verb. **up and about** (*informal*) out of bed and active (e.g after being ill). **up against s.o/ s.t** having s.o/s.t as one's enemy; faced by s.o/s.t who/that causes trouble. **up and down (a)** higher and then lower: *We climbed up and down. Prices went up and down during last month.* **(b)** in one direction and then in the opposite direction: *We drove up and down looking for a place to park the car.* **up in s.t** knowing a lot about s.t; having a lot of information about s.t. **up in arms** ⇒ arms. **up on s.t** more than s.t: *Profits are up on last year.* **up till s.t** ⇒ up until s.t. **up to s.o (to do s.t)** the duty, job, responsibility of s.o (to do s.t): *It's up to you to find out the cost of the ticket.* **up to s.t (a)** busy doing s.t, usu bad or secret: *What's that boy up to with that knife?* **(b)** experienced enough to know about s.t: *The teacher was up to all the children's tricks.* **up to date** ⇒ date¹(n). **up to one's eyes in s.t** ⇒ eye(n). **up to no good** ⇒ good(n). **up to the mark** ⇒ mark(n). **up to the minute** ⇒ minute²(n). **up to strength** ⇒ strength. **up until/ till s.t** as far as s.t in time or place: *We waited up until 4 o'clock.* **Up with s.o/s.t** I support, am in favour of, s.o/s.t: *Up with the* prime minister*!* Opposite down with s.t. **what is up with s.o** why s.o is sad, angry, feeling unwell etc: *Tell me, what's up with Emma today.* **what is up with s.t** why a tool, machine etc is not working properly: *What's up with your car?*

▷ *n* **20** (*informal*) high or more encouraging point: *I'm on an up at work at the moment.* **on the up-and-up** (*informal*) improving steadily and quickly. **ups and downs** periods of good fortune with periods of bad fortune: *We all have our ups and downs.*

▷ *prep* **21** at or to a higher position or level in, on, (s.o/s.t): *We went up several mountains. She climbed up the ladder. He lives three flights of stairs up.* Compare up(1). Opposite down¹(17). **22** along (a road, river, coastline etc): *Let's walk up the street and look in the shop windows.* Compare up(6), down¹(18), along(3). **23** at or towards a place or position further away from the mouth of a river: *Ships can go up the river as far as London.* Compare up(9). Opposite down¹(19). **up country** ⇒ country. **up river** ⇒ river(*n*). ⇒ upstream.

▷ *tr.v* (-pp-) **24** (*informal*) increase (a price etc): *They've upped their offer for the car from £500 to £600.* **s.o upped and did s.t** s.o suddenly did s.t: *She upped and left the room as soon as he arrived.*

‚up-and-'coming *adj* likely to be successful: *an up-and-coming young lawyer.*

‚up-and-'up *def.n* ⇒ up(*n*).

'up‚bringing *sing.n* (way of) caring for and educating a child as he/she becomes older.

up-'country *adj* **1** belonging to, coming from, a part of the country that is not near the sea.

▷ *adv* **2** in or to a place far from the sea: *live up-country.*

up'date *tr.v* bring (s.t that was old-fashioned or out-of-date) up to date (⇒ date¹(*n*)): *update information on a file³(2).*

up'end *tr.v* turn (s.t) so that the part that was (or is usu) downwards is now at the top or on one side: *upend a boat.*

up'grade *tr.v* move (s.o/s.t) up into a higher rank or position; improve (s.t): *Our airline is going to upgrade its services by having wider and more comfortable seats.* Opposite downgrade.

up'hill *adj* **1** in a direction that slopes upwards. Opposite downhill. **2** (usu — *struggle/task*) (*fig*) causing difficulty or hard work.

▷ *adv* **3** in a direction that slopes upwards. Opposite downhill.

up'hold *tr.v* (*p.t,p.p* upheld /ʌp'held/) **1** support (s.t); prevent (s.t) being lost: *The law upholds everybody's right to be fairly treated.* **2** agree with (s.t); confirm (s.t) as right: *When the man was found guilty, he appealed(6) but the higher court upheld the lower court's judgment.* Opposite overturn.

up'holder *c.n* (usu — *of s.t*) person who upholds(1,2) s.t.

up'holster *tr.v* **1** provide (a room etc) with carpets, curtains and other furnishings. **2** make (a chair etc) soft and comfortable by putting padding, springs, cloth etc on it.

up'holsterer *c.n* **1** person whose job is upholstering. **2** (also **up'holsterer's**) shop, business etc of an upholsterer(1).

up'holstery *u.n* **1** job of upholstering. **2** carpets, curtains and other furnishings.

'up‚keep *u.n* (usu *the — of s.t*) (cost of) keeping s.t in a good state by repairing it when necessary.

upland /'ʌplənd/ *u.n* (often *the — of s.t*) land (in a place) that is higher than other land near it.

uplands /'ʌpləndz/ *pl.n* = upland.

'up‚lift *c/u.n* **1** (*old use*) feeling of feeling (morally) better or happier: *The church service gave me a moral uplift.*

▷ *tr.v* (/‚ʌp'lift/) **2** make (s.o/s.t) feel (morally) better or happier.

upon /ə'pɒn/ *prep* (*formal*) on (*prep*). (Notice that there is no adverb 'upon'.)

'upper *attrib.adj* **1** higher than s.t else: *the upper floors of a building.* **2** (often *the — reaches* (*of a river*)) nearer the beginning and further from the mouth. **3** higher in rank, importance etc. Opposite lower.

▷ *c.n* **4** (often *pl*) part of a shoe or boot that is over the top of one's foot. **5** (*slang*) drug(2) used to make s.o excited, interested, lively(1) etc. Compare downer.

‚upper 'arm *c/def.n* part of the arm that is between the shoulder and the elbow.

‚Upper 'Chamber *c/def.n* = Upper House.

‚upper 'class *adj* (**'upper-‚class** when *attrib*) **1** belonging to the highest ranks of society. ⇒ U, non-U.

▷ *c/def/def.pl.n* **2** (also *pl*) highest ranks of society.

‚upper 'hand *def.n* (usu *gain/get/have the — (over s.o)*) stronger or more powerful position (than s.o): *Mary began by losing the first set of her tennis match but then quickly got the upper hand over the other girl and won 4–6, 6–1, 6–2.*

‚Upper 'House *c/def.n* higher of two parts of parliament with fewer members and less power than the other: *In Britain the* House of Lords *is the Upper House.* ⇒ Lower House.

'upper‚most *adj* **1** highest: *the uppermost layer of soil.*

▷ *adv* **2** in or into the highest position. **be/come uppermost (in one's mind)** be or become the thing one thinks of most.

'up‚right *adj* **1** vertical; standing straight up, not lying down or bent: *upright books on a shelf.* **2** (*formal*) honest: *He is always upright with me.*

▷ *adv* **3** in or into a position where he/she/it is upright(1): *standing/sitting upright.*

▷ *c.n* **4** vertical support for s.t: *The uprights of a gate.*

'upright pi'ano *c.n* piano in which the strings are vertical. Compare grand piano.

'up‚rightly *adv.* **'up‚rightness** *u.n.*

'up‚rising *c.n* attack(s) by people against their ruler(s); rising(2); revolt(1), usu a small local one.

up'root *tr.v* **1** pull (a plant etc) out of the ground with its roots. **2** (*fig*) make (a person) leave her/his home, way of life etc and move to new ones.

‚ups and 'downs ⇒ up(*n*).

‚upside 'down *adv* **1** with the part that is usu on the top underneath: *The bread and butter landed upside down on the floor.* **2** in or into a state of disorder. **turn s.t upside down** (**a**) turn s.t over so that the top becomes the bottom. (**b**) go through s.t (e.g a cupboard) in an untidy way, usu when searching.

up'stage adv **1** at or towards the back of a theatre stage. Opposite downstage.

▷ tr.v **2** (informal) draw people's attention away from (the person they are supposed to be watching etc) and towards oneself, usu by being more attractive, interesting etc.

up'stairs adj **1** who/that is, works etc upstairs(2). Opposite downstairs.

▷ adv **2** to a higher floor; (to a floor) above the ground floor. Opposite downstairs.

▷ c/def.n **3** floor(s) above the ground floor. Opposite downstairs.

up'standing adj (of a person) having good moral qualities; honest, truthful etc: a fine upstanding student.

'up,start c.n (derog) person who has quickly become important, rich etc and behaves too proudly: young upstarts in the management team.

up'stream adj/adv further towards the beginning of the river and away from its mouth. Opposite downstream.

'up,surge c.n (often — of s.t) sudden (often violent) increase (in s.t): There was an upsurge of interest in football after the international matches.

,up-to-the-'minute attrib.adj ⇨ minute²(n).

up'town adj/adv (that is) away from the part(s) of a town/city where the offices, big shops etc are and in the part(s) where people have their homes. Opposite downtown.

'up,turn c.n (usu — in s.t) improvement (in one's fortune, health etc or financial affairs etc).

up'turned adj **1** that bends upwards at the end: an upturned nose. **2** that has been turned upside down.

upward(s) /'ʌpwəd(z)/ adj **1** moving or pointing up: an upward movement of one's eyes; an upward movement of prices.

▷ adv **2** rising; in a direction that goes up. Opposite downward(s). **upward(s) of s.t** more than s.t: Upwards of 100 people were waiting.

upbringing, up-country, update, up-end, upgrade ⇨ up.

upheaval /ʌp'hiːvl/ c/u.n disturbance caused by big changes.

uphill, uphold(er), upholster(er), upholstery, upkeep, upland, uplift, upon, upper(most), upright(ly, ness), uprising ⇨ up.

uproar /'ʌpˌrɔː/ c/u.n noisy disturbance by a number of people in which different people shout different things.

up'roarious adj **1** noisy, usu because of a lot of people laughing. **2** so amusing that it makes people laugh loudly.

up'roariously adv.

uproot ⇨ up.

ups and downs ⇨ up(n).

upset (/ʌp'set/, when attrib /'ʌpˌset/) adj **1** disturbed or not happy (about s.t): She's feeling upset (about losing the match). **2** not very well; rather sick(2): The food gave the children upset stomachs.

▷ c/u.n /'ʌpˌset/ **3** rather sick(2) feeling: a stomach upset. **4** act of disturbing plans or expectations: The loss of the game was a surprising upset. **5** (informal) quarrel: an upset in a family.

▷ v /ʌp'set/ (-tt-, p.t,p.p upset) **6** tr.v cause (s.o) to feel upset(1). **7** tr.v cause (s.o/s.t) to be upset(2): The food upset our stomachs. **8** tr/intr.v (cause (s.t) to) (turn over and) spill out: You've upset that (cup of) coffee on the carpet. **9** tr.v disturb (plans etc) so much that they fail: The bad weather upset the arrangements for the holiday.

upshot /'ʌpˌʃɒt/ def.n (informal) (often the — of s.t) final result (of s.t): The upshot was that no one accepted responsibility.

upside down, upstage, upstairs, upstanding, upstart, upstream, up-surge ⇨ up.

uptake /'ʌpˌteɪk/ def.n **quick/slow on the uptake** quick/slow to understand what is being suggested, taught etc.

uptight /ʌp'taɪt/ adj (informal) tense¹(2); feeling worried, nervous etc.

uptown, upturn(ed), upward(s) ⇨ up.

uranium /jʊ'reɪnɪəm/ u.n kind of metal that looks silvery, is heavier than a lot of the other metals and is radioactive, used to produce atomic power, chem.symb U.

Uranus /jʊ'reɪnəs/ unique n seventh planet from the sun.

urban /'ɜːbən/ adj of or referring to a town or city: an urban district council. Opposite rural.

urbanization, -isation /ˌɜːbənaɪˈzeɪʃən/ u.n becoming, or causing s.t to become, urbanized.

'urba,nize, -ise tr.v change (a place) from being rural (i.e from having the ways of life of the country) to being urban.

urbane /ɜː'beɪn/ adj (sometimes derog) behaving or talking (too) politely.

ur'banely adv.

urbanity /ɜː'bænɪtɪ/ u.n (formal) **1** fact of being urbane. **2** urbane behaviour.

urchin /'ɜːtʃɪn/ c.n **1** small (and usu dirty, untidy and/or naughty) boy. **2** = sea urchin.

urge /ɜːdʒ/ c.n **1** strong desire to do s.t: I wish I could travel every time I feel/get the urge.

▷ tr.v **2** (often — s.o to do s.t) force or strongly encourage (s.o to do s.t): We urged her to see a doctor. **3** (often — s.t on s.o) say (s.t) very strongly (to s.o): I must again urge on you the need for speed if we are to succeed. **urge s.o/s.t on** try to make (s.o, an animal) move forward more quickly, work with more energy(1) etc.

urgency /'ɜːdʒənsɪ/ u.n fact or state of being urgent(1,2).

urgent /'ɜːdʒənt/ adj **1** very much needing to be done (now). **2** (often — in s.t) showing that s.t very much needs to be done (now): The electricity company are becoming urgent in their demands for payment.

'urgently adv.

urine /'jʊərɪn/ u.n waste liquid that comes out of an animal's or person's body through the bladder(1).

urinal /jʊə'raɪnl/ c.n **1** lavatory where men can urinate. **2** bottle etc into which men can urinate, usu in a hospital bed.

urinary /'jʊərɪnərɪ/ adj of or referring to the parts of a person's or animal's body in which there is urine: a urinary infection.

urinate /'jʊərɪˌneɪt/ intr.v cause or allow urine to come out of one's body.

urination /jʊərɪ'neɪʃən/ u.n.

urn /ɜːn/ c.n **1** big container, usu made of metal,

for making hot liquids (e.g tea) in. **2** big container for the ashes of a body after it has been cremated.

us (strong form /ʌs/, weak form /əs/) *pron* (form of 'we' used when it is the object[1](4) of a verb or preposition, or (*informal*) when it is a subjective complement): *We saw him and he saw us. He went with us. It was us that saw him.* (Notice that we use 'we', not 'us', in formal English when it is the subjective complement, e.g *It was we that saw him.*)

US /ˌjuː ˈes/ *abbr* **1** *def.n/abbr* United States: *the US army.* **2** *abbr* (*informal*) so badly damaged that it can no longer be used.

USA /ˌjuː ˌes ˈeɪ/ *def.n abbr* United States of America.

use¹ /juːs/ *n* **1** *u.n* act of doing of s.t for a purpose; act or fact of using[1](3) (s.o/s.t) or being used: *The use of guns is not allowed in these woods.* **2** *c/u.n* usefulness; purpose or reason: *Is this paper any use to you or shall I throw it away?* (**be**) (**of**) **no earthly use** be no use(2) at all to anyone. **give s.o the use of s.t** allow s.o to use[1](3) s.t. **go out of use** stop being used[1](3). **have a , any** *etc* **use for s.o/s.t** consider s.o/s.t to be useful: *Do you have any use for this old bicycle?* **have no use for s.o/s.t** (*informal*) not like s.o/s.t: *We have no use for lazy students.* **have the use of s.t** be allowed or able to use[1](3) s.t: *The manager has the use of a company car whenever she wants it.* **in use** being used[1](3) (now): *You can't have the car now because it's in use.* **it's no use (s.o/s.t)** doing s.t it's useless (for s.o/s.t) to do s.t. **lose the use of s.t** no longer be able to use[1](3) s.t: *As a result of the accident he lost the use of his left arm.* **make use of s.o/s.t** use[1](3) s.o/s.t. **of (no, some** *etc*) **use** useful (in no, some etc way): *Is this coat of any use to you?* **What's the use of doing s.t?** In what way is it useful to do s.t?

▷ *tr.v* /juːz/ (*p.t,p.p used* /juːzd/) **3** employ (s.o/s.t) for a reason or purpose: *We use a spoon to eat soup.* **4** (often — *s.t up*) completely finish (s.t): *I need some more envelopes; I've used (up) all the ones I had.* **5** cheat (s.o) by getting her/him to do s.t one wants while letting her/him think one is not doing this.

usable /ˈjuːzəbl/ *adj* that can be used[1](3); that is good enough to use[1](3). Compare useful(1). Opposite unusable.

usage /ˈjuːzɪdʒ/ *c/u.n* way of using[1](3) s.t, often the way in which most people use it: *'Between you and I' is not good English usage; you should say 'Between you and me'.*

used¹ /juːzd/ *adj* that has been used[1](3) before and is therefore not clean, new etc: *a used razor blade.* Opposited unused. ⇒ ill-used.

useful /ˈjuːsful/ *adj* Opposite useless. **1** helpful and able to be used[1](3): *a useful machine that opens cans easily.* Compare usable. **2** having a chance of success: *a useful suggestion.* **3** (of a person) able to do something well: *a useful teacher.* **come in useful** become useful(1): *Take your coat; it will come in useful if it rains.* **ˈusefully** *adv*. **ˈusefulness** *u.n*.

useless /ˈjuːslɪs/ *adj* Opposite useful. **1** not able to be used[1](3), esp because of a low standard, broken etc: *a useless dictionary.* Compare unusable. **2** having no chance of success: *a useless attempt.* **3** (*derog*) (of a

person) not able to do anything well: *a useless worker.*
ˈuselessly *adv*. **ˈuselessness** *u.n*.

user /ˈjuːzə/ *c.n* person, country, industry etc using[1](3) s.t, esp often: *a dictionary user*; *the main users of coal for heating.*

use² /juːs/ *v* (*p.t used* /juːst/) (only used in the infinitive and p.t; negative *usen't to, usedn't to* or *didn't use to*; 'use' is always followed by the infinitive of a verb with *to*; questions usually formed by using *did*) was in the habit (of doing or having s.t): *We used to go dancing every Friday evening. He didn't use to be so rude. Didn't she use to own a blue car? Used they to have a lot of problems with their house?* **used to be** was formerly: *There used to be a good restaurant in our village.*

used¹ /juːst/ *p.t,p.p* of use[1].
used² /juːst/ *p.t, p.p* of use[2].
used³ /juːst/ *pred.adj* (usu be/get — to s.o/s.t) accustomed (to s.o/s.t): *I didn't like the colour of her kitchen at first but now I am getting used to it.* Opposite unused[2].

usher /ˈʌʃə/ *c.n* **1** man who shows people where to sit, usu in church at weddings. **2** person who stops people behaving badly in a court of law.
▷ *tr.v* **3** (often — *s.o in*(*to* s.t), *out* (*of* s.t)) help/cause (s.o) to come/go in(to s.t), out (of s.t): *When the guests arrive, the doorman has to usher them in.* **4** (often — *s.t in*) cause (s.t) to begin; happen at the same time as the beginning of (s.t): *April ushered in a few weeks of warm weather.*

usherette /ˌʌʃəˈret/ *c.n* woman who works in a cinema, theatre etc to show customers where their seats are and to sell them ice cream etc.

USSR /ˌjuː ˌes ˌes ˈɑː/ *def.n/abbr* Union of Soviet Socialist Republics.

usu *written abbr* usually.

usual /ˈjuːʒuəl/ *adj* that one has, does etc (nearly) always: *Someone was sitting in my usual seat in the train.* Compare unusual. **as usual** as happens (nearly) always: *That day we had lunch at one o'clock as usual.*

ˈusually *adv* in most cases; on most occasions: *It usually rains a lot here in December.* Compare unusually.

usurp /juːˈzɜːp/ *tr.v* take, usu by force, (a position etc that one has no right to).
usurpation /ˌjuːzɜːˈpeɪʃən/ *u.n*.
uˈsurper *c.n* (*derog*) person who usurps (s.t).

usury /ˈjuːʒərɪ/ *u.n* act of lending money at rates of interest that are considered too high.

utensil /juːˈtensl/ *c.n* thing that one uses for doing s.t: *cooking utensils.*

uterus /ˈjuːtərəs/ *c.n* (*pl -es,* or less usu, *uteri* /ˈjuːtəˌraɪ/) (*medical*) place in a female in which babies grow before they are born; womb.

utility /juːˈtɪlɪtɪ/ *n* (*pl -ies*) (*formal*) **1** *u.n* usefulness. **2** *c.n* thing that is a service to people: *Our town's public utilities include a very good children's library and playground.*

utilitarian /ˌjuːtɪlɪˈteərɪən/ *adj* useful for practical purposes, often without being attractive to look at etc.

utilizable, -isable /ˈjuːtɪˌlaɪzəbl/ *adj* (*formal*) that can be utilized.

utilization, -isation /ˌjuːtɪlaɪˈzeɪʃən/ *u.n* (*formal*) act or fact of making use of/ utilizing (s.o/s.t).

'uti,lize, -ise *tr.v* (*formal*) make use of (s.o/s.t); use (s.o/s.t).

utmost /'ʌt,məʊst/ *attrib.adj* (also **'utter,most**) **1** (*formal*) greatest possible: *using our utmost effort.* **2** farthest: *utmost ends/limits.*
▷ *n* **3 do one's utmost** make the greatest possible effort.

'utter¹ /'ʌtə/ *attrib.adj* complete; absolute: *utter nonsense/madness.*

'utterly *adv*: *utterly stupid.*

'utter,most *attrib.adj* = utmost(1,2).

utopia /juː'təʊpɪə/ *c/unique n* (often with capital **U**) (imaginary) place where everything is perfect and everyone is absolutely happy.

u'topian *adj* (often with capital **U**) (of an idea, plan) considered worth doing or having but not practical or possible because idealistic.

utter¹ *attrib.adj* ⇒ utmost.

utter² /'ʌtə/ *tr.v* make (sounds, e.g cries, a sigh, words) out loud. ⇒ unutterable.

utterance /'ʌtərəns/ *c.n* (*formal*) thing that one says. **give utterance to s.t** say s.t out loud.

uttermost ⇒ utmost.

U-turn ⇒ U.

uvula /'juːvjʊlə/ *c.n* (*pl* -s or, less usu, *uvulae* /'juːvjʊˌliː/) (*technical*) small narrow back end of the soft palate(1) which hangs down towards the throat and is used for making some sounds.

'uvular *adj* **1** (*technical*) pronounced with the back of one's tongue touching or near one's uvula.
▷ *c.n* **2** (*technical*) consonant sound pronounced in this way.

V v

V, v /viː/ *c/unique n* **1** 22nd letter of the English alphabet.
▷ *written abbr* **2** (**v**) verb. **3** (**v**) verse. **4** (**v**) versus: *The match tomorrow is France v Italy.* ⇒ vs. **5** (usu **V**) very. ⇒ VG. **6** (**V**) Vice³. **7** (**V**) Viscount.
▷ *symb* **8** (**v**) velocity. **9** (**V**) victory. ⇒ V-sign(1). **10** (**V**) volt(s). **11** (**V**) volume(3). **12** Roman numeral for 5.

'V-,neck *c.n* neck of a piece of clothing shaped like a V.

'v-,necked *adj* having a V-neck: *a V-necked jumper.*

'V-,sign *c/def.n* **1** sign (made with two fingers of the hand up and the palm¹(1) outwards) meaning 'Victory' or 'We shall win'. **2** (do not use!) rude sign (made with two fingers of the hand up and the palm¹(1) inwards) meaning 'fuck off' (i.e go away).

vac /væk/ *abbr* vacation.

vacant /'veɪkənt/ *adj* **1** not being used by anyone: *a vacant seat. This room's vacant if you'd like to move in.* **2** in which no one is working at present:

When John retired, his job remained vacant for several weeks. **3** showing that s.o is not thinking or interested: *a vacant expression. The boy was looking quite vacant.*

vacancy /'veɪkənsɪ/ *c.n* (*pl* -ies) place (e.g in a hotel, school, office) which is waiting to be filled by s.o wanting a room, job etc: *There's a vacancy in our office for a clerk.*

'vacantly *adv* looking vacant(3): *She was staring vacantly at the floor.*

vacate /və'keɪt/ *tr.v* (*formal*) leave (s.t); stop being, living or working in (s.t): *Will you please turn the electricity off when you vacate your flat.*

vacation /və'keɪʃən/ *n* **1** *c.n* (esp US) holiday. **2** *c.n* time when a university etc is closed to students: *the summer vacation.* **3** *u.n* act of vacating a house, room etc. **on vacation (a)** having a holiday. **(b)** having one of one's regular holidays from university, college etc.

vaccine /'væksiːn/ *c/u.n* liquid containing living or dead bacteria or viruses put into s.o's or an animal's body to protect her/him/it from illnesses caused by such bacteria or viruses.

vaccinate /'væksɪˌneɪt/ *tr.v* (often — s.o/s.t against s.t) put a vaccine into (s.o/an animal) (to stop her/him/it getting a certain disease).

vaccination /ˌvæksɪ'neɪʃən/ *c/u.n* (often — against s.t) act or fact of putting in a vaccine (to stop s.o getting a certain disease).

vacillate /'væsɪˌleɪt/ *intr.v* (*formal*) (often — between s.t and s.t) change again and again from one idea, plan, feeling etc to another and then back again because one cannot decide what to think, do or feel.

vacillation /ˌvæsɪ'leɪʃən/ *u.n.*

vacuum /'vækjʊəm/ *c.n* **1** state of being (almost) completely empty of everything including air. **2** (fig) (feeling of) complete emptiness or loneliness: *Nobody can live in a vacuum, we all have to live with the world as it is.*
▷ *tr.v* **3** clean or empty (s.t) by using a vacuum cleaner.

'vacuum ,cleaner *c.n* machine used to suck dust, dirt etc from floors etc.

'vacuum ,flask = flask(1).

'vacuum-,packed *adj* (of food in shops) packed in an airtight bag from which (nearly) all the air has been taken out.

'vacuum ,pump *c.n* (*technical*) pump that sucks air etc out or up by making a vacuum(1) that the air etc rushes in to fill.

vagabond /'væɡəˌbɒnd/ *c.n* (also *attrib*) (often *derog*) person with no home and no job (often because he/she is lazy or useless): *a vagabond life.* Compare tramp(1), vagrant(1).

vagary /'veɪɡərɪ/ *c.n* (*pl* -ies) (*formal*) unexpected behaviour; behaviour that does not follow any regular pattern: *the vagaries of the British climate; the vagaries of s.o's mind.*

vagina /və'dʒaɪnə/ *c.n* tube in female human beings and animals between the outside sex organs and the womb.

va'ginal *adj* of or referring to the vagina: *a vaginal irritation(2).*

vagrant /'veɪɡrənt/ *c.n* **1** person with no home or job who often begs. Compare tramp(1), vagabond. **2** (law) person arrested by the police for wandering about without any money etc.

'vagrancy *u.n* **1** state or fact of being a vagrant(1,2). **2** (*law*) offence of being a vagrant(2).

vague /veɪg/ *adj* **1** not clear when one looks at it or tries to understand it: *I could see the vague shape of a building through the fog. His answers were too vague to be of any help to me.* **2** not speaking, writing or thinking clearly: *She was vague about what the man had said.* **not have the vaguest idea (what, who, why etc . . .)** (*informal*) not know at all (what etc . . .): *I haven't the vaguest idea where George is.*
'vaguely *adv.* **'vagueness** *u.n.*

vain /veɪn/ *adj* **1** (*derog*) having too high an opinion of one's own beauty, ability etc. **2** (*attrib*) not having the result one had hoped; useless: *He died in a vain attempt to save his son from drowning.* **in vain** without getting the result one had hoped for: *He tried in vain to save his son.* **take God's name in vain** use God's name in a bad or evil way.
'vainly *adv.* **'vainness** *u.n.*

vanity /'vænɪtɪ/ *n* (*pl -ies*) **1** *u.n* fact or state of being vain(1). **2** *c.n* thing, action etc that is not really important or valuable but that s.o has/does because it makes her/him feel important etc.
'vanity ,bag/,case *c.n* bag/case in which a woman carries things she uses to make herself look more beautiful.

valance /'væləns/ *c.n* strip of cloth hanging round the edge of a shelf, bed etc for decoration.

vale /veɪl/ *c.n* (*poetry* or in names with capital **V**) valley.

valentine /'vælən,taɪn/ *c.n* **1** person chosen as one's boyfriend/girlfriend on Saint Valentine's Day (February 14). **2** card sent to s.o on Saint Valentine's Day saying one loves her/him.

valet /'vælɪt or 'væleɪ/ *c.n* **1** worker in a hotel who cleans and presses the hotel guests' clothes. **2** male servant who usu looks after his master (cooking, cleaning his clothes etc).
▷ *v* **3** *tr/intr.v* clean, press etc (s.o's clothes). **4** *tr.v* act as a valet(2) to (s.o).

valiant /'vælɪənt/ *adj* (*formal*) very brave: *a valiant person/action.* ⇨ valour.
'valiantly *adv.*

valid /'vælɪd/ *adj* Opposite invalid[2]. **1** that can be accepted (often by a court of law); good enough to be accepted: *What valid excuse/reason can David have for not coming to such an important meeting?* **2** (often — *for s.t*) that can legally be used (for the purpose of s.t): *Is your ticket valid? This pass is only valid for travel in France.*
validate /'vælɪ,deɪt/ *tr.v* (*formal*) make (s.t) valid(1,2). Opposite invalidate.
validation /,vælɪ'deɪʃən/ *c/u.n.*
validity /və'lɪdɪtɪ/ *u.n* (*formal*) state or fact of being valid(1,2).
'validly *adv.*

valise /və'liːz/ *c.n* (*formal*) small piece of luggage.

valley /'vælɪ/ *c/u.n* (with capital **V** in names) low area or stretch of land between two (lines of) mountains or hills, usu with a river: *the Nile Valley.*

valour /'vælə/ *u.n* (US **'valor**) (*formal*) great bravery. ⇨ valiant.
'valorous *adj* (*formal*) very brave.

'valorously *adv.*

value /'væljuː/ *n* **1** *c/u.n* amount s.t is worth in money or in comparison with other things: *They are asking £1000 for this car but its real value is nearer £500.* **2** *u.n* measure of how useful s.o/s.t is, usu when compared to s.o/s.t else: *One can see the value of this new medicine from the number of people it has already cured.* **3** *c.n* (*technical*) number a sign stands for: *In 10 + x = 12, x has the value 2.* **4** *c.n* (*music*) length of a note. **(be/ get) (good) value for (one's) money** (be or get s.t) well worth what one pays for it: *When I buy clothes I always look for value for money.* **of (great** etc**) value** (very etc) valuable(1,2): *Articles of value should be put in the hotel safe. I am afraid the painting you bought is of little value. The pen is of great personal value.* **set a (high, low** etc**) value on s.t** state a value(1,2) for s.t (that is high, low etc). **take s.o/s.t at face value** ⇨ face(*n*).
▷ *tr.v* **5** find or give the value(1) of (s.t): *Before you decide how much to ask for that carpet, you should have it valued by someone who really knows about such things.* **6** consider (s.o/s.t) to be valuable(1,2): *I value Denise's advice highly.* **value s.t at s.t** consider that s.t is worth an amount of money: *I value this watch at £45.* Compare undervalue.
valuable /'væljuəbl/ *adj* **1** worth a lot of money, useful etc: *a valuable ring; a valuable educational course. My assistant is very valuable to me.* Compare invaluable.
▷ *c.n* **2** (usu *pl*) valuable(1) thing: *You should keep your valuables in the bank.*
valuation /,væljuː'eɪʃən/ *n* **1** *u.n* action or fact of valuing(5) s.t. **2** *c.n* suggested or estimated value(1) for s.t: *I didn't know how much to insure the watch for so I took it to a shop for a valuation.* **3** *c.n* idea a person has of s.o's value(2): *My valuation of Adrian is that he has the brains to become a* first-class *lawyer.*
,Value 'Added ,Tax *c.n* (usu as *abbr* VAT) tax that the person buying s.t has to pay to the person selling it, who then has to pay it to the government.
'valued *adj* considered to be important, useful etc: *Graham has always been a valued friend of mine.*
'valueless *adj* having no value(1,2).
valuer /'væljuə/ *c.n* person who says what s.t is worth. ⇨ evaluate.
'values *pl.n* idea a person has concerning the value(1,2) of different things, e.g material possessions, ideals and things of the mind: *Have we got our values wrong — are we too interested in material things?*

valve /vælv/ *c.n* **1** kind of flap(1) or door in a tube allowing liquid, air etc to go through in one direction but not in the other: *a heart valve.* **2** glass container with no air in it (formerly) in radios etc, used to control the flow of electric current.

vampire /'væmpaɪə/ *c.n* **1** evil spirit supposed to be in some dead human bodies and to come out at night to suck people's blood while they are asleep. **2** (*derog*) evil person who forces others to give her/him money or to work for her/him etc. **3** (also **'vampire ,bat**) kind of bat from South America which sucks the blood of animals and people.

van¹ /væn/ *c.n* **1** vehicle with a covered area at the back, used for carrying goods and sometimes people: *a delivery van*; *a police van*. **2** covered railway truck usu for carrying goods: *the guard's van.*

van² /væn/ *def.n* (often *be in the —* (*of s.t*)) front or leading part (of s.t): *Whenever the army moved our company was in the van.* Compare vanguard(2).

vandal /'vændl/ *c.n* (*derog*) person who enjoys damaging beautiful or useful things.
  vandalism /'vændə,lɪzəm/ *u.n* actions or behaviour of a vandal.
  vandalize, -ise /'vændə,laɪz/ *tr.v* **1** damage (s.t) intentionally. **2** treat (s.t) as a vandal does.

vane /veɪn/ *c.n* **1** one of certain parts of a machine turned round and round by water or air and so driving s.t: *the vanes of a propeller.* **2** = weather vane.

vanguard /'væn,gɑːd/ *def.n* **1** part of a group of people (e.g soldiers) which is at the front when the group is moving forward: *The army set off with the tanks in the vanguard.* Compare van². Opposite rearguard. **2** (often *in the — of s.t*) part which is in the front or leading position for progress (in s.t): *Britain was once in the vanguard of industrial progress.*

vanilla /və'nɪlə/ *n* **1** *c.n* kind of plant from the hot parts of America whose flowers smell sweet. **2** *u.n* (also *attrib*) powder, liquid etc from the beans of the vanilla(1) plant: *vanilla ice-cream.*

vanish /'vænɪʃ/ *intr.v* disappear; stop being able to be seen.
  'vanishing ,cream *u.n* thick cream(4) rubbed into the skin of people's faces etc to make it soft.
  'vanishing ,point *unique n* (in drawing, painting etc) point where lines that are really parallel(1) seem to meet in the distance.

vanity ⇒ vain.

vanquish /'væŋkwɪʃ/ *tr.v* (*formal*) overcome, beat, win against, (s.o/s.t).

vantage /'vɑːntɪdʒ/ *c.n* (*formal*) position from which one can do s.t particularly well: *From my vantage on the top of the hill, I could see every movement the men made.*
  'vantage ,point *c.n* (*fig*) way one considers s.t: *From my vantage point there is no excuse for his behaviour but some people do not agree.*

vapour /'veɪpə/ *c/u.n* (US **'vapor**) thing like a gas, formed from a liquid when it is heated or when it is affected by weather conditions: *Clouds, fog, mist(1) and steam are kinds of vapour.*
  vaporization, -isation /,veɪpəraɪ'zeɪʃən/ *u.n* act or fact of changing into vapour.
  vaporize, -ise /'veɪpə,raɪz/ *tr/intr.v* (cause (s.t) to) become vapour.
  'vaporous *adj* (*technical*) made of, like, vapour.

var *written abbr* variant.

variable, variance, variant, variation ⇒ vary.

varicose vein /,værɪkəʊs 'veɪn/ *c.n* vein(1), usu in a person's leg, so swollen that it cannot be made better.

varied, variegated, variegation, variety, various ⇒ vary.

varnish /'vɑːnɪʃ/ *n* **1** *c/u.n* liquid mixture of oil etc which people put on wood etc and that dries

and becomes hard, shiny and transparent. ⇒ nail varnish. **2** *c/u.n* shiny appearance that is, or looks like, the result of varnishing(3).
  ▷ *tr.v* **3** (often *— s.t over (with s.t)*) cover (s.t) with varnish(1).

varsity /'vɑːsɪtɪ/ *c.n* (*pl -ies*) (*informal*) university.

vary /'veərɪ/ *v* (*-ies, -ied*) **1** *tr/intr.v* change (s.t) from one thing to another (and then to another etc); change from one thing to another and then back to the first thing etc: *I don't like to eat the same things every day so I vary my meals a lot.* **2** *intr.v* (often *— in s.t*) show changes (in a particular thing); differ (in certain ways); not be the same (in s.t): *The quality of the fruit in this shop never varies (in quality).* **vary between s.t and s.t**; **vary from s.t to s.t** be anything between s.t at one end of the range and s.t at the other end: *The weather here varies between wet and very wet.*
  'variable *adj* **1** that varies(1,2) often. Opposite invariable.
    ▷ *c.n* **2** (*technical*) thing that varies(1,2).
  'variance *u.n* **be at variance (with s.o/s.t)** (*formal*) be disagreeing (with s.o/s.t): *Your report of the meeting is at variance with mine.*
  'variant *c.n* (also *attrib*) form of s.t that is different from the usual one or from the one a particular person knows: *This flower is usually red but there is a white variant. 'Color' is a variant form of 'colour'.* Compare variation(3).
  variation /,veərɪ'eɪʃən/ *n* **1** *u.n* act or fact of varying. **2** *c.n* thing showing one example of varying or one amount by which s.t varies: *There are a lot of variations of this car and a lot of variations of their prices too!* **3** *c/u.n* form of an animal, plant etc different from the usual form or from the form a particular person knows. Compare variant. **4** *c.n* one of several ways in which a piece of music is changed.
  'varied *adj* **1** not all of the same kind: *This place provides varied amusements.* **2** changing: *These animals can't just live on grass, they need a varied diet(1).*
  variegated /'veərɪ,geɪtɪd/ *adj* having different patterns and/or colours: *variegated leaves.*
  variegation /,veərɪ'geɪʃən/ *u.n.*
  variety /və'raɪtɪ/ *n* (*pl -ies*) **1** *u.n* state or fact of varying: *I like variety of scenery when I am on holiday.* **2** *c.n* (often *— of s.t*) kind (of s.t) that is different in one or more ways from other things of the same kind: *This is a new variety of potato which is ready to eat sooner than other varieties.* **3** *c.n* (often *— of s.t*) various different kinds (of s.t): *This restaurant serves a variety of soups.* **4** *u.n* (also **va'riety ,show**) (also *attrib*) show in a theatre or on television etc made up of several short funny or exciting acts by different people: *a variety performance.* **lack variety** be too much the same; not have enough differences: *My job lacks variety.*
  various /'veərɪəs/ *adj* **1** of different kinds: *We have various kinds of wild birds in our woods.* **2** several different: *We had various visitors on various days last month.*
  'variously *adv* in more than one different way; at more than one different time: *Heights are variously shown on different maps.*

vascular /'væskjʊlə/ *adj* (*technical*) having to

do with blood vessels and other vessels carrying liquids in one's body: *the vascular system.*

vase /vɑːz/ *c.n* container, usu made of glass or china(1), often with flowers put in for decoration.

vasectomy /væ'sektəmɪ/ *c/u.n* (*pl* *-ies*) (operation of) cutting of the tubes carrying the sperm in a man, done to prevent him from being able to become a father.

Vaseline /'væsɪˌliːn/ *u.n* (*t.n*) soft greasy substance made from petroleum, used for putting on sore skin etc.

vast /vɑːst/ *adj* very big; covering a very big area: *a vast desert.*
'vastly very; very much: *Asia is vastly bigger than Europe.*
'vastness *u.n.*

vat /væt/ *c.n* very big container, mostly for a liquid while it is being made into s.t, e.g in a factory.

VAT /ˌviː'eɪ 'tiː: or væt/ *u.n abbr* Value Added Tax.

vaudeville /'vɔːdəˌvɪl/ *u.n* (also *attrib*) (US) = variety(4): *vaudeville theatre.*

vault¹ /vɔːlt/ *c.n* **1** room under the ground, used for keeping things cool: *a wine vault.* **2** room under a church where dead human bodies and/or bones are put. **3** room, often in a bank, with thick walls and a strong door, where money etc is kept. **4** roof or ceiling made of two or more arches.
'vaulted *adj* having a roof shaped like a vault¹(4).
'vaulting *u.n* arches etc forming the roof or ceiling of a vault¹(4).

vault² /vɔːlt/ *c.n* **1** jump over s.t by putting one's hands on it but without touching it with one's feet. ⇨ pole vault.
▷ *tr/intr.v* **2** (often — *over s.t*) do a vault²(1) (over s.t): *He vaulted (over) the fence.* **3** jump over (s.t) by using a pole. ⇨ pole vault.
'vaulting ˌhorse *c.n* wooden shape over which people vault²(2) as a sport; horse(4).

VC /ˌviː 'siː:/ *c/def.n abbr* Victoria Cross.

VD /ˌviː 'diː:/ *u.n abbr* venereal disease.

VDU /ˌviː ˌdiː: 'juː:/ *c.n abbr* visual display unit.

've /v/ ⇨ have.

veal /viːl/ *u.n* (also *attrib*) meat from a calf(1): *veal pie.*

veer /vɪə/ *tr/intr.v* (often — *away* (*from s.t*); — *off/round* (*to s.t*)) (sometimes *fig*) change direction (away from s.t etc); change (from the direction of one thing or from one subject) (to another direction or subject): *The wind veered round to the north. Whenever the conversation seemed to be coming round to politics, it quickly veered away to safer subjects.*

veg /vedʒ/ *c/u.n* (*pl veg*) (also *attrib*) (*informal*) vegetable(s): *The only food that old man enjoys is meat and two veg. I love veg stew.*

vegan /'viːgən/ *c.n* (also *attrib*) person who does not eat anything that comes from animals, including eggs, milk and cheese. Compare vegetarian.

vegetable /'vedʒtəbl/ *adj* **1** (*informal veg*) of, referring to, coming from, plants: *vegetable oil*; *vegetable soup.*
▷ *c.n* **2** (*informal veg*) (part of a) plant eaten by people and not considered by ordinary people

to be a fruit: *A tomato is a vegetable but an apple is a fruit.* **3** person who, usu as a result of an accident, illness etc, cannot use (much of) her/his brain (and cannot move her/his body).

'vegetable ˌkingdom *def.n* all the substances that are not animals or minerals. ⇨ animal kingdom, mineral kingdom.

ˌvegetable 'marrow *c/u.n* ⇨ marrow(2).

vegetarian /ˌvedʒɪ'teərɪən/ *adj* **1** of or referring to vegetarianism; who/that is a vegetarian(3). **2** made up only of vegetables, eggs and milk products: *a vegetarian* diet(1). Compare vegan.
▷ *c.n* **3** person who does not eat any meat or fish.

ˌvege'tariaˌnism *u.n* **1** belief that one should not eat meat and fish, usu for religious, moral or health reasons. **2** practice of not eating meat and fish.

vegetate /'vedʒɪˌteɪt/ *intr.v* (*derog*; *informal*) live a very quiet life where nothing interesting happens, where one does not use one's brain (or one's body) much.

vegetation /ˌvedʒɪ'teɪʃən/ *u.n* **1** plants in general. **2** plants in a particular place: *The hills around us are covered in thick vegetation.*

vehement /'viːɪmənt/ *adj* **1** (of feelings or the way they are expressed) very strongly felt and/or expressed: *It was a vehement defence of his political opinions.* **2** (*formal*) very (usu unpleasantly) strong (and sudden): *a vehement storm.*
'vehemence *u.n.* **'vehemently** *adv.*

vehicle /'viːɪkl/ *c.n* **1** (also **'motor ˌvehicle**) thing with an engine that is used for carrying people, animals and/or things usu along roads. **2** means used for carrying people etc on land, e.g a bicycle, cart. **3** (often — *for/of s.t*) thing used (by s.o) for spreading s.t or for showing what a person can do: *The play was written specially as a vehicle for the actor's particular skills. Many countries use the radio and television as vehicles for mass education.*
vehicular /vɪ'hɪkjʊlə/ *adj* (*formal*) having to do with, made up of, vehicles: *vehicular traffic.*

veil /veɪl/ *c.n* **1** (often — *of s.t*) thing (made of s.t) covering s.o/s.t, often so that he/she/it cannot be seen (clearly) or to protect her/him/it from insects, dust etc: *In some countries women have to wear veils when they go out in public. The river was hidden under a veil of fog.* **draw a veil over s.t** (*fig*) not talk about, try to hide, s.t one does not like. **take the veil** become a nun. **under the veil of s.t** (*fig*) using s.t to hide one's real actions, behaviour or intentions.
▷ *tr.v* **2** (often — *s.o/s.t in s.t, from s.t*) cover (s.o/s.t) (with s.t) (as if) with a veil(1) (as a protection from s.t): *The women had to veil themselves as soon as a strange man came in.* ⇨ unveil.
veiled *adj* covered, protected or hidden (as if) with a veil(1).
ˌveiled 'threat *c.n* threat which is not expressed openly but only suggested.
ˌveil of 'secrecy *c.n* (often *do s.t under a —*) silence intended to hide s.t.

vein /veɪn/ *c.n* **1** tube in a body carrying blood towards the heart. Compare artery(1). **2** rib(4) on a leaf or the wing of some kinds of insect. **3** (often — *of s.t*) **(a)** layer(1) in rock etc (made of s.t) of a different colour from the rest of it: *We found veins of gold in the rock.* **(b)** (*fig*) small but clearly

existing amount (of s.t):*There is a vein of sadness in all his writings.* **in a happy** etc **vein** (*fig*) in a happy etc way or mood(1): *She answered all my questions in a thoughtful vein.*
veined *adj* having veins in it.
venous /ˈviːnəs/ *adj* (*technical*) of or referring to veins(1).

veld /velt/ *c*/*def.n* (also **veldt**) open area in southern Africa which has not got many trees on it.

vellum /ˈveləm/ *u.n* **1** kind of fine leather as used for the covers of books, lampshades etc. **2** kind of very good quality thick smooth paper for writing on.

velocity /vɪˈlɒsɪtɪ/ *c*/*u.n* (*pl -ies*) (often *technical*; *formal*) speed, *symb* v. (**at**) **a velocity of s.t** (moving with) a speed of s.t: *This plane can travel at a velocity of 1000 kilometres an hour.*

velour /vəˈlʊə/ *u.n* (also *attrib*) (also **velours**) (*French*) fairly thick cloth that feels like velvet: *a velour collar.*

velvet /ˈvelvɪt/ *u.n* (also *attrib*) kind of cloth, usu made of silk and with a short thick pile³ on one side: *a velvet jacket.*

velveteen /ˌvelvɪˈtiːn/ *u.n* (also *attrib*) kind of cloth that looks like velvet but is cheap and made of cotton.
velvety *adj.*

venal /ˈviːnl/ *adj* **1** (*derog*) (of a person) who can be bribed. **2** (of an action) done in return for a bribe.
venality /vɪˈnælɪtɪ/ *u.n* fact of being venal(1).
venally *adv.*

vend /vend/ *tr.v* (*formal*) sell (small things), usu in a street or public market.
vending ma,chine *c.n* machine from which one can get things like cigarettes or cups of coffee by putting money into it.
vendor /ˈvendɔː/ *c.n* (*formal*) person selling s.t, esp in a market.

vendetta /venˈdetə/ *c.n* **1** serious quarrel between two families which goes on for many years (and sometimes in which each family feels that its members must kill members of the other family). **2** quarrel between two people or groups in which each side tries to damage the other.

vending machine, vendor ⇒ vend.

veneer /vəˈnɪə/ *n* **1** *c*/*u.n* thin slice of more expensive and beautiful wood stuck over cheaper less beautiful wood, plastic etc. **2** *c.n* (*fig*) outer appearance hiding s.t different (usu unpleasant) underneath: *Her veneer of being a caring mother hid her true personality — she was really a cruel parent.*
▷ *tr.v* **3** cover (s.t) with veneer(1).

venerable /ˈvenərəbl/ *adj* **1** (*usu attrib*) (*formal*) (treated as) deserving to be respected and/or honoured: *a venerable statesman.* **2** (with capital **V**) title given to an archdeacon in the Church of England: *the Venerable Henry Smith.*
venerate /ˈvenəreɪt/ *tr.v* (*formal*) treat (s.o/s.t) as venerable(1).
veneration /ˌvenəˈreɪʃən/ *u.n.*

venereal /vəˈnɪərɪəl/ *adj* **1** caused or passed from one person to another by sexual activity. **2** of or referring to a venereal disease.
ve,nereal di'sease *c.n* (*abbr* **VD**) disease caused or passed from one person to another by sexual activity.

venetian blind /vəˌniːʃən ˈblaɪnd/ *c.n* blind² made of strips of wood, metal etc joined together by pieces of string, cloth etc; it can be pulled up or let down and the strips can be turned to let in, or keep out, light.

vengeance /ˈvendʒəns/ *u.n* (*formal*) (often violent) action taken against another person in order to pay her/him back for s.t (one thinks) she/he has done against one: *The way his enemies treated him was cruel but his vengeance was much worse.* Compare revenge(1). **take vengeance (up)on s.o** get one's revenge for s.t (one thinks) s.o has done. ⇒ avenge. **with a vengeance** very strongly or violently: *When the insects began to eat the plants the farmers attacked them with a vengeance.*
vengeful *adj* (*formal*) **1** feeling that one wants vengeance. **2** caused by a desire for vengeance.
vengefully *adv.* **vengefulness** *u.n.*

venial /ˈviːnɪəl/ *adj* (*formal*) (of s.t wrong that s.o has done) not serious so that one can easily forgive it: *Pride may be a venial fault if it leads to good work.*

venison /ˈvenɪzən/ *u.n* (also *attrib*) flesh or meat of a deer: *venison steak.*

venom /ˈvenəm/ *u.n* **1** liquid poison used by some snakes etc when they bite. **2** (*fig*) great anger, hatred etc: *Whenever she spoke of Stephen, the venom in her voice showed how much she hated him.*
venomous *adj* **1** poisonous; containing venom(1). **2** showing venom(2): *venomous remarks.*
venomousness *u.n.*

venous ⇒ vein.

vent /vent/ *c.n* **1** open place through which air, gas, liquid etc can get into or out of a room, machine etc. **2** slit(1) at the bottom of the back of a coat or jacket: *This jacket(1) has one vent in the middle.*
▷ *tr.v* **3** (*esp — one's anger, feelings* etc *on s.o/s.t*) allow (one's anger etc) to come out (by attacking s.o/s.t); not keep one's feelings secret.

ventilate /ˈventɪleɪt/ *tr.v* **1** let or make fresh air go into and through (a place) to clean the air already in it: *ventilate a room.* **2** (*formal*) allow or cause (a subject) to be discussed by anyone who wants to do so: *The government's policy of selling farms for building houses must be widely ventilated.*
ventilation /ˌventɪˈleɪʃən/ *u.n* **1** (system used for) ventilating(1) a place. **2** (*formal*) ventilating(2) of people's ideas.
ventilator /ˈventɪleɪtə/ *c.n* thing used for ventilating(1) a place.

ventricle /ˈventrɪkl/ *c.n* (*technical*) cavity in a human or animal body, esp in the brain or heart.

ventriloquism /venˈtrɪləkwɪzəm/ *u.n* skill of speaking or singing in such a way that the mouth does not seem to move and the sounds seem to come from somewhere else.
ventriloquist *c.n* person with the skill of ventriloquism.

venture /ˈventʃə/ *c.n* **1** piece of work, scheme(1) etc that includes some risk: *a business/commercial venture.*
▷ *v* (*formal*) **2** *tr.v* (usu — *to do s.t*) attempt (to do) (s.t that may or may not be successful); attempt

(to do) (s.t risky): *He ventured to explain the cause of the accident.* **3** *intr.v* dare to do s.t that is risky: *When most of the smoke had gone, I ventured into the room.* **4** *tr.v* offer/give (s.t) that may be unpopular: *venture an opinion.* ***Nothing ventured, nothing gained*** (*proverb*) Unless one is willing to take risks, one cannot expect to win. ***venture to say***, ***suggest*** etc (***that***) ... be bold enough to say etc (that) ... although one thinks it might not be accepted.

venturesome /'ventʃəsəm/ *adj* (*formal*) **1** (of a person) daring to do dangerous things; willing to take risks. **2** (of actions etc) risky.

venue /'venjuː/ *c.n* (often — *or s.t*) place where people have agreed to meet (for s.t): *The venue of the lecture is the central hall of the university.*

Venus /'viːnəs/ *unique n* **1** (*astronomy*) second planet from the sun. **2** (in Roman mythology) goddess of love.

veracious /və'reɪʃəs/ *adj* (*formal*) **1** (of a person) telling the truth. **2** (of a story etc) true.
veracity /və'ræsɪtɪ/ *u.n* truthfulness.

verandah /və'rændə/ *c.n* (also **ve'randa**) open part on the outside of a building with a roof and a floor.

verb /vɜːb/ *c.n* (*grammar*) one of the parts of speech; it can be composed of one word only, e.g 'is'; or of two or more, e.g 'has done', 'would have been doing'; it shows what the subject[1](4) is, does or undergoes.
'verbal *adj* **1** of or referring to verbs. **2** of, using etc words: *verbal games.* **3** in a spoken, not a written, form: *a verbal answer only.* **4** referring to the words used and not their meanings: *A parrot's command of a language is purely verbal.* **5** (of translations, equivalents etc) exact; word for word: *He can do verbal translations from French but he often misses the real meaning.*
verbalize, -ise /'vɜːbəˌlaɪz/ *tr/intr.v* put (s.t) into words: *At last Alan verbalized his fears.*
'verbally *adv* **1** in the form of a verb. **2** in spoken words, not in writing: *reply verbally.*
ˌverbal 'noun *c.n* noun ending in '-ing' and describing an action or state or s.t that s.o/s.t undergoes; gerund: *In 'I like reading', 'reading' is a verbal noun.*

verbatim /vɜː'beɪtɪm/ *adj/adv* using exactly the same words as the original that one is repeating: *a verbatim account; an account giving verbatim her reasons for refusing.*

verbiage /'vɜːbɪdʒ/ *u.n* (*derog*) excessive number of spoken or written words.

verbose /vɜː'bəʊs/ *adj* (*derog*; *informal*) using too many words to express s.t: *a verbose speaker/ statement.*
ver'bosely *adv.* **ver'boseness** *u.n.*
verbosity /vɜː'bɒsɪtɪ/ *u.n* (*derog*; *formal*) fact or quality of being verbose.

verdant /'vɜːdənt/ *adj* (*formal*) covered with bright fresh green grass, leaves etc.

verdure /'vɜːdʒə/ *u.n* (*formal*) verdant grass or other plants.

verdict /'vɜːdɪkt/ *c.n* **1** (*law*) decision by a jury(1), e.g 'Guilty' or 'Not guilty'. **2** decision or opinion (supposed to have been) reached after long and careful thought: *What is your own verdict about the quality of his work?* ***bring in a verdict of*** (***not***) ***guilty*** (*law*) (of a jury(1)) say that s.o is (not) guilty of a crime.

open verdict ⇒ open. ***unanimous verdict*** ⇒ unanimous.

verdure ⇒ verdant.

verge /vɜːdʒ/ *c.n* **1** edge, usu of a road, path etc: *grass verges.* ***on the verge of*** (***doing***) ***s.t*** very near to (doing) s.t; about to do s.t: *The telephone rang as we were on the verge of leaving. After reading the letter, Mary was on the verge of tears.*
▷ *intr.v* **2** (usu — (*up*)*on s.t*) be very close (to s.t); almost be the same (as s.t): *His behaviour verges on rudeness.*

verger /'vɜːdʒə/ *c.n* person who works in a church and shows people where to sit etc.

verify /'verɪˌfaɪ/ *tr.v* (*-ies, -ied*) (*formal*) **1** check (s.t) to make sure it is true or correct: *I need all your receipts so that I can verify the bill for the work.* **2** show that (s.t one had only suspected) is in fact true or correct: *Her confession verified my opinion of her as a thief.*
verifiable /'verɪˌfaɪəbl/ *adj* that can be verified.
verification /ˌverɪfɪ'keɪʃən/ *u.n* act or fact of verifying s.t.
'veritable *attrib.adj* real; that can fairly be described as: *After our advertisement we received a veritable flood of replies.*
'veritably *adv* really; truly.

vermicelli /ˌvɜːmɪ'selɪ/ *u.n* (*Italian*) food like spaghetti but with thinner strings.

vermilion /və'mɪlɪən/ *u.n* (also *attrib*) bright orange-red colour: *vermilion paint.*

vermin /'vɜːmɪn/ *u/pl.n* **1** harmful or damaging animal, bird or insect that people therefore try to get rid of: *Fleas and mice are vermin.* **2** (*derog*) people considered to be useless, unpleasant, harmful etc.
'verminous *adj* **1** full of or covered with vermin(1). **2** (*derog*) (of a person) useless, unpleasant, harmful, etc.

vermouth /'vɜːməθ/ *u.n* kind of bitter-sweet alcoholic(1) drink made from red or white wine and certain plants.

vernacular /və'nækjʊlə/ *adj* **1** in the language used locally by ordinary people.
▷ *c/def.n* **2** vernacular(1) language.

vernal /'vɜːnl/ *adj* ⇒ equinox.

versa ⇒ vice versa.

versatile /'vɜːsəˌtaɪl/ *adj* having several skills and/or abilities so that he/she/it can change quickly and easily from one to another: *This bird can fly, swim and dive so it is very versatile.*
versatility /ˌvɜːsə'tɪlɪtɪ/ *u.n* fact of being versatile.

verse /vɜːs/ *n* **1** *c.n* section of a poem made up of an arrangement of lines; often a poem has several verses. ⇒ blank verse. **2** *u.n* poetry; system of writing s.t in lines, each of which usu has the same number and pattern of stressed and unstressed syllables in it. Compare prose. **3** *c.n* small section of a chapter(1) of the Bible. ***blank verse*** ⇒ blank. (***give/quote*** etc) ***chapter and verse*** (***for s.t***) ⇒ chapter. ***in verse*** spoken or written in the form of verse(2).

versed /vɜːst/ *adj* (***well-***)***versed in s.t*** having a (very good) knowledge or skill in s.t.

version /'vɜːʃən/ *c.n* one of various forms s.t is described, is done etc in: *His version of what happened at the match is quite different from mine. I have only read the French version of the poem.*

versus /'vɜːsəs/ *prep* (*abbr* v) (*Latin*; *formal*) against: *The next match is France versus Germany* (or *France v Germany*).

vertebra /'vɜːtɪbrə/ *c.n* (*pl* -e /'vɜːtɪˌbriː/) bone that is part of the backbone of a person or animal.

'vertebral *adj* of or referring to one or more vertebrae.

vertebrate /'vɜːtɪbrət/ *adj* 1 having a backbone: *vertebrate creatures.*

▷ *c.n* 2 animal that has a backbone. Compare invertebrate.

vertex /'vɜːteks/ *c.n* (*pl* -es, *vertices* /'vɜːtɪˌsiːz/) (*technical*) 1 angle at the top of a triangle, cone(1) etc. 2 point where the two lines forming an angle meet.

vertical /'vɜːtɪkl/ *adj* 1 at an angle of (about) 90° with the thing it is standing on, usu the ground; upright: *When you are standing your body is vertical and when you are lying down it is horizontal.* 2 (moving) in a direction straight up or down: *an almost vertical graph.* ⇨ horizontal(1).

▷ *c.n* 3 thing (e.g a line) that is vertical(1).

vertigo /'vɜːtɪˌɡəʊ/ *u.n* (*formal*) feeling of giddiness; dizziness, esp because of being high up and looking down: *She suffers from vertigo.*

verve /vɜːv/ *u.n* strong feeling for experiencing life fully and joyfully.

very /'verɪ/ *adj* 1 (used after 'the', 'this', 'that', 'these', 'those', to emphasize them) exact: *I've got the very thing you need* (= I've got exactly the thing you need). *We'll go to the park this very day if that's what you want. Come in this very minute, you bad boy!*

▷ *adv* 2 to a high degree; much more than a little: *very small; very quickly.* (Notice 'very' is not used with a comparative(4); instead we use 'much', e.g 'very big', 'much bigger'.) 3 (usu *the — first, last, best* etc (*s.t*)) absolutely; quite: *the very biggest; for the very last time.* (**s.o/s.t**) **of one's very own** s.o/s.t belonging only to oneself: *I was happy when at last I got a bedroom of my very own!* **not very** . . . not at all . . .: *She wasn't very pleased when he dropped paint on her dress.* **very many more** (**people** etc); **very much** (**smaller books** etc) (used before 'many', 'much' for emphasis): *There were very many more workers at the gate than we had predicted. It was a very much bigger meeting than the last one.* **the very same** (**person**, **thing** etc) (used to make 'the same' stronger) exactly: *'Are you Elton John, the singer?' 'The very same.'* **very well** (used to express agreement when not really wanting to): *'You'll have to stop playing now and come inside.' 'Oh, very well.'*

,very ,high 'frequency *c/u.n* (usu as *abbr* VHF) (sending of) radio waves at a frequency(2) of between 30 000 and 300 000 kilohertz.

vespers /'vespəz/ *u/pl.n* evening service in some kinds of Christian(1) church.

vessel /'vesl/ *c.n* 1 (*formal*) ship or big boat: *a fishing vessel; a motor vessel.* 2 (*formal*) container (e.g pan, bottle, bucket, barrel) usu for liquids: *drinking vessels.* 3 tube in a human or animal body or in a plant along which a liquid, e.g blood, flows. ⇨ blood vessel.

vest¹ /vest/ *c.n* piece of underclothing covering the upper part of the body and usu without sleeves(1).

vest² /vest/ *intr.v* (usu passive, *be —ed in* s.o/ s.t) (*formal*, usu *law*) (of a right, power etc) be the property (of s.o) as her/his legal right: *The power to appoint and dismiss prime ministers is vested in the king or queen.*

,vested 'interest *c.n* thing a person possesses or has a right to which influences her/his behaviour (sometimes making her/him behave unfairly) because she/he does not want to lose it: *John has a vested interest in an increase in rents because he owns a lot of houses.*

,vested 'interests *pl.n* all the people who possess a vested interest in s.t and who therefore sometimes behave unfairly to protect it: *Vested interests in the business world made it impossible for him to keep his small shop open.*

vestibule /'vestɪˌbjuːl/ *c.n* (*formal*) hall at the entrance to a (big) building through which one gets to the other rooms.

vestige /'vestɪdʒ/ *c.n* (often — *of* s.t) 1 thing still existing which is a sign (of s.t else that existed in the past although this has now disappeared): *One can still find vestiges of an ancient civilization on some of the desert islands.* 2 very small piece (of s.t) which is still left: *Hungry dogs were licking the last vestiges of food off the plates.* 3 (*technical*) small part of the body which is all that is now left (of s.t that was bigger and more important in the past): *We have a small bone at the base of our backbone which is a vestige of the tail we used to have millions of years ago.*

vestigial /ve'stɪdʒɪəl/ *adj* (*technical*) that is a vestige(3): *a vestigial tail.*

vestment /'vestmənt/ *c.n* (often *pl*) piece of clothing worn for certain ceremonies, usu by priests in a church.

vestry /'vestrɪ/ *c.n* (*pl* -ies) small room in, or belonging to, a church in which things are kept and/or business is done.

vet /vet/ *c.n* 1 (*informal*) veterinary surgeon.

▷ *tr.v* (-*tt*-) 2 give medical treatment to (an animal). 3 examine (a person) medically, e.g to find whether he/she is fit for a certain job. 4 examine (s.o/s.t) carefully to find out all (the truth) about her/him/it: *You'd better vet these accounts before you send them off.*

veterinary /'vetərɪnərɪ/ *adj* of or referring to medical treatment for animals: *veterinary science.*

,veterinary 'surgeon *c.n* (*informal* vet) doctor for animals, not people.

veteran /'vetərən/ *attrib.adj* 1 who/that is a veteran(*n*): *a veteran soldier/speaker/machine.*

▷ *c.n* 2 person who was a soldier (during a particular war or period). 3 person who has been doing a certain thing for a long time: *As a member of the club he is our oldest veteran.* 4 thing made a long time ago (and used a lot since then): *This motorbike is a veteran belonging to Mr Green.* **a veteran of s.t** a person/thing who/that took part or was used in s.t: *Fred is a veteran of the last war.*

,veteran 'car *c.n* (in Britain) car made before 1919 (or 1905). Compare vintage car.

veterinary ⇨ vet.

veto /'viːtəʊ/ *c.n* (*pl* -es) 1 (often *power/right of* —) authority(1) to forbid s.t absolutely: *She used her veto to stop the plan from being accepted.* (**put**) **a veto on s.t** (give) an order forbidding s.t absolutely.

▷ *tr.v* (*-es, -ed*) **2** forbid (s.t) absolutely.

vetoer /'viːtəʊə/ *c.n* person who vetoes(2) s.t.

vex /veks/ *tr.v* (*formal*) **1** annoy (s.o); make (s.o) angry: *The children vexed the new teacher with silly questions.* **2** puzzle (s.o); make (s.o) think hard: *We had some very vexing questions to answer in our test.*

‚vexed 'question *c.n* problem people discuss a lot and have difficulty deciding.

vexation /vek'seɪʃən/ *u.n* (*formal*) **1** fact or feeling of being vexed (⇒ vex(1,2)). **2** *c.n* vexing (⇒ vex(1)) thing.

vexatious /vek'seɪʃəs/ *adj* (*formal*) causing vexation(1).

VG *written abbr* very good.

VHF /ˌviː ˌeɪtʃ 'ef/ *abbr* very high frequency.

via /'vaɪə/ *prep* **1** by way of; passing through (s.w) on one's way s.w: *You can go from Britain to Australia via America or via Asia.* **2** using; through the medium(3) of: *I hear all your family news via your brother Tom.*

viable /'vaɪəbl/ *adj* **1** good enough, able to, succeed: *Your plan isn't viable unless there is more money.* **2** able to develop normally: *The last kitten was very weak and soon died because it was not viable.*

viability /ˌvaɪə'bɪlɪtɪ/ *u.n*. **viably** *adv*.

viaduct /'vaɪədʌkt/ *c.n* high bridge carrying a road, railway etc over a valley etc.

vibrate /vaɪ'breɪt/ *tr/intr.v* (cause (s.t) to) shake slightly and very fast: *The strings on a guitar vibrate when it is played.* **vibrate to s.t. (a)** vibrate because of s.t: *Whenever a train passed the whole house vibrated to its movement.* **(b)** (*fig*) feel excited by s.t: *The whole audience vibrated to the sound of the singer's voice.* Compare vibrant(2). **vibrate with s.t** vibrate because of s.t: *vibrating with the sound of insects.*

vibrancy /'vaɪbrənsɪ/ *u.n* fact or state of being vibrant(1,2).

vibrant /'vaɪbrənt/ *adj* (*formal*) **1** strong; bright: *a vibrant shade of yellow.* **2** lively: *a vibrant personality.* **3** vibrating strongly: *the vibrant notes of a violin.*

vibration /vaɪ'breɪʃən/ *n* **1** *c.n* single act of vibrating. **2** *c/u.n* numerous acts of vibrating, one immediately after the other.

vibrator /vaɪ'breɪtə/ *c.n* instrument used to produce vibrations(1) in order to massage(2) a person's body.

vibro-massage /ˌvaɪbrəʊ 'mæsɑːʒ/ *c/u.n* massage(1) done with a vibrator.

vicar /'vɪkə/ *c.n* priest in charge of a parish and the church in it.

vicarage /'vɪkərɪdʒ/ *c.n* house supplied for a vicar to live in.

vicarious /vɪ'keərɪəs/ *adj* (*formal*) not felt or done etc oneself but experienced only through hearing, seeing etc other people feeling it etc: *A lot of people who hate being hurt themselves get vicarious pleasure out of seeing violence against others on television.*

vi'cariously *adv*. **vi'cariousness** *u.n*.

vice¹ /vaɪs/ *c.n* (US **vise**) tool with metal jaws that open and/or close, used for holding s.t tight while one is cutting or shaping it etc.

'vice‚like *adj* (usu — *grip*) very tight or firm.

vice² /vaɪs/ *n* **1** *u.n* badness; wickedness; immorality: *Can you get rid of vice in our cities?* **2** *c.n*

thing that is wicked or immoral: *sexual vices.* **3** *c.n* thing considered wrong or bad: *Laziness is not among my vices.* Compare virtue.

'vice ‚squad *c.n* section of the police whose job is to see that people obey the laws against vice²(1).

vicious /'vɪʃəs/ *adj* **1** cruel; evil: *a vicious attack.* **2** dangerous; who/that can cause harm: *a vicious dog.*

‚vicious 'circle *c.n* (*fig*) situation in which one thing causes another, which causes another etc until the last thing is again the cause of the first: *He's not able to get a job because he has no experience but he cannot get experience without getting a job — it's a vicious circle.*

'viciously *adv*. **'viciousness** *u.n*.

vice³ /vaɪs/ *c.n* (*abbr* V) (often *vice-*) next in rank below the one in the second part of the word: *vice-president. The vice-captain takes the place of the captain and does her/his work when she/he is absent.*

‚vice-'chancellor *c.n* chief official of a British university who does the real work of the head of the university. ⇒ chancellor.

‚vice-'regal *adj* of or referring to a viceroy.

vicereine /'vaɪsˌreɪn/ *c.n* wife of a viceroy.

viceroy /'vaɪsˌrɔɪ/ *c.n* person representing a king, queen, emperor or empress in another part of his/her empire: *When India was part of the British Empire, its ruler was called the Viceroy of India.*

vice versa /ˌvaɪsɪ 'vɜːsə/ *adv* (*Latin*) (usu *and* —) the opposite to: *Bill likes Kate and vice versa* (i.e and Kate likes Bill).

vicinity /vɪ'sɪnɪtɪ/ *u.n* (usu *in the, this* etc —; *in the* — of s.t) (*formal*) area that is near: *Is there a hospital in this vicinity? We live in the vicinity of the school. The vicinity of the park is a good thing for people with children here.*

vicious(ness) ⇒ vice².

victim /'vɪktɪm/ *c.n* (often — *of s.o/s.t*) person, animal or thing suffering s.t unpleasant, dangerous or fatal (caused by s.o/s.t): *Old people are victims of very cold weather in winter.* **fall victim to s.o/s.t** become the victim(1) of s.o/s.t: *My mother fell victim to the flu epidemic and died.*

victimization, -isation /ˌvɪktɪmaɪ'zeɪʃən/ *u.n*.

victimize, -ise /'vɪktɪˌmaɪz/ *tr.v* make (s.o) a victim(1) by accusing her/him of s.t bad that she/he did not do or did not do alone.

victor /'vɪktə/ *c.n* (*formal*) winner.

victorious /vɪk'tɔːrɪəs/ *adj* **1** winning; successful: *a victorious team/army.* Opposite losing, vanquished. **2** showing one has won: *victorious cries.*

victory /'vɪktərɪ/ *c/u.n* (*pl -ies*) act or fact of defeating an opponent, enemy etc: *She won a victory over her great rival in the tennis competition. It was a victory for common sense.* **a narrow victory** a win by a very small margin(5).

Victoria Cross /vɪkˌtɔːrɪə 'krɒs/ *c/def.n* (usu *abbr* VC) highest decoration(3) for bravery which can be won in battle in the British armed forces.

Victorian /vɪk'tɔːrɪən/ *adj* **1** referring to, dating from, the time (1837–1901) when Queen Victoria was Queen of England.

▷ *c.n* **2** person of that time.

victoria plum /vɪkˌtɔːrɪə 'plʌm/ *c.n* kind of red plum (*n*).

victorious, victory ⇨ victor.

vide /'vaɪdi:/ *tr.v* (*formal*; *Latin*) (used only in commands) look at; see: *Vide page 5, above.*

video /'vɪdɪˌəʊ/ *attrib.adj* **1** made on videotape: *a video recording.* **2** (*formal*) referring to pictures shown on a television set. Compare audio.

▷ *c.n* **3** = videotape(1).

'video cas,sette *c.n* cassette(1) holding videotape.

'video,tape *c/u.n* **1** (also *attrib*) tape(2) used for recording¹(2) pictures and sound: *a videotape recorder.*

▷ *tr.v* **2** record¹(2) (s.t) on videotape(1).

vie /vaɪ/ *intr.v* (*pres.p* vying /'vaɪɪŋ/, *p.t,p.p* vied) (usu — (with s.o/s.t) (for s.t/to do s.t)) compete (against s.o) (to try to get or do s.t): *The two footballers were vying for the ball. She vied with her sister for a place in the team.*

view /vjuː/ *c.n* (often — of s.o/s.t) **1** sight(3) (of s.t); what can be seen (of s.t) from a particular place: *We have a wonderful view of the sea from this window. The trees blocked our view of the lake.* **2** opinion (of s.o/s.t); what one thinks (of s.o/s.t): *What is your view of her/his work?* **come into view** reach a position where one/it can be seen. **have/keep s.o/s.t in view** (manage to) keep one's eyes on s.o/s.t so that he/she/it does not disappear from one's sight. **hidden from (s.o's) view** in a position where s.o/s.t cannot be seen (by s.o). **in full view (of s.o)** where one/it can be completely seen (by s.o). **in view** where he/she/it can be seen. **in view of s.t** because of s.t: *In view of the late arrival of the train, we shall have to change our meeting to tomorrow.* **lost to (s.o's) view** no longer in a position where one/it can be seen (by s.o). **on view (to s.o)** being shown (where s.o can see her/him/it); in a position where people can see her/him/it: *The paintings will be on view to the public today and tomorrow.* **point of view** ⇨ point. **take a dim/poor view of s.o/s.t** (*informal*) have a low opinion of s.o/s.t. **view of s.o/s.t (a)** ⇨ view(1,2). **(b)** picture or photograph of s.o/s.t: *a postcard with a view of the mountains.* **with a view to (doing) s.t** with the purpose of (doing) s.t: *I am going to look at the house today with a view to buying it if I like it.*

▷ *tr.v* **3** look at (s.o/s.t) carefully; examine (s.o/s.t): *I am going to view the house tomorrow to see whether I want to buy it.* **4** consider (s.t); think of (s.t): *How do you view your daughter's plans to start her own business? She viewed his behaviour as an insult. He viewed the international economic(1) situation with anxiety.* **5** (*formal*) watch (television etc).

'viewer *c.n* **1** person who watches television. **2** thing used for viewing(3) slides(6).

'view-,finder *c.n* part of a camera etc looked through to see exactly what one is trying to photograph.

'view,point *c.n* way one looks at or thinks of s.t; opinion; point of view: *My viewpoint on the tax is not the same as other people's.* ⇨ point of view (⇨ point).

vigil /'vɪdʒɪl/ *c/u.n* act of staying awake and watchful, usu to guard or look after s.o/ s.t or to pray; an all-night vigil. **keep vigil (over s.o/s.t)** be awake and watchful (over s.o/s.t).

'vigilance *u.n* (*formal*) being vigilant.

'vigilant *adj* (*formal*) watchful; ready for anything that may happen.

vigilante /ˌvɪdʒɪ'lænti/ *c.n* person who is not an official but joins with others to try to keep order, fight crime etc in a country or community where there is political or social unrest.

vigour /'vɪgə/ *u.n* (US **'vigor**) (*formal*) energy¹(1); strength with which one grows, behaves etc: *Although Joe is small, he plays all games with great vigour and determination. The plants grew with vigour after the rain.*

'vigorous *adj* showing vigour: *a vigorous defence of one's beliefs; the vigorous growth of some plants.*

'vigorously *adv.*

vile /vaɪl/ *adj* (*derog*) very nasty, unpleasant or evil: *a vile smell; vile crimes; a vile person.*

'vilely /'vaɪllɪ/ *adv.* **'vileness** *u.n.*

vilification /ˌvɪlɪfɪ'keɪʃən/ *c/u.n* (*formal*) act or fact of vilifying s.o/s.t.

vilify /'vɪlɪˌfaɪ/ *tr.v* (*-ies, -ied*) (*formal*) tell nasty things about (s.o/s.t) to make other people hate her/him/it.

villa /'vɪlə/ *c.n* (with capital **V** in names) **1** pleasant, expensive house in the country surrounded by its own land: *a country villa.* **2** house in a big town or city which has a garden: *I live at 3 Sunview Villas, Brighton.* **3** small house in the country, a seaside town etc, used for holidays: *a holiday villa.*

village /'vɪlɪdʒ/ *n* (also *attrib*) **1** *c.n* place, not in a town or city, where people have houses and often shops etc: *village life.* **2** *def.pl.n* all the people who live in a village(1): *All the village are going to the meeting this afternoon.*

'villager *c.n* person living in a village.

villain /'vɪlən/ *c.n* **1** (esp in stories) person who is very bad, evil etc. Compare hero(2). **2** (*informal*) criminal.

'villainous *adj* **1** behaving like a villain. **2** very unpleasant: *We had to walk home through villainous black mud.*

'villainy *n* (*pl -ies*) (*formal*) **1** *u.n* villainous(1) behaviour. **2** *c.n* villainous(1) act.

vim /vɪm/ *u.n* (*informal*) vigour.

vinaigrette ⇨ vinegar.

vindicate /'vɪndɪˌkeɪt/ *tr.v* (*formal*) prove (s.o) is not in fact guilty of s.t he/she was accused of; prove s.o/s.t was right after all: *The new evidence vindicated her. It vindicated my trust in her.*

vindication /ˌvɪndɪ'keɪʃən/ *c/u.n.*

vindictive /vɪn'dɪktɪv/ *adj* (*formal*) **1** (of a person) wanting or determined to get revenge for s.t: *Vindictive people are never happy.* **2** showing one is vindictive(1): *a vindictive act/comment.*

vin'dictively *adv.* **vin'dictiveness** *u.n.*

vine /vaɪn/ *c.n* plant with long stems that climbs or spreads along the ground: *a grapevine.*

vinery /'vaɪnərɪ/ *c.n* (*pl -ies*) glass building where vines are grown in cold countries, usu to produce grapes.

vineyard /'vɪnjəd/ *c.n* area or field where vines are planted to produce grapes for wine. ⇨ viticulture.

vinous /'vaɪnəs/ *adj* (*formal*) of or referring to wine.

vintage /'vɪntɪdʒ/ *adj* (usu *attrib*) **1** (of a wine) so good that it is not mixed with wines made from grapes harvested in other years: *A vintage* *wine has a* label(1) *showing the year the grapes were harvested.* **2** dating from a time when things were particularly good in quality: *The 1920s were vintage years for silent films.* **3** having all the best qualities of the person whose name follows: *This film is vintage Charlie Chaplin.*

▷ *c.n* **4** (wine made in a certain) year when the wines are particularly good: *I think this year's vintage will be the best for many years.* **5** (often (*of*) *a year, period* —) (from) a particular year or period: *My house is (of) Victorian/1930s vintage.*

ˌvintage ˈcar *c.n* (in Britain) car made between 1919 and 1930. Compare veteran car.

vintner /ˈvɪntnə/ *c.n* person who buys and sells wine as a job.

vinegar /ˈvɪnɪgə/ *u.n* kind of liquid made from sour wine or other things used on food or in sauces etc to give a pleasantly sour taste: *I like lots of vinegar on my chips.*

vinaigrette /ˌvɪneɪˈgret/ *u.n* (also *attrib*) kind of mixture of oil, vinegar etc, put on salad(1) etc to produce a strong, sour taste: *vinaigrette dressing(1).*

vinegary /ˈvɪnɪgrɪ/ *adj* **1** having vinegar in it. **2** tasting (usu unpleasantly) sour like vinegar. **3** (*derog; fig*) (of a person or behaviour) unkind; nasty.

vinery, vinous, vintage, vintner ⇒ vine.

vinyl /ˈvaɪnɪl/ *u.n* (also *attrib*) kind of strong plastic(3) that can bend without breaking, used for covering floors, making clothes etc: *a vinyl floor.*

viola¹ /vɪˈəʊlə/ *c.n* kind of musical instrument with strings which is a little bigger than a violin.

viola² /ˈvaɪələ/ *c.n* small plant grown in gardens for its pretty flowers.

violate /ˈvaɪəˌleɪt/ *tr.v* (*formal*) **1** break (a promise etc): *You have violated the rules of the society.* **2** enter by force (a religious place that should not be entered). **3** spoil (s.t): *Noisy motor-boats violate the peace of our river every weekend.* **4** (*old use*) rape(3) (a girl/woman).
violation /vaɪəˈleɪʃən/ *c/u.n.*

violence /ˈvaɪələns/ *u.n* **1** great force or strength, usu considered dangerous or bad: *The violence of the storm surprised us. He spoke with such violence that we were afraid he was going to attack us.* **2** rough and often cruel behaviour: *violence on television.* **robbery with violence** ⇒ robbery.

ˈviolent *adj* **1** using violence: *violent behaviour/ prisoners; a violent death.* **2** (of a thing) showing violence(1): *a violent wind.* **3** very (usu unpleasantly) strong: *a violent argument.*
ˈviolently *adv.*

violet /ˈvaɪələt/ *adj* **1** *u.n* (also *attrib*) having the colour that is blue with little red in it: *violet paper. The curtains are violet.*

▷ *n* **2** *c.n* kind of plant with violet(1) or sometimes white flowers that usu have a sweet smell. **3** *c/u.n* violet(3) colour.

violin /ˌvaɪəˈlɪn/ *c.n* (also *attrib*) kind of musical instrument with strings, played with a bow³(2): *a violin lesson. Can you play the violin?*
vioˈlinist *c.n* person who plays the violin.

violoncello /ˌvaɪələnˈtʃeləʊ/ *c.n* (*formal*) = cello.
ˌvioloncellist *c.n* (*formal*) = cellist.

VIP /ˌviː ˌaɪ ˈpiː/ *c.n abbr* (*informal*) Very Important Person.

viper /ˈvaɪpə/ *c.n* **1** kind of small poisonous snake. Compare adder. **2** (*derog; fig*) evil or ungrateful person who harms other people.

virgin /ˈvɜːdʒɪn/ *attrib.adj* **1** not having had sexual experience. **2** (*fig*) not having been touched, spoilt etc by anything, esp by human beings: *virgin snow; virgin soil.*

▷ *c.n* **3** person (usu female) who has not had sexual intercourse.
ˌvirgin ˈbirth *def.n* belief that Jesus was not conceived(3) in the ordinary way, but by God's power.
ˌVirgin ˈMary *def.n* (often *the Blessed* —) (in Christian belief) mother of Jesus.
ˈvirginal *adj* referring to, suitable for, a virgin.
virˈginity *u.n* state of being a virgin(3). **lose one's virginity** have sexual intercourse for the first time.

Virgo /ˈvɜːgəʊ/ *n* (*pl* -s) **1** *unique n* one of the groups of stars people have mapped out in the sky. **2** *unique n* one of the 12 signs of the zodiac. **3** *c.n* person born under this sign.

virile /ˈvɪraɪl/ *adj* **1** (of a man) having the strength and tough qualities a lot of people expect from a man. **2** (of a man) having strong sexual powers. **3** (of behaviour etc) showing strength and tough qualities: *a virile voice.*
virility /vɪˈrɪlɪtɪ/ *u.n* quality or fact of being virile (esp 2).

virtual /ˈvɜːtʃʊəl/ *attrib.adj* almost what is described by the noun that follows: *We had met once but we were virtual strangers to each other. She's the virtual manager now that her husband is so ill.*
ˈvirtually *adv* nearly; in all important ways: *The business is virtually bankrupt(1).*

virtue /ˈvɜːtjuː/ *n* **1** *u.n* morality: *acts of virtue.* **2** *c.n* thing that is good or moral: *Being kind is one of her great virtues.* **3** *c.n* thing considered right or useful: *One of the virtues of a university education is that it gives the chance of getting an interesting job. Do you think there is really any virtue in being a vegetarian(3)?* Compare vice². **by/ in virtue of s.t** as a result of s.t; because of s.t: *You can use our club by virtue of your membership of the students' union.* **make a virtue of necessity** pretend one wants to do s.t one is really forced to do; try to get some advantage from a thing one did not want to do but is forced to do.

virtuous /ˈvɜːtjʊəs/ *adj* showing virtue(1).
ˈvirtuously *adv.*

virtuoso /ˌvɜːtjʊˈəʊzəʊ/ (*pl* -s, *virtuosi* /ˌvɜːtjʊˈəʊziː/) *c.n* person who is extremely good at s.t artistic, usu playing a musical instrument.
virtuosity /ˌvɜːtjʊˈɒsɪtɪ/ *u.n* skill shown by a virtuoso.

virtuous ⇒ virtue.

virulent /ˈvɪrʊlənt/ *adj* (*formal*) **1** (of an illness, poison etc) very strong, rapid and dangerous. **2** (of a feeling, way of speaking or way of writing) showing strong hatred: *a virulent attack on an enemy.*
ˈvirulence *u.n.* **ˈvirulently** *adv.*

virus /ˈvaɪərəs/ *c.n* (also *attrib*) very small living thing much smaller than a bacterium that can cause diseases such as the common cold: *a virus injection(1).*

virologist /ˌvaɪəˈrɒlədʒɪst/ *c.n* person whose job is in virology.

vi'rology *u.n* study of viruses and the diseases they cause.

visa /ˈviːzə/ *c.n* permission stamped in a person's passport allowing her/him to enter a country (entry visa), to pass through it (transit visa) or to leave it (exit visa).

visage /ˈvɪzɪdʒ/ *c.n* (*formal*) (appearance or expression of a) person's face. ⇨ envisage.

vis-à-vis /ˌviːz ɑː ˈviː/ *prep* (*French*; *formal*) with reference to; as regards; when he/she/it is compared to: *Our relations vis-à-vis our teachers are friendly but rather distant.*

viscount /ˈvaɪkaʊnt/ *c.n* (*abbr* V) (with capital V in names) rank of a lord in Britain and some other countries below an earl or count[2] and above a baron(1).

'viscountcy *c.n* (*pl* -ies) rank, title, of a viscount(ess).

'viscountess *c.n* 1 wife of a viscount. 2 woman who has the same rank as a viscount because she has inherited(1) it.

viscous /ˈvɪskəs/ *adj* (*formal*) (of a liquid) thick and not running easily: *dirty viscous oil.*

viscosity /vɪsˈkɒsɪtɪ/ *u.n.*

vise /vaɪs/ *c.n* ⇨ vice[1].

visible /ˈvɪzɪbl/ *adj* 1 who/that can be seen: *Is the coffee stain visible? There is a visible improvement in his health.* Opposite invisible. 2 that can be shown: *The man was arrested because he had no visible means of support.*

visibility /ˌvɪzɪˈbɪlɪtɪ/ *n* 1 *u.n* fact of being visible(1): *The visibility of the scar worried her.* 2 *sing/u.n* distance or degree to which the things around can be seen: *When visibility is poor, you should drive slowly. We had a visibility of only twenty kilometres because of the rain.*

'visibly *adv* in a way that can be seen: *The boys were visibly frightened by the speed of the car.*

vision /ˈvɪʒən/ *n* 1 *u.n* ability to see: *Vision is one of our five senses. Sally has poor vision so she has to wear glasses.* 2 *u.n* ability to understand things clearly so that one can plan cleverly for the future: *Mary has vision (or is a person of vision) and that is what we need in our future director.* 3 *c.n* person or thing not seen with one's eyes but with one's mind, usu when one is asleep but sometimes when one is awake as a religious experience. **field of vision** ⇨ field. **have a (clear etc) vision of (doing) s.t** have a (clear etc) idea of s.t: *While I swam, I had a clear vision of winning the race and collecting the gold medal. Before his birthday, John had visions of (getting) lots of presents and he was not disappointed.*

visionary /ˈvɪʒənrɪ/ *adj* (*formal*) 1 showing vision(2): *a visionary thinker.* 2 not close to reality; imagined, but impossible or very unlikely: *visionary ideas/plans.*
▷ *c.n* (*pl* -ies) 3 person having clever ideas about the future although these ideas may not be practical.

visit /ˈvɪzɪt/ *c.n* 1 act of going to spend time in a place with s.o: *a visit to the doctor.* **a flying visit** ⇨ flying(*adj*). **go on, pay, a visit (to s.o/s.t)** visit s.o/s.t.
▷ *v* 2 *tr/intr.v* (go to and) spend time in (a place) or with (s.o): *We've come here to visit friends. I visit London several times a year. Jane doesn't* live here; she's only visiting. 3 *tr.v* go to (a place or person) to do a particular job there: *I visited my dentist three times last month.*

visitation /ˌvɪzɪˈteɪʃən/ *c.n* (*formal*) official visit(1) (by an important person).

'visiting *attrib.adj* 1 not permanent but on loan from s.w else: *a visiting professor.*
▷ *u.n* 2 act or fact of making visits(1): *prison visiting* (i.e going regularly to a prison to help the prisoners with advice etc).

'visiting ,card *c.n* (*old use*) small card with one's name, address, telephone number etc printed on it which one can give people when first meeting them. ⇨ business card.

'visiting ,hours *pl.n* hours when one is allowed to visit museums, people in hospital etc.

visitor /ˈvɪzɪtə/ *c.n* 1 person who visits(2) (s.o/s.t). 2 bird etc that is not a native of a place but comes from s.w else.

'visitors' ,book *c.n* book in which visitors(1) to an official place or to a private house can write their names, addresses and sometimes remarks.

visor /ˈvaɪzə/ *c.n* 1 (also **'sun ,visor**) flap (*n*) above the windscreen in a car that can be put down to protect one's eyes from very bright light. 2 front part of a helmet that can be put down to protect a person's face: *The motorcyclist pulled his visor up so that he could wipe his face.*

vista /ˈvɪstə/ *c.n* (often — of s.t) 1 view (of s.t) into the distance between narrow limits (e.g between rows of trees or buildings). 2 (*formal*) long line (of events) seen in one's mind following each other, either in the past or in the future: *My grandmother often looks back at the long and happy vista of her life.*

visual /ˈvɪʒʊəl/ *adj* 1 received through one's sense of sight: *visual images(4).* 2 of or referring to the sense of sight: *visual difficulties.*

,visual 'aid *c.n* thing using one's sense of sight to help one learn, remember etc: *Television is one of the most powerful visual aids.*

,visual 'arts *pl.n* arts using one's sense of sight, e.g painting, sculpture(1), rather than one's sense of hearing etc.

visualization, -isation /ˌvɪʒʊəlaɪˈzeɪʃən/ *u.n* (*formal*) act or fact of visualizing s.o/s.t.

visualize, -ise /ˈvɪʒʊəˌlaɪz/ *tr.v* (*formal*) imagine (s.o/s.t); have an idea of (s.o/s.t): *Try to visualize a world without wars.* **visualize s.o/s.t as s.o/s.t** imagine s.o/s.t to be s.o/s.t: *Can you visualize me as a painter?*

'visually *adv* 1 to the sight of a person looking at her/him/it: *This bay is visually beautiful but it is a dangerous place to swim in.* 2 by using visual aids: *Have you tried teaching some of the new words in the lesson visually?*

vital /ˈvaɪtl/ *adj* 1 (often — for s.o/s.t; — that . . .) essential (for s.o/s.t, that . . .); of the greatest importance or highly necessary (if one is to have s.t): *It is vital for you to (or that you) pass the examination. If our attack is to succeed, absolute secrecy is vital.* 2 full of vitality(1): *a vital person/personality.*

vitality /vaɪˈtælɪtɪ/ *u.n* cheerful or healthy energy: *Climate can affect one's vitality. He works with great vitality.*

vitalize, -ise /ˈvaɪtəˌlaɪz/ *tr.v* (*formal*) give vitality to (s.o/s.t): *Her plans have vitalized her assistants/department.* ⇨ revitalize.

vitally /'vaɪtɪlɪ/ adv extremely; highly; absolutely: It is vitally important to keep our plans secret if our attack is to succeed.

,vital 'organ c.n one of the organs[1](1) inside a human or animal body (e.g the heart) without which it cannot live.

,vital sta'tistics pl.n **1** measurements round a person's chest, waist and hips(1) used when buying clothes etc. **2** statistics(1) about births, marriages, deaths etc in a population.

vitamin /'vɪtəmɪn/ c.n (also attrib) one of a group of substances made up of carbons(1) which living things need in order to live and be healthy: Vitamins A and B are found in fruit and vegetables. She takes vitamin pills/tablets to improve her health.

viticulture /'vɪtɪ,kʌltʃə/ u.n (science of) growing grapes, usu for making wine.

vitreous /'vɪtrɪəs/ adj (usu attrib) **1** made from glass: vitreous china. **2** (technical) like glass: vitreous rocks.

vitriolic /,vɪtrɪ'ɒlɪk/ adj (derog; formal) very cruel; intended to hurt s.o: a vitriolic speech attacking the qualities of the president.

vituperative /vɪ'tjuːpərətɪv/ adj (formal) (of a speech) using angry words and curses.
vi'tuperatively adv.

viva /'vaɪvə/ c.n (Latin) (informal) oral(2) examination.
viva voce /,vaɪvə 'vəʊsɪ/ adj/adv **1** oral(ly).
▷ c.n **2** = viva.

vivacious /vɪ'veɪʃəs/ adj (usu of a woman or girl) gay; full of life and spirit.
vi'vaciously adv. **vi'vaciousness** u.n. **vivacity** /vɪ'væsɪtɪ/ u.n.

viva voce ⇒ viva.

vivid /'vɪvɪd/ adj **1** (of colour or light) strong; bright. **2** able to produce very clear exact pictures in one's mind: a vivid description; a vivid imagination.
'vividly adv. **'vividness** u.n.

vivisect /'vɪvɪ,sekt/ tr/intr.v operate on (a living animal), not for its own good but to increase knowledge of (esp human) diseases.
vivisection /,vɪvɪ'sekʃən/ c/u.n (one example of the) science and practice of vivisecting.
,vivi'sectionist c.n person who performs vivisections.

vixen /'vɪksən/ c.n **1** female fox(1). **2** (derog) nasty rude woman.

viz /vɪz/ adv namely; and that is; and those are; in other words: England has two favourite sports, viz football and cricket[1].

V-neck ⇒ V.

vocabulary /və'kæbjʊlərɪ/ c.n **1** list of words, usu in alphabetical order and sometimes with explanations of their meanings: A vocabulary sometimes lists the new words to be found in a language exercise. **2** total number of words a particular person etc knows: Our parrot(1) has a vocabulary of about twenty words. **3** total number of (special) words used in a particular kind of job etc.
vocab /'vəʊkæb/ c.n (informal) vocabulary.

vocal /'vəʊkl/ adj **1** (usu attrib) of or referring to the voice; used when one speaks, sings etc. **2** (often pred) (informal) (of a person) able to express himself/herself freely in speech, and in the habit of doing so, sometimes loudly and too much: She's often vocal at meetings.
▷ c.n **3** words of a song, usu in a musical(4).

,vocal 'cords pl.n organs[1](1) in the throat producing the musical sounds in speech and singing by vibrating very fast.

,vocal 'organs pl.n organs[1](1) such as the tongue and lips, used for speaking.

'vocalist c.n singer, usu of popular songs.

vocalize, -ise /'vəʊkə,laɪz/ tr/intr.v put (ideas, feelings etc) into spoken words: She wouldn't vocalize her anger.

vocation /vəʊ'keɪʃən/ c.n **1** work done out of a sense of duty (as well as to earn money): Nursing old people is a vocation. **2** feeling that one has a call from God to become a priest, monk, nun etc. **3** (formal) job a person does as her/his main way of earning money. **have a vocation for s.t** especially suitable for a particular kind of work etc, esp when it is a vocation(1): Tom has always had a vocation for teaching in poor countries because he is a very sympathetic person.
vo'cational adj having to do with or preparing one for a vocation(3): vocational training.

vociferous /və'sɪfərəs/ adj (formal) loud, full of force and usu angry: vociferous criticism.
vo'ciferously adv. **vo'ciferousness** u.n.

vodka /'vɒdkə/ u.n strong alcoholic(1) drink with no colour which comes from Russia and Poland.

vogue /vəʊg/ attrib.adj **1** fashionable, usu for a short time: The vogue word for 'roughage' is 'fibre'.
▷ c.n **2** fashion, usu for a short time: I didn't like the vogue of last year for wearing black. **be (all) the vogue** be (very) fashionable, usu for a short time: Coloured hair was (all) the vogue in the 1980s. **come into vogue** become fashionable. **go out of vogue** stop being fashionable. **in vogue** fashionable, usu for a short time: Short hair is in vogue at the moment. **out of vogue** no longer fashionable.

voice /vɔɪs/ n **1** c.n sound(s) a person makes when he/she speaks or sings: Can you hear voices in the next room? **2** c.n ability to sing etc well: John has a trained voice. **3** c.n person who sings with other people in a group, each person singing a different set of notes: All the songs we sing are arranged for four voices. **4** c.n (grammar) one of (usu two) ways in which a verb is used, to show whether its subject[1](4) does the action of the verb, or the action is done to the subject[1](4). ⇒ active voice, passive voice. **5** u.n (technical) quality of sound produced by vibration(2) of the vocal cords: The sound /z/ has voice but the sound /s/ does not. **give voice to s.t** say what one is thinking etc aloud: She gave voice to her disapproval. **have a voice in s.t** be allowed to give one's opinion about s.t: As a parent I ought to have a voice in how the school should spend the money. **have little, no** etc **voice in s.t** not be allowed to give one's opinion about s.t (much). **have no voice**; **have lost one's voice**; **lose one's voice** be unable to speak or speak easily, e.g because one has a cold. **lower one's voice** speak less loudly. **raise one's voice** speak more loudly (and angrily). **s.o's voice is breaking** a male's voice is changing from the high tones of a boy to the lower tones of a man. **(shout etc) at the**

top of one's voice ⇨ top¹. **the voice of reason** reasonable ideas, either spoken or only thought: *I wish you'd listen to the voice of reason and decide not to buy that big house.* **with one voice** (*formal*) all saying the same thing: *They agreed with one voice.*

▷ *tr.v* **6** put (s.t) into the form of spoken words; say (s.t) (often strongly): *At last one of the boys dared to voice what we had all been feeling.*

voiced *attrib.adj* (*technical*) pronounced with voice(5). Opposite unvoiced(2).

-voiced having a voice like the first part of the word: *loud-voiced.*

'voiceless *adj* **1** pronounced without voice(5). **2** not producing any sound. **3** unable or not allowed to have a voice in s.t: *Unfortunately, as observers(2) we were voiceless.*

void /vɔɪd/ *adj* **1** (*pred*) (usu — *of s.t*) (*formal*) not having (s.t) in it: *The play was void of interest.* ⇨ devoid. **null and void** ⇨ null.

▷ *n* **2** *c.n* large empty gap or space: *There were many voids on the map where no one had travelled.* **3** *def.n* space around our world or universe. **4** *c.n* feeling that one needs s.t, often s.t one has lost: *His retirement from his job left a void in his life.*

▷ *tr.v* **5** (*law*) make (s.t) void(1).

voile /vɔɪl/ *u.n* very thin material used mostly for making clothes for women to wear when it is hot.

vol *written abbr* volume(2).

volatile /'vɒlə,taɪl/ *adj* **1** (*technical*) (of a liquid) easily turned into a gas: *The better the petrol, the more volatile it is.* **2** (often *derog*) (of a person) whose feelings, interests etc change very easily (often so that one cannot trust her/ him). **3** changing very easily and often: *a volatile political situation.*

volatility /,vɒlə'tɪlɪtɪ/ *u.n.*

vol-au-vent /'vɒl əʊ ,vɒŋ/ *c.n* (*French*) kind of food made by putting meat etc into a small light pastry case.

volcano /vɒl'keɪnəʊ/ *c.n* (*pl* -(e)s) mountain that has one or more big holes (craters(1)) out of which lava comes when the mountain erupts(1): *An active volcano is one that still erupts(1) sometimes but the volcano on this island is extinct(2).*

volcanic /vɒl'kænɪk/ *adj* **1** of, referring to, coming from, a volcano: *volcanic ash.* **2** (*fig*) very strong and violent: *a volcanic temper.*

vole /vəʊl/ *c.n* small animal of the same family as a mouse but with a short tail and thicker body.

volition /və'lɪʃən/ *u.n* (esp *of one's own* —) (*formal*) free will: *You came here of your own volition — no one forced you to come.*

volley /'vɒlɪ/ *c.n* **1** (often — *of s.t*) number (of bullets, shells, arrows, stones etc) fired or thrown at (about) the same time. **2** (often — *of s.t*) number (of blows, words etc) directed against s.o with force. **3** kick or hit given to a ball before it has dropped to the ground.

▷ *v* **4** *tr.v* send (many bullets, stones, questions etc) at the same time. **5** *tr/intr.v* kick or hit (a ball) s.o else has kicked, hit or thrown before it has time to touch the ground.

'volley ,ball *u.n* game between two teams who hit a big ball with the hands over a high net.

volt /vəʊlt/ *c.n* (*technical*) unit used for measuring the pressure of electricity, *symb* V: *One volt is the amount needed to produce one ampere of*

electrical current when the resistance(4) *of the wire through which it flows is one* ohm.

'voltage *c/u.n* (*technical*) force of an electrical current measured in volts.

volte-face /,vɒlt 'fɑːs/ *c.n* (*French*; *formal*) (often *do a* —) complete change from one opinion, way of behaving etc to the opposite one. Compare U-turn.

voluble /'vɒljʊbl/ *adj* (*formal*) **1** (of a person) talking a lot or too much. **2** (of a way of speaking) using a lot of, or too many, words.

volubility /,vɒljʊ'bɪlɪtɪ/ *u.n.* **'volubly** *adv.*

volume /'vɒljuːm/ *n* **1** *c.n* (*formal*) book: *a library with many volumes.* **2** *c.n* (often with capital **V**; *abbr* vol or Vol) one book in a particular collection: *Volume 3 of the complete works of Shakespeare.* **3** *c.n* amount s.t can contain; length multiplied by width multiplied by depth, *symb* V: *This case has a volume of 5* cubic(2) *metres.* **4** *c/u.n* amount; quantity: *The volume of traffic in London's streets is huge.* **5** *c/u.n* (also *attrib*) (level of) loudness or richness of a sound: *the volume knob.* **turn the volume down/ up** make the sound (e.g of a radio or television set) quieter/louder.

'volumes *pl.n* **1** books etc. ⇨ volume(1). **2** large amounts or quantities: *When the wall broke, volumes and volumes of water flowed out.* **speak volumes (for s.t)** (*formal*) show (s.t) very clearly and completely: *Her children's behaviour speaks volumes for the wonderful way she has brought them up.*

voluminous /və'ljuːmɪnəs/ *adj* (*formal*) **1** able to contain a large amount or number: *a voluminous bag; a voluminous pocket.* **2** (of s.t made of cloth etc) very loose and made of a lot of material: *a voluminous skirt.* **3** using too many words: *a voluminous statement; a voluminous speaker.*

vo'luminously *adv.* **vo'luminousness** *u.n.*

voluntary /'vɒləntrɪ/ *adj* **1** done of one's own free will; because one chooses to do it and not because one has to do it: *voluntary work.* **2** doing s.t of her/his own free will: *a voluntary worker.* **3** organized and/or paid for by people who work of their own free will without being paid for it. **4** that one can control oneself: *voluntary movements of the* muscles(1). Opposite involuntary.

voluntarily /'vɒləntrɪlɪ/ *adv* of one's own free will; without being forced: *I came voluntarily.*

volunteer /,vɒlən'tɪə/ *c.n* **1** person who volunteers(2,3) to join or do s.t: *We need two volunteers to help count the money. We've no volunteers for* (or *to do*) *these jobs.*

▷ *v* **2** *intr.v* (often — *for s.t*) offer to do s.t (e.g to join the armed forces) of one's own free will: *Mary has volunteered to help us tomorrow.* **3** *tr.v* offer (advice, information etc) without being asked for it: *While I was trying to start the car, several people in the crowd volunteered advice.*

voluptuous /və'lʌptjʊəs/ *adj* (*formal*) **1** giving pleasure through the senses of touch, sight, hearing etc, esp making one feel, or reminding one of, sexual pleasure: *voluptuous music.* **2** (of a woman's shape) that is pleasantly large and sexually attractive.

vo'luptuously *adv.* **vo'luptuousness** *u.n.*

vomit /'vɒmɪt/ *n* **1** *u.n* substance vomited(3). **2** *c.n* example or act of vomiting(3).

▷ *v* **3** *intr.v* be sick; bring up what is in one's stomach and pour it out of one's mouth. **4** *tr.v* (often — *s.t out*) bring (s.t) up, e.g out of one's stomach, and pour it out: *The volcano vomited (out) melted rock and smoke.*

voodoo /'vu:du:/ *u.n* (also **'voodoo₁ism**) kind of religion based on magic(3), found mostly in the West Indies.

voracious /və'reɪʃəs/ *adj* (*formal*) **1** wanting to eat, making one want to eat, a very great amount: *a voracious eater/ appetite.* **2** very eager to do s.t, e.g to learn as much as possible: *a voracious reader.*
vo'raciously *adv.* **vo'raciousness** *u.n.*
voracity /vɒ'ræsɪtɪ/ *u.n.*

vortex /'vɔːteks/ *c.n* (*pl* -es, **vortices** /'vɔːtɪˌsiːz/) water or air going round and round very fast in a spiral(1) so that it pulls anything that gets into it towards its centre. Compare tornado, whirlpool, whirlwind.

vote /vəʊt/ *n* **1** *c.n* example of voting(8) by one person: *John will have my vote tomorrow.* **2** *c.n* example of voting(8) by a group of people: *As the members could not agree, they had to have a vote.* **3** *c.n* piece of paper etc on which s.o marks how he/she votes(8). **4** *c.n* total number of votes(1,2) of a particular group or side: *the miners' vote.* **5** *c.n* result of a vote(2): *We won the vote yesterday quite easily.* **6** *def.n* right to vote(8) in elections to parliament etc: *There are still countries in the world where women do not have the vote.* **7** *c.n* money that parliament decides to spend on s.t: *The Ministry of Defence is asking for a vote of fifteen million pounds more this year.* **cast one's vote** = vote(8). **casting/deciding vote** vote(1) given by the chairperson of a meeting when both sides have voted equally. **give s.o the vote** allow s.o to vote(1) in elections etc: *Women were given the vote in Britain in 1918.* (**propose**) **a vote of** (**no**) **confidence** (**in s.o/s.t**) (suggest formally) a vote(2) (to be) taken to decide to express (lack of) confidence in s.o/s.t. (**propose**) **a vote of thanks** (**to s.o**) (suggest formally) a vote(2) (to be) taken to decide to thank s.o. **put s.t to the vote** allow people to decide s.t by voting(8). **take a vote** (**on s.t**) allow people to decide (about s.t) by voting(8).

▷ *v* **8** *intr.v* show which person, side etc one supports in an election etc, usu by putting a mark on a piece of paper, putting up one's hand or saying s.t. **9** *tr.v* vote in favour or in support of (a person, party etc): *Vote for Smith! Vote Labour(4)!* **10** *tr.v* (usu — *s.o/s.t s.t*) give (money) to s.o, an organization etc as a result of a vote(2): *The committee voted the Sports Club an extra £1000.*
vote against/for s.o/s.t vote(8) to show that one does not, does, support or favour s.o/s.t.
vote on s.t vote(8) to decide s.t.
vote s.o/s.t down defeat s.o/s.t in a vote(2).
vote s.o/s.t in vote(8) in such a way that s.o/s.t comes in (e.g as the government).
vote s.o into office vote(8) in such a way that s.o wins an election to a government position.
vote s.o off s.t vote(8) in such a way that s.o stops being on (a committee etc).
vote s.o out of office vote(8) in such a way that s.o loses re-election to a government position.
vote s.t through manage to have s.t (e.g a law) accepted as a result of a vote(2).

vote to do s.t decide by a vote(2) to do s.t: *The children voted to have their sports meeting on Saturday morning.*
'voter *c.n* person who votes(8) or is allowed to vote(8).

vouch /vaʊtʃ/ *intr.v* **1** **vouch for s.o** say one knows s.o and can guarantee(7) that he/she is honest etc. **2** **vouch for s.t** say one is sure about s.t: *I can vouch for the truth of Brian's story because I saw it all myself.*

voucher /'vaʊtʃə/ *c.n* **1** receipt (often on an attractive card) showing that money has been paid for s.t, (to be) given to s.o to pay for s.t: *a gift/book/travel voucher.* **2** piece of paper used to get certain things free or at less than the full price: *a government milk voucher.* ⇨ token(4).
a voucher for s.t (**a**) a voucher(2) allowing one to do s.t: *a voucher for travelling free on a bus.* (**b**) a voucher(1) worth a certain amount of money: *a voucher for £5.*

vouchsafe /ˌvaʊtʃ'seɪf/ *tr.v* (*formal*) be kind or gracious enough to do, offer, give etc (s.t): *She vouchsafed to look after the children while the parents were in prison.*

vow /vaʊ/ *c.n* **1** solemn promise or statement that one is going to do s.t. **take vows** become a monk or nun by making vows(1). **under a vow of s.t** having vowed(2) to do s.t: *Some monks live under a vow of silence.* **under a vow to do s.t** (*formal*) having vowed to do s.t: *Mary is under a vow to look after her mother in her old age.*

▷ *tr.v* **2** (often — *to do s.t; — that ...*) (*formal*) promise (s.t, to do s.t, that ...) seriously: *She vowed her revenge* (or *to be revenged*, or *that she would be revenged*).

vowel /'vaʊəl/ *c.n* **1** (also *attrib*) sound made in speaking without narrowing or blocking the passage through which the air comes out of the mouth. The vowel sounds in English are /iː/, /ɪ/, /e/, /æ/, /ʌ/, /ɑː/, /ɒ/, /ɔː/, /ʊ/, /uː/, /ə/ and /ɜː/. Compare consonant, diphthong. **2** letter representing one of the vowel sounds (in English A, E, I, O, U and sometimes Y, e.g in 'my' but not in 'yes').

voyage /'vɔɪɪdʒ/ *c.n* **1** journey on the sea (usu long) or through space(3). **go on, make, a voyage** travel in a ship or spacecraft.

▷ *intr.v* **2** (*formal*) travel on a ship (usu for a long distance) or in a spacecraft.
'voyager *c.n* **1** person who travels (usu for a long distance and often under difficult and/or dangerous conditions) by sea. **2** person travelling in a spacecraft.

voyeur /vwɑː'jɜː/ *c.n* (*French*) person getting sexual pleasure from watching other people's sexual behaviour, usu secretly.

vs *written abbr* versus. ⇨ v.

V-sign ⇨ V.

vulgar /'vʌlgə/ *adj* **1** (*derog*) (of a person, behaviour, speech etc) not decent, pleasant, polite etc; showing bad manners: *vulgar language/expressions. He has a vulgar sense of humour(1). It is vulgar to spit in public.* **2** (*derog*) (of things, colours, designs(1) etc) not of an acceptable (artistic) standard; not showing good judgement or taste(4): *vulgar wallpaper/jewellery.* **3** (*formal*) of or referring to ordinary people: *a vulgar accent(1).*

₁vulgar 'fraction *c.n* fraction(2) in which the

number to be divided is above the line and the dividing number is below the line, e.g $\frac{5}{8}$.

vulgarity /vʌlˈgærɪtɪ/ c/u.n (often — of s.t) (example of the) fact or state of being vulgar: *vulgarities in his behaviour*; *the vulgarity of her behaviour*.

ˈvulgarly adv.

vulnerable /ˈvʌlnərəbl/ adj (often — to s.t) easily hurt, wounded, attacked etc (by s.t): *David seems very confident but he is very vulnerable to criticism. Children are vulnerable to many illnesses.* ⇒ invulnerable.

vulnerability /ˌvʌlnərəˈbɪlɪtɪ/ u.n (often — to s.t) fact of being vulnerable (to s.t): *vulnerability to disease.*

ˈvulnerably adv.

vulture /ˈvʌltʃə/ c.n 1 kind of big bird in hot countries which eats dead bodies. 2 (derog) nasty greedy cruel person, esp when dealing with people who cannot defend themselves.

vulva /ˈvʌlvə/ c.n (pl -s, vulvae /ˈvʌlviː/) (technical) outer part of the female sex organs.

vying /ˈvaɪɪŋ/ pres.p of vie.

W w

W, w /ˈdʌblˌjuː/ c/unique n 1 23rd letter of the English alphabet.

▷ written abbr 2 week. 3 width.

▷ symb (**W**). 4 watt. 5 west.

wad /wɒd/ c.n (often — of s.t) 1 lump (of soft material) used to fill holes etc: *When the boat began to leak, we pushed wads of cotton into the holes.* 2 thick collection (of bank notes, letters etc): *When the woman opened her bag, I saw a fat wad of five-pound notes in it.*

ˈwadding u.n material used for making wads(1), often for packing s.t that breaks easily: *cotton wadding.*

waddle /ˈwɒdl/ c.n 1 way of walking in which the body bends awkwardly from side to side.

▷ intr.v 2 walk with a waddle(1): *Ducks waddle.*

wade /weɪd/ intr.v walk in water that is not so deep that one has to swim. **wade in** (fig; informal) attack s.o/s.t strongly; start doing s.t strongly: *The soldiers waded in and soon defeated the enemy.*

ˈwader c.n 1 person who wades. 2 wading bird.

ˈwading ˌbird c.n (any) kind of bird that wades to get its food.

wafer /ˈweɪfə/ c.n very thin kind of biscuit, often eaten with ice-cream.

ˌwafer-ˈthin adj very thin.

waffle¹ /ˈwɒfl/ c.n kind of light cake with a pattern of squares (made by the waffle iron in which it is cooked).

ˈwaffle ˌiron c.n thing that one cooks waffles¹ in, which makes the pattern of squares in them.

waffle² /ˈwɒfl/ u.n 1 (informal) talk that may sound reasonable but is really stupid and not to the point.

▷ intr.v 2 (often — (on) (about s.t)) (informal) talk waffle²(1) (about s.t) (for a long time).

waft /wɒft/ c.n 1 (often — of s.t) passing smell (of s.t) carried by moving air: *When I opened the window, wafts of scent came in from the roses outside.*

▷ tr/intr.v 2 carry s.t (or be carried) gently (as if) on the wind or waves: *A light wind wafted the smell of cooking to us from the shore. The wind wafted the leaves across the grass.*

wag /wæg/ c.n 1 shake.

▷ tr/intr.v (-gg-) 2 shake or move (s.t) from side to side: *Dogs wag their tails when they are happy.*

ˈwagˌtail c.n kind of small bird that moves its tail up and down while it is walking.

wage¹ /weɪdʒ/ c.n amount of money one earns, usu in a day or week. **ˈliving wage** ⇒ live². Compare salary.

ˈwage ˌearner c.n person earning wages.

ˈwage ˌfreeze c.n situation in which wages are not allowed to rise to try to prevent prices rising too.

ˈwage ˌlevel c.n average wage¹ for a particular industry, time etc with which one can compare the average wage¹ for other industries, times etc.

ˈwage reˌstraint c.n agreement to keep rises in wages down or not to have any increases.

ˈwages pl.n money one earns, usu in a day or week.

ˈwage ˌscale c.n range of wages for a particular kind of job, starting at the bottom and going up to the top: *The wage scale starts at £100 a week and goes up by £10 stages to £200 a week.*

ˈwage ˌslave c.n (informal) wage earner who is considered to have to work like a slave(3) to get her/his wage.

ˌwages of ˈsin pl.n punishment one gets for sinning(3).

ˈwages ˌfreeze = wage freeze.

wage² /weɪdʒ/ tr.v **wage war** (against/on s.o/s.t) fight (s.o/s.t): *It is better to wage war on poverty and disease than on people.*

wager /ˈweɪdʒə/ c.n 1 = bet(1). **make a wager that** ... bet(3) that ...: *I have just made a wager that my brother will win tomorrow's race.*

▷ tr/intr.v 2 (often — (s.o) (s.t) that ...) make a bet(3,4) (of a certain amount of money etc) (with s.o) that ...: *He wagered £5 that I wouldn't get a higher score than him.* **wager (s.t) on s.o/s.t** bet(3) (a certain amount of money etc) about s.o/s.t: *I sometimes wager money on horses.*

waggle /ˈwægl/ c.n 1 movement from side to side; wag(1): *The dog's tail gave a quick waggle and then stopped.*

▷ tr/intr.v 2 (often — (s.t) about) move (s.t) from side to side; wag(2) (s.t): *The back of the cart waggled about as it moved over the rough road.*

wagon /ˈwægən/ c.n (also **ˈwaggon**) 1 cart with four wheels pulled by animals, usu horses or oxen. 2 vehicle travelling on rails and used for carrying goods, not people: *goods wagon.* **on the wagon** (fig; informal) no longer drinking alcoholic(1) drinks.

ˈwaggoner c.n man who drives a wagon(1).

wagon-lit /ˌvægɒn ˈliː/ (pl **wagons-lits**

/ˌvægɒnˈliː/) c.n (French) carriage on a train which has beds during the night for passengers to sleep in; sleeping car.

wagtail ⇨ wag.

waif /weɪf/ c.n (also (pl) **waifs and 'strays**)child with no home and/or no one to look after it.

wail /weɪl/ c.n **1** loud unhappy cry. **2** long loud sound, e.g of a siren(1).

▷ tr/intr.v **3** cry (s.t) loudly and unhappily; make a loud sound or sounds like an unhappy person: The child wailed because her toy was broken. She's wailing over her lost doll. The wind wailed through the trees. Bob wailed that his bicycle was gone. She wailed out the sad news. 'It's gone!' she wailed.

wainscot /ˈweɪnskət/ u.n narrow pieces of wood along the lower edge of a wall; skirting boards.
'wainscoting u.n = wainscot.

waist /weɪst/ c.n **1** (narrower) part of a person's body that is between the chest and the top of the hips[1]. **2** part of a dress or pair of trousers etc that fits a person's waist(1). **3** size of a waist(1,2): 'What's your waist?' '85 centimetres.' **4** narrow part in the middle of s.t: the waist of a violin.
'waist,band c.n part of a piece of clothing that goes round a waist(1).
'waist,coat c.n short coat coming down as far as the waist(1) and having no sleeves, usu worn under a jacket(1).
'waisted adj having a waist(2,4).
-waisted having a waist(1,2,4) like the thing that is the first part of the word: wasp-waisted.
'waist,line c.n distance round a waist(1,2); position of a waist(1): When people become middle-aged, their waistlines usually get larger.

wait /weɪt/ c/u.n **1** (often a — of an hour etc) state or time of waiting(2) (lasting an hour etc). **lie in wait (for s.o/s.t)** wait in a place where one is hidden (until s.o/s.t comes): The robbers used to lie in wait for people crossing the park in order to stop them and take their money.

▷ intr.v **2** stay s.w; not go away: Wait a few minutes — I am sure Mary will be here soon. **3** stay without being done, said, heard etc: Let's go and have lunch now; the rest of the work can wait until the afternoon.
keep s.o/s.t waiting cause s.o/s.t to wait: I'm sorry I kept you waiting; I had an urgent phone call.
wait and see stay without doing anything until one has more information on which to base one's actions.
wait at table ⇨ table(n).
wait for s.o/s.t wait until s.o/s.t comes or until s.t happens. **wait for s.o/s.t to do s.t** wait until s.o/s.t does s.t: Let's wait for the rain to stop before we go out.
wait on s.o hand and foot ⇨ hand(n).
wait one's chance (to do s.t) ⇨ chance(n).
wait one's turn (to do s.t) ⇨ turn(n).
wait up (for s.o) not go to bed while one waits (for s.o): You needn't wait up (for me); I'll be very late and I've got my own key.
'waiter c.n man or woman who brings food etc to people in a restaurant etc.
'waiting ,list c.n list of people or things, in the order in which they came or are to be dealt with: There is a long waiting list for operations in our hospital.

'waiting-,room c.n place where people wait to be seen by a doctor, official etc.

waitress /ˈweɪtrɪs/ c.n woman who brings food etc to people in a restaurant etc.

waive /weɪv/ tr.v allow s.o not to do or take (s.t he/she has a right to do or take): We do not pay back money we have received for tickets but our manager has the power to waive this rule in cases of sudden illness.

wake¹ /weɪk/ c.n **1** meeting of people to eat, drink, look at a dead body and show their sorrow before the body is buried.

▷ v (p.t woke /wəʊk/, p.p woken /ˈwəʊkən/) **2** tr/intr.v (often — (s.o) up) (cause s.o/s.t to) stop sleeping: There was a lot of noise in the street but luckily the baby did not wake up (or it did not wake the baby). **3** intr.v become fully conscious again after daydreaming etc. **4** tr.v cause (s.t) to be felt: An open drawer in the office woke my suspicions and that is how I discovered that we had been robbed. **wake from s.t** wake(2,3) after s.t: I woke suddenly from a deep sleep with the feeling that there was someone else in the room.
wake s.o from, out of, s.t wake(2,3) s.o so that he/she stops doing s.t: It was only the news of his grandson's success in his examinations that woke the old man from his sad thoughts. **wake up (a)** ⇨ wake¹(2). **(b)** (fig) pay attention; stop daydreaming: Wake up, it's your turn to answer a question! **wake up to s.t** (fig) begin to realize or understand s.t; become conscious of s.t: John is just waking up to the fact that he won't pass his examinations unless he starts working much harder.
'wakeful adj not sleeping; not able to sleep: My wife often has wakeful nights.
'wakefully adv. **'wakefulness** u.n.
'waken tr/intr.v (often — (s.o) up) (formal) wake(2).
wakey wakey /ˌweɪkɪ ˈweɪkɪ/ interj (informal) Wake up!
'waking attrib.adj during which one is not asleep: During her waking hours that woman thinks only of her child.

wake² /weɪk/ c.n signs left behind s.t moving, usu through water, and showing where it has passed: the wake of a ship. Compare wash(3). **in the wake of s.t** (fig) following s.t; behind s.t: Hundreds of children followed in the wake of the procession, singing and waving flags.

walk /wɔːk/ c.n **1** (for people and animals with two legs) way of going forwards, backwards or sideways by moving one foot after another in such a way that both feet are never off the ground at the same time. **2** (for animals with four legs) way of going forwards, backwards or sideways by moving the feet in such a way that there are always two or three feet on the ground at the same time. **3** way of walking(7) of a particular (kind of) person or animal: People who ride horses a lot have a special walk that one can recognize at once. **4** journey on foot, usu done for exercise or pleasure: Our walk this morning did me a lot of good. **5** place where one can walk(7): Our local council is building some beautiful walks along the top of the cliffs. **6** distance people walk(7): The post office is only five minutes' walk from here. **go for a walk**; **have/take a walk** (go out and) walk(7) for pleasure or exercise.

▷ *v* **7** *tr/intr.v* go or move on foot (along s.t) at the speed of a walk(1,2): *I walked the streets for hours looking for a hotel which was not full.* **8** *tr.v* carry or move (s.t heavy) while walking: *This piano is very heavy but I think the four of us can walk it across to the other side of the hall.* **9** *tr.v* walk with (s.o) to a place: *I'll walk you home. He walked me to the front gate.* **walk a dog** etc take a dog etc (out) for a walk, usu for exercise. **walk (all) over s.o/s.t** (*fig*) treat s.o badly, rudely or arrogantly: *Don't let that man walk all over you; tell him to shut up.* **walk away/off with s.t** (a) steal s.t. (b) (*fig*) win easily. ⇨ walkover(1). **walk out** strike(5). ⇨ walkout. **walk out (of s.t)** leave (s.t) when one is not expected to do so, usu to show that one does not like s.t: *When the speaker said rude things about the staff, I walked out (of the meeting).* **walk out on s.o** (*fig*) leave s.o when one is not expected to do so, and often when this action causes her/him difficulties. ⇨ walkout. **walk s.o off her/his feet** ⇨ foot(*n*).

'**walka,bout** *c.n* (*informal*) walk through a crowd by an important person so that he/she can meet and talk to ordinary people. **go (on a) walkabout** walk in this way.

'**walker** *c.n* person who walks, usu for exercise or pleasure.

,**walkie-'talkie** *c.n* (*informal*) radio carried by police officers etc which allows them to send as well as to receive spoken messages.

'**walk-,in** *adj* big enough for people to walk into it: *One thing I liked about our hotel room was that it had a walk-in cupboard for my clothes.*

'**walking** *attrib.adj* **1** done on foot: *a walking holiday.* **2** suitable for walking in or with: *walking shoes.*

,**walking 'dictionary** *c.n* (*fig; informal*) person who knows a great number of words and their meanings.

'**walking ,holiday** *c.n* holiday during which one goes on foot because one enjoys walking.

'**walking ,stick** *c.n* stick with a curved end which acts as a handle, used by s.o who is lame(1), old, ill etc when walking.

,**walk of 'life** *c.n* (*pl* walks of life) position in society; social position; kind of job. (**in**) **all walks of life; in every walk of life** in every kind of social position, job etc: *One finds nice people and nasty people in all walks of life.*

'**walk,out** *c.n* **1** strike(1). **2** act of leaving work or a meeting etc because one disagrees with s.t.

'**walk,over** *c.n* **1** easy victory: *The match was a walkover for our team.* **2** victory when the other side does not play: *Our boys were given a walkover when the team they were supposed to be playing did not arrive.*

wall /wɔːl/ *c.n* **1** side of a room or building. **2** thing like the side of a building but open on top, used to divide spaces: *There is a high wall between our garden and the road outside.* **3** thing covering the inside of s.t hollow: *The walls of our stomachs are lined with something that resists acids.* **4** (*fig*) thing that divides or stops s.t: *When the firemen tried to get into the house they met a wall of fire. The police met a wall of silence because of fear of being injured by the robbers.* **come up against a blank wall** (*fig*) find it impossible to get information, permission, agreement etc. **drive s.o up the wall** (*fig*;

informal) make s.o very angry. **go to the wall** (*fig*) lose in a struggle or fight: *I'm afraid it is a fact of life that the weak usually go to the wall.* **have one's back to the wall** ⇨ back(*n*). **Walls have ears** (*proverb*) (One has to be very careful to keep one's secrets, because) people are always listening even in places one thinks quite safe.

▷ *tr.v* **5** make a wall for or round (s.t). **wall s.o/s.t up (in s.t)** close s.o/s.t up (in s.t) so that he/she/it cannot get, be taken, out. **wall s.t off (from s.t)** separate s.t (from s.t) with a wall.

walled *adj* (usu *attrib*) having walls round it: *a walled garden.*

'**wall,flower** *c.n* **1** kind of flower with a sweet smell which is grown in gardens. **2** (*fig; informal*) woman at a dance etc whom none of the men ask to dance.

'**wall ,painting** *c/u.n* picture painted on a wall; painting or pictures on walls; fresco.

'**wall,paper** *u.n* **1** paper with a pattern on it, stuck on walls to make them look nice.
▷ *tr/intr.v* **2** = paper(6).

'**Wall ,Street** *unique n* **1** street in the US city of New York in which the Stock Exchange(1) is. **2** the New York Stock Exchange(1) itself.

,**wall-to-'wall** *attrib.adj* **1** stretching from the bottom of one wall right across to the bottom of the opposite wall: *wall-to-wall carpeting.*
▷ *adv* **2** so that it stretches from the bottom of one wall right across to the bottom of the opposite wall.

wallaby /'wɒləbɪ/ *c.n* (-*ies*) kind of small Australian animal belonging to the same family as the kangaroo.

walled ⇨ wall.

wallet /'wɒlɪt/ *c.n* case in which people carry bank notes, credit cards etc and which is small enough to fit into a pocket.

wallflower ⇨ wall.

wallop[1] /'wɒləp/ *c.n* **1** (*informal*) hard hit.
▷ *tr.v* (*informal*) **2** hit (s.o/s.t) hard. **3** (often — *s.o at s.t*) beat s.o (at a game etc): *Joe is cleverer than I am but I can wallop him at tennis.*

'**walloping** *attrib.adj* **1** (*informal*) very big; huge: *My friend arrived on a walloping great horse.*
▷ *c.n* **2** (*informal*) (often *get a* — (*from s.o*); *give s.o a* —) beating (from s.o): *Our team got a walloping last time they played a match.*

wallop[2] /'wɒləp/ *u.n* (*informal*) beer.

wallow /'wɒləʊ/ *c.n* **1** act of sitting, lying or rolling about (in mud, water etc). **2** place where some animals go to roll in mud. (**have**) **a wallow in s.t** (*have*) a lie or roll in s.t: *There's nothing I like more after a hard game of football than a good wallow in a hot bath.*
▷ *intr.v* **5** (often — *in s.t*) **3** lie or roll about (in mud or water, in the sea etc): *Elephants love wallowing in muddy water.* **4** (*fig*) (seem to) get pleasure (from feeling sad etc): *She was wallowing in misery(1).* **be wallowing in it/money** (*informal*) be very rich.

wall painting, wallpaper, Wall Street, wall-to-wall ⇨ wall.

walnut /'wɔːl,nʌt/ *n* (also *attrib*) **1** *c.n* kind of large nut with a wrinkled surface that can be eaten: *a walnut cake.* **2** *c.n* (also '**walnut ,tree**) tree on which walnuts(1) grow. **3** *u.n* brown-red colour.

walrus /'wɔːlrəs/ *c.n* kind of big animal that lives

in the sea and has two long teeth in its top jaw pointing downwards.

,walrus mou'stache *c.n* man's long moustache like that of a walrus.

waltz /wɔːls/ *n* **1** *c/def.n* kind of dance in which the steps are divided up into groups of three. **2** *c.n* music for such a dance.
▷ *v* **3** *intr.v* dance a/the waltz(1). **4** *tr/intr.v* (*informal*) (cause (s.o/s.t) to) move quickly: *As the argument began, my father waltzed me out of the room.* **waltz away/off with s.t** (*informal*) get s.t easily: *Mary has waltzed off with the prize for history again this year.* **waltz up to s.o** (*informal*) go towards s.o in a showy or arrogant way: *You can't just waltz up to the manager and invite her to lunch!*

wan /wɒn/ *adj* (*-nn-*) pale; looking tired and/or ill.
'wanly *adv.* **wanness** /'wɒnnɪs/ *u.n.*

wand /wɒnd/ *c.n* thin stick used by a magician when he/she is doing tricks, or by a fairy when he/she is doing magic(3).

wander /'wɒndə/ *c.n* **1** example of wandering (⇨ wander(2)): *We had a pleasant wander through the park before dinner.*
▷ *v* **2** *intr.v* (often — *about, around, along* etc) walk about without trying to get to any particular place or because one is lost. **3** *tr.v* go about (in s.t) in this way: *We spent a lot of our holiday wandering the beautiful forests around our hotel.* **4** *intr.v* wind²(3): *A pretty stream wanders through our valley.* **5** *intr.v* fail to keep one's mind, attention, thoughts etc under control: *She tried to follow the story of the film but her attention kept wandering.* **wander off** go away in a wandering (⇨ wander(5)) way: *Now children, don't wander off or you may get lost.* **wander off s.t** leave s.t during one's wandering (⇨ wander(5)): *It was not a good discussion because everybody kept wandering off the point.*
'wanderer *c.n* person who wanders(2).
'wanderings *pl.n* travels to various places without any special plan, usu without any special purpose except pleasure or discovery.
'wander,lust *sing/u.n* love of wandering (⇨ wander(2)).

wane /weɪn/ *def.n* **1 on the wane** slowly becoming less big or strong: *I'm afraid your father's very ill and his strength is on the wane. The moon is on the wane at present.*
▷ *intr.v* **2** (esp of the moon) slowly become less big or strong: *The moon wanes until it disappears completely and then waxes again until it is full.* Opposite wax²(2).

wangle /'wæŋgl/ *c.n* **1** (*informal*) act or example of wangling(2): *Colin didn't really have a right to a day off yesterday but he managed to get one by a wangle.*
▷ *tr/intr.v* **2** (*informal*) get (s.t) by using tricks or by being clever or cunning(1): *How did you manage to wangle a ticket to the big show?* **wangle one's way, oneself, s.o into, out of, s.t** use cunning(2) etc to get oneself/s.o into s.t/out of s.t: *He wangled himself into the meeting by saying he was a journalist.* **wangle s.t out of s.o** succeed in getting s.t from s.o by being cunning(1).

want /wɒnt/ *n* **1** *c.n* thing one wants(3); thing one would like to have: *Now that George is old he has only one want — a quiet life.* **2** *u.n* lack; absence; poverty: *Many people in the poorer countries of the world have a life of want.* (**die**) **for/from want of s.t** (die) because of the absence or lack of s.t. **in want** in a state of poverty. **in want (of s.t)** lacking/needing/wanting s.t; not having s.t: *This house is in want of repair.*
▷ *v* **3** *tr.v* wish or desire to have (s.o/s.t): *I want a new pen because my old one has broken.* **4** *tr.v* need (s.t): *Your shoes want a good clean. Tell me what wants doing and I'll do it for you.* **5** *tr.v* welcome (s.o): *Never go anywhere where you're not wanted.* **6** *tr.v* (often — *s.o* for *s.t*) look for (s.o), try to catch (s.o) (because one thinks he/she has done s.t bad): *Why do the police want that man?* **want (for anything/s.t/nothing)** need (essential things/nothing): *As long as she has such good children she will never want for anything* (or *she'll want for nothing*). **not want s.o/s.t doing s.t** object to s.o/s.t doing s.t: *We've built a high wall round our garden because we don't want people watching us all the time.* **say what you want** = say(v). **want in/out** (*informal*) want to get in/out: *I don't like this university any more and I want out as soon as possible.* **want doing** need to be done: *This door wants painting; it will rot if you don't do something about it soon.* **want s.o to do s.t** wish s.o to do s.t; wish that s.o would do s.t. **want to do s.t (a)** wish or desire to do s.t: *I want to watch television.* **(b)** ought to do s.t; should do s.t: *Look, you've broken that glass; you want to be more careful!*
'want ,ad *c.n* advertisement saying that s.o wants (to buy) s.t.
'wanting *pred.adj* lacking; not having; needing: *This old jacket(1) will do; only the buttons are wanting.* **find s.o/s.t (to be) wanting (in s.t)** find that s.o/s.t does not have (enough of) s.t (e.g intelligence or strength): *I'm sorry but I find your soup wanting in flavour.*
wants *pl.n* things one wants, needs or lacks: *Now that Jack is old, he has few wants.*

wanton /'wɒntən/ *adj* (*formal*) **1** (*attrib*) not having a good reason or excuse: *Wanton cruelty to animals is a thing I hate.* **2** immoral in a sexual way: *The wanton behaviour of the young girl encouraged men to think she was older than she really was.*
'wantonly *adv.* **'wantonness** *u.n.*

war /wɔː/ *n* **1** *u.n* fighting with weapons (guns, bombs etc). **2** *c.n* example of war(1). (Notice that a *battle* is one part of a war.) **3** *c/u.n* (often — *against/on s.t*) (example of a) struggle (against s.t bad): *a war against poverty; be involved in a war on dangerous diseases.* **4** *c/u.n* (example of a) strong argument or quarrel. **act of war** act that is part of a war or that may start a war: *If the navy of one country sinks a ship belonging to another country that is an act of war.* **at war (with s.o/s.t)** engaged(4) in fighting a war (against s.o/s.t): *When they did not reply to our letter, our prime minister declared that we were at war with them.* **civil war** ⇨ civil. **class war** ⇨ class. **cold war** ⇨ cold. **declare war (on s.o/s.t)** say officially that one is going to start fighting (s.o/s.t): *I have decided to declare war on waste and inefficiency in our company.* **declaration of war** statement that one is going to start a war. **go to war (against/with s.o/s.t)** begin a war (against s.o). **in the wars** (*fig; informal*) suffering as a result of having been hurt, damaged etc, or of having been accused of s.t: *I see that Johnny has been in the wars again; look at those bruises on his arms!* **make/wage war (against/(up)on s.o/s.t)** fight (against s.o/s.t): *We must wage war against dangerous* drugs(2). **prisoner of war** ⇒ prisoner. **war of nerves** ⇒ nerves. **war of words** ⇒ word(*n*).

▷ *intr.v* (-rr-) **5** fight with weapons: *Those countries warred for many years.* **6** quarrel seriously: *We've been warring with the neighbours about who should mend the fence.*

'**war ,cloud** *c.n* (*fig*) danger or threat that war will start.

'**war ,crime** *c.n* crime against one or more members of the enemy committed (⇒ commit) by members of the armed forces, politicians, officials etc during a war.

warfare /'wɔː,feə/ *u.n* war; fighting.

'**war,head** *c.n* front part of a bomb or missile(1) which is where the explosive is.

'**war,like** *adj* ready and/or eager to fight.

warmonger /'wɔː,mʌŋgə/ *c.n* person who wants war or who tries to get people to start a war.

'**war,path** *c/def.n* (often *on the* —) (*fig*) (following the sort of) course taken by s.o who is going to fight, usu with words.

'**warring** *adj* (always) fighting each other, either with real weapons or with words, thoughts etc: *As I watched the wedding, warring feelings of happiness and jealousy filled my heart.*

warrior /'wɒrɪə/ *c.n* person who fights.

warship /'wɔː,ʃɪp/ *c.n* ship intended for fighting.

'**war,time** *u.n* (also *attrib*) (often *in* —) time when a war is happening: *wartime regulations.*

'**war ,zone** *c.n* area in which a war is going on.

warble /'wɔː,bl/ *c.n* **1** (sound like the) song of a bird; sound of warbling(2,3).

▷ *tr/intr.v* **2** (of a bird) sing (s.t) in such a way that one produces several notes one after the other without stopping. **3** (of a person) sing (s.t) in a way that is like the sound of a bird warbling(2). **warble s.t out** sing s.t in a warbling(1,2) way.

'**warbler** *c.n* kind of bird that warbles(2).

ward[1] /wɔːd/ *c.n* **1** room in a hospital in which patients have their beds. **2** one part of a town or city which elects a political representative(3). **3** one of the main parts into which a prison is divided. **4** (also ,**ward of 'court**) young person for whom another person (not her/his parent), or a court of law, has responsibility: *After the girl's parents died, she was made a ward of her uncle and aunt.* **casualty ward** ⇒ casualty(4). **isolation ward** ⇒ isolation.

,**ward of 'court** person for whom a court of law has responsibility. ⇒ ward[1](4).

ward[2] /wɔːd/ *tr.v* **ward s.o/s.t off (s.o/s.t)** keep or prevent s.o/s.t from attacking or hitting (s.o/s.t): *He tried to hit me but I warded his blows off. One can sometimes ward off a cold by going to bed for a day.*

warden /'wɔːdn/ *c.n* person who guards or looks after (s.o/s.t): *My friend Jack is a warden of a youth hostel.* **traffic warden** ⇒ traffic.

warder /'wɔːdə/ *c.n* man who guards prisoners: *prison warders.*

wardress /'wɔːdrɪs/ *c.n* woman who guards prisoners: *a prison wardress.*

wardrobe /'wɔːdrəʊb/ *c.n* **1** cupboard for

hanging clothes in. **2** clothes belonging to one person or used for one purpose: *My mother had a summer wardrobe and a winter wardrobe.* **3** clothes a theatre or an actor etc has for use in plays, films etc: *Our theatre has a big wardrobe of historical costumes.*

-**ware** /-weə/ *u.n* things made of, for, or used in, the thing shown in the first part of the word: earthenware; kitchenware.

warehouse /'weə,haʊs/ *c.n* (*pl* /'weə,haʊzəz/) place where wares are stored; place where one's furniture etc is stored when there is no room for it in one's own home, or when one has sold one's home and has not yet moved into another one.

wares *pl.n* things one is trying to sell.

warfare, warhead ⇒ war.

warily, wariness ⇒ wary.

warlike ⇒ war.

warm /wɔːm/ *adj* **1** pleasantly hot; not too hot, but also not at all cold. Opposite cool(1). **2** preventing one from feeling or getting cold: *It's cold outside today so you'd better put on your warmest coat.* **3** making one feel warm: *I felt cold at first but a warm run across the park soon made me feel fine again.* **4** (of a person, action etc) having or showing friendly feelings: *a warm welcome.* Opposite cold(2). **5** showing anger, excitement etc: *As the argument became warmer people began to shout and threaten each other.* **6** sounding or looking friendly or cheerful: *Orange is such a warm colour.* **7** not yet having had time to get cold; fresh: *When we found the body, it was still warm. We must try to find the thieves while their* trail(1) *is still warm.*

▷ *def.n* **8** warm place; opportunity to get warm(1): *You look frozen; come into the warm.* **have a warm** (*informal*) warm oneself: *Have a warm in front of the fire before you go out into the snow again.*

▷ *tr/intr.v* **9** (often — (s.o/s.t) up) (cause (s.o/s.t) to) become warm: *After playing in the snow the children warmed their hands (up) by rubbing them together. I'll warm up some soup for you.* ⇒ heat(5). **warm to(wards) s.o/s.t** begin to feel (more) friendly towards s.o/s.t. **warm up (a)** ⇒ warm(9). **(b)** become readier to do s.t successfully by doing exercises or practice first: *Before a race it is wise to warm up for a few minutes to loosen your muscles(1).* ⇒ warm-up.

,**warm-'blooded** *adj* **1** having blood that is always warm even when the outside temperature is very cold or very hot: *People, cows and mice are warm-blooded animals.* **2** (*fig*) (of a person) having strong, enthusiastic feelings. Compare cold-blooded, hot-blooded.

,**warm 'front** *c.n* warm(1) air that is rising up below an area of cold air. Compare cold front.

,**warm-'hearted** *adj* kind; friendly; having or showing kind warm(6) feelings. Opposite cold-hearted.

,**warm-'heartedness** *u.n.*

'**warmish** *adj* rather warm.

'**warmly** *adv.* '**warmness** *u.n.*

warmth /wɔːmθ/ *u.n* fact or state of being warm(*adj*) or of showing that one is warm: *Our friends greeted us with great warmth and soon made us comfortable in their home.*

'**warm-,up** *c.n* time during which one warms up

before starting a race, performance etc; actions done to warm up.

warmonger ⇨ war.

warmth, warm-up ⇨ warm.

warn /wɔːn/ *tr/intr.v* (often — *s.o* (*not*) *to do s.t*) give information (to s.o) that is intended to help her/him to do s.t she/he ought to do, or to avoid s.t dangerous, bad etc: *She warned her little daughter to keep away from strange dogs.* **warn s.o away/off** warn s.o not to come s.w. **warn** (**s.o**) **against/of/off s.o/s.t** warn (s.o) that s.o/ s.t should be avoided or treated cautiously.

'warning *attrib.adj* **1** given to warn s.o: *The army gave a warning shot before their shooting practice in the woods.*

▷ *c/u.n* **2** spoken or written word(s) whose purpose is to warn: *There is now a government warning on all our cigarette packets that smoking may damage one's health.* **give s.o a warning** warn s.o. **give s.o** (**a week's** etc) **warning that** . . . warn s.o (a week etc before s.t is going to happen) that . . . . **without warning** when one is not expecting it: *They arrived without warning.*

warp /wɔːp/ *n* **1** *c/def.n* threads running along the length of a piece of cloth. ⇨ weft. **2** *c.n* (often— *in s.t*) twist (in wood etc) caused by some parts getting drier or wetter than others.

▷ *tr/intr.v* **3** (cause (s.t) to) twist so that it is no longer of the correct shape. **4** (*fig*) (cause (s.o/s.t) to) become evil or impossible to trust: *I'm afraid that all those nasty films Joe has been watching have warped his mind.*

‚warped 'mind *c.n* mind that has been warped(4).

warpath ⇨ war.

warrant /'wɒrənt/ *n* **1** *c.n* written permission: *The police arrived with a warrant for his arrest. Do you have a warrant to use this building for a meeting?* **2** *u.n* (often (*have*) — *for s.t*) (*formal*) thing giving s.o a good respectable reason (for doing s.t): *You have no warrant for saying such cruel things about her.* **search warrant** ⇨ search. **take out a warrant** (**for s.t**) get a warrant(1) (to do s.t).

▷ *tr.v* **3** serve as a good reason for (s.t); justify(2) (s.t): *Nothing could possibly warrant such rudeness to one's guests.* ⇨ unwarranted. **I'll warrant you** (*formal*) I myself feel sure: *Don't worry, he'll bring your car back by dinner time, I'll warrant you.* **warrant s.o doing s.t** give s.o a good reason or excuse for doing s.t: *His having broken your pen doesn't warrant you giving him such a hard kick.*

'warrant ‚officer *c.n* (*written abbr WO*) (*military*) officer who is lower in rank than a commissioned officer(1) but higher than a non-commissioned officer(1).

‚warran'tee *c.n* person who has been given a legal(2) warrant(1).

‚warran'tor *c.n* person who gives a legal(2) warrant(1).

'warranty *c/u.n* (*pl -ies*) (*law*) guarantee(1) that what the warrantor is selling is exactly as described. **under warranty** with a warranty to prove that it is as described: *If you bought that car under warranty and it is not as it should be, you can demand your money back or have things put right.*

warren /'wɒrən/ *c.n* **1** piece of ground in which

there are a lot of rabbits: *rabbit warren.* **2** (*fig*) very crowded place. **3** (*fig*) place with many routes: *The village was a warren of little streets.*

warring, warrior, warship ⇨ war.

wart /wɔːt/ *c.n* small hard rough lump on a person's or animal's skin, or on a tree.

'wart‚hog *c.n* kind of wild African pig with warts on its face.

'warty *adj* (*-ier, -iest*) having warts on her/him/ it.

wartime ⇨ war.

wary /'weərɪ/ *adj* (*-ier, -iest*) cautious; careful before doing anything; not taking any risks. **wary of s.o/s.t** not trusting s.o/s.t until one is sure he/ she/it is safe. **wary of doing s.t** careful not to do s.t until one is sure it is safe.

'warily *adj.* **'wariness** *u.n.*

was (strong form /wɒz/, weak form /wəz/) *1st and 3rd pers sing p.t* of be.

wash /wɒʃ/ *n* **1** *c.n* one example of washing(5,6) or being washed(6). **2** *def.n* clothes etc that are washed(6). **3** *c.n* disturbed water behind a moving ship, boat etc. Compare wake². **4** *c.n* movement of water caused by waves etc: *I love to listen to the wash of the water against the river bank at night.* **come out in the wash** (*fig; informal*) (**a**) finish up satisfactorily after looking as if it would not: *Don't worry; it will all come out in the wash.* (**b**) (of s.t secret or bad) become known: *She tried to hide what had happened but it all came out in the wash when her friend arrived.* **do the wash** wash the clothes etc that are waiting to be washed. **give s.t a wash** wash(6) s.t. **have a wash** wash(5). **in the wash** being, waiting to be, washed(6) with other clothes etc.

▷ *v* **5** *intr.v* clean oneself by using water or some other liquid: *Have you washed yet?* **6** *tr.v* clean (s.o/s.t) with water or some other liquid: *Wash your hands, please. Can I wash these socks with the shirts?* **7** *intr.v* be able to be washed: *Does this suit wash well or do I have to send it to be cleaned?* **8** *tr.v* (of the sea, a river etc) touch (s.t) with its water: *The steps of our garden are washed by the river when it is high.* **9** *tr.v* (of water) carry (s.o/ s.t); move (s.o/s.t): *One of the sailors was washed over the side of the ship by the waves.* **10** *tr.v* (of water) make (s.t): *The sea has washed a big hole in the bottom of the cliff here.*

s.t won't wash with s.o (*fig; informal*) s.t cannot be believed (by s.o): *That story just won't wash (with me).*

wash against s.o/s.t (of a liquid) hit s.o/s.t: *The waves continually washed against my legs as I stood in the lake.*

wash s.t away remove s.t by washing.

wash s.t clean wash all the dirt off s.t.

wash s.t down (**with s.t**) wash s.t all over from top to bottom (with s.t).

wash one's hands of s.o/s.t ⇨ hand(*n*).

wash off (**s.t**) come off (s.t) if it is washed: *Don't worry about that dirt on the car; it will wash off easily.* **wash s.t off** (**s.t**) remove s.t (from s.t) by washing it.

wash over s.o/s.t (**a**) (of a liquid) pass over s.o/ s.t: *When the tide is high it washes over these rocks.* (**b**) (*fig*) pass over s.o without affecting her/him: *When she gets angry I just sit quietly and let it all wash over me without getting upset.*

wash s.t out (**of s.t**) (**with s.t**) remove s.t from inside (s.t) (by washing s.t). **wash s.t out** (**with s.t**) clean the inside of s.t (by using s.t).

wash (**s.t**) **up** wash the plates etc after cooking and/or eating.

-wash liquid used to wash(6) the thing shown in the first part of the word: *mouthwash.* ⇨ *whitewash.*

'washable *adj* able to be washed(6) safely.

'wash,basin *c.n* basin in which one washes(6) one's face and hands.

'wash,bowl *c.n* bowl in which one washes(6) one's hands, face, plates etc.

'wash,cloth *c.n* cloth with which one washes(6) one's face etc.

'wash,day *c/unique n* day (usu the same each week) on which one does one's washing(2).

,washed-'out *adj* **1** having lost (most of) its colour. **2** (*fig*) feeling very tired.

,washed-'up *adj* (often *all* —) (*informal*) finally unsuccessful; having failed finally: *I'm sorry but after that last month of poor sales the business is all washed-up.*

'washer *c.n* **1** person or thing who/that washes(5,6). **2** ring put between two surfaces before they are joined together to prevent a leak or to make the joint tighter or better: *Put a metal washer on each bolt²(2) before you screw the nut on.*

'washer,woman *c.n* (*pl* -,women) woman who washes(6) clothes for other people to earn money.

'wash,house *c.n* (*pl* /'woʃ,hauzəz/) building or room in which clothes are washed(6) or in which people wash(5). Compare bathroom.

'washing *u.n* **1** action of washing (⇨ wash(5,6)): *After washing, she got dressed. Who does the washing in this house?* **2** clothes etc that have to be or have been washed(6): *When it is raining, we have to hang our washing up to dry inside the house.*

'washing ,day *c/unique n* = washday.

'washing ,line *c.n* length of rope, string etc used for wet washing(2) to hang on and dry.

'washing ma,chine *c.n* machine that washes(6) clothes.

'washing ,powder *u.n* powder used for washing (⇨ wash(6)) clothes etc.

,washing-'up *u/def.n* (often *do the* —) washing (⇨ wash(6)) of the dishes etc after cooking and eating.

'wash,out *c.n* (*informal*) thing or person that fails: *Our party was a complete washout because hardly anyone came.*

washroom /'woʃ,rum/ *c.n* (US) lavatory.

'wash,stand *c.n* piece of furniture with a bowl and jug of water on it which are used for washing (⇨ wash(5)), brushing one's teeth etc.

'washy *adj* (*-ier, -iest*) (of liquid food) having too much water in it or not having enough taste. ⇨ *wishy-washy.*

wasn't /'woznt/ = was not. ⇨ be.

wasp /wosp/ *c.n* kind of insect (usu having black and yellow rings round its body) with a sting: *A wasp is different from a bee because a bee makes honey that we eat but a wasp does not.*

'waspish *adj* (*derog*) (of people and the things they say or write) nasty; unpleasant: *I don't like that woman because she is always making waspish remarks about other people.*

'waspishly *adv.* **'waspishness** *u.n.*

,wasp-'waisted *adj* having a very small waist, like a wasp(1).

waste /weɪst/ *attrib.adj* **1** not needed, no longer needed, and therefore able to be thrown away: *We burn all our waste paper.* **2** (of land) on which nothing is grown, and on which there are no buildings: *There is an area of waste land behind our house where the local children play.* **3** used for taking away s.t that is waste(1): *waste pipes.* **lay s.t waste** destroy everything that is on s.t: *In the last war, bombs laid waste whole towns.*

▷ *n* **4** *u.n* useless material left after s.t has been done: *After we have finished a day's work in our factory there is a lot of waste to get rid of.* **5** *c.n* (usu *sing, a* — of *s.t*) act of wasting(7) (s.t); not using s.t fully or in an economical way: *Look at those empty bottles; what a terrible waste; they could be used again and that would save a lot of glass. It is a waste of money to buy food here when the supermarket is much cheaper.* **6** *c.n* area of land not used for anything (often because it cannot be): *As we looked out of the train, huge wastes spread out on both sides as far as our eyes could see.* **go/run to waste** be or become wasted: *Look at all that water going to waste; isn't it sad that it can't be used for something?*

▷ *tr.v* **7** use (s.o/s.t) in a way that is not economical; not make full or efficient use of (s.o/s.t): *If you waste money when you are young, you may be sorry when you are old and need it.* **8** slowly make (s.o/s.t) weak and/or thin: *This is a disease that wastes the body until one dies.* **9** damage (s.t) until it becomes useless: *Twenty years of bad farming have wasted this land.* **Waste not, want not** (*proverb*) If you are careful not to waste anything, you will always have enough of what you need. **waste** (**one's**) **breath** (**doing s.t, on s.o/s.t**) ⇨ breath. **waste s.t on s.o/s.t** waste s.t by giving it to s.o or using it on s.t.

'wastage *sing/u.n* (often — of *s.t*) a/the waste(5) (of *s.t*); wasting(7) (of *s.t*): *The wastage of electricity in this building is terrible because all the lights are left on all the time.*

'wasted *adj* not used in an economical way; not needed or wanted. **s.t is wasted on s.o** it is useless to give s.t to s.o: *Good advice is wasted on Brian because he never listens to it.*

'wasteful *adj* causing waste(5): *It is wasteful to leave good food out in the hot sun to go bad.*

'wastefully *adv.* **'wastefulness** *u.n.*

,waste 'paper *u.n* paper that is not needed (any more).

'waste,paper ,basket/,bin *c.n* basket/bin into which one puts waste paper.

'waste ,pipe *c.n* pipe carrying waste(1) materials away.

'waste ,product *c.n* thing produced while making s.t else but not itself wanted or not thought to be useful for anything: *Ashes are a waste product of the fires in our fireplaces.*

wastrel /'weɪstrəl/ *c.n* (*derog; literary*) person who wastes money etc in a very foolish way.

watch[1] /wotʃ/ *c.n* thing worn on one's wrist or carried in one's pocket etc to show the time. **put a watch back, forward, on** change the time shown by a watch to an earlier, a later, time. **set a watch** change the time shown by a watch.

'watch,band *c.n* = watchstrap.

'watch,maker *c.n* person who makes and/or repairs watches¹ and/or clocks.

'watch,strap *c.n* (also **'watch,band**) piece of leather, cloth, metal chain etc that has a watch¹ fixed to it and is worn round the wrist.

watch² /wɒtʃ/ *c.n* **1** person or people whose job is to guard a place or person. **2** part of the night during which a person or people must guard a place or person. *keep (a) careful/close watch (on s.o/s.t)* guard (s.o/s.t) carefully. *keep watch (for s.o/s.t)* be on guard (waiting for s.o/s.t). *on the watch (for s.o/s.t)* waiting and looking carefully (for s.o/s.t). *on watch* guarding (s.o/s.t). *set a watch (on s.o/s.t)* arrange for one or more people to form a watch²(1) (to guard s.o/s.t).

▷ *v* **3** *tr/intr.v* look (at (s.o/s.t)), for a length of time and not just for a moment. **4** *tr.v* take care of (s.o/s.t); pay attention to (s.o/s.t); make oneself responsible for (s.o/s.t); be careful about (s.o/s.t): *Will you please watch the milk for a minute and see that it doesn't boil over?* **5** *tr/intr.v* look (at s.o/s.t) carefully: *The lion's coming down to the water; now watch and you'll see how it drinks.* **6** *intr.v* (*formal*) remain awake when others are sleeping: *There was always someone watching beside the sick woman's bed.*
watch one's chance/moment to do s.t wait carefully until one gets a chance (to do s.t): *The soldier watched his chance to get into the building while the guard was looking the other way.*
watch the clock ⇨ clock(*n*).
watch s.o/s.t do s.t watch from start to finish while s.o/s.t does s.t. *watch s.o/s.t doing s.t* watch while s.o/s.t does s.t but perhaps not during the whole time that he/she/it does it.
watch how etc (to do s.t) look in order to see how etc (to do s.t): *Look, there's a man fishing; watch how he throws his line. Before you paint that door, you'd better watch what to do.* ⇨ watch²(5).
watch (out) (for s.o/s.t) keep looking carefully (so as to see s.o/s.t when he/she/it appears): *Watch out for bicycles in Oxford, especially when you open your car door.*
watch over s.o/s.t guard or protect s.o/s.t.
watch one's step ⇨ step(*n*).

'watch,dog *c.n* **1** dog that is used to keep people away from s.w and to bark if a stranger tries to come there. **2** (*fig*) person who watches²(4) to see that officials etc do not behave badly: *We have a few watchdogs to see that shops do not sell cigarettes to children.*

'watcher *c.n* person who watches²(3–5) (s.o/s.t).

'watchful *adj* (often — *for s.o/s.t*) watching (⇨ watch²(*v*)) and ready (in case s.o/s.t comes or s.t happens): *When you are in a crowd, you should always be watchful for pickpockets.*

'watchfully *adv.* **'watchfulness** *u.n.*

'watchman *c.n* (*pl* **-men**) man whose job is to guard a place. ⇨ nightwatchman.

'watch,tower *c.n* tower from which people watch²(4) the country around in order to give warning in case of danger or attack.

'watch,word *c.n* short way of expressing the important things a political party, company etc

believes in: *The watchword in our shop is 'The customer is always right'.*

water /'wɔːtə/ *n* **1** *u.n* kind of liquid that, when it is clean and pure, has no colour, taste or smell and that changes to steam when it is made very hot and to ice when it is made very cold, *chem. form* H_2O. **2** *u.n* liquid made up mostly of water(1) (e.g the sea, the liquid in a lake, the waste liquid coming out of human beings and animals). *(at) high/low water* (at) the time when the tide is high/low. *by water* on the sea, a lake or a river: *It is possible to go/travel from Oxford to London by water along the River Thames. be in, get into, deep water* (*fig*) be in, get into, a situation that one does not understand properly; get into a situation that is difficult to get out of again safely. *be in, get into, hot water* ⇨ hot(*adj*). *(flow etc) like water* (of drinks) (be served) very generously: *At Helen's wedding party, the wine flowed like water. hold water* (*fig*) be possible to believe: *No, I'm sorry but that argument doesn't hold water.* *(keep one's head) above water* (*fig*) (keep oneself) out of difficulties, esp ones caused by not having enough money. *(like) a fish out of water* ⇨ fish(*n*). *like water off a duck's back* ⇨ duck¹. *of the first water* of the highest quality. *on the water* in a boat etc floating or moving on water. *open water* area in which there is only water and no islands, rocks etc. *pass water* cause waste liquid to come out of one's bladder(1); urinate. *throw cold water on s.t* (*fig*) try to stop s.t, usu by pointing out the difficulties and/or disadvantages: *Peter wanted to spend Saturday by the sea but his wife threw cold water on the idea because there was a lot of work to be done in the garden. tread water* remain floating in an upright position in the same place in the sea etc by moving one's feet up and down as if walking. *water on the brain, knee* etc liquid on the brain, knee etc caused by disease or damage.

▷ *v* **3** *tr/intr.v* put water on/in (s.t): *We must water (the plants) this evening or everything will die in this heat.* **4** *tr.v* give water to (animals or an area of land): *We water our horses twice a day. The River Nile waters parts of Egypt.* **5** *intr.v* (esp of the eyes and mouth) fill with liquid, which then sometimes comes out: *The blow on my nose made my eyes water. When I saw the beautiful cakes, my mouth watered. make one's mouth water* ⇨ mouth. *water s.t down* (**a**) make s.t weaker by adding water: *This tea is too strong for me — could you please water it down a little?* (**b**) (*fig*) make s.t less strong: *This report is too critical and should be watered down before being given to the newspapers.*

-,water *u.n* **1** liquid made from the thing that is the first part of the word: lavender(3) *water*; rosewater. **2** water used for the thing that is the first part of the word: bathwater.

'water ,bird *c.n* (any) kind of bird that spends a lot of its time near and/or on water.

'water ,biscuit *c.n* biscuit with little or no sugar in it so that it is good to eat with cheese and other things that are not sweet.

'water ,blister *c.n* blister(1) with liquid but no blood or poison in it.

waterborne /'wɔːtəbɔːn/ *adj* (usu *attrib*) carried by water: *waterborne diseases.*

'water ,bottle *c.n* bottle in which one carries water, esp during journeys. ⇒ hot-water bottle.

'water ,buffalo (*pl -es*) *c.n* kind of black animal that comes from Asia and looks like a cow or bull(1), kept for its milk, to pull carts etc.

'water ,butt *c.n* kind of barrel used for collecting the water that comes down from a roof when it rains.

'water ,cannon *c.n* machine used, e.g by the police, for attacking people etc with a strong jet¹(1) of water to stop them causing trouble, esp in the streets.

'water ,closet *c.n* (*usu abbr WC*) lavatory using water to wash away the waste materials that go into it.

'water,colour *n* (US **'water,color**) **1** *c/u.n* (*usu pl*) paint that one mixes with water, not oil, before using it. **2** *c.n* painting done using colours mixed with water, not oil.

'water,course *c.n* **1** bed(3) along which water is flowing or sometimes flows. **2** stream or small river.

'water,cress *u.n* (*also attrib*) plant with rather a hot taste which grows in water and is eaten in salads(1) etc: *watercress soup*.

'water,fall *c.n* (place with) water that falls (almost) straight down from a high place.

'water,fowl *c.n* (*pl -(s)*) kind of bird (esp one that people shoot) that spends most of its time on or near water.

'water,front *c/def.n* (often *on the* —) part of a town etc which is at the edge of the sea, a lake or a river, esp when it is a place to which boats and/or ships come.

'water,hole *c.n* hole in a dry area which contains water and to which animals come to drink.

'water ,ice *c/u.n* ice for eating which does not have any milk or cream in it. Compare ice-cream.

'watering ,can *c.n* can that one fills with water and then uses to water plants in a garden etc.

'watering ,place *c.n* place in a dry area that animals come to to drink. Compare waterhole.

'water ,level *c/def.n* height of the surface of an area of water: *The water level in our well has gone down a lot because of the dry weather.*

'water ,lily *c.n* (*pl -ies*) **1** kind of plant growing in water which has leaves and flowers floating on the surface. **2** flower of this plant.

'water,line *def.n* (often *above/below/on the* —) line where the surface of the water touches s.t (e.g the side of a ship): *The explosion caused a hole below the waterline so the ship quickly began to sink.*

waterlogged /'wɔ:tə,lɒgd/ *adj* **1** (of a boat etc) so full of water that it cannot float properly any more. **2** (of earth etc) so full of water that it cannot take in any more.

'water ,main *c.n* big pipe bringing water to a building etc.

'waterman *c.n* (*pl -men*) man who earns his living on a river, lake etc, usu by rowing people on it in a boat.

'water,mark *c.n* **1** mark in paper which one can only see when one holds the paper up and looks through it with a light behind it. **2** mark showing the level of a river, the sea etc. **high/low watermark** mark showing the highest/lowest level a river, the sea etc reaches.

'water,melon *n* **1** *c.n* large fruit with juicy red flesh inside a thick green skin. **2** *u.n* (also *attrib*) flesh of this fruit.

'water,mill *c.n* mill whose machinery is driven by water.

'water ,pipe *c.n* pipe that carries water in, to or from buildings.

'water ,polo *u.n* game in water in which two teams try to score goals against each other by throwing a ball into each other's goal.

'water,power *u.n* mechanical power produced by water falling or moving.

'water,proof *adj* **1** that water cannot get through.
▷ *c.n* **2** coat that water cannot get through.
▷ *tr.v* **3** make (s.t) waterproof(1).

'water ,rate *c/def.n* amount of money one has to pay regularly for the water supplied to one's home, factory etc.

'waters *pl.n* **1** part of a sea or lake which belongs to a particular country: *The government declared that any foreign ship fishing in its waters would be arrested.* **2** water from a particular river: *The waters of the Nile flow out into the sea over a wide area.* **3** water coming out of the ground in a particular place which people drink because it is supposed to be good for the health. **fish in troubled waters** (*fig*) try to profit from other people's difficulties. **territorial waters** ⇒ territorial.

'water,shed *c.n* **1** imaginary line along high land dividing the waters(2) which run down to two different rivers or seas. **2** (*fig*) point in time at which there is, or ought to be, a big change in s.t, e.g in political systems: *The 1960s were a watershed in African history.*

'water,side *def.n* (often *at/by the* —) place near the side of the sea, a river etc.

'water ,skiing *u.n* sport in which one slides over the water on one or two skis and is pulled by a motorboat.

'water ,softener *n* **1** *u.n* substance put into water to make it soft(9). **2** *c.n* machine into which one puts water softener to make the water in a house etc soft(9).

'water,spout *c.n* column of cloud spinning round and round and down and down very fast until it reaches the surface of the sea and draws up a column of water that also spins round as it rises.

'water sup,ply *c/def.n* (*pl -ies*) **1** act of providing and storing water for a house, town etc. **2** water provided and stored in this way.

'water ,table *c/def.n* level at which one can first find water if one digs down into the ground.

'water,tight *adj* **1** fixed or fitted so tightly that water cannot get through: *Unless a ship has water-tight joints, it leaks.* **2** (*fig*) having no mistakes in it; in which one cannot find any fault: *The men thought they had a watertight plan for robbing the bank. You had better find a watertight excuse for not coming to school yesterday.*

'water ,tower *c.n* tower at the top of which water is stored so that it can run down easily to places which are lower.

'water ,vapour *u.n* water that has changed into vapour(1).

'water,way c.n stretch of water along which ships, boats etc can go from one place to another with land on both sides: *England has a lot of canals which form a system of waterways through large parts of the country.*

'water,wheel c.n wheel turned by falling or running water to produce power. Compare water-power.

'water,wings pl.n things like balloons fixed to the arms of people learning to swim so that they will not sink.

'water,works c.n (pl waterworks) **1** company whose job is to supply water to the public. **2** everything such a company uses to do this job. **3** (pl) (*informal*) system in a person's body that deals with waste liquid: *Anne went to the doctor yesterday because she had waterworks trouble.* **turn on the waterworks** (fig; informal) begin to cry, esp when one is not really in trouble, but only wants to get s.t by crying.

watery /ˈwɔːtərɪ/ adj (-ier, -iest) **1** having too much water in it: *watery soup.* **2** (of eyes, lips etc) wetter than usual: *I always get watery eyes when I go out in very strong sunshine.* **3** pale; showing that there is going to be rain soon: *a watery moon/sun/sky.*

Waterloo /ˌwɔːtəˈluː/ **meet one's Waterloo** ⇨ meet¹.

watt /wɒt/ c.n (*technical*) unit measuring the rate at which electrical energy(2) is used or produced, *symb* W: *1 watt = 1 volt × 1 ampere.*

wattage /ˈwɒtɪdʒ/ sing/u.n power of s.t measured in watts.

wattle¹ /ˈwɒtl/ u.n material for making walls and/or fences which is made by weaving thin sticks together over thicker sticks.

,wattle and 'daub u.n material made from wattle¹ and mud or clay, used for making walls.

wattle² /ˈwɒtl/ c.n red thing growing on the head of a cock or the neck of a turkey(1).

wave /weɪv/ c.n **1** high moving line of water on the sea, a lake etc: *As water rises and falls along a level, it looks as if waves are moving along as well as up and down.* **2** movement up and down in gas, liquid etc by which light, sound, radio signals etc travel. **3** movement of the hand when one waves(8). **4** line of people or things which is one of several following each other: *We could see wave after wave of enemy soldiers advancing across the open ground.* **5** curve like a wave(1) in s.o's hair: *That girl has beautiful natural waves in her hair.* **6** sudden increase in feeling or way of behaving which does not last very long: *As he saw the woman hit her child, a wave of anger swept over him.* **be/ride on the crest of a wave** ⇨ crest. **crime wave** ⇨ crime. **heat wave** ⇨ heat. **permanent waves** ⇨ permanent.

▷ v **7** tr/intr.v (cause (s.t) to) move up and down and/or from side to side without leaving the place in which it is: *If you wave your handkerchief like that, people will think that we are in trouble.* **8** intr.v (often — to s.o) move one's hand as a sign, esp of greeting (to s.o): *Sarah hasn't seen us yet, so let's wave to her.* **9** tr.v make (s.t) into waves(5): *I'm going to the hairdresser now to have my hair waved.* **wave (s.o) goodbye; wave goodbye to s.o.** ⇨ goodbye. **wave s.o aside/away/on** give s.o a signal by waving(8) one's hand to tell her/him to get out of the way, go away or to come/go

forward. **wave s.t aside/away** give s.o a signal by waving(8) one's hand to tell her/him to take s.t out of the way or away. **wave s.t at s.o** use s.t as a signal to s.o by waving(7) it.

'wave,band c.n all the wavelengths within certain limits: *The medium waveband on my radio set is from 187 to 566 metres.*

'wave,length c.n distance from the top of one wave to the top of the next, esp in radio signals. **on a (certain) wavelength** (fig) thinking in a particular way: *I'm sorry but I can't understand your feelings about this at all as we seem to be on completely different wavelengths.*

'waviness u.n fact of being wavy.

'wavy adj (-ier, -iest) having the shape of waves(1); having curves which are at regular distances from each other: *She has wavy hair.*

waver /ˈweɪvə/ intr.v not be steady or certain: *Although I liked his offer, I wavered a little before accepting it because I thought my family might not approve.*

'waverer c.n person who wavers.

waviness, wavy ⇨ wave.

wax¹ /wæks/ u.n **1** yellow/white substance made by bees which they store their honey in. **2** solid material made from fats and/or oils, used for making candles etc; when it is heated it melts. **3** soft yellow material that collects in people's ears.

▷ tr.v **4** cover (s.t) with wax¹(1,2); soak (s.t) in wax¹(1,2).

'wax,works n (pl waxworks) **1** pl.n models of people made of wax. **2** c.n place in which such models are on show.

'wax ,paper u.n (also **'waxed ,paper**) paper with wax¹(2) in it to make it waterproof(1) so that one can wrap greasy things etc in it.

'waxen adj (old use) = waxy.

'waxiness u.n fact or state of being waxy.

'waxy adj (-ier, -iest) **1** looking, behaving or feeling like wax¹(2). **2** (esp of people who are very ill) very pale.

wax² /wæks/ intr.v **1** (*literary*) become: *wax sentimental.* **2** (esp of the moon) become bigger: *The moon waxes for 14 days and then wanes(2) for 14.* Opposite wane(2).

way /weɪ/ adv **1** a long distance: *Our house is way above the village.*

▷ c.n **2** road or path for people, animals or things to go along: *There is a covered way from the car park to the shops so that people can go from one to the other without getting wet when it is raining.* **3** direction: *Which way is the station from here? If you want to go to the park, you must go that way.* **4** method; manner: *What's the way to draw an exact circle? That's the right/wrong way to do it. That is his way of saying sorry. You can open the bottle this way* (using this method). **5** custom; habit: *the friendly ways of people living on the island. It's difficult to learn their ways.* **6** distance (in space or time): *The hotel is a long way from here. Christmas is still quite a long way away/off.* **ask (s.o) the way** ask s.o how one can get to the place one is trying to reach. **be on one's way** start or continue a walk, journey etc: *Well, I must be on my way — it's late.* **bite, eat etc one's way into/through s.t** make a hole or holes in or through s.t by biting etc. **by the way** (used when one wants to change the subject one is talking about): *It will cost you £2, and by the way you still owe me £5 from last week.* **by way of s.t** (a) passing by or through s.t: *I came home by way of Joan's house to see how she is.* (b) in order to serve as an example of s.t: *Fred gave his secretary some beautiful flowers by way of thanks for all she had done for him.* (c) as an example of s.t: *What have you got by way of sweets on your menu?* **clear the way (for s.o/s.t)** move anyone or anything that is preventing s.o/s.t from making progress. (**do it/ s.t, learn (s.t)) the hard way** ⇒ hard(*adj*). **each way** (in betting) in such a way that one wins some money if the horse is first, second or third. **edge one's way forward, through, in(to s.t)** move cautiously forward etc: *He edged his way to the front of the crowd.* **feel one's way** (*fig*) learn how to do something or how something works, e.g in a new job. **find one's/the way (about, (to) s.w)** find how to get to a place one is trying to reach: *Please don't trouble to come to the station with me; I'll find the way.* **get in s.o's way**; **get in the way of s.o/s.t** get into a position that interferes with the movements of s.o/s.t. **get one's own way** = have one's own way. **get out of s.o's way**; **get out of the way of s.o/s.t** get out of a position that interferes with the movements of s.o/s.t. **give way (to s.o/s.t)** (a) allow s.o/s.t else to go first; allow s.o to do what he/she wants, instead of doing what one wants oneself: *At this crossing, cars must give way to ones coming from the right. It is polite to give way to people who are older than oneself.* (b) break because of. too much weight or pressure: *The rope gave way and the man fell down the mountain.* (c) do (s.t) because one cannot control oneself, one's feelings any longer: *She gave way to tears/crying.* (d) be followed by s.t: *Her tears gave way to anger.* **go a long, some, way (towards s.t)** be very useful or helpful (when trying to do or achieve(1) s.t): *The money will go a long way towards paying our debts.* **go (on) one's way** go where one planned to go: *Well, I'll go my way and you go yours.* **go out of one's/the way to do s.t** take trouble to do s.t. **have a way with one** have charm which makes it possible for one to get what one wants from people. **have (it all) one's own way** succeed in doing or having what one wants in spite of other people. **in a bad way** (*informal*) not well or happy: *Poor Chris is in a bad way; she fell and broke her leg.* **in a big etc way** on a large etc scale: *Tony is a hairdresser but only in a small way.* **in a way** not completely; to some extent: *In a way I like Alex, but I wouldn't really trust him.* **in any way (at all)** to any extent: *Can I help you in any way?* (**in) every way** ⇒ every. **in s.o's/the way** in a position that prevents s.o doing what he/she wants to do: *I can't get out of the car park because there's a bus in the way.* **in such a way as to do s.t; in such a way that** . . . in a way that will have as its result that . . .: *You must open the door in such a way as not to wake anyone up.* **in the family way** ⇒ family. **in the way of s.t** as far as s.t is concerned: *What will you have in the way of vegetables in your shop tomorrow?* **keep out of s.o's way** avoid being s.w where s.o prevents one doing s.t freely; avoid being s.w where s.o can see one: *Keep out of her way this morning.* **know one's way about (s.t)** be familiar with a

town, region etc and know where to go, how to find things etc. **lead the way** (a) go first and show the route. (b) go first and show how to do s.t. **lose one's way** (a) stop knowing one's route(1): *I've lost my way and I don't know which road to take.* (b) (*fig*) stop being certain about one's career(1), ambitions etc. **make one's way (in life, in the world** etc) make progress; get on: *Friends can be very helpful when one is trying to make one's way in life.* **make way (for s.o/s.t)** get out of the way, clear the way, so that s.o/s.t can pass freely. **no way** ⇒ no(*det*). **on one's/the way (to s.w)** while one is going s.w. **once in a way** occasionally; not often. **out of harm's way** ⇒ harm(*n*). **out of the way (out-of-the-'way** when *attrib*) (a) far from busy places. (b) (*fig*) not common; not known by many people. **pave the way (for s.t)** make preparations (for s.t): *The invention of the steam engine paved the way for the development of industry in the 19th century.* **pay one's way** pay for everything one gets: *I never borrow money because I believe one ought always to pay one's way.* **put s.o in the way of s.t** (*informal*) give s.o a chance to get s.t: *Because Sarah's uncle is in business, he put her in the way of getting a small shop of her own.* **right of way** ⇒ right[1]. **rub s.o up the wrong way** (*informal*) annoy s.o: *Saying that will only rub him up the wrong way.* **see one's way (clear) to doing s.t** not see anything that would stop one doing s.t: *After his old mother died, he at last saw his way clear to going to live in a warmer place.* **smooth the way for s.t** get rid of any problems connected with achieving(1) s.t: *Agreement about the agenda will smooth the way for useful discussions.* **some way away/off** at some distance away (in place or time). **some way (from s.w)** not near (s.w). **stand in s.o's way** (a) stand in a position where one is preventing s.o moving freely. (b) (*fig*) be in a position where one is preventing s.o doing s.t: *If you want to become a lawyer, your father will not stand in your way.* **stand in the way (of s.o/s.t)** prevent s.o/s.t acting or moving freely: *You should never stand in the way of progress if it is for the good of others.* **the other/opposite way round** with the other/opposite side or face showing. **the right/wrong way round** with the right/wrong side or face in front or on the top. **There's no way (that)** . . . (*informal*) It is impossible (that) . . .: *There's no way (that) your father's going to agree to your going abroad alone at your age.* **to s.o's way of thinking** in s.o's opinion: *To Joe's way of thinking, buses and trains should be free.* **under way** (of a ship etc) moving. **way ahead (of s.o/s.t)** etc a long distance ahead (of s.o/s.t) etc. **way in** entrance(1). **way out** exit(1). **Where there's a will, there's a way** ⇒ will[3]. **work one's way (through) (to s.t)** get s.w by making an effort or efforts: *The boy worked his way to the front of the crowd so that he could see the soldiers.* **worm one's way in(to s.t)**; **worm s.t out (of s.o)** ⇒ worm(*v*).

'**way,bill** *c.n* list of passengers and/or goods carried by the person or persons responsible for taking them from one place to another.

way'lay *tr.v* (*p.t,p.p* waylaid /weɪˈleɪd/) wait for (s.o/s.t) and stop her/him/it when she/he/ it arrives, usu for the purpose of robbery or in order to talk, ask questions etc: *The* journalist waylaid the famous singer at the airport to get an article about her for his newspaper.

,way of 'life c.n (pl ways of life) manner in which one lives: Some people manage to have a very easy way of life.

,way-'out adj (informal) extreme; very far from the normal or average: way-out clothes/ inventions.

ways pl.n manners; customs. **both ways** (in betting) so that one wins some money if the horse comes first in the race but also if it comes second or third. **go our, their** etc **separate ways** go in different directions. **have it both ways** get the advantage of one thing and at the same time of the opposite thing: If you're old enough to dance till three in the morning you're also old enough to get a job; you can't have it both ways. **in some ways** not completely; to some extent: In some ways Peter is still very young but in others he is already a man. **mend one's ways** ⇒ mend(v). **set in one's ways** always behaving in the same ways and being unable and/or unwilling to change. **the parting of the ways** ⇒ parting(n).

,ways and 'means pl.n methods of doing or getting s.t (sometimes not honest): It is very difficult to get tickets for that play but there are ways and means if you know the right people.

'way,side def.n side of a road. **fall by the wayside** (fig) stop doing s.t because one is unsuccessful or unable to continue: Many new students start the year at university but some fall by the wayside before a year has passed.

wayward /'weɪwəd/ adj (derog) behaving in a manner that is not responsible; behaving like a child that does whatever it wants to do.

WC /,dʌblju: 'si:/ c.n abbr water closet.

we (strong form /wi:/, weak form /wɪ/) pron (used as the subject'(4) of verbs or the subjective complement(3) in formal English)) I and you; I and one or more other persons including you; I and one or more persons but not including you: We are still waiting for you. Are we also included? 'Who did that?' 'We did.' It is we who should be helping you! Compare our, ours, ourselves, us.

weak /wi:k/ adj 1 not strong in body; easily broken, bent, defeated or tired: The branches of that tree are too weak to support your weight. John was still feeling very weak after his illness. 2 (derog) not strong in character; not able to resist temptation: He tried to give up smoking several times but was always too weak to do so. 3 not able to be believed; not convincing: He wasn't able to persuade anyone because his arguments were too weak. 4 (of drinks) containing more water than normal: I like my tea weak, please. 5 (often — in s.t) not clever or successful (in s.t): Mary is good at most subjects but she is rather weak in mathematics. 6 (grammar) (of verbs) having '-(e)d' in the p.t and p.p, e.g fix, fixed; stop, stopped; hope, hoped.

'weak ,form c/def.n (technical) form of a word used when it is not stressed(4): the weak form of 'of' is /əv/, and its strong form is /ʌv/.

'weaken tr/intr.v (cause (s.o/s.t) to) become weak(er)(1,2).

,weaker 'sex def.pl.n (derog) women.

weak-kneed /,wi:k 'ni:d/ adj (derog) = weak(2).

'weakling c.n (usu derog) person who is weak(1,2).

'weakly adv.

'weakness n 1 c/u.n state of being weak(1–5). 2 c.n weak part or point; bad quality; fault: Ted has one weakness — he drives too fast. **a weakness for s.t** a great liking for s.t that is not good for one: A lot of children have a weakness for too many chocolates, chips and ice-cream.

,weak 'verb c.n (grammar) ⇒ weak(6).

wealth /welθ/ n 1 u.n state or fact of being rich; riches: Is wealth more important than happiness? 2 sing.n (often a — of s.t) great amount (of s.t): Between them, the members of this company have a wealth of experience. There is an extraordinary wealth of detail in all his paintings.

'wealthy adj (-ier, -iest) rich; having a lot of money (and possessions).

wean /wi:n/ tr.v teach (s.o/s.t) to feed in other ways than from a woman's or a female animal's breast(1): At what age do you usually wean babies in your country? **wean s.o (away) from s.o/s.t** (fig) persuade s.o to stop a habit etc; get s.o used to not doing s.t or not being with s.o: She hoped to wean her husband away from his friends so that he would spend more time at home.

weapon /'wepən/ c.n 1 thing made or used for hurting and/or killing people and/or animals, e.g a sword, gun, knife, stick. 2 thing used for attacking other people or defending oneself, but not causing material damage, e.g tears, a personal secret, sarcasm.

'weaponless adj without any weapons(1,2).

'weaponry u.n collection of weapons(1).

wear /weə/ u.n 1 (often as the second part of a word) things one wears(5): leisure wear; sportswear; underwear. 2 use as clothing: This is the latest fashion for holiday wear. 3 normal damage resulting from being used for some time: His tie was already showing signs of wear after one month. ⇒ wear and tear. 4 ability to resist normal damage resulting from being used for some time: There is still a lot of wear in this old coat, so don't throw it away yet. **evening wear** ⇒ evening. **the worse for wear** ⇒ worse(adj).

▷ v (p.t wore /wɔ:/, p.p worn /wɔ:n/) 5 tr.v be dressed in (s.t); have (s.t) on one's body as clothing or as a sign or decoration: What shall I wear to the party? Was she wearing a lot of jewellery when you saw her? 6 tr.v (of expressions on one's face) have (s.t): She always wore a sweet smile. 7 tr.v (informal) be willing to agree to (s.t): She tried to persuade her father to buy her a car but he wouldn't wear it.

wear away/off (a) disappear as a result of being rubbed or used a lot: The paint on this metal is wearing away. **(b)** (fig) disappear slowly as time goes on: Your headache will wear off soon. **wear s.t away** destroy s.t by rubbing or using it a lot. **wear badly/well** show many/few signs of damage as a result of normal use: These trousers have worn well.

wear s.o down tire s.o, usu so that he/she agrees to do s.t he/she did not want to do before: The children wore their mother down by complaining again and again until she finally agreed to buy them sweets. **wear (s.t) down** (cause (s.t) to) become thinner by rubbing at it or using it a lot: The tyres of a car slowly wear *down until they become dangerous to drive on.*

wear a hole etc **in**, **through**, s.t make a hole etc in or through s.t by rubbing: *I wore holes in my shoes by walking so much. The river has worn a* channel(1) *through the rocks over the centuries.*

wear on (of time) continue slowly: *The days wore on and at last the holidays were there.*

wear s.o out tire s.o completely. **wear (s.t) out** (cause (s.t) to) become useless as a result of rubbing or using it: *The man wore out several pairs of shoes during his 2000 kilometre walk.* ⇨ hard-wearing.

wear thin (a) become thin as a result of being rubbed or used. **(b)** (*fig*) become less: *My patience is wearing thin after having had to listen to that noise for so long.*

wear (s.t) through (cause s.t to) be rubbed or used until there are one or more holes in it.

'wearable *adj* able to be worn (⇨ wear(5)): *Is that* jumper *still wearable?*

,wear and 'tear *u.n* ordinary damage caused by normal use: *You can insure your clothes against fire and* theft(2) *but not against normal wear and tear.*

'wearing *adj* very tiring: *Old people often find living with small children wearing.* ⇨ wearisome.

worn /wɔːn/ *adj* **1** showing signs of having been worn(5) or used a lot: *a worn coat; an old worn bicycle.* **2** looking tired: *a worn face.* **worn to a frazzle** ⇨ frazzle.

,worn 'out *adj* **1** so worn(1), used so often, that it has become useless: *worn out shoes; a typewriter that is worn out.* **2** very tired: *You look worn out.* ⇨ well-worn (⇨ well¹).

wearily, weariness, wearisome ⇨ weary.

wearing ⇨ wear.

weary /'wɪərɪ/ *adj* (-ier, -iest) **1** very tired. (**grow**) **weary of s.o/s.t** (become) very tired of s.o/s.t: *When the old man grows weary of all the talk, he goes for a walk.*

▷ *tr/intr.v* (-ies, -ied) **2** (often — of s.o/s.t) (cause (s.o) to) become very tired or weary(1) (of s.o/s.t). **weary s.o with s.t** cause s.o to become weary(1) by telling her/him of s.t: *I won't weary you with all the details.*

'wearily *adv.* **'weariness** *u.n.*

wearisome /'wɪərɪsəm/ *adj* very tiring; making one very weary(1): *wearisome problems.*

'wearisomely *adv.*

weasel /'wiːzl/ *c.n* **1** kind of small long thin animal that has fur and kills small animals, chickens etc for its food.

▷ *intr.v* **2 weasel out of s.t** (*informal; derog*) get out of doing s.t one ought to do: *Don't try to weasel out of doing the shopping for me today or I'll be angry.*

weather /'weðə/ u/def.n **1** conditions of heat or cold, dryness or rain, sunshine or cloud etc in a place at a certain time or over a limited length of time. Compare climate. **make heavy weather of s.t** ⇨ heavy(*adj*). **under the weather** (*fig; informal*) not feeling well or happy.

▷ *v* **2** *tr/intr.v* (cause (s.t) to) become affected by rain, wind, heat, cold etc: *Before using the wood to build our hut, we weathered it for a year so that it would not change its shape later on. Even the hardest rocks weather over the centuries.* **3** *tr.v* manage to get through (s.t) safely: *Our small*

boat weathered the storm surprisingly well. Their marriage passed through difficult times but once they had weathered these, they lived many happy years together.

'weather-,beaten *adj* **1** showing signs of having been affected by the weather, e.g by being damaged or made rough. **2** (of people's skin, esp the skin of their faces) showing signs (e.g being brown and/or rough) of having often been out in various kinds of weather.

'weather ,bureau *c.n* (*pl* -x /-z/) office that finds out what the weather is (going to be) and passes this information on to people who are interested.

'weather,cock *c.n* device (often shaped like a cock(1)) turned by the wind in such a way that it points to the direction from which the wind is coming. Compare weather vane.

'weather ,eye *c.n* **keep a/one's weather eye open (for s.t)** (*fig*) always be ready (for s.t that may happen, usu s.t nasty).

'weather ,fore,cast *c.n* statement, often in a newspaper, or on the radio or television, of what weather is expected.

'weather ,fore,caster *c.n* person who prepares and/or gives weather forecasts.

'weather,man *c.n* (*pl* -men) man who studies the weather and or gives the weather forecasts.

'weather,proof *adj* **1** that does not allow rain, wind etc to get through: *weatherproof material for a tent.*

▷ *tr.v* **2** make (s.t) weatherproof(1): *I've weatherproofed my walking boots.*

'weathers *pl.n* **in all weathers** whatever the weather may be: *Modern planes are built to fly in all weathers.*

'weather ,station *c.n* place in which people collect information about the weather.

'weather ,vane *c.n* thing that turns to show which direction the wind is coming from. Compare weathercock.

weave /wiːv/ *c.n* **1** way in which s.t is woven (⇨ weave(2)): *This shirt is quite cool because it has a loose weave.*

▷ *v* (*p.t* wove /wəʊv/, *p.p* woven /'wəʊvn/) **2** *tr/intr.v* make (s.t) by putting threads etc over and under other ones in a regular way: *These women are weaving mats out of grass.* **3** *tr.v* (*fig*) make (a story, plan etc): *That child has a wonderful imagination and weaves beautiful stories out of her own head for her little brother.* **weave in and out (of s.t)** move forward, going first to one side and then to the other (to get through s.t): *It is dangerous when people on* motorbikes *weave in and out of the traffic.* **weave one's way through s.t** go through s.t by turning first one way and then the other: *As she was in a hurry, she wove her way quickly through the crowd.* **weave s.t together** make s.t by weaving (⇨ weave(2)) parts into each other.

'weaver *c.n* **1** person who weaves(2). **2** kind of bird that weaves(2) its nest out of grass etc.

'weaver-,bird *c.n* = weaver(2).

'weaving *adj* **get weaving** (*informal*) (hurry up and) start doing s.t: *If you want to arrive early, you'd better get weaving.*

'woven *adj* that has been woven (⇨ weave(2)): *a woven* scarf.

web /web/ *c.n* **1** network of very fine sticky

threads made by a spider to catch flies etc.
2 skin between the toes of some birds, e.g
ducks, that helps them to swim in the water.
3 (usu — *of s.t*) (*fig*) network (of s.t); carefully
arranged collection (of s.t): *a web of lies*; *a* spy(1)
web.

,web 'off,set *u.n* (*technical*) way of printing
using a long roll of paper instead of separate
sheets.

webbed /webd/ *adj* having webs(2): *webbed
feet*.

,web-'footed *adj* having webs(2) between the
toes.

wed /wed/ *tr/intr.v* (*-dd-*) (*old use*) marry.

'wedded *adj* (*old use*) married. (one's) (*lawful*) *wedded husband/wife* (one's) husband/
wife whom the law accepts as married to one.
wedded to s.t (*fig*) extremely interested in s.t;
not willing to give s.t up: *Mary is wedded to the
idea of going to poor countries to help the children
there*.

'wedding *c.n* ceremony of marriage, often with
a party as well as a church service. *diamond*,
golden, *silver wedding* ⇨ diamond, golden,
silver.

'wedding ,band *c.n* = wedding ring.

'wedding ,breakfast/re,ception *c.n* party or
meal following a wedding ceremony.

'wedding ,ring *c.n* ring that the bridegroom puts
on the finger of the bride, or the bride on the finger
of the bridegroom, during a wedding ceremony.

'wedlock *u.n* (*formal*) state of being a married
man/woman. *born out of wedlock* born to a
woman who is not married.

Wed *written abbr* Wednesday.

we'd (strong form /wiːd/, weak form /wɪd/) **1** =
we had. ⇨ have. **2** = we would. ⇨ will², would.

wedded, wedding ⇨ wed.

wedge /wedʒ/ *c.n* **1** piece of wood, metal etc,
thin at one end and thick at the other, used
either to split s.t (e.g a log of wood), or to fill a
space between two things (e.g the space between
the bottom of a door and the floor) to stop s.t
moving. *the thin end of the wedge* (*fig*) the thing
that does not seem important but prepares the
way for other bigger, more important or worse
things: *When her son asked if he could learn to
drive, she did not realize this was the thin end of
the wedge and that soon her son would use her
car every evening*.

▷ *tr/intr.v* **2** (cause (s.o/s.t) to) be unable to move
because of a wedge(1). *wedge s.o/s.t in*(*to s.t*)
put s.o into a position where he/she cannot
move, or it cannot be moved. *wedge s.t open/
shut* keep s.t open/shut by using a wedge(1) to
stop it moving.

,wedge 'heels *pl.n* heels on shoes which look
like wedges(1).

wedlock ⇨ wed.

Wednesday /'wenzdɪ/ *c/unique n* (also *attrib*)
(*written abbr* Wed) third working day of the
week in Christian(1) (and some other) countries;
day after Tuesday and before Thursday. *last
Wednesday* the last Wednesday before today.
next Wednesday the first Wednesday after
today. *on a Wednesday* on a day of one
week that was/is a Wednesday. *on Wednesday*
on the nearest Wednesday before/after today
or on the Wednesday of the week being referred

to: *We met on Wednesday. on Wednesdays* every
Wednesday: *We play football on Wednesdays*.
Wednesday after next the second Wednesday after today. *Wednesday before last* the
Wednesday before last Wednesday. *Wednesday
morning*, *afternoon* etc the morning, afternoon
etc of last, next, every Wednesday.

wee¹ /wiː/ *adj* little; very small: *a wee child. a wee
bit* (*cold* etc) a little (cold etc).

wee² /wiː/ *c.n* (also 'wee-,wee) **1** (usu *do/have
a* —) (used by children) waste liquid out of the
body; example of urinating. *do/have a wee*(-*wee*)
= wee².

▷ *intr.v* (also 'wee-,wee) **2** pass waste liquid out of
the body; urinate.

weed /wiːd/ *n* **1** *c.n* wild plant that is not wanted
in a garden, field etc: *We went round the garden
pulling out all the weeds and now it looks nice
and tidy*. **2** *c.n* (*derog*; *informal*) person who
(looks weak and) has a weak character. **3** *u/
def.n* (*informal*) tobacco; cigarettes, esp ones
with marijuana in them.

▷ *tr/intr.v* **4** remove weeds(1) (from s.t). *weed s.o/
s.t out* (*from/of s.t*) (*fig*) remove s.o/s.t (from
s.t) in order that he/she/it should no longer form
part of it: *As all the officers in our company have
to learn to fly, we are weeding out all those with
poor eyesight*.

'weediness *u.n* **1** state of being weedy(1).
2 (*derog*; *informal*) fact of looking or behaving
like a weed(2).

'weedy *adj* (*-ier*, *-iest*) *adj* **1** having (too many)
weeds(1) in it. **2** (*derog*; *informal*) having a weak
body or a weak character: *She wants a big strong
boyfriend, not a weedy one like that fellow*.

week /wiːk/ *c.n* **1** seven days, one following
the other, esp when the first is Sunday and
the last Saturday: *This job has taken six
weeks. He's only five weeks old. We meet
twice a week*. **2** five days from Monday
to Friday: *I've had a lot of work to do
all week*. ⇨ weekday. *a week last/next/this
Friday* etc; *last/next/this Friday* etc *week*
exactly seven days after last/next/this Friday
etc. *on Friday* etc *week* on the Friday etc
after the next one: *My birthday is on Sunday
week. a week today*, *tomorrow*, *Monday* etc;
today, *tomorrow*, *Monday* etc *week* seven
days after today, tomorrow, next Monday etc.
week in, *week out* during every week without
any rest etc. *a/the working week* the days/
hours of the week on which one works.

'week,day *c.n* **1** Monday, Tuesday, Wednesday, Thursday or Friday (but not Saturday or
Sunday). **2** any day of the week except Sunday.
on a weekday; *on weekdays* during any day
except Sunday (and Saturday): *The bus only
runs on weekdays. We have lunch at the office
on a weekday*.

,week'end *c/def.n* **1** period of Saturday, Sunday
and sometimes also Friday evening, after one has
finished work. *at the weekend* during Saturday,
Sunday and sometimes also Friday evening, after
one has finished work: *I work in my garden at the
weekend*.

▷ *intr.v* **2** pass the weekend(1) (s.w, doing s.t etc):
They always weekend on their boat.

,week'ender *c.n* person who spends one or
more weekends in a certain place: *We get*

a lot of weekenders here during the summer because they come to swim and sail.

'weekly *adj* **1** happening, appearing etc once in every week: *a weekly magazine.*

▷ *c.n* (*pl* -**ies**) **2** magazine, newspaper etc that appears once in every week.

weeny /'wiːnɪ/ *adj* (-**ier**, -**iest**) (*informal*) very small. Compare teeny.

weep /wiːp/ *c.n* **1** example of weeping (⇨ weep(2)). **have a (good) weep** weep(2) (a lot).

▷ *tr/intr.v* (*p.t,p.p* wept /wept/) **2** allow (tears) to come out of one's eyes, usu because one is very sad. **3** give out (liquid) slowly and in small quantities: *Because of the dirt in it, the wound wept for some time.* **weep for/over s.o/s.t** weep(2) because of s.o/s.t.

'weeping *adj* (of a tree) whose branches hang down.

,weeping 'willow *c.n* kind of willow(1) whose branches hang down.

'weepy *adj* (-**ier**, -**iest**) **1** who weeps(2) easily or often. **2** making one want to weep(2): *a weepy film.* **3** that weeps(3): *The cat has a weepy eye.*

wee-wee ⇨ wee².

w.e.f. *written abbr* with effect from.

weft /weft/ *c/def.n* threads of a piece of material running from one side of it to the other and woven in among the threads running along from one end of the cloth to the other. Compare warp(1).

weigh /weɪ/ *v* **1** *tr.v* (try to) find the weight(1) of (s.o/s.t), usu by putting it on a weighing machine. **2** *tr.v* have (a certain weight(1)): *This parcel weighs 534 grams.* ⇨ overweight, underweight. **3** *tr.v* think about (s.t) carefully; compare (s.t): *Thank you for all your suggestions; after I have weighed them all carefully, I shall decide what to do.* **4** *intr.v* (*formal*) be regarded as being important when deciding: *Such excuses won't weigh at all* (or *will weigh against you*, or *will weigh in your favour*).

weigh s.t against s.t compare s.t to s.t: *If you weigh the cost of going against the losses you will suffer if you don't go, you will certainly decide to go.*

weigh s.o/s.t down (with s.t) load s.o/s.t heavily (with s.t): *The donkey was so weighed down that it could not move. The woman was weighed down with worries about her children.*

weigh in (*informal*) enter a fight, argument etc.

weigh in (at 120 kilos etc) find out one's weight before a boxing match etc (and find that it is 120 kilos etc).

weigh on s.o/s.t worry s.o/s.t; make s.o feel ashamed, guilty etc.

weigh on s.o's mind ⇨ mind¹.

weigh s.t out measure amounts of s.t by weighing it: *The shop assistant weighed(1) out 250 grams of sweets.*

weigh s.o/s.t up examine s.o/s.t carefully in one's mind; compare s.o/s.t carefully: *The boss is very good at weighing people up to decide what jobs to give each of them. After weighing up the different possibilities, she decided to buy the expensive coat because it would last longer.*

weigh with s.o be important for s.o: *What weighs with our boss is not only how clever a person is, but how pleasant he or she is.*

weight /weɪt/ *n* **1** force with which a person,

animal, thing is pulled downwards by gravity²; amount s.o/s.t weighs(2): *The weight of this parcel is 550 grams.* ⇨ overweight, underweight. **2** *u.n* system of measuring how much things or people weigh(2): Metric *weight is taking the place of older systems in most countries.* ⇨ avoirdupois, metric, troy. **3** *c.n* piece of metal etc whose weight(1) is known and which is used for weighing(1) other things and sometimes people. **4** *c.n* heavy thing whose weight(1) is known and which one lifts, either to strengthen one's body or in a competition to see who can lift the heaviest amount. **5** *c.n* heavy thing used to hold s.t (e.g sheets of paper) down. **6** *c.n* load that has to be held up or carried: *I am afraid the floor won't support the weight of any more machinery.* **7** *u.n* importance. **a weight off s.o's mind; a weight on s.o's mind** ⇨ mind(*n*). **carry weight (with s.o)** be important (to s.o). **gain weight** become heavier. Opposite lose weight. **give weight to s.t (a)** consider s.t to be important. **(b)** cause s.t to seem (more) important. **lose weight** become lighter in weight. Opposite gain weight, put on weight. **pull one's weight** do a fair share of the work: *Anyone who does not pull his weight in our office is soon disliked by the others.* **put on weight** become heavier. Opposite lose weight. **take the weight of s.t (a)** be/become the person or thing supporting the weight of s.t: *This wall takes the weight of the whole of the next floor.* **(b)** (*fig*) be/become responsible for s.t: *When her husband died, she had to take the full weight of the work on herself.* **take the weight off one's feet** (*informal*) sit down to rest (one's feet or legs). **throw one's weight about/around** (*informal*) behave as if one was more important than one really is, usu by ordering other people to do things one really has no right to order them to do; behave in an arrogant way.

▷ *tr.v* **8** make (s.t) heavy by putting a weight(3–5) on it: *The bottom of the net is weighted with lead and the top is held up by floats(2).* **9** *tr.v* make (s.t) unequal. **weight s.o/s.t down (with s.t)** load s.o/s.t heavily with s.t: *The ship was so weighted down with coal that it sank in the first storm.* **weight s.t against, in favour of, s.o/s.t** ⇨ weight(9). **worth one's weight in gold** ⇨ gold(*n*).

'weighted *adj* made unequal. ⇨ weight(9).

'weightily *adv* in a weighty way.

'weightiness *u.n* condition or fact of being weighty.

'weighting *c/u.n* (also *attrib*) extra pay etc given to s.o so that he/she can be at the same level as other people who are in the same job etc but live and/or work in less expensive places: *Most things in London are more expensive than they are in the rest of the country, so many workers get London weighting* (or *a London weighting allowance*) *if they work there.*

'weightless *adj* not weighing(2) anything, esp because one/it is flying in space, where there is no gravity².

'weightlessness *u.n.*

'weight,lifter *c.n* person who takes part in the sport of weightlifting.

'weight,lifting *u.n* sport in which people compete to see who can lift the heaviest weight.

'weighty *adj* (-**ier**, -**iest**) *adj* **1** heavy. **2** (*fig*) important: *weighty arguments against a strike.*

weir /wɪə/ *c.n* kind of wall built across a river or stream, used to stop the water running further down or to control the amount of water that goes further down.

weird /wɪəd/ *adj* strange; not normal: *weird clothes*; *weird behaviour*.
'weirdly *adv.* **'weirdness** *u.n.*
weirdo /'wɪədəʊ/ *c.n* (*pl* -s/-dəʊz/) (*informal*) person who acts, dresses etc in ways that are not normal or expected.

welch /welʃ/ *intr.v* (also **welsh**) (often — *on s.t*) **1** avoid paying what one owes. **2** not do what one has promised.

welcome /'welkəm/ *adj* **1** wanted; met or accepted with pleasure. **bid s.o welcome** say to s.o that he/she is welcome(1). **make s.o welcome** treat s.o in a way that shows that he/she is welcome(1); welcome(4) s.o. **You're welcome (a)** I am pleased you have been able to come. **(b)** (as an answer to 'thank you') it was a pleasure to do, give etc it. **you're welcome to (do) s.t, to s.o** I am happy (and relieved) for you to do, have, take etc s.o/s.t: *You're welcome to John; I don't want to do anything with him!*
▷ *interj* **2** you are welcome(1). **Welcome to s.w** I am pleased that you are here: *Welcome to London! Welcome to our little home!*
▷ *c.n* **3** act of greeting s.o/s.t in a glad and/or kind way. **give a (warm etc) welcome to s.o/s.t** welcome(4) s.o/s.t (warmly etc).
▷ *tr.v* **4** greet (s.o/s.t) with pleasure; tell/show (s.o) that one is glad to see her/him. **Welcome back/home** I am pleased that you have come back/home. **welcome s.o in** ask s.o to come inside in a manner that shows that one is glad he/she has come. **welcome s.o with open arms** ⇔ arm¹.

weld /weld/ *c.n* **1** join in metal etc made by heating and then pressing, or by heating until it melts.
▷ *tr/intr.v* **2** (often — *s.t together*) (cause (metal etc) to) join together by making a weld(1).
'welder *c.n* person who welds(2) (s.t).

welfare /'welfeə/ *u.n* **1** satisfactory state of health, comfort, happiness etc. **2** (also *attrib*) help and advice given by the government or by officials of a company etc to help people's welfare(1): *welfare workers*. **on welfare** receiving help (e.g money) from the government because one is poor.
wel,fare 'state *c/def.n* country that looks after people's welfare(1) without their having to pay anything except their taxes, or very little money; the system for doing this.

well¹ /wel/ *adj* (*comp* **better**, *superl* **best**) **1** not ill; in good health: *He's almost well again.* Opposite **unwell**. **all is well (with s.o/s.t)** everything is all right (with s.o/s.t); nothing is wrong (with s.o/s.t). **it is all very well (for s.o) (to do s.t), but** . . . (way of not accepting a suggestion that may seem a good one but is really not): *It's all very well for you to say that the injection won't hurt but I know it will.* **it would be (just) as well (to do s.t)** it would be a good idea (to do s.t); the best thing to do would be to do s.t. **may/might just as well do s.t**; **just as well** ⇔ just².
▷ *adv* (*comp* **better**, *superl* **best**) **2** in a good, the right, way or manner; in a way that is accepted as being good. **3** thoroughly; completely; carefully; enough for it to be accepted: *Wash yourself well*

before you put your clothes on again. **as well** also; too: *I'd like some meat and some potatoes as well.* **as well as s.o/s.t** in addition to s.o/s.t: *I want to see David as well as Mary.* **s.o can't/couldn't very well do s.t** it would not be, was not, right or suitable for s.o to do s.t: *I know you're tired but I can't very well tell our guests to go, can I?* **come off well** be successful or fortunate in the end. **do well by s.o** treat s.o generously. **do well out of s.o/s.t** make a profit because of s.o/s.t; gain from s.o/s.t. **do well to do s.t** be wise if one does s.t: *You would do well to buy some shares in that company; it is going to be very successful.* **doing well** making good progress, esp after an illness or accident. **s.o may/might (just) as well (do s.t)** ⇔ may. **mean well** ⇔ mean³. **pretty well** ⇔ pretty. **speak well of s.o/s.t** say nice things about s.o/s.t: *He always speaks well of his family.* **well and truly** completely: *She was well and truly beaten.* **well away (a)** making good progress. **(b)** (*informal*) drunk(1). **Well done!** (a way of congratulating s.o who has been successful in s.t): *You won the race, did you? Well done!* Compare well-done. **well out of s.t** (*informal*) lucky to have escaped (from) s.t: *John said it was the dullest party he had ever been to so we were well out of it.* **well outside** etc **s.t** quite a long way outside etc s.t: *You can get the jar down from the shelf; it's well within your reach. It was a slow race; the winning time was well outside four minutes.* **well up in s.t** (*informal*) knowing a lot about s.t: *Whenever I want to know something about animals, I ask Betty because she's well up in the subject.* **wish s.o well** ⇔ wish(v). **You etc may well ask** I don't know the answer either (and have been trying to find it): *'Where's Doris?' 'You may well ask! I've been waiting for her since 10 o'clock.'*
▷ *interj* **4** (word used when one wants time to think before speaking): *'Would you like to come to the cinema?' 'Well, I'll have to ask my mother first.'*
,well-ad'vised *pred.adj* wise; sensible: *You would be well-advised not to go into the boss's office just now as she is in a bad temper.*
,well-'balanced *adj* **1** (*formal*) (of people) sensible; reasonable; not doing anything at all extreme. **2** (of food or a meal) having in it a healthy choice of the things the body needs and in the right amounts.
,well-be'haved *adj* behaving in a good or correct way: *well-behaved children.*
,well-'being *u.n* (of bodily feelings) comfort; health.
,well-'bred *adj* behaving in a polite way, usu because one has been taught to do this while still a child.
,well-'chosen *adj* chosen in such a way as to be quite suitable for the purpose: *At the end of the dinner my uncle thanked our hostess in a few well-chosen words.*
,well-con'nected *adj* having important or powerful relatives and/or friends.
,well-dis'posed *pred.adj* (usu — *towards s.o/s.t*) having good intentions or kind feelings (for s.o/s.t): *The teacher was well-disposed towards students who worked hard.*
,well-'done *adj* having been cooked for longer than the average time: *I like my meat well-done.* Opposite **underdone**. Compare well done (⇔ well(*adv*)). ⇔ overdone, rare(3).

,well-'earned *adj* that has been fully earned or deserved: *After working hard at his mathematics for a whole year, Henry is having a well-earned rest.*

,well-e'quipped *adj* having everything that is necessary for a particular purpose: *a well-equipped hospital.*

,well-e'stablished *adj* 1 having been in existence long enough to be really successful: *Jane has a well-established business selling fruit and vegetables.* 2 that can be proved: *It is a well-established fact that smoking is bad for one's health.*

,well-'founded *adj* based on facts; that can be proved: *It was soon discovered that the man's accusations were well-founded and that the children had really taken his bicycle.*

,well-'groomed *adj* (*formal*) looking very neat, tidy and clean, usu because s.o has taken care: *A well-groomed appearance is helpful when one is trying to get a job in a big office.*

,well-'grounded *adj* = well-founded. ⇒ ground³(10).

,well-'heeled *adj* ⇒ -heeled(2) (⇒ heel).

,well-in'formed *adj* (*formal*) having a lot of information stored in one's mind; able to get a lot of information when one needs it.

,well-in'tentioned *adj* having or showing good intentions even if they are not successful: *My advice was well-intentioned but it proved to be useless because he had already sold his house.*

,well 'known *adj* (**'well-,known** when *attrib*) known by a lot of people.

,well-'lined *adj* (*fig*; *informal*) having plenty of money, food etc in it: *well-lined pockets.* ⇒ lined².

,well-'mannered *adj* ⇒ -mannered.

,well-'meaning *adj* (also **,well-'meant**) = well-intentioned. ⇒ meaning(1) (⇒ mean³).

,well-'nigh *adv* (*formal*) almost or nearly: *It's well-nigh impossible to swim that far.*

,well-'off *adj* 1 rich. 2 lucky; fortunate. **s.o does not know when he/she is well-off** s.o thinks he/she is poor or unfortunate when he/she is really the opposite.

,well-'oiled *adj* (*informal*) drunk(1).

,well-'planned *adj* that s.o has planned carefully so that it works well.

,well-pre'served *adj* (*informal*) (of a person) who does not look or seem as old as he/she is.

,well-pro'portioned *adj* having a physical(1) shape, relationship of parts in a group or set etc that is balanced(1), pleasing etc.

,well-'read *adj* (*formal*) knowing a lot because one has done a lot of reading in one's life.

,well-'spoken *adj* speaking in a pleasing way that shows good education. ⇒ -spoken (⇒ speak).

well-thought-of /,wel 'θɔːt ,ɒf/ *adj* (often *pred*) whom/that people like and/or respect.

,well-,thought-'out *adj* (often *pred*) having been carefully arranged after one has thought about it a lot.

,well-'timed *adj* coming at a very suitable time: *His appearance was well-timed because it was his turn to speak.* ⇒ -timed.

,well-to-'do *adj* comfortably rich; having enough money to live comfortably.

,well-'trained *adj* who/that has been trained well.

,well-'tried *adj* known to work well because it has often been done, used, before.

,well-'turned *attrib.adj* ⇒ -turned.

'well-,wisher *c.n* person who gives s.o good wishes.

,well-'worn *adj* 1 showing signs that it has been used a lot: *He came out to meet us wearing a well-worn coat and trousers.* 2 (of a way of saying s.t) used so often that it no longer has much meaning: *Our meeting with him was boring because we did nothing but exchange well-worn remarks about the weather.*

well² /wel/ *n* 1 *c.n* place where water, oil etc comes up from under the ground. 2 *c.n* hole made in the ground by people to reach water, oil etc. 3 *c.n* upright space in a building that is taller than one floor and often has stairs and/or a lift in it. **stair well** ⇒ stair.

▷ *intr.v* 4 (of a liquid) come out strongly. **well out (of s.t)** come up out (of s.t): *They dug for hours and then suddenly oil welled out (of the hole).* **well over** rise so high that it spills over the edge: *They filled their glasses with wine until it welled over.* **well up (from s.t)** rise (from/in s.t); rise out of s.t: *As she realized what the news meant, tears welled up in her eyes.*

we'll /wiːl/ 1 = we shall. ⇒ shall. 2 = we will. ⇒ will¹.

wellies /'weliz/ *pl.n* (*informal*) wellington boots.

wellington /'welɪŋtən/ *c.n* (also **,wellington 'boot**) (*informal pl* **wellies**) high boot, usu made of rubber so that it keeps water out.

welsh /welʃ/ *intr.v* = welch.

Welsh /welʃ/ *adj* 1 belonging to, coming from, Wales.

▷ *def.pl.n* 2 Welsh(1) people as a group.

,Welsh 'rabbit /,welʃ 'ræbɪt/ (also **,Welsh 'rarebit** /,welʃ 'reəbɪt/) *c/u.n* kind of food made by putting cheese on bread and then melting it under a grill.

welter /'weltə/ *c.n* (often *a* — *of s.t*) confused mixture (of s.t): *Because so many parties shared in the government of the country, there was a welter of different policies¹ that were often the opposite of each other.*

welterweight /'weltə,weɪt/ *c.n* (also *attrib*) boxer weighing between about 61 and 67 kilograms.

wend /wend/ *tr.v* **wend one's way** (*formal*; *literary*) leave; go, usu slowly: *Well, it's midnight, so I'd better be wending my way (home).*

went /went/ *p.t* of go.

wept /wept/ *p.t* of weep.

were (strong form /wɜː/, weak form /wə/) 1 *2nd pers sing p.t* of be. 2 *pl p.t* of be.

we're /wɪə/ = we are. ⇒ be.

weren't /wɜːnt/ = were not. ⇒ be.

west /west/ *adj* 1 in or coming from the direction in which the sun goes down, *abbr* W: *a west wind.*

▷ *adv* 2 towards a west(1) direction: *We travelled west to get to the river.* **out west** (*informal*) in/ towards a west(1) direction. Opposite out east (⇒ east(*adv*)).

▷ *n* (often with capital **W**) 3 *def/unique n* direction that is west(1). 4 *def.n* part of a country or of the world that is further west(1) than the rest of it: *The west of America was populated much later than the east.* **go west** (**a**) go/travel towards the west(3). (**b**) (*slang*) be damaged or destroyed: *Many houses went west in the fire.* **in the west** (**a**) in the direction that is west(1): *The sun sets in the west.* (**b**) in that part of the country or the world which is further west(1) than the rest: *People living in the west sometimes find life in eastern countries difficult to imagine.* **in the west of s.t** in the western(1) part of s.t. (**to the**) **west of s.t** further west(1) than s.t.

'**west,bound** *adj* going towards the west(3): *westbound traffic.*

,**West ,Country** *def.n* southwest England.

,**West 'End** *def.n* western part of London with the most expensive shops, hotels etc.

westerly /'westəlɪ/ *adj* from, in, towards the west(3): *a westerly wind. We travelled in a westerly direction.*

western /'westən/ *adj* (often with capital **W**) **1** of, belonging to, the west(3) of a place: *Western Europe.*

▷ *c.n* **2** exciting film or book about adventures, usu of cowboys, in the western(1) part of the US.

'**Westerner** *c.n* person who lives in or comes from the western(1) part of a place or country.

,**Western 'Hemi,sphere** *def.n* ⇒ hemisphere.

westernization, -isation /,westənaɪ'zeɪʃən/ *u.n* action or state of becoming, making s.o/s.t, (more) like the West(4).

'**wester,nize, -ise** *tr.v* cause (s.o/s.t) to become (more) like the West(4) by changing ways of doing things, beliefs etc.

'**western,most** *adj* that is furthest to the west(3).

'**west,facing** *adj* that looks towards, faces, the west(3): *a westfacing window.*

westward /'westwəd/ *adj* towards the west(3).

westwards /'westwədz/ *adv* (US '**westward**) towards the west(3).

wet /wet/ *adj* (-*tt*-) **1** covered or filled with liquid. Opposite dry(1). ⇒ soaked. **2** during which rain falls, either continuously or for part of the time: *We had a wet ten minutes' walk to get home from the station. This wet weather is unusual for the time of year.* Opposite dry(2). **3** (*derog; informal*) (of a person) weak in character; afraid to do things that are difficult or dangerous: *Don't be so wet — tell him you don't like it.* (**be**) **wet behind the ears** ⇒ ear. **soaking wet** very wet. **wet through** so wet that one cannot become any wetter.

▷ *c.n* **4** (*derog*) person who is wet(3). **in the wet** in a wet place or situation: *Don't walk in the wet in those light shoes or you will spoil them.*

▷ *tr.v* (-*tt*-, *p.t,p.p* **wet**(ted)) **5** make (s.o/s.t) wet(1); cause (s.o/s.t) to become wet(1): *You should wet that shirt a little before ironing it.* **wet one's/the bed** ⇒ bed(*n*).

,**wet 'blanket** *c.n* (*derog; informal*) person who stops (or tries to stop) people enjoying themselves often by being boring or not cheerful.

,**wet 'dock** *c.n* dock¹(1) in which ships can float. Opposite dry dock.

'**wetness** *u.n.*

'**wet ,suit** *c.n* rubber clothes a person wears to keep her/him warm when she/he swims under water.

'**wetting** *c.n* (often *get, give s.o/s.t, a —*) example of being made wet, or of making s.o/s.t wet: *When we went too close to the edge of the rough sea, we got a wetting.*

wether /'weðə/ *c.n* male sheep, esp a castrated one.

we've (strong form /wiːv/, weak form /wɪv/) = we have. ⇒ have.

whack /wæk/ *c.n* **1** heavy blow, usu with a stick. **2** sound (like one) made by a whack(1). **3** (*informal*) (often *get/have one's — (of s.t)*) share (of s.t): *He's old and tired now but he had his whack of fun when he was younger.*

▷ *tr.v* **4** hit (s.o/s.t) hard, usu with a stick and in a way that makes a loud noise.

whacked *adj* (also ,**whacked 'out**) (*informal*) very tired.

'**whacking** *attrib.adj* **1** (usu — *great…*) very big *…: After falling on the floor she had a whacking great bruise for a week.* Compare whopping.

▷ *c.n* **2** (often *give s.o, get/receive, a —*) punishment by beating, usu with a stick.

whale /weɪl/ *c.n* biggest animal that exists in the sea which looks like a fish but has warm blood and comes to the surface to breathe air. **have a whale of a (good) time** (*informal*) enjoy oneself very much; have great fun.

'**whaler** *c.n* **1** kind of ship or boat used for hunting whales. **2** person who hunts whales.

'**whaling** *u.n* hunting of whales.

wham /wæm/ *c.n* = whack(1).

wharf /wɔːf/ *c.n* (*pl* **wharves** /wɔːvz/) special place built at the edge of, or built out into, the sea, a lake or a river, so that ships can load and unload there.

what /wɒt/ *adv* **1** how (much): *What does it matter whether we get there at 10 or 11 provided we get there in the end?*

▷ *det/pron* **2** (in questions, asking s.o to choose out of a number or amount of things (not persons) that are not known to the person who asks the question: *What (clothes) are you going to wear today?* (Compare: Which (of these) clothes are you going to wear today?) *What time is it?* (or *What is the time?*). *He asked me what the time was.* **3** (way of expressing surprise, admiration etc): *What a big nose he has! What lovely flowers!* **What a pity** ((**that**) *…*) it is a great pity (that) *…: 'We can't go to the party on Saturday.' 'What a pity!' What a pity (that) your new house hasn't got a better view.* **What the blazes/devil/hell** (*slang*) (a way of showing angry or annoyed surprise): *What the blazes! There's a police car in our garden! 'What the hell does that fool want now?'*

▷ *pron* **4** (in questions that ask s.o to say what a person's job, character etc is): *'What was your father?' 'He was a policeman.'* (Compare 'Who was your father?' 'He was John Smith.') **5** that which; the thing that/which: *Tell me what you want.* (Compare 'Tell me who you want'.) (**and**) **what's more** *…* in addition *…*; also (and this is more important *…*: *I'm not going for a walk with you because I'm tired — and what's more, I think it's going to rain.* **come what may/will** (*formal*) whatever happens; whatever may happen. **give s.o what for** (*informal*) punish and/or scold s.o. **Guess what** (*informal*) guess what has happened, what is going to happen etc: *Guess what — Mary's going to marry Fred!* **have (got) what it takes (to do s.t)** (*informal*) have the necessary skill, character, knowledge, beauty etc to do s.t: *Don't worry about Sue; she'll succeed in life because she has what it takes.* **know what's what** (*informal*) know the things that are really necessary and/or important. **So what?** (*informal*) (a rude way of answering what s.o has said) what is the use and/or importance of what you have just said?: *'Jack says you were rude to him.' 'So what?'* **What?** (word used (**a**) to ask s.o to repeat what he/she has just said because one did not hear it. (Compare: '(I beg your) pardon?' which some people consider more polite); (**b**) (to show surprise and sometimes anger at the same time): *'John's absent.' 'What? He was absent yesterday too.'* **what about s.o/s.t** (**a**) (asking for information): *'Peter's coming.' 'And what about Mary?'* (i.e 'And is Mary coming too?'); (**b**) (making a suggestion): *'I need something to cut this string with.' 'What about a knife from the kitchen?'* (i.e 'Would a knife from the kitchen be suitable?'). **What did you say?** (a way of asking s.o to repeat what he/she said because one did not hear it). (Compare: '(I beg your) pardon?' which some people consider more polite.) **What (. . .) for?** for what reason (. . .)? Why (. . .)?: *'I've asked Helen to come.' 'What for?' 'What did you invite John for?'* **What if . . .?** what will/would happen if . . .?: *'Joan promised to look after the children.' 'What if she can't come?'* **What is s.o/s.t for?** What is the purpose of s.o/s.t? **What is s.o/s.t like?** How would you describe s.o/s.t?: *'What's your new teacher like?' 'He's very nice.'* **What of it?** (rude way of suggesting that what s.o has just said is not useful or important) What does it matter?: *'Your hair isn't very tidy.' 'What of it? I like it like that.'* **what with s.o/s.t (and s.o/s.t)** because of s.o/s.t; as a result of s.o/s.t: *What with the rise in the cost of wood and the increased wages, we are having to charge more for our furniture this month.*

what'ever *det/pron* **1** any(thing) that/which: *In this hotel you can order whatever (food) you want and you will get it.* Compare whichever(1). **2** it does not matter what: *Whatever you do, you won't be able to get in. The children won't be able to break those toys, whatever else they may do to them.* Compare whichever(2). **or whatever** (*informal*) or anything (else) of the same kind: *Bring some beer or lemonade or whatever for the picnic.* **Whatever next!** (a way of showing shocked surprise) If that is possible, what may be the next thing to happen?: *'The police have arrested Alan!' 'Whatever next!'*

▷ *adj* **3** (following a noun in questions and negative statements) of any kind; at all: *Mary has no wish whatever to leave home yet.* Compare whatsoever.

,what 'ever . . .? (a way of making 'what' stronger and of showing surprise, anger or annoyance): *What ever did you say that to him for, you fool? Now he'll never help us.*

,what 'have you *unique n* (*informal*) anything else of that kind: *The room was full of broken old chairs, tables and what have you.*

'what,not *unique n* (*informal*) anything (else): *His desk was covered with papers and books and whatnot.*

,whatso'ever *adj* (following a noun in questions and negative statements) of any kind; at all: *I have no food whatsoever in the house.* Compare whatever(3).

wheat /wiːt/ *u.n* (also *attrib*) kind of plant grown for making bread etc; the grain from this plant before it is made into flour: *The US produce very great quantities of wheat flour every year.*

'wheat ,germ *u.n* thing on the outside of a grain of wheat from which the new plant grows, used in making some health foods.

'wheaten *adj* made from wheat.

wheedle /'wiːdl/ *tr.v* **wheedle s.o, into, out of, doing s.t** (try to) persuade s.o (not) to do s.t by being very nice to her/him but only for the purpose of getting what one wants: *She knew just how to wheedle her mother into letting her stay home from school.* **wheedle s.t out of s.o** get information etc from s.o by being very nice to her/him.

wheel /wiːl/ *c.n* **1** circular thing that goes round and round and is used for a car etc to run on, or in a machine for driving one or more parts of it: *a bicycle wheel.* **2** way of turning in which one end or part, e.g one foot, remains in the same position while the other end or part, e.g the other foot, goes round with a circular motion. Compare wheel(5). **at the wheel (of s.t)** driving or steering (a car etc): *Who was at the wheel of the car when it crashed?* **meals on wheels** ⇒ meal. **put a spoke in s.o's wheel** ⇒ spoke[1]. **put one's shoulder to the wheel** ⇒ shoulder(*n*). **take the wheel** begin to drive/steer a car etc, usu after s.o else has been doing it: *When Dick was tired of driving I took the wheel.* **wheels within wheels** (*fig*) things that one cannot see but which influence the things one can see, often dishonestly: *Unless you work in our organization you will have no idea why things happen because there are wheels within wheels.*

▷ *v* **3** *tr.v* move (s.t that has wheels) by pushing it: *When he got to a red light, he got off his bicycle and wheeled it across the road.* **4** *tr.v* move (s.o/s.t that is on s.t with wheels) by pushing the thing he/she/it is on: *When the patient got to the hospital, she was put in a chair and wheeled to the lift.* **5** *intr.v* (*military*) change direction by doing a wheel(2): *If a line of soldiers is marching northwards and their officer wants them to march westwards in line instead, he gives the order 'Left wheel!'* **6** *intr.v* turn suddenly: *When he heard the shout behind him, he wheeled round.* **7** *intr.v* fly in circles: *In the desert one sometimes sees big birds wheeling in the sky above a dying animal.*

'wheel,barrow *c.n* thing with a wheel at one end and two legs and handles at the other, used to carry earth, stones etc in gardens or when one is building.

'wheel,base *c.n* distance between the front axle of a car etc and its back axle.

'wheel,chair *c.n* chair with wheels in which people who are too old or ill to walk can be wheeled(4) from one place to another: *When I broke my leg I needed a wheelchair.*

-'wheeler *c.n* thing having the number of wheels shown in the first part of the word: *a threewheeler.*

,wheeler-'dealer *c.n* (*informal*) person who makes (business) deals (esp for her/his own advantage).

,wheeling and 'dealing *u.n* ways of making

(business) deals by using any means, whether they are honest or not.

'wheel,wright *c.n* person who makes and mends wheels(1), esp ones for carts.

wheeze /wi:z/ *c.n* **1** (sound heard when s.o is) breathing noisily, usu because there is s.t wrong with (the pipes going down to) her/his lungs.

▷ *v* **2** *intr.v* make the sound of a wheeze(1). **3** *tr.v* (often — *s.t out*) say s.t while wheezing(3): *'Get me a doctor,' the old man wheezed* (*out*).

'wheezily *adv* in a wheezy way.

'wheeziness *u.n* fact or state of being wheezy.

'wheezy *adj* (*-ier, -iest*) who/that wheezes(2).

whelk /welk/ *c.n* kind of shellfish that is eaten.

whelp /welp/ *c.n* **1** very young dog or animal belonging to the same family as dogs or cats.

▷ *intr.v* **2** (*technical*) give birth to a whelp(1).

when /wen/ *adv* **1** (in questions) at what time; how long ago; on what occasion: *When are your English lessons? When did you see him last? When will you be ready? I asked him when he wore that strange hat.* **2** (of time) at/on which: *the day when I saw him.* **Say when** (*informal*) Tell me when to stop pouring the drink into your glass etc. **when to do s.t** when one should do s.t: *Will you please tell me when to turn off this road to get to your house?*

▷ *conj* **3** at any/the time that; as soon as; on any/the occasion that: *When I feel hungry I eat. We'll start when you're ready. When I meet a lady I know, I take off my hat.* **4** although; when one considers that: *How can you say such things about Jim when you know he's so ill! He died at the age of 50, when he could have lived another 30 years if he had been more careful.* **5** if: *It's useless to try to play tennis when it is raining.* **6** after which; as a result of which; and/but then: *We began to play, when it soon became clear that none of the boys knew the rules of the game. The boys had scarcely got out into the street when it began to rain hard.* **when doing s.t** while one is doing s.t: *When drying glasses it is best to use a cotton cloth.*

▷ *def.n* **7 the when and how/where** the time and method/place: *I know you plan to start your own business, but what I don't know is the when and how.*

▷ *pron* **8** (after a preposition, in questions) (**a**) what time: *Till when are you going to be here?* (**b**) which time: *Mary passed her examinations last month, since when she has been on holiday.*

when'ever *adv* **1** (*informal*) = when ever. **or whenever** (*informal*) or at any other time: *Come and visit us next summer or in the autumn, or whenever.*

▷ *conj* **2** at any time that; at whatever time; on any occasion that: *Come whenever you like. Whenever there is a public holiday, I go fishing. We'll have lunch whenever we've all finished work.*

ˌwhen 'ever *adv* (also **when'ever**) (used to ask a question about time while showing surprise, anger etc): *When ever will you be able to meet Anne again now that she lives on the other side of the world from you?*

ˌwhenso'ever *adv/conj* (*old use*) = whenever.

whence /wens/ *adv* (*old use*) **1** (in questions) from where; how; why: *Whence comes it that* (How is it that) *the people of this country are so good at business?* **2** from which: *We visited*

the place whence our family had come several hundred years before.

▷ *pron* (*old use*) **3** (after a preposition, in questions) what place: *From whence do you come?* **4** which place: *This is the village from whence my family came.* (Notice that some people consider 'from whence' to be bad English and use only 'whence'.)

where /weə/ *adv* **1** (in questions) in, to, what place or position; in what direction: *Where's the bathroom? Where are you going? He asked her where she was looking.* **2** (in questions) in what situation/condition: *Where will the children be if their father loses his job?* **3** in which: *This is the place where I saw all those lions last year.*

▷ *conj* **4** in, to, any place, position, or situation that: *Sit where you like. Tell him to go where he wants.* Compare wherever(2). **5** in, to, the place, position, situation, that: *After losing his job, he is back where he was ten years ago.* **6** but: *He prefers a quiet evening where his wife wants to go out dancing.* Compare whereas.

▷ *def.n* **7 the where and how/when** the place and manner/time: *I'm willing to come and help you if you'll tell me the where and how/when* (i.e where and how/when) *I can help you*).

▷ *pron* **8** (when qualified by a preposition, in questions) what place: *Where does this animal come from?* **9** (when qualified by a preposition) (*informal*) which place: *This is the place where my family come from.* **where it's at** (*informal*) in the place where interesting or exciting things are happening: *New York is where it's at!* **Where to?** To what place?: *'We're going now.' 'Where to?'*

where'abouts /'weərəˌbaʊts/ *adv* **1** (in questions often when one does not expect the person one is asking to be able to give an exact answer) where; in, to, what place: *Whereabouts do you think you may have left your umbrella?*

▷ *u/pl.n* **2** place where s.o/s.t is: *Her daughter disappeared last month and her whereabouts are still not known.*

where'as /weər'æz/ *conj* but on the contrary: *John likes funny films whereas his wife likes serious ones. Whereas July was hot and dry, August has been cold and wet.* Compare where(6).

ˌwhere 'ever *adv* (also **wher'ever**) (used when one wants to ask a question about a place etc while showing surprise): *Where ever did you find that beautiful coat in a small town like this?*

where'fore /'weəˌfɔ:/ *adv* **1** (*old use*) (in questions) for what reason; why.

▷ *conj* **2** (*old use*) for which reason.

▷ *c.n* **3 the whys and** (**the**) **wherefores** ⇒ whys.

where'in /weər'ın/ *adv* **1** (*old use*) (in questions) in what (part); where; how: *Wherein do you see the problem?*

▷ *adv/conj* **2** (*old use*) in which: *The hole wherein the money had been buried could not be found.*

where'of /weər'ɒv/ *adv* **1** (*old use*) (in questions) of what: *Whereof does he speak?*

▷ *adv/conj* **2** (*old use*) of which: *The material whereof it is made is very expensive now.*

where'on /weər'ɒn/ *adv* **1** (*old use*) (in questions) on what. **2** on which.

▷ *conj* **3** (*old use*) = whereupon(3).

ˌwhereso'ever *adv/conj* (*old use*) = wherever.

whereto /weə'tuː/ *adv* **1** (*old use*) (in questions) for what purpose/reason; why; in what direction; to what place.
▷ *adv/conj* **2** (*old use*) to which.
whereupon /ˌweərə'pɒn/ *adv* **1** (*old use*) (in questions) on what. **2** on which.
▷ *conj* **3** (*old use*) (immediately) after (and as a result of) which: *Suddenly the teacher came into the room, whereupon the boys quickly went back to their seats.*
wherever /weər'evə/ *adv* **1** = where ever. **or wherever** (*informal*) or at/in any other place: *I don't want to see him again at college, or in my house, or wherever.*
▷ *conj* **2** at, to, any place that; at, to, all the places that: *Sit wherever you like.* **3** in all the situations in which (it is); in any situation in which (it is): *Wherever possible, you should avoid drinking the local water.*
wherewithal /'weəwɪðˌɔːl/ *def.n* thing necessary (in order to do s.t): *The poor old man did not even have the wherewithal to buy himself a loaf of bread.*
whet /wet/ *tr.v* (-tt-) make (s.t) sharp: *If your knife is blunt, try whetting it on a stone.* **whet s.o's appetite (for s.t)** ⇨ appetite.
whether /'weðə/ *conj* **1** (word used to introduce reported questions of the kind that can be answered with 'yes' or 'no') if: *He asked you whether you wanted to come in.* **2** it does not matter if; regardless if: *Whether it rains or not, I am going to the match. He's going to do it whether it's right or not.* **whether or not** (. . .) if (. . .) or not: *I don't know whether or not he is coming.* **whether . . . or not** regardless of . . .: *She's going to become the head of the business whether you like it or not.* **whether to do s.t (or not)** whether one ought to do s.t: *I don't know whether to write to him about it (or not).*
whew /hjuː/ *interj* (sound people make by breathing in or out quickly to show surprise, tiredness, relief etc): *Whew, I'm glad that's over and I hope I'll never have to do it again!*
whey /weɪ/ *u.n* **curds and whey** ⇨ curd.
which /wɪtʃ/ *det/pron* **1** (in questions, asking for a choice to be made between two or more things that are known): *Which of these (two, three etc) books do you want? 'Here are the pencils I bought. Which do you want?' 'I'll have this one.' I asked her which way she wanted to go.* Compare what(1). **2** and that/them/they/this: *He missed the lecture, which was a pity, because it was very useful. Our two schools, which we were both proud of, often played matches against each other. All you need is a couple of sticks and a ball, which you can find in most houses.* (Notice that in which(2) commas are used to separate the clauses(1).) **at which** and when this/that happened: *Suddenly a bell rang, at which all the children in the class began to put their books away.* **in which case** ⇨ case¹. **Which is which?** Which of them is . . . and which is . . .?: *I know that one of the twins must be Julia and that the other must be Jane, but which is which?* **which to do, take** etc which one ought to do etc: *There are so many beautiful kinds of fruit here that I don't know which to choose first.*
▷ *pron* **3** (word used to join two clauses(1) together by replacing a noun or pronoun in one of them

so that it does not have to appear twice) that; the one(s) that; the . . . that: *The shoes which you bought are too tight. The house which is behind ours has a beautiful garden.* (Notice that in which(3) one does not use a comma to separate the two clauses(1).)
which'ever *det/pron* **1** (giving a choice between two or more things that one knows): *Take whichever (of these) pens you want.* Compare whatever(1). **2** it does not matter which: *Whichever way you go, you will get to the sea.* Compare whichever(1). **3** (*informal*) = which ever.
,which 'ever *det/pron* (word used to ask the same kinds of questions as which(1) but with the addition of surprise): *I can't see her anywhere; which ever way did she go?*
whiff /wɪf/ *c.n* **1** smell (often an unpleasant one); movement of air or smoke that passes quickly: *As the car passed, there was a whiff of petrol.* **2** breath that one takes in: *I'm going out for a few whiffs of fresh air. The dentist gave me a whiff of gas before he took my tooth out.*
'whiffy *adj* (-ier, -iest) (*derog; informal*) having a bad smell.
while /waɪl/ *conj* **1** during the whole of the time that; at the same time as; for as long as: *I'll stay here while you're away so that the children won't be alone.* **2** during the time that: *I'm sorry you came while I was out because I wanted to see you.* **3** although; even though: *While I quite understand why he refused to help her, I cannot agree that he was right not to do so.* **4** but (on the contrary): *Mary plays tennis while her husband prefers football.* **5** and (this is more important): *John only broke a leg in the accident while his wife was more seriously hurt.*
▷ *sing.n* **6** (usu a short) time: *Let's stay here (for) a while and see what happens.* **all the/this while** during all the/this time: *I've been waiting here for nearly an hour and all this while you were watching television.* **(make it) worth s.o's while (to do s.t)**; **worth s.o's while (to do s.t)** ⇨ worth(*prep*). ⇨ worthwhile. **once in a while** ⇨ once.
▷ *tr.v* (also **wile**) **7** **while s.t away** pass (a period of time) in a quiet pleasant way without doing anything hard: *They whiled the summer days away by eating, drinking and sleeping.*
whilst /waɪlst/ *conj* (*old use*) = while(1–5).
whim /wɪm/ *c.n* sudden wish to do s.t, often s.t not sensible or reasonable.
whimsical /'wɪmzɪkl/ *adj* strange; having ideas or wishes that are not sensible or reasonable: *whimsical behaviour.*
whimsicality /ˌwɪmzɪ'kælɪtɪ/ *c/u.n.*
'whimsically *adv.*
whine /waɪn/ *c.n* **1** sound made by a person or an animal when he/she/it whines.
▷ *v* **2** *intr.v* make a high long complaining noise like a dog that is not happy: *The dog whined at the door until I let it in.* **3** *tr/intr.v* complain, usu a lot, in a whining(2) way; say (s.t) in a whining(2) voice: *I hate whining children.*
'whiner *c.n* (*derog*) person who complains a lot.
whip /wɪp/ *c.n* **1** instrument used for hitting horses etc and made of a piece of rope, leather etc fixed to the end of a stick. **2** official of a party in Parliament whose job is to control the other members of the party in certain ways, e.g

to persuade them to vote (in the ways that the party wants). **3** mixture of eggs, cream, sugar etc made by beating the various things together.

▷ *v* (*-pp-*) **4** *tr.v* beat (s.o/s.t) with a whip(1). **5** *tr.v* (*fig*) beat (s.o, a team etc) thoroughly in a match, game etc. **6** *intr.v* move suddenly and quickly: *I tried to come up behind the man quietly and catch him, but he whipped round while I was still five metres away and ran.* **7** *intr.v* move strongly or violently: *We decided to stay at home because the wind and rain were whipping past the door.* **8** *tr.v* sew (the edge of a hem(1)) over to make it stronger. **9** *tr.v* beat (eggs, cream etc) to make a smooth mixture. **whip s.t out** (*informal*) take s.t out suddenly and quickly: *The man whipped out a knife.* **whip s.t up** (**a**) (*informal*) make s.t quickly: *You have ten minutes before you must go — time for me to whip you up something to eat.* (**b**) cause s.t to become stronger, more violent etc: *The wind was beginning to whip up waves on the lake. The man was trying to whip up some interest in his plans.*

'whip,lash *c.n* **1** part of a whip(1) that is made of rope, leather etc. **2** blow with a whip(1). **3** damage to one's body, esp one's neck, caused by the shock of stopping suddenly, e.g when a car crashes.

,whipped 'cream *u.n* cream made stiff by whipping(9) it.

'whipping *c.n* (often *get, give s.o, a —*) **1** punishment by beating with a whip or other instrument. **2** (*fig*) fact of being beaten easily in a game or match.

'whip,round *c.n* (often *have a —* (*for s.o/s.t*)) collection of money etc from a group of people (to be given to s.o or to be used to buy s.t for s.o because he/she is in hospital, leaving a job, retiring(1) etc).

whirl /wɜːl/ *c.n* **1** going round and round, usu very fast and often in a confused or confusing way. (**be**) **a whirl of s.t** (be) very busy because of s.t: *Our house is a whirl of activity because we are preparing for tomorrow's wedding.* **give s.t a whirl** (*fig; slang*) try s.t; give s.t a try to see how good it is. **in a whirl** in a state of confusion: *After doing all those sums my head is in a whirl.*

▷ *v* **2** *tr/intr.v* (often — (*s.o/s.t*) *about/round*) (cause (s.o/s.t) to) go round and round, usu very fast and often in a confused or confusing way. **3** *intr.v* feel as if one is going round and round: *My brain is still whirling from all the noise at the party.*

'whirl,pool *c.n* place in the sea or a river etc where the water goes round and round.

'whirl,wind *c.n* wind that goes round and round very fast in a circle and sometimes goes up high into the air. **like a whirlwind** very fast.

whirr /wɜː/ *c.n* **1** sound heard when s.t whirrs(2).

▷ *intr.v* **2** make a long low sound like that of a machine turning.

whisk /wɪsk/ *c.n* **1** instrument used to beat eggs, cream etc by hand: *an egg whisk.* **2** instrument made of hairs etc on the end of a stick and used to drive away flies etc. **3** sudden quick movement, often for the purpose of brushing s.t away: *There was a whisk of a curtain and suddenly Mary was in the room.*

▷ *tr.v* **4** (often — *s.o/s.t away/off*) move, take, (s.o/ s.t) (away) suddenly and quickly: *Freddie arrived*

and whisked Nora off to a restaurant. **5** beat (eggs etc) with a whisk(1).

whisker /'wɪskə/ *c.n* hair, usu one of the long stiff ones a cat etc has at the side of its face. **by a whisker** (*informal*) only just; by a very narrow amount: *We won the match but only by a whisker — 32 points to 31.*

'whiskers *pl.n* **1** long stiff hairs on the face of a cat etc. ⇨ whisker. **2 =** sidewhiskers.

whisky /'wɪskɪ/ *n* (*pl -ies*) (also **'whiskey**) **1** *u.n* (also *attrib*) kind of brown strong alcoholic(1) drink made from grain: *a whisky bottle.* **2** *c.n* amount of whisky(1) served to one person at one time.

whisper /'wɪspə/ *n* **1** *c.n* sound heard when s.o whispers(4). **2** *c.n* sound like that of s.t whispering(5): *I love to hear the whisper of the wind in the autumn leaves.* **3** *c.n* news or information s.o gives secretly to s.o else; secret suggestion or rumour: *I have heard a whisper that Jill is going to marry Ted soon.* Compare whisper(6). **in a whisper** quietly by or while whispering: *When I spoke to her, she told me in a whisper to be quiet because her baby was asleep.*

▷ *v* **4** *tr/intr.v* speak, say s.t, quietly and without the vibration(2) in one's throat that produces full sounds: *We whisper when we do not want to be heard except by someone who is quite close to us. 'Come in,' she whispered, 'but don't make a noise.'* **5** *intr.v* make a noise that sounds like a person whispering(4): *The wind was whispering in the trees above her head.* **6** *tr.v* pass on (information, news, a rumour etc) secretly: *The news that an attack was coming was whispered around the village and everyone got ready to defend themselves.*

whistle /'wɪsl/ *c.n* **1** instrument that a referee(2) etc blows with the mouth to stop or call s.o. **2** noise that is (or sounds like) that of a whistle(1). **blow the whistle on s.o/s.t** (*slang*) tell the secret of s.o's crime, bad behaviour etc or s.t wrong that is being done. **wet one's whistle** (*informal*) have a drink (usu an alcoholic(1) one). **wolf whistle** ⇨ wolf.

▷ *v* **3** *intr.v* make the sound of, like, a whistle(1), either with one's lips or with two fingers in one's mouth, or with an instrument such as a whistle(1). **4** *intr.v* (of a bird or animal) make a noise like that of a whistle(1) with the voice. **5** *tr.v* produce (a tune) by whistling(3,4). **6** *intr.v* (of the wind, an engine, a bullet etc) make a noise like a whistle(1) by the movement of or through air, steam etc. **s.o can, will have to, whistle for it/ s.t** (*fig; informal*) s.o is not going to get what he/she wants, however much he/she wants it: *She was tired of bringing her husband tea in bed every morning so she told him that in future he could whistle for it.* **whistle s.o/s.t back** call s.o/s.t back by whistling to her/ him/it: *When his dog ran after rabbits, he whistled it back and it came at once.* **whistle s.t up** (*informal*) call s.t by whistling: *If you want a taxi I can whistle one up for you.*

Whit /wɪt/ *adj* **=** Whitsun.

,Whit 'Monday *unique n* day after Whit Sunday, usu a holiday in England.

Whitsun /'wɪtsən/ *unique n* **1** the seventh Sunday after Easter. **2** the days of public holiday that include this Sunday.

,**Whit 'Sunday** *unique n* seventh Sunday after Easter.

'**Whitsun,tide** *unique n* = Whitsun(2).

,**Whit week'end** *def/unique n* weekend of which Whit Sunday is part.

white /waɪt/ *adj* **1** having the colour of clean snow or the part of a boiled egg that is just under the shell. **2** pale, often because of fear or illness. **3** (of coffee etc) having milk or cream in it. **4** (of a person) of a race that has pale skin. Compare black(3). **5** (of wine) pale yellow in colour or almost without any colour. Compare red(3), rosé. **(go) white (as a sheet)** (become) white, usu because of fear.

▷ *n* **6** *c/u.n* white(1) colour: *If you mix the colours of the rainbow together in equal parts you get white.* **7** *c.n* (often with capital **W**) white(4) person. **8** *c/ u.n* part of an egg that is between the shell and the yellow yolk: *egg white.* **in black and white** ⇒ black(*n*). **in white** having white clothes on: *At the wedding all the young girls were (dressed) in white.*

,**white 'ant** *c.n* common name for termite.

'**white,bait** *u.n* small young fish that are cooked and eaten.

,**white 'blood ,cell** *c.n* (also ,**white cor'puscle**) one of the two kinds of blood cell (the other kind is the red blood cell): *White blood cells fight disease.*

,**white-'collar** *adj* (usu *attrib*) **1** working with her/his brain rather than her/his hands: *Mark is a white-collar worker because he works in an office.* **2** done by people who work with their brains rather than their hands: *My students are looking for white-collar jobs.* Compare blue-collar.

,**white cor'puscle** *c.n* = white blood cell.

,**white 'elephant** *c.n* something that cost a lot of money but is useless or not wanted.

'**white-,faced** *adj* having a white face because of fear, illness etc.

,**white 'flag** *c/def.n* flag showing that one is surrendering(2); flag showing one wants to stop fighting.

,**white-'hot** *adj* so hot that it has changed from red to white in colour.

'**White ,House** *def.n* official home of the President of the US.

,**white 'lie** *c.n* lie that is better than telling the truth because it does not hurt people so much: *I did not like the meal at all but when my hostess asked me whether I had enjoyed it I told a white lie and said that I had.*

'**white ,meat** *u.n* **1** meat from the breast(2) of a bird, which is paler than the meat from the legs (the dark meat). **2** meat from animals which is pale in colour, e.g chicken, veal and pork. Compare red meat.

'**whiten** *tr/intr.v* (cause (s.t) to) become white(1) or whiter (⇒ white(1)) than before.

'**whiteness** *u.n.*

whitening /'waɪtnɪŋ/ *u.n* substance used to make things white: *Your tennis shoes are getting grey so you had better put some whitening on them.*

,**white of 'egg** *c/u.n* (*pl* whites of egg) white(8).

,**white 'paper** *c.n* report produced by the British Government to give information on a particular subject.

,**white 'pepper** *u.n* pepper that is very pale

because the dark covering of the seeds was taken off before they were crushed.

,**white 'sauce** *c/u.n* thick white sauce made with white flour.

,**white 'spirit** *u.n* liquid made from petrol and used to clean paint, grease etc off brushes, clothes etc or to make paint thinner.

'**white,wash** *n* **1** *u.n* white liquid made from lime or whitening and put on walls etc to make them white and clean. **2** *c.n* (*fig*) attempt to hide s.t bad by pretending that it is really good: *After the complete failure of the president's plan, there was a whitewash to try to make people believe that it had really been successful.*

▷ *tr.v* **3** cover (s.t) with whitewash(1).

,**white 'wedding** *c.n* wedding at which the bride wears white clothes.

,**white 'wine** *u.n* wine that is (pale) yellow in colour. Compare red wine, rosé wine.

'**whitish** *adj* rather white.

whither /'wɪðə/ *adv* (*old use*) **1** (in questions) to what place: *Whither did those men go?* **2** to which (place): *That was the town whither we were hoping to go.*

whiting /'waɪtɪŋ/ *c.n* kind of fish that is cooked and eaten.

Whitsun(tide) ⇒ Whit.

whittle /'wɪtl/ *tr.v* make (wood) thinner by cutting strips off, usu starting at one end and often just for amusement, without intending to make anything. **whittle s.t away** (a) whittle s.t until nothing remains. (b) (*fig*) wear s.t away: *Too much drink and not enough exercise whittled his health away until he died at the early age of 41.* **whittle s.t down** (a) make s.t smaller by whittling it. (b) (*fig*) reduce s.t: *We shall have to whittle down our costs because we are losing money.*

whizz /wɪz/ *intr.v* (also **whiz**) (-zz-) go very fast, usu with a buzz(1): *We drove along slowly, letting the other cars whizz past us.*

'**whizz ,kid** *c.n* very clever and/or successful young person, esp in business and esp because he/she has new ideas.

who (strong form /huː/, weak form /hʊ/) *pron* **1** (in questions in which 'who' is the subject'(4) or the subjective complement(3)) what person(s): *Who live(s) in this house? I asked him who his father was.* Compare what(1). **2** (in questions in which 'who' is the object'(4)) (*informal*) what person(s): *Who did you see yesterday? Who does this bicycle belong to?* (Notice that in formal English 'whom' can take the place of 'who' when it is the object'(4).) **3** (used to join two clauses(1) by replacing a noun (phrase(1)/pronoun) in one of them so that it does not have to appear twice) the person(s) that: *I have seen the man who you saw yesterday.* (Notice that in formal English 'whom' can take the place of 'who' when it is the object'(4), e.g 'This is the man whom I saw yesterday'. Notice also that 'who' can be left out when it is the object'(4), e.g 'This is the man I saw yesterday'.) **4** and, but, he/she/they: *Her father, who is a doctor, lives in London. That's Denis, who isn't a member of a club in spite of what you say.* (Notice that in formal English 'whom' can take the place of 'who' when it is the object'(4), e.g 'That's Sharon, whom you met at the party yesterday'.)

who'd (strong form /huːd/, weak form /hʊd/) **1** = who had. ⇨ have. **2** = who would.

whodunit /huːˈdʌnɪt/ c.n (informal) detective story, film etc.

who'ever pron **1** (in questions) anyone who: ask whoever happens to be there. **2** it does not matter who: 'Someone's ringing the doorbell.' 'Whoever it is, tell them I'm ill and can't come down.' **3** (informal) = who ever.

who 'ever pron (also **who'ever**) (way of asking about a person or persons while at the same time showing surprise): Who ever can have said such a nasty thing about such a nice girl?

who'll (strong form /huːl/, weak form /hʊl/) = who shall/will.

whom (strong form /huːm/, weak form /hʊm/) pron (used instead of 'who' in formal English when it is the object): Whom did you see yesterday? Whom does this belong to? Those are the people whom I gave the books to. That's Peter, whom I met yesterday. (Notice that 'whom' can be left out when it is used instead of who(3).)

who're (strong form /ˈhuːə/, weak form /hʊə/) = who are. ⇨ be.

who's (strong form /huːz/, weak form /hʊz/) = who is. ⇨ be.

whose (strong form /huːz/, weak form /hʊz/) det/pron **1** (in questions) belonging to who: Whose book is this? He asked her whose garden that was. **2** (used to join two clauses(1) by replacing 'her/his/its/their' in one of them) the person(s) that own(s) the: This is the woman whose bicycle I borrowed last week. **3** and his/her/its/their (or, more rarely, my/your/our): That's Fred whose house we are living in.
▷ pron **4** (in questions) belonging to who: Whose is this book? He asked me whose those flowers were.

whosoever /ˌhuːsəʊˈevə/ pron (old use) (also **whomso'ever**) = whoever; anyone who.

who've (strong form /huːv/, weak form /hʊv/) = who have. ⇨ have.

WHO /ˌdʌbljuː ˌeɪtʃ ˈəʊ/ abbr World Health Organization (a department of the United Nations).

whoa /wəʊ/ interj (usu said to a horse) Stop!

who'd, whodunit, whoever ⇨ who.

whole /həʊl/ attrib.adj **1** complete; not broken and not having any parts missing: We spent the whole day on the beach yesterday. **swallow s.t whole** swallow s.t without chewing it and without cutting or breaking it into pieces: The bird swallowed the fish whole.
▷ c.n **2** (often the — of s.t) complete unit (of s.t), not just part of it; thing that is complete in itself; all that there is (of s.t): The whole of the cake was wet. **3** complete thing (from various parts): All the parts can be put together in five minutes to make a whole. **as a whole; on the whole** when it is, they are, taken all together; in general, not separately: The people of this country as a whole work hard. She likes sports on the whole but there are some that she finds boring.

whole'hearted adj (usu attrib) done, given etc with no hesitation or doubt: You have my wholehearted support.

whole'heartedly adv.

whole,meal adj/u.n (using) flour made without removing any part of the grain: wholemeal biscuits/bread.

whole,sale adj/adv **1** (sold) in large quantities and therefore more cheaply than if it is sold one by one or in small quantities; (sold) to shops etc and not to individual buyers: I am sorry but we can't sell you one of our machines because we are only wholesale dealers. Opposite retail(1).
▷ u.n **2** selling of things to retailers. Opposite retail(2).

whole,saler c.n person who sells things wholesale(1). Opposite retailer.

wholly /ˈhəʊllɪ/ adv completely.

wholesome /ˈhəʊlsəm/ adj **1** good for one's health; clean and harmless: The food we got at school was simple but wholesome. **2** (formal) morally clean and good: What these children need is some wholesome books to read instead of watching television for hours.

wholesomeness u.n.

who'll, whom ⇨ who.

whoop /wuːp/ c.n **1** (often —s of joy) loud shout, usu because one is happy or excited. **2** noisy cough during which one finds it difficult to breathe, usu because one has whooping cough.
▷ tr/intr.v **3** shout (s.t) loudly, usu because one is happy or excited. **whoop it up** (informal) have a very enjoyable (often noisy) time.

whooping cough /ˈhuːpɪŋ ˌkɒf/ u.n disease, mostly of small children, in which one coughs a lot and finds it difficult to draw breath in again after each cough. Compare whoop(2).

whoopee /wʊˈpiː/ interj (shout showing that one is happy or excited).

whoosh /wʊʃ/ c.n sound made by air or water when it comes out of s.t very quickly.

whopper /ˈwɒpə/ c.n (informal) **1** very big thing: The little boy asked for a big sweet, and his mother gave him a real whopper. **2** big lie: Don't believe what Bill says; he tells real whoppers.

whopping attrib.adj (informal) (usu — great) very big: I saw a whopping great plane at the airport yesterday. Compare whacking(1).

whore /hɔː/ c.n = prostitute.

whorehouse /ˈhɔːˌhaʊs/ c.n (pl /ˈhɔːˌhaʊzəz/) (old use) = brothel.

who're ⇨ who.

whorl /wɜːl/ c.n circular pattern in the shape of a spiral(3) seen in some fingerprints and in some seashells.

who's, whose, whoso(ever), who've ⇨ who.

why /waɪ/ adv **1** for what reason(s): 'Why did you come in?' 'Because it was raining.' I asked her why she was wearing new shoes while working in the garden.
▷ conj **2** the reason(s) for which: Jane hasn't arrived yet; that's why we haven't started dinner. **the reason why** why(2): Can you tell me the reason why we are waiting here? **Why not?** (a) What reasons are there for not doing it?: 'I don't want to go to school today.' 'Why not?' 'Because I feel ill.' (b) (informal) All right; I agree: 'Let's go for a walk.' 'Why not?'
▷ interj **3** (word showing surprise): Where's the baby? Why, here he is!

whys *pl.n* **the whys and (the) wherefores** the reasons (for s.t).

WI /ˌdʌblju: 'aɪ/ *def.n abbr* Women's Institute.

wick /wɪk/ *c.n* **1** twisted material in a candle which burns and melts the candle. **2** piece of woven etc material in an oil lamp through which the oil burns. **get on s.o's wick** (*fig*; *informal*) make s.o (often) angry.

wicked /'wɪkɪd/ *adj* **1** morally very bad; cruel; evil: *Cruelty to animals is wicked.* **2** naughty; behaving badly: *Stop that, you wicked boy!*
'wickedly *adv.* **'wickedness** *u.n.*

wickerwork /'wɪkəˌwɜːk/ *u.n* (also *attrib*) (also **'wicker**) work done, or thing made, by weaving sticks or reeds(1) together.

wicket /'wɪkɪt/ *c.n* (in cricket¹) **1** thing that the bowler(1) tries to hit with the ball, made up of three vertical stumps(4) and two horizontal bails². **2** pitch(1). **3** one player's turn to go out on to the pitch(1) and try to hit the ball. **keep wicket** be the wicketkeeper. **lose a wicket** (in cricket¹) be in a position in which one of the players is out(19). **on a good wicket** (*fig*; *informal*) in a favourable situation. **on a sticky wicket** (*fig*; *informal*) in a difficult or dangerous situation.
'wicket,keeper *c.n* player in a cricket¹ team who stands behind the wicket(1) and tries to catch the ball.

wide /waɪd/ *adj* **1** in which the distance from one side or edge to the other is big: *The Amazon is a very wide river.* **2** very open: *The children watched the man's tricks with wide eyes.* **3** spreading over a great area or distance: *He enjoyed sailing over the wide oceans of the world. Diana has a wide knowledge of birds.*
▷ *adv* **4** completely; so that it is as open as possible: *Open your mouth wide, please.* **5** in such a way that it misses by a considerable distance: *Luckily all the stones went wide so that the window was not damaged.* **far and wide** ⇒ far(*adv*). **wide awake** (**a**) completely awake. (**b**) (*fig*) not easily cheated or tricked. ⇒ wide-awake. (**fall**) **wide of the mark** ⇒ mark(*n*). **wide open** open as far as possible: *The door was wide open.* **wide open (to s.t)** (*fig*) in a situation where one/he/she/ it can easily be attacked or criticized etc: *If you write things like that in the newspaper, you will be wide open to accusations of dishonesty.*
▷ *c.n* **6** (in cricket¹) ball that is bowled²(3) so far to the left or right of the wicket(1) that the other side gets one run(8) for it.
,wide-'angle *attrib.adj* giving a wider view than usual: *a wide-angle lens for a camera.*
,wide-a'wake *attrib.adj* completely awake and/ or ready for anything.
,wide-'eyed *adj* having one's eyes wide open, usu because one is surprised.
'widely *adv* **1** over a wide area; in such a way as to include very many things: *Alison is widely known as an excellent artist. Harry reads widely.* **2** very: *There are widely different kinds of students in our college.*
'widen *tr/intr.v* (cause (s.t) to) become wider: *They are going to widen the street by knocking down those houses.*
'wide,spread *adj* covering a wide area; found etc in many places: *widespread diseases.*
width /wɪdθ/ *n* **1** *u.n* (often — of s.t) distance from one side or edge of s.t to the other. **2** *c.n*

piece of material that has not had anything cut off from either of its sides: *To make each of these curtains I'll need two widths of this material.*

widow /'wɪdəʊ/ *c.n* woman whose husband has died and who has not married again.
'widowed *adj* no longer having a husband/wife because he/she has died.
'widower *c.n* man whose wife has died and who has not married again.
'widow,hood *u.n* fact or state of being a widow.

width ⇒ wide.

wield /wiːld/ *tr.v* (*old use*) hold and use (a weapon etc). ⇒ unwieldy. **wield power (over s.o/ s.t)** rule, have control, (over a person, country): *The old kings wielded absolute power over their peoples.*

wife /waɪf/ *c.n* (*pl* wives /waɪvz/) woman who is married to a man. ⇒ husband.
'wife,like *adj* (also **'wifely**) behaving in the ways in which a (good) wife behaves.

wig /wɪg/ *c.n* artificial hair worn either to hide one's own hair or to cover one's head if one has little or no hair: *In England judges and lawyers wear wigs in court.*

wiggle /'wɪgl/ *c.n* **1** small movement from side to side, up and down or in a circle: *The fish gave a wiggle and then disappeared into the weeds.*
▷ *tr/intr.v* **2** (cause (s.t) to) move a short distance or short distances from side to side, up and down or in a circle or circles: *The baby lay on its back and wiggled its toes in the air.*

wild /waɪld/ *adj* **1** not tame or civilized; not grown intentionally by people; not kept by people as pets or for their milk, meat etc; living in its natural condition: *wild animals/birds/flowers/ plants.* **2** (of places, scenery etc) in the natural state; not having been interfered with by human beings. **3** violent; strong; angry; not controlled; not well thought out: *I did not know the answer to the question so I made a wild guess at it.* **4** (*informal*) really enjoyable, exciting etc: *What a wild time we had at the party last night!* **be wild about s.o/s.t** (*informal*) like s.o/s.t very much. **go wild** become wild(1,2). **go wild (about s.o/s.t)** (*informal*) become very excited or angry (about s.o/s.t). **sow one's wild oats** ⇒ oat.
▷ *adv* **5** without paying attention; without care. **run wild** (start to) become wild; (start to) live or grow without control: *After he died, the weeds ran wild in his garden.*
▷ *def.n* **6** areas of land not interfered with by human beings. **in the wild** under natural conditions, when not interfered with by human beings: *These plants grow much bigger in the wild than they do in our gardens.*
,wild 'boar *c.n* kind of wild pig (male or female) hunted and eaten in Europe.
,wild 'cat *c.n* **1** kind of cat that does not live with people but is wild and dangerous. **2** (*derog*) person (esp a woman) who becomes very angry suddenly and is sometimes also violent.
,wild,cat 'strike *c.n* sudden strike(1) by workers which has not been planned or agreed.
wildebeest /'wɪldɪˌbiːst/ *c.n* (*pl* -(s)) = gnu.
wilderness /'wɪldənɪs/ *c.n* **1** wild(2) place. **2** (*fig*) place that shows no signs of planning or control: *The poorer parts of the town were a wilderness of small dirty streets.*

'wild,fire *u.n* **spread like wildfire** spread extremely fast.

'wild,fowl *pl.n* birds shot for sport and/or food.

,wild-'goose ,chase *c.n* (*fig*) search that is not, and probably never can be, successful (because the thing one is looking for is not there).

'wild,life *u.n* wild animals, birds and sometimes also plants.

'wildly *adv* very much: *His guess at the number of beans in the pot was wildly out* (very wrong).

'wildness *u.n.*

wilds *pl.n* (usu *the — of s.w*) wild(2) parts (of a place): *the wilds of Africa.*

wile /waɪl/ = while(7).

wiles /waɪlz/ *pl.n* tricks; clever ways of trying to persuade s.o to do s.t, usu by being deceitfully charming.

wilful(ness) ⇒ will³.

wilily, wiliness ⇒ wily.

will¹ /wɪl/ *aux. v* (*p.t would* (strong form /wʊd/, weak form /wəd/); negative forms *will not* or *won't* /wəʊnt/, *would not* or *wouldn't* /'wʊdnt/; 'I will' can be *I'll* /aɪl/, 'you will' can be *you'll* /juːl/, 'he/she will' can be *he'll/she'll* /hiːl, ʃiːl/, 'it will' can be *it'll* /'ɪtl/, 'we will' can be *we'll* /wiːl/; 'will' is followed by the infinitive form of a verb without *to*) Compare shall. **1** (used to show that the action or state is in the future): *I will see you at the lecture tomorrow.* (Notice that 'will + verb' is often replaced by 'am/are/is going to + verb', e.g 'It's going to rain soon', except in formal English and in the main clause(1) of conditional(2) sentences; e.g 'I will see him if he comes here'. Notice also that 'will + verb' is sometimes replaced by 'am/are/is -ing', e.g 'I am leaving at 9 o'clock tomorrow' or by the present tense of the verb, e.g 'Our train leaves at 14.02 hours this afternoon'. 'I/we will' is sometimes replaced by 'I/we shall', esp in formal English; ⇒ shall.) **2** (in questions and answers) am/are/is willing to: '*Will you help me, please?*' '*No, I will not!*' **3** (in questions) want to: '*Will you have some more tea?*' '*Yes, please.*' **4** (as a way of making a request stronger with the suggestion that, if it is not obeyed, the person will be punished): *Will you stop arguing and do what I tell you?* **5** have/ has the habit of doing s.t; always do/does s.t, often in an annoying way: *The children will leave their dirty clothes lying about the house. If you will stay up till 2 a.m every morning, you must expect to be tired at work.* (Notice that the main stress is on 'will'.) **6** have/has the ability to (do s.t): *These stockings are elastic so they will fit anybody.* **7** (in question tags) **(a)** ('will' is used after a statement with 'won't' in it, and 'won't' after a statement with 'will' in it): '*You won't forget, will you?*' '*No, I won't.*' '*You'll remember to come early, won't you?*' '*Yes, I will.*' **(b)** ('will' can be used in a question tag following a command to make the command stronger): '*Stop that noise, will you!*' **(c)** ('won't' can be used in a question tag after an invitation or offer to make it more polite): '*Come in, won't you?*'

will² /wɪl/ *c.n* **1** document(1) that a person signs in order to tell s.o what to do with her/his possessions after she/he dies. **make a will** have a will²(1) made about one's possessions. **(last) will and testament** = will²(1).

▷ *tr.v* **2** (usu *— s.t to s.o*) leave (s.t) (to s.o) in one's will²(1).

will³ /wɪl/ *c/u.n* **1** force of mind, often combined with the wish to do s.t by means of it; ability to make one's body and mind do what one wants: *It is difficult to get that child to do what one wants because he has a very strong will.* **at will** when and how one wants: *The officer told his men to fire at will.* **do s.o's will** (*formal*) do what s.o wants. **force of will** = will³(1). **free will** ⇒ free. **God's etc will** whatever God etc wants us to do. **ill will** ⇒ ill. **the will to do s.t** the wish or desire to do s.t; wanting to do s.t. **Where there's a will, there's a way** (*proverb*) If one wants (to do) s.t very much, a method will be found to achieve(1) it. **with a will** willingly and strongly: *When the men realized that a child was buried under the ruins, they set to work to clear the bricks away with a will.*

▷ *tr.v* **2** try to make (s.t) happen by using one's will-power. **will s.o to do s.t** (try to) make s.o do s.t by using only one's will-power.

'wilful *adj* (*derog*) **1** (*attrib*) (of behaviour) done because one wants to do it, usu in spite of the fact that it is wrong or bad: *wilful damage.* **2** (of a person) behaving in a wilful(1) manner.

'wilfully *adv.* **'wilfulness** *u.n.*

-willed *adj* having a will³(1) of the kind shown in the first part of the word: *strong-willed; weak-willed.*

'willing *adj* (often *— to do s.t; — that...*) ready and glad (to do s.t; that s.t should be done): *willing hands/helpers. Are you willing to help?* Opposite unwilling. **God willing** if God is willing.

'willingly *adv.* **'willingness** *u.n.*

'will-,power *u.n* strength of a person's will³(1).

willies /'wɪlɪz/ *def.pl.n* **give s.o the willies** (*informal*) make s.o feel frightened, nervous etc.

willow /'wɪləʊ/ *n* **1** *c.n* (also **'willow ,tree**) kind of tree with long thin branches which usu grows near water. ⇒ weeping willow. **2** *u.n* (also *attrib*) wood from this tree.

'willow ,pattern *u.n* picture painted (usu in blue) on some plates, cups etc and showing a Chinese scene with one or more willows(1) in it.

'willowy *adj* pleasantly thin; slim(1).

willy-nilly /,wɪlɪ 'nɪlɪ/ *adv* (*informal*) whatever may happen; whatever anyone thinks; without considering whether it is harmful: *It may be raining but we must walk to the station willy-nilly.*

wilt /wɪlt/ *tr/intr.v* (cause (s.t) to) become less fresh or strong; (cause (s.t) to) become tired: *Flowers wilt if they get no water. After working for several hours in the heat, we began to wilt.*

wily /'waɪlɪ/ *adj* (*-ier, -iest*) (*derog*) cunning(1); clever in a bad way; having the habit of getting what one wants by tricks.

'wilily *adv.* **'wiliness** *u.n.*

win /wɪn/ *c.n* **1** victory; success; act or fact of being the winner(1): *There was a win for his horse in the last race.*

▷ *v* (*-nn-, p.t,p.p* **won** /wʌn/) **2** *intr.v* be the most successful in s.t: '*We had a match against another school on Saturday.' 'Who won?'* Opposite lose(4). **3** *tr.v* be successful in (a race etc): *Our boys won the match yesterday.* Opposite lose(4). **4** *tr.v* get (s.t) as a result of being successful in a competition, race, fight etc: *Mary has won a prize* *for history.* **5** *tr.v* get (s.t) as a result of guessing s.t correctly: *I won £10 on the last race by* betting(4) *on the black horse.* **6** *intr.v* get the most correct answer to s.t one is arguing about: *'Who said there were 200 beans in the jar?' 'I did.' 'Well, you win. There are 215.'* **7** *tr.v* get (s.t) as a result of hard work and/or effort: *After several weeks the boy at last won the approval of his teacher.*

win at s.t win when one plays a game etc.

win s.t back manage, after losing s.t, to get it back by winning it.

win (s.t) hands down ⇒ hand(*n*).

win out win in the end after a lot of effort etc.

win s.o over/round (to s.t) manage, after trying hard, to persuade s.o (to believe, do etc s.t).

win through (s.t) manage to get through (s.t) successfully after a lot of effort. -

'**winner** *c.n* **1** (often — *of s.t*) person, animal or thing that wins(2–7) (s.t). **2** thing that is (expected to be) very successful: *Her idea of hiring out bicycles just outside the station was a real winner.*

'**winning** *attrib.adj* **1** who/that wins. **2** attractive; helping to make people one's friends: *a winning smile.*

'**winningly** *adv.*

'**winnings** *pl.n* things (usu money) one wins(3–5): *After the races had finished we met and shared out our winnings.*

winsome /'wɪnsəm/ *attrib.adj* (*formal*) attractive; winning(2).

'**winsomely** *adv.* '**winsomeness** *u.n.*

wince /wɪns/ *c.n* **1** action of wincing(2).

▷ *intr.v* **2** show that one is hurt, shocked, worried etc by making a sudden small movement. **3** (*fig*) feel suddenly hurt, shocked or worried in one's mind but without making any movement with one's body. **wince at s.t** wince(2,3) because of s.t.

winch /wɪntʃ/ *c.n* **1** machine used for pulling things along or up, or for letting things down, by turning a wheel etc round which there is a rope, wire etc.

▷ *tr.v* **2** move (s.o/s.t) with the help of a winch(1): *The firemen tied a rope under the man's shoulders and winched him down the cliff.*

wind¹ /wɪnd/ *n* **1** *c/u.n* air blowing or moving rather fast, usu as a result of natural weather conditions. ⇨ breeze, gale. **2** *u.n* breathing; breath. **3** *u.n* gas or air in the stomach or bowels, often causing pain. **4** *u.n* (*derog; informal*) things said which have no real meaning. **5** *def.pl.n* all the people playing the wind instruments in a band²(2) or orchestra. **break wind** make gas come out of one's anus. **fling/throw caution to the winds** ⇒ caution(*n*). **get one's (second) wind** be able to breathe (again) comfortably after having become breathless, usu as a result of taking exercise. **get/have the wind up** (*informal*) become/be afraid. **get wind of s.t** hear information from a person about s.t. **in the wind** being prepared secretly: *I know something is in the wind in our college but I haven't yet been able to find out what it is.* **like the wind** very quickly: *My new car goes like the wind.* **put the wind up s.o** (*informal*) frighten s.o. (**sail**) **close to the wind** (*fig; informal*) (do things) that are very nearly dishonest or bad. **see how the wind blows** wait to see what happens before deciding what to do. **take the wind out of s.o's sails** (*fig; informal*)

prevent s.o doing s.t by doing the same thing, or s.t more successful, oneself first; do s.t that makes s.o feel less important, proud etc than he/she was before.

▷ *tr.v* **6** *tr.v* cause (s.o) to lose her/his breath: *If you hit someone in the stomach you will probably wind her or him.* **7** give (a horse etc) time to get its breath back to normal after it has been working hard.

'**wind,bag** *c.n* (*derog; slang*) person who talks too much, usu about things that are not interesting to others.

'**wind,break** *c.n* thing built or put up to protect s.o/s.t from strong winds.

'**wind,cheater** *c.n* short coat worn to protect one's body (but not one's legs) from the wind.

'**wind,fall** *c.n* **1** apple or other fruit that has been blown to the ground by the wind. **2** (*fig*) piece of good luck one was not expecting, usu money got from s.o who has died.

'**wind ,gauge** *c.n* instrument for measuring the strength of the wind.

'**windiness** *u.n* fact or state of being windy.

'**wind ,instrument** *c.n* musical instrument played by blowing air into it.

'**windless** *adj* without any wind: *a windless day.*

'**wind,mill** *c.n* **1** mill with four or more sails(3) that the wind turns to drive a machine that grinds(2) corn. **2** kind of toy for children that is on a stick and goes round and round when the wind blows it.

'**wind,pipe** *c.n* pipe joining one's throat to one's lungs.

'**wind,screen** *c.n* window on the front of a car, plane etc through which the driver or pilot can see.

'**wind,screen ,wiper** *c.n* long device on the windscreen of a car, plane etc used to remove rain, snow etc by moving across or from side to side.

'**wind,shield** *c.n* windscreen of a motorbike.

'**wind,storm** *c.n* storm in which there is a lot of wind but little or no rain.

'**wind,swept** *adj* (often) swept by winds, usu in such a way that damage is caused (e.g trees cannot grow well): *windswept hills.*

'**wind ,tunnel** *c.n* tunnel built to test how new kinds of cars, planes etc behave when they are going very fast.

windward /'wɪndwəd/ *adj/adv* **1** towards the direction from which the wind is coming. Opposite leeward(1).

▷ *u.n* **2** (often *to* —) direction from which the wind is coming. Opposite leeward(2).

'**windy** *adj* (*-ier, -iest*) having a lot of wind(1).

wind² /waɪnd/ *v* (*p.t,p.p* wound /waʊnd/) **1** *tr/intr.v* turn (a handle etc) round and round. **2** *tr.v* make (s.t) into a round shape by winding(1): *Wind the rope tidily after you have pulled the anchor up.* Opposite unwind(1). **3** *intr.v* go along in a way that bends from side to side: *the path winds through beautiful valleys.* **4** *tr.v* (often — *s.t up*) make (a clock, watch etc) able to work by tightening its spring or raising its weights, usu with a key. **wind (s.t) down** (*fig*) (cause s.t to) become calmer or slower; (cause s.t to) do less work until it finally stops working completely: *We are winding down our factory and selling the* machines. **wind s.t round s.o/s.t** put a bandage etc round s.o/s.t two or more times. **wind s.o up** make s.o angry. ⇨ unwind(3). **wind s.t up (a)** ⇨ wind(4). **(b)** (*fig*) cause s.t to come to an end: *Our company is losing too much money so we shall have to wind it up.* **wind up s.w** (*fig*; *informal*) finish s.w: *After dinner we went for a walk and wound up at Jean's house at midnight.*

'**winding** *attrib.adj* not going straight but bending or turning from side to side: *We followed the winding path down to the beach.*

windbag, windbreak, windcheater, windfall, wind gauge, windiness, wind instrument, windless, windmill ⇨ wind¹.

window /'windəu/ *c.n* 1 opening in a wall of a house or the side of a car etc through which one can see, get air etc. 2 glass, usu with a frame round it, in a window(1).

'**window ,box** *c.n* box filled with earth and put outside or inside a window so that one can grow plants in it, usu for decoration.

'**window ,dressing** *u.n* 1 ways of arranging examples of what a shop is selling in its window(s) so that people are attracted to come in and buy. 2 (*fig*) thing used, sometimes dishonestly, to try to persuade people to believe, buy or do s.t: *All that talk by the government about human rights is just window dressing, as you would see if you were allowed into their prisons.*

'**window ,pane** *c.n* complete piece of glass which is part of a window(2).

'**window ,shop** *intr.v* (-pp-) act of looking into shop windows for pleasure or out of interest and not because one intends to buy anything.

'**window ,shopper** *c.n* person who window shops.

'**window ,shopping** *u.n* looking into shop windows for pleasure or out of interest and not because one intends to buy something.

'**window,sill** *c.n* ⇨ sill.

windpipe, windscreen, windshield, windstorm, windswept, wind tunnel, windward, windy ⇨ wind¹.

wine /wain/ *c/u.n* 1 kind of alcoholic(1) drink usu made from grapes, but sometimes also from other fruits or plants: *red/white wine.* ⇨ vineyard.

▷ *tr/intr.v* 2 **wine and dine (s.o)** (cause (s.o) to) have dinner and wine.

'**wine ,glass** *c.n* glass(2) used for wine.

wing /wiŋ/ *c.n* 1 (often — *of s.t*) part (of a bird, insect, plane or building) that is not in the main body but sticks out on one side and is usu used for flying. 2 (*military*) unit in the Royal Air Force with three squadrons(1) in it. 3 player who plays in the furthest left/right position in the front line of her/his football/hockey etc team; the position in which he/she plays. ⇨ -winger. **(on) the left/right wing (of s.t)** (the part) having more radical(2)/conservative(1) beliefs than the average members of one's political party. **take s.o under one's wing** (*fig*) begin to help or protect s.o regularly. **under s.o's wing** (*fig*) helped or protected by s.o.

▷ *tr.v* 4 wound (s.o/s.t) in an arm or wing: *The soldiers winged the man who had shot at them but he managed to escape.*

,**Wing Co'mmander** *c.n* (*military*) rank in the Royal Air Force just below a Group Captain and just above a Squadron Leader.

'**wing ,nut** *c.n* nut(2) with two things like wings on it which enable one to turn the nut with one's fingers more easily.

-**winger** *c.n* person on the left/right wing (of football etc team, a political party etc), as shown by the first part of the word: *left-winger*; *right-winger*.

'**wingless** *adj* not having wings(1): *wingless insects.*

wings *pl.n* 1 one or both sides of a stage in a theatre which cannot be seen by the audience. 2 badge one is allowed to wear after one has passed one's examination to pilot a plane. **in the wings (a)** at the side of the stage, where one cannot be seen but can see what is happening on the stage. **(b)** (*fig*) in a position where one can have an influence on what happens without being seen to be doing so.

'**wing,span** *c.n* (also '**wing,spread**) distance from the end of one wing to the end of the other when both are fully extended.

wink /wiŋk/ *c.n* 1 quick closing and then opening of one eye, usu as a sign to s.o. Compare blink(1). **not have a wink of sleep; not sleep a wink** not sleep even for a second: *I didn't have a wink of sleep until three last night because of the party in the flat above.*

▷ *v* 2 *intr.v* close and then open one eye quickly, usu as a sign to s.o, often to show one is only joking when one says or does s.t. Compare blink(2). 3 *tr.v* cause (a light) to flash one or more times, usu as a signal: *When a driver in this country winks his lights, it may mean that he is allowing you to pass in front of him.* 4 *intr.v* flash one or more times: *I love to sit beside the sea and watch the lights of the fishing boats winking in the distance.* **wink at s.o** give s.o a signal by winking(2,3).

'**winkers** *pl.n* (*informal*) small yellow lights on a car which flash to show that one wants to turn left/right; indicators(1).

winkle /'wiŋkl/ *c.n* 1 kind of small shellfish that one can eat.

▷ *tr.v* 2 **winkle s.o/s.t out (of s.t)** (*informal*) get s.o/s.t out (of s.t) by force or after a lot of effort: *The teacher managed to winkle all the children out of the* exhibition(1) *after an hour. He didn't want to tell her what had happened but she finally winkled it out of him.*

winner, winning(s) ⇨ win.

winnow /'winəu/ *tr.v* remove the chaff(1) from (grain) by blowing air over it.

winsome(ness) ⇨ win.

winter /'wintə/ *c/u/def.* (also *attrib*) 1 (often with capital **W**) season of the year between autumn and spring when one has the coldest weather: *winter snow. Does this tree lose its leaves in (the) winter?*

▷ *intr.v* 2 (usu — (*in*) *s.w*) spend the winter (s.w): *My grandmother hated the cold so she always wintered abroad, in Tunisia.*

,**winter 'sports** *pl.n* sports done in winter on snow and/or ice.

'**winter,time** *u/def.n* (often *in* (*the*) —) winter(1); (during the) time when the climate is cold.

'**wintry** *adj* (also '**wintery**) of, like, winter; cold: *It is unusual to get such wintry weather in September.*

wipe /waɪp/ *c.n* **1** action or example of wiping(2). **give s.t a wipe** wipe(2) s.t: *You had better give your shoes a wipe before you go into the house.*
▷ *tr.v* **2** clean or dry (s.t) by rubbing it once or more than once with one's hand, a cloth etc. **wipe s.t away** remove s.t by wiping(2). **wipe s.t clean/dry** clean/dry s.t by wiping(2) it. **wipe s.o/s.t down** clean s.o/s.t from top to bottom by wiping(2) her/him/it. **wipe one's feet, shoes** etc **(on s.t)** clean one's shoes etc by rubbing them (on a mat etc). **wipe the floor with s.o** ⇒ floor(*n*). **wipe one's nose (on/with s.t)** ⇒ nose(*n*). **wipe s.t off (s.o/s.t)** **(a)** remove s.t (from s.o/s.t) by wiping(2). **(b)** (*fig*) get rid of s.t completely: *We have at last managed to wipe off all our debts.* **wipe s.o out** destroy s.o. **wipe s.t out (a)** clean the inside of s.t by wiping. **(b)** (*fig*) destroy s.t; get rid of s.t. **wipe the slate clean** ⇒ slate(*n*). **wipe s.t up** remove s.t that has been spilt or dropped by wiping.

¹wiper *c.n* thing that wipes(1) s.t: *a windscreen wiper.*

wire /waɪə/ *n* **1** *c/u.n* (piece of) metal in the shape of a piece of string. **2** *c.n* (*informal*) telegram. **barbed wire** ⇒ barb. **live wire** ⇒ live¹.
▷ *tr.v* **3** fasten or strengthen (s.t) with one or more wires. **4** supply (s.t) with the necessary system of wires: *It was such an old house that it did not have electricity so we had to have all the rooms wired (for it).* **5** send a telegram (to s.o) (telling s.t): *Please wire (us) (the time of your arrival).*

¹wire,cutters *pl.n* kind of tool like a big pair of scissors, used for cutting wire(1).

¹wire,haired *adj* (of some kinds of dogs) having stiff smooth hair.

¹wireless *adj* **1** not having or using wires(1). Compare **cordless**. **2** of or referring to (a) wireless(3).
▷ *c/u.n* **3** (*old use*) radio(1,2). **on the wireless** during a radio broadcast: *I heard that piece of news on the wireless.*

¹wireless ,set *c.n* (*old use*) radio(1).

,wire-¹netting *u.n* net made of wire and used to make a fence etc.

,wire ¹wool *u.n* material made of fine wires woven together to make a kind of pad, used to clean or polish metal objects like pots and pans.

¹wiriness *u.n* state or fact of being wiry.

¹wiring *u.n* system of wires(1) needed or used for a particular purpose, esp for supplying a building with electricity.

¹wiry *adj* (-ier, -iest) thin and strong: *He's small and wiry and can lift one of these sacks easily.*

wise /waɪz/ *adj* Opposite unwise. **1** (of ideas, behaviour etc) sensible; based on reason and experience. **2** (of people) thinking and/or behaving in wise(1) ways. **get wise to s.o/s.t** get the information about s.o/s.t and so think or behave sensibly. **none the wiser (for s.t)** not knowing any more than before (in spite of s.t): *He told her what the word meant but she was none the wiser (for his explanation) because she didn't understand some of the words he used.* **put s.o wise (to s.o/s.t)** (*informal*) give s.o (the right) information about s.o/s.t when he/she had not

known it before. **wise after the event** ⇒ event. **wise (of s.o) to do s.t** wise that s.o did (or should do etc) s.t: *It was wise of you to take an umbrella because it's beginning to rain.*

¹wise,crack *c.n* (*informal*) joke.

wisdom /'wɪzdəm/ *u.n* quality or state of being wise(1,2).

¹wisdom ,tooth *c.n* one of the four back teeth that (usu) appear when a person has stopped growing.

¹wise ,guy *c.n* (*derog*; *informal*) person who thinks he/she is cleverer than he/she really is, or that he/she knows more than he/she really does.

¹wisely *adv.*

wish /wɪʃ/ *c.n* **1** feeling or statement that one wants s.t even if one does not really need it. (Notice that 'want' has almost the same meaning but often it means that one does really need the thing.) **a wish for s.t** a wish that one may get s.t. **a wish to do s.t** a wish that one might do s.t. **make a wish** say (to oneself) that one wants s.t to happen, usu by magical means: *It is our custom to make a wish when we cut our birthday cake.*
▷ *v* **2** want (often s.t one cannot have just now or at all). **3** *intr.v* = make a wish. **wish s.o s.t** hope that s.o will get or have s.t: *Before the examinations her friends wished her success.* ⇒ well-wisher. **wish (s.o) to do s.t** want (s.o) to do s.t. (Notice that 'wish' is here more polite than 'want'.) **wish for s.t** want s.t; ask for s.t; would like to have s.t: *Here we have everything we could wish for. I wish for a little more time to myself.* **wish (that) . . .** want s.t to happen that cannot happen (just now): *I'm hungry and I wish I had one of my mother's cakes.* **wish s.o well** hope s.o will be happy, successful etc.

¹wish,bone *c.n* bone in the middle of a chicken, duck etc which is shaped like the letter V, used to wish(2) for s.t by two persons pulling it and the person with the biggest part being allowed to wish(2).

,wishful ¹thinking *u.n* thinking that s.t is true, or behaving as if it was, but only because one wishes it was true.

wishy-washy /'wɪʃɪ ,wɒʃɪ/ *adj* (-ier, -iest) (*derog*) **1** (of a liquid) weak; thin: *wishy-washy soup.* **2** (of ideas) not clear or definite; not strongly expressed. **3** (of a person) not having a strong character.

¹wishy-,washily *adv.*

wisp /wɪsp/ *c.n* **1** small thin piece: *Some wisps of hair could be seen sticking out under her hat. Wisps of smoke were still coming out of the building.* **2** small bunch of thin pieces: *I picked up a wisp of straw and cleaned the mud off my shoes with it.*

¹wispy *adj* (-ier, -iest) thin and small.

wistful /'wɪstfʊl/ *adj* (showing that one is) feeling one wants s.o/s.t one cannot have or (that one is) remembering s.o/s.t one no longer has.

¹wistfully *adv.* **¹wistfulness** *u.n.*

wit /wɪt/ *adv* **1 to wit** (*formal*; *joking*) namely; that is to say.
▷ *n* **2** *u.n* intelligent humour: *Her stories are filled with wit.* **3** *c/u.n* ability to think of things to say and/or write that are both clever and amusing: *Her writing shows her wit.* **4** *c.n* person who shows wit(2): *He's quite a wit!* **at one's wit's**

end no longer knowing what to say or do because one has tried everything one knows and found it is not suitable or enough. **frighten/scare s.o out of her/his wits** frighten s.o very much; give s.o a big fright. **have/keep one's wits about one** be/remain alert(2) and ready to deal with whatever happens. **have the wit to do s.t** think quickly and do s.t: *He hadn't the wit to say he was busy when his father asked him to do the shopping.* **live by one's wits** get money etc to live on by clever tricks instead of by working.

-witted *adj* having a brain or mind of the kind shown in the first part of the word: *quick-witted*; *slow-witted*.

witticism /'wɪtɪˌsɪzəm/ *c.n* witty thing s.o says or writes.

'wittily *adv* in a witty manner.

'wittiness *u.n* fact or quality of being witty.

'witty *adj* (*-ier*, *-iest*) showing wit(3).

witch /wɪtʃ/ *c.n* **1** woman who is supposed to be able to do (usu bad) things by magic(3). ⇒ bewitch. **2** (*derog*) bad (ugly) old woman.

'witch,craft *u.n* use of magic(3) to make (usu bad) things happen.

'witch,doctor *c.n* man in some societies, esp in Africa, who is supposed to be able to cure a person, make the rain fall etc by magic(3).

'witch,hunt *c.n* search for people one thinks dangerous because one does not agree with their ideas, in order to get them out of positions in which they have power and/or influence.

'witch,hunting *u.n.*

with /wɪð, wɪθ// *prep* **1** by use of; (by) using: *Cover her with this blanket. Make a hole with this stick.* **2** in the company of; bringing or taking: *Our teacher goes for a walk with us every Friday. They managed to escape from the fire with their lives but they lost all their things. Jane still lives with her parents.* **3** living in the house of; working for: *Peter is still with Ann. John has been with his company for 25 years.* **4** in the care or possession of: *After they separated, all the furniture remained with his wife.* **5** having or possessing: *We want a room with two beds. With the results of the tests, we can do something about the illness. It's a large box with a green lid.* **6** because of having or being full of: *The cinema was crowded with people. The tree was alive with insects.* **7** because of: *Joe is in bed with a bad cold. The little boy was crying with pain after falling. The prisoner was charged with causing a disturbance. Are you pleased with your present?* **8** at the same rate, speed, time etc as: *the size of the balloon increases with the temperature.* **9** in the course of: *Skill comes with experience. Good wine improves with age/time.* **10** When . . . comes or happens: *With his death all his property goes to his wife.* **11** in the same direction as: *They were swimming with the current.* Opposite against(4). **12** in: *We started our journey with beautiful weather.* **13** (joining people or things whose position, standard etc is being compared): *The surface of the lake was on a level with the third step. She ranks with the best tennis players. His skill cannot be compared with hers.* **14** accompanied by; including: *The judge sentenced him to five years' imprisonment with hard labour. They earn £70 a week with all meals.* **15** on acceptance of (a condition): *I agree to your plan with the* proviso *that . . . .* **16** in the

case of; as far as (s.o/s.t is concerned): *I agreed with everything he said. Such mistakes would be impossible with a trained worker. I wish I could do something with my hair — it looks terrible!* **17** in spite of: *With all his rough manners, he is really a kind man.* **18** on the side of; in favour of: *'We should all help the poor!' 'I'm with you, there.'* **19** (introducing expressions of thanks, love etc, usu at the end of a letter): *With many thanks for your kindness, Your loving daughter, Alice.* **with it** (*informal*) in the latest fashion. **with that/this** then; after (saying) that/this: *With that he walked out of the room.* For verb or noun + 'with', e.g *get away with s.t, bear with s.o, have nothing/s.t etc to do with s.o/s.t, put up with s.o/s.t, trust s.o/s.t with s.o/s.t, with an eye to s.t, with a view to s.t*, or adv + 'with', e.g *off with s.o.s.t/you, out with it, through with s.o/s,t, up with s.o/s.t,* ⇒ the verb, noun or adv.

withdraw /wɪð'drɔː/ *v* (*p.t* withdrew /wɪð'druː/ *p.p* withdrawn /wɪð'drɔːn/) **1** *tr/intr.v* (often — s.o/s.t from s.t) (cause (s.o/s.t) to) move aside, away or back (from s.t): *A cat can withdraw its claws but a dog cannot. He has withdrawn from the race because of a cold.* **2** *tr.v* take back (s.t one has said) so that it is as if it had not been said at all: *If a Member of Parliament says something that is against the rules, he/she is made to withdraw it.*

withdrawal /wɪð'drɔːəl/ *c/u.n* act of withdrawing s.t; state of being withdrawn.

with'drawal ,symptoms *pl.n* feelings of pain when one stops having s.t one has become addicted to (e.g cigarettes or a drug(2)).

with'drawn *adj* quiet and (seeming to be) interested only in one's own thoughts.

wither /'wɪðə/ *tr/intr.v* (often — (s.t) up) **1** (cause (a plant etc) to) become dry and/or brown because it is dying or because it has too little water, too much heat etc. **2** (*fig*) (cause (s.t) to) become less strong, fresh or important; (cause (s.t) to) become less full of life. **wither (s.t) away** (cause (s.t) to) wither until it is dead.

'withering *attrib.adj* (of the way in which s.o looks at or speaks to s.o) causing, trying to cause, or-e to feel shame; scornful: *She gave me a withering look.*

withhold /wɪð'həuld/ *tr.v* (*p.t,p.p* withheld /wɪð'held/) (often — s.t from s.o/s.t) keep (s.t) back (from s.o/s.t); not give (s.o/s.t) (a thing one would normally expect to give him/her/it): *I am going to withhold payment for the goods until they actually reach me.*

within /wɪ'ðɪn/ *adv* **1** (*formal*) inside: *While one dog stayed outside the house at night, the other was kept within.* **apply/inquire within** (on notices) ask inside (the building etc): *There was a notice outside the shop which said 'Salesmen wanted: apply within.'*

▷ *prep* **2** (in) not more than (a distance, time etc): *We chased the car and caught it within five kilometres.* **3** before the end of (a certain time); since the beginning of (a time): *We shall finish this work within the next few days. She had seen him ten times within the past hour.* **4** (*fig*) inside (the limits of s.o's ability etc): *It was within her power to make him very rich. The examination is well within her ability.* Opposite beyond(3). **5** inside; in the inner part of: *This secret must stay within* *the family/this house.* **within s.o's reach**; **within (easy) reach (of s.o/s.t)** ⇨ reach(n). **within reason** ⇨ reason(n). **within sight (of s.o/s.t)** ⇨ sight(n).

without /wɪ'ðaʊt/ *adv* **1** (*old use*) outside. (Notice that 'without' is used in many verbs, e.g 'do without', 'go without'; for explanations, ⇨ the entry for the verb.)
▷ *prep* **2** in a state of not having (with one); not using; with absence or lack of: *I can say without hesitation that I enjoyed the play very much.* **3** with no help or support from: *I can do this job without you, thank you.* **4** if there is not; if one has not got: *One can't live for long without water.* **5** not including: *There were five without the baby.* **6** with no possibility of; beyond; having gone too far for: *His case was without hope.* **do without (s.t)** ⇨ do(v). **go without s.t** ⇨ go(v). **it goes without saying (that . . .)** ⇨ say(v). **not without s.t** with a certain amount of s.t: *We managed to get in but not without some trouble.* **without fail** ⇨ fail(n). **without number** ⇨ number(n).

withstand /wɪð'stænd/ *tr.v* (*p.t,p.p* **withstood** /wɪð'stʊd/) resist; fight against (s.o/s.t) instead of surrendering(2); not be damaged by (s.o/s.t): *These toys withstand very rough treatment by young children.*

witness /'wɪtnɪs/ *c.n* **1** (often — *to s.t*) person who sees, or has seen, or hears or has heard, s.t: *I know what happened because I was a witness (to it).* **2** (*law*) person called to say in a court of law what he/she has seen or heard, or what he/she knows about s.o/s.t. **3** person who signs s.o else's will² etc to show that he/she has seen that person signing it too. **bear/give (false) witness** (*formal*) say that one has seen or heard s.t (but not speak the truth). **material witness** ⇨ material.
witness of s.t person who actually saw or heard s.t: *Were you yourself a witness of the accident or did you hear about it from someone else?*
▷ *tr.v* **4** see or hear (s.t) oneself: *Did you actually witness the attack?* **5** act as a witness(3) to (a will² etc): *Could you please witness my signature?* **6** show (s.t): *The redness of her cheeks witnessed the shame she felt.* Compare bear/give (false) witness. **witness to s.t (a)** act as a witness(2) to help prove s.t. **(b)** witness(6) s.t.
'witness ,box *c.n* (also *law*) place in a court of law in which a witness(2) stands when he/she is giving evidence.

-witted, witticism, wittily, wittiness, witty ⇨ wit.

wives /waɪvz/ *pl* of wife.

wizard /'wɪzəd/ *c.n* **1** man who can do magic(3). **2** (often — *at s.t*) person who is very clever or skilful (at s.t): *Nick is a wizard at making model trains.*

'wizardry *u.n* **1** doing of magic(3). **2** great skill or cleverness.

wizened /'wɪznd/ *adj* **1** (of fruit etc) dried up, usu because it is old: *There were only a few wizened old apples there.* **2** (of people, human skin etc) looking as if he/she/it is dried up.

wk *written abbr* week.

WNW *abbr* West North West.

WO *written abbr* Warrant Officer.

wobble /'wɒbl/ *c.n* **1** example of wobbling(2): *After a few wobbles the child managed to ride the bicycle quite well.*
▷ *tr/intr.v* **2** (cause (s.t) to) move from side to side, up and down etc in a dangerous or unpleasant way: *Stop wobbling the table or you'll spill the tea!*
'wobbler *c.n* person who wobbles(2).
'wobbly *adj* (*-ier, -iest*) not steady: *a wobbly jelly.*

woe /wəʊ/ *n* **1** *u.n* (*old use*) sadness. **2** *c.n* trouble: *People often go to their doctor to tell her or him all their woes.* **tale of woe** ⇨ tale.

woebegone /'wəʊbɪ,gɒn/ *adj* (*formal*) very sad and miserable.

'woeful *adj* **1** (*formal*) sad: *There was a woeful look on her face as she watched her bag fall down the mountain.* **2** (*attrib*) unfortunate; that is to be regretted: *a woeful lack of equipment(2); woeful ignorance.*
'woefully *adv.* **'woefulness** *u.n.*

woke /wəʊk/ *p.t* of wake¹.

woken /'wəʊkən/ *p.p* of wake(v).

wolf /wʊlf/ *c.n* (*pl* **wolves** /wʊlvz/) **1** kind of wild animal that looks like a big dog and hunts in groups. **2** (*derog; informal*) man who makes a habit of trying to attract women so that he can have sex with them. **a wolf in sheep's clothing** (*derog; fig*) a person who seems, or pretends to be, good but is really bad. **cry wolf** (*fig*) call for help when one does not really need it with the result that another time people do not come when one is really in danger. **keep the wolf from the door** (*fig*) manage, with difficulty, to get enough money, food etc to live on.
▷ *tr.v* **3** (often — *s.t down*) eat or swallow (s.t) very quickly and/or hungrily.

'wolf ,whistle *c.n* sound a man sometimes makes by whistling with his mouth when he sees a pretty woman.

'wolf,hound *c.n* kind of big dog that used to be used to hunt wolves(1) or to protect sheep etc from them.

'wolfish *adj* **1** (*derog*) cruel; fierce. **2** looking like a wolf(1). **3** eating very quickly and/or hungrily.

wolves /wʊlvz/ *pl.n* ⇨ wolf(n).

woman /'wʊmən/ *attrib.adj* **1** (of human beings) female: *a woman judge.*
▷ *n* (*pl* **women** /'wɪmɪn/) **2** *c.n* adult female human being. **3** *unique n* female human beings in general: *Woman is different from man in being able to give birth to children.* **4** *c.n* female human being with whom s.o lives as her husband, lover etc: *Who is the woman in your son's life now?*

,woman of the 'world *c.n* woman with a lot of experience of life, business etc. ⇨ man of the world.

'woman,hood *u.n* **1** time or state of being a woman after one is no longer a child. **2** female qualities: *She shows her womanhood in everything she does.* ⇨ manhood.

'womanish *adj* (*derog*) (of a man, or a man's way of behaving, speaking etc) like a woman instead of a man.

womanize, -ise /'wʊmə,naɪz/ *intr.v* (*derog*) (of a man) spend a lot of time with different women in order to have sex with them.

'woma,nizer, -iser *c.n* (*derog*) man who womanizes.

'woman,kind *unique n* women in general. ⇨ mankind.

'womanliness *u.n* fact or quality of being womanly.

'womanly *adj* (who behaves, talks etc in ways) that one expects from a woman(1).

,woman-to-'woman *adj* (of a conversation between two women) speaking openly about s.t without keeping anything back. ⇨ man-to-man.

'women,folk *pl.n* **1** female human beings in general. **2** female relatives of a man or men.

womb /wuːm/ *c.n* part of a female human being or animal in which a baby grows before it is born.

wombat /'wɒmbæt/ *c.n* Australian animal that looks rather like a small bear, has soft fur and keeps its babies in a pouch(2).

women(folk) ⇨ woman.

won /wʌn/ *p.t,p.p* of win.

wonder /'wʌndə/ *attrib.adj* **1** surprisingly good, successful etc: *a wonder cure.*

▷ *n* **2** *u.n* feeling that s.o/s.t is strange, surprising and usu also beautiful, pleasant etc: *I was filled with wonder when I saw his paintings.* **3** *c.n* thing that people think strange, surprising and usu also beautiful, pleasant etc. **4** *c.n* (*informal*) person or action who/that is strange, surprising and usu also beautiful, pleasant, skilful, clever etc: *Linda is a real wonder when it comes to giving big parties; I don't know how she does it.* **It's a wonder (that)** . . . It's very surprising (that) . . .: *It's a wonder that he hasn't discovered the truth.* **Small wonder (that . . .)** ⇨ small(*adj*).

▷ *v* **5** *tr/intr.v* (feel surprised and) want to know (why, where etc . . .): *Where ever has he put the key, I wonder. 'Mary's gone!' 'I don't wonder after all the things you said to her.'* **6** *intr.v* (often — about s.o/s.t) feel doubtful (about s.o/s.t): *'Is he ill or just pretending?' 'I wonder.' 'Is Eric really a trained teacher?' 'Well, I sometimes wonder about that myself.'* **wonder at s.t** be surprised by s.t: *I often wonder at the way some children talk to their parents.* **wonder what, why** etc want to know what, why etc: *I wonder why the train is late this time.* **wonder what to do, where** etc **to do s.t** would like to know what to do, where etc to do (s.t): *I am wondering what to wear today — do you think it's going to be cold?*

'wonderful *adj* very good; better than one expected: *What wonderful news!*

'wonder,land *n* **1** *c.n* place that is very beautiful, fertile(1) etc. **2** *unique n* magic(1) place where fairies etc live.

'wonderment *u.n* (often *in —*) (*formal*) state of wonder(2); feeling of wonder(2): *I looked in wonderment at their beautiful garden.*

'wonders *pl.n* things that are surprisingly good. **do/work wonders** do things that people did not think possible: *If you are feeling sick, try some of this medicine; it works wonders with me.* **Wonders will never cease** (*proverb*) That is very surprising: *'Peter has passed his examination after all!' 'Wonders will never cease.'*

'wondrous /-rəs/ *adj* (*poetical*) wonderful.

wonky /'wɒŋkɪ/ *adj* (-ier, -iest) (*informal*) badly made; unsteady: *a wonky shelf.*

won't /wəʊnt/ = will not. ⇨ will¹.

woo /wuː/ *tr.v* **1** try to persuade (s.o) to love and/or marry one. **2** try to persuade (s.o) to support one: *The manager successfully wooed the committee so that they did what he wanted.*

wooer /'wuːə/ *c.n* person who woos(1).

wood /wʊd/ *n* **1** *u.n* (also *attrib*) material of which trees are made; this material when it is cut etc and used to make things like tables and ships or to burn in a fire. **2** *c.n* group of trees that is large but not as large as a forest. **3** *c.n* kind of golf club with a wooden head, used when one wants to hit the ball a long way. **from/in the wood** from/in a barrel, not a bottle: *In this pub you can get wine from the wood.* **out of the wood** (*fig*) no longer in the danger or trouble one has been in before: *Don't get too excited; we aren't out of the wood yet.* **s.o can't see the wood for the trees** (*proverb*) s.o is looking at the small details of s.t so much that he/she fails to notice its general meaning, which is more important.

'wood,carver *c.n* person who carves(1) objects in wood.

'wood,craft *u.n* knowledge of forests and how to live, hunt etc in them.

'wood,cut *c.n* picture printed from a design(1) cut in wood.

'wood,cutter *c.n* person who cuts trees down; person who cuts wood.

'wooded *adj* having trees or woods(2) on it: *wooded hills.*

'wooden *adj* **1** made of wood(1). **2** (*derog; fig*) stiff and/or awkward; lacking expression.

'woodenness *u.n* state or condition of being wooden(2).

,wooden 'spoon *c.n* (*fig*) prize said to be given to the person, team etc that is last in a competition (although that person etc is not given a wooden spoon).

'woodland /-lənd/ *u.n* (also *attrib*) area of land with trees or woods on it.

'wood,pecker *c.n* kind of bird that gets insects out of wood by hitting it with its long beak.

'wood ,pigeon *c.n* kind of large pigeon with white areas on its wings.

'wood,pile *c.n* pile of wood.

'wood ,pulp *u.n* wood that has been cut up and crushed in order to make paper out of it.

'woods *pl.n* woodland; one or more woods(2).

'wood,shed *c.n* shed in which wood is stored, usu for burning in a fire.

'woodsman *c.n* (*pl* -men) man working in a forest or woodland; man skilled in woodcraft.

'wood,wind *n* **1** *u/def.n* (also *attrib*) musical instruments made of wood(1) and played by blowing with the mouth: *the woodwind section of the orchestra.* **2** *pl.n* people in an orchestra who play such instruments.

'wood,work *u.n* **1** (also *attrib*) work or skill of making things out of wood(1); carpentry. **2** things made out of wood(1). **3** parts of a building etc that are made of wood(1).

'wood,worm *n* **1** *c.n* larva of a kind of insect that eats wood(1). **2** *u.n* damage caused by woodworms(1): *Don't put that table in your house until you get rid of the woodworm in it.*

'woody *adj* (-ier, -iest) **1** hard like wood(1). **2** having a wood(2) in or on it.

wooer ⇨ woo.

woof /wʊf/ *interj* **1** (sound made by a dog when it barks).

▷ *c.n/intr.v* **2** (of a dog) bark.

woofer /'wuːfə/ *c.n* part of a loudspeaker that gives the low notes. Compare tweeter.

wool /wʊl/ *u.n* (also *attrib*) **1** kind of soft wavy hair that sheep and some other kinds of animals have. **2** material spun into long threads from wool(1), used in knitting or weaving. **3** cloth made by knitting or weaving wool(2). ⇨ cotton-wool, wire wool. *pull the wool over s.o's eyes* (*fig*) cheat or trick s.o; hide the truth from s.o.

‚**woollen** /ˈwʊlən/ *adj* made of wool(2).

‚**woollens** *pl.n* clothes made of wool(2).

ˈ**woolliness** *u.n* state or fact of being woolly.

ˈ**woolly** *adj* (*-ier, -iest*) **1** of, like, wool; smooth and soft. **2** (*derog*; *fig*) not clear: *I can never follow his woolly ideas.*

▷ *c.n* (*pl -ies*) **3** article of clothing made of wool(2), worn on the upper half of the body.

‚**woolly-ˈheaded** *adj* (*derog*) whose thoughts or ideas are woolly(2): *a woolly-headed thinker.*

woozy /ˈwuːzɪ/ *adj* (*-ier, -iest*) (*informal*) dizzy(1); confused in one's mind, often because one has drunk too much alcoholic(1) drink or because one has been hit on the head.

ˈ**woozily** *adv.* ˈ**wooziness** *u.n.*

Worcester sauce /ˌwʊstə ˈsɔːs/ *u.n* kind of dark sauce that has a strong sharp taste.

word /wɜːd/ *c.n* **1** unit of meaning in written language which has a space before and after it; one of these units when it is spoken: *Thousands of words are explained in this dictionary. a man/ woman of his/her word* a man/woman who keeps the promises he/she makes. *a play on words* = wordplay. *as good as one's word* absolutely honest in doing what one has said one is going to do. *break one's word* fail to do what one has promised to do. (*by*) *word of mouth* ⇨ mouth(*n*). *eat one's words* (*fig*; *informal*) admit that s.t one has said was wrong. *from the word go* ⇨ go(*n*). *hardly/not get a word in edgeways* ⇨ edgeways. *give one's word* (*to s.o*) make a promise (to s.o). *give the word* say s.t that one or more persons have been waiting for: *Don't put the lights out till I give the word; then we'll surprise your mother.* (*have*) *a word in s.o's ear* (*about s.o/s.t*) (usu *fig*) (say) s.t private or secret to s.o (about s.o/s.t). *have a word with s.o* (*about s.o/s.t*) (*informal*) speak to s.o (about s.o/s.t). (*have*) *the last word* (*on s.t*) (succeed in making) the final remark or speech (about s.t) in an argument so that one has (or appears to have) won it. *have words* (*with s.o*) have an argument or quarrel (with s.o). *in other words* saying it in a different way: *Joe doesn't work but he manages to live very well; in other words he is clever but useless. in s.o's own words* said using the exact words s.o used herself/himself. *keep one's word* (*to s.o*) do what one has promised (s.o). *leave word with s.o* leave a message with s.o. *a man of one's word* ⇨ man(*n*). *My word!* (an expression showing surprise, admiration etc). *not believe a word of s.t* not believe any part of s.t. *not have a good word* (*to say*) *for s.o/s.t* not have anything that one is willing to say in favour of s.o/s.t. (*not*) *in so many words* (not) actually said or written as clearly or definitely as that (but certainly suggested): *He didn't tell me in so many words that he was going to vote for us, but it was clear that he was. put in a good word for s.o* (*with s.o*) recommend s.o (to s.o). *put s.t into words* express in speech or writing s.t that was only felt or thought before. *put words into s.o's mouth* ⇨ mouth(*n*). *not say a word* (*of*

s.t) (*to s.o*) keep (s.t) a complete secret (from s.o). *say the word* give the order; tell s.o to do or start s.t: *I'm ready; just say the word and I'll start. send word* (*about/of s.o/s.t*) (*to s.o*) send (s.o) information (about s.o/s.t). *send word* (*to s.o*) *to do s.t* send (s.o) orders to do s.t. *take s.o at her/his word* do exactly what s.o has said: *A lot of people say 'Come and see me any time', but if you take them at their word few of them are glad to see you! take s.o's word for it/s.t* believe s.o when he/she says s.t, without wanting any more proof. *take the words out of s.o's mouth* ⇨ mouth(*n*). *the last word in s.t* the most modern example of s.t; the person or thing that is in the very latest fashion in s.t. *war of words* serious argument. *word by word* one word after another, separately: *The small boy read the story to me word by word. word for word* (**a**) exactly; without any changes: *The examiner was surprised to find two answer papers which were the same, word for word.* (**b**) translating each word as a separate unit. *Words fail me* I am so surprised, shocked etc that I cannot say anything.

▷ *tr.v* **2** use words to say or write (s.t): *How shall I word the letter so as not to hurt his feelings?*

ˈ**word ‚blindness** *u.n* (*informal*) dyslexia.

ˈ**wordiness** *u.n* (*derog*) fact of being wordy.

ˈ**wording** *c/u.n* way(s) in which one chooses one's words in order to say or write what one means.

‚**word-ˈperfect** *adj* (usu *pred*) speaking or writing in a way that contains no wrong words; spoken or written without any mistakes in the words used.

ˈ**word‚play** *u.n* using words in a joking way; making puns(1).

‚**word-ˈprocessor** *c.n* machine like a typewriter but with a computer and a monitor(3), used to type, esp business, things.

ˈ**wordy** *adj* (*-ier, -iest*) (*derog*) using too many words to say s.t.

wore /wɔː/ *p.t* of wear.

work /wɜːk/ *n* **1** *u.n* thing(s) one does in order to earn money or because one thinks one ought to do it/them or because one is forced to. **2** *u.n* thing that a machine etc is made to, is supposed to, do: *This new kind of digging machine does its work well.* Compare work(6). **3** *c/u.n* thing(s) produced as a result of s.o's work(1): *Is that painting all your own work? There is an interesting work by the painter Giotto there. I think this damage is the work of small boys.* **4** *u.n* (*technical*) force multiplied by distance. *all in a/the day's work* not unusual; normal for that situation: *Rescuing cats that have climbed trees and cannot get down again is all in the day's work for firemen. at work* (*on s.t*) busy (doing s.t). *get/go/set to work* (*on s.t*) start (doing s.t). *have one's work cut out* (*to do s.t*) find it very difficult (to do s.t). *in work* having a job; employed. *make hard work of s.t* have difficulty in doing s.t. *make short work of s.o/ s.t* (*informal*) deal with s.o/s.t, finish etc s.t quickly: *You made short work of that meal! out of work* not having a job; unemployed.

▷ *v* **5** *intr.v* do s.t in order to earn money, because one thinks one ought to do it or because one is forced to. ⇨ overwork. **6** *tr/intr.v* (cause (s.t) to) do what it is supposed to do; (cause (s.t) to) do its work successfully: *My typewriter isn't working properly. I don't think that idea of yours will work. Do you know how to work this machine? The government is working the coal mines here.* Compare work(2). **7** *tr/intr.v* (cause (s.o) to) work(1): *Our teacher works us hard.* **8** *tr.v* go through (a place) doing s.t: *Those thieves work any place where there are crowds, stealing things out of people's bags and pockets.* **9** *tr.v* (informal) manage to do (s.t) successfully: *Can you work it/things so that we get home early this evening?* **10** *tr.v* press (s.t) with one's hands to make it into s.t: *Before a potter¹ uses clay, he works it with his hands.* **11** *tr.v* operate (s.t) with one's hands etc: *This toy is worked by metal rods.*

work against s.o/s.t have a bad result for s.o/s.t: *He wants a job as a bank clerk but the fact that he is bad at mathematics works against him.*

work (away) at s.t try or work hard to do s.t: *Fred isn't good at languages but he's working (away) at learning enough French for his holiday.*

work by s.t use s.t as its means of working(6): *That bell works by electricity.*

work one's fingers to the bone ⇨ finger(*n*).

work (s.t) free ⇨ free(*adv*).

work like a horse ⇨ horse(*n*).

work (s.t) loose (cause (s.t) to) become loose by moving (it) a little in one direction, a little in another direction etc: *After the screws that held the door had been in place for a few months, they worked loose and the door fell off.*

work miracles ⇨ miracle.

work on s.o/s.t gradually try to influence s.o/s.t.

work out (a) be able to come to a clear answer: *This sum won't work out; I think there must be a mistake in it somewhere.* (b) have the result one wants: *Their marriage didn't work out so now they have separated.* (c) have a result: *How did your plan work out when you tried it?* (d) have or take exercise; have a workout. **work out at/to s.t** reach a certain amount after one has made all the calculations: *With taxes and service, our hotel bill worked out at £102.13.* **work itself out** succeed, in the end, in doing what it is supposed to do. **work s.t out** (a) think about s.t until one reaches the answer: *I can't work this sum out. Can you work out why Mary wants these papers?* ⇨ working-out. (b) take things from a mine etc until nothing is left in it. ⇨ workings.

work s.o over (informal) attack s.o seriously with several blows.

work one's passage (to s.w) ⇨ passage.

work round to s.o/s.t gradually reach a subject of conversation etc after mentioning others: *After a lot of unimportant talk, Sarah finally worked round to telling her parents that she was leaving home.* **work s.o round to s.t** gradually persuade s.o to do s.t.

work to rule ⇨ rule(*n*). ⇨ work-to-rule.

work s.o up make s.o angry, sad etc. **work s.t up** bring s.t gradually to a better, or a finished, state. **work up an appetite** ⇨ appetite. **work up to s.t** make gradual progress towards a subject of conversation etc: *The politician had some unpleasant news to give his listeners but he worked up to it by talking about all the good things he had done for the country first.*

work one's way (through) (to s.t) ⇨ way(*n*).

work wonders ⇨ wonders (⇨ wonder).

-work *u.n* thing done or made by using the thing mentioned in the first part of the word: *metalwork; needlework.*

'workable *adj* **1** that one can work(6) or use; that will work(6): *a workable machine, a workable plan.* **2** that can be worked(9). Opposite unworkable.

'worka,day *attrib.adj* concerning daily life and/or events; not at all unusual; not very interesting or exciting: *workaday matters.*

'work,basket *c.n* basket in which one keeps the needles, thread etc one uses for sewing.

'work,bench *c.n* table or flat surface on which a person works (e.g cutting wood or metal) with tools.

'work,book *c.n* **1** book that gives a student work to do herself/himself. **2** = handbook. **3** book in which a student makes notes of things he/she does in each lesson etc.

'work,day *c.n* **1** day on which people work(5); day that is not a holiday. **2** (number of) hours during which one works(5) in a day.

,worked 'up *adj* (often *all* —) very excited or worried.

'worker *c.n* **1** person or animal who/that works(5). **2** person who works(5) with her/his hands more than with her/his brain. **3** person who works(5) hard: *For this job we need people who are workers.*

'work ,force *c/def.n* all the workers(1,2) employed by a person, factory etc, or in a country, a city etc.

'work-,in *c.n* kind of strike(1) by workers(1,2) during which they refuse to leave the place where they work (and continue to work) instead of stopping work(1).

'working *attrib.adj* **1** who/which is working (work(5,6)). **2** who works(5) with her/his hands rather than with her/his brain. **3** during which one works(5): *a working holiday.* **4** used for work(1), not for pleasure, decoration etc: *working clothes.*

,working 'class *adj* (**'working-,class** when *attrib*) **1** belonging to the class of society which works(5) for wages in a manual(1) or industrial context(2).

▷ *def/def.pl.n* **2** people who belong to this class. **,working 'classes** *def.pl.n* = working class(2).

,working 'day *c/def.n* hours of a day during which one works(5).

,working 'knowledge *c.n* (usu — *of s.t*) just enough knowledge (of s.t) for s.o to be able to use it for what he/she wants to do: *I have a working knowledge of German — enough for my needs when I travel.*

,working 'order *u.n* **in** (**good** etc) **working order** in a condition that allows it to do its work(2) (well etc).

,working-'out *c.n* **1** way in which one works s.t (e.g a problem) out(a). **2** way in which s.t, e.g a plan, develops.

'working ,party *c.n* (*pl -ies*) group of people formed for a particular purpose, e.g to try to find the answer to a certain problem and then make recommendations to the people who set the group up.

'workings *pl.n* **1** ways in which s.t does its work(2): *I just can't understand the workings of*

that man's mind — he says the strangest things.
2 parts of a mine which have been worked out.

ˌ**working ˈweek** *c/def.n* hours or days in a week during which one works(5).

ˈ**work,load** *c.n* amount of work(5) one or more persons, animals, machines etc have to do: *My workload is heavier this week because two of the people in the office are ill.*

ˈ**workman** *c.n* (*pl* -*men*) **1** man who works(5) with his hands rather than with his brain. **2** man who has the amount of skill in s.t (esp in work(1) with his hands) shown by another word in the sentence: *a bad/good/skilled/trained workman.*

ˈ**workman,like** *adj* efficient; done in a way that produces the result one wants with the least waste of time, effort etc.

ˈ**workman,ship** *u.n* **1** skill in making s.t. **2** things that show the amount of skill with which s.t has been made. **3** thing(s) that has/have been made.

ˌ**work of ˈart** *c.n* (*pl* works of art) **1** picture etc painted etc by an artist. **2** (*fig*) thing made, arranged or done very beautifully or skilfully: *The cakes Wendy makes are real works of art.*

ˈ**work,out** *c.n* taking of exercise in order to prepare for a game, sport, match, race etc.

ˈ**work,room** *c.n* room used for doing work(1) in.

works *n* (*pl* works) **1** *c/def.pl.n* (also *attrib*) factory; place where a particular kind of work(5) is done, or a particular kind of thing is made, on a commercial scale: *a gas works*; *the works canteen*(1). **2** parts of s.t, e.g a clock, which move. **a spanner in the works** ⇨ spanner. **give s.o the works** (*informal*) (**a**) give s.o all the information about s.o/s.t. (**b**) attack s.o violently. **gum up the works** ⇨ gum¹ (*v*).

ˈ**work,shop** *c.n* **1** = workroom. **2** place in a factory, big garage etc where machines are repaired. **3** group of people who are all interested in the same thing and who join together to study it.

ˈ**work,shy** *adj* (*derog*) not liking work(1); avoiding work(1) whenever one can.

ˈ**work,study** *c.n* (*pl* -*ies*) study of how people are working (⇨ work(5)) in order to find faster, better or more efficient methods.

ˈ**work,top** *c.n* top of a low cupboard etc which is flat so that one can do one's work(1) on it, e.g in a kitchen.

ˌ**work-to-ˈrule** *c.n* kind of strike(1) in which workers(1,2) do their work(1) but slower than usual because they follow every rule carefully even when it is not necessary in a particular case.

world /wɜ:ld/ *n* **1** *c.n* planet or group of stars, esp one where there may be life. **2** *def.n* our universe(1). **3** *def.n* (also *attrib*) our planet; earth(1): *The United Nations tries to help the peoples of the world to understand each other better. I'm studying world politics.* **4** *def.n* all the people interested in a particular thing; the thing such people are interested in: *the business world*; *the fashion world*; *the world of music.* **5** *def.n* all the people of a particular kind; the place or condition such people live in: *the world of film-stars.* **6** *c/def.n* all the living creatures of a particular kind, or the place or condition they live in: *the world of the ant.* **be/mean all the world to s.o** be more important to s.o than anyone or anything else. **bring s.o/s.t into the**

world give birth to s.o/s.t. **come down in the world** lose the high social or financial status(1) one has had. **come into the/this world** be born. **come up in the world** gain a higher social or financial status(1) than one has had. **dead to the world** ⇨ dead. **do s.o a/the world of good** do s.o a great amount of good. **for all the world as if . . .** exactly or just as if . . . . **go down (in the world)** ⇨ go down. (**have**) **the best of both worlds** (have) the advantages or benefits(1) of two possibilities in a situation instead of having to choose only one of them: *In this job I have the best of both worlds — a job with a good salary and the chance to travel.* **live in a world of one's own** have an imaginary world in one's head which one treats as if it was the real world one lives in. **make a world of difference (to s.o/s.t)** make a very big difference (to s.o/s.t). **make one's way (in the world)** ⇨ way. **man of the world** ⇨ man(*n*). **not for the world** not for any reason at all: *I wouldn't for the world give Sally the idea that I don't like her clothes.* **on top of the world** ⇨ top¹(*n*). **out of this world** (*informal*) wonderful; extremely pleasant, attractive etc. **the animal/mineral/plant world** animals/minerals/plants in general. **the New World** ⇨ new. **the Old World** ⇨ old. **Third World** ⇨ three. **think the world of s.o/s.t** have a very high opinion of s.o/s.t; like s.o/s.t very much. **What etc in the world . . .?** (a way of showing surprise or impatience when one is asking a question) *What etc ever . . .?*: *Where in the world can Jane have put the key?* **woman of the world** ⇨ woman. **the whole world** (**a**) every part of the world. (**b**) everybody: *The whole world must have heard about that film star's private life.* **worlds apart** extremely different.

ˌ**World ˈBank** *def.n* international bank whose job is to help the poorer (developing) nations of the world.

ˈ**world-,beater** *c.n* person/animal/thing (said or thought to be) better than any other in the world.

ˌ**world-ˈclass** *adj* good enough to compete against the best ones in the world.

ˌ**World ˈHealth ˌOrgani,zation** *def.n* = WHO.

ˈ**worldliness** *u.n* state or fact of being worldly(2).

ˈ**worldly** *adj* (-*ier*, -*iest*) **1** (of things) in or of our world(3) and not the place we are supposed to go to after we die. **2** (of people or their ideas etc) concerned with material things, not spiritual(1) ones. Opposite unworldly.

ˌ**worldly ˈgoods** *pl.n* material possessions in this world(3), not spiritual(1) possessions that will help us in the place we are supposed to go to after we die: *All that old man's worldly goods are the clothes he is wearing.*

ˌ**worldly-ˈwise** *adj* having plenty of experience of life.

ˌ**world ˈpower** *c.n* one of the strongest and most important countries which can influence what happens in most parts of the world.

ˈ**world-,shaking** *attrib.adj* very important; having a very great effect.

ˌ**world ˈwar** *c/u.n* war in which some of the strongest and most important nations fight each other, and which is fought in more than one part of the world.

,**world-'weary** adj (informal) bored with life.

,**world'wide** adj/adv (existing) in every part of the world.

worm /wɜːm/ c.n **1** small long creature with no legs or bones and that lives in the ground, or in the bodies of people or animals etc. **have worms** have worms inside one's body, usu in one's stomach or bowels.

▷ tr.v **2** give (a person or animal a) medicine etc to get rid of the live worms inside her/him/it. **worm one's way in(to s.t)** (informal) get in(to s.t) gradually by moving from side to side, or (fig) by behaving very nicely: At first she did not like the child much, but he wormed his way into her affections during the following months. **worm s.t out (of s.o)** (informal) get s.t, e.g a secret, out (of s.o) by cunning(1) means or by behaving very nicely.

'**worm-,eaten** adj having been partly eaten by worms(1) so that s.t is rotten or has holes in it.

'**worm-,hole** c.n hole in the ground or in wood which has been made by a worm(1).

'**wormy** adj (-ier, -iest) **1** having worms(1) in s.t. **2** having holes in s.t which were made by worms(1). **3** like a worm(1).

worn(-out) ⇒ wear.

worry /'wʌrɪ/ n (pl -ies) **1** u.n feeling of being anxious; feeling of not being happy or satisfied because of s.t that makes one rather afraid. **2** c.n (often a — to s.o) person or thing causing s.o worry(1).

▷ v (-ies, -ied) **3** tr/intr.v (cause (s.o) to) feel anxious, unhappy, dissatisfied or rather afraid. **4** tr.v (of dogs etc) chase and bite (other animals): The farmers here have a lot of trouble with dogs that worry their sheep at night. **be worried sick** feel worry(1) (almost) to the point of being sick. **worry (one's head) about/over s.o/s.t** worry because of s.o/s.t. **worry s.o for s.t** try again and again to get s.o to give one s.t: She worried him for a decision about the dates of their holiday until he finally decided.

'**worried** adj **1** feeling worry(1): a worried father. **2** ,showing worry(1): a worried look on one's face.

worrisome /'wʌrɪsəm/ adj causing worry(1).

worse /wɜːs/ adj **1** (comp of 'bad'/'ill'): Too much rain is bad but too little is worse. He began to feel ill that evening and in the morning he was worse. Opposite better. **a change for the worse** ⇒ change(n). **even worse (than s.o/s.t)** (a way of making 'worse' stronger): The soup was horrible but the meat was even worse. **for better or for worse** ⇒ better² (adj). **go from bad to worse** ⇒ go. **none the worse (for s.t)** not having suffered in any way because of s.t. (**and**) **to make matters worse** ⇒ matter(n). **the worse for wear** showing signs of wear(3). **worse at s.t (than s.o)** not able to do s.t so well (as s.o else can). **worse at s.t (than at s.t)** not able to do s.t so well (as one can do s.t else). **worse luck** (informal) unfortunately: Joan hurt her leg before the match, worse luck, so she wasn't able to play. **worse still** . . . and this was even worse (than what I have already said): It rained all day on Saturday and, worse still, the electricity went off so that we couldn't even watch television.

▷ adv **2** (comp of 'badly') in a way that is less good, more unpleasant or more painful: That girl sings

worse than her sister. The second injection hurt worse than the first. Opposite better.

'**worsen** tr/intr.v (cause (s.t) to) become worse(1).

worship /'wɜːʃɪp/ u.n **1** (showing of) great respect for (and often praying to) s.o/s.t, esp God, a god, or s.t one thinks sacred. **divine worship** ⇒ divine. **her/his/your Worship** (way of speaking about or to a magistrate, mayor(ess) etc).

▷ v (-pp-, US -p-) **2** tr.v show great respect to (s.o/s.t, esp God, a god or s.o/s.t one thinks sacred). **3** tr.v admire or love (s.o/s.t) very much. **worship the ground s.o walks on** ⇒ ground(n).

'**worshipful** adj (often with capital **W**) (title given to mayor(esse)s and certain other groups of people in England): the Worshipful the Mayor; the Worshipful Company of . . . .

'**worshipper** c.n (US '**worshiper**) person who worships(2,3) (s.o/s.t).

worst /wɜːst/ adj **1** (superl of 'bad'/'ill') least good or well: If one has a fever, one usually feels worst in the evening. Opposite best. **at (the) worst** even if everything is as bad as it can be; the worst thing that can happen is (that . . .): Well, we may miss the last bus, but at (the) worst we shall have to spend the night here in Aunt Mabel's spare room. **do one's worst** do the worst thing(s) one can do (the suggestion is that even that will not be enough to hurt s.o etc): Let him do his worst — I will never do what he wants. **if the worst comes to the worst** if the worst possible situation arises. **the worst of s.t is** the part or result of s.t that is the worst is: Mike is late, and the worst of that is that our team will not be ready when the match starts.

▷ adv **2** (superl of 'badly') most unpleasantly or badly: I always sleep worst when I have eaten too much. Opposite best. **come off worst** lose (in a fight, argument etc).

▷ def.n **3** least good person, animal or thing.

▷ tr.v **4** (formal) defeat or beat (s.o) in a fight, argument etc.

worsted /'wʊstɪd/ u.n (also attrib) kind of cloth made of wool.

worth /wɜːθ/ prep **1** having the value of; of the value of: That house is worth £60 000 now. **2** owning things that have a total value of: That old woman is worth half a million pounds now that her husband has died. **3** (often — doing; — it/s.t) good enough to deserve (to be done): Don't run to catch the bus; it isn't worth the effort because there'll be another one in five minutes. I don't think those old bottles are worth keeping. It isn't worth arguing because he'll never do what you want. **for all s.o is worth** as hard or strongly as s.o can: Even though Mary ran for all she was worth, she couldn't reach the bus in time. **for what it's worth** although it may not be worth much; although it may not be true: Here's the story Margaret told me, for what it's worth. (**make it**) **worth s.o's while (to do s.t)** (make sure that) s.o is rewarded with enough money, benefits etc. ⇒ worthwhile. **worth one's weight in gold** ⇒ gold(n). **worth s.o's while (to do s.t)** useful enough to s.o for her/him to do it: I'm not working late next week; it isn't worth my while because the extra money goes on tax. ⇒ worthwhile.

▷ *u.n* **4** value; amount s.t is worth(1).

-worth as much as is worth(1) the first part of the word or phrase(1): *I need a hundred pounds-worth of dollar traveller's cheques, please.*

worthily /'wɜːðɪlɪ/ *adv* in a worthy(1) way.

worthiness /'wɜːðɪnɪs/ *u.n* state or fact of being worthy(1).

worthless /'wɜːθlɪs/ *adj* having no value or worth(4).

'worthlessness *u.n.*

,worth'while *adj* that is worth(3) doing; that is worth(3) the money, time, trouble etc that it costs: *Anything we can do to send food to hungry children is worthwhile.*

'worthy /'wɜːðɪ/ *adj* (-ier, -iest) **1** who/that one should admire, respect or support: *Although this is a gambling game, it is in a worthy cause because all the profits go to our local hospital.* Opposite unworthy. **worthy of s.o** of the high standard expected of s.o: *At the end of his speech he made some rude remarks about our town which I did not think were worthy of him.* **worthy of s.t** deserving s.t: *I don't agree with his views but I think they are worthy of respect.* **worthy to do s.t** good enough to be allowed to do s.t: *I don't think he is worthy to become our mayor.*

▷ *c.n* (*pl -ies*) **2** (*joking*) important person.

-worthy deserving the thing that is given in the first part of the word: praiseworthy; blameworthy.

would (strong form /wʊd/, weak form /wəd/) *aux.v* (no *pres.p*; negative forms would not or wouldn't /'wʊdnt/; he/she would can be he'd /hiːd/, she'd /ʃiːd/; it would can be it'd /'ɪtəd/; would have can be would've /'wʊdəv/; 'would' is followed by the infinitive of a verb without *to*) **1** *p.t* of 'will' in reported speech: *'What did he say?' 'He said he would be there at 10'.* Compare should(1). **2** (used in the main clause(1) of some conditional sentences): *If you had asked, he would have apologized.* ⇒ should(2). **3** (used to show that the action of the main verb annoys one because it is the kind of thing that the person or thing ought not to do but often does): *Oh, you would drop my best plate, of course! Oh, it would rain just when we want to play tennis!* (Notice that the main stress(2) is on 'would'.) **would rather do s.t** (**than** (**do**) **s.t**) prefer to do s.t (instead of (doing) s.t). **would you do s.t** (polite way of asking s.o to do s.t): *Would you hold this for me, please?*

'would-,be *attrib.adj* who is not (s.t) but would like to be it: *Fred is a would-be writer but he still hasn't had a book accepted.*

wouldn't /'wʊdnt/ = would not. ⇒ will[1].

wouldst /wʊdst/ *aux.v* (*old use*) 2nd pers sing of would.

would've /'wʊdəv/ = would have. ⇒ would.

wound[1] /wuːnd/ *c.n* **1** damage to the body of a person or animal (often caused by a bullet or weapon) which breaks the skin. **2** (often *a — to s.t*) (*fig*) damage (to a person's feelings, e.g her/his pride). **flesh wound** ⇒ flesh. **lick one's wounds** (*fig*) take time to recover from a bad experience. **rub salt into s.o's wounds** ⇒ salt(*n*).

▷ *tr.v* **3** give a wound(1,2) to (s.o or an animal).

wound[2] /waʊnd/ *p.t* of wind[2].

wove /wəʊv/ *p.t* of weave.

woven /'wəʊvn/ *adj* **1** ⇒ weave.

▷ *v* **2** *p.p* of weave.

wow /waʊ/ *interj* **1** (*informal*) (sound showing admiration or surprise).

▷ *n* (*informal*) **2** *c.n* great success. **3** *u.n* unsteady sound heard when the motor of a machine that plays music etc does not always run at the same speed. Compare flutter(1).

WRAC /,dʌblju: ,ɑːr ,eɪ 'siː/ *abbr* Women's Royal Army Corps.

wrangle /'ræŋgl/ *c.n* **1** quarrel; unpleasantly angry, noisy or rude argument between two or more people.

▷ *intr.v* **2** (often — *with s.o*) quarrel (with s.o); have an unpleasantly angry, noisy or rude argument (with s.o).

'wrangler *c.n* person who wrangles(2).

wrap /ræp/ *c.n* **1** piece of cloth or clothing to cover or wrap(1) (part of) one's body. **under wraps** hidden so that it cannot be seen by people one does not want to see it: *The car factory kept their new model under wraps until yesterday.*

▷ *tr.v* (*-pp-*) **2** (often — *s.o/s.t up* (*in s.t*)) cover (s.o/s.t) by putting s.t right round her/him/it once or more than once: *I'm going to wrap* (*up*) *the Christmas presents now.* Opposite unwrap. **wrap s.t (a)round s.o/s.t** put s.t right round s.o/s.t once or more than once. **Wrap up!** (*informal*) Be quiet! Shut up! **wrap s.t up** (**a**) ⇒ wrap(2). (**b**) (*fig*) finish s.t, e.g a piece of work, completely. **wrap up** (**in s.t**) cover oneself right round (with s.t) once or more than once. **wrapped up in s.o/s.t** (*fig*) very busy with s.o/s.t; thinking only of s.o/s.t.

'wrapper *c.n* **1** thing in which one wraps s.t, e.g a magazine one is going to send. **2** thing, e.g a loose paper cover round a book, in which s.t is wrapped (⇒ wrap(2)).

'wrapping *c/u.n* thing(s) in which s.t is wrapped (⇒ wrap(2)), usu to protect it when it is sent s.w.

wrath /rɒθ/ *u.n* (*literary*) great anger.

'wrathful *adj* (*literary*) very angry.

'wrathfully *adv.* **wrathfulness** *u.n.*

wreak /riːk/ *tr.v* (usu — *havoc, vengeance* etc (*on s.o/s.t*)) (*literary*) cause (havoc etc) or get (revenge etc) (on s.o/s.t).

wreath /riːθ/ *c.n* (often — *of s.t*) **1** (circle (of flowers and/or leaves fixed or tied together) put on or near a grave, or on the head (or round the neck) of a person one wants to honour. **2** line (of smoke etc) moving in an irregular way.

wreathe /riːð/ *v* **1** *tr.v* surround (s.o/s.t) completely (as if) with a wreath(1,2). **2** *intr.v* (of or like a snake) move forward by twisting from side to side. **3** *intr.v* (of smoke etc) form wreaths(2). **wreathed in smiles** smiling very much.

wreck /rek/ *c.n* **1** thing (esp a ship or boat) that has been badly damaged and/or sunk. **2** ruin; destruction: *The change of government meant the wreck of all the company's plans.* **3** (sometimes *fig*) part(s) left after s.t has been ruined or almost destroyed: *After losing the big race, all his hopes of becoming famous were a wreck.* **4** person who is very weak after an illness etc.

▷ *tr.v* **5** cause (s.o/s.t) to become a wreck.

wreckage /'rekɪdʒ/ *u.n* thing(s) left after s.t has been wrecked(5).

wrecked *adj* **1** made, turned into, a wreck. **2** (of people) made or caused to be in a wreck(1): *We were wrecked on some hidden rocks.*

'wrecker *c.n* (*derog*) person who wrecks(5) things.

wren /ren/ *c.n* kind of very small bird.

wrench /rentʃ/ *c.n* **1** twist and at the same time pull, often causing one pain and/or damage. **2** thing causing a lot of sorrow: *Leaving home was a great wrench for her.* **3** tool used for turning nuts(2) etc which can be changed and adjusted(1) to fit different sizes. **give s.t a wrench** wrench(5) s.t: *While I was trying to lift the boat I gave my right shoulder a nasty wrench.* **monkey wrench** ⇨ monkey.

▷ *tr.v* **4** pull (s.t) hard, and at the same time twist or turn it. **5** damage (s.t) by twisting it and at the same time pulling: *When I jumped, I fell awkwardly and wrenched my knee.* **wrench s.t from s.o/s.t** pull s.t away from s.o/s.t while at the same time twisting or turning it. **wrench s.t off** etc **(s.t)** pull s.t off etc (s.t) while at the same time twisting or turning it. **wrench s.t open** open s.t by pulling and at the same time twisting or turning it.

wrest /rest/ *tr.v* (usu — *s.t from, out of, s.o/s.t*) (*literary*) pull (s.t) violently away (from s.o/s.t) get s.t, e.g the truth, from s.o by strong means: *The man had a gun but the policeman managed to wrest it from him.*

wrestle /'resl/ *tr/intr.v* fight (s.o) without hitting or kicking, not only by catching, holding and throwing. **wrestle with s.t** (*fig*) (a) try very hard to overcome s.t, e.g an illness or a failure. (b) try very hard to succeed in s.t: *She wrestled with the problem for an hour before she finally solved it.*

'wrestler *c.n* person who wrestles.

'wrestling *u.n* sport of wrestling (⇨ wrestle).

wretch /retʃ/ *c.n* (*derog*) unlucky, unhappy or poor person.

wretched /'retʃɪd/ *adj* **1** miserable; very sad or unhappy. **2** (*informal*) making one feel miserable, unhappy or very sad: *Sally has a wretched cold again.* **3** (*informal*) whom/that one does not like; whom/that one is angry with: *That wretched boy has broken my necklace now! We had wretched weather during our holidays.*

'wretchedly *adv.* **'wretchedness** *u.n.*

wriggle /'rɪgl/ *c.n* **1** example of wriggling(2). **give a wriggle** wriggle(2) once.

▷ *tr/intr.v* **2** (cause (s.t) to) twist about while, or without, moving from the place where it is: *The boy sat on the beach wriggling his toes in the soft sand.* **wriggle (s.t) about** (cause (s.t) to) twist from side to side without moving from the place where one/it is. **wriggle out (of s.t)** (*fig; informal*) escape (from s.t unpleasant) by being clever or by using tricks: *Joe was very good at wriggling out of jobs he did not want to do.*

wring /rɪŋ/ *c.n* (usu **give s.t a —**) twist, usu to get water out of it.

▷ *tr.v* (*p.t,p.p* **wrung** /rʌŋ/) **2** give (s.t) a wring(1): *I always wring the clothes before I hang them up to dry.* **wring one's hands**; **wring s.o's hand** ⇨ hand(*n*). **wring s.o's neck** ⇨ neck(*n*). **wring s.t out** get the liquid out of s.t by twisting it: *Wring your shirt out before you hang it up to dry.* **wring s.t out of s.o** (*fig*) get s.t, e.g money or the truth, out of s.o by force or threats, or after a lot of trouble. **wring s.t out of s.t** get s.t, e.g water, out of s.t by twisting it.

'wringer *c.n* (part of a) machine that gets the water out of s.t by pressing it.

'wringing *adv* **wringing wet** very wet.

wrinkle /'rɪŋkl/ *c.n* **1** fold, esp in the skin of the forehead or in cloth that has been crushed.

▷ *tr/intr.v* **2** (often — (*s.t*) *up*) (cause (s.t) to) become full of wrinkles(1).

'wrinkly *adj* (-*ier*, -*iest*) full of wrinkles(1).

wrist /rɪst/ *c.n* **1** joint between the hand and the arm. **2** part of a shirt, blouse etc that is at the bottom of the arm.

'wrist,band *c.n* **1** narrow strip of s.t used to fasten s.t (e.g a watch) round one's wrist. **2** piece of a shirt, blouse etc that goes round one's wrist.

wristlet /'rɪstlɪt/ *c.n* wristband(1) made of pieces of metal joined together in such a way that they can move separately.

'wrist,watch *c.n* watch worn on one's wrist.

writ /rɪt/ *c.n* (*law*) paper given or sent to s.o by a law court to tell her/him that she/he must (not) do a particular thing.

write /raɪt/ *v* (*p.t* **wrote** /rəʊt/, *p.p* **written** /'rɪtn/) **1** (*tr/intr.v* (often — (*s.t*) *down*) put (s.t) down on paper etc with a pen, pencil, typewriter etc in the form of letters and/or numbers. **2** *tr/intr.v* be a writer (of s.t): *'What does Judy do?' 'She writes (poetry).'* **3** *tr.v* produce (s.t) using letters and/or numbers: *I am going to write some letters and postcards now.*

write s.o s.t write s.t to s.o and send it to her/him.

write away/in/off (for s.t) write to a person, company etc to order or ask for s.t.

write back write an answer to s.o who has already written to one.

write s.t down ⇨ write(1).

write s.t in add s.t in writing: *All you need to do with this application form is to write your name and address in just here.*

write s.o/s.t off (as s.t) (*fig*) consider s.o/s.t to be s.t bad (e.g s.t useless or harmful): *After meeting David several times, Sarah wrote him off as a fool.* Compare write-off.

write s.t out write s.t in full; write s.t completely.

write s.o/s.t up write a story of s.o/s.t, e.g for an article for a newspaper.

'write-,off *c.n* (*derog*) thing that is so badly damaged that it is not worth repairing: *Our insurance company agreed that our car was a write-off after the accident and paid its full value.*

'writer *c.n* person who writes books etc usu as her/his job; author. **the writer of s.t** the person who writes or wrote s.t.

,writer's 'cramp *u.n* (*informal*) stiffness one sometimes gets in one's hand as a result of writing a lot.

'write-,up *c.n* (favourable) report in writing about s.t a lot of people buy or go to see etc.

'writing *u.n* **1** thing that is written. ⇨ writings. **2** way of forming (and joining) one's letters when one writes(1) by hand: *Can you read that man's writing?* **3** activity of writing (⇨ write(2)): *He lives by writing.* **piece of writing** thing that has been written. **in writing** in(to) a written form: *If you will put your request in writing, I can put it on the manager's desk for his attention.*

'writing ,desk *c.n* desk made or used for sitting at when one wants to write.

'writing ,materials *pl.n* things used when one wants to write, e.g pens, paper and ink.

'writing ,paper *u.n* paper that is made for, or is suitable for, writing on.

'writings *pl.n* (often *the — of s.o*) things (e.g stories and plays) that have been written by s.o.

writhe /raɪð/ *intr.v* (often *— with s.t*) twist about (because of s.t, e.g great pain).

writing(s) ⇒ write.

written /'rɪtn/ *attrib.adj* **1** in writing: *a written apology.* ⇒ unwritten.

▷ *v* **2** *p.p* of write.

wrong /rɒŋ/ *adj* Opposite right. **1** not correct, accurate or right: *You've put the wrong address on this letter. This is the wrong side of the cloth.* **2** morally bad; evil; against the rules of morality: *It is wrong to spread nasty stories about people when you don't know whether they are true or not.* **3** not suitable: *This is the wrong time to ask your father for money because he's just had his* income tax *demand.* **be caught on the wrong foot** ⇒ foot(*n*). **get (hold of) the wrong end of the stick** ⇒ stick(*n*). **get on the wrong side of s.o** ⇒ side(*n*). **get out of bed on the wrong side** ⇒ bed. **on the wrong side of 40** etc ⇒ side(*n*). **rub s.o up the wrong way** ⇒ way(*n*). **wrong side out** ⇒ side(*n*).

▷ *adv* **4** not in the correct, accurate or right way: *The clerk's spelt my name wrong again.* Opposite right(4). **get s.o wrong** (*informal*) misunderstand s.o. **get s.t wrong** make one or more mistakes in s.t. **go wrong** (a) start to make a mistake or mistakes: *We're not going the right way; now we must try to find out where we went wrong.* (b) stop behaving as one/it ought to behave: *My watch has gone wrong; it says 5.31 but it is really 6.05. Ted was such a nice boy but he went wrong somehow when he was at university.* (c) begin not to go as one had planned or hoped it would: *We thought that we had a really good plan but it went wrong.* (**not, never** etc) **put a foot wrong** ⇒ foot(*n*).

▷ *c/u.n* **5** morally bad or evil action; action that is against the rules of morality. Opposite right(12). **in the wrong** on the wrong side of an argument etc: *After a long argument, Joan managed to get Vanessa to admit that she had been in the wrong when she had accused the children of breaking her window.* Opposite in the right. **know the difference between right and wrong** ⇒ right(12).

▷ *tr.v* **6** (*formal*) treat (s.o) unfairly: *If you think it was John's fault that you failed, you wrong him because he had nothing to do with it.*

'wrong,doer *c.n* (*derog*; *formal*) person who does bad, evil or immoral things.

'wrong,doing *c/u.n* (*formal*) bad, evil or immoral (piece of) behaviour.

wrote /rəʊt/ *p.t* of write.

wrought /rɔːt/ *adj* **1** (*old use*) (often *— of s.t*) made (of s.t).

▷ *v* **2** (*old use*) *p.t,p.p* of work.

,wrought 'iron *u.n* iron that has been rolled and hammered into shape.

,wrought-'iron *adj* made of wrought iron.

,wrought-'up *adj* very excited, nervous or worried. Compare overwrought.

wrung /rʌŋ/ *p.t,p.p* of wring.

wry /raɪ/ *adj* showing that one does not like s.t (often the taste of s.t): *He had a wry expression on his face.*

'wryly *adv.* **'wryness** *u.n.*

WSW *abbr* West South West.

wt *written abbr* weight.

X, x /eks/ *n* **1** *c/unique n* 24th letter of the English alphabet. **2** *unique n* Roman numeral for 10.

▷ *symb* **3** (x) (*mathematics*) one axis(2) of a graph: *the x-axis.* **4** (*x*) (*mathematics*) unknown number e.g '$2x + 1 = 7$' means 'if you add twice a certain number to 1, the answer is 7' (here $x = 3$). **5** (x) unknown person or thing. **6** (X) person whose name is kept secret, usu in a law case: *During the trial of the man accused of trying to* blackmail *a lady, she was referred to only as Mrs X so that people would not know who she really was.* **7** (X) kiss: *When my children write to me, they always put 'XXX' at the bottom of their letters.*

'X-,chromo,some *c.n* one of the two kinds of chromosome; it occurs in cells of a female person or animal and forms a pair with the Y-chromosome in males.

'X ,film *c.n* (*old use*) film that people under the age of 18 are not allowed to see in a cinema.

xenophobia /ˌzenəˈfəʊbɪə/ *u.n* strong fear and/or dislike of foreigners and/or strangers.

,xeno'phobic *adj* feeling and/or showing xenophobia.

xerox /'zɪərɒks/ *c.n* (*t.n*) **1** copy (of s.t written, typed, drawn etc) by xeroxing(2).

▷ *tr.v* (*t.n*) **2** make a copy of (s.t written, typed, drawn etc) by photographing it on a kind of machine that works by electricity.

Xmas /'krɪsməs/ *c/unique n* (*informal*) Christmas.

X-ray /'eks ,reɪ/ *c.n* (also *attrib*) **1** (usu *pl*) kind of ray of light used to photograph the insides of solid objects because it can pass through these and produce a photograph or image(2): *X-rays are used to examine and treat people who are ill or have broken a bone.* **2** photograph taken by the use of X-rays(1): *an X-ray photograph.* **3** examination of part of s.o's body using X-rays(1): *The doctor did not know what was wrong with the man's stomach so she asked him to come for an X-ray.*

▷ *tr.v* **4** photograph, examine or treat (s.o/s.t) by means of X-rays(1): *We've X-rayed your arm to see if it is broken.*

xylophone /'zaɪləˌfəʊn/ *c.n* kind of musical instrument made of pieces of wood etc of different lengths in a frame and played by hitting the pieces with small wooden hammers.

Yy

Y, y /waɪ/ n 1 c/unique n 25th letter of the English alphabet.
▷ symb 2 (y) (mathematics) one axis(2) of a graph: the y-axis. 3 unknown number, e.g $2x + y = 7$. ⇒x(4).
'Y-,chromo,some c.n one of two kinds of chromosome. ⇒ X-chromosome.

yacht /jɒt/ c.n 1 kind of sailing boat used for pleasure, racing or private voyages. 2 kind of big expensive motor boat used for pleasure.
'yachting u.n hobby of sailing, racing or travelling in a yacht(1,2). **go yachting** go out on the sea etc in a yacht(1,2).
'yachtsman c.n (pl -men) man whose hobby is yachting.
'yachts,woman c.n (pl -,women) woman whose hobby is yachting.

yak¹ /jæk/ c.n kind of animal from Central Asia like a cow or bull but with long black hair.
yak² /jæk/ intr.v (-kk-) (often — (on) about s.o/ s.t) (informal) talk too much, usu about things other people do not consider important.

yam /jæm/ n 1 c.n kind of climbing plant that grows in hot damp countries. 2 c/u.n (also attrib) root of this plant which people cook and eat like a potato: yam chips.

yank /jæŋk/ c.n (informal) 1 sudden hard pull. **give (s.t) a yank** suddenly pull (s.t) hard: He gave his sister's hair a yank when no one was looking.
▷ tr/intr.v 2 (often — s.o/s.t out) (informal) suddenly pull (s.o/s.t) hard: She fell into the pool but her father soon yanked her out again.

yap /jæp/ c.n 1 short bark given by a small dog.
▷ intr.v (-pp-) 2 (of a small dog) give one or more sharp barks.

yard¹ /jɑːd/ c.n 1 area of land surrounded by walls or buildings (i.e it is not made to be a garden). ⇒ dockyard. 2 (US) garden.
yard² /jɑːd/ c.n (written abbr yd) unit of measure of length equalling three feet(4) or about 92 centimetres: There are 1760 yards in a mile.
yardage /'jɑːdɪdʒ/ c/u.n length of s.t when it is measured in yards²: What yardage of cloth do we need to make the curtains?
'yard,stick c.n 1 stick one yard long with smaller divisions (feet(4) and inches(1)) marked on it, used for measuring length. 2 (fig) thing whose size or qualities is/are known so that it can be used to measure or compare other things: My yardstick for judging a meal in a restaurant is my wife's excellent cooking at home.
yard³ /jɑːd/ c.n pole¹ fixed to the mast of a ship or boat to carry sails, flags etc.

yarn¹ /jɑːn/ u.n thread used for making cloth etc.
yarn² /jɑːn/ c.n (informal) story. **spin (s.o) a yarn** (informal) tell (s.o) a story that is not true.

yashmak /'jæʃmæk/ c.n veil used by some Muslim women to hide (most of) their faces.

yawn /jɔːn/ c.n 1 act of yawning(2).
▷ intr.v 2 open one's mouth, tighten one's throat and breathe deeply because of being tired or bored. 3 be or become wide open: A deep hole yawned a few metres in front of the car.
'yawning attrib.adj wide open: After the fire there was a yawning gap between our house and the corner.

yd written abbr yard².

ye /jiː/ det 1 (used to make s.t sound old) the: The café is called 'Ye Olde Coffee Shoppe'.
▷ pron 2 (old use) you.

yea /jeɪ/ adv 1 (old use) yes.
▷ c.n 2 (formal) yes; vote in favour of s.t. Opposite nay.

yeah /jeə/ adv (informal) yes.

year /jɪə/ c.n time the earth takes to go round the sun once; between 365 and 366 days; 365 days (or in a leap year 366 days). ⇒ calendar year, leap year. **a year last/next/this Friday** etc exactly one year after last/next/this Friday etc. **a year on Friday** etc exactly one year after next Friday. **a year today, tomorrow** etc exactly one year after today, tomorrow etc. Compare week. **all the year round; the whole year round** during the whole of the year: The sea is so warm here that you can bathe all the year round. **put years on s.o** be a great worry to s.o so that he/she feels worn out. **the year dot** (informal) a very long time ago: People have lived in this place since the year dot. **year in, year out** for a very long time without stopping: That old man wears exactly the same clothes year in, year out.
'year-,book c.n book that is published once a year and tells people what happened during the year before.
'yearling c.n animal, esp a horse, that is more than one year old but less than two.
'year,long adj/adv (continuing) during a whole year: a yearlong enquiry.
'yearly adj/adv (happening, coming etc) once a year or every year; in a year: I make a yearly payment of £25 to the sports club. That plant flowers twice yearly.

yearn /jɜːn/ intr.v (usu — for s.t) want (s.t) very strongly, often with a feeling of sadness because one does not have it now.

yeast /jiːst/ u.n kind of living substance like a fungus, used to make bread light and full of holes or to change sugar into alcohol(1) when making beer etc.
'yeasty adj (-ier, -iest) smelling, tasting, of or like yeast.

yell /jel/ c.n 1 loud cry or shout: a yell of pain; an angry yell. **give a yell** shout loudly: When she saw her brother fall into the river, Sue gave a yell and then ran for help.
▷ tr/intr.v 2 (often — (s.t) out) shout (s.t) loudly; give a loud cry (of (s.t)): He yelled out an angry remark. **yell (s.t) at s.o** shout (abuse(1), a warning etc) at s.o loudly.

yellow /'jeləʊ/ adj 1 having the colour of the middle part of an egg. 2 (informal) cowardly; not brave. **in yellow** having yellow clothes on: She was (dressed) in yellow.
▷ c/u.n 3 yellow colour(1); it is one of the three main colours used in printing. ⇒ cyan, magenta.
▷ tr/intr.v 4 (cause (s.t) to) become yellow(1): The leaves are yellowing.
'yellow-,bellied adj (derog; slang) cowardly; not brave.

'yellowish *adj* a little yellow(1).

,yellow 'line *c.n* (UK) place at the side of a road (marked with a yellow line) where parking is not allowed or is restricted.

,yellow 'pages *def.pl.n* (part of a) telephone book giving addresses and telephone numbers of businesses and services.

yelp /jelp/ *c.n* **1** sudden short sharp bark by a dog because of pain, surprise or fear. **2** similar sound made by s.o because of pain, surprise etc. *give a yelp* yelp(3) once.
▷ *intr.v* **3** make the sound of a yelp(1,2). *yelp with s.t* yelp(3) because of pain, surprise etc.

yen /jen/ *sing.n* (often *a — for s.t*) (*informal*) feeling of wanting (s.t) very much: *She doesn't often eat chocolate but occasionally she gets a yen for some. a yen to do s.t* a strong desire to do s.t.

yeoman /'jəumən/ *c.n* (*pl* yeomen /'jəumən/) (*old use*) **1** farmer who farms his own land. **2** man of high rank who serves a king or a nobleman of high rank.

'yeomanry *def.pl.n* **1** group of yeomen(1). **2** (in history) unit(s) of soldiers who join the army of their own free will and fight on horses.

yes /jes/ *interj* **1** (used to say that s.t is true, correct, wanted etc): *'Would you like another cake?' 'Yes, please.' 'Is that your pen?' 'Yes, it is.' 'Do you like it?' 'Yes, I do.' 'Can I help you?' 'Yes, you can.' 'Do you agree?' 'Yes.' 'Do you love me, yes or no?'* Opposite no(5). **2** (used with a rising tone(3) of voice to show that one has heard s.o and is waiting to hear what he/she wants): *'George!' 'Yes?'* (or *'Yes, dear?'*) *'Can you come here, please?'*
▷ *c.n* **3** vote for s.t: *After the discussion there were 22 yeses and only 3 noes.* Opposite no(6). **4** expression of agreement: *When he asked if we would support him he got a loud yes! She demanded a clear yes or no.* Opposite no(7).

yes-man /'jes ,mæn/ *c.n* (*pl* yes-men /'jes ,men/) man who always says 'Yes' to anything that his boss, or anyone else he wants to get s.t from, says or asks.

yesterday /'jestədɪ/ *adv* **1** on or during the day before today: *We finished the work yesterday.* **2** (*old use*) in the recent past: *Typewriters were widely used yesterday, but not now. s.o was not born yesterday* s.o is not stupid (usu because of lack of experience): *That man tried to sell me his old car for £1000 but I wasn't born yesterday. yesterday afternoon, evening* etc the afternoon, evening etc of yesterday.
▷ *unique n* **3** the day before today: *Yesterday was a Sunday.* **4** (usu of — or *pl*) the recent past: *songs of yesterday; all our yesterdays.*

yet /jet/ *adv* **1** (used in negative statements and in questions) already; up to this or that time; still: *We were expecting him at 11 but it's half past now and he hasn't come yet. 'Is it time to leave yet?'* **2** (used in affirmative statements; often *old use*) still (not): *I have yet to meet a person who can read a doctor's writing.* **3** (usu with comparatives) even; still: *We gave the man a great amount of food but he kept asking for more and yet more. I've had yet another letter from your teacher. as yet* (used in negative sentences) still; up to this time: *I wrote to the bank a week ago but have received no reply as yet. not just yet* ⇒ just². *yet again* still; another

time: *I told the children not to climb that tree but now they are doing it yet again!*
▷ *conj* **4** but (in spite of that): *She's fat yet full of energy*(1). *It rained during most of our holiday* (*and/but*) *yet we managed to enjoy ourselves.*

yeti /'jetɪ/ *c.n* (*pl* -s) = abominable snowman.

yew /ju:/ *n* **1** *c.n* (also **'yew ,tree**) kind of tree that does not lose its leaves in winter. **2** *u.n* (also *attrib*) wood of this kind of tree, used to make furniture.

YHA /,waɪ ,eɪtʃ 'eɪ/ *abbr* Youth Hostels Association.

yield /ji:ld/ *c.n* **1** amount produced (naturally): *a yield of 20 boxes of apples/of several* litres *of milk.*
▷ *v* **2** *tr.v* produce (s.t); have (s.t) as a crop; give (s.t): *Our garden yields excellent tomatoes. £1000 at 5% per year yields £50 every year.* **3** *intr.v* (often *— to s.o/s.t*) surrender(3): *He refused to yield* (*to their demands*). **4** *intr.v* (*formal*) bend or break as a result of a heavy weight etc: *The branches of the tree yielded under the weight of the snow. yield s.o s.t* provide s.o with s.t: *Those trees yield us several hundred* litres *of oil every year. yield s.t up* (*to s.o*) give s.t up (to s.o); surrender(2) s.t (to s.o): *After a brave defence, the general finally had to yield the town up to the enemy.*

'yielding *adj* **1** bending easily, so that s.t does not break: *the yielding branches of a young tree.* **2** not arguing or resisting: *She has a sweet yielding nature.*

yippee /jɪ'pi:/ *interj* (*informal*) (kind of cry to express excited pleasure).

YMCA /,waɪ ,em ,si: 'eɪ/ *abbr* Young Men's Christian Association.

yob /'jɒb/ *c.n* (also **'yobbo**) (*derog*; *informal*) rude unpleasant (usu young) man: *Some yobs scratched our car.*

yodel /'jəudl/ *c.n* **1** sound(s) made by s.o who is yodelling(2).
▷ *tr/intr.v* (*-ll-*, US *-l-*) **2** sing (s.t) in such a way that one's voice changes often and suddenly from its natural sounds to very high sounds and then back again.

yoga /'jəugə/ *u.n* (also *attrib*) system of exercises for the body and mind which comes from India and is used to make or keep the body and the mind healthy and happy: *yoga classes.*

yogi /'jəugɪ/ *c.n* (*pl* -s) person who does and/ or teaches yoga.

yoghurt /'jɒgət/ *u.n* (also **'yogurt**) kind of food made from milk that has been made sour and thick by bacteria.

yogi ⇒ yoga.

yoke /jəuk/ *c.n* **1** piece of wood fixed on the necks of two animals, usu oxen, so that they can pull a cart etc together. **2** pair of animals joined together with a yoke(1). **3** piece of wood etc across a person's shoulders to help her/him carry two buckets etc, one on each end. **4** part of a shirt etc which is on the shoulders and to which the rest of the shirt etc is joined. **5** (*fig*) thing that ties people together: *For many years he and I were joined together by the yoke of working in the same office.* **6** (*fig*) thing preventing people doing what they want to do: *Most countries in Africa have known many years of being under a foreign yoke.* (*under*) *the yoke of s.o/s.t* (suffering) the control of s.o/s.t not wanted: *under the yoke of poverty.*

▷ *tr.v* **7** (often — *s.o/s.t to s.o/s.t*) join (s.o/s.t) (to s.o/s.t) (as if) with a yoke(1).

yokel /ˈjəʊkl/ *c.n* (*derog*) person who lives in the country and is thought of as uneducated, stupid or simple.

yolk /jəʊk/ *c/u.n* yellow part in the centre of an egg. ⇨ white(8).

yonder /ˈjɒndə/ *adj/adv* (also **yon**) (*old use*) (who/that is) over there or in that place: *Can you see yonder mountain? Can you see that ship yonder?*

yore /jɔː/ *u.n* (*old use*; *literary*) (often (*in days*) *of* —) belonging to a time or times that finished long ago: *In days of yore battles were fought with swords and not guns.*

you (strong form /juː/, weak form /jʊ/) *pron* **1** person(s) to whom one is speaking or writing: *You can have it if you like it. Does it belong to you? Hallo, Gordon. How are you? All of you have passed the examination. Can you all help to start my car by pushing it?* (Notice that 'you' can be followed by a noun, a number or a phrase(1), esp when one is speaking angrily or giving a command, e.g 'Come here, you boys!' 'You two, what are you doing here?' 'You with the glasses, sit down!' **2** (*informal*) any person; one(3): *You have to stop your car when you come to a red light.* ⇨ your, yours.

you'd (strong form /juːd/, weak form /jʊd/) **1** = you had. ⇨ have. **2** you would.

you'll (strong form /juːl/, weak form /jʊl/) you shall/will.

you're /jʊə/ you are. ⇨ be. ⇨ your.

you've (strong form /juːv/, weak form /jʊv/) = you have.

young /jʌŋ/ *adj* (*comp* younger /ˈjʌŋɡə/, *superl* youngest /ˈjʌŋɡɪst/) **1** having lived or existed for a short time: *a young child/cat. I'd like to take you with me but you are too young. These young beans are sweet and tender. This is a young college that opened only five years ago. Kenya is a young country.* Opposite old(1). **2** having the qualities of a young(1) person: *She looks very young for her age. Some older parents have young minds.* Opposite old(3). **3** suitable for young(1) people: *young fashions/styles/designs.* Compare old(8). **4** (*pred*; *formal*) (of a period of time) at an early stage: *The night/afternoon is still young.* Opposite old(4). **5** (*attrib*) not experienced: *a young member of the committee.* Opposite old(7). **young at heart** ⇨ heart. **young in s.t** young(1) in respect to s.t: *young in years; young in mind.*

▷ *def.pl.n* **6** young people: *The young of today have a much easier life than those of my day.* **7** *pl.n* young animals: *Even a duck will fight when it is defending its young.* **with young** (usu of animals) pregnant.

Young Men's/Women's Christian Association *def.n* (*abbr* YMCA, YWCA) Christian(1) association that runs clubs for young men/women.

younger /ˈjʌŋɡə/ *adj* **1** *comp* of young. **2** (usu *s.o the* —) younger of two in the same family or group: *David Owen the younger was the nephew of David Owen the elder.* Opposite elder¹.

youngish /ˈjʌŋɪʃ/ *adj* rather young.

youngster *c.n* young person.

youth /juːθ/ *n* (*pl* /juːðz/) **1** *u.n* early part of one's life; time when one is no longer a child but is not yet an adult: *In her youth she was a very good swimmer.* **2** *c.n* young person, usu male. **3** *unique n* = youthfulness. **the youth of s.t** (**a**) the young people of (a place, period of time): *The youth of today have much more money than those of my young days.* (**b**) the time during which s.o is young.

youth hostel *c.n* place where young people can stay cheaply when they are travelling.

Youth Hostels Association *def.n* (*abbr* YHA) association providing and running youth hostels.

youthful *adj* **1** young(1): *a youthful assistant.* **2** looking or behaving like a young person: *Some people manage to remain youthful even when they become quite old.*

youthfully *adv.* **youthfulness** *u.n.*

your /jɔː/ *possessive adj* belonging to, for, you: *this your bus/pen? Your wife is waiting for you.*

yours /jɔːz/ *possessive pron* the one(s) belonging to, for, you: *This pen is yours. Yours is the one with the red lid.* **of yours** of, belonging to, you: *I still have a book of yours. It's a nasty habit of yours.* **Yours ever/faithfully/sincerely/truly** ways of ending a letter ⇨ ever, faithfully, sincerely, truly.

yourself *pron* (*pl* your**selves**) **1** *reflex.pron* (used when the object of the verb or preposition is the same (people, animals, things) as the subject): *You ought to look at yourselves in the mirror and see how dirty you all are! You are too interested in yourself to care about others.* **2** (used to emphasize 'you'): *You yourself know who is telling the truth.* **3** without help: *Did you do it yourself or did someone help you?* (**all**) **by yourself** (**a**) without help: *Can you carry that box by yourself?* (**b**) alone: *You've been (all) by yourself this afternoon but Jim will soon be free to join you. Hallo, David and Mary, are you all by yourselves?*

do it yourself *u.n* (also *attrib*) (*abbr* DIY) practice of doing jobs (e.g repairs and painting) oneself instead of paying professionals to do them: *a do-it-yourself shop.*

you're ⇨ you.

youth, youthful, youthfulness ⇨ young.

you've ⇨ you.

yowl /jaʊl/ *c.n* **1** long sad cry, usu of an animal, caused by pain, sudden unhappiness etc.

▷ *intr.v* **2** (often — *at s.o/s.t*) give one or more yowls(1).

yo-yo /ˈjəʊ jəʊ/ *c.n* toy made of a round flat piece of wood etc which runs up and down on a string when one pulls the string. **like a yo-yo** (*informal*) (of prices, amounts etc) going up and down again and again.

yule /juːl/ *unique n* (often with capital **Y**) (*old use*) Christmas.

yule log *c.n* **1** piece of wood burnt on the evening before Christmas. **2** Christmas cake that looks like a log.

yuletide *unique n* (often with capital **Y**) (*old use*) Christmas (and the time round it).

YWCA /ˌjuː waɪ ˌdʌbljuː siː ˈeɪ/ *abbr* Young Women's Christian Association.

Zz

Z, z /zed/ *c/unique n* 26th and last letter of the English alphabet.

zany /'zeını/ *adj* (*-ier*, *-iest*) silly, often in an amusing way: *zany clothes.*

zeal /zi:l/ *u.n* strong interest and effort: *Too much zeal as an official can actually annoy other people.*

zealot /'zelət/ *c.n* (usu *derog*) person who is too zealous, esp concerning religion.

zealous /'zeləs/ *adj* trying very hard to do or get s.t: *a zealous member of a political party.* ⇒ overzealous. **zealous in doing s.t** trying very hard (while doing one's work, searching etc). **'zealously** *adv.* **'zealousness** *u.n.*

zebra /'zi:brə/ *c.n* (*pl* -(s)) kind of African animal like a horse but with black and white stripes. **,zebra 'crossing** *c.n* place in a road with black and white lines where people can cross and where traffic has to let them cross first.

zen /zen/ *unique n* (also *attrib*) kind of Buddhism that comes from Japan: *He's a zen Buddhist.*

zenith /'zenıθ/ *def.n* **1** highest point in the sky: *When will the sun reach its zenith over the desert?* **2** (often the — of s.t) highest point reached by (s.o/s.t): *Winston Churchill reached the zenith of his* career(1) *in 1941.* Opposite nadir.

zero /'zıərəʊ/ *c/unique n* (*pl* -s) **1** 0; nought; nothing; nil; love(7): *The temperature today is zero degrees* Centigrade (or 0°C). (Notice that in most games scores 'nil' is used instead of 'zero', e.g 'We won our last football match five nil'. Compare love(7).) **above zero** higher than zero: *The temperature today is five degrees above zero* (i.e +5°). **absolute zero** ⇒ absolute. **below zero** lower than zero: *The temperature today is five degrees below zero* (i.e −5°).
▷ *tr/intr.v* **2** zero (s.t) in (on s.o/s.t) (a) aim (s.t, e.g a gun) as exactly as possible (at s.o/s.t). (b) focus(4) (s.t, e.g a camera) as exactly as possible (on s.o/s.t).
,zero 'growth *unique n* no growth at all: *Production in our factory increased by 15% in 1986 but in 1987 we had zero growth.*
'zero ,hour *unique n* time at which s.t (usu an attack) is due to begin.

zest /zest/ *n* **1** *u.n* strong sharp pleasure: *A bit of danger can add zest to a sport for many people.* **2** *c.n* piece of orange or lemon peel(1) put in a drink or in food to give it a more exciting taste. **zest for s.t** eagerness to get pleasure out of s.t: *In spite of their age, some old people still have a great zest for living.*

zigzag /'zıg,zæg/ *attrib.adj* **1** having sharp bends: *a zigzag path/line.*
▷ *c.n* **2** line or course with many sharp bends and corners while always leading in the same general direction. **go in a zigzag** follow a zigzag(1) course.
▷ *intr.v* (*-gg-*) **3** follow a zigzag(1) course.

zinc /zıŋk/ *u.n* kind of pale metal often mixed with other metals or used to cover other metals, *chem.symb* Zn.

zip /zıp/ *n* **1** *c.n* strip of cloth with two rows of metal or plastic teeth which can lock together, used for closing the front of trousers, the side of a skirt etc. **2** *c.n* sound like a zzzzz or sssss made by s.t moving very fast: *I heard the zip of a bullet passing my ear.* **3** *u.n* energy; speed: *I like the way your brother plays football — he always shows plenty of zip.*
▷ *v* (*-pp-*) **4** *tr.v* close (s.t) with a zip(1). Opposite unzip. **5** *intr.v* move fast and with a noise like a zzzzz or sssss: *When I looked out from behind the tree, a bullet zipped past my ear.* **zip s.o up** close part of s.o's clothing with a zip: *Will you please zip me up? I can't reach.* **zip s.t up** close s.t by pulling the zip down/up.
'zip ,code *c/def.n* (US) post code.
,zip 'fastener *c.n* = zip(1).

zizz /zız/ *c.n* (often have a —) (*informal*) short sleep.

zodiac /'zəʊdı,æk/ *def.n* (also with capital **Z**) imagined area across the sky divided into 12 equal parts, each of which is called 'a sign of the zodiac' and named after a group of stars. **zodiacal** /zəʊ'daıəkl/ *adj* of or referring to the zodiac.

zombie /'zɒmbı/ *c.n* (*pl* -ies) (often *derog*) person who is stupid or who behaves as if her/his brain was controlled by a force outside her/his power.

zone /zəʊn/ *c.n* particular area or part of s.t that has qualities that make it different from other areas or parts of the same thing: *The world is divided into a number of time zones and the time is different in each one.* **danger zone** ⇒ danger. **war zone** ⇒ war.

zoo /zu:/ *c.n* (*pl* -s) place where various kinds of wild animals are kept so that people can walk about and look at them and scientists can study them.
'zoo-,keeper *c.n* person whose job is to look after the animals in a zoo.
zoological /,zəʊə'lɒdʒıkl/ *adj* of or referring to zoology.
,zoo,logical 'garden(s) *c.n* (*formal*) = zoo.
zoologist /zəʊ'ɒlədʒıst/ *c.n* person who is skilled in, or a student of, zoology.
zoology /zəʊ'ɒlədʒı/ *u.n* science dealing with animals; study of animals.

zoom /zu:m/ *sing.n* **1** long loud sound as from a very fast plane.
▷ *intr.v* **2** (often — *past*) move very quickly, esp making a long loud sound. **3** change the focus(2) of a camera to move from a more distant to a closer view, or the opposite. **zoom in** (on s.o/s.t) change the focus(2) of a camera so that s.o/s.t appears to come closer and therefore look larger.
,zoom 'lens *c.n* lens on a camera which allows one to zoom(3).

Appendix 1 Irregular verbs

Infinitive	Past tense	Past participle	Infinitive	Past tense	Past participle
abide	abided, abode	abided, abode	creep	crept	crept
arise	arose	arisen	curse (⇒ *Note 4 below*)		
awake	awoke, awakened	awoken	cut	cut	cut
			dare (⇒ *Note 5 below*)		
be	was, were	been (⇒ *Note 1 below*)	deal	dealt	dealt
			dig	dug	dug
			do	did	done (⇒ *Note 6 below*)
bear	bore	borne			
beat	beat	beaten			
become	became	become	draw	drew	drawn
befall	befell	befallen	dream	dreamt, dreamed	dreamt, dreamed
beget	begot	begotten			
begin	began	begun	drink	drank	drunk (⇒ *Note 7 below*)
behold	beheld	beheld			
bend	bent	bent			
bereave	bereft, bereaved	bereft, bereaved	drive	drove	driven
			dwell	dwelt, dwelled	dwelt, dwelled
beseech	beseeched, besought	beseeched, besought	eat	ate	eaten
			fall	fell	fallen
beset	beset	beset	feed	fed	fed
bet	bet, betted	bet, betted	feel	felt	felt
bethink	bethought	bethought	fight	fought	fought
bid	bad, bade, bid	bid, bidden	find	found	found
bind	bound	bound	flee	fled	fled
bite	bit	bitten	fling	flung	flung
bleed	bled	bled	fly	flew	flown
bless	blessed, blest	blessed, blest (⇒ *Note 2 below*)	forbear	forbore	forborne
			forbid	forbad, forbade	forbidden
blow	blew	blown	forecast	forecast	forecast
break	broke	broken	foreknow	foreknew	foreknown
breed	bred	bred	foresee	foresaw	foreseen
bring	brought	brought	foretell	foretold	foretold
broadcast	broadcast	broadcast	forget	forgot	forgotten
build	built	built	forgive	forgave	forgiven
burn	burnt, burned	burnt, burned	forsake	forsook	forsaken
burst	burst	burst	forswear	forswore	forsworn
buy	bought	bought	freeze	froze	frozen
can (⇒ *Note 3 below*)			gainsay	gainsaid	gainsaid
cast	cast	cast	get	got	got
catch	caught	caught	gird	girded, girt	girded, girt
chide	chided, chid	chided, chid, chidden	give	gave	given
			go	went	gone
choose	chose	chosen	grave	graved	graven, graved
cleave	cleft, cleaved, clove	cleft, cleaved, cloven	grind	ground	ground
			grow	grew	grown
cling	clung	clung	hamstring	hamstringed, hamstrung	hamstringed, hamstrung
clothe	clothed	clothed, clad (*formal*)			
			hang	hung, hanged	hung, hanged (⇒ *Note 8 below*)
come	came	come			
cost	cost	cost			

Infinitive	Past tense	Past participle	Infinitive	Past tense	Past participle
have	had	had (⇒ Note 9 below)	overfeed	overfed	overfed
			overhang	overhung	overhung
			overhear	overheard	overheard
hear	heard	heard	overlay	overlaid	overlaid
heave	heaved, hove	heaved, hove	overleap	overleapt, overleaped	overleapt, overleaped
hew	hewed	hewn, hewed			
hide	hid	hidden	overlie	overlay	overlain
hit	hit	hit	override	overrode	overridden
hold	held	held	overrun	overran	overrun
hurt	hurt	hurt	oversee	oversaw	overseen
inlay	inlaid	inlaid	overset	overset	overset
keep	kept	kept	overshoot	overshot	overshot
kneel	knelt, kneeled	knelt, kneeled	oversleep	overslept	overslept
knit	knitted, knit	knitted, knit	overtake	overtook	overtaken
know	knew	known	overthrow	overthrew	overthrown
lay	laid	laid	partake	partook	partaken
lead	led	led	pay	paid	paid
lean	leant, leaned	leant, leaned	prove (⇒ Note 19 below)		
leap	leapt, leaped	leapt, leaped	put	put	put
learn	learnt, learned	learnt, learned (⇒ Note 10 below)	read	read /red/	read /red/
			rebind	rebound	rebound
			rebuild	rebuilt	rebuilt
leave	left	left	recast	recast	recast
lend	lent	lent	redo	redid	redone (⇒ Note 20 below)
let	let	let			
lie	lay	lain (⇒ Note 11 below)	relay	relaid	relaid (⇒ Note 21 below)
light	lit, lighted	lit, lighted	remake	remade	remade
lose	lost	lost	rend	rent	rent
make	made	made	repay	repaid	repaid
may (⇒ Note 12 below)			rerun	reran	rerun
mean	meant	meant	reset	reset	reset
meet	met	met	retell	retold	retold
melt (⇒ Note 13 below)			rewind	rewound	rewound
miscast	miscast	miscast	rewrite	rewrote	rewritten
misdeal	misdealt	misdealt	rid	rid, ridded	rid, ridded
misgive	misgave	misgiven	ride	rode	ridden
mislay	mislaid	mislaid	ring	rang	rung
mislead	misled	misled	rise	rose	risen
misspell	misspelt, misspelled	misspelt, misspelled	run	ran	run
			saw	sawed	sawn, sawed
misspend	misspent	misspent	say	said	said
mistake	mistook	mistaken	see	saw	seen
misunderstand	misunderstood	misunderstood	seek	sought	sought
mow	mowed	mown, mowed	sell	sold	sold
must (⇒ Note 14 below)			send	sent	sent
need (⇒ Note 15 below)			set	set	set
ought (⇒ Note 16 below)			sew	sewed	sewn, sewed
outbid	outbid	outbidden, outbid	shake	shook	shaken
			shall (⇒ Note 22 below)		
outdo	outdid	outdone (⇒ Note 17 below)	shave (⇒ Note 23 below)		
			shear	sheared	shorn, sheared
outgrow	outgrew	outgrown			
outride	outrode	outridden	shed	shed	shed
outrun	outran	outrun	shine	shone	shone (⇒ Note 24 below)
outshine	outshone	outshone			
overbear	overbore	overborne			
overcast	overcast	overcast	shit	shitted, shat	shitted, shat
overcome	overcame	overcome	shoe	shod	shod
overdo	overdid	overdone (⇒ Note 18 below)	shoot	shot	shot

Infinitive	Past tense	Past participle	Infinitive	Past tense	Past participle
show	showed	shown, showed	underbid	underbid	underbid, underbidden
shrink	shrank, shrunk	shrunk (⇒ Note 25 below)	undergo	underwent	undergone (⇒ Note 28 below)
shut	shut	shut	understand	understood	understood
sing	sang	sung	undertake	undertook	undertaken
sink	sank, sunk	sunk (⇒ Note 26 below)	undo	undid	undone (⇒ Note 29 below)
sit	sat	sat			
slay	slew	slain	unwind	unwound	unwound
sleep	slept	slept	uphold	upheld	upheld
slide	slid	slid	upset	upset	upset
sling	slung	slung	wake	woke, waked	woken, waked
slink	slunk	slunk	waylay	waylaid	waylaid
slit	slit	slit	wear	wore	worn
smell	smelt, smelled	smelt, smelled	weave	wove	woven
smite	smote	smitten	wed	wedded, wed	wedded, wed
sow	sowed	sown, sowed	weep	wept	wept
speak	spoke	spoken	wet	wet, wetted	wet, wetted
speed	sped, speeded	sped, speeded	will (⇒ Note 30 below)		
spell	spelt, spelled	spelt, spelled	win	won	won
spend	spent	spent	wind /waɪnd/	wound /waʊnd/	wound /waʊnd/ (⇒ Note 31 below)
spill	spilt, spilled	spilt, spilled			
spin	spun, span	spun			
spit	spat	spat	withdraw	withdrew	withdrawn
split	split	split	withhold	withheld	withheld
spoil	spoilt, spoiled	spoilt, spoiled	withstand	withstood	withstood
spread	spread	spread	wring	wrung	wrung
spring	sprang	sprung	write	wrote	written
stand	stood	stood			
steal	stole	stolen			
stick	stuck	stuck			
sting	stung	stung			
stink	stank, stunk	stunk			
strew	strewed	strewn, strewed			
stride	strode	stridden			
strike	struck	struck (⇒ Note 27 below)			
string	strung	strung			
strive	strove, strived	striven, strived			
swear	swore	sworn			
sweep	swept	swept			
swell	swelled	swollen, swelled			
swim	swam	swum			
swing	swung	swung			
take	took	taken			
teach	taught	taught			
tear	tore	torn			
tell	told	told			
think	thought	thought			
thrive	thrived, throve	thrived, thriven			
throw	threw	thrown			
thrust	thrust	thrust			
tread	trod	trodden, trod			
unbend	unbent	unbent			
unbind	unbound	unbound			

Notes

1 Infinitive 'be': *pres.t*: I am, you are, he/she/it is, we/you/they are; *p.t*: I was, you were, he/she/it was, we/you/they were; *p.p* been.

2 The adj is 'blessed' /ˈblesɪd/ when it is *attrib* and /blest/ in the *pred* position.

3 No infinitive; *pres.t*: I/you/he/she/it/we/you/they can; *p.t* could; no *p.p*.

4 The adj 'cursed' /ˈkɜːsɪd/ exists.

5 *Pres.t* when followed by an infinitive without 'to': I/you/he/she/we/you/they dare; I/you/he/she/we/you/they daren't; Dare I/you/he/she/we/you/they? *Pres.t* when followed by an infinitive with 'to': I/you/we/you/they dare; he/she/it dares.

6 *Pres.t*: he/she/it does /dʌz/.

7 The adj 'drunken' exists.

8 'hanged' is used only for the punishment of humans by hanging.

9 *Pres.t*: I/you/we/you/they have; he/she/it has.

10 The adj 'learned' /ˈlɜːnɪd/ exists.

11 When 'lie' means 'tell a lie', it is a regular verb.

12 No infinitive; *pres.t*: I/you/he/she/it/we/you/they may; *p.t*: might; no *p.p*.

13 The adj 'molten' exists.

14 No infinitive; *pres.t*: I/you/he/she/it/we/you/they must; *p.t* had to.

15 There is a regular verb 'need' and also an irregular verb that is followed by 'to' without infinitive and has no infinitive; *pres.t*: I/you/he/she/it/you/they need, I/you/he/she/it/we/you/they need not; Need I/you/he/she/it/we/you/they? *p.t*: needn't have or didn't need.

16 No infinitive; *pres.t*: I/you/he/she/it/we/you/they ought; *p.t*: ought to have.

17 *Pres.t*: I/you/we/you/they outdo; he/she/it outdoes.

18 *Pres.t*: I/you/we/you/they overdo; he/she/it overdoes.

19 The adj 'proven' exists.

20 *Pres.t*: I/you/we/you/they redo; he/she/it redoes.

21 'relay' meaning 'send on' is a regular verb.

22 No infinitive; *pres.t*: I/you/he/she/it/we/you/they shall; *p.t* should.

23 The adj 'shaven' occurs in compounds, e.g 'cleanshaven'.

24 The verb 'shine' meaning polish (shoes etc) is regular.

25 The adj 'shrunken' exists.

26 The adj 'sunken' exists.

27 The adj 'stricken' exists.

28 *Pres.t*: I/you/we/you/they undergo; he/she/it undergoes.

29 *Pres.t*: I/you/we/you/they undo; he/she/it undoes.

30 'Will' meaning 'try to make something happen by using one's will', or 'leave s.t to s.o in one's will' is a regular verb. The auxiliary verb 'will' has no infinitive; *pres.t*: I/you/he/she/it/we/you/they will; *p.t*: would.

31 The verb 'wind' /wɪnd/ is regular.

Appendix 2 Common affixes and roots

a-¹ /ə-/ in a -*ing* state: *ablaze*; *asleep*.
a-² /eɪ-/, /ə-/ without: *amoral*; *amorphous*; *atheist*.
-a /-ə/ forming the plural of certain words borrowed from Greek or Latin: *addenda*; *criteria*.
ab- /əb-/, /æb-/ from: *abduct*; *aboriginal*.
-able /-əbl/ which can be (changing a verb/ noun into an adj): *acceptable*; *readable*.
ac- /-ək/ (before *c*) (added) to: *acclimatize*; *accompaniment*; *accustom*.
acro- /ækrə-/ relating to height: *acrobat*.
acu- /ək'ju:-/, /'ækjʊ-/ sharp: *acupuncture*; *acute*.
-acy /-əsɪ/ forming abstract and collective nouns: *delicacy*; *democracy*.
ad- /əd-/, /'æd-/ (added) to: *adrenal*; *adverb*.
-ade¹ /-eɪd/ forming nouns (sometimes also verbs): *blockade*; *escapade*; *lemonade*; *serenade*.
-ade² /-eɪd/ forming verbs (the noun has -*asion*): *dissuade*; *persuade*.
aer(o)- /eə(rə)-/, /'eə(rəʊ)-/ relating to air: *aerate*; *aeroplane*.
af- /əf-/, /æf-/ (before *f*) in a -*ing* state: *affect*; *afforest*.
Afro- /æfrəʊ-/ relating to Africa: *Afro-American*.
ag- /əg-/, /æg-/ (before *g*) (put) in a -*ing* state: *aggravate*; *aggressive*.
-age /-ɪdʒ/ forming nouns and sometimes meaning 'collection of'; 'the whole of': *acreage*; *coinage*.
agr(i)- /ægrɪ-/, /ægr(ə)-/ relating to the land: *agriculture*.
al- /əl-/ (before *l*) (put) in a -*ing* state: *allege*; *alleviate*.
-al /-(ə)l/ **-al-** /-æl/ referring to (forming adjs, sometimes used also as nouns): *accidental*; *capital*; *original*.
alim- /ælɪm-/ relating to food or maintenance: *alimentary*; *alimony*.
altern- /ɔ:ltɜ:n-/, /'ɔ:ltən-/ other: *alternate*; *alternatively*.
alt(i)- /'ælt(ɪ)-/ relating to height: *altimeter*; *altitude*.
ambi- /æmbɪ-/ both; around; two-sided: *ambidextrous*; *ambivalent*.
ami(c)- /ˌeɪmɪ-/, /'æmɪ(k)-/ friendly: *amiability*; *amicable*; *amity*.
amphi- /æmfɪ-/ both: *amphibian*.
ampl- /'æmpl-/ increase: *amplifier*; *amplitude*.
an- /ən-/, /'æn-/ (before *n*) (put) in a -*ing* state: *annihilate*; *annotation*.

-an /-ən/ person (noun or attrib): *African*; *comedian*.
-ance /-əns/ forming (usu abstract) nouns: *acceptance*; *appliance*; *disappearance*; *tolerance*.
angli- /'ænglɪ-/ relating to England and the English: *anglicize*.
anglo- /ænglʊ-/ relating to England and the English: *Anglo-Saxon*.
anim- /'ænɪm-/ relating to life: *animate*.
ann(i), ann(u), /'æn(ɪ)-/, /'ænjʊ-/, /ən'ju:-/ year: *annals*; *anniversary*; *annual*.
-ant /-ənt/ forming nouns or sometimes adjs, and meaning '(person/thing) that does s.t': *accountant*; *defendant*; *ignorant*.
ante- /æntɪ-/ before: *antedate*.
anthropo- /ænθrə'pɒ-/, /-pə-/ relating to man: *anthropology*.
ant(i)- /ænt(ɪ)-/ against; opposite: *antibiotic*; *antonym*.
ap- /əp-/ (before *p*) (put) in a -*ing* state: *append*; *applaud*.
aqu(a)-, aqu(e)- /ækw(ə)-/, ækw(ɪ)- relating to water: *aquarium*; *aqualung*; *aqueous*.
ar- /ər-/ (before *r*) (put) in a -*ing* state: *arrange*.
-ar /-ə/ forming adjs from nouns: *circular*; *vulgar*.
arch(e)- /ɑ:tʃ-/, /ɑ:kɪ-/ chief: *archbishop*; *archetype*.
ard- /ɑ:d-/ burning; difficulty: *ardent*; *arduous*.
-ard /-əd/ person: *drunkard*.
-arious /-eərɪəs/ forming adjs from nouns and meaning 'having a tendency towards': *gregarious*; *hilarious*.
-arity /-ærɪtɪ/ forming nouns: *barbarity*; *hilarity*.
-ary /-(ə)rɪ/ forming adjs and nouns: *imaginary*; *revolutionary*; *secretary*.
astro- /æstro-/, /æstrə(ʊ)-/ relating to the stars: *astrologer*; *astronaut*.
at- /ət-/ (before *t*) (put) in a -*ing* state: *attach*; *attend*.
-ate¹ /-ɪt/ forming adjs and sometimes nouns: *affectionate*; *triplicate*.
-ate² /-eɪt/ forming verbs: *circulate*; *irritate*.
-atic /-ætɪk/ forming adjs from nouns (sometimes the adj can also be used as a noun): *automatic*; *diplomatic*.
-ation /-eɪʃən/ forming nouns usually from verbs: *accommodation*; *collaboration*.
-ative /-ətɪv/ forming adjs (sometimes the adj can also be used as a noun): *administrative*; *representative*.

-ator /-eɪtə/, /-ətə/ forming nouns and meaning 'person/thing that does the action': *administrator*; *conspirator*.

-ature /-ɪtʃə/ forming nouns or sometimes adjs: *curvature*; *miniature*.

audi(o)- /ɔːdɪ(əʊ)-/ relating to hearing: *audibility*; *audio-visual*.

auto- /ɔːtə(ʊ)-/ relating to self: *autobiography*; *auto-suggestion*.

avi- /eɪvɪ-/ relating to birds or flying: *avian*; *aviator*.

belli- /belɪ-/ relating to war: *bellicose*; *belligerent*.

bene- /benɪ-/ good: *benediction*; *benefactor*.

bi- /baɪ-/ twice; two: *biannual*; *bicycle*.

by-¹ /baɪ-/ subsidiary; local: *by-law*; *by-product*.

by-² /baɪ-/ passing by: *by-pass*.

carn(i)- /kɑːn(ɪ)-/ relating to flesh: *carnivorous*; *incarnation*.

-ceive /-siːv/ various verb meanings: *conceive*; *deceive*; *receive*.

centen(n)- /senten-/, /sen'tiːn-/ relating to a hundred years: *centenarian*; *centennial*.

cent(i)- /sent(ɪ)-/ relating to a hundred or hundredth: *centigrade*; *centimetre*.

-cep- /-sep-/ various verb meanings: *conception*; *deception*; *reception*.

(-)chron(o)- /krɒn-/, /-krən(ɒ)-/ relating to time: *chronometer*; *synchronous*.

cine- /sɪnɪ-/ relating to filming: *cine-camera*; *cinema*.

circum- /sɜːkəm-/ around: *circumcise*; *circumnavigate*.

civ- /sɪv-/ relating to a city or citizen: *civic*; *civilize*.

-clude /-kluːd/ forming verbs and meaning approximately 'keep': *exclude*; *preclude*.

co- /kə(ʊ)-/ together (with): *co-education*; *cooperation*.

contra- /kɒntrə-/ against: *contraception*; *contradictory*.

counter- /kaʊntə(r)-/ against: *counteract*; *counterweight*.

-cy /-sɪ/ forming abstract nouns: *accuracy*; *presidency*.

de- /dɪ-/, /diː-/ away from: *decentralize*; *defrost*.

deci- /desɪ-/ relating to ten or a tenth: *decigramme*; *decimal*.

(-)dict- /(-)dɪkt-/, /dɪkʃ/ relating to speaking: *contradict*; *diction*; *predict*.

dis- /dɪs-/ away (from): *disconnect*; *discomfort*.

-dom /-dəm/ forming nouns and meaning 'area belonging to, or fact concerning': *freedom*; *kingdom*.

-duc(e)- /-djuːs-/ forming verbs and meaning approximately 'bring': *introduce*; *produce*.

-duc(t) /-dʌk(t)/ carry; bring: *abduct*; *aqueduct*.

dynam- /daɪ'næm-/, /'daɪnəm-/ relating to force: *dynamic*; *dynamo*.

e-, ec-, ef- /ɪ-, ɪk-, ɪf/, /e-, ek, ef-/ from; out (of): *eccentric*; *efflorescence*; *eject*.

-ed /t/, /-(ɪ)d/ forming the *p.t* or *p.p*, or adj meaning 'having': *looked*; *redheaded*.

-ee /-'iː/ person who undergoes an action (sometimes who does an action): *employee*; *trainee*.

-eer /-ɪə/ person who does, or is concerned with, s.t: *auctioneer*; *engineer*.

en-¹ /en-/, /ɪn-/ in: *enclose*; *entomb*.

en-² /en-/, /ɪn-/ make; cause to (have): *encourage*; *enforce*.

-en¹ /-(ə)n/ forming the *p.p* or an adj based on it: *broken*; *given*.

-en² /-(ə)n/ forming a plural ending: *brethren*; *oxen*.

-en³ /-(ə)n/ ending forming a verb and meaning 'make': *dampen*; *gladden*.

-ence /-əns/ forming (usu abstract) nouns: *coincidence*; *interference*.

-ency /-ənsɪ/ forming (usu abstract) nouns: *fluency*; *tendency*.

-ent /-ənt/ forming adjs and sometimes also nouns showing persons having the quality of the adj: *adherent*; *irreverent*.

equi- /iːkwɪ-/, /ɪkwɪ-/ equal(ly): *equidistant*; *equivalent*.

-er¹ /-ə/ forming the comp of some adjs and advs: *bigger*; *easier*.

-er² /-ə/ person, or sometimes thing, that does s.t: *farmer*; *heater*.

-ern /-ən/ forming adjs: *eastern*; *southern*.

-eous /-ɪəs/ forming adjs and meaning 'giving/having s.t': *courageous*; *outrageous*.

-ery /-ərɪ/ forming (mostly abstract or collective) nouns: *cookery*; *machinery*.

-es /-ɪz/ forming the plural or *3rd pers pres.t* ending after *s*, *z*, *sh* or *ch*: *masses*; *buzzes*; *pushes*; *watches*.

-esce, -esc- /-es-/ become: *acquiesce*; *obsolescence*.

-ese /-iːz/ forming adjs or noun of nationality, city of origin etc: *Chinese*; *Viennese*.

-ess /-ɪs/, /-es/ female: *actress*; *lioness*.

-est /-ɪst/ forming the superl of adjs and some advs: *biggest*; *easiest*.

-eth /-əθ/ forming ordinal numbers: *twentieth*.

-etic /-etɪk/ forming adjs: *aesthetic*; *sympathetic*.

-ette /-et/ small: *kitchenette*; *statuette*.

-ety /-ətɪ/ forming (usu abstract or collective) nouns: *anxiety*, *variety*.

eu- /juː-/ good; well: *eulogy*; *euphoric*.

-eur /-(j)ə/ forming (usu abstract) nouns: *connoisseur*; *grandeur*.

Euro- /'jʊərəʊ-/ relating to Europe: *Eurocheque*.

ex- /eks-/ former: *ex-husband*; *ex-minister*.

ex(e)- /ɪks-/, /eks(ɪ)-/, /ɪgz(e)-/ out (of); away; completely: *excavate*; *exclude*; *executive*; *exhale*.

extra- /ekstr(ə)-/, /ek'streɪ-/ out(side): *extradite*; *extraneous*; *extraordinary*.

-faction /-fækʃən/ forming nouns meaning 'making': *rarefaction*; *stupefaction*.

-fer- /-fɜː-/, /-fər-/ move (really or metaphorically): *confer*; *preferential*; *reference*.

-fication /-fɪkeɪʃən/ forming nouns and meaning 'making': *magnification*.

-fin- /-faɪn-/, /-fɪn-/ relating to an end: *finite*; *infinitesimal*.

-flu- /-flʊ-/, /-fluː-/ relating to flowing: *confluence*; *fluent*.

(-)fore- /-fɔː-/ ahead; in/to the front: *aforesaid*; *before*; *foreground*; *forewarn*.

Franco /ˈfræŋkəʊ-/ relating to France: *Francophone*.

-ful¹ /-f(ə)l/ full of: *artful*; *tuneful*.

-ful² /-fʊl/ as much as s.t can hold: *armful*; *mouthful*.

-fy /-ˌfaɪ/ forming verbs and meaning 'make': *beautify*; *glorify*.

(-)gene-; (-)gen(er)- /-dʒenə(r)-/, **geni-** /dʒenɪ-/, **geno-** /dʒenə-/ produce; people or things produced: *congenital*; *genealogical*; *generate*; *genocide*.

(-)graph(-) /-grɑːf/, /(-)græf(-)/, /-grəf(-)/ relating to writing, drawing etc: *autograph*; *cartographer*; *graphic*.

(-)grav- /-grəv-/, /(-)græv-/ heavy: *gravitational*; *aggravate*.

-gress(-) /-gres/, /-gref-/ relating to movement: *egress*; *progression*.

-hood /-hʊd/ forming abstract or collective nouns: *adulthood*; *brotherhood*.

(-)hydr(o)- /(-)haɪdr(əʊ)-/ relating to water: *dehydrate*; *hydroelectric*.

hyper- /haɪpə-/ excessively: *hyper-critical*.

hypo- /haɪpə-/, /hɪpə-/, /haɪˈpɒ-/ below; defectively: *hypocritical*; *hypodermic*.

-ia /-ɪə/ forming nouns, often showing a medical condition or treatment: *amnesia*; *anaesthesia*; *intelligentsia*.

-iac /-ˌæk/ forming adjs and nouns and meaning 'concerning or who/that experiences s.t': *cardiac*; *insomniac*.

-ial /-(ə)l/, /-ɪəl/ changing nouns into adjs although the adj that is formed can sometimes also be used as a noun: *adverbial*; *provincial*.

-ian /-ɪən/, /-ən/ forming adjs and nouns and meaning '(person/thing) of a certain kind': *Arabian*; *electrician*.

-iance /-(ɪ)əns/ forming (usu abstract) nouns: *allegiance*; *radiance*.

-iant /-(ɪ)ənt/ forming adjs and sometimes nouns: *brilliant*; *radiant*.

-ibility /-ɪˈbɪlɪtɪ/ forming nouns showing that s.t can be done or made s.t: *contemptibility*; *perfectibility*.

-ible /-ɪbl/ forming adjs and meaning 'that can be done or made': *admissible*; *collapsible*.

-ic /-ɪk/ forming adjs and sometimes nouns and meaning 'relating to, or having the property of, s.t': *academic*; *alcoholic*; *prehistoric*.

-ical /-ɪkl/ forming adjs: *anatomical*; *surgical*.

-ically /-ɪklɪ/ forming advs: *chronologically*; *practically*.

-ication /-ɪkeɪʃən/ forming nouns indicating actions: *application*; *simplification*.

-icide /-ˌsaɪd/ relating to killing: *infanticide*; *insecticide*; *suicide*.

-icity /-ɪsɪtɪ/ forming abstract nouns: *multiplicity*; *simplicity*.

-ics /-ɪks/ forming nouns and meaning 'study, performance or science of s.t': *dramatics*; *ethics*; *politics*.

-id /-ɪd/ forming adjs or sometimes nouns: *fluid*; *splendid*.

-idity /-ɪdɪtɪ/ forming abstract nouns: *frigidity*; *validity*.

-ie /-ɪ/ forming nouns and often meaning 'small', or used by children: *birdie*; *doggie*.

-ience /-(ɪ)əns/ forming abstract nouns: *convenience*; *impatience*.

-iency /-(ɪ)ənsɪ/ forming abstract nouns: *efficiency*; *sufficiency*.

-ient /-(ɪ)ənt/ forming adjs: *insufficient*; *subservient*.

-ier /-ɪə/ forming nouns and meaning 'person/thing that does s.t': *barrier*; *furrier*.

-iety /-ˈaɪətɪ/ forming abstract nouns: *anxiety*; *variety*.

-ific /-ɪfɪk/ forming adjs and meaning 'causing or connected with': *horrific*; *scientific*.

-ify /-ˌfaɪ/ forming verbs and meaning 'make': *fortify*; *horrify*.

-ility /-ɪlɪtɪ/ forming nouns indicating conditions: *facility*; *mobility*.

im-¹ /ɪm-/ (before *b*, *m* or *p*) not: *imbalance*; *immature*; *impossibility*.

im-² /ɪm-/ (before *b*, *m* or *p*) in(to); towards s.t: *immigrate*; *imprison*.

in-¹ /ɪn-/ not: *inability*; *indestructible*.

in-² /ɪn-/ in(to); towards s.t: *inborn*; *inject*.

-inal /-ɪnəl/ forming nouns and adjs: *criminal*; *nominal*.

Indo- /ˌɪndəʊ-/ relating to India: *Indo-European*.

inter- /ɪntə-/ between: *interact*; *international*.

intro- /ɪntrə-/ in(to): *introduce*; *introspective*.

-ion /-(ɪ)ən/ forming abstract nouns: *oblivion*; *separation*.

-ior /-ɪə/ forming nouns and adjs: *junior*; *superior*.

-ious /-(ɪ)əs/ forming adjs: *glorious*; *seditious*.

ir-¹ /ɪr-/ (before *r*) not: *irrational*; *irresolution*.

ir-² /ɪr-/ (before *r*) in(to); towards s.t: *irradiate*; *irrupt*.

-ise, -ize, -is-, -iz- /-(a)ɪz/ forming verbs and meaning 'cause to be': *colonize* (-ise); *synthesize* (-ise).

-ish¹ /-ɪʃ/ forming verbs: *embellish*; *finish*.

-ish² /-ɪʃ/ forming adjs and meaning 'like (s.o/s.t)' or 'in origin': *blackish*; *Swedish*.

-ism /-ɪzəm/ forming abstract nouns: *absenteeism*; *patriotism*.

-ist /-ɪst/ forming nouns and meaning 'person who does or is s.t': *artist*; *extremist*; *terrorist*.

-ite /-ɪt/, /-aɪt/ forming nouns and adjs: *composite*; *meteorite*.

-ition- /-ɪʃən-/ forming (mostly abstract) nouns and usually meaning 'act or fact of doing s.t': *acquisition*; *additional*.

-itious /-ɪʃəs/ forming adjs: *expeditious*; *suppositious*.

-itis /-aɪtɪs/ disease of: *appendicitis*; *tonsillitis*.

-itive, -itiv- /-ɪtɪv(-)/ forming adjs and nouns: *additive*; *insensitivity*.

-itude /-ɪtjuːd/ forming abstract nouns: *aptitude*; *magnitude*.

-ity /-ɪtɪ/ forming mostly abstract nouns: *ability*; *severity*; *university*.

-ium /-ɪəm/ forming nouns: *gymnasium*; *tedium*.

-ive, -iv /-ɪv(-)/ forming adjs and nouns: *abusive*; *festivity*.

-ize ⇒ -ise.

-ject(-) /-dʒek(t)-/ relating to throwing: *eject*; *projectile*.

(-)judic- /-ˈdʒuːdɪk-/, /dʒuːˈdɪʃ-/ relating to judging: *adjudicate*; *judicious*.

(-)junct- /(-)dʒʌŋkt-/, /-dʒʌŋʃ-/ joined; joining: *adjunct*; *conjunction*.

-less /-lɪs/ forming adjs and meaning 'without': *ageless*, *shapeless*.

-let¹ /-lɪt/ forming nouns and meaning 'small': *islet*; *ringlet*.

-let² /-lɪt/ way: *inlet*; *outlet*.

-like /-laɪk/ forming adjs and meaning 'like': *childlike*; *warlike*.

-ling /-lɪŋ/ forming nouns and meaning 'small or subordinate': *duckling*; *princeling*.

-log- /-lɒdʒ-/, /-lədʒ-/ relating to study: *psychology*; *physiologist*.

-ly¹ /-lɪ/ forming advs from adjs and sometimes nouns: *beautifully*; *easily*.

-ly² /-lɪ/ forming adjs: *daily*; *friendly*.

mal(e)- /mæl(ɪ)-/, /mɒl(e)-/ bad(ly): *maladjusted*; *malefactor*; *maltreat*.

(-)memor- /(-)memər-/, /(-)məˈmɔːr-/ relating to remembering: *immemorial*; *memorize*.

-ment¹ /-mənt/ forming (mostly abstract) nouns: *achievement*; *encouragement*.

-ment² /-ˈment/ forming verbs: *impleˈment*; *suppleˈment*.

micro- /maɪkrə(ʊ)-/, /maɪˈkrɒ-/ small: *microbiology*; *micrometer*.

mid- /mɪd-/ relating to middle: *midday*; *midsummer*; *midway*.

mis- /mɪs-/ bad(ly); wrong(ly): *misapply*; *mistrust*.

mono- /ˈmɒnə(ʊ)-/, /məˈnɒ-/ relating to one: *monochrome*; *monopoly*.

(-)mort- /-mɔːt-/ relating to death or dying: *immortal*; *mortuary*.

multi- /mʌltɪ-/ relating to many: *multimillionaire*; *multi-purpose*; *multitude*.

(-)naut- /(-)nɔːt-/ relating to travel by sea or in space: *nautical*; *astronaut*.

-ness /-nɪs/ forming (mostly abstract) nouns from adjs: *bitterness*; *weariness*.

non- /nɒn-/ not: *nonsense*; *non-stick*.

-oid /-ɔɪd/ forming adjs and nouns and meaning 'having the form of s.t': *celluloid*; *tabloid*.

omni- /ɒmnɪ-/ relating to all: *omnipotent*; *omnivorous*.

-or /-ə/ forming nouns and meaning 'person/thing that does s.t': *actor*; *adaptor*.

-or- /-ər-/ form of *-our* when *-ous* follows: *amorous*.

-ory¹ /-ɔrɪ/ forming adjs: *advisory*; *satisfactory*.

-ory² /-ɔrɪ/ forming nouns: *directory*; *factory*.

-our(-) /-ə(-)/ forming nouns and (rarely) verbs: *armour*; *favourite*.

-ous /-əs/ forming adjs: *joyous*; *victorious*.

pan- /pæn-/ relating to all: *pan-American*; *pandemic*.

p(a)ed- /ped-/, /piːd-/ relating to child(ren): *pedagogic*; *paediatrics*.

-pect- /-pekt-/ (same as *-spect-* but after *ex-*) relating to looking: *expectant*; *expectation*.

(-)ped- /(-)ped-/ relating to the foot or base: *pedestal*; *pedestrian*.

-pel, -pell- /-pel-/ drive: *compel*; *dispelled*.

-pend- /-pend-/ hang; attach: *append*; *depend*; *suspend*.

peri- /perɪ-/, /pəˈrɪ-/ around: *perimeter*; *periscope*.

-phile /-faɪl/, **(-)phil(o)-** /fɪˈlɒ-/, /fɪlə-/ relating to liking or studying: *anglophile*; *philanthropy*; *philosopher*; *philosophical*.

-phobia /-fəʊbɪə/ relating to fear or dislike: *anglophobia*; *claustrophobia*.

(-)port- /-pɔːt-/ relating to carrying: *export*; *porter*; *support*.

-pose /-pəʊz/, **-pos-** /-pɒz-/, /-pəʊʒ-/ place, put: *depose*; *depositor*; *exposure*.

post- /pəʊst-/, /pɒst-/, /pəs-/ after: *post-date*; *posthumous*; *postpone*.

pre- /priː-/, /prɪ-/, /pre-/ before: *precede*; *prejudice*.

pro-¹ /prəʊ-/ in favour of: *pro-British*.

pro-² /prəʊ-/ instead of; on behalf of: *pro-consul*.

pro-³ /prə(ʊ)-/, /prɒ-/ forward: *progress*; *propose*.

pseudo- /sjuːdəʊ-/ seeming(ly) but falsely so: *pseudo-intellectual*; *pseudonym*.

-pulse /-pʌls/, **-puls-** /-pʌls-/, /-pʌlʃ-/ relating to driving; pushing: *compulsive*; *repulse*.

re-¹ /ˌriː-/ again: *redo*; *reopening*.

re-² /rɪ-/ back: *repel*; *revert*.

retro- /retrə(ʊ)-/ relating to going backwards: *retroactive*; *retro-rocket*.

(-)rupt- /-rʌpt(ʃ)-/ relating to break(ing): *disruptive*; *rupture*.

Russo- /ˈrʌsəʊ-/ relating to Russia: *Russophile*.

-ry /-rɪ/ forming (mostly abstract or collective) nouns: *artistry*; *chemistry*; *weaponry*.

-s¹ /-(ə)z/, /-s/ forming the plural of nouns: *bells*; *sizes*.

-s² /-z/, /-s/ forming the possessive of some prons: *ours*; *yours*.

-s³ /-(ə)z/, /-s/ forming the 3rd pers sing pres.t: *gives*; *puts*.

-s⁴ /-z/ forming some advs: *always*; *backwards*; *besides*.

-'s /-(ə)z/, /-s/ forming the possessive of sing nouns and pl nouns that do not end in -s: *girl's*; *horse's*; *women's*.

-s' /-(ə)z/, /-s/ forming the possessive plural of most nouns: *cats'*; *girls'*; *horses'*.

sacr- /ˈsækr-/, /ˈseɪkr-/, **-secr-** /-sɪkr-/ holy: *consecrate*; *sacrament*; *sacred*; *sacrosanct*.

(-)sect- /-sekt-/, /-sekʃ-/ relating to cutting: *bisect*; *section*; *sector*.

semi- /semɪ-/ relating to half: *semicircle*; *semiconscious*.

-semin- /-semɪn-/ relating to seed: *inseminate*; *seminal*.

(-)sent(-) /-sent(-)/, /-zent(-)/ relating to feeling: *resent*; *sentient*; *sentimental*.

-ship /-ʃɪp/ forming nouns and meaning 'fact or state of having or being s.t': *citizenship*; *studentship*.

Sino- /ˌsaɪnəʊ-/ relating to China: *sinology*.

-sist- /-sɪst-/ act; exist: *assist*; *insist*; *persist*.

(-)soc(i)- /-səʊʃ(ɪ)-/, /-səˈsaɪ-/ **-socio-** /-səʊsɪ(ˈɒ)-/, /-səʊsɪə-/ relating to gathering together: *associate*; *society*; *sociable*; *sociological*.

-some /-səm/ forming adjs meaning 'having (the quality of)': *adventuresome*; *quarrelsome*.

(-)soph- /-səf-/, /-sɒf-/ relating to knowledge of wisdom: *philosophy*; *sophism*.

(-)spect- /-spekt-/, /-spekʃ-/ relating to looking: *inspection*; *spectroscope*.

(-)struct- /-strʌkt-/, /(-)strʌkʃ-/ relating to building or creating: *construct*; *instruction*; *structure*.

sub- /sʌb-/, /səb-/ under; down: *subcommittee*; *submarine*.

-sume /-sjuːm/, /-zjuːm/, **-sump-** /-sʌmp-/, /-zʌmp-/ take: *assume*; *consumer*; *presumption*.

super- /suːpə-/ over; above; too: *superabundant*; *superhuman*; *superstructure*.

tele- /telɪ-/, /tɪˈle-/ over a long distance: *telecommunications*; *telegraphy*.

-tempor- /-tempə(r)-/ relating to time: *contemporary*; *extemporize*.

-th /-θ/ forming ordinal numbers: *fourth*; *hundredth*.

therm(o)- /θɜːmə(ʊ)-/, /θəˈmɒ-/ relating to heat: *thermal*; *thermometer*.

-tial /-ʃəl/ forming adjs: *circumstantial*; *martial*.

-tion /-ʃən/ forming abstract nouns: *reception*; *subscription*.

tran(s)- /trɑːn(z)-/, /trɑːns-/ relating to movement (across): *transatlantic*; *transpire*; *transport*.

tri- /ˈtraɪ-/, /trɪ-/ relating to three: *triangle*; *tricolour*.

-tude, -tud- /-tjuːd-/ forming nouns: *disquietude*; *servitude*.

-ture /-tʃə/, **-tur-** /-tʃə-/ forming nouns and sometimes verbs: *capture*; *fixture*; *fracture*.

-ty /-tɪ/ forming nouns: *admiralty*; *certainty*.

-ual /-(j)ʊəl-/, /-ˈjʊæl-/ forming adjs: *actual*; *sensuality*.

ultra- /ʌltrə-/ beyond: *ultrasonic*; *ultraviolet*.

un-[1] /ʌn-/ not: *uncomfortable*; *unworthy*.

un-[2] /ʌn-/ do the opposite of s.t: *unbutton*; *unzip*.

uni- /juːnɪ-/ relating to one: *unicellular*; *unify*.

-uous /-jʊəs/ forming adjs: *continuous*; *virtuous*.

-ure /-(j)ə/, **-ur-** /-ər-/ forming nouns: *closure*; *cultural*; *failure*.

-ution(-) /-juːʃən(-)/ forming nouns: *evolution*; *revolutionary*.

(-)val- /(-)vəl-/, /(-)ˈvæl-/ worth; value: *ambivalent*; *evaluate*; *valid*.

-vent- /-vent-/, /-vənt-/, /-venʃ/ come; move: *advent*; *circumvention*; *prevent*.

-verse /-vɜːs/, **-vers-** /-vɜːs-/, /-vɜːʃ-/ opposite; turn: *adversary*; *aversion*; *reverse*.

-vert- /-vɜːt-/, /-vət-/ turn: *advertise*; *avert*.

vice- /vaɪs-/ in place of s.o; deputizing for s.o: *vice-captain*; *vice-chairman*.

-vise /-ˌvaɪz/, **-vis-** /-vɪz-/, /-vɪʒ-/ relating to seeing: *televise*; *visible*; *vision*.

(-)voc- /-və(ʊ)k-/, /-vɒk-/, **-voke** /-vəʊk/ call: *invoke*; *vocalist*.

(-)vol- /(-)vɒl-/, /-vəl-/ relating to one's will or wish: *benevolence*; *voluntary*.

-ward- /-wəd-/ in a (certain) direction: *backward*; *eastward*; *windward*.

-y[1] /-ɪ/ forming adjs: *dirty*; *funny*.

-y[2] /-ɪ/ forming nouns, often meaning 'small' or used by children: *mummy*; *pussy*.

Appendix 3 **Punctuation**

.   **full stop 1** put at the end of sentences: *'Oh.'* *'Do come in.'* *'I'm ready now.'* *'Please help yourself.'* **2** put after a letter or letters to show that it is, or they are, an abbreviation: *Ph.D.*

,   **comma** showing a short pause, usually for a grammatical purpose: *'This is Peter, who used to be our children's teacher.'*

?   **question mark** put at the end of a direct question: *'Oh?'* *'This way?'* *'It's cold today, isn't it?'* *'Where's Helen?'* *'Do you live here?'*

!   **exclamation mark** put at the end of an exclamation, order or statement to show loudness or strong feeling: *'Hi!'* *'Stop!'* *'Don't do that!'* *'You're standing on my foot!'* *'Oh, I'm so sorry!'*

. . .   **dots/dash** showing an interruption or un-
—   finished sentence: *'I'm looking for what's-her-name — er — Mary.'* *'Do you know where . . .?'*

;   **semi-colon** used to separate important parts of a sentence, especially when these parts have commas inside them: *'The girls, Helen, Mary and Jane, always play hockey; and the boys, Fred, David and Harry, play football.'*

:   **colon** showing that a list, an explanation or an example follows: *'We need the following: 4 eggs, ½ kg flour, 1 tsp sugar.'* *'I'm not going swimming today: it's too cold.'*

Appendix 4 **The family**

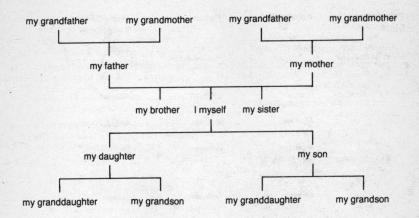

My father and mother are my **parents.**

My daughter and son are my **children.**

My grandfathers and grandmothers are my **grandparents.**

My children's children are my **grandchildren.** *They are my* **granddaughters** *and my* **grandsons.**

My granddaughters and grandsons are my **grandchildren.**

My grandparents' parents are my **great-grandparents.** *They are my* **great-grandfathers** *and my* **great-grandmothers.**

My husband's/wife's parents are my **parents-in-law.** *They are my* **father-in-law** *and my* **mother-in-law.**

My brother's wife is my **sister-in-law** *and my sister's husband is my* **brother-in-law.**

My daughter's husband is my **son-in-law** *and my son's wife is my* **daughter-in-law.**

My father's/mother's brother is my **uncle** *and my father's/mother's sister is my* **aunt.**

My father's/mother's aunt is my **great-aunt** *and my father's/mother's uncle is my* **great-uncle.**

My brother's/sister's daughter is my **niece** *and my brother's/sister's son is my* **nephew.**

My nephew's/niece's daughter is my **grandniece** *and my nephew/niece's son is my* **grandnephew.**

My aunt's/uncle's daughter/son is my **first cousin.**

The children of first cousins are each other's **second cousins.**

If my father marries again, or had a wife before my mother, his other wife is my **stepmother.**

If my mother marries again, or had another husband before my father, he is my **stepfather.**

If my father has a daughter by a woman who is not my mother, or my mother has a daughter by a man who is not my father, this daughter is my **stepsister** *or* **half-sister.**

If it is a son instead of a daughter, he is my **stepbrother** *or* **half-brother.**

If my husband/wife has a daughter by a person other than me, she is my **stepdaughter.**

If it is a son instead of a daughter, he is my **stepson.**

Appendix 5 **Geographical names**

Country or State	Adjective	Person	Main/Official Language
Afghanistan /æfˈgænɪˌstɑːn/	Afghan /ˈæfgæn/	Afghani, Afghanistani /æfˈgɑːnɪ, æfˌgænɪˈstɑːnɪ/	Pashto
Albania /ælˈbeɪnɪə/	Albanian /ælˈbeɪnɪən/	Albanian /ælˈbeɪnɪən/	Albanian
Algeria /ælˈdʒɪərɪə/	Algerian /ælˈdʒɪərɪən/	Algerian /ælˈdʒɪərɪən/	Arabic, French
America, the United States of America /əˈmerɪkə/	American /əˈmerɪkən/	American /əˈmerɪkən/	English
Andorra /ænˈdɔːrə/	Andorran /ænˈdɔːrən/	Andorran /ænˈdɔːrən/	Catalan
Angola /æŋˈgəʊlə/	Angolan /æŋˈgəʊlən/	Angolan /æŋˈgəʊlən/	Portuguese
Argentina, the Argentine /ˌɑːdʒənˈtiːnə, ˈɑːdʒənˌtiːn/	Argentinian /ˌɑːdʒənˈtɪnɪən/	Argentinian /ˌɑːdʒənˈtɪnɪən/	Spanish
Australia /ɒˈstreɪlɪə/	Australian /ɒˈstreɪlɪən/	Australian /ɒˈstreɪlɪən/	English
Austria /ˈɒstrɪə/	Austrian /ˈɒstrɪən/	Austrian /ˈɒstrɪən/	German
Bahama Islands, the Bahamas /bəˈhɑːməz/	Bahamian /bəˈheɪmɪən/	Bahamian /bəˈheɪmɪən/	English
Bahrain /bɑːˈreɪn/	Bahraini /bɑːˈreɪnɪ/	Bahraini /bɑːˈreɪnɪ/	Arabic
Bangladesh /ˌbæŋgləˈdeʃ/	Bangladeshi /ˌbæŋgləˈdeʃɪ/	Bangladeshi /ˌbæŋgləˈdeʃɪ/	Bengali
Barbados /bɑːˈbeɪdɒs/	Barbadian /bɑːˈbeɪdɪən/	Barbadian /bɑːˈbeɪdɪən/	English
Belgium /ˈbeldʒəm/	Belgian /ˈbeldʒən/	Belgian /ˈbeldʒən/	Flemish, French
Belize /bəˈliːz/	Belizean /bəˈliːzɪən/	Belizean /bəˈliːzɪən/	English
Benin /beˈnɪn/	Beninese /ˌbenɪˈniːz/	Beninese /ˌbenɪˈniːz/	French
Bermuda, the Bermudas /bəˈmjuːdə(z)/	Bermudan /bəˈmjuːdən/	Bermudan /bəˈmjuːdən/	English
Bhutan /buːˈtɑːn/	Bhutanese /ˌbuːtəˈniːz/	Bhutani /buːˈtɑːnɪ/	Dzongka

Country or State	Adjective	Person	Main/Official Language
Bolivia /bəˈlɪvɪə/	Bolivian /bəˈlɪvɪən/	Bolivian /bəˈlɪvɪən/	Spanish, Quechua, Aymara
Botswana /bɒtˈswɑːnə/	Botswanan /bɒtˈswɑːnən/	Motswana c.n /mɒtˈswɑːnə/ Batswanna pl.n /bætˈswɑːnə/	English, Tswana
Brazil /brəˈzɪl/	Brazilian /brəˈzɪlɪən/	Brazilian /brəˈzɪlɪən/	Portuguese
Britain /ˈbrɪtn/ ⇒ Great Britain			
Brunei /bruːˈnaɪ/	Bruneian /bruːˈnaɪən/	Bruneian /bruːˈnaɪən/	Malay
Bulgaria /bʌlˈgeərɪə/	Bulgarian /bʌlˈgeərɪən/	Bulgarian /bʌlˈgeərɪən/	Bulgarian
Burkina-Faso /bɜːˌkiːnə ˈfæsəu/	Burkinese /ˌbɜːkɪˈniːz/	Burkinian /bɜːˈkɪnɪən/	French, Mossi
Burma /ˈbɜːmə/	Burmese /bɜːˈmiːz/	Burmese /bɜːˈmiːz/	Burmese
Burundi /bəˈrundɪ/	Burundian /bəˈrundɪən/	Burundian /bəˈrundɪən/	French, Kirundi
Cambodia /kæmˈbəudɪə/ = Kampuchea			
Cameroon /ˌkæməˈruːn/	Cameroonian /ˌkæməˈruːnɪən/	Cameroonian /ˌkæməˈruːnɪən/	French, English
Canada /ˈkænədə/	Canadian /kəˈneɪdɪən/	Canadian /kəˈneɪdɪən/	English, French
Central African Republic /ˌsentrəl ˌæfrɪkən rɪˈpʌblɪk/	Central African Republican /ˌsentrəl ˌæfrɪkən rɪˈpʌblɪkən/		French, Sangho
Chad /tʃæd/	Chadian /ˈtʃædɪən/	Chadian /ˈtʃædɪən/	French
Chile /ˈtʃɪlɪ/	Chilean /ˈtʃɪlɪən/	Chilean /ˈtʃɪlɪən/	Spanish
China /ˈtʃaɪnə/	Chinese /tʃaɪˈniːz/	Chinese /tʃaɪˈniːz/	Mandarin, Chinese
Colombia /kəˈlɒmbɪə/	Colombian /kəˈlɒmbɪən/	Colombian /kəˈlɒmbɪən/	Spanish
Congo, the Congo Republic /ˈkɒŋgəu/	Congolese /ˌkɒŋgəˈliːz/	Congolese /ˌkɒŋgəˈliːz/	French
Costa Rica /ˌkɒstə ˈriːkə/	Costa Rican /ˌkɒstə ˈriːkən/	Costa Rican /ˌkɒstə ˈriːkən/	Spanish
Cuba /ˈkjuːbə/	Cuban /ˈkjuːbən/	Cuban /ˈkjuːbən/	Spanish
Cyprus /ˈsaɪprəs/	Cypriot /ˈsɪprɪət/	Cypriot /ˈsɪprɪət/	Greek, Turkish
Czechoslovakia /ˌtʃekəsləuˈvækɪə/	Czech, Czechoslovakian /tʃek/, /ˌtʃekəsləˈvækɪən/	Czech, Czechoslovak /ˌtʃekəˈsləuvæk/	Czech, Slovak
Denmark /ˈdenmɑːk/	Danish /ˈdeɪnɪʃ/	Dane /deɪn/	Danish
Dominica /dəˈmɪnɪkə/	Dominican /dəˈmɪnɪkən/	Dominican /dəˈmɪnɪkən/	English

Country or State	Adjective	Person	Main/Official Language
Dominican Republic /dəˈmɪnɪkən/	Dominican /dəˈmɪnɪkən/	Dominican /dəˈmɪnɪkən/	Spanish
East Germany = German Democratic Republic			
Ecuador /ˈekwə,dɔː/	Ecuadorian /ˌekwəˈdɔːrɪən/	Ecuadorian /ˌekwəˈdɔːrɪən/	Spanish
Egypt /ˈiːdʒɪpt/	Egyptian /ɪˈdʒɪpʃən/	Egyptian /ɪˈdʒɪpʃən/	Arabic
Eire /ˈeərə/ ⇒ Ireland			
El Salvador /el ˈsælvə,dɔː/	Salvadorian /ˌsælvəˈdɔːrɪən/	Salvadorian /ˌsælvəˈdɔːrɪən/	Spanish
England /ˈɪŋglənd/	English /ˈɪŋglɪʃ/	Englishman, Englishwoman; /ˈɪŋglɪʃmən, -ˌwumən/ the English (people)	English
Equatorial Guinea /ˌekwɪˈtɔːrɪəl ˈgɪnɪ/	Equatorial Guinean /ˈgɪnɪən/	Equatorial Guinean /ˈgɪnɪən/	Spanish
Ethiopia /ˌiːθɪˈəupɪə/	Ethiopian /ˌiːθɪˈəupɪən/	Ethiopian /ˌiːθɪˈəupɪən/	Amharic
Federal Republic of Germany ⇒ Germany			
Fiji /ˈfiːdʒɪ/	Fijian /fɪˈdʒiːən/	Fijian /fɪˈdʒiːən/	English
Finland /ˈfɪnlənd/	Finnish /ˈfɪnɪʃ/	Finn /fɪn/	Finnish, Swedish
France /frɑːns/	French /frentʃ/	Frenchman, Frenchwoman; /ˈfrentʃmən, -ˌwumən/ the French (people)	French
Gabon /gæˈbɒn/	Gabonese /ˌgæbəˈniːz/	Gabonese /ˌgæbəˈniːz/	French
Gambia /ˈgæmbɪə/	Gambian /ˈgæmbɪən/	Gambian /ˈgæmbɪən/	English
Germany: /ˈdʒɜːmənɪ/			
Federal Republic of Germany	West German /ˌwest ˈdʒɜːmən/	West German /ˌwest ˈdʒɜːmən/	German
German Democratic Republic	East German /ˌiːst ˈdʒɜːmən/	East German /ˌiːst ˈdʒɜːmən/	German
Ghana /ˈgɑːnə/	Ghanaian /gɑːˈneɪən/	Ghanaian /gɑːˈneɪən/	English
Gibraltar /dʒɪˈbrɔːltə/	Gibraltarian /ˌdʒɪbrɔːlˈteərɪən/	Gibraltarian /ˌdʒɪbrɔːlˈteərɪən/	English
Great Britain /ˌgreɪt ˈbrɪtn/ = England, Scotland and Wales. ⇒ United Kingdom.			
Greece /griːs/	Greek /griːk/	Greek /griːk/	Greek
Grenada /grəˈneɪdə/	Grenadian /grəˈneɪdɪən/	Grenadian /grəˈneɪdɪən/	English
Guatemala /ˌgwɑːtəˈmɑːlə/	Guatemalan /ˌgwɑːtəˈmɑːlən/	Guatemalan /ˌgwɑːtəˈmɑːlən/	Spanish

Country or State	Adjective	Person	Main/Official Language
Guiana, the Guianas /gɪˈɑːnə(z)/	Guianian, Guianese /gɪˈɑːnɪən, ˌgɪəˈniːz/	Guianian, Guianese /gɪˈɑːnɪən, ˌgɪəˈniːz/	French
Guinea /ˈgɪnɪ/	Guinean /ˈgɪnɪən/	Guinean /ˈgɪnɪən/	French
Guyana /gaɪˈɑːnə/	Guyanese, Guyanan /ˌgaɪəˈniːz, gaɪˈɑːnən/	Guyanese, Guyanan /ˌgaɪəˈniːz, gaɪˈɑːnən/	English
Haiti /ˈheɪtɪ/	Haitian /ˈheɪʃən/	Haitian /ˈheɪʃən/	French
Holland /ˈhɒlənd/ = the Netherlands			
Honduras /hɒnˈdjʊərəs/	Honduran /hɒnˈdjʊərən/	Honduran /hɒnˈdjʊərən/	Spanish
Hungary /ˈhʌŋgərɪ/	Hungarian /hʌŋˈgeərɪən/	Hungarian /hʌŋˈgeərɪən/	Hungarian
Iceland /ˈaɪslənd/	Icelandic /aɪsˈlændɪk/	Icelander /ˈaɪsˌlændə/	Icelandic
India /ˈɪndɪə/	Indian /ˈɪndɪən/	Indian /ˈɪndɪən/	Hindi, English
Indonesia /ˌɪndəˈniːzjə/	Indonesian /ˌɪndəˈniːzjən/	Indonesian /ˌɪndəˈniːzjən/	Bahasa Indonesia
Iran /ɪˈrɑːn/	Iranian /ɪˈreɪnɪən/	Iranian /ɪˈreɪnɪən/	Iranian
Iraq /ɪˈrɑːk/	Iraqi /ɪˈrɑːkɪ/	Iraqi /ɪˈrɑːkɪ/	Arabic
Ireland, Eire /ˈaɪələnd, ˈeərə/ Irish Republic	Irish /ˈaɪərɪʃ/	Irishman, Irishwoman; /ˈaɪərɪʃmən, -ˌwʊmən/ the Irish (people)	Irish, English
Israel /ˈɪzreɪl/	Israeli /ɪzˈreɪlɪ/	Israeli /ɪzˈreɪlɪ/	Hebrew
Italy /ˈɪtəlɪ/	Italian /ɪˈtælɪən/	Italian /ɪˈtælɪən/	Italian
Jamaica /dʒəˈmeɪkə/	Jamaican /dʒəˈmeɪkən/	Jamaican /dʒeˈmeɪkən/	English
Japan /dʒəˈpæn/	Japanese /ˌdʒæpəˈniːz/	Japanese /ˌdʒæpəˈniːz/	Japanese
Jordan /ˈdʒɔːdən/	Jordanian /dʒɔːˈdeɪnɪən/	Jordanian /dʒɔːˈdeɪnɪən/	Arabic
Kampuchea /ˌkæmpʊˈtʃɪə/	Kampuchean /ˌkæmpʊˈtʃɪən/	Kampuchean /ˌkæmpʊˈtʃɪən/	Khmer
Kenya /ˈkenjə/	Kenyan /ˈkenjən/	Kenyan /ˈkenjən/	English, Swahili
Korea: /kəˈrɪə/ North Korea, Democratic People's Republic of Korea	Korean /kəˈrɪən/	Korean /kəˈrɪən/	Korean
South Korea	Korean /kəˈrɪən/	Korean /kəˈrɪən/	Korean
Kuwait /kʊˈweɪt/	Kuwaiti /kʊˈweɪtɪ/	Kuwaiti /kʊˈweɪtɪ/	Arabic

Country or State	Adjective	Person	Main/Official Language
Laos /ˈlɑːɒs/	Laotian /ˈlaʊʃɪən/	Laotian /ˈlaʊʃɪən/	Lao
Lebanon /ˈlebənən/	Lebanese /ˌlebəˈniːz/	Lebanese /ˌlebəˈniːz/	Arabic
Lesotho /ləˈsəʊtəʊ/	Sotho /ˈsuːtuː/	Mosotho *c.n*, /məˈsuːtuː/ Basotho *pl.n* /bəˈsuːtuː/	Sesotho, English
Liberia /laɪˈbɪərɪə/	Liberian /laɪˈbɪərɪən/	Liberian /laɪˈbɪərɪən/	English
Libya /ˈlɪbɪə/	Libyan /ˈlɪbɪən/	Libyan /ˈlɪbɪən/	Arabic
Luxemburg /ˈlʌksəmˌbɜːg/	Luxemburg /ˈlʌksəmˌbɜːg/	Luxemburger /ˈlʌksəmˌbɜːgə/	French, German
Madagascar /ˌmædəˈgæskə/	Madagascan /ˌmædəˈgæskən/	Malagasy /ˌmæləˈgæsɪ/	Malagasi
Malawi /məˈlɑːwɪ/	Malawian /məˈlɑːwɪən/	Malawian /məˈlɑːwɪən/	English
Malaysia /meˈleɪzɪə/	Malaysian /məˈleɪzɪən/	Malaysian /məˈleɪzɪən/	Malay, English
Mali /ˈmɑːlɪ/	Malian /ˈmɑːlɪən/	Malian /ˈmɑːlɪən/	French
Malta /ˈmɔːltə/	Maltese /mɔːlˈtiːz/	Maltese /mɔːlˈtiːz/	Maltese, English
Mauritania /ˌmɒrɪˈteɪnɪə/	Mauritanian /ˌmɒrɪˈteɪnɪən/	Mauritanian /ˌmɒrɪˈteɪnɪən/	Arabic, French
Mauritius /məˈrɪʃəs/	Mauritian /məˈrɪʃən/	Mauritian /məˈrɪʃən/	English
Mexico /ˈmeksɪkəʊ/	Mexican /ˈmeksɪkən/	Mexican /ˈmeksɪkən/	Spanish
Monaco /ˈmɒnəˌkəʊ/	Monegasque /ˌmɒnɪˈgæsk/	Monegasque /ˌmɒnɪˈgæsk/	French
Mongolia /mɒŋˈgəʊlɪə/	Mongolian /mɒŋˈgəʊlɪən/	Mongol, Mongolian /ˈmɒŋgɒl, mɒŋˈgəʊlɪən/	Mongolian (Khalkha)
Morocco /məˈrɒkəʊ/	Moroccan /məˈrɒkən/	Moroccan /məˈrɒkən/	Arabic, Berber, French
Mozambique /ˌməʊzəmˈbiːk/	Mozambiquean /ˌməʊzəmˈbiːkən/	Mozambiquean /ˌməʊzəmˈbiːkən/	Portuguese
Namibia /nəˈmɪbɪə/	Namibian /nəˈmɪbɪən/	Namibian /nəˈmɪbɪən/	English
Nepal /nəˈpɔːl/	Nepalese /ˌnepəˈliːz/	Nepalese /ˌnepəˈliːz/	Nepali
The Netherlands /ˈneðələndz/	Dutch /dʌtʃ/	Dutchman, Dutchwoman /ˈdʌtʃmən, -ˌwʊmən/ the Dutch (people)	Dutch
New Zealand /ˌnjuːˈziːlənd/	New Zealand /ˌnjuːˈziːlənd/	New Zealander /ˌnjuːˈziːləndə/	English
Nicaragua /ˌnɪkəˈrægjʊə/	Nicaraguan /ˌnɪkəˈrægjʊən/	Nicaraguan /ˌnɪkəˈrægjʊən/	Spanish

Country or State	Adjective	Person	Main/Official Language
Niger /ˈnaɪdʒə/	Nigerien /nɪˈdʒɛərɪən/	Nigerien /nɪˈdʒɛərɪən/	French
Nigeria /naɪˈdʒɪərɪə/	Nigerian /naɪˈdʒɪərɪən/	Nigerian /naɪˈdʒɪərɪən/	English, Hausa, Ibo, Yoruba
Norway /ˈnɔːweɪ/	Norwegian /nɔːˈwiːdʒən/	Norwegian /nɔːˈwiːdʒən/	Norwegian
Oman /əʊˈmɑːn/	Omani /əʊˈmɑːnɪ/	Omani /əʊˈmɑːnɪ/	Arabic
Pakistan /ˌpɑːkɪˈstɑːn/	Pakistani /ˌpɑːkɪˈstɑːnɪ/	Pakistani /ˌpɑːkɪˈstɑːnɪ/	Urdu
Palestine /ˈpælɪˌstaɪn/	Palestinian /ˌpælɪˈstɪnɪən/	Palestinian /ˌpælɪˈstɪnɪən/	Arabic
Panama /ˌpænəˈmɑː/	Panamanian /ˌpænəˈmeɪnɪən/	Panamanian /ˌpænəˈmeɪnɪən/	Spanish, English
Papua New Guinea /ˌpɑːpʊə ˌnjuː ˈgɪnɪ/	Papuan /ˈpɑːpʊən/	Papuan /ˈpɑːpʊən/	Papuan, English
Paraguay /ˈpærəˌgwaɪ/	Paraguayan /ˌpærəˈgwaɪən/	Paraguayan /ˌpærəˈgwaɪən/	Spanish, Guarani
Peru /pəˈruː/	Peruvian /pəˈruːvɪən/	Peruvian /pəˈruːvɪən/	Spanish, Quechua
Philippines /ˈfɪlɪˌpiːnz/	Philippine /ˈfɪlɪˌpiːn/	Filipino /ˌfɪlɪˈpiːnəʊ/	Filipino, English
Poland /ˈpəʊlənd/	Polish /ˈpəʊlɪʃ/	Pole /pəʊl/	Polish
Portugal /ˈpɔːtjʊgəl/	Portuguese /ˌpɔːtjʊˈgiːz/	Portuguese /ˌpɔːtjʊˈgiːz/	Portuguese
Romania /ruːˈmeɪnɪə/	Romanian /ruːˈmeɪnɪən/	Romanian /ruːˈmeɪnɪən/	Romanian
Russia /ˈrʌʃə/ ⇒ Soviet Union			
Saudi Arabia /ˌsaʊdɪ əˈreɪbɪə/	Saudi Arabian /ˌsaʊdɪ əˈreɪbɪən/	Saudi, Saudi Arabian /ˌsaʊdɪ (əˈreɪbɪən)/	Arabic
Scotland /ˈskɒtlənd/	Scottish, Scots /ˈskɒtɪʃ, ˈskɒts/	Scotsman, Scotswoman /ˈskɒtsmən, -ˌwʊmən/ the Scots (people) /skɒts/	English
Senegal /ˌsenɪˈgɔːl/	Senegalese /ˌsenɪgəˈliːz/	Senegalese /ˌsenɪgəˈliːz/	French
Seychelles /seɪˈʃelz/	Seychellois /ˌseɪʃelˈwɑː/	Seychellois /ˌseɪʃelˈwɑː/	English, French
Sierra Leone /sɪˌerə lɪˈəʊn/	Sierra Leonean /sɪˌerə lɪˈəʊnɪən/	Sierra Leonean /sɪˌerə lɪˈəʊnɪən/	English
Singapore /ˌsɪŋəˈpɔː/	Singaporean /ˌsɪŋəˈpɔːrɪən/	Singaporean /ˌsɪŋəˈpɔːrɪən/	Malay, English, Chinese, Tamil
Somalia /səˈmɑːlɪə/	Somali, Somalian /səˈmɑːlɪ(ən)/	Somali /səˈmɑːlɪ/	Arabic, Somali, Italian, English

Country or State	Adjective	Person	Main/Official Language
South Africa /ˌsaʊθ ˈæfrɪkə/	South African /ˌsaʊθ ˈæfrɪkən/	South African /ˌsaʊθ ˈæfrɪkən/	Afrikaans, English
Soviet Union /ˌsəʊvɪət ˈjuːnɪən/	Soviet, Russian /ˌsəʊvɪət, ˈrʌʃən/	Soviet, Russian /ˌsəʊvɪət, ˈrʌʃən/	Russian
Spain /speɪn/	Spanish /ˈspænɪʃ/	Spaniard /ˈspænjəd/	Spanish
Sri Lanka /ˌsriː ˈlæŋkə/	Sri Lankan /ˌsriː ˈlæŋkən/	Sri Lankan /ˌsriː ˈlæŋkən/	Sinhalese, Tamil, English
Sudan /suːˈdɑːn/	Sudanese /ˌsuːdəˈniːz/	Sudanese /ˌsuːdəˈniːz/	Arabic
Surinam /ˌsʊərɪˈnæm/	Surinamese /ˌsʊərɪnəˈmiːz/	Surinamese /ˌsʊərɪnəˈmiːz/	Dutch, English
Swaziland /ˈswɑːzɪˌlænd/	Swazi /ˈswɑːzɪ/	Swazi /ˈswɑːzɪ/	English, Swazi
Sweden /ˈswiːdən/	Swedish /ˈswiːdɪʃ/	Swede /swiːd/	Swedish
Switzerland /ˈswɪtsələnd/	Swiss /swɪs/	Swiss /swɪs/	German, French, Italian
Syria /ˈsɪrɪə/	Syrian /ˈsɪrɪən/	Syrian /ˈsɪrɪən/	French, Arabic
Tahiti /tɑːˈhiːtɪ/	Tahitian /tɑːˈhiːʃən/	Tahitian /tɑːˈhiːʃən/	French
Taiwan /taɪˈwɑːn/	Taiwanese /ˌtaɪwəˈniːz/	Taiwanese /ˌtaɪwəˈniːz/	English, Chinese
Tanzania /ˌtænzəˈnɪə/	Tanzanian /ˌtænzəˈnɪən/	Tanzanian /ˌtænzəˈnɪən/	English, Swahili
Thailand /ˈtaɪlənd/	Thai /taɪ/	Thai /taɪ/	Thai
Tibet /tɪˈbet/	Tibetan /tɪˈbetən/	Tibetan /tɪˈbetən/	Tibetan, Chinese
Togo /ˈtəʊgəʊ/	Togolese /ˌtəʊgəˈliːz/	Togolese /ˌtəʊgəˈliːz/	French
Tonga /ˈtɒŋə/	Tongan /ˈtɒŋən/	Tongan /ˈtɒŋən/	Tongan, English
Trinidad & Tobago /ˈtrɪnɪˌdæd, təˈbeɪgəʊ/	Trinidadian, Tobagan /ˌtrɪnɪˈdædɪən, təˈbeɪgən/	Trinidadian, Tobagan /ˌtrɪnɪˈdædɪən, təˈbeɪgən/	English
Tunisia /tjuːˈnɪzɪə/	Tunisian /tjuːˈnɪzɪən/	Tunisian /tjuːˈnɪzɪən/	Arabic, French
Turkey /ˈtɜːkɪ/	Turkish /ˈtɜːkɪʃ/	Turk /tɜːk/	Turkish
Uganda /juːˈgændə/	Ugandan /juːˈgændən/	Ugandan /juːˈgændən/	English, Swahili, Lugando, Luo
United Kingdom of Great Britain and Northern Ireland	British /ˈbrɪtɪʃ/	Briton /ˈbrɪtən/ the British (people)	English
United States of America /juːˌnaɪtɪd ˌsteɪts əv əˈmerɪkə/ ⇒ America			
Uruguay /ˈjʊərəˌgwaɪ/	Uruguayan /ˌjʊərəˈgwaɪən/	Uruguayan /ˌjʊərəˈgwaɪən/	Spanish
Venezuela /ˌvenɪˈzweɪlə/	Venezuelan /ˌvenɪˈzweɪlən/	Venezuelan /ˌvenɪˈzweɪlən/	Spanish
Vietnam /ˌvjetˈnɑːm/	Vietnamese /ˌvjetnəˈmiːz/	Vietnamese /ˌvjetnəˈmiːz/	Vietnamese

Country or State	Adjective	Person	Main/Official Language
Wales /weɪlz/	Welsh /welʃ/	Welshman, Welshwoman, /ˈwelʃmən, -ˌwʊmən/ the Welsh (people)	English, Welsh
Western Samoa /ˌwestən səˈməʊə/	Western Samoan /ˌwestən səˈməʊən/	Samoan /səˈməʊən/	Samoan, English

West German = Federal Republic of Germany ⇒ Germany

Country or State	Adjective	Person	Main/Official Language
Yemen /ˈjemən/ North Yemen, Yemen Arab Republic	Yemeni /ˈjemənɪ/	Yemeni /ˈjemənɪ/	Arabic
South Yemen	Yemeni /ˈjemənɪ/	Yemeni /ˈjemənɪ/	Arabic
Yugoslavia /ˌjuːgəˈslɑːvɪə/	Yugoslavian /ˌjuːgəˈslɑːvɪən/	Yugoslav /ˈjuːgəˈslɑːvɪən/	Serbo-Croatian, Slovene, Macedonian
Zaïre /zaɪˈɪə/	Zaïrean /zaɪˈɪərɪən/	Zaïrean /zaɪˈɪərɪən/	French
Zambia /ˈzæmbɪə/	Zambian /ˈzæmbɪən/	Zambian /ˈzæmbɪən/	English
Zimbabwe /zɪmˈbɑːbwɪ/	Zimbabwean /zɪmˈbɑːbwɪən/	Zimbabwean /zɪmˈbɑːbwɪən/	English

Continent	Adjective and Person	Continent	Adjective and Person
Africa /ˈæfrɪkə/	African /ˈæfrɪkən/	North America /ˌnɔːθ əˈmerɪkə/	North American /ˌnɔːθ əˈmerɪkən/
Antarctica /ænˈtɑːktɪkə/	Antarctican /ænˈtɑːktɪkən/	Oceania /ˌəʊʃɪˈeɪnɪə/	Oceanian /ˌəʊʃɪˈeɪnɪən/
Asia /ˈeɪʃə/	Asian /ˈeɪʃən/	South America /ˌsaʊθ əˈmerɪkə/	South American /ˌsaʊθ əˈmerɪkən/
Europe /ˈjʊərəp/	European /ˌjʊərəˈpiːən/		
Latin America /ˌlætɪn əˈmerɪkə/	Latin American /ˌlætɪn əˈmerɪkən/		

Some other areas of the world

The Antarctic /ænˈtɑːktɪk/
Arabia /əˈreɪbɪə/
The Arctic /ˈɑːktɪk/
Asia Minor /ˌeɪʃə ˈmaɪnə/
Australasia /ˌɒstrəˈleɪʒɪə/
The Caribbean /ˌkærɪˈbiːən/

The Far East /ˌfɑːr ˈiːst/
The Iberian Peninsula /aɪˌbɪərɪən pəˈnɪnsjʊlə/
The Middle East /ˌmɪdl ˈiːst/
The Near East /ˌnɪər ˈiːst/
Scandinavia /ˌskændɪˈneɪvɪə/

Oceans

Antarctic /ænˈtɑːktɪk/
Arctic /ˈɑːktɪk/
Atlantic /ətˈlæntɪk/ (North and South)

Indian /ˈɪndɪən/
Pacific /pəˈsɪfɪk/ (North and South)

Some seas

Adriatic /ˌeɪdrɪˈætɪk/
Aegean /əˈdʒiːən/
Arabian /əˈreɪbɪən/
Baltic /ˈbɔːltɪk/
Black /blæk/
Caribbean /ˌkærɪˈbiːən/
Caspian /ˈkæspɪən/

China /ˈtʃaɪnə/
Irish /ˈaɪrɪʃ/
Japan /dʒəˈpæn/
Mediterranean /ˌmedɪtəˈreɪnɪən/
North /nɔːθ/
Red /red/
Yellow /ˈjeləʊ/

Appendix 6 **Numbers**

(For pronunciations, look up the entry in the dictionary.)

Cardinal	Ordinal	Fraction
1 one	first **1st**	
2 two	second **2nd**	$\frac{1}{2}$ half
3 three	third **3rd**	$\frac{1}{3}$ third
4 four	fourth **4th**	$\frac{1}{4}$ quarter; fourth
5 five	fifth **5th**	$\frac{1}{5}$ fifth
6 six	sixth **6th**	$\frac{1}{6}$ sixth
7 seven	seventh **7th**	$\frac{1}{7}$ seventh
8 eight	eighth **8th**	$\frac{1}{8}$ eighth
9 nine	ninth **9th**	$\frac{1}{9}$ ninth
10 ten	tenth **10th**	$\frac{1}{10}$ tenth
11 eleven	eleventh **11th**	$\frac{1}{11}$ eleventh
12 twelve	twelfth **12th**	$\frac{1}{12}$ twelfth
13 thirteen	thirteenth **13th**	$\frac{1}{13}$ thirteenth
14 fourteen	fourteenth **14th**	$\frac{1}{14}$ fourteenth
15 fifteen	fifteenth **15th**	$\frac{1}{15}$ fifteenth
16 sixteen	sixteenth **16th**	$\frac{1}{16}$ sixteenth
17 seventeen	seventeenth **17th**	$\frac{1}{17}$ seventeenth
18 eighteen	eighteenth **18th**	$\frac{1}{18}$ eighteenth
19 nineteen	nineteenth **19th**	$\frac{1}{19}$ nineteenth
20 twenty	twentieth **20th**	$\frac{1}{20}$ twentieth
21 twenty-one	twenty-first **21st**	$\frac{1}{21}$ twenty-first
22 twenty-two	twenty-second **22nd**	$\frac{1}{22}$ twenty-secondth
23 twenty-three etc	twenty-third **23rd**	$\frac{1}{23}$ twenty-third
30 thirty	thirtieth **30th**	$\frac{1}{30}$ thirtieth
31 thirty-one etc	thirty-first **31st**	$\frac{1}{31}$ thirty-first
40 forty	fortieth **40th**	$\frac{1}{40}$ fortieth
50 fifty	fiftieth **50th**	$\frac{1}{50}$ fiftieth
60 sixty	sixtieth **60th**	$\frac{1}{60}$ sixtieth
70 seventy	seventieth **70th**	$\frac{1}{70}$ seventieth
80 eighty	eightieth **80th**	$\frac{1}{80}$ eightieth
90 ninety	ninetieth **90th**	$\frac{1}{90}$ ninetieth
100 a/one hundred	hundredth **100th**	$\frac{1}{100}$ hundredth
(⇒ *Note below*)		
200 two hundred etc	two hundredth **200th**	$\frac{1}{200}$ two hundredth
1000 a/one thousand	thousandth **1000th**	$\frac{1}{1000}$ thousandth
(⇒ *Note below*)		
1 000 000 a/one million	millionth **1 000 000th**	$\frac{1}{1\,000\,000}$ millionth
(⇒ *Note below*)		

Note:

In the plural, when **hundred, thousand** or **million** has a number immediately before it and a noun immediately after it, it does not have an -s: three hundred students; five thousand houses; two million people. We use *-s* if we are thinking of a hundred etc as a unit: In 2 008 600, there are two millions, eight thousands and six hundreds. **hundreds/thousands** etc **of** = a lot of: I've been there hundreds of times.

When telephoning or reading numbers aloud, each number is spoken separately, except that, if the same number is repeated, one can say double . . ., e.g double five (55).

32216: we would usually say ',three double ,two one 'six'.

0 (zero) is usually pronounced 'oh' /əʊ/, e.g in 602.

Appendix 7 **Times and dates**

60 seconds ('')	= 1 minute (')
60 minutes (*min*)	= 1 hour (*hr*)
24 hours	= 1 day
7 days	= 1 week (*wk*)
30 or 31 days	= 1 month (*mth*)

(⇒ Note below)

12 months	= 1 year (*yr*)
10 years	= 1 decade
100 years	= 1 century (*C*)

(*Note: February has 28 or 29 days.*)

British times
from midnight to midday

1.00	*one (o'clock)* or *one a.m*
2.01	*one (minute) past two* or *two oh one*
4.10	*ten (minutes) past four* or *four ten*
5.15	*a quarter past five* or *five fifteen*
6.25	*twenty-five (minutes) past six* or *six twenty-five*
8.30	*half past eight* or *eight-thirty* or (*informal*) *half eight*
9.35	*twenty-five (minutes) to ten* or *nine thirty-five*
10.45	*a quarter to eleven* or *ten forty-five*
11.59	*one minute to twelve* or *eleven fifty-nine*

from midday to midnight

As above, except that p.m replaces a.m.

USA times

In the USA, 'after' is used instead of 'past' and 'of' instead of 'to':
4.10 *ten after four*; 9.55 *five of ten*.

The twenty-four hour clock
(used in airports, timetables etc)

05.00	(*oh*) *five hundred hours*
06.32	(*oh*) *six thirty-two*
11.00	*eleven hundred hours*
12.00	*twelve hundred hours*
13.05	*thirteen oh five*
21.00	*twenty-one hundred hours*
24.00	*twenty-four hundred hours.*

Years

5000 BC	*five thousand BC* /ˌbiː ˈsiː/
21 BC	*twenty-one BC* /ˌbiː ˈsiː/
AD 21	*AD* /ˌeɪ ˈdiː/ *twenty-one.*

AD is rarely used except for the years nearest to the end of BC.

Months and days

British system

6(th) January 1992	
6 Jan 92	*the sixth of January nineteen ninety-two*
6/1/92	

USA system

January 6 1992	
Jan 6 1992	*January sixth, nineteen ninety-two*
1/6/92	

The months are abbreviated *Jan, Feb, Mar, Apr, May, Jun, Jul, Aug, Sep(t), Oct, Nov, Dec.*

Appendix 8 **Money**

British

100 pennies/pence (p) = one pound (£)

1p	*a/one p* or *a/one penny* (coin: *one p* or *one penny piece*)
2p	*two p* or *two pence* (coin: *two p* or *two penny piece*)
5p	*five p* or *five pence* (coin: *five p* or *five pence piece*)
50p	*fifty p* or *fifty pence* (coin: *fifty p* or *fifty pence piece*)
£1	*a/one pound* (slang: *a/one quid*) (coin: *one pound (coin)*)
£5	*five pounds* (slang: *five quid*) (note: *five pound note*)
£10	*ten pounds* (slang: *ten quid*) (note: *ten pound note*)
£20	*twenty pounds* (slang: *twenty quid*) (note: *twenty pound note*)
£50	*fifty pounds* (slang: *fifty quid*) (note: *fifty pound note*)
£1.01	*one pound one*
£1.50	*one pound fifty*

USA

100 cents (c) = 1 dollar ($)

1c	*one cent* (coin: *penny*)
5c	*five cents* (coin: *nickel*)
10c	*ten cents* (coin: *dime*)
25c	*twenty-five cents* (coin: *quarter*)
50c	*fifty cents* (coin: *half-dollar* or *fifty cent piece*)
$1	*a/one dollar* (slang: *a/one buck*) (coin: *(silver) dollar*; note: *dollar bill*)
$5	*five dollars* (slang: *five bucks*) (note: *five dollar bill*)
$10	*ten dollars* (slang: *ten bucks*) (note: *ten dollar bill*)
$20	*twenty dollars* (slang: *twenty bucks*) (note: *twenty dollar bill*)
$50	*fifty dollars* (slang: *fifty bucks*) (note: *fifty dollar bill*)
$100	*a/one hundred dollars* (slang: *a/one hundred bucks*) (note: *hundred dollar bill*)
$1.34	*a dollar thirty-four*
$4.35	*four (dollars) thirty-five (cents)*

Appendix 9 **Weights and measures**

Weight

Metric

10 milligrams (*mg*)	= 1 centigram (*cg*)
10 centigrams	= 1 decigram (*dg*)
10 decigrams	= 1 gram (*g*)
100 grams	= 1 hectogram (*hg*)
10 hectograms	= 1 kilogram (*kg*)
1000 kilograms	= 1 tonne

Avoirdupois

16 ounces (*oz*)	= 1 pound (*lb*)
14 pounds	= 1 stone (*st*)
28 pounds	= 1 quarter (*qtr*)
4 quarters	= 1 hundredweight (*cwt*)
20 hundredweight	= 1 (long) ton

Troy weight

12 ounces (*oz*)	= 1 pound (*lb*)

1 kilogram = 2.205 pounds.
1 pound = 0.4536 kilograms.

1 tonne = 0.984 (long) ton.
1 (long) ton = 1.016 tonnes.

Length

Metric

10 millimetres (*mm*)	= 1 centimetre (*cm*)
10 centimetres	= 1 decimetre (*dm*)
10 decimetres	= 1 metre (*m*)
10 metres	= 1 decametre (*dam*)
10 decametres	= 1 hectometre (*hm*)
10 hectometres	= 1 kilometre (*km*)

Imperial

12 inches (*in*)	= 1 foot (*ft*)
3 feet	= 1 yard (*yd*)
22 yards	= 1 chain (*ch*)
10 chains	= 1 furlong (*fur*)
8 furlongs	= 1 mile (*ml*)
6076.12 feet	= 1 nautical/sea mile

1 metre = 39.37 inches.
1 yard = 0.9144 metre.
1 kilometre = 0.6214 mile.
1 mile = 1.609 kilometres.
1 kilometre is about $\frac{5}{8}$ mile. To change miles into kilometres multiply by 8 and divide by 5. To change kilometres into miles, multiply by 5 and divide by 8.

Square measure

Metric

100 square millimetres (mm²)	= 1 square centimetre (*cm²*)
100 square centimetres	= 1 square decimetre (*dm²*)
100 square decimetres	= 1 square metre (*m²*)
100 square metres	= 1 are
100 ares	= 1 hectare (*ha*)
100 hectares	= 1 square kilometre (*km²*)

Imperial

144 square inches (*in²*)	= 1 square foot (*ft²*)
9 square feet	= 1 square yard (*yd²*)
4840 square yards	= 1 acre
640 acres	= 1 square mile (*ml²*)

1 square metre = 1.196 square yards.
1 square yard = 0.8361 square metre.
1 hectare = 2.47 acres.
1 acre = 0.4047 hectare.

Cubic measure

Metric

1000 cubic centimetres (*cm³*)	= 1 cubic decimetre (*dm³*)
1000 cubic decimetres	= 1 cubic metre (*m³*)

Imperial

1728 cubic inches (*in³*)	= 1 cubic foot (*ft³*)
27 cubic feet	= 1 cubic yard (*yd³*)

Liquid Measure

Metric

10 millilitres (*ml*)	= 1 centilitre (*cl*)
10 centilitres	= 1 decilitre (*dl*)
10 decilitres	= 1 litre (*l*)
10 litres	= 1 decalitre (*dal*)
10 decalitres	= 1 hectolitre (*hl*)
10 hectolitres	= 1 kilolitre (*kl*)

Imperial

4 gills	= 1 pint (*pt*)
2 pints	= 1 quart (*qt*)
4 quarts	= 1 gallon (*gal*)

1 litre = 0.22 UK gallon.
1 UK gallon = 4.5435 litres.

Circular measure

60 seconds ('')	= 1 minute (')
60 minutes	= 1 degree (°)
360 degrees	= 1 circle.

Temperatures

	Freezing	Boiling
Fahrenheit	32°	212°
Centigrade, Celsius	0°	100°

To change Fahrenheit into Centigrade or Celsius,
take away 32, multiply by 5 and then divide by 9.
To change Centigrade/Celsius into Fahrenheit,
multiply by 9, divide by 5 and then add 32.

Weighing and measuring people

72 kg	*I weigh seventy-two kilos*
11st 4lb	*I weigh eleven stone four (pounds)*
158 lb	*I weigh a/one hundred and fifty-eight pounds*
1.77m	*I am one metre seventy-seven (tall)*
5' 9''	*I am five foot/feet nine (inches) (tall)*
99–70–99	*I am ninety-nine, seventy, ninety-nine* (centimetres round the bust, waist, hips)
39–29–39	*I am thirty-nine, twenty-nine, thirty-nine* (inches round the bust, waist, hips)

Sports and games

100m	the (men's/women's) hundred metres race (running, hurdles, swimming etc)
1500m	the fifteen hundred metres
4 × 200m	the four by two hundred metres (relay race)
11.25 sec	(a time of) eleven point two five seconds
12.05m	(a jump etc of) twelve point oh five metres
5–3	(*We won the match*) *five three* or (*We won the match by*) *five goals to three*

6–1, 6–0, 6–3	(in tennis) (*He won the game*) *six one, six love, six three*
30–30	*thirty all*
40–40	(in tennis) deuce
15–0	(in football, rugby, hockey etc) fifteen nil
10–1	(in betting) ten to one

Appendix 10 **Mathematical signs and symbols**

$+$	plus	∞	infinity
$-$	minus	π	pi /paɪ/
$\times$	multiplied by	r	/ɑ:/ radius (of a circle)
$\div$	divided by	$2\pi r$	two pi r /ˌtu: ˌpaɪ 'ɑ:/ circumference of a circle
$\sqrt{\ }$	square root	Πr^2	pi r squared /ˌpaɪ 'ɑ: ˌskweəd/ area of a circle
$\sqrt[3]{\ }$	cube root	$\parallel$	is parallel to
x^2	x squared	$\perp$	is perpendicular to
x^3	x cubed	$\angle$	angle
x^4 etc	x to the power of 4	$\llcorner$	right angle
$=$	equals	$\triangle$	triangle
$\neq$	is not equal to	$°$	degree
$>$	is more than	$'$	minute, foot
$<$	is less than	$''$	second, inch
$\%$	per cent		

Appendix 11 **Ranks in the armed forces**

	British Royal Navy (*RN*)	**US Navy** (*USN*)
Officers	Admiral of the Fleet	Fleet Admiral
	Admiral (*Adm*)	Admiral (*ADM*)
	Vice-Admiral (*Vice-Adm*)	Vice-Admiral (*VADM*)
	Rear-Admiral (*Rear-Adm*)	Rear-Admiral (*RADM*)
	Commodore (*Cdre*)	Commodore (*CDRE*)
	Captain (*Capt*)	Captain (*CAPT*)
	Commander (*Cdr*)	Commander (*CDR*)
	Lieutenant-Commander (*Lt-Cdr*)	Lieutenant-Commander (*LCDR*)
	Lieutenant (*Lt*)	Lieutenant (*LT*)
	Sub-Lieutenant (*Sub-Lt*)	Lieutenant Junior Grade (*LTJG*)
	Acting Sub-Lieutenant (*Actg Sub-Lt*)	Ensign (*ENS*)
		Chief Warrant Officer (*CWO*)
	Midshipman	Midshipman
Warrant Officers, Petty Officers and Seamen	Fleet Chief Petty Officer (*FCPO*)	Warrant Officer (*WO*)
		Master Chief Petty Officer of the Navy (*MCPO*)
	Chief Petty Officer (*CPO*)	Chief Petty Officer (*CPO*)
	Petty Officer (*PO*)	Petty Officer (*PO*)
	Leading Seaman (*LS*)	Seaman (SN)
	Able Seaman (*AB*)	
	Ordinary Seaman (*OD*)	
	Junior Seaman (*JS*)	Seaman Apprentice (*SA*)

	British Army (also Royal Marines, except without Field Marshal)	**US Army (and Marines, except without General of the Army)**
Officers	Field Marshal (*FM*)	General of the Army (*GEN*)
	General (*Gen*)	General (*GEN*)
	Lieutenant-General (*Lt-Gen*)	Lieutenant-General (*LTG*)
	Major-General (*Maj-Gen*)	Major-General (*MG*)
	Brigadier (*Brig*)	Brigadier-General (*BG*)
	Colonel (*Col*)	Colonel (*COL*)
	Lieutenant-Colonel (*Lt-Col*)	Lieutenant-Colonel (*LTC*)
	Major (*Maj*)	Major (*MAJ*)
	Captain (*Capt*)	Captain (*CPT*)
	Lieutenant (*Lieut*)	First-Lieutenant (*1LT*)
	Second-Lieutenant (*2nd-Lt*)	Second-Lieutenant (*2LT*)
Warrant Officers, Non-Commissioned Officers and Soldiers	Warrant Officer, First Class (*WO1*)	Chief Warrant Officer (*CWO*)
	Warrant Officer, Second Class (*WO2*)	Warrant Officer (*WO*)
	Staff-Sergeant (*Staff-Sgt*)	Sergeant-Major of the Army (*SGM*)
		Command Sergeant-Major (*CSM*)
	Sergeant (*Sgt*)	First-Sergeant (*1SG*)
		Master-Sergeant (*MSG*)
		Sergeant First Class (*SFC*)
		Staff-Sergeant (*SSG*)
		Sergeant (*SGT*)

Corporal (*Cpl*)
Lance-Corporal (*Lance-Cpl*)
Private (*Pte*)

(**Note:** In the Artillery and
Guards Regiments, Corporals,
Lance-Corporals and Privates
are called by other names, e.g.
Bombardier, Lance-Bombardier
and Gunner in the Artillery)

Corporal (*CPL*)
Private First Class (*PFC*)
Private (*PVT*)

(**Note:** In the Marines, some
ranks are given different names)

	(British) Royal Air Force	**US Air Force**
Officers	Marshal of the Royal Air Force	General of the Air Force (*GEN*)
	Air Chief Marshal	General (*GEN*)
	Air Marshal	Lieutenant-General (*LTG*)
	Air Vice-Marshal	Major-General (*MG*)
	Air Commodore (*Air-Cdre*)	Brigadier-General (*BG*)
	Group Captain (*Gp Capt*)	Colonel (*COL*)
	Wing Commander (*Wing Cdr*)	Lieutenant-Colonel (*LTC*)
	Squadron Leader (*Sqn Ldr*)	Major (*MAJ*)
	Flight Lieutenant (*Flt Lt*)	Captain (*CAPT*)
	Flying Officer (*FO*)	First-Lieutenant (*1LT*)
	Pilot Officer (*PO*)	Second-Lieutenant (*2LT*)
Warrant Officers, Non-Commissioned Officers and Airmen	Warrant Officer (*WO*)	Chief Warrant Officer (*CWO*)
		Warrant Officer (*WO*)
		Chief Master-Sergeant (*CMSGT*)
		Senior Master-Sergeant (*SMSGT*)
		Master-Sergeant (*MSGT*)
	Chief Technician (*Chf Tech*)	Technical-Sergeant (*TSGT*)
	Sergeant (*Sgt*)	Staff-Sergeant (*SSGT*)
	Corporal (*Cpl*)	Sergeant (*SGT*)
	Junior Technician (*Jnr Tech*)	
	Senior Aircraftsman (*SAC*)	Airman First Class (*A1C*)
	Leading Aircraftsman (*LAC*)	
	Aircraftsman	Airman Basic (*AB*)